CECIL
Textbook
of Medicine

Associate Editors

Principles of Immunology and Inflammation
Diseases of Allergy and Clinical Immunology
Rheumatic Diseases

William P. Arend, MD
Scoville Professor of Medicine
Department of Medicine
Director, Rheumatology Clinical Programs
University of Colorado School of Medicine
Denver, Colorado

Hematologic Diseases
Oncology

James O. Armitage, MD
Dean, University of Nebraska College of Medicine
Joe Shapiro Professor of Internal Medicine
University of Nebraska Medical Center
Omaha, Nebraska

Respiratory Diseases
Critical Care Medicine

Jeffrey M. Drazen, MD
Professor of Medicine
Harvard Medical School
Editor-in-Chief, New England Journal of Medicine
Boston, Massachusetts

Metabolic Diseases
Nutritional Diseases
Endocrine Diseases
Women's Health
Diseases of Bone and Mineral Metabolism

Gordon N. Gill, MD
Professor of Medicine
Chair, Faculty of Basic Biomedical Sciences
University of California, San Diego
La Jolla, California

Neurology

Robert C. Griggs, MD
Chair, Department of Neurology
Professor of Neurology, Medicine, Pathology and
*   Laboratory Medicine, and Pediatrics*
Edward A. and Alma Vollersten Professor in
*   Neurophysiology*
University of Rochester School of Medicine and
*   Dentistry*
Rochester, New York

Gastrointestinal Diseases
Diseases of the Liver, Gallbladder, and Bile Ducts

Don W. Powell, MD
Professor of Internal Medicine
Professor of Physiology and Biophysics
Associate Dean for Research
University of Texas Medical Branch at Galveston
Galveston, Texas

Infectious Diseases
HIV and the Acquired Immunodeficiency Syndrome

W. Michael Scheld, MD
Professor of Internal Medicine
Clinical Professor of Neurosurgery
University of Virginia Health System
Charlottesville, Virginia

CECIL
Textbook
of Medicine

22nd Edition

VOLUME 1

EDITED BY

Lee Goldman, MD

Julius R. Krevans Distinguished Professor and Chair
Department of Medicine
Associate Dean for Clinical Affairs
University of California, San Francisco, School of Medicine
San Francisco, California

Dennis Ausiello, MD

Jackson Professor of Clinical Medicine
Harvard Medical School
Chief, Medical Service
Massachusetts General Hospital
Boston, Massachusetts

SAUNDERS
An Imprint of Elsevier

SAUNDERS
An Imprint of Elsevier

The Curtis Center
Independence Square West
Philadelphia, Pennsylvania 19106

CECIL TEXTBOOK OF MEDICINE, 22ND EDITION

Single Volume	0–7216–9652–X
Set (Vols. 1 and 2)	0–7216–9653–8
International Edition	0–8089–2292–0

The following chapters are in the public domain (except borrowed figures or tables): Chapter 11, "The Periodic Health Examination," by David Atkins; Chapter 16, "Immunization," by Walter A. Orenstein; Chapter 29, "Pain," by Mitchell B. Max; Chapter 34, "Complementary and Alternative Medicine," by Stephen E. Straus; Chapter 55, "Heart Failure: Pathophysiology and Diagnosis," by Barry M. Massie; Chapter 140, "Pancreatic Endocrine Tumors," by Robert T. Jensen; Chapter 198, "Lung Cancer and Other Pulmonary Neoplasms," by York E. Miller; Chapter 224, "Wilson's Disease," by Stephen G. Kaler; Chapter 257, "Mineral and Bone Homeostasis," by Stephen J. Marx; Chapter 260, "The Parathyroid Glands, Hypercalcemia, and Hypocalcemia," by Allen M. Spiegel; Chapter 272, "Mastocytosis," by Dean D. Metcalfe; Chapter 301, "Introduction to Bacterial Disease," by David A. Relman; Chapter 309, "Rheumatic Fever," by Alan L. Bisno; Chapter 314, "Infections Caused by *Haemophilus* Species," by Michael S. Simberkoff; Chapter 317, "Diphtheria," by Roland W. Sutter; Chapter 373, "Enteroviruses," by Michael N. Oxman; Chapter 374, "Viral Gastroenteritis," by Albert Z. Kapikian; Chapter 378, "Introduction to Mycoses," by Carol A. Kauffman; Chapter 379, "Histoplasmosis," by Carol A. Kauffman; Chapter 381, "Blastomycosis," by Carol A. Kauffman; Chapter 382, "Paracoccidioidomycosis," by Carol A. Kauffman; Chapter 383, "Cryptococcosis," by Carol A. Kauffman; Chapter 384, "Sporotrichosis," by Carol A. Kauffman; Chapter 385, "Candidiasis," by Carol A. Kauffman; Chapter 394, "American Trypanosomiasis (Chagas' Disease)," by Franklin A. Neva.

Notice

Medicine is an ever-changing field. Standard safety precautions must be followed, but as new research and clinical experience broaden our knowledge, changes in treatment and drug therapy become necessary or appropriate. Readers are advised to check the product information currently provided by the manufacturer of each drug to be administered to verify the recommended dose, the method and duration of administration, and contraindications. It is the responsibility of the treating physician, relying on experience and knowledge of the patient, to determine dosages and the best treatment for each individual patient. Neither the Publisher nor the editors assume any responsibility for any injury and/or damage to persons or property arising from this publication.

The Publisher

Library of Congress Cataloging-in-Publication Data

Cecil textbook of medicine / edited by Lee Goldman, Dennis Ausiello.—22nd ed.
    p. ; cm.
    Includes bibliographical references and index.
    ISBN 0–7216–9652–X
    1. Internal medicine.   I. Title: Textbook of medicine.   II. Cecil, Russell L. (Russell La Fayette), 1881–1965.   III. Goldman, Lee, MD.   IV. Ausiello, D. A.
    [DNLM: 1. Medicine. WB 100 C3888 2004]
RC46.C423 2004
616–dc21

2003044631

Executive Publisher, Global Medicine: Kim Murphy
Executive Director of Development: Lynne Gery
Publishing Services Manager: Frank Polizzano
Senior Project Manager: Robin E. Davis
Associate Developmental Editor: Joanie Milnes
Interior Design: Karen O'Keefe Owens

Printed in the United States of America.

Last digit is the print number: 9   8   7   6   5   4   3   2   1

Contributors

Nezam H. Afdhal, MD, FRCPI
Associate Professor of Medicine, Harvard Medical School; Director, Liver Center, Beth Israel Deaconess Medical Center, Boston, Massachusetts
Diseases of the Gallbladder and Bile Ducts

Masood Akhtar, MD
Clinical Professor of Medicine, University of Wisconsin Medical School, Milwaukee, Wisconsin
Cardiac Arrythmias with Supraventricular Origin

Robert H. Allen, MD
Professor of Medicine and Cleo Meador and George Ryland Scott Professor of Hematology Research, University of Colorado Health Sciences Center, Denver, Colorado
Megaloblastic Anemias

David Altshuler, MD, PhD
Assistant Professor of Genetics and Medicine, Harvard Medical School and Massachusetts General Hospital, Boston, Massachusetts; Director, Medical and Population Genetics, Whitehead Institute, MIT Center for Genome Research, Cambridge, Massachusetts
The Inherited Basis of Common Diseases

Michael J. Aminoff, MD, DSc
Professor of Neurology, University of California, San Francisco, School of Medicine, San Francisco, California
Approach to the Patient with Neurologic Disease; Mechanical and Other Lesions of the Spine, Nerve Roots, and Spinal Cord

Jeffrey L. Anderson, MD
Professor of Medicine, University of Utah School of Medicine; Associate Chief of Cardiology, LDS Hospital, Salt Lake City, Utah
ST-Elevation Acute Myocardial Infarction and Complications of Myocardial Infarction

Karl E. Anderson, MD
Professor of Preventive Medicine and Community Health, Medicine, and Pharmacology and Toxicology, University of Texas Medical Branch at Galveston, Galveston, Texas
The Porphyrias

Nicholas Anthonisen, MD, PhD
Professor Emeritus of Medicine, University of Manitoba, Winnipeg, Manitoba, Canada
Chronic Obstructive Pulmonary Disease

Michael A. Apicella, MD
Professor and Head, Department of Microbiology, University of Iowa, Iowa City, Iowa
Meningococcal Infections

Gerald B. Appel, MD
Professor of Clinical Medicine, Columbia University College of Physicians and Surgeons; Director of Clinical Nephrology, Presbyterian Division of the New York Presbyterian Hospital, New York, New York
Glomerular Disorders

Frederick R. Appelbaum, MD
Professor and Head, Division of Medical Oncology, University of Washington School of Medicine; Member and Director, Clinical Research Division, Fred Hutchinson Cancer Research Center, Seattle, Washington
The Acute Leukemias

Gordon L. Archer, MD
Professor of Medicine, Microbiology, and Immunology, and Chair, Division of Infectious Diseases, Department of Medicine, Virginia Commonwealth University School of Medicine, Richmond, Virginia
Staphylococcal Infections

William P. Arend, MD
Scoville Professor of Medicine, Department of Medicine; Director, Rheumatology Clinical Programs, University of Colorado School of Medicine, Denver, Colorado
Approach to the Patient with Rheumatic Disease

James O. Armitage, MD
Dean, University of Nebraska College of Medicine; Joe Shapiro Professor of Internal Medicine, University of Nebraska Medical Center, Omaha, Nebraska
Approach to the Patient with Lymphadenopathy and Splenomegaly; Non-Hodgkin's Lymphomas; Venomous Snake Bites

Cheryl Armstrong, MD
Associate Professor, Northwestern University Feinberg School of Medicine, Chicago, Illinois
Examination of the Skin and Approach to Diagnosing Skin Diseases

M. Amin Arnaout, MD
Professor of Medicine, Harvard Medical School; Chief, Nephrology Division, Massachusetts General Hospital, Boston, Massachusetts
Cystic Kidney Diseases

David Atkins, MD, MPH
Chief Medical Officer, Center for Outcomes and Evidence, Agency for Healthcare Research and Quality, Rockville, Maryland
The Periodic Health Examination

Dennis Ausiello, MD
Jackson Professor of Clinical Medicine, Harvard Medical School; Chief, Medical Service, Massachusetts General Hospital, Boston, Massachusetts
Approach to Medicine, the Patient, and the Medical Profession: Medicine as a Learned and Humane Profession

David E. Avrin, MD, PhD
Professor of Radiology and Chief, Abdominal Imaging, Department of Radiology, University of Utah, Salt Lake City, Utah
Applications and Limitations of Diagnostic Imaging

Bruce R. Bacon, MD
Professor of Internal Medicine and James F. King, MD Endowed Chair in Gastroenterology; Director, Division of Gastroenterology and Hepatology, Saint Louis University School of Medicine, St. Louis, Missouri
Iron Overload (Hemochromatosis)

Grover C. Bagby, Jr., MD
Professor of Medicine and Molecular and Medical Genetics; Director, Cancer Institute, Oregon Health and Science University, Portland, Oregon
Leukopenia and Leukocytosis

Robert W. Baloh, MD
Professor of Neurology and Head and Neck Surgery, University of California, Los Angeles, David Geffen School of Medicine, Los Angeles, California
Neuro-Ophthalmology; Smell and Taste; Hearing and Equilibrium

Alan F. Barker, MD
Professor of Medicine, Division of Pulmonary and Critical Care, Oregon Health and Science University, Portland, Oregon
Bronchiectasis and Localized Airway/Parenchymal Disorders

A. James Barkovich, MD
Professor of Radiology, Neurology, Pediatrics, and Neurosurgery and Chief, Pediatric Neuroradiology, University of California, San Francisco, San Francisco, California
Congenital, Developmental, and Neurocutaneous Disorders

Richard J. Barohn, MD
Professor and Chairman, Department of Neurology, University of Kansas Medical Center, Kansas City, Kansas
Approach to Muscle and Nerve Disease; Muscle Diseases

Murray G. Baron, MD
Professor of Radiology, Emory University School of Medicine, Atlanta, Georgia
Radiology of the Heart

Michael J. Barry, MD
Associate Professor of Medicine, Harvard Medical School; Chief, General Medicine Unit, Massachusetts General Hospital, Boston, Massachusetts
Benign Prostatic Hyperplasia and Prostatitis

Bruce A. Barshop, MD, PhD
Associate Professor, Department of Pediatrics, University of California, San Diego, School of Medicine, La Jolla, California
Homocystinuria

Robyn J. Barst, MD
Professor of Pediatrics, Columbia University College of Physicians and Surgeons; Attending Pediatrician, New York Presbyterian Hospital, New York, New York
Pulmonary Hypertension

John A. Bartlett, MD
Professor of Medicine, Duke University School of Medicine, Durham, North Carolina
Management and Counseling for Persons with HIV Infection

John G. Bartlett, MD
Professor of Medicine and Chief, Division of Infectious Diseases, Johns Hopkins University School of Medicine and Johns Hopkins Hospital, Baltimore, Maryland
Botulism; Tetanus; Gastrointestinal Manifestations of AIDS

Hasan Bazari, MD
Instructor in Medicine, Harvard Medical School; Assistant Chief, Department of Medicine, Massachusetts General Hospital, Boston, Massachusetts
Approach to the Patient with Renal Disease

George A. Beller, MD
Ruth C. Heede Professor of Cardiology, University of Virginia Health System; Chief, Cardiovascular Division and Co-Director, Heart Center, University of Virginia Medical Center, Charlottesville, Virginia
Nuclear Cardiology and Computed Tomography

John M. Bennett, MD
Professor Emeritus of Medicine, School of Medicine and Dentistry, University of Rochester Medical Center, Rochester, New York; Executive Officer, Southwest Oncology Group, San Antonio, Texas
The Peripheral Blood Smear

Robert M. Bennett, MD, FRCP
Professor of Medicine, Oregon Health and Science University, Portland, Oregon
Fibromyalgia

Neal L. Benowitz, MD
Professor of Medicine, Psychiatry, and Biopharmaceutical Sciences, University of California, San Francisco; Chief, Division of Clinical Pharmacology and Experimental Therapeutics, San Francisco General Hospital, San Francisco, California
Tobacco

Joseph R. Berger, MD
Professor and Chair, Department of Neurology, University of Kentucky College of Medicine, Lexington, Kentucky
Approach to Viral Infections of the Nervous System; Acute Viral Meningitis and Encephalitis; Poliomyelitis; The Herpesviruses; Rabies; Cytomegalovirus, Epstein-Barr Virus, and Slow Virus Infections of the Central Nervous System; Prion Diseases

Timothy Berger, MD
Professor of Clinical Dermatology and Executive Vice Chair, Department of Dermatology, University of California, San Francisco, San Francisco, California
Skin Disease in Patients with HIV Infection

Paul D. Berk, MD
Professor of Molecular, Cell, and Developmental Biology and Lillian and Henry M. Stratton Professor of Molecular Medicine; Emeritus Chief, Division of Liver Disease, Mount Sinai School of Medicine, New York, New York
Approach to the Patient with Jaundice or Abnormal Liver Tests

Joseph R. Bertino, MD
Professor of Medicine and Pharmacology, University of Medicine and Dentistry of New Jersey, Robert Wood Johnson Medical School; Associate Director, Cancer Institute of New Jersey, New Brunswick, New Jersey
Principles of Cancer Therapy

Bruce Beutler, MD
Professor of Immunology, The Scripps Research Institute, La Jolla, California
The Pathogenesis of Fever

Steven M. Beutler, MD
Associate Director, Division of Infectious Diseases, Arrowhead Regional Medical Center, Colton, California
The Pathogenesis of Fever

Philip J. Bierman, MD
Associate Professor of Medicine, Department of Internal Medicine, University of Nebraska Medical Center, Omaha, Nebraska
Non-Hodgkin's Lymphomas

J. Andrew Billings, MD
Associate Professor and Co-Director, Center for Palliative Care, Harvard Medical School; Director, Palliative Care Service, Massachusetts General Hospital, Boston, Massachusetts
Care of Dying Patients and Their Families

Alan L. Bisno, MD
Professor and Vice Chair, Department of Medicine, Department of Veterans Affairs Medical Center, Miami, Florida
Rheumatic Fever

Bruce R. Bistrian, MD, MPH, PhD
Professor of Medicine, Harvard Medical School; Chief, Clinical Nutrition, Beth Israel Deaconess Medical Center, Boston, Massachusetts
Nutritional Assessment

David J. Bjorkman, MD, MSPH/HSA, SM (Epi)
Professor of Medicine, Department of Internal Medicine, Division of Gastroenterology and Senior Associate Dean, University of Utah School of Medicine; Executive Medical Director, University of Utah Medical Group, University of Utah Health Sciences Center, Salt Lake City, Utah
Gastrointestinal Hemorrhage and Occult Gastrointestinal Bleeding

William A. Blattner, MD
Professor of Medicine; Associate Director, Institute of Human Virology and Director of the Division of Epidemiology and Prevention, University of Maryland Medical Biotechnology Center, Baltimore, Maryland
Retroviruses Other Than HIV

Thomas P. Bleck, MD
Louise Nerancy Eminent Scholar in Neurology and Professor of Neurology, Neurological Surgery, and Internal Medicine; Director, Neuroscience Intensive Care Unit, University of Virginia, Charlottesville, Virginia
Arthropod-Borne Viruses Affecting the Central Nervous System

William J. Blot, PhD
Professor, Vanderbilt University Medical Center, Nashville, Tennessee; Chief Executive Officer, International Epidemiology Institute, Rockville, Maryland
Epidemiology of Cancer

Henry M. Blumberg, MD
Professor of Medicine and Program Director, Division of Infectious Diseases, Emory University School of Medicine; Hospital Epidemiologist, Grady Memorial Hospital, Atlanta, Georgia
Anthrax

Jean Bolognia, MD
Professor, Department of Dermatology, Yale University School of Medicine, New Haven, Connecticut
Infections, Hyper- and Hypopigmentation, Regional Dermatology, and Distinctive Lesions in Black Skin

James R. Bonner, MD
Professor of Medicine, University of Alabama at Birmingham School of Medicine, Birmingham, Alabama
Drug Allergy

Dennis W. Boulware, MD
Professor of Medicine, University of Alabama at Birmingham School of Medicine, Birmingham, Alabama
Bursitis, Tendinitis, and Other Periarticular Disorders

Robert C. Bourge, MD
Professor of Medicine, Radiology, and Surgery, University of Alabama at Birmingham School of Medicine; Director, Division of Cardiovascular Disease; Head, Section of Advanced Heart Failure and Transplantation, University of Alabama at Birmingham Hospital, Birmingham, Alabama
Cardiac Transplantation

Laurence A. Boxer, MD
Professor and Director, Pediatric Hematology/Oncology, C. S. Mott Children's Hospital, University of Michigan Health System, Ann Arbor, Michigan
Disorders of Phagocyte Function

Randall Brand, MD
Associate Professor of Medicine, Evanston-Northwestern University Feinberg School of Medicine and Evanston-Northwestern Health Care, Evanston, Illinois
Pancreatic Cancer

Lawrence J. Brandt, MD
Professor of Medicine and Surgery, Albert Einstein College of Medicine; Chief of Gastroenterology, Montefiore Medical Center, Bronx, New York
Vascular Disorders of the Intestine

Barry D. Brause, MD
Clinical Professor of Medicine, Weill Medical College of Cornell University; New York Presbyterian, Cornell Medical Center, and the Hospital for Special Surgery, New York, New York
Osteomyelitis

William J. Britt, MD
Professor, Departments of Pediatrics, Microbiology, and Neurobiology, University of Alabama at Birmingham School of Medicine; Attending Physician, Children's Hospital of Alabama, Birmingham, Alabama
Infections Associated with Human Cytomegalovirus

Itzhak Brook, MSc, MD
Professor of Pediatrics, Georgetown University School of Medicine, Washington, D.C.; Attending Physician for Infectious Diseases, National Naval Medical Center, Bethesda, Maryland
Actinomycosis

Philip A. Brunell, MS, MD
Special Volunteer, Laboratory of Clinical Investigation, National Institute of Allergy and Infectious Diseases, National Institutes of Health, Bethesda, Maryland
Measles; Rubella (German Measles); Varicella (Chickenpox, Shingles)

Robert C. Brunham, MD
Professor, University of British Columbia; Consultant, Vancouver Hospital and Health Sciences Center, Vancouver, British Columbia, Canada
Diseases Caused by Chlamydiae

John C. M. Brust, MD
Professor of Clinical Neurology, Columbia University College of Physicians and Surgeons; Director, Department of Neurology, Harlem Hospital Center, New York, New York
Nutritional and Alcohol-Related Neurologic Disorders

Joseph A. Buckwalter, MS, MD
Professor and Chair, Orthopaedics, University of Iowa, Iowa City, Iowa
Surgical Treatment of Joint Diseases

Daniel Burkhoff, MD, PhD
Associate Professor of Medicine, Columbia University; New York Presbyterian, New York, New York
Cardiac Function and Circulatory Control

Thomas Butler, MD
Professor of Internal Medicine and of Microbiology and Immunology, Texas Tech University Health Sciences Center; Chief of Infectious Diseases, Texas Tech University Medical Center, Lubbock, Texas
Typhoid Fever; Shigellosis

Joel N. Buxbaum, MD
Professor and Director, Division of Rheumatology Research and W. M. Keck Autoimmune Disease Center, Scripps Research Institute, La Jolla, California
The Amyloidoses

Hugh Calkins, MD
Professor of Medicine and Director, Arrhythmia Service and Clinical Electrophysiology Laboratory, Division of Cardiology, Johns Hopkins University School of Medicine and Johns Hopkins Hospital, Baltimore, Maryland
Principles of Electrophysiology

Michael Camilleri, MD
Atherton and Winifred W. Bean Professor of Medicine and Physiology, Mayo Medical School and Foundation, Rochester, Minnesota
Disorders of Gastrointestinal Motility

Blase A. Carabello, MD
Professor of Medicine, Vice Chair, Department of Medicine, Veterans Affairs Medical Center, Houston, Texas
Valvular Heart Disease

Edgar M. Carvalho, MD, PhD
Full Professor of Internal Medicine and Clinical Immunology, Federal University of Bahia Medical School; Chief, Immunology Service, Hospital Universitário Professor Edgard Santos, Salvador, Bahia, Brazil
Schistosomiasis (Bilharziasis)

Hugo Castro-Malaspina, MD
Associate Professor of Medicine, Cornell University Medical College; Memorial Sloan-Kettering Cancer Center, New York, New York
Aplastic Anemia and Related Disorders

Stephen D. Cederbaum, MD
Professor of Psychiatry, Pediatrics, and Human Genetics, University of California, Los Angeles, David Geffen School of Medicine, Los Angeles, California
Disorders of Phenylalanine and Tyrosine Metabolism; Diseases of the Urea Cycle

Bartolome R. Celli, MD
Professor of Medicine, Tufts University; Chief of Pulmonary, Critical Care, and Sleep, Caritas–St. Elizabeth's Medical Center, Boston, Massachusetts
Diseases of the Diaphragm, Chest Wall, Pleura, and Mediastinum

Henry F. Chambers, MD
Professor of Medicine, University of California, San Francisco, School of Medicine; Chief of Infectious Diseases, San Francisco General Hospital, San Francisco, California
Infective Endocarditis

Russell W. Chesney, MD
Professor, Department of Pediatrics, University of Tennessee Health Science Center College of Medicine; Senior Vice President, Academic Affairs, LeBonheur Children's Medical Center, Memphis, Tennessee
Specific Renal Tubular Disorders

Dennis L. Cooper, MD
Professor of Medicine, Yale University School of Medicine, New Haven, Connecticut
Tumor Markers

Max D. Cooper, MD
Professor of Medicine, Pediatrics, Microbiology, and Pathology, University of Alabama at Birmingham; Investigator, Howard Hughes Medical Institute, Birmingham, Alabama
Diseases of the Thymus

Ralph Corey, MD
Professor of Medicine and Infectious Diseases, Duke University Clinical Research Institute, Durham, North Carolina
Venomous Snake Bites

Joseph E. Craft, MD
Professor of Medicine and Immunobiology, Yale University School of Medicine; Chief, Section of Rheumatology, Yale–New Haven Hospital, New Haven, Connecticut
Diagnostic Tests in Rheumatic Diseases

William A. Craig, MD
Professor of Medicine, Head, Section of Clinical Pharmacology, University of Wisconsin Medical School; W. S. Middleton Memorial Veterans Affairs Hospital, Madison, Wisconsin
Antibacterial Therapy

Michael H. Criqui, MD, MPH
Professor and Vice Chair, Department of Family and Preventive Medicine; Professor, Department of Medicine, University of California, San Diego, School of Medicine, La Jolla, California
Epidemiology of Cardiovascular Disease

Jeffrey L. Cummings, MD
Augustus S. Rose Professor of Neurology; Professor of Psychiatry and Biobehavioral Sciences, University of California, Los Angeles, David Geffen School of Medicine; Director, Alzheimer's Disease Center, University of California, Los Angeles, Medical Center, Los Angeles, California
Diagnosis of Regional Cerebral Dysfunction; Alzheimer's Disease and Other Disorders of Cognition

Charlotte Cunningham-Rundles, MD, PhD
Professor of Medicine, Pediatrics, and Immunobiology, Mount Sinai School of Medicine, New York, New York
Primary Immunodeficiency Diseases

David T. Curiel, MD, PhD
Director, Gene Therapy Center, University of Alabama at Birmingham, Birmingham, Alabama
Gene Therapy

F. Michael Cutrer, MD
Assistant Professor of Neurology, Mayo Clinic, Rochester, Minnesota
Headaches and Other Head Pain

David C. Dale, MD
Professor of Medicine, University of Washington School of Medicine, Seattle, Washington
The Febrile Patient

Troy E. Daniels, MS, DDS
Professor, University of California, San Francisco, Schools of Dentistry and Medicine, San Francisco, California
Diseases of the Mouth and Salivary Glands

Lisa M. DeAngelis, MD
Professor of Neurology, Weill Medical College of Cornell University; Chair, Department of Neurology, Memorial Sloan-Kettering Cancer Center, New York, New York
Tumors of the Central Nervous System and Intracranial Hypertension and Hypotension

Haile Debas, MD
Professor of Surgery and Dean, School of Medicine; Vice Chancellor, Medical Affairs, University of California, San Francisco, San Francisco, California
Peptic Ulcer Disease: Surgical Therapy

Leonard J. Deftos, MD, JD
Professor of Medicine, University of California, San Diego, School of Medicine, La Jolla, California; Physician, San Diego Veterans Affairs Medical Center, San Diego, California
Medullary Thyroid Carcinoma and Calcitonin

Anthony N. DeMaria, MD
Professor of Medicine, University of California, San Diego, School of Medicine, La Jolla, California; Chief, Division of Cardiology, University of California, San Diego, Medical Center, San Diego, California
Echocardiography

Robert H. Demling, MD
Professor of Surgery, Harvard Medical School; Director, Burn Center, Brigham and Women's Hospital, Boston, Massachusetts
Medical Aspects of Trauma and Burn Care

Anastacio de Queiroz-Sousa, MD
Professor of Medicine, Universidade Federal do Rio Grande do Norte; Secretary of Health, Ceara State, Fortaleza, Ceara, Brazil
Leishmaniasis

Richard D. deShazo, MD
Professor of Medicine and Pediatrics; Director, Division of Allergy and Immunology; Chair, Department of Medicine, University of Mississippi Medical Center, Jackson, Mississippi
Allergic Rhinosinusitis

Robert J. Desnick, MD, PhD
Professor of Human Genetics and Pediatrics, Mount Sinai School of Medicine, New York, New York
Lysosomal Storage Diseases

Lisa L. Dever, MD
Associate Professor of Medicine, University of Medicine and Dentistry of New Jersey, New Jersey Medical School, Newark, New Jersey; Staff Physician; Veterans Affairs New Jersey Health Care System, East Orange, New Jersey
Pneumonia Caused by Aerobic Gram-Negative Bacilli; Aspiration Pneumonia

Robert B. Diasio, MD
Professor of Pharmacology and Medicine and Chair, Department of Pharmacology and Toxicology; Director, Division of Clinical Pharmacology, University of Alabama at Birmingham School of Medicine; Associate Director of Basic Sciences, University of Alabama at Birmingham Comprehensive Cancer Center, Birmingham, Alabama
Principles of Drug Therapy

Anna Mae Diehl, MD
Professor of Medicine and Director of Hepatology, Gastroenterology Division, Johns Hopkins University School of Medicine and Johns Hopkins Hospital, Baltimore, Maryland
Alcoholic and Nonalcoholic Steatohepatitis

Wolfgang H. Dillmann, MD
Professor of Medicine, Division of Endocrinology and Metabolism, University of California, San Diego, School of Medicine, La Jolla, California
The Thyroid

Charles A. Dinarello, MD
Professor of Medicine, University of Colorado School of Medicine and University Hospital, Denver, Colorado
The Acute Phase Response

Jeffrey M. Drazen, MD
Professor of Medicine, Harvard Medical School; Editor-in-Chief, New England Journal of Medicine, Boston, Massachusetts
Asthma

Marc K. Drezner, MD
Professor of Medicine and Chief, Endocrinology, Diabetes, and Metabolism Section, University of Wisconsin, Madison, Wisconsin
Osteomalacia and Rickets

Raymond N. DuBois, MD, PhD
Professor of Medicine and Cancer Biology, Vanderbilt University Medical Center; Director of Gastroenterology, Vanderbilt University Hospital, Nashville, Tennessee
Neoplasms of the Large and Small Intestine

Thomas D. DuBose, Jr., MD
Professor and Chair, Department of Internal Medicine; Professor, Physiology and Pharmacology, Wake Forest University Health Sciences; Chief of Internal Medicine Service, North Carolina Baptist Hospital, Winston-Salem, North Carolina
Vascular Disorders of the Kidney

Thomas P. Duffy, MD
Professor of Medicine, Yale University School of Medicine, New Haven, Connecticut
Microcytic and Hypochromic Anemias; Nonhemolytic Normochromic, Normocytic Anemias

Herbert L. DuPont, MD
Clinical Professor and Vice Chair, Department of Medicine; H. Irving Schweppe, Jr., Chair and Vice Chair, Baylor College of Medicine; Mary W. Kelsey Chair, University of Texas–Houston; Director, Center for Infectious Diseases, University of Texas–Houston School of Public Health; Chief, Internal Medicine Service, St. Luke's Episcopal Hospital, Houston, Texas
Introduction to Enteric Infections

Madeleine Duvic, MD
Professor and Deputy Department Chair, Dermatology, University of Texas M. D. Anderson Cancer Center, Houston, Texas
Urticaria, Drug Hypersensitivity Rashes, Nodules and Tumors, and Atrophic Diseases

Paul H. Edelstein, MD
Professor of Pathology and Laboratory Medicine, University of Pennsylvania School of Medicine; Director, Clinical Microbiology Laboratory, University of Pennsylvania Medical Center, Philadelphia, Pennsylvania
Legionellosis

Lawrence H. Einhorn, MD
Distinguished Professor of Medicine, Indiana University, Indianapolis, Indiana
Testicular Cancer

Garabed Eknoyan, MD
Professor of Medicine, Department of Medicine, Renal Section, Baylor College of Medicine, Houston, Texas
Tubulointerstitial Diseases and Toxic Nephropathies

Ronald J. Elin, MD, PhD
A. J. Miller Professor and Chair, Department of Pathology and Laboratory Medicine, University of Louisville; Medical Director, Pathology and Laboratory Medicine, University of Louisville Hospital, Louisville, Kentucky
Reference Intervals and Laboratory Values

Diane L. Elliot, MD
Professor of Medicine, Division of Health Promotion and Sports Medicine, Oregon Health and Science University, Portland, Oregon
Pregnancy: Hypertension and Other Common Medical Problems

Louis J. Elsas II, MD
Professor of Pediatrics and Biochemistry and Director, Division of Medical Genetics, Department of Pediatrics, University of Miami School of Medicine; Director, Dr. John T. Macdonald Foundation Center for Medical Genetics, Miami, Florida
Inborn Errors of Metabolism; Galactosemia; Branched-Chain Aminoacidurias

Ezekiel J. Emanuel, MD, PhD
Chair, Department of Clinical Bioethics, Warren G. Magnuson Clinical Center, National Institutes of Health, Bethesda, Maryland
Bioethics in the Practice of Medicine

Stephen H. Embury, MD
Professor of Medicine, University of California, San Francisco; Director, Hematology Research Laboratory, San Francisco General Hospital, San Francisco, California
Sickle Cell Anemia and Associated Hemoglobinopathies

Andrew G. Engel, MD
McKnight-3M Professor of Neuroscience, Mayo Medical School, Mayo Clinic, Rochester, Minnesota
Disorders of Neuromuscular Transmission

Gregory F. Erickson, PhD
Professor of Medicine, University of California, San Diego, La Jolla, California
Ovaries and Development; Menstrual Cycle and Fertility

Luis R. Espinoza, MD
Professor and Chief, Section of Rheumatology, Department of Internal Medicine, Louisiana State University Health Sciences Center, New Orleans, Louisiana
Infectious Arthritis

Michael Fallon, MD
Associate Professor of Medicine, University of Alabama at Birmingham School of Medicine, Birmingham, Alabama
Hepatic Tumors

Barry M. Farr, MSc, MD
William S. Jordan, Jr. Professor of Medicine and Epidemiology, University of Virginia School of Medicine; Hospital Epidemiologist, University of Virginia Health System, Charlottesville, Virginia
Prevention and Control of Hospital-Acquired Infections

David P. Faxon, MD
Professor of Medicine and Chief of Cardiology, University of Chicago, Chicago, Illinois
Catheterization and Angiography

Aaron Fay, MD
Instructor in Ophthalmology, Harvard Medical School; Assistant in Ophthalmology, Massachusetts Eye and Ear Infirmary, Boston, Massachusetts
Diseases of the Visual System

Judith E. Feinberg, MD
Professor of Medicine, University of Cincinnati, Cincinnati, Ohio
Pneumocystis carinii *Pneumonia*

Eva L. Feldman, MD, PhD
Professor of Neurology, University of Michigan, Ann Arbor, Michigan
Hereditary Cerebellar Ataxias and Spastic Paraplegias; Amyotrophic Lateral Sclerosis and Other Motor Neuron Diseases

Sydney M. Finegold, MD
Professor of Medicine and of Microbiology, Immunology, and Molecular Genetics, University of California, Los Angeles, David Geffen School of Medicine, Los Angeles, California
Lung Abscess

Joel S. Finkelstein, MD
Associate Professor of Medicine, Harvard Medical School; Associate Physician, Massachusetts General Hospital, Boston, Massachusetts
Osteoporosis

Gary S. Firestein, MD
Professor of Medicine and Chief, Division of Rheumatology, Allergy, and Immunology, University of California, San Diego, School of Medicine, La Jolla, California
Mechanisms of Inflammation and Tissue Repair

Garret A. FitzGerald, MD
Robinette Foundation Professor of Cardiovascular Medicine, Chair, Department of Pharmacology, University of Pennsylvania School of Medicine, Philadelphia, Pennsylvania
Prostaglandins, Aspirin, and Related Compounds

Marsha D. Ford, MD
Clinical Professor of Emergency Medicine, University of North Carolina at Chapel Hill School of Medicine, Chapel Hill, North Carolina; Director, Carolinas Poison Center; Director, Division of Medical Toxicology, Department of Emergency Medicine, Carolinas Medical Center, Charlotte, North Carolina
Acute Poisoning

Jay W. Fox, PhD
Professor of Microbiology and Assistant Dean for Research, University of Virginia School of Medicine and Health System, Charlottesville, Virginia
Venoms and Poisons from Marine Organisms

Michael M. Frank, MD
Professor and Chair, Department of Pediatrics, Duke University Medical Center, Durham, North Carolina
Urticaria and Angioedema

David O. Freedman, MD
Professor of Medicine and Public Health, University of Alabama at Birmingham School of Medicine; Director, University of Alabama at Birmingham Travelers Health Clinic, Birmingham, Alabama
Filariasis

Victoria H. Freedman, PhD
Assistant Professor, Department of Microbiology and Immunology; Associate Director, Sue Golding Graduate Division, Albert Einstein College of Medicine, Bronx, New York
Leprosy (Hansen's Disease)

Linda P. Fried, MS, MPH
Professor of Medicine, Epidemiology, and Health Policy, Johns Hopkins University School of Medicine and Johns Hopkins Hospital, Baltimore, Maryland
Epidemiology of Aging: Implications of the Aging of Society

Scott L. Friedman, MD
Fishberg Professor of Medicine, Mount Sinai School of Medicine; Chief, Division of Liver Diseases, Mount Sinai Hospital, New York, New York
Cirrhosis and Its Sequelae

Valentin Fuster, MD, PhD
Richard Gorlin, MD Heart Research Foundation Professor of Cardiology, Mount Sinai School of Medicine; Director, Zena and Michael A. Wiener Cardiovascular Institute; Director, Marie-Josée and Henry R. Kravis Cardiovascular Health Center, Mount Sinai Medical Center, New York, New York
Atherosclerosis, Thrombosis, and Vascular Biology

Robert F. Gagel, MD
Professor and Head, Division of Internal Medicine, University of Texas M. D. Anderson Cancer Center, Houston, Texas
Endocrine Manifestations of Tumors: "Ectopic" Hormone Production; Medullary Thyroid Carcinoma and Calcitonin

John N. Galgiani, MD
Professor of Medicine and Director, Valley Fever Center of Excellence, University of Arizona; Program Director for Infectious Diseases, Southern Arizona Veterans Affairs Health Care System, Tucson, Arizona
Coccidioidomycosis

Jonathan D. Gates, MD
Assistant Professor of Surgery, Harvard Medical School; Vascular Surgeon and Director, Trauma Center, Brigham and Women's Hospital, Boston, Massachusetts
Medical Aspects of Trauma and Burn Care

Robert M. Genta, MD
Professor of Pathology, Chief of Anatomic Pathology, Division of Clinical Pathology, University of Geneva, Geneva Cantonal Hospital, Geneva, Switzerland; Adjunct Professor of Pathology and Medicine, Baylor College of Medicine, Houston, Texas
Gastritis and Helicobacter pylori

M. Eric Gershwin, MD
Professor of Medicine and Chief, Division of Rheumatology, Allergy, and Clinical Immunology, University of California, Davis, School of Medicine, Davis, California
Sjögren's Syndrome

Gordon N. Gill, MD
Professor of Medicine; Chair, Faculty of Basic Biomedical Sciences, University of California, San Diego, La Jolla, California
Principles of Endocrinology

D. Gary Gilliland, MD, PhD
Associate Professor of Medicine, Harvard Medical School; Associate Investigator, Howard Hughes Medical Institute; Physician, Brigham and Women's Hospital, Boston, Massachusetts
Myelodysplastic Syndrome

John W. Gnann, Jr., MD
Professor of Medicine, Pediatrics, and Microbiology, Division of Infectious Diseases, Department of Medicine, University of Alabama at Birmingham School of Medicine and the Birmingham Veterans Affairs Hospital, Birmingham, Alabama
Mumps

Nelson Goes, MD
Instructor in Medicine, Harvard Medical School; Assistant Physician, Massachusetts General Hospital, Boston, Massachusetts
Treatment of Irreversible Renal Failure

David E. Golan, MD, PhD
Professor of Medicine, Biological Chemistry, and Molecular Pharmacology; Co-Director, MD-PhD Program, Harvard Medical School; Physician, Brigham and Women's Hospital and Dana-Farber Cancer Institute, Boston, Massachusetts
Hemolytic Anemias: Red Cell Membrane and Metabolic Defects

Lee Goldman, MD
Julius R. Krevans Distinguished Professor and Chair, Department of Medicine; Associate Dean for Clinical Affairs, University of California, San Francisco, School of Medicine, San Francisco, California
Approach to Medicine, the Patient, and the Medical Profession: Medicine as a Learned and Humane Profession; Approach to the Patient with Possible Cardiovascular Disease

Nora Goldschlager, MD
Professor of Clinical Medicine, University of California, San Francisco, School of Medicine; Co-Director, Division of Cardiology and Director, Coronary Care Unit, ECG Laboratory and Pacemaker Clinic, San Francisco General Hospital, San Francisco, California
Electrocardiography

Ellie J. C. Goldstein, MD
Clinical Professor of Medicine, University of California, Los Angeles, David Geffen School of Medicine, Los Angeles, California; Director, R. M. Alden Research Laboratory, Santa Monica, California
Diseases Caused by Non–Spore-Forming Anaerobic Bacteria

Duncan A. Gordon, MD
Professor of Medicine, University of Toronto Faculty of Medicine; Senior Rheumatologist, Toronto Western Hospital, University Hospital Group, Toronto, Ontario, Canada
Approach to the Patient with Rheumatic Disease

Jörg J. Goronzy, MD, PhD
Professor of Medicine and Immunology, Mayo Medical and Graduate School, Rochester, Minnesota
The Innate and Adaptive Immune Systems

David Y. Graham, MD
Professor of Medicine and Molecular Virology and Microbiology, Baylor College of Medicine; Chief of Gastroenterology, Veterans Affairs Medical Center, Houston, Texas
Gastritis and Helicobacter pylori; *Peptic Ulcer Disease*

F. Anthony Greco, MD
Medical Director, Sarah Cannon Cancer Center, Nashville, Tennessee
Cancer of Unknown Primary Origin

Harry L. Greene, MD
Vice President and Medical Director, SlimFast Foods Company
Glycogen Storage Diseases; Fructose Intolerance

William B. Greenough III, MD
Professor of Medicine, School of Medicine; Professor of International
Health, Bloomberg School of Public Health, Johns Hopkins University;
Attending Physician, Johns Hopkins Bayview Medical Center, Baltimore,
Maryland
Cholera

Xylina Gregg, MD
Clinical Instructor, Baylor College of Medicine, Houston, Texas
*Hemoglobinopathies: Methemoglobinemias, Polycythemias,
and Unstable Hemoglobins*

Edward C. Grendys, Jr., MD
Associate Professor, University of South Florida School of Medicine, Tampa,
Florida
Pregnancy: Neoplastic Diseases

John W. Griffin, MD
Professor of Neuroscience and Pathology and Director, Department of
Neurology, Johns Hopkins University School of Medicine; Neurologist-in-
Chief, Johns Hopkins Hospital, Baltimore, Maryland
Peripheral Neuropathies

Robert C. Griggs, MD
Professor of Neurology, Medicine, Pathology and Laboratory Medicine, and
Pediatrics; Edward A. and Alma Vollersten Professor in Neurophysiology;
Chair, Department of Neurology, University of Rochester School of
Medicine and Dentistry, Rochester, New York
Approach to the Patient with Neurologic Disease; Neurogenetics

Jerome E. Groopman, MD
Professor of Medicine, Harvard Medical School; Chief, Division of
Experimental Medicine, Beth Israel Deaconess Medical Center, Boston,
Massachusetts
Hematology and Oncology in AIDS

Robert I. Grossman, MD
Louis Marx Professor and Chair, Department of Radiology; Professor of
Neurology, Neurosurgery, and Physiology and Neuroscience, New York
University School of Medicine, New York, New York
Radiologic Imaging Procedures

Lisa M. Guay-Woodford, MD
Pediatric Nephrologist, Professor of Medicine, and Director, Genetic and
Translational Medicine, University of Alabama at Birmingham,
Birmingham, Alabama
Anomalies of the Urinary Tract

Richard L. Guerrant, MD
Thomas H. Hunter Professor of International Medicine; Director, Center for
Global Health, Division of Infectious Diseases and International Health,
University of Virginia School of Medicine and Health System,
Charlottesville, Virginia
Campylobacter Enteritis; Enteric Escherichia coli Infections

John D. Hainsworth, MD
Director, Clinical Research, Sarah Cannon Cancer Center, Nashville,
Tennessee
Cancer of Unknown Primary Origin

William Hait, MD, PhD
Professor of Medicine and Pharmacology, University of Medicine and
Dentistry of New Jersey, Robert Wood Johnson Medical School; Director,
Cancer Institute of New Jersey, New Brunswick, New Jersey
Principles of Cancer Therapy

Judith Hall, MD
Professor, Departments of Pediatrics and Medical Genetics, University of
British Columbia, Vancouver, British Columbia, Canada
Single Gene and Chromosomal Disorders

Kenneth R. Hande, MD
Professor of Medicine and Pharmacology, Vanderbilt University School of
Medicine; Chief, Medical Oncology, Nashville Veterans Affairs Medical
Center, Nashville, Tennessee
Multiple-Organ Syndromes: Carcinoid Syndrome

H. Hunter Handsfield, MD
Professor of Medicine, University of Washington; Director, STD Control
Program, Public Health - Seattle & King County; Division of Infectious
Diseases, Harborview Medical Center, Seattle, Washington
Gonococcal Infections

Nancy Lee Harris, MD
Professor, Harvard Medical School; Austin L. Vickery, Jr. Professor of
Pathology and Editor, Case Records, Massachusetts General Hospital,
Boston, Massachusetts
Non-Hodgkin's Lymphomas

Raymond C. Harris, MD
Ann and Roscoe R. Robinson Professor of Medicine and Chief, Division of
Nephrology and Hypertension, Vanderbilt University School of Medicine,
Nashville, Tennessee
Diabetes and the Kidney

Frederick G. Hayden, MD
Professor of Internal Medicine and Pathology, Stuart S. Richardson
Professor of Clinical Virology, University of Virginia School of Medicine,
Charlottesville, Virginia
Influenza

Barton T. Haynes, MD
Frederic M. Hanes Professor of Medicine, Duke University School of
Medicine; Professor of Immunology, Duke University Human Vaccine
Institute, Durham, North Carolina
Diseases of the Thymus

Douglas C. Heimburger, MS, MD
Professor of Nutrition Sciences and Medicine, Schools of Medicine and
Health Related Professions, University of Alabama at Birmingham,
Director, Medical Nutrition Services, University of Alabama at
Birmingham Hospital and Birmingham Veterans Affairs Medical Center,
Birmingham, Alabama
Nutrition's Interface with Health and Disease

Akseli Hemminki, MD, PhD
Group Leader, Cancer Gene Therapy Group, Rational Drug Design
Program, University of Helsinki; Department of Oncology, Helsinki
University Central Hospital, Helsinki, Finland
Gene Therapy

J. Owen Hendley, MD
Professor of Pediatrics, University of Virginia School of Medicine,
Charlottesville, Virginia
The Common Cold

Janet B. Henrich, MD
Associate Professor of Medicine and Obstetrics and Gynecology, Yale
University School of Medicine, New Haven, Connecticut
Approach to Women's Health

Michael S. Hershfield, MD
Professor of Medicine and Biochemistry, Duke University School of
Medicine, Durham, North Carolina
Disorders of Purine and Pyrimidine Metabolism

William R. Hiatt, MD
Professor of Medicine, University of Colorado Health Sciences Center,
Denver, Colorado
Atherosclerotic Peripheral Arterial Disease

Richard E. Hillman, MD
Professor of Child Health, Biochemistry, and Pathology, University of
Missouri; Director of Metabolic Genetics, University of Missouri Hospital
and Clinics, Columbia, Missouri
Primary Hyperoxaluria

Jack Hirsh, CM, MD, DSc
Professor Emeritus, McMaster University, Hamilton, Ontario, Canada
Antithrombotic Therapy

Charles J. Hodge, MD
Professor and Chair, Department of Neurosurgery, Upstate Medical University, Syracuse, New York
Spinal Cord Injury; Head Injury

Craig J. Hoesley, MD
Assistant Professor of Medicine, Division of Infectious Diseases, University of Alabama at Birmingham School of Medicine, Birmingham, Alabama
Disease Caused by Bartonella *Species*

V. Michael Holers, MD
Professor of Medicine and Immunology and Head, Division of Rheumatology; Smyth Professor of Rheumatology, University of Colorado Health Sciences Center, Denver, Colorado
Complement in Health and Disease

David R. Holmes, MD
Professor of Medicine, Mayo Medical School; Consultant, Cardiovascular Disease, Mayo Clinic, Rochester, Minnesota
Cardiogenic Shock

Jay H. Hoofnagle, MD
Director, Division of Digestive Diseases and Nutrition, National Institute of Diabetes and Digestive and Kidney Diseases, National Institutes of Health, Bethesda, Maryland
Acute Viral Hepatitis; Chronic Hepatitis

Edward W. Hook III, MD
Professor of Medicine, Microbiology, and Epidemiology, University of Alabama at Birmingham School of Medicine; Medical Director, Sexually Transmitted Diseases Control Program, Jefferson County Department of Health, Birmingham, Alabama
Granuloma Inguinale (Donovanosis); Chancroid; Syphilis; Nonsyphilitic Treponematoses

Keith A. Hruska, MD
Professor of Pediatrics, Medicine, and Cell Biology, Washington University School of Medicine; Director, Pediatric Nephrology Division, St. Louis Children's Hospital, St. Louis, Missouri
Renal Calculi (Nephrolithiasis)

Laurence Huang, MD
Associate Professor of Medicine, University of California, San Francisco, School of Medicine; Medical Director, Inpatient AIDS Unit and AIDS Consultation Service and Chief, AIDS Chest Clinic, San Francisco General Hospital, San Francisco, California
Pulmonary Manifestations of HIV/AIDS

Leonard D. Hudson, MD
Professor of Medicine and Endowed Chair in Pulmonary Disease Research, University of Washington, Seattle, Washington
Acute Respiratory Failure

Molly A. Hughes, MD, PhD
Assistant Professor of Internal Medicine, Division of Infectious Diseases, University of Virginia Health Sciences System, Charlottesville, Virginia
Relapsing Fever

Russell D. Hull, MBBS, MSc
Professor of Medicine and Director, Thrombosis Research Unit, University of Calgary; Professor of Medicine, Foothills Hospital, Calgary, Alberta, Canada
Peripheral Venous Disease

Christopher D. Huston, MD
Assistant Professor of Medicine, University of Vermont College of Medicine; Fletcher Allen Healthcare, Burlington, Vermont
Leptospirosis

Robert D. Inman, MD
Professor of Medicine and Immunology, University of Toronto; Director, Arthritis Center of Excellence, Toronto Western Hospital, Toronto, Ontario, Canada
The Spondyloarthropathies

Sharon K. Inouye, MD, MPH
Professor of Medicine, Yale University School of Medicine, New Haven, Connecticut
Neuropsychiatric Aspects of Aging; Delirium and Other Mental Status Problems in the Older Patient

Michael D. Iseman, MD
Professor of Medicine, University of Colorado School of Medicine; Division of Pulmonary Sciences and Critical Care Medicine, University of Colorado Health Sciences Center, Denver, Colorado
Tuberculosis

Eric M. Isselbacher, MD
Assistant Professor of Medicine, Harvard Medical School; Medical Director, Thoracic Aortic Center, Massachusetts General Hospital, Boston, Massachusetts
Diseases of the Aorta

Mark A. Jacobson, MD
Professor of Medicine, University of California, San Francisco, School of Medicine; San Francisco General Hospital, San Francisco, California
Ophthalmologic Manifestations of AIDS

Frederick A. Jakobiec, MD
Department of Ophthalmology, Massachusetts Eye and Ear Infirmary, Boston, Massachusetts
Diseases of the Visual System

Joseph Jankovic, MD
Professor of Neurology and Director, Parkinson's Disease Center and Movement Disorders Clinic, Baylor College of Medicine, Houston, Texas
Extrapyramidal Disorders; Parkinsonism; Tremors, Tics, Myoclonus, and Stereotypies; Dystonias, Choreas, Athetosis, and Ballism

Michael D. Jensen, MD
Professor of Medicine, Mayo Clinic and Foundation, Rochester, Minnesota
Obesity

Robert T. Jensen, MD
Director, Digestive Diseases Branch, National Institute of Diabetes and Digestive and Kidney Diseases, National Institutes of Health, Bethesda, Maryland
Pancreatic Endocrine Tumors

Selma M. B. Jeronimo, MD, PhD
Professor of Biochemistry, Universidade Federal do Rio Grande do Norte, Natal, Rio Grande do Norte, Brazil
Leishmaniasis

Waldemar G. Johanson, Jr., MD, MPH
Professor Emeritus of Medicine, University of Medicine and Dentistry of New Jersey, New Jersey Medical School, Newark, New Jersey
Pneumonia Caused by Aerobic Gram-Negative Bacilli; Aspiration Pneumonia

Richard B. Johnston, Jr., MD
Professor of Pediatrics and Associate Dean for Research Development, University of Colorado School of Medicine, Denver, Colorado
Whooping Cough (Pertussis)

Keith A. Joiner, MD, MPH
Professor of Medicine, Yale University School of Medicine, New Haven, Connecticut
Introduction to Protozoan and Helminthic Diseases

Howard W. Jones III, MD
Professor of Obstetrics and Gynecology and Director, Gynecologic Oncology, Vanderbilt University School of Medicine, Nashville, Tennessee
Gynecologic Cancers

Nathalie Josso, MD
Investigator, École Normale Supérieure, Montrouge, France
Disorders of Sexual Differentiation

Ralph F. Józefowicz, MD
Professor of Neurology and Medicine and Associate Chair for Education, University of Rochester School of Medicine and Dentistry, Rochester, New York
Approach to the Patient with Neurologic Disease

Irmantas Juknevicius, MD
Assistant Professor of Medicine, Washington University School of Medicine, St. Louis, Missouri
Renal Calculi (Nephrolithiasis)

Stephen G. Kaler, MD, MPH
Clinical Director, Intramural Research Program and Head, Unit on Pediatric Genetics, National Institute of Child Health and Human Development, National Institutes of Health, Bethesda, Maryland; Children's National Medical Center, George Washington University School of Medicine, Washington, D.C.
Wilson's Disease

John A. Kanis, MD
Professor of Human Metabolism and Clinical Biochemistry, University of Sheffield Medical School, Sheffield, United Kingdom
Paget's Disease of Bone (Osteitis Deformans)

Hagop Kantarjian, MD
Professor and Chair, Leukemia Department, University of Texas M. D. Anderson Cancer Center, Houston, Texas
The Chronic Leukemias

Albert Z. Kapikian, MD
Head, Epidemiology Section, Laboratory of Infectious Diseases, National Institute of Allergy and Infectious Diseases, National Institutes of Health, Bethesda, Maryland
Viral Gastroenteritis

Gilla Kaplan, PhD
Full Member, Laboratory of Mycobacterial Immunity and Pathogenesis, Public Health Research Institute, Newark, New Jersey
Leprosy (Hansen's Disease)

David R. Karp, MD, PhD
Associate Professor of Internal Medicine and Chief, Rheumatic Diseases Division; Harold C. Simmons Chair of Arthritis Research, University of Texas Southwestern Medical Center at Dallas, Dallas, Texas
Complement in Health and Disease

Paul Katz, MD
Professor of Medicine, University of Miami School of Medicine, Miami, Florida; Vice President, Academic and Research Affairs and Chief Medical Officer, Mount Sinai Medical Center and Miami Heart Institute, Miami Beach, Florida
Glucocorticosteroids in Relation to Inflammatory Disease

Carol A. Kauffman, MD
Professor of Internal Medicine, University of Michigan Medical School; Chief, Infectious Diseases Section, Veterans Affairs Ann Arbor Healthcare System, Ann Arbor, Michigan
Introduction to the Mycoses; Histoplasmosis; Blastomycosis; Paracoccidioidomycosis; Cryptococcosis; Sporotrichosis; Candidiasis

Donald Kaye, MD
Professor of Medicine, Drexel University College of Medicine, Philadelphia, Pennsylvania
Salmonella *Infections Other Than Typhoid Fever*

Keith S. Kaye, MD, MPH
Assistant Professor of Medicine, Duke University School of Medicine; Hospital Epidemiologist, Duke University Medical Center, Durham, North Carolina
Salmonella *Infections Other Than Typhoid Fever*

James W. Kazura, MD
Professor, Center for Global Health and Diseases, Case Western Reserve University School of Medicine; Physician, University Hospitals of Cleveland, Cleveland, Ohio
Nematode Infections

Michael J. Keating, MBBS
Professor of Medicine, Department of Leukemia, University of Texas M. D. Anderson Cancer Center, Houston, Texas
The Chronic Leukemias

Emmet B. Keeffe, MD
Professor of Medicine, Stanford University School of Medicine; Chief of Hepatology and Co-Director, Liver Transplant Program, Stanford University Medical Center, Stanford, California
Hepatic Failure and Liver Transplantation

Craig M. Kessler, MD
Professor of Medicine and Pathology, Georgetown University School of Medicine; Chief, Division of Hematology-Oncology and Director, Division of Coagulation, Georgetown University Hospital, Washington, D.C.
Hemorrhagic Disorders: Coagulation Factor Deficiencies

Catarina I. Kiefe, MD, PhD
Professor of Medicine and Biostatistics and Director, Division of Preventive Medicine; Director, Center for Outcomes and Effectiveness Research and Education, University of Alabama at Birmingham; Director, Targeted Research Enhancement Program (TREP), Birmingham, Alabama
Applications of Statistics

Elliott D. Kieff, MD, PhD
Albee Professor of Medicine and of Microbiology and Molecular Genetics, Harvard University School of Medicine; Director, Infectious Disease, Brigham and Women's Hospital, Boston, Massachusetts
Infectious Mononucleosis: Epstein-Barr Virus Infection

Charles H. King, MS, MD
Associate Professor of International Health, Case Western Reserve University School of Medicine; Attending Physician, University Hospitals of Cleveland, Cleveland, Ohio
Cestode Infections

Beth D. Kirkpatrick, MD
Assistant Professor of Medicine, Unit of Infectious Diseases, University of Vermont College of Medicine, Burlington, Vermont
Cryptosporidiosis

Saulo Klahr, MD
John E. and Adaline Simon Professor of Medicine, Washington University School of Medicine; Physician, Barnes-Jewish Hospital of St. Louis, St. Louis, Missouri
Obstructive Uropathy

Samuel Klein, MD
William H. Danforth Professor of Medicine and Nutritional Science and Director, Center for Human Nutrition, Washington University School of Medicine, St. Louis, Missouri
Protein-Energy Malnutrition

Juha P. Kokko, MD, PhD
Professor of Medicine, Emory University School of Medicine, Atlanta, Georgia
Rhabdomyolysis; Fluids and Electrolytes

D. P. Kontoyiannis, MD, ScD
Assistant Professor of Medicine, Department of Infectious Diseases, Infection Control and Employee Health, University of Texas M. D. Anderson Cancer Center, Houston, Texas
Mycetoma

Bruce R. Korf, MD, PhD
Wayne H. and Sara Crews Finley Professor of Medical Genetics and Chair, Department of Genetics, University of Alabama at Birmingham School of Medicine, Birmingham, Alabama
Principles of Genetics: Overview of the Paradigm of Genetic Contribution to Health and Disease

Neil J. Korman, MD, PhD
Associate Professor, Case Western Reserve University; Attending Physician, University Hospitals of Cleveland, Cleveland, Ohio
Macular, Papular, Vesiculobullous, and Pustular Diseases

Donald J. Krogstad, MD
Henderson Professor and Chair, Department of Tropical Medicine; Director, Tulane Center for Infectious Diseases, School of Public Health and Tropical Medicine, Tulane University Health Sciences Center, New Orleans, Louisiana
Malaria

Henry M. Kronenberg, MD
Professor of Medicine, Harvard Medical School; Chief, Endocrine Unit, Massachusetts General Hospital, Boston, Massachusetts
Polyglandular Disorders

Ruben I. Kuzniecky, MD
Professor of Neurology, University of Alabama at Birmingham Medical Center, Birmingham, Alabama
Congenital, Developmental, and Neurocutaneous Disorders

Robert A. Kyle, MD
Professor of Medicine, Laboratory Medicine, and Pathology, Mayo Medical School; Consultant, Hematology and Laboratory Medicine, Mayo Clinic, Rochester, Minnesota
Plasma Cell Disorders

Philip J. Landrigan, MSc, MD
Ethel H. Wise Professor of Pediatrics and Chair, Department of Community and Preventive Medicine, Mount Sinai School of Medicine; Director, Collaborating Center in Environmental Epidemiology, World Health Organization, New York, New York
Principles of Occupational and Environmental Medicine

Nancy E. Lane, MD
Associate Professor of Medicine, University of California, San Francisco, School of Medicine; Co-Director, Rheumatology Outpatient Clinic, San Francisco General Hospital, San Francisco, California
Osteoarthritis

Thomas H. Lee, MSc, MD
Associate Professor of Medicine, Harvard Medical School; Chief Medical Officer, Partners Community Healthcare, Boston, Massachusetts
Interpretation of Data for Clinical Decisions

William M. Lee, MD
Meredith Mosle Distinguished Professor in Liver Disease, University of Texas Southwestern Medical Center at Dallas; Attending Physician, Parkland Memorial Hospital, Dallas, Texas
Toxic and Drug-Induced Liver Disease

Bruce B. Lerman, MD
H. Altschul Master Professor of Medicine, Cornell University Medical College; Chief, Division of Cardiology and Director, Cardiac Electrophysiology Laboratory, Cornell University Medical Center New York Presbyterian Hospital, New York, New York
Ventricular Arrhythmias and Sudden Death

Stuart Levin, MD, FACP
Ralph C. Brown, MD Professor of Medicine, Rush Medical College; Chair, Department of Internal Medicine, Rush-Presbyterian-St. Luke's Medical Center, Chicago, Illinois
Zoonoses

Lawrence M. Lichtenstein, MD, PhD
Professor of Medicine, Johns Hopkins University School of Medicine and Johns Hopkins Hospital, Baltimore, Maryland
Insect Sting Allergy

Oliver Liesenfeld, MD
Professor of Medical Microbiology and Immunology of Infection, Institute for Infection Medicine, Department of Medical Microbiology and Immunology of Infection, Benjamin Franklin Medical Center, Free University of Berlin, Berlin, Germany
Toxoplasmosis

Henry W. Lim, MD
Professor of Dermatology, Case Western Reserve University School of Medicine, Cleveland, Ohio; C. S. Livingood Chair, Department of Dermatology and Director, Academic Programs, Henry Ford Medical Group, Detroit, Michigan
Eczemas, Photodermatoses, Papulosquamous (Including Fungal) Diseases, and Figurative Erythemas

Aldo A. M. Lima, MD, PhD
Professor Titular, Universidade Federal do Ceará; Coordenador Geral da Unidade de Pesquisas Clínicas, Hospital Universitário Walter Cantídio, Fortaleza, Ceará, Brazil
Schistosomiasis (Bilharziasis)

Andrew H. Limper, MD
Professor of Medicine, Mayo Medical School; Director, Thoracic Diseases Research Unit, Mayo Clinic and Foundation, Rochester, Minnesota
Overview of Pneumonia

Karen L. Lindsay, MD
Associate Professor of Medicine, University of Southern California, Los Angeles, California
Acute Viral Hepatitis; Chronic Hepatitis

Edison T. Liu, MD
Professor, National University of Singapore; Executive Director, Genome Institute of Singapore, Singapore
Oncogenes and Suppressor Genes: Genetic Control of Cancer

Rogerio A. Lobo, MD
Professor of Obstetrics and Gynecology and Reproductive Medicine, Columbia University College of Physicians and Surgeons; Attending Physician, New York Presbyterian Hospital, New York, New York
Menopause

Richard F. Loeser, MD
Professor of Medicine (Rheumatology) and Biochemistry, Rush Medical College of Rush-Presbyterian-St. Luke's Medical Center, Chicago, Illinois
Connective Tissue Structure and Function

Bennett Lorber, MD, DSc (Hon)
Professor of Microbiology and Immunology and Thomas M. Durant Professor of Medicine, Temple University School of Medicine; Chief, Section of Infectious Diseases, Temple University Hospital, Philadelphia, Pennsylvania
Listeriosis

D. Lynn Loriaux, MD
Professor and Chair, Department of Medicine; Chief, Division of Endocrinology, Diabetes, and Clinical Nutrition, Oregon Health and Science University, Portland, Oregon
The Adrenal Cortex

John M. Luce, MD
Professor of Medicine and Anesthesia, University of California, San Francisco, School of Medicine; Associate Director, Medical and Surgical Intensive Care Units, San Francisco General Hospital, San Francisco, California
Approach to the Patient in a Critical Care Setting; Respiratory Monitoring in Critical Care; Ventilator Management in the Intensive Care Unit

Michael R. Lucey, MD
Professor of Medicine, University of Wisconsin–Madison Medical School; Chief, Section of Gastroenterology and Hepatology, Department of Medicine, University of Wisconsin–Madison Medical School Clinical Science Center, Madison, Wisconsin
Diseases of the Peritoneum, Mesentery, and Omentum

Robert G. Luke, MD
Chair, Department of Internal Medicine, University of Cincinnati College of Medicine; Physician-in-Chief, University Hospital, Cincinnati, Ohio
Chronic Renal Failure

Bruce W. Lytle, MD
Surgeon, Department of Thoracic and Cardiovascular Surgery, Cleveland Clinic Foundation, Cleveland, Ohio
Surgical Treatment of Coronary Artery Disease

Jacquelyn J. Maher, MD
Associate Professor of Medicine, University of California, San Francisco, School of Medicine; San Francisco General Hospital, San Francisco, California
Inherited, Infiltrative, and Metabolic Disorders Involving the Liver

Adel A. F. Mahmoud, MD, PhD
President, Merck Vaccines, Merck and Company, Incorporated, Whitehouse Station, New Jersey
Liver, Intestinal, and Lung Fluke Infections

Stephen E. Malawista, MD
Professor of Medicine, Yale University School of Medicine, New Haven, Connecticut
Lyme Disease

Hartmut H. Malluche, MD
Professor and Robert G. "Robin" Luke Chair in Nephrology, University of Kentucky, Lexington, Kentucky
Renal Osteodystrophy

Gerald L. Mandell, MD
Professor of Medicine and Owen R. Cheatham Professor of the Sciences, University of Virginia Health System, Charlottesville, Virginia
Introduction to Microbial Disease

Lionel Mandell, MD
Professor of Medicine and Chief, Division of Infectious Diseases, McMaster University and Hamilton Health Science Corporation Henderson Hospital, Hamilton, Ontario, Canada
Pneumococcal Pneumonia

Warren J. Manning, MD
Associate Professor of Medicine and Radiology, Harvard Medical School; Section Chief, Noninvasive Cardiac Imaging, Beth Israel Deaconess Medical Center, Boston, Massachusetts
Cardiovascular Magnetic Resonance Imaging; Pericardial Disease

Ariane J. Marelli, MD
Assistant Professor of Medicine, McGill University; Director, Adult Congenital Heart Disease Unit, McGill University Health Center, Montreal, Quebec, Canada
Congenital Heart Disease in Adults

George M. Martin, MD
Professor Emeritus of Pathology, University of Washington, Seattle, Washington
Biology of Aging

Manuel Martínez-Maldonado, MD
President and Dean, Ponce School of Medicine, Ponce, Puerto Rico
Hereditary Chronic Nephropathies: Glomerular Basement Membrane Diseases

Stephen J. Marx, MD
Chief, Metabolic Diseases Branch and Chief, Genetics and Endocrinology Section, National Institute of Diabetes and Digestive and Kidney Diseases, National Institutes of Health, Bethesda, Maryland
Mineral and Bone Homeostasis

Jay W. Mason, MD
Professor of Medicine, University of Utah, Salt Lake City, Utah; Professor of Medicine, University of Kentucky, Lexington, Kentucky; Medical Director, Covance Central Diagnostics, Reno, Nevada
Electrophysiologic Diagnostic Procedures

Joel B. Mason, MD
Associate Professor of Medicine and Nutrition, Tufts University; Director, Vitamins and Carcinogenesis Laboratory, United States Department of Agriculture Human Nutrition Research Center on Aging at Tufts University, Boston, Massachusetts
Consequences of Altered Micronutrient Status

Barry M. Massie, MD
Professor of Medicine, University of California, San Francisco, School of Medicine; Chief, Cardiology Division, San Francisco Veterans Affairs Medical Center, San Francisco, California
Heart Failure: Pathophysiology and Diagnosis

Henry Masur, MD
Chief, Critical Care Medicine Department, Clinical Center, National Institutes of Health, Bethesda, Maryland
Treatment of HIV Infection and AIDS

Mitchell B. Max, MD
Senior Investigator, Pain and Neurosensory Mechanisms Branch, National Institute of Dental and Craniofacial Research, National Institutes of Health, Bethesda, Maryland
Pain

Margaret M. McGovern, MD, PhD
Associate Professor of Human Genetics and Pediatrics, Mount Sinai School of Medicine, New York, New York
Lysosomal Storage Diseases

Elizabeth McLoughlin, ScD
Director of Programs, Trauma Foundation, San Francisco, California
Violence and Injury

M. Molly McMahon, MD
Associate Professor of Medicine, Mayo Medical School; Director of Clinical Nutrition, Division of Endocrinology, Diabetes, Metabolism, Nutrition, and Internal Medicine, Mayo Clinic, Rochester, Minnesota
Parenteral Nutrition

Mary McNaughton Collins, MD, MPH
Assistant Professor of Medicine, Harvard Medical School; Assistant Physician, Massachusetts General Hospital, Boston, Massachusetts
Benign Prostatic Hyperplasia and Prostatitis

Mario F. Mendez, MD, PhD
Professor of Neurology and Psychiatry and Biobehavioral Sciences, University of California, Los Angeles, David Geffen School of Medicine; Director, Neurobehavior Unit, Veterans Affairs Greater Los Angeles Healthcare Center, Los Angeles, California
Alzheimer's Disease and Other Disorders of Cognition

Jay E. Menitove, MD
Clinical Professor of Medicine, University of Missouri–Kansas City School of Medicine, Kansas City, Missouri, and University of Kansas School of Medicine, Kansas City, Kansas; Executive Director and Medical Director, Community Blood Center, Kansas City, Missouri
Transfusion Medicine

Steven J. Mentzer, MD
Associate Professor of Surgery, Harvard Medical School; Division of Thoracic Surgery, Brigham and Women's Hospital, Boston, Massachusetts
Surgical Approach to Lung Disease

Dean D. Metcalfe, MD
Chief, Laboratory of Allergic Diseases, National Institute of Allergy and Infectious Diseases, National Institutes of Health, Bethesda, Maryland
Mastocytosis

Frederick W. Miller, MD, PhD
Chief, Environmental Autoimmunity Group, Office of Clinical Research, National Institute of Environmental Health Sciences, National Institutes of Health, Bethesda, Maryland
Polymyositis and Dermatomyositis

York E. Miller, MD
Thomas L. Petty Professor of Lung Research, Division of Pulmonary
Sciences and Critical Care Medicine, Department of Medicine, University of
Colorado School of Medicine; Staff Physician, Denver Veterans Affairs
Medical Center; Leader, Tobacco-Related Malignancy Program, University
of Colorado Cancer Center, Denver, Colorado
Lung Cancer and Other Pulmonary Neoplasms

Kenneth L. Minaker, MD
Associate Professor of Medicine, Harvard Medical School; Chief, Geriatric
Medicine Unit, Massachusetts General Hospital, Boston, Massachusetts
Common Clinical Sequelae of Aging

Daniel R. Mishell, Jr., MD
Lyle G. McNeile Professor and Chair, Department of Obstetrics and
Gynecology, Keck School of Medicine, University of Southern California;
Chief of Women's Services, Los Angeles County and University of Southern
California Medical Center, Los Angeles, California
Contraception

William E. Mitch, MD
Edward Randall Distinguished Professor of Medicine and Chair,
Department of Medicine, University of Texas Medical Branch at
Galveston; Chair, Department of Medicine, John Sealy Hospital, Galveston,
Texas
Acute Renal Failure

Beverly S. Mitchell, MD
Professor of Medicine and Pharmacology and Wellcome Professor of
Cancer Research, University of North Carolina at Chapel Hill, Chapel Hill,
North Carolina
Disorders of Purine and Pyrimidine Metabolism

Mark E. Molitch, MD
Professor of Medicine, Division of Endocrinology, Metabolism, and
Molecular Medicine, Northwestern University Feinberg School of Medicine,
Chicago, Illinois
Neuroendocrinology and the Neuroendocrine System; Anterior Pituitary

Kelly L. Molpus, MD
Associate Professor and Director of Gynecologic Oncology; Vice Chair,
Department of Obstetrics and Gynecology, University of Nebraska Medical
Center, Omaha, Nebraska
Gynecologic Cancers

Marie-Claude Monier-Faugere, MD
Research Professor, Internal Medicine and Pathology, University of
Kentucky, Lexington, Kentucky
Renal Osteodystrophy

Fred Morady, MD
Professor of Medicine, University of Michigan; Director, Clinical
Electrophysiology Laboratory, University of Michigan Health System, Ann
Arbor, Michigan
Electrophysiologic Interventional Procedures and Surgery

J. Glenn Morris, Jr., MD, MPH&TM
Professor of Medicine (Infectious Diseases) and of Microbiology and
Immunology; Chair, Department of Epidemiology and Preventive Medicine,
University of Maryland School of Medicine, Baltimore, Maryland
Yersinia Infections

Michael A. Moskowitz, MD
Professor of Neurology, Harvard Medical School; Director, Stroke and
Neurovascular Regulation Laboratory, Massachusetts General Hospital,
Boston, Massachusetts
Headaches and Other Head Pain

Maurice A. Mufson, MD
Professor of Medicine and Chair Emeritus, Marshall University School of
Medicine, Huntington, West Virginia
Viral Pharyngitis, Laryngitis, Croup, and Bronchitis

Hyman B. Muss, MD
Professor of Medicine, University of Vermont College of Medicine and
Fletcher Allen Health Care, Burlington, Vermont
Breast Cancer and Differential Diagnosis of Benign Lesions

Stanley Naguwa, MD
Clinical Professor of Medicine, University of California, Davis, School of
Medicine, Davis, California
Sjögren's Syndrome

Stanley J. Naides, MD
Professor of Microbiology and Immunology, Penn State; Chief, Division of
Rheumatology, Milton S. Hershey Medical Center, Hershey, Pennsylvania
Arthropod-Borne Viruses Causing Fever and Rash Syndromes

Avindra Nath, MD
Professor, Department of Neurology, Johns Hopkins University School of
Medicine and Johns Hopkins Hospital, Baltimore, Maryland
*Approach to Viral Infections of the Nervous System; Acute Viral Meningitis
and Encephalitis; Poliomyelitis; The Herpesviruses; Rabies;
Cytomegalovirus, Epstein-Barr Virus, and Slow Virus Infections of the
Central Nervous System; Prion Diseases*

Heidi Nelson, MD
Professor of Surgery, Mayo Medical School; Chair, Division of Colon and
Rectal Surgery, Mayo Clinic, Rochester, Minnesota
Diseases of the Rectum and Anus

Jeffrey Nelson, MD
Associate Professor of Biology, North Park University; Associate Professor
of Medicine, Rush Medical College, Chicago, Illinois
Zoonoses

Brent A. Neuschwander-Tetri, MD
Associate Professor of Internal Medicine, Saint Louis University, St. Louis,
Missouri
Bacterial, Parasitic, Fungal, and Granulomatous Liver Diseases

Franklin A. Neva, MD
Head, Section on Opportunistic Parasitic Diseases, Laboratory of Parasitic
Diseases; Staff Member, Clinical Center, National Institutes of Health,
Bethesda, Maryland
American Trypanosomiasis (Chagas' Disease)

Maria I. New, MD
Harold and Percy Uris Professor of Pediatric Endocrinology and
Metabolism, Weill Medical College of Cornell University; Professor,
Department of Pediatrics, New York Presbyterian Hospital–Cornell Medical
Center, New York, New York
Disorders of Sexual Differentiation

Ragnar Norrby, MD, PhD
Director General, Swedish Institute for Infectious Disease Control,
Solna, Sweden
Urinary Tract Infections

David A. Norris, MD
Professor and Chair, Department of Dermatology, University of Colorado
Health Sciences Center, Denver, Colorado
Structure and Function of the Skin

John A. Oates, MD
Professor of Pharmacology and Thomas F. Frist, Sr. Professor of Medicine,
Vanderbilt University School of Medicine, Nashville, Tennessee
Multiple-Organ Syndromes: Carcinoid Syndrome

Albert Oberman, MD, MPH
Professor Emeritus, University of Alabama at Birmingham School of
Medicine, Birmingham, Alabama
Principles of Preventive Health Care

Daniel T. O'Connor, MD
Professor of Medicine, University of California, San Diego, School of
Medicine, La Jolla, California; Chief, Hypertension, Veterans Affairs San
Diego Healthcare System, San Diego, California
The Adrenal Medulla, Catecholamines, and Pheochromocytoma

Patrick G. O'Connor, MD, MPH
Professor of Medicine, Yale University School of Medicine; Chief, Section of
General Internal Medicine, Yale–New Haven Hospital, New Haven,
Connecticut
Alcohol Abuse and Dependence

James R. O'Dell, MD
Professor and Vice Chair of Internal Medicine and Chief, Rheumatology, University of Nebraska Medical Center and Omaha Veterans Affairs Hospital, Omaha, Nebraska
Rheumatoid Arthritis

Jeffrey W. Olin, DO
Professor of Medicine, Mount Sinai School of Medicine; Director, Vascular Medicine, Zena and Michael A. Wiener Cardiovascular Institute, Mount Sinai Medical Center, New York, New York
Other Peripheral Arterial Diseases

Gilbert S. Omenn, MD, PhD
Professor of Internal Medicine, Human Genetics, and Public Health, University of Michigan Medical School, Ann Arbor, Michigan
Cancer Prevention

Richard J. O'Reilly, MD
Professor of Pediatrics, Weill Medical College of Cornell University; Chair, Department of Pediatrics and Chief, Bone Marrow Transplantation Service, Memorial Sloan-Kettering Cancer Center, New York, New York
Aplastic Anemia and Related Disorders

Walter A. Orenstein, MD
Director, National Immunization Program, Centers for Disease Control and Prevention, Atlanta, Georgia
Immunization

Roy C. Orlando, MD
Professor of Medicine and Adjunct Professor of Physiology, Tulane University Medical School; Chief, Gastroenterology and Hepatology, Tulane University Health Sciences Center, New Orleans, Louisiana
Diseases of the Esophagus

Susan Orloff, MD
Associate Professor of Surgery, Oregon Health and Science University; Staff Surgeon, Portland Veterans Affairs Medical Center, Portland, Oregon
Peptic Ulcer Disease: Surgical Therapy

Joseph G. Ouslander, MD
Professor of Medicine and Director, Division of Geriatric Medicine and Gerontology, Emory University School of Medicine; Chief Medical Officer, Wesley Woods Center of Emory University, Atlanta, Georgia
Urinary Incontinence

Chung Owyang, MD
Professor of Internal Medicine; H. Marvin Pollard Collegiate Professor and Chief, Division of Gastroenterology, University of Michigan Medical Center, Ann Arbor, Michigan
Pancreatitis

Michael N. Oxman, MD
Professor of Medicine and Pathology, University of California, San Diego, School of Medicine, La Jolla, California; Staff Physician in Infectious Diseases, Veterans Affairs San Diego Healthcare System, San Diego, California
Enteroviruses

Milton Packer, MD
Dickinson W. Richards, Jr. Professor of Medicine and Chief, Division of Circulatory Physiology, Columbia University College of Physicians and Surgeons; Director, Heart Failure Center, Columbia-Presbyterian Medical Center, New York, New York
Heart Failure: Management and Prognosis

Stephen A. Paget, MD
Professor of Medicine, Weill Medical College of Cornell University; Physician-in-Chief and Chair of the Division of Rheumatology, Hospital for Special Surgery, New York, New York
Polymyalgia Rheumatica and Temporal Arteritis

Peter G. Pappas, MD
Professor of Medicine, Division of Infectious Diseases, University of Alabama at Birmingham School of Medicine, Birmingham, Alabama
Dematiaceous Fungal Infections

Joseph E. Parrillo, MD
Professor of Medicine, University of Medicine and Dentistry of New Jersey, Robert Wood Johnson Medical School; Head, Division of Cardiovascular and Critical Care Services, Cooper Health System, Camden, New Jersey
Approach to the Patient with Shock; Shock Syndromes Related to Sepsis

Pankaj Jay Pasricha, MD
Professor of Anatomy, Neurosciences, and Biomedical Engineering; Bassel and Frances Blanton Distinguished Professor in Internal Medicine; Chief, Division of Gastroenterology and Hepatology, University of Texas Medical Branch at Galveston, Galveston, Texas
Gastrointestinal Endoscopy

Steven Z. Pavletic, MD
Head, Graft-Versus-Host and Autoimmunity Unit, National Cancer Institute Experimental Transplantation and Immunology Branch, National Institutes of Health, Bethesda, Maryland
Hematopoietic Stem Cell Transplantation

Richard D. Pearson, MD
Professor of Medicine and Pathology, University of Virginia School of Medicine and Health System, Charlottesville, Virginia
Advice to Travelers; Leishmaniasis; Other Protozoan Diseases

Timothy A. Pedley, MD
Henry and Lucy Moses Professor of Neurology and Chair, Department of Neurology, Columbia University; Neurologist-in-Chief, Neurological Institute of New York, Columbia-Presbyterian Medical Center, New York, New York
The Epilepsies

William A. Petri, Jr., MD, PhD
Wade Hampton Frost Professor of Medicine and Chief, Division of Infectious Disease, University of Virginia School of Medicine and Health System, Charlottesville, Virginia
Relapsing Fever; Leptospirosis

James M. Phang, MD
Chief, Metabolism and Cancer Susceptibility Section, Basic Research Laboratory, National Cancer Institute at Frederick, National Institutes of Health, Frederick, Maryland
The Hyperprolinemias and Hydroxyprolinemia

Claude A. Piantadosi, MD
Professor of Medicine, Assistant Professor in Anesthesiology, Pulmonary and Critical Care Medicine, Duke University Medical Center, Durham, North Carolina
Physical, Chemical, and Aspiration Injuries of the Lung

Reuven Porat, MD
Associate Professor of Medicine, Sackler School of Medicine, Tel Aviv University; Director, Internal Medicine, Ichilov Hospital, Sourasky Medical Center, Tel Aviv, Israel
The Acute Phase Response

Carol S. Portlock, MD
Professor of Clinical Medicine, Weill Medical College of Cornell University; Memorial Sloan-Kettering Cancer Center, New York, New York
Hodgkin's Disease

Marshall Posner, MD
Associate Professor of Medicine, Harvard Medical School; Medical Director, Head and Neck Oncology Program, Dana-Farber Cancer Institute, Boston, Massachusetts
Head and Neck Cancer

Don W. Powell, MD
Professor of Internal Medicine, Professor of Physiology and Biophysics, Associate Dean for Research, University of Texas Medical Branch at Galveston, Galveston, Texas
Approach to the Patient with Gastrointestinal Disease; Approach to the Patient with Diarrhea and Malabsorption; Approach to the Patient with Liver Disease

Michael Pratt, MS, MD, MPH
Principal Investigator, World Health Organization Collaborating Center for Physical Activity and Health Promotion, Centers for Disease Control and Prevention Physical Activity and Health Branch, Atlanta, Georgia
Physical Activity

Josef T. Prchal, MD
Professor of Medicine, Cell Biology, and Pediatrics, Baylor College of Medicine, Houston, Texas
Hemoglobinopathies: Methemoglobinemias, Polycythemias, and Unstable Hemoglobins

Laurel C. Preheim, MD
Professor of Medicine, Medical Microbiology and Immunology, Creighton University School of Medicine, University of Nebraska College of Medicine; Chief, Infectious Diseases, Department of Veterans Affairs Medical Center, Omaha, Nebraska
Other Myobacterioses

Richard W. Price, MD
Professor of Neurology, University of California, San Francisco, School of Medicine; Chief, Neurology Service, San Francisco General Hospital, San Francisco, California
Neurologic Complications of HIV Type 1 Infection

Basil A. Pruitt, Jr., MD
Clinical Professor of Surgery, University of Texas Health Science Center at San Antonio, San Antonio, Texas; Professor of Surgery, Uniformed Services University of the Health Sciences, Bethesda, Maryland; Consultant Surgeon, U. S. Army Institute of Surgical Research, Fort Sam Houston, Texas
Electric Injury

Reed E. Pyeritz, MD, PhD
Professor of Medicine and Genetics, University of Pennsylvania School of Medicine; Chief, Division of Medical Genetics, Hospital of the University of Pennsylvania, Philadelphia, Pennsylvania
Inherited Diseases of Connective Tissue

Peter J. Quesenberry, MD
Professor of Medicine, Boston University School of Medicine, Boston, Massachusetts; Chair, Department of Research and Head, Center for Stem Cell Biology, Roger Williams Medical Center, Providence, Rhode Island
Hematopoiesis and Hematopoietic Growth Factors

Thomas C. Quinn, MSc, MD
Professor of Medicine, International Health, Epidemiology, and Molecular Microbiology and Immunology, Johns Hopkins University School of Medicine and Johns Hopkins Hospital, Baltimore, Maryland
African Trypanosomiasis (Sleeping Sickness); Epidemiology of HIV Infection and AIDS

S. Vincent Rajkumar, MD
Associate Professor of Medicine, Mayo Medical School; Consultant, Division of Hematology, Mayo Clinic, Rochester, Minnesota
Plasma Cell Disorders

Didier Raoult, MD, PhD
Full Professor of Medicine, Faculté de Médecine de Marseille, Université de la Méditerranée; Chief, Department of Clinical Microbiology, Hôpital de la Timone, Marseille, France
Rickettsioses

Jonathan I. Ravdin, MD
Nesbitt Professor and Chair, Department of Medicine, University of Minnesota Medical School, Minneapolis, Minnesota
Amebiasis

Robert W. Rebar, MD
Clinical Professor, Department of Obstetrics and Gynecology, University of Alabama at Birmingham School of Medicine; Executive Director, American Society for Reproductive Medicine, Birmingham, Alabama
Ovaries and Development; Menstrual Cycle and Fertility

Annette C. Reboli, MD
Professor of Medicine, University of Medicine and Dentistry of New Jersey, Robert Wood Johnson Medical School; Head, Infectious Diseases Division and Hospital Epidemiologist, Cooper Health System, Camden, New Jersey
Erysipeloid

John J. Reilly, Jr., MD
Associate Professor of Medicine, Harvard Medical School; Brigham and Women's Hospital, Boston, Massachusetts
Surgical Approach to Lung Disease

Michael F. Rein, MD
Professor of Medicine, Division of Infectious Diseases, University of Virginia School of Medicine; Medical Director, Sexually Transmitted Disease Clinic, Thomas Jefferson District Health Department, Charlottesville, Virginia
Introduction to Sexually Transmitted Diseases and Common Syndromes

David A. Relman, MD
Associate Professor of Medicine and of Microbiology and Immunology, Stanford University School of Medicine, Stanford, California; Chief, Infectious Diseases, Veterans Affairs Palo Alto Healthcare System, Palo Alto, California
Introduction to Bacterial Disease; Disease Caused by Bartonella *Species*

Steven M. Reppert, MD
Professor and Chair, Department of Neurobiology; Higgins Family Professor of Neuroscience, Program in Neuroscience, University of Massachusetts Medical School, Worcester, Massachusetts
Chronobiology (Circadian Rhythms)

Herbert Y. Reynolds, MD
Professor Emeritus, Department of Medicine, Pennsylvania State College of Medicine, Milton S. Hershey Medical Center, Hershey, Pennsylvania; Division of Lung Diseases, National Heart, Lung, and Blood Institute, National Institutes of Health, Bethesda, Maryland
Respiratory Structure and Function

Paul N. Reynolds, MBBS, PhD
Clinical Senior Lecturer, University of Adelaide; Senior Consultant Physician and Director of Basic Research, Department of Thoracic Medicine, Royal Adelaide Hospital, Adelaide, South Australia, Australia
Gene Therapy

Robert R. Rich, MD
Executive Associate Dean and Professor of Medicine and of Microbiology and Immunology, Emory University School of Medicine, Atlanta, Georgia
The Major Histocompatibility Complex and Disease Susceptibility

Roger S. Rittmaster, MD
Adjunct Professor of Physiology and Biophysics, Dalhousie University, Halifax, Nova Scotia, Canada
Hirsutism

Robert A. Rizza, MD
Professor of Medicine, Mayo Clinic and Foundation, Rochester, Minnesota
Hypoglycemia/Pancreatic Islet Cell Disorders

William O. Robertson, MD
Professor of Pediatrics, University of Washington School of Medicine; Medical Director, Washington Poison Center, Seattle, Washington
Chronic Poisoning: Trace Metals and Others

Alan G. Robinson, MD
Associate Vice Chancellor, Medical Sciences and Executive Associate Dean, University of California, Los Angeles, David Geffen School of Medicine, Los Angeles, California
Posterior Pituitary

Cheryl L. Rock, RD, PhD
Professor, Department of Family and Preventive Medicine, University of California, San Diego, School of Medicine, La Jolla, California
Nutrition in the Prevention and Treatment of Disease

Griffin P. Rodgers, MD
Chief, Molecular and Clinical Hematology Branch and Deputy Director,
National Institute of Diabetes and Digestive and Kidney Diseases, National
Institutes of Health, Bethesda, Maryland
Hemoglobinopathies: The Thalassemias

John L. Rombeau, MD
Professor of Surgery, University of Pennsylvania School of Medicine,
Philadelphia, Pennsylvania
Enteral Nutrition

Daniel I. Rosenthal, MD
Professor of Radiology, Harvard Medical School; Associate Radiologist-in-
Chief, Massachusetts General Hospital, Boston, Massachusetts
Bone Tumors

Michael C. Rowbotham, MD
Professor of Clinical Neurology and Anesthesia, Department of Neurology,
University of California, San Francisco, School of Medicine; Director,
University of California, San Francisco, Pain Clinical Research Center, San
Francisco, California
Specific Pain Syndromes

Robert H. Rubin, MD
Osborne Professor of Health Sciences and Technology and Professor of
Medicine, Harvard Medical School; Associate Director, Division of
Infectious Disease, Brigham and Women's Hospital, Boston, Massachusetts;
Director, Center for Experimental Pharmacology and Therapeutics,
Harvard–Massachusetts Institute of Technology Division of Health Sciences
and Technology, Cambridge, Massachusetts
The Compromised Host

Richard A. Rudick, MD
Professor of Neurology, Cleveland Clinic Lerner College of Medicine, Case
Western Reserve University; Chair, Division of Clinical Research and
Director, Mellen Center for Multiple Sclerosis Treatment and Research,
Cleveland Clinic Foundation, Cleveland, Ohio
*Multiple Sclerosis and Demyelinating Conditions of the Central
    Nervous System*

Hope S. Rugo, MD
Associate Clinical Professor of Medicine and Director, Breast Medical
Oncology Clinical Trials, University of California, San Francisco,
Comprehensive Cancer Center, San Francisco, California
Paraneoplastic Syndromes and Other Non-neoplastic Effects of Cancer

Anil K. Rustgi, MD
T. Grier Miller Associate Professor of Medicine and Genetics,
University of Pennsylvania School of Medicine, Philadelphia, Pennsylvania
Neoplasms of the Stomach

Michael S. Saag, MD
Professor of Medicine, University of Alabama at Birmingham School of
Medicine, Birmingham, Alabama
*Prevention of HIV Infection; Renal, Cardiac, Endocrine, and Rheumatologic
    Manifestations of HIV Infection*

R. Bradley Sack, MS, MD, ScD
Professor of International Health, Johns Hopkins University Bloomberg
School of Public Health; Director, International Travel Clinic, Johns
Hopkins Hospital, Baltimore, Maryland
The Diarrhea of Travelers

Robert A. Salata, MD
Professor of Medicine and Chief, Division of Infectious Diseases, Case
Western Reserve University; Attending Physician, University Hospitals of
Cleveland, Cleveland, Ohio
Brucellosis

Jane E. Salmon, MD
Professor of Medicine, Weill Medical College of Cornell University;
Attending Physician and Senior Scientist, Hospital for Special Surgery, New
York, New York
Mechanisms of Immune-Mediated Tissue Injury

Jeffrey H. Samet, MA, MD, MPH
Professor of Medicine and Public Health, Boston University Schools of
Medicine and Public Health; Chief, Section of General Internal Medicine,
Boston Medical Center, Boston, Massachusetts
Drug Abuse and Dependence

Jonathan M. Samet, MS, MD
Professor and Chair, Department of Epidemiology, Johns Hopkins
University Bloomberg School of Public Health, Baltimore, Maryland
Occupational Pulmonary Disorders

Clifford B. Saper, MD, PhD
James Jackson Putnam Professor of Neurology and Neuroscience, Harvard
Medical School; Neurologist-in-Chief, Beth Israel Deaconess Medical
Center, Boston, Massachusetts
Autonomic Disorders and Their Management

Fred R. Sattler, MD
Professor of Medicine, University of Southern California School of
Medicine; LAC-USC Medical Center, Los Angeles, California
Pneumocystis carinii Pneumonia

Paul E. Sax, MD
Assistant Professor of Medicine, Harvard Medical School; Clinical
Director, HIV Program and Division of Infectious Diseases, Brigham and
Women's Hospital, Boston, Massachusetts
Immunology Related to AIDS

David T. Scadden, MD
Associate Professor of Medicine, Harvard Medical School; Director, Center
for Regenerative Medicine and Technology and Co-Director, AIDS Research
Center, Massachusetts General Hospital, Boston, Massachusetts
Hematology and Oncology in AIDS

Andrew I. Schafer, MD
Frank Wister Thomas Professor of Medicine and Chair, Department
of Medicine, University of Pennsylvania School of Medicine,
Philadelphia, Pennsylvania
*Approach to the Patient with Bleeding and Thrombosis; Hemorrhagic
    Disorders: Disseminated Intravascular Coagulation, Liver Failure,
    and Vitamin K Deficiency; Thrombotic Disorders:
    Hypercoagulable States*

William Schaffner, MD
Professor of Medicine (Infectious Diseases); Professor and Chair,
Department of Preventive Medicine, Vanderbilt University School of
Medicine; Nashville, Tennessee
Tularemia

W. Michael Scheld, MD
Professor of Internal Medicine, Clinical Professor of Neurosurgery,
University of Virginia Health System, Charlottesville, Virginia
*Introduction to Microbial Disease; Typhoid Fever; Shigellosis; Introduction
    to HIV and Associated Disorders*

Thomas D. Schiano, MD
Associate Professor of Medicine, Mount Sinai School of Medicine;
Medical Director, Adult Liver Transplantation and Director, Clinical
Hepatology, Division of Liver Diseases, Mount Sinai Hospital, New York,
New York
Cirrhosis and Its Sequelae

R. B. Schiffer, MD
Haggerton Professor and Chair, Department of Neuropsychiatry and
Behavioral Science, Texas Tech University School of Medicine; Service
Chief, Neurology and Psychiatry, University Medical Center Hospital,
Lubbock, Texas
Psychiatric Disorders in Medical Practice

Stephen C. Schimpff, MD
Professor of Medicine and Interim Director, Greenebaum Cancer Center;
Executive Vice President, University of Maryland Medical Center,
Baltimore, Maryland
Diseases Caused by Pseudomonads

Frank V. Schiødt, MD
Assistant Professor of Gastroenterology, Rigshospitalet, Copenhagen, Denmark
Toxic and Drug-Induced Liver Disease

David Schlossberg, MD
Professor of Medicine, Temple University School of Medicine; Adjunct Professor of Medicine, Jefferson Medical College, Thomas Jefferson University, Philadelphia, Pennsylvania; Director, Medical Services, Merck and Company, Incorporated, North Wales, Pennsylvania
Mycoplasmal Infection; Arthropods and Leeches

Thomas J. Schnitzer, MD, PhD
Professor of Medicine and Assistant Dean for Clinical Research, Northwestern University Feinberg School of Medicine, Chicago, Illinois
Osteoarthritis

Alan D. Schreiber, MD
Professor of Medicine, University of Pennsylvania School of Medicine, Philadelphia, Pennsylvania
Autoimmune and Intravascular Hemolytic Anemias

Steven Schroeder, MD
Distinguished Professor of Health and Health Care, Department of Medicine; Director, Smoking Cessation Leadership Center, University of California, San Francisco, School of Medicine, San Francisco, California
Social and Economic Issues in Medicine

Lynn Schuchter, MD
Associate Professor of Medicine, University of Pennsylvania School of Medicine, Philadelphia, Pennsylvania
Melanoma and Nonmelanoma Skin Cancers

Peter H. Schur, MD
Professor of Medicine, Harvard Medical School; Senior Physician, Brigham and Women's Hospital, Boston, Massachusetts
Systemic Lupus Erythematosus

Lawrence B. Schwartz, MD, PhD
Charles and Evelyn Thomas Professor of Medicine, Virginia Commonwealth University School of Medicine, Richmond, Virginia
Systemic Anaphylaxis

Charles R. Scriver, MD, CM
Alva Professor of Human Genetics, Professor of Pediatrics and Biology, McGill University; Physician and Director (Retired), DeBeve Laboratory of Biochemical Genetics, Montreal Children's Hospital Research Institute, Montreal, Quebec, Canada
Disorders of Phenylalanine and Tyrosine Metabolism

Cynthia L. Sears, MD
Professor of Medicine, Divisions of Infectious Disease and Gastroenterology, Johns Hopkins University School of Medicine, Baltimore, Maryland
Cryptosporidiosis; Giardiasis

Margretta R. Seashore, MD
Professor of Genetics and Pediatrics, Yale University School of Medicine, New Haven, Connecticut
Genetic Risk Assessment

Julian L. Seifter, MD
Associate Professor of Medicine, Harvard Medical School; Physician, Renal Division, Brigham and Women's Hospital, Boston, Massachusetts
Acid-Base Disorders

Carol E. Semrad, MD
Associate Professor of Medicine, University of Chicago, Chicago, Illinois
Approach to the Patient with Diarrhea and Malabsorption

F. John Service, MDCM, PhD
McDonough Professor of Medicine, Mayo Medical School, Rochester, Minnesota
Hypoglycemia/Pancreatic Islet Cell Disorders

George M. Shaw, MD, PhD
Professor, Division of Hematology/Oncology, University of Alabama at Birmingham School of Medicine; Investigator, Howard Hughes Medical Institute, Birmingham, Alabama
Biology of Human Immunodeficiency Viruses

Steven A. Shea, PhD
Associate Professor of Medicine, Harvard Medical School; Associate Director, Sleep Disorders Program, Division of Sleep Medicine, Brigham and Women's Hospital, Boston, Massachusetts
Disorders of Ventilatory Control

Robert S. Sherwin, MD
C. N. H. Long Professor of Medicine, Section of Endocrinology, Department of Internal Medicine, Yale University School of Medicine, New Haven, Connecticut
Diabetes Mellitus

Robert E. Shope, MD
Professor of Pathology, University of Texas Medical Branch at Galveston, Galveston, Texas
Introduction to Hemorrhagic Fever Viruses

Jonas A. Shulman, MD
Professor of Medicine, Division of Infectious Diseases; Executive Associate Dean of Medical Education and Student Affairs, Emory University School of Medicine, Atlanta, Georgia
Anthrax

Marc Shuman, MD
Professor of Medicine, University of California, San Francisco, School of Medicine; Co-Chief, Division of Hematology-Oncology, Moffitt and Long Hospitals, San Francisco, California
Hemorrhagic Disorders: Abnormalities of Platelet and Vascular Function

Wilmer L. Sibbitt, Jr., MD
Professor of Internal Medicine, Division of Rheumatology, University of New Mexico Health Sciences Center School of Medicine, Albuquerque, New Mexico
Idiopathic Multifocal Fibrosclerosis

Michael S. Simberkoff, MD
Associate Professor of Medicine and Assistant Dean for Veterans Affairs, New York University School of Medicine; Chief of Staff, Veterans Affairs New York Harbor Healthcare System, New York, New York
Infections Caused by Haemophilus *Species*

David L. Simel, MD, MHS
Professor of Medicine, Duke University School of Medicine; Associate Chief of Staff for Ambulatory Care, Durham Veterans Affairs Medical Center, Durham, North Carolina
Approach to the Patient: History and Physical Examination

Roger P. Simon, MD
Adjunct Professor of Neurology, Physiology, and Pharmacology, Oregon Health and Science University School of Medicine; Robert Stowe Dow Chair of Neurology and Director, Dow Neurobiology Laboratories, Legacy Research, Portland, Oregon
Syncope; Coma and Disorders of Arousal; Persistent Vegetative States and Brain Death; Disorders of Sleep and Arousal; Parameningeal Infections

Arthur S. Slutsky, MD
Professor of Medicine, Surgery, and Biomedical Engineering, Director, Interdepartment Division of Critical Care, University of Toronto; Vice President (Research), St. Michael's Hospital, Toronto, Ontario, Canada
Acute Respiratory Failure

Eric J. Small, MD
Professor of Medicine and Urology, University of California, San Francisco, School of Medicine; San Francisco, California
Prostate Cancer

Delia Smith West, PhD
Professor of Public Health, College of Public Health, University of Arkansas Medical Sciences, Little Rock, Arkansas
The Eating Disorders

P. Frederick Sparling, MD
Professor and Chair, Department of Medicine, University of North Carolina School of Medicine, Chapel Hill, North Carolina
Gonococcal Infections

Stephen A. Spector, MD
Professor and Vice Chair, Department of Pediatrics; Member, Center for Molecular Genetics and Center for AIDS Research; Chief, Division of Infectious Diseases, University of California, San Diego, School of Medicine, La Jolla, California
HIV in Pregnancy

Allen M. Spiegel, MD
Director, National Institute of Diabetes and Digestive and Kidney Diseases, National Institutes of Health, Bethesda, Maryland
The Parathyroid Glands, Hypercalcemia, and Hypocalcemia

Sally P. Stabler, MD
Professor of Medicine, Division of Hematology, University of Colorado Health Sciences Center, Denver, Colorado
Megaloblastic Anemias

Daniel Steinberg, MD, PhD
Research Professor, Department of Medicine, University of California, San Diego, School of Medicine, La Jolla, California
The Hyperlipoproteinemias

Theodore Steiner, MD
Assistant Professor of Medicine, Division of Infectious Diseases, University of British Columbia, Vancouver, British Columbia, Canada
Pseudomembranous Colitis

William F. Stenson, MD
Professor of Medicine, Washington University School of Medicine, St. Louis, Missouri
Inflammatory Bowel Disease

David A. Stevens, MD
Professor of Medicine, Stanford University School of Medicine, Stanford, California; Chief, Division of Infectious Diseases, Santa Clara Valley Medical Center, San Jose, California
Aspergillosis; Mucormycosis

Dennis L. Stevens, MD, PhD
Professor of Medicine, University of Washington School of Medicine, Seattle, Washington; Chief, Infectious Disease Section, Veterans Affairs Medical Center, Boise, Idaho
Streptococcal Infections; Clostridial Myonecrosis and Other Clostridial Diseases

John H. Stone, MD, MPH
Associate Professor of Medicine and Director, Johns Hopkins Vasculitis Center, Division of Rheumatology, Johns Hopkins University School of Medicine, Baltimore, Maryland
The Systemic Vasculitides

Stephen E. Straus, MD
Director, National Center for Complementary and Alternative Medicine, National Institutes of Health, Bethesda, Maryland
Complementary and Alternative Medicine

Kingman P. Strohl, MD
Professor of Medicine, Case Western Reserve University School of Medicine; Director, Center for Sleep Disorders Research, Louis Stokes Cleveland Veterans Affairs Medical Center, Cleveland, Ohio
Obstructive Sleep Apnea-Hypopnea Syndrome; Upper Airway Diseases

Wadi N. Suki, MD
Clinical Professor of Medicine, Baylor College of Medicine; Senior Physician, Kidney Institute, Houston, Texas
Phosphorus Deficiency and Hypophosphatemia; Disorders of Magnesium Metabolism

Maria J. Sunseri, MD
Sleep Disorders Center, Pittsburgh, Pennsylvania
Disorders of Sleep and Arousal

Roland W. Sutter, MD, MPH&TM
Medical Officer, Vaccines and Biologicals Department, World Health Organization, Geneva, Switzerland
Diphtheria

Morton N. Swartz, MD
Professor of Medicine, Harvard Medical School; Chief, Jackson Firm, Department of Medicine, Massachusetts General Hospital, Boston, Massachusetts
Bacterial Meningitis

Ronald S. Swerdloff, MD
Professor of Medicine, University of California, Los Angeles, David Geffen School of Medicine, Los Angeles, California; Chief, Division of Endocrinology, Harbor–University of California, Los Angeles Medical Center, Torrance, California
The Testis and Male Sexual Function

Nicholas J. Talley, MD, PhD
Professor of Medicine, Mayo Medical School, Rochester, Minnesota
Functional Gastrointestinal Disorders: Irritable Bowel Syndrome, Nonulcer Dyspepsia, and Noncardiac Chest Pain

Victor Tapson, MD
Associate Professor of Medicine, Duke University School of Medicine, Durham, North Carolina
Pulmonary Embolism

Ayalew Tefferi, MD
Professor of Medicine and Hematology, Mayo Medical School and Mayo Clinic, Rochester, Minnesota
Polycythemia Vera and Related Disorders; Chronic Myeloproliferative Disorders: Essential Thrombocythemia and Myelofibrosis with Myeloid Metaplasia

Paul S. Teirstein, MD
Associate Clinical Professor, University of California, San Diego, School of Medicine; Director of Interventional Cardiology, Scripps Clinic, La Jolla, California
Percutaneous Coronary Interventions

Margaret Tempero, MD
Professor and Chief, Medical Oncology, University of California, San Francisco, School of Medicine; Deputy Director, University of California, San Francisco, Comprehensive Cancer Center, San Francisco, California
Pancreatic Cancer

Robert Terkeltaub, MD
Professor of Medicine, University of California, San Diego, School of Medicine, La Jolla, California; Chief, Rheumatology Section, Veterans Affairs Medical Center, San Diego, California
Crystal Deposition Diseases

Pierre Théroux, MD
Professor of Medicine, University of Montreal; Cardiologist, Montreal Heart Institute, Montreal, Quebec, Canada
Angina Pectoris

Charles Thornton, MD
Associate Professor of Neurology, University of Rochester School of Medicine and Dentistry; Neurologist, Strong Memorial Hospital, Rochester, New York
Neurogenetics

C. Craig Tisher, MD
Professor of Medicine and Pathology, Folke H. Peterson Dean's Distinguished Professorship, Dean, University of Florida College of Medicine; Attending Physician, Shands Hospital, Gainesville, Florida
Structure and Function of the Kidneys

Galen B. Toews, MD
Professor of Internal Medicine, University of Michigan Medical School;
Chief, Division of Pulmonary and Critical Care Medicine, University of
Michigan Health System, Ann Arbor, Michigan
Interstitial Lung Disease

Nina E. Tolkoff-Rubin, MD
Associate Professor of Medicine, Harvard Medical School; Medical Director,
Dialysis Services; Medical Director, Renal Transplantation; Director, End
Stage Renal Disease Program; Chief, Hemodialysis and Continuous
Ambulatory Peritoneal Dialysis, Massachusetts General Hospital, Boston,
Massachusetts
Treatment of Irreversible Renal Failure; The Compromised Host

John J. Treanor, MD
Associate Professor of Medicine and of Microbiology and Immunology,
University of Rochester School of Medicine and Dentistry,
Rochester, New York
Adenovirus Diseases

Gerard M. Turino, MD
John H. Keating, Sr. Professor Emeritus of Medicine, Columbia
University College of Physicians and Surgeons; Director, James P. Mara
Center for Lung Disease, St. Luke's-Roosevelt Hospital, New York,
New York
Approach to the Patient with Respiratory Disease

Arthur C. Upton, MD
Clinical Professor of Environmental and Community Medicine,
University of Medicine and Dentistry of New Jersey, Robert Wood
Johnson Medical School, Piscataway, New Jersey; Professor Emeritus,
Department of Environmental Medicine, New York University Medical
School, New York, New York
Radiation Injury

Ronald Victor, MD
Professor of Internal Medicine and Chief, Hypertension Division,
University of Texas Southwestern Medical Center, Dallas, Texas
Arterial Hypertension

Nicholas J. Vogelzang, MD
Fred C. Buffett Professor of Genitourinary Oncology and Director, Cancer
Research Center, University of Chicago, Chicago, Illinois
Tumors of the Kidney, Bladder, Ureters, and Renal Pelvis

Julie M. Vose, MD
Professor of Internal Medicine, University of Nebraska Medical Center,
Omaha, Nebraska
Hematopoietic Stem Cell Transplantation

Bruce D. Walker, MD
Professor of Medicine, Director, Division of AIDS, Harvard Medical School;
Director, Partners AIDS Research Center, Massachusetts General Hospital,
Boston, Massachusetts
Immunology Related to AIDS

Richard J. Wallace, Jr., MD
John Chapman Professor and Chair, Department of Microbiology,
University of Texas Health Center, Tyler, Texas
Nocardiosis

Edward E. Walsh, MD
Professor of Medicine, University of Rochester School of Medicine and
Dentistry; Rochester General Hospital, Rochester, New York
Respiratory Syncytial Virus; Parainfluenza Viral Disease

Christina Wang, MD
Professor of Medicine, University of California, Los Angeles, David Geffen
School of Medicine, Los Angeles, California; Physician Specialist,
Harbor–University of California, Los Angeles Medical Center, Torrance,
California
The Testis and Male Sexual Function

Lynne Warner Stevenson, MD
Associate Professor of Medicine, Harvard Medical School; Co-Director,
Cardiomyopathy and Heart Failure Program, Brigham and Women's
Hospital, Boston, Massachusetts
Diseases of the Myocardium

Stephen I. Wasserman, MD
Professor of Medicine and Head, Section of Allergy and Immunology,
Division of Rheumatology, Allergy, and Immunology, Department of
Medicine, University of California, San Diego, School of Medicine,
La Jolla, California
Approach to the Patient with Allergic or Immunologic Disease

David D. Waters, MD
Professor of Medicine, University of California, San Francisco,
School of Medicine; Chief of Cardiology, San Francisco General Hospital,
San Francisco, California
*Acute Coronary Syndrome: Unstable Angina and Non–ST Segment
Elevation Myocardial Infarction*

Steven E. Weinberger, MD
Professor of Medicine and Faculty Associate Dean for Education, Harvard
Medical School; Executive Vice Chair, Department of Medicine, Beth Israel
Deaconess Medical Center, Boston, Massachusetts
Sarcoidosis

Myron L. Weisfeldt, MD
William Osler Professor of Medicine and Director, Department of Medicine,
Johns Hopkins University School of Medicine; Physician-in-Chief, Johns
Hopkins Hospital, Baltimore, Maryland
Cardiac Function and Circulatory Control

Peter F. Weller, MD
Professor of Medicine, Harvard Medical School; Chief, Allergy and
Inflammation Division; Co-Chief, Infectious Diseases Division, Department
of Medicine, Beth Israel Deaconess Medical Center, Boston, Massachusetts
Eosinophilic Syndromes

Michael J. Welsh, MD
Professor of Medicine, University of Iowa Roy J. and Lucille A. Carver
College of Medicine; Investigator, Howard Hughes Medical Institute,
University of Iowa Health Care, Iowa City, Iowa
Cystic Fibrosis

Victoria P. Werth, MD
Associate Professor of Dermatology and Medicine, University of
Pennsylvania School of Medicine; Chief, Division of Dermatology,
Philadelphia Veterans Affairs Hospital, Philadelphia, Pennsylvania
Principles of Therapy

Sterling G. West, MD
Professor of Medicine, University of Colorado Health Sciences Center,
Denver, Colorado
Systemic Diseases in Which Arthritis Is a Feature

Cornelia M. Weyand, MD, PhD
Barbara Woodward Lips Professor of Medicine and Immunology, Mayo
Medical and Graduate School, Rochester, Minnesota
The Innate and Adaptive Immune Systems

David P. White, MD
Associate Professor of Medicine, Harvard Medical School; Associate
Director, Division of Sleep Medicine, Brigham and Women's Hospital,
Boston, Massachusetts
Disorders of Ventilatory Control

Richard J. Whitley, MD
Professor of Pediatrics, Microbiology, Medicine, and Neurosurgery,
University of Alabama at Birmingham School of Medicine,
Birmingham, Alabama
*Introduction to Viral Diseases; Antiviral Therapy (Non–AIDS); Herpes
Simplex Virus Infections*

Michael P. Whyte, MD
Professor of Medicine, Pediatrics, and Genetics, Division of Bone and Mineral Diseases, Washington University School of Medicine at Barnes-Jewish Hospital; Medical-Scientific Director, Center for Metabolic Bone Disease and Molecular Research, Shriners Hospitals for Children, St. Louis, Missouri
Osteonecrosis, Osteosclerosis/Hyperostosis, and Other Disorders of Bone

Fredrick M. Wigley, MD
Professor of Medicine, Johns Hopkins University School of Medicine and Johns Hopkins Hospital, Baltimore, Maryland
Scleroderma (Systemic Sclerosis)

C. Mel Wilcox, MD
Professor of Medicine, Director, Division of Gastroenterology and Hepatology, University of Alabama at Birmingham School of Medicine; Chief of Endoscopy, University of Alabama at Birmingham Hospital, Birmingham, Alabama
Appendicitis, Diverticulitis, and Miscellaneous Intestinal Inflammatory Conditions

Gerhard R. Wittich, MD
Professor of Radiology, University of Texas Medical Branch at Galveston, Galveston, Texas; Chair, Department of Radiology, Bayshore Medical Center, Pasadena, Texas
Diagnostic Imaging Procedures in Gastroenterology

Joseph L. Witzum, MD
Professor of Medicine, Division of Endocrinology and Metabolism; Director, Specialized Center of Research in Molecular Medicine and Atherosclerosis, University of California, San Diego, School of Medicine, La Jolla, California
The Hyperlipoproteinemias

Raymond L. Woosley, MD, PhD
Professor of Medicine and Pharmacology and Vice President for Health Sciences, University of Arizona Health Sciences Center, Tucson, Arizona
Antiarrhythmic Drugs

Albert W. Wu, MD, MPH
Associate Professor of Health Policy and Management, Epidemiology, and International Health, Johns Hopkins University Bloomberg School of Public Health; Associate Professor of Medicine, Johns Hopkins University School of Medicine, Baltimore, Maryland
Principles of Outcome Assessment

Joshua Wynne, MD, MBA, MPH
Professor of Medicine, Wayne State University School of Medicine; Physician, Harper University Hospital Detroit Medical Center, Detroit, Michigan
Miscellaneous Conditions of the Heart: Tumor, Trauma, and Systemic Disease

Joachim Yahalom, MD
Professor of Radiation Oncology, Weill Medical College of Cornell University; Memorial Sloan Kettering Cancer Center, New York, New York
Hodgkin's Disease

Ernest Yoder, MD, PhD
Clinical Associate Professor of Medicine, Wayne State University School of Medicine, Detroit, Michigan; Chair, Department of Internal Medicine, Providence Hospital and Medical Centers, Southfield, Michigan
Disorders Due to Heat and Cold

Justin A. Zivin, MD, PhD
Professor of Neurosciences, University of California, San Diego, School of Medicine, La Jolla, California; Staff Neurologist, San Diego Veterans Affairs Medical Center, San Diego, California
Approach to Cerebrovascular Diseases, Ischemic Cerebrovascular Disease; Hemorrhagic Cerebrovascular Disease

Kenneth S. Zuckerman, MD
Professor of Oncology, Internal Medicine, and Biochemistry/Molecular Biology; Harold H. Davis Professor of Cancer Research, University of South Florida H. Lee Moffitt Cancer Center and Research Institute, Tampa, Florida
Approach to the Anemias

Reviewers

The Publisher wishes to acknowledge the following individuals, who previewed advance materials from *Cecil Textbook of Medicine,* 22nd Edition.

L. Arisz, MD, PhD
Professor of Internal Medicine, University of Amsterdam, Amsterdam, The Netherlands

Masharip Atadzhanov, MD, PhD
Professor of Neurology, Department of Clinical Medicine, University of Zambia School of Medicine, Lusaka, Zambia

Samy Azer, MD, PhD
Associate Chair and Senior Lecturer, Faculty Education Unit, Faculty of Medicine, Dentistry & Health Sciences, University of Melbourne, Parkville, Victoria, Australia

Vincent Barba, MD
Assistant Professor of Medicine, New Jersey Medical School, Newark, New Jersey

David L. Battinelli, MD
Professor of Medicine, Internal Medicine, Program Director, Boston University School of Medicine, Boston, Massachusetts

Richard V. Birtwhistle, MD
Associate Dean, School of Medicine, Queen's University, Kingston, Ontario

Jan C. C. Borleffs, MD, PhD
Department of Internal Medicine, University Medical Center Utrecht School of Medical Science, Utrecht, The Netherlands

Mary L. Forsling, PhD, DSc
Professor of Neuroendocrinology, Guy's, King's, and St. Thomas' School of Medicine, Guy's Campus, London, United Kingdom

A. B. J. Groeneveld, MD, PhD
Department of Intensive Care, Vrije University Medical Center, Amsterdam, The Netherlands

Alan A. Harris, MD
Professor of Internal Medicine and Preventive Medicine, University of Illinois at Chicago; Senior Assistant Chairman and Program Director, Department of Internal Medicine, Rush-Presbyterian-St. Luke's Medical Center, Chicago, Illinois

I. M. Hoepelman, MD
Professor in Medicine, Head, Division of Acute Medicine and Infectious Disease, Utrecht, The Netherlands

Harry Hollander, MD
Professor of Clinical Medicine and Director, Medical Residency Program, Department of Medicine, University of California, San Francisco, School of Medicine, San Francisco, California

Byron J. Hoogwerf, MD
Director, Internal Medicine Residency Program, Department of Endocrinology, Metabolism and Diabetes, Cleveland Clinic Foundation, Cleveland, Ohio

William D. Kaehny, MD
Professor of Medicine, University of Colorado School of Medicine; Associate Chief, Medical Service, Veterans Affairs Medical Center, Denver, Colorado

C. G. M. Kallenberg, MD, PhD
Department of Clinical Immunology, University Hospital Groningen, Groningen, The Netherlands

Gregory Kane, MD
Associate Professor of Medicine, Program Director, Internal Medicine Residency, Jefferson Medical College, Philadelphia, Pennsylvania

Kiyoshi Kurokawa, MD
Director and Professor, Institute of Medical Science, Tokai University, Kanagawa, Japan

Mitchell Lhara, MD
Associate Professor of Clinical Medicine, New York University School of Medicine, New York, New York

Gerald Logue, MD
Professor of Medicine, Program Director, Internal Medicine Residency Program, School of Medicine and Biomedical Sciences, State University of New York at Buffalo, Buffalo, New York

Diana McNeill, MD
Associate Clinical Professor of Medicine, Program Director, Internal Medicine Residency Training Program, Duke University Medical Center, Durham, North Carolina

M. R. Moosa, MD
Associate Professor of Medicine, University of Stellenbosch, Cape Town, South Africa

Catherine Popadiuk, MD
Assistant Professor, Department of Women's Health, Memorial University of Newfoundland, Canada

Jay Rosenfield, MD
Associate Professor of Pediatrics, Director, Undergraduate Medical Education, University of Toronto, Toronto, Ontario, Canada

Martin Schreiber, MD
Associate Professor of Medicine, University of Toronto, Toronto, Ontario, Canada

Janet L. Seggie, MD
Professor of Medicine, Faculty of Health Sciences, University of Cape Town, Cape Town, South Africa

Ramesh M. Shah, MD
Director of Primary Care and Medical Service, Associate Chief of Staff for Education, VA Medical Center, Wilkes-Barre, Pennsylvania

Peter Speelman, MD, PhD
Resident Director, Chief, Division of Infectious Diseases, Tropical Medicine and AIDS, University of Amsterdam, Amsterdam, The Netherlands

Jos W. M. van der Meer, MD, PhD
Professor of Medicine, University Medical Centre St. Radboud, Nijmegen, The Netherlands

James F. Wallace, MD
Professor of Medicine, Director, Internal Medicine Residency Program, University of Washington, Seattle, Washington

Preface

The 22nd Edition of the *Cecil Textbook of Medicine* symbolizes a time of extraordinary advances in medicine and in the methods for the dissemination of information. This hardbound, published textbook and its associated electronic products incorporate the latest medical knowledge in formats that are designed to be appealing to physicians who prefer to access information in a variety of ways.

The contents of *Cecil* have remained true to the tradition of a comprehensive textbook of medicine that carefully explains the *why* (the underlying normal physiology and pathophysiology of disease, now at the cellular and molecular as well as the organ level) and the *how* (now frequently based on Grade A evidence from randomized controlled trials). Descriptions of physiology and pathophysiology include the latest genetic advances in a practical format that strives to be useful to the non-expert. Grade A evidence is now specifically highlighted in the text and referenced at the end of each chapter. The electronic version provides an immediate link to the cited reference and will be continuously updated to incorporate subsequent Grade A information.

The sections for each organ system begin with a chapter that summarizes an approach to patients with key symptoms, signs, or laboratory abnormalities associated with dysfunction of that organ system. As summarized in Table 1–1, the text specifically provides clear, concise information regarding how a physician should approach over 100 common symptoms, signs, and laboratory abnormalities, usually with a flow diagram and/or table for easy reference. In this way, *Cecil* remains a comprehensive text to guide diagnosis and therapy not only for patients with suspected or known diseases but also for patients who may have undiagnosed abnormalities that require an initial evaluation.

Perhaps the most obvious innovation of this edition is the full-color format. Color not only makes a text easier to read but also permits inclusion of hundreds of new figures, especially color photographs of patients with a wide range of physical findings.

Just as each edition brings new authors, it also reminds us of our gratitude to past editors and authors. Previous editors of the *Cecil Textbook of Medicine* include a short but remarkably distinguished group of leaders of American medicine: Russell Cecil, Paul Beeson, Walsh McDermott, James Wyngaarden, H. Lloyd Smith, Fred Plum, and J. Claude Bennett. As we welcome three new associate editors—William P. Arend, James O. Armitage, and W. Michael Scheld—we also express our appreciation to editors from the previous edition on whose foundation we have built. We specifically would like to thank Juha P. Kokko who served as consulting editor for the renal section for two editions, Gerald L. Mandell who served as consulting editor for infectious diseases for three editions, and Andrew I. Schafer who served as consulting editor for hematology and oncology for the 21st Edition. Our returning consulting editors for this edition—Jeffrey M. Drazen, Gordon N. Gill, Robert C. Griggs, and Don W. Powell—continue to make critical contributions to the selection of authors and the review of and approval of all manuscripts. The editors, however, are fully responsible for the book as well as the integration among chapters.

This edition includes new parts on Genetics, Immunology and Inflammation, and Clinical Pharmacology, as well as substantially expanded parts on Oncology and on Preventive and Environmental Medicine. Twenty-three chapters make their debuts in this edition: "Approach to the Patient: History and Physical Examination,"

"Common Clinical Sequelae of Aging," "Complementary and Alternative Medicine," "Principles of Genetics," "Single Gene and Chromosomal Disorders," "The Inherited Basis of Common Diseases," "The Innate and Adaptive Immune Systems," "Mechanisms of Immune-Mediated Tissue Injury," "Mechanisms of Inflammation and Tissue Repair," "Medical Aspects of Trauma and Burn Care," "Benign Prostatic Hyperplasia and Prostatitis," "Approach to the Patient with Jaundice or Abnormal Liver Tests," "Alcoholic and Nonalcoholic Steatohepatitis," "Hepatic Failure and Liver Transplantation," "The Peripheral Blood Smear," "Testicular Cancer," "Prostate Cancer," "Melanoma and Nonmelanoma Skin Cancers," "Chronobiology (Circadian Rhythms)," "Diagnostic Tests in Rheumatic Diseases," "Fibromyalgia," "Surgical Treatment of Joint Diseases," and "Prion Diseases." Of the other 455 chapters, 129 have new authors.

The tradition of *Cecil Textbook of Medicine* is that all chapters are written by distinguished experts in each field. We would also like to take this opportunity to thank several colleagues who assisted these individuals on specific chapters: Shao-Lee Lin ("Mechanisms of Inflammation and Tissue Repair"), Roy Kwak ("Applications and Limitation of Diagnostic Imaging"), Jacqueline M. Moline ("Principles of Occupational and Environmental Medicine"), George Juang ("Principles of Electrophysiology"), Michael Kilborn ("Antiarrhythmic Drugs"), James S. Zebrack ("ST-Elevation Acute Myocardial Infarction and Complications of Myocardial Infarction"), Tabo Sikaneta ("Cystic Kidney Diseases"), Jean A. Shafer ("The Peripheral Blood Smear"), Ivan Maillard ("Autoimmune and Intravascular Hemolytic Anemias"), Guillermo Garcia-Manero ("The Chronic Leukemias"), Miguel R. Arguedas ("Hepatic Tumors"), H. Shawn Hu ("Tumors of the Kidney, Bladder, Ureters, and Renal Pelvis"), Michael Ming ("Melanoma and Nonmelanoma Skin Cancers"), Timothy Quan and Insoo Kang ("Diagnostic Tests in Rheumatic Diseases"), W. Timothy Ballard ("Surgical Treatment of Joint Diseases"), Carolyn Calfee ("Infective Endocarditis"), John Ringman ("Diagnosis of Regional Cerebral Dysfunction"), Tomoko V. Nakawatase ("Alzheimer's Disease and Other Disorders of Cognition"), Andrea M. Vincent ("Amyotrophic Lateral Sclerosis and Other Motor Neuron Diseases"), and Gary Bellus and William Hahn ("Structure and Function of the Skin"). We are also most grateful for the editorial assistance in San Francisco of Vida Lynum and in Boston of Clinton Sours and Jane Newman; these individuals have shown extraordinary dedication and equanimity in managing the unending flow of manuscripts, disks, figures, and permissions. At Elsevier, Lynne Gery, Robin Davis, Karen O'Keefe Owens, and Pat Morrison have been critical to the planning and production process under the direction of Kimberly Murphy, to whom we are also most indebted. Many of the clinical photographs were supplied by Charles D. Forbes and William F. Jackson, authors of *Color Atlas and Text of Clinical Medicine*, Third Edition, published in 2003 by Elsevier Science Ltd. We thank them for graciously permitting us to include their pictures in our book. Finally, we would like to thank our families—Jill, Jeff, Daniel, and Robyn Goldman, and the Ausiello famiglia—for their understanding of the time and focus required to edit a book that attempts to sustain the tradition of our predecessors and to meet the needs of today's physician.

LEE GOLDMAN, MD
DENNIS AUSIELLO, MD

Features of the New Edition

- **Consistent internal chapter headings give quick access to the information you need.**

- ℞ **Treatment boxes summarize therapeutic options.**

Table 89–2 • PRINCIPAL OCCUPATIONS ASSOCIATED WITH SILICON EXPOSURE

Abrasives workers	Silica flour workers
Foundry workers	Silica millers
Glass makers	Stone workers
Pottery workers	Surface mine drillers
Quarriers	Underground miners
Sandblasters	

Etiology

Crystalline silicon dioxide, the causal agent, is abundant and ubiquitous in the earth's crust and is used in a variety of industrial applications. Quartz is the most common form. Consequently, large numbers of workers, probably millions in the United States, are still exposed (Table 89–2).

Epidemiology

As for the other pneumoconioses, the risk of developing disease increases with the level and duration of exposure. Although the hazard posed by silica exposure has long been recognized and exposure standards have been promulgated, new cases continue to occur, even of acute silicosis, which has been recently reported in sandblasters, ground silica workers, and rock drillers.

Pathology

Like coal workers' pneumoconiosis, chronic silicosis occurs in a simple form and as progressive massive fibrosis. The earliest lesions are collections of dust-laden macrophages in the peribronchiolar and paraseptal or subpleural areas. The silicotic nodule has an acellular core composed of collagen surrounded by a cellular capsule with macrophages, lymphocytes, and fibroblasts. Silicotic nodules may also involve the hilar lymph nodes. Silicotic nodules coalesce to form the lesions of progressive massive fibrosis, masses of dense hyalinized connective tissue with little inflammation. Accelerated silicosis progresses rapidly to progressive massive fibrosis, whereas acute silicosis has a distinct pattern with few or no nodules and alveolar filling with proteinaceous material. Polarized light microscopy may show birefringent particles indicative of silica in the lungs of silica-exposed persons, including those with silicosis.

Clinical Manifestations

Chronic silicosis without progressive massive fibrosis is associated with little physiologic impairment. Cough and sputum production may reflect underlying bronchitis related to dust exposure or cigarette smoking. As in coal workers' pneumoconiosis, progressive massive fibrosis can be associated with significant impairment on lung function testing and clinically significant dyspnea. Both airflow obstruction and lung restriction may be present. Acute silicosis presents with rapidly progressive dyspnea. Persons with silicosis are at increased risk for mycobacterial infection (Chapter 341), and they may present with manifestations of infection such as fever and weight loss.

In chronic silicosis, the chest radiograph shows small nodules that tend to predominate in the upper lobes (Fig. 89–3). Calcification of the nodules is rare, as is so-called eggshell calcification of enlarged hilar nodes. In progressive massive fibrosis, the mass lesions are typically in the upper lobes and are often associated with compensatory hyperinflation of the lower lobes. Widespread consolidation is present on the chest radiograph in acute silicosis. Caplan's syndrome may also occur in silica-exposed workers, but it is rare.

Diagnosis

The diagnosis of chronic silicosis is made on the basis of characteristic radiographic findings and history of employment in a job associated with exposure to silica-containing dust. Before accepting a diagnosis of progressive massive fibrosis in a silica-exposed worker, other causes of lung masses should be considered, including, specifically, lung cancer and mycobacterial infection. Acute silicosis should be considered in heavily exposed individuals with a diffuse consolidating process. Unless the epidemiologic features of the case make the diagnosis of acute silicosis certain, lung biopsy may be indicated to establish the diagnosis and to exclude other diseases.

℞ Treatment

As in any chronic lung disease, supportive therapy, oxygen, and rehabilitation may be indicated. One report suggested possible short-term benefits of corticosteroid therapy, but steroid therapy cannot be recommended at present. Because of the increased risk of mycobacterial diseases, particularly *Mycobacterium tuberculosis*, all persons with silicosis should receive yearly tuberculin skin tests and evaluation for active tuberculosis if the test is positive. Isoniazid prophylaxis is recommended if the test is positive and active disease is not present. Some studies indicate that prolonged antituberculous therapy may be indicated in patients with silicosis and active tuberculosis (Chapter 341).

Prognosis

The prognosis of accelerated and acute silicosis is poor; both are associated with progressive loss of function, and acute silicosis may be rapidly fatal. Progressive massive fibrosis has a more variable course, which may also lead to progressive impairment and respiratory failure. Factors determining progression from chronic silicosis to progressive massive fibrosis are uncertain.

OTHER PNEUMOCONIOSES

Inhaling other minerals and metals may also cause pneumoconioses (see Table 89–1). Silicates other than asbestos have been linked to interstitial lung disease, including talc, kaolinite, mica, and vermiculite. Benign pneumoconioses are associated with inhaling forms of barium (baritosis) and tin (stannosis). Hard-metal disease occurs in workers exposed to cobalt in applications involving its use in alloys and abrasives. This diffuse interstitial disease, which can be associated with clinically significant impairment, should be considered in workers in foundries and in industries involving grinding of metals, gems, and other materials. Some workers exposed to man-made fibers develop small opacities, but a distinct pneumoconiosis has not yet been identified from exposure to these newer fibers. *Mixed-dust pneumoconiosis* is a nonspecific label often used for the presence of both rounded and irregular opacities on the chest radiograph of a worker with exposure to several types of dust. Typically, there is exposure to silica and to an additional mineral.

BERYLLIUM DISEASE

Beryllium disease is a granulomatous lung disease that results from inhaling beryllium, a rare metal now widely used in high-technology applications (Table 89–3). The typical cases currently observed present with gradual onset and are referred to as *chronic beryllium disease*; a more acute form was reported with past higher levels of exposure. When first recognized, the disease was found in workers who extracted and produced beryllium and in workers making fluorescent lamps containing a beryllium phosphor. Cases have been reported in bystanders not working directly with the metal and in persons

Table 89–3 • CURRENT INDUSTRIES USING BERYLLIUM

Aerospace	Nuclear reactors
Beryllium extraction, fabrication, smelting	Nuclear weapons
Ceramics	Plating
Dental alloys and prostheses	Telecommunications
Electronics	Tool and die
Foundries	

- **Clinical Manifestations boxes describe key signs and symptoms, aiding accurate diagnosis.**

- **Color-coded algorithms outline strategies for diagnosing and treating common complaints and diseases.**

  - **Blue boxes indicate diagnostic tests.**

  - **Green boxes indicate treatments.**

  - **Red boxes are used for all other steps.**

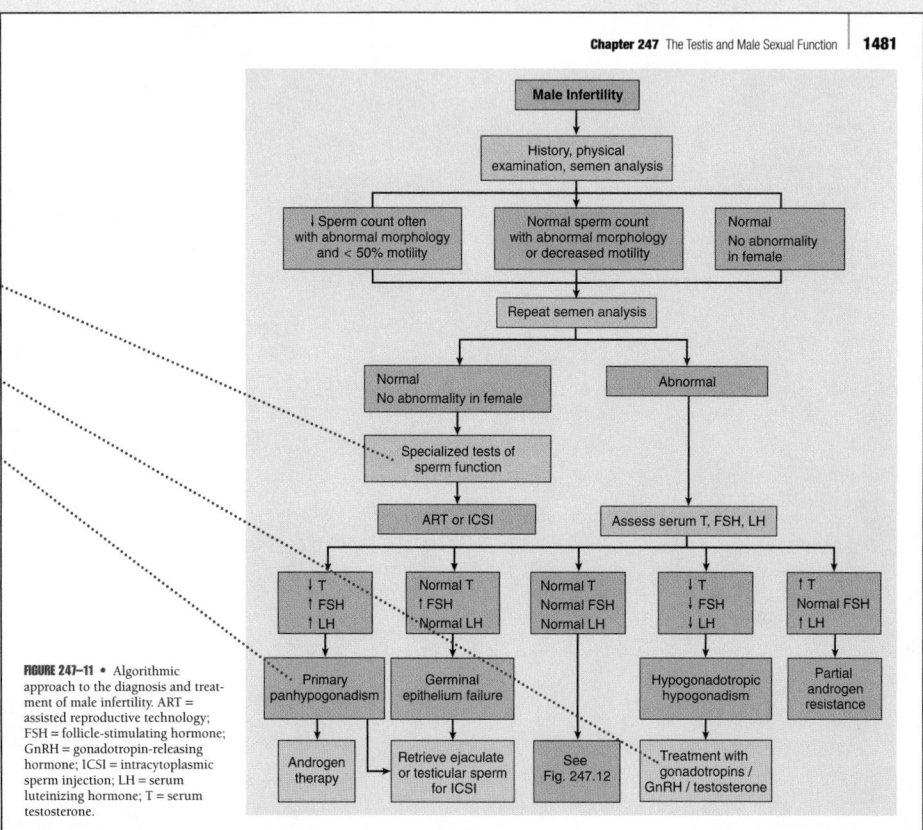

FIGURE 247–11 • Algorithmic approach to the diagnosis and treatment of male infertility. ART = assisted reproductive technology; FSH = follicle-stimulating hormone; GnRH = gonadotropin-releasing hormone; ICSI = intracytoplasmic sperm injection; LH = serum luteinizing hormone; T = serum testosterone.

Table 26–3 • DELIRIUM RISK FACTORS AND POTENTIAL INTERVENTIONS

RISK FACTOR	INTERVENTIONS
Cognitive impairment	Reality orientation program (reorienting techniques, communication)
	Therapeutic activities program
Sleep deprivation	Noise reduction strategies
	Scheduling of nighttime medications, procedures, and nursing activities to allow uninterrupted period of sleep
Immobilization	Early mobilization (e.g., ambulation or bedside exercises)
	Minimizing immobilizing equipment (e.g., bladder catheters)
Psychoactive medications	Restricted use of "as needed" sleep and psychoactive medications (e.g., sedative-hypnotics, narcotics, anticholinergic medications)
	Nonpharmacologic protocols for management of sleep and anxiety
Vision impairment	Provision of vision aids (e.g., magnifiers, special lighting)
	Provision of adaptive equipment (e.g., illuminated phone dials, large-print books)
Hearing impairment	Provision of amplifying devices
	Repair of hearing aids
Dehydration	Early recognition and volume repletion

to have greater deleterious effects in patients with underlying cognitive impairment. The long-term detrimental effects most probably are related to the duration, severity, and underlying cause of the delirium and the vulnerability of the patient.

Prevention

The most effective intervention strategy to reduce delirium and its associated complications is primary prevention of delirium before it occurs. Preventive strategies should address important delirium risk factors and target patients at a moderate to high risk for delirium at baseline (Table 26–3). Randomized trials have shown that a geriatrics consultation or a multidisciplinary intervention aimed at the risk factors for delirium can reduce the incidence of delirium by 40%. On a larger scale, preventive efforts for delirium require system-wide changes to educate physicians and nurses to improve recognition and heighten awareness of the clinical implications, provide incentives to change practice patterns that lead to delirium (e.g., immobilization, use of sleep medications, bladder catheters, and physical restraints), and create systems that enhance high-quality geriatric care (e.g., geriatric expertise, case management, clinical pathways, and quality monitoring).

Future Directions

It is hoped that future research will elucidate the pathophysiology of delirium using neuroimaging modalities, neuropsychological testing, and laboratory markers; clarify the contribution of delirium to irreversible cognitive impairment; and improve the management of delirium.

1. Inouye SK, Bogardus ST, Charpentier PA, et al: A multicomponent intervention to prevent delirium in hospitalized older patients. N Engl J Med 1999;340:669.
2. Marcantonio ER, Flacker JM, Wright RJ, Resnick NM: Reducing delirium after hip fracture: A randomized trial. J Am Geriatr Soc 2001;49:516.
3. Britton A, Russell R: Multidisciplinary team interventions for delirium in patients with chronic cognitive impairment. Cochrane Review. The Cochrane Library, Issue 4. Oxford, Update Software, 2003.

SUGGESTED READINGS
Carnes M, Howell T, Rosenberg M, et al: Physicians vary in approaches to the clinical management of delirium. J Am Geriatr Soc 2003;51:234–239. *This study documents the broad variability in pharmacologic management of delirium, in the absence of sound clinical evidence.*
Marcantonio ER, Simon SE, Bergmann MA, et al: Delirium symptoms in post-acute care: prevalent, persistent, and associated with poor functional recovery. J Am Geriatr Soc 2003;51:4–9. *This study reveals that delirium is a frequent complication of post-acute care that is associated with poor functional recovery.*
Roche V: Etiology and management of delirium. Am J Med Sci 2003;325:20–30. *An up-to-date review of literature on delirium.*

- **Highlighted Grade A Evidence references emphasize evidence-based treatments, to foster cost-effective, best practice in clinical medicine.**

- **Suggested Readings provide sources for further information.**

Part XXVI Eye, Ear, Nose, and Throat Diseases

Part XXVII Skin Diseases

Part XXVIII Reference Intervals and Laboratory Values

CECIL
Textbook
of Medicine

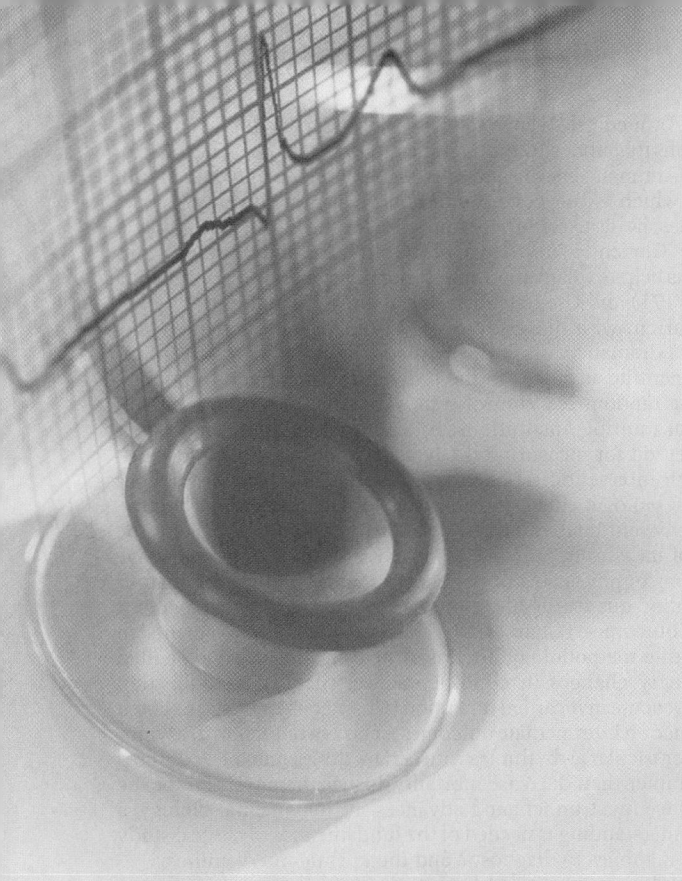

part I

Social and Ethical Issues in Medicine

1 APPROACH TO MEDICINE, THE PATIENT, AND THE MEDICAL PROFESSION: MEDICINE AS A LEARNED AND HUMANE PROFESSION

Lee Goldman

Dennis Ausiello

APPROACH TO MEDICINE

Medicine is a profession that incorporates science and the scientific method with the art of being a physician. The art of tending to the sick is as old as humanity itself. Even in modern times, the art of caring and comforting, guided by millennia of common sense as well as a more recent, systematic approach to medical ethics (Chapter 2), remains the cornerstone of medicine. Without these humanistic qualities, the application of the modern science of medicine is suboptimal, useless, or even detrimental.

The caregivers of ancient times and premodern cultures tried a variety of interventions to help the afflicted. Some of their potions contained what are now known to be active ingredients that form the basis for proven medications (Chapter 27). Others (Chapter 34) have persisted into the present era despite a lack of convincing evidence. Modern medicine should not dismiss the possibility that these unproven approaches may be helpful, but it should adopt a guiding principle that all interventions, whether traditional or newly developed, can be tested vigorously, with the expectation that any beneficial effects can be explored further to determine their scientific basis.

Compared with its long and generally distinguished history of caring and comforting, the scientific basis of medicine is remarkably recent. Other than an understanding of human anatomy and the later description, albeit widely contested at this time, of the normal physiology of the circulatory system, almost all of modern medicine is based on discoveries made within the last 150 or so years. Until the late 19th century, the paucity of medical knowledge perhaps was exemplified best by hospitals and hospital care. Although hospitals provided caring that all but well-to-do people might not be able to obtain elsewhere, there is little if any evidence that hospitals improved health outcomes. The term *hospitalism* referred not to expertise in hospital care, but rather to the aggregate of iatrogenic afflictions that were induced by the hospital itself.

The essential humanistic qualities of caring and comforting can achieve little if they are not coupled with an understanding of how medical science can and should be applied to patients with known or suspected diseases. Without this knowledge, comforting may be inappropriate or misleading, and caring may be ineffective or counterproductive if it inhibits the sick person from obtaining appropriate, scientific medical care. The *Cecil Textbook of Medicine* focuses on the discipline of *internal medicine*, from which neurology and dermatology, which also are covered in substantial detail in this text, are relatively recent evolutionary branches. The term *internal medicine*, which is often misunderstood by the lay public, was developed in 19th century Germany. *Inneren medizin* was to be distinguished from clinical medicine because it emphasized the physiology and chemistry of disease, not just the patterns or progression of clinical manifestations. The *Cecil Textbook of Medicine* follows this tradition by showing how pathophysiologic abnormalities cause symptoms and signs and by emphasizing how therapies can improve the underlying pathophysiology and make the patient feel better.

Modern medicine has moved rapidly past organ physiology to an increasingly detailed understanding of cellular, subcellular, and genetic mechanisms. Understanding of microbial pathogenesis (Chapter 294) and many inflammatory diseases (Chapter 273) is guided now by a detailed understanding of the human immune system and its response to foreign antigens (Chapters 41–45).

Health, disease, and an individual's interaction with the environment also are determined substantially by genetics. In addition to many conditions that may be determined by a single gene (Chapters 37 and 38), medical science increasingly understands the complex interactions that underlie multigenic traits (Chapter 39). The description of the human genome and ongoing attempts to understand proteomics, which is the normal and abnormal protein expression of these genes, holds extraordinary promise for the future of health and medicine. Currently, knowledge of the structure and physical forms of proteins helps explain abnormalities as diverse as sickle cell anemia (Chapter 171) and Creutzfeldt-Jakob disease (Chapter 456).

Concurrent with these advances in fundamental human biology has been a dramatic shift in the methods for evaluating the application of scientific advances to the individual patient and to populations. The randomized control trial, sometimes with thousands of patients at multiple institutions, has replaced anecdote as the preferred method for measuring the benefits and uses of diagnostic or therapeutic interventions (Chapter 6). As studies progress from those that show biologic effect, to those that elucidate dosing schedules and toxicity, and finally to those that assess true clinical benefit, the metrics of measuring outcome also have improved from subjective impressions of physicians or patients to reliable and valid measures of morbidity, quality of life, functional status, and other patient-oriented outcomes (Chapter 8). These marked improvements in the scientific methodology of clinical investigation have expedited extraordinary changes in clinical practice, such as recanalization therapy for acute myocardial infarction (Chapter 69), and have shown that reliance on intermediate outcomes, such as a reduction in asymptomatic ventricular arrhythmias with certain drugs, unexpectedly may increase rather than decrease mortality. Just as the physician for the 21st century must understand advances in fundamental biology, a similar understanding is needed of the fundamentals of clinical study design as it applies to diagnostic and therapeutic interventions.

The explosion in medical knowledge has led to increasing specialization and subspecialization, defined initially by organ system and more recently by locus of principal activity (inpatient compared with outpatient), reliance on manual skills (proceduralist compared with nonproceduralist), or participation in research. More recently, however, it is becoming increasingly clear that the same fundamental molecular and genetic mechanisms are broadly applicable across all organ systems and that the scientific methodologies of randomized trials and careful clinical observation span all aspects of medicine.

APPROACH TO THE PATIENT

Patients commonly present with complaints (symptoms). These symptoms may or may not be accompanied by abnormalities on examination (signs) or on laboratory testing. Conversely, asymptomatic patients may have signs or laboratory abnormalities, and laboratory abnormalities can occur in the absence of symptoms or signs.

Symptoms and signs commonly define *syndromes,* which may be the common final pathway of a wide range of pathophysiologic alterations. The fundamental basis of internal medicine is that diagnosis should elucidate the pathophysiologic explanation for symptoms and signs so that therapy may improve the underlying abnormality, not just attempt to suppress the abnormal symptoms or signs.

When patients present to physicians, they may have manifestations or exacerbations of known conditions, or they may have symptoms and signs that suggest malfunction of a particular organ system. Sometimes the pattern of symptoms and signs is highly suggestive or even pathognomonic for a particular disease process. In these situations, in which the physician is focusing on a particular disease, the *Cecil Textbook of Medicine* has always been easy to use. Whether a patient has an acute myocardial infarction (Chapters 68 and 69), chronic obstructive lung disease (Chapter 85), an obstructive uropathy (Chapter 121), inflammatory bowel disease (Chapter 142), gallstones (Chapter 158), rheumatoid arthritis (Chapter 278), hypothyroidism (Chapter 239), tuberculosis (Chapter 341), or virtually any known medical condition, this text covers its presentation, pathophysiology, diagnosis, treatment, and prognosis.

Many patients, however, present with undiagnosed symptoms, signs, or laboratory abnormalities that cannot be ascribed immediately to a particular disease or cause. Whether the initial presentation is chest pain (Chapter 46), diarrhea (Chapter 141), neck or back pain (Chapter 429), or a variety of more than 100 common symptoms, signs, or laboratory abnormalities, the *Cecil Textbook of Medicine* also provides tables, figures, and entire chapters to guide the approach to diagnosis and therapy (Table 1–1). By virtue of this dual approach

Table 1–1 • GUIDE TO THE APPROACH TO COMMON SYMPTOMS, SIGNS, AND LABORATORY ABNORMALITIES

	CHAPTER	SPECIFIC TABLES OR FIGURES		CHAPTER	SPECIFIC TABLES OR FIGURES
SYMPTOMS			**SIGNS**		
Constitutional			**Vital Signs**		
Fever	295, 296	Table 295–1	Fever	295, 296	Table 295–1
Weight loss	227, 228, 232		Hypothermia	105	Table 105–4
Obesity	233	Table 233–1	Tachycardia/bradycardia	50, 58, 59	
Sleep disturbances	96, 236, 438	Table 96–1	Hypertension	63	Table 63–4
Snoring	96, 438		Hypotension/shock	102	Figure 102–1
			Altered respiration	83, 99	Table 83–1, Table 99–2
Head, Eyes, Ears, Nose, Throat			**Head, Eyes, Ears, Nose, Throat**		
Headache	428	Table 428–1	Red eye	465	Table 465–4
Visual loss, transient	466	Table 466–1	Dilated pupil	466	Figure 466–3
Painful eye	465		Strabismus	466	Figure 466–4
Hearing loss	470	Figure 470–1	Jaundice	149	Figure 149–2
Ringing in ears (tinnitus)	470	Figure 470–2	Otitis	468	Table 468–1
Vertigo	470	Figure 470–3	Sinusitis	268	
Nasal congestion	268	Table 268–1	Oral ulcers	467	Tables 467–1, 467–3, 467–4
Dry mouth	467	Table 467–7			
Hoarseness	468		**Neck**		
Loss of smell or taste	469	Table 469–1	Lymphadenopathy	164	Tables 164–1, 164–2, 164–5
Cardiopulmonary			Thyroid nodules	239	Figure 239–5
Chest pain	46	Table 46–2	Thyromegaly/goiter	239	Figure 239–4
Shortness of breath	46, 81	Figure 46–1, Figure 81–1	**Breast**		
Palpitations	46, 58	Table 46–3, Table 58–2	Breast mass	204	
Dizziness	46, 470	Table 58–2, Table 470–1			
Syncope	58, 435	Table 58–2, Table 435–1	**Lungs**		
Cardiac arrest	60	Table 60–2, Figure 60–5	Wheezes	84	Table 84–2
Cough	81				
Hemoptysis	81		**Cardiac**		
			Heart murmur or extra sounds	46	Figure 46–4, Table 46–6
Gastrointestinal					
Nausea and vomiting	130		Jugular venous distention	46	Table 46–5
Dysphagia	136		Carotid pulse abnormalities	46	Figure 46–3
Hematemesis	133, 156	Table 133–1, Figure 133–3, Figure 156–2	**Abdomen**		
Heartburn/dyspepsia	135, 136	Figure 135–2, Figure 136–3	Hepatomegaly	148	
			Splenomegaly	164	Tables 164–6, 164–8
Abdominal pain:			Acute abdomen	143	
Acute	130, 143		Abdominal swelling/ascites	148, 156	
Chronic	135	Figure 135–1	Rectal bleeding/positive stool	133, 200	Figure 133–4
Diarrhea	141	Figures 141–2, 141–3, 141–8, 141–9, 141–10	**Genitourinary**		
Melena	133	Table 133–4, Figure 133–4	Scrotal mass	206	
Constipation	134	Figure 134–4	Vaginal discharge	345	
Fecal incontinence	147	Figure 147–3	**Musculoskeletal**		
Genitourinary			Monarticular arthritis	273	
Dysuria	344		Polyarticular arthritis	273	
Incontinence	24	Figure 24–1			
Frequency	129		**Extremities**		
Female infertility	250	Table 250–7	Edema	46	Figure 46–6
Vaginal discharge	345		Cyanosis	46	
Menstrual irregularities	250, 256	Figure 250–8, Tables 250–5, 250–6	Clubbing	46	
Erectile dysfunction	247		**Neurologic**		
Male infertility	247	Figures 247–10, 247–11	Delirium/altered mental states	26	Figure 26–1
Urinary obstruction	121	Table 121–31, Figure 121–2	Psychiatric disturbances	426	Tables 426–1, 426–3, 426–4, 426–5, 426–7, 426–8, 426–9
Musculoskeletal			Coma	436	Table 436–1
Neck or back pain	429	Tables 429–1, 429–2, 429–4, 429–5			
Painful joints	273	Table 273–2	**COMMON LABORATORY ABNORMALITIES**		
			Hematology/Urinalysis		
Extremities			Anemia	160	Figure 160–1
Swollen feet, ankles, or legs	46	Figure 46–6	Polycythemia	176	Figure 176–1
Claudication	76	Figure 76–2	Leukopenia	163	Figure 163–2
			Leukocytosis	163	Figure 163–9
Neurologic			Neutropenia with fever	163	Table 163–5
Weakness	423, 463, 464	Tables 423–1, 461–2	Thrombocytosis	183	Figure 183–3
Sensory loss	461, 462	Tables 461–8, 461–9, 461–10	Thrombocytopenia	177	Figure 177–2
Memory loss	433	Tables 433–6, 433–7	Urinalysis	110	Figures 110–2, 110–3, 110–7, 110–8, 110–9, 110–10, Table 110–4
Abnormal gait	423	Table 423–2			
Integumentary			**Chemistries**		
Abnormal bleeding	162	Table 162–1	Prolonged PT or PTT	162	Figures 162–3, 162–4
Rash	472	Table 472–1, Figure 472–1			
Hirsutism	255	Figure 255–1, Table 255–1			

Table 1–1 • GUIDE TO THE APPROACH TO COMMON SYMPTOMS, SIGNS, AND LABORATORY ABNORMALITIES—cont'd

	CHAPTER	SPECIFIC TABLES OR FIGURES		CHAPTER	SPECIFIC TABLES OR FIGURES
Abnormal liver enzymes	149	Figures 149–3, 149–4	Acid-base disturbances	113	Tables 113–1, 113–2, 113–3, 113–4, 113–5
Elevated BUN/creatinine					
Acute	116	Tables 116–1, 116–2, 116–5	**Chest Radiograph/ECG**		
Chronic	117	Table 117–1	Cardiomegaly	49, 51	Figure 51–6
Hyperglycemia	243	Table 243–1	Pulmonary congestion	49, 99	Table 99–5
Hypoglycemia	243	Figure 243–2, Table 243–1	Interstitial lung disease	88	Tables 88–1, 88–2
Electrolyte abnormalities	112	Tables 112–10, 112–11, 112–12, 112–13	Solitary pulmonary nodule	81	Figure 81–2
			ECG abnormalities	50	Figures 50–5, 50–6

BUN = blood urea nitrogen; ECG = electrocardiogram; PT = prothrombin time; PTT = partial thromboplastin time.

to known disease and to undiagnosed abnormalities, this textbook, similar to the modern practice of medicine, applies directly to patients regardless of their mode of presentation or degree of prior evaluation.

The patient-physician interaction proceeds through many phases of clinical reasoning and decision making. The interaction begins with an elucidation of complaints or concerns, followed by inquiries or evaluation to address these concerns in increasingly precise ways. The process commonly requires a careful history or physical examination, ordering of diagnostic tests, integration of clinical findings with the test results, understanding of the risks and benefits of the possible courses of action, and careful consultation with the patient and family to develop future plans. Physicians increasingly can call on a growing literature of evidence-based medicine to guide the process so that benefit is maximized, while respecting individual variations among different patients.

The increasing availability of evidence from randomized trials to guide the approach to diagnosis and therapy should not be equated with "cookbook" medicine. Evidence and the guidelines that are derived from it emphasize proven approaches for patients with specific characteristics. Substantial clinical judgment is required to determine whether the evidence and guidelines apply to individual patients and to recognize the occasional exceptions. Even more judgment is required in the many situations in which evidence is absent or inconclusive. Evidence also must be tempered by patients' preferences, although it is a physician's responsibility to emphasize evidence when presenting alternative options to the patient. The adherence of a patient to a specific regimen is likely to be enhanced if the patient also understands the rationale and evidence behind the recommended option.

To care for a patient as an individual, the physician must understand the patient as a person. This fundamental precept of doctoring includes an understanding of the patient's social situation, family issues, financial concerns, and preferences for different types of care and outcomes, ranging from maximum prolongation of life to the relief of pain and suffering (Chapters 2 and 3). If the physician does not appreciate and address these issues, the science of medicine cannot be applied appropriately, and even the most knowledgeable physician fails to achieve appropriate outcomes.

Even as physicians become increasingly aware of new discoveries, patients can obtain their own information from a variety of sources, some of which are of questionable reliability. The increasing use of alternative and complementary therapies (Chapter 34) is an example of patients' frequent dissatisfaction with prescribed medical therapy. Physicians should keep an open mind regarding unproven options but must advise their patients carefully if such options may carry any degree of potential risks, including the risk that they may relied on to substitute for proven approaches. It is crucial for the physician to have an open dialogue with the patient and family regarding the full range of options that either may consider.

The physician does not exist in a vacuum but rather as part of a complicated and extensive system of medical care and public health. In premodern times and even today in some developing countries, basic hygiene, clean water, and adequate nutrition have been the most important ways to promote health and reduce disease. In developed countries, the adoption of healthy lifestyles, including better diet (Chapter 12) and appropriate exercise (Chapter 13), are cornerstones to reducing the epidemics of obesity (Chapter 233), coronary disease (Chapter 66), and diabetes (Chapter 242). Public health

interventions to provide immunizations (Chapter 16) and to reduce injuries (Chapter 15) and the use of tobacco (Chapter 14), illicit drugs (Chapter 30), and excess alcohol (Chapter 17) collectively can produce more health benefit than nearly any other imaginable health intervention (Chapter 10).

APPROACH TO THE MEDICAL PROFESSION

In a profession, the practitioner puts the welfare of the client or patient above his or her own welfare. Professionals have a duty that may be thought of as a contract with society. The American Board of Internal Medicine and the European Federation of Internal Medicine jointly have proposed that medical professionalism should emphasize three fundamental principles: the primacy of patient welfare, patient autonomy, and social justice. As modern medicine brings a plethora of diagnostic and therapeutic options, the interactions of the physician with the patient and society become more complex and potentially fraught with ethical dilemmas (Chapter 2). To help provide a moral compass that not only is grounded in tradition, but also adaptable to modern times, the primacy of patient welfare emphasizes the fundamental principle of a profession. The physician's altruism, which begets the patient's trust, must be impervious to the economic, bureaucratic, and political challenges that are faced by the physician and the patient (Chapter 4).

The principle of patient autonomy asserts that physicians make recommendations, but patients make the final decisions. The physician is an expert advisor who must inform and empower the patient to decide based on scientific data and how these data can and should be integrated with a patient's preferences.

The importance of social justice symbolizes that the patient-physician interaction does not exist in a vacuum. The physician has a responsibility to the individual patient and to broader society to promote access and to eliminate disparities in health and health care.

To promote these fundamental principles, a series of professional responsibilities has been suggested (Table 1–2). These specific responsibilities represent practical, daily traits that benefit the physician's own patients and society as a whole.

Table 1–2 • PROFESSIONAL RESPONSIBILITIES

Commitment to:
  Professional competence
  Honesty with patients
  Patient confidentiality
  Maintaining appropriate relations with patients
  Improving the quality of care
  Improving access to care
  A just distribution of finite resources
  Scientific knowledge
  Maintaining trust by managing conflicts of interest
  Professional responsibilities

From Brennan T, Blank L, Cohen J, et al: Medical professionalism in the new millennium: A physician charter. Ann Intern Med 2002;1136:243–246.

The changing medical care environment places increasing emphasis on standards, outcomes, and accountability. As purchasers of insurance become more cognizant of value rather than just cost, outcomes ranging from rates of screening mammography (Chapter 204) to mortality rates with coronary artery bypass graft surgery (Chapter 71) become metrics by which rational choices can be made. Clinical guidelines and critical pathways derived from randomized control trials and evidence-based medicine potentially can lead to more cost-effective care and better outcomes.

These major changes in many Western health care systems bring with them many major risks and concerns. If the concept of limited choice among physicians and health care providers is based on objective measures of quality and outcome, the channeling of patients to better providers is one reasonable definition of better selection and enlightened competition. If the limiting of options is based overwhelmingly on cost rather than on measures of quality, outcomes, and patient satisfaction, it is likely that the historic relationship between the patient and the truly professional physician will be fundamentally compromised.

In this new environment, the physician often has a dual responsibility: to the health care system as an expert who helps create standards, measures of outcome, clinical guidelines, and mechanisms to ensure high-quality, cost-effective care and to individual patients who entrust their well-being to that physician to promote their best interests within the reasonable limits of the system. A health insurance system that emphasizes cost-effective care, that gives physicians and health care providers responsibility for the health of a population and the resources required to achieve these goals, that must exist in a competitive environment in which patients can choose alternatives if they are not satisfied with their care, and that places increasing emphasis on health education and prevention can have many positive effects. In this environment, however, physicians must beware of overt and subtle pressures that could entice them to underserve patients and abrogate their professional responsibilities by putting personal financial reward ahead of their patients' welfare. The physician's responsibility to represent the patient's best interests and avoid financial conflicts by doing too little in the newer systems of capitated care provides different specific challenges but an analogous moral dilemma to the historic American system in which the physician could be rewarded financially for doing too much.

In the current health care environment, all physicians and trainees must redouble their commitment to professionalism. At the same time, the challenge to the individual physician to retain and expand the scientific knowledge base and process the vast array of new information is daunting. In this spirit of a profession based on science and caring, the *Cecil Textbook of Medicine* seeks to be a comprehensive approach to modern internal medicine.

SUGGESTED READING

Brennan T, Blank L, Cohen J, et al: Medical professionalism in the new millennium: A physician charter. Ann Intern Med 2002;1136:243–246. *A brief but powerful discussion of professionalism in medicine and how it is a crucial part of the health care system.*

2 BIOETHICS IN THE PRACTICE OF MEDICINE

Ezekiel J. Emanuel

It commonly is argued that modern advances in medical technology, antibiotics, dialysis, transplantation, and intensive care units have created the bioethical dilemmas that confront physicians in the 21st century. Concerns about ethical issues are as old as the practice of medicine itself, however. The Hippocratic Oath, composed sometime around 400 BC, attests to the need of ancient Greek physicians for advice on how to address the many bioethical dilemmas that they confronted. The Oath addresses issues of confidentiality, abortion, euthanasia, sexual relations between physician and patient, divided loyalties, and, at least implicitly, charity care and executions. Other Hippocratic works address issues such as terminating treatments to dying patients and telling the truth. Whether we agree with the advice dispensed or not, the important point is that many bioethical issues are not created by technology but are inherent in medical practice.

Technology may make these issues more common and may change the context in which they arise, but there are underlying bioethical issues that seem timeless.

Many physicians have been educated that four main principles can be invoked to address bioethical dilemmas: autonomy, nonmaleficence, beneficence, and justice. Autonomy is the idea that people should have the right and freedom to choose, pursue, and revise their own life plans. Nonmaleficence is the idea that people should not be harmed or injured knowingly; this principle is encapsulated in the frequently repeated phrase that a physician has an obligation to "first do no harm"—*primum non nocere.* This phrase is not found either in the Hippocratic Oath or in other Hippocratic writing; the only related, but not identical, Hippocratic phrase is "at least, do not harm." Although nonmaleficence is about avoiding harm, beneficence is about the positive actions that the physician should undertake to promote the well-being of his or her patients. In clinical practice, this obligation usually arises from the implicit and explicit commitments and promises surrounding the physician-patient relationship. Finally, there is the principle of justice as the fair distribution of benefits and burdens.

Although helpful in providing an initial framework, these principles have limited value. They are broad and open to diverse and conflicting interpretations. In addition, as is clear with the principle of justice, they frequently are underdeveloped. In any difficult case, the principles are likely to conflict. Conflicting ethical principles are precisely why there are bioethical dilemmas. The principles themselves do not offer guidance on how they should be balanced or specified to resolve the dilemma. These principles are focused on the individual physician-patient context; they are not particularly helpful when the bioethical issues are institutional and systemic, such as setting priorities or policies. Finally, these four principles are not comprehensive. There are other fundamental ethical principles and values, such as communal solidarity, duties to future generations, trust, and professional integrity, that are important in bioethics but not encapsulated except by deformation in these four principles.

There is no formula or small set of ethical principles that mechanically or magically gives answers to bioethical dilemmas. Instead, medical practitioners should follow an orderly analytic process. First, practitioners need to obtain the facts relevant to the situation. Second they must delineate the basic bioethical issue. Third, it is important to identify all the crucial principles and values that relate to the case and how they might conflict. Fourth, because many ethical dilemmas have been analyzed previously and subjected frequently to empirical study, practitioners should examine the relevant literature, whether it is commentaries or studies in medical journals, legal cases, or books. With these analyses, the particular dilemma should be reexamined; this process might lead to reformulating the issue and identifying new values or new understandings of existing values. Fifth, with this information, it is important to distinguish clearly unethical practices from a range of ethically permissible actions. Finally, it is important not only to come to some resolution of the case, but also to state clearly the reasons behind the decisions; that is, the interpretation of the principles used and how values were balanced. Although unanimity and consensus may be desirable ideals, reasonable people frequently disagree about how to resolve ethical dilemmas without being unethical or malevolent.

A multitude of bioethical dilemmas arise in medical practice, including issues of genetics, reproductive choices, and termination of care. In clinical practice, the most common issues revolve around informed consent, terminating life-sustaining treatments, euthanasia and physician-assisted suicide, and conflicts of interest.

Physician-Patient Relationship: Informed Consent

HISTORY. It commonly is thought that the requirement for informed consent is a more recent phenomenon. Suggestions about the need for patient informed consent can be found as far back as Plato, however. The first recorded legal case involving informed consent is the 1767 English case of *Slater v. Baker and Sapleton,* in which two surgeons refractured a patient's leg after it had healed improperly. The patient claimed they had not obtained consent. The court ruled:

[I]t appears from the evidence of the surgeon that it was improper to disunite the callous without consent; this is the usage and law of surgeons: then it was ignorance and unskillfulness in that very particular, to do contrary to the rule of the profession, what no surgeon ought to have done.

Although there may be some skepticism about the extent of the information disclosed or the precise nature of the consent obtained, the notable fact is that an 18th century court declared that obtaining prior patient consent is not only the usual practice, but also the ethical and legal obligation of surgeons. Failure to obtain consent is incompetence and inexcusable. In contemporary times, the 1957 case of *Salgo v. Leland Stanford Junior University Board of Trustees* constitutes a landmark by stating that physicians have a positive legal obligation to disclose information about risks, benefits, and alternatives to patients; this decision popularized the term *informed consent*.

DEFINITION AND JUSTIFICATION. Informed consent is when a person autonomously authorizes a physician to undertake diagnostic or therapeutic interventions for himself or herself. In this view, the patient understands that he or she is taking responsibility for the decision, while empowering someone else, the physician, to implement it. Not any agreement to a course of medical treatment qualifies as informed consent, however. There are three fundamental requirements for valid informed consent: disclosure, understanding, and voluntariness. Crucial information relevant to the decision must be disclosed, usually by the physician, to the patient. The patient must understand the information and its implications for his or her interests and life goals. Finally, the patient must make a voluntary decision (i.e., one without coercion or manipulation by the physician). It is a mistake to view informed consent as an event, such as the signing of a form. Informed consent is viewed more accurately as a process that evolves over the course of diagnosis and treatment.

Informed consent assumes people have the mental capacity to make decisions; disease, development, or medications can compromise patients' mental capacity to provide informed consent. Technically, adults are presumed to have the legal competence to make medical decisions, and determining whether an adult is incompetent to make medical decisions is a legal determination. Practically, physicians usually decide whether patients are competent or not based on whether patients can understand the information disclosed, appreciate its significance for their own situation, and use logical and consistent thought processes in decision making. Incompetence in medical decision making does not mean a person is incompetent in all types of decision making and vice versa. If patients are deemed incompetent, family members—beginning with spouse, children, parents, siblings, then more distant relatives—usually are selected as surrogates or proxies, although there may be concerns about conflicting interests or knowledge of the patients' wishes. In the relatively rare circumstance in which a patient formally designated a proxy, that person has decision-making authority.

Typically, patient autonomy is the value invoked to justify informed consent. Other values, such as bodily integrity and beneficence, also have been cited, especially in early legal rulings.

EMPIRIC DATA. Fairly extensive research has been done on informed consent. In general, studies show that physicians frequently do not communicate all relevant information for informed decision making. In a study of audiotapes from 1057 outpatient encounters, physicians mentioned alternatives in only 11.3% of cases, provided pros and cons of interventions in only 7.8% of situations, and assessed the patient's understanding of the information in only 1.5% of decisions. The more complex the medical decisions, the more likely it was that the elements of informed consent would be fulfilled. Similarly, studies show that patients frequently fail to recall crucial information disclosed, although they usually feel they have sufficient information for decision making. Whether patients fail to recall key information because they are overwhelmed by the information or because they do not find much of it salient to their decision is unclear. The issue is what patients understand at the point of decision making, not what they recall later.

One of the most important results of empiric research on informed consent is the information–decision making gap. Many studies show that most patients want information, but far fewer prefer decision-making authority. One study showed that most patients wanted information, but only about one third desired decision-making authority, and patients' decision-making preferences were not correlated with their information-seeking preferences. Several investigators found that patients' preference for decision-making authority increases with higher educational levels and declines with advancing age. Most importantly, the more serious the illness, the more likely patients are to prefer that physicians make the decisions. Several studies suggest that patients who have less of a desire to make their own decisions generally are more satisfied with how the decisions were made.

Finally, surrogate decision making has been studied most thoroughly in relationship to terminating care. In general, studies show that surrogates cannot predict patients' care preferences much better than chance. Surrogates' predictions about a patient's own assessment of quality of life are poor; surrogates tend to underestimate patients' functional status and satisfaction. Similarly, surrogate predictions are inaccurate regarding life-sustaining preferences when the patient is mentally incompetent. In one study, families agreed with patients only 68% of the time in deciding whether to provide cardiopulmonary resuscitation (CPR) to the patient if the patient became demented, when chance alone would generate agreement in 50% of the cases.

PRACTICAL CONSIDERATIONS. Implementing informed consent raises concerns about the extent of information to be disclosed and exceptions to the general requirement. What information to disclose and how has been a major area of ethical and legal disagreement. As a practical matter, physicians should disclose at least six fundamental elements of information to patients: (1) the diagnosis and prognosis, (2) the nature of the proposed intervention, (3) alternative interventions, (4) the risks associated with each alternative, (5) the benefits of each alternative, and (6) the likely outcomes of these alternatives (Table 2–1). Because risk is usually the key worry of physicians, it generally is recommended that physicians disclose (1) the nature of the risks, (2) their magnitude, (3) the probability that each risk will occur, and (4) when the consequence might occur. Some argue that minor risks need not be disclosed. In general, serious risks, even if rare, should be disclosed, as should common risks.

The central problem is that the physician should provide this detailed information within reasonable time constraints and yet not overwhelm patients with complex information in technical language. The result has been various legal standards defining how much information should be disclosed. The *physician* or *customary* standard, adapted from malpractice law, states that the physician should disclose that information "which a reasonable medical practitioner would make under the same or similar circumstances." Conversely the *reasonable person* or *lay oriented* standard states that physicians should disclose all information that a "reasonable person in the patient's circumstances would find material to" their medical decision. The physician standard is factual and can be determined empirically, but the patient-oriented standard, which is meant to engage physicians with patients, is hypothetical. Currently, each standard is used by about half the states.

There are exceptions to the requirements of informed consent. In emergency situations, consent can be assumed because reasonable persons would want treatment. In some circumstances, physicians may believe the process of informed consent could harm the patient. In rare cases, the "therapeutic privilege" promoting patient well-being trumps autonomy, but physicians should be wary of invoking this exception too readily.

How surrogates decide appropriate treatments for mentally incompetent patients is a matter of much controversy. The *substituted judgment* standard states that the surrogate should choose what the patient would choose if he or she were competent. The *best interests* standard states that the surrogate should choose what is best for the patient. Frequently, it is not clear how the patient would have decided because the situation was not discussed with the patient and he or she left no living will. Similarly, what is best for a patient is controversial because there are usually tradeoffs between quality of life and survival. These problems can be reflected in conflicts among family members or between the family and medical providers. In such circumstances, an ethics consultation may be helpful.

Table 2–1 • FUNDAMENTAL ELEMENTS FOR DISCLOSURE TO PATIENTS

Diagnosis and prognosis
Nature of proposed intervention
Reasonable alternative interventions
Risks associated with each alternative intervention
Benefits associated with each alternative intervention
Probable outcomes of each alternative intervention

Terminating Medical Interventions

HISTORY. Since the start of medicine, it has been viewed as ethical to withhold medical treatments from the terminally ill and "let nature take its course." Hippocrates argued that physicians should "refuse to treat those [patients] who are overmastered by their disease." In the 19th century, prominent American physicians advocated withholding cathartic and emetic "treatments" from the terminally ill and using ether to ease pain at the end of life. In 1900, editors of *The Lancet* argued that physicians should intervene to ease the pain of death but did not have an obligation to prolong a clearly terminal life. The contemporary debate on terminating care began in 1976 with the *Quinlan* case, in which the New Jersey Supreme Court ruled that patients had a right to refuse life-sustaining interventions based on a right of privacy and that the family could exercise the right for a patient in a persistent vegetative state.

DEFINITION AND JUSTIFICATION. It generally is agreed that all patients have a right to refuse medical interventions. Ethically, this right is based on patient autonomy and is implied by the doctrine of informed consent. Legally, state courts have cited the right to privacy, right to bodily integrity, or common law to justify the right to refuse medical treatment. In the 1990 *Cruzan* case and in the subsequent physician-assisted suicide cases, the U.S. Supreme Court affirmed that there is a "constitutionally protected right to refuse lifesaving hydration and nutrition." The Court stated that "[A] liberty interest [based on the 14th Amendment] in refusing unwanted medical treatment may be inferred from our prior decisions." All patients have a constitutional and an ethical right to refuse medical interventions.

EMPIRIC DATA. Data show that terminating medical treatments is now the norm. More than 85% of Americans die without CPR, with more than 90% of decedents in intensive care units not receiving CPR. Of decedents in intensive care units, 90% die after the withholding or withdrawal of medical treatments, with an average of 2.6 interventions being withheld or withdrawn per decedent. Since the 1990s, the trend has been to stop interventions more frequently.

Despite extensive public support for use of advance care directives and the passage of the Patient Self-Determination Act mandating that health care institutions inform patients of their right to complete such documents, only about 20% of Americans have completed one. Efforts to improve completion of advance care directives have generated mixed results; even successful pilot efforts have not been adopted or reproduced widely. A persistent problem has been that even when patients complete advance care directives, the documents frequently are not available, physicians do not know they exist, or they tend to be too general or vague to guide decisions.

Just as surrogates are poor at predicting patients' wishes, data show that physicians are probably even worse at determining patients' preferences for life-sustaining treatments. In many cases, life-sustaining treatments are continued even when patients or their proxies desire them to be stopped; conversely, most physicians discontinue or never begin interventions unilaterally without the knowledge or consent of patients or their surrogate decision makers. These discrepancies emphasize the importance of engaging patients early in their care about treatment preferences.

PRACTICAL CONSIDERATIONS. There are many practical considerations in enacting this right (Table 2–2). First, patients have a right to refuse any and all medical interventions, from blood transfusions and antibiotics to respirators, artificial hydration, and nutrition. Although initiating CPR was the focus of the early court cases, this issue is viewed best as addressing just one of the many medical interventions that can be stopped or withheld. The attempt to distinguish ordinary from extraordinary or heroic treatments has been unhelpful in determining which treatments may be stopped.

Second, there is no ethical or legal difference between withholding an intervention and withdrawing it. If a respirator or other treatment is started because physicians are uncertain whether a patient would have wanted it, they always can stop it later when information clarifies the patient's wishes. Although physicians and nurses might find stopping a treatment to be more difficult psychologically, withdrawal is ethically and legally permitted—and required—when it is consonant with the patient's wishes.

Third, competent patients have the exclusive right to decide about terminating their own care. If there is a conflict between a competent patient and his or her family, the patient's wishes are to be followed. It is the patient's right to refuse treatment, not the family's right. For incompetent patients, the situation is more complex; if the patients

Table 2–2 • PRACTICAL CONSIDERATIONS IN TERMINATING MEDICAL TREATMENTS

PRACTICAL QUESTION	ANSWER
Is there a legal right to refuse medical interventions?	Yes, the U.S. Supreme Court declared that competent people have a constitutionally protected right to refuse unwanted medical treatments based on the 14th Amendment.
What interventions can be legally and ethically terminated?	Any and all interventions (including respirators, antibiotics, intravenous or enteral nutrition, and hydration) can be legally and ethically terminated.
Is there a difference between withholding life-sustaining interventions and withdrawing them?	No, the consensus is that there is no important legal or ethical difference between withholding and withdrawing medical interventions. Stopping a treatment already begun is just as ethical as never having started it.
Whose view about terminating life-sustaining interventions prevails if there is a conflict between the patient and family?	The views of a competent adult patient prevail. It is the patient's body and life.
Who decides about terminating life-sustaining interventions if the patient is incompetent?	If the patient appointed a proxy or surrogate decision maker when competent, that person is legally empowered to make decisions about terminating care. If no proxy was appointed, there is a legally designated hierarchy, usually (1) spouse, (2) adult children, (3) parents, (4) siblings, and (5) available relatives.
Are advance care directives legally enforceable?	Yes, as a clear expression of the patient's wishes they are a constitutionally protected method for patients to exercise their right to refuse medical treatments.

left clear indications of their wishes, whether as oral statements or as written advance care directives, these wishes should be followed. Physicians should not be overly concerned about the precise form patients use to express their wishes; because patients have a constitutional right to refuse treatment, the real concern is whether the wishes are clear and relevant to the situation. If an incompetent patient did not leave explicit indications of his or her wishes or designate a proxy decision maker, the physician should identify a surrogate decision maker and rely on the decision maker's wishes, while being cognizant of the potential problems noted.

Fourth, the right to refuse medical treatment does not translate into a right to demand any treatment, especially treatments that have no pathophysiologic rationale, have already failed, or are known to be harmful. Attempts by physicians to invoke futility as a rationale for stopping treatments have been fraught with problems, however. Initially, some commentators advocated that an intervention was futile when the probability of success was 1% or lower. Although this threshold seems to be based on empiric data, it is a covert value judgment. Because the declaration of futility is meant to justify unilateral determinations by physicians, it generally has been viewed as an inappropriate assertion that undermines physician-patient communication and violates the principle of shared decision making. Similar to the ordinary/extraordinary distinction, futility is viewed increasingly as more obfuscating than clarifying, and it is being invoked much less often.

Assisted Suicide and Euthanasia

HISTORY. Since Hippocrates, euthanasia and physician-assisted suicide have been controversial issues. In 1905, a bill was introduced into the Ohio legislature to legalize euthanasia; it was defeated. In

Table 2–3 • DEFINITIONS OF ASSISTED SUICIDE AND EUTHANASIA

TERM	DEFINITION
Voluntary active euthanasia	Intentionally administering medications or other interventions to cause the patient's death with the patient's informed consent
Involuntary active euthanasia	Intentionally administering medications or other interventions to cause the patient's death when the patient was competent to consent but did not (e.g., the patient may not have been asked)
Nonvoluntary active euthanasia	Intentionally administering medications or other interventions to cause the patient's death when the patient was incompetent and was mentally incapable of consenting (e.g., the patient might have been in a coma)
Passive euthanasia	Withholding or withdrawing life-sustaining medical treatments from a patient to let him or her die (terminating life-sustaining treatments)
Indirect euthanasia	Administering narcotics or other medications to relieve pain with the incidental consequence of causing sufficient respiratory depression to result in the patient's death
Physician-assisted suicide	A physician provides medications or other interventions to a patient with the understanding that the patient can use them to commit suicide

the mid-1930s, similar bills were introduced and defeated in the British Parliament and the Nebraska legislature. Today, physician-assisted suicide is legal in Oregon, and euthanasia and physician-assisted suicide are legal in the Netherlands.

DEFINITION AND JUSTIFICATION. There has been much terminologic confusion about euthanasia and physician-assisted suicide. Table 2–3 provides accepted definitions. So-called passive and indirect euthanasia are not cases of euthanasia, and both are deemed ethical and legal.

There are four arguments against permitting euthanasia and physician-assisted suicide. First, Kant and Mill thought that autonomy did not permit the voluntary ending of the conditions necessary for autonomy, and as a result, both philosophers were against voluntary enslavement and suicide. Consequently the exercise of autonomy cannot include the ending of life because that would mean ending the possibility of exercising autonomy. Second, many dying patients may have pain and suffering because they are not receiving appropriate care, and it is possible that adequate care would relieve much pain and suffering (Chapter 3). Although a few patients still may suffer uncontrolled pain and suffering despite optimal end-of-life care, it is unwise to use the condition of these few patients as a justification to permit euthanasia and/or physician-assisted suicide for any dying patient. Third, there is a clear distinction between intentionally ending a life compared with terminating life-sustaining treatments. The actual acts are different—injecting a life-ending medication, such as a muscle relaxant, or providing a prescription for one is not the same as removing or refraining from introducing an invasive medical intervention. Finally, adverse consequences of permitting euthanasia and physician-assisted suicide must be considered. There are disturbing reports of involuntary euthanasia in the Netherlands, and many worry about coercion of expensive or burdensome patients to accept euthanasia and/or physician-assisted suicide. Permitting euthanasia and physician-assisted suicide is likely to lead to further intrusions of lawyers, courts, and legislatures into the physician-patient relationship.

There are four parallel arguments for permitting euthanasia and physician-assisted suicide. First, it is argued that autonomy justifies euthanasia and physician-assisted suicide. To respect autonomy requires permitting individuals to decide when it is better to end their lives by euthanasia and/or physician-assisted suicide. Second, beneficence—furthering the well-being of individuals—supports permitting euthanasia and physician-assisted suicide. In some cases, living can create more pain and suffering than death; ending a painful life relieves more suffering and produces more good. Just the

reassurance of having the option of euthanasia and/or physician-assisted suicide, even if people do not use it, can provide "psychological insurance" and be beneficial to people. Third, euthanasia and physician-assisted suicide are no different from terminating life-sustaining treatments that are recognized as ethically justified. In both cases, the patient consents to die; in both cases, the physician intends to end the patient's life and takes some action to end the patient's life; and in both cases, the final result is the same: the patient's death. With no difference in patient consent, physician intention, or the final result, there can be no difference in the ethical justification. Fourth, the supposed slippery slope that would result from permitting euthanasia and physician-assisted suicide is not likely. The idea that permitting euthanasia and physician-assisted suicide would undermine the physician-patient relationship or lead to forced euthanasia is completely speculative and not borne out by the available data.

In its 1997 decisions, the U.S. Supreme Court stated that there is no constitutional right to euthanasia and physician-assisted suicide, but that there also is no constitutional prohibition against states legalizing these interventions. Consequently, Oregon's legalization of physician-assisted suicide was constitutional. In more recent years, however, voters consistently have defeated referenda to legalize physician-assisted suicide in other states, and bills have been defeated in state legislatures.

EMPIRIC DATA. Attitudes and practices related to euthanasia and physician-assisted suicide have been studied extensively. First, surveys indicate that 60 to 70% of Americans support euthanasia and/or physician-assisted suicide for terminally ill patients who suffer intractable pain, but public support declines significantly for euthanasia and/or physician-assisted suicide in other circumstances. American physicians are much less likely to support euthanasia and/or physician-assisted suicide, with oncologists being even more opposed than other types of physicians. Second, approximately 18 to 25% of American physicians have received requests for euthanasia and/or physician-assisted suicide; 43 to 63% of oncologists have received requests. Third, multiple studies indicate that less than 5% of American physicians have performed euthanasia and/or physician-assisted suicide. Among oncologists, 4% have performed euthanasia and 11% have performed physician-assisted suicide during their careers. Fourth, in many cases, the safeguards are violated. One study found that in 54% of euthanasia cases it was the family who made the request; in 39% of euthanasia and 19% of physician-assisted suicide cases the patient was depressed; in only half of the cases was the request repeated.

Counterintuitively, data indicate that it is not pain that motivates requests for euthanasia and/or physician-assisted suicide, but rather psychological distress, especially depression and hopelessness. In Oregon's first year, only 15% of patients who received physician-assisted suicide had uncontrolled pain. Interviews with physicians and with patients with amyotrophic lateral sclerosis, cancer, or infection with human immunodeficiency virus show that pain is not associated with interest in euthanasia and/or physician-assisted suicide; instead, depression and hopelessness are the strongest predictors of interest.

Finally, data from the Netherlands and the United States suggest there are significant problems in performing euthanasia and/or physician-assisted suicide. Dutch researchers reported that physician-assisted suicide causes complications in 7% of cases, and in 15% of cases, the patients did not die, awoke from coma, or vomited up the medication. Ultimately, in nearly 20% of physician-assisted suicide cases, the physician ended up injecting the patient with life-ending medication, converting physician-assisted suicide to euthanasia. These data raise serious questions about how to address complications of physician-assisted suicide when euthanasia is illegal or unacceptable.

PRACTICAL CONSIDERATIONS. There is widespread agreement that if euthanasia and physician-assisted suicide are used, they should be considered only after all attempts at physical and psychological palliation have failed. A series of safeguards have been developed and embodied in the Oregon and the Dutch procedures, as follows: (1) The patient must be competent and must request euthanasia and/or physician-assisted suicide repeatedly and voluntarily; (2) the patient must have pain and suffering that cannot be relieved by optimal palliative interventions; (3) there is a waiting period to ensure the patient's desire for euthanasia and/or physician-assisted suicide is stable and sincere; and (4) the physician should obtain a second opinion from an independent physician. Oregon requires patients to be terminally ill, whereas the Netherlands has no such safeguard. Although there have been some prosecutions, there have been no convictions—except for Dr. Kevorkian—when physicians and others have participated in euthanasia and/or physician-assisted suicide.

Financial Conflicts of Interest

HISTORY. Worrying about how payment and fees affect medical decisions is not new. In 1899, a physician reported that more than 60% of surgeons in Chicago were willing to provide a 50% commission to physicians for referring cases. He subsequently argued that in some cases this fee splitting led to unnecessary surgical procedures. A 1912 study by the American Medical Association confirmed that fee splitting was a common practice. Selling patent medicines and patenting surgical instruments were other forms of financial conflicts of interest thought to discredit physicians a century ago. In the 1990s, the ethics of capitation for physician services and pharmaceutical prescriptions and payments by pharmaceutical and biotechnology companies to clinical researchers raised the issue of financial conflicts of interest.

DEFINITION AND JUSTIFICATION. It commonly is argued that physicians have certain primary interests: (1) to promote the well-being of their patients, (2) to advance biomedical research, (3) to educate future physicians and, more controversially, (4) to promote public health (Table 2–4). Physicians also have other, secondary interests, such as earning income, raising a family, and pursuing avocational interests. These secondary interests are not evil; they are legitimate and admirable. A conflict of interest occurs when one of these secondary interests compromises pursuit of a primary interest, especially patient well-being.

Conflicts of interest are problematic because they can or appear to compromise the integrity of physicians' judgment, compromising patient well-being. Conflict of interest can induce a physician to do something—perform a procedure, fail to order a test—that would not be in a patient's best interest. These conflicts can undermine the trust of patients and the public, not only in an individual physician, but also in the entire medical profession. The appearance of conflicts of interest can be damaging because it is difficult for patients and the public "to determine what motives have influenced a professional decision." The focus on financial conflicts of interest is not because they are worse than other types of conflicts, but because they are more pervasive and more easily identified and regulated compared with other conflicts. Since ancient times, the ethical norm on conflicts has been clear: The physician's primary obligation is to patients' well-being, and a physician's personal financial well-being should not compromise this duty.

EMPIRIC DATA. Financial conflicts are not rare. In Florida, it was estimated that nearly 40% of physicians were involved as owners of freestanding facilities to which they referred patients. Studies in the early 1990s consistently showed that self-referring physicians ordered more services, frequently charged more per service, and referred patients with less established indications. In one study, 4 to 4.5 times more imaging examinations were ordered by self-referring physicians than by physicians who referred patients to radiologists. Similarly, patients referred to joint-venture physical therapy facilities have an average of 16 visits compared with 11 at non–joint-venture facilities. Of greatest concern, licensed physical therapists at joint-venture facilities spent about 28 minutes per patient per visit compared with 48 minutes at non–joint-venture facilities. There are no comparable data on the influence of capitation on physician judgment.

Similarly, multiple studies have shown that interaction with pharmaceutical representatives can lead to prescribing of new drugs, nonrational prescribing, and decreased use of generic drugs by physicians. Industry funding for continuing medical education payment for travel to educational symposia increases prescribing of the sponsor's drug.

PRACTICAL CONSIDERATIONS. First, it is important to recognize that financial conflicts of interest are inherent in any profession when the professional earns income from rendering a service. Second, conflicts come in many different forms, from legitimate payment for services rendered, to investments in medical laboratories and facilities, to drug company dinners and payment for attendance at meetings, to payment for enrolling patients in clinical research trials, to consultation with companies.

Third, in considering how to manage conflicts, it is important to note that people are poor judges of their own potential conflicts. Individuals often cannot distinguish the various influences that guide their judgments, do not think of themselves as bad, and do not imagine that payment shapes their judgments. Physicians tend to be defensive regarding charges of conflicts of interest. In addition, conflicts tend to act insidiously, subtly changing practice patterns so that they then become what appear to be justifiable norms.

Fourth, rules—whether laws, regulations, or professional standards—to regulate conflicts of interest are based on two considerations: (1) the likelihood that payment or other secondary interests would create a conflict and (2) the magnitude of the potential harm if there is compromised judgment. Rules tend to be of three types: (1) disclosure of conflicts, (2) management of conflicts, and (3) outright prohibition. Federal law bans certain types of physician self-referral in the Medicare program. The American Medical Association and the Pharmaceutical Research and Manufacturers of America have established joint rules that permit physicians to accept gifts of minimal value but "refuse substantial gifts from drug companies, such as the costs of travel, lodging, or other personal expenses . . . for attending conferences or meetings."

Fifth, although there is much emphasis on disclosure of conflicts, which may be useful in publications, it is unclear whether this is a suitable safeguard in the clinical setting. Disclosure just may make patients worry more. Patients may have no context in which to place the disclosure or evaluate the physician's clinical recommendation, and patients may have few other options in selecting a physician or getting care, especially in an acute situation.

Finally, some conflicts can be avoided by a physician's own action. Physicians can refuse to engage in personal investments in medical facilities or to accept gifts from pharmaceutical companies at relatively little personal cost. In other circumstances, the conflicts may be institutionalized, and minimizing them can occur only by changing the way organizations structure reimbursement incentives. Capitation encourages physicians to limit medical services, and its potentially adverse effects are likely to be managed by institutional rules, rather than by personal decisions.

Future Directions

In the near future, as genetics moves from the research to the clinical setting, practicing physicians are likely to encounter issues surrounding genetic testing, counseling, and treatment (Chapter 36). The use of genetic tests without the extensive counseling so common in research studies would alter the nature of the bioethical issues. Because these tests have serious implications for the patient and others, scrupulous attention to informed consent must occur. The bioethical issues raised by genetic tests for somatic cell changes, such as tests that occur commonly in cancer diagnosis and risk stratification, are no different than the issues raised with the use of any laboratory or radiographic test.

In some cases, ethics consultation services may be of assistance in resolving bioethical dilemmas, although current data suggest that consultation services are used mainly for problems that arise in individual cases and are not used for more institutional or policy problems.

Table 2–4 • PRIMARY INTERESTS OF PHYSICIANS
Promoting the health and well-being of their patients
Advancing biomedical knowledge through research
Educating future physicians and health care providers
Promoting the public health

SUGGESTED READINGS

Bauchamp TL, Childress JF: Principles of Biomedical Ethics, 5th ed. New York, Oxford University Press, 2001. *An excellent review.*

Berg JW, Applebaum PS, Lidz CW, Parker LS: Informed Consent: Legal Theory and Clinical Practice, 2nd ed. New York, Oxford University Press, 2001. *Principles and guidelines for obtaining informed consent.*

Crawley LM, Marshall PA, Lo B, et al: Strategies for culturally effective end-of-life care. Ann Intern Med 2002;136:673–679. *Emphasizes differences in preferences based on cultural background.*

Partnership for Caring: Available at www.partnershipforcaring.org. *A frequently updated website.*

3 CARE OF DYING PATIENTS AND THEIR FAMILIES

J. Andrew Billings

What can a physician offer when a patient is dying? No procedure, no medicine, and no words can thwart death, and the physician is faced with a morass of difficult emotions in the patient, family, staff, and self. Death may be viewed as the physician's personal failure. The dying person also may be an unwelcome reminder of the limitations of medicine, of the inevitability of loss and suffering in life, and of mortality. Few clinicians have been trained in providing good end-of-life care, and many feel uneasy, uncertain, or helpless about their role in these settings. Many physicians tend to avoid terminally ill patients, contributing to the isolation and loneliness regularly experienced by the dying.

Patients and families facing a terminal condition report hearing from clinicians, "There is nothing more we can do," a terrible dismissal that is never true. Physicians have a vital, active, and often satisfying role in the final stages of illness, assuring safe passage for the patient and family and guiding them through an often complicated, frightening, unfamiliar, and difficult process. Good care for a person with an advanced, fatal condition means the physician, although recognizing the impossibility of cure, engages enthusiastically in the many opportunities to be helpful, primarily through preventing and treating physical, emotional, and spiritual suffering and by assisting in defining and achieving appropriate goals for the end of life. Shifting from a familiar focus on cure and life prolongation to a focus on comfort and quality of life—maintaining a focus on both—often proves difficult for physicians and for patients and families.

Talking with Dying Patients

How does one talk with a dying person? More important than anything that is said is the ability to listen carefully—to let patients express their understanding of the situation and their concerns and hopes. All the issues outlined in this chapter are likely to tumble out of the patient's mouth when the physician sits down with the dying person in a quiet, private setting; attends in a relaxed, unhurried manner; facilitates and encourages discussion and elaboration; tolerates occasional silences; pays close attention to verbal and nonverbal communication; discreetly encourages expression of emotion; provides empathic responses; tactfully probes difficult topics; and gently guides the discussion toward the common concerns of a person facing a fatal illness. The discussion often begins with the physician asking some introductory questions (Table 3–1). In the next sections, four key issues in end-of-life care are addressed: pain and symptom control, shared decision making, psychosocial and spiritual support, and alternative sites of care.

IS THE PATIENT COMFORTABLE? (PAIN AND SYMPTOM CONTROL)

A first step in good end-of-life care is meticulous attention to the management of a variety of disagreeable symptoms faced by the dying person—attending to "all that hurts," including physical distress, emotional suffering, functional limitations, and any other factors impairing quality of life. Assessment should precede treatment, although many symptoms in advanced disease do not require further diagnostic investigation to guide initial management, and sometimes the discomfort of such procedures outweighs their benefit. Treatment of pain in terminally ill patients does not need to await determination of the cause of pain (Chapter 29). Some symptoms are predictable and preventable (e.g., dyspnea from an enlarging pleural effusion), so the physician should anticipate and plan for alleviating such conditions before they cause serious distress, sometimes rehearsing next steps with the patient: "If the shortness of breath worsens, you can turn up the oxygen to 5 liters per minute and double the dosage of the morphine." Additionally, patients and family members regularly harbor unrealistic fears about the future (e.g., of intractable pain or other severe suffering), so eliciting and addressing concerns about anticipated suffering can be as important as managing symptoms: "No, I don't think you have to worry about suffocating or choking with this sort of condition."

Table 3–1 • SUGGESTED QUESTIONS FOR THE CLINICAL INTERVIEW WITH PATIENTS FACING THE END OF LIFE

Tell me the story of your illness. [the patient's perspective]
Tell me how you first found out about your illness. [hearing bad news]
　　How were you told?
　　What was it like? How did you feel then?
What is your understanding now about the illness? [patient's understanding]
　　What have you been told? What do the doctors say? Your family?
　　How did it begin? What caused it? Why did it happen?
　　How has it been treated?
　　What is happening with the illness now? What is likely to happen?
　　What are your expectations and concerns about the future?
What do you want to be told about your illness? [shared decision making and information preferences]
　　Part of my job is to assure that you have as much information as you wish about your health and that all your questions are answered in understandable terms. But people vary enormously in how much they want to know about their medical condition and their options for treatment—some want to hear as many of the details as possible, while others prefer to leave these matters to the doctors or their family
　　How much do you want to be told?
　　If there is bad news, how do you want to be informed?
　　How do you want us to communicate about these matters with your family?
How has the illness affected you? [patient's coping]
　　What has it been like for you?
　　How has it affected you physically?
　　　Have you had pain?
　　　Other disagreeable physical problems?
　　How are you doing emotionally?
　　　Have you been upset?
　　　　Nervous? Frightened? Worried?
　　　　Angry? Irritable?
　　　　Sad or depressed?
　　What has been most difficult about the illness?
　　What are your main worries now?
　　Has there been any good side to what has happened?
How have your family (or close friends) been affected? [family's coping]
　　What have you discussed with them?
How have you been helped? [supports]
　　What gives you strength in facing these problems?
　　How have you been helped by family and friends?
　　　What do they say or do?
　　　How are they not helpful or disappointing?
　　How have you been helped by doctors and nurses?
　　　Other health care workers?
　　　How are they not helpful or disappointing?
Have there been other tough times you have had to face? [previous coping]
　　Have there been other serious illnesses or losses?
　　What was it like for you then?
　　How did you manage? What helped?
Do you have a religious or spiritual practice or set of beliefs? [existential and spiritual concerns]
　　Were you brought up in a religious tradition? Do you continue in this tradition? Are you connected to a minister (priest, rabbi)? To a church or congregation?
　　How have your religious background and current religious or spiritual beliefs affected your experience of this illness?
　　How have you made sense of this serious illness?
　　How has your faith been important to you?
　　Do you pray? What about? To whom?
　　Do you believe in a life after death?
Have you been thinking about dying? [addressing death and dying]
　　What kinds of thoughts have you had? What worries?
　　Have you made plans because of it?

From Billings JA, Block SD: Program in palliative care education and practice. 2002. Available at http://www.hms.harvard.edu/cdi/pallcare/

Numerous studies in a variety of settings show a high incidence of inadequately treated pain in many terminal illnesses (Chapter 29). An "epidemic of unnecessary pain" has been attributed to poor clinical education about pain management, a focus on diagnosis and treatment of underlying conditions rather than on patients' suffering, and inappropriate fears of opioids among laypersons and health professionals (Chapters 29 and 30). Relatively simple pharmacologic management can control about 75% of pain in advanced cancer, whereas

Table 3–2 • COMMON SYMPTOMS IN SERIOUSLY ILL HOSPITALIZED PATIENTS (% OF TOTAL PATIENTS)

	AT ANY TIME	SEVERE AND FREQUENT*
Pain	51%	23%
Dyspnea	49%	23%
Anxiety	47%	16%
Depression	45%	14%
Nausea	34%	6%

*Moderately or extremely severe symptoms occurring half to all the time.
After Desbiens NA, Mueller-Rizner N, Connors AF Jr, et al for the SUPPORT investigators: The symptom burden of seriously ill hospitalized patients. J Pain Symptom Manage 1999;17:248–255.

Table 3–3 • PATIENT'S PERSPECTIVE ON A "GOOD DEATH"

Control pain and other symptoms
Avoid inappropriate prolongation of dying when life no longer enjoyable
Relieve burden on the family
Achieve a sense of control
Strengthen relationships with loved ones

After Singer PA, Martin DK, Kelner M: Quality end-of-life care: patients' perspective. JAMA 1999;218:163–168.

more specialized interventions are successful for all but a small proportion of the remaining patients (see Fig. 29–3).

Similar disturbingly high rates of untreated nonpain symptoms, including dyspnea and anxiety, have been shown in adults and children with terminal illness (Table 3–2). Most patients report multiple disturbing symptoms. Depression (Chapter 426) and delirium (Chapter 26) often are underrecognized and inadequately managed.

Encouraging progress in the relief of many nonpain symptoms of advanced, terminal disease (e.g., nausea and vomiting) has occurred over the past few decades, and all of these symptoms can be alleviated, although not eradicated. Common, underused interventions include opioids and benzodiazepines for dyspnea; antimuscarinics for excessive secretions and "death rattle"; glucocorticosteroids and progestational agents for anorexia; prokinetic agents for gastroparesis; glucocorticosteroids for fatigue and obstruction of a viscus; neuroleptics (rather than benzodiazepines) for confusional states; artificial saliva for xerostomia; and psychostimulants for depression, fatigue, and sedation. The physician, working closely with nurses and other allied health practitioners, should become familiar with nonpharmacologic approaches to providing comfort, including careful skin and mouth care, adapting the home to the needs of a debilitated patient, and dealing with issues such as bowels and bladder when a patient is bed bound.

Unnecessary and disagreeable treatments and diagnostic maneuvers that hold little promise of improving a patient's quality of life should be avoided. Many routines of hospital care, including venipunctures, endotracheal suction, noisy monitors, and obtaining vital signs or turning the patient in bed, especially when patients are trying to sleep, often can be discontinued, whereas heightened attention may be required for mouth comfort and regular bowel movements. The clinician may promote well-being and reduce suffering by choosing conservative management of selected conditions (e.g., managing partial small bowel obstruction without nasogastric suction); using simpler, less painful interventions in the place of complex, disagreeable approaches (e.g., sublingual administration of medications rather than starting intravenous catheters); and forgoing inappropriate treatments (e.g., use of feeding tubes for advanced dementia).

IS THE PATIENT WELL INFORMED, AND HAS AN INDIVIDUALIZED PLAN OF CARE BEEN DEVELOPED? (SHARED DECISION MAKING)

WHAT IS A "GOOD DEATH"? There is no right way to die except for the way an informed patient desires. The patient's view of a "good death" is highly individualized and often different than the perspective held by physicians (Table 3–3). Psychosocial and spiritual goals often trump biomedical goals. Good end-of-life care requires a shared understanding of the patient's values and aspirations. Physicians tend to see their role as prolonging life at any reasonable cost, whereas patients may place higher priority on being at home; having meaningful time with their family; and avoiding unnecessary, expensive, or physically distressing prolongation of life. Family members, although hoping for a cure or prolonged survival, may recognize that communicating love and enjoying relationships are usually more important than having the patient endure extra days in discomfort.

INFORMATION SHARING AND HOPE. End-of-life care for a chronic, progressive illness inevitably places the physician in the role of repeatedly sharing bad news. No expertise in communication skills can make the conveying of distressing information painless for the patient and family or easy for the physician, but clinical guidelines can promote a humane process (Table 3–4).

Patients cannot make good choices and participate intelligently in setting goals and making decisions unless they are reasonably well informed about their condition. Major gaps in terminally ill persons' understanding about their condition, especially about prognosis and alternatives to treatment, have been documented repeatedly. Almost all dying patients report that they want to be informed about their medical condition, although excess frankness or a presentation of information that is perceived as uncaring can be viewed as cruel or as taking away hope. Many patients seem to have unrealistically optimistic expectations about the value of treatments, regardless of what they have been told. At the same time, patients and their health care professionals may "collude" in avoiding discussions of troubling topics or disagreeable information. A few patients, reflecting their personal or cultural preferences, do not want to be informed fully and instead prefer to delegate decisions to their family or physicians.

The sharing of information and the making of decisions in the face of a life-threatening illness often are not totally rational processes, and neither the provision of better prognostic estimates nor the encouragement to share information has been shown to reduce pain or potentially unnecessary discomfort.■ How much information a terminally

Table 3–4 • SHARING BAD NEWS

1. *Find an appropriate setting and adequate time.* Ensure comfort, privacy, quiet, absence of interruptions
2. *Prepare yourself.* Rehearse key points. Monitor your personal reactions
3. *Consider involving the family* (especially key decision makers) and other health professionals. Ask the patient who should be present
4. Unless the conversation occurs in the context of a well-established relationship, *begin by "aligning."* What does the patient and family know? What do they want to know? Let them ask questions and absorb information at their own pace
5. *Be brief and simple,* giving the key message in a few sentences. Give plain, clear explanations in jargon-free language. Set realistic goals for the initial discussion, avoiding information overload. Tailor the information to the listener. Grade exposure to upsetting material. Keep in mind key objectives: What does the patient really need to know? Repeat key points and write them down. Beware of euphemisms
6. *Honesty—exert a firm pressure for candor.* Avoid false reassurance and false optimism *versus* excess bluntness. Respect cultural and personal preferences about information sharing. Avoid false certainty or precision, but give patients needed prognostic information
7. *Listen.* Attending to the patient is often more important than what you say. Listen for and respond to concerns and emotions. Tolerate silence. Encourage questions. Clarify. What is "hope" for this patient?
8. *Support.* Convey your caring. Respond to affect. Actively elicit and encourage emotional reactions. Empathize. Acknowledge difficulty. Identify current supports and offer additional resources
9. *Offer next steps* that convey continued attention and, if reasonable, helpfulness (e.g., referral for treatment). Plan for follow-up for information sharing and support. Guarantee availability and continued attention. Conveying bad news is a process, not an event
10. *Document* information sharing, and communicate about it to the health care team.

ill patient wants to know or is able to appreciate about his or her medical condition varies enormously from person to person and from moment to moment for each individual. Requests for information may be requests for reassurance—pleas for offering hope. Especially when bad news is involved, a patient may deal with matters with deep ambivalence or denial—at one moment, eager to absorb new information and, at a later moment, acting as if the conversation never occurred. Family members may behave similarly or differ from the patient in terms of preferences for information or ability to grasp distressing facts. The physician should not use the patient's reluctance to hear bad news as an excuse for avoiding difficult discussions.

Discussions about prognosis may be particularly treacherous because physicians usually can offer only an educated guess. Nevertheless, laypersons may ascribe great certainty to the physician's estimates: "The doctor says he only has 3 months to live." Patients are entitled to a physician's best guesses, but speculations should be phrased in terms that reflect uncertainty and probabilities: "The course of this cancer can be quite unpredictable. I think you should be aware of the possibility that your health may deteriorate quickly, and plan accordingly. We probably are dealing with a few months, while hoping that the disease stabilizes and allows us even longer. As time goes on, the course may become clearer and, if you wish, I might be able to be a little more precise about what we are facing."

The physician's duty is neither to protect the patient from bad news nor to confront denial, but rather to tailor the sharing of information to a particular person at a particular time, while conveying realistic hopes and applying a firm, but gentle pressure toward full appreciation of current facts. Honesty is a requisite for a relationship of trust, but truth can be shaded to meet the patient's needs of the moment. The challenge for most clinicians is turning conversations toward a recognition that death is likely without leaving the patient and family feeling hopeless or abandoned: "I see how you are striving to overcome this illness and to focus on the bright side of things, but I wonder if part of you doesn't also sometimes think about things not working out so well?" The physician can help change the focus from exclusively curative or life-prolonging interventions to making the best of the remaining time, while striving to reassure the patient and family that everything reasonable will be done, that comfort is a priority, and that they will not be neglected. When a patient's expectations for cure or prolonged survival are unrealistic, the physician can reinforce realistic optimism on such matters as hopes for acceptable physical well-being and level of function, enjoying the love of one's family or friends, and developing a sense of completing a meaningful life. A shift toward comfort as the goal of care does not mean helplessness, hopelessness, or loss of the physician's commitment to making the best of the situation. The physician's acceptance of the inevitability of death, combined with expectations for and enthusiastic engagement in achieving the best possible dying and death, can lead the patient and family toward better coping and can support their maintenance of hope.

DIFFICULT DECISIONS. A common observation since the middle of the 20th century has been that advances in medical science lead to difficult new clinical and ethical decisions, such as whether to initiate cardiopulmonary resuscitation (CPR) or withdraw ventilatory support in situations in which these technologic interventions seem to prolong or contribute to suffering without offering clear benefit (Chapter 98). Such decisions constitute some of the most difficult judgments in medical practice and will become more frequent and complex in the future. Interventions that at one time were considered routine and even morally required, such as the provision of intravenous fluids for patients unable to drink on their own, are seen increasingly as matters of choice. Even now, few patients with one of the chronic fatal illnesses that cause most deaths in the United States can die without some judgments being made about whether to prolong dying by providing cardiopulmonary support, hospitalization, intensive care, blood products, antibiotics, pressors, nutritional support, and fluids. The nostalgic notion of a "natural death"—a death not involving difficult decisions about the use of technology or at least free of modern medical interventions—is limited to sudden deaths and patients who do not have access to good medical care. About a quarter of deaths now occur in intensive care units (ICUs), and in one study of ICU deaths, 90% involved the withholding and withdrawing of life support (Chapter 98). Death has been "medicalized."

Complicating matters further, studies of decision making in ICUs reveal conflicts between staff and family in half of cases and among family members about a quarter of the time, with such conflicts centering primarily on decisions to limit life-sustaining treatment. Clinicians express high rates of dissatisfaction about burdensome treatments in end-of-life care. A frequently discussed intervention in this setting is CPR (Chapters 2 and 98). Patients and families often have unrealistic notions of the utility of this procedure, which can be a life-saving measure in some settings but in terminally ill patients is unlikely to result in return of satisfactory cardiopulmonary function, survival to discharge from the hospital, or ability to return home.

ADVANCE CARE PLANNING. Many terminally ill patients, especially patients hospitalized or facing the last few days of life, cannot participate meaningfully in health care decisions owing to confusion or other barriers to understanding and communication. In anticipation of difficult decisions when the patient lacks decisional capacity, patients have been encouraged to designate health care proxies and to create advance care planning documents, typified by the use of living wills (Chapter 2). These documents are meant to protect patients against unwanted treatments, and the courts, at times, have considered them essential if life-sustaining treatments are to be withheld or withdrawn. Discussions of such documents among family members generally provoke important conversations about end-of-life care decisions and encourage patients to name a substitute decision maker, proxy, or "surrogate" who, should the patient become seriously ill and incapacitated, ideally can represent the patient's wishes and identify treatment preferences in specific situations. The potential utility of a health care proxy seems incontrovertible. Advance care directives are prepared infrequently by patients, however, and rarely are documented in accessible medical records, even on hospital admission for a serious illness. Earlier decisions made by patients in a time of relative stability may not reflect their true wishes in a later situation when they are faced by a serious illness, so documents must be reviewed regularly. When advance care directives, including do not resuscitate orders, are obtained, patients frequently have serious misunderstandings. Finally, physicians often do not understand or follow such directives. In one large multi-institutional study, physicians did no better than chance in identifying their seriously ill hospitalized patients' wishes to forgo CPR, and such wishes, even when known, rarely were respected when the physician believed that another course was appropriate.[1]

ARE THE PSYCHOSOCIAL AND SPIRITUAL CONCERNS OF THE PATIENT AND FAMILY BEING ADDRESSED? (PSYCHOSOCIAL AND SPIRITUAL SUPPORT)

Emotional, social, economic, and spiritual distresses among patients and their families near the end of life are even more complex phenomena than physical suffering, and they generally are even less well understood.

EMOTIONAL SUFFERING. Patients commonly face issues such as isolation and loneliness, fear and anxiety, being a burden on loved ones, a sense of loss of control and vulnerability, diminished self-esteem associated with inability to perform normal roles, worries about the future of dependents, adaptation to disfigurement, unrecognized or untreated depression, wishes for a hastened death, economic pressures, and existential or spiritual crises. For the universal crises of dying, death, and loss, deep feelings and strong beliefs about the nature of good psychosocial care are common, but surprisingly little research has been conducted, and few interventions have been examined systematically. In general, successful psychosocial interventions promote quality of life without influencing survival.[2] Social connectedness and a related concept—maintaining a sense of a valuable self despite the alterations in functioning attendant to the illness—have emerged as important factors in how patients cope with dying. For some families, a terminal illness allows for greater cohesion and support; for others, it accentuates tensions and promotes distancing.

Dying patients experience considerable isolation and harbor many concerns that may not be shared with family members. An attentive physician or other member of the health care team can counter this loneliness and provide valued support through careful listening and empathy. Key interventions include combating isolation and identifying important goals by offering opportunities for open communication about all aspects of the illness, conveying nonabandonment, facilitating life review, identifying and addressing fears and worries, providing appropriate reassurance, recognizing and treating depression, helping adults attend to the special needs of younger children affected by the illness, showing equanimity and honesty in the face of frightening events, promoting reconciliation and forgiveness, and attending to the possibilities of personal growth in the face of dying. Consultation with a mental health clinician should be considered for selected patients, especially when there is evidence of major psychosocial dysfunction, when there is a history of psychiatric problems or dysfunctional relationships, or when patients simply seek more time and expertise in exploring their coping with the crisis of dying.

SPIRITUALITY. For patients and families facing the crisis of dying, existential or spiritual concerns are inevitable. Spirituality can provide a source of comfort and support—or provoke further distress. Taking a spiritual history allows clinicians to understand patients more fully, and most patients indicate an interest in sharing this important aspect of their lives with clinicians. The physician's role is not to answer unanswerable questions or to provide premature reassurance, but rather to help the dying person explore spiritual issues and find supportive resources (e.g., the hospital chaplain), while clarifying how spirituality influences decision making and coping.

FAMILY COPING AND THE BURDEN OF CARE. Families and friends of patients with a terminal illness suffer as surely as the patient, and any rational health care system should address this suffering. Often neglected are the special needs for age-appropriate support for young children. Depression causes significant, preventable morbidity. Families also are regularly burdened with the physical care of the patient. Families may receive assistance from a variety of relatives, friends, formal caregivers, and volunteers, but the social and financial burden of a terminal illness—needing to quit work or take off significant time, losing a major source of income, or using up savings—is often disastrous for families and underappreciated by health care professionals. Simply listening empathically to the family about their struggles is helpful, but arranging for a variety of concrete services and for more formal counseling also should be considered.

BEREAVEMENT. Bereavement care is a neglected field of medicine. Family grief may be associated with serious deterioration in psychological and social function and increased rates of substance abuse that may lead to premature death. At the same time, most bereaved persons adjust to loss over months and years without any formal help, albeit usually after considerable suffering.

The physician has an important role in assessing and assisting in bereavement through sensitive attention to the family before and at the time of death, attending funeral rituals, writing a letter of condolence, following up with the family and being available for later questions about the illness and death, and providing appropriate information and referral regarding bereavement. Individual counseling and support groups improve outcomes for family and friends who are at high risk of complicated grief. Many other survivors benefit from opportunities to understand and express their distress through the assistance of family, friends, clergy and other professional counselors, and support groups.

WHERE DOES THE PATIENT PREFER TO RECEIVE CARE?

An important theme in the hospice approach to death is that patients and families are generally happier when cared for in the home. In the United States, where about half of deaths occur in hospitals, the hospice movement has contributed to renewed attention to managing a terminal illness in the home when appropriate resources allow patients to feel well cared for and safe.

For about a quarter of patients in the United States, the site of death is a nursing home. High levels of pain and other symptoms, low support, excess use of tube feeding, and excess hospitalization have been shown in this setting, and access to palliative care is limited.

Palliative Care and Hospice

State-of-the-art end-of-life care is synonymous with *palliative care,* a term describing comprehensive (physical, psychosocial, and spiritual), interdisciplinary services that focus on alleviating suffering and promoting quality of life for patients and their families facing a life-threatening or terminal illness. The term *palliative* literally means "to cloak" and can be used derisively to describe measures that merely cover up a problem, but the term has become widely accepted as a description of approaches to providing comfort for dying persons without necessarily modifying the underlying medical condition (e.g., reducing pain or dyspnea from metastatic lung cancer without affecting the tumor burden).

Many aspects of palliative care, as with any specialty, are relevant to the general practice of medicine and to all clinicians who tend to dying persons. Palliative care has a role in the earliest phases of a life-threatening illness but assumes a more prominent or even dominant role in the final 3 to 6 months of common terminal conditions: advanced cancer, heart and lung failure, end-stage liver and renal disease, acquired immunodeficiency syndrome, and life-limiting neurologic diseases.

Hospice programs offer a widely recognized form of palliative care in the United States. Hospice in the United States refers to a specific, government-regulated form of end-of-life care, first available under Medicare but then adopted by Medicaid and many third-party insurers. Hospice care typically is given at home or in a nursing home—less commonly in an acute care hospital or specialized acute care unit—and is provided by an interdisciplinary team, which usually includes a physician, nurse, social worker, chaplain, volunteers, bereavement coordinator, and home health aides, all of whom work with the primary care physician, patient, and family. Bereavement services are offered to the family for a year after the death.

Hospice regulations in the United States require that a patient agree to forgo measures with curative intent and focus on comfort. Although hospice programs vary in their policies, many "aggressive," expensive interventions, such as surgery, radiation therapy, total parenteral nutrition, and transfusions, tend to be excluded. To many patients and families, hospice seems to signify "giving up," rather than being viewed as a model of compassionate care and of making the best of a situation with limited options. Also, to be eligible for a Medicare-certified hospice program, the primary physician must certify that the patient is likely to die within 6 months if the illness runs its usual course. No penalties exist, however, for referring a patient too early to hospice, and physicians generally use hospice care much later in the course of an illness than appropriate.

Another option is palliative care in inpatient units, which are furnished in a homelike fashion; are quieter than the typical noisy hospital ward; are decorated with personally important objects from each patient; and typically lack, minimize, or obscure hospital paraphernalia. Patients are encouraged to wear their own clothes, pets are allowed, and families (including children) have unlimited visiting privileges and are encouraged to stay overnight and to cook there or bring food.

Strains and Rewards in End-of-Life Care

No discussion of palliative care would be complete without touching on the importance of the inner life of clinicians and their personal relationships with the patient and family. Even with the best informed and most proactive consumers of health care, clinicians must shepherd patients and families through an often terrifying, unfamiliar trajectory, attempting to provide safe passage, not only by applying their technical skills to prevent and reduce suffering, but also by a reassuring presence—an intimate, individualized relationship that communicates concern, connectedness, equanimity in the face of death, realistic hope, nonabandonment, and an eagerness to address a broad range of psychosocial and spiritual concerns. More accurately, palliative care should involve a team of professionals and a relationship that provides the patient and family with a variety of opportunities for supportive interactions with skilled, professional caregivers.

Seriously ill and dying persons may evoke strong emotional reactions in clinicians, thrusting them into often intense, intimate relationships at a major crisis point in the lives of patients and their families. Clinicians may report a wearying sense of grief and depletion over recurrent losses and an exhilarating sense of privilege in witnessing how some patients and families cope using extraordinary dignity, acceptance, and love.

Staff support programs, which are routine aspects of most palliative care services, can help all clinicians develop and maintain a working environment that attends to emotional reactions, addresses staff conflict, and bolsters a personal capacity to deal with multiple losses without becoming hardened to suffering. The camaraderie and support that can accompany interdisciplinary teamwork is an important antidote to clinician burnout.

1. SUPPORT Principal Investigators: A controlled trial to improve care for seriously ill hospitalized patients. The Study to Understand Prognoses and Risks of Treatments (SUPPORT). JAMA 1995;274:1591–1598.
2. Goodwin PJ, Leszca M, Ennis M, et al: The effect of group psychosocial support on survival in metastatic breast cancer. N Engl J Med 2001;345:1719–1726.

SUGGESTED READINGS

American Academy of Hospice and Palliative Medicine: Available at www.aahpm.org.

Back AL, Arnold RM, Quill TE: Hope for the best, and prepare for the worst. Ann Intern Med 2003;138:439–443. *A practical approach end-of-life care.*

Christakis NA, Lamont EB: Extent and determinants of error in doctors' prognoses in terminally ill patients: Prospective cohort study. BMJ 2000;320:469–472. *Physicians are inaccurate and systematically optimistic in their opinions about dying patients' prognoses.*

Doyle D, Hanks GWC, MacDonald N: Oxford Textbook of Palliative Medicine, 2nd ed. New York, Oxford University Press, 1999. *A comprehensive review of the scientific basis of palliative care and an outstanding clinical resource.*

Ellershaw J, Ward C: Care of the dying patient: The last hours or days of life. BMJ 2003;326:30–34. *A recent overview of end-of-life care and of barriers to good care, focusing on the difficulties of "diagnosing dying" and its consequences.*

End of Life/Palliative Education Resource Center. *Peer-reviewed instructional and evaluation materials on end-of-life care, core resources for educators, and opportunities for training and funding. Available at www.eperc.mcw.edu/*

Steinhauser KE, Christakis NA, Clipp EC, et al: Factors considered important at the end of life by patients, family, physicians, and other care providers. JAMA 2000;284:2476–2482. *Patients, families, and clinicians share many goals for end-of-life care (e.g., rating pain management as highly important), but patients and families strongly value quality-of-life issues, whereas physicians tend to focus on physical care.*

The AM, Hak T, Koeter G, van der Wal G: Collusion in doctor-patient communication about imminent death: An ethnographic study. BMJ 2000;321:1376–1381. *Physicians and patients in this study were reluctant to talk about dying and colluded in producing and sustaining "false optimism."*

Truog RD, Cist AFM, Brackett SE, et al: Recommendations for end-of-life care in the intensive care unit: The Ethics Committee of the Society of Critical Care Medicine. Crit Care Med 2001;29:2332–2348. *Detailed guidelines on end-of-life care in the ICU, including discontinuation of life supports.*

4 SOCIAL AND ECONOMIC ISSUES IN MEDICINE

Steven Schroeder

Medicine is practiced in a social, economic, and political context. It takes more than excellent medical care to improve the health of patients because many of the determinants of the health of individuals and populations lie outside traditional clinical activity. As shown in Figure 4–1, only 10% of premature deaths result from inadequate medical care. By contrast, 40% of premature deaths are attributed to personal behaviors, including patterns of eating and physical activity and decisions about smoking, drinking, illicit drug use, and sexual behavior (Chapters 12 through 17). Genetics (Chapters 35 through

39) account for an additional 30%, and social factors and environmental factors account for about 15% and about 5% (Chapters 18 through 20).

Social Issues

Socioeconomic status, which is determined by a person's income, education, and occupation, also exerts a strong influence on health status, in part by influencing patterns of behavior. In the United States, people in lower socioeconomic groups have higher rates of smoking, and there is a continuous gradient between health and socioeconomic status that persists well above the poverty line. British male transportation workers in the lowest social quintile have standardized mortality rates almost three times as high as those in the upper quintile, and there is a continuous gradient with progressively better survival as socioeconomic status improves. The relationship of mortality with socioeconomic status is widening rather than narrowing. During a 50-year period in the United Kingdom, the mortality ratios between the highest and lowest social class quintiles widened from 1.2 to 2.5 (Fig. 4–2). Although some of these trends can be attributed to differential access to medical care, these differences persist even after adjusting for access and are found in countries such as Great Britain that have universal access to a national health system. Some of the relationship between socioeconomic status and mortality also can be attributed to behavioral differences, but a person in the top quintile of wealth can expect on average a healthier and longer life span than a person in the next lowest (but still economically comfortable) quintile, even after correcting for differences in access to medical care or health-related behavior and even in the wealthiest countries and states.

Some have advanced the theory of allostatic load to explain how social status contributes to health, even among the relatively well-to-do population. Individuals in the highest social class presumably have more control over their lives at work and at home and consequently suffer less stress. *Allostatic load* refers to biochemical and neurologic adaptations to stress, which, although beneficial over the short-term, may exert a toll on immunologic and metabolic systems over the long-term, increasing the risks of morbidity and mortality resulting from conditions such as cardiovascular diseases and cancer.

Another way in which social determinants influence health is the degree to which a person is connected with others. Evidence is mounting that people who are isolated socially are at higher risk of premature deaths. Of patients with a serious illness, such as acute myocardial infarction or breast cancer, patients with better social networks have better survival and function than patients who are socially disconnected. It is speculated that social relationships help buffer the deleterious effects of stress and may stimulate more healthy behavior,

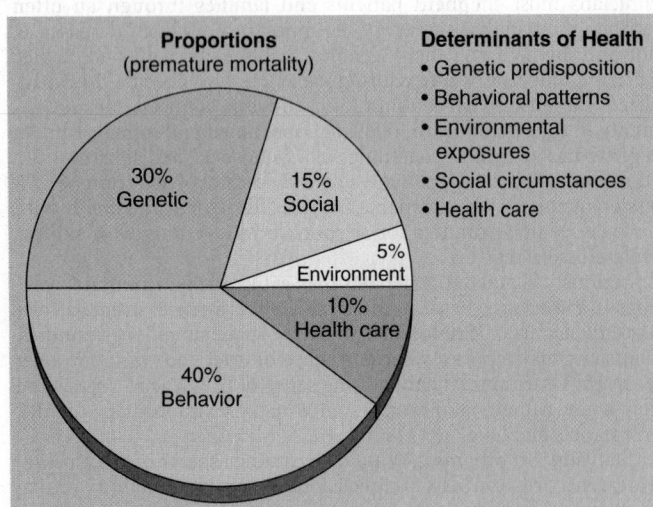

FIGURE 4–1 • Determinants of health. Health is influenced by genetic predisposition, behavioral patterns, environmental exposures, social circumstances, and health care. (Data from McGinnis MJ, Williams-Russo P, Knickman JR: The case for more active policy attention to health promotion. Health Aff [Millwood] 2002;21:78–93.)

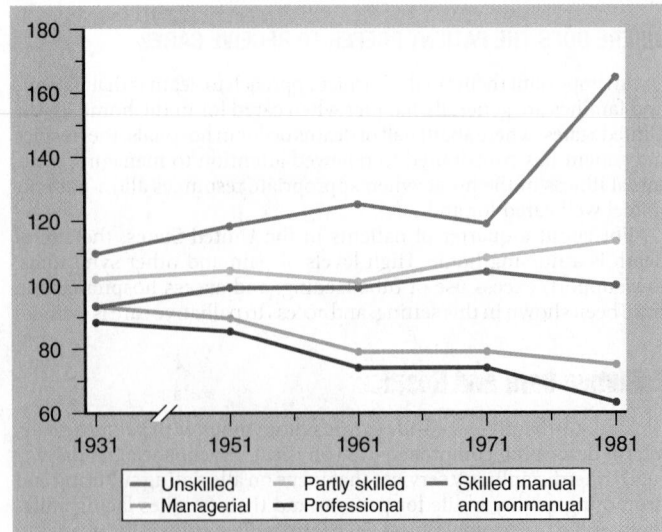

FIGURE 4–2 • Comparison of standardized mortality ratios of men 15 to 64 years old by social class, England and Wales, 1931 to 1981. (From McCally M, Haines A, Fein O, et al: Poverty and ill health. Ann Intern Med 1998;129:726–733.)

such as regular physical exercise. In contrast to the linear association between health and social class, however, there seems to be little health difference between individuals with moderate compared with high levels of social support.

What can physicians do with this information? First, they can look for ways to encourage healthy behavior. Second, at key times of transition, such as during discharge planning for hospitalized patients, physicians should be attentive to the patient's social circumstances. For patients who are likely to be socially isolated, clinicians should encourage or arrange interactions with family, neighbors, religious organizations, or community agencies to improve the likelihood of an optimal outcome.

Economic Issues in Medical Care Delivery

Medical care today is on a collision course. An ever-expanding science base continuously yields new drugs and technologies with the promise of extending and improving life. An increasingly sophisticated public, armed with information available in the press and over the internet, is eager to obtain the best and newest medical care. Payers for medical care—the government, health insurance companies, and employers who contract with them—are reluctant to absorb the costs.

All countries now wrestle with how to pay for medical care, but the United States leads the world in health care expenditures. In 2002, health care consumed about $1.5 trillion, or about 13.9% of gross domestic product. Germany and Switzerland are the only other countries with double-digit health expenditures, but both are less than 11%. In the 1990s, however, the United States managed to restrain health care expenditure growth after a decade of double-digit inflation. This slowing in the growth rate was accomplished under the general strategy of managed care, which includes reductions in reimbursement rates, decreases in in-hospital capacity, controls over usage, and administrative delays in processing payments; little actual managing of care occurs. A public backlash against the perceived constraints on access to desired medical services has led insurance companies to weaken their usage controls, and as a result, large increases in annual insurance premiums are occurring.

The reason that the United States leads the world in medical care expenditures can be found in a potent combination of supply and demand. On the supply side, the United States far exceeds other countries in its supply and use of expensive diagnostic technologies, such as magnetic resonance imaging and computed tomography. The United States has five times as many magnetic resonance imaging imagers and computed tomography scanners per capita as Canada (Table 4–1). Similarly the United States outstrips all other nations in its rates of performance of expensive treatments, such as coronary angiography, coronary artery bypass graft surgery, and carotid thromboendarterectomy. The United States has twice as many coronary angioplasty procedures and 2.5 times as many coronary artery bypass graft procedures per capita as Canada, which itself does more than most developed nations. These differences generally are found across all age groups but are most apparent in elderly persons. In the 65- to 69-year age group, the United States performs 1.87-fold more angiograms per capita than Canada. The ratio increases to 7.68 for the greater than 80-year age group.

Other supply factors that drive high medical expenditures in the United States include a fee-for-service payment system, especially for most patients who are older than age 65 and are covered by Medicare insurance, which compensates physicians far more when they use expensive interventions than when they do not and stimulates the use of more costly services; a medical professional work force that depends more on specialists and less on generalists than most other countries; accelerated development of new and costly medications and their direct marketing to consumers; and a high rate of medical malpractice litigation, with resultant defensive medicine.

Not only does the United States lead the world in the supply and use of medical services, but also it probably sets the pace in demand. The extent to which the media feature medical "breakthroughs" is extensive and one-sided. New promising treatments merit front-page stories, whereas disappointing subsequent results are buried or simply ignored. The cumulative result has been to whet the appetite of U.S. patients and to leave the impression that cure depends only on finding a better-informed physician. This same quest for better health explains the more than $30 billion annual expenditures for alternative medical treatments (Chapter 34), few of which are covered by health insurance.

Patterns of health care use in the United States and elsewhere are not homogeneous. There is a two-fold difference in the supply of acute care hospital beds in metropolitan regions across the United States, even when adjusted for illness, age, and sex. Similarly, there is a almost four-fold regional difference in the likelihood of being hospitalized in an intensive care unit at the end of life, and similar regional variations exist for surgical procedures, such as transurethral prostatectomy, hysterectomy, or coronary artery bypass graft surgery. There is no evidence, however, that, on a regional basis, "more is better." Some data indicate that geographical areas with higher consumption of medical care may have worse outcomes for some illnesses, such as acute myocardial infarction.

Health insurance coverage in the United States is an incomplete patchwork, consisting of government-sponsored programs for the elderly (Medicare), the poor (Medicaid), and veterans, plus employer-based coverage for most but not all working persons and their families. Medicare covers acute care services in the hospital and the physician's office, but it does not cover prescription drugs or long-term care. More than half of Medicare subscribers purchase supplemental insurance that helps pay for additional care not covered by Medicare. Medicaid covers more services than Medicare, but in many states Medicaid pays physicians and hospitals so little that patients are restricted in their choices for care. More than 40 million Americans remain uninsured; this number rises and falls with unemployment rates and employers' decisions about coverage. The uninsured essentially depend on charity care, often at so-called safety net institutions, such as community clinics and public hospitals. As a result, they often forego needed treatment entirely or have potentially dangerous delays in care, such as presenting with later stage cancers.

Why the United States, which is one of the wealthiest countries in the world, tolerates such a large proportion of uninsured citizens has long puzzled policy analysts. The reasons are complex and include the myths that the uninsured get all the care they need anyway and that many people choose not to be covered because they anticipate staying healthy. Other explanations include the lack of political power among the uninsured, a cultural distrust of government solutions, and disagreement about how to extend coverage.

Political pressures currently exist to reduce taxes, to avoid budget deficits, to add a prescription drug benefit to Medicare and other benefits to private insurance coverage, to increase spending for the military and for homeland security, and to contain medical costs. It is not clear how these conflicting pressures will be resolved.

It is likely that physicians will become more involved in issues of medical economics. As pressures for cost containment force patients to assume more of the expense of their care, patients will become more cost conscious and more demanding about the value and price of services. Informed clinical decision making will require that physicians have better information about the risks and benefits of the myriad of interventions in medical care and better ways to communicate what is known.

Table 4–1 • RATES OF CARDIOVASCULAR PROCEDURES IN THE UNITED STATES AND CANADA

PROCEDURE	RATIO U.S. TO CANADA	
	Age 65-69	Age >80
Angioplasty	1.87	7.68
Coronary artery bypass graft surgery	1.36	7.16
Carotid endarterectomy	1.95	8.68

From Verrilli DK, Berenson R, Katz SJ: A comparison of cardiovascular procedure use between the United States and Canada. Health Serv Res 1998;33:467–487.

SUGGESTED READINGS

Fisher E, Wennberg D, Stukel T, et al: The implications of regional variations in Medicare spending. Part 2: Health outcomes and satisfaction with care. Ann Intern Med 2003;138:288–299. *Provocative study showing that Medicare enrollees in higher spending geographic regions receive more medical care but do not have better outcomes.*

Institute of Medicine, National Academy of Sciences: Health and Behavior: The Interplay of Biological, Behavioral, and Societal Influences. Washington, DC, National Academy Press, 2001. *In-depth review of the relationship between behavior and health.*

McGinnis MJ, Williams-Russo P, Knickman JR: The case for more active policy attention to health promotion. Health Aff [Millwood]. 2002;21:78–93. *Reviews the determinants of health and makes the case for nonclinical factors.*

Schroeder SA: Prospects for expanding health insurance coverage. N Engl J Med 2001;344:847–852. *Why the United States has so many uninsured citizens and how coverage expansion might occur.*

Wennberg JE, Cooper MM (eds): The Dartmouth Atlas of Health Care 1998. Chicago, American Hospital Publishing, 1998. *Shows extent of regional variations in health care services.*

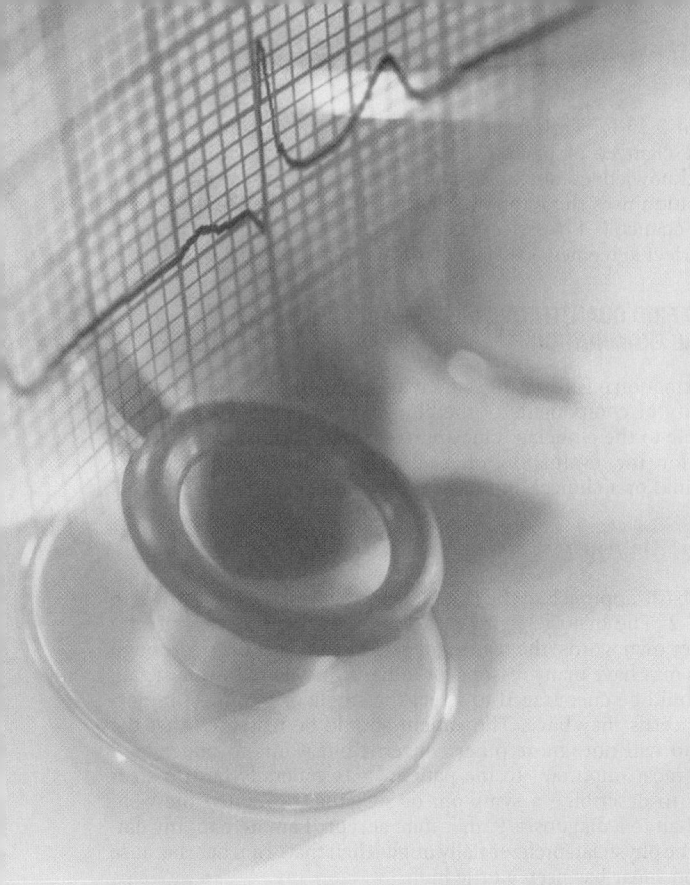

part II

Principles of Evaluation and Management

5 APPROACH TO THE PATIENT: HISTORY AND PHYSICAL EXAMINATION

David L. Simel

Overview

Physicians have several specific medical goals that assume varying degrees of importance in the patient encounter depending on the patient's individual characteristics and the patient care setting. These goals include but are not limited to the translation of symptoms and signs into diagnoses, the assessment of stability or change in known conditions, the provision of information and counseling for future prevention, and the reaffirmation or alteration of therapeutic interventions.

In the context of these medical goals, the physician also should strive to address several related social goals, whose achievement synergistically can improve medical outcomes, such as establishing a relationship and measure of trust. The interaction between the patient and physician represents not only a scientific encounter, but also a social ritual centered on locus of control and meeting each other's expectations. Patients may not be able to express their needs fully and may fear a loss of control in determining their own medical fate. Conversely, physicians also have expectations that they must consider and answer sometimes for themselves: a need to feel that they have not missed something important in addressing diagnostic challenges, a need to put limits on the time available for each interaction, and a need to maintain objectivity so that their evaluation and recommendations are not clouded by their emotional feelings about the patient. When the patient's needs are to establish the presence of health or the diagnosis for a symptom, the expertise of the physician is expressed through the performance and interpretation of a rational clinical examination.

PHYSICAL EXAMINATION BEGINS WITH THE HISTORY

It is almost impossible to consider the history as distinct from the physical examination because the clinical examination begins as soon as the physician sees or hears the patient. Cynics contend that physical diagnosis skills have eroded because most diagnoses are made during the history, then confirmed by a more objective test, such as a laboratory value or a radiographic image. It is perhaps unfair to assume that clinical diagnosis skills have deteriorated because scientific principles were not applied to the clinical examination until the mid-1970s. Before then, the sparse literature that addressed the clinical examination was dominated by case reports and case series that provided anecdotal evidence, which often overstated the usefulness of the physical examination. Even proponents of the clinical examination now demand proof of reasonable reproducibility and accuracy before they accept the value of specific components of the history and physical examination.

QUANTITATIVE PRINCIPLES OF THE CLINICAL EXAMINATION

The clinical examination can be studied with the same principles as those applied to more traditional tests, such as laboratory results or diagnostic images. For each component of the history and physical examination, there is an associated sensitivity (the percentage of patients with a disorder who have an abnormal finding), specificity (the percentage of patients without a disorder who have a normal finding), and measure of precision (the agreement beyond chance between two observers) (Chapter 6). Current research on the clinical examination uses likelihood ratios (LRs) that inform clinicians how likely they are to observe a particular finding in a patient with a given condition compared with a patient without the condition. When it is estimated that an older patient who "shuffles her feet" when she walks has an LR of 3.0 for Parkinson's disease (Chapter 443), it means that the shuffling patient is three times as likely to have the disorder as a patient who does not shuffle. Similarly, if a patient who insists that he does not have "shaking in his arms" has

an LR of 0.25 for Parkinson's disease, he is one fourth as likely (a reduced chance) of having the disease compared with a patient who acknowledges shaking. Evaluation of the precision of the examination uses the Kappa (κ) statistic to describe the agreement beyond chance (−1 = perfect disagreement, 0 = random agreement, +1 = perfect agreement) (Chapter 8).

HOW TO FIND QUANTITATIVE INFORMATION ABOUT THE CLINICAL EXAMINATION

Information regarding the sensitivity, specificity, LRs, and observer variability of components of the clinical examination is not easily accessible to the clinician. One approach is to perform a MEDLINE search for the evaluation of a disease-specific condition (e.g., melanoma) or a clinical finding (e.g., splenomegaly) (Table 5–1).

Medical History

The basic approach to the complete medical history is outlined in Table 5–2. The history begins by asking the patient to describe, in his or her own words, the reason for seeking medical care. Although patients may have many reasons for initiating a visit to the physician, they should be encouraged to select the single or two most important concerns they have. The patient should be reassured that the physician will not ignore other concerns but wants to understand what is most important to the patient. It is generally best to steer patients to describing a symptom or sign that prompted the visit, rather than to a diagnosis. Rather than accept "I am here for my diabetes," the physician preferentially might elicit that "I am here because my blood sugar has been a little high."

HISTORY OF THE PRESENTING PROBLEM

Initially, patients should be asked open-ended questions to permit a description of their problems in their own words. This initial process can be followed with a series of specific questions to fill in any gaps or to clarify important points. These questions should be asked in an order dictated by the story the patient tells and targeted to suit the individual problem. When the patient is acutely ill, the physician should limit the amount of time in open-ended discussion, moving promptly to the most important features that allow quick evaluation and management. In general, the history of the presenting problem includes the following:

- Description of onset and chronology
- Location of symptoms

Table 5–1 • MEDLINE SEARCH STRATEGY FOR IDENTIFYING QUANTITATIVE INFORMATION ON THE CLINICAL EXAMINATION USING THE OVID SEARCH SYSTEM*

1 exp physical examination/or physical exam$.mp
2 medical history taking.mp
3 professional competence.mp
4 (sensitivity and specificity).mp or (sensitivity and specificity).tw
5 (reproducibility of results or observer variation).mp
6 diagnostic tests, routine/
7 (decision support techniques or Bayes theorem).mp
8 1 or 2 or 3 or 4 or 5 or 6 or 7
9 limit 8 to (Ovid full text available and human and English language)
10 exp knee injuries
11 10 and 9
12 exp splenomegaly
13 9 and 12

*OVID Technologies, Inc. A condition and a physical finding are given as examples. Abbreviations or search term abbreviations are as follows: "exp" indicates that the topic is "exploded" to include all subheadings for the topic. The "$" is a wildcard designator, so "exam$" would include the words *examination, examining,* and *examiner.* "mp" searches for the word or phrase in the title, abstract, registry number word, or mesh subject heading. Step 9 limits the search to studies that were of humans only and where the full manuscript is available on-line and is written in English. If the search yields too few topics, the limitation of full text available can be removed and the search repeated. If too many results are obtained, some of the items from Step 8 can be eliminated.

Table 5-2 • PATIENT'S MEDICAL HISTORY

Description of the patient
    Age, gender, ethnic background, occupation
Chief reason for seeking medical care
    State the purpose of the evaluation (usually in the patient's words)
Other physicians involved in the patient's care
    Include the clinician the patient identifies as his or her primary
    provider or the physician who referred the patient. Record the
    contact information for all physicians who should receive informa-
    tion about the visit
History of the presenting reason for seeking medical care
    In a chronologic fashion, determine the evolution of the indication
    for the visit, then each major symptom. It is best first to address
    the patient's reason for seeking care, rather than what the physician
    ultimately believes is most important
    Be careful to avoid "premature closure," in which a diagnosis is
    assumed before all the information is collected
Past medical and surgical history
    List other illnesses and/or prior surgeries not related to the current
    problem
    List all prescribed and over-the-counter medications with dose
    Remember to ask about vitamin and herbal supplements
Allergies and adverse reactions
    List allergic reactions to medications and food. Record the specific
    reaction (e.g., hives). Distinguish allergies from adverse reactions
    or intolerance to medication (e.g., dyspepsia from nonsteroidal
    anti-inflammatory agents)
Social and occupational history
    Describe the patient's current family and a typical day for patient. The
    occupational history should focus on current and past employment
    as it might relate to the current problem. For veterans, inquire
    about their military history including combat exposure, years of
    service, and areas of deployment
Risk factors
    Include history of tobacco use, illegal drug use, and risk factors for
    sexually transmitted disease (including human immunodeficiency
    virus and hepatitis)
Family history
    History of any diseases in first-degree relatives and a listing of family
    members with any conditions that could be risk factors for the
    patient (e.g., cardiovascular disease at young age, malignancy,
    known genetic disorders, longevity)
Review of systems
    Systematic review of items not covered already: skin, hematopoietic,
    head, eyes, ears, nose, throat, cardiovascular, respiratory, breast,
    gastrointestinal, genitourinary, musculoskeletal, nervous,
    endocrine, and psychiatric systems. In particular, address sexual
    function because patients typically may be reluctant to volunteer
    information

- Character (quality) of symptoms
- Intensity
- Precipitating, aggravating, and relieving factors
- Inquiry into whether the problem or similar problems occurred before and, if so, was there a diagnosis established at that time?

Finally, it is often helpful to ask the patient to express what he or she believes is the cause of the problem or what concerns the patient the most. This approach often uncovers other pertinent factors and helps establish that the physician is trying to meet the patient's needs.

PAST MEDICAL AND SURGICAL HISTORY

Much of the past medical history and surgical history is obtained when the patient relates the history of the presenting problem. The astute clinician should not rely on patients to divulge all their prior problems, however: Patients may forget, they may assume that prior events are unrelated to their current problem, or they simply may not want to discuss past events. An open-ended statement, such as "Tell me about other medical illnesses you have had that we did not discuss" and "Tell me about any operations you have had," prompts the patient to consider other items. During the physical examination, the physician should ask the patient about unexplained surgical or traumatic scars.

A list of current medications should include not only prescriptions, but also over-the-counter medications, vitamins, and herbal preparations. When a patient is uncertain about the names of

medications, the patient or family member should be asked to bring all medication bottles to the next visit. Patients may not consider topical medications (e.g., skin preparations or eye drops) as important, so they may need prompting.

Information about allergies (Chapter 28) is particularly important to collect but also challenging. Patients may attribute adverse reactions or intolerances to allergies, but many supposed allergic reactions are not truly drug allergies. Less than 20% of patients who claim a penicillin allergy are allergic on skin testing. Eliciting the patient's actual response to medications facilitates a determination of whether the response was a true allergic reaction.

SOCIAL AND OCCUPATIONAL HISTORY AND RISK FACTORS

The social history not only gathers important data, but also improves understanding of the patient's unique values, support systems, and social situation. The social history should be tailored to the individual patient and allow for physician-centered questioning and patient-centered expression of values and concerns.

Data that may influence risk factors for disease should be gathered, including a nonjudgmental assessment of substance abuse. Tobacco history should include use of snuff, chewing tobacco, and cigars and cigarette smoking (Chapter 14). Alcohol use should be determined quantitatively and by the effect it has had on the patient's life (Chapter 17). Past or present use of illicit substances, prescription pain medications or sedatives, and intravenous drug use history should be assessed (Chapter 30). Sexual history should include current sexual activity, including number of partners and past history. Employment history should include current employment and past employment history, military experiences, and any significant hobbies. Information should be elicited from military veterans regarding their combat history, years of service, and areas of deployment.

The physician also should obtain information on socioeconomic status, insurance, the ability to afford or obtain medications, and past or current barriers to health care because of their impact on patient care (Chapter 4). Marital status and living situation (i.e., whom the patient lives with, what are the significant stressors for that patient) are important as risk factors for disease and to determine how best to care for a patient. A patient's values should be known, including any advance directives (Chapter 3). The physician should elicit explicitly and record information regarding next of kin; surrogate decision makers; emergency contacts; social support systems; and financial, emotional, and physical support available to the patient.

The social history should be tailored to the individual patient and to the physician-patient encounter. An understanding of a patient's habits and social situation furthers understanding of risk factors, is crucial to developing an appropriate patient-physician relationship, and allows for planning of optimal care.

FAMILY HISTORY

The patient's family history is of increasing importance given the rapid expansion of knowledge about genetics in medicine. The family history is never diagnostic, but it allows risk stratification that affects the pretest probability for an increasing number of disorders (e.g., heart disease, breast cancer, or Alzheimer's disease). For common diseases such as heart disease, additional inquiry into the age of onset in first-degree relatives and death attributed to the disease should be obtained (Chapter 47). When a patient reports that a first-degree relative had a myocardial infarction, the LR is 19 that the patient has a family history of myocardial infarction. Patients may lack appropriate information as to the absence of disease, however, so a reported lack of a family history of myocardial infarction reduces the likelihood only by one third. In general, the specificity of the reported family history far exceeds its sensitivity; for example, only two thirds of patients with essential tremor (Chapter 444) report a family history, but 95% of such patients have first-degree relatives with tremor. The expansion of knowledge about genetic diseases requires clinicians not only to improve their skills in eliciting the family history, but also to develop methods for confirming the information.

REVIEW OF SYSTEMS

The review of systems is the structural assessment of each of the major organ systems. It generally focuses on topics not covered in the history of the present illness and allows the examiner a standardized method for eliciting symptoms that may have been overlooked. In practice, the review of systems may be accomplished by direct questioning or by having the patient fill out a previsit questionnaire. When directly obtained, the best approach is not to use open-ended questions but rather to proceed efficiently and effectively by asking direct questions. The physician may ask the patient, "has there been any recent change in your vision" or "have you recently had shortness of breath, wheezing, or cough?" The relative value of these approaches has not been investigated fully. One estimate is that the review of systems yields a new important diagnosis about 10% of the time. Nevertheless, the review of systems is an efficient mechanism for detecting issues and for obtaining a complete understanding of the patient's overall status.

Physical Examination

CHAPERONES

When asked in surveys, most patients of either sex and all ages report a lack of preference for a chaperone; it is not clear if this response is their true feeling or a desire to give a "correct" response. Nevertheless, many adult women (29%) and adolescent girls (46%) do express a preference for a chaperone during a breast, pelvic, or rectal examination by a male physician (especially during their first examination). Examiners should offer patients the option of a chaperone, and a chaperone should be considered when the clinician and patient are of different genders. Many examiners prefer a chaperone to allay their own anxieties attributable to gender differences or to achieve a perceived need for protection should the patient develop concerns during the procedure.

VITAL SIGNS

A nurse or assistant often obtains the vital signs. Traditionally the vital signs include pulse rate, blood pressure, respiratory rate, and body temperature. More recently, advocates of various causes have advocated for a "fifth vital sign." The most cogent of these "new" vital signs is the patient's quantitative assessment of pain.

The pulse should be recorded as not just the rate but also the rhythm. Physicians may prefer to initiate the examination by holding the patient's hand while palpating the pulse. This nonthreatening initial contact with the patient allows the physician to determine whether the patient has a regular or irregular rhythm.

When the blood pressure is abnormal, many physicians repeat the measurement. The instrument error that contributes to the greatest variability is the cuff size of the sphygmomanometer (Chapter 63). Many adults require a large-size adult cuff; using a narrow cuff can alter systolic/diastolic blood pressure by −8 to +10/+2 to +8 mm Hg. The appearance of repetitive sounds (Korotkoff sounds, phase 1) constitutes the systolic pressure. After the cuff is inflated about 20 to 30 mm Hg above the palpated pressure, the Korotkoff sounds muffle and disappear as pressure is released (phase 5). The level at which the sounds disappear is the diastolic pressure. The American Heart Association recommends that each measure should be rounded upward to the nearest 2 mm Hg.

The respiratory rate should be assessed at the same time the patient is observed to determine whether there is any respiratory discomfort (dyspnea) (Chapter 81). The subjective sensation of dyspnea is caused by an increased work of breathing. The examiner should decide whether patients have tachypnea (a rapid rate of breathing) or hypopnea (a slow or shallow rate of breathing). Tachypnea is not always associated with hyperventilation, which is defined by increased alveolar ventilation resulting in a lower arterial carbon dioxide level (Chapter 100). In the evaluation of patients suspected of having pneumonia, examiners agree on the presence of tachypnea only 63% of the time.

The body temperature of adults usually is measured with an oral electric thermometer. These thermometers correlate well with the traditional mercury thermometer and are safer to use. Rectal thermometers reliably record temperatures 0.4° C higher than oral thermometers. By comparison, newer tympanic thermometers may vary too much compared with oral thermometers (−1.2° C to +1.6° C versus the oral temperature) to be reliable among hospitalized patients.

The Joint Commission on Accreditation of Healthcare Organizations has been a leading advocate of the systematic measurement of self-assessed pain, typically rated on a 0-to-10 scale (no pain to worst pain ever) (Chapters 29 and 427) in all hospitalized patients. The validity, usefulness, and value of the adopted scales as a screening tool for clinical diagnosis are uncertain, however.

HEAD AND NECK

Face

When looking at the face, the examiner can simplify the assessment by carefully judging for symmetry. Asymmetrical facial features should be noted and explained. Examples of asymmetry include skin lesions (Chapter 472), cranial nerve palsies (Chapter 423), parotid enlargement (Chapter 467), or the ptosis of Horner's syndrome (Chapter 460). A variety of disorders may cause symmetrical, abnormal facies; examples include acromegaly (Chapter 237), Cushing's syndrome (Chapter 240), and Parkinson's disease (Chapter 443).

Ears

Physicians may not recognize hearing loss unless they pay special attention (Chapter 470). When patients do not appreciate the whispered voice, the likelihood of hearing loss increases considerably (LR 6.0). Cerumen impaction is an easily treated cause of diminished hearing. Otoscopic evaluation of the tympanic membranes should reveal a translucent membrane and an obvious cone of light reflected where the eardrum meets the malleolus. Few data exist to determine the observer variability of the otoscopic examination in adult patients.

Nose

Patients frequently present with nasal symptoms, such as a self-diagnosis of sinusitis or snoring. The nares should be examined for the presence of polyps, which can be seen as obstructing, glistening mucosal masses. Transillumination performed in a dark room is useful for diagnosing sinusitis, especially when combined with visualization of a purulent discharge, a patient's report of a poor response to decongestants or antihistamines, maxillary toothache, and the presence of discolored rhinorrhea (Chapter 468). These patients have an LR greater than 6 for bacterial sinusitis.

Mouth

The quality of the patient's dentition directly affects his or her nutrition. Generalist physicians can be confident that the patient requires dental care if periodontal disease or dental caries are detected (LR >4.0). The need for dental care cannot be excluded even in the absence of such findings (LR 0.7), however, and all patients should be encouraged to seek regular dental evaluations. Premalignant oral lesions (e.g., leukoplakia, nodules, ulcerations) found by generalist physicians usually are verified by dentists (LR >6.5) (Chapter 467). Patients who use smokeless tobacco products are at significantly increased risk of premalignant and malignant oral lesions (Chapter 14). A bimanual palpation of the cheeks and floor of the mouth facilitates identification of potentially malignant lesions (Chapter 467).

Eyes

The eye examination begins with simple visual inspection to look for symmetry in the lids, extraocular movements, pupil size and reaction, and whether or not there is redness (Chapters 465 and 466). Abnormalities in extraocular movements should be grouped into nonparalytic (usually chronic with onset in childhood) or paralytic (third, fourth, or sixth cranial nerve palsy) causes. Pupillary abnormalities may be symmetrical or asymmetrical (anisocoria). Red eyes should be categorized by the pattern of ciliary injection, presence of pain, effect on vision, and papillary abnormalities. When the eye examination is approached systematically, the generalist physician can evaluate the likelihood of conjunctivitis, episcleritis or scleritis, iritis, and acute glaucoma.

Routine determination of visual acuity can help confirm or refute a patient's report of diminished vision but does not replace the need for formal ophthalmologic evaluation in patients with visual complaints (Chapter 465). Cataracts can be detected with direct ophthalmoscopy, but the generalist's proficiency in this evaluation is uncertain.

After identifying the optic disc by ophthalmoscopy, the examiner should note the border of the disc for clarity, color, and the size of the central cup in relation to the total diameter (usually less than half the diameter of the disc). A careful observer sees spontaneous venous pulsations that indicate a normal intracranial pressure. Abnormalities of the optic disc include optic atrophy (a white disc), papilledema (blurry margins with a pink, hyperemic disc), and glaucoma (a large, pale cup with retinal vessels that dive underneath and that may be displaced toward the nasal side). The generalist's examination inadequately detects early glaucomatous changes, so high-risk patients should have routine ophthalmologic examinations for glaucoma.

After inspecting the disc, the examiner should inspect the upper and lower nasal quadrants for the appearance of the vessels and presence of any retinal hemorrhages or lesions. Proceeding from the nasal quadrants to the temporal quadrants decreases the risk of papillary constriction from the bright light focused on the fovea. Dilating the pupils leads to an improved examination. Despite the improved results in direct ophthalmoscopy after dilation, patients with diabetes (Chapter 242) should have routine examination by ophthalmologists to detect diabetic retinopathy because the sensitivity of the generalist examination is not adequate to exclude diabetic retinopathy or follow it over time.

Neck

CAROTID PULSES. The carotid pulses should be palpated for contour and timing in relation to the cardiac impulse. Abnormalities in the carotid pulse contour reflect underlying cardiac abnormalities (e.g., aortic stenosis) but generally are appreciated only after detecting an abnormal cardiac impulse or murmur (Chapter 46).

Many physicians listen for bruits over the carotid arteries because asymptomatic carotid bruits are associated with an increased incidence of cerebrovascular and cardiac events in older patients (Chapters 439 and 440). The poor predictive power of the bruit for high-grade stenosis (LR for predicting high-grade stenosis is 1.5 in the presence of a bruit and 0.67 in its absence) raises questions, however, about the utility of this part of the physical examination.

THYROID. The thyroid gland is felt best when standing behind the patient and using both hands to palpate the thyroid gland gently (Chapter 239). The palpatory examination is enhanced by asking the patient to swallow sips of water, allowing the thyroid to glide underneath the fingers, but the quantitative improvement of this maneuver for detecting thyroid enlargement or nodules has not been evaluated rigorously. Inspection of the gland from the side is useful because lateral prominence of the thyroid between the cricoid cartilage and the suprasternal notch indicates thyromegaly. The generalist physician should estimate the thyroid gland as normal or enlarged; the impression of an enlarged thyroid gland by a generalist physician has an LR of almost 4.0, whereas the assessment of a normal-sized gland makes thyromegaly less likely (LR 0.4).

LYMPHATIC SYSTEM. While palpating the thyroid, the examiner also may identify enlarged cervical lymph nodes (Chapter 164). Lymph nodes also can be palpated in the supraclavicular area, axilla, epitrochlear area, and inguinofemoral region. Simple lymph node enlargement confined to one region is common and as a single finding does not usually represent an important underlying disorder. Unexpected gross lymph node enlargement in a single area or diffuse lymph node enlargement is more important. Patients with febrile illnesses, underlying malignancy, or inflammatory diseases routinely should have an examination in each of the above-mentioned areas for lymph node enlargement.

CHEST

Inspection of the patient's posture may reveal lateral curves in the back (scoliosis) or kyphosis that may be associated with loss of vertebral height from osteoporosis (Chapter 258). When patients have back pain, the spine and paravertebral muscles should be palpated in search of spasm and tenderness (Chapter 429). The patient may be placed through maneuvers to assess loss of mobility associated with ankylosing spondylitis (Chapter 279), but the history of loss of lateral mobility may be just as efficient in the early stages of spondylitis.

LUNGS

Examination of the lungs begins with inspection of the shape of the chest, although a barrel chest, thought to be typical of obstructive airways disease, is present only in severely affected patients (Chapters 81 and 85). The incremental value of palpation and percussion of the chest to supplement the history, auscultation, and eventual chest radiograph is unknown. Medical students show more consistency than do pulmonary specialists in recording auscultatory abnormalities. The presence or absence of adventitial sounds (wheezes, crackles, or rubs) has good interobserver reliability ($\kappa = 0.30$ to 0.70). The best piece of information for increasing the likelihood of chronic obstructive pulmonary disease is a history of more than 40 pack-years of smoking (LR 19). The presence of wheezing (LR about 3.0) or downward displacement of the larynx to within 4 cm of the sternum (distance between the top of the thyroid cartilage and the suprasternal notch; LR about 3.5) increases the likelihood of obstructive pulmonary disease.

HEART

The patient should be examined in the sitting and lying positions (Chapter 46). Typically the examination begins with auscultation of the precordium while the patient is sitting. Most examiners progress as follows: aortic area, pulmonic area, left sternal border, apex. For auscultation over the aortic area, having the patient lean forward may increase the intensity of aortic murmurs. Palpation of the apical impulse when the patient lies down in the left lateral decubitus position helps detect a displaced apical impulse and can reveal a palpable S_3. When the apical impulse is lateral to the midclavicular line, the likelihood of radiographic cardiomegaly and the likelihood of an ejection fraction less than 50% increase appreciably (LR about 3.5 and 6.0).

A systematic approach to auscultation helps organize the examination. First, the physician should listen to the heart sounds and concentrate on the timing, intensity, and splitting with respiration. The first and second heart sounds are heard best with the diaphragm, as are pericardial rubs. Gallops (S_3 and S_4) are heard best with the stethoscope bell. Murmurs, depending on their origin, vary in pitch and may require switching from the diaphragm to the bell to assess their characteristics (Table 46–6). The location, timing, intensity, radiation patterns, and respiratory variation of murmurs should be noted. Special maneuvers during auscultation (e.g., Valsalva, auscultation during sudden squat/stand) usually do not need to be performed if the routine precordial examination is entirely normal.

There is considerable concern about the reliability and accuracy of the cardiac examination. When performed on patients (as opposed to cardiac simulators), the reliability of perceiving an S_3 or S_4 is no better than chance, and agreement on the finding among examiners does not seem to improve with the examiner's experience. Nevertheless, the presence of an S_3 on any examination is useful for detecting left ventricular systolic dysfunction (LR >4.0 for identifying patients with an ejection fraction <30%). Reliability is better for cardiologists' evaluation for systolic (κ 0.3) and diastolic murmurs (simple agreement 94%). There is evidence that the detection of abnormalities in a "laboratory" setting improves with the experience of the observer, but the same information is not available for patients.

BREAST

The most important determinants of the accuracy of the breast examination are duration of the examination; the patient's position; the careful evaluation of breast boundaries; the pattern of the examination; and the position, movement, and pressure of the examiner's fingers (Chapter 204). Interobserver variability is substantial (κ about 0.3 to 0.6) because these aspects of the examination vary among physicians. To obtain the best sensitivity, the duration of the breast examination needs to be 5 to 10 minutes total time, but few generalist physicians perform such a lengthy examination. Clinicians should recognize that the examination may make them (or their patient) feel uncomfortable—the presence of a chaperone may allow the clinician the confidence to perform an intensive examination.

The patient should be examined with the pads of the fingers while she is supine, holding her hand first on the forehead (to flatten the lateral border of the breast) and then on the shoulder (to flatten the medial border). The examiner should make small circular motions with his or her fingers, moving up and down in parallel rows spanning the entire breast—clavicle to the bra line. Cancerous breast lumps are difficult to distinguish from benign breast lumps on examination, but the presence of a fixed mass or a mass 2 cm in diameter has an LR of about 2 to 2.5 for cancer.

ABDOMEN

Palpation and percussion of the abdomen of patients with no risk factors or symptoms of an abdominal disorder rarely reveal important abnormalities (Chapter 130). The only caveat would be palpation of the older patient for asymptomatic widening of the abdominal aorta, which is useful when found (LR of 15 for detecting aneurysms >4 cm in diameter) but misses a substantial proportion of small-sized to medium-sized aneurysms (Chapter 75). After specific training for palpation techniques, general internists have good agreement on the presence or absence of an aortic aneurysm ($\kappa = 0.53$).

When patients have potential abdominal symptoms, the examination should be guided by the symptoms. If the history suggests an acute problem, the examination should focus initially on identifying patients who may require a surgical evaluation.

Auscultation of the abdomen in patients with acute symptoms is directed toward listening for bowel sounds to evaluate possible intestinal obstruction. For patients without gastrointestinal symptoms or abnormalities on palpation, auscultation for bruits is important primarily to detect renal bruits in patients with hypertension (Chapters 63 and 124). The presence of an abdominal bruit in a hypertensive patient, if heard in systole and diastole, strongly suggests renovascular hypertension (LR approximately 40).

LIVER

The detection of liver disease depends mostly on the history and on laboratory evaluations (Chapter 148). By the time signs are present on physical examination, the patient usually has advanced liver disease. The first abnormalities on physical examination associated with liver disease are extrahepatic. The clinician should assess the patient for ascites, peripheral edema, jaundice, or splenomegaly as signs of liver disease. The presence of an enlarged liver itself should begin with palpation of the liver edge, but the presence of a palpated edge below the costal margin increases the likelihood of hepatomegaly only slightly (LR 1.7). The upper border of the liver may be detected by percussion, and a span of less than 12 cm reduces the likelihood of hepatomegaly. In the absence of a known diagnosis (e.g., a hepatoma, which may cause a hepatic bruit), auscultation of the liver rarely is helpful.

SPLEEN

Examination for splenomegaly in patients who have no suspicion of a disorder associated with splenomegaly almost always reveals nothing (Chapter 164). Approximately 3% of healthy teenagers may have a palpable spleen. The examination for an enlarged spleen begins first with percussion in the left upper quadrant to detect dullness. Percussion is performed over the lowest left anterior axillary line in inspiration and expiration, while the patient is supine. In the absence of dullness, the results of palpation do not establish or exclude splenomegaly, so a radiographic image (ultrasound or nuclear scintigraphy) is required. The presence of a palpable splenic edge in patients with dullness to percussion and a clinical suspicion of splenomegaly confirms enlargement. Palpation can be performed using any of the following three approaches (κ about 0.2 to 0.4): by palpating with the right hand, while providing counter pressure with the left hand behind the spleen; by palpating with one hand without counter pressure (with the patient in the right lateral decubitus position for both techniques); or by placing the patient supine with the left fist under the left costovertebral angle, while the examiner tries to hook the spleen with his or her hands.

MUSCULOSKELETAL

The musculoskeletal examination in adult patients is almost always driven by symptoms (Chapters 273 and 277). Regional musculoskeletal complaints are ubiquitous, and the limited formal clinical training most physicians receive on the evaluation and management of

such disorders belies their impact on the generalist's daily professional activities.

Most patients have back pain at some point during their lives (Chapter 429). Back pain is second only to upper respiratory illness as a reason for seeking outpatient care. The goal is to be sure that the back pain is not representative of systemic disease and to exclude neurosurgical emergencies. The patient's history helps assess the likelihood of an underlying systemic disease (age, history of systemic malignancy, unexplained weight loss, duration of pain, responsiveness to previous therapy, intravenous drug use, urinary infection, or fever). The most important physical examination findings for lumbar disc herniations among patients with sciatica all have excellent reliability, including ipsilateral straight leg raising causing pain, contralateral straight leg raising causing pain, and ankle or great toe dorsiflexion weakness (all with $\kappa > 0.6$).

The generalist physician should evaluate the adult patient with knee discomfort for torn menisci or ligaments. The best maneuvers for showing an anterior cruciate ligamentous tear is the anterior drawer or Lachman maneuver, in which the examiner detects the lack of a discrete end point as the tibia is pulled toward the examiner while the femur is stabilized. A variety of maneuvers that assess for pain, popping, or grinding along the joint line between the femur and tibia are used to assess for meniscal tears. As with many musculoskeletal disorders, no single finding has the accuracy of the orthopedist's examination that factors in the history and a variety of clinical findings.

The shoulder examination is directed toward determining the range of motion, maneuvers that cause discomfort, and an assessment of functional disability. Hip osteoarthritis is detected through evidence of restriction of internal rotation and abduction of the affected hip. Generalist physicians often rely on radiographs to determine the need for referral to orthopedic physicians, but routine radiographs are not needed early in the course of disease. The degree of pain and disability experienced by the patient may prompt confirmation of the diagnosis and referral to evaluate for surgery.

The hands and feet may show evidence of osteoarthritis (local or as part of a systemic process) (Chapter 287), rheumatoid arthritis (Chapter 278), gout (Chapter 288), or other connective tissue diseases. In addition to regional musculoskeletal disorders, such as carpal tunnel syndrome, a variety of medical and neurologic conditions should prompt routine examination of the distal extremities to prevent complications (e.g., diabetes [neuropathy or ulcers] or hereditary sensorimotor neuropathy [claw toe deformity]).

SKIN

The skin should be examined systematically and under good lighting (Chapter 472). It is best to ask the patient to point out any spots on the skin that concern them. Examiner agreement on some of the most important features of melanoma (asymmetry, haphazard color, border irregularity) is fair to moderate (Chapter 476). The physician's overall assessment of the likelihood of melanoma has not been studied well. The specificity of greater than or equal to 95% for lesions exhibiting any of the aforementioned signs or a diameter greater than 6 mm is high enough to warrant referral to a dermatologist. Conversely the sensitivity of generalist physicians may not be adequate (50 to 97%), so patients with risk factors for melanoma should be examined frequently or referred to a dermatologist.

Basal cell carcinomas and squamous cell carcinoma occur even more frequently than melanomas (Chapter 476). These lesions can be detected during routine examinations, paying careful attention to the sun-exposed areas of the nose, face, forearms, and hands.

NEUROLOGIC EXAMINATION

Full details of the neurologic examination are given in Chapter 423.

PSYCHIATRIC EVALUATION

During the general examination, much of the psychiatric assessment (including cognition) is accomplished while eliciting the routine history and the review of systems (Chapter 426). Observation of the patient's mannerisms, affect, facial expression, and behaviors may suggest underlying psychiatric disturbances. When a screening questionnaire and review of systems is obtained by a patient questionnaire, the clinician should review the responses carefully to determine if the patient exhibits symptoms of depression. Specific questioning for symptoms of depression is appropriate for all adult patients.

GENITALIA AND RECTUM

Pelvic Examination

A complete examination should result in descriptions of the external genitalia, appearance of the vagina and cervix as seen through a speculum, and bimanual palpation of the uterus and ovaries (Chapters 205 and 248). The precision of the pelvic examination is uncertain. In the emergency setting, there is poor agreement between resident physicians and emergency physicians on the presence of cervical motion tenderness, uterine tenderness, adnexal tenderness, and adnexal masses (κ 0.2 to 0.25) (Chapters 345 through 348). Among gynecologists, the assessment of uterine size by examination correlates reasonably well with measurement by pelvic ultrasound. Among asymptomatic women, 10 to 15% have some abnormality on examination, and 1.5% have abnormal ovaries. Screening for ovarian cancer is limited by the low sensitivity of the physical examination for detecting early stage ovarian carcinoma (Chapter 205).

Male Genitalia

Examination of the male genitalia should begin with a description of whether the penis is circumcised and whether there are any visible skin lesions (e.g., ulcers or warts). Palpation should confirm the presence of bilateral testes in the scrotum. The epididymis and testes should be palpated for nodules. As for ovarian carcinoma, the low incidence of testicular carcinoma means than most nodules are benign (Chapters 206 and 247).

The prostate should be examined in all quadrants with attention focused on surface irregularities or differences in consistency throughout the prostate (Chapter 207). An estimate of the prostate size may be confounded by the size of the examiner's fingers. It may be best to estimate the size of the prostate in centimeters of width and height.

Rectum

Patients can be examined while lying on their side, although this approach may place the examiner in an awkward stance (Chapters 130 and 147). The rectal examination in women can be performed as part of a bimanual examination, with the index finger in the vagina and third finger in the rectum, allowing palpation of the rectovaginal fault. Men may be asked to stand and lean over the examining table; alternatively, they may be examined while on their back with their hips and knees flexed. This latter maneuver is not used often, although it may facilitate examination of the prostate, which falls into the finger in this position.

The rectal examination begins with inspection of the perianal area for skin lesions. Using a well-lubricated gloved finger, the examiner places the finger on the anus and, while applying gentle pressure, asks that the patient bear down as if having a bowel movement. This maneuver facilitates entry of the finger into the rectum. A normal rectal response includes tightening of the anal sphincter around the finger. The examiner should palpate circumferentially around the length of the fully inserted finger for masses. On withdrawing the gloved finger, the finger should be wiped on a stool guaiac card for fecal blood testing. As a screening test for colorectal carcinoma (Chapter 200), the digital examination does not replace the need for testing stool samples collected by the patient (or using alternative screening strategies, such as flexible sigmoidoscopy or colonoscopy) but is necessary for ill patients who may have gastrointestinal hemorrhage.

Summarizing the Findings for the Patient

The physician should summarize the pertinent positive and negative findings for the patient and be willing to express uncertainty to the patient, provided that it is accompanied by a plan of action (e.g., "I will reexamine you on your next visit"). The rationale for subsequent laboratory, imaging, or other tests should be explained. A plan should be established for providing further feedback and results to the patient, especially when there is a possibility that bad news may need to be delivered. Some physicians ask the patient if there is "anything else" to be covered. Patients who express additional new concerns at the end of the visit may have been fearful to address them earlier (e.g., "by the way, doctor, I'm getting a lot of chest pain"), although this does not make them any less important. When the problems seem inconsequential, however, it is acceptable to reassure the patient and offer the promise of evaluating them further in a follow-up phone call or at the next visit.

Future Directions

The common assumption that physicians' diagnostic skills are deteriorating is not based on prior rigorous assessment. There is considerable evidence that the scientific approach to understanding what is worthwhile and what is not worthwhile during the clinical examination identifies a core set of skills for clinical diagnosticians. Because good patient outcomes at good value are driven primarily by the quality of the information obtained during the clinical examination, continued application of scientific principles to the history and physical examination should improve diagnostic skills.

SUGGESTED READINGS

Bates B, Bickley LS, Hoekelman RA: A Guide to Physical Examination and History Taking, 7th ed. Philadelphia, JB Lippincott, 1999. *Traditional textbook, nicely illustrated, for the general clinical examination.*

Oboler SK, Prochazka AV, Gonzalez R, et al: Public expectations and attitudes for annual physical examinations and testing. Ann Intern Med 2002;136:652–659. *The public generally wants annual examinations if the cost to them is acceptable.*

Society of General Internal Medicine: Website for Clinical Examination Research Groups. Available at http://www.sgim.org/clinexam.cfm. *Facilitates personal literature searches for topics on the clinical examination and a bibliography of the "Rational Clinical Examination Series" published in the* Journal of the American Medical Association.

6 INTERPRETATION OF DATA FOR CLINICAL DECISIONS

Thomas H. Lee

Key functions in the professional lives of all physicians are the collection and analysis of clinical data. Decisions must be made on the basis of these data, including which therapeutic strategy is most appropriate for the patient or whether further information should be gathered before the best strategy can be chosen. This decision-making process is a blend of science and art, in which the physician must synthesize a variety of concerns, including what is the patient's most likely outcome with various management strategies, what is the patient's worst possible outcome, and what are the patient's preferences among these strategies.

Only rarely does the physician enjoy true certainty regarding any of these issues, so a natural inclination for physicians is to seek as much information as possible before making a decision. This approach ignores the dangers inherent in the collection of information. Some of these dangers are direct, such as the risk of cerebrovascular accident associated with coronary angiography. Other dangers are indirect, such as the possibility that performance of a blood culture might lead to a contaminant result that might lead in turn to further blood cultures, unnecessary antibiotic therapy, and prolongation of hospitalization.

An additional concern is the cost of information gathering, including the direct costs of the tests themselves and the indirect costs that flow from decisions made on the basis of the test results. Standards of medical professionalism endorse the need for physicians to exert their influence to minimize inefficiency and for good reason. The available pool of resources for health care is not expanding as quickly as the demands posed by medical advances and the aging of the population. If resources are to be available to care for the sick patients who are most likely to benefit from them, physicians must be skillful at identifying low-risk patients and exercise discretion on the use of resources for them.

For the physician, there are three key questions in this sequence: Should I order a test to improve my assessment of diagnosis or prognosis? Which test is best? Which therapeutic strategy is most appropriate for this patient?

Should I Order a Test?

The decision of whether to order a test depends on the physician's and the patient's willingness to pursue a management strategy with the current degree of uncertainty. This decision is influenced by several factors, including the patient's attitudes toward diagnostic and therapeutic interventions (e.g., a patient with claustrophobia might prefer an angiogram to magnetic resonance imaging) and the information provided by the test itself. The personal tolerance of the patient and physician for uncertainty also frequently influences test-ordering approaches. A decision to watch and wait rather than to obtain a specific test also should be considered as an information-gathering alternative because the information obtained while a patient is being observed often reduces uncertainty about the diagnosis and outcome. Even as medicine increasingly becomes evidence-based, randomized trials are not available to guide physicians in most of their choices about diagnostic strategies and many of their choices among therapeutic options.

The impact of information from tests often is expressed as *probabilities* (Table 6–1). A probability of 1.0 implies that an event is certain to occur, whereas a probability of 0 implies that the event is impossible. When all the possible events for a patient are assigned probabilities, these estimates should sum to 1.0.

It is often useful to use *odds* to quantify uncertainty instead of probability. Odds of 1:2 suggest that the likelihood of an event is only half the likelihood that the event will not occur. The relationship between odds and probability is expressed in the following formula:

$$Odds = P/(1 - P)$$

where *P* is the probability of an event.

PERFORMANCE CHARACTERISTICS

Sensitivity and *specificity* are key terms for the description of test performance. These parameters describe the test and are in theory true regardless of the patient population to which the test is applied. Research studies that describe test performance often are based, however, on highly selected patient populations; test performance may deteriorate when tests are applied in clinical practice. The result of a test for coronary artery disease, such as an electron beam computed tomography scan, rarely may be abnormal if evaluated in a low-risk population, such as high school students. False-positive abnormal results secondary to coronary calcification in the absence of

obstructive coronary disease are common when the test is performed in middle-aged and elderly people.

Although researchers are interested in the performance of tests, the true focus of medical decision making is the patient. Physicians are more interested in the implications of a test result on the probability that a patient has a specific disease or outcome, that is, the predictive values of positive or negative test results. These predictive values are extremely sensitive to the population from which they are derived. An abnormal lung scan result in an asymptomatic patient has a much lower positive predictive value than that same test result in a patient with dyspnea and a diminished oxygen saturation. Bayes' theorem (see later) provides a framework for analyzing the interaction between test results and a patient's pretest probability of a disease.

As useful as the performance characteristics may be, they are limited by the fact that few tests truly provide dichotomous (i.e., positive or negative) test results. Tests such as exercise tests have several parameters (e.g., ST-segment deviation, exercise duration, hemodynamic response) that provide insight into the patient's condition, and the normal range for many blood tests (e.g., prostate-specific antigen) varies markedly depending on the age of the tested population and one's willingness to "miss" patients with disease. Tests that require human interpretation (e.g., radiologic studies) are particularly subject to variability in the reported results.

BAYES' THEOREM

The impact of a test result on a patient's probability of disease was first quantified by Bayes, an 18th century English clergyman who developed a formula for the probability of disease in the presence of a positive test result. The classic presentation of Bayes' theorem is complex and difficult to use. A more simple form of this theorem is known as the *odds ratio* form, which describes the impact of a test result on the pretest odds (see Table 6–1) of a diagnosis or outcome for a specific patient.

To calculate the post-test odds of disease, the pretest odds are multiplied by the *likelihood ratio* (LR) for a specific test result. The mathematical presentation of this form of Bayes' theorem is as follows:

$$\text{Post-test odds} = (\text{Pretest odds}) \times (\text{LR})$$

The LR is the probability of a particular test result in patients with the disease divided by the probability of that same test result in patients without disease. In other words, the LR is the test result's sensitivity divided by the false-positive rate. A test of no value (e.g., flipping a coin and calling "heads" an abnormal result) would have an LR of 1.0 because half of patients with disease would have positive test results, as would half of patients without disease. This test would have no impact on a patient's odds of disease. The further a likelihood ratio is above 1.0, the more that test result raises a patient's probability of disease. For LRs less than 1.0, the closer the LR is to 0, the more it lowers a patient's probability of disease.

When displayed graphically (Fig. 6–1), a test of no value (dotted line) does not change the pretest probability, whereas an abnormal or normal result from a useful test moves the probability up or down. For a patient with a high pretest probability of disease, an abnormal test result changes the patient's probability only slightly, but a negative test result leads to a marked reduction in the probability of disease. Similarly, for a patient with a low pretest probability of disease, a normal test result has little impact, but an abnormal test result markedly raises the probability of disease.

Consider how various exercise test results influence a patient's probability of coronary disease (Table 6–2). For a patient whose clinical history, physical examination, and electrocardiographic findings suggest a 50% probability of disease, the pretest odds of disease are 1.0. LRs for various test results are developed by pooling data from published literature. The sensitivity of an exercise test with no ST-segment changes is the rate of such test results in patients with coronary disease, and the specificity is the percentage of patients without coronary disease who do *not* have this test result.

When the LRs for various test results are multiplied by the pretest odds to calculate post-test odds, the odds decrease for patients without ST-segment changes but increase for patients with 1 or 2mm of ST-segment change. Post-test odds can be converted to post-test probabilities according to the following formula:

Table 6–1 • KEY DEFINITIONS*

Probability = A number between 0 and 1 that expresses an estimate of the likelihood of an event
Odds = The ratio of [the probability of an event] to [the probability of the event not occurring]

TEST PERFORMANCE CHARACTERISTICS
Sensitivity = Percentage of patients with disease who have an abnormal test result
Specificity = Percentage of patients without disease who have a normal test result
Positive predictive value = Percentage of patients with an abnormal test result who have disease
Negative predictive value = Percentage of patients with a normal test result who do not have disease

BAYESIAN ANALYSIS
Pretest (or prior) probability = The probability of a disease before the information is acquired
Post-test (or posterior) probability = The probability of a disease after new information is acquired
Pretest (or prior) odds = (Pretest probability of disease) ÷ (1 − pretest probability of disease)
Likelihood ratio = (Probability of result in diseased persons) ÷ (Probability of result in nondiseased persons)

*Disease can mean a condition, such as coronary artery disease, or an outcome, such as postoperative cardiac complications.

Table 6–2 • EXAMPLE OF ODDS RATIO FORM OF BAYES' THEOREM

Question: What is the probability of coronary disease for a patient with a 50% pretest probability of coronary disease who undergoes an exercise test if that patient develops (a) no ST-segment changes, (b) 1 mm of ST-segment depression, or (c) 2 mm of ST-segment depression?

Step 1. Calculate the pretest odds of disease:

$$p/(1-p) = 0.5/(1-0.5)$$
$$= 0.5/0.5$$
$$= 1.0$$

Step 2. Calculate the likelihood ratios for the various test results, using the formula LR=Sensitivity/(1−specificity). (Data from pooled literature)

TEST RESULT	SENSITIVITY	SPECIFICITY	LIKELIHOOD RATIO
No ST-segment changes	0.34	0.15	0.4
1-mm ST-segment depression	0.66	0.85	4.4
2-mm ST-segment depression	0.33	0.97	11

Step 3. Calculate the post-test odds of disease, and convert those odds to post-test probabilities:

TEST RESULT	PRETEST ODDS	LIKELIHOOD RATIO	POST-TEST ODDS	POST-TEST PROBABILITY
No ST-segment changes	1	0.4	0.4	0.29
1-mm ST-segment depression	1	4.4	4.4	0.81
2-mm ST-segment depression	1	11	11	0.92

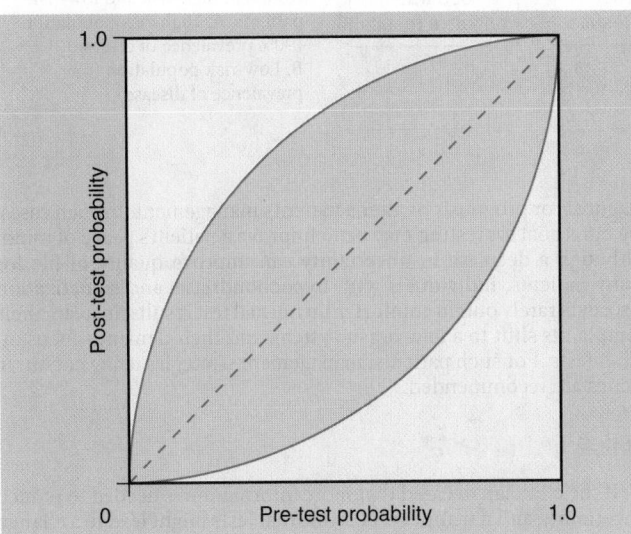

FIGURE 6–1 • Impact of various test results on the patient's probability of disease. The *x* axis depicts a patient's probability of disease before a test. If the test is of no value, the post-test probability (*dotted line*) is no different from the pretest probability. An abnormal test result raises the post-test probability of disease, as depicted by the concave-downward arc, whereas a normal test result lowers the probability.

$$\text{Probability} = \text{Odds}/(1 + \text{odds})$$

The calculations quantify how the absence of ST-segment changes reduces a patient's probability of disease, whereas ST-segment depression raises the probability of disease.

This form of Bayes' theorem is useful for showing how the post-test probability of disease is influenced by the patient's pretest probability of disease. If a patient's clinical data suggest a *probability* of coronary disease of only 0.1, the *pretest odds* of disease would be only 0.11. For such a low-risk patient, an exercise test with no ST-segment changes would lead to post-test probability of coronary disease of 4%, whereas 1-mm or 2-mm ST-segment changes would lead to a post-test probability of disease of 33 or 55%.

Even if clinicians rarely perform the calculations that are described in Bayes' theorem, there are important lessons from this theorem that are relevant to principles of test ordering (Table 6–3). The most crucial of these lessons is that the interpretation of test results must incorporate information about the patient. An abnormal test result in a low-risk patient may not be a true indicator of disease. Similarly a

Table 6–3 • PRINCIPLES OF TEST ORDERING AND INTERPRETATION

1. The interpretation of test results depends on what is already known about the patient
2. No test is perfect; clinicians should be familiar with their diagnostic performance (see Table 6–1) and never believe that a test "forces" them to pursue a specific management strategy
3. Tests should be ordered if they may provide *additional* information beyond that already available
4. Tests should be ordered if there is a reasonable chance that the data will influence patient care
5. Two tests that provide similar information should not be ordered
6. When choosing between two tests that provide similar data, use the test that has lower costs and/or causes less discomfort and inconvenience to the patient
7. Clinicians should seek all of the information provided by a test, not just a positive or negative result
8. The cost-effectiveness of strategies using noninvasive tests should be considered in a manner similar to that of therapeutic strategies

normal test result in a high-risk patient should not be taken as evidence that disease is not present.

Figure 6–2 provides an example of the post-test probabilities for positive and negative results for a test with a sensitivity of 85% and a specificity of 90% (e.g., thallium scintigraphy for diagnosis of coronary artery disease). In a high-risk population with a 90% prevalence of disease, the positive predictive value of an abnormal result is 0.99 compared with 0.31 for the same test result obtained in a low-risk population with a 5% prevalence of disease. Similarly the negative predictive value of a normal test result is greater in the low-risk population than in the high-risk population.

MULTIPLE TESTING

Clinicians frequently obtain more than one test aimed at addressing the same issue and at times are confronted with conflicting results. If these tests are truly independent (i.e., the tests do not have the same basis in pathophysiology), it may be appropriate to use the post-test probability obtained through performance of one test as the pretest probability for the analysis of the impact of the second test result.

If the tests are not independent, this strategy for interpretation of serial test results can be misleading. Suppose a low-risk patient has an abnormal lung ventilation-perfusion scan. Obtaining that same test result over and over would not raise that patient's probability of coronary disease further and further. In this extreme case, the tests are identical; serial testing adds no information. More commonly,

Principles of Evaluation and Management

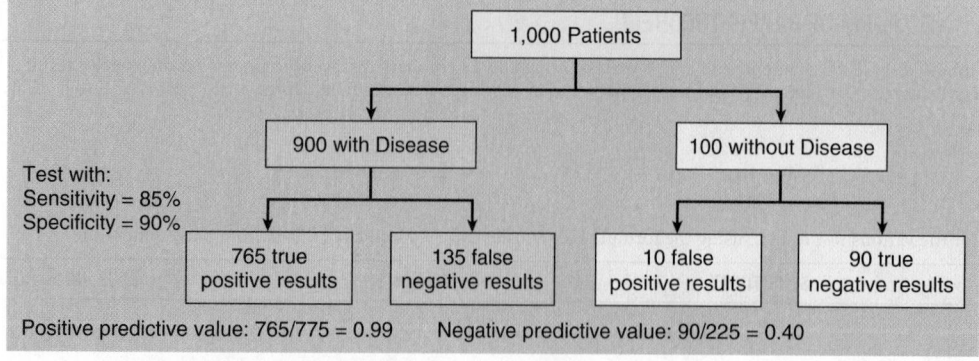

A

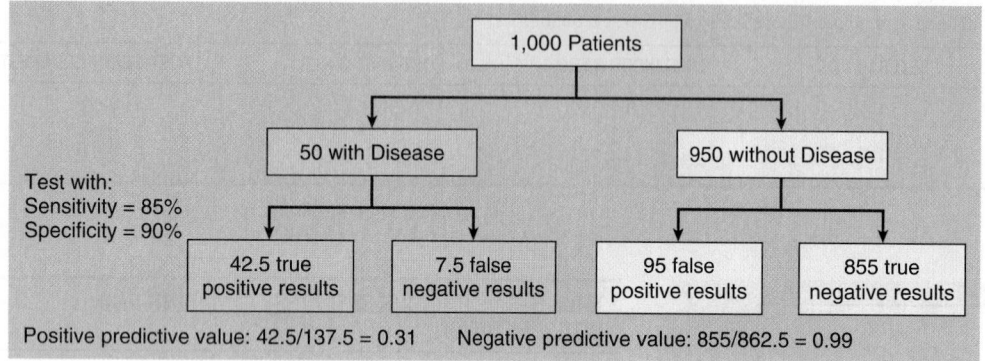

B

FIGURE 6–2 • Interpretation of test results in high-risk and low-risk patients. *A,* High-risk population (90% prevalence of disease). *B,* Low-risk population (5% prevalence of disease).

clinicians are faced with results from tests with related but not identical bases in pathophysiology, such as ventilation-perfusion scintigraphy and pulmonary angiography.

Regardless of whether tests are independent, the performance of multiple tests increases the likelihood that an abnormal test result will be obtained in a patient without disease. If a chemistry battery includes 20 tests and the normal range for each test has been developed to include 95% of healthy individuals, the chance that a healthy patient will have a normal result for any specific test is 0.95. However, the probability that all 20 tests will be normal is $(0.95)^{20}$, or 0.36. Most healthy people can be expected to have at least one abnormal result. Unless screening test profiles are used thoughtfully, false-positive results can subject patients to unnecessary tests and procedures.

THRESHOLD APPROACH TO DECISION MAKING

Even if a test provides information, that information may not change care. A radiograph of a knee in a patient who is not willing to undergo surgery may reveal the severity of osteoarthritis but not be a useful expenditure of health care resources. Similarly a test that merely confirms a diagnosis that already is recognized is a waste of resources (see Table 6–3).

Before ordering a test, clinicians should consider whether that test result could change the choice of management strategies. This approach is called the *threshold approach to medical decision making,* and it requires the physician to be able to estimate the threshold probability at which one strategy will be chosen over another. The management of a clinically stable patient with a high probability of coronary disease might not be changed by any of the post-test probabilities shown in Table 6–2. If that patient had no ST-segment changes, the post-test probability of 0.29 still would be too high for a clinician to consider that patient free of disease. A positive test result that strengthened the diagnosis of coronary disease might not change management, unless the abnormal results suggested a greater severity of disease that might warrant another management strategy.

TESTING FOR PEACE OF MIND

Physicians frequently order tests even when there is little chance that the outcomes will provide qualitatively new insights into a patient's

diagnosis or prognosis or alter a patient's management. In such cases, the cited goal for testing may be to improve a patient's peace of mind. Although a decrease in uncertainty can improve quality of life for many patients, individuals with hypochondriasis and somatization disorders rarely obtain comfort from normal test results; instead, their complaints shift to a new organ system, and their demands focus on other tests. For such patients, management strategies using cognitive tactics are recommended.

Which Test Is Best?

If the clinician decided that more information is needed to reduce uncertainty, and if it appears possible that tests might lead to a change in management strategies, the question arises as to which test is most appropriate. Several factors influence this decision, including patients' preferences, the risk associated with the tests, and the diagnostic performance of the alternative tests.

Diagnostic performance of a test often is summarized in terms of sensitivity and specificity, but, as shown in the example in Table 6–2, these parameters depend on which threshold (e.g., 1 mm vs. 2 mm of ST-segment change) is used. A low threshold for calling a test abnormal might lead to excellent sensitivity for detecting disease, but at the expense of a false-positive rate. Conversely a threshold that led to few false-positive results might cause a clinician to miss many cases of true disease.

The receiver operating characteristic (ROC) curve is a graphic form of describing this tradeoff and providing a method for comparing test performance (Fig. 6–3). Each point on the ROC curve describes the sensitivity and the false-positive rate for a different threshold for abnormality for a test. A test of no value would lead to an ROC curve with the course of the dotted line, whereas a misleading test would be described by a curve that was concave upward (not shown).

The more accurate the test, the closer its ROC curve comes to the upper left corner of the graph, which would indicate a test threshold that had excellent sensitivity and a low false-positive rate. The closer an ROC curve comes to the upper left corner, the greater the area under the curve. The area under ROC curves can be used to compare the information provided by two tests.

Even if one test is superior to another as shown by a greater area under its ROC curve, the question still remains as to what value of

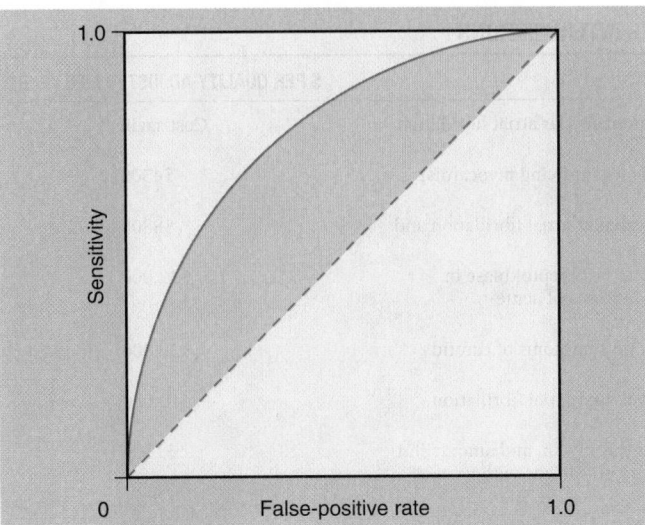

FIGURE 6–3 • Receiver operating characteristic curve. The points on the curve reflect the sensitivity and false-positive (1 – specificity) rates of a test at various thresholds. As the threshold is changed to yield greater sensitivity for detecting the outcome of interest, the false-positive rate rises. The better the test, the closer the curve comes to the upper left-hand corner. A test of no value (e.g., flipping a coin) would lead to a curve with the course of the dotted line. The area under the curve is used often to compare alternative testing strategies.

that test should be considered abnormal. The choice of threshold depends on the purpose of testing and on the consequences of a false-positive or false-negative diagnosis. If the goal is to screen the population for a disease that is potentially fatal and potentially curable, a threshold with excellent sensitivity is appropriate even if it leads to frequent false-positive results. In contrast, if a test is used to confirm a diagnosis that is likely to be treated with an invasive procedure, a threshold with high specificity is preferred. Only 1 mm of ST-segment depression might be the appropriate threshold when exercise electrocardiography was used to evaluate the possibility of coronary disease in a patient with chest pain. If the question were whether to perform coronary angiography in search of severe coronary disease that might benefit from revascularization, a threshold of 2 mm or more would be more appropriate.

Choosing a Strategy

Physicians and patients ultimately must use clinical information to make decisions. These choices usually are made after consideration of a variety of factors, including information from the clinical evaluation, patients' preferences, and expected outcomes with various management strategies. Insight into the impact of these considerations can be improved through the performance of decision analysis (Table 6–4).

Table 6–4 • STEPS IN PERFORMANCE OF DECISION ANALYSIS

1. Frame the question
2. Create the decision tree
   a. Identify the alternative strategies
   b. List the possible outcomes for each of the alternative strategies
   c. Describe the sequence of events as a series of decision nodes and chance nodes
3. Choose a time horizon for the analysis
4. Determine the probability for each chance outcome
5. Assign a value to each outcome
6. Calculate the expected utility for each strategy
7. Perform sensitivity analysis

The first step in a decision analysis is to define the problem clearly; this step often requires writing out a statement of the issue so that it can be scrutinized for any ambiguity. After the problem is defined, the next step is to define the alternative strategies.

Consider the question of which management strategy is most appropriate to screen patients for colorectal cancer: fecal occult blood testing, flexible sigmoidoscopy, or colonoscopy. The expected outcomes for these strategies depend on each test's sensitivity for detecting colorectal cancer, which is influenced in turn by other factors, such as the frequency with which the test is performed and whether fecal occult blood testing is used annually during intervals between endoscopic procedures. Patients' outcomes also are influenced by their compliance with the screening program, the age-specific incidence of colonic polyps, and the likelihood that earlier detection of polyps reduces the risk for cancer and for death resulting from cancer.

Each of these variables must be known or estimated to make calculations for each strategy's predicted life expectancy and direct medical costs. These outcomes usually differ for patients of different ages and with different underlying risks for the outcomes of interest—in this case, death resulting from colorectal cancer. Optimal strategies are unlikely to be the same for an elderly patient with a short life expectancy and low risk of cancer as for a younger patient with a long life expectancy except for a high risk of cancer resulting from familial colonic polyposis.

The credibility of the decision analysis depends on the credibility of these estimates. Published reports often do not provide information on the outcomes of interest for specific patient subsets, or there may not have been sufficient statistical power within patient subsets for the findings to be statistically significant. Randomized trial data are relevant to the populations included in the trial; the extension of the findings to other genders, races, and age groups requires assumptions by individuals performing the analysis. For many issues, expert opinion must be used to derive a reasonable estimate of the outcome.

For many diseases, the potential outcomes are more complex than perfect health or death. With chronic diseases, patients may live many years in a condition somewhere between these two, and the goal of medical interventions may be to improve quality of life rather than to extend survival. The value of life in imperfect health must be reflected in decision analyses. These values by convention are expressed on a scale of 0 to 100, where 0 indicates the worst outcome and 100 indicates the best outcome.

Life-expectancy and quality-of-life estimates are combined in many decision analyses to calculate *quality-adjusted life years*. A strategy that leads to a 10-year life expectancy with such severe disability that utility of the state of health is only half that of perfect health would have a quality-adjusted life expectancy of 5 years. With such adjustments to life-expectancy data, the impact of interventions that improve quality of life but do not extend life can be compared with interventions that extend life but do not improve its quality.

After the value and the probability of the various outcomes have been estimated, the expected utility of each strategy can be calculated. In comparing the different strategies available at a decision node, the analysis generally selects the option with the highest expected utility. At chance nodes, the expected utility is the weighted average of the utility of the various possible branches.

After the analysis has been performed with the baseline assumptions, *sensitivity analyses* should be performed in which these assumptions are varied over a reasonable range. These analyses can reveal which assumptions have the most influence over the conclusions and identify threshold probabilities at which the conclusions would change. The decision analysis comparing various strategies for screening for colorectal cancer found that screening with fecal occult blood testing is more sensitive to changes in compliance rates by patients and was clearly inferior to colonoscopy when less than perfect compliance was assumed.

COST-BENEFIT AND COST-EFFECTIVENESS ANALYSIS

For clinicians and health care policymakers, the choices that must be addressed go beyond the choices within any single decision analysis. Because resources available for health care are limited, policymakers may have to choose among many competing "investments" in health. Although such decisions frequently are made on the basis

Table 6–5 • ESTIMATED COST-EFFECTIVENESS OF COMMON HEALTH INTERVENTIONS

DISEASE CATEGORY	INTERVENTION VS. COMPARATOR IN TARGET POPULATION	$ PER QUALITY-ADJUSTED LIFE YEAR*
Circulatory system	Warfarin vs. no therapy in 65-year-old patients with nonvalvular atrial fibrillation and medium risk for stroke	Cost saving
	Captopril therapy vs. no captopril in 80-year-old patients surviving myocardial infarction	$4300
	Warfarin vs. aspirin in 65-year-old patients with nonvalvular atrial fibrillation and medium risk for stroke	$8800
	Thrombolytic therapy with tissue plasminogen activator vs. streptokinase in patients presenting within 6 hours after onset of symptoms of acute myocardial infarction	$32,000
	Screening for carotid disease in 65-year-old men with no symptoms of carotid disease	$130,000
	Warfarin vs. aspirin in 65-year-old patients with nonvalvular atrial fibrillation and low risk for stroke	$410,000
Digestive system	Eradicate *H. pylori* empirically using omeprazole, clarithromycin, and amoxicillin vs. no treatment in adults presenting to primary care physicians with dyspepsia	$1300
	Check serum *H. pylori* titer; if positive, eradicate *H. pylori* vs. eradicate *H. pylori* using omeprazole, clarithromycin, and amoxicillin in adults presenting to primary care physicians with dyspepsia	$57,000
	Give omeprazole alone empirically vs. check serum *H. pylori* titer in adults presenting to primary care physicians with diagnosis of dyspepsia	$780,000
Genitourinary	One-time screening with magnetic resonance angiography at 50 years old vs. no screening in patients with rapidly progressive renal insufficiency who have no symptoms of vascular disease	$2500
	One-time screening with conventional angiography vs. one-time screening with magnetic resonance angiography in 50-year-old patients with rapidly progressive renal insufficiency who have no symptoms of vascular disease	$9400
Infectious	Pneumococcal pneumonia vaccination vs. no vaccination in people >65 years old	Cost saving
Injury	Driver-side air bags vs. no air bags	$27,000
	Dual air bags vs. driver-side air bag only	$69,000
Nervous system	CT of the head vs. no imaging tests with clinical follow-up for diagnosis in 35-year-old women presenting to physicians for a single episode of an asymmetrical neurologic symptom suggesting a possible neurologic disorder	$23,000
	Magnetic resonance imaging of the head vs. CT in 35-year-old women presenting to physicians for a single episode of an asymmetrical neurologic symptom suggesting a possible neurologic disorder	$110,000

*1998 dollars.
CT = computed tomography.
From: Chapman RH, Stone PW, Sandberg EA, et al: A comprehensive league table of cost-utility ratios and a sub-table of "panel-worthy" studies. Med Decis Making 2000;20:451–467.

of political considerations, cost-benefit and cost-effectiveness analyses can be informative in making the choices.

The methodology of these techniques is similar to that of decision analysis except that costs for the various possible outcomes and strategies also are calculated. *Discounting* is used to adjust the value of future benefits and costs because resources saved or spent currently are worth more than resources saved or expended in the future. In *cost-benefit* analyses, all benefits are expressed in terms of economic impact. Extensions in life expectancy are translated into dollars by estimating societal worth or economic productivity.

Because of the ethical discomfort associated with expressing health benefits in financial terms, *cost-effectiveness* analyses are used more commonly than cost-benefit analyses. In these analyses, the ratio of costs to health benefits is calculated; one frequently used method for evaluating a strategy is calculation of cost-per-quality-adjusted life year ($/QALY). These estimates can be used to compare strategies and identify settings in which strategies that may be more expensive (e.g., coronary angiography) may "purchase" quality-adjusted life years at a lower cost than less aggressive strategies (e.g., observation). A cost-effectiveness analysis indicates that, compared with fecal occult blood testing, colonoscopy improves survival with a cost-effectiveness of about $11,000 per year of life saved.

Cost-effectiveness analyses can provide important insights into the relative attractiveness of different management strategies and can help guide policymakers in decisions about which technologies to make available on a routine basis. No medical intervention can have an attractive cost-effectiveness if its effectiveness has not been proved. The cost-effectiveness of an intervention depends heavily on the patient population in which it is applied. An inexpensive intervention would have a poor cost-effectiveness ratio if it were used in a low-risk population unlikely to benefit from it. In contrast, an expensive technology can have an attractive cost-effectiveness ratio if used in patients with a high probability of benefiting from it. Table 6–5 shows cost-effectiveness estimates from published literature for some common medical and nonmedical interventions. Such estimates should be used only with understanding of the population for which they are relevant.

SUGGESTED READINGS

Barsky AJ: The patient with hypochondriasis. N Engl J Med 2001;345:1395–1399. *This review of therapeutic strategies for patients who are hypochondriacs and somaticizers notes that additional testing to achieve "peace of mind" has not been shown to provide reassurance for this patient population.*

Sonnenberg A, Delco F, Inadomi JM: Cost-effectiveness of colonoscopy in screening for colorectal cancer. Ann Intern Med 2000;133:573–584. *Colonoscopy is a cost-effective means of screening for colorectal cancer because it reduces mortality at relatively low incremental costs, in part because of low compliance rates with other screening strategies for colorectal cancer.*

Stern JA, Davey Smith G: Sifting the evidence—what's wrong with significance tests? BMJ 2001;322:226–231. *This thoughtful discussion seeks to help physicians move beyond thinking about P values when reading the literature and to use a flexible Bayesian approach in which insights into the patient's prior probability of specific diagnoses or outcomes guide the interpretation of test results.*

7 APPLICATIONS AND LIMITATIONS OF DIAGNOSTIC IMAGING

David E. Avrin

The traditional evaluation of the patient includes the history and physical examination (Chapter 5) and a well-planned set of diagnostic tests, often including imaging. Dramatic advances in imaging not only supplement the physical examination, but also now may begin to substitute for part of it. Medical imaging provides an approach for dividing patients into patients who have an acute compared with a chronic medical problem and patients who have an anatomic compared with a "biochemical" illness. These determinations are crucial for prompt and effective medical and surgical therapy.

A key issue for clinicians is determining the appropriate role for imaging in a patient. Ultrasonography is highly accurate for the diagnosis of cholelithiasis, but it is less clear how to decide when a patient with right upper quadrant pain (Chapter 130) needs ultrasonography, computed tomography (CT), an upper gastrointestinal radiographic series (Chapter 131), endoscopy (Chapter 132), or no imaging study whatsoever. Optimum choices among the armamentarium of tests guide efficient and cost-effective care.

Radiographic Techniques

CONVENTIONAL RADIOGRAPHY

Traditional projection plain radiography is a shadow picture formed by illuminating the portion of the body being imaged with x-rays from a small source or focal spot. X-rays are attenuated to varying degrees by body tissues, depending on type and thickness. The terms *posteroanterior* and *anteroposterior* refer to the direction of the x-ray beam from source to detector. In many institutions, the detector is now electronic, rather than conventional film screen. *Film screen* refers to the fact that traditional film radiographs result from their exposure by visible light produced by the "bread of the sandwich," in which the film is covered on both sides by phosphor plates that capture the x-rays more efficiently, convert them to visible light, and expose the adjacent film, which has photographic emulsions on both sides.

Often, when the images are captured electronically, they also are viewed electronically at a computer workstation attached to a digital medical imaging system. Images also can be made available through web browsers with secure techniques.

Plain radiographs are able to distinguish four basic material attenuations: air (none), fat (intermediate, but less than water), non-adipose tissue and body fluids such as blood (intermediate, but greater than water), and bone or metallic foreign bodies (high). The traditional chest radiograph (Chapters 49 and 81) is of high diagnostic value because abnormalities in the lung are identified most commonly when the normal air is replaced by soft tissue density material or fluid. Fluid density can be identified in the pleural space, displacing or compressing lung. The structures of the mediastinum (heart and great vessels, including the pulmonary hila) form distinct tissue density contours outlined by the minimally attenuating lungs; the bony thorax also can be visualized.

The same physical facts that make the chest radiograph of such high diagnostic value also cause the plain films of the abdomen to be less so. As a result, CT has nearly totally replaced the plain film of the abdomen.

ULTRASOUND

Medical ultrasound imaging grew out of the *SONAR* (*SO*nic *Na*vigation *A*nd *R*anging) technology developed during World War II for submarine warfare. Images are created based on the time delay and intensity of echos returned from tissue after a short pulse of ultrasonic energy, emitted and received by a transducer held in contact with the body. Ultrasound is nonionizing radiation and considered safe for the unborn fetus and other sensitive tissues.

With appropriate instrumentation, it is possible to create "tomographic" or slice images, with real-time motion, of body parts if the path of the sound does not hit gas or bone, both of which severely attenuate the sound. Gray-scale ultrasound enables some degree of tissue characterization. Ultrasound with Doppler instrumentation can measure blood flow. As with all of the technologies discussed in this section, the images are created within a computer component of the imaging device.

COMPUTED TOMOGRAPHY

Of all advances, CT has had the most profound effect since the 1970s. Using x-rays emitted from a fairly conventional x-ray tube, but which now rotates around the patient in a circular ring, sets of attenuation data are collected. One to 16 (new helical scanners) sections or tomographic slices, perpendicular to the long axis of the patient's body, are measured at a time. These measured data are processed by an algorithm that essentially calculates the most likely pattern of tissue density that could give rise to the data set. The combination of true cross-sectional imaging (which yields three-dimensional information) with exquisite soft tissue density of less than 1% of the attenuation of water gave birth to a new era of medical imaging.

MAGNETIC RESONANCE IMAGING

Magnetic resonance imaging (MRI) became clinically useful a few years after CT. MRI provides exquisite detail, without ionizing radiation, of the neuraxis, musculoskeletal structures, and the female and male pelvis. Success also has been achieved in cardiovascular imaging; this technology has the inherent ability to visualize blood vessels even without intravenously administered contrast material. Compared with CT, MRI is limited by longer imaging times and respiratory motion image artifacts. Gadolinium often is used as an additional contrast-enhancing agent.

MRI is based on the nuclear magnetic resonance phenomenon of atoms with an unpaired electron, principally hydrogen, which is ubiquitous within water molecules in biologic tissues. When subjected to an aligning constant magnetic field, the atom can be made to resonate similar to a toy top in response to excitation by an external radiofrequency electromagnetic pulse when the frequency equals the resonant frequency. Imaging is achieved by the fact that the resonant frequency is proportional to the strength of the local magnetic field. Beginning with a strong and uniform constant field, position-dependent changes are created with additional gradient field electromagnets. Slight but detectable changes in resonant frequency can be used to determine the location of the resonant hydrogen atoms within water molecules. Images can be reconstructed from this data set by spectral processing and techniques similar to those used for CT.

NUCLEAR IMAGING AND POSITRON EMISSION TOMOGRAPHY

Nuclear imaging is achieved by intravenously injecting radioactive isotopes, usually bound to an organic or biologic molecular carrier. The carriers are designed to have affinity for a particular tissue (e.g., bone). In contradistinction to x-ray techniques, the body parts examined emit the radiation, rather than external radiation passing through the region examined. Cameras are designed to measure the amount of radiation emitted as a function of location and time.

The development of positron emission tomography (PET) yields two advantages over conventional nuclear medicine. First, the positron emitted by the isotope quickly finds an electron, and they annihilate each other, producing two gamma rays in 180-degree opposite direction. A specially designed "coincidence" detector can calculate a linear path on which the event occurred. This data set can be reconstructed in a computer using mathematical techniques similar to CT. Second, fluorodeoxyglucose, the isotope commonly used, is an analogue of glucose, and regions of high radioactivity (concentration) indicate regions of high metabolic activity. This approach yields extremely sensitive, but not specific, images for evaluation of metastatic disease. Two limitations of this technology are that the isotope currently has to be produced in a cyclotron, a device that requires expensive construction for radiation safety, and the isotopes are short-lived (a few hours), requiring proximity to a cyclotron.

ANGIOGRAPHY AND INTERVENTIONAL RADIOLOGY

Angiography, the imaging of blood vessels, remains at the focus of the field of vascular and interventional radiology and cardiology.

Images are achieved by placing a small, steerable catheter within the arterial or venous system, usually by way of a needle puncture of the femoral artery or vein. Small quantities of iodine-containing radiographic contrast material can be injected by way of the tip of the catheter, yielding detailed x-ray images of the downstream vascular flow from the location of the tip. Images are captured digitally, using a subtraction technique that enhances the image quality, in a rapid time sequence.

The same minimally invasive catheter techniques can be used for examination and drainage of an obstructed biliary system and for intra-abdominal abscess drainage. Other therapeutic interventions include most prominently the use of angioplasty balloon catheters and catheter-delivered intravascular stents to treat vascular and biliary stenoses.

Principles of Ordering Imaging Tests

ONE EXAMINATION OR TWO, AND WHEN TO ORDER THE MORE EXPENSIVE TEST FIRST: EXAMPLE OF ABDOMINAL PAIN

As a general rule, when confronted with two reasonable alternatives, it is advisable to choose the least expensive, safest, and least uncomfortable imaging examination first. For acute right upper quadrant abdominal pain (Chapter 130), ultrasonography is usually the procedure of choice because it is less expensive than CT, primarily because the imaging equipment is cheaper. Although ultrasound is more subjective and operator dependent than CT, ultrasound can yield exquisite visualization of the biliary tree, including the gallbladder and the pericholecystic space, in which fluid can be a sign of acute cholecystitis (Chapter 158). Ultrasonography also confirms or denies the presence of gallstones in the gallbladder with high accuracy that at least equals that of CT, and ultrasonography can detect biliary dilations and masses in the liver and pancreas (Chapter 201)

(Fig. 7–1). Ultrasonography works well in the right upper quadrant because there is little bowel gas, which obscures underlying structures on ultrasound but not on CT, and the liver provides an excellent acoustic window for ultrasound visualization of the underlying structures.

Ultrasonography can be difficult and suboptimal in patients who are obese or who have a distended abdomen. Ultrasonography is generally less accurate in surveying the remainder of the abdomen, an important issue when the pain is less localized.

How should the choice between CT or ultrasonography be made in a patient who presents with acute abdominal pain? More specifically, when is it appropriate to move directly to CT? In general, if the pain is not biliary in character, is not localized to the right upper quadrant, or occurs in an obese patient, CT is preferred because it often reveals previously unsuspected abnormalities. At least three other imaging choices exist: (1) no imaging study, (2) a plain radiographic series of the abdomen (technically and economically similar to the chest radiograph but generally not as useful), and (3) MRI of the abdomen or pelvis (usually reserved for more complex situations or after failure to diagnose with other methods). Other than identifying free intraperitoneal air (perforated viscus), gas patterns of bowel obstruction, and radiodense ureteral calculi, the traditional abdominal series, although the least expensive test, is considered generally inferior to CT and has been largely replaced by CT. A current-generation multislice helical CT scanner can generate 5-mm sections of the entire abdomen and pelvis in about 1 minute. It is helpful to use oral and intravenous contrast material to opacify (and identify) loops of bowel and vascular structures.

MRI can be useful for the cooperative patient in renal failure who cannot receive intravenous contrast material because it can provide tissue and vascular detail not achievable without contrast-enhanced CT. Patient cooperation is required because of the longer imaging times and respiratory motion artifacts. MRI is also useful in specific

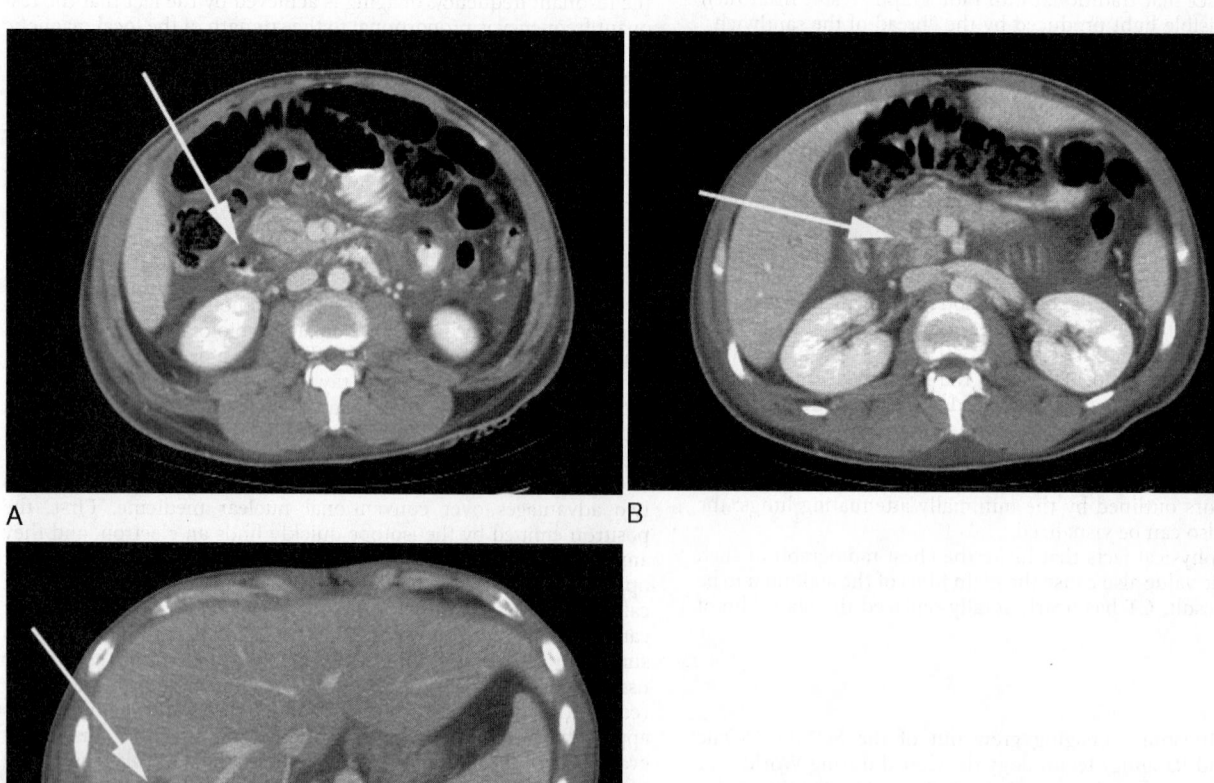

FIGURE 7–1 • Pancreatic carcinoma. Computed tomographic scans of the abdomen show infiltration of the duodenal wall evidenced by thickening (*A*, arrow), associated involvement of the body and tail of the pancreas (*B*, arrow), and a liver lesion (*C*, arrow). Complete anatomic staging was achieved by this single study.

situations to image the biliary tree, liver parenchyma, and male and female pelvis.

EXPENSES OF IMAGING PROCEDURES

In the inpatient environment, charges must be distinguished from actual costs. *Charges* are the price that the institution requests from patients and insurers for providing a service. *Reimbursement* is what is paid. *Costs* are the expenses associated with providing the service. For imaging procedures, costs include the fixed costs related to the use of expensive equipment, variable costs related to each individual test (e.g., technologists' time, contrast material), and indirect costs (e.g., facility overhead for building and maintenance). Although useful as a guideline, the charge for an examination may not reflect its cost accurately, particularly for the marginal or incremental test. If an institution owns a CT scanner, the incremental cost of performing an additional test is much lower than the average cost (and the charge) for all tests. These marginal assumptions or calculations break down, however, when the incremental studies trigger a decision to purchase an additional scanner to satisfy the needs of the institution to provide timely service.

SCREENING

For a screening program to be beneficial, the radiation risk to the population must be significantly less than the benefit achieved by early detection of resectable (curable) lesions. The most widely accepted screening imaging procedure is mammography (Chapter 204). Imaging also can be used to screen for coronary artery calcification, although its usefulness is subject to debate (Chapter 52). Newer screening modalities that are under evaluation include CT for early detection of lung cancer (Chapter 198) and CT colonography (Chapter 200). Whole body screening for the early detection of neoplasm is widely advertised but of unproven utility.

The portable chest radiograph is crucial in the serial evaluation of patients in the intensive care environment. Routine daily screening portable chest radiographs are inappropriate, however, and not cost-effective. Every portable chest radiograph should be ordered for a specific clinical indication, such as change in status.

Imaging Approach to Selected Common Clinical Problems

CHEST PAIN

The chest radiograph is a valuable initial imaging step for patients with chest pain (Chapter 46). The common entities that are identifiable are atelectasis or collapse, pneumonia or consolidation, pulmonary mass, pleural effusion, pneumothorax, and chest wall trauma. Evidence of aortic dissection and pulmonary emboli often can be subtle or absent on plain radiograph. The most common chest radiograph appearance in patients with known pulmonary emboli is "normal." For aortic dissection, transesophageal echocardiography, CT, and MRI are nearly equivalent diagnostic options (Chapter 75). For pulmonary embolus, ventilation-perfusion scanning, helical CT, and angiography are useful for diagnosis (Chapter 94) (Fig. 7–2).

SHORTNESS OF BREATH

The routine two-view or single anteroposterior examination of the chest can be the most valuable routine radiographic study for patients with shortness of breath (Chapter 81). It is crucial to base the choice of imaging examination on the presenting problem of the patient to gain the most information on which to narrow the differential diagnostic possibilities. For many, but not all, abnormalities (pulmonary embolism being the most prominent exception), a conventional radiograph can help distinguish among pulmonary, cardiac, and thoracic causes.

The most common pulmonary causes of shortness of breath are consolidative pneumonia, atelectasis (collapse), pleural effusion with or without atelectasis, pneumothorax, and pulmonary embolism. For otherwise healthy patients with documented pulmonary embolism, the chest radiograph is often normal.

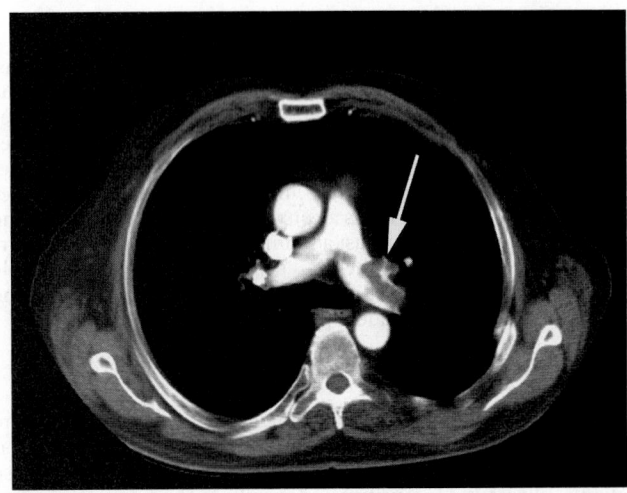

FIGURE 7–2 • Asymptomatic pulmonary embolus. Contrast-infused sections through the chest show embolus (arrow) straddling the major bifurcation of the left pulmonary artery, with a strand of clot extending into the right pulmonary artery.

Bacterial pneumonia classically presents radiographically with a portion of previously normally aerated lung that is replaced by a fluid density that usually follows a segmental or lobar anatomic distribution (Chapter 92). With classic pneumonia, volume loss or collapse is minimal, but the larger, air-filled bronchi are silhouetted by the fluid-filled lung, resulting in the air bronchogram sign, which is a reliable sign of consolidation. With pneumonia and atelectasis, certain regions of the chest can be difficult to evaluate, including the retrocardiac left lower lobe, the medial portion of the right middle lobe (against the right heart border), the entire right middle lobe (best evaluated on the lateral radiograph), and the medial portions of the upper lobes. Viral pneumonia can present with these same classic changes or with only subtle interstitial abnormalities on the chest radiograph.

Patients who are being evaluated for chronic shortness of breath often have nonspecific evidence of interstitial lung disease on the routine chest radiograph. High-resolution, thin-slice CT allows the classification of the various subtypes of interstitial lung disease (Chapter 88) (Fig. 7–3).

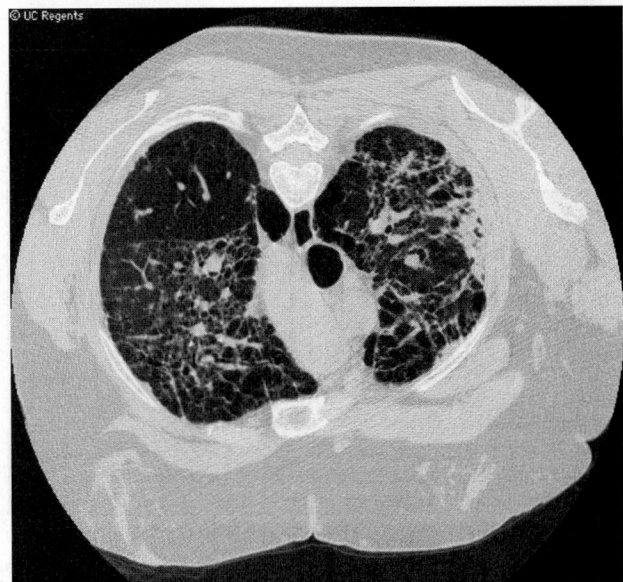

FIGURE 7–3 • Thin-section, high-resolution computed tomographic study in a patient with sarcoidosis.

Principles of Evaluation and Management

SOLITARY PULMONARY NODULE

In the evaluation of a solitary pulmonary nodule, the most valuable piece of information is a prior chest radiograph to determine whether the nodule is old, stable, and of no clinical concern or whether it represents a new finding and requires further evaluation (Chapter 81). Any prior chest radiographs should be reviewed because pre-existing small pulmonary nodules may have been missed. Further evaluation most often includes a computed tomographic scan of the chest with intravenous contrast administration to confirm and characterize the nodule, detect the presence of other nodules (multiple new nodules raise suspicion of metastatic disease), and evaluate the hila and mediastinum for adenopathy.

ACUTE RENAL FAILURE

Imaging can be helpful in determining whether acute renal failure is due to obstruction and can determine the level, chronicity, and cause of the obstruction (Chapter 121). In all but the most obese patients, ultrasound is sensitive and specific for hydronephrosis, but visualization of the ureters with ultrasound is difficult. Ultrasound is also useful for evaluating the size of the renal parenchyma and for determining the presence of medical renal disease. In larger patients, CT may be required. CT, which has the added benefit of visualizing all of the urinary structures to the base of the bladder, yields better visualization of the ureters and retroperitoneal masses.

PAINLESS HEMATURIA

Either ultrasonography or CT can best detect and characterize renal masses. Simple renal cysts are a common finding with a sufficiently typical CT appearance that no further evaluation is necessary (Chapter 127). By comparison, complex cysts or cysts with intrinsically high CT density require further evaluation with ultrasonography.

Renal cell carcinoma (Chapter 203), a process of the renal parenchyma, has typical CT appearances (Fig. 7–4) but occasionally can be difficult to distinguish from benign processes, such as xanthogranulomatous pyelonephritis and hamartoma. Transitional cell carcinoma, either of the renal collecting structures or of the ureter, can be difficult to identify on CT because the masses are smaller and do not usually enhance with radiographic contrast material. Transitional cell carcinomas of the bladder are easier to identify because they present as a polypoid or focal protrusion of the bladder mucosa, outlined by contrast material mixed with urine.

HEMATURIA WITH FLANK PAIN

The most common cause of hematuria with acute flank pain is a renal or ureteral calculus (Chapter 126). In many centers, CT

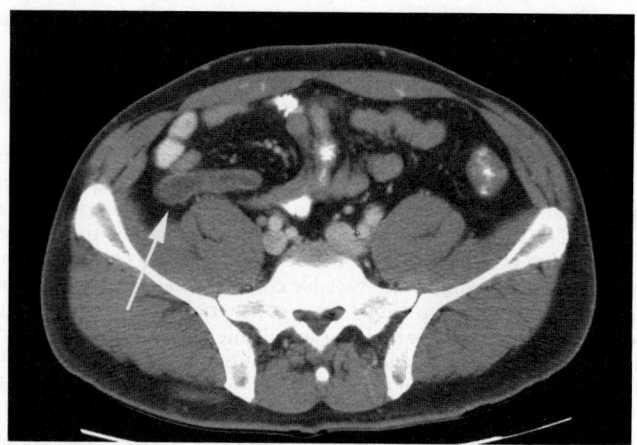

FIGURE 7–5 • Appendicitis, with the classic appearance on computed tomography (arrow) of a dilated tubular structure arising from the cecum distinct from the terminal ileum with or without surrounding inflammatory changes.

is replacing intravenous urography for evaluating this problem. Often the CT protocol does not require intravenous radiographic contrast material because obstruction is often readily visible on CT. The existence of radiopaque renal or ureteral calculi can be confirmed or denied with a high degree of accuracy. The level of obstruction can be determined and, when combined with the presence of a calculus, is diagnostic. If no calculus or other cause of the patient's hematuria and flank pain is found initially, a repeat abdominal/pelvic scan can be performed with contrast administration to evaluate for other causes.

Appendicitis can present with flank pain without hematuria. CT is particularly valuable for dealing with this diagnosis (Chapter 143) (Fig. 7–5).

STAGING OF ONCOLOGIC DISEASES

Diagnostic imaging is a principal method for presurgical staging of neoplastic disease and is essential for evaluating the response to therapy and long-term surveillance. Extent of the primary tumor, invasion or encasement of adjacent structures, presence of regional or distant lymphadenopathy, and distant metastases can be evaluated by cross-sectional imaging with great accuracy. PET is highly sensitive but nonspecific for neoplastic disease.

The search for an unknown primary tumor in the presence of metastatic disease is challenging (Chapter 210). With the advent of MRI and high-resolution multislice CT, more than 50% of initially unknown primary tumors now can be found (Fig. 7–6).

ADRENAL GLAND

CT is the primary imaging modality for evaluating the adrenal glands, which are a common site for metastatic disease. Because of their typical leaflike shape, adrenal gland hypertrophy usually can be distinguished readily from an adrenal mass. Benign adrenal adenomas, similar to renal cysts, are a relatively common finding with typical CT characteristics, including low Hounsfield unit density, and are usually of no clinical significance (Chapter 240). Adrenal masses that are less than 3 cm in diameter and that have typical CT characteristics can be classified reliably as adenomas and require no further follow-up. Masses that are greater than 3 cm in size, have high density or a complex appearance, or show an increase in size from a prior imaging study require further evaluation, usually with MRI.

Pheochromocytoma, a relatively uncommon lesion, usually is associated with clinical and biochemical findings (hypertension) that precipitate a search for this endocrine tumor (Chapter 241). Pheochromocytomas can present in extra-adrenal sites in the retroperitoneum so that careful inspection of this area is required even with normal-appearing adrenal glands.

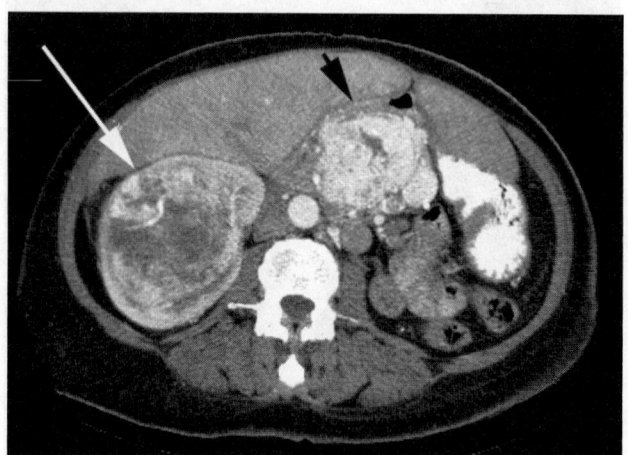

FIGURE 7–4 • Renal cell carcinoma (white arrow). Primary renal cell carcinoma usually shows enhancement with intravenous contrast administration on computed tomography. This study also shows metastatic involvement of the pancreas (black arrow).

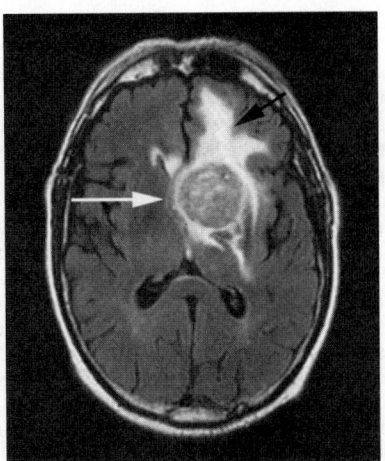

A

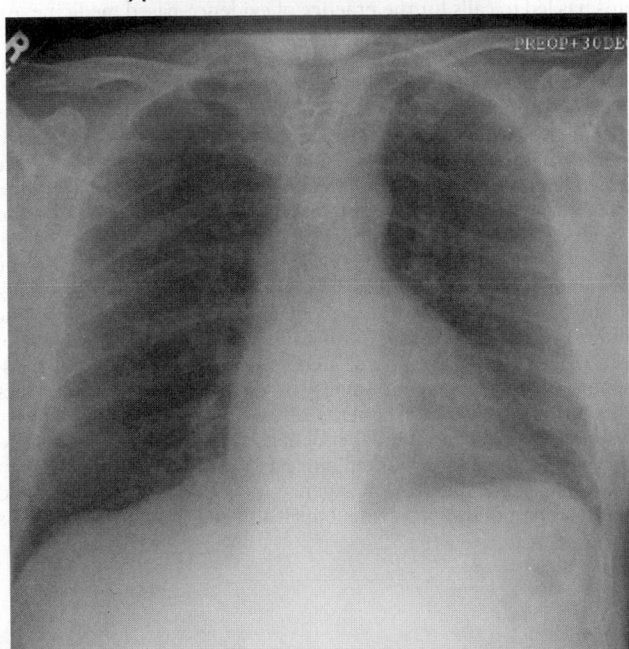

B

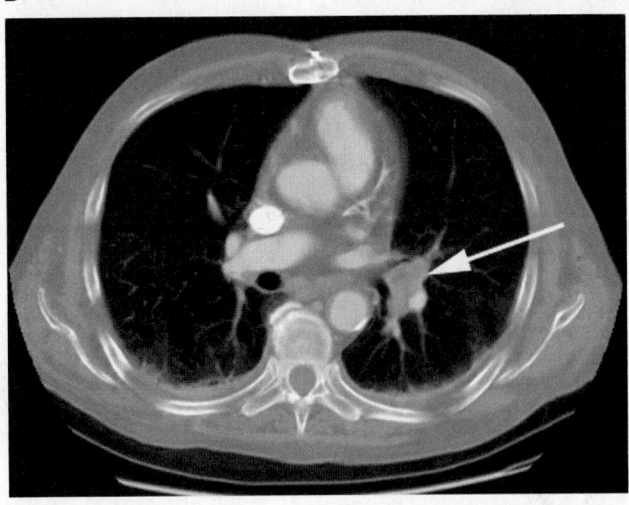

C

FIGURE 7–6 • Metastatic disease, unknown primary. Magnetic resonance imaging (A) shows a solitary lesion of the brain (white arrow) with mass effect and edema (black arrow). The preoperative chest radiograph (B) is negative. After craniotomy and biopsy, which showed adenocarcinoma rather than glioma, computed tomographic scan (C) of the chest, abdomen, and pelvis shows a left hilar mass (white arrow) not visible by conventional radiography.

Digital Image Storage and Teleradiology

Most medical images today are inherently digital by origin, produced by computerized analysis. With the decreasing cost of digital storage, picture archiving and communications systems (PACS), sometimes known as digital medical imaging systems, has led to filmless radiology. PACS is a cost-effective technology relative to film and the associated expenses of handling and storing it. Most important, image data and reports can be made available anytime and anywhere within the health care environment, simultaneously in multiple locations. In addition, web servers can provide secure web access to imaging studies and reports by way of personal computers using standard browsers.

SUGGESTED READINGS

ACR Appropriateness Criteria, 2000, American College of Radiology. W. Max Cloud, MD, Chairman. 2000;215(Suppl.):1–1511. *Current consensus guidelines for selection of imaging studies for specific clinical presentations and suspected diagnoses.*

Brant-Zawadzki M: CT screening: why I do it. AJR 2002;179:319–326. *Review of a controversial topic.*

Gore GM, Miller FH, Pereles FS, et al: Helical CT in the evaluation of the acute abdomen. Am Roentgen Ray Soc 2000;174:901–913. *Excellent review with image examples of the use of computed tomographic evaluation of the acute abdomen.*

Hopper KD, Singapuri K, Finkel A: Body CT and oncologic imaging—how I do it. Radiology 2000;215:27–40. *Current state of the art of the use of computed tomography for diagnosis, staging, therapy response, and follow-up surveillance of thoracic, abdominal, and pelvic neoplasms.*

Smith TP: Pulmonary embolism: What's wrong with this diagnosis? Am Roentgen Ray Soc 2000;174:1489–1497. *Thorough analysis of the use of computed tomographic scan versus ventilator-perfusion scans and pulmonary angiography for definitive diagnosis of pulmonary embolism.*

8 PRINCIPLES OF OUTCOME ASSESSMENT

Albert W. Wu

Physicians treat patients to improve or maintain their health. For some complaints, such as an isolated symptom, it is evident when the patient's health has improved. In other cases, the effects of treatment may not be immediately apparent. For a given patient, it is often difficult to know what treatment or course of action is likely to lead to the best outcome. Several kinds of outcomes may be important in evaluating a treatment.

Traditionally, data obtained from a medical history, physical examination, and laboratory tests form the basis of treatment evaluation and include parameters such as clinical events, physical findings, laboratory abnormalities, symptoms, and mortality. These conventional measures represent only a portion of the effects of treatment, however, on the patient's overall health because much of the emphasis in medicine has shifted from delivering acute care to treating chronic diseases. New approaches use standardized questions to assess quality of life and patient satisfaction and use insurance claims data to examine costs. As issues of cost-effectiveness and quality improvement become increasingly important, so does outcome assessment.

Definitions

Outcomes research, which is a comprehensive approach to determining the effects of medical care, entails the use of a variety of data sources and measurement methods. Outcomes research includes the rigorous determination of what does and does not work in medical care and how different providers compare with regard to their effects on patient outcome.

In outcomes research, *efficacy* refers to how a treatment works in ideal circumstances when delivered to selected patients by providers most skilled at providing it. *Effectiveness* refers to how a treatment works under ordinary conditions by the average practitioner for the typical patient. Efficacy often is evaluated in clinical trials, whereas effectiveness is better evaluated in observational studies.

Outcome assessment plays an important role in studies of quality of care. Excellent quality care maximizes the benefits and minimizes the risks to the patient, adheres to professional standards, is consistent with patient expectations and preferences, and achieves efficiency in the use of resources. According to Donabedian's widely accepted model of quality of care, it is necessary to assess the "structure, process, and outcomes" of care when monitoring quality. *Structure* refers to stable elements that form the basis of the health system, such as the type of facility, administrative organization, and provider qualifications. *Process* refers to what happens in the medical interaction and includes the technical and interpersonal skills of the physician and other providers. Process measures compare care with relevant standards. In this framework, *outcomes* are the measurable events and observations that are presumed to occur in part as a result of the structure and process of medical care.

Importance of Outcome Assessment

Factors that have led to the current interest in patient outcomes include the rising cost of health care, changes in the organization and financing of care, findings of unexplained variation in physicians' practice patterns, recognition of the limitations of available information about the effects of many treatments, and increased adoption of a model of shared patient and physician decision making. The cost of medical care in the United States has grown from $250.1 billion and 9.2% of the gross domestic product in 1980 to a projected $1.8 trillion and nearly 15% of the gross domestic product by 2004. Desire to control the growth rate in medical expenditure, coupled with evidence that some medical procedures may be performed inappropriately, has created incentives to assess the relative effectiveness of different treatments. Elimination of treatments deemed less effective could result in reductions or reallocation of resources to treatments that produce greater benefits.

The growth of prepaid care and prospective payment for hospital care has promoted increased competition among health care providers. Managed care organizations and insurers now compete for corporate buyers, and individual physicians compete for inclusion on preferred provider lists. Most of the competition currently involves price and services offered, but "report cards" detailing the performance of health plans, institutions, and individual physicians on a variety of outcomes can show value and improve consumers' choices. The emergence of managed care as the predominant model of practice in the United States also has led to concern about erosion in the quality of care to achieve cost savings.

Researchers have documented substantial geographic differences in the use of medical procedures for apparently similar patients. In 1999, rates of percutaneous coronary interventions varied markedly in different parts of the United States (Fig. 8–1). Related studies have shown that the per capita costs of hospitalization for residents of Boston, Massachusetts, are about twice the costs for residents of New Haven, Connecticut. There is growing evidence for the simultaneous underuse, overuse, and misuse of common treatments and procedures. Striking differences also may be seen in outcomes depending on whom the patient sees for care. Five additional deaths per 100 are related to which cardiac surgeon performs coronary artery bypass graft surgery. Although some patients receive unneeded procedures, it is estimated that 25% of patients with serious coronary artery disease are not offered indicated revascularization.

Recognition of the considerable uncertainty facing practicing physicians has led to calls for the practice of evidence-based medicine. An evidence-based approach combines pathophysiologic rationale, caregiver experience, and patients' preferences with a synthesis of valid and current evidence from clinical research.

The traditional model of clinical decision making, in which patients delegate choice to the physician, is being replaced by a model of shared decision making, in which patients actively participate in the choice of treatment. In choosing among treatment options, this model requires increased emphasis on patient preferences for risks and outcomes and increased patient understanding (Chapter 6).

For all of the aforementioned reasons, activity directed at outcome assessment has grown rapidly. In 1986, the Health Care Financing Administration began reporting hospital mortality rates for specific conditions. Since 1987, the Joint Commission on Accreditation of Health Care Organizations has shifted from traditional structural measures of quality assurance to quality assessment based on outcomes adjusted for the severity of patients' disease. The National Committee on Quality Assurance, an independent accrediting body for managed care organizations, has worked since 1989 to develop measures of health plan performance. The Agency for Healthcare Research and Quality, as part of the Department of Health and Human Services, has

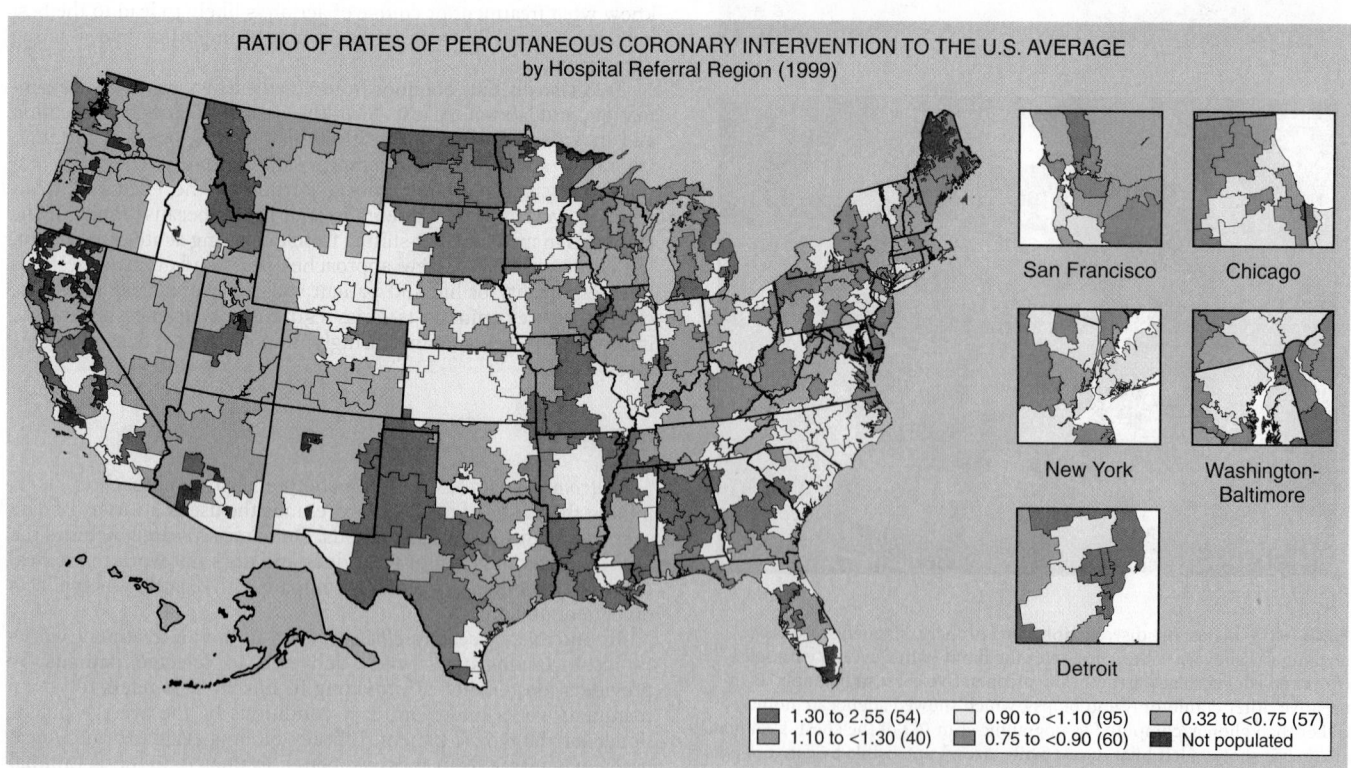

FIGURE 8–1 • Rates of percutaneous coronary intervention vary markedly in different regions of the United States. (From Wennberg JE, Cooper MM [eds]: Dartmouth Atlas of Health Care. © Trustees of Dartmouth College, 1999.)

taken the lead on generating evidence-based information on health care outcomes, quality, cost, use, and access.

Types of Health Outcomes

Outcomes research considers a broad range of indicators, including conventional clinical measures, such as mortality, complications of disease or treatment, persistence of pathology, physiologic or laboratory abnormalities, deformity, signs and symptoms, and adverse clinical events. In addition, outcomes research considers the patient's perspective of quality of life and satisfaction with care. Other relevant outcomes include the use of health care resources and the costs and economic losses caused by disability or death (Table 8–1).

Measurement Standards

To be useful, a measurement instrument must meet standards for reliability, validity, responsiveness, and interpretability (Table 8–2). *Reliability* concerns the extent to which a measuring procedure yields consistent results on repeated trials. *Validity* is the degree to which a test measures what it is intended to measure (e.g., whether a pain questionnaire measures pain rather than the patient's mood). *Responsiveness* is the ability of a test to detect clinically meaningful changes. If a treatment results in an important improvement in health-related quality of life, a measure should be able to detect that difference. For results to be useful, measurements also must be expressed in terms that clinicians can understand.

Patient-Assessed Outcomes

QUALITY OF LIFE. Several terms are used almost interchangeably to refer to the concept of health, including *health status, functional status,*

quality of life, and *health-related quality of life.* In 1948, the World Health Organization defined health as "a state of complete physical, mental, and social well-being, and not merely the absence of disease and infirmity." Bergner identified five dimensions of *health status:* (1) genetic and inherited characteristics; (2) biochemical, physiologic, and anatomic condition, including impairment of systems, disease, signs, and symptoms; (3) *functional status,* which includes performance of the usual activities of life, such as self-care, physical activities, and work; (4) mental condition, which includes positive and negative feelings; and (5) health potential, including longevity and prognosis.

Quality of life is a broad concept that encompasses a person's assessment of all aspects of his or her experience. Because quality of life includes important dimensions of life that are distant from conventional medical concern (e.g., achievement and spiritual fulfillment), it is useful to focus on aspects of quality of life that may be affected by therapeutic measures. *Health-related quality of life* encompasses several dimensions of health status that are experienced directly by the person (e.g., physical functioning, mental health, cognitive functioning, social and role functioning, energy, general health perceptions, symptoms, sexual functioning, and sleep) (Table 8–3).

STRUCTURE OF MEASURES AND MODES OF ADMINISTRATION. Measurements of health-related quality of life require indicators of different dimensions. Some measures consist of a single global health item, such as the question, "Would you say your health is excellent, very good, good, fair, or poor?" Most instruments consist, however, of a series of questions or items that are summed to yield a score for each specific concept.

Questionnaires can be self-administered or given by trained interviewers. Interviews are labor intensive but ensure compliance and minimize misinterpretation. Interviews may be conducted in person, by telephone, or by computerized platforms. Sometimes a surrogate respondent is used to estimate the responses that would be obtained from an unreliable or inarticulate patient.

TYPES OF QUALITY-OF-LIFE MEASURES. Two basic approaches are used to assess quality of life: generic and disease-specific. The format of measures may be indices, health profiles, or utility measures.

Generic instruments are designed for use across different diseases, treatments, settings, and patient groups. The major advantage is that they can be used in any population and allow comparisons of the

Table 8–1 • HEALTH OUTCOMES

OUTCOME	EXAMPLE FOR A PATIENT WITH MYOCARDIAL INFARCTION
CLINICAL	
Mortality	Death in hospital
Pathology	Coronary artery narrowing
Nonfatal clinical event	Stroke
Hospital readmission	Readmission within 30 days of hospital discharge
Complication of disease or treatment	Sternal wound infection after coronary artery bypass graft surgery
Physiologic test	Ejection fraction
Laboratory test	Troponin level
Symptom	Angina pectoris
PATIENT REPORTED	
Health-related quality of life	Ability to perform usual physical activities
Satisfaction with care	Patient ratings of overall quality of care
COST	
Use of health services	Number of physician visits
Direct cost	Cost of physician visits and prescription medications
Indirect cost	Loss of income from missed days of work

Table 8–3 • DIMENSIONS OF HEALTH-RELATED QUALITY OF LIFE

DIMENSION	DESCRIPTION
Physical functioning	Activities of daily living, strenuous activities
Mental health	Anxiety, depression, well-being, behavioral and emotional control
Social functioning	Quantity and quality of social contacts
Role functioning	Ability to perform work or usual activities
Cognitive functioning	Attention, memory, concentration
Energy	Energy and fatigue
General health perceptions	Global self-assessment of health
Pain	Severity and frequency of pain
Symptoms	Nausea, headache, dizziness
Sexual functioning	Performance and satisfaction
Sleep	Quantity and quality of sleep

Table 8–2 • MEASUREMENT STANDARDS

STANDARD	DEFINITION	EXAMPLE
Reliability	Does the instrument produce the same results if reapplied to the same situation?	CD4 lymphocyte counts repeated for the same individual yield the same results
Validity	Does the instrument measure what it purports to?	Scores on a pain questionnaire are highly correlated with scores on established pain measures
Responsiveness	Is the instrument capable of identifying small but clinically significant changes?	The mean score on a functional status questionnaire increases significantly with the use of inhaled corticosteroids for asthma

relative impact of various health interventions. They may be unresponsive to changes in specific conditions, however, and may be too general to guide clinical decision making. *Disease-specific* measures focus on dimensions of health related to a particular disease, population, symptom, or problem and may be more responsive to a change in the patient's condition than a generic instrument. The Health Assessment Questionnaire, widely used in studies of arthritis, includes questions about handgrip strength and pain. Disease-specific measures are understood more easily by clinicians but are frequently less well tested than generic instruments.

Indices attempt to reduce several concepts to a single, unidimensional scale. The Karnofsky Performance Status score, which is used commonly in cancer trials, combines information about the ability to work, to perform normal activities without assistance, and to care for personal needs. Single indices are brief but are less reliable than multi-item scales and generally yield limited information.

Health profiles attempt to measure all important dimensions of health-related quality of life. The *Sickness Impact Profile* assesses a physical dimension (including ambulation, mobility, body care, and movement), a psychosocial dimension (including social interaction, alertness behavior, communication, and emotional behavior), and additional domains, including eating, work, home management, sleep and rest, and recreation and pastimes. The *SF-36 Health Survey* is a relatively brief (36-item), widely used questionnaire that assesses several dimensions of health, including general health perceptions, physical functioning, role limitations because of physical health, role limitations because of mental health, social functioning, pain, mental health, and energy (Fig. 8–2).

Utility measures are derived from economic and decision theory. The term *utility* refers to the value placed by the individual on a particular health state. Utility is summarized as a score ranging from 0.0, representing death, to 1.0, representing perfect health. In economic analyses, utilities are used to justify devoting resources to a treatment. Because utility measures weight the duration of life according to its quality, they can be used to generate quality-adjusted life years. Because they are expressed as a single score, however, they do not provide details about how specific aspects of patients' lives are affected. The standard gamble and time tradeoff methods are used most commonly to assess utilities.

PATIENT SATISFACTION. *Patient satisfaction* refers to patients' subjective evaluations of their health care. Patient ratings of care reflect what

Table 8–4 • TYPES OF COST STUDIES

TYPE	DESCRIPTION
Cost-identification	Enumerates cost of applying a treatment to a specified population under a particular set of conditions
Cost-benefit	Compares the costs of treatment and cost savings resulting from benefits of the treatment in dollar terms
Cost-effectiveness	Compares the costs and benefits of a treatment in terms of reduced mortality or morbidity, such as years of life saved or quality-adjusted life years saved
Cost-utility	Compares the cost and benefits of a treatment in terms of utility scores

patients think is important about the quality of care, including the physician-patient relationship and their perception of the adequacy of diagnosis and therapy. They also predict patients' subsequent behavior, including how well they comply with the medications prescribed, whether they return to the same physician or go elsewhere, and whether they recommend a physician to others. The method used to elicit a patient's judgments about care can affect the results dramatically. When the response choices use the word *satisfied,* most patients choose the best possible answer. Rating scales (e.g., excellent to poor) result in a better distribution of responses. The Consumer Assessment of Health Plans survey asks consumers to rate their experience with their health plans; the results are used to help consumers and purchasers assess and select health plans.

Cost Studies

The basic formula of a cost study is a cost-benefit ratio. Studies most often examine direct costs (the costs of treatment itself) but also may include estimates of indirect costs (the costs of disability or loss of livelihood, actual and potential) (Table 8–4). *Cost-identification* studies enumerate the cost of applying a treatment to a specified population under a particular set of conditions. These studies describe the natural history of costs without comparing the benefits of one intervention with the benefits of alternatives. *Cost-benefit* studies compare the monetary costs of a treatment with the cost savings that result from the benefits of that treatment. A limitation is that all benefits, including decreased mortality, are expressed in dollar terms. Techniques for assigning value to a human life are controversial. *Cost-effectiveness* analysis compares the costs and benefits of a treatment in terms of reduced mortality or morbidity, such as years of life saved. A rough rule of thumb considers a treatment to be cost-effective if the cost is less than $50,000 per year of life saved. *Cost-utility* analysis expresses the costs and benefits of treatment in terms of utility scores, such as cost per quality-adjusted life year gained.

Study Design

Outcome assessments use a variety of research designs, including experiments (e.g., randomized controlled trials) and observational studies (e.g., cross-sectional, cohort, and case-control studies) (Chapter 6). Meta-analysis is used to pool data from many studies. Appropriateness studies examine whether treatments are used on patients who are likely to benefit from them and are not used on patients unlikely to benefit. Each of these study designs has strengths and limitations (Table 8–5).

RANDOMIZED CONTROLLED TRIALS. The randomized controlled trial involves selecting representative subjects, randomly assigning them to treatment and control groups, and monitoring them for the outcomes of interest. The randomized double-blind, placebo-controlled trial is considered the "gold standard" for evaluating the efficacy of a treatment. The experimental design allows the greatest control over the influence of confounding variables and permits causal inferences. Randomized controlled trials also have shortcomings, however. Data collection is time-consuming and costly. Many research questions are not suitable for experimental designs, such as when ethical concerns prohibit placebo controls or when outcomes are rare. Although

ACTIVITIES	(circle one number on each line)		
	Yes, limited a lot	**Yes, limited a little**	**No, not limited at all**
a. Vigorous activities, such as running, lifting heavy objects, participating in strenuous sports	1	2	3
b. Moderate activities, such as moving a table, pushing a vacuum cleaner, bowling, or playing golf	1	2	3
c. Lifting or carrying groceries	1	2	3
d. Climbing several flights of stairs	1	2	3
e. Climbing one flight of stairs	1	2	3
f. Bending, kneeling, or stooping	1	2	3
g. Walking more than a mile	1	2	3
h. Walking several blocks	1	2	3
i. Walking one block	1	2	3
j. Bathing or dressing yourself	1	2	3

FIGURE 8–2 • Sample questions assessing physical functioning from the SF-36 Health Survey. (From Ware JE, Snow KK, Kosinski M, et al: SF-36 Health Survey: Manual and Interpretation Guide. Boston, The Health Institute, 1993.)

Principles of Evaluation and Management

Table 8–5 • STUDY DESIGNS

DESIGN	STRENGTHS	WEAKNESSES
Experiment	Strongest evidence for cause and effect	Expensive Long duration Unsuitable for many questions Not useful for rare outcomes Limited generalizability
Cross-sectional	Short duration May study several outcomes Controls subject selection Controls measurements Yields prevalence	Does not establish causal relationships Unmeasured differences between groups
Cohort	Establishes sequence of events Avoids bias in measuring predictors Yields incidence, relative risk, excess risk	Relatively expensive Long duration Requires large sample size Not useful for rare outcomes
Case-control	Useful for rare conditions Relatively inexpensive Short duration Yields odds ratio	Potential sampling bias Limited to one outcome variable Does not yield prevalence, incidence, or relative risk
Meta-analysis	Increases statistical power for outcomes Helpful when studies disagree	Quality of secondary data varies Requires combining data from different studies

blinding study subjects and physicians to treatment assignment is possible in studies of medications, it is more difficult when studying medical and surgical procedures. Although randomized controlled trials provide data on treatment efficacy, their inclusion and exclusion criteria and the selected nature of study volunteers often limit their generalizability.

OBSERVATIONAL STUDIES. Rather than assigning patients to a treatment of interest, observational studies examine the outcomes of medicine as it is practiced. In *cross-sectional studies,* all variables are measured at a single point in time. Although cross-sectional studies are relatively inexpensive and can provide useful descriptions of the prevalence of diseases, treatments, and outcomes, they provide weak evidence for causal associations because they do not account for temporal relationships.

In *cohort studies,* patients are monitored over a certain period. Prospective cohort studies can provide evidence for cause-and-effect relationships between predictors and outcomes because the predictors are measured before the outcomes occur. If some patients receive a treatment and some do not, evidence for effectiveness also can be estimated. In some cases, observational studies may use a *quasi-experimental design* to take advantage of "natural experiments," such as introducing a new treatment or changing insurance coverage. As in clinical trials, prospective data collection is expensive and time-consuming, and cohort studies are not useful when outcomes are rare.

In *case-control studies,* the prevalence of risk factors in a sample of subjects who have a disease or outcome (the cases) is compared with the prevalence in a sample who do not (the controls). Case-control studies are inexpensive and uniquely efficient for studying rare conditions. A case-control study can examine only one outcome, however, because cases are selected on this basis. In addition, because cases and controls are selected separately, and data on predictors are collected retrospectively, these studies are susceptible to bias.

All observational studies are subject to significant confounding effects because groups may differ with regard to measured or unmeasured characteristics. Risk-adjustment methods are used to control for factors that are unequally distributed between groups and that may be related to patient outcomes, such as patient demographics and severity of illness. Inferences must be made cautiously, however, because unmeasured variations in patients, practitioners, and processes may be the real explanation for differences in outcomes.

META-ANALYSIS LITERATURE SYNTHESIS. Literature synthesis can be used to characterize the extent and quality of medical evidence and to summarize findings of existing studies. *Meta-analysis* is a systematic synthesis of the literature that uses standardized statistical methods (Chapter 9) to obtain a quantitative estimate of the effect of a particular intervention by aggregating the effects reported in many studies. Its main purposes are to identify gaps in knowledge, increase

statistical power for primary outcomes by combining studies that are too small to be conclusive, and resolve controversy when studies disagree. Its primary disadvantage is that it relies on secondary data. If the data are inadequate, little additional information can be generated. It may be difficult to combine data from studies conducted at different times and using different methods on different patient populations.

APPROPRIATENESS STUDIES. Appropriateness studies establish standard indications against which the use of a particular medical intervention is judged. Methods to develop indications involve careful analysis of what is known and the use of expert physicians to fill in gaps in knowledge and come to consensus about indications. Appropriateness studies can be incorporated into guidelines to help practicing physicians decide under what circumstances a procedure should or should not be performed.

Data Sources

Outcomes research uses a variety of sources of data, including patient questionnaires, medical records, and claims and administrative data files (Table 8–6).

PATIENT QUESTIONNAIRES. Outcomes research frequently uses a questionnaire-based approach to assess patient outcomes. Patients commonly are asked about their ability to function, how they feel, and their satisfaction with the care received. Sometimes, subjective data from patients can provide valuable information that may not be evident from physiologic measurements. Studies have shown that patient-reported measures can be at least as reliable as conventional biochemical or physiologic indices. Although patient reports provide a unique perspective, measures must be chosen with care. Data collection requires the cooperation of patients and providers, and selective non-participation can threaten generalizability. Study designs must recognize the limitations of patient recall and the fact that patients' evaluations of outcome may be affected by their expectations.

MEDICAL RECORD REVIEW. Detailed clinical information can be collected unobtrusively by retrospective review of medical records. To maximize reliability, abstraction must be done by trained reviewers with a clinical background. Data obtained by this method are limited by the level and accuracy of documentation, the completeness of the medical record, and the availability of the records themselves.

CLAIMS AND ADMINISTRATIVE DATA. Claims data analysis uses data files, such as those maintained by the Medicare program, to explore patterns of care and clinical outcomes. The database on all Medicare beneficiaries and providers includes demographics, characteristics of hospitals and other providers, expenditures, diagnoses, procedures, dates of service, and complications. Available data include a longitudinal record of health care use and medical costs for all claims submitted since 1991.

Table 8–6 • DATA SOURCES FOR OUTCOME ASSESSMENTS

DATA SOURCE	ADVANTAGES	DISADVANTAGES
Patient surveys	Provide the patient's perspective Provide reliable data	Labor intensive Requires cooperation of patient with or without providers Selective nonparticipation Patient may have trouble with recall Evaluations of outcome affected by expectation
Chart abstraction	Unobtrusive Detailed clinical information Can be performed retrospectively	Costly Labor intensive May be unreliable Variables may not be recorded consistently
Claims data	Unobtrusive Low cost Large number Broad cross section of patients	Data lack clinical detail for identifying patient groups or risk adjustment May be inaccurate

Medicare data have revealed striking variations in clinical practice, particularly in the performance of diagnostic and therapeutic procedures. They also provide population-based descriptions of the frequency of death and complications associated with various diagnoses and procedures and are used to monitor trends over time. Several problems limit the value of claims data, however, for assessing medical effectiveness or evaluating the quality of care. Claims data may not contain enough detail about clinical features thought to affect prognosis, such as the stage of colon cancer. It may be difficult to identify clinically relevant patient groups and control adequately for clinical factors likely to affect outcome.

Challenges

Many challenges remain before outcome assessment can be applied to full advantage. In particular, there are large gaps in the understanding of how the structure and process of care influence patient outcomes.

Clinical trials are needed to examine the effectiveness and the efficacy of existing and newly developed treatments and procedures. Studies that measure the effectiveness of treatments must examine short-term and long-term outcomes. To examine the effectiveness of services, to disseminate information, and to evaluate the quality of medical care, data systems must be able to characterize variation in treatments and outcomes. Better research tools and measurement techniques are needed, including more reliable, valid, and understandable measures of patient-reported outcomes tested in more diverse populations. Better risk-adjustment models are needed to facilitate valid reports and comparisons of patient outcomes. Finally, to improve decision making in the care of individual patients, students and clinicians must learn to understand and integrate evidence for effective practices with clinical expertise, pathophysiologic knowledge, and patient preferences.

SUGGESTED READINGS

Berwick DM: Disseminating innovations in health care. JAMA 2003;289:1969–1975. *Explores why some innovations are adopted and how to promote effective change.*

Committee on the Quality of Health Care in America, Institute of Medicine: Crossing the Quality Chasm: A New Health System for the 21st Century. Washington, DC, National Academy Press, 2001. *Cites problems with underuse, overuse, and misuse of medical care; calls for immediate action to improve care; and offers a comprehensive strategy to do so.*

Hays J, Ockene JK, Brunner RL, et al: Effects of estrogen plus progestin on health-related quality of life. N Engl J Med 2003;348:1839–1854. *Estrogen plus progestin did not have a meaningful benefit on health-related quality of life.*

Hulley SB, Cummings SR, Browner WS, Grady DE: Designing Clinical Research: An Epidemiologic Approach, 2nd ed. Baltimore, Lippincott Williams & Wilkins, 2001. *Highly accessible primer that walks the reader step by step from conceiving a research question, through designing a study, to writing a grant proposal.*

Kohn LT, Corrigan JM, Donaldson MS (eds): To Err Is Human: Building a Safer Health System. Washington, DC, National Academy Press, 2000. *Synthesis of theory and research on patient safety, pointing out that medical errors are an important public health problem, that they stem primarily from systems rather than individuals, and that blaming health care providers is counterproductive.*

9 APPLICATIONS OF STATISTICS

Catarina I. Kiefe

The sound practice of medicine requires the ability to use scientific evidence that is based on data and is published in the peer-reviewed medical literature. In this literature, investigators publish their findings using *descriptive statistics* to summarize data and *inferential statistics* to test hypotheses. Judgment is required in the choice of statistical tools and in the interpretation of statistical analyses. Physicians must have a basic understanding of statistics to benefit their patients by being informed and critical users of the medical literature.

Epidemiologic concepts of study design, data quality, and validity of inferences are key to understanding and using the medical literature. Statistics allow a scientific approach to dealing with data subject to *random variation*. The appropriate use of statistical tools is a necessary but insufficient component of a good study. Statistics always need to be understood in the wider context of overall study quality.

Descriptive Statistics

Many clinical variables, such as systolic blood pressure (SBP), are measured on a continuous numeric scale. For these continuous variables, appropriate measures of "central location" include a *mean* (average), *median* (50th percentile or middle value), and *mode* (most common value). Measures of dispersion quantify the amount of variability exhibited by variables. For continuous variables distributed in a bell-shaped fashion (*gaussian or normal distribution*), the mean ±1.96 *standard deviations* (SDs) defines an interval *containing 95% of the observed values*. The *standard error of the mean* (SEM) measures the precision of the estimate of the mean itself. The SEM is always smaller than the SD, and it is not appropriate to use the SEM directly as a measure of dispersion. When a variable has a bell-shaped distribution, the sample mean ±1.96 SEM represents the 95% *confidence interval* for the mean. The length of this confidence interval describes the precision of the mean estimate. Consider a study reporting that the mean SBP is 123 mm Hg, with SD = 10 mm Hg and SEM = 2 mm Hg. Assuming SBP is normally distributed, 95% of the population represented by this study should have SBP between 103 mm Hg and 143 mm Hg, and if 100 similar studies were performed, 95 of them would be expected to yield a mean SBP within the interval estimated from each study's data by the same process that yielded the interval 119 to 125 mm Hg. Asserting that the mean is within its 95% confidence interval is true 95% of the time.

Many variables of clinical interest are not continuous. Vital status after a myocardial infarction is a *dichotomous (nominal)* variable taking on only the two values "alive" or "dead." Major blood group (A, B, AB, or O) is also a nominal variable with individuals classified into one of four categories, without intrinsic order to the categories. Stage of breast cancer is an *ordinal variable* because values are "ordered" in a meaningful manner (e.g., stage IV breast cancer is more advanced than stage II). The progression from stage I to stage II is quite different, however, from the progression from stage III to stage IV. In contrast to what would be true for a continuous variable, each one-unit increment in an ordinal, noncontinuous variable is not equivalent. As a result, the statistical tools used to analyze ordinal variables are different from the tools used for continuous variables. Nominal and ordinal variables usually are summarized by computing the proportions of individuals in each category; means and SDs are not appropriate in these situations.

Hypothesis Testing

Much clinical research is concerned with detecting associations between an exposure (e.g., tobacco smoking) and a disease (e.g., lung cancer) or between an intervention and a clinical response or outcome (Chapter 6). For a typical study, investigators first develop a hypothesis, for example, that the mean SBP in a group given an antihypertensive agent is lower than the mean SBP in a group given a placebo. Next the investigators sample the populations of interest (treatment and control groups) and measure the variable of interest (SBP). A *null hypothesis* of no effect, or no difference between groups is formulated. In this case, the null hypothesis would be that the two groups (treatment and control) were drawn from the same underlying population. If the null hypothesis is true, and the study is well designed, any observed difference in mean SBPs between the two groups is due to random sampling. Rejecting the null hypothesis becomes the goal.

With a well-designed study, inferences based on population samples apply to the entire population. The underlying assumption is that the samples (treatment and control groups) are selected at random. Any systematic violation of this assumption, such as preferentially including individuals on a low-salt diet in the treatment group, would introduce bias and jeopardize the validity of inferences to be drawn from the study. Statistics would not speak to this study flaw, however. If a difference between two population samples is observed (e.g., SBP is lower in the treatment than in the control group), the key statistical question is whether this difference could have been due to random sampling (i.e., chance).

The likelihood that an observed difference or an even more extreme difference is due to chance alone is called the *P value*. If a certain difference between mean SBPs in treatment and control groups were observed, $P < .05$ would mean: Given that the null hypothesis is true, there is a less than 5% likelihood that this (or a larger) difference is due to chance. If the P value is small, it is unlikely that an observed difference is due to chance, the null hypothesis is rejected, and it is inferred that there are real population differences (i.e., a real association between treatment and response).

Although an association may be shown with statistical tools, this association does not establish causality. One study reported a statistical association between pancreatic cancer and coffee drinking; however, based on the weight of scientific evidence, coffee is not considered to be a cause of pancreatic cancer. The decision of whether an association is due to cause and effect involves much more than statistics. Factors contributing to this decision include biologic plausibility, temporal plausibility (cause precedes effect), strength of association, consistency of association across well-designed studies performed in different settings, and dose-response effect.

A small P value (the conventional level for "small" traditionally has been accepted, arbitrarily, as .05) safeguards against chance leading to rejection of a null hypothesis that is true. A low P value strongly suggests that the observed data are inconsistent with the null hypothesis. The error of rejecting a true null hypothesis is called a *type I error*. This error occurs when chance leads to inferring differences or associations that do not exist (e.g., ascertaining that SBP was lowered by treatment, when in reality we observed only random variation). The probability of a type I error is usually called α or significance level. Traditionally the acceptable upper limit for α is .05. In contrast, a *type II error* occurs when a large P value leads to the incorrect conclusion that a difference does not exist (incorrectly not rejecting a null hypothesis) (e.g., concluding that SBP was not lowered by treatment, when in reality treatment works but a random sample did not show it). The probability of a type II error usually is called β. A type II error may occur because the study lacks the statistical power (i.e., it has insufficient sample size) to show a true association or difference.

Table 9–1 • SAMPLE SIZE REQUIREMENTS FOR TESTING THE EFFICACY OF A NEW ANTIHYPERTENSIVE AGENT, BY CLINICALLY SIGNIFICANT EFFECT SIZE AND DESIRED POWER*

MINIMUM DIFFERENCE IN MEAN SBP BETWEEN TWO GROUPS TO BE DETECTED (CLINICALLY SIGNIFICANT EFFECT SIZE) (mm Hg)	POWER (%)	REQUIRED SAMPLE SIZE IN EACH GROUP
10	80	36
5	80	142
10	90	48
5	90	190
10	95	59
5	95	234

*Based on $\alpha = .05$, Student *t*-test, equal size, and standard deviation (SD) of 15 mm Hg in both groups and mean systolic blood pressure (SBP) of 130 mm Hg in group receiving the proven agent.

The sample size in each group is calculated for means by the following formula:

$$n = 2\left[\frac{(z \text{ of desired two-sided } \alpha \text{ error} + z \text{ of desired } \beta \text{ error}) \text{ SD}}{\text{mean expected difference between the two groups}}\right]^2$$

where z can be found in a standardized table. The total sample size needed is twice the sample size in each group. The formulas for calculating sample size in these and other situations can be found in standard statistical tests.

The *power* of the study (i.e., the probability of detecting a difference or an association that really exists) is $1 - \beta$. The power of the study increases with sample size, with α, and with the magnitude of the difference that is considered clinically significant. Power also decreases with increasing variability in the data. While designing a study, researchers should plan the sample size required to test their hypothesis in an attempt to minimize type II errors to a clinically acceptable level.

To illustrate this principle, assume that a study proposes to test whether a new antihypertensive agent is more efficacious than a proven agent by randomly allocating patients to equal-size groups, one group receiving the new agent and the other receiving the proven agent. The decision on sample size (i.e., how many patients to study) is based on desired power, on estimates of what would be a clinically significant difference (i.e., the minimum difference in mean SBP between the groups that the investigator wishes to be able to detect), and on the known variability in SBP (its SD). If a clinically significant difference between the two groups should be at least 10 mm Hg, and a power of at least 80% is desired, 36 patients need to be randomized to each group (Table 9–1). Conversely, if a 5 mm Hg reduction in SBP attributable to the new agent would be clinically significant and an 80% power is desired, 142 patients would be needed in each group.

One of the most common statistical misinterpretations is concluding that an effect does not exist because a study with low power failed to show it. The critical reader of medical journals should beware of type I errors when a study is *positive* (shows an effect) and should consider the possibility of type II errors when a study is *negative*. Impressive (very small) P values may correspond to effects of small magnitude in studies with large sample sizes. If a study reports a mean drop in 1 mm Hg, $P < .001$ for a certain medication, this result possesses high statistical significance but limited clinical significance. Studies with large sample sizes may detect statistically significant but clinically irrelevant differences.

Testing of statistical significance safeguards against the possibility that chance threatens a study's validity. Other threats, such as bias, confounding variables, or collecting faulty data, are not addressed by statistical significance testing. Frequently, investigators overestimate their study's external validity (i.e., they generalize the results shown by their data to a population inadequately represented in their study sample). The benefits of thrombolytic agents initially were shown only in patients younger than 65 to 70 years old. Because these initial studies were well designed and conducted, their internal validity was not questioned. The extent to which these results can be extrapolated to older individuals has been the object of extensive debate and additional research, however.

Table 9–2 • RECOMMENDED STATISTICAL APPROACHES TO VARIOUS TYPES OF VARIABLES AND SITUATIONS

WHO OR WHAT IS BEING STUDIED?	CHARACTERISTICS OF THE VARIABLE		
	Continuous*	Ordinal	Nominal
Same variable measured in two groups of different persons	Unpaired *t*-test	Mann-Whitney rank-sum test	Chi-square test or Fisher exact test
Same variable measured in three or more groups of different persons	Analysis of variance	Kruskal-Wallis statistic	Chi-square test
Same variable measured before and after in the same persons	Paired *t*-test	Wilcoxon signed-rank test	McNemar test
Association of two different variables measured in same person†	Linear regression and Pearson correlation coefficient	Spearman correlation coefficient	Contingency coefficients

*With a distribution that at least approximates a bell-shaped curve.
†If *both* do not meet the criteria for the type of data, choose the column farther to the right that is consistent with both variables.

Tests of Statistical Significance

When a hypothesis is clearly formulated and data have been collected to test that hypothesis, statistical procedures are used to interpret the data and assign P values. These procedures are called *tests of statistical significance*. The choice of statistical tests depends on the nature of the data. Consider the previous example of the antihypertensive trial in which the goal is to compare the mean SBP for subjects given placebo versus subjects given active drug. Assuming that the SBP distributions are bell-shaped, the appropriate test of statistical significance for this situation is the unpaired Student *t*-test. Expanding the antihypertensive trial to include three (or more) randomization groups, such as diet, drugs, and placebo, means that analysis of variance (ANOVA) is the most appropriate test of statistical significance. Student *t*-test and ANOVA assign P values to the differences across randomized groups.

ANOVA and Student *t*-test are parametric tests in that they assume that data follow certain distributions described by parameters, such as the traditional bell-shaped curves. Alternatively, nonparametric tests do not assume that data follow specified distributions. Table 9–2 provides a summary of the parametric and nonparametric tests that generally are recommended for specific indications.

The study assessing effectiveness of an antihypertensive medication could have been designed differently, using each subject as his or her own control rather than a placebo group. SBP before and after administering the antihypertensive agent are compared. Observations in the two groups of SBP are now paired and not independent. This situation calls for the use of the *paired Student t-test*.

A different situation arises when a dichotomous variable is the outcome of interest. Investigators studying the effect of β-blockers on mortality after myocardial infarction might randomize subjects into two groups: one receiving a β-blocker and the other receiving a placebo. The null hypothesis would be that the proportion of deaths is the same in both groups. The appropriate test of statistical significance in this case is the *chi-square*.

Certain situations call for evaluating the association between two continuous variables. One might hypothesize that SBP increases linearly with age. Mathematically, this may be represented by the following model:

$$SBP = a + b \times age$$

with SBP and age varying with the individual and fixed values *a* (regression constant) and *b* (regression slope or regression coefficient) to be determined. *Linear regression* provides a P value for the null hypothesis that b = 0 and supplies estimates for the coefficients a and b. Linear regression determines whether this model fits a given data set reasonably well. Assuming normally distributed data, the *Pearson correlation coefficient*, usually denoted by R, is a measure of the strength of linear association between age and SBP; R is always between −1 and 1, and R^2 (always between 0 and 1) measures how much of the variability in SBP is explained by age. A Pearson correlation coefficient of 0.6 would mean that approximately 36% (0.6 squared) of the variability in SBP is explained by age.

Multivariable Methods

Frequently the complexity of clinical phenomena defies reduction to a simple equation with only one independent variable (age). For the above-mentioned study, other factors, such as weight, may affect blood pressure while also being associated with age. The linear regression model described neglects this confounding variable (weight) and may distort the association between SBP and age. A more sophisticated method is needed to adjust for confounding variables, modeling the relationship more precisely (Table 9–3). Here, SBP is the dependent (outcome) variable, and age and weight are independent variables:

$$SBP = a + b \times age + c \times weight$$

Multiple linear regression allows determination of the coefficients *a*, *b*, and *c*. The model is assessed by a P value for each coefficient and an overall R or R^2 for the entire model.

When the dependent variable is dichotomous rather than continuous, and several continuous and/or nominal independent variables are being considered, *multiple logistic regression* is a popular option. Multiple logistic regression has been developed for polytomous (nominal with more than two categories) dependent variables as well. *Discriminant analysis* accomplishes a similar purpose of modeling a polytomous outcome variable that is determined by several independent variables.

Another multivariable analytic tool frequently found in the medical literature is *Cox proportional hazards regression*, in which the outcome variable is time to occurrence of a certain event. A randomized controlled trial evaluating two different treatments for lung cancer might take survival time as its outcome variable. Cox regression allows one to model the effect of the treatment on survival time, while adjusting for variables such as age, gender, and stage at diagnosis. One difference between Cox regression and multiple logistic regression is that the outcome variable in Cox regression is continuous (e.g., survival time) and the outcome in multiple logistic regression is dichotomous (e.g., survival at 5 years). The randomized controlled trial evaluating two different treatments for lung cancer may have been

Table 9–3 • COMMONLY USED MULTIVARIABLE METHODS AND THEIR DEPENDENT (OUTCOME) VARIABLES

MULTIVARIABLE METHODS	DEPENDENT VARIABLE
Multiple linear regression	Continuous
Multiple logistic regression	Dichotomous
Cox proportional hazards	Time to outcome event
Discriminant analysis	Nominal
Classification and regression trees	Dichotomous (but can be nominal or time to outcome event)

conducted at different sites, with patients at each site sharing characteristics attributable to the site (e.g., unmeasured practice patterns of the physicians at the site). This situation would result in lack of independence of the observations within each site, requiring more advanced analytic approaches, such as *hierarchical linear models* or *mixed models*.

Multivariable modeling has become deceptively easy because of the availability of powerful statistical software, which has led to its frequent misuse. Suppose that multiple logistic regression is used to study the effect of β-blockers on mortality after myocardial infarction, and 20 deaths in a group of 200 subjects are observed. The outcome variable is vital status (alive or dead) at the end of the study. Investigators may be tempted to include in the model as independent variables, in addition to the use of β-blockers versus placebo, age, gender, comorbidity, left ventricular ejection fraction, and a few other clinically relevant variables. Although no exact method is available to calculate the required number of outcome events (deaths), this modeling situation may lead to *overfitting*. This means that the number of outcome events (deaths) is so low that the model is unreliable. In general, fewer than 5 to 10 outcome events per independent variable may result in a model that is inaccurate. Other issues, such as violating the assumptions of normality and linearity, also plague multivariable models in the clinical literature. These models are powerful tools that are easily misused; they need to be handled with care.

Statistics play an important role in interpreting and applying clinical data. Statistics only safeguard, however, against random sampling error causing erroneous inferences. Statistics cannot compensate for other threats to the validity of clinical research, such as bias or collecting faulty data.

SUGGESTED READINGS

Hosmer DW, Lemeshow S: Applied Logistic Regression, 2nd ed. New York, John Wiley & Sons, 2000. *Assumes familiarity with linear regression methods and contingency table analysis. This is a hands-on guide to the use of logistic regression and includes many examples using different popular statistical software packages.*

Rosner B: Fundamentals of Biostatistics, 5th ed. Pacific Grove, CA, Duxbury, 2000. *A concise and rigorous introductory biostatistics textbook with many clinical examples that provides useful information on most statistical tools used in clinical research, including multivariable analysis.*

Principles of Evaluation and Management

part III

Preventive and Environmental Medicine

10 PRINCIPLES OF PREVENTIVE HEALTH CARE

Albert Oberman

A growing body of evidence links personal health behavior and preventive services to reductions in mortality from the leading causes of death and disability in the United States. Advances in understanding the determinants of risk, the demand for preventive measures, and the mortality trend in several leading causes of death provide the momentum for continuing preventive efforts. Table 10–1 depicts the changes in mortality for the leading causes of death over a decade and the ranking of these causes by sex and by selected ethnic groups. Reductions in cardiovascular mortality accounted for much of the decline in total mortality. Life expectancy at birth in the United States reached a record high of 76.9 years in 2000. Life expectancy in the United States is only at the median for developed countries, however. People with annual household incomes of at least $25,000 live an average of 3 to 7 years longer, depending on gender and race, than people with a household income less than $10,000. Men have higher age-adjusted death rates for every cause, especially for human immunodeficiency virus infection. Death rates vary by geographic locale, correlate inversely with socioeconomic status, and are higher for blacks than for whites for most leading causes of death.

There is a broad spectrum of health care delivery and prevention within the United States. Use of clinical preventive services is lower among people without a usual source of health care, people in lower income and education groups, and older adults. Access to preventive care involves barriers relating to the patient, provider, and health care system. In addition to access to health care, determinants of health status include health care policies and interventions, personal behavior, the physical and social environment, and individual biology (Fig. 10–1).

Prevention Strategies

The two complementary strategies for prevention are a population approach and a clinical, high-risk approach. A strong rationale exists for the population approach, in which interventions are offered on a broad scale to all segments of the population. This approach is attractive because much of the current burden of ill health comes from the large numbers of individuals at moderate individual risk, rather than from the few who show marked abnormalities. The

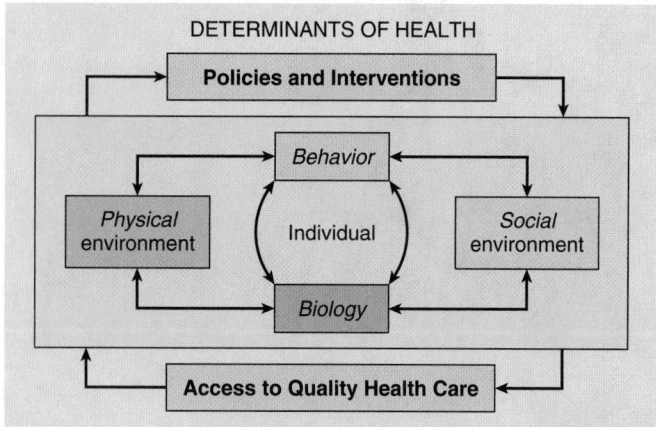

FIGURE 10–1 • Determinants of health involve a complex interplay among health policies and interventions with health behavior, the environment, and individual biology. (From U.S. Department of Health and Human Services: Healthy People 2010. With Understanding and Improving Health and Objectives for Improving Health, 2 vols, 2nd ed. Washington, DC, U.S. Government Printing Office, 2000.)

challenge is to shift the entire population risk factor distribution to the left so that a larger proportion of the population is at a low risk level.

Chronic diseases commonly arise from the interaction of multiple risk factors at moderate levels rather than from a single aberrant risk factor. Because the risk for chronic diseases from a given determinant is generally continuous and often curvilinear, the population approach shifts everyone's risk to a lower level. For example, most complications and preventable deaths from hypertension occur in the many individuals with stage I to stage II hypertension (Chapter 63) rather than in the relatively few individuals with more severe stage III hypertension. The efficacy of treating hypertension has been clearly established.■ Estimates indicate that a 3 mm Hg downward shift in the average systolic blood pressure in the United States might reduce the annual mortality from all causes by 4%, from coronary heart disease by 5%, and from stroke by 8%.

The high-risk strategy targets individuals in whom disease is judged most likely to develop and who would benefit from intervention. This strategy, which is more compatible with usual medical practice, avoids

Table 10–1 • U.S. DEATH RATES AND % CHANGE IN RATES, 1990–1999; RANK AND PERCENT OF TOTAL DEATHS FOR LEADING CAUSES OF DEATH BY SEX AND BY RACE, 1999

CAUSE OF DEATH*	DEATH RATE ALL PERSONS 1999 Rate†	DEATH RATE ALL PERSONS % Change 1990–1999	MALE Rank	MALE %	FEMALE Rank	FEMALE %	WHITE Rank	WHITE %	BLACK Rank	BLACK %	HISPANIC Rank	HISPANIC %
Diseases of heart	267.7	−16.8	1	29.9	1	30.7	1	30.8	1	27.6	1	24.9
Malignant neoplasms	202.6	−6.2	2	24.3	2	21.7	2	23.2	2	21.7	2	19.5
Cerebrovascular diseases	61.8	−5.6	3	5.5	3	8.5	3	7.0	3	6.6	4	5.7
Accidents (unintentional injuries)	35.7	−4.8	4	5.4	7	2.8	5	4.0	4	4.5	3	8.3
Chronic lower respiratory disease	45.8	23.1	5	5.3	4	5.1	4	5.6	6	2.8	8	2.8
Diabetes mellitus	25.2	21.7	6	2.7	5	3.1	7	2.6	5	4.2	5	5.0
Influenza and pneumonia	23.5	−36.1	7	2.4	6	3.0	6	2.8	10	2.1	9	2.2
Intentional self-harm (suicide)	10.6	−15.2	8	2.0	—	0.5	10	1.3	—	0.7	—	1.6
Chronic liver disease and cirrhosis	9.7	−12.6	9	1.5	—	0.8	—	1.1	—	1.0	6	2.9
Nephritis, nephrotic syndrome, and nephrosis	—	—	10	1.4	9	1.5	9	1.4	9	2.4	—	1.5
Alzheimer's disease	—	—	—	1.1	8	2.6	8	2.0	—	0.8	—	0.9
Septicemia	—	—	—	1.1	10	1.4	—	1.2	—	2.0	—	—
Assault (homicide)	—	—	—	—	—	—	—	0.4	8	2.7	7	2.8
Human immunodeficiency virus disease	5.4	−47.1	—	—	—	—	—	0.3	7	2.8	—	1.9
Certain conditions originating in the perinatal period	—	—	—	—	—	—	—	—	—	—	10	2.1

*Based on the *Tenth Revision, International Classification of Diseases,* 1992.
†Per 100,000 standard population; preliminary data.
— = category not applicable.
Adapted from National Vital Statistics Report 2001;49:10.

the inefficiency of the population approach with its need to intervene in many who neither desire such help nor are likely to benefit. The ability to approach symptomatic patients in a medical care setting offers opportunities for screening and intervening for prevention. Preventive policies that focus on high-risk individuals offer substantial benefits for these individuals, but the potential impact on the total burden of disease is often disappointing.

Despite the rationale for emphasizing prevention in clinical settings, studies indicate that major gaps exist in the delivery of preventive health care services. The lack of reimbursement for the required time, the skepticism toward attempting behavioral change, the difficulty in judging efficacy over the long-term, and a health care system geared toward illness all discourage widespread use of clinical preventive measures.

Clinical Preventive Services

Clinical preventive services include counseling, immunization, screening tests, and reduction of the susceptibility to disease by interventions such as therapeutic lifestyle changes and pharmacotherapy. Preventive services often are classified as primary, secondary, or tertiary. Primary prevention is directed toward preventing disease or injury before it develops, whereas secondary prevention deals with early detection and treatment to impede the progress of overt disease. In contrast, tertiary prevention refers to rehabilitative activities after the onset of disease to minimize complications and disability. Because of considerable overlap, distinguishing among these phases of prevention may be confusing. Detecting and treating hypertension could be considered secondary prevention of hypertensive cardiovascular disease but primary prevention of heart failure and stroke. Prevention may be perceived best along a continuum from modification of predisposing factors, to preventing a disease, to avoiding premature death and disability. The sooner the prevention, the more likely unnecessary illness, disability, and premature death can be avoided. Increasing emphasis has been placed on preventing risk factors themselves. The term *primordial prevention* has been introduced for this concept.

Indiscriminate screening for risk factors or disease without adequate advice and follow-up serves no useful purpose. The periodic health examination (Chapter 11) has evolved from an annual, broad-based, uniform protocol to an approach that targets the prevention, detection, and treatment of specific diseases or risk factors for particular age, gender, and ethnic groups at appropriate intervals. Current recommendations by the U.S. Preventive Services Task Force are based on systematic evidence reviews that distinguish procedures likely to prove effective and to have substantially more benefit than harm.

Changes in the health care system and the development of national guidelines for management of disease are likely to draw greater attention to health promotion, disease prevention, and the interface of physician-based medical care with the public health care system. Physicians should consider each disorder in terms of the potential for prevention, including the possibility of adverse effects and cost-effectiveness. A concept useful for clinical decision making is the number of patients needed to treat to prevent one adverse event, which is based on absolute risk reduction. This number is based on efficacy and is calculated as the reciprocal of the difference in event rates between control and treatment groups for a specified period.

Ample evidence connects identifiable and often preventable factors to the morbidity and mortality associated with major health problems. About half of all deaths, morbidity, and disability can be attributed to such nongenetic factors. Many lifestyle changes benefit multiple systems and disorders. Cigarette smoking has been estimated to contribute to one in five deaths in the United States (Chapter 14); dietary habits (Chapter 12) may affect the occurrence of cardiovascular disease, diabetes, osteoporosis, and cancer. Other important personal behavior factors influencing health include physical activity, alcohol intake, illicit drug use, sexual practices, and exposure to environmental toxins. The identification of informative DNA polymorphisms (e.g., single nucleotide polymorphisms) and further elucidation of candidate genes allow for detection of susceptible individuals and possible institution of measures to prevent the expression of these harmful genetic traits.

Several common misconceptions impede preventive health care. Many believe that diseases with a strong heritable component cannot be altered, but susceptibility to disease often requires the interaction of multiple genes and environmental factors for expression (Chapter 39). In addition, chronic diseases are multifactorial, so other factors can be changed to compensate for an elevated genetic risk. Although gene therapy holds much promise, preventive measures currently offer the best possibilities for limiting gene expression and avoiding disease. The notion that prevention is less useful in older persons excludes many who would benefit most from prevention because elderly patients generally have a greater absolute risk of disease and have been shown to adhere and respond favorably to preventive measures. Also, life expectancy frequently is underestimated in the elderly; individuals who reach age 75 now can expect to live an average of 11 more years.

With an expanding aging population, decreasing fatality rates, earlier detection of disease, and improved treatment of many disorders, it is essential that the focus be on primary prevention. Otherwise, the prevalence and associated morbidity of major diseases will escalate and further consume available medical resources. On average, U.S. citizens spend 85% of their more than 75 years of life expectancy in a healthy state unimpaired by disabilities, disease, or injuries. The leading causes of disability-adjusted loss of years in life in developed countries over the next 25 years probably will continue to be atherosclerotic diseases, but the impact of depression, smoking-related disease, accidents, alcohol, and degenerative neurologic and rheumatologic diseases also will be substantial (Table 10–2). The purpose of prevention is not only to prolong life, but also to postpone illness and disability to a later age, so as to implement the "compression of morbidity" principle.

Much of the downward trend in the leading causes of death and the increase in life expectancy can be attributed to preventive efforts

Table 10–2 • TEN PROJECTED LEADING CAUSES OF DISABILITY-ADJUSTED LIFE YEARS IN 2020 ACCORDING TO BASELINE PROJECTION BY REGION

DEVELOPED REGIONS		DEVELOPING REGIONS	
Rank/Disease or Injury	DALYs* (×10⁶)	Rank/Disease or Injury	DALYs (×10⁶)
All causes	160.5	All causes	1228.3
1. Ischemic heart disease	18.0	1. Unipolar major depression	68.8
2. Cerebrovascular disease	9.9	2. Traffic accidents	64.4
3. Unipolar major depression	9.8	3. Ischemic heart disease	64.3
4. Trachea, bronchus, and lung cancers	7.3	4. Chronic obstructive pulmonary disease	52.7
5. Traffic accidents	6.9	5. Cerebrovascular disease	51.5
6. Alcohol use	6.1	6. Tuberculosis	42.4
7. Osteoarthritis	5.6	7. Lower respiratory infections	41.1
8. Dementia and other degenerative and hereditary CNS disorders	5.5	8. War injuries	40.2
9. Chronic obstructive pulmonary disease	4.9	9. Diarrheal diseases	37.0
10. Self-inflicted injuries	3.9	10. Human immunodeficiency virus	34.0

*Sum of the years of life lost to death and reduction in the value of years of life lived because of disability.
DALYs = disability-adjusted life years; CNS = central nervous system.
From Murray CJL, Lopez AD: Alternative projections of mortality and disability by cause 1990–2020: Global Burden of Disease Study. Lancet 1997;349:1498–1504.

and to improved medical technology and health care. Despite the advances in these areas, the health status of the United States lags substantially behind that of other developed countries. Ample opportunities exist to improve health care, especially by means of prevention. A compilation of health objectives, Healthy People 2010, provides a framework for health promotion in the community and in clinical practice for this decade.

1. Chobanian A, Bakris G, Black H, et al: The Seventh Report of the Joint National Committee on Prevention, Detection, Evaluation and Treatment of High Blood Pressure. The JNC 7 Report. JAMA 2003;289:2560–2572.

SUGGESTED READINGS
Murray CJL, Lopez AD: Alternative projections of mortality and disability by cause 1990–2020: Global Burden of Disease Study. Lancet 1997;349:1498–1504. *One of a four-part series by the authors on the Global Burden of Disease Study, which predicts worldwide trends in mortality and morbidity.*
National Center for Health Statistics: Health, United States, 2001, with Socioeconomic and Health Status Chartbook. Hyattsville, MD, Public Health Service, 2002. *A report on the health status and trends of the nation.*
U.S. Department of Health and Human Services: Healthy People 2010. With Understanding and Improving Health and Objectives for Improving Health, 2 vols, 2nd ed. Washington, DC, U.S. Government Printing Office, 2000. *A compilation of health improvement opportunities for the next decade, encompassing objectives for 28 focus areas.*
U.S. Preventive Services Task Force Web Site. Available at http://www.ahrq.gov/clinic/uspstfix.htm. *Provides the latest available reviews and recommendations for prevention, plus resource links to major references, including the* Guide to Clinical Preventive Services.

11 THE PERIODIC HEALTH EXAMINATION

David Atkins

Clinicians and patients increasingly accept primary and secondary prevention as an important part of adult primary health care (Chapter 10). The traditional concept of an annual visit structured around a physical examination and a standard battery of screening tests has given way, however, to an emphasis on a set of clinical preventive services targeted to each individual. The appropriate services vary with age, gender, and the individual risk factors of each patient and can be delivered as a part of ongoing care.

A wide array of clinical prevention guidelines are available from the National Guideline Clearinghouse (http://www.guideline.gov). The most comprehensive recommendations are produced by the U.S. Preventive Services Task Force (USPSTF) (http://preventiveservices.ahrq.gov), an ongoing panel of experts supported by the federal Agency for Healthcare Research and Quality, and by the Canadian Task Force on Preventive Health Care (http://www.ctfphc.org). USPSTF recommendations are used by major primary care subspecialty groups (American College of Physicians and American Academy of Family Physicians), many health plans, and organizations such as the National Committee for Quality Assurance (http://www.ncqa.org) that develop measures to assess the quality of health care. The USPSTF recommendations require evidence that a service can reduce disease-specific mortality or morbidity. Grade A recommendations generally require direct evidence from high-quality studies (e.g., large screening trials) and benefits that substantially exceed harms. USPSTF recommendations are more conservative than recommendations of some subspecialty organizations, which may be based on less direct evidence, such as earlier detection of disease without a proven effect on long-term outcomes. Among the conclusions of USPSTF are that clinicians should be more selective in their use of screening tests; clinicians and patients should share decision making about specific services, especially when benefits must be balanced against harms; and clinicians need to take advantage of opportunities to deliver services outside of the specifically scheduled prevention visit.

Specific components of the periodic health examination include the following:

• History and risk assessment
• Screening for early disease or modifiable risk factors
• Counseling and behavioral interventions to promote healthy behaviors
• Immunizations
• Discussions about chemoprevention

History

The history and risk assessment are important tools to guide decisions about other preventive interventions. Risk assessment can identify individuals who may benefit from additional services (e.g., screening tests or immunizations not generally recommended for their age group) and individuals in need of specific behavioral counseling:

• Use of tobacco, alcohol, and other drugs (especially injection drugs) (Chapters 14, 17, and 30)
• Diet (Chapter 12)
• Physical activity (Chapter 13)
• Sexual behavior that may increase risk of sexually transmitted diseases (including human immunodeficiency virus) or unintended pregnancy
• Family history for cancer and heart disease
• Residence (community risk of infectious diseases)
• Presence of chronic diseases and cardiovascular risk factors

Screening for Early Disease or Asymptomatic Risk Factors

Every year, new screening tests are introduced and marketed on the basis of their ability to detect reliably unrecognized diseases or risk factors for disease. Other conditions need to be fulfilled, however, for a screening test to be worthwhile for routine use (Table 11–1). Benefits of screening must be balanced against the potential harms, including false-positive and false-negative results and the risks and costs of follow-up procedures or treatments. Even when tests have high specificity, most positive results are false-positives if the test is used to screen healthy populations for uncommon conditions such as cancer (Chapter 6). There is convincing evidence for only a relatively small number of screening tests for the entire population (Table 11–2), whereas other tests and interventions can be reserved for higher risk populations (Table 11–3). Finally, despite their popularity, some commonly used tests are generally not recommended for routine screening (Table 11–4). For most other potential screening tests, inadequate data are available to make a convincing case for or against screening.

DEPRESSION. Depression is common and frequently undetected in primary care (Chapter 426). Simple screening instruments can increase the detection of patients with major depression. Two questions—"Over the past 2 weeks have you felt down, depressed, or hopeless?" and "Over the past 2 weeks, have you felt little interest or pleasure in doing things?"—may be as sensitive as longer instruments. Screening must be linked, however, to interventions to improve follow-up and treatment if the outcomes for depressed patients are to be improved.

HIGH BLOOD PRESSURE. Blood pressure should be measured periodically (Chapter 63). Intensity of treatment should be tailored to cardiovascular risk status rather than blood pressure alone, considering other risk factors such as age, lipid levels, and presence and severity of other risk factors (Chapter 47).

ABNORMAL LIPIDS. The USPSTF recommends measuring total and high-density lipoprotein cholesterol, which can be performed on nonfasting samples, beginning in middle-aged adults. The National Cholesterol Education Program guidelines recommend fasting lipoprotein analysis beginning at age 20 (Chapter 211). Either strategy detects the high-risk patients who are most in need of specific interventions, such as lipid-lowering therapy. Treatment with statins can reduce

---

Table 11–1 • REQUIREMENTS OF AN EFFECTIVE SCREENING TEST

Disease is an important cause of morbidity and mortality
Screening can detect disease in early, presymptomatic phase
Screening and treating patients with early disease or risk factors produces better health outcomes than treating patients when they present with symptoms
Screening test is acceptable to patients and clinicians—safe, convenient, acceptable false-positive rate, acceptable costs
Benefits of early detection and treatment are sufficient to justify potential harms and costs of screening

Table 11–2 • RECOMMENDATIONS OF THE U.S. PREVENTIVE SERVICES TASK FORCE INTERVENTIONS FOR THE GENERAL POPULATION

SCREENING
Height and weight—periodically
Blood pressure—every 2 years
Screen for problem drinking
Brief screen for depression*
Total blood cholesterol and HDL cholesterol—men age ≥35, women ≥45, and others with CVD risk factors; every 5 years
Colorectal cancer screening: Age ≥50 (see above for options)
Mammogram every 1–2 years (±clinical breast examination)—women age ≥40
Papanicolaou (Pap) test—at least every 3 years until age 65
Chlamydia—sexually active women ≤25 and older women at risk
Bone mineral density test: women age ≥65 and at-risk women ages 60–64
Vision screening: Age ≥65
Assess for hearing impairment: Age ≥65

Sexual Behavior
Unintended pregnancy: contraception
STD prevention: avoid high-risk behavior,[†] condoms/female barrier with spermicide[†]

Injury Prevention
Lap/shoulder belts
Motorcycle/bicycle/ATV helmets[†]
Smoke detector[†]
Safe storage/removal of firearms[†]

Dental Health
Regular visits to dental care provider[†]
Floss, brush with fluoride toothpaste daily[†]

IMMUNIZATIONS
Pneumococcal immunization (age ≥65)
Influenza immunization (annual, age ≥50)
Tetanus-diphtheria (Td) boosters (every 10 years)
Rubella (susceptible women of childbearing age)[‡]

COUNSELING

Substance Use
Tobacco cessation
Reduce risky or harmful alcohol use
Avoid alcohol/drug use while driving, swimming, boating[†]

Diet and Exercise
Limit saturated fat; maintain caloric balance; emphasize grains, fruits, and vegetables
Adequate calcium intake (women)
Regular physical activity[†]

CHEMOPREVENTION
Multivitamin with folic acid (women planning or capable of pregnancy)
Discuss benefits and harms of aspirin to prevent myocardial infarction in middle-aged adults and others at increased risk of heart disease

*Depression screening most effective where systems exist to improve management of depression.
[†]The ability of clinician counseling to influence this behavior is unproven.
[‡]Serologic testing, documented vaccination history, and routine vaccination (preferably with MMR) are equally acceptable alternatives.
HDL = high-density lipoprotein; CVD = cardiovascular disease; STD = sexually transmitted disease; ATV = all-terrain vehicle.

Table 11–3 • RECOMMENDED SCREENING AND INTERVENTIONS FOR HIGH-RISK POPULATIONS

POTENTIAL INTERVENTIONS	POPULATION
HIV test	High-risk sexual behavior or IV drug use; consider local epidemiology*
Syphilis (RPR/VDRL)	High-risk sexual behavior; consider local epidemiology*
Gonorrhea screen	High-risk sexual behavior; consider local epidemiology*
PPD	Immigrants, tuberculosis contacts, alcoholics; consider local epidemiology*
Hepatitis B vaccine	Exposure to blood products; IV drug use; high-risk sexual behavior; travelers to specific countries
Hepatitis A vaccine	Persons living in or traveling to high-risk areas; institutionalized persons and workers in these institutions. Certain chronic medical conditions
MMR, varicella vaccine	Susceptible to measles, mumps, or varicella
Discuss breast cancer chemoprevention	Women at increased risk for breast cancer and low risk of thromboembolic complications
Diabetes screen	Persons with elevated blood pressure or high cholesterol

*Routine screening may be indicated in communities or settings where infection is prevalent.
HIV = human immunodeficiency virus; IV = intravenous; RPR = rapid plasma reagin; VDRL = Venereal Disease Research Laboratory; PPD = Purified protein derivative; MMR = measles, mumps, rubella.

Table 11–4 • INTERVENTIONS NOT RECOMMENDED FOR ROUTINE USE IN ASYMPTOMATIC AVERAGE-RISK ADULTS*

Resting or exercise electrocardiogram or helical CT for asymptomatic coronary disease
Ultrasound for asymptomatic carotid artery disease
Chest radiograph or helical CT for early detection of lung cancer
Routine blood tests for anemia
Routine urine tests
Blood tests or ultrasound for ovarian cancer
Whole body CT
Brief tests of mental status
Vitamin supplements

*These tests are not recommended for routine use because they are not supported by evidence that they improve clinical outcomes. Any of the tests may be appropriate for selected patients based on clinical judgment, and some are under investigation for more widespread use.
CT = computed tomography.

coronary events by an estimated 30%. Treatment decisions should be based on estimates of coronary heart disease risk.

COLORECTAL CANCER. Screening for colorectal cancer can reduce the incidence of and mortality from this disease.∎ Options for screening men and women older than age 50 include annual fecal occult blood test (FOBT), flexible sigmoidoscopy every 5 to 10 years, FOBT and sigmoidoscopy, colonoscopy every 10 years, or barium enema every 5 to 10 years (Chapter 200). The choice should consider local resources and patients' preferences. Strategies that are more sensitive (colonoscopy, combined FOBT and sigmoidoscopy) increase false-positive results, invasive procedures, and costs, and no single strategy has been documented to be more effective or cost-effective.

48 | **Chapter 11** The Periodic Health Examination

Preventive and Environmental Medicine

BREAST CANCER. In large trials, mammography screening (with or without clinical breast examination) reduced breast cancer mortality by 15 to 20% (Chapter 204). The decision of when to begin screening should be shared between a woman and her physician. Most but not all trials suggest benefits extend to women screened in their 40s, but the benefits are smaller and risks of false-positive results are higher than in women older than age 50 years. The marginal benefits of annual (versus biennial) mammography and of the clinical breast examination are uncertain: They increase the detection rate for cancer but at the expense of more false-positive results. Although many cancers are discovered by the patient, teaching breast self-examination has not been proved to improve outcomes.

CERVICAL CANCER. Despite the prevalence of annual Papanicolaou (Pap) screening, there is general consensus that less frequent screening (every 2 to 3 years) is adequate in women with previous normal test results (Chapter 205). Low-risk women should be offered the option of discontinuing screening after age 65. Advances such as liquid-based cytology specimens and automated methods for interpreting Pap smears may increase the sensitivity of testing but have not been proved to improve clinical outcomes significantly. Testing for human papillomavirus has been approved as a part of primary screening but has not been proved to be more effective than regular screening with Pap alone. It may help in managing borderline Pap smear results, such as atypical squamous cells of undetermined significance.

OSTEOPOROSIS. Tests of bone mineral density, using central or peripheral tests, can identify women who are at high risk of fracture and who may benefit from medications proved to lower the risk of fractures in women with osteoporosis (Chapter 258). Because age is the strongest risk factor for osteoporosis and fracture, the benefits of screening and treatment are clearer for women older than age 65 and for younger postmenopausal women with specific risk factors for fracture, such as low body weight or family history of fracture.

PROSTATE CANCER. Screening with prostate-specific antigen can increase the detection of organ-confined prostate cancer, but proof that prostate cancer screening can lower morbidity or mortality from prostate cancer is still lacking (several trials of screening are currently under way in the United States and Europe) (Chapter 207). The prognosis of untreated prostate cancer varies with the grade of the tumor, and the benefits of aggressive treatments, such as prostatectomy or irradiation, are uncertain for cancers found by screening. Screening may increase morbidity by leading to treatment of indolent cancers, especially in men older than age 70. If early detection is effective, men who are between ages 50 and 70 and in good health are most likely to benefit. Neither the USPSTF nor other organizations recommend widespread screening. The American Cancer Society and other specialty groups recommend offering prostate-specific antigen screening after discussing potential benefits and harms to men who have a life expectancy of at least 10 years.

THYROID DISEASE. Routine thyroid testing in high-risk groups can identify patients with symptomatic but undiagnosed hypothyroidism (Chapter 239) but the benefits of detecting and treating subclinical hypothyroidism (elevated thyroid stimulating hormone but normal thyroxine) are not well established. Screening is recommended by some groups, but not the USPSTF, for populations in which symptomatic disease is prevalent but often may go undetected (e.g., postmenopausal women).

DIABETES. Routine screening for diabetes beginning at age 45 is recommended by some groups but not the USPSTF (Chapter 242). Although tight glucose control can reduce the incidence of microvascular disease, the benefits of early detection on retinopathy, neuropathy, and nephropathy are likely to be small. More substantial benefits are achieved by screening for diabetes among patients who have hypertension or elevated lipids because more aggressive treatment of cardiovascular risk factors produces significant benefits over a relatively short period. ▪

SEXUALLY TRANSMITTED DISEASE. Screening for chlamydia is recommended for all sexually active women younger than age 25 and for older women at risk, based on the high prevalence of disease and the benefits of early detection in reducing pelvic inflammatory disease (Chapter 345). ▪ Similar benefits are likely from screening women for gonorrhea, but the risk of infection is more concentrated in urban and Southeastern rural populations. New DNA- and RNA-based tests, which can be performed on urine or cervical specimens, have largely supplanted culture techniques.

VISION AND HEARING. In older patients, testing visual acuity and asking about hearing problems can identify correctible but undiagnosed problems.

Behavioral Interventions

Lifestyle factors, such as tobacco use, alcohol use, diet, lack of physical activity, and other risky behaviors, contribute to a large proportion of preventable deaths in the United States. There is good evidence that brief interventions can have measurable effects on some behaviors such as smoking and problem drinking, but changing other behaviors usually requires more intensive interventions. The 5 As framework—ask, advise, agree, assist, and arrange—that developed out of smoking cessation research provides a useful framework for other behavioral interventions.

TOBACCO USE. Brief interventions can produce small but clinically important increases in quit rates among smokers. Effects increase with more intensive counseling and support, including use of medication (Chapter 14).

PROBLEM DRINKING. A variety of screening instruments can detect patients with problems resulting from alcohol and patients with risky patterns of alcohol consumption. Brief interventions can reduce alcohol consumption successfully in at-risk drinkers (Chapter 17).

DIET. Diet counseling can reduce intake of saturated fat and increase consumption of fruits and vegetables, but effects are most consistent with more intensive counseling (multiple sessions with trained counselors) and in higher risk patients (e.g., patients with elevated lipids) (Chapter 12).

PHYSICAL ACTIVITY. Moderate physical activity reduces the risk of obesity, diabetes, and coronary heart disease, among other benefits. Studies of counseling in the primary care setting have produced mixed effects, however, on long-term physical activity levels (Chapter 13).

INJURY PREVENTION. Motor vehicle injuries are the leading cause of years of potential life lost before age 65 (Chapter 15). In older persons, falls are a leading cause of unintentional injury and can be reduced with targeted interventions (Chapter 23).

Immunizations

Recommendations regarding immunization are updated regularly by the Centers for Disease Control and Prevention's Advisory Committee on Immunization Practices (Chapter 16).

INFLUENZA IMMUNIZATION. The most severe complications of influenza occur in adults older than age 50 and others at high risk as a result of chronic conditions or immunodeficiency, but annual immunization is also effective in healthy adults. The benefits in preventing lost work time may make immunization of healthy adults cost-effective.

PNEUMOCOCCAL IMMUNIZATION. Pneumococcal immunization is recommended at least once at age 65 years or after for all adults and for younger adults with asplenia, chronic heart or lung disease, and other immune disorders. Revaccination generally is not recommended unless initial immunization was before age 65.

TETANUS-DIPHTHERIA BOOSTER. Tetanus is rare in persons who have received a complete series of primary vaccinations. The more important benefit of revaccination, which is recommended every 10 years, is likely to be maintaining levels of immunity against diphtheria.

Discussions about Chemoprevention

Aspirin, hormone replacement, and breast cancer chemopreventive drugs carry benefits and risks. Decisions need to consider the likely benefits (which increase with the underlying risk of the disease being prevented), the probability of harm, and the individual preferences of each patient.

ASPIRIN. Aspirin reduces coronary heart disease by 30% in persons who are at increased risk of heart disease, but it also increases risk of serious gastrointestinal bleeding and hemorrhagic stroke. Benefits exceed risks as 5-year risk of heart disease reaches 3 to 5%, but individual preferences should be considered (Chapters 67, 68, and 69). At 81 mg per day, aspirin can also reduce the risk of colorectal adenomas.

CHEMOPREVENTION OF BREAST CANCER. Tamoxifen and possibly raloxifene can reduce the incidence of invasive breast cancer by nearly

50% in women at increased risk, but both agents increase risk of thromboembolic events (including stroke) and worsen menopausal symptoms; tamoxifen also increases risk of endometrial cancer (Chapter 204). The balance of benefits and harm is most favorable in women younger than age 60 who have an increased risk of breast cancer as a result of family history or previous abnormalities on breast biopsy. Tools are available to calculate risk of breast cancer based on age and individual risk factors (http://cancer.gov/bcrisktool).

POSTMENOPAUSAL HORMONE THERAPY. Estrogen therapy can relieve menopausal symptoms, but more recent trials have forced a reassessment of the benefits and harms of hormone therapy over extended periods of 5 years or more (Chapter 256). Long-term benefits include improved bone density, reduced risk of fracture, and probably a reduced risk of colon cancer. A large trial of daily conjugated equine estrogen plus medroxyprogesterone in generally healthy women was stopped because of an increased risk of breast cancer and heart disease observed after 5 years of follow-up. ◼ Hormone therapy also increased the risk of venous thromboembolism and stroke. Ongoing studies should clarify whether unopposed estrogen has a similar balance of benefits and harms for women without a uterus.

Quality Measurement and Improvement

Clinicians are increasingly accountable for delivering recommended preventive care. Health plans collect and report data on the delivery rates of many preventive services, including smoking cessation, immunizations, and cancer screening. These performance data are being extended to groups and individual clinicians. Improving regular delivery of preventive care requires a systems approach. Among the most effective interventions for increasing the delivery of preventive care is reminders aimed at patients and physicians. Automated reminders can identify opportunities to deliver services when patients are being seen outside of a periodic examination. Standing orders (especially for immunizations) and feedback to clinicians about specific performance are also effective, but educational material alone does not have a consistent effect on patients or clinicians.

Future Directions

Genetic screening has the potential to change the delivery of preventive care significantly. A better understanding of genetic factors that modify the risk of disease may allow clinicians to target screening, preventive treatments, or lifestyle interventions to individuals at greatest risk. Although the number of mutations associated with specific diseases is growing steadily, their value for routine use in primary care is limited by incomplete understanding of the predictive value of specific genotypes in the general population, the uncertain role of the information on clinical decisions, and concerns about the possible adverse effects of screening (anxiety or "labeling," false reassurance, or discrimination). Many genetic screens for cancer risk are now commercially available and may become a useful part of counseling individuals from high-risk families, but their role in the general population is not resolved (Chapter 36).

Other technologic advances, such as helical computed tomography, will increase the ability to detect early disease and persons at increased risk of disease. Determining the clinical benefits of early detection often may be difficult, however. Unless newer tests increase specificity and sensitivity, they will generate more false-positive results, which may lead to invasive diagnostic testing. They also increase the likelihood of detecting disease that might never have come to clinical attention, especially in older populations.

1. Pignone M, Rich M, Teutsch SM, et al: Screening for colorectal cancer in adults at average risk: Summary of the evidence for the U.S. Preventive Services Task Force. Ann Intern Med 2002;137:132–141.
2. Harris R, Donahue K, Rathore S, et al: Screening adults for type 2 diabetes: A review of the evidence for the U.S. Preventive Services Task Force. Ann Intern Med 2003;138:215–229.
3. Nelson HD, Helfand M: Screening for chlamydial infection. Am J Prev Med 2001;20:95–107. Available at http://www.elsevier.com/locate/ajpmonline.
4. Writing Group for the Women's Health Initiative Investigators: Risks and benefits of estrogen plus progestin in healthy postmenopausal women: Principal results from the Women's Health Initiative randomized controlled trial. JAMA 2002;288:321–333.

SUGGESTED READINGS
Burke W, Atkins D, Gwinn M, et al: Genetic test evaluation: Information needs of clinicians, policy makers, and the public. Am J Epidemiol 2002;156:311–318. *Recommendations for standardized communication.*

Canadian Task Force on Preventive Health Care. Available at http://www.ctfphc.org.
National Committee for Quality Assurance. Available at http://www.ncqa.org. *This site provides information on the quality measures for preventive care reported by many health plans and annual data on how well health plans are delivering individual preventive services.*
National Guideline Clearinghouse. Available at http://www.guideline.gov. *This site provides access to standardized descriptions of more than 1000 guidelines, with full text access to many of them. Guidelines can be searched by condition, intervention, or organization, and the site constructs a comparison of different guidelines on a given topic.*
Task Force on Community Preventive Services and the Guide to Community Preventive Services. Am J Prev Med 2000;18(Suppl. 1):1. Available at http://www.thecommunityguide.org. *This site, sponsored by the Centers for Disease Control and Prevention, provides access to a wide array of recommendations, reviews, and background articles on community-based preventive interventions, including interventions in clinical settings to improve the delivery of preventive services such as immunizations, cancer screening, and smoking cessation.*
U.S. Preventive Services Task Force: Available at http://www.preventiveservices.ahrq.gov. *This site, sponsored by the Agency for Healthcare Research and Quality, includes all the recommendations of the USPSTF, supporting reviews of the scientific evidence, and background articles on methods and history of the USPSTF.*

12 NUTRITION'S INTERFACE WITH HEALTH AND DISEASE

Douglas C. Heimburger

Old and New Paradigms

Nutritional science was characterized by two major phases in the 20th century. During the first phase, nutritional scientists discovered, characterized, and synthesized the various vitamins and described their deficiency syndromes in detail. The dietary requirements for these nutrients were estimated and have been updated periodically by the National Academy of Sciences, most recently as the *Dietary Reference Intakes*. In addition to recommended intakes for individuals (Table 12–1) that are judged to be sufficient to meet the nutrient requirements of nearly all healthy individuals, the dietary reference intakes include estimates of tolerable upper intake levels (Table 12–2), representing the highest intake level likely not to pose any adverse health risks.

The second phase of modern nutritional science focused on the relationship of diet and nutritional status to the diseases that plague Western societies, such as coronary heart disease (CHD), cancer, and the other leading causes of death. This focus has led to expansion of the perspectives of nutritional scientists and the evolution of new paradigms for understanding nutrition.

Nutrition's Influence on Mortality and Morbidity

The causal connections between diet and chronic disease are difficult to tease out of the complex network of other risk factors, including social and behavioral variables, so a wide variety of studies must be relied on to establish these connections with reasonable certainty. The first links between diet and disease often are derived from epidemiologic studies, but such studies are unable to infer causal relationships and may be confounded by variables that have not been examined. Epidemiologic studies also are challenged by the difficulty of accurately assessing the diets of free-living individuals. Animal and in vitro studies can overcome some of these drawbacks but may be confounded by experimental conditions that differ from conditions encountered by humans. Many prospective, randomized human intervention trials have been undertaken to test the effects of dietary change on the risk for disease. Even these trials may not always be conclusive, however, because of pitfalls associated with selecting study populations and isolating individual dietary factors.

Nevertheless, taken together, epidemiologic, animal, in vitro, and intervention studies are proving that human dietary habits contribute importantly to the pathogenesis of most of the major causes of death in developed countries. Some of the leading causes of death in the United States are listed in Table 12–3, along with other morbid conditions that have well-established dietary links.

CORONARY HEART DISEASE

Nutritional influences on the most common cause of death in the United States, CHD, have been the subject of a great deal of

Table 12–1 • DIETARY REFERENCE INTAKES: RECOMMENDED INTAKES FOR INDIVIDUALS

LIFE STAGE GROUP	CALCIUM (mg/day)	PHOSPHORUS (mg/day)	MAGNESIUM (mg/day)	VITAMIN D (μg/day)[a,b]	FLUORIDE (mg/day)	THIAMINE (mg/day)	RIBOFLAVIN (mg/day)	NIACIN (mg/day)
Infants								
0–6 mo	210*	100*	30*	5*	0.01*	0.2*	0.3*	2*
7–12 mo	270*	275*	75*	5*	0.5*	0.3*	0.4*	4*
Children								
1–3 yr	500*	460	80	5*	0.7*	0.5	0.5	6
4–8 yr	800*	500	130	5*	1*	0.6	0.6	8
Males								
9–13 yr	1300*	1250	240	5*	2*	0.9	0.9	12
14–18 yr	1300*	1250	410	5*	3*	1.2	1.3	16
19–30 yr	1000*	700	400	5*	4*	1.2	1.3	16
31–50 yr	1000*	700	420	5*	4*	1.2	1.3	16
51–70 yr	1200*	700	420	10*	4*	1.2	1.3	16
>70 yr	1200*	700	420	15*	4*	1.2	1.3	16
Females								
9–13 yr	1300*	1250	240	5*	2*	0.9	0.9	12
14–18 yr	1300*	1250	360	5*	3*	1.0	1.0	14
19–30 yr	1000*	700	310	5*	3*	1.1	1.1	14
31–50 yr	1000*	700	320	5*	3*	1.1	1.1	14
51–70 yr	1200*	700	320	10*	3*	1.1	1.1	14
>70 yr	1200*	700	320	15*	3*	1.1	1.1	14
Pregnancy								
≤18 yr	1300*	1250	400	5*	3*	1.4	1.4	18
19–30 yr	1000*	700	350	5*	3*	1.4	1.4	18
31–50 yr	1000*	700	360	5*	3*	1.4	1.4	18
Lactation								
≤18 yr	1300*	1250	360	5*	3*	1.4	1.6	17
19–30 yr	1000*	700	310	5*	3*	1.4	1.6	17
31–50 yr	1000*	700	320	5*	3*	1.4	1.6	17

NOTE: This table presents recommended dietary allowances (RDAs) in **bold type** and adequate intakes (AIs) in ordinary type followed by an asterisk (*). RDAs and AIs may be used as goals for individual intake. RDAs are set to meet the needs of almost all (97 to 98%) individuals in a group. For healthy breast-fed infants, the AI is the mean intake. The AI for other life-stage and gender groups is believed to cover needs of all individuals in the group, but lack of data or uncertainty in the data prevent being able to specify with confidence the percentage of individuals covered by this intake.

[a]As calciferol. 1 μg calciferol = 40 IU vitamin D.
[b]In the absence of adequate exposure to sunlight.
[c]As niacin equivalents (NE). 1 mg of niacin = 60 mg of tryptophan; 0–6 months = preformed niacin (not NE).
[d]As dietary folate equivalents (DFE). 1 DFE = 1 μg food folate = 0.6 μg of folic acid from fortified food or as a supplement consumed with food = 0.5 μg of a supplement taken on an empty stomach.
[e]Although AIs have been set for choline, there are few data to assess whether a dietary supply of choline is needed at all stages of the life cycle, and it may be that the choline requirement can be met by endogenous synthesis at some of these stages.

Table 12–2 • DIETARY REFERENCE INTAKES: TOLERABLE UPPER INTAKE LEVELS (UL[a])

LIFE STAGE GROUP	CALCIUM (g/day)	PHOSPHORUS (g/day)	MAGNESIUM (mg/day)[b]	VITAMIN D (μg/day)	FLUORIDE (mg/day)	NIACIN (mg/day)[c]	VITAMIN B6 (mg/day)	FOLATE (μg/day)[c]	CHOLINE (g/day)	VITAMIN C (mg/day)	VITAMIN E (mg/day)[d]	SELENIUM (μg/day)
Infants												
0–6 mo	ND[e]	ND	ND	25	0.7	ND	ND	ND	ND	ND	ND	45
7–12 mo	ND	ND	ND	25	0.9	ND	ND	ND	ND	ND	ND	60
Children												
1–3 yr	2.5	3	65	50	1.3	10	30	300	1.0	400	200	90
4–8 yr	2.5	3	110	50	2.2	15	40	400	1.0	650	300	150
Males, females												
9–13 yr	2.5	4	350	50	10	20	60	600	2.0	1200	600	280
14–18 yr	2.5	4	350	50	10	30	80	800	3.0	1800	800	400
19–70 yr	2.5	4	350	50	10	35	100	1000	3.5	2000	1000	400
>70 yr	2.5	3	350	50	10	35	100	1000	3.5	2000	1000	400
Pregnancy												
≤18 yr	2.5	3.5	350	50	10	30	80	800	3.0	1800	800	400
19–50 yr	2.5	3.5	350	50	10	35	100	1000	3.5	2000	1000	400
Lactation												
≤18 yr	2.5	4	350	50	10	30	80	800	3.0	1800	800	400
19–50 yr	2.5	4	350	50	10	35	100	1000	3.5	2000	1000	400

[a]UL = The maximum level of daily nutrient intake that is likely to pose no risk of adverse effects. Unless otherwise specified, the UL represents total intake from food, water, and supplements. Because of lack of suitable data, ULs could not be established for thiamin, riboflavin, vitamin B₁₂, pantothenic acid, biotin, or any carotenoids. In the absence of ULs, extra caution may be warranted in consuming levels above recommended intakes.
[b]The ULs for magnesium represent intake from a pharmacologic agent only and do not include intake from food and water.
[c]The ULs for niacin, folate, and vitamin E apply to synthetic forms obtained from supplements, fortified foods, or a combination of the two.
[d]As α-tocopherol; applies to any form of supplemental α-tocopherol.
[e]ND = Not determinable because of lack of data of adverse effects in this age group and concern with regard to lack of ability to handle excess amounts. Source of intake should be from food only to prevent high levels of intake.

From the Food and Nutrition Board, Institute of Medicine: Dietary Reference Intakes. Washington, DC, National Academy Press, 2000. Copyright 2000 by the National Academy of Sciences. All rights reserved.

VITAMIN B₆ (mg/day)	FOLATE (µg/day)^d	VITAMIN B₁₂ (µg/day)	PANTOTHENIC ACID (mg/day)	BIOTIN (µg/day)	CHOLINE^e (mg/day)	VITAMIN C (mg/day)	VITAMIN E^f (mg/day)	SELENIUM (µg/day)
0.1*	65*	0.4*	1.7*	5*	125*	40*	4*	15*
0.3*	80*	0.5*	1.8*	6*	150*	50*	5*	20*
0.5	150	0.9	2*	8*	200*	15	6	20
0.6	200	1.2	3*	12*	250*	25	7	30
1.0	300	1.8	4*	20*	375*	45	11	40
1.3	400	2.4	5*	25*	550*	75	15	55
1.3	400	2.4	5*	30*	550*	90	15	55
1.3	400	2.4	5*	30*	550*	90	15	55
1.7	400	2.4^g	5*	30*	550*	90	15	55
1.7	400	2.4^g	5*	30*	550*	90	15	55
1.0	300	1.8	4*	20*	375*	45	11	40
1.2	400^h	2.4	5*	25*	400*	65	15	55
1.3	400^h	2.4	5*	30*	425*	75	15	55
1.3	400^h	2.4	5*	30*	425*	75	15	55
1.5	400	2.4^g	5*	30*	425*	75	15	55
1.5	400	2.4^g	5*	30*	425*	75	15	55
1.9	600^i	2.6	6*	30*	450*	80	15	60
1.9	600^i	2.6	6*	30*	450*	85	15	60
1.9	600^i	2.6	6*	30*	450*	85	15	60
2.0	500	2.8	7*	35*	550*	115	19	70
2.0	500	2.8	7*	35*	550*	120	19	70
2.0	500	2.8	7*	35*	550*	120	19	70

^{f}As α-tocopherol. α-Tocopherol includes *RRR*-α-tocopherol, the only form of α-tocopherol that occurs naturally in foods, and the 2*R*-stereoisomeric forms of α-tocopherol (*RRR*-, *RSR*-, *RRS*-, and *RSS*-α-tocopherol) that occur in fortified foods and supplements. It does not include the 2*S*-stereoisomeric forms of α-tocopherol (*SRR*-, *SSR*-, *SRS*-, and *SSS*-α-tocopherol), also found in fortified foods and supplements.

^{g}Because 10 to 30% of older people may malabsorb food-bound B₁₂, it is advised that those older than 50 years meet their RDA mainly by consuming foods fortified with B₁₂ or a supplement containing B₁₂.

^{h}In view of evidence linking folate intake with neural tube defects in the fetus, it is recommended that all women capable of becoming pregnant consume 400 µg from supplements or fortified foods in addition to intake of food folate from a varied diet.

^{i}It is assumed that women will continue consuming 400 µg from supplements or fortified foods until their pregnancy is confirmed and they enter prenatal care, which ordinarily occurs after the end of the periconceptional period—the critical time for formation of the neural tube.

From the Food and Nutrition Board, Institute of Medicine: Dietary Reference Intakes. Washington, DC, National Academy Press, 2000.

Table 12–3 • DIETARY INFLUENCES ON MAJOR CAUSES OF DEATH AND MORBIDITY IN THE UNITED STATES

	POSSIBLE BENEFICIAL INFLUENCES	POSSIBLE DELETERIOUS INFLUENCES
CAUSE OF DEATH		
Coronary heart disease	Complex carbohydrates, particular fatty acids (e.g., monounsaturated, polyunsaturated, and ω-3 fatty acids from fish), soluble fiber, antioxidants (vitamins E, C; β-carotene, selenium), folic acid, moderate alcohol, soy protein, isoflavones	Saturated fat, cholesterol; excess calories, sodium, animal protein; abdominal distribution of body fat
Cancer	Fruits and vegetables (for β-carotene, vitamins A, C, D, E, folic acid, calcium, selenium, phytochemicals), fiber	Excess calories, fat, alcohol, red meat, salt- and nitrite-preserved meats, possibly grilled meats; abdominal distribution of body fat
Stroke	Potassium, calcium, ω-3 fatty acids	Sodium, alcohol (as with hypertension)
Accidents		Alcohol
Diabetes mellitus	Fiber	Excess calories, fat, alcohol; abdominal distribution of body fat
Suicide		Alcohol
Chronic liver disease		Alcohol
Atherosclerosis (peripheral)	Particular fatty acids (e.g., monounsaturated and ω-3 fatty acids), soluble fiber, antioxidant vitamins	Saturated fat, cholesterol
CAUSE OF MORBIDITY		
Obesity		Excess calories and fat
Hypertension	Potassium, calcium, ω-3 fatty acids, fruits and vegetables	Sodium, alcohol, excess calories, and saturated and total fat; abdominal distribution of body fat
Osteoporosis	Calcium, vitamin D, magnesium	Sodium, protein
Diverticular disease, constipation	Fiber	
Neural tube defects	Folic acid	

productive research. The overall U.S. mortality rate from CHD peaked in the 1960s and, in a trend that surprised medical science, has declined steadily ever since. Changes in lifestyle, including diet, are responsible for a substantial proportion of this decline. Elevated plasma low-density lipoprotein (LDL) cholesterol levels are a major risk factor for CHD and peripheral atherosclerosis and correlate strongly with dietary saturated fat intake and less strongly with cholesterol intake.[◼] Intake of both of these substances in the United States is derived largely from foods of animal origin, such as meats, dairy products, and eggs. Attempts to produce less atherogenic substitutes for some of these foods have not always proved beneficial. For instance, hydrogenation of vegetable oils to create margarine and shortening results in the formation of *trans* fatty acids, which affect serum cholesterol levels in a manner similar to, and perhaps worse than, the saturated fatty acids found in butter and lard. LDL cholesterol levels can be lowered modestly by increasing the intake of soluble fiber from legumes, fruits, vegetables, and flax seed and by consuming proteins and isoflavones from soy foods. LDL must be oxidized before it induces injury to arterial wall epithelial cells; adequate dietary levels of the antioxidant vitamins C and E and β-carotene have been shown to inhibit LDL oxidation, but pharmacologic doses of these vitamins have not reduced CHD events when tested in randomized trials.

Epidemiologic evidence suggests that fish consumption may reduce CHD risk, perhaps through the action of ω-3 fatty acids. Evidence also indicates that moderate consumption of alcohol, especially wine, is associated with decreased risk for CHD, possibly through increasing high-density lipoprotein (HDL) cholesterol levels and/or preventing oxidation of LDL. Polyphenols in red wine also are apparently beneficial. Circulating levels of the amino acid homocysteine, which are asymptomatically elevated in 20 to 25% of Americans, have been strongly correlated with risk for CHD. Homocysteine levels can be reduced by increasing the intake of folic acid (mainly from legumes, vegetables, and fortified grain) and decreasing the intake of methionine (principally from animal protein). A conservative estimate suggests that moderate dietary modification by the U.S. population consisting mainly of replacing saturated fats with complex carbohydrates, fiber, monounsaturated fats, and fish could lead easily to another 10% reduction in serum cholesterol levels and a 20% or greater reduction in CHD.

CANCER

Nutrients, non-nutritive dietary constituents, and nutritional status can influence the risk for cancer in a variety of ways. Nutrition interacts with each step of carcinogenesis (carcinogen activation and tumor initiation, promotion, and progression). Humans are exposed to countless potential carcinogens and to many anticarcinogens each day through dietary and other means. Excess caloric intake may favor the generation of free radicals and reduce the body's ability to detoxify carcinogens. By contrast, antioxidant nutrients scavenge free radicals and other (pre)carcinogens and inhibit their activation and/or their ability to initiate mutations. Folic acid may improve a cell's ability to preserve, repair, and methylate its DNA, either preventing or reversing the tendency toward mutation. Obesity, excess dietary fat intake, and excess alcohol seem to promote tumor growth.

Much evidence indicates that the number one cancer killer, lung cancer, is influenced strongly by diet. Although the most important causal factor is cigarette smoking, consumption of fruits and vegetables is inversely associated with lung cancer risk in smokers and non-smokers. It is probable that many nutrients in fruits and vegetables are partly responsible for the protective effects. In view of the disappointing results of randomized trials of supplementation with β-carotene, however, antioxidant supplements should not be relied on to reduce disease risk. Plasma levels of antioxidant nutrients (β-carotene and vitamins C and E) and folic acid are lower in smokers than nonsmokers and intermediate in persons passively exposed to smoke. Probably caused by oxidants in cigarette smoke and poorer dietary habits in smokers, this difference is an example of an interaction between nutritional factors and environmental exposure that explains more of the variation in cancer incidence than does either factor alone.

The second largest cause of cancer deaths in women, breast cancer, is positively associated with dietary fat intake and obesity, especially when the latter predominantly affects the abdomen. Because of the inconsistencies between ecologic and cohort studies noted earlier, however, it is unclear whether dietary fat per se, total calorie intake, or other factors are responsible for the associations. Epidemiologic evidence suggests that alcohol intake also may be a risk factor for this disease, especially in women with lower intakes of folic acid. Prostate cancer, the most common cancer and second leading cause of cancer deaths in men, is associated with intake of animal fats and red meats. Colorectal cancer is the third leading cause of cancer mortality in men and women. Its risk correlates positively with dietary fat intake and obesity and inversely with intake of calcium and folic acid, whereas evidence regarding the effect of dietary fiber is equivocal. Higher physical activity is associated with 30 to 50% lower risk for colon cancer and may reduce breast cancer risk.

The interaction of all these influences is powerful enough to indicate that diet contributes to about 35% of cancer deaths in Western countries. Although the independent influences of potentially protective nutrients, such as carotenoids, vitamins C and E, folic acid, and fiber, are not known because they are all present in vegetables and fruits, the evidence that liberal intake of fruits and vegetables reduces cancer risk is compelling.

HYPERTENSION

Elevated blood pressure is a major risk factor for stroke, CHD, heart failure, peripheral vascular disease, and renal disease. It is often associated with obesity, especially abdominal obesity, and weight reduction in obese hypertensives usually leads to improvement in blood pressure. Sodium restriction also usually reduces blood pressure levels. A diet rich in fruits, vegetables, and low-fat dairy products and with reduced saturated and total fat content also can decrease blood pressure levels, and reduced sodium intake provides additional benefit.[◼] Because alcohol intake elevates blood pressure, its use should be minimized in hypertensive patients.

DIABETES MELLITUS

Type 2 diabetes mellitus is strongly associated with obesity. This relationship is especially true for abdominal obesity and less so for peripheral obesity. Sugar consumption does not lead to diabetes except to the extent that it may promote weight gain. Past recommendations to restrict total carbohydrate intake in diabetics have been abandoned; 55 to 60% of a diabetic's energy intake should come from carbohydrates, preferably unrefined carbohydrates that include fiber. Because higher fat diets tend to promote obesity and CHD, for which diabetics are at high risk, dietary fat intake should be kept low. Alcohol can cause hypoglycemia, hyperglycemia, and increased triglyceride levels in diabetics, and its use should be minimized. In diabetics and non-diabetics, excess alcohol intake is responsible for many deaths, particularly from accidents and liver disease, and is a factor in some suicides.

OSTEOPOROSIS

Osteoporosis is influenced by several dietary factors. Inadequate calcium intake during adolescence may result in suboptimal peak bone mass in early adulthood, and during later life it may lead to more rapid bone loss, increasing the risk for osteoporosis. Other nutrients that influence bone mass have received less attention. Sodium and protein, which are consumed by Americans in greater quantities than required, may promote excess bone loss. Vitamin D and magnesium assist in maintaining optimal bone mass.

OTHER ISSUES

The causes and health effects of obesity, the most prevalent nutritional disorder in the United States, are reviewed in Chapter 233. A constellation of obesity with elevated waist circumference, increased serum glucose, triglyceride level, hypertension, and low HDL cholesterol level is often termed the *metabolic syndrome* or *syndrome X* and is increasingly prevalent in the United States.

Low dietary fiber intake causes constipation, and although not conclusively established, it is thought to be a cause of intestinal diverticular disease. Inadequate maternal folic acid intake has been proved conclusively to be a major risk factor for congenital neural tube defects such as spina bifida and myelomeningocele. For this reason, cereal and grain products in the United States have been fortified with folic acid since 1998.

Translating Evidence into Dietary Change

Strong evidence has surfaced that dietary habits can influence the incidence and severity of many potentially incapacitating or lethal diseases in the United States. No justification exists for the belief that modification of the "usual" American diet is unnecessary or futile. The only questions are whether it is feasible and what is required to effect change. Various health agencies and the U.S. government have used public education, particularly the publication of dietary goals,

as their primary means. The U.S. Department of Agriculture (USDA) and the Department of Health and Human Services developed the food guide pyramid (Fig. 12–1A) and the Dietary Guidelines for Americans (Table 12–4) to educate the public.

Even these recommendations do not typify an ideal diet based on the available evidence; instead, they reflect a consensus on what can be realistically expected of the American public. A potentially more "ideal" pyramid, based on observations of low rates of chronic disease and high adult life expectancies in the Mediterranean region in 1960, has been promulgated (Fig. 12–1B). In this pyramid, sources of monounsaturated fatty acids, such as olive oil and nuts, are given a more prominent place in the diet, as are beans and other legumes.

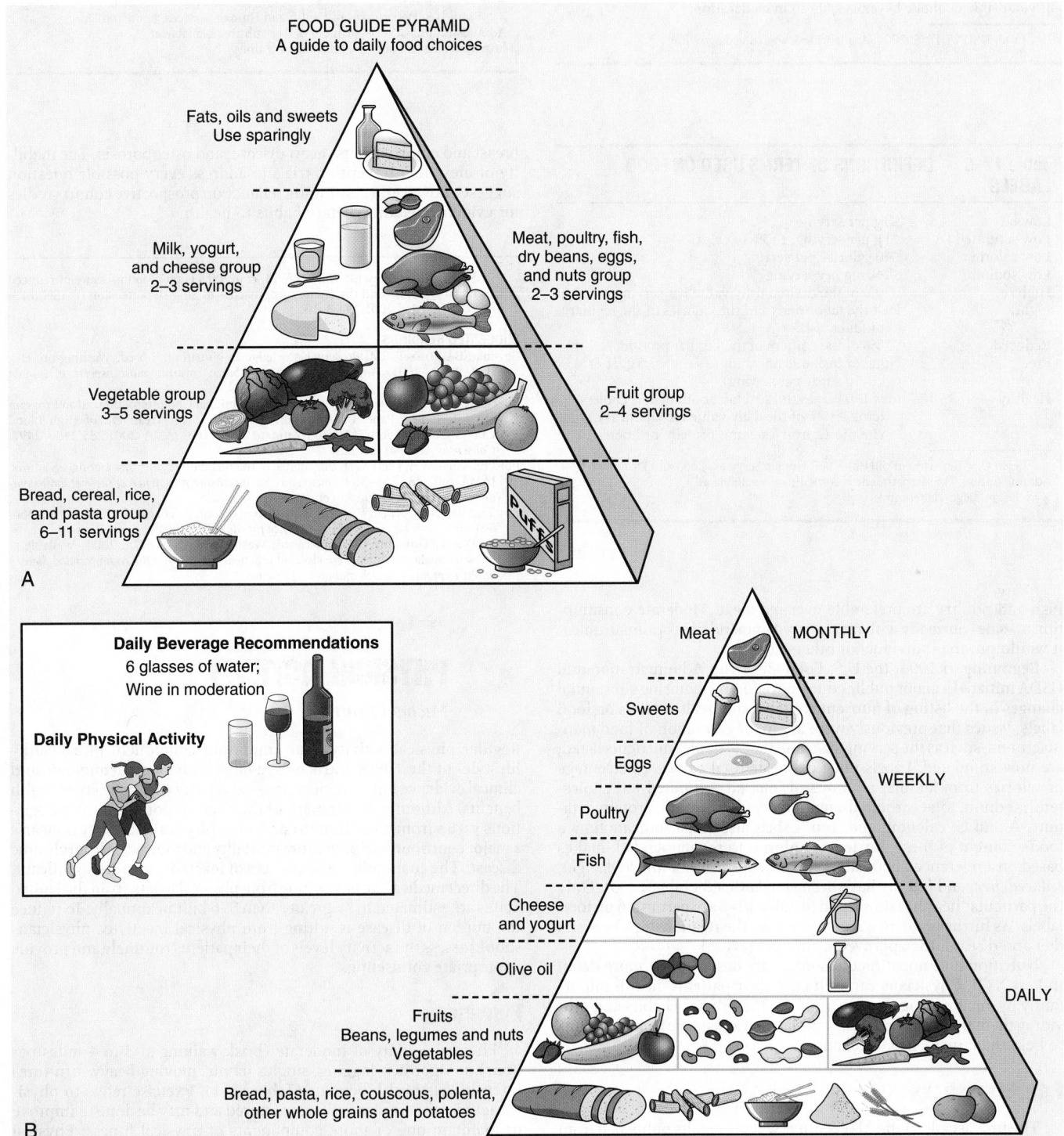

FIGURE 12–1 • *A*, U.S. Department of Agriculture/Department of Health and Human Services Food Guide Pyramid. *B*, Healthy Food Pyramid, emphasizing the Mediterranean diet. (*A*, From USDA/DDHS. Available at www.nal.usda.gov/fnic. *B*, From Oldways Preservation & Exchange Trus. Used by permission.)

Preventive and Environmental Medicine

Table 12–4 • DIETARY GUIDELINES FOR AMERICANS, 2000

AIM FOR FITNESS
Aim for healthy weight
Be physically active each day

BUILD A HEALTHY BASE
Let the food pyramid guide your food choices
Choose a variety of grains daily, especially whole grains
Choose a variety of fruits and vegetables daily
Keep food safe to eat

CHOOSE SENSIBLY
Choose a diet that is low in saturated fat and cholesterol and moderate
   in total fat
Choose beverages and foods to moderate intake of sugars
Choose and prepare foods with less salt
If you drink alcoholic beverages, do so in moderation

From USDA/DHHS, 2000. Available at www.nal.usda.gov/fnic.

Table 12–6 • PERMISSIBLE HEALTH CLAIMS FOR FOOD LABELS

Calcium	May lower risk for osteoporosis
Fat	May increase risk for cancer
Fiber-containing grain products, fruits, and vegetables	May reduce risk for coronary disease and cancer
Fruits and vegetables	May reduce risk for cancer
Folic acid supplementation	Reduces risk for neural tube defects
Plant sterol/stanol esters	May reduce the risk of heart disease
Saturated fat and cholesterol	Increase risk for coronary heart disease
Sodium	May increase risk for high blood pressure
Soy protein	May reduce risk of heart disease
Sugar	Promotes tooth decay

From U.S. Department of Health and Human Services, Food and Drug Administration, U.S. Department of Agriculture. Available at http://www.cfsan.fda.gov/~dms/hclaims.html.

Table 12–5 • DEFINITIONS OF TERMS USED ON FOOD LABELS

Low fat	≤3 g per serving
Low saturated fat	≤1 g per serving, ≤15% of calories
Low calorie	≤40 calories per serving
Low sodium	≤140 mg per serving
High	≥20% of the desired daily value per serving
Light	Half the fat or one third the calories of the regular product
Reduced	≤75% of the content of the regular product
Free	None or insignificant amount (e.g. <0.5 g fat or <0.5 g sugar per serving)
Healthy	Low total and saturated fat, sodium, and cholesterol: ≥10% of the daily value for vitamin A, vitamin C, iron, calcium, protein, or fiber

From U.S. Department of Health and Human Services, Food and Drug Administration, U.S. Department of Agriculture. Available at www.cfsan.fda.gov/label.html.

breast and colon cancers, heart disease, and osteoporosis. The inability of lifestyle intervention trials to address every possible question suggests, however, a continuing reliance on prospective cohort studies for evidence relating dietary habits to health.

 1. Sacks FM, Svetkey LP, Vollmer WM, et al: Effects on blood pressure of reduced dietary sodium and the Dietary Approaches to Stop Hypertension (DASH) diet. N Engl J Med 2001;344:3–10.

SUGGESTED READINGS
Bowman BA, Russell RM: Present Knowledge in Nutrition, 8th ed. Washington, DC, ILSI Press, 2001. *A general reference resource covering most aspects of human nutrition.*
Executive Summary of the Third Report of the National Cholesterol Education Program (NCEP) Expert Panel on Detection, Evaluation, and Treatment of High Blood Cholesterol in Adults (Adult Treatment Panel III). JAMA 2001;285:2486–2497. *Consensus recommendations.*
Ford ES, Giles WH, Dietz WH: Prevalence of the metabolic syndrome among US adults. JAMA 2002;287:356–359. *Documents the increasing prevalence of the metabolic syndrome, presumably related to obesity.*
Key TJ, Allen NE, Spencer EA, et al: The effect of diet on risk of cancer. Lancet 2002;360: 861–868. *Concise review of the evidence for the effects of diet on cancer risk.*
USDA: Dietary Guidelines for Americans. Washington, DC, USDA, 2000. Available at www.nal.usda.gov/fnic. *A concise and practical summary of the recommended dietary habits to promote health and prevent disease.*

Fish and poultry are preferable over red meat. Moderate consumption of wine (normally with meals) is recommended as optional, unless it would put the individual or others at risk.

Beginning in 1994, the U.S. Food and Drug Administration and USDA initiated a major public education effort by requiring substantial changes in the listing of nutrient contents and health claims on food labels. Issues that previously were left to the discretion of food manufacturers, such as the serving sizes and the particular nutrients listed, are now stipulated. Labels must delineate total calories, percentage of calories from fat, and amounts of total fat, saturated fat, cholesterol, sodium, total carbohydrates, dietary fiber, sugars, protein, vitamins A and C, calcium, and iron. Labels also must indicate how a food's content of these nutrients conforms to recommended intakes based on a reference 2000-calorie diet. Definitions for *low, high, light, reduced, free,* and *healthy* have been standardized (Table 12–5). Only the particular health claims listed in Table 12–6 are permitted on food labels. As further evidence accumulates on the relationships between diet and disease, the approved claims are revised.

Nutrition and nutritional disorders are described in more detail in Part XVII. Physicians can influence their patients' health importantly by encouraging them to optimize their dietary habits and providing them with instructional materials and assistance from dietitians to help them make needed changes.

Future Directions

The first decade of the 21st century will see results published from several large randomized dietary intervention trials, including the Women's Health Initiative, which is testing the effects of reduced dietary fat, calcium supplementation, and hormone replacement therapy on

13 PHYSICAL ACTIVITY

Michael Pratt

Regular physical activity is an important component of a healthy lifestyle. In the 1980s and 1990s, a large body of epidemiologic and clinical evidence linked regular physical activity with a variety of health benefits. Although the strength of the data supporting these associations varies from condition to condition, physical inactivity is clearly a major contributor to premature mortality and morbidity from chronic disease. The economic consequences of inactivity also are significant. The direct medical costs resulting from physical inactivity in the United States are estimated to be greater than $76 billion annually. To reduce the burden of disease resulting from physical inactivity, physicians should assess the activity levels of their patients routinely and provide appropriate counseling.

Definitions

Physical activity of moderate (brisk walking at 3 to 4 miles per hour) or vigorous (jogging, singles tennis, moving heavy furniture) intensity has health benefits (Table 13–1). Exercise refers to physical activity that is planned or structured and may be done to improve or maintain one or more components of physical fitness. Physical activity and exercise are behaviors, whereas physical fitness refers to an individual's capacity to perform physical activity. Physical fitness generally is considered to consist of five components: aerobic or

Table 13–1 • DEFINING THE INTENSITY OF PHYSICAL ACTIVITY

ACTIVITY TYPE	METS*	HEART RATE†	AEROBIC CAPACITY‡
Moderate	3–6	50–70%	40–60%
Vigorous	>6	>70%	>60%

*Ratio of the metabolic rate during activity to the resting metabolic rate. One MET is defined as the energy expended while sitting quietly.
†Percentage of maximum heart rate.
‡Percentage of maximum aerobic capacity.

Table 13–2 • MECHANISMS BY WHICH PHYSICAL ACTIVITY PREVENTS CORONARY HEART DISEASE

Reduces elevated systolic blood pressure
Reduces elevated diastolic blood pressure
Raises HDL cholesterol
Reduces triglycerides
Reduces weight gain and enhances weight maintenance and fat distribution
Increases glucose uptake and insulin sensitivity
Reduces platelet adhesion
Enhances fibrinolysis
May reduce thrombosis
Decreases sympathetic and increases parasympathetic drive, which reduces myocardial oxygen demand
May reduce ventricular arrhythmias
May increase myocardial oxygen supply

HDL = high-density lipoprotein.

endurance capacity, muscular strength, muscular endurance, flexibility, and body composition.

Epidemiology

National and state-based surveys indicate that approximately 30% of American adults are completely sedentary during their leisure time, and another 30 to 40% are minimally active. Fewer than 40% of adults report being physically active at the recommended levels (≥ 20 minutes of vigorous activity at least three times per week or ≥ 30 minutes of moderate-intensity activity five or more times per week). Participation in leisure time physical activity seemed to increase from the 1960s through the 1980s but reached a plateau in the 1990s. Declining levels of routine or incidental physical activity may be a major contributor to the marked increases in obesity observed in the 1980s and 1990s. Participation in physical activity declines with age and tends to be slightly higher among men than women and among whites than among members of other racial or ethnic groups. Higher levels of education and income are associated with greater participation in physical activity and account for most of the racial and ethnic differences observed for leisure time physical activity.

Health Benefits of Physical Activity

The physiologic and metabolic responses to exercise are at the root of the multiple health benefits associated with physical activity. Physical activity requires increased energy expenditure and imposes demands and stresses on multiple organ and enzyme systems. These demands lead to acute responses and to long-term adaptations of the circulatory, respiratory, nervous, endocrine, and skeletal systems. The most direct benefits of physical activity are cardiovascular and musculoskeletal adaptations, which increase functional capacity in these organ systems. Increased aerobic capacity and muscular strength and endurance have been well documented after training programs in individuals of all ages. Maintenance of functional capacity and strength may be especially important for preventing disability and maintaining independence among older adults. Many disease-specific and risk factor–specific benefits of physical activity also have been postulated. Convincing data link regular physical activity to lower rates of coronary heart disease (CHD) and colon cancer and to improvements in mental health, glucose metabolism, and bone density, but much research is needed to evaluate other possible health consequences of physical activity.

CORONARY HEART DISEASE

Classic epidemiologic studies showed that heart disease was less likely to develop in conductors on double-decker buses in London than in less active drivers and that the risk of CHD among longshoremen was inversely correlated with their activity level at work. Longitudinal studies of college alumni have shown a reduced incidence of CHD and lower CHD and all-cause mortality among regularly active men compared with their sedentary counterparts. Previously sedentary men who initiated regular physical activity in middle age also reduced their risk of death from CHD and all causes compared with men who remained sedentary. Overall, the risk of CHD in sedentary men is about twice that of men who are habitually active, and increased physical fitness has been linked with lower all-cause and CHD mortality for women and men. To date, no randomized clinical trial of physical activity has been conducted for the primary prevention of CHD. The association of regular physical activity with reductions in CHD meets strict epidemiologic criteria for causality, however—the association is strong, consistent, graded, temporally appropriate, and biologically plausible (Table 13–2).

The evidence for a causal role of regular physical activity in the secondary prevention of CHD is at least as strong as the evidence for primary prevention. Patients with CHD who engage in regular physical activity as part of a cardiac rehabilitation program have lower all-cause and CHD mortality than do nonparticipants 1 to 3 years after initial hospitalization. Exercise-based cardiac rehabilitation programs also have been shown to increase functional capacity and reduce CHD symptoms and may improve quality of life. Appropriate physical activity should be a part of the management and rehabilitation of most patients with CHD (Chapters 67, 68, and 69).

WEIGHT CONTROL

Individuals who are regularly active tend to weigh less and have a lower percentage of body fat than do sedentary individuals despite the fact that physically active persons are consistently observed to consume more calories than sedentary individuals. Regular physical activity increases caloric expenditure indirectly by raising the resting metabolic rate after activity and directly by the activity itself. A combined program of diet and regular physical activity seems to be the most effective means of maintaining ideal body weight. Regular physical activity seems to alter body fat distribution beneficially, independent of its effects on body weight and total adiposity. Higher levels of physical activity are associated with the primary prevention of weight gain and obesity.

DIABETES

Physical activity increases muscle glucose uptake directly and increases insulin sensitivity. Physical activity commonly is prescribed for managing type 2 diabetes mellitus. Physical activity also may prevent type 2 diabetes through its effects on insulin and glucose metabolism and maintenance of body weight (Chapter 242). In well-conducted longitudinal studies, the incidence of type 2 diabetes has been lower in regularly active male college alumni, physicians, and female nurses than their sedentary counterparts. Clinical trials have shown conclusively that a combined program of moderate physical activity, diet, and weight control can reduce the incidence of type 2 diabetes by 50% or more among high-risk patients with impaired glucose tolerance.∎

OSTEOPOROSIS

Physical activity may play an important role in maintaining bone mineral density, preventing osteoporosis, and reducing fractures (Chapter 257). Bone density is reduced by bed rest and can be increased by weight-bearing activity. Regular physical activity increases bone mass in young women, reduces the decline in bone mass seen in postmenopausal women, and may increase bone density in patients with osteoporosis. Postmenopausal women who walk approximately 1 mile per day have higher bone mineral density and slower rates of bone loss than do sedentary women. Regular physical activity also increases muscle mass and strength, perhaps reducing the risk of falls and protecting against fractures when falls do occur.

CANCER

Regular physical activity and physical fitness have been associated with lower mortality from cancer in longitudinal studies. Although data for most specific cancers are limited, studies of occupational and leisure time activity indicate that physical activity is protective against colon cancer. The evidence is strongly suggestive of a reduced risk of breast cancer in regularly active women, but this relationship is complicated and may be modified by age, body weight, and patterns of activity over the lifespan. The protective effects may be mediated by reduced intestinal transit time (colon cancer) and altered endocrine function.

MENTAL HEALTH

Regular physical activity and physical fitness are positively associated with mental health and well-being. Persons who are regularly active report less anxiety and depression and lower levels of stress than do sedentary persons. Exercise programs may be useful as an adjunctive therapy for treating mild-to-moderate depression.

Health Risks

Physical activity is associated with risks and benefits. Musculoskeletal overuse injuries of the lower extremity are the most common negative consequences of physical activity. Three factors are strongly associated with a risk of musculoskeletal injury: previous injuries, increased duration of activity, and exercise intensity. The risk of injury is considerably higher with vigorous activity than with moderate activity. The clinician can reduce patients' risk of injury by making them aware of these associations and by advocating moderate physical activity and gradual increases in duration of activity.

Major cardiac events, although rare, have been associated with vigorous physical activity. The risk of cardiac arrest is elevated transiently during exercise for individuals who are regularly active and to a greater extent for individuals who are irregularly active. The overall risk of cardiac arrest is reduced in men who are regularly active, however. The incidence of sudden cardiac arrest associated with exercise has been estimated at 1 per 565,000 person hours in the general population and 1 per 60,000 person hours among individuals with known heart disease. Most of these deaths are due to underlying CHD. Physical activity also may exacerbate medical conditions such as asthma, and irregular exercise may make insulin dosing more challenging in diabetic patients. Nevertheless, most individuals with underlying disease or disability still may exercise safely if appropriate precautions are taken.

Medical Evaluation

Appropriate medical evaluation depends on the individual's age and health status and the type of activity undertaken. Individuals who are free of disease and who are initiating moderate-intensity physical activity, such as regular walking, do not require medical evaluation. Men older than 40 years and women older than 50 who wish to become vigorously active should undergo a medical examination. Persons of any age with symptomatic cardiovascular disease or multiple risk factors for cardiovascular disease require medical evaluation. Evaluation of patients with known cardiovascular disease should include a physician-supervised, symptom-limited exercise test with blood pressure and electrocardiogram monitoring; this testing is not generally thought to be mandatory in asymptomatic adults without known cardiovascular disease.

Assessment and Counseling

Health professionals should counsel patients routinely to adopt and maintain an active lifestyle. Evidence-based reviews show that primary care–based counseling is, at best, of only modest effectiveness in increasing physical activity in the short-term[2] and works best when tailored to patient characteristics. More research is required to assess long-term efficacy and optimal implementation strategies. The exercise prescription should consider an individual's age, health, current activity level, and readiness to initiate behavior change. Research on quitting smoking and initiating physical activity has shown that patients move along a behavioral continuum from precontemplation, to contemplating change, to making a change, and finally to maintaining the new behavior. Physicians have greater success in changing their patient's physical activity practices if they can target their counseling to the patient's current activity level and behavioral stage. Brief, specific physical activity counseling reinforced by other providers, follow-up appointments, and educational materials can increase physical activity.

How much and what type of physical activity should be prescribed? The traditional exercise prescription calls for 20 or more minutes of continuous aerobic activity three to five times per week at moderate-to-vigorous intensity (60% of maximum heart rate or 50% of aerobic capacity). This prescription is appropriate for increasing fitness and improving health status. Assessment of epidemiologic and clinical data on the health aspects of physical activity reveals that many of the health benefits attributable to physical activity are associated with the total quantity of activity performed even if the activity is discontinuous and of only moderate intensity. Moderate activities, such as brisk walking, gardening, and stair climbing, on a daily basis can have major health impacts. The Centers for Disease Control and Prevention, National Institutes of Health, Surgeon General, and American College of Sports Medicine currently recommend that American adults participate in 30 minutes or more of moderate-intensity physical activity on most and preferably all days of the week.

The physical activity prescription can take the traditional vigorous exercise approach or follow the recommendation for daily moderate physical activity (Table 13–3). Both provide significant health benefits. Tailoring recommendations for physical activity to the patient's individual goals, interests, skills, available time, and barriers to activity increases the chance for success.

Most persons are aware that they should be more active. The physician can encourage patients to become regularly active by

Table 13–3 • EXERCISE PRESCRIPTION

TYPE OF PHYSICAL ACTIVITY
Continuous or intermittent
Primarily aerobic
Stretching for flexibility
Resistance exercise for strength

INTENSITY
Moderate (40–60% relative to capacity, "brisk walk")
or
Vigorous (>60% relative to capacity)

DURATION
20–60 min/day
150–300 kcal/day

FREQUENCY
Daily for intermittent moderate activity
Three or more times per week for continuous, vigorous activity

SESSION
For planned exercise:
 Warm-up, 3–5 min
 Conditioning, 15–40 min
 Cool-down, 2–5 min
For lifestyle activity: Incorporate activity into the daily routine. "Pulses" of activity should be at least 10 min long and at an intensity equal to brisk walking

PROGRESSION
Increase duration, intensity, and frequency gradually
Evaluate progress each visit

WARNING SIGNS
Severe musculoskeletal pain
Claudication
Chest pressure, pain, or discomfort
Unusual shortness of breath
Dizziness, nausea, vomiting

reinforcing the importance of physical activity to health, working with the patient to help build the skills and self-confidence needed to be active, and designing a program of physical activity that fits into the individual's lifestyle. Primary care providers play an important part in promoting physical activity, but increasing overall levels of physical activity in the United States and other developed countries also requires widespread community programs. Effective community-based interventions include school physical education, social support, point-of-decision prompts to use stairs, community-wide campaigns, and enhancing access to places for physical activity.

1. Tuomilehto J, Lindstrom J, Eriksson JG, et al: Prevention of type 2 diabetes mellitus by changes in lifestyle among subjects with impaired glucose tolerance. N Engl J Med 2001;344:1343–1350.
2. Eden KB, Orleans CT, Mulrow CD, et al: Does counseling by clinicians improve physical activity? A Summary of the evidence for the U.S. Preventive Services Task Force. Ann Intern Med 2002;137:208–215.
3. Centers for Disease Control and Prevention: Increasing physical activity: A report on recommendations of the Task Force on Community Preventive Services. MMWR Morb Mortal Wkly Rep 2001;50(RR-18):1–14.

SUGGESTED READINGS

Dunn AL, Marcus BH, Kampert JB, et al: Comparison of lifestyle and structured interventions to increase physical activity and cardiorespiratory fitness: A randomized trial. JAMA 1999;281:327–334. *Lifestyle changes are as effective as a structured exercise program.*

Fletcher GF, Balady GJ, Amsterdam EA, et al: Exercise standards for testing and training: A statement for healthcare professionals from the American Heart Association. Circulation 2001;104:1694–1740. *Updated guidelines and the evidence behind them for exercise testing and prescription for healthy adults and cardiac patients.*

Kesaniemi YA, Danforth E, Jensen MD, et al: Dose-response issues concerning physical activity and health: An evidence-based symposium (consensus statement). Med Sci Sports Exerc 2001;33:s351–s398. *A review of the health benefits of physical activity and dose-response relationships between physical activity and key health outcomes. Additional articles in this supplement address physical activity and CHD, cancer, diabetes, obesity, and other health outcomes in depth.*

14 TOBACCO

Neal L. Benowitz

Epidemiology

Currently, about 46 million individuals in the United States are cigarette smokers, including 26% of men and 22% of women. People who are less well educated and/or have unskilled occupations are more likely to smoke. Smoking is responsible for about 430,000 preventable U.S. deaths annually. A lifelong smoker has about a one in three chance of dying prematurely from a complication of smoking. Smoking is the major preventable cause of death in developed countries.

Other forms of tobacco use include pipes and cigars (used by 8.7% of men and 0.3% of women) and smokeless tobacco (5.5% of men and 1% of women). Smokeless tobacco use in the United States is primarily oral snuff and chewing tobacco, whereas nasal snuff is used to a greater extent in the United Kingdom. Oral snuff (snus) is widely used by men in Sweden.

Harmful Constituents of Tobacco

Tobacco smoke is an aerosol of droplets (particulates) containing water, nicotine and other alkaloids, and tar. Tobacco smoke contains several thousand different chemicals, many of which may contribute to human disease. Major toxic chemicals in the particulate phase of tobacco include nicotine, benzo(a)pyrene and other polycyclic hydrocarbons, N′-nitrosonornicotine, β-naphthylamine, polonium-210, nickel, cadmium, arsenic, and lead. The gaseous phase contains carbon monoxide, acetaldehyde, acetone, methanol, nitrogen oxides, hydrogen cyanide, acrolein, ammonia, benzene, formaldehyde, nitrosamines, and vinyl chloride. Tobacco smoke may produce illness by way of systemic absorption of toxins and/or cause local pulmonary injury by oxidant gases.

Tobacco Addiction

Tobacco use is motivated primarily by the desire for nicotine. Drug addiction is defined as compulsive use of a psychoactive substance, the consequences of which are detrimental to the individual or society. Understanding addiction is useful in providing effective smoking cessation therapy. Nicotine is absorbed rapidly from tobacco smoke into the pulmonary circulation; it then moves quickly to the brain, where it acts on nicotinic cholinergic receptors to produce its gratifying effects, which occur within 10 to 15 seconds after a puff. Smokeless tobacco is absorbed more slowly and results in less intense pharmacologic effects. With long-term use of tobacco, physical dependence develops as a result of an increased number of nicotinic cholinergic receptors in the brain. When tobacco is unavailable, even for only a few hours, withdrawal symptoms often occur, including anxiety, irritability, difficulty concentrating, restlessness, hunger, craving for tobacco, disturbed sleep, and, in some people, depression.

Addiction to tobacco is multifactorial, including a desire for the direct pharmacologic actions of nicotine, relief of withdrawal symptoms, and learned associations. Smokers report a variety of reasons for smoking, including pleasure, arousal, enhanced vigilance, improved performance, relief of anxiety or depression, reduced hunger, and control of body weight. Environmental cues, such as a meal, a cup of coffee, talking on the phone, an alcoholic beverage, or friends who smoke, often trigger an urge to smoke. Smoking and depression are strongly linked. Smokers are more likely than nonsmokers to have a history of major depression. Smokers with a history of depression are also likely to be more highly dependent on nicotine and to have a lower likelihood of quitting. When they do quit, depression is more apt to be a prominent withdrawal symptom.

Most tobacco use begins in childhood or adolescence. Risk factors for youth smoking include peer and parental influences; behavioral problems (e.g., poor school performance); personality characteristics, such as rebelliousness or risk taking, depression, and anxiety; and genetic influences. Adolescent desire to appear older and more sophisticated, such as emulating more mature role models, is another strong motivator. Environmental influences such as advertising also are thought to contribute. Although smoking rates among adults have been declining since the 1970s, initiation rates for youth have remained constant since the mid-1980s. Approaches to preventing tobacco addiction in youth include educational activities in schools, aggressive anti-tobacco media campaigns, taxation, changing the social and environmental norms, and deglamorizing smoking (restricting indoor smoking, educating parents not to smoke around children).

Tobacco-Related Diseases

Tobacco use is a major cause of death from cancer, cardiovascular disease, and pulmonary disease (Table 14–1). Smoking is also a major risk factor for osteoporosis, reproductive disorders, and fire-related and trauma-related injuries.

CANCER

Smoking, although the largest preventable cause of cancer (Table 14–2), is responsible for about 30% of cancer deaths. Many chemicals in tobacco smoke may contribute to carcinogenesis as tumor initiators, cocarcinogens, tumor promoters, or complete carcinogens. Cigarette smoking induces specific patterns of p53 mutations that are associated with squamous cell carcinomas of the lung, head, and neck. Lung cancer (Chapter 198) is the leading cause of cancer deaths in the United States and is predominantly attributable to cigarette smoking. The risk of lung and other cancers is proportional to how many cigarettes are smoked per day and the duration of smoking. Workplace exposure to asbestos or α-radiation (the latter in uranium miners) (Chapter 19) synergistically increases the risk of lung cancer in cigarette smokers. Alcohol use (Chapter 17) interacts synergistically with tobacco in causing oral, laryngeal, and esophageal cancer (Chapters 136, 197, and 467). The mechanism of interaction may involve alcohol-solubilizing tobacco carcinogens and/or alcohol-related induction of liver or gastrointestinal enzymes that metabolize and activate tobacco carcinogens. The tobacco-related risks of bladder and kidney cancer (Chapter 203) are enhanced by occupational exposure to aromatic amines, such as found in the dye industry. Cervical cancer (Chapter 205) is more common in women who smoke, presumably the result of exposure to carcinogens in cervical secretions. Smoking seems to be involved in 20 to 30% of leukemia cases in adults (Chapters 192 and 193), including lymphoid and myeloid leukemia, and in 20% of colorectal cancers (Chapter 200).

Table 14–1 • HEALTH HAZARDS OF TOBACCO USE (RISKS INCREASED BY SMOKING)

CANCER
See Table 14–2

CARDIOVASCULAR DISEASE
Sudden death
Acute myocardial infarction
Unstable angina
Stroke
Peripheral arterial occlusive disease (including thromboangiitis obliterans)
Aortic aneurysm

PULMONARY DISEASE
Lung cancer
Chronic bronchitis
Emphysema
Asthma
Increased susceptibility to pneumonia
Increased susceptibility to pulmonary tuberculosis and desquamative interstitial pneumonitis
Increased morbidity from viral respiratory infection

GASTROINTESTINAL DISEASE
Peptic ulcer
Esophageal reflux

REPRODUCTIVE DISTURBANCES
Reduced fertility
Premature birth
Lower birth weight
Spontaneous abortion
Abruptio placentae
Premature rupture of membranes
Increased perinatal mortality

ORAL DISEASE (SMOKELESS TOBACCO)
Oral cancer
Leukoplakia
Gingivitis
Gingival recession
Tooth staining

OTHER
Non–insulin-dependent diabetes mellitus
Earlier menopause
Osteoporosis
Cataract
Tobacco amblyopia
Age-related macular degeneration
Premature skin wrinkling
Aggravation of hypothyroidism
Altered drug metabolism or effects

Table 14–2 • SMOKING AND CANCER MORTALITY

TYPE OF CANCER	RELATIVE RISK AMONG SMOKERS		MORTALITY ATTRIBUTABLE TO SMOKING	
	Current	Former	Percentage	Number
Lung				
Male	22.4	9.4	90	82,800
Female	11.9	4.7	79	40,300
Larynx				
Male	10.5	5.2	81	2400
Female	17.8	11.9	87	700
Oral cavity				
Male	27.5	8.8	92	4900
Female	5.6	2.9	61	1800
Esophagus				
Male	7.6	5.8	78	5700
Female	10.3	3.2	75	1900
Pancreas				
Male	2.1	1.1	29	3500
Female	2.3	1.8	34	4500
Bladder				
Male	2.9	1.9	47	3000
Female	2.6	1.9	37	1200
Kidney				
Male	3.0	2.0	48	3000
Female	1.4	1.2	12	500
Stomach				
Male	1.5	?	17	1400
Female	1.5	?	25	1300
Leukemia				
Male	2.0	?	20	2000
Female	2.0	?	20	1600
Cervix				
Female	2.1	1.9	31	1400

Adapted from Newcomb PA, Carbone PP: The health consequences of smoking: Cancer. Med Clin North Am 1992;76:305–331.

CARDIOVASCULAR DISEASE

Cigarette smoking accounts for about 20% of cardiovascular deaths in the United States (Chapter 47). Risks are increased for coronary heart disease (Chapters 67, 68, and 69), sudden death (Chapter 60), cerebrovascular disease (Chapters 439 and 440), and peripheral vascular disease (Chapter 78), including aortic aneurysm (Chapter 75). Cigarette smoking accelerates atherosclerosis (Chapter 66) and promotes acute ischemic events. The mechanisms of the effects of smoking are not fully elucidated but are believed to include (1) hemodynamic stress (nicotine increases the heart rate and transiently increases blood pressure; Chapter 63), (2) endothelial injury and dysfunction (nitric oxide release and resultant vasodilation are impaired), (3) development of an atherogenic lipid profile (smokers have on average higher low-density lipoprotein, more oxidized low-density lipoprotein, and lower high-density lipoprotein cholesterol than nonsmokers do; see Chapter 211), (4) enhanced coagulability (Chapter 162), (5) arrhythmogenesis (Chapter 57), and (6) relative hypoxemia because of the effects of carbon monoxide (Chapter 81). Carbon monoxide reduces the capacity of hemoglobin to carry oxygen and impairs the release of oxygen from hemoglobin to body tissues, both of which combine to result in a state of relative hypoxemia. To compensate for this hypoxemic state, polycythemia develops in

smokers, with hematocrits often 50% or more (Chapter 176). The polycythemia and the increased fibrinogen levels that are found in cigarette smokers also increase blood viscosity, which adds to the risk of thrombotic events. Cigarette smoking also induces a chronic inflammatory state, as evidenced by increased levels of C-reactive protein in the blood of smokers. Chronic inflammation is thought to contribute to atherogenesis.

Cigarette smoking acts synergistically with other cardiac risk factors to increase the risk of ischemic heart disease. Although the risk of cardiovascular disease is roughly proportional to cigarette consumption, the risk persists even at low levels of smoking (e.g., one to two cigarettes per day). Cigarette smoking reduces exercise tolerance in patients with angina pectoris (Chapter 67) and intermittent claudication (Chapter 76). Vasospastic angina is more common, and the response to vasodilator medication is impaired in patients who smoke. The number of episodes and total duration of ischemic episodes as assessed by ambulatory electrocardiogram monitoring in patients with coronary heart disease are substantially increased by cigarette smoking. The increase in relative risk of coronary heart disease because of cigarette smoking is greatest in young adults, who in the absence of cigarette smoking would have a relatively low risk. Women who use oral contraceptives and smoke have a synergistically increased risk of myocardial infarction and stroke.

After acute myocardial infarction (Chapters 68 and 69), the risk of recurrent myocardial infarction is higher and survival is half over the next 12 years in persistent smokers compared with quitters. Smoking also interferes with revascularization therapy for acute myocardial infarction. After thrombolysis, the reocclusion rate is four-fold higher in smokers who continue than in quitters. The risk of reocclusion of a coronary artery after angioplasty or occlusion of a bypass graft is increased in smokers. Cigarette smoking is not a risk factor for hypertension per se but does increase the risk of complications, including the development of nephrosclerosis and progression to malignant hypertension. Cigarette smoking has been shown to be a substantial contributor to morbidity and mortality in patients with left ventricular dysfunction (Chapter 56). The mortality benefit of stopping smoking in such patients is equal to or greater than the benefit of therapy with angiotensin-converting enzyme inhibitors, β-blockers, or spironolactone.

PULMONARY DISEASE

More than 80% of chronic obstructive lung disease in the United States is attributable to cigarette smoking (Chapter 85). Cigarette smoking also increases the risk of respiratory infection, including pneumonia, and results in greater disability from viral respiratory tract infections. Pulmonary disease from smoking includes the overlapping syndromes of chronic bronchitis (cough and mucus hypersecretion), emphysema, and airway obstruction. The lung pathology produced by cigarette smoking includes loss of cilia, mucous gland hyperplasia, increased number of goblet cells in the central airways, inflammation, goblet cell metaplasia, squamous metaplasia, mucus plugging of small airways, destruction of alveoli, and a reduced number of small arteries. The mechanism of injury is complex and seems to include direct injury by oxidant gases, increased elastase activity (a protein that breaks down elastin and other connective tissue), and decreased antiprotease activity. A genetic deficiency of α_1-antiprotease activity produces a similar imbalance between pulmonary protease and antiprotease activity and is a risk factor for early and severe smoking-induced pulmonary disease. Cigarette smoking also is associated with an increased risk of desquamative interstitial pneumonitis (Chapter 88).

OTHER COMPLICATIONS

Cigarette smoking increases the risk of duodenal and gastric ulcers, delays the rate of ulcer healing, and increases the risk of relapse after ulcer treatment (Chapter 138). Smoking also is associated with esophageal reflux symptoms (Chapter 136). Smoking produces ulcer disease by increasing acid secretion, reducing pancreatic bicarbonate secretion, impairing the gastric mucosal barrier (related to decreased gastric mucosal blood flow and/or inhibition of prostaglandin synthesis), and reducing pyloric sphincter tone.

Cigarette smoking is an independent risk factor for the development of non–insulin-dependent diabetes mellitus (Chapter 242), which is a consequence of development of resistance to the effects of insulin. The effects of nicotine seem to contribute at least in part to insulin resistance, and insulin resistance has been described in users of smokeless tobacco, who are not exposed to tobacco combustion products.

Cigarette smoking is a risk factor for osteoporosis in that it reduces the peak bone mass attained in early adulthood and increases the rate of bone loss in later adulthood (Chapter 258). Smoking antagonizes the protective effect of estrogen replacement therapy on the risk of osteoporosis in postmenopausal women.

Cigarette smoking is a major cause of reproductive problems and results in approximately 4600 U.S. infant deaths annually. Growth retardation from cigarette smoking has been termed the *fetal tobacco syndrome*. Cigarette smoking causes reproductive complications by causing placental ischemia mediated by the vasoconstricting effects of nicotine, the hypoxic effects of chronic carbon monoxide exposure, and the general increase in coagulability produced by smoking.

Other adverse effects of cigarette smoking include premature facial wrinkling, an increased risk of cataracts (Chapter 465), olfactory dysfunction (Chapter 469), and fire-related injuries (Chapters 15 and 108); the last-mentioned contribute significantly to the economic costs of tobacco use. Smoking reduces the secretion of thyroid hormone in women with subclinical hypothyroidism and increases the severity of clinical symptoms of hypothyroidism in women with subclinical or overt hypothyroidism, the latter effect reflecting antagonism of thyroid hormone action (Chapter 239). Cigarette smoking also potentially interacts with a variety of drugs by accelerating drug metabolism or by the antagonistic pharmacologic actions that nicotine and/or other constituents of tobacco have with other drugs (Table 14–3).

Health Hazards of Smokeless Tobacco

Smokeless tobacco refers to snuff and chewing tobacco. Oral snuff is placed (as a "pinch") between the lip and gum or under the tongue; chewing tobacco is actively chewed and generates saliva that is spit out ("spit tobacco"). Smokeless tobacco products are usually flavored, many with licorice, and also contain sodium bicarbonate to keep the local pH alkaline to facilitate buccal absorption of nicotine. Nicotine absorption from smokeless tobacco is similar in magnitude to that absorbed from cigarette smoking. Other chemicals, including sodium, glycyrrhizinic acid (from licorice), and potentially carcinogenic chemicals such as nitrosamines also are absorbed systemically.

Smokeless tobacco is addictive and is associated with an increased risk of oral cancer at the site where the tobacco is usually placed (inside the lip, under the cheek or tongue) or nasal cancer in nasal snuff users (Chapter 197). Other oral diseases also associated

Table 14–3 • INTERACTION BETWEEN CIGARETTE SMOKING AND DRUGS

DRUG(S)		INTERACTION (EFFECTS COMPARED WITH NONSMOKERS)	SIGNIFICANCE
Antipyrine	Imipramine	Accelerated metabolism	May require higher doses in smokers, reduced doses after quitting
Caffeine	Lidocaine		
Chlorpromazine	Olanzapine		
Clozapine	Oxazepam		
Desmethyldiazepam	Pentazocine		
Estradiol	Phenacetin		
Estrone	Phenylbutazone		
Flecainide	Propranolol		
Fluvoxamine	Tacrine		
Haloperidol	Theophylline		
Oral contraceptives		Enhanced thrombosis, increased risk of stroke and myocardial infarction	Do not prescribe to smokers, especially if >35 years old
Cimetidine and other H$_2$ blockers		Lower rate of ulcer healing, higher ulcer recurrence rates	Consider using mucosal protective agents
Propranolol		Less antihypertensive effect, less antianginal efficacy; more effective in reducing mortality after myocardial infarction	Consider the use of cardioselective β-blockers
Nifedipine (and probably other calcium blockers)		Less antianginal effect	May require higher doses and/or multiple-drug antianginal therapy
Diazepam, chlordiazepoxide (and possibly other sedative-hypnotics)		Less sedation	Smokers may need higher doses
Chlorpromazine (and possibly other neuroleptics)		Less sedation, possibly reduced efficacy	Smokers may need higher doses
Propoxyphene		Reduced analgesia	Smokers may need higher doses

Table 14–4 • HEALTH HAZARDS OF ENVIRONMENTAL TOBACCO SMOKE IN NONSMOKERS

CHILDREN	ADULTS
Hospitalization for respiratory tract infection in first year of life	Lung cancer
	Myocardial infarction
Wheezing	Reduced pulmonary function
Middle ear effusion	Irritation of eyes, nasal congestion, headache
Asthma	
Sudden infant death syndrome	Cough

with smokeless tobacco include leukoplakia, gingivitis, gingival recession, and staining of the teeth. Cardiovascular effects of smokeless tobacco include acute aggravation of hypertension or angina pectoris as a result of the sympathomimetic effects of nicotine, hypokalemia, hypertension secondary to the effects of glycyrrhizinic acid (a potent mineralocorticoid; Chapter 63), and excessive sodium absorption resulting in aggravated hypertension or sodium-retaining disorders.

Second Hand Smoke

Considerable evidence indicates that exposure to second hand smoke is harmful to the health of nonsmokers (Table 14–4). The U.S. Environmental Protection Agency classifies second hand smoke as a class A carcinogen, which means that it has been shown to cause cancer in humans.

Second hand smoke consists of smoke that is generated while the cigarette is smoldering and mainstream smoke that has been exhaled by the smoker. Of the total combustion product from a cigarette, 75% or more enters the air. The constituents of environmental tobacco smoke are qualitatively similar to those of mainstream smoke. However, some toxins, such as ammonia, formaldehyde, and nitrosamines, are present in much higher concentrations in second hand smoke than in mainstream smoke. The Environmental Protection Agency has estimated that second hand smoke is responsible for approximately 3000 lung cancer deaths annually in nonsmokers in the United States, is causally associated with 150,000 to 300,000 cases of lower respiratory tract infection in infants and young children up to 18 months of age, and is causally associated with the aggravation of asthma in 200,000 to 1 million children. Second hand smoke exposure is also responsible for about 40,000 cardiovasular deaths per year. An appreciation of the hazards of second hand smoke is important to the physician because it provides a basis for advising parents not to smoke when children are in the home, for insisting that child care facilities be smoke-free, and for recommending smoking restrictions in work sites and other public places.

Benefits of Quitting

The benefits of quitting smoking are substantial for smokers of any age. A person who quits smoking before age 50 has half the risk of dying in the next 15 years compared with a continuing smoker. Smoking cessation reduces the risks of developing lung cancer, with the risk falling to half that of a continuing smoker by 10 years and one sixth that of a smoker after 15 years' cessation. Quitting smoking in middle age substantially reduces lung cancer risk, with a 50% reduction in risk if a lifelong smoker quits at age 55 compared with age 75. The risk of acute myocardial infarction falls rapidly after quitting smoking and approaches nonsmoking levels within 1 year of abstinence. Cigarette smoking produces a progressive loss of airway function over time that is characterized by an accelerated loss of forced expiratory volume in 1 second (FEV_1) with increasing age. FEV_1 loss to cigarette smoking cannot be regained by cessation, but the rate of decline slows after smoking cessation and returns to that of nonsmokers. Women who stop smoking during the first 3 to 4 months of pregnancy reduce the risk of having a low-birth-weight infant to that of a woman who has never smoked.

After quitting, smokers gain an average of 5 to 7 lb, which is perceived as undesirable and a reason not to quit by some smokers. Smokers tend to be thinner because of the effects of nicotine to increase energy expenditure and reduce compensatory increases in food consumption. After they quit smoking, ex-smokers tend to reach the weight expected had they never smoked. On balance, the benefits of quitting far outweigh the risks associated with weight gain, and patients should be counseled accordingly.

Treatment of Nicotine Addiction

Of cigarette smokers, 70% would like to quit, and 46% try to quit each year. Spontaneous quit rates are about 1% per year. Simple physician advice to quit increases the quit rate to 3%. Minimal-intervention programs increase quit rates to 5 to 10%, whereas more intensive treatments, including smoking cessation clinics, can yield quit rates of 25 to 30%. A practical office smoking cessation program developed by the U.S. Public Health Service consists of 5 As: (1) *ask* about smoking at every opportunity, (2) *advise* all smokers to stop, (3) *assess* willingness to make a quit attempt, (4) *assist* the patient in stopping and maintaining abstinence, and (5) *arrange* follow-up to reinforce nonsmoking. Assistance in quitting should include providing self-help material or quit kits, which are widely available from governmental health agencies; professional societies; and local organizations, such as cancer, heart, and lung associations. The physician may offer additional education and counseling through the office (most efficiently provided by office staff and by teaching aids such as videotapes) or through referral to community smoking cessation programs. Smokers who are interested should be offered nicotine replacement or other pharmacologic therapy.

Currently, two medications have been approved for smoking cessation: nicotine and bupropion. All types of smoking cessation medications, if used properly, double smoking cessation rates compared with placebo treatments. Nicotine replacement medications include 2- and 4-mg nicotine polacrilex gum, transdermal nicotine patches, nicotine nasal spray, and nicotine inhalers. All seem to have comparable efficacy, but in a randomized study, compliance was greatest for the patch, lower for gum, and very low for the spray and the inhaler.[1] A smoker should be instructed to quit smoking entirely before beginning nicotine replacement therapies. Optimal use of nicotine gum includes instructions not to chew too rapidly, to chew 8 to 10 pieces per day for 20 to 30 minutes each, and to use it for an adequate period for the smoker to learn a lifestyle without cigarettes, usually 3 months or longer. Side effects of nicotine gum are primarily local and include jaw fatigue, sore mouth and throat, upset stomach, and hiccups.

Several different transdermal nicotine preparations are marketed—three deliver 21 or 22 mg over a 24-hour period, and one delivers 15 mg over 16 hours. Most have lower dose patches for tapering. Patches are applied in the morning and removed either the next morning or at bedtime, depending on the patch. Full-dose patches are recommended for most smokers for the first 1 to 3 months, followed by one to two tapering doses for 2 to 4 weeks each. Nicotine nasal spray, one spray into each nostril, delivers about 0.5 mg of nicotine systemically and can be used every 30 to 60 minutes. Local irritation of the nose commonly produces burning, sneezing, and watery eyes during initial treatment, but tolerance develops to these effects in 1 to 2 days. The nicotine inhaler delivers nicotine to the throat and upper airway, from where it is absorbed similarly to nicotine from gum. It is marketed as a cigarette-like plastic device and can be used *ad libitum.*

Nicotine medications seem to be safe in patients with cardiovascular disease and should be offered to cardiovascular patients.[2] Although smoking cessation medications are recommended by the manufacturer for relatively short-term use (generally 3 to 6 months), the use of these medications for 6 months or longer is safe and may be helpful in smokers who fear relapse without medications. Combination therapy—combining bupropion and nicotine or combining slow-release nicotine patches with preparations with more rapid release, such as gum, inhaler, or nasal spray—increases the likelihood of cessation compared with single-drug therapy.

Bupropion, also marketed as an antidepressant drug, is dosed at 150 to 300 mg/day for 7 days before stopping smoking, then at 300 mg/day for the next 6 to 12 weeks; sustained release preparation should be used. Bupropion also can be used in combination with a nicotine patch.[3] Bupropion in excessive doses can cause seizures and should not be used in individuals with a history of seizures or with eating disorders (bulimia or anorexia). On average, nicotine medications or bupropion treatment doubles the cessation rates found with placebo treatment, and absolute rates of smoking cessation have increased from 12% (placebo) to 24% (active medication) in clinical trials.

Follow-up office visits and/or telephone calls during and after active treatment increase long-term smoking cessation rates. Even in the best treatment circumstances, 70% or more of smokers relapse. Most smokers go through a quitting process three or four times before they finally succeed. When a quit attempt fails, the health care provider should encourage patients to try again as soon as they are ready. Cost-effectiveness studies find average costs per year of life saved of $400 to $900 for brief physician counseling alone and an incremental cost for adding a course of nicotine patch therapy of $2000 to $4000, depending on the individual's gender and age, to aid cessation. Smoking cessation treatment is much less costly per year of life saved than other widely accepted preventive therapies, including treatment of mild-to-moderate hypertension or hypercholesterolemia.

1. Hajek P, West R, Foulds J, et al: Randomized comparative trial of nicotine polacrilex, a transdermal patch, nasal spray, and an inhaler. Arch Intern Med 1999;159:2033–2038.
2. Joseph AM, Norman SM, Ferry LH, et al: The safety of transdermal nicotine as an aid to smoking cessation in patients with cardiac disease. N Engl J Med 1996;335:1792–1798.
3. Jorenby DE, Leischow SJ, Nides MA, et al: A controlled trial of sustained-release bupropion, a nicotine patch, or both for smoking cessation. N Engl J Med 1999;340:685–691.

SUGGESTED READINGS

Lancaster T, Stead L, Silagy C, Sowden A: Effectiveness of interventions to help people stop smoking: Findings from the Cochrane Library. BMJ 2000;321:355–358. *A meta-analysis of effectiveness of various interventions to promote smoking cessation.*

Peto R, Darby S, Deo H, et al: Smoking, smoking cessation, and lung cancer in the UK since 1950: Combination of national statistics with case-control studies. BMJ 2000;321:323–329. *Case-control studies show that smoking cessation even in middle age substantially reduces lung cancer risk.*

Rigotti NA: Treatment of tobacco use and dependence. N Engl J Med 2002;346:506–512. *A review of interventions includes behavioral and pharmacologic approaches to promote tobacco use cessation.*

Suskin N, Sheth T, Negassa A, Yusuf S: Relationship of current and past smoking to mortality and morbidity in patients with left ventricular dysfunction. J Am Coll Cardiol 2001;37:1677–1682. *An analysis of the Study of Left Ventricular Dysfunction (SOLVD) prevention and intervention trial shows that smoking is associated with increased morbidity and mortality and that smoking cessation is as or more effective than standard pharmacotherapy for left ventricular dysfunction in reducing morbidity and mortality.*

Tobacco Use and Dependence Clinical Practice Guideline Panel, Staff, and Consortium Representatives: A clinical practice guideline for treating tobacco use and dependence. A US Public Health Service Report. JAMA 2000;282:3244–3254. *Consensus recommendations on implementing smoking cessation for primary care physicians, smoking cessation specialists, and health care administrators.*

15 VIOLENCE AND INJURY

Elizabeth McLoughlin

Definitions

Serious violence and injury have life-altering consequences for victims and their families that often cannot be reversed. Prevention and treatment must be priorities. *Violence* in the United States is a public health epidemic that is caused by institutional and personal actions. The root causes of violence include inequitable social and economic conditions. *Personal violence* is the intentional use of physical or psychological force against another person or against oneself that may result in injury or death. An *injury* is damage to tissue usually caused by excessive energy transfer. Energy can be kinetic (causing fractures, lacerations, and contusions), thermal (burns and scalds), electrical (electrocutions), or chemical (poisonings). The mechanism is different for drowning and suffocation, which result when tissue is deprived of oxygen. Injuries may be classified in many ways, primarily by type, by cause, and by intent. *Type* of injury includes a fracture, laceration, or burn. *Cause* groupings distinguish among injuries caused by a car crash, a bullet, poisons, or a fall. *Intent* categories address whether the injury was unintentional, intentionally self-inflicted (the most severe outcome being suicide), or intentionally inflicted by another (the most severe outcome being homicide). Violent injuries such as homicide and suicide are positioned at the intersection of violence in general and all injuries.

Epidemiology

In 2000, 6% of all deaths in the United States were caused by an injury; 6% of all hospital discharges had a first listed diagnosis of

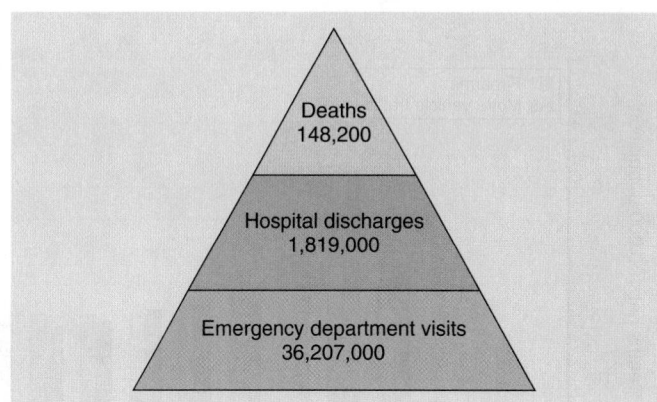

FIGURE 15–1 • Injury data (counts and estimates) for 2000. Data for deaths are from the National Vital Statistics System, hospitalizations are from the National Hospital Discharge Survey, and emergency department visits are from the National Hospital Ambulatory Medical Care Survey. (From National Center for Health Statistics, Hyattsville, MD, 2003.)

injury, and 35% of all emergency department visits were for injuries. Figure 15–1 presents the burden of injury at three levels of severity. Suicide and homicide account for about 31% of deaths from injury (Table 15–1).

The leading external causes of injury death in 2000, regardless of intent, were motor vehicle traffic crashes, firearms, poisoning (primarily by drug overdose), falls, suffocation (which includes suicide by hanging), drowning, and fire. As a result of the 29% decrease in firearm deaths between 1993 and 1998, motor vehicle crashes now exceed firearms as the leading cause of injury deaths for males of almost all age groups except among adults 25–29 and 70–74 years of age (Fig. 15–2). High rates of traffic deaths among elders are due in large part to their inability to survive serious injury. Among causes of firearm deaths, the peak in young men is primarily homicide, whereas the peak in older men is primarily suicide. Falls are the leading cause of injuries requiring hospitalization and, among the elderly, are a major cause of disability and loss of independent living (Chapter 23).

Violence in families is an increasingly recognized and complex problem. Being exposed to childhood abuse or living in a dysfunctional household has been found to produce a 12-fold increase in adult health risks for alcoholism, drug abuse, depression, and suicide attempts. An estimated 880,000 children were victims of substantiated maltreatment in 2000. Almost three fifths suffered neglect, whereas one fifth suffered physical abuse, and approximately 10% were sexually abused. In a 1998 national survey, almost one third of female respondents reported being physically or sexually abused by a husband or boyfriend at some point in their lives. Another national survey estimated that at least 0.5 million older persons in domestic settings were abused and/or neglected or experienced self-neglect and that for every reported incident, approximately five go unreported.

Alcohol consumption is a major risk factor for all types of injury, although estimates of involvement vary widely, and hospital-based medical records do not routinely document levels of blood alcohol. One review found evidence of alcohol involvement in 21 to 77% of fatal falls, 18 to 53% of nonfatal falls, 21 to 47% of drowning deaths, and 9 to 86% of burn deaths. The findings of the various studies were difficult to compare because they varied greatly in the age groups examined and the way they tested for alcohol involvement. The U.S. Department of Transportation reported alcohol involvement in about 40% of all traffic fatalities in 2001.

The terrorist attacks in September 2001 and anthrax-related deaths and illnesses have drawn increased awareness to the vulnerability of the U.S. population and infrastructure and the importance of public health agencies and emergency medical services. After these attacks, gun purchases and alcohol consumption, two factors known to increase the incidence of injury and violence, have increased. Physicians also may find an increase in the prevalence of anxiety and post-traumatic stress disorders among patients.

Secular Trends in Injuries

Injuries are preventable. Data on injury deaths from 1910 to 2000 show a significant decrease in unintentional injury death rates

Preventive and Environmental Medicine

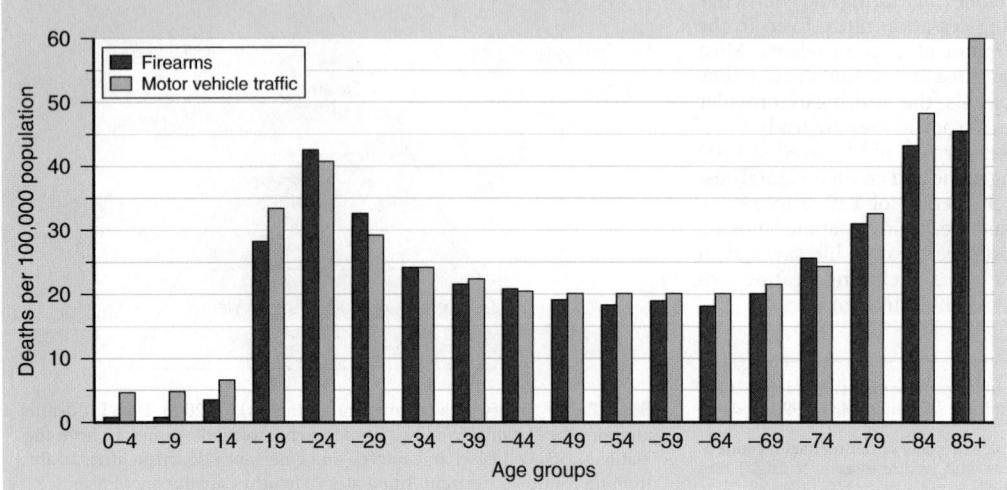

FIGURE 15–2 • Firearms and motor vehicle traffic crashes: male death rates by age groups, United States, 2000. (Data from 2000 Injury Mortality Data. Available on WISQUARS, http://www.cdc.gov/ncipc/.)

Table 15–1 • NUMBERS* AND RATES† OF INJURY DEATHS IN THE UNITED STATES (2000) BY INTENTIONALITY AND MECHANISM

	BOTH SEXES	RATE	MALE	RATE	FEMALE	RATE	%
All injury deaths	148,209	53.69	103,254	79.63	44,955	29.97	
DISTRIBUTION BY INTENTIONALITY							
Unintentional	97,900	35.47	63,817	50.02	34,083	22.29	66.1
Suicide	29,350	10.64	23,618	18.08	5732	4.03	19.8
Homicide	16,765	6.06	12,820	9.33	3945	2.81	11.3
Undetermined and other	4194	1.52	2999	2.23	1195	0.85	2.8
DISTRIBUTION BY MECHANISM							
Motor vehicle traffic	41,994	15.22	28,352	21.33	13,642	9.53	28.3
Firearms	28,663	10.38	24,582	18.54	4081	2.89	19.3
Poisoning	20,230	7.33	13,695	10.13	6535	4.61	13.6
Falls	14,002	5.08	7605	6.87	6395	3.72	9.4
Suffocation	12,098	4.39	8110	6.39	3988	2.58	8.2
Drowning	4073	1.47	3127	2.30	946	0.67	2.7
Fire/flame	3907	1.42	2322	1.82	1585	1.07	2.6
All other	23,242	8.44	15,459	11.48	7783	5.53	15.7

*Excludes adverse-related deaths (International Classification of Diseases, Injuries and Causes of Death codes [Y40-Y98]).

†Per 100,000 population; age-adjusted rates are based on the 2000 standard population.

From the National Vital Statistics System, 2000. Hyattsville, MD, National Center for Health Statistics, Centers for Disease Control and Prevention, 2003.

secondary to causes other than motor vehicles (Fig. 15–3). This decrease was due in part to improved safety design of occupational machinery and other protective measures, the mechanization of agriculture and industry, labeling and packaging of drugs and toxic products, and improved medical care. Between 1912 and 1995, unintentional work deaths per 100,000 population were reduced by 90%, from 21 to 2. In 1912, an estimated 18,000 to 21,000 workers' lives were lost; in 2000, in a work force that had more than tripled in size and produced 13 times more goods and services, there were only 5915 work-related deaths.

The death rate from motor vehicle crashes increased 10-fold from 1910 to 1930 as cars became the primary form of transportation. This death rate decreased by 30% in the 1980s and 1990s owing in part to improved safety features in vehicles and roads, temporary lowering of speed limits, increased legal drinking age, and public intolerance of drinking and driving.

The homicide rate had two major fluctuations in the 20th century. It increased from 6 per 100,000 population in 1910 to 9 per 100,000 population in 1930, decreased during World War II and the postwar period (1940s to 1960s) to approximately 5, then increased to greater than 10 in the 1980s and early 1990s, attributable in part to drug trafficking and the enormous number of guns in circulation. Between 1993 and 2000, however, there was an estimated 44% decrease in

violent crimes, but the numbers now seem to be increasing. The suicide rate has shown less variability but has been consistently higher than the homicide rate throughout the 20th century.

Ways to Reduce Injury

An example of the effectiveness of a public policy to prevent injury is the reduction in deaths and nonfatal head injuries in motorcyclists after enactment of the mandatory helmet laws. Hospital charges for injuries to California motorcyclists declined markedly in the 2 years (1992 to 1993) after enactment of the law, with charges related to head injuries decreasing by 58%. Certain personal and family actions can prevent injury from known hazards (Table 15–2), and enactment of public policies has the potential to reduce injury.

ALCOHOL-RELATED INJURY

BEHAVIORS. Avoid binge drinking; promote alcohol moderation; provide nonalcoholic beverages at social gatherings; drive sober.

POLICIES. Permit community control over the number and location of alcohol outlets in neighborhoods; restrict alcohol advertising that is attractive and available to children.

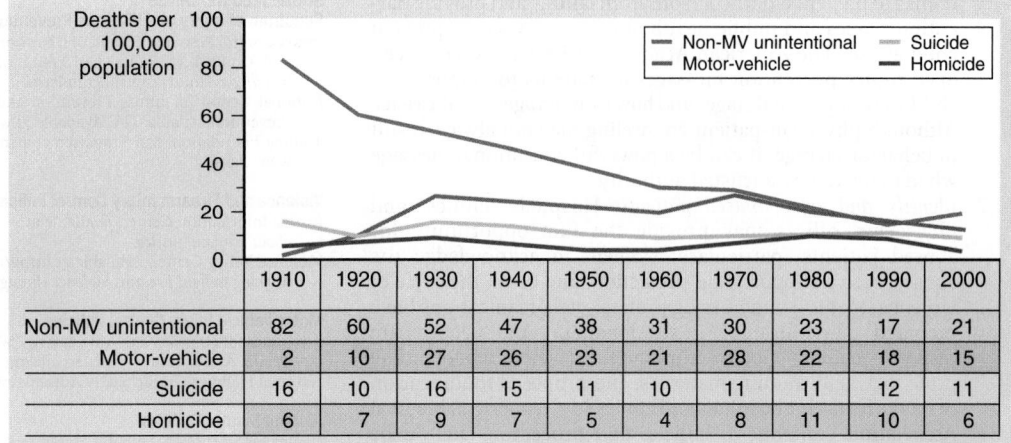

FIGURE 15–3 • Trends in injury death rates, United States, 1910 to 2000. (Updated from Baker SP, O'Neill B, Ginsburg MJ, et al: The Injury Fact Book, 2nd ed. New York, Oxford University Press, 1992, using 1990 and 2000 data from the National Vital Statistics System. National Center for Health Statistics, Hyattsville, MD, 2001.)

	1910	1920	1930	1940	1950	1960	1970	1980	1990	2000
Non-MV unintentional	82	60	52	47	38	31	30	23	17	21
Motor-vehicle	2	10	27	26	23	21	28	22	18	15
Suicide	16	10	16	15	11	10	11	11	12	11
Homicide	6	7	9	7	5	4	8	11	10	6

Table 15–2 • SOME KEY MEASURES TO PREVENT INJURY

INJURY	FOR PUBLIC POLICY	FOR PATIENTS
Motor vehicle	Enact and enforce seat belt, child restraint, and motorcycle helmet laws	Use seat belts, child restraints Use helmets when riding bicycles and motorcycles
Firearms	Ban assault weapons Enforce waiting period for firearm purchase	Remove firearms from home If gun in home, store locked and unloaded
Fire and burns	Mandate fire-safe cigarettes	Maintain smoke detectors; install sprinklers
Drowning	Mandate 4-sided fencing of pools	Wear flotation devices when boating
Falls		Install guards on balconies, windows; install handrails in elders' homes
Alcohol	Advocate for local control of alcohol outlets Restrict alcohol advertising that appeals to children	Drive sober Avoid binge drinking
Actions for physicians	Counsel patients about injury and prevention (see above) Identify and refer abused patients to social/legal services Insist on adequate physical/occupational rehabilitation Improve injury databases and use them to design preventive strategies Become knowledgeable about and advocate sound public policies	

MOTOR VEHICLE CRASHES

BEHAVIORS. Wear seat belts to maximize the protection offered by air bags; keep children properly restrained in the back seat; wear helmets while riding motorcycles and bicycles; drive sober.

POLICIES. Enact or maintain motorcycle helmet laws; improve public transportation to reduce dependence on cars; support "traffic easing" interventions in urban areas.

FIREARMS

BEHAVIORS. Remove guns from the home (or at least store unloaded, locked, and out of reach of children).

POLICIES. Restrict the purchase and possession of handguns in the home, up to and including bans (official policy of the American Academy of Pediatrics and the American Public Health Association).

FIRE AND BURN INJURIES

BEHAVIORS. Install and maintain smoke detectors or residential sprinklers; reduce the temperature settings in residential hot water heaters to 125°F.

POLICIES. Establish mandatory flammability performance standards for cigarettes to prevent furniture ignition.

DROWNING

BEHAVIORS. Wear flotation devices while boating.

POLICIES. Require four-sided isolation fences with self-latching gates on all residential pools.

FALLS

BEHAVIORS. Develop and/or maintain flexibility and agility among elders; improve lighting and install handgrip devices in the home; install guards on balconies and windows in high-rise buildings.

POLICIES. Install suicide-guards on places known to invite suicides, such as bridges and tall buildings.

Violence and injuries are complex, pervasive problems that must be reduced through comprehensive, multidisciplinary interventions. As is the case with preventing diseases such as acquired immunodeficiency syndrome and smoking-associated cancers, preventing violence and injuries requires that physicians intervene at the individual level and in the social and political processes that determine the prevalence of these conditions.

Implications for Medical Practice

Traditionally, physicians have focused on treating and counseling individual patients and have concentrated on knowledge, attitudes, and behaviors. Evidence from successful injury prevention efforts suggests that equal attention should be given to public policies to prevent injury. To reduce violence and injuries, physicians can do the following:

1. *Counsel patients about injury risk and prevention.* All physicians, regardless of specialty, have the opportunity to advise patients and families about actions they can take to prevent injury. Physicians should refer patients to community resources that can assist them to prevent injury, such as programs that teach proper placement of children in car seats, show how to modify

Preventive and Environmental Medicine

homes to prevent elderly persons from falling, and provide parenting classes and public health nurse home visits to prevent child abuse. The American Academy of Pediatrics has developed injury prevention messages for parents to emphasize a child's developmental stages and how to avoid age-specific risks. Although physician-patient counseling may not always result in behavior change, it can be a powerful educational message when delivered by a trusted authority.

2. *Identify and refer abused patients.* Hospitals, clinics, and physicians' offices may provide the first opportunity for abused patients, particularly women, to acknowledge the abuse, receive support, find protection, and break the cycle of violence. Medical and nursing professional organizations have prepared guidelines for institutionalizing the health care response to family violence through the development of model protocols, staff training materials, and proposed modification of intake forms for hospitals and clinics (e.g., American Medical Association guidelines). Policies and procedures should be adapted to individual hospital needs and address state-specific regulations about reporting abuse to authorities. Health care providers can assist abused patients best by working collaboratively with local social and legal services and by referring patients to these resources.

3. *Emphasize rehabilitation and community follow-up.* Tertiary prevention involves minimizing functional disability, a consequence of serious injury. Physicians can help their patients return to productive lives by ensuring that patients receive appropriate physical and occupational therapy and that they have access to community services after discharge. The independent living movement and local centers for independent living and state departments of rehabilitation can provide role models and resources for people with disabilities. Because community social and mental health services are essential for prevention and rehabilitation, physicians can serve patients by publicly speaking out in support of these services.

4. *Improve the injury database for research and prevention.* Information about the mechanisms and intentionality of injury must be gathered by coroners, medical examiners, and health care providers, and these findings must be documented in official records. The usefulness of nonfatal injury data would be increased if all states established centralized hospital and emergency department databases that included codes for external cause of injury.

5. *Advocate for public policy solutions to the violence and injury problem.* Physicians have played a leadership role in injury control in such diverse areas as traffic safety, burns from tap water and clothing ignition, and firearms policy. Today's injury problems call for augmented medical leadership in policy areas. Legislators and journalists turn to physicians for information about disease and injury because physicians have daily contact with sick and injured people and can speak from personal experience about the problem. Informed physicians can advocate for solutions by testifying at legislative hearings, by granting media interviews, by making presentations at professional meetings, and by teaching medical students and residents about injury prevention principles and strategies. The Internet sites listed in the reference section provide the most recent data on statistics, policies, and programs related to violence and injury.

Future Directions

Globalization offers opportunities and challenges. One challenge is to balance the priorities of free trade with the priorities of national health and safety, a subject that may seem distant from the practice of medicine but that affects the health of populations in the United States and abroad. One opportunity is to support international efforts to regulate the small weapons trade, which supplies arms to combatants and escalates deadly conflicts around the world.

1. Harborview Medical Center, Injury Prevention and Research Center: Systematic reviews of childhood injury prevention interventions. Available at http://depts.washington.edu/hiprc/childinjury/. *Data from the Cochrane Collaborative reviews of research on the prevention of injuries to children.*

SUGGESTED READINGS
Spectrum of Injury and Violence Prevention Resources
Injury Control Resource Information Network, sponsored by the Center for Injury Research and Control (CIRCL), University of Pittsburgh, Pittsburgh, PA. Available at http://www.injurycontrol.com/icrin.
National Center for Injury Prevention and Control, Centers for Disease Control and Prevention, Atlanta, GA. Available at www.cdc.gov/ncipc.
Trauma Foundation, San Francisco General Hospital, San Francisco, CA. Available at www.tf.org.

Violence and Firearm Injury Control Policies
Justice Information Center. Available at www.ncjrs.org. *Federal government information about criminal justice.*
Violence Policy Center. Available at http://www.vpc.org. *National nonprofit organization working to fight firearms violence through research, education, and advocacy.*

Motor Vehicle Injury Control Policies
Advocates for Highway and Auto Safety, 750 First Street, NE, Suite 901, Washington, DC 20002. Available at www.saferoads.org.
National Highway Traffic Safety Administration. Available at www.nhtsa.dot.gov.

Alcohol Control Policies
Center for Science in the Public Interest. Available at http://www.cspinet.org/booze/index.html.
National Institute on Alcohol Abuse and Alcoholism. Available at http://www.niaaa.nih.gov/.

Textbook
Rivara FP, Cummings P, Koepsell TD, et al: Injury Control: A Guide to Research and Program Evaluation. Cambridge, UK, Cambridge University Press, 2001.

16 IMMUNIZATION

Walter A. Orenstein

Immunization is one of the most cost-effective means of preventing morbidity and mortality from infectious diseases. Routine immunization, particularly of children, has resulted in decreases of 90% or more in reported cases of measles, mumps, rubella, congenital rubella syndrome, polio, tetanus, diphtheria, and pertussis. In many circumstances, immunization not only prevents morbidity and mortality, but also, in the long run, reduces health care costs.

General Characteristics of Immunizations

Immunization protects against disease or the sequelae of disease through the administration of an immunobiologic—vaccines, toxoids, immune globulin preparations, and antitoxins. Protection induced by immunization can be active or passive.

ACTIVE IMMUNIZATION. Administering a vaccine or toxoid causes the body to produce an immune response against the infectious agent or its toxins. Vaccines consist of suspensions of live (usually attenuated) or inactivated microorganisms or fractions thereof. Toxoids are modified bacterial toxins that retain immunogenic properties but lack toxicity. Active immunization generally results in long-term immunity, although the onset of protection may be delayed because it takes time for the body to respond. With live attenuated vaccines, small quantities of living organisms multiply within the recipient until an immune response cuts off replication. In contrast, inactivated vaccines and toxoids contain large quantities of antigen. In most recipients, a single dose of a live vaccine generally induces an immune response that closely parallels natural infection and induces long-term immunity. Killed vaccines, in contrast, often require multiple doses.

PASSIVE IMMUNIZATION. Passive immunization using immune globulins or antitoxins delivers preformed antibodies to provide temporary immunity. Immune globulins obtained from human blood may contain antibodies to a variety of agents, depending on the pool of human plasma from which they are prepared. Specific immune globulins are made from the plasma of donors with high levels of antibodies to specific antigens, such as tetanus immune globulin. Most immune globulins must be injected intramuscularly. Antitoxins are solutions of antibodies derived from animals immunized with specific antigens (e.g., diphtheria antitoxin). Passive immunization usually is indicated to protect individuals immediately before anticipated exposure or shortly after known or suspected exposure to an infectious agent (Table 16–1), when active immunization either is not possible or has not been adequate.

ROUTE AND TIMING OF VACCINATION. Each immunobiologic has a preferred site and route of administration. In adults, vaccines containing adjuvants should be injected intramuscularly, preferably in the

Table 16–1 • PASSIVE IMMUNIZATIONS FOR ADULTS

DISEASE	NAME OF MATERIAL	COMMENTS AND USE
Tetanus	Tetanus immune globulin, human	Management of tetanus-prone wounds in persons without adequate prior active immunization and treatment of tetanus
Cytomegalovirus	Cytomegalovirus immune globulin, intravenous	Prophylaxis for bone marrow and kidney transplant recipients
Diphtheria	Diphtheria antitoxin, equine	Treatment of established disease, high frequency of reactions to serum of nonhuman origin. In the U.S., available only from CDC
Rabies	Rabies immunoglobulin, human	Postexposure prophylaxis of animal bites
Measles	Immune globulin, human	Prevention or modification of disease in contacts of cases, not for control of epidemics
Hepatitis A	Immune globulin, human	Protection of household contacts, pre-exposure prophylaxis for travelers who need protection before immunity can be achieved with hepatitis A vaccine
Hepatitis B	Hepatitis B immune globulin, human	Prophylaxis for needlestick or mucous membrane contact with HBsAg-positive persons, for sexual partners with acute hepatitis B or hepatitis B carriers, for infants born to mothers who are carriers of HBsAg, for infants whose mother or primary caregiver has acute hepatitis B
Varicella	Varicella-zoster immune globulin	Persons with underlying disease and at risk of complications from chickenpox who have not had varicella or varicella vaccine and who are exposed to varicella. May be given postexposure to known susceptible adults, particularly if antibody-negative
Vaccinia	Vaccinia immune globulin	Treatment of eczema vaccinatum, vaccinia necrosum, and severe inadvertent inoculations such as ocular vaccinia after vaccinia (smallpox) vaccination
Erythroblastosis fetalis	Rh immune globulin	Rh-negative women who give birth to Rh-positive infants or who abort
Hypogammaglobulinemia	Immune globulin, intravenous	Maintenance therapy
Idiopathic thrombocytopenic purpura	Immune globulin, intravenous	Therapy for acute episodes
Botulism	Trivalent A, B, and E antitoxin, equine	Treatment of botulism; available through CDC
Snakebite	Antivenin, equine (North American coral snake antivenin)	Specific for North American coral snake, *Micrurus fulvius*
	Crotalidae, polyvalent	Effective for viper and pit viper bites, including rattlesnakes, copperheads, moccasins
Spider bite	Antivenin, equine	Specific for black widow spider, *Latrodectus mactans*, and other members of the genus

HBsAg = hepatitis B surface antigen.

deltoid muscle. For most adults, intramuscular injections should be administered using a 1–1½ inch, 22–25 gauge needle. Use of the buttocks is discouraged except when large volumes are required because of the potential for damage to the sciatic nerve and because of diminished immune response to some vaccines, such as hepatitis B. Subcutaneous vaccines also are usually administered in the deltoid area, and intradermal vaccines are usually given on the volar surface of the forearm. In general, inactivated vaccines and toxoids can be given simultaneously at different sites. With vaccines that frequently cause side effects, it may be best to separate administration by at least 1 week. Live and inactivated vaccines usually can be administered at the same time. Measles, mumps, and rubella (MMR) vaccine can be administered at the same time as inactivated polio vaccine and live attenuated varicella vaccine. With the exception of a parenterally administered vaccine, such as MMR, and an orally administered live vaccine, such as oral typhoid vaccine, which can be administered at any interval, live vaccines not delivered on the same day should be separated by at least 1 month to avoid interference. Immune globulin also may interfere with the take of live vaccines; ideally, most live vaccines should be administered at least 2 weeks before or 3 to 11 months after immune globulin. Immune globulin does not interfere with the response to yellow fever vaccine.

ADVERSE REACTIONS. No vaccine is completely safe or completely effective. Suspected adverse events temporally related to vaccinations should be reported to the Vaccine Adverse Events Reporting System (1-800-822-7967 or *www.vaers.org*). Hypersensitivity to vaccine components, such as animal proteins, antibiotics, preservatives, and stabilizers, can lead to local and systemic reactions ranging from mild to severe. The egg protein contained in vaccines grown in chicken eggs (influenza and yellow fever vaccines) may cause reactions in persons allergic to eggs. In general, persons without anaphylactic-type allergies to eggs can be given these vaccines safely, but persons with anaphylactic reactions to eggs generally should not receive these

vaccines except when absolutely necessary and then only under established protocols by physicians who are expert in such situations. Although measles and mumps vaccines are grown in chick embryo tissue culture, the risk of anaphylaxis even in persons with severe hypersensitivity to eggs is low, so they can be vaccinated without prior testing.

GENERAL CONSIDERATIONS. Two major groups make comprehensive, detailed recommendations regarding immunization of adults: (1) the Task Force on Adult Immunization of the American College of Physicians (ACP) and the Infectious Diseases Society of America (IDSA), which publishes the *Guide for Adult Immunization*, and (2) the Advisory Committee on Immunization Practices of the U.S. Public Health Service. The latter group publishes its information in *Morbidity and Mortality Weekly Report* (also available at *www.cdc.gov/nip*). Immunizations for adults depend on age, lifestyle, occupation, and medical conditions (Table 16–2). All adults should have a primary series of tetanus and diphtheria toxoids with boosters of combined toxoids (Td) every 10 years. Persons born in or after 1957 should have evidence of immunity to measles, mumps, and rubella. Vaccination of susceptible adolescents and adults against varicella is desirable. Pneumococcal vaccine and annual vaccination against influenza are indicated for all adults 65 years old and older and younger adults with certain medical conditions that place them at high risk of complications. Influenza vaccine also is recommended for all adults 50 to 64 years of age. People caring for patients at high risk of complications from influenza should receive annual vaccination. Health care workers exposed to blood or blood products should receive hepatitis B vaccine. Health care workers likely to come in contact with persons transmitting measles, mumps, rubella, or varicella should be immune to those diseases.

IMMUNOCOMPROMISE. Patients with conditions that compromise their immune systems should not receive live attenuated vaccines. Such patients include those with immunodeficiency diseases, leukemia,

Text continued on page 70.

Preventive and Environmental Medicine

Table 16–2 • SELECTED IMMUNIZING AGENTS INDICATED FOR ADULTS*

DISEASE	IMMUNIZING AGENT	INDICATIONS	SCHEDULE	MAJOR CONTRAINDICATIONS AND PRECAUTIONS	COMMENTS
Anthrax	Anthrax vaccine, adsorbed, an inactivated vaccine	Pre-exposure prophylaxis of persons at high risk of exposure (e.g., military, certain laboratory workers), consider with antibiotics for post-exposure prophylaxis	0.5 mL dose SC at 0, 2, and 4 wk and 6, 12, and 18 mo. Manufacturer recommends booster annually thereafter. If used postexposure, 3 doses at 0, 2, and 4 wk with antibiotics for at least 7–14 days after third dose	Previous anaphylaxis to a prior dose or to a vaccine component	Effectiveness against aerosol exposure inferred primarily from animal data. Limited data on the benefits of postexposure use
Diphtheria	Tetanus and diphtheria toxoids combined	All adults	Two doses IM 4 wk apart, third dose 6–12 mo after second dose for primary series, booster every 10 yr, no need to repeat if schedule is interrupted	History of neurologic or severe hypersensitivity reaction after a previous dose	
Hepatitis A	Inactivated hepatitis A vaccine	Travelers to highly or intermediately endemic countries, men who have sex with men; illegal drug users (injectors and noninjectors); persons who work with hepatitis A virus–infected primates or who do research with the virus; persons with chronic liver disease; recipients of clotting factors	Two doses at least 6 mo apart for persons ≥2 yr old	Hypersensitivity to vaccine components	Recommended for children and adolescents in states or communities with high hepatitis A incidence. Should be considered for outbreak control
Hepatitis B	Inactivated hepatitis B virus subunit vaccine containing HBsAg	Adolescents; health care and public safety workers potentially exposed to blood; clients and staff of institutions for the developmentally disabled; hemodialysis patients; men who have sex with men; users of illicit injectable drugs; recipients of clotting factors; household and sexual contacts of HBV carriers; inmates of long-term correctional facilities; heterosexuals treated for sexually transmitted diseases or with multiple sexual partners; travelers with close contact for ≥6 mo with populations with high prevalence of HBV carriage	IM; three doses at 0, 1, and 6 mo		Pregnancy should not be considered a contraindication if the woman is otherwise eligible. Health care workers who have contact with patients or blood, sexual contacts of persons with chronic HBV infection, hemodialysis patients, and recipients of clotting factor concentrates should be tested 1–2 mo after vaccination to determine serologic response
Influenza	Inactivated influenza virus vaccine	All adults ≥50 years old; with greatest priority for those ≥65 years old; other adults with high-risk conditions; adults caring for persons with high-risk conditions, including medical personnel (see text); women who will be in second or third trimester of pregnancy during influenza season	Annual vaccination; see annual ACIP recommendation	Anaphylactic hypersensitivity to eggs	

Table 16–2 • SELECTED IMMUNIZING AGENTS INDICATED FOR ADULTS*—cont'd

DISEASE	IMMUNIZING AGENT	INDICATIONS	SCHEDULE	MAJOR CONTRAINDICATIONS AND PRECAUTIONS	COMMENTS
Japanese encephalitis	Inactivated Japanese encephalitis virus vaccine	Travelers to Asia spending at least 1 mo in endemic areas during transmission season	Three 1-mL doses SC on days 0, 7, 30; shortened schedule of 0, 7, 14 days may be used when necessary. Booster doses may be given after 2 yr	Persons with a history of urticaria are at greater risk of adverse reactions to vaccine; pregnancy	No data exist on concurrent administration with vaccines other than DTP, drugs (e.g., chloroquine, mefloquine), or other biologics
Measles	Live-virus vaccine	All adults born after 1956 without history of live vaccine on or after first birthday, physician-diagnosed measles, or detectable measles antibody; persons born before 1957 generally can be considered immune	One dose sufficient for most adults; 2 doses at least 1 mo apart indicated for persons entering college or medical facility employment, traveling abroad, or at risk of measles during outbreaks	Altered immunity (e.g., leukemia, lymphoma, generalized malignancy, congenital immunodeficiency suppressive therapy), immune globulin or other blood products within prior 3–11 mo depending on dose of immune globulin or blood product received, untreated tuberculosis, anaphylactic hypersensitivity to neomycin or gelatin, pregnancy, thrombocytopenia	Persons with anaphylactic allergies to eggs may be vaccinated (see text). Vaccine should be administered to persons with asymptomatic HIV infection and should be considered for patients except those with severe immunocompromise
Meningococcal disease	Polysaccharide vaccine containing tetravalent A, C, W135, and Y	Terminal complement component deficiencies, anatomic or functional asplenia, travelers who will live in areas with hyperendemic or epidemic diseases; may be useful during localized oubreaks. College freshmen living in dormitories are at increased risk of disease; offer vaccine, if desired by the patient and parent	One dose		Consider revaccination after 3–5 yr for adults at increased risk of disease
Mumps	Live-virus vaccine	All adults born after 1956 without history of live vaccine on or after first birthday, physician-diagnosed mumps, or detectable mumps antibody; persons born before 1957 generally can be considered immune	One dose	Altered immunity (e.g., leukemia, lymphoma, generalized malignancy, congenital immunodeficiency, immunosuppressive therapy), immune globulin or other blood products within prior 3–11 mo, anaphylactic hypersensitivity to neomycin or gelatin, pregnancy, thrombocytopenia if adminstered with measles vaccine	Although persons born after 1957 are generally immune, vaccine can be given to adults of all ages and may be particularly indicated for postpubertal males who are thought to be susceptible. Persons with anaphylactic allergies to eggs may be vaccinated

Continued on page 68.

Table 16–2 • SELECTED IMMUNIZING AGENTS INDICATED FOR ADULTS*—cont'd

DISEASE	IMMUNIZING AGENT	INDICATIONS	SCHEDULE	MAJOR CONTRAINDICATIONS AND PRECAUTIONS	COMMENTS
Pneumococcal disease	23-valent polysaccharide vaccine	Adults with cardiovascular disease, pulmonary disease, diabetes mellitus, alcoholism, cirrhosis, cerebrospinal fluid leaks, splenic dysfunction or anatomic asplenia, Hodgkin's disease, lymphoma, multiple myeloma, chronic renal failure, nephrotic syndrome, immunosuppression, HIV infection; high-risk populations such as certain Native Americans and *all* adults ≥65 years old	One dose IM or SC. A second dose should be considered ≥5 yr later for adults at high risk of disease (e.g., asplenic patients) and those who lose antibody rapidly (e.g., nephrotic syndrome, renal failure, transplant recipients). Revaccinate adults who received a first dose when <65 years old who are now ≥65 years old and who received their vaccine at least 5 years earlier		A 7-valent conjugate pneumococcal vaccine is not indicated for adults
Poliomyelitis	Inactivated poliovirus vaccine (IPV)	Certain adults who are at greater risk of exposure to wild poliovirus than the general population, including travelers to countries where polio is epidemic or endemic, members of community or specific populations with disease caused by wild poliovirus, laboratory workers handling specimens that may contain poliovirus, health care workers in close contact with wild poliovirus	For unvaccinated adults, two doses SC 4 wk apart and a third dose 6–12 mo after the second; if <4 wk available before protection is needed, a single dose of IPV. For incompletely immunized adults, complete primary series that consists of three doses of IPV or prior oral polio vaccine (OPV); no need to restart interrupted series. A single dose of IPV can be given to adults who previously received a primary series but now are at high risk, such as travel to an endemic area.	On theoretical grounds, pregnant women should not receive IPV. If immediate protection is needed, IPV can be used	
Rabies	Inactivated vaccine, HDCV, PCEC, or RVA	High-risk persons, including animal handlers, selected laboratory and field workers, and persons traveling for ≥1 mo to areas with high risk of rabies	Pre-exposure prophylaxis: three doses of 1.0 mL IM for HDCV, PCEC, or RVA on days 0, 7, and 21 or 28.	History of severe hypersensitivity reaction	Further doses needed after exposure. If to be given concurrently with chloroquine, only IM route should be used
Rubella	Live-virus vaccine	Adults, particularly women of childbearing age, who lack history of rubella vaccine and detectable rubella-specific antibodies in serum; males and females in institutions where rubella outbreaks may occur, such as hospitals, the military, and colleges. Persons born before 1957, except women who can become pregnant, generally can be considered immune	One dose SC	Pregnancy, altered immunity (e.g., leukemia, lymphoma, generalized malignancy, congenital immunodeficiency, immunosuppressive therapy), immune globulin or other blood products within the 3–11 mo before vaccination, anaphylactic hypersensitivity to neomycin. Administration of blood products should not contraindicate postpartum vaccination; thrombocytopenia if administered with measles vaccine	Women should be counseled to avoid pregnancy for 1 mo

Table 16–2 • SELECTED IMMUNIZING AGENTS INDICATED FOR ADULTS*—cont'd

DISEASE	IMMUNIZING AGENT	INDICATIONS	SCHEDULE	MAJOR CONTRAINDICATIONS AND PRECAUTIONS	COMMENTS
Smallpox	Live vaccinia virus	Persons working with orthopox viruses, members of public health and health care response teams	One dose intracutaneously using a bifurcated needle. Boosters every 10 yr and perhaps every 3 yr for persons working with virulent orthopox viruses	History or presence of eczema or other acute, chronic, or exfoliative skin condition, immunosuppression, pregnancy, in patient or a close household or personal contact. Breast feeding. Age < 1 year. Allergy to a vaccine component. No contraindications if exposed to smallpox	Some complications of vaccination are treatable with VIG. Vaccine is effective 3–4 days postexposure to variola and perhaps longer to prevent or modify the illness. Serious adverse events rare but significant, including eczema vaccinatum, progressive vaccinia, myopericarditis, and autoinoculation, encephalitis. Vaccinia is transmissible
Tetanus	Tetanus and diphtheria toxoids combined	All adults	Three doses IM needed for primary series: two doses 4 wk apart, third dose 6–12 mo after second dose, booster every 10 yr; no need to repeat if schedule is interrupted	History of neurologic or severe hypersensitivity reaction after a previous dose	Special recommendations for wound treatment (see text). Persons with GBS within the first 6 wk after immunization, particularly adults who received a prior primary series, probably should not be revaccinated in most circumstances
Typhoid fever	Vi capsular polysaccharide vaccine, live attenuated Ty21a oral vaccine	Travelers to areas where the risk of prolonged exposure to contaminated food and water is high; may be considered for family and intimate contacts of carriers and laboratory workers who work with *Salmonella typhi*	Vi polysaccharide vaccine: one dose IM 0.5 mL, boosters every 2 yr *Oral vaccine:* 4 doses on alternate days, boosters every 5 yr	Severe local or systemic reaction to a prior dose. Ty21A vaccine should not be administered to persons with altered immunity or those receiving antimicrobial agents	Efficacy only 50–77%. Food and water precautions essential
Varicella	Attenuated varicella vaccine, OKA strain	Persons, including health care workers, who have contact with patients, at high risk of complications from varicella; persons who work with children (e.g., teachers), persons in institutions that may have outbreaks (e.g., colleges), nonpregnant women of childbearing age, international travelers; desirable for other susceptible adolescents and adults	Two 0.5-mL SC doses 4–8 wk apart for persons ≥13 years old	Immunocompromise, pregnancy, allergy to vaccine components. Manufacturer recommends to avoid salicylate use for 6 wk after vaccination	Adults with a history of prior varicella should be considered immune. Vaccine virus has rarely been transmitted to contacts from healthy vaccinees in whom rash developed. Women who receive vaccine should not become pregnant for 1 mo
Yellow fever	Live attenuated virus (17D strain)	Persons living or traveling in areas where yellow fever exists	One dose; booster every 10 yr	Immunocompromised persons; history of anaphylactic allergies to eggs; pregnancy on theoretical grounds, although may be given if risk is high	Fever, jaundice, and multiple organ system failure (viscerotropic disease) have been rarely reported in recipients of 17D-derived yellow fever vaccinations. Vaccinate only persons traveling to areas endemic to yellow fever

*See the text and package inserts for further details, particularly regarding indications, dosage, mode of administration, side effects, and adverse reactions and contraindications.

SC = subcutaneously; IM = intramuscularly; ID = intradermally; HBV = hepatitis B virus; ACIP = Advisory Committee on Immunization Practices; DTP = diphtheria-tetanus-pertussis; HIV = human immunodeficiency virus; IPV = inactivated polio vaccine; OPV = live-virus trivalent oral polio vaccine; HDCV = human diploid cell vaccine for rabies; RVA = rabies vaccine absorbed; PCEC = purified chick embryo cell culture rabies vaccine; GBS = Guillain-Barré syndrome.

lymphoma, and generalized malignancy and those who are immuno-suppressed from therapy with corticosteroids, alkylating agents, antimetabolites, and radiation. An exception is infection with human immunodeficiency virus (HIV). Asymptomatic patients should receive MMR vaccine. MMR should be considered for symptomatic patients with HIV; however, severely immunocompromised persons should not be vaccinated. Patients with leukemia in remission who have not been receiving any chemotherapy for at least 3 months may receive live-virus vaccines. Short-course therapy (<2 weeks) with corticosteroids, alternate-day regimens with low-to-moderate doses of short-acting corticosteroids, and topical applications or tendon injections are not ordinarily contraindications to the administration of live vaccines.

Immunocompromised patients can receive inactivated vaccines and toxoids, although the efficacy of such preparations may be diminished. Patients with known HIV infection should receive pneumococcal vaccine and annual influenza vaccination.

PREGNANCY. In general, live vaccines should not be given to pregnant women because of the theoretical concern that the vaccines could adversely affect the fetus. No significant adverse events attributable to vaccination of pregnant women with MMR or varicella have been documented; nevertheless, pregnant women should not receive MMR or varicella vaccine, and women who do receive these vaccines should wait 1 month before becoming pregnant. Polio and yellow fever vaccines usually should not be given to pregnant women unless the risk of disease is substantial. Td vaccination is especially indicated for pregnant women who are not appropriately vaccinated to prevent neonatal tetanus in their infants. Vaccination is done best after the first trimester. All pregnant women should be screened for hepatitis B surface antigen (HBsAg). Offspring of HBsAg carrier mothers should receive hepatitis B vaccine and hepatitis B immune globulin within 12 hours of birth. Women who will be in the second or third trimester of pregnancy during the influenza season should receive influenza vaccine.

Individual Immunobiologics

HEPATITIS A

Two inactivated hepatitis A (Chapter 151) vaccines are available in the United States. Seroconversion rates after a single dose of either vaccine in persons older than 2 years exceed 95%. Antibody levels shown to be protective in animals develop in almost all persons.

The vaccine is indicated primarily for persons traveling to countries, generally the developing world, with high or intermediate endemicity for hepatitis A, but it is also recommended for other groups at high risk for developing severe hepatitis. In addition, children living in communities with high rates of endemic hepatitis A (anti–hepatitis A prevalence of 30 to 40% by 5 years of age) should be vaccinated. Health care workers have not been shown to be at higher risk than the general population for hepatitis A and do not need routine immunization. Although food handlers are not at increased risk of hepatitis A compared with the general population, the consequences of infection or suspected infection in this group, which can lead to extensive public health investigations, may make vaccination cost-effective in some settings. Hepatitis A vaccine should be given to children 2 years of age or older to control outbreaks in communities with high rates of prior infection and be considered for communities with intermediate levels of prior infection (anti–hepatitis A seroprevalence of 10 to 25% by 5 years of age). In 1999, the Advisory Committee on Immunization Practices recommended universal vaccination of children who reside in states or counties with an average annual incidence rate of hepatitis A between 1987 and 1997 of greater than 20/100,000 population. Universal vaccination also may be considered for areas with average annual incidence rates between 10 and 20/100,000. Doses vary by age and product. All schedules call for a second dose at least 6 months after the first dose with a permissible range for one of the products 18 months after the initial dose. Vaccines are not indicated for children younger than 2 years because adequate data on safety and efficacy are lacking.

The most common side effect has been tenderness and soreness at the injection site. Although rare and more serious adverse events have been reported in temporal association with vaccination, a causal relationship has not been established.

HEPATITIS B

Hepatitis B (Chapter 151) vaccine is the first vaccine that can prevent cancer (an estimated 800 persons per year in the United States die of hepatitis B–related liver cancer; many times more die in the developing world). It also can prevent acute and chronic complications of hepatitis B, including an estimated 4000 deaths annually from cirrhosis and 250 deaths annually from fulminant hepatic disease in the United States. The original hepatitis vaccine in the United States consisted of purified, inactivated, alum-adsorbed, 22-nm HBsAg particles obtained from human plasma. Currently produced vaccines are derived from inserting the gene for HBsAg into *Saccharomyces cerevisiae*. Hepatitis B vaccine, the first licensed vaccine made by using recombinant techniques, produces adequate antibody responses in more than 90% of normal adults and more than 95% of normal infants, children, and adolescents when administered in a three-dose series. The dosage depends on the product, the age group, and the underlying clinical condition and can be determined by consulting the package insert. The duration of vaccine-conferred immunity is not known, although follow-up of vaccinees for more than 16 years indicates persistence of protection against clinically significant infections (i.e., detectable viremia and clinical disease). Booster doses are not currently recommended. Vaccine must be injected intramuscularly, preferably in the deltoid.

Hepatitis B vaccine is indicated for adults at high risk of infection (see Table 16–2). Because strategies targeting hepatitis B vaccine use only to high-risk populations have not had a significant impact on hepatitis B incidence, universal vaccination is now recommended for infants and for all adolescents who have not been previously vaccinated. Universal screening for HBsAg is recommended for all pregnant women, with administration of three doses of vaccine and one dose of hepatitis B immune globulin recommended for infants of carrier mothers.

The major side effect is soreness at the injection site. Alopecia, which is usually reversible, has been reported rarely. Hepatitis B vaccine has not been shown to induce multiple sclerosis in controlled studies and has not been shown to exacerbate illness in patients with multiple sclerosis who are vaccinated. There is no risk of acquiring HIV infection from either the recombinant or the plasma-derived vaccine.

INFLUENZA

Annual influenza (Chapter 363) vaccination is indicated for adults at high risk of complications from the disease: persons with chronic cardiopulmonary disorders, residents of nursing homes or other long-term care facilities, persons aged 65 or older, patients with other chronic diseases (e.g., diabetes mellitus, kidney dysfunction, hemoglobinopathies, and immunosuppression) who have required regular medical follow-up or hospitalization in the prior year, and children receiving long-term aspirin therapy. Women who will be in the second or third trimester of pregnancy during the influenza season (usually late December through mid-March) also should be vaccinated. Transmission of influenza to high-risk patients can be reduced by annually vaccinating health care workers and household contacts of high-risk patients. Vaccination has been recommended for all adults 50 to 64 years old to reduce influenza. Influenza vaccine can be considered for providers of essential community services and anyone who wants to avoid disease.

The efficacy of influenza vaccine varies with the host's condition and the degree to which antigens in the vaccine match viruses in circulation the following season. Current vaccines contain split inactivated viruses of three major antigenic types—A (H3N2), A (H1N1), and B. Provided that the match is good, vaccine efficacy is usually 70 to 90% in normal healthy young adults. Efficacy is substantially lower, often between 20 and 40%, in the institutionalized elderly; nevertheless, it seems to be 60 to 80% protective against pneumonia and death. Ideally, vaccines should be administered between October and November of each year, although earlier in the autumn suffices if circumstances require. If vaccine is available in December and January, vaccination should continue because it still can offer protection for many individuals. A review of 25 consecutive influenza seasons documented peak activity did not occur until January or later in 21 seasons and until February or later in 15 seasons.

Persons with anaphylactic allergies to eggs should not be immunized. The most common side effect is soreness at the injection site. Fever, malaise, and myalgia may begin 6 to 12 hours after vaccination and persist for 1 to 2 days, although such reactions are most common in children exposed to vaccine for the first time. Severe allergic reactions are rare. If current influenza vaccines cause Guillain-Barré syndrome, it is likely to be rare, on the order of 1 case per 1 million doses. A live attenuated trivalent influenza vaccine for intranasal administration may become available soon.

MEASLES

Measles (Chapter 365) immunization is recommended for all persons born in or after 1957 who lack evidence of prior physician-diagnosed measles or laboratory evidence of immunity or appropriate vaccination. Before 1989, appropriate vaccination consisted of a single dose of live vaccine administered on or after the first birthday. Now a routine two-dose schedule is recommended: the first dose, which is 93 to 98% effective, at 12 to 15 months of age and the second dose at entry to primary school. All children from kindergarten through the 12th grade should have a second dose. Most adults are considered to have been appropriately vaccinated if they received one dose of vaccine administered on or after their first birthday. Some adults who are at increased risk of measles (health care workers with direct patient contact, students in college, international travelers) should receive a second dose of vaccine, however, unless they have documentation of prior physician-diagnosed measles or serologic evidence of immunity. Persons embarking on foreign travel ideally should have received two doses or have other evidence of measles immunity. Persons born before 1957 are usually immune as a result of natural infection and do not require vaccination, although vaccination is not contraindicated if they are believed to be susceptible.

During outbreaks of measles in institutions, all persons at risk who have not received two doses or who lack other evidence of measles immunity should be vaccinated. Measles vaccine is usually administered along with MMR to ensure immunity against all three diseases. Individuals already immune to one or more of the components may receive MMR without harm.

Measles vaccine is contraindicated for pregnant women on theoretical grounds, for persons with moderate-to-severe acute febrile illnesses, and for persons with altered immunocompetence except persons with HIV infection who are not severely immunocompromised. Patients with anaphylactic reactions to eggs can be vaccinated without prior skin testing.

In approximately 5 to 15% of susceptible recipients of measles vaccine, temperatures of 39.4° C or higher develop 5 to 12 days after vaccination and last 1 to 2 days. Transient rashes develop in about 5%. Thrombocytopenic purpura has been reported rarely after MMR. The overall rate of reactions after the second dose of a measles-containing vaccine is substantially lower than after the first dose. Encephalopathy or encephalitis after measles vaccination has been reported at a rate lower than the background or expected rate.

MENINGOCOCCAL POLYSACCHARIDE VACCINE

A quadrivalent meningococcal polysaccharide vaccine containing serogroups A, C, Y, and W135 is available. These groups account for approximately 50% of meningococcal disease in the United States (Chapters 312 and 313). Serogroup A and C vaccines have had 85 to 100% efficacy in epidemic settings, whereas vaccines for the other groups have documented good immunogenicity in adults. The duration of immunity is unknown, although protection in older children and adults probably persists for at least 3 years. Protection in preschool children may be shorter. Routine vaccination is not recommended in the United States because of the low risk of infection. A single dose is indicated for high-risk persons. Vaccination also may be useful during localized epidemics of serogroups in the vaccine. Meningococcal vaccine may be offered to travelers and persons who will live in areas with hyperendemic or epidemic disease (e.g., the "meningitis belt" of sub-Saharan Africa, stretching from Mauritania to Ethiopia).

Although the incidence of meningococcal disease is low in the United States, college freshmen living in dormitories have been shown to be at a higher risk of disease than other persons of the same age. Although disease is still rare in such students, parents and the student should be made aware of the risk and offered vaccine if they want it.

Revaccination should be considered 2 to 3 years after primary immunization for children younger than 4 years at the initial vaccination. Revaccination 3 to 5 years after the initial dose also may be considered for older adolescents and adults at continued risk. College students other than freshmen are not at increased risk, and revaccination is not needed for older college students. The major side effects are local reactions lasting 1 to 2 days.

MUMPS

Mumps (Chapter 368) vaccine is indicated for all persons, especially susceptible males, without a prior history of vaccination on or after the first birthday, physician-diagnosed mumps, or laboratory evidence of immunity. Most persons born before 1957 can be considered immune as a result of natural infection, although vaccination is not contraindicated if such persons are thought to be susceptible. In clinical trials, a single dose of vaccine has induced seroconversion in more than 90% of recipients.

Adverse events after the Jeryl Lynn strain of mumps vaccine, the strain used in the United States, are uncommon—fever, parotitis, and allergic manifestations. Thrombocytopenic purpura has been reported rarely in persons administered MMR. Mumps vaccine is contraindicated for pregnant women on theoretical grounds, for persons with moderate-to-severe acute febrile illnesses, and for persons with altered immunocompetence. When combined with measles vaccine, it may be given to persons with asymptomatic HIV infection and considered for persons with symptomatic infection if they are not severely immunocompromised. Patients with anaphylactic reactions to eggs can be vaccinated without skin testing (see Measles earlier).

PNEUMOCOCCAL VACCINE

Pneumococcal polysaccharide vaccine consists of purified polysaccharide capsular antigens from the 23 types of *Streptococcus pneumoniae* that are responsible for 85 to 90% of the bacteremic disease in the United States (Chapter 303). Most adults, including the elderly and patients with alcoholic cirrhosis and diabetes mellitus, have a twofold or greater rise in type-specific antibodies within 2 to 3 weeks of vaccination. Although the serologic response is generally acceptable, estimates of vaccine efficacy in preventing disease vary widely. Efficacy may be lower in some patients, such as patients with alcoholic cirrhosis or Hodgkin's disease. There is good evidence that vaccination is approximately 60% effective against bacteremic pneumococcal disease, which accounts for an estimated 50,000 cases annually. Evidence regarding efficacy against pneumonia in high-risk populations is not clear, however. Regardless, the preponderance of information supports the use of pneumococcal vaccine in high-risk populations, including all persons older than 65 years. Special efforts should target hospitalized patients. Approximately two thirds of patients who are admitted later with pneumococcal disease had been hospitalized for other reasons within the preceding 5 years.

Immunity may decrease 5 or more years after initial vaccination; a single booster dose should be considered at that time for adults at highest risk of disease, such as asplenic patients, and for adults who lose antibody rapidly, such as patients with nephrotic syndrome or renal failure. Persons older than 65 years who received a dose more than 5 years earlier when they were younger than 65 years should be revaccinated.

Local reactions are frequent. Fewer than 1% of vaccinees experience severe local reactions or systemic illness, such as fever and malaise. Severe events such as anaphylaxis are rare. Because of the rarity of severe reactions in revaccinated patients, persons with indications for vaccination but with unknown histories of prior vaccination should be vaccinated.

A pneumococcal conjugate vaccine in which the polysaccharides of seven types are covalently linked to a protein carrier was licensed and recommended for universal use in children in 2000. This vaccine, which covers substantially fewer types than the 23-valent polysaccharide vaccine, is not indicated for persons 9 years of age or older.

POLIOMYELITIS

The last documented cases of indigenously acquired poliomyelitis (Chapters 373 and 452) caused by wild polioviruses in the United States were reported in 1979. In 2000, an all inactivated polio vaccine (IPV) schedule was recommended in the United States, and this vaccine replaced the live attenuated oral polio vaccine (OPV), which, although it had eliminated wild poliovirus in the United States, caused about eight cases per year on average among OPV recipients or their contacts. IPV is the only vaccine available in the United States. OPV is still the vaccine used in most countries around the world, however. A goal has been established to certify the eradication of wild poliovirus from the world by the end of 2005, a goal that requires a 3-year period free of disease from wild viruses. Between 1988, when the goal was announced, and 2000, cases of polio worldwide decreased by an estimated 99%, and indigenous wild poliovirus transmission has been eliminated from the Americas since late 1991.

Routine vaccination of adults is not warranted given the small risk of exposure to wild virus in the United States. The major indication for adult vaccination is travel to areas where wild poliovirus is endemic or epidemic. Previously unvaccinated adults should receive IPV. Adult travelers who have histories of partial vaccination should complete a primary series of three doses with IPV. Adults who formerly received three doses of OPV or IPV should receive a single booster of IPV. Health care personnel who come in contact with wild viruses should be immune to polio.

A primary series of IPV consists of three doses. A fourth dose is administered to children at school entry. No serious side effects of IPV have been reported.

RABIES

Rabies (Chapter 454) vaccine is indicated for pre-exposure prophylaxis of high-risk persons, including animal handlers, selected laboratory and field workers, and persons traveling for more than 1 month to areas where rabies is a constant threat. The pre-exposure regimen consists of either three 1-mL intramuscular injections on days 0, 7, and 21 or 28 for all rabies vaccines. Testing for serum antibody or a booster every 2 years is indicated for persons with continuing risk. Postexposure treatment depends on prior exposure to vaccine (Chapter 454). Human rabies immune globulin is indicated for previously unvaccinated persons who are exposed.

RUBELLA

Rubella (Chapter 366) vaccine is indicated for susceptible adults born in 1957 or later and for susceptible women of any age who are considering becoming pregnant. Persons without a prior history of vaccination on or after the first birthday or laboratory evidence of immunity should be considered susceptible. A single dose of vaccine is 95% or more effective. Many persons receive two doses of rubella vaccine via the two-dose schedule of MMR.

Follow-up of susceptible pregnant women who received rubella vaccines within 3 months of the estimated date of conception has failed to reveal any evidence of defects compatible with congenital rubella syndrome in their offspring. Nevertheless, vaccine is contraindicated in pregnant women on theoretical grounds, and conception should be delayed for 1 month after rubella vaccination.

Reactions occur only in susceptible persons. Arthralgia, usually of the small peripheral joints, develops in 40% of susceptible adults, and frank arthritis develops in 10 to 20%. Joint symptoms usually begin 1 to 3 weeks after vaccination and persist for 1 day to 3 weeks. Chronic recurrent or persistent joint symptoms have developed rarely after vaccination, but controlled studies have shown that the incidence of these events in vaccinees is similar to that of nonvaccinees. Other infrequent adverse events include transient peripheral neuritis and pain in the arms and legs. Thrombocytopenic purpura has been reported rarely when rubella vaccine is administered as MMR. Rubella vaccine is contraindicated for persons with moderate-to-severe acute febrile illnesses and for persons with reduced immunocompetence. When given with measles vaccine, it may be administered to persons with asymptomatic HIV infection and considered for persons with symptomatic infection without severe immunocompromise. Rubella vaccine is grown in human diploid cells and can be administered without problems to persons with allergy to eggs.

TETANUS AND DIPHTHERIA

Tetanus (Chapter 321) toxoid is one of the most effective immunizations, with greater than 95% protection after a primary series. The adsorbed preparation is preferred over the fluid preparation because it induces protective levels of antitoxin that persist longer after fewer doses. A primary series consists of three doses. In persons aged 7 years or older, it should always be used in combination with diphtheria (Chapter 317) toxoid (Td), which is more than 85% effective in preventing disease. Doses need not be repeated if the schedule is interrupted. Boosters are recommended every 10 years. An easy way to remember is to schedule immunization at the middle of each decade (e.g., 25 years, 35 years). The ACP/IDSA Task Force on Adult Immunization has suggested that a single Td booster at age 50 may be sufficient to maintain protective antibody levels in older adults who have received a primary series with boosters as a teenager and young adult.

After a wound, persons of unknown immunization status or persons who have received fewer than three doses of tetanus toxoid should receive a dose of Td regardless of the severity of the wound. Td also is indicated for persons who have previously received three or more doses if more than 10 years has elapsed since the last dose, in the case of clean, minor wounds, and if more than 5 years has elapsed for all other wounds. Tetanus immune globulin should be administered simultaneously at a separate site to persons who have not received at least three doses of toxoid and who have wounds that are not clean and minor. Most reactions to Td consist of local inflammation and low-grade fever. Guillain-Barré syndrome and brachial neuritis rarely have been associated with tetanus toxoid.

VARICELLA

A live attenuated varicella vaccine (Oka strain) was licensed in March 1995. The vaccine protects 70 to 90% of recipients against any disease and more than 95% of recipients against severe disease. Breakthrough infections in persons who have previously seroconverted have been reported in 2 to 4% per year after vaccination with the licensed product. Such breakthroughs are typically mild and average fewer than 50 lesions compared with several hundred lesions in unvaccinated persons with varicella. Breakthrough illnesses do not seem to increase in incidence or severity with increasing time since vaccination, a finding compatible with long-term protection after initial vaccination. Persons 13 years or older require two doses at least 4 weeks apart to achieve seroconversion rates of approximately 99%, a rate comparable to that in younger children after one dose.

Varicella vaccine is indicated routinely for all children. Persons with a prior history of varicella disease can be considered immune and do not need vaccination. Although a negative or unknown history of disease is predictive of susceptibility in children, many adults with such histories are immune. Serologic screening of adults in some situations may be cost-effective, provided that identified susceptible adults are vaccinated. The vaccine is contraindicated in the immunocompromised, persons with anaphylactic allergies to vaccine components, and pregnant women. Varicella vaccine is more temperature sensitive than other vaccines used in the United States. It must be stored frozen at −15° C or colder to retain potency, and it should be discarded if not used within 30 minutes of reconstitution.

The most common side effect is soreness at the injection site, which is reported in 25 to 35% of recipients 13 years or older. Varicella-like rashes at the injection site (median of two lesions) have been reported in 3% of recipients in this age group after the first dose and in 1% after the second dose. Nonlocalized rashes with a median of five lesions have been reported in 5.5% of recipients after the first dose and in 0.9% after the second dose. Although the vaccine can cause herpes zoster (shingles), the incidence is substantially lower than would be expected after natural varicella (Chapter 367). More severe events occurring in temporal relation to the vaccine have been reported rarely, although a causal relationship has not been established. Transmission of vaccine virus to a contact is extremely rare and seems to take place only with vaccinees in whom a varicella-like rash has developed.

Vaccines Intended Primarily for International Travelers

CHOLERA

At present, the manufacture and sale of the only licensed cholera vaccine in the United States has been discontinued. No cholera vaccination requirement exists for entry into or exit from any country. Cholera vaccine has not been recommended for travelers because of the brief and incomplete immunity it offers (Chapter 328).

JAPANESE ENCEPHALITIS VACCINE

Japanese encephalitis (Chapter 377) vaccine is indicated primarily for travelers to Asia who will spend a month or longer in endemic areas during the transmission season, especially if travel will include rural areas. In all instances, travelers should be advised to take personal precautions to reduce exposure to mosquito bites. The vaccine seems to be 80 to 91% effective in preventing clinical disease. The primary series consists of three subcutaneous 1-mL doses given on days 0, 7, and 30 (Table 16–2). A shortened schedule given on days 0, 7, and 14 may be used when necessary. Booster doses may be given after 2 years. The vaccine is contraindicated for pregnant women on theoretical grounds, but if such women travel to an endemic, high-risk area, they may be vaccinated. Local reactions are common and occur in about 20% of vaccinated persons, and systemic symptoms of fever, headache, chills, nausea, and abdominal pain have been noted in about 10%. A delayed urticaria-angioedema syndrome may occur a median of 12 hours after the first dose of vaccine and 2 weeks after the second dose. Vaccinees should be observed for at least 30 minutes after inoculation and, during the subsequent 10 days, should remain in areas with ready access to medical care.

TYPHOID VACCINE

Two types of vaccines, a live attenuated Ty21a oral vaccine and a capsular polysaccharide vaccine (ViCPS), seem to be of comparable efficacy (50 to 77%). Typhoid (Chapter 324) vaccine is indicated primarily for travelers to areas where the risk of prolonged exposure to contaminated food and water is high. The vaccine is not optimally effective; food and water precautions are still essential. The vaccine also may be considered for family or other intimate contacts of typhoid carriers and laboratory workers who work with *Salmonella typhi*. For adults and children 6 years and older, either of the vaccines may be used. For Ty21a, one enteric-coated capsule is taken every other day for four doses. Alternatively a single dose of the ViCPS vaccine may be given. The duration of protection with Ty21a is not known; repetition of the primary series is recommended every 5 years for persons at risk. Boosters are recommended every 2 years for the ViCPs vaccine if persons continue to be at risk. The ViCPS vaccine can be given to children 2 years of age. Adverse reactions are rare.

YELLOW FEVER

Yellow fever (Chapter 375) now occurs only in areas of South America and Africa. Vaccination with a single dose of the live attenuated 17D strain of virus confers protection to almost all recipients for at least 10 years. Boosters are recommended every 10 years for persons at risk. Side effects are uncommon. A rare syndrome of yellow fever vaccine "febrile multiple organ system failure" or viscerotropic disease has been reported, with high rates of mortality, primarily among older adults. Yellow fever vaccine should be administered with caution and only after careful counseling to elderly patients who are going to spend time in yellow fever endemic zones. Yellow fever vaccine should not be given to immunocompromised persons or persons with anaphylactic allergies to eggs. The vaccine is contraindicated in pregnant women on theoretical grounds, although if pregnant women must travel to a high-risk area, they may be vaccinated.

Vaccines for Possible Bioterrorism Agents

ANTHRAX

Anthrax vaccine adsorbed (AVA) is prepared from a cell-free filtrate of a nonencapsulated strain of anthrax and contains many cell products including protective antigen. Protective antigen is responsible for binding to cells, allowing transport of lethal factor and edema factor into host cells. Pre-exposure prophylaxis consists of six doses subcutaneously at 0, 2, and 4 weeks and 6, 12, and 18 months followed by annual boosters. Protective efficacy of an earlier form of the vaccine against cutaneous anthrax was 92.5%. Animal models suggest efficacy against inhalation anthrax. Pre-exposure vaccination is recommended for persons engaged in work involving exposure to high concentrations of *Bacillus anthracis* or in activities with high potential for aerosol production. Vaccine may be given with antibiotics for postexposure prophylaxis (Chapter 333); the antibiotics

should be continued for 7–14 days after the third dose of vaccine is given. The most common adverse events are local reactions, including subcutaneous nodules, which are thought to be due to the deposition of the aluminum-containing adjuvant in subcutaneous tissue.

SMALLPOX

Smallpox vaccine uses vaccinia virus, an orthopox virus that is distinct from variola and cowpox viruses and that provides cross-protection from smallpox. With successful eradication of natural transmission and laboratory containment, variola virus is known to be in only two sites, the Centers for Disease Control and Prevention in Atlanta, Georgia, and the Russian State Research Center for Virology and Biotechnology, Koltsovo, Novosibirsk. Allegations that the former Soviet Union was engaged in using variola virus in weapons and concerns that with the break-up of the Soviet Union, some scientists may have given the virus to other countries or terrorist groups have raised the potential of a bioterrorist event using variola. Smallpox vaccine is close to 100% effective when administered properly, using a bifurcated needle. Vaccination also prevents or modifies disease when administered within 3 to 4 days of exposure and perhaps even after greater delays. The skin usually does not need any special preparation. If alcohol is used for cleaning, the skin should be allowed to dry before vaccination to avoid inactivating the vaccine. The needle is held perpendicular to the skin; 3 punctures for primary vaccination and 15 punctures for revaccination are made rapidly with enough vigor to ensure that a trace of blood appears within 15 to 20 seconds. With a primary take, the vaccination site should become reddened and pruritic by 3 to 4 days after vaccination; a large vesicle with a red areola forms and becomes pustular by 7 to 11 days. The lesion scabs by the third week. Fever is the most common adverse event. Other more serious complications include eczema vaccinatum, a local or disseminated vaccinia infection in persons with a history of eczema or other exfoliative dermatitis; vaccinia necrosum, which occurs in immunocompromised persons; autoinoculation, especially of the eye, which can cause keratitis and scarring; generalized vaccinia; myopericarditis, and encephalitis. The risk of death from vaccinia has been estimated to be approximately 1 per 1 million primary vaccinations. The vaccine is indicated for persons who work with orthopox viruses. To increase preparedness for a smallpox attack, vaccination is often recommended for persons who will serve on public health or health care response teams. The duration of immunity is unclear. Revaccination is recommended at least every 10 years for persons who continue to be at risk. Contraindications include history or presence of eczema, other chronic or exfoliative skin conditions, immunosuppression or pregnancy in the patient or a close household or other contact. Persons who are younger than 1 year, are breast feeding, or have allergies to vaccine components should not be vaccinated. Because of reports of postvaccination cardiac events, vaccination should be deferred in persons with ischemia or other severe heart diseases or at high risk for ischemic heart disease events (*www.cdc.gov/smallpox*). In the event of exposure to variola, there are no contraindications. Should variola be introduced into a community, vaccination would be indicated for all exposed persons and their close contacts to prevent further spread, and recommendations for more widespread vaccination would have to be evaluated on a case-by-case basis.

OTHER AGENTS

Other organisms or products that have been considered potential bioterrorism threats include plague (Chapter 331) and botulinum toxin (Chapter 320). An inactivated whole cell plague vaccine had been available in the United States for persons whose occupation places them at risk; it is no longer being produced. Although the vaccine seemed to be effective against bubonic plague, animal studies suggest poor efficacy against pneumonic disease. At present, vaccine is not considered a major part of the response to a bioterrorist attack with *Yersinia pestis*.

Poisoning with botulinum toxin can be treated with a trivalent antitoxin, available from the Centers for Disease Control. An experimental pentavalent botulinum toxoid can be obtained from the Centers for Disease Control and Prevention for laboratory workers at high risk of exposure to toxin. Pre-exposure vaccination is not warranted or feasible for the general population.

Preventive and Environmental Medicine

Other Vaccines

Many other vaccines are used in selected circumstances, including BCG (bacille Calmette-Guérin) vaccine, which has limited use in the United States, to prevent tuberculosis (Chapter 341). BCG vaccination of health care workers should be considered on an individual basis in settings in which (1) a high percentage of tuberculosis patients are infected with *Mycobacterium tuberculosis* strains resistant to isoniazid and rifampin, (2) transmission of drug-resistant *M. tuberculosis* strains to health care workers and subsequent infection are likely, and (3) comprehensive tuberculosis infection control has been implemented but has not been successful.

Future Directions

Although not available today, many vaccines are under development and may be licensed in the future. Extensive field trials have occurred or are planned with meningococcal conjugate vaccines, acellular pertussis vaccines in adults, and HIV vaccines.

SUGGESTED READINGS

ACP Task Force on Adult Immunization and Infectious Diseases Society of America: Guide for Adult Immunization, 3rd ed. Philadelphia, American College of Physicians, 1994. *An excellent comprehensive guide covering all aspects of adult immunization. A must for the physician who cares for adults, whether in primary, secondary, or tertiary care (to be revised and published in 2002).*

Centers for Disease Control and Prevention: Recommendations of the Advisory Committee on Immunization Practices. *Comprehensive coverage on vaccine-preventable diseases, vaccines, indications, schedules, and adverse events. Published as available in the Morbidity and Mortality Weekly Report as "Recommendations and Reports" supplements and available at www.cdc.gov/nip.*

Centers for Disease Control and Prevention: General recommendations on immunization: Recommendations of the Advisory Committee on Immunization Practices (ACIP) and the American Academy of Family Physicians (AAFP). Morb Mortal Wkly Rep MMWR 2002;51(RR-2):1–35. *A comprehensive review of vaccination schedules, precautions, contraindications, and adverse events and information about federal laws on injury compensation and record keeping.*

Centers for Disease Control and Prevention: Health Information for International Travel. *A complete guide for the international traveler, including required and recommended vaccinations. Revised every 1 to 2 years. Available online at www.cdc.gov/travel. Hard copy versions can be obtained from the Public Health Foundation (1-877-252-1200) or order online at http://bookstore.phf.org.*

Centers for Disease Control and Prevention: Recommendations for using smallpox vaccine in a pre-event vaccination program. Morb Mortal Wkly Rep MMWR 2003;52(Dispatch):1–16. *Latest recommendations for increasing preparedness against a bioterrorist attack with variola.*

Centers for Disease Control and Prevention: Notice to Readers: Recommended Adult Immunization Schedule—United States, 2002–2003. Morb Mortal Wkly Rep MMWR 2002;51:904–908. *The schedule is divided in two parts: 1) vaccine, recommended by age group and 2) vaccines recommended by underlying medical condition.*

Committee on Infectious Diseases, American Academy of Pediatrics: Report of the Committee on Infectious Diseases, 23rd ed. Elk Grove Village, IL, American Academy of Pediatrics, 2000. *The "Red Book" is published every 2 to 3 years and addresses in a comprehensive manner vaccination of children and adolescents and other issues relating to prevention, control, and treatment of infectious diseases.*

National Immunization Program (NIP), Centers for Disease Control and Prevention. *The NIP has established toll-free numbers for answering questions from the general public and physicians: 1-800-232-2522 (English), 1-800-232-0233 (Spanish). Inquiries can be made to the NIP by e-mail: nipinfo@cdc.gov or the NIP web site at www.cdc.gov/nip.*

17 ALCOHOL ABUSE AND DEPENDENCE

Patrick G. O'Connor

Definitions

A variety of terms have been used to describe the spectrum of medical, psychological, behavioral, and social problems associated with excessive consumption of alcohol (*alcohol problems*). *Alcoholism* is perhaps the most widely used term to describe patients with alcohol problems. In an attempt to define *alcoholism* more precisely, a panel of 23 experts convened by the National Council on Alcoholism and Drug Dependence and the American Society of Addiction Medicine developed a definition of alcoholism that included: ". . . a primary chronic disease with genetic psychosocial and environmental factors . . . often progressive and fatal . . . characterized by impaired control over drinking, preoccupation with the drug alcohol, use of alcohol despite future consequences, and distortions of thinking most notably denial. . . ." Because the term

alcoholism is so broad, it also can be imprecise in defining the entire spectrum of alcohol problems.

Abstainers are individuals who consume no alcohol. *Moderate drinking* is defined by the National Institute on Alcohol Abuse and Alcoholism as the average number of drinks consumed daily that places an adult at low risk for alcohol problems. There is some epidemiologic evidence to suggest that moderate drinking may have some health benefits by reducing the risk of cardiovascular disease (see Chapter 47). The scope of alcohol consumption that imparts this benefit may be quite low, however (e.g., less than one drink per day).

At-risk drinking is a level of alcohol consumption that imparts health risks (Table 17–1). This category of drinking behavior has been identified on the basis of epidemiologic evidence that certain threshold levels of alcohol consumption are associated with increased risk of specific health problems. At-risk drinking is defined differently for men younger than age 65 than for women of all ages because of generally lower body weights and lower rates of metabolizing alcohol in women; the definition in men older than age 65 years is the same as in women because of the age-related increased risk of alcohol problems, in part owing to changes in alcohol metabolism in older individuals. *Binge drinking* is the episodic consumption of large amounts of alcohol, usually five or more drinks per occasion for men and four or more drinks per occasion for women. One standard drink contains 12 g of pure alcohol, an amount equivalent to that contained in 5 oz of wine, 12 oz of beer, or 1.5 oz of 90 proof of spirits. *Problem drinking* refers to a level of alcohol consumption that causes any problems for the patient (medical, psychiatric, behavioral, or social—*alcohol problems*).

Alcohol abuse and *alcohol dependence*, which are alcohol use disorders defined in the *Diagnostic and Statistical Manual of Mental Disorders*, 4th edition, require the presence of specific social or clinical phenomena (see Table 17–1). *Alcohol abuse* includes criteria that indicate social dysfunction or use in high-risk situations (e.g., driving). *Alcohol dependence* includes social consequences along with criteria related to physiologic aspects of dependence (e.g., tolerance, loss of control) and use despite physical or psychological problems. The distinction between *alcohol abuse* and *alcohol dependence* is important given the general need for more intensive treatment services for patients who are alcohol dependent.

Table 17–1 • TERMS AND CRITERIA FOR PATTERNS OF ALCOHOL USE

At-risk drinking
Men < age 65: >14 drinks/wk or >4 drinks/occasion
Men > age 65 and all women: >7 drinks/wk or >3 drinks/occasion

Alcohol abuse
Maladaptive pattern of alcohol use leading to clinically significant impairment or distress, manifested within a 12-mo period by one or more of the following:
  Failure to fulfill role obligations at work, school, or home
  Recurrent use in hazardous situations
  Legal problems related to alcohol
  Continued use despite alcohol-related social or interpersonal problems
Symptoms have never met criteria for alcohol dependence

Alcohol dependence
Maladaptive pattern of alcohol use leading to clinically significant impairment or distress, manifested within a 12-mo period by three or more of the following:
  Tolerance (either increasing amounts used or diminished effects with the same amount)
  Withdrawal (withdrawal symptoms or use to relieve or avoid symptoms)
  Use of larger amounts over a longer period than intended
  Persistent desire or unsuccessful attempts to cut down or control use
  Great deal of time spent obtaining, using, or recovering from use
  Important social relationships, occupations, or recreational activities given up or reduced
  Use despite knowledge of alcohol-related physical or psychological problems

Epidemiology

In national surveys, 64% of American adults reported that they use alcoholic beverages (liquor, wine, or beer), whereas 36% reported that they were abstinent. Among individuals who use alcohol, many experience problems because of their drinking. It has been estimated that more than $100 billion is spent by American society each year to treat alcohol use disorders and to recover the costs of alcohol-related economic losses. Excessive alcohol consumption ranks as the third leading preventable cause of death in the United States after cigarette smoking and obesity. More than 100,000 deaths per year in the United States are attributed to alcohol use disorders.

Population-based epidemiologic studies have shown that alcohol use disorders are among the most prevalent medical behavioral or psychiatric disorders in the general population. An epidemiologic survey of the general population in the United States documented a prevalence of alcohol abuse and dependence estimated to be between 7.4 and 9.7%. The lifetime prevalence of abuse and dependence is estimated to be even higher. Despite higher thresholds and tolerance, men are at least twice as likely to meet criteria for alcohol abuse and dependence using standard diagnostic survey techniques. Although sociodemographic features, such as young age, low income, and low education level, have been associated with an increased risk for problem drinking, alcohol use disorders are prevalent throughout all sociodemographic groups, and all individuals should be screened carefully. The "skid row" stereotype of the alcohol-dependent patient is much more the exception than the rule.

The prevalence of alcohol use disorders is higher in most health care settings than it is in the general population because alcohol problems often result in treatment-seeking behaviors. The prevalence in alcohol abuse and dependence in general outpatient and inpatient medical settings has been estimated between 15 and 40%. These data strongly support the need for physicians to screen all patients for alcohol use disorders.

Pathobiology

Beverage alcohol contains ethanol, which acts as a sedative-hypnotic drug. Alcohol is absorbed rapidly into the bloodstream from the stomach and intestinal tract. Because women have lower levels of gastric alcohol dehydrogenase, the enzyme primarily responsible for metabolizing alcohol, they experience higher blood alcohol concentrations than men who consume similar amounts of ethanol per kilogram of body weight. The absorption of alcohol can be affected by other factors, including the presence of food in the stomach and the rate of alcohol consumption. By means of metabolism in the liver, alcohol is converted to acetaldehyde and acetate (Fig. 17–1). Metabolism is proportional to an individual's body weight, but a variety of other factors can affect how alcohol is metabolized. A genetic variation in a significant proportion of the Asian population alters the structure of an acetaldehyde, aldehyde hydrogenase isoenzyme, resulting in the development of an "alcohol flush reaction," which includes facial flushing, hot sensations, tachycardia, and hypotension.

In the brain, alcohol seems to affect a variety of receptors, including γ-aminobutyric acid (GABA), N-methyl-D-aspartate, and opioid receptors. Glycinuric and serotoninergic receptors also are thought to be involved in the interaction between alcohol and the brain. The

phenomena of "reinforcement" and "cellular adaptation" are thought, at least in part, to influence alcohol-dependent behaviors. Alcohol is known to be reinforcing because withdrawal from ethanol and ingestion of ethanol itself are known to promote further alcohol consumption. After chronic exposure to alcohol, some brain neurons seem to adapt to this exposure by adjusting their response to normal stimuli. This adaptation is thought to be responsible for the phenomenon of tolerance, whereby increasing amounts of alcohol are needed over time to achieve desired effects. Although much has been learned about the variety of effects alcohol can have on various brain receptors, no single receptor site has been identified. A variety of neuropsychological disorders are seen in association with chronic ethanol use, including impaired short-term memory, cognitive dysfunction, and perceptual difficulties.

Although the brain is the primary target of alcohol's actions, a variety of other tissues have a major role in the pathobiology of how alcohol affects the human body. Direct liver toxicity may be among the most important consequences of acute and chronic alcohol use (Chapter 155). A variety of histologic abnormalities have been described, ranging from inflammation to scarring and cirrhosis. The pathophysiology of these effects is thought to include the direct release of toxins and the formation of free radicals, which can interact negatively with liver proteins, lipids, and DNA. Alcohol also has substantial negative effects on the heart and cardiovascular system. Direct toxicity to myocardial cells frequently results in heart failure (Chapter 73), and chronic heavy alcohol consumption is considered to be a major contributor to hypertension (Chapter 63). Other organ systems that experience significant direct toxicity from alcohol include the gastrointestinal tract (e.g., esophagus, stomach), immune system (e.g., bone marrow, immune cell function), and endocrine system (e.g., pancreas, gonads).

Clinical Manifestations

> Alcohol has a variety of specific acute and chronic effects. The acute effects seen most commonly are alcohol intoxication and alcohol withdrawal. Chronic clinical effects of alcohol include almost every organ system.

ACUTE EFFECTS

ALCOHOL INTOXICATION. After entering the bloodstream, alcohol rapidly passes through the blood-brain barrier. The clinical manifestations of alcohol intoxication are related directly to the blood level of alcohol. Because of tolerance, individuals chronically exposed to alcohol generally experience less severe effects at a given blood alcohol level than individuals who are not chronically exposed to alcohol. The symptoms of mild alcohol intoxication in nontolerant individuals typically occur at blood alcohol levels of 20 to 100 mg/dL and include euphoria, mild muscular incoordination, and mild cognitive impairment. At higher blood alcohol levels (100 to 200 mg/dL), more substantial neurologic dysfunction occurs, including more severe mental impairment, ataxia, and prolonged reaction time. Individuals with blood alcohol levels in these ranges can be obviously intoxicated with slurred speech and incoordination. These effects progress as the blood alcohol level rises to higher levels, to the point where stupor,

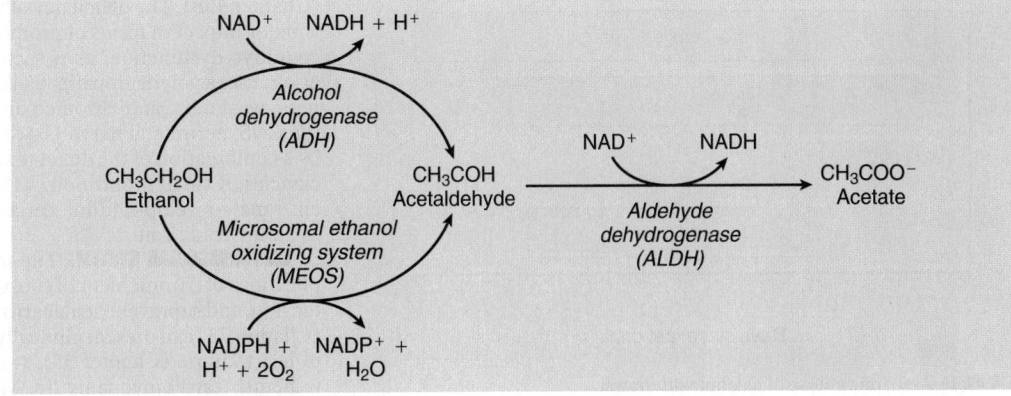

FIGURE 17–1 • Ethanol metabolism. Alcohol dehydrogenase (ADH) predominates at low-to-moderate ethanol doses. The microsomal ethanol-oxidizing system (MEOS) is induced at high ethanol levels of chronic exposure and by certain drugs. Aldehyde dehydrogenase (ALDH) inhibition (genetic or drug induced) leads to acetaldehyde accumulation.

coma, and death can occur at levels equal to or greater than 400 mg/dL, especially in individuals who are nontolerant to the effects of alcohol. Respiratory depression and hypotension are the usual cause of death in individuals with very high blood levels of alcohol.

ALCOHOL WITHDRAWAL SYNDROME. Alcohol withdrawal can occur when individuals decrease their alcohol use or stop using alcohol altogether. The severity of symptoms can vary greatly: Many individuals experience alcohol withdrawal without seeking medical attention, whereas others require hospitalization for severe illness. Because ethanol is a central nervous system (CNS) depressant, the body's natural response to withdrawal of the substance is a hyperexcitable neurologic state. This state is thought to be the result of adaptive neurologic mechanisms being unrestrained by alcohol, with an ensuing release of a variety of neurohumoral substances, including norepinephrine. In addition, chronic exposure to alcohol results in a decrease in the number of GABA receptors and impairs their function.

The clinical manifestations of alcohol withdrawal include hyperactivity resulting in tachycardia and diaphoresis. Patients also experience tremulousness, anxiety, and insomnia. More severe alcohol withdrawal can result in nausea and vomiting, which can exacerbate metabolic disturbances. Perceptual abnormalities, including visual and auditory hallucinations and psychomotor agitation, are common manifestations of more moderate-to-severe alcohol withdrawal. Grand mal seizures commonly occur during alcohol withdrawal, although they do not generally require treatment beyond the acute withdrawal phase.

The time course of the alcohol withdrawal syndrome can vary within an individual and by symptom complex, and the overall duration of symptoms can be a few to several days (Fig. 17–2). Tremor is typically among the earliest symptoms and can occur within 8 hours of the last drink. Symptoms of tremulousness and motor hyperactivity typically peak within 24 to 48 hours. Although mild tremor typically involves the hands, more severe tremors can involve the entire body and greatly impair a variety of basic motor functions. Perceptual abnormalities typically begin within 24 to 36 hours after the last drink and resolve within a few days. When withdrawal seizures occur, they are typically generalized tonic-clonic seizures and most often occur within 12 to 24 hours after reduction of alcohol intake. Seizures can occur, however, at later time periods as well.

The most severe manifestations of the alcohol withdrawal syndrome are delirium tremens. This symptom complex includes disorientation, confusion, hallucination, diaphoresis, fever, and tachycardia. Delirium tremens typically begin after 2 to 4 days of abstinence, and the most severe form can result in death.

CHRONIC EFFECTS

Acute manifestations, including intoxication and withdrawal, are generally stereotypical in their appearance and time course, but chronic manifestations tend to be more varied. Many patients with alcohol dependence may be without evidence of any chronic medical manifestations for many years. As time goes on, however, the likelihood that one or more of these manifestations will occur increases considerably. All major organ systems can be affected, but the primary organ systems involved include the nervous system, cardiovascular system, liver, gastrointestinal system, pancreas, hematopoietic system,

Table 17–2 • ALCOHOL-RELATED COMPLICATIONS

SYSTEM/REALM OF PROBLEM	COMPLICATIONS
Nervous system	Intoxication Withdrawal Cognitive impairment Cerebellar degeneration Peripheral neuropathy
Cardiovascular system	Cardiac arrhythmias Chronic cardiomyopathy Hypertension
Liver	Fatty liver Alcoholic hepatitis Cirrhosis
Gastrointestinal tract Esophagus	Chronic inflammation Malignancies Mallory-Weiss tears Esophageal varices
Stomach	Gastritis Peptic ulcer disease
Pancreas	Acute pancreatitis Chronic pancreatitis
Other medical problems	Cancers: mouth, oropharynx, esophagus Hepatoma Pneumonia Tuberculosis
Psychiatric	Depression Anxiety Suicide
Behavioral and psychosocial	Injuries Violence Crime Child/partner abuse Tobacco, other drug abuse Unemployment Legal problems

and endocrine system (Table 17–2). Patients who drink are at risk for a variety of malignancies, such as head and neck, esophageal, and liver cancers (Chapters 136, 197, and 202). Excessive alcohol use often causes significant psychiatric and social morbidity that can be more common and more severe than the direct medical effects, especially earlier in the course of problem drinking.

NERVOUS SYSTEM. In addition to the acute neurologic manifestations of intoxication and withdrawal, alcohol has major chronic neurologic effects. Approximately 10 million Americans have identifiable nervous system impairment from chronic alcohol use. Individual predisposition to these disorders is highly variable and is related to genetics, environment, sociodemographic features, and gender; the relative contribution of these factors is unclear. In the CNS, the major effect is cognitive impairment. Patients may present with mild-to-moderate short-term or long-term memory problems or may have severe dementia resembling Alzheimer's disease (Chapter 433). The degree to which the direct toxic effect of alcohol is responsible for these problems or the impact of alcohol-related nutritional deficiencies is uncertain (Chapter 458). The deficiency of vitamins such as thiamine may have a major impact in terms of promoting alcoholic dementia and severe cognitive dysfunction, as is seen in Korsakoff's syndrome. Alcohol also causes a polyneuropathy that can present with paresthesias, numbness, weakness, and chronic pain (Chapters 458 and 462). As with the CNS, peripheral nervous system effects are thought to be caused by a combination of the direct toxicity of alcohol and nutritional deficiencies. A small proportion (<1%) of patients with alcohol dependence may develop midline cerebellar degeneration, which presents as an unsteady gait.

CARDIOVASCULAR SYSTEM. The most common cardiovascular complications of chronic alcohol consumption are cardiomyopathy, hypertension, and supraventricular arrhythmias. Alcoholic cardiomyopathy (Chapter 73) can present clinically in a manner similar to other causes of heart failure (Chapter 55). It is the most common cause of nonischemic cardiomyopathy in Western countries, accounting for

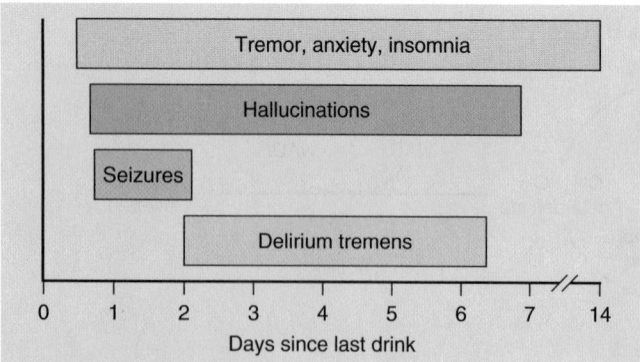

FIGURE 17–2 • Time course of alcohol withdrawal.

Tremor, anxiety, insomnia

Hallucinations

Seizures

Delirium tremens

0 1 2 3 4 5 6 7 14

Days since last drink

approximately 45% of cases. As with these other causes, alcoholic cardiomyopathy also responds to conventional treatments for heart failure (Chapter 56). Abstinence from alcohol can result in significant improvement in cardiomyopathy in some patients. Increasing levels of alcohol consumption also are associated with increasing levels of systolic and diastolic hypertension (Chapter 63). The most common arrhythmias associated with chronic alcohol use include atrial fibrillation and supraventricular tachycardia; these are seen commonly in the setting of acute intoxication and withdrawal (Chapter 59). The prevalence of alcohol-induced arrhythmias is unclear. Alcoholic cardiomyopathy also is associated with arrhythmias, in particular, ventricular arrhythmias (Chapter 60).

LIVER. Alcohol abuse is the major cause of morbidity and mortality from liver disease in the United States. It has been estimated that there are more than 2 million people with known alcoholic liver disease in the United States. Factors that predispose to early liver disease include the quantity and duration of alcohol exposure, female gender, and malnutrition. The range of clinical manifestations includes acute fatty liver, alcoholic hepatitis, and cirrhosis (Chapter 155). Fatty liver associated with alcohol ingestion can be asymptomatic or associated with nonspecific abdominal discomfort; it generally improves with abstinence from alcohol. Alcoholic hepatitis can present as an asymptomatic condition identified through abnormalities in liver enzymes or as an acute episode with abdominal pain, nausea, vomiting, and fever. Patients with alcoholic hepatitis have particularly high levels of aspartate aminotransferase levels in the blood and elevated levels of γ-glutamyltransferase. Alcoholic hepatitis typically improves with abstinence from alcohol.

Alcohol-related cirrhosis is a major cause of death in the United States (Chapter 156). Although patients are often asymptomatic, patients with more advanced cirrhosis may present with a variety of symptoms and signs, including jaundice, ascites, and coagulopathy. Cirrhosis also is associated with gastrointestinal bleeding from esophageal varices (Chapter 133). Although there is some controversy about the use of liver transplantation to treat patients with alcoholic cirrhosis, many believe that patients in established recovery are good candidates for liver transplantation (Chapter 157).

GASTROINTESTINAL DISEASE. Chronic alcohol use is associated with a variety of esophageal problems, including esophageal varices, Mallory-Weiss tears, and squamous cell carcinoma of the esophagus. The risk of squamous cell carcinoma is increased further in patients who smoke tobacco and drink alcohol (Chapter 136). Patients with these problems can present with difficulty swallowing, chest pain, gastrointestinal blood loss, and weight loss. Acute alcoholic gastritis typically presents with abdominal discomfort, nausea, and vomiting (Chapter 137).

PANCREAS. The risk of pancreatitis in individuals with alcohol dependence is approximately four times that in the general population. Quantity and duration of alcohol exposure and a history of pancreatitis are predictive of future episodes. Acute alcoholic pancreatitis, which may present with severe abdominal pain, nausea, vomiting, fever, and hypotension, can be life-threatening (Chapter 145). Individuals who have recurrent acute pancreatitis may develop chronic pancreatitis, which typically presents with chronic abdominal pain, malabsorption, weight loss, and malnutrition.

HEMATOPOIETIC SYSTEM. The anemia that commonly is seen in patients with chronic alcohol problems can be multifactorial (e.g., blood loss, nutrient deficiency, secondary to liver disease and hypersplenism). Studies of selected inpatients with alcohol dependence showed the prevalence of anemia to range from approximately 10 to 60%. Gastrointestinal blood loss owing to Mallory-Weiss tears (Chapter 136), alcoholic gastritis (Chapter 137), or esophageal varices (Chapters 136 and 156) may be a key factor, and many patients develop subsequent iron deficiency. Dietary folate deficiency can be associated with megaloblastic anemias (Chapter 174). Alcohol also has a direct toxic effect on the bone marrow, which can lead to sideroblastic anemia that resolves after abstinence (Chapter 173). Alcohol can suppress megakaryocyte production and cause thrombocytopenia, which may manifest as petechiae or bleeding (Chapter 162); the thrombocytopenia is particularly sensitive to abstinence, with platelet counts usually rebounding or returning to normal within 5 to 7 days after cessation of alcohol intake. Alcohol also appears to interfere directly with platelet function. Alcohol-related immune dysfunction, as evidenced by decreased production and function of white blood cells and derangement in humoral and cell-mediated immunity, explains why alcohol-dependent individuals are at higher risk for infectious diseases, such as pneumonia and tuberculosis. The hypersplenism that occurs in combination with cirrhosis also may contribute to the increased risk of serious infection seen in these patients (Chapters 156 and 164).

MALIGNANCIES. Alcohol intake has been associated with upper digestive, respiratory, and liver malignancies. Alcohol use is associated with squamous cell carcinomas of the esophagus (Chapter 136) and of the head and neck (Chapter 197). The co-occurrence of alcohol and tobacco abuse seems to be synergistic. Either heavy alcohol use or smoking individually increases the rate of oropharyngeal cancer by about six to seven times that of the general population, whereas the risk for people with both risk factors is about 40 times that of the general population. Patients with alcohol-induced liver disease who also have a history of hepatitis B or C are at particularly increased risk for hepatocellular carcinoma (Chapter 202).

Chronic alcohol use also has been associated with malignancies of the breast (Chapter 204), prostate (Chapter 207), pancreas (Chapter 201), cervix (Chapter 205), lung (Chapter 198), and colon (Chapter 200). Women who have more than one to two alcoholic drinks per day may increase their breast cancer risk 1.5-fold or more. Hormonal mechanisms and direct carcinogenic effects of alcohol have been postulated as causes of this association. The association of cervical cancer with alcohol dependence may be due to alcohol-associated, high-risk sexual behaviors that are thought to increase the risk of cervical cancer.

OTHER MEDICAL ISSUES. Gout has been associated with alcohol abuse, and flares can occur at lower serum urate levels than in nonalcoholic patients (Chapter 288). Alcoholic ketoacidosis (Chapter 113), which usually follows an alcoholic binge, presents as nausea, vomiting, abdominal pain, and volume depletion. Typically, ketoacidosis is seen with low or normal glucose readings. Mild or nonspecific abnormalities in thyroid function, especially in patients with underlying liver disease, may reflect abnormalities in the clearance of thyroid-stimulating hormone or the impact of elevated circulating estrogens (Chapter 239). Infertility and menstrual irregularities have been associated with chronic alcohol consumption, presumably owing to alcoholic-induced disruption in hypothalamic-pituitary dysfunction, gonadal toxicity, and impaired hepatic metabolism of circulating hormones (Chapter 250). Hypogonadism is highly prevalent in male alcoholics with cirrhosis (Chapter 247). Alcohol dependence also is associated with higher rates of dental and periodontal disease (Chapter 467) and with a variety of dermatologic problems, including spider angiomas (see Fig. 148–1) and, in patients with poor hygiene, skin infestations.

PSYCHIATRIC ISSUES. Psychiatric symptoms and illnesses (Chapter 426) are exceedingly common among individuals with alcohol problems. The prevalence of anxiety disorders is about 40%, and the prevalence of affective disorders is about 30%. Antisocial personality disorder is also more common in individuals with alcohol problems than in the general population. These psychiatric problems are more prevalent during periods of heavy drinking and withdrawal. All patients with alcohol use disorders require careful screening for psychiatric illnesses. Effective treatment of underlying psychiatric disorders may result in improved drinking behaviors.

OTHER BEHAVIORAL AND PSYCHOSOCIAL ISSUES. Alcohol commonly is the underlying cause of domestic abuse injuries, trauma, motor vehicle accidents, and burns (Chapters 15 and 108). Patients presenting with injuries should be questioned carefully about their alcohol use. Tobacco (Chapter 14) and other drug abuse (Chapter 30) are more prevalent in people with alcohol problems than in the general population.

Diagnosis

Data from the history, physical examination, and laboratory generally are needed to provide a complete picture of the extent of alcohol problems in affected patients (Table 17–3).

HISTORY

A four-step approach to the alcohol history includes comprehensive questions about alcohol use and a thorough evaluation for alcohol-related problems.

STEP 1: ASK ALL PATIENTS ABOUT CURRENT AND PAST ALCOHOL USE. A single question—"Do you currently or have you ever used alcohol?"—can identify quickly patients who are not lifetime abstainers and who require further screening. Patients who answer yes to this question

Table 17–3 • DIAGNOSIS OF ALCOHOL PROBLEMS

HISTORY

Step 1: Ask all patients about current and past use
1. Do you drink alcohol (ever or currently)?
2. Do you have a family history of alcohol problems?

Step 2: Obtain detailed history regarding quantity and frequency of alcohol use
1. What types of alcohol do you consume?
2. How often do you drink?
3. How much do you usually drink?
4. Do you ever drink more and, if so, how much?

Step 3: Standardized questionnaire

CAGE QUESTIONS
1. Have you ever felt that you should Cut down on your drinking?
2. Have people Annoyed you by criticizing your drinking?
3. Have you ever felt bad or Guilty about drinking?
4. Have you ever taken a drink first thing in the morning (Eye-opener) to steady your nerves or get rid of a hangover?

Step 4: Assess specific areas in suspected or known problem drinkers
1. Criteria for alcohol abuse and dependence
2. Evidence of medical and psychiatric problems
3. Evidence of behavioral or social problems
4. Use of other substances:
   a. Tobacco
   b. Mood-altering prescription drugs
   c. Illicit drugs (e.g., heroin, cocaine)
5. Prior alcohol/substance abuse treatment

PHYSICAL EXAMINATION
1. Thorough and complete examination important in all patients
2. Focus attention to system with identified problems
3. In all patients, carefully examine
   a Central and peripheral nervous systems
   b. Cardiovascular system
   c. Liver
   d. Gastrointestinal tract

LABORATORY STUDIES
(IN SELECTED PATIENTS)
1. Liver enzymes
2. Coagulation studies
3. Complete blood count
4. Carbohydrate deficient transferrin

should proceed through the subsequent three steps. Patients who answer no can be classified as lifetime abstainers from alcohol and require no further questioning unless their answer changes over time. It is crucial to ask about current and past alcohol use because many patients who meet lifetime criteria for alcohol dependence but who are currently in recovery answer no to the question about current use; unless specifically asked about, important past use information may be missed.

STEP 2: OBTAIN DETAILED HISTORY REGARDING QUANTITY AND FREQUENCY OF ALCOHOL USE. Questions to be asked routinely include "What type or types of alcoholic drinks (beer, wine, spirits) do you consume?" Many patients do not consider the use of beer or wine "drinking." Quantity should be determined for typical use—"How much do you usually drink on a typical drinking day?"—and for range of use—"Do you ever drink more than your usual amount and, if so, how much?" This second question can be particularly important for identifying binge drinking. Quantity questions offer easy identification of at-risk drinking. Asking about the frequency of alcohol consumption—"How often do you drink?"—helps to distinguish daily from nondaily alcohol users. Binge drinkers who drink only on weekends tend to have significant alcohol problems yet not be daily drinkers. A major goal of step 2 is to acquire a complete characterization of current alcohol use behaviors and the pattern of quantity and frequency of alcohol use over the patient's lifetime.

STEP 3: USE STANDARDIZED SCREENING INSTRUMENTS. Many standardized questionnaires have been developed to detect alcohol abuse and dependence. The two questionnaires that have been evaluated most extensively in medical settings are the CAGE (Cut down, Annoyed, Guilty, and Eye opener; see Table 17–3) questionnaire and the Alcohol Use Disorder Identification Test (AUDIT). The CAGE questionnaire includes four questions and is scored by giving 1 point for each pos-

itive response. Given that the word *ever* is used in each CAGE question, by definition this instrument is designed to detect lifetime alcohol problems and does not distinguish between lifetime problems and current problems. To screen for alcohol abuse and dependence, the CAGE has a sensitivity of 43 to 94% and a specificity of 70 to 97% when a cutoff score of 2 is used to indicate a "positive" result.

The AUDIT's 10 questions cover the quantity and frequency of alcohol use, drinking behaviors, adverse psychological symptoms, and alcohol-related problems. It was developed by the World Health Organization to identify "hazardous" (e.g., at risk) drinking and "harmful" (e.g., alcohol use that results in physical or psychological harm) drinking. In contrast to the CAGE questionnaire, the AUDIT focuses on recent (current to past year) drinking behaviors. Each question is scored from 0 to 4 (range for total score is 0 to 40), and a total score of 8 is considered to be a positive result.

STEP 4: ASSESS SPECIFIC AREAS IN SUSPECTED OR KNOWN PROBLEM DRINKERS. Questions asked in step 4 are based on the results of the questions asked in steps 2 and 3 so as to obtain more detailed information in patients with potential alcohol problems. Even patients who do not screen positive on the CAGE may warrant detailed questioning about alcohol abuse and dependence (see Table 17–1), especially if they are drinking at or above at-risk levels or there is other evidence of possible alcohol problems. A detailed review for evidence of alcohol-related medical and psychiatric problems should occur, and the need for further medical and psychiatric evaluation should be determined. The physician should look for evidence for behavioral and social problems commonly associated with alcohol use and screen for family and occupational dysfunction and other problems, such as domestic violence. Patients should be asked about their use of tobacco, mood-altering prescription medications, and illicit drugs such as heroine and cocaine.

Finally, many patients with alcohol problems have prior treatment episodes that should be detailed. The inquiry should include questions not only about "formal" alcohol treatment (including number of episodes, duration of treatment, and inpatient versus outpatient treatment), but also about more "informal" treatments, such as attendance at self-help groups (e.g., Alcoholics Anonymous [AA]). For patients who require a referral for treatment, knowledge of prior treatment experience is a crucial determinant of future referral recommendations.

PHYSICAL EXAMINATION

Patients with potential alcohol use disorders require a detailed physical examination to complement the history. In addition, attention should be focused to detect common alcohol-related problems, including the nervous system, cardiovascular system, liver, and gastrointestinal system (see Table 17–2).

LABORATORY STUDIES

A variety of laboratory tests have been proposed to aid screening for alcoholic abuse and dependence. Aminotransferase levels, red blood cells, mean corpuscular volume, and carbohydrate deficient transferrin, alone or in combination, are not as effective as screening questionnaires, such as the CAGE and the AUDIT.

Laboratory tests do have a role in diagnosis and assessment of patients with potential alcohol problems. Routine laboratory testing including liver enzymes (Chapter 149), bilirubin, complete blood count, and prothrombin time should be obtained in all patients with alcohol problems on a regular basis so that an appropriate and complete picture of the effects of alcohol on the individual can be obtained.

DISCUSSING THE DIAGNOSIS WITH PATIENTS

When discussing alcohol problems, it is crucial that physicians be sensitive to the stigma and shame, which may be felt by patients with alcohol use and by their families. Alcohol-related diagnoses or problems should be discussed in a nonjudgmental manner, which forges a partnership and indicates commitment to helping with whatever problems the patients might have. Setting the stage for the discussion should include educating patients about the various levels of alcohol problems (e.g., at-risk drinking, alcohol abuse, alcohol dependence) so that patients have an understanding of the spectrum of alcohol problems. Many patients may have a skewed view of what qualifies

Table 17–4 • ADVICE FOR PATIENTS WITH ALCOHOL PROBLEMS

State your medical concern:
1. Be specific about your patient's drinking patterns and related health risks
2. *Ask* "How do you feel about your drinking?"

Agree on a plan of action:
1. *Ask:* "Are you ready to try to cut down or abstain?"
2. Talk with patients who are ready to make a change in their drinking about a specific plan of action

For patients who are not alcohol dependent:
1. Advise to cut down if drinking is at or above at-risk drinking amounts (see Table 17–1) and no evidence of alcohol dependence
2. *Ask* patient to set a specific drinking goal: "Are you ready to set a drinking goal?" Some patients choose to abstain for a period of time or for good; others prefer to limit the amount they drink. "What do you think will work best for you?"
3. Provide patient education materials and tell patient: "It helps to think about your reasons for wanting to cut down and examine what situations trigger unhealthy drinking patterns. These materials will give you some useful tips on how to maintain your drinking goal."

For patients with evidence of alcohol dependence:
1. Advise to abstain if:
   a. Evidence of alcohol dependence
   b. History of repeated failed attempts to cut down
   c. Pregnant or trying to conceive
   d. Contraindicated medical condition or medication
2. Refer for additional diagnostic evaluation or treatment. Procedures for patient in making referral decisions:
   a. Involve your patient in making referral decisions
   b. Discuss available alcohol treatment services
   c. Schedule a referral appointment while the patient is in the office

as problem drinking and may believe that only individuals with severe alcohol problems are truly problem drinkers. The history, physical examination, and laboratory studies should be provided as "proof" that a problem may or does exist.

 Prevention and Treatment

The relationship of change in alcohol use with prevention of subsequent problems has been well established. Treating alcohol use disorders should be based on the severity of potential or actual alcohol problems and tailored to meet the needs of individual patients. Separate advice and management approaches are suggested for nondependent at-risk or problem drinkers compared with individuals who are alcohol dependent (Table 17–4).

TREATMENT OF AT-RISK DRINKERS

Evidence confirms that generalist physicians, in a cost-effective manner, can help patients reduce their alcohol intake and prevent subsequent alcohol-related problems by using brief (5 to 20 minutes), focused counseling techniques (brief interventions) that are well suited for primary care and other medical settings. The brief counseling strategy includes four main components: motivational techniques, feedback about the problems with alcohol use, discussion of the adverse effects of alcohol, and setting recommended drinking limits. Motivational techniques are designed to motivate patients to change their alcohol use behavior by identifying potential or actual problems with which their alcohol use is associated. Feedback about these problems can make it clear to the patient that the problems exist. For at-risk and problem drinkers who do not meet criteria for alcohol dependence, setting recommended drinking limits below at-risk levels (e.g., less than one drink per day for women and less than two drinks per day for men) is a realistic and suitable goal. Epidemiologic evidence suggests that drinking below these levels is less likely to be associated with problems. Several randomized clinical trials confirm that patients who receive brief interventions significantly decrease their alcohol intake, often to "safe" levels, and can decrease health care use as well.∎

TREATMENT OF ALCOHOL DEPENDENCE

Patients who meet criteria for alcohol dependence typically require more intensive services than patients who meet criteria for at-risk drinking. Most patients can be managed in outpatient treatment settings, whereas patients with more severe alcohol dependence or comorbid problems initially may require inpatient management, specific counseling programs, and pharmacologic therapy. Before entering a formal program to maintain remission, many patients first require medical management of alcohol withdrawal. Professional organizations have published practice guidelines that provide useful recommendations for how to select among treatment options for patients with alcohol dependence.

Management of Alcohol Withdrawal

Many patients may not present for medical management of alcohol withdrawal and deal with it on their own. A substantial subset do present for alcohol withdrawal treatment, however. Patients with mild-to-moderate withdrawal generally can be managed safely as outpatients with close follow-up. Patients with moderate-to-severe withdrawal, as manifested by hypertension, tremor, and any mental status changes, especially patients with significant comorbid medical or psychiatric illnesses, generally are treated best as inpatients. Patients who have a history of severe withdrawal in the past (e.g., delirium tremens) or who have a history of alcohol withdrawal seizures also generally should be managed as inpatients. The three major goals of medical management of alcohol withdrawal are to minimize the severity of withdrawal-related symptoms; prevent specific withdrawal-related complications, such as seizures and delirium tremens; and provide referral to relapse-prevention treatment.

A wide variety of medications have been evaluated for their effectiveness in managing the alcohol withdrawal syndrome (Table 17–5). Longer acting benzodiazepines are preferred because they provide a smoother withdrawal. Shorter acting benzodiazepines, such as oxazepam, may be indicated in individuals with severe liver disease. The most common approach is to administer a standing dose of a benzodiazepine, with additional medication being given "as needed" on the basis of withdrawal symptoms. The specific benzodiazepine and dose often depend on the experience of the prescribing physician and the characteristics of the patient, including the severity of withdrawal (higher doses used if more severe), the presence of liver disease (patients with severe liver disease should receive lower doses or shorter acting medications), and the response to prior doses of medication (higher doses if symptom control is inadequate; lower doses if adverse effects, such as oversedation, have occurred). Generally, the amount of medication per dosing period is decreased gradually as the withdrawal syndrome abates. An individualized "symptom-triggered" dosing approach, in which benzodiazepines are administered on a dose-by-dose basis (e.g., 25 to 100 mg of chlordiazepoxide hourly) as guided by withdrawal symptoms, is safe and effective in certain patients and can reduce the total doses of benzodiazepines needed to treat withdrawal.∎ β-Blockers (atenolol and propranolol), α-agonists (clonidine), and antiepileptics (carbamazepine) improve signs and symptoms of alcohol withdrawal but are viewed best as adjunctive medications to be used in addition to benzodiazepines.

Prevention of Relapse

COUNSELING STRATEGIES USED BY ALCOHOL TREATMENT PROGRAMS. Three commonly used psychotherapeutic techniques include motivational enhancement therapy, 12-step facilitation, and cognitive behavioral coping skills. Two of these techniques are designed to give patients specific tools to help them avoid relapse to alcohol use. In motivational enhancement therapy, patients identify reasons for staying away from alcohol. The 12-step facilitation therapy uses the principles of AA to help patients focus their attention on abstinence. In cognitive behavioral coping skills therapy, the patient identifies triggers to alcohol use and develops strategies to help deal with the triggers when they are present.

Project MATCH (Matching Alcohol Treatments to Client Heterogenicity) showed equivalence among three counseling approaches (cognitive behavioral coping skills therapy, motivational enhancement therapy, or 12-step facilitation therapy) to treat alcohol dependence. At 1-year follow-up, most enrolled patients either remained abstinent or significantly decreased their alcohol use.

Table 17–5 • MEDICATIONS FOR THE TREATMENT OF ALCOHOL DEPENDENCE*

MEDICATION	DOSE, ROUTE(S)	FREQUENCY‡	EFFECTS	MAJOR COMMON ADVERSE EFFECTS
ALCOHOL WITHDRAWAL				
Benzodiazepines‡				
Chlordiazepoxide*	25–100 mg, PO/IV/IM†	Every 4–6 hr	Decreased severity of withdrawal; stabilization of vital sings; prevention of seizures and delirium tremens	Confusion, oversedation, respiratory depression
Diazepam†	5–10 mg, PO/IV/IM†	Every 6–8 hr		
Oxazepam†	15–30 mg, PO†	Every 6–8 hr		
Lorazepam†	1–4 mg, PO/IV/IM†	Every 4–8 hr		
β-Blockers				
Atenolol	25–50 mg, PO	Once a day	Improvement in vital signs; reduction in craving	Bradycardia, hypotension
Propranolol	10–40 mg, PO	Every 6–8 hr		
α-Agonists				
Clonidine	0.1–0.2 mg, PO	Every 6 hr	Decreased withdrawal symptoms	Hypotension, fatigue
Antiepileptics				
Carbamazepine	200 mg, PO	Every 6–8 hr	Decreased severity of withdrawal; prevention of seizures	Dizziness, fatigue, red blood cell abnormalities
PREVENTION OF RELAPSE				
Disulfiram†	125–500 mg, PO	Daily	Decreased alcohol use among those who relapse	Disulfiram-alcohol reaction, rash, drowsiness, peripheral neuropathy
Naltrexone†	50 mg, PO	Daily	Increased abstinence, decreased drinking days	Nausea, abdominal pain, myalgias/arthralgias
Acamprosate	1300–2000 mg, PO	Daily	Increased abstinence	Diarrhea

*Most commonly used medications listed.
†Currently approved by Food and Drug Administration for the indication noted.
‡Dose and routes given for standard fixed-dose regimens, which include dose tapers over time.

SELF-HELP GROUPS. Self-help groups such as AA and Rational Recovery are an important source of support and treatment for many patients with alcohol dependence. AA has the advantage of being widely available throughout the United States and free of charge. The overall approach to treatment is based on the 12 steps for maintaining abstinence and dealing with the various effects of alcohol. AA meetings can be either "open" to anybody in the community or "closed" to active members. The meetings vary in format, size, location, and demographic makeup. When counseling patients about attending AA, it is important for physicians to make them aware that variations in the nature of specific meetings, especially location and demographics of participants, require patients to be willing to attend more than one meeting site on a trial basis so that they find a comfortable setting.

Research of the effectiveness of AA has been limited, and there are no large controlled studies. Indirect evidence suggests, however, a significant improvement in alcohol use behaviors.

PHARMACOTHERAPY TO PREVENT RELAPSE TO ALCOHOL USE. The addition of medication to enhance the effectiveness of counseling therapies has been the subject of research for the past 40 years. As the neurobiology of alcohol use disorders has become more clearly understood, the potential to develop medications that may promote abstinence or decreased alcohol use has grown. Two medications, disulfiram and naltrexone, are approved for the treatment of alcohol dependence in the United States, and a third (acamprosate, which has been used extensively in Europe), is likely to be approved in the future (see Table 17–5).

Disulfiram. Disulfiram is designed to prevent alcohol use by causing a severe adverse reaction when patients use alcohol. The disulfiram reaction, which includes flushing, nausea, vomiting, and diarrhea, is mediated by the inhibition of alcohol dehydrogenase and the resulting increase in serum levels of acetaldehyde and acetate after ingestion of alcohol. Disulfiram also affects monoamine metabolism, and the alcohol-disulfiram reaction may be related to changes in central monoamine functioning. Although disulfiram offers little benefit to most patients, it is effective in reducing alcohol intake in highly motivated patients who are supervised in an alcohol treatment program.[3]

Naltrexone. Naltrexone is thought to decrease alcohol use by diminishing the euphorigenic effects of alcohol and by decreasing craving in alcohol-dependent patients. Randomized, placebo-controlled trials generally have shown that alcohol-dependent patients who receive naltrexone (50 mg/day) are more likely to remain abstinent compared with patients who receive placebo, and the effects persist after discontinuation of treatment,[4] although one randomized trial did not show benefit in male veterans with severe alcohol dependence. Side effects of naltrexone are infrequent, most notably self-limited nausea in about 10% of patients. Dose-related hepatotoxicity has been reported in patients treated for obesity with high-dose naltrexone (300 mg/day). Mild liver enzyme abnormalities are not a contraindication to naltrexone, but patients should be followed with repeat liver enzymes. Patients with acute hepatitis or liver failure should not use naltrexone.

Acamprosate. Although not approved by the Food and Drug Administration at this time, acamprosate (calcium acetylhomoaurinate) has been identified as a potentially effective agent for treating alcohol dependence. The precise mechanism of action of acamprosate is uncertain, but it may be related to its effects on neuroexcitatory amino acids and the inhibitory GABA system. In a randomized, placebo-controlled clinical trial, subjects who received acamprosate were more likely to remain abstinent compared with subjects who received placebo.[5] Side effects are minimal and typically include diarrhea. As with naltrexone, acamprosate is given as an adjunctive therapy to psychological treatments for alcohol dependence.

Other Pharmacologic Treatments to Prevent Relapse. Other medications that have shown promise include ondansetron,[6] bromocriptine, and sodium valproate. Other drugs have shown possible benefits in patients with concurrent depression (e.g., fluoxetine) or anxiety (e.g., buspirone) or no effect (e.g., lithium).

Prognosis

Alcohol abuse and dependence are chronic disorders that are characterized by exacerbations and remissions. The prognosis is better for patients who seek treatment and receive it in a systematic way (Table 17–6), but it can be poor for patients with advanced liver disease and continued alcohol use. In addition, the use of combinations of medications (e.g., naltrexone plus acamprosate) is under investigation.

Future Directions

To date, most studies have focused on shorter term outcomes, from a few months to a year. It is important to understand more clearly what happens to these patients over time, especially the need for "booster sessions" to sustain improvements provided by brief interventions. Acamprosate and other newer pharmacologic therapies may help many patients.

Table 17–6 • OVERVIEW OF TREATMENT APPROACH FOR PATIENTS WITH ALCOHOL PROBLEMS

Evaluate all patients
For patterns of problem alcohol use (Table 17–1).
For alcohol-related complications, if indicated (Table 17–2)
Using data collected from history, physical examination, and laboratory testing (Table 17–3)

For at-risk and nondependent problem drinkers:
Advise to decrease alcohol use to below at-risk levels (Table 17–4)
Advise patients who cannot decrease use to below at-risk levels to abstain

For patients who are alcohol dependent:
Assess for need for withdrawal management medications (Table 17–5)
Refer to an alcohol treatment program
Consider medication to prevent relapse (Table 17–5)

1. Fleming MF, Barry KL, Manwell LB, et al: Brief physician advice for problem alcohol drinkers: A randomized controlled trial in community-based primary care practices. JAMA 1997;277:1039–1045.
2. Saitz R, Mayo-Smith MF, Roberts MS, et al: Individualized treatment for alcohol withdrawal: A randomized double-blind controlled trial. JAMA 1994;272:519–523.
3. Fuller RK, Branchey L, Brightwell DR, et al: Disulfiram treatment of alcoholism: A Veterans Administration cooperative study. JAMA 1986;256:1449–1455.
4. Chick J, Anton R, Checinski K, et al: A multicentre, randomized, double-blind, placebo controlled trial of naltrexone in the treatment of alcohol dependence or abuse. Alcohol Alcohol 2000;35:587–593.
5. Tempesta E, Janiri L, Bignamini A, et al: Acamprosate and relapse prevention in the treatment of alcohol dependence: A placebo-controlled study. Alcohol Alcohol 2000;35:202–209.
6. Johnson BA, Roache JD, Javors MA, et al: Ondansetron for reduction of drinking among biologically predisposed alcoholic patients: A randomized controlled trial. JAMA 2000;284:963–971.

SUGGESTED READINGS

American Psychiatric Association Practice Guidelines for the Treatment of Psychiatric Disorders: Compendium 2002. Washington, DC, American Psychiatric Association, 2002. *Includes guidelines for treating alcohol dependence.*
Fiellin DA, Reid MC, O'Connor PG: New therapies for alcohol problems: Application to primary care. Am J Med 2000;108:227–237. *An evidence-based evaluation of the literature focusing on the treatment of alcohol-related problems in primary care settings.*
Kosten TR, O'Connor PG: Management of drug and alcohol withdrawal. N Engl J Med 2003;348:1786–1795. *Overview of inpatient and outpatient options.*
Kranzler HR, Van Kirk J: Efficacy of naltrexone and acamprosate for alcoholism treatment: A meta-analysis. Alcohol Clin Exp Res 2001;25:1335–1341. *Both seem to be equally effective.*
Saitz R, Horton NJ, Sullivan LM, et al: Addressing alcohol problems in primary care: A cluster randomized, controlled trial of a systems intervention. Ann Intern Med 2003;138:372–382. *When physicians are provided information and recommendations about their patients' alcohol habits, subsequent discussions may lead to decreased alcohol use.*

18 PRINCIPLES OF OCCUPATIONAL AND ENVIRONMENTAL MEDICINE

Philip J. Landrigan

In their work, people can be exposed to dangerous chemicals, hazardous physical agents, emotional stress, and trauma. Any of these occupational exposures can cause disease—sometimes immediately and sometimes after an interval of years or decades. In addition, tens of millions of people of all ages are exposed to environmental toxins. Some are exposed to high levels in well-publicized disasters, but many more are exposed chronically to lower levels. Air pollution, lead, radon, and pesticides are examples of environmental agents that can cause illness and death.

Occupational and environmental exposures cause a broad range of illnesses, and these diseases can involve virtually every organ system. They include classic, well-described diseases, such as lung cancer and malignant mesothelioma in workers exposed to asbestos, cancer of the bladder in dye workers, pneumoconiosis in coal miners, leukemia and lymphoma in people exposed to benzene, skin cancer in farmers and sailors chronically exposed to the sun, and chronic bronchitis in workers exposed to dust particles. Occupational illnesses also include more recently recognized entities, such as dementia in persons exposed to solvents; sterility in men and women exposed to certain pesticides; asthma and bronchitis in children and adults chronically exposed to particulate air pollution; and carpal tunnel syndrome in workers engaged in repetitive, stressful wrist motion. Some of these diseases are

acute; others are chronic. Some are manifested through obvious symptoms, whereas others involve more subtle degrees of dysfunction.

In the United States, occupational exposure accounts each year for approximately 6500 traumatic deaths from injury, 13.2 million nonfatal injuries, 60,000 deaths from disease, and 860,000 cases of work-related illness. The total costs, direct medical expenses plus indirect economic losses, are estimated to be $171 billion annually, nearly 3% of the gross domestic product of the United States. In the environment, the Centers for Disease Control and Prevention estimate that nearly 1 million children have lead poisoning and that tens of thousands have asthma induced by indoor and outdoor air pollution. The total costs of disease of environmental origin in American children are estimated annually to be $55 billion.

Diagnosis

Occupational and environmental exposures always need to be considered in the differential diagnosis. Because of the enormous numbers exposed and the wide range of illnesses, the possibility of occupational or environmental exposure to toxins needs to be considered in the evaluation of every patient.

Occupational and environmental diseases are underdiagnosed. Many are attributed incorrectly to other causes because frequently these diseases are not distinct in their clinical features and can resemble closely chronic diseases caused by other factors. Examples include (1) lung cancer caused by asbestos or radon, which is attributed to cigarette smoking; (2) severe abdominal pain caused by lead poisoning, which is diagnosed erroneously as acute appendicitis (some cases have resulted in unnecessary laparotomy); (3) dementia caused by organic solvents, which is attributed to "old age" or to ethanol ingestion; (4) renal failure caused by chronic exposure to lead or cadmium, which is ascribed to "idiopathic factors"; (5) hearing loss caused by noise, which is incorrectly attributed to presbycusis; and (6) asthma resulting from an occupational exposure, which is diagnosed incorrectly as intrinsic asthma.

A correct diagnosis can be made in these cases only if a careful history of toxic occupational and environmental exposure is taken. A barrier to accurate diagnosis is the long latency that commonly must elapse between some occupational or environmental exposure and the appearance of disease. For some occupational and environmental cancers (e.g., mesothelioma caused by asbestos or lymphoma caused by benzene), this latency may span decades. Another impediment to diagnosis is that many people have had multiple toxic exposures at work or in the environment. Until more recently, workers often were not given the names of the materials with which they worked or provided adequate information about the hazards of these materials.

The keys to diagnosing occupational and environmental disease are (1) obtaining an adequate history of occupational and environmental exposure for every patient, (2) possessing basic knowledge about the pathogenesis and clinical features of the major types of occupational and environmental disease, and (3) knowing how to report suspected cases of occupational and environmental illness to public health authorities so that additional cases caused by the same exposure can be recognized or prevented. Clusters of disease in a workplace can be an important clue to a common cause. Physicians should be especially knowledgeable about the occupational and environmental diseases that commonly occur in their practice areas, such as asbestosis and malignant mesothelioma in port cities with shipyards, pesticide intoxication in agricultural areas, and poisonings from solvents and exotic metals in regions that produce computer components.

OCCUPATIONAL AND ENVIRONMENTAL HISTORY

The history is the most important instrument for obtaining information on the role of occupational and environmental factors in causing disease (Chapter 5). Information about current and past exposure routinely should be sought in every patient at several logical points when taking a history. At each juncture, a few brief screening questions should be asked systematically. Then if suspicious information is elicited, more detailed follow-up questions are needed. A routine screen for occupational and environmental disease consists of the following items:

1. In the *history of the present illness,* pay attention to any temporal relationship between the onset of illness and toxic exposure in the workplace or the environment. Did symptoms begin shortly after the patient started a new job? Did the symptoms

abate during vacation, then recrudesce after the patient resumed work? Were the symptoms related to the introduction of a new chemical or process? Did the symptoms correlate with episodes of pollution? Were there similar illnesses among coworkers or neighbors? Were individuals who were exposed more heavily affected more severely? A possible occupational cause should be sought in every case of acute trauma (in children and adolescents as well as adults) and in every case of repetitive trauma (e.g., carpal tunnel syndrome).

2. In the *medical history,* obtain a list of current and principal past occupations and industries of employment. Each patient should be asked whether illness ever developed as a consequence of the work.

3. In the *review of systems,* routinely ask every patient: "Do you now or have you previously had occupational or environmental exposure to asbestos, lead, fumes, chemicals, dust particles, loud noise, radiation, or other toxic factors?" Also ask all patients whether they believe that any of these factors may have caused or contributed to their illness. Even if a postulated connection between exposure and disease initially seems tenuous, these suspicions always need to be considered carefully.

DETAILED EXPOSURE HISTORY. If information from the routine interview suggests an occupational or environmental cause, the physician should obtain a more detailed history of toxic exposure. Data on the duration and intensity of exposure are particularly important. It is necessary to learn how the patient worked with the suspected toxin and to consider how the material may have been absorbed. Information should be obtained on all jobs ever held, places of employment, products manufactured, and materials with which the patient worked.

If toxic exposure is identified or strongly suspected and an occupational or environmental cause seems likely, further follow-up inquiries may need to be made through the patient's labor union, companies where the patient has been employed, company physicians, or state or local health departments. Information on toxic substances used in a workplace should be legally available to patients under the Records Access Standard and Hazard Communication Standard of the Occupational Safety and Health Administration and under state and local "right-to-know" laws.

REPORTING AND REFERRAL. If the diagnostic interview indicates or strongly raises suspicion that disease is due to toxic occupational or environmental exposure, the physician is required in most jurisdictions to report the case to state or local public health authorities. Many episodes of these diseases are in essence common-source outbreaks of highly preventable illness. Prompt reporting can lead to identification of additional cases earlier and to prevention by abating a common exposure source.

The physician may require access to specialized referral sources in occupational and environmental medicine. Two national organizations that maintain listings of occupational and environmental specialist physicians are the American College of Occupational and Environmental Medicine (Arlington Heights, IL) and the Association of Occupational and Environmental Clinics (Washington, DC). Other valuable resources are the U.S. Public Health Service's National Institute for Occupational Safety and Health (Cincinnati, OH), the Centers for Disease Control and Prevention (Atlanta, GA), and the Agency for Toxic Substances and Disease Registry (Atlanta, GA).

If the history suggests an occupational or environmental cause, the following fundamental principles help make a diagnosis of occupational or environmental disease:

1. *Biologic plausibility.* The likelihood that a disease is of occupational or environmental origin increases if the disease has been seen previously in other patients with the same or similar exposure, if a biologic mechanism is known, or if the disease has been seen in laboratory animals experimentally exposed to the chemical (or to a similar chemical). Many thousands of chemicals to which workers are exposed regularly in industry and that have been dispersed into the environment have never been laboratory tested for their toxicity, however. The possibility always exists of diagnosing a disease entity that has never been recognized previously. That was the sequence of events in the initial clinical recognition of malignant mesothelioma in workers exposed to asbestos, hepatic angiosarcoma in workers exposed to vinyl chloride, and cancer of the bladder in aniline dye workers.

2. *Dose response.* The likelihood of occupational or environmental causation increases if the disease occurs more commonly and seriously in more heavily exposed members of a population. In the case of occupational and environmental carcinogens, however, there are no threshold levels of exposure below which safety is ensured; any exposure to these agents is potentially carcinogenic, although heavier exposure carries greater risk. In addition, agents that are allergens or chemical sensitizers can cause symptoms at low exposure levels.

SENTINEL HEALTH EVENTS. To help physicians establish linkages between occupational exposure and disease, a sentinel health event is defined as an unnecessary disease, disability, or untimely death that is occupationally related. By scanning the list in Table 18–1, physicians can identify work-related illnesses or exposures that may occur in their patients. Additionally, they can identify occupations and industries that may be pertinent to their local practice areas. This selected list also represents an accessible starting point for developing competence in the differential diagnosis of occupational and environmental disease.

Table 18–1 • SELECTED LIST OF SENTINEL HEALTH EVENTS (OCCUPATIONAL)—OCCUPATIONALLY RELATED UNNECESSARY DISEASE, DISABILITY, AND UNTIMELY DEATH

CONDITION	INDUSTRY/PROCESS/OCCUPATION	AGENT
Pulmonary tuberculosis	Medical personnel, medical laboratory workers	*Mycobacterium tuberculosis*
Plague, tularemia, anthrax, rabies, and other infections	Farmer, rancher, hunter, veterinarian, laboratory worker, bioterrorist	Various infectious agents
Fish fancier's finger	Aquarium worker/cleaner, longshoreman	*M. tuberculosis*
Herpetic whitlow	Health care personnel	Herpes simplex virus
Tetanus	Farmer, rancher	*Clostridium tetani*
Human immunodeficiency virus	Health care worker	Human immunodeficiency virus
Rubella	Medical personnel, intensive care personnel	Rubella virus
Hepatitis	Day care staff, orphanage staff, health care worker, sewage worker	Hepatitis A, B, and C viruses
Ornithosis	Bird breeder, pet shop staff, veterinarian, zoo staff, duck processing	*Chlamydia psittaci*
Rocky Mountain spotted fever	Laboratory technician, tick breeder, microbiologist, hiker	*Rickettsia rickettsii*
Leptospirosis	Farmer, laborer	*Leptospira*
Histoplasmosis	Bridge maintenance worker	*Histoplasma capsulatam*
Sporotrichosis	Nursery worker, forest worker, florist	*Sporothrix schenckii*

Table 18–1 • SELECTED LIST OF SENTINEL HEALTH EVENTS (OCCUPATIONAL)—OCCUPATIONALLY RELATED UNNECESSARY DISEASE, DISABILITY, AND UNTIMELY DEATH—cont'd

CONDITION	INDUSTRY/PROCESS/OCCUPATION	AGENT
Malignant neoplasm of nasopharynx	Carpenter, cabinet maker, sawmill worker, lumberjack, electrician, fitter	Chlorophenols
Hemangiosarcoma of the liver	Vinyl chloride polymerization industry	Vinyl chloride monomer
Mesothelioma	Asbestos industry and utilizer	Asbestos (all types)
Malignant neoplasm of nasal cavities	Woodworker, cabinet and furniture maker	Hardwood dusts
	Boot and shoe industry	Unknown
	Radium chemists and processors	Radium
	Nickel smelting and refining worker	Nickel
	Chromium producer and user	Chromates
Malignant neoplasm of larynx	Asbestos industry and utilizer	Asbestos
Malignant neoplasm of trachea, bronchus, and lung	Asbestos industry and utilizer	Asbestos
	Topside coke oven worker	Coke oven emissions
	Uranium and fluorspar miner	Radon daughters
	Smelter, processor, user, welder	Chromates, nickel, arsenic
	Mustard gas formulator	Mustard gas
	Ion exchange resin maker, chemist	Bis(chloromethyl) ether, chloromethyl ether
	Foundry-floor molder and caster	Polycyclic aromatic hydrocarbons
Malignant neoplasm of bone	Radium chemist and processor, dial painter	Radium
Malignant neoplasm of scrotum	Automatic lathe operator, metalworker	Mineral/cutting oils
	Chimney sweep	Soot
Malignant neoplasm of bladder	Rubber and dye worker	Benzidine, α- and β-naphthylamine, magenta, auramine, 4-aminobiphenyl, 4-nitrophenyl
Malignant neoplasm of kidney, other and unspecified urinary organs	Coke oven worker	Coke oven emissions
Lymphoid leukemia	Rubber industry, chemical industry	Benzene, 1,3-butadiene, ethylene oxide
	Radiologist	Ionizing radiation
Myeloid leukemia	Rubber worker, chemist, and other occupations with exposure to benzene	Benzene
	Radiologist	Ionizing radiation
Erythroleukemia	Occupations with exposure to benzene	Benzene
Nonautoimmune hemolytic anemia	Whitewashing and leather industry	Copper sulfate
	Electrolytic processes, arsenical ore smelting	Arsine
	Plastics industry	Trimellitic anhydride
	Dye, celluloid, resin industry	Naphthalene
Aplastic anemia	Explosives manufacture	Trinitrotoluene (TNT)
	Rubber worker, chemist, and other occupations with exposure to benzene	Benzene
	Radiologist, radium chemist, and dial painter	Ionizing radiation
Agranulocytosis or neutropenia	Explosives and pesticide industries	Arsenic
	Pesticides, pigments, pharmaceuticals	Phosphorus
	Rubber worker, chemist, and other occupations with exposure to benzene	Benzene
Methemoglobinemia	Explosives and dye industries	Aromatic amino and nitro compounds (e.g., aniline, TNT, nitroglycerin)
	Rubber worker	Aniline, o-toluidine, nitrobenzene
Toxic encephalitis	Battery, smelter, and foundry workers	Lead
	Electrolytic chlorine production, battery maker, fungicide formulator	Inorganic and organic mercury
Parkinson's disease (secondary)	Manganese processing, battery maker, welder	Manganese
	Internal combustion engine industries	Carbon monoxide
Cerebellar ataxia	Chemical industry using toluene	Toluene
	Electrolytic chlorine production, battery marker, fungicide formulator	Organic mercury
Carpal tunnel syndrome	Meat packer, deboner, computer operator	Cumulative trauma
Mononeuritis of upper limb and mononeuritic multiplex	Dental technician	Methylmethacrylate monomer
	Poultry processing turkey	Cumulative trauma
	Meat packer, deboner	Cumulative trauma
Inflammatory and toxic neuropathy	Pesticide industry, pigments, pharmaceuticals formulator	Arsenic/arsenic compounds
	Furniture refinisher, degreasing operation	Hexane
	Plastic-coated–fabric worker	Methyl n-butyl ketone
	Explosives industry	TNT
	Rayon manufacturing	Carbon disulfide
	Plastics, hydraulics, coke industries	Tri-o-cresyl phosphate
	Battery, smelter, and foundry workers	Inorganic lead
	Dentist, chloralkali workers	Inorganic mercury
	Chloralkali plants, fungicide maker, battery maker	Organic mercury

Continued on page 84.

Table 18–1 • SELECTED LIST OF SENTINEL HEALTH EVENTS (OCCUPATIONAL)—OCCUPATIONALLY RELATED UNNECESSARY DISEASE, DISABILITY, AND UNTIMELY DEATH—cont'd

CONDITION	INDUSTRY/PROCESS/OCCUPATION	AGENT
	Plastics industry, paper manufacturing	Acrylamide
	Ethylene oxide sterilizer operator	Ethylene oxide
Cataract	Microwave and radar technicians	Microwaves
	Explosives industries, trinitrotoluene worker	TNT
	Radiologist	Ionizing radiation
	Blacksmith, glass blower, baker	Infared radiation
	Moth repellant formulator, fumigator	Naphthalene
	Explosives, dye, herbicide and pesticides industries	Dinitrophenol dinitro-o-cresol
	Ethylene oxide sterilizer operator, microbiology supervisor, inspector	Ethylene oxide
Hearing loss	Occupations with exposure to excessive noise	Excessive noise
Raynaud's phenomenon (secondary)	Lumberjack, chain sawyer, grinder, chipper, rock driller, stone cutter, jackhammer operator, riveter	Whole body or segmental vibration
	Vinyl chloride polymerization industry	Vinyl chloride
Extrinsic asthma	Jewelry, alloy, and catalyst makers	Platinum
	Polyurethane, adhesive, and paint workers	Isocyanates
	Alloy, catalyst, and refinery workers	Chromium, cobalt
	Solderer	Aluminum soldering flux
	Plastic, dye, and insecticide maker	Phthalic anhydride
	Foam worker, latex maker, biologist	Formaldehyde
	Printing industry	Gum arabic
	Nickel plater	Nickel sulfate
	Baker	Flour
	Plastics industry, organic chemical manufacture	Trimellitic anhydride
	Woodworker, furniture maker	Red cedar (plicatic acid) and other wood dusts
	Detergent formulator	*Bacillus*-derived exoenzymes
	Snow crab processing worker	Unknown
	Hospital worker	Latex
Maltworker's lung	Maltworker	*Aspergillus clavatus*
Mushroom worker's lung	Mushroom farm/spawning shed, farmer	Pasteurized compost
Grain handler's lung	Grain handler	*Erwinia herbicola* (*Enterobacter agglomerans*)
Sequoiosis	Red cedar mill worker, woodworker, sawmill, joinery	Redwood sawdust *Thuja plicata*
Unspecified allergic alveolitis	Cinnamon processing worker	Cinnamon dust, cinnamaldehyde
	Distillery, vegetable compost plant worker	*Aspergillus fumigatus*
	Sawmill worker	Wood dust
	Paper manufacture/wood room	*Alternaria*, wood dust
	Snow crab processing worker	Unknown
Coalworker's pneumoconiosis	Coal miner, power plant worker	Coal dust
Asbestosis	Asbestos industry and utilizer	Asbestos
Silicosis	Quarryman, sandblaster, silica processor, mining, metal, and ceramic industries	Silica
	Cryolite refining	Cryolite (Na_3AlF_6), quartz dust
Talcosis	Talc processor, soapstone mining/milling, polishing, cosmetics industry	Talc
Chronic beryllium disease of the lung	Beryllium alloy worker, ceramic and cathode ray tube maker, nuclear reactor worker	Beryllium
Byssinosis	Cotton industry worker	Cotton, flax, hemp, and cotton-synthetic dusts
Acute bronchitis, pneumonitis, and pulmonary edemia owing to fumes and vapors	Refrigeration, fertilizer, oil refining industries	Ammonia
	Alkali and bleach industries	Chlorine
	Silo fillers, arc welders, nitric acid industry	Nitrogen oxides
	Paper and refrigeration industries, oil refining	Sulfur dioxide
	Cadmium smelter, processor	Cadmium
	Plastics industry	Trimellitic anhydride
	Boilermaker	Vanadium pentoxide
	Organic chemicals manufacture	Trimellitic anhydride
Toxic hepatitis	Solvent utilizer, dry cleaner, plastics industry	Carbon tetrachloride, chloroform, tetrachloroethane, trichloroethylene, tetrachlorethylene
	Explosives and dye industries	Phosphorus, TNT
	Fire and waterproofing additive formulators	Chloronaphthalenes
	Plastics formulator	Methylenedianiline
	Fumigator, gasoline and fire extinguisher formulators	Methyl bromide Ethylene dibromide
	Disinfectant, fumigant, synthetic resin formulators	Cresol

Table 18–1 • SELECTED LIST OF SENTINEL HEALTH EVENTS (OCCUPATIONAL)—OCCUPATIONALLY RELATED UNNECESSARY DISEASE, DISABILITY, AND UNTIMELY DEATH—cont'd

CONDITION	INDUSTRY/PROCESS/OCCUPATION	AGENT
Acute or chronic renal failure	Battery maker, plumber, solderer	Inorganic lead
	Electrolytic processes, arsenical ore smelting	Arsine
	Battery maker, jeweler, dentist	Inorganic mercury
	Fluorocarbon formulator, fire extinguisher maker	Carbon tetrachloride
	Antifreeze manufacture	Ethylene glycol
Infertility, male	Chlordecone (Kepone) formulator	Chlordecone
	DBCP producer, formulator, and applicator	Dibromochloropropane
Contact and allergic dermatitis	Leather tanning, poultry dressing plants, fish packing, adhesives and sealants industry, boat building and repair	Irritants (e.g., cutting oils, phenol, solvents, acids, alkalis, detergents); allergens (e.g., nickel, chromates, formaldehyde, dyes, rubber products)
Skeletal fluorosis	Cryolite worker (grinding room), cryolite refining worker	Cryolite (Na_3AlF_6)

Adapted from Mullan RJ, Murthy LI: Occupational sentinel health events: An updated list for physician recognition and public health surveillance. Am J Ind Med 1991;19:775–799.

SUGGESTED READINGS

Levy B, Wegman D: Occupational Health: Recognizing and Preventing Work-Related Disease and Injury, 4th ed. Philadelphia, Lippincott Williams & Wilkins, 2000. *A prevention-based guide to occupational medicine.*

Rosentock L, Cullen M: Clinical Occupational Medicine, 3rd ed. Philadelphia, WB Saunders, 2003. *The definitive text in occupational and environmental medicine.*

19 RADIATION INJURY

Arthur C. Upton

The term *radiation injury* denotes any abnormality of form or function caused by electromagnetic waves or accelerated atomic particles. The term also often is applied to the harmful effects of high-intensity ultrasound and electromagnetic fields. Because the different types of radiation differ markedly in their biologic effects, each must be dealt with separately in terms of the injuries that they can cause.

IONIZING RADIATION

Ionizing radiation occurs as electromagnetic waves of extremely short wavelength (Fig. 19–1) and as accelerated atomic particles (e.g., electrons, protons, neutrons, α-particles). The injuries caused by ionizing radiation include mutagenic, carcinogenic, and teratogenic effects and various acute and chronic tissue reactions, such as erythema, cataract of the lens, sterility, and depression of hematopoiesis.

Etiology

The biologic effects of ionizing radiation result from damage to DNA and other vital molecules by locally deposited energy. Doses of ionizing radiation are measured in terms of energy deposition (Table 19–1).

All humans are exposed continuously to natural background ionizing radiation from (1) cosmic rays; (2) radium and other radioactive elements in the earth's crust; (3) potassium-40, carbon-14, and other radionuclides normally present in human tissues; and (4) inhaled radon and its daughter elements (Table 19–2). In people residing at mile-high elevations, as in Denver, Colorado, the contribution from cosmic rays may be increased 2-fold, and at jet aircraft altitudes it may be increased more than 100-fold, exceeding 0.005 mSv (1 Sv = 100 rem) per hour. Likewise, in regions where the earth's crust is rich in radium, the contribution from this radionuclide may be substantially increased.

Among man-made sources of radiation, the largest source is the use of x-rays in medical diagnosis. Smaller amounts of radiation are received from radioactive minerals in building materials, phosphate fertilizers, and crushed rock; radiation-emitting components of tele-

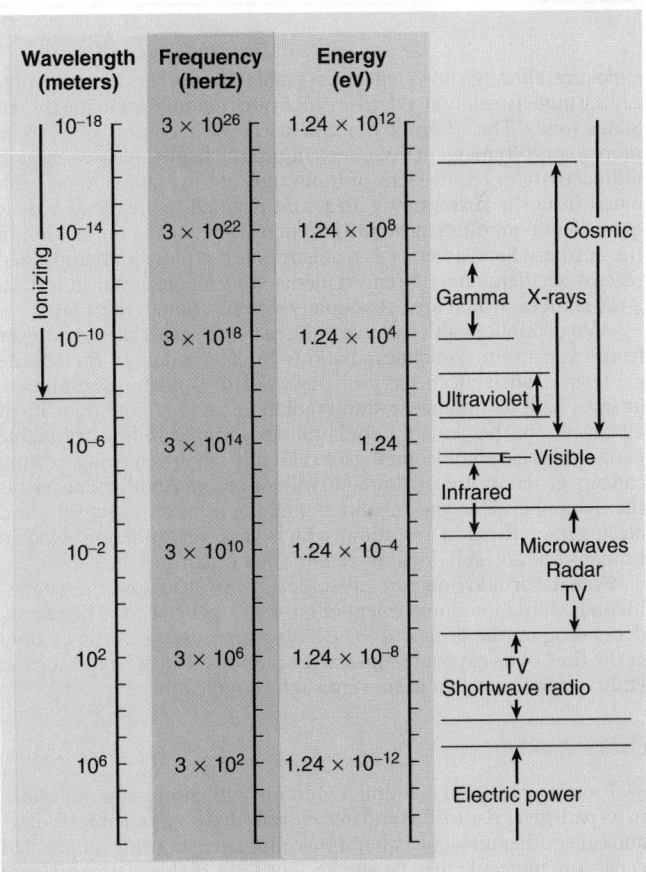

FIGURE 19–1 • The electromagnetic spectrum. (From Mettler FA, Upton AC: Effects of Ionizing Radiation, 2nd ed. Philadelphia, WB Saunders, 1995.)

vision sets, smoke detectors, and other consumer products; radioactive fallout from atomic weapons; and nuclear power.

Workers in various occupations are exposed to additional doses of ionizing radiation, depending on their job assignments and working conditions. The average annual effective dose received by monitored radiation workers in the United States is less than 1 mSv, and fewer than 1% approach the maximum permissible dose limit (50 mSv) in any given year.

Incidence, Prevalence, and Epidemiology

Precise data on the frequency of injuries caused by ionizing radiation are not available. Injuries attributable to excessive occupational

Table 19–1 • RADIATION QUANTITIES AND DOSE UNITS

QUANTITY	DOSE UNIT	DEFINITION
Radioactivity	Becquerel (Bq)	One disintegration per second
Absorbed dose	Gray (Gy)	Energy deposited in tissue (1 J/kg)
Equivalent dose	Sievert (Sv)	Absorbed dose weighted for quality (potency) of the radiation
Effective dose	Sievert (Sv)	Equivalent dose weighted for sensitivity of the exposed organs
Collective effective dose	Person—Sv	Effective dose applied to a population
Committed effective dose	Sievert (Sv)	Effective dose from a given intake of radioactivity to be received over a period extending into the future

Modified from Phillips TL: Radiation injury. *In* Wyngaarden JB, Smith LH Jr, Bennett JC (eds): Cecil Textbook of Medicine, 19th ed. Philadelphia, WB Saunders, 1992, p 2351.

Table 19–2 • AVERAGE AMOUNTS OF IONIZING RADIATION RECEIVED ANNUALLY FROM DIFFERENT SOURCES BY A RESIDENT OF THE UNITED STATES

SOURCE	DOSE*	
	mSv	%
Natural		
Radon[†]	2.0	55
Cosmic	0.27	8
Terrestrial	0.28	8
Internal	0.39	11
Total natural	2.94	82
Artificial		
X-ray diagnosis	0.39	11
Nuclear medicine	0.14	4
Consumer products	0.10	<0.3
Occupational	<0.01	<0.03
Nuclear fuel cycle	<0.01	<0.03
Nuclear fallout	<0.01	<0.03
Miscellaneous[‡]	<0.01	<0.03
Total artificial	0.63	18
Total natural and artificial	~3.6	100

*Average effective dose.
[†]Average effective dose to bronchial epithelium.
[‡]Department of Energy facilities, smelters, and transportation.
Modified from Health Effects of Exposure to Low Levels of Ionizing Radiation: BEIR V. Washington, DC, National Academy of Sciences, National Academy Press, 1990.

exposure, although prevalent among radiation workers in the era preceding modern safety standards, seldom are encountered in the United States today. The Chernobyl accident caused radiation sickness in more than 200 emergency workers, injured 28 fatally, released enough radioactivity to require tens of thousands of inhabitants to be evacuated from the surrounding area, and resulted in a collective dose equivalent commitment of 600,000 person-Sv for the population of the northern hemisphere. Less catastrophic but more numerous than reactor accidents have been accidents with medical and industrial γ-ray sources, which are occasionally serious enough to be fatal.

Also of public health concern is the risk to the population of cancer from exposure to ionizing radiation. To date, although no definite evidence of such effects has been observed in populations residing in areas of high natural background radiation, and no more than 3% of all cancers in the general population are thought to be attributable to natural background ionizing irradiation, a larger percentage of lung cancers generally are attributed to indoor radon. Another concern is the risk of heritable abnormalities resulting from the mutagenic and clastogenic effects of radiation, which have yet to be observed in humans but are well documented in other organisms.

Prenatal irradiation can cause death, malformations, cataracts, mental retardation, impairment of growth, and behavioral disorders, depending on the dose and the developmental stage of the embryo at the time of its exposure. Special precautions to avoid exposing the embryo now are taken to prevent such complications.

Pathogenesis

Ionizing radiation colliding randomly with atoms and molecules in its path gives rise to ions and free radicals that break chemical bonds and cause other molecular alterations, ultimately injuring the affected cells. Any molecule may be altered, but DNA is the critical biologic target because of the limited redundancy of its genetic information. A dose of radiation large enough to kill the average dividing cell (2 Sv) causes hundreds of lesions in its DNA molecules. Most lesions are reparable, but lesions produced by a densely ionizing radiation (e.g., proton or α-particle) are generally less reparable than lesions produced by a sparsely ionizing radiation (e.g., x-ray or γ-ray).

Unrepaired or misrepaired damage to DNA may be expressed in the form of mutations, the frequency of which approximates 10^{-5} to 10^{-6} per locus per sievert. Because the mutation rate tends to increase in proportion to the dose, it is inferred that a single ionizing particle traversing a genetic target may suffice to cause a mutation. Radiation damage also can cause changes in chromosome number and structure, the yields of which are characterized well enough that their frequency in lymphocytes can serve as a biologic dosimeter.

Radiation damage to genes, chromosomes, and other vital organelles may kill cells, especially dividing cells, which are radiosensitive as a class. Measured in terms of proliferative capacity, the survival of dividing cells tends to decrease exponentially with increasing dose; rapid exposure to 1 to 2 Sv generally reduces the surviving population of such cells by about 50%. Except for lymphocytes and oocytes, which tend to die in interphase, most cells killed by irradiation die in mitosis.

Although the killing of cells is a stochastic process, too few cells are killed by a dose less than 0.5 Sv to cause clinically detectable injury in most organs other than the testis and organs of the embryo. The killing of dividing progenitor cells, if sufficiently extensive, can interfere with the orderly replacement of senescent cells, especially in tissues such as the epidermis, bone marrow, and intestinal epithelium, which normally are characterized by high rates of cell turnover. The timing of the resulting atrophy (Fig. 19–2) varies, depending on the cell population dynamics within the tissue in question; in organs such as the liver and vascular endothelium, which are characterized by slow cell turnover, expression of the injury is delayed. Also, if the volume of tissue exposed is small or if the dose is accumulated slowly enough, the effects of irradiation may be counteracted in part by compensatory regenerative hyperplasia of surviving cells.

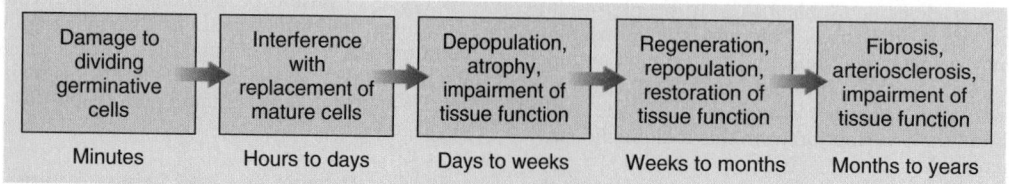

Damage to dividing germinative cells	Interference with replacement of mature cells	Depopulation, atrophy, impairment of tissue function	Regeneration, repopulation, restoration of tissue function	Fibrosis, arteriosclerosis, impairment of tissue function
Minutes	Hours to days	Days to weeks	Weeks to months	Months to years

FIGURE 19–2 • Characteristic sequence of events in the pathogenesis of the nonstochastic effects of ionizing radiation. (From Upton AC: Radiological science. *In* Detels R, Holland W, McEwen J, Omenn GS [eds]: Oxford Textbook of Public Health, 3rd ed. New York, Oxford University Press, 1997, by permission of Oxford University Press.)

Table 19–3 • APPROXIMATE THRESHOLD DOSES OF CONVENTIONALLY FRACTIONATED THERAPEUTIC RADIATION FOR CLINICALLY DETRIMENTAL NONSTOCHASTIC EFFECTS IN VARIOUS TISSUES

ORGAN	INJURY AT 5 YEARS	THRESHOLD DOSE (Gy)*	IRRADIATION FIELD (AREA)
Fetus	Death	2	Whole
Bone marrow	Hypoplasia	2	Whole
Ovary	Permanent sterility	2–3	Whole
Lens	Cataract	5	Whole
Testes	Permanent sterility	5–15	Whole
Cartilage, child	Arrested growth	10	Whole
Breast, child	Hypoplasia	10	5 cm^2
Bone, child	Arrested growth	20	10 cm^2
Bone marrow	Hypoplasia, fibrosis	20	Localized
Muscle, child	Hypoplasia	20–30	Whole
Kidney	Nephrosclerosis	23	Whole
Lymph nodes	Atrophy	33–45	—
Liver	Liver failure, ascites	35	Whole
Lung	Pneumonitis, fibrosis	40	Lobe
Heart	Pericarditis, pancarditis	40	Whole
Stomach, small intestine, colon	Ulcer, perforation	45	100 cm^2
Thyroid	Hypothyroidism	45	Whole
Pituitary	Hypopituitarism	45	Whole
Lymphatics	Sclerosis	50	—
Central nervous system (brain)	Necrosis	50	Whole
Spinal cord	Necrosis, transaction	50	5 cm^2
Salivary glands	Xerostomia	50	50 cm^2
Cornea	Keratitis	50	Whole
Capillaries	Telangiectasis, fibrosis	50–60	—
Breast, adult	Atrophy, necrosis	>50	Whole
Rectum	Ulcer, stricture	55	100 cm^2
Skin	Ulcer, severe fibrosis	55	100 cm^2
Eye	Panophthalmitis, hemorrhage	55	Whole
Oral mucosa	Ulcer, severe fibrosis	60	50 cm^2
Esophagus	Ulcer, stricture	60	75 cm^2
Cartilage, adult	Necrosis	60	Whole
Urinary bladder	Ulcer, contracture	60	Whole
Bone, adult	Necrosis, fracture	60	10 cm^2
Ear (inner)	Deafness	>60	Whole
Adrenal	Hypoadrenalism	>60	Whole
Vagina	Ulcer, fistula	90	5 cm
Muscle, adult	Atrophy	>100	Whole
Uterus	Necrosis, perforation	>100	Whole

*Dose causing effect in 1 to 5% of exposed persons.
Adapted from Rubin P, Casarett GW: A direction for clinical radiation pathology: The tolerance dose. In Vaeth JM (ed): Frontiers of Radiation Therapy and Oncology. Basel, Karger, 1972; and Nonstochastic effects of ionizing radiation. ICRP Publication 41. Ann ICRP 14:1, 1984, with permission from Elsevier Science Ltd.

Clinical Manifestations

Ionizing radiation injuries encompass a diversity of tissue reactions that vary markedly in dose-response relationships, manifestations, timing, and prognosis (Table 19–3). Except for mutagenic and carcinogenic effects, the reactions generally result from the killing of sizable numbers of cells in the exposed tissues and are not detectable unless the dose of radiation exceeds a substantial threshold. For this reason, the reactions are called *nonstochastic* (or *deterministic*) effects, in contrast to mutagenic and carcinogenic effects, which are presumed to have no thresholds and are considered to be *stochastic* in nature. The existing data do not exclude the possibility, however, that the latter effects may have thresholds in the millisievert dose range, and the existence of adaptive responses to radiation (e.g., DNA repair processes) has been interpreted by some observers to support the hypothesis that the net effects of small doses may be beneficial ("radiation hormesis").

Tissues in which cells proliferate rapidly are generally the first to exhibit radiation injury. In such tissues, mitotic inhibition and cytologic abnormalities may be detectable immediately after irradiation, whereas ulceration, fibrosis, and other degenerative changes may not appear until months or years later (see Fig. 19–2).

SKIN. After rapid exposure to a dose of 6 Sv or more, erythema typically appears within 1 day, lasts a few hours, and is followed 2 to 4 weeks later by one or more waves of deeper and more prolonged erythema and epilation. Brief exposure to a dose greater than 10 to 20 Sv may cause transepithelial injury, with moist desquamation, necrosis, and ulceration within 2 to 4 weeks. The ensuing fibrosis of the underlying dermis and vasculature may lead to atrophy and a second wave of ulceration months or years later.

BONE MARROW AND LYMPHOID TISSUE. A dose of 2 to 3 Sv delivered rapidly to the whole body destroys enough lymphocytes to depress the lymphocyte count and immune response within hours. Such a dose also can damage enough hematopoietic cells to cause profound leukopenia and thrombocytopenia within 3 to 5 weeks. If the dose exceeds 5 Sv, fatal infection or hemorrhage or both are likely to result (Table 19–4).

INTESTINE. The killing of epithelial stem cells is sufficiently extensive after an acute dose of 10 Sv to cause rapid denudation of the overlying intestinal villi. If the area affected is large, death from a fatal dysentery-like syndrome may ensue within days.

RESPIRATORY TRACT. Rapid exposure of the lung to a dose of 6 to 10 Sv damages alveolar cells and the pulmonary vasculature sufficiently to result in acute pneumonitis within 1 to 3 months. If extensive, the process may lead to fatal respiratory failure within 6 months or pulmonary fibrosis and cor pulmonale months or years later.

GONADS. Spermatozoa are relatively radioresistant, but spermatogonia are highly radiosensitive; a dose of 0.15 Sv delivered rapidly to both testes causes oligospermia after a latent period of about 6 weeks, and a dose of 2 to 4 Sv may cause permanent sterility. Oocytes

Continued

also are radiosensitive; a dose of 1.5 to 2.0 Sv delivered to both ovaries causes temporary sterility, and a larger dose causes permanent sterility, depending on the woman's age at the time of exposure.

LENS OF THE EYE. Acute exposure of the lens to more than 0.5 Sv may lead within months to a microscopic posterior polar opacity, and 2 to 3 Sv received in a single brief exposure or 5.5 to 14 Sv accumulated over months may result in a vision-impairing cataract.

OTHER TISSUES AND ORGANS. Other tissues and organs, except for those of the embryo, are relatively less radiosensitive. All tissues are relatively more radiosensitive when rapidly growing, however.

WHOLE BODY RADIATION INJURY

Brief exposure of a major part of the body to more than 1 Sv may cause the acute radiation syndrome, which is characterized by (1) an initial prodromal stage of malaise, anorexia, nausea, and vomiting; (2) an ensuing latent period; (3) a second (main) phase of illness; and (4) either recovery or death (see Table 19–4). The main phase of the illness usually takes one of four primary forms: (1) hematologic, (2) gastrointestinal, (3) neurovascular, or (4) pulmonary, depending on the size and anatomic distribution of the dose.

LOCALIZED OR REGIONAL RADIATION INJURY

In contrast to the acute radiation syndrome, manifestations of which are dramatic and relatively prompt, reactions to localized irradiation in most tissues tend to evolve more slowly and not to produce symptoms or signs unless the volume of tissue irradiated or the dose is large. When the injury is produced by a radionuclide, it follows the anatomic distribution of the radionuclide and the resulting radiation, which may be influenced by the physicochemical state in which the radionuclide is encountered and its portal of entry into the body.

HERITABLE (GENETIC) EFFECTS OF RADIATION

Radiation-induced heritable mutations and chromosomal abnormalities, although well documented in other organisms, have yet to be observed in humans. The intensive study of more than 76,000 children of Japanese atomic bomb survivors has failed to reveal definite evidence of heritable radiation effects detectable in terms of untoward outcomes of pregnancy, neonatal deaths, malignancies, balanced chromosomal rearrangements, sex chromosome aneuploidy, alterations in serum or erythrocyte protein phenotypes, changes in gender ratio, or disturbances in growth and development. On the basis of the existing evidence, it is inferred that a dose of at least 1 Sv is required to double the rate of heritable mutations in human germ cells and that, consequently, less than 1% of all genetically determined disease is attributable to natural background irradiation.

CARCINOGENIC EFFECTS OF RADIATION

Many but not all types of benign and malignant growths have been observed to be inducible by irradiation; however, the induced growths characteristically take years or decades to appear and possess no features to distinguish them from growths arising through other causes. With few exceptions, growths have been detectable only after relatively large doses (>0.5 Sv) and have varied in frequency with the type of neoplasm and the age and gender of the exposed population. Because the existing data do not suffice to describe the dose-incidence relationship precisely or define how long after irradiation the risk of cancer may remain elevated in an exposed population, assessment of the risks of low-level irradiation must be based on assumptions about these parameters. Assessments (Table 19–5) have depended heavily on findings in atomic bomb survivors, whose overall incidence of cancer seems to have increased as a linear nonthreshold function of their radiation dose. These estimates cannot be assumed to predict the risk of cancer attributable to a dose accumulated over weeks, months, or years, however, because experiments with laboratory animals have shown the carcinogenic potency of x-rays or γ-rays to decrease by a factor of 2 to 10 if the exposure is sufficiently prolonged. The estimates tabulated represent averages for a nominal population of males and females of all ages, and the estimates for breast cancer in women and for thyroid cancer in persons irradiated during childhood are substantially higher than those shown.

EFFECTS ON LIFESPAN

Mortality from cardiovascular, respiratory, and other nonneoplastic diseases and from various forms of cancer is increased in heavily irradiated populations. In lightly irradiated populations, these effects have not been evident, and survival has appeared to be enhanced in some instances. This finding has prompted some to infer that the effects of small doses may be beneficial on balance (radiation hormesis), but this hypothesis remains to be validated.

EFFECTS OF PRENATAL IRRADIATION

The embryo is especially vulnerable to death if exposed before implantation, it is susceptible to malformations and other developmental disturbances if exposed during subsequent stages in organogenesis, and it is sensitive to the carcinogenic effects of radiation. Among various disturbances in growth and development, the dose-dependent increase in frequency of severe mental retardation and the dose-dependent decrease in IQ test scores in atomic bomb survivors who were irradiated between the 8th and the 15th week and, to a lesser extent, the 16th and the 25th week after conception are particularly noteworthy.

Table 19–4 • SYMPTOMS, THERAPY, AND PROGNOSIS OF WHOLE BODY IONIZING RADIATION INJURY

	0–1 Sv	1–2 Sv	2–6 Sv	6–10 Sv	10–20 Sv	>50 Sv
Therapeutic needs	None	Observation	Specific treatment	Possible treatment	Palliative	Palliative
Vomiting	None	5–50%	>3 Gy, 100%	100%	100%	100%
Time to nausea, vomiting	—	3 hr	2 hr	1 hr	30 min	<30 min
Main locus of injury	None	Lymphocytes	Bone marrow	Bone marrow	Small bowel	Brain
Symptoms and signs	—	Moderate leukopenia, epilation	Leukopenia, hemorrhage, epilation	Leukopenia, hemorrhage, epilation	Diarrhea, fever, electrolyte imbalance	Ataxia, coma, convulsions
Critical period	—	—	4–6 wk	4–6 wk	5–14 days	1–4 hr
Therapy	Reassurance	Observation	Transfusion of granulocytes, platelets	Transfusion, antibiotics, bone marrow transplant	Fluids and salts, possible bone marrow transplant	Palliative
Prognosis	Excellent	Excellent	Guarded	Guarded	Poor	Hopeless
Lethality	None	None	0–80%	80–100%	100%	100%
Time of death	—	—	2 mo	1–2 mo	2 wk	1–2 days
Cause of death	—	—	Infection, hemorrhage	Hemorrhage, infection, pneumonitis	Enteritis, infection	Cerebral edema

Modified from Phillips TL: Radiation injury. *In* Wyngaarden JB, Smith LH Jr, Bennett JC (eds): Cecil Textbook of Medicine, 19th ed. Philadelphia, WB Saunders, 1992, p 2354.

Table 19–5 • ESTIMATED LIFETIME RISK OF CANCER OF VARIOUS ORGANS ATTRIBUTABLE TO 0.1-Sv RAPID IRRADIATION

TYPE OR SITE OF CANCER	EXCESS CANCER DEATHS PER 100,000	
	No.	%*
Stomach	110	17
Lung	85	2
Colon	85	7
Leukemia (excluding CLL)	50	14
Urinary bladder	30	12
Esophagus	30	8
Breast	20	2
Liver	15	8
Gonads	10	3
Thyroid	8	40
Bone	5	12
Skin	2	30
Remainder	50	1
Total	*500*	*3*

*Percent increase in the expected risk of death from cancer of the same organ in a nonirradiated population.
CLL = chronic lymphocytic leukemia.
Modified from 1990 Recommendations of the International Commission on Radiological Protection. ICRP Publication 60. Ann ICRP 21:3, 1991, with permission from Elsevier Science Ltd.

Diagnosis

Any facility likely to deal with radiation injuries should be able to cope with these injuries and should have personnel on call who are trained and equipped appropriately for the purpose. At the outset, to evaluate the dose and to determine whether the patient has been contaminated with radionuclides, the nature of the exposure and any measurements by film badges or other detectors should be reviewed in detail. If exposure to radionuclides is known or suspected, radioactivity measurements of the whole body, skin, other tissue, blood, urine, and body fluid may be indicated to identify the isotope and evaluate the dose. Malaise, anorexia, nausea, and vomiting suggest a total body dose larger than 1 Sv, as do signs of erythema; hemorrhage; or infection in the skin, conjunctivae, or mucous membranes. The depth of lymphopenia within the first 24 hours also varies with the size of the total body dose. Although the granulocyte count may be elevated temporarily during the first 24 to 48 hours, the rapidity with which it and the platelet count fall in the ensuing 2 to 4 weeks also varies with the total body dose. Cytogenetic analysis of cultured lymphocytes for chromosomal aberrations can provide another useful index of exposure.

 Treatment

In managing radiation injury, good medical judgment and first aid are the priorities. Even if the patient has been heavily irradiated, the patient should be evaluated for other forms of injury, such as burns, mechanical trauma, and smoke inhalation. If radioactive contamination is known or suspected, rescue and medical personnel who handle the patient should wear gloves and other protective clothing and take precautions to isolate all contaminated objects.

Apart from symptomatic treatment, management of the hematologic form of acute radiation syndrome is similar to that used for pancytopenic leukemia, including reverse isolation, antibiotics to combat infection, granulocyte and platelet transfusions as needed, and intravenous fluids as required to combat dehydration and electrolyte loss (Chapter 193). Colony-stimulating factors and interleukin may be beneficial in patients exposed to 6 to 10 Sv. Bone marrow transplantation (Chapter 166) may be life-saving after a dose of 7 to 10 Sv if a suitably matched donor is available; specimens of marrow and peripheral blood should be obtained for tissue typing as early as possible.

For localized injuries, treatment depends on the anatomic location and severity. Dry and moist desquamation of the skin, which are the most common injuries requiring treatment, usually are managed adequately by simple cleansing. Large or ulcerated lesions should be covered with lanolin and closed dressings that are changed regularly; severe injuries may require resection of necrotic tissue and skin grafting.

In the event of radioactive contamination, steps should be taken to minimize the uptake and retention of isotope. Contaminated areas should be rinsed; the mouth, nose, and bronchial tree should be lavaged; and the gastrointestinal tract should be purged, if necessary. Additional measures to inhibit the uptake and retention of specific radionuclides may be indicated. Radioactive iodine may be released in a radiation accident or nuclear detonation and can pose a significant risk of thyroid cancer, especially in children. Stable potassium iodide should be administered to potentially exposed persons, except persons who are sensitive to iodine, to inhibit the uptake of radioactive iodine by the thyroid. The protective effect of a given dose persists for about 24 hours, and the optimal effect is achieved when potassium iodide can be given before exposure or concurrently with exposure. The recommended dose varies, depending on the recipient's age, expected level of thyroid exposure to radioactivity, and pregnancy or lactation status; recommendations range from 130 mg for adults to 16 mg for neonates.

Prognosis

After a total body dose of 2 Sv or less, survival is probable with little or no treatment; in the 2-Sv to 10-Sv range, appropriate treatment can afford a high rate of survival. If the injury is localized, the prognosis depends on the nature and severity of the reaction. Although recovery is the rule after minor, acute reactions, delayed reactions tend to be irreversible and progressive.

Prevention

Because the mutagenic and carcinogenic effects of ionizing radiation may have no thresholds, unnecessary exposure should be avoided, and any doses to radiation workers and patients should be kept as low as reasonably achievable, with particular care that they not exceed the relevant maximum permissible doses (e.g., 50 mSv/year occupational whole body radiation). Facilities using radiation or radiation sources should be designed and equipped appropriately and should provide specialized training and supervision for all workers who may be occupationally exposed. Because indoor radon accounts for the bulk of the public's exposure to ionizing radiation, measures to limit excessive doses from this source also are warranted.

NONIONIZING RADIATION

ULTRAVIOLET RADIATION

The ultraviolet (UV) radiation spectrum (see Fig. 19–1) is subdivided, for convenience, into three bands: UVA, or "black light," 315 to 400 nm; UVB, 280 to 315 nm; and UVC, which is germicidal, 200 to 280 nm. UV radiation does not penetrate deeply into human tissues, so the injuries it causes are confined chiefly to the skin and eyes.

Etiology

The largest source of UV radiation for the public is sunlight, which varies in intensity with latitude, elevation, and season. Important man-made sources include sun and tanning lamps, welding arcs, plasma torches, germicidal and black-light lamps, electric arc furnaces, hot-metal operations, mercury-vapor lamps, and some lasers. Low-intensity sources include fluorescent lamps and certain laboratory equipment.

Incidence and Prevalence

Reactions of the skin to UV radiation, common among fair-skinned people, include sunburn, skin cancers (basal cell and squamous cell carcinomas and to a lesser extent melanomas), aging of the skin, solar elastosis, and solar keratosis. Injuries of the eye include photokeratitis, which may result from brief exposure to a high-intensity UV radiation source ("welder's flash") or more prolonged exposure to intense sunlight ("snow blindness"); cortical cataract; and pterygium.

Pathogenesis

The effects of UV radiation are primarily attributable to its absorption in DNA; pyrimidine dimers are produced and cause mutational changes in exposed cells. Sensitivity to UV radiation may be increased by DNA repair defects (as in xeroderma pigmentosum), by agents (e.g., caffeine) that inhibit repair enzymes, and by photosensitizing agents (e.g., psoralens, sulfonamides, tetracyclines, nalidixic acid, sulfonylureas, thiazides, phenothiazines, furocoumarins, and coal tar) that produce UV radiation–absorbing DNA photoproducts. The carcinogenic action of UV radiation is mediated through direct effects on the exposed cells and depression of local immunity. UVB in sunlight, although far less intense than UVA, plays a more important role in sunburn and skin carcinogenesis, but UVA also contributes to skin carcinogenesis, tanning, some photosensitivity reactions, and aging of the skin.

Clinical Aspects

See Chapters 465, 471–474, 476, and 477.

Prevention

Excessive exposure to sunlight or other sources of UV radiation should be avoided, especially in fair-skinned individuals. Protective clothing, UV radiation–screening lotions or creams, and UV radiation–blocking sunglasses should be used. To protect occupationally exposed workers, the National Institute of Occupational Safety and Health has recommended a limit of 1 mW/cm² for periods longer than 1000 seconds and 1000 mW/cm² (1 J/cm²) for periods of 1000 seconds or less. Globally the protective layer of ozone in the stratosphere is being depleted by chlorofluorocarbons and other air pollutants, and every 1% decrease in ozone is expected to increase the UV radiation reaching the earth by 1 to 2% and increase the rates of nonmelanotic skin cancer by 2 to 6%.

VISIBLE LIGHT

Visible light consists of electromagnetic waves varying in wavelength from 380 nm (violet) to 760 nm (red) (see Fig. 19–1). Too little illumination can cause eyestrain or seasonal affective disorder, whereas too bright a light can injure the retina.

Etiology

Bright, continuously visible light normally elicits an aversion response to protect the eye against injury, so few sources of light other than a laser or the sun in a solar eclipse are large or bright enough to cause a retinal burn under normal viewing conditions.

Pathogenesis

Photochemical reactions in the retina from sustained exposure to intensities exceeding 0.1 mW/cm², such as can result from fixing on a bright source of light, may suffice to produce photochemical blue-light injury, and brief exposure of the retina to intensities exceeding 10 W/cm², depending on image size, may cause a retinal burn.

Clinical Aspects

See Chapter 465.

Prevention

Common sense usually suffices to prevent excessive exposure of the retina to light; however, in situations involving potential exposure to high-intensity sources, such as carbon arcs or lasers, appropriate training, proper design of equipment, and protective eye shields are important.

INFRARED RADIATION

Infrared radiation consists of electromagnetic waves ranging in wavelength from 7×10^{-5} m to 3×10^{-2} m. The injuries caused by infrared radiation are chiefly burns of the skin and cataracts of the lens of the eye.

Etiology

Potentially hazardous sources include furnaces, ovens, welding arcs, molten glass, molten metal, and heating lamps.

Incidence and Prevalence

The warning sensation of heat usually prompts aversion in time to prevent burning of the skin by infrared radiation; however, the lens of the eye is vulnerable because it lacks the ability to sense or dissipate heat. As a result, glass blowers, blacksmiths, oven operators, and people working around heating and drying lamps are at increased risk of infrared radiation–induced cataracts.

Clinical Aspects

See Chapter 465.

Prevention

Control of infrared radiation hazards requires appropriate shielding of its sources, training of potentially exposed persons, and use of protective clothing and goggles.

MICROWAVE RADIATION

Microwave and radiofrequency radiation consists of electromagnetic waves ranging in frequency from about 3 kHz to 300 GHz. The injuries caused by microwave and radiofrequency radiation are primarily burns of the skin and other tissues. Microwave and radiofrequency radiation also can interfere with cardiac pacemakers and other medical devices.

Etiology

Sources of microwave and radiofrequency radiation are used widely in radar, televisions, cellular phones, radios, other telecommunications systems, various industrial operations (e.g., heating, welding, and melting of metals; processing of wood and plastic; high-temperature plasma), household appliances (e.g., microwave ovens), and medical applications (e.g., diathermy and hyperthermia).

Incidence and Prevalence

Isolated cases of skin burns, thermal injury to deeper tissues, and death from hyperthermia have been caused by industrial microwave and radiofrequency radiation sources. Burns also have resulted from faulty or improperly used household microwave ovens and from the overexposure of patients with impaired cutaneous pain and temperature senses that usually warn of impending injury. Other effects reported in the literature but not as yet conclusively documented include cataract of the lens, impairment of fertility, developmental disturbances, neurobehavioral abnormalities, depression of immunity, and increased risk of cancer.

Pathogenesis

The biologic effects of microwave and radiofrequency radiation are primarily thermal in nature. Because of the deep penetration of these types of radiation, the cutaneous burns they cause tend to involve dermal and subcutaneous tissues and heal slowly.

Clinical Aspects

See Chapters 61 and 108.

Prevention

Microwave and radiofrequency radiation sources must be designed and shielded properly, and potentially exposed persons, especially persons with cardiac pacemakers or other sensitive devices, must be trained and supervised properly. In general, detectable heating of tissue requires microwave and radiofrequency radiation power densities greater than 10 W/cm²; avoidance of such exposure, as prescribed by existing federal standards, suffices to prevent injury.

EXTREMELY LOW-FREQUENCY ELECTROMAGNETIC FIELDS

Extremely low-frequency electromagnetic fields range in frequency from 1 to 3000 Hz, including the 50-Hz to 60-Hz fields associated with alternating currents in electric power distribution systems and appliances. Exposure to such fields is not known to be hazardous, but data suggesting that it may cause reproductive abnormalities and carcinogenic effects have aroused public health concern.

Etiology

The earth is surrounded by a naturally occurring electromagnetic field ranging in frequency from the low end of the extremely low-frequency region to radiofrequencies that exist briefly as a result of lightning discharges. Localized electromagnetic fields also are generated by electric power lines, transformers, motors, household appliances, video display tubes, and various medical devices, notably nuclear magnetic resonance imaging systems. These localized fields are generally stronger than naturally existing ones; electromagnetic field flux densities near common household appliances may range up to 270 mG compared with the average value of 0.6 mG for the earth's magnetic field.

Incidence and Prevalence

Exceptionally strong fields may affect electrically active tissues (nerves, neuromusculature, heart) and cardiac pacemakers and may raise body temperature. Conflicting epidemiologic studies have evaluated the possibility that (1) residential exposure of children to weaker electromagnetic fields may increase their risk of leukemia, (2) occupational exposure of male utility workers may increase their risk of brain cancer and leukemia, and (3) chronic exposure of pregnant women to video display tubes may increase their risk of miscarriage and of bearing children with birth defects; none of these links have been established.

Pathogenesis

Evaluation of epidemiologic data is complicated by the lack of any known biologic basis for the effects of extremely low-frequency electromagnetic fields on tissue, especially because the currents emanating from normal nerve and muscle activity are far stronger than the currents attributable to 1-mG to 10-mG external 60-Hz fields. Such fields nevertheless have been reported to influence ion transport, melatonin secretion, and tumor promotion in some model systems.

Prevention

Persons with pacemakers should avoid electromagnetic fields stronger than 0.5 mT, such as exist around transformers, accelerators, nuclear magnetic resonance systems, and other electrical devices; areas containing such fields should be posted with warning signs. Exposure of workers also should be limited, in accordance with national guidelines.

ULTRASOUND

Although frequently classified with nonionizing radiation, ultrasound consists of mechanical vibrations at inaudibly high frequencies (i.e., >16 kHz) and is not a component of the electromagnetic spectrum. Deleterious effects from prolonged exposure to high-power ultrasound include headache, malaise, tinnitus, vertigo, hypersensitivity to light and sound, and peripheral neuritis. Low-level exposure to ultrasound has not been shown conclusively to cause injury; the possibility of adverse effects on embryos has been speculated but not documented.

Etiology

High-power, low-frequency ultrasound is used widely in science and industry for cleaning, degreasing, plastic welding, liquid-extracting, atomizing, homogenizing, and emulsifying operations and in medicine for lithotripsy. Low-power, high-frequency ultrasound is used widely in analytic work and in medical diagnosis (e.g., ultrasonography).

Incidence and Prevalence

Low-frequency ultrasound, transmitted through the air or through bodily contact with the generating source, has been observed to cause a variety of problems in occupationally exposed workers, including headache, earache, tinnitus, vertigo, malaise, photophobia, hyperacusis, peripheral neuritis, and autonomic polyneuritis. Similar complaints may result from excessive exposure to high-frequency ultrasound through bodily contact with the source; however, adverse effects have not been shown to result from exposure to high-frequency ultrasound at the low power levels used in medical ultrasonography.

Pathogenesis

The biologic effects of ultrasound are similar in mechanism to those of mechanical vibration.

Prevention

Protection against ultrasound injury requires appropriate isolation and insulation of generating sources and proper training and ear protective devices for persons working around such sources. Yearly audiometric and neurologic examinations of workers are advisable.

SUGGESTED READINGS

American Conference of Governmental Industrial Hygienists: 2000 Threshold Limit Values and Biological Exposure Indices. Cincinnati, American Conference of Governmental Industrial Hygienists, 2000. *An authoritative listing of recommended maximum permissible occupational exposure limits of radiation of all types.*

Mettler FA, Voelz GL: Major radiation exposure—what to expect and how to respond. N Engl J Med 2002;346:1554–1561. *Overview of the consequences of a possible terrorist attack.*

National Academy of Sciences/National Research Council: Possible Health Effects of Exposure to Residential Electric and Magnetic Fields. Washington, DC, National Academy Press, 1997. *An authoritative review of the possible health hazards of residential electric and magnetic fields.*

United Nations Scientific Committee on the Effects of Atomic Radiation (UNSCEAR): Sources and Effects of Ionizing Radiation: UNSCEAR 2000 Report to the General Assembly, with Scientific Annexes. New York, United Nations, 2000. *An extensive review of the sources and levels of ionizing radiation in various parts of the world and of the biologic effects of ionizing radiation, including the effects of the Chernobyl accident.*

U.S. Food and Drug Administration Center for Drug Evaluation and Research (CDER): Potassium Iodide as a Thyroid Blocking Agent in Radiation Emergencies. Rockville, MD, U.S. Food and Drug Administration Center for Drug Evaluation and Research, 2001. *A review of the rationale for and guidance on the safe and effective use of potassium iodide as a protective measure in the event of the release of radioactive iodine into the environment.*

20 CHRONIC POISONING: TRACE METALS AND OTHERS

William O. Robertson

Definition

The chemical environment was recognized as a threat to health early in history. Well-documented outbreaks of occupational mercury and lead "poisonings" had been recorded and preventive measures implemented by 200 BC. In the Middle Ages, arsenic poisoning was used as a political weapon. In more recent times, industrial toxins, "accidental poisoning" in childhood, purposeful overdoses in adults, adverse reactions to drugs, medication mix-ups in hospitals, and environmental hazards increasingly have been recognized. The patient's metabolic and genetic variability determine the impact of a given molecule in hereditary disorders such as phenylketonuria, glucose-6-phosphate dehydrogenase deficiency, and others. As understanding of life has expanded, the connotation of poisoning has undergone substantial evolution. Nonetheless, it is the dose and not simply the chemical that makes the poison—witness the popularity of Botox.

Etiology

New analytical techniques can identify poisonings promptly and completely and have uncovered the causes of diverse entities such as Minamata disease (teratogenesis consequent to methyl mercury), an outbreak of ascending paralysis affecting more than 4000 with more than 400 deaths in Iraq (also caused by methyl mercury), the "gray syndrome" in premature infants (caused by chloramphenicol), mesotheliomas induced by asbestos, and an epidemic of angiosarcoma of the liver among industrial workers (caused by vinyl chloride). Nevertheless, many unknowns remain and justify careful prospective monitoring of industry, of the home, and of the environment. The combination of more "synthetic chemicals," vastly more precise testing techniques, a press more devoted to Rachel Carson's *Silent Spring* than to DuPont's "better living through chemistry," and an increasingly litigious society has created an era of "toxic torts" and its consequences, plus an anxious and concerned public and profession.

Many metals and nonmetals in trace amounts are capable of causing human disease, especially after chronic or repetitive exposure. In some cases, poisoning is a consequence of workplace exposure. In others, the disease results from using prescription or nonprescription medicines or as an adverse effect of medical procedures such as hemodialysis. Occasionally, poisoning results from attempts at suicide or homicide.

Increased awareness of the health consequences of industrial substances, more stringent federal and state regulations, and fear of lawsuits all have resulted in a healthier workplace. However, most of the potentially exposed workforce is employed by small industries, which may not have implemented protective measures.

Knowledge of the subtle consequences of chronic, low-level trace element exposure is still grossly inadequate. Acute lead poisoning in children or adults is readily diagnosed, but the consequences of increased body lead burdens in the absence of anemia, colic, or clinically apparent encephalopathy and their clinical significance, if any, are not well understood.

The interrelationships among trace elements also are poorly understood. Copper smelter workers are exposed not only to copper, but also to lead, zinc, arsenic, gold, silver, cadmium, and mercury; in these workers, pneumonitis or other acute illnesses may result from two or more metals acting in concert. In other instances, excesses or deficits of a trace element may act indirectly by inducing deficiency or toxicity of another trace element.

LEAD

Etiology

In the past, lead poisoning was ascribed to pica (abnormal ingestion) among children living in dilapidated houses with peeling layers of lead-based paints. In the 1980s and 1990s, lead intoxication occurred with decreasing frequency, in part related to less use of lead in paint and far more to the disappearance of leaded gasoline. Several studies related environmental lead contamination to traffic density patterns, with leaded gasoline the major culprit.

It is estimated that more than 800,000 American workers have potentially significant lead exposure. Lead and other metal smelter workers or miners, welders, storage battery workers, and pottery makers are particularly heavily exposed. Workers in automobile manufacturing, shipbuilding, paint manufacture, and printing industries also are at substantial risk, as are house painters and people who repair old houses.

Lead-soldered kettles and cans and lead-glazed pottery can release lead when acidic fluids are stored or cooked in them. Demolition workers and people employed in firing ranges have become poisoned from intensive aerosol exposure. In the southern United States, moonshine whiskey is an important cause of poisoning. The stills are connected with lead solder, and old radiators containing lead are used as condensers; 20 to 90% of moonshine samples contain lead in the potentially toxic range.

In past centuries, lead acetate was added to wine to sweeten it, a deception that eventually was made punishable by death. More recently, adding lead to various herbal and folk medicines has resulted in poisoning. Retained bullets can result in lead poisoning, especially if a joint is involved because synovial fluid seems to be a good solvent for lead. The interval between lodging of the bullet and clinical evidence of lead poisoning has ranged from 2 days to 40 years. Lead poisoning also has occurred in adults who have eaten fowl and inadvertently ingested lead pellets. Children have been poisoned by swallowing lead household objects, such as lead curtain weights, that are retained in the gastrointestinal tract for a prolonged time. Gasoline sniffing can produce lead poisoning; the organic tetraethyl lead seems to have a proclivity for the nervous system.

In a sense, we are all lead poisoned; before the Industrial Revolution, the total body burden of lead was about 2 mg, whereas currently in industrialized societies, the whole body content is about 200 mg. Each day, an average of 150 to 250 μg is ingested, 5 to 10% of which is absorbed. In children, the percentage is higher.

Clinical Manifestations

The major toxic effects of lead are referable to the abdomen, the blood, and the nervous system.

GASTROINTESTINAL TRACT. The exact pathogenesis of lead colic is uncertain. The crampy, diffuse, often intractable abdominal pain may be accompanied by nausea, vomiting, anorexia, constipation, or occasionally diarrhea. The pain may be confined to the epigastric, periumbilical, or other areas of the abdomen and may simulate a variety of surgical and nonsurgical diseases.

BLOOD. Lead interferes with a variety of red blood cell enzyme systems, including aminolevulinate dehydratase and ferrochelatase. The former is needed to conjugate δ-levulinic acid to form porphobilinogen; the latter facilitates the incorporation of iron into protoporphyrin IX. The red blood cell abnormalities include punctate basophilic stippling. Anemia is frequent in severe acute lead poisoning and may be normocytic normochromic but usually is microcytic hypochromic. An inherited deficiency in aminolevulinate dehydratase can cause lead intoxication at modest blood lead levels.

NERVOUS SYSTEM. The central nervous system (CNS) symptoms at first are vague and often mistakenly are disregarded. These manifestations include irritability, incoordination, memory lapses, labile affect, sleep disturbances, restlessness, listlessness, paranoia, headache, lethargy, and dizziness. In more serious cases, manifestations include syncope-like attacks, disorientation, flaccidity, severe mental impairment, ataxia, vomiting, cranial nerve palsies, localized neurologic signs, psychosis, somnolence, seizures, blindness, and coma. Severe lead encephalopathy is not restricted to children. Occasionally the brain manifestations mimic a space-occupying lesion. The cerebrospinal fluid may be under increased pressure and may show an increased protein content. Papilledema has been reported, as have grayish deposits surrounding the optic disc and optic atrophy. Frank encephalopathy is an ominous prognostic sign for mortality and persistent brain damage. Most children who experience clinically evident encephalopathy have neurologic residua. Tetraethyl lead (organic lead) poisoning causes euphoria, nervousness, insomnia, hallucinations, convulsions, and frank psychosis.

Peripheral nerve involvement is seen more often in adults than in children. Wristdrop and footdrop occur most often; the former, depending on type of occupation, may be asymmetrical, and there may be paresthesias. The spinal cord also may be involved, with manifestations having some similarity to those of amyotrophic lateral sclerosis.

Since the 1980s, increasing evidence has arisen of subtle brain damage in the absence of clinical evidence of encephalopathy. Inordinate body burdens of lead may result in mentation difficulties, emotional lability, deficits in intelligence and memory, impaired psychomotor and visual motor function, slowed nerve conduction, and behavioral aberrations in children and adults, even in the absence of overt evidence of poisoning. These changes are postulated to occur at blood levels of 40 μg/dL in adults and 10 μg/dL in children. The scientific community is sharply divided, however, about the clinical significance of these latter observations.

OTHER CLINICAL MANIFESTATIONS. In adults, the kidneys are often involved (Chapter 120), the characteristic lesion being interstitial nephritis; as the disease progresses, glomerular filtration rate falls. Polyarthralgias, mild hepatic dysfunction, and dysuria also may occur. Occasionally, arrhythmias and cardiomegaly have been reported, as have abnormalities of liver function. Lead readily crosses the placenta and is thought to be responsible for an increased incidence of spontaneous abortion and miscarriage and possibly for impairing the fetal CNS.

Diagnosis

In adults, a high index of suspicion and a careful examination of the peripheral blood for basophilic stippling are mandatory; for occupational workers, lead screening is warranted. Blood lead level, which is determined by atomic absorption spectrophotometry or anodic

Table 20–1 • POSITIVE SCREENING TESTS INDICATING UNDUE LEAD ABSORPTION

Whole blood lead	Children	>10 µg/dL
	Adults	>30 µg/dL*
Whole blood erythrocyte	Children	>35 µg/dL*
protoporphyrin or	Adults	>50 µg/dL
zinc protoporphyrin		

*This value is unsettled; do not use for screening.

stripping voltometry, is currently the preferred method for detecting lead toxicity (Table 20–1). Urinary coproporphyrin levels are increased because lead interferes with incorporation of iron into heme. Erythrocyte protoporphyrin can be measured rapidly fluorometrically; erythrocyte protoporphyrin and zinc protoporphyrin are reliable indicators of lead poisoning when the blood lead level exceeds 30 µg/dL but also are elevated in iron-deficiency anemia.

Additional industrial exposure should not be permitted if blood levels exceed 25 to 40 µg/dL. Currently, 26 states have lead registries to monitor all lead analytic determinations in the state in an attempt to curtail problems.

Rx Treatment

At least four agents have been used to form tight complexes with lead and promote its biologic inactivation and elimination from tissues (Table 20–2). Dimercaprol (British antilewisite [BAL]) is given in oil intramuscularly; calcium disodium edetate (calcium versenate) can be given either intramuscularly or intravenously; and D-pencillamine is administered orally. Chelation should be undertaken only after careful consideration for patients with milder evidence of poisoning because each of the agents may be associated with significant adverse effects. Because most of the body lead is stored in the bones, clinical improvement and reduction in blood lead levels (or reduction in erythrocyte protoporphyrin or zinc protoporphyrin) may be temporary, to be followed by increases in blood lead concentrations and clinical evidence of repoisoning owing to mobilization of lead from bone. In these cases, chelating agents may need to be readministered. Newer, less toxic oral dimercaprol analogues (2,3-dimercaptosuccinic acid [DMSA] and dimercaptopropanesulfonate [DMPS]) have been introduced for easy oral administration with the hope of enhancing efficacy and reducing complications.

Treatment is usually successful in extra-CNS disease but may not be successful in patients with encephalopathy. Various degrees of mentation deficits may remain in children and adults.

Although the Centers for Disease Control and Prevention (CDC) has said the acceptable blood concentration of lead for children is 10 µg/dL, debate continues about that specific number. Blood lead levels have decreased dramatically in the United States (and some other countries) since the 1970s with the elimination of lead from gasoline. The percentage of children with blood lead levels >10 µg/dL has fallen from 88% in 1978–1980 to less than 3% in 2002. However, no measurable increase in IQ has followed; if anything, hyperactivity, aggressiveness, and antisocial behavior all have increased.

MERCURY

Etiology

Mercury has been used for at least 2000 years. More than 60 occupations involve mercury exposure, including chloralkali work; manufacture of pesticides, insecticides, and fungicides; manufacture of mercury-containing instruments, lamps, neon lights, batteries, paper, paint, dye, electrical equipment, and jewelry; and dentistry. Exposure in dental offices has diminished substantially, however.

In addition to occupational or industrial exposure, poisoning has resulted from inadvertent contamination of grains by mercury-containing pesticides and from accidental or intentional ingestion or injection of elemental mercury or mercury-containing compounds. In the past, mercury was administered medicinally as a component of cathartics, teething powders, and antihelminthics. Today, mercury compounds have no bona fide place in therapeutic medicine.

Clinical Manifestations and Treatment

The biologic effects, tissue distribution, and toxicity of mercury depend on the form in which it is introduced into the body.

METALLIC MERCURY. Elemental mercury is a liquid at environmental temperatures but vaporizes with agitation and gentle heating. Bulk mercury is used in dental amalgams; 10% of dental offices used to have excessive mercury vapor levels; and accidental spillage can lead to mercury poisoning. The greatest exposure to metallic mercury is in industry. Heavy aerosol exposure to mercury produces chills, fever, cough, chest pain, and hemoptysis; radiographs show diffuse pulmonary infiltrates. Oxidized elemental mercury is absorbed readily from the alveoli; subsequently, it can enter the brain. With mild exposure, the manifestations are likely to be subtle, and diagnosis is difficult. Insomnia, nervousness, mild tremor, impaired judgment and coordination, decreased mental efficiency, emotional lability, headache, fatigue, loss of sexual drive, and depression are early manifestations and often mistakenly are ascribed to psychogenic causes. Abdominal cramps, dermatitis, and diarrhea also may occur, and the victim may complain of a metallic taste. As the poisoning becomes more severe, persistent involuntary tremors of the extremities are noted. Thereafter, other signs of mercury poisoning may appear, including amblyopia, polyneuropathy, erythroderma, acrodynia, joint pains, swollen gums with a blue line around the teeth, sialorrhea, and paresthesias. The major manifestation of chronic mercury vapor exposure may be renal damage, including nephrotic syndrome. The wide range of clinical findings after elemental mercury exposure seems to relate in part to the rate of oxidation of mercury to its salts and the rapidity of their subsequent excretion through the kidneys, saliva, and urine. Chelation therapy is of uncertain value.

Because of the body's metabolism of mercury, levels of mercury in the blood and urine may be unreliable. In most cases, improvement occurs after removal from exposure or treatment with appropriate chelating agents.

In contrast, ingesting even large amounts of metallic mercury usually produces no clinical disturbance. Aspiration of liquid

Continued

Table 20–2 • CHELATION REGIMENS

	CHILDREN*	ADULTS*	DURATION
CaNa₂ EDTA	50 mg/kg/d IM† or IV, or 1500 mg/m²/24 hr (severe disease); 1000 mg/m²/day (mild-moderate intoxication)	1.0 g IV in 5% dextrose twice daily, or 2.0 g/day IM in divided doses; longer term, 1 g IM 3× per week† until lead burden reduced to satisfactory levels	3–5 days
BAL	3 mg/kg/dose IM, or 300–450 mg/m²/24 hr IM (Given in divided doses every 4 hr)	2.5 mg/kg/dose IM	3–5 days
2,3-Dimer- captosuccinic acid (DMSA)‡	10 mg/kg tid for 5 days 10 mg/kg then bid for 14 days	4–7 mg/kg bid for 5 days 4–7 mg/kg bid for 14 days	

*CaNa₂ EDTA and BAL are ordinarily used together for symptomatic illness.
†Procaine must be used for IM injections of CaNa₂ EDTA.
‡Orphan drug approved only for children but being used in adults.

mercury into the lungs is also usually benign, although radiographic visualization of mercury globules may be evident for many years. Even after intravenous injection of mercury, there may be no abnormalities other than radiographic densities in the lungs, which may persist for decades, or subcutaneous tissue abnormalities or mild respiratory distress.

INORGANIC MERCURY. Exposure to the salts of mercury (i.e., $HgCl_2$ and Hg_2Cl_2) occurs primarily in industry and results from ingestion. $HgCl_2$ is far more toxic than Hg_2Cl_2. The major manifestations are gastrointestinal and renal, with proteinuria, granular casts in the urinary sediment, nephrotic syndrome, and pyuria from tubular damage. In some cases, severe oliguria and anuria may occur. Additionally, diarrhea, abdominal pain, hepatic dysfunction, and lesser evidence of CNS disease may be found. Rhabdomyolysis with striking muscle enzyme elevation and acrodynia also have been reported. DMSA is the preferred chelation therapy because older agents may increase the penetration of inorganic mercury into the CNS.

ORGANOMERCURIALS. Methyl mercury—a devastating teratogen found in fungicides—is well absorbed from the intestinal tract, is distributed widely in the body, and readily passes through the placenta into the fetus and into breast milk. About 10% localizes in the brain, and the ensuing damage is largely irreversible. Major epidemics have resulted from industrial contamination of water, with subsequent biotransformation of elemental and inorganic mercury into methyl mercury that was ingested by fish that subsequently were consumed by humans. Other epidemics have resulted from using grains contaminated by organic mercurial pesticides or animal ingestion of seeds treated with mercury. The epidemics in the Minamata and Niigata regions of Japan and in Iraq, Guatemala, and Pakistan have resulted in a high death rate and an appalling amount of permanent brain damage. In addition to the milder symptoms listed under elemental mercury poisoning, CNS manifestations include severe paresthesias, dysarthria, ataxia, visual field constriction, hearing loss, blindness, microcephaly, spasticity, paralysis, and coma. Prevention or avoidance is far more effective than any form of treatment.

ARSENIC

Etiology

Arsenic is ubiquitous in nature; it is present in the earth's crust in concentrations of 2 to 5 parts per billion. It is found in inordinately high concentrations in some well water. It is used in the glass, pigment, textile, tanning, and bronze-plating industries; in wood preservation; in a variety of metal alloys; in veterinary medicines; in some herbicides, insecticides, and rodenticides; in fire salts to produce multicolored flames; and by farmers and vintners. American industry uses about one half of the world's production of arsenic trioxide. Arsenic poisoning also has resulted from using certain herbal preparations, from ingesting illegal (moonshine) whiskey, from burning arsenate-treated wood, and from administering arsenic-containing folk and prescription medicines. In contrast to mercury, organic arsenic is far less toxic to humans than the inorganic form. For coastal inhabitants who consume large amounts of shellfish (e.g., clams, oysters, mussels), urinary excretion of arsenic may be elevated to three to four times normal values, but the arsenic is typically organic and not an important risk.

Elemental arsenic is not toxic even if ingested in substantial amounts. There are three toxic forms of arsenic: pentavalent salts, trivalent salts, and arsine gas. The arsenic in the earth's crust and in most foods is in the pentavalent form, the least toxic form. Trivalent arsenic, which is more toxic, accumulates in the body more readily than the pentavalent form. Arsenic gas (arsine) is extraordinarily toxic; it is formed by the hydrolysis of metallic arsenide or by the action of acids or nascent hydrogen on arsenical compounds, especially in the refining of certain metals. Arsine is used in the electronics industry and can be liberated in sewage plants.

Clinical Manifestations

Arsine gas poisoning is usually overwhelming and frequently fatal. The onset of symptoms after exposure is usually 1 to 6 hours. Fever, headache, muscle pains, nausea, vomiting, epigastric pain, dysuria, and explosive diarrhea characterize acute episodes. Because arsenic preferentially binds to red blood cells, hemolytic anemia and hemoglobinuria occur early, and red blood cell ghosts may be seen in the peripheral blood. There also may be profound hypoxia and cyanosis. Renal failure resulting from acute tubular necrosis (occasionally caused by cortical necrosis) occurs in the first few days after onset of symptoms. Renal failure may be accompanied by shock and encephalopathy, characterized by agitation and disorientation. Bone marrow depression and myocardial damage may occur. Persons who do not die of intractable vascular collapse often develop subacute manifestations of arsenic poisoning (see later). Persons who recover may develop chronic renal failure.

ARSENIC INGESTION. Depending on dose and form, arsenic ingestion can be insidious or overwhelming with cramping abdominal pain and diarrhea. Other acute manifestations include nausea, vomiting, dysphagia, cyanosis, headache, hematuria, and weakness. Hyperesthesia, muscle cramps, conjunctivitis, syncope, excessive thirst, periorbital swelling, epistaxis, and tinnitus also may occur. The patient may complain of a metallic taste, and there may be a garlic odor to the breath, which also can occur with selenium, tellurium, phosphorus, and dimethyl sulfoxide poisoning. Other manifestations that may occur in the first week include jaundice, hematuria, and hepatomegaly with hepatic enzyme abnormalities; electrocardiogram abnormalities; a cardiomyopathy that can be lethal; pericarditis; rhabdomyolysis; pulmonary edema; evidence of encephalopathy; seizures; renal dysfunction; kidney failure with acute tubular necrosis; and respiratory muscle paralysis.

The most prominent manifestation after the first week of illness is symmetric polyneuropathy. At first, sensory manifestations predominate; the patient complains of a burning sensation in a stocking-glove distribution. Motor involvement follows almost immediately with diminished or absent reflexes and severe weakness. Occasionally, neuropathy is unilateral. Prolonged encephalopathy and/or psychosis have been reported in a few instances. In cases of subacute poisoning, Aldrich-Mees lines (transverse white bands) may be seen in the nails; similar to the garlic odor, these may be seen in other trace element intoxications.

Chronic exposure is associated with cutaneous lesions, particularly hyperpigmentation (arsenic melanosis) and hyperkeratoses located primarily on the palms and soles. Alopecia and so-called raindrop depigmentation also may occur. In 5 to 10% of patients chronically exposed, skin cancers appear after latent periods of 5 to more than 25 years; these tend to be multiple and are situated mainly on the trunk and upper extremities. An epidemic of skin cancers is under way in India and Bangladesh after arsenic-contaminated deep well waters replaced bacteriologically contaminated surface water. In the United States, the most frequent cause of these skin lesions in past years was the medicinal use of Fowler's solution, an inorganic trivalent arsenical. Currently, most cases arise after occupational exposure, but a few have been ascribed to chronic exposure to well water with high arsenic content. Epidemiologic studies on gold ore and tin miners, vineyard workers, laborers in sheep-dip factories, and smelter workers show a clear increase in the incidence of squamous cell carcinoma of the lung, the risk of bronchogenic cancer correlating with the intensity and duration of arsenic trioxide exposure, and all are potentiated by smoking. Considerable debate continues regarding federal actions to mandate lowering the tolerable levels of arsenic in drinking water supplies from 50 ppm to 10 ppm—based almost exclusively on extrapolations of data from India, Bangladesh, Chile, and Taiwan about both levels of arsenic in drinking water as well as illnesses virtually never seen in the U.S.

Diagnosis

Skin, nails, and hair usually do not contain arsenic until 2 to 4 weeks after exposure, but occasionally hair accumulation can occur more rapidly. If the diagnosis is suspected, arsenic concentrations can be measured in blood, urine, hair, or nails by atomic absorption spectrophotometry or neutron activation techniques, but, as with mercury, accurate interpretation can be difficult. Hair analysis usually is reserved for studying epidemics and not for assessing individuals.

 Treatment

> The treatment of choice is BAL. It should be given within the first 24 hours after exposure. If BAL is given later, improvement is less likely to be observed, and in many cases the peripheral neuropathy is refractory to treatment. Exchange transfusion or dialysis shortly after the onset of acute illness also has been reported to be beneficial. Orally administered DMSA is another alternative.

TRACE ELEMENTS WHOSE TOXICITY IS ASSOCIATED IN LARGE PART WITH HEMODIALYSIS

ZINC. The normal adult body zinc content is 1.5 to 3.0 g. Usually, daily intake ranges from 5 to 35 mg. Over the past several decades, dietary deficiency in humans has been well established and corrected by zinc supplements to regional diets. In turn, the use of zinc as a treatment for the common cold has skyrocketed in popularity in developed countries despite the paucity of supportive data. Acute zinc ingestion can lead to emesis and, rarely, other transient bowel symptoms, but usually with no permanent damage. Zinc is not considered a reproductive risk or a carcinogen. Ethylenediaminetetraacetic acid chelation or whole bowel lavage may hasten elimination, but evidence for toxic damage in nondialysis patients is no firmer than is evidence for therapeutic benefits.

Zinc is bound to metallothioneins synthesized in the liver and is excreted by the urine and the gastrointestinal tract. It has a strong affinity for red blood cells and plasma proteins. Consequently, there is no loss across dialysis membranes; instead, depending on the dialysate, blood zinc concentrations may increase markedly during hemodialysis. There seem to be two well-documented zinc sources: adhesive plaster (containing zinc oxide) used to prevent dialysis coils from unwinding and the water of the dialysis fluid.

The manifestations of zinc toxicity do not correlate well with plasma or whole blood zinc levels. Nausea, vomiting, anorexia, lethargy, irritability, weakness, abdominal pain, and anemia are the most frequent manifestations. Other manifestations may include diarrhea, muscle pain, lymphadenopathy, hyperamylasemia with or without pancreatitis, intestinal bleeding, thrombocytopenia, oliguria, hypotension, and renal failure with tubular necrosis. Injecting large amounts of zinc has resulted in death. Intestinal manifestations may supervene after either orally or parenterally induced zinc intoxication.

Welders, smelter workers, and solderers are exposed to aerosolized zinc and may experience "metal (zinc) fume fever" (Chapter 89), characterized by chills, fever, myalgias, a metallic taste, cough, nausea, lethargy, and occasionally hemoptysis. There may be diffuse radiographic infiltrates and pulmonary dysfunction. Ordinarily, all manifestations disappear rapidly after cessation of exposure. If more prolonged pulmonary dysfunction occurs, it is thought to result from the effects of other metals to which the workers are exposed simultaneously.

ALUMINUM. Aluminum-induced dialysis dementia can be a fatal disease. The tap water used during dialysis is often to blame. Some waters naturally contain high concentrations of aluminum. In other cases, aluminum sulfate had been added to the community water supply to remove organic materials. In still other cases, the dialysis fluid seemed to be less responsible than aluminum-containing gels administered by mouth to reduce phosphate levels. If oral aluminum hydroxide is administered to nondialyzed patients with renal failure, the encephalopathy syndrome rarely occurs in adults, but young children seem to be particularly at risk. Dialysis encephalopathy occurs only after repeated dialyses, usually spanning months or years. Peritoneal dialysis also be can complicated by encephalopathy.

Early manifestations include malaise, memory loss, and a characteristic speech disturbance. As the disease progresses, dysarthria, asterixis, myoclonic twitches, dementia, somnolence, and seizures occur. The electroencephalogram shows slowing, together with bursts of delta activity and high-voltage, symmetrical spikes. Using reverse osmosis or deionization treatment has reduced markedly the

incidence of severe dialysis dementia, but there is increasing evidence of a mild form of encephalopathy in long-term dialysis patients, characterized by psychomotor dysfunction, memory defects, weakness, and mild myoclonus.

Unusual manifestations of aluminum intoxication include myalgias, proximal myopathy, and severe skeletal pain caused by profound osteodystrophy that is unresponsive to vitamin D and is followed by fractures. Aluminum is deposited at the calcified bone-osteoid junction, and bone formation is impaired (Chapters 257, 259, and 262). Aluminum also interferes with parathyroid function, and it may be associated with cardiomyopathy. Aluminum toxicity also is characterized by a poorly understood microcytic anemia that may be related in part to aluminum binding to transferrin and interfering with iron incorporation into heme.

Persons involved in aluminum processing or manufacturing, pottery or explosive making, or welding may be exposed to aluminum aerosols. Pulmonary granulomas, fibrosis, and, in some cases, post-fibrosis emphysema may supervene. In bauxite smelters, this is called *Shaver's disease*. Workers involved in aluminum smelting may develop wheezing, chest tightness, and evidence of airway obstruction (potroom asthma).

Serum aluminum levels often do not reflect body loads. Intoxication may be documented by a deferoxamine mobilization test, but it can exacerbate the encephalopathy temporarily.

Although frequently lethal, in some cases the encephalopathy has regressed after intake of oral aluminum is curtailed. Treatment with deferoxamine, which complexes with aluminum, may be beneficial. Patients with uremia should be wary of community water supplies with inordinately high concentrations of aluminum.

COPPER. Copper levels may be inordinately high in the dialysis water if the water is supplied through copper plumbing. Copper is a potent red blood cell toxin, damaging cell membranes and inhibiting a variety of red blood cell enzymes. Major manifestations of toxicity include hemolysis and gastrointestinal disturbances. Nausea, vomiting, diarrhea, abdominal pain, fever, chills, hemolytic anemia, jaundice, hemoglobinuria, and severe myalgias all occur frequently. Myoglobinemia, necrotizing pancreatitis, hepatic necrosis, and profound leukocytosis also may occur.

Copper poisoning may occur after intentional or accidental ingestion. Hematemesis, melena, hepatic necrosis, and shock may supervene.

Persons exposed to metallic copper industrially may develop transient pulmonary manifestations (metal fume fever) and, rarely, green hair. These disappear rapidly when exposure is stopped.

COBALT. Patients with renal failure may have elevated tissue cobalt levels, often as a result of oral intake to combat anemia. Toxicity includes nausea, vomiting, anorexia, tinnitus, peripheral neuropathy, goiter resulting from blockage of iodine uptake, neurogenic deafness, hyperlipidemia, optic atrophy, and renal tubular damage.

Persons exposed to cobalt industrially occasionally may develop cardiomyopathy. Workers exposed to finely powdered cobalt may develop pulmonary interstitial fibrosis and cor pulmonale. Cobalt is often a component of alloys that are used in joint prostheses. Cases have been reported of joint pains, spontaneous dislocation of the prosthesis, and bone necrosis starting 9 months to 4 years postoperatively, apparently caused by a reaction to the cobalt in the alloy.

OTHER METALS. Tissue tin concentrations, especially in the liver, also are increased in patients undergoing hemodialysis. Tin levels are even higher, however, in uremic patients who have not been dialyzed. As of yet, no definite clinical disease has been associated with these increased body tin burdens.

Patients undergoing maintenance hemodialysis often are treated with iron for anemia. In these patients, parenteral and occasionally oral iron administration may be followed by hemosiderosis and occasionally by hemochromatosis. Serum ferritin concentrations may exceed 500 ng/mL. A proximal myopathy also has been described. Treatment with deferoxamine may reduce the body iron burden in impending or actual hemosiderosis.

CADMIUM

Etiology

More than 10 million pounds of cadmium are used industrially every year in the United States. The metal is a component of alloys; it is used to manufacture electrical conductors and in electroplating;

and it is present in ceramics, pigments, dental prosthetics, plastic stabilizers, and storage batteries. Cadmium is also a byproduct of zinc smelting and is used in the photographic, rubber, motor, and aircraft industries. Smelters, metal-processing furnaces, and the burning of coal and oil are responsible for much of the cadmium in air.

Clinical Manifestations

Acute intoxication by cadmium fumes produces a characteristic clinical picture (called "ouch-ouch" disease in Japan). Four to 10 hours after exposure, dyspnea, cough, and substernal discomfort supervene, often accompanied by prominent myalgias, fatigue, headache, and vomiting. In more severe cases, wheezing, hemoptysis, and pulmonary edema may occur and may be accompanied by hypotension and renal failure.

In most cases, the pulmonary manifestations resolve rapidly, but pulmonary function abnormalities may not disappear for months; in these cases, vital capacity is reduced, and there is a restrictive defect. Occasionally, pulmonary edema is lethal.

Ingesting large amounts of cadmium results in nausea, vomiting, and abdominal pain, often accompanied by weakness, prostration, and myalgias. The onset of the gastroenteritis occurs shortly after ingestion and usually lasts for less than 24 hours.

Chronic cadmium exposure by aerosol for at least 10 years has resulted in emphysema in a few cases. The emphysema is not accompanied by bronchitis and may appear many years after industrial exposure has stopped. Workers exposed for at least 10 years also may suffer olfactory nerve damage; in some cases, this progresses to total anosmia.

The most frequent long-term consequence of aerosol or oral exposure is proteinuria. After prolonged and heavy contact, cadmium urinary excretion continues for years and is associated with damage to the proximal tubule. On occasion, the proteinuria may be accompanied by glycosuria and aminoaciduria. Only infrequently are the proteinuria and tubular damage followed by progressive renal failure.

NICKEL

Etiology

Nickel is used in various alloys, iron shell casings, ball bearings, and heart and joint prostheses. It also is used in nickel plating; as a catalyst; in magnetic tapes, dyes, and paints; and in acrylic plastics. It is found in petroleum and coal, in diesel fuels, and in soil and air. Municipal incinerators may contribute to the ambient air nickel concentrations.

Nickel is a potent contact allergen; the most frequent adverse effect for humans is nickel dermatitis, which may be persistent and severe. Serious systemic reactions have occurred in allergic persons from nickel-containing dental prostheses, jewelry, pacemakers, or fluids given intravenously through a nickel-containing needle. Prosthetic joints and heart valves have failed because of a reaction to the nickel in the prosthesis. In cases of recalcitrant nickel dermatitis, restriction in dietary nickel may be helpful.

Clinical Manifestations and Treatment

The most toxic of the nickel compounds is nickel carbonyl, created by a reaction between nickel and carbon monoxide. Industrial aerosol exposure is followed immediately by headache, drowsiness, substernal pain, nausea, and vomiting. After a latent period of 1 to 5 days, the victim experiences fever, chills, dyspnea, a feeling of chest tightness, cough that is sometimes productive of blood-tinged sputum, muscle pains, weakness, and fatigue. Hepatic enzyme concentrations may be elevated considerably. In severe cases, cyanosis, progressive respiratory difficulties, and convulsions ensue, and death may follow. The treatment of choice is diethyldithiocarbamate (Dithiocarb); BAL is an alternative therapeutic agent, but neither agent has proven effectiveness in humans. Although overwhelming pneumonitis caused by nickel carbonyl is now rare, milder pulmonary toxicity in occupations such as welding probably goes unrecognized under the general rubric of *metal fume fever*.

Carcinogenesis

Nickel is considered a potent respiratory tract carcinogen. Studies of nickel refinery workers have shown a 5-fold increase in risk of lung cancer, a 150-fold increase in the risk of nasal cancer, and a substantially increased risk of laryngeal cancer. Occupations most at risk among nickel workers are roasting, smelting, and electrolysis. Workers developing lung, laryngeal, and nasal cancers usually have been exposed for at least 10 years. Biopsy specimens of nasal mucosa show potentially precancerous epithelial dysplasia in a substantial percentage of nickel workers. The cancer risk is so great that workers heavily exposed for more than 10 years probably should have annual nasal mucosa biopsies and sputum cytologic studies and radiographic examinations every 4 to 6 months in an attempt at secondary prevention. The incidence of respiratory tract cancer in nickel workers depends on the extent of nickel exposure and the effects of cocarcinogens, in particular, cigarette tobacco. Except for nickel miners and refinery workers, industrial nickel exposure has not been associated convincingly with increased risk of cancer.

THALLIUM

Etiology and Pathogenesis

Thallium is used in optical lenses, jewelry, low-temperature thermometers, semiconductors, luminescent tubes, dyes and pigments, scintillation counters, and fireworks. It forms a stainless alloy with silver and a corrosion-resistant alloy with lead and may be a byproduct of lead and zinc production. In some areas, it is still a component of rodenticides, pesticides, and insecticides. Thallium can enter the body through the respiratory tract, gastrointestinal tract, or skin. Similar to many other trace metals, thallium has a strong affinity for sulfhydryl groups and interferes with many enzyme systems. Additionally, it enters the cell, exchanging for intracellular potassium.

Clinical Manifestations

Poisoning can be acute and overwhelming after suicidal ingestion, or it can be chronic and subtle. In acute poisoning, manifestations include nausea, vomiting, hematemesis, headache, lethargy, abdominal pain, diarrhea that may be bloody, insomnia, myalgias, muscle weakness, fever, hyperhidrosis, excessive thirst, confusion, delirium, seizures, coma, and respiratory failure. At least 10% of acutely poisoned persons die.

Among persons who survive at least 1 week or who are exposed to smaller amounts of thallium, the most predictable manifestations are a combined sensory and motor, often painful, peripheral neuropathy and alopecia. Although the head alopecia is total, the facial, axillary, and pubic hair are spared, as is the inner one third of the eyebrows. Motor manifestations may predominate, and the ascending, predominantly motor paralysis may mimic Guillain-Barré syndrome. Abdominal colic, nausea, and vomiting occur frequently in the acute and the subacute forms of thallium toxicity and may dominate the clinical picture so that a diagnosis of acute appendicitis is made. Other manifestations of subacute intoxication include dementia, headache, fatigue, sleep disorders, intractable thirst, hallucinations, blindness caused by optic neuritis, impotence, amenorrhea, a blue discoloration of the gingivae, centrilobular hepatic necrosis, renal tubular necrosis, orthostatic hypotension, paralytic ileus, and myoclonic twitches. Multiple cranial nerves may be involved, but the eighth nerve almost always is spared. The electrocardiogram may show arrhythmias and changes similar to those associated with hypokalemia.

Diagnosis

Thallium can be measured in blood and urine, but blood levels are often deceptively low even during clinically apparent poisoning. Because thallium is excreted in the urine, thallium determinations on 24-hour specimens are more reliable.

In some cases, there is no history of occupational, environmental, or intentional exposure. Unexplained abdominal pain, neurologic abnormalities, and alopecia suggest the diagnosis.

Rx Treatment

Treatment consists of hemodialysis, which can remove half the thallium body burden, and probably administration of Prussian blue. Prussian blue (which is not approved by the U.S. Food and Drug Administration for this purpose) or activated charcoal given by mouth adsorbs thallium so that fecal thallium concentrations increase, but there are no data to confirm improved outcomes in humans. The half-life of thallium in the body is about 1 month, and repeated dialyses usually are needed.

Prognosis

Of individuals poisoned, 30% suffer some residual effects. The neuropathy may persist for many months before resolving. Some patients are left with variable amounts of dementia, neuropathy, ataxia, visual impairment, alopecia, and myoclonus.

SELENIUM

Etiology

Selenium is well absorbed from the gastrointestinal tract and the lungs. The amount normally ingested varies markedly, depending on the local soil selenium content and on the geographic origins of foods consumed. The element is used widely in pigment, glass, electronics, ceramics, and steel industries, and it has gained popularity with traditional and alternative medicine for its antioxidant properties.

Clinical Manifestations

In humans, a *selenium deficiency syndrome* has been defined clearly in human toddlers. In the Republic of China, diffuse cardiomyopathy (Keshan disease) has been associated with low soil and blood selenium levels, and the incidence of the disease apparently has been reduced strikingly by selenium supplementation.

Selenium toxicity syndromes in humans can be divided into acute and chronic poisoning. Subjects with inordinate exposure to selenium fumes experience one or more of the following: intestinal disturbances, giddiness, apathy, lassitude, pallor, nervousness, depression, hair and nail loss, a garlic odor to the breath, and a metallic taste. Sore throat, dyspnea, and cough also may be noted. Symptoms usually disappear after removal from the occupational exposure. In persons ingesting excessive selenium, symptoms and signs include nausea, vomiting, abdominal pain, diarrhea, anorexia, fatigue, sore throat, arthralgias, emotional lability, a metallic taste, a garlic odor to the breath, brittle nails, brittle hair, hair loss, a bronze color to the skin, hepatic dysfunction, and diffuse dermatitis. Increased selenium burdens may be associated with an increased prevalence of dental caries. To date, no treatment of selenium excess or poisoning—save supportive measures—has been documented as beneficial; chelation therapy is currently not advised.

Epidemiology

An epidemic of chronic selenium intoxication was observed in China in the 1960s. Subacute and chronic selenium toxicity may be seen with an increasing frequency because selenium is being promoted as a nonprescription dietary supplement.

OTHER TOXIC METALS

MANGANESE. Manganese toxicity occurs primarily in miners who have been exposed to manganese dioxide aerosols for prolonged periods. The manifestations, known as *manganic madness,* are limited to the CNS. The manganese is concentrated primarily in the basal ganglia and cerebellum, accounting for the extrapyramidal Parkinson-like facies, rigidity, and difficulty in walking. Other manifestations include compulsive behavior (including singing, dancing, fighting, and running), explosive and involuntary laughter, headache, muscular weakness, tremors, somnolence, dystonia, hypotonia, retropulsion and propulsion, dementia, speech disturbances, irritability, sialorrhea, impotence, hypersomnia, and memory defects. In some cases, psychosis may be the dominant feature. Manganese contamination of dialysates or ingestion has been associated with abdominal pain, liver dysfunction, and evidence of pancreatitis. The molecular mechanism is unclear, and no effective therapy exists.

BARIUM. Barium compounds are used in printing; in the production of paints, glass, paper, leather, soap, and rubber; in ceramics, plastic, steel, oil, textile, and dye industries; as fuel additives; and in insecticides, rodenticides, and depilatories. After accidental or intentional ingestion of large amounts, abdominal pain, vomiting, and increased peristalsis occur. If enough is absorbed, potassium is displaced intracellularly, resulting in profound hypokalemia, which may produce flaccid paralysis, potentially dangerous cardiac arrhythmias, renal failure, and respiratory paralysis. Poisoning also has been described after barium chloride skin burn. Treatment consists of potassium administration and efforts to promote barium excretion. Severe allergic reaction has followed barium enema; whether this is due to the barium or preservatives is not clear.

Contact with barium also causes a benign pneumoconiosis that may occur after 1 or more years of aerosol exposure. Chest radiographs show extensive, dense bilateral nodules 4 to 5 mm in diameter. There is no prominent fibrosis and no clinically significant disease; the nodules often regress after occupational exposure is stopped.

BORON. Few reports of boron toxicity exist despite significant acute exposures. Ingesting boric acid can result in nausea; vomiting; diarrhea; anemia; seizures; a variety of skin eruptions characterized by intense erythema, desquamation, and exfoliation; and striking alopecia. Additionally, occupational aerosol exposure to diborane (B_2H_6) in high-energy fuels can produce acute pulmonary edema that resolves after the exposure is discontinued. Exposure to liquid boron hydride (B_5H_9) can produce dementia, cortical blindness, deafness, seizures, acidosis, and cardiac arrest. A subacute mild organic brain syndrome also has been observed.

ANTIMONY. Industrial antimony toxicity is rare, as is intentional ingestion or inadvertent poisoning from antimony released from inexpensive enamelware. Manifestations of acute poisoning include nausea, abdominal pain, weakness, headache, vomiting, diarrhea, hematemesis, myalgias, liver function abnormalities, acute renal tubular dysfunction, electrolyte abnormalities, and circulatory collapse. Gaseous stibine (SbH_3) is as toxic as arsine, producing CNS toxicity and hemolysis. After antimonial injection for medicinal purposes, adverse effects include nausea, vomiting, cough, and muscle and joint pain. Hepatic dysfunction can occur, as can cardiac arrhythmias, including Adams-Stokes syndrome. Antimony also is considered one of the metals capable of causing metal fume fever. Treatment of oral ingestion consists of lavage, administration of activated charcoal, and administration of dimercaprol or the less toxic analogues dimercaptosuccinic acid or dimercaptopropanesulfonic acid.

CHROMIUM. Chromium is used extensively in metal and galvanizing industries and in the manufacture of dyes, enamel, and paints. Chromate exposure is associated with an increased incidence of lung and certain upper respiratory tract cancers. Chromium-exposed workers may show evidence of proximal renal tubule dysfunction and commonly suffer nasal septum perforations.

MOLYBDENUM. In animals, molybdenum produces diarrhea, anemia, alopecia, diminished growth, and bone and joint abnormalities. No clearly defined molybdenum toxicity syndrome has been reported in humans.

PLATINUM. The major adverse effects observed in platinum workers are allergic pulmonary reactions, including bronchial asthma.

PLUTONIUM. In experimental models, plutonium, because of its radioactivity, is a potent carcinogen. Workers generally have been well protected, but data suggest that occupational exposure may be a significant problem. Some controversial epidemiologic studies have suggested that accidental community exposure has resulted in an increase in frequency of certain cancers and fetal malformations.

TELLURIUM. Used particularly in rubber, metallurgic, and electronics industries, tellurium can cause giddiness, headache, nausea, a metallic taste, and a garlic smell to the breath. In animals, tellurium causes neuropathy, but this has not been shown convincingly in humans.

TIN. Tin can be released into beverages or foods from tin cans; ingestion can produce nausea, vomiting, abdominal pain, and diarrhea. This toxicity occurs infrequently. There also have been occasional reports of neurologic abnormalities after exposure to organic tin, including the triethyl, trimethyl, and triphenyl tins, which are used primarily in agriculture for their bactericidal, fungicidal, antiparasitic, and molluscacidal properties. Manifestations include ataxic dysmetria, disorientation, seizures, nystagmus, impaired vision, hearing loss, headache, vertigo, paresthesias, intracranial hypertension, paresis, and polyneuropathy. Aerosol exposure to tin may result in stannosis, which is a mild pneumoconiosis with dense bilateral infiltrates but usually no pulmonary dysfunction.

VANADIUM. Vanadium is used in alloys and in the steel and chemical industries. Inhalation of vanadium can result in neurasthenia, anorexia, vertigo, throat pain, nasal irritation (even nasal hemorrhage), and acute bronchitis characterized by a cough that sometimes is accompanied by a whoop. The nasal mucosa of vanadium-exposed workers shows vascular hyperemia and round cell infiltration.

SUGGESTED READINGS

Centers for Disease Control and Prevention. Second National Report on Human Exposure to Environmental Chemicals 2003, Atlanta, Georgia. *The first normative data available from 2500 normal healthy people.*

Goldfrank LR, Flomenbaum NE, Leavin NA, et al: Goldfrank's Toxicologic Emergencies. New York, McGraw Hill, 2002. *Comprehensive text.*

Klaassen CD (ed): Casarett and Doull's Toxicology: The Basic Science of Poisons, 6th ed. New York, McGraw Hill, 2001. *Comprehensive text.*

Sullivan JB, Krieger GR: Clinical Environmental Health and Toxic Exposures, 2nd ed. Philadelphia, Lippincott Williams & Wilkins, 2001. *Comprehensive text.*

part IV

Aging and Geriatric Medicine

21 EPIDEMIOLOGY OF AGING: IMPLICATIONS OF THE AGING OF SOCIETY

Linda P. Fried

Demographic Revolution: Transition to an Aging Society

Society is aging. There are now more than 35 million persons age 65 and older in the United States, representing more than 13% of the population; in contrast, in 1900, there were 3 million persons age 65 years and older, representing just 4% of the population. By 2030, about 20% of the U.S. population will be older than age 65. These increases represent similarly dramatic increases in life expectancy over the last century: in 1900, at birth, men could expect to live to 48 years and women could expect to live to 51 years, on the average; by 1997, life expectancy had increased to 74 and 79 years. Substantial years are now lived after the age of 65 by a large proportion of the population.

With this significant demographic shift, older adults have become the majority users of health care. One index of this statement is that a substantial proportion of persons with most chronic diseases are older than age 65 (Table 21–1). As a result of this burden of disease, people 65 years old and older account for one third of U.S. health care expenditures. Older adults make, on average, 11 outpatient visits per year and use a wide spectrum of health services, including hospital care, home care, and nursing home care.

Changes in Health Status of Older Adults

By many measures, overall well-being is improving for the current generation of older adults compared with prior birth cohorts. In 1995,

39% of persons age 65 and older reported being in excellent or very good health. Educational status, a strong predictor of health behaviors and health outcomes, also is increasing. In 1950, 17.7% of persons age 65 and older had a high school diploma or higher, and 3.6% had a bachelor's degree or higher; by 1998, these percentages had increased to 67% and 14.8%. Physical disability, which is an adverse outcome of chronic diseases and aging, is reported by 40% of older adults; however, the remaining 60% are not disabled, and disability rates appear to have declined in the last 10 years.

In 1900, pneumonia and influenza, tuberculosis, diarrhea, and enteritis were the leading causes of death, accounting for 30% of all deaths in persons older than age 65. In 1997, heart disease was the leading cause of death in persons age 65 and older, followed by cancer, stroke, chronic obstructive pulmonary diseases, pneumonia and influenza, and diabetes (Table 21–2); the first three diseases accounted for 60% of all deaths. Among persons age 85 and older, heart disease alone is responsible for 40% of all deaths. Alzheimer's disease is the sixth leading cause of death among white women age 85 and older, but it is a less common cause among black women and men of either race.

From 1980 through 1997, actual death rates declined by 30% for heart disease and by 36% for stroke. Both of these declines are due to a combination of improved medical care, risk factor reductions, and changes in lifestyle. Conversely, mortality resulting from cancer, pneumonia, and influenza increased slightly, and death rates for chronic obstructive pulmonary diseases and diabetes increased 57% and 32%. Evidence for improvements in health status and declines in mortality rates indicates that either many of the outcomes associated with aging are not inevitable or their onset potentially can be delayed until later in a person's life by means of effective prevention or treatment.

Multiple Causes of Death in Older Adults

Mortality in older adults seems to result from multiple contributing causes, even if one cause can be considered primary. One study of the predictors of 5-year mortality in older adults found that numerous types of health indices contribute: sociodemographic characteristics, health habits, cardiovascular risk factors, clinical and subclinical diseases, physical disability, and cognitive impairment (Table 21–3). After taking these risk factors and conditions into account, age itself becomes substantially less important as a predictor of mortality.

Disease Frequencies Rise with Increasing Age

Given the substantial number of years that are lived after age 65, patients and clinicians must focus on the conditions with which people live. After age 65 years, 80% of persons report one or more chronic diseases, with almost all chronic diseases increasing with age. Arthritis is reported by 2% of men and 4% of women younger than age 45, by 18% of men and 29% of women age 45 to 64, by 39% of men and 50% of women age 65 to 74, and by 44% of men and 62% of women age 75 or older. For conditions such as severe memory impairment, prevalence also rises rapidly with aging (Fig. 21–1). In the oldest age groups, arthritis, diabetes, hypertension, and possibly cerebrovascular disease are substantially more frequent in African Americans than whites. Overall, the proportion who report very good or excellent health decreases with increasing age, from 82% of persons age 18, to 68% of persons age 18 to 64, to 39% of persons age 65 and older.

Table 21–1 • PROPORTION OF ALL CASES OF A DISEASE REPORTED BY PERSONS 65 YEARS AND OLDER (COMMUNITY-DWELLING), UNITED STATES, 1996

	NUMBER OF PERSONS 65 YEARS AND OLDER WITH THE DISEASE (IN THOUSANDS)	PERCENT OF ALL INDIVIDUALS REPORTING THE DISEASE WHO ARE 65 YEARS AND OLDER
Arthritis	15,335	45.6
Hypertension	11,547	40.8
Hearing impairment	9638	43.7
Heart disease	8535	41.3
Diabetes	3178	41.7
Visual impairment	2674	32.3
Asthma and emphysema	2475	13.4
Cerebrovascular disease	2067	68.9

From NCHS Vital and Health Statistics: Current Estimates from the National Health Interview Survey. Series 10, No. 200, U.S. GPO, October 1999.

Table 21–2 • DEATH RATES (PER 100,000) FOR LEADING CAUSES OF DEATH AMONG PERSONS AGE 65 OR OLDER, 1980–1997

	HEART DISEASE	CANCER	STROKE	COPD	PNEUMONIA AND INFLUENZA	DIABETES
1980	2629	1052	669	179	214	107
1997	1832	1133	426	281	237	141
Percent Change from 1980–1997	−30.3	7.7	−36.3	57.0	10.7	31.8

COPD = chronic obstructive pulmonary disease.
From National Vital Statistics System.

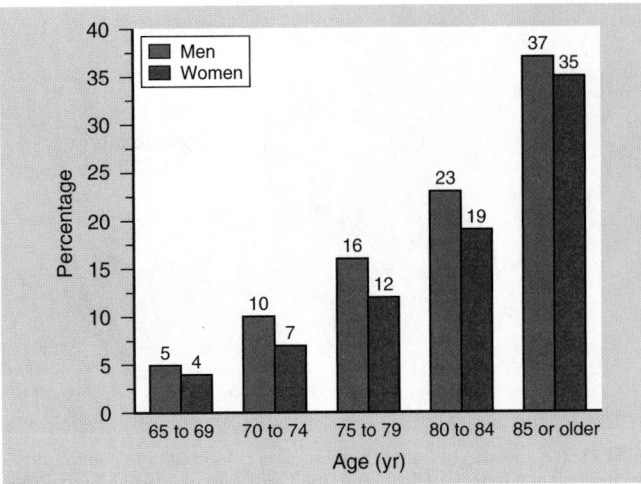

FIGURE 21–1 • Percentage of persons age 65 or older with moderate or severe memory impairment (defined as ≤4 words recalled, out of 20, on combined immediate and delayed recall tests). (Data from Older Americans 2000: Key Indicators of Well-being. Federal Interagency Forum on Aging Related Statistics, Washington, DC, U.S. Government Printing Office.)

Table 21–4 • MOST PREVALENT CONDITIONS AMONG COMMUNITY-DWELLING PERSONS AGE 65 YEARS AND OLDER

DISEASE OR CONDITION	ANNUAL PREVALENCE (PER 1000)
Arthritis*	48.3
Disability†	40.0
Hypertension*	36.4
Falls†	30.0
Hearing impairment†	30.3
Heart disease*	26.9
Influenza*	21.4
Disabled in IADL and/or ADL†	21.0
Cataracts*	17.2
Orthopedic impairment†	15.8
Depression*	14.7
Malignant neoplasms*	14.5
Chronic sinusitis*	11.7
Diabetes mellitus*	10.0
Urinary incontinence†	8.8
Visual impairment†	8.4
Asthma, emphysema*	7.7
Alzheimer's disease*	7.0
Frailty†	6.9
Cerebrovascular disease*	6.5

*Clinical diseases.
†Conditions not associated with specific diseases.
IADL = instrumental activities of daily living; ADL = activities of daily living.

Table 21–3 • PREDICTORS OF 5-YEAR MORTALITY IN MEN AND WOMEN 65 YEARS AND OLDER IN THE CARDIOVASCULAR HEALTH STUDY*

Sociodemographic	
	Age (older)
	Gender (male)
	Income (<$50,000/yr)
Anthropometric	
	Weight (lower)
Health habits	
	Physical activity (low)
	Smoking (pack years)
Cardiovascular risk factors	
	Brachial systolic blood pressure (elevated)
	Posterior tibial artery blood pressure (reduced)
	Diuretic use (in persons with severe CHF or liver disease)
	Fasting blood glucose (higher)
Serum measures	
	Albumin (lower)
	Creatinine (higher)
Clinically manifest disease	
	CHF
Subclinical disease, measured noninvasively	
	Forced vital capacity, mL (lower)
	Ejection fraction abnormal
	Aortic stenosis (moderate-severe)
	Major ECG abnormality
	Stenosis (maximal) of internal carotid artery (greater)
Consequences of disease	
	Difficulty with instrumental activities of daily living (≥2)
	Cognitive impairment (greater)
	Poor self-assessed health

*Persons without cancer at the time of enrollment.
CHF = congestive heart failure; ECG = electrocardiogram.
From Fried LP, Kronmal RA, Newman AB, et al: Risk factors for 5-year mortality in older adults: The Cardiovascular Health Study. JAMA 1998;279:585–592.

In addition to prevalent clinical disease (Table 21–4), subclinical disease is common in older adults. Among the 6000 men and women age 65 and older participating in the Cardiovascular Health Study, 31% had evidence of clinical cardiovascular disease, whereas another 37% had subclinical disease by a variety of noninvasive measures.

This subclinical disease in some circumstances may have manifestations that are not yet diagnosed or diagnosable. Infarct-like lesions were found on magnetic resonance imaging in 28% of Cardiovascular Health Study participants without a known history of stroke. These imaging findings were associated with falling, balance problems, and cognitive decline but not with clinically diagnosed stroke. Overall, subclinical cardiovascular disease is a stronger predictor of which older adults will develop clinical cardiovascular disease than are other classic risk factors. These epidemiologic data suggest that the detection of subclinical disease should become a focus of diagnostic attention and preventive interventions.

Onset of Geriatric Conditions

Health status in aging is a result of many factors, including the chronic diseases of aging and many other prevalent conditions that cannot be defined as classic "diseases" because they do not result from a single pathologic cause (see Table 21–4). Falls, which occur in one third of older adults, result in injuries, fractures, and high risk for disability and mortality (Chapter 23). Severe cognitive impairment (Chapters 25 and 26) and urinary incontinence (Chapter 24) have a substantial adverse impact on an elderly person, as does sensory isolation resulting from hearing and visual impairment; all of these conditions are frequent with aging.

Why Geriatric Patients Are Different

Older patients differ from young or middle-aged adults with the same disease in many ways, one of which is the frequent occurrence of comorbidities and of subclinical disease. As a function of the high prevalence of disease, comorbidity (or the co-occurrence of two or more diseases in the same individual) is also common. Of people age 65 and older, 50% have two or more chronic diseases, and these diseases can confer additive risk of adverse outcomes, such as mortality. In some patients, cognitive impairment may mask the symptoms of important conditions. Treatment for one disease may affect another adversely, as in the use of aspirin to prevent stroke in individuals with a history of peptic ulcer disease. The risk for becoming disabled or dependent also increases with the number of diseases present. Specific pairs of diseases can increase synergistically the risk of disability. Arthritis and heart disease coexist in 18% of older adults; although the odds of developing disability are increased by three-fold to four-fold with either disease alone, the risk of disability increases 14-fold if both are present.

A second way in which older adults differ from younger adults is the greater likelihood that their diseases present with nonspecific symptoms and signs. Pneumonia and stroke may present with nonspecific changes in mentation as the primary symptom. Similarly, the frequency of silent myocardial infarction increases with increasing age, as does the proportion of patients who present with a change in mental status, dizziness, or weakness rather than typical chest pain (Chapter 69). As a result, the diagnostic evaluation of geriatric patients must consider a wider spectrum of diseases than generally would be considered in middle-aged adults.

A third condition that is found primarily in older adults is frailty. Frailty is thought to be a wasting syndrome that presents with multiple symptoms and signs, including reduced muscle mass, weight loss, weakness, poor exercise tolerance, slowed motor performance, and low physical activity. Some estimates indicate that the full syndrome is found in 7% of community-dwelling people age 65 and older, and in 25% of community-dwelling people age 85 and older. Many institutionalized older adults also are frail. Frailty is a state of decreased reserve and increased vulnerability to all kinds of stress, from acute infection or injury to hospitalization, and may identify individuals who cannot tolerate invasive therapies. The syndrome of frailty is associated with high risk of falls, need for hospitalization, disability, and mortality. There is early evidence that a core component of frailty is sarcopenia, or loss of muscle mass associated with aging, which occurs in 13 to 24% of persons age 65 to 70 and in 60% of persons age 80 and older. It is likely that dysregulation of multiple physiologic systems, including inflammation, hormonal status, and glucose metabolism, underlies the syndrome, with resulting decreased ability to maintain homeostasis in the face of stress. Subclinical disease (e.g., atherosclerosis), end-stage chronic disease (e.g., heart failure), or a combination of comorbid diseases may precipitate the syndrome. Evidence from randomized, controlled trials shows that resistance exercise, with or without nutritional supplements,[1] and home-based physical therapy[2] can increase lean body mass and strength in even the frailest older adults. This evidence suggests that earlier stages of frailty may be remediable, although end-stage frailty likely presages death.

Fourth, cognitive impairment increases in prominence as people age (Chapters 25 and 26). Cognitive impairment is a risk factor for a wide range of adverse outcomes, including falls, immobilization, dependency, institutionalization, and mortality. Cognitive impairment complicates diagnosis and requires additional care giving to ensure safety.

Finally, a serious and common outcome of chronic diseases of aging is physical disability, defined as having difficulty or being dependent on others for the conduct of essential or personally meaningful activities of life, from basic self-care (e.g., bathing or toileting) to tasks required to live independently (e.g., shopping, preparing meals, or paying bills) to a full range of activities considered to be productive and/or personally meaningful. Of older adults, 40% report difficulty with tasks requiring mobility, and difficulty with mobility predicts the future development of difficulty in instrumental activities of daily living (IADL; household management tasks) and activities of daily living (ADL; basic self-care tasks) (Table 21–5). In persons age 65 and older, difficulty with IADL is reported by 20%, and difficulty with ADL is reported by 11%; for both, the prevalence increases with age. People who have difficulty with tasks of IADL and ADL are at high risk of becoming dependent. Of persons older than age 65, 5% reside in nursing homes, largely as a result of dependency in IADL and/or ADL secondary to severe disease. Generally, women live more years with disability, whereas men who become similarly disabled are more likely to die at a younger age. Although physical disability is primarily a result of chronic diseases and geriatric conditions, its onset and severity are modified by other factors, including treatments that control the underlying diseases, physical activity, nutrition, and smoking. Many intervention trials indicate that disability can be prevented or its severity decreased; one trial showed improvements in functioning with resistance and aerobic exercise[3] in older adults with osteoarthritis of the knee.

Comorbidity, frailty, and disability are recognized as distinct clinical entities (Fig. 21–2), although they are related in the same causal pathway. Comorbidity may be a risk factor for frailty, and both are risk factors for disability. A vicious cycle may exist, whereby inactivity resulting from disability precipitates or worsens frailty.

The health status of older adults includes a broader spectrum of issues than is found for middle-aged or younger patients, including

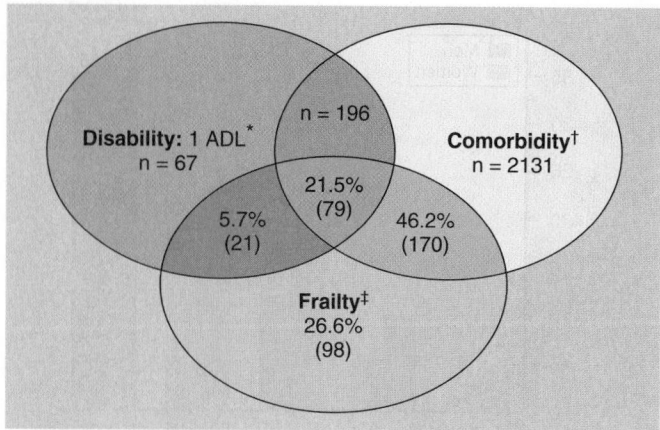

FIGURE 21–2 • Overlap of frailty, disability, and comorbidity in community-dwelling older adults participating in the Cardiovascular Health Study. The total represented was 2762 subjects who had comorbidity and/or disability and/or frailty. *n = 363 with an ADL disability; of these, 100 were frail. †n = 2576 with two or more of the following nine diseases: myocardial infarction, angina, heart failure, claudication, arthritis, cancer, diabetes, hypertension, and chronic obstructive pulmonary disease. Of these, 249 were also frail. ‡n = 368 frail subjects. ADL = activities of daily living. (From Fried LP, Tangen CM, Walston J, et al. Frailty in older adults: Evidence for a phenotype. J Gerontol A Biol Sci Med Sci 2001;56: M146–156.)

Table 21–5 • **ASSESSMENT OF PHYSICAL DISABILITY IN OLDER ADULTS**

DISABILITY TYPE	DESCRIPTOR
Ambulation	Difficulty in walking
Instrumental activities of daily living	Difficulty in Preparing meals Doing housework Using telephone Shopping Medication management Financial management
Basic activities of daily living	Difficulty in Bathing Dressing Grooming Toileting Transfers Eating

For full assessment instrument, see Reuben DB, Herr KA, Pacala JT, et al: Geriatrics at Your Fingertips. Maiden, MA, Blackwell Science, Inc, for the American Geriatrics Society, 2002.

prevalent chronic disease, recurrent disease, comorbidity, and geriatric conditions, each of which can be an independent problem or interact with other problems to cause disability, dependency, or death. There is also, however, great heterogeneity in health status among older adults, with robust, independent individuals even in the oldest age ranges. Because of this heterogeneity, older patients may require primary, secondary, or tertiary preventive health care (Table 21–6), tailored to their individual health status and inherent risk. Overall, preventive health care is effective in older adults (Chapter 11), and attention to clinical practices and health habits, from immunization to physical activity, can prevent adverse outcomes into the oldest ages. Preventive measures also should be targeted to situations of acute stress (e.g., hospitalization or immobilization) when the risk of decline in function is high. Health status can change rapidly as people age so that clinical care and services must evolve in concert with the health and function of the patient.

Table 21–6 • SPECTRUM OF HEALTH CARE AND PREVENTIVE CARE NEEDS AMONG OLDER ADULTS

LEVEL OF PREVENTION	TARGETED HEALTH ISSUES
Primary	Incident disease, geriatric conditions
Secondary	Screening, early detection of prevalent disease and geriatric conditions
	Treatment of morbidity
	Prevention of recurrent disease
Tertiary	Impact of disease and geriatric conditions
	Disability and dependency
	Hospitalization
	Institutionalization
	Death

Future Directions

Clinical care of older adults will become more effective in improving health outcomes as new evidence emerges regarding how best to identify the subsets of older individuals who are at risk of adverse outcomes. The range of outcomes for which more effective screening methods are being developed includes cardiovascular disease, hip fractures, disability, and susceptibility to medical procedures or polypharmacy.

1. Fiatarone MA, O'Neill EF, Ryan ND, et al: Exercise training and nutritional supplementation for physical frailty in very elderly people. N Engl J Med 1994;330:1769–1775.
2. Gill TM, Baker DI, Gottschalk M, et al: A program to prevent functional decline in physically frail, elderly persons who live at home. N Engl J Med 2002;347:1068–1074.
3. Ettinger WH, Burns R, Messier SP, et al: A randomized trial comparing aerobic exercise and resistance exercise with a health education program in older adults with knee osteoarthritis. The Fitness Arthritis and Seniors Test (FAST). JAMA 1997;277:25–31.

SUGGESTED READINGS

Burke GL, Arnold AA, Bild DE, et al: Factors associated with healthy aging: The Cardiovascular Health Study. J Am Geriatr Soc 2001;49:254–262. *Many modifiable behavioral risk factors (physical activity, smoking, and obesity) and cardiovascular risk factors (diabetes, high-density lipoprotein cholesterol, and blood pressure) are associated with maintenance of good health in older adults, whereas subclinical disease, such as inflammation and atherosclerosis, are adverse predictors.*

Fried LP, Tangen CM, Walston J, et al: Frailty in older adults: Evidence for a phenotype. J Gerontol Med Sci 2001;M 56:146–156. *Validation of a phenotype of frailty and its outcomes, including falls, disability, hospitalization, and mortality.*

22 BIOLOGY OF AGING

George M. Martin

The Life Course Approach to the Understanding of Aging

It is useful to think of organisms as protein-synthesizing factories. If that factory is to function at very high levels of efficiency and stability for very long periods of time, the builder should start with an excellent set of blueprints (hence the importance of understanding the constitutional genomes of individual patients), hire engineers and supervisors to oversee its construction and maturation (hence the relevance of understanding how development impacts upon the adult phenotypes of our patients), ensure that the factory functions in a safe environment (hence the importance of protecting patients from teratogens, mutagens, carcinogens, and candidate "gerontogens," such as tobacco smoke), and, finally, initiate rigorous regimens of quality control throughout the life span of the factory (hence the importance of such biologic processes as DNA repair and the detection, reconstitution, and turnover of aberrant proteins). This same rationale underlies the view of many biologists that aging begins at conception.

Operationally, however, gerontologists typically use the terms *aging* and *senescing* interchangeably to refer to the slow, insidious declines in structure and function that unfold after the achievement of sexual maturation and the young adult phenotype. Given large populations of individuals, this process eventually translates into exponential increases in age-specific death rates, although the rate of increase has been shown to decline in exceedingly old organisms. The mechanisms underlying this paradoxical terminal slowing of mortality rates is not fully understood; because slowing can be observed even in genetically homogeneous experimental animals, it cannot be attributed solely to genetic differences.

Some postmaturational changes in structure and function are compensatory and therefore adaptive. Physicians contemplating interventions in their aging patients should first consider if a given biochemical, metabolic, or physiologic change is indeed acting to maintain homeostasis. Such compensatory changes may be considered part of a process of "sageing" rather than senescing. Examples include the essentially full-time use of the Frank-Starling phenomenon to increase diastolic filling so as to maintain cardiac output. Another example of "sageing" is the neuritic sprouting that maintains dendritic arborization in the brains of old subjects, particularly those with neurodegenerative processes that result in focal neuronal loss.

Although genes and the environment play major roles in a person's life course, stochastic processes also influence longevity and morbidity, especially during the later half of the life span. Consider, for example, somatic mutational mechanisms of aging. Two individuals may be subject to exactly the same flux of somatic mutation, that is, the same probability that a certain number of mutations will occur over a certain period of time. One person may be quite lucky, with all or most of the "hits" occurring in pseudogenes—dead, nonfunctional relics of genes where mutations would have absolutely no functional consequences. Another person might be quite unlucky, however, with "hits" preferentially involving tumor suppressor genes such as *p53* or activating oncogenes such as *Ras*. Consider also two individuals who have a comparable degree of coronary artery atherosclerosis or amyloid deposits in cerebral blood vessels. Physicians are not surprised by the fact that such individuals may differ substantially in the age at which a fatal event (coronary artery thrombosis or cerebral hemorrhage) occurs. Although future discoveries may elucidate all of the interacting variables that determine the probability of such events, chance juxtapositions of sets of such variables are likely to be responsible for much of the variance. These considerations provide great difficulties for investigators interested in performing a genetic analysis of longevity, such as the genetic contributions to achieving centenarian celebrity.

The Evolutionary Biological Theory of Aging Provides a Satisfactory Explanation for *Why* We Age

Why do animal species evolve such striking differences in their life history strategies? The answer appears to lie in an understanding of the different ecologies in which they have evolved. Consider, for example, an exceptionally hazardous environment—one with unreliable sources of food and water and a rich supply of predators, infectious agents, and dangerous terrains conducive to fatal accidents. In such ecologies, there is strong selective pressure to "get the job over with quickly"; that "job," of course, is reproduction. Natural selection sculpts the genome so as to provide the maximum opportunity for enhancing reproductive fitness in a given ecologic niche. For the niche just described, natural selection will favor a life history characterized by rapid development, large numbers of progeny during a relatively short course of reproductively active adult life, and an abbreviated longevity. There is no need for nature to have designed energetically expensive quality control systems to maintain the soma for long periods of time. Such gene variations might well appear spontaneously and potentially benefit a rare long-lived individual within an age-structured population, but the chances of that individual passing on that allelic variant to the gene pool of the next generation is negligible, as the bulk of the alleles would be derived from the much larger cohort of younger animals. Older animals would be much less frequent even in the absence of senescence, as they are likely to have been eliminated by disease, predators, starvation, and so on. Thus, limited life spans occur because the alleles that have the potential to provide enhanced life spans escape the force of natural selection. Both laboratory and field experiments have proved, however, that when animals are provided with a much more benign ecology that has low hazards, a different life history strategy can emerge, one characterized by a slower rate of development and fewer progeny per gestation but longer periods of fecundity and longer life spans. Various classes of gene actions conspire to modulate life spans, including some that escape the force of natural selection.

Classes of Gene Action that Escape the Force of Natural Selection

A summary of the several classes of gene action that escape the force of natural selection is given in Table 22–1. The term *good allele* refers to a variety of a gene that functions well and is adaptive—that is to say, it contributes to organismal viability and durability. Of course, some good alleles may be better than others. The first category involves alleles that are often termed *longevity assurance genes*. These alleles are beneficial both early and late in the life course. Examples could include alleles at an array of DNA repair loci, alleles that function efficiently to scavenge reactive oxygen species, and alleles that reduce methionine sulfoxides. The second category involves genes that function at high levels early in the life course but whose expressions are decreased during certain developmental epochs, presumably to enhance reproductive fitness. There is evidence in murine models, for example, of downregulation of sets of ribosomal DNA genes at about the time animals reach sexual maturity and the fully adult phenotype, after which there is no requirement for rapid somatic growth. Another example that may function adaptively to modulate rates of somatic growth is the gradual downregulation of the paternal *IGF2* allele, a change that ensures markedly decreased function of this gene product so that the maternal allele is imprinted. In humans, there is evidence that this process may well begin at about puberty or shortly thereafter. Once such a process is initiated, it "has a life of its own." In both of these examples, there is continuing downregulation, eventually reaching very low levels late in the life span, when the deficiency may well have deleterious effects but when such phenotypic expression will have escaped the force of natural selection.

A number of genetic loci may become upregulated during the process of "sageing" mentioned earlier, but genetic loci may also become inappropriately upregulated late in the life span. This process, which has been called "loss of gene silencing," occurs, for example, when the inactive X chromosome becomes activated in aging mice. The molecular mechanisms for such loss of silencing have not been fully elucidated but may sometimes involve changes in the regulation of enzymes such as NAD^+-dependent histone deacetylase, an enzyme required for chromatin-dependent gene silencing in yeast. Homologues of the responsible gene, *Sir2*, occur in mammals. Increased dosages of a *Sir2* gene have been shown to extend the life span of *Caenorhabditis elegans*.

The fourth class in Table 22–1 is one of the two classic examples of gene action that escape the force of natural selection. The phenomenon of *antagonistic pleiotropy* refers to alleles that are associated with adaptive effects early in the life span but with deleterious effects late in the life span. This class of gene action has received a great deal of recent attention in connection with evidence that levels of the tumor suppressor gene, *p53*, have been "fine-tuned" by evolution both to decrease the risk of cancer and to decrease the rate of aging. In mouse models, putative excessive functioning of *p53* protects against cancer but is associated with decreased life spans and conditions such as osteopenia, multiple organ atrophy, and poor wound healing.

Another possible example of antagonistic pleiotropic gene action is the gradual loss of telomeric repeat units of most replicating types of human somatic cells as a consequence of a basic molecular flaw in the process of semiconservative DNA replication. An enzyme complex called telomerase, consisting of both an RNA template subunit and a catalytic protein subunit, compensates for this intrinsic end-replication problem by maintaining the telomeric caps of chromosomes. However, nature has seen fit to turn off that enzyme, apparently when cells leave a stem cell compartment, thus setting the stage for an eventual loss of replicative potential, a process known as *replicative senescence*. Many investigators believe that this programmed loss of telomerase expression is adaptive in that it protects the organism from cancers. An alternative possibility is that it evolved for the fine-tuning of organ growth during fetal development. Late in the life span, however, replicative senescence might, in some organs, be partially responsible for atrophic changes. There is even some evidence that short telomeres correlate with regions of the vasculature with heightened susceptibility to atherosclerosis.

Somatic mutations, which are stochastic alterations in the primary nucleotide sequences or copy numbers of gene loci, clearly occur during the aging of mammals. Mutations likely accumulate exponentially with age and are proved causes of various age-related cancers. Less is known about what has been termed *epimutation*, which involves stochastic alterations in such epinucleic chemical changes as methylation and acetylation. Given that somatic mutations make their greatest impact late in the life span, they in large part escape the force of natural selection.

Another class of gene action that also escapes the force of natural selection involves inborn, constitutional mutations that have neutral, or nearly neutral, effects early in the life course but deleterious effects late in the life course. The prototypic example is Huntington disease, which typically does not reach a level of expression until after the peak of reproduction. Although individually rare, there are potentially thousands of such examples. All patients are likely to have one or more such "private" modulations that can have an impact on patterns of aging. Moreover, all patients also are likely to carry a private array of suppressor mutations at other loci to postpone the age of phenotypic expression.

Environmentally Triggered Diapause and Caloric Restriction Can Increase the Life Spans of Diverse Organisms

Research has implicated a homologous pathway of neuroendocrine modulation of life span in diverse organisms. The most detailed understanding has come from mutational studies of *C. elegans*, but research with *Drosophila melanogaster*, Monarch butterflies, and unusually long-lived dwarf mice strongly suggests that comparable pathways may be involved (Fig. 22–1). In humans, a counterpart to one of the dwarf mouse mutations involves the growth hormone receptor and is a variant of the Laron syndrome, but there is insufficient information to know whether this syndrome is also associated with enhanced longevity. The pathways observed in nematodes appear to have evolved to implement a mechanism for what might be called a *diapause*, or "time out," in the usual progression of the life history. Some investigators believe that this pathway may also contribute to the well-known ability of caloric restriction to enhance life span in a wide range of organisms. Most such research has been conducted in laboratory mice and rats, in which life span extensions of about 50% have been observed with a nutritionally balanced diet containing 60% fewer calories than fed control animals on an unrestricted diet. The same common causes of death, such as cancer and chronic renal disease, occurred in the experimental animals, but they were substantially postponed. Ongoing experiments in rhesus monkeys are encouraging in that a number of physiologic changes seen in calorically restricted mice are also observed in the calorically restricted monkeys, including a lowering of the levels of oxidative damage to skeletal muscle. However, it is clearly premature to conclude that caloric restriction is a viable mechanism for the extension of the human life span. The effects of caloric restriction may be another example of diapause; in the face of nutritional hard times, it pays to decrease reproductive efforts and concentrate on maintaining the soma until new nutritional opportunities appear.

Human Progeroid Mutations

Progress in understanding the nature of gene action associated with differential rates of aging and longevity in experimental organisms did not come from a study of genes that shortened life span; it has been difficult to be certain that the associated phenotypes were valid models of accelerated normative aging. Real progress came only with the isolation and characterization of long-lived mutants, although in many cases, such mutations may merely have comple-

---

Table 22–1 • SEVEN CLASSES OF GENE ACTION THAT CAN ESCAPE THE FORCE OF NATURAL SELECTION

1. Good alleles with good effects early and late ("longevity assurance genes")
2. Good alleles downregulated for good reasons
3. Good alleles inappropriately upregulated in late life (loss of "silencing")
4. Good alleles with bad late effects ("antagonistic pleiotropy")
5. Good alleles that go bad via somatic mutation or epimutation
6. Bad alleles that do not reach a phenotypic level of expression until late in the life course (constitutional "mutation accumulation")

Modified from Martin GM: Gene action in the aging brain: An evolutionary biological perspective. Neurobiol Aging 2002;23:647–654.

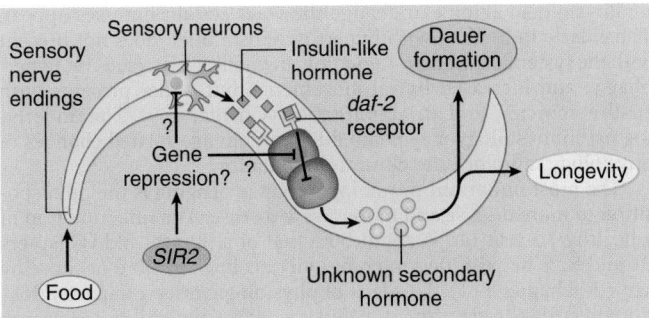

FIGURE 22–1 • Gene variation at an insulin-like growth factor signal transduction pathway regulates diapause and modulates longevity in multiple species. The most detailed analysis comes from research on the simple nematode, *Caenorhabditis elegans*, illustrated in this figure. The pathway responds to the degree of availability of sources of nutrition via sensory nerve endings. With limited food, the wild-type function leads to a dauer phenotype, a sort of hibernation state that is associated with a degree of motility sufficient for the discovery of a new food source during a larval stage, which then triggers exit from the dauer stage. Dauers are resistant to a variety of stresses, including oxidative stress. Certain leaky mutations at a receptor for an insulin-like growth factor (*daf-2*) permit development beyond the dauer larval stage and are also associated with enhanced longevity, although with a wide range of ages of death. The pathway has an impact on a forkhead transcription factor (*DAF-16*) to modulate its expression. Under wild-type conditions, the transcription factor is negatively regulated; it appears to function, in association with signals from the gonad, to integrate developmental and environmental signals so as to modulate life span, perhaps via downstream genes responsive to various stresses, including oxidative stress. A homologue of an NAD$^+$-dependent histone deacetylase (*SIR-2*) is thought to participate in the regulation of gene expression. (From Strauss E: Growing old together. Science 2001;292:41–43, with permission.)

mented some special vulnerability of a clonal strain. Research in humans on the discovery of gene mutations and polymorphic alleles that may lead to unusually robust structure and function during the latter half of the life span is in its infancy.

Putative linkages of longevity to a region on chromosome 4 and to a variety of polymorphisms await confirmation. Perhaps the best-documented example is the triallellic polymorphism at the apolipoprotein E locus: an unusual polymorphic allele (*APOε2*) is found disproportionately in centenarians, in whom the *APOε2* allele is unusual. The latter is also known to be a risk factor for Alzheimer-type dementia and cardiovascular disorders. This deleterious allele, however, may have evolved among ancestors of some extant populations because it provided enhanced reproductive fitness in particular environments. If that was indeed the case, this type of gene action can be viewed as an example of antagonistic pleiotropy (class 4 of Table 22–1).

The gene action responsible for the abbreviated life spans of at least a subset of human subjects can be divided into two types of syndromes. One type involves gene actions that appear to lead to the premature onset and accelerated rate of development of numerous senescent phenotypes. The prototypic example is the Werner syndrome (Chapter 37), sometimes known as progeria of the adult, which is caused by homozygosity for null mutations at a member of the *RecQ* family of DNA helicases. The responsible gene is an unusual member of the *RecQ* family in that it has exonuclease as well as helicase functions. Its definitive role in pathophysiology remains to be defined, but the wild-type function probably acts to recognize and resolve unusual DNA structures during DNA replication and recombination, such as nucleotide mismatch "bubbles" and Holliday junctions. Deficient function results in high frequencies of somatic mutations, especially deletions and chromosomal rearrangements. Deficient function also leads to marked limitations of the replicative potentials of somatic cells. These cellular and molecular phenotypes may explain the striking progeroid features, which include bilateral ocular cataracts, atherosclerosis, medial calcinosis, calcification of heart valves, type 2 diabetes mellitus, osteoporosis, gonadal atrophy, atrophy of skin and subcutaneous tissues, and premature thinning and graying of hair. These patients also experience a variety of benign and malignant neoplasms. The syndrome differs, however, from usual aging.

For example, patients with Werner syndrome develop a disproportionate number of mesenchymal neoplasms and have an unusual distribution of their osteoporosis. It therefore seems prudent to continue to refer to this syndrome as a progeroid syndrome rather than as a "premature aging" syndrome. Nevertheless, research on Werner syndrome has drawn attention to a potentially key role for somatic mutations and replicative senescence in the pathogenesis of a wide array of geriatric disorders.

A second category of progeroid syndromes appears to involve only a single tissue or organ. Prototypic examples include the several forms of early-onset familial dementias of the Alzheimer type, such as the autosomal dominant mutations at the *presenilin 1* locus on chromosome 14 and the *presenilin 2* locus on chromosome 1, as well as the *beta amyloid precursor* locus on chromosome 21. Alzheimer pathology may be part of normative aging because varying degrees of plaques, tangles, and amyloid deposits are seen in the central nervous systems of virtually all very old humans. In addition, because the age-specific incidence of the Alzheimer form of dementia increases exponentially after age 65 years and because the clinical diagnosis of probable Alzheimer disease has been made in about 50% of all human subjects over 85 years of age in a community-based population of Americans (see Chapter 433), it could be concluded that Alzheimer pathology goes hand-in-hand with aging in a very large proportion of humanity. The advantage of studying unimodal progeroid syndromes is that it may help define biochemical pathways that operate to produce an array of specific geriatric disorders, thus opening the door to the development of interventions tailored to the individual needs of each geriatric patient.

Summary

A genetic and evolutionary biology approach to aging emphasizes that, in age-structured populations such as humans, phenotypes whose expressions are delayed can escape the forces of natural selection because most reproducing individuals have been young. Seven classes of gene action can escape the force of natural selection, including the two "classic" types: antagonistic pleiotropy and the accumulation of constitutional mutations. Research in diverse species points to an important role for signal transduction pathways involving insulin-like growth factors and their receptors in the modulation of the life span. Finally, research on genetic causes of progeroid syndromes can help elucidate mechanisms of aging, with the hope that such research may eventually lead to rational interventions tailored to the specific vulnerabilities of geriatric patients.

SUGGESTED READINGS

Hekimi S, Guarente L: Genetics and the specificity of the aging process. Science 2003;299:1351–1354. *The biology of reactive oxygen species in the mitochondria and elsewhere appears to be a critical determinant of life span.*

Martin GM: Gene action in the aging brain: An evolutionary biological perspective. Neurobiol Aging 2002;23:647–654. *An elaboration of the several classes of gene action that escape the force of natural selection, with examples relevant to the aging brain.*

Martin GM, Oshima J: Lessons from human progeroid mutations. Nature 2000;408:263–266. *A brief review of selected segmental progeroid mutations classified according to proposed biochemical and molecular mechanisms.*

Strauss E: Growing old together. Science 2001;292:41–43. *Commentary on research described in Figure 22–1.* http://sageke.sciencemag.org. The Science of Aging Knowledge Environment, sponsored by *Science* magazine and the American Association for the Advancement of Science. *An intellectual home for scientists interested in research and teaching on the biology of aging that will report relevant clinical issues and include links to other sites of interest to biogerontologists and geriatricians.*

23 COMMON CLINICAL SEQUELAE OF AGING

Kenneth L. Minaker

Epidemiology and Pathobiology of Aging

Increased longevity throughout the world is influencing medical care dramatically as more older individuals develop or survive with various medical conditions. Although some elderly present typically with single-system disease, they often have presentations and responses to treatments that are different from their younger counterparts. This variation in behavior of illnesses, which is due to the combined effect of aging and comorbid disease, must be understood if the elderly are to receive successful care.

Age-associated changes in health and disease are the result of (1) variations in the underlying physiologic changes that occur with age; (2) the presence of other diseases and medical conditions that have developed over time; (3) genetic predispositions for certain diseases; (4) lifestyle factors, including health-seeking behavior, diet, exercise, and exposure to medications and toxins; and (5) the variability intrinsic to diseases and medical conditions in general. No single hypothesis fully explains the process of aging (Chapter 22). Two major theories have emerged (Table 23–1). The first concerns programmed causes, which are dominated by genetic theories. The second concerns stochastic causes, so-called process-of-living theories, in which genetic or environmental influences limit viability.

SPECTRUM OF CHANGES PRODUCED BY AGING PROCESSES

Perhaps the most important observation regarding normal aging is how much does not change. Most hormone levels, liver enzymes, electrolytes, body temperature, and basal glucose remain constant throughout the lifespan. Long-term studies have indicated there is no age-related anemia (Chapter 160), although the hematocrit declines slightly in men presumably because of the age-related decline in testosterone.

Physiology also is affected by the passage of time. More prolonged exposure results in the emergence of abnormalities and illnesses, such as skin cancer owing to cumulative sun exposure (Chapter 209). Much of the lifetime exposure to sun is received before age 20 years, yet the resulting cancers follow decades later. Another example is polycystic kidney disease, which is an inheritable condition that does not appear until well into adulthood (Chapter 127); the passage of time, not aging, is the key factor.

Some conditions become less likely with advancing age. Immune disorders, such as systemic lupus erythematosus (Chapter 280) and multiple sclerosis (Chapter 448), rarely appear in late life, presumably because changes in the immune system lead to less aggressive autoimmune disease. Similarly, although many cancers are more common in the elderly, many of the most aggressive tumors occur at a young age, suggesting that immune tolerance develops with advancing age.

Physiologic aging can change the ways certain illnesses appear. The elderly individual with hyperthyroidism often does not present with the systemic findings of agitation, irritability, hyperactivity, hyperphagia, and increased bowel movements, but rather presents with apathy, anorexia, and atrial fibrillation (Chapter 239). The underlying pathophysiology may be no different, but age-related changes in physiology influence the clinical presentation.

The most important physiologic change of aging is the predisposition to more disease and more severe disease. The lung function of a healthy 70-year-old is about 50% that of a 30-year-old (Chapters 81 and 82). Renal function commonly declines by 50% or more by age 70 (Chapter 111). This lack of physiologic reserve capacity does not affect day-to-day function but can affect the ability to recover from an extreme illness.

Geriatric syndromes emerge from these age-related findings. The many systems that support the ability to maintain an upright posture are compromised by age, leading to postural sway; as a result, an older individual is much more likely to fall after a slip or a push. The consequences of that fall are more serious owing to the age-related loss of bone mass (Chapter 258), which can predispose to fall-related fractures.

Some physiologic changes imitate illness when they may be a normal part of aging. Diabetes mellitus may "appear" and "disappear" in the elderly (Chapter 242). The ability of insulin to stimulate glucose uptake declines with age and usually is manifested as postprandial hyperglycemia with a maintenance of normal fasting insulin and glucose levels. Under stress situations, older individuals can appear to be diabetic, but when the stressful situation is relieved, they no longer have chemical evidence of diabetes. Nevertheless, this loss of physiologic reserve understandably contributes to the increasing prevalence of diabetes with advancing age.

The age-related changes that make the elderly more vulnerable in daily life are more subtle. Older individuals are more likely to develop hypothermia or hyperthermia (Chapter 105) during extreme environmental exposure because of a variety of neurologic and thermoregulatory changes. The loss of brainstem neurotransmitters in older persons not only may cause a senile gait pattern, but also predisposes to genetically determined conditions such as Parkinson's disease (Chapter 443).

Some age-related changes cause specific medical sequelae. Menopause (Chapter 256) is a normal aging process that produces symptoms and predisposes to future bone loss and atherosclerosis.

Table 23–1 • PATHOBIOLOGY OF AGING

THEORY	DEFINITION	CAUSE	GENETIC (G) ENVIRONMENT (E)
PROGRAMMED THEORIES			
Programmed senescence	Aging results from gene interference with the ability of the cells to reproduce	Master clock	G
Hormonal	Biologic clock alters hormone secretion, resulting in tissue changes	Decrease in levels of insulin-like growth factor-1 and the hormones estrogen, testosterone, DHEA, and melatonin	G
Immunologic	T-cell function declines, increasing the chances of developing infections and cancer	Alteration in the (cytokines) that are responsible for communication between immune cells	G
Telomere shortening	Shortening of telomeres in somatic cells lessens the ability of cells to divide	Cells cannot divide	G/E
STOCHASTIC THEORIES			
Metabolic rate	The higher the basal metabolic rate (the rate at which the body, at rest, uses energy), the shorter the lifespan	Energy demands to maintain basal metabolism	G
Glycation	Glycation (browning) causes proteins to be joined, resulting in rigidity and decreased function	Elevated glucose	G/E
Somatic mutation	Mutations in genes occur with aging, eventually causing cells to stop functioning	Errors in the transmission of genetic messages over time	G
Wear and tear	Parts of cells wear out over time	Accumulated debris mechanically disrupts cell function	E
Oxygen free radicals	Tissue damage is caused by free radicals, such as superoxide or hydroxl radicals; this is a specific form of the wear-and-tear theory	Oxygen free radicals are unstable chemical compounds that can oxidize cell components such as DNA and proteins	E

DHEA = dehydroepiandrosterone.

Another example is senile cataracts, which are caused by post-translational modifications in lens proteins combined with the inability of the lens to dispose of breakdown products; as a result, the lens becomes stiffer, thicker, and more opaque with age (Chapter 465).

Effects of Aging on Specific Organs and Systems

CARDIOVASCULAR SYSTEM

AGING AND ITS CLINICAL SEQUELAE. Many important physiologic changes occur in the aging heart and help explain some common age-associated cardiac disorders. Perhaps the most important physiologic change is the delay in left ventricular filling, which declines 50% between ages 20 and 80. Cardiac filling becomes more dependent on active filling late in diastole during atrial contraction (Chapter 48). This phenomenon commonly is related to thickening and stiffening of the left ventricular wall. Under normal conditions, systolic function remains unchanged.

The resting heart rate tends to slow with advancing age, and maximum and submaximum exercise-induced heart rates show an age-related decline. The loss of a substantial proportion of sinus node pacemaker cells—90% up to age 80 years—contributes to these changes. There also are changes in central and baroreflex-mediated heart rate control (Chapter 57). Heart valves thicken and stiffen, particularly in the mitral and aortic locations (Chapter 72). The functional significance of heart valve stiffening is minimal, but 25% of older individuals have flow murmurs (Chapter 46). The aorta dilates and its walls thicken as medial walls calcify; with this loss of elasticity, there is a secondary increase in systolic blood pressure (Chapter 63). The arteriosclerosis that occurs as arterial walls thicken, calcify, and lose their elasticity also may predispose aging vessels to atherosclerosis (Chapter 66).

In most industrialized countries, there is a progressive increase in blood pressure with advancing age (Chapter 63). In general, systolic blood pressure increases after age 30 years, continues to rise until the mid-70s, then tends to fall slightly through the 80s and 90s. Diastolic blood pressure tends to parallel the usual increase in body weight that peaks in the early 50s in men and the early 60s in women; diastolic pressures subsequently fall slightly in older age. These changes in blood pressure are not universal, suggesting varied genetic and environmental causes, such as stress, sodium and potassium intake, and obesity.

AGE-RELATED CARDIOVASCULAR SYNDROMES. Although atherosclerosis is the most important cause of symptomatic cardiac disease in the elderly, age-associated vascular stiffness predisposes to left ventricular stiffness, impaired diastolic filling, and the clinical syndrome of diastolic heart failure (Chapter 55). The most common arrhythmia seen in older individuals is atrial fibrillation (Chapter 59), which may occur in one third of older individuals undergoing surgery and may affect 4% of community-dwelling elderly. Although thyroid disease, coronary artery disease, valvular heart disease, and ischemic heart disease are known causal agents, atrial fibrillation in the elderly is often "lone" atrial fibrillation without a detectable underlying illness.

The combination of sensitivity to filling volumes and impaired heart rate response to stress may explain the increasingly prevalent syndrome of postural hypotension that is present in 20% of older individuals (Chapter 435). Postural hypotension is also common in the elderly after large meals; during infections severe enough to depress salt and water intake; and during volume-depleting stresses, such as diarrhea, diuretic therapy, or bowel preparation for colonoscopy. Stiffening of vessels in which baroreceptors reside may accentuate the tendency for autoregulation of blood pressure to be less robust with advancing age.

Perhaps the most important principle in the approach to cardiovascular signs and symptoms with advancing age is to recognize the narrowed homeostatic capacity of the elderly. Volume status must be managed carefully, attention should be paid to standing as opposed to sitting blood pressure in patients predisposed to postural hypotension, side effects of medications must be anticipated and monitored, and cardiovascular instability must be anticipated during almost any major illness that an older person may experience.

RESPIRATORY SYSTEM

The most characteristic change in the chest wall with advancing age is stiffening (Chapter 82). Not only do cartilages thicken and calcify, but also spinal ligaments and joints become stiffer. The primary internal change in the lungs is the loss of the elastic recoil. The result is a modest expansion of the chest wall with the appearance of a mild barrel chest. Although resting lung mechanics do not seem to change in any major way, the loss of maximum breathing capacity declines by approximately 40%. At the alveolar level, the capacity to exchange oxygen and carbon monoxide decreases by approximately 50% between ages 30 and 65 years. Although these changes are not noticeable at rest, individuals experience fatigue or shortness of breath when the respiratory system is under stress (e.g., during exercise or major illness). Pulmonary reflexes, such as coughing and cilial function, decrease, predisposing elderly individuals to the pooling of secretions and to aspiration pneumonia.

All these changes do not produce substantial abnormalities in resting oxygen saturation, but they produce a steady decline in arterial PO_2. The arterial PO_2 of many individuals older than age 80 is about 70 to 75 mm Hg. As with other age-related physiologic findings, these changes do not interfere with function under resting conditions but dramatically affect survival during severe respiratory illness.

AGE-RELATED RESPIRATORY SYNDROMES. The major clinical impact of normal physiologic aging in the lungs is an earlier appearance of shortness of breath as a warning signal of underlying disease. Myocardial infarction and heart failure can present primarily with shortness of breath, owing mainly to age-related mechanical changes, an inability to clear blood from the lungs, and a decline in resting pulmonary function to near the threshold for clinical hypoxia.

GASTROINTESTINAL SYSTEM

A broad series of changes occur in gastroenterologic tissues, but the redundancy of overall gastrointestinal function usually prevents clinical symptoms. Age-related changes in the mouth include slower production of dentine, shrinkage of the root pulp, and decreasing bone density of the jaw. Taste and smell decline progressively with advancing age, with rising thresholds for salt, sweet, and certain proteins (Chapter 469). The overall net effect is that food may taste more bitter, and more sugar is required before something tastes sweet. Salivary gland function normally does not change with age (Chapter 467). The loss of bone and tongue musculature makes the tongue appear to be enlarged.

The esophagus seems to function relatively normally. The strength of muscular contraction declines, however, and peristaltic waves slow with advancing age. There is also a tendency for the lower esophageal sphincter to become lax with advancing age (Chapter 136).

The gastric mucosa secretes less acid with advancing age. Although these changes do not seem to affect digestion in most individuals, associated conditions, such as atrophic gastritis, may decrease the absorption of nutrients (Chapter 137). Most studies suggest delayed gastric emptying is a feature of aging, leading to a sense of false or early satiety, which can impair subsequent food ingestion (Chapter 134).

Liver weight declines by one third between ages 30 and 90 years owing primarily to the loss of hepatocytes. The result is a decreased ability to process medications, such as benzodiazepines, and dietary components, such as alcohol and vitamin K–blocking agents. Doses of drugs often must be adjusted, and their blood levels should be monitored when possible.

Aging is associated with a significant reduction in small intestinal surface area with the consequence of reduced absorption of some dietary components, such as calcium. Colonic function seems to decline with advancing age. Motility up to the rectosigmoid area, measured by passage of markers, does not seem to decline with advancing age (Chapter 134). Distal to this point, however, evacuation is characteristically slower with advancing age. Stool frequency tends to decline, and hardness of stools seems to increase with advancing age. Diverticuli are present in approximately 50% of people older than age 80 and likely are related to reduced dietary fiber and the resulting greater pressure on colonic tissues (Chapter 143).

AGE-RELATED GASTROENTEROLOGIC SYNDROMES. The most important age-related symptom is constipation, which may affect 60% of individuals in late life. Obstipation can present atypically with confusion,

nausea, and vomiting or as obscure fevers resulting from stercoral ulcerations. Perhaps the most common abnormality related to declining hepatic function is increased sensitivity to medications that require hepatic metabolism.

RENAL AND URINARY EXCRETORY SYSTEM

Overall kidney size declines by approximately one third, and blood flow through the kidney declines by about 1% per year. Beginning in the late 30s, cortical nephrons appear to drop out and sclerose at a much higher rate than medullary nephrons, creating a hyperfiltration syndrome that limits maximum concentrating capacity (Chapter 111). Resulting functional changes include a decreased ability to excrete a salt load, a declining glomerular filtration rate, a delayed ability to regain sodium and potassium balance during deprivation states, and difficulty in conserving water under situations of dehydration.

The bladder tends to become more irritable with advancing age and may generate less power during contraction. Because of the delay in sodium excretion and orthostatic changes, nocturia is common; older individuals seem to produce more urine at night than during the day. The most important bladder change may be the slight increase in residual bladder urine volume. Atrophy of vaginal and urethral tissues owing to postmenopausal estrogen deprivation predisposes women to urinary tract infections (Chapters 256 and 344).

AGE-RELATED RENAL AND URINARY TRACT SYNDROMES. The age-related increases in asymptomatic bacteriuria and urinary tract infections are almost certainly due to increased residual bladder volume and loss of protective factors in the normal anatomic structures. As the prostate gland grows with advancing age, benign prostatic hypertrophy causes urinary retention in men (Chapter 129). Urinary incontinence (Chapter 24) is more prevalent in women. The kidney is more susceptible to the effects of medications, particularly nonsteroidal anti-inflammatory drugs, which can result in sodium and fluid retention and subsequent hypertension. Dehydration or volume depletion, which is increasingly more prevalent with advancing age, often accompanies acute infections and increases the morbidity of pneumonia or urinary tract infections.

Dehydration is the most common fluid and electrolyte disorder in the frail elderly, owing to decreased fluid intake and increased fluid losses (Chapter 112). Vomiting and diarrhea are the most common causes of isotonic dehydration. Fever associated with delirium is the leading cause of hypertonic dehydration. Hypotonic dehydration is seen most commonly with overuse of diuretics. Signs and symptoms of dehydration are notoriously vague or absent. Serial weights are helpful to quantify fluid therapy. Orthostatic tachycardia and hypotension are important clinical findings. Perhaps the most useful clinical parameter is a history of having missed one or more meals. Laboratory tests should measure the electrolytes, osmolality, creatinine, and blood urea nitrogen levels; a blood urea nitrogen-to-creatinine ratio greater than or equal to 25 is suggestive of dehydration.

Anticipation and prevention are crucial. Adequate food intake should be maintained, with 30 mL of daily fluid intake per kg of body weight recommended. For an acute event, it is important to review any long-term medications, particularly diuretics, that may have contributed to dehydration and to define the ethically appropriate approach to future episodes. In terminally ill patients, death from dehydration becomes a natural event in which symptom-focused care relieves discomfort from dry mucous membranes (Chapter 3).

ENDOCRINE SYSTEM

Growth hormone levels fall with advancing age, with initial loss of nocturnal growth hormone spikes (Chapter 237). These declines may contribute to the decreased muscle strength, thinning of bones and skin, and increased fat associated with aging. It is currently unclear whether replacement of growth factors can induce a permanent reversal of muscle, bone, and skin changes with advancing age.

The production rates and clearance rates of thyroxine, triiodothyronine, and calcitonin seem to be constant with advancing age despite the increased prevalence of thyroid disease in late life (Chapter 239). There is an increase in parathyroid hormone levels, particularly in women, with advancing age, perhaps in compensation for the age-related decline of the kidney's ability to maintain normal levels of phosphorus and calcium in the blood (Chapter 260).

The adrenal glands maintain their ability to secrete cortisone with advancing age (Chapter 240). Dehydroepiandrosterone declines 85 to 90% by age 70, however, perhaps contributing to impaired immune or cardiovascular function with advancing age. Renin and aldosterone secretion rates decline progressively with advancing age and do not contribute to the increased rates of hypertension with advancing age.

The insulin content of the elderly pancreas is increased, but the release of insulin in response to stimulation may be blunted with advancing age (Chapter 242). There is also a concomitant decline in insulin clearance with advancing age, with the net result that plasma insulin levels in response to glucose seem to be relatively preserved. Insulin resistance may increase with advancing age, but glucagon secretion seems to be well preserved.

The ovaries show dramatic declines in estrogen and progesterone as fibrosis and scarring occur. Menopause occurs at an average age of 51 years with subsequent hot flashes, accelerated bone loss, and atrophy of estrogen-sensitive tissues (Chapter 256). Levels of testosterone decrease in some men beginning around age 50 years, but declines do not seem to affect the potency of semen. Sexual function is relatively well preserved, albeit with an increase in the refractory period and time to arousal and a loss of tissue turgor (Chapter 247).

AGE-RELATED ENDOCRINE SYNDROMES. The most important age-related endocrine syndrome occurring with advancing age is menopause (Chapter 256). Most other endocrine changes with age may enhance the prevalence of common disorders seen with aging, especially diabetes.

IMMUNE SYSTEM

Normal aging produces an obvious decrease in the size of the thymus gland between puberty and age 50 or 60 years (Chapter 266), at which time the gland becomes difficult to identify anatomically. This decrease in size is accompanied by a corresponding drop in thymosin levels, which are related directly to the number of functional T cells found in older adults. T cells also seem to be less active in responding to the presence of foreign proteins, and they tend to reproduce more slowly than those in younger adults. Functional studies of immune responsiveness suggest that although antibody responses are mounted in older individuals, they tend to be less robust and less long lasting than in younger individuals (Chapters 41 and 265).

CLINICAL SYNDROMES OF AGING. There are increased morbidity and mortality associated with influenza and pneumonia with advancing age and reactivation of infections such as tuberculosis and herpes zoster. The decline in immune function also may make it less likely that older adults will develop autoimmune diseases, such as systemic lupus erythematosus.

HEMATOPOIETIC SYSTEM

The pluripotent stem cell and the erythroid and myeloid progenitor cells show no age-related reduction, indicating that there is minimal or no change in basal hematopoiesis during aging (Chapter 159). The aging hematopoietic system is less able to respond to increased demands, however, as evidenced by a slower recovery from anemia and less of a rise of hemoglobin during hypoxia. The older marrow also seems to respond less well to erythropoietin.

Neutrophils from elderly individuals show less prekilling activity and lower levels of lysozyme (Chapters 163 and 191), with a significant reduction in signal transduction and less release of IP$_3$ and diacylglycerol during stimulation. During nutritional deprivation, there seems to be an impairment in the reserve capacity to kill phagocytosed bacteria, a change that may contribute to the high prevalence of serious bacterial infections among the nutritionally compromised elderly.

AGE-RELATED HEMATOPOIETIC SYNDROMES. There are no specific syndromes of impaired hematopoiesis, aside from the clinical observation that during a comparable illness stress, hematologic abnormalities are more likely in the elderly.

MUSCULOSKELETAL SYSTEM

Bone mass and density decrease with age after reaching maximum in the 20s. In women, this loss may be about 1% per year until

menopause, when it can increase to 2 to 3% per year (Chapters 256 and 258). After 5 to 10 years postmenopause, bone loss returns to a rate of loss of 1% per year, but it may accelerate again in the late 80s. Because men have more bone mass than women and lose bone mass at a similar rate of about 1% per year, the clinical effects in men are not seen until advanced age.

Tendons and ligaments become less elastic with advancing age, contributing to a higher incidence of rupture, especially of the Achilles tendon, in older individuals. Cartilage and ligaments of the ribs and spine are more prone to become calcified and less elastic.

Muscles reach their ultimate size and strength in the 20s and 30s. By age 70 years, muscle mass declines by approximately 25% for men and women unless offset by exercise. By age 80 years, muscle size and strength in most sedentary adults decrease by 30 to 40% from the mid-30s peak. Muscle mass in late life depends on exercise earlier in life to reach a higher early mass and exercise late in life to stimulate muscle preservation.

AGE-RELATED MUSCULOSKELETAL SYNDROMES. The most important age-related clinical syndrome associated with advancing age is osteoporosis (Chapter 258). Sarcopenia, or diminished muscle mass, is a clear predisposing factor for falling, which is the leading cause of death at home in older individuals. Bone and muscle mass respond well to exercise, even in the oldest age ranges.

Falls are a major age-related syndrome, involving neural, musculoskeletal, and cardiovascular systems. Most falls in older adults are due to a combination of several factors rather than a single event. Internal contributors to falls include sensory impairment from poor eyesight, hearing loss, and balance disturbances; diseases of the brain, including motor and sensory disorders, cognitive impairment, and depression; cardiovascular, respiratory, and metabolic diseases; and musculoskeletal conditions, such as lower limb weakness, poor grip strength, osteoporosis, rheumatoid arthritis, osteoarthritis, and foot disorders. External causes of falls include medications and environment inside and outside of the home. The risk of falling increases in patients who receive four or more prescription medications; drugs specifically shown to increase the risk of falling include hypnotics, muscle relaxants, antihypertensives, diuretics, and antidepressants. Inside the home, risks include stairs (coming down is more hazardous than climbing up); loose objects, such as furniture, cords, and rugs; poor lighting, particularly in areas with dark/light variability; poorly fitting shoes; surfaces with glare or patterning; and lack of bathroom safety equipment. Outdoor risks include uneven pavements and surface roads made slippery from ice, water, or fallen leaves.

For a person who has fallen, the evaluation should include a detailed history of the circumstances surrounding the fall, medications, medical problems, and mobility; an examination of vision, gait, balance, and lower extremity joint function; an examination of neurologic function, including muscle strength; and an examination of the cardiovascular system. The investigations for falls and syncope (Chapter 435) are similar. Tests are needed only if the history and physical examination do not reveal the cause of falling or if they point to a particular abnormality that requires laboratory evaluation. These tests may include the following:

- Blood tests to exclude anemia, infection, and metabolic problems such as diabetes and thyroid disease
- An electrocardiogram to evaluate heart disease
- A 24-hour electrocardiogram recording or loop monitor to evaluate arrhythmias (Chapter 58)
- An echocardiogram for patients with significant heart murmurs (Chapter 51)
- Drug levels to check if a patient is being undertreated or overtreated with a particular drug
- If focal neurologic signs or symptoms are present, a computed tomography scan of the brain
- If suggestive symptoms are present, a radiograph of the neck or spine looking for spinal stenosis (Chapter 429)

Prevention of Fractures

The prevention of fractures includes three components. First, persons with lower bone densities are more likely to fracture a bone, given the same amount of trauma, than are persons with higher bone densities. Women should be assessed for osteoporosis and treated accordingly (Chapter 258). Osteoporosis often is underdiagnosed in men, and men with fractures or repeated falls should be evaluated

for possible osteoporosis; however, screening strategies for elderly men have not been defined.

Fractures can be prevented if falls can be prevented. Risk factors for falls include a previous fall, muscle weakness, polypharmacy, sedative or hypnotic medications, balance and gait abnormalities, cognitive impairment, arthritis, visual impairment, and foot problems. Reduction in falls requires a targeted attempt to minimize any treatable abnormalities. Older people who have recurrent falls should have regular exercise and balance training. The optimal type, duration, and intensity of exercise are unclear, but balance training for 10 weeks or more has the best-proven benefit.[1] Exercise must be sustained for continued benefit.

When someone falls, the damage may be reduced by the intrinsic padding of fat or by devices such as mechanical hip protectors. Randomized controlled trials of hip protectors to reduce fractures in nursing home patients and in ambulatory older individuals in Europe have shown mixed results.[2,3] Compliance with these cumbersome devices is only 25 to 70%, and some of these hip protectors that have been studied are not yet available in the United States.

NERVOUS SYSTEM

Anatomically the brain shrinks in size with advancing age; after age 60 years, its size declines by 5 to 10%. The decrease in size is caused primarily by a decrease in brain tissue in the cerebral cortex. Novel adjustments made by the brain include the formation of new connections between remaining neurons. Aging is associated with a progressive decline in the synthesis of neurotransmitters and a decline in their corresponding receptors. A major functional change is slower reaction times, which may be the result of a slower nerve conduction or transsynaptic speed.

The farsightedness of aging is caused by the diminished ability of the lens to focus on nearby objects because of its thickening and stiffening (Chapter 465). There is reduced ability to distinguish colors, particularly blue, owing to yellowing of the lens. Overall transmission of light through the lens may decline by 50 to 65% between ages 25 to 60 years; as a result, individuals require more ambient light. Older individuals experience more glare because light scatters through the thickened lens. Older individuals also notice more floaters as the vitreous jelly becomes slightly more liquefied and mobile with advancing age. Tear production is decreased, leading to a sense of grittiness in the older eye. Overall visual acuity tends to decrease with age, and by age 65 years, 40% of men and 60% of women have a visual acuity of 20/70 or worse.

Approximately 25% of individuals older than age 65 experience hearing loss with age (Chapter 470), with men affected more than women. The degeneration of neural transmission from the ear to the brain results in difficulty identifying a voice or understanding a spoken message when there is background noise. Presbycusis results in high-frequency sound loss and more difficulty distinguishing high-pitched consonants and voices compared with lower pitched vowels and sounds.

Sleep patterns change with advancing age (Chapter 438). Functionally, older adults are more wakeful during the night and spend much more time in bed. The pattern of sleep characteristically changes from the fairly regular stepwise patterns of childhood and young adulthood to a more fragmented pattern, with frequent awakenings in late life.

AGE-RELATED NEUROLOGIC SYNDROMES. Age-associated memory dysfunction is common (Chapters 25 and 433), and delirium may occur, especially in response to illness or stress. Prevention of delirium is possible with a proactive consultation intervention, which can reduce the incidence of delirium by about 40 to 50%.[4]

Sleep cycle disturbances are increasingly important with advancing age, and sleep-disordered breathing associated with sleep apnea seems to rise in prevalence with advancing age (Chapter 96). Anatomic changes, such as tissue laxity and diseases of the nose and sinuses, may contribute to sleep-disordered breathing. Sleep apnea may have a neurologic basis either in the sleep cycling center, leading to central sleep apnea, or in neurologic control of pharyngeal tissues.

INTEGUMENTARY SYSTEM

Thinning of the subcutaneous tissue begins in most people in their mid-40s independent of the degree of sun exposure or protection from injury. The epidermis and dermis adhere less tightly, making

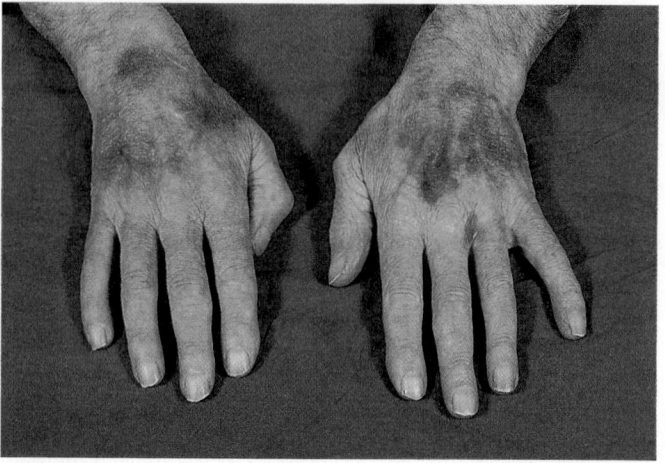

FIGURE 23–1 • Senile purpura is a common and benign condition that results from impaired collagen production and capillary fragility in the elderly. In the absence of other signs of disease, no investigation is necessary. (From Forbes CD, Jackson WF: Color Atlas and Text of Clinical Medicine, 3rd ed. London, Mosby, 2003, with permission.)

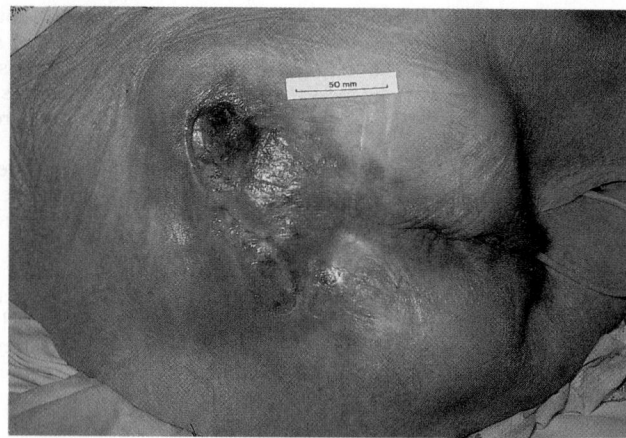

FIGURE 23–2 • Severe sacral pressure sore, one of the serious but preventable complications of immobility. (From Forbes CD, Jackson WF: Color Atlas and Text of Clinical Medicine, 3rd ed. London, Mosby, 2003, with permission.)

the skin feel looser and increasing its tendency to blister and to be subject to friction burns or pressure ulceration (Chapter 471). This phenomenon also leads to senile purpura (Fig. 23–1) that results from tears in small venules when the skin is bumped or abraded (Chapter 476).

Environmental exposures, including ultraviolet sunlight, wind, and smoking, help promote the development of wrinkles by damaging the subcutaneous tissues and the epidermis, especially the elastin fibers. The process of photo injury (Chapter 474) leads to slow repair, particularly of tissues of the distal forearm and lower leg. Ultraviolet light exposure also predisposes to the development of skin cancer, the most common of which is basal cell cancer, but squamous cell cancer and melanoma are also age dependent (Chapter 209). Approximately two thirds of aging individuals experience at least one skin problem, and about 40% have two underlying skin disorders.

The most profound consequence of environmental exposure and age-related changes is that wound repair rates are significantly prolonged. In individuals older than age 65 years, healing takes about 50% longer compared with individuals in their 30s; complete skin healing can take 5.5 weeks instead of 3.5 weeks.

Rates of epithelial cell regeneration decrease by about 50% from maturity to age 70. A similar pattern is seen in hair, which grows more slowly. With advancing age, graying is variable but universal because the number of melanocytes within hair bulbs declines with age (Chapter 477). Changes in skin cell size and shape cause irregular patterning and may predispose to water-induced or environmental-induced cracking.

AGE-RELATED INTEGUMENTARY SYNDROMES. Specific illnesses affecting the skin include basal cell cancer and rosacea (Chapters 474 through 477). Aging skin syndromes also include xerosis, thermoregulatory changes, skin thinning, and hair loss. The primary therapy for xerosis is the external application of treatments to protect and moisturize the skin (Chapter 473).

Diminished sweating poses a threat during times of high ambient and environmental temperatures or in the context of fever (Chapter 105). The absence of sweating lessens heat loss by conduction and evaporation, and it diminishes the urge to move to a more protected environment. Environmental protection from temperature extremes is crucial (Chapter 105).

Pressure sores are necrotic areas of muscle, subcutaneous fat, and skin as a result of compression and subsequent ischemia (Fig. 23–2). Pressure sores usually occur between underlying bone and a hard surface or a soft surface over a prolonged time. Among elderly patients in acute care hospitals, the incidence rate is 8%, and the prevalence rate is 16%. Rates are even higher in patients who are in intensive care units or who have hip fractures.

Pressure sores develop only when there is continuing pressure exceeding 30 to 35 mm Hg; pressures of 150 mm Hg may be generated by a standard mattress. In addition to pressure injury, shear injury is important. Shear injury, which occurs when local blood vessels are stretched and separated from underlying perforating vessels, is more likely when the patient is in a sloped position or is rubbing constantly against underlying surfaces. Burning injury also can result from friction of the superficial skin layers. A complicating feature of all pressure ulcers is moisture, which leads to softening of the skin, sticking to underlying surfaces, and easy access for infection.

Individuals at higher risk include those who are immobile; are incontinent of bowel or bladder; or have compromised circulation owing to hypotension, dehydration, or vascular disease. Neurologic disease, particularly peripheral neuropathy that impairs sensation, can predispose to pressure ulcers, as can any neurologic condition that causes spasticity, contractures, or poor mobility.

Preventive strategies encourage safe positioning, regular turning, and avoidance of direct pressure. Judicious use of pressure-reducing beds may reduce the incidence of pressure ulcers after hip fractures. Deep foam mattresses or air suspension beds are even more effective.

When pressure sores appear, they should be photographed to establish a baseline. Nutrition should be improved, all pressure on the wound should be removed, and active vigilance should be focused to prevent additional pressure ulcers. Débridement of necrotic tissue should be considered; wet to dry dressings and surgical or chemical débridement are often used. Infections may require topical or systemic antibiotics. Semiocclusive and occlusive dressings also can be helpful. Most pressure ulcers heal within 6 months, but operative repair is sometimes necessary.

CLINICAL PHARMACOLOGY

Of all prescription medications (Chapter 27), about 30% are taken by the elderly even though they comprise only 14% of the population. Nonprescription medications, which often are used as much as or more than prescription medications, also are disproportionately consumed by older individuals.

The gastrointestinal absorption of medications generally does not change with advancing age, despite the theoretical possibility that medications requiring acidification in the stomach may be absorbed less well because of the higher frequency of atrophic gastritis and reduced gastric acid. Drug distribution changes significantly with advancing age because medications distribute to fat or muscle. As muscle mass declines with advancing age, fat increases as a proportion of total body weight. As a result, older individuals are more sensitive to the effects of water-soluble drugs and have prolonged effects from lipophilic drugs.

The decline in renal function with normal aging reduces the clearance of many drugs, especially digoxin, aminoglycosides, and cimetidine. Hepatic metabolism also may decline with age. Oxidative reactions, so-called phase 1 reactions, become impaired with normal aging, whereas phase 2 reactions (conjugation and glucuronidization) are relatively spared. A clinical example is that diazepam, which requires phase 1 and phase 2 metabolism, has a prolonged half-life with advancing age, but oxazepam, which requires only phase 2 reactions to be metabolized, does not.

The overall impact of these pharmacokinetic changes is that the half-life, which is proportional to the volume of distribution divided by drug clearance, increases for many lipophilic drugs. Poorly nourished or frail elderly persons may have a low serum albumin level. The normal age-related decline in the serum albumin level is clinically insignificant. When the albumin level is less than 3 g/dL, however, drug levels have to be interpreted based on their binding to albumin.

The elderly are more sensitive to many medications after they are absorbed. The brain appears to be increasingly sensitive to many compounds, including opiates, benzodiazapines, and neuroleptics. As a result, lower doses create equivalent effects to higher doses in younger individuals. Warfarin, which acts primarily on the liver, should be used at lower doses in the elderly to maintain normal anticoagulation profiles because the aging liver is increasingly sensitive to blockage of vitamin K–dependent systems.

The elderly are at higher risk for nonadherence to prescribed regimens. Factors influencing nonadherence include the cost of medications, inadequate patient education about their medications, unacceptable side effects, and the complexity of the medical regimen. Individuals who take more than three prescription drugs have lower compliance.

Perhaps the most important phenomenon in multiple drug regimens in older individuals is the progressive accumulation of anticholinergic effects, including dry mouth, constipation, poor vision, urinary retention, balance disorders, and cognitive difficulties. Drug classes include neuroleptics, antispasmodics, antianxiety agents, antihistamines, and medications used for urinary incontinence.

1. Tinetti ME, Baker DI, McAvay G, et al: A multifactorial intervention to reduce the risk of falling among elderly people living in the community. N Engl J Med 1994;331:821–827.
2. Kannus P, Parkkari J, Niemi S, et al: Prevention of hip fracture in elderly people with use of a hip protector. N Engl J Med 2000;343:1506–1513.
3. van Schoor NM, Smit JH, Twisk JW, et al: Prevention of hip fractures by external hip protectors: A randomized controlled trial. JAMA 2003;289:1957–1962.
4. Marcantonio ER, Flacker JM, Wright JR, Resnick NM: Reducing delirium after hip fracture: A randomized trial. J Am Geriatr Soc 2001;49:516–522.

SUGGESTED READINGS

Cohen HJ, Feussner JR, Weinberger M, et al: A controlled trial of inpatient and outpatient geriatric evaluation and management. N Engl J Med 2002;346:905–912. *Significant reductions in functional decline and improvements in mental health were achieved at no increase in costs.*

Cuddigan J, Berlowitz DR, Ayello EA, for the National Pressure Ulcer Advisory Panel: Pressure ulcers in America: Prevalence, incidence, and implications for the future. An executive summary of the National Pressure Ulcer Advisory Panel Monograph. Adv Skin Wound Care 2001;14:208–215. *A definitive review of this common problem is presented.*

Juurlink DN, Mamdani M, Kopp A, et al: Drug-drug interactions among elderly patients hospitalized for drug toxicity. JAMA 2003;289:1652–1658. *Many admissions for drug toxicity occur after administration of a drug known to cause drug-drug interactions.*

Tinetti ME: Clinical practice. Preventing falls in elderly persons. N Engl J Med 2003;348:42–49. *A thorough, case-based review.*

24 URINARY INCONTINENCE

Joseph G. Ouslander

Definition and Scope of the Problem

Urinary incontinence is defined as involuntary loss of urine of sufficient severity to be a health and/or social problem. Although it is commonly hidden and not discussed with health professionals, urinary incontinence is a prevalent, morbid, and expensive condition. Half of young and middle-aged women experience urinary incontinence, often in association with childbirth. Urinary incontinence is a common manifestation of benign and malignant prostate enlargement in middle-aged and older men. The prevalence and incidence of urinary

incontinence are higher in women and increase with age. Among relatively healthy community-dwelling adults age 60 years and older, about one third of women and nearly 20% of men have some degree of urinary incontinence. About 10% of both sexes have frequent (at least weekly) episodes and/or use protective padding. The prevalence is nearly 40% in hospitalized older adults and is 70 to 80% in adults in long-term care institutions.

Urinary incontinence causes considerable physical and psychosocial morbidity and health care costs. The condition is uncomfortable and predisposes to skin problems and falls in older patients rushing to the bathroom. It is a social stigma and can lead to embarrassment, isolation, and depression. Urinary incontinence is commonly an important precipitating factor in the decision to enter a long-term care facility. The annual health care costs of managing urinary incontinence and its complications have been estimated to be more than $20 billion.

Pathogenesis

Continence requires effective lower urinary tract functioning; adequate mobility, dexterity, cognition, and motivation to be continent; and absence of environmental and iatrogenic barriers (Table 24–1). From a lower urinary tract standpoint, incontinence results from (1) failure to store urine because of bladder overactivity and/or low urethral resistance, (2) failure to empty the bladder because of anatomic or physiologic obstruction and/or inadequate bladder contractility, or (3) a combination of these factors.

Aging per se does not cause urinary incontinence, but age-related changes can predispose to it. Among women, urethral resistance declines because of diminished estrogen effects and weakened periurethral and pelvic muscles. Among men, urethral resistance increases, and the urine flow rate decreases in association with prostatic enlargement. In both sexes, the bladder tends to become overactive and is affected by involuntary detrusor contractions (more so in men than women). In many older individuals, impaired bladder contractility develops and can result in a condition termed *detrusor hyperactivity with impaired contractility*. Finally, age-related declines in renal concentrating mechanisms and loss of the normal diurnal rhythm of arginine vasopressin can predispose older patients to nocturnal polyuria and incontinence.

Several potentially reversible factors may cause or contribute to urinary incontinence, especially in geriatric patients (Table 24–2). The common reversible factors can be remembered by the mnemonic *DRIP* (delirium; restricted mobility, retention; infection, inflammation [atrophic vaginitis], impaction of stool; polyuria, pharmaceuticals).

Table 24–1 • **REQUIREMENTS FOR CONTINENCE**

Effective lower urinary tract function
  Storage
    Accommodation by bladder of increasing volumes of urine under low pressure
    Closed bladder outlet
    Appropriate sensation of bladder fullness
    Absence of involuntary bladder contractions
  Emptying
    Bladder capable of contraction
    Lack of anatomic obstruction to urine flow
    Coordinated lowering of outlet resistance with bladder contractions
Adequate mobility and dexterity to use toilet or toilet substitute and to manage clothing
Adequate cognitive function to recognize toileting needs and to find a toilet or toilet substitute
Motivation to be continent
Absence of environmental and iatrogenic barriers, such as inaccessible toilets or toilet substitutes, unavailable caregivers, or drug side effects

From Kane RL, Ouslander JG, Abrass IB: Essentials of Clinical Geriatrics, 4th ed. New York, McGraw-Hill, 1998. Copyright © by McGraw-Hill, Inc. Used by permission of McGraw-Hill Book Company.

Table 24–2 • REVERSIBLE CONDITIONS THAT CAUSE OR CONTRIBUTE TO URINARY INCONTINENCE

CONDITION	MANAGEMENT
CONDITIONS AFFECTING THE LOWER URINARY TRACT	
Urinary tract infection (symptomatic with frequency, urgency, dysuria)	Antimicrobial therapy
Atrophic vaginitis/urethritis	Topical estrogen
Postprostatectomy, postpartum	Behavioral interventions. Further evaluation if condition does not resolve over a few months
Stool impaction	Disimpaction; appropriate use of stool softeners, bulk-forming agents, and laxatives if necessary; high fiber intake; adequate exercise and fluid intake
DRUG SIDE EFFECTS	
Diuretics	Discontinue or change therapy if clinically
Anticholinergics	appropriate. Dosage reduction or modification
α-Adrenergic agents	(e.g., flexible scheduling of rapid-acting
Psychotropics	diuretics) also may help
Narcotics	
INCREASED URINE PRODUCTION	
Metabolic (hyperglycemia, hypercalcemia)	Better control of diabetes mellitus. Therapy for hypercalcemia depends on the underlying cause
Excess fluid intake	Reduction in intake of caffeinated beverages
Volume overload	
Venous insufficiency with edema	Support stockings
	Leg elevation
	Sodium restriction
	Diuretic therapy
Congestive heart failure	Medical therapy
IMPAIRED ABILITY OR WILLINGNESS TO REACH A TOILET	
Delirium	Diagnosis and treatment of underlying cause of acute confusional state
Chronic illness, injury, or restraint that interferes with mobility	Regular toileting
	Environmental alterations (e.g., bedside commode, urinal)
Psychological	Pharmacologic and/or nonpharmacologic treatment

From Kane RL, Ouslander JG, Abrass IB: Essentials of Clinical Geriatrics, 4th ed. New York, McGraw-Hill, 1998. Copyright © by McGraw-Hill, Inc. Used by permission of McGraw-Hill Book Company.

Clinical Manifestations

Urinary incontinence may be of sudden onset. In geriatric patients, a sudden onset commonly is associated with an acute medical illness and/or one or more potentially reversible factors (see Table 24–2). More commonly, urinary incontinence is a chronic problem, and patients often delay for years after its onset before discussing it with a health professional. For this reason, the physician periodically should ask screening questions specifically about bladder control problems.

Persistent types of urinary incontinence can be categorized into four basic types (Table 24–3). *Stress* incontinence is far more common in women than men, among whom it occurs only after sphincter damage from surgery or radiation. *Urge* incontinence is the most common and bothersome symptomatic type of incontinence in the geriatric population and usually is associated with other symptoms of bladder overactivity, such as daytime frequency (voiding every 2 hours or more often) and nocturia (awakening to void during normal sleeping hours). The symptoms and signs of *overflow* incontinence are nonspecific and may mimic symptoms and signs of the stress and urge types. Men, patients with diabetes mellitus, and patients with neurologic disorders are at highest risk for overflow urinary incontinence. *Functional* incontinence refers to patients whose involuntary urine loss is related predominantly to impaired mobility and/or cognition. These basic types of urinary incontinence commonly coexist. A substantial proportion of women have symptoms of urge *and* stress incontinence (generally referred to as a *mixed* type). Frail geriatric patients commonly have urge incontinence with bladder overactivity and functional impairments that contribute to the incontinence problem.

Diagnosis

The basic evaluation of incontinent patients includes a focused history (which can be enhanced by a voiding diary), a targeted physical examination, urinalysis, and a postvoid residual determination (Fig. 24–1). Postvoid residual determination is essential in almost all patients because the symptoms of overflow incontinence are nonspecific, and the physical examination alone is not sensitive in detecting significant urinary retention (i.e., postvoid residual >200 mL). A portable ultrasound device is available and can provide noninvasively an accurate estimate of bladder volume. The objectives of this basic evaluation are to (1) identify potentially reversible factors (see Table 24–1); (2) determine, if possible, the most likely types and underlying causes (see Table 24–2); and (3) identify patients who may require further evaluation.

Selected patients may benefit from further urologic, gynecologic, and urodynamic evaluation. Patients with sterile hematuria should be considered for urine cytology and cystoscopy. Women with severe pelvic prolapse should be referred to a gynecologist for consideration of pessary placement or surgery. Women or men with severe stress incontinence should be considered for referral for surgical intervention. Patients with significant urinary retention, patients with a neurologic disorder that may underlie the incontinence, and patients who fail initial treatment interventions should be considered for urodynamic evaluation. Complex urodynamic tests (multichannel cystometry, pressure-flow studies, leak point pressure) can assist in determining the precise underlying lower urinary tract pathophysiology and in targeting specific treatment based on the findings.

Aging and Geriatric Medicine

Table 24–3 • **BASIC TYPES, CAUSES, AND TREATMENT OF PERSISTENT URINARY INCONTINENCE**

TYPE	CLINICAL MANIFESTATIONS	COMMON CAUSES	PRIMARY TREATMENTS
Stress	Involuntary loss of urine (usually small amounts) with increases in intra-abdominal pressure (e.g., cough, laugh, exercise); with sphincter weakness, symptoms may be constant wetting	Weakness of pelvic floor musculature and urethral hypermobility Bladder outlet or urethral sphincter weakness	Pelvic muscle exercises and other behavioral interventions α-Adrenergic agonists (pseudoephedrine, 30–60 mg tid) Periurethral injections Surgical bladder neck suspension or sling
Urge	Leakage of urine (variable but often larger volumes) because of inability to delay voiding after sensation of bladder fullness is perceived	Detrusor overactivity, isolated or associated with one or more of the following: Local genitourinary condition such as tumors, stones, diverticuli, or outflow obstruction CNS disorders such as stroke, dementia, parkinsonism, or spinal cord injury	Bladder training and other behavioral interventions Bladder relaxants (tolterodine, 4 mg qd; other anticholinergics)
Overflow	Leakage of urine (usually small amounts without warning) resulting from mechanical forces on an overdistended bladder or from other effects of urinary retention on bladder and sphincter function	Anatomic obstruction by prostate, stricture, or cystocele Acontractile bladder associated with diabetes mellitus or spinal cord injury Neurogenic (detrusor-sphincter dyssynergy), associated with multiple sclerosis and other suprasacral spinal cord lesions	Surgical removal of obstruction Intermittent or chronic catheterization
Functional	Urinary accidents associated with inability to toilet because of impairment of cognitive and/or physical functioning, psychological unwillingness, or environmental barriers	Severe dementia and other neurologic disorders Psychological factors such as depression and hostility	Prompted voiding and other behavioral intervention Absorbent padding Drug treatment for bladder overactivity (selected patients)

CNS = central nervous system.
From Kane RL, Ouslander JG, Abrass IB: Essentials of Clinical Geriatrics, 4th ed. New York, McGraw-Hill, 1998. Copyright © by McGraw-Hill, Inc. Used by permission of McGraw-Hill Book Company.

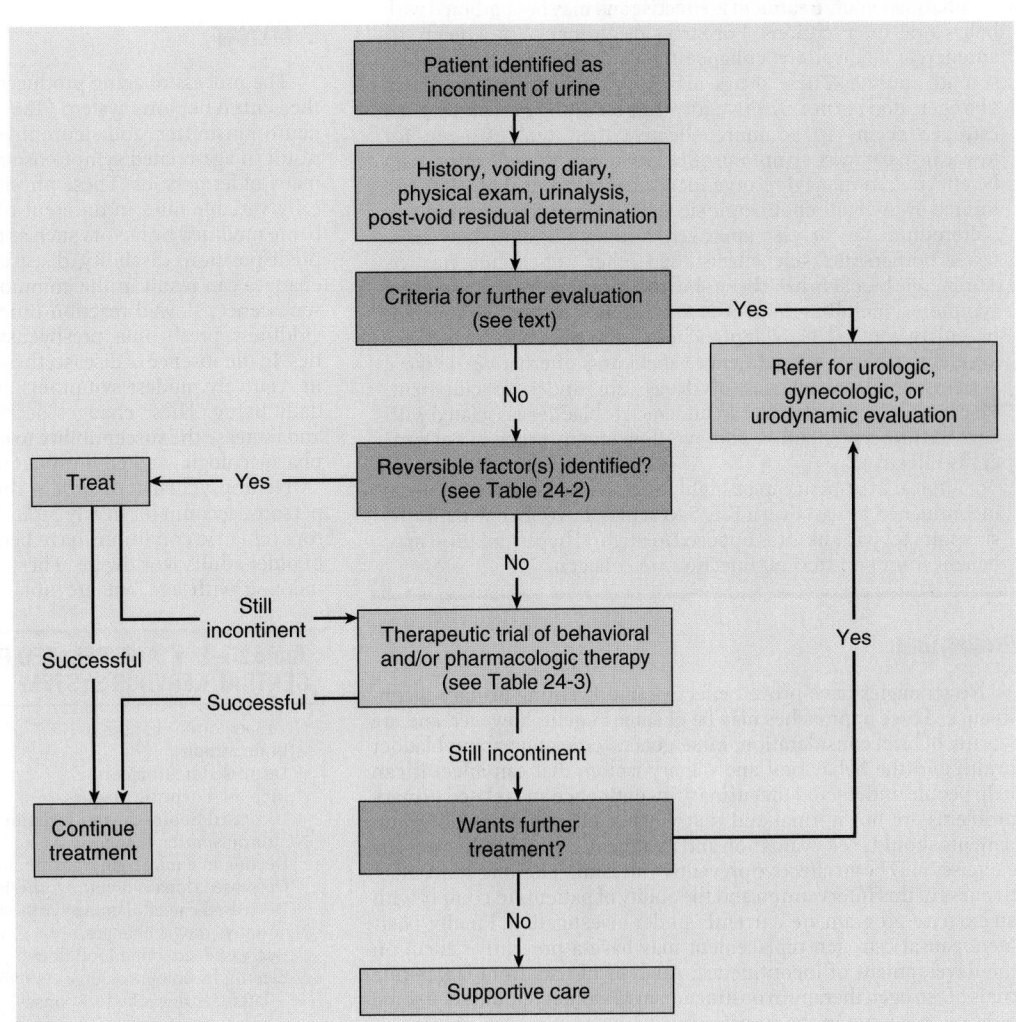

FIGURE 24–1 • Flow diagram for the evaluation and treatment of urinary incontinence in primary care practice. Criteria for further evaluation are outlined in the text.

Rx Treatment

The most common method of managing urinary incontinence is adult diapers and pads. Although many of these products are well designed and helpful, they are nonspecific and expensive. Many patients cannot afford these products and instead design their own, often poorly hygienic substitutes. Use of adult diapers and pads may serve simply to hide a curable or potentially serious problem or foster dependency in frail geriatric patients. These products generally should be used as adjuncts to more specific interventions, and patients should be encouraged to undergo at least a basic evaluation of their condition.

Reversible factors identified by the basic evaluation outlined here should be treated (see Table 24–2). In some patients, the urinary incontinence resolves after treating one or more of these factors. Primary therapies for persistent types of urinary incontinence are listed in Table 24–3. A variety of behavioral therapies have been shown in randomized, controlled clinical trials to be highly effective for targeted patients.[1] Functional, motivated patients with stress, urge, and mixed incontinence generally respond well to behavioral interventions. These interventions include education, self-monitoring with a voiding diary, modifications of fluid intake, various bladder training techniques (e.g., timed voiding and strategies to manage urgency), and pelvic muscle exercises. Many patients have difficulty isolating the appropriate pelvic muscles and benefit from adjunctive techniques, such as biofeedback (using surface electromyography of sphincteric and abdominal muscles), vaginal weights, and electrical stimulation (which can help identify and exercise pelvic muscles and help inhibit bladder activity, depending on the frequency of the stimulus). For some mobility-impaired and/or cognitively impaired patients in long-term care institutions and at home, reminders to void (or some other form of systematic toileting assistance) can be highly effective in managing urinary incontinence during the daytime.

Pharmacologic treatment is effective and may be combined with behavioral interventions. For stress incontinence in women, α-adrenergic medications enhance the contraction of periurethral smooth muscle. These drugs may be combined with estrogen. Estrogen alone is not effective for stress incontinence, and topical estrogen seems to be more effective than oral estrogen for lower urinary tract symptoms. Bladder relaxant medications can be effective in managing urge incontinence,[2] but they often are limited by their anticholinergic side effects (especially dry mouth). Tolterodine, the newest approved bladder relaxant, may have fewer bothersome side effects than other anticholinergics. α-Adrenergic blockers have been shown to improve irritative voiding symptoms, including frequency and urgency, in men with prostatic enlargement.[3] New approaches to the pharmacologic management of urge incontinence, including alternative delivery systems and new classes of drugs, are under development. Pharmacologic treatment of an underactive bladder associated with chronic urinary retention and overflow incontinence is not generally effective.

Surgical treatment can be highly effective in women with stress incontinence, at least over a 1- to 5-year period. Women with intrinsic sphincter weakness (as opposed to urethral hypermobility) may benefit from periurethral injections of collagen.

Prevention

No strategies have proved effective in preventing urinary incontinence. Three approaches may be of some benefit, however, and are worthy of brief consideration. First, general education about bladder health and the behavioral and dietary factors that can affect it can help people understand that urinary incontinence and related urinary problems are not normal and that when such symptoms do occur, patients should seek evaluation and treatment. Second, pelvic muscle exercises may be an effective preventive measure. The long-term effectiveness of this intervention and the ability of patients to comply with an exercise program are currently under investigation. Finally, postmenopausal estrogen replacement may have a preventive effect on the development of incontinence. Analysis of data from large-scale trials of estrogen therapy in postmenopausal women should shed some light on this issue in the future.

Future Directions

Defining the basic abnormalities that cause detrusor hyperactivity, including the role of sensory afferent innervation, is a crucial goal. New drugs and drug delivery systems to treat detrusor hyperactivity but minimize bothersome anticholinergic side effects will have a major impact on the treatment of urinary incontinence.

1. Burgio KL, Locher JL, Goode PS, et al: Behavioral vs. drug treatment for urge urinary incontinence in older women. JAMA 1998;280:1995–2000.
2. Appell RA, Sand P, Dmochowski R, et al: Prospective randomized controlled trial of extended-release oxybutynin chloride and tolterodine tartrate in the treatment of overactive bladder: Results of the OBJECT Study. Mayo Clin Proc 2001;76:358–363.
3. Lepor H, Williford WO, Barry MJ, et al: The efficacy of terazosin, finasteride, or both in benign prostatic hyperplasia. Veterans Affairs Cooperative Studies Benign Prostatic Hyperplasia Study Group. N Engl J Med 1996;335:533–539.

SUGGESTED READINGS

Boyles SH, Weber AM, Meyn L: Procedures for urinary incontinence in the United States, 1979–1997. Am J Obstet Gynecol 2003;189:70–75. *From 1979 to 1997, the rate of surgery for urinary incontinence in women has nearly doubled.*

Burgio KL, Locher JF, Goode PS: Combined behavioral and drug therapy for urge incontinence in older women. J Am Geriatr Soc 2000;48:370–374. *The combination has added benefits.*

Dugan E, Cohen SJ, Bland DR, et al: The association of depressive symptoms and urinary incontinence among older adults. J Am Geriatr Soc 2000;48:413–416. *The two are clearly related.*

Goode PS, Burgio KL, Locher JL, et al: Effect of behavioral training with or without pelvic floor electrical stimulation on stress incontinence in women: A randomized controlled trial. JAMA 2003;290:345–352. *Pelvic floor electrical stimulation did not add incremental benefit to a behavioral program.*

25 NEUROPSYCHIATRIC ASPECTS OF AGING

Sharon K. Inouye

Overview

The process of aging produces important physiologic changes in the central nervous system (Table 25–1), including neuroanatomic, neurotransmitter, and neurophysiologic changes. These processes result in age-related symptoms and manifestations (Table 25–2) for many older persons. These physiologic changes develop at dramatically variable rates in different older persons, however, the decline being modified by factors such as diet, environment, lifestyle, genetic predisposition, disability, disease, and side effects of drugs. These changes can result in the common age-related symptoms of benign senescence, slowed reaction time, postural hypotension, vertigo or giddiness, presbyopia, presbycusis, stiffened gait, and sleep difficulties. In the absence of disease, these physiologic changes usually result in relatively modest symptoms and little restriction in activities of daily living. These changes decrease physiologic reserve, however, and increase the susceptibility to challenges posed by disease-related, pharmacologic, and environmental stressors.

Neuropsychiatric disorders, the leading cause of disability in older persons, account for nearly 50% of functional incapacity. Severe neuropsychiatric conditions have been estimated to occur in 15 to 25% of older adults worldwide. These conditions are due to diseases that increase with age but are not part of the normal aging process.

Table 25–1 • AGE-RELATED PHYSIOLOGIC CHANGES IN THE CENTRAL NERVOUS SYSTEM

Neuroanatomic changes
  Brain atrophy
  Decreased neuron counts
  Increased neuritic plaques
  Increased lipofuscin and melanin
Neurotransmitter changes
  Decline in cholinergic transmission
  Decreased dopaminergic synthesis
  Decreased catecholamine synthesis
Neurophysiologic changes
  Decreased cerebral blood flow
  Electrophysiologic changes (slowing of alpha rhythm, increased latencies in evoked responses)

Table 25–2 • NEUROPSYCHIATRIC MANIFESTATIONS OF AGE-RELATED PHYSIOLOGIC CHANGES

SYSTEM	MANIFESTATION
Cognition	Forgetfulness
	Processing speed declines throughout adult life
	Neuropsychological declines: selective attention, verbal fluency, retrieval, complex visual perception, logical analysis
Reflexes	Stretch reflexes lose sensitivity
	Decreased or absent ankle reflexes
	Decreased autonomic and righting reflexes, postural instability
Sensory	Presbycusis (high-frequency hearing loss), tinnitus
	Deterioration of vestibular system, vertigo
	Presbyopia (decreased lens elasticity)
	Slowed pupil reactivity, decreased upgaze
	Olfactory system deterioration
	Decreased vibratory sensation
Gait/balance	Gait stiffer, slowed, forward flexed
	Increased body sway and mild unsteadiness
Sleep	Decreased sleep efficiency, fatigue
	Increased awakenings, insomnia
	Decrease in sleep stages 3 and 4
	Sleep duration more variable, more naps

Table 25–3 • GERIATRIC DEPRESSION SCALE—SHORT FORM

1. Are you basically satisfied with your life?	yes/NO
2. Have you dropped many of your activities and interests?	YES/no
3. Do you feel that your life is empty?	YES/no
4. Do you often get bored?	YES/no
5. Are you in good spirits most of the time?	yes/NO
6. Are you afraid that something bad is going to happen to you?	YES/no
7. Do you feel happy most of the time?	yes/NO
8. Do you feel helpless?	YES/no
9. Do you prefer to stay home rather than going out and doing new things?	YES/no
10. Do you feel you have more problems with memory than most?	YES/no
11. Do you think it is wonderful to be alive now?	yes/NO
12. Do you feel pretty worthless the way you are now?	YES/no
13. Do you feel full of energy?	yes/NO
14. Do you feel that your situation is hopeless?	YES/no
15. Do you think that most people are better off than you are?	YES/no

Scoring: Answers indicating depression are **highlighted**; six or more highlighted answers indicate depressive symptoms.

Adapted from Yesavage J, Brink T, Rowe T, et al: Development and validation of a geriatric depression screening scale: A preliminary report. J Psychiatr Res 1983;17:37–49.

Alzheimer's disease and related dementias occur in approximately 10% of adults age 65 and older and 40% of adults older than 85 (Chapter 433). Delirium occurs in 5 to 10% of all persons age 65 and older, usually in the setting of acute illness and hospitalization. Severe depression (Chapter 426) occurs in approximately 5% of older adults, with 15% having significant depressive symptoms. Anxiety disorders occur in 10% of older adults. Older individuals also are subject to substantial morbidity and functional disability from cerebrovascular disease (Chapters 439, 440, and 441), Parkinson's disease (Chapters 442 and 443), peripheral neuropathies (Chapter 462), degenerative myelopathies (Chapters 463 and 464), spinal stenosis and disc disease (Chapter 429), seizure disorders (Chapter 434), sleep apnea (Chapter 96), falls (Chapter 23), incontinence (Chapter 24), and impotence (Chapter 247). To diagnose these conditions, physicians must understand and perform a mental status examination and an assessment of functional capacity and know the uses and side effects of psychoactive drugs in geriatric patients.

MENTAL STATUS EXAMINATION

In addition to a detailed neurologic examination, evaluation of neuropsychiatric disturbances in older persons requires a careful mental status examination, including an assessment of mood, affect, and cognition. Brief screening tests are available to evaluate these domains and to assist in the detection of potential problems requiring further evaluation and treatment. For depression screening, scores of 6 or more on the 15-item short-form Geriatric Depression Scale (Table 25–3) indicate substantial depressive symptoms requiring further evaluation. Alternative depression screening instruments include the General Health Questionnaire; for cognitively impaired patients, observer-rated depression scales, such as the Hamilton Depression Scale, are recommended.

Early cognitive deficits can be missed easily during conversation because intellectual impairment can be masked with intact social skills. Given the high frequency of cognitive impairment, formal cognitive screening is recommended for all older persons. Ideally, cognitive testing should evaluate at least the general domains of attention, orientation, language, memory, visuospatial ability, and conceptualization. To exclude delirium, attention should be assessed first by asking the patient to perform a task such as repeating five digits or reciting the months backwards; the remainder of cognitive testing would not be useful in an inattentive patient. For further cognitive testing, many brief, practical screening instruments are available. The most widely used instrument is the Mini Mental State Examination, a 19-item, 30-point scale that can be completed in 10 minutes (Table 25–4). A score of 25 or more generally indicates intact cognitive function, whereas a score of 24 or less requires further evaluation for potential dementia. Further bedside testing can include asking the patient to draw a clock with the hands at a set time to assess visuospatial ability

Table 25–4 • MINI-MENTAL STATE EXAMINATION

COGNITIVE DOMAIN	MAXIMUM SCORE
ORIENTATION	
What is the (year) (season) (date) (day) (month)?	5
Where are we (city) (state) (county) (hospital) (floor)?	5
REGISTRATION	
Name 3 objects: 1 sec to say each. Ask the patient for all 3 after you have said them. Given 1 point for each correct answer. Repeat them until all 3 are learned. Count the trials and record the number	3
ATTENTION AND CALCULATION	
Serial 7s backward from 100 (stop after 5 answers) Alternatively, spell WORLD backward	5
RECALL	
Ask for the 3 objects repeated above. Give 1 point for each correct answer	3
LANGUAGE AND PRAXIS	
Show a pencil and watch, and ask the patient to name them	2
Ask the patient to repeat the following: "No ifs, ands, or buts"	1
Three-stage command: "Take this paper in your right hand, fold it in half, and put it on the floor"	3
"Read and obey the following: Close your eyes."	1
"Write a sentence"	1
"Copy this design" (interlocking pentagons)	1

A score of 25 or greater signifies intact cognitive function.

Adapted from Folstein MF, Folstein SE, McHugh PR: "The Mini-Mental State": A practical method for grading the cognitive state of patients for the clinician. J Psychiatr Res 1975;12:189–198.

and higher cortical functions. Questions to evaluate judgment and problem-solving ability in hypothetic situations, such as in a fire or when driving, can provide crucial insight into the patient's ability to function safely and independently.

FUNCTIONAL ASSESSMENT

Functional impairment, defined as difficulty in performing daily activities, is common among elderly persons. Although not routinely

Aging and Geriatric Medicine

evaluated in the standard medical assessment, determination of the patient's degree of functional incapacity based on their medical and neuropsychiatric conditions is crucial to understanding the burden of disease and its impact on the individual's daily life. The important relationship of functional status with health in older persons is reflected in the finding that functional measures are stronger predictors of mortality after hospitalization than are admitting diagnoses. Functional measures strongly predict other important hospital outcomes in the elderly, such as length of stay, functional status at discharge, future care needs, caregiver burden, risk for institutionalization, and long-term prognosis.

The functional assessment should include an assessment of the patient's ability to perform basic self-care activities of daily living and instrumental activities of daily living, the higher level activities needed for independent living. Performance of activities of daily living reflects the ability of the patient to perform basic self-care activities, including feeding, grooming, bathing, dressing, toileting, transferring, and walking. Performance of instrumental activities of daily living reflects the ability of the patient to perform more complex tasks, including shopping, preparing meals, managing finances, housekeeping, using the telephone, taking medications, driving, and using transportation. The functional assessment is conducted with the patient or the family, and the questions ascertain whether the patient can perform these activities independently. Other related domains that should be assessed include vision, hearing, continence, nutritional status, safety, falls, living situation, social supports, and socioeconomic status.

The onset of acute cognitive or functional decline is often the first and sometimes the only sign of serious acute illness in older persons and warrants immediate medical attention. Similarly the onset or worsening of related conditions, such as delirium, falls, incontinence, depression, or failure to thrive, heralds the need for prompt medical evaluation.

Psychoactive Effects of Drugs in Older Patients

ADVERSE DRUG EVENTS IN THE ELDERLY. Iatrogenic complications occur in 29 to 38% of older hospitalized patients, with a three-fold to five-fold increased risk in older compared with younger patients. Adverse drug events, the most common type of iatrogenic complication, account for 20 to 40% of all complications. The elderly are particularly vulnerable to adverse drug reactions because of multiple-drug regimens, multiple chronic diseases, relative renal and hepatic insufficiency, decreased physiologic reserve, and altered drug metabolism with aging. Inappropriate drug use has been reported in about 40% of hospitalized older patients, with more than one quarter of these patients having absolute contraindications to the drug and the others being given a drug that was unnecessary. Because 50% of adverse drug events occur in patients receiving inappropriate drugs, the potential for reducing these adverse events is substantial.

DRUGS WITH PSYCHOACTIVE EFFECTS. Nearly every class of drugs has the potential to cause delirium in a vulnerable patient, but specific drugs have been most commonly implicated (Table 25–5) and should be used with caution in older patients. Many cases of delirium or cognitive decline in older patients may be preventable through avoidance, substitution, or dose reduction of these psychoactive drugs. Long-acting benzodiazepines (e.g., flurazepam and diazepam) are particularly problematic medications for the elderly and should be avoided whenever possible. If nonpharmacologic approaches to the management of insomnia are unsuccessful, short-term use of an intermediate-acting benzodiazepine without active metabolites (e.g., lorazepam, 0.5 mg, half-life of 10 to 15 hours) is recommended. Drugs with anticholinergic effects (e.g., antihistamines, antidepressants, neuroleptics, antispasmodics) produce a panoply of poorly tolerated side effects in older patients, including delirium, postural hypotension, urinary retention, constipation, and dry mouth. Of the narcotics, meperidine causes delirium more frequently than other agents because of an active metabolite, normeperidine. Cardiac drugs, such as digitalis and antiarrhythmic agents, have prolonged half-lives, narrowed therapeutic windows, and decreased protein binding in older patients. The clinician should be aware that toxicity with these agents (e.g., digoxin) can occur even at therapeutic drug levels. The H_2-receptor antagonists (e.g., cimetidine, ranitidine, famotidine, nizatidine) are among the most common causes of drug-induced delirium in the elderly because of their frequent use; clinicians should strongly consider the use of less toxic alternatives (e.g., sucralfate or antacids) or dosage reduction for older patients, especially when the medication

Table 25–5 • DRUGS WITH PSYCHOACTIVE EFFECTS

Sedative/hypnotics
  Benzodiazepines (especially flurazepam, diazepam)
  Barbiturates
  Sleeping medications (chloral hydrate)
Narcotics (especially meperidine)
Anticholinergics
  Antihistamines (diphenhydramine, hydroxyzine)
  Antispasmodics (belladonna, Lomotil)
  Heterocyclic antidepressants (amitriptyline, imipramine, doxepin)
  Neuroleptics (chlorpromazine, haloperidol, thioridazine)
  Antiparkinsonian (benztropine, trihexyphenidyl)
  Atropine/scopolamine
Cardiac
  Digitalis glycosides
  Antiarrhythmics (quinidine, procainamide, lidocaine)
  Antihypertensives (β-blockers, methyldopa)
Gastrointestinal
  H_2-antagonists (cimetidine, ranitidine, famotidine, nizatidine)
  Metoclopramide (Reglan)
Miscellaneous
  Nonsteroidal anti-inflammatory drugs
  Corticosteroids
  Anticonvulsants
  Levodopa
  Lithium
Over-the-counter drugs
  Cold/sinus preparations (antihistamines, pseudoephedrine)
  Sleep aids (diphenhydramine, alcohol-containing elixirs)
  Stay Awake (caffeine)
  Nausea/gastrointestinal (Donnagel, meclizine, H_2-antagonists, loperamide)

is being used for prophylaxis rather than treatment of active disease. Proton-pump inhibitors have been associated with delirium in case reports; however, the overall rate of this adverse effect has not been systematically determined.

Psychoactive drugs account for nearly 50% of preventable adverse drug events, often in patients in whom three or more psychoactive drugs are prescribed, frequently at inappropriately high doses. Delirium and cognitive impairment are the most frequent adverse outcomes of psychoactive drugs. The use of any psychoactive drug is associated with a four-fold increased risk of delirium or cognitive decline, but the outcomes of delirium and cognitive decline depend on the type or class of drug administered and total number of drugs received. Sedative-hypnotic drugs are associated with a three-fold to 12-fold increased risk for delirium or cognitive decline, narcotics are associated with a two-fold to three-fold increased risk, and anticholinergic drugs are associated with a five-fold to 12-fold increased risk. When more drugs are used, not only does each carry its own individual risk for adverse outcomes, but also the overall risk is compounded by the heightened potential for drug-drug interactions. If more than three drugs are added in a 24-hour period, the risk of delirium increases four-fold. Similarly the risk of cognitive decline increases directly with the number of drugs prescribed, from a three-fold increased risk with two or three drugs to a 14-fold increased risk with six or more drugs.

PRINCIPLES OF DRUG THERAPY IN THE ELDERLY. Physicians always should consider whether nonpharmacologic approaches are appropriate alternatives to medications in older persons. Relaxation techniques, massage, and music are highly effective for the treatment of insomnia and anxiety; localized pain often can be managed effectively with local measures, such as injection, heat, ultrasound, and transcutaneous electrical stimulation.

When drug therapy is required in the elderly, physicians should choose the drug with the least toxic potential and emphasize drugs that have been well tested in older populations (Table 25–6). When the drug is chosen, it is often wise to start with 25 to 50% of the standard adult dosage for psychoactive drugs and increase the dose slowly. Drug regimens should be kept as simple as possible, with the fewest drugs and the fewest number of pills possible. Most importantly, the medication list should be reassessed frequently.

Even long-standing medications should be re-evaluated because the host is changing with age and illness. Long-term usage does not justify continued usage. The physician should review with the patient all prescribed and over-the-counter medications on a regular basis,

Table 25–6 • GUIDELINES FOR DRUG THERAPY IN THE ELDERLY

General principles:
   Remember that the elderly are highly sensitive to the psychoactive effects of all drugs
   Know the pharmacology of the drugs you prescribe. Know a few drugs well
Recommended approach:
  1. Use nonpharmacologic approaches whenever possible
  2. Avoid *routine* use of "as needed" drugs for sleep, anxiety, pain
  3. Choose the drug with the least toxic potential
  4. Substitute less toxic alternatives whenever possible (antacid or sucralfate for an H_2-blocker, Metamucil/Kaopectate for Lomotil, scheduled acetaminophen/choline magnesium salicylate regimen for pain management)
  5. Reduce the dosage
  6. "Start low and go slow"
     Start with 25–50% of the standard dose of psychoactive drugs in the elderly
     Titrate the drug slowly
     Set realistic end points: titrate to improvement, not elimination of symptoms
  7. Keep the regimen simple
  8. Regularly reassess the medication list. Have the patient bring in all bottles and review what is being taken
  9. Re-evaluate long-time drug use since the patient is changing
 10. Review over-the-counter medication use

preferably by having the patient bring in all medication bottles and indicate how each is being taken. Patients frequently underestimate the toxic potential of over-the-counter medications and herbal remedies, and they may be using a variety of such agents that could potentiate the side effects or directly counteract the desired effects of prescription medications (Chapter 27).

Future Directions

Screening methods for cognitive and functional decline in older persons will continue to be refined and simplified. An important future direction will be to incorporate these screening measures into the routine care of all older persons in physicians' offices, clinics, hospitals, nursing homes, and other settings.

SUGGESTED READINGS
Drugs that may cause cognitive disorders in the elderly. Med Lett Drugs Ther 2000;42:111–112. *A comprehensive listing of drugs with potential psychoactive effects.*
Dufouil C, Clayton D, Brayne C, et al: Population norms for the MMSE in the very old: Estimates based on longitudinal data. Neurology 2000;55:1609–1613. *Norms for the Mini-Mental State Examination in subjects age 75 and older from longitudinal, population-based data.*
Hanlon JT, Schmader KE, Boult C, et al: Use of inappropriate prescription drugs by older people. J Am Geriatr Soc 2002;50:26–34. *Inappropriate drug use, as defined by expert national consensus panel criteria, is common among community-dwelling older persons and persists over time.*
Karlawish JHT, Clark CM: Diagnostic evaluation of elderly patients with mild memory problems. Ann Intern Med 2003;138:411–419. *Case-based discussion emphasizing a stepwise approach.*

26 DELIRIUM AND OTHER MENTAL STATUS PROBLEMS IN THE OLDER PATIENT

Sharon K. Inouye

EVALUATION OF MENTAL STATUS CHANGE IN THE OLDER PATIENT

Mental status change, one of the most common presenting symptoms in acutely ill elders, is estimated to account for 30% of emergency evaluations for older patients. Mental status often serves as a barometer of the overall underlying health of an elderly patient and is commonly the only symptom of serious underlying disease. A broad range of medical, neurologic, and psychiatric conditions can lead to mental status changes (Chapters 426 and 433), and a systematic approach aids in the evaluation of suspected mental status change in an older patient (see Fig. 26–1).

The first step in evaluating suspected altered mental status in an older patient is to obtain a detailed history from a reliable informant to establish the patient's baseline level of cognitive function and the clinical course of any cognitive changes. Chronic changes (i.e., changes occurring over months to years) most likely represent an underlying dementing illness, which should be evaluated accordingly (Chapter 433). Acute changes (i.e., changes occurring over days to weeks)—even if superimposed on an underlying dementia—should be evaluated further by detailed cognitive assessment to determine whether delirium is present. If features of delirium (e.g., inattention, disorganized thinking, altered level of consciousness, fluctuating symptoms) are not present, further evaluation for depression, acute nonorganic psychotic disorders, or other psychiatric conditions is indicated.

DELIRIUM

Delirium, a clinical syndrome characterized as an acute disorder of attention and cognitive function, is the most frequent complication of hospitalization for elders and a potentially devastating problem. Delirium often is unrecognized despite sensitive methods for its detection, and its complications may be preventable.

Definitions

The definition and diagnostic criteria for *delirium* are evolving. The *Diagnostic and Statistical Manual of Mental Disorders,* fourth edition, has been used widely (Table 26–1), but development of the criteria in this manual was based on expert consensus, and their diagnostic sensitivity and specificity have not been determined. The Confusion Assessment Method provides a simple, operationalized diagnostic algorithm with a sensitivity of 94 to 100%, a specificity of 90 to 95%, and a high interrater reliability.

Etiology

Similar to other common geriatric syndromes (Chapter 23), delirium usually has a multifactorial cause. A search for the innumerable potential underlying contributors requires clinical astuteness and a thorough medical evaluation, especially because many of these factors are treatable but, if untreated, may result in substantial morbidity and mortality. The process is made more challenging by the frequently nonspecific, atypical, or muted features of the underlying illness in older persons. Delirium is commonly the only initial sign of underlying life-threatening illness, such as pneumonia, urosepsis, or myocardial infarction, in the older population.

The development of delirium usually involves a complex interrelationship between a vulnerable patient with pertinent predisposing factors and exposure to noxious insults or precipitating factors. Delirium may develop in patients who are highly vulnerable to delirium, such as cognitively impaired or severely ill patients, after a relatively benign insult, such as a single dose of sleeping medication. Conversely, patients who are not vulnerable would be relatively resistant, and delirium would develop only after exposure to multiple noxious insults. Previous studies have shown that the effects of these risk factors may be cumulative. The importance of this multifactorial causation to the clinician is that removing or treating one factor in isolation usually is not sufficient to resolve the delirium. The full spectrum of vulnerability and precipitating factors should be addressed.

Predisposing, or vulnerability, factors identified consistently in previous studies include preexisting cognitive impairment or dementia, severe underlying illness, high levels of comorbidity, functional impairment, advanced age, chronic renal insufficiency, dehydration, malnutrition, and vision or hearing impairment. Dementia is an important and consistent risk factor for delirium, with demented patients having a two-fold to five-fold increased risk for delirium. Of delirious patients, 30 to 50% have underlying dementia. Delirious patients commonly

Table 26–1 • DIAGNOSTIC CRITERIA FOR DELIRIUM

DSM-IV DIAGNOSTIC CRITERIA

A. Disturbance of consciousness (i.e., reduced clarity of awareness of the environment) with reduced ability to focus, sustain, or shift attention

B. A change in cognition (e.g., memory deficit, disorientation, language disturbance) or the development of a perceptual disturbance that is not better accounted for by a preexisting, established, or evolving dementia

C. The disturbance develops over a short period (usually hours to days) and tends to fluctuate during the course of the day

D. Evidence from the history, physical examination, or laboratory findings indicates that the disturbance is caused by the direct physiologic consequences of a general medical condition

CAM DIAGNOSTIC ALGORITHM*

Feature 1. Acute onset and fluctuating course

This feature is usually obtained from a family member or nurse and is shown by positive responses to the following questions: Is there evidence of an acute change in mental status from the patient's baseline? Did the (abnormal) behavior fluctuate during the day, that is, tend to come and go, or increase and decrease in severity?

Feature 2. Inattention

This feature is shown by a positive response to the following question: Did the patient have difficulty focusing attention, for example, being easily distractible, or have difficulty keeping track of what was being said?

Feature 3. Disorganized thinking

This feature is shown by a positive response to the following question: Was the patient's thinking disorganized or incoherent such as rambling or irrelevant conversation, unclear or illogical in flow of ideas, or unpredictable and switching from subject to subject?

Feature 4. Altered level of consciousness

This feature is shown by any answer other than "alert" to the following question: Overall, how would you rate this patient's level of consciousness (alert [normal], vigilant [hyperalert], lethargic [drowsy, easily aroused], stupor [difficult to arouse], or coma [unarousable])?

*The diagnosis of delirium by CAM requires the presence of features 1 and 2 and either 3 or 4.

DSM-IV = American Psychiatric Association: *Diagnostic and Statistical Manual of Mental Disorders*, fourth edition. Washington, DC, American Psychiatric Association, 1994; CAM = Confusion Assessment Method.

From Inouye SK, van Dyck CH, Alessi CA, et al: Clarifying confusion: The Confusion Assessment Method. A new method for detection of delirium. Ann Intern Med 1990;113:941–948.

have evidence of underlying chronic brain disease, particularly conditions associated with cognitive impairment, such as Alzheimer's disease, Parkinson's disease, cerebrovascular disease, and space-occupying lesions.

Medications, the most common remediable cause of delirium, contribute to delirium in 40% of cases (Chapter 25). Insufficiency or failure of any major organ system, particularly renal or hepatic failure, can precipitate delirium. Hypoxemia and hypercarbia have been associated with delirium. Clinicians must be attuned to occult respiratory failure, which in the elderly often lacks the usual signs and symptoms of dyspnea and tachypnea and can be missed by measuring oxygen saturation alone. Acute myocardial infarction or heart failure can be manifested as delirium in an elderly patient without the usual symptoms of chest pain or dyspnea. Occult infection is a particularly notable cause of delirium. Older patients frequently fail to mount the febrile or leukocytotic response to infection, and clinicians must assess carefully for signs of pneumonia, urinary tract infection, endocarditis, abdominal abscess, or infected joints. A variety of metabolic disorders may contribute to delirium, including hypernatremia or hyponatremia, hypercalcemia, acid-base disorders, hypoglycemia and hyperglycemia, and thyroid or adrenal disorders. Immobilization and immobilizing devices (e.g., indwelling bladder catheters, physical restraints) have been shown to be important factors in precipitating delirium. Dehydration and volume depletion and nutritional decline during hospitalization (e.g., decline in weight, fall in serum albumin) are well-documented factors contributing to delirium. Drug and alcohol withdrawal are important and often unsuspected causes of delirium in the elderly. Environmental factors, such as unfamiliar surroundings, sleep deprivation, deranged schedule,

frequent room changes, sensory overload, or sensory deprivation, may aggravate delirium in the hospital. Psychosocial factors, such as depression, psychological stress, pain, or lack of social supports, also may precipitate delirium.

Incidence and Prevalence

In the elderly, the prevalence of delirium at hospital admission is 10 to 40%. Delirium develops anew in 25 to 56% of patients during hospitalization. Higher rates are found when frequent surveillance is performed in older, surgical, and intensive care populations. Delirium occurs in 60 to 80% of patients in medical intensive care units.

Epidemiology

The associated hospital mortality rates for delirium are 25 to 33%, rates as high as those associated with acute myocardial infarction and sepsis. The problem of delirium in hospitalized elderly patients has assumed particular prominence because patients aged 65 years and older currently account for more than 40% of all inpatient days of hospital care. Based on U.S. vital health statistics and a conservative delirium rate of 20%, delirium complicates hospital stays for more than 2.3 million older persons, involves more than 17.5 million inpatient days, and accounts for greater than $4 billion of hospital expenditures each year. Substantial additional costs are incurred after hospital discharge because of the increased need for rehabilitation services, nursing home placement, and home care. These extrapolations highlight the extensive economic and health policy implications of delirium.

Pathogenesis

The basic pathogenesis of delirium is unclear. Most investigators agree that delirium seems to be a functional rather than structural lesion. Electroencephalographic studies showed global functional derangements in patients with delirium, characterized by generalized slowing of cortical background (α) activity. The leading current hypotheses view delirium as the final common pathway of many different pathogenic mechanisms culminating in a widespread reduction in cerebral oxidative metabolism with resultant impairment of cholinergic transmission. Proposed mediators examined in previous studies have included β-endorphin, somatostatin, lymphokines, tryptophan, phenylalanine metabolites, and cortisol. Although delirium has long been considered a transient syndrome, several of these basic mechanisms may not be completely reversible, particularly mechanisms resulting in hypoxic damage. The dose and duration of the noxious insults, along with the degree of vulnerability of the patient, also may exert great influence on the ultimate reversibility of the delirium.

Clinical Manifestations

The cardinal features of delirium include acute onset and inattention. Establishing the acuity of onset requires accurate knowledge of the patient's baseline cognitive function. Patients are inattentive; that is, they have difficulty focusing, maintaining, and shifting attention. They appear easily distracted and have difficulty maintaining conversation and following commands. Objectively, patients may have difficulty with simple repetitive tasks, digit spans, and recitation of months backward. Other key features include disorganization of thought processes, which is usually a manifestation of underlying cognitive or perceptual disturbances; an altered level of consciousness, which typically is lethargy with reduced clarity of awareness of the environment; and fluctuation of cognitive symptoms. Although not cardinal elements, other features frequently occurring during delirium include disorientation, cognitive deficits, psychomotor agitation or retardation, perceptual disturbances such as hallucinations and illusions, paranoid delusions, and sleep-wake cycle reversal.

Diagnosis and Evaluation

The cornerstone of evaluation of delirium is a comprehensive history and physical examination. The first step in evaluation (Table

Table 26–2 • EVALUATION OF DELIRIUM IN ELDERLY PATIENTS

1. Cognitive testing and determination of baseline cognitive functioning. Establish the diagnosis of delirium
2. Comprehensive history and physical examination, including careful neurologic examination for focal deficits and search for occult infection
3. Review the medication list: discontinue or minimize all psychoactive medications. Check the side effects of all medications
4. Laboratory evaluation (tailored to the individual): complete blood count, electrolytes, blood urea nitrogen, creatinine, glucose, calcium, phosphate, liver enzymes, oxygen saturation
5. Search for occult infection: physical examination, urinalysis, chest radiography, selected cultures (as indicated)
6. When no obvious cause is revealed from the above steps, further targeted evaluation is considered in selected patients:
   Laboratory tests:
      Magnesium, thyroid function tests, B_{12} level, drug levels, toxicology screen, ammonia level
   Arterial blood gas:
      Indicated in patients with dyspnea, tachypnea, any acute pulmonary process, or history of significant respiratory disease
   Electrocardiogram:
      Indicated in patients with chest or abdominal discomfort, shortness of breath, or cardiac history
   Cerebrospinal fluid examination:
      Indicated when meningitis or encephalitis is suspected
   Brain imaging:
      Indicated in patients with new focal neurologic signs or with a history or signs of head trauma
   Electroencephalogram:
      Useful in diagnosing occult seizure disorder and differentiating delirium from nonorganic psychiatric disorders

26–2) should be to establish the diagnosis of delirium through cognitive assessment and determine whether the present condition represents an acute change from the patient's baseline cognitive function. Because cognitive impairment may not be apparent during conversation, brief cognitive screening tests, such as the Mini-Mental Status Examination and the Confusion Assessment Method, should be used. Attention should be assessed further with simple tests, such as a forward digit span (inattention indicated by an inability to repeat five digits forward) or recitation of the months backward. A delirium assessment for nonverbal (e.g., intubated) patients has been developed. The history, which should be obtained from a reliable informant, is targeted to establish the patient's baseline cognitive function and the time course of any mental status change and to obtain clues about potential precipitating factors, such as recent medication changes, intercurrent infections, or medical illness. Physical examination should include a detailed neurologic examination for focal deficits and a careful search for signs of occult infection or an acute abdominal process.

A crucial difficulty in the differential diagnosis of delirium is distinguishing a long-standing confusional state (dementia) from delirium alone or delirium superimposed on dementia (Fig. 26–1). These two conditions are differentiated by the acute onset of symptoms in delirium (dementia is much more insidious) and the impaired attention and altered level of consciousness associated with delirium. The differential diagnosis also includes depression and nonorganic psychotic disorders. Although paranoia, hallucinations, and affective changes can occur with delirium, the key features of acute onset, inattention, altered level of consciousness, and global cognitive impairment assist in the recognition of delirium. At times, the differential diagnosis can be difficult, particularly with an uncooperative patient or when an accurate history is unavailable. Because of the potentially life-threatening nature of delirium, it is prudent to manage the patient as having delirium and search for underlying precipitants (e.g., intercurrent illness, metabolic derangements, drug toxicity) until further information can be obtained.

Review of the medication list, including over-the-counter medications, is crucial, and use of medications with psychoactive effects should be discontinued or minimized whenever possible. In the elderly, these medications may cause psychoactive effects even at doses and measured drug levels that are within the "therapeutic range."

Consideration should be given to the possibility that withdrawal from alcohol or other medications is a contributor to delirium.

Laboratory evaluation must be tailored to the individual situation (see Table 26–2). In patients with preexisting cardiac or respiratory diseases or related symptoms, an electrocardiogram or arterial blood gas determination may be indicated. The need for cerebrospinal fluid examination is controversial except when clearly indicated, such as in a febrile delirious patient. Brain imaging should be reserved for patients with new focal neurologic signs, for patients with a history or signs of head trauma, or for patients without another identifiable cause of the delirium. The electroencephalogram, with a false-negative rate of 17% and false-positive rate of 22% for distinguishing delirious from nondelirious patients, has a limited role and is most useful for detecting an occult seizure disorder and differentiating delirium from psychiatric disorders.

Rx Treatment

In general, nonpharmacologic approaches should be used in all delirious patients and usually are successful for symptom management. Pharmacologic approaches should be reserved for patients in whom the delirium symptoms may result in interruption of needed medical therapies (e.g., intubation, intravenous lines) or may endanger the safety of the patient or other persons. No drug is ideal for the treatment of delirium symptoms, however; any choice may cloud the patient's mental status further and obscure efforts to monitor the course of the mental status change. Any drug chosen should be given in the lowest dose for the shortest time possible. Neuroleptics are the preferred agents of treatment, with haloperidol being the most widely used agent. Haloperidol causes less orthostatic hypotension and fewer anticholinergic side effects than thioridazine does and is available in parenteral form; however, it has a higher rate of extrapyramidal side effects and acute dystonias. If parenteral administration is required, intravenous use results in rapid onset of action with a short duration of effect, whereas intramuscular use has a more optimal duration of action and is preferred. The recommended starting dose is 0.5 to 1 mg of haloperidol orally or parenterally, repeated every 30 minutes after the vital signs have been rechecked until sedation has been achieved. The end point should be an awake but manageable patient. The average elderly patient who has not been treated previously with neuroleptics should require a total loading dose of no more than 3 to 5 mg of haloperidol. Subsequently a maintenance dose consisting of half of the loading dose should be administered in divided doses over the next 24 hours, with doses tapered over the next few days as the agitation resolves.

Benzodiazepines are not recommended for the first-line treatment of delirium because of their tendency to cause oversedation and exacerbate the confusional state. They remain the drugs of choice, however, for treatment of withdrawal syndromes from alcohol and sedative drugs (Chapters 17 and 30).

Nonpharmacologic management techniques recommended for every delirious patient include encouraging the presence of family members, using "sitters" to be orienting influences, or transferring a disruptive patient to a private room or closer to the nurse's station for increased supervision. Interpersonal contact and communication, including verbal reorientation strategies, simple instructions and explanations, and frequent eye contact, are vital. Patients should be involved in their own care and allowed to participate in decision making as much as possible. Eyeglasses and hearing aids may reduce sensory deficits. Mobility, self-care, and independence should be encouraged, and physical restraints should be avoided, if possible, because of their tendency to increase agitation, their questionable efficacy, and their potential to cause injury. Attention must be focused on minimizing the disruptive influences of the hospital environment. Clocks and calendars should be provided to assist with orientation. Room and staff changes should be kept to a minimum. A quiet environment with low-level lighting is optimal for delirious patients. Perhaps the most important intervention is to schedule vital signs, medications, and procedures to allow an uninterrupted period for sleep at night. Nonpharmacologic approaches to relaxation, including music, relaxation tapes, and massage, can be highly effective.

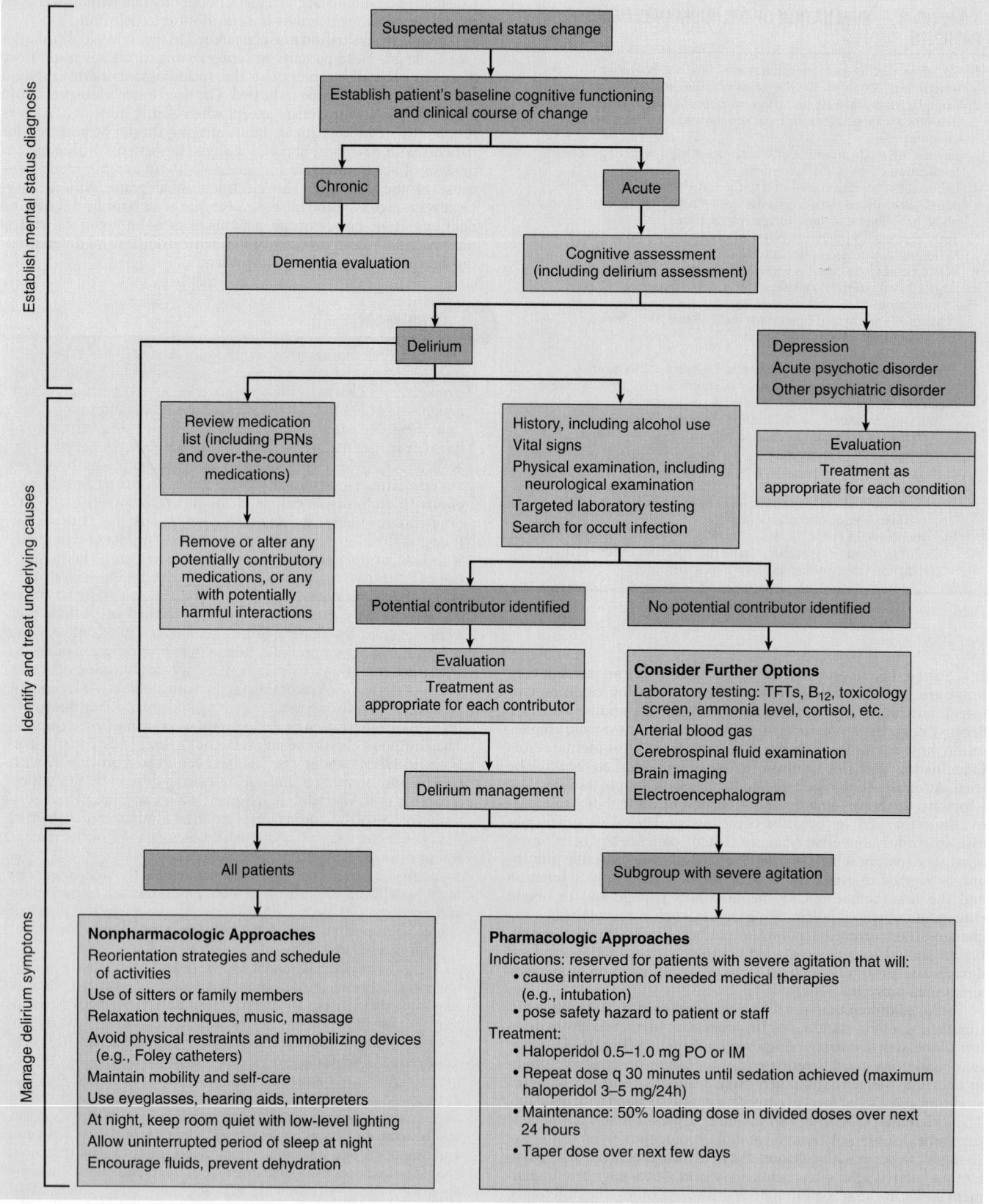

FIGURE 26–1 • Algorithm for evaluation of suspected mental status change in an older patient.

Prognosis

Delirium is an important independent determinant of prolonged hospital stay, increased mortality, increased rates of institutional placement, and functional and cognitive decline—even after controlling for age, gender, dementia, illness severity, and baseline functional status.

Delirium previously had been considered to be a reversible, transient condition, but more recent studies on the duration and persistence of delirium symptoms document that delirium may be much more persistent than previously believed. Delirium typically persists for 30 days or more, and only 20% of patients may have complete resolution of all delirium symptoms at 6-month follow-up. Delirium seems

Table 26–3 • DELIRIUM RISK FACTORS AND POTENTIAL INTERVENTIONS

RISK FACTOR	INTERVENTIONS
Cognitive impairment	Reality orientation program (reorienting techniques, communication)
	Therapeutic activities program
Sleep deprivation	Noise reduction strategies
	Scheduling of nighttime medications, procedures, and nursing activities to allow uninterrupted period of sleep
Immobilization	Early mobilization (e.g., ambulation or bedside exercises)
	Minimizing immobilizing equipment (e.g., bladder catheters)
Psychoactive medications	Restricted use of "as needed" sleep and psychoactive medications (e.g., sedative-hypnotics, narcotics, anticholinergic medications)
	Nonpharmacologic protocols for management of sleep and anxiety
Vision impairment	Provision of vision aids (e.g., magnifiers, special lighting)
	Provision of adaptive equipment (e.g., illuminated phone dials, large-print books)
Hearing impairment	Provision of amplifying devices
	Repair of hearing aids
Dehydration	Early recognition and volume repletion

to have greater deleterious effects in patients with underlying cognitive impairment. The long-term detrimental effects most probably are related to the duration, severity, and underlying cause of the delirium and the vulnerability of the patient.

Prevention

The most effective intervention strategy to reduce delirium and its associated complications is primary prevention of delirium before it occurs. Preventive strategies should address important delirium risk factors and target patients at a moderate to high risk for delirium at baseline (Table 26–3). Randomized trials have shown that a geriatrics consultation or a multidisciplinary intervention aimed at the risk factors for delirium can reduce the incidence of delirium by 40%. On a larger scale, preventive efforts for delirium require system-wide changes to educate physicians and nurses to improve recognition and heighten awareness of the clinical implications, provide incentives to change practice patterns that lead to delirium (e.g., immobilization, use of sleep medications, bladder catheters, and physical restraints), and create systems that enhance high-quality geriatric care (e.g., geriatric expertise, case management, clinical pathways, and quality monitoring).

Future Directions

It is hoped that future research will elucidate the pathophysiology of delirium using neuroimaging modalities, neuropsychological testing, and laboratory markers; clarify the contribution of delirium to irreversible cognitive impairment; and improve the management of delirium.

Grade *A*

1. Inouye SK, Bogardus ST, Charpentier PA, et al: A multicomponent intervention to prevent delirium in hospitalized older patients. N Engl J Med 1999;340:669–676.
2. Marcantonio ER, Flacker JM, Wright RJ, Resnick NM: Reducing delirium after hip fracture: A randomized trial. J Am Geriatr Soc 2001;49:516–522.
3. Britton A, Russell R: Multidisciplinary team interventions for delirium in patients with chronic cognitive impairment. Cochrane Review. The Cochrane Library, Issue 4. Oxford, Update Software, 2003.

SUGGESTED READINGS

Carnes M, Howell T, Rosenberg M, et al: Physicians vary in approaches to the clinical management of delirium. J Am Geriatr Soc 2003;51:234–239. *This study documents the broad variability in pharmacologic management of delirium, in the absence of sound clinical evidence.*

Marcantonio ER, Simon SE, Bergmann MA, et al: Delirium symptoms in post-acute care: prevalent, persistent, and associated with poor functional recovery. J Am Geriatr Soc 2003;51:4–9. *This study reveals that delirium is a frequent complication of post-acute care that is associated with poor functional recovery.*

Roche V: Etiology and management of delirium. Am J Med Sci 2003;325:20–30. *An up-to-date review of literature on delirium.*

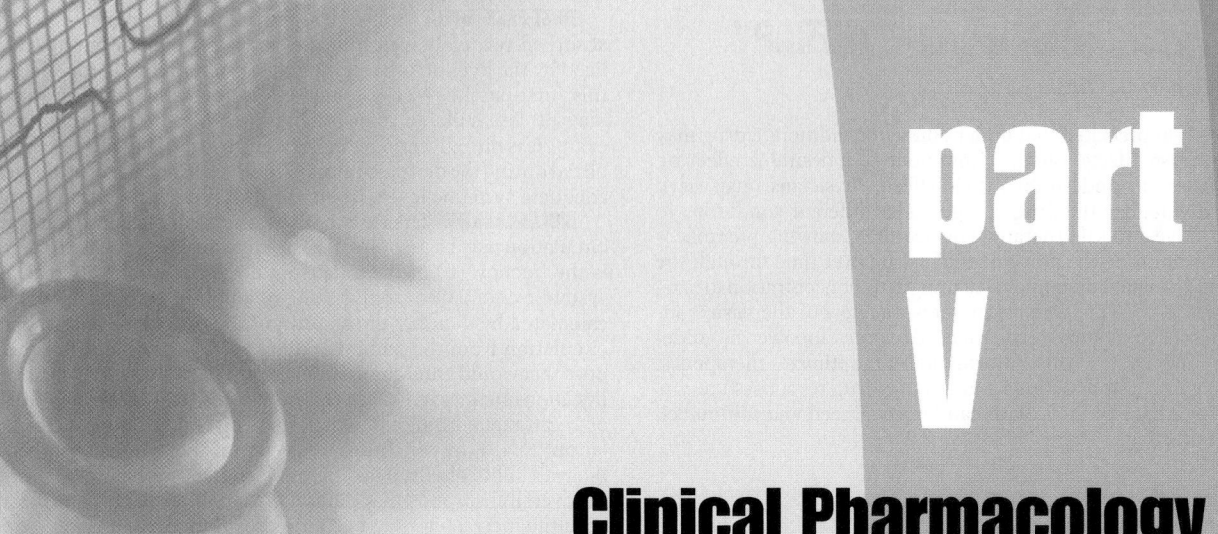

part V

Clinical Pharmacology

27 PRINCIPLES OF DRUG THERAPY

Robert B. Diasio

It is generally appreciated that under different conditions a drug may produce diverse effects, ranging from none to a desirable effect or, in other cases, an undesirable, toxic effect. Physicians must learn how to individualize the drug dosage under different conditions to ensure effective and safe therapy. This requires knowing pharmacokinetics—examining the movement of a drug over time through the body—and pharmacodynamics—relating drug concentration to drug effect (Fig. 27–1). This chapter presents a review of the basic concepts of pharmacokinetics and pharmacodynamics, followed by guidelines on how to use this information to optimize therapeutic applications. Drug interactions and adverse drug responses are discussed with advice on how both can be recognized and minimized in clinical practice.

PHARMACOKINETIC PRINCIPLES

ADMINISTERING DRUGS. The most straightforward means of administering a drug into the systemic circulation is by intravenously injecting it as a bolus. With this route, the full amount of a drug is delivered to the systemic circulation almost immediately. The same dose also may be administered as an intravenous infusion over a longer time, resulting in a decrease in the peak plasma concentration and an increase in the time the drug is present in the circulation. Many other routes of administration can be used, including sublingual, oral, transdermal, rectal, inhalation, subcutaneous, and intramuscular; each of these routes carries not only a potential delay in the time it takes the drug to enter the circulation, but also the possibility that a large fraction of it will never reach the circulation.

ABSORPTION. Absorption refers to the transfer of a drug from the site where it was administered to the systemic circulation. Most drugs use passive diffusion to cross a membrane barrier and enter the systemic circulation. Because passive diffusion in this setting depends on the concentration of the solute at the membrane surface, the rate of drug absorption is affected by the concentration of free drug at the absorbing surface. Factors that influence the availability of free drug affect drug absorption from the administration site; this effect can be exploited to design medications that provide a slow release of drug into the circulation by prolonging drug absorption. With certain sustained-released oral preparations, the rate of dissolution of the drug in the gastrointestinal tract determines the rate at which the drug is absorbed (e.g., timed-release antihistamines). Similarly a prolonged drug effect can be obtained by using transdermal medications (e.g., nitroglycerin) or intramuscular depot preparations (e.g., benzathine penicillin G).

FIRST-PASS EFFECT. Some drugs that are administered orally are absorbed relatively well into the portal circulation but are metabolized by the liver before reaching the systemic circulation. Because of this "first-pass" or "presystemic" effect, for some drugs, the oral route may be less suitable than other routes of administration. A good example is nitroglycerin, which is well absorbed but efficiently metabolized during the first pass through the liver. The same drug can achieve adequate systemic levels when given sublingually or transdermally.

BIOAVAILABILITY. The extent of absorption of drug into the systemic circulation may be incomplete. The bioavailability of a particular drug is the fraction (F) of the total drug dose that ultimately reaches the systemic circulation from the site of administration. This fraction is calculated by dividing the amount of the drug dose that reaches the circulation from the administration site by the amount of the drug dose that would enter the systemic circulation after direct intravenous injection into the circulation (essentially the total dose). Bioavailability, or F, can range from 0, in which no drug reaches the systemic circulation, to 1.0, in which essentially all of the drug is absorbed. The bioavailability of a drug in different formulations may change because the overall absorption may differ. This variability has become a concern with the increasing use of generic preparations.

DISTRIBUTION. After delivery of a drug into the systemic circulation either directly by intravenous injection or after absorption, the drug is transported throughout the body, initially to the well-perfused tissues and later to areas that are less perfused. The distribution phase can be assessed best by plotting the drug's plasma concentration on a log scale versus time on a linear scale (Fig. 27–2). The initial phase, from immediately after administration through the rapid fall in concentration, represents the distribution phase, during which a drug rapidly disappears from the circulation and enters the tissues. This is followed by the elimination phase (see later), when drug in the plasma is in equilibrium with drug in the tissues. During this latter phase the drug's plasma concentration is thought to be related to drug effect.

VOLUME OF DISTRIBUTION. The volume of distribution (VD) is a term used to relate the amount of drug in the body to the concentration of drug in the plasma. It is calculated by dividing the dose that ultimately gets into the systemic circulation by the plasma concentration at time zero (C_{p0}):

$$VD = \{\{\text{dose} \mathbin{/\mkern-5mu/} C_{p0}\}\} \tag{1}$$

The C_{p0} can be calculated by extrapolating the elimination phase back to time zero (see Fig. 27–2). The VD is best considered the "apparent VD" because it represents the apparent volume needed to contain the entire amount of the drug, assuming that the drug is distributed throughout the body at the same concentration as in the plasma. Table 27–1 lists pharmacokinetic data for 20 commonly used drugs from

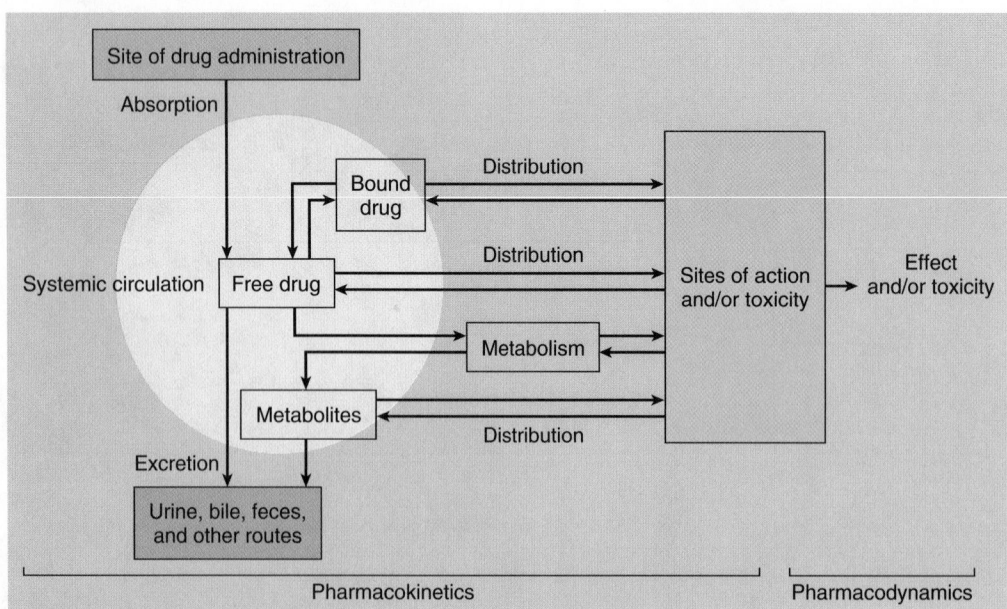

FIGURE 27–1 • Schematic of drug movement through the body, from site of administration to production of drug effect. The relationship between pharmacokinetics and pharmacodynamics is shown.

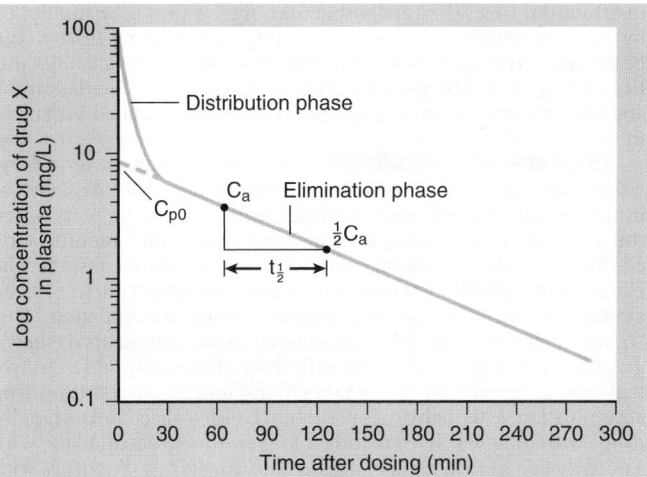

FIGURE 27–2 • Representative concentration versus time plot used in pharmacokinetic studies, in which concentration of drug is plotted with a logarithmic scale on the ordinate, and time is plotted with a linear scale on the abscissa. The resultant curve is seen to have two phases: the distribution phase, the initial portion of the plotted line when the concentrations of drug decrease rapidly, and the elimination phase, the later phase when there is exponential disappearance of drug from the plasma with time. The dotted line extrapolated from the elimination phase back to time zero is used to calculate C_{p0}. During the elimination phase, the half-life can be calculated as the time it takes to decrease the concentration by half (shown here as the time needed to decrease from concentration C_a to 1/2 C_a).

several drug classes, showing the wide variation in VD. Digoxin can be seen to have a large VD (>5 L), whereas valproic acid has a relatively small VD (0.15 L). As discussed later, the VD is a useful pharmacokinetic term for calculating the loading dose and appreciating how various changes can affect a drug's half-life.

ELIMINATION. Drugs are removed from the body by two major mechanisms: hepatic elimination, in which drugs are metabolized in the liver and excreted through the biliary tract, and renal elimination, in which drugs are removed from the circulation by either glomerular filtration or tubular secretion. For most drugs, the rates of hepatic and renal elimination are proportional to the plasma concentration of the drug. This relationship often is described as a "first-order" process. Two measurements are used to evaluate elimination: clearance and half-life.

CLEARANCE. The efficiency of elimination can be described by assessing how fast the drug clears from the circulation. Drug clearance is a measure of the volume of plasma cleared of drug per unit of time. It is similar to the measurement used clinically to assess renal function—the creatinine clearance, which is the volume of plasma from which creatinine is removed per minute. Total drug clearance (Cl_{tot}) is the rate of elimination by all processes (El_{tot}) divided by the plasma concentration of the drug (C_p):

$$Cl_{tot} = \{\{El_{tot} /\!/ C_p\}\} \qquad (2)$$

Drugs may be cleared by several organs, with renal and hepatic clearance being the two major mechanisms. Total drug clearance (Cl_{tot}) can be described best as the sum of clearances by each organ. For most drugs, this is essentially the sum of the renal and hepatic clearance:

$$Cl_{tot} = Cl_{Ren} + Cl_{Hep} \qquad (3)$$

Table 27–1 shows the wide variation in clearance values among commonly used medications, with some drugs (e.g., ethosuximide and phenobarbital) having relatively low clearances (<5 mL/min) and other drugs (e.g., aspirin and mexiletine) having relatively high clearances (>500 mL/min). Amikacin, gentamicin, and tobramycin are cleared almost entirely by the kidneys, whereas aspirin, carbamazepine, and phenytoin are cleared less than 5% by the kidneys.

Drug clearance is affected by several factors, including (1) blood flow through the organ of clearance, (2) protein binding to the drug, and (3) the activity of the clearance processes in the organs of elimination (e.g., glomerular filtration rate [GFR] and tubular secretion in the kidney or enzyme activity in the liver). Drug clearance is not affected by distribution of drug throughout the body (VD) because clearance mechanisms act only on drug in the circulation.

HALF-LIFE. The amount of time needed to eliminate a drug from the body depends on the clearance and the VD. The first-order elimination constant (k_e) represents the proportion of the apparent VD that

Table 27–1 • PHARMACOKINETIC PARAMETERS FOR SOME COMMONLY USED DRUGS

	V_D (L/kg)	PROTEIN BINDING (%)	TOTAL Cl (mL/min)	% OF Cl_{tot} AS RENAL Cl	HALF-LIFE (hr)	THERAPEUTIC RANGE (mg/L)
Amikacin	0.25	<10	100	94–98	2–3	5–20 (TR) 20–30 (PK)
Aspirin (acetylsalicylic acid)	0.14–0.18	80–90	575–725	<2	0.2–0.3	20–250
Carbamazepine	1.2	75–90	50–125	1–3	12–17	4–12
Digoxin	5–7.3	20–30	75	50–70	34–44	0.5–2.0
Disopyramide	0.6–1.4	50–65	1.3–1.4	40–60	4–10	2–4
Ethosuximide	0.7	<10	3	20	60	40–100
Gentamicin sulfate	0.22–0.3	<10	60	>95	1.5–4 4–8 (PK)	0.5–2.0 (TR)
Lidocaine	3	60–80	700	<10	1.5–2.0	1–5
Lithium carbonate	0.7–1	0	20–40	95–99	20–270	4–1.4*
Mexiletine	5.4	75	500–850	15	8–10	0.7–2.0
Penicillin G	0.5–0.7	45–68	—	20	0.4–0.9	Variable
Phenobarbital	0.6–0.7	20–45	4	25	2–6 days	<10–40*
Phenytoin	0.4–0.8	88–93	—	<5	7–26	10–20
Primidone	0.6	<20	45–100	15–25	10–12	5–12
Procainamide	2.2	14–23	470–600	40–70	2.5–4.7	4–8
Quinidine sulfate	2	80	180–300	10–20	6–8	0.3–6.0
Theophylline	0.3–0.7	60	36–50	<10	4–16	5–20
Tobramycin	0.25–0.30	<10	70	>95	2–4 4–8 (PK)	0.5–2.0 (TR)
Valproic acid	0.15	80–95	7	<10	5–20	50–100
Vancomycin	0.4–1.0	52–60	65	85	4–6	5–10 (TR) 25–35 (PK)

TR = trough value; PK = peak value.
*Therapeutic range varies depending on indication for drugs (e.g., lithium carbonate—range 0.4–1.3 mg/L, appropriate for affective schizophrenia disorder; whole range 1.0–1.4 mg/L appropriate for mania; phenobarbital—concentration <10 mg/mL appropriate for anticonvulsant, 40 mg/L appropriate as hypnotic.

is cleared of drug per unit of time during the exponential disappearance of drug from the plasma over time (elimination phase):

$$k_e = \{\{Cl /\!/ VD\}\} \tag{4}$$

The value of this constant for a particular drug can be determined by plotting drug concentration versus time on a log-linear plot (see Fig. 27–2) and measuring the slope of the straight line obtained during the exponential (elimination) phase.

The time needed to eliminate the drug is described best by the drug half-life ($t_{1/2}$), which is the time required during the elimination phase (see Fig. 27–2) to decrease the plasma concentration of the drug by half. Mathematically the half-life is equal to the natural logarithm of 2 (representing a reduction of drug concentration to half) divided by k_e. Substituting for k_e from Equation 4 and calculating the natural logarithm of 2, the half-life can be represented by the following equation:

$$t_{1/2} = \{\{0.693\ VD /\!/ Cl\}\} \tag{5}$$

From this equation, one can predict that at a given clearance, as the VD increases, the half-life increases. Similarly at a given VD, as the clearance increases, the half-life decreases. Clinically, many disease states (see later) can affect VD and clearance. Because disease affects the VD and clearance differently, the half-life may increase, decrease, or not change much. By itself, the half-life is not a good indicator of the extent of abnormality in elimination.

The half-life is useful to predict how long it takes for a drug to be eliminated from the body. For any drug that has a first-order elimination, one would expect that by the end of the first half-life the drug would be reduced to 50%; by the end of the second half-life, to 25%; by the end of the third half-life, to 12.5%; by the end of the fourth half-life, to 6.25%; and by the end of the fifth half-life, to 3.125%. In general, a drug can be considered to be essentially eliminated after three to five half-lives when less than 10% of the effective concentration remains. Table 27–1 shows the wide variation in half-life for several commonly used drugs.

APPLYING PHARMACOKINETIC PRINCIPLES

USING A LOADING DOSE. To attain a desired therapeutic concentration rapidly, a loading dose often is used. In determining the amount of drug to be given, the physician must consider the "volume" within the body into which the drug may distribute. This volume is described best by the apparent VD. The loading dose can be calculated by multiplying the desired concentration by the VD:

$$\text{Loading dose} = \text{desired concentration} \times \text{VD} \tag{6}$$

Administering the entire loading dose rapidly may produce an initially high peak concentration that results in toxicity. This problem can be avoided either by administering the loading dose as a divided dose or by varying the rate of access to the circulation (e.g., by administering the drug as an infusion [with intravenous drug] or by taking advantage of the slower access to the circulation from various other routes [oral dose]). This approach is illustrated by phenytoin (see Table 27–1), which may need to be administered with a loading dose to achieve a therapeutic level (10 to 20 mg/L) rapidly. Because the VD for phenytoin is approximately 0.6 L/kg, the loading dose calculated from Equation 6 would be 420 mg/L to attain a minimally therapeutic level of 10 mg/L in a 70-kg adult. Administering 420 mg of phenytoin by intravenous bolus carries the risk of cardiac arrest and death. By taking advantage of the reduced bioavailability (F = 0.8) and slow absorption of oral phenytoin, the loading dose can be administered safely as an oral dose of 500 mg.

The equation for the loading dose also can be used to calculate the dose needed to "boost" an inadequate blood level of drug to a desired therapeutic range. If the phenytoin level is observed on therapeutic monitoring to be 5 mg/L and the desired level is 15 mg/L, it is necessary to multiply the difference needed to achieve the desired concentration (10 mg/L) by the VD (0.6 L/kg) to determine the dose (in milligrams per kilogram) necessary to achieve this drug level after

distribution. In a 70-kg individual, 0.6 mg/kg would be multiplied by 70 kg to obtain the calculated loading dose (420 mg) that could be administered safely. A 500-mg oral dose with a bioavailability less than 1 (e.g., F = 0.8) would deliver to the systemic circulation the approximate amount needed and avoid the risks associated with rapid intravenous administration.

DETERMINING DRUG ACCUMULATION. Continuing to administer a drug, either as a prolonged infusion or as repeated doses, results in accumulation until a steady state occurs. Steady state is the point when the amount of drug being administered equals the amount being eliminated so that the plasma and tissue levels remain constant. The elimination half-life determines not only the time course of drug elimination, but also the time course of drug accumulation. This "mirror image" pattern of drug accumulation and elimination is shown graphically in Figure 27–3. As with drug elimination, three to five half-lives determine the time it takes to reach steady state during drug accumulation. Although drugs with short half-lives accumulate rapidly, drugs with long half-lives require a longer time to accumulate, with a potential delay in achieving therapeutic drug levels. For drugs with long half-lives, a loading dose may be needed to achieve drug accumulation rapidly and a more rapid therapeutic effect.

With each change in drug dose or rate of infusion, a change in steady state occurs. Although not obvious for drugs with short half-lives, the effects of dose adjustments for drugs with longer half-lives are delayed, with the time varying directly with the drug's half-life.

USING A MAINTENANCE DOSE. After steady state is reached in three to five half-lives with either a continuous infusion or intermittent doses, the rate of drug administered equals the rate of drug eliminated. For an intravenous drug, the administration rate is the infusion rate (I), whereas for a drug administered by another route (e.g., oral dose), the administration rate is the dose per unit time (D/t). From Equation 3, the rate of elimination (total) can be seen to equal the $Cl_{tot} \times C_p$. It follows with an intravenously administered drug, because the infusion rate equals the elimination rate at steady state, that:

$$I = Cl_{tot} \times C_p \tag{7}$$

Similarly, with an orally administered drug, the dose administered per unit time equals the elimination rate at steady state, with the result that:

$$D/t = Cl_{tot} \times C_p \tag{8}$$

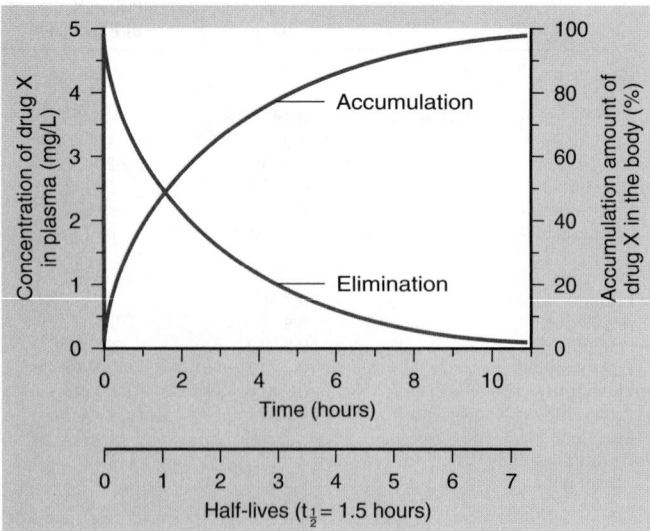

FIGURE 27–3 • Representative plot of the "mirror image" relationship between elimination of drug (after drug is discontinued) and accumulation of drug (during infusion). The plot shows the concentration on the left y-axis and time on the upper x-axis. The lower x-axis shows the time in half-lives, and the y-axis on the right shows the percentage of drug in the body. After three to five half-lives, elimination is essentially complete, and accumulation is essentially at a steady state.

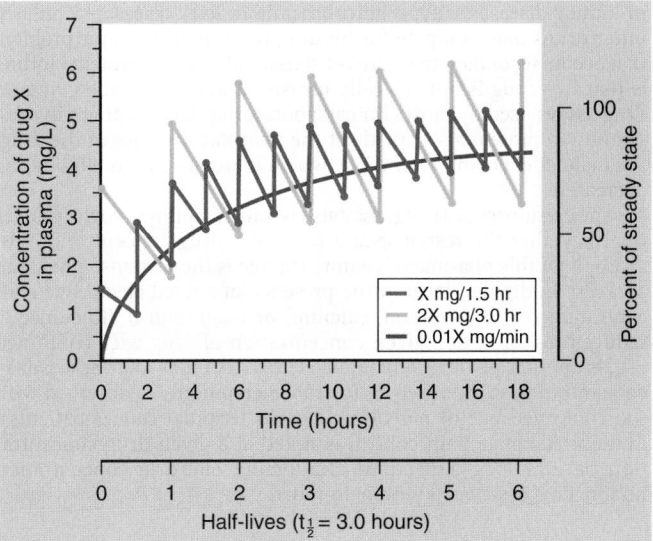

FIGURE 27–4 • The accumulation of drug over time approaching a steady state is shown. Time is depicted in hours (upper *x*-axis) and half-lives (lower *x*-axis, showing that in three to five half-lives steady state is reached). The *solid line* depicts the pattern produced by an infusion of a hypothetical drug at a dose of 0.01X. The *solid circles* with the *hatched line* show the pattern resulting from orally administering a 2X dose every 3 hours, and the *open circles* with the *solid line* represent the pattern produced by orally administering a dose X every 1.5 hours.

These equations show the direct relationship between the dose and the resultant plasma concentration at steady state. This relationship is independent of the distribution of the drug. By using these equations, it is possible to determine the infusion rate or the interval and dose needed to achieve and maintain a specified drug concentration in the plasma.

When administered intermittently, a drug approaches steady-state concentration over time with a pattern similar to that observed with continuous infusion (Fig. 27–4). With intermittent drug administration, such as with an oral dose, the drug concentration fluctuates; the magnitude of fluctuation between the peak and trough concentrations depends on the interval of administration, drug half-life, absorption characteristics, and site of administration. The effect of a change in the interval of administration for an oral drug is shown in Figure 27–4. As the intervals decrease below the half-life, the fluctuation decreases and approaches the curve produced by an intravenous infusion. Orally administered drugs may reach the bloodstream more rapidly, attaining a higher peak concentration with one formulation, whereas the same drug administered as a timed-release formulation is absorbed more slowly, with a lower peak concentration but lasting longer in the plasma. Finally, the same drug administered by different routes may have different plasma profiles not only because of differing absorption characteristics, but also because of other effects, such as first-pass metabolism.

DECREASING THE DRUG LEVEL. At times it may be necessary to decrease the plasma drug level while maintaining therapy (e.g., when signs of toxicity become apparent or a potentially dangerously high concentration of drug is noted when monitoring drug levels; see later). The most effective and rapid response is to discontinue the drug, with the length of time off the drug determined by the estimated drug half-life in the specific patient. After discontinuing the drug for a time based on the drug's half-life, the total clearance (Cl_{tot}) of the drug can be used to determine what infusion rate (I) (Equation 7) or dose and interval (D/t) (Equation 8) must be used to achieve the new desired concentration (C_p).

DOSE-DEPENDENT PHARMACOKINETICS

Although the previously discussed pharmacokinetic principles can be a guide to the dose of most drugs, not all drugs behave the same when the dose is increased. Most drugs are eliminated following first-order or linear kinetics, with the amount of drug eliminated directly proportional to the concentration of drug in the plasma (Fig. 27–5A). A few drugs have a different pattern when eliminated. Three of the most commonly used drugs that exhibit this different pharmacokinetic pattern are ethanol, phenytoin, and salicylate. These drugs have dose-dependent, nonlinear, saturation kinetics. As the dose of drug increases and the concentration of drug in the plasma rises, the relative amount of drug being eliminated falls (i.e., the clearance decreases) until the rate of drug metabolism is at its maximum. At this point, drug elimination is said to be zero-order, and the drug concentration in plasma starts to increase much more (no longer a linear relationship) with each subsequent increase in dose (Fig. 27–5B).

MONITORING DRUG CONCENTRATION AS A GUIDE TO THERAPY

Although published pharmacokinetic data (usually population averages), such as are listed in Table 27–1, are useful to determine initial drug dosing, dose modification still may be needed in the individual patient. For some drugs (e.g., certain antihypertensives or anticoagulants), the therapeutic effects (e.g., blood pressure or coagulation) can be quantified easily over a range of concentrations, permitting adequate drug adjustment. For many other drugs (e.g., some antiarrhythmics or antiseizure medications), therapeutic effects over a range of concentrations are not readily detectable. With these drugs, the plasma concentration of the drug may be used to provide further guidance in optimizing therapy if the plasma drug concentration is a reflection of the concentration at the site of action and the drug effects are reversible. A third, much smaller group of drugs produces irreversible effects (e.g., aspirin inhibition of platelet aggregation). With these drugs, plasma drug concentration does not correlate with drug effect, and drug monitoring is not useful.

To use drug concentrations as a guide to therapy, it is necessary to establish a range of concentrations from minimally to maximally efficacious with tolerable toxicity. This range of concentrations, or *therapeutic window,* usually is determined from a dose-response curve generated from a population of patients who have been examined

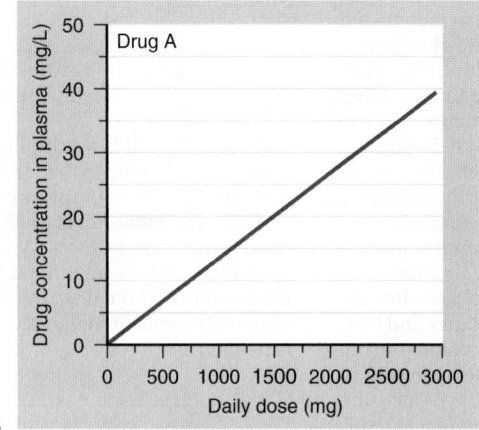

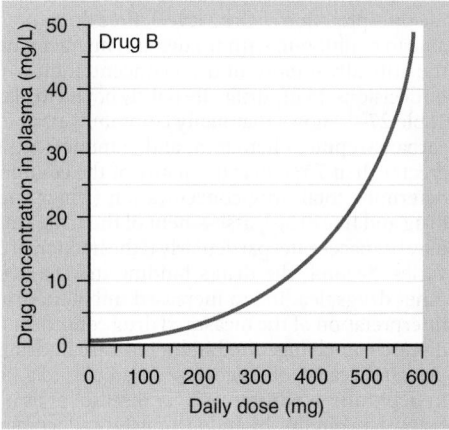

FIGURE 27–5 • The effect of increasing dose on serum concentration for drug *A*, which follows first-order or linear kinetics, and drug *B*, which follows zero-order or non-linear (or saturable) kinetics.

Clinical Pharmacology

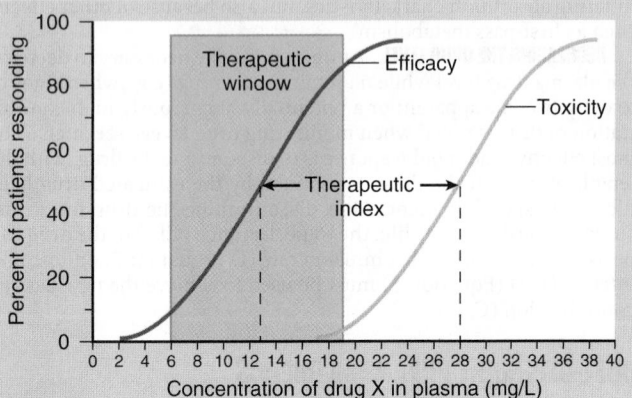

FIGURE 27–6 • The pattern produced in a dose-response population study in which both effect and toxicity are measured. The therapeutic window is shown as the range of therapeutically effective concentrations, which includes most of the efficacy curve and less than 10% of the toxicity curve. The therapeutic index is calculated by dividing the 50% value on the toxicity curve by the 50% value on the efficacy curve.

closely for therapeutic and toxic effects (Fig. 27–6). This graph also may be used to determine the *therapeutic index*. This useful measure of drug toxicity is calculated by dividing the 50% value from the toxicity curve by the 50% value of the efficacy curve. Because these curves are generated from population data, the values may not be applicable for all individuals.

Table 27–1, in addition to providing useful pharmacokinetic data, lists therapeutic ranges for several commonly used drugs for which measuring the drug concentration and knowing the therapeutic range may be useful in clinical management. Many of these drugs typically are used to treat serious or life-threatening diseases. It is essential to avoid inadequate doses because therapeutic effect is needed. Excessive doses also must be avoided because of the risk of toxicity with many of these drugs that have a small therapeutic index. In contrast, it is not necessary to assay drug levels for other drugs used in noncritical diseases (no problem if inadequately treated) or for which the therapeutic index is large (overtreatment is not likely to produce toxicity).

Problems with Interpreting Drug Concentration

The time of blood collection, perhaps more than any other factor, contributes to the misinterpretation of drug levels. As can be seen from Figure 27–2, if sampling is performed too early, while the drug is still in the distribution phase, the drug level may be high and not reflect drug concentration at the site of action. It is important to sample after the distribution phase.

For many drugs administered intermittently, a trough level, obtained immediately before administering the next dose, is most useful for making decisions regarding dose adjustments (see Table 27–1). For drugs that are administered by infusion or intermittently at short intervals (see Fig. 27–4), the best time to draw blood is during steady state.

Protein binding is another major factor that contributes to the misinterpretation of drug levels. Free drug (not bound to protein and able to equilibrate with tissues and interact with the site of action) is the critically important drug concentration when making therapeutic decisions. Many drugs are tightly bound to plasma protein, however. Table 27–1 shows that many commonly used drugs, such as aspirin, carbamazepine, phenytoin, and valproic acid, have protein binding greater than 75%. Because many of the commonly used drug assays determine total drug concentration (which includes protein-bound drug and free drug), assessment of the "true" free drug concentration may be inaccurate, particularly if the fraction of drug bound to protein varies. Second, the drug's binding may be decreased by disease or other drugs, leading to increased unbound drug levels that alter the interpretation of the measured drug concentrations. Kidney and liver disease can change the binding of certain drugs (e.g., phenytoin) to protein because of a decrease in protein (e.g., decreased albumin as in nephrotic syndrome or liver disease) or as a result of competition for protein binding by endogenously produced substances (e.g., uremia

in kidney disease or hyperbilirubinemia in liver disease). Similarly, other drugs may compete for binding to protein. A major problem that occurs secondary to the just-discussed changes in protein binding is that free drug is not typically measured in many of the common drug assays used by most clinical laboratories. Last, changes in drug binding to protein also can affect the pharmacokinetics of the drug, the main effect being on the VD, which increases as protein binding decreases.

The usefulness of a drug assay also is limited by physiologic changes that may alter the response at a particular drug concentration. An example of this pharmacodynamic change is the response produced at a certain digoxin level in the presence of altered electrolyte concentration (e.g., potassium, calcium, or magnesium). Tolerance, a reduced response to a given concentration of drug with continued use, is another pharmacodynamic change that may alter how a drug concentration is interpreted. Tolerance commonly is observed with the continued use of narcotics (e.g., in terminal cancer patients); initially, adequate pain control is noted at a given drug concentration, but after long-term administration the same drug concentration no longer is associated with pain relief.

ADJUSTING DRUG DOSE WITH DISEASE

Kidney Disease

The major questions to be answered in determining whether drug dosage needs to be adjusted in the setting of kidney disease include: (1) Is the drug primarily excreted through the kidneys? (2) Are increased drug levels likely to be associated with toxicity? If the answer to both is yes, it is likely that with decreased renal clearance a drug will accumulate and become toxic. With renal failure, it is necessary to adjust the dosing regimen of such drugs, particularly for a drug with a long half-life and small therapeutic index (e.g., digoxin).

To obtain the desired concentration over time in the presence of decreased clearance, adjustments can be made by (1) decreasing the dose while maintaining the dose interval (DD), (2) maintaining the dose but increasing the interval between doses (II), or (3) a combination of both (DD and II). Table 27–2 shows how these three different methods are used for several commonly used drugs (previously characterized in Table 27–1 as to their pharmacokinetic properties with normal renal function) that require dosage adjustment with renal dysfunction. Although it may be possible with these adjustments to achieve an average concentration similar to that with normal renal function, there may be concomitant marked changes in the magnitude of peak and trough values. In choosing the type of drug adjustment, the physician should consider not only the therapeutic index of the drug, but also (1) whether an effective concentration needs to be achieved quickly and maintained within a narrow range (i.e., there is a need to maintain an average drug concentration and avoid trough levels when the drug is ineffective) and (2) whether toxicity is associated with elevated drug concentrations (i.e., toxicity with peak drug concentration).

Renal drug clearance has been shown to correlate with creatinine clearance (whether the drug uses glomerular filtration or tubular secretion); any adjustment of drug dose in kidney disease can use the creatinine clearance to calculate the dose needed because the renal drug clearance is proportional to the creatinine clearance. The creatinine clearance, which is used as an estimate of GFR, may be calculated directly from the serum creatinine using the following equation:

$$\mathrm{Cl_{Cr}} = \{[(140 - \mathrm{age}) \times \mathrm{weight\ (kg)} // 72 \times \mathrm{serum\ creatinine\ (mg/dL)}]\} \qquad (9)$$

The value should be multiplied by 0.85 for females. (*Note:* This calculation applies only when the serum creatinine is <5 mg/dL and the renal function is not rapidly changing.)

USING CLEARANCE FOR DOSE ADJUSTMENT. The dose of a drug used in renal insufficiency ($\mathrm{dose_{D-RI}}$) can be shown to be proportional to the dose used with normal renal function ($\mathrm{dose_D}$) in the same ratio as the clearance of the drug in renal insufficiency ($\mathrm{Cl_{D-RI}}$) to the clearance with normal renal function ($\mathrm{Cl_D}$). By rearranging, the $\mathrm{Dose_{D-RI}}$ is defined as:

$$\mathrm{Dose_{D-RI}} = \mathrm{dose_D} \times \{[\mathrm{Cl_{D-RI}} // \mathrm{Cl_D}]\} \qquad (10)$$

Table 27-2 • ADJUSTMENT OF DRUG DOSAGE IN RENAL FAILURE

DRUG	TYPE OF ELIMINATION	HALF LIFE (hr) Normal	End-Stage Renal	Method*	GFR (mL/min) >50	10-50	<10	Removed By Dialysis†
Amikacin	Renal	2–3	30	DD II	60–90% 12 hr	30–70% 12–18 hr	20–30% 24 hr	Yes
Aspirin	Hepatic (renal)	2–19	Unchanged	II	4 hr	4–6 hr	Avoid	Yes
Carbamazepine	Hepatic (renal)	35	?	DD	Unchanged	Unchanged	75%	No
Digoxin	Renal (nonrenal 15–40%)	36–44	80–120	DD II	Unchanged 24 hr	25–75% 36 hr	10–25% 48 hr	No
Disopyramide	Renal + hepatic	5–8	10–18	II	Unchanged	12–24 hr	24–40 hr	No
Ethosuximide	Hepatic, renal	55	60	DD	Unchanged	Unchanged	75%	Yes
Gentamicin sulfate	Renal	2	24–48	DD II	60–90% 8–12 hr	30–70% 12 hr	20–30% 24 hr	Yes
Lidocaine	Hepatic (renal <20%)	1.2–2.2	1.3–3.0	DD	Unchanged	Unchanged	Unchanged	No
Lithium carbonate	Renal	14–28	Prolonged	DD	Unchanged	50–75%	25–50%	Yes
Mexiletine	Hepatic (renal)	8–13	16	DD	Unchanged	Unchanged	50–75%	Yes
Penicillin G	Renal (hepatic)	0.5	6–20	DD II	Unchanged 6–8 hr	75% 8–12 hr	25–50% 12–16 hr	Yes
Phenobarbital	Hepatic (renal 30%)	60–150	117–160	II	Unchanged	Unchanged	12–16 hr	Yes
Phenytoin	Hepatic (renal)	24	8	DD	Unchanged	Unchanged	Unchanged	No
Primidone	Hepatic (renal <20%)	8	12	II	8 hr	8–12 hr	12–24 hr	Yes
Procainamide	Renal (hepatic 7–24%)	2.5–4.9	5.3–5.9	II	4 hr	6–12 hr	8–24 hr	Yes
Quinidine sulfate	Hepatic (renal 10–50%)	5.0–7.2	4–14	II	Unchanged	Unchanged	Unchanged	Yes
Theophylline	Hepatic	3–12	?	DD	Unchanged	Unchanged	Unchanged	Yes
Tobramycin	Renal	2.5	56	DD II	60–90% 8–12 hr	30–70% 12 hr	20–30% 24 hr	Yes
Valproic acid	Hepatic	Biphasic 1 and 12	10	DD	Unchanged	Unchanged	Unchanged	No
Vancomycin	Renal	6–8	200–250	II	24–72 hr	72–240 hr	240 hr	No

GFR = glomerular filtration rate.
*Method: DD (alone)—decrease dose (maintain same interval).
II (alone)—increase interval between doses (maintain dose).
DD and II (together)—combination of both approaches.
†Dialysis refers to hemodialysis.

One can estimate the Cl_{D-RI} by multiplying the Cl_D by the ratio of the creatinine clearance in renal insufficiency (Cl_{Cr-RI}) over the Cl_{Cr} with normal renal function:

$$Cl_{D-RI} = Cl_D \times \{\{Cl_{Cr-RI} \, // \, Cl_{Cr}\}\} \qquad (11)$$

As shown in Equation 3, total clearance is the sum of clearance by renal and nonrenal (typically hepatic) mechanisms. Any nonrenal clearance is assumed to remain normal, and only the renal clearance is adjusted, with total clearance being reduced only to the extent that renal clearance is reduced. The dose may be calculated from the total (adjusted) clearance and the desired plasma concentration using either Equation 7 or Equation 8. The calculated dose is only an initial guide to the dose needed, however. By monitoring the drug response and/or the plasma drug concentration at various times after initial dosing, further dose adjustments can be made as necessary. From a practical perspective, most clinical dose adjustment of drugs in the presence of renal dysfunction can be guided by published tables that recommend reductions based on changes in GFR (see Table 27–2) and the effectiveness of dialysis in removing the drug. Computerized decision support systems are particularly effective in guiding medication dosing for inpatients with renal insufficiency.

LOADING DOSE IN RENAL INSUFFICIENCY. For drugs that typically are administered with a loading dose with normal renal function, the same approach may be used with renal insufficiency to ensure that the desired concentration is achieved rapidly. For other drugs that typically are administered without a loading dose with normal renal function, the presence of a prolonged half-life resulting from renal insufficiency may delay drug accumulation to steady state. In this setting, a loading dose (equal to the amount needed to reach steady state with normal renal function) would be required.

ADDITIONAL CONSIDERATIONS IN RENAL INSUFFICIENCY. Because of individual differences among patients, the approaches outlined earlier should be considered only initial approximations to prevent ineffective (too low) or toxic (too high) doses. In planning further maintenance therapy, it is desirable to monitor blood levels to guide further dosing.

If a metabolite of the drug is responsible for effect or toxicity and accumulates in renal failure, the drug level alone may not provide sufficient guidance for planning therapy in the setting of renal insufficiency. The major metabolite of procainamide is N-acetylprocainamide, which has similar toxicity to the parent drug but only modest antiarrhythmic activity. In the setting of renal failure, N-acetylprocainamide may accumulate dramatically because it is more dependent on renal elimination. Measuring procainamide levels alone does not assess accurately either the levels needed for antiarrhythmic effect or the risk of toxicity.

Liver Disease

Although many drugs are biotransformed in the liver, it is not possible to make any general recommendations for drug dose adjustments in liver disease. In contrast to renal disease, no useful laboratory test is available on which to base dose adjustments. It has been suggested that if the liver's capacity to produce protein (reflected by albumin concentration and the prothrombin time) is reduced significantly, the clearance of drugs metabolized by the P-450 enzymes probably also is reduced.

One special situation that can develop with chronic liver disease and may require dose adjustment is the presence of portacaval shunts. This condition produces not only a potential hemodynamic alteration, leading to decreased hepatic blood flow with accompanying decreased clearance, but also possible bypassing of a first-pass effect, resulting in higher concentrations of drug reaching the systemic circulation. Drugs with a large hepatic extraction that typically are administered orally (e.g., propranolol) may appear in the systemic circulation with higher, potentially toxic concentrations.

Hemodynamic Diseases

Decreased cardiac output or hypotensive conditions lead to decreased perfusion of the organs, including those responsible for eliminating drugs. As noted earlier with primary kidney disease, the dose can be adjusted for decreased renal perfusion by using the creatinine clearance. The effect of decreased hepatic blood flow on pharmacokinetics is more difficult to assess. For drugs that have a high hepatic extraction (e.g., lidocaine), decreased hepatic blood flow suggests a need to reduce doses.

Altered hemodynamics also may affect the distribution of selected drugs. Drugs that have a relatively large VD (e.g., lidocaine, procainamide, and quinidine) may be affected by conditions leading to hypotension, such as shock resulting in a decrease in the apparent VD. With a reduced VD, the loading dose of a drug should be reduced to avoid potentially toxic drug levels.

In general, in the setting of severely compromised hemodynamics, it is advisable to be conservative, avoiding potentially toxic loading and maintenance doses of drugs. Drug levels and the clinical status should be monitored closely, and drug doses should be adjusted as necessary.

APPROACH TO DRUG OVERDOSE

The pharmacokinetic principles discussed earlier can be used to determine the best approach to drug removal in the setting of a drug overdose, particularly if hemodialysis or hemoperfusion is contemplated. The major goal is to increase the overall clearance of drug, removing a substantial fraction of the total body load of drug. Examining the VD and clearance values can provide some guidance. For drugs with a large VD (e.g., digoxin in Table 27–1), only a small amount of drug can be removed because clearance affects only the amount of drug present in the plasma, and a large portion of the drug in the body is outside the plasma compartment. Similarly, for drugs with high clearance values, hemoperfusion may increase the overall clearance only minimally and is not indicated. Table 27–2 provides data for determining whether hemodialysis is likely to be useful to remove several commonly used drugs.

USING DRUGS IN THE ELDERLY

Administering drugs to the elderly is perhaps the most challenging area in adult therapeutics because of several factors, including (1) the increasing likelihood of multiple illnesses, often with multisystemic involvement; (2) the need for these patients to be on multiple drugs (often prescribed by different physicians); and (3) the increasing probability of altered pharmacokinetics and pharmacodynamics. These factors together contribute to significantly increased frequency of drug interactions and adverse drug responses in this group of patients.

PHARMACOKINETIC CHANGES WITH AGE. These changes can be secondary to the effects of general physiologic changes of aging, such as the change in body composition, or to specific changes in pharmacokinetically important organs (e.g., kidneys or liver). The distribution of drugs tends to change dramatically with age, mainly because of changes in body composition. Most typical is the increase in total body fat with the accompanying decrease in lean body mass and total body water. Changes also may occur in the concentration of plasma proteins, particularly albumin, which decreases as the liver ages. The changes in distribution are manifest as a change in the apparent VD. For water-soluble drugs that are not bound to plasma proteins, the apparent VD is reduced, in contrast to lipid-soluble drugs, for which the VD is increased. Minimal changes in metabolism accompany aging, but these alone cannot typically account for altered pharmacokinetics.

Excretion can be altered in the elderly. The clearance of many drugs is decreased. Cardiac output and blood flow to the kidneys and liver also may be decreased. GFR may be reduced by 50%. Hepatic elimination of drugs is less affected except for drugs with a high hepatic clearance (e.g., lidocaine). The elimination half-life of many drugs is increased with aging as a consequence of a larger apparent VD and a decreased hepatic or renal clearance (see Equation 5).

PHARMACODYNAMIC CHANGES WITH AGE. These changes are a result of changes in the responsiveness of the target organ. They require using smaller drug doses in the elderly, even if the pharmacokinetics are unchanged. Many examples exist of such changes with drugs commonly used in the elderly; for example, antianxiety drugs and drugs from the sedative-hypnotic class may produce increased central nervous system depression in the elderly at concentrations that are well tolerated in younger adults. Similarly, anticoagulants (e.g., warfarin) may produce hemorrhage in the elderly at concentrations that are well tolerated in younger adults.

GENERAL RECOMMENDATIONS. Several general principles apply to drug use in the elderly: (1) The clearance of drugs eliminated by the kidneys may be reduced by 50%; (2) drugs that are eliminated primarily by the liver typically do not require adjustment for age except for drugs with high hepatic clearances, which may be affected by age-related decrease in hepatic blood flow; (3) because of potential for increased target-organ sensitivity in the elderly, only the lowest effective dose should be used; and (4) frequent reviews of the patient's drug history should be conducted, including not only prescription medications, but also over-the-counter medications, keeping in mind the increased potential risk for drug interactions and adverse drug responses.

INTERACTIONS BETWEEN DRUGS

Because patients typically are treated today with multiple agents for a single disease, the possibilities for drug interactions are great. In general, most clinically important drug interactions typically involve a drug with a low therapeutic index (e.g., warfarin) and an easily detectable pharmacologic effect (e.g., bleeding), such that a small increase in the amount of drug produces a significant effect (toxicity).

Epidemiology

It is difficult to assess accurately the prevalence of drug interactions in either the inpatient or ambulatory settings, particularly because no formal surveillance mechanism is currently available. The risk for drug interactions seems to be increasing, particularly for critically ill, hospitalized patients who frequently are taking more than 10 medications.

Etiology

There are basically two types of drug interaction: (1) pharmacokinetic drug interactions, caused by a change in the amount of drug or active metabolite at the site of action, and (2) pharmacodynamic drug interactions (without a change in pharmacokinetics), caused by a change in drug effect.

PHARMACOKINETIC DRUG INTERACTIONS

Less Drug at the Site of Action

DECREASED ABSORPTION. The gastrointestinal lumen is perhaps the best example of an area where two or more drugs have the opportunity to interact, resulting in decreased drug absorption. Several examples, including some commonly used drugs, illustrate this type of interaction. For many of these drugs, a physicochemical interaction prevents the drug from being absorbed. Drugs such as colestipol and cholestyramine (resins used to lower cholesterol and bind bile acids) also can bind other drugs simultaneously present in the gastrointestinal lumen. Among the drugs that can be bound are digoxin and warfarin. Because of the potential for many other drugs also to be bound, it generally is recommended that other drugs not be administered within 2 hours of colestipol or cholestyramine. Metal ions (e.g., aluminum, calcium, and magnesium that are present in antacids and iron in supplements to treat iron deficiency) may form insoluble complexes with tetracyclines, which can act as chelating agents. Other commonly used medications that decrease absorption include kaolin-pectin suspensions used to treat diarrhea. These medications can inhibit significantly the absorption of coadministered drugs (e.g., digoxin).

Drugs that are particularly susceptible to pH changes may have decreased absorption when coadministered with drugs that either affect gastric acidity or alter the extent of exposure to low pH. H_2-receptor antagonists, such as cimetidine, ranitidine, and famotidine, may elevate gastric pH, which can inhibit the dissolution and subsequent absorption of drugs that are weak bases (e.g., ketoconazole). Medications that delay gastric emptying (e.g., belladonna alkaloids) can increase the degradation of a coadministered acid-labile drug (e.g., levodopa), resulting in decreased absorption.

ALTERED DISTRIBUTION. Drugs that use the same active transport process to reach their site of action can compete at the level of transport, resulting in lower levels of drug reaching the site of action. The classic example of this type of interaction is guanidinium-type antihypertensives coadministered with tricyclic antidepressants, phenothiazines, and certain sympathomimetic amines (e.g., ephedrine), which block the antihypertensive effects of the former.

INCREASED METABOLISM. Many drugs (e.g., barbiturates such as phenobarbital, phenytoin, ethanol, glutethimide, griseofulvin, rifampin, and toxic compounds such as cigarette smoke and certain chlorinated hydrocarbons) can increase hepatic metabolism of other drugs (e.g., corticosteroids, cyclophosphamide, cyclosporine, certain β-adrenergic blockers, theophylline, and warfarin) by inducing the activity of the cytochrome P-450 mixed-function oxidase (CYP) system.

More Drug at the Site of Action

INCREASED ABSORPTION. Any drug that increases the rate of gastric emptying (e.g., metoclopramide) potentially can increase the absorption of acid-unstable drugs. Also, drugs that decrease intestinal motility (e.g., anticholinergics) may increase the absorption of drugs that are relatively poorly absorbed (e.g., digoxin tablets) by increasing the contact time of the drug with the absorbing surface.

ALTERED DISTRIBUTION. Drugs bound to protein are limited in their distribution (particularly to the site of action) and are not available for metabolism or excretion. Drugs can compete with each other for binding to plasma proteins, resulting in drug interactions. Sulfonamides can displace barbiturates bound to serum albumin, leading to increased levels of free barbiturates with possible toxicity.

DECREASED METABOLISM. One of the most impressive drug interactions is produced when one drug inhibits the metabolism of another drug, leading to the second drug accumulating and significantly risking toxicity. This type of interaction results from using 6-mercaptopurine, an antileukemic drug with a low therapeutic index, with allopurinol, often used in this setting to control hyperuricemia. The interaction may result in potentially life-threatening toxicity.

Some drugs can inhibit the metabolism of many other drugs. Cimetidine can inhibit the metabolism of diazepam, imipramine, lidocaine, propranolol, quinidine, theophylline, and warfarin. Amiodarone inhibits the metabolism of calcium channel blockers, flecainide, phenytoin, quinidine, and warfarin. Of particular importance with amiodarone is its half-life of 1 to 2 months so that it continues to inhibit drug metabolism for several months after being discontinued.

Other drugs are notable in that their metabolism is inhibited by a variety of different drugs. The metabolism of the commonly used anticoagulant warfarin is inhibited not only by cimetidine and amiodarone, but also by many other drugs, including alcohol, allopurinol, disopyramide, disulfiram, metronidazole, phenylbutazone, sulfinpyrazone, and trimethoprim-sulfamethoxazole. Similarly the metabolism of phenytoin also is inhibited by additional drugs, including chloramphenicol, clofibrate, dicumarol, disulfiram, isoniazid (slow acetylators), phenylbutazone, and valproic acid.

Although most of the examples just noted involved enzymes metabolizing the drug in the liver, drug-metabolizing enzymes located outside the liver also may be affected by certain drugs. The best-known example is monoamine oxidase, which can be affected by nonspecific monoamine oxidase inhibitors, resulting in the accumulation of catecholamines at multiple sites after their release in response to eating tyramine-containing foods.

DECREASED EXCRETION. Drugs can compete for the active transporters present in the kidney. Most of these interactions involve the acid transporters. The best-known interaction is the probenecid inhibition of penicillin transport, leading to decreased penicillin clearance with resultant increased plasma levels—an interaction that was used in the past to maximize penicillin therapy. A similar inhibitory effect on renal excretion of methotrexate can be produced by salicylates, phenylbutazone, and probenicid. The active transport of basic drugs (e.g., procainamide) also can be inhibited by other drugs (e.g., cimetidine or amiodarone).

PHARMACODYNAMIC DRUG INTERACTIONS

With pharmacodynamic interactions, drugs interact at the level of the receptor or may produce additive effects by acting at separate sites on cells. An example of the first is the interaction of propranolol and epinephrine, which blocks β-adrenergic receptors with the result that the α-adrenergic effects of epinephrine are unopposed. This undesirable interaction can result in severe hypertension.

Many examples exist of additive effects between drugs. Aspirin, which can produce increased bleeding time by acting on platelets, can interact with warfarin, which affects clotting. The result is an

increased risk of hemorrhage. Similarly, cardiac drugs, such as β-adrenergic blockers and calcium channel blockers, when coadministered have additive negative inotropic effects, resulting in an increased risk of cardiac failure.

Diagnosing and Preventing Drug Interactions

To recognize the presence of a drug interaction, the index of suspicion must be high whenever multiple drugs are used together. Because of the ever-increasing list of known and suspected drug interactions, it is impossible for a clinician to remember all or even many of the possible interactions.

Several clinical settings should raise concern about the possibility of drug interactions: (1) The use of any drug with a low therapeutic index (Table 27–3) should be suspect. (2) As the number of drugs being used concurrently increases, there is a disproportionately greater risk of drug interactions, particularly with more than 10 drugs. (3) Critically ill patients who have multisystemic disease with compromised renal, hepatic, cardiac, or pulmonary function have an increased risk of drug interactions. This risk may be higher for patients with acquired immunodeficiency syndrome, who have an immunocompromised state as well as being on a great number of drugs. (4) Patients with various behavioral and psychiatric disorders (e.g., drug abusers taking not only a large number of prescription drugs, but also illicit drugs and alcohol) are at risk to develop drug interactions. Another type of drug interaction that is becoming increasingly important is the interaction of components of food (e.g., grapefruit juice) or natural products (e.g., herbs) with drugs. Concomitant use of grapefruit juice, through its inhibition of the intestinal cytochrome P-450 3A4 enzyme system, can raise levels of drugs (e.g., saquinavir, cyclosporine, or verapamil) metabolized by this pathway and result in toxicity or adverse drug effects.

Several steps can be taken to prevent drug interactions: (1) In taking the medical history, it is important to document all the drugs the patient is taking (and has recently taken), including prescription, over-the-counter, and other addictive drugs. (2) It is desirable to minimize the number of drugs the patient is taking by frequently reviewing the patient's drug list to ensure that each drug continues to be needed. (3) There should be a high degree of suspicion when medications with a low therapeutic index known to have a high risk of drug interactions (see Table 27–3) are used. (4) High-risk clinical settings, such as occur with critically ill patients, should raise suspicion of adverse drug interactions. (5) Adverse drug interactions should be considered in the differential diagnosis whenever any change occurs in a patient's course.

ADVERSE REACTIONS TO DRUGS

An adverse drug response is an undesired effect produced by a drug at standard doses, which typically necessitates reducing or stopping the suspected agent and may require treatment for the noxious effect produced. Further harm may occur with continued or future therapy with the drug.

EPIDEMIOLOGY. The actual incidence of adverse drug responses is difficult to quantify because many cases are either not recognized or not reported. Several large studies have shown that the incidence may approach 20% for outpatients (even higher for patients on >15 drugs) and 2 to 7% for inpatients. Meta-analyses of several prospective studies suggest that adverse drug reactions may be the fourth to sixth leading cause of death in hospitalized patients. It is clear from more recent surveys that a relatively small group of drugs (see Table 27–3)

Table 27–3 • DRUGS WITH LOW THERAPEUTIC INDICES AT HIGH-RISK FOR ADVERSE DRUG RESPONSE AND DRUG INTERACTIONS

Anticoagulants
Antiarrhythmics
Anticonvulsants
Digoxin
Lithium carbonate
Oral hypoglycemics
Theophylline

continues to be implicated in most of the reported adverse drug responses. Current trends suggest that the incidence of adverse drug responses is likely to increase as a result of an increase in the number of prescribed and over-the-counter medications.

ETIOLOGY. Most adverse drug responses are caused by (1) exaggerated (but predictable) pharmacologic effect of the drug or (2) toxic or immunologic effect of drug or metabolite (not typically expected).

EXAGGERATED (PREDICTABLE) RESPONSE TO A DRUG

Exaggerated drug responses that cause adverse drug effects may be due to any condition that causes either altered pharmacokinetics or pharmacodynamics (discussed earlier). There has been interest in the role of genetic factors as a cause of increased susceptibility to adverse drug responses, primarily through an effect on drug metabolism. Genetic polymorphism of drug-metabolizing enzymes can account for variability in pharmacokinetics and drug effect observed in population studies. Three of the best-studied polymorphisms are the debrisoquine/sparteine, N-acetylation, and mephenytoin polymorphisms. These are each associated with an autosomal recessive inheritance and together are responsible for the metabolism of approximately 40 drugs (Table 27–4). Individuals with autosomal recessive genes are "poor metabolizers" with potentially altered pharmacokinetics that result in elevated plasma drug concentrations and can lead to toxicity. A particularly impressive example occurs with certain cancer chemotherapy agents that have a relatively narrow therapeutic window and the potential to produce severe cytotoxicity (e.g., deficiency in dihydropyrimidine dehydrogenase activity can result in life-threatening toxicity after administration of 5-fluorouracil). These defects typically are not recognized until the patient is given the drug. They often are described as being "pharmacogenetic" syndromes.

Other genetic defects do not affect metabolism specifically and do not produce a range of quantitative changes. These defects can produce "qualitative" defects and often are associated with structural defects. The classic example is glucose-6-phosphate dehydrogenase (G6PD). Individuals who are deficient in this enzyme cannot tolerate oxidative stress that is produced by some drugs, leading to hemolysis (Chapter 170). Drugs that can produce this clinical picture include aspirin, nitrofurantoin, primaquine, probenecid, quinidine, quinine, sulfonamides, sulfones, and vitamin K. Another similar defect is deficiency of methemoglobin reductase, which results in an inability to maintain iron in hemoglobin in the ferrous state, causing methemoglobinemia after exposure to oxidizing drugs, such as nitrites, sulfonamide, or sulfones.

TOXIC OR IMMUNOLOGIC (UNPREDICTABLE) RESPONSE TO DRUG

A toxic or immunologic adverse drug response is not predictable and is not obviously due to an increase in drug concentration (pharmacokinetic) or drug effect (pharmacodynamic). Toxic responses include direct reactions between drug and a specific organ (e.g., platinum-containing drugs, such as cisplatin, can produce direct toxicity in the kidney and the eighth cranial nerve). With other drugs,

metabolism of the drug to an active intermediate must occur first. With a standard dose of acetaminophen, no untoward effects occur because the relatively small amount of reactive metabolite formed by oxidative metabolism is detoxified rapidly by reduced glutathione. In the presence of an overdose, the glutathione is depleted, and the remaining reactive metabolite can damage the liver. Understanding the mechanism of this toxicity has provided a rationale for treating acetaminophen overdose. Sulfhydryl-containing compounds (e.g., N-acetylcysteine), which can complex with the reactive metabolite, can be administered to reduce the amount of free toxic metabolite present, protecting the liver.

Immunologic reactions to drugs (Table 27–5) in general are not produced by the drug alone. Similar to other small-molecular-weight compounds (<1000 D), they are typically not antigenic themselves. When a drug or reactive metabolite combines with a protein to form a drug-protein complex, it can become antigenic, capable of eliciting an immune response.

Perhaps the most impressive form of drug allergy is anaphylaxis, which is due to an IgE-mediated hypersensitivity. Many drugs from different classes have been shown to produce this type of drug allergy (see Table 27–5). The best-known example is the anaphylactic response produced by penicillin, which can occur after administering penicillin by any route. Skin testing with penicillin G, penicilloic acid, or penicilloyl polylysine can identify patients at risk and should be used in patients with suspected penicillin allergy who need to be treated with penicillin. If the skin test is positive, the patient must undergo desensitization before receiving penicillin. If the skin test is negative, penicillin can be administered with caution.

Diagnosis

Although many of the well-known adverse drug effects are due to a relatively small group of drugs, every drug potentially can cause an adverse drug response. The physician always should consider the possibility of an adverse drug response in the differential diagnosis even if none has been reported previously for the particular drug. Table 27–5 lists many diverse clinical presentations associated with adverse drug responses. In many instances, it is readily apparent that a specific drug has produced an adverse drug response, such as the appearance of a rash in an otherwise healthy patient who recently has been started on a single drug (e.g., penicillin). In other cases, the effect produced by the drug may be difficult to discern from other disease states. In still other cases, the adverse effect may mimic the illness being treated (e.g., an arrhythmia developing in a patient being treated with an antiarrhythmic drug).

From a public health perspective, it is highly desirable to have a mechanism available for detecting, cataloging, and tracking the incidence and severity of adverse drug responses not only for drugs at various stages of development, but also for drugs that were approved earlier. The Food and Drug Administration tries to track adverse drug events through a voluntary reporting program, MedWatch. Health care professionals are encouraged to report any adverse events or product problems on a one-page form that can be sent by mail, fax,

---

Table 27–4 • GENETIC POLYMORPHISMS OF DRUG-METABOLIZING ENZYMES

TYPE	PRIMARY DRUG EXAMPLES	OTHER DRUGS THAT ARE SUBSTRATES	INCIDENCE OF "POOR METABOLIZERS" IN WHITES (%)	ENZYME INVOLVED
Debrisoquine-sparteine polymorphism	Debrisoquine, sparteine, bufuralol	Antidepressants, antiarrhythmics, β-adrenergic-receptor blocking drugs, codeine, dextromethorphan, neuroleptics	5–10	Cytochrome P-450 IID6 (CYP2D6)
Mephenytoin polymorphism	Mephenytoin	Mephobarbital, hexobarbital, diazepam, omeprazole	4 (Japanese, Chinese, 15–20)	Cytochrome P-450 IIC (CYP2C)
Acetylation polymorphism	Isoniazid, sulfadiazine	Isoniazid, hydralazine, phenelzine, procainamide, dapsone, sulfamethazine, sulfapyridine, aminoglutethimide, aminosalicylic acid, sulfadiazine, sulfasalazine	40–70 (Japanese, 10–20)	N-Acetyltransferase (NAT₂)
Methyl-conjugation polymorphism	Catecholamines	L-Dopa, methyldopa	25–30	Catechol-Q-methyltransferase (COMT)

Table 27–5 • SOME NOTABLE ADVERSE DRUG REACTIONS

I. Multisystemic manifestations
  A. Anaphylaxis
    1. Macromolecules
      Allergenic extracts
      Dextrans (including iron dextran)
      Enzymes
        Asparaginase
        Chymopapain
        Trypsin
      Heparin
      Hormones (e.g., ACTH, insulin)
      Human gamma globulin
      Monoclonal antibodies
      Protamine
      Vaccines
      Antisera
    2. Diagnostic agents
      Fluorescein
      Iodinated contrast media
    3. Antimicrobials
      Aminosalicylic acid
      Amphotericin B
      Cephalosporins
      Cinoxacin
      Clindamycin
      Demeclocycline
      Ethambutol
      Kanamycin
      Lincomycin
      Nalidixic acid
      Pencillins
      Streptomycin
      Sulfonamides
      Tetracyclines
      Vancomycin
    4. Other drugs, including nonsteroidal anti-inflammatory drugs (NSAIDs)
      Aspirin
      Benzyl alcohol
      Bleomycin
      Cisplatin
      Colchicine
      Cromolyn
      Cytarabine
      Dantrolene
      Ethylenediamine
      Etoposide
      Flucytosine
      Glucocorticoids
      Indomethacin
      Lidocaine
      Local anesthetics
      Mephyton
      Meprobamate
      Niacin
      Opiates
      Pentamidine
      Probenecid
      Procainamide
      Sulfite
      Thiopental
      Tolmetin
      Triamterene
      Tubocurarine and other muscle-relaxing agents
      Vitamin B_{12}
  B. Serum sickness
    1. Macromolecules
      Dextrans
      Heparin
      Hormones (e.g., insulin, ACTH)
      Vaccines
      Antisera
    2. Antimicrobials
      Cephalosporins
      Griseofulvin
      Lincomycin

      Minocycline
      Penicillins
      Streptomycin
      Sulfonamides
    3. Other drugs
      Barbiturates
      Hydralazine
      Phenylbutazone
      Phenytoin
      Procarbazine
      Propylthiouracil
  C. Drug fever
    1. Antimicrobials
      5-Aminosalicylic acid
      Amphotericin B
      Cephalosporins
      Erythromycin
      Isoniazid
      Kanamycin
      Nitrofurantoin
      Norfloxacin
      Penicillins
      Pyrazinamide
      Quinine
      Streptomycin
      Sulfonamides
      Tetracyclines
    2. Other drugs
      Allopurinol
      Captopril
      Heparin
      Hydantoins
      Hydralazine
      Hydrochlorothiazide
      Methyldopa
      Penicillamine
      Phenobarbital
      Pneumococcal vaccine
      Procainamide
      Propylthiouracil
      Quinine
  D. Vasculitis
      Allopurinol
      Atenolol
      Busulfan
      Carbamazepine
      Colchicine
      Diphenhydramine
      Ethionamide
      Furosemide
      Hydantoins
      Hydroxyurea
      Ibuprofen
      Indomethacin
      Isoniazid
      Meprobamate
      Methamphetamine
      Naproxen
      Penicillins
      Phenothiazines
      Phenylbutazone
      Propranolol
      Propylthiouracil
      Streptokinase
      Sulfonamides
      Tetracyclines
      Thiazide diuretics
      Vaccines
  E. Systemic lupus erythematosus syndrome
      5-Aminosalicylic acid
      Chloroquine
      Chlorpromazine
      Ethosuximide
      Griseofulvin
      Hydralazine
      Isoniazid
      Methyldopa
      Nitrofurantoin

      Penicillamine
      Penicillins
      Phenytoin
      Procainamide
      Propylthiouracil
      Quinidine
      Tetracycline
      Tocainide
      Trimethadione
II. Skin
  A. Urticaria and angioedema
    1. Antimicrobials
      5-Aminosalicylic acid
      Aminoglycosides
      Cephalosporins
      Isoniazid
      Metronidazole
      Miconazole
      Nalidixic acid
      Penicillins
      Quinine
      Rifampin
      Spectinomycin
      Sulfonamides
    2. Other drugs
      Asparaginase
      Aspirin and other NSAIDs
      Calcitonin
      Chloral hydrate
      Chorambucil
      Cimetidine
      Cyclophosphamide
      Daunorubicin
      Doxorubicin
      Ergotamine
      Ethchlorvynol
      Ethosuximide
      Ethylenediamine
      Glucocorticoids
      Melphalan
      Penicillamine
      Phenothiazines
      Procainamide
      Procarbazine
      Quinidine
      Tartrazine
      Thiazide diuretics
      Thiotepa
  B. Morbilliform-maculopapular rash
    1. Antimicrobials
      5-Aminosalicylic acid
      Cephalosporins
      Erythromycin
      Gentamicin
      Penicillins
      Streptomycin
      Sulfonamides
    2. Other drugs
      Allopurinol
      Barbiturates
      Captopril
      Coumarin
      Gold salts
      Hydantoins
      Thiazide diuretics
  C. Toxic epidermal necrolysis, erythroderma, and exfoliative dermatitis
      Allopurinol
      Amikacin
      Captopril
      Carbamazepine
      Chloral hydrate
      Chlorambucil
      Chloroquine
      Chlorpromazine
      Cyclosporine
      Diltiazem
      Ethambutol
      Ethylenediamine
      Glutethimide

      Gold salts
      Griseofulvin
      Hydantoins
      Hydroxychloroquine
      Minoxidil
      Nifedipine
      NSAIDs
      Penicillin
      Phenobarbital
      Rifampin
      Spironolactone
      Streptomycin
      Sulfonamides
      Trimethadione
      Trimethoprim
      Tocainide
      Vancomycin
      Verapamil
  D. Erythema multiforme
      Acetaminophen
      Barbiturates
      Carbamazepine
      Chloroquine
      Chlorpropamide
      Clindamycin
      Ethambutol
      Ethosuximide
      Gold salts
      Hydantoins
      Hydralazine
      Hydroxyurea
      Mechlorethamine
      Meclofenamate
      Penicillins
      Phenolphthalein
      Phenylbutazone
      Rifampin
      Streptomycin
      Sulfonylureas
      Sulindac
      Vaccines
  E. Photosensitive
    1. Topical
      Fluorouracil
      Hexachlorophene
      Para-aminobenzoic acid esters
      Promethazine
      Sulfanilamide
    2. Systemic
      Carbamazepine
      Chlorpromazine
      Griseofulvin
      Imipramine
      Lincomycin
      Nalidixic acid
      Naproxen
      Norfloxacin
      Phenothiazines
      Piroxicam
      Quinethazone
      Sulfonamides
      Sulfonylureas
      Thiazide diuretics
      Triamterene
  F. Fixed drug eruptions
      Acetaminophen
      5-Aminosalicylic acid
      Aspirin
      Barbiturates
      Benzodiazepines
      Chloroquine
      Dapsone
      Dimenhydrinate
      Diphenhydramine
      Gold salts
      Hydralazine
      Hyoscine
      Ibuprofen
      Iodides
      Meprobamate
      Methenamine

Continued

Clinical Pharmacology

Table 27–5 • SOME NOTABLE ADVERSE DRUG REACTIONS—cont'd

Metronidazole
Penicillins
Phenobarbital
Phenolphthalein
Phenothiazines
Phenylbutazone
Procarbazine
Pseudoephedrine
Quinine
Saccharin
Streptomycin
Sulfonamides
Tetracyclines
G. Erythema nodosum
Bromides
Oral contraceptives
Penicillin
Sulfonamides
H. Contact dermatitis
Ambroxol
Amikacin
Antihistamines
Bacitracin
Benzalkonium chloride
Benzocaine
Benzyl alcohol
Cetyl alcohol
Chloramphenicol
Chlorpromazine
Clioquinol
Colophony
Ethylenediamine
Fluorouracil
Formaldehyde
Gentamicin
Glucocorticoids
Glutaraldehyde
Heparin
Hexachlorophene
Iodochlorhydroxyquin
Lanolin
Local anesthetics
Minoxidil
Naftin
Neomycin
Nitrofurazone
Opiates
Para-aminobenzoic acid
Parabens
Penicillins
Phenothiazines
Proflavine
Propylene glycol
Streptomycin
Sulfonamides
Thimerosal
Timolol
III. Lungs
A. Asthma
Aspirin and other NSAIDs
Cromolyn

Sulfite
Tartrazine
Occupational exposures to:
Cephalosporins
Glutaraldehyde
Pancreatic enzymes
Papain
Penicillins
Psyllium
Thimerosal
B. Eosinophilic pneumonitis
5-Aminosalicylic acid
Azathioprine
Captopril
Carbamazepine
Chlorpropamide
Cromolyn
Desipramine
Gold salts
Imipramine
Nitrofurantoin
Penicillins
Phenytoin
Sulfonamides
L-Tryptophan
C. Fibrotic and pleural reactions
Bleomycin
Busulfan
Cyclophosphamide
Gold salts
Hydralazine
Hydrochlorothiazide
Melphalan
Methotrexate
Methysergide
Mitomycin
Nitrofurantoin
Procarbazine
IV. Liver
A. Cholestatic
Chlorzoxazone
Erythromycin estolate
Ethchlorvynol
Imipramine
Nalidixic acid
Nitrofurantoin
Phenothiazines
Sulfamethoxazole
Sulfonylureas
Troleandomycin
B. Hepatocellular
5-Aminosalicylic acid
Amphotericin B
Azapropazone
Ethacrynic acid
Furosemide
Gold salts
Griseofulvin
Halothane
Hydantoins
Isoniazid

Methyldopa
Monoamine oxidase inhibitors
Nitrofurantoin
Propylthiouracil
Pyrazinamide
Quinidine
Rifampin
Sulfonamides
Trimethadione
C. Chronic active hepatitis
Methyldopa
Nitrofurantoin
V. Kidney
A. Glomerulitis
Allopurinol
Captopril
Gold salts
NSAIDs
Penicillamine
Penicillins
Phenytoin
Probenecid
Sulfonamides
Thiazide diuretics
B. Interstitial nephritis
Allopurinol
Aztreonam
Captopril
Carbamazepine
Cephalosporins
Chloramphenicol
Cimetidine
Ciprofloxacin
Colistin
Furosemide
Minocycline
NSAIDs
Penicillins, especially
methicillin
Phenytoin
Polymyxin B
Rifampin
Sulfonamides
Tetracycline
Thiazide diuretics
VI. Bone marrow and blood cells
A. Bone marrow aplasia
Chloramphenicol
Gold salts
Mephenytoin
Penicillamine
Phenylbutazone
Trimethadione
B. Anemia
Acetaminophen
5-Aminosalicylic acid
Captopril
Cephalosporins
Chlorpromazine
Cisplatin

Hydantoins
Ibuprofen
Insulin
Isoniazid
Levodopa
Mefenamic acid
Melphalan
Methyldopa
Methylsergide
Penicillins
Quinidine
Quinine
Rifampin
Sulfonamides
Sulfonylureas
C. Thrombocytopenia
Acetaminophen
Acetazolamide
Acetylsalicylic acid
5-Aminosalicylic acid
Carbamazepine
Chloramphenicol
Chlorpheniramine
Cimetidine
Digitoxin
Diltiazem
Ethchlorvynol
Gold salts
Heparin
Hydantoins
Isoniazid
Levodopa
Meprobamate
Methyldopa
Penicillamine
Phenylbutazone
Procainamide
Quinidine
Quinine
Ranitidine
Rauwolfia alkaloids
Rifampin
Sulfonamides
Sulfonylureas
Thiazide diuretics
D. Granulocytopenia
Captopril
Cephalosporins
Chloral hydrate
Chlorpropamide
Penicillins (semisynthetic)
Phenothiazines
Phenylbutazone
Phenytoin
Procainamide
Propranolol
Tolbutamide
E. Lymphoid hyperplasia
Phenytoin
Mephenytoin

Adapted from Reed CE: Drug allergy. *In* Wyngaarden JB, Smith LH Jr, Bennett JC (eds): Cecil Textbook of Medicine, 19th ed. Philadelphia, WB Saunders, 1992, pp 1480–1481.

or modem to the Food and Drug Administration. Although various methods for surveying adverse drug responses have been proposed, ultimately the cooperation of alert clinicians and health care professionals must be encouraged.

SUGGESTED READINGS

Chertow GM, Lee J, Kuperman GJ, et al: Guided medication dosing for inpatients with renal insufficiency. JAMA 2001;286:2839–2844. *Shows the value of using a real-time computerized decision support system for prescribing drugs in inpatients with renal insufficiency.*

Evans WE, McLeod HL: Pharmacogenomics—drug disposition, drug targets, and side effects. N Engl J Med 2003;348:538–549. *Describes how genetic differences affect drug metabolism.*

Izzo AA, Ernst E: Interactions between herbal medicines and prescribed drugs: A systematic review. Drugs 2001;61:2163–2175. *Review of clinically important drug interactions that occur with commonly used herbal medicines and prescribed drugs.*

Kane GC, Lipsky JJ: Drug-grapefruit interactions. Mayo Clin Proc 2000;75:933–942. *Review of clinically important drug interactions that occur with commonly used herbal medicines and prescribed drugs.*

Kim RB: The Medical Letter Handbook of Adverse Drug Interactions. New Rochelle, NY, The Medical Letter, 2001. *This paperback handbook provides a relatively comprehensive listing of drugs thought to produce interactions, with a description of adverse effects, their probable mechanisms, clinical recommendations, and original references.*

Pirmohamed M, Park BK: Genetic susceptibility to adverse drug reactions. Trends Pharmacol Sci 2001;22:298–305. *Genetic variability may lead to susceptibility to adverse drug reactions.*

28 DRUG ALLERGY

James R. Bonner

The designation *drug allergy* should be reserved for adverse drug reactions caused by immunologic mechanisms. Although drug allergies are responsible for only a few adverse drug effects, the possibility of such reactions is a daily concern of most physicians. Drug allergy has a great variety of clinical manifestations and has been attributed to most categories of therapeutic agents. Because specific diagnostic tests are not usually available, physicians most often base decisions on probabilities and the patient's need for treatment. This chapter provides an overview of drug allergy with an emphasis on pathogenic mechanisms, diagnostic considerations, and preventive measures. Nonallergic reactions are discussed in Chapter 27.

Epidemiology and Etiology

Complications of drug therapy are the most common adverse events among hospitalized patients, and 10 to 14% of drug reactions have an allergic basis. An estimated 5% of adult patients have at least one drug allergy, and many more patients incorrectly believe that they are allergic to medications. Drug allergy may be more common in women and may be expected to occur more frequently in patients given multiple courses of treatment. Atopic patients are not predisposed to drug allergy but may have more severe reactions. Drug allergy seems to be less common at the extremes of age—a reflection of fewer sensitizing exposures in the very young and a decline in immune responsiveness in the very old. Risk factors for drug allergy are complex and include individual genetic differences in drug metabolism and immunologic reactivity.

Most drugs are capable of causing allergic reactions; the agents listed in Table 28–1 are among the most frequent offenders. Table 27–5 provides a more comprehensive listing of individual drugs by type of reaction. Topical application of drugs is associated with a higher risk of sensitization than is oral or parenteral administration, although reactions occur most frequently when medications are given parenterally.

Pathogenic Mechanisms

The process by which patients become immunologically sensitized to therapeutic agents is complex and for most drugs poorly understood. It generally is accepted that to be an effective immunogen, a drug must have a molecular weight greater than 4000 or, for polypeptides, have at least seven amino acids. Some large-molecular-weight therapeutic agents, such as antisera, vaccines, enzymes, and hormones, are potentially immunogenic, but most drugs are much smaller and to elicit an immune response must form large hapten-carrier complexes by binding to tissue proteins. These carrier proteins may be free in plasma, intracellular, or incorporated into cell-surface membranes. A high hapten density on the carrier proteins strengthens the immune response, which can be directed against the haptenated drug itself, a complex of hapten and protein, or a tissue protein conformationally changed by the binding of hapten. The binding of hapten to carrier proteins must be covalent rather than the reversible binding by which drugs usually are associated with plasma proteins. Allergy to β-lactam antibiotics may occur frequently because these drugs and the products of their spontaneous in vivo degradation readily can form covalent bonds with proteins. Most drugs do not bind well to proteins and initially must be enzymatically metabolized to reactive forms by processes such as oxidation. Reactive forms can lose their ability to bind proteins by undergoing further metabolism through processes such as acetylation and conjugation with glutathione. Risk factors for drug allergy in individual patients may include not only the ability to respond immunologically to hapten-carrier complexes, but also the balance of genetically variable, drug-metabolizing enzymes.

All categories of immunologic hypersensitivity, as classified by Gell and Coombs, have been implicated in drug allergy (Chapter 265); for many presumed allergic reactions, however, the mechanism is unknown. Most hypersensitivity reactions require multivalent antigens to cross-link antibody, such as IgE molecules bound to the high-affinity receptors on the surface of mast cells. Large-molecular-weight drugs may be inherently multivalent, and smaller drugs become

Table 28–1 • DRUGS FREQUENTLY CAUSING ALLERGIC AND PSEUDOALLERGIC REACTIONS

ANTIMICROBIALS
β-Lactams
Sulfonamides
Vancomycin
Nitrofurantoin
Antituberculous drugs
Quinolones

ANTICONVULSANTS
Phenytoin
Carbamazepine
Barbiturates

CARDIOVASCULAR AGENTS
Procainamide
Hydralazine
Quinidine
Methyldopa
ACE inhibitors
Heparin
Protamine

MACROMOLECULES
Heterologous antisera
Enzymes
Hormones

ANTI-INFLAMMATORY AGENTS
Aspirin
Other nonsteroidal anti-inflammatory drugs
Gold salts
Penicillamine

ANTINEOPLASTIC AGENTS
Azathioprine
Procarbazine
Asparaginase
Cisplatin
Doxorubicin

OTHER
Allopurinol
Radiographic contrast media
Opiates
Sulfasalazine
Neuromuscular blocking drugs
Antithyroid drugs
Phenothiazines

ACE = angiotensin-converting enzyme.

effectively multivalent by binding to tissue proteins. To cause a generalized anaphylactic reaction, small drugs must bind rapidly to protein. Rapid protein binding is not as important in eliciting a primary immune response, which might explain why some drugs that frequently evoke an antibody response are associated less commonly with clinical reactions. The specific organ location of some reactions may be due to hapten binding to particular tissue proteins or the production of reactive drug metabolites in specific locations, such as the liver.

Some drug reactions that clinically resemble an allergic response have been shown not to involve specific immune recognition. Such *pseudoallergic* reactions can result from direct histamine release from mast cells and basophils, complement activation, generation of inflammatory mediators from arachidonic acid metabolism, or activation of the contact coagulation system. Examples of pseudoallergic reactions include aspirin-induced asthma, anaphylactoid reactions to radiographic contrast media, and angioedema attributed to angiotensin-converting enzyme (ACE) inhibitors (see later).

Classification

Allergic drug reactions can be classified as generalized or organ specific (Table 28–2). Descriptions of these reactions can be found elsewhere in this text. Urticaria, eosinophilia, cutaneous exanthems, contact dermatitis, and drug fever are the most common clinical manifestations of drug allergy.

Table 28–2 • CLINICAL MANIFESTATIONS OF DRUG ALLERGY

GENERALIZED
Anaphylaxis
Serum sickness
Drug fever
Vasculitis
Drug-induced systemic lupus erythematosus

ORGAN SPECIFIC
Cutaneous
  Urticaria, angioedema, exanthems, hypersensitivity vasculitis, fixed
  eruptions, contact dermatitis, exfoliative dermatitis, erythema
  multiforme, toxic epidermal necrolysis, Stevens-Johnson syndrome
Renal
  Acute interstitial nephritis, glomerulonephritis
Pulmonary
  Asthma, acute infiltrates
Hematologic
  Hemolytic anemia, granulocytopenia, thrombocytopenia, eosinophilia
Hepatic
  Cholestatic hepatitis, hepatocellular damage

Diagnosis

The following criteria should be considered when diagnosing drug allergy:

1. Enough time has elapsed for an immune response. For the initial use of most drugs, sufficient time is at least 7 to 10 days. Reactions with a more rapid onset are considered pseudoallergic or depend on prior sensitization during previous administration of the drug or a cross-reacting agent.
2. The character of the reaction does not suggest a pharmacologic or toxic effect of the drug.
3. The reaction does not seem to be dose dependent and is not caused by drug interaction or abnormalities of absorption or elimination.
4. The reaction has characteristics that suggest a hypersensitivity response, such as skin rash, fever, and eosinophilia.
5. Clinical improvement occurs promptly after use of the suspect drug is discontinued. For most reactions, improvement is evident within 48 to 72 hours after stopping use of the drug.

Although it is not necessary that all these criteria be met, all should be considered when a patient is evaluated for possible drug allergy. The serum tryptase level, which may be elevated for 4 to 6 hours after a reaction, can help confirm the diagnosis of anaphylaxis.

Patients suspected of having drug allergy are often receiving multiple drugs, and identification of the agent responsible can be difficult. It sometimes is helpful to make a flow chart listing the starting dates and times of all medications, including drug therapy that has been discontinued recently. The likely allergen may be recognized by considering the above-mentioned criteria and the drug categories most commonly implicated in allergic reactions (see Table 28–1). An allergic reaction to drugs that have been given continuously for long periods is much less likely than a reaction to recently introduced therapy. If the offending drug cannot be identified confidently, it may be necessary to discontinue all nonessential therapy and substitute treatment with chemically unrelated drugs.

Specific tests to evaluate drug allergy include skin tests, measurement of serum antibody (IgE) levels, and challenge administration of suspect drugs. *Skin testing* to detect specific IgE involves pricking the skin or intradermal injection with dilute solutions of the drug in question. If the test solution contains antigen able to cross-link IgE molecules on cutaneous mast cells, histamine and other mediators of inflammation are released and produce a wheal-and-flare response. The significance of a skin response must be evaluated by comparison with control testing using histamine and diluent solutions. This testing method can be used only to predict or confirm drug reactions of the immediate hypersensitivity type, such as urticaria or systemic anaphylaxis. To obtain valid results, testing must be done with relevant antigens, which for most low-molecular-weight drugs are unknown metabolites. The lack of knowledge of the immunochemistry of most drugs severely limits the usefulness of skin testing. Negative tests are often uninterpretable, and false-positive reactions can result from non-specific skin irritation. Skin testing has proved useful for evaluating penicillin allergy in cases in which the relevant antigens are well known (see later) and for allergic reactions associated with anesthetic agents. Large-molecular-weight therapeutic agents, such as heterologous antisera, peptide hormones (e.g., insulin), and vaccines, are complete antigens that can be used appropriately for skin testing. Treatment with antihistamines must be discontinued before skin testing, and for safety, testing always should begin with the prick method. In vitro tests for drug-specific IgE, such as the radioallergosorbent test, also are limited by incomplete knowledge of drug immunochemistry. Skin tests are generally more sensitive than measurement of specific IgE and have the advantage of immediately available results.

Challenge administration of a suspect drug offers the possibility of specific diagnosis or exclusion of drug allergy. Challenges are inherently dangerous, however, and usually should be avoided, especially if possible anaphylaxis or other potentially life-threatening complications, such as exfoliative dermatitis, are of concern. When the drug in question is considered essential and the history is vague or suggests a mild reaction, challenge testing might be justified. Challenges should begin with a low dose considered unlikely to cause a reaction.

Rx Treatment

Discontinuing the use of the responsible drug is often the only treatment necessary. Some reactions may require supportive measures directed at relieving symptoms and reducing inflammation. Antihistamines, such as diphenhydramine, 25 to 50 mg every 4 to 6 hours, or hydroxyzine, 25 mg four times daily for adults, can relieve pruritus and may lessen the duration of some reactions. Corticosteroids should be reserved for the most severe or prolonged reactions. Treatment of anaphylaxis is discussed in Chapter 270.

In exceptional circumstances, it may be acceptable to continue drug treatment despite mild reactions, such as delayed-onset urticaria, exanthems, and fever. Patients who continue to take the drug should receive supportive measures and should be monitored closely; if the reaction increases in severity, the drug should be stopped.

Patients with a history of allergic reactions to multiple drugs, particularly antibiotics, present a difficult management problem. These reactions sometimes can be attributed to immunologic cross-reactivity, but often patients claim sensitivity to chemically dissimilar agents. In some cases, a careful history reveals that allergy has been confused with other types of adverse drug reactions, such as side effects or drug toxicity. Some patients who have experienced severe allergic reactions become fearful of all drug use and experience reactions attributable to anxiety. The possibility of true allergy to multiple, chemically dissimilar drugs also must be considered, however. A prospective study showed that patients with a history of allergic reactions to any antimicrobial agent were 10 times more likely to react to unrelated antimicrobial drugs than were history-negative controls. This finding suggests the existence of a group of patients predisposed to respond immunologically to drug haptens. Special care should be taken for patients with a history of multiple drug allergies, including administering the initial dose of any new drug in a physician's office or other supervised environment.

Another group of patients at risk for multiple drug sensitivities are individuals with human immunodeficiency virus (HIV) infection (Part XXIV). Patients with acquired immunodeficiency syndrome (AIDS) are reported to be at increased risk for reaction to multiple antimicrobial agents, including sulfonamides, amoxicillin, pentamidine, clindamycin-primaquine, foscarnet, zidovudine, carbamazepine, dapsone, quinolones, acyclovir, probenecid, thalidomide, and antituberculosis drugs. Most drug reactions in HIV-infected patients are manifested by delayed onset of maculopapular rash and fever rather than the early onset of urticaria or cardiorespiratory symptoms that characterizes type I hypersensitivity. The predisposition to drug reactions in HIV-infected patients may be due to immune dysregulation or changes in drug metabolism caused by the retroviral infection. The risk of drug reactions in HIV-infected patients can create difficult management problems. Successful rechallenge or desensitization of AIDS patients has been reported with trimethoprim-sulfamethoxazole, zidovudine, pentamidine, acyclovir, and dapsone. Although such procedures are inherently dangerous and have caused severe systemic reactions, the risk sometimes is justified for patients with opportunistic infections. Sensitivity to multiple antimicrobial agents also has been reported in patients with humoral immunodeficiency and in patients with systemic lupus erythematosus.

Prevention

The most effective preventive measures are taking a careful history of previous drug reactions and avoiding unnecessary drug use. The history should be adequate to allow classification of the type of reaction experienced, and physicians should educate patients to distinguish allergy from other types of adverse reactions (Chapter 27). Reactions attributable to drug toxicity or side effects do not preclude future use of the same or chemically similar agents.

Before prescribing any new drug, physicians should inquire again about past drug reactions. Skin tests can predict a type I hypersensitivity response to some drugs and should be done routinely before heterologous antisera is given. Patients should be kept under observation for 20 to 30 minutes after receiving parenteral medication.

When newly marketed drugs are used, physicians should be alert for unexpected complications, including allergic reactions. New drugs are not routinely evaluated for immunogenicity, and animal studies may not predict human hypersensitivity. Premarketing clinical trials seldom include adequate numbers of patients to detect problems of low incidence such as drug allergy.

When treatment is considered essential despite well-documented allergic hypersensitivity, the drug sometimes can be administered by following a desensitization protocol. Successful desensitization regimens have been published for β-lactam antibiotics (see later), trimethoprim-sulfamethoxazole, vancomycin, allopurinol, tetanus toxoid, acyclovir, sulfasalazine, insulin, aspirin, and heterologous antisera. These regimens start with a low drug dose, which is increased slowly as the patient is monitored closely. Reactions often occur during desensitization, and it is frequently necessary to reduce the dose to a previously tolerated level before proceeding. The mechanism of desensitization is uncertain but for some drugs may involve the gradual neutralization of IgE antibody with low drug doses. Desensitization is always a high-risk procedure that is undertaken only after obtaining informed consent from the patient or family and only by physicians who are prepared to treat severe reactions.

SPECIFIC DRUG ALLERGIES

β-LACTAM ANTIBIOTICS

β-Lactam antibiotics, including penicillins, carbapenems, cephalosporins, and monobactams, are the most common cause of drug-induced immediate hypersensitivity reactions. The immunochemistry of penicillin is the best studied of any drug. Most protein-bound penicillin is in the form of penicilloyl, which is designated the major determinant. Other products of penicillin degradation, including penicilloate and penilloate, and penicillin itself are designated the minor determinants, which indicates that these haptens are present in relatively small amounts. This terminology is confusing because most patients who have had immediate reactions to penicillin are found to have IgE antibody to minor determinants rather than to penicilloyl alone.

Most patients with a history of penicillin allergy have no reaction if given the drug. This observation can be attributed to inaccurate histories and the loss of sensitivity with time. The significance of a history of penicillin allergy can be clarified by skin testing. If skin testing is done with penicilloyl (Pre-Pen) and minor determinants, the test has about a 99% sensitivity for identifying patients at risk for immediate-type reactions. Although minor determinants other than penicillin itself are not commercially available, skin testing with just penicilloyl and penicillin identifies about 95% of patients at risk. Details of penicillin skin testing are given in Table 28-3.

Whenever possible, alternative antimicrobial agents should be chosen for patients with a history of penicillin allergy of any type. If use of a penicillin or another β-lactam agent is considered essential for patient care, however, the decision to use a β-lactam usually can be based on the patient's history and skin test results. If the prior

Table 28-3 • PENICILLIN SKIN TESTING

TESTING MATERIALS
Penicilloyl polylysine (Pre-Pen)
Penicillin G, 10,000 U/mL
Histamine, 1 mg/mL (positive control)
Diluent (negative control)

PROCEDURE
Testing usually is done on the volar surface of the forearm or lateral surface of the upper part of the arm. Begin the prick test by using a 26-gauge needle to prick through a drop of test material. If the prick test is negative, proceed with intradermal testing and raise a bleb by intradermal injection of 0.02 mL of test material. Read the test results at 15 min. For a patient with a history of a recent severe reaction to penicillin, begin testing with a 100-fold dilution of test antigens

INTERPRETATION
Skin tests can be interpreted only if the histamine control produces a wheal-and-flare response. A positive reaction includes a wheal of at least 4 mm accompanied by erythema. If the patient has dermatographism, manifested by a significant response to the diluent control, skin test results may not be interpretable. Questionable results should be repeated

reaction is recalled as a delayed appearance of a morbilliform rash, which is the most common manifestation of penicillin sensitivity, a β-lactam may be administered cautiously starting with a low dose. If the history is one of rapid-onset urticaria or anaphylaxis, skin testing can help determine the risk. Patients with a history of immediate-type hypersensitivity in the distant past and negative skin testing with penicillin and penicilloyl can be given a β-lactam agent starting with a low dose under a physician's observation. For patients with positive skin tests or a recent history of anaphylaxis with penicillin, a formal desensitization protocol should be used (Table 28-4). Oral desensitization may be safer and is preferred in most situations.

The reliability of skin testing with β-lactam antibiotics other than penicillin has not been established, and the degree of cross-reactivity among different classes of β-lactams varies. Published reports of patients with a history of penicillin allergy and positive penicillin skin tests who were given a cephalosporin antibiotic indicate a reaction risk of less than 10%, but many reported reactions have been severe. The carbapenem antibiotic imipenem has considerable cross-reactivity with penicillin, but the monobactam antibiotic aztreonam has no significant cross-reactivity and can be used safely in patients with penicillin allergy. Aztreonam and the third-generation cephalosporin ceftazidime have the same side chain on the β-lactam ring and may have significant clinical cross-reactivity.

INSULIN

The incidence of significant allergic reactions to insulin has declined with the availability of recombinant human insulin. Most patients suspected of insulin allergy are found to have idiopathic urticaria or sensitivity to other medications. True immediate-type hypersensitivity reactions to human insulin do occur, however; such reactions are particularly likely in patients whose insulin therapy has been interrupted by attempts at management with diet and oral hypoglycemic agents. Sensitive patients usually have rapid onset of local reactions at insulin injection sites, and the presence of specific IgE antibody can be confirmed by skin testing. Effective desensitization regimens are available; after desensitization, patients should receive insulin treatment continuously.

LOCAL ANESTHETICS

Immediate-type hypersensitivity to local anesthetics is rare. Most adverse reactions to these agents can be attributed to toxicity, anxiety, contact dermatitis, or coadministration of other drugs, such as epinephrine. True allergy to local anesthetics is perhaps more common with benzoic acid esters, such as procaine and benzocaine. When the history of past reactions is unclear or suggests immediate-type hypersensitivity, skin testing with dilute solutions of local anesthetics can be diagnostically useful. Skin testing usually is done with one of the amide local anesthetics, such as lidocaine and mepivacaine. If skin

Table 28–4 • β-LACTAM DESENSITIZATION

PENICILLIN ORAL DESENSITIZATION PROTOCOL*

Dose[†]	Penicillin V Elixir	Amount mL	Amount U	Cumulative Dose (U)
1	1000	0.1	100	100
2	1000	0.2	200	300
3	1000	0.4	400	700
4	1000	0.8	800	1500
5	1000	1.6	1600	3100
6	1000	3.2	3200	6300
7	1000	6.4	6400	12,700
8	10,000	1.2	12,000	24,700
9	10,000	2.4	24,000	48,700
10	10,000	4.8	48,000	96,700
11	80,000	1.0	80,000	176,700
12	80,000	2.0	160,000	336,700
13	80,000	4.0	320,000	656,700
14	80,000	8.0	640,000	1,296,700

β-LACTAM INTRAVENOUS DESENSITIZATION PROTOCOL[‡]

Dose No.	Concentration of Stock Solution[§] (mg/mL)	Concentration of Infused Solution (mg/mL)	Amount of Antibiotic Administered (mg)
1	0.0005	0.00001	0.0005
2	0.005	0.0001	0.005
3	0.05	0.001	0.05
4	0.5	0.01	0.5
5	5	0.1	5
6	50	1	50
7	500	10	500

*From Wendel GD Jr, Stark BJ, Jamison RB, et al: Penicillin allergy and desensitization in serious infections during pregnancy. N Engl J Med 1985;312:1229–1232.

[†]Patients should be observed for 15 minutes between doses and for 30 minutes after the last dose before parenteral drug administration.

[‡]From Borish L, Tamir R, Rosenwasser LJ: Intravenous desensitization to beta-lactam antibiotics. J Allergy Clin Immunol 1987;80:314–319.

[§]Stock solution is prepared by solubilizing the antibiotic with nonbacteriostatic saline to a final concentration of 500 mg/mL. Dilutions are prepared by adding 1 mL of each preceding dilution to 9 mL of diluent. One milliliter of stock solution is further diluted into 50 mL of saline and infused over 20 minutes.

tests are negative, incremental challenge doses of the anesthetic are usually well tolerated.

ANGIOTENSIN-CONVERTING ENZYME INHIBITORS

Angioedema of the face and oropharyngeal structures is an important complication of ACE inhibitor therapy. Patients with these reactions seem to be sensitive to alternative ACE inhibitors that have the same pharmacologic action but different chemical structures. Such a response suggests a pseudoallergic reaction not mediated by a specific immune response but possibly resulting from the drug's effect on kinin metabolism. The angioedema is characterized by nonpruritic swelling that is usually not accompanied by urticaria. Most reactions occur within the initial week of therapy, but reactions have been reported many years after the start of drug use. These reactions may be more common in women, blacks, and patients who have experienced idiopathic angioedema. Fatal episodes have been reported, and therapy with alternative ACE inhibitor drugs should not be attempted. The angioedema associated with these drugs is unrelated to ACE inhibitor–induced cough. Angiotensin receptor antagonists are usually well tolerated by patients who have experienced angioedema with ACE inhibitors, but there are case reports of patients who have reacted to both categories of drugs.

ASPIRIN AND OTHER NONSTEROIDAL ANTI-INFLAMMATORY DRUGS

Of asthmatic patients, 2 to 6% have a history of aspirin-induced symptoms, and challenge studies have shown airflow obstruction in 20% of unselected asthmatics. Asthmatic patients with chronic

rhinosinusitis and nasal polyps are at particularly high risk for aspirin sensitivity. Aspirin also can exacerbate symptoms in patients with chronic urticaria. Aspirin-sensitive patients with asthma or chronic urticaria also react to most other nonsteroidal anti-inflammatory drugs (NSAIDs). This cross-reactivity between drugs with chemically different structures but similar pharmacologic action suggests that these reactions are not immunologically mediated. Reactions in asthmatics may be related to inhibition of cyclooxygenase with concomitant enhancement of leukotriene synthesis or to hyperresponsiveness to leukotrienes, which are potent bronchoconstrictors. Desensitization regimens have been effective for patients with aspirin-induced bronchospasm and produce cross-desensitization to other NSAIDs. For the most sensitive asthmatic patients, aspirin and NSAIDs are easily avoided. Patients with asthma and chronic rhinosinusitis/polyposis probably should avoid these drugs regardless of past history of aspirin sensitivity. Patients who have experienced exacerbations of asthma or chronic urticaria with conventional NSAIDs often tolerate cyclooxygenase-2 antagonists such as rofecoxib,[1,2] but the initial challenge dose of these agents should be given under the direct supervision of a physician.

1. Stevenson D, Simon R: Lack of cross reactivity between rofecoxib and aspirin in aspirin-sensitive patients with asthma. J Allergy Clin Immunol 2001;108:47–51.
2. Sanchez-Borges M, Capriles-Hulett A, Caballero-Fonseca F, et al: Tolerability to new COX-2 inhibitors in NSAID sensitive patients with cutaneous reactions. Ann Allergy Asthma Immunol 2001;87:201–204.

SUGGESTED READINGS
Bernstein I, Gruchalla R, Lee R, et al: Disease management of drug hypersensitivity: A practice parameter. Ann Allergy Asthma Immunol 1999;83:665–700. *Authoritative guidelines.*
Gruchalla RS: Drug allergy. J Allergy Clin Immunol 2003;111(2 Suppl):S548–S559. *An updated review.*
Gruchalla RS: Drug metabolism, danger signals, and drug-induced hypersensitivity. J Allergy Clin Immunol 2001;108:475–488. *Review of basic mechanisms and suggestions for patient evaluation and management.*
Kelkar PS, Li JT: Cephalosporin allergy. N Engl J Med 2001;345:804–809. *A review of cephalosporin allergy with special attention to the use of cephalosporins when there is a history of penicillin allergy.*

29 PAIN

Mitchell B. Max

Pain is the main symptom for which patients seek relief and is often a key clue for diagnosis. Given this importance, it is paradoxical that, until recently, the study of pain and its treatment were of relatively marginal interest to medical science and limited to anesthesiology, neurology, and a few other specialties. Basic neuroscientists now are expanding the understanding of pain processing rapidly, making it possible for any interested clinician to translate these mechanistic insights into better diagnosis and treatment.

Pain Mechanisms and Their Implications for Practice

PAIN PATHWAYS AND MECHANISMS

TRANSMISSION. A conscious experience of pain generally requires signaling by two neurons in sequence (Fig. 29–1, *left panel*). The peripheral *nociceptor* has specialized tissue endings that transduce strong mechanical, thermal, or chemical stimuli into action potentials. This nerve fiber, which is nourished by a cell body in the dorsal root ganglion in the spinal canal, sends its central process into the dorsal horn of the spinal cord to synapse on a secondary neuron. The peripheral neuron releases excitatory neurotransmitters, such as glutamate and substance P, which cause the secondary neuron to discharge, sending impulses into its projections to the brain stem and thalamus. Projection of nociception to this level is sufficient to evoke pain experience and behavior, but additional processing by projections to the cerebral cortex contribute to the distinct sensory qualities, mood, and motor responses associated with the pain experience.

MODULATION. A comparison of a crying child with a minor scrape of the knee, a college football hero running full speed on a broken ankle, and a depressed adult with multiple pain complaints and

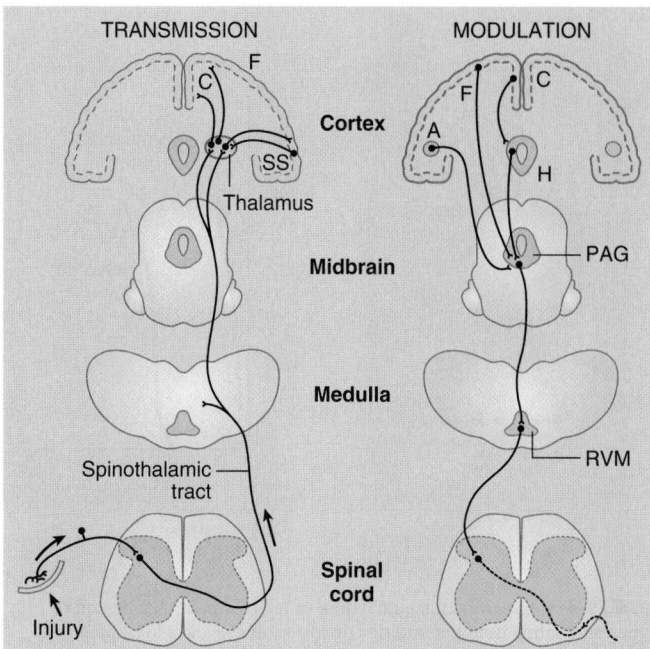

FIGURE 29–1 • Pain transmission and modulation pathways. *Left,* A noxious stimulus applied to the skin *(lower left)* elicits a train of impulses beginning in peripheral nociceptors and propagated to the dorsal horn of the spinal cord, where they activate the nerve cells of origin of the spinothalamic tract. The spinothalamic tract activates thalamic neurons, which project to and activate neurons in the cingulate cortex (C), frontal cortex (F), and somatosensory cortex (SS). *Right,* A variety of stimuli can activate pain modulation circuits. Frontal and cingulate cortex projections and afferents from the amygdala (A) and hypothalamus (H) converge on midbrain periaqueductal gray (PAG) neurons, which, through a relay in the rostral ventromedial medulla (RVM), control spinothalamic pain transmission neurons. (Redrawn from Fields HL: Pain modulation: Expectation, opioid analgesia and virtual pain. Progr Brain Res 2000;122:245–253. © 2000, with permission from Elsevier Science.)

negative evaluations makes it clear that there is not a one-to-one correspondence between a peripheral lesion and the experience of pain. Such reflections led to the hypothesis that higher brain centers could modulate incoming pain signals. Decades of animal studies have elucidated systems that descend to the spinal dorsal horn (Fig. 29–1, *right panel*) and either can inhibit or can amplify pain signals, depending on the importance of pain to the organism in that situation. Neurophysiologic studies in nonhuman primates whose state of attention is modified during painful stimulation suggest mechanisms by which a variety of clinical interventions, such as reassurance, cognitive-behavioral therapy, or placebo effects associated with drug treatments may not only change patients' interpretation of incoming pain messages, but also markedly decrease the number of pain impulses arising at the spinal dorsal horn projection neuron.

PLASTICITY OF PAIN-PROCESSING CIRCUITS. Injuries to peripheral tissues or nerve and the resulting painful input alter subsequent pain processing. In the uninjured state (Fig. 29–2), noxious and innocuous stimuli trigger modest numbers of impulses in nociceptors and A β mechanoreceptors. Only the noxious stimuli result in pain. After injury to any kind of tissue, release of inflammatory mediators, such as prostaglandins, cytokines, bradykinin, and protons, sensitizes nociceptors (Fig. 29–2) so that light touch can trigger impulses in these fibers, and noxious stimuli cause higher rates of firing than before. If nerve is injured, new sodium channels at sites of repair or regeneration give rise to spontaneous discharges, which can lead to steady or episodic pain in the absence of peripheral stimulation. In some cases, adrenoreceptors at the injury site trigger pain when activated by norepinephrine released by local sympathetic nerves or by circulating catecholamines (see Fig. 29–2). A barrage of painful impulses from either injured nerve or tissue can sensitize the central neuron (see Fig. 29–2) so that light touch signals carried by A β fibers can trigger a central discharge sufficient to generate pain.

Additional mechanisms have been described in animals to explain the development of pain with light touch. One day or more after tissue

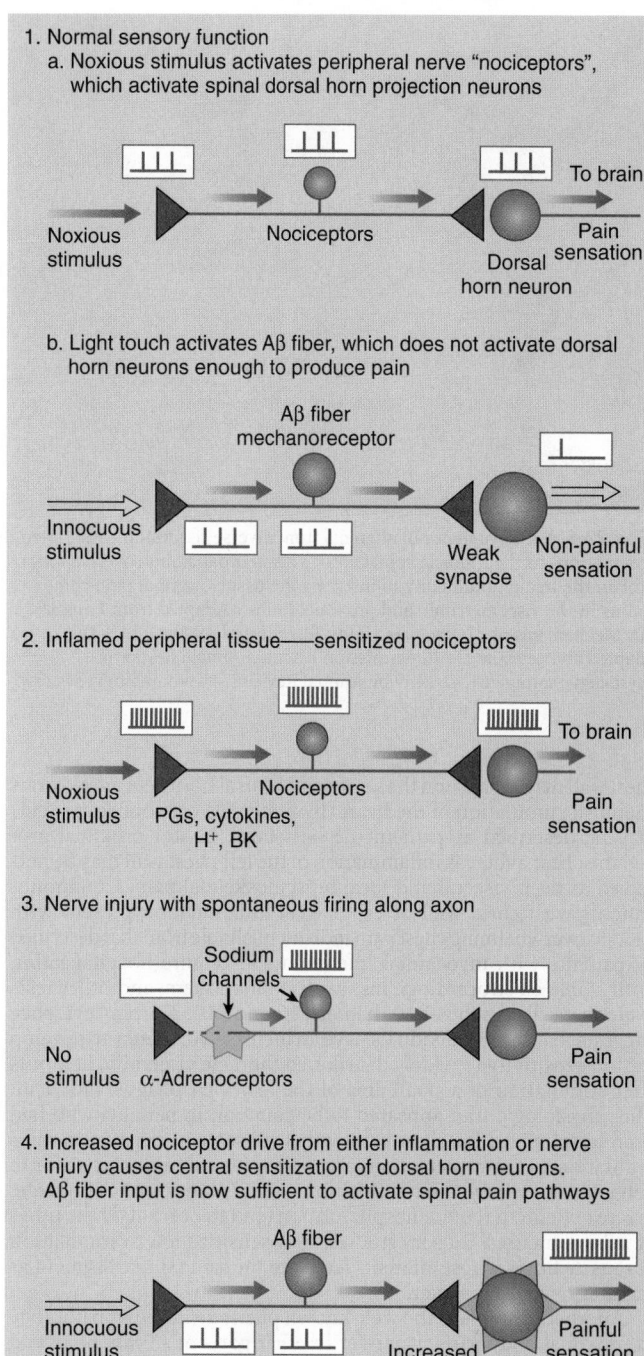

FIGURE 29–2 • Plasticity of pain-processing circuits. See text for explanation. PG = prostaglandins; BK = bradykinin. (Adapted from Woolf CJ, Mannion RJ: Neuropathic pain: Etiology, symptoms, mechanisms, and management. Lancet 1999;353:1959–1964.)

injury, A β mechanoreceptors may begin to make a neurotransmitter, substance P, that is otherwise confined to pain-signaling fibers and excites central pain projection neurons. After nerve injury, A β mechanoreceptors, which normally synapse in a deep layer of the spinal cord that processes light touch, may grow new sprouts that synapse on pain projection neurons in the superficial dorsal spinal cord.

IMPLICATIONS FOR DIAGNOSIS OF PAINFUL COMPLAINTS

PROXIMAL LIMBS, TRUNK, AND VISCERA HAVE HEAVILY OVERLAPPING INPUT ON A FEW SPINAL NEURONS. Patients' description of pain arising from many of these structures may be similar. Figure 29–3 shows that nociceptors from heart, esophagus, and deep tissues in the left shoulder and

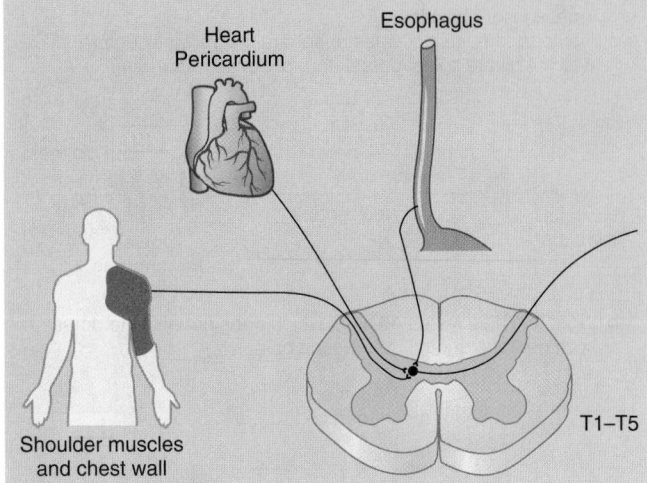

FIGURE 29-3 • Convergence of afferents from diverse tissues on pain projection neurons in the thoracic spinal cord. This neuroanatomic overlap may explain the frequent difficulty in inferring the tissue origin of pain complaints in the viscera, trunk, and proximal limbs. (Adapted from Foreman RD: Mechanisms of cardiac pain. Annu Rev Physiol 1999;61:143–167. Adapted and reprinted with permission from the *Annual Review of Physiology*, Volume 61. © 1999 by Annual Reviews www.annualreviews.org)

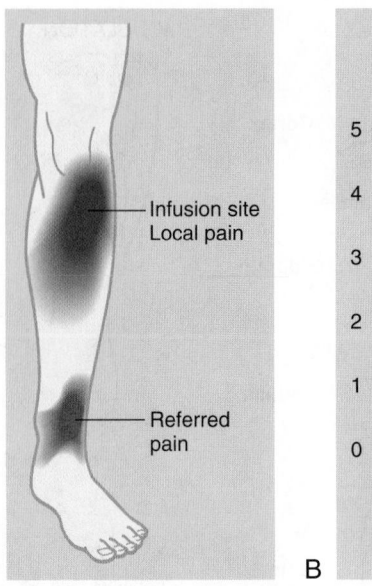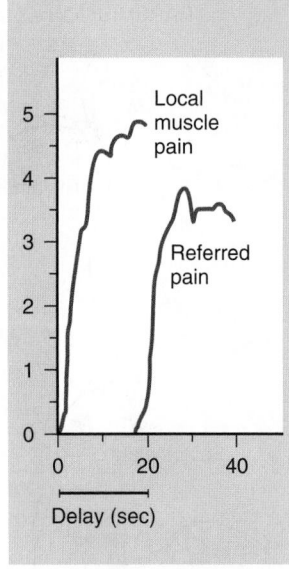

FIGURE 29-4 • Experimental elucidation of referred pain. *A,* Infusion of hypertonic saline in upper anterior tibialis muscle evokes local pain and pain referred to the ankle region. *B,* A 20-second delay in the appearance of the referred pain suggests an explanation other than simple convergence of afferents from upper and lower leg, which would cause immediate referral of pain. The investigators hypothesized that sensitization of the spinal neuron occurs over the first 20 seconds, eventually giving rise to a discharge pattern mimicking what would occur with distal muscle injury as well. (Reprinted from Graven-Nielsen T, Arendt-Nelson L, Svensson P, et al: Stimulus-response functions in areas with experimentally induced referred muscle pain—a psychophysical study. Brain Res 1997;744:121–128. © 1997, with permission from Elsevier Science.)

chest wall may synapse on the same spinal dorsal horn neuron. Noxious chemical stimulation of the heart (by ischemia) or esophagus (acid) may be described as pain in the left shoulder and proximal arm and the chest, whereas inflammation of the left chest wall may be perceived as deep visceral and local musculoskeletal pain. Commonly, patients with chest wall or esophageal inflammation present with sudden overwhelming chest pain indistinguishable from that described by patients with myocardial infarction and require hospitalization until stable electrocardiograms, cardiac biomarkers, and other tests exclude cardiac ischemia (Chapters 46 and 68). Current evidence suggests that some individuals have an increased tendency to develop central sensitivity to widely distributed thoracic visceral pain inputs after stimulation of a small area of the lower esophagus with acid. This physiologic trait appeared to be common in patients who had been hospitalized for chest pain with a subsequent negative cardiac evaluation. Similar interactions among noxious stimuli may occur in pelvic disease. In women with chronic renal stones, attacks of colic severe enough to require hospitalization tend to occur near the times of painful menses. Sensory studies show sensitization to stimulation of muscle fibers whose afferents feed into the same spinal segment as the uterine and renal pain.

Another example is the well-known phenomenon that pathology in proximal body parts may refer to other parts of a limb. Bone and soft tissue pathology in the spine often refers pain to the buttock or hip, and pathology in the hip often refers pain to the knee. Figure 29-4 illustrates the timing and location of pain after the experimental infusion of hypertonic saline into the upper anterior tibialis muscle of normal volunteers. Local pain is described near the upper tibial injection site, but pain also is referred to an area just above the ankle (Fig. 29-4A). The local muscle pain begins immediately (Fig. 29-4B), whereas the referred pain is not reported for another 20 seconds. This sequence argues against the simple "converging input" model of referred pain illustrated in Figure 29-3. With the former model, one would expect the referred pain to be felt as soon as the local pain begins. The delay suggests that an additional process intervenes (e.g., that it takes 20 seconds for the pain input from the saline infusion to sensitize central neurons, after which they can be activated by low-level innocuous input from the ankle area).

IMPLICATIONS FOR PAIN TREATMENT

Most of the important knowledge about the range of effectiveness of new analgesics can be gained only after drugs are approved for use. Studies usually used in development are limited to a few types of pain—most commonly postoperative pain and osteoarthritis—yet different types of clinical pain may have different mechanisms.

Randomized trials of substance P receptor antagonists in postoperative pain showed little or no benefit, but most of these studies occurred immediately after tissue injury, whereas new neurons are known to express substance P a day or more after injury. When substance P antagonists reach the market for nonpain indications, alert clinicians try them in a range of chronic pain conditions and may discover a new analgesic niche. Such anecdotal reports led to the formal evaluation of the anticonvulsant gabapentin, which became a first-line treatment for nerve injury pain.

The pain mechanisms outlined in Figures 29-1 to 29-4 also may assist the choice of treatment. Because a brief barrage of pain impulses may cause central sensitization that persists for several days, long-acting suppression of peripheral discharge by means of sustained release or slowly metabolized anti-inflammatory drugs may be desirable. Combination treatments may work at different sites of the pain pathways. Anti-inflammatory drugs and local anesthetics predominantly block peripheral sensitization, whereas opioids have their strongest effects at the central spinal synapse (although opioids and nonsteroidal anti-inflammatory drugs [NSAIDs] have peripheral and central effects). Gabapentin reduces central sensitization. The blockade of norepinephrine and serotonin reuptake at spinal synapses by tricyclic antidepressants (TCAs) and tramadol enhances descending pain-inhibiting systems.

Approach to the Patient with Pain

Table 29-1 lists some of the principles of assessing and treating the patient with pain.

Believe the patient's complaint of pain. Despite decades of effort, there is no neurophysiologic or chemical test that can measure pain in individual patients. The most promising technique, functional brain imaging, so far shows only rough correlation with reports of acute pain and has been disappointing for chronic pain. Objective observations of grimacing, limping, and tachycardia may be useful in assessing the patient, but these signs are often absent in patients with chronic pain caused by large structural lesions. The clinician can acknowledge the patient's report of pain before understanding its cause. Acceptance of the patient's reality of pain does not

Table 29–1 • CLINICAL ASSESSMENT OF PAIN

1. Believe the patient's complaint of pain
2. Take a careful history of the pain
3. Assess the characteristics of each pain, including site, referral pattern, and aggravating and relieving factors
4. Clarify the temporal aspects of the pain: acute, subacute, chronic, episodic, intermittent, breakthrough, or incident
5. List and prioritize each pain complaint
6. Evaluate the response to previous and current analgesic therapies
7. Assess the patient's current level of functioning in work and family life, including what are his or her priorities for increasing function
8. Record the severity of pain and functional impairment with a scale simple enough for repeated use
9. Evaluate the psychological state of the patient, asking specifically about suicidal thoughts
10. Ask if the patient has a past history of alcohol or drug dependence
11. Perform a careful medical and neurologic examination
12. Develop a series of diagnosis-related hypotheses
13. Order and personally review the appropriate diagnostic procedures
14. In patients with multiple chronic symptoms that are unexplained despite a full diagnostic evaluation, consider the possibility of multisomatoform disorder
15. Design the diagnostic and therapeutic approach to suit the individual
16. Provide continuity of care from evaluation to treatment to optimize adherence to treatment and to reduce anxiety
17. Reassess the patient's response to pain therapy
18. In patients with advanced illness, discuss advance directives for managing pain and other symptoms

Adapted from Foley KM: Pain. In Goldman L, Bennett C (eds): Cecil Textbook of Medicine, 21st ed. Philadelphia, WB Saunders, 2000, p 104.

obligate the physician to provide strong opioids or other particular types of treatments.

Clarify the temporal aspects of the pain. The circumstances and speed of onset of the pain not only are pertinent to diagnosis, but also guide the choice of treatment methods whose onset and duration of effect should correspond to the true cause of pain.

Evaluate the response to previous and current analgesic therapies. The dose and duration of each previous treatment should be recorded. Optimal doses of the best medication for a particular syndrome often produce gratifying results in patients who failed a brief trial with lower doses.

Record the severity of pain and functional impairment with a measure simple enough for repeated use. Extensive work in many diseases has shown that changes in a 0-to-10 scale for pain intensity are valid and sensitive for detecting meaningful relief. Pain-related functional limitations can be assessed either by using the patient's choice of important activities or by asking the patient how much, on a 0-to-10 scale, pain has interfered with domains such as general activity, mood, walking, work, relations with other people, sleep, and enjoyment of life.

Evaluate the psychological state of the patient. Unrecognized depression and anxiety disorders are common in patients with chronic pain. Patients readily tell the clinician about these if asked, and these mood disorders are readily treatable. The presence of suicidal thoughts and the pain's effect on the patient's sexual activities should be assessed. It is often helpful to ask patients how they are coping in the face of the pain or what keeps them from giving up because these responses identify sources of strength on which the clinician can build.

Develop a series of diagnosis-based hypotheses. Because pain may result from disease at the pain site or be referred from other parts of the body, it may be helpful to list all the possibilities for the site of origin, particularly when the pain has been resistant to therapy. Persistent rib pain in a patient with metastatic cancer despite radiation therapy to the lesion in that rib would raise the possibility of referred pain from thoracic epidural tumor, which can be imaged and treated. For each potential site of the lesion, the list of the common disease processes in that area can be considered.

Personally review the diagnostic procedures. In the re-evaluation of difficult pain diagnoses, it is remarkable how often lesions had been missed previously on imaging procedures, particularly when the radiologist was not given a specific diagnostic hypothesis.

In patients with multiple chronic symptoms that are unexplained despite a full diagnostic evaluation, consider the possibility of multisomatoform disorder. This more recently proposed diagnosis, which applies to one tenth of primary care visits, is defined by the presence of three bothersome and unexplained complaints, some of which have troubled the patient on most days in the previous 2 years. Depending on the presenting complaint or the clinician's specialty, many of these patients are said to have fibromyalgia, chronic fatigue, irritable bowel syndrome, idiopathic low back pain, or chronic tension-type headaches, but most of these patients have multisystem complaints. Laboratory studies suggest that generalized amplification of symptoms by the central nervous system is common in these patients. Recognition of multisomatoform disorder alerts the clinician to look closely for depressive or panic disorders, whose prevalence is high in these patients; to treat with antidepressants or cognitive behavioral treatment, shown to reduce symptoms; and to limit elaborate diagnostic testing or potentially hazardous medical treatments.

Reassess the patient's response to pain therapy. The principles of analgesic treatment are simple, but dose requirements and adverse effects vary widely. The key to successful treatment is often a daily phone call until the patient's treatment has been optimized.

Rx Treatment of Pain

Mastery of the principles of analgesic drug prescribing yields gratifying results (Figure 29–5). Three key classes of analgesic drugs are traditional *nonopioid analgesics*, including acetaminophen, NSAIDs, and selective cyclooxygenase-2 (COX-2) inhibitors; *opioid analgesics*; and *miscellaneous analgesics*, including some antidepressant and anticonvulsant drugs.

NONOPIOID ANALGESICS

The chief advantage of nonopioid analgesics is that they do not cause sedation or other central nervous system side effects. Unless the patient has contraindications to these drugs or has been shown not to respond to several of them, any analgesic regimen should include a nonopioid drug even if pain is severe enough to require the addition of an opioid. *Acetaminophen* optimally is prescribed in doses approaching 4000 mg/day. Higher doses, or standard doses in patients who are fasting or who drink alcohol heavily, may cause hepatic necrosis. Acetaminophen lacks the antiplatelet or gastric erosive effects of the NSAIDs. NSAIDs and COX-2 inhibitors often provide better analgesia than acetaminophen (Chapter 32).

OPIOID ANALGESICS

The μ receptor opioid agonists include morphine, codeine, oxycodone, hydrocodone, fentanyl, hydromorphone, methadone, and meperidine. More than a century of research has failed to reveal significant differences in the relative ratios of analgesia to side effects offered by different members of this class, although clinical anecdote suggests that individual patients may respond to one drug better than the other. The one exception is meperidine, which has a toxic metabolite that accumulates after several days of treatment and causes myoclonus anxiety and, with higher doses, confusion and seizures. The key differences among the available opioids are in speed of onset and duration of action.

Tramadol is an opioid-like drug that has weak opioid analgesic properties and opioid-like side effects of sedation and nausea, but it is less constipating and has less risk of abuse than the μ receptor agonists. Tramadol should be avoided in patients with epilepsy because it rarely can trigger seizures. Opioid agonist-antagonists include butorphanol, nalbuphine, and pentazocine. These drugs produce analgesia by binding to κ opioid receptors but antagonize the action of μ receptor agonists. The κ stimulatory actions of these drugs may cause psychotomimetic reactions, and their blockade of the μ receptor may cause withdrawal symptoms in patients already on strong μ agonists. Apart from a possibly reduced risk of respiratory depression and fewer regulatory controls, there is no convincing evidence that agonist-antagonists offer any advantage over the μ agonists. Buprenorphine, a partial agonist at the μ receptor, does not cause psychotomimetic reactions, but there are few studies directly comparing it with full μ agonists.

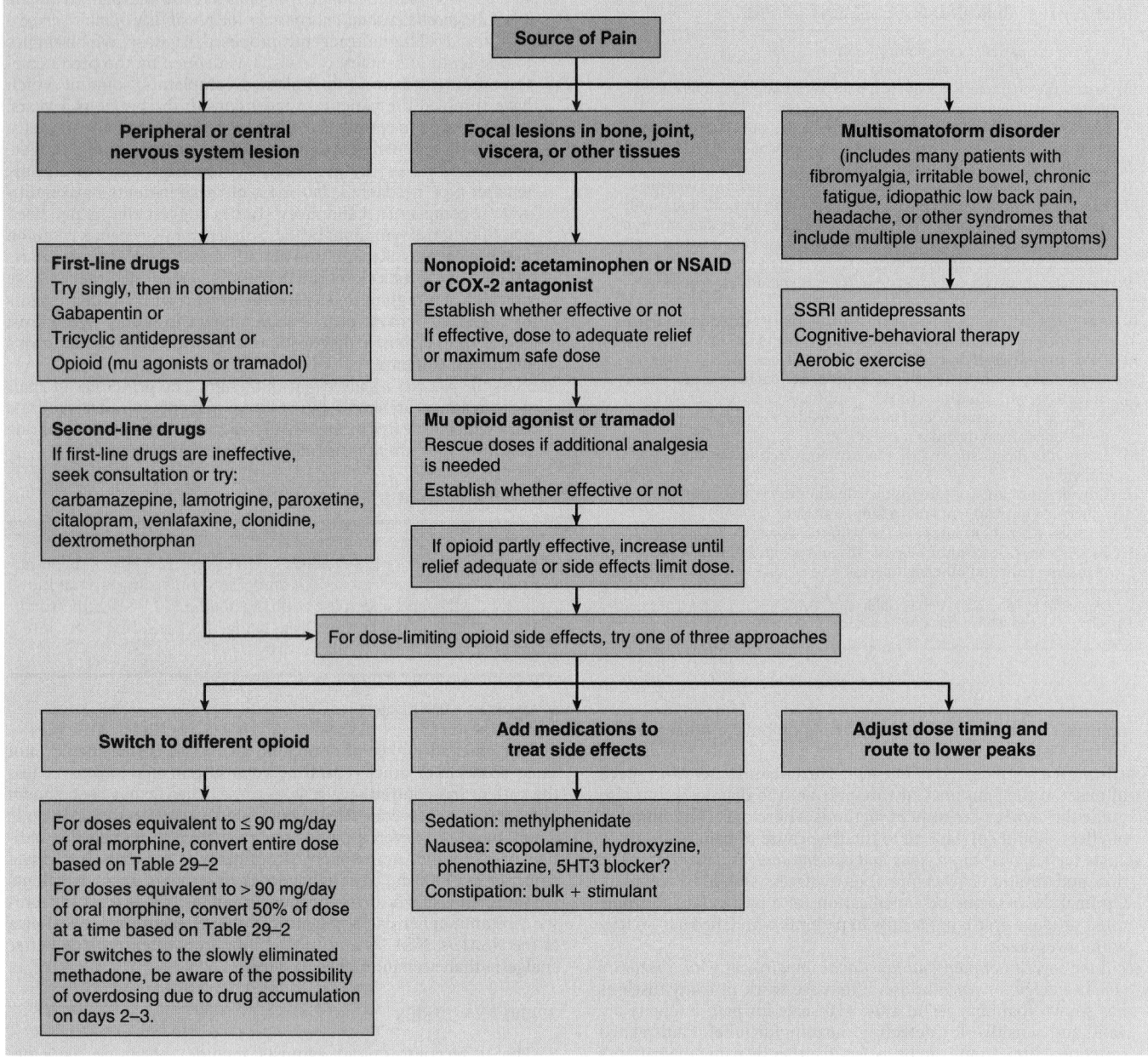

FIGURE 29-5 • Algorithm for the treatment of pain. NSAID = nonsteroidal anti-inflammatory drug; COX = cyclooxygenese; SSRI = selective serotonin reuptake inhibitor.

Opioid-naive patients with acute pain are far more susceptible to respiratory depression than patients on long-term opioid treatment, and they must be monitored more closely. Table 29–2 and the following principles should guide the tailoring of a regimen to the needs of an individual patient:

1. **Individualize the route, dosage, and schedule.**
   a. *Routes of administration*
      (1) *Oral (PO).* The oral route usually is preferred because of its convenience. For patients who cannot swallow tablets, many opioids are available in suspensions. Peak drug effects occur 1.5 to 2 hours after oral administration. Patients may take a second dose safely 2 hours after the first dose if side effects are mild. The need to wait this long can be a drawback, however, in treating rapidly fluctuating pain.
      (2) *Intramuscular* use, although still common, is discouraged because of painful administration, wide fluctuations in absorption from muscle, a 30- to 60-minute lag to peak effect, and rapid falloff of action compared with oral administration.

(3) *Intravenous (IV) bolus.* IV bolus administration provides the most rapid onset of effect and clarity of titration. Time to peak effect varies with drug lipid solubility, ranging from 1 to 5 minutes for fentanyl to 15 to 30 minutes for morphine. Although morphine is the traditional treatment for the pain of myocardial infarction and other acute syndromes, its slow penetration into the brain may delay the onset of pain relief and predispose toward relative overdosage 1 to 2 hours later. For initial dosing in acute pain, many experts use one half the doses listed in the second column of Table 29–2. Duration is shorter than after intramuscular administration. If severe pain persists but side effects are minimal at the time of expected peak effect, another bolus may be given. Opioids with long elimination half-lives, such as methadone or levorphanol, are not recommended for rapid opioid titration because drug levels remain elevated for many hours if too high a dose is given.

(4) *IV infusion.* Continuous IV infusions provide steady blood levels, which should provide the most effective analgesia with the fewest side effects. Subcutaneous infusion is an alternative to IV infusion and produces equivalent blood

Table 29–2 • OPIOID ANALGESICS COMMONLY USED FOR SEVERE PAIN

NAME	EQUIANALGESIC DOSE (mg)		COMMENTS	PRECAUTIONS AND CONTRAINDICATIONS
	ORAL	PARENTERAL*		
MORPHINE-LIKE AGONISTS				
Morphine	30	10	Standard of comparison for opioid analgesics. Sustained-release preparations (MS Contin, Oramorph SR, or generic morphine sulfate ER) release drug over 8–12 hr. Recent addition of once-a-day sustained-release formulation (Kadian)†	For all opioids, caution in patients with impaired ventilation, bronchial asthma, increased intracranial pressure, liver failure
Hydromorphone (Dilaudid)	7.5	1.5	Slightly shorter duration than morphine	
Oxycodone	20	—	Sustained-release 8–12 hr preparation (OxyContin)	
Methadone (Dolophine)	20 acute 2–4 long-term	10 acute 2–4 long-term	Good oral potency, long plasma half-life (24–36 hr)	Accumulates with repeated dosing, requiring decreases in dose size and frequency, especially on days 2–5
Levorphanol (Levo-Dromoran)	4 acute 1 long-term	2 acute 1 long-term	Long plasma half-life (12–16 hr)	Accumulates on days 2–3
Fentanyl	—	0.1	Transdermal fentanyl (Duragesic), 25 µg/hr, roughly equivalent to sustained-release morphine, 45 mg/day. Oral transmucosal fentanyl citrate now available for treatment of breakthrough pain in chronic cancer pain patients already taking around-the-clock opioids	Because of skin reservoir of drug, 12-hr delay in onset and offset of transdermal patch; fever increases dose rate
Oxymorphone (Numorphan)	—	1	5 mg rectal suppository = 5 mg morphine IM	Same as IM morphine
Meperidine (Demerol)	300	75	Slightly shorter acting than morphine	Normeperidine (toxic metabolite) accumulates with repetitive dosing, causing central nervous system excitation; avoid in children and in all patients who have impaired renal function or who are receiving monoamine oxidase inhibitors‡
MIXED AGONIST-ANTAGONISTS				
Nalbuphine (Nubain)	—	10	Not available orally, not scheduled under Controlled Substances Act	Incidence of psychotomimetic effects lower than with pentazocine; may precipitate withdrawal in narcotic-dependent patients
Butorphanol (Stadol)	—	2	Same as nalbuphine	Same as nalbuphine
PARTIAL AGONISTS				
Buprenorphine (Buprenex)	—	0.4	Sublingual preparation (0.6 mg) now available in United States to treat addiction; lower abuse liability than morphine; does not produce psychotomimetic effects	May precipitate withdrawal in narcotic-dependent patients; not readily reversed by naloxone; avoid in labor

*These are standard intramuscular (IM) doses for acute pain in adults and can be used to convert doses for intravenous (IV) infusions and repeated small IV boluses. For single IV boluses, use half the IM dose. For total 24-hour dose, IV and IM doses are similar.

†Once-a-day formulation (Kadian) available as 20-, 50-, or 100-mg capsules. Sustained-release formulation not destroyed by breaking capsule and sprinkling over food, such as applesauce.

‡Irritating to tissues with repeated IM injection.

Adapted from Max MB, Payne R, Edwards WT, et al: Principles of Analgesic Use in the Treatment of Acute Pain and Cancer Pain, 4th ed. Glenview, IL, American Pain Society, 1999.

levels at steady state. Subcutaneous boluses have slower onset and offset, however, and a lower peak effect than IV boluses.

(5) *IV, patient-controlled analgesia.* A popular and effective method for treating severe acute pain is to titrate the patient to temporary comfort with IV boluses, then start a patient-controlled analgesia machine. Usual patient-triggered bolus doses of morphine are 0.5 to 2 mg every 5 to 10 minutes.

(6) *Transdermal.* Fentanyl is available in a transdermal drug delivery system, providing a steady opioid infusion without pumps or needles. Several clinical trials suggest that

constipation is reduced by using the transdermal route, which avoids the local slowing effects of opioids in the gut. There is a 12- to 24-hour lag to analgesia after initial application of the patch as opioid is transferred to subcutaneous fat and a 24-hour offset after the patch is removed. Fever of greater than 39°F or a local heating pad accelerates absorption and may cause overdose.

(7) *Oral transmucosal.* Oral transmucosal fentanyl citrate is absorbed rapidly through the oral mucosa, giving this route a rapidity of onset comparable to IV morphine.

(8) *Rectal suppositories.* Suppositories of hydromorphone, oxymorphone, and morphine are available and well

Clinical Pharmacology

absorbed but are used rarely in the United States because of patients' preferences.

b. *The optimal analgesic dose varies widely among patients.* Studies have shown enormous variability in opioid doses required for pain relief, even among opioid-naive patients with identical surgical lesions. Regimens and orders should include provisions for supplementary doses or decreases in dose if needed.

c. *Each analgesic should be given an adequate trial by increasing the dose with the onset of side effects before switching to another drug.*

2. **Administer analgesic around-the-clock if pain is present most of the day.** Clinicians often begin opioid therapy with preparations that combine acetaminophen or an NSAID with small doses of codeine, hydrocodone, or oxycodone. Data from single-dose postoperative pain studies suggest that the following doses have similar effects: codeine, 60 mg; hydrocodone, 10 mg; oxycodone, 7 mg; tramadol, 50 mg; and dextropropoxyphene, 100 mg. Patients should be cautioned not to surpass the safe dosing limits for the nonopioid, particularly the 4000 mg/day total acetaminophen dose. In pain too severe to respond to these moderate opioid doses, treatment may be started with an immediate-release preparation of one of the opioids in Table 29–2.

When the optimal dose requirements for a 24-hour period have been established by titrating with a short-acting opioid preparation, the analgesics can be administered on a scheduled around-the-clock basis with better pain relief and fewer side effects. An as-needed order for a supplementary opioid dose between regular doses is an essential backup.

Special mention must be made of methadone, whose low cost and long duration make it the opioid of choice in health settings where sustained-release opioids are not affordable. Methadone's elimination half-life of 24 hours or more poses the risk of drug accumulation and overdose on days 2 to 4 of treatment if a fixed dosing schedule is maintained. A reasonable approach is to prescribe doses of methadone as needed for the first 3 to 7 days. By that time, most patients are approaching steady-state levels. An around-the-clock regimen, based on the duration of action reported by the patient, is then established. The interdose interval may vary from 4 to 12 hours.

3. **When changing to a new opioid or a different route, first use the equianalgesic doses in Table 29–2 to estimate the new dose, then modify the estimate based on the clinical situation and the specific drugs.** Changing from one opioid to another in patients already on moderate-to-large doses can be challenging. Estimates must take into account the wide interindividual variability, any differences in the time course of absorption and metabolism, the expected course of the pain condition, and the possibility of incomplete cross-tolerance between opioids. For this reason, the general recommendation (see Fig. 29–5) is to convert only half of the dose of the old opioid to the new opioid at one time, in case the estimate in Table 29–2 is too high or too low for that patient.

4. **Anticipate and treat opioid side effects.** Sedation, constipation, nausea, itching, and respiratory depression are the most common side effects, and they may be treated by changing the dosing regimen to provide lower or more steady blood concentrations, by switching to a different opioid, or by adding a treatment that counteracts the adverse effect. Sedation may be counteracted partly by adding a stimulant such as caffeine, dextroamphetamine, (2.5 to 10 mg PO) or methylphenidate (5 to 10 mg PO). To prevent constipation, patients should be given stool softeners and agents to increase bowel motility. A useful regimen includes dioctyl sodium sulfosuccinate, 100 to 300 mg/day, combined with senna, 2 to 6 tablets twice a day; laxative suppositories; or lactulose. Opioid-related nausea and vomiting often abate after the first few days of treatment but may be treated with transdermal scopolamine, hydroxyzine, or a phenothiazine antiemetic.

Although respiratory depression is rare in patients on long-term opioid treatment, even when doses are increased, it is a risk in the treatment of opioid-naive patients who require high opioid doses for severe pain. When pain is relieved, the patient may fall asleep, which considerably augments the opioid depressant effect and predisposes to closure of the airway by the tongue. In such situations, patients should be stimulated to keep them awake. If an opioid antagonist is required to reverse respiratory depression or coma in a patient on long-term opioids, the physician must be

Table 29–3 • GUIDELINES FOR USING CONTROLLED SUBSTANCES FOR THE TREATMENT OF CHRONIC NONMALIGNANT PAIN*

1. Conduct and record a complete history and physical examination, including nature and intensity of pain, current and past pain treatments, effect of pain on physical and psychological function, and whether there is a history of substance abuse. Document one or more recognized medical indications for use of a controlled substance

2. Record objectives that will determine treatment success, such as pain relief and improved physical and psychosocial function, and indicate if further diagnostic evaluations or treatments are planned

3. Discuss the risks and benefits of the prescribing of controlled substances with the patient or persons designated by the patient. The patient should receive prescriptions from one physician and one pharmacy whenever possible. If the patient is assessed to be at high risk for medication abuse, consider a written agreement outlining the patient's responsibilities, including urine/blood level screening when requested, the number and frequency of prescription refills, and circumstances, such as violation of the agreement, in which drug therapy may be stopped

4. Review the course of treatment and reconsider the cause of the pain at reasonable intervals depending on the individual patient. If treatment goals are not being met despite medication adjustments, reconsider the appropriateness of the treatment. Monitor the patient's compliance with medication and other treatment plans

5. Make referrals as indicated for additional evaluation or treatment. Consider consultation with a psychiatrist or substance abuse expert for patients with a history of substance abuse or a comorbid psychiatric disorder

6. Keep records current and accessible, and document through the course of treatment how points 1–5 have been addressed

7. Comply with state and federal controlled substance regulations

*Abridged from Federation of State Medical Boards, 1998. The unabridged version of these guidelines and a wealth of other information about state and U.S. Federal opioid regulatory policies are available at the website of the University of Wisconsin Pain and Policy Group, http://www.medsch.wisc.edu/painpolicy/.

aware that these patients are exquisitely sensitive to antagonists. Experts often start with small doses of naloxone (e.g., one twentieth of a 0.4-mg ampule IV every 2 minutes).

5. **Carefully consider the risk-benefit balance and treatment alternatives before starting long-term opioid treatment for nonmalignant pain.** Large case series suggest that many patients with chronic malignant pain benefit from long-term opioid treatment. Patients often develop tolerance to opioid side effects (except constipation) without losing analgesia. In typical series of patients followed by pain specialists for 10 years or more, behaviors raising concerns about abuse have arisen in only 5 to 10% of patients—most commonly unauthorized dose increases—and usually responded to renegotiation of treatment between clinician and patient. Compared with most other drug classes, opioids are remarkably free of major organ toxicity, with the possible exception of decreased gonadotropic function, which may require estrogen or testosterone replacement (Chapter 30). Surgical pain specialists have reported that the use of opioids has reduced the need for surgical procedures in some chronic pain conditions. Many medical specialty societies and Federal and state drug regulators have emphasized that the long-term prescription of opioids in nonmalignant pain is a legitimate medical option.

There are no controlled trials of opioid therapy in nonmalignant pain beyond 2 months, and the increase in prescribing for nonmalignant pain may create new problems, including opioid abuse and diversion. Table 29–3 summarizes guidelines for appropriate prescribing that have been adopted by the Federation of State Medical Boards of the United States.

Medication therapy alone rarely provides complete relief of pain. Most pain clinicians agree that the best results may be obtained from combinations of analgesic treatments with psychological and physical approaches to rehabilitation.

MISCELLANEOUS ANALGESICS

FIRST-LINE DRUGS FOR PAIN FROM NERVE LESIONS. Systematic reviews have suggested that three classes of medication have similar effectiveness in 1- to 2-month clinical trials in a variety of neuropathic pain syndromes: opioids (µ agonists and tramadol), TCAs, and gabapentin. Each of these approaches provides clinically significant relief, defined as a 50% reduction in pain beyond that seen with placebo treatment, for one in every two or three patients.■ For refractory pain, higher doses of oral opioids provide incremental benefit.■ Of the TCAs, nortriptyline and imipramine probably have the best efficacy-to-side effect ratio. Amitriptyline is equally effective but sedating, and it should be reserved for bedtime dosing in patients with poor sleep. Desipramine may be less effective but has the least sedation. Specific serotonin reuptake inhibitors seem less effective than the first-generation TCAs. For treating pain, TCAs should be initiated at low dosages (10 to 25 mg in a single dose at bedtime) and increased weekly by the same amount as tolerated. Limited dose-response information suggests that an average dose of 125 to 150 mg/day is optimal, but because of interindividual variability in the cytochrome P450 2D6 isoenzymes that metabolize TCAs, some patients need much lower or higher doses. Side effects include sedation; postural hypotension; weight gain; and anticholinergic effects, such as dry mouth, constipation, and urinary hesitancy. Because TCAs have a quinidine-like proarrhythmic effect in the presence of cardiac ischemia, they are contraindicated in patients with suspected coronary disease.

Gabapentin has similar efficacy to TCAs and opioids in neuropathic pain, but it is safer than TCAs because it has no cardiovascular effects or drug interactions. Treatment is started at 100 to 300 mg in a single dose at bedtime, then three times daily, and then titrated to 1800 to 3600 mg/day, which are the doses shown to be effective in randomized trials. Side effects include somnolence, dizziness, and peripheral edema. Dosage must be reduced in patients with renal impairment.

SECOND-LINE DRUGS FOR PAIN FROM NERVE LESIONS. Second-line drugs include lamotrigine (which must used with caution because of the uncommon complication of Stevens-Johnson syndrome), carbamazepine, selective serotonin reuptake blockers and venlafaxine, epidural or systemic clonidine, and high-dose dextromethorphan.

SECOND-LINE DRUGS FOR CANCER PAIN. High-dose steroids temporarily shrink many tumors and may be helpful in intractable pain secondary to malignant infiltration of nerves or the spinal cord. Rapid withdrawal of steroids may exacerbate pain. Pamidronate and other bisphosphonates and strontium 89 reduce pain caused by bony metastases.

PHYSICAL THERAPY

Restoration of physical function is crucial in treating patients with pain. When pain limits physical activities, nerve blocks or coverage with extra analgesic doses may be especially valuable. Injecting painful soft tissue "trigger points" with local anesthetic or saline may be helpful, although controlled studies are scarce.

COGNITIVE AND BEHAVIORAL THERAPIES

Cognitive-behavioral interventions (including training in coping skills and modification of thoughts, feelings, and behaviors) can increase function and reduce distress caused by pain. Some patients may be able to use relaxation techniques, biofeedback, meditation, imagery, or self-hypnosis to reduce muscular tension and emotional arousal or to enhance pain tolerance (Chapter 34). Experienced clinicians sometimes work with family members to encourage the patient to increase function, overriding the natural inclination to relieve the loved one of pain-provoking activities.

NERVE BLOCKS, SPINAL INFUSIONS, AND NEUROSURGICAL INTERVENTIONS

Anesthetic and neurosurgical procedures are occasionally helpful in intractable pain (Chapter 427). Nerve blocks are limited because motor, light touch, and position sense fibers accompany pain fibers in most nerves. Local anesthetics and permanent neurolytic treatments with alcohol or phenol usually cause unacceptable motor loss along with pain blockade. Temporary nerve blocks sometimes provide a window for physical therapy, however, which itself may give sustained relief. Selective blockade of sympathetic nerves may be helpful in pain conditions such as reflex sympathetic dystrophy or complex regional pain syndrome types I and II (Chapter 427). Injection of the celiac plexus may provide selective analgesia of the pancreas and

transverse colon by interrupting the afferent fibers that run through the ganglion.

Epidural or intrathecal infusion of opioids and/or local anesthetics may relieve pain below the midthorax with fewer cerebrally mediated side effects than systemic opioids. Electrical spinal cord stimulators, which may activate endogenous pain modulating systems, can be implanted as an outpatient procedure and have been shown to be moderately effective in complex regional pain syndrome.

Destructive neurosurgical procedures, such as anterolateral cordotomy, dorsal root entry zone destruction, midline myelotomies, and destruction of nerve roots with alcohol, have become uncommon since the more widespread use of systemic and epidural opioids. The exception is trigeminal neuralgia, in which neurosurgery remains an important option (Chapter 428). As with any major surgical procedure, benefits are greatest and complications minimized when these procedures are performed by experts who do them frequently.

MANAGEMENT OF PAIN IN TERMINAL ILLNESS

Pain may become severe in the final weeks of cancer and other illnesses (Chapters 2 and 3). Expert consultation should be sought early to prepare for possible worsening. Clinicians should not be reluctant to give as much opioid analgesic as needed, even though there is a possibility that major increases in dose may slow respiration and hasten death by hours or, rarely, days (Chapter 3). Regulatory authorities, medical societies, and ethicists are unanimous in their written policies stating that in this situation, pain relief is the prime concern, and clinicians should not be criticized or disciplined if death is hastened as a byproduct of this effort. Occasionally, opioid tolerance develops to the point where opioids are unhelpful. At doses above several hundred milligrams per hour, morphine infusions may cause neuroexcitation or seizures, necessitating a switch to a different opioid. If opioids, NSAIDs, local anesthetics, and other measures are insufficient, sedation with barbiturates, benzodiazepines, propofol, or other anesthetic agents may provide comfort for the remaining hours of life.

Future Directions

Many novel analgesics are in early clinical development, and ongoing studies will define better the benefit-risk ratio of long-term opioid treatment in subsets of patients with nonmalignant pain. The greatest opportunity for advance may rest with medical and surgical specialists outside of the traditional pain research community who test current theories about pain physiology and treatment.

---

 1. Raja SN, Haythornthwaite JA, Pappagallo M, et al: Opiods versus antidepressants in postherpetic neuralgia: a randomized placebo-controlled trial. Neurology 2002;59:1015–1021.
2. Rowbotham MC, Twilling L, Davies PS, et al: Oral opioid therapy for chronic peripheral and central neuropathic pain. N Engl J Med 2003;348:1223–1232.

SUGGESTED READINGS
Federation of State Medical Boards of the United States, Inc: Model guidelines for the use of controlled substances for the treatment of pain. Available at http://www.medsch.wisc.edu/painpolicy/domestic/model.htm. *The most commonly used standards by which state medical boards judge whether prescription of opioids for chronic nonmalignant pain is within the standard of care.*
Kroenke K, Laine C (eds): Investigating symptoms: Frontiers in primary care research. Ann Intern Med 2001;134(9 Pt 2):801–930. *A symposium on the current state of research into unexplained pain and other symptoms in primary care.*
Max MB, Lynn J (eds): Symptom Research: Methods and Opportunities. Available at http://symptomresearch.nih.gov. *A web-based interactive textbook that uses real data sets and research scenarios to teach clinical research approaches to pain, nausea, fatigue, constipation, anorexia, dyspnea, and other common symptoms.*
Max MB, Payne R, Edwards WT, et al: Principles of Analgesic Use in the Treatment of Acute Pain and Cancer Pain, 4th ed. Glenview, IL: American Pain Society, 1999. *A pocket-sized guide to analgesic prescribing that supplements the material in this chapter.*

30 DRUG ABUSE AND DEPENDENCE

Jeffrey H. Samet

Drug abuse increasingly is recognized as an important mainstream health problem as a consequence of several factors: Injection drug use remains a major transmission risk for human immunodeficiency virus (HIV) infection; more than 1 million drug arrests occur in the United States each year; and costs are enormous, estimated as greater than $110 billion in the United States in 1995. About 15 million people older than 12 years of age have used illicit drugs at least once during the past month, and about 3.5 million people are classified as drug dependent. Medical complications of drug abuse are predominantly infectious but span organ systems and range from cocaine-related cardiac arrhythmia to neuropsychiatric effects of hallucinogens.

Definitions

The terms *drug* (or *substance*) *dependence* and *drug abuse* have specific clinical meanings (Table 30–1). Dependence is the more severe disorder and frequently is associated with physiologic and psychological manifestations. *Tolerance* and *withdrawal* are the major physiologic manifestations of drug dependence. Tolerance is defined as either a need for increased amounts of the substance to achieve the desired effect or a diminished effect with continued use of the same amount of the substance. Withdrawal is manifested by a characteristic syndrome with sudden abstinence, but it may be relieved or avoided if the same or a closely related substance is taken. The other criteria for dependence relate to the pattern of drug use (i.e., taken in a larger amount or longer period than intended); effects on life activities (i.e., great deal of time spent on activities to obtain, use, or recover from the substance; reduction in social, occupational, or recreational activities as a result of substance use); and the psychological need to use the substance (i.e., use despite awareness of adverse consequences, persistent desire for the substance, or inability to control its use).

A diagnosis of substance abuse requires the recurrent use of a substance over 12 months with subsequent adverse consequences (e.g., failure to fulfill a major role at work, school, or home; legal problems; persistent interpersonal problems) or placement of an individual in high-risk, physically hazardous situations. Addiction is a chronic, relapsing illness characterized by compulsive drug seeking and use.

The degree of harm associated with occasional drug use or "experimentation" is difficult to quantify, and no definition has been assigned formally to the use of illicit drugs with consequences less than those associated with the abuse definition. Fear of progression to abuse or dependence, the potential morbidity of use of drugs such as cocaine, the criminality associated with drug use, and the high-risk behavior while under the influence of a drug are the basis of recommendations to proscribe use of these substances.

Etiology

A minority of people who ever experiment with an illicit drug progress to a clinical drug abuse diagnosis. The cofactors responsible for progression to dependence and abuse are only partially defined. Genetic susceptibility, social context of the drug use, and comorbid psychiatric conditions are considered important factors affecting an individual's potential for subsequent problems. Twin studies suggest that genetics plays a role in a person's positive or negative perception of a drug's effect. The social context in which drug abuse develops and is expressed is important. Returning Vietnam War veterans addicted to heroin were relatively easy to treat compared with addicts on the streets of the United States, in part because the veterans had become addicted in a setting different from the one they found on return home and were exposed to few enduring environmental cues. Psychiatric comorbidity, particularly depression and panic disorders, seems to be a high-risk condition for the development of drug abuse and possible consequences of this abuse.

DRUG OF ABUSE: HEROIN AND OTHER OPIOIDS

Classification

Opioids, including naturally occurring alkaloids (opiates derived from the poppy plant *Papaver somniferum*), semisynthetic compounds (chemically altered alkaloids), and synthetic agents, are potent analgesics and produce an intense euphoria associated with nausea; drowsiness; miosis; and a decrease in respiration, pulse, and blood pressure. Opioids also are valued for their calming, antitussive, and antidiarrheal properties. Depending on the particular effect on opioid cell membrane receptors, they may be classified as agonists (morphine, heroin, methadone), partial agonists-antagonists (buprenorphine), or antagonists (naloxone, naltrexone). These drugs have led to many medical complications because of their abuse potential and their parenteral route of administration.

History

In the 19th century, opioids were used commonly in many settings in the United States. The drug was supplied freely by physicians to treat symptoms of pain, anxiety, cough, and diarrhea. Opiates also were available without restriction in commercial medicinal remedies.

In 1806, a pure substance was isolated from opium and named *morphine* after the Greek god of dreams Morpheus. By the middle of the 19th century, the advent of the hypodermic needle allowed this inexpensive, standard-strength agent to become a highly effective pain-killing and calming therapy. Smoking opium, which has no medicinal value, also rose in the latter half of the 19th century. In 1898, heroin was introduced commercially by the Bayer Company as an antitussive and was used as therapy for morphine addiction. The increasing recognition of the perils of opiate addiction, its identification with foreign groups and internal minorities, and concern over the estimated prevalence of 250,000 opiate users in 1900 led to a series of state and federal measures culminating in the Harrison Narcotic Act in 1914, which legislated controls over the importation and distribution of opiates.

Opiate use remained a problem in the early 20th century despite interdiction efforts and the development and dismantling of narcotic clinics that maintained narcotic addicts with prescription drugs. In the 1920s, narcotic abuse became a predominantly underground activity. Efforts to treat narcotic addiction as a medical problem were limited until the advent of methadone maintenance therapy in the 1960s.

Epidemiology

In the United States, an estimated 3 million people have reported prior use of heroin. About 170,000 of the estimated 810,000 opioid-dependent persons are enrolled in opioid treatment programs.

An estimated 150,000 individuals become new heroin users each year, an upward trend comparable with increases seen in the epidemic associated with the Vietnam War in the late 1960s. New users are likely to be young (72% <26 years old), noninjecting (63%), and urban dwellers (89%). Polysubstance abuse is increasingly common, with

---

Table 30–1 • DIAGNOSTIC CRITERIA FOR DEPENDENCE AND DRUG ABUSE

DEPENDENCE (≥3 NEEDED)	ABUSE (≥2 FOR 12 MO)
1. Tolerance	1. Recurrent substance use resulting in failure to fulfill major role obligations at work, school, or home
2. Withdrawal	2. Recurrent substance use in situations in which it is physically hazardous
3. The substance is often taken in larger amounts over a longer period than intended	3. Recurrent substance-related legal problems
4. Any unsuccessful effort or a persistent desire to cut down or control substance use	4. Continued substance use despite having persistent or recurrent social or interpersonal problems caused or exacerbated by the effects of the substance
5. A great deal of time is spent in activities necessary to obtain the substance or recover from its effects	5. Never met criteria for dependence
6. Important social, occupational, or recreational activities given up or reduced because of substance use	
7. Continued substance use despite knowledge of having had persistent or recurrent physical or psychological problems that are likely to be caused or exacerbated by the substance	

50% of male and 25% of female narcotic addicts meeting the criteria for alcohol dependence. Nicotine is the most common substance used together with opiates.

Biomolecular Mechanisms of Action

Opioids exert their effects on specific receptors for three distinct families of endogenous opioid peptides: enkephalins, endorphins, and dynorphins. In the central nervous system, three major classes of opioid receptors with unique selectivity and pharmacologic profiles have been identified: μ, κ, and δ. Subtypes of these major classes ($\mu 1$, $\mu 2$, $\kappa 1$, $\kappa 2$, $\kappa 3$, $\delta 1$, $\delta 2$) have been elucidated primarily by the use of selective receptor antagonists. μ receptor activity is associated with the most prominent manifestations of morphine and heroin: respiratory depression, analgesia, euphoria, and the development of dependence. It is thought that opioid peptides acting as neurotransmitters or neuromodulators exert their actions at neuronal synapses.

Clinical Pharmacology

Heroin may be injected intravenously or subcutaneously, snorted, smoked, or ingested. The parenteral and inhaled routes of administration result in the most rapid delivery of drug to the brain and are the most potentially addicting. As the purity of street heroin has increased from less than 5% in the 1960s to 80% in the 1990s, its nonparenteral administration has risen. Heroin may be used intermittently or regularly. Intermittent users generally either quit or become regular users within 1 to 3 years. Given the drug's short half-life, regular users require two to four daily doses to avoid withdrawal symptoms.

Heroin's initial effect is an intense euphoria described as a "rush" or "kick," compared in intensity and pleasure with an orgasm, that lasts 45 seconds to several minutes. The initial effects may be perceived as a turning in the stomach with tingling and warmth. A user's first experience may be unpleasant because of nausea, vomiting, and anxiety, but these effects decrease or become less of a concern to the user over time. The intense euphoria is followed by an intoxicated pleasant feeling referred to as "nodding," with decreased respiration and peristalsis. The depressant effect of heroin on the central nervous system is marked, particularly after parenteral administration. Sedation, mental clouding, decreased visual acuity, heavy feeling in the extremities, light sleep with vivid dreams, and reduction in anxiety are typical, at least until tolerance develops. Physical signs include

Table 30–2 • SIGNS AND SYMPTOMS OF WITHDRAWAL FROM OPIOIDS AND COCAINE

OPIOID WITHDRAWAL	
Vital signs	Tachycardia, hypertension, fever
Central nervous system	Craving, restlessness, insomnia, muscle cramps, yawning, miosis
Eyes, nose	Lacrimation, rhinorrhea
Skin	Perspiration, piloerection
Gastrointestinal	Nausea, vomiting, diarrhea
COCAINE WITHDRAWAL	
Crash	Depression, fatigue
Withdrawal	Anxiety, high craving
Extinction	Normalization of mood, episodic craving

miosis, decreased heart rate, and lowered blood pressure. In addition to these effects on opioid receptors, heroin causes the release of histamine, which may result in itching, scleral injection, and hypotension.

High levels of tolerance develop rapidly with regard to respiratory depression, analgesia, sedation, vomiting, and euphoric properties. Little tolerance develops for miosis or constipation, so a heroin addict with an acutely painful medical condition may complain of insufficient analgesia despite pinpoint pupils. Cross-tolerance is common among opioids.

From the patient's perspective, withdrawal from heroin is a dreaded clinical condition, a mix of emotional, behavioral, and physical signs and symptoms (Table 30–2). Although unpleasant, it is not life-threatening. The timing of withdrawal symptoms, which are related directly to clearance of the drug, begins 4 to 8 hours after the last dose of heroin. The acute withdrawal syndrome peaks in intensity after 36 to 72 hours and resolves over 5 to 7 days.

In addition to the acute abstinence syndrome, a protracted abstinence syndrome occurs and lasts 6 months or more. In contrast to the hyperadrenergic characteristics of the primary withdrawal syndrome (tachycardia, hypertension, elevated temperature, mydriasis, and diaphoresis), the period afterward can consist of sluggishness, sleep disturbance, and malaise. Craving can recur for years after cessation of drug use. An understanding of the nature of recovery from heroin use is important for setting appropriate expectations for the patient and the health care provider.

Clinical Complications

Deaths from heroin overdose have been increasing in several countries. Nevertheless, most opioid-related medical complications occur as a result of the spread of infectious agents by injection drug use among heroin addicts (Fig. 30–1). The manifestations of these medical complications are protean but frequently nonspecific, such as fever, malaise, weight loss, pain, or dyspnea. The underlying causes include endocarditis, cellulitis, HIV disease, hepatitis, pneumonia, and a variety of abscesses. Additionally, specific syndromes have been attributed to direct toxic effects of the opioid itself.

Reports of infectious complications of intravenous drug use before 1970 included falciparum malaria, tetanus, endocarditis, and acute hepatitis. Although falciparum malaria and tetanus are now rare, hepatitis B and C are exceedingly common and serologically detectable in most heroin addicts in the United States and abroad.

The major cardiac complication of opioid abuse is bacterial endocarditis (Chapter 310) caused by injection drug use. *Staphylococcus aureus* is the most frequently reported bacterial isolate, and the tricuspid valve is the most common valve involved. Left-sided valvular infection is associated with a worse prognosis, as are the uncommon gram-negative and fungal infections.

Opioid abusers normally have acute rather than subacute endocarditis. The initial clinical finding can be fever alone in half the cases, or fever may be associated with pulmonary infiltrates from right-sided emboli or systemic embolic phenomena, such as arthritis, abscess, and osteomyelitis. The diagnosis of endocarditis in a febrile injection drug user is difficult because of the poor sensitivity and specificity of readily available clinical and laboratory data. Blood cultures are essential for these patients. If adequate outpatient follow-up is not possible, hospitalization generally is recommended until initial blood culture results are known. The sensitivity and specificity of echocardiography vary greatly among different studies but are not adequate to exclude endocarditis. Other cardiac complications associated with opioid abuse include toxic cardiomyopathy, perivalvular abscess, abnormalities of the conduction system such as QT prolongation and ST-T wave changes, and cor pulmonale.

The most common pulmonary complication is bacterial pneumonia, which is present in one third of injection drug users evaluated for fever. The risk for this infection probably results from a combination of factors, including hypoventilation, immune dysfunction, suppression of coughing, and aspiration during periods of clouded sensorium. Pulmonary hypertension can result from "talc granulomatosis," the development of diffuse pulmonary granulomas caused by the intravenous injection of foreign substances, most notably talc. Other pulmonary complications associated with opioid abuse include acute pulmonary edema, bronchospasm, septic pulmonary emboli, and infectious or chemical mediastinitis.

Renal complications of opioid abuse include acute diseases (myoglobinuria, necrotizing angiitis, glomerulonephritis associated with endocarditis or hepatitis) and chronic diseases (nephrotic syndrome, renal failure, renal amyloidosis). The pathology most commonly found in heroin-associated nephrotic syndrome is focal and

Continued

diffuse glomerulosclerosis (Chapter 119). In HIV-infected patients, HIV-associated nephropathy also is found (Chapter 420).

Of patients in methadone maintenance clinics, 50 to 90% have positive serologic studies for hepatitis B and C. Complications of these infections (Chapter 152) range from chronic asymptomatic antigenemia to cirrhosis and hepatocellular carcinoma.

Neurologic complications of opioid abuse are infectious and noninfectious. Seizures, most often generalized, are the most common noninfectious complication. The cause of seizures includes overdose, with centrally mediated respiratory depression and hypoxia, and cerebral infarction. Meningitis, mycotic aneurysm, and abscesses (epidural, subdural, and brain) are well-described infectious conditions resulting from injection drug use. In HIV-infected patients, HIV-associated neurologic infectious and noninfectious diseases occur (Chapter 414).

Psychiatric conditions among opioid abusers are common and include alcohol abuse/dependence, major depression, phobic disorders, and antisocial personality, all of which have a greater than 15% lifetime prevalence. Men are four to seven times more likely to have an antisocial personality than women are; women more commonly have depression. Women abusers are at high risk of being victims of violence.

Immunologic abnormalities among heroin addicts were described before the acquired immunodeficiency syndrome epidemic. In vitro, morphine decreases the number of T lymphocytes, and naloxone, an opiate antagonist, can reverse this decrease. The hypergammaglobulinemia of addicts, presumably resulting from repeated antigenic stimulation, is the explanation given for a high rate of false-positive indirect syphilis serologic test results. The long-term consequences of opioid-related immunologic effects are not clear. The most prominent clinical endocrine effect is amenorrhea.

The associated medical complications of HIV infection in drug users mirror those of noninjection drug users with HIV infection with a few caveats. HIV-infected drug users have an increased frequency of bacterial pneumonia and a decreased frequency of Kaposi's sarcoma. HIV testing with appropriate counseling should be recommended strongly for all opioid abusers. Behavioral changes to promote the use of condoms and the avoidance of sharing of needles can reduce HIV transmission. Needle exchange programs are efficacious in reducing the harm of heroin addiction.

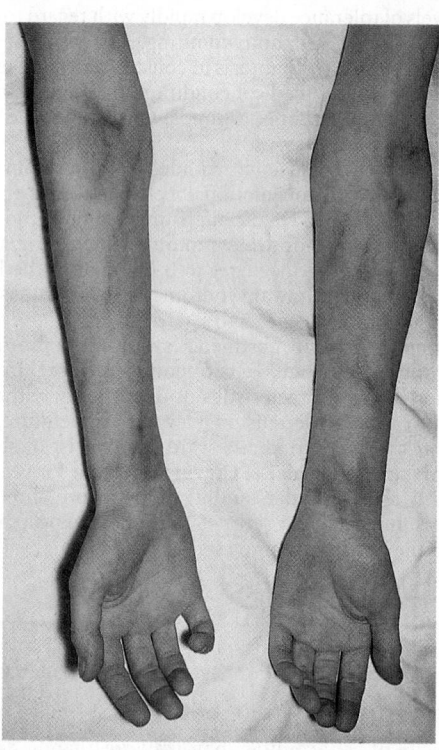

FIGURE 30–1 • Injection drug use typically leads to this appearance, which results from repeated superficial thrombophlebitis of accessible veins in the arm or elsewhere in the body. Sharing and reuse of syringes and needles puts these patients at risk of a wide range of infections, including bacterial septicemia, systemic fungal infection, hepatitis B, hepatitis C, and HIV infection. Right-sided endocarditis is a common complication. (From Forbes CD, Jackson WF: Color Atlas and Text of Clinical Medicine, 3rd ed. London, Mosby, 2003, with permission.)

PRESCRIPTION OPIOIDS

Opioids are prescribed appropriately for acute and chronic pain. These analgesic medications vary in their potency and bioavailability and include oxycodone (Percodan, Percocet), hydrocodone (Vicodin), hydromorphone (Dilaudid), and meperidine (Demerol). A new slow-release formulation of oxycodone, OxyContin, has gained great popularity among recreational and dependent opioid users since its approval in 1995. By crushing these pills and destroying the slow-release matrix in which the opioid is embedded, oxycodone is abused orally, parenterally, and intranasally, yielding effects comparable to heroin. An estimated 2.6 million Americans misuse pain relievers each year. Despite these abuses, it is important for the physician to understand that it is uncommon for appropriate use of these medications in the treatment of pain to lead to opioid dependence (Chapter 29).

DRUG OF ABUSE: COCAINE AND OTHER PSYCHOSTIMULANTS

Classification

Cocaine, an alkaloid extracted from coca leaves, and other psychostimulants (e.g., amphetamine, methamphetamine) rapidly increase the concentration of several neurotransmitters in synaptic junctions and stimulate the sympathetic and central nervous systems. Topical cocaine is used in otolaryngologic procedures, and psychostimulants are used either for their stimulant effects or for their paradoxical calming effect in some patients with attention-deficit hyperactivity disorder.

History

The earliest recorded use of cocaine in the form of ingested coca leaf occurred around 3000 BC. In 1860, cocaine was isolated and incorporated into tonics, teas, and wines. In the 1880s, an Atlanta druggist patented a product that contained two naturally occurring stimulants, cocaine and caffeine, which eventually became known as Coca-Cola; until 1903, it contained approximately 60 mg of cocaine per 8-oz serving. In the late 19th century, reports of cocaine addiction surfaced, and its use was restricted after passage of the Harrison Narcotic Act of 1914. The abuse potential of amphetamines led to their being listed as schedule II drugs, which are defined as having a high potential for abuse with severe liability to cause psychic or physical dependence.

Epidemiology

An estimated 1.5 million Americans, representing 0.8% of the population aged 12 years and older, have used cocaine in the past month. More than 900,000 Americans use cocaine for the first time each year, and more than 30 million Americans have used cocaine at least once. Use is higher in the 18- to 34-year-old age group (1.5 to 2.0%), in men than in women (1.1 versus 0.5%), in urban areas, and among individuals with less education. Although current cocaine use is highest in the unemployed (2.4%), 73% of adult users are employed full-time or part-time. Current cocaine use is similar for whites (0.8%), blacks (1.0%), and Hispanics (1.1%).

Biomolecular Mechanisms Of Action

Cocaine increases neurotransmitter concentrations at the synaptic terminal by blocking the reuptake of norepinephrine, dopamine, and serotonin and by potentiating the release of these monoamines. In the heart, α-adrenergic and β-adrenergic receptors are stimulated.

Dopamine activates the ventral tegmental-nucleus accumbens pathway, a major component of the brain's reward system. The system is complex, with at least five dopamine receptor subtypes with distinct molecular and pharmacologic properties. D_1, D_2, and D_3 receptors have been implicated in the reinforcing actions of cocaine. Cocaine's ability to block sodium channels in neuronal cells accounts for its local anesthetic actions. Chronic use of cocaine leads to dysregulation of the brain's dopaminergic systems. Possible degeneration of dopaminergic terminals in the brains of cocaine addicts is suggested by positron emission tomographic studies in which the binding of cocaine to dopamine transporters in the basal ganglia and thalamus is decreased.

Clinical Pharmacology

Cocaine can be smoked, ingested orally, applied to mucous membranes, or injected intravenously. Cocaine hydrochloride, a water-soluble powder often mixed with adulterants, can be used by all routes except that it cannot be smoked because it decomposes when burned. Freebase or crack cocaine, a chemically altered form of cocaine, vaporizes before decomposition and can be smoked.

The route of administration determines the amount of cocaine absorbed and the rapidity of its uptake in the brain. Swallowed or snorted (intranasal) cocaine penetrates biologic membranes poorly and undergoes 70 to 80% hepatic transformation. Cocaine administered intravenously or smoked is absorbed. The onset of action varies according to the route of administration: oral, peak effect in 1 hour; intranasal, 3 to 5 minutes for onset with a peak effect in 30 to 60 minutes; intravenous, onset in 12 to 16 seconds, with 10 to 20 minutes' duration of effect; and smoked, onset in 6 to 8 seconds with 5 to 10 minutes' duration of effect. Cocaine has an elimination half-life of 30 to 60 minutes. Less than 5% of cocaine appears unchanged in urine. Cocaine's two major metabolites are benzoylecgonine and ecgonine methyl ester. Both are inactive, and the former is the main target in urine testing (Table 30–3). Casual users can progress to high-dose users with compulsive and uncontrollable bingeing. During a binge, cocaine is administered every 10 to 30 minutes, generally over 4 to 24 hours or more.

The acute effects of cocaine include intense euphoria, increased energy and self-confidence, enhanced mental acuity and sensory awareness (including sexual), and decreased appetite. Sympathetic signs include tachycardia, mydriasis, and hyperthermia. Withdrawal symptoms are the inverse of the acute effects: depressed mood, lack of energy, limited interest in the environment, hyperphagia, hypersomnia, anxiety, and craving. The withdrawal syndromes of cocaine-dependent individuals are not as consistent as those of alcohol or opioid withdrawal. Chronic users become tolerant to its acute effects; symptoms of anxiety, agitation, inability to concentrate, and loss of sexual drive predominate. Beyond the initial withdrawal period, craving

leading to relapse can be precipitated by conditioned cues in which the pleasurable effects of cocaine use are associated with particular settings.

Clinical Manifestations

The most common medical complications of cocaine use involve the brain and the heart and include altered mental status, seizures, chest pain, palpitations, and syncope. Sudden death can occur by a variety of mechanisms, including arrhythmias, status epilepticus, intracerebral hemorrhage, and centrally mediated respiratory arrest.

Cocaine use leads to ischemia and myocardial infarction as a result of increased myocardial demand because of tachycardia and hypertension, diffuse and local coronary spasm in normal or atherosclerotic arteries, and a propensity to thrombus formation secondary to blood stasis in narrowed arteries and increased platelet aggregability. Myocardial infarction is unrelated to the dose of cocaine ingested, the frequency of use, or the route of administration; first-time, recreational, and habitual users are all at risk. Almost 90% of cocaine-associated myocardial infarctions occur in men. Most chest pain develops within minutes, but pain can be delayed 15 hours after use.

Other cardiac complications include supraventricular and ventricular arrhythmias, cardiomyopathy, and myocarditis. Arrhythmias are attributed to direct toxic effects and a cocaine-induced hyperadrenergic state. Myocardial damage may be similar to that seen in pheochromocytoma, in which norepinephrine excess results in a nonspecific pathologic finding, contraction band necrosis.

Cocaine addiction frequently is associated with psychiatric diseases, such as depression, anxiety, phobia, attention-deficit disorder, and antisocial personality disorder. High doses can result in transient psychosis, delirium, paranoid ideation, bizarre behavior, and suicide attempts.

Other complications of cocaine use include vascular headaches, rhabdomyolysis with acute renal failure, placental abruption, erosion of dental enamel, gingival ulceration, chronic rhinitis, perforated nasal septum, pulmonary edema, and sexual dysfunction. Sexually transmitted diseases, including HIV, have been associated strongly with cocaine use; HIV testing should be pursued in any patient with a cocaine abuse diagnosis. Ingested packets of cocaine can rupture and cause acute toxic reactions and cardiovascular collapse.

OTHER SPECIFIC DRUGS: METHAMPHETAMINE, METHYLPHENIDATE

The synthetic psychostimulant methamphetamine, a particularly potent form of amphetamine, is highly addictive, cheaper, and longer lasting than cocaine. Nicknames include "speed," "crank," and "zip"; the smokable form is called "ice" or "crystal." Chronic use has been associated with violent behavior.

Methylphenidate (Ritalin), a central nervous system stimulant, is prescribed primarily for treatment of attention-deficit hyperactivity disorder in children because of its paradoxical calming effect. About 3% of high school seniors report using it in a nontherapeutic setting. Illicit users take the drug tablets orally, crush them for intranasal use, or dissolve and inject them.

DRUG OF ABUSE: MARIJUANA AND OTHER CANNABINOIDS

Marijuana is the common name applied to the leaves, stems, and tops of the plant *Cannabis sativa*, which contains cannabinoids, the most active of which is Δ^9-*trans*-tetrahydrocannabinol (THC). It generally is smoked but can be ingested, mixed in food or tea. Tolerance and physical dependence are not major clinical problems. The changes in the brain, cardiovascular system, and lungs are acute and reversible. Marijuana or purified oral THC may be effective therapy for nausea in some patients.

Cannabinoids are the most commonly used illicit drugs in the world. An estimated 19.5 million Americans, or about 9% of the population aged 12 and older, have used cannabinoids within the

Table 30–3 • URINE TESTING FOR ABUSED DRUGS

DRUG	COMPOUND DETECTED	URINE DETECTION TIME
Heroin	Morphine 6-Acetylmorphine	1–3 days
Codeine	Codeine Morphine	1–3 days
Methadone	Methadone	2–4 days
Cocaine	Benzoylecgonine	1–3 days
Amphetamine	Amphetamine	2–4 days
Methamphetamine	Methamphetamine, amphetamine	2–4 days
Marijuana	Tetrahydrocannabinol	1–3 days for casual use, up to 30 days for chronic use
Phencyclidine	Phencyclidine	2–7 days for casual use, up to 30 days for chronic use
Benzodiazepines	Oxazepam, diazepam, other benzodiazapines	Up to 30 days
Barbiturates	Amobarbital, secobarbital, other barbiturates	2–4 days for short acting, up to 30 days for long acting

Clinical Pharmacology

past year, and more than 75 million have used marijuana in their lifetime.

Cannabinoids bind to specific receptors for the endogenous ligand anandamide: CB1 in the brain and CB2 in the periphery. G-protein activation occurs as a result of the receptor binding and has three effects: inhibition of adenylate cyclase, increased potassium ion conductance, and decreased calcium ion conductance. CB1 receptors are concentrated in the globus pallidus, hippocampus, cerebral cortex, cerebellum, and striatum.

Smoked marijuana results in a variety of acute changes within 3 minutes that peak within 20 to 30 minutes; when ingested, onset takes 30 to 60 minutes, and the peak effect occurs after 2 to 3 hours. An average cigarette contains 2.5 to 5 mg of THC, and 50 to 60% of it is absorbed. THC is lipophilic and distributed rapidly throughout the body. Because of slow release from adipose tissue, THC or its metabolites can be found in urine 1 to 3 days after use in nonchronic users and 30 days after use in chronic users (see Table 30–3).

Most effects last 2 to 3 hours after inhalation; psychomotor effects can last 11 hours. Effects include conjunctival injection, mild euphoria, impaired memory, dry mouth, motor incoordination, time-space distortion, increased visual and auditory awareness, increased hunger, sleepiness, and spontaneous laughter; some may experience nausea, headaches, tremors, decreased muscle strength, and increased anxiety. Few chronic effects have been attributed to marijuana use, but an amotivational syndrome has been described in which young people lose goal-directed behavior with regard to school or work.

DRUG OF ABUSE: LSD AND OTHER HALLUCINOGENS

Hallucinogen use results predominantly in changes in thought, perception, and mood. Minimal impairment occurs in memory or intellect. This class of drugs is not generally associated with stupor, narcosis, or excessive stimulation. Users do not exhibit craving. The two major categories of hallucinogens are indolamines (e.g., lysergic acid diethylamide [LSD], dimethyltryptamide, psilocybin) and phenylethylamines (e.g., methylenedioxyamphetamine, methylenedioxymethamphetamine [MDMA], mescaline). Related drugs include phencyclidine (PCP), nutmeg, morning glory seeds, catnip, nitrous oxide, and amyl or butyl nitrite. These drugs have no appropriate clinical role.

In the United States, the lifetime prevalence of hallucinogen use is about 11%; more than 25 million individuals have used hallucinogens at least once. LSD was used widely on college campuses in the 1960s. The 1970s and early 1980s saw a decline in the use of most hallucinogens. Hallucinogen use increased in the 1990s, however, and by 1998 there were 1.2 million new users, twice the average in the 1980s.

The classic hallucinogens are structurally similar to many major neurotransmitters, but serotonin (5-hydroxytryptamine [5-HT]) agonist or partial agonist properties have been associated most consistently with its actions. These drugs bind at $5-HT_{2A}$ and $5-HT_{2C}$ receptors with high affinity. These receptors are found in greatest density in brain cortical regions (cerebral cortex, claustrum, caudate putamen, globus pallidus, ventral pallidum, islands of Calleja, mammillary nuclei, and inferior olive) and may have a role in depression and suicide.

Hallucinogen use results in an altered perception of one's environment marked by a subjective feeling of enhanced mental activity, perceptual distortions, visual hallucinations, sharpened sense of hearing, and a reduced ability to tell the difference between one's self and one's surroundings. These drugs can produce sympathomimetic effects, including mydriasis, flushed face, fine tremor, piloerection, high blood pressure, hyperthermia, and hyperglycemia. Panic attacks and psychosis are the two major adverse effects. Clinically "desired" effects and adverse effects vary by specific hallucinogen. Altered perceptions can be associated with paranoid delusions, manic or depressed behavior, and confusion. Aggressive behavior has been described with psychosis; in particular, PCP has been implicated in violent crimes. The psychotic episodes can last hours or days, and flashbacks can occur. Precipitants for flashbacks are anxiety, stress, fatigue, emergence into a dark environment, and marijuana.

Although tolerance can develop with hallucinogens, the clinical syndrome is unusual inasmuch as chronic use is uncommon. No clinically significant withdrawal symptoms are known. Concerns about chronic use include prolonged psychotic episodes, decreased

intellect, organic brain syndrome, and possibly "chromosomal damage," although definitive correlations have not been established.

The use of hallucinogens may be detected in the acute setting when examining a patient with toxic manifestations or may be noted when obtaining a history of drug use. After diagnosis, it is important to obtain a history of other substance abuse and psychiatric illness and a neurologic evaluation. No specific laboratory tests are required; a urine toxicologic screen for other drugs of abuse is recommended (see Table 30–3).

LSD often is sold as postage stamp–size papers impregnated with varying doses of LSD, from 50 μg to more than 300 μg. Doses of 20 μg can lead to psychological effects, with doses of 100 μg causing hallucinogenic psychoactive manifestations within 1 to 2 hours. Clearing of symptoms begins in 10 to 12 hours, although symptoms of fatigue and tension can persist for an additional 24 hours.

PCP, also known as "phencyclidine" or "angel dust," originally was developed as an anesthetic in the 1950s but was abandoned because of frequent postoperative delirium and hallucinations. It can be obtained in various forms (powder, liquid, tablet, capsule, or sprayed on other drugs such as marijuana) and administered by several routes (smoked, ingested, snorted, or injected intravenously). The drug is water soluble and lipophilic, so it penetrates fat stores and has a long half-life, up to 3 days. Casual use by smoking on a weekly basis is most common, although some have reported continuous intake lasting 2 days or longer. A pronounced pharmacologic characteristic of PCP is its analgesia and amphetamine-like stimulation in addition to hallucination. Ataxia, slurred speech, nystagmus, and numbness commonly are observed at doses of 1 to 10 mg. Emotional withdrawal, catatonic posturing resembling schizophrenia, and physical violence can result from its use.

DRUG OF ABUSE: BENZODIAZEPINES AND OTHER SEDATIVES

Benzodiazepines and the less commonly used barbiturates are legitimate therapeutic drugs with abuse potential. These drugs are designated as schedule IV substances by the Drug Enforcement Agency and the Food and Drug Administration. Schedule IV drugs have a low potential for abuse and lead to limited physical or psychological dependence.

Nonmedical use of tranquilizers and sedatives occurs in fewer than 2% of U.S. adults annually. The magnitude of the problem is substantially less than that of opioids, psychostimulants, and marijuana. This problem occurs largely in individuals who also abuse other substances. This finding is consistent with the experience in laboratory animals, which do not exhibit repeated self-administration, a standard measure of addictive potential, when exposed to benzodiazepines.

All benzodiazepines studied are capable of producing physiologic dependence even when used in low doses over prolonged periods as may be seen in clinical practice. The key to the diagnosis of benzodiazepine or other sedative abuse is evidence of inappropriate drug-taking behavior, including escalation in dose, obtaining prescriptions from multiple physicians, or taking the drug for reasons other than those for which it was prescribed. Physiologic dependence should not imply that inappropriate drug-taking behavior exists. Before initiating clinical use of benzodiazepines and other sedatives, a careful medical history must be obtained regarding current and prior substance abuse. Although not absolutely contraindicated, particular caution and extra monitoring are appropriate in patients with such a history.

NEW DRUGS OF ABUSE: CLUB DRUGS

Newer drugs of abuse, such as 3,4 methylenedioxymethamphetamine (MDMA), γ-hydroxybutyrate (GHB), and ketamine, are used in a variety of settings. When ingested in association with inadequate fluid intake, vigorous exercise, or a hot, humid environment, these drugs are particularly likely to cause complications.

MDMA (ECSTASY)

MDMA, commonly referred to as "Ecstasy," is a synthetic analogue of amphetamine and shares properties with amphetamine and hallucinogenic drugs. It acts on the serotonin transporter, stimulating serotonin release and inhibiting its reuptake. Although usually taken in the pill form, MDMA also can be snorted, injected, or administered per rectum. The purity of MDMA tablets may vary 70-fold, and tablets may include caffeine, heroin, or mescaline. More than 8% of high school seniors report using MDMA.

MDMA's clinical effects are predominately sensory enhancement with distortion and decreased inhibitions. The onset of action is 30 to 60 minutes, the peak effects occur at 90 minutes, and the duration is 8 hours or more. Common adverse effects, which are similar to effects found with amphetamines and cocaine, include sweating, muscle spasms, involuntary teeth clenching, faintness, chills, and tachycardia. Psychological manifestations include confusion, depression, sleep problems, severe anxiety, and paranoia. High temperatures and muscle exertion from dancing seem to lower the threshold for serious MDMA-associated adverse effects, especially rhabdomyolysis; other reported adverse effects in the club setting include hyponatremia, dehydration, hypothermia, hypertensive crisis, and cardiac arrhythmias.

GHB

GHB, or "liquid ecstasy," is a metabolite of the neurotransmitter γ-aminobutyric acid. It is thought to function as a neurotransmitter, producing a dopaminergic response and release of an opiate-like substance. Its half-life is approximately 30 minutes. GHB is used for its euphoric and anabolic effects. Behavioral changes include increased aggression, and neurologic changes range from mild ataxia to apnea. Withdrawal symptoms are similar to those of sedative abuse and persist for 3 to 7 days. There is no antidote for GHB overdoses, and treatment is limited to nonspecific supportive care.

KETAMINE

Ketamine, commonly referred to as "Special K," is a fast-acting intravenous or intramuscular anesthetic that delivers hypnotic, analgesic, and amnesic effects. Most of ketamine's activity is associated with N-methyl-D-aspartate receptors. Because it causes an intense dissociative state and loss of physical control, ketamine use is associated with a high risk of injuries. Ketamine usually is acquired from veterinary clinics.

TREATMENT OF DRUG ABUSE AND PREVENTION OF RELAPSE

Patients who use illicit drugs benefit from treatment if they recognize that their substance use is a problem. The transtheoretical model considers a patient on a continuum from precontemplation (denial) toward maintenance (abstinence/recovery) (Fig. 30–2). The clinical approach should be tailored to the patient's readiness to change behavior and enter treatment. For all abused drugs, medical follow-up after any acute toxic presentation is essential to address substance abuse issues and possible coexisting medical and psychiatric problems.

The major goals of drug abuse treatment are detoxification, abstinence initiation, and relapse prevention. Treatment can be pharmacologic and nonpharmacologic. Pharmacologic approaches are offered by physicians specializing in addiction and increasingly by primary care physicians.

Some form of psychosocial treatment is the backbone of substance abuse treatment, be it psychotherapy, behavioral therapy, or counseling. Issues addressed in these encounters include teaching coping skills, changing reinforcement contingencies, fostering management

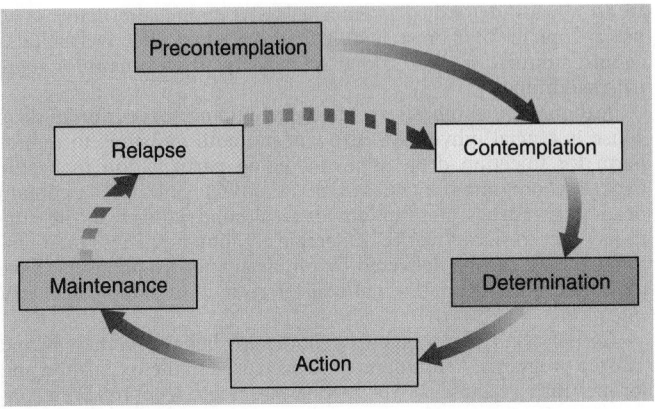

FIGURE 30–2 • Graphic depiction of the Prochaska and DiClemente model for readiness for behavioral change.

of painful effects, addressing motivation, improving interpersonal functioning, enhancing social supports, and encouraging compliance with and retention in pharmacotherapy. Much of this work is done by substance abuse care providers. Physicians are in an excellent position to detect drug abuse, however, by exploring this history when confronted by a possible drug abuse–related clinical manifestation. Primary care physicians also can make significant contributions. Individuals with substance abuse–related medical conditions were more likely to remain abstinent when randomized to an integrated medical care and substance abuse treatment program.

The active ingredients of brief intervention have been summarized by the acronym *FRAMES*: (1) *feedback* of personal risk or impairment (e.g., sharing abnormal test results, discussing medical complications), (2) emphasis on personal *responsibility* to change, (3) clear *advice* to change, (4) a *menu* of different options for change, (5) provider *empathy,* and (6) enhancement of patient *self-efficacy* or optimism. Physicians can refer to substance abuse treatment specialists; self-help groups (e.g., Narcotics Anonymous) are often part of a successful abstinence maintenance program.

Pharmacologic treatment of opioid abuse includes agonist, antagonist, mixed agonist-antagonist, or symptomatic treatment. With detoxification, the goal is amelioration of the symptoms of heroin or other opioid withdrawal by agonist substitution (e.g., methadone) or symptomatic treatment (e.g., clonidine). A new treatment involves the use of buprenorphine, which has agonist and antagonist properties. It has a better safety profile and produces less physical dependence. Hospitalized opioid-dependent patients may be treated with methadone for withdrawal symptoms by any physician. Methadone for the postdischarge treatment of opioid addiction is currently available only via specially licensed treatment facilities.

Prevention of relapse to active heroin abuse has been attempted most commonly by substitution of a safer drug (e.g., methadone, buprenorphine, or the second-line agent, l-acetyl-α-methadol) with similar pharmacologic properties to relieve the craving and withdrawal and to block some of the euphoric effects of heroin (Table 30–4). These medications (i.e., high-dose methadone [60 to 100 mg], buprenorphine [16 to 32 mg], and levomethadyl acetate [75 to 115 mg]) substantially reduced use of illicit opioids compared with low-dose methadone (20 mg) in a randomized controlled trial.

Table 30–4 • RELAPSE PREVENTION FOR OPIOID ABUSE

MEDICATION	DOSE	DOSING INTERVAL	MECHANISM	PRESCRIBING REGULATIONS	WITHDRAWAL*
Methadone	60–100 mg orally	Daily	Agonist	Yes	++
LAAM	30–115 mg orally	q2–3d	Agonist	Yes	++
Buprenorphine	8–32 mg sublingually	q1–2d	Agonist/antagonist	Yes	+
Naltrexone	50 mg orally	Daily	Antagonist	No	–

LAAM = l-acetyl-α-methadol; FDA = Food and Drug Administration.
*++ = moderate; + = mild; – = none.

Clinical Pharmacology

In an already detoxified patient, a less common alternative is to use an opioid antagonist (e.g., naltrexone) that effectively blocks agonist stimulation. Methadone is not adequate treatment for acute pain syndromes.

Although an emphasis on the treatment and prevention of drug abuse is crucial, physicians also can promote measures to reduce harm for injection drug users, including participation in needle exchange programs, avoidance of "shooting galleries" to obtain or administer drugs, prescriptions for needles and syringes, and instructions never to share "works" (injection equipment). These interventions, which can be delivered by physicians to drug abusers, have played a crucial role in international efforts to limit the spread of HIV infection.

Cocaine abuse is treated by psychotherapy, behavioral therapy, and 12-step programs. Acupuncture has been used for detoxification and for preventing relapse. As yet, no pharmacologic agent has been consistently effective in reducing cocaine use or craving. Dopamine agonists, antidepressants, and other drugs have been studied, but none are currently recommended. No antidote is known for acute cocaine overdose.

Marijuana use rarely requires acute treatment in the medical setting. Reassurance generally is sufficient to manage the occasional dysphoric manifestations. Occasionally, anxiety reactions require specific therapy with benzodiazepines; rarely, psychotic reactions are treated with haloperidol.

Specific therapy for the complications of *hallucinogen* use is nonpharmacologic and involves emotional reassurance and a calm supportive environment. No specific antagonists are clinically available for any of the hallucinogens. Medications are required only if the patient cannot be controlled adequately, in which case anxiolytic drugs are recommended.

Discontinuation of *benzodiazepines* can be accomplished in dependent patients by prescribing a regimen of gradual dose reduction. Alternatively, another long-acting sedative-hypnotic can be substituted for the drug of abuse and gradually withdrawn. It is important to attempt to verify that the patient has no alternative sources for these medications.

Future Directions

With current understanding of the associated morbidities and costs of drug use, increasing emphasis will be placed on the contributions that physicians can make in the care of patients with drug abuse and dependence. Opportunities to work with substance abuse providers to treat opioid-dependent patients in the primary medical care setting with pharmacologic therapy, including buprenorphine and methadone, will become widely available. Such future opportunities will increase the need for physicians to obtain skills to screen for drug abuse, address use of illicit drugs, and intervene to reduce the harm of these addictive behaviors.

1. Weisner C, Mertens J, Parthasarathy S, et al: Integrating primary medical care with addiction treatment: A randomized controlled trial. JAMA 2001;286:1715–1723.
2. Johnson RE, Chutuape MA, Strain EC, et al: A comparison of levomethadyl acetate, buprenorphine, and methadone for opioid dependence. N Engl J Med 2000;343:1290–1297.

SUGGESTED READINGS

Fiellin DA, O'Connor PG: Office-based treatment of opioid-dependent patients. N Engl J Med 2002;347:817–824. *A useful guide to ambulatory care.*

Kosten TR, O'Connor PG: Management of drug and alcohol withdrawal. N Engl J Med 2003;348:1786–1795. *Overview of inpatient and outpatient options.*

McLellan AT, Lewis DC, O'Brien CP, Kleber HD: Drug dependence, a chronic medical illness: Implications for treatment, insurance, and outcomes evaluation. JAMA 2000;284:1689–1695. *Drug dependence is portrayed as a mainstream medical problem, and its treatment is associated with efficacy and adherence comparable with other common chronic conditions.*

Samet JH, Friedmann P, Saitz R: Benefits of linking primary medical care and substance abuse services: Patient, provider, and societal perspectives. Arch Intern Med 2001;161:85–91. *A new paradigm of collaboration between physicians and substance abuse professionals is described, and potential benefits of such interactions are outlined.*

31 GLUCOCORTICOSTEROIDS IN RELATION TO INFLAMMATORY DISEASE

Paul Katz

For more than 50 years, glucocorticosteroids have been important agents in treating diseases characterized by inflammation and exaggerated immune responses. The pioneering work of Hench and colleagues in rheumatoid arthritis showed the possible potency of these agents in such pathologic states. Although substantial advances have been made in understanding the mechanisms by which glucocorticosteroids exert beneficial effects, considerable gaps in knowledge remain. Despite extensive data regarding the in vitro and in vivo activities of these drugs, it is probable that glucocorticosteroids have different beneficial activities in different diseases.

The challenge of glucocorticosteroid therapy continues to be the counterbalancing of desirable anti-inflammatory and immunosuppressive actions versus undesirable pharmacologic activities. More precise understanding of the mechanisms of action of glucocorticosteroids has not resulted in the development of regimens with minimal toxicity.

Pharmacology

The glucocorticosteroid preparations available for systemic use (Table 31–1) differ in their relative anti-inflammatory potency, potential for sodium retention, and plasma and biologic half-lives. In general, shorter acting preparations, such as prednisone and prednisolone, are preferable to longer acting agents, such as dexamethasone, because tapering to an alternate-day schedule cannot be accomplished with drugs with prolonged (i.e., >24 hours) biologic half-lives. Additionally, hydrocortisone and cortisone rarely are used to treat inflammatory and immunologically mediated diseases because of the considerable mineralocorticoid activity that accompanies their use.

Mechanisms of Action

Glucocorticosteroids exert anti-inflammatory and immunosuppressive actions through several pathways. Nonetheless, all effects

Table 31–1 • GLUCOCORTICOSTEROID PREPARATIONS

	ANTI-INFLAMMATORY POTENCY	EQUIVALENT DOSE (mg)	SODIUM-RETAINING POTENCY	PLASMA HALF-LIFE (min)	BIOLOGIC HALF-LIFE (h)
Hydrocortisone	1	20	2+	90	8–12
Cortisone	0.8	25	2+	30	8–12
Prednisone	4	5	1+	60	12–36
Prednisolone	4	5	1+	200	12–36
Methylprednisolone	5	4	0	180	12–36
Triamcinolone	5	4	0	300	12–36
Betamethasone	20–30	0.6	0	100–300	36–54
Dexamethasone	20–30	0.75	0	100–300	36–54

From Garber EK, Targoff C, Paulus HE: In Paulus HE, Furst DE, Droomgoole SH (eds): Drugs for Rheumatic Diseases. New York, Churchill Livingstone, 1987, p 446.

Clinical Pharmacology

Table 31–2 • EFFECT OF GLUCOCORTICOSTEROIDS ON INFLAMMATORY AND IMMUNE RESPONSES

EFFECTS ON LEUKOCYTE CIRCULATORY KINETICS (TRANSIENT AND MAXIMAL 4–6 HOURS AFTER ADMINISTRATION)
1. Neutrophilia
2. Monocytopenia
3. Lymphocytopenia—selective depletion of CD4+ T cells
4. Eosinopenia
5. Basophilopenia

EFFECTS OF LEUKOCYTE FUNCTION
1. Neutrophils: Little effect on chemotaxis, phagocytosis, and killing
2. Monocytes: Suppression of chemotaxis, cidal activity, and surface receptor expression
3. Eosinophils: Decreased chemotaxis and killing
4. T lymphocytes: Cutaneous anergy; suppression of activation, proliferation, and differentiation; reduced cytotoxic (CD8) responses
5. B lymphocytes: Reduction in serum immunoglobulins; no effect on response to injected antigens; decreased activation and proliferation
6. Natural killer cells: No effect on cytotoxic activity.

EFFECTS ON SOLUBLE MEDIATORS
1. Decreased production of prostaglandins, histamine, and leukotrienes
2. Decreased production of IL-1, IL-2, interferon-γ, and tumor necrosis factor-α
3. Little effect on complement
4. Decreased clearance of antigen-antibody complexes from circulation

are mediated by changes in the circulatory kinetics of leukocytes, alterations in the function of inflammatory cells, and modification of soluble mediators (Table 31–2).

Regardless of which of the mechanisms is examined, the initial subcellular events are initiated by glucocorticosteroid binding to cytoplasmic receptors that are reasonably comparable, although heterogeneous, among different leukocytes. The 800-amino acid receptor consists of three domains that differ in function: a hormone-binding or ligand-binding carboxyl terminal region, a DNA-binding domain, and an amino terminal immunogenic area. After glucocorticosteroid-receptor interaction, the complex traverses nuclear pores, binds to DNA at specific sites, leads to changes in the transcription rates of glucocorticosteroid-sensitive genes, and results in regulation of the synthesis of the proteins participating in the inflammatory response.

EFFECTS ON LEUKOCYTE CIRCULATORY KINETICS. The profound but transient effects of glucocorticosteroids on leukocyte trafficking differ depending on cell type. Regardless of white blood cell type and regardless of duration of therapy or dosing interval, these effects are maximal at 4 to 6 hours after administration. In part, these effects derive from glucocorticosteroid action on vascular endothelial cells, including alterations in the expression of adhesion molecules, changes in cytokine secretion, and decreased expression of major histocompatibility complex (MHC) class II antigens (Chapter 42).

A significant neutrophilia is observed 4 to 6 hours after glucocorticosteroids because neutrophils have an increased intravascular half-life, increased bone marrow release, and decreased egress from the circulation to extravascular sites of inflammation. By 24 hours, the neutrophilia resolves, unless further doses are given. Although glucocorticosteroids induce a transient increase in circulating neutrophils, these cells have a decreased ability to migrate to extravascular sites.

Neutrophilia (Chapter 163) is accompanied by lymphopenia because of the temporary migration of selected lymphocytes to bone marrow and spleen. A significant T lymphocytopenia occurs with a selective egress from the circulation of CD4+ "helper-inducer" T cells, whereas CD8+ "cytotoxic-suppressor" T cells are relatively resistant to these effects (Chapter 41). B lymphocytes are less susceptible to glucocorticosteroid-induced effects than T cells, with little alteration in intravascular number or composition. Natural killer cells, identified by CD16 expression, are similarly resistant. Monocytes migrate to extravascular locales, however, within the time frame of other glucocorticosteroid-associated changes. Eosinophils and basophils transiently exit the circulation, although the exact sites of migration are

unknown; eosinophils are reduced at areas characterized by immediate hypersensitivity reactions.

These glucocorticosteroid-induced transient changes in the intravascular leukocyte pool occur regardless of dosing intervals or duration of therapy. These effects mitigate the ability of inflammatory cells to participate in inflammatory and immunologically mediated reactions, inducing a favorable effect, but also diminish leukocyte participation in eliminating microbial invaders.

CHANGES IN LEUKOCYTE FUNCTION. Just as leukocytes vary in responsiveness to glucocorticosteroid-induced circulatory changes, similar variability is observed in their intrinsic functional capabilities. Although neutrophils are sensitive to changes in trafficking after glucocorticosteroid administration, these cells are relatively refractory to glucocorticosteroid-associated changes in function. Chemotaxis, lysosomal enzyme release, and killing are either resistant to glucocorticosteroid effects or affected only with high doses. Conversely, cells of the monocyte-macrophage series are functionally sensitive to glucocorticosteroid effects with reduced chemotaxis, killing activity, and surface receptor expression of class II antigens, Fc receptors, and receptors for the third component of complement (C3). Eosinophil chemotactic and cytotoxic functions also are reduced by glucocorticosteroids.

A variety of lymphocyte functions, including activation, proliferation, and differentiation, are sensitive to glucocorticosteroids. Although glucocorticosteroids do not affect T-cell activation, downregulation of RNA synthesis decreases proliferation, which can be reversed in vitro with exogenous interleukin (IL)-2. Mitogen-induced and antigen-induced proliferative responses are reduced in vitro; the in vivo counterpart of these responses, cutaneous delayed-type hypersensitivity, is similarly impaired within 2 weeks of starting drug therapy. Similar effects on the mixed lymphocyte reaction occur and may explain in part the utility of glucocorticosteroids in reversing allograft rejection. Cytotoxic T-cell (CD8+) responses are depressed by in vivo glucocorticosteroids.

In contrast to T cells, B-lymphocyte function is affected only modestly by glucocorticosteroids. Within 1 month of glucocorticosteroid therapy, reduction in serum immunoglobulins is noted because of increased catabolism. Antibody responses to injected antigens are not impaired. In vitro, glucocorticosteroids suppress B-cell activation with abrogation of cell enlargement, expression of activation antigens, and responses to B-cell activators. After in vitro activation and proliferation have occurred, immunoglobulin and antibody production are unaffected by glucocorticosteroids. The cytotoxic activities of natural killer cells are resistant to in vitro and in vivo glucocorticosteroids.

EFFECTS ON SOLUBLE MEDIATORS. Glucocorticosteroids may mediate some of the aforementioned activities by affecting soluble mediators. Prostaglandins arise from arachidonic acid after the action of phospholipase A_2 on phospholipids. Glucocorticosteroids block prostaglandin production through effects on the inhibitors of phospholipase A_2, called *lipocortins,* or directly on enzyme production. Transcription of the enzyme cyclooxygenase, which catalyzes the metabolism of arachidonic acid to prostaglandins, also may be blocked by glucocorticosteroids (Chapter 32).

IL-1, interferon-γ, IL-6, and tumor necrosis factor-α production and release are suppressed by glucocorticosteroids. Other monocyte-derived cytokines, such as migration inhibitory factor, are unaffected by glucocorticosteroids, however. Substantial effects on the T cell–derived cytokine IL-2 are observed. Glucocorticosteroids inhibit IL-2 synthesis, likely through effects on gene expression by suppressing RNA transcription, translation, and degradation, resulting in decreased production of this cytokine. Additionally, glucocorticosteroids block IL-2-directed protein phosphorylation and the release of other T cell–derived mediators.

Basophil-derived histamine and leukotriene secretion are abrogated by glucocorticosteroids. In general, complement metabolism is clinically unaffected, although these drugs may have some effects on release of C3 and factor B. Glucocorticosteroids inhibit the production of a variety of fibroblast-derived mediators, including prostaglandins, glycosaminoglycans, and IL-1. These effects may be clinically relevant in the inflammatory arthritides. The clearance of antigen-antibody (i.e., immune) complexes from the circulation is decreased by glucocorticosteroids; this effect, which may be important in the therapy for autoimmune diseases, seems to be mediated by downregulation of reticuloendothelial Fc receptor activity.

CLINICAL USE OF GLUCOCORTICOSTEROIDS

General Principles of Therapy

The decision to implement therapy with glucocorticosteroids must be derived from a precise understanding of these agents and the often formidable adverse reactions that accompany their use. These drugs have important roles in treating entities such as hypoadrenalism (Chapter 240) and malignancy (Chapter 191), in which the replacement is physiologic or aimed at a life-threatening disease. For inflammatory and immunologically related disorders, it is incumbent on the treating physician to determine that glucocorticosteroids are the appropriate form of treatment and that other nonglucocorticosteroid approaches are unlikely to be equally beneficial. When glucocorticosteroid treatment becomes desirable, if not mandatory, efforts must focus on minimizing glucocorticosteroid side effects, while maintaining therapeutic efficacy. Generally, these goals can be attained at least partially by using short-acting glucocorticosteroid medications at the lowest possible dose and the greatest dosing interval for the shortest period of time.

Systemic Glucocorticosteroid Therapy

INITIATING AND TAPERING THERAPY. For most inflammatory and immunologically mediated diseases, short-acting glucocorticosteroid preparations are desirable (see Table 31–1). In general, plasma half-life correlates with biologic half-life; use of preparations with longer half-lives, such as dexamethasone, is associated with a greater likelihood of adverse effects. Shorter acting glucocorticosteroids, such as prednisone or prednisolone, are preferable to longer acting preparations. These agents also are more amenable to being tapered to alternate-day regimens to reduce side effects.

Therapy usually is initiated as a single oral morning dose of prednisone (0.5 to 1.0 mg/kg). A morning dose is preferable to dosing later in the day because morning administration mimics the natural diurnal variation in cortisol levels. When more potent anti-inflammatory and immunosuppressive effects are desired, the total daily dose can be divided into three to four doses, given the short half-life of this drug. This regimen is associated with a greater likelihood of adverse effects and hypothalamic-pituitary-adrenal axis suppression; as quickly as possible, efforts should be undertaken to consolidate the split-dose schedule to a single morning dose. For example, 15 mg of prednisone given four times per day is reduced to 20 mg three times daily, then to 30 mg twice daily, and, finally to a single dose of 60 mg. The duration of each of these steps is dictated by the patient's tolerance and by control of the underlying disease; in general, this consolidation of dose should be accomplished within 3 weeks.

The once-daily regimen is maintained until the disease is stable and clinical improvement is recognized or deemed unlikely or side effects develop. Tapering should not be undertaken until the disease process is clinically quiescent, at which time reduction to an alternate-day regimen should be initiated with the goal of administering enough prednisone on the high-dose, or "on," day to suppress disease activity on the low-dose, or "off," day. This approach permits a return to normal hypothalamic-pituitary-adrenal axis function, while reducing the risk of glucocorticosteroid side effects, especially opportunistic infection.

The possibility of hypothalamic-pituitary-adrenal suppression in patients receiving long-term glucocorticosteroid therapy is particularly problematic, especially around times of stress, such as surgery. Although hypothalamic-pituitary-adrenal suppression generally depends on daily and cumulative doses and duration of treatment, it may be impossible to anticipate which patients will require supplemental glucocorticosteroids. A variety of tests have been proposed to determine the integrity of the hypothalamic-pituitary-adrenal axis, but the impact of exogenous corticotropin on serum cortisol may be the most valuable. More recent work has suggested that the amount of supplemental glucocorticosteroids required during surgery can be estimated by ascertaining the "amount" of stress (minor, moderate, or severe) anticipated in the perioperative period, with an upward adjustment of daily hydrocortisone (25 mg for minor stress; 50 to 75 mg for moderate stress, 100 to 150 mg for major stress) for 3 days.

Several protocols for tapering to an alternate-day regimen have been used. The single daily dose may be reduced in 5- to 10-mg decrements to one half of the initial dose. The dose on the "on" day can be doubled, while the dose on the "off" day is gradually decreased. When a daily dose of 30 mg of prednisone is achieved, the patient is changed to a regimen of 60 mg/day alternated with 30 mg/day, with subsequent 5-mg reductions on the low-dose day weekly until a 15-mg daily level is reached. This dose is then reduced in 2.5-mg amounts until discontinuation, at which point a 60-mg alternate-day regimen has been attained. When alternate-day therapy has been realized, gradual reductions in glucocorticosteroids should be attempted. An alternate approach is to reach a total daily dose of 30 mg/day, then reduce the drug on the low-dose day. These tapering schemes are feasible only when relatively short-acting glucocorticosteroids are used; longer acting drugs have biologic half-lives of more than 24 hours, negating the beneficial effects of an alternate-day regimen.

This protocol is not uniformly effective. Failures may occur if the attempt to begin tapering is premature because the disease is still active, if the dose is reduced too rapidly, if the decrements in dose are too large, if not enough prednisone is administered on the "on" day, or if glucocorticosteroid "withdrawal" symptoms (e.g., myalgias, arthralgias, fever) are confused with a recrudescence of the disease. In some instances, tapering can be facilitated by using glucocorticosteroid-sparing drugs that help control the primary disease as glucocorticosteroids are reduced. Nonsteroidal anti-inflammatory agents, cytotoxic drugs (e.g., methotrexate, azathioprine, and cyclophosphamide), and other agents may permit tapering to alternate-day glucocorticosteroid regimens. These agents also may have associated toxicities that limit utility, however.

One review has underscored the benefits of short-term glucocorticosteroid use in acute exacerbations of chronic obstructive pulmonary disease. Although pulmonary function improves during the initial 3 days of treatment, benefits decrease after this time, whereas side effects increase.∎

ALTERNATIVES TO ORAL THERAPY. In many circumstances, it may be appropriate to administer glucocorticosteroids locally or to use systemic regimens that may reduce the likelihood of adverse effects. Topical and ophthalmic preparations often can control cutaneous (Chapter 473) and ocular (Chapter 465) disease, without appreciable systemic absorption of the preparation. Similarly, glucocorticosteroids administered nasally for allergic rhinitis (Chapter 268), by inhalation for asthma or lower airway disease (Chapter 84), and intra-articularly or by soft tissue injection for musculoskeletal inflammatory conditions may control the underlying disease without the adverse effects of systemic therapy. These methods of delivering drugs also can cause local toxicity, however, and must be used with caution. Deflazacort, an oral glucocorticosteroid preparation not currently available in the United States, has been reported to have fewer adverse reactions, particularly osteoporosis, than conventional glucocorticosteroids.

When local glucocorticosteroid therapy and systemic daily oral treatment are inadequate to control the underlying disease, intermittent, short-term, high-dose intravenous methylprednisolone can be used in inflammatory and immunologically mediated diseases, using 3- to 5-day regimens at 20 mg/kg/day or 1 g/m²/day. Pulse regimens have been used successfully in systemic lupus erythematosus with renal disease, some forms of vasculitis, rheumatoid arthritis, ankylosing spondylitis, and Goodpasture's syndrome. The precise mechanism of the beneficial actions of "pulse" therapy is unclear, particularly because these protocols are often efficacious even when superimposed on daily glucocorticosteroid usage.

Pulse therapy has been associated with arrhythmias and sudden death, probably because of shifts in electrolytes in patients with underlying electrolyte abnormalities, conduction system disturbances, or diuretic therapy. In these settings, electrocardiographic monitoring is advisable while the drug is administered slowly over 1 to several hours. Other reported adverse reactions with pulse therapy include seizures and systemic infections, but the precise relationship of the reactions to pulse glucocorticosteroids is unclear because the therapy commonly is given to critically ill patients. Current indications for pulse regimens have included recrudescence of disease despite long-term glucocorticosteroid therapy, a flare of disease activity in the setting of glucocorticosteroid side effects, the need to control disease until another modality (e.g., cytotoxic drug) becomes effective, and the onset of a rapidly progressive glucocorticosteroid-responsive syndrome.

Table 31–3 • SIDE EFFECTS OF GLUCOCORTICOSTEROID THERAPY

Characteristic early in therapy; essentially unavoidable
  Insomnia
  Emotional lability
  Enhanced appetite or weight gain or both
Common in patients with underlying risk factors or other drug toxicities
  Hypertension
  Diabetes mellitus
  Peptic ulcer disease
  Acne vulgaris
Anticipated with use of sustained and intense treatment: minimize risk by conservative dosing regimens and steroid-sparing agents when possible
  Cushingoid habitus
  Hypothalamic-pituitary-adrenal suppression
  Infection diathesis
  Osteonecrosis
  Myopathy
  Impaired wound healing
Insidious and delayed: likely dependent on cumulative dose
  Osteoporosis
  Skin atrophy
  Cataracts
  Atherosclerosis
  Growth retardation
  Fatty liver
Rare and unpredictable
  Psychosis
  Pseudotumor cerebri
  Glaucoma
  Epidural lipomatosis
  Pancreatitis

From Boumpas DT, Chrousos GP, Wilder RL, et al: Glucocorticoid therapy for immune-mediated diseases: Basic and clinical correlates. Ann Intern Med 1993;19:1198.

Complications of Glucocorticosteroid Therapy

Prolonged systemic glucocorticosteroid therapy is invariably associated with toxicity (Table 31–3). In general, side effects depend on daily dose, dosing frequency, and duration of treatment and emphasize the need to treat with alternate-day regimens or the lowest daily dose possible for as briefly as feasible. Hypothalamic-pituitary-adrenal axis suppression may occur with less than 2 weeks of systemic therapy and may be persistent despite cessation of the drug. The integrity of the hypothalamic-pituitary-adrenal axis in the setting of glucocorticosteroid therapy can be determined by measuring the change in serum cortisol level after cosyntropin infusion (Chapter 240).

In general, the most effective way of preventing or minimizing the adverse effects of glucocorticosteroids is to reduce their dosage; this may not always be feasible. It is particularly important to monitor patients closely for the development of infection; typical signs of infection may be masked by glucocorticosteroid treatment. Glucocorticosteroid-induced osteoporosis (Chapter 258) is especially problematic in older individuals, particularly those who are estrogen deficient. Calcium supplementation and postmenopausal estrogen repletion are also helpful. Cyclical, oral bisphosphonates prevent glucocorticosteroid-induced loss of bone mineral density in the spine and hip and may be the preferred therapy.

1. Wood-Baker R, Walters EH, Gibson P: Oral corticosteroids for acute exacerbations of chronic obstructive pulmonary disease. Cochrane Database Syst Rev 2000;2:CD001288.

SUGGESTED READINGS

Buchman AL: Side effects of corticosteroid therapy. J Clin Gastroenterol 2001;33:289–294. *Excellent summary of short-term and long-term effects of treatment in inflammatory bowel disease.*
Saag KG: Glucocorticoid-induced osteoporosis. Endocrinol Metab Clin North Am 2003;32:135–157. *Recent summary including dilemmas in diagnosis and prevention.*

32 PROSTAGLANDINS, ASPIRIN, AND RELATED COMPOUNDS

Garret A. FitzGerald

Arachidonic acid (AA) is an unsaturated fatty acid that contains 20 carbon atoms and 4 double bonds (Δ5,8,11,14: C20:4). It circulates in plasma in free and esterified forms and is a natural constituent of the phospholipid domain of cell membranes, bound to the glycerol backbone in the sn:2 position. AA is mobilized for release from the membrane by the action of various phospholipases A_2 (PLA_2), but particularly a type IV cytosolic (c) PLA_2, which has high affinity for AA as a substrate. Diverse stimuli, including physical perturbation and hormones, mediate a calcium-dependent translocation of $cPLA_2$ to the nuclear membrane and the endoplasmic reticulum, where it catalyzes the release of AA. The lipid substrate is subject to metabolism by three major groups of enzymes—prostaglandin G/H synthase, which catalyzes the formation of prostaglandins; lipoxygenases, which result in the formation of leukotrienes; and cytochrome P-450 isozymes, which generate epoxyeicosatrienoic acids. Collectively, these products are known as *eicosanoids*, derived from the Greek έικώσι for the 20 carbons. Isoeicosanoids are free radical catalyzed isomers of prostaglandins, leukotrienes, and epoxyeicosatrienoic acids formed by direct peroxidation of AA in situ in cell membranes.

Cyclooxygenase Pathway

The best-known products of AA are the prostaglandins, formed by the action of prostaglandin G/H synthase on AA to form bisenoic products containing two double bonds, denoted by a subscript $_2$, such as prostaglandin E_2 (PGE_2). Prostaglandin G/H synthase catalyzes the formation of monoenoic (Δ13) prostaglandins (e.g., PGE_1) from eicosatrienoic acid (C 20:3; n-6) and of trienoic (Δ5,13,17) prostaglandins (e.g., PGE_3) from eicosapentaeonic acid (C 20:5; n-3), which is prevalent in fatty fish.

Prostaglandin G/H synthase is expressed as a dimer, homotypically inserted into the endoplasmic reticulum membrane. Prostaglandin G/H synthase contains cyclooxygenase (COX) and hydroperoxidase activities, sequentially catalyzing the transformation of AA into the unstable cyclic endoperoxides, prostaglandin G_2 and prostaglandin H_2 (Fig. 32–1). Prostaglandin H_2 is delivered to downstream isomerases and synthases that are expressed in a cell-specific manner and that generate evanescent products, the prostaglandins. It is presently not understood how AA is delivered specifically to prostaglandin G/H synthase (colloquially known as *COX*) or how prostaglandin H_2 is presented to downstream enzymes. Prostaglandins activate G-protein–coupled membrane receptors. Two COX genes have been identified: *COX-1* is expressed constitutively in most cells; *COX-2* is upregulated by cytokines, shear stress, and tumor promoters. These observations suggest that *COX-1* accounts for prostaglandin formation that subserves housekeeping functions, such as gastric epithelial cytoprotection and hemostasis (see later), whereas *COX-2* is the dominant source of prostaglandin formation in inflammation and cancer. Both isozymes are subject to developmental regulation, however, and both may contribute to prostaglandin formation in human inflammation; they are coexpressed in human atherosclerotic plaque and in synovial tissue in patients with rheumatoid arthritis.

Deletion of *COX-2* results in multiple defects of implantation and reproduction; it is difficult for these animals to breed. Offspring variably have had cardiac fibrosis, renal defects, and impairment of inflammatory responses. The extent to which these phenotypes are modulated by genetic background is presently unclear, however. *COX-1* deletion has been reported to impair certain inflammatory responses. Deletion of the *COX-2* gene results in an increased frequency of patent ductus arteriosus. Although *COX-1* deletion alone does not result in a patent ductus arteriosus, coincidental deletion of *COX-1* increases the frequency of the *COX-2* knockout patent ductus arteriosus phenotype. Uses of COX knockouts and isozyme-specific inhibitors suggest that *COX-1* and *COX-2* are expressed in a spatially segregated manner at different times during thymic development and that they influence T-cell maturation. Deleting one isozyme seems to have a variable, tissue-dependent impact on expression of the other.

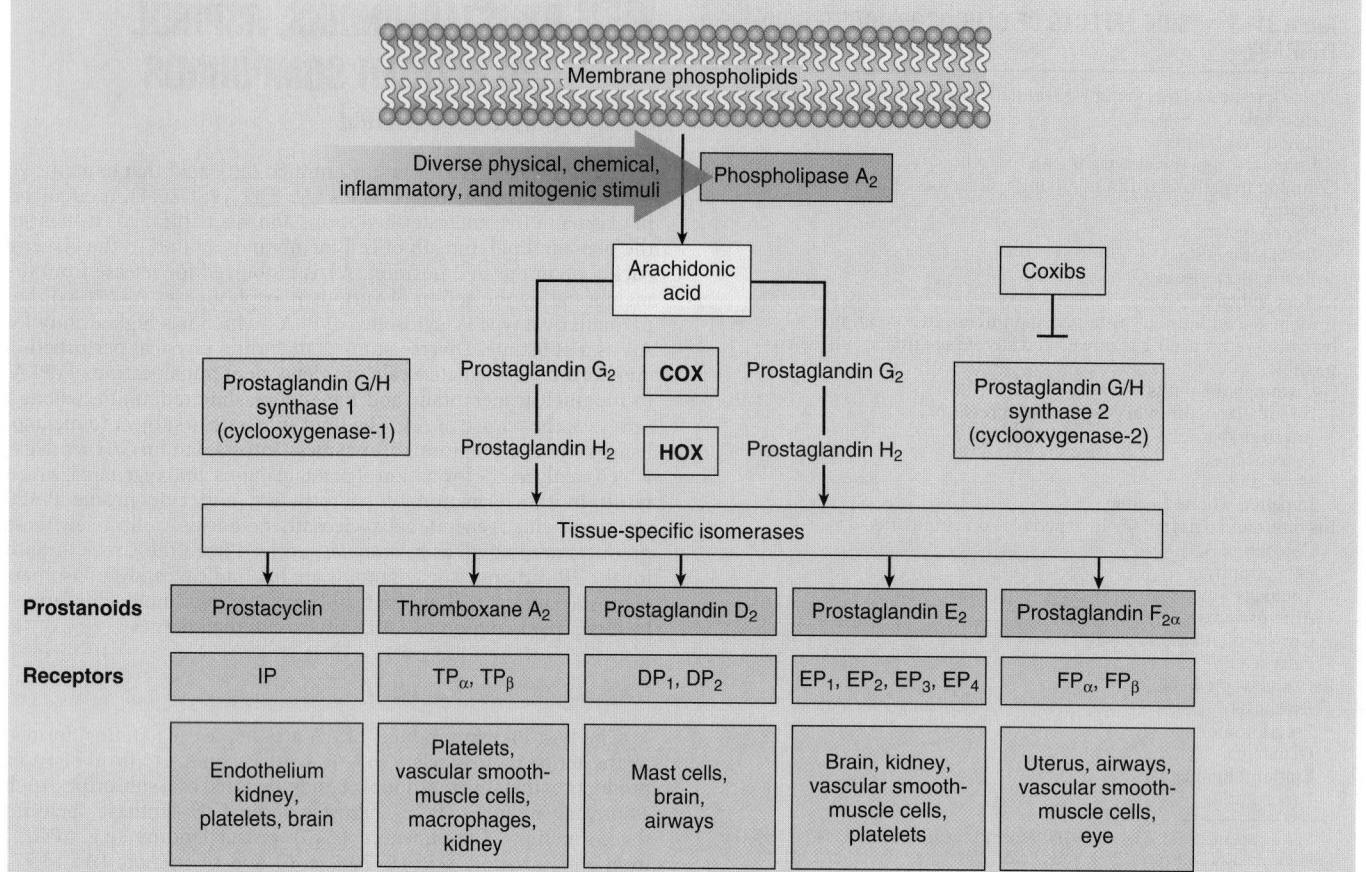

FIGURE 32–1 • Production and actions of prostaglandins and thromboxane. Arachidonic acid (AA), a 20-carbon fatty acid containing four double bonds, is liberated from the *sn*2 position in membrane phospholipids by phospholipase A_2, which is activated by diverse stimuli. AA is converted by cytosolic prostaglandin G/H synthases, which have cyclooxygenase (COX) and hydroperoxidase (HOX) activity, to the unstable intermediate prostaglandin H_2. The synthases are colloquially termed *cyclooxygenases* and exist in two forms, cyclooxygenase-1 and cyclooxygenase-2. Coxibs selectively inhibit cyclooxygenase-2. Prostaglandin H_2 is converted by tissue-specific isomerases to multiple prostanoids. These bioactive lipids activate specific cell-membrane receptors of the superfamily of G-protein-coupled receptors. Some of the tissues in which individual prostanoids exert prominent effects are indicated. EP = prostaglandin E_2 receptor; FP = prostaglandin $F_{2\alpha}$ receptor; P = prostacyclin receptor; P = prostaglandin D_2 receptor; TP = thromboxane receptor. (From FitzGerald GA, Patrono C: The coxibs, selective inhibitors of cyclooxygenase-2. N Engl J Med 2001;345:433–442.)

COX-1 and *COX-2* have been crystallized and bear a remarkable similarity at the atomic level (Fig. 32–2). One difference is a more accommodating hydrophobic tunnel for substrate access to the COX catalytic site in *COX-2*, reflected by a broader range of substrate specificity for this isozyme. Another is the existence of a side pocket in the hydrophobic channel of *COX-2*, which has afforded the structural basis for the development of selective inhibitors of this isozyme. Although immunogold studies suggest a similar subcellular distribution of both isoenzymes, each exhibits a preference for coupling with different downstream enzymes in heterologous expression systems and, apparently, in vivo. *COX-1* preferentially couples with thromboxane synthase and prostaglandin F synthase, whereas *COX-2* prefers prostaglandin I synthase. Two classes of prostaglandin E synthases have been cloned. One is a microsomal family of m-prostaglandin E synthase isoenzymes that belong to the *MAPEG* (membrane associated proteins in eicosanoid and glutathione metabolism) superfamily; these colocalize with *COX-2* in several systems and are induced by cytokines and tumor promoters. A second is a cytosolic family of c-prostaglandin E synthase isoenzymes that colocalize with *COX-1* and seem to favor this isozyme in heterologous coexpression systems. Two forms of prostaglandin D synthase and prostaglandin F synthase also have been identified. It seems likely that understanding of the diversity, function, and localization of the isomerases and synthases will expand dramatically in the near future.

Because of their short half-lives (seconds to minutes), prostaglandins act as autacoids rather than circulating hormones. They activate membrane receptors at, or close to, the site of their formation, perhaps following their export by dodecahelical transporters. Specific heptahelical receptors have been cloned for all of the prostaglandins (see Fig. 32–1). Single receptors have been identified

for prostacyclin (prostaglandin I_2 [PGI_2]; the I prostanoid receptor), prostaglandin $F_{2\alpha}$ ($PGF_{2\alpha}$) (the F prostanoid receptor), and thromboxane A_2 (the T prostanoid receptor). Four receptors have been cloned for PGE_2 (the E prostanoid receptors 1 through 4) and two for prostaglandin D_2 (PGD_2) (D prostanoid receptor 1 and D prostanoid receptor 2). All except for D prostanoid receptor 2 seem to derive from an ancestral E prostanoid receptor and share high homology. The D prostanoid receptor 2, by contrast, is unrelated to the others and belongs to the N-formyl Met-Leu-Phe receptor superfamily. It seems likely that other prostaglandin receptors will emerge. There is pharmacologic evidence for two functionally distinct forms of the T prostanoid receptor; however, this distinction is not attributable to the two carboxy terminal variants of the cloned receptor (T prostanoid receptor α and T prostanoid receptor β), which presently have been identified. Receptor deletion studies in mice revealed the diversity prostaglandin function in mammals.

THROMBOXANE A_2

Thromboxane A_2 is the major product of *COX-1*, the only isoform expressed in mature human platelets. Both COX isoforms have been identified in developing megakaryocytes. *COX-2* is detectable in immature platelets released into the circulation in syndromes of accelerated platelet turnover. Its contribution to platelet thromboxane formation even under such circumstances seems trivial, however. Thromboxane A_2 is a potent vasoconstrictor and induces platelet activation in vitro. Deletion of the T prostanoid receptor reveals a mild hemostatic defect and resistance to AA-induced platelet activation. Despite the diversity of platelet agonists, inhibition of platelet thromboxane formation is thought to account for cardioprotection from

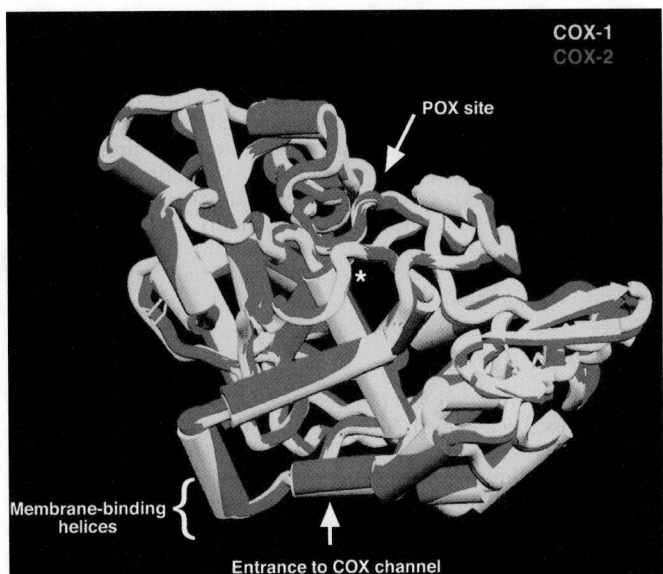

FIGURE 32–2 • The *COX-1* and *COX-2* backbones, overlaid. *COX-1* is shown in yellow, and *COX-2* is shown in red. The two structures are almost perfectly superimposable. The amphiphatic helices that form the site of monotopic membrane attachment are indicated. The peroxidase (POX) active site lies on the opposite side of the molecule from the entrance to the COX active site channel. The actual position of the COX active center is marked by the asterisk, found near the center of the molecule. (From FitzGerald GA, Loll P: COX in a crystal ball: Current status and future promise of prostaglandin research. J Clin Invest 2001;107:1335–1337.)

aspirin (see later). This finding may reflect the importance of thromboxane A_2 as an amplification signal for continuing the process of platelet aggregation induced by more potent agonists, such as thrombin and adenosine diphosphate (ADP). Thromboxane A_2 is also a major product of macrophage *COX-2* and has been shown to contribute to atherogenesis in mouse models. Deletion of the T prostanoid receptor also modulates the proliferative response to vascular injury in mice. Overexpression of the T prostanoid receptor in vascular tissues results in a syndrome reminiscent of intrauterine growth retardation, probably secondary to placental ischemia.

Two forms of the T prostanoid receptor have been segregated pharmacologically: one mediating platelet shape change, the other mediating aggregation. The cloned splice variants do not seem to account for this distinction, however, and only T prostanoid receptor α is expressed in platelets. The only differences that have emerged between the splice variants to date have related to affinity for coupling with downstream guanosine triphosphate (GTP) binding (G) proteins and the rate of agonist-induced desensitization. Given the identification of distinct purinergic receptors of low homology, which mediate either ADP-induced platelet shape change or aggregation, it seems likely that at least one more T prostanoid receptor remains to be identified.

The cloned T prostanoid receptor isoforms couple via G_q, $G_{12/13}$, and G_h (which is also tissue transglutaminase II) to activate phospholipase C–dependent inositol phosphate generation and an elevation in intracellular calcium. Activation of the T prostanoid receptor also may inhibit adenylate cyclase via G_i and signal via G_q and related proteins to membrane associated protein kinase signaling pathways. Analogous to its role in vascular proliferation, T prostanoid receptor activation also may mediate hypertrophy of myometrial cells and cardiomyocytes. The T prostanoid receptor is expressed abundantly in the thymus, but its role in lymphocyte development and function is presently unclear. A naturally occurring mutation in the first intracellular loop of the T prostanoid has been associated with a mild bleeding diathesis and resistance to platelet aggregability by T prostanoid receptor agonists. A polymorphism in the T prostanoid has been linked to bronchodilator resistance in asthma.

PROSTACYCLIN (PROSTAGLANDIN I₂)

PGI_2, the major product of *COX-2* in healthy individuals, is a potent inhibitor of platelet aggregation reduced by all recognized agonists

and a vasodilator. Mice deficient in the I prostanoid receptor, although normotensive, have an exaggerated response to hypertensive stimuli, such as dietary salt. Similarly, findings in I prostanoid receptor–deficient mice implicated PGI_2 in the mediation of pain and inflammation. These consequences seem conditioned, however, by genetic background. Platelets of I prostanoid receptor knockout mice reveal resistance to disaggregation by I prostanoid receptor agonists. These mice exhibit an enhanced proliferative response to vascular injury. Biosynthesis of PGI_2 is increased in syndromes of platelet activation, such as severe atherosclerosis and unstable angina (Chapters 66 and 68), perhaps as a homeostatic response to accelerated platelet vascular interactions. Evidence has emerged in mice that PGI_2 specifically limits the effects of thromboxane A_2 on platelets and the vessel wall in vivo.

Prostaglandin I synthase appears uniquely sensitive among the AA biosynthetic enzymes to nitrative inactivation. Deletion of the I prostanoid receptor undermines the atheroprotective effect of female gender in apolipoprotein-E-deficient mice. Female sex hormones upregulate prostaglandin I synthase and may protect it from free radical–based inactivation. Prostaglandin I synthase gene transfer diminishes the response to vascular injury in rodents and the response to thrombotic stimuli in dogs. Prostaglandin I synthase knockout mice have a phenotype—severe hypertension and renal lesions—that is distinct from I prostanoid receptor knockout mice. *COX-2*-dependent PGI_2 formation also limits oxidant injury in cardiomyocytes, reduces the pulmonary vasoconstriction induced by hypoxia, and blocks angiotensin II–induced renal vasoconstriction and systemic hypertension.

PROSTAGLANDIN D₂

PGD_2 is the major *COX* product formed by mast cells. It is released during allergic responses, including asthma and systemic mastocytosis. Infusion of PGD_2 in humans results in flushing, nasal stuffiness, and hypotension, although subsequent formation of F-ring metabolites may result in hypertension, presumably owing to activation of the F prostanoid receptor. PGD_2 activates a G-protein-coupled receptor, the D prostanoid receptor 1, which is related closely to the other prostanoid receptors. Deletion of the D prostanoid receptor 1 sharply reduces the infiltration of lymphocytes and eosinophils and decreases the airway's reactivity induced by ovalbumin in rodents, suggesting that PGD_2 may have a role in the mediation of asthma. A chemoattractant receptor-homologous molecule (CRTH2) expressed on T helper type 2 cells has been recognized to function as a D prostanoid receptor 2. PGD_2 induces chemotaxis and migration of T helper type 2 cells through the D prostanoid receptor 2. D prostanoid receptor 2 and prostaglandin D synthase are expressed coordinately at the fetal-maternal interface in human deciduas, where they may participate in lymphocyte recruitment. Overexpression of the prostaglandin D synthase increases the cellular and functional response to bronchial challenge with ovalbumin in mice.

PGD_2 is an abundant COX product in brain, where its functional significance is presently incompletely understood. Data from knockout mice suggest, however, that PGD_2 acts on arachnoid trabecular cells in the basal forebrain to mediate an increase in extracellular adenosine, which facilitates induction of sleep. Elevated levels of PGD_2 occur in African sleeping sickness (Chapter 393) and meningitis (Chapter 312). Localized infusions of PGE_2 into the third ventricle counter the effects of PGD_2 and induce wakefulness through E prostanoid receptor 1 and E prostanoid receptor 3. When infused into the subarachnoid space of the basal forebrain, PGE_2 also induces sleep, however, via the E prostanoid 4 receptor. Prostaglandin D synthase is highly expressed in the leptomeninges and the choroid plexus, and it is a major protein in cerebrospinal fluid. Expression seems to be increased in meningiomas. Deletion of prostaglandin D synthase abolishes allodynia (sensitivity to pain) in mice. A second form of prostaglandin D synthase is found in blood cells, and abnormal levels have been described in the circulation in patients with coronary disease.

PGD_2 may be metabolized in vitro to prostaglandin J_2, from which the metabolite 15-deoxy Δ (12,14) prostaglandin J_2 is formed. Considerable interest has revolved around the possibility that the metabolite might function as a natural ligand for perioxisomal proliferator activator receptor γ and contribute to the resolution phase of inflammation. Although prostaglandin J_2 and its metabolite can

Clinical Pharmacology

activate the nuclear receptor in vitro, however, it is presently unclear whether sufficient concentrations are formed to exert this effect in vivo. *COX-2*-derived PGD_2 and its putative J_2 metabolite have been suggested to contribute to the resolution phase in inflammation in several animal models.

PROSTAGLANDIN E_2

PGE_2 is coupled to two receptors—the E prostanoid receptor 2 and the E prostanoid receptor 4—which activate adenylate cyclase through coupling to the GTP binding protein, Gs. Mice deficient in the E prostanoid receptor 2 are normotensive but have an increased sensitivity to salt and can develop pressor hormone—induced hypertension. PGE_2 and PGI_2 play crucial roles in maintaining renal blood flow under conditions of increased vasoconstrictor tone associated with activation of the sympathoadrenal and renin-angiotensin systems. *COX-2* is induced in the proximal tubule under conditions of salt loading, and PGE_2 activates the E prostanoid receptor 2 to inhibit tubular sodium reabsorption. Inhibition of these prostanoids does not compromise renal blood flow under physiologic conditions, but COX inhibition may result in impairment of blood flow under renoprival conditions, with a consequent rise in systemic blood pressure, fluid retention, or deterioration in renal function. Experiments in mice suggest that *COX-2* is the dominant source of these autoregulatory prostaglandins. It is unclear whether E prostanoid receptor 2 or E prostanoid receptor 4 plays a dominant role in mediating the PGE_2's vasodilator effects in this setting and its ability to inhibit tubular sodium reabsorption.

Selective E prostanoid receptor 2 agonists inhibit myometrial contractility and are being investigated for use in the treatment of premature labor. *COX-2*-dependent PGE_2 activates the E prostanoid 2 to enhance the development of intestinal polyposis in mice, apparently by inducing release of vascular endothelial growth factor and consequent angiogenesis. PGE_2 plays a complex role in the switch from the fetal to adult circulation. Inactivation of the E prostanoid receptor 4, but not the E prostanoid receptor 2, results in a patent ductus arteriosus and neonatal death, suggesting that PGE_2 is the major product mediating *COX-2*-dependent ductal remodeling and closure. An abrupt decline in the perinatal period results from induction of 15-PGE_2 dehydrogenase, the major inactivating enzyme of PGE_2. Low levels of PGE_2 signal via the EP4 receptor to induce remodeling. Deletion of this enzyme sustains high levels of PGE_2 throughout the perinatal period. By contrast, these high levels of the prostaglandin mediate ductal patency through the E prostanoid 4 receptor. E prostanoid receptor 2 and E prostanoid receptor 4 also seem relevant to immune function; E prostanoid 2 receptors inhibit T-cell proliferation, and E prostanoid 2 and E prostanoid 4 receptors regulate antigen presenting function in vivo. Both receptors mediate T-cell factor (Tcf)/lymphoid enhancer factor (Lef)–mediated transcriptional activation. Finally, E prostanoid receptor 2 and E prostanoid receptor 4 interact in bone development and remodeling; E prostanoid receptor 4 antagonists limit osteoclastogenesis and bone resorption in vitro, whereas E prostanoid receptor 2 deletion reduces bone biomechanical strength in vivo. E prostanoid 4 receptor agonists limit bone loss and stimulate osteoblastogenesis in rodents, suggesting potential utility in osteoporosis.

E prostanoid receptor 1 and E prostanoid receptor 3 are coupled via G_q to phospholipase C activation and an inositol phosphate–mediated increase in intracellular calcium, similar to the T prostanoid and the F prostanoid receptors (see later). E prostanoid receptor 3 also inhibits adenylate cyclase via G_i. Activation of these receptor subtypes may result in a metalloproteinase-dependent transactivation of the epidermal growth factor receptor, also of potential relevance to proliferative effects of PGE_2 in cancer. Circulating levels of the cytokine interleukin-1β induce coordinate expression of *COX-2* and m-prostaglandin E synthase at the blood-brain barrier, permitting activation of E prostanoid receptors in the brain and spine. The pyrexial response to a range of endogenous and exogenous pyrogens seems to be mediated by activation of the E prostanoid receptor 3 in neurons of the organum vasculosum of lamina terminalis, at the midline of the preoptic area. Spinal E prostanoid receptor 1 mediates allodynia, similar to the I prostanoid receptor and products of prostaglandin D synthase (see earlier), whereas E prostanoid receptor 3 seems to mediate hyperalgesia in mice. The implications of these findings in murine models for human syndromes of pain remain to be determined, however. E prostanoid 1 and 3 receptors seem to mediate the

myometrial contractility caused by prostaglandin E analogues, such as misoprostol, used to induce labor.

The E prostanoid 3 also mediates platelet aggregation, similar to the T prostanoid receptor. High concentrations of PGE_2 can inhibit platelet function by activating the I prostanoid receptor. Such issues of functional redundancy and their implications for drug development are only beginning to be explored. Similarly the role of E prostanoid subtypes may be conditioned by differential tissue expression. The cytoprotective effects of prostaglandin E analogues are mediated by E prostanoid receptor 1 in the murine stomach but by E prostanoid receptors 3 and 4 in the intestine and by E prostanoid receptor 4 in the colon.

PROSTAGLANDIN $F_{2\alpha}$

So far, one G-protein-coupled receptor for $PGF_{2\alpha}$, the F prostanoid receptor, has been cloned. It is coupled to G_q and can activate phospholipase C–dependent increases in intracellular calcium culminating in activation of protein kinase C or a rho-dependent kinase. Activation of the F prostanoid receptor is crucial to parturition. Mice deficient in the F prostanoid receptor do not deliver normal fetuses at term because of failure to induce the oxytocin receptor and absence of the normal decline in elevated progesterone levels. Ovariectomy restores responsiveness to oxytocin and permits successful parturition. *COX-1*-derived $PGF_{2\alpha}$ seems to interact with the F prostanoid receptor to induce luteolysis. *COX-2* is upregulated subsequently, and its products, including $PGF_{2\alpha}$ and thromboxane A_2, play a role in the final stages of parturition. $PGF_{2\alpha}$ and its 15-hydroxy metabolite function as male pheromones in fish.

The F prostanoid receptor also is expressed in the ciliary body of the eye, and F prostanoid receptor agonists have shown clinical utility in the treatment of increased intraocular pressure in patients with glaucoma. Activation of the F prostanoid receptor results in vasoconstriction, bronchoconstriction, vascular smooth muscle cell proliferation, and cardiomyocyte hypertrophy. The role of this prostaglandin in cardiopulmonary disease is poorly characterized, however. Similarly, activation of the F prostanoid receptor blocks preadipocyte differentiation in vitro, but the role of the F prostanoid receptor, if any, in obesity is poorly understood.

Prostaglandin F synthase is a member of the aldo-keto reductase (*AKR*) family of enzymes. It catalyzes the reduction of prostaglandin H_2 to $PGF_{2\alpha}$ and of PGD_2 to 9α 11β-prostaglandin F_2, and it has been shown to reduce retinal to retinol. Prostaglandin F synthase exists in at least two isoforms, identified initially in liver and lung. Prostaglandin F synthase is related closely to 20α-hydroxysteroid dehydrogenase, an aldo-keto reductase that inactivates progesterone to 20α progesterone; is crucial to the maintenance of pregnancy; and is inhibited by nonsteroidal anti-inflammatory drugs (NSAIDs). Prostaglandin F synthase is expressed in contractile tissues of the lung and in lymphocytes, the spinal cord, and the liver.

ISOEICOSANOIDS

Isoeicosanoids are free radical–catalyzed isomers of the enzymatic products of AA. Isoprostanes, isomers of the prostaglandins, are formed initially in situ in the membrane after peroxidation of AA. Because they are inflexible molecules, they may contribute to membrane injury induced by oxidants. After formation, they are cleaved by phospholipases. The endogenous phospholipases that fulfill this function are unknown, but secretory type II PLA_2s and the platelet activating factor acetyl hydrolase exhibit this function in vitro. The isoprostanes are a much more complex family than the prostaglandins. Theoretically, 64 isomers, divided into 4 chemical classes (isoprostanes III, IV, V, and VI), may be formed for each prostaglandin by this mechanism.

Perhaps the most studied isoprostane is isoprostane $F_{2\alpha}$-III, a prostaglandin F isomer also known as 8-*iso* $PGF_{2\alpha}$. This compound acts as an incidental ligand at the T prostanoid receptor to modulate platelet function and induce vascular smooth muscle cell contraction. Other isoprostanes exhibit diverse biologic actions by activating other eicosanoid G-protein-coupled receptors or by acting as ligands for nuclear perioxisomal proliferator activator receptors in vitro. It is unknown, however, if the concentrations attained in vivo evoke these responses and contribute to the clinical manifestations of oxidant stress in human disease. Because isoprostanes are chemically stable, circulate, and are cleared into urine, they have attracted much attention as indices of lipid peroxidation in vivo. Urinary isoprostanes are elevated in syndromes of oxidant stress, such as during tissue reperfusion after ischemia. Elevated levels have been detected in atherosclerotic plaque, circulating low-density lipoprotein, and urine of hypercholesterolemic patients and in the senile plaques, cerebrospinal fluid, plasma, and urine of patients with Alzheimer's disease. Because isoprostane $F_{2\alpha}$-III is a minor urinary isoprostane and may be formed in a COX-dependent mechanism, attention has focused on members of the more abundant VI series, such as 8,12-*iso* isoprostane $F_{2\alpha}$-VI, as a preferable anylate. Quantification of urinary isoprostanes may facilitate a rational basis to select doses and patients for clinical trials of antioxidants.

Inhibitors of Cyclooxygenase

Three classes of COX inhibitors include aspirin, traditional NSAIDs, and a subset of the NSAIDs, the coxibs, which specifically target *COX-2*.

ASPIRIN

Aspirin irreversibly acetylates a serine (Ser[529]) residue close to, but not at, the COX catalytic site in prostaglandin G/H synthase. Interpolation of the bulky acetyl residue prevents access of the substrate to the catalytic site (Fig. 32–3). The anucleate platelet retains minimal capacity to generate new protein and is rendered a unique cellular target for aspirin action. This effect has two major clinical implications. First, doses of aspirin that incompletely block the capacity of platelet *COX-1* to generate thromboxane A_2 have a cumulative effect until they produce maximal inhibition after repeated daily administration. This principle underlies the use of low doses of aspirin, such as 75 to 80 mg/day, for cardiac protection (Chapters 67, 68, and 69). These doses take 3 to 4 days to reach a steady state and would be expected to provide similar protection as high doses of aspirin, while simultaneously reducing drug exposure and drug-related side effects. Complete inhibition of platelet *COX-1* can be achieved with a single loading dose of 160 mg or more of aspirin. By comparison, nucleated cells, such as endothelial cells, generate PGI_2 and recover from aspirin exposure within hours owing to synthesis of new prostaglandin G/H synthase.

The second implication of aspirin's mechanism of action is that when platelet thromboxane A_2 is completely inhibited, new platelets must be generated to overcome aspirin's effects. Recovery of platelet function requires regeneration of only 10% of the normal platelet count,

but there is a 1- to 2-day lag thought to reflect the impact of aspirin on marrow megakaryocytes. Platelet function begins to recover 4 to 5 days after inhibition by aspirin and is complete within 12 to 14 days, corresponding to platelet turnover time. This principle underlies the use of aspirin every other day, which would be expected, under steady-state conditions, to be equally effective for cardiac protection.

So far, there are no large-scale prospective trials to assess the relative effectiveness of higher and lower doses of aspirin in cardiovascular disease. Doses of 81 mg/day, 324 mg/day, and 1300 mg/day all reduce myocardial infarction (MI) and death, however, each by 50%, in placebo-controlled trials in patients with unstable angina (Chapter 68). Meta-analyses suggest that doses greater than and less than 325 mg are similarly effective in the secondary prevention of MI and stroke. No difference was seen in the effectiveness of daily doses of 30 mg versus 283 mg in the secondary prevention of these events in patients presenting with a transient ischemic attack or minor stroke. Insufficient data are available, however, to permit a rigorous analysis of the relative impact of lower dosing regimens on clinical outcomes. Because PGI_2 modulates the cardiovascular biology of thromboxane A_2 in vivo, one might speculate that lower doses might be more efficacious if PGI_2 were spared. Even low doses of conventionally formulated aspirin reduce biosynthesis of PGI_2 coincident with that of thromboxane A_2, however. Aspirin acetylates platelets as they circulate through the portal circulation. A slow-release, low-dose aspirin preparation takes advantage of the high first-pass metabolism of aspirin to its deacetylation product, salicylic acid, a weak reversible COX inhibitor, and confines aspirin's action to the presystemic circulation. Because the systemic vasculature is protected from aspirin exposure, PGI_2 formation is not depressed coincident with thromboxane A_2 with this formulation; it is unknown if this confers a clinical advantage.

Overview analyses suggest that aspirin reduces the secondary incidence of important vascular events—nonfatal stroke, nonfatal MI, and vascular death—by about 25%. Aspirin reduces the secondary incidence of MI by about 30% and of stroke by about 15%. This disparity in aspirin action is explained partly by the reduction in thrombotic strokes being offset by an increase in the less common hemorrhagic strokes. Relatively short-term studies (follow-up approximately 1 month) showed that aspirin reduces mortality in patients presenting with either acute stroke or acute MI. Benefit from aspirin is a function of the incidence of thrombotic events. The magnitude of the absolute benefit decreases as one moves from unstable angina to MI to stroke to chronic stable angina, all conditions in which aspirin

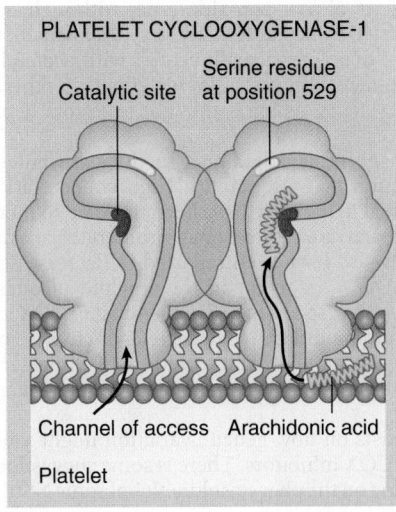 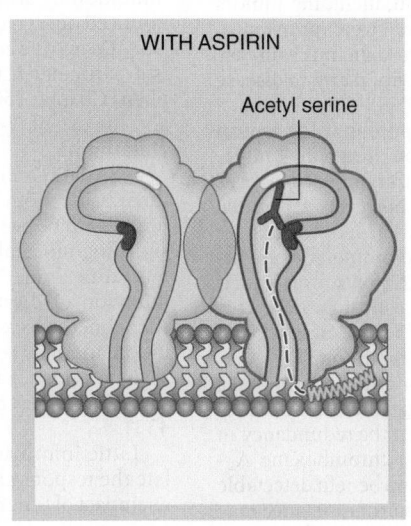 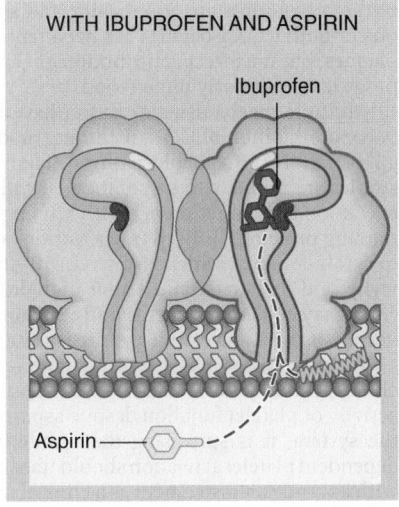

FIGURE 32–3 • The platelet prostaglandin G/H synthase-1 (cyclooxygenase-1) is depicted as a dimer. The arachidonic acid (AA) substrate gains access to the catalytic site (orange area) through a hydrophobic channel that leads into the core of the enzyme (A). Aspirin blocks the access of AA to the catalytic site by irreversibly acetylating a serine residue at position 529 in platelet cyclooxygenase-1, near but not within the catalytic site (B). Interpolation of the bulky acetyl residue prevents metabolism of AA into the cyclic endoperoxide prostaglandin G_2 and prostaglandin H_2 for the lifetime of the platelet. Because prostaglandin H_2 is metabolized by thromboxane synthase into thromboxane A_2, aspirin prevents the formation of thromboxane A_2 by the platelets until new platelets are generated. Nonsteroidal anti-inflammatory drugs, such as ibuprofen, are reversible, competitive inhibitors of the catalytic site whose use results in the reversible inhibition of thromboxane A_2 formation during the dosing interval. Prior occupancy of the catalytic site by ibuprofen prevents aspirin from gaining access to its target serine (C). (From Catella-Lawson F, Reilly MP, Kapoor SC, et al: Cyclooxygenase inhibitors and the antiplatelet effects of aspirin. N Engl J Med 2001;345:1809–1837.)

Clinical Pharmacology

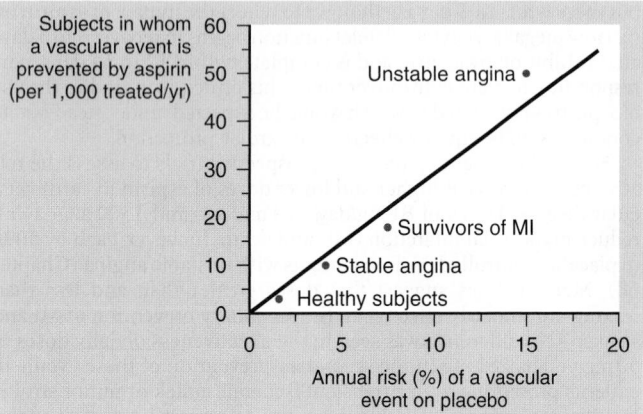

FIGURE 32–4 • The absolute risk of vascular complications is the major determinant of the absolute benefit of antiplatelet prophylaxis. Data are plotted from placebo-controlled aspirin trials in different clinical settings. For each category of patients, the abscissa denotes the absolute risk of experiencing a major vascular event as recorded in the placebo arms of the trials. The absolute benefit of antiplatelet treatment is reported on the ordinate axis as the number of subjects in whom an important vascular event (i.e., nonfatal myocardial infarction [MI], nonfatal stroke, or vascular death) is prevented by treating 1000 subjects with aspirin for 1 year. (From Patrono C, Coller B, Dalen JE, et al: Platelet-active drugs: The relationships among dose, effectiveness, and side effects. Chest 2001;119:39S–63S.)

is more effective than placebo (Fig. 32–4). The place of aspirin in primary prevention is less clear. Controlled trials indicate that low-dose aspirin reduces the incidence of nonfatal MI, but the number of MIs prevented corresponds almost precisely to the number of serious upper gastrointestinal bleeds attributable to aspirin therapy.[2]

Multiple epidemiologic studies have associated aspirin consumption with a reduced incidence of colon cancer (Chapter 200). Similar data have been obtained for NSAIDs. COX-2 expression is upregulated in many colonic cancers, and the intensity of protein expression has been related to tumor survival. COX-2 deletion and inhibition delays the development of intestinal polyps in mouse models of human familial polyposis coli, a precancerous condition. Deletion of COX-1 has a similar effect, however, and the interplay of the two enzymes in carcinogenesis is poorly understood. The inverse relationship between aspirin/NSAID consumption and tumor progression has been reported for tumors in sites other than the colon, including tumors of the breast, prostate, esophagus, and stomach. Overexpression of one or both COX isozymes has been reported in Alzheimer's disease plaques, but the direct contribution of COX activity, if any, to disease progression is poorly understood.

Multiple mechanisms of action have been proposed for aspirin beyond inhibition of COX, including modulation of signaling molecules of the NFκB signaling pathway. The concentrations used in these studies are unlikely to be compatible with life, however. A possible exception is the interference with binding of the CCAAT—enhancer binding protein (CEBP) β transcription factor to promoter elements in cytokine genes, which is observed in vitro at concentrations of salicylic acid that are attained after high doses of aspirin in vivo. This effect may explain in part the anti-inflammatory actions of salicylate, despite its weak reversible properties as a COX inhibitor.

Aspirin resistance is a term variably used for patients who have clinical thrombotic events or evidence of failed inhibition of COX activity or platelet function despite aspirin. Given the redundancy in the system, it is surprising that inhibiting just thromboxane A$_2$–dependent platelet activation should translate into a benefit detectable with as crude an instrument as a clinical trial. Aspirin resistance may reflect the relative importance of other pathways of platelet activation in some individuals, but it also may cover drug interactions, noncompliance, and pharmacokinetic or pharmacogenetic differences. The incidence of cardiovascular events is elevated in individuals who sustain high levels of urinary excretion of thromboxane metabolites despite being prescribed aspirin. All drugs are subject to such heterogeneous causes of "resistance" or "treatment failure." A molecular basis for this phenomenon remains to be identified.

NONSTEROIDAL ANTI-INFLAMMATORY DRUGS

NSAIDs are isoform nonselective, reversible active site inhibitors of COX. The class includes arylpropionic acids (ibuprofen, naproxen, flurbiprofen, ketoprofen), indole acetic acids (indomethacin, etodolac), heteroaryl acetic acids (diclofenac, ketorolac), enolic acids (piroxicam, phenylbutazone), and alkanones (nabumetone).

As a result of the reversible action of NSAIDs, they attain maximal inhibition of platelet COX-1 only transiently during the dosing interval. Owing to a nonlinear relationship between the inhibition of COX capacity to generate thromboxane A$_2$ and thromboxane A$_2$–dependent platelet function, the offset of their effects on platelet function is even more striking. Inhibition of greater than 95% of platelet COX is thought to be necessary to provide cardiac protection. An exception to these generalities regarding NSAIDs may be naproxen, which some investigators have found to have an extended pharmacodynamic half-life. Epidemiologic analyses have yielded conflicting information as to the association of naproxen consumption with a reduced incidence of MI.

NSAIDs are anti-inflammatory, antipyretic, and analgesic. These effects are attributed largely to suppression of PGE$_2$ and PGI$_2$ formation. These same prostaglandins provide cytoprotection when made by gastric epithelial COX-1. Gastropathy, which is the most common adverse effect of NSAIDs (Chapters 137 and 138), has two components: bleeding, owing to inhibition of platelet COX-1, and impairment of gastric cytoprotection, which is attributed largely to epithelial COX-1. The recognition that COX-2 was readily induced by cytokines suggested that it might represent a discrete target for inhibition, bypassing inhibition of COX-1 and minimizing gastropathy. This conjecture is referred to as the "COX-2 hypothesis."

NSAIDs may prevent access of aspirin to its target in platelet COX-1. Predosing with ibuprofen, the most commonly consumed NSAID in the United States, 2 hours before aspirin administration provides a rapidly reversible inhibition of platelet thromboxane A$_2$ and aggregation, an effect not observed with a selective COX-2 inhibitor because mature human platelets express only COX-1. This interaction is evident in volunteers taking ibuprofen three times a day, even when the morning dose follows the daily low dose of aspirin.

Acetaminophen is also a nonspecific COX inhibitor. This effect is partial at 1000 mg, a dose commonly taken for mild pain and pyrexia. Epidemiologic studies suggest, however, that higher doses (≥2000 mg) trigger adverse gastrointestinal effects indistinguishable from traditional NSAIDs. The degree of COX inhibition would be expected to be dose related. It has been speculated that acetaminophen, which is a good reducing agent, might act to reduce COX from its active, oxidized form. If this were the basis for COX inhibition by acetaminophen, it would be expected to be most pronounced under conditions of low peroxide tone. Although other NSAIDs may be complicated by hepatotoxicity (e.g., diclofenac), this is a particular feature of overdose (usually >10 g) with acetaminophen (Chapter 150). Treatment is by gastric lavage, supportive therapy, and the use of N-acetylcysteine, which is thought to restore hepatic glutathione.

NSAIDs, similar to aspirin, have had many actions attributed to them aside from inhibition of COX activity. High concentrations, unlikely to be ever attained in patients, have been reported to modify signaling molecules and activate perioxisomal proliferator activator receptors. Some NSAIDs also have been reported to decrease accumulation of the toxic Aβ$_{(1-42)}$ fragment in the amyloid plaques of Alzheimer's disease. This effect seems to be independent of COX inhibition and may result from modulation of γ-secretase activity. There is some evidence from epidemiologic studies and small clinical trials that NSAIDs may delay the progression of Alzheimer's disease (Chapter 433).

Little information exists on how genetic variation might modulate the response to any COX inhibitors. There is some suggestion of an impact of time of dosing on the pharmacokinetics of some NSAIDs.

SELECTIVE INHIBITORS OF *COX-2* (THE COXIBS)

The relative selectivity of NSAIDs is evaluated in whole blood assays based on the capacity of platelet COX-1 to generate thromboxane A$_2$ in serum and of bacterial lipopolysaccharide induction of monocyte COX-2-dependent PGE$_2$ formation in plasma, pretreated with aspirin to inhibit COX-1, which is expressed constitutively. Currently, three

Clinical Pharmacology

Table 32–1 • CLINICAL PHARMACOLOGY OF COXIBS

	VALDECOXIB	CELECOXIB	ROFECOXIB
Formulation	Oral	Oral	Oral
Selectivity ratio	30×	7.6×	35×
Onset of action (min)	60	60	≤45*
T_{max} (hr)	2.25	3	2–3
Half-life (hr)	8.11	11	17
Bioavailability (%)	83	—	93
Protein binding (%)	98	97	87
Metabolism	P450 (3A4 and 2C9) and glucuronidation	P450 2C9	Reduced by cytosolic enzymes
Excretion	90% in urine (changed); 10% in feces	27% in urine; 57% in feces (changed)	72% in urine; 14% in feces (unchanged)

*In some studies, rofecoxib was shown to provide pain relief in 27 minutes.
T_{max} = time of maximum concentration.
Sources of data: Prescribing information for rofecoxib (Merck & Co, Inc); prescribing information for celecoxib and valdecoxib (Pharmacia); unpublished data.

coxibs have been approved as selective *COX-2* inhibitors in the United States: celecoxib, rofecoxib, and valdecoxib (Table 32–1). All three drugs have established efficacy in inflammatory syndromes, such as the chronic arthritides, and are effective in the treatment of pain (Chapter 29). Overall, the coxibs seem to be similarly effective as the traditional NSAIDs, a finding that is compatible with the notion that *COX-2* is the dominant source of prostaglandin formation in pain and inflammation. Both COX isoenzymes are coexpressed in inflammatory tissues, however, such as the synovial lining of rheumatoid joints and in atherosclerotic plaque. Also, *COX-1* contributes roughly 10 to 15% of the prostaglandin formation induced by bacterial lipopolysaccharide administered to volunteers, and both isoenzymes are expressed in circulating cells ex vivo.

Given these caveats, the trials that led to clinical approval of the *COX-2* inhibitors were based on endoscopic evidence of less gastrointestinal ulceration at doses that were equally efficacious to doses of a traditional NSAID. Celecoxib, rofecoxib, and valdecoxib all have fared well in these comparisons, compatible with the "*COX-2* hypothesis." In one study, the incidence of complicated ulcers, mainly gastrointestinal bleeding and perforations, was reduced significantly from roughly 4 to 2% in patients on rofecoxib compared with naproxen, a traditional NSAID.**3** In another trial, celecoxib was compared with two NSAIDs, diclofenac and ibuprofen. Of note was that celecoxib was not significantly better than diclofenac with respect to the prespecified gastrointestinal end point. Analysis of the ex vivo assays suggests that celecoxib is similarly selective to diclofenac and to two other older drugs, nimesulide and meloxicam. Diclofenac and celecoxib depress serum thromboxane B_2 by 50% and 30%, respectively, on average. Because of the nonlinear relationship between inhibition of platelet *COX-1* and thromboxane A_2–dependent platelet aggregation, however, neither drug inhibits platelet function. In contrast to ibuprofen, rofecoxib also does not interact with aspirin, compatible with its preference for *COX-2*. Diclofenac is the most commonly consumed NSAID in Western Europe.

In comparisons of rofecoxib with naproxen, naproxen-treated patients had only one fifth the incidence of MI, a finding that may have been due to chance because there were less than 80 events in the study. It may be, however, that naproxen has a cardiac protective effect (see earlier) or that rofecoxib has cardiovascular toxicity because of substantial depression of PGI_2 without the coincident platelet inhibition that would occur with aspirin. Deletion of the I prostanoid receptor, which enhances the effects of thromboxane A_2 on platelets and the vasculature in mice, does not induce spontaneous thrombosis, but rather enhances the response to prothrombotic stimuli. This mechanism would be expected to pertain to the class of drugs, but to be relevant only to patients at increased risk of thrombosis. This hypothesis is compatible with reassuring overviews of the cardiovascular safety of rofecoxib and celecoxib in patients at low to medium risk of cardiovascular events. Little information is available in patients at high risk.

Presently the possibility of a cardiovascular hazard of coxibs remains a hypothesis, rather than an established reality. Should coxibs need to be combined with an antiplatelet drug in high-risk patients, it would be necessary to establish how the gastrointestinal profile of a coxib or an NSAID with low-dose aspirin might differ or how either regimen might compare with high, anti-inflammatory, and cardioprotective doses of aspirin.

Experience to date suggests that the renal adverse effect profile for coxibs and NSAIDs—fluid retention and a rise in blood pressure—is similar. PGE_2 plays a crucial role in tubular reabsorption of salt and water, whereas PGI_2 modulates potassium reabsorption. As discussed earlier, both prostanoids modulate renal blood flow, especially in renoprival conditions. Adverse event reports suggest that the incidence of hypertension and fluid retention are dose dependent in patients receiving *COX-2* inhibitors. The preservation of renal blood flow becomes critically dependent on vasodilator prostanoids, such as PGI_2 and PGE_2, only when vasoconstrictor tone is enhanced, however, such as in secondary hyperaldosteronism in patients with cardiac, hepatic, or renal failure (see earlier). Few of these patients have been included in studies of *COX-2* inhibitors to date, and no comparative analysis with NSAIDs in these patients is currently available.

Patients receiving aspirin, even at low doses, or traditional NSAIDs occasionally develop an asthmatic hypersensitivity syndrome. It has been suggested that this reaction may be the result of depression of prostaglandins that serve an antiallergic role or from rediversion of the AA substrate to bronchoconstrictor lipoxygenase products in some individuals. Although the cause of this syndrome is poorly understood, a controlled comparison suggests that it does not occur when aspirin-sensitive patients are switched to the selective *COX-2* inhibitor rofecoxib. *COX-1* seems to be the source of prostaglandins relevant to this syndrome.

As with NSAIDs, there is considerable interest in the potential efficacy of coxibs in the chemoprevention of cancer and in the treatment of patients with Alzheimer's disease. Celecoxib already has been approved for the treatment of patients with familial adenomatous polyposis, a precancerous condition of the colon (Chapter 200), based on the outcome of a placebo controlled trial. It is presently unclear, however, how selective inhibition of *COX-2* might compare with coincident inhibition of both isoenzymes or what place these drugs might have in the prevention of cancer.

1. Antithrombotic Trialists' Collaboration: Collaborative meta-analysis of randomized trials of antiplatelet therapy for prevention of death, MI, and stroke in high risk patients. BMJ 2002;324:71–86.
2. Patrono C, Coller B, Dalen JE, et al: Platelet-active drugs: The relationships among dose, effectiveness, and side effects. Chest 2001;119:39S–63S.
3. Bombardier C, Laine L, Reicin A, et al: Comparison of upper gastrointestinal toxicity of rofecoxib and naproxen in patients with rheumatoid arthritis. N Engl J Med 2000;343:1521–1528.

SUGGESTED READINGS

FitzGerald GA, Patrono C: The coxibs, selective inhibitors of cyclooxygenase-2. N Engl J Med 2001;345:433–442. *A review of coxibs, with particular attention to their adverse gastrointestinal effects and their cardiorenal profiles.*

FitzGerald GA: Parsing an enigma: The pharmacodynamics of aspirin resistance. Lancet 2003;361:542–544. *An overview of the NSAIDs and their possible interactions.*

Narumiya S, FitzGerald GA: Genetic and pharmacologic analysis of prostanoid receptor function. J Clin Invest 2001;108:25–30. *A review of prostanoid receptor biology.*

33 ANTITHROMBOTIC THERAPY

Jack Hirsh

Antithrombotic therapy alters the natural hemostatic mechanisms (Chapter 162) and is especially useful for patients with abnormalities of platelet or vascular function (Chapter 177) or with thrombotic disorders or a hypercoagulable state (Chapter 180). A variety of medications can interfere with various aspects of the coagulation system, sometimes with synergistic effects. In recent years, numerous randomized clinical trials have produced a substantial evidence-based literature to guide the use of antithrombotic therapy for a wide range of clinical conditions.

Clinical Pharmacology

PHARMACOLOGIC AGENTS

ORAL ANTICOAGULANTS

For more than 50 years, vitamin K antagonists have been the only oral anticoagulants available for clinical use. With the development and clinical evaluation of novel oral agents that target single enzymes in the coagulation sequence, the situation is likely to change in the near future, however. Vitamin K antagonists are coumarin derivatives, of which warfarin is the most widely used. Coumarins produce their anticoagulant effect by inhibiting a vitamin K reductase that catalyzes the reduction of 2,3 epoxide (vitamin K epoxide), leading to the depletion of vitamin KH_2. This reduced form of vitamin K is required for the production of functionally active (γ-carboxylated) coagulation proteins (factors VII, IX, and X) and anticoagulant proteins (protein C and protein S) (Chapters 178 and 179). Vitamin K_1 in food sources can reverse these effects of coumarins because it is reduced to vitamin KH_2 by a warfarin-insensitive vitamin K reductase (Fig. 33–1).

Warfarin is absorbed rapidly and almost completely from the gastrointestinal tract. It has a half-life of about 40 hours, a delayed onset of action (2 to 7 days, depending on dose), and an anticoagulant effect that is not reversed completely for 5 days after treatment is discontinued. The dose-response relationship of warfarin varies widely among individuals, and the drug's effects must be monitored closely to prevent overdosing or underdosing. Laboratory monitoring is performed by measuring the prothrombin time and is reported as an international normalized ratio (INR). The INR is responsive to depression of three of the four vitamin K–dependent procoagulant clotting factors (prothrombin and factors VII and X). During initiation of warfarin therapy, the INR reflects primarily the depression of factor VII, which has a half-life of only approximately 6 hours, whereas during maintenance therapy, the INR is elevated by all three vitamin K–dependent factors. The dose response to warfarin is influenced by many factors, including age, liver disease, dietary vitamin K_1, genetic factors, concomitant drug use, patient compliance, and

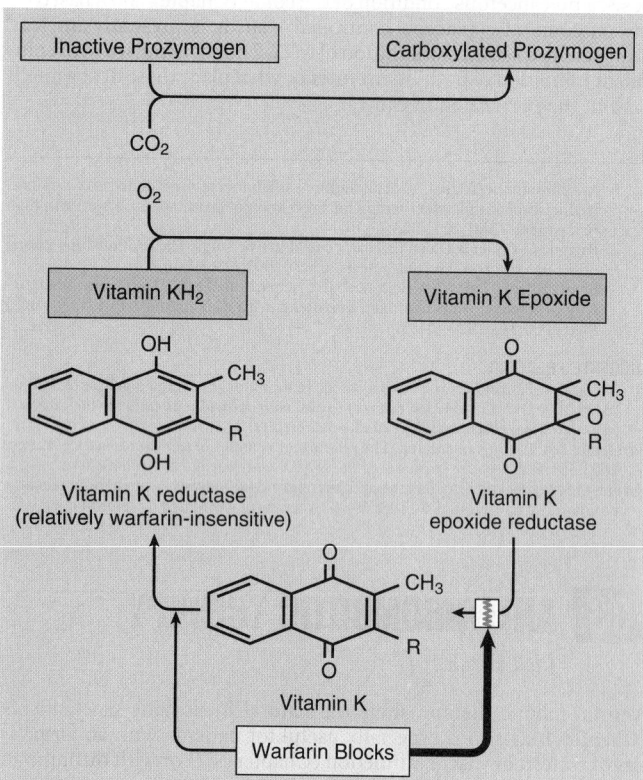

FIGURE 33–1 • Warfarin inhibits vitamin K epoxide reductase and leads to the intracellular depletion (in the hepatocyte) of vitamin KH_2. Vitamin KH_2 is required for the conversion (by γ carboxylation) of functionally inactive to active coagulation proteins. The anticoagulant effect of warfarin can be reversed by vitamin K_1 in food because it is reduced to vitamin KH_2 by a warfarin-insensitive vitamin K reductase.

Table 33–1 • RECOMMENDED THERAPEUTIC RANGE FOR ORAL ANTICOAGULANT THERAPY

INDICATION	INR
Prophylaxis of venous thrombosis (high-risk surgery)	
Treatment of venous thrombosis	
Treatment of pulmonary embolism	
Prevention of systemic embolism	2.0–3.0
Tissue heart valves	
Valvular heart disease	
Atrial fibrillation	
Recurrent systemic embolism	
Cardiomyopathy	
Mechanical prosthetic valves (high risk)	2.5–3.5
Acute myocardial infarction	

INR = international normalized ratio.

inappropriate dosage adjustments. Of these factors, inappropriate dosage adjustment and improved compliance through patient education are the most readily correctable. Overanticoagulation during initiation of warfarin can be avoided by using an average daily dose of 5 mg, with the expectation that a stable anticoagulant (and antithrombotic) effect will be achieved in 5 or 6 days. The starting dose should be reduced to 3 or 4 mg/day in the elderly because they are more sensitive to warfarin.

There is evidence that the reliability of warfarin monitoring is improved by having the dosage controlled by an anticoagulation management service and by using computer-assisted algorithms. The convenience of monitoring is increased, particularly in busy patients who travel frequently, by using point-of-care testing with portable finger-prick monitors.

Indications for Warfarin

Warfarin is effective in the prevention of recurrent systemic embolism in patients with atrial fibrillation (AF) (Chapter 59); in the prevention of systemic arterial embolism in patients with valvular heart disease (native and prosthetic tissue and mechanical heart valves; Chapter 72); in the primary and secondary prevention of venous thromboembolism (Chapters 78 and 94); in the prevention of acute myocardial infarction (MI) in high-risk patients (Chapter 69); and in the prevention of stroke, recurrent MI, and death in patients with acute MI (Chapter 69). A target INR of 2.5 (range 2.0 to 3.0) is recommended for all indications except for patients with mechanical prosthetic heart valves, for which an INR of 3.0 (range 2.5 to 3.5) is recommended, and in certain patients with thrombosis owing to the antiphospholipid syndrome, who may require a higher targeted INR than 2.0 to 3.0 (Chapter 180) (Table 33–1).

Dosing and Monitoring

If a rapid anticoagulant effect is required, heparin and warfarin should be started simultaneously and overlapped for at least 5 days. A loading dose of warfarin should not be used because it is safer to start with the estimated maintenance dose, of about 5 mg/day, which usually results in patients reaching an INR of 2.0 in 4 to 5 days. Heparin treatment is discontinued when the INR has been in the therapeutic range for 2 days. If treatment is not urgent (e.g., chronic stable AF), warfarin treatment can be started outside the hospital at this same dose.

If treatment is started with a maintenance dose, the first INR measurement can be delayed until day 2 or 3, then be performed daily until the INR is in the therapeutic range. The INR is performed two or three times weekly for 1 to 2 weeks, then less often, depending on the stability of INR results.

If the INR response remains stable, the frequency of testing can be reduced to intervals of every 4 weeks. If adjustments to the dose are required because the INR drifts out of the therapeutic range, the adjustments should be gradual and based on the weekly dose (e.g., a 10 to 20% change in weekly dose). The practice of stopping treatment for 1 or 2 days, then restarting it with the same dose is illogical and should be avoided. Patients should be encouraged to keep a log of their dose and their INR response.

Adverse Effects

Warfarin-related bleeding is increased by the level of the INR, with the risk of bleeding increasing noticeably when the INR reaches 4.0 and even more sharply when the INR is higher than 5.0. Compared with an INR of 2.0 to 3.0, the risk of a major bleeding episode is increased 2-fold to 3-fold at an INR of 4.5, about 5-fold at an INR of 5.5, and 8-fold to 10-fold at an INR of greater than 6.0. The risk of bleeding also is increased with concomitant aspirin use, in patients older than age 65 years, and in patients with a history of stroke, gastrointestinal bleeding, or serious comorbid conditions. Elderly patients are more sensitive to warfarin, requiring lower doses to reach the therapeutic range, and have an increased tendency to bleed, including intracranial bleeding, even when their INR is in the therapeutic range. The elderly also are more likely to be receiving one or more of the many drugs that interact with warfarin. When treatment with any new drug is indicated in a patient who is being treated with warfarin, the INR should be monitored more frequently during the initial stages of combined drug therapy.

Reversing the Effect of Warfarin

The anticoagulant effect of warfarin can be reversed in one of three ways: by discontinuing therapy, with the expectation that the INR will return to baseline in about 5 days; by administering vitamin K_1, with the expectation that the anticoagulant effect will be reduced in 6 hours and reversed in 24 hours; and by an infusion of fresh-frozen plasma, which produces immediate reversal.

Patients whose INR is elevated to 5.0 can be treated by appropriate dosage reduction. Patients with bleeding or whose INR is elevated to greater than 5.0 may require more rapid reversal with vitamin K_1 treatment. Patients with serious bleeding commonly require fresh-frozen plasma in addition to vitamin K_1. When the INR is elevated to potentially dangerous levels and the patient is not bleeding, vitamin K_1 should be administered in a dose of 1 to 10 mg, depending on the level of the INR. For an INR of 5.0 to 10.0, an oral dose of 1 to 2 mg of vitamin K_1 usually brings the INR down to the range of 2.0 to 3.0 in less than 24 hours. The oral and intravenous (IV) routes give a predictable response, whereas the response to subcutaneous vitamin K_1 can be unpredictable. The oral route is recommended unless rapid reversal of warfarin is necessary, in which case vitamin K is administered by slow IV infusion.

PLATELET-ACTIVE DRUGS

The platelet-active drugs inhibit different steps in either platelet activation (aspirin, ticlopidine, clopidogrel, and dipyridamole) or platelet recruitment (glycoprotein [GP] IIb/IIIa antagonists, abciximab, tirofiban, and eptifibatide) (Fig. 33–2).

Aspirin and Other Cyclooxygenase Inhibitors

ASPIRIN. Based on the results of a meta-analysis of more than 50 secondary prevention cardiovascular trials, there is evidence that aspirin prevents vascular death by approximately 15% and nonfatal vascular events by about 30% in patients with cardiovascular disease (Table 33–2).[1] Aspirin is also effective in preventing venous thromboembolism, including fatal pulmonary embolism in patients after surgery for hip fracture, but it is less effective than low-molecular-weight heparins (LMWHs) or warfarin for this indication.[1,2]

Mechanism of Action. Aspirin permanently inactivates cyclooxygenase-1 and cyclooxygenase-2, isoenzymes that catalyze the conversion of arachidonic acid to prostaglandin H_2, a precursor of a variety of prostaglandins, including thromboxane A_2 and prostacyclin (prostaglandin I_2). Thromboxane A_2 is a potent inducer of platelet aggregation and vasoconstriction, whereas prostaglandin I_2 induces vasodilation. Aspirin is approximately 50-fold to 100-fold more potent at inhibiting platelet cyclooxygenase-1 than cyclooxygenase-2. Consequently the cyclooxygenase-2-dependent anti-inflammatory effects of aspirin require larger doses of the drug (Chapter 32). The effect of aspirin on thromboxane A_2 production in platelets lasts for

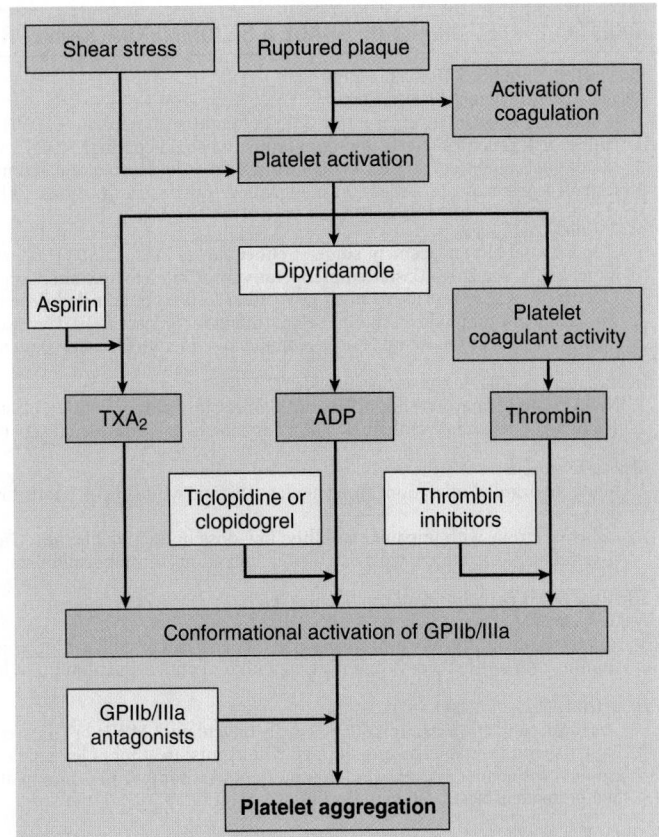

FIGURE 33–2 • Sites of action of platelet inhibitors.

the lifespan of the platelet. In contrast to platelets, vascular endothelial cells process prostaglandin H_2 to produce prostaglandin I_2. Low and even moderate doses of aspirin do not inhibit prostaglandin I_2 synthesis substantially because the effect of aspirin on endothelial cell–derived cyclooxygenase-1 is short-lived.

Pharmacology. Aspirin is absorbed rapidly in the stomach and upper intestine, attaining peak plasma levels at about 30 minutes after ingestion; it has a half-life of about 15 minutes. Inhibition of platelet function is evident by 1 hour with uncoated aspirin but can be delayed after administration of enteric-coated aspirin. If only enteric-coated tablets are available when a rapid effect is required, the tablets should be chewed.

Aspirin potentiates the antithrombotic effects of warfarin (in high-risk patients), dipyridamole (in patients with ischemic stroke), clopidogrel (in patients with coronary stents or acute myocardial ischemia), and heparin (in the prevention of recurrent miscarriages in pregnant women with antiphospholipid antibody syndrome and in patients with acute coronary ischemia). Aspirin produces a small increase in major bleeding and a small increase in the risk of cerebral hemorrhage. It also potentiates bleeding when added to another antithrombotic agent.

Aspirin causes gastrointestinal side effects that are dose dependent and reduced by using low doses (≤325 mg/day). Aspirin is contraindicated in patients with peptic ulcer disease or aspirin-induced asthma or if gastrointestinal side effects are severe.

Clinical Uses. Aspirin reduces the incidence of MI and/or death in patients with silent myocardial ischemia or stable angina, unstable angina, non–ST segment elevation MI, ST segment elevation MI, and ischemic cerebrovascular disease.[1,3] Aspirin is also effective in patients after coronary angioplasty or coronary artery bypass graft (CABG) surgery[1,4,5] and in preventing symptomatic coronary events in asymptomatic men and women older than age 50.[1,3] Aspirin has a favorable risk-to-benefit ratio for secondary prevention in patients with overt vascular disease, but the risk-to-benefit ratio is marginal when aspirin is used as primary prevention in asymptomatic individuals.

Aspirin is less effective than oral anticoagulants in the prevention of recurrent stroke in AF and less effective than LMWH or warfarin in preventing venous thromboembolism.[2,6]

Table 33–2 • SUMMARY OF GRADE A RECOMMENDATIONS FOR ANTITHROMBOTIC THERAPY

PREVENTION OF VENOUS THROMBOEMBOLISM
General, Gynecologic, and Urologic Surgery
1. Moderate-risk general surgery: low-dose unfractionated heparin, LMWH, elastic stockings, or intermittent pneumatic compression
2. Higher risk general surgery: low-dose unfractionated heparin, LMWH, or intermittent pneumatic compression
3. Major gynecologic surgery for benign disease: low-dose unfractionated heparin every 12 hr
4. Extensive gynecologic surgery for malignancy: low-dose unfractionated heparin every 8 hr

Major Orthopedic Surgery
1. Elective total hip replacement surgery: either subcutaneous LMWH (started 12 hr before or 12–24 hr after surgery) or adjusted-dose warfarin (INR target 2.5, range 2.0–3.0; started preoperatively or immediately after surgery)
2. Elective total knee replacement surgery: either LMWH or adjusted-dose warfarin
3. Anticoagulant prophylaxis should be continued for at least 7–10 days. Routine duplex ultrasonography screening at the time of hospital discharge or during outpatient follow-up is not recommended in asymptomatic patients after total hip replacement or total knee replacement

Neurosurgery, Trauma, and Acute Spinal Cord Injury
1. Neurosurgery: intermittent pneumatic compression with or without elastic stockings for intracranial neurosurgery
2. Trauma patients: LMWH therapy started as soon as it is considered safe to do so

Medical Conditions
1. Acute myocardial infarction: anticoagulant therapy with subcutaneous low-dose unfractionated heparin or IV heparin in prophylactic or therapeutic doses
2. Ischemic stroke with impaired mobility: low-dose unfractionated heparin or LMWH or the heparinoid danaparoid
3. General medical patients with risk factors for venous thromboembolism: low-dose unfractionated heparin or LMWH.

TREATMENT OF VENOUS THROMBOEMBOLIC DISEASE
Acute Treatment
1. Acute treatment: LMWH or unfractionated IV heparin or adjusted-dose subcutaneous heparin
2. Continue for at least 5 days and overlap with oral anticoagulation for at least 4–5 days

Long-Term Anticoagulation
1. Oral anticoagulation contraindicated or inconvenient: LMWH or adjusted-dose heparin in therapeutic doses
2. Patients with reversible or time-limited risk factors: treat for at least 3 mo
3. Patients with a first episode of idiopathic venous thromboembolism: treat for at least 6 mo
4. Symptomatic isolated calf vein thrombosis: treat for at least 6–12 wk

ATRIAL FIBRILLATION
1. High-risk patients
   Standard approach: warfarin anticoagulation (INP 2.5; range 2.0–3.0)
   Warfarin contraindicated or declined by patient: aspirin (80–325 mg)
   Aspirin plus low, fixed-dose warfarin: should not be used
2. Moderate-risk patients: either oral anticoagulation or aspirin

ANTITHROMBOTIC THERAPY IN CORONARY ARTERY DISEASE (INCLUDING CORONARY THROMBOLYSIS)
Coronary Thrombolysis
1. All patients with acute myocardial infarction who receive fibrinolytic therapy: should receive aspirin (165–325 mg), chewed and swallowed, on arrival to the hospital and daily thereafter
2. Patients with ischemic symptoms for <12 hr who have ST-segment elevation or left bundle-branch block on the electrocardiogram: should receive fibrinolytic therapy
3. Choice of fibrinolytic agent for patients with symptom duration <12 hr: streptokinase, reteplase, tenecteplase, or alteplase
4. Choice of fibrinolytic agent for patients with symptom duration <6 hr: alteplase is superior to streptokinase

Acute Myocardial Infarction
1. Low-dose heparin therapy (5000 U subcutaneously every 12 hr) or LMWH until ambulatory (as a minimum)
2. Aspirin: initial dose of 162.5 mg of nonenteric-coated aspirin to chew and swallow as soon as possible after the clinical impression of evolving acute myocardial infarction is formed
3. Maintenance dose of 75–162.5 mg should be continued indefinitely
4. Patients who have contraindications to aspirin: should receive clopidogrel (75 mg/day) indefinitely

UNSTABLE ANGINA
Antiplatelet Therapy
1. Aspirin at an initial dose 162.5 mg of nonenteric-coated aspirin to chew and swallow as soon as possible after the clinical impression of unstable angina is formed. Aspirin by mouth should be continued indefinitely
2. In cases of aspirin allergy or intolerance, ticlopidine (250 mg twice daily), or triflusal in countries where it is available

Glycoprotein IIb–IIa Antagonists
1. IV tirofiban or eptifibatide, in addition to aspirin and heparin, to patients with continuing ischemia or other high-risk features. The indication is strengthened by the detection of elevated troponin T or I. The infusion should continue for 48–72 hours or until PCI
2. Abciximab for 12–24 hours in patients who will undergo PCI within the following 24 hr

Anticoagulants
1. IV heparin (about 75 U/kg IV bolus, initial maintenance 1250 U/hr IV, APTT 1.5–2× control) or LMWH (dose regimens from trials) in patients hospitalized with unstable angina for at least 48 hr or until the unstable pain pattern resolves

INCREASED RISK
Chronic Coronary Artery Disease
1. Aspirin for patients with stable angina (indefinitely)

Coronary Artery Bypass Grafts
1. Aspirin (325 mg) starting 6 hr after operation
2. In most patients, aspirin is indicated for life

ANTITHROMBOTIC THERAPY IN PATIENTS UNDERGOING PERCUTANEOUS CORONARY INTERVENTION
Oral Antiplatelet Agents
1. Aspirin should be administered >2 hr before PCI
2. Aspirin (80–325 mg daily) should be used for secondary prevention of cardiovascular events
3. For patients who cannot tolerate aspirin, clopidogrel, 300 mg oral loading and 75 mg daily for 14–30 days after the procedure

Table 33–2 • SUMMARY OF GRADE A RECOMMENDATIONS FOR ANTITHROMBOTIC THERAPY—cont'd

Platelet Glycoprotein IIb-IIa Antagonists
1. Abciximab, eptifibatide, or tirofiban should be considered in all patients undergoing PCI, particularly patients with refractory unstable angina or with other high-risk features

Anticoagulant Therapy
1. Heparin: When abciximab therapy is used, the heparin bolus should be reduced to 50–70 IU/kg to achieve a target ACT of >200 sec with either the HemoTec or Hemochron device. Femoral sheaths should be removed after the procedure when the ACT falls to <150–180 sec

ANTITHROMBOTIC THERAPY IN PERIPHERAL ARTERIAL OCCLUSIVE DISEASE
1. Patients with clinical evidence of cerebrovascular disease or coronary artery disease should be treated with aspirin

Peripheral Vascular Reconstructive Surgery
1. Reconstruction of low-flow arteries: Patients having prosthetic, femoropopliteal bypass operations: aspirin (81–325 mg/day) begun preoperatively
2. Anticoagulation: Patients undergoing infrainguinal bypass who are at high risk of graft thrombosis: warfarin and aspirin
3. Intraoperative anticoagulation therapy: Patients undergoing major vascular reconstructive operations should be systemically anticoagulated with heparin at the time of application of cross-clamps

ANTITHROMBOTIC AND THROMBOLYTIC THERAPY FOR ISCHEMIC STROKE
Acute Ischemic Stroke: Treatment within 3 Hours of Onset of Symptoms
1. Thrombolytic therapy: In eligible patients, IV tissue plasminogen activator in a dose of 0.9 mg/kg (maximum of 90 mg), with 10% of the total dose given as an initial bolus and the remainder infused over 60 min
2. Streptokinase is not recommended except within the confines of a clinical trial

Acute Ischemic Stoke: Patients Not Receiving Thrombolysis or Anticoagulation
1. Aspirin (160–325 mg/day)
2. Aspirin may be used safely in combination with low doses of subcutaneous heparin for DVT prophylaxis.

DVT/Pulmonary Embolism Prophylaxis
1. For acute stroke patients with restricted mobility: low-dose subcutaneous heparin or LMWHs or the heparinoid danaparoid, provided that there are no contraindications to anticoagulation

Stroke Prevention
1. Antiplatelet agents and anticoagulation: Noncardioembolic cerebral ischemic events (stroke or TIA; atherothrombotic, lacunar, or cryptogenic): aspirin (50–325 mg/day). The combination of aspirin and extended-release dipyridamole (25/200 mg twice daily) or clopidogrel (75 mg daily) is an acceptable option for initial therapy
2. The combination of aspirin and extended-release dipyridamole (25/200 mg twice daily) is more effective than aspirin alone for the prevention of stroke
3. Long-term oral anticoagulation at an INR of 3.0–4.5 should not be used
4. Cardioembolic ischemic events: long-term oral anticoagulation (target INR of 2.5, range 2.0–3.0) for atrial fibrillation
5. Carotid endarterectomy: aspirin (81–325 mg/day) before carotid endarterectomy and continued long-term after the procedure

Cerebral Sinus Thrombosis
1. Unfractionated heparin during the acute phase (even in the presence of hemorrhagic infarction).

LMWH = low-molecular-weight heparin; INR = international normalized ratio; IV = intravenous; PCI = percutaneous coronary intervention; APTT = activated partial thromboplastin time; ACT = activated clotting time; DVT = deep venous thrombosis; TIA = transient ischemic attack.

DIPYRIDAMOLE. Dipyridamole is a pyrimidopyrimidine derivative with vasodilator and antiplatelet properties. It inhibits platelet function by elevating platelet cyclic adenosine monophosphate (AMP) levels. The absorption of conventional dipyridamole is variable but has been improved by a modified-release formulation. Dipyridamole has a terminal half-life of 10 hours and is eliminated primarily by biliary excretion. Results of clinical trials with conventional dipyridamole, either used alone or in combination with aspirin, have been disappointing. Favorable results were obtained, however, with the modified-release preparation in patients with prior stroke or transient ischemic attack, in whom the risk of stroke was reduced by 16% with dipyridamole alone and by 37% with aspirin and dipyridamole compared with placebo.[17] Whether these favorable results reflect the use of a higher dose (400 mg versus 225 mg daily) of dipyridamole than in prior trials or the improved systemic bioavailability of modified-release dipyridamole is uncertain.

THIENOPYRIDINES. Ticlopidine and clopidogrel are thienopyridines that inhibit adenosine diphosphate (ADP)–induced platelet aggregation through the action of their active metabolites. Both drugs are administered orally, but their onset of action is delayed until their active metabolites are formed. Similarly, recovery of platelet function is delayed until the active thienopyridine metabolites are cleared and the circulating affected platelets are replaced by newly formed, unaffected platelets.

Ticlopidine is more effective than aspirin in reducing stroke in patients with transient cerebral ischemia or minor stroke and more effective than placebo in patients with thromboembolic stroke, unstable angina, or peripheral vascular disease and after CABG surgery. The combination of ticlopidine and aspirin is more effective than aspirin alone or aspirin plus warfarin in preventing thrombotic

complications after coronary artery stent placement. Ticlopidine has many important side effects, however, including hypercholesterolemia and neutropenia. Its use also has been associated with thrombocytopenia, aplastic anemia, and thrombotic thrombocytopenic purpura.

The better safety profile and equal efficacy of clopidogrel has resulted in its substitution for ticlopidine for essentially all indications. Clopidogrel is absorbed and metabolized rapidly, and the onset of the inhibition of platelet aggregation with clopidogrel is more rapid than with ticlopidine. Inhibition of platelet aggregation is detectable 90 minutes after an oral loading dosing of 300 mg. With repeated daily administration of low doses (75 mg), there is cumulative inhibition of platelet function with a return to normal 7 days after the last dose of clopidogrel.

Clopidogrel is more effective than aspirin in patients who have experienced a recent stroke or recent MI and patients presenting with symptomatic peripheral arterial disease.[1,3,7,8] The additional benefit over aspirin is modest and similar to that observed with ticlopidine (about 10% relative risk reduction). The combination of clopidogrel and aspirin is also more effective than aspirin alone in patients with unstable angina and non–ST segment elevation MI (20% risk reduction) but at a cost of a modest increase in bleeding. Clopidogrel seems to be as well tolerated as aspirin.[1]

Integrin IIbβ₃ (Glycoprotein IIb/IIIa) Receptor Antagonists

The final common pathway of platelet aggregation is mediated by the binding of fibrinogen to the functionally active integrin $_{IIb}\beta_3$ (GP IIb/IIIa) on the platelet surface. Inhibitors of this process include monoclonal antibodies, synthetic Arg-Gly-Asp (RGD)–containing or Lys-Gly-Asp (KGD)–containing peptides, and peptidomimetic and nonpeptide RGD mimetics. These compounds are administered intravenously and inhibit platelet function by competing with fibrinogen (and von Willebrand factor) for occupancy on the platelet integrin receptor.

Abciximab (ReoPro), a mouse/human chimeric 7E3 Fab antibody, inhibits platelet aggregation in a concentration-dependent manner. Abciximab is unique among the GP IIb/IIIa antagonists because it also blocks binding to the $_v\beta_3$ receptor on endothelial cells and to an activated form of the leukocyte $\alpha M\beta 2$ receptor. The role of these two unique actions in the antithrombotic effects of abciximab is unclear. Platelet function is impaired rapidly after an IV bolus of abciximab and gradually recovers over 24 to 48 hours. Because of its tight binding to its integrin receptor, however, small amounts of abciximab can be detected on circulating platelets 14 days after administration.

Tirofiban (MK-383; Aggrastat) is a nonpeptide derivative of tyrosine. It has a plasma half-life of 1.6 hours, and its effect on hemostasis is reversed within 4 hours of stopping treatment.

Eptifibatide (Integrilin) is a synthetic disulfide-linked cyclic heptapeptide. It has a rapid onset and offset of action, and its effect on platelet function is reduced by more than 50% after 4 hours.

All three GP IIb/IIIa receptor antagonists are effective IV agents in patients undergoing percutaneous coronary interventions (PCI), and tirofiban and eptifibatide are effective in patients with unstable angina or non–ST segment elevation MI.[1,4] The GP IIb/IIIa receptor antagonists are administered in combination with heparin and aspirin. Orally active nonpeptide GP IIb/IIIa inhibitors have been developed for long-term use, but the results of clinical trials have been disappointing.

HEPARIN AND LOW-MOLECULAR-WEIGHT HEPARINS

Heparin

Heparin acts as an anticoagulant by activating the plasma cofactor, antithrombin (AT), increasing the rate at which the plasma cofactor inactivates thrombin, activated factor X (factor Xa), and other coagulation enzymes. Heparin accelerates the inactivation of thrombin by AT by providing a template to which the enzyme and the inhibitor bind to form a ternary complex (Fig. 33–3). In contrast, the inactivation of factor Xa by AT/heparin complex does not require ternary complex formation and is achieved by binding of the activated AT to factor Xa. Although effective clinically, heparin has biophysical limitations caused by the reduced ability of heparin to bind to and inactivate thrombin that is bound to fibrin and factor Xa that is bound to the platelet surface.

Heparin binds to many plasma-derived, platelet-derived, and endothelial cell–derived proteins that compete with AT III for heparin binding. Binding of heparin to plasma proteins contributes to the variability of its anticoagulant response, whereas binding to hepatic macrophages is responsible for its dose-dependent clearance. Both properties contribute to the unpredictable anticoagulant effect of heparin and the need for laboratory monitoring.

Heparin is effective for the prevention and treatment of venous thromboembolism [2,9,10] for the early treatment of patients with unstable angina and acute MI [3,9] and for patients who have cardiac surgery under cardiopulmonary bypass, [5] for patients undergoing vascular surgery, [8] and for patients during and after coronary angioplasty and coronary stents. [4] The anticoagulant effects of heparin usually are monitored by the activated partial thromboplastin time (APTT). A therapeutic effect is achieved when the APTT ratio is equivalent to a heparin level of 0.3 to 0.7 U of antifactor Xa, which for many reagents is an APTT ratio of 2.0 to 3.0. The risk of bleeding complications is increased with increasing heparin dosage, which is related to the anticoagulant response. Other clinical factors, such as recent surgery, trauma, and invasive procedures, are also important, however, as predictors of bleeding during heparin treatment.

For the treatment of venous thromboembolism, heparin is given in doses of 80 U/kg followed by 18 U/kg per hour by continuous infusion, and the dose is adjusted according to the APTT result at 6 hours using a validated nomogram (see Table 78–5). Lower doses (70 U/kg followed by 1000 U/hr) of heparin are used in patients with acute myocardial ischemia who also receive aspirin and GP IIb/IIIa antagonists or thrombolytic therapy.

The main complications of heparin are bleeding and heparin-induced thrombocytopenia (HIT). Less common complications are heparin-induced osteoporosis and hyperkalemia. Heparin-related bleeding is dose related, and the risk is increased in patients who undergo an invasive procedure and if heparin is used in combination with a GP IIb/IIIa antagonist or a thrombolytic agent.

HIT, which is an antibody-mediated adverse reaction to heparin, can be complicated by venous or arterial thrombosis. The diagnosis should be considered when a patient treated with heparin experiences an unexplained fall in the platelet count of 50% or more or develops skin lesions at sites of subcutaneous heparin injection. The fall in platelet count almost always occurs between day 5 and day 15 after the introduction of heparin, but it can develop earlier in patients who had been exposed to heparin during the previous 3 months. Venous thrombosis is a more common complication than arterial thrombosis, which occurs more commonly in surgical patients than in medical patients.

The HIT antigen is a complex between platelet factor 4 and heparin; HIT antibodies bind to regions of the platelet factor 4 molecule that have been modified conformationally by its interaction with heparin. A minimum of 12 to 14 saccharides are required to form the antigenic complex with platelet factor 4, so heparin molecules with a molecular weight greater than approximately 4000 Da have the potential to cause HIT, and HIT occurs less commonly with LMWH than with unfractionated heparin. Documentation of the HIT antibody confirms the diagnosis.

If HIT is suspected on clinical grounds and anticoagulant treatment is indicated, heparin should be stopped and replaced with a thrombin inhibitor, either hirudin (lepirudin) or argatroban. Patients with acute HIT without clinical thrombosis often have silent venous thrombosis (detected by compression ultrasound) or are at high risk of developing venous thrombosis and should be considered for treatment with a thrombin inhibitor. Warfarin should not be used alone to treat acute HIT because it can aggravate the thrombotic process, but it is safe when used in combination with a thrombin inhibitor after the platelet count has risen to greater than 100×10^9/L.

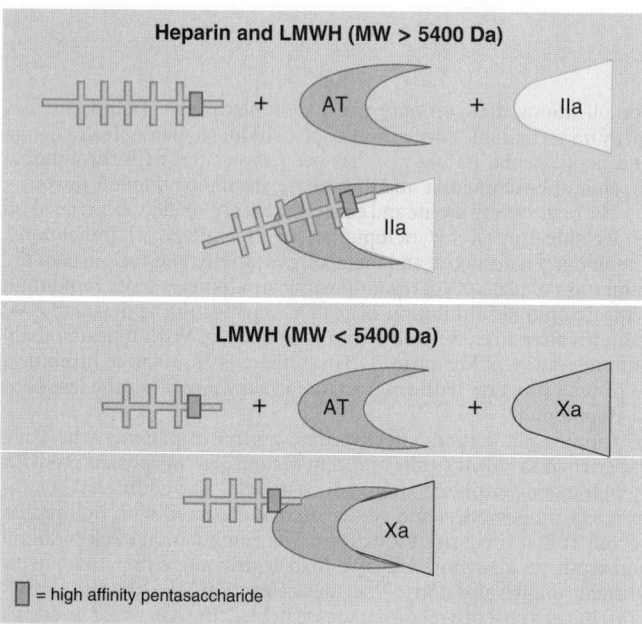

Heparin and LMWH (MW > 5400 Da)

LMWH (MW < 5400 Da)

◼ = high affinity pentasaccharide

FIGURE 33–3 • Only one third of high-affinity pentasaccharide-containing heparin molecules and one fifth of pentasaccharide-containing low-molecular-weight heparin (LMWH) molecules activate antithrombin (AT) Virtually all of the high-affinity heparin molecules are large enough to bridge between AT and factor IIa (thrombin). In contrast, only 25 to 50% of LMWH molecules have a molecular weight of 5400 or more, and although these smaller molecules inactivate factor Xa (Xa), they do not inactivate IIa. Although heparin has equal anti-IIa and anti-Xa activity, LMWH has reduced anti-IIa activity.

Low-Molecular-Weight Heparins

LMWHs are fragments produced by either chemical or enzymatic depolymerization of heparin. LMWHs are approximately one third the size of heparin (Table 33–3). Depolymerization of heparin changes

Clinical Pharmacology

Table 33–3 • ANTICOAGULANT PROFILES, MOLECULAR WEIGHTS, PLASMA HALF-LIVES, AND RECOMMENDED DOSES OF COMMERCIAL LOW-MOLECULAR-WEIGHT HEPARINS

AGENT	ANTI-Xa–TO–ANTI-IIa RATIO	MOLECULAR WEIGHT	PLASMA HALF-LIFE (min)	RECOMMENDED DOSE (INTERNATIONAL ANTI-Xa UNITS) General Surgery Prophylaxis	Orthopedic Surgery Prophylaxis	Acute Treatment
Enoxaparin	2.7:1	4,500	129–180	2000 U SC daily	4000 U SC daily or 3000 U SC bid	7000 U SC bid*
Dalteparin	2.0:1	5,000	119–139	2500 U SC daily	2500 U SC bid or 5000 U SC daily	8400 U SC bid*
Nadroparin	3.2:1	4,500	132–162	7500 U/IC SC daily†		31,500 U/IC daily†
Tinzaparin (Innohep)	1.9:1	4,500	111	3500 U SC daily	50 U/kg SC daily	12,250 U daily*
Ardeparin	2.0:1	6,000	200		50 U/kg SC bid	
Danaparoid†	20:1	6,500	1100		750 U SC bid	1250 U SC bid

*Weight-adjusted dose; stated dose for 70-kg patient.
†U/IC = Institute Choay units; 3 ICU = 1 IU.
†Danaparoid sodium is a heparinoid.
SC = subcutaneously.

the anticoagulant profile. As a result, LMWHs have less protein and cellular binding and, as a consequence, have a more predictable dose response, better bioavailability, and a longer plasma half-life than regular heparin.

Compared with heparin, which has a ratio of anti–factor Xa to anti–factor IIa activity of approximately 1:1, the various commercial LMWHs have anti–factor Xa to anti–factor IIa ratios varying between 4:1 and 2:1, depending on their molecular size distribution. LMWHs bind much less avidly to heparin-binding proteins than heparin, a property that contributes to superior bioavailability at low doses and to a more predictable anticoagulant response. LMWHs are cleared principally by the renal route. LMWHs are associated with a lower incidence of HIT and heparin-induced osteoporosis than heparin. LMWHs have a longer plasma half-life and a more predictable anticoagulant response than heparin, allowing LMWH to be administered once daily without laboratory monitoring, a property that facilitates out-of-hospital management of patients with venous thrombosis or unstable angina.

LMWHs are effective in the prevention and treatment of venous thrombosis (Chapter 78), [2,9,10] in the treatment of patients with unstable angina and non–ST segment elevation MI (Chapters 67 and 68), [3,9] and as an adjunct to fibrinolytic therapy in patients with acute ST segment elevation MI (Chapter 69). [11]

FIBRINOLYTIC AGENTS

Fibrinolytic agents convert plasminogen to the enzyme plasmin, which then degrades fibrin to soluble fragments, lysing the thrombus. Of the available fibrinolytic agents, streptokinase and urokinase are not fibrin specific; in contrast, recombinant tissue-type plasminogen activator (rtPA) (alteplase), saruplase (prourokinase), and the rtPA variant tenecteplase (TNK-tPA) are relatively fibrin specific. In addition, the rtPA variants tenecteplase and reteplase (t-PA) have been engineered to have a longer plasma half-life than rtPA, allowing the variants to be administered as a bolus injection (see Table 69–5).

Streptokinase is an indirect fibrinolytic agent. It binds to plasminogen, converting it into a plasmin-like molecule, which converts plasminogen to plasmin. Streptokinase has many disadvantages. It is antigenic, rendering its repeated use problematic, and allergenic, producing chills, fever, and rigors in some patients and, in rare instances, anaphylaxis. Anistreplase (APSAC) is an acylated complex of streptokinase and lys-plasminogen. Compared with streptokinase, it is more fibrin specific, has a longer plasma half-life, and is inactive until it is activated selectively by deacylation on the fibrin surface. Its side-effect profile, antigenicity, and efficacy are similar to streptokinase.

Urokinase is a naturally occurring plasminogen activator that differs from streptokinase in that it directly activates plasminogen and is not antigenic. Urokinase was used extensively for treating peripheral vascular occlusions, but production problems have curtailed its availability.

Saruplase (prourokinase), a single-chain precursor to urokinase, has little intrinsic enzymatic activity in the fluid phase but expresses its fibrinolytic activity in the presence of fibrin. Saruplase has relative fibrin specificity, similar to tissue plasminogen activator (t-PA).

In its natural state, t-PA is produced by vascular endothelium. *rt-PA (alteplase)* is produced by recombinant DNA technology. Alteplase is not antigenic or allergenic, and it has greater fibrin specificity than streptokinase. It has a short half-life of about 3.5 minutes and is given as a continuous IV infusion.

Truncated forms of rt-PA have been developed; the first, *r-PA (reteplase)*, is a single-chain deletion mutant that lacks certain domains. As a result, its half-life is about twice that of rt-PA, permitting double-bolus therapy 30 minutes apart. r-PA has lower affinity for fibrin than rt-PA, but fibrinogen depletion with r-PA is less than that with streptokinase. No antigenicity has been reported with this compound.

TNK-tPa (tenecteplase) is a mutant tPA with amino acid substitution at three sites. Compared with rt-PA, it has a longer half-life, allowing single bolus administration, increased fibrin specificity, and increased resistance to inhibition by plasminogen activator inhibitors-1.

NEW ANTICOAGULANTS

The limitations of established anticoagulants have prompted the development of a variety of new anticoagulant agents that target various specific steps in the coagulation mechanism.

DIRECT THROMBIN INHIBITORS. Direct thrombin inhibitors act independently of AT III to inactivate free thrombin and thrombin bound to fibrin. The direct thrombin inhibitors include hirudin, synthetic hirudin fragments (hirugen and hirulog), and low-molecular-weight inhibitors that react with the active site of thrombin (melagatran and its oral prodrug and argatroban). Although all of these inhibitors bind directly to thrombin, their sites of interaction are different. Hirulog is approved for use in coronary angioplasty, and argatroban and hirudin are approved in patients with HIT. Hirudin is more effective than heparin in the prevention of venous thrombosis and in patients with acute coronary syndromes, but it causes more bleeding. [3,12] Although the results of a meta-analysis suggested that bivalirudin is safer and possibly more effective than heparin in acute coronary syndromes, [12] this more favorable safety efficacy profile was not confirmed in a more recent HERO 2 study in patients with acute MI. [13] Data comparing argatroban with heparin are too limited currently to draw conclusions.

FACTOR XA INHIBITORS. Based on knowledge of the AT-binding sequence on heparin, a pentasaccharide with high affinity for AT has been synthesized. In a randomized trial in high-risk orthopedic patients, pentasaccharide was more effective than LMWH (about a 50% relative risk reduction) in preventing venous thrombosis in patients having major orthopedic procedures. [14] Many specific small-molecular-weight, active site–directed factor Xa inhibitors have been designed and are in early clinical development.

ACTIVATED PROTEIN C AND SOLUBLE THROMBOMODULIN. Activated protein C, a naturally occurring anticoagulant, is available in plasma-derived and recombinant forms. Soluble thrombomodulin is available through recombinant DNA technology. Both are effective antithrombotic agents in a variety of experimental animal models, and activated protein C is effective in reducing mortality in severe sepsis. [12,15]

TISSUE FACTOR PATHWAY INHIBITOR. Tissue factor pathway inhibitor is a naturally occurring inhibitor that blocks thrombin generation by inactivating factor Xa and factor VIIa. Tissue factor pathway inhibitor failed to show benefit in the treatment of disseminated intravascular coagulation that complicates severe sepsis.

CLINICAL INDICATIONS

CORONARY ARTERY DISEASE

Coronary artery disease usually is caused by coronary atherosclerosis with or without complicating coronary thrombosis (Chapter 66). Patients with symptomatic coronary artery disease present with stable angina, an acute coronary syndrome (unstable angina or non–ST segment elevation MI), acute ST segment elevation MI, and sudden cardiac death.

ASYMPTOMATIC INDIVIDUALS AND PATIENTS WITH STABLE ANGINA. Platelet-active agents, including aspirin and clopidogrel, are effective in reducing the risk of acute coronary events in high-risk patients with asymptomatic coronary artery disease and in patients with stable angina (Chapter 67). [1,3]

UNSTABLE ANGINA/NON–ST SEGMENT ELEVATION MYOCARDIAL INFARCTION. In patients with unstable angina, the combination of either aspirin and unfractionated heparin or aspirin and LMWH is effective in preventing progressive symptoms, progression to MI, and sudden death (Chapter 68). [3,9] The effects of aspirin and heparin seem to be additive. [3] The addition of an IV GP IIb/IIIa antagonist, abciximab, tirofiban, or eptifibatide, to aspirin and heparin produces further modest benefit (odds ratio 0.91) in patients with unstable angina treated without PCI and a substantial benefit in patients who undergo percutaneous coronary revascularization (odds ratio 0.62). [4,16] Abciximab is particularly effective in patients with unstable angina who require coronary angioplasty when it is given before and during the procedure.

ST SEGMENT ELEVATION MYOCARDIAL INFARCTION. Fibrinolytic therapy and aspirin are effective in reducing mortality in patients with acute ST segment elevation MI (Chapter 69). Fibrinolytic therapy should be given within 12 hours of the onset of chest pain. [11] It restores coronary patency, salvaging myocardium that otherwise would have become infarcted. Patients with ST segment depression only or with a normal electrocardiogram do not seem to benefit from fibrinolytic therapy. Streptokinase produces about a 20 to 25% reduction in mortality, and the effect of streptokinase and aspirin is additive, with the combination producing a 42% relative reduction compared with neither treatment. [11,17] Aspirin is effective because it prevents progressive thrombosis or rethrombosis. Accelerated rtPA (alteplase) and IV heparin provide a 14% reduction in relative risk (1% reduction in absolute risk) in 30-day mortality compared with streptokinase (plus either subcutaneous or IV heparin), which translates into an additional 10 lives saved per 1000 treated with alteplase. Intracranial hemorrhage occurs in 0.5% of patients treated with streptokinase compared with 0.7% of patients treated with accelerated alteplase. Reteplase administered in two boluses given 30 minutes apart has efficacy and safety similar to alteplase. Tenecteplase given as a single bolus in weight-adjusted doses is as effective and possibly safer than accelerated alteplase. [11] Although mortality and stroke rates were virtually identical with the two agents, major bleeding and overall bleeding rates were significantly lower with tenecteplase.

Although adjunctive heparin is used routinely, its addition to fibrinolytic therapy increases bleeding with uncertain clinical benefit. After successful fibrinolytic therapy, either aspirin or warfarin is effective in maintaining patency and in preventing recurrent events. [11]

LONG-TERM TREATMENT. There is good evidence that aspirin and warfarin reduce the incidence of reinfarction, death, and stroke when used long-term in patients after MI (Chapters 67, 68, and 69). [3] The results of trials comparing aspirin with warfarin for long-term treatment of acute MI indicate that warfarin is more effective. [18,19]

PERCUTANEOUS CORONARY INTERVENTION. PCI is effective for the treatment of stable and unstable coronary disease, but the procedure can be complicated by abrupt early closure and late restenosis (Chapter 70). Coronary stents are effective in preventing abrupt closure and reducing late restenosis. Periprocedural use of aspirin (80 to 325 mg) and unfractionated heparin (50 to 70 U/kg to achieve a targeted activated clotting time of >200 seconds) reduces the frequency of early ischemic complications after PCI. [4] Even with this treatment, abrupt closure and longer term restenosis remain problematic, however. Acute complications have been reduced further by the use of IV GP IIb/IIIa antagonists [4] and clopidogrel. The risk of excessive bleeding with abciximab is reduced without compromising efficacy by adopting a low-dose heparin regimen (50 to 70 U/kg).

The direct thrombin inhibitor bivalirudin has been approved as a replacement for heparin during PCI. Its efficacy is similar to heparin, but bivalirudin produces significantly less bleeding. The current recommendation for patients undergoing PCI is as follows: A GP IIb/IIIa antagonist should be used during and immediately after the procedure; when abciximab (the preferred GP IIb/IIIa antagonist) is used, heparin is given as a bolus of 50 to 70 U/kg to achieve a target activated clotting time greater than 200 seconds. Aspirin (80 to 325 mg) is given before treatment. After PCI, aspirin is continued, and for patients having stents, clopidogrel is given orally, 300 mg followed by 75 mg/day for 10 to 14 days.

CORONARY ARTERY BYPASS GRAFT SURGERY. CABG surgery can be complicated by early thrombotic occlusion or late occlusion owing to atherosclerotic narrowing (Chapter 71). Saphenous vein grafts are more thrombogenic than internal mammary artery grafts. Saphenous veins are more vulnerable to early thrombotic occlusion. Aspirin, 325 mg/day, begun within 6 hours after operation increases early saphenous vein graft patency but does not influence the long-term patency rate after 1 year. [5]

Even without treatment, the patency of internal mammary grafts is 96 to 100% at 3 months to 1 year after CABG surgery and 92% at 3 years. Studies with antiplatelet agents have failed to show improved patency.

PERIPHERAL ARTERIAL OCCLUSIVE DISEASE

Atherosclerosis is the major cause of chronic peripheral arterial occlusive disease (Chapter 76). Because arteriosclerosis usually is generalized, patients with peripheral arterial disease have a two-fold to three-fold increased risk of cardiovascular mortality.

Antiplatelet therapy with either aspirin or clopidogrel is effective in patients with peripheral vascular disease, but clopidogrel is more effective than aspirin in reducing acute MI and vascular-related deaths in patients with symptomatic peripheral arterial vascular disease. [8] Preoperative aspirin is also effective in maintaining patency of lower extremity vascular prosthetic bypasses. [8]

Thrombolytic therapy administered as an intra-arterial infusion is effective in achieving lysis and reversing acute thromboembolic occlusion. This approach is reserved for selected patients, however, who have acute lower extremity ischemia and who cannot tolerate emergency surgical therapy.

CEREBROVASCULAR DISEASE

Atherosclerosis of small and large arteries supplying the brain is the most common cause of ischemic stroke (Chapter 440). About 20% of ischemic strokes are due to cardiogenic embolism, most commonly from AF. Lipohyalinosis and other occlusive diseases of the small penetrating brain arteries are the most frequent causes of small, subcortical "lacunar" infarcts. Some strokes occur in patients without obvious cause. Most of these cryptogenic infarcts are thought to be cardioembolic.

ACUTE STROKE. Thrombolytic therapy and antithrombotic therapy are effective in selected patients with stroke. Most stroke patients are not eligible for IV rtPA therapy and are treated with antithrombotic agents. When administered to selected patients within 3 hours of acute ischemic stroke onset, IV t-PA improves outcome at 3 months. [7] Although the benefit occurs at the cost of symptomatic cerebral hemorrhage, there is a net benefit in terms of a reduction in the incidence of severe disability or death and an increase in the number of patients with a good functional outcome. In contrast to results with tPA, streptokinase is associated with an increased incidence of adverse outcomes.

A low-dose heparin regimen (5000 U subcutaneously twice daily) yields a small but significant reduction in the composite of early death or nonfatal stroke, with only a slight, nonsignificant excess of bleeding. Patients who receive low-dose heparin and aspirin have the lowest rate of stroke recurrence or pulmonary embolism without a significant increase in bleeding risk (compared with patients who received low-dose heparin without aspirin). [7]

Aspirin reduces the stroke recurrence risk and mortality, with no excess of hemorrhagic strokes and a trend toward a reduction in death or dependence at 6 months. For every 1000 acute strokes treated with aspirin, about 9 deaths or nonfatal stroke recurrences are prevented in the first few weeks, and approximately 13 fewer patients will be dead or dependent at 6 months. [7]

By comparison, neither moderate-dose heparin or LMWH is effective in the treatment of acute stroke. Subcutaneous heparin (12,500 U twice daily) not only is ineffective, but also is associated with more systemic bleeding, hemorrhagic strokes, and a significantly increased risk of death or nonfatal stroke at 14 days.

STROKE PREVENTION. Aspirin, ticlopidine, clopidogrel, and dipyridamole (particularly when combined with aspirin) are effective for prevention of stroke and other vascular events in patients with cerebrovascular disease. [7] Oral anticoagulant therapy is effective for primary and secondary prevention of stroke in patients with AF. [6] In contrast, there is no evidence that oral anticoagulants are effective in noncardioembolic stroke, but there is evidence that when used at a targeted INR of 3.0 to 4.5, oral anticoagulant therapy causes unacceptably high rates of intracranial hemorrhage.

CEREBRAL VENOUS SINUS THROMBOSIS. Cerebral venous sinus thrombosis can present as headache, focal neurologic deficits, seizures, alterations of consciousness, and papilledema with a sudden or progressive onset. Risk factors include pregnancy, estrogens, and inherited thrombophilic disorders. The diagnosis is made by imaging studies. The prognosis is good with treatment but poor without treatment. Unfractionated heparin and LMWHs are safe and effective in these patients.

VENOUS THROMBOEMBOLIC DISEASE

Prevention

Despite advances in prophylaxis, venous thromboembolism remains a major cause of morbidity and mortality among hospitalized patients (Chapter 78). The important clinical risk factors include advanced age, prolonged immobility or paralysis, previous venous thromboembolism, cancer, extensive surgery, orthopedic surgery of lower limb, hip or pelvic fracture, major trauma, stroke, obesity, varicose veins, and heart failure. Many patients have multiple risk factors, and the risks are cumulative.

Venous thromboembolism can be prevented by reducing venous stasis with external pneumatic compression or graduated compression stockings or by counteracting increased blood coagulability with oral anticoagulants, heparin, or LMWHs. Low-dose heparin, external pneumatic compression, graduated compression stockings, LMWHs, and oral anticoagulants all have been shown to be highly effective in reducing the incidence of venous thrombosis, but only low-dose heparin and LMWHs have been shown to reduce mortality. [2] LMWHs and low-dose heparin are also effective in preventing venous thrombosis and fatal pulmonary embolism in high-risk medical patients (see Table 33–2). [2]

In general surgical patients, LMWH preparations seem to be equivalent or only slightly better than low-dose heparin, with slightly less bleeding. [2] For elective total hip replacement patients, LMWHs and oral anticoagulants are most effective, with reported risk reductions of 60 to 80%. [2] Low-dose heparin and aspirin are less effective. Patients undergoing elective hip replacement remain at substantial risk of postoperative thrombosis after discharge from the hospital. Continuing LMWH for 35 days postoperatively is effective in reducing the incidence of these delayed thrombi. For patients with hip fracture, combined LMWH or warfarin is most effective with risk reductions of about 50%. LMWHs are most effective for elective major knee (total knee replacement) surgery patients, for stroke patients, and for patients with spinal cord injury.

Graduated compression stockings augment the effectiveness of low-dose heparin. External pneumatic compression and LMWH are effective in preventing thrombosis in neurosurgery patients, but the first approach is preferred because it does not carry an increased risk of bleeding.

 Treatment

ANTICOAGULANTS. Patients with venous thromboembolic disease have a high risk of recurrence if treated inadequately but respond well to anticoagulant therapy (Chapters 78 and 94). In most cases, initial treatment is with either LMWH or heparin. LMWHs have the advantage that they do not require laboratory monitoring and can be given to selected patients in an outpatient setting.

If LMWH is used, it should be administered in a dose of 100 U/kg of anti–factor Xa twice daily or 150 to 200 U/kg of anti–factor Xa daily (depending on manufacturers' dosing instructions). If heparin is used, it should be administered either as a 5000-U IV bolus followed by 32,000 U every 24 hours by continuous infusion or by the weight-adjusted regimen (see Table 78–5). Warfarin can be started on the first day, overlapped with heparin for a minimum of 5 days, and continued for 3 months or longer if indicated. Heparin or LMWH should be administered for about 10 days in patients with major pulmonary embolism or extensive iliofemoral vein thrombosis. Laboratory monitoring is not required if LMWH is used, but monitoring with the APTT is necessary if heparin is used. The platelet count and hematocrit also should be measured daily.

If the clinical suspicion is high and there is a delay before diagnosis can be confirmed by objective tests, treatment should be started while awaiting confirmation. Patients with a reversible risk factor and proximal vein thrombosis should be treated for at least 3 months, whereas patients with idiopathic venous thromboembolism should be treated for at least 6 months. Some patients with continuing risk factors, such as patients with AT III deficiency, a lupus anticoagulant, malignancy, or recurrent venous thromboembolism, should be treated with warfarin indefinitely. Patients with idiopathic proximal vein thrombosis or pulmonary embolism and deficiencies of protein C or S or patients with activated protein C resistance should be treated for at least 6 months. In patients who have already received 6 months of regular anticoagulant therapy, continued low-intensity therapy for 4–5 years with an INR target of 1.5–2.0 can reduce adverse events by about 50% compared with placebo, [20] but such therapy is not yet standard. Patients' preferences should be taken into account when considering duration of anticoagulant therapy.

THROMBOLYTIC THERAPY. Thrombolytic therapy should be used in patients with massive pulmonary embolism and be considered for patients with recent-onset (≤3 days) extensive proximal vein thrombosis who are relatively young, provided that there are no contraindications.

ATRIAL FIBRILLATION

AF, an important risk factor for stroke, is present in more than 2 million people in the United States (Chapter 59). Its prevalence rises rapidly with age to about 10% in people older than age 80. Although the overall incidence of stroke in AF is about 5% per year, it is much lower in young people without risk factors and higher in people with associated risk factors. People with AF at high risk of stroke include individuals with prior systemic embolism, history of hypertension, poor left ventricular function, age greater than 75 years, rheumatic mitral valve disease, and prosthetic heart valves. Moderate risk factors are age 65 to 75 years, diabetes mellitus, and coronary artery disease.

Warfarin (INR 2.0 to 3.0) reduces the risk of stroke or recurrent stroke in AF patients by about 70%. [6] Lower intensity warfarin is much less effective. Aspirin is less effective than warfarin, producing a risk reduction in stroke of about 25%. [6] When compared directly with aspirin, warfarin is about 40% more effective in reducing stroke. Aspirin is more convenient to use and is associated with less bleeding than warfarin.

Anticoagulant therapy is indicated in patients with AF who have either one major risk factor or more than one moderate risk factor. The decision to use either anticoagulants or aspirin is optional when only one moderate risk factor is present. Aspirin is indicated in low-risk patients or patients in whom anticoagulants are contraindicated. The risk of systemic embolism is increased during electrical cardioversion and can be reduced by the use of prophylactic warfarin administered before and after cardioversion (Chapter 61).

MECHANICAL AND BIOPROSTHETIC VALVES

Patients with prosthetic heart valves are at risk of systemic embolism (Chapter 72). The risk is greater with mechanical than bioprosthetic valves, with prosthetic mitral than aortic valves, and if there is associated AF. Newer mechanical valves seem to be less thrombogenic than older valves. The risk of embolism is confined mainly to the first 3 months for patients with tissue prosthetic valves but is lifelong for patients with mechanical prosthetic valves.

Warfarin is effective in reducing the risk of systemic embolism in patients with mechanical prosthetic valves and is indicated for life at a targeted INR of 3.0 (range 2.5 to 3.5). The addition of aspirin to warfarin reduces the risk of stroke and vascular death by 67% and 40% compared with warfarin alone but at a 65% increase in the risk of bleeding and a 250% increased risk of major gastrointestinal hemorrhage.[21] The combination of warfarin and aspirin is indicated for patients who fail on warfarin therapy. Warfarin is also effective in patients with bioprosthetic valves when used at a targeted INR of 2.0 to 3.0, but in these patients its use usually is limited to 3 months unless there are other risk factors, such as AF.

VALVULAR HEART DISEASE

RHEUMATIC MITRAL VALVE DISEASE. Patients with rheumatic mitral valve disease have about a 20% lifetime risk of developing systemic embolism (Chapter 72). The incidence of systemic embolism increases dramatically with the development of AF and is thought to be 50% higher in mitral stenosis than in rheumatic mitral regurgitation. Risk factors for systemic embolism include age, the presence of a left atrial thrombus, low cardiac output, and significant aortic regurgitation. The risk is reduced by mitral valvuloplasty.

Patients who suffer a first embolus are at high risk of recurrent embolism. Although never evaluated by randomized trial, there is a strong impression that long-term anticoagulant therapy is effective in reducing the incidence of systemic emboli in patients with rheumatic mitral valve disease and AF, but the use of long-term anticoagulation in patients with sinus rhythm is controversial.

Percutaneous balloon mitral valvuloplasty is being used with increasing frequency to treat mitral stenosis. In some centers, it is common practice to treat all patients with warfarin for a minimum of 3 weeks before balloon valvuloplasty, regardless of the presence or absence of AF.

MITRAL VALVE PROLAPSE. Mitral valve prolapse is the most common form of valve disease in adults, occurring in about 5% of the population. The risk of stroke in young adults with mitral valve prolapse is only about 1 in 6000 per year, so the condition is usually benign. Aspirin is indicated in patients who develop a transient ischemic attack, whereas long-term warfarin therapy is indicated in patients with associated AF and for patients who continue to have cerebral ischemic events despite aspirin therapy.

INFECTIVE ENDOCARDITIS

Although patients with infective endocarditis are at risk of systemic embolism, treatment with anticoagulants is problematic because they are also at high risk of intracranial bleeding (Chapter 310). Emboli occur more frequently in patients with acute endocarditis than in patients with subacute endocarditis, in mitral compared with aortic valve endocarditis, and with mechanical prosthetic valve endocarditis than with native or bioprosthetic valve endocarditis.

In general, anticoagulants are not indicated in patients with native valve or bioprosthetic valve endocarditis because the risk of intracranial bleeding is thought to outweigh the benefits of treatment. In higher risk patients with mechanical bioprosthetic valve endocarditis, discontinuation of anticoagulant therapy is not recommended, however, because the risk of cerebral embolism in untreated patients is thought to be greater than the risk of intracranial hemorrhage.

NONBACTERIAL THROMBOTIC ENDOCARDITIS

Nonbacterial thrombotic endocarditis (NBTE) occurs in malignancies, in other chronic debilitating diseases, and in patients with acute fulminant diseases, such as septicemia or burns. Systemic embolism occurs in about 40% of patients with NBTE. The diagnosis of NBTE is difficult to document. Cardiac murmurs are often absent, and echocardiography is less sensitive for the detection of NBTE than it is for bacterial endocarditis. Heparin seems to be effective in preventing embolic events in these patients, whereas limited data suggest that warfarin is ineffective.

1. Patrono C, Coller B, Dalen JE, et al: Platelet-active drugs: The relationships among dose, effectiveness, and side effects. Chest 2001;119(suppl 1):39S–63S.
2. Geerts WH, Heit JA, Clagett GP, et al: Prevention of venous thromboembolism. Chest 2001;119(suppl 1):132S–175S.
3. Cairns JA, Theroux P, Lewis HD, et al: Antithrombotic agents in coronary artery disease. Chest 2001;119(suppl 1):228S–252S.
4. Popma JJ, Ohman EM, Weitz JI, et al: Antithrombotic therapy in patients undergoing percutaneous coronary intervention. Chest 2001;119(suppl 1):321S–336S.
5. Stein PD, Dalen JE, Goldman S, et al: Antithrombotic therapy in patients with saphenous vein and internal mammary artery bypass grafts. Chest 2001;119(suppl 1):278S–282S.
6. Albers GW, Dalen JE, Laupacis A, et al: Antithrombotic therapy in atrial fibrillation. Chest 2001;119(suppl 1):194S–209S.
7. Albers GW, Amarenco P, Easton JD, et al: Antithrombotic and thrombolytic therapy for ischemic stroke. Chest 2001;119(suppl 1):300S–320S.
8. Jackson MR, Clagett GP: Antithrombotic therapy in peripheral arterial occlusive disease. Chest 2001;119(suppl 1):283S–299S.
9. Hirsh J, Warkentin TE, Shaughnessy S, et al: Heparin and low-molecular-weight heparin: Mechanisms of action, pharmacokinetics, dosing, monitoring, efficacy and safety. Chest 2001;119(suppl 1):64S–94S.
10. Hyers TM, Agnelli G, Hull RD, et al: Antithrombotic therapy for venous thromboembolic disease. Chest 2001;119(suppl 1):176S–193S.
11. Ohman EM, Harrington RA, Cannon CP, et al: Intravenous thrombolysis in acute myocardial infarction. Chest 2001;119(suppl 1):253S–277S.
12. Weitz JI, Hirsh J: New anticoagulant drugs. Chest 2001;119(suppl 1):95S–107S.
13. White H, the Hirulog and Early Reperfusion or Occlusion (HERO)-2 trial investigators: Thrombin-specific anticoagulation with bivalirudin versus heparin in patients receiving fibrinolytic therapy for acute myocardial infarction: The HERO-2 randomised trial. Lancet 2001;358:1855–1863.
14. Turpie AGG, Bauer KA, Bengt I, et al: Fondaparinux versus enoxaparin for the prevention of venous thromboembolism in major orthopedic surgery: A meta-analysis of four randomized double-blind studies. Arch Intern Med 2002;162:1806–1808.
15. Bernard GR, Vincet JL, Laterre PF, et al: Efficacy and safety of recombinant human activated protein C for severe sepsis. N Engl J Med 2001;344:699–709.
16. Bosch X, Marrugat J: Platelet glycoprotein IIb/IIIa blockers for percutaneous coronary revascularization, and unstable angina and non-ST-segment elevation myocardial infarction. Cochrane Review. Cochrane Database Syst Rev 2001;4:CD002130.
17. ISIS-2 (Second International Study of Infarct Survival) collaborative group: Randomised trial of intravenous streptokinase, oral aspirin, both, or neither among 17,187 cases of suspected acute myocardial infarction: ISIS-2. Lancet 1988;2:349–360.
18. Van Es RF, Jonker JCJ, Verheugt FWA, et al: Aspirin and coumadin after acute coronary syndromes: Results of the ASPECT-2 trial. Lancet 2002;360:109–113.
19. Hurlen M, Abdelnoor M, Smith P, et al: Warfarin, aspirin, or both after myocardial infarction. N Engl J Med 2002;347:969–974.
20. Ridker PM, Goldhaber SZ, Danielson E, et al: Long-term, low-intensity warfarin therapy for the prevention of recurrent venous thromboembolism. N Engl J Med 2003;348:1425–1434.
21. Stein PD, Alpert JS, Bussey HI, et al: Antithrombotic therapy in patients with mechanical and biological prosthetic heart valves. Chest 2001;119(suppl 1):220S–227S.

SUGGESTED READINGS

Anand SS, Yusuf S: Oral anticoagulants in patients with coronary artery disease. J Am Coll Cardiol 2003;41(4 Suppl):62S–69S. *A practical review.*

Antithrombotic Trialists' Collaboration: Collaborative meta-analysis of randomized trials of antiplatelet therapy for prevention of death, myocardial infarction, and stroke in high-risk patients. BMJ 2002;324:71–86. *Aspirin is protective in most types of patients at increased risk of occlusive vascular events.*

Dalen JE, Hirsh J, Guyatt JH (eds): Sixth ACCP Consensus Conference on Antithrombotic Therapy. Chest 2001;119:1S–370S. *A comprehensive review of the pharmacology of antithrombotic agents and an evidence-based appraisal of the results of the clinical trials with antithrombotic agents in venous and arterial thromboembolic disease.*

34 COMPLEMENTARY AND ALTERNATIVE MEDICINE

Stephen E. Straus

Despite dramatic advances in medical science and evidence-based practice, many people turn to other healing approaches, some derived from ancient medical traditions and others from new-age concepts. Although extraordinarily diverse in their nature and purpose, these approaches share enormous appeal, often despite the lack of compelling evidence that they are safe or effective. The term *alternative medicine* is used to indicate practices that are used instead of mainstream approaches, whereas *complementary medicine* refers to practices that are used as adjuncts to conventional medicine. The most recent term for these approaches, *integrative medicine*, signals the hope that conventional medicine can embrace any modality that proves to be safe and effective, regardless of its origins, under a more inclusive health care umbrella. Complementary and alternative medicine commonly emphasizes therapies, many of which are based on unproven hypotheses regarding pathophysiology, and rarely focuses on specific diagnostic strategies.

Definitions and Disciplines

Complementary and alternative medicine includes healing approaches that presently are not considered an integral part of conventional medicine as practiced in developed nations. Its many forms can be divided conveniently into five major but overlapping categories: alternative medical systems, biologically based therapies, manipulative and body-based methods, mind-body interventions, and energy therapies.

ALTERNATIVE MEDICAL SYSTEMS

Alternative medical systems aim to prevent or treat disease without relying on any elements of conventional Western medicine. Included are traditional Chinese medicine, Ayurveda (meaning "science of life") of India, and various Native American healing approaches. Each is a complex system that incorporates natural products, diet, spiritual elements, and other modalities. Of the various elements that are specific to some traditional medical systems, Americans are most familiar with herbal medicines and acupuncture, approaches that evolved over thousands of years through careful observation and empirical refinement. As practiced in traditional healing systems, herbs and acupuncture are but two of several tools commonly advised for relief of a particular condition, but in the United States, they typically are prescribed as stand-alone modalities. Many other alternative approaches similarly have been adapted to the tastes and interests of the broader American populace.

Newer, European-based or American-based alternative systems include homeopathic medicine and naturopathic medicine. Homeopathy was founded in the late 18th century as a reaction to the toxic and unsuccessful normative practices of the day, such as purging and leeching. The theory of homeopathy is that infinitesimal doses of a substance that causes particular symptoms in higher concentrations relieve similar symptoms, regardless of their cause. Previously a widely respected field that inspired some of the first placebo-controlled experiments and from which the original theory leading to allergen desensitization was derived, homeopathy is a small field today in the United States. Only four states provide licenses for the practice of homeopathy. By contrast, homeopathy remains widely practiced in Germany and is well accepted within the National Health Service in the United Kingdom.

Naturopathic medicine derived from the early 19th century German concept of natural healing (i.e., the body possesses an inherent ability to heal itself). The purpose of this approach is to guide the patient toward self-healing with gentle and nontoxic measures, proper diet, and a variety of other approaches. The emphasis is on outpatient-based primary care and family medicine. Training involves 4 years of postgraduate education leading to the Doctorate of Naturopathic Medicine (N.D.) degree. Practitioners are licensed for individual practice in 13 states in the United States.

BIOLOGICALLY BASED THERAPIES

Because numerous drugs are of natural origin, it is presumed that nature harbors yet more medicinal gems awaiting discovery and characterization. Countless natural products and mixtures of products have been described in ancient medical texts, and contemporary versions of many of these products are sold to eager consumers as dietary supplements. The extraordinary popularity of these products, for which Americans spend billions of dollars each year, rests at least in part on

the prevalent assumption that a natural product is healthy, whereas synthetic chemicals often are not. Under the Dietary Supplements Health and Education Act passed by the U.S. Congress in 1994, dietary supplements include vitamins, minerals, and all natural herbal and chemical products that are ingested for the maintenance of wellness or for the prevention and treatment of symptoms that arise from normal bodily processes, such as menopause, rather than from pathologic causes. These products are not deemed to be drugs and are not regulated as such; as a result, they do not require premarket review or approval by the Food and Drug Administration (FDA).

MANIPULATIVE AND BODY-BASED METHODS

Therapeutic massage, chiropractic, and osteopathic manipulation are the best known of the manual therapies. Massage is widely practiced and licensed in 25 states. Manipulation procedures are practiced largely within chiropractic and osteopathic systems that emerged in the American heartland in the late 19th century. Both fields originally proposed that vertebral misalignments contribute to many diseases, each of which could be treated by appropriate manipulations. There were strong efforts by allopathic organizations to discredit chiropractic and osteopathic medicine. In part as reactions to these challenges, chiropractic medicine evolved as a discrete discipline that primarily uses spinal manipulation, most often to address musculoskeletal problems. Four years of postgraduate education lead to a Doctor of Chiropractic (D.C.) degree, and chiropractic physicians are licensed to practice in all states.

Osteopathic medicine also may use manipulative techniques, but historical differences between osteopathic medicine and allopathic medicine otherwise have disappeared. Other than teaching manipulation, undergraduate medical training for an osteopathic degree (D.O.) is now virtually indistinguishable from that which leads to the M.D. degree. Osteopathic physicians complete conventional residencies in osteopathic or allopathic hospitals and training programs; are licensed in all states; and have rights and responsibilities, such as military service, that are identical to allopathic physicians and surgeons.

MIND-BODY INTERVENTIONS

Complementary and alternative medicine is based on the premise that the mind influences bodily functions, and vice versa, and that the interactions between them can be affected for salutary purposes. This belief is a remarkably ancient and strikingly modern concept that conflicts with the cartesian dissociation of mind from body that dominated Western philosophical thought for more than 300 years. Some uses for hypnosis, cognitive therapies, and biofeedback are well integrated within conventional medicine. Other approaches involving meditation; dance, music, and art therapy; and prayer are considered complementary or alternative.

ENERGY THERAPIES

Ancient peoples postulated that health depends on the proper balance and flow of life energies, termed *Qi* (pronounced "Chee") in Chinese systems or the *doshas* in Ayurveda. Many strategies were developed with the goal of restoring the vitality and balance of a person's energies. In the aggregate, these approaches are controversial complementary and alternative medicine practices because neither these internal energy fields nor the activities they are assumed to possess have been shown convincingly. There are two general classes of energetic approaches. One involves the application of external electromagnetic fields, as with magnets inserted into clothing and mattresses. The other purports to manipulate a person's fields, such as by having a healer place hands in or through them. Therapeutic touch derives from the ancient practice of "laying on of hands" with the goal of allowing the therapist's healing force to restore that of the patient. Other related approaches include Qi gong and Reiki.

Acupuncture is a widely practiced energy healing art whose traditional justification may be less important than what contemporary science teaches about it. Acupuncture involves insertion of needles into empirically derived points on the body, or meridians, across which streams of energy are said to flow. Modern versions of acupuncture include attachment of electrodes to the needles and the application of small currents through them. Whatever the style of practice, acupuncture has moved progressively mainstream. Reports in the early 1970s of its use in China to substitute for general anesthetics excited the curiosity and fascination of Americans. Today, formal training leads to a license in acupuncture degree (L.Ac.) that permits either independent practice or practice under the supervision of a physician in about 34 states.

Appeal and Use of Complementary and Alternative Medicine

Widely cited estimates suggest that 42% of Americans employ complementary and alternative medicine therapies to help satisfy their personal health care needs. The appeal is sufficient for Americans to spend billions of dollars on these therapies annually without any prospect of reimbursement from insurance companies.

Surveys indicate that patients choose complementary and alternative medicine approaches to sustain or restore their health and well-being, primarily to relieve symptoms of chronic or terminal illnesses that are not addressed adequately by conventional medical treatments. In general, its use is not a reaction against or fundamental dissatisfaction with conventional medicine. Most use is as an adjunct to conventional treatment. Complementary and alternative medicine approaches are sought more frequently by women, people born after World War II, people with more years of formal education, people who think more about emotional stress and the environment, more affluent people, and people who are chronically ill.

Clinical Approach

A full inquiry into what ails patients includes an attempt to understand not only the clinical problems themselves, but also what the patients believe the problems to represent and how they have attempted to address them. The physician must ask specifically about complementary and alternative medicine practices that patients may use. The broad range of complementary and alternative options available and the inundation of the public with unsubstantiated claims about them challenge physicians' abilities to guide their patients' choices. Merely to pontificate that none of these practices are meritorious may alienate a patient whose personal experience and firm convictions indicate otherwise. Yet a physician cannot accede to all preferences of all patients. Ultimately a conscious decision must be made whether to prescribe a complementary and alternative treatment; endorse a patient's own choices for complementary and alternative medicine; accept his or her choices, provided that they do not interfere with the prescribed conventional approaches; or advise against the complementary and alternative approach. First and foremost, the decision should be based on whether the approach could be harmful.

Risks

That many complementary and alternative medicine practices are rooted in ancient health care systems and may involve natural products has been taken as ample proof of at least their safety if not also their effectiveness. This assumption is frequently incorrect. Few complementary and alternative medicine approaches have been studied rigorously, and some have not held up to scientific scrutiny at all. Despite millennia of empirically derived practices regarding which herbal medicines should be considered for a given condition (and in what form, quantity, and duration), Americans consume many such agents with impunity. It is common for individuals to self-medicate with dozens of different tablets, capsules, and liquid extracts daily. In the United States, there are no accepted standards for the manufacture, composition, or purity of herbal medicines. Occasionally, products have been withdrawn when shown by the FDA to be inherently toxic, contaminated with toxic materials, or adulterated with proprietary drugs. The Federal Trade Commission also has cited manufacturers for making unsubstantiated claims about their products. Many of the most popular dietary supplements have been shown to interact with conventional drugs and affect their potential clinical effectiveness (Table 34–1).

A major concern regarding complementary and alternative medicine approaches is that an individual might choose them instead of mainstream practices that are known to be effective. Because few patients inform physicians about their consumption of dietary supplements and few physicians inquire about them, potential problems emerge in many clinical settings. Patients who consume medicinal herbs known to interfere with coagulation may be at increased risk

Table 34–1 • SOME NATURAL MEDICINES THAT POTENTIATE OR INTERFERE WITH DRUGS

NATURAL MEDICINE	APPROVED DRUG
Ephedra	Theophylline (P)
Garlic	Anticoagulants (P); saquinavir (I)
Ginkgo leaf extract	Anticoagulants (P)
Glucosamine	Antidiabetic drugs (I)
Panax ginseng	Anticoagulants (P)
Saw palmetto	Hormone replacement therapies (P)
Soy	Estrogenic drugs (P)
St. John's wort	Antidepressants (P), HIV protease inhibitors (I), cyclosporine (I)
Valerian	Sedatives (P)
Yohimbe	Antihypertensives (I)

P = potentiate; I = interfere; HIV = human immunodeficiency virus.

of hemorrhage after surgery. With the increased awareness of the use and potential hazards of complementary and alternative medicine, more practitioners and institutions have begun to incorporate relevant questions into routine patient interactions. By knowing what a patient is using and considering its potential hazards, the physician can begin to address the level of evidence supporting or negating a complementary and alternative medicine approach.

Evidence Base

If a modality were rigorously proven and widely accepted as such, it would no longer be considered complementary or alternative. The basis for claims regarding complementary and alternative medicine is frequently anecdotal, an aggregate of empirical observations, or a retrospective case series. Nonetheless, there have been hundreds of prospective controlled studies involving selected complementary and alternative medicine approaches. Thoughtful reviews of the data regarding some complementary and alternative medicine modalities have been conducted, including dozens by the members of the Cochrane Collaboration (http://www.update-software.com/cochrane/). Many complementary and alternative medicine studies are flawed because of inadequate sample size, poor design, lack of blinding even when feasible, and the failure to incorporate objective or standardized outcome instruments.

Credible information resources for the patient and the practitioner are accruing. Public databases such as PubMed of the National Library of Medicine now highlight a complementary medicine subset with more than 250,000 articles. The National Cancer Institute and the National Center for Complementary and Alternative Medicine of the National Institutes of Health (NIH) maintain active websites (www.nih.gov) that post relevant complementary and alternative medicine information. The database ClinicalTrials.gov lists all NIH-supported clinical studies of complementary and alternative medical approaches that are actively accruing patients.

Failed Approaches

Desperation has long driven people to seek alternative and even radical therapies. A glimmer of hope, however faint, can be appealing; a mere anecdote can prove persuasive. Nonetheless, there is no justification for people to elect unconventional treatments when there is abundant evidence that such therapies are unsafe (Table 34–2) or ineffective.

An instructive example of a failed approach is that of laetrile, a cyanide-containing extract of apricot seeds. Through the 1970s, anecdotes and media reports that laetrile cured thousands of patients with inoperable cancers fanned public demand for the product. Finally, the National Cancer Institute funded two substantive prospective studies showing no clear evidence that laetrile could induce a partial or complete remission from cancer; these findings led to a dramatic reduction in requests for the product. Although laetrile remains available to determined and desperate patients, far fewer seek it today than in the 1970s. In the open-market environment in which alternative treatments are widely available, the fact that clear evidence affects

Table 34–2 • SOME NATURAL PRODUCTS WITH POTENTIALLY SERIOUS ADVERSE EFFECTS

PRODUCT	EFFECT
Aristolochia	Nephrotoxicity, carcinogenicity
Chaparral	Cholestatic hepatitis
Comfrey	Acute and chronic hepatitis
Digitalis leaf	Arrhythmias
Ephedra	Hypertension, stroke
Germander	Acute and chronic hepatitis
Khat	Tachycardia, psychosis
Kombucha	Hepatotoxicity, lactic acidosis
Mistletoe	Anaphylaxis
Skullcap	Seizures, acute and chronic hepatitis

consumers' demand may be as good a public health outcome as could be expected.

Acceptable Approaches

In considering complementary and alternative medicine approaches, patients and physicians must look to practices that at least make sense based on clinical experience and what might be known of their mechanisms of action. Healthy skepticism must be balanced with thoughtful empiricism. Two categories of potentially acceptable complementary and alternative therapies exist: supportive approaches and specific therapies.

SUPPORTIVE APPROACHES

Many complementary and alternative medicine practices are based on core elements that always have been a part of good medicine, what is known as "the three Ts"—talk, touch, and time. It is unworthy of good medicine to have abandoned these core elements under the pressure of limited time or because of the emergence of more powerful technologies. Most current physicians cannot auscultate the chest or palpate a spleen as well as leading practitioners of prior generations, and modern imaging techniques are far better than physical diagnosis for detecting many pathologic changes. For reasons that might be cultural or even biologic, however, patients respond better to practitioners who listen well, care enough to touch them, and explain their findings and decisions. In the aggregate, these facets of the traditional physician-patient relationship may contribute to the placebo effect that facilitates healing. Rather than being a pejorative concept that once implied a patient who recovers while receiving an inert substance was never really ill, the placebo increasingly is viewed as a way to increase the patient's own will to recover. The concept of the placebo is a sensitive one for the complementary and alternative medicine field. On the one hand, some complementary and alternative medicine approaches are based on the desire to harness the power of the mind as a healing force. On the other hand, there is a reluctance to accept that some part of the success of complementary and alternative medicine rests on the placebo rather than on a particular procedure or herb.

Anything that can relieve or distract a person suffering from severe pain can be a sensible approach (Chapter 29). Only in more recent years has pain management emerged as a distinct specialty, and its tools extend well beyond the wise and adequate use of narcotic analgesics. Increasingly, massage, relaxation, and meditative approaches have found their way into mainstream pain management. As indicated subsequently, the evidence supporting acupuncture for some forms of pain is fairly good, but similar evidence is not available for many other complementary and alternative approaches to pain. Nonetheless, it is sensible to pursue some of these approaches in a logical and coherent sequence.

Contemporary medicine has acknowledged its historical shortcomings not only in pain management, but also in the broader arena of palliative and end-of-life care (e.g., the success of the hospice movement) (Chapter 3). Dying patients not only need relief from pain or nausea, but also they may seek spiritual guidance and a means to bring closure to their careers and their interactions with family and friends. Dying patients fear isolation, dependency, and the loss of

intellectual and physical faculties. Hospitals have long housed chaplains, psychiatric social workers, and physical therapists. Increasingly, hospitals also are providing massage, art or music therapy, group counseling with patients who are similarly afflicted, and supportive services for the caretaker and the patient. These and other approaches to palliative care may be viewed as complementary and alternative medicine, but they are sensible, even if unproven.

SPECIFIC THERAPIES

Ubiquitous advertising might be all that some individuals need to be enticed to buy and use medicinal herbs. When published case series and pilot trials suggest that the product might be beneficial and there is little to indicate it is unsafe, the physician might be comfortable with the patient's wish to use it, especially if the patient is not neglecting more important health issues and proven effective therapies, if the patient can afford it, and if the complementary and alternative medicine seems to help and not cause side effects.

Valerian is an herb often consumed as a tea for improved sleep. Melatonin is a pineal hormone touted for the same purposes. Small studies suggest they might relieve insomnia, and there may be little harm in a trial course of either agent. Echinacea has long been taken to treat or prevent colds, just as are zinc lozenges or spray or high doses of vitamin C. As yet, only moderate-sized studies have been conducted with echinacea or zinc, and their outcomes have been conflicting. Large trials of high doses of oral vitamin C showed little if any benefit in preventing or treating the common cold.◻ Although there is no reason to recommend these agents, there also is no great urgency to demand they be abandoned. In talking with a patient, the physician instead might emphasize important health measures, such as avoidance of addictive substances; timely vaccination; and compliance with prescribed diet, exercise, and medications, rather than try to influence the patient's use of unproven but apparently safe complementary and alternative measures.

Encouraging Approaches

Physician and patients should be most comfortable in advising or accepting a complementary and alternative medicine approach when data from one or more fairly well-designed, randomized controlled trials support it. Table 34–3 highlights some encouraging approaches that are now under increasingly rigorous scrutiny.

HERBAL AND BIOCHEMICAL MEDICINE

Nature has long been the inspiration for and source of medicines, many of which are derived from plants, molds, or bacteria, including digoxin, morphine, aspirin, quinine, vincristine, taxol, the statins, penicillin, and cyclosporine. Although combinatorial chemistry provides more efficient ways to discover active agents, the screening of natural product repositories, especially if guided by claims of native practitioners, still yields promising compounds for drug development. One example is a new class of antimalarial drugs based on artemisinin, an extract of a plant used for treatment of fevers for more than 2000 years in southern China. Although plants serve as sources for discrete new chemical entities, it is also possible that, as believed by

Table 34–3 • SOME COMPLEMENTARY AND ALTERNATIVE MEDICINE APPROACHES WITH ENCOURAGING CLINICAL RESULTS

MODALITY	POSSIBLE INDICATION
Artemisinin	Malaria
Acupuncture	Pain of dental extraction; nausea from chemotherapy
Chiropractic manipulation	Uncomplicated low back pain
Ginkgo biloba leaf extract	Dementia
Glucosamine	Osteoarthritis
Horse chestnut	Chronic venous insufficiency
S-adenosyl methionine	Osteoarthritis; depression
Saw palmetto	Benign prostatic hypertrophy
St. John's wort	Mild depressive illnesses

herbal medicine advocates, the aggregate of chemicals in an herb is superior to any of its constituents.

There are several medicinal herbs and natural substances for which existing data are encouraging. Extracts of *Ginkgo biloba* are well standardized and prescribed as drugs in Germany and most other European Union countries for prevention and treatment of dementia. This practice is supported by small but placebo-controlled, double-blind trials that, in the aggregate, show a significant improvement in cognitive performance in patients with Alzheimer's disease.

Glucosamine and chondroitin sulfate are found in the ground substance of cartilage. Crude extracts containing these agents are administered widely alone or in combination for the treatment and prevention of osteoarthritis, not only in humans, but also in dogs and horses. Among 13 randomized controlled trials, 12 have found glucosamine to be superior to placebo for osteoarthritis. In one study of 212 randomized subjects followed for 3 years, benefits were reported not only in pain and function, but also in preservation of the joint space.[2]

Many small or poorly designed trials concluded that St. John's wort effectively treats a range of depressive conditions. More recent, well-designed trials showed that St. John's wort does not benefit patients with major depression of moderate severity.[3]

ACUPUNCTURE

Thousands of publications attest to the benefits of acupuncture, but few are scientific. Nonetheless, careful laboratory investigations have shown the induction of opioid-dependent brain pathways by which acupuncture might mediate an analgesic effect. In the aggregate, there are sufficient encouraging findings to support its consideration in selected settings, such as pain associated with dental extraction and nausea associated with cancer drugs.[4] A wristband that applies pressure to an "acupoint" associated with nausea was approved for management of seasickness by the FDA.

SPINAL MANIPULATION

Manipulation is practiced most frequently by chiropractic and osteopathic physicians. Massage therapists practice their own specific forms of manipulation. Among all of the target indications for manipulation, its merits for treatment of back pain have been addressed the most. Although the conclusions from these studies are controversial, the aggregate data suggest that spinal manipulation is superior to bed rest and at least equivalent to results with nonsteroidal drugs or back training exercises.[5]

Prospects

Conventional medical practice may not evolve, as some have espoused, to a system in which patients are greeted routinely in a multimodality practice by a team of homeopaths, chiropractic and Ayurvedic physicians, herbalists, and spiritual counselors as well as by conventional physicians and nurses. There is no question, however, that patients increasingly are offered a menu of choices that is greater and more diverse than ever before. Witness the emergence of specialties and allied health professions that were unforeseen a generation ago. Today's patients interact with legions of medical technologists, therapists, counselors, dietitians, and hygienists, not to mention interventional radiologists, clinical psychopharmacologists, or cellular and molecular biologists in the guise of gene and stem cell therapists.

The question is what elements of today's complementary and alternative medicine should become tomorrow's normative practice? The willingness of practitioners to commit adequate time, to listen carefully to patients, and to touch them physically and emotionally must remain part of conventional medicine. There are no longer any doubts that proper diet, exercise, intellectual and social engagement, and avoidance of stress and addictive substances are beneficial practices. Physicians must be trained to incorporate these messages into their routine interactions with patients. It also is appropriate that physicians acquaint themselves with other practices to which their patients might be drawn and to negotiate thoughtfully and openly about their use to achieve the best outcome. It is unreasonable to expect physicians to master the rudiments of disciplines such as acupuncture or Ayurveda, but they should understand the essential claims of these disciplines and know how to access the evidence base.

Complementary and alternative medicine, in some incarnation, is here to stay. It is preferable to comprehend the movement and address its tenets as fairly and rigorously as possible, rather than risk alienating from mainstream health care institutions people who find it appealing.

Future Directions

The encouraging existing reports regarding several products, such as *Ginkgo biloba* and glucosamine, are under scrutiny in large, placebo-controlled, randomized multicenter trials involving thousands of patients each. Studies such as these will help transform the question from does it work, to should one recommend it?

1. Karlowski TR, Chalmers TC, Frenkel LD, et al: Ascorbic acid for the common cold: A prophylactic and therapeutic trial. JAMA 1975;231:1038–1042.
2. Reginster JY, Deroisy R, Rovati LC, et al: Long-term effects of glucosamine sulphate on osteoarthritis progression: A randomized, placebo-controlled clinical trial. Lancet 2001;357:251–256.
3. Hypericum Depression Trial Study group: Effect of *Hypericum perforatum* (St. John's Wort) in major depressive disorder: A randomized controlled trial. JAMA 2002;287:1807–1814.
4. Shen J, Wenger N, Glaspy J, et al: Electroacupuncture for myeloablative chemotherapy-induced vomiting: A randomized controlled trial. JAMA 2000;284:2755–2761.
5. Cherkin D, Deyo RA, Battie M, et al: A comparison of physical therapy, chiropractic manipulation, and provision of an educational booklet for the treatment of patients with low back pain. N Engl J Med 1998;339:1021–1029.

SUGGESTED READINGS

Cochrane Library: Available at http://www.update-software.com/cochrane/.

De Smet PA: Herbal remedies. N Engl J Med 2002;347:2046–2056. *A critical review of the hazards and potential benefits of herbal medicines.*

Ernst E: The role of complementary and alternative medicine. BMJ 2000;321:1133–1135. *A thoughtful essay on the place of complementary and alternative medicine in contemporary medical practice.*

Kessler RC, Davis RB, Foster DF, et al: Long-term trends in the use of complementary and alternative medical therapies in the United States. Ann Intern Med 2001;135:262–268. *An extensive analysis of who uses various complementary and alternative medicine approaches.*

Niggemann B, Gruber C: Side-effects of complementary and alternative medicine. Allergy 2003;58:707–716. *Cautions about the many potential hazards.*

part VI

Genetics

35 PRINCIPLES OF GENETICS: OVERVIEW OF THE PARADIGM OF GENETIC CONTRIBUTION TO HEALTH AND DISEASE

Bruce R. Korf

The elucidation of the structure and function of the genome is one of the great scientific triumphs of the 20th century. The relevance of inheritance to health and disease probably has been recognized throughout history, but it is only during the 20th century that the rules that govern inheritance and the mechanisms whereby genetic information is stored and used have come to light. The application of this knowledge to medical practice so far has focused on relatively rare monogenic and chromosomal disorders. Major contributions have been made in these areas in the form of approaches to genetic counseling, genetic testing, prenatal diagnosis, newborn screening, carrier screening, and, to a limited extent, treatment. As important as these contributions are, however, their impact has been limited by the rarity of these disorders. New powerful tools resulting from the Human Genome Project are changing this situation rapidly. Genetic factors that contribute to common and rare disorders are being identified and will result in new approaches to diagnosis, prevention, and treatment. Genetics and genomics increasingly are going to occupy center stage in medical practice, guiding treatment decisions and preventive strategies. This chapter reviews the paradigm whereby genetics will be integrated into the routine practice of medicine.

Genetic Contribution to Disease

It may be argued that there is no disorder that is either completely determined genetically or completely determined by nongenetic factors. Even monogenic conditions, such as phenylketonuria, are modified by the environment, in this case by dietary intake of phenylalanine. Genetically determined host factors are known to modify susceptibility to infection or other environmental agents. Even individuals who are victims of trauma may find themselves at risk in part because of genetic traits that affect behavior or ability to perceive or escape from danger.

The overall scheme whereby genes contribute to disease is described best by the concept of multifactorial inheritance, in which multiple genes interact with one another and with the environment to alter homeostasis in a manner that can be defined as *disease* (Fig. 35–1). In some cases, individual genes or environmental factors contribute overwhelmingly to the cause of a disorder, as with a genetic condition, such as neurofibromatosis or Down syndrome, or an acquired

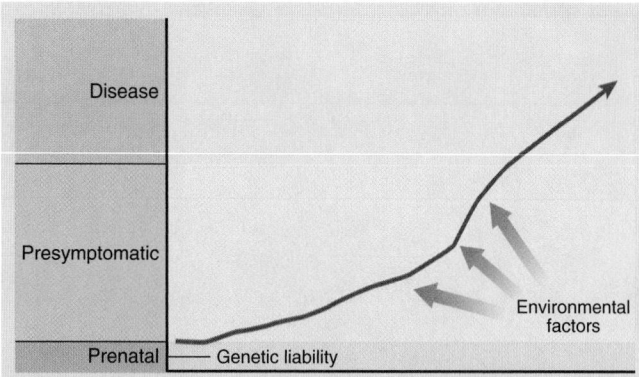

FIGURE 35–1 • Multifactorial etiology of disease. An individual is born with a genetic liability but remains in a presymptomatic state for some time, until additional events occur, including exposure to environmental factors, that result in crossing a threshold that is identified as *disease*. In instances of high-penetrance monogenic disorders, the genetic liability may be overwhelming. In other instances, genetic factors may contribute only slightly to disease risk.

disorder, such as bacterial infection or trauma. Other times there may be a complex interplay among many factors, making it difficult to dissect out the specific genes or environmental exposures.

From a medical perspective, it is helpful to divide the genetic contribution to disease into three categories: high-penetrance monogenic or chromosomal disorders, monogenic versions of common disorders, and complex multifactorial disorders. Each of these has an impact on medical practice in distinctive ways.

HIGH-PENETRANCE MONOGENIC OR CHROMOSOMAL DISORDERS

High-penetrance monogenic or chromosomal disorders are the disorders that most clinicians think of as "genetic conditions." They include rare but familiar single gene disorders, such as neurofibromatosis, Marfan syndrome, and cystic fibrosis, and chromosomal abnormalities, such as trisomy 21 (Down syndrome). At present, several thousand distinct human genetic disorders have been described and cataloged in *Mendelian Inheritance in Man* (available at www.ncbi.nlm.nih.gov/Omim/). These include mendelian dominant or recessive disorders, sex-linked disorders, and more recently discovered conditions that are due to mutations within the 16.6 kb mitochondrial genome. They also include major chromosomal aneuploidy syndromes and syndromes resulting from duplication or deletion of small regions of the genome that result in either reproducible syndromes, such as Williams syndrome (deletion of the elastin locus on chromosome 7), or nonspecific mental retardation.

The internist or primary care physician plays a crucial role in the care of individuals with these disorders and faces significant challenges. Because of the rarity of many of these conditions, most practitioners have limited experience with a given disorder and are likely to need to refer the patient to an appropriate specialist for assistance with diagnosis and management. Nevertheless, the nonspecialist has many distinct roles in the care of these patients. These roles begin with the recognition of the fact that the patient may have a disorder and arrangement for appropriate diagnostic evaluation. Many genetic disorders produce obvious signs or symptoms, which, even if not immediately suggestive of a diagnosis, at least prompt referral. Others can be more subtle, with nevertheless significant consequences if the diagnosis is missed. An example is Marfan syndrome. The physician needs to be alert to the physical characteristics of patients with Marfan syndrome because life-threatening aortic dissection can be avoided with appropriate monitoring and treatment with β-blockers or surgery. Table 35–1 lists examples of some adult-onset monogenic conditions with which the internist should be familiar.

The treatment of patients with genetic disorders may require the assistance of a specialist, but the nonspecialist is likely to be the first contact when an affected individual is ill. The primary care physician needs to be familiar with the disorder and major potential complications. For example, the patient with neurofibromatosis who experiences chronic back pain may be presenting with a malignant peripheral nerve sheath tumor, requiring more aggressive evaluation than would be typical for an unaffected individual with back pain. Formation of a good working relationship between the specialist and nonspecialist is crucial to ensure effective care.

The nonspecialist also has a crucial role in supporting the patient and helping to explain the difficult choices that may be offered for management. This includes providing support for patients who have disorders that cannot be treated and for the emotional impact that accompanies knowledge that a disorder may be transmitted to one's offspring or shared with other relatives. Most patients have little understanding of the mechanisms of genetics and genetic disease. Although the responsibility to explain these issues may reside with specialists and counselors, the primary care provider has an important supportive role.

Although many of the disorders in this group have been known for a long time, more recent advances in genetics have had a substantial impact on approaches to diagnosis and management. Genetic testing has been refined with the advent of molecular diagnostic tests that detect mutations within individual genes. Even rare disorders may be amenable to diagnostic testing; a database of testing laboratories can be found on the Internet (available at www.genetests.org). Population screening for carrier status of some disorders now is offered routinely. Some tests are targeted to particular ethnic groups, such as Ashkenazi Jews (Tay-Sachs disease, Canavan's disease, cystic fibrosis, Gaucher's disease) or individuals of African, Mediterranean, or Asian ancestry (hemoglobinopathies) (Table 35–2). Panethnic

Table 35–1 • HIGH-PENETRANCE SINGLE GENE DISORDERS THAT MAY PRESENT IN ADULTHOOD, WITH SOME MAJOR MEDICAL IMPLICATIONS*

DISORDER	INHERITANCE	MAJOR MEDICAL IMPLICATIONS
CARDIOVASCULAR		
Marfan syndrome	AD	Risk of aortic dissection; lens dislocation
Long QT syndrome	AD, AR	Arrhythmia, sudden death
RENAL		
Adult polycystic kidney disease	AD	Renal failure
PULMONARY		
α-Antitrypsin deficiency	AR	Emphysema, cirrhosis
NEUROLOGIC		
NF1	AD	Benign and malignant nerve sheath tumors; gliomas
NF2	AD	Schwannomas (especially vestibular), meningiomas
Von Hippel–Lindau	AD	Hemangioblastoma of cerebellum, brainstem, eye; pheochromocytoma; renal cell carcinoma
Huntington disease	AD	Movement disorder, psychiatric disorder, dementia
HEMATOLOGIC		
Globin disorders	AR	Stroke, iron overload
ENDOCRINE		
MEN syndromes	AD	Tumors of thyroid, parathyroid, pheochromocytoma

*See Table 35–3 for examples of lower penetrance disorders.
AD = autosomal dominant; AR = autosomal recessive; MEN = multiple endocrine neoplasia; NF = neurofibromatosis.

Table 35–2 • MAJOR RECESSIVE DISORDERS FOR WHICH CARRIER SCREENING COMMONY IS OFFERED IN THE UNITED STATES

DISORDER	MAJOR AT-RISK POPULATION	CARRIER FREQUENCY
Cystic fibrosis	Caucasian	1:25
	Ashkenazi Jewish	1:29
Sickle cell anemia	African American	1:10
β-Thalassemia	Mediterranean	1:60
α-Thalassemia	Southeast Asian, Chinese	1:50
Tay-Sachs disease	Ashkenazi Jewish	1:30
	French Canadian	1:30
Canavan's disease	Ashkenazi Jewish	1:40

screening is now being made available for cystic fibrosis, although risks differ in different ethnic groups. Newborn screening is being expanded beyond inborn errors of metabolism such as phenylketonuria and galactosemia. Some states now include hemoglobinopathies, cystic fibrosis, and hearing loss. Metabolic screening also is being expanded using the technology of tandem mass spectrometry. Finally, treatment of some monogenic disorders is becoming feasible. Life expectancy for patients with cystic fibrosis has been increasing gradually with better treatments for chronic lung disease; dietary therapy is available for many inborn errors of metabolism; novel therapies that use either pharmaceuticals or gene replacement strategies are beginning to be tested for many conditions. The principles of management of genetic disorders are evolving rapidly so that care of patients increasingly requires active partnership of appropriate specialists and primary care providers.

MONOGENIC VERSIONS OF COMMON DISORDERS

Not all monogenic disorders produce obscure phenotypes, and not all common disorders are due to complex multifactorial causes. In more recent years, it has been recognized that some common disorders occur in some families as single gene traits (Table 35–3). Usually this is true for only a few affected individuals, but in some cases it is a significant minority and represents an important group of patients to recognize.

An example is breast cancer. About 7% of cases of this common form of cancer can be attributed to mutation in one of two genes, *BRCA1* or *BRCA2*. Women who inherit a mutation in one of these genes face a high risk of eventually developing breast or ovarian cancer—80% by age 70 years, depending in part on the specific mutation. Women at risk because of mutation do not look different from women with sporadic breast cancer but can be distinguished by many features, including family history of breast or ovarian cancer in multiple relatives, early age of onset of cancer, and multifocality of the cancer (e.g., bilateral breast cancer or breast and ovarian cancer).

Another example from cancer genetics is colon cancer. Two syndromes, familial adenomatous polyposis and hereditary nonpolyposis colon cancer, are autosomal dominantly inherited and convey a high risk of colon cancer. Other noncancer examples are hemochromatosis, in which cirrhosis, cardiomyopathy, diabetes, joint disease, and other problems ensue from excessive iron absorption; 10% of whites carry an allele that predisposes to this recessive disorder. Mutations in the factor V gene or the prothrombin gene occur commonly and predispose to deep vein thrombosis. Rarer examples include inherited forms of cardiomyopathy, hypertension, and familial hypercholesterolemia.

The physician may be called on to address these disorders in many ways. There is a compelling reason to make an early diagnosis of hemochromatosis because the complications can be prevented, but not reversed, by phlebotomy and subsequent monitoring of iron stores. Individuals at risk of colon cancer can be offered surveillance with colonoscopy or surgical resection of the colon to reduce the risk of cancer. Individuals at risk of breast and ovarian cancer likewise can be offered surveillance or surgery, although the benefits of surveillance are less well established in this monogenic disorder. The benefits of knowledge of genetic risks are less clear in some instances. Carriers of the factor V Leiden mutation would not be treated with anticoagulation until after an event of thrombosis, and the treatment may not be different for a carrier versus a noncarrier. In some cases, knowledge of carrier status might help to ensure prompt diagnosis, however.

Monogenic disorders have drawn public attention toward genetics in more recent years. In particular, major ethical and legal issues

Table 35–3 • SINGLE GENE DISORDERS WITH INCOMPLETE PENETRANCE THAT MAY ACCOUNT FOR INHERITED FORMS OF SELECTED COMMON DISORDERS

DISORDER	INHERITANCE— GENE(S)	MAJOR MEDICAL IMPLICATIONS
Hemochromatosis	AR—*HFE*	Cirrhosis, cardiomyopathy, diabetes mellitus
Thrombophilia	AD/AR—multiple genes	Deep vein thrombosis
Breast/ovarian cancer	AD—*BRCA1,2*	Breast and ovarian cancer
Familial adenomatous polyposis	AD—*APC*	Multiple colonic polyps, colon cancer
Hereditary nonpolyposis colorectal cancer	AD—DNA mismatch repair genes	Colorectal cancer; endometrial cancer
MODY	AD—multiple genes	Diabetes mellitus
Cardiomyopathy	AD—genes involved in cardiac contractile apparatus	Arrhythmia, heart failure

AD = autosomal dominant; AR = autosomal recessive; MODY = maturity = noset diabetes of the young.

have been raised. Although there may be benefits to genetic testing, the benefits of surveillance are not clear. The risks include anxiety, stigmatization, guilt, and possibly discrimination for insurance or employment. Some of these risks may be addressed by legislation to maintain privacy of genetic information, but the risks of anxiety, guilt, and stigmatization cannot be legislated away. To some extent, further research may improve the basis for surveillance or lead to effective treatments. For now, many of these monogenic disorders present a double-edged sword of potentially useful knowledge and potentially harmful information.

The role of the physician in dealing with monogenic disorders includes recognition of individuals at risk and participation in formulation of a care plan. Individuals at risk cannot be identified by physical appearance and usually are not evident from medical history or physical examination. The most valuable screening tool is the family history. Directed questioning about a family history of major monogenic disorders, especially breast, ovarian, and colon cancer, as well as hypercholesterolemia, hypertension, deep vein thrombosis, cirrhosis, and diabetes can identify the relatively rare patient with mendelian segregation of these common disorders. Even if the information is of uncertain reliability, eliciting a family history can prompt referral for further evaluation, documentation of the family history, and consideration for genetic testing. The physician's job is not only to identify individuals at risk; some people believe they are at high risk even in the absence of well-documented risk factors. Addressing these misconceptions can bring peace of mind and usually does not require genetic testing.

In some instances, there may be a role for tests to screen for inherited disorders. The utility of screening for hemochromatosis has been under study, based on the argument that diagnosis before the onset of complications can avoid major morbidity and mortality. It is unclear whether diagnosis is best accomplished by genetic testing for the major *HFE* gene mutations responsible for hemochromatosis, or whether testing of iron stores and transferrin saturation is a better approach. Not all individuals who are homozygous for an *HFE* mutation develop clinical hemochromatosis. Testing of iron metabolism may be more specific, but also may result in instances of false-negative results.

It is likely that the number of disorders in this category will increase in the coming years, as genes that predispose to other common disorders are discovered. Although most affected individuals have only a small genetic contribution to their condition, a subset has a much more substantial genetic component. Discussions about the appropriateness of testing, surveillance, screening, and treatment are likely to increase in intensity in the near future.

COMPLEX, MULTIFACTORIAL DISORDERS

Understanding the genetics of common disorders is one of the great challenges of modern medicine, with the promise of major returns in terms of prevention, diagnosis, and treatment. The etiology of these disorders is complex in that they result from an interaction of multiple genes with one another and with environmental factors. The specific genes that are relevant may be different from one person to the next. Identification of these genes is difficult given this heterogeneity and the relatively small impact that any particular gene may have in a particular person.

Dissection of the genetic contribution to common disease cannot be accomplished using the standard genetic approaches involving study of rare variants or family-based linkage studies. Most recent efforts have focused on study of large groups of patients, comparing the prevalence of particular genetic markers in cases and controls. The availability of markers has been boosted enormously by the identification of single nucleotide polymorphisms (SNPs). These are differences in single DNA bases between individuals that occur every few hundred bases. Some of these account for common genetic differences between people, including differences that may contribute to disease. The map of SNPs currently includes more than 2 million variants; it has been found that the genome has evolved as blocks of clusters of genes, making it possible to use only a limited number of SNPs within a given region to determine whether there is a gene in that region that is associated with a disease.

The problem of establishing disease associations is made more difficult by differences between affected individuals and especially between large ethnic groups. This can be an obstacle to case-control studies, in which spurious associations may occur or in which

associations that occur only in a subset of patients may be missed. To some extent, this problem is ameliorated by study of triads of an affected child and parents, but these studies are limited to instances in which nuclear families can be recruited for study.

It is likely that genetic risk factors for common disorders will come to light gradually over the next several years. The information derived from this effort probably will be used in a variety of ways, but especially in risk assessment, disease stratification, and developing new approaches to treatment.

The goal of genetic risk assessment is the identification of individuals at risk of disease before the onset of signs or symptoms. In principle, the genetic factors could be identified at birth, or any time in life, by testing a DNA sample. Individuals found to be at risk might be offered treatment in advance of onset of the disease to avoid complications or might be advised to modify their lifestyle to avoid exposure to environmental factors that might increase their risk of disease.

Although this would appear to be an attractive paradigm, many questions may be raised regarding its practicality and implementation. First, predictive testing would be useful only insofar as it guides further management. This is likely to be a moving target because ability to test for risk can be developed more quickly than ability to modify that risk. The utility of interventions may be valued differently by different people. This already has been the case for testing disorders such as breast cancer. Some women at risk choose not to know their *BRCA1* status because the options, including surveillance or prophylactic surgery, are unacceptable to them. If there were a low-cost, safe, and effective treatment that would neutralize any risk, the decision to test would be simple, but short of that, there are reasonable arguments on both sides of the issue of whether to test or not. For many disorders, it will take a long time to show the efficacy of any intervention because there may be a period of many years between the time of testing and the time of onset of a disorder. Unless surrogate markers can be identified and followed, the task of proving a benefit to predictive testing may require years to decades in some instances.

A second issue surrounds the degree to which genetic testing would be predictive. Most genetic tests are likely to involve detection of relatively common polymorphic alleles that account for small increments of relative risk of disease. The predictive value of these tests would be modest, perhaps too low to induce an individual to modify behavior or take medication. Here, again, much depends on the efficacy of any intervention that can be offered. There may be some disorders for which testing would have substantial predictive value and clinical utility and others for which testing would not be justified.

A third concern relates to social and ethical issues. Will people use test results as an excuse to pursue self-destructive behaviors having received what may be false reassurance of "immunity"? Will genetic testing further exacerbate the divide between individuals who can afford to pay for their care and those who cannot? Will individuals found to be at risk of disease on the basis of genetic testing become part of an underclass in terms of employability or insurability? Will people misinterpret results of testing in terms of a simplistic notion of genetic determinism, erroneously believing that their futures have been written, leaving them no recourse but to meet their fate? The rapid pace of technologic change is going to challenge the ability of the social and legal systems to keep pace.

A second application of genomics in medical practice entails stratification of disease. Even if genetic testing is not used to predict individuals at risk, it may well be used to determine the most appropriate treatment for a clinically diagnosed disorder. Probably most common disorders, such as hypertension or diabetes, are symptom complexes that result from a variety of causes. The particular combination of causes may differ in different individuals and may respond to different types of treatments. Choice of antihypertensive drug may depend at some point in time on genetic testing to determine the specific cause of hypertension in a patient. There are already examples of genotypes that predict response to commonly used drugs, for example, in asthma. Although not yet ready for routine clinical use, eventually it is possible that genetic tests will accompany many, if not most, treatment decisions.

Aside from helping to choose the most efficacious drug, genetic testing may play a role in avoidance of side effects and in appropriate dosing. Many drugs are known to be associated with rare side effects, some of which are sufficiently severe as to lead the drug to be withdrawn from use. Some of these side effects may occur only in

Genetics

Table 35–4 • GENES IN WHICH COMMON POLYMORPHISMS AFFECT RATES OF DRUG METABOLISM

GENE	MEDICATIONS (EXAMPLES)
CYP2C9	Phenytoin, warfarin
CYP2D6	Debrisoquin, β-blockers, antidepressants
Thiopurine methyltransferase	Mercaptopurine, azathioprine
N-acteyltransferase	Isoniazid, hydralazine

individuals who are susceptible on the basis of having a particular allele at a polymorphic locus. An example is the association of a mitochondrial DNA polymorphism with susceptibility to aminoglycoside-induced hearing loss. Genetic testing may be used to identify individuals at risk of these side effects, allowing the drug to be used in nonsusceptible individuals without risk. This testing not only would make treatment safer, but also would allow drugs that otherwise might be withdrawn from use to be reintroduced.

Absorption and metabolism of drugs is largely under genetic control. Several polymorphisms are known to lead to particularly rapid or slow metabolism, accounting for individuals who experience dose-related side effects or lack of efficacy at standard dosages (Table 35–4). Detection of these polymorphisms would allow customization of drug dosage to an individual's pattern of metabolism, increasing the likelihood of efficacy without a prolonged period of trial-and-error dosing.

The greatest gift of genetics and genomics to medicine may be in the ability to identify new drug targets and develop new approaches to treatment. Identification of genes that contribute to common disorders is revealing the cellular mechanisms that lead to disease. This knowledge offers the opportunity to develop new pharmaceutical agents that would target the physiologic mechanisms more precisely, leading to drugs that work better and cause fewer side effects. New approaches to gene replacement or insertion of genes into cells as localized drug delivery systems also may be developed. The treatment of common disorders likely would entail use of treatments developed as a result of genomics even in cases in which genetic testing is not used to predict individuals who are at risk.

Conclusion

The Human Genome Project began after most practicing physicians completed their medical training, and few are familiar with the methods and approaches of medical genetics and genomics. Nevertheless, physicians will be using the products of the genome project increasingly in their day-to-day practice during the coming years. Whether they are providing care for a patient with a rare genetic disorder or for a patient with a common condition not usually regarded as genetic, management choices increasingly will be informed by tests and treatments that in some way are based on information from the genome sequence.

The essence of the encounter between a physician and a patient can be distilled to two questions: Why this person? Why this time? A person who seeks medical care is doing so as the product of human evolution, as a member of an ethnic group with certain genetic vulnerabilities, because of inheritance of certain familial risk factors, because of exposure to some environmental factors, because of a particular physiologic process gone awry, because of behavioral traits that lead the person to seek medical care, because of prompting by family or friends to go to the doctor, because society makes medical services available, and because the person can afford to seek care. Genetics cannot answer all of these questions, but it is providing the key to addressing many of the biologic questions that underlie the medical mysteries that have puzzled humankind for generations.

SUGGESTED READINGS

Collins FS, Green ED, Guttmacher AE, Guyer MS: A vision for the future of genomics research. Nature 2003;422:835–847.

Collins FS, McKusick VA: Implications of the human genome project for medical science. JAMA 2001;285:540–544.

Subramanian G, Adams MD, Ventor JC, Broder S: Implications of the human genome for understanding human biology and medicine. JAMA 2001;286:2296–2307. *Three overviews of the future of genomics.*

36 GENETIC RISK ASSESSMENT
Margretta R. Seashore

Advances in genetics and genomics are making profound changes in medical practice. Using these advances, the physician can identify individuals at genetic risk and provide appropriate assessment and testing to aid in prevention and management of illness. The physician's response to questions and concerns about genetic risks depends on understanding how to identify these risks. Genetic factors confer an increased risk of developing a specific disorder compared with the prevalence of that disorder in the general population. Factors that result in increased genetic risk include genetic mutations that determine single-gene disorders, balanced chromosomal rearrangements, and genotypes that confer disease susceptibility. Multiple genes and environmental factors contribute to susceptibility to disease.

The challenge to the physician is to identify individuals and families who incur risks in time to provide information and interventions that may mitigate the risks or allow persons and families to make informed choices about them. Few well-controlled, prospective studies on genetic risk assessment exist. Current decision making depends on clinical observation and expert opinion. Nevertheless, a body of knowledge supports the utility of genetic assessment. Preventive therapy may enhance the medical care the physician can provide. Genetic risk information may offer the opportunity for reproductive decisions that enhance the chance for the birth of a healthy infant. Genetic testing can provide information that refines these risks. Ethnic background, medical history, and family history provide indicators of increased genetic risk and direct the kind of genetic testing to be done. When the physician and patient have decided that genetic testing will have a role in management of the patient, specific tests are selected and decisions about whom to test are made. This chapter addresses the use of genetic testing, ethnic background, and family history to refine the assessment of genetic risk in individuals and families.

Genetic Risk Assessment Using Genetic Testing

Genetic testing has been defined in the literature as the "analysis of a specific gene, gene product or function, or other DNA or chromosome analysis to detect or exclude an alteration likely to be associated with a genetic disorder." This definition places the emphasis on the genetic test and the correlation of the test result with the presence of or predisposition to a genetic disorder. The benefit of gene-based testing depends on many factors, including the characteristics of the test, the selection of whom to test and when to test, and an understanding of how to use the results of the test.

The development of gene-based diagnostic techniques for any disorder depends on understanding the disorder at the genetic level. The characteristics and the utility of the test are important factors in making the decision to use testing for assessment of genetic risk. The precision and predictive value of gene-based testing determine whether a test is suitable or not. After investigators identify a new molecular or biochemical observation that correlates with disease, testing for the disease is developed on a research basis. Before research results can move into the clinical realm, tests for clinical use must undergo rigorous validation. The usual criteria to judge the validity of a medical test, including sensitivity, specificity, positive predictive value, and negative predictive value, must be determined. Technical standards and guidelines for performance and interpretation of genetic tests are in place. Laboratory testing in clinical use must conform to the requirements of the Clinical Laboratory Improvement Amendments of 1988 (CLIA). The Joint Test and Technology Transfer Committee Working Group of the American College of Medical Genetics (ACMG) and the College of American Pathologists have developed programs to help maintain quality assurance and proficiency standards for genetic testing. The ACMG provides position statements on the use of genetic testing in certain disorders. When a test is known to provide reproducible results, the clinical utility of the test must be considered.

Individual genetic testing may be helpful to confirm clinical findings when signs and symptoms suggest a genetic diagnosis. Genetic testing can provide assessment of increased risk for presymptomatic diagnosis. Finally, genetic testing can identify heterozyosity for genes that confer increased risk for adverse reproductive outcome when both members of the couple carry a mutation.

An understanding of the molecular pathology and the genetic heterogeneity of the disorder is crucial to the selection of an appropriate gene-based test. For some disorders, only a few mutations in a specific gene cause disease; these can be tested using DNA-based methods. DNA-based methods of gene testing include linkage studies of DNA haplotypes associated with disease segregating with the disorder in a family, nucleic acid hybridization methods between DNA probes of normal and mutant sequences, polymerase chain reaction techniques that define specific DNA changes, and direct sequencing of DNA to identify mutations. Some DNA changes within a gene are normal polymorphisms and are not associated with increased disease risk. Some genetic alterations cannot be detected easily with today's technology. In conditions in which there are hundreds of different mutations or in which each affected family has a unique mutation, DNA-based methods may not be practical, and protein-based testing, such as enzymology and protein truncation studies, may provide more specific and accurate information. In the future, expression testing based on microchip assays that show which proteins are being expressed may revolutionize genetic testing again, but for today this approach does not exist for most inherited disorders.

In populations in which specific mutations and their frequencies are known, testing is highly accurate and predictive. For conditions in which a few specific mutations account for nearly all the mutations within that population, gene-based testing can be straightforward, and detection of gene carriers may reach 90% to 95% or higher. When these correlations are not high, the utility of genetic testing is considerably less.

Prediction of clinical outcome based on genetic testing depends on how well the genotype correlates with the phenotype. This correlation varies from one genetic disorder to another. Many single-gene disorders that present in childhood have a high correlation between genotype and phenotype. Examples include the four base-pair insertion in exon 11 (4-bp ins, ex11) of the hexosaminidase A gene, which causes classic Tay-Sachs disease (TSD) in affected children of Ashkenazi Jewish ancestry. Another example is the glutamine-to-arginine substitution at protein position 188 (Q188R) in galactose-1-phosphate uridyltransferase, which is the classic, severe galactosemia allele.

In selecting a genetic test, the physician must be aware of consequences of genetic locus heterogeneity, in which similar clinical disorders can result from mutations in different genes. This heterogeneity complicates genetic testing. In breast cancer, mutations in *BRCA1*, *BRCA2*, and *TP53* can be associated with familial breast cancer. Before genetic testing can be of use to persons at risk for breast cancer in such a family, the associated mutation in an affected individual in the family must be established. Even in the single-gene disorders that are inherited in a mendelian fashion, this kind of genetic heterogeneity adds to the complexity of testing. Genetic locus heterogeneity plays a role in such diverse conditions as Charcot-Marie-Tooth neuropathy, retinitis pigmentosa, and sensorineural deafness, each of which has multiple different genetic causes.

The patient and the physician must consider the purpose of genetic testing when deciding whether or not to use a genetic test. They must have realistic expectations about the kind of information the test will provide and must decide whether or not multiple family members will need or wish to be tested. Integral to the process are communication of relevant information, obtaining consent, and providing results. For conditions in which there is a strong correlation between homozygosity or heterozygosity for specific mutations and clinical outcome, gene testing can provide clear guidance for selection of treatment options. To make the decision to use a genetic test, the patient and physician need to ask how well the test result predicts clinical outcome and what kind of action the physician or the patient can take based on the test result. Is there an effective treatment, a need for directed surveillance, or a reproductive option to select? Will a negative test result reduce the need for surveillance or invasive medical testing?

Considerable ethical, legal, and social issues surround the use of genetic testing in individuals and families. Gene-based testing may uncover information about family members other than the individual who is being tested, and these persons frequently are not part of the decision to perform testing. If multiple family members are being tested, the results may reveal the fact that family biologic relationships are not what the family has believed. In families with multiple affected members, the results of testing may reveal who is and who is not at risk, and this information may cause grief or guilt in some tested members. Testing may not provide an answer in a particular family. Because these issues are complex, careful informed consent is an essential part of the process of obtaining genetic testing, and privacy of results must be assured. Communication of results requires sensitivity to all of these concerns.

Genetic testing can involve entire populations rather than single individuals or families. Population screening should identify treatable disease before symptoms occur, especially if outcome is improved by early identification. This screening also can identify risk for adverse reproductive outcome. Population-based screening can be a public health measure, as in newborn screening; community-based testing, as in Tay-Sachs carrier screening; or practice-based testing, as in testing offered prenatally to all women.

The experience gained in 40 years of newborn screening shows a paradigm for widely based population genetic screening. Phenylketonuria (PKU), a disorder of phenylalanine metabolism that results in severe mental retardation, was the first disorder identified by newborn screening programs. The observation that early diagnosis of siblings of children with PKU and treatment of them with a phenylalanine-restricted diet resulted in normal cognitive development led, in 1962, to the establishment of newborn screening for PKU. These programs became the prototype for the development of newborn screening for an increasing number of disorders. New methodology using tandem mass spectrometry has expanded the list of disorders that can be identified to more than 30. The success of newborn screening programs depends on the tracking and treatment programs that provide confirmatory testing, effective follow-up, and treatment for the disorders identified. Experience has shown that what was thought to be a well-defined disorder also had variant, usually less severe forms not previously understood. In addition to variant forms of PKU, further newborn screening outcome studies have shown that most of the disorders screened show similar degrees of variation. Examples include the milder Duarte variant of galactosemia and the variability in age of onset of symptoms in medium-chain, acyl-coenzyme A dehydrogenase deficiency. Newborn screening programs have enhanced understanding of long-term outcome of the disorders screened and identified surprising consequences, such as the teratogenic effects of high concentrations of blood phenylalanine in untreated maternal PKU. These programs have raised new questions, such as the preservation of Guthrie cards for later use for other purposes, including identification in the event of kidnapping, diagnosis in the event of sudden death, or later research on genetic factors affecting health. The experience gained from newborn screening will provide important guidance in the development of wider population-based genetic screening programs for adult-onset disorders.

The adoption of screening panels for pregnant women or women contemplating pregnancy is another example of population-based genetic screening. This screening is offered to assess reproductive risk by identifying women who are heterozygous for genes that would be deleterious in the homozygous state. The tests offered are chosen based on population frequency of the disorder, ability to identify a substantial percentage of heterozygotes, severity of the disorder, and availability of reproductive options. Some tests are offered on the basis of increased risk based on ethnic background of the woman or her partner. Other tests are offered on the basis of maternal age, family history, or outcome of previous pregnancy. The American College of Obstetricians and Gynecologists and the ACMG have offered guidelines for prenatal screening. One recommendation is to offer testing for a panel of mutations in the *CFTR* gene that can identify at least 90% of heterozygotes for the alleles responsible for cystic fibrosis in a multiethnic population.

Broad application of screening for genetic risks in the unselected general population is not yet practical. This screening would have the greatest value if it were inexpensive and could provide information about the risk of developing disease that could be mitigated by appropriate preventive action. Possible disorders amenable to screening include hemochromatosis and α_1-antitrypsin deficiency. Specific alleles in the apolipoprotein E locus may be associated with an increased risk of developing Alzheimer's disease. Pharmacogenomic traits that confer a high risk of adverse reaction to particular drugs would be candidates. Before any of this new information would be of practical use, however, investigators need to define the lifetime risk of disease or adverse outcome that such alleles confer. So far, the identification of variant alleles that confer this kind of increased susceptibility is in its infancy, and this testing is not yet practical. New models must take genetic and environmental contributions to disease into account. Loci associated with an increased risk for common complex disorders, such as diabetes and hypertension, are not yet well defined; mutations in *MTHFR* that confer increased risk for neural tube defects are being investigated, but no practical testing for increased risk for these conditions is available yet. In some disorders, such as hemochromatosis, mutations do not predict the clinical course well enough to warrant the use of population-based genetic testing. The lessons learned from newborn screening and from prenatal genetic testing suggest, however, that when population screening on this level becomes available, attention to defining the genotype-phenotype correlations and the variability in phenotype within classes of genetic variations will play an important role in effective use of population testing. Testing children for alleles that confer a risk for adult-onset disease if no intervention is available or necessary in childhood is controversial. New developments will increase its power, but genetic testing is already an effective tool that, when properly used with appropriate expectations, can guide clinical decisions and provide information that leads to action that can mitigate disease. Figure 36–1 is an algorithm for selecting genetic testing.

Genetic Risk Assessment Based on Ethnic Background

Genetic testing based on ethnic background is used commonly to assess susceptibility to disease and to provide information for reproductive choices. Ethnic background and race frequently are misconstrued to mean the same thing. The concept of "race" is a social construct, whereas information about ethnic origin can convey genetic information. *Race*, as generally used, even by the U.S. Census, is a vague term without a scientific definition. Within the races that are so construed, there is more genetic variation between individuals than there is genetic variation between the racial groups. *Race* as so defined is not helpful as a criterion for the use of genetic testing. Founder effects, geographic isolation, social isolation, genetic drift, and similar factors can result, however, in enrichment of particular disease-causing alleles within specific populations. Because of this, ethnic background, insofar as it represents these factors, may stand for increased risk of having mutations that result in susceptibility to disease or increased risk of adverse reproductive outcome. When the full scope of human genomics and proteomics is understood and can be measured, identification of individual genetic risk based on gene expression or multiplex allelic testing may be possible. Until then, the use of ethnic background as a proxy for geographic origin or other isolating factors that imply an increased risk of specific mutations is useful. For this reason and within these limits, the physician can offer genetic testing based on self-reported ethnic origin.

All ethnic groups have mutations that increase disease frequency in that group compared with the rest of the population; no ethnic group is exempt from this liability. Frequency of mutations that cause or predispose to disease varies between ethnic groups. Ethnic groups that should be considered in genetic risk assessment include northern European whites, southern European whites, sub-Saharan Africans, native indigenous peoples, Ashkenazi Jews, Jews of other

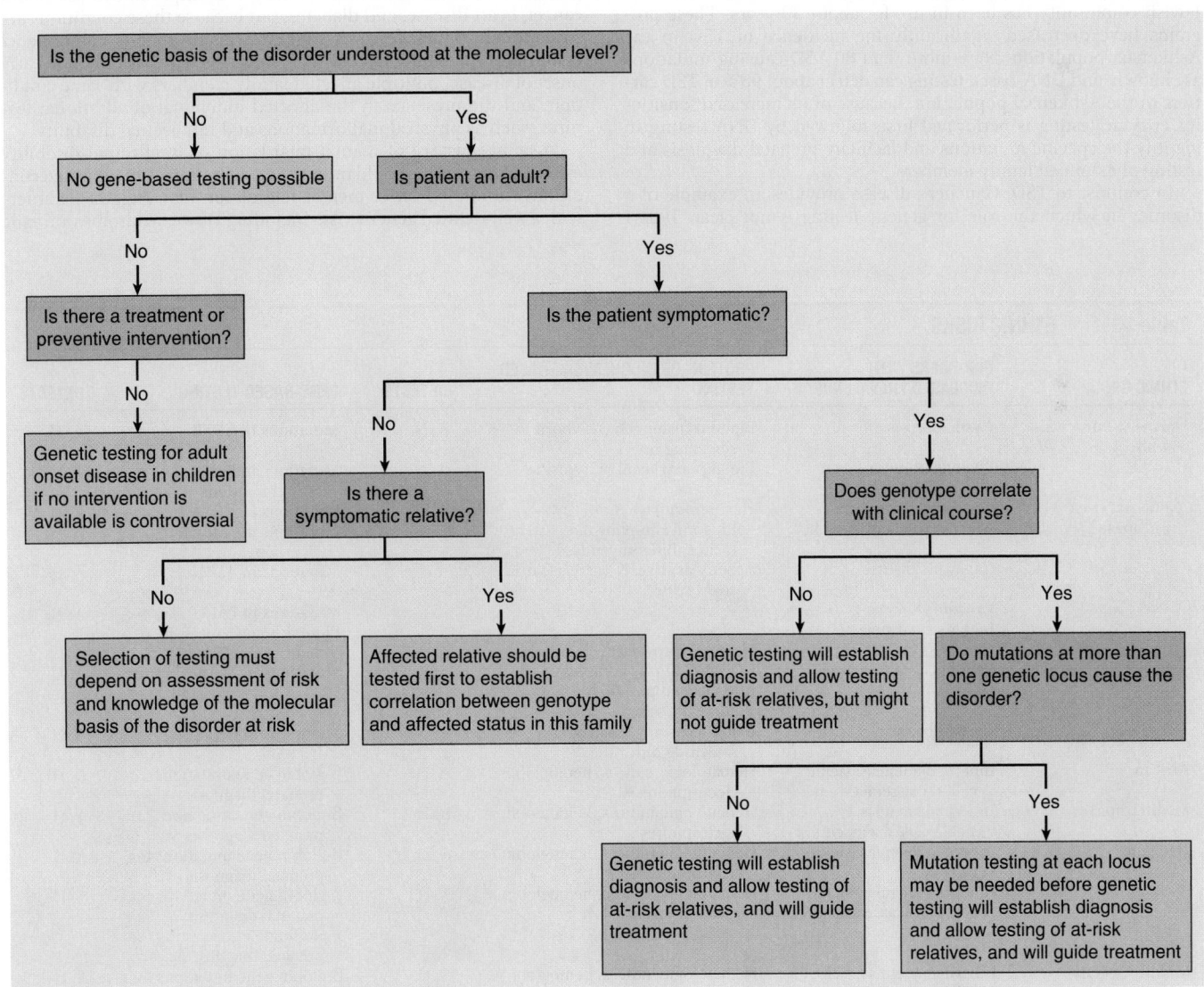

FIGURE 36–1 • Strategy for gene-based testing. The utility of gene-based testing depends on the knowledge of the molecular pathology of the disorder. The correlation between genotype and clinical course guides use of this testing. Testing may be able to confirm diagnosis, provide guidance for treatment, and offer assessment to relatives at risk.

geographic origin, Asians including Indians and Southeast Asians, Middle Eastern peoples, and Mediterranean peoples.

The goal of genetic testing based on ethnic origin is to obtain information to guide medical interventions. Testing prospective parents for heterozyosity for recessive alleles that cause serious disease in the homozygous state provides information for making reproductive decisions. Testing for mutations that cause or increase susceptibility to disease provides the basis for treatment or prevention of disease. In both cases, the utility of genetic testing depends on technical factors and on the correlation between mutation status and clinical outcome. Medical problems for which the genetic contribution has not yet been established also occur in certain ethnic groups, such as hypertension in people of African origin. Although specific genetic testing for these disorders is not yet available, clinical monitoring can be performed in an effort to identify disease in time to prevent serious complications.

Testing for heterozygosity for TSD in individuals of Ashkenazi Jewish ancestry can serve as a model for the use of genetic testing in particular ethnic groups. TSD as it occurs in the Ashkenazi population is a recessively inherited neurologic condition that causes severe impairment and death in the early childhood years. The abnormality in the lysosomal enzyme hexosaminidase A that causes TSD was identified in the 1970s, and measurement of that enzyme activity was shown to distinguish heterozygotes from those who did not carry this genetic mutation. This measurement is nearly 100% sensitive in detecting heterozygotes. Educational programs for the population at risk, accurate testing, and sensitive prenatal testing provide reproductive options for couples in which both members carry a TSD mutation. Community-based heterozygote screening for TSD in the Ashkenazi Jewish community has been in use for about 30 years. These programs have decreased significantly the incidence of TSD in the Ashkenazi population. Now more than 80 TSD-causing mutations are known, and DNA-based testing can detect about 98% of TSD carriers in the Ashkenazi population. Because of its increased sensitivity, enzyme testing is performed first, followed by DNA testing to identify the specific mutations and facilitate prenatal diagnosis and testing of extended family members.

In contrast to TSD, Gaucher's disease provides an example of a disorder in which the role for genetic testing is not clear. Type I Gaucher's disease, the adult-onset form, occurs in about 1:1000 Ashkenazi Jews, a higher risk than in other ethnic groups. Four mutations in the glucocerebrosidase gene account for about 97% of the mutations in the Ashkenazi Jewish population. Nevertheless, clinical expression varies considerably among individuals with the same genotype. Detection programs such as those used for TSD testing do not have a clear role because of the poor correlation between the genotype and the onset and clinical course of the disease. Although genetic testing may identify individuals at highest risk for developing symptoms, the genetic change is not sufficient to cause symptoms. Genetic testing alone does not provide sufficient information to decide on clinical intervention, and other kinds of clinical and laboratory data must complement the decision making.

Confounding factors may complicate the use of ethnic background as a criterion for selecting genetic testing. Patients and families may not know this background with accuracy. Adoption may obscure ethnic origin. More recently, there have been social reasons for concealing ethnic background. Because religious conversion occurs in many populations, religious preference cannot serve accurately as a proxy for ethnic background. American society is composed widely of multi-ethnic families. Risk calculations using ethnic risks for recessive disorders depend on the ethnic background of both parents. Table 36–1 provides a model for genetic testing based on ethnic origin.

Genetic Risk Assessment Based on Family History

The family history may provide important clues to the presence of an increased risk for a disorder with a significant genetic component. In obtaining a family history, it is important to ask about cancer, heart disease, and diabetes, but because these conditions are so common, which features suggest a major genetic component? Features of the family history that suggest genetic risk include early onset of disease, multiple affected family members with same condition, and the presence in the affected individual of additional features, such as physical malformations and intellectual disability.

A family history of mental retardation or intellectual disability including dementia should prompt consideration of an inherited condition. Childhood-onset mental retardation may suggest disorders with a well-defined genetic risk, including Down syndrome or fragile

Table 36–1 • ETHNIC RISKS

ETHNIC GROUP	DISORDERS WITH INCREASED PREVALENCE	PROTEIN- OR BIOCHEMICAL-BASED TESTING	DETECTS	GENE-BASED TESTING	DETECTS
Northern European white	Cystic fibrosis	Blood trypsinogen (newborn screening only)	A, N	Mutations in *CFTR*	A, H
	Phenylketonuria	Blood phenylalanine, tyrosine	A, N	Mutations in *PAH*: >600 mutations	A, H
Ashkenazi (east European) Jewish	Tay-Sachs disease	Hexosaminidase A	A, H	Mutations in *HEXA*	A, H
	Niemann-Pick disease A	Sphingomyelin phosphodiesterase (acid sphingomyelinase)	A	Mutations in *SMPD1*	A, H
	Canavan's disease	Aspartylacylase; N-acetylaspartic acid (urine)	A	Mutations in *ASPA*	A, H
	Fanconi's anemia C			Mutations in *FACC*	A, H
	Bloom's syndrome			BlmAsh mutations in *BLM*	A, H
	Gaucher's disease	Glucocerebrosidase	A	Mutations in *GBA*	A, H
	Familial dysautonomia	IKAPPAB kinase complex–associated protein but not clinical testing		Mutations in *IKAP*	A, H
	Cystic fibrosis	Blood trypsinogen (newborn screening only)	A, N	Mutations in *CFTR*	A, H
African	Inherited anemias: sickle cell, thalassemias	Hematologic indices, hemoglobin electrophoresis	A, H	β-globin gene mutations for prenatal diagnosis	A, H
Mediterranean	Inherited anemias: sickle cell, thalassemias	Hematologic indices, hemoglobin electrophoresis	A, H	β-globin gene mutations for prenatal diagnosis	A, H
Hispanic	Inherited anemias: sickle cell	Hematologic indices, hemoglobin electrophoresis	A, H	β-globin gene mutations for prenatal diagnosis	A, H
Asian	Inherited anemias: sickle cell, α-thalassemias	Hematologic indices, hemoglobin electrophoresis	A, H	β-globin gene mutations for prenatal diagnosis x-globin deletion testing for prenatal diagnosis	A, H
Middle Eastern	Inherited anemias: sickle cell, thalassemias	Hematologic indices, hemoglobin electrophoresis	A, H	β-globin gene mutations for prenatal diagnosis	A, H

A = testing for affected; H = testing for heterozygote; N = newborn screening for affected infant.

X syndrome. Adult-onset dementia may suggest a different group of disorders with defined genetic risk, such as Huntington's disease and early-onset Alzheimer's disease. A family history of mental retardation, neonatal death, or unexplained stillbirths, especially if associated with congenital malformations, may be the result of a chromosomal rearrangement in the family. Unexplained early or sudden death in children or adults may result from diverse genetic conditions such as Marfan syndrome, long QT syndrome, and disorders of fatty acid oxidation and transport.

An unusual reaction to medications should raise the question of an inherited abnormality in the metabolism, transport, or activation of a drug. Polymorphisms in the *CYP* cytochrome P-450 genes alter the metabolism of a broad variety of medications, including coumarin anticoagulants, antihypertensives, and antiarrhythmic drugs. Although specific genetic tests are not yet widely available to confirm risk in an individual, a family history of an abnormal reaction to a specific medication should prompt concern and consideration of an alternative class of medications if possible. The 1555A-G mutation in mitochondrial DNA alters metabolism of some aminoglycoside antibiotics. People carrying this mutation can be tested for sensorineural hearing loss after exposure to these antibiotics.

The family history may reveal the presence of consanguinity. Genetic risks on the basis of consanguinity derive from the fact that in a consanguineous couple, both individuals share a common ancestor from whom both have inherited genes, identical by descent from the common ancestor. If that ancestor passed on to them an abnormal allele for a recessively inherited condition, the consanguineous couple has a risk for having a child affected with that recessive disorder. The magnitude of this risk is significant if the members of the couple are first cousins or closer. If the couple belongs to an ethnic group with an increased chance of carrying abnormal alleles for recessive conditions, testing for those mutations is useful.

Family history of colon cancer is an example of how family history of genetic disorders can provide guidance for evaluation and management. The family history alerts the physician to the possibility of genetic risk. Properly defining that risk enhances the ability to target surveillance and provide presymptomatic treatment (e.g., colectomy) in some patients. Genetic testing can help identify other family members at risk. Because many genes are involved in the development of colon cancer, testing must be targeted to the appropriate ones.

Certain mutations are associated with cancer in other organs besides the colon, such as uterine cancer, thyroid cancer, or duodenal cancer, and the identification of these mutations suggests the need for wider surveillance. Still other mutations are associated with a predisposition to cancer, but are not the only factors involved. The ACMG and the American Society of Human Genetics have developed a position statement on genetic testing for colon cancer that reviews the use of specific testing and counseling when there is a family history of colon cancer. Table 36–2 lists molecular testing used to identify risk for colon cancer.

The taking of a family history should begin with obtaining a three-generation pedigree and learning about the health of each family member. Any time two or more people in the family have what seems to be the same condition, genetic factors should be considered, especially if the condition is relatively rare. When a clear mendelian pattern is seen or the disorder is a recognized mendelian condition, further assessment and testing can follow. When the family history fails to show a mendelian pattern, the diagnosis is reviewed and the medical literature consulted to determine if familial cases of the specific disorder have been reported. In autosomal recessive conditions, the birth of an affected child may be the first signal that a set of parents is heterozygous for a rare recessive condition. Here the genetic model depends on the correct diagnosis and the known inheritance pattern for that disorder.

For X-linked conditions, the decision must be made whether the affected individual has a new mutation or has inherited a mutation from a heterozygous mother who by chance has no affected relatives. In the past, bayesian calculations based on the pedigree have been the mainstay of this kind of analysis. Today, however, molecular diagnostic tools have refined the ability to determine heterozygosity in this situation.

For autosomal dominant conditions, the literature must be consulted to determine the proportion of patients who represent new mutations, a figure that can approach 50%. When a new mutation seems to be the explanation in these dominant conditions, others in the family are not at risk, but each offspring of the affected individual has a 50% risk of inheriting the gene. Variable expression can confound the analysis in a family showing an autosomal dominant condition. Gonadal mosaicism for the mutation accounts for rare recurrences in families in which neither parent is affected with the

Table 36–2 • GENETIC TESTS FOR SUSCEPTIBILITY TO COLON CANCER

CANCER TYPE	TEST NAME	METHOD (REFERENCE)*	ESTIMATED ANALYTIC SENSITIVITY/SPECIFICITY	SAMPLE	INDICATION
HNPCC	MSI, IHC	Microsatellite instability analysis (22) and immunohistochemical staining (38-40)	85%/85%	Paraffin block (tumor)	Affected individuals with colon or uterine cancer in families with ≥3 cases of colon cancer or uterine cancer or early-onset colon cancer; if tumor manifests MSI, germline mutation analysis should be considered
HNPCC	MSH2, MLH1	DNA sequencing (i.e., 31)	70%/99%	Whole blood (14-mL lavender-top tube)	Affected individuals in families with ≥3 cases of colon or uterine cancer; if prior MSI tumor assay done, probability of germline mutation is low if tumor was microsatellite stable
HNPCC	MSH2	Protein truncation (28-30)	50%/99%	Whole blood (7-mL lavender-top tube)	Affected individuals in families with ≥3 cases of colon cancer tested first; unaffected at-risk relatives tested only if affected patient mutation detected
FAP	APC	Protein truncation (26-27)	75%/99%	Whole blood (7-mL lavender-top tube)	Affected individuals tested first; unaffected at-risk relatives tested only if affected patient mutation detected
Familial colon	APC11307K	ASO (17)	99%/99%	Whole blood (7-mL lavender-top tube)	Affected and unaffected individual of Ashkenazi Jewish ethnicity with family history of colon cancer

*References refer to article in Genet Med.
APC = adenomatous polyposis coli; ASO = allele-specific oligonucleotide; FAP = familial adenomatous polyposis; HNPCC = hereditary nonpolyposis colorectal cancer; IHC = immunohistochemistry; MSI = microsatellite instability.
From Joint Test and Technology Transfer Committee Working Group, American College of Medical Genetics: Genetic testing for colon cancer: Joint statement of the American College of Medical Genetics and American Society of Human Genetics. Joint Test and Technology Transfer Committee Working Group. Genet Med 2000;2:362–366.

dominant condition and no test can exclude it. In general, however, the absence of the condition in any other family member makes it likely that the patient represents a new mutation.

Frequently, no mendelian hypothesis can be sustained, yet there is familial aggregation of the disorder. Many conditions, such as neural tube defects, cleft lip and palate, pyloric stenosis, and multiple sclerosis, seem to be multifactorial in origin and have genetic and other, undefined components. Quantitative traits, such as hypertension, and common disorders, such as diabetes and heart disease, have familial aggregation. Genes governing these disorders are undergoing intense research. Genetic counseling for these conditions must rely on empirical figures for the specific condition until association with specific alleles is defined.

Reproductive Planning and Prenatal Diagnosis

The use of information obtained from genetic testing, ethnic background, and family history depends on the interventions available for the condition under consideration. Actions can include informed reproductive decision making, presymptomatic surveillance or treatment to mitigate the risk or prevent the onset of disease, prompt treatment of the newly diagnosed condition, or a refined understanding of the cause of the disease even if no further action is available. When the family has the genetic information, putting the risk in perspective is an important step. The perception of risk may be more important in family decision making than the actual numerical value of the risk. This perception depends on at least two factors: (1) risk compared with background risk and (2) overall burden, a combination of risk and severity. A risk of 1 in 4 of recurrence in a second child, in the case of PKU, for example, is much greater than a risk of 1 in 10,000 in the general population. Conversely a risk of 1 in 10,000 may sound high to a couple who believe that the chances of something being wrong with an unborn child are 1 in a million. The presentation of such risk figures can change the perception of that risk. A 1 in 4 chance of recurrence of PKU is also a 3-to-1 chance against recurrence. The judgment of burden is a personal one. Physical handicap may be a severe burden for one family, whereas another may find physical handicap tolerable but mental handicap unacceptable. Helping families to think about risks in these ways is an important component of genetic counseling. Families often are helped by being provided a description of the disorder that has been diagnosed or for which an increased risk has been determined. Many persons go to their local library in an attempt to find literature about the disorder or ask friends in the medical profession to do so. Often this results in misinformation or information that is out of date. Physicians can provide reliable, up-to-date written material and website information about the disorder. Medical genetics clinics have pamphlets, booklets, and other literature to provide. The family also should be furnished with a written report of the counseling summarizing the important points. Thoughtful genetic counseling challenges the skills of the physician in diagnosis, analysis, communication, and support. From the initial evaluation through development of the genetic model and identification of those at risk to completion of the transfer of information, the use of these skills enables patients and their families to make intelligent, informed, and reasoned decisions for their futures.

If risk to future unborn children is at issue, the family at risk for a genetic disorder needs to know about the reproductive options available. Prenatal diagnosis and preconception diagnosis are important

Table 36–3 • REPRODUCTIVE OPTIONS FOR FAMILIES WITH GENETIC RISKS
Adoption
Reproductive assistance
In vitro fertilization with a donor egg
Artificial insemination by donor
Preimplantation genetic diagnosis
Prenatal diagnosis

reproductive options that must be discussed, along with appropriate referral to experts in areas of assisted reproductive technologies. For the family at risk, these options can enhance the chances of having healthy children (Table 36–3).

The methods in prenatal diagnosis depend on imaging the fetus, examining DNA in cells of fetal origin, analyzing chromosomes in fetal cells, examining analytes, and measuring proteins and enzymes in cells of fetal origin. The major autosomal and sex chromosomal aneuploidies can be diagnosed in this way, along with chromosomal rearrangements, deletions, insertions, and the like. Prenatal DNA-based diagnosis uses fetal cells. Preimplantation genetic diagnosis uses embryo biopsy to examine one cell from a zygote obtained using in vitro fertilization, followed by implantation of an unaffected embryo. Testing depends on knowing the specific mutation or DNA change involved, and interpretation requires the assumption that one cell is representative of the entire fetus. For inherited single-gene disorders, this is a reasonable assumption, but it may be more difficult to exclude mosaicism in the case of chromosomal analysis. The range of single-gene disorders that have been identified using preimplantation genetic diagnosis includes autosomal recessive, autosomal dominant, and X-linked conditions. Multiplex testing for several disorders is a much bigger challenge and is still under development.

Measurement of α-fetoprotein, human chorionic gonadotropin, and unconjugated estrogen in maternal serum (triple screen) allows detection of an estimated 70% of fetuses with Down syndrome regardless of maternal age and is recommended regardless of prior risk. The addition of serum measurement of inhibin A (the quadruple screen) or addition of the measurement of pregnancy-associated plasma protein A and of ultrasound measurement of nuchal thickness may improve this detection rate and are actively under investigation. Table 36–4 lists prenatal diagnostic tests with indications and risks.

Indications, diagnostic uses, and risks of preimplantation diagnosis, midtrimester amniocentesis, chorionic villus sampling, and fetal blood sampling by cordocentesis are shown in Table 36–4. Studies of chorionic villus sampling suggest a small (1:3000 to 1:1000) risk of limb hypoplasia in infants born after that procedure. Fetoscopy is done only when other diagnostic avenues have failed and is used to visualize fetal anatomy and to perform biopsy of fetal tissues, such as liver or skin.

It is crucial that the pregnant woman undergoing prenatal diagnosis have extremely clear counseling. Spelling out clearly the expectations and limitations of the testing before any procedures is crucial. The diagnoses that are being sought must be explained, and it must be made clear that a normal result does not guarantee a normal infant. If the result of the test is not normal, the options for the woman are to terminate the pregnancy or to carry it to term. Rarely, surgical or

Table 36–4 • PRENATAL DIAGNOSIS METHODS

METHOD	USE	RISK
Preimplantation genetic diagnosis	Identify genetic abnormalities before implantation	Requires in vitro fertilization protocol
Ultrasonography	Estimate fetal age	None recognized
	Assess growth	
	Evaluate anatomy and organ function	
Amniocentesis or chorionic villus sampling	Amniotic fluid: analyze proteins, measure analytes of fetal origin	
	Fetal cells: analyze DNA, chromosomes, proteins	
Amniocentesis (15-20 wk)		<0.5% risk miscarriage
Chorionic villus sampling (9-11 wk)		<2% risk miscarriage
Periumbilical blood sampling	Fetal blood: analyze cells, measure serum analytes	<2% risk miscarriage

medical treatment of the identified fetus can be offered, but this may be experimental, uncertain, and risky. The decision to terminate a pregnancy must be made in collaboration with the obstetrician who will perform the procedure so that the process can be described and possible complications reviewed, and appropriate psychosocial support should be provided.

SUGGESTED READINGS

Geller GBJ, Green MJ, Press N, et al: Genetic testing for susceptibility to adult-onset cancer: The process and content of informed consent: Consensus Development Conference. JAMA 1997;277:1467-1474. *Informative about the psychological aspects of genetic counseling, the impact of genetic information, and the challenge of information transfer.*

Human Genome Project Information on Gene Testing: Available at http://www.ornl.gov/hgmis/medicine/genetest.html. *Website with reviews of genetic testing and links to sites providing testing information.*

Lloyd FJ, Reyna VF, Whalen P: Accuracy and ambiguity in counseling patients about genetic risk. Arch Intern Med 2001;161:2411-2413. *Case-based review of the use of genetic testing and counseling.*

Milunsky A: Genetic Disorders and the Fetus: Diagnosis, Prevention and Treatment, 3rd ed. New York, Plenum Press, 1998. *Extensive textbook on prenatal diagnosis.*

Online Mendelian Inheritance in Man (OMIM): Available at http://www.ncbi.nlm.nih.gov/Omim/searchomim.html. *Website of the catalog of known human mendelian traits with links to the genome database.*

37 INBORN ERRORS OF METABOLISM

Louis J. Elsas II

Metabolism is a collective term for integrated biochemical processes of the intact organism, differentiated organ, cell, and subcellular organelle. Normal metabolism enables homeostasis for the organism by maintaining anabolic and catabolic flow of substrates to products. In the early 20th century, Garrod recognized heritable blocks in normal human metabolic flow that conformed to Mendelian mechanisms of inheritance. He first coined the term *inborn error of metabolism* in his Croonian Lectures of 1908, in which he described four diseases—alkaptonuria, albinism, cystinuria, and pentosuria. Garrod presumed that the patient expressing the full abnormality was homozygous for mutant alleles affecting a specific metabolic flow, whereas the parents were heterozygous for this same inherited block but were clinically normal. When he gave patients with alkaptonuria proteins or other precursors of homogentisic acid, excretion of alkaptones increased, as evidenced by a darkening of the urine on standing. He theorized that this "block-in-reaction sequence" was controlled genetically because pedigree analyses were consistent with an *autosomal recessive* mode of inheritance. The enzyme defect in alkaptonuria was not discovered until 50 years later, when homogentisic acid oxidase was found impaired in the liver and kidneys of patients with this disease. More recently, the gene for homogentisate-1,2-dioxygenase was cloned, and mutations causing altered function were defined.

First proof that abnormal protein function led to disease came from Gibson's observation in 1948 that erythrocyte methemoglobin reductase was decreased in patients with *methemoglobinemia*. By 1952, Pauling and Ingram had identified an abnormal hemoglobin structure in *sickle cell anemia*. During this same period, Cori and Cori identified a deficiency of hepatic glucose-6-phosphatase in *von Gierke's disease* or *type I glycogen storage disease* and confirmed Garrod's theory by defining a block in the flow of hepatic glucose production from its stored glycogen.

Variations in human proteins do not usually produce disease. Heritable diversity in hemoglobins, phosphoglucomutase, lactate dehydrogenase, red blood cell acid phosphatase, haptoglobins, and immunoglobins was discovered and defined for normal populations. In some cases, diversity is required for optimal health, for example, the switch from fetal to adult hemoglobins. Nucleotide sequence variations may produce different amino acid changes in the primary protein structure without producing a functional change. When no functional change occurs, the alteration is considered a *polymorphism*. There are many molecular mechanisms producing normal protein diversity. Normal protein variation can occur through gene rearrangements, as exemplified by the formation of immunoglobins, giving rise to required variations in response to foreign antigens (Chapter 265). Here, gene rearrangements occur in response to antigens to produce protein diversity. Post-transcriptional, alternative splicing of RNA is another mechanism for protein variation. There are many examples, including the

insulin receptor, elastin, thyroid peroxidase, and tyrosine hydroxylase. Post-translational modification of proteins produces diversity and is important in directing proteins to subcellular organelles, to the cell surface, or for secretion. Glycosylation of proteins directed to the plasma membrane receptors is an example of this post-translational mechanism. As an example of the importance of these mechanisms, consider that humans have more than 200,000 functions of proteins but only 37,000 genes predicted from the human genome sequence.

The relatively rare circumstance in which a change in a protein impairs function is called a *mutation* and may produce an inborn error of metabolism. Naturally occurring mutations that produce pathology also provide insight into the functional role of normal proteins in human metabolism. Inborn errors of metabolism are classified here in accordance with the organ, cell, and subcellular location of normal protein function (Table 37–1) and the abnormal mechanisms that interfere with the normal metabolic flow resulting from impaired proteins (Table 37–2). Therapy of inborn errors of metabolism is aimed at returning homeostasis to the intact organism.

One important clinical aspect in defining the genetic component of a metabolic disease is that one can predict, intervene in, and prevent irreversible pathology by a variety of stratagems before the disease is expressed. In general, the severity of an inborn error of metabolism depends on the degree of protein impairment rendered by the genetic mutation and the trauma induced by the environment. A "leaky" mutation may not be expressed until adulthood, whereas a complete block in the same metabolic pathway is lethal in infancy. The age of onset also is predicated on the severity of environmental effects superimposed on genetic susceptibility. The pathophysiologic mechanisms outlined in Table 37–2 may occur individually or combine to produce loss in homeostasis and a disease state. The clinical manifestations are usually *pleiotropic*, which means one blocked reaction produces multiple dysfunctions at the organ level. An example is galactosemia, which causes cataracts, ovarian failure, liver disease, and central nervous system dysfunction. The phenotype (clinical outcome) also is affected not only by the specific genetic block, but also by alternate metabolic pathways (*epigenetic* phenomena) that may remove toxic precursors or supply deficient products of a blocked reaction. Outcome may be affected adversely by an alternate pathway, and a pathophysiologic mechanism may differ among organs. In galactosemia, the accumulation of galactose can produce excess intracellular galactitol through the alternate pathway catalyzed by aldose reductase and consequently cell death owing to the osmotic effect of

---

Table 37–1 • CLASSIFICATION OF PROTEIN FUNCTION BY LOCATION IN ORGANISM

Proteins act as follows:
1. Catalyze plasma membrane functions
   a. Substrate transport
   b. Cellular signaling (receptors)
2. Catalyze integrated metabolic pathways in the cytosol, lysosome, peroxisome, mitochondria, nucleus, and endoplasmic reticulum
3. Circulate in blood and provide and maintain various functions (clotting; metal, lipid, and vitamin transport; immunity; oxygen transport; regulation of proteases, hormones, and adhesion proteins)
4. Maintain structural integrity of organs and organelles (collagen, elastin, actin, dystrophin, fibrillins)

Table 37–2 • CLASSIC PATHOLOGIC MECHANISMS FOR INBORN ERRORS OF METABOLISM

1. Accumulation to toxic concentrations of substrates in a blocked catabolic reaction. *Examples*: maple syrup urine disease, galactosemia, glucose-galactose malabsorption, Fabry, Gaucher, urea cycle defects
2. Production of toxic byproducts through a normally minor pathway. *Examples*: tyrosinemia type I, adenosine deaminase deficiency
3. Deficiency of an end product in an anabolic pathway. *Examples*: albinism, orotic aciduria, scurvy
4. Loss of regulation resulting in overproduced intermediates to toxic levels. *Examples*: congenital adrenal hyperplasia, intermittent porphyria, familial hypercholesterolemia

Table 37–3 • DISEASES CAUSED BY PLASMA MEMBRANE TRANSPORTER PROTEIN MUTATIONS

DISEASE	TISSUE AFFECTED	SUBSTRATE	MODE OF INHERITANCE	CLINICAL EXPRESSION
B_{12} malabsorption	Ileum	Vitamin B_{12}	Autosomal recessive	Juvenile
Blue diaper syndrome	Gut	Tryptophan	Autosomal recessive	Hypercalcemia
Primary carnitine deficiency	Kidney/gut	Carnitine	Autosomal recessive	Hypoglycemia, hyptotomia
Congenital chloridorrhea	Gut	Chloride	Autosomal recessive	Diarrhea, alkalosis
Cystic fibrosis	Apical epithelia	Chloride	Autosomal recessive	Lung, intestinal obstruction
Cystinuria	Kidney + gut	Cystine + lysine, arginine, ornithine	Autosomal recessive	Renal lithiasis (cystine)
Familial hypophosphatemic rickets	Kidney + gut	Phosphate	X-linked dominant	Rickets
Folate deficiency	Lymphocyte, erythrocyte	Methyl tetrahydrofolate	Autosomal recessive	Aplastic anemia
Glucose-galactose malabsorption	Gut + kidney	Glucose and galactose	Autosomal recessive	Refractory diarrhea
Hartnup's syndrome	Gut + kidney	Neutral amino acids	Autosomal recessive	Nicotinic acid deficiency (pellagra)
Hereditary hypophosphatemic rickets	Kidney	Phosphate	Autosomal dominant	Growth restriction, rickets, hypercalciuria
Hereditary renal hypouricemia	Kidney	Uric acid	Autosomal recessive	Urolithiasis (uric acid)
Hereditary spherocytosis	Erythrocyte	Sodium	Autosomal recessive	Hemolytic anemia
Hyperdibasic aminoaciduria (type I)	Kidney	Lysine, arginine, ornithine	Autosomal dominant	?Symptoms
Iminoglycinuria	Kidney + gut	Glycine, proline, hydroxyproline	Autosomal recessive	Benign ?
Isolated lysinuria	Kidney + gut	Lysine	Autosomal recessive	Growth failure, seizures
Lysinuric protein intolerance (type II)	Kidney, fibroblasts, hepatocytes, gut	Lysine	Autosomal recessive	Growth restriction, hyperammonemia, mental retardation
Methionine malabsorption (oasthouse disease)	Gut	Methionine	Autosomal recessive?	Mental retardation, white hair, failure to thrive
Renal glycosuria	Kidney	Glucose	Autosomal recessive	Benign glycosuria
Renal tubular acidosis (type I)	Distal renal tubule	H^+ secretion, citrate, calcium	Autosomal dominant	Hypokalemia, growth restriction, nephrocalcinosis
Renal tubular acidosis (type II)	Proximal renal tubule	Bicarbonate	"Familial"	Hyperchloremic metabolic acidosis

intracellular galactitol. Galactitol accumulation causes cataracts, whereas galactose-1-phosphate accumulation produces hepatic cell death.

Many disorders are produced by mutant proteins that impair the transport of nutrients into cells (Table 37–3). *Familial glucose-galactose malabsorption syndrome* exemplifies defective transporter protein, resulting in accumulation of nontransported glucose in the intestinal lumen and refractory diarrhea secondary to its osmotic effects. Direct evidence for the genetic control of intestinal glucose transport in humans was obtained by in vitro studies of jejunal biopsy material from families in which the affected members express refractory diarrhea on ingesting D-galactose or D-glucose but not fructose. Pedigree analysis conformed to autosomal recessive inheritance. These data predicted a gene coded for a stereospecific, sodium-dependent, and energy-dependent transporter protein in human jejunal (and proximal renal tubular) microvilli. Expression cloning of active glucose transport now has confirmed the presence of a family of glucose transporter genes, their deduced amino acid sequences, and specific codon changes producing syndromes of familial glucose-galactose malabsorption and renal glycosuria.

There are many inherited defects involving the plasma membrane transport of glucose caused by mutations of either active or facilitative glucose transport. Glucose transporters are a family of proteins whose definitions of function evolved after their cloning and molecular genetic analyses (Table 37–4). Comparing the data from families with renal glycosuria and glucose-galactose malabsorption, it became evident that different Na+-dependent, active glucose transporters were present in kidney and gut epithelium. The SGLT1 is shared by kidney and gut, whereas SGLT2 functions predominantly in kidney alone and causes renal glycosuria without glucose-galactose malabsorption (see Table 37–4). An insulin-responsive, facilitative glucose transporter (GLUT4) is not Na+-dependent and is expressed primarily in insulin-responsive tissues (fat cells, skeletal muscle). More than one glucose transporter are expressed by most cells. The jejunal epithelial cell uses SGLT1 to concentrate glucose

from its luminal surface into the cytosol, then effluxes glucose at its basal-lateral surfaces through GLUT2. GLUT2 also is involved in regulating the amount of glucose transported into β cells of the pancreas, a process that regulates glucose stimulation of insulin release. Indirect evidence suggests that mutations in the GLUT2 gene are "sensitivity genes" involved in regulating insulin secretion.

Many diseases characterized by "hormone resistance" are caused by a family of proteins that function as receptors in the plasma membrane and postreceptor transmitters of signals located in the cytosol and nucleus. The concept of failure to respond to hormone stimulation originated in the early 1940s with a description of *pseudohypoparathyroidism* (Chapter 260). Heritability of resistance to parathormone was suggested before the existence of parathormone receptors, hormone-sensitive adenylate cyclases, or guanine nucleotide–binding proteins were known.

Diseases caused by defective transmembrane binding and signaling include *Laron dwarfism*, which results from growth hormone receptor (GHR) defects. Phenotypic characteristics are *proportionate dwarfism*, hypoglycemia, craniofacial dysmorphology with a doll-like face, balding, frontal bossing, truncal obesity, and wrinkled skin. In this disorder, growth hormone concentration is elevated in blood, peripheral tissue responses are decreased, and insulin-like growth factor-1 concentrations in blood are low. An autosomal recessive mode of inheritance is defined. Causes for dominant or polygenic symmetrical growth restriction may result from mutations in nuclear transproteins, hypothalamic pituitary trophic proteins, growth hormone, GHR, and postreceptor signaling. The *GHR* gene is found on chromosome 5p13-p12, and many different mutations account for disorders of stature in this gene. *Familial hypercholesterolemia* defines a phenotype of autosomal dominant hypercholesterolemia and early-onset heart disease. This disorder affects an estimated 1 in 500 individuals in the general population. An autosomal dominant mode of inheritance for early-onset adult heart disease is caused by many different mutations in the low-density cholesterol (LDL) cholesterol receptor. The dysfunction of LDL receptors results in a loss in the cell's ability

Table 37–4 • HUMAN GLUCOSE TRANSPORTERS

PROTEIN	kD (AA)	mRNA SIZE (kb)	CHROMOSOMAL LOCALIZATION	EXPRESSION IN TISSUE AND CELLS	FUNCTION	DISORDER
GLUT1	55 (492)	2.8	lp35 → p31.3	Blood-brain barrier, erythrocyte fibroblast	Basal glucose transport across most cells, including blood-brain barrier	Seizures with low cerebrospinal fluid and normal blood glucose
GLUT2	58 (524)	2.8 3.4 5.4	3q26.1 → q26.3	Liver, kidney, intestine, beta cell of the pancreas	Low-affinity glucose transport	Defective insulin secretion in diabetes
GLUT3	54 (496)	2.7 4.1	12p13.3	Neurons, fibroblast, placenta, testes	Basal glucose transport, high affinity	?
GLUT4	55 (509)	2.8 3.5	17p13	Fat, skeletal muscle, heart	Insulin-stimulated glucose transport	Defective insulin-stimulated transport, ? NIDDM
GLUT5	50 (501)	2.0	1p32 → p22	Small intestine	Fructose transport	?
GLUT7 (rat)	52 (528)	?	?	Liver microsome	Glucose release from endoplasmic reticulum	Type 1d glycogen storage disease
CONCENTRATIVE GLUCOSE TRANSPORTERS						
SLGT1	75 (664)	2.2 2.6 4.8	22q11 → qter	Intestine, kidney (medulla)	Intestinal absorption, renal reabsorption, high affinity (2 Na: 1 glucose)	Glucose-galactose malabsorption
SLGT2	76 (672)	2.4 3.0 3.5 4.5	16p11.2	Kidney (cortex)	Low affinity, high capacity (1 Na: 1 glucose)	Renal glycosuria

NIDDM = non–insulin-dependent diabetes mellitus.

to downregulate endogenous cholesterol synthesis and to incorporate LDL cholesterol into cells. Increased intravascular accumulation of LDL cholesterol results in atherosclerosis and heart disease before the sixth decade of life (see Table 37–2). The gene for the LDL cholesterol receptor is found on chromosome 19p13.1-13.2. *Leprechaunism* has become a prototypic inborn error of severe insulin resistance and loss of cellular signal transduction through the insulin receptor. Affected infants have low birth weight, acanthosis nigricans, cystic changes in organs, and loss of glucose homeostasis. Affected patients have remarkably elevated plasma insulin concentrations greater than 500 mIU/mL. Specific impairment in iodine-125-labeled insulin binding is evident in cells cultured from patients, and a spectrum of mutations produces a spectrum of severe insulin-resistant syndromes (leprechaunism, Rabson-Mendenhall, and type A diabetes with acanthosis nigricans). Obligate heterozygotes (parents) of patients with leprechaunism have partially impaired insulin binding and glucose tolerance curves suggesting type II diabetes mellitus. The insulin receptor transfers its signal by phosphotransfer to the insulin

receptor signal protein 1 (IRS-1), and a cascade of anabolic signals occurs.

In *Albright's hereditary osteodystrophy* or *pseudohypoparathyroidism* (Chapter 260), a heterogeneous group of mutations affect the gene for the parathormone receptor's guanine nucleotide-binding protein (G$_s$a), which links the receptor to adenylate cyclase and stimulates cyclic adenosine monophosphate when the receptor is occupied by parathormone. This gene for G$_s$a is located on chromosome 20q13, and deletions and missense mutations are defined that produce Albright's hereditary osteodystrophy. Somatic mutations in arginine 201 of the same gene turn the G$_s$a protein constitutively "on" and produce another disease, McCune-Albright-Sternberg syndrome. Cells are *mosaic* for the mutation, and the syndrome includes nonossifying bone tumors and premature puberty.

Inborn errors affecting proteins of the cytosolic compartment within a cell are the more "traditional" inborn errors of metabolism (Table 37–5). They impair the catalytic reactions of anabolic or catabolic pathways and usually are classified by the class of biochemical involved.

Table 37–5 • SOME DISEASES CAUSED BY IMPAIRED CYTOSOLIC ENZYMES

DISORDER	ENZYME DEFECT	PHENOTYPE	INHERITANCE
CARBOHYDRATES			
Fructosuria	Fructokinase	Benign	Autosomal recessive
Hereditary fructose intolerance	Fructose 1-phosphate aldolase	Liver dysfunction, early death	Autosomal recessive
Galactosemia	Galactose-1-P-uridyl transferase	Liver dysfunction, cataracts, sepsis, mental retardation, death	Autosomal recessive
Hereditary fructose 1,6-*bis*-phosphate deficiency	Fructose 1,6-*bis*-phosphatase	Apnea, ketosis, lactic acidosis	Autosomal recessive
AMINO ACIDS			
Phenylketonuria	*p*-Hydroxyphenylalanine hydroxylase	Mental retardation (teratogenic)	Autosomal recessive
Tyrosinemia			
Type II	Tyrosine aminotransferase	Palmar bullae, corneal lesions	Autosomal recessive
Type I	Fumarylacetoacetate hydrolase	Succinyl acetone accumulation	Autosomal recessive
Homocystinuria	Cystathionine B synthase	Marfanoid habitus, arterial thrombosis, lens dislocation, mental retardation	Autosomal recessive
Hyperornithinemia	Ornithine aminotransferase	Gyrate atrophy of the retina	Autosomal recessive
Lesch-Nyhan syndrome	Hypoxanthine phosphoribosyltransferase	Neurologic dysfunction with self-destructive tendency	X-linked

Classifications of disorders are of glucose, lipid fatty acid, amino acid, purine, organic acid, vitamin, and drug metabolism.

Phenylalanine is essential for growth, and its anabolic products include tyrosine, thyroid hormone, adrenergic neurotransmitters, and melanin. *Phenylketonuria* (PKU) (Chapter 217) is caused by mutations in the gene encoding phenylalanine hydroxylase, the first enzyme in this anabolic flow that catalyzes tyrosine production. PKU also may occur if coenzymes are deficient in this reaction, such as dihydropteridine reductase or enzymes involved in biopterin biosynthesis.

Albinism is an example of an inborn error in an anabolic pathway in which the pathophysiologic mechanism is related directly to the lack of an end product (see mechanism 3, Table 37–2). Tyrosine is converted by the action of a cytosolic tyrosinase first to dopa and then to dopamine. Dopamine can be converted either to the red-yellow pigment pheomelanin or to the black-brown pigment eumelanin. These reactions occur in the melanosomes produced in the melanocytes and exported to the keratinocytes. Color of skin is an inherited factor that depends on many genes (polygenic) and is a function of the intensity of the pigment in the skin and not the number of melanocytes, which is constant for all humans. Although skin color is a polygenic trait, single genes can have a profound effect on this color, as evidenced by the albino phenotype. In humans, *oculocutaneous albinism* (OCA) is inherited as an autosomal recessive trait. X-linked forms of *ocular albinism* also exist. Individuals with OCA are classified as tyrosinase negative or positive for tyrosine activity in hair bulbs. Tyrosinase-negative individuals form no pigment. The gene for tyrosinase has been localized to chromosome 11q14, and many mutations are defined. A tyrosine-positive OCA has been associated with an autosomal recessive gene located on chromosome 15q11-13 (the P gene) and X-linked ocular albinism caused by *OCA-1* gene mutations. A wide variation in phenotypic expression of albinism is reported ranging from severe neurologic deficiency with ocular and sarcomatous skin cancers to mild cosmetic problems.

Inborn errors of the urea cycle (Chapter 219) are represented by defects in the integration of anabolic and catabolic pathways and the distribution of catalytic proteins between mitochondria and cytosol. The role of the urea cycle is to convert ammonia, a byproduct of protein breakdown, to urea and to synthesize arginine and ornithine. Reactions to complete this anabolic cycle require three mitochondrial enzymes, three cytosolic enzymes, and two mitochondrial transporter proteins. Inherited disorders affecting the function of each of these proteins are known. Individuals with defects in any of the enzymes present with varying degrees of hyperammonemia caused by protein ingestion or a nutritional state in which muscle is catabolized. With the exception of the gene for ornithine transcarbamylase found on the short arm of chromosome X, the other proteins are encoded on autosomes, and defects are inherited as autosomal recessive traits. Many principles of diagnosis and therapy for inborn errors of metabolism are exemplified by disorders of the urea cycle.

A group of inborn errors of metabolism is caused by mutations in nuclear genes that encode mitochondrial proteins. Collectively, they are considered disorders of organic acid metabolism (Table 37–6). Branched-chain α-ketoacid dehydrogenase is a multienzyme complex located on the matrix side of the mitochondrial inner membrane in all tissues. When any of these proteins is impaired, the autosomal recessive disorder *maple syrup urine disease* may result (Chapter 220). In addition to nuclear-encoded genes, 13 proteins of mitochondrial complexes involved in oxidative phosphorylation are encoded in the mitochondrial DNA genome. Only complex II is encoded entirely by the nuclear genome. A wide range of disorders affecting the eye, brain, and muscle are caused by mutations in mitochondrial DNA that impair oxidative phosphorylation. The inheritance pattern of disorders encoded by the mitochondrial genome is distinguished from disorders caused by mutations in nuclear DNA by being transmitted through an affected mother to all of her offspring. Males do not transmit mitochondrial mutations to their offspring, thus the term *maternal inheritance*. Since there are about 10,000 mitochondrial genomes per cell, variation in disease expression is caused by differences in the ratio of mutant to normal mitochondrial genomes (*heteroplasmy*) and the environment.

Another group of inborn errors of metabolism is collectively categorized as *lysosomal disorders* (Chapter 222) to indicate the subcellular localization of these enzymes that function in this acidic environment. Most of these enzymes are involved in breakdown of endocytosed membrane components and when defective result in accumulation of their nondegraded substrates in the lysosomes and macrophages of affected organs.

I-cell disease is an inborn error of post-translational processing of proteins directed to the lysosome. Clarification of this pathophysiology led to an understanding of the mechanisms by which lysosomal enzymes are polarized through phosphorylation to remain in the acidic lysosomes. Patients with I-cell disease have inherited defects in the recognition markers required to direct enzymes to the endocytic receptor of plasma membrane and to its capture in the acidic milieu of the lysosome. Patients lack all cellular lysosomal enzymes. Instead, empty lysosomes look like inclusion bodies ("I cell"). The misdirected lysosomal enzymes are secreted and are present in excess in plasma but are missing from cells. These extracellular enzymes were found to lack mannose 6-phosphate residues, and this observation led to an understanding of the post-translational mechanisms by which enzymes are directed to the lysosome and recaptured into endosomes by adding phosphorylated mannose to their protein structure. Individuals with I-cell disease lack this phosphotransferase activity.

Inborn errors affecting single enzymes in the degradative pathway for mucopolysaccharides and gangliosides helped define the steps required for the breakdown of these complex macromolecules. Disorders of mucopolysaccharide metabolism include Hurler's syndrome; Scheie's syndrome; Hunter's syndrome; Sanfilippo's syndrome types A, B, C, and D; Morquio's syndrome types A and B; and Sly's syndrome. Disorders of ganglioside metabolism include Fabry's disease, Gaucher's disease, Niemann-Pick disease, Tay-Sachs disease, I-cell disease, fucosidosis, mannosidosis, sialidosis, and aspartylglycosaminuria.

Table 37–6 • ORGANIC ACIDEMIAS: DISORDERS OF METABOLISM BY MITOCHONDRIAL PROTEINS

DISORDER	ENZYME DEFECT	INHERITANCE
Isovaleric acidemia	Isovaleryl CoA dehydrogenase	Autosomal recessive
Methylcrotonic aciduria	3-Methylcrotonyl CoA carboxylase	Autosomal recessive
Glutoconic aciduria	3-Methylglutaconyl CoA hydralatase	Autosomal recessive
Glutaric aciduria (1)	3-Hydroxy-3-methylglutaryl CoA lyase	Autosomal recessive
Mevalonic aciduria	Mevalonate kinase	Autosomal recessive
Thiolase deficiency	2-Methylacetoacetyl CoA thiolase	Autosomal recessive
Isobutyric aciduria	3-Hydroxyisobutyryl CoA deacylase	Autosomal recessive
Propionic aciduria	Propionyl CoA carboxylase	Autosomal recessive
Methylmalonic aciduria	Methylmalonyl CoA mutase	Autosomal recessive
Lactic acidosis	Pyruvate dehydrogenase Pyruvate decarboxylase	Autosomal recessive
Acyl-CoA dehydrogenase deficiencies	Short-, medium-, and long-chain fatty acyl CoA dehydrogenase	Autosomal recessive
Branched-chain α-ketoacidemia	Branched-chain α-ketoacid dehydrogenase	Autosomal recessive
Glutaric acidemia type II	Electron transfer factor deficiency	Autosomal recessive
Leber's optic atrophy	Mitochondrial oxidative phosphorylation complexes	Maternal
Myoclonic epilepsy and ragged red fibers	Mitochondrial oxidative phosphorylation complexes	Maternal
Leigh's disease	Mitochondrial oxidative phosphorylation complexes	Maternal

Table 37–7 • INBORN ERRORS OF PEROXISOMES

Disorders of peroxisomal biogenesis
    Zellweger's syndrome (cerebrohepatorenal syndrome)
    Neonatal adrenoleukodystrophy
    Infantile Refsum's disease
    Hyperpipecolic acidemia
    Leber's amaurosis
    Rhizomelic chondrodysplasia punctata (Conradi's syndrome)
    Peroxisomal 3-oxoacyl CoA thiolase deficiency
    Peroxisomal acyl-CoA oxidase deficiency
    X-linked adrenoleukodystrophy (impaired lignoceroyl CoA and
        hexacosanoyl CoA ligase)
    Adult Refsum's disease (phytanic acid α-hydroxylase deficiency)
    Acatalasemia (H_2O_2 oxidoreductase deficiency)

Table 37–8 • SOME INBORN ERRORS OF PROTEINS THAT CIRCULATE IN BLOOD

FUNCTIONAL CLASS	PROTEIN	PHENOTYPE
Transport	Ceruloplasmin	Wilson's disease
	Albumin	Analbuminemia
	Hemoglobin	Hemoglobinopathies
	α-Lipoprotein	Analphalipoproteinemia
	β-Lipoprotein	Abetalipoproteinemia
	Transcobalamin II	Megaloblastic anemia
Hormones	Growth hormone	Pituitary dwarfism
	Insulin	Diabetes mellitus (insulin-dependent)
	Somatomedin	Pituitary dwarfism
Coagulation	Factors I–XIII	Coagulopathies
	Kininogen	Kininogen deficiency
	Prekallikrein	Prekallikrein deficiency
Immune system	Complement components	Hypocomplementemias
	Immunoglobulins	Hypogammaglobulinemias
Inhibitors	$α_1$-Antitrypsin	Pulmonary emphysema and/or cirrhosis
	G'1 esterase inhibitor	Angioneurotic edema
Drugs	Pseudocholinesterase	Prolonged paralysis after succinylcholine exposure (Anectine)

Another group of inborn errors of metabolism defined by altered organelle function are *peroxisomal diseases* (Table 37–7). Peroxisomes are radiodense organelles of 0.5 to 1 nm diameter bounded by a single trilaminar membrane. Anabolic and catabolic reactions occur in this organelle. Primary pathways synthesize plasmalogens (unique fatty acids containing vinyl ethers), cholesterol, and bile acids. Other biosynthetic reactions include gluconeogenesis from amino acids and the formation of oxalic acid by the action of alanine-glyoxylate aminotransferase (Chapter 215). Catabolic reactions include breakdown of hydrogen peroxide by peroxisomal catalase, a traditional protein of the peroxisome; polyamine oxidation; purine breakdown; ethanol oxidation; phytanic acid hydroxylation; and pipecolic acid degradation. A major function of the peroxisome is β-oxidation of very-long-chain fatty acids (>24 carbons). Diagnosis of these disorders is by finding excess very-long-chain fatty acids but reduced plasmalogen in blood.

An understanding of the importance of many reactions that occur in the peroxisome has come from identifying patients with either defects in individual biochemical pathways or lack of peroxisomes. The targeting signal for peroxisomal proteins may lie in their carboxyl terminal end, and mutations in the alanine-glyoxylate aminotransferase have resulted in mistargeting of this enzyme to mitochondria with consequent *familial hyperoxaluria* (Chapter 215).

Several inborn errors are caused by abnormalities in proteins that function in the nucleus and are involved in DNA repair (see class 2, Table 37–1). Patients expressing these inherited disorders carry a high risk for developing cancers. Among these inborn errors of DNA repair are rare disorders, such as *xeroderma pigmentosum*, *Bloom syndrome*, *ataxia-telangiectasia*, *Fanconi's anemia*, and diseases associated with early aging such as *progeria* and *Werner syndrome*, and more common adult-onset *nonpolyposis colon cancer*. Collectively the disorders show an increased sensitivity and delayed repair of damaged DNA owing to ultraviolet, x-ray, alkylating cross-links, or "normal" DNA report requirements.

Many inborn errors involve proteins that circulate in blood (see class 3 of Table 37–1). Stable circulating proteins in blood perform a variety of functions, including immunologic, hemostatic, regulatory, hormonal, and interorgan transport of trace metals, lipids, and other nutrients. Some inherited disorders affecting circulating proteins are tabulated in Table 37–8. Proteins involved in oxygen transport, coagulation, and immunity are detailed in other chapters, but the pathophysiologic mechanisms and genetic approaches of screening, diagnosis, and intervention to return homeostasis and prevent an expected disease state make them appropriate to consider here as inborn errors of metabolism.

Abnormal matrix proteins produce inborn errors, such as Marfan syndrome (fibrillin), osteogenesis imperfecta (collagen type I), spondyloepiphyseal dysplasia (collagen type II), and Sach's disease (collagen type III) (Chapter 276). These disorders exemplify class 4 of inborn errors of metabolism (see Table 37–1). The enzymes involved in post-translational processing of these proteins also may cause these syndromes. An example is Ehlers-Danlos syndrome type VI, in which collagen lysylhydroxylase deficiency produces excess poorly hydroxylated lysyl residues in collagen. Inborn errors of matrix proteins are exemplified by disorders of collagen metabolism. More than 20 different genes dispersed on nine chromosomes are currently known to code for more than 13 different types of collagen. These disorders are detailed in Chapters 215 to 218 and 283.

Treatment of Inherited Disease

Because the metabolic diseases considered in this chapter have in common that they are caused by genes of large effect, which disrupt normal homeostasis, we can consider a general approach to their treatment. These approaches are outlined in Table 37–9. The level at which therapy is rendered depends on the level or understanding of the pathophysiologic mechanisms producing disease and the interventional methods available. Genetic counseling is used for all inherited diseases, even those whose mechanisms are not yet understood and for which no other treatment is available.

Genetic counseling is a unique and fundamental aspect of management in inherited metabolic diseases. Patients, their parents, and relatives usually ask the following questions: Why did this disease

Table 37–9 • APPROACHES TO TREATING INBORN ERRORS OF METABOLISM

Genetic counseling: prospective therapy
Diagnosis, risk assessment, informational transfer, support for resource allocation
Reproductive alternatives: Contraception, abstinence, artificial insemination, in vitro fertilization, risk taking with or without prenatal monitoring
Environmental engineering
Avoiding the offending agent
Supplemental physical, speech, occupational therapy
Nutritional management
    Promote anabolism
    Limit toxic precursor
    Detoxify through alternative metabolic route
    Provide feedback inhibitor
    Provide supraphysiologic amounts of vitamin precursor
    Induce protein (enzyme) production
    Chemoprevention
Protein and enzyme replacement
Infuse engineered enzyme
Provide clotting factors and peptide hormones
Transplantation
    Organ transplant
    Bone marrow transplant
Genetic engineering
Somatic gene therapy
    Random insertion
    Homologous recombination (site specific)
Germline therapy

occur? Will this disease happen to me or my children? Can it be cured or prevented? Genetic counseling tries to answer these questions through processes involving several elements. One cannot overemphasize the importance of an accurate clinical diagnosis and prognosis. A genetic discriminant is necessary for other family members before entering into formal genetic counseling. The genetic discriminant can be at the clinical, histologic, biochemical, or molecular level and must define whether or not an individual family member has or has not inherited the mutant allele or alleles.

Surgical intervention may be a useful adjunct for treating heritable disorders. Stabilizing hypoplastic cervical vertebrae may prevent quadriparesis or death in a variety of *chondrodysplasias* and *mucopolysaccharidoses* accompanied by hypoplasia of the odontoid process or atlantoaxial instability. In Marfan syndrome, careful monitoring of aortic root diameter with surgical removal of the aorta and prosthesis may prevent a lethal aortic dissection. Evaluation of polyps and early colectomy may prevent disseminated adenocarcinoma in families with the autosomal dominant forms of *familial polyposis coli*. Molecular diagnosis of mutations in the *APC* gene help identify at-risk family members and reassure members who did not inherit the mutant allele. Preventing heritable cancer by surveillance and early surgical excision is therapeutic for *medullary thyroid carcinoma, Wilms' tumors,* and neurofibromas of *von Recklinghausen's disease*. Other examples of the benefit of preventive surgery for inborn errors include splenectomy for hemolytic anemias associated with spherocytosis, pyloroplasty in pyloric stenosis, and mastectomy and oophorectomy for patients with *BRCA-1* or *BRCA-2* mutations.

Environmental engineering is the most commonly used approach to preventing disease in patients affected by inherited metabolic disease. The environment (nutritional intake, exposure to toxins, sun, stress, climatic variation, and drug therapy) may produce a disease state in individuals who have inherited single genes or polygenic susceptibility to specific environmental stress. Newborn screening for galactose-1-P-uridyltransferase deficiency identifies infants susceptible to galactose-1-phosphate accumulation if they ingest human or cow's milk. Restriction and replacement of lactose with sucrose saves the lives of infants with galactosemia. Pharmacogenetic disorders exemplify the simple treatment of *avoidance* when the genetic susceptibility is identified. Health can be viewed as a continual adaptation between the individual and the environment. Environmental engineering is a form of genetic therapy in which individual genetic susceptibility is identified and the environment is altered to provide optimal health for the individual's unique genetic constitution. The frequency of diseases caused by genetic susceptibility to the environment varies from rare to 100%. *Scurvy* develops in all humans unless ascorbate is provided in the diet because we are all unable to convert glucuronic acid to glucuronolactone and ascorbate. Humans and primates lost this anabolic pathway during evolution. By contrast, humans usually can synthesize tetrahydrobiopterin, a cofactor in many hydroxylase reactions, including phenylalanine hydroxylase. In some rare diseases (about 1 in 500,000) of increased blood phenylalanine and severe neurodegeneration, biopterin is not synthesized.

Nutritional management and chemoprevention involve correction of the metabolic imbalance and return of the patient to homeostasis through diet manipulation and drug therapy. Many of the diseases listed in this chapter are amenable to several concurrent therapeutic approaches listed in Table 37–9. For example, in disorders of the urea cycle, protein intake is limited, and anabolism is encouraged to reduce ammonia accumulation from either protein intake or catabolism of lean body mass. Arginine is supplemented to provide deficient product of the blocked reaction, and alternative pathways are induced for nitrogen excretion. The latter therapy is made possible by a ubiquitous enzyme, N-glycine-acylase, that forms adducts with benzoic acid and glycine to produce hippuric acid, which is excreted, eliminating one nitrogen molecule. Phenylacetylglutamine transferase also is used by giving phenylacetate to produce and excrete two nitrogens as phenylacetylglutamate. Orotic aciduria is caused by mutations in the bifunctional enzyme orotate phosphoribosyl transferase-orotidine-5′-monophosphate decarboxylase. The disease process, which includes severe anemia and immune deficiency, is caused by a deficient end product, uridine, and is treated by replacing 100 to 200 mg/kg/day of uridine (orally). Feedback inhibition of pituitary adrenocorticotropic hormone production is important in treating congenital adrenal hypertrophy with replacement doses of hydrocortisone to prevent virilization from testosterone overproduction. Vitamin dependency disorders require supraphysiologic amounts of a specific vitamin as the

precursor for an active cofactor required for holoenzyme function. Many vitamin-dependent metabolic disorders are known and include pyridoxine (vitamin B_6)-dependent homocystinuria and vitamin C-dependent Ehlers-Danlos syndrome type VI. In vitamin B_6-dependent homocystinuria, mutant cystathionine synthase is stabilized to biologic degradation when saturated with pyridoxal phosphate. Others include vitamin B_{12}-dependent methylmalonic aciduria, thiamine-dependent maple syrup urine disease, biotin-dependent multiple carboxylase deficiency, and biopterin-dependent hyperphenylalaninemia. Some blocked metabolic reactions can be augmented by inducing transcription of their gene. Phenobarbital and several other drugs induce hepatic uridine diphosphate glucuronyl transferase gene expression and reduce the accumulation of unconjugated bilirubin in Gilbert's syndrome. In tyrosinemia type I, a drug NTBC blocks the catabolic pathway by which tyrosine produces the toxin succinylacetone and successfully prevents hepatotoxicity.

If the specific protein or enzyme has been purified and engineered to function in its specified organ or subcellular organelle, it can be used to treat an inherited metabolic disease. One good example is glucocerebrosidase, the enzyme that is impaired in Gaucher's disease. This enzyme has been purified in large quantities from placenta and from recombinant mammalian cells. The secreted enzyme is biochemically engineered to contain the mannose recognition site for cellular uptake into lysosomal compartments. It has been used successfully to prevent and reverse the hypersplenism, pancytopenia, and bone disease of *type I Gaucher's disease* (Chapter 222). Many proteins now are made through recombinant techniques to treat metabolic disease and reduce the risks of viral disease attendant on using human-derived biologic agents. These enzymes now include *glucocerebrosidase*, factor VIII for *hemophilia type A*, growth hormone for *growth hormone deficiency*, α-galactosidase to treat *Fabry's disease*, iduronidase for *Hurler-Scheie syndrome*, and acid maltase for *Pompe disease*. Several other engineered proteins used to treat inherited metabolic disease include 1-deamino-8-D-arginine vasopressin to treat *X-linked recessive diabetes insipidus* and recombinant α_1-antitrypsin made stable by inactivating methionine 385 in the treatment of α_1-antitrypsin deficiency. Some enzymes, such as adenosine deaminase, have been modified with polyethylene glycol to reduce immunogenicity and prolong their biologic half-life in blood. It is used to treat *severe combined immunodeficiency*. Chemoprevention is being developed for heritable cancers. Cyclooxygenase II inhibitors may prevent progression of colon polyps to adenocarcinoma, and estrogen receptor inhibitors may prevent some forms of breast cancer.

For metabolic disorders that are lethal and have no other available therapy, organ transplantation may be life-saving. Transplantation with histocompatible organs is clinically available because of advances in immunology that not only allow for better tissue typing, but also enable long-term immunosuppression with drugs such as cyclosporine, azathioprine, and prednisone to prevent rejection. Cloned embryonic cells or stem cells that are still naïve to adult antigens are promising therapeutic agents in this category.

Several principles are required for successful treatment of an inherited metabolic disorder by organ transplantation: (1) The normal enzyme, protein, or function must be provided by the transplanted organ. (2) Usually the affected organ must be removed. (3) The host must be immunologically tolerant to the gene product being introduced in addition to the transplanted organ itself. These principles are particularly relevant when displacement bone marrow transplantation is used. In the latter, normal donor stem cells differentiate and provide their enzymes to the recipient's reticuloendothelial system. Diseases associated with accumulation of products in the central nervous system are not yet ameliorated by bone marrow transplantation, although accumulation in bone, liver, and spleen is reduced. One group of metabolic diseases uses stem cell bone marrow transplantation to prevent leukemia caused by inherited syndromes that are associated with defective DNA repair, such as *Fanconi's anemia, Bloom's syndrome,* and *ataxia-telangiectasia*. Liver or kidney transplantation can reverse growth and developmental delay in type I glycogen storage disease, cystinosis, acute intermittent porphyria, type I tyrosinemia, Fabry's disease, oxalosis, and non-neuronotropic lysosomal storage diseases. Lung transplantation has been successful in cystic fibrosis and α_1-antitrypsin deficiency, and prophylactic aortic transplantation has prevented aortic dissection in Marfan syndrome.

Somatic cell gene therapy to treat patients with genetic disease has entered the arena of clinical research. Numerous laboratories throughout the world are actively designing strategies by which exogenous

DNA can be incorporated into the genomic DNA of specific organs to provide a missing gene function. *Somatic gene therapy* for many inherited metabolic diseases continues to be a goal of the future and awaits a nontoxic, stable vector with which to transfer normally transcribed genes.

SUGGESTED READINGS

Elsas LJ, Acosta P: Nutritional support of inherited metabolic disease. In Shils M, Olson J, Shike M, Ross C (eds): Modern Nutrition in Health and Disease, 9th ed. Baltimore, Williams & Wilkins, 1999. *A review of metabolic pathways and pathophysiologic mechanisms and an emphasis on nutritional approaches to returning homeostasis. A practical resource for intervention.*

GeneTests and GeneClinics: Available at http://www.genetests.org/cgi-bin. *This newly merged website offers updated information for physicians and investigators on availability of diagnostic tests and reviews of diagnosis and intervention for many inherited metabolic disorders.*

National Center for Biotechnology: Available at http://www3.ncbi.nlm.nih.gov/Omim. *The database can be searched by disease name and contains updated information on the history, biochemistry, and molecular biology of all inherited disorders caused by mutations in single genes.*

Scriver CR, Beaudet AL, Sly WS, Vallee D (eds): The Metabolic and Molecular Bases of Inherited Disease, 8th ed. New York, McGraw-Hill, 2001. *A comprehensive biochemical and molecular review of inherited metabolic disorders.*

Society for Inherited Metabolic Disorders: Available at http://www.simd.org. *This website has linkages to an international collection of websites dealing with diagnosis and treatment guidelines for inherited metabolic disorders. Includes patient support groups.*

38 SINGLE GENE AND CHROMOSOMAL DISORDERS

Judith Hall

Single gene disorders are disorders in which inheritance is due to a single mutant gene. Genes are "units of heredity," now known to be based in DNA. The concept of units of heredity first was described by Mendel in 1865. Consequently, this type of inheritance often is called *mendelian inheritance*. Mendel's work describing these invisible factors, which are passed from generation to generation and determine various traits or characteristics, was largely ignored until Bateson translated Mendel's work and reintroduced these concepts in the early 1900s.

Mendel's work was based on the characteristics he observed in his monastery's garden peas and led to four important conclusions:

1. Genes come in pairs, one from each parent.
2. The individual genes can have different forms (alleles) that can exert their effect on each other, being dominant or recessive. These various forms of the gene are transmitted entirely unchanged from generation to generation.
3. When germ cells are made, the two genes segregate/separate from each other so that the resultant gamete receives only one of the two alleles present in the parent.
4. The segregation/separation of a given gene (and the trait it produces) is independent of other traits.

What is remarkable about Mendel is that he was able to deduce these characteristics about the units of heredity from observing the transmission of characteristics that we now understand to have a basis in the physical nature of DNA. Although exceptions to each of Mendel's rules are now recognized, the concept of genes has been an extremely useful one. The idea that these units of heredity were arranged in linear sequence on each chromosome was anticipated long before the DNA basis of inheritance had been defined.

Chromosomes are nuclear structures that become visible as cells divide. They represent the condensation of the cell's nuclear DNA together with histones and proteins. They can be seen readily through special preparation and staining techniques. Disorders of single genes have been observed clinically because of a phenotypic change related to alterations in a protein or protein pathway that the gene normally would influence. Today, it is possible to define the exact change in the DNA (genotype) that leads to the change in phenotype. These changes are too small to see through a microscope, however, and require a specialized molecular technique to define. By contrast, disorders of chromosomes almost always involve multiple genes and are a reflection of the absence or excess created by numerical or positional changes of chromosome material.

Molecular techniques have enabled dramatic advances in the understanding of how genes and chromosomes function. The techniques allow amplification, sequencing, and even visualization of extremely small changes in genetic material. Most of what is inherited in humans resides along the 46 chromosomes; however, the mitochondria (inherited solely from the mother) also carry DNA. Other cell structures originally transferred from the egg and coming from the mother serve as templates for future cells, such as the cell wall and various organelles.

The Human Genome Project is in the process of defining the sequence, the normal position, and variations of all human genes. A great deal of additional work will be needed to refine the variations and annotate unique areas. A major surprise of the project has been that there appear to be only about 30,000 genes. As there are more than 100,000 human proteins, it was anticipated that there would be a gene for each protein. It is now recognized, however, that one gene may produce more than one protein by using different parts of the gene's sequence in what is called *alternative splicing*. With a little more than 30,000 genes, it can be expected that the genes and their gene products will fall into something in the range of 1000 pathways and that the pathways will interact in a variety of ways. It also can be anticipated that gene expression will occur in a time-specific and tissue-specific manner; however, the mechanisms of control of that orchestration are not yet understood. Clearly gene expression would be modified by environmental interactions.

SINGLE GENE DISORDERS

Single gene disorders have been recognized because of a change in the phenotype of the affected individual. In the case of diseases of adulthood, the phenotypic changes may not become obvious until long after puberty, although the abnormal gene has been present since conception. Classically, genetic disorders have been described on the basis of the presence of physical or functional abnormalities (phenotype). Only more recently has the DNA change (genotype) from "normal" and molecular basis been understood. Consequently the first descriptions of single gene disorders came as a list of signs or symptoms that were inherited together, within a family, in recognizable patterns of inheritance (i.e., autosomal or X-linked, dominant or recessive).

In more recent years, the most useful listing of genes and genetic diseases for the clinician has been OMIM (Online Mendelian Inheritance in Man), spearheaded by McKusick (available at http://www.ncbi.nlm.nih.gov/Omim/). Analysis of the mutations and the types of DNA changes that lead to the disease phenotypes has given much insight into (1) the mechanisms of disease, (2) the parts of the gene that lead to disease when changed, and (3) the complex biochemical pathways leading to disease.

Single gene disorders are separated into autosomal versus X-linked. This classification is determined by whether the responsible gene is carried on one of the autosomal chromosomes (chromosomes that are homologous in males and females) or on the X chromosome (females have two X chromosomes and males have an X and a Y chromosome).

Patterns of Inheritance

Genes carried on the autosomes display different patterns of inheritance, as seen from the pedigree or family history (Table 38–1), compared with genes inherited on the X chromosome. *Dominant* and *recessive* refer to whether the disease phenotype produced by the mutant allele is manifested or observed when only a single copy of the abnormal allele is present (dominant) or whether expression requires, as in the case of recessively inherited traits, that no normal allele is present.

The terms *dominant* and *recessive* refer to the phenotypic expression. Now that the molecular basis of most genes is understood or at least clearer, it has become obvious that there are many mechanisms that can lead to the phenotypic expression. There are many molecular ways for a mutant allele to exert an effect, such as by blocking a pathway or by overproduction or underproduction. *Codominant* is the term used to describe the situation in which the products of both alleles exert an observable effect (e.g., hemoglobin S and hemoglobin C can be observed at the same time). Traditionally, recessive inheritance implied that both alleles must be mutant to produce a phenotypic effect, but today, using molecular techniques, most carriers can be identified and often have subtle or late-onset phenotypic features.

Table 38–1 • CHARACTERISTICS OF SINGLE GENE INHERITANCE

	AUTOSOMAL DOMINANT	AUTOSOMAL RECESSIVE	X-LINKED DOMINANT	X-LINKED RECESSIVE
Transmission	Vertical	Usually horizontal	Daughters of affected males always inherit the disorder	Mainly inherited by males through carrier women
	Successive generations	Multiple sibs affected	Sons of affected males never inherit the disorder	
		Usually only one generation	Affected females can transmit the disorder to offspring of both sexes	
			An excess of affected females exists in the pedigree	
Consanguinity	No increase	Parents often consanguineous	Consanguinity not increased	Affected males are at risk of transmission through their obligate carrier daughter
Risk of affected offspring	50% (both sexes)	25% affected 50% carriers	50% affected	Males affected almost exclusively Females affected only when affected father and carrier mother (affected 50% of the time) or with skewed X-inactivation
Females affected	50%	Half of affected expected to be female	50% of daughters; however, twice as many affected women as affected men in family	Females are rarely affected; however, are obligate carriers of affected men
Males affected	50% (expect male-to-male transmission)	Half of affected expected to be male	50% (no male-to-male transmission)	50% of sons of carrier females Male-to-male transmission not observed

Most single gene disorders are rare. If they are common, it reflects (1) selection during evolution (because of an advantage for survival); (2) that a population came from a few founders, one of whom carried the mutation; or (3) that the gene has a high mutation rate.

Because single gene diseases have been described on a phenotypic basis, we refer to the abnormalities as *traits*. When the genes responsible for a trait are on one of the autosomes, they are called *autosomally inherited traits*. There are normally two of each autosomal chromosome, one inherited from the father and one from the mother. The traits represent the expression of genes; the two different genes (alleles) on the two different chromosomes may express in a manner such that one of the genes produces a trait that is dominant or, in other words, is observed as the phenotype. This sometimes is called *dominant inheritance* of the trait. If the abnormal gene expresses itself in the phenotype only when it is present in a double dose, or homozygous state, this is called *recessive inheritance* of the trait. Because over the years disorders have been described on the basis of their phenotype rather than really understanding what was happening on a gene level, the terms that have been used actually were describing the characteristics of the phenotype rather than the gene.

AUTOSOMAL INHERITANCE PATTERNS. When we talk about *autosomal dominant* inheritance, implying that the trait is expressed so that it is observable, each of the affected individuals usually has an affected parent from whom the gene for the condition has been passed on (see Table 38–1). Occasionally a mutation arises and is present in the germ cell that formed the affected individual. In this case, neither parent manifests the disorder, and the situation is described as a new "mutation."

In autosomal dominant disorders, males and females are affected in equal numbers. An affected individual would be expected to have equal numbers of affected and unaffected offspring. Males and females can transmit the trait to males and females. The normal children of an affected individual have only normal offspring. The transmission of a trait is vertical through successive generations if the trait does not impair reproductive capacity or viability.

Many well-known autosomal dominant traits affect several organ systems. This is called a *pleiotropic* effect. There can be a great deal of variability from individual to individual even within the same family as to the age of onset of abnormalities and the degree of involvement. This is called *variable expressivity*. In other words, an abnormal gene is present, but it expresses in a variable way. *Penetrance* refers to whether or not there is *any* expression of the gene. Some individuals carry an abnormal (usually dominant) gene but show no phenotypic features; this is called *nonpenetrance*.

In autosomal dominantly inherited traits, there is a 50% (1 in 2) chance that a child will inherit the trait. It does not matter whether the child is male or female. The normal individual in these families does not bear affected children unless it is a trait in which nonpenetrance occurs.

In classic autosomal dominant inheritance, in a homozygous state, that is, when there are two abnormal genes, the phenotype is said to be no worse than when one abnormal gene is present (heterozygous state). There are, however, few examples because in almost all conditions, "double" dominant (homozygous mutant) is phenotypically more severe. There are many genes that are *sex-influenced* or *sex-limited* but that are inherited as autosomal traits. Baldness (usually only affects males) and menstrual irregularities (only in females) would be two such traits.

It is important to make a distinction between genotype and phenotype because *genotype* refers to the actual gene and *phenotype* refers to the clinical expression of that gene in a functional or structural trait. Classically, genotypes are described as *homozygous* or *heterozygous*, implying that there are two genes and if they are identical genes, the person is said to be homozygous, and if they are two different genes (if one is normal), they are said to be heterozygous. Most of the time each family has a unique mutation in the gene, and unless the parents are related, the actual mutations are not exactly the same. If the affected person has two abnormal genes, however, they still usually called are homozygous mutations.

AUTOSOMAL RECESSIVE INHERITANCE PATTERNS. Autosomal recessive disorders are clinically apparent when the gene responsible is in the homozygous state (i.e., both alleles are mutant). Often being a carrier for that mutant gene produces a phenotype that appears to be normal, but as more is learned about gene function, carriers often can be identified on a biochemical or molecular basis.

A characteristic of an autosomal recessively inherited trait is that the parents are usually phenotypically normal. Males and females are affected in equal proportions, and multiple sibs can be affected. There is a 25% risk that each sib will be affected. Should the affected individuals (who have a homozygous mutant genotype) marry a normal individual who is homozygous normal, none of their children will be affected, but all will be heterozygote carriers of a mutant gene. If two individuals who are homozygous mutants marry, all of their children will be homozygous and affected. Homozygous-recessive traits are seen more commonly with consanguineous unions because relatives are more likely to carry the same mutant genes. Because the mutant genes often have slightly different mutations, such autosomal recessive inheritance can be described as heteroallelic (i.e., with two different alleles, both of which are abnormal).

X-LINKED INHERITANCE. X-linked inheritance refers to genes located on the X chromosome. Females have two X chromosomes; they may be heterozygous or homozygous for mutant genes. Males have only one X chromosome and thus one set of X-linked genes (called *hemizygous*), so if that allele is abnormal, they are affected. X-linked dominant diseases are disorders in which the female is affected with only one copy of the abnormal gene. Because males have only one X chromosome, they would be expected to express an X-linked trait whether it is recessive or dominant. Most X-linked traits and diseases are recessive, and consequently females usually do not manifest these disorders or disease states. If a woman's father has the disorder and her mother is a carrier, however, she has a 50% chance of being affected.

Women carry two X chromosomes that are both active early in development; however, as tissue differentiation occurs, one of the X chromosomes becomes inactive. This process of X inactivation is thought to be random, and there is an equal chance that the paternal or maternally derived X chromosome will be inactivated. When one of the X chromosomes has been inactivated, it remains inactivated throughout all subsequent cell divisions. The cells of the placenta usually inactivate the paternally inherited X chromosome and have an active maternally inherited chromosome. There also are situations of skewed X inactivation in which one or the other paternally derived X chromosome is disproportionately inactivated. Occasionally, this leads to females manifesting X-linked recessive disorders, such as hemophilia or color blindness.

X-linked dominant traits are traits in which the gene on the X chromosome is expressed in males and females. Usually these are disorders that are dominant in females but lethal in males. X-linked recessive traits are traits that are fully expressed in the hemizygous affected male. With X-linked recessive traits, heterozygote females are usually normal; however, because they can have skewed X inactivation, females occasionally are mildly affected but only rarely may be as affected as a male.

Gene Function

Because descriptions of disorders have been on a phenotypic basis, when the mutations within the gene responsible have been found, it turns out that a specific gene may be responsible for more than one disease. Sometimes these diseases are a part of a spectrum as in the case of achondroplasia and thanatophoric dysplasia, both having mutations in the fibroblast growth factor receptor 3 (*FGFR-3*) gene. Other times, the disorders were apparently quite different disorders, as in the case of Greig's cephalopolysyndactyly and polydactyly alone, both of which are mutations of the *GLI 3* gene. The differences in expression of specific genes are not entirely understood as yet but seem to relate to the fact that genes are complex in their structures such that different domains of the gene deal with different functions. A mutation in one domain may affect one biochemical pathway, and a mutation in another domain may affect a different process.

Gene Organization

As the structure of genes has become clearer, it is recognized that there are noncoding parts of genes that are important (i.e., the parts other than the *exons* whose sequence is transcribed into RNA). These include DNA sequences, distant from the gene, that enhance expression and determine whether or not the gene will be transcribed. There are also promoter elements close to the gene. As part of the gene, there are a beginning sequence and a clear ending sequence that signal the point at which transcription should begin and end. In addition, there are intervening sequences called *introns* that are transcribed into the RNA and then must be excised. The excision (splice) junctions are critical points. It is now clear that in large genes there can be several different combinations of exons (sequences that express) that are transcribed. This is called *alternative splicing* and produces different proteins from the same gene. The DNA is copied to RNA, which is transcribed into proteins using the genetic code.

When a protein is expressed, there are still modifications that need to be made to it so that it is folded properly and made functional. How control of the transcription process occurs is not clear for most genes. There many transcription factor genes that seem to be responsible for turning on other genes. These seem to be essential to the cascades of events occurring in differentiation, organ formation, and tissue-specific processes. Such a gene would have a major effect on many different pathways. For gene products to have an effect, not only do the proteins have to be made and properly processed, but also other protein receptors for that protein need to be produced in a tissue-specific, time-specific way. In addition, the protein needs to

"find" its proper place on the cell membrane, in the cytoplasm, or in an organelle. A great deal of work is needed to understand all of these processes and what controls their orderly, timely production.

The molecular techniques for identifying abnormalities in genes are discussed elsewhere; however, the abilities to isolate DNA and then amplify it so that there is enough material to work with and then to recognize changes in the sequence or deletions of the sequence to determine that a particular gene is in fact abnormal are now fundamental to determining single gene disorders. The newer technologies to recognize shortening (truncation) of a protein, which reflects mutations or alterations in triplet repeats, or other changes in gene structure will enhance the ability to identify the particular change in genetic information that has led to a disease. Most recently, the development of molecular "chips" that can run thousands of tests simultaneously will change dramatically the approach to diagnosis of single gene disorders.

Mutations

Until more recently, mutations producing changes in a gene that lead to a disease phenotype were thought of as nucleotide changes or deletions. Several new classes of mutations, including expansion of genes through triple repeats and the presence of transposable elements that can disrupt a sequence but also can be removed, require the consideration of a new classification of the types of mutations that can lead to phenotypic changes in individuals.

There are markedly variable mutation rates for different genes. Until more recently, new mutations were thought to occur in the range of 1 in 30,000 to 1 in 50,000 individuals. Each time cell division occurs and the DNA of the cell is replicated, it has been estimated that there are one or two errors during the replication of the total DNA of the cell. Because most of those errors occur in noncoding regions, they are not considered to be detrimental. These errors are the source of somatic mosaicism, however, in which individuals have some cells that are normal and some cells with an abnormality. Somatic mosaicism may be seen in individuals with patchy or streaky pigment or asymmetrical expression of abnormalities (as in segmented neurofibromatosis). They may be expressed in milder manifestations, so mild that they may appear to be a different disorder (arthritis in the parent and severe spondyloepiphyseal dysplasia in the child).

There does seem to be a wide range of mutation rates: For some genes, such as the neurofibromatosis gene, mutations seem to occur approximately in 1 of 6000 individuals, whereas in other genes, the rate of new mutation may be 1 in 50,000 individuals. It is not clear why these differences exist. Some of the variation may relate to the size of genes (i.e., large genes are more likely to have more mutations). Some of it may relate to the type of mutation (i.e., deletions seem to occur when there are repeat segments within the gene such that there is a slippage of one area of repeat sequences to another). Most mutations of a single nucleotide within the gene seem to occur during paternal meiosis when the paternal DNA is methylated, and they are particularly related to CpG islands. The processes of mutation also seem to be specific for specific disorders so that somatic mutation in pseudoachondroplasia is relatively common, whereas somatic mutation in achondroplasia is rare. Mutations of the paternal germline gene in achondroplasia are extremely common (on an order of 1000 times the mutation rate of other genes). The reasons for these variable mutation rates are not yet understood.

Gene expression occurs in a time-specific, tissue-specific way. Some genes are used and reused in different tissues at different times in development and in normal physiology. They can have a detrimental effect, at one time, if they misexpress, whereas at another time or in another tissue, there is no ill effect. The same gene product may be attracting other cells and a day later in development be repelling cells, as in development of the nervous system.

Mosaicism

Mosaicism is common in any multicellular organism (single gene mutations and chromosomal abnormalities). The question is whether it occurs in a tissue that will lead to a phenotype that will cause disease. Mutations that occur in stem cells give rise to many daughter cells with the same abnormality. Perhaps the most important consideration is whether the mutation has occurred in the germline. This would give the parent's germline more than one germ cell carrying the mutation so that a phenotypically normal parent may have more than one affected child. This situation has been well documented in the case of osteogenesis imperfecta. Occasionally a parent has some mild manifestation suggesting that he or she has some somatic cells that are affected, but germ cells that have the mutation produce a fully affected child. This situation is seen in individuals with pseudoachondroplasia, in which the parent has minimal expression, such as limitation of elbow extension, but the child has the full-blown disease.

In addition to mosaicism for mutations that develop during embryologic and fetal development of the individual, it is now clear that microchimerism also occurs, in which an individual received some cells (including stem cells) from the mother or dizygotic twin during pregnancy. A woman also may receive cells from her children, and those cells may find a niche where they become permanently housed and produce their own daughter cells, causing the individual to manifest chimerism.

Many mutations result in proteins that are not functional. Mutations lead to dysfunction in many ways, including an increased expression of the gene with more product being produced such that it "clogs" up a pathway. This also occurs as part of autosomal trisomies and in chromosomal duplications. Normal expression of genetic products either at the wrong time or in the wrong place can lead to abnormalities. Many of these dysfunctions relate to the promoter/control regions of the gene (rather than the gene product sequence). Also increased or decreased protein activity can relate to a protein that cannot be broken down or is cleared too rapidly or to a protein that is not inhibited in the usual way so that the protein action cannot be reversed. *Dominant negative* mutations are mutations that interfere with the activity of the normal wild-type allele. These are particularly common in multimeric proteins, in which a mutation of one of the subunits interacts in a way that binds and alters the catalytic activity of the rest of the protein so that it affects the entire multimere. In these situations, most or all of the protein produced would be abnormal. Toxic protein alterations include those in which there is disruption of function or in which new functions are produced that give totally new pathways. There are mutations that would be considered recessive, such as that seen in a retinoblastoma gene mutation, since both alleles must be abnormal to produce a retinoblastoma. Because the mutation rate of the second allele is high during the course of development, however, the homozygous abnormality (including deletion or loss of the normal allele) is frequent.

Nontraditional Epigenetic and "Parent of Origin" Effects

Epigenetic refers to effects on inheritance that are not part of the gene itself, but that rather reflect other mechanisms leading to differential control, such as the gender of the parent from whom something is inherited. There is a new class of genes, particularly related to development, growth, and behavior, in which although two alleles are present, only the allele inherited from one parent is expressed. This is called *genomic imprinting*. It produces an unusual pattern of inheritance in the pedigree. What is observed is that expression of the abnormal phenotype occurs only when the gene is inherited from the parent of one gender.

Expression or exposure during development may have long-lasting effects. The growing understanding of developmental genetics reflects that there is an orderly hierarchy of processes in the course of development, including patterning information, tissue differentiation, organ development, and interdependent tissue function. If there are abnormalities that occur during the process of formation, these are called *malformations*. If the structures have formed and are lost because of some mechanical force or loss of vascular supply, these are called *disruptions*. If one organ or tissue is formed and compression deforms the tissue, these are called *deformations*. *Dysplasias* are abnormalities of growth related to a specific tissue type. It is important in evaluating congenital anomalies to consider what type of process has led to the structural abnormalities. Different mechanisms underlie these different processes and reflect genetic versus environmental influences, recurrent risks, preventive strategies, and responses to therapy.

CHROMOSOMAL DISORDERS

The DNA of genes is packaged into chromosomes. In humans, there are 44 nonsex autosomes that come in 22 pairs. Normally, one of each pair is inherited from the father and one from the mother. There are normally two sex chromosomes. In addition to the 22 pairs of autosomes, females have two X chromosomes, and males have an X and a Y chromosome. Normally, humans have 46 chromosomes in the nucleus of every cell carrying, for practical purposes, the same (99.9%) genetic information (DNA) from one individual to the next. The Y chromosome in males carries little genetic information but is important for determining the phenotypic sex of the individual. Extra chromosomes, missing chromosomes, parts of missing chromosomes, duplications, and rearrangements all can present a problem. There is an increased occurrence of chromosomal abnormalities among spontaneous abortions and stillborns. Chromosomal abnormalities are a major cause of infertility. Chromosomal rearrangements occur in most cancers. A chromosomal anomaly is present in 0.5% of live-born infants, and at least half of these chromosomal abnormalities present clinically as recognizable syndromes. It is important to be aware of the problems related to the mechanisms that underly chromosomal abnormalities because they can have long-term effects on health in the adult.

Chromosomes are normally visible only through the microscope when they are in a contracted state going through cell division; however, a variety of new methods allow the visualization of chromosomes and chromosomal material at other times. Advances in molecular technology show submicroscopic deletions even during interphase. Microdeletions frequently are seen with many relatively common syndromes. In these deletions, more than one gene is lost, and usually affected individuals have multiple system involvement.

Nomenclature

Karyotype is the term used for the visual display of chromosomes (Fig. 38–1). This display is obtained by growing cells, usually fibroblast or lymphocytes, and arresting them during cell division at the specific cell cycle stage of metaphase. The cells are photographed, and the chromosomes are arranged in order according to size. This type of visual display also can be produced by computer.

In describing a karyotype, there are three elements to be defined:

1. The number of chromosomes
2. The sex chromosome constitution
3. Any abnormalities that are found

The normal karyotype for females is 46,XX and for males, 46,XY. Any abnormality observed is noted after the sex chromosome constitution. In a male with Wolf-Hirschhorn syndrome, in which a piece of the short arm of chromosome 4 is missing, the karyotype is 46,XY,4p–.

In a female with Down syndrome, in which there is an extra chromosome 21, the karyotype is 47,XX,+21. Other types of abnormalities are noted by an abbreviation (e.g., *t* for translocation and the chromosomes that are involved). For instance, a male carrier with translocation between the long arms of 13 and 15 would be represented by 45,XY,t(13q15q). If a chromosome breaks along the arm of a chromosome, the band position in which the breaks occur also is indicated within the brackets [e.g., 45,XX,t(13q2.3,15q3.2)].

Types of Cell Division

Normally, there are two types of cell division: mitosis and meiosis. In *mitosis*, there are two genetically identical daughter cells produced from a single parent cell. Most cells in the body are produced by mitosis. During mitosis, there are several stages. During the first stage, the chromosomes become condensed and are visible and easy to identify for karyotyping. Before the cell division and condensation, the DNA replicates so that there is already double the normal amount of DNA when the chromosomes condense. These chromosomes containing two identical copies of the DNA are called *sister chromatids*. The next phase of mitotic cell division is characterized by the chromosome threads coiling to form recognizable chromosomes. The nuclear membrane and the nucleolus disappear, and a mitotic spindle forms. In the next stage, metaphase, the chromosomes condense and become clearly visible. The center structure of the chromosomes (centromere) attaches to microtubules of the mitotic spindle, and the chromosomes align in the middle of the cell along with the spindle.

In the next phase, called *anaphase*, the chromosomes separate along their longitudinal axis, and one of each pair of the sister chromatids is drawn into what will be the two daughter cells. The next phase,

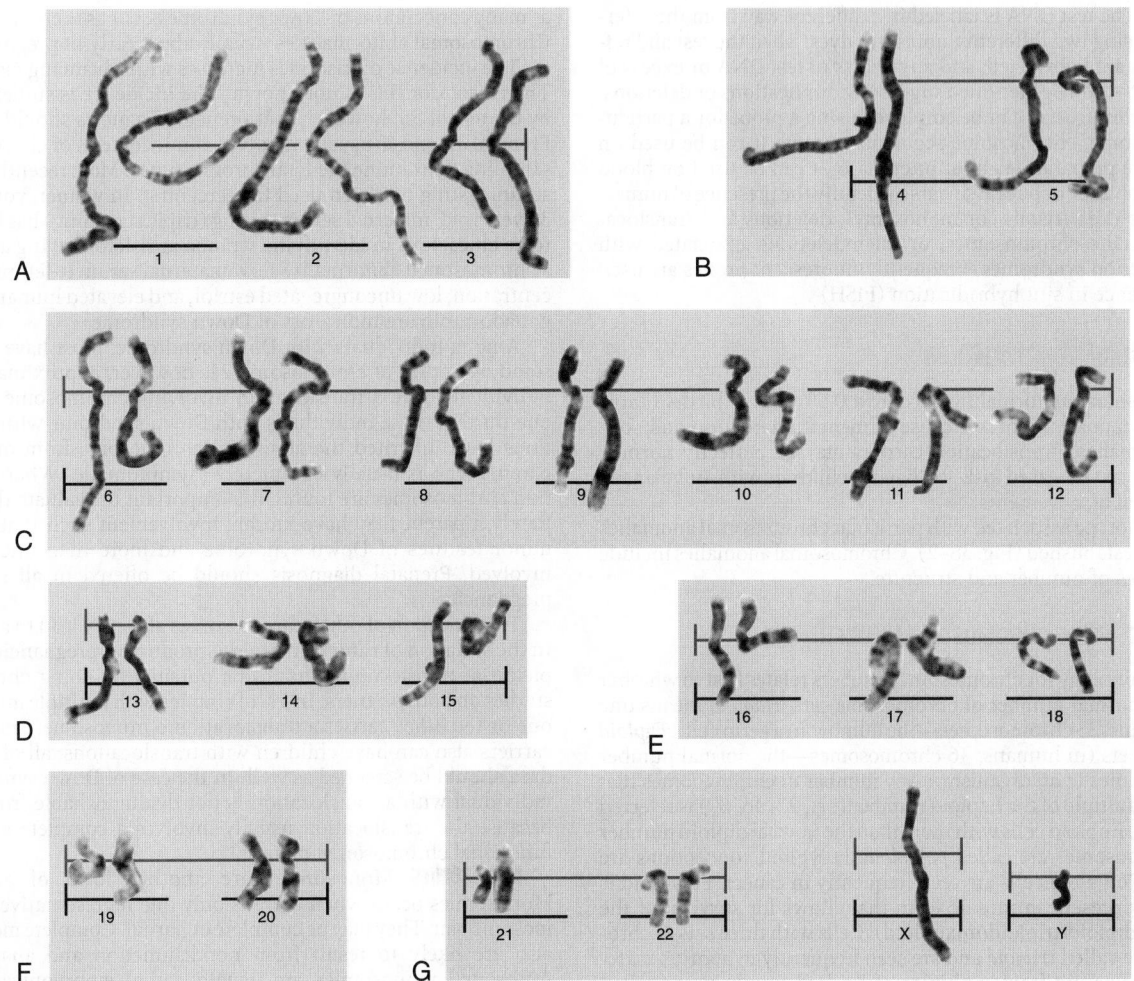

FIGURE 38-1 • Normal Giemsa-banded (G-band) male karyotype at the 850-band stage. This band level is the best to look for microdeletions, although the long chromosomes tend to curve, and overlapping of chromosomes is frequent.

telophase, completes mitosis, and during this stage, the nuclear membrane and the nucleoli reappear to form the two new daughter cells.

The second form of cell division is *meiosis,* which is involved in the formation of germ cells or gametes (sperm and egg). In this process, the normal set of 46 chromosomes is reduced to a half (haploid) set or 23 chromosomes so that with fertilization the normal number of chromosomes can be reestablished. Meiosis is divided into two parts; the first is meiosis I, in which the DNA replicates. During the early stages of meiosis, the future germ cell replicates the DNA to have two times the normal amount of DNA.

Male meiosis takes place after puberty. In male meiosis during this first cell division, each of these first daughter cells gets one of the duplicated chromosomes of a pair. In males, at the beginning of the second cell division of meiosis (meiosis II), each cell contains 23 chromosomes the DNA of which has been duplicated, and during meiosis II, the duplicated pairs separate so that each of the daughter cells ends up with 23 chromosomes. There are four daughter cells, each with half the normal number (haploid) set of chromosomes.

In the female, meiosis begins during embryogenesis, and rather than going through cell divisions, the extra sets of duplicated chromosomes clump together on the side of the cell and form *polar bodies.* During meiosis I, one set of duplicated chromosomes condenses and forms the first polar body. Then, during meiosis II in females (which is not completed until after puberty), one of the other half sets of chromosomes forms the second polar body. The egg has two polar bodies and one set of half the normal number of chromosomes.

In the process of meiosis, there is the exchange of segments of chromosomes (*crossing over* of chromosomes segments). This leads to new alignments and new combinations of genes and their various allele states along the chromosomal DNA.

The two common errors in cell division that occur during meiosis and lead to abnormal numbers of chromosomes are nondisjunction,

in which the pair of chromosomes fails to separate so that one new cell will have two copies of a particular chromosome and one cell will have no copy. The second type of problem is anaphase lag, in which a chromatid is lost because it fails to move quickly enough during anaphase to become incorporated into one of the new daughter cells and is lost.

Techniques

Chromosome studies producing a karyotype can be obtained from any dividing nucleated cell. Because blood is readily accessible, cytogenetic studies usually are performed on lymphocytes, but studies of fibroblasts should be considered if there is a suspicion of mosaicism.

Chromosome studies for prenatal diagnosis are obtained from amniotic fluid, chorionic villus sampling, and fetal blood and, when preimplantation prediagnosis is used, by analyzing blastomeres. In cancer, chromosome studies are done to provide prognosis and identify the most appropriate therapy.

In routine karyotyping, the stains used allow 400 to 600 bands to become visible (see Fig. 38-1). Trypsin-Giemsa staining reveals G-bands and quinacrine staining reveals Q-bands. Other special stains are used to show other chromosome structures, such as centromeres. If finer detail is necessary, prophase chromosomes may be examined. These are longer with less condensation, and they may show 600 to 1200 bands. Usually, chromosome studies done during prenatal diagnosis do not reveal as many bands as 1000, and it may be necessary when looking for fine deletions to repeat the chromosome studies if the first set was done for prenatal diagnosis.

Comparative genomic hybridization is a molecular technique that allows simultaneous enumeration of every chromosome. Test DNA is isolated from a single cell, then, using polymerase chain reaction, duplicated many times and paired with reference DNA from a normal individual. The test DNA is labeled in a different way from the reference DNA using two different fluorescent dyes. Then the test and reference DNA are hybridized, and any excess of test DNA or excess of reference DNA can be identified suggesting duplications or deletions.

In situ hybridization can be employed using a probe for a particular chromosome, chromosome segment, or gene. It can be used on chromosome preparations or at interphase. It can be used on blood smears, fibroblasts, or buccal smears to identify the presence of numerical changes (i.e., trisomy or monosomy), deletions and translocations of specific chromosomes, or microdeletions associated with specific deletion syndromes. Frequently, fluorescent probes are used for fluorescence in situ hybridization (FISH).

Chromosomal Abnormalities

Chromosomal abnormalities occur in 0.5% of live births (Table 38–2). They are an important cause of mental retardation and congenital anomalies. Translocation carriers may be perfectly normal, but they are at increased risk for having children with unbalanced chromosomal arrangements.

The phenotype associated with particular chromosomal anomalies is often well established (Fig. 38–2). Chromosomal anomalies include abnormalities of number and structure.

ABNORMALITIES OF CHROMOSOME NUMBER

The terminology for chromosome numbers relates first to whether there are a normal number of chromosome sets. *Haploid* means one set (in humans, 23 chromosomes—the number in a germ cell). *Diploid* means two sets (in humans, 46 chromosomes—the normal number of chromosomes in an organism). Any number of chromosomes that is an exact multiple of the haploid number (i.e., 23, 46, 69) is referred to as *euploid*. Euploid cells with more than the normal diploid number of 46 chromosomes are called *polyploid*. Polyploid conceptions are not viable. Polyploid cells are seen frequently in cancer. Polyploid is occasionally present in mosaic form that allows for survival of the individual (diploid/triploid/mixoploid). Cells with three sets of chromosomes are called *triploid* and are seen frequently in abortus material. Cells deviating from multiples of haploid numbers are called *aneuploid* (i.e., not euploid), which include all the variations of missing or extra chromosomes and deletions and duplications.

TRISOMIES. Trisomies are the most common aneuploidy. *Trisomy* occurs when there are three representatives of a particular chromosome rather than the normal two (i.e., trisomy 21, trisomy 18). Trisomies are usually the result of a meiotic nondisjunction and most frequently are associated with meiosis I defects in the mother. They also are associated with advanced maternal age. Trisomy may be present in all the cells of an individual or may occur in mosaic form with some normal cells or some cells with the additional chromosome. Most individuals with trisomy exhibit a consistent and specific phenotype depending on the chromosome involved. The most frequent and best-known trisomy in humans is trisomy 21, or Down syndrome. Trisomies of chromosomes 18, 13, and X also occur relatively frequently. The incidence of trisomies among miscarriages is much higher than among live births. In the case of Down syndrome, at least twice

as many conceptions of Down syndrome occur as there are live births. Chromosomal abnormalities usually abort early in pregnancy.

The incidence of trisomies increases with advancing maternal age. The reason for this is not known. The incidence is sufficiently high by the age of 35, however, that prenatal diagnosis should be offered. Prenatal diagnosis usually involves amniocentesis or chorionic villus sampling to examine the fetal chromosomes. Most recently, maternal serum testing has been used for screening. In women younger than 35 years old, maternal serum testing (triple screening) has been found to be efficacious in identifying women at risk for having a child with a chromosomal abnormality. Low maternal serum α-fetoprotein concentration, low uncongregated estriol, and elevated human chorionic gonadotropin are indicators of Down syndrome.

Among individuals with Down syndrome, most have three freestanding copies of chromosome 21; however, approximately 3% of individuals have a translocation involving chromosome 21. About one third of these individuals with Down syndrome with translocations have inherited the abnormal chromosome from one of their parents who is usually completely asymptomatic. When translocation chromosomes are found, it is important to evaluate the parents. Rarely a parent may have mosaic involvement such that they have minor features of Down syndrome and more than one germ cell involved. Prenatal diagnosis should be offered in all subsequent pregnancies.

Translocation of other chromosomes also may lead to aneuploidy. In the situation of three or more nonproductive pregnancies, the suspicion of translocation should be pursued by doing chromosomal studies on both partners. In 5% of couples with multiple miscarriages, one or the other carries a translocation chromosome. Translocation carriers also can have children with translocations; all of their children should be screened as well. In the case of Down syndrome, the individual with a translocation is not distinguishable from trisomy because the translocation usually involves a complete extra set of functional chromosomal material.

MONOSOMIES. Monosomies are another form of aneuploidy. Monosomies occur when there is only one representative of a chromosome pair. They may be complete or partial. Complete monosomies also are likely to result from nondisjunction and anaphase lag. Autosomal monosomies are usually lethal embryonically. Partial monosomies frequently occur in the offspring of individuals with translocations.

ABNORMALITIES OF CHROMOSOME STRUCTURE

DELETIONS. Visible chromosomal deletions indicate that part of the chromosome is missing. They can occur as simple deletions or as a deletion with a duplication (i.e., with a duplication of another segment). Deletions can be located at the end of a chromosome or in an interstitial segment of the chromosome. Visible deletions usually are associated with mental retardation and/or malformations. Small telomeric deletions are relatively common in nonspecific mental retardation (10% of cases). The most commonly observed deletions in humans are 4p–, 5p–, 9p–, 11p–, 13q–, 18p–, and 18q–. These are associated with well-defined phenotypes. More recently, microdeletions have been found associated with specific syndromes most of which also have been well described. About half of these microdeletions are so small that they are not seen with microscopic studies and must be defined using DNA probes.

MICRODELETIONS. Microdeletions involve several genes, and the affected individuals can be expected to have a phenotype involving several organ systems. Known microdeletions identifiable with fluorescent probes include Williams syndrome, Langer Giedion syndrome, Prader-Willi syndrome, Angelman syndrome, Rubinstein-Taybi syndrome, Smith-Magenis syndrome, Miller-Dieker syndrome, Alagille syndrome, and velocardiofacial (DiGeorge) syndrome (Table 38–3).

TRANSLOCATIONS. Translocations involve the transfer of chromosomal material from one chromosome to another and occur because of a break in the chromosomes. They occur with a frequency of about 1 in 500 live births and can be inherited from a parent or can occur de novo. When translocations are transmitted to children, there can be imbalances with missing and/or extra chromosomal material. The two main types of translocations are robertsonian translocation and reciprocal translocation. *Robertsonian translocation* involves acrocentric chromosomes (i.e., chromosomes in which the centromere is located near the end of the chromosome). This type of translocation involves

Table 38–2 • FREQUENCY OF CHROMOSOME DISORDERS AMONG NEWBORN INFANTS DETERMINED BEFORE AVAILABILITY OF PRENATAL DIAGNOSIS

DISORDER	FREQUENCY AT BIRTH
AUTOSOMAL	
Trisomy 21	1/600
Trisomy 18	1/5000
Trisomy 13	1/15,000
SEX CHROMOSOME	
Klinefelter syndrome (47, XXY)	1/700 males
XYY syndrome	1/800 males
XXX syndrome	1/1000 females
Turner syndrome	1/4000 females

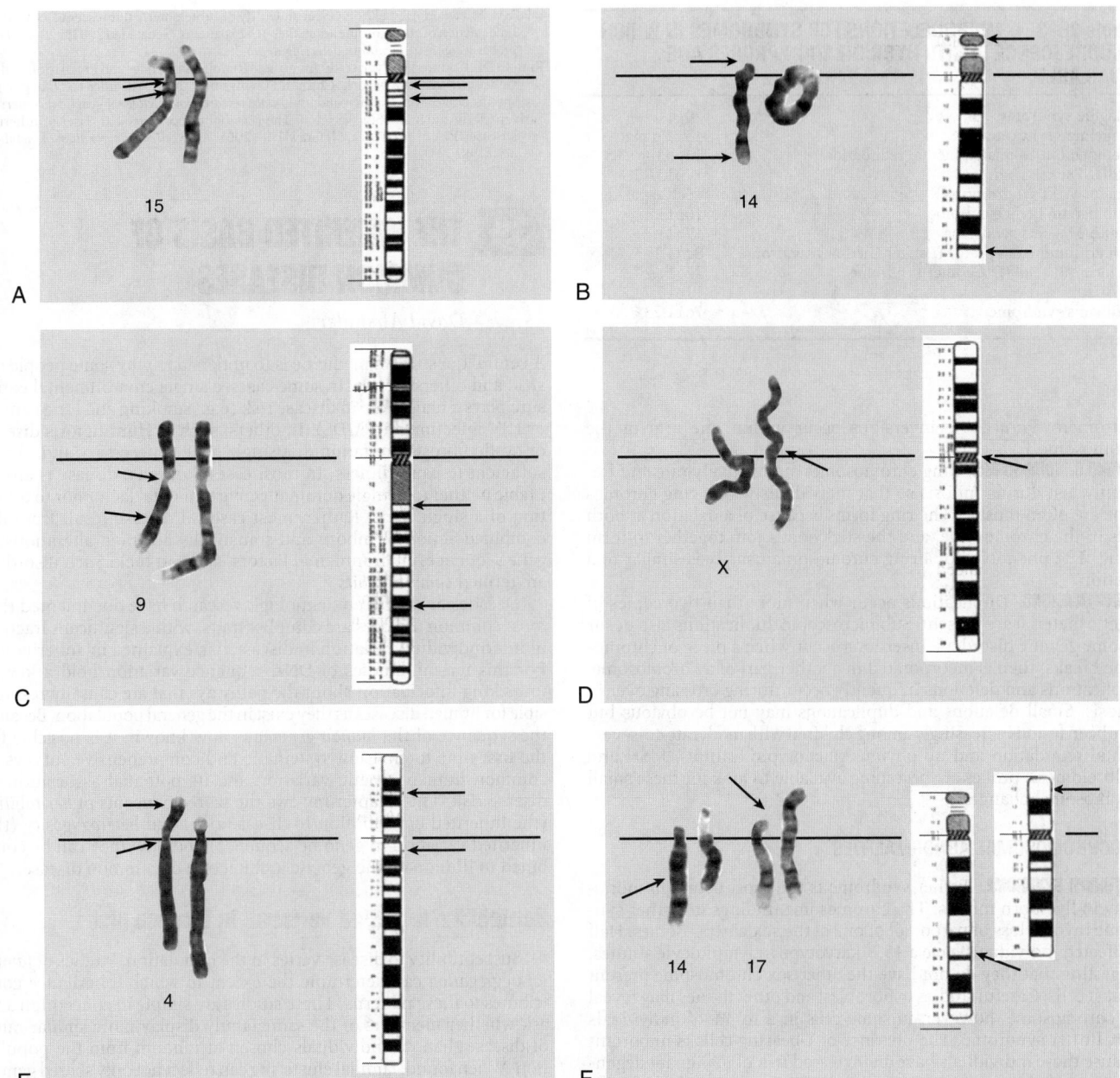

FIGURE 38–2 • Partial karyotypes illustrating several types of structural chromosome aberrations. The abnormal chromosomes are placed on the right of each pair. *A*, Interstitial deletion: Chromosomes 15 from a patient with Angelman syndrome. Ideogram and chromosomes are at the 850-band stage. Arrows on the ideogram and normal 15 indicate the small segment deleted. This same deletion is seen in 75 to 80% of patients with Prader-Willi syndrome. *B*, Ring chromosome: Chromosomes 14 from a patient with nonspecific mental retardation. Both ends of the abnormal chromosome have small deletions; the broken ends are joined in the form of a ring. Chromosomes are at the 550-band stage. *C*, Duplication: Chromosomes 9 at about the 850-band level. In the right-hand chromosome 9, there is an interstitial duplication of a large segment on the long arm, delineated by the arrows on the normal chromosome. The patient had multiple minor anomalies and mental retardation. *D*, Isochromosomes with duplication-deficiency: X chromosomes from a patient with Turner syndrome. Chromosomes at the 550-band stage show a deletion duplication, in this case resulting from isochromosome formation. Both arms of the abnormal chromosome are long arms; the short arm is missing. One explanation for this recurring characteristic abnormality is centromere misdivision. The arrow points to the centromere of the abnormal chromosome. *E*, Inversion: Balanced chromosome 4 pericentric inversion delineated by arrows, from a normal woman. This inversion chromosome segregated throughout her family. Chromosomes are at the 550-band stage. *F*, Translocation: Balanced reciprocal translocation between chromosomes 14 and 17 from a normal individual. Arrows indicate breakpoints. Ideogram is at the 550-band level, as are the chromosomes 14; the chromosomes 17 are between the 550-band and 850-band length. This likely is due to position in the metaphase spread; chromosomes at the periphery are often longer than chromosomes at the center.

fusion near the centromeric region, and consequently there is not loss of functional DNA. Robertsonian translocations comprise the fusion of the two long arms of two such chromosomes, and the individual carrying a robertsonian translocation only has 45 chromosomes. Individuals with robertsonian translocations are usually phenotypically normal; however, they are at increased risk to have offspring with translocation and trisomy.

Reciprocal translocations are the result of breaks of nonhomologous chromosomes and a reciprocal exchange of the broken segments.

Carriers of various reciprocal translocations are usually phenotypically normal. Designation for reciprocal translocation includes the break points along the chromosome; an individual with 45,XY, t(13q2.1-14q1.3) indicates a male carrier for translocation within the long arms of chromosome 13 and chromosome 14.

INVERSIONS. Inversions require the chromosome to break at two points. The broken piece then inverts and rejoins the chromosome. It can be *pericentric,* meaning that the breaks are in the two opposite arms of a chromosome so that the inverted portion contains the

Genetics

Table 38–3 • MICRODELETIONS FOR SYNDROMES IN WHICH FLUORESCENCE IN SITU HYBRIDIZATION PROBES ARE AVAILABLE

Alagille syndrome	20p11.2
Angelman syndrome	15.12q mat
Hemoglobin H–related mental retardation	16pter–p13.3
Miller-Dieker syndrome	17p13.12
Prader-Willi syndrome	15.12q pat
Rubinstein-Taybi syndrome	16p13.3
Smith-Magenis syndrome	17p11.2
Trichorhinophalangeal II (Langer Giedion) syndrome	8q24.1
Velocardiofacial (DiGeorge) syndrome	22q11.2
WAGR	11p13
Williams syndrome	7q11.23

Jalal SM, Harwood AR, Sekhon GS, et al: Utility of subtelomeric fluorescent DNA probes for detection of chromosome anomalies in 425 patients. Genet Med 2003;5:28–34. *These probes were instrumental in detecting anomalies.*

Rimoin DL, Connor JM, Pyeritz RE: Emery and Rimoin's Principles and Practice of Medical Genetics, 4th ed. New York, Churchill Livingstone, 2001. *A detailed text that provides specific clinical information and up-to-date research knowledge on genetic disorders.*

Scriver CR, Beaudet AL, Sly WS, et al: The Metabolic and Molecular Bases of Inherited Disease, 8th ed. New York, McGraw-Hill, 2001. *An excellent compendium of metabolic disorders.*

39 THE INHERITED BASIS OF COMMON DISEASES

David Altshuler

A central question in medicine is to understand why some people get sick, and others do not. In some cases, a single environmental exposure plays a major role in disease risk (e.g., smoking and lung cancer, or HIV infection and AIDS). In others, such as Huntington's disease or cystic fibrosis, mutation of a single gene is necessary and can be sufficient to cause illness. In most cases, however, disease is attributable neither to a single dominant environmental factor nor to mutation of a single gene. Rather, most cases of disease result from the combined action of inborn and somatically acquired alterations in gene sequence, environmental factors, and bad luck. Such disorders are termed *complex traits*.

Decades of careful epidemiologic research have documented that most common diseases are complex traits, with a significant fraction of interindividual variation in disease risk explained by inheritance. For this reason, studies of DNA sequence variation hold a key to unlocking information about the pathways that are causally responsible for human diseases as they exist in the general population. Because the sequence of the *human genome* is now known, it is possible for the first time to envision systematic and comprehensive surveys of common human genetic variation and its potential association to disease risk. This chapter reviews the paired concepts of *heritability* (the inherited contribution to disease risk) and *heterozygosity* (the inherited variation in genome sequence) and how they can be combined to illuminate the genetic architecture of common disease.

Heritability: Inherited Variation in Disease Risk

Susceptibility to disease varies in the population. Studies of *familial aggregation* can determine the extent to which inheritance contributes to these patterns. These studies are simple in conception and ask whether members of the same family display more similar rates of disease than do individuals chosen at random from the population. When found, familial clustering can reflect not only shared genes, but also shared environment. The contribution of shared genotype can be dissected further by comparing rates of disease within families as a function of the extent of genetic relatedness. The cleanest such design involves the comparison of disease concordance among dizygotic compared with monozygotic twin pairs. For common diseases such as type I and II diabetes mellitus, obesity, hypertension, coronary artery disease, autoimmune diseases, common cancers, schizophrenia, and bipolar disease, twin studies have documented that rates of concordance are significantly higher in monozygotic compared with dizygotic twin pairs. For many other traits of clinical interest (e.g., most drug responses), formal tests of heritability have not yet been performed, and the role of inheritance in these characteristics is less clear.

Data about familial aggregation allow the calculation of *heritability*, the fraction of interindividual variability in disease risk attributable to additive genetic influences. The remaining variability among individuals is due to all other contributions: environmental influences on disease, nonadditive (*epistatic*) genetic effects (e.g., gene-gene interactions or gene-environmental interactions), error in the measurement of relatedness or disease, and random chance. For most clinically important traits (diseases and risk factors), empirical estimates of heritability range from 20 to 80% (see Online Mendelian Inheritance in Man, available at http://www.ncbi.nlm.nih.gov:80/entrez/query.fcgi?db=OMIM, for comprehensive information).

When interpreting estimates of heritability, it is important to consider two crucial factors: the effect of measurement errors and the

---

centromere. *Paracentric* inversions occur within one arm of the chromosome.

RING CHROMOSOMES. Ring chromosomes are relatively rare and frequently lost during mitosis so that individuals with a ring chromosome are often mosaic. The ring forms because of a deletion at both ends of the chromosome, and the sticky ends join together to form a ring. The phenotype of a ring chromosome usually is similar to a deletion.

DUPLICATIONS. Duplications occur when more than two copies of genetic material are present. Submicroscopic duplications also occur in some genetic disorders. Insertions occur when a piece of chromosome breaks, then is incorporated in another part of a chromosome. Duplications and deletions frequently occur during crossing over in meiosis. Small deletions and duplications may not be obvious but have been found increasingly among children with moderate-to-severe mental retardation and no obvious phenotypic features. FISH and multitelomeric probes are becoming available to look for these small chromosomal changes.

SEX CHROMOSOMAL ABNORMALITIES

TURNER SYNDROME. Turner syndrome is the most common monosomy in live-born infants. The chromosome findings in Turner syndrome involve loss of part or all of one of the sex chromosomes. Half of affected individuals have a 45,X karyotype in lymphocyte studies, suggesting that they do not have the other sex chromosome present in most cells. Careful studies in fibroblast and other tissues may reveal a Y chromosome, however, in some cells in 2 to 3% of individuals with Turner syndrome. The presence of Y-bearing cells is important because these individuals have an increased risk of malignant degeneration of their gonads or masculinization at puberty. Half of individuals with Turner syndrome have a variety of abnormalities of their other sex chromosome and may be mosaic. Turner syndrome occurs in about 1 in 4000 live-born females. The phenotype is almost always female, characterized by short stature and underdeveloped ovaries.

KLINEFELTER SYNDROME. Individuals with Klinefelter syndrome are males with one or more extra X chromosomes, usually 47,XXY. The phenotype is male; they are usually relatively tall, they may have gynecomastia, and they almost always have azoospermia and small testes. Secondary sex characteristics may be late, and many men benefit from testosterone therapy.

OTHER SYNDROMES WITH EXTRA X CHROMOSOMES. There are many syndromes described in which additional X chromosomes are observed. Males with an increasing number of X chromosomes are likely to be mentally retarded with radioulnar synostoses and genital anomalies. Women with 47,XXX, are usually phenotypically normal and fertile.

47,XYY MALE. The frequency of 47,XYY males is said to be about 1 in 1000 live births. Because XYY males do not have striking phenotype abnormalities, they often are not recognized, although they are said to be relatively tall and may have behavioral problems.

SUGGESTED READINGS

Am J Med Genet 2003;119C(1):1–86 [whole volume]. *A complete volume dedicated to the subject of congenital abnormalities.*

Gorlin RJ, Cohen MM, Hennekam RCM: Syndromes of the Head and Neck, 4th ed. New York, Oxford University Press, 2002. *The most comprehensive text available on summaries of syndromes of the head and neck.*

environmental context. *Measurement errors* can decrease the estimate of the heritability of a trait. A single measurement of blood pressure is much less heritable than a composite score based on serial measures of blood pressure over time. That is, day-to-day variability and imprecision in clinical measures can obscure an underlying biologic susceptibility that is entrained by inheritance. For the patient and physician, this means that although the blood pressure on a given day may not be particularly heritable, the blood pressure over time (which is the risk factor for vascular disease) is heritable to a much greater extent.

Second, estimates of heritability have meaning only in the context of the environment in which the study was performed. In the case in which environmental triggers of disease are relatively constant across a study population, inherited factors may explain much of the variation in rates of disease. In contrast, in the case in which exposure to environmental causes of disease is highly varied across the study population, nongenetic factors may outweigh the contribution of inborn susceptibility. The rate and diversity of smoking histories have a major impact on how much of the variability in rates of lung cancer (in any given study or patient cohort) may be explained by inheritance. It is impossible to interpret or extrapolate measures of heritability without considering the environmental context in which the study was performed and that of the patients' population of interest.

For these reasons, heritability is not a fixed characteristic of a disease, but an assessment of a given population, set of measurements, and the extent to which variability in genetic and environmental exposures explains disease risk. This explains the apparent (but nonexistent) contradiction between rates of disease being highly heritable (in a given population) and yet varying dramatically across populations separated by time, geography, or socioeconomic status. In broad comparisons across groups, environmental exposures and methods of clinical ascertainment can vary substantially and contribute to secular changes in patterns of disease. Conversely, within a group exposed to a relatively uniform environment and studied in a uniform manner, genetic susceptibility may play a major role in determining individual risk. *Heritability* expresses the patterns of inherited variation in rates of disease; its doppelganger is *heterozygosity,* the pattern of inherited variation in genome sequence.

Heterozygosity: Inherited Variation in Genome Sequence

To what extent is there variation in the individual copies of the human genome sequence that we each inherit from our parents (Table 39–1)? A traditional measure of genetic variation is *heterozygosity,* defined as the proportion of sites on the chromosome at which two randomly chosen copies differ in DNA sequence. Because cells are *diploid* (carry two copies of the genome sequence), and because these two copies were selected in a semirandom manner from the population, heterozygosity is also equivalent to the fraction of base pairs that vary between the two copies in each of our own cells. That is, heterozygosity is the rate of genetic variation in the individual.

Table 39–1 • CHARACTERISTICS OF HUMAN GENOME SEQUENCE VARIATION

Length of the human genome sequence (base pairs)	3,000,000,000
Number of human genes (estimated)	30,000
Fraction of base pairs that differ between the genome sequence of a human and a chimpanzee	1.3% (1:80)
Fraction of base pairs that vary between the genome sequence of any two humans	0.08% (1:1,250)
Fraction of coding region base pairs that vary in a manner that alters the sequence of the encoded protein	0.02% (1:5,000)
Number of sequence variants present in each individual as heterozygous sites	2,400,000
Number of amino acid–altering variants present in each individual as heterozygous sites	12,000
Number of sequence variants in the human population with a population frequency >1%	10,000,000
Number of amino acid polymorphisms present in the human genome with a population frequency >1%	75,000
Fraction of all human heterozygosity attributable to variants with frequency >1%	90%

There is limited heterozygosity in the human population. On average, less than 1 in 1200 positions in the human genome sequence vary between any two copies that are compared. In the coding regions of genes, rates of genetic variation are lower—less than 1 of every 2000 bases compared secondary to darwinian selection against changes that alter amino-acid sequence. These numbers are the same whether the two copies were sampled from a single geographic region or from groups whose ancestors lived in widely dispersed parts of the globe. The low rate of genetic diversity in the human population is quite unusual: Chimpanzees, gorillas, and orangutans, primates closely related to humans, have 3 to 10 times as much genetic variation as do humans.

Approximately 90% of the heterozygosity in the human population is due to single nucleotide polymorphisms (SNPs)—sites at which a single letter in the DNA code has been swapped for a single alternate letter. The remaining variation is due to insertions and deletions of nucleotides, variation in the number of copies of repeat sequences, and larger scale alterations.

Among the limited fraction of sites that are heterozygous in any individual, approximately 90% are due to sequence variants that are *common* in the population (see Table 39–1). In cases in which the two copies in a single person differ, it is exceedingly likely that both versions would be found at an appreciable frequency in the population at large; only 10% of heterozygous sites in each individual are due to variants that exist at a frequency less than 1% in the global human population. Because most human heterozygosity is due to common variants, it is possible to build catalogues that contain a substantial fraction of all human genetic diversity. A database containing all common (>1% frequency) sequence variants in the human population could be constructed by sequencing the genomes of only a few hundred individuals (drawn from all over the world) but would capture perhaps 90% of the heterozygous sites present in any individual on the planet.

Sparked by the human genome project, efforts have sought to create such catalogues of common variants in the human genome sequence. At the time of this writing, the public database of SNPs contains 2.6 million candidate SNPs in the human genome (http://www.ncbi.nlm.nih.gov:80/SNP/index.html), and when combined with SNP discovery efforts by private companies, more than 4.5 million SNPs have been discovered. The existing collection represents a substantial fraction of the 10 million or so common SNPs thought to exist in the entire human population, with more than half of human genetic variants that have a population frequency greater than 10%.

The preponderance of common variation is explained by the unique demographic history of the human population. Despite the global distribution of the current human population, it is now clear that all people on the planet are the descendants of a single population that lived in Africa only 10,000 to 40,000 years ago. The ancestral population was small (with an effective size of perhaps 10,000 individuals), lived a hunter-gatherer existence at low population densities (relative to other humans and later domesticated animals), and had evolved in Africa over millions of years. Most human genetic variation arose in this phase of human history, before the more recent migrations, expansions, and invention of technologies (e.g., farming) that resulted in widespread population of the globe. Most common human genetic variation predates the diaspora and is shared by all populations on earth.

The shared ancestry of human populations explains another aspect of human genetic variation: the correlations among nearby variants known as *linkage disequilibrium,* or *haplotypes.* Empirically, individuals who carry a particular variant at one site in the genome are much more likely than expected by chance to carry a particular set of variants at nearby positions along the chromosome. That is, not all combinations of nearby variants are observed in the population, but rather only a small subset of the possible combinations is observed. These correlations reflect the fact that most variants in our genomes arose once in human history (typically long ago) and did so on an arbitrary but unique copy carried by some individual in the population. The ancestral copy of the genome on which the mutation occurred can be recognized in the current population as a stretch of particular alleles (known as a *haplotype*) that track together in the population. That is, although most variations in our genomes arose before written human history, the DNA sequence in each of us carries a record of the evolution and demographic history of the human population.

Studies have shown that these ancestral haplotypes, passed down from shared prehistoric ancestors in Africa, can be recognized in the current human population and explain the bulk of heterozygosity in each human. The relatively simple (modular) haplotype structure of the human genome offers a practical advantage in association studies of human disease. These haplotypes are typically long (spanning, on average, the size of a typical gene) and carry multiple variants always coinherited in the population. It is possible to treat the haplotype (rather than the individual variant) as a unit for the purposes of association testing. This may reduce dramatically the number of variants that need to be typed to assess comprehensively common genetic variation across a region. Developing a public database of human haplotypes is the goal of the recently launched International Haplotype Map Project.

Monogenic and Polygenic Forms of Disease

With most diseases found to cluster in families, and given increasingly powerful information and tools to query human genetic variation, there is great interest in identifying genetic risk factors that contribute to common human diseases. The design of studies to find these variations—and the likely implementation of any discoveries in clinical practice—depends on the underlying *genetic architecture* of each disease.

The genetic architecture of a disease refers to the number and magnitude of genetic risk factors that exist in each patient and in the population and their frequencies and interactions. Diseases can be due to a single gene (*monogenic*) in each family or to multiple genes (*polygenic*). It is easiest to identify genetic risk factors when only a single gene is involved, and this gene has a major impact on disease. In cases in which a single gene is necessary and sufficient to cause disease, the condition is termed a *mendelian* disorder. This is because the disease tracks perfectly with a mutation (in the family) that obeys Mendel's simple laws of inheritance.

Some single-gene disorders are caused by the same gene in all affected families: For example, cystic fibrosis is always caused by mutations in *CFTR*. Alternatively, a mendelian disorder can be due to a single genetic lesion in any given family, but in different families can be due to mutations in a variety of genes. This phenomenon, termed *locus heterogeneity,* is illustrated by retinitis pigmentosa. Although mutation in a single gene is typically necessary and sufficient to cause retinitis pigmentosa, there are dozens of different genes in which retinitis pigmentosa mutations have been found (Online Mendelian Inheritance in Man #268000). In each family, however, only one such gene is mutated to cause disease.

Most single-gene disorders are rare (present in <1% of the population) and manifest early in life. Many are severe and cause death before reproduction in the absence of modern medical care. The fact that most monogenic disorders are severe in childhood and rare in the population is likely not a coincidence, but rather reflects the impact of *natural selection*. The deleterious effect of these mutations results in a decrease in reproductive fitness (in individuals unlucky enough to inherit them), and the mutations and the disease are unlikely to drift to high frequency in the population. There are exceptions to this general idea: cases in which the mutation causing a severe monogenic disease (such as *HbS*, the cause of sickle cell anemia, or the δ-508 mutation in *CFTR*) is common in the population at large. These cases appear as a result of a different kind of selection, known as *balancing selection*: situations in which a gene mutation is beneficial in one circumstance (a genotype or environment) but deleterious in another. It is believed that heterozygous carriers for *HbS* and δ-508 are relatively protected against infectious diseases and that this benefit balances the deleterious effect of the disease in homozygotes.

There has been spectacular success identifying the specific genetic mutations that cause mendelian disorders, with hundreds of genes identified for clinically important conditions (for comprehensive information, see http://www.ncbi.nlm.nih.gov:80/entrez/query.fcgi?db= OMIM). Progress was sparked by the development of a suite of powerful research techniques—*family-based linkage analysis* and *positional cloning*—in which the causal gene first is localized to a chromosomal region, then that chromosomal neighborhood is scoured for the genetic culprit. In most, but not all, cases, the causal mutations are rare in the population, with each family carrying a different and novel mutation that severely alters the function of the encoded protein. The bias toward low-frequency mutations that are relatively unique to each family argues for the role of natural selection against the disease-causing mutations.

Similar to mendelian disorders, most common diseases also are influenced by inheritance. In contrast to mendelian disorders, the genetic contribution to common diseases seems to be due to the action of many genes, rather than a single gene in each family and a limited number of genes in the population. Empirical evidence in favor of this model comes from efforts to use the same approach (positional cloning) for complex traits that was applied successfully to monogenic disorders. In the 1990s, the tools of family-based linkage analysis were applied to nearly all common disorders of the industrialized world. In many of these studies, dozens or hundreds of families were studied, and hundreds of genetic markers were typed in each individual. Despite this heroic effort and except for a few notable successes, these studies revealed few strong signals that localized the genes responsible for disease. In most of the dozens of such studies that have been published, there are many weak statistical signals (none statistically significant) and little agreement between different studies of the same disease.

Given the well-understood statistical power of family-based linkage methods (based on their extensive use for monogenic disorders) and their relatively limited success despite extensive efforts in common diseases, it is reasonable to conclude that no single gene explains a large fraction of risk of common diseases. If a single gene contained mutations that explained 30% of the inherited risk of type II diabetes, hypertension, or schizophrenia, it is extremely likely its location long since would have been found. Supporting this idea is the observation that the HLA, which explains approximately 50% of the genetic risk for type I diabetes, has been identified strongly in every linkage study performed to date in that disease. The fact that few such findings (outside the HLA) have been found for common diseases suggests that few single genetic risk factors (of this magnitude) are likely operative in complex traits. Rather the typical situation seems to be a larger number of susceptibility factors each of which more modestly contributes to disease.

Monogenic Forms of Common Diseases

One potential shortcut to understanding the genetic determinants of common diseases is to identify and study rare, early-onset forms of diseases that display mendelian patterns of inheritance. Because these diseases display mendelian patterns of inheritance, the powerful tools of positional cloning can be and have been employed successfully to identify the genes responsible. Important examples include the role of *BRCA1* and *BRCA2* in early-onset breast cancer, maturity-onset diabetes of the young as a form of type II diabetes, many monogenic disorders of blood pressure and electrolyte regulation, and early-onset Alzheimer's disease.

These successes are important because they provide diagnostic information for families burdened with severe, early-onset forms of disease, and because they provide insight into the underlying pathways responsible for disease. More than a dozen genes have been identified that, when mutated, cause rare, mendelian disorders of blood pressure and electrolyte regulation. So far, every one of these genes is active in the kidney, and most are involved in the renin-angiotensin-aldosterone pathway. This result is a spectacular confirmation of the central importance of the kidney in human blood pressure regulation and has suggested new therapeutic targets of substantial promise.

It had long been hoped that the genes identified as responsible for early-onset, monogenic forms of common diseases would contribute to the more common forms of disease in the population. In this scenario, severe mutations might cause early-onset forms, and more prevalent but subtle alterations in the same genes might contribute to common forms of disease. To date, convincing evidence in support of this hypothesis does not exist. Genes identified for the above-mentioned, early-onset diseases have not yet been shown to contribute more generally to the population risk of disease. The hypothesis remains viable, however, because comprehensive evaluation of the genetic variation at any given gene is only now becoming possible, owing to developments in knowledge from the human genome and improved methods for genetic epidemiologic analysis.

Models for the Genetic Architecture of Common Disease

Although there is little specific knowledge about the genes and mutations responsible for most common diseases, two broad classes of models have been proposed to explain the genetic architecture of common disorders. In the first class of model, common diseases are not a single, homogeneous entity, but rather composites of many different rare disorders. Each of these disorders may be caused by mutations in different genes, with the mutations having characteristics (of low frequency and large magnitude of effect) similar to that in traditional mendelian disorders. In this model, which is reminiscent of retinitis pigmentosa, the failure to achieve linkage (see earlier) is simply because the signal for any single gene is diluted by the large number of cases caused by mutations at other loci.

The second prominent model suggests that each case of disease is due to the combined influence of many different mutations and that disease ensues when the sum of susceptibility alleles outweighs the sum of alleles that are protective. In this scenario, many of these mutations must be common in the population because it is necessary for each case to inherit more than one such mutation, and the diseases are common in the population. In this model, the relative risk attributable to any single mutation would be modest because disease would result only when each variant was inherited in concert with other such changes.

Two models are based on different precedents: the former from human genetics and the latter from epidemiology. Beyond argument by analogy, however, it is possible to base these arguments on the foundation of well-understood evolutionary principles and hypotheses about the evolutionary history of common diseases. Because most human genetic variation arose—and evolution took place—before the more recent expansions in the population and invention of modern society, it is likely that the relevant epoch of human history is that of the small, prehistorical ancestral population, rather than the large, technologically advanced modern population.

If the disease (or other characteristic influenced by the genotype) had been neutral from the point of natural selection, the bulk of genetic variation contributing to the trait is expected to be common. If the mutations led to traits that were evolutionarily disadvantageous (even mildly so), the bulk of disease-causing variants would be largely rare (as in most monogenic diseases). Finally, if the sum of evolutionary effect of the disease-causing class of mutations was beneficial, the mutations likely will be more common than the genome-wide pattern.

One thing is certain: There will be no single answer, but rather examples of all such scenarios among the variety of common human diseases. It seems unlikely that mutations causing infertility would be found to be common in the population because the negative effect on reproduction is disadvantageous from an evolutionary perspective. In contrast, mutations that protected against infections or other major killers (e.g., famine or surviving the neonatal period) may well be common and could influence common diseases in the modern world. Mutations that cause a disease in the current environment may have had a different evolutionary impact in the environment in which humans evolved.

Association Studies

Despite this uncertainty, there has been limited progress identifying genes that contribute significantly to the population risk of common diseases. Nearly all examples have been discovered through epidemiologic association studies of common genetic variation. Genetic association studies are simple in conception. One or more putative causal variants are identified, and their frequency is compared between populations with the disease of interest and well-matched controls (drawn from the population at large or unaffected family members). Because association studies are a direct test of each allele, they offer the greatest sensitivity to detect the relationship between a variant and disease.

The *HLA* locus on chromosome 6 is likely the largest single determinant of susceptibility to common diseases, playing a major (if complex) role in infectious and autoimmune diseases. Other robust and reproducible associations include the contribution of Apoε4 to Alzheimer's disease, factor V^Leiden to deep venous thrombosis, a 32-base deletion in the chemokine receptor CCR5 to risk of AIDS, the insulin VNTR to type I diabetes, and the PPARγ Pro12Ala variant to risk of type 2 diabetes (Table 39–2). A comprehensive survey of all published genetic association studies showed that although many published associations have been nonreproducible (likely owing to inappropriate statistical thresholds for declaring or rejecting associations), true associations have been identified through this approach.

Table 39–2 • EXAMPLES OF INHERITED SEQUENCE VARIANTS THAT INFLUENCE COMMON, POLYGENIC HUMAN DISEASES

Apoε4	Alzheimer's disease
Factor V^Leiden	Deep venous thrombosis
HLA (many)	Autoimmunity (many)
Insulin VNTR	Type I diabetes
PPARγ Pro12Ala	Type II diabetes
CCR5 δ32	Protection against HIV infection
CTLA4 Thr17Ala	Graves' disease
TPMT	Response to thiopurine

Nearly all known genetic influences on common disease are, themselves, common in the population. It is much too early to conclude, however, whether this will be a general feature of the genetic basis of common disease. On the one hand, it is possible that the high frequency of the common diseases is a byproduct of their evolutionary history. In this scenario, many common variants would be found, with many individually rare alleles that contribute a fraction to the overall genetic influence on the disease. On the other hand, the preponderance of common mutations identified so far could reflect *ascertainment bias*. That is, it is possible that only a small subset of the mutations influencing common disease is common (with the rest being rare), but only those that are common could be found with the available information, tools, and methodologies. Only more data can resolve this question.

Challenges to the Identification of Genetic Factors for Common Diseases

Regardless of the specific model, it seems that common diseases are due to genetic effects that are modest: either highly heterogeneous across individuals (and modest in the population) or multiple and modest in each individual. Under the assumption of modest effects, nearly all studies to date have been drastically underpowered. The challenge of finding such genes is the large universe of candidates that might play a role in disease and the low probability that any particular gene and variant (tested in a study) actually is involved.

The low likelihood of finding a gene and variant that plays a role in disease requires that more stringent statistical thresholds be applied than is usually the case in epidemiologic research. This often is described as a problem of "multiple hypothesis testing," with the investigative community searching for associations between multiple genes, multiple variants in each gene, and multiple diseases. Given a large-scale and broad search, it becomes likely that a statistical fluctuation would be encountered (absent any true association), leading to the false interpretation of a relationship between the exposure and disease of interest.

This problem is illuminated most clearly in a Bayesian statistical framework. The human genome contains approximately 25,000 to 40,000 genes. Each of these genes harbors dozens of common variants, and many more changes that are rare. Absent any other knowledge of biology, each of these changes would have an equal (and exceedingly low) *a priori* likelihood of containing variation that confers risk of disease. Similar to the use of a screening test in a population that has a low rate of disease, the number of false-positive results is expected to outnumber true-positive results unless dramatically more stringent statistical thresholds are employed. It is possible to increase the prior probability by guessing about candidate genes based on hypotheses about gene function, but these studies are by their nature limited and prone to bias. These concerns are supported by the published association literature, in which perhaps only 5 to 10% of the many hundreds of published genetic associations are found to be reproducible on repeated testing.

The statistical challenges increase exponentially when gene-gene or gene-environment interactions are considered. Although it is clear that gene-gene and gene-environment interactions exist, there is a huge potential universe of gene-gene or gene-environment pairs, and the prior probability of any given pair explaining a large degree of disease risk is correspondingly small. In the absence of a strong prior hypothesis (e.g., a known biochemical or physical interaction between proteins) or an extremely impressive statistical result, associations of this nature are more likely to represent a false-positive result arising from aggressive dredging of data, rather than a biologically meaningful relationship to disease.

There is no simple, straightforward or general answer to these challenges. As in most rapidly evolving fields of medical research, individual clinicians need to have access to reliable guidance as to the interpretation of genetic studies and to extrapolate from the available literature to their own clinical practice.

Future Directions

Decades of epidemiology have shown that inherited factors contribute substantially to common human diseases. Progress in population genetics and genomics has revealed that most human heterozygosity is due to genetic variants that are common, old, and shared broadly across the planet. There is a narrow but deep universe of less common variation that arose more recently in human history. Genome-wide catalogues of human genetic variation are increasingly complete and offer an approach to testing the bulk of human heterozygosity for a contribution to disease.

The exact path to applying these tools is uncertain because the evolutionary history and the genetic architecture of common diseases have not yet been defined. It is likely, however, that in the years and decades to come the answers to these questions will come into much clearer focus. Over time, the tools of human genetics will help elucidate the pathways that cause common human diseases and, similar to the discovery of cholesterol and its association with vascular diseases, point toward the development of therapeutics of broad value to human health.

SUGGESTED READINGS

Lohmueller K, Pearce CL, Pike M, et al: Meta-analysis of genetic association studies supports a contribution of common variants to susceptibility to common disease. Nat Genet 2003;33:177–182. *Many common variants likely have modest but real effects.*

Risch NJ: Searching for genetic determinants in the new millennium. Nature 2000;405:847–856. *Strategies for approaching the hunt for polygenetic diseases.*

40 GENE THERAPY

Paul N. Reynolds
Akseli Hemminki
David T. Curiel

The Concept of Gene Therapy

Gene therapy is an experimental form of treatment whereby sequences of nucleic acids (i.e., genes) are delivered to cells to change their biologic function. The concept initially arose as replacement therapy for monogenic inherited disorders. For these disorders, the aim is to replace a defective gene with the normal counterpart. The delivered genetic material undergoes transcription and translation using the host cell's machinery, leading to in situ production of the normal protein and thereby correction of the phenotypic defect. The concept of gene therapy has since broadened from that of replacement to one of using genes as an indirect method for delivering a variety of therapeutic proteins. These proteins may be identical to the natural human protein, whereby therapy occurs via the magnitude and location of expression, or the delivered genes may be engineered to produce novel proteins with distinct therapeutic properties.

Delivering therapies as genes has several potential advantages over the use of proteins. Depending on the gene delivery technique used, long-term, sustained protein production can be achieved. For inherited disorders this would be ideal; gene delivery approaches that result in integration of the delivered genes into the host chromosomes can potentially result in lifelong correction. The prospect of such a therapy provided a powerful incentive during the early years of gene therapy development, although the achievement of this goal has been much harder than initially envisaged. Even strategies that do not lead to integration of the genes can result in a much longer therapeutic impact than delivery of the corresponding protein, especially for those that

are rapidly metabolized. In situ production of protein may also allow for tighter control of biodistribution than do standard administration techniques, allowing the use of potent agents too toxic to administer by conventional means. The nature of certain proteins precludes conventional delivery, including membrane-bound receptors or proteins confined to the intracellular compartment. Also, some soluble proteins may be difficult and expensive to produce using standard pharmaceutic techniques. Nucleic acids thus offer cheaper production alternatives and are also more stable than proteins, thereby cutting costs relating to storage and shipment (having implications for developing countries, especially for the use of DNA-based vaccines). In view of these potential advantages, gene-based therapies have been proposed for virtually the whole spectrum of serious human disease. At this time, given the experimental nature of the approach, the major efforts are devoted to conditions for which conventional therapies are nonexistent or poorly efficacious.

The Clinical Spectrum

The first human trials of gene therapy began in 1989. The U.S. Recombinant DNA Advisory Committee (RAC), the principal review authority for U.S. federally funded recombinant DNA trials, lists 484 trials at various stages (Fig. 40–1). The U.S. Food and Drug Administration gives final approval of U.S. trials. Approximately 700 gene therapy trials have been presented to regulatory authorities worldwide. Thirty-nine of the RAC-listed trials used gene delivery as a cell-marking strategy (e.g., in bone marrow transplantation), and two are listed as "nontherapeutic" (using normal volunteers). The remaining 443 trials have some ultimate therapeutic intent. The majority of these trials are for cancer. More than 60% (189 of 303) of these

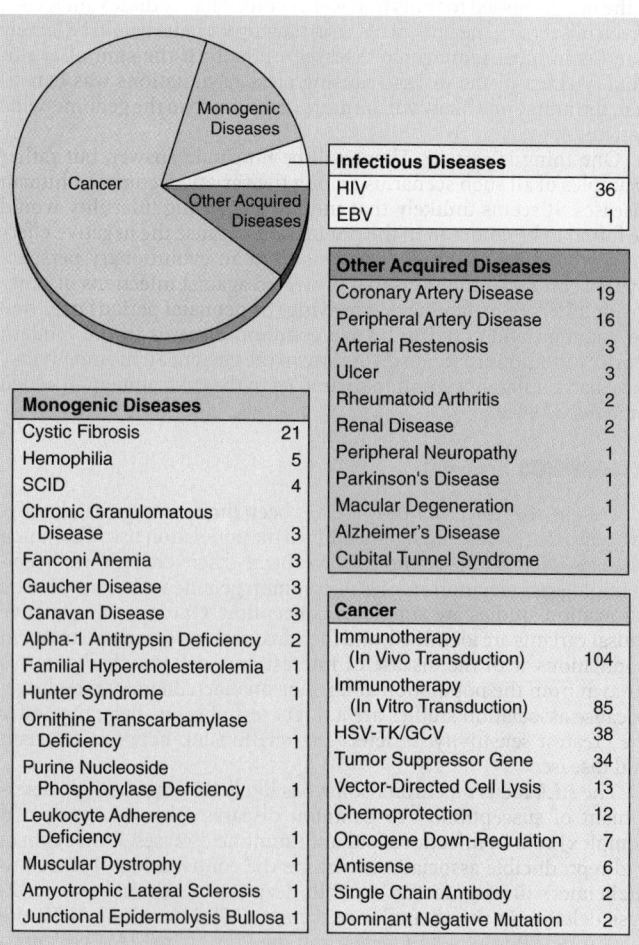

Monogenic Diseases	
Cystic Fibrosis	21
Hemophilia	5
SCID	4
Chronic Granulomatous Disease	3
Fanconi Anemia	3
Gaucher Disease	3
Canavan Disease	3
Alpha-1 Antitrypsin Deficiency	2
Familial Hypercholesterolemia	1
Hunter Syndrome	1
Ornithine Transcarbamylase Deficiency	1
Purine Nucleoside Phosphorylase Deficiency	1
Leukocyte Adherence Deficiency	1
Muscular Dystrophy	1
Amyotrophic Lateral Sclerosis	1
Junctional Epidermolysis Bullosa	1

Infectious Diseases	
HIV	36
EBV	1

Other Acquired Diseases	
Coronary Artery Disease	19
Peripheral Artery Disease	16
Arterial Restenosis	3
Ulcer	3
Rheumatoid Arthritis	2
Renal Disease	2
Peripheral Neuropathy	1
Parkinson's Disease	1
Macular Degeneration	1
Alzheimer's Disease	1
Cubital Tunnel Syndrome	1

Cancer	
Immunotherapy (In Vivo Transduction)	104
Immunotherapy (In Vitro Transduction)	85
HSV-TK/GCV	38
Tumor Suppressor Gene	34
Vector-Directed Cell Lysis	13
Chemoprotection	12
Oncogene Down-Regulation	7
Antisense	6
Single Chain Antibody	2
Dominant Negative Mutation	2

FIGURE 40–1 • The spectrum of clinical gene therapy trials. All therapeutic trial applications presented to the Recombinant DNA Advisory Committee (RAC) since 1989 are shown, along with the number of applications by disease type, or for cancer trials by therapeutic strategy. (From http://www4.od.nih.gov/oba/rac/aboutrdagt.htm)

use gene delivery to enhance antitumor immunity (including 42 of 60 cancer trials during 2000-2001). Fifty-two trials are for monogenic disease (with 21 for cystic fibrosis, 5 for hemophilia), 37 for infectious disease (all but one for human immunodeficiency virus [HIV] and acquired immunodeficiency syndrome [AIDS]), 22 for coronary artery disease, and 16 for peripheral artery disease, with a broad spectrum of conditions comprising the remainder. Most trials are phase I (304), designed to assess safety rather than efficacy. Fifty-nine trials are phase I-II and 58 are phase II, where there is intent to get efficacy data. Only four trials, all in cancer patients, are listed as phase III (i.e., a controlled comparison of gene therapy, sometimes with conventional therapy vs. conventional therapy alone), and only one of these trials involves previously untreated patients. These data are a reflection of gene therapy trials since 1990 and may not include all trials conducted by non–federally funded institutions, but the spectrum is representative. A problem with many of the early trials is that little information was gained about the efficiency of gene delivery. Newer trials, even those designated as phase I, now typically aim to obtain some information about the efficacy of gene transfer. This new emphasis is in recognition of the fact that the main impediment to progress is inefficiency of gene delivery, per se, rather than a lack of potentially therapeutic genes. At present no gene therapy approach has entered standard clinical practice. Nevertheless, a limited number of settings have seen early efficacy. Strategies for inherited immunodeficiency disease, hemophilia, and ischemic vascular disease are the closest to being incorporated into mainstream therapeutics.

Gene Delivery Strategies

THE EXPRESSION CASSETTE

Genes are delivered into cells as engineered expression cassettes. Cassettes are a stretch of nucleic acid comprised of a promoter region, the gene itself, followed by a polyA sequence. The promoter region controls attachment of cellular transcription machinery. The gene is typically a complementary DNA (cDNA) sequence containing only those nucleic acids coding for protein and lacking the intron regions found in most natural genes. The polyA sequence directs the addition of multiple adenosine residues onto the end of the transcribed RNA. As for natural genes, the polyA sequence promotes transport of the RNA to the cytoplasm, enhances stability, and promotes translation. Use of cDNA rather than natural, intron-containing genes dramatically shortens the length of the nucleic acid sequence required, improving manipulation and delivery. The delivered genes are typically referred to as transgenes. The promoter region determines control of gene expression. Most often, strong, constitutively active promoters are used to maximize expression levels. Examples of such promoters are the cytomegalovirus (CMV) immediate early and Rous sarcoma virus (RSV) promoters. These sequences are conveniently short and drive expression in most human cells. However, cell-specific promoters are increasingly being used. These sequences are derived from the upstream regions of naturally occurring genes known to be active in the target cell. For example, vascular endothelial growth factor (VEGF) receptors are expressed in endothelial cells; thus, the promoter for VEGF receptors can be placed upstream of a transgene of interest to restrict expression to endothelium, even if other cells take up the delivered DNA. In practice, the degree of specificity is not absolute, and promoters vary widely in their fidelity when placed in expression cassettes. Thus, promoters can be artificially engineered by sequence manipulation to improve specificity, strength, and duration of expression. Promoter systems have also been developed that can be switched on or off with drugs (e.g., the tetracycline responsive system). Some promoter elements respond to physical stresses (such as hypoxia or temperature) rather than being restricted by cell type. These latter developments are mostly at the preclinical stage.

THE DELIVERY VECTOR

Once a rational expression cassette has been determined, a strategy is designed to deliver the nucleic acids into the target cell. This requires a delivery device or "vector." In practice, the efficient, safe delivery of genes is the major obstacle to clinical gene therapy. The simplest vectors are those in which the expression cassette is incorporated into a circular, double-stranded piece of DNA, a plasmid, which is then amplified by bacterial culture. Plasmids alone (after

being purified from the bacteria, and sometimes referred to as "naked DNA") are taken up by cells. However, the use of naked DNA approaches is inefficient for many applications. Although this technique is generally safe, recent data show that certain motifs contained within the bacterially derived plasmid backbone (CpG motifs) incite an inflammatory response. Thus, newer agents are engineered to remove these sequences.

To improve the efficacy of cellular uptake, plasmid DNA may be incorporated into various chemical formulations, typically comprising a combination of various cationic lipids, which fall under the generic term of nonviral vectors. Positively charged lipids spontaneously form complexes (lipoplexes) with negatively charged plasmid DNA and then interact with the cell surface, which is normally negatively charged. The cationic lipid then fuses with the cell membrane, allowing the cytoplasmic release of the plasmid DNA. Polycationic polymers (e.g., polylysine) have also been used to deliver DNA (in which case the complexes are termed polyplexes). Although improvements in efficiency over naked DNA are achieved by these techniques, efficacy remains low. As for naked DNA, in the current form, nonviral approaches may be best suited for delivery of genes for highly potent, secreted proteins or as a basis for DNA vaccines. One of the key limitations of nonviral delivery approaches relates to intracellular trafficking. Most of the DNA that enters the cell is unable to reach the nucleus as a result of sequestration into endosomes and eventual degradation.

The use of viruses to deliver transgenes (called viral vectors) is also under development. This strategy exploits the capacity of viruses to enter (infect) cells and deliver viral genes to the cell nucleus as part of their natural life cycle. The construction of viral vectors is based on the manipulation of their genomes to remove genes essential for viral replication (thereby preventing death of the infected cell and spread of infectious virus) and replacing these genes with the transgene expression cassette. The merits of basic viral vectors thus stem from the properties of the wild-type viruses from which they are derived. This includes the natural tropism of the virus for various cell types depending on the level of expression of the appropriate viral receptors (note that these are normal cellular membrane components to which the virus is evolutionarily adapted to use). However, considerable efforts are being made to modify viral vectors so that they infect via cell-specific markers rather than natural viral receptors. Most viral vector work has involved retroviruses, adenoviruses, adeno-associated viruses (AAVs), herpesviruses, and lentiviruses (HIV based).

RETROVIRAL VECTORS. Retroviral vectors for gene therapy are typically based on the Moloney murine leukemia virus (Mo-MLV). These viruses can carry transgenes of up to 8 kilobases (kb) in length. Generally, the envelope protein of these vectors are modified from the wild-type virus by replacing the Mo-MLV protein with that of either amphotropic virus 4070A or vesicular-stomatitis virus glycoprotein (VSVG), which greatly broadens the range of cells that can be infected. After infection, linear, double-stranded DNA is generated from the RNA viral genome by the viral enzyme reverse transcriptase. The viral DNA then forms a preintegration complex that migrates to the cell nucleus—but can enter only when the nuclear membrane breaks down during mitosis. Thus, retroviral vectors are only capable of transducing dividing cells. If the DNA does reach the nucleus, integration of the viral genome into the host cell chromosome can occur, leading to stable, long-term transgene expression. Therefore, if long-term correction of a genetic disorder is required, the target cells must first be induced to replicate. The integration is a random event, so there is some concern that disruption of normal cell function (including the activation of oncogenes) could occur. On the other hand, the selectivity for dividing cells is advantageous if one is aiming to deliver a toxin gene to a growing tumor surrounded by quiescent normal parenchyma.

Retroviral vectors have been particularly suited to ex vivo gene therapy approaches. These approaches involve the removal of cells from the body (e.g., bone marrow), followed by gene delivery to the cells in the laboratory, then return of the modified cells to the patient. Trials of this nature were the first human clinical trials conducted. Newer agents are now being used for direct in vivo administration. Efforts have been made to impart specific targeting properties to these vectors by incorporating cell-specific ligands or antibody fragments into the protein coat. A recent innovation has been to target retroviruses to the milieu of damaged vessels or tumor vasculature by directing attachment to exposed elements of extracellular matrix. The proximity of the viruses to tumor cells facilitates infection and has been shown to have therapeutic benefit in animal models.

ADENOVIRAL VECTORS. Adenoviral vectors (mostly based on serotype 2 and 5 viruses) are the most commonly used viral agent in clinical trials. These agents can transduce both dividing and nondividing cells; however, they do not achieve integration of the transgene, so expression is transient. They contain a double-stranded DNA genome and can carry transgenes of up to 10 kb. They are stable on systemic administration and have achieved the highest efficiencies of transduction in vivo compared to other vectors. Their short-term expression profile makes them more suited to the treatment of malignancy or acquired disease rather than inherited disorders. Furthermore, the induction of antiadenoviral antibodies generally makes readministration difficult. Nevertheless, these agents have been evaluated in a wide variety of early trials for genetic diseases, including cystic fibrosis. The natural cellular receptor for adenovirus is the Coxsackie and adenovirus receptor (CAR), a member of the immunoglobulin superfamily, which appears to have a role in cell-cell adhesion. The ability of adenovirus to infect many tissues including tumors is dependent on CAR expression. The virus has a natural tropism for the liver that relates to many factors, including the fenestrations of hepatic sinusoids and high CAR expression in hepatocytes (although non-CAR factors are also involved). Short-term transgene expression from adenoviral vectors is not only due to the lack of integration of the transgene but also because early-generation adenoviral vectors contain many natural viral genes that are expressed at low levels and lead to a T-cell-mediated immune response with loss of the transduced cells. Expression from adenoviral vectors can be greatly prolonged (≥2 years in some models) by replacing native viral genes in the vector with "stuffer" DNA (so-called gutless vectors, which also enlarge capacity to carry transgenes). Despite these improvements, there is an issue with direct toxicity of the viral particles and the innate immune response. The only vector-related death in gene therapy trials to date occurred acutely following infusion of a high dose of adenovirus into the hepatic artery. Efforts to improve the cell specificity, safety, and efficacy of adenoviral vectors are being made by imparting targeting properties to the vector. These strategies involve genetic modification of the capsid proteins or the use of separate adapter molecules to attach cell-specific ligands and thereby avoid the virus's reliance on CAR. This is especially relevant for tumor therapy, because most tumors tend to have low CAR levels. More efficient vectors should allow for a reduction in the necessary dose, thus reducing direct, vector-related toxicity. Targeting approaches have been shown to achieve substantial improvements in the efficacy and specificity of infection in preclinical animal models.

ADENO-ASSOCIATED VIRUS. Adeno-associated virus (AAV) is a small, single-stranded DNA, nonpathogenic virus. Viral replication requires coinfection with a helper virus—typically adenovirus, but others, including herpes, can provide this function. The advantages of AAV are its lack of toxicity and ability to achieve long-term transgene expression. For this reason applications have focused on inherited disease. AAV vectors contain no native viral genes, just the inverted terminal repeats and the transgene cassette. Although wild-type virus integrates into a specific site in chromosome 19 of the host cell (in the absence of adenoviral helper), AAV vectors appear to achieve long-term expression most often as a persistent episomal form rather than transgene integration, although this can occur. The principal disadvantage of the vector is the small amount of room for inserting the expression cassette, which is approximately 4 kb. The virus infects cells via attachment to heparan sulfates and fibroblast growth factor (FGF) receptors. A recent discovery found that the single-stranded genome of AAV could lead to abnormal "DNA repair" attempts in certain tumor cells, leading to apoptosis. This discovery may lead to broader application of AAV for cancer gene therapy.

HERPESVIRUS VECTORS. Herpesvirus vectors are large, double-stranded DNA viruses. Up to 44 kb of the virus's 152-kb genome can be removed and replaced with expression cassettes, often several in the one vector. These viruses have natural tropism for neuronal tissue, and clinical application has focused principally on their use in treating brain tumors and neurodegenerative disease.

LENTIVIRAL VECTORS. Lentiviral vectors are retroviral vectors based on modifications of the HIV. Typically, they are enveloped using the VSVG. Thus, the repertoire of cells they infect is similar to that of standard retroviral vectors. However, a major advantage is that they can transduce and achieve transgene integration into nondividing cells. During production, only certain HIV components and helper

functions are used to avoid the possibility of recombination and generation of wild-type HIV. These agents may be ideal for the treatment of inherited disorders, but safety issues are still being evaluated and none have yet entered into clinical trials.

OTHERS. The development of new gene delivery strategies is a rapidly expanding field. In addition to the viruses mentioned, others such as polio, Semliki Forest virus, and Sindbis virus are at various stages of preclinical development. Vaccinia has been used in immunomodulary/DNA vaccine strategies. The use of cells is being considered for gene delivery. A clinical trial has been proposed using *Salmonella* bacteria for cancer therapy. The use of various genetically modified human cells as "cell vehicles" is being developed as a distinct endeavor from ex vivo correction of genetic defects in hematopoietic cells.

Selected Disease Applications

SEVERE COMBINED IMMUNODEFICIENCY

Severe combined immunodeficiency (SCID) resulting from adenosine deaminase (ADA) deficiency was the first disease in which gene therapy was attempted. An ex vivo, retroviral approach delivered the *ADA* gene to autologous T cells of two patients. A major limitation was the inefficiency of the gene transfer technology, although the patients' requirements for ADA enzyme replacement therapy were reduced after the gene transfer. More recently, the application of ex vivo gene therapy for a different form of SCID (X-linked [SCID-XI]) has been heralded as the first unequivocal success for gene therapy. Fischer and colleagues used a highly optimized ex vivo approach to achieve efficient transduction of autologous hematopoietic stem cells from several infants using a retroviral vector to deliver the gene for the common cytokine receptor γc-chain (which is mutated in SCID-XI). These patients remained well and off treatment 2 years after therapy. Efficient transduction, plus a selective advantage conferred by the delivered gene, contributed to the success. However, concerns remain that viral integration could lead to activation of oncogenes. Such an occurrence has led to the development of T-cell leukemia in one clinical trial for SCID where a retroviral vector inserted in the *LM02* gene linked to T-cell leukemia.

CYSTIC FIBROSIS

The discovery of the mutated gene in cystic fibrosis, the gene for a chloride channel (the cystic fibrosis transmembrane regulator) in conjunction with the beginnings of clinical gene therapy research, led to expectations during the 1990s that a cure would be developed. This has been much more difficult to implement than hoped. Despite the fact that genetic correction of only 5% of airway epithelium could correct the net chloride transport abnormality, even this seemingly modest goal has been beyond current gene delivery techniques in human trials. Airway epithelium lacks accessible CAR and receptors for AAV. Newer approaches, combining viral vectors and nonviral vectors, show some promise in animal models, but whether these approaches will be of any benefit in the infected airways of patients with established cystic fibrosis is uncertain.

HEMOPHILIA

The relationships between clinical hemophilia A and B and the responsible genes (for factors VIII and IX, respectively) are well understood. Factor levels of 5 to 10% of normal are sufficient to prevent spontaneous hemorrhages and do not need to be tightly regulated. Treatment is helped by the fact that clotting factors are secreted; thus, the nature of the transduced cell is not critical. In vivo gene delivery to liver and skeletal muscle cells has been used. In view of the need for long-term correction, recent trials focus on the use of AAV and gutless adenoviral vectors. Early evidence of clinical efficacy is emerging; nevertheless, there remains a concern that patients will develop antifactor antibodies (as seen when the factors themselves are given), which may undermine therapy.

MYOCARDIAL AND PERIPHERAL ISCHEMIA

In the setting of inoperable ischemia, gene therapy is being used to stimulate the growth of new vessels (angiogenesis) into myocardium or limbs. Genes for angiogenic factors such as VEGF and FGF have been delivered by direct injection of either naked plasmid DNA or adenoviral vectors. These strategies are facilitated by the high potency and secreted nature of the factors delivered, which means that highly efficient transduction is not necessary. Phase I-II studies have been conducted, with some evidence of efficacy based on improvements in exercise tolerance. Other gene therapy applications for vascular disease include the delivery of genes having antiproliferative effects in the settings of angioplasty restenosis and in vein grafts and to promote endothelialization of artificial grafts.

HIV INFECTION AND AIDS

Despite advances in antiretroviral therapy, many patients progress to AIDS. Thus, there is a rationale for considering a gene-based approach, and several trials have been presented to the RAC, including a DNA vaccine approach using the HIV-1 IIIB glycoprotein as the antigen. Owing to the rapid antigenic shift of the HIV, it has been extremely difficult to generate protective antibodies that prevent infection of an exposed individual. However, the generation of cell-mediated immunity, which, while not preventing infection, will dramatically lower viral load (and consequently the risk of further transmission), appears feasible with current technology. Other approaches seek to directly attack the viral DNA via the delivery of antisense oligonucleotides or ribozymes, or to reconstitute the CD4 cell population with cells genetically manipulated ex vivo.

CANCER

In view of the paucity of effective therapies for many common malignancies, novel treatments are continually being sought. For this reason, as well as the large number of patients willing to be involved in trial, cancer has emerged as the most common clinical application of gene therapy. Several gene-based strategies have been applied, with all seeking to achieve amplification of therapeutic impact beyond the initially transduced cells.

GENETIC IMMUNOMODULATION. It is clear that tumors contain mutations that not only lead to dysregulated cell growth but also lead to the expression of cellular proteins that differ from their counterparts in normal tissues and thus can be recognized by the immune system as foreign antigens. The reason tumors are not ordinarily eliminated by the immune system, despite the presence of these antigens, is both unclear and likely multifactorial; an entire field of cancer immunotherapy has evolved based on the development of strategies to solve this problem. Many gene-based approaches have now been incorporated into this field. As with gene therapy for other acquired diseases, the rationale for their use here relates to overcoming the limitations of protein-based approaches: issues of duration of expression, localization of product, systemic toxicity, and often technical limitations in the pharmaceutic production of the relevant protein, per se. Strategies involve the delivery of genes encoding tumor-specific antigens, immunostimulatory cytokines, or a combination thereof. In vivo and ex vivo approaches have been tried, in the latter case via manipulation of T lymphocytes (to promote killing efficacy) or tumor cells (to improve antigenicity). The attraction of a strategy that has the theoretical capacity for systemic efficacy is clear, especially when most cancer deaths are due to disseminated disease. Although clinical efficacy has been limited, a small number of dramatic responses have provided encouragement.

MUTATION COMPENSATION. Cancers arise following a series of acquired genetic mutations leading to dysregulated cell growth. Such mutations may lead to the activation of an oncogene or the inactivation of an antioncogene (tumor suppressor gene). Thus, direct genetic correction, analogous to the situation for monogenic inherited disorders, has been proposed. However, because the goal is to kill the cell rather than achieve "normality," complete correction of all mutations within the cell is not needed. It has been established that correction of only one key defect (e.g., via delivery of a normal tumor suppressor gene to replace the function of its mutated counterpart) can be enough to induce cell death. Furthermore, in several cases this strategy has been shown to achieve a "bystander effect" beyond the initially transduced cell. The delivery of tumor suppressor genes is now the second most common cancer gene therapy. Most of these trials involve delivery of the *P53* tumor suppressor gene, which is mutated in many tumors. Aside from inducing cell growth arrest and apoptosis of the transduced cell, *P53* gene delivery is associated with an antiangiogenesis effect and may inhibit the antiapoptosis effect of insulin-like growth factor 1. Local inflammation induced by the vector

agents themselves may add to the therapeutic effect via immune stimulation. Thus, the effects of tumor suppressor gene therapy extend beyond the initial hypothesis in complex and often ill-defined manners. Despite these bystander effects, however, clinical trials of tumor suppressor genes have had disappointing efficacy, albeit with minimal toxicity. The basic issue of gene delivery efficiency remains a significant problem.

MOLECULAR CHEMOTHERAPY. In molecular chemotherapy the rationale is to achieve tumor expression of enzymes that convert nontoxic systemically administered prodrugs into their toxic counterparts, to achieve high tumor concentrations while avoiding systemic side effects. An example is herpes simplex virus type I thymidine kinase (HSV-TK), which catalyzes the phosphorylation of the relatively nontoxic prodrug ganciclovir (GCV). GCV-triphosphate incorporates into DNA, interferes with polymerases, and leads to cell death. GCV-triphosphate can spread from the transduced cells to adjacent cells via gap junctions and confer a bystander effect. Other prodrug-converting systems include bacterial cytosine deaminase (CD, which converts 5-flurocytidine to the chemotherapeutic and radiosensitizing agent 5-fluorouracil), carboxypeptidase G2, purine nucleoside phosphorylase, and nitroreductase. Enzymes of human origin include deoxycytidine kinase and cytochrome P450.

A limitation of molecular chemotherapy is the promiscuity of the vector systems used. Although the mechanism of action of the HSV-TK system was postulated to limit toxicity to replicating cells, this has not proven to be the case in preclinical studies. Significant morbidity and mortality were seen in animal models due to the transduction of normal hepatocytes by adenoviral vectors, followed by TK/GCV toxicity. This is especially concerning given the natural tropism of adenoviral vectors for the liver. Human trials of HSV-TK have been conducted using direct injection of adenoviral vectors to tumors. Even in this setting, mild elevations of hepatic transaminases have been noted, presumably owing to escape of the vector from the injection site and localization to the liver. Conversely, the efficiency of gene delivery by direct injection to tumor cells has been poor. Combination approaches with radiation therapy and chemotherapy are being pursued. Strategies to develop more efficient, tumor-specific vectors (including the use of tumor-specific promoters that have low activity in the liver) are being pursued, as are strategies to improve the efficacy of the bystander effect (e.g., by increasing gap junctions) and to improve transduction by targeting and infectivity enhancement. Preclinical studies using transductional or transcriptional targeting approaches have been shown to reduce HSV-TK/GCV hepatic toxicity while maintaining good antitumor effects.

ANTIANGIOGENESIS. Tumor growth relies on the development of new blood vessels; thus, efforts are being directed toward strategies to inhibit tumor angiogenesis. Key aspects differentiate this approach from the direct killing of cancer cells, per se. One is the amplification effect; that is, the destruction of a defined number of vascular cells leads to the death of many more tumor cells by ischemia. The other is that the cells being directly attacked (i.e., the vessel cells) are not themselves malignant and therefore have a much lower capacity for mutation and subsequent development of resistance to therapy than tumor cells. Pharmacologic agents with specific antiangiogenic properties, including endostatin and angiostatin, have been developed and shown to have efficacy in animal models. These agents are currently being evaluated in human trials. Delivering the genes for these antiangiogenic agents, as well as others such as soluble "dominant negative" VEGF receptors (which compete with natural receptors on tumor vessels for VEGF), has been shown to have efficacy in animal models but has not yet progressed to clinical trial. Gene-based approaches may help to circumvent production difficulties of antiangiogenic factors as well as achieve high local concentrations of these agents at the tumor site.

CHEMOPROTECTION. Difficulties in the use of conventional cytotoxic chemotherapy agents relate not just to limited efficacy in tumor cells but to toxicity in normal tissues, especially the bone marrow. Efforts have been made to improve the therapeutic window for chemotherapy agents by delivering protective genes (such as the multidrug resistance gene, *MDR*) to bone marrow cells ex vivo, then reinfusing the cells. To date this strategy has been limited by the low level of efficiency of transduction of the marrow cells. Thus, improvements in vector design are necessary.

REPLICATION-COMPETENT VIRUSES ("VIROTHERAPY"). The observation that cancer gene therapy is limited by poor gene delivery efficacy to tumors and inadequate bystander effects has lead to a re-emergence of the concept of using viruses, per se, as therapeutic agents, and several phase I-II studies have been conducted. Although different approaches are being taken, the studies to date share a common theme—the manipulation (or attenuation) of viruses to limit replication and toxicity to tumor cells and avoid toxicity to normal cells, or alternatively, to seek natural viruses that already possess such a differential. With regard to natural viruses, agents proposed include reovirus, Newcastle disease virus, vesicular stomatitis virus, and autonomous parvovirus. The basis for the selectivity of these agents varies but relies on defects in cell-cycle regulation in tumor versus normal cells, for example, aberrant interferon/*RAS/PKR* pathway signaling, regularly seen in tumors. However, these associations need to be clarified.

Several strategies to engineer tumor-selective oncolytic viruses have been evaluated. One general approach relies on the deletion of viral genes or parts of genes that are ordinarily required for replication in normal cells but are dispensable for replication in tumors because of their disordered cell cycle. The first demonstration of utility with this approach was seen with herpesvirus. A multimutated virus with deletions in the ribonucleotide reductase gene and/or neurovirulence gene showed selective replication in tumor versus normal cells in preclinical studies. These agents have entered phases I and II studies for glioblastoma multiforme or colorectal cancer.

Most replicative approaches under evaluation involve adenoviruses. A key requirement for adenoviruses to replicate is the inactivation of *P53*, a feat accomplished by the product of the viral *E1B-55kd* gene. In the absence of this gene, the actions of *P53* lead to apoptosis of the cell and thus prevent efficient replication and spread. However, because *P53* is either mutated or functionally deficient (due to mutations in associated genes) in many tumors, viral inactivation of *P53* is not required, and thus a virus with an *E1B-55kd* deletion (Ad*dl*1520) can selectively replicate in these tumor cells (although other mechanisms may also be involved). Other strategies based on mutations in the E1 region include mutations that block the normal viral inhibition of the RB pathway (thus limiting replication to cancer cells in which the RB pathway is disordered). This virus, AdΔ24, is currently in preclinical development. An alternate strategy to the mutation approach is to place the expression of genes essential for viral replication under the control of tumor-specific promoters. Thus, for example, a virus in which the essential *E1* gene is controlled by the prostate-specific antigen (PSA) promoter should replicate only in prostate and prostate tumor cells. This approach, and one using the osteocalcin promoter (for both prostate cancer and osteosarcoma), are in phase I-II trial.

The progression of replicative agents to clinical trial has been rapid, with most investigations involving Ad*dl*1520. Applications include squamous cell carcinoma of the head and neck (SCCHN), ovarian, pancreatic, and colorectal tumors. Virus has been administered by direct tumor injection, intraperitoneally, via the hepatic artery and peripheral vein. More than 200 patients have received this agent. Toxicities were mild, including fevers and flulike symptoms predominantly following vascular administration. However, clinical efficacy has been disappointing, limited to partial responses after repeated injection of SCCHN tumors. There was no correlation between circulating antiadenovirus antibody levels and response in this study, although the impact in the vascular administration studies has not been adequately determined. Barriers to effective oncolysis include areas of fibrosis and necrosis within tumors, lack of CAR, and ultimately limitation by the host immune system.

New clinical protocols combining replicative agents with chemotherapy and radiation therapy are being developed. Other strategies include manipulation of the adenovirus genome to incorporate toxin genes and tropism modification to improve tumor infection. A difficulty in the development of replicative viral agents is the lack of good animal models to address safety and efficacy. For most studies, preclinical evaluation is conducted in mice. However, adenovirus does not replicate efficiently in normal mouse tissues. Thus, it is not possible to determine the true specificity of replication. Furthermore, tumor studies are conducted using human tumor xenografts in immunocompromised mice, largely precluding assessment of the impact of the immune system on viral oncolysis. Assays to quantify viral replication in vivo also need further development.

Future Directions

The development of gene therapy began in the early 1990s with considerable publicity, high expectations, and rapid attempts to achieve clinical translation. These efforts largely failed due to an underappreciation of the basic science complexities involved. The last 5 to 7 years has seen a significant maturation of the science, most notably with respect to the issues of efficiency of gene delivery and vector design. Modulation of host immune responses, particularly against viral agents, remains a concern. However, meaningful clinical results are now being achieved, and in a few selected areas (SCID, hemophilia, ischemia, vaccines, and cancer therapy with replicative agents) gene-based medicines may enter mainstream therapeutics within the next 5 years. Nevertheless, further developments are required before gene therapy reaches its full potential.

SUGGESTED READINGS
Bloomberg P, Smith CE: Gene therapy of monogenic and cardiovascular disorders. Expert Opin Biol Ther 2003;3:941–949. *Review of disorders for which gene therapy is an option and has been attempted, with a discussion of existing vector systems, including their advantages and drawbacks.*
Cavazzana-Calvo M, Hacein-Bey S, de Saint Basile G, et al: Gene therapy of human severe combined immunodeficiency (SCID)-X1 disease. Science 2000;288:669–672. *Key milestone in the successful therapeutic application of gene therapy.*
Kay MA, Glorioso JC, Naldini L: Viral vectors for gene therapy: The art of turning infectious agents into vehicles of therapeutics. Nat Med 2001;7:33–40. *Review of vector strategies.*
Koehler DR, Hitt MM, Hu J: Challenges and strategies for cystic fibrosis lung gene therapy. Mol Ther 2001;4:84–91. *Review of cystic fibrosis gene therapy, one of the earliest hopes, yet most difficult challenges, for this treatment.*

part VII

Principles of Immunology and Inflammation

41 THE INNATE AND ADAPTIVE IMMUNE SYSTEMS

Jörg J. Goronzy
Cornelia M. Weyand

GENERAL PRINCIPLES OF THE IMMUNE SYSTEM

The immune system has evolved as a complex network of molecules, cells, and organs to defend against pathogenic microorganisms and noninfectious foreign substances. Beyond its role in host protection, it regulates tissue homeostasis and tissue repair by screening cell surfaces for the expression of specific molecules. Cells of the immune system identify and remove injured, dead, or malignant cells. Immune cells derive from hematopoietic stem cells in the bone marrow, circulate in the blood and lymph, form complex microstructures in specialized lymphoid organs, and infiltrate virtually every tissue. Their anatomic organization in lymphoid organs and their ability to circulate throughout the body and to migrate between blood and lymphoid tissues are crucial components of host defense.

Principally, host protection is accomplished by two types of immunity, innate and adaptive. These two arms of the immune system are not independent but are closely interlinked. The *innate immune system* is the older system, is present in all vertebrates, and is widely conserved among species. It provides the first line of defense and functions through immediate responses that use preformed proteins and preexisting cells. *Innate immunity*, broadly defined, includes physical barriers, such as epithelial layers, and chemical impediments, such as antimicrobial substances at these surfaces. Using a more narrow definition, the innate immune system mediates nonspecific protection through a diverse set of cells, including monocytes, macrophages, dendritic cells, natural killer (NK) cells, eosinophils, basophils, neutrophils, and mast cells. A variety of chemical mediators, such as members of the complement system, acute phase reactants, and cytokines, contribute to inflammatory responses that develop to prevent tissue invasion by pathogens. The immediacy of the responses makes it impossible to use highly specific and adaptive mechanisms. Instead, response patterns are broad and lack specificity; collateral tissue damage is often unavoidable. Despite the lack of specificity, innate immunity is highly effective—microbial invasion frequently is controlled, and pathogens often are eliminated. The pathogenicity of microorganisms largely is related to their ability to resist and overcome the first line of defense mounted by the innate immune system.

If invading microorganisms succeed in escaping nonspecific host-defense mechanisms, a second line of defense, *adaptive immunity*, secures host survival. Adaptive immune responses depend on innate immunity for supplementation and augmentation and providing crucial information on the nature of the attacker. The term *adaptive* relates to the ability of the system to adapt to the microbial challenge; it is also called *acquired* or *specific immunity*. The adaptive immune system is characteristic of higher vertebrates; is evolutionarily younger than innate immunity; and has unique attributes, such as specificity, diversity, memory, specialization, tolerance, and homeostasis.

Immune specificity relies on two major cell types, B cells and T cells. These cells possess receptors that specifically recognize antigenic determinants and that distinguish subtle differences on small protein structures. To contend with the gamut of possible antigens, the adaptive immune system requires an enormous spectrum of specific receptors. An extremely high degree of discriminatory specificity is achieved by clonally distributing the recognition structures; each T cell and B cell expresses a unique receptor.

The diversity of the adaptive immune system is not inherited; it is acquired somatically and is called the *lymphocyte repertoire*. The lymphocyte repertoire is estimated to discriminate 10^9 to 10^{11} antigenic structures. On recognition of antigen, the adaptive immune system reacts with clonal expansion of antigen-responsive cells. These antigen-specific cells increase in frequency and acquire new functional characteristics. Because memory for the antigen is being generated, a second challenge from the same antigen elicits a faster and more efficient response. Specificity and memory are prerequisites for heightened reactivity to recurrent or persistent infections and provide the basis for vaccination. Another example of the adaptive power

of the specific immune system lies in specialized responses to different classes of microbes (e.g., parasites versus viral infections). Specialization is a consequence of differentiation during evolving immune responses and results in the selection of the most appropriate effector pathway for a particular microbial challenge.

Generating immunity adapted to the invading pathogen inevitably involves the risk to mount responses directed against self-antigens. To prevent injury to the host, the adaptive immune system discriminates between self and nonself. Nonreactivity to self is actively acquired and maintained by several mechanisms collectively called *self-tolerance*. Distinguishing self and nonself is individualized for each host and requires the selection of an individual set of nonself-reactive receptors. Consequently the outcome of self/nonself discrimination is not transferred from generation to generation and is devoid of evolutionary pressure. In contrast, innate immunity relies on genetically programmed recognition structures that exclusively respond to foreign antigens. Evolutionary selection of receptors that recognize pathogens but not self potentially should avoid autoimmunity. It generally is believed that the likelihood of autoimmune disease resulting from a failure in the adaptive immune system is indefinitely higher.

Together with the capability of generating tremendous diversity and specificity, the adaptive immune system has a built-in ability to self-limit responses and to regain homeostasis. This mechanism is crucial in preventing excessive immunity and in providing space for emerging lymphocytes that are required for a new specific immune response.

Although the innate immune system is the more ancient and the adaptive immune system is phylogenetically younger, the most recent evolution has been the formation of lymphoid organs. In the highly specialized microenvironment of lymphoid tissues, both arms of the immune system can interact intimately and collaborate efficiently to augment and optimize immune reactions. The earliest organized lymphoid structures detected during evolution are the gut-associated lymphoid tissues. More sophisticated secondary lymphoid organs, such as the spleen, thymus, and lymph nodes, are found only in higher vertebrates.

LEUKOCYTE MIGRATION AND HOMING

Mobility of the cellular constituents is fundamental to innate and adaptive immunity. To home to the site of tissue injury or to enter lymphoid organs, cells use a multistep process of adherence and activation. Initially, leukocytes roll on activated endothelial cells, activate chemokine receptors, increase their adhesiveness, and eventually migrate through the endothelial layer across a chemokine gradient. The selectin family of proteins mediates the first steps of leukocyte migration. Selectins have a lectin domain and bind to carbohydrate ligands. L-selectin is present on virtually all leukocytes, P-selectin and E-selectin are expressed on activated endothelial cells, and P-selectins are stored in platelets. Selectins capture floating leukocytes and initiate their attachment and rolling on activated endothelial cells. To transform attachment and rolling into firm adhesion, the concerted action of chemokines, chemokine receptors, and integrins is necessary. Integrins are heterodimers formed of many different α-chains and β-chains; different α-β combinations are expressed on different cell subsets. Only after activation can integrins interact with ligands on endothelial cells. Activation involves modification of the cytoplasmic domain of the β-chain, which leads to a structural change of the extracellular domains. This process is termed *inside-out signaling*. Integrin activation can be mediated by chemokines binding to leukocytes. The last step of homing is transendothelial migration. Here the firmly attached leukocytes migrate through the endothelial cell monolayer and the basement membrane. Leukocytes need to be released from the endothelial cell contact and directed to migrate toward the tissue. Molecular components governing this process have not been identified.

INNATE IMMUNE SYSTEM

Activation of the Innate Immune System

Neutrophils, eosinophils, basophils, macrophages/monocytes, dendritic cells, and NK cells are the cellular constituents of the innate immune system. These cells depend on a variety of soluble factors, such as serum and tissue proteins, to generate nonspecific immune responses. Of particular importance is the complement system, a group of plasma enzymes and regulatory proteins that are converted from inactive proenzymes to active enzymes in a controlled and systematic cascade (Chapter 45). Cells of the innate immune system sense infection, cellular damage, and threat to tissue integrity with a variety of receptors and respond with an activation program. They possess surface receptors for complement factors. They are activated when binding antibody molecules through immunoglobulin Fc receptors. Finally, they express pattern recognition receptors (PRRs) that are instrumental in recognizing microbial invasion. Beyond its response to soluble factors, the innate immune system is able to screen cells for intactness by surveying cell surface molecules. In principle, recognition of membrane molecules provides inhibitory signals for constitutively activated cells of the innate immune system. Loss of these membrane molecules on the tissue abrogates inhibition and allows the generation of protective effector functions.

ACTIVATION BY PATTERN RECOGNITION RECEPTORS

The strategy of the innate immune system is to focus on the recognition of a few, highly conserved structures preserved in large groups of microorganisms. It currently is estimated that the system uses a few hundred receptor structures to identify microbial invaders. This set of receptors is insufficient to cover the entire spectrum of infectious antigens. Innate responses are directed against structures that are shared by entire classes of pathogens and are essential for their survival and pathogenicity. Determinants targeted by the innate immune system are expressed exclusively on microbes and not by the host, avoiding autoimmune injury. Structures recognized by PRRs are collectively referred to as *pathogen-associated molecular patterns* (PAMPs). Examples of PAMPs are bacterial lipopolysaccharides, peptidoglycans, mannans, bacterial DNA, double-stranded RNA, and glucans.

PAMP-binding receptor families share structural characteristics, such as leucine-rich repeated domains, calcium-dependent lectin domains, and scavenger-receptor protein domains, and they use several different pathways to identify their microbial target. They can be secreted to act as opsonins; the best-characterized receptor of this class is the mannan-binding lectin that binds to microbial carbohydrates and activates the lectin pathway of complement activation.

Another functional class of PRRs is expressed on the surface of phagocytes and facilitates endocytosis. The macrophage mannose receptor and the macrophage scavenger receptor are the best-known examples. These receptors are essential for the clearance of microbes from the circulation. A third class of PRRs controls cell activation (Fig. 41–1); the most important members are toll-like receptors. Initially described in *Drosophila*, at least 10 toll-like receptors have been identified in mammals. Toll-like receptors function by regulating the activity of NF-κB signaling pathways and control the expression of many inflammatory cytokines and cell surface molecules. Prominent members of the toll-like receptor family are the toll-like receptor 4, which, in conjunction with other cell surface molecules, binds bacterial lipopolysaccharides; the toll-like receptor 2, which recognizes bacterial peptidoglycans and lipoproteins; and the toll-like receptor 9, which binds to bacterial DNA motifs.

PRRs used by the innate immune system are fundamentally different from the antigen-specific receptors generated in the adaptive immune system. The receptors of the innate immune system are encoded in the germline and are under evolutionary pressure. They are shared by many different effector cells, including macrophages and dendritic cells, and are not clonally distributed (i.e., different cell types display identical specificity). Finally, they cannot recognize self and should not be dangerous to the host.

REGULATION BY MAJOR HISTOCOMPATIBILITY COMPLEX CLASS I–RECOGNIZING RECEPTORS

PRRs dominate cell activation for some cell types and under certain conditions. Other cells of the innate immune system require reversal of inhibition to enter the activation cycle. Loss of inhibitory signals in constitutively activated cells is particularly important for NK cells. NK cells are poised constantly to attack, but they are held in check by inhibitory receptors that recognize major histocompatibility complex (MHC) class I or MHC class I–like molecules. The observation that NK cells kill target cells lacking MHC class I molecules led to the *missing-self hypothesis*. The principle that immune cells are kept in check by recognizing self-determinants is appreciated now as fundamental in the immune system. Besides NK cells, other cells of the innate immune system and the adaptive immune system use this principle. Provision of negative signals seems to be linked closely to the recognition of MHC class I molecules.

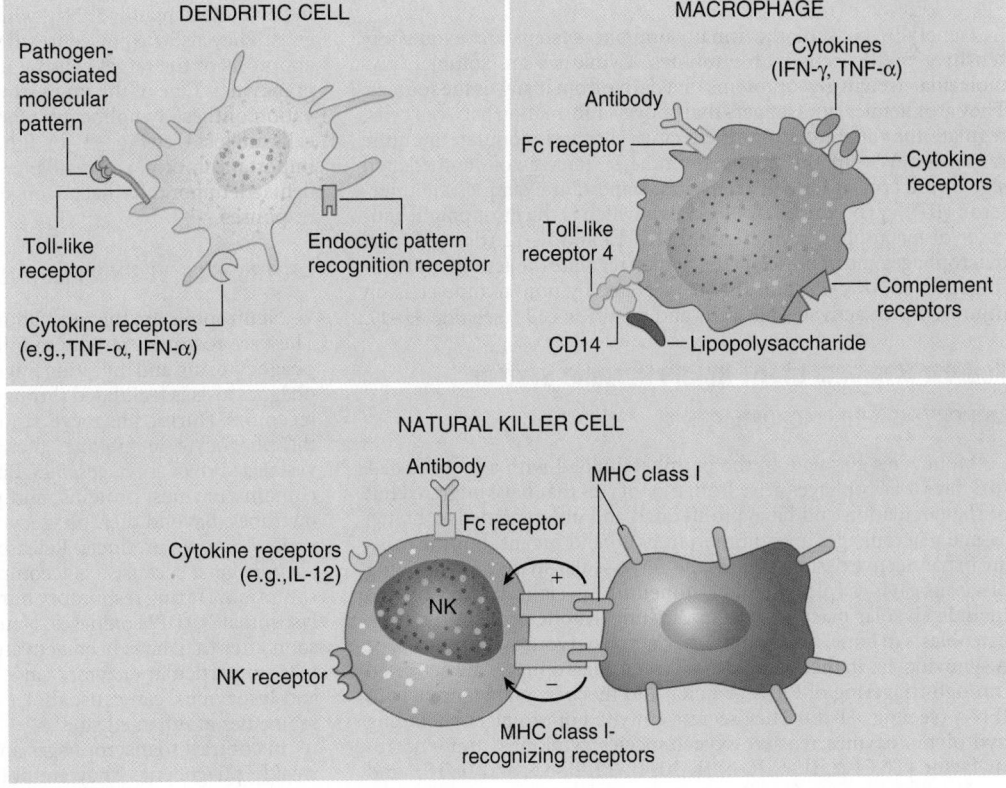

FIGURE 41–1 • Activation pathways in the innate immune system. Cells of the innate immune system recognize microorganisms and tissue damage caused by either infection or malignancy. Dendritic cells and monocytes/macrophages use a multitude of receptors to sense constituents of pathogens, often bacterial molecules common to many classes of microorganisms, and respond to cytokines and endogenous stimulators released from injured cells. Binding of complement factors also can trigger cell activation. Self-recognition of major histocompatibility complex (MHC) class I molecules by natural killer (NK) cells can deliver positive or negative signals. Lack of MHC class I molecules on the target cell surface activates NK cells to kill the target.

Currently, three different types of MHC class I–recognizing receptors are known. C-type lectin receptors (predominantly expressed on NK cells) recognize HLA-E. Killer cell immunoglobulin-like receptors are specific for HLA-C and, to a lesser extent, HLA-A and HLA-B. Immunoglobulin-like transcript receptors are found preferentially on cells of the innate immune system other than NK cells. Immunoglobulin-like transcript receptor 2 is expressed on B cells, monocytes, dendritic cells, and macrophages. Immunoglobulin-like transcript receptors 3 and 4 have a more restrictive expression pattern and are encountered on monocytes, dendritic cells, and macrophages. By screening cell surfaces for the expression of MHC class I molecules, the innate immune system collects information about the intactness of tissues, emphasizing the crucial role of MHC class I molecules as markers of tissue integrity.

Recognition of MHC class I molecules often provides a negative signal that suppresses cell activity. All receptor families also include stimulatory isoforms, however, that mediate an activating signal. The current paradigm assumes that the balance between these opposing signals is finely tuned, ultimately determining whether innate immunity is initiated or not.

ACTIVATION BY FC RECEPTORS

Most cells of the innate immune system possess Fc receptors (FcRs) and can bind antibodies attached to antigens (see Fig. 41–1). FcRs specifically interact with the constant region (Fc portion) of immunoglobulins. Each member of the FcR family displays specificity for one or a few immunoglobulin isotypes. The isotype of the antibody determines which cell type is activated in a given response. Triggering of most FcRs transmits activating signals; however, inhibitory FcRs do exist. Phagocytic cells, such as neutrophils and macrophages, are equipped with FcγRs that are activated by IgG antibodies, particularly IgG1. Ligation of an FcγR triggers phagocytosis of the antigen, activation of respiratory burst, and induction of cytotoxicity. On eosinophils, FcγRs mainly regulate granule release. On NK cells, FcγRs initiate antibody-dependent, cell-mediated cytotoxicity. In this process, the cytolytic machinery of NK cells is triggered by the binding of IgG1-coated or IgG3-coated target cells. FcRs on mast cells, basophils, and activated eosinophils are specific for IgE. In contrast to other FcRs, they bind monomeric antibody molecules with extremely high affinity. Cross-linking of the constitutively cell-surface bound IgE induces cell activation and the release of cytoplasmic granules.

ACTIVATION BY CYTOKINES

Generally, cells of the innate immune system are exquisitely sensitive to the action of cytokines. Cytokines are soluble, low-molecular-weight glycoproteins that derive from many tissue sources. They are chemical messengers that convey information between cells, regulate the differentiation of effector cells, and modulate immune responses. Within the innate immune system, cytokine-mediated signals are crucial for cell activation. Important examples are interferon (IFN)-γ (produced by NK cells), which is the most potent activator of macrophages; interleukin (IL)-15 and IL-12 (derived from macrophages and dendritic cells), which regulate the activity and proliferation of NK cells; and IFN-α (secreted by nonimmune cells on injury), which activates NK cells and dendritic cells (see Fig. 41–1).

Cellular Elements of the Innate Immune System

MONOCYTES AND MACROPHAGES

Monocytes circulate in the peripheral blood with a half-life of 1 to 3 days. Macrophages arise from monocytes that have migrated out of the circulation and have proliferated and differentiated in tissue. Tissue macrophages are common in lymphoid organs, but they also are in connective tissues, such as the perivascular space, and the lining of serous cavities (pleura and peritoneum). Specialized macrophages include alveolar macrophages in the lung, Kupffer cells in the liver, osteoblasts in bone, microglia in the central nervous system, and type A synoviocytes in the synovial membrane. Macrophages are activated through triggering of PRRs or FcRs, and they respond vigorously to IFN-γ (see Fig. 41–1). They secrete a myriad of products, including hydrolytic enzymes, reactive oxygen species, cytokines (tumor necrosis factor [TNF]-α, IL-1, IL-6, IL-10, IL-12, IL-15, and IL-18), and

chemokines. They can phagocytose and expose the engulfed microorganism to a wide range of toxic intracellular molecules, including reactive oxygen species, nitric oxide, antimicrobial cationic proteins and peptides, and lysosomal enzymes. In addition to attacking microbial organisms, macrophages remove dying and dead host cells. They recognize molecules expressed on apoptotic cells and eliminate them without initiating an inflammatory response. Finally, they play a crucial role in the recruitment of adaptive immune responses. After capturing antigen, they function as antigen-presenting cells for T lymphocytes. In this function, however, they are less important than dendritic cells. As a partner for IFN-γ-releasing T cells, they mediate effector functions; contribute to tissue repair; and orchestrate immune responses through their release of cytokines, chemokines, and growth factors.

DENDRITIC CELLS/LANGERHANS CELLS

Dendritic cells represent the major cell type linking innate immunity to the adaptive immune system. Their primary function is the presentation of antigen to T cells. They are the only cell type that can activate naive T cells and initiate adaptive immune responses. Dendritic cells are derived from lymphoid and myeloid lineages. When positioned in the skin and under the mucosal surface, dendritic cells are referred to as *Langerhans cells*. They constantly endocytose and digest extracellular molecules but usually do not display these molecules at a sufficient density to activate T cells. On receiving a stimulatory signal, they convert into highly efficient antigen-presenting cells. Activation signals can derive from PAMP and from host cells that react to injury and secrete mediators, such as TNF-α, IFN-α, or heat-shock proteins (see Fig. 41–1). Activation causes dendritic cells to change their expression profile of chemokine receptors and to migrate from the local tissue to lymph nodes. In parallel, they begin expressing accessory molecules on their cell surface, a prerequisite for T-cell activation. When they arrive in the T-cell zone of the lymph node, they display MHC/peptide complexes with peptides derived from endocytosed and digested antigens. With high surface expression of MHC and accessory molecules, dendritic cells optimize the process of antigen presentation and T-cell priming (Fig. 41–2).

NATURAL KILLER CELLS

The current paradigm holds that NK cells provide the first line of defense against viral infections and other intracellular pathogens while adaptive responses are generated. NK cells are sensitized by cytokines released from macrophages and dendritic cells. They function by secreting cytokines, mainly IFN-γ, which activates macrophages and other cells. They also are poised to kill virus-infected cells. NK cells induce apoptosis of the target cells by injecting pore-forming enzymes and granzymes. One of the interesting features of NK biology is the activation of these lymphocytes when MHC class I molecules on target cells are lost (see Fig. 41–1). It has been postulated that NK cells are important in tumor surveillance by being able to kill MHC class I–deficient tumor cells that no longer are susceptible to adaptive immune responses.

NEUTROPHILS, EOSINOPHILS, AND BASOPHILS

Neutrophils are the most abundant circulating white blood cells. They are recruited rapidly to inflammatory sites and are capable of phagocytosing and digesting microbes. Activation of neutrophils and phagocytosis is facilitated through triggering of FcRs or complement receptors. During phagocytosis, the pathogen first is surrounded by the phagocyte membrane, then internalized in membrane-bound vesicles known as *phagosomes*. Phagosomes fuse with lysosomes that contain enzymes, proteins, and peptides that inactivate and digest microbes. Beyond their phagocytic capability, neutrophils produce a variety of toxic products. Release of toxic products is known as *respiratory burst* because it is accompanied by an increase in oxygen consumption. During respiratory burst, oxygen radicals are generated by lysosomal NADPH oxidases. Neutrophils are short-lived cells, dying soon after they have been activated. Secretion of their granule products, in particular enzymes (myeloperoxidase, elastase, collagenase, and lysozyme), can cause direct cellular injury and damage macromolecules at inflamed sites.

In contrast to macrophages and neutrophils, eosinophils are only weakly phagocytic. They are potent cytotoxic effector cells against

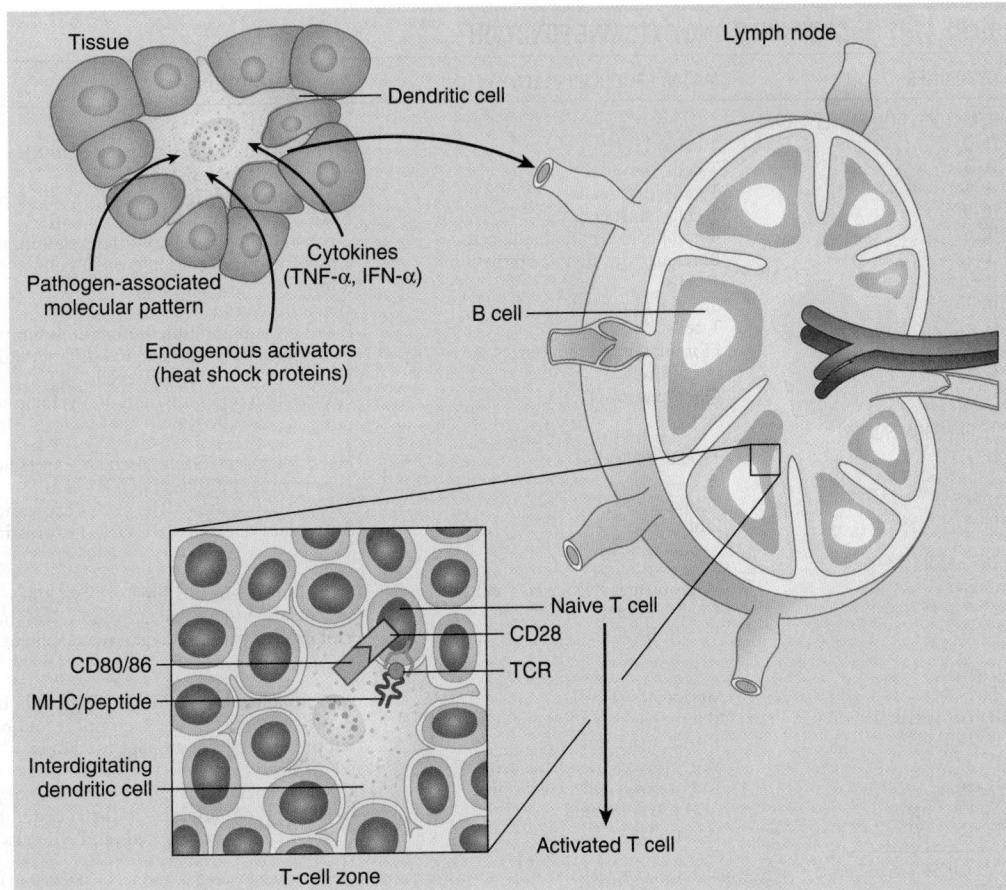

FIGURE 41-2 • The interface of the innate and adaptive immune systems. Dendritic cells reside in the tissue, where they recognize and ingest antigens. If they also receive an activating signal (e.g., by binding pathogen-associated molecular patterns or cytokines), they enter lymph vessels to travel to regional lymph nodes. In parallel, they mature into efficient antigen-presenting cells that express high levels of cell surface major histocompatibility complex and costimulatory molecules. In the T-cell zones, dendritic cells present the antigen engulfed in the peripheral tissue to primed naive T cells. By capturing and transporting antigen and priming naive T cells, dendritic cells integrate responses of the innate and adaptive immune systems.

parasites. Their major effector mechanism is the secretion of various cationic proteins (major basic protein, eosinophil cationic protein, and eosinophil-derived neurotoxin) that are released into the extracellular space where they directly destruct the invading microorganism, but these proteins also can attack host tissue.

Basophils and tissue mast cells are important reservoirs of inflammatory mediators, such as histamines, prostaglandins, leukotrienes, and selected cytokines, including IL-4. Basophils and tissue mast cells have high-affinity receptors for monomeric IgE. They play a role in atopic allergies in which allergens bind IgE and cross-link FcεRs. Their function in normal immune responses is incompletely understood.

Soluble Factors in Innate Defenses

Effector functions of the cells of the innate immune system are complemented by many circulating proteins. A particularly important contribution derives from the complement system, which holds a crucial position in linking microbial recognition to cellular effector functions. The mannose-binding lectin circulates in the plasma, functioning as an opsonin, and is involved in the activation of the complement pathway. C-reactive protein, an acute phase protein, participates in opsonization by binding to bacterial phospholipids. Finally the innate immune system could not work without cytokines that regulate recruitment and activation of leukocytes (Table 41-1). Cells of the innate immune system are not only the principal producers of such cytokines, but also their targets.

ADAPTIVE IMMUNE SYSTEM

Activation of the Adaptive Immune System: Recognition of Antigen

STRUCTURE OF ANTIGEN-SPECIFIC RECEPTORS

The innate immune system recognizes structural patterns common in the microbial world, whereas the adaptive immune system is designed to respond to the entire continuum of antigens. This goal is achieved through two principal types of antigen recognition receptors, antibodies and T-cell receptors (TCRs). These receptors distinguish antigens through subtle changes in shape. The antigen recognition structures are complementary to the shape of antigens and bind the antigen noncovalently. Antibodies are expressed as cell surface receptors on B cells or are secreted. They recognize conformational structures, determinants formed by the tertiary configuration of proteins. In contrast, α-β TCRs fit specifically to epitopes formed by a small linear peptide embedded into MHC molecules on the surface of antigen-presenting cells.

Antibodies consist of two identical heavy chains and two identical light chains, which are covalently linked by disulfide bonds. The N-terminal domain of each chain is variable and represents the recognition structure that interacts with the antigen. Each antibody has two binding arms of identical specificity. The C-terminal ends of the heavy and the light chains form the constant region that defines the subclass of the antibody (κ or λ for light chains and IgM, IgA, IgD, IgE, or IgG for heavy chains). Additional subclasses can be distinguished for IgG and IgA. The constant region of antibodies includes the Fc region. Fc regions can polymerize (IgA) or penterize (IgM) in the presence of a J (joining) chain. Fc regions also are the ligand for the FcRs on cells of the innate immune system.

TCRs are dimers of α-chains and β-chains or of γ-chains and δ-chains, each of which contains three complementary-determining binding sites in the N-terminal domain. These complementary-determining sites define the specificity by contacting antigenic shapes. α-β TCRs exclusively recognize peptide fragments in the context of MHC molecules. γ-δ TCRs are more variable and can recognize certain glycolipid antigens in the context of MHC-like molecules or even unprocessed antigen, functioning similar to antibodies. The repertoires of antibodies and TCRs are extremely diverse and have been estimated to be on the order of 10^{15} unique combinations. This enormous diversity cannot be genetically encoded; it must be acquired. The basis of this enormous diversity consists of fewer than 400 genes that are recombined and modified. Immunoglobulin heavy chains are formed from four gene segments encoded on chromosome 14—the variable, diversity, joining, and constant region gene segments. Also,

Table 41–1 • CYTOKINES AND CYTOKINE FUNCTION

CYTOKINES	MAJOR PRODUCER CELLS	PRINCIPAL ACTION
HEMATOPOIETIN FAMILY		
IL-2	T cells	Proliferation of T cells, B cells, and NK cells
IL-3	T cells	Early hematopoiesis
IL-4	T cells, mast cells	B-cell activation, IgE switch, inhibition of TH1 cells
IL-5	T cells, mast cells	Eosinophil growth and differentiation
IL-6	Macrophages, endothelial cells	T-cell and B-cell growth differentiation, induction of acute phase proteins
IL-7	Bone marrow, thymic epithelium	Growth of pre-B cells and pre-T cells
IL-9	T cells	Stimulates mast cells and TH2 cells
IL-11	Stromal fibroblasts	Hematopoiesis
IL-13	T cells	B-cell growth and differentiation, inhibition of TH1 cell and macrophages
G-CSF	Fibroblasts and monocytes	Neutrophil development and differentiation
IL-15	Non–T cells	Growth of T cells and NK cells
GM-CSF	Macrophages, T cells	Growth and differentiation of myelomonocytic lineage cells
INTERFERON FAMILY		
IFN-γ	T cells, NK cells	Macrophage activation, increase expression of MHC molecules, Ig class switching, inhibition of TH2 cells
IFN-γ	Leukocytes	Antiviral, increases MHC class I expression
IFN-γ	Fibroblasts	Antiviral, increases MHC class I expression
TNF FAMILY		
INF-α	Macrophages, NK cells, T cells	Induction of proinflammatory cytokines, endothelial cell activation, apoptosis
TNF-β (TL-a)	T cells, B cells	Cell death, endothelial activation, lymphoid organ development
LT-β	T cells, B cells	Cell death, lymphoid organ development
OTHERS		
TGF-β	Monocytes, T cells	Anti-inflammatory, inhibits cell growth, induces IgA secretion
IL-1α, IL-1β	Macrophages, endothelial cells	Acute phase response, macrophage and neutrophil migration
IL-10,IL-1β	T cells, macrophages	Suppression of macrophage functions
IL-12	Macrophages, dendritic cells	NK cell activation, TH1 cell differation
IL-16	T cells, mast cells, eosinophils	Chemoattractant for CD4 T cells, monocytes, and eosinophils
IL-17	CD4 memory cells	Cytokine production by epithelia endothelia, and fibroblasts
IL-18	Macrophages	IFN-γ production by T cells and NK cells

G-CSF = granulocyte colony-stimulating factor; GM-CSF = granulocyte-macrophage colony-stimulating factor; IFN = interferon; IL = interleukin; LT = leukotriene; MHC = major histocompatibility; NR = natural killer; TGF = transforming growth factor.

TCR β-chains and δ-chains are assembled by the recombination of variable, diversity, joining, and constant region segments of TCR genes. Immunoglobulin light chains and TCR α-chains and γ-chains lack the diversity segment and are composed of three gene segments. During antibody or TCR rearrangement, gene segments are cut out by nucleases and spliced together at the DNA level to form linear coding units for each receptor gene. By combining several different mechanisms, an enormous diversity of receptors is generated. First, the genome contains multiple forms of gene segments; each receptor or antibody uses a different combination of these gene segments. Second, the splicing process is imprecise, introducing nucleotide variations at the variable/diversity, diversity/joining, or variable/joining junctions. These inaccuracies lead to frame shifts and result in completely different amino acid sequences. Finally, random nucleotides can be inserted at the junctional region by an enzyme, deoxyribonucleotidyl transferase.

When recombined, TCR sequences remain unchanged. This rule does not apply to immunoglobulins, which can undergo editing. Immunoglobulin editing can include replacement of an entire variable region (receptor editing); class switching during immune responses, in which the variable/diversity/joining unit can combine with different constant region genes; or somatic hypermutation, in which the complementary-determining regions undergo mutations during an immune response.

ANTIGEN PROCESSING

T cells do not recognize native antigens but peptide fragments that are displayed in the context of either MHC class I or class II molecules. The two classes of MHC molecules are used as restriction elements by two different subsets of T cells. CD4 T cells recognize antigen peptide embedded into MHC class II molecules, whereas CD8 T cells are directed against peptides complexed with MHC class I. Generally, MHC class II molecules are expressed only on specialized antigen-presenting cells, such as dendritic cells, monocytes, macrophages, and B cells. Peptides bound to MHC class II molecules derive from extracellular antigens that are captured and internalized into endosomes to be digested by proteinases, notably cathepsin. Occasionally, intracellular proteins or membrane proteins also are funneled into this pathway. MHC class II molecules are assembled in the endoplasmic reticulum in association with a protein called the *invariant chain* (Fig. 41–3). The molecules are transported to the endosome, where the invariant chain is removed from the peptide-binding cleft, making the cleft accessible to peptides derived from extracellular proteins. MHC class II molecules, stabilized by peptides of 10 to 30 amino acids, are displayed on the cell surface, where they can be recognized by CD4 T cells.

MHC class I–associated peptides are produced in the cytosol by the proteosome, a large cytoplasmic multiprotein enzyme complex (see Fig. 41–3). Specialized transporter proteins, called *transporter associated with antigen processing proteins*, facilitate translocation from the cytosol to the endoplasmic reticulum. Here the peptides bind to newly formed MHC class I molecules and are transported to the cell surface, where they are recognized by antigen-specific CD8 T cells.

The nature of the antigen-processing pathway determines the sequence of events in immune responses. Extracellular antigens, in general, enter the endosomal pool and associate with MHC class II molecules to stimulate CD4 T cells. Cytosolic antigens, including antigens from intracellular infectious agents, are degraded and displayed in the context of MHC class I molecules to initiate CD8 T-cell responses.

Cellular Elements of the Adaptive Immune System

T CELLS

T-CELL DEVELOPMENT. T cells derive from the hematopoietic stem cell in the fetal liver or in the bone marrow. Precursor cells already committed to T-cell development are seeded into the thymus, where all the subsequent stages of T-cell maturation occur (Fig. 41–4). Pre-T cells express recombinase activating genes and terminal deoxynucleotidyl transferase, enabling them to recombine TCR genes. The

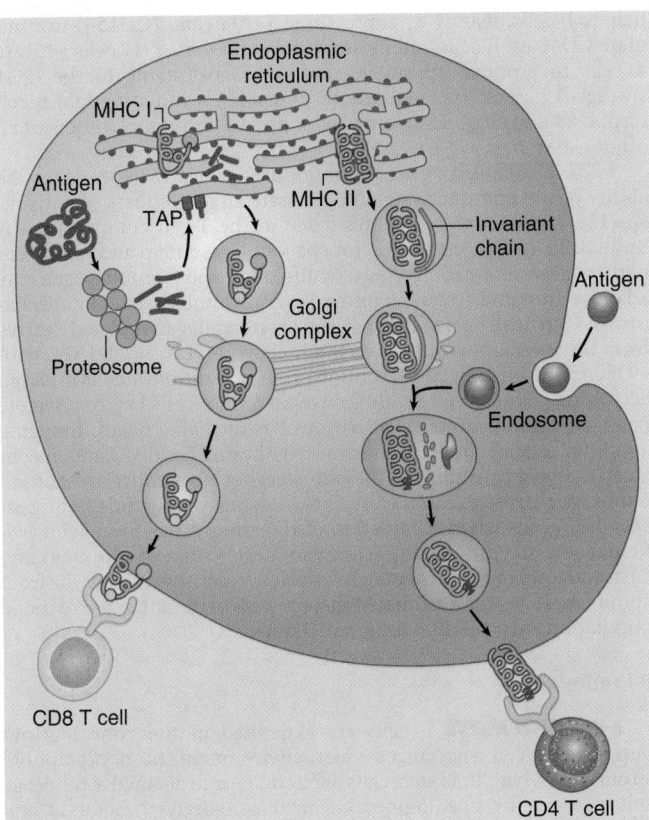

FIGURE 41–3 • Pathways of antigen processing and delivery to major histocompatibility complex (MHC) molecules. Cytosolic proteins are degraded by the proteosome to generate peptide fragments that are transported into the endoplasmic reticulum by specialized peptide transporters (TAP). After peptides are bound to MHC class I molecules, MHC/peptide complexes are released from the endoplasmic reticulum to travel to the cell surface by the Golgi apparatus. MHC class I/peptide complexes are ligands for T-cell receptors (TCRs) of CD8 T cells. Extracellular foreign antigens are taken into intracellular vesicles, endosomes. As the pH in the endosomes gradually decreases, proteases are activated that digest antigens into peptide fragments. After fusing with vesicles that contain MHC class II molecules, antigenic peptides are placed into the antigen-binding groove. Loaded MHC class II/peptide complexes are transported to the cell surface, where they are recognized by the TCRs of CD4 T cells.

β-chain of the TCR is rearranged first and is expressed together with pre-TCR α-chain. Signals from the immature TCR complex inhibit rearrangement of the second β-chain allele and induce proliferation and expression of the CD4 and CD8 molecules. Subsequently the TCR α-chain is recombined, and low levels of TCRs appear on the cell surface. From here, the T cell undergoes many differentiation and selection steps modulated by the thymic microenvironment, in particular, by thymic epithelial cells, macrophages, and dendritic cells. Early stages of thymocytes reside in the thymic cortex, where they mostly interact with epithelial cells. They then migrate toward the medulla, encountering dendritic cells and macrophages at the corticomedullary junction. Thymic stromal cells regulate T-cell proliferation by secreting lymphopoietic growth factors, such as IL-7. Interaction of the TCR with MHC molecules expressed on epithelial cells and on dendritic cells/macrophages determines the fate of the thymocyte. Low-avidity recognition of peptide/MHC complexes on thymic epithelial cells by the TCR results in positive selection. This recognition event rescues cells from apoptotic cell death and ensures that only T cells with functional receptors survive. Thymocytes that express a receptor not fitting to any MHC antigen complex die by neglect. High-affinity interaction between the TCR and peptide/MHC complex induces apoptotic cell death of the recognizing T cell. This process of negative selection eliminates T cells with specificity for self-antigens and is responsible for central tolerance to many autoantigens. It has been estimated that approximately 1% of thymocytes survive the stringent selection process. While

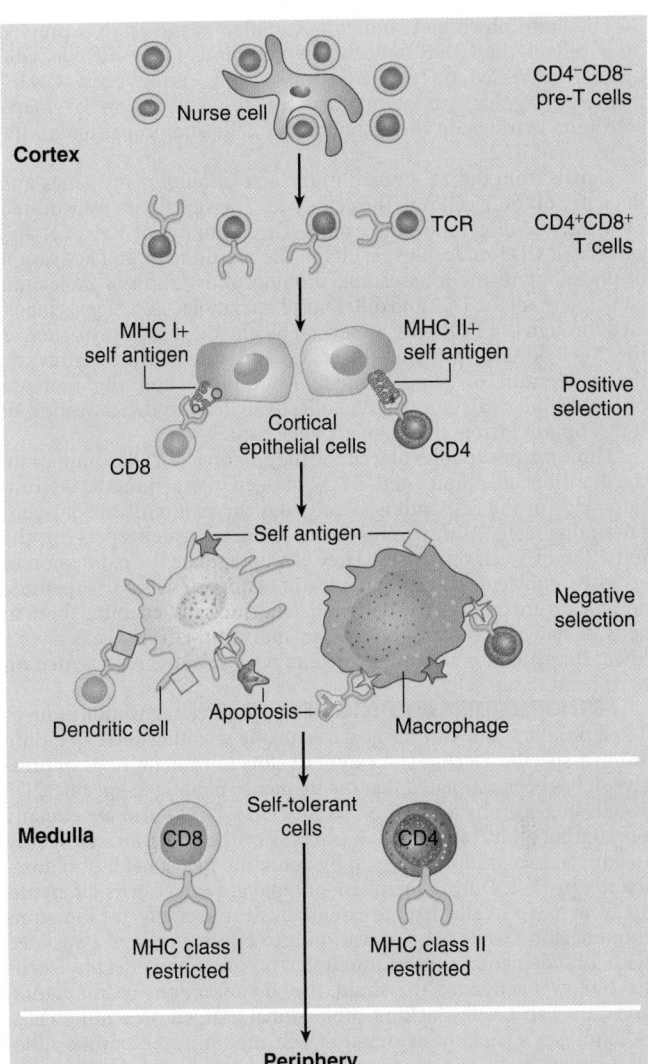

FIGURE 41–4 • Maturation of T cells in the thymus. Precursors committed to the T-cell lineage arrive in the thymus and begin to rearrange their T-cell receptor genes. Immature T cells with receptors binding to self—major histocompatibility complex (MHC) on cortical epithelial cells receive signals for survival (positive selection). At the corticomedullary junction, surviving T cells probe self-antigens presented by dendritic cells and macrophages. T cells reacting strongly to self-antigens are deleted by apoptosis (negative selection). T cells released into the periphery are tolerant toward self and recognize foreign antigens in the context of self-MHC.

undergoing selection, T cells continue to differentiate with orderly expression of cell surface molecules. Thymocytes expressing CD4 and CD8 molecules develop into single-positive CD4+ helper T cells that have been selected on MHC class II complexes and CD8 cytotoxic T cells that are restricted to MHC class I complexes.

T-CELL STIMULATION AND ACCESSORY MOLECULES. T-cell activation is initiated when TCR complexes recognize antigenic peptides in the context of the appropriate MHC molecule on the surface of an antigen-presenting cell. Antigen recognition by T cells results in proliferation and differentiation and triggers different effector functions. Stimulation of the TCR is not sufficient and needs to be complemented by the interaction of accessory molecules on the T cell and their ligands on the antigen-presenting cell. A spectrum of accessory molecules is known. The coreceptors, CD4 and CD8, interact with MHC class II and class I molecules and support activation signals through the TCR. Adhesion molecules (integrins) stabilize the interactions between T cells and antigen-presenting cells. Finally, specialized costimulatory molecules provide a second signal in addition to the TCR signal. In the absence of such a second signal, T cells undergo apoptosis or are rendered nonresponsive and anergic.

Principles of Immunology and Inflammation

The best-known and studied costimulatory molecule expressed on T cells is the CD28 molecule, which binds to the CD80/CD86 ligands expressed on activated antigen-presenting cells. CD28-mediated signals are mandatory for the expression of many activation markers on the responding T cells and, in particular, the secretion of IL-2.

Signals from the TCR result in the activation of many genes and the entry of the T cell into the cell cycle. The signals are transmitted by a cascade of cytoplasmic events. Cross-linking of the TCR and associated CD3 molecules results in the recruitment and activation of phosphotyrosine kinases and the phosphorylation of molecular constituents of the TCR and different adapter molecules. Signals mediated through the TCR activate several biochemical pathways, such as the MAP kinase, protein kinase C, and calcineurine pathways; the generation of phosphoinositol products; and the increase of intracellular calcium, which collectively lead to the activation of transcription factors that regulate gene expression.

Three major variables determine the outcome of TCR stimulation: the duration and affinity of the TCR/antigen interaction, the maturation stage of the responding T cell, and the nature of the antigen-presenting cell. Antigen-presenting cells are gatekeepers in the initiation of T-cell responses. They can upregulate the expression of accessory molecules that provide costimulatory signals. MHC/peptide complexes are particularly dense on dendritic cells, enabling them to activate naive T cells. In contrast, memory and effector cells have a lower threshold for activation and can react to antigen presented on peripheral tissue cells.

T-CELL DIFFERENTIATION AND EFFECTOR FUNCTIONS. T-cell activation induces T-cell proliferation with the goal of clonally selecting and expanding antigen-specific T cells. The extent of clonal proliferation is impressive. It has been estimated that the frequency of antigen-specific CD8 T cells increases by a factor of 50,000. CD4 T cells also are clonally selected but proliferate to a lesser extent. T-cell proliferation in response to antigen recognition is driven by autocrine mechanisms, predominantly by IL-2. During the phase of rapid growth, T cells differentiate from naive T cells that are essentially devoid of effector functions into effector T cells. The transition into effector cells is associated with a fundamental shift in functional profile. First, effector T cells have a lower activation threshold; they do not require costimulation and can scan tissues lacking professional antigen-presenting cells. Second, they switch the expression of chemokine receptors and adhesion molecules to gain access to peripheral tissues. Finally, they gain effector functions. The principal effector function of CD8 cells is to lyse antigen-bearing target cells. CD4 T cells produce many cytokines and express cell surface molecules important in the activation of phagocytes and other lymphocytes. CD8 T cells are committed to differentiate into cytotoxic T cells as they emerge from the thymus; the spectrum of options for CD4 T cells is larger. Different subsets of CD4 effector T cells can be distinguished based on the preferential production of certain cytokines (see Table 41–1). TH1 T cells predominantly produce IFN-γ and TNF-α and are involved in cell-mediated immunity, such as delayed-type hypersensitivity reactions. TH2 T cells preferentially produce IL-4, IL-5, and IL-13, cytokines that regulate B-cell responses and the activation of eosinophils. The decision as to which differentiation pathway to take is made during the early stages of T-cell activation and depends on many factors, including the cytokines produced by cells of the innate immune system in the microenvironment, the nature of costimulatory signals, and the avidity of the TCR-MHC/antigen interaction.

T-cell effector functions are triggered by antigen recognition by the TCR. On recognizing the appropriate MHC class I/peptide complex, CD8 T cells induce apoptosis in target cells. The T cell polarizes toward the area of antigen contact; specialized lytic granules are clustered in the contact area. A pore-forming protein, perforin, is released from the lytic granules and inserted into the target cell membrane. Proteases (granzymes) are injected into the target cells to initiate the apoptotic process by activating enzyme cascades. Mechanisms deployed by CD8 T cells are essentially identical to those of NK cells. CD4 T cells also can induce apoptosis but by a different mechanism and only in target cells expressing the cell-surface molecule, Fas (CD95). Triggering of Fas by Fas ligand (CD178), which is expressed on activated CD4 T cells, initiates the apoptotic cascade. Cytokine release by CD4 effector T cells is induced by the recognition of antigen in the context of MHC class II molecules. T cells polarize to the target cell followed by the secretion of cytokines and the expression of stimulatory cell surface molecules. TH1 and TH2 lymphocytes can provide help to B cells, mainly by expressing CD40 ligand (CD154) to stimulate CD40 on B cells and by secreting cytokines. TH1 cells activate B cells to produce opsonizing antibodies belonging to the IgG1 and IgG3 classes; TH2 cells are responsible for initiating IgM B-cell responses and supporting the production of immunoglobulins of all other classes.

T-CELL HOMEOSTASIS. Effective immunity critically depends on the ability of the immune system to generate large numbers of antigen-specific T cells rapidly, yet the space in the T-cell compartment is limited. To avoid competition for space and resources and to prevent perturbation of T-cell diversity by lifelong exposure to antigen, the adaptive immune system employs several counterbalancing mechanisms. During the activation process, a strong negative signal derives from the interaction of the T-cell molecule, CTLA-4 (CD152), with CD80/CD86 on antigen-presenting cells. In addition, T cells undergo activation-induced cell death. Activated CD4 T cells begin to secrete Fas ligand and acquire sensitivity to Fas-mediated death, inducing apoptotic suicide and fratricide in neighboring T cells. These mechanisms impose constraints in the early stages of T-cell antigen responses. Other mechanisms control the rapid decline of expanded antigen-specific T cells when elimination of the antigen has been achieved. Removal of the driving antigen causes deprivation of cytokines and costimulatory molecules, and growth factor–deprived T cells die from apoptosis. It has been estimated that only 5% of the antigen-expanded population survives after antigen clearance.

B LYMPHOCYTES

B-CELL DEVELOPMENT. B cells are generated in the bone marrow. Supported by a specialized microenvironment of nonlymphoid stromal cells, lymphoid stem cells differentiate into distinctive B-lineage cells. Driven by chemokines (stromal cell–derived factor-1) and cytokines (IL-7), precursor B cells enter a process of tightly controlled sequential rearrangements of heavy-chain and light-chain immunoglobulin genes. On pre-B cells, the membrane μ-chain is associated with a surrogate light chain to form a pre-B-cell receptor (BCR). Signals provided through this receptor are believed to induce proliferation of a progeny that subsequently rearranges different light-chain gene segments.

It is estimated that only 10% of B cells generated in the bone marrow reach the recirculating pool. Losses are mostly due to negative selection and clonal deletion of immature B cells that express receptors directed against self-antigens. Cross-linking of surface IgM by multivalent self-antigens causes immature B cells to die. Such self-reactive B cells can be rescued from death by replacing the light chain with a newly rearranged light chain that is no longer self-reactive (receptor editing). On maturation, B cells begin to express surface IgD. IgD-positive and IgM-positive B cells are exported from the bone marrow and seed peripheral lymphoid tissues (Fig. 41–5).

B-CELL STIMULATION. Mature B cells are activated by soluble and cell-bound antigen to develop into antibody-secreting effector cells. B cells respond to a large variety of antigens, including proteins, polysaccharides, and lipids. Binding of antigen to cell surface IgM molecules induces BCR clustering. Besides the antigen-binding immunoglobulin, the BCR comprises two proteins, Ig-α and Ig-β. The Ig-α/Ig-β heterodimer functions to transduce a signal and initiates the intracellular signaling cascade. The composition of the BCR with a ligand-binding and signal-transducing unit and the subsequent signaling events leading to gene induction are similar to those of the TCR. BCR triggering can be enhanced by coreceptors. This coreceptor complex is composed of CD81, CD19, and CD21; CD21 binds to complement fragments on opsonized antigens.

Naive B cells require accessory signals in addition to the triggering of the immunoglobulin receptor. They receive second signals either from helper T cells or from microbial components. Microbial constituents, such as bacterial polysaccharides, can induce antibody production in the absence of helper T cells (thymus-independent antigens). In the case of protein antigens (thymus-dependent antigens), the initial BCR stimulation prepares the cell for subsequent interaction with helper T cells. These activated B cells start to enter the cell cycle; upregulate cell surface molecules, such as CD80 and CD86 that provide costimulatory signals to T cells; and upregulate certain cytokine receptors. These B cells are prepared to activate helper T cells and to respond to cytokines secreted by these T cells, but they cannot differentiate into antibody-producing cells in the absence of T-cell help.

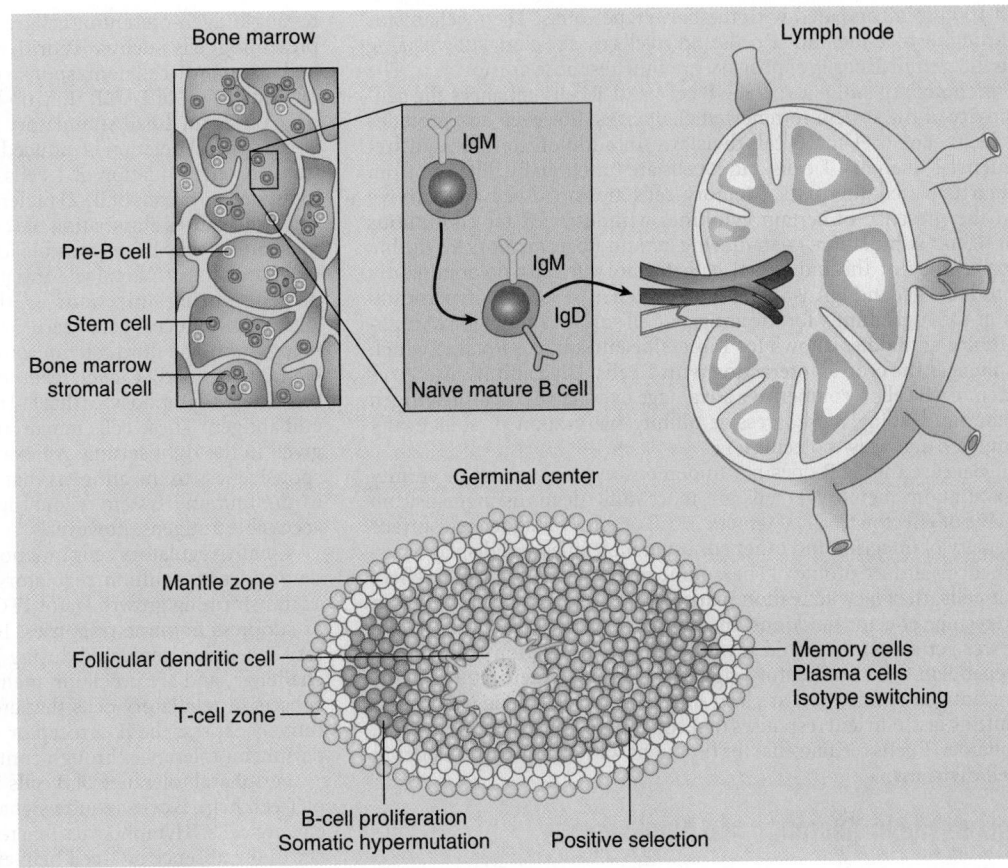

FIGURE 41–5 • B-cell development and B-cell differentiation. The early stages of B-cell development occur in the bone marrow, with cells progressing along a developmental program determined by the rearrangement and expression of immunoglobulin genes. Immature B cells with receptors for multivalent self-antigens die in the bone marrow. Surviving B cells coexpress IgD and IgM surface receptors. They are seeded into peripheral lymphoid organs, where they home to selected locations and receive signals to survive and become longer lived naive B cells. Antigen-binding B cells and antigen-presenting B cells that receive help from antigen-specific T cells are activated through membrane-bound and secreted molecules. Activated B cells migrate into the follicles, leading to the formation of germinal centers. B cells in germinal centers undergo somatic hypermutation of immunoglobulin genes; cells with high affinity for antigen presented on the surface of follicular dendritic cells are selected to differentiate into either memory B cells or plasma cells.

B-CELL DIFFERENTIATION. Subsequent differentiation of antigen-activated B cells depends on interaction with helper T cells. B cells use their antigen receptor not only to recognize antigen, but also to internalize it. After processing endocytosed antigen, MHC class II/peptide complexes appear on the cell surface, where antigen-specific CD4 T cells detect them. Also, B cells express costimulatory molecules and provide optimal conditions for T-cell activation. On activation, CD4 T cells express CD154 on their surface and are able to stimulate the CD40 molecule on their B-cell partner. CD40/CD154 interaction is essential for subsequent B-cell proliferation and differentiation. Cytokines secreted by the helper T cells act in concert with CD154 to amplify B-cell differentiation and to determine the antibody type by controlling isotype switching. Isotypes greatly influence the versatility of antibodies as effector molecules, and cytokines drive switching by stimulating the transcriptional activation of heavy-chain constant region genes. The late events of T cell–dependent B-cell differentiation and maturation take place in germinal centers, specialized structures in secondary lymphoid tissues (see Fig. 41–5). Here B cells undergo important modifications, finally leading to the production of large amounts of high-affinity antibodies. The variable regions of B cells are altered by somatic hypermutation. Subsequently, B cells that possess immunoglobulin receptors with high affinity are selected for survival (affinity maturation).

LYMPHOCYTES AND LYMPHOID TISSUE

The initiation of adaptive immune responses depends on rare antigen-specific T cells and B cells to meet antigen-presenting cells and their relevant antigen. It is unlikely that antigen recognition occurs in tissue, and sufficient numbers of antigen-presenting cells and lymphocytes can be brought together to provide crucial momentum. The immune system uses specialized lymphoid microstructures to bring antigen to the site of lymphocyte traffic and accumulation. Secondary lymphoid organs include the spleen for blood-borne antigens, the lymph nodes for antigens that are encountered in peripheral tissues, the mucosa-associated lymphoid tissue, the bronchial-associated lymphoid tissue, and the gut-associated lymphoid tissue where antigens from epithelial surfaces are collected. Lymphocytes recirculate

through secondary lymphoid organs, constantly searching for their antigen. Their homing to secondary lymphoid organs is facilitated by specialized microvessels, high endothelial venules. Different forms of secondary lymphoid tissue have developed different strategies to sequester the relevant antigen. Antigens in peripheral tissue are encountered first by dendritic cells that, after activation, are mobilized to transport antigen into the local lymph nodes by the draining lymph. These antigen-bearing dendritic cells enter the lymph nodes through the afferent lymphatic vessel and settle in the T cell–rich zones to present processed antigens to T cells. The net result of this process is an accumulation and concentration of the antigen in an environment that can be readily screened by infrequent antigen-specific T cells (see Fig. 41–2).

B cells are segregated from T cells in the lymph nodes and are localized in follicles. If B cells find their cooperating T cells, they can enter germinal centers. Germinal centers contain a network of follicular dendritic cells that capture particulate antigen or immune complexes on the cell surface. This unprocessed antigen is taken up by antigen-specific B cells, processed and presented, and recognized by antigen-specific T cells. These T cells provide cytokines and cell-cell contact signals to support the germinal center reaction, a process that leads to somatic hypermutation, affinity selection, and eventual isotype switching (see Fig. 41–5). Germinal centers are essential to generate antibody-secreting plasma cells and memory B cells.

Memory

An important consequence of adaptive immunity is the generation of immunologic memory, the basis for long-lived protection after a primary infection. Memory induction by vaccination is one of the landmark successes in medicine. Immunologic memory is defined as the ability to respond more rapidly and effectively to pathogens that have been encountered previously. The basis of immunologic memory is qualitative and quantitative changes in antigen-specific T cells and B cells. As a direct result of clonal expansion and selection in antigen-driven responses, the frequencies of antigen-specific memory B cells and memory T cells are increased 10-fold to 100-fold and 100-fold to 1000-fold compared with the naive repertoires. The mechanisms through which memory T cells and B cells escape clonal downsizing in the terminal stages of primary immune response are not clear. The enrichment of antigen-specific B cells and T cells enhances the sensitivity of the system to renewed challenges, however, and provides a head start of 4 to 10 cell divisions. In addition to increased frequencies, memory T cells and B cells are functionally different from their naive counterparts. Memory cells are long-lived and survive in the presence of certain cytokines without need for continuous antigenic stimulation, guaranteeing immunologic memory for the life expectancy of the individual cell. Memory B cells predominantly produce IgG and IgA isotypes with evidence of somatic hypermutation and high affinity for the antigen. Cell surface expression of high-affinity antibodies allows for more efficient antigen uptake, which enhances the crucial interaction with T cells. High affinity also gives memory B cells a competitive advantage over naive B cells in antigen binding, leading to progressive affinity maturation of somatically mutated antibody molecules.

Because the TCR does not undergo isotype switching or affinity maturation, memory T cells are more difficult to distinguish from naive or effector T cells. Memory T cells express a higher cell surface density of integrins and other adhesion molecules and display a distinct cell surface profile of chemokine receptors. In contrast to effector cells, they lack activation markers and need antigen stimulation to resume effector functions. In contrast to naive T cells, they have a lower activation threshold toward antigen stimulation and are less dependent on costimulatory signals. In essence, their requirements for antigen stimulation are less, and their clonal size is larger, permitting fast, efficient responses to secondary antigen encounters. Also, memory T cells resume effector functions without having to undergo cell divisions.

Immunologic Tolerance and Autoimmunity

Unresponsiveness to self is a fundamental property of the immune system and a condition sine qua non to maintain tissue integrity of the host. Self/nonself distinction is relatively straightforward for the innate immune system, in which receptors to nonself molecules are genetically encoded and evolutionarily selected. Self/nonself discrimination is much more complex for the adaptive immune system, in which antigen-specific receptors are generated randomly, and the entire spectrum of antigens theoretically can be recognized. The adaptive immune system must acquire the ability to distinguish between self and nonself. Several different mechanisms are used, collectively called *tolerance*. Tolerance is antigen specific; its induction requires the recognition of antigen by lymphocytes in a defined setting. Failure of self-tolerance results in immune responses against self-antigens. Such reactions are called *autoimmunity* and may give rise to chronic inflammatory autoimmune disease.

Several tolerance mechanisms exist, some of which are shared between T cells and B cells. In central tolerance, self-reactive lymphocytes are deleted during development. Central tolerance implies that developing immature lymphocytes respond differently to antigen contact than do mature lymphocytes. This process of negative selection is particularly important for T cells. During thymic development, T cells that recognize antigen with high affinity are deleted. Negative selection ensures that T cells that recognize abundant antigen with high affinity, in particular, antigens that are constitutively expressed on antigen-presenting cells, are deleted from the repertoire. Central tolerance for B cells follows the same principles. Recognition of antigen by developing B cells in the bone marrow induces apoptosis. Negative selection is particularly important for B cells that recognize multivalent antigens because they do not depend on T-cell help and cannot be controlled peripherally.

Not all self-reactive T cells are centrally purged from the repertoire; certain antigens are not encountered at sufficient densities in the thymus. T cells are selected on self (positive selection) and have some degree of self-reactivity necessary for their survival. Additional mechanisms of peripheral T-cell tolerance exist, such as anergy, peripheral deletion, clonal ignorance, and suppression. T-cell anergy is transient and actively maintained. It is induced if CD4 T cells recognize antigens without receiving costimulatory signals. In general, costimulatory molecules are restricted to antigen-presenting cells, and their expression is activation dependent. Antigen recognition on any cell other than peripheral antigen-presenting cells or on immature or

resting antigen-presenting cells results in anergy. In the tissue, antigen-presenting cells, such as dendritic cells, are usually immature or resting and maintain T-cell nonresponsiveness. On activation with cytokines or recognition of PAMP, they no longer anergize T cells and instead have powerful T-cell stimulatory capabilities.

Peripheral deletion is induced as a consequence of hyperstimulation. Hyperstimulation of T cells (e.g., by high doses of antigen and high concentrations of IL-2) preferentially activates proapoptotic pathways and causes elimination of the responding T-cell specificity. This mechanism may be responsible for the elimination of T cells specific for abundant peripheral self-antigens and foreign antigens abundantly present during infections. Although induction of anergy and activation-induced cell death are active consequences of antigen recognition, the third tolerance mechanism, clonal ignorance, is less well understood. *Clonal ignorance* is defined as the presence of self-reactive lymphocytes that fail to recognize or to respond to peripheral antigen. These cells remain responsive to antigenic challenge if given in the right setting. An example of clonal ignorance is nonresponsiveness to the antigens that are sequestered and not accessible to the immune system. Clonal ignorance also has been shown for accessible antigens, however.

Finally, regulatory cells function to maintain peripheral tolerance. On antigen recognition, regulatory cells may produce cytokines, such as transforming growth factor (TGF)-β, IL-10, or IL-4, that dampen or suppress immune responses. It currently is believed that regulatory T cells are generated during T-cell differentiation, after antigen challenge, and are crucial in maintaining T-cell homeostasis. Other subsets of regulatory cells that are generated in the thymus constitutively express the IL-2 receptor without prior activation and guard peripheral tolerance through contact-dependent mechanisms.

Peripheral tolerance of B cells is maintained through the absence of T-cell help. B cells require signals from T cells to differentiate into effector cells. B lymphocytes that recognize self-antigens in the periphery in the absence of T-cell help are rendered anergic or are not able to enter lymphoid follicles, where they could receive T-cell help, effectively excluding them from immune responses.

Generating and maintaining self-tolerance for T cells and B cells is complex. This system can fail, and autoimmune responses are generated. One may argue that autoimmune diseases are infrequent, given the complexity of regulation. It currently is thought that most autoimmune diseases result from dysfunction of the adaptive immune system. Many models of autoimmunity rely on the hypothesis that peripheral anergy is broken. Aberrant expression of costimulatory molecules on nonprofessional antigen-presenting cells or inappropriate activation of tissue-residing dendritic cells would set the stage for the induction of "forbidden" T-cell responses. Autoreactive B cells that recognize self-antigen complexed with foreign antigen may engulf this complex and receive help from T cells specific for the foreign antigen. Autoimmunity also may emerge if peripheral ignorance is broken. This could happen if antigens that usually are sequestered from the immune system become accessible, such as antigens from the central nervous system or from the eye. Tolerance mechanisms of anergy or clonal ignorance also can fail if foreign antigen is sufficiently different from self-antigen to initiate an immune response, but it is sufficiently similar for activated T cells to elicit T-cell and B-cell effector functions (molecular mimicry).

Immunocompetence and Immunodeficiencies

Defects in any of the components of the immune system can compromise host protection and lead to increased susceptibility for infections. Patients with immune deficiencies also are prone to develop certain types of malignancies. Immunodeficiency can be inherited or acquired. Genetic defects have been instructive in defining the biologic relevance of different pathways in the immune system. Inherited defects that interfere with the development of the cellular components of the innate immune system have not been described, emphasizing that these deficiencies may not be compatible with survival. Few genetic defects exist that impair effector functions in innate immunity. Of these, complement deficiencies are most common. They increase susceptibility for certain infections and, more so, predispose the host toward autoimmune disease (Chapter 45). Leukocyte adhesion deficiencies affect all cellular components of the innate and the adaptive immune systems and are associated with bacterial and fungal infections and impaired wound healing. Chédiak-Higashi syndrome is caused by a defect in a gene encoding a protein involved in intracellular vesicle formation. Lysosomes cannot fuse properly, and intracellular killing is impaired. Clinical consequences are those of persistent bacterial infections. Another example of defective phagocytic cells is chronic granulomatous disease, in which phagocytes fail to produce reactive oxygen intermediates, and intracellular bacteria are inefficiently eliminated.

For the adaptive immune system, the underlying molecular defects for many types of inherited immunodeficiencies are now understood. As a common denominator, these immunodeficiencies severely impair the host's resistance to infection. Combined immunodeficiencies, affecting T cells and B cells, are rare and have been attributed to mutations in the cytokine receptor γ-chain or its proximal signaling molecules, defects in the recombination machinery of TCRs and BCRs, or a deficiency of the enzyme adenosine deaminase. Children born with severe combined immunodeficiencies often die from infections early in childhood (Chapter 267). Other primary immunodeficiency syndromes selectively target the T-cell or B-cell arm or interfere with T-cell and B-cell triggering. DiGeorge syndrome (Chapter 267) is characterized by congenital malformation of the thymus. Congenital abnormalities in T-cell or B-cell activation and defects in MHC class I or II expression increasingly are defined at a molecular level. X-linked hyper-IgM syndrome results from mutations that disrupt T cell–mediated B-cell activation by CD40/CD154 interaction. The most frequent congenital immunodeficiencies are selective immunoglobulin isotype deficiencies, in which serum concentrations of one or more immunoglobulin subclasses are reduced. Affected individuals may not have any clinical manifestations or may present with recurrent bacterial infections.

More frequent than inherited immunodeficiency syndromes are acquired immunocompromised states. These conditions can be divided into infectious immunodeficiencies, iatrogenic immunodeficiencies, and immunoincompetence of the elderly. Infection with human immunodeficiency virus (HIV) causes the best-known acquired immunodeficiency. The virus paralyzes the immune system by targeting CD4-expressing helper T cells, macrophages, and dendritic cells (Chapter 410). More subtle strategies of subverting host immune responses are employed by other viruses. Cytomegalovirus is able to interfere with antigen processing and antigen presentation at several levels and compromises adaptive immune responses. Chemotherapy is regularly associated with acquired immunodeficiency, in particular in adult hosts. Although the innate immune system has a high degree of regenerative capacity, the adaptive immune system has limitations in its potential to repopulate. The ability to produce T cells progressively declines with age, and chemotherapy in adults frequently is associated with permanent defects in T-cell numbers and T-cell function. Other forms of iatrogenic immunodeficiencies are found in patients who require immunosuppressive therapy for transplant rejection or autoimmune diseases. The acquired immunodeficiency associated with aging is termed *immunosenescence*. Age-related degeneration mostly affects functions of the adaptive immune system. The decline in T-cell diversity and function with advancing age leads to increased susceptibility to infections, reduced efficacy of vaccinations, increased risk of malignancies, and reactivation of viral infections. The dysfunction of the adaptive immune system in the elderly not only manifests as insufficient T-cell and B-cell responses, but also it impairs the maintenance of self-tolerance and predisposes these individuals to autoimmunity.

SUGGESTED READINGS

Abbas AK, Janeway CA Jr: Immunology: Improving on nature in the twenty-first century. Cell 2000;100:129–138. *A lucid review of immunologic concepts and landmark discoveries.*

Bancherau J, Steinman RM: Dendritic cells and the control of immunity. Nature 1998;392:245–252. *Describes the emerging role of dendritic cells as a central regulatory cell in immune responses.*

Dykstra M, Cherukuri A, Sohn HW, et al: Location is everything: Lipid rafts and immune cell signaling. Ann Rev Immunol 2003;21:457–481. *Emphasizes the role of lipids in membrane microdomains as signaling receptors.*

Goldrath AW, Bevan MJ: Selecting and maintaining a diverse T-cell repertoire. Nature 1999;402:255–262. *Review on how the receptor diversity of T cells is generated and how T-cell homeostasis is maintained.*

Goodnow CC: Pathways for self-tolerance and the treatment of autoimmune diseases. Lancet 2001;357:2115–2121. *Discusses the premises and limitations of immunosuppressive treatments in the context of tolerance and autoimmunity models.*

Medzhitov R, Janeway C Jr: Innate immunity. N Engl J Med 2000;343:338–344. *Excellent summary of the most recent concepts of how innate immunity is regulated.*

42 THE MAJOR HISTOCOMPATIBILITY COMPLEX AND DISEASE SUSCEPTIBILITY

Robert R. Rich

It has been more than 30 years since the first report that susceptibility to a disease was associated with inheritance of a specific HLA allele. Since the discovery of a statistically significant increase in the incidence of Hodgkin's disease in patients inheriting certain HLA-B genes, such associations have been recorded for more than 500 different diseases. In many of these cases, the reported increase in susceptibility is quite weak and, in some, may represent faulty statistical analysis or a chance occurrence. In others, however, the association is very strong and impels a conclusion that genes within the HLA complex have a role in disease pathogenesis.

The importance of HLA genes in predisposition to disease is commonly expressed as *relative risk*, or the ratio of the frequency with which a disease occurs in individuals carrying a particular HLA gene divided by its frequency in those not carrying it. As illustrated in Table 42–1, the relative risk between particular diseases and HLA molecules is reported to vary from marginally significant (e.g., approximately 2.0 for Hodgkin's disease in individuals who express the HLA molecule DP3) to a preponderant role in determining disease susceptibility (e.g., a relative risk of greater than 500 for celiac disease developing in individuals who are HLA-DQA1*0501, DQB1*0201). Inspection of a table of HLA inheritance and disease susceptibility

Table 42–1 • SELECTED HLA AND DISEASE ASSOCIATIONS

DISEASE	HLA MOLECULE	APPROXIMATE RELATIVE RISK*
Ankylosing spondylitis	B27	70-150[†]
Reactive arthritis	B27	37-40
Acute anterior uveitis	B27	8-20
Hereditary hemochromatosis	A3, B14[‡]	90
Behçet's disease	B5	3-6
Sporadic narcolepsy	DR2, DQ6	130
Multiple sclerosis	DR2	3-6
	DR2, DQ6	12
Celiac disease	DR3	10-13
	DQ2	>250
Graves' disease	DR3	4
Idiopathic membranous glomerulonephritis	DR3	6-12
Chronic active hepatitis	DR3	7-9
Systemic lupus erythematosus	DR3	3-6
Type I diabetes mellitus	DR3	3-5
	DR4	3-6
	DR3/DR4[§]	14-20
	DR3, DQ8	35-100
	DR2	0.2
	DQ6	0.02
Seropositive rheumatoid arthritis	DR4	4-10
Pauciarticular juvenile rheumatoid arthritis	DR5	3-5
Pemphigus vulgaris	DR4	14-21
	DR8	5-8
Dermatitis herpetiformis	DR3	15-18
Goodpasture's syndrome	DR2	16-20
Hodgkin's disease	DP3	2

*Relative risk = {(% of patients with disease-associated HLA molecule) × (% of controls lacking disease-associated HLA molecule)} ÷ {(% of patients lacking disease-associated HLA molecules) × (% of controls with disease-associated HLA molecules)}.

[†]Ranges of relative risk are from different studies in the published literature, with significant differences commonly reflecting studies in different ethnic populations, perhaps with differing frequency of disease-associated molecular subtypes.

[‡]Denotes relative risk of extended haplotype.

[§]Denotes relative risk in heterozygotes.

reveals some general conclusions. Among these are that HLA-associated disease has been identified in virtually every major organ system and that most of these diseases are regarded as autoimmune. However, because the principal biologic role of the immune system is in defense against infectious diseases, it is not surprising that susceptibility to (or the course of) several infectious diseases is also HLA-associated. A further conclusion is that the majority of disease associations are with class II HLA-DR and HLA-DQ genes, but with some notable exceptions, particularly the class I gene HLA-B27. Finally, in some cases, inheritance of a specific HLA allele is associated with protection from rather than susceptibility to a disease. The best known of these cases is the negative association of HLA-DR2 and DQ6 with susceptibility to insulin-dependent (type I) diabetes mellitus. Together, these observations lead to a conclusion that the genes of the HLA complex are critically involved in the pathogenesis of autoimmune diseases. A reasonable corollary is that the role of HLA molecules in pathogenesis probably relates to their role in normal functioning of the immune system.

Structure and Function of HLA Molecules

HLA (for *Human Leukocyte Antigen*) is the designation in humans for the major histocompatibility complex (MHC). The MHC is a series of linked genes that are critically important in the presentation of antigens to T lymphocytes and for the discrimination by T cells of molecules that are self constituents from those of non-self (Chapter 41). It is in this manner that the immune system differentiates molecules and tissues that must be protected from immunologic attack from those that are possibly derived from pathogenic organisms and are thus appropriate targets. Based on this concept, it is a reasonable conclusion that ambiguity or mistakes in self/non-self discrimination could lead to autoimmunity, namely, immunologic attack directed against one or more of the body's own molecular constituents. To understand how this process might occur, it is important to appreciate the basic molecular principles underlying T-cell recognition of antigen, which differ dramatically from those that determine antigen recognition by antibodies.

HLA GENES. The HLA complex resides on the short arm of the sixth chromosome, where it is distributed over more than 3.5 megabases of DNA (approximately the size of the *Escherichia coli* genome). At defined loci within this large amount of DNA are two classes of genes critically involved in T-cell recognition (Fig. 42–1). This activity is based on the capacity of the gene products (HLA molecules) to bind antigen fragments (which are, with few exceptions, oligopeptides) and then to present them on the surface of antigen-presenting cells (APCs) to T cells. Three genetic loci encode distinct class Ia MHC genes (HLA-A, HLA-B, and HLA-C; hereafter designated class I for simplicity), and three loci encode the class II genes involved in antigen presentation (HLA-DR, HLA-DQ, and HLA-DP). In addition to the six class Ia and class II loci, the HLA complex includes many other

genes, some of which are involved in effector functions of the immune system (e.g., tumor necrosis factor α; the C4, C2, and properdin factor B components of the complement system; and heat shock protein HSP-70). Other genes imbedded within HLA have no specific known role in the immune system, such as the 21-hydroxylase genes involved in steroid biosynthesis.

The HLA complex also contains a series of class Ib genes that are thought to serve a more specialized role (e.g., HLA-G, which is distinguished by its limited placental expression and has been hypothesized to be involved in protection of the maternal-fetal interface against immune attack, and HLA-E, which is involved in inhibition of natural killer cell–mediated cytotoxicity), as well as a series of pseudogenes. At least one group of class I–like molecules, designated CD1, is not encoded on the sixth chromosome but nevertheless probably plays an important role in defenses through binding and presentation of nonpeptide (particularly glycolipid) antigens. At least two sets of class II–like genes, HLA-DM and HLA-DO, encode proteins involved in the intracellular loading of exogenous peptide antigens into the classic class II molecules. Also within the class II region are several genes, designated *LMP* and *TAP*, that encode molecules that lack structural features of MHC molecules but play an important role in the hydrolysis and transport, respectively, of intracellular (endogenous) antigens to class I molecules.

CLASS I MOLECULES. A major conceptual advance in understanding the biologic function of MHC molecules was accomplished in 1987 with the solution by x-ray crystallography of the structure of a class I HLA molecule (Fig. 42–2). A 45-kD heavy (A) chain of these molecules consists of three extracellular domains of approximately 90 amino acids each connected to a transmembrane segment and a short intracytoplasmic tail (Fig. 42–3A). The class I heavy chains are noncovalently associated with a light chain (approximately 12 kD), designated β_2-microglobulin, that is not genetically encoded within the MHC. Both β_2-microglobulin and the membrane-proximal α_3-domain of the heavy chain have structural features that define them as members of the immunoglobulin superfamily, including an intrachain disulfide bond and a secondary structure of antiparallel β-pleated sheets with loop connections. The α_1 and α_2 domains form two α-helical loops mounted upon a platform of β-pleated sheet with a groove between the helical loops. The crystallographic surprise, and new insight, are derived from the presence of an amorphous material bound within the cleft formed by the opposing helical loops.

It has since been shown that this cleft at the exterior-most surface of the class I molecule serves as a binding site for peptide fragments of partially digested proteins, usually eight to nine amino acids in length. These peptides are loaded into newly synthesized class I molecules and then, together with β_2-microglobulin, are presented to T cells at the surface of APCs. MHC class I molecules are now known to present oligopeptide antigens to T cells that express the accessory molecule CD8. The peptide thus presented may be derived either from self proteins, in which case it is either not recognized or is

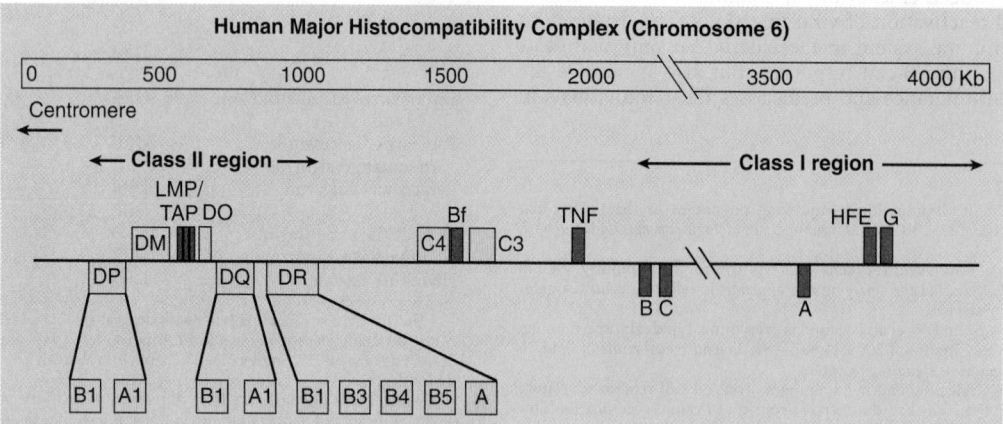

FIGURE 42–1 • Simplified schematic of the HLA complex. Illustrated below the line are MHC class I and class II genes, the products of which are involved in presentation of antigen to T lymphocytes. Above the line, within the class II region, are genes involved in antigen transport and processing. Between the class II and class I regions are several genes involved in effector functions of the immune system. And in the class I region are three class Ib genes: HLA-E, HLA-G, and HLA-H (also known as HFE, a candidate gene for hereditary hemochromatosis). Not shown are several additional expressed class Ib genes, as well as a large number of class I and class II pseudogenes. Approximate genetic distances are given in thousands of base pairs (Kb).

FIGURE 42–2 • Crystallographic structure of an HLA class I molecule. β-Strands are depicted as thick arrows in the amino-to-carboxy direction, and α-helices are presented as helical ribbons with connecting loops shown as thin lines. The disulfide bonds are illustrated as connected spheres. *A,* Side view of the molecule showing the three domains of the heavy chain noncovalently associated with β₂-microglobulin. *B,* Top view of the antigen-binding cleft with the α-helices on top of a β-pleated sheet platform. (From Bjorkman PJ, Spaer MA, Samraoui B, Bennett WS, Strominger JL, Wiley DC: Structure of the human class I histocompatibility antigen, HLA-A2. Nature 1987;329:506–512.)

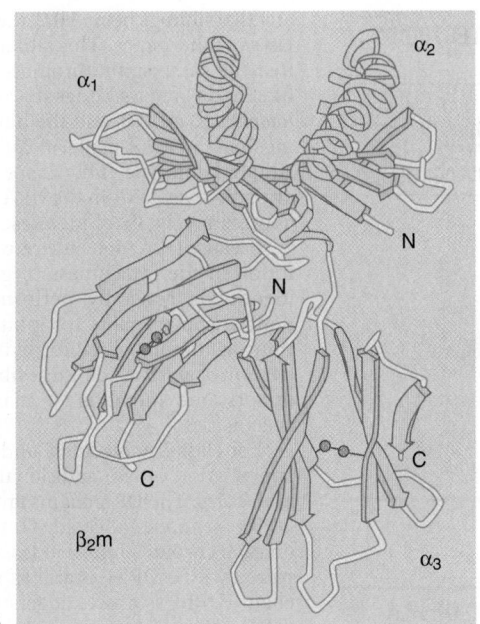
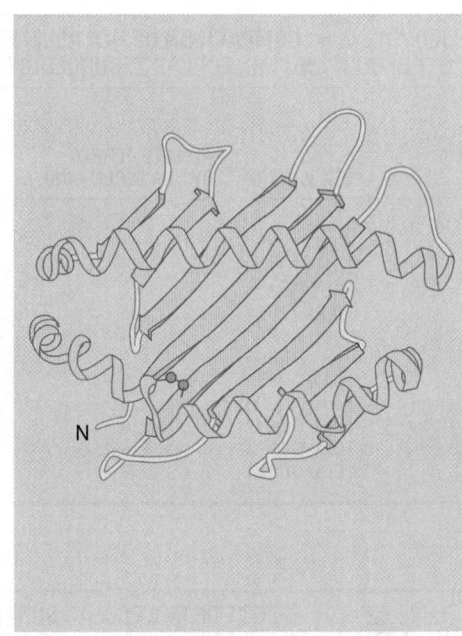

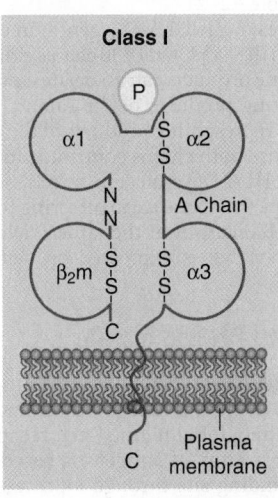
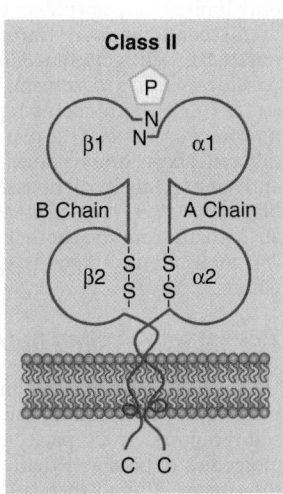

FIGURE 42–3 • Schematic representation of HLA molecules. *A,* A class I molecule illustrating the three-domain heavy chain, which penetrates the cell membrane and is noncovalently associated with β₂-microglobulin. An antigenic peptide (P) is illustrated in the antigen-binding groove formed by the α₁ and α₂ domains. *B,* A class II molecule illustrating the noncovalently associated A and B chains of the molecule. Both chains are integral membrane proteins. The amino terminal domains of both chains together form an intermolecular antigen-binding groove.

tolerated, or from a non-self protein, in which case it may lead to activation of CD8+ T cells of appropriate binding specificity. Antigens presented by class I molecules are usually derived from endogenous proteins (i.e., proteins synthesized within the APC). "Foreign" endogenous antigens include such molecules as viral proteins, proteins from intracytosolic bacteria and "tumor-specific" antigens. T-cell receptors for antigen have been selected within the thymus gland to recognize, within a single binding site, specific elements of both the self-MHC molecule and the peptide within the antigen-binding groove. Consequently, antigens presented (in an experimental system) by non-self MHC molecules are not recognized, a phenomenon known as *MHC-restriction* of antigen recognition by T cells.

CLASS II MOLECULES. The overall structure of MHC class II molecules is very similar to that of class I molecules (Fig. 42–3B). Class II molecules also are composed of two noncovalently associated chains, A and B. In contrast to class I molecules, however, both chains of class

II molecules are encoded within the MHC and both are integral membrane proteins that penetrate the cell membrane. The A and B class II polypeptide chains are of approximately equal size (about 34 and 29 kD, respectively) and consist of two rather than three extracellular domains. The membrane-proximal α₂ and β₂ domains, like the α₃ domain of the class I heavy chain, are composed of antiparallel β-pleated sheets and contain a single intrachain disulfide bond. The α₁ and β₁ (amino terminal) domains come together to form an intermolecular β-pleated sheet platform that is also surmounted by two α-helical coils, one contributed by each chain. These coils, together with the β-pleated sheet floor, again form an antigen-binding cleft into which peptide fragments are bound for presentation to T lymphocytes. In the case of class II molecules, however, antigen presentation is exclusively to T cells for which the antigen receptor is characterized by coexpression of the accessory molecule CD4. Moreover, the proteins from which class II binding peptides are derived are generally synthesized extracellularly (e.g., most bacterial pathogens). They are then processed into oligopeptides and bound into a ternary complex with the class IIA and B chains within endosomal granules, whereupon the complex is transported to the cell surface. The newly synthesized class II molecules are transported from the endoplasmic reticulum to the granules by a process that protects their antigen-binding grooves from premature (endogenous) antigen–peptide encounter before arrival within the granules, where exogenous peptides are available.

The peptides that bind to MHC class II molecules are longer than those binding to class I molecules, usually 13 to 20 amino acids in length, because the ends of the helices are open to allow the peptide to extend outside the groove in either direction and also to slip back and forth to accomplish binding of the highest possible affinity. In contrast, the α-helices of class I molecules come together to close the antigen-binding groove at both ends. Recognition of oligopeptide antigens bound to class II molecules is also MHC-restricted and requires the T-cell receptors of CD4+ T cells to recognize simultaneously the self class II MHC molecule and the peptide antigen. Furthermore, again like class I molecules, although peptides derived from both self and non-self exogenous proteins may bind to class II molecules, processes of receptor selection normally ensure that only T cells with receptors that recognize a foreign peptide are available for activation.

HLA Polymorphism

The HLA genes are the most polymorphic of the human genome, particularly in the case of molecules that have a major role in antigen presentation, namely, the class I molecules HLA-A and HLA-B and the class II molecules HLA-DR and HLA-DQ. Moreover, polymorphism defined serologically by antibodies has proved on subsequent

Table 42–2 • COMPARISON OF HLA ALLELES DETECTED BY SEROLOGIC AND MOLECULAR TECHNOLOGIES

	HLA ISOTYPE	ALLELES DEFINED BY DNA SEQUENCING, *n*	ALLELIC PRODUCTS DEFINED SEROLOGICALLY, *n*
CLASS I	HLA-A	50	39
	HLA-B	97	46
	HLA-C	34	15
CLASS II	HLA-DRA	2	0
	HLA-DRB1	106	14
	-DRB3	4	1
	-DRB4	5	1
	-DRB5	5	1
	HLA-DQA1	15	0
	HLA-DQB1	26	7
	HLA-DPA1	8	0
	HLA-DPB1	59	6

Table 42–3 • EFFECT OF MOLECULAR SUBTYPING OF HLA HAPLOTYPES ON RELATIVE RISK OF TYPE 1 DIABETES MELLITUS

DRB1	DQA1	DQB1	RELATIVE RISK
0403	0301	0302	0.7
0406	0301	0302	0.2
0405	0301	0302	34.0
0405	0301	0301	2.1
0405	0301	0401	2.5
0401	0301	0302	3.0
0301	0501	0201	7.7
0901	0301	0303	1.2
1201	0501	0301	0.2

Data predominantly from Chinese subjects, abstracted from She J-X; Susceptibility to type I diabetes: HLA-DQ and DR revisited. Immunol Today 1996;17:323.

Relative risk: See footnote to Table 42–1.

typing by DNA sequencing to substantially underestimate true molecular polymorphism (Table 42–2). The definition of molecular subtypes is quite relevant to understanding of HLA and disease associations inasmuch as most such associations were initially based on serologic associations with a specific HLA type. Thus, determination of associations with specific molecular variants has often resulted in a significant increase in relative risk (Table 42–3). A nomenclature has been developed to distinguish related molecular subtypes of major alleles. The specific gene designated is separated by an asterisk from a four-digit number, the first two digits of which denote the major allelic specificity and the last two, the molecular subtype. For example, DRB1*0301 defines the B chain of a molecular variant (split) of HLA-DR3 (which is also described by serologic typing as HLA-DR17).

For both class I and class II molecules, polymorphism is largely restricted to amino acid residues on the floor or the surrounding α-helices of the antigen-binding groove. Polymorphism thus serves two distinct purposes. First, polymorphisms within the binding groove determine the peptide binding specificity (motif). This motif defines which few peptides any given MHC molecule will bind from among the many available in the cellular microenvironment. Second, polymorphisms within the α-helices also serve as the markers of "self" upon which T-cell receptors are selected. Polymorphisms of MHC molecules outside the antigen-binding groove are far more limited.

The high degree of polymorphism at the HLA gene loci has several consequences. First, it is only rarely that two unrelated individuals are HLA identical. Second, the vast majority of individuals are heterozygous at each HLA locus, having inherited one set of alleles from their mother and a second (different) set from their father. Third, because all of the genes of the HLA complex are inherited as a single unit on the sixth chromosome, termed a *haplotype*, the likelihood of

any two siblings being HLA identical is 25%, in accord with Mendel's laws of inheritance. This situation would occur when siblings inherited the same sixth chromosome from both parents. Similarly, the likelihood of two siblings sharing one such chromosome, termed *haploidentical*, is 50%, and the likelihood of sharing neither sixth chromosome, or *HLA nonidentical*, is again 25%. The exception to this simple haplotype inheritance is the occasional interchromosomal crossing-over. Within the HLA complex, crossing-over is observed in approximately 3% of meioses.

Because HLA molecules are the most important elements in recognition of the foreignness of grafted tissues, tissue typing for HLA identity is generally performed to identify the most favorable donor-recipient pairs for grafting of bone marrow and solid organ transplantation, which for living related donors often means identification of an HLA-identical sibling; for unrelated (usually cadaveric) donors, the intent is to maximize the number of shared HLA specificities.

For class II molecules, understanding of polymorphism requires appreciation of two additional phenomena. The first applies to DR molecules. The DRA chains are essentially nonpolymorphic, and the DRB genes are duplicated. Thus, every individual expresses products on each chromosome of at least two sets of DR genes, the DRA chain paired with a DRB1 chain, as well as with a DRB3, DRB4, or DRB5 chain (DRB2 is a pseudogene). Polymorphism of DR molecules is predominantly a product of the DRB1 polypeptide, for which more than 100 alleles have been identified by DNA sequencing. The products of DRB3, DRB4, and DRB5 are expressed in combination with specific DRB1 alleles and, although differing from one another, exhibit only limited polymorphism (see Table 42–2).

A second important feature relates to the HLA-DQ genes. In contrast to HLA-DR, genes encoding both the DQA and DQB chains exhibit considerable polymorphism. The gene products can associate equally either in *cis* (both chains representing products of the same chromosome) or in *trans* (the two chains representing products of the two different sixth chromosomes). Because both chains contribute to the antigenic specificity of the assembled HLA-DQ molecule, novel assemblages that are expressed by neither parent can arise in offspring (e.g., an A chain from the mother and a B chain from the father yields a DQ molecule of antigenic specificity that is expressed by neither parent).

The Antigen Binding Groove and Peptide Motifs

The MHC molecules are one of three basic types involved in antigen binding and recognition, the others being immunoglobulins and T-cell receptors. The capacity of immunoglobulin and T-cell receptor molecules to bind a virtually limitless array of antigens is based on the construction of their antigen binding site through a process of DNA rearrangements between two or three gene segments that encode the site, together with nucleotide insertions at junctions between rearranged segments. MHC molecules, in contrast, do *not* rearrange. The capacity of MHC molecules to present a large number of different antigens thus depends on different strategies. First, the high degree of polymorphism at the various loci along with the multiplicity of loci within the HLA complex provides an organism with a considerable number of distinct antigen-presenting MHC molecules. The heart of the strategy, however, is that each MHC molecule has a distinct peptide-binding "motif" that consists of pockets into which antigen-peptide amino acid side chains of a particular type (e.g., aromatic, hydrophobic, or charged) can be anchored (Fig. 42–4). Most peptides will be bound by two to three high-affinity major anchors and a similar number of minor anchors (of lower affinity). Thus, a large number of different peptides derived from different proteins can be presented by any particular MHC molecule. The peptides interact with T-cell receptors via side chains of amino acids other than the anchors, which point out of the groove. As a consequence, any particular protein usually generates one or more peptides that can bind to one or more of the MHC molecules expressed by an individual. Nevertheless, the T-cell response to a complex protein antigen may be dominated by the response to one or a few specific peptides derived from that antigen.

The fact that peptides derived from single proteins have limited immunogenicity for T cells has obvious consequences when the design of T-cell vaccines is considered. The antigenic epitopes for one individual may differ from those of another, depending on the peptide binding specificity of their particular MHC molecules. When dealing

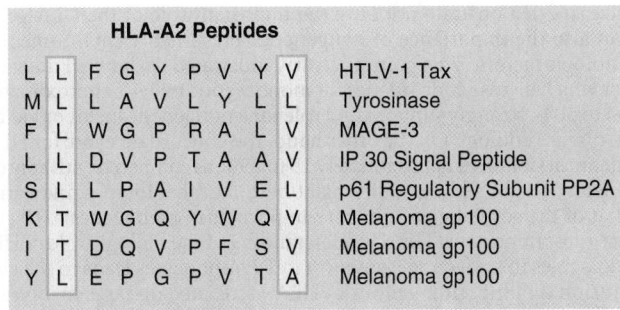

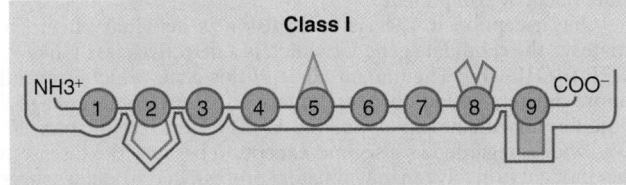

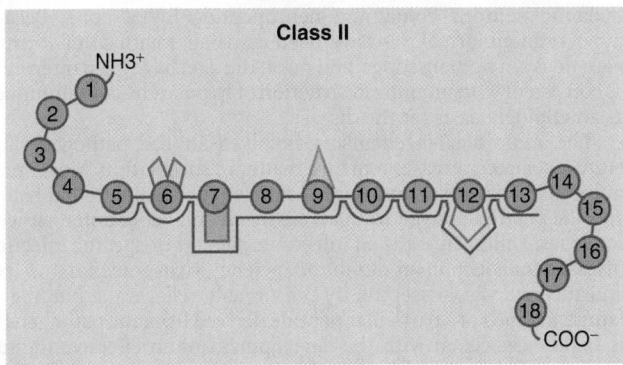

FIGURE 42–4 • Peptide binding motifs of HLA molecules. *A,* Nonamer peptides, which have been shown to bind into the antigen-binding groove of HLA-A2, illustrate the strong anchors at positions 2 (leucine) and 9 (valine or leucine). The high degree of variability of peptides available for interacting with the T-cell receptor is apparent. Proteins from which these peptides are derived are listed to the right of the sequence. Sequences are denoted with the single letter amino acid code. Also shown are three peptides from the melanoma gp 100 antigen that appear to violate the canonic motif with a threonine at position 2 or an alanine at position 9. In these exceptional cases, weak anchors, illustrated in part *B* as interactions with amino acids 1 and 3, are thought to contribute importantly to peptide binding. *B,* Peptide binding of HLA-A2 showing strong anchors at positions 2 and 9, minor anchors at positions 1 and 3, and closure of the binding groove ends with electrostatic interactions at both the NH_3^+ and COO^- termini. Side chains of residues at positions 5 and 8 are shown pointing up for interaction with the T-cell receptor. *C,* Peptide binding motif of a typical class II MHC molecule with strong anchors at positions 7 and 12 and weak anchors at positions 6, 10, and 11 and with positions 6 and 9 directing the side chain outward for interaction with the T-cell receptor. In contrast to class I, the ends of the class II binding groove are open, which allows for binding of a longer peptide and for movement back and forth to optimize interaction with MHC pocket anchors.

with highly complex antigenic structure (e.g., from attenuated viral vaccines), such specificity is not of particular importance because there are almost always some antigen peptides that can bind to one or more MHC molecules from every individual. As antigens are simplified, however, specificity does become a matter of practical concern. For example, with recombinant hepatitis B surface antigen vaccines, 4 to 10% of vaccine recipients fail to mount a substantial immune response. This failure is associated with the inheritance of specific HLA haplotypes.

Expression and Distribution of HLA Molecules

HLA genes are codominantly expressed: cells display the products of both sixth chromosomes on their surface. This codominance is

another important distinction from the products of immunoglobulin and T-cell receptor genes, which express the products of only one or the other chromosome. Moreover, cells express complete haplotypes of MHC molecules. That is, the products of both complete haplotypes (HLA-A, B, and C and HLA-DR, DQ, and DP) are displayed. A fully competent APC thus expresses at least six different class I molecules and 10 different class II molecules (the larger number of class II molecules reflecting multiple DRB chains and *trans*-complementation of DQ).

The distribution of class I and class II molecules differs considerably. Class I molecules are expressed on almost all nucleated cells of the body (exceptions being very low or absent expression on neurons and spermatozoa). Expression of class II molecules is much more limited. Under normal circumstances (in the absence of an acute inflammatory process), class II molecules are expressed only on cells that are specialized for antigen presentation (i.e., APCs), including such cells as monocytes, macrophages, dendritic cells (including Langerhans' cells in skin), B lymphocytes, and (in humans) activated T lymphocytes. APCs are distinguished not only by their capacity to present peptide antigens to CD4+ T cells but also by their surface expression of costimulatory molecules essential to T-cell activation (Chapter 41). In the presence of acute inflammation, however, other cell types can be induced by the T-cell cytokine interferon-γ to express class II molecules. Induced expression on endothelial cells and on the parenchymal cells of endocrine organs may be important in the pathogenesis of immunologic diseases involving such tissues.

Linkage Disequilibrium

Analysis of HLA susceptibility to diseases is complicated by the phenomenon of linkage disequilibrium, which is the observation of an increased frequency with which a specific allele at one HLA locus is inherited in combination with a specific allele or alleles at some other HLA locus. Linkage disequilibrium results in considerable difficulty in determining which specific HLA locus is causally associated with a given disease, because more than one locus may show a statistically significant association. The phenomenon is most consistently observed with closely linked genes, such as the association of DRB1 alleles determining DR3, DR5, DR6, and DR8 with the DRB3 alleles that determine DRw52 and the association of DRB1 alleles encoding DR4, DR7, and DR9 with the DRB4 allele that encodes DRw53. A very high level of association is also noted between certain DR and DQ specificities, such as DR2 with DQ1 and DQ6, DR3 with DQ2, DR7 with DQ2, and DR4 with DQ3. Linkage disequilibrium can operate over the substantial genetic distance of the entire HLA complex. For example, the frequent haplotypes of HLA-A1, B8, DR3 and A3, B7, and DR2 are several times more frequent in white populations than their individual allelic gene frequencies would predict.

Several non-mutually exclusive mechanisms are advanced to explain the phenomenon of linkage equilibrium. The simplest, and perhaps the most common, is the lack of sufficient evolutionary time since the emergence of alleles for them to have come into equilibrium by the process of crossing-over. Other mechanisms may pertain, however, especially when the linked genes are at substantial distance from one another and the alleles (or series of alleles) in question are known to be relatively old. These include a selective advantage of certain combinations of allelic products in defenses against specific pathogens and possible physical impediments to DNA crossing-over between chromosomes bearing specific alleles.

Molecular Definition of HLA-Associated Disease Susceptibility

The availability of molecular subtyping of serologically related HLA specificities during the past decade has enabled definition of HLA-associated disease susceptibility in considerably greater detail. Disease association defined at a molecular level can generally be associated with polymorphisms at specific sites within the HLA antigen-binding groove. For example, in the case of type I diabetes (Chapter 242), the protective effect associated with DQ6 (as well as several other DQ alleles) is highly associated with the presence of an aspartic acid at residue 57 of the DQB chain. In contrast, susceptibility to type I diabetes is highly associated with an alanine at this position, and valine and serine are associated with a modest increase in susceptibility. In fact, DQ8, which has an alanine in this position, is associated with type I diabetes in 65 to 70% of cases. Moreover, individuals inheriting the DQ7 molecule do not have an increase in susceptibility to type I diabetes despite the fact that DQ7 and DQ8 share an identical DQA chain and differ in only four amino acids in the peptide-binding portion of their B chain, including position 57, which is an aspartic acid in DQ7 and a noncharged amino acid (alanine) in DQ8. DQB57 lies on the α-helix of the B chain in pocket 9 of the peptide-binding cleft, which implies a specific role of this pocket in the binding and presentation of a peptide involved in the pathogenesis of type I diabetes.

Disease association for type I diabetes, however, is more complex than simply the definition of a critical amino acid at DQB position 57. Of particular interest is the observation that heterozygosity for HLA-DR3/4 is more highly associated with disease than is homozygosity at either allele. This observation may reflect DR/DQ linkage disequilibrium and the formation of DQ trans-dimers in heterozygotes that are responsible for the increased susceptibility. Certain molecular polymorphisms of the DRB1 chain are also independently associated with disease susceptibility. This role of DRB1 alleles is illustrated in Table 42–3, which demonstrates significant differences in the susceptibility of individuals with identical DQ genes who differ for DRB1.

Molecular studies of disease association in cases of seropositive rheumatoid arthritis have focused attention on a specific segment of the DRB1 chain. DRB1*0401, *0404, *0405, and *0408 are all strongly associated with the development of rheumatoid arthritis. Indeed, approximately 70% of patients with rheumatoid arthritis are HLA-DR4 positive. On the other hand, DR4-positive individuals with the molecular subtype DRB1*0402 are not at increased risk for rheumatoid arthritis. Each of the rheumatoid arthritis–associated HLA-DR molecules has an identical or very similar sequence of amino acids in positions 67 to 74 of the third hypervariable region of the B chain of the molecule. Most notably, at position 71, the disease-associated genes encode the positively charged amino acids lysine or arginine. In contrast, DRB1*0402 encodes a negatively charged glutamic acid at this site. Because DRB1 position 71 is an important constituent of pocket 4 of the peptide-binding cleft, this observation provides strong evidence of the role of a negatively charged peptide that may be accommodated into pocket 4 in the pathogenesis of rheumatoid arthritis.

Molecular analysis of the effect of HLA genes on the progression of human immunodeficiency virus infection to acquired immunodeficiency syndrome provides a striking example of how changes in the peptide-binding groove can affect the course of an infectious disease. Rapid progression to acquired immunodeficiency syndrome has been associated positively with inheritance of the class I allele HLA-B*35. But not all molecular subtypes of B*35 exhibited this effect. HLA-B*3501 and -B*3508, which share a binding motif in pocket 9 that prefers peptides with a carboxy-terminal tyrosine, did not demonstrate rapid progression. In contrast, rapid progression to acquired immunodeficiency syndrome was observed with those subtypes (HLA-B*3502, -B*3503, -B*3504) that did not bind peptides with a carboxy-terminal tyrosine in pocket 9 but did not otherwise demonstrate a clear carboxy-terminal preference.

Similar molecular studies have been carried out or are in progress for other HLA-associated diseases, particularly those for which molecular subtyping has revealed significant differences in susceptibility associated with minor molecular variants. Because such studies will also clarify the true disease-associated allele or alleles for isotypes in linkage disequilibrium, it is likely that future analyses of HLA and disease susceptibility will reveal increases in relative risk associated with specific HLA subtypes that are substantially greater than those based on analysis of serologically defined specificities.

Interpretation of HLA and Disease Associations

Observations of HLA and disease association lead to several conclusions and to theoretic speculation regarding pathogenetic mechanisms. First, it must be appreciated that none of the HLA-associated diseases occur as mendelian monogenic diseases. Indeed, the vast majority of individuals inheriting a specific disease-associated allele never exhibit manifestations of the disease. Such is the case even with the associations of greatest statistical significance. For example, ankylosing spondylitis or one of the other HLA-B27–associated diseases do not develop in most individuals inheriting HLA-B27. Second, inheritance patterns within families with certain of the HLA-associated

diseases demonstrate not only the important role of the HLA genes but also the importance of nongenetic (presumably environmental) etiologic factors. This point is clearly illustrated with type I diabetes, for which disease concordance for monozygotic twins is approximately 35 to 50%, strongly supporting a role for a nongenetic factor or factors in disease etiology. On the other hand, the concordance rate for HLA-identical siblings is approximately 15 to 25%, as compared with approximately 1% for siblings differing at both HLA haplotypes, indicating that of the several genes that are important in pathogenesis, HLA is the most important. Third, understanding of the biologic role of HLA molecules in antigen presentation to T lymphocytes leads to the conclusion that the pathogenesis of HLA-associated diseases involves T-cell activation in the vast majority of such diseases with a clear inflammatory component.

One exception to the last conclusion is hereditary hemochromatosis, the candidate gene for which is a defective class I–like gene HFE (or HLA-H). The mutant allele of this gene, which is encoded approximately 300 kilobases telomeric of HLA-A, is in linkage disequilibrium with the haplotype HLA-A3, B14. Until recently, narcolepsy was widely regarded as a second exception because the disease was not thought to involve an inflammatory process. Recent studies suggest, however, that the disease is associated with the destruction of hypothalamic neurons containing neuropeptide hypocretins. Because hypocretin abnormalities have been associated with some forms of narcolepsy in humans, dogs, and mice, the data have been interpreted as consistent with immune destruction of hypocretin-containing cells as an etiologic basis for the disease.

The molecular mechanisms involved in the pathogenesis of HLA-associated diseases remain a matter of speculation. Most immunologists believe that an essential nongenetic element is probably a specific peptide derived from an environmental encounter, either as food, as an allergen, or as an infectious agent. For specific infectious diseases such as human immunodeficiency virus infection, malaria, and tuberculosis, susceptibility presumably reflects the binding (or failure to bind) of a particular peptide derived from the pathogen that is highly associated with the development of an effective immune response. Other than known infectious diseases, however, in most cases no convincing etiologic agent has been discovered. It has been suggested that the pathogenesis of such diseases may also involve common infectious agents encountered at some critical time in the maturation and/or activation of the immune system. In such cases, immunologic attack might not be limited to the etiologic agent; it might also be directed perversely against autologous tissue constituents. Recent data suggesting a possible role for Epstein-Barr virus in the etiology of systemic lupus erythematosus in some patients support the notion of infection with a ubiquitous pathogen leading to development of an autoimmune disease in a small minority of susceptible individuals.

A specific etiologic antigen has been implicated in at least one disease, celiac disease. In this case, the antigen is the gliadin component of gluten, present as a dietary component derived from wheat and several other cereal grains. Patients with celiac disease have been shown to have gliadin-reactive T cells that are specifically activated when the antigen is presented by the disease-associated HLA-DQ molecule (DQ2 or DQ8, depending on the allele expressed by the specific patient).

An important mystery is the pathogenetic basis of an inflammatory lesion following an encounter with an etiologic environmental peptide. To re-emphasize, the vast majority of DQ2 and DQ8 individuals ingest gluten-containing foods throughout their lives and celiac disease never develops. Moreover, it remains unclear in the case of tissue-specific autoimmune diseases why a particular etiologic event is associated with destruction of the specific target tissue. A frequently advanced hypothesis is that of "molecular mimicry," in which the structure of a particular autologous peptide is antigenically cross-reactive with an etiologic peptide when bound by chance by a disease-associated HLA molecule. In such cases, it is argued, T-cell tolerance for self tissues may be broken by an ambiguity in self/non-self discrimination, with an immune response initiated against the etiologic peptide, and then being directed (and perhaps amplified and perpetuated) as an immunologic response against the autologous self-peptide/MHC complex. Such a hypothesis gains credence with the recognition that tolerance for self proteins is not only determined by T-cell receptor selection in the thymus but also involves mechanisms of anergy or active suppression of potentially self-reactive T cells in peripheral lymphoid organs. It is further supported by the recent concept that with minor structural changes, a T-cell–activating peptide bound to a particular MHC molecule can be converted from a T-cell agonist to antagonist and vice versa.

Diagnostic Considerations

With the very strong association between HLA inheritance and disease susceptibility for a considerable number of diseases, it is reasonable to ask whether HLA tissue typing has a role in the diagnostic tool kit or in assessing the future likelihood of development of an HLA-associated disease. Because HLA-associated disease does not develop in most individuals with the appropriate HLA inheritance, the general answer to this question is emphatically *no*. Moreover, in no instance can the presence of an appropriate HLA allele positively establish a diagnosis. For example, one cannot make the diagnosis of ankylosing spondylitis in an HLA-B27–positive patient with low back pain in the absence of compatible radiologic findings (Chapter 279). On the other hand, in selected cases, the *absence* of a highly associated marker may be of diagnostic usefulness. Thus, a B27-negative patient with low back pain and equivocal or absent radiologic findings is unlikely to have incipient ankylosing spondylitis as an explanation for the symptoms. Similarly, a patient complaining of excessive daytime sleepiness in the absence of HLA-DQ6 is unlikely to have sporadic narcolepsy as an explanation.

One intriguing possibility for future diagnostic use is the identification of individuals at risk within families with an HLA-associated disease in which evidence of immunologic attack predictably antedates the development of clinical disease. For example, in type I diabetes, several studies are now in progress in families in whom HLA-identical siblings of a patient with disease are being monitored for immunologic signs of pancreatic β-cell destruction, which may occur years before the development of clinical diabetes. It is hoped that with the development of increasingly safe and effective immunosuppressive agents, the possibility of therapeutic intervention in the preclinical phase of such diseases may make prevention a possibility.

SUGGESTED READINGS

Gao X, Nelson GW, Karacki P, et al: Effect of a single amino acid change in MHI class I molecules rate of progression to AIDS. N Engl J Med 2001;344:1668–1675. *A well-executed study demonstrating the association of minor changes in the peptide-binding groove of a class I HLA molecule with the clinical progression of acquired immunodeficiency syndrome.*

Klein J, Sato A: The HLA system. N Engl J Med 2001;343:702,782–786. *A two-part review by a leading authority on the evolution, genetic organization and biology of the major histocompatibility complex.*

Onengut-Gumuscu S, Concannon P: Mapping genes for autoimmunity in humans: Type 1 diabetes as a model. Immunol Rev 2002;190:182–194. *Summarizes current understanding of the genetic basic of type 1 diabetes, emphasizing the HLA and insulin gene regions and the power of consortium efforts with pooled data in susceptibility-gene identification.*

Ramos M, DeCastro JA: HLA-B27 and the pathogenesis of spondyloarthritis. Tissue Antigens 2002;60:191–205. *An interesting and provocative analysis of the strong association between HLA-B27 and a predisposition to spondyloarthropathies.*

Undlien DE, Thorsby E: HLA associations in type 1 diabetes: Merging genetics and immunology. Trends Immunol 2001;22:467–469. *A brief review of the complex relationships between multiple genes of the HLA complex and susceptibility to or protection from type I diabetes, particularly as revealed by studies in transgenic mice.*

Yu D, Kuipers JG: Role of bacteria and HLA-B27 in the pathogenesis of reactive arthritis. Rheum Dis Clin North Am 2003;29:21–36. *A review of spondyloarthropathies induced by infection with five species of gram-negative bacteria and the role of HLA-B27 in the disease pathogenesis.*

43 MECHANISMS OF IMMUNE-MEDIATED TISSUE INJURY

Jane E. Salmon

The adaptive immune response is a crucial component of host defense against infection. Its distinguishing and unique feature is the ability to recognize pathogens specifically, based on clonal selection of lymphocytes bearing antigen-specific receptors. Antigens unassociated with infectious agents also may elicit adaptive immune responses. Many clinically important diseases are characterized by normal immune responses directed against an inappropriate antigen, typically in the absence of infection. Immune responses directed at noninfectious antigens occur in allergy, in which the antigen is an innocuous foreign substance, and in autoimmunity, in which the response is to self-antigen.

Effector mechanisms that eliminate pathogens in adaptive immune responses are essentially identical to those of innate immunity. The specific antigen recognition feature of the adaptive immune response seems to have been appended to the preexisting innate defense system. As a result, the inflammatory cells and molecules of the innate immune system are essential for the effector functions of B and T lymphocytes. In addition to initiating protective responses, they mediate tissue injury in allergy, hypersensitivity, and autoimmunity.

Effector Mechanisms

Effector actions of antibodies depend almost entirely on recruiting cells and molecules of the innate immune system. Antibodies are adapters that bind antigens to nonspecific inflammatory cells and direct their destructive effector responses. Antibodies also activate the complement system, which enhances opsonization of antigens, recruits phagocytic cells, and amplifies (or "complements") antibody-triggered damage. The isotype or class of antibodies produced determines which effector mechanisms are engaged.

Cell-bound receptors for immunoglobulin constitute the link between humoral and cellular aspects of the immune cascade and play an integral part in the process by which foreign and endogenous opsonized material is identified and destroyed. These cell-based binding sites for antibodies, termed *Fc receptors,* interact with the constant region (Fc portion) of the immunoglobulin heavy chain of a particular antibody class or subclass regardless of its antigen specificity. Accessory cells that lack intrinsic specificity, such as neutrophils, macrophages, and mast cells, are recruited to participate in inflammatory responses through the interaction of their Fc receptors with antigen-specific antibodies. Distinct receptors for different immunoglobulin isotypes are expressed on different effector cells.

Receptors for IgG (FcγRs) are a diverse group of receptors expressed as hematopoietic cell surface molecules on phagocytes (macrophages, monocytes, neutrophils), platelets, mast cells, eosinophils, and natural killer (NK) cells. FcγRs often are expressed as stimulatory and inhibitory pairs. Triggering stimulatory FcγRs initiates phagocytosis; antibody-dependent, cell-mediated cytotoxicity; secretion of granules; and release of inflammatory mediators, such as cytokines, reactive oxidants, and proteases. Extensive structural diversity among FcγR family members leads to differences in binding capacity, signal transduction pathways, and cell type–specific expression patterns. This diversity allows IgG complexes to activate a broad program of cell functions relevant to inflammation, host defense, and autoimmunity. Phagocyte activation is triggered by stimulatory FcγRs, facilitating the recognition, uptake, and destruction of antibody-coated targets, whereas multivalent IgG binding to FcγRs on platelets leads to platelet aggregation and thrombosis, and binding to FcγRs on NK cells mediates cytotoxicity of antibody-coated targets.

IgE binds to high-affinity FcεRs on mast cells, basophils, and activated eosinophils. In contrast to FcγRs, which are low affinity and bind multivalent IgG to antigens rather than to circulating individual IgG molecules, FcεRs can bind monomeric IgE. A single mast cell may be armed with IgE molecules specific for many different antigens, all bound to surface FcεRs. Mast cells, localized beneath the mucosa of the gastrointestinal and respiratory tracts and the dermis of the skin, await exposure to multivalent antigens, which cross-link surface IgE bound to FcεRs and cause release of histamine-containing granules and generation of cytokines and other inflammatory mediators. IgE-mediated activation of eosinophils, cells normally present in the connective tissue of underlying respiratory, urogenital, and gut epithelium, leads to the release of highly toxic granule proteins, free radicals, and chemical mediators, such as prostaglandins, cytokines, and chemokines. These amplify local inflammatory responses by activating endothelial cells and recruiting and activating more eosinophils and leukocytes. Prepackaged granules and high-affinity FcεRs that bind to free monomeric IgE enable an immediate response to pathogens or allergens at the first site of entry, a location where FcεR-bearing cells reside.

Inhibitory FcγRs, which modulate activation thresholds and terminate stimulating signals, are key elements in the regulation of effector function. Given that inhibitory and stimulatory Fc receptors are often coexpressed on the same cells, the effector response to a specific stimulus in a particular cell represents the balance between stimulatory and inhibitory signals. Inhibitory FcγRs can dampen

Table 43–1 • FOUR MAJOR TYPES OF IMMUNOLOGICALLY MEDIATED HYPERSENSITIVITY REACTIONS*

IMMUNOLOGIC SPECIFICITY	TYPE I IgE ANTIBODY	TYPE II IgG ANTIBODY	TYPE III IgG ANTIBODY	TYPE IV T CELLS		
				T$_H$1 cells	T$_H$2 cells	T cells
Antigen	Soluble antigen allergen	Cell- or matrix-associated antigen	Soluble antigen	Soluble antigen	Soluble antigen	Cell-associated antigen
Effector mechanism	FcεRI or FcγRIII-dependent mast cell activation, with release of mediators/cytokines	FcγR+ cells (phagocytes, NK cells), complement	FcγR+ cells, complement	Macrophage activation	Eosinophil activation	Direct cytotoxicity
Examples	Systemic anaphylaxis, asthma, allergic rhinitis, urticaria, angioedema	Certain drug reactions and reactions to incompatible blood transfusions	Arthus reaction and other immune complex–mediated reactions (serum sickness, subacute bacterial endocarditis)	Contact dermatitis, tuberculin reaction	Chronic allergic inflammation (chronic asthma, chronic allergic rhinitis)	Contact dermatitis (poison ivy), reactions to certain viral infected cells, some graft rejection

*Hypersensitivity reactions were classified into four types by Coombs and Gell (1963) and modified by Janeway and Colleagues (2001).

responses triggered by FcεRs on mast cells and FcγR-mediated inflammation at sites of immune complex deposition.

Effector activities targeted by IgG and IgM also may be mediated by components of the complement system (Chapter 45). Antigen-bound multimeric immunoglobulin can initiate activation of the classic pathway of complement causing enhanced phagocytosis of antigen-antibody complexes, increased local vascular permeability, and recruitment and activation of inflammatory cells. The target of injury is specified by the antibody, and the extent of damage is determined by the synergistic activities of immunoglobulin and complement.

Antigen-specific effector T cells also may initiate tissue injury. On exposure to an appropriate antigen, memory T cells are stimulated to release cytokines and chemokines that activate local endothelial cells and recruit and activate macrophages and other inflammatory cells. The effector cells directed by T cell–derived cytokines, or cytolytic T cells themselves, mediate tissue damage. T$_H$1 cells produce IFN-γ and activate macrophages to cause injury, whereas T$_H$2 cells produce IL-4, IL-5, and eotaxin (an eosinophil-specific chemokine) and trigger inflammatory responses in which eosinophils predominate.

Hypersensitivity Reactions

In predisposed individuals, innocuous environmental antigens may stimulate an adaptive immune response, immunologic memory, and, on subsequent exposure to the antigen, inflammation. These "over-reactions" of the immune system to harmless environmental antigens

(allergens), called *hypersensitivity* or *allergic reactions*, produce tissue injury and may cause serious disease. Hypersensitivity reactions are grouped into four types according to the effector mechanisms by which they are produced (Table 43–1). The effectors for types I, II, and III hypersensitivity reactions are antibody molecules, whereas type IV reactions are antigen-specific effector T cells.

Autoimmune disease is characterized by the presence of antibodies and T cells specific for self-antigens expressed on target tissues. The mechanisms of antigen recognition and effector function that lead to tissue damage in autoimmune disease are similar to the mechanisms elicited in response to pathogens and environmental antigens. These mechanisms resemble certain hypersensitivity reactions and may be classified accordingly (Table 43–2). Autoimmune disease caused by antibodies directed against cell surface or extracellular matrix antigens corresponds to type II hypersensitivity reactions; disease caused by formation of soluble immune complexes that subsequently are deposited in tissue corresponds to type III hypersensitivity; and disease caused by effector T cells corresponds to type IV hypersensitivity. Typically, several of these pathogenic mechanisms are operative in autoimmune disease. IgE responses are not associated, however, with damage in autoimmunity.

TYPE I HYPERSENSITIVITY REACTIONS

Type I hypersensitivity reactions (Fig. 43–1) are triggered by the interaction of antigen with antigen-specific IgE bound to FcεRs on

Table 43–2 • CLASSIFICATION OF AUTOIMMUNE DISEASES ACCORDING TO MECHANISM OF TISSUE INJURY

HYPERSENSITIVITY REACTION	AUTOIMMUNE DISEASE	AUTOANTIGEN
TYPE II		
Antibody against cell-surface antigens	Autoimmune hemolytic anemia	Rh blood group antigens, I antigen
	Autoimmune thrombocytopenic purpura	Platelet integrin glycoprotein IIb:IIIa
Antibody against receptors	Graves' disease	Thyroid-stimulating hormone receptor (agonistic antibodies)
	Myasthenia gravis	Acetylcholine receptor (antagonistic antibodies)
Antibody against matrix antigens	Goodpasture's syndrome	Basement membrane collagen (α$_3$ chain of type IV collagen)
	Pemphigus vulgaris	Epidermal cadherin (desmoglein)
TYPE III		
Immune complex diseases	Mixed essential cryoglobulinemia	Rheumatoid factor IgG complexes (with or without hepatitis C antigens)
	Systemic lupus erythematosus	DNA, histones, ribosomes, ribonuclear proteins
TYPE IV		
T cell–mediated diseases	Insulin-dependent diabetes mellitus	Pancreatic β-cell antigen
	Rheumatoid arthritis	Unknown synovial joint antigen
	Multiple sclerosis	Myelin basic protein, proteolipid protein

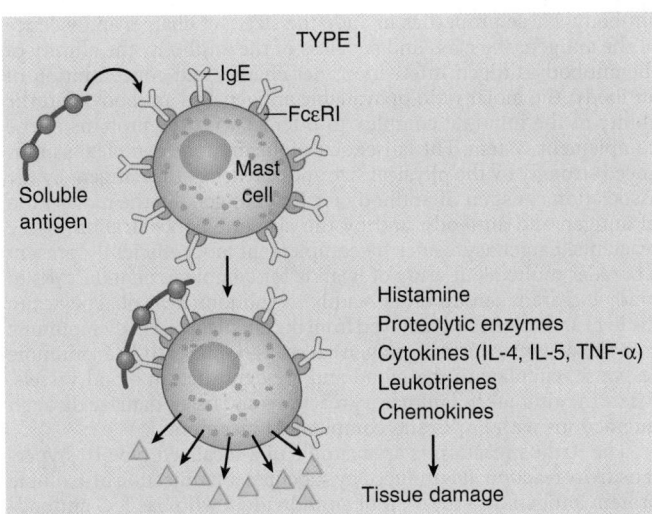

FIGURE 43–1 • Type I hypersensitivity. Type I responses are mediated by IgE, which induces mast cell activation. Cross-linking FcεR on mast cells, triggered by the interaction of multivalent antigen with antigen-specific IgE bound to FcεR, causes the release of preformed granules containing histamine and proteases. Cytokines, chemokines, and lipid mediators are synthesized after cell activation.

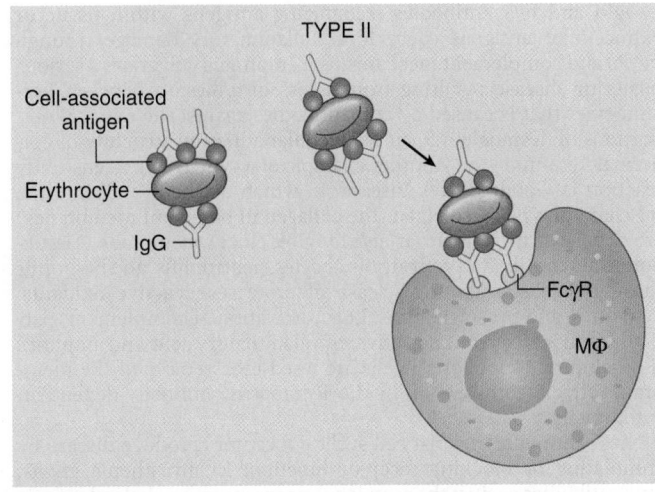

FIGURE 43–2 • Type II hypersensitivity. Type II responses are mediated by IgG directed against cell surface or matrix antigens, which initiates effector responses through FcγR and complement. The relative contribution of these pathways varies with the IgG subclass and the nature of the antigen. Only FcγR-mediated phagocytosis by macrophages (MΦ) is depicted in this figure. Activation of complement components would result in binding of C3b to the red blood cell membrane, rendering red blood cells susceptible to phagocytosis and leading to formation of the membrane attack complex and cell lysis.

mast cells, causing mast cell activation. Proteolytic enzymes and toxic mediators, such as histamine, are released immediately from preformed granules, and chemokines, cytokines, and leukotrienes are synthesized after activation. Together, these mediators increase vascular permeability; break down tissue matrix proteins; promote eosinophil production and activation (interleukin [IL]-3, IL-5, granulocyte-macrophage colony-stimulating factor [GM-CSF]); and cause influx of effector leukocytes (tumor necrosis factor [TNF]-α, platelet-activating factor, macrophage inflammatory protein [MIP-1]), constriction of smooth muscle, stimulation of mucus secretion, and amplification of T_H2 cell responses (IL-4, IL-13). Eosinophils and basophils, activated through cell surface FcεRs, rapidly release highly toxic granular proteins (major basic protein, eosinophil peroxidase, and collagenase) and, over a longer period, produce cytokines (IL-3, IL-5, GM-CSF), chemokines (IL-8), prostaglandins, and leukotrienes that activate epithelial cells, leukocytes, and eosinophils to augment local inflammation and tissue damage.

FcεR-bearing effectors act in a coordinated fashion. The immediate allergic inflammatory reaction initiated by mast cell products is followed by a late-phase response that involves recruitment and activation of eosinophils, basophils, and T_H2 cell lymphocytes. The manifestations of IgE-mediated reactions depend on the site of mast cell activation. Mast cells reside in vascular and epithelial tissue throughout the body. In a sensitized host (an individual with IgE responses to antigens), re-exposure to antigen leads to type I hypersensitivity responses only in the mast cells exposed to the antigen. Inhalation of antigens produces bronchoconstriction and increased mucus secretion (asthma and allergic rhinitis), and ingestion of antigens causes increased peristalsis and secretion (diarrhea and vomiting), whereas the presence of subcutaneous antigens initiates increased vascular permeability and swelling (urticaria and angioedema). Blood-borne antigens cause systemic mast cell activation, increased capillary permeability, hypotension, tissue swelling, and smooth muscle contraction—the characteristics of systemic anaphylaxis.

TYPE II HYPERSENSITIVITY REACTIONS

Type II hypersensitivity reactions (Fig. 43–2) are caused by chemical modification of cell surface or matrix-associated antigens generating "foreign" epitopes to which the immune system is not tolerant. B cells respond to this antigenic challenge by producing IgG that binds to these modified cells and renders them susceptible to destruction through complement activation, phagocytosis, and antibody-dependent cytotoxicity.

This phenomenon is seen clinically when drugs interact with blood constituents and alter their cellular antigens. Hemolytic anemia caused by immune-mediated destruction of erythrocytes and thrombocytopenia caused by destruction of platelets, both type II hypersensitivity reactions, are adverse effects of certain drugs. Chemically reactive drug molecules bind covalently to the surface of red blood cells or platelets. This modification of human proteins creates new epitopes that, in a small subset of individuals, are recognized as foreign antigens by the immune system and stimulates production of IgM and IgG antibodies reactive with the conjugate of drug and cell surface protein. Penicillin-specific IgG binds to penicillin-modified proteins on red blood cells. The binding of these antibodies to blood cells triggers activation of the complement cascade. Activation of complement components C1 through C3 results in covalent binding of C3b to the red blood cell membrane and renders circulating red blood cells susceptible to phagocytosis by FcγR-bearing and complement receptor–bearing macrophages in the spleen or liver. Activation of complement components C1 through C9 and formation of the membrane attack complex causes intravascular lysis of red blood cells. The factors that predispose only some people to drug-induced type II hypersensitivity reactions are unknown. Penicillin, quinidine, and methyldopa have been associated with hemolytic anemia and/or thrombocytopenia through this mechanism. Another example is heparin-induced thrombocytopenia/thrombosis, a severe, life-threatening complication that occurs in 1 to 3% of patients exposed to heparin. Interactions between heparin, human platelet factor 4, antibodies to the human platelet factor 4/heparin complex, platelet FcγRIIA, and splenic FcγRs (which remove opsonized platelets) are involved in the pathogenesis of this disease.

Autoantibodies directed at antigens on the cell surface or extracellular matrix cause tissue damage by mechanisms similar to type II hypersensitivity reactions. IgG or IgM antibodies against erythrocytes lead to cell destruction, in autoimmune immune hemolytic anemia, because opsonized cells (coated with IgG or IgM and complement) are removed from the circulation by phagocytes in the liver and spleen or lysed by formation of the membrane attack complex. Platelet destruction in autoimmune thrombocytopenic purpura occurs through a similar process. Because nucleated cells express membrane-bound complement regulatory proteins (Chapter 45), they are less sensitive to lysis through the membrane attack complex, but when coated with antibody, they become targets for phagocytosis or antibody-dependent cytotoxicity. This mechanism is responsible for autoimmune and alloimmune neutropenia.

IgM and IgG antibodies recognizing antigens within tissue or extracellular antigens cause local inflammatory damage through FcγRs and complement mechanisms. Pemphigus vulgaris is a serious blistering disease resulting from a loss of adhesion between keratinocytes that is caused by autoantibodies against the extracellular portions of desmoglein 3, an intercellular adhesion structure of epidermal keratinocytes. Another example of a type II hypersensitivity reaction is Goodpasture's disease, in which antibodies against the α3 chain of type IV collagen (the collagen in basement membranes) are deposited in glomerular and lung basement membrane. Tissue-bound autoantibodies activate monocytes, neutrophils, and basophils through FcγRs, initiating release of proteases, reactive oxidants, cytokines, and prostaglandins. Local activation of complement, particularly C5a, recruits and activates inflammatory cells and amplifies tissue injury. Neighboring cells are lysed by assembly of the membrane attack complex or by FcγR-initiated, antibody-dependent cytotoxicity.

Autoantibodies against cell surface receptors produce disease by stimulating or blocking receptor function. In myasthenia gravis, autoantibodies against the acetylcholine receptors on skeletal muscle cells bind the receptor and induce its internalization and degradation in lysosomes, reducing the efficiency of neuromuscular transmission and causing progressive muscle weakness. In contrast, Graves' disease is characterized by autoantibodies that act as agonists. Autoantibodies to thyroid-stimulating hormone receptors bind the receptor mimicking the natural ligand, inducing thyroid hormone overproduction, disrupting feedback regulation, and causing hyperthyroidism.

TYPE III HYPERSENSITIVITY REACTIONS

Type III hypersensitivity reactions (Fig. 43–3) are caused by tissue deposition of small soluble immune complexes, containing antigens and high-affinity IgG antibodies directed at these antigens. Localized deposition of immune complexes activates FcγR-bearing mast cells and phagocytes and initiates the complement cascade, all effectors of tissue damage.

Immune complexes are generated in all antibody responses. The formation and the fate of immune complexes depend, however, on the biophysical and immunologic properties of the antigen and the

antibody. These properties include the size, net charge, and valence of the antigen; the class and subclass of the antibody; the affinity of the antibody-antigen interaction, net charge, and concentration of antibody; the molar ratio of available antigen and antibody; and the ability of the immune complex to interact with the proteins of the complement system. The lattice size of the immune complex is influenced strongly by the physical size and valence of the antigen, by the association constant of antibody for that antigen, by the molar ratio of antigen and antibody, and by the absolute concentration of the reactants. Larger aggregates fix complement more efficiently, present a broader multivalent array of ligands for complement and FcγRs to bind, and are taken up more readily by mononuclear phagocytes in the liver and spleen and removed from the circulation. Smaller immune complexes, which form in antigen excess as occurs early in an immune response, circulate in the blood and are deposited in blood vessels, where they initiate inflammatory reactions and tissue damage through interactions with FcγRs and complement receptors.

The Arthus reaction is an example of a localized type III hypersensitivity reaction. It is induced by subcutaneous injection of a soluble protein antigen into the skin of an individual who has IgG antibodies against the sensitizing antigen. Local immune complexes form and bind to FcγRs on mast cells and phagocytes, causing release of inflammatory mediators that increase vascular permeability and induce influx and activation of leukocytes, further propagating injury. Complement also is activated and amplifies inflammation.

Serum sickness is a systemic type III hypersensitivity reaction, historically described in patients injected with therapeutic horse antiserum for the treatment of bacterial infections. Generally, serum sickness occurs after the injection of large quantities of a soluble antigen. Clinical features include chills, fever, rash, urticaria, arthritis, and glomerulonephritis. Disease manifestations become evident 7 to 10 days after exposure, when antibodies are generated against the foreign protein and form immune complexes with these circulating antigens. Immune complexes are deposited in blood vessels, where they activate phagocytes and complement, producing widespread tissue injury and clinical symptoms. The effects are transient, however, and resolve when the antigen is cleared.

A syndrome similar to serum sickness occurs in chronic infections in which pathogens persist in the face of continued immune response. In subacute bacterial endocarditis, antibody production continues but fails to eliminate the infecting microbes. As the pathogens multiply, generating new antigens, immune complexes form in the circulation and are deposited in small blood vessels, where they lead to inflammatory damage of skin, kidney, and nerve. Hepatitis B virus infection may be associated with immune complex deposition early in its course, during a period of antigen excess because antibody production in response to hepatitis B surface antigen is as yet relatively insufficient; some anicteric patients present with acute arthritis. Mixed essential cryoglobulinemia, which may be associated with hepatitis C viral infection, is an immune complex–mediated vasculitis in which deposition of complexes containing IgG, IgM, and hepatitis C antigens causes inflammation in peripheral nerves, kidneys, and skin. Serum sickness also can develop in transplant recipients treated with mouse monoclonal antibodies specific for human T cells used to prevent rejection and in patients with myocardial infarction treated with the bacterial enzyme streptokinase to effect thrombolysis.

Systemic lupus erythematosus, the prototypical immune complex–mediated autoimmune disease, is characterized by circulating IgG directed against common cellular constituents, typically DNA and DNA-binding proteins. Small immune complexes are deposited in skin, joints, and glomeruli with FcγRs playing a dominant role in initiating local tissue damage.

TYPE IV HYPERSENSITIVITY REACTIONS

Type IV hypersensitivity reactions (Fig. 43–4), also known as *delayed-type hypersensitivity reactions,* are mediated by antigen-specific effector T cells. They are distinguished from other hypersensitivity reactions by the lag time from exposure to antigen until the response is evident (1 to 3 days). Antigen is taken up, processed, and presented by macrophages or dendritic cells. T_H1 effector cells that recognize the specific antigen (these are scarce and take time to arrive) are stimulated to release chemokines, which recruit macrophages to the site and release cytokines, which mediate tissue injury. IFN-γ activates macrophages and enhances their release of

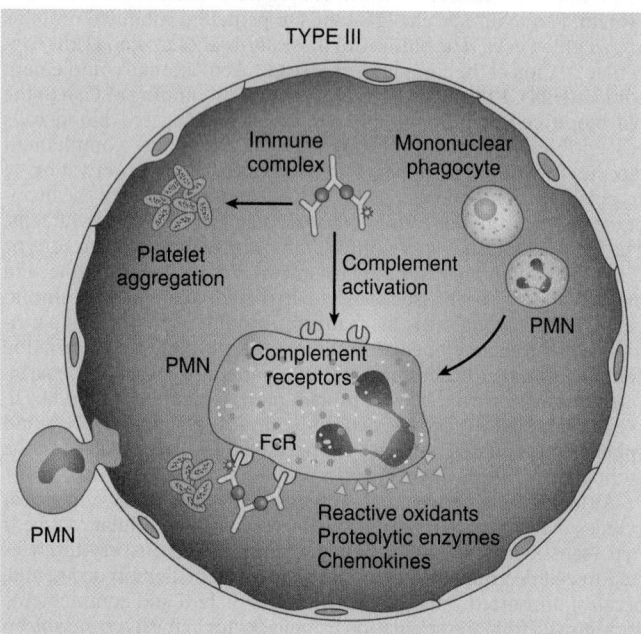

FIGURE 43–3 • Type III hypersensitivity. Type III responses are mediated by IgG directed against soluble antigens. Localized deposition of immune complexes activates FcγR-bearing mast cells, monocytes, neutrophils, and platelets and initiates the complement cascade, all effectors of tissue damage. Generation of C3a and C5a recruits and stimulates inflammatory cells and amplifies effector functions. PMN, polymorphonuclear leukocyte (also called neutrophil).

Figure labels: TYPE III; Immune complex; Mononuclear phagocyte; Platelet aggregation; Complement activation; PMN; Complement receptors; PMN; FcR; Reactive oxidants, Proteolytic enzymes, Chemokines; PMN

Principles of Immunology and Inflammation

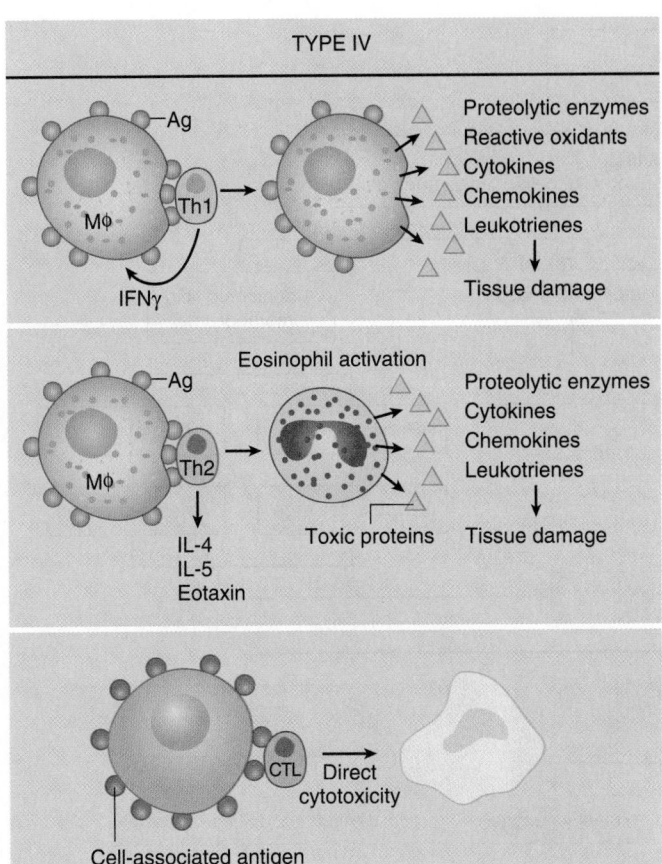

TYPE IV

FIGURE 43–4 • Type IV hypersensitivity. Type IV responses are mediated by T cells through three different pathways. In the first, T_H1 cells recognize soluble antigens and release IFN-γ to activate effector cells, in this case macrophages, and cause tissue injury. In T_H2-mediated responses, eosinophils predominate. T_H2 cells produce cytokines to recruit and activate eosinophils, leading to their degranulation and tissue injury. In the third pathway, damage is caused directly by cytolytic T cells.

inflammatory mediators, whereas TNF-α and TNF-β activate endothelial cells, enhance vascular permeability, and damage local tissue. The prototypical type IV hypersensitivity reaction is the tuberculin test, but similar reactions occur with contact sensitizing antigens (e.g., poison ivy or certain metals) and lead to epidermal reactions characterized by erythema, cellular infiltration, and vesicles. CD8 T cells also may mediate damage by direct toxicity.

In contrast to T_H1-mediated hypersensitivity reactions, in which the effectors are macrophages, in T_H2-mediated responses eosinophils predominate. T_H2 effector T cells are associated with tissue damage in chronic asthma. T_H2 cells produce cytokines to recruit and activate eosinophils (IL-5 and eotaxin), leading to degranulation, further tissue injury, and chronic, irreversible airway damage.

In some autoimmune diseases, effector T cells specifically recognize self-antigens to cause tissue damage, either by direct cytotoxicity or by inflammatory responses mediated by activated macrophages. In type I insulin-dependent diabetes mellitus, T cells mediate destruction of β cells of the pancreatic islets. IFN-γ-producing T cells, specific for myelin basic proteins, have been implicated in multiple sclerosis. Rheumatoid arthritis is another autoimmune disease caused, at least in part, by activated T_H1 cells.

SUGGESTED READINGS

Janeway C, Travers P, Walport M, Shlomchick M: Immunobiology: The Immune System in Health and Disease, 5th ed. New York, Garland Publishing, 2001. *A superb description of the principles of immunology and immunopathology.*

McIntyre TM, Prescott SM, Weyrich AS, Zimmerman GA: Cell-cell interactions: leukocyte-endothelial interactions. Curr Opin Hematol 2003;10:150–158. *How these cells are part of a multistep paradigm of inflammation.*

44 MECHANISMS OF INFLAMMATION AND TISSUE REPAIR

Gary S. Firestein

Inflammation is a complex, highly regulated sequence of events that can be triggered by a variety of stimuli including pathogens, noxious mechanical and chemical agents, and autoimmune responses. The subsequent cascade of events is characterized by the classically described signs and symptoms of "rubor et tumor cum calore et dolore," or redness and swelling with heat and pain. This corresponds with increased microvascular caliber, enhanced vascular permeability, leukocyte recruitment, and release of inflammatory mediators. In the normal physiologic state, this tightly controlled response protects against further injury and clears damaged tissue. In disease states, pathologic inflammation can lead to marked destruction of the extracellular matrix (ECM) as well as organ dysfunction.

Initiation of the Inflammatory Response

Tissue injury from direct trauma is associated with microvascular damage, extravasation of leukocytes through vascular walls, and leakage of plasma and proteins into the tissue (Fig. 44–1). The initial event caused by a wound or noxious stimulus is blood clotting at the site of damaged vessels. During this process, platelets release fibrinogen, fibronectin, thrombospondin, and von Willebrand factor, which permit homotypic aggregation as well as adherence to collagen. The resulting thrombus not only serves as a mechanical plug but also begins the inflammatory cascade through the release of vasoactive amines (e.g., serotonin), release of lysosomal proteases, and formation of eicosanoid products. The platelets can also initiate the process of healing with release of growth factors such as platelet-derived growth factor (PDGF) and transforming growth factor-beta (TGF-β).

When inflammation is triggered by a pathogen, resident phagocytes are stimulated by pattern recognition receptors expressed on their cell membranes as part of the innate immune response. These receptors include the Toll-like receptor (TLR) family of proteins and can recognize molecular structures on microbial pathogens that are normally not found in mammalian hosts. Of the TLRs identified to date, perhaps the best studied are TLR2, which is activated primarily by peptidoglycan and lipoproteins, and TLR4, which is activated by lipopolysaccharide (LPS, or endotoxin) and lipoteichoic acid. In addition, TLR9 is activated by unmethylated bacterial sequences that are enriched for CpG. This primitive immune response can activate a sterotypic sequence that includes activation of the transcription factor NF-κB along with an array of proinflammatory genes. The range of recognized microbial stimulants and the wide range of signaling pathways is increased through the structural diversity of the TLR intracytoplasmic domains, their ability to heterodimerize, and their associations with tissue-specific accessory molecules.

In addition to the innate immune response via TLRs, bacteria can be opsonized by specific immunoglobulins by activating the classic complement pathway, or by direct interaction (e.g., LPS) with complement through the alternative pathway. Other components of the humoral immune response can also initiate inflammation. For instance, common inhaled proteins, known as *aeroallergens*, can trigger immediate hypersensitivity reactions by binding to IgE antibodies and initiating mast cell degranulation. Soluble mediators of inflammation, such as histamine, are thus released and can initiate intense, acute airway inflammation with bronchial smooth muscle hyperreactivity in patients with asthma. In addition, there are instances, such as with rheumatoid arthritis, in which aberrant release of acute inflammatory mediators contributes to chronic destructive processes even in the absence of identifiable triggers.

Mediators of Tissue Damage

After the initial stimulus, a massive influx of inflammatory cells to the site of injury begins. Resident cells, such as vascular endothelial cells (ECs), dendritic cells, and interstitial fibroblasts, respond by releasing soluble mediators, including the eicosanoids and

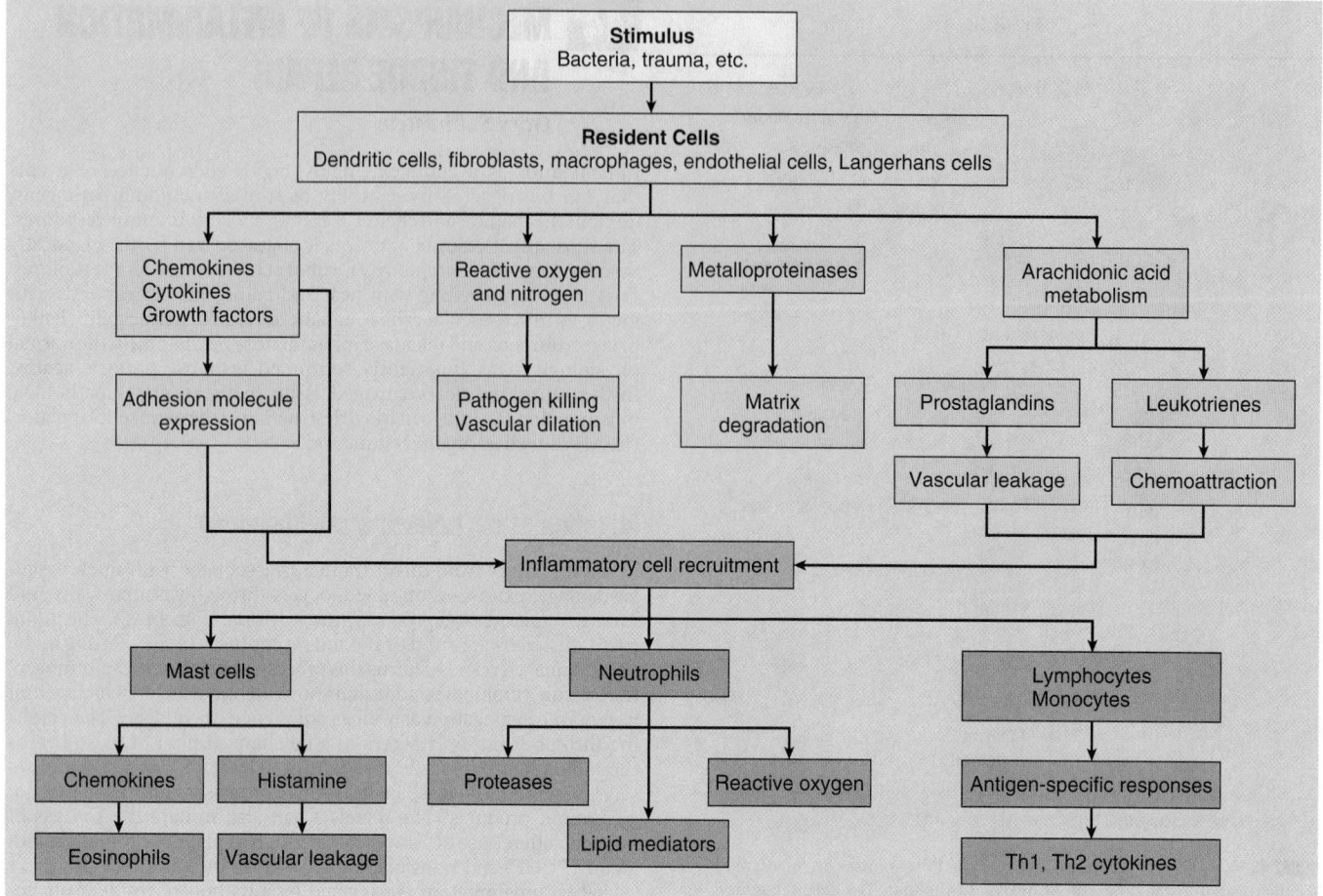

FIGURE 44–1 • Pathways for initiation of inflammation. Multiple pathways converge to recruit and activate cells in the affected tissue.

proinflammatory cytokines. These mediators amplify the inflammatory response and recruit additional leukocytes. Locally stimulated cells, together with the newly arrived inflammatory cells, subsequently release direct effector molecules. These include highly toxic small molecule reactive intermediates of nitrogen and oxygen as well as a myriad of proteases, principally matrix metalloproteinases (MMPs), serine proteases, and cysteine proteases. The role of these molecules is to destroy infectious agents and damaged cells, thus clearing the injured site for tissue repair. Ordinarily, carefully balanced and controlled, prolonged stimulation of acute inflammatory mechanisms can lead to severe tissue destruction. However, in most situations, the normal physiologic response is an exquisitely coordinated program that uses proteolytic enzymes to remodel the ECM and promote a supportive environment for wound healing rather than tissue damage.

CELLULAR RESPONSE

Inflammatory cell infiltration at the site of initial tissue damage progresses in an orderly fashion. The process begins with release of chemokines and soluble mediators from locally residing cells, including interstitial fibroblasts and vascular ECs. Signaling from these events alters the local adhesion molecule profile and creates a chemotactic gradient that recruits cells from the bloodstream. Polymorphonuclear leukocytes (PMNs) are the first inflammatory cells to extravasate and arrive at the site of injury. Specialized mononuclear cells are then recruited by further downstream signals.

Before this onslaught, tissue fibroblasts and vascular ECs are generally quiescent. However, they can be triggered to proliferate and migrate toward injury as well as synthesize large amounts of cytokines, proteases, and ECM components. Growth factors are released, such as basic fibroblast growth factor and vascular endothelial growth factor, which stimulate angiogenesis, or new blood

vessel formation. Together with granulocyte-macrophage colony-stimulating factor (GM-CSF), these locally released growth factors contribute to cellular proliferation and amplification of the inflammatory response. In addition, fibroblasts and ECs secrete new ECM proteins, such as collagen, fibronectin, and laminins, as well as matrix metalloproteinases and other ECM-digesting enzymes. The balance of protease and ECM production varies as tissue is remodeled during the course of inflammation. Initially, the response favors proteolytic activity to clear damaged infrastructure. This is followed by a shift to increased production of new ECM to allow tissue repair and wound healing.

Coordinated with the proteolytic changes in ECM, alterations are made in endothelial morphology that affect their barrier function. Increased vascular permeability by disruption of EC tight junctions allows blood-borne provisional ECM proteins, such as fibrinogen, fibronectin, and vitronectin, to access the perivascular ECM. Interaction with preexisting ECM allows the assembly of new ligands for a subset of adhesion molecules (e.g., integrins $\alpha5\beta1$ and $\alpha v\beta3$). This increased vascular permeability and change in the adhesion molecule protein and ligand profile, in conjunction with release of chemoattractant molecules, leads to recruitment and retention of leukocytes to sites of inflammation. Some of the chemokines involved include monocyte chemotactic protein-1 (MCP-1), IL-8 (for neutrophils), RANTES (for monocytes and eosinophils), and IL-16 (for CD4+ T cells).

The precise combination of chemokines and adhesion molecules determines time and event specificity to recruit specialized subsets of inflammatory cells. For example, in the synovial lining and microvasculature of patients with rheumatoid arthritis, induction of the adhesion molecule ICAM-1 on ECs and fibroblasts, in combination with chemokines like IL-8 and MCP-1, serves to recruit neutrophils and monocytes through the $\beta2$ integrins. Similarly, induction of VCAM-1 results in recruitment of T cells and macrophages through their surface expression of integrin α4β1. Ligation of these integrins on leukocytes leads to prolonged cell survival through protection from the apoptosis pathway. In addition, direct contact between T cells and fibroblasts can enhance cytokine, metalloproteinase, and prostanoid production and serve to enhance chronic inflammation and subsequent tissue destruction.

Increased expression of the adhesion molecules, ICAM-1 and VCAM-1, as well as increased chemokine expression, is also evident in the airway epithelium after allergen challenge in asthma. A rapid and transient influx of neutrophils occurs, along with activation of the local T cells and mast cells. These neutrophils produce lipid mediators, reactive oxygen intermediates (ROIs), and proteases such as elastase, which may contribute to airflow obstruction, epithelial damage, and remodeling. In addition, the neutrophil elastase, together with chemokines released by both recruited and allergen-activated T cells and mast cells, serves to recruit eosinophils. The overall population of eosinophils is chronically elevated in the inflamed asthmatic airway, where eosinophils function as central effector cells. Chemoattractants for this specific inflammatory cell type include IL-5, RANTES, and eotaxin. Their activation and recruitment results in release of toxic basic proteins and lipid mediators, such as the cysteinyl-leukotrienes, together causing significant bronchial epithelial damage and airflow obstruction in asthma.

SOLUBLE MEDIATORS

In addition to the activation of local cells and the recruitment of leukocytes, the inflammatory response requires production of soluble mediators (Table 44–1). In some cases, as with cytokines, these products form a primary communication system between cells, orchestrating subsequent infiltration and activation. Other mediators, such as reactive oxygen, serve as direct effectors that can kill pathogens. However, damage of normal tissues can be an unfortunate by-product of these events.

Proinflammatory Cytokines

Proinflammatory cytokines, mainly derived from macrophages and fibroblasts, are primary mediators that activate the immune system. Dozens of factors have been identified, but IL-1 and tumor necrosis factor (TNF)-α are perhaps the most important. IL-1 and TNF-α have pleiotropic activities and can enhance adhesion molecule expression on ECs, induce proliferation, and stimulate antigen presentation. IL-1 and TNF-α also increase expression of matrix degrading enzymes, such as collagenase and stromelysin. In addition, they stimulate synthesis of inflammatory mediators such as prostaglandin E$_2$ (PGE$_2$) from fibroblasts. Direct injection of these cytokines into animals induces local inflammatory responses, and IL-1 or TNF-α blockade abrogates damage in many animal models of inflammatory disease. In humans, inhibitors of IL-1 and TNF-α are available for use in inflammatory diseases such as rheumatoid arthritis.

IL-1 and TNF-α comprise only a small portion of the acute cytokine response. Many other factors also participate, including IL-6, which induces acute phase reactants and T-cell cytokines that can bias an immune response toward a Th1 or Th2 phenotype (Chapter 41). GM-CSF can increase HLA-DR expression and thereby enhance antigen-specific responses, in addition to increasing bone marrow production of myeloid cells. Specialized chemoattractant cytokines called *chemokines* recruit specific cell types to the site of injury. Through G-coupled receptors, some of these molecules directly activate neutrophil effector functions. The T-cell lymphokine, IFN-γ, although generally considered part of the secondary wave that ensues after T-cell activation, can also induce HLA-DR, increase EC adhesion molecule expression, and inhibit collagen production. Leukemia inhibitory factor, IL-17 (a T-cell–derived proinflammatory factor), IL-18, and many others participate in this complex cytokine network.

In some disease states, such as rheumatoid arthritis, these autocrine and paracrine cytokine networks are thought to play a critical role in the perpetuation of inflammation. In rheumatoid arthritis in particular, this is manifest as ongoing joint inflammation, or synovitis. Effects of IL-1 and TNF-α are central to continued synovitis, and there is increasing evidence that IL-15 participates by enhancing TNF-α production. IL-17 contributes to synoviocyte activation, and IL-18 can trigger T-cell differentiation toward a Th1 phenotype. In allergic asthma, IL-13 is emerging as a central inflammatory cytokine. IL-13 functions through binding to cell surface IL-4 receptors, and IL-4Rα deficient mice are found to be relatively resistant to the development of asthma. In addition, overexpression of IL-13 in murine lung causes inflammation, mucus hypersecretion, subepithelial fibrosis, and eotaxin production. Administration of IL-13 directly into the airways of mice induces hyperreactivity, eosinophilia, and increased immunoglobulin E (IgE) production. Finally, administration of soluble IL-13 receptor can function as an antagonist and reduces bronchial hyperreactivity and mucus production in the mouse model of asthma.

Immune Complexes and Complement

The complement system is an ancient defense mechanism comprised of two pathways that link innate and humoral immunity. Both the classic pathway, activated by IgG- and IgM-containing immune complexes, and the alternative pathway, activated directly by bacterial products, converge at the third component of complement, C3, with proteolytic release of fragments that amplify the inflammatory response and mediate tissue injury. The anaphylotoxins, C3a and C5a, directly increase vascular permeability and contraction of smooth muscle. C3a and C3a desArg participate in the regulation of TNF-α and IL-1β in peripheral blood mononuclear cells. In addition, C5a induces mast cell release of histamine, thereby mediating increased vascular permeability through an indirect pathway. C5a also activates leukocytes and enhances their chemotaxis, adhesion, and degranulation, with release of proteases and toxic metabolites. C5b attaches to the surface of cells and microorganisms and is the first component in the assembly of the C5b-9 membrane attack complex, which can

Table 44–1 • SIGNALS FOR INDUCTION AND REPAIR OF INFLAMMATION

INDUCTION	REPAIR
CYTOKINES AND GROWTH FACTORS	
TNF-α	TGF-β
IL-1	IL-10
IL-6	FGF
IL-13	
IL-15	
IL-17	
IL-18	
VEGF	
Chemokines	
PROTEASES/INHIBITORS	
Matrix metalloproteinases (MMP)	Tissue inhibitors of
Collagenases	metalloproteinase (TIMP)
Gelatinase	Inhibitory receptors and binding
Stromelysins	proteins
Serine proteases	IL-1RII
Trypsin	IL-1Ra
Chymotrypsin	IL-18 binding protein
Cysteine proteases	Osteoprotegerin
A disintegrin and metalloproteinase	α$_2$-macroglobulins
family (ADAM)	Inhibitors of serine
ADAM-related family with	proteases (SERPIN)
thrombospondin-1 repeats	
(ADAMT)	
SMALL MOLECULES	
Prostaglandins (esp., PGE$_2$)	Lipoxins
Leukotrienes (esp., LTC4, -D4, -E4)	Cyclopentenone prostaglandins
C3a and C5a	Antioxidants
Histamine	
Bradykinin	
Reactive oxygen	
Reactive nitrogen	
APOPTOSIS REGULATORS	
Soluble Fas ligand	Fas ligand
	Reactive oxygen
	Reactive nitrogen

TNF = tumor necrosis factor; TGF = transforming growth factor; IL = interleukin; FGF = fibroblast growth factor; VEGF = vascular endothelial growth factor.

be found deposited in inflammatory states such as immune vasculitis and infarcted myocardium.

In systemic lupus erythematosus, uncontrolled activation of complement proteins occurs with disease exacerbations and, despite increased synthesis, is typically accompanied by decreases in total plasma levels of C3 and C4 due to increased consumption. Subsequent activation of neutrophils and ECs leads to induction of neutrophil-EC adhesion and predisposes to the leuko-occlusive vasculopathy seen during systemic lupus erythematosus disease flares. Systemic complement and EC activation can thus promote microvascular injury in the absence of immune complex deposition and can lead to pathologic manifestations in the kidney (glomerulonephritis), in the gut (enteritis, due to events in the mesenteric circulation), in the lungs (acute hypoxemia, due to leukosequestration), and in the brain (microinfarctions with inflammation).

Eicosanoids

In addition to cytokines and immune complexes, local inflammatory responses lead to the release of eicosanoids, which are lipid-derived molecules. Because lipids are present in the cell membrane, they are readily available substrates for the synthesis of protective molecules. These mediators signal at or immediately adjacent to sites of synthesis, because their half-lives are short, ranging from seconds to minutes. They are not stored, but rather are produced de novo from membranes when cell activation by mechanical trauma, cytokines, growth factors, and other stimuli lead to release of arachidonic acid (AA). Cytosolic phospholipase A2 (cPLA2) is the key enzyme in eicosanoid production. Cell-specific and agonist-dependent events coordinate translocation of cPLA2 to the nuclear envelope, endoplasmic reticulum, and Golgi, where interaction with cyclooxygenase (in the case of prostaglandin synthesis) or 5-lipoxygenase (in the case of leukotriene synthesis) can occur. The temporal sequence of events in acute inflammation may be governed by eicosanoid profile switching. This shift can be mediated, in part, by the induction of inducible cyclooxygenase (COX-2) in macrophages and fibroblasts after exposure to IL-1 or TNF-α.

PROSTAGLANDINS. Prostanoids are produced when AA is released from the plasma membrane of injured cells by phospholipases and metabolized by cyclooxygenases and specific isomerases. These molecules act at both peripheral sensory neurons and at central sites within the spinal cord and brain to evoke pain and hyperalgesia. Their production is increased in most acute inflammatory conditions, including arthritis and inflammatory bowel disease. In response to exogenous (bacterial LPS) and endogenous (cytokine) pyrogens, PGE_2 derived from COX-2 mediates a central febrile response. In addition, PGs synergize with bradykinin and histamine to enhance vascular permeability and edema. The levels of PG are generally very low in normal tissues and increase rapidly with acute inflammation, well before leukocyte recruitment. Levels further increase with cellular infiltration and local cytokine production. COX-2 induction with inflammatory stimuli likely accounts for the high levels of prostanoids in chronic inflammatory lesions.

LEUKOTRIENES. In addition to prostaglandins, a distinct set of enzymes direct arachidonic acid metabolites toward the synthesis of leukotrienes. Their relative importance depends on the specific target organ of an inflammatory response. For instance, leukotriene receptor antagonists have demonstrated efficacy in asthma whereas similar approaches have been less impressive in rheumatoid arthritis. Unlike PGs, leukotrienes are primarily produced by inflammatory cells such as neutrophils, macrophages, and mast cells. Activation of these cells by immune complexes, bacterial peptides, and other stimuli elicit translocation of cPLA2 and 5-lipoxygenase to the nuclear membrane. 5-Lipoxygenase is the key enzyme in this cascade, transforming released AA to the epoxide leukotriene A4 (LTA4) in concert with 5-lipoxygenase–activating protein (FLAP). LTA4 can be hydrolyzed by cytosolic LTA4 hydrolase to LTB4, a potent neutrophil chemoattractant and stimulator of leukocyte adhesion to ECs. LTA4 can also conjugate with glutathione to form LTC4 by LTC4 synthase at the nuclear envelope. LTC4 migrates out of the cell using transporters such as the multidrug resistance-associated protein and can be metabolized extracellularly to LTD4 and LTE4. These three cysteinyl leukotrienes comprise the "slow-reacting substance of anaphylaxis" for their slow and sustained smooth muscle contracting abilities. They promote plasma leakage from postcapillary venules, upregulation of cell adhesion molecules, and bronchoconstriction.

Histamine

One of the hallmarks of allergic inflammation is the activation of mast cells with release of histamine. This mediator is a vasoactive amine produced by basophils and mast cells that markedly increases capillary leakage. In basophils, histamine is released in response to bacterial f-MLP sequences, complement fragments C3a and C5a, and IgE. The resultant edema can be readily observed clinically in urticaria and allergic rhinitis. Despite the production of histamine in asthma and synovitis, histamine blockers have minimal therapeutic effect in these conditions. The stimulus for release from mast cell granules is the same, except for the absence in this cell type of f-MLP receptors. Histamine can also synergize with locally produced LTB4 and LTC4. In addition, it enhances leukocyte rolling and firm adhesion and induces gaps in the EC lining, enhancing its capacity for promoting leukocyte extravasation.

Kinins

Pain plays a key role in host responses as a mechanism to protect damaged sites from subsequent trauma by modulating behavior. The kinins participate in vasodilation, edema, and smooth muscle contraction, as well as pain and hyperalgesia through stimulation of C fibers. They are formed from high- and low-molecular-weight kininogens by the action of serine protease kallikreins in plasma and peripheral tissues. The primary products of kininogen digestion are bradykinin and lysyl-bradykinin. These products have high affinity for the B2 receptor, which is widely expressed and is responsible for the most common effects of kinins. Carboxypeptidase generated peptides desArg-BK and Lys-desArg-BK bind the kinin B1 receptor subtype, which is not expressed in normal tissues but is rapidly upregulated by LPS and cytokines. The B2 receptor is internalized rapidly and desensitized, whereas the kinin B1 receptor remains highly responsive. Both receptors belong to the G-coupled receptor superfamily; they signal through phospholipase C with activation of protein kinase C and subsequent flux of intracellular calcium. Kinin actions are associated with the secondary production of other mediators of inflammation, including nitric oxide, mast cell derived products, and the proinflammatory cytokines IL-6 and IL-8. In addition, kinins can increase IL-1α production through initial stimulation of TNF-α and can increase prostanoid production through activation of phospholipase A2 and AA release.

DIRECT EFFECTORS

Small Molecules: Reactive Oxygen and Nitrogen Intermediates

Macrophages, neutrophils, and other phagocytic cells can generate large amounts of highly toxic ROIs and reactive nitrogen intermediates (RNI) that can directly kill pathogens. These molecules can damage DNA, oxidize membrane lipids, and nitrosylate proteins. Hence, their utility in inflammatory responses due to infections is obvious. The ability of reactive species to serve as critical signal transduction molecules that regulate inflammatory gene expression is no less important.

Uncontrolled production of reactive oxygen and nitrogen can also lead to tissue damage. Release of reactive intermediates is initiated by microbial products such as LPS and lipoproteins, by cytokines such as IFN-γ or IL-8, or by engagement of Fc receptors. These events cause translocation of several cytosolic proteins including Rac2 and Rho-family GTPase to the membrane-bound complex carrying cytochrome C with subsequent activation of NADPH oxidase. The reaction catalyzed by NADPH oxidase leads primarily to superoxide production, which can be converted to hydrogen peroxide, hydroxyl radicals and anions, hypochlorous acid, and chloramines. ROIs are critically important to the antimicrobial activity of neutrophils, but it is not clear to what extent other phagocytes use ROIs for control of intracellular bacteria in vivo.

Nitric oxide synthases (NOS) convert L-arginine and molecular oxygen to L-citrulline and nitric oxide (NO). There are three known isoforms of NOS: neuronal NOS (ncNOS or NOS1) and EC NOS (ecNOS or NOS3) are both constitutively expressed, whereas macrophage NOS (macNOS, iNOS, or NOS2) is induced by inflammatory cytokines such as TNF-α and IFN-γ. The expression of NOS2 is suppressed by TGF-β. Products of viruses, bacteria, protozoa, and

Binding to RANK ligand (RANK-L) or TNF-related activation-induced cytokine (TRANCE) leads to protection against bone resorption by osteoclasts.

Prostanoids/COX

COX-2 induced by proinflammatory mediators appears early and can contribute to inflammatory responses. However, late COX-2 expression has led to speculation that it can also function in the resolution of inflammation. This regulation might occur through the formation of the cyclopentenone prostaglandins (CyPG). CyPG, which are suppressed by COX inhibition, may be anti-inflammatory by inhibition of proinflammatory gene transcription. They can serve as a ligand for peroxisome proliferator-activated receptor gamma (PPARγ). PPARγ is associated with the suppression of AP-1 and STAT transcriptional pathways in macrophages. In addition, CyPG can inhibit IKKβ, thus preventing NF-κB activation.

INHIBITORS OF DIRECT EFFECTORS

Antioxidants

Free radicals are produced as part of normal cellular metabolism and as part of host defenses. Excess free radical production from endogenous or exogenous sources may induce uncontrolled tissue damage by reacting indiscriminately. Hence an extensive array of antioxidant defenses exists to protect cellular components. In animal models, such as adjuvant arthritis in rats, treatment with antioxidants helps attenuate the disease process. Human diseases appear to be more complex and use of these agents has not met with universal success. Antioxidants can be divided into the antioxidant enzymes, chain-breaking antioxidants, and transition-metal–binding proteins.

The antioxidant enzymes include catalase and superoxide dismutase. Catalase is a peroxisomal enzyme that catalyzes the conversion of hydrogen peroxide to water and oxygen. Most catalase activity is found in liver and erythrocytes. Superoxide dismutases catalyze the dismutation of superoxide to hydrogen peroxide, which is then removed by catalase or glutathione peroxidase. Glutathione peroxidases and glutathione reductase are additional mechanisms for maintaining redox balance and removal of toxic metabolites. Insufficient production of intracellular antioxidants such as glutathione can suppress lymphocyte responses and could account for defective T-cell receptor signaling and blunted immunity in T cells derived from rheumatoid arthritis synovium.

Interactions of free radicals with surrounding molecules can generate secondary radical species in a self-propagating chain reaction. Chain-breaking antioxidants are small molecules that can receive or donate an electron and thus form a stable by-product with a radical. These antioxidant molecules are categorized as aqueous phase (vitamin C, albumin, reduced glutathione) and lipid phase (vitamin E, ubiquinol-10, carotenoids, and flavonoids). In addition, transition metal-binding proteins (ceruloplasmin, ferritin, transferrin, and lactoferrin) can serve as antioxidants by sequestering cationic iron and copper and thereby inhibiting hydroxyl radical propagation.

Protease Inhibitors

As noted earlier, tissue destruction mediated by proteases is a hallmark of inflammation. Mechanisms to protect the host and prevent unregulated tissue destruction using a complex system of protease inhibitors have developed as part of the repair process. Protease inhibitors regulate the function of endogenous proteases and reduce the likelihood of collateral damage to tissues. These proteins form two functional classes, active site inhibitors and α2-macroglobins (α2M). The latter class acts by covalently linking the protease to the α2M chain and thereby blocking access to substrates. The basic function of α2M is to bind all classes of proteases and convey them through receptor-mediated endocytosis and inactivation by cleavage. The SERPIN family, inhibitors of the serine proteases, are the most abundant members of the former class and play a major role in regulation of blood clot resolution and inflammation, as indicated by many of their names: antithrombin III, plasminogen activator inhibitors 1 and 2, α₂-antiplasmin, α₁-antitrypsin, and kallistatin. In addition to direct inactivation via protease inhibitors, serine proteases can be inactivated by oxidation, such as in the inflammatory setting of synovial

fluid in rheumatoid arthritis. In contrast, MMPs are activated by this type of hostile environment.

A specialized mechanism for inhibiting MMP function has also evolved and can be induced during the reparative phase of inflammation. A family of TIMPs are capable of inhibiting most members of the MMP family. The TIMPs bind to activated MMPs and irreversibly block their catalytic sites. Examples of disease states with an unfavorable balance between TIMP and MMP levels include loss of cartilage with osteoarthritis and rheumatoid arthritis and invasion and metastasis of tumor cells. TIMP expression is similar in the synovium of patients with rheumatoid arthritis and osteoarthritis, whereas MMP expression is considerably higher in the former. The imbalance might be related to the limited capacity to produce the protease inhibitors, which is overwhelmed by the prodigious ability to release MMPs by the rheumatoid synovium. Whereas IL-1 and TNF-α induce MMPs, TGF-β and several other growth factors suppress MMPs and increase TIMPs. In addition, TGF-β increases production of matrix proteins such as collagen. Therefore, the cytokine profile provides a pivotal influence on the status of remodeling. When proinflammatory cytokines predominate, the balance favors matrix destruction. In the presence of proinflammatory cytokine inhibitors and growth factors, matrix protein production increases and MMPs are inhibited by TIMPs.

Summary

Inflammation is a carefully orchestrated sequence of events designed to be self-limited and to lead to the efficient removal of pathogens and the healing of wounds. Under normal circumstances, this process occurs without lasting tissue injury. A high degree of plasticity exists within the system that allows multiple avenues for an appropriate tissue response and resolution. However, there clearly exist circumstances in which these safeguards fail, and inflammation continues unchecked leading to end-organ damage over time. In these situations, therapeutic interventions involving modulation of the effector cell, cytokine, or small molecule mediator milieu may abrogate the process and redirect the tissue to normal repair mechanisms.

SUGGESTED READINGS

Bogdan C, Rollinghoff M, Diefenbach A: Reactive oxygen and reactive nitrogen intermediates in innate and specific immunity. Curr Opin Immunol 2000;12:64–76. *Functions of oxygen metabolites include the modulation of the cytokine response of adaptive immunity and lymphocytes and the regulation of immune cell apoptosis.*

Funk CD: Prostaglandins and leukotrienes: Advances in eicosanoid biology. Science 2001;294:1871–1875. *Insights into the mechanisms of inflammatory responses, pain, and fever.*

Mantovani A, Locati M, Vecchi A, et al: Decoy receptors: A strategy to regulate inflammatory cytokines and chemokines. Trends Immunol 2001;22:328–336. *The use of decoy receptors is a general strategy to regulate the action of primary pro-inflammatory cytokines and chemokines.*

Mengshol JA, Mix KS, Brinckerhoff CE: Matrix metalloproteinases as therapeutic targets in arthritis diseases: Bull's-eye or missing the mark? Arthritis Rheum 2002;46:13–20. *An examination of the expression of MMPs in arthritis.*

Soberman RJ, Christmas P: The organization and consequences of eicosanoid signaling. J Clin Invest 2003;111:1107–1113. *An overview of arachidonic acid biology.*

Tak PP, Zvaifler NJ, Green DR, et al: Rheumatoid arthritis and p53: How oxidative stress might alter the course of inflammatory diseases. Immunol Today 2000;21:78–82. *Oxidative stress at sites of chronic inflammation can cause permanent genetic changes.*

45 COMPLEMENT IN HEALTH AND DISEASE

David R. Karp
V. Michael Holers

Historical Perspective

In 1919, the Nobel Prize in Physiology or Medicine was awarded to the Belgian microbiologist Bordet for his "discoveries concerning immunity." This award followed more than a quarter century of work by Bordet and others that defined the existence and function of what is now referred to as the *complement system*. The bactericidal nature of immune serum had been shown in the 1880s and 1890s. The term *alexin* was used by Buchner for this protective substance found in cell-free serum. Alexin was thought to be a heat-labile enzyme that destroyed bacteria.

In 1894, Pfeiffer reported that cholera vibrios injected into the peritoneum of immune guinea pigs were killed rapidly and that immune serum could transfer this effect to normal animals. Bordet and Metschnikoff showed that this transfer could occur in vitro and developed a novel, noninfectious method to investigate this phenomenon by immunizing guinea pigs with rabbit erythrocytes, then monitoring the release of hemoglobin when the cells were lysed. Based on these studies, Bordet was able to identify the heat-stabile specific antibody fraction of immune serum and the heat-labile bactericidal fraction that "complemented" the antibody.

From the 1920s to the 1970s, the study of complement was largely biochemical. The 11 proteins of the classical pathway of complement activation and their interactions were described. In 1954, Pillemer reported the existence of an alternative pathway that activates complement in the absence of specific antibody. Although the controversy over this finding contributed to Pillemer's suicide, he ultimately was vindicated. The alternative pathway is not only recognized as older evolutionarily than the classic pathway, but also it is responsible for complement activation by a diverse set of compounds, such as bacterial endotoxin and biomaterials.

Since the 1970s, the focus has been on the identification of the regulatory proteins of the complement cascades. Almost as many serum and cell surface proteins are involved in the regulation of complement function as are involved in its activation. In addition, an entirely new pathway of complement activation, the mannan-binding lectin pathway, has been described. This pathway combines features of the classic and alternative pathways.

The complement system serves many protective functions ascribed to the innate immune system. As originally described, it helps to maintain blood sterility by depositing the membrane attack complex (MAC) in bacterial cell walls and lysing them. It also participates in the opsonization of pathogens for phagocytic removal. The peptide *anaphylatoxins* produced during complement activation promote inflammatory responses with microbicidal effects. The deposition of complement on immune complexes helps to keep them soluble and remove them from the circulation.

There also is increasing evidence that complement can shape the adaptive immune response. Antigens decorated by complement proteins are taken up by B cells and other antigen-presenting cells, resulting in T-cell activation. Studies from mice deficient in various complement proteins have shown that complement activation is needed for optimal antibody production by B cells. Lastly, it is well known that humans and experimental animals that are deficient in early complement components are often predisposed to autoimmune diseases, particularly systemic lupus erythematosus. This observation suggests that complement is required in some way to identify soluble self-antigens and eliminate self-reactive B cells.

Complement is activated immediately on exposure to immune complexes but lacks the immunologic memory of T or B cells with clonotypic receptors that discriminate between self and nonself. Activated complement can be deposited on host and pathogenic surfaces. This potentially dangerous situation is controlled by a series of genetically, structurally, and functionally similar proteins termed the *regulators of complement activation* (RCA). These proteins provide species-specific downregulation of complement activation on host tissues.

Inappropriate complement action occurs when the nondiscriminating activating proteins function in excess of the regulatory proteins that limit damage on self-tissues. This can be seen in almost any inflammatory disease. Some conditions are obvious, such as autoimmune hemolytic anemia, lupus nephritis, and immune complex vasculitis. In other diseases, the role of complement may be contributory but is less clear. These include myocardial infarction, stroke, cardiopulmonary bypass, and hemodialysis. Table 45–1 lists conditions in which complement activation is associated with pathology rather than protection.

In each of these conditions, inhibition of complement activation potentially would limit tissue damage. Many strategies have been developed to discover inhibitors that can work at different parts of the complement activation cascades. These include small molecules designed similar to traditional drugs and newer, biologic agents. The latter are antibodies that inhibit complement activation and versions of human complement regulatory proteins. None of these compounds is available yet, although several are in advanced clinical trials.

Table 45–1 • PATHOLOGIC CONDITIONS ASSOCIATED WITH COMPLEMENT ACTIVATION

Alzheimer's disease	Ischemia-reperfusion injury
Allotransplantation	Immune complex vasculitis
Asthma	Multisystem organ failure
ARDS	Multiple sclerosis
Arthus reaction	Myasthenia gravis
Bullous pemphigoid	Post–cardiopulmonary bypass
Burns	Psoriasis
Crohn's disease	Rheumatoid arthritis
Glomerulonephritis (many causes)	Septic shock
Hemolytic anemia	Systemic lupus erythematosus
Hemodialysis	Stroke
Hereditary angioedema	Xenotransplantation

ARDS = adult respiratory distress syndrome.

Activation of Complement

As an essential component of the innate immune system, complement is endowed with redundant, yet carefully controlled activation pathways. The molecular events that occur during activation are not only responsible for the pathology of complement-associated disease states, but also offer opportunities for the rational design of inhibitors. For simplicity, it is convenient to think of the different parts of the complement activation pathways as *recognition*, *convertase/amplification*, and *effector*.

CLASSICAL PATHWAY

Although traditionally thought of as activated only by IgM-containing or IgG-containing immune complexes, the classical pathway has been shown to be activated by targets other than immune complexes (Fig. 45–1). Notably, apoptotic cells bind C1q and activate the C1 proteases. C1 also is activated by the accumulated Aβ protein found in the neuritic plaques of Alzheimer's disease. C-reactive protein (CRP) and serum amyloid protein bind to chromatin and other ribonucleoprotein complexes released from apoptotic cells. The CRP/nuclear antigen complexes bind and activate C1. C1q and the classical pathway seem to play a role in the opsonization and removal of nuclear materials that frequently contain autoantigens. The few patients with hereditary C1q deficiency all eventually develop systemic lupus erythematosus. Similarly, mice that have been engineered to lack C1q develop a lupus-like illness and have deposition of apoptotic bodies in their glomeruli. The addition of CRP and enzymatically modified low-density lipoprotein to human serum causes the activation of complement as determined by nearly quantitative conversion of C3 to C3b. Finally, deposits of CRP and activated C1 have been shown in infarcted human myocardium. Together, these observations suggest that antibody-independent classical pathway activation is important in protective immune responses and pathogenic inflammatory reactions.

Regulation of classical pathway activation occurs at several levels. First is the serine protease inhibitor (serpin), C1-inhibitor (C1-INH). C1-INH blocks the activity of many proteases, including factor XIIa,

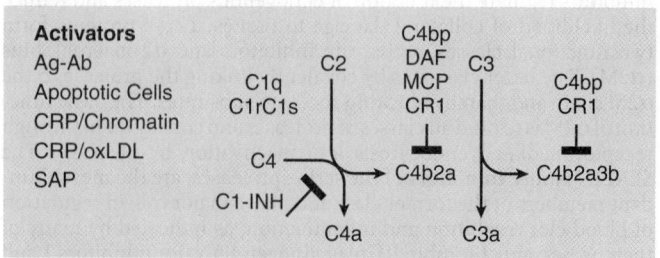

FIGURE 45–1 • Schematic representation of the activation of the classical pathway and generation of its C3 convertase. Included are naturally occurring regulators (inhibitors) of this pathway.

kallikrein, and factor XIa of the clotting system and C1r and C1s of the complement system. The importance of C1-INH is seen in the disease hereditary angioedema. In this instance, the heterozygous deficiency of C1-INH allows uncontrolled proteolysis of C2 and C4 after minor trauma. A vasoactive peptide is released from C2 leading to painless (but occasionally life-threatening) soft tissue swelling. Treatment of acute attacks of hereditary angioedema includes purified C1-INH and antifibrinolytic drugs such as ε-aminocaproic acid.

Classical pathway activation also is regulated by RCA proteins. These proteins form the basis for the ability of the complement system to discriminate self from nonself targets. They are discussed in depth subsequently. The RCA proteins C4-binding protein (C4-bp) and complement receptor 1 (CR1) are specific to classical pathway regulation.

ALTERNATIVE PATHWAY

The alternative pathway is much less stringent in its recognition requirements. It takes advantage of the fact that C3 undergoes spontaneous low-grade activation in the fluid phase (Fig. 45–2). Based on estimates of the glomerular filtration of C3a and its steady-state serum concentration, it has been suggested that 1 to 2% of serum C3 is activated in serum each hour. This allows the covalent attachment of C3 to the polysaccharides of fungi and bacteria and to other appropriately charged targets, such as endotoxin and virally infected cells. Other alternative pathway activators include IgA immune complexes and biomaterials, such as cardiopulmonary bypass and hemodialysis membranes.

When bound to a surface, C3 acquires a C3b-like conformation and binds factor B that is cleaved by the serine protease factor D to form the alternative pathway C3 convertase C3bBb. This complex has a short half-life. It is stabilized by properdin (factor P) during physiologic complement activation. It also can be stabilized by the autoantibody, C3-nephritic factor, which is associated with type I membranoproliferative glomerulonephritis. The alternative pathway C3 convertase is negatively regulated by the RCA proteins factor H, DAF, and CR1 (see later).

LECTIN PATHWAY

The latest complement recognition and activation pathway to be described is the lectin pathway (Fig. 45–3). The protein mannose binding lectin (MBL) is a member of the collectin family that includes pulmonary surfactants A (SP-A) and D (SP-D). MBL has a structure similar to C1q, in that it consists of several subunits each having a globular recognition domain and a collagen-like portion that interacts with serine proteases. In the case of MBL, the globular domain is a lectin that binds to repeating carbohydrates (mannose and N-acetylglucosamine) on the surface of pathogens. Many microorganisms are recognized by MBL, including gram-positive and gram-negative bacteria, mycobacteria, fungi, parasites, and viruses, including human immunodeficiency virus (HIV)-1. In general, mammalian glycoproteins and glycolipids are not recognized by MBL. One notable exception is agalactosyl-IgG. The levels of this modified immunoglobulin are increased in inflammatory conditions such as

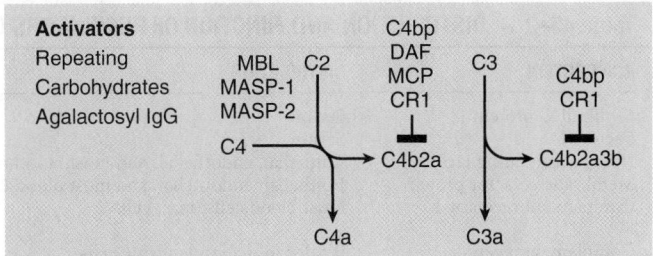

FIGURE 45–3 • Schematic representation of the activation of the lectin pathway and generation in concert with the classic pathway of a C3 convertase. Included are naturally occurring regulators (inhibitors) of this pathway.

rheumatoid arthritis, raising the possibility that excessive activation of the lectin pathway is clinically relevant.

Two serine proteases, MASP-1 and MASP-2, associate with MBL, presumably through the collagen-like domain. Although not formally proven, this is analogous to the association of C1r and C1s with C1q. Activation of MASP-1 and MASP-2 results in cleavage of C2 and C4, with the subsequent formation of the classical pathway C3 convertase (C4b2a).

Variation in the structural and regulatory portions of the MBL gene leads to wide individual differences in serum levels. Low levels have been associated with recurrent infections in children and adults and have been shown to be a minor risk factor for the development of systemic lupus erythematosus. More striking is the association of low levels of MBL with infection in systemic lupus erythematosus. In a study of Danish lupus patients, heterozygous MBL deficiency was associated with a 4-fold increase in the risk of bacterial pneumonia, whereas homozygous deficiency carried a greater than 100-fold risk.

C3 AND C5 CONVERTASES

The three activation pathways converge at C3. C3 (and C4) contains a reactive glutamic acid residue buried within the three-dimensional structure of the protein. Normally the γ-carboxy group of the reactive glutamic acid in C3 or C4 is linked to a nearby cysteine in an "internal thiolester." On activation, the thiolester is exposed to the surface of the protein, where it can react with amino or hydroxyl groups. Most of the thiolesters are hydrolyzed by water to form inactive C3 or C4. Some form amide or ester bonds to proteins or carbohydrates, covalently attaching C3b (and C4b) to target surfaces. This enables cells bearing CR1 to bind these targets and opsonize them, representing one of the effector mechanisms of complement.

The covalently bound C3b associates with C4b2a (classical or lectin pathways) or C3bBb (alternative pathway) to form a convertase for C5. C3b is part of the alternative pathway C3 convertase, and its product generates an amplification loop that can deposit thousands of C3b molecules on a target, regardless of the initial activation step.

REGULATORS OF COMPLEMENT ACTIVATION

A significant advance in the area of complement research has been the description of RCA proteins (Fig. 45–4). The major function of these proteins as a group is to limit the production of C3b by either the classic or the alternative C3 convertases. Because the addition of C3b to a C3 convertase makes it a C5 convertase, regulation of the two enzyme complexes is linked. Modulation of their activity on host cells limits tissue destruction and the production of inflammatory mediators.

There are six RCA proteins that control the C3/C5 convertases (Table 45–2). They are factor H, C4 binding protein (C4bp), membrane cofactor protein (MCP; CD46), decay accelerating factor (DAF; CD55), complement receptor 1 (CR1; CD35), and complement receptor 2 (CR2; CD21). The genes for all of these proteins are found in a cluster on human chromosome 1.q32. Structurally, they are composed of repeating subunits termed *short consensus repeats* (SCR), sometimes referred to as *complement control protein* modules. Each SCR has approximately 60 amino acids with four invariant cysteine residues. The pairing of the disulfides leads to a four to five

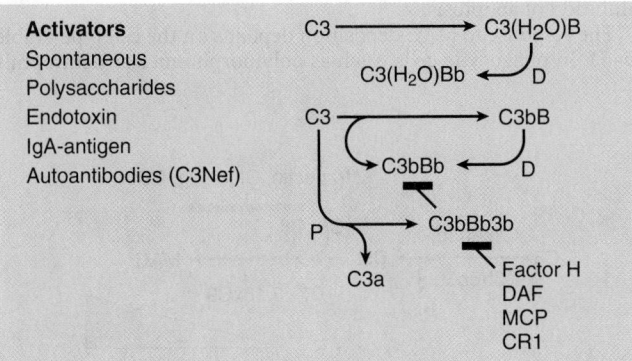

FIGURE 45–2 • Schematic representation of the activation of the alternative pathway and generation of its C3 convertase. Included are naturally occurring regulators (inhibitors) of this pathway.

Table 45–2 • DISTRIBUTION AND FUNCTION OF REGULATORS OF COMPLEMENT ACTIVATION (RCA) PROTEINS

RCA PROTEIN	DISTRIBUTION	FUNCTION
C4 binding protein	Serum	Cofactor for C4b; decay of classic C3/C5 convertases
Factor H	Serum	Cofactor for C3b; decay of alternative C3/C5 convertases
Decay accelerating factor	Epithelial, endothelial, and most blood cells	Decay of classic and alternative C3/C5 convertases
Membrane cofactor protein	Epithelial, endothelial, and most blood cells (not RBCs)	Cofactor for C3b and C4b
Complement receptor 1	Most blood cells; mast cells	Cofactor for C3b and C4b; decay of C3/C5 convertases; receptor for C3b/C4b
Complement receptor 2	B cells; follicular dendritic cells	Receptor for C3b fragments; regulation of B cells

RBCs = red blood cells.

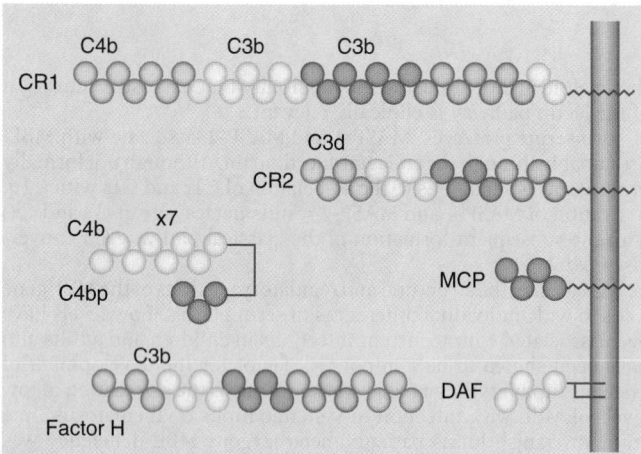

FIGURE 45–4 • Schematic representation of the regulators of complement activation (RCA) proteins. Circles represent individual short consensus repeats (SCRs), whereas shading indicates higher organizational units composed of several SCRs. The approximate locations of C3 and C4 fragment binding are indicated.

β pleated sheet structure causing the SCRs to appear like beads on a string.

Although the SCRs are structurally related, the individual RCA proteins may recognize different parts of the C3 molecule. They do so using specific combinations of SCRs. The RCA proteins function to control complement activation by two processes. First is *decay acceleration*. This refers to the process whereby the RCA protein binds to C3b in the convertase and dissociates the other members of the complex, rendering it enzymatically inactive. The second effect is *cofactor* activity. Some of the RCA proteins facilitate the recognition of C3b or C4b by a serum protease, factor I. Cleavage of C3b or C4b by factor I also renders the convertase inactive.

Despite their relatedness, the RCA proteins exhibit differences in their overall structure, distribution, and function. All of the RCA proteins except MCP and CR2 have decay acceleration activity; it is the only function of DAF. This glycosyl phosphatidylinositol–linked protein is widely expressed and causes the removal of C2a or Bb from the C3 and C5 convertases. DAF lacks the cofactor activity seen by the other RCA proteins (except CR2). Factor H and C4bp are serum proteins. MCP and DAF are ubiquitously expressed membrane proteins. CR1 and CR2 are membrane proteins expressed primarily on hematopoietic cells.

RCA proteins have been linked to several disease states. DAF is missing from the abnormal erythrocytes of patients with paroxysmal nocturnal hemoglobinuria. Although the hemolysis of these cells is ultimately due to the fact that the cells also lack CD59 (see later), the DAF deficiency promotes complement activation on these cells. Genetic factor H deficiency has been associated with type II membranoproliferative glomerulonephritis in humans and a strain of Yorkshire pigs. Renal biopsy specimens in both cases showed evidence of robust alternative pathway activation. There is also evidence that mutations in factor H are responsible for some of the pathology seen in either sporadic or familial hemolytic-uremic syndrome. Lastly, low levels of CR1

and/or CR2 have been seen in patients with systemic lupus erythematosus. CR1 has cofactor and decay activity, and its major role is in the removal of immune complexes from the circulation. CR2 is necessary for optimal B-cell regulation, including the down modulation of autoreactive B cells.

MEMBRANE ATTACK COMPLEX

The cleavage of C5 by either convertase generates C5a, the most potent of the complement anaphylatoxins, and C5b. C5b associates with C6 and C7 to create a lipophilic trimer as part of the MAC (Fig. 45–5). On the surface of a target cell, less than 1% of the C5b67 trimers formed insert into the lipid bilayer and serve as binding sites for C8. This attracts C9 to the membrane, and C9 has the capacity to self-polymerize. A total of 12 to 18 C9 molecules form a ring structure, completing the MAC. In its complete form, the MAC appears like a doughnut with a 10-nm pore running through the center. This pore can allow water and ions to enter the cells, ultimately leading to cell lysis. A MAC with only one or two C9 molecules also can cause lysis, however, suggesting the MAC disrupts the lipid integrity in its general vicinity, rather than creating holes in the membrane.

The MAC itself appears to be largely redundant in terms of protection against infection. It seems to be essential only for efficient elimination of *Neisseria* species. Individuals who are homozygous deficient for C6, C7, C8, or C9 are at risk for meningococcal and gonococcal infection. C9 deficiency is the most common immunodeficiency in Japan, with a heterozygote frequency of 3 to 5%. Absence of an efficient MAC is not deleterious to the population in general and may have some selective advantage.

Extensive complement activation during an inflammatory response can result in sufficient MAC deposition to cause host cell lysis. Most nucleated cells have mechanisms to resist the osmotic changes caused by the MAC, however, and may "disassemble" the MAC as it is formed. Rather the nonlethal effects of sublytic MAC deposition are more likely to contribute to pathology. In most cells, this occurs by a general activation of multiple cell signaling pathways. Calcium enters the cell activating protein kinases and phospholipase C and upregulates cyclic adenosine monophosphate (cAMP) production. G proteins and their associated factors are concentrated at the cell membrane, perhaps localized to C9 directly. The mitogen activated protein kinase pathways (ERK, JNK, and p38) are activated, resulting in the induction of transcription factors such as c-jun and fos, cell proliferation, and inhibition of apoptosis.

The response to MAC deposition depends on the cell type (Table 45–3). In phagocytic cells, such as polymorphonuclear neutrophils

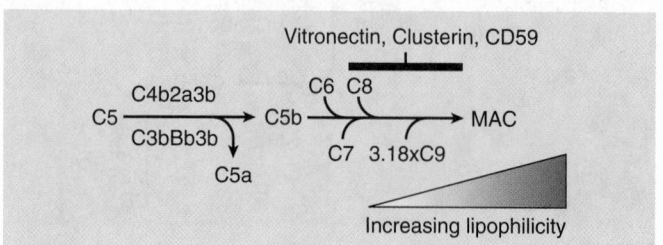

FIGURE 45–5 • Schematic representation of the assembly of the membrane attack complex (MAC) on a cell membrane.

Table 45–3 • RESPONSES TO SUBLYTIC MEMBRANE ATTACK COMPLEX ACTIVATION

CELL TYPE	EFFECTS
Most cells	Increased intracellular calcium flux
	G protein activation
	Activation of protein kinases
	Activation of transcription factors
	Proliferation
Neutrophils and macrophages	Release of reactive oxygen species
	Activation of phospholipase A_2
	Release of prostaglandins, thromboxane, and leukotrienes
Platelets	ATP release
	Increased P-selectin expression
	Procoagulant membrane changes
Endothelial cells	Increased IL-1α synthesis
	Increased tissue factor release
	Increased von Willebrand factor release
	Increased basic fibroblast and platelet-derived growth factor synthesis
Synoviocytes	Increased prostaglandin synthesis
	Increased IL-6 synthesis
	Increased matrix metalloproteinase production
Glomerular epithelium	Phospholipase A_2 activation
	Prostaglandin synthesis
	Increased collagen and fibronectin synthesis
Oligodendrocytes	Increased myelin basic protein and proteolipid synthesis
	Increased proliferation

ATP = adenosine triphosphate; IL = interleukin.

or macrophages, sublytic MAC activation leads to the production of reactive oxygen species, such as superoxide and hydrogen peroxide, and prostaglandins and leukotrienes. Platelets undergo the exposure of phosphatidylserine on their outer membrane, resulting in greater formation of blood coagulation enzyme complexes. This has a potentially procoagulant effect. On endothelial cells, MAC deposition leads to many important events. It induces the synthesis of interleukin (IL)-1α, which leads to further autocrine and paracrine endothelial cell activation. It stimulates a procoagulant state by altering the phospholipid composition of the endothelial membrane, inducing the synthesis of tissue factor and upregulating the synthesis of plasminogen activator inhibitor. MAC treatment of endothelial cells causes an increase in the expression of adhesion molecules, including intercellular adhesion molecule (ICAM)-1 and E-selectin. Finally, the MAC stimulates endothelial cells to proliferate through growth factor production. Despite the fact that cell lysis does not occur, deposition of the MAC leads to a potentially more dangerous situation with increased inflammation, coagulation, and cellular proliferation.

Regulation of MAC formation is important clinically and has become an area of therapeutic research. Two fluid-phase proteins, clusterin and S-protein (vitronectin), bind the C5b-7 complex and prevent its association with the lipid membrane. C8 and usually two to four C9 molecules bind to this soluble complex, termed *sC5b-9*, that is lytically inactive. CD59 is a membrane-bound inhibitor of MAC formation. This small glycoprotein is attached to the cell membrane through a glycosyl phosphotidylinositol tail. It binds tightly to C5b-8, preventing the binding and polymerization of C9. CD59 shows strong species restriction. That is, it is most effective in the inhibition of MAC formation by the same or closely related species. Lastly, the expression of CD59 is defective in patients with paroxysmal nocturnal hemoglobinuria, owing to failure to synthesize the glycosyl phosphotidylinositol tail on this and many other cell-surface proteins, including DAF. The clinical features of paroxysmal nocturnal hemoglobinuria are protean. The hemolysis is believed to be due to low-grade complement activation on red cells, however; without CD59, MAC formation proceeds and allows hemolysis.

ANAPHYLATOXINS

In addition to the MAC, the other major source of pathologic damage resulting from complement activation comes from the action of the anaphylatoxins. These are the peptides C3a, C4a, and C5a cleaved from their respective proteins during activation. They were named by Friedberger in 1910 to describe the toxic effects after the transfer of complement activated serum into laboratory animals. They are 77 (C3a and C4a) or 74 (C5a) amino acids long and contain a carboxy terminal arginine. The structures of C3a and C5a have been determined by x-ray crystallography and nuclear magnetic resonance; they exhibit a compact amino terminal region that is held together by conserved disulfide bonds. This part of the molecule contains cationic amino acids that are believed to interact with the anaphylatoxin receptors. The carboxy terminal regions of the anaphylatoxins are extended sequences. Only the last five amino acids are required for activity. In plasma, the C-terminal arginine is removed rapidly by carboxypeptidase N from anaphylatoxins not bound to their receptors. Depending on the response studied, this removal totally inactivates the anaphylatoxin or reduces its potency by 1000-fold.

Understanding of anaphylatoxin effects has been aided greatly by the identification of their receptors. This identification has been done by a combination of molecular cloning and immunochemical techniques. The C5a receptor (C5aR, CD88) was the first anaphylatoxin receptor characterized. It is a seven-transmembrane spanning protein that couples ligand binding to G protein signaling. Traditionally, it was thought to be expressed only on myeloid cells, particularly neutrophils and eosinophils. It mediates the potent chemoattractant property of C5a for both of these cell types. Signaling through CD88 leads to rapid secretion of all granule contents. These include proteases, peroxidases, and lactoferrin from neutrophils and peroxidase, major basic protein, and eosinophil cationic protein from eosinophils. C5a also induces the release of cytokines, such as tumor necrosis factor (TNF), IL-1, IL-6, and IL-8, and adhesion molecules, promoting the inflammatory response.

The C5aR also has been found on numerous other tissues (Table 45–4). These include hepatocytes; bronchial and alveolar epithelium; vascular endothelium; renal mesangial and tubular epithelial cells; and brain astrocytes, microglia, and neurons. The function of C5a in these tissues is not clear. In vitro experiments have shown that these cells are activated by exposure to the anaphylatoxins, leading to production of cytokines, chemokines, and prostaglandins and to cell proliferation.

The C3a receptor has been identified; it is also a seven-transmembrane domain protein. Similar to the C5aR, the tissue distribution of the C3aR is much greater than previously thought. It is expressed on nearly all myeloid cells, including mast cells, where it mediates allergic mediator release. The C3aR also has been detected on many tissues, including in the brain by Northern blot analysis for RNA expression. Detailed functional studies on the C3aR have not been carried out.

The anaphylatoxins have many biologic effects. In general, they cause smooth muscle contraction and recruitment of granulocytes, monocytes, and mast cells. In theory, they can contribute to the

Table 45–4 • DISTRIBUTION OF ANAPHYLATOXIN RECEPTORS AND THEIR CELLULAR RESPONSES

CELL TYPE	RESPONSES
C5aR (CD88)	
Neutrophils	Chemotaxis
Eosinophils	Enzyme release
Basophils	Generation of reactive oxygen species
Mast cells	Upregulation of adhesion molecules
Monocytes	Increased IL-1, IL-6, and IL-8 synthesis
	Prostaglandin/leukotriene synthesis
Hepatocytes	Increased synthesis of acute phase reactants
Pulmonary epithelium	Increased IL-8
Neuronal cells	?
Endothelial cells	Increased expression of P-selectin
Renal epithelial/mesangial cells	Proliferation
	Synthesis of growth factors
C3aR	
Eosinophils	Chemotaxis
Mast cells	Enzyme release
Platelets	Generation of reactive oxygen species
	Upregulation of adhesion molecules
CNS (multiple cells)	?

pathophysiology of any inflammatory condition. C3a and C5a have been shown to play a role in diseases including adult respiratory distress syndrome, multisystem organ failure, septic shock, myocardial ischemia-reperfusion injury, rheumatoid arthritis, systemic lupus erythematosus, and inflammatory bowel disease. The anaphylatoxin peptides also are responsible for the "postpump" syndrome seen in patients undergoing cardiopulmonary bypass or hemodialysis. Exposure of blood to dialysis or perfusion membranes leads to complement activation. Within minutes of starting bypass, there is a sharp increase in the level of C3a and C5a in the extracorporeal circuit being returned to the patient. This increase can be associated with respiratory distress, pulmonary hypertension, and pulmonary edema. It has been shown that the length of time that patients stay on the ventilator after bypass surgery depends on the level of C3a generated during reperfusion.

C3a and C5a have been implicated in the initiation and prolongation of adult respiratory distress syndrome and multisystem organ failure. After severe trauma, levels of C3a have been measured that suggest activation of the entire circulating C3 pool. This activation leads to bronchoconstriction, increased vascular permeability, and vascular plugging with leukocytes. The activation of white blood cells continues the cycle of tissue damage with further complement activation. Continued elevation of C3a in shock or adult respiratory distress syndrome is a poor prognostic sign.

The role of C5a in pulmonary pathology has been shown using C5aR knockout mice. A model of immune complex damage to the lung was studied. The wild-type mice had expected increases in lung permeability and leukocyte infiltration after induction of intrapulmonary ovalbumin/antiovalbumin complexes. These effects were not seen in the C5aR-deficient animals. In other animal models, antibodies to C5a have been shown to limit infarct size owing to myocardial ischemia-reperfusion and tissue damage in experimental septic shock.

Complement Inhibitors

Given the many disease states in which complement is one of the central mediators of pathology, it is no surprise that several complement inhibitors are in preclinical or clinical development. These take several different forms. Some are variations of physiologic inhibitors, whereas others are the products of molecular biologic searches for novel compounds.

It is important to consider where in the complement pathway to design an inhibitor. Inhibition of the activation pathways limits the production of biologically active peptides. All three pathways need to be inhibited, however, for this to be effective. Inhibiting the activation of C3 not only prevents the generation of the C3a anaphylatoxin, but also may leave the patient susceptible to infection by limiting the deposition of C3b on targets as an opsonin. Inhibition of C3b deposition also theoretically would decrease the patient's ability to clear immune complexes, resulting in renal, pulmonary, and vascular damage. It also may promote the development of antibodies to self-antigens.

Inhibition of the C5 convertases is an attractive goal because it would prevent the generation of the C5a anaphylatoxin and the MAC. This strategy would inhibit complement activation from any cause without the potentially immunosuppressive effects of limiting C3b deposition. Inhibitors based on this concept are the farthest along in clinical trials.

Other concerns about complement inhibition include the questions whether it is short-term or long-term and whether it is systemic or localized. Long-term inhibition of complement, particularly at early steps, is likely to predispose the patient to infection. Short-term (hours to days) inhibition at any step is unlikely to cause problems. Given that inflammation is usually a local phenomenon, there are several mechanisms being tested to target complement inhibitors to these sites. In this way, higher levels of inhibition can be achieved where needed with lower doses of inhibitor.

NATURAL COMPLEMENT INHIBITORS

There is a large literature on naturally occurring compounds that control complement activation. These include products or extracts of plants, fungi, insects, venoms, and cell lines. The mechanism of complement inhibition by some of these natural products is known and is of clinical and experimental importance. Cobra venom factor

isolated from *Naja naja* is a 144,000 D glycoprotein that forms an alternative pathway convertase in association with Bb; this leads to massive activation of complement that causes pulmonary microvascular injury in experimental animals. This injury is usually not fatal, however, and the end result is a total depletion of complement that lasts 4 to 6 days. During this window, it has been possible to show the importance of the complement system in animal models of immune complex vasculitis, glomerulonephritis, multiple sclerosis, and graft rejection.

Perhaps the most widely used natural inhibitor of complement activation is heparin. Although heparin has been known to inhibit complement since 1929, the mechanism is not clear. It decreases activation of the classical and the alternative pathways. It has been reported to block association of C3b with Bb, inhibit binding of C4 to C1s and C2, and inactivate C1q. In clinical practice, the anticomplementary effect of heparin has been used to prevent complement activation during cardiopulmonary bypass. Measurement of complement activation products such as C3a or soluble C5b-9 after bypass showed decreases of 35 to 70% for adult and pediatric patients when heparin-coated extracorporeal circuits (e.g., Duraflo II) were used. Although numerous studies have looked at the decrease in complement activation by heparin-coated bypass circuits, there have been few attempts to correlate this with clinical outcome.

SOLUBLE CR1

Soluble CR1 (sCR1) was the first rationally designed complement inhibitor to undergo extensive testing. The idea behind the use of this RCA protein was that it had multiple mechanisms of action. It has two separate binding sites for C3b and one for C4b. It not only serves as a cofactor for the enzymatic degradation of C3b and C4b, but also it can dissociate the classic (C3b4b) and the alternative (C3b$_2$) C5 convertases. It is produced by recombinant methodology in animal cells. It consists of the entire extracellular portion of CR1 (30 SCRs). A modified version is produced in a manner that decorates the protein with the carbohydrate sialyl Lewis^x, the ligand for P-selectin and E-selectin. This modification targets sCR1 directly to activated (inflamed) endothelium. Another modified form of sCR1 has been developed that, rather than the entire 30-SCR protein, contains just the first three SCRs that retain complement-inactivating capacity in association with a cationic peptide at the carboxy terminus followed by a myristyl group. This sCR1 targets the protein to the lipid membrane of cells. This technique has been shown to be effective in situations in which sCR1 can be delivered locally, such as intra-articular injections or the perfusion of donor organs before transplantation.

Similar to its membrane-bound counterpart, sCR1 binds C3b and C4b and blocks human classical and alternative pathway activation. It also blocks activation of complement in many experimental animals, leading to almost 100 publications describing its utility in a wide number of disease models.

The first disease model that was tested with sCR1 was myocardial ischemia-reperfusion injury in rats. These disease models include intestinal ischemia in mice and rats and middle cerebral artery ligation in mice. In each case, the administration of sCR1 was associated with decreased tissue injury, less neutrophil accumulation, and lower concentrations of inflammatory mediators, such as leukotriene B$_4$. In allograft transplantation, the donor organ undergoes significant ischemia-reperfusion injury. Animal models of allogeneic renal and lung transplantation have shown that sCR1 prolongs graft survival, which may prevent early rejection episodes. In pig-to-primate cardiac xenotransplantation, sCR1 prolongs graft survival remarkably. In one study of human lung transplantation, patients were randomized to receive a single infusion of 10 mg/kg of sCR1 before restoration of blood flow in the graft. Complement activation was suppressed for 2 days after surgery. There were trends for all patients toward decreased time on the ventilator and in the intensive care unit that did not reach statistical significance. For patients who had been on cardiopulmonary bypass during surgery (and may have had more complement activation), however, there was a 56% decrease ($P = .035$) in time spent on the ventilator postoperatively if they were treated with sCR1.

sCR1 has been tested in models of autoimmune disease. Given intravenously, sCR1 delays the onset of collagen-induced arthritis in rats and inhibits the progression of established disease. In experimental autoimmune neuritis, a model for Guillain-Barré syndrome, daily sCR1 administration prevented the development of paresis and sciatic nerve damage. Similar beneficial results were seen in models of myasthenia gravis, multiple sclerosis, and glomerulonephritis.

CD55-CD46

Another soluble RCA protein under development as a therapeutic complement inhibitor is based on DAF and MCP. As stated earlier, DAF acts as only a decay accelerator of C3 and C5 convertases, whereas MCP acts as a cofactor for the degradation of C3. A recombinant fusion protein has been made that combines the four SCRs of MCP followed by the four SCRs of DAF. This protein now has decay-accelerating and cofactor activity, similar to sCR1.

TRANSGENIC ANIMALS

Xenotransplantation offers a solution to the chronic lack of solid organs for transplantation. The most studied donor animal is the pig because swine have many desirable experimental and practical characteristics, such as size and ease of production. Although immunosuppression and other strategies may be able to overcome cellular immune barriers, the immediate problem facing xenotransplantation is hyperacute rejection. This is the immediate (within minutes) cessation of graft function owing to natural IgM antibodies that react with the vascular endothelium of the xenograft. The target of these antibodies is mainly the carbohydrate moiety galactose-(α1,3)-galactose present on the graft. These antibodies quickly activate complement, leading to intravascular coagulation, tissue edema, hemorrhage, and endothelial activation. Prevention of hyperacute rejection would require reducing the levels of antibodies or their antigen, inhibiting complement activation, or a combination of all three.

Because complement regulatory proteins display species specificity, the approach to limit complement activation in xenografts has been to make transgenic pigs expressing one or more membrane proteins of human origin. In one approach, pigs were generated that were transgenic for human CD55 (DAF), CD59, and the enzyme α1,3-fucosyltransferase. This enzyme modifies the carbohydrate antigen and has been shown to prolong orthotopic heart transplants in mice. Kidneys from the triple transgenic pigs were transplanted into bilaterally nephrectomized baboons. No immunosuppression or pretreatment of the recipients was given. Under these circumstances, the function of a nontransgenic pig kidney ceases within 3 minutes, and the graft rapidly becomes nonviable. The function of transgenic kidneys was maintained with good urine output for 3 to 5 days in the six baboons that received these grafts.

C3A AND C5A RECEPTOR ANTAGONISTS

The profound biologic effects of the anaphylatoxins and the many conditions in which C3a and/or C5a are believed to play a pathologic role make the development of specific inhibitors attractive. Because the active portion of the anaphylatoxins is contained in the carboxyl terminal part of the protein, it is possible that small molecule antagonists could be developed that may be orally available, easy to synthesize, and inexpensive. These are all advantages over the use of biologics such as monoclonal antibodies or recombinant RCA proteins.

To date, there have been several synthetic C5a antagonists described. One is a cyclic analogue of C5a, acetyl-Phe[L-ornithine-Pro-D-cyclohexylalanine-Trp-Arg]. This compound inhibits C5a binding to CD88 with an IC_{50} of 20 nM. In vivo, it inhibits an Arthus-type reaction, completely blocking vascular permeability, cellular efflux, and systemic IL-6 and TNF production. The other C5a antagonist that has been studied is a mutant version of C5a itself, selected using random phage methodology. This compound also was effective in inhibition of Arthus reactions in mice and prevention of ischemia-reperfusion injury. Neither of these C5a inhibitors is in human clinical trials. Finally, a potent small molecule inhibitor of C3a has been reported in an abstract. This compound is active in vitro as an inhibitor of C3a-mediated cellular activation, chemotaxis, and smooth muscle contraction.

COMPSTATIN

Because the proteolytic cleavage of C3 and its subsequent attachment to target surfaces is the central event of complement activation, it seems rational to look for inhibitors of this step. In one approach,

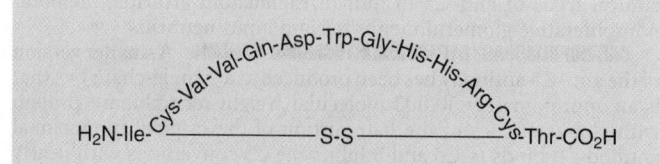

FIGURE 45–6 • Schematic representation of the structure of the cyclic peptide compstatin.

the technique of random peptide libraries was used to address this question. Phages that bound specifically to C3b were selected and amplified, and using the strategy, a single clone was identified. It contained a cyclic peptide, by virtue of two cysteines that formed a disulfide bond. The core sequence that retained C3 binding was found in a 13-amino acid cyclic peptide, termed *compstatin* (Fig. 45–6).

Compstatin inhibits the classic and alternative pathways of complement activation with IC_{50} values of 63 and 12 μM. The mechanism of compstatin action is not clear. It seems to bind to native C3 at a site distinct from the C3a/C3b cleavage site and alters the protein so that it is not recognized by either C3 convertase. Compstatin has been tested in several disease models, including an ex vivo model of porcine renal transplantation, extracorporeal circulation–induced complement activation, and the activation of complement after heparin/protamine complexes. Each showed benefit. These data indicate that compstatin is an effective and apparently safe inhibitor of C3 activation. It should be possible to use either compstatin or drugs based on its structure to design more potent, orally bioavailable compounds for conditions such as organ transplantation.

ANTI-C5

The complement inhibitor that has achieved the widest attention as a potential therapeutic agent is a monoclonal antibody to C5. The advantage to this strategy is that it prevents the generation of C5a, the most potent of the anaphylatoxins, and of the MAC. The generation of C3b and C4b opsonins still would occur, allowing proper clearance of pathogens and immune complexes even if C5 conversion were inhibited chronically. Because there is evidence that activation of early complement components is important for the maintenance of tolerance to self-antigens, inhibition of C5 activation would be less worrisome than inhibition of C3 activation. Lastly, there seems to be little detrimental effect of genetic C5 deficiency. Certain inbred mouse strains are C5 deficient with no apparent increase in infections or decrease in lifespan. The only consequence of C5 deficiency in humans seems to be an increased risk of *Neisseria* infection.

Several groups have reported the use of an anti-C5 monoclonal antibody in either complement activation assays or animal model systems. All of these antibodies block the formation of the MAC, whereas a subset of them also blocks the generation of C5a. These are the proteins that have been selected for clinical development.

ARTHRITIS. The availability of naturally C5-deficient mice has enabled the generation of monoclonal mouse antimouse C5 to test some of these therapies. Collagen-induced arthritis is a model for human rheumatoid arthritis. Mice are immunized with bovine type II collagen in complete Freund's adjuvant, resulting in an inflammatory peripheral arthritis with histopathology similar to rheumatoid arthritis. Treatment of the mice with anti-C5 for 3 weeks before the first immunization with collagen decreased the level of total hemolytic complement by about 60%. It totally prevented the appearance of arthritis in the mice. Histology of mice with arthritis that received a control antibody showed the typical proliferative synovitis with neutrophil and monocyte infiltration along with cartilage loss and bone erosion. In contrast, the anti-C5–treated mice had normal joints with smooth articular surfaces. The investigators then looked at the ability of anti-C5 to ameliorate established disease. Either anti-C5 or control antibody was not given until arthritis was evident clinically. The mice that received control antibody exhibited continued increases in paw thickness, clinical score, and number of joints involved. The mice treated with anti-C5 showed a halt in the progression of the arthritis and some indication of regression of disease with a significant decrease in the number of joint erosions. These and other results have led to clinical trials of anti-C5 in human rheumatoid arthritis, membranoproliferative glomerulonephritis, and lupus nephritis.

CARDIOPULMONARY BYPASS AND MYOCARDIAL ISCHEMIA. A smaller version of the anti-C5 antibody has been produced as a "single-chain Fv" that is an approximately 30,000 molecular weight recombinant protein with characteristics of the Fab portion of the original monoclonal antibody. It binds to C5 and inhibits the C5 convertases with nearly identical effectiveness as the intact antibody. This reagent is being developed for unstable angina, thrombolysis/angioplasty after myocardial infarction, and myocardial damage after cardiopulmonary bypass.

GRAFT REJECTION. Similar to soluble CR1 and the other complement inhibitors described, anti-C5 treatment has been used to prolong xenograft survival. These results suggest that anti-C5 could play a role in managing acute graft rejection in humans.

OTHER INFLAMMATORY CONDITIONS. Anti-C5 has several other therapeutic uses. It has been shown to delay the onset of proteinuria and prolong survival in the (NZB × NZW)F$_1$ mouse model of systemic lupus erythematosus.

Future Directions

Understanding of the complement system is evolving. It is no longer a simple antimicrobial effector of the humoral immune system. Although the complement system plays important roles in infection and inflammatory responses, it also has many deleterious effects that must be controlled in conditions ranging from immune complex injury to reproduction. More than half of the proteins associated with the complement system are dedicated to the control of activation or effector functions.

Knowledge of how complement is activated and how it can be controlled offers new opportunities for the development of therapeutic agents for human diseases. It is anticipated that within the next few years many of these drugs will be approved for clinical use. The most likely successful therapeutic target will be antibodies to C5/C5a, and the diseases most likely to be improved by complement inhibition are ischemic injury to the heart and brain and autoimmune/inflammatory injury to joints and the kidney.

SUGGESTED READINGS

Barilla-LaBarca ML, Atkinson JP: Rheumatic syndromes associated with complement deficiency. Curr Opin Rheumatol 2003;15:55–60. *Overview of the recognized manifestations of complement deficiency and how targeted gene deletions of complement proteins are providing new insights.*

Bhole D, Stahl GL: Therapeutic potential of targeting the complement cascade in critical care medicine. Crit Care Med 2003;31(1 Suppl):S97–S104. *Review of the clinical applications of complement inhibitors and antagonists.*

Carroll MC: A protective role for innate immunity in autoimmune disease. Clin Immunol 2000;95:S30–S38. *Deficiencies in components of the innate immune system are risks for autoimmune diseases.*

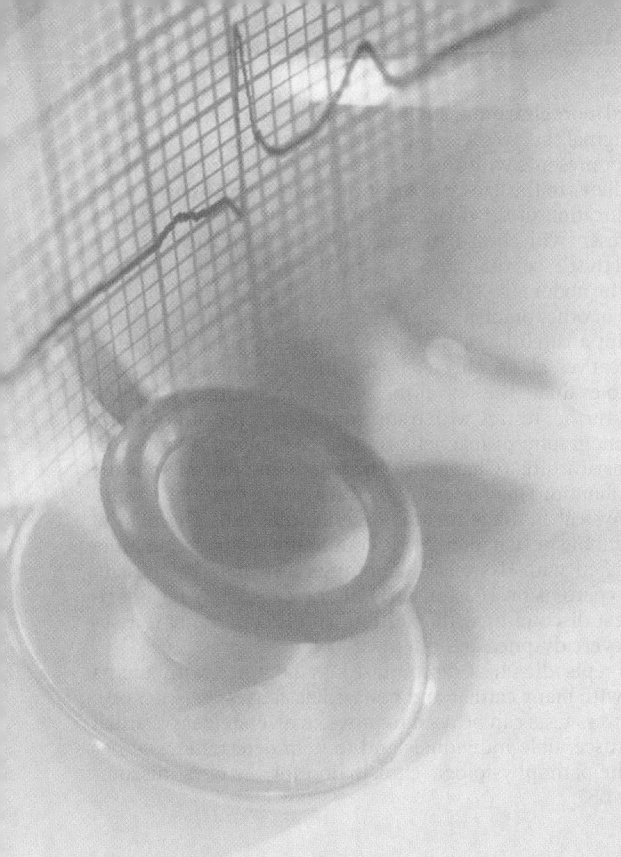

part VIII

Cardiovascular Disease

46 APPROACH TO THE PATIENT WITH POSSIBLE CARDIOVASCULAR DISEASE

Lee Goldman

Patients with cardiovascular disease may present with a wide range of symptoms and/or signs, each of which may be caused by noncardiovascular conditions. Conversely, patients with substantial cardiovascular disease may be asymptomatic. Because cardiovascular disease is the leading cause of death in the United States and other developed countries, it is crucial that patients be evaluated carefully to detect early cardiovascular disease, that symptoms or signs of cardiovascular disease be evaluated in detail, and that appropriate therapy be instituted. Improvements in diagnosis, therapy, and prevention have contributed to an impressive decline in age-adjusted cardiovascular death rates in the United States since the late 1960s. Because of the increase in the number of persons older than 40 years, however, the absolute number of deaths from cardiovascular disease in the United States has not declined.

In evaluating a patient with known or suspected heart disease, the physician must determine quickly whether a potentially life-threatening condition exists. In these situations, the evaluation must focus on the specific issue at hand and be accompanied by the rapid performance of appropriately directed additional tests. Examples of potentially life-threatening conditions include acute myocardial infarction (Chapter 68), unstable angina (Chapter 68), suspected aortic dissection (Chapter 75), pulmonary edema (Chapter 56), and pulmonary embolism (Chapter 94).

History for Detection of Cardiovascular Symptoms

Patients may complain spontaneously of a variety of cardiovascular symptoms (Table 46–1), but sometimes these symptoms are elicited only by obtaining a careful, complete medical history. In patients with known or suspected cardiovascular disease, questions about cardiovascular symptoms are key components of the history of present illness; in other patients, these issues are a fundamental part of the review of systems.

CHEST PAIN

Chest discomfort or pain is the cardinal manifestation of myocardial ischemia resulting from coronary artery disease or any condition that causes myocardial ischemia via an imbalance of myocardial oxygen demand compared with myocardial oxygen supply (Chapter 68). New, acute, often ongoing pain may indicate an acute myocardial infarction, unstable angina, or aortic dissection; a pulmonary cause, such as acute pulmonary embolism or pleural irritation; a musculoskeletal condition of the chest wall, thorax, or shoulder; or a gastrointestinal abnormality, such as esophageal reflux or spasm, peptic ulcer disease, or cholecystitis (Table 46–2). The chest discomfort of myocardial infarction commonly occurs without an immediate or obvious precipitating clinical cause and builds in intensity over at least several minutes; the sensation can range from annoying discomfort to severe pain (Chapter 68). Although a variety of adjectives may be used by patients to describe the sensation, physicians must be suspicious of any discomfort, especially if it radiates to the neck, shoulder, or arms. The chest discomfort of unstable angina is clinically indistinguishable from that of myocardial infarction except that the former may

be precipitated more clearly by activity and may be more rapidly responsive to antianginal therapy (Chapter 68). Aortic dissection (Chapter 75) classically presents with the sudden onset of severe pain in the chest that radiates to the back; the location of the pain often provides clues to the location of the dissection: Ascending aortic dissections commonly present with chest discomfort radiating to the back, whereas dissections of the descending aorta commonly present with back pain radiating to the abdomen. The presence of back pain or a history of hypertension or other predisposing factors, such as Marfan syndrome, should prompt a careful assessment of peripheral pulses, to determine if the great vessels are affected by the dissection, and of the chest radiograph, to evaluate the size of the aorta. If this initial evaluation is suspicious, further testing with transesophageal echocardiography, computed tomography, or magnetic resonance imaging is indicated. The pain of pericarditis (Chapter 74) may simulate that of an acute myocardial infarction, may be primarily pleuritic, or may be continuous. Key physical findings include a pericardial rub. The pain of pulmonary embolism (Chapter 94) is commonly pleuritic in nature and is associated with dyspnea; hemoptysis also may be present. Pulmonary hypertension (Chapter 64) of any cause may be associated with chest discomfort with exertion, and it commonly is associated with severe dyspnea and often with cyanosis.

Recurrent, episodic chest discomfort may be noted with angina pectoris and with many cardiac and noncardiac causes (Chapter 68). A variety of stress tests can be used to provoke reversible myocardial ischemia in susceptible individuals and to help determine whether ischemia is the pathophysiologic explanation for the chest discomfort (Chapter 68).

DYSPNEA

Dyspnea, which is an uncomfortable awareness of breathing, is commonly due to cardiovascular or pulmonary disease. A systematic approach nearly always reveals the cause (Fig. 46–1). Acute dyspnea can be caused by myocardial ischemia, heart failure, severe hypertension, pericardial tamponade, pulmonary embolism, pneumothorax, upper airway obstruction, acute bronchitis or pneumonia, or some drug overdoses (e.g., salicylates). Subacute or chronic dyspnea is also a common presenting or accompanying symptom in patients with pulmonary disease (Chapter 81). Dyspnea also can be caused by severe anemia (Chapter 160) and can be confused with the fatigue that often is noted in patients with systemic and neurologic diseases (Chapters 273 and 423).

In heart failure, dyspnea typically is noted as a hunger for air and a need or an urge to breathe. The feeling that breathing requires increased work or effort is more typical of airway obstruction or neuromuscular disease. A feeling of chest tightness or constriction during breathing is typical of bronchoconstriction, which is commonly caused by obstructive airway disease but also may be seen in pulmonary edema. A feeling of heavy breathing, a feeling of rapid breathing, or a need to breathe more is classically associated with deconditioning.

In cardiovascular conditions, chronic dyspnea usually is caused by increases in pulmonary venous pressure as a result of left ventricular failure (Chapters 55 and 56) or valvular heart disease (Chapter 72). Orthopnea, which is an exacerbation of dyspnea when the patient is recumbent, is due to increased work of breathing because of either increased venous return to the pulmonary vasculature or loss of gravitational assistance in diaphragmatic effort. Paroxysmal nocturnal dyspnea is severe dyspnea that awakens a patient at night and forces the assumption of a sitting or standing position to achieve gravitational redistribution of fluid.

PALPITATIONS

Palpitations describe a subjective sensation of an irregular or abnormal heartbeat. Palpitations may be caused by any arrhythmia (Chapters 59 and 60) with or without important underlying structural heart disease. Palpitations should be defined in terms of the duration and frequency of the episodes; the precipitating and related factors; and any associated symptoms of chest pain, dyspnea, lightheadedness, or syncope. It is crucial to use the history to determine whether the palpitations are caused by an irregular or a regular heartbeat. The feeling associated with a premature atrial or ventricular contraction, often described as a "skipped beat" or a "flip-flopping of the heart," must be distinguished from the irregularly irregular rhythm of atrial fibrillation and the rapid but regular rhythm of

---

Table 46–1 • CARDINAL SYMPTOMS OF CARDIOVASCULAR DISEASE

Chest pain or discomfort
Dyspnea, orthopnea, paroxysmal nocturnal dyspnea, wheezing
Palpitations, dizziness, syncope
Cough, hemoptysis
Fatigue, weakness
Pain in extremities with exertion (claudication)

Table 46–2 • CAUSES OF CHEST PAIN

CONDITION	LOCATION	QUALITY	DURATION	AGGRAVATING OR RELIEVING FACTORS	ASSOCIATED SYMPTOMS OR SIGNS
CARDIOVASCULAR CAUSES					
Angina	Retrosternal region; radiates to or occasionally isolated to neck, jaw, epigastrium, shoulder, or arms—left common	Pressure, burning, squeezing, heaviness, indigestion	<2–10 min	Precipitated by exercise, cold weather, or emotional stress; relieved by rest or nitroglycerin; atypical (Prinzmetal's) angina may be unrelated to activity, often early morning	S_3 or murmur of papillary muscle dysfunction during pain
Rest or unstable angina	Same as angina	Same as angina but may be more severe	Usually <20 min	Same as angina, with decreasing tolerance for exertion or at rest	Similar to stable angina, but may be pronounced; transient cardiac failure can occur
Myocardial infarction	Substernal and may radiate like angina	Heaviness, pressure burning, constriction	≥30 min but variable	Unrelieved by rest or nitroglycerin	Shortness of breath, sweating, weakness, nausea, vomiting
Pericarditis	Usually begins over sternum or toward cardiac apex and may radiate to neck or left shoulder; often more localized than the pain of myocardial ischemia	Sharp, stabbing, knifelike	Lasts many hours to days; may wax and wane	Aggravated by deep breathing, rotating chest, or supine position; relieved by sitting up and leaning forward	Pericardial friction rub
Aortic dissection	Anterior chest; may radiate to back	Excruciating, tearing, knifelike	Sudden onset, unrelenting	Usually occurs in setting of hypertension or predisposition such as Marfan's syndrome	Murmur of aortic insufficiency, pulse or blood pressure asymmetry; neurologic deficit
Pulmonary embolism (chest pain often not present)	Substernal or over region of pulmonary infarction	Pleuritic (with pulmonary infarction) or angina-like	Sudden onset; minutes to <1 hr	May be aggravated by breathing	Dyspnea, tachypnea, tachycardia; hypotension, signs of acute right ventricular failure, and pulmonary hypertension with large emboli; rales, pleural rub, hemoptysis with pulmonary infarction
Pulmonary hypertension	Substernal	Pressure; oppressive	Similar to angina	Aggravated by effort	Pain usually associated with dyspnea; signs of pulmonary hypertension
NONCARDIAC CAUSES					
Pneumonia with pleurisy	Localized over involved area	Pleuritic, localized	Brief or prolonged	Painful breathing	Dyspnea, cough, fever, dull to percussion, bronchial breath sounds, rales, occasional pleural rub
Spontaneous pneumothorax	Unilateral	Sharp, well localized	Sudden onset, lasts many hours	Painful breathing	Dyspnea; hyperresonance and decreased breath and voice sounds over involved lung
Musculoskeletal disorders	Variable	Aching	Short or long duration	Aggravated by movement; history of muscle exertion or injury	Tender to pressure or movement
Herpes zoster	Dermatomal in distribution	Burning, itching	Prolonged	None	Vesicular rash appears in area of discomfort
Esophageal reflux	Substernal, epigastric	Burning, visceral discomfort	10–60 min	Aggravated by large meal, postprandial recumbency; relief with antacid	Water brash
Peptic ulcer	Epigastric, substernal	Visceral burning, aching	Prolonged	Relief with food, antacid	
Gallbladder disease	Epigastric, right upper quadrant	Visceral	Prolonged	May be unprovoked or follow meals	Right upper quadrant tenderness may be present
Anxiety states	Often localized over precordium	Variable; location often moves from place to place	Varies; often fleeting	Situational	Sighing respirations, often chest wall tenderness

From Andreoli TE, Bennett JC, Carpenter CCJ, Plum F: Evaluation of the patient with cardiovascular disease. *In* Cecil Essentials of Medicine 4th ed. Philadelphia, WB Saunders, 1997, pp. 11–12.

supraventricular tachycardia. Associated symptoms of chest pain, dyspnea, lightheadedness, dizziness, or diaphoresis suggest an important effect on cardiac output and mandate further evaluation. In general, evaluation begins with ambulatory electrocardiography (ECG) (Table 46–3), which is indicated in patients who have palpitations in the presence of structural heart disease or substantial accompanying symptoms. Depending on the series, 9 to 43% of patients have important underlying heart disease.

Lightheadedness or *syncope* (Chapters 58 and 435) can be caused by any condition that decreases cardiac output (e.g., bradyarrhythmia, tachyarrhythmia, obstruction of the left ventricular or right ventricular inflow or outflow, cardiac tamponade, aortic dissection, or

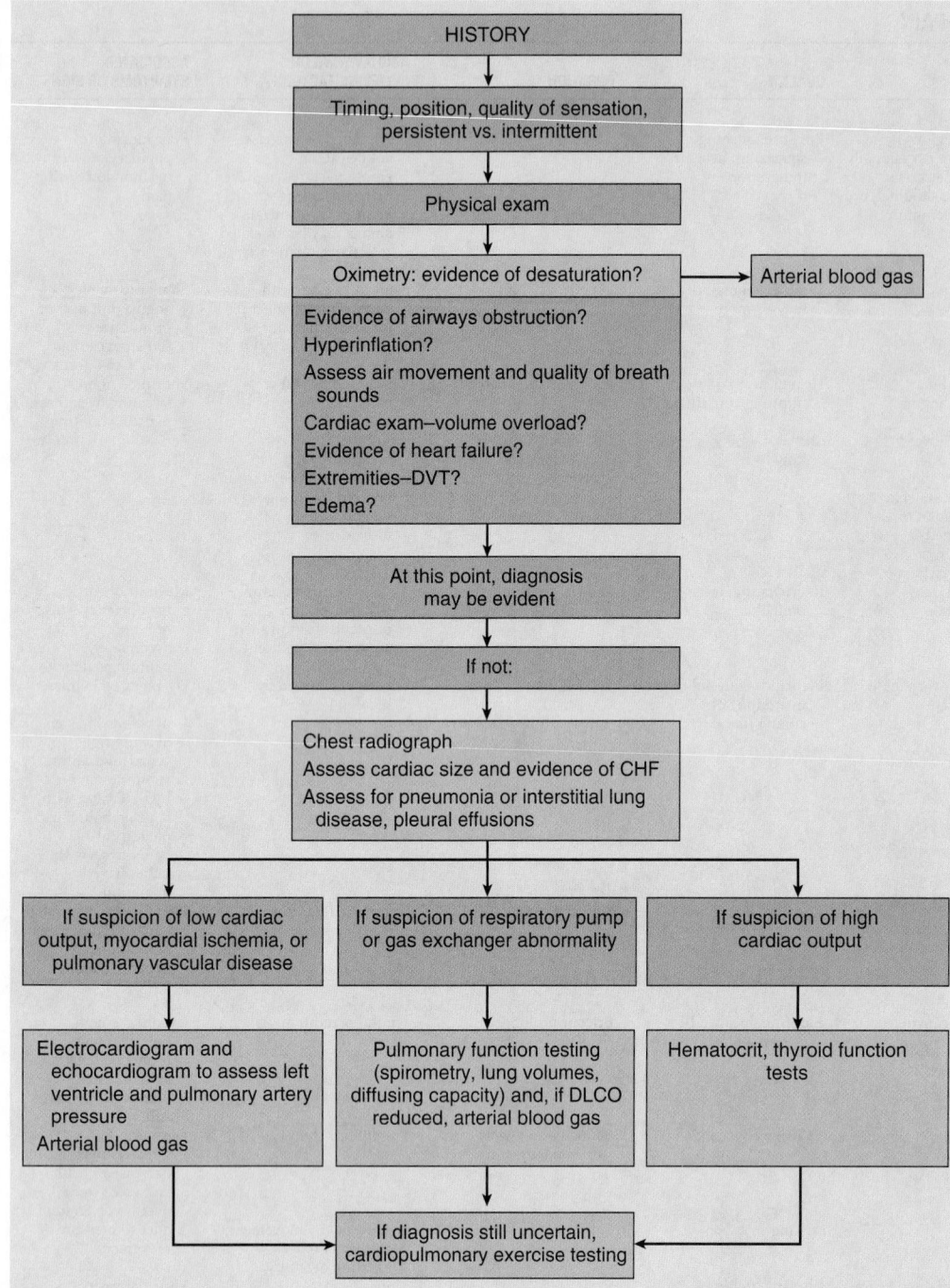

FIGURE 46–1 • Algorithm for the evaluation of a patient with dyspnea. The pace and completeness with which one approaches this framework depend on the intensity and acuity of the patient's symptoms. In a patient with severe, acute dyspnea, an arterial blood gas measurement may be one of the first laboratory evaluations, whereas it might not be obtained until much later in the work-up of a patient with chronic breathlessness of unclear cause. A therapeutic trial of a medication, such as a bronchodilator, may be instituted at any point if one is fairly confident of the diagnosis based on the data available at that time. CHF, congestive heart failure; DLCO, diffusing capacity of the lung for carbon monoxide; DVT, deep venous thrombosis. (From Schwartzstein RM, Feller-Kopman D: Approach to the patient with dyspnea. *In* Braunwald E, Goldman L [eds]: Primary Cardiology, 2nd ed. Philadelphia, WB Saunders, 2003.)

severe pump failure), by reflex-mediated vasomotor instability (e.g., vasovagal, situational, or carotid sinus syncope), or by orthostatic hypotension. Neurologic diseases (e.g., migraine headaches, transient ischemic attacks, or seizures) also can cause transient loss of consciousness. The history, physical examination, and ECG are often diagnostic of the cause of syncope. Syncope caused by a cardiac arrhythmia usually occurs with little warning. Syncope with exertion or just after concluding exertion is typical of aortic stenosis and hypertrophic obstructive cardiomyopathy. In many patients, additional testing is required to document central nervous system disease, the cause of reduced cardiac output, or carotid sinus syncope. When the history, physical examination, and ECG do not provide helpful diagnostic information that points toward a specific cause of syncope, it is imperative that patients with heart disease or an abnormal ECG be tested with continuous ambulatory ECG monitoring to diagnose a possible arrhythmia (see Fig. 435–1); in selected patients, formal electrophysiologic testing may be indicated (Chapter 58). In patients with no evident heart disease, tilt testing (Chapters 58 and 435) can help detect reflex-mediated vasomotor instability.

OTHER SYMPTOMS

Nonproductive *cough* (Chapter 81) is often an early manifestation of elevated pulmonary venous pressure and otherwise unsuspected heart failure. *Fatigue* and *weakness* are common accompaniments of advanced cardiac disease and reflect an inability to perform normal activities. A variety of approaches have been used to classify the severity of cardiac limitations ranging from class I (little or no limitation) to class IV (severe limitation) (Table 46–4). *Hemoptysis* is a classic presenting finding in patients with pulmonary embolism, but it is also common in patients with mitral stenosis, pulmonary edema, bronchiectasis, and bronchitis. *Claudication*, which is pain in the extremities with exertion, should alert the physician to possible peripheral arterial disease (Chapters 76 and 77).

COMPLETE MEDICAL HISTORY

The complete medical history should include a thorough review of systems, family history, social history, and past medical history

Table 46–3 • AHA/ACC GUIDELINES FOR USE OF DIAGNOSTIC TESTS IN PATIENTS WITH PALPITATIONS*

AMBULATORY ELECTROCARDIOGRAPHY

Class I	Palpitations, syncope, dizziness
Class II	Shortness of breath, chest pain, or fatigue (not otherwise explained, episodic and strongly suggestive of an arrhythmia as the cause because of a relation of the symptom with palpitation)
Class III	Symptoms not reasonably expected to be due to arrhythmia

ELECTROPHYSIOLOGIC STUDY

Class I	1. Patients with palpitations who have a pulse rate documented by medical personnel as inappropriately rapid and in whom electrocardiographic recordings fail to document the cause of the palpitations
	2. Patients with palpitations preceding a syncopal episode
Class II	Patients with clinically significant palpitations, suspected to be of cardiac origin, in whom symptoms are sporadic and cannot be documented; studies are performed to determine the mechanisms of arrhythmias, to direct or provide therapy, or to assess prognosis
Class III	Patients with palpitations documented to be due to extracardiac causes (e.g., hyperthyroidism)

ECHOCARDIOGRAPHY

Class I	Arrhythmias with evidence of heart disease
	Family history of genetic disorder associated with arrhythmias
Class II	Arrhythmias commonly associated with, but without evidence of, heart disease
	Atrial fibrillation or flutter
Class III	Palpitations without evidence of arrhythmias
	Minor arrhythmias without evidence of heart disease

*Class I, general agreement the test is useful and indicated; class II, frequently used, but there is a divergence of opinion with respect to its utility; class III, general agreement the test is not useful.

AHA/ACC = American Heart Association/American College of Cardiology.

From Goldman L, Braunwald E (eds): Primary Cardiology. Philadelphia, WB Saunders, 1998, p 126.

(Chapter 11). The review of systems may reveal other symptoms that suggest a systemic disease as the cause of any cardiovascular problems. The family history should focus on premature atherosclerosis or evidence of familial abnormalities, such as may be found with various causes of the long QT syndrome (Chapter 57) or hypertrophic cardiomyopathy (Chapter 73).

The social history should include specific questioning about cigarette smoking, alcohol intake, and use of illicit drugs. The past medical history may reveal prior conditions or medications that suggest systemic diseases, ranging from chronic obstructive pulmonary disease, which may explain a complaint of dyspnea, to hemochromatosis, which may be a cause of restrictive cardiomyopathy. A careful history to inquire about recent dental work or other procedures is crucial if bacterial endocarditis is part of the differential diagnosis.

Physical Examination for Detection of Signs of Cardiovascular Disease

The cardiovascular physical examination, which is a subset of the complete physical examination, provides important clues to the diagnosis of asymptomatic and symptomatic cardiac disease and may reveal cardiovascular manifestations of noncardiovascular diseases. The cardiovascular physical examination begins with careful measurement of the pulse and blood pressure. If aortic dissection (Chapter 75) is a consideration, blood pressure should be measured in both arms and, preferably, in at least one leg. When coarctation of the aorta is suspected (Chapter 65), blood pressure must be measured in at least one leg and in the arms. Discrepancies in blood pressure between the two arms also can be caused by atherosclerotic disease of the great vessels. Pulsus paradoxus, which is a decrease in the systolic blood pressure of more than the usual 10 mm Hg drop in inspiration, is typical of pericardial tamponade (Chapter 74).

GENERAL APPEARANCE

The respiratory rate may be increased in patients with heart failure. Patients with pulmonary edema are usually markedly tachypneic and

Table 46–4 • A COMPARISON OF THREE METHODS OF ASSESSING CARDIOVASCULAR DISABILITY

CLASS	NEW YORK HEART ASSOCIATION FUNCTIONAL CLASSIFICATION	CANADIAN CARDIOVASCULAR SOCIETY FUNCTIONAL CLASSIFICATION	SPECIFIC ACTIVITY SCALE
I	Patients with cardiac disease but without resulting limitations of physical activity. Ordinary physical activity does not cause undue fatigue, palpitation, dyspnea, or anginal pain	Ordinary physical activity, such as walking and climbing stairs, does not cause angina. Angina with strenuous or rapid or prolonged exertion at work or recreation	Patients can perform to completion any activity requiring ≥7 metabolic equivalents, e.g., can carry 24 lb up 8 steps; carry objects that weigh 80 lb; do outdoor work (shovel snow, spade soil); do recreational activities (skiing, basketball, squash, handball, jog/walk 5 mph)
II	Patients with cardiac disease resulting in slight limitation of physical activity. They are comfortable at rest. Ordinary physical activity results in fatigue, palpitations, dyspnea, or anginal pain	Slight limitation of ordinary activity. Walking or climbing stairs rapidly, walking uphill, walking or stair climbing after meals, in cold, in wind, or when under emotional stress, or only during the few hours after awakening. Walking >2 blocks on the level and climbing >1 flight of ordinary stairs at a normal pace and in normal conditions	Patient can perform to completion any activity requiring ≥5 metabolic equivalents but cannot and does not perform to completion activities requiring ≥7 metabolic equivalents, e.g., have sexual intercourse without stopping, garden, rake, weed, roller skate, dance fox trot, walk at 4 mph on level ground
III	Patients with cardiac disease resulting in marked limitation of physical activity. They are comfortable at rest. Less than ordinary physical activity causes fatigue, palpitations, dyspnea, or anginal pain	Marked limitation of ordinary physical activity. Walking 1 to 2 blocks on the level and climbing >1 flight in normal conditions	Patient can perform to completion any activity requiring ≥2 metabolic equivalents but cannot and does not perform to completion any activities requiring ≥5 metabolic equivalents, e.g., shower without stopping, strip and make bed, clean windows, walk 2.5 mph, bowl, play golf, dress without stopping
IV	Patient with cardiac disease resulting in inability to carry on any physical activity without discomfort. Symptoms of cardiac insufficiency or of the anginal syndrome may be present even at rest. If any physical activity is undertaken, discomfort is increased	Inability to carry on any physical activity without discomfort—anginal syndrome *may be* present at rest	Patient cannot or does not perform to completion activities requiring ≥2 metabolic equivalents. *Cannot* carry out activities listed above (Specific Activity Scale, class III)

From Goldman L, et al: Comparative reproducibility and validity of systems for assessing cardiovascular functional class: Advantages of a new specific activity scale. Circulation 1981;64:1227–1234. Reproduced by permission of the American Heart Association.

may have labored breathing. Patients with advanced heart failure may have Cheyne-Stokes respirations.

Systemic diseases, such as hyperthyroidism (Chapter 239), hypothyroidism (Chapter 239), rheumatoid arthritis (Chapter 278), scleroderma (Chapter 281), and hemochromatosis (Chapter 225), may be suspected from the patient's general appearance. Marfan syndrome (Chapter 276), Turner's syndrome (Chapter 249), Down syndrome (Chapter 38), and a variety of congenital anomalies also may be readily apparent.

OPHTHALMOLOGIC EXAMINATION

Examination of the fundi may show diabetic or hypertensive retinopathy or Roth's spots typical of infectious endocarditis. Beading of the retinal arteries is typical of severe hypercholesterolemia. Osteogenesis imperfecta, which is associated with blue sclerae, also is associated with aortic dilation and mitral valve prolapse. Retinal artery occlusion may be caused by an embolus from clot in the left atrium or left ventricle, a left atrial myxoma, or atherosclerotic debris from the great vessels. Hyperthyroidism may present with exophthalmos and typical stare, whereas myotonic dystrophy, which is associated with atrioventricular block and arrhythmia, often is associated with ptosis and an expressionless face.

JUGULAR VEINS

The external jugular veins help in assessment of mean right atrial pressure, which normally varies between 5 and 10 cm H_2O; the height (in centimeters) of the central venous pressure is measured by adding 5 cm to the height of the observed jugular venous distention above the sternal angle of Louis. The normal jugular venous pulse, best seen in the internal jugular vein (and not seen in the external jugular vein unless insufficiency of the jugular venous valves is present), includes an a wave, caused by right atrial contraction; a c wave, reflecting carotid artery pulsation; an x descent; a v wave, which corresponds to isovolumetric right ventricular contraction and is more marked in the presence of tricuspid insufficiency; and a y descent, which occurs as the tricuspid valve opens and ventricular filling begins (Fig. 46–2). Abnormalities of the jugular venous pressure and pulse are useful in detecting conditions such as heart failure, pericardial disease, tricuspid valve disease, and pulmonary hypertension (Table 46–5).

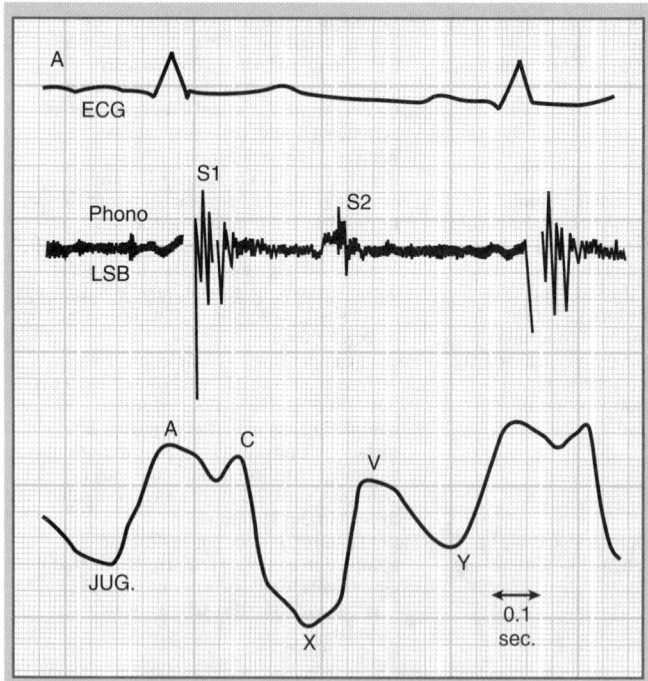

FIGURE 46–2 • Normal jugular venous pulse. ECG = electrocardiogram; JUG = jugular vein; LSB = left sternal border; phono = phonocardiogram; S_1 = first heart sound; S_2 = second heart sound; Sec = second.

Table 46–5 • ABNORMALITIES OF VENOUS PRESSURE AND PULSE AND THEIR CLINICAL SIGNIFICANCE

1. Positive hepatojugular reflux—suspect congestive heart failure, particularly left ventricular systolic dysfunction (echocardiography recommended)
2. Elevated systemic venous pressure without obvious "x" or "y" descent and quiet precordium and pulsus paradoxus—suspect cardiac tamponade (echocardiography recommended)
3. Elevated systemic venous pressure with sharp "y" descent, Kussmaul's sign and quiet precordium—suspect constrictive pericarditis (cardiac catheterization and MRI or CT recommended)
4. Elevated systemic venous pressure with a sharp brief "y" descent, Kussmaul's sign, and evidence of pulmonary hypertension and tricuspid regurgitation—suspect restrictive cardiomyopathy (cardiac catheterization and MRI or CT recommended)
5. A prominent "a" wave with or without elevation of mean systemic venous pressure—exclude tricuspid stenosis, right ventricular hypertrophy due to pulmonary stenosis, and pulmonary hypertension (echo-Doppler study recommended)
6. A prominent "v" wave with a sharp "y" descent—suspect tricuspid regurgitation (echo-Doppler or cardiac catheterization to determine etiology)

CT = computed tomography; MRI = magnetic resonance imaging.
From Braunwald E (ed): Heart Disease: A Textbook of Cardiovascular Medicine, 5th ed. Philadelphia, WB Saunders, 1997.

CAROTID PULSE

The carotid pulse should be examined in terms of its volume and contour. The carotid pulse (Fig. 46–3) may be increased in frequency and may be more intense than normal in patients with a higher stroke volume secondary to aortic regurgitation, arteriovenous fistula, hyperthyroidism, fever, or anemia. In aortic regurgitation or arteriovenous fistula, the pulse may have a bisferious quality. The carotid upstroke is delayed in patients with valvular aortic stenosis (Chapter 72) and has a normal contour but diminished amplitude in any cause of reduced stroke volume.

CARDIAC INSPECTION AND PALPATION

Inspection of the precordium may reveal the hyperinflation of obstructive lung disease or unilateral asymmetry of the left side of the chest because of right ventricular hypertrophy before puberty. Palpation may be performed with the patient either supine or in the left lateral decubitus position; the latter position moves the left ventricular apex closer to the chest wall and increases the ability to palpate the point of maximal impulse and other phenomena. Low-frequency phenomena, such as systolic heaves or lifts from the left ventricle (at the cardiac apex) or right ventricle (parasternal in the third or fourth intercostal space), are felt best with the heel of the palm. With the patient in the left lateral decubitus position, this technique also may allow palpation of an S_3 gallop in cases of advanced heart failure and/or an S_4 gallop in cases of poor left ventricular distensibility during diastole. The left ventricular apex is more diffuse and sometimes may be frankly dyskinetic in patients with advanced heart disease. The distal palm is best for feeling thrills, which are the tactile equivalent of cardiac murmurs. By definition, a thrill denotes a murmur of grade 4/6 or louder. Higher frequency events may be felt best with the fingertips; examples include the opening snap of mitral stenosis or the loud pulmonic second sound of pulmonary hypertension.

AUSCULTATION

The first heart sound (Fig. 46–4), which is largely produced by closure of the mitral and—to a lesser extent—the tricuspid valves, may be louder in patients with mitral valve stenosis and intact valve leaflet movement and less audible in patients with poor closure owing to mitral regurgitation (Chapter 72). The second heart sound is caused primarily by closure of the aortic valve, but closure of the pulmonic valve is also commonly audible. In normal individuals, the louder aortic closure sound occurs first, followed by pulmonic closure. With expiration, the two sounds are virtually superimposed, whereas with inspiration the increased stroke volume of the right ventricle commonly leads to a discernible splitting of the second sound. This splitting may

Cardiovascular Disease

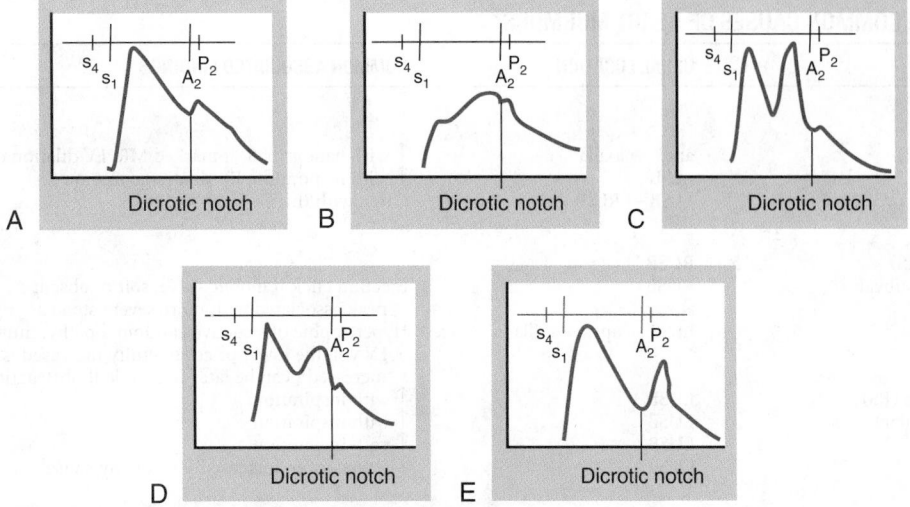

FIGURE 46–3 • Schematic diagrams of the configurational changes in the carotid pulse and their differential diagnosis. Heart sounds also are illustrated. *A*, Normal. *B*, Anacrotic pulse with slow initial upstroke. The peak is close to the second heart sound. These features suggest fixed left ventricular outflow obstruction, such as valvular aortic stenosis. *C*, Pulsus bisferiens, with percussion and tidal waves occurring during systole. This type of carotid pulse contour is observed most frequently in patients with hemodynamically significant aortic regurgitation or combined aortic stenosis and regurgitation with dominant regurgitation. It rarely is observed in patients with mitral valve prolapse or in normal individuals. *D*, Pulsus bisferiens in hypertrophic obstructive cardiomyopathy. This finding rarely is appreciated at the bedside by palpation. *E*, Dicrotic pulse results from an accentuated dicrotic wave and tends to occur in sepsis, severe heart failure, hypovolemic shock, cardiac tamponade, and after aortic valve replacement. A_2 = aortic component of the second heart sound; P_2 = pulmonary component of the second heart sound; S_1 = first heart sound; S_4 = atrial sounds. (From Chatterjee K: Bedside evaluation of the heart: The physical examination. *In* Chatterjee K, et al [eds]: Cardiology: An Illustrated Text/Reference. Philadelphia, JB Lippincott, 1991, pp 3.11–3.51.)

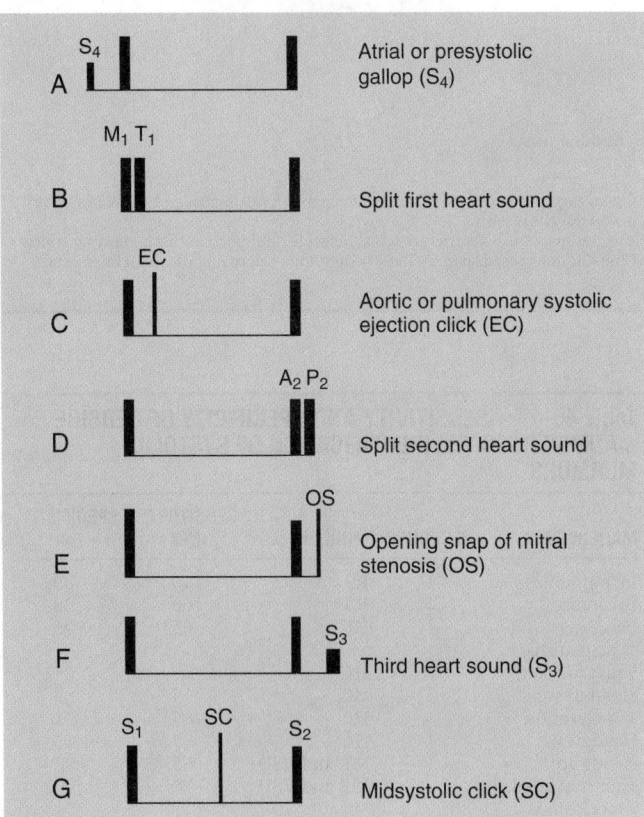

FIGURE 46–4 • Timing of the different heart sounds and added sounds. (Modified from Wood P: Diseases of the Heart and Circulation, 3rd ed. Philadelphia, JB Lippincott, 1968, with permission.)

be fixed in patients with an atrial septal defect (Chapter 65) or a right bundle-branch block. The split may be paradoxical in patients with left bundle-branch block or other causes of delayed left ventricular emptying. The aortic component of the second sound is increased in intensity in the presence of systemic hypertension and decreased in intensity in patients with aortic stenosis. The pulmonic second sound is increased in the presence of pulmonary hypertension.

Early systolic ejection sounds are related to forceful opening of the aortic or pulmonic valve. These sounds are common in congenital aortic stenosis, with a mobile valve; in hypertension, with forceful opening of the aortic valve; and in healthy young individuals, especially when cardiac output is increased. Midsystolic or late systolic clicks are caused most commonly by mitral valve prolapse (Chapter 72). Clicks are relatively high-frequency sounds that are heard best with the diaphragm of the stethoscope.

S_3 corresponds to rapid ventricular filling during early diastole. It may occur in normal children and young adults, especially if stroke volume is increased. After about age 40 years, however, an S_3 should be considered abnormal; it is caused by conditions that increase the volume of ventricular filling during early diastole (e.g., mitral regurgitation) or that increase pressure in early diastole (e.g., advanced heart failure). A left ventricular S_3 gallop is heard best at the apex, whereas the right ventricular S_3 gallop is heard best at the fourth intercostal space at the left parasternal border; both are heard best with the bell of the stethoscope. An S_4 is heard rarely in young individuals but is common in adults older than 40 or 50 years because of reduced ventricular compliance during atrial contraction; it is a nearly ubiquitous finding in patients with hypertension, heart failure, or ischemic heart disease.

The opening snap of mitral and, less commonly, tricuspid stenosis occurs at the beginning of mechanical diastole, before the onset of the rapid phase of ventricular filling. An opening snap is high-pitched and is heard best with the diaphragm; this differential frequency should help distinguish an opening snap from an S_3 on physical examination. An opening snap commonly can be distinguished from a loud pulmonic component of the second heart sound by the differential location (mitral opening snap at the apex, tricuspid opening snap at the left third or fourth intercostal space, pulmonic second sound at the left second intercostal space) and by the longer interval between S_2 and the opening snap.

Table 46–6 • SOME COMMON CAUSES OF HEART MURMURS*

	USUAL LOCATION	COMMON ASSOCIATED FINDINGS
SYSTOLIC		
Holosystolic		
Mitral regurgitation (MR)	apex → axilla	↑ with handgrip; S₃ if marked MR; LV dilation common
Tricuspid regurgitation (TR)	LLSB	↑ with inspiration; RV dilation common
Ventricular septal defect (VSD)	LLSB → RLSB	Often with thrill
Early-mid Systolic		
Aortic valvar stenosis (AS)	RUSB	
Fixed supravalvar or subvalvar	RUSB	Ejection click if mobile valve; soft or absent A₂ if valve immobile; later peak associated with more severe stenosis
Dynamic infravalvar	LLSB → apex + axilla	Hypertrophic obstructive cardiomyopathy; murmur louder if LV volume lower or contractility increased, softer if LV volume increased†; can be later in systole if obstruction delayed
Pulmonic valvar stenosis (PS)	LUSB	↑ with inspiration
Infravalvar (infundibular)	LUSB	↑ with inspiration
Supravalvar	LUSB	↑ with inspiration
"Flow murmurs"	LUSB	Anemia, fever, increased flow of any cause‡
Mid-late Systolic		
Mitral valve prolapse (MVP)	LLSB or apex → axilla	Preceded by click; murmur lengthens with maneuvers that ↓ LV volume*
Papillary muscle dysfunction	Apex → axilla	Ischemic heart disease
DIASTOLIC		
Early Diastolic		
Aortic regurgitation (AR)	RUSB, LUSB	High-pitched, blowing quality; endocarditis, diseases of the aorta, associated AS; signs of low peripheral vascular resistance
Pulmonic valve regurgitation (PR)	LUSB	Pulmonary hypertension as a causative factor
Mid-late Diastolic		
Mitral stenosis (MS), tricuspid stenosis (TS)	Apex, LLSB	Low-pitched; in rheumatic heart disease, opening snap commonly precedes murmur; can be due to increased flow across normal valve‡
Atrial myxomas	Apex (L), LLSB (R)	"Tumor plop"
Continuous		
Venous hum	Over jugular or hepatic vein or breast	Disappears with compression of vein or pressure of stethoscope
Patent ductus arteriosis (PDA)	LUSB	
Arteriovenous (AV) fistula		
Coronary	LUSB	
Pulmonary, bronchial, chest wall	Over fistula	
Ruptured sinus of Valsalva aneurysm	RUSB	Sudden onset

*See also Chapters 65 and 72.

†LV (left ventricular) volume is decreased by standing or during prolonged, forced expiration against a closed glottis (Valsalva maneuver); it is increased by squatting or by elevation of the legs; contractility is increased by adrenergic stimulation or in the beat after a postextrasystolic beat.

‡Including a left-to-right shunt through an atrial septal defect for tricuspid or pulmonic flow murmurs and a ventricular septal defect for pulmonic or mitral flow murmurs.

LLSB = left lower sternal border (4th intercostal space); LUSB = left upper sternal border (2nd–3rd intercostal spaces); RLSB = right lower sternal border (4th intercostal space); RUSB = right upper sternal border (2nd–3rd intercostal spaces).

Heart murmurs may be classified as systolic, diastolic, or continuous (Table 46–6). Murmurs are graded by intensity on a scale of 1 to 6. Grade 1 is faint and appreciated only by careful auscultation; 2, readily audible; 3, moderately loud; 4, loud and associated with a palpable thrill; 5, loud and audible with the stethoscope only partially placed on the chest; and 6, loud enough to be heard without the stethoscope on the chest. Systolic ejection murmurs usually peak in early to mid systole when left ventricular ejection is maximal; examples include fixed valvar, supravalvar, or infravalvar aortic or pulmonic stenosis. The murmur of hypertrophic obstructive cardiomyopathy has a similar ejection quality, although its peak may be later in systole when dynamic obstruction is maximal (Chapter 73). Pansystolic murmurs are characteristic of mitral or tricuspid regurgitation or with a left-to-right shunt from conditions such as a ventricular septal defect (left ventricle to right ventricle). A late systolic murmur is characteristic of mitral valve prolapse (Chapter 72) or ischemic papillary muscle dysfunction. Ejection quality murmurs also may be heard in patients with normal valves but increased flow, such as occurs with marked anemia, fever, or bradycardia secondary to congenital complete heart block; they also may be heard across a valve that is downstream from increased flow owing to an intracardiac shunt. Maneuvers such as inspiration, expiration, standing, squatting, and hand gripping can be especially useful in the differential diagnosis of a murmur; however, echocardiography commonly is required to make a definitive diagnosis of cause and severity (Table 46–7).

Table 46–7 • SENSITIVITY AND SPECIFICITY OF BEDSIDE MANEUVERS IN THE IDENTIFICATION OF SYSTOLIC MURMURS

MANEUVER	RESPONSE	MURMUR	SENSITIVITY (%)	SPECIFICITY (%)
Inspiration	↑	RS	100	88
Expiration	↓	RS	100	88
Valsalva maneuver	↑	HC	65	96
Squat to stand	↑	HC	95	84
Stand to squat	↓	HC	95	85
Leg elevation	↓	HC	85	91
Handgrip	↓	HC	85	75
Handgrip	↑	MR and VSD	68	92
Transient arterial occlusion	↑	MR and VSD	78	100

HC = hypertrophic cardiomyopathy; MR = mitral regurgitation; RS = right-sided; VSD = ventricular septal defect.

Modified with permission from Lembo NJ, Dell'Italia IJ, Crawford MH, et al: Bedside diagnosis of systolic murmurs. N Engl J Med 1988;318:1572–1578. Copyright 1988 Massachusetts Medical Society. All rights reserved.

High-frequency, early diastolic murmurs are typical of aortic regurgitation and pulmonic regurgitation from a variety of causes. The murmurs of mitral and tricuspid stenosis begin in early to mid diastole and tend to diminish in intensity later in diastole in the absence of effective atrial contraction, but they tend to increase in intensity in later diastole if effective atrial contraction is present.

Continuous murmurs may be caused by any abnormality that is associated with a pressure gradient in systole and diastole: Examples include a patent ductus arteriosis, ruptured sinus of Valsalva aneurysm, arteriovenous fistula (of the coronary artery, pulmonary artery, or thoracic artery), or a mammary soufflé. In some situations, murmurs of two coexistent conditions (e.g., aortic stenosis and regurgitation; atrial septal defect with a large shunt and resulting flow murmurs of relative mitral and pulmonic stenosis) may mimic a continuous murmur.

ABDOMEN

The most common cause of hepatomegaly in patients with heart disease is hepatic engorgement from elevated right-sided pressures associated with right ventricular failure of any cause. Hepatojugular reflux is elicited by pressing on the liver and showing an increase in the jugular venous pressure; it indicates advanced right ventricular failure or obstruction to right ventricular filling. Evaluation of the abdomen also may reveal an enlarged liver caused by a systemic disease, such as hemochromatosis or sarcoidosis, which also may affect the heart. In more severe cases, splenomegaly and ascites also may be noted. Large, palpable, polycystic kidneys commonly are associated with hypertension. A systolic bruit suggestive of renal artery stenosis or an enlarged abdominal aorta is a clue of atherosclerosis.

EXTREMITIES

Extremities should be evaluated for peripheral pulses, edema, cyanosis, and clubbing. Diminished peripheral pulses suggest peripheral arterial disease (Chapters 76 and 77). Delayed pulses in the legs are consistent with coarctation of the aorta and are seen after aortic dissection.

Edema (Fig. 46–5) is a cardinal manifestation of right-sided heart failure. When caused by heart failure, pericardial disease, or pulmonary hypertension, the edema is usually symmetrical and progresses upward from the ankles; each of these causes of cardiac edema commonly is associated with jugular venous distention and often with hepatic congestion. Unilateral edema suggests thrombophlebitis or proximal venous or lymphatic obstruction (Fig. 46–6). Edema in the absence of evidence of right-sided or left-sided heart failure suggests renal disease, hypoalbuminemia, myxedema, or other noncardiac causes. Among unselected patients with bilateral edema, about 40% have an underlying cardiac disease, about 40% have an elevated pulmonary blood pressure, about 20% have bilateral venous disease, about 20% have renal disease, and about 25% have idiopathic edema.

Cyanosis (Fig. 46–7) is a bluish discoloration caused by reduced hemoglobin exceeding about 5 g/dL in the capillary bed. Central cyanosis is seen in patients with poor oxygen saturation resulting from a reduced inspired oxygen concentration or inability to oxygenate the blood in the lungs (e.g., as a result of advanced pulmonary disease, pulmonary edema, pulmonary arteriovenous fistula, or right-to-left shunting); it also may be seen in patients with marked erythrocytosis. Methemoglobinemia (Chapter 172) also can present with cyanosis. Peripheral cyanosis may be caused by reduced blood flow to the extremities secondary to vasoconstriction, heart failure, or shock. *Clubbing* (Fig. 46–8), which is loss of the normal concave configuration of the nail as it emerges from the distal phalanx, is seen in patients with pulmonary abnormalities such as lung cancer (Chapter 198) and in patients with cyanotic congenital heart disease (Chapter 65).

EXAMINATION OF THE SKIN

Examination of the skin may reveal bronze pigmentation typical of hemochromatosis, jaundice characteristic of severe right-sided heart failure or hemochromatosis, or capillary hemangiomas typical of Osler-Weber-Rendu disease, which also is associated with pulmonary arteriovenous fistulas and cyanosis. Infectious endocarditis may be associated with Osler's nodes, Janeway's lesions, or splinter hemorrhages (Chapter 310). Xanthomata are subcutaneous deposits of

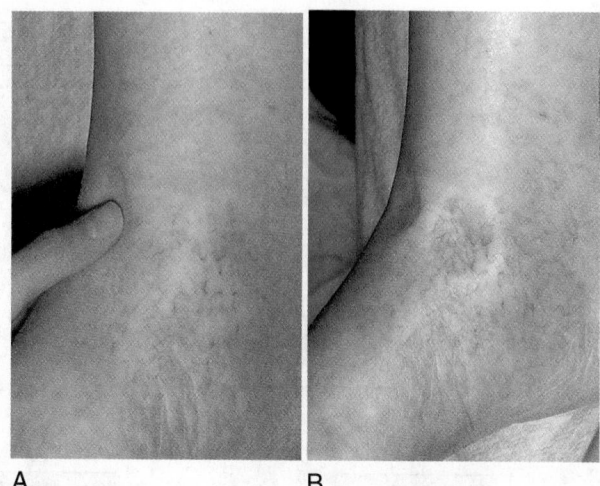

A   B

FIGURE 46–5 • Pitting edema in a patient with cardiac failure. A depression ("pit") remains in the edema for some minutes after firm fingertip pressure is applied. (From Forbes CD, Jackson WD: Color Atlas and Text of Clinical Medicine, 3rd ed. London, Mosby, 2003, with permission.)

cholesterol seen on the extensor surfaces of the extremities or on the palms and digital creases; they are found in patients with severe hypercholesterolemia.

LABORATORY STUDIES

All patients with known or suspected cardiac disease should have an ECG and chest radiograph. The ECG (Chapter 50) helps identify rate, rhythm, conduction abnormalities, and possible myocardial ischemia. The chest radiograph (Chapter 49) yields important information on chamber enlargement, pulmonary vasculature, and the great vessels.

Blood testing in patients with known or suspected cardiac disease should be targeted to the conditions in question. In general, a complete blood cell count, thyroid indices, and lipid levels are part of the standard evaluation.

Echocardiography (Chapter 51) is the most useful test to analyze valvar and ventricular function. Using Doppler flow methods, stenotic and regurgitant lesions can be quantified. Transesophageal echocardiography is the preferable method for evaluating possible aortic dissection and for identifying clot in the cardiac chambers. Radionuclide studies (Chapter 52) can measure left ventricular function, assess myocardial ischemia, and determine whether ischemic myocardium is viable.

Stress testing using exercise or pharmacologic stress is useful to precipitate myocardial ischemia that may be detected by ECG abnormalities, perfusion abnormalities on radionuclide studies, or transient wall motion abnormalities on echocardiography. These tests are often crucial in diagnosis of possible myocardial ischemia (Chapter 77) and in establishment of prognosis in patients with known ischemic heart disease.

Cardiac catheterization (Chapter 54) can measure precisely gradients across stenotic cardiac valves, judge the severity of intracardiac shunts, and determine intracardiac pressures. Coronary angiography provides a definitive diagnosis of coronary disease and is a necessary prelude to coronary revascularization with percutaneous transluminal coronary angioplasty (Chapter 70) or coronary artery bypass graft surgery (Chapter 71).

Continuous ambulatory ECG monitoring can help diagnose arrhythmias. A variety of newer technologies allow for longer term monitoring in patients with important but infrequently occurring symptoms (Chapter 58). Formal invasive electrophysiologic testing can be useful in the diagnosis of ventricular or supraventricular wide-complex tachycardia, and it is crucial for guiding a wide array of new invasive electrophysiologic therapies (Chapter 61).

Summary

The history, physical examination, and laboratory evaluation should help the physician to establish the cause of any cardiovascular

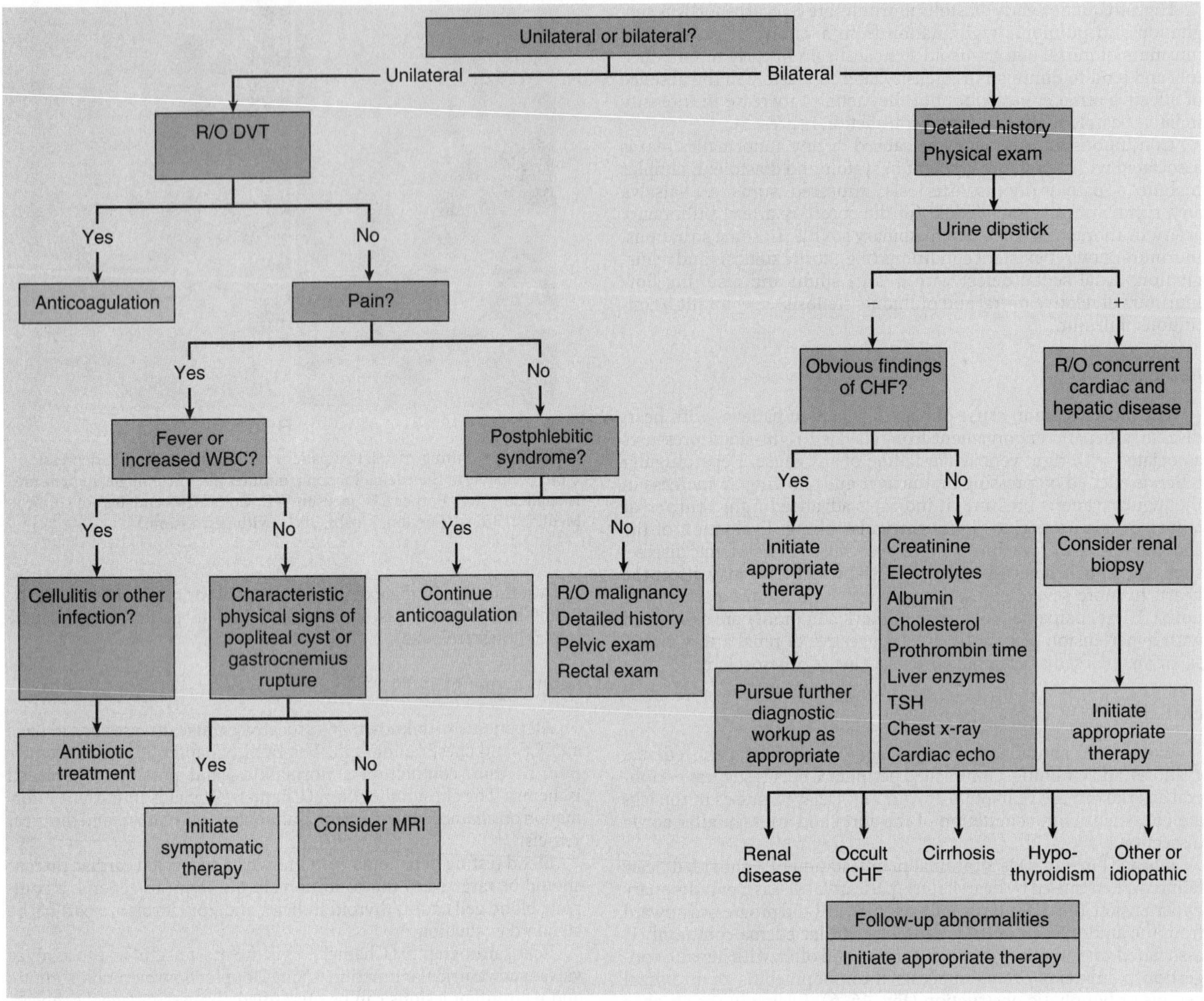

Cardiovascular Disease

Unilateral or bilateral?

— Unilateral — | — Bilateral —

Unilateral branch:

R/O DVT

Yes → Anticoagulation

No → Pain?

Pain? Yes → Fever or increased WBC?

Pain? No → Postphlebitic syndrome?

Fever or increased WBC? Yes → Cellulitis or other infection? → Antibiotic treatment

Fever or increased WBC? No → Characteristic physical signs of popliteal cyst or gastrocnemius rupture → Yes → Initiate symptomatic therapy; No → Consider MRI

Postphlebitic syndrome? Yes → Continue anticoagulation

Postphlebitic syndrome? No → R/O malignancy; Detailed history; Pelvic exam; Rectal exam

Bilateral branch:

Detailed history; Physical exam

Urine dipstick

− → Obvious findings of CHF?

+ → R/O concurrent cardiac and hepatic disease → Consider renal biopsy → Initiate appropriate therapy

Obvious findings of CHF? Yes → Initiate appropriate therapy → Pursue further diagnostic workup as appropriate

Obvious findings of CHF? No → Creatinine; Electrolytes; Albumin; Cholesterol; Prothrombin time; Liver enzymes; TSH; Chest x-ray; Cardiac echo

→ Renal disease | Occult CHF | Cirrhosis | Hypo-thyroidism | Other or idiopathic

Follow-up abnormalities

Initiate appropriate therapy

FIGURE 46–6 • Diagnostic approach to patients with edema. CHF = congestive heart failure; DVT = deep venous thrombosis; MRI = magnetic resonance imaging; R/O = rule out; TSH = thyroid-stimulating hormone; WBC = white blood cell count. (From Chertow G: Approach to the patient with edema. *In* Braunwald E, Goldman L [eds]: Primary Cardiology, 2nd ed. Philadelphia, WB Saunders, 2003, with permission.)

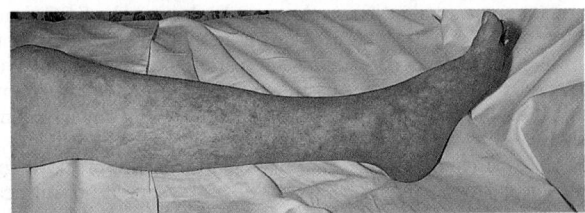

FIGURE 46–7 • Arterial embolism causing acute ischemia and cyanosis of the leg. Initial pallor of the leg and foot was followed by cyanosis. (From Forbes CD, Jackson WD: Color Atlas and Text of Clinical Medicine, 3rd ed. London, Mosby, 2003, with permission.)

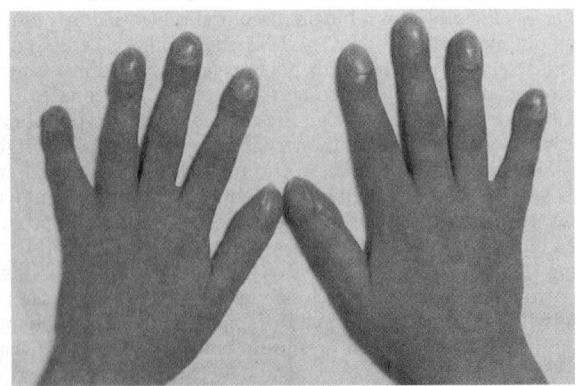

FIGURE 46–8 • Severe finger clubbing in a patient with cyanotic congenital heart disease. (From Forbes CD, Jackson WD: Color Atlas and Text of Clinical Medicine, 3rd ed. London, Mosby, 2003, with permission.)

Cardiovascular Disease

problem; identify and quantify any anatomic abnormalities; determine the physiologic status of the valves, myocardium, and conduction system; determine functional capacity; estimate prognosis; and provide primary and/or secondary prevention. Key preventive strategies, including diet modification, recognition and treatment of hyperlipidemia, cessation of cigarette smoking, and adequate physical exercise, should be part of the approach to every patient, with or without heart disease.

SUGGESTED READINGS

Braunwald E: The clinical examination. *In* Braunwald E, Goldman L (eds): Primary Cardiology, 2nd ed. Philadelphia, WB Saunders, 2003, pp 29–46.

Braunwald E: The history and physical examination of the heart and circulation. *In* Braunwald E, Zipes DP, Libby P (eds): Heart Disease, 6th ed. Philadelphia, WB Saunders, 2001, pp 27–81. *These textbook chapters give more detailed descriptions of the cardiac history and physical examination.*

Cho S, Atwood EJ: Peripheral edema. Am J Med 2002;113:580–586. *An overview of pathophysiology, diagnosis, and treatment.*

47 EPIDEMIOLOGY OF CARDIOVASCULAR DISEASE

Michael H. Criqui

Types of Cardiovascular Disease

The three major clinical manifestations of atherosclerotic cardiovascular disease (CVD) are coronary heart disease (CHD) (Chapters 67 through 71), stroke (Chapters 439, 440, and 441), and peripheral arterial disease (PAD) (Chapter 76). Atherosclerosis also can be found in other arterial beds, especially the renal arteries, where it causes about two thirds of cases of renal artery stenosis (Chapters 63 and 124).

Importance of Cardiovascular Disease

DISEASE IMPACT. More than 60 million Americans are estimated to have some form of CVD: 50 million have hypertension, 12.4 million have CHD, and 4.5 million have had a stroke. More than one in five Americans currently have some form of CVD.

CVD accounts for about 950,000 deaths annually in the United States and constitutes more than 40% of all deaths. About 35% of CVD deaths occur prematurely (i.e., in persons <75 years old). Each year, about 1.1 million Americans have a new or recurrent myocardial infarction (MI), and more than 40% of these events are fatal. The annual incidence of stroke is about 600,000 per year, and about 180,000 Americans die from a stroke each year.

SECULAR TRENDS. The death rate from heart disease has decreased more than 40% since 1968 (Fig. 47–1), and stroke mortality has con-

tinued to decline throughout the 20th century. These observations have raised the question of whether this decline in mortality is due to a true reduction in incidence at the population level, which logically could be attributed to improved prevention, or simply to a decline in case-fatality rates, which presumably would be attributable mostly to better treatment. Several studies have evaluated this question, and the consensus is that both prevention and therapy have contributed and that both population incidence rates and case-fatality rates have declined.

Despite this decline, CVD is still the leading cause of death in developed countries by a considerable margin. CHD and stroke are the second and third leading causes of mortality in developing nations.

ECONOMIC IMPACT. Despite the age-adjusted decline in mortality from CVD in the United States and many Western countries, CVD paradoxically poses an increasing economic burden, owing largely to two factors: (1) an aging population, which keeps the actual numbers of CVD cases relatively stable, and (2) technologic improvements, which allow more aggressive and extensive therapy. Hospital discharges and deaths from heart failure (Chapters 55 and 60), which is a frequent consequence of chronic CHD, increased substantially in the 1990s, as did the number of CVD operations and procedures (Chapters 70 and 71).

Natural History of Cardiovascular Disease

Arterial lesions begin as fatty streaks, often early in life (Chapter 66). Autopsies of teenagers and young adults who were victims of accidental and other non-CVD causes of mortality show early fatty streaks, and these changes have correlated with traditional CVD risk factors. These fatty streaks can progress to raised lesions, which progressively can occlude the lumen of the artery.

Symptoms that typically occur in vascular beds well before the lesions completely occlude the lumen include angina pectoris from lesions in the coronary arteries (Chapters 67 and 68), transient ischemic attacks from lesions in the cerebrovascular arteries (Chapter 440), and intermittent claudication from lesions in the arteries in the lower extremities (Chapter 76). Although each of these pain syndromes has a classic prototype, patients can present with atypical symptoms despite significant disease. Many patients do not experience symptoms or ignore warning symptoms, and their first presentation may be a severe or fatal MI or stroke.

Risk Factors for Cardiovascular Disease

TYPES OF STUDIES. The epidemiology of CVD has been evaluated in many study designs including ecologic, case-control, cross-sectional survey, prospective cohort, and clinical trial designs (Chapters 6 and 8). In general, the strength of the causal inference one can draw from a study increases along this continuum, with policy changes typically appropriate only when supported by solid evidence from clinical trials.

UNMODIFIABLE CARDIOVASCULAR DISEASE RISK FACTORS. Several CVD risk factors are essentially immutable, including older age, male gender, and a family history of CVD. Nonetheless, these risk factors are important to consider in evaluating risk in an individual patient.

CIGARETTE SMOKING. Cigarette smoking, along with dyslipidemia and hypertension, is considered one of the three major risk factors for CHD, thromboembolic stroke, and PAD. Event rates are three to four times higher in regular smokers, with a dose-response relationship. In contrast to most other CVD risk factors, cigarette smoking can be eliminated entirely, but not easily (Chapter 14). For CHD, the benefits of quitting smoking are dramatic: CHD incidence in ex-smokers falls to near nonsmoking levels in 2 years.

DYSLIPIDEMIA. *Dyslipidemia* is probably a better term than *hyperlipidemia* because it includes all lipid and lipoprotein abnormalities, such as low levels of high-density lipoprotein (HDL) cholesterol (hypoalphalipoproteinemia), which can be a potent risk factor (Chapter 211). An elevated serum cholesterol level is an independent risk factor for CVD, with a strong dose-response relationship that is exponential at higher levels of cholesterol. Although much of the interindividual variability in cholesterol is genetic, dietary consumption of cholesterol, saturated fat, and trans-fatty acids (typically formed by partial hydrogenation [saturation] of unsaturated vegetable fat) increases serum cholesterol.

Total cholesterol is carried on three lipoproteins in the blood, resulting in three separate cholesterol fractions with differing prognostic significance: very-low-density lipoprotein (VLDL) cholesterol,

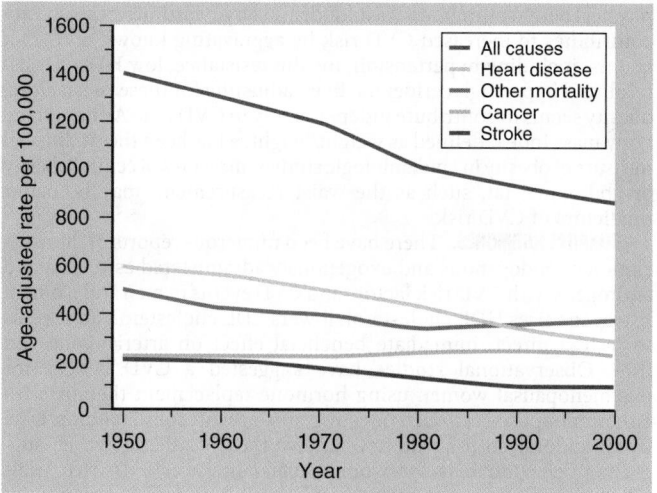

FIGURE 47–1 • Age-adjusted rates per 100,000 for five categories of mortality.

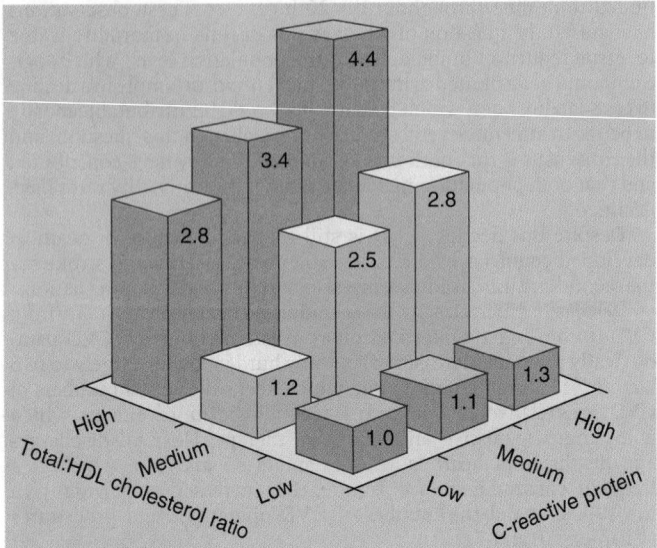

FIGURE 47-2 • Relative risks of first myocardial infarction among apparently healthy men associated with high (>5.01), middle (3.78 to 5.01), and low (<3.78) tertiles of the total cholesterol–to–high-density lipoprotein cholesterol ratio and high (>1.69 mg/L), middle (0.72 to 1.69 mg/L), and low (<0.72 mg/L) tertiles of C-reactive protein. (From Ridker PM, Glynn RJ, Hennekens CH: C-reactive protein adds to the predictive value of total and HDL cholesterol in determining risk of first myocardial infarction. Circulation 1998;97:2007–2011.)

low-density lipoprotein (LDL) cholesterol, and HDL cholesterol. LDL cholesterol is positively related and HDL cholesterol is inversely related to CVD incidence. VLDL cholesterol is a close surrogate for serum triglycerides when the triglyceride level is less than 400 mg/dL. Triglycerides may be related independently to CVD in some subgroups in the population, such as persons with diabetes or low HDL cholesterol levels.

Lp(a) is a lipoprotein identical to LDL except for the addition of a highly glycosylated protein, apolipoprotein (a). The similarity of the amino acid sequences of Lp(a) and plasminogen suggests the possibility of a connection between atherogenesis and thrombosis. Lp(a) has been associated with elevated CHD risk in most, but not all, epidemiologic studies. Intervention is problematic, however, with only niacin and estrogen showing some effect in lowering Lp(a).

The best single lipid measure in predicting risk is the total cholesterol–to–HDL cholesterol ratio (Fig. 47–2). Total cholesterol includes LDL cholesterol, VLDL cholesterol (a triglyceride surrogate), and HDL cholesterol, whereas the denominator is the protective HDL cholesterol. Ratios less than 3 are ideal, 3 to 5 are average, and greater than 5 represent elevated risk, but risk continues to rise throughout the range of total cholesterol–to–HDL cholesterol values. Evidence from randomized trials confirms the benefits of treating dyslipidemia in patients with CVD and individuals at increased risk of developing CVD.[1] In addition to being the best predictor of CVD outcomes in epidemiologic studies, a decrease in the total cholesterol–to–HDL cholesterol ratio has been a better predictor of treatment benefit in clinical trials than are changes in any other lipid or lipoprotein parameter.

HYPERTENSION. Elevated blood pressure is a potent risk factor for all forms of atherosclerotic CVD and is the dominant risk factor for stroke (Chapters 439, 440, and 441). In epidemiologic studies, there is a graded relation between the level of blood pressure, even at the lowest levels, and CVD outcomes (Chapter 63). In general, systolic blood pressure is related more strongly to incident CVD than is diastolic blood pressure, particularly in the elderly. In some studies of older adults, pulse pressure (systolic blood pressure – diastolic blood pressure) shows the strongest association. Early trials in severe hypertension unequivocally showed the benefits of reducing very high blood pressure levels, with a sharp reduction in morbidity and mortality from CVD. Meta-analyses of pharmacologic treatment of mild hypertension also showed benefit. Multiple classes of antihypertensive drugs are now available, and extensive research is needed to determine the optimal drug regimen for a given patient because some evidence suggests different drugs affect CVD outcomes differently despite similar

reductions in blood pressure. The short-acting dihydropyridine calcium channel blockers may increase the risk of CHD events. The angiotensin-converting enzyme inhibitor ramipril reduces fatal and nonfatal CVD and diabetic complications in patients with CVD or diabetes plus one additional CVD risk factor.[2] In most patients, blood pressure and other CVD risk factors can be improved to a greater or lesser degree by lifestyle changes, including weight loss, exercise, and a diet that is rich in fruits and vegetables and avoids excess sodium and alcohol (Chapters 12 and 13).

Systolic pressure rises with age throughout life in Western populations, whereas diastolic pressure plateaus in late midlife and decreases thereafter. Trials of blood pressure lowering in isolated systolic hypertension in the elderly have shown dramatic benefits for reducing stroke and CHD, with the absolute benefit of treatment remaining stable or rising with increasing age.

PHYSICAL INACTIVITY. Persons who exercise more or are better conditioned are at lower CVD risk (Chapter 13). Evidence shows significant changes in multiple risk factors with exercise, including improved insulin resistance, blood pressure, HDL cholesterol, triglycerides, and fibrinolysis. Randomized trials of cardiac rehabilitation for secondary prevention also suggest benefit. Physical inactivity now commonly is considered one of the four major risk factors for CVD. Prior concerns about the possible acute risk of exercise for cardiac ischemia in susceptible persons are outweighed by the benefits for most individuals; nevertheless, high-risk individuals should be evaluated carefully before beginning an exercise program.

DIABETES MELLITUS. Patients with either type I or II diabetes mellitus are at increased risk of CVD (Chapter 242). In type II diabetes, CVD risk is approximately doubled in men and increased four-fold in women, sharply attenuating the typical relative CVD protection in women. In type I diabetes, the risks are higher, particularly in patients with proteinuria.

Patients with type II diabetes mellitus commonly exhibit evidence of insulin resistance well before the onset of chemical diabetes. Insulin resistance and type II diabetes usually are accompanied by one or more of many metabolic abnormalities: elevated insulin, glucose, blood pressure, and triglyceride levels and lower HDL cholesterol levels. Although LDL cholesterol levels are often normal, the LDL particles tend to be smaller and more dense and may be more atherogenic, although it is not yet known if this effect is independent of accompanying hypertriglyceridemia. Evidence suggests that correction of the lipid abnormalities in type II diabetes substantially decreases CHD risk. Controversy persists, however, as to whether reduction of glucose levels would improve macrovascular risk. New oral agents that lower glucose and insulin and improve insulin resistance may help resolve this issue. With weight loss and exercise, insulin resistance improves, triglyceride levels decrease, LDL particles become larger and less dense, HDL cholesterol increases, and hypertension tends to improve. Diet and exercise can reduce dramatically the likelihood of new-onset diabetes in high-risk patients. Angiotensin-converting enzyme inhibitors can reduce the risk of progressive renal disease and CHD events in patients with existing diabetes mellitus.

OBESITY. Obesity (Chapter 233) has increased dramatically in recent years in the United States for unclear reasons. Possible causes include the automobile, television, the Internet, a decrease in school-based physical activity programs, fast food, and large portion sizes. Obesity contributes to increased CVD risk by aggravating known CVD risk factors, including hypertension, insulin resistance, low HDL cholesterol, and hypertriglyceridemia. Even adjusting for these risk factors, obesity seems to contribute independently to CVD risk. Although the body mass index, defined as weight/height,[2] has been the traditional measure of obesity in epidemiologic studies, measures of central obesity or abdominal fat, such as the waist measurement, may be better predictors of CVD risk.

GONADAL HORMONES. There have been numerous reports of the association of endogenous and exogenously administered estrogens and androgens with CVD risk factors and CVD events in men and women. Estrogen raises HDL cholesterol, lowers LDL cholesterol, and seems to have a direct, immediate beneficial effect on arterial tone and flow. Observational studies have suggested a CVD benefit for postmenopausal women using hormone replacement therapy with either unopposed estrogen or estrogen/progestin combinations. Data from randomized trials do not confirm these results, however, suggesting selection bias for women using hormones. In two trials of estrogen for the secondary prevention of events in women with preexisting CVD, one in women with CHD and the other in women with cerebrovascular disease, no benefit was detected, and the estrogen-progestin arm of a large primary prevention trial, the Women's Health Initiative, was stopped prematurely because of an increased hazard for CVD and breast cancer.[3] New "designer estrogens," such as raloxifene, are now available and are being studied in long-term clinical trials.

ANTIOXIDANTS. Intake of supplemental antioxidants, such as vitamins C or E, has been associated with a significant CVD risk reduction in observational studies, but several clinical trials have shown no benefit of antioxidants for reducing CVD.[4] As a result, there is currently no role for their prescription to reduce or prevent CVD.

ALCOHOL. Alcohol consumption (Chapter 17) at less than one drink and up to three drinks per day is associated with protection against CHD in epidemiologic studies. Thrombotic stroke and PAD show similar associations. This protective effect seems to be mediated by increases in HDL cholesterol and by possible effects on coagulation and fibrinolytic factors. Some of the apparent benefit of moderate alcohol consumption could reflect selection bias. Clinical trials of alcohol for CVD end points have not and likely will not be conducted, however, owing to technical and ethical difficulties with study design. For nonatherosclerotic CVD, such as hemorrhagic stroke (Chapter 44) and cardiomyopathy (Chapter 73), risk is increased by alcohol consumption. At higher levels of alcohol consumption (three or more drinks per day), blood pressure increases, arrhythmias may be induced, rebound hypercoagulability may develop, direct myocardial damage can occur, and total CVD risk is increased. Maximum overall benefit for alcohol is reached at a single drink per day, and consumption of more than two drinks per day is associated with increases in morbidity and mortality from total cardiovascular causes, cirrhosis, accidents and violence, and certain cancers. Of particular concern is the consistent increase in breast cancer observed in women in epidemiologic studies even with only modest levels of drinking. The benefit of alcohol for CHD is essentially limited to older persons at relatively high risk of CHD, whereas younger persons and persons at lower risk of CHD have minimal CHD benefit but easily could suffer alcohol-related harm. For these reasons and the high abuse potential of alcohol, it seems unwise to recommend alcohol for cardioprotection.

THROMBOTIC AND FIBRINOLYTIC FACTORS. Increasing attention has been paid to factors influencing thrombosis and fibrinolysis. The most consistent and reproducible risk factor in this group is fibrinogen, and epidemiologic studies have reported consistent and independent associations of fibrinogen with CHD, stroke, and PAD. Several other coagulation factors showed associations in some studies, including factor VII, factor VIII, and various measures of platelet aggregability. Aspirin therapy inhibits platelet aggregation and, as a result, reduces CVD risk. Low-dose aspirin generally seems as efficacious as a higher dose, but the lower dose shows fewer side effects, such as bleeding.

Plasminogen activator inhibitor 1 has been correlated with MI and carotid disease. Tissue-type plasminogen activator has shown positive and inverse associations with CVD, with the counterintuitive positive associations possibly explained by ongoing fibrinolysis, which similarly may explain the findings of an elevated D-dimer level in CVD patients.

HOMOCYSTEINE. Numerous studies have shown homocysteine to be a strong, independent risk factor for CVD, including CHD, stroke, and PAD. The potential for intervention is theoretically good because folic acid supplementation alone or in combination with other B vitamins is known to lower total plasma homocysteine levels. Many individuals with normal homocysteine levels may show hyperhomocysteinemia after methionine loading. A small trial suggested benefit of folate for reducing coronary restenosis and events, and larger clinical trials are in progress. Positive trial results would indicate an inexpensive, relatively safe intervention for patients with, or at risk for, CVD.

INFECTION. Research has given support to an old theory that infectious agents may be involved in the pathogenesis of atherosclerosis (Chapter 66). The evidence is strongest for *Chlamydia pneumoniae*, which has been isolated from atherosclerotic plaques. *C. pneumoniae* titer levels after MI may predict CVD events, and treatment with macrolide antibiotics may reduce recurrent CVD events. In animals, herpesviruses can stimulate atherosclerosis, and cytomegalovirus titers have been reported to be increased in some studies of CVD patients. Evidence for other infectious agents, such as *Helicobacter pylori*, is weaker than for cytomegalovirus and *C. pneumoniae*. Some data suggest that the total burden of several infections may be more predictive than any single infectious agent alone.

INFLAMMATION. Inflammatory markers, such as C-reactive protein, may reflect ongoing atherogenic inflammation at the level of the vessel wall. In this sense, such inflammatory markers can be thought of as measures of subclinical CVD. The C-reactive protein is a strong, independent predictor of future fatal and nonfatal CHD events (see Fig. 47–2). Data suggest aspirin and statin therapy may reduce the CVD risk associated with elevated C-reactive protein levels.

PSYCHOSOCIAL FACTORS. Psychosocial factors, such as anger, anxiety, depression, hostility, type A behavior, and various measures of social support, have been associated with the occurrence or recurrence of CVD. In addition, measures of cardiovascular physiologic reactivity have been correlated with CVD outcomes. Currently, data are inadequate to prove whether or not psychosocial interventions can reduce CVD risk.

SYNERGY OF RISK FACTORS. CVD risk factors seem to interact synergistically in producing risk. The observed rate of CHD death in men who smoke, have serum cholesterol levels greater than or equal to 250 mg/dL, and have diastolic blood pressures greater than or equal to 90 mm Hg is nearly twice as great as would be predicted by adding the risk attributable to each of these three risk factors to the baseline risk. Multivariate statistical models have confirmed the multiplicative effect of CVD risk factors acting in concert. These data also imply that control of one risk factor would provide a substantial preventive benefit in persons with multiple risk factors.

RISK FACTORS IN PRIMARY AND SECONDARY PREVENTION. Primary prevention refers to preventing CVD in healthy persons. Secondary prevention refers to preventing recurrent CVD and death in patients with extant CVD (Chapter 10). The major difference between primary and secondary CVD prevention is that event rates are much greater in secondary prevention, approximately five-fold higher, and the proportion of morbidity and mortality resulting from CVD is much higher. These simple facts have major clinical implications. First, the short-term benefit of intervention for a given patient is much greater in absolute terms in secondary prevention. Second, if a given intervention has any hazard, such as bleeding from antiplatelet therapy, such a hazard is likely to be of greater importance in primary prevention, in which CVD event rates in the near term are relatively low.

In general, CVD risk factors and preventive interventions have similar effects on outcomes in primary and secondary prevention. Smoking cessation after MI cuts recurrent CHD risk in half, and cholesterol lowering after MI can reduce new CHD events by about 35% (Chapter 69).

GENDER ISSUES. The epidemiology of CVD in women and men is similar. Except for gonadal hormones, risk factors produce similar relative risks in men and women. The major gender difference is the greater absolute age-specific CVD risk of men, particularly at younger ages. Because absolute CVD risk is lower overall in women, the incremental risk produced by a given risk factor tends to be less except for diabetes, in which the relative and the incremental risks for heart disease are greater in women.

ETHNIC ISSUES. Minority ethnic groups are increasing as a proportion of the total U.S. population, with Hispanics being the fastest growing group. Considerable evidence exists for differences in CVD epidemiology between whites and African Americans and Native Americans. African Americans have higher blood pressures and worse hypertensive outcomes than whites, and some Native American groups have a sharp excess of diabetes. Data also suggest excess obesity and diabetes in Hispanics and a high risk of insulin resistance and CHD among immigrants from the Indian subcontinent.

RISK FACTOR DIFFERENCES FOR CORONARY HEART DISEASE, STROKE, AND PERIPHERAL ARTERIAL DISEASE. Table 47–1 shows comparative associations of established and newer risk factors with CHD, stroke, and PAD. Important differences include the strength of inflammatory factors in CHD, the dominance of hypertension for stroke, and the importance of cigarette smoking and diabetes for PAD.

Subclinical Cardiovascular Disease

Tests for subclinical CVD include cerebral magnetic resonance imaging, retinal photography, and carotid duplex imaging in the cerebral circulation (Chapters 424 and 439); cardiac magnetic resonance imaging, echocardiography, ambulatory electrocardiography, and computed tomography for calcium in the coronary circulation (Chapters 51, 52, and 53); computed tomography for calcium in the aorta (Chapter 75); and reactive hyperemia, duplex imaging, and systolic blood pressures at the ankle (ankle-brachial index) and toe relative

Cardiovascular Disease

Table 47–1 • RELATIVE STRENGTH OF ESTABLISHED AND NEWER CARDIOVASCULAR DISEASE RISK FACTORS FOR CORONARY HEART DISEASE, STROKE, AND PERIPHERAL ARTERIAL DISEASE

	CHD	STROKE	PAD
ESTABLISHED			
Advanced age	+++	++++	++++
Male gender	++	+	+
Cigarette smoking	+++	+	++++
Hypertension	++	++++	++
LDL cholesterol	++	+	+
Low HDL cholesterol	+++	+	+++
Triglycerides	++	+	+++
Diabetes mellitus	+++	+	++++
NEWER			
Homocysteine	++	++	+++
Fibrinogen	++++	++	+++
C-reactive protein	++++	++	+++
Lp(a)	++	++	++
Chlamydia pneumoniae	++	+?	?

CHD = coronary heart disease; PAD = peripheral arterial disease; LDL = low-density lipoprotein; HDL = high-density lipoprotein.

to the arm systolic pressure in the lower extremity arteries (Chapters 76 and 77). Current evidence for prognostic significance is strongest for carotid duplex imaging and the ankle-brachial index; significant carotid stenosis or an ankle-brachial index less than or equal to 0.9 independently predicts a four-fold or greater increase in future CVD events. Coronary calcification on computed tomography correlates well with anatomic coronary stenosis and predicts CVD events in the short-term. Long-term studies of coronary calcium are not yet available (Chapter 52).

Future Directions

It is unclear why some persons can tolerate higher levels of CVD risk factors, whereas others develop clinical CVD despite "normal" risk factor levels. Now that numerous traditional and newer CVD risk factors have been identified, research will focus on the transition from risk factors to subclinical disease to clinical disease and on the key factors in this transition.

1. Heart Protection Study Collaborative Group: MRC/BHF Heart Protection Study of cholesterol lowering with simvastatin in 20,536 high-risk individuals: A randomized placebo-controlled trial. Lancet 2002;360:7–22.
2. Heart Outcomes Prevention Evaluation Study investigators: Effects of an angiotensin-converting-enzyme inhibitor, ramipril, on cardiovascular events in high-risk patients. N Engl J Med 2000;342:145–153.
3. Writing Group for the Women's Health Initiative investigators: Risks and benefits of estrogen plus progestin in healthy postmenopausal women: Principal results from the Women's Health Initiative randomized controlled trial. JAMA 2002;288:321–333.
4. Heart Protection Study Collaborative Group: MRC/ BHF Heart Protection Study of antioxidant vitamin supplementation in 20,536 high-risk individuals: A randomized placebo-controlled trial. Lancet 2002;360:23–33.

SUGGESTED READINGS

Chobanian AV, Bakris GL, Black HR, et al: The Seventh Report of the Joint National Committee on Prevention, Detection, Evaluation, and Treatment of High Blood Pressure: The JNC 7 report. JAMA 2003;289:2560–2572. *Updated consensus guidelines.*
Executive Summary of the Third Report of the National Cholesterol Education Program (NCEP) Expert Panel on Detection, Evaluation, and Treatment of High Blood Cholesterol in Adults (Adult Treatment Panel III) final report. Circulation 2002;106:3143–3421. *Latest recommendations from a U.S. consensus panel.*
Greenland P, Abrams J, Aurigemma GP, et al: Prevention Conference V: Beyond secondary prevention: Identifying the high-risk patient for primary prevention: Noninvasive tests of atherosclerotic burden: Writing Group III. Circulation 2000;101:e16–e22. *Approaches to assessing high-risk patients for more aggressive primary prevention.*
Sever PS, Dahlöf B, Poulter NR, et al: Prevention of coronary and stroke event with atorvastatin in hypertensive patients who have average or lower-than-average cholesterol concentrations in the Anglo-Scandinavian Cardiac Outcomes Trial—Lipid Lowering Arm (ASCOT-LLA). Lancet 2003;361:1149–1158. *Lowering cholesterol with atorvastatin significantly reduced events in hypertensive patients with normal cholesterol levels, thereby emphasizing the need to assess overall risk as a guide to intervention.*
Strauss RS, Pollack HA: Epidemic increase in childhood overweight, 1986–1998. JAMA 2001;286:2845–2848. *Emphasizes this increasing public health problem.*

48 CARDIAC FUNCTION AND CIRCULATORY CONTROL

Daniel Burkhoff
Myron L. Weisfeldt

The heart is a muscular pump connected to the systemic and pulmonary vascular systems. Working together, the job of the heart and vasculature is to maintain adequate circulation of blood to the organs at rest and during periods of exercise. To understand perturbations that cause symptoms and disease, it is first necessary to understand the normal anatomy and physiology of the heart, its interaction with the vascular system, and its regulation by the autonomic nervous system.

Anatomy of the Heart

The left ventricle, which is an axisymmetrical, truncated ellipsoid with walls approximately 1 cm thick, is constructed from billions of cardiac muscle cells (myocytes) connected end to end at their *gap junctions* to form a network of branching muscle fibers that wrap around the chamber in an organized manner. The right ventricle is a roughly crescent-shaped structure formed by a 3- to 5-mm-thick sheet of myocardial fibers (the *right ventricular free wall*) that interdigitate at the anterior and posterior insertion points with the muscle fibers of the outer layer of the left ventricle. The right and left ventricular (LV) chambers share a common wall, the *interventricular septum*, that divides the chambers. Both the right and left atria are thin-walled muscular structures that receive blood from a low-pressure venous system. The *tricuspid valve* in the right heart and the *mitral valve* in the left heart separate each atrium from its associated ventricle, prohibit backward flow during forceful contraction of the ventricles, and are attached to fibrous rings that encircle each valve annulus. The central regions of these valves attach via *chordae tendineae* to *papillary muscles* that emerge from the ventricular walls. The predominant factor that determines valve opening and closure is the pressure gradient that exists between the ventricle and the atrium. However, the papillary muscles contract synchronously with the other heart muscles and aid in maintaining proper valve leaflet position, thus helping to prevent regurgitant flow during contraction. A second set of tissue valves, the *aortic valve* and the *pulmonary valve*, separate each ventricle from its accompanying arterial connection and ensure unidirectional flow by preventing blood from flowing from the artery back into the ventricle. Pressure gradients across these valves are the major determinants of whether they are open or closed.

Cardiac Muscle Physiology

The ability of the ventricles to generate blood flow and pressure derives from the ability of individual myocytes to shorten and generate force. Myocytes are tubular structures. During contraction, the muscles shorten and generate force along their long axis. Force production and shortening of cardiac muscle are created by regulated interactions among contractile proteins, which are assembled in an ordered and repeating structure called the *sarcomere* (Fig. 48–1). The lateral boundaries of each sarcomere are defined on both sides by a band of structural proteins at the Z lines to which the so-called *thin filaments* attach. The *thick filaments* are centered between adjacent Z lines and are held in register by a strand of proteins at the central M line. Alternating light and dark bands, as seen in cardiac muscle under light microscopy, result from the alignment of thick and thin filaments and give cardiac muscle its typical striated appearance.

The thin filaments are composed of linearly arranged globular actin molecules. The thick filaments are composed of bundles of myosin strands, with each strand having a tail, a hinge, and a head region. The tail regions bind to each other in the central portion of the filament, and the strands are aligned along a single axis. The head regions extend out from the center of the thick filament in both directions to create a central bare zone and head-rich zones on both ends of the thick filament. Each actin globule has a binding site for the myosin head. The hinge region allows the myosin head to protrude from the thick filament and make contact with the actin filament. In addition to the actin binding site, the myosin head contains an enzymatic site that cleaves the terminal phosphate molecule of adenosine triphos-

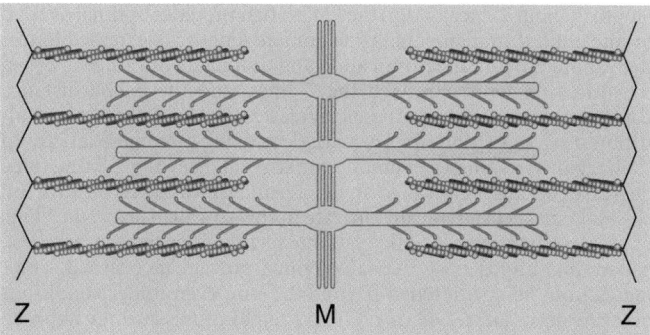

FIGURE 48–1 • Basic structure of the sarcomere. Thin filaments composed of actin with the associated regulatory proteins tropomyosin and troponin insert into structural proteins at the Z line, which define the boundaries of the sarcomere. Thick filaments composed of myosin sit between the thin filaments and send their heads out in proximity to the actin molecules. During diastole (state of low intracellular calcium), tropomyosin strands block the interactions between actin and myosin. The thick filaments are kept in register at their centers by structural proteins at the M line. During systole (state of high calcium), calcium binds to troponin, which causes tropomyosin to shift away from the myosin binding site on actin, thus allowing the actin-myosin interactions that underlie force generation.

phate (ATP, myosin ATPase) to provide the energy used for repeatedly generating force. Force is produced when myosin binds to actin and, with the hydrolysis of ATP, the head rotates and extends the hinge region. The force generated by a single sarcomere is proportional to the number of actin-myosin bonds. The state of actin-myosin binding following ATP hydrolysis is referred to as the *rigor state* because in the absence of additional ATP the actin-myosin bond will persist and maintain high muscle tension. Relaxation, which requires uncoupling of the actin-myosin bond, occurs when a new ATP molecule binds to the ATPase site on the myosin head.

Actin-myosin interactions are regulated by troponin and tropomyosin. Tropomyosin is a thin protein strand that sits on the actin strand and, under normal resting conditions, covers the actin-myosin binding site, inhibits the interaction of actin and myosin,

and prevents force production. Troponin, which is associated with tropomyosin, has calcium binding sites. When calcium binds to troponin, a conformational change causes the tropomyosin molecule to be pulled away from the actin-myosin binding site; as a result, inhibition of the actin-myosin interaction is eliminated, thus allowing force to be produced. This arrangement of proteins provides a means by which variations in intracellular calcium can readily modify instantaneous force production. The rise and fall of calcium levels during each beat is the basis for the cyclic rise and fall of muscle force. The greater the peak calcium, the greater the number of potential actin-myosin bonds and the greater the amount of force production.

In addition to the structural and regulatory proteins described, it is becoming increasingly clear that a multitude of other proteins are important for normal sarcomere structure, for the attachment of sarcomeres to the sarcolemma, and for proper transmission of force between sarcomeres and cells. These include, among others, titin, desmin, dystrophin, α-actinin, talin, vinculin and muscle LIM protein (MLP). Titin runs through the thick filaments, connects to adjacent Z-lines, and helps maintain proper thick filament alignment within sarcomeres. Dystrophin links the sarcomere to the sarcolemma by binding sarcomeric and cytoskeletal actin to a glycoprotein complex on the sarcolemma. Desmin is a filamentous cytoskeletal protein found throughout the cell and at the Z-lines; it appears to stabilize the sarcomeric actin via α-actinin, which in turn associates with the actin filament via talin, vinculin, and MLP. The physiologic roles of these structural proteins in maintaining normal contractile function has become clear recently by the use of murine models in which these genes are under-expressed and by the identification of specific inherited human cardiomyopathies that are due to point mutations of the genes encoding each of these proteins.

EXCITATION-CONTRACTION COUPLING. The sequence of events that lead to myocardial contraction is triggered by electrical depolarization of the cell; electrical depolarization increases the probability of sarcolemmal calcium channel opening, which in turn results in calcium influx into the cell (Fig. 48–2). An increase in calcium concentration then occurs in the subsarcolemmal space near the *lateral cisternae* of the sarcoplasmic reticulum. This increase in local calcium concentration causes the release of a larger pool of calcium stored in the sarcoplasmic reticulum through calcium release channels called *ryanodine receptors*, which are found in high concentration near the lateral cisternae. The mechanisms by which the subsarcolemmal increase in calcium concentration results in calcium

FIGURE 48–2 • Important features of the cardiac cell with an emphasis on aspects related to calcium metabolism. Arrows indicate calcium fluxes. The contraction cycle begins with calcium entering the cell via calcium channels and inducing the release of calcium from the lateral cisternae of the sarcoplasmic reticulum. This calcium binds to myofilaments and allows cross-bridge interactions that lead to force generation. A majority of the cytosolic systolic calcium is sequestered at the middle portion of the sarcoplasmic reticulum by the adenosine triphosphate (ATP)-dependent calcium pump; the activity of these pumps is modified by the phosphorylation status of phospholamban. The sodium-calcium exchanger removes an amount of calcium during diastole equal to what entered through calcium channels to maintain calcium homeostasis. The sodium-

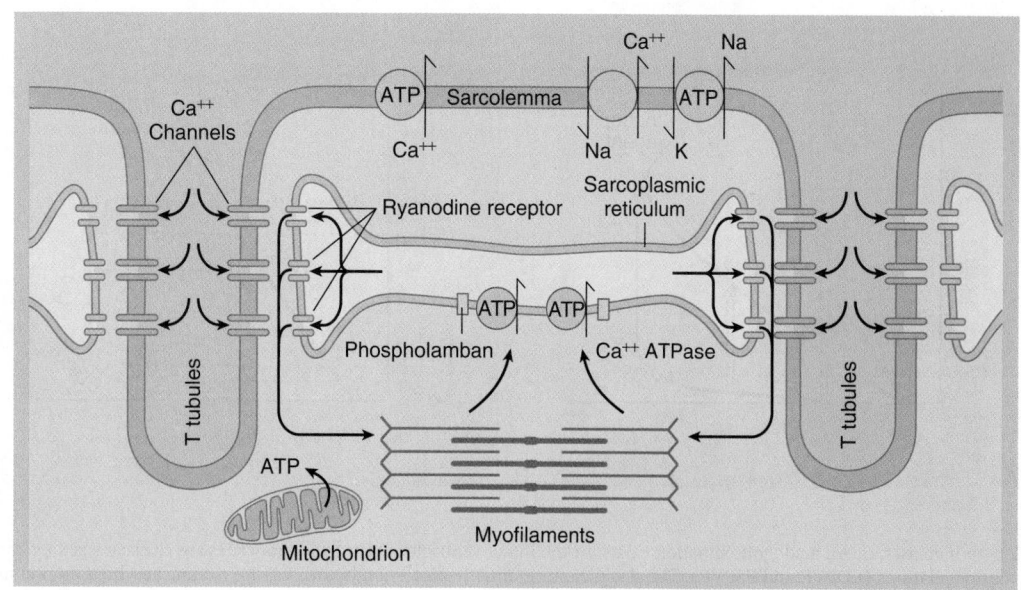

potassium pump (an ATP-dependent pump) influences intracellular sodium concentrations, which in turn can influence the activity of the sodium-calcium exchanger and thus influence intracellular calcium and contractility.

release from the sarcoplasmic reticulum, a process referred to as *calcium-induced calcium release*, are not fully elucidated; a tight anatomic coupling between the sarcolemmal calcium channels and ryanodine receptors has suggested that conformational changes of calcium channel proteins can directly influence the properties of the ryanodine receptor. The calcium released from the sarcoplasmic reticulum diffuses through the myofilament lattice and is available for binding to troponin, which disinhibits actin and myosin interactions and results in force production.

Calcium release is rapid and does not require energy because of the large calcium concentration gradient between the sarcoplasmic reticulum and the cytosol during diastole. In contrast, removal of calcium from the cytosol and from troponin occurs up a concentration gradient and is an energy-requiring process. Calcium sequestration is primarily accomplished by pumps on the sarcoplasmic reticulum membrane that consume ATP (sarcoplasmic reticulum Ca^{2+}-ATPase pumps); these pumps are located in the central portions of the sarcoplasmic reticulum and are in close proximity to the myofilaments. Sarcoplasmic reticulum Ca^{2+}-ATPase activity is regulated by the phosphorylation status of another sarcoplasmic reticulum protein, phospholamban. To maintain calcium homeostasis, an amount of calcium equal to what entered the cell through the sarcolemmal calcium channels must also exit with each beat. This equilibrium is accomplished primarily by the sarcolemmal sodium-calcium exchanger, a transmembrane protein that translocates calcium across the membrane down its concentration gradient in exchange for sodium ions moved in the opposite direction. Sodium homeostasis is in turn regulated largely by the ATP-requiring sodium-potassium pump on the sarcolemma.

As suggested earlier, the amount of calcium released and the rate of calcium uptake are regulated by the β-adrenergic pathway, which provides a ready means of enhancing contractile force under settings of stress. β-agonist (e.g., epinephrine or norepinephrine) binding to the β-receptor activates membrane-bound adenylyl cyclase, which results in the generation of cyclic adenosine monophosphate and then the activation of phosphokinase A (PKA). PKA activation results in phosphorylation of phospholamban, the calcium channel, the ryanodine receptor, and sarcomeric regulatory proteins. The modification of protein function caused by such phosphorylations results in a coordinated increase in calcium entry, uptake, and release, with an associated increase in contractile strength.

FORCE-LENGTH RELATIONS. In addition to calcium, cardiac muscle length exerts a major influence on force production (Fig. 48–3). Because each muscle is composed of a linear array of sarcomere bundles from one end of the muscle to the other, muscle length is directly proportional to the average sarcomere length. Changes in sarcomere length alter the geometric relationship between thick and thin filaments. For myofilaments in general, optimal force is achieved when sarcomere length is about 2.2 to 2.3 µm, the length that provides optimal overlap of thick and thin filaments. As sarcomere length is decreased to less than about 2.0 µm, the tips of apposing thin filaments hit each other, the thick filaments approach the Z lines, and the lateral distance between thick and thin filaments increases. Each of these factors contributes to a reduction in force with decreasing sarcomere length. In skeletal muscle, when sarcomeres are stretched beyond 2.3 µm, force decreases because fewer myosin heads can reach and bind with actin; skeletal muscle can typically operate in this so-called *descending limb* of the sarcomere force-length relationship. In cardiac muscle, however, constraints imposed by the sarcolemma prevent myocardial sarcomeres from being stretched beyond 2.3 µm, even under conditions of severe heart failure when very high stretching pressures are imposed on the heart.

Force-length relationships are conveniently used to characterize systolic and diastolic contractile properties of cardiac muscle. These relationships are measured by holding the ends of an isolated muscle strip and measuring the force developed at different muscle lengths while preventing the muscle from shortening (*isometric contractions*). As the muscle is stretched from its slack length (the length at which no force is generated), both the resting (end-diastolic) tension and the peak (end-systolic) tension increase. The end-diastolic force-length relationship is nonlinear and exhibits a shallow slope at small lengths and a steeper slope at larger lengths, which is a reflection of the nonlinear mechanical restraints imposed by the sarcolemma and extracellular matrix to prevent overstretch of the sarcomeres. End-systolic force increases with increasing muscle length to a much greater degree than does end-diastolic force. The difference in force at end-diastole as compared with end-systole increases as muscle length increases and indicates a greater amount of developed force as the muscle is stretched. This fundamental property of cardiac muscle is called the *Frank-Starling law of the heart* in recognition of its two discoverers. If a drug increases the amount of calcium released to the myofilaments (e.g., epinephrine, which belongs to a class of drugs referred to as *inotropic* agents), the end-systolic force-length relationship shifts upward and at any given length the muscle can generate more force. Inotropic agents typically do not affect the end-diastolic force-length relationship. In view of the prominent effect of muscle length on force generation, the intrinsic strength of cardiac muscle, commonly referred to as muscle *contractility*, should be indexed by the end-systolic force-length relationship and not simply by peak force generation.

FROM MUSCLE TO CHAMBER. Muscle length and the force generated by muscles in the walls of the ventricles are interrelated with the volume and pressure of the chambers. It is intuitively clear that, as ventricular chamber volume varies, so too do muscle and sarcomere lengths. Ventricular pressure is related to the force within the walls and the geometry of the chamber. For the left ventricle, which has a

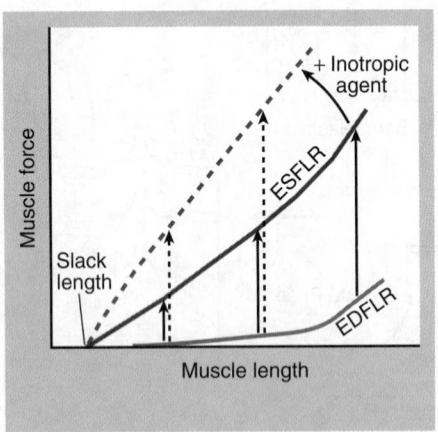

A

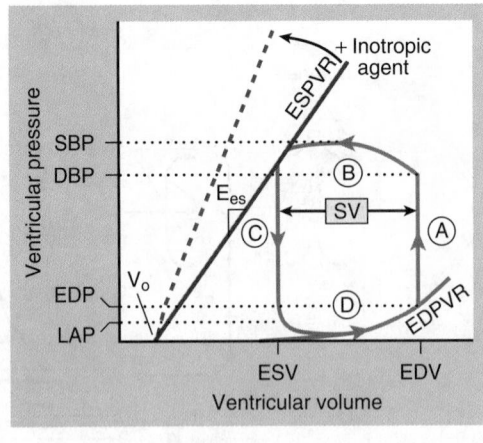

B

FIGURE 48–3 • *A*, Relationship between muscle length and force. When stretched from the slack length (the length at which no force is generated), both diastolic and systolic forces increase and result in the end-diastolic force-length relationship (EDFLR) and the end-systolic force-length relationship (ESFLR). ESFLR increases much more steeply than the EDFLR, so the force developed (difference between the two curves, indicated by the arrows) increases as the muscle is stretched. Pharmacologic agents that acutely increase contractile strength (contractility) have little effect on the EDFLR, but the ESFLR increases and consequently the force developed at any given length increases. *B*, An analogous situation exists for the intact ventricle: Contractile properties are characterized by end-diastolic and end-systolic pressure-volume relations (EDPVR and ESPVR). The slack length in muscle corresponds with V_0, the volume at which no pressure is generated. The ESPVR is nearly linear and characterized by a slope, E_{es}, that varies in relation to contractility. The pressure-volume loop sits within the boundaries defined by the EDPVR and ESPVR. The four phases of the cardiac cycle are indicated by isovolumic contraction (*A*), ejection (*B*), isovolumic relaxation (*C*), and filling (*D*). EDV = end-diastolic volume; ESV = end-systolic volume; DBP = diastolic aortic blood pressure; SBP = peak systolic blood pressure; EDP = end-diastolic pressure; LAP = left atrial pressure; SV = stroke volume.

roughly circular cross section, the Laplace law for thick-walled structures provides an approximation of this relationship: P ≈ 2 · T · h/R, where P is the pressure within the chamber, T is the tension developed by the muscle (force/unit cross-sectional area), h is the wall thickness, and R is the internal radius of the chamber. From this equation, it follows that chamber pressure depends on both tension and muscle length (because muscle length is related to chamber volume, which in turn is related to chamber radius). Because of the complex structure and geometry of the right ventricle, no simple analytic equation can describe this interrelationship; however, the underlying principle is the same.

Just as end-systolic and end-diastolic force-length relationships can be used to characterize the systolic and diastolic properties of cardiac muscle fibers, so too can end-systolic and end-diastolic *pressure-volume relationships* be used to characterize the peak systolic and end-diastolic properties of the ventricular chambers. Analogous to muscle, the end-diastolic pressure-volume relationship is nonlinear, with a shallow incline at low pressures and a steep rise at pressures in excess of 20 mm Hg. However, the end-systolic pressure-volume relationship is typically linear, and as for muscle, ventricular pressure-generating capability is increased as ventricular volume is increased. Also analogous to muscle, the end-systolic pressure-volume relationship is used to index ventricular chamber *contractility*. Because the end-systolic pressure-volume relationship is roughly linear, it can be characterized by a slope and volume axis intercept. The slope of the line, which has units of myocardial stiffness or volume elastance (mm Hg/mL) is called E_{es} (*end-systolic elastance*), and the volume axis intercept (analogous to slack length of the muscle) is referred to as V_0. When muscle *contractility* is increased (e.g., by administration of an *inotropic* agent), the slope of the end-systolic pressure-volume relationship (E_{es}) increases, whereas little change occurs in V_0 (discussed later).

THE CARDIAC CYCLE. The heart beats roughly once every second and repeatedly cycles through a sequence of hemodynamic events that can be divided into four phases. This cycle can be summarized by tracking the time course of change in ventricular pressure and volume along with atrial and aortic pressures in relation to events noted on the electrocardiogram (Fig. 48–4). At end-diastole, ventricular pressure is at its resting level (*end-diastolic pressure*) and ventricular volume is at its maximal value (*end-diastolic volume*). Aortic pressure declines gradually during this period as the blood ejected into the aorta during the prior ventricular contraction discharges to the peripheral circulation. Just before the onset of ventricular systole, atrial contraction provides a final boost to ventricular volume. As ventricular contraction begins about 120 milliseconds later, pressure increases inside the ventricular chamber and exceeds the pressure in the atrium; this pres-

sure differential causes the mitral valve to close. Ventricular pressure is still less than that of the aorta, so the aortic valve remains closed. Because both valves are closed, no blood enters or leaves the ventricle during this time; this first phase of the cardiac cycle is called *isovolumic contraction*. As systole progresses, ventricular pressure eventually exceeds that of the aorta, so the aortic valve opens. As muscular contraction continues, blood is ejected from the ventricle into the aorta, and ventricular volume decreases during the *ejection* phase of the cycle. As contraction of the cardiac muscle reaches its maximal effort (end of systole), ejection ends as ventricular volume reaches its lowest point (*end-systolic volume*). The amount of blood ejected is called the stroke volume (SV) and equals the difference between end-diastolic and end-systolic volume. The *ejection fraction* (EF), defined as the percentage of end-diastolic volume (EDV) ejected during a contraction (EF = 100 · SV/EDV), provides a practical means of indexing heart strength in the clinical setting. As the muscles relax, ventricular pressure falls below that in the aorta, and the aortic valve closes. Muscular relaxation proceeds, and pressure continues to decrease. Ventricular volume is constant during this phase of *isovolumic relaxation* because both the mitral and aortic valves are closed. Eventually, ventricular pressure falls below the pressure in the left atrium; the mitral valve opens and blood can flow from the atrium into the ventricle during the *filling* phase.

The four phases of the cardiac cycle are also illustrated by a *pressure-volume diagram* (see Fig. 48–3). The plot of instantaneous ventricular pressure versus volume for one cardiac cycle forms a loop called the *pressure-volume loop*, which sits within the boundaries defined by the end-diastolic and end-systolic pressure-volume relationships. The right ventricle, coupled with the right atrium and the pulmonary artery, undergoes a sequence of events nearly identical to that of the left ventricle except that the magnitudes of the peak pressures are approximately one sixth that of the left ventricle (Table 48–1).

DETERMINANTS OF CARDIAC PERFORMANCE. Two primary measurements of overall cardiovascular performance are arterial blood pressure and cardiac output (mean arterial blood flow) because both adequate blood pressure and adequate cardiac output are necessary to maintain life. In general terms, these aspects of cardiac performance depend on four fundamental factors: *preload, afterload, ventricular contractility,* and *heart rate* (Chapter 55).

Preload, which refers to the degree to which sarcomeres are stretched just before the onset of systole, is generally defined for the ventricle as either end-diastolic pressure or end-diastolic volume—two parameters that are interrelated by the nonlinear end-diastolic pressure-volume relationship. As for myocytes, ventricular pressure and flow-generating capacity vary with the *preload* (Frank-Starling law of the heart); a decrease in preload corresponds to a decrease in both end-diastolic volume and pressure, which are associated with decreases in peak pressure and stroke volume (Fig. 48–5). An increase in preload leads to an increase in ventricular pressure and flow generation, but there are limits to how high preload pressures can be increased; LV end-diastolic pressures in excess of about 20 to

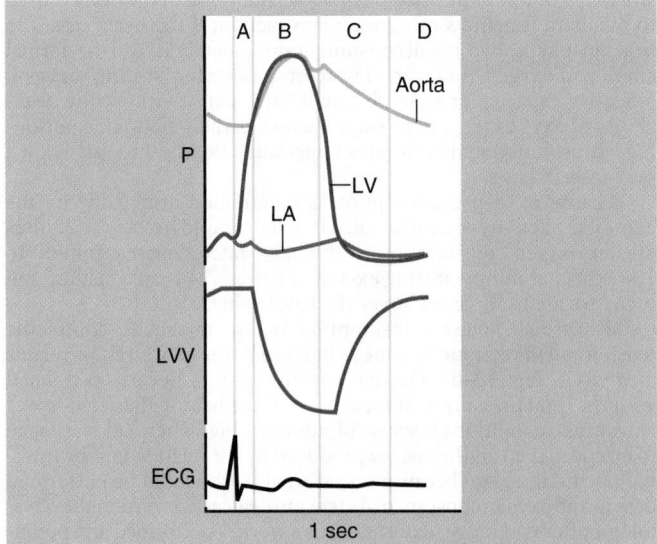

FIGURE 48–4 • Time sequence of events during a single cardiac cycle. Pressures (P) in the aorta, left ventricle (LV), and left atrium (LA) are shown. The four phases of the cardiac cycle are also illustrated: isovolumic contraction (*A*), ejection (*B*), isovolumic relaxation (*C*), and filling (*D*).

Table 48–1 • RANGE OF NORMAL RESTING VALUES

PRESSURE
Central venous (mean): 0–5 mm Hg
Right atrial (mean): 0–5 mm Hg
Right ventricular (systolic/diastolic): 20–30/0–5 mm Hg
Pulmonary artery (systolic/diastolic): 20–30/8–12 mm Hg
Left atrial (mean): 8–12 mm Hg
Left ventricular (systolic/diastolic): 100–150/8–12 mm Hg
Aortic (systolic/diastolic): 100–150/70–90 mm Hg

VOLUME-RELATED MEASURES
Right ventricular end-diastolic volume: 70–100 mL
Left ventricular end-diastolic volume: 70–100 mL
Stroke volume: 40–70 mL
Cardiac index: 2.5–4.0 L/min/m²
Ejection fraction: 55–70%

ARTERIAL RESISTANCE
Systemic vascular resistance: 10–20 mm Hg · min/L
Pulmonary vascular resistance: 0.5–1.5 mm Hg · min/L

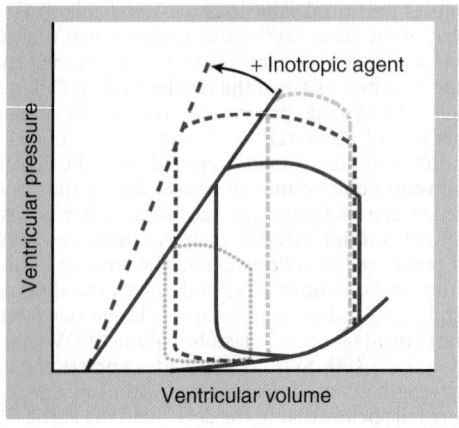

A

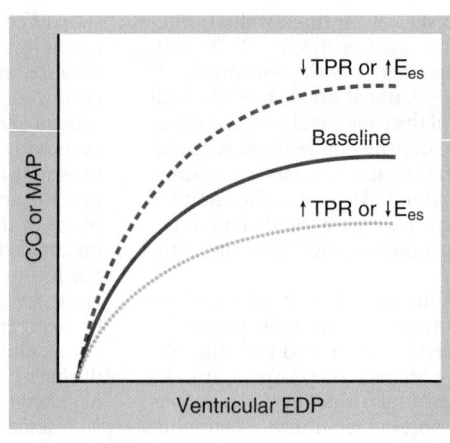

B

FIGURE 48–5 • *A*, Baseline end-systolic pressure-volume relationship (ESPVR) and pressure-volume loop shown by the solid red lines. The effect of a decrease in filling volume (but constant vascular resistance) on the loop is shown by the dotted yellow line. The effect of increased afterload resistance (but nearly constant preload volume) on the loop is shown by the green dotted-dashed line. The effect of a positive inotropic agent on the ESPVR and on the pressure-volume loop with constant afterload resistance and nearly constant preload is shown by the blue dashed line. With the exception of the inotropic agent, the changes in pressure and stroke volume do not reflect changes in intrinsic cardiac function. *B*, The interdependence between indices of ventricular pump performance (e.g., cardiac output [CO] and mean arterial pressure [MAP]) are summarized by Frank-Starling curves that plot these indices as a function of filling pressure and vary with changes in heart contractile strength (E_{es}) and with total systemic peripheral resistance (TPR). The nature of this interdependence is summarized according to modern theories of ventricular vascular coupling according to the following equations: $CO \approx HR \cdot [EDV - V_0]/[1 + TPR/(T \cdot E_{es})]$, and $MAP \approx [EDV - V_0]/[T/TPR + 1/E_{es}]$, where T is the duration of the cardiac cycle (i.e., $T = 60/HR$), HR is heart rate, and EDV is end-diastolic volume.

25 mm Hg typically cause exudation of fluid into the alveoli, and the resulting pulmonary edema limits blood oxygenation.

Afterload refers to the physical forces that must be overcome for myocytes to shorten and for the ventricle to eject blood. From the point of view of myocardium, peak arterial pressure provides a measure of the peak stress experienced by myocytes because stress is related to pressure according to Laplace's law. In the absence of LV outflow obstruction, arterial pressure is an appropriate index for quantifying myocyte afterload in vivo. Another parameter that characterizes the ventricular afterloading properties of the arterial system is *total peripheral resistance (TPR)*, which predominantly relates to the vasomotor tone of the resistance vessels.

TPR is calculated as the ratio between the mean pressure decrease across the arterial system (mean arterial pressure [MAP] minus mean central venous pressure [CVP]) and cardiac output (CO): TPR = (MAP – CVP)/CO. When compared with the baseline pressure-volume loop, the loop obtained with increased TPR (but a similar preload volume) exhibits a higher peak pressure and a decrease in stroke volume and ejection fraction (see Fig. 48–5).

Contractility refers to the intrinsic strength of the cardiac muscle (*myocardial contractility*) or the ventricle (*ventricular contractility*), independent of external conditions imposed by either preload or afterload. Inotropic agents such as epinephrine change muscle contractility and therefore induce shifts of the end-systolic pressure-volume relationship and changes in cardiac performance. When compared with the baseline pressure-volume loop, the loop obtained at increased contractility exhibits a greater pressure, stroke volume, and ejection fraction despite a constant preload volume and arterial resistance. Although the end-systolic pressure-volume relationship fundamentally provides a load-independent index of ventricular contractility, it is difficult to measure in patients and is usually limited to the research setting. Although ejection fraction is influenced by afterload resistance as well as by changes in contractility, the ejection fraction can help assess response to therapy and is a strong correlate of survival in cardiac disease. Thus, despite theoretical limitations, the ejection fraction provides a simple and useful clinical indicator of overall LV contractile strength.

The importance of *heart rate* in determining cardiac performance is appreciated by noting that cardiac output measured in liters per minute is equal to the amount of blood ejected at each heartbeat (stroke volume in liters per beat) multiplied by the number of beats per minute. Because blood pressure is related to cardiac output and TPR, heart rate variations also provide a means of influencing mean arterial pressure. Thus, the ability to vary the heart rate provides an effective means of influencing cardiovascular performance.

Cardiac output and mean arterial pressure can be related to the measures of preload, afterload, contractility, and heart rate (see Fig. 48–5B) by Frank-Starling curves. These curves plot end-diastolic pressure versus either cardiac output or mean arterial pressure to provide an overall characterization of LV pump function in practical terms and to demonstrate the dependence of pump function on afterload resistance and contractility.

DETERMINATION OF MYOCARDIAL OXYGEN CONSUMPTION AND ENERGY METABOLISM. The heart relies almost exclusively on oxidation of fatty acids and glucose as an immediate source of energy. The heart normally extracts free fatty acids preferentially from the coronary perfusion for oxidative energy production. Under conditions of limited oxygen supply, this preference is changed to glucose. Greater energy is consumed in metabolizing free fatty acids than in metabolizing glucose. Under most conditions, anaerobic metabolism provides very limited energy. Severe hypoxia with high coronary flow produces lactate and anaerobic ATP. The much more common condition of ischemia with acidosis results in little anaerobic energy. Under most steady-state circumstances, the heart is dependent on the availability of oxygen to continue its function.

The oxygen and energy consumption of the heart is determined principally by its contractile activity. Three major independent hemodynamic or mechanical factors contribute to myocardial oxygen consumption by the heart: heart rate, the tension developed by the heart during systole, and the contractile state (contractility) of the heart. Only 10% or less of the total oxygen consumption of the heart is used to maintain functions other than contraction; if the heart ceases to beat but is kept alive, it will consume approximately 10% of the normal amount of oxygen. A very modest reserve exists for "storing" oxygen, oxidative capacity, or anaerobic substrate. Thus, without the availability of oxygen (e.g., hypoxia, ischemia, carbon monoxide poisoning), heart function deteriorates remarkably rapidly, essentially on a beat-to-beat basis.

Because oxygen consumption is determined principally by the contractile activity of cardiac muscle, a more rapid heart rate requires greater oxygen consumption. If the heart rate increases from 60 to 180 beats per minute during exercise or stress, oxygen consumption increases about three-fold over the basal value.

Myocardial oxygen consumption is also related to contractile tension and the contractile state as indexed by the total *pressure-volume area* (PVA; Fig. 48–6). Oxygen consumption is linearly correlated with the total pressure-volume area, so if the heart contracted under isovolumic conditions because of infinitely high afterload resistance to ejection, then all the energy produced by the heart would be internal potential energy because no external work would be performed despite the oxygen consumed. As tension decreases to within the physiologic afterload range, external stroke work is performed and potential energy is also produced; oxygen consumption is proportional to the sum of the two.

A simpler index of myocardial oxygen consumption for an intact heart is the *rate-pressure product*. With this index, the heart rate is

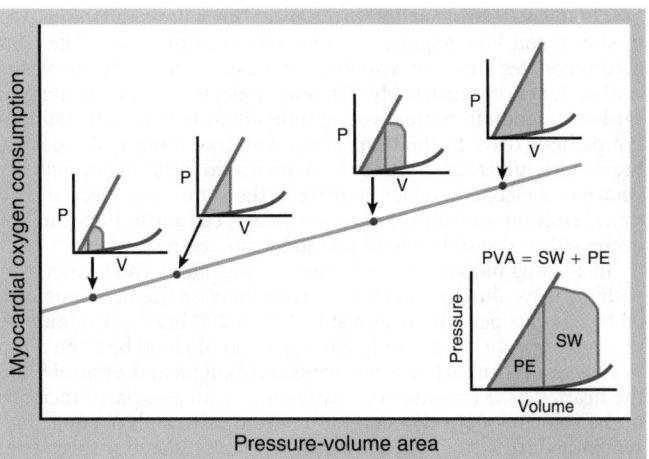

FIGURE 48–6 • The total pressure-volume area (PVA), which equals the sum of the stroke work ([SW] area contained within the pressure-volume loop [PVL]) and the potential energy ([PE] area contained between the end-systolic and end-diastolic pressure-volume relationships and the isovolumic relaxation portion of the PVL), is linearly related to oxygen consumption. The insets show various PVLs and their corresponding PVA-oxygen consumption point on the curves. An ejecting beat at low filling volume (left) has a lower oxygen consumption than an isovolumic beat at the same filling volume (second from the left). For isovolumic contractions, there is no external SW; all generated energy is PE. When filling is increased, the PVA increases for both ejecting and isovolumic contractions in proportion to the increase in PVA. The non-zero y-axis intercept indicates the substantial energy requirements for basal metabolism and for calcium cycling, which are not directly related to energy for force generation. At increased contractility, the PVA-oxygen consumption curve shifts upward in a parallel manner, which is related largely to the fuel required for cycling the increased amount of calcium present at the increased contractility.

multiplied by the peak systolic pressure and used as an index of oxygen demand or consumption. Although this index ignores the contribution of the contractile state, the rate-pressure product provides a reasonable index of oxygen consumption when the contractile state is unchanged or relatively stable.

With an increase in the contractile state, an additional obligatory increase in oxygen consumption is produced above what is related to heart rate and tension. Evidence suggests that the increased oxygen consumption with an increase in the contractile state is due to the increased sarcoplasmic reticular ATPase activity required to sequester the increased amount of cycling calcium that underlies the increase in contractility.

CORONARY BLOOD FLOW: METABOLIC AND NEUROHORMONAL REGULATION. The volume of coronary or myocardial blood flow under normal conditions is largely regulated by myocardial oxygen demands. Because the heart extracts 90% or more of the oxygen needed from the coronary blood, the striking increases in oxygen consumption that occur with high tension development, higher heart rates, and/or high contractility are met almost entirely by increases in coronary blood flow. High myocardial oxygen consumption and high coronary flow are characteristic of exercise.

The predominant mechanisms involved in this augmentation of coronary blood flow from normal values of 60 to 100 mL/100 g/minute to values that are six-fold higher are metabolic factors, especially adenosine released from mildly ischemic myocardial and other cells. Adenosine is the byproduct of the breakdown of ATP to adenosine monophosphate and then to adenosine. A second control of the magnitude of coronary blood flow under increased workload or demand conditions is nitric oxide, which is produced by coronary vascular endothelial cells and has a direct local vasodilating effect on coronary arteries and the more distal bed. Nitric oxide is a byproduct in a number of reactions that lead to an increase in the activity of nitric oxide synthase, an enzyme that produces nitric oxide from the amino acid L-arginine. In addition to adenosine and nitric oxide, other longer-acting coronary vasodilators such as bradykinin, prostaglandins, and

CO_2 may have a direct effect in maintaining coronary artery blood flow.

Coronary artery mechanical changes also contribute to regulation of coronary flow. As coronary arteries are stretched by higher luminal pressure, they constrict; as pressure within the coronary artery is reduced, the artery dilates. These very potent changes, which help maintain coronary blood flow under circumstances of altered coronary flow hemodynamics but maintained oxygen demands, are termed *autoregulatory* mechanisms for coronary blood flow.

In addition to the metabolic and other factors that lead to coronary vasodilatation, a series of factors can lead to coronary arterial vasoconstriction. The exact roles of these vasoconstricting factors in health are unclear, but in disease these factors may have a profoundly important effect. A local regulating factor is the endothelin system, which consists of peptides that are synthesized and controlled locally within small arteries or arterioles and that have a profound vasoconstricting effect on the resistance arteries within the coronary circulation. Constricting endothelins may be produced at the site of coronary artery atherosclerotic lesions and lead to vasoconstriction at those sites. In addition, at sites of coronary artery atherosclerosis where the endothelium is disrupted or abnormal, circulating vasoconstrictor substances gain access to smooth muscle receptors that are ordinarily covered by coronary arterial endothelium. These substances include circulating serotonin, 5-hydroxytryptamine, and other serotonin-like substances, as well as thromboxane, which may be produced by platelets or adjacent endothelium (Chapter 66). In addition, angiotensin II and sympathetic α_1-adrenergic stimulation cause vasoconstriction in coronary arteries.

CORONARY BLOOD FLOW: CHAMBER MECHANICAL REGULATION. The coronary arteries originate from the aorta and spread over the outer surface of the heart or epicardium (Chapter 54). From this epicardial position the arteries penetrate the myocardium from epicardium to endocardium and arborize to form the capillary network. Coronary collateral channels are 25 to 100 μm in diameter and link one major epicardial coronary artery with its adjacent neighbor. The collateral circulation in the coronary bed is not like other vascular beds, in which collateralization is through overlapping arborization of small blood vessels originating from adjacent major arteries.

The head of pressure at the origin of the coronary artery and the pressure within the large epicardial coronary arteries directly reflect the central aortic pressure. During diastole, the resistance to blood flow from the coronary arteries is largely from the tone of resistance vessels. During systole, coronary perfusion pressure (which equals aortic pressure) is determined by the LV intracavitary pressure. In turn, cavitary pressure equals the pressure within the inner myocardial wall. It is not surprising, then, that the endocardial coronary arteries are remarkably compressed during systole. The systolic pressure within the thick LV wall toward the epicardial surface is not nearly as high as the endocardial portion of the wall. Therefore, coronary blood flow occurs both during systole and diastole toward the epicardium but is essentially exclusively limited to diastole in the subendocardium.

In addition, if LV workload is increased or myocardial contractility or function is decreased, then LV diastolic pressure will increase. This increase in diastolic pressure acts as a compressor force on the subendocardial vessels and limits myocardial blood flow during this critical period of diastole. Finally, the influence of heart rate on coronary blood flow, particularly to the subendocardium, is important and dramatic. As the heart rate increases, the period of diastole between beats becomes shorter and shorter. This limitation of coronary flow to the subendocardium during tachycardia can have profound effects in the setting of coronary artery disease and heart failure such that drugs that block tachycardia during exercise may be very useful therapeutically.

NEUROHORMONAL REGULATION OF THE CARDIOVASCULAR SYSTEM. The major components of the neurohormonal systems that regulate cardiovascular function are the sympathetic and parasympathetic components of the autonomic nervous system and the renin-angiotensin system (Chapter 55). The major attributes of the sympathetic nervous system in responding rapidly to stress are the ability to increase the heart rate, to increase myocardial contractility, and to regulate vascular tone in the various organs. Most of these functions are performed by the sympathetic nervous system through release of norepinephrine at the nerve endings throughout the circulation. Under more profound stress, the sympathetic nervous system elaborates epinephrine from the adrenal gland. Norepinephrine and epinephrine act through the α-adrenergic vasoconstricting mechanisms in the periphery, but both increase contractility by stimulating α- and β-adrenergic receptors in the heart. Epinephrine has a more striking β-adrenergic effect than norepinephrine does, especially at low circulating levels. Through these β-adrenergic actions, epinephrine profoundly increases the heart rate and, at the same time, induces vasodilatation of the central arterial bed, thereby reducing impedance to LV ejection. The coronary circulation operates in a mixed fashion, with evidence of coronary artery vasoconstriction occurring in response to α-adrenergic stimulation and vasodilation in response to lower doses of epinephrine.

The most important parasympathetic innervation is that of the sinoatrial and atrioventricular nodes, where these nerves slow the firing rate of pacemaker tissue and slow conduction in the atrioventricular node (Chapter 57). The neurotransmitter for the parasympathetic nervous system is acetylcholine. Ventricular muscle is poorly innervated by the parasympathetic nervous system and vagal tone has very little effect on contractility under normal resting conditions; however, increased vagal tone depresses myocardial contractility when sympathetic tone is high. At rest, the heart rate is under control of the parasympathetic nervous system rather than the sympathetic system. Thus β-adrenergic blocking drugs have little effect on the heart rate at rest but markedly reduce augmentation of the heart rate particularly at high levels of exercise.

The sympathetic nervous system also has a profound vasoconstrictive effect on the venous system, particularly the capacitance bed within the splanchnic or abdominal circulation. Thus, in forms of stress that are associated with rapid loss of blood or fluids, the venous constriction effects of sympathetic stimulation can be life saving.

The renin-angiotensin system is a second coordinated system that regulates blood pressure, peripheral vasoconstriction, and contractility in a fashion complementary to the sympathetic nervous system. Generally, action of the renin-angiotensin system is not nearly as immediate or profound as that of the sympathetic nervous system, but it operates principally as an intermediate- and long-term regulator. Under pathologic conditions such as heart failure, the system can remain chronically activated (Chapter 55). Renin is a hormone released by macula densa cells within the juxtaglomerular apparatus of the kidney under conditions of decreased perfusion to the kidney, decreased delivery of sodium to the macula densa, or increasing sympathetic activity (Chapter 111). Once renin is released, it acts exclusively through production of angiotensin II, a potent peripheral vasoconstrictor and coronary arterial constrictor, within the circulation and at individual organ sites. Angiotensin II induces release of the sodium-retaining hormone aldosterone from the adrenal gland (Chapter 241). All these actions tend to retain sodium in the circulation and increase arterial blood pressure. Angiotensin, which is also a potent stimulus to both myocardial and peripheral vessel hypertrophy, promotes the release of norepinephrine from peripheral sympathetic nervous system sites.

CARDIOVASCULAR RESPONSE TO EXERCISE. High levels of exercise require truly remarkable augmentation of heart function and performance, as well as adaptation of the peripheral circulation. Enhanced blood flow is needed to the exercising muscles and restriction of blood flow away from those parts of the body that are not essential during the period of exercise. Blood flow is also augmented to the skin and oral mucosa for dissipation of the heat produced by exercising muscles.

Oxygen consumption for the entire body during strenuous exercise increases approximately 18-fold. Two thirds of this increase in oxygen consumption results from greater cardiac output and the remaining one third from an increase in oxygen extraction from arterial blood. Arterial oxygen saturation usually remains near 100%, whereas venous oxygen saturation decreases from approximately 75% to 25%. This increase in oxygen extraction is mostly related to the increase in blood flow to the exercising muscle, which essentially extracts most of the oxygen within the blood. The increase in blood flow to the exercising muscle occurs as a result of an increase in arterial pressure and perfusion of the exercising limbs and profound vasodilation of the arteries of the exercising muscle. Arterial dilation is a consequence of the release of potassium and other vasodilating substances from the exercising muscle. Whereas overall cardiac output may increase six-fold, blood flow to the exercising muscle may increase 40- or 50-fold from rest to exercise.

This increase in blood flow to the exercising muscle and the increase in skin blood flow augment venous return to the heart. The heart accommodates this augmentation in venous return by increasing cardiac function remarkably. The major element in this increase in cardiac function in normal young individuals is an augmentation in sympathetic drive to the heart and a withdrawal of vagal tone. The heart rate is increased, contractility is increased (resulting in increased ventricular ejection and an increase in the ventricular ejection fraction), ejection and filling rates are increased, aortic impedance is decreased, and systolic blood pressure is increased.

In a young individual, withdrawal of vagal tone and greater sympathetic drive during maximal exercise increase the heart rate from 60 to 70 beats per minute at rest to 170 to 200 beats per minute. At this rapid heart rate, not only must ejection of blood be more rapid, but it is also essential to use mechanisms to augment the rate of filling the heart. These increases in contractility with associated increases in the velocity of ejection and filling occur as a result of augmented sympathetic drive to the heart, which increases the amount of calcium cycling within the cell and increases the rate of sarcoplasmic reticulum ATPase activity to hasten calcium sequestration.

Another sympathetic adaptation during exercise is arterial vasodilation of the aorta and central arteries. This β-sympathetic central arterial vasodilation decreases the impedance to LV ejection, but the augmentation in cardiac output is so great that even though impedance is lowered, systolic arterial blood pressure rises. The final mechanism available to the heart to augment cardiac function beyond that created by the withdrawal of vagal tone and the increase in sympathetic tone is an enhancement of preload (the Frank-Starling mechanism). A young individual at maximum exercise uses this mechanism very little, but when the sympathetic nervous system is blocked or when the sympathetic response is limited by aging or chronic heart failure, then preload recruitment operates as a reserve mechanism to augment cardiac output during exercise. With increased preload, the left ventricle (and presumably the right ventricle) dilate acutely to a larger diastolic volume. This increase in diastolic volume results in stretching of myocardial fibers and augmentation of pump function.

PHYSIOLOGIC PRINCIPLES UNDERLYING HEART FAILURE. Heart failure is an inability of the heart to provide sufficient blood flow to meet the metabolic demands of the body (Chapter 55). Heart failure can occur by three primary physiologic mechanisms: increased work, decreased function of the heart, and altered filling of the heart. For many types of chronic increase in workload, the heart adapts significantly by increasing its size or volume and by increasing its muscle mass through hypertrophy. The ventricles dilate in response to volume overload from endurance exercise or aortic and mitral regurgitation, anemia, and hyperthyroidism. With long-term pressure overload such as in hypertension (Chapter 63) or aortic or pulmonary valve obstruction (Chapter 72), pressure overload hypertrophy occurs. The ventricle can generate greater pressure at the same volumes. This same type of hypertrophy also occurs in athletes who perform exercises that increase blood pressure but do not increase volume, such as weight lifting.

AGE CHANGES IN THE CARDIOVASCULAR SYSTEM. In the cardiovascular system, intrinsic cardiac muscle function, the inotropic response to nonsympathetic mediators, and coronary perfusion are well maintained with age (Chapter 22). With age, however, cellular hypertrophy occurs because of both cell dropout and increased stiffening of the vascular tree; the result is increased afterload on the left ventricle. As a result of the hypertrophy, systole is prolonged.

Large arteries stiffen with age. Thus, even without hypertension, an age-related increase in impedance to ejection, a greater systolic load, and an increased pulse wave velocity occur. In addition, the chronotropic (i.e., heart rate response) and inotropic response to sympathetic mediation is diminished, so conditions that put sudden loads on the left ventricle, such as acute hypertension or myocardial infarction (Chapter 69), have more severe consequences in the elderly. Also, disease and stress may produce less compensatory hypertrophy in the elderly and therefore place more stress on the left ventricle with age.

With exercise or other forms of stress, the effects of a decreased β-sympathetic response in the elderly are dominant. Older individuals have less of an increase in heart rate and contractility and a larger increase in impedance. Fortunately, the intrinsic cardiac muscle reserve is adequate to compensate for these limitations in exercise response if no cardiac disease is present. In the presence of disease, however, cardiac reserve is diminished. Therefore, older individuals or victims of acute myocardial infarction or heart failure have much greater difficulty during exercise because the heart rate increases less, load or impedance is greater, and preload recruitment may already be near the maximally tolerated level.

SUGGESTED READINGS

Bers DM: Cardiac excitation-contraction coupling. Nature 2002;415:198–205. *A review of the role of calcium and its influence on contractility.*

Marx SO, Reiken S, Hisamatsu Y, et al: PKA phosphorylation dissociates FKBP12.6 from the calcium release channel (ryanodine receptor): Defective regulation in failing hearts. Cell 2000;101:365–376. *How local regulation of phosphorylation regulates contractility.*

Towbin JA, Bowles NE: The failing heart. Nature 2002;415:227–233. *The role of structural proteins in normal and abnormal contractility.*

49 RADIOLOGY OF THE HEART

Murray G. Baron

The heart casts a homogeneous shadow on the chest film. No internal detail can be seen within its contours because the radiodensities of blood, myocardium, and other cardiac tissues are so similar that one cannot be distinguished from the others. Only two borders of the heart, where it contacts the radiolucent, air-containing lung, can be discerned in any one projection. Changes in the size and/or shape of the chambers of the heart and the great vessels usually alter the shape of the cardiac silhouette. However, because the heart is a three-dimensional structure, multiple views are required for complete radiographic evaluation. With the advent of echocardiography, the need for this "cardiac series" has disappeared. However, a remarkable amount of information regarding the heart is contained on standard frontal and lateral chest films, which remain a useful tool for detecting disease, evaluating the severity of known disease, documenting the progress of disease, and assessing the efficacy of treatment.

Radiologic Anatomy

Except for the more complex cardiac anomalies, which are rare, especially in the adult, the positions and spatial relationships of the cardiac chambers and the great vessels are the same from one patient to the next and are not significantly affected by disease. On a frontal chest film, the right cardiac border is composed of a straight vertical upper half formed by the superior vena cava and a gently convex lower half representing the lateral wall of the right atrium (Fig. 49–1). The break in the contour of this border of the heart indicates the

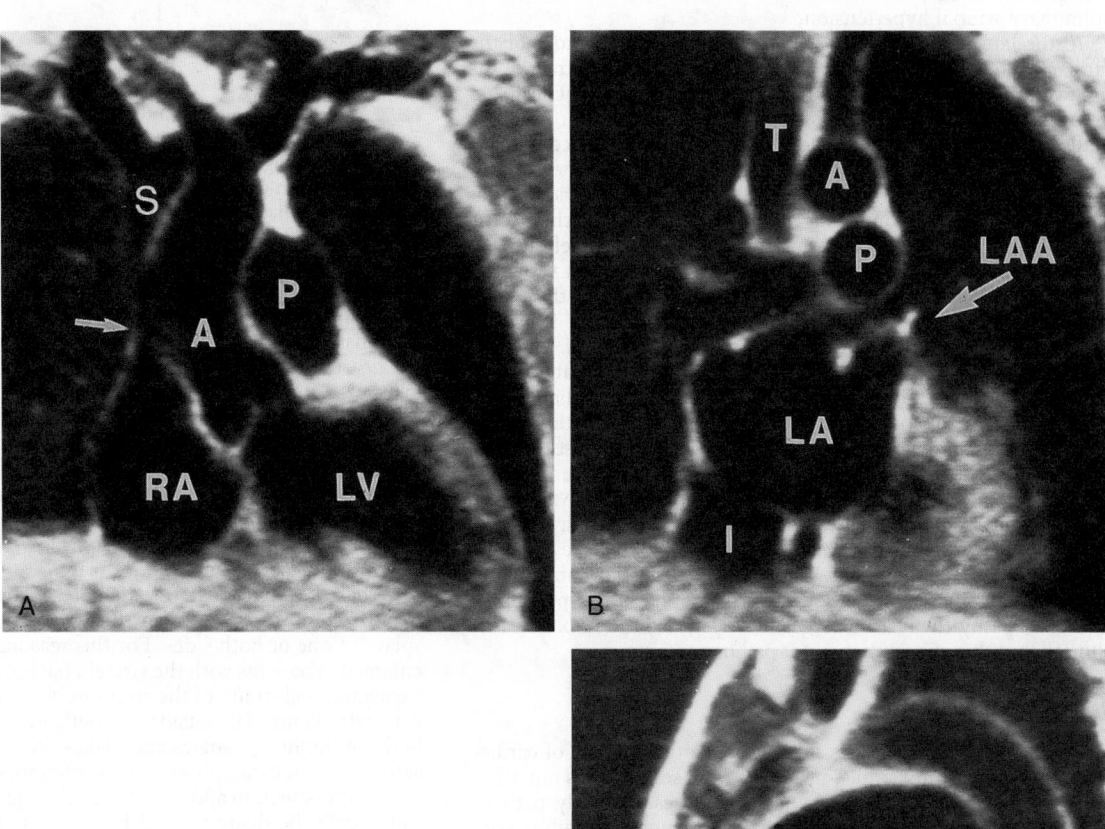

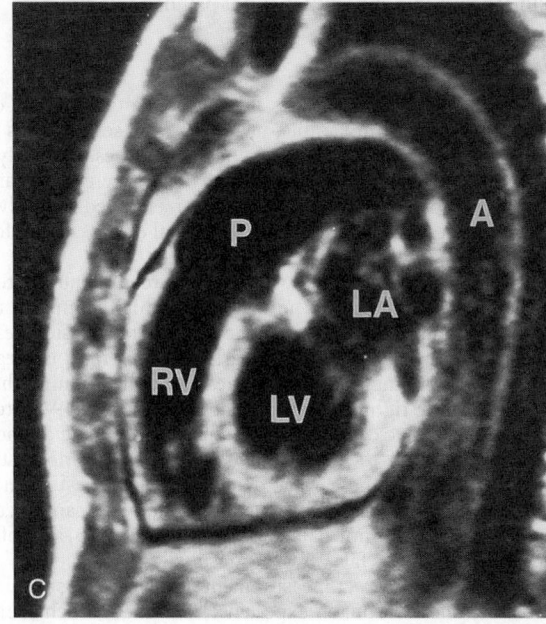

FIGURE 49–1 • Normal radiographic anatomy, magnetic resonance images. *A,* Coronal section at the level of the aortic valve. The right border of the cardiac silhouette is formed by the superior vena cava (S) and the right atrium (RA). The arrow indicates the caval-atrial junction. The lower portion of the left cardiac border is formed by the left ventricle (LV). A = ascending aorta; P = main pulmonary artery. *B,* Coronal section at the level of the left atrium. The upper portion of the left cardiac border is formed by the aorta (A), main pulmonary artery (P), and left atrial appendage (LAA). LA = left atrium; I = inferior vena cava; T = trachea. *C,* Sagittal section near the midline. The right ventricle (RV) forms the anterior surface of the heart, which abuts the sternum. The pulmonary artery (P) extends upward and posteriorly from the ventricle. The posterior border of the heart is formed by the left atrium (LA) and left ventricle (LV).

caval-atrial junction. Some patients are able to inhale deeply enough to uncover a small, straight segment of the inferior vena cava between the diaphragm and the right atrium.

Abnormalities of the caval segment are usually due to dilatation of the ascending aorta. A localized bulge of its midportion usually indicates post-stenotic dilatation secondary to aortic valve stenosis, whereas aortic insufficiency is commonly associated with a more generalized dilatation of the aorta. A bulge in the region of the caval-atrial junction may be due to an aneurysm of the right, or noncoronary sinus of Valsalva, or a markedly enlarged left atrium. Dilatation of either atrium tends to extend the cardiac silhouette to the right, whereas dilatation of either ventricle enlarges the silhouette to the left.

The left cardiac border is composed of four distinct segments. The uppermost bulge represents the aortic knob, the most distal portion of the aortic arch where it turns downward to become the descending aorta. The prominence below the knob is formed by the main pulmonary artery and the subvalvular portion of the outflow tract of the right ventricle. The lowermost third of this border represents the anterolateral wall of the left ventricle. Between this bulge and that of the pulmonary artery is a short, flat, or slightly concave, segment where the left atrial appendage reaches the border of the heart.

Aneurysms of the descending thoracic aorta commonly involve its most proximal portion in the region of the ligamentum arteriosum and present as a dilated aortic knob. Prominence of the pulmonary artery segment is common in younger individuals; but after the age of 35 to 40 years, dilatation is almost always an indicator of pulmonary arterial hypertension.

In the lateral view (see Fig. 49–1C), the anterior border of the cardiac silhouette is formed by the body and the outflow tract of the right ventricle. The heart lies in the anterior portion of the chest, and the right ventricle abuts the lower third of the sternum. Both the outflow tract and pulmonary artery slope posteriorly. Air-containing lung interposed between this portion of the heart and the anterior chest wall forms the "retrosternal clear space." The posterior border of the heart extends from the level of the pulmonary carina to the diaphragm. Its upper half is formed by the back of the left atrium, and the lower half represents the posterior wall of the left ventricle. The shadow of the inferior vena cava is usually seen in the lateral projection extending obliquely upward and anteriorly from the diaphragm to enter the posterior aspect of the right atrium. The lowermost contour of the normal left ventricle curves anteriorly and crosses the inferior vena cava about 2 cm above the left side of the diaphragm.

Alterations in the contour of the heart usually reflect dilation and/or hypertrophy of the chambers. Many times the pattern of these changes, together with the appearance of the pulmonary vasculature, points to a specific underlying cardiac abnormality. Chest films are most sensitive for detecting chamber dilation. Cardiac hypertrophy is more difficult to recognize as the thickened myocardium tends to encroach on the ventricular lumen more than extending outward and enlarging the cardiac silhouette. With severe hypertrophy, as in hypertrophic cardiomyopathy, the heart enlarges to the left and the apex becomes blunted, but this appearance is not pathognomonic.

Heart Size

A normal-sized heart does not guarantee the absence of cardiac disease. Angina, for example, no matter how severe, does not affect heart size until the left ventricle decompensates. Similarly, patients with restrictive cardiomyopathy may be in severe heart failure with a normal-appearing heart. Conversely, an enlarged heart always indicates the presence of cardiac or pericardial disease. Therefore, accurate evaluation of heart size is important.

Heart size, in the absence of disease, is directly related to the habitus of the patient. The cardiothoracic ratio, which compares the transverse diameter of the heart with the width of the chest, gives a readily obtainable, rough estimate of heart size. This ratio is measured by dropping a vertical line through the heart and summing the greatest distance to the right and left cardiac borders (Fig. 49–2) to give the transverse cardiac diameter. The transverse thoracic diameter is the greatest width of the chest, measured from the inner surfaces of the ribs. Dividing the cardiac diameter by the chest diameter gives the cardiothoracic ratio. A value of less than 0.6 can be considered within the limits of normal. Setting this value at 0.5, as is often done, produces too many false-positive results.

In most cases, exact measurement of the cardiac silhouette is not necessary, and a reasonably experienced observer can achieve an accept-

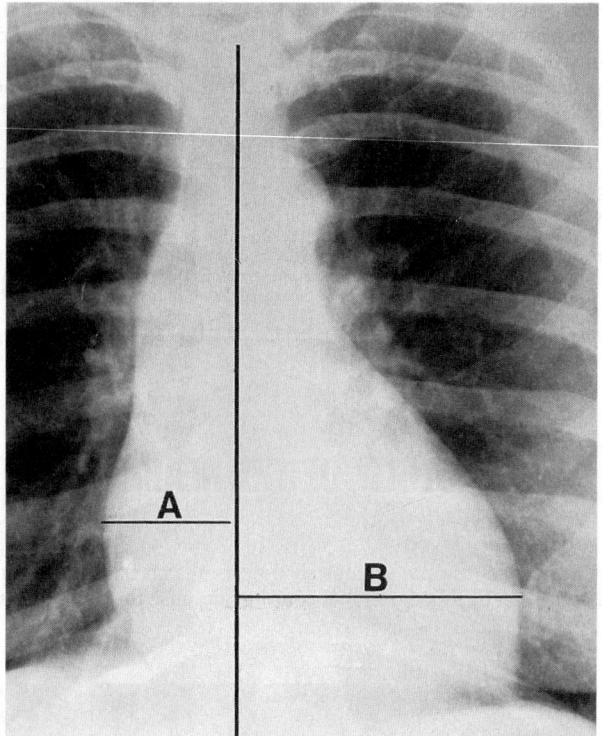

FIGURE 49–2 • Measurement of the transverse cardiac diameter. Severe aortic stenosis with a 95-mm systolic gradient across the valve is present. The heart, although considerably hypertrophied, is normal in size and configuration. A vertical line is drawn through the heart. The greatest distances to the right cardiac border (A) and to the left cardiac border (B) are then measured. Transverse cardiac diameter = A + B.

able degree of accuracy by visual estimation. The single greatest effect on apparent cardiac size is the degree of inspiration. The volume of the heart is essentially constant throughout the cardiac cycle. With expiration, the diaphragm moves up; as a result, the vertical diameter of the heart is shortened and its transverse diameter increases. Because heart size is estimated primarily from its width, the heart appears larger on expiratory films. The degree of inspiration can be determined from the relationship of the diaphragm to the ribs. On a properly positioned frontal chest film, a reasonable degree of inspiration is indicated if the diaphragm is lowered to at least the level of the posterior portion of the ninth rib.

When the anteroposterior diameter of the chest is small, the heart may be compressed between the sternum and the spine so that it splays to one or both sides. For this reason, the heart often appears enlarged in patients with the straight back syndrome or with a pectus excavatum deformity of the sternum. An epicardial fat pad (actually it is extrapleural fat outside the pericardium) can occur in one or both cardiophrenic angles and makes the heart appear larger than it actually is. The cardiophrenic angle often appears obtuse or the cardiac apex is indistinct. In addition, the slightly greater density of the heart can usually be distinguished from the more radiolucent image of the fat.

A change in size of the cardiac silhouette can also occur between systole and diastole. This point is important because chest films are exposed at random with reference to the cardiac cycle, and the apparent size of the heart may be different on two films of the same patient made at different times. In the majority of cases, the difference in the transverse cardiac diameter between systole and diastole is small, no more than several millimeters. However, in younger patients, especially the more athletic with a slow heart rate and a large stroke volume, phasic change in the normal cardiac diameter can be as much as 2 cm.

Chamber Enlargement

LEFT ATRIUM. Dilation of the left atrium alone, in the absence of a left-to-right shunt, is most often due to disease of the mitral valve, although it can also result simply from atrial fibrillation. The two

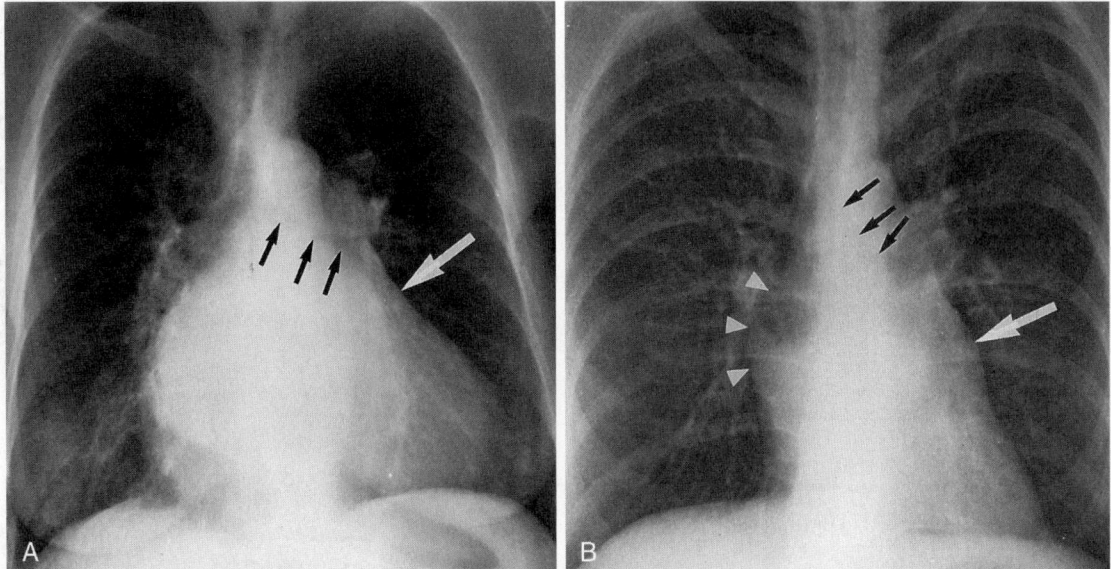

FIGURE 49–3 • Left atrial enlargement in mitral valve disease. *A*, Patient 1: The enlarged left atrium causes the central portion of the cardiac silhouette to be abnormally dense. The right border of the atrium is seen within the right side of the cardiac silhouette. The left main bronchus (small arrows) is elevated. The region of the left atrial appendage (white arrow) is slightly concave because this structure was resected at a previous mitral commissurotomy. *B*, Patient 2: The enlarged left atrial appendage bulges from the left side of the heart (white arrow), whereas the body of the atrium (arrowheads) extends beyond the right atrium to form a part of the right heart border. No double density is seen within the heart, and the left main bronchus (small arrows) is not elevated.

"popular" radiologic signs of left atrial enlargement—a double contour within the right cardiac border and elevation of the left main bronchus—are accurate when present, but they are insensitive and are seen in only about half the cases of mitral valve disease. To produce a discernible margin within the cardiac silhouette in the frontal projection, the thickness of the heart must increase sharply at some point. This increase in thickness occurs in mitral disease when the left atrium enlarges and protrudes posteriorly from the back of the heart. The right border of the left atrium is then silhouetted where it abuts the right lung, and its contour is seen within the cardiac silhouette (Fig. 49–3*A*). This pattern is not apparent with lesser degrees of left atrial enlargement. Conversely, when the right atrium also enlarges, as is common in long-standing mitral valve disease, it forms a continuous curve on the posterior cardiac border with the enlarged left atrium. Thus, the double contour is not seen with mild left atrial enlargement or in severe cases of mitral valve disease. Furthermore, the radiologic technique used for chest films is chosen to provide optimal images of the lungs. The heart, when enlarged, is underexposed, and the double contour may be hidden within its opaque silhouette. For the same reason, the position of the left main bronchus often cannot be clearly visualized through the mediastinal shadow.

A more sensitive sign of left atrial enlargement in the frontal projection is dilation of the left atrial appendage. The appendage extends anteriorly from the atrium along the left side of the heart, below the level of the pulmonary artery (see Fig. 49–1*B*). It forms the part of the left heart border between the pulmonary artery segment and the left ventricular segment. Normally, the border of the appendage is flat or slightly concave. Any convexity is abnormal and usually indicates left atrial enlargement.

LEFT VENTRICLE. The shape of the dilated left ventricle depends to a large extent on the underlying cause. When it is due to insufficiency of the aortic or mitral valve, the ventricle elongates and its apex is displaced downward, to the left, and posteriorly (Fig. 49–4). When the dilatation is due to coronary artery disease or primary myocardial disease, the ventricle tends to assume a more globular shape. In the lateral view, the downward extension of the enlarged left ventricle covers more of the vena caval shadow than normal, and the crossing point of their posterior borders occurs nearer to the diaphragm than normal. Unfortunately, the usefulness of this sign is limited because of the distortion produced by even slight rotation of the patient from the true lateral position.

Enlargement of the left ventricle produces a smoothly curved dilatation of the lower portion of the cardiac silhouette. A localized bulge in this contour most often represents a ventricular aneurysm (Fig.

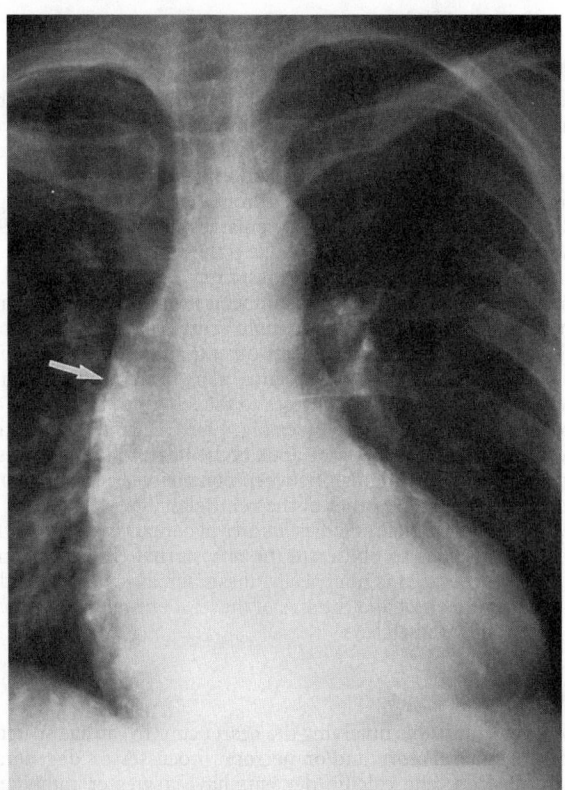

FIGURE 49–4 • Left ventricular dilatation, aortic insufficiency. The apex of the heart is displaced downward and to the left. The ascending aorta (arrow) is diffusely dilated. The pulmonary vasculature is normal.

49–5). Dilatation of the left ventricle is usually associated with elevation of left ventricular end-diastolic pressure. The latter increases the resistance to left atrial emptying and can result in dilation of the atrium. Therefore, left atrial enlargement in the presence of a large left ventricle does not necessarily indicate the presence of mitral valve disease.

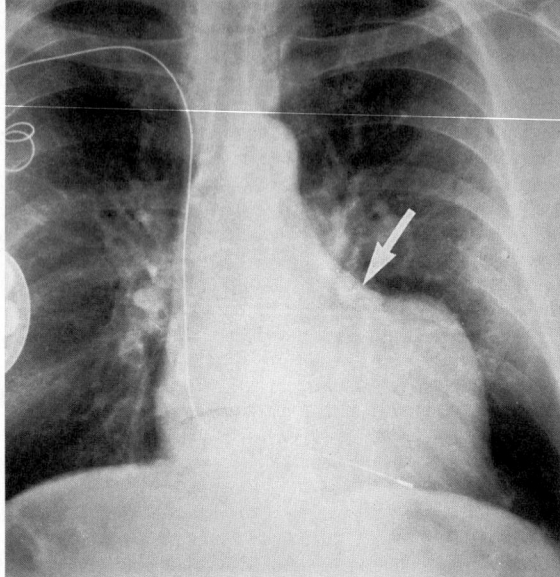

FIGURE 49–5 • Left ventricular aneurysm. A bulge on the lower portion of the left cardiac border, formed by the anterolateral wall of the left ventricle, represents a ventricular aneurysm. The patient had suffered a myocardial infarct 1 year previously. The left atrial appendage segment (arrow) is normal. A transvenous pacemaker has been inserted through the right subclavian vein. The electrode tip is situated in the apex of the right ventricle.

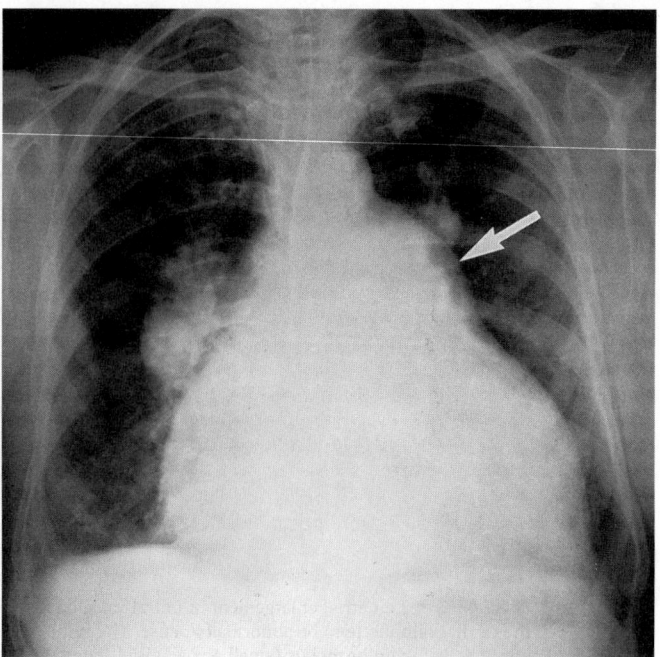

FIGURE 49–6 • Right ventricular enlargement seen in a patient with resistive pulmonary hypertension secondary to an atrial septal defect. The main pulmonary artery (arrow) and the right pulmonary artery are markedly dilated. The left pulmonary artery was also dilated but is hidden by the heart in this view. The sudden "cutoff" of the vascular shadows just beyond the hila is characteristic of resistive pulmonary hypertension. Enlargement of the right ventricle is elevating the cardiac apex and displacing it to the left. Accentuation of the curvature of the lower right cardiac border and enlargement of the cardiac silhouette to the right are caused by dilatation of the right atrium.

RIGHT ATRIUM. Enlargement of only the right chambers of the heart is seen in severe pulmonary hypertension without coexisting left heart failure, in bacterial endocarditis of the tricuspid and/or pulmonic valve, and in the carcinoid syndrome. Dilatation of the right atrium causes an accentuation and outward bowing of the curvature on the lower half of the right cardiac contour in the frontal view. With greater degrees of dilatation, the cardiac silhouette enlarges to the right (Fig. 49–6).

RIGHT VENTRICLE. The right ventricle is the most difficult of the four cardiac chambers to evaluate on chest films. Except for a small area in the subpulmonic region, the chamber is not border forming in the frontal projection. Even moderate right ventricular enlargement may produce no abnormality in this view other than some elevation of the main pulmonary artery. As right ventricular size increases, the transverse diameter of the heart enlarges to the left, and the cardiac apex becomes blunted and elevated (see Fig. 49–6). Enlargement of either or both ventricles displaces the apex of the heart to the left. It is not often possible to distinguish between biventricular enlargement or dilatation of one or the other of the ventricles.

As the right ventricle enlarges, its area of contact with the sternum increases and tends to obliterate the retrosternal clear space in the lateral view. This sign is nonspecific inasmuch as it also depends on the shape of the chest and the size of the left ventricle, as well as the size of the right ventricle.

Calcification

Most calcifications involving the heart occur in cardiac structures owing to inflammatory and/or necrotic processes or degenerative disease. Because the calcific deposits have a greater radiodensity than the cardiac tissues, they can often be seen within the cardiac silhouette.

The aortic and mitral valves abut each other, both inserting on the central fibrous tendon of the heart. On a frontal chest film, the two valves lie next to each other in the midportion of the cardiac silhouette, to the left of the spine (Fig. 49–7A), the aortic valve being slightly higher. It is often difficult to determine which valve is calcified in this view. They can be separated by fluoroscopy as the aortic valve tends to move in a vertical direction as the heart beats, while the motion of the mitral valve approximates the horizontal. This distinction can also be accurately made from the lateral chest film. If a line is drawn from the left main bronchus, seen as a dark circular shadow over the lower extreme of the trachea, to the anterior costophrenic angle, then

the mitral valve lies below the line and the aortic valve is above it (see Fig. 49–7B).

In the United States, calcification of the aortic valve is most likely to represent degenerative disease of the cusps (a process in older patients akin to coronary artery calcification) or deterioration of a congenitally bicuspid valve (Chapter 72). In developing countries, calcification of the aortic and/or mitral valves is usually a late sequela of rheumatic fever. Calcification of the mitral annulus, which is seen in patients older than age 70 years and which is about four times more frequent in women than men, is only rarely of clinical significance. The pattern of calcification is characteristic and should not be confused with that of the mitral valve. Calcium is deposited mainly between the base of the posterior mitral leaflet and the posterior wall of the left ventricle. It is seen as a broad, curvilinear band of calcium in a "C" shape, open superiorly and to the right on the frontal film and anteriorly on the lateral. In severe cases, the calcific deposits may also extend across the base of the anterior mitral leaflet and then form an "O" encircling the mitral orifice.

Calcification of the myocardium almost always indicates a previous transmural infarction and, frequently, a ventricular aneurysm. The calcified scar appears as a fine, curvilinear density, most commonly on the anterolateral aspect of the heart, best seen in the frontal view (Fig. 49–8A), or in the lower portion of the interventricular septum, best seen in the lateral projection (see Fig. 49–8B). Calcification of the pericardium is usually coarser and tends to occur in clumps. Often, pericardial calcium is distributed primarily over the interventricular sulcus and the atrioventricular grooves, but when extensive, the deposits may coalesce and completely surround the heart (Fig. 49–9).

Calcification of the coronary arteries is a specific sign of complicated atheromatous plaques in which previous hemorrhage has occurred. Not uncommonly, this type of plaque, which may not produce significant narrowing of the vessel, is the site of acute thrombosis and vascular occlusion leading to myocardial infarction. There is no correlation between the sites of calcium deposition and the sites of greatest stenosis, but a strong correlation exists between the extent of coronary artery calcification and the extent of coronary arterial sclerosis.

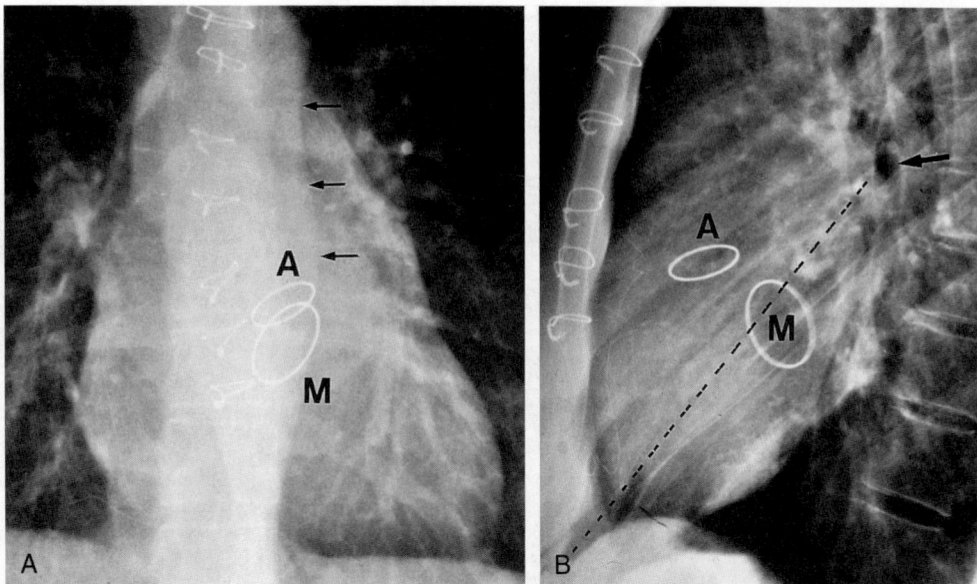

FIGURE 49–7 • Location of the mitral and aortic valves. Both the mitral and aortic valves have been replaced by porcine heterografts. The circular stents indicate the location and tilt of each valve. M = mitral valve; A = aortic valve. *A*, Frontal projection. The two valves are normally in contact with each other, and it is difficult to separate them in the frontal projection. Furthermore, on a routinely exposed film, calcific deposits are not easily seen because of the overlapping shadows of the descending aorta (arrows) and the spine. *B*, Lateral projection. The valves can be differentiated on the lateral view by drawing a line from the left main bronchus (arrow) to the anterior costophrenic sulcus. The aortic valve lies above this line and the mitral valve below it.

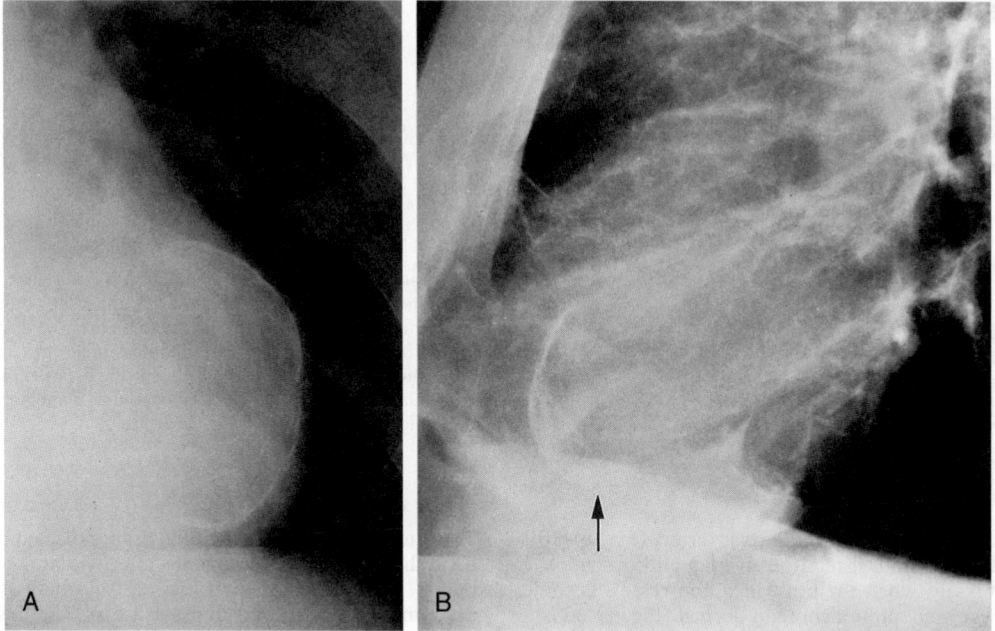

FIGURE 49–8 • Calcified myocardial infarcts. *A*, Patient 1: Frontal projection of an anterolateral left ventricular aneurysm. The fine calcific line outlines an anterolateral aneurysm of the left ventricle. The calcific deposit is much finer than that seen with pericardial calcification. The patient had suffered a myocardial infarction several years earlier. *B*, Patient 2: Lateral projection of a septal infarction. The curvilinear calcific deposit is within the scarred lower portion of the ventricular septum. The infarct extended posteriorly along the base of the heart to involve the diaphragmatic wall of the left ventricle (arrow).

Calcification of the coronary arteries is difficult to visualize on chest films because the deposits are thin and their shadows are blurred by the motion of the heart. Ultrafast computed tomography (CT) scanning, using either an electron beam CT or a helical CT, is very sensitive and accurate for detecting and quantifying the extent of coronary arterial calcification (Chapter 52). However, the accumulated data to date have not clearly shown a correlation between the volume of coronary calcification and the clinical status of the patient. Although high calcium scores indicate severe atherosclerosis, acute events, such as myocardial infarction or sudden death, can occur in patients with little or no calcification of their coronary arteries.

Pericardial Effusion

The pericardium completely invests the heart, except for a small area on its posterior surface between the entrances of the pulmonary veins and the superior and inferior venae cavae. When fluid accumulates in the pericardium, the sac distends smoothly to enlarge the cardiac silhouette and give it a flask-shaped appearance. A similar shape can occur with a dilated, failing heart.

Differentiation of the two conditions is readily made from the appearance of the pulmonary hila on a frontal chest film. The pericardial sac extends onto the great vessels and up to or slightly above

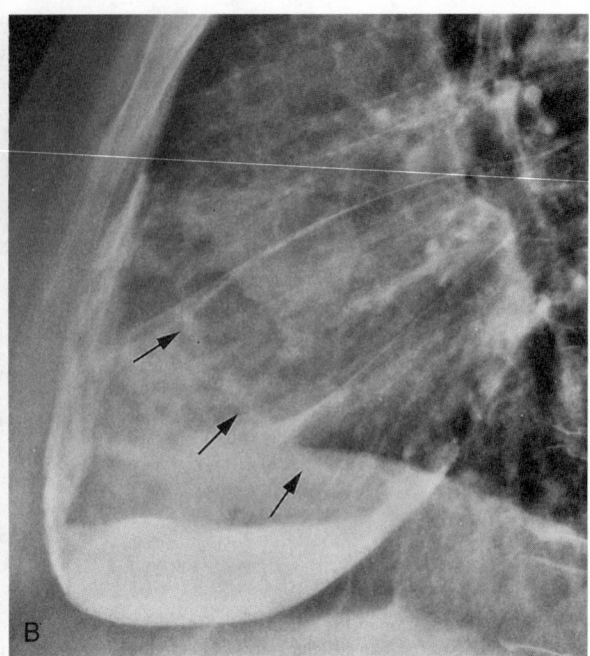

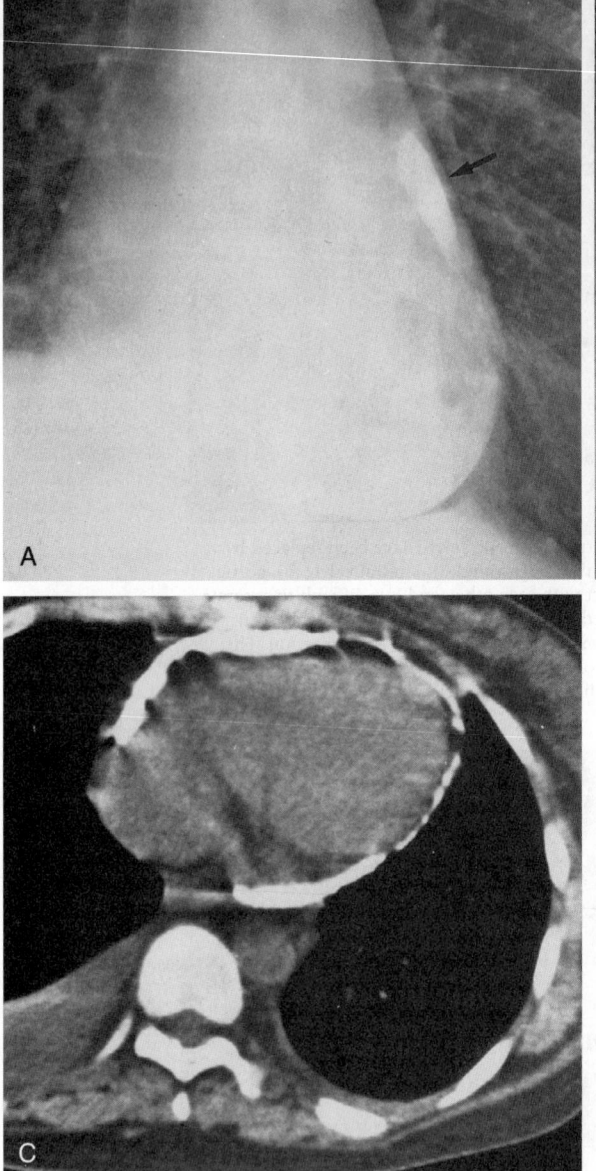

FIGURE 49–9 • Calcific pericarditis. *A*, Frontal projection. A large, thick, calcific plaque (arrow) lies just below the level of the left upper lobe bronchus. More caudad, the calcific deposits become confluent and cover the diaphragmatic surface of the heart. *B*, The dense calcific peel around the cardiac apex and the diaphragmatic aspect of the heart is better seen. Linear calcific deposits (arrows) lie within the atrioventricular sulcus. *C*, Nonenhanced computed tomography shows the irregular, thick, calcific peel almost encircling the heart.

the level of the bifurcation of the main pulmonary artery (Fig. 49–10). As the sac distends with fluid, it tends to overlap and obscure the hilar vessels. Conversely, when the heart fails, the vessels become congested and appear more prominent than normal (Fig. 49–11).

Posterior displacement of the epicardial fat line is a second reliable sign of pericardial effusion (Chapter 74). In adults, fat is often insinuated between the myocardium and the visceral pericardium (the epicardium) and is sometimes seen in the lateral projection as a curvilinear, radiolucent shadow paralleling the anterior aspect of the heart. The anterior surface of the parietal pericardium borders the retrosternal mediastinal fat. The soft tissue density between these two fat lines therefore represents the pericardium, the epicardium, and the fluid between them. When normal, this stripe is no more than 1 to 2 mm thick. As fluid accumulates in the pericardial sac, the epicardial fat line is displaced posteriorly and the pericardial stripe widens (Fig. 49–12).

Pulmonary Vasculature

Almost all of the linear shadows in the lung represent large and medium-sized pulmonary arteries and veins. The terminal branches of the vessels are too small to be visualized as individual structures.

The same is true of the interstitial tissues that support the alveoli and form the primary and secondary interlobular septa. However, summation of the minimal densities cast by these structures gives the pulmonary fields an overall grayish cast. The large vessels are seen because their soft tissue density is set off against the surrounding air-containing alveoli.

The caliber of the pulmonary vessels reflects the volume of blood flowing through the lungs. When this volume is diminished because of a right-to-left shunt, venous blood bypasses the pulmonary vessels and consequently these vessels are smaller in caliber and the lungs appear abnormally radiolucent. Increased size and prominence of the pulmonary vessels, both central and peripheral, usually indicate an increase in pulmonary blood flow secondary to a left-to-right shunt (Fig. 49–13A). The vessels in the lower as well as the upper lung fields are dilated. Although pulmonary arteries and veins also become abnormally prominent in heart failure, the vessels are not usually sharply outlined, and additional signs of pulmonary venous hypertension or interstitial edema are present (Chapter 64).

The vessels to the lower lobes carry about 60 to 70% of the pulmonary blood flow and are normally of greater caliber than the vessels to the upper lobes. As pulmonary venous pressure increases, the lower lobe vessels become constricted, so more blood is distributed to the

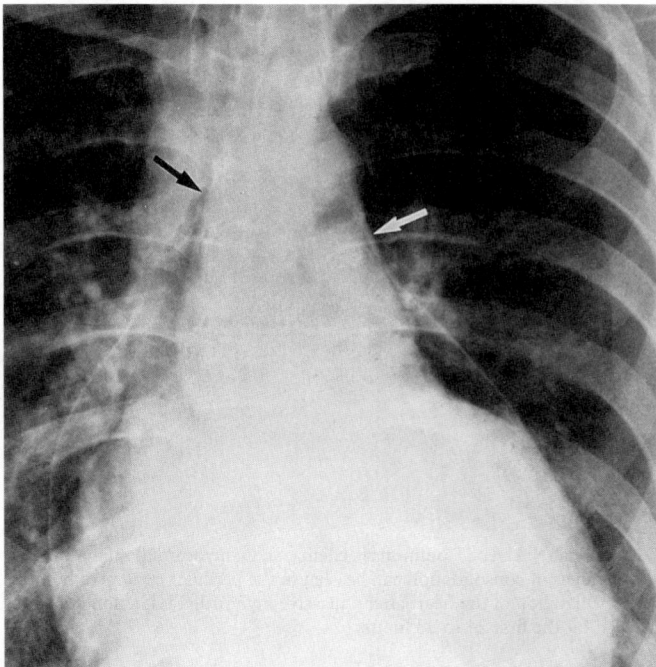

FIGURE 49–10 • The superior pericardial reflection with effusion following a tap. During pericardiocentesis, some of the withdrawn fluid was replaced with air. The normal pericardium is now outlined between the intrapericardial air and the air in the lungs and is seen as a thin linear shadow along the outer border of the cardiac silhouette. The film is made in the erect position and the air has risen to the highest point of the pericardial cavity (arrows), above the level of the pulmonary hila and almost reaching the aortic arch.

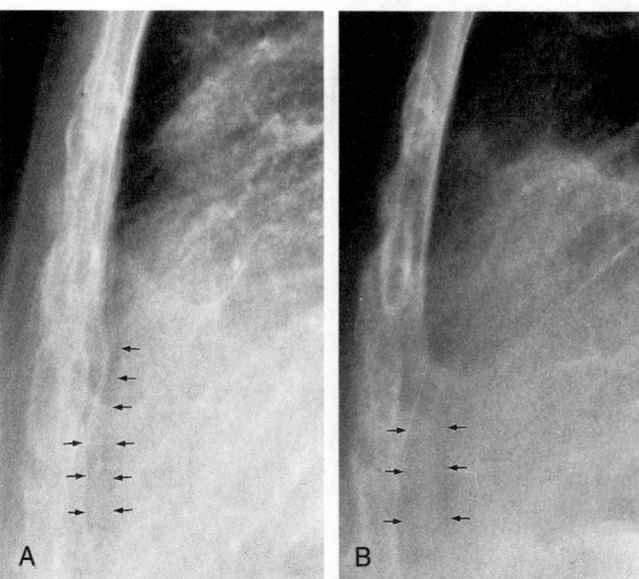

FIGURE 49–12 • Pericardial effusion with posterior displacement of the epicardial fat line. The two lines of arrows point to the substernal fat and the subepicardial fat layers. *A*, Normal. The fine line of soft tissue density between the fat layers represents the epicardium, the pericardium, and the fluid between them. *B*, Same patient with a pericardial effusion. The epicardial fat line is displaced posteriorly, and the pericardial stripe is abnormally wide.

upper lobes, which makes their vessels more prominent. This redistribution of the pulmonary vasculature is a reliable sign of pulmonary venous hypertension (see Fig. 49–13B), although it is often difficult to recognize unless quite marked. With a sufficient further increase in venous pressure, pulmonary edema develops.

PULMONARY EDEMA. Normally, extravascular circulation of fluid in the lungs from the capillaries through the interstitium and back to the blood stream by way of the lymphatics is constant. When pulmonary venous pressure increases, more and more fluid leaks from the capillary bed, the capacity of the lymphatics to remove the fluid is exceeded, and the interstitium becomes waterlogged. Because the

interlobular septa in the outer portions of the lung bases are oriented parallel to the x-ray beam on an erect film, when thickened, they are seen as parallel, short horizontal lines extending to the pleural surfaces (Kerley B lines). Kerley A lines also represent thickened interlobular septa, but they are longer and are seen in the upper lung fields. These lines are within the depth of the lung and usually do not reach the pleural surface. Most of the other septa, even when thickened, are too fine to be identified as individual structures. However, the summation pattern creates random "noise" on the film that obscures the shadows of the pulmonary vessels (Fig. 49–14). A ground-glass appearance of the lung fields without identifiable vascular markings within them is characteristic of interstitial pulmonary edema (Chapter 56). The patient is usually severely tachypneic at this stage, but rales may not be present. Interstitial edema also causes thickening of the bronchial walls and peribronchial connective tissue best seen where they are projected on end. This "peribronchial cuffing"

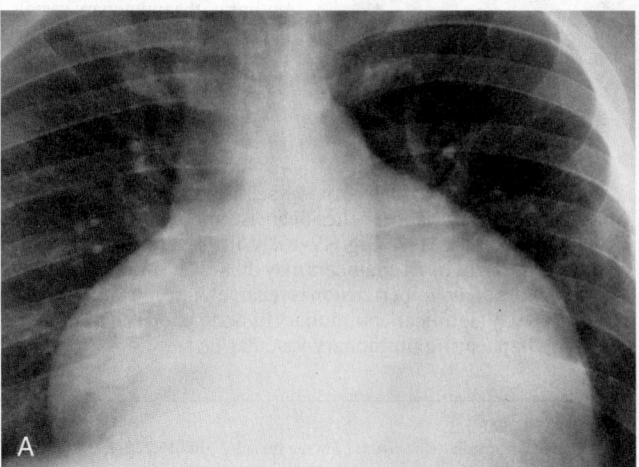

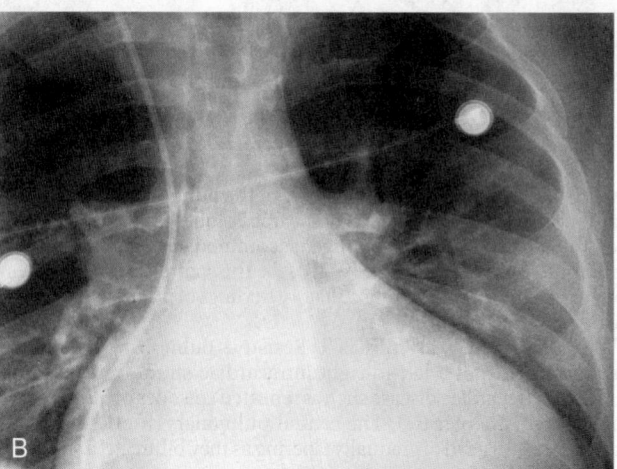

FIGURE 49–11 • Hilum overlay sign. *A*, Pericardial effusion. The heart is diffusely enlarged. Its silhouette extends outward and obscures the hilar shadows in each lung. *B*, Dilated cardiomyopathy. The heart is diffusely enlarged. The failing left ventricle has caused congestion of the hilar vessels and they are more prominent than normal.

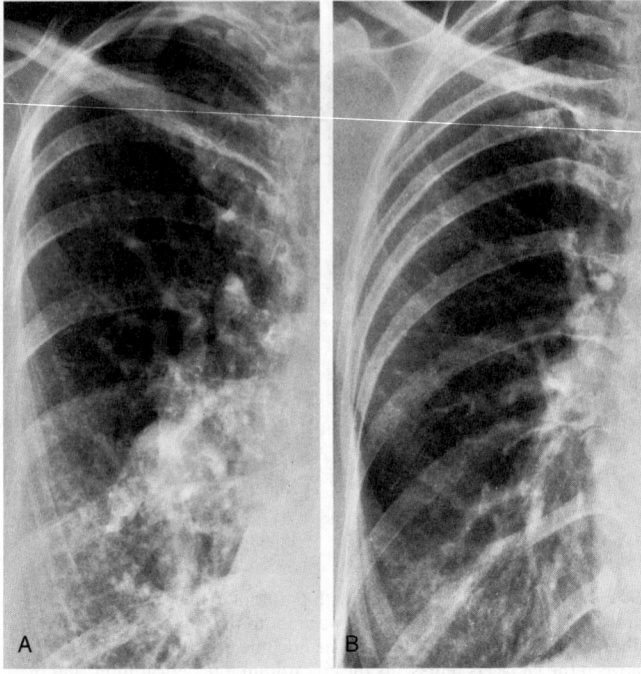

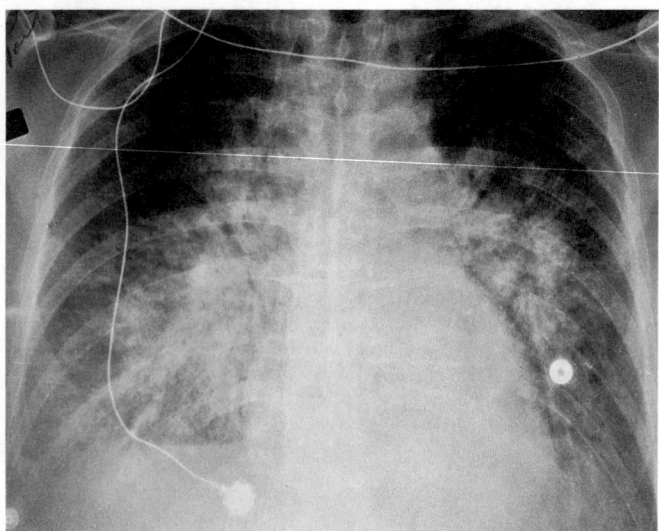

FIGURE 49–15 • Alveolar pulmonary edema, acute myocardial infarction. Patchy areas of consolidation can be seen in the perihilar regions of both lungs. Dilatation of the heart after a massive myocardial infarction may not be seen for the first 24 to 48 hours.

FIGURE 49–13 • Pulmonary vasculature. A, Atrial septal defect, left-to-right shunt. All pulmonary vessels, to the lower lobes as well as the upper lobes, are dilated, which is indicative of increased blood flow. B, Mitral stenosis, pulmonary venous hypertension with redistribution of the pulmonary vasculature. The lower lobe vessels are constricted and the upper vessels, which now carry more blood, are of greater caliber.

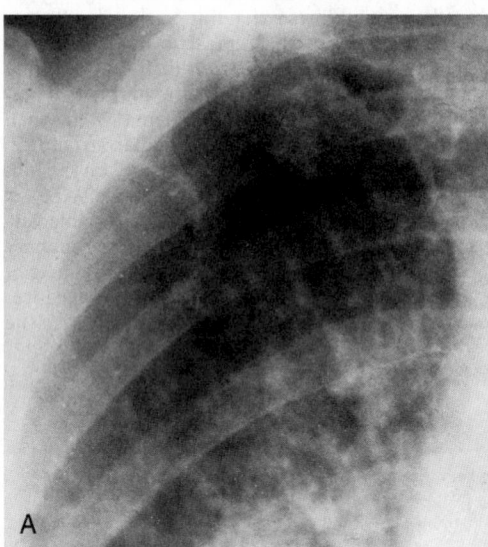

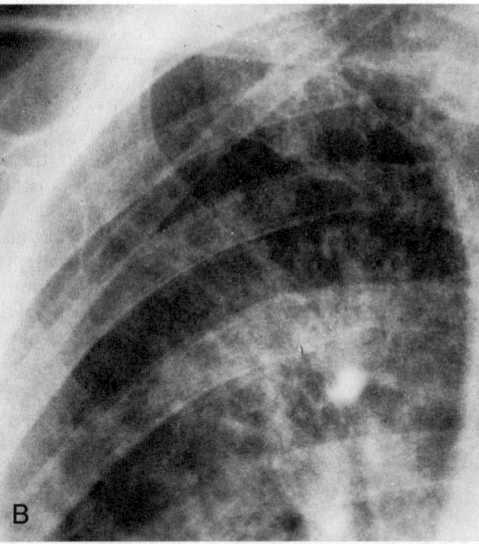

FIGURE 49–14 • Interstitial pulmonary edema. A, Close-up of the right upper lobe; portable film of a patient with an acute myocardial infarct. The pulmonary vessels are well outlined. B, Two days later, the patient became tachypneic. No abnormal auscultatory findings were present in the lungs. Radiographically, the lung fields are noisy, with numerous random shadows obscuring the outline of the pulmonary vessels. The appearance and the time sequence of the changes are characteristic of interstitial pulmonary edema.

is best visualized in the superior portion of the pulmonary hila, where the anterior segmental bronchus of the upper lobes is viewed on end. When the interstitium can no longer accommodate the excess fluid, it spills into the alveoli (Fig. 49–15). At this point, as air bubbles through the fluid, the typical auscultatory findings of pulmonary edema appear.

PULMONARY ARTERIAL HYPERTENSION. Resistive pulmonary hypertension can result from a left-to-right intracardiac shunt, mitral valve disease, or extracardiac disease such as repeated episodes of pulmonary embolization (Chapter 64). The central pulmonary arteries become grossly dilated. Instead of gradually tapering as they bifurcate, a sudden, sharp change in the caliber of the vessels is noted. The size and number of the smaller arterial branches decrease and take on the appearance of a "pruned tree" (see Fig. 49–6). With severe pulmonary hypertension, the right heart chambers may dilate. The radiographic appearance of pulmonary hypertension is relatively specific but not sensitive, and clinically significant pulmonary hypertension can be present with a normal-appearing pulmonary vascular bed.

SUGGESTED READING
Baron MG: The cardiac silhouette. J Thorac Imaging 2000;15:230–242.

50 ELECTROCARDIOGRAPHY

Nora Goldschlager

The electrocardiogram (ECG) is a recording of the electrical potentials produced by cardiac tissue. Formation of electrical impulses occurs within the conduction system of the heart. When excited, or depolarized, atrial and ventricular myocardial muscle fibers contract. The electrical currents produced by these electrical impulses spread through the body and are recorded from the body surface by applying electrodes at various body surface points and connecting them to a recording apparatus.

The ECG is a valuable diagnostic tool to evaluate conduction delay of atrial and ventricular electrical impulses, origin of arrhythmias, myocardial ischemia and infarction, atrial and ventricular hypertrophy, pericarditis, the effect of cardiac drugs (especially digitalis and certain antiarrhythmic agents), disturbances in electrolyte balance (especially potassium), the function of electronic cardiac pacemakers, and systemic diseases that affect the heart. A patient with heart disease may have a normal ECG, and a normal individual may have an abnormal ECG.

LEAD SYSTEMS

12-Lead Electrocardiogram (I, II, III, aVR, aVL, aVF, V₁₋₆)

Bipolar standard leads (I, II, and III) record electrical potentials in the frontal plane. Electrodes are applied to the arms and legs; the right leg electrode serves as the ground. Lead I reflects the potential difference between the left and right arms, lead II reflects the potential difference between the left leg and right arm, and lead III reflects the potential difference between the left leg and left arm. The electrical potential recorded from any one extremity is the same regardless of where the electrode is placed on the extremity. In a patient with tremor, an ECG relatively free of muscle "noise" can be obtained by applying the electrodes to the upper portions of the limbs. In exercise testing and in ambulatory ECG recordings, the electrodes are applied near or on the torso. Similar electrode placements are used in patients with bandaged extremities and in patients who have had amputations.

A *unipolar* lead records electrical potentials from the small area of tissue underlying the lead and all the electrical events of the cardiac cycle as viewed from that recording site. The frontal plane unipolar leads (aVR, aVL, and aVF) are related to the standard bipolar leads (I, II, and III). The precordial (V) leads record potentials in the horizontal plane without being influenced by potentials from an "indifferent" electrode. The recording of right ventricular and posterior leads (Table 50–1 and Fig. 50–1) has become important in the evaluation of patients with suspected acute ischemic symptoms involving these areas. Esophageal leads record atrial and ventricular potentials as seen from the esophagus, and intracardiac leads record potentials from the chamber or site in which they are positioned.

Cardiac Vector

The frontal plane vector, or axis, is the sum of the electrical potentials of the cardiac cycle as reflected in the frontal plane of the body. By combining frontal plane bipolar leads I, II, and III with frontal

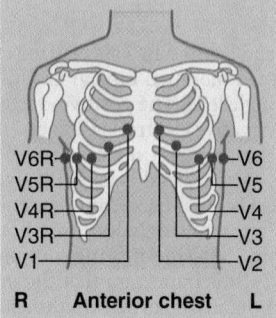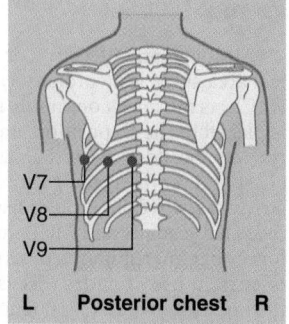

FIGURE 50–1 • Position of unipolar precordial leads on the body surface. The standard V leads (*A*) are placed in the anterior chest and routinely include V₁ (fourth intercostal space, right sternal border), V₂ (fourth intercostal space, left sternal border), V₃ (equidistant between V₂ and V₄), V₄ (fifth intercostal space, left midclavicular line), V₅ (anterior axillary line, in the same horizontal plane as V₄), and V₆ (midaxillary line). Supplemental leads include V₇ (posterior axillary line), V₈ (posterior scapular line), and V₉ (left border of the spine). The right-sided leads, V₃₋₉, are used when right ventricular myocardial infarction is suspected (Chapter 69) or in patients with situs inversus (Chapter 65). Posterior leads, V₇₋₉ (*B*), are reserved for suspected posterior wall myocardial infarction (Chapter 69).

plane unipolar leads aVR, aVL, and aVF, a hexaxial reference system that illustrates all six leads of the frontal plane can be constructed (Fig. 50–2); the mean QRS, P, and T wave vectors in the frontal plane can be approximated by determining their net magnitudes and direction in any two of the three standard leads. The normal QRS axis lies between 0 and +90 degrees; superior axis deviation (between −45 and −90 degrees) and right axis deviation (between +90 and ±180 degrees) are considered abnormal. Leftward deviation of the mean frontal plane QRS axis can occur with advancing age in the absence of clinically overt heart disease. The normal frontal plane P wave and T wave axes usually correspond to the normal QRS axis and point in the same general direction. The unipolar precordial leads approximate the electrical potentials (vectors) in the horizontal plane.

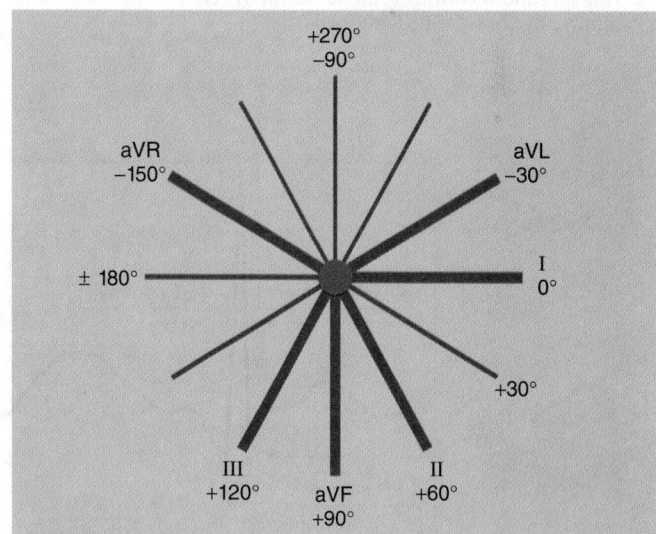

FIGURE 50–2 • Hexaxial reference system depicting frontal plane ECG leads. By convention, the positive pole of lead I is designated as 0 degrees and the negative pole as ±180 degrees; the positive pole of aVF is designated as +90 degrees and the negative pole as +270 degrees or −90 degrees; the positive pole of aVR is designated as +210 degrees or −150 degrees; and the positive pole of aVL is designated as +330 degrees or −30 degrees. If a perpendicular line is drawn through the center of a given lead axis, any electrical force (vector) oriented in the positive half of the electrical field records an upright deflection in that lead; any force oriented in the negative half of the electrical field records a downward deflection. (Adapted from Goldschlager N, Goldman MJ: Principles of Clinical Electrocardiography, 13th ed. Norwalk, CT, Appleton & Lange, 1989. The McGraw-Hill Co, Inc.)

Table 50–1 • **SOME CAUSES OF LOW VOLTAGE* IN THE ELECTROCARDIOGRAM**

Anasarca
Pneumothorax
Pleural effusion
Pericardial effusion
Obesity
Emphysema
Hypothyroidism
Infiltrative myocardial diseases (e.g., amyloid)

---

*QRS complexes less than 5 mm in limb leads or less than 10 mm in precordial leads.

Monitor Leads

Although any ECG lead or leads can be used in a specialized clinical area such as a coronary care unit, a modified bipolar chest lead (MCL) is the most commonly used single lead. The positive electrode is placed in the V_1 position, and the negative electrode is placed near the left shoulder; a third electrode is placed at a remote area of the chest and serves as the ground. This "MCL_1" lead is useful to evaluate cardiac rhythm. Bipolar lead II also is often used. Simultaneously recorded leads II and MCL_1 are preferred to single lead monitoring for proper interpretation of arrhythmias. Most monitoring equipment in current use provides this capability. It is important that the monitoring lead or leads be documented on any recorded rhythm strips so as to avoid erroneous diagnoses based on improper interpretation of P-QRS morphologies depicted in that lead. To monitor the patient for ST and T wave abnormalities resulting from ischemia, the positive electrode can be placed in any position that has been noted previously to show the abnormality.

Electrocardiogram Grid

ECG paper is graph paper with horizontal and vertical lines at 1-mm intervals (Fig. 50–3) with a heavier line every 5 mm. Time is measured along the horizontal lines with 1 mm = 0.04 second. Voltage is measured along the vertical lines and is expressed as millimeters (10 mm = 1 mV). In routine clinical practice, the recording speed is 25 mm per second. The usual calibration is a 1-mV signal that produces a 10-mm deflection. "Double standard," sometimes useful for identifying the atrial rhythm in patients with tachycardia or for evaluating PQRST complexes in patients with low voltage, produces a 20-mm deflection; "half standard," useful when a markedly increased voltage precludes optimal visualization of QRS morphology, produces a 5-mm deflection; and "quarter standard," useful when recording intracardiac electrograms, produces a 2.5-mm deflection. Every ECG should be accompanied by a standard to interpret the tracing properly, particularly because low voltage can suggest important clinical conditions (see Table 50–1); currently available page-writing ECG machines, which record multiple leads simultaneously, automatically inscribe the selected standard. The recording speed also is inscribed automatically in currently available page-writing machines and should be noted: 50 mm/second recordings can be misinterpreted as bradycardia or as abnormally long PQRST intervals, whereas 12.5 mm/second recordings can be misinterpreted as tachycardia or as abnormally short PQRST intervals.

CELLULAR ELECTROPHYSIOLOGY OF THE HEART

See also Chapter 57.

Cell Depolarization and Repolarization

Four electrophysiologic events are involved in generating the ECG: (1) impulse formation in the primary pacemaker of the heart (usually the sinoatrial [SA] node); (2) impulse transmission through specialized conduction fibers; (3) activation (depolarization) of myocardial tissue; and (4) repolarization (recovery) of the myocardium. The potential difference between the inside and outside of the cell is known as the resting membrane potential, which is determined mainly by the 30:1 intracellular-to-extracellular potassium gradient across the membrane. The resting potential in most cardiac cells, with the exception of cells of the SA and atrioventricular (AV) nodal areas, is −80 to −90 mV.

When cell depolarization begins, an abrupt change occurs in membrane permeability to sodium. Sodium and, to a lesser extent, calcium ions enter the cell through their respective channels, resulting in a sharp rise of intracellular potential to about ±20 mV. This phase of depolarization is designated *phase 0* and reflects the sodium-dependent fast inward current typical of working myocardial cells and Purkinje fibers. The maximum rate of depolarization of ventricular cells is 200 volts/second, and that of atrial cells is 100 to 200 volts/second. Pacemaker cells in the SA and AV nodes are depolarized by a calcium-dependent slow inward current. Under some abnormal conditions, such as ischemia, cells whose fast inward sodium current is inhibited are depolarized by slow inward calcium currents.

After cell depolarization, the potential gradually returns to resting potential. This repolarization process is characterized by *phase 1*—an initial rapid return of intracellular potential to 0 mV, largely the result of sodium channels closing; *phase 2*—a plateau resulting from calcium entering slowly into the cell and potassium exiting slowly from the cell; and *phase 3*—return of the intracellular potential to resting level, resulting from potassium extruding out of the cell. At the end of phase 3, the normal resting potential is re-established, and the excess of sodium and deficit of potassium ions are rectified by a sodium pump. In calcium-dependent cells (SA and AV nodal cells), the phases of repolarization are less well demarcated.

The summation of all phase 0 potentials of atrial myocardial cells results in the P wave inscribed in the surface ECG. Phase 2 corresponds to the PR segment, which follows the P wave, and phase 3 corresponds to the T_a wave of atrial repolarization. The summation

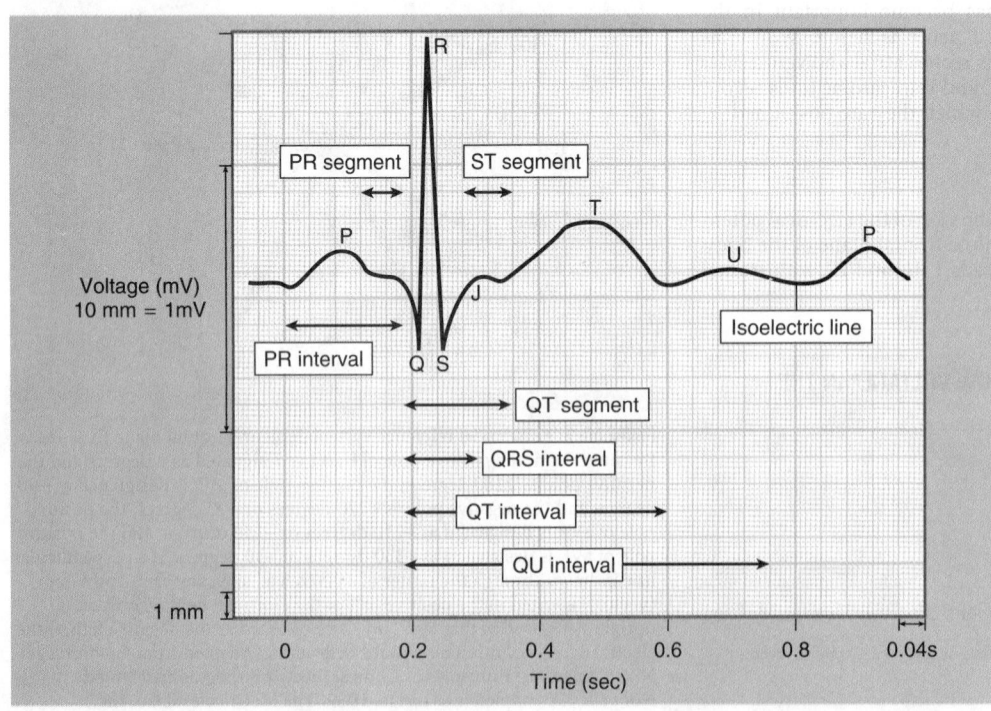

FIGURE 50–3 • Schematic illustration of the ECG grid and normal complexes, intervals, and segments. (Adapted from Goldschlager N, Goldman MJ: Principles of Clinical Electrocardiography, 13th ed. Norwalk, CT, Appleton & Lange, 1989. The McGraw-Hill Co, Inc.)

of phase 0 potentials of ventricular myocardial cells results in the QRS complex in the surface ECG. Phase 2 corresponds to the ST segment, and phase 3 corresponds to the T wave.

Excitation and Threshold Potential

Excitation of a cardiac cell occurs when a stimulus reduces the transmembrane potential to threshold potential (about −60 mV in atrial and ventricular muscle cells and about −40 mV in SA and AV nodal cells). If the resting membrane potential is raised toward the level of the threshold potential, a relatively weak stimulus can evoke a response. Conversely, if the resting potential is lowered away from the threshold potential, a relatively stronger stimulus is required to produce a response.

Refractoriness

The refractory period of myocardial cells and tissue consists of the absolute refractory period, during which no stimulus of any intensity can evoke a response, and a relative (effective) refractory period, during which only a strong stimulus can evoke a response. The relative refractory period begins at about the time the membrane potential reaches the threshold potential and ends just before the end of phase 3; it is followed by a period of supernormal excitability, during which a relatively weak stimulus can evoke a response. Factors that alter the duration of the action potential generally also alter the duration of the refractory period. In some circumstances (e.g., ischemia, hyperkalemia, and use of some antiarrhythmic agents), the duration of the refractory period can exceed the duration of the action potential.

Conduction Velocity

The velocity at which electrical impulses spread through the heart depends on the intrinsic properties of different portions of the conduction system and myocardium, including size, shape, and orientation of muscle cells, and presence and type of connective tissue. Conduction of action potentials from cell to cell occurs over specialized intercellular channels or gap junctions. Conduction velocity is most rapid in the His bundle and Purkinje system (about 2 m/second) and slowest in the SA and AV nodes (0.01 to 0.02 m/second); conduction in atrial and ventricular muscle is about 1 m/second.

NORMAL ELECTROCARDIOGRAM

Normal Complexes

The *P wave* is the deflection produced by atrial depolarization; it is normally 0.12 second long or less and is directed leftward and inferiorly in the frontal plane (see Fig. 50–3). An abnormally long P wave signifies an interatrial conduction delay, which could be due to conduction system disease or to atrial enlargement or hypertrophy. The QRS complex represents ventricular depolarization. The *Q* (*q*) *wave* is the initial negative deflection resulting from the onset of ventricular depolarization; the *R* (*r*) *wave* is the first positive deflection resulting from ventricular depolarization; and the *S* (*s*) *wave* is the negative deflection of ventricular depolarization that follows the first positive (R) wave. A *QS wave* signifies a negative deflection that does not rise above the baseline. An *R′* (*r′*) *wave* is a second positive deflection and follows an S wave; a negative deflection that follows the r′ is termed the s′ wave; if an s wave does not follow the initial R wave, the second positive deflection is still termed an R′ (r′) wave, and the QRS complex is described as an Rr′ (rR′) complex. Capital letters (Q, R, S) refer to waves greater than 5 mm; lowercase letters (q, r, s) refer to waves less than 5 mm. The morphology and axis of the QRS complex provide information regarding ventricular hypertrophy, myocardial infarction, and conduction delays in the bundle branches and myocardium. The *T wave* is the deflection produced by ventricular repolarization. The *U wave* is the (usually positive) deflection following the T wave and preceding the subsequent P wave; it is thought to be due to repolarization of the intraventricular (Purkinje) conduction system and often is accentuated in left ventricular hypertrophy. In some circumstances, such as hypokalemia and hypomagnesemia, the U wave is thought to represent an oscillatory membrane potential, called an *afterdepolarization*. Negative U waves, best seen in leads V_{4-6}, can be seen in acute myocardial ischemia (where they are insensitive but relatively specific markers of left anterior descending coronary artery disease) and left ventricular hypertrophy from any cause.

Normal Intervals

The *RR interval* is the interval between two consecutive R waves. If the ventricular rhythm is regular, this interval in seconds (or fractions of a second) divided into 60 (seconds) equals the heart rate per minute. If the ventricular rhythm is irregular, the number of R waves in a specific number of seconds is counted and converted into number per minute. The *PP interval* is the interval between two consecutive P waves. In regular sinus rhythm, the PP interval is the same as the RR interval. When the ventricular rhythm is irregular or when atrial and ventricular rhythms are regular but their rates are different from each other, the PP interval, measured from the same point (the onset of the P wave is preferred) on two successive P waves, is computed in the same manner as the ventricular rate. The *PR interval* measures the AV conduction time and includes the time required for atrial depolarization, normal conduction delay in the AV node (approximately 0.07 second), and impulse propagation through the His bundle and bundle branches to the onset of ventricular depolarization. The normal PR interval is 0.12 to 0.20 second and is related to heart rate and to prevailing autonomic tone (Table 50–2).

The *QRS interval* or duration represents ventricular depolarization time. The upper limit of normal is 0.11 second. Conduction delay in the bundle branches or in myocardial tissue results in a prolonged QRS interval. If the conduction delay is in one of the bundle branches, a specific ECG pattern of right or left bundle-branch block is recorded (Table 50–3 and Fig. 50–4).

Table 50–2 • COMMON CAUSES OF ATRIOVENTRICULAR CONDUCTION DELAYS

Hypervagotonia (often associated with sinus bradycardia or sinus arrhythmia)
Digitalis
β-Blocking drugs
Some calcium channel–blocking drugs (verapamil, diltiazem)
Class III antiarrhythmic agents (sotalol, amiodarone)
Coronary artery disease
Lenegre's disease (diffuse fibrosis of the conduction system)
Infiltrative heart disease
Aortic root disease (syphilis, spondylitis)
Calcification of the mitral and/or aortic annulus
Acute infectious disease
Myocarditis

Table 50–3 • SOME CAUSES OF BUNDLE-BRANCH BLOCK PATTERN

Clinically normal individual
Lenegre's disease (idiopathic fibrosis of the conduction tissue)
Lev's disease (calcification of the cardiac skeleton)
Cardiomyopathy
  Dilated
  Hypertrophic (concentric or asymmetric)
  Infiltrative
    Tumor
    Chagas' disease
    Myxedema
    Amyloidosis
Ischemic heart disease
  Acute myocardial infarction
  Remote myocardial infarction
  Coronary artery disease without myocardial infarction
Aortic stenosis
Infective endocarditis with abscesses in the conduction system
Cardiac trauma
Hyperkalemia
Ventricular hypertrophy
Rapid heart rates
Massive pulmonary embolism

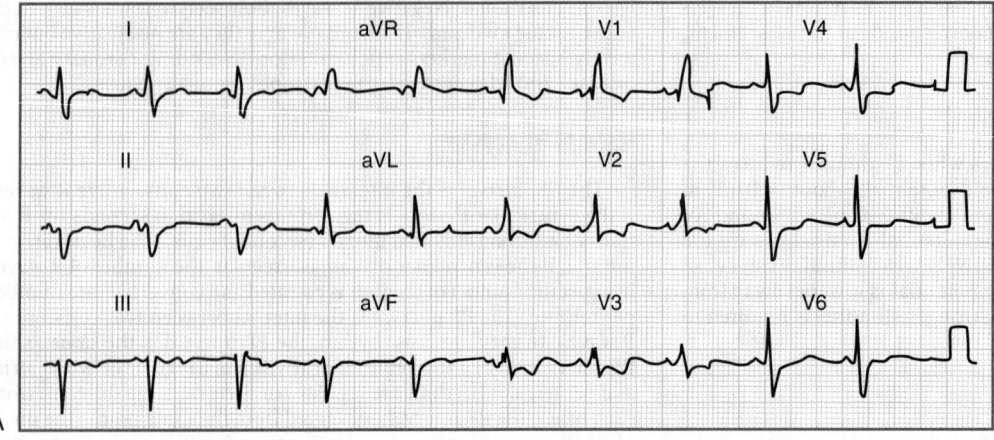

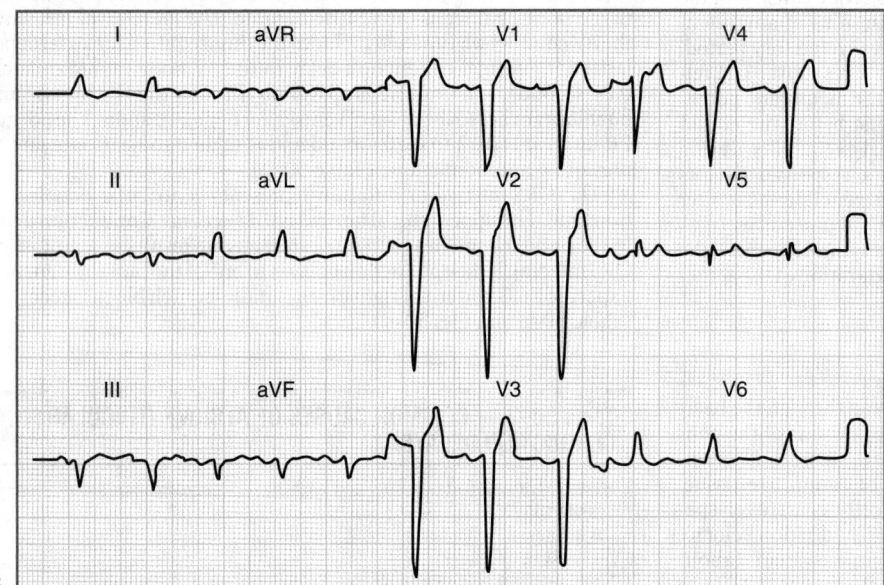

FIGURE 50-4 • *A,* A 12-lead ECG illustrates a markedly superior mean frontal plane QRS axis and right bundle-branch block (deep, wide S wave in leads I, aVL, and V$_{5-6}$ and rSR′ in V$_1$). The ST segments are downsloping and depressed in leads overlying the region of conduction delay and may represent secondary abnormalities. The QU interval also is abnormally prolonged. *B,* A 12-lead ECG illustrates left bundle-branch block, indicated by the notched broad QRS complex in leads overlying the left ventricle (I, aVL, V$_{5-6}$). The QRS axis is about −30 degrees, perhaps because of the left bundle-branch block.

The *QT interval* represents the duration of electrical systole and varies with heart rate and autonomic nervous system input. It includes the *QT segment,* which reflects calcium balance: A prolonged QT segment suggests hypocalcemia, whereas a short QT segment indicates hypercalcemia. The *QU interval* represents total ventricular repolarization time, including that of the Purkinje fibers. When the end of the T wave is not distinguished owing to superimposition of a U wave, the QT interval can be measured by extrapolating the apex of the T wave and its visible downsloping portion to the baseline. Alternatively the *QU interval* can be measured in place of the QT interval. An abnormally prolonged QU interval is potentially clinically significant in patients with ischemia, syncope, or ventricular arrhythmias and potassium and magnesium imbalance.

Normal Segments and Junctions

The *PR segment* is measured from the end of the P wave to the onset of the QRS complex; it is normally isoelectric but is often depressed in patients with ventricular hypertrophy or chronic pulmonary disease. PR-segment depression can carry over into the subsequent ST segment, mimicking true ST-segment depression. The *J junction* defines the point at which the QRS complex ends and the ST segment begins; it may not be easily discernible during rapid heart rates and in patients with hyperkalemia. It can be depressed or elevated relative to the isoelectric baseline.

The *ST segment* begins at the J point and ends at the onset of the T wave. This segment is usually isoelectric but may vary from −0.5 to +2 mm in the precordial leads; it is considered elevated or depressed compared with the portion of the baseline between the end of the T wave and the beginning of the P wave (TP segment). ST-segment abnormalities are important diagnostically in acute myocardial ischemia and infarction and pericarditis. The *TP segment* defines the portion of the tracing between the end of the T wave and the beginning of the next P wave; at normal heart rates, it is usually isoelectric. At rapid heart rates, the P wave encroaches on the T wave, eliminating the TP segment.

In addition to the standard 12-lead ECG, recordings are used during exercise or pharmacologic stress testing to document myocardial ischemia, for ambulatory monitoring to detect arrhythmias or ischemic ST-segment abnormalities, and for transtelephonic monitoring in patients with cardiac pacemakers or frequent rhythm disturbances. Newer ECG techniques such as body surface mapping (in which instantaneous depolarization and repolarization are plotted) and signal-averaged electrocardiography (in which the P wave and QRS complex are filtered to assess the presence of abnormal low-amplitude terminal potentials to predict the risk of an arrhythmic event) are now available (Chapter 58). The availability of computerized ECG interpretation allows for rapid initial screening, which may be useful in some clinical circumstances; however, physician over-read is mandatory for accurate interpretation.

STEPS IN ANALYZING AN ELECTROCARDIOGRAM

Identify the atrial rhythm and measure its rate (Fig. 50–5). Establishing the rate allows the atrial rhythm to be characterized as bradycardia (rate <50 beats per minute), normal (rate between 50 and 100 beats per minute), and tachycardia (rate >100 beats per minute). If atrial and ventricular rates are different from each other, their rates must be determined separately. Determine the regularity or irregularity of the rate. Irregular rhythms should be described further as totally irregular ("irregularly" irregular as in atrial fibrillation) or

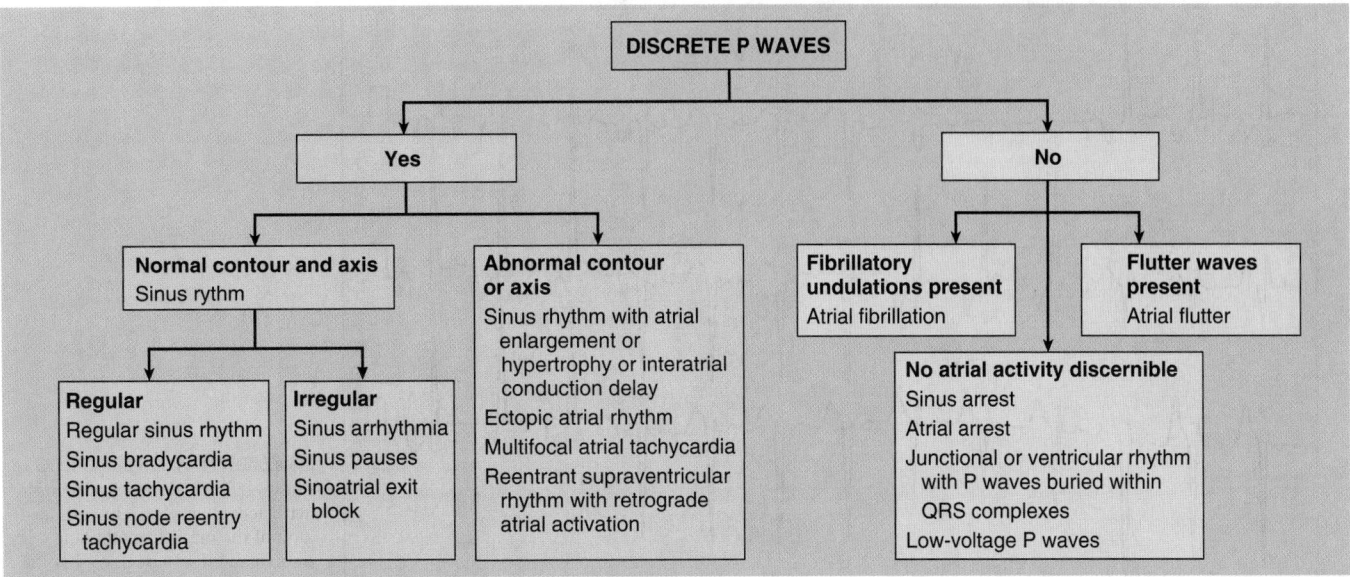

FIGURE 50–5 • An approach to the interpretation of the ECG rhythm based on the presence and type of P waves.

regular with periods of irregularity ("regularly" irregular as in atrial bigeminy).

Determine the P wave axis, duration, and morphology to provide information about the focus of origin of the atrial rhythm and whether the atria are being depolarized antegradely or retrogradely. If the atrial rhythm is sinus, the P wave morphology and duration can suggest the presence of atrial enlargement or hypertrophy or interatrial conduction delay (Fig. 50–6).

Identify the ventricular rate and whether it is regular or irregular. Ascertain whether the ventricular rate is associated with the atrial rhythm and what their relationships are: Is there one P wave for each QRS complex? Do the P waves precede or follow the QRS complexes? If the P wave follows the QRS complex, is it inverted in the inferior leads (II, III, and aVF), signifying retrograde atrial depolarization? What is the PR interval? Is it constant, or does it change?

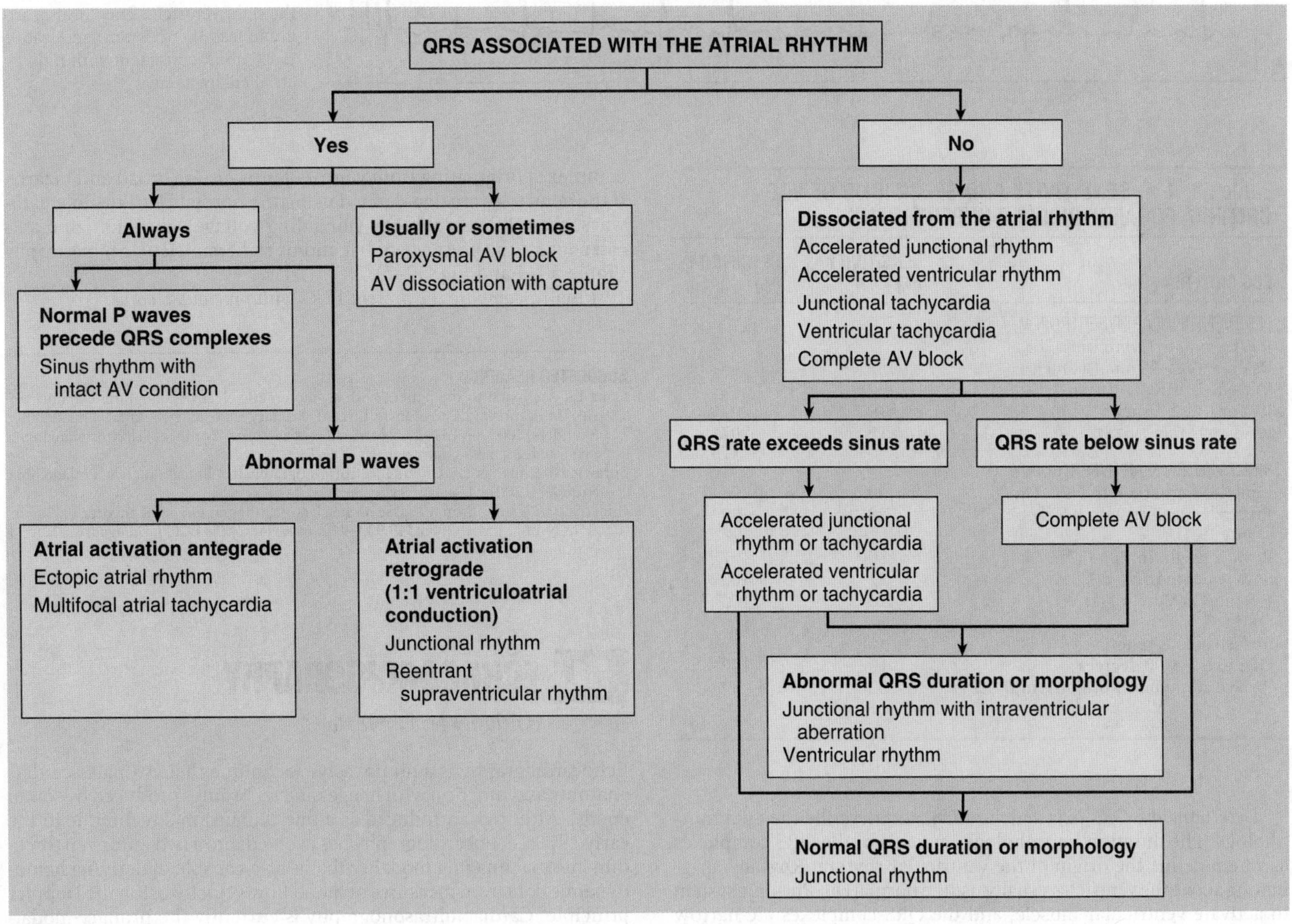

QRS ASSOCIATED WITH THE ATRIAL RHYTHM

Yes

Always

Normal P waves precede QRS complexes
Sinus rhythm with
  intact AV condition

Usually or sometimes
Paroxysmal AV block
AV dissociation with capture

Abnormal P waves

Atrial activation antegrade
Ectopic atrial rhythm
Multifocal atrial tachycardia

Atrial activation retrograde (1:1 ventriculoatrial conduction)
Junctional rhythm
Reentrant
  supraventricular rhythm

No

Dissociated from the atrial rhythm
Accelerated junctional rhythm
Accelerated ventricular rhythm
Junctional tachycardia
Ventricular tachycardia
Complete AV block

QRS rate exceeds sinus rate

Accelerated junctional
  rhythm or tachycardia
Accelerated ventricular
  rhythm or tachycardia

QRS rate below sinus rate

Complete AV block

Abnormal QRS duration or morphology
Junctional rhythm with intraventricular
  aberration
Ventricular rhythm

Normal QRS duration or morphology
Junctional rhythm

FIGURE 50–6 • An approach to the interpretation the ECG rhythm based on the relationship between the P wave and the QRS complex.

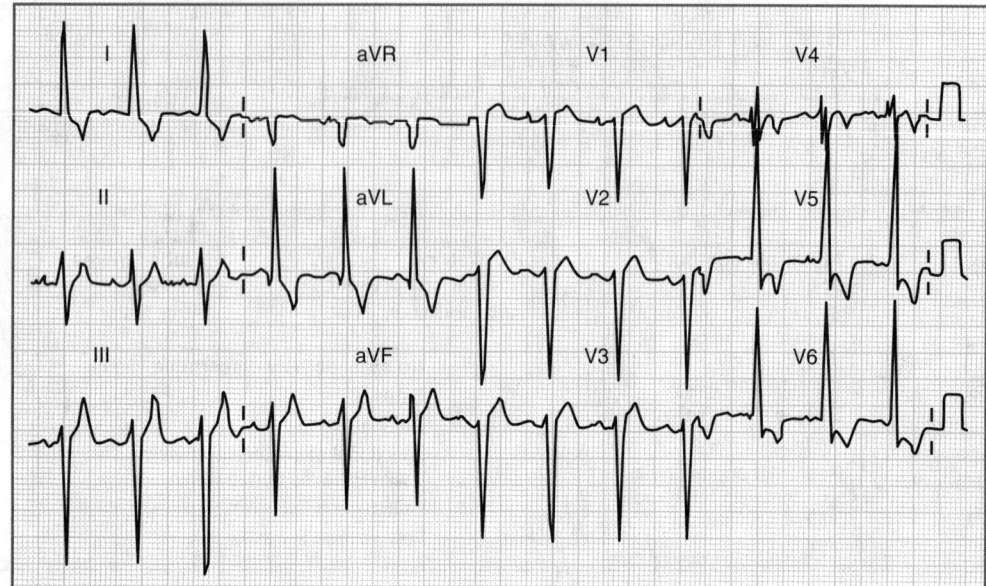

A

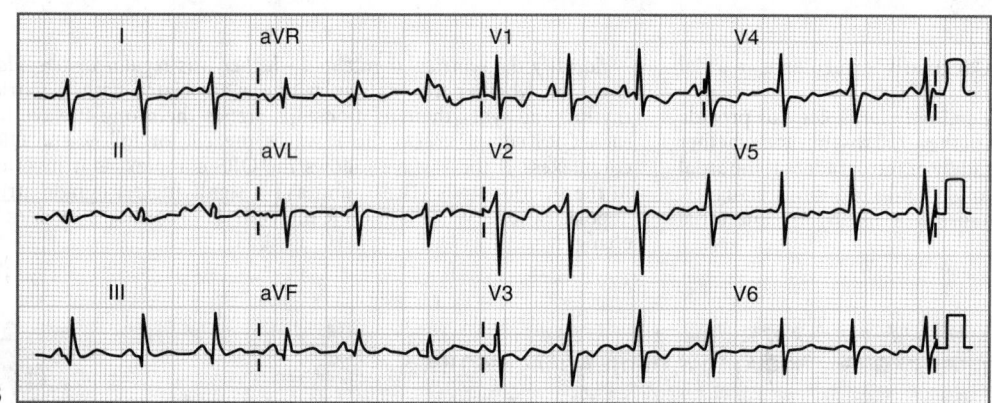

B

FIGURE 50–7 • *A,* A 12-lead ECG shows left ventricular hypertrophy with accompanying leftward deviation of the mean frontal plane QRS axis to about −40 degrees, J point and ST-segment elevation in precordial leads V_{1-3}, and depressed downsloping ST-T waves in leads overlying the left ventricle. The P waves are broad and notched, consistent with left atrial enlargement, a common accompaniment of left ventricular hypertrophy. *B,* A 12-lead ECG shows right ventricular hypertrophy with accompanying rightward deviation of the mean frontal plane QRS axis to greater than 120 degrees, a QRS complex in lead V, and depressed downsloping ST-T waves in leads overlying the right ventricle. The P waves are tall in lead II (>2.5 mm) and lead V (>1.5 mm), consistent with right atrial enlargement.

Table 50–4 • SENSITIVITY AND SPECIFICITY OF ECG CRITERIA FOR VENTRICULAR HYPERTROPHY

ECG CRITERIA	SENSITIVITY (%)	SPECIFICITY (%)
LEFT VENTRICULAR HYPERTROPHY		
RaVL + SV$_3$ > 25 mm (men) or		
RaVL + SV$_3$ > 20 mm (women)	42	95
SV$_1$ + RV$_5$ or RV$_6$ > 35 mm	29	93
RV$_5$ or RV$_6$ ≥ 25 mm	19	97
RaVL > 11 mm	18	97
RIGHT VENTRICULAR HYPERTROPHY		
Limb lead criteria R in I ≤ 0.2 mV	40	98
Precordial lead criteria R/S ratio in V$_1$ > 1	28	99
R wave height in V$_1$ > 0.7 mV	30	97
S wave depth in V$_1$ < 0.2 mV	22	100
R/S ratio in V$_5$ or V$_6$ < 1.0	10	100
QR in V$_1$	—	100
Miscellaneous criteria		
QRS axis > + 90 degrees	16	100
P wave amplitude > 0.25 mV in II, III, aVF, V$_1$, or V$_2$	22	99

Determine the QRS axis and duration, and describe the QRS morphology. The duration, morphology, and axis of the QRS complexes can help define the origin of the ventricular rhythm. Rhythms originating above the ventricles usually use the normal His-Purkinje system to activate ventricular muscle, and the QRS complexes are narrow and normal appearing unless bundle-branch block is present. QRS complexes originating from ventricular tissue are broad and bizarre. If the ventricles are depolarized using the normal His-Purkinje pathways, the QRS morphology (including voltage), duration, and axis can suggest the presence of left and/or right ventricular hypertrophy (Table 50–4 and Fig. 50–7).

Finally, *compare the present ECG with previous records.*

SUGGESTED READINGS

Ganz LI: Approach to the patient with asymptomatic electrocardiographic abnormalities. *In* Braunwald E, Goldman L (eds). Primary Cardiology, 2nd ed. Philadelphia, Saunders, 2003, pp 169–192. *A focused overview of a wide range of electrocardiographic abnormalities, with clear examples of each.*

Surawicz B, Knilanas TK: Chou's Electrocardiography in Clinical Practice. Philadelphia, Saunders, 2001. *A concise text.*

Zimetbaum PJ, Josephson ME: Use of the electrocardiogram in acute myocardial infarction. N Engl J Med 2003;348:933–940. *Overview of the ECG for diagnosis, choice of therapy, and prognosis.*

51 ECHOCARDIOGRAPHY

Anthony N. DeMaria

Echocardiography is a noninvasive technique that evaluates cardiac anatomy and function with images and recordings produced by sound energy. Although introduced as a one-dimensional technique in the early 1970s, echocardiography has evolved into a two- and even three-dimensional imaging modality that is also capable of deriving hemodynamic data from measures of blood flow velocity using the Doppler principle. Cardiac ultrasonography is currently the primary modality used for assessing valvular, pericardial, and congenital heart diseases, as well as cardiac masses. It also has an established role in the assessment of left ventricular (LV) structure and performance, the evaluation of myocardial infarction (MI), and the detection of coronary artery disease (CAD).

PHYSICAL PRINCIPLES

Sound energy produces a series of sinusoidal cycles of alternating compression and rarefaction as it travels through a medium. Sound of a frequency above the audible range of 20,000 cycles/second is termed *ultrasound*; it travels as a beam that obeys the laws of reflection and refraction. When directed into the thorax and aimed at the heart, a sound beam travels in a straight line until it encounters a boundary between structures with different acoustical impedance, such as between blood and tissue. At such surfaces, a portion of the energy is reflected or refracted, and the remaining attenuated signal is transmitted distally. A cardiac image is then constructed from the reflected energy, or echoes.

In practice, the ultrasound signal is both produced and received by a single handheld transducer that converts electrical to mechanical (sound) energy and vice versa. The central component of the transducer is a piezoelectric crystal whose ionic structure changes shape to produce sound waves when exposed to an electric current. This same crystal is deformed by the reflected sound wave to produce an electrical signal. Echocardiographic images and recordings are constructed in the form of a display of the distance between individual cardiac structures and the transducer. Specifically, electronic circuitry within the instrument measures the transit time for the beam to travel from the transducer to a given structure and back again, and then it calculates distance from transit time using the velocity of sound in soft tissue of 1540 m/second. The structure is then displayed on the image at the calculated distance. Because interrogating beams can be repetitively transmitted at rates of up to 1000 per second, the movement of structures can be tracked as they change their positions relative to the transducer over time.

The earliest echographs used a single beam to record the structure and motion of a small region of the heart over time, so-called M-mode echocardiography. Subsequently, multiple ultrasound beams were combined to produce a wedge-shaped tomographic image of cardiac anatomy, referred to as two-dimensional echocardiography. The spatial orientation provided by two-dimensional echocardiography was a marked advance, but the typical frame rates of 20 to 30 per minute provide less temporal resolution than M-mode. Miniaturization of ultrasonic transducers enabled incorporation into standard gastroscopes to perform transesophageal echocardiography (TEE) or into cardiac catheters to yield intravascular ultrasound images. TEE has been of particular value in studying posteriorly located cardiac structures such as the left atrial appendage or in supplying high-resolution images in patients who are difficult to examine by the transthoracic approach. Echocardiography has been performed in conjunction with exercise or pharmacologic stress to evaluate CAD or, most recently, with the administration of contrast agents to facilitate endocardial definition and evaluate myocardial perfusion.

The sound energy reflected by blood cells is not of sufficient amplitude to be detected by conventional methods. Therefore, blood flow recordings are performed using the Doppler principle. Specifically, when a sound signal is reflected by moving blood cells, the frequency of the signal is changed (the Doppler shift). The resultant frequency shift depends on the direction and velocity of blood flow relative to the transducer. Frequency shift signals can be recorded for a single range-gated point along the beam (pulsed Doppler) or all composite points along the beam (continuous-wave Doppler) and can be displayed as a graphic record of velocity plotted against time (spectral Doppler). Pulsed Doppler enables localized assessment of flow velocity and turbulence but cannot record high velocities due to an artifact termed *aliasing*. Continuous-wave Doppler cannot localize flow but can accurately measure the high velocities produced by disturbed flow. The velocity and direction of flow can also be estimated for multiple points along multiple beams and be displayed as color signals superimposed on standard black and white tissue images (color Doppler flow imaging). Flow velocity, which is related to the pressure gradient across any orifice, provides a mechanism to calculate pressures from velocities within the central circulation using a simplification of the Bernoulli equation. In addition, instruments can be adjusted so that Doppler signals can record the velocity of myocardial movement to assess segmental

systolic and diastolic function, which is relatively independent of loading conditions.

Several technical factors limit echocardiography in clinical practice. Air and bone present an impediment to ultrasound transmission, and good image quality requires that the ultrasound beam have clear access to cardiac structures. Thus, echocardiographic imaging may be limited or impossible in some patients, such as those with severe lung disease or marked obesity. In addition, structures that are not perpendicular to the beam may not reflect adequate energy to be recorded, a phenomenon referred to as *dropout*. Artifacts may also be produced by high levels of background noise or by the increasing width of the imaging beam as it propagates away from the transducer. In regard to Doppler recordings, velocity is a vectorial entity that has magnitude and direction; the beam must be parallel to or within 20 degrees of the direction of flow to record velocity accurately.

ECHOCARDIOGRAM IMAGES AND MEASUREMENTS

The conventional two-dimensional echocardiographic examination consists of wedge-shaped sector images acquired from a number of standard views obtained with different transducer orientations. Doppler recordings can be obtained in any view but are of greatest value when the beam is parallel to flow direction (e.g., transmitral and transaortic flow is best evaluated from the apical view).

A variety of measurements can be derived from echocardiographic recordings. Because the images are tomographic, any individual view may not be representative of the whole. Areas of dropout may limit measurements based on the entire perimeter of the chamber, but this problem usually can be obviated by the use of ultrasonic contrast agents. Simple one-dimensional measurements (e.g., LV dimension, LV wall thickness, left atrial dimension) are easy to obtain and can be used to calculate measures of fractional shortening and wall thickening. LV volumes and ejection fraction, which usually can be calculated using a variety of algorithms based on assumed LV geometry, correlate well with measures obtained by other techniques such as angiography.

Echocardiography enables the derivation of a number of hemodynamic parameters. Flow volume through an orifice can be calculated as the product of the orifice cross-sectional area derived from echocardiographic images multiplied by velocity measurements provided by pulsed Doppler. Such measurements can be made for flow through any valve or in the ascending aorta or pulmonary artery. Volumetric flow calculations are applied in estimating stroke volume and cardiac output. In normal persons, the volume of blood entering the left ventricle through the mitral valve (LV inflow) equals that exiting the left ventricle through the aortic valve (LV outflow). In the presence of isolated mitral or aortic regurgitation, a greater volume of blood will inflow or outflow the ventricle, respectively; the difference between inflow and outflow measures represents regurgitant volume. A similar approach underlies the calculation of valve area by the continuity equation. The continuity equation is based on the fact that the volume of flow proximal to a stenotic valve is equal to that through the orifice. Since the area and velocity can be measured proximal to the orifice and the velocity can be measured through the orifice, the continuity equation yields the orifice area. Transmitral LV filling patterns by pulsed Doppler can be analyzed for evidence of diastolic dysfunction, manifested by a marked increase in either early or atrial flow velocities or a change in early deceleration rate. Diminished velocities with a slow early diastolic deceleration indicate impaired relaxation, whereas increased velocity and rapid deceleration in early diastole indicate augmented stiffness and a restrictive pattern of filling. Doppler recordings of pulmonary vein flow into the left atrium are of value in distinguishing diastolic abnormalities and estimating left atrial pressure in conjunction with transmitral velocities. A simplification of the Bernoulli equation as $4 \times (\text{peak velocity})^2$ can be used to measure the pressure gradient across any orifice. Gradient measurement is useful not only in quantifying valve stenosis but also in evaluating pulmonary artery, left atrial, and LV pressures from tricuspid, mitral, and aortic regurgitant jets, respectively. Color flow recordings yield qualitative and quantitative evidence of the severity of valvular regurgitation.

CLINICAL APPLICATIONS

Echocardiography is useful to evaluate patients with a murmur that might be indicative of an important cardiac condition, for

Table 51–1 • INDICATIONS FOR ECHOCARDIOGRAPHY BY SIGNS AND SYMPTOMS

Murmur (not functional)
Dyspnea
Edema
Systemic embolus
Evaluation of abnormal electrocardiogram (question of old myocardial
   infarction or pericarditis)
Unexplained syncope of potential cardiac etiology
Abnormal heart size on chest radiograph
Chest pain

Table 51–2 • INDICATIONS FOR ECHOCARDIOGRAPHY BY DISORDERS

Valvular stenosis Valvular regurgitation Infectious endocarditis Mitral prolapse Prosthetic valves	For diagnosis or to assess hemodynamic severity or ventricular function
Myocardial ischemia Myocardial infarction	To assess presence, area, and complications
Chronic coronary artery disease	To assess left ventricular dysfunction
Heart failure	To determine etiology and ventricular function
Pericardial disease Cardiac masses Great vessel abnormalities Pulmonary disease	To identify and for follow-up
Hypertension	If left ventricular function will influence decision
Arrhythmias	If heart disease is suggested

evaluation of unexplained dyspnea or edema, to detect a potential source of systemic emboli, to evaluate an abnormal electrocardiogram that may be suggestive of an old MI or pericardial disease, to evaluate unexplained syncope of potential cardiac etiology, and sometimes to evaluate patients with chest pain (Table 51–1). It is also useful for the evaluation of a variety of suspected specific disorders of cardiac valves, cardiac muscle, the pericardium, and the great vessels (Table 51–2).

Valvular Heart Disease

STENOSIS. Echocardiography is unsurpassed in its ability to detect and quantify valvular heart disease (Chapter 72). Normal valve leaflets are well visualized by echocardiography and appear as thin, rapidly moving structures with an excursion extending to the borders of the chamber or great vessel into which they open. Doppler examination of normal valves depicts forward blood flow of maximal velocities less than 1.7 m/second, without evidence of regurgitation. Flow through the semilunar valves exhibits a progressive rise and fall in systole, whereas that through the atrioventricular valves is characterized by a bimodal pattern, with high flow velocities on valve opening in early diastole and after atrial contraction just before the next systole.

Stenotic valves are invariably apparent on an echocardiogram (Fig. 51–1) and are characterized by marked thickening and an obvious decrease in the extent of opening excursion. High-intensity echocardiographic signals indicative of calcification are usually observed. Two-dimensional echocardiographic images of the mitral orifice are readily obtainable, and planimetry of these structures yields estimates of valve area in mitral stenosis that correlate well with values obtained by cardiac catheterization and surgery. However, the orifice of the aortic valve leaflets is often difficult to identify with certainty by transthoracic echocardiography, and aortic stenosis severity cannot be accurately assessed by ultrasound imaging. The quantification of aortic

stenosis typically relies on Doppler measurements. Measurements of peak and mean transvalvular aortic gradient can be readily derived from the maximal transvalve Doppler velocity when subjected to the simplified Bernoulli equation. Similar Doppler approaches can be taken to measure mitral stenosis severity, although peak gradient is a less physiologic measure of the severity of mitral obstruction than aortic obstruction. An alternative approach to assessing the severity of mitral stenosis uses the rate of transmitral flow deceleration in early diastole by Doppler, calculated as the time for the Doppler velocity to decrease to one half of the pressure equivalent (pressure half-time). Although encountered less frequently, tricuspid and pulmonic stenosis can be quantitatively assessed using the same techniques.

The accuracy of echocardiography in the assessment of valvular stenosis is so high that cardiac catheterization currently is believed to be indicated only in those patients with technically poor ultrasound examination, in those whom the echocardiographic data are not consistent with signs and symptoms of disease, or to define coronary artery anatomy.

REGURGITATION. With valvular regurgitation, there often is a divergence between anatomy and function (Chapter 72). Thus, anatomically abnormal valves may not be regurgitant, whereas normal-appearing valves may be accompanied by severe regurgitation. Accordingly, two-dimensional ultrasonic imaging is of greatest value in establishing the specific etiology of valvular regurgitation, whereas Doppler techniques provide the primary method for the detection and quantitation of these abnormalities. Echocardiographic images are also of value in providing evidence of ventricular or atrial volume overload. Of the etiologies of mitral regurgitation identifiable by echocardiography, mitral prolapse and torn chordae tendineae are of particular significance. Mitral prolapse, or superior/posterior displacement of the mitral leaflets behind the annulus into the left atrium in systole, is usually midsystolic and best diagnosed by echocardiography. Associated abnormalities include valvular thickening and redundancy, annular dilatation, and perhaps aortic enlargement. Although it was initially believed to be quite common, application of strict diagnostic criteria to the parasternal long-axis view has revised estimates of prevalence downward. In torn chordae, the flail portion of the mitral apparatus can usually be visualized and typically signifies a large regurgitant volume. With the refinement of mitral valve repair surgery (Chapter 72), detection of these anatomic lesions has assumed greater importance for early therapy.

The presence of regurgitation is readily identifiable by the retrograde flow of blood emanating from the affected valve into the receiving chamber by color flow Doppler (Figs. 51–2 and 72–2). Regurgitant jets may be observed in normal subjects, most commonly for the tricuspid and pulmonic valves, but are rarely observed with normal aortic or mitral valves. Quantitation of valvular regurgitation is based on four basic approaches: (1) the documentation of differences between LV inflow and LV outflow as determined by volumetric calculations; (2) detection of retrograde flow in the descending aorta for aortic regurgitation and into the pulmonary veins with mitral regurgitation; (3) assessment of the size of the regurgitant jet by color Doppler imaging; and (4) derivation of regurgitant flow rate, volume, and effective orifice area from volume calculations or analysis of the convergence signal proximal to the regurgitant leaflets. The rate of jet deceleration may also be of value in quantifying regurgitation, particularly for the aortic valve. Each of these approaches is limited by imprecision of measurement and the influence of confounding variables. Therefore, the quantitation of valvular regurgitation by echocardiography is less accurate than that of valvular stenosis and is best achieved as the cumulative result of analyzing all possible criteria.

The noninvasive evaluation of prosthetic heart valves has long been fraught with difficulty. The foreign materials with which prosthetic valves are made characteristically result in reverberation artifacts and in severe attenuation and shadowing of ultrasound signals, rendering ultrasound images difficult to interpret. Two-dimensional echocardiographic imaging is of greatest value in determining that artificial valves are properly seated, exhibit free movement of the mechanical occluder device or bioprosthetic leaflets, and are free from external masses such as thrombi or vegetations. Doppler, the predominant modality for the assessment of prosthetic valves by ultrasound, provides data regarding abnormalities of transvalvular velocity, gradient, and the presence or absence of valvular regurgitation. Because of artifacts, TEE may be required for adequate examination of prosthetic valves, particularly those in the mitral position.

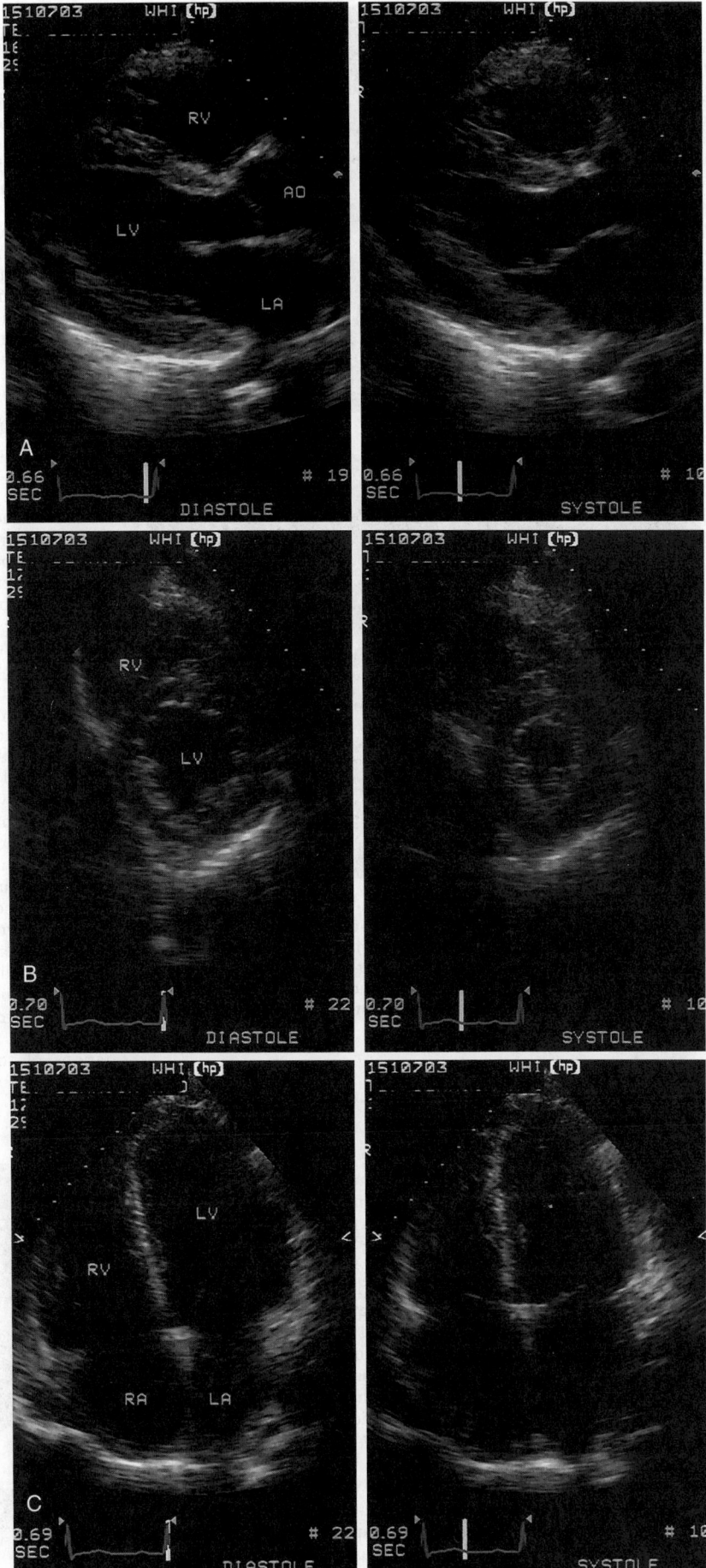

FIGURE 51–1 • Normal two-dimensional transthoracic echocardiogram in systole and diastole. *A,* With the transducer in the left parasternal location, images can be obtained parallel to the longitudinal axis of the left ventricle. This long-axis view depicts an elliptical left ventricle as visualized from the left shoulder, with the apex to the left and the base to the right. *B,* With the transducer in the left parasternal location, a perpendicular (short-axis) view of the left ventricle is obtained. The left ventricle appears as a circular cross section in the short-access view. *C,* Positioning the transducer at the apical impulse provides images of the perimeter of all four cardiac chambers and both the mitral and tricuspid valves (four-chamber view).

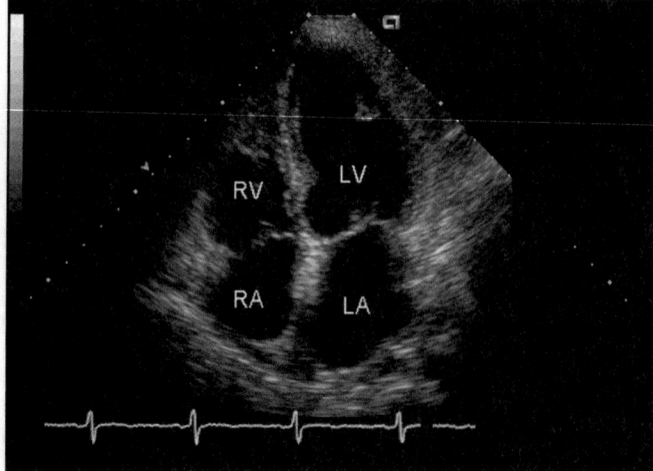

A

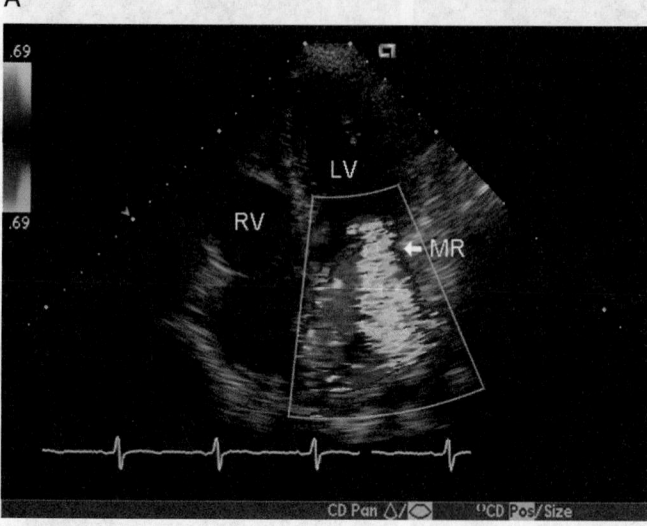

B

FIGURE 51–2 • Mitral regurgitation. *A,* The four-chamber apical view in systole is demonstrated with (left panel) and without (right panel) superimposed color Doppler flow imaging. *B,* A clear-cut mitral regurgitant jet can be seen emanating from a preacceleration area in the mitral orifice and penetrating backward into the left atrium (arrows). LV = left ventricle; LA = left atrium; RA = right atrium.

Infective Endocarditis

Echocardiography has assumed an important role in diagnosing and assessing the hemodynamic consequences, complications, prognosis, and need for surgery in patients with infective endocarditis (Chapter 310). The hallmark of infective endocarditis on echocardiography is a vegetation (see Fig. 72–4), which can be detected in more than 80% of cases as a focal valvular thickening without restrictive leaflet motion. The presence of vegetation is associated with an increase in heart failure, emboli, and need for surgical intervention. Echocardiography is also extremely valuable in detecting complications of infective endocarditis such as periannular abscess and valve perforation or tear. TEE is more accurate than transthoracic echocardiography in assessing endocarditis, particularly in regard to complications and prosthetic valves.

Ischemic Heart Disease

Disease of the coronary arteries is by far the most common cause of heart disease, and echocardiography is assuming an emerging role in assessing this disorder. Although echocardiography cannot regularly visualize the coronary arteries, it provides important information about CAD through the evaluation of LV performance. Detection of regional dyssynergy is of value in identifying and sizing acute MI

(Chapter 69). Furthermore, cardiac ultrasound is the modality of choice for assessing the complications of acute MI such as ventricular septal defect, ruptured papillary muscle, pseudoaneurysm, and thrombi.

The provocation of regional contractile abnormalities by treadmill or bicycle exercise or by pharmacologic stress imposed by inotropic or vasodilator drugs can be applied to diagnose and assess the physiologic significance of CAD. Stress echocardiography is superior to stress electrocardiography in the identification of CAD, yields similar results to radionuclide techniques, and provides prognostic information (Chapter 67).

Documentation of enhanced contraction of hypokinetic or akinetic segments by cardiac ultrasound in response to low-dose inotropic stimulation with dobutamine is a good marker of viable myocardium, especially when high-dose stimulation induces recurrent contractile dysfunction.

Cardiomyopathy

Primary disease of the myocardium independent of other cardiovascular structures such as coronary arteries or valves (cardiomyopathy) has multiple causes, is often idiopathic, and is generally a diagnosis of exclusion. Echocardiography forms the cornerstone of the diagnostic strategy for cardiomyopathy (Chapter 73). The approach aims first to classify the pathophysiology of the disorder as dilated (myocyte necrosis, profound dilation, and systolic dysfunction), hypertrophic (disproportionate septal thickening, obstructive or nonobstructive), or restrictive (generalized wall thickening with both systolic and diastolic impairment). Classification is based on LV cavity size, wall thickness, and systolic contraction. Dilated cardiomyopathy (Fig. 51–3) is characterized by dilation, near-normal wall thickness, and severe global hypokinesis. Hypertrophic cardiomyopathy may be concentric hypertrophy (Fig. 51–4) or asymmetrical septal hypertrophy (Fig. 51–5) with normal contraction and often LV outflow tract obstruction due to systolic anterior movement of the mitral valve. Restrictive cardiomyopathy is characterized by generalized wall thickening, modest generalized hypokinesis, and evidence of impaired diastolic function. Causes associated with dilated myopathy include infection, inflammation, toxins, collagen vascular disease, and musculoskeletal disease. Hypertrophic cardiomyopathy is familial, whereas restrictive cardiomyopathy is associated with infiltrative processes such as amyloidosis and hemochromatosis. Echocardiography can establish and assess the severity of cardiomyopathy in nearly all cases, although cardiac catheterization or biopsy is occasionally necessary.

Echocardiography plays a particularly important role in hypertrophic obstructive cardiomyopathy. Because asymmetrical septal hypertrophy and systolic anterior motion are fundamental manifestations of the disorder and are best detected by tomographic

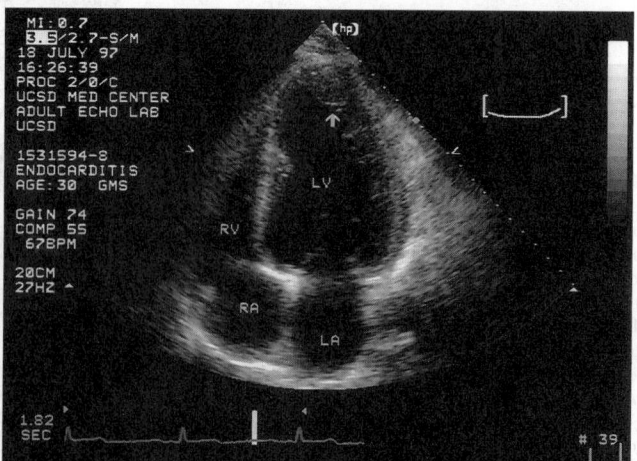

FIGURE 51–3 • Dilated left ventricle with clot. An apical view of a four-chamber echocardiogram in a patient with dilated cardiomyopathy. The left ventricle is enlarged and spherical; a thrombus is seen at the cardiac apex (arrow). LV = left ventricle; LA = left atrium; RA = right atrium.

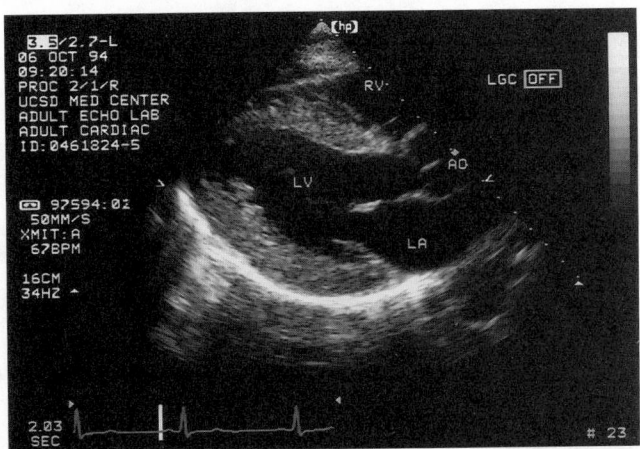

FIGURE 51-4 • Concentric hypertrophy. The parasternal long-axis view obtained in a patient with concentric hypertrophy resulting from systemic hypertension. The distance between calibration dots on the right is 10 mm so the wall thickness is 13 mm for both the septum and the posterior wall. Ao = aorta.

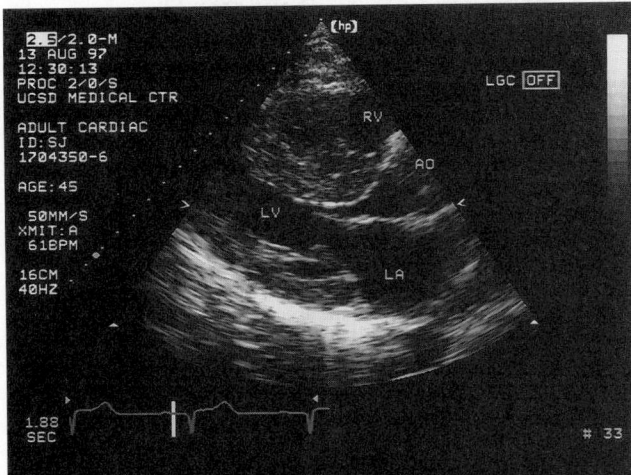

FIGURE 51-5 • Hypertrophic cardiomyopathy. The parasternal long-axis view obtained in a patient with hypertrophic cardiomyopathy in diastole. As can be seen, the thickness of the interventricular septum exceeds that of the posterior basal left ventricular wall by a factor of 2.

techniques, echocardiography is the modality of choice for diagnosis. The presence of mitral regurgitation and extent of hypertrophy can also be defined. In addition, echocardiography can detect dynamic subvalvular obstruction and quantify the gradient by virtue of the Bernoulli approach.

Congenital Heart Diseases

Congenital heart diseases represent fundamental distortions of cardiac anatomy (Chapter 65). Echocardiography is a particularly valuable technique to assess these disorders and has largely eliminated the need for cardiac catheterization. Echocardiography can distinguish the anatomic right ventricle from the left ventricle by the presence of a moderator band, coarser trabeculae, an infundibulum, and an atrioventricular valve positioned closer to the cardiac apex. An oval orifice is readily identified by echocardiography in patients with bicuspid aortic valves. Atrial septal defects are characterized by right ventricular enlargement and paradoxical anterior motion of the septum in systole; in the absence of pulmonary hypertension, both the orifice and shunt of an atrial septal defect may be visualized by two-dimensional echocardiography and color Doppler imaging. In ventricular septal defects, the primary presentation often consists of shunt flow depicted by color Doppler imaging. Measurement of cardiac

chamber size and pulmonary artery pressure enables a comprehensive evaluation of these disorders.

Cardiac Masses

Echocardiography is the modality of choice for the diagnosis and evaluation of cardiac mass lesions such as tumors and clots (see Fig. 51-3). Cardiac masses must be distinguished from ultrasonic artifacts, which manifest inappropriate motion, lack border definition, and are often unattached to a cardiac surface.

Cardiac thrombi may be located in the left atrium or left ventricle. Most left atrial clots are due to atrial fibrillation or mitral valve disease and are found in the left atrial appendage, which is not well visualized by transthoracic echocardiography. Therefore, left atrial clots are best evaluated by TEE, which may also detect spontaneous contrast due to extreme stasis of blood flow. Conversely, LV thrombi are characteristically caused by CAD or cardiomyopathy, are located in the LV apex, and are easily identified by transthoracic echocardiography. The presence of wall motion abnormalities helps distinguish these lesions from artifacts. An increase in the size and mobility of thrombi on an echocardiogram appears to increase the risk of embolization.

Cardiac tumors (Chapter 79) occur uncommonly and may be intracavitary or intramural. Myxoma, the most common form of cardiac tumor, is located in the atrium in more than 75% of cases. Left atrial myxoma is usually manifested by the presence of a pedicle and broad movement into and out of the mitral valve orifice during diastole and systole, respectively. Intramyocardial tumors typically present as asymmetrical localized thickening of one area of the ventricular wall.

Pericardial Disease

Pericarditis often occurs in the absence of any detectable abnormalities on an echocardiogram and is usually recognized only when accompanied by effusion, which is readily identified as a clear space surrounding the heart between epicardium and pericardium (Chapter 74). The severity of pericardial effusion may be generally assessed by the size of the space and the presence of right ventricular and right atrial compression. However, optimal evaluation of the physiologic significance of pericardial effusion is obtained by demonstrating a greater than 25% decrease in transmitral flow velocity during inspiration by Doppler. On occasion, fibrin strands, clots, or tumors may be visualized in the fluid. Echocardiography also provides an excellent guide for performing pericardiocentesis by identifying the site of the greatest fluid accumulation.

Pericardial constriction is both less common and less well detected by echocardiography than is effusion. Although cardiac ultrasound may occasionally provide evidence of pericardial thickening or calcification, it is not as accurate for this purpose as is computed tomography. The predominant abnormality observed with constrictive pericarditis is inappropriate septal motion (perhaps due to restrained cardiac movement) and a greater than 20% variation of peak transmitral velocity with respiration. As with other manifestations of constrictive pericarditis, these findings may also be seen in severe chronic obstructive pulmonary disease.

Unexplained Cardiomegaly

Echocardiography is the procedure of choice to evaluate unexplained cardiomegaly detected by chest radiography (Fig. 51-6). It can readily discriminate a large left ventricle, with or without right ventricular enlargement, and detect pericardial effusions. Echocardiography is also very helpful in determining the causes of enlargement of the left and right ventricles.

Role of Echocardiography in Clinical Syndromes
(see Table 51-2)

The decision to perform echocardiography is often prompted by the presence of symptoms or signs consistent with heart disease. Echocardiography is a key study for assessing the potential cardiovascular causes of shortness of breath and for determining the diagnosis, prognosis, and optimal therapy of patients with heart failure (Chapter 56). Based on its ability to detect abnormal valve function

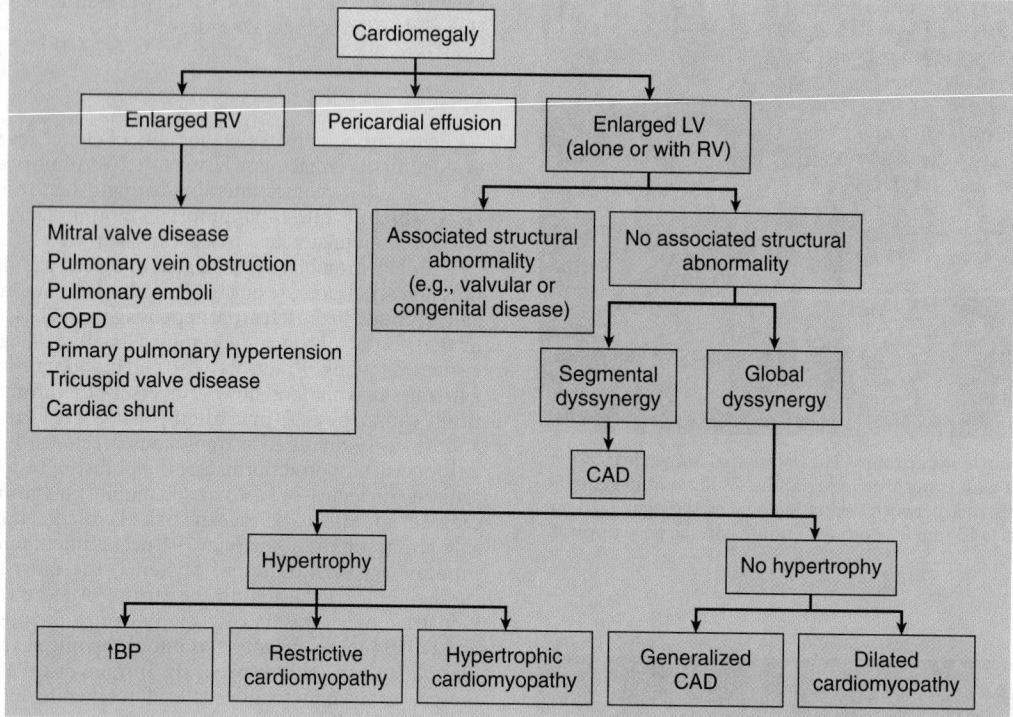

FIGURE 51–6 • Echocardiographic approach to cardiomegaly. The initial step in the evaluation of a patient with evidence of cardiomegaly involves examining the echocardiogram to determine whether the enlargement is due to pericardial effusion or whether it involves the right ventricle or left ventricle alone or in combination. If isolated right ventricular enlargement is present, the potential causes are enumerated. If left ventricular enlargement is found, the physician must next determine whether there are associated structural abnormalities such as valvular or congenital heart disease. If no associated anatomic abnormalities are present, the observation of segmental dyssynergy points strongly toward underlying coronary artery disease. If generalized global dyssynergy is present, the echocardiogram should distinguish the presence or absence of increased wall thickening. Conditions associated with increased wall thickening include infiltrative processes associated with restrictive cardiomyopathy and hypertrophy associated with hypertension or hypertrophic cardiomyopathy. A dilated left ventricle with global dyssynergy in the absence of hypertrophy may represent dilated cardiomyopathy or generalized left ventricular dysfunction caused by widespread coronary artery disease (sometimes referred to as *ischemic cardiomyopathy*).

and intracardiac shunting, echocardiography is the cornerstone for assessing cardiac murmurs. The utility of cardiac ultrasound to detect intracardiac masses and shunts makes it the primary modality for the assessment of a potential source of emboli. The ability to detect vegetations has made an abnormal echocardiogram one of the major diagnostic criteria for endocarditis.

Future Directions

A number of technical advances are expanding the role of echocardiography in clinical practice. Real-time three-dimensional imaging will enhance the precision of quantitative measurements derived by ultrasound and may provide a basis for using the technology to guide procedures such as catheterization. Contrast agents have increased the yield of diagnostic studies and provided a method from which to derive information regarding myocardial perfusion. Perhaps most strikingly, miniaturization of ultrasound instrumentation has resulted in the introduction of handheld echocardiographs that are the size of laptop computers. Such devices are already being used in intensive care units and emergency departments to assess ventricular and valvular function, in essence creating an "ultrasonic stethoscope" to augment the physical examination.

SUGGESTED READINGS

ACC/AHA Practice Guidelines: ACC/AHA Guidelines for the Clinical Application of Echocardiography: Executive Summary: A report of the American College of Cardiology/American Heart Association Task Force on Practice Guidelines (Committee on Clinical Application of Echocardiography). J Am Coll Cardiol 1997;29:862–879. *Consensus guidelines for appropriate ordering of echocardiograms.*
Gottdiener JS: Overview of stress echocardiography: Uses, advantages, and limitations. Prog Cardiovasc Dis 2001;43:315–334. *A practical review.*
Otto CM: The Practice of Clinical Echocardiography, 2nd ed. Philadelphia, WB Saunders, 2002. *A concise text.*

52 NUCLEAR CARDIOLOGY AND COMPUTED TOMOGRAPHY

George A. Beller

NUCLEAR CARDIOLOGY

The techniques of nuclear cardiology permit the noninvasive imaging of myocardial perfusion under stress and resting conditions and of resting regional and global function using radionuclide imaging agents and gamma or positron cameras with associated computer processing. All these techniques are based on acquiring images of radioactivity emanating from tracers localized in heart muscle or in the blood pools of the left and right ventricle. Myocardial perfusion imaging is the most commonly performed nuclear cardiology technique, and it is employed most often in conjunction with either exercise or pharmacologic stress intended to produce flow heterogeneity between relatively hypoperfused and normally perfused myocardial regions. Radionuclide angiography, in which technetium-99m (^{99m}Tc)–labeled red blood cells or other ^{99m}Tc-labeled agents are injected intravenously, is used for measurement of left ventricular ejection fraction (LVEF) and assessment of regional wall motion. This technique is used most commonly to monitor changes in global left ventricular function in patients undergoing chemotherapy for cancer when drugs with the potential for cardiac toxicity are administered. Positron emission tomography (PET) is used predominantly to assess regional myocardial metabolism to estimate myocardial viability, most often using fluorine-18-labeled 2-deoxyglucose (FDG).

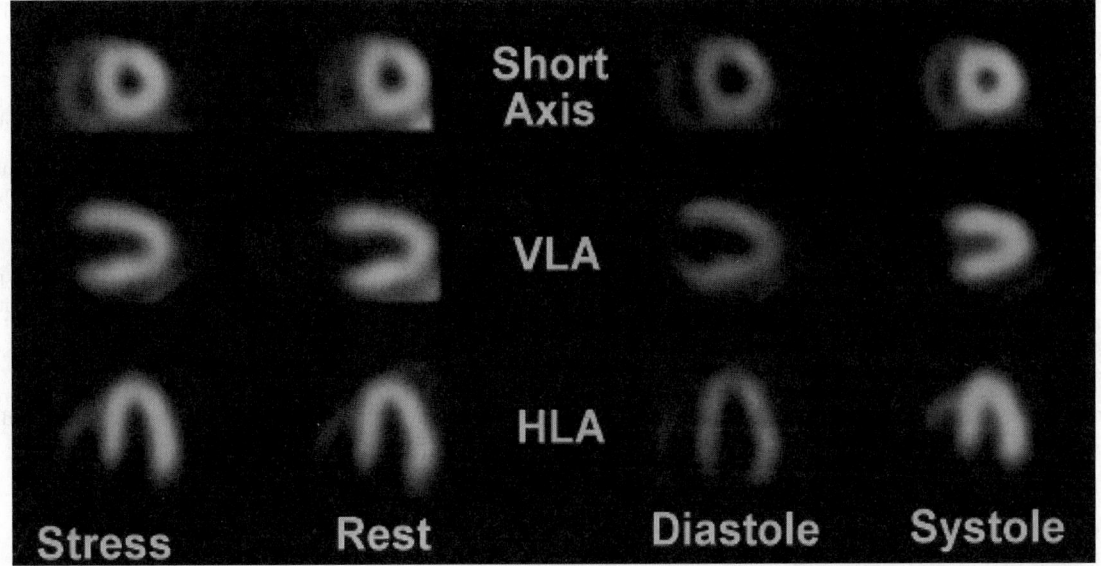

FIGURE 52–1 • Stress and rest single-photon emission computed tomography (SPECT) studies (left two columns) in a normal patient, showing representative short-axis, vertical long-axis (VLA), and horizontal long-axis (HLA) images. Note the uniform uptake of ^{99m}Tc-sestamibi on the stress and the rest tomograms consistent with homogeneous regional myocardial blood flow. The right two columns show the end-diastolic and end-systolic images acquired during stress and show uniform systolic thickening in all myocardial segments. The left ventricular cavity size is greater on images acquired during diastole compared with systole, consistent with a normal left ventricular ejection fraction. The "brightness" of the images at end-systole correlates directly with the degree of systolic thickening.

MYOCARDIAL PERFUSION IMAGING

Imaging Agents

Thallium-201 (^{201}Tl), a monovalent cation that is biologically similar to potassium, was the most commonly employed radionuclide agent for the assessment of myocardial perfusion using either planar imaging or single-photon emission computed tomography (SPECT) techniques. The initial uptake of intravenously administered ^{201}Tl (usually 2 to 3 mCi) is directly proportional to regional myocardial blood flow and to the extraction fraction of ^{201}Tl by the myocardium. The extraction fraction is an index of the ability of the myocardium to extract the tracer from the blood pool in the first pass through the coronary circulation. The extraction fraction for ^{201}Tl under normal conditions is approximately 85%. After the initial phase of myocardial uptake, there is continuous exchange of myocardial ^{201}Tl and ^{201}Tl in the blood pool that recirculates from the systemic compartment. ^{201}Tl continually is washed out of normally perfused myocardium and replaced by circulating ^{201}Tl from residual activity in the blood compartment. This process of continuous exchange forms the basis of the phenomenon of ^{201}Tl *redistribution*, which is defined as total or partial reversibility (i.e., resolution) of initial poststress defects by the time of repeat imaging at 3 to 4 hours after initial tracer administration. Defects that show no redistribution between the stress and the delayed images are designated as being *persistent* or *nonreversible* and most often represent myocardial scar. Some nonreversible defects at 4 hours improve or resolve with reinjection of a second dose of ^{201}Tl in the resting state, however, which indicates ischemia.

^{99m}Tc-labeled perfusion agents now are used more commonly than ^{201}Tl for exercise stress testing to evaluate patients with suspected or known coronary heart disease (CHD) (Fig. 52–1). Of the various ^{99m}Tc-labeled agents, ^{99m}Tc-sestamibi and ^{99m}Tc-tetrofosmin are the most common. ^{99m}Tc-sestamibi, an isonitrile, is superior in many ways to ^{201}Tl for myocardial perfusion imaging. The 140-keV photon energy peak of ^{99m}Tc is optimal for gamma camera imaging and produces higher quality images than those generated using ^{201}Tl. Because of its short half-life (6 hours), 10 to 15 times larger doses of ^{99m}Tc than of ^{201}Tl can be administered, yielding superior images in a shorter time.

For clinical imaging, the major advantage of ^{99m}Tc perfusion imaging is the improved specificity for detecting CHD because its higher energy reduces attenuation artifacts and permits the images to be gated with the electrocardiogram (ECG) to assess regional systolic thickening on tomographic images throughout the cardiac cycle. Mild nonreversible defects that represent attenuation artifacts show normal systolic thickening, whereas if these areas represent scar, abnormal systolic thickening is observed. ^{99m}Tc agents provide simultaneous assessment of regional and global left ventricular function using the gated SPECT technology. LVEF and end-diastolic and end-systolic volumes are measured accurately on gated SPECT images.

Some laboratories use dual-isotope rest ^{201}Tl/stress ^{99m}Tc-sestamibi imaging in which patients undergo ^{201}Tl imaging at rest, then immediately afterward undergo ^{99m}Tc-sestamibi imaging during stress. Reversibility is identified by comparing the perfusion pattern on the stress ^{99m}Tc-sestamibi images with the pattern on the baseline resting ^{201}Tl images. The major advantage of this technique is the marked decrease in total imaging time.

Detection of Coronary Heart Disease

The current indications for stress and rest myocardial perfusion imaging are to diagnose CHD and myocardial infarction, assess prognosis, and detect myocardial viability (Table 52–1). Exercise or pharmacologic stress ^{201}Tl or ^{99m}Tc-sestamibi SPECT imaging in patients with chest pain yields a sensitivity for detecting CHD in the 85% to 90% range. The specificity for excluding CHD is in the 85% range for ^{99m}Tc-sestamibi SPECT imaging and increases to 90% when using gated images. Exercise or pharmacologic SPECT ^{201}Tl and exercise or pharmacologic SPECT ^{99m}Tc perfusion imaging have sensitivities and specificities that are superior to exercise ECG testing alone. The specificity of gated SPECT for detecting CHD using one of the ^{99m}Tc-labeled perfusion agents is 20 to 30% higher than ^{201}Tl SPECT in women. Radionuclide stress perfusion imaging is of particular value compared with exercise ECG testing alone in (1) patients with resting ECG abnormalities, such as those seen with left ventricular hypertrophy, digitalis effect, Wolff-Parkinson-White syndrome, and intraventricular conduction abnormalities, and (2) patients who fail to achieve more than 85% of maximum predicted heart rate. Approximately 40% of patients with a low-to-intermediate pretest likelihood of CHD who manifest equal to or greater than 1.0 mm of horizontal or downsloping ST-segment depression have no evidence for CHD (false-positive findings). The addition of stress perfusion imaging can assist in differentiating true-positive from false-positive ST depression. Detection of proximal left anterior descending stenoses and proximal multivessel CHD is enhanced by identifying regional systolic thickening or wall motion abnormalities on the gated SPECT images compared with assessment based on perfusion alone.

Table 52–1 • RADIONUCLIDE TESTING TO DIAGNOSE ISCHEMIC HEART DISEASE

INDICATION	TEST	CLASS
1. Diagnosis of symptomatic and selected patients at high risk for asymptomatic myocardial ischemia	Exercise or pharmacologic myocardial perfusion imaging, including PET*	I
	Exercise RNA	IIa
2. Assessment of ventricular performance (rest or exercise)	RNA[†]	I
	Gated sestamibi imaging	IIb
3. Assessment of myocardial viability in patients with left ventricular dysfunction in planning revascularization	Rest-distribution Tl-201 imaging	I
	Stress-redistribution-reinjection Tl-201 imaging	I
	PET imaging with FDG	I
	Dobutamine RNA	IIb
	Postexercise RNA	IIb
	Post-NTG RNA	IIb
4. Planning PTCA—identifying lesions causing myocardial ischemia, if not otherwise known	Exercise or pharmacologic myocardial perfusion imaging	I
	Exercise RNA	IIa
5. Risk stratification before noncardiac surgery	Pharmacologic or exercise perfusion imaging	I
6. Screening of asymptomatic patients with low likelihood of disease	All tests	III

Class I = usually appropriate and considered useful; class II = acceptable but usefulness less well established; class IIa = weight of evidence in favor of usefulness; class IIb = can be helpful but not well established by evidence; class III = generally not appropriate.

*The relative cost of positron emission tomography (PET) and thallium (Tl)-201 or technetium (Tc)-99m agents and lesser availability of PET must be considered when selecting this technique.

[†]RNA can be accomplished by first-pass imaging of a technetium-based myocardial perfusion agent.

FDG = ^{18}F-2-deoxyglucose; RNA = radionuclide angiography; NTG = nitroglycerine; PTCA = percutaneous transluminal coronary angioplasty.

Adapted with permission from Ritchie JL, Bateman TM, Bonow RO, et al: Guidelines for clinical use of cardiac radionuclide imaging. Report of the American College of Cardiology/American Heart Association Task Force on Assessment of Diagnostic and Therapeutic Cardiovascular Procedures (Committee on Radionuclide Imaging), developed in collaboration with the American Society of Nuclear Cardiology. J Am Coll Cardiol 1995;25:521–547.

Table 52–2 • HIGH-RISK RESULTS IN EXERCISE MYOCARDIAL PERFUSION SCANNING

Abnormal regional perfusion in regions supplied by two or more coronary arteries (e.g., defects in the left anterior descending artery and left circumflex artery territories)

Extensive reversible defects, even if only in the region of one major coronary artery (e.g., defects in the anterior wall, septum, and apex corresponding to the left anterior descending coronary artery territory)

Large defect size (>20% of the left ventricular myocardium) on quantitative single-photon emission computed tomography

Increased lung thallium-201 uptake best assessed by quantitating the lung-to-heart thallium-201 ratio

Transient ischemic left ventricular cavity dilation in the stress compared with the resting state

Extensive regional systolic thickening or wall motion abnormalities on gated technetium-99m single-photon emission computed tomographic (SPECT) images

A left ventricular ejection fraction of <40%

with intravenous aminophylline, an adenosine antagonist that immediately reverses these side effects.

Assessment of Prognosis

One of the chief applications of stress myocardial perfusion imaging is the identification of patients at either high or low risk for future ischemic cardiac events. Numerous studies have shown that the extent of hypoperfusion on poststress SPECT perfusion images provides important incremental prognostic information when added to clinical variables, the resting LVEF, exercise ECG stress test variables, and even coronary artery anatomy. Patients with chest pain and a normal myocardial perfusion scan at peak exercise or under vasodilator stress have a subsequent cardiac death or infarction rate of less than 1% per year and are generally appropriate candidates for medical therapy or require further diagnostic evaluation for a noncardiac cause of chest pain (Chapters 46 and 67). Conversely, patients with high-risk imaging results (Table 52–2), such as depicted in Figure 52–2, may benefit from early referral for invasive strategies, including revascularization, even if symptoms are mild. Patients who have diabetes and who show inducible ischemia have a higher cardiac event rate than nondiabetics who have a similar extent and severity of perfusion abnormalities

Pharmacologic Stress Imaging

Certain patients are unable to exercise to adequate heart rates and workloads on exercise stress testing protocols. Pharmacologic stress testing using vasodilators, such as dipyridamole or adenosine, or inotropic agents, such as dobutamine, is an alternative to exercise for detecting physiologically significant coronary artery stenoses. The basis for vasodilator perfusion imaging relates to the concept of coronary flow reserve. When blood flow is maximally increased with an intravenously administered vasodilator, an impairment in the flow reserve capacity in a stenotic artery compared with the large flow increase in a normal nonstenotic vascular bed results in a "relative" inhomogeneity of myocardial perfusion between normal and stenotic beds. If ^{201}Tl or ^{99m}Tc-sestamibi is injected during peak vasodilation in the presence of a hemodynamically significant coronary stenosis with reduced flow reserve, a heterogeneity of tracer uptake is observed as defects on poststress images acquired soon after tracer injection. Sensitivity and specificity for CHD detection are comparable for dipyridamole and adenosine. The addition of limited exercise to dipyridamole or adenosine imaging can prevent the vasodilator-induced hypotension, improve the ECG detection of ischemia, and enhance image quality by increasing the heart-to-liver ratio of tracer uptake. Dobutamine stress is preferred in patients who have bronchospasm or a history of asthma or who have consumed caffeine, which is an adenosine receptor antagonist, within 12 hours before testing. Patients who experience side effects such as hypotension and chest pain during dipyridamole or adenosine infusion should be treated

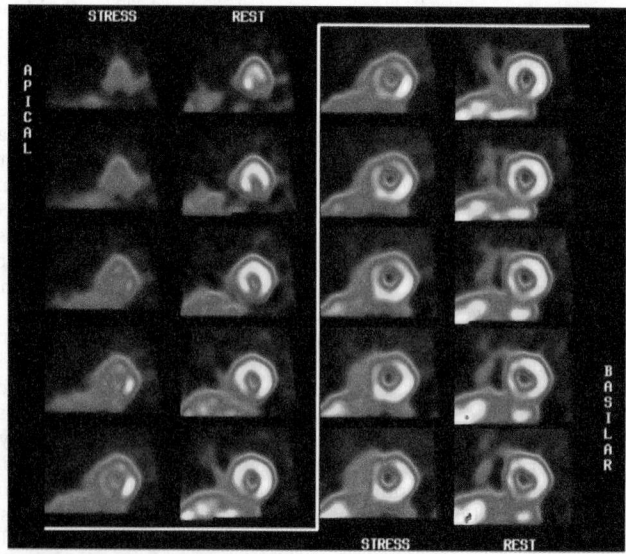

FIGURE 52–2 • Stress and rest short-axis ^{99m}Tc-sestamibi tomograms in a patient with chest pain and 3 mm of upsloping ST-segment depression on exercise electrocardiogram stress testing. Note a large defect involving the anterior wall, septum, and inferior wall; the defect is reversible on the resting study. These findings indicate significant inducible ischemia in the region of a proximal left anterior descending coronary artery stenosis. This patient was referred for further invasive evaluation.

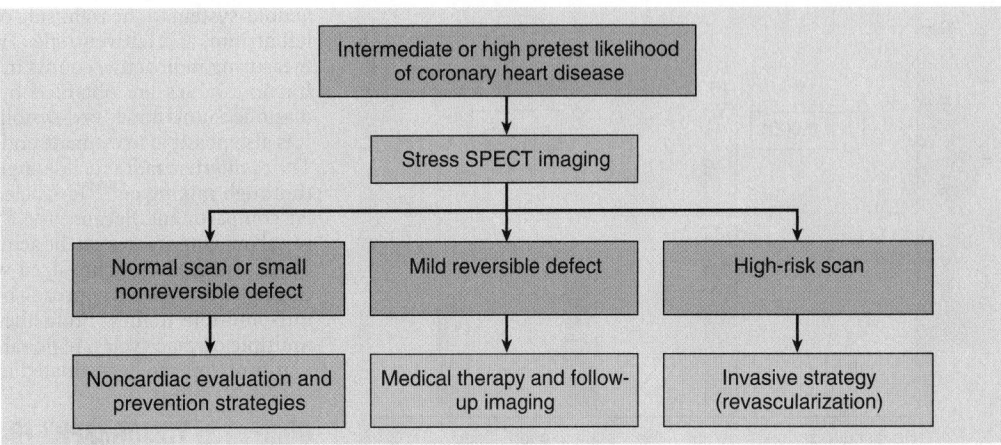

FIGURE 52–3 • Decision-making algorithm after stress single-photon emission computed tomography (SPECT) myocardial perfusion imaging in patients with intermediate or high pretest clinical likelihood of coronary heart disease. (A mild reversible defect is one that is confined to one coronary artery region and does not include the entire risk zone of the left anterior descending coronary artery [apex, anterolateral wall, and septum].)

on exercise or pharmacologic stress SPECT images. Patients with a non–high-risk scan or mild perfusion defects (e.g., a single-vessel disease pattern) and a normal LVEF can be treated medically without initially pursuing an invasive strategy (Fig. 52–3).

Transient ischemic left ventricular cavity dilation, by which the left ventricular cavity appears more dilated on stress images compared with rest images, is a particularly high-risk finding on SPECT. This finding occurs when subendocardial ischemia after stress causes a decrease in tracer uptake in the subendocardium, yielding what appears to be a larger left ventricular cavity than was observed on the resting images. Assessment of regional left ventricular function on poststress gated SPECT images enhances the detection of three-vessel CHD. The presence of stress-induced reversibility in patients with an LVEF less than 40% is a high-risk finding. Lipid-lowering therapy with or without anti-ischemic therapy (e.g., nitrates, β-blockers) is associated with improvement in poststress ischemic defects during follow-up, presumably owing to improved endothelial function and enhanced flow reserve.

Exercise or pharmacologic stress perfusion imaging also provides useful prognostic information for predischarge risk stratification in patients who have experienced an uncomplicated myocardial infarction or unstable angina. Demonstration of defects remote from the zone of infarction, which indicate underlying multivessel disease; evidence for residual ischemia within the infarct zone; or both identifies patients with an increased risk of reinfarction and subsequent cardiac death. Patients with only a nonreversible defect within the zone of infarction have a better long-term outcome unless the total defect size exceeds 15% of the left ventricular myocardium. Diabetic patients with inducible ischemia on exercise or adenosine SPECT images have a higher cardiac event rate than nondiabetic individuals with a similar extent of ischemia.

Patients with peripheral vascular disease may be limited by claudication and not manifest exertional angina despite substantial CHD. Preoperative pharmacologic stress perfusion imaging offers a noninvasive strategy for the detection of physiologically important coronary stenoses that may be associated with an increased risk of early and late cardiac events after peripheral vascular or aortic surgery. Patients who benefit most from preoperative risk assessment using pharmacologic stress perfusion imaging are patients at an intermediate or high risk of having underlying CHD based on clinical and resting ECG variables and who are scheduled to undergo intermediate-risk or high-risk operations. Patients with evidence for inducible ischemia on preoperative perfusion imaging are likely to benefit from preoperative β-blocker therapy. Some patients also may benefit from coronary angiography and coronary revascularization performed before the planned elective vascular surgical operation.

Exercise or pharmacologic stress perfusion imaging is superior to exercise ECG testing alone for detection of coronary restenosis in patients presenting with recurrence of symptoms after a percutaneous coronary intervention. Stress perfusion imaging also has proved useful for identifying high-risk patients who have undergone previous coronary artery bypass graft surgery. Ischemia induced at a low workload in patients with depressed left ventricular function merits an invasive evaluation in postbypass patients.

Determination of Myocardial Viability with Single-Photon Emission Computed Tomography or Positron Emission Tomography

SPECT perfusion imaging, particularly with ^{201}Tl, is performed only in the resting state to identify residual myocardial viability in zones corresponding to severe regional wall motion abnormalities in patients with CHD and depressed left ventricular function. When severe left ventricular dysfunction is caused by "hibernation," which is a state of chronic reduced contractility because of substantial ischemia, and not by irreversible myocardial necrosis, ^{201}Tl uptake is preserved at rest. [201]Tl is injected at rest, and images are acquired 10 minutes and 4 hours later. Areas of resting hypoperfusion that are viable and contributing to hibernation show initial defects on early images and delayed redistribution or mild nonreversible defects on delayed images. If ^{201}Tl uptake ultimately exceeds 50% or 60% of peak uptake in these regions, there is a high probability (65 to 75%) that regional myocardial function would improve after successful revascularization. Myocardial zones of asynergy showing less than 50% [201]Tl uptake on resting ^{201}Tl images have only a 10 to 20% probability of showing improved regional function after revascularization. Resting ^{99m}Tc-sestamibi or ^{99m}Tc-tetrofosmin gated SPECT after nitroglycerin administration also can assess viability.

Regional myocardial metabolism can be assessed noninvasively using PET with FDG and a flow tracer such as ^{13}N ammonia. FDG is a glucose analogue that is taken up initially in myocardial cells and is trapped by conversion to FDG-6 phosphate. FDG is impermeable to the cell membrane and remains within viable cells at high concentrations for more than 40 to 60 minutes. Increased FDG activity on clinical PET images in areas of diminished regional blood flow as determined by ^{13}N ammonia imaging is characteristic of myocardial viability. These areas of blood flow/FDG mismatch usually show improved regional function after coronary revascularization. Regions of the heart that show diminished ^{13}N uptake and FDG uptake (a "match" pattern) represent predominantly nonviable myocardium, and these segments have only a 10 to 15% probability of showing improved systolic function after revascularization.

Patients with CHD with predominantly viable myocardium as the cause of left ventricular dysfunction have better survival (Fig. 52–4) and more improvement of heart failure symptoms after revascularization than with medical therapy. Patients who have an ischemic cardiomyopathy with poor viability on either resting SPECT or PET have a worse outcome after coronary revascularization compared with patients with predominantly viable myocardium. Figure 52–5 is a proposed decision-making algorithm for identifying patients with CHD and depressed LVEF who would benefit most from revascularization.

IMAGING OF VENTRICULAR FUNCTION

Global and segmental left and right ventricular function can be evaluated accurately using gated cardiac blood pool imaging with either the *first-pass* method or the *equilibrium* method to provide a radionuclide angiogram or ventriculogram. A uniform diminution of

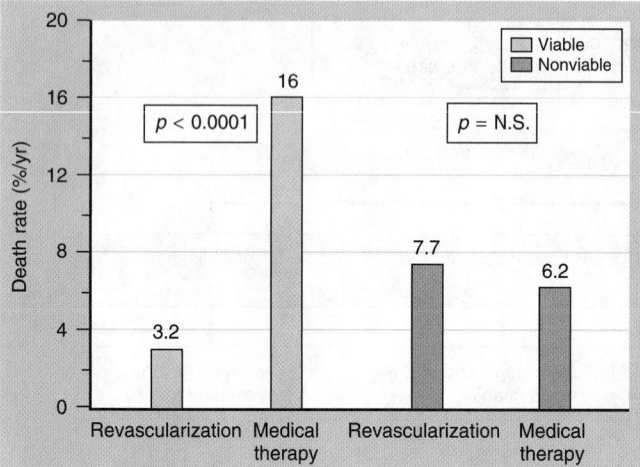

FIGURE 52–4 • Death rates for patients with and without myocardial viability treated by revascularization (Revsc) or medical therapy (Med Rx). There was a significant, approximately 80%, reduction in mortality for patients with viable myocardium treated by revascularization. In patients with nonviable myocardium, there was no significant difference in mortality with revascularization versus medical therapy. Patients with nonviable myocardium had almost twice the death rate with revascularization compared with patients with viable myocardium who underwent revascularization (7.7% versus 3.2%; $P < .0001$). (Reprinted with permission from the American College of Cardiology Foundation, J Am Coll Cardiol 2002;39:1151-1158.)

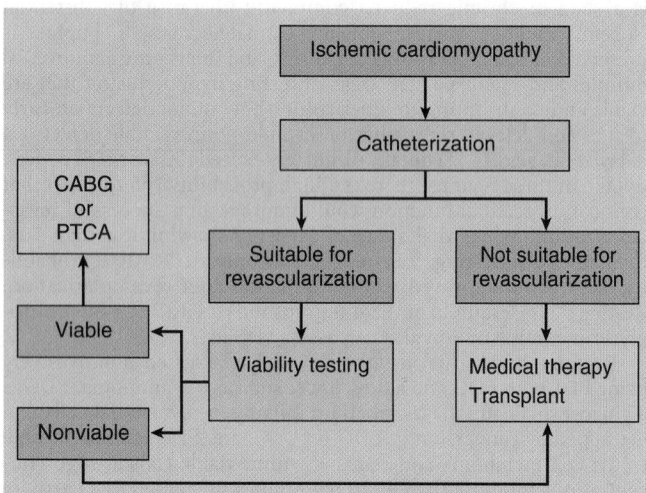

FIGURE 52–5 • Decision-making algorithm for the assessment of patients with ischemic cardiomyopathy. All patients should undergo coronary angiography and ventriculography, and patients not suitable for revascularization should undergo vigorous medical treatment and subsequent transplantation if criteria for such an intervention are met. In patients whose coronary vessels are suitable for revascularization, a resting single-photon emission computed tomography (SPECT) study, positron emission tomography (PET) study, or low-dose dobutamine echocardiogram can help identify hibernating but viable myocardium that may benefit from coronary revascularization. In contrast, patients with poor viability in areas of abnormal myocardial function would be treated best medically or considered for cardiac transplantation. An exception to this strategy is in patients who have severe angina and who usually should undergo revascularization to alleviate symptoms and improve quality of life without a prior assessment of myocardial viability. CABG = coronary artery bypass graft surgery; PTCA = percutaneous transluminal coronary angioplasty.

left ventricular systolic function without segmental wall motion abnormalities suggests nonischemic dilated cardiomyopathy, whereas depressed global left ventricular function associated with segmental wall motion abnormalities suggests ischemic heart disease.

First-pass radionuclide angiography analyzes rapidly acquired image frames to observe the fate of a bolus of ^{99m}Tc as it traverses the

venous system to the right side of the heart, pulmonary artery, lungs, left atrium, and left ventricle. Time-activity curves are generated by measuring radioactive counts in the blood pools over time. Ejection fraction values are obtained by dividing the stroke counts (end-diastolic counts minus end-systolic counts) by the end-diastolic counts. It is also possible to estimate end-systolic and end-diastolic volumes. The *equilibrium* radionuclide angiographic approach is performed after thorough mixing of ^{99m}Tc-labeled blood cells within the intravascular compartment. Because the ^{99m}Tc remains within the blood pool, serial imaging studies can be acquired over several hours. Acquisition of the images is synchronized with the QRS complex on the ECG through a multigated approach by which each cardiac cycle is divided into multiple frames. From the frame images accumulated during multiple cardiac cycles, regional wall motion and global left ventricular function can be evaluated in a cine mode.

COMPUTED TOMOGRAPHY FOR DETECTING AND QUANTIFYING CORONARY ARTERY CALCIUM

Ultrafast computed tomography (CT), also referred to as electron beam CT, images calcification associated with atherosclerotic plaques in coronary arteries. Coronary calcium also can be detected using multislice CT scanners permitting rapid cardiac imaging during a single breath hold. Autopsy studies have shown a significant relationship between the amount of calcium deposited in coronary arteries and the severity of underlying coronary atherosclerotic disease. Ultrafast CT can measure coronary calcification accurately with a high degree of reproducibility (Fig. 52–6). Coronary calcification is measured using a radiographic density of 130 Hounsfield units (HU) in at least one pixel as a threshold for a calcified lesion. The calcium-scoring algorithm from Agaston is the one most often used. Calcium densities of 130 to 200 HU are assigned a score of 1; densities of 201 to 300 HU, a score of 2; densities of 301 to 400 HU, a score of 3; and densities greater than 401 HU, a score of 4. Peak calcium density values are multiplied by the area of calcification in mm^2 per coronary tomographic segment to derive the score. Adding the scores for the individual coronary arteries yields a score for the entire coronary tree. Often, results of electron beam CT are represented as a percentile (e.g., 75th percentile). Ultrafast CT can identify obstructive coronary

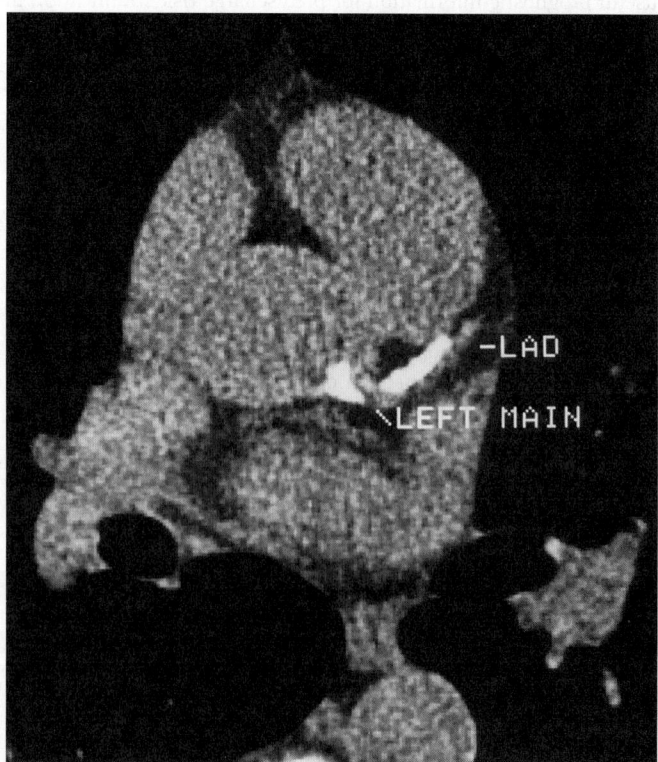

FIGURE 52–6 • Example of an electron beam computed tomography (CT) scan (ultrafast CT) showing heavy calcium deposits in the left main and left anterior descending (LAD) coronary arteries. (Courtesy Alan D. Guerci, MD, The Heart Center, St. Francis Hospital, Roslyn, NY.)

disease with an approximate 75% sensitivity and 80% specificity in *symptomatic* patients. The extent of calcification does not correlate with the severity of stenosis, however, so CT for coronary calcification has limited value in the evaluation of symptomatic patients (e.g., patients with chest pain). The presence and extent of coronary calcium predict an increased risk of future cardiac events in asymptomatic individuals, but controversy exists regarding whether calcium-scanning information provides incremental prognostic information over clinical variables. Event-free survival is significantly higher for patients with a coronary artery calcification score of less than 100 than for those with scores of 100 or higher. Some observers have suggested that asymptomatic patients in the 45- to 60-year age group with risk factors for CHD and high calcium scores might be candidates for more aggressive lipid-lowering therapy than asymptomatic patients with low scores. Whether electron beam CT scanning is effective in motivating asymptomatic patients with abnormal scans to change their lifestyle in modifying CHD risk factors is unclear, but one randomized trial showed no incremental benefit.■ Ultrafast CT also may be useful for detecting myocardial fat infiltration and diagnosing arrhythmogenic right ventricular dysplasia.

CONVENTIONAL COMPUTED TOMOGRAPHY

Perhaps the most frequently used clinical application of conventional CT in patients with cardiovascular disease is the assessment of disorders of the aorta, such as suspected dissecting aortic aneurysm (Chapter 75). Conventional CT with contrast medium enhancement has a high sensitivity for diagnosing an aneurysm, can measure its diameter accurately, and can determine the presence or absence of intraluminal thrombus. CT is also highly accurate for identifying the intimal flap and differentiating the true from the false lumen. Conventional CT can detect accurately pericardial cysts, neoplastic pericardial infiltration, pericardial effusion, and pericardial thickening as seen in chronic constrictive pericarditis.

New-generation multislice CT scanners have the capability of imaging the coronary arteries noninvasively. The ability to evaluate coronary plaque morphology is also a promising application of this technology.

1. O'Malley PG, Feuerstein IM, Taylor AJ: Impact of electron beam tomography, with or without case management, on motivation, behavioral change, and cardiovascular risk profile: A randomized controlled trial. JAMA 2003;289:2215–2223.

SUGGESTED READINGS

Allman KC, Shaw LJ, Hachamovitch R, Udelson JE: Myocardial viability testing and impact of revascularization on prognosis in patients with coronary artery disease and left ventricular dysfunction: A meta-analysis. J Am Coll Cardiol 2002;39:1151–1158. *The data show a significantly higher mortality with medical treatment versus revascularization for patients with coronary heart disease and left ventricular dysfunction. Patients with poor viability had a worse outcome after revascularization than patients with good viability.*

Beller GA, Zaret BL: Contributions of nuclear cardiology to diagnosis and prognosis of patients with coronary artery disease. Circulation 2000;101:1465–1478. *This article reviews the clinical applications of nuclear cardiology techniques and new imaging techniques being investigated.*

Berman DS, Hayes SW, Shaw LJ, Germano G: Recent advances in myocardial perfusion imaging. Curr Probl Cardiol 2001;26:1–140. *A review of clinical applications of nuclear cardiology.*

Hachamovitch R, Berman DS, Kiat H, et al: Value of stress myocardial perfusion single photon emission computed tomography in patients with normal resting electrocardiograms: An evaluation of incremental prognostic value and cost-effectiveness. Circulation 2002;105:823–829. *Data show incremental value of stress SPECT imaging in patients with a normal resting ECG and an intermediate likelihood of CHD.*

O'Rourke RA, Brundage BH, Froelicher VF, et al: American College of Cardiology/American Heart Association Expert Consensus Document on electron-beam computed tomography for the diagnosis and prognosis of coronary artery disease. J Am Coll Cardiol 2000;36:326–340. *Guidelines for use of coronary calcium scanning are presented.*

53 CARDIOVASCULAR MAGNETIC RESONANCE IMAGING

Warren J. Manning

More than any other imaging technique, cardiovascular magnetic resonance (CMR) offers the potential for dramatically changing current imaging strategies for the evaluation of patients with known or suspected cardiovascular disease. The combined attributes of superior image quality and flexibility for assessment of cardiac anatomy, ventricular function, great vessel and coronary anatomy and blood flow,

Table 53–1 • CLINICAL APPLICATIONS FOR CARDIOVASCULAR MR

1. Diagnosis and serial evaluation of thoracic aorta
   Aneurysm
   Dissection
   Hematoma
   Coarctation
2. Assessment of simple and complex congenital heart disease
   Spatial relationships of aorta, pulmonary arteries, cardiac chambers, venous system
   Identification of anomalous coronary arteries
   Quantitation of intracardiac shunt
3. Quantitation of ventricular volumes, ejection fraction, mass
   Quantitative left and right ventricle volumes, ejection fraction, mass
   Regional and global systolic function
4. Primary or secondary cardiac tumors
   Especially tumors that involve extracardiac structures
5. Pericardial disease
   Constriction
   Pericardial effusions—especially loculated effusions
6. Assessment of specific cardiomyopathies
   Hypertrophic cardiomyopathy—distribution of hypertrophy
   Sarcoidosis
   Hemochromatosis
   Right ventricular dysplasia
   Discrimination of ischemic vs. nonischemic etiology with coronary magnetic resonance angiography
7. Coronary artery disease
   Multivessel proximal/mid coronary artery disease
   Regional myocardial viability
   Regional myocardial contractility

myocardial viability, and myocardial perfusion give CMR tremendous potential for evaluation of the cardiovascular system. Current clinical applications of CMR are expanding rapidly (Table 53–1), but are not "mainstream" at most institutions. Given the relative cost disadvantage of CMR in comparison with other noninvasive technologies such as ultrasound (echocardiography, Chapter 51) and nuclear cardiology (Chapter 52), the ultimate clinical role of CMR will likely depend on strategies that eliminate the need for other imaging tests such as echocardiography or diagnostic x-ray coronary angiography (Chapter 54).

The most common CMR approaches are *spin-echo* (black blood) imaging, used for mediastinal and cardiac anatomy, and *gradient-echo* (bright blood) techniques, used for cine imaging (e.g., ventricular function). Regions of local turbulence are depicted as low signal intensity techniques on the latter. For most CMR applications, electrocardiographic (ECG) gating is essential. Exogenous intravenous contrast (gadolinium-diethylenetriamine pentaacetic acid) may be helpful in some situations (e.g., magnetic resonance angiography [MRA] of the aorta or assessment of myocardial viability) but is not needed for most anatomic and functional assessments.

Thoracic Aorta and Great Vessels

Over the past decade, CMR has had its greatest clinical impact on assessment of the thoracic aorta in patients with known or suspected thoracic aortic aneurysm or aortic dissection (Fig. 53–1) (Chapter 75). ECG-gated spin-echo transverse, coronal, and sagittal images are typically acquired along with oblique three-dimensional contrast-enhanced MRA. The "sine qua non" of aortic dissection (Chapter 75) is the identification of an intimal "flap" separating the true and false lumens. Cine gradient-echo imaging often helps to define flap mobility and blood flow in both lumens. Eccentric aortic wall thickening may also be seen and possibly represents an early dissection or intramural hematoma. In experienced hands, CMR, helical computed tomography (CT), and multiplane transesophageal echocardiography (TEE) all have similarly high sensitivity, specificity, and accuracy for the identification of thoracic aortic dissection. CMR and CT have specific advantages (vs. TEE) for providing information regarding the full extent of the dissection, specific involvement of the great vessels, entry and exit points, and the presence of a thrombosed lumen. Both TEE and CMR permit assessment of aortic valve involvement and aortic regurgitation, although valve morphology and the severity of aortic regurgitation are better appreciated by TEE. Both TEE and CMR

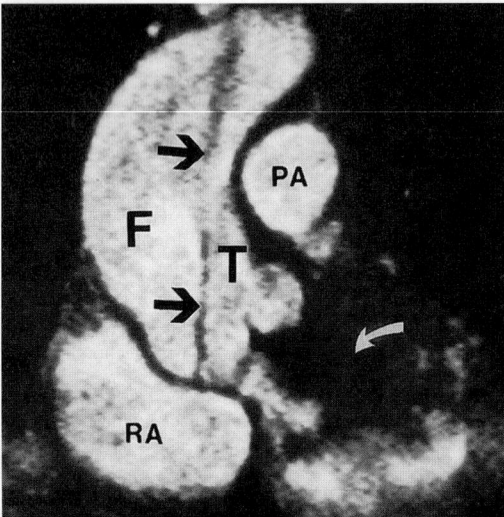

FIGURE 53–1 • Ascending aortic dissection: coronal orientation, gradient-echo sequence. Note that the dissection flap (black arrows) begins immediately superior to the aortic valve leaflet. Flow (white signal) is seen in both the true (T) and false (F) lumen. Signal void (turbulence) is seen in the left ventricular cavity immediately below the aortic valve and is caused by associated aortic insufficiency (curved white arrow). PA = pulmonary artery; RA = right atrium.

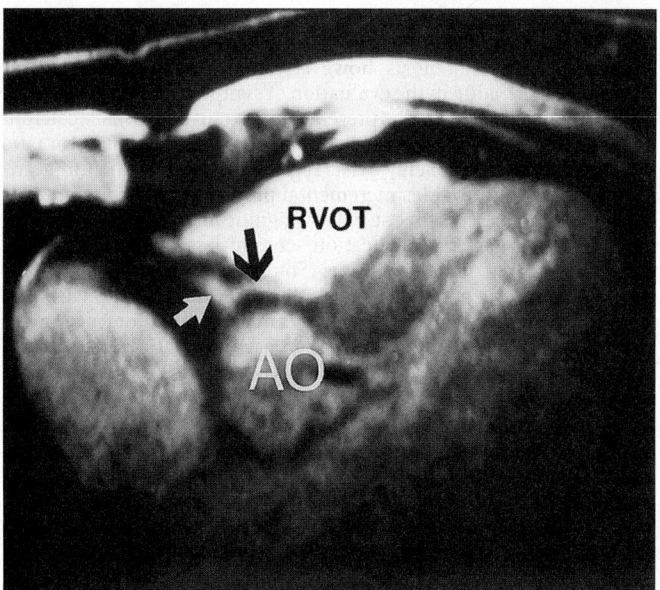

FIGURE 53–2 • Anomalous left coronary artery: transverse image, gradient-echo sequence. The normal right coronary artery (white arrow) may be seen with the anomalous left coronary artery (black arrow) traversing between the aorta (Ao) and right ventricular outflow tract (RVOT).

can often provide information regarding the involvement of the proximal coronary arteries. With current techniques, CMR assessment can be safely completed within 30 minutes. Both ECG rhythm monitoring and noninvasive blood pressure monitoring are strongly recommended during the examination.

CMR is also useful for delineation of aortic coarctation, patent ductus arteriosus, and more complex congenital abnormalities involving the great vessels (Chapter 65). In general, patients with congenital lesions are referred for CMR to confirm and/or define better an abnormality already identified or suspected on prior imaging by echocardiography or invasive x-ray angiography.

Cardiac Tumors and Masses

Although the high spatial resolution of CMR allows for depiction of intracavitary tumors/masses (e.g., myxoma, left ventricular thrombi; Chapter 79), these "masses" are generally well appreciated by echocardiographic methods. CMR adds information primarily in situations in which a mass extends into the myocardium and/or neighboring mediastinal structures (e.g., venae cavae, pulmonary veins, pericardial space). The three-dimensional representation of the mass by CMR often helps guide the surgical approach in such situations.

Although rarely difficult to diagnose from echocardiographic images, benign lipomatous hypertrophy of the interatrial septum as visualized on echocardiography may sometimes lead to the misdiagnosis of an atrial septal "tumor." The characteristic, very bright signal from fatty tissue on T1-weighted spin-echo magnetic resonance imaging (MRI) readily allows for the diagnosis of this benign disorder.

Pericardium and Pericardial Effusions

The normal pericardium is seen as a thin black line between visceral and parietal pericardial fat on spin-echo MRI. Normal pericardial thickness is less than 3 mm. In patients with constrictive cardiomyopathy, the thickened (>6 mm) pericardium is readily appreciated by MRI. CT is also valuable in this situation and is better for specific assessment of pericardial *calcifications* (Chapters 73 and 74). However, even though both MRI and CT accurately quantify focal pericardial thickening, the isolated presence of global or focal pericardial thickening is not diagnostic of constrictive physiology.

Congenital Heart Disease

CMR is useful for the assessment of both simple and complex congenital heart disease (Chapter 65). Although atrial septal defects and ventricular septal defects in adults are generally well appreciated by

transthoracic echocardiography and/or TEE, phase contrast MRI allows for quantification of blood flow through the major blood vessels, thereby facilitating quantification of the ratio of pulmonary to systemic flow. CMR is particularly valuable for assessing congenital heart disease outside the cardiac chambers, such as aortic coarctation or anomalous pulmonary venous drainage, and in patients with complex congenital heart disease who have undergone corrective or palliative surgery.

Newer breath-hold two-dimensional or navigator three-dimensional coronary MRA approaches can also be used to readily identify anomalous coronary arteries (Fig. 53–2; Chapter 65). Although uncommon, with a prevalence of only 1 to 2%, an anomalous vessel that courses between the aorta and pulmonary artery is associated with an increased risk of sudden death and myocardial infarction in young adults. Even among patients with anomalous coronary arteries identified by invasive x-ray angiography, the course of the anomalous vessel may be misinterpreted because of the projection method, thus making MRI a preferred technique.

Quantitative Assessment of Ventricular Volumes and Mass

Although rarely used clinically because of its relative cost disadvantage in comparison with echocardiography, CMR is considered the "gold standard" for the *quantitative* assessment of left and right ventricular volumes and ejection fraction, as well as regional systolic function. When compared with echocardiography, which has suboptimal results in many patients, breath-hold cine-MRI can be readily performed in nearly all patients in less than 10 minutes. Modern methods provide superior definition of the endocardial border. Semiautomated methods allow for delineation of the endocardial and epicardial borders with very high accuracy/reproducibility for determination of ventricular volumes, stroke volume, and ejection fraction. CMR may be especially valuable for eliciting *quantitative* data regarding left ventricular mass and regression of hypertrophy in response to antihypertensive therapy or aortic valve replacement. The accurate evaluation of *right* ventricular volumes and ejection fraction is also relatively unique to CMR.

Cardiomyopathies

The ability of MRI to acquire images of the entire heart in true tomographic planes makes it ideal for the evaluation of patients with hypertrophic cardiomyopathies, especially patients with focal hypertrophy (Chapter 73). Investigative CMR "tagging" methods may also be helpful in the further assessment of patients with hypertrophic cardiomyopathy, but this application remains to be more fully elucidated.

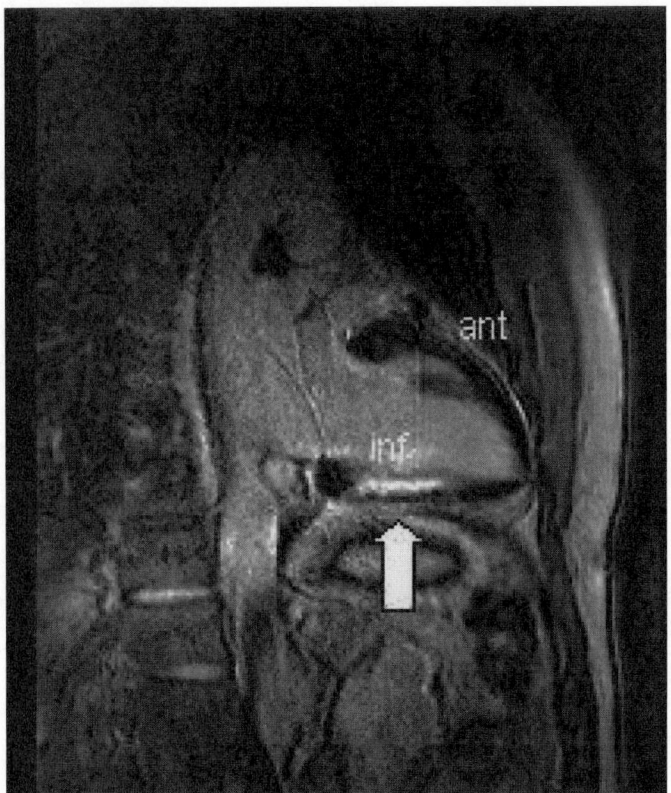

FIGURE 53–3 • Delayed-imaging, contrast-enhanced cardiovascular magnetic resonance in a patient with prior infarction. Note the near transmural enhancement of the inferior wall consistent with a low likelihood of functional improvement with mechanical revascularization. (Courtesy of Susan B. Yeon, MD.)

In specific conditions, CMR is also useful in the assessment of patients with dilated cardiomyopathy. In addition to biventricular volumetric and mass data, CMR may confirm excess iron deposition as the cause of depressed systolic function in a patient with suspected hemochromatosis (Chapter 225). With spin-echo imaging, depressed T2* correlates with impaired systolic function and with the severity of iron deposition. In contrast, focal signal enhancement may be found with other diseases such as sarcoidosis (Chapter 91) or myocarditis (Chapter 73). In the absence of clinical suspicion, however, routine CMR to assess iron in patients with a dilated cardiomyopathy is currently not suggested.

Spin-echo CMR can be used to identify transmural or focal fatty infiltration in the right ventricular free wall of patients with suspected right ventricular dysplasia, a condition associated with ventricular arrhythmias and sudden death and in which the right ventricular free wall myocardium is diffusely or focally replaced with fatty or fibrous tissue (Chapter 60). Associated focal wall thinning and systolic dysfunction are also often present.

Coronary Artery Disease

In addition to the quantification of global ventricular volumes and mass and the assessment of regional systolic function, there appears to be an increasing role for the use of CMR for the depiction of proximal/mid native coronary artery disease and for the identification of viable myocardium (Fig. 53–3). Patients likely to benefit from coronary MRA include those presenting with a dilated cardiomyopathy in the absence of prior clinical infarction. Delayed-imaging, contrast-enhanced CMR accurately discriminates patients with an ischemic myopathy from those with a nonischemic myopathy. Delayed-imaging CMR may also be used to identify regional myocardium that will demonstrate functional improvement following mechanical revascularization.

Special Considerations for CMR in Cardiac Patients

In addition to general restrictions regarding MRI (e.g., intracranial clips, transcutaneous electrical nerve stimulation units, intra-auricular implants), special considerations are also needed when performing MRI in cardiac patients. Nearly all current clinical CMR strategies use ECG gating to minimize artifacts (blurring) related to bulk cardiac motion. Although the presence of an irregular rhythm (atrial fibrillation, frequent ventricular or atrial ectopic activity) is not a contraindication to CMR, image quality often may be suboptimal in these settings.

MRI is considered safe for all bioprosthetic and mechanical heart valves, but signal loss and image distortion occur in the region immediately surrounding the prosthesis. Similarly, sternotomy wires and thoracic vascular clips are not a contraindication to imaging, but localized artifacts are common. CMR appears to be safe in patients with intracoronary stents.

Patients with cardiac pacemakers and implantable cardioverter-defibrillators should *not* undergo MRI because of concern regarding reprogramming of the device, direct stimulation of the heart during gradient switching, and/or localized heating in the lead system. Similarly, patients with retained permanent pacemaker leads or patients with pulmonary artery catheters that include pacing or thermistor wires should not undergo MRI.

Future Directions

"Real-time" CMR imaging is likely to become routinely available, and its clinical and prognostic value, either alone or in comparison with more established noninvasive imaging methods, will be defined.

SUGGESTED READINGS

Kim RJ, Wu E, Rafael A, et al: The use of contrast-enhanced magnetic resonance imaging to identify reversible myocardial dysfunction. N Engl J Med 2000;343:1445–1453. *Report demonstrating the predictive value of delayed, contrast-enhanced CMR for the identification of regional myocardium dysfunction that will (or will not) improve after mechanical revascularization.*

Kim WY, Danias PG, Stuber M, et al: Three-dimensional coronary magnetic resonance angiography for the detection of coronary artery stenoses. N Engl J Med 2001;345:1863–1869. *First multicenter prospective study comparing coronary MRA with x-ray angiography for the detection of proximal/mid coronary artery disease.*

Kwong RY, Schussheim AE, Rekhraj S, et al: Detecting acute coronary syndrome in the emergency department with cardiac magnetic resonance in aging. Circulation 2003;107:531–537. *MR may be useful for discriminating ischemic from nonischemic causes of acute chest pain.*

Manning WJ and Pennell DJ (eds): Cardiovascular Magnetic Resonance. New York, Churchill-Livingstone, 2002. *A general reference for nearly all aspects of cardiac MR.*

54 CATHETERIZATION AND ANGIOGRAPHY

David P. Faxon

Cardiac catheterization and angiography provide the detailed assessment of anatomy and physiology of the heart and vasculature and are the gold standard for assessment of cardiac disease. The technique first was applied to humans by Forssmann in 1929, but it was expanded into a diagnostic tool by Cournand and Richards; in 1956, all three physicians shared the Nobel Prize for their discovery. Selective coronary angiography was introduced by Sones in 1963 and modified further by Judkins. Cardiac catheterization is now the second most common operative procedure in the United States, with nearly 2 million procedures performed annually.

Indications

Cardiac catheterization is performed most commonly to determine the nature and extent of a suspected cardiac problem in a symptomatic patient in whom surgical or interventional therapy is anticipated (Table 54–1). It is also used to exclude the presence of significant disease when findings from other modalities, such as stress testing or echocardiography, are equivocal or when the patient continues to be severely symptomatic and a definitive diagnosis is important in the patient's management.

Because coronary angiography is the only technique capable of accurately defining the severity and extent of coronary disease, it is essential in the assessment of patients being considered for revascularization. If coronary disease is unlikely and noninvasive testing can define accurately the cardiac abnormality, cardiac catheterization

Table 54–1 • INDICATIONS FOR CARDIAC CATHETERIZATION AND ANGIOGRAPHY

CORONARY ARTERY DISEASE
Asymptomatic or symptomatic
  High risk for adverse outcome based on noninvasive testing
  After resuscitation from cardiac arrest or sustained ventricular
    tachycardia
Symptomatic
  Severe angina on medical therapy
  Unstable angina (high or intermediate risk)
  Acute myocardial infarction
    Primary reperfusion with angioplasty
    Recurrent ischemic episodes during hospitalization
    Shock or hemodynamic instability
    Mechanical complications such as mitral regurgitation or
      ventricular septal defect
  Chest pain of uncertain origin and noninvasive testing is equivocal
  High-risk patients undergoing noncardiac surgery

VALVULAR HEART DISEASE
Aortic stenosis
  Symptomatic patients (angina, heart failure, syncope) with suspected
    severe aortic stenosis
  Hypertrophic cardiomyopathy with angina
Aortic regurgitation
  Symptomatic patients (angina, heart failure, syncope) with suspected
    severe aortic regurgitation
  Asymptomatic patients with progressive cardiac enlargement or
    reduction of ejection fraction
Mitral stenosis
  Symptomatic patients (dyspnea, heart failure, emboli) with suspected
    severe mitral stenosis
Mitral regurgitation
  Symptomatic patients (dyspnea, heart failure, emboli) with suspected
    severe mitral regurgitation

OTHER
Congenital heart disease
  Before cardiac surgery or percutaneous correction
Pericardial disease
  Symptomatic patients with suspected constrictive pericarditis or
    tamponade
Vascular disease
  Aortic dissection or aneurysm with suspected concomitant coronary
    disease
Congestive heart failure
  New onset
  Suspected to be secondary to coronary artery disease
Cardiac transplantation
  Presurgical and postsurgical evaluation

Adapted from American College of Cardiology/American Heart Association Ad Hoc Task Force on Practice Guidelines: ACC/AHA Guidelines for Coronary Angiography. Circulation 1999;99:2345–2357.

may not be necessary in young adults or children with simple congenital anomalies, such as atrial septal defect, or young adults with valvular heart disease, such as aortic stenosis or mitral stenosis. Even then, valuable prognostic information often can be gathered from the hemodynamic measurements at the time of cardiac catheterization.

Contraindications and Risks

The risks of cardiac catheterization and coronary angiography are low, with a 0.05% risk of myocardial infarction, 0.07% risk of stroke, and a reported mortality of 0.1%. These risks are increased substantially, however, in certain subsets of patients, such as patients undergoing an emergency procedure, patients having an acute myocardial infarction, and patients who are hemodynamically unstable. In patients who require catheterization as a prelude to a potentially life-saving intervention, there are no absolute contraindications, but relative contraindications include acute renal failure, pulmonary edema, bacteremia, acute stroke, active gastrointestinal bleeding, and documented anaphylactic reaction to contrast dye.

Of all the potential complications, contrast medium–induced allergic reactions and contrast medium–induced renal failure are particularly important because they are common, even in relatively healthy patients, and precautions can reduce these risks. The frequency of

allergic reactions is 5%, and life-threatening anaphylactic reactions occur in 0.1% of patients undergoing angiographies. Pretreatment of patients with prior allergic reactions with corticosteroids, antihistamines, and H_2 antagonists can reduce substantially the risk of a subsequent reaction. Contrast medium–induced renal failure occurs in 3 to 7% of all patients but is most common in patients with diabetes and/or preexisting renal failure, in whom the incidence is 12 to 30%. Preprocedural and postprocedural hydration for 12 hours with 0.5 normal saline at 50 mL/hr reduces the risk of subsequent renal failure. Pretreatment and post-treatment for 2 days with acetylcysteine has been shown in randomized trials to reduce the incidence of contrast-induced nephropathy in patients with moderate renal failure. Diabetics on metformin should have the drug withdrawn 48 hours before the procedure to reduce the risk of contrast-induced lactic acidosis.

Technique

Patients should be fasting and sedated, but awake, for the procedure. Antibiotics are not necessary. Oral anticoagulation should be stopped before the procedure, but emergent cardiac catheterization can be performed on full anticoagulation or even after the recent administration of thrombolytic agents.

Vascular Access

Most procedures are performed percutaneously through the femoral artery and vein. A brachial (or radial or, rarely, axillary) approach is used when peripheral vascular disease precludes access from the lower extremity or when early ambulation after the procedure is crucial. After the femoral approach, 4 to 6 hours of local compression and bed rest is desirable before the patient ambulates and is discharged. If percutaneous closure devices are used, earlier ambulation is possible.

Right-Sided Heart Catheterization

The most commonly used catheter is a balloon flotation catheter that is introduced into the femoral, brachial, subclavian, or internal jugular vein, then passed with or without fluoroscopic guidance into the right atrium, right ventricle, and pulmonary artery. If necessary, hemodynamic measurement of oxygen saturations can be obtained as the catheter is passed into the pulmonary artery. When in the pulmonary artery, inflation of the balloon at the tip of the catheter occludes the smaller pulmonary arteries and allows for measurement of the pulmonary capillary wedge pressure, which is nearly always an accurate reflection of left atrial pressure. With a thermistor-tipped balloon, thermal dilution cardiac output also can be obtained.

Left-Sided Heart Catheterization

The left-sided cardiac structures can be accessed from the femoral, brachial, radial, or axillary artery. The catheters are passed retrograde under fluoroscopic guidance into the ascending aorta. Because embolization of a clot from a catheter in the arterial circulation could lead to a stroke, heparin frequently is used. Hemodynamic measurements and oxygen saturations also are obtained.

Occasionally, left-sided heart catheterization can be accomplished by a needle-tipped catheter that punctures the atrial septum from the right atrial side to enter the left atrium; the needle is withdrawn, and the catheter is advanced to the left ventricle. This technique is reserved for situations in which the left ventricle cannot be accessed by the retrograde approach, such as in patients who have aortic valve prostheses, or when mitral valvuloplasty or invasive electrophysiology studies are being done.

Hemodynamic Assessment

PRESSURE MEASUREMENTS

The measurement of intracardiac pressure is an essential component of cardiac catheterization and is performed through fluid-filled catheters that are attached to an external pressure transducer (Table 54–2). The shape and magnitude of the waveforms provide important diagnostic information. An elevated mean right atrial pressure

Table 54–2 • NORMAL HEMODYNAMIC MEASUREMENTS

	RANGE
PRESSURES (mm Hg)	
Right heart	
Right atrium (mean, a wave, v wave)	0–5, 1–7, 1–7
Right ventricle (peak systole, end-diastole)	17–32, 1–7
Pulmonary artery (peak systole, diastole, mean)	17–32, 4–13, 9–19
Pulmonary capillary wedge (mean)	4–12
Left heart	
Left atrium (mean, a wave, v wave)	4–12, 4–15, 4–15
Left ventricle (peak systole, end-diastole)	90–140, 5–12
Aorta (peak systole, diastole, mean)	90–140, 60–90, 70–105
CARDIAC OUTPUT AND RESISTANCES	
Cardiac index (L/min/m²)	2.8–4.2
Arteriovenous oxygen difference (vol%)	3.5–4.8
Systemic vascular resistance (dyne-sec-cm⁻⁵)	900–1400
Pulmonary vascular resistance (dyne-sec-cm⁻⁵)	40–120
Oxygen consumption (mL/min)	115–140

associated with a rapid y descent and an early rise (square root sign), with equalization of right atrial, right ventricular diastolic, left atrial, and left ventricular diastolic pressures is characteristic of *constrictive pericarditis*. *Cardiac tamponade* (Chapter 74) results in equalization of diastolic chamber pressures but without a prominent y descent. A large v wave (two times greater than the mean pressure) in the right atrium or left atrium suggests severe *tricuspid* or *mitral regurgitation*. Simultaneous recording of pressures in the proximal and distal cardiac chambers can allow for assessment of valvular stenosis. A pressure gradient in diastole between the pulmonary capillary wedge pressure or left atrial pressure and the left ventricle is found in patients with *mitral stenosis*. A gradient between the aorta and left ventricular systolic pressure is present when *aortic stenosis* (Chapter 72) occurs (Fig. 54–1). Simultaneous measurement of blood flow is important in assessment of valvular disease. In the presence of regurgitation, an increasing gradient is evident because of an increase in blood flow across the valve. When a premature ventricular contraction induces a large pressure gradient between the aorta and left ventricle and a reduction in pulse pressure in the aorta (Brockenbrough effect), *hypertrophic obstructive cardiomyopathy* (Chapter 73) is suggested. *Severe aortic regurgitation* (Chapter 72) causes an elevation in aortic systolic pressure, a

fall in aortic diastolic pressure, and equalization of the end-diastolic pressures in the ventricle and aorta.

CARDIAC OUTPUT

Cardiac output can be measured by the direct Fick method, by indicator dilution methods, or by angiographic techniques. The Fick method is the most accurate in low cardiac output states, whereas the indicator dilution method is most accurate in high-output conditions. When an accurate assessment of cardiac output is essential (e.g., when assessing the degree of valvular stenosis), Fick and indicator dilution techniques are frequently used. The Fick principle states that the amount of a substance taken up or released by an organ is the product of its blood flow and the arterial-venous difference in the concentration of the substance. Because oxygen can be measured reliably, the Fick method determines oxygen consumption by measuring inhaled and exhaled oxygen content and the arterial and venous blood oxygen content. The formula for calculating Fick cardiac output is:

$$\text{Cardiac output (L/min)} = \left\{\frac{\text{oxygen consumption (mL O}_2/\text{min)}}{\text{arterial-venous oxygen difference (vol \% } \times 10)}\right\}$$

where the arterial-venous oxygen difference is 1.39 (oxygen carrying capacity of blood) × hemoglobin (g/dL) × (arterial-oxygen saturation difference).

The indicator dilution method is based on the Stewart-Hamilton equation, in which cardiac output is determined by the following formula:

$$\text{Cardiac output} = \left\{\frac{I \times 60}{cm \times t}\right\}$$

where *I* is amount of indicator injected, *60* is sec/min, *cm* is mean indicator concentration (mg/L), and *t* is total indicator circulatory time in seconds. The indicator dilution method involves injection of a substance that can be measured in blood. The indicator is injected at one site and sampled at another. Because the completeness of the mixing of the indicator is crucial, injection and sampling optimally are done in cardiac chambers that are not adjacent to each other, for example, injection into the right atrium and sampling in the pulmonary artery. Thermodilution techniques are most common: Temperature is the indicator, and the mean change in temperature is the indicator concentration that is sampled distally. Because cardiac output varies with body size, it is customary to calculate the cardiac index (L/min/m²) by dividing cardiac output by body surface area.

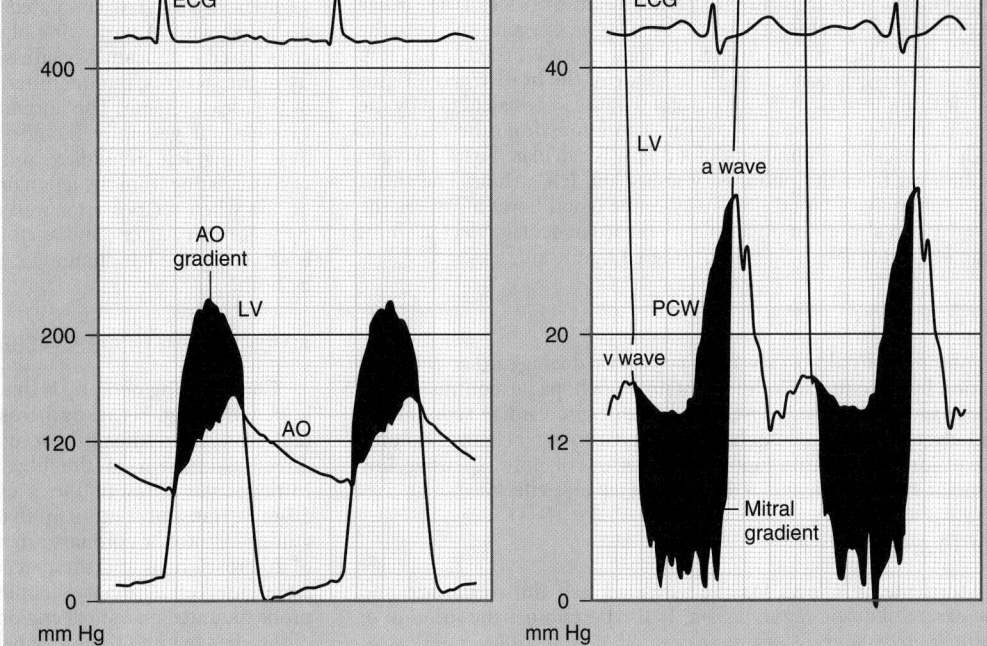

FIGURE 54–1 • Examples of the hemodynamic findings in aortic and mitral stenosis. *Left panel,* Simultaneous recording of aortic (AO) and left ventricular (LV) pressure shows a 50-mm Hg systolic pressure gradient. *Right panel,* There is a 15-mm Hg diastolic gradient between the pulmonary capillary wedge pressure (PCW) and left ventricular pressure (LV). The a wave in the PCW tracing is larger than the v wave, indicating increased resistance to left ventricular filling in this patient.

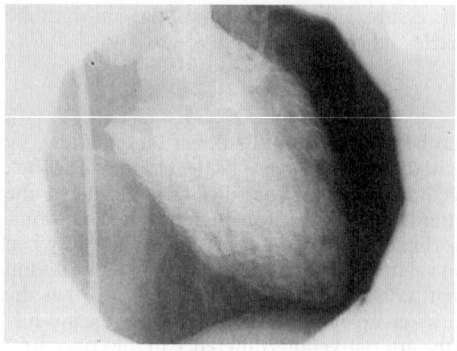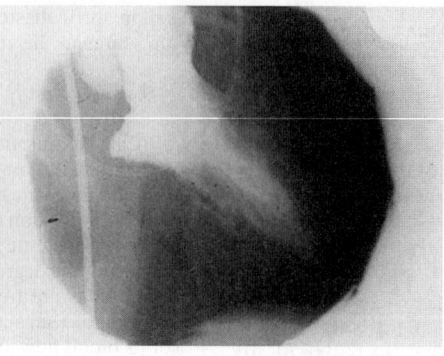

FIGURE 54–2 • An example of left ventriculography. The ventricular contour is seen in diastole (left panel) and in systole (right panel).

VALVE AREAS AND RESISTANCES

The resistance to blood flow can be calculated in a manner similar to Ohm's law of electrical resistance, as the ratio of the mean pressure gradient to the flow:

$$Resistance = \{\{mean\ pressure\ gradient//mean\ flow\}\}$$

The resistance through the systemic circulation is calculated as the mean aortic pressure minus the mean right atrial pressure, divided by cardiac output, multiplied by 80 to convert to dynes-seconds-cm^{-5}. Likewise, pulmonary vascular resistance is calculated as mean pulmonary artery pressure minus mean pulmonary capillary wedge pressure multiplied by 80 divided by cardiac output. The valve area in stenotic valves is the inverse of resistance. The most commonly used formula for calculation of valve stenosis is the Gorlin formula, where K is the constant (44.3 for aortic valve and 37.7 for mitral valve):

$$Valve\ area = \{\{flow\ across\ the\ valve//K \times \sqrt{valvular\ gradient}\}\}$$

Severe aortic stenosis is considered to be present when the mean valvular gradient is greater than 50 mm Hg and the aortic valve area is less than or equal to $0.8\ cm^2$. For the mitral valve, a valve area of less than $1.0\ cm^2$ is considered severe.

SHUNTS

Patients with known or suspected congenital heart disease (Chapter 65) should have hemodynamic assessment and estimation of the location and degree of cardiac shunting if present. Estimation of the shunt can be made by changes in oxygen saturation and by angiography. Measurement of oxygen saturation in each of the cardiac chambers and vessels can detect a "step up" in oxygen content in the right side of the heart when a left-to-right shunt is present or a "step down" in oxygen content in the left side of the heart when a right-to-left shunt is present. Systemic blood flow can be calculated by the Fick principle by obtaining oxygen saturations from the aorta and both venae cavae. Pulmonary blood flow is calculated using oxygen saturations from the pulmonary artery and left atrium. The shunt ratio (pulmonary blood flow-to-systemic blood flow) measures the severity of a shunt; for an atrial or ventricular septal defect, a shunt ratio of greater than 1.5 : 1 is considered significant.

Cardiac Angiography

Angiography almost always is performed during cardiac catheterization by injecting an iodine-containing radiopaque contrast agent. These agents are highly viscous and can cause cardiac arrhythmias and adverse hemodynamic changes secondary to ionic changes, volume expansion, and negative inotropic effects. Use of more expensive, low osmolar, nonionic agents reduces these adverse effects.

AORTOGRAPHY

Aortography allows for the assessment of the aortic size and the extent of aortic regurgitation. It also determines the location of coronary bypass grafts, if present.

LEFT VENTRICULOGRAPHY

Left ventriculography frequently is performed with coronary angiography because it allows for assessment of left ventricular size and function and the presence and extent of mitral regurgitation (Fig. 54–2). Left ventricular volume in end-diastole and end-systole can be calculated by the area-length method (normal = 70 ± 20 mL and 25 ± 10 mL). The difference between end-diastole and end-systole is the stroke volume. Cardiac output is calculated by multiplying the stroke volume by the heart rate. The ratio of angiographic stroke volume to end-diastolic volume is the ejection fraction, which is an estimate of contractile function. Normal ejection fraction ranges from 0.5 to 0.7. Wall motion abnormalities, which are usually indicative of coronary artery disease, also can be assessed during angiography and classified as hypokinetic (reduced motion), akinetic (no motion), or dyskinetic (paradoxical motion). Estimation of mitral regurgitation by angiography uses a semiquantitative technique by which 1+ is minimal regurgitation into the left atrium in systole, 2+ is mild-to-moderate regurgitation of contrast material to outline the left atrium, 3+ is moderate-to-severe regurgitation from which the left atrium becomes as dense as the left ventricle, and 4+ is severe regurgitation from which the left atrium becomes more dense than the left ventricle. Usually 3 to 4+ mitral regurgitation is considered to be hemodynamically significant and a relative indication for mitral valve surgery.

CORONARY ANGIOGRAPHY

Coronary angiography defines the coronary anatomy, the degree of obstruction of the coronary arteries, and the states of any coronary artery bypass grafts by means of injection of a contrast agent selectively in the ostium of the right or left coronary artery or bypass conduit (Figs. 54–3 and 54–4). The degree of obstruction is expressed as the percent stenosis, which is the ratio of the most severely narrowed segment in any view compared with the "normal" proximal and/or distal segment. A narrowing of greater than 50% of the diameter is considered significant. Visual assessments can overestimate the severity of the stenosis, but quantitative techniques reduce the variability of the measurement. The normal coronary vasculature can be highly variable but generally includes three major vessels: left anterior descending, left circumflex, and right coronary artery, with the first two emanating from the left main artery. A *right dominant* circulation occurs when the posterior wall of the left ventricle is served by the right coronary artery, and a *left dominant* circulation occurs when it is served by the left circumflex artery; it is *codominant* when served by both.

ADJUNCTIVE METHODS TO ASSESS CORONARY STENOSIS

Coronary angiography is limited to assessment of changes in the lumen diameter. Because atherosclerosis is a diffuse process, angiography can underestimate the severity of the disease and does not provide direct assessment of the physiologic significance of a stenosis. Intravascular ultrasound uses a small, flexible catheter with a 20- to 30-mHz transducer at its tip that can be passed over an angioplasty guidewire into the coronary artery. Accurate assessment of the degree of atherosclerosis and the percent stenosis can be obtained by this technique. Intracoronary Doppler flow measurements use a Doppler probe mounted on a small angioplasty-type guidewire. Measurement of the change in flow velocity before and after coronary vasodilation

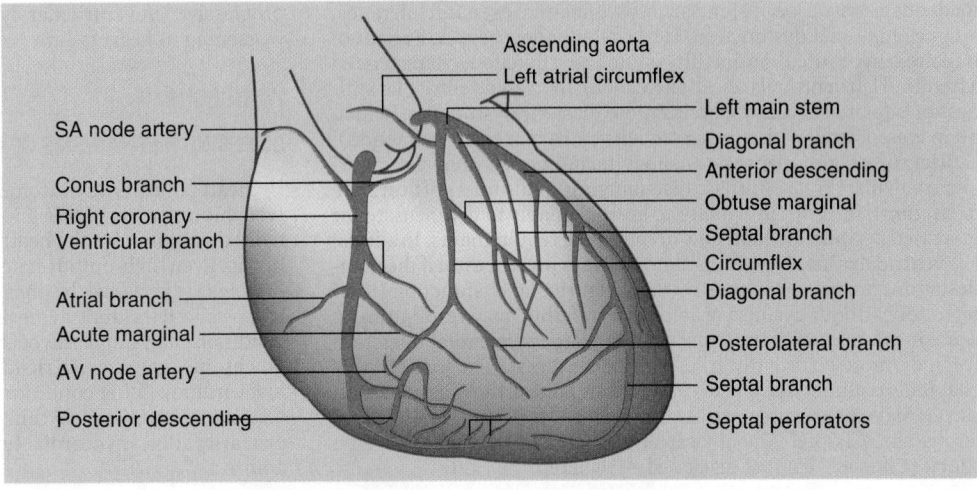

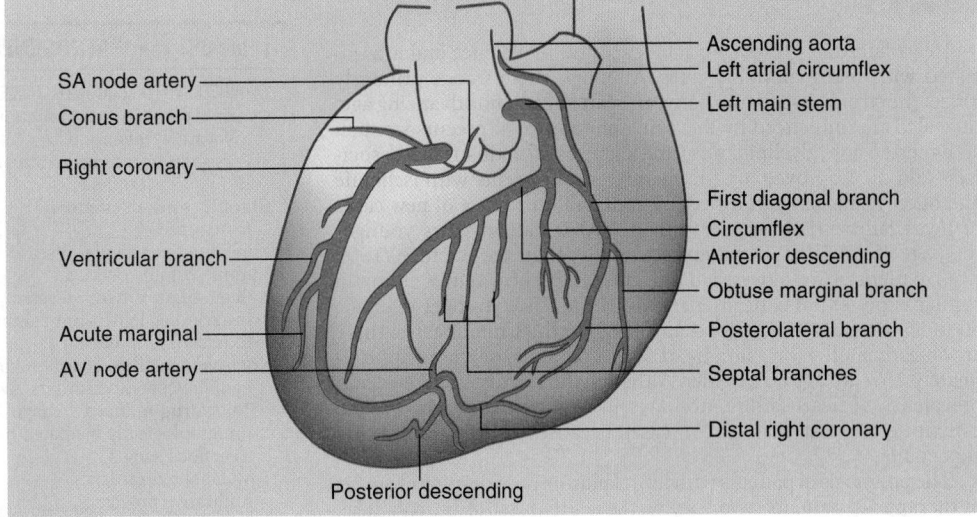

FIGURE 54–3 • The coronary vessels in the right anterior oblique (**A**) and left anterior oblique (**B**) view are shown. The major arteries are the left main, left anterior descending, circumflex, and right coronary arteries. (From Yang SS, Bentivoglio LG, Maranhao V, Goldberg H [eds]: From Cardiac Catheterization Data to Hemodynamic Parameters. Philadelphia: Oxford University Press, 1988. Used by permission of Oxford University Press, Inc.)

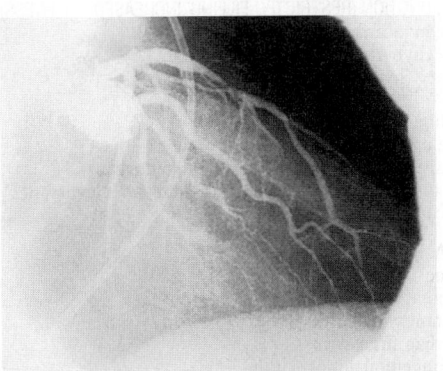

FIGURE 54–4 • An example of a significant stenosis in the left anterior descending coronary artery.

with agents such as adenosine can provide an estimate of coronary flow reserve and help assess the severity of the stenosis. A significant reduction in coronary flow reserve is present when the ratio of flow at rest to flow after vasodilation is less than 2 : 1. Measurement of the pressure gradient across a stenosis using a small wire transducer also can assess functional severity. Fractional flow reserve is the ratio of the distal pressure to proximal pressure after maximum vasodilation. A fractional flow reserve of less than 0.75 indicates a significant stenosis. Measurement of blood flow velocity and coronary artery diameter before and after administration of acetylcholine can assess the possibility that coronary vasospasm or abnormalities in coronary endothelial function are present. Intravascular ultrasound, fractional flow reserve, and Doppler flow studies are used most commonly in conjunction with interventional procedures.

Future Directions

The cardiac catheterization laboratory of the future is likely to incorporate new methods of cardiac imaging, real-time magnetic resonance angiography, and the imaging of atherosclerotic plaques with magnetic resonance techniques.

SUGGESTED READING

American College of Cardiology/American Heart Association Ad Hoc Task Force on Practice Guidelines: ACC/AHA guidelines for coronary angiography. Circulation 1999;99:2345–2357. *Review of coronary angiography and indications for the procedure.*

55 HEART FAILURE: PATHOPHYSIOLOGY AND DIAGNOSIS

Barry M. Massie

HEART FAILURE

Definition

Heart failure is a heterogeneous syndrome in which an abnormality of cardiac function is responsible for the inability of the heart to pump blood at an output sufficient to meet the requirements of metabolizing tissues or to do so only at abnormally elevated diastolic pressures or volumes. The heart failure syndrome is characterized by signs and symptoms of intravascular and interstitial volume overload, including shortness of breath, rales, and edema, and/or manifestations of inadequate tissue perfusion, such as impaired exercise tolerance, fatigue, and renal dysfunction. Heart failure may occur as a result of impaired myocardial contractility (systolic dysfunction, characterized as reduced left ventricular ejection fraction); increased ventricular stiffness or impaired myocardial relaxation (diastolic dysfunction, which often is associated with a preserved left ventricular ejection fraction); a variety of other cardiac abnormalities (including obstructive or regurgitant valvular disease, intracardiac shunting, or disorders of heart rate or rhythm); or states in which the heart is unable to compensate for increased peripheral blood flow or metabolic requirements. In adults, left ventricular involvement is almost always present even if the manifestations are primarily those of right ventricular dysfunction (fluid retention without dyspnea or rales). Heart failure may result from an acute insult to cardiac function, such as a large myocardial infarction (MI), or, more commonly, from a chronic process. The focus in this chapter is on the syndrome of *chronic* heart failure; the most common causes of de novo acute heart failure, such as MI (Chapter 69), valvular disease (Chapter 72), myocarditis (Chapter 73), and cardiogenic shock (Chapter 103), are discussed elsewhere.

Epidemiology

Heart failure is growing in incidence and prevalence and is associated with rising mortality rates. Although these trends primarily reflect the strong association between heart failure and advancing age, they also are influenced by the rising prevalence of precursors such as hypertension, dyslipidemia, and diabetes in industrialized societies and the improved long-term survival of patients with ischemic and other forms of heart disease. The annual incidence of new cases of heart failure rises from less than 1/1000 patient-years younger than age 45, to 10/1000 patient-years older than age 65, to 30/1000 (3%) patient-years older than age 85. Prevalence figures follow a similar exponential pattern, increasing from 0.1% younger than age 50 to 55 to nearly 10% older than age 80. In the United States, there are an estimated 4.8 million heart failure patients, of whom approximately 75% are age 65 or older. Although the relative incidence and prevalence of heart failure are lower in women than men, women constitute at least half of the cases because of their longer life expectancy.

The prognosis of patients with heart failure is poor despite advances in therapy. Of patients who survive the acute onset of heart failure, only 35% of men and 50% of women are alive after 5 years. Although it is difficult to predict prognosis in individual patients, patients with symptoms at rest (class IV) have a 30 to 70% annual mortality rate, patients symptomatic with mild activity (class III) have mortality rates of 10 to 20% annually, and patients with symptoms only with moderate activity (class II) have a 5 to 10% annual mortality rate. Mortality rates are higher in older patients, men, and patients with reduced ejection fractions and underlying coronary heart disease. In the United States, nearly 1 million hospitalizations each year with a primary diagnosis of heart failure account for 6 million hospital days. The estimated cost of heart failure management ranges from $15 to $40 billion annually, depending on the formula used.

Etiology and Prevention

Any condition that causes myocardial necrosis or produces chronic pressure or volume overload can induce myocardial dysfunction and heart failure. In developed countries, the causes of heart failure have changed greatly over several decades. Valvular heart disease, with the exception of calcific aortic stenosis, has declined markedly, whereas coronary heart disease has become the predominant cause in men and women, being responsible for 60 to 75% of cases. Hypertension, although less frequently the primary cause of heart failure than in the past, continues to be a factor in 75%, including most patients with coronary disease.

Treatment of hypertension, with a focus on the systolic pressure, reduces the incidence of heart failure by 50%. This intervention remains effective even in patients older than 75 years of age (Chapter 63). Any intervention that reduces the risk of a first or recurrent MI also reduces the incidence of heart failure (Chapter 47). In post-MI patients, β-blockers, antihyperlipidemic agents, antithrombotic therapy, and coronary revascularization can prevent the development of heart failure. In patients with reduced ejection fractions, angiotensin-converting enzyme (ACE) inhibitors and β-blockers prevent or delay

progressive left ventricular dysfunction and dilation and the onset or worsening of heart failure.

Pathogenesis

DIFFERING MECHANISMS OF HEART FAILURE

Heart failure is a syndrome that may result from many cardiac and systemic disorders (Table 55–1). Some of these disorders, at least initially, do not involve the heart, and the term *heart failure* may be confusing. Even high-output states may present, however, with the classic findings of exertional dyspnea and edema—*high-output heart failure*—that resolve if the underlying disorder is eliminated. If persistent, these conditions may impair myocardial performance secondarily as a result of chronic volume overload or direct deleterious effects on the myocardium. Other conditions, including mechanical abnormalities, disorders of rate and rhythm, and pulmonary abnormalities, do not primarily affect myocardial function but are frequent causes of heart failure.

Table 55–1 • PATHOGENESIS OF HEART FAILURE

IMPAIRED SYSTOLIC (CONTRACTILE) FUNCTION
Ischemic damage or dysfunction
 Myocardial infarction
 Persistent or intermittent myocardial ischemia
 Hypoperfusion (shock)
Chronic pressure overloading
 Hypertension
 Obstructive valvular disease
Chronic volume overload
 Regurgitant valvular disease
 Intracardiac left-to-right shunting
 Extracardiac shunting
Nonischemic dilated cardiomyopathy
 Familial/genetic disorders
 Toxic/drug-induced damage
 Immunologically mediated necrosis
 Infectious agents
 Metabolic disorders
 Infiltrative processes
 Idiopathic conditions

DIASTOLIC FUNCTION (RESTRICTED FILLING, INCREASED STIFFNESS)
Pathologic myocardial hypertrophy
 Primary (hypertrophic cardiomyopathies)
 Secondary (hypertension)
Aging
Ischemic fibrosis
Restrictive cardiomyopathy
 Infiltrative disorders (amyloidosis, sarcoidosis)
 Storage diseases (hemochromatosis, genetic abnormalities)
Endomyocardial disorders

MECHANICAL ABNORMALITIES
Intracardiac
 Obstructive valvular disease
 Regurgitant valvular disease
 Intracardiac shunts
 Other congenital abnormalities
Extracardiac
 Obstructive (coarctation, supravalvular aortic stenosis)
 Left-to-right shunting (patent ductus)

DISORDERS OF RATE AND RHYTHM
Bradyarrhythmias (sinus node dysfunction, conduction
 abnormalities)
Tachyarrhythmias (ineffective rhythms, chronic tachycardia)

PULMONARY HEART DISEASE
Cor pulmonale
Pulmonary vascular disorders

HIGH-OUTPUT STATES
Metabolic disorders
 Thyrotoxicosis
 Nutritional disorders (beriberi)
Excessive blood flow requirements
 Chronic anemia
 Systemic arteriovenous shunting

Table 55–2 • MAJOR DETERMINANTS OF CARDIAC PERFORMANCE

Ventricular systolic function (contractility)
Ventricular diastolic function
Relaxation
Stiffness
Ventricular preload
Ventricular afterload
Cardiac rate and conduction
Myocardial blood flow

ABNORMALITIES OF CARDIAC FUNCTION

SYSTOLIC FUNCTION. In the normal ventricle, stroke volume increases over a wide range of end-diastolic volumes (the Frank-Starling effect). If contractility (or the inotropic state of the myocardium) is enhanced, such as during exercise or catecholamine stimulation, this increase is correspondingly greater (Table 55–2). In the failing heart with depressed contractility, there is relatively little increment in systolic function with further increases in left ventricular volume, and the ventricular function curve is shifted downward and flattened (Chapter 48). In the clinical setting, systolic dysfunction is characterized by depressed stroke volume despite elevated ventricular filling pressures. The resulting symptoms are those of pulmonary or systemic congestion, activity intolerance, and organ dysfunction.

Assessment of systolic function clinically is more problematic. The most useful measure is the left ventricular ejection fraction (stroke volume/end-diastolic volume, usually expressed as a percent), which reflects a single point on the ventricular function curve. The ejection fraction is "load dependent," however, meaning that alterations in afterload (see later) can affect it independent of contractility. In addition, mitral regurgitation, which facilitates ejection into the low-pressure left atrium, may lead to an overestimation of systolic function by the ejection fraction. Nonetheless, with the exceptions indicated earlier, when the ejection fraction is normal (>50% in most laboratories), systolic function is usually adequate. Ejection fractions that are mildly (40 to 50%), moderately (30 to 40%), and severely (<30%) depressed are associated with reduced survival and, in the severe range, with reduced functional reserve if not overt symptoms of heart failure. Cardiac output, in contrast, is a poor measure of systolic function because it can be affected markedly by heart rate, systemic vascular resistance, and the degree of left ventricular dilation.

DIASTOLIC FUNCTION. Diastole is the portion of the cardiac cycle between aortic valve closure and mitral valve closure. Diastole consists of three phases: (1) active relaxation, (2) the conduit phase, and (3) atrial contraction. If relaxation is delayed or if the myocardium is abnormally stiff (e.g., a steeper relationship between change in pressure to change in volume; $\Delta P/\Delta V$ is excessively steep), passive filling may be impaired and atrial pressures are abnormally elevated. In this setting of a noncompliant ventricle (compliance is the inverse of stiffness, e.g., the change in volume for a given change in pressure), atrial contraction is responsible for a disproportionately large amount of diastolic filling.

The importance of abnormalities of diastolic function in the pathogenesis of heart failure is increasingly appreciated. Because relaxation is energy dependent, it frequently is impaired in the presence of ischemia or hypoxemia. Recurring myocardial ischemia, pathologic myocardial hypertrophy, chronic volume overload, and aging all are associated with increased interstitial fibrosis and poor relaxation.

In the left ventricle with diastolic dysfunction, left ventricular filling pressures rise because of the compliance changes, with resulting left atrial hypertension and pulmonary congestion. Cardiac output may be reduced if ventricular filling is sufficiently impaired. With activity, these abnormalities are exaggerated, with resulting exertional dyspnea and exercise intolerance.

VENTRICULAR PRELOAD. In the intact heart, preload is characterized best by the end-diastolic volume or pressure, which are indirect indicators of end-diastolic fiber length (Chapter 48). The performance of the normal ventricle is highly preload dependent, but the failing heart operates at high preloads and on the flat part of the ventricular function curve (see Fig. 48–3). In contrast to the normal ventricle, a

modest decrease in preload has little effect on left ventricular filling pressures, whereas an increase in preload does not improve systolic function but worsens pulmonary congestion further. Preload reduction by diuresis or by reducing venous return with venodilating agents generally has a beneficial clinical effect in heart failure.

VENTRICULAR AFTERLOAD. Left ventricular afterload frequently is equated with arterial pressure or systemic vascular resistance, but a more accurate measurement of afterload is systolic wall stress (Chapter 48), defined as: [Pressure × the radius of the left ventricle] ÷ [2 × the thickness of the left ventricle]. At any given arterial pressure, afterload is increased in a dilated thin ventricle and decreased with a smaller or thicker ventricle. Increased afterload has an effect similar to that of depressed contractility, so afterload reduction can improve cardiac performance.

HEART RATE AND RHYTHM. Heart rate affects cardiac performance by two mechanisms. First, increasing heart rate enhances the inotropic state by upregulating cytosolic calcium concentrations. Second, heart rate is an important determinant of cardiac output and is the primary mechanism by which cardiac output is matched to demand in situations such as exercise. Because stroke volume is relatively fixed in the failing heart, heart rate becomes the major determinant of cardiac output. Chronic tachycardia impairs ventricular performance, however, and cardiac function often improves with control of tachyarrhythmias such as atrial fibrillation.

Optimal cardiac performance depends on a well-coordinated sequence of contraction. Normal atrioventricular conduction times (0.16 to 0.20 second) enhance the contribution of atrial contraction to left ventricular filling, which is particularly important in the noncompliant ventricle. Patients with heart failure frequently have intraventricular conduction abnormalities, which result in dyssynchronous contractions, such that the septum and parts of the anterior wall begin contracting only after systole has ended in other regions.

MYOCARDIAL BLOOD FLOW AND OXYGEN REQUIREMENTS. In the normal heart, myocardial blood flow is closely coupled to oxygen requirements, and it is not ordinarily considered a determinant of cardiac performance. Myocardial ischemia is associated, however, with a rapid decline in contractile function that may persist long beyond the episode (myocardial stunning). Chronically inadequate blood flow may lead to a reduction in contractility, which re-establishes the balance between oxygen delivery and demands (hibernation). Low arterial diastolic pressures may interfere with the autoregulatory reserve of the coronary circulation, which is limited at diastolic pressures less than 60 mm Hg. Endothelial dysfunction, which is common in heart failure patients, also may limit blood flow. At the same time, tachycardia, increased afterload, and substantial left ventricular hypertrophy increase myocardial oxygen requirements. Inadequate myocardial blood flow plays an important role in the pathogenesis of cardiac dysfunction, sometimes even in patients without obstructive coronary disease.

GENETIC CAUSES OF DILATED CARDIOMYOPATHY

Although much less is known about the genetics of dilated cardiomyopathy than hypertrophic cardiomyopathy, several forms of familial cardiomyopathy have been recognized, most of which are inherited in an autosomal dominant pattern. Mutations of genes encoding for nuclear membrane proteins (emerin, lamin) or for contractile or cytoskeletal proteins (desmin, a cardiac myosin, vinculin) have been identified. Cardiomyopathy also is associated with muscular dystrophies (Duchenne's, Becker's, and limb-girdle dystrophies; Chapter 463) and other forms of myopathy. As research in this area burgeons, it is estimated that genetic abnormalities may be involved in 20 to 30% of patients with idiopathic dilated cardiomyopathy.

HEART FAILURE SYNDROME

Chronic heart failure is a multifaceted syndrome with diverse presentations (Fig. 55–1). The initial manifestations of hemodynamic dysfunction are a reduction in stroke volume and a rise in ventricular filling pressures, perhaps in the basal state but consistently under conditions of increased systemic demand for blood flow. These changes have downstream effects on cardiovascular reflexes and systemic organ perfusion and function, which in turn stimulate a variety of interdependent compensatory responses involving the cardiovascular system,

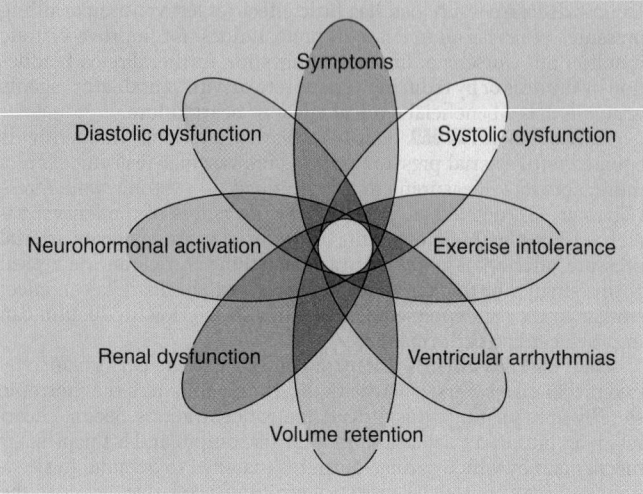

FIGURE 55-1 • Pathophysiology of heart failure, illustrated by Venn diagram.

neurohormonal systems, and alterations in renal physiology. It is this constellation of responses that leads to the characteristic pathophysiology of the heart failure syndrome. Recognition of the role of neurohormonal activation in heart failure has grown with the increasing understanding of its pathophysiology and with evidence that blockade of some of these responses can have a profound effect on the natural history of the disease (Table 55–3). The number of hormonal systems that are known to be activated in heart failure continues to grow.

Neurohumoral Responses

SYMPATHETIC NERVOUS SYSTEM

Initial activation of the sympathetic nervous system probably results from reduced pulse pressures, which stimulate arterial baroreceptors, and renal hypoperfusion. Evidence for its activation comes from elevated levels of circulating norepinephrine, direct sympathetic nerve recordings showing increased activity, and increased norepinephrine release by several organs, including the heart. As cardiac function deteriorates, responsivity to norepinephrine diminishes, as evidenced by baroreceptor desensitization and downregulation of cardiac adrenergic receptors and signal transduction. This densensitization may stimulate sympathetic responses further.

The adaptive role of norepinephrine is to stimulate heart rate and myocardial contractility and to produce vasoconstriction. All of these actions reverse the depression of cardiac output and blood pressure. Elevated levels of plasma norepinephrine are associated with a worse

Table 55-3 • NEUROHORMONES THAT MAY BE INCREASED IN CHRONIC HEART FAILURE

Norepinephrine
Epinephrine
Plasma and tissue renin activity
Angiotensin II
Aldosterone
Prostaglandins
Vasopressin
Neuropeptide Y
Vasoactive intestinal peptides
Natriuretic peptides
Endothelin
Endorphins
Calcitonin gene–related peptide
Growth hormone
Cortisol
Proinflammatory cytokines
Neurokinin A
Substance P

prognosis, although it is unclear whether this is a cause-and-effect relationship. There is also convincing, albeit circumstantial, evidence that norepinephrine has adverse effects on the myocardium. In this regard, β-adrenoceptor blockade, which for many years has been considered dangerous in heart failure because it deprives the heart of important compensatory stimulation, consistently improves left ventricular function and prognosis. The role of other catecholamines in heart failure remains undefined.

RENIN-ANGIOTENSIN-ALDOSTERONE SYSTEM

Elements of the renin-angiotensin-aldosterone system are activated relatively early in heart failure. The presumptive mechanisms of induction include renal hypoperfusion, β-adrenergic system stimulation, and hyponatremia. All may be activated further by diuretic therapy. Angiotensin II increases blood pressure by vasoconstriction and enhances glomerular filtration by increasing renal pressure and maintaining glomerular flow by its intrarenal hemodynamic effects. Aldosterone causes sodium retention, which restores normal cardiac output by enhancing intravascular volume. These adaptations have deleterious consequences, however. Excessive vasoconstriction can depress left ventricular function, and sodium retention worsens the already elevated ventricular filling pressures. There also is experimental evidence indicating that angiotensin II may have pathologic effects on the myocardium and induce vascular hypertrophy, whereas aldosterone induces myocardial fibrosis. The striking success of ACE inhibitors and, more recently, spironolactone in improving the natural history of heart failure suggests that the adverse effects of renin-angiotensin-aldosterone activation may outweigh their benefit.

OTHER NEUROHORMONAL SYSTEMS

Levels of several natriuretic peptides are elevated consistently in heart failure, and they may counterbalance the vasoconstricting and sodium-retaining actions of the renin-angiotensin-aldosterone and sympathetic nervous systems. It does seem, however, that responses to these natriuretic hormones are downregulated so that they do not have the same diuretic effects in chronic heart failure that they manifest in normal individuals. Elevated circulating and tissue levels of vasodilating prostaglandins may improve glomerular hemodynamics, and inhibitors of prostaglandin synthesis (including aspirin and other nonsteroidal anti-inflammatory agents) interfere with the hemodynamic and renal actions of ACE inhibitors.

Endothelin and arginine vasopressin are elevated in many heart failure patients, and interference with their actions may promote vasodilation and diuresis. Arginine vasopressin induces vasoconstriction through a vascular (V-1) receptor and reduces free water clearance through a renal tubular (V-2) receptor. The endothelins cause prolonged vasoconstriction, reductions in glomerular filtration, mesangial hypertrophy, bronchoconstriction, and pulmonary arteriolar constriction. The endothelins are particularly attractive targets for therapy.

CYTOKINE ACTIVATION

Circulating levels of many proinflammatory cytokines, including tumor necrosis factor-α, interleukin-1β, and interleukin-6, are elevated in patients with relatively severe heart failure and may be involved in the syndrome of cardiac cachexia. These cytokines also may induce contractile dysfunction, myocardial fibrosis, and myocyte necrosis, perhaps by mediating some of the deleterious responses to catecholamines and angiotensin II.

Altered Renal Physiology

In most patients with chronic heart failure, the kidneys are anatomically and structurally normal. Reduced blood pressure, diminished stroke volume, and reduced renal perfusion pressure and flow are sensed as reduced blood volume by the high-pressure baroreceptors and the juxtaglomerular apparatus that maintain cardiovascular homeostasis. In chronic heart failure, these receptors become desensitized, generating reduced afferent responses. The low-pressure intracardiac pressure and volume receptors also are desensitized. Thirst and fluid intake may be increased as a result of activation of the cerebral thirst center. Although heart failure usually is associated with a normal or increased blood volume, it paradoxically is characterized by activation of the same homeostatic responses as those to hemorrhage and shock; the result is abnormal retention of sodium and water. In advanced heart failure, usually characterized by low cardiac output and/or hypotension (or with coexisting renal vascular disease), the glomerular filtration rate may become so severely reduced that sodium and fluid retention becomes refractory to diuretic therapy.

Left Ventricular Remodeling and Progression of Heart Failure

After an initial insult precipitates heart failure, progressive alterations occur in myocardial structure and function owing to continuing damage by the underlying process and responses to hemodynamic stresses and neurohormonal activation. The left ventricle progressively dilates and changes from the normal ellipsoid shape to a more spherical geometry. This "remodeling" is accompanied by changes in the cardiac interstitium, leading to altered orientation of the myofibrils and progressive fibrosis. The result is more discoordinate and less effective contraction. ACE inhibitors and β-blockers slow, halt, or reverse this remodeling process, preventing left ventricular dilation, geometric distortion, and deterioration in contractile function.

CLINICAL PRESENTATION OF HEART FAILURE

Heart failure may present acutely in a de novo manner, chronically, or as an acute exacerbation of chronic heart failure.

Acute Heart Failure

Acute heart failure usually presents as shortness of breath, culminating, sometimes in a matter of minutes, with pulmonary edema. A more subacute presentation is of progressive dyspnea associated with systemic fluid retention over days to a few weeks. The precipitous form usually suggests extensive acute damage, most commonly as an ongoing or recent MI. Other insults include the acute development of valvular regurgitation from ruptured chordae tendineae, bacterial endocarditis, or aortic dissection or of rapidly progressive myocarditis or toxic damage. The syndrome may progress to cardiogenic shock (Chapter 103).

Rapid diagnosis by noninvasive testing, early cardiac catheterization, and, in some cases, endomyocardial biopsy is crucial. Treatment is cause specific and may include early coronary revascularization, valve repair or replacement, or supportive care (e.g., inotropic support, intra-aortic balloon pumping, ventricular assist devices). If not reversed, cardiac transplantation (Chapter 80) may be the best option for appropriate candidates.

Chronic Heart Failure

LEFT-SIDED AND RIGHT-SIDED HEART FAILURE

Most adult patients with heart failure have abnormalities of the left ventricle as the underlying cause. Nonetheless, the clinical presentation may be variable, sometimes suggesting predominantly or even exclusively right ventricular dysfunction. The manifestations of left ventricular dysfunction are related to elevated filling (diastolic) pressures, which are transmitted backward to the left atrium and pulmonary veins, or inadequate cardiac output. The former results in dyspnea, sometimes at rest but usually with activity, and, when severe, pulmonary edema, classically associated with rales and possibly pleural effusions. The cardiac output may be insufficient to support peripheral organ function, causing exertional muscle fatigue, impaired renal function and salt excretion, or depressed mentation.

Right-sided heart failure results from either chronic right ventricular pressure overload (e.g., pulmonary hypertension resulting from cor pulmonale or pulmonary vascular disease) or intrinsic dysfunction of the right ventricle or its valves. The most common cause of right ventricular pressure overload is left-sided heart dysfunction, however, resulting in pulmonary hypertension. When the symptoms and signs of left-sided heart failure are absent or difficult to elicit, the physician inappropriately may seek a primarily right-sided pathology. The primary manifestations of right-sided failure are related to chronically elevated right atrial and systemic venous pressures: jugular venous distention, peripheral edema, ascites, hepatic and bowel edema, and varied gastrointestinal complaints.

HEART FAILURE WITH PRESERVED SYSTOLIC FUNCTION

Myocardial mechanisms that lead to the syndrome of heart failure can be differentiated into conditions that depress left ventricular systolic function and conditions that occur despite preserved contractility. Although arbitrary, a left ventricular ejection fraction threshold of 45 to 50% often is employed for this distinction.

Until the widespread use of noninvasive assessments of left ventricular function, heart failure with preserved systolic function was considered unusual in the absence of valvular abnormalities or other specific and uncommon causes. It is now recognized, however, that 20 to 40% of heart failure patients have normal ejection fractions. In the ongoing Cardiovascular Health Study, a population-based study of more than 5000 patients age 65 and older, more than 70% of patients developing heart failure had normal or only mildly impaired systolic function. It is likely that more elderly heart failure patients have diastolic dysfunction as the primary cause of their symptoms.

Although there are many potential causes of heart failure with preserved systolic function, most patients have current hypertension or a history of treated hypertension; the resulting left ventricular hypertrophy and increased fibrosis are probably responsible for increased chamber stiffness. Ischemic heart disease also may contribute to heart failure with preserved systolic function, probably by virtue of subendocardial fibrosis or as a result of acute, intermittent ischemic dysfunction. Diabetes mellitus is often present, especially in women. Age itself is a crucial predisposing factor because it causes loss of myocytes (apoptosis), increased fibrosis with shifts to more rigid forms of collagen, and loss of vascular compliance.

The mortality rates of patients with preserved systolic function are lower than those with low ejection fractions but remain higher than the general population, even in comparison with similarly older aged individuals. Hospitalization and rehospitalization rates for these patients are comparable to rates for patients with reduced ejection fractions, and there are few data on treatment to guide physicians in the management of these patients.

Although heart failure patients with preserved systolic function often are considered to have *diastolic dysfunction*, there are many other explanations for this presentation, some of which are reversible or warrant specific therapy (Table 55–4). The first two questions are whether the patient's symptoms are due to heart failure of any type

---

Table 55–4 • CAUSES OF (AND ALTERNATIVE EXPLANATIONS FOR) HEART FAILURE WITH PRESERVED SYSTOLIC FUNCTION (LEFT VENTRICULAR EJECTION FRACTION > 45 TO 50%)

Inaccurate diagnosis of heart failure (e.g., pulmonary diseases, obesity)
Inaccurate measurements of ejection fraction
Systolic function overestimated by ejection fraction (e.g., mitral regurgitation)
Episodic, unrecognized systolic dysfunction
Intermittent ischemia
Arrhythmia
Severe hypertension
Alcohol
Diastolic dysfunction
Abnormalities of myocardial relaxation
   Ischemia
   Hypertrophy
Abnormalities of myocardial compliance
   Hypertrophy
   Aging
   Fibrosis
   Diabetes
   Infiltrative diseases (amyloidosis, sarcoidosis)
   Storage diseases (hemachromatosis)
   Endomyocardial diseases (endomyocardial fibrosis, radiation, anthracyclines)
Pericardial diseases (constriction, tamponade)

and whether important valvular abnormalities were missed. Ejection fraction measurements may be inaccurate, particularly when their technical quality is suboptimal. Regurgitant valve diseases may lead to a dissociation between the ejection fraction and underlying myocardial dysfunction because in this setting the afterload may be low. There also are many conditions in which left ventricular function is impaired transiently, but subsequently measured ejection fractions may be normal; intermittent ischemia, presenting as episodic heart failure ("flash pulmonary edema") is the most important because revascularization may be indicated. Severe hypertension with subsequent treatment and transient arrhythmias also may have temporary effects on ejection fraction. Some patients with alcoholic cardiomyopathy may exhibit rapid recovery in ejection fraction when they cease drinking.

The remaining patients most likely have diastolic dysfunction as the underlying disorder. The noninvasive measurement of diastolic function remains problematic. The most common test used, Doppler echocardiography, is neither sensitive nor specific for diastolic dysfunction. Particularly in the elderly, Doppler mitral valve filling patterns show impaired early diastolic filling in most subjects, whether or not they have evidence of heart failure. Diastolic dysfunction is basically a diagnosis of exclusion based on accompanying conditions and circumstantial evidence.

FACTORS PRECIPITATING ACUTE DECOMPENSATION OF CHRONIC HEART FAILURE

Many patients with chronic heart failure maintain a stable course, then abruptly present with acutely or subacutely worsening symptoms. Although this decompensation may reflect unrecognized gradual progression of the underlying disorder, many precipitating events must be considered and, if present, addressed (Table 55–5). An important focus is on changes in medications (by patient or physician), diet, or activity. Superimposed new or altered cardiovascular conditions, such as arrhythmias, ischemic events, hypertension, or valvular abnormalities, should be considered. Systemic processes, such as fever, infection, or anemia, also may cause cardiac decompensation.

EVALUATION OF THE PATIENT WITH POSSIBLE HEART FAILURE

Symptoms of Heart Failure

The common symptoms of heart failure are well known but are frequently absent and variably specific for this condition. The symptoms generally reflect, but may be dissociated from, the hemodynamic derangements of elevated left-sided and right-sided pressures and impaired cardiac output or cardiac output reserve.

DYSPNEA

Dyspnea, or perceived shortness of breath, is the most common symptom of patients with heart failure. In most patients, dyspnea is present only with activity or exertion. The underlying mechanisms are multifactorial. The most important is pulmonary congestion with increased interstitial or intra-alveolar fluid, which activates juxta-capillary J receptors, which stimulate a rapid and shallow pattern of breathing. Increased lung stiffness may enhance the work of breathing, leading to a perception of dyspnea. Central regulation of respiration may be disturbed in more severe heart failure, resulting in disordered sleep patterns and sleep apnea. Cheyne-Stokes respiration, or periodic breathing, is common in advanced heart failure, is usually associated with low output states, and may be perceived by the patient (and the patient's family) as either severe dyspnea or transient cessation of breathing. Hypoxia, which is uncommon in heart failure patients unless there is accompanying pulmonary disease, suggests the presence of pulmonary edema. Dyspnea is a relatively sensitive symptom of heart failure, provided that a careful history is taken of the patient's level of activity, but dyspnea may become less prominent with the onset of right ventricular failure and tricuspid regurgitation, which may lead to lower pulmonary venous pressures. Dyspnea is a common symptom of patients with pulmonary disease, obesity, and anemia and of sedentary individuals.

ORTHOPNEA AND PAROXYSMAL NOCTURNAL DYSPNEA

Orthopnea is dyspnea that is positional, occurring in the recumbent or semirecumbent position. It occurs as a result of the increase in venous return from the extremities and splanchnic circulation to central circulation with changes in posture, with resultant increases in pulmonary venous pressures and pulmonary capillary hydrostatic pressure. Nocturnal cough may be a manifestation of this process and is an underrecognized symptom of heart failure. Orthopnea is a relatively specific symptom of heart failure, although it may occur in patients with pulmonary disease who breathe more effectively in an upright posture and in individuals with significant abdominal obesity or ascites. Most patients with mild or moderate heart failure do not experience orthopnea, however, when they are treated adequately.

Paroxysmal nocturnal dyspnea is an attack of acute, severe shortness of breath awakening the patient from sleep, usually 1 to 3 hours after the patient retires. Symptoms usually resolve over 10 to 30 minutes after the patient arises, often gasping for fresh air from an open window. Paroxysmal nocturnal dyspnea results from increased venous return and mobilization of interstitial fluid from the extremities and elsewhere, with accumulation of alveolar edema. Paroxysmal nocturnal dyspnea almost always represents heart failure, but it is a relatively uncommon finding.

ACUTE PULMONARY EDEMA

Pulmonary edema results from transudation of fluid into the alveolar spaces as a result of acute rises in capillary hydrostatic pressures owing to an acute depression of cardiac function or to an acute rise in intravascular volume. The initial symptoms may be cough or progressive dyspnea. Because alveolar edema may precipitate bronchospasm, wheezing is common. If the edema is not treated, the patient may begin coughing up pink (or blood-tinged), frothy fluid and become cyanotic and acidotic.

EXERCISE INTOLERANCE

Activity or exercise intolerance is, together with dyspnea, the most characteristic symptom of chronic heart failure. Intuitively, it might be assumed that exercise would be limited by shortness of breath because of rising pulmonary venous pressures and pulmonary congestion. Although this mechanism may contribute, it is only one of many operating. Blood flow to exercising muscles is impaired, as a result of reduced cardiac output reserve and impaired peripheral vasodilation; oxygen delivery is limited, and early fatigue ensues. Heart failure is associated with additional abnormalities of skeletal muscle itself, including biochemical changes and alterations in fiber types, which increase muscle fatigue and impair muscle function. Finally, heart failure may affect adversely respiratory muscle function and ventilatory control.

FATIGUE

Fatigue is a common, if nonspecific, complaint of patients with heart failure. Perhaps the most common origin of this complaint is

---

Table 55–5 • FACTORS THAT MAY PRECIPITATE ACUTE DECOMPENSATION OF CHRONIC HEART FAILURE

Discontinuation of therapy (patient noncompliance or physician initiated)
Initiation of medications that worsen heart failure (calcium antagonists, β-blockers, nonsteroidal anti-inflammatory drugs, antiarrhythmic agents)
Iatrogenic volume overload (transfusion, fluid administration)
Dietary indiscretion
Alcohol consumption
Increased activity
Pregnancy
Exposure to high altitude
Arrhythmias
Myocardial ischemia or infarction
Worsening hypertension
Worsening mitral or tricuspid regurgitation
Fever or infection
Anemia

muscle fatigue. Fatigue also may be a nonspecific response to the systemic manifestations of heart failure, such as chronic increases in catecholamines and circulating levels of cytokines, sleep disorders, and anxiety.

EDEMA AND FLUID RETENTION (ASCITES, PLEURAL EFFUSION, PERICARDIAL EFFUSION)

Elevated right atrial pressures increase the capillary hydrostatic pressures in the systemic circulation, with resultant transudation. The location of edema fluid is determined by position (e.g., dependent) and accompanying pathology. Most commonly, edema accumulates in the extremities and resolves at night when the legs are not dependent. Edema may occur only in the feet and ankles, but if it is more severe, it may accumulate in the thighs, scrotum, and abdominal wall. Edema is more likely and more severe in patients with accompanying venous disease (or who have had veins harvested for coronary bypass surgery) and patients on calcium channel blockers, which themselves cause edema.

Fluid also may accumulate in the peritoneal cavity and in the pleural or pericardial space. Ascites occurs as a result of elevated pressures in the hepatic, portal, and systemic veins draining the peritoneum. Ascites is unusual in heart failure and almost always is associated with peripheral edema. Most commonly, there is severe tricuspid regurgitation, with potential damage to the liver. Otherwise, significant primary liver disease should be suspected as an exacerbating factor or cause of ascites. Pleural effusions are fairly common in chronic heart failure, especially when they are accompanied by left-sided and right-sided manifestations. The effusions result from an increase in transudation of fluid into the pleural space and impaired lymphatic drainage owing to elevated systemic venous pressures. Pericardial effusions are far less frequent but may occur.

ABDOMINAL AND GASTROINTESTINAL SYMPTOMS

Passive congestion of the liver may lead to right upper quadrant pain and tenderness and mild jaundice. Usually only mild elevations of transaminase levels and modest increases in bilirubin levels are observed. With severe, acute rises in central venous pressures, especially when associated with systemic hypotension, a severe congestive and ischemic hepatopathy may occur with striking elevations in liver function tests and hypoglycemia. Recovery is usually rapid and complete if the hemodynamic abnormalities are corrected.

Bowel wall edema may lead to early satiety (a common symptom in heart failure), nausea, diffuse abdominal discomfort, malabsorption, and a rare form of protein-losing enteropathy. The potential role of heart failure in producing these nonspecific gastrointestinal symptoms is often overlooked, leading to extensive diagnostic testing or unnecessary discontinuation of medications.

SLEEP DISORDERS AND CENTRAL NERVOUS SYSTEM MANIFESTATIONS

Periods of nocturnal oxygen desaturation to less than 80 to 85% are relatively common in patients with heart failure, coincide with episodes of apnea, and often are preceded or followed by episodes of hyperventilation. These are similar to, and may represent truncated forms of, Cheyne-Stokes respiration. These episodes reflect altered central nervous system ventilatory control and have been associated with diminished heart rate variability. Supplemental oxygen seems to reverse some of the ventilatory disorders, and the apneic spells respond to nasal positive-pressure ventilation. In some patients, these interventions may have a striking beneficial effect on fatigue and other symptoms of heart failure.

Aside from the common complaint of fatigue, which may be in part central nervous system in origin, brain function is not affected in most patients with heart failure. In advanced heart failure, cerebral hypoperfusion may cause impairment of memory, irritability, limited attention span, and altered mentation.

CARDIAC CACHEXIA

In chronic, severe heart failure, unintentional chronic weight loss may occur, leading to a syndrome of cardiac cachexia. The cause of this syndrome is unclear, but it may result from many factors, including elevated levels of proinflammatory cytokines (e.g., tumor necrosis factor), elevated metabolic rates, loss of appetite, and malabsorption. Cardiac cachexia carries a poor prognosis.

Physical Findings

The physical findings associated with heart failure generally reflect elevated ventricular filling pressures and, to a lesser extent, reduced cardiac output. In chronic heart failure, many of these findings are absent, often obscuring the correct diagnosis.

APPEARANCE AND VITAL SIGNS

Compensated patients may be comfortable, but patients with more severe symptoms are often restless, dyspneic, and pale or diaphoretic. Although the heart rate is usually at the high end of the normal range or above (>80 beats per minute), it may be lower in chronic, stable patients. Premature beats or arrhythmias are common. Pulsus alternans (alternating amplitude of successive beats) is a sign of advanced heart failure (or a large pericardial effusion). The blood pressure may be normal or high, but in advanced heart failure it is usually on the low end of normal or below.

JUGULAR VEINS AND NECK EXAMINATION

Examination of the jugular veins is one of the most useful aspects of the evaluation of heart failure patients. The jugular venous pressure should be quantified in centimeters of water (normal ≤8 cm) estimating the level of pulsations above the sternal angle (and arbitrarily adding 5 cm in any posture). The presence of abdominal-jugular reflux should be assessed by putting pressure on the right upper quadrant of the abdomen for 30 seconds and avoiding an induced Valsalva maneuver; a positive finding is a rise in the jugular pressure of at least 1 cm. Either an elevated jugular venous pressure or an abnormal abdominal-jugular reflux has been reported in 80% of patients with advanced heart failure. No other simple sign is nearly as sensitive.

An additional important finding in the neck is evidence of tricuspid regurgitation—a large cv wave, usually associated with a high jugular venous pressure. This finding is confirmed by hepatic pulsations, which can be detected during the abdominal-jugular reflux determination. The carotid pulses should be evaluated for evidence of aortic stenosis, and thyroid abnormalities should be sought.

PULMONARY EXAMINATION

Although dyspnea is the most common symptom of patients with heart failure, the pulmonary examination is usually unremarkable. Rales, representing alveolar fluid, are a hallmark of heart failure; when present in patients without accompanying pulmonary disease, they are highly specific for the diagnosis. In chronic heart failure, they are usually absent, however, even in patients known to have pulmonary capillary wedge pressures greater than 20 mm Hg (normal <12 mm Hg). Left ventricular failure cannot be excluded by the absence of rales. Pleural effusions, which are indicative of bilateral heart failure in patients with appropriate symptoms, are relatively rare.

CARDIAC EXAMINATION

The cardiac examination is a crucial part of the evaluation of the patient with heart failure, but more for identification of associated cardiac abnormalities than the assessment of its severity (Chapter 46). Assessment of the point of maximal impulse may provide information concerning the size of the heart (enlarged if displaced below the fifth intercostal space or lateral to the midclavicular line) and its function (if sustained beyond one third of systole or palpable over two interspaces). Additional precordial pulsations may indicate a left ventricular aneurysm. A parasternal lift is valuable evidence of pulmonary hypertension.

The first heart sound (S_1) may be diminished in amplitude when left ventricular function is poor, and the pulmonic component of the second heart sound (P_2) may be accentuated when pulmonary hypertension is present. An apical third heart sound (S_3) is a strong indicator of significant left ventricular dysfunction but is present only in a few patients with low ejection fractions and elevated left ventricular filling pressures. A fourth heart sound (S_4) is not a specific indicator of heart failure, but it is usually present in patients with diastolic dysfunction. An S_3 at the lower left or right sternal border or below the xiphoid indicates right ventricular dysfunction. Murmurs may indicate the presence of significant valvular disease as the cause of heart failure, but mitral and tricuspid regurgitation also are common secondary manifestations of severe ventricular dilation and dysfunction.

EXAMINATION OF THE ABDOMEN AND EXTREMITIES

The size, pulsatility, and tenderness of the liver should be evaluated as evidence of passive congestion and tricuspid regurgitation. Ascites and edema should be sought and quantified.

Diagnosis

The diagnosis of heart failure is straightforward when a patient presents with classic symptoms and accompanying physical findings. In patients with chronic heart failure, however, the diagnosis is often delayed or missed entirely because no single sign or symptom is diagnostic (Table 55–6).

The most frequent symptoms, dyspnea and fatigue, are not specific for heart failure, especially in the older population, although their presence always should lead to a more complete evaluation. The more specific symptoms of orthopnea, paroxysmal nocturnal dyspnea, and edema are much less common. Although the physical examination may be helpful, characteristic physical findings may be absent. The chest radiograph, on which many physicians rely, adds relatively little to the clinical evaluation.

The key to making the timely diagnosis of chronic heart failure is to maintain a high degree of suspicion, particularly in high-risk patients (patients with coronary artery disease, chronic hypertension, diabetes, histories of heavy alcohol use, and advanced age). When these patients present with any of the symptoms or physical findings suggestive of heart failure, additional testing (see later) should be undertaken, generally beginning with echocardiography.

DIAGNOSTIC TESTING

CHEST RADIOGRAPHY. Although the standard posteroanterior and lateral chest radiograph provides limited information about chamber size, the presence of overall cardiomegaly (a cardiothoracic ratio >0.50 and especially >0.60) is a strong indicator of heart failure or another cause of cardiomegaly (especially valvular insufficiency) (Chapter 49).

Nearly 50% of heart failure patients do not have this high a cardiothoracic ratio, however.

Most patients with acute heart failure, but only a few with chronic heart failure, have evidence of pulmonary venous hypertension (upper lobe redistribution, enlarged pulmonary veins) or interstitial (haziness of the central vascular shadows or increased central interstitial lung markings) or pulmonary (perihilar or patchy peripheral infiltrates) edema. The absence of these findings reflects the subjectivity of interpretation and the increased capacity of the lymphatics to remove interstitial and alveolar fluid in chronic heart failure. This absence of radiographic findings is consistent with the absence of rales in most patients with chronic heart failure despite markedly elevated pulmonary venous pressures. Pleural effusions are important adjunctive evidence of heart failure. Characteristically these are more common and larger on the right than left side, reflecting the greater pleural surface area of the right lung.

ELECTROCARDIOGRAPHY. The major importance of the electrocardiogram is to evaluate cardiac rhythm, identify prior MI, and detect evidence of left ventricular hypertrophy (Chapter 50). Prior MIs suggest that the cause is ischemic cardiomyopathy with systolic dysfunction. Left ventricular hypertrophy is a nonspecific finding but may point toward left ventricular diastolic dysfunction if the ejection fraction is not depressed.

ECHOCARDIOGRAPHY. Noninvasive cardiac imaging is a crucial part of the diagnosis and evaluation of heart failure. The most useful procedure is the transthoracic echocardiogram (Chapter 51), which provides a quantitative assessment of left ventricular function and can confirm, in the presence of appropriate symptoms and signs, the presence of heart failure owing to systolic dysfunction or indicate whether the patient has heart failure with preserved systolic function. The echocardiogram also provides a wealth of additional valuable information, including assessment of left and right ventricular size, regional wall motion (as an indicator of prior MI), evaluation of the heart valves, and diagnosis of left ventricular hypertrophy. The echocardiogram generally has replaced the chest radiograph in the diagnostic assessment of heart failure.

NATRIURETIC PEPTIDE MEASUREMENTS. Serum levels of natriuretic peptides can be measured quickly and accurately, including point-of-care testing at the bedside. B-type natriuretic peptide and N-terminal pro–B natriuretic peptide are relatively sensitive and specific markers of clinically confirmed heart failure, whether secondary to left ventricular systolic or diastolic dysfunction. These peptides also seem to be useful adjuncts in the diagnosis of patients presenting with possible heart failure, although further experience is required to define their appropriate use. Levels also increase with age, especially in women, and may be elevated slightly in patients with chronic obstructive pulmonary disease. These elevations may reflect diastolic dysfunction or right ventricular dysfunction but nonetheless may lead to a false-positive clinical diagnosis of heart failure. Serial natriuretic peptide measurements seem to be helpful in assessing the response to therapy, in guiding the management of individual patients, and in assessing prognosis.

DIFFERENTIAL DIAGNOSIS

Although it is not difficult to make the definitive diagnosis of heart failure in a patient presenting with the classic symptoms and signs, several alternative diagnoses need to be considered in less clear-cut situations, such as in the patient with normal left ventricular function and less definitive clinical evidence. The most important differentiation is between heart failure and pulmonary disease. In this setting, pulmonary function testing or additional tests to characterize lung pathology may be helpful. When left ventricular systolic function is normal, it sometimes may be difficult to make a conclusive determination of the relative role of heart failure compared with other concomitant conditions, such as severe obesity, chronic anemia, or other systemic illnesses; in some patients, a therapeutic trial (Chapter 56) may be diagnostic.

EVALUATION AND FOLLOW-UP OF THE HEART FAILURE PATIENT

When the diagnosis of heart failure is made, the goal of additional testing is to identify potentially correctable or specifically treatable cases and to obtain further information necessary for future management.

Table 55–6 • SENSITIVITY, SPECIFICITY, AND PREDICTIVE VALUE OF SYMPTOMS AND PHYSICAL FINDINGS FOR DIAGNOSING HEART FAILURE

SYMPTOM OR SIGN	SENSITIVITY* (%)	SPECIFICITY* (%)	PREDICTIVE ACCURACY* (%)
Exertional dyspnea	66	52	23
Orthopnea	21	81	2
Paroxysmal nocturnal dyspnea	33	76	26
History of edema	23	80	22
Resting heart rate >100 beats/min	7	99	6
Rales	13	91	21
Third heart sound	31	95	61
Jugular venous distention†	10	97	2
Edema (on examination)	10	93	3

*See Chapter 6 for definitions.
†Reported to have much higher sensitivity (57%) and predictive accuracy (67%) at rest and better sensitivity (81%) and predictive accuracy (81%) with abdominal jugular reflux in another series (Butman SM, et al: Bedside cardiovascular examination in patients with severe chronic heart failure: Importance of direct or inducible jugular venous distention. J Am Coll Cardiol 1993;22:968–974).

Adapted from Harlan WR, et al: Chronic congestive heart failure in coronary artery disease: Clinical criteria. Ann Intern Med 1977;86:133–138.

Routine Diagnostic Assessment

LABORATORY TESTING. An extensive battery of laboratory tests is not required for most patients with heart failure. Routine testing should include a complete blood cell count (to detect anemia and systemic diseases with hematologic manifestations), measurement of renal function and electrolytes including magnesium (to exclude renal failure and to provide a baseline for subsequent therapy), liver function tests (to exclude accompanying liver pathology and provide a baseline), and blood glucose and lipid testing (to diagnose diabetes and dyslipidemia, both of which should be managed aggressively in heart failure patients).

A few additional tests may be indicated. Thyrotoxicosis, and to a lesser extent hypothyroidism, may cause heart failure and may be difficult to diagnose clinically, especially in older patients (Chapter 239). Many guidelines recommend thyroid function tests in all patients, or at least in elderly patients and patients with atrial fibrillation. Hemochromatosis (Chapter 225) is a potentially treatable cause of heart failure; particularly if there is accompanying diabetes or hepatic disease, serum ferritin levels are indicated. Sarcoidosis (Chapter 91) is another potentially treatable cause, although it would be unusual not to have evidence of accompanying lung disease. Amyloidosis (Chapter 290) should be considered in patients with other manifestations, but treatment of the cardiac manifestations is rarely successful except with heart transplantation.

ASSESSMENT OF LEFT VENTRICULAR FUNCTION. Although heart failure is a syndrome with many pathogenic mechanisms, the most common are left ventricular systolic dysfunction and left ventricular diastolic dysfunction. In some patients, it may be nearly impossible to distinguish between these two forms of heart failure by clinical evaluation because both may present with the same symptoms and with only subtle differences on physical examination. It is essential to distinguish between these two entities, however, because they may require different diagnostic evaluations and different therapeutic approaches (Chapter 56). The most useful and practical test is the echocardiogram (Chapter 51); alternative approaches include radionuclide measurements of ejection fraction (Chapter 52) and left ventriculography if cardiac catheterization (Chapter 54) is being performed. All these tests allow the detection of significant systolic dysfunction; diastolic dysfunction sometimes can be documented (Chapter 51) but often is identified primarily as a process of exclusion in patients with preserved systolic function.

Additional Diagnostic Evaluation

ASSESSMENT FOR CORONARY ARTERY DISEASE. Coronary artery disease is the most common cause of heart failure in industrialized societies. Although it often is known whether a patient has coronary disease based on a prior history of MI or positive results in an angiogram or noninvasive test, in some patients it may be silent. There are two reasons to identify the coexistence of heart failure and coronary disease: first, to treat symptoms that may be due to ischemia and, second, to improve prognosis (Chapters 67, 68, and 69). A prudent approach is to subdivide heart failure patients into three groups: (1) patients with clinical evidence of ongoing ischemia (active angina or a possible ischemic equivalent), (2) patients who have had a prior MI but do not currently have angina, and (3) patients who may or may not have underlying coronary disease. The first group of patients may be evaluated most expeditiously by coronary angiography because they stand to benefit in terms of symptoms and probably have more extensive ischemia. In the second group are patients with heart failure and prior MI who by other criteria (age, absence of other major comorbid conditions) are otherwise good candidates for coronary revascularization; they generally should undergo noninvasive stress testing in conjunction with nuclear myocardial perfusion imaging or echocardiography. These procedures identify individuals with extensive ischemic but viable myocardium, whose prognosis and symptoms also may be improved with revascularization. The third group, patients without either angina or prior MI, are much less likely to benefit from an evaluation for asymptomatic coronary disease.

MYOCARDIAL BIOPSY. There is no rationale for routine myocardial biopsy in patients with heart failure, even in the subgroup without apparent coronary disease. Few entities that might be detected are amenable to specific therapy, and those that are (hemochromatosis, sarcoidosis) usually can be detected by their other manifestations or

other procedures. A possible exception is acute fulminant myocarditis (Chapter 73), particularly eosinophilic and giant cell myocarditis, which may respond to immunosuppressive therapy. Another potential exception is the patient being evaluated for cardiac transplantation (Chapter 80) because the presence of some entities may preclude this procedure.

ASSESSMENT OF EXERCISE CAPACITY. Quantitative assessment of exercise capacity provides additional insight into prognosis over the clinical evaluation and measurements of cardiac function, particularly when a detailed history of activity tolerance cannot be obtained. Exercise testing with measurements of peak oxygen uptake by respiratory gas exchange has become a routine part of the transplant evaluation (Chapter 80) because it provides an indication of need for early intervention and an additional method for follow-up. In most patients, testing is not necessary, however. Emphasis should be placed on eliciting each patient's maximum tolerated activity and the minimum activity associated with symptoms; both can be followed from visit to visit, as a guide to management.

ASSESSMENT OF ARRHYTHMIAS. Ventricular arrhythmias are extremely common in patients with chronic heart failure, with 50 to 80% of patients exhibiting nonsustained ventricular tachycardia during 24-hour monitoring. Because approximately 50% of cardiac deaths in these patients are sudden, these arrhythmias have been viewed with concern. In multivariate analyses, asymptomatic ventricular arrhythmias carry little independent prognostic significance when the severity of symptoms, ejection fraction, and presence of concurrent coronary disease are taken into account. Arrhythmias are no more predictive of sudden death than of total mortality. Further evaluation of asymptomatic arrhythmias is not warranted. In contrast, ventricular arrhythmias associated with syncope or hemodynamic compromise must be taken seriously and require further evaluation and treatment (Chapter 52).

Follow-Up Evaluation

After the diagnosis of heart failure is confirmed and the initial evaluation is complete, there is little need for further testing beyond the laboratory tests (primarily renal function and electrolytes) necessary to monitor therapy. When the status of ventricular function is known, there are few indications for retesting. Exceptions are monitoring for transplantation and important changes in clinical status (e.g., marked deterioration in a patient previously known to have preserved left ventricular function, occurrence of new murmurs in conjunction with declining status).

Instead the key to successful follow-up is the careful tracking of clinical symptoms and patient weights, which often involves interviewing not only the patient, but also family members, who may be more aware of changes in status than the patient. Continuity of care and seamless transitions from the inpatient to outpatient setting are crucial aspects of optimal management. Patients with advanced heart failure and patients requiring frequent hospitalization require special handling. Programs that provide telephone-based tracking of daily weights and symptoms can detect deterioration in time to intervene before the need for hospitalization. Although these programs may be costly, several evaluations have found them to be cost-effective. Because the management of these patients requires considerable experience and expertise, specialized heart failure programs and clinics have been developed and may provide additional benefit compared with traditional care.

SUGGESTED READINGS

Angeja BG, Grossman W: Evaluation and management of diastolic heart failure. Circulation 2003;107:659–663. *Excellent review of the pathophysiology, diagnosis, and management of this important and often underappreciated group of patients.*

Drazner MH, Rame JE, Stevenson LW, Dries DL: Prognostic importance of elevated jugular venous pressure and a third heart sound in patients with heart failure. N Engl J Med 2001;345:574–581. *Both were associated with adverse outcomes.*

Jessup M, Brozena S: Heart failure. N Engl J Med 2003;348:2007–2018. *Concise review of the societal impact, pathophysiology, and management of chronic heart failure.*

Maisel AS, Krishnaswamy P, Nowak RM, et al: Rapid measurement of B-type natriuretic peptide in the emergency diagnosis of heart failure. N Engl J Med 2002;347:161–167. *Prospective study of 1586 patients presenting to the emergency department with dyspnea, demonstrating the value of serum B-type natriuretic peptide measurements in the diagnosis of heart failure.*

Olson TM, Illenberger S, Kishimoto NY, et al: Metavinculin mutations alter actin interaction in dilated cardiomyopathy. Circulation 2002;105:431–437. *Example of a gene that is associated with dilated cardiomyopathy.*

56 HEART FAILURE: MANAGEMENT AND PROGNOSIS

Milton Packer

The cardinal manifestations of heart failure (Chapter 55) are (1) dyspnea and fatigue, which may limit exercise tolerance, and (2) fluid retention, which may lead to pulmonary and peripheral edema. Both abnormalities can impair the functional capacity and quality of life of affected individuals. In addition, by its very nature, heart failure is a progressive disorder. With time, the functional limitations imposed by the disease become increasingly apparent, and eventually patients experience symptoms at rest or on minimal exertion. This progression is directly related to the inexorable deterioration of cardiac structure and function, which can occur without any recurrence of the initial injury to the heart. Once initiated, heart failure advances (often silently) and leads inevitably to a recurrent need for medical care and hospitalization and, finally, to the death of the patient.

Approach to the Patient with Heart Failure

DEFINING THE CAUSE OF HEART FAILURE

The primary step in the management of heart failure is to identify and characterize the nature of the underlying cardiac disorder. A careful history may reveal the past occurrence of a myocardial infarction (MI) (Chapter 69), valvular disease (Chapter 72), hypertension (Chapter 63), myocarditis (Chapter 73), thyroid disease (Chapter 239), or the ingestion of cardiotoxic substances. Direct inquiry may also identify any associated disorders (e.g., anemia, arrhythmias, ischemia, or renal dysfunction) or concomitant medications (e.g., calcium channel blockers, antiarrhythmic drugs, and nonsteroidal anti-inflammatory drugs) that can exacerbate the syndrome of heart failure or complicate its management. The physical examination may indicate the presence of cardiac enlargement, valvular disorders, or congenital heart disease (Chapter 65) or evidence of a systemic disease that may lead to or contribute to heart failure.

Although the history and physical examination may provide important clues about the nature of the underlying cardiac abnormality, such information may occasionally be misleading, because patients with risk factors for one specific cause of heart failure may prove to have an unrelated cardiac disorder. Hence, regardless of the clinical impressions formed during the initial evaluation, the physician should define the precise nature of the underlying disorder by performing an invasive or a noninvasive imaging test of the cardiac chambers. The most useful diagnostic test is the two-dimensional Doppler flow echocardiogram. This test allows the physician to determine if the primary abnormality is pericardial, myocardial, valvular, or vascular and, if it is myocardial, whether the dysfunction is primarily systolic or diastolic (Chapter 55). This distinction is critical, because surgery is the primary approach to the management of most pericardial, valvular, or vascular disorders, whereas pharmacologic strategies are the primary approaches to the management of myocardial disorders.

The focus in this chapter is on the management of patients with left ventricular systolic dysfunction, which is the cause of heart failure in 70% of patients presenting with the syndrome. The management of patients with a hypertrophic cardiomyopathy (Chapter 73) or with disorders of the pericardium (Chapter 74), valves (Chapter 72), or great vessels (Chapter 75) is discussed in the chapters specifically devoted to these topics.

MECHANISMS LEADING TO HEART FAILURE

There are four distinct phases in the evolution of heart failure (Fig. 56–1): (1) the initial cardiac injury, (2) neurohormonal activation and cardiac remodeling, (3) fluid retention and peripheral vasoconstriction, and (4) contractile failure.

CAUSES OF CARDIAC INJURY. A variety of disorders can injure the myocardium and lead to systolic dysfunction. About two thirds of patients with systolic dysfunction have coronary artery disease; in these patients, the occurrence of an acute MI is usually the injurious event that triggers the decline in ejection fraction. These patients characteristically show regional abnormalities of wall motion in the myocardial segments that are perfused by the obstructed coronary arteries,

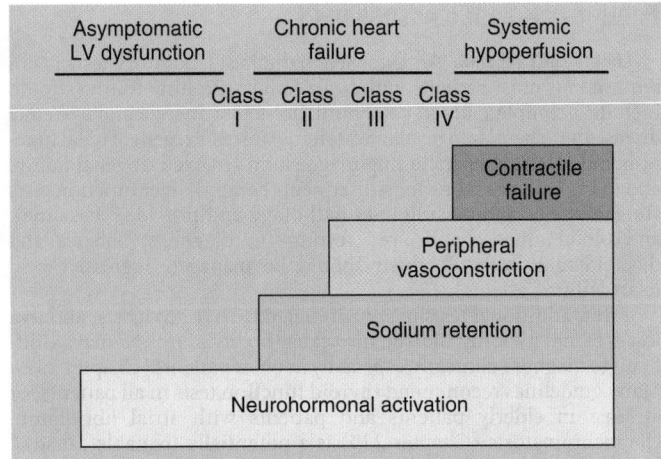

FIGURE 56–1 • Mechanisms contributing to the development of heart failure at each stage of the disease. This diagram should be used in conjunction with Figure 56–2; see text for details. The classes designated at the top of the page refer to the functional classification developed by the New York Heart Association. According to this classification system, patients may have symptoms at rest (class IV), on less than ordinary exertion (class III), on ordinary exertion (class II), or only at levels that would cause symptoms in normal individuals (class I).

and the left ventricle is typically more severely affected than the right. In the remaining third of patients, the coronary vessels appear normal; the ventricle is globally (rather than regionally) hypokinetic; and the right and left ventricles are generally affected to a similar degree. The source of myocardial injury in patients with a nonischemic cardiomyopathy may be a prior infection (e.g., myocarditis), exposure to a cardiac toxin (e.g., alcohol, cocaine, or cancer chemotherapeutic agent), or a systemic disorder (e.g., hypothyroidism or hyperthyroidism). However, no cause of myocardial injury may be found; such patients are considered to have idiopathic dilated cardiomyopathy.

Is it important to identify the cause of myocardial injury in a patient with systolic dysfunction due to a cardiomyopathy? Coronary arteriography and noninvasive imaging studies can indicate the presence and functional consequences of coronary artery disease, and myocardial biopsy may identify the presence of inflammatory or infiltrative disorders of the heart. Yet, it remains unclear how the information generated by these tests should be used. There is little evidence that anti-ischemic interventions can improve clinical outcomes in patients who have heart failure due to advanced systolic dysfunction but who do not have angina, and most infiltrative or inflammatory disorders are not reversible. Indeed, most treatable causes of myocardial injury can be identified by history or by simple blood tests (e.g., thyroid function tests).

NEUROHORMONAL ACTIVATION AND CARDIAC REMODELING. Regardless of the source of myocardial injury, once a critical mass of the left ventricle is injured, heart failure becomes a progressive, self-reinforcing process, regardless of whether the initial insult recurs or is adequately treated. The principal manifestation of such progression is a change in the geometry of the left ventricle such that the chamber enlarges and becomes more spherical; this process is termed *cardiac remodeling*. This change in chamber size not only increases the hemodynamic stresses on the walls of the failing heart and depresses its performance but also increases the magnitude of regurgitant flow through the mitral and tricuspid valves. These effects in turn serve to sustain and exacerbate the remodeling process, leading to a progressive decline in the left ventricular ejection fraction. Remodeling is an essential step in the transition from the initial cardiac injury to asymptomatic ventricular dysfunction to symptomatic heart failure.

What factors are responsible for, or accelerate, the process of left ventricular remodeling? Although many mechanisms may be involved, there is substantial evidence that the activation of endogenous neurohormonal systems (Chapter 55) plays a critical role in cardiac remodeling and thereby in the progression of heart failure. These systems are activated early after an acute myocardial injury, and their activity is progressively enhanced as the disorder advances. Elevated circulating or tissue levels of norepinephrine and angiotensin II can act, alone or in concert, to affect adversely the structure and function of the failing heart. These neurohormonal factors not only increase the hemodynamic stresses on the heart by causing peripheral vasoconstriction but also may exert a direct toxic effect on the heart by causing myocytes to undergo a process of programmed cell death (apoptosis). Neurohormonal factors can also stimulate the process of myocardial fibrosis, which can further alter the architecture and impair the performance of the failing heart. Interestingly, the initial activation of neurohormonal systems and cardiac remodeling that follows a myocardial injury is commonly asymptomatic. Although the ejection fraction is depressed and may further deteriorate, the patient commonly shows no evidence of symptoms or fluid retention for long periods of time. This is the phase referred to as *asymptomatic left ventricular dysfunction.*

FLUID RETENTION AND PERIPHERAL VASOCONSTRICTION. As the process of physiologic deterioration continues, the activation of neurohormonal systems not only adversely affects the heart but also begins to exert a deleterious effect on the kidneys and peripheral blood vessels. The sympathetic nervous system and renin-angiotensin system act on the kidneys to retain sodium and water and act on peripheral blood vessels to cause vasoconstriction. Both of these mechanisms increase the loading conditions in the failing heart, which can in turn lead to symptoms of pulmonary congestion and exercise intolerance—a phase termed *chronic heart failure.* As cardiac function deteriorates, hemodynamic factors can exacerbate the functional derangements of the kidneys and peripheral vessels produced by neurohormonal systems. A decline in renal blood flow impairs the ability of the kidneys to excrete salt and water, and an increase in the sodium content of peripheral vessels can impair their dilatory capacity. Similarly, a decline in regional blood flow can attenuate the physiologic actions of endogenous natriuretic peptides that normally counteract vasoconstrictor mechanisms. Over time, the interplay of hemodynamic and neurohormonal factors leads to worsening of symptoms and a deterioration of clinical status, often with little additional decrease in the left ventricular ejection fraction.

CONTRACTILE FAILURE. As the process that causes heart failure progresses, the myocardium eventually loses a critical mass of functioning myocytes and no longer can sustain forward flow and peripheral perfusion. Despite the decline in cardiac performance, the patient survives because the inotropic and vasoconstrictor effects of the sympathetic nervous system and the renin-angiotensin system act to support cardiac contractility and systemic pressures, at least in the short term. The renal retention of salt and water is intense, but the resulting expansion of intravascular volume fails to support the circulation and acts only to exacerbate pulmonary and peripheral congestion. This precarious state cannot be sustained; the threat to the circulation is so immediate that the patient can be stabilized only by intensive medical care in a hospital. The phase of contractile failure frequently characterizes the terminal stages of the disorder.

The evolution through these four stages of heart failure may occur slowly or rapidly, with the rate of progression being determined by the severity of the initial cardiac injury and the intensity of neurohormonal activation. Death may occur during any of the four phases, although it is commonly sudden in patients with minimal or mild symptoms and is usually related to pump failure in patients with advanced symptoms.

DEFINING AN APPROPRIATE THERAPEUTIC STRATEGY

Each of the four phases of heart failure requires a specific therapeutic approach (Fig. 56–2). For patients who have not yet experienced an initial cardiac insult, every effort should be made to minimize the occurrence and impact of diseases that can injure the heart. For patients who have developed left ventricular dysfunction but remain asymptomatic, physicians should interfere with the neurohormonal systems that can cause cardiac remodeling and lead to the development of clinical heart failure. For patients who have developed symptoms, the primary goals are to alleviate fluid retention, lessen disability, and reduce the risk of further progression and death. These goals generally require a strategy that combines diuretics (to control salt and water retention) with neurohormonal interventions (to minimize the deleterious effects of the sympathetic nervous system and renin-angiotensin system) and that frequently adds hemodynamic interventions (to enhance cardiac performance and reduce peripheral vasoconstriction). Finally, for patients hospitalized with immediately life-threatening heart failure, the principal objectives are to stabilize the precarious state of the circulation and to maintain end-organ

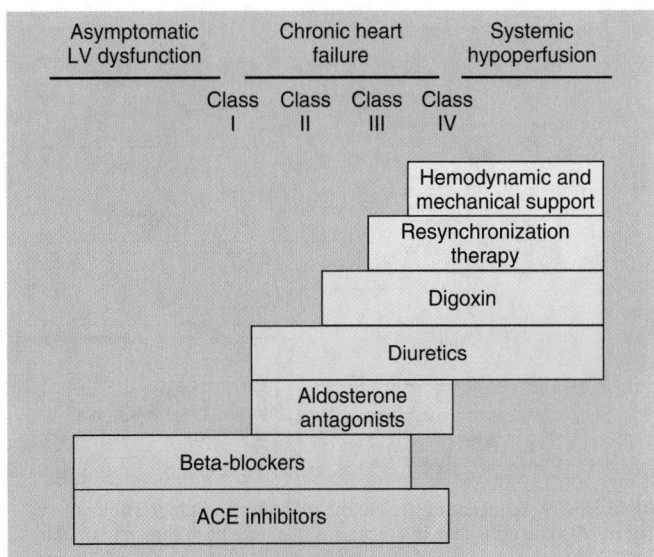

FIGURE 56–2 • Treatment strategies appropriate to each stage of heart failure. This diagram should be used in conjunction with Figure 56–1; see text for details. The classes designated at the top of the page refer to the functional classification developed by the New York Heart Association (see legend to Fig. 56–1). ACE = angiotensin-converting enzyme.

function until precipitating factors have resolved or until a definitive solution can be formulated to treat the underlying disease. Such patients generally require intensive hemodynamic or mechanical support (Chapter 103). These observations suggest that neurohormonal mechanisms are dominant in the early phases of heart failure, whereas hemodynamic mechanisms play an increasingly critical role as the disease advances to its terminal phase.

Both neurohormonal and hemodynamic interventions can improve the performance of the failing heart, but they do so in distinct ways. On the one hand, drugs can increase ejection fraction by directly stimulating the contractility of individual myocyte cells. This approach (used by positive inotropic agents) can produce immediate hemodynamic benefits but may exacerbate the deleterious actions of neurohormonal systems and thereby the process of cardiac remodeling. As a result, positive inotropic agents may be useful in the short-term management of patients hospitalized with immediately life-threatening disease, but long-term treatment with these agents may increase morbidity and mortality. On the other hand, drugs can increase ejection fraction by antagonizing the neurohormonal activation that can impair the function and viability of cardiac cells. This approach (used by angiotensin-converting enzyme [ACE] inhibitors and β-adrenergic receptor blockers) can slow the progression of heart failure and reduce the risk of major cardiac events in patients with asymptomatic left ventricular dysfunction or established symptoms of heart failure. However, in patients with end-stage disease, neurohormonal antagonists can undermine the homeostatic mechanisms that are critical for the support of cardiac contractility and systemic pressures. These observations indicate that the treatment of heart failure should be targeted to the mechanisms that drive the disease process during each phase of the disorder.

Prevention of Heart Failure

Heart failure can be prevented by decreasing the risk of the initial cardiac injury or, if the injury has already occurred, by decreasing the early and continuing loss of myocardium. Specific interventions can alter the development and progression of heart failure during each phase of the disease (Fig. 56–3).

DECREASE THE RISK OF THE INITIAL CARDIAC INJURY. The treatment of hyperlipidemia and hypertension in high-risk patients can reduce the risk of MI and, as a result, the likelihood of developing heart failure. In patients with hypercholesterolemia and a history of angina or MI, treatment with a lipid-lowering agent has been shown to decrease the risk of heart failure and of death (Chapters 67 and 69). In patients with systolic or diastolic hypertension, antihypertensive therapy

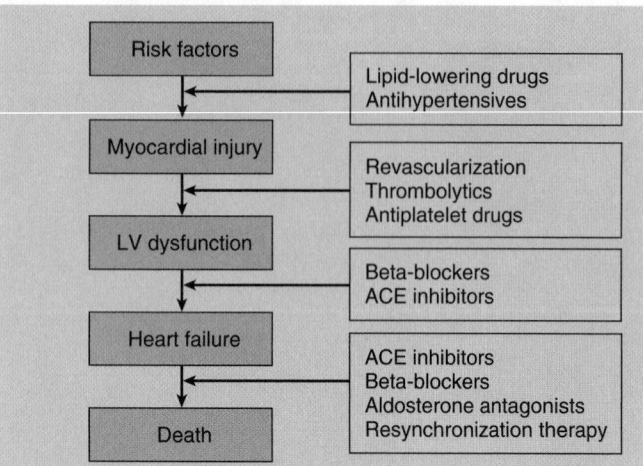

FIGURE 56–3 • Sequence of steps in the evolution and progression of heart failure. Also identified are interventions that have been shown to inhibit each step in the process and thus can favorably affect the natural history of the disease. ACE = angiotensin-converting enzyme.

decreases the risk of stroke and of heart failure (Chapter 63); these benefits are particularly marked in patients with a previous MI.

DECREASE THE LIKELIHOOD OF DEVELOPING HEART FAILURE AFTER CARDIAC INJURY. The aggressive treatment of patients *during* an acute MI can reduce the *extent* of the initial myocardial injury. In patients who are experiencing an acute MI, reperfusion with percutaneous transluminal coronary angioplasty and thrombolytic agents can minimize the loss of myocardium and can thereby reduce the risk of developing subsequent heart failure in patients with an uncomplicated MI and decrease the risk of death in patients whose MI is complicated by heart failure (Chapter 69).

Furthermore, the aggressive treatment of patients after an acute MI can reduce the extension of the initial injury to other segments of the myocardium. In patients with a recent MI, treatment with a β-blocker reduces the risk of reinfarction and of death, especially in those with left ventricular dysfunction or heart failure at the start of treatment (Chapter 69). Similarly, use of an ACE inhibitor in patients with a recent MI reduces the risk of reinfarction, heart failure, and death, especially in those with left ventricular dysfunction at the start of treatment. Combined neurohormonal blockade (ACE inhibitors and β-blockers) may produce complementary benefits. Finally, in patients with established ischemic or nonischemic left ventricular systolic dysfunction (ejection fraction, <35 to 40%) with no or minimal symptoms of heart failure, treatment with an ACE inhibitor can reduce the risk of developing heart failure.

Outpatient Treatment of Heart Failure

The goals of outpatient management of patients with symptoms of heart failure due to systolic dysfunction of the left ventricle are (1) the control of fluid retention, (2) the control of neurohormonal activation (to reduce morbidity and mortality), and (3) the control of symptoms and disability.

GENERAL MEASURES

Several general measures are advisable for most patients with chronic heart failure. Obese patients should lose weight, smokers should stop using tobacco products, and those concomitant cardiac conditions and risk factors (e.g., hyperlipidemia) should have their conditions actively managed. Moderate sodium restriction is usually indicated to permit the use of lower doses of diuretic drugs, but water restriction is generally unnecessary unless patients have moderate or severe hyponatremia. Although most patients should not participate in heavy labor or exhaustive sports, exercise should be encouraged, and bed rest should be avoided (except during periods of acute decompensation), because the restriction of activity promotes physical deconditioning and increases disability.

Specific interventions are indicated and contraindicated in patients with heart failure. Hypertension (Chapter 63) should be treated

aggressively, because a reduction in cardiac load can improve both systolic and diastolic function. In patients with chronic atrial fibrillation, every effort should be made to control the ventricular response, both at rest and during exercise. Anticoagulants are indicated in patients with atrial fibrillation (Chapter 59) or a history of an embolic event. Asymptomatic ventricular arrhythmias (Chapter 60) require no therapy, but electrophysiologic devices may reduce the risk of death in patients who have sustained ventricular tachycardia or ventricular fibrillation or who have been resuscitated from or at high risk of sudden death. Patients with heart failure are predisposed to the proarrhythmic effects of antiarrhythmic drugs and the cardiodepressant effects of calcium channel blockers, and such agents should be avoided. Nonsteroidal anti-inflammatory drugs (NSAIDs) inhibit the effects of diuretics and ACE inhibitors and can worsen both cardiac and renal function.

DRUGS FOR THE CONTROL OF FLUID RETENTION

The first step in the treatment of patients with chronic heart failure is the control of fluid retention. This step is generally not necessary in patients with asymptomatic left ventricular systolic dysfunction.

Diuretics

Diuretics interfere with the sodium retention of heart failure by inhibiting the reabsorption of sodium and chloride at specific sites in the renal tubules. Of the commonly used agents, furosemide, torsemide, and bumetanide act at the loop of Henle (i.e., loop diuretics); thiazides and metolazone act in the distal tubule; and potassium-sparing diuretics act at the level of the collecting duct.

All diuretics increase urine volume and sodium excretion, but these agents differ in their pharmacologic properties. The loop diuretics increase the fractional excretion of sodium up to 20% to 25% of the filtered load, enhance the clearance of free water, and maintain efficacy even when renal perfusion and function are impaired. In contrast, the thiazide diuretics increase the fractional excretion of sodium to only 5% to 10% of the filtered load, tend to decrease free water clearance, and lose their effectiveness in patients with only moderately impaired renal perfusion and function. Consequently, the loop diuretics are the preferred diuretic agents for patients with heart failure.

CLINICAL EFFECTS. Controlled trials have shown that diuretic drugs can decrease signs and symptoms of fluid retention, but diuretics alone cannot maintain the clinical stability of patients with heart failure for long periods of time. However, the risk of clinical decompensation can be reduced if diuretics are combined with a neurohormonal antagonist (e.g., an ACE inhibitor). These observations indicate that diuretics are a necessary, but not sufficient, component of any successful therapeutic strategy for heart failure.

CLINICAL USE. Diuretics play a pivotal role in the treatment of heart failure for three reasons. First, diuretics are the only drugs that can adequately control the fluid retention of heart failure. Few patients with heart failure can maintain sodium balance without the use of diuretic drugs, and attempts to substitute ACE inhibitors for diuretics can lead to pulmonary and peripheral congestion. Second, diuretics produce symptomatic benefits more rapidly than any other drug for heart failure, because they can relieve pulmonary and peripheral edema within hours or days, whereas the effects of digitalis, ACE inhibitors, or β-blockers may require weeks or months to become apparent. Third, diuretics modulate the responses to other drugs used for the treatment of heart failure, because the effects of neurohormonal antagonists are highly dependent on sodium balance. If diuretics are prescribed in doses that are too low, the expansion of intravascular volume inhibits the response to ACE inhibitors and enhances the risks of treatment with β-blockers.

Diuretics are generally initiated in low doses (Table 56–1), and the dose is increased until signs and symptoms of fluid retention are alleviated. Once this goal has been achieved, treatment with the diuretic is continued on a long-term basis to prevent the recurrence of salt and water retention. Although diuretics are commonly prescribed at a constant daily dose, the doses of these drugs should ideally be adjusted based on changes in the patient's body weight. As heart failure advances and renal function declines, patients become resistant to the effects of low doses of these drugs and respond only when high doses are used or when diuretics with different renal tubular sites of action are used in combination. NSAIDs can decrease the efficacy and increase the risk of diuretics and should be avoided.

DRUGS THAT ANTAGONIZE NEUROHORMONAL MECHANISMS

Drugs that interfere with the actions of endogenous neurohormonal systems (e.g., the renin-angiotensin system and the sympathetic nervous system) can relieve the symptoms of heart failure by antagonizing the vasoconstriction caused by an increase in neurohormonal activity. However, their major advantage over traditional treatments is their ability to inhibit the cardiotoxic effects of the neurohormonal system and thereby retard the progression of heart failure. As a result, neurohormonal interventions have emerged as essential agents in the management of heart failure. Several types of neurohormonal antagonists have been approved for the treatment of heart failure by the U.S. Food and Drug Administration (FDA): (1) ACE inhibitors, (2) β-adrenergic receptor blockers, and (3) angiotensin receptor blockers.

Angiotensin-Converting Enzyme Inhibitors

ACE inhibitors interfere with the renin-angiotensin system by inhibiting the enzyme responsible for the conversion of angiotensin I to angiotensin II. However, the benefits of these drugs may not be entirely explained by their actions on the renin-angiotensin system. Because the ACE is identical to kininase II, ACE inhibition not only interferes with the formation of angiotensin II but also enhances the action of kinins; kinin potentiation may add importantly to angiotensin suppression in mediating the effects of ACE inhibitors. The favorable effects of ACE inhibitors on cardiac remodeling may be greater than those of angiotensin II receptor antagonists, and this advantage of ACE inhibitors is abolished by the coadministration of kinin antagonists. Moreover, the hemodynamic and prognostic benefits of ACE inhibitors may be attenuated by the coadministration of aspirin, which blocks kinin-mediated prostaglandin synthesis.

Five ACE inhibitors have been approved for the treatment of chronic heart failure by the FDA: captopril, enalapril, lisinopril, quinapril, and fosinopril (see Table 56–1). Ramipril is approved for the treatment of heart failure after an acute MI.

CLINICAL EFFECTS. All ACE inhibitors approved for the treatment of heart failure have been shown in double-blind, placebo-controlled trials to produce hemodynamic and clinical benefits. Treatment with these drugs improves left ventricular ejection fraction and decreases left ventricular chamber size; both actions suggest a favorable effect on the process of cardiac remodeling. ACE inhibitors relieve dyspnea, prolong exercise tolerance, and reduce the need for emergency care for worsening heart failure. These benefits are seen in patients with mild, moderate, and severe symptoms, regardless of whether they are treated with digitalis. However, ACE inhibitors should not be used before (or instead of) diuretics in patients with a history of fluid retention, because diuretics are needed to maintain sodium balance and prevent the development of peripheral and pulmonary edema. Nevertheless, ACE inhibitors may reduce the need for large doses of diuretics and potassium supplements and may attenuate many of the adverse metabolic effects of aggressive diuretic therapy (e.g., hypokalemia and hyponatremia).

In addition, several long-term trials have shown that ACE inhibitors can reduce the risk of death and retard the progression of heart failure in patients with an ischemic or a nonischemic cardiomyopathy who are already receiving digitalis and diuretics.[1,2] In the Studies of Left Ventricular Dysfunction (SOLVD) Treatment Trial, the use of enalapril in patients with mild-to-moderate symptoms was associated with a 16% reduction in all-cause mortality ($P = .004$) and a 26% decrease in the risk of death or hospitalization for heart failure ($P < .001$). In the Cooperative North Scandinavian Enalapril Survival Study (CONSENSUS), the use of enalapril in patients with severe symptoms was associated with a 27% reduction in the risk of death ($P = .003$). When the results of all studies are combined, ACE inhibitors appear to reduce both the risk of death and the risk of hospitalization for heart failure by 20% to 30%. Furthermore, ACE inhibitors produce greater effects on survival than a combination of direct-acting vasodilators (e.g., hydralazine and isosorbide dinitrate). ACE inhibitors have also been shown to reduce mortality rates in patients with impaired left ventricular function or heart failure after an acute MI (Chapter 60).

CLINICAL USE. Because of their ability to improve the natural history of heart failure, all patients with heart failure due to left ventricular systolic dysfunction should receive an ACE inhibitor unless they are unable to tolerate the drug or have a contraindication to it. Physicians

---

Table 56–1 • DRUGS RECOMMENDED FOR GENERAL USE IN CHRONIC HEART FAILURE

	STARTING DOSE	SUBSEQUENT DOSES
DIURETICS		
Furosemide	20–40 mg qd or bid	Titrate to achieve dry weight (up to 400 mg/day)
Torsemide	10–20 mg qd or bid	Titrate to achieve dry weight (up to 200 mg/day)
Bumetinide	0.5–1.0 mg qd or bid	Titrate to achieve dry weight (up to 10 mg/day)
Metolazone	2.5–5.0 mg qd or bid	Titrate to achieve dry weight (up to 20 mg/day)
ANGIOTENSIN-CONVERTING ENZYME INHIBITORS		
Captopril	6.25 mg tid	Titrate to target dose (50 mg tid)
Enalapril	2.5 mg bid	Titrate to target dose (10–20 mg bid)
Lisinopril	2.5-5.0 mg qd	Titrate to target dose (20–35 mg qd)
Ramipril*	1.25-2.5 mg bid	Titrate to target dose (5 mg bid)
Quinapril	10 mg bid	Target dose not established (not >40 mg bid)
Fosinopril	5–10 mg qd	Target dose not established (not >40 mg qd)
β-RECEPTOR BLOCKERS		
Carvedilol	3.125 mg bid	Titrate to target dose (25 mg bid)
Bisoprolol*	1.25 mg qd	Titrate to target dose (10 mg qd)
Metoprolol tartrate*	6.25 mg bid	Titrate to target dose (50 mg bid)
Metoprolol succinate (extended-release)	12.5–25 mg qd	Titrate to target dose (200 mg qd)
ALDOSTERONE ANTAGONISTS		
Spironolactone	12.5–25 mg qd	Titrate to target dose (25 mg qd)
DIGITALIS GLYCOSIDES		
Digoxin	0.125–0.25 mg qd	Target dose not established (≤0.375 mg/day)

*Drugs not approved by the U.S. Food and Drug Administration for use in the management of chronic heart failure, July 2002.

CLINICAL PRECAUTIONS. The principal adverse effects of diuretics include (1) electrolyte depletion, (2) neurohormonal activation, and (3) hypotension and azotemia. Other types of side effects may occur (e.g., rash, hearing difficulties), but these are generally idiosyncratic reactions or occur with the use of very large doses.

Electrolyte Depletion. Diuretics can cause the depletion of potassium and magnesium, which can predispose patients to serious cardiac arrhythmias, particularly in the presence of digitalis therapy. The loss of electrolytes is related to enhanced delivery of sodium to distal sites in the renal tubules and the exchange of sodium for other cations, a process that is potentiated by activation of the renin-angiotensin-aldosterone system. Concomitant administration of ACE inhibitors, angiotensin II receptor blockers, or aldosterone antagonists can prevent the loss of electrolytes caused by diuretics.

Neurohormonal Activation. Diuretic drugs may increase the activation of endogenous neurohormonal systems in patients with heart failure. Such activation may increase the risk of disease progression, unless patients are receiving concomitant treatment with a neurohormonal antagonist (ACE inhibitor or sympathetic antagonist).

Hypotension and Azotemia. Although the use of diuretics can lower blood pressure or cause azotemia, these changes are generally asymptomatic and require no specific treatment. The dose of diuretic should not be reduced for asymptomatic changes in blood pressure or renal function if the patient has signs of fluid overload.

should not withhold treatment with an ACE inhibitor until the patient becomes resistant to treatment with other drugs, because such patients might die during the period of delay and such deaths might have been prevented if treatment with the ACE inhibitor had been initiated earlier. The available data do not justify withholding ACE inhibitors from any specific subset of patients, even patients with low blood pressures or impaired renal function. Treatment is generally maintained even in patients who do not experience symptomatic benefits.

Treatment with an ACE inhibitor is generally initiated in low doses followed by gradual increments in dose if lower doses have been well tolerated. In general, the dose of ACE inhibitor is increased until the doses are similar to those used in the clinical trials that established the ability of these drugs to reduce morbidity and mortality. Examples of starting dosages of ACE inhibitors include captopril 6.25 mg three times a day, enalapril 2.5 mg twice daily, or lisinopril 2.5 to 5.0 mg once daily (see Table 56–1). Examples of target dosages of ACE inhibitors include captopril 50 mg three times a day, enalapril 10 to 20 mg twice daily, and lisinopril 20 to 35 mg once daily. High doses are more effective than low doses in reducing the risk of hospitalization. The clinical effects of therapy may take weeks or months to become apparent.

Because fluid retention can attenuate the effects of ACE inhibitors, physicians should ensure that the dose of diuretics is optimized before initiating treatment. Close monitoring of diuretic therapy is also needed after initiation of treatment, because the dose of diuretic may need to be reduced if the patient experiences symptomatic decreases in blood pressure or clinically important declines in renal function. NSAIDs can decrease the efficacy and increase the risks of ACE inhibitors and should be avoided.

CLINICAL PRECAUTIONS. The adverse effects of ACE inhibitors can be attributed to the two principal pharmacologic actions of these drugs: (1) those related to the effects of angiotensin suppression and (2) those related to the effects of kinin potentiation.

Adverse Effects Related to Angiotensin Suppression. Decreases in blood pressure or increases in blood urea nitrogen may be seen early in treatment but are generally asymptomatic and require no specific therapy. However, if hypotension is accompanied by dizziness or blurred vision or if renal function deteriorates significantly, the physician should reduce the dose of the diuretic, unless fluid retention is present. Potassium retention may be seen if the patient is receiving potassium supplements or potassium-sparing diuretics but usually resolves after a change in these background medications. Most patients with hypotension, azotemia, or hyperkalemia can be managed without the withdrawal of the ACE inhibitor; thus, most patients (about 90%) who experience these early reactions remain excellent candidates for, and tolerate, long-term ACE inhibition.

Adverse Effects Related to Kinin Potentiation. Angioedema occurs in less than 1% of patients, but because it may be life threatening, its occurrence justifies avoidance of all ACE inhibitors for the lifetime of the patient. A nonproductive cough is observed in 5% to 15% of patients receiving ACE inhibitors; it usually appears within the first several months of therapy, disappears within 1 to 2 weeks of discontinuation of treatment, and recurs within days of rechallenge. When a patient receiving an ACE inhibitor complains of cough, other causes should be considered (especially pulmonary congestion), and the ACE inhibitor should be implicated only after the physician confirms that the cough disappears after withdrawal of the drug and recurs after rechallenge. Because the cough is related to a common action of all ACE inhibitors, its occurrence frequently requires the withdrawal of the ACE inhibitor and the use of alternative approaches to interfering with the renin-angiotensin system (e.g., angiotensin II receptor antagonists; see Drugs Used in Patients Intolerant of Angiotensin-Converting Enzyme Inhibitors).

β-Adrenergic Receptor Blockers

Although most physicians were formerly taught to avoid the use of β-blockers in patients with heart failure, these drugs can produce important clinical benefits in this disorder. Like ACE inhibitors, β-blockers interfere with the deleterious actions of an endogenous neurohormonal system, which can adversely affect the failing heart by promoting cell death, hypertrophy, ischemia, and arrhythmias. Although these deleterious effects are mediated through three distinct adrenergic receptors (α_1, β_1, and β_2), evidence suggests that agents that block multiple receptors may provide greater protection against

catecholamine-induced cardiomyopathy than drugs that block only one receptor. Of available β-blockers, only carvedilol and metoprolol have been approved by the FDA for the treatment of heart failure.

CLINICAL EFFECTS. Several β-blockers have been shown in double-blind, placebo-controlled trials to produce hemodynamic and clinical benefits. Treatment with these drugs improves left ventricular ejection fraction and decreases left ventricular chamber size; both actions suggest a favorable effect on the process of cardiac remodeling. β-Blockers relieve symptoms and improve clinical status; these benefits have been seen in patients with mild, moderate, and severe symptoms, regardless of whether they are treated with digitalis. β-Blockers are generally used together with ACE inhibitors in clinical practice; combined use of both neurohormonal antagonists can be expected to produce additive benefits.

In addition, several long-term trials have shown that β-blockers can reduce the risk of death and retard the progression of heart failure in patients with an ischemic or nonischemic cardiomyopathy who are already receiving digitalis, diuretics, and ACE inhibitors.[3,4] In the U.S. Carvedilol Program, the use of carvedilol in patients with mild-to-moderate symptoms was associated with a 65% reduction in all-cause mortality ($P < .001$) and a 36% decrease in the risk of death or hospitalization for a cardiovascular reason ($P < .001$). In the Metoprolol CR/XL Randomized Trial in Heart Failure (MERIT-HF) study, the use of metoprolol in mild-to-moderate heart failure was associated with an approximately 35% reduction in the risk of death ($P < .001$) and a 31% lower risk of death or hospitalization for heart failure ($P < .001$). In the Second Cardiac Insufficiency Bisoprolol Study (CIBIS II), the use of bisoprolol in moderate-to-severe heart failure was associated with a 32% reduction in the risk of death ($P < .001$) and a 32% decrease in the frequency of being hospitalized for heart failure ($P < .0001$). In the Carvedilol Prospective Randomized Cumulative Survival (COPERNICUS) study, the use of carvedilol in patients with severe symptoms was associated with a 35% reduction in all-cause mortality ($P < .001$) and a 31% lower risk of death or hospitalization for heart failure ($P < .001$). When the results of all studies are combined, β-blockers appear to reduce both the risk of death and the risk of hospitalization for heart failure by 30% to 40% in patients already receiving ACE inhibitors. The magnitude of the effects is similar regardless of the cause or severity of heart failure. β-Blockers have also been shown to reduce mortality rates in patients with impaired left ventricular function or heart failure after an acute MI (Chapter 69). Recent data suggest that carvedilol is significantly more efficacious than metoprolol in reducing mortality, presumably because it provides more comprehensive sympathetic antagonism.[5]

CLINICAL USE. Because β-blockers can favorably modify the natural history of heart failure, all patients with heart failure due to left ventricular systolic dysfunction should receive a β-blocker unless they have a contraindication to its use or are unable to tolerate treatment with the drug. β-Blockers should not be withheld until the patient is shown to be resistant to treatment with other drugs, because such patients might die or experience worsening of their disease during the period of delay and such progression might have been prevented if treatment with the β-blocker had been initiated earlier. Treatment is generally maintained even in patients who do not experience symptomatic benefits. However, there are insufficient data on the efficacy and safety of β-blocker use in patients in an intensive care unit or receiving intravenous positive inotropic drugs for heart failure to recommend the use of β-blockers in those with clinical instability or end-stage disease. In addition, patients with bronchospastic disease or advanced heart block should not receive treatment with these drugs.

Treatment with a β-blocker is generally initiated in very low doses followed by gradual increments in dose if lower doses have been well tolerated (see Table 56–1). In general, the dose of these drugs is increased until doses are achieved similar to those used in the clinical trials that established the ability of these drugs to reduce morbidity and mortality. Examples of starting dosages of β-blockers include carvedilol 3.125 mg twice daily, bisoprolol 1.25 mg/day, and metoprolol (sustained-release) 12.5 mg/day. Examples of long-term dosages of β-blockers include carvedilol 25 mg twice daily, bisoprolol 10 mg/day, and metoprolol (sustained-release) 200 mg/day. As in the case of ACE inhibitors, the clinical effects of therapy may take weeks or months to become apparent.

Because fluid retention can increase the risks of β-blockade, physicians should ensure that the dose of diuretics is optimized before initiating treatment. Close monitoring of diuretic therapy is also needed after initiation of treatment, because an increase in the dose of diuretic may be required if the patient experiences a significant increase in body weight or worsening symptoms of heart failure.

CLINICAL PRECAUTIONS. Like ACE inhibitors, β-blockers can produce unwanted side effects that result directly from changes in neurohormonal activity. These adverse reactions occur during initiation of therapy but are generally mild in severity, can be managed by changes in concomitant therapy, usually subside after several days or weeks of treatment, and, thus, infrequently lead to the withdrawal of treatment. In clinical trials, most patients (>85%) with heart failure were able to tolerate short- and long-term therapy with these drugs.

Hypotension. Vasodilatory side effects may be seen within 24 to 48 hours of initiation of therapy or after increments in dose but usually subside with repeated dosing without any change in the dose of the β-blocker or background medications. Physicians can minimize the risk of hypotension by administering the β-blocker and the ACE inhibitor at different times of the day.

Fluid Retention. Initiation of therapy with a β-blocker can produce fluid retention, which is usually manifested as an asymptomatic increase in body weight but may be severe enough to cause worsening symptoms of heart failure. Increases in body weight are generally seen within 3 to 5 days of initiation of therapy or after increments in dose. Physicians should ask patients to weigh themselves daily, and asymptomatic increases in weight should be treated promptly by increasing the dose of concomitantly administered diuretics until the patient's weight is restored to pretreatment levels.

Bradycardia and Heart Block. Therapy with a β-blocker can decrease heart rate and alter cardiac conduction, thereby leading to bradycardia or heart block. These changes are usually asymptomatic but may be severe enough to cause symptomatic hypotension. If the heart rate declines to less than 50 beats per minute or second or third heart block is observed, the dose of β-blocker should be decreased. Cardiac pacing might be considered to allow the use of β-blockade in selected patients.

Aldosterone Antagonists

Although generally classified in the category of potassium-sparing diuretics, drugs that block the actions of aldosterone (e.g., spironolactone) act to antagonize an endogenous neurohormonal mechanism that may adversely affect the heart independent of its effects on sodium balance. In the Randomized Aldactone Evaluation Study (RALES) trial, the addition of low dosages of spironolactone (12.5 to 25 mg/day) to patients with current or recent class IV symptoms receiving ACE inhibitors decreased the risk of death by 25% to 30% and the risk of hospitalization for heart failure by approximately 35% (P < .001). ◻ This principle has been reinforced by a recent study in which another aldosterone antagonist, eplerenone (50 mg per day) reduced the risk of death by 15% in patients with left ventricular dysfunction after myocardial infarction. ◻ Therefore, the use of low doses of spironolactone merits consideration in patients with advanced heart failure. Such use, however, is not approved by the FDA.

DRUGS USED TO RELIEVE SYMPTOMS AND LESSEN DISABILITY

Digitalis

The digitalis glycosides exert their effects in patients with heart failure by virtue of their ability to inhibit sodium-potassium adenosine triphosphatase (Na^+, K^+-ATPase). Inhibition of this enzyme in the heart results in an increase in cardiac contractility, and for many decades, the benefits of digitalis in heart failure were ascribed to this positive inotropic action. However, by inhibiting Na^+, K^+-ATPase in vagal afferents, digitalis acts to sensitize cardiac baroreceptors, which, in turn, reduce the outflow of sympathetic impulses from the central nervous system. In addition, by inhibiting Na^+, K^+-ATPase in the kidney, digitalis reduces the renal tubular reabsorption of sodium; the resulting increase in the delivery of sodium to the distal tubules leads to the suppression of renin secretion. These observations have led to the hypothesis that, in addition to increasing contractile force, digitalis may produce important vasodilatory effects by attenuating the activation of neurohormonal systems.

Although a variety of digitalis glycosides have been used in the treatment of heart failure for the past 200 years, the most commonly used preparation in the United States is digoxin. Digoxin is the principal glycoside that has been evaluated in placebo-controlled trials.

CLINICAL EFFECTS. Controlled studies have shown that digoxin can improve symptoms, quality of life, and exercise tolerance in patients with mild-to-moderate heart failure. These benefits are seen regardless of the underlying rhythm (sinus rhythm or atrial fibrillation), cause of heart failure (ischemic or nonischemic cardiomyopathy), or concomitant therapy (with or without ACE inhibitors). The addition of digoxin produces favorable effects on clinical status and ejection fraction, and the withdrawal of digoxin is followed by hemodynamic and clinical deterioration. However, in a long-term controlled clinical trial, digoxin did not reduce the risk of death and was associated with only a modest reduction in the combined risk of death and hospitalization. ◻ These results indicate that the primary benefit of digoxin in heart failure is to alleviate symptoms and improve clinical status.

CLINICAL USE. Digoxin provides a convenient, inexpensive, and well-tolerated means of improving the clinical status of patients with heart failure. However, the finding that the drug has little effect on the progression of heart failure has minimized any mandate for its early use; thus, it can be prescribed at any time if symptoms persist after the use of other drugs. Digoxin is a preferred agent in patients with heart failure who have atrial fibrillation and a rapid ventricular response (Chapter 59). The drug is not recommended for use in patients who have no symptoms or for the stabilization of patients with acutely decompensated heart failure.

Digoxin is usually initiated and maintained at a dosage of 0.25 mg/day (see Table 56–1). Lower doses are indicated in patients who are elderly (>70 years old) or in those with impaired renal function (serum creatinine >1.5 mg/dL). Higher doses may be needed to control the ventricular response in patients with atrial fibrillation. Although serum digoxin levels are commonly used to guide the administration of digoxin, there is little evidence to support this approach. There is no relation between drug levels and efficacy in patients in sinus rhythm, and patients with atrial fibrillation are better monitored by their heart rate response than by drug levels.

CLINICAL PRECAUTIONS. The principal adverse effects of digoxin include (1) cardiac arrhythmias (e.g., ectopic and reentrant cardiac rhythms and heart block), (2) gastrointestinal symptoms (e.g., anorexia, nausea and vomiting), and (3) neurologic complaints (e.g., visual disturbances, disorientation, and confusion). These side effects are commonly associated with serum digoxin levels greater than 2 ng/mL, but digitalis toxicity may occur with lower digoxin levels, particularly if hypokalemia or hypomagnesemia coexist. The concomitant use of quinidine, verapamil, spironolactone, flecainide, propafenone, and amiodarone can increase serum digoxin levels and may increase the risk of adverse reactions. Patients with advanced heart block should not receive the drug unless a pacemaker is in place.

Low doses of digoxin are well tolerated by most patients with heart failure. Adverse effects occur primarily when the drug is administered in large doses, but large doses are generally not needed to produce clinical benefits. Nevertheless, there is persistent concern that digitalis may exert deleterious cardiovascular effects in the long term at doses that appear to be well tolerated in the short term. In a large-scale trial, the use of digoxin in doses that produced serum levels below the toxic range appeared to increase the frequency of hospitalizations and deaths related to cardiovascular events other than heart failure. These observations raise the possibility that even low doses of digoxin can adversely affect the heart.

ALGORITHM FOR THE MANAGEMENT OF CHRONIC HEART FAILURE

The evidence summarized in this section can be synthesized into an algorithm that can guide the management of patients with symptoms of heart failure (Fig. 56–4).

Step 1: Establish the Diagnosis of Heart Failure

Patients who are limited in their ability to exercise or perform activities of daily living because of dyspnea or fatigue should be evaluated for the presence of heart failure. During the initial evaluation, the clinician should obtain a two-dimensional echocardiogram, which can identify disorders of the valves, pericardium, or great vessels that may be corrected surgically and can quantify the type and magnitude of ventricular dysfunction. Patients with systolic dysfunction (ejection fraction <40%) should be distinguished from patients with preserved left ventricular function (>40%).

Every effort should be made to identify and treat concomitant conditions (e.g., anemia, thyroid disorders) or withdraw concomitant

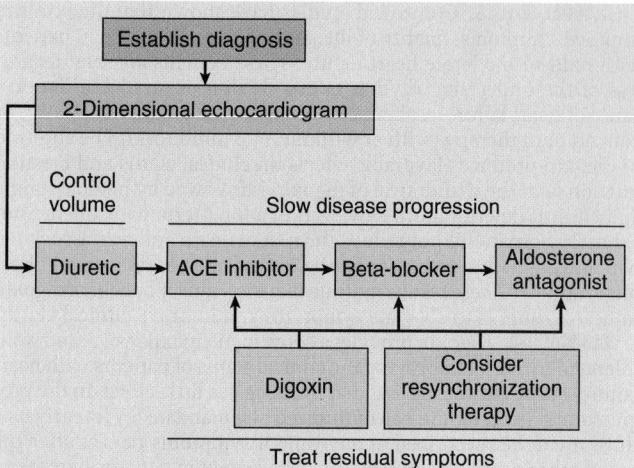

FIGURE 56–4 • Algorithm for the management of chronic heart failure. *Step 1: Establish the diagnosis.* A two-dimensional echocardiogram can quantify the type and magnitude of ventricular dysfunction and can identify disorders of the valves, pericardium, or great vessels that may be corrected surgically. *Step 2: Control volume with the use of diuretics.* The dose of diuretic should be adjusted until there is no evidence of fluid retention, as reflected either by resolution of peripheral edema or normalization of jugular venous pressure. *Step 3: Slow disease progression with the use of ACE inhibitors, β-blockers, and an aldosterone antagonist.* Even if symptoms are controlled with a diuretic, ACE inhibitors, β-blockers, and usually an aldosterone antagonist should be used together to reduce the risk of death and hospitalization. *Step 4: Treat any residual symptoms with digoxin.* Some physicians prescribe digoxin to all symptomatic patients with systolic dysfunction receiving a diuretic, whereas others reserve digoxin for patients who remain symptomatic despite the use of a diuretic, ACE inhibitor, β-blocker, and aldosterone antagonist. Resynchronization therapy may be considered in patients with a widened QRS who have persistent symptoms despite other therapies. ACE = angiotensin-converting enzyme.

medications (e.g., calcium channel blockers, antiarrhythmic drugs, and NSAIDs) that may exacerbate the syndrome of heart failure. Patients who are in respiratory distress, have evidence of poor end-organ perfusion or fluid overload, or have a serious complicating illness should be hospitalized for treatment with intravenous agents (e.g., diuretics, vasodilators and/or positive inotropic agents) to achieve rapid stabilization of their clinical condition.

Step 2: Initiate Therapy with a Diuretic to Stabilize the Symptoms

Because of the critical importance of fluid retention, the use of diuretics is warranted in most patients with symptoms of heart failure, together with a moderate degree of sodium restriction. The dose of diuretic should be adjusted until there is no evidence of fluid retention, as reflected either by resolution of peripheral edema or by normalization of jugular venous pressure. After these early goals are achieved, treatment with the diuretic should be continued in the long term to prevent the recurrence of fluid retention, and the doses of diuretics should be continually reevaluated to maintain patients free of edema and at dry weight. If this approach is not followed, the resulting underuse of diuretics not only undermines the ability of these drugs to relieve symptoms but also adversely affects the patient's ability to respond favorably and safely to ACE inhibitors and β-blockers. As heart failure advances and renal function declines, patients may become resistant to the effects of low doses and respond only when high doses are used or a second diuretic (e.g., metolazone) is added.

Step 3: Use Angiotensin-Converting Enzyme Inhibitors and β-Blockers to Stabilize the Disease

Because diuretics do not prevent disease progression, patients with heart failure due to systolic dysfunction should not be treated with a diuretic alone, even if their symptoms are alleviated with the use of diuretic drugs. Patients who respond favorably to diuretics should receive additional therapy with agents that block the actions of neurohormonal systems (ACE inhibitors and β-blockers). The use of

neurohormonal inhibitors should not be reserved for patients who are refractory to diuretics, because patients might die during the period of delay and patients with end-stage heart failure and persistent fluid retention often respond poorly to ACE inhibitors and β-blockers. In patients with mild, moderate, or severe heart failure, treatment with the ACE inhibitor should be started first, initially in low doses, and every effort should be made to maintain treatment if patients experience early intolerance. Changes in diuretics may be needed to minimize the risk of adverse reactions. In stable patients with mild, moderate, or severe heart failure, treatment with a β-blocker should be added to the ACE inhibitor, regardless of the degree of clinical improvement with the ACE inhibitor. Therapy should be initiated in low doses followed by appropriate increments in dose, and every effort should be made to maintain treatment if patients experience early intolerance. As with ACE inhibitors, changes in diuretics may be needed to minimize the risk of adverse reactions. In patients with recent or current class IV symptoms, the addition of spironolactone to the ACE inhibitor merits consideration.

Optimal effects on disease progression can be achieved only by using both an ACE inhibitor and a β-blocker in combination. ACE inhibition appears to reduce the risk of death and of hospitalization by 20 to 30%, and the addition of a β-blocker to the ACE inhibitor produces a further 30 to 40% reduction in the risk of a major clinical event. However, treatment with ACE inhibitors and a β-blocker should not be initiated at the same time. Therapy with a β-blocker should be started after the patient has been stabilized on appropriate doses of the ACE inhibitor.

Step 4: Add Therapy with Digoxin in Patients with Persistent Symptoms

Because the benefits of digoxin are largely related to its ability to improve symptoms and clinical status, the drug may be used at any time to alleviate symptoms. Some physicians prescribe digoxin to all symptomatic patients with systolic dysfunction receiving a diuretic, whereas others reserve digoxin for patients who remain symptomatic despite the use of diuretics, ACE inhibitors, and β-blockers. Digoxin should be a preferred agent in patients whose heart failure is associated with atrial arrhythmias (e.g., atrial fibrillation).

OTHER THERAPEUTIC STRATEGIES IN PATIENTS WITH HEART FAILURE

Drugs Used in Patients Intolerant of ACE Inhibitors

Two types of drugs are available for patients who cannot tolerate treatment with an ACE inhibitor. Neither approach is recommended in patients who can tolerate an ACE inhibitor without difficulty.

ANGIOTENSIN RECEPTOR BLOCKERS. Angiotensin II receptor antagonists (e.g., losartan, valsartan, irbesartan, eprosartan, candesartan) interfere with the actions of the renin-angiotensin system by blocking the interaction of angiotensin II with its receptor. This mechanism, distinct from that of ACE inhibitors, is not associated with the accumulation of kinins; thus, the effects of these drugs in heart failure may differ from those reported for ACE inhibitors. In the Losartan Heart Failure Survival Study (ELITE II), the angiotensin II antagonist losartan was somewhat less effective than the ACE inhibitor captopril in modifying survival, especially in patients receiving a β-blocker. In the Valsartan Heart Failure Trial (Val-HeFT), the angiotensin II antagonist valsartan was shown to reduce the risk of death or hospitalization for heart failure in patients not receiving an ACE inhibitor, but had little effect when added to patients already receiving an ACE inhibitor and may have exerted an adverse effect in patients receiving both an ACE inhibitor and β-blocker. Accordingly, angiotensin II receptor antagonists should not be used for the treatment of heart failure in patients who have no prior exposure to an ACE inhibitor, and these drugs should not be substituted for ACE inhibitors in patients who are tolerating ACE inhibitors without difficulty. Furthermore, these agents cause hypotension and renal insufficiency as frequently as ACE inhibitors. Angiotensin II antagonists may be used in patients who cannot tolerate an ACE inhibitor because of cough or angioedema.[9,10]

HYDRALAZINE AND ISOSORBIDE DINITRATE. Although direct-acting vasodilators can produce favorable short-term hemodynamic effects in patients with heart failure, their long-term use has not improved symptoms and has increased the risk of heart failure and death in controlled clinical trials. Of the agents evaluated, only a combination of isosorbide dinitrate and hydralazine has produced some encouraging results. The combination of these two direct-acting vasodilators reduces the risk of death in patients with heart failure receiving digitalis and diuretics. However, this vasodilator combination has no effect on the frequency of hospitalizations, and many patients fail to tolerate long-term treatment with these drugs. Furthermore, when compared with ACE inhibitors, the nitrate-hydralazine combination is associated with a higher risk of death, despite greater benefits on exercise fraction and exercise tolerance. Finally, there is little experience with the use of hydralazine and isosorbide dinitrate in patients receiving an ACE inhibitor or a β-blocker. For all of these reasons, neither hydralazine nor isosorbide dinitrate (alone or in combination) is approved by the FDA for the treatment of heart failure.

Therefore, the combination of hydralazine and isosorbide dinitrate is not used for the treatment of heart failure in patients who have no prior exposure to an ACE inhibitor, and these drugs should not be substituted for ACE inhibitors in patients who are tolerating ACE inhibitors. The combined use of hydralazine and isosorbide dinitrate may be used in patients who cannot tolerate an ACE inhibitor because of hypotension or renal insufficiency. There is no good evidence to support the use of nitrates alone or hydralazine alone in the management of chronic heart failure.

Drugs and Devices Used for the Treatment of Coexistent Cardiac Disorders

Many patients with heart failure have coexistent cardiac disorders that require active management. Revascularization should be strongly considered in patients with heart failure who have angina, because it may reduce the risk of major cardiac events (Chapter 67). Nitrates and β-blockers may be used if revascularization cannot be performed or is unsuccessful. Diuretics, ACE inhibitors, and β-blockers are excellent choices for the treatment of patients who have heart failure and hypertension (Chapter 63).

Atrial arrhythmias are common in patients with heart failure, and if accompanied by a rapid ventricular response, they can exacerbate the severity of symptoms and possibly accelerate progression of the underlying disease. Although the prevention of atrial arrhythmias would be highly desirable, this goal cannot be effectively or safely achieved with most antiarrhythmic drugs. The agent most likely to suppress atrial arrhythmias in patients with heart failure is amiodarone, but the substantial toxicity of the drug has justifiably discouraged its widespread use. As a result, many physicians do not attempt to restore sinus rhythm in patients with an established atrial arrhythmia but instead focus on controlling the rate of the ventricular response with digitalis and β-blockers and reducing the risk of embolic events with anticoagulants. If a slow ventricular response cannot be achieved in this manner, amiodarone or radiofrequency ablative procedures (Chapter 59) should be considered.

Most patients with heart failure have frequent and complex ventricular arrhythmias, but when asymptomatic, these do not presage or contribute to the occurrence of sudden death and thus do not require therapy. The appearance of ventricular arrhythmias in these patients is likely to reflect the severity of the underlying cardiac disease and thus may respond to interventions that reduce the risk of disease progression. In addition, every effort should be made to correct electrolyte imbalances if these are found. In patients who have an immediate life-threatening ventricular arrhythmia (sustained ventricular tachycardia or ventricular fibrillation) or who have been resuscitated from or are at high risk of sudden death, use of an implantable cardioverter-defibrillator may reduce the risk of a lethal recurrence (Chapter 60). In addition, implantation of a cardioverter-defibrillator may decrease the risk of death in survivors of an acute MI who have a depressed ejection fraction with or without symptoms of heart failure. [11] In the second Multicenter Automatic Defibrillator Implantation Trial (MADIT-II), prophylactic use of a cardioverter-defibrillator reduced the risk of death by 31% ($P = .016$) in post-MI patients who had no or mild symptoms of heart failure and who were not selected based on the findings of electrophysiological testing. However, questions remain about the applicability of these results to patients with more severe symptoms or without coronary artery disease, and concerns remain about the potential of these devices to increase the risk of hospitalization for heart failure. Additional studies are in progress to address these issues.

About one third of patients with moderate-to-severe heart failure have a widened QRS complex on the surface electrocardiogram owing to asynchronous activation of the right and left ventricles. Such asynchrony may contribute to the hemodynamic abnormalities and symptoms experienced by some patients. Asynchronous contraction can be ameliorated by electrically activating the right and left ventricles in a synchronized manner with a pacemaker to enhance ventricular contraction and to reduce the degree of secondary mitral regurgitation that results from delayed septal activation. Patients randomized to cardiac resynchronization have improvement in their symptoms and a significant reduction in mortality. [12] Resynchronization therapy can be combined with an implantable cardiovertor defibrillator in appropriate patients.

Because of stasis of blood in dilated hypokinetic cardiac chambers, patients with a dilated cardiomyopathy are at increased risk of cardiac thrombi and embolic events. However, it is unclear whether all patients with a depressed ejection fraction should receive treatment with anticoagulant drugs, even if they are known to harbor a cardiac thrombus. Most cardiac thrombi detected by echocardiography do not embolize, and most embolic events are related to thrombi that were not visualized. Anticoagulation is recommended primarily for patients with a previous embolic event or atrial fibrillation.

Drugs to be Avoided in Patients with Heart Failure

Patients with heart failure can improve dramatically after the withdrawal of drugs that are known to affect cardiac function adversely or that interact unfavorably with drugs of established benefit.

ASPIRIN AND NSAIDS. Prostaglandins play an important role in circulatory homeostasis and in the action of many drugs used to treat heart failure. These substances are endogenous vasodilators that act to unload the heart when peripheral vessels are constricted and can support glomerular filtration when renal perfusion is compromised. The natriuretic actions of diuretics and the vasodilatory effects of ACE inhibitors are mediated in part by the release of endogenous prostaglandins. For all of these reasons, the administration of agents that block prostaglandin synthesis can produce worsening cardiac and renal function and can lead to clinical deterioration, particularly in patients with compromised renal perfusion who are receiving diuretics and ACE inhibitors. As a result, most patients with heart failure should not receive NSAIDs.

Whether the recommendation to avoid inhibitors of prostaglandin synthesis applies to aspirin remains controversial. Aspirin is widely prescribed to patients with heart failure, either to reduce the risk of recurrent myocardial ischemic events in patients with coronary artery disease or to decrease the frequency of systemic embolic events in patients with normal coronary arteries. However, by interfering with kinin-mediated prostaglandin synthesis, aspirin can attenuate the hemodynamic actions of ACE inhibitors in patients with heart failure. In large multicenter trials, the use of aspirin was associated with a loss of the effects of ACE inhibitors on survival and an attenuation of the effects of these drugs on cardiovascular morbidity. As a result, some physicians prefer to use a nonaspirin platelet inhibitor (e.g., clopidogrel) (Chapter 33) in patients with heart failure who are receiving ACE inhibitors.

CYTOKINE ANTAGONISTS. Antagonists of the actions of tumor necrosis factor are approved for use in the treatment of several chronic inflammatory diseases, including rheumatoid arthritis and Crohn's disease. Two types of antagonists are commercially available: a soluble receptor (etanercept) and a chimeric antibody (infliximab). Both agents have been shown to exacerbate the course of patients with chronic heart failure in controlled clinical trials. As a result, both etanercept and infliximab should be avoided in patients with heart failure, even if they are being used for a noncardiovascular indication.

ENDOTHELIN ANTAGONISTS. Drugs that interfere with the interaction between endothelin and its receptors produce notable vasodilatory effects, in both the systemic and pulmonary circulations. Only one endothelin receptor antagonist is approved by the FDA for clinical use, specifically for the treatment of patients with pulmonary arterial hypertension (Chapter 64). However, most patients with pulmonary hypertension have elevated pulmonary artery pressures as a result of left heart failure, a condition in which long-term treatment has been associated with an early risk of worsening heart failure. As a result, physicians contemplating the use of bosentan for pulmonary hypertension should confirm that systolic function is preserved before the drug is initiated.

CALCIUM CHANNEL BLOCKERS. Although calcium channel blockers are peripheral vasodilators, these agents have not improved the symptoms of heart failure or enhanced exercise tolerance. Instead, the short- and long-term administration of these drugs has caused serious adverse cardiovascular reactions, including profound hypotension, worsening heart failure, pulmonary edema, and cardiogenic shock. These deleterious responses have been observed with short- or long-acting formulations of the same drug (e.g., nifedipine) as well as with the older and newer members of this class (e.g., felodipine and mibefradil). As a result, clinicians should not use calcium channel blockers for the treatment of heart failure, and most calcium channel blockers should be avoided for the treatment of angina, atrial fibrillation, or hypertension in patients with heart failure.

ANTIARRHYTHMIC AGENTS. Antiarrhythmic agents can suppress ventricular arrhythmias in patients with heart failure, but these agents have not been shown to reduce the risk of sudden death. Instead, the short- and long-term administration of these drugs has caused serious adverse cardiovascular reactions, including worsening heart failure, life-threatening proarrhythmia, and death. These deleterious responses have been observed with most types of antiarrhythmic agents, including class I (encainide, flecainide, and mexiletine) and class III (D-sotalol) drugs (Chapter 62). Mixed results have been reported with amiodarone. As a result, antiarrhythmic therapy should not be used to treat patients with heart failure who have asymptomatic ventricular arrhythmias, regardless of their frequency or complexity. Antiarrhythmic drugs may be useful for patients with rapid atrial fibrillation or for those with hemodynamically destabilizing ventricular tachycardia or ventricular fibrillation.

OUTPATIENT INTRAVENOUS POSITIVE INOTROPIC THERAPY. Although positive inotropic agents (e.g., dobutamine and milrinone) can produce striking hemodynamic benefits when given intravenously for short periods of time, long-term use of these drugs has not been shown to produce symptomatic benefits and has been associated with an increase in the risk of death. Such toxicity has been reported with all types of agents of this class (except for digitalis), whether these have been prescribed orally or intravenously or administered continuously or intermittently. Because of the lack of data demonstrating efficacy and important concerns about toxicity, the use of intermittent intravenous positive inotropic therapy cannot be recommended as a long-term treatment strategy, even in patients with end-stage heart failure.

Treatment of Patients Hospitalized for Heart Failure

Most patients with heart failure can be managed as outpatients, but nearly one third of patients with heart failure require hospitalization each year. The major syndromes requiring hospitalization include (1) fluid overload resistant to orally administered diuretics (e.g., refractory peripheral edema), (2) severe respiratory distress with or without hypoxemia (e.g., acute pulmonary edema), and (3) refractory symptoms with poor end-organ perfusion requiring intravenous therapy. Each syndrome represents an exaggerated expression of each of the pathophysiologic mechanisms that play a role in the evolution of heart failure. Refractory edema reflects excessive sodium and water retention, acute pulmonary edema is the result of extreme vasoconstriction, and refractory symptoms associated with systemic hypoperfusion are the ultimate consequences of contractile failure. Aspects of these syndromes frequently coexist in the same patient.

These syndromes share a common therapeutic approach: because of their immediate life-threatening nature, physicians must rely on short-term hemodynamic interventions to achieve clinical stability as rapidly as possible. If the syndromes are the result of changes in diet or medications or the advent of a treatable complicating illness (e.g., arrhythmia, pneumonia, or renal failure), the hemodynamic support can be gradually withdrawn, and a long-term outpatient strategy can be implemented. However, if these syndromes represent the end stage of a terminal disease that is refractory to medical therapy, hemodynamic support must be continued until a definitive mechanical solution can be devised (e.g., cardiac transplantation; Chapter 80). In either case, neurohormonal activation is not a therapeutic target in patients who are hospitalized for the treatment of decompensated heart failure. Indeed, by supporting cardiac contractility and systemic blood pressure, the activation of the sympathetic nervous system and renin-angiotensin system may help to maintain circulatory homeostasis in acutely ill patients. The administration of neurohormonal antagonists (ACE inhibitors and β-blockers) in this setting is frequently ineffective and may be deleterious.

FLUID OVERLOAD REFRACTORY TO ORAL DIURETICS (REFRACTORY PERIPHERAL EDEMA)

Patients with heart failure are frequently hospitalized for the treatment of edema that persists despite the use of diuretics. These patients typically present with a marked increase in body weight, associated with pleural effusions, ascites, and massive peripheral edema. The degree of fluid retention can become so severe that the edema itself becomes incapacitating and may require mechanical removal of fluid for relief of symptoms. A frequent cause of this syndrome is noncompliance with diet or medications; when such is the case, clinical stability can usually be achieved rapidly by restoring the patient's earlier therapeutic regimen. However, in some patients, the occurrence of refractory edema is indicative of advancing right and left ventricular failure. By causing mesenteric congestion, right ventricular failure can impair the rate of absorption of diuretics; by causing renal hypoperfusion, left ventricular failure can impede the delivery of diuretics to active sites in the renal tubules. As a result, as heart failure advances, patients become increasingly resistant to the effects of diuretic drugs and require increasingly larger doses to achieve a therapeutic response.

Management of Refractory Peripheral Edema

Several strategies should be considered in the management of patients with refractory edema. NSAIDs, which can decrease the efficacy and increase the risk of diuretics, should be withdrawn. Vasodilators (especially ACE inhibitors) may reduce renal perfusion pressure and attenuate the effects of furosemide; they should be used cautiously. Diuretics acting on the loop of Henle (e.g., furosemide) should be selected and administered intravenously to ensure their rapid entry into the bloodstream in high concentrations. If the patient fails to respond to the intravenous administration of large dosages of furosemide (e.g., 160 to 200 mg/day), the physician may add a second diuretic with a different renal tubular site of action (e.g., metolazone). A combination of two diuretics can produce a dramatic increase in urine output, but such a regimen is commonly accompanied by striking (and occasionally life-threatening) degrees of hypokalemia. If a combination of intravenous furosemide and oral metolazone proves ineffective, these diuretics should be coadministered with drugs that increase renal blood flow (e.g., dopamine alone or combined with dobutamine). Finally, if the edema becomes refractory to all pharmacologic interventions, hemofiltration or peritoneal dialysis may be useful in restoring fluid balance in selected patients.

Regardless of the severity of fluid retention, every effort should be made to achieve dry weight, even if achievement of this goal requires a prolonged hospitalization. Patients discharged prematurely with residual edema due to an inadequate diuresis are commonly readmitted to the hospital for refractory edema within several weeks. In contrast, patients who achieve dry weight frequently become responsive to conventional treatments for heart failure and have a lower risk of recurrent hospitalization.

PULMONARY CONGESTION (ACUTE PULMONARY EDEMA)

One of the most common clinical presentations of advanced left ventricular failure is the syndrome of pulmonary congestion. These patients complain of dyspnea at rest and have pulmonary rales on physical examination. Pulmonary congestion may be the first evidence of heart failure in patients without a history of cardiac disease; it may appear in patients who are already hospitalized for an acute cardiac disorder (e.g., MI); or it may complicate the course of a patient with long-standing heart failure. If severe, abrupt, and accompanied by clinical evidence of sympathetic overactivity (tachycardia, diaphoresis, and vasoconstriction), the syndrome is designated as acute pulmonary edema. Acute pulmonary edema may also be triggered by noncardiac disorders, including direct injury to the alveolar-capillary membrane, high-altitude stress, catastrophes of the central nervous system, narcotic overdose, or pulmonary embolism.

Regardless of its cause, pulmonary edema reflects the transudation of fluid into the alveolar space and arises from an imbalance in the factors that regulate the transport of fluid from the pulmonary microcirculation to the interstitial space of the lung. When the cause of the syndrome is cardiac, pulmonary edema results from the rapid onset of intense peripheral vasoconstriction that leads to a marked increase in pulmonary venous pressures. The profound constriction of systemic arteries and veins causes a sudden and dramatic redistribution of blood from peripheral reservoirs to the pulmonary circuit, causing the pulmonary capillary hydrostatic pressure in the lung to exceed the capillary colloid osmotic pressure. However, the transudation of fluid into the alveoli cannot occur if pulmonary blood flow is impaired; thus, patients with an elevated pulmonary vascular resistance or depressed right ventricular function rarely develop acute pulmonary edema.

Management of Pulmonary Edema

Several general measures are advisable for most patients with pulmonary congestion. Every effort should be made to identify an underlying precipitating factor, because its correction is often critical to the success of treatment. Patients usually feel most comfortable resting in bed in the upright position with the legs dependent. Special attention should be devoted to maintaining adequate oxygenation, which can be achieved by increasing the concentration of inspired oxygen or (if necessary) by endotracheal intubation and mechanical ventilation.

Given the importance of peripheral vasoconstriction in the pathogenesis of pulmonary edema, pharmacologic dilation of peripheral vessels represents the critical element in any successful approach to management. This goal can be achieved with the use of (1) morphine, (2) loop diuretic drugs (e.g., furosemide), and (3) direct-acting vasodilators (e.g., nitroglycerin, nitroprusside, and nesiritide). Because of the need for rapid and reliable treatment, these interventions are generally administered intravenously.

MORPHINE. Morphine remains the most effective single agent for the treatment of acute cardiogenic pulmonary edema. The drug acts specifically to antagonize the peripheral vasoconstrictor effects of the sympathetic nervous system; the resultant vasodilatation leads to an immediate and dramatic decline in pulmonary arterial and venous pressures, leading directly to symptomatic improvement. The precise site of the vasodilation produced by morphine is uncertain. The magnitude of venodilation produced by the drug in the limbs is insufficient to explain its effects on pulmonary flow and pressures; instead, morphine appears to act primarily to increase the pooling of blood in the splanchnic circulation. In addition, morphine blunts the chemoreceptor-mediated ventilatory reflexes that trigger the severe tachypnea that accompanies pulmonary edema; by doing so, the drug reduces the work of breathing and thereby oxygen demand.

Morphine is administered in intermittent dosages of 2 to 4 mg IV (up to 10 to 15 mg) until dyspnea is relieved and diaphoresis subsides. The former reflects the acute decline in pulmonary blood flow and pulmonary venous pressures; the latter indicates a decline in the activity of the sympathetic nervous system. Patients should be monitored for respiratory depression, which can be reversed by narcotic antagonists.

LOOP DIURETICS. All diuretics increase urine output in patients with pulmonary edema, but loop diuretics can produce dramatic clinical benefits even before a diuresis has materialized. These immediate benefits are related to the peripheral arterial and venous dilatation produced by these drugs, which results from their ability to enhance the release of prostaglandins from the kidney. Nonloop diuretics do not exert this direct vasodilator action. Although loop diuretics act quickly to increase sodium excretion, the rapidity of diuresis does not determine the clinical response to treatment, because vasodilation (not diuresis) is the principal mechanism of symptom relief. Indeed, an increase in urine output in general is not seen until peripheral signs of vasoconstriction have resolved.

Furosemide is the loop diuretic most commonly used in the treatment of pulmonary edema. The dose of the drug is determined by the prior exposure of the patient to diuretic therapy. In patients who have not received loop diuretics, treatment is usually begun with low dosages (40 to 80 mg IV), whereas patients who have received long-term therapy may require large dosages of the drug (120 to 200 mg IV). Furosemide is usually well tolerated, but hypotension may occur when the drug is administered to patients with acute heart failure after an acute MI. In such patients, pulmonary congestion may be primarily related to diastolic dysfunction rather than volume overload.

NITROPRUSSIDE, NITROGLYCERIN, AND NESIRITIDE. By stimulating guanylate cyclase within the vascular smooth muscle cell, nitroprusside, nitroglycerin, and nesiritide exert dilating effects on arterial resistance and venous capacitance vessels and thereby lower pulmonary

blood flow and pulmonary venous pressures. Of the three, nitroprusside has the greatest effects and nitroglycerin has the least effects on arterial resistance vessels, and thus nitroprusside is most likely and nitroglycerin is the least likely to produce hypotension. Prolonged infusion of nitroglycerin (but not nitroprusside or nesiritide) may be accompanied by a loss of the drug's hemodynamic effects (pharmacologic tolerance). Although nesiritide has natriuretic properties in normal subjects, it does not increase sodium excretion in heart failure and has not been shown to replicate or potentiate the effects of diuretics.

Therapy with nitroprusside, nitroglycerin, and nesiritide is usually initiated as a continuous low-dose intravenous infusion, the rate of which is increased to achieve specific hemodynamic or clinical goals. Nitroglycerin (1 to 50 μg/kg/min) is a reasonable first choice for most patients and may have advantages in patients with underlying ischemic heart disease. Nesiritide (2 μg/kg bolus followed by 0.01 to 0.03 μg/kg/min) or nitroprusside (0.2 to 5.0 μg/kg/min) may be used in patients who have not responded well to nitroglycerin, but nitroprusside is preferred for patients who have severe hypertension or valvular regurgitation. Hypotension is the most common side effect of all three vasodilators; thus, infusions of the drugs require close continuous monitoring of vital signs. Symptomatic hypotension is frequently associated with bradycardia (not tachycardia), particularly when nitroglycerin is used. All three drugs can cause pulmonary vasodilatation, which can aggravate arterial hypoxemia in patients with ventilation-perfusion abnormalities. Long-term (>48-hour) infusions of all three drugs is fraught with difficulties (i.e., the development of hemodynamic tolerance with nitroglycerin, the risk of cyanide and thiocyanate toxicity with nitroprusside, and renal impairment and possibly increased mortality with nesiritide). Hence, these drugs should be used generally only for brief periods.

MECHANICAL VENTILATION AND PHLEBOTOMY. If dyspnea, diaphoresis, and peripheral vasoconstriction persist or if the syndrome becomes immediately life threatening, mechanical ventilation can improve oxygenation and reduce the redistribution of blood into the pulmonary circuit. If this approach fails to stabilize the course of the patient, the removal of 250 to 500 mL of blood by phlebotomy can produce a rapid reduction in pulmonary blood volume and dramatic clinical improvement.

REFRACTORY SYMPTOMS ASSOCIATED WITH SYSTEMIC HYPOPERFUSION

The most serious presentation of heart failure in the hospitalized patient is the syndrome of refractory heart failure, which is characterized by hemodynamic instability and systemic hypotension. Patients complain of dyspnea and fatigue at rest and have objective evidence of poor peripheral perfusion, as reflected by low systemic blood pressure, diminished mental alertness, cool extremities, and decreased urine output. Laboratory evaluation frequently reveals hyponatremia and azotemia. Refractory heart failure may represent the first evidence of heart disease; it may appear in patients who are already hospitalized for an acute cardiac disorder (e.g., MI), or it may complicate the course of a patient with long-standing heart failure. If severe, abrupt, and accompanied by clinical evidence of sympathetic overactivity, the syndrome is designated as cardiogenic shock (Chapter 103).

The central feature of refractory heart failure is a deterioration of cardiac performance to a level incompatible with adequate perfusion of peripheral organs. Although patients characteristically present with very low blood pressures, the level of systemic pressure may not accurately reflect the adequacy of perfusion. Some patients have very low blood pressures but maintain excellent end-organ perfusion and function (e.g., patients with heart failure receiving ACE inhibitors). In others, blood pressure is preserved by intense peripheral vasoconstriction even though cerebral and renal function is severely compromised. In either case, the degree of circulatory compromise is so profound and the state of the circulation is so precarious that small changes in physiologic variables can readily provoke end-organ failure or death. The primary goal of treatment is the restoration of clinical stability and adequate perfusion to all organs of the body.

Management of Refractory Heart Failure

Several general measures are indicated in all patients with refractory heart failure. Immediate hospitalization (usually in a critical care unit) is essential. Noninvasive assessment of ventricular function may be useful to quantify the magnitude of ventricular dysfunction and to allow the diagnosis of surgically correctable lesions (e.g., papillary muscle rupture, ventricular septal defect, prosthetic valve thrombosis). Invasive hemodynamic monitoring may be helpful in characterizing the hemodynamic derangement and guiding the use of pharmacologic agents. Daily measurements of urine output and body weight are useful in monitoring fluid balance.

The most important therapeutic measures in the treatment of refractory heart failure are (1) fluid management, (2) the use of intravenous positive inotropic agents, (3) the use of intravenous vasoconstrictor agents, and (4) mechanical and surgical interventions.

FLUID MANAGEMENT. In general, patients should be maintained at dry weight as long as this goal can be achieved without compromising peripheral perfusion. Although fluids are commonly administered with the goal of maintaining the pulmonary capillary wedge pressure at a specific level, there is little evidence that this approach improves the outcome of patients. Similarly, although pulmonary artery balloon flotation catheters are frequently used to perform hemodynamic measurements, physicians should recognize that the level of cardiac output does not assess the adequacy of peripheral perfusion and that the level of pulmonary capillary wedge pressure is influenced not only by intravascular volume but also by changes in cardiac contractility, diastolic function, mitral valve function, and the peripheral circulation. Hence, the clinical response to fluid administration may provide more useful information than isolated measurements of cardiac output or ventricular filling pressures.

INTRAVENOUS POSITIVE INOTROPIC AGENTS. Positive inotropic drugs can produce hemodynamic and clinical benefits not only by stimulating cardiac contractility but also by exerting dilatory effects on peripheral blood vessels. Cardiac output is increased and pulmonary wedge pressures are decreased, usually with little change in systemic blood pressure. All positive inotropic agents used in the treatment of refractory heart failure act by increasing myocardial levels of cyclic adenosine monophosphate, either by increasing its synthesis (e.g., dobutamine) or by decreasing its degradation (e.g., milrinone). However, milrinone differs from dobutamine in several ways: (1) because it is a more effective vasodilator, milrinone produces greater decreases in pulmonary wedge pressure and greater decreases in blood pressure than dobutamine; (2) because it is a long-acting agent, adverse effects persist for longer periods with milrinone than dobutamine; and (3) pharmacologic tolerance may occur with dobutamine, but this is less of a problem with milrinone. A combination of dobutamine and milrinone may be particularly useful in selected patients with nonischemic cardiomyopathy, but such a regimen should be used cautiously because both drugs can produce tachycardia, myocardial ischemia, and serious arrhythmias.

Dobutamine is administered as a continuous intravenous infusion, initially at a rate of 3 to 6 µg/kg/min (without a bolus), and the rate may be increased up to 10 to 15 µg/kg/min. Milrinone is generally initiated with a bolus dose of 0.5 µg/kg, followed by a continuous infusion at a rate of 0.375 to 0.75 µg/kg/min. Short-term infusions of both drugs (alone or in combination) can be effective in the treatment of refractory heart failure, especially when systemic blood pressures are relatively preserved. However, long-term continuous or intermittent infusions can increase the risk of cardiac events (including death) and should be avoided.

INTRAVENOUS VASOCONSTRICTOR AGENTS. Two vasoconstrictor agents are commonly used to support systemic blood pressure in patients with refractory heart failure: dopamine and levarterenol. Dopamine is an endogenous catecholamine that interacts with dopamine receptors (both DA_1 and DA_2 subtypes), β_1 (but not β_2) adrenergic receptors, and α-adrenergic receptors in the heart and peripheral circulation. As a result of these interactions, the drug causes vasodilation (owing to its agonist effects on DA_1 receptors), stimulates cardiac contractility (owing to its agonist effects on β_1 receptors), and causes constriction of peripheral arterial and venous vessels (owing to its agonist effects on α_1-receptors). The hemodynamic effects of dopamine depend largely on the dose of the drug administered. Low dosages (<2 µg/kg/min), which stimulate DA_1 and DA_2 receptors, act to dilate the renal and splanchnic circulations. Moderate dosages (2 to 5 µg/kg/min), which activate β_1-receptors, increase cardiac output but produce little change in pulmonary wedge pressure, heart rate, or systemic vascular resistance. High dosages (>5 µg/kg/min), which stimulate α_1-receptors, increase pulmonary wedge pressure, blood pressure, and heart

rate and may reduce renal blood flow. Dopamine may be useful in the treatment of both pulmonary congestion and peripheral hypoperfusion. In normotensive patients with pulmonary congestion, low doses of dopamine increase renal blood flow and are used alone (or in combination with dobutamine) to potentiate the diuretic actions of furosemide. In hypotensive patients with peripheral hypoperfusion, large doses of dopamine are used to support systemic blood pressure (Chapter 103).

Levarterenol is the commercial preparation of the endogenous catecholamine norepinephrine, which stimulates both α_1- and β_1-receptors when administered in therapeutic doses. Because of its lack of DA_1-receptor effects, levarterenol increases systemic vascular resistance and blood pressure more than does dopamine, and the degree of systemic vasoconstriction may be sufficient to reduce renal blood flow even though cardiac output is increased as a result of β_1-receptor stimulation. Consequently, levarterenol is used only in patients with shock whose blood pressure cannot be supported adequately with dopamine (Chapter 103). Levarterenol is generally infused in dosages ranging from 0.03 to 0.12 µg/kg/min.

Both dopamine and levarterenol can cause serious adverse effects. Stimulation of α-receptors can cause intense peripheral vasoconstriction, which may reduce peripheral perfusion and (if extravasated during infusion) can cause local tissue necrosis. Stimulation of β-receptors can lead to serious atrial and ventricular arrhythmias and myocardial ischemia. Stimulation of DA_1-receptors may cause nausea and vomiting.

MECHANICAL AND SURGICAL INTERVENTIONS. If pharmacologic interventions fail to stabilize the patient with refractory heart failure, mechanical and surgical interventions may provide effective circulatory support (Chapter 71). These include intra-aortic balloon counterpulsation, left ventricular assist device, and cardiac transplantation (Chapter 80). A number of experimental surgical procedures have also been developed to support the failing heart (cardiomyoplasty and partial resection of the left ventricle), but despite a high level of initial enthusiasm, the results to date have been variable, unpredictable, and largely disappointing.

Intra-aortic balloon counterpulsation has been useful in the management of cardiogenic shock that is caused by acute myocardial ischemia or infarction (Chapter 103), particularly when there is a coexisting mechanical defect (e.g., ventricular septal defect or papillary muscle rupture). Short-term use of ventricular assist devices has produced dramatic hemodynamic and clinical benefits, but long-term use of these devices has been associated with a high risk of infection and thromboembolic events. Ventricular assist devices have been primarily used to provide temporary circulatory support for patients awaiting transplantation, but they may have a limited role as a long-term treatment strategy. In the Randomized Evaluation of Mechanical Assistance for the Treatment of Congestive Heart Failure (REMATCH), patients with end-stage heart failure who were randomized to a permanent left ventricular assist device had a 48% lower risk of death than a control group. However, treatment was frequently complicated by infection, bleeding, and device malfunction, and the mortality advantage at 2 years was marginal. Cardiac transplantation (Chapter 80) is an effective treatment for refractory heart failure, with a survival rate of 80% to 90% at 1 year and 60% to 70% at 5 years, usually with a markedly improved quality of life, despite the risks of organ rejection, immunosuppression, and allograft vasculopathy. These outcomes exceed the results with any medical or surgical intervention available for the management of patients with advanced heart failure, but such outcomes are comparable (and perhaps somewhat inferior) to the results with medical therapy in patients with mild or moderate heart failure. Hence, cardiac transplantation should be considered only for patients with refractory symptoms. The usefulness of transplantation is limited by the small number of donor hearts.

1. The CONSENSUS Trial Study Group: Effects of enalapril on mortality in severe congestive heart failure. Results of the Cooperative North Scandinavian Enalapril Survival Study (CONSENSUS). N Engl J Med 1987;316:1429–1435.
2. The SOLVD Investigators: Effect of enalapril on survival in patients with reduced left ventricular ejection fractions and congestive heart failure. N Engl J Med 1991;325:293–302.
3. Metoprolol CR/XL Randomised Intervention Trial in Congestive Heart Failure (MERIT-HF): Effect of metoprolol CR/XL in chronic heart failure. Lancet 1999;353:2001–2007.

4. Packer M, Coats AJ, Fowler MB, et al, for the Carvedilol Prospective Randomized Cumulative Survival Study Group: Effect of carvedilol on survival in severe chronic heart failure. N Engl J Med 2001;344:1651–1658.
5. Poole-Wilson PA, Swedberg K, Cleland JG, et al: Comparison of carvedilol and metoprolol on clinical outcomes in patients with chronic heart failure in the Carvedilol Or Metoprolol European Trial (COMET): randomised controlled trial. Lancet 2003;362:7–13.
6. Pitt B, Zannad F, Remme WJ, et al, for the Randomized Aldactone Evaluation Study Investigators: The effect of spironolactone on morbidity and mortality in patients with severe heart failure. N Engl J Med 1999;341:709–717.
7. Pitt B, Remme W, Zannad F, et al: Eplerenone, a selective aldosterone blocker, in patients with left ventricular dysfunction after myocardial infarction. N Engl J Med 2003;348:1309–1321.
8. The Digitalis Investigation Group: The effect of digoxin on mortality and morbidity in patients with heart failure. N Engl J Med 1997;336:525–533.
9. Pitt B, Poole-Wilson PA, Segal R, et al: Effect of losartan compared with captopril on mortality in patients with symptomatic heart failure: Randomised trial—the Losartan Heart Failure Survival Study ELITE II. Lancet 2000;355:1582–1587.
10. Cohn JN, Tognoni G, for the Valsartan Heart Failure Trial Investigators: A randomized trial of the angiotensin-receptor blocker valsartan in chronic heart failure. N Engl J Med 2001;345:1667–1675.
11. Moss AJ, Zareba W, Hall WJ, et al: Prophylactic implantation of a defibrillator in patients with myocardial infarction and reduced ejection fraction. N Engl J Med 2002;346:877–883.
12. Bradley DJ, Bradley EA, Baughman KL, et al: Cardiac resynchronization and death from progressive heart failure: A meta-analysis of randomized controlled trials. JAMA 2003;289:730–740.

SUGGESTED READINGS

Anker SD, Negassa A, Coats AJ, et al: Prognostic importance of weight loss in chronic heart failure and the effect of treatment with angiotensin-converting enzyme inhibitors: an observational study. Lancet 2003;361:1077–1083. *Weight loss is independently linked to impaired survival.*
Jong P, Demers C, McKelvie RS, et al: Angiotensin receptor blockers in heart failure: meta-analysis of randomized controlled trials. J Am Coll Cardiol 2002;39:463–470. *ARBs are promising as monotherapy and may add to ACE inhibitors but are not better alone than ACE inhibitors alone.*
McMurray J, Pfeffer MA: New therapeutic options in congestive heart failure. Circulation 2002;105:2099–1106 and 2223–2228. *A two-part overview.*
Rose EA, Gelijns AC, Moskowitz AJ, et al: Randomized Evaluation of Mechanical Assistance for the Treatment of Congestive Heart Failure (REMATCH) Study Group. Long-term mechanical left ventricular assistance for end-stage heart failure. N Engl J Med 2001;345:1435–1443. *These devices provided a marginal improvement in outcome.*

57 PRINCIPLES OF ELECTROPHYSIOLOGY

Hugh Calkins

The function of the human heart requires rhythmic beatings occurring on the average 70 times a minute, 24 hours a day, for 80 or more years. The close to 3 billion contractions of the cardiac musculature that must occur without fail are coordinated by an intricate network of specialized electrically active cells that are integrated with the myocytes that comprise the predominant mass of the heart. Any loss of electrical activity, even for a few seconds, results in syncope (Chapter 435); loss of electrical activity for a few minutes may end in death.

Cardiac Electrophysiology

Ion channels are integral membrane-spanning proteins, which allow the rapid movement of specific ions, most importantly Na^+, K^+, Cl^-, and Ca^{2+}, across the cell membrane at rates of 10^8 ions per second. The opening and closing of the channels occur through a process of gating, whereby changes in the voltage, ligand, or receptor associated with the channel lead to alterations in the conformation of the proteins that activate or inactivate the channel pore. Voltage gating is the predominant method of regulating ion channels in the heart and is found in sodium and various potassium channels. Ligand-gated ion channels use ligands such as neurotransmitters, ions such as intracellular calcium, and metabolic products such as adenosine triphosphate (ATP) to activate a variety of channels, including those for potassium. Receptor-gated channels use changes in the physical environment, such as stretch, to activate channels, including those for chloride, which regulate intracellular volume.

The coordinated activity of numerous ion channels contributes to the creation of the cardiac action potential (Figs. 57–1 and 57–2). There are five phases to the cardiac action potential. At rest, the transmembrane potential of the cell exists close to −90 mV (the inside of the cell is positive with respect to the outside). With depolarization of the cell either from depolarization of adjacent cells or from an

external change in voltage, sodium channels change from a closed to an open state and rapidly move sodium ions down a gradient into the interior of the cell, creating the sodium current I_{Na} and the rapid upstroke of phase 0 of the action potential. At the peak of depolarization, approximately +40 mV, the sodium current is inactivated, and the transient outward current I_{to} is activated with the opening of various

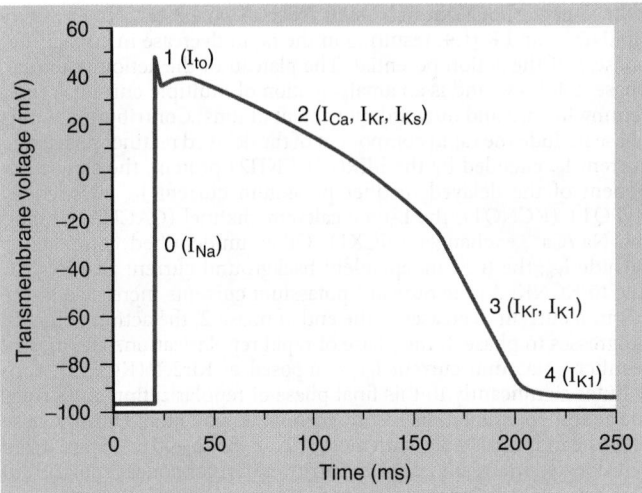

FIGURE 57–1 • The cardiac action potential. (From Keating MT, Sanguinetti MC: Molecular and cellular mechanisms of cardiac arrhythmias. Cell 2001;104:569.)

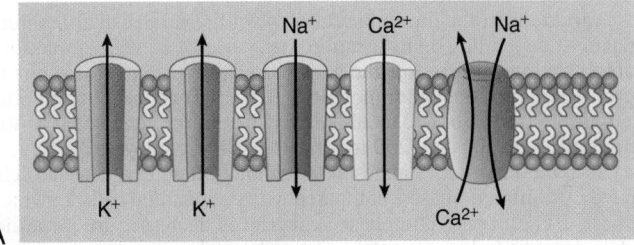

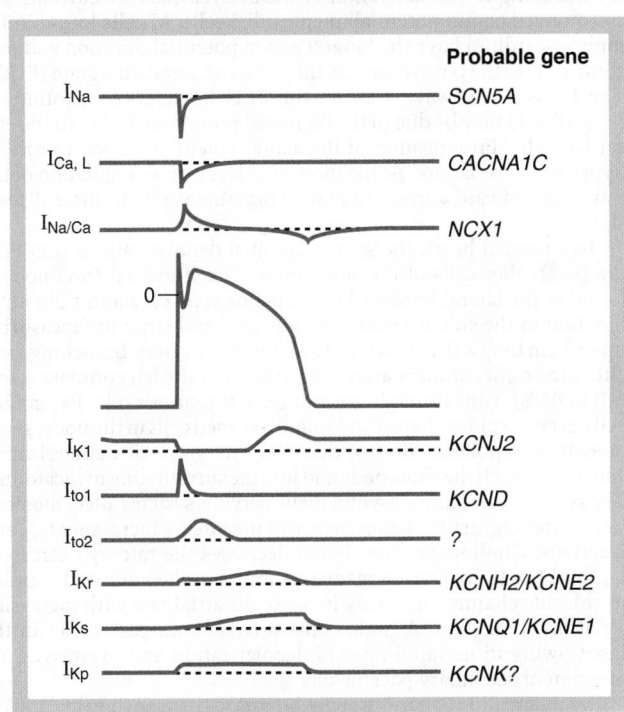

FIGURE 57–2 • Components of the cardiac action potential. *A,* Key ion channels. *B,* Ionic currents underlying the action potential. (From Marban E: Cardiac channelopathies. Nature 2002;415:213.)

Cardiovascular Disease

voltage-gated potassium channels, such as Kv4.2 (KCND2), Kv4.3 (KCND3), and Kv1.4, resulting in the rapid decrease in voltage and phase 1 of the action potential. The plateau of the action potential, phase 2, follows and is an amalgamation of multiple currents representing inward and outward movement of ions. Contributors to this phase include the rapid component of the delayed rectifier potassium current I_{Kr} encoded by the hERG (KCNH2) protein, the slow component of the delayed rectifier potassium current I_{Ks} encoded by KvLQT1 (KCNQ1), the L-type calcium channel (CACNA1C), and the Na^+/Ca^{2+} exchanger (NCX1). Other unidentified components include I_{Kp}, the time-independent background current that may be due to KCNK. As the outward potassium currents increase and the calcium current decreases at the end of phase 2, the action potential progresses to phase 3, the phase of rapid repolarization. The inward rectifier potassium current I_{K1}, composed of Kir2.1 (KCNJ2), contributes significantly to this final phase of repolarization and brings the action potential to its resting membrane potential. During phase 4, the heart is in diastole, with most cells at -85 to $-90\,mV$. Specialized cells located in the sinoatrial and atrioventricular nodes repolarize to approximately $-60\,mV$ and contain currents that contribute to spontaneous depolarization during phase 4. These pacemaker cells contain the inward activation, or funny, current I_f activated by hyperpolarization and carried by sodium, and the background sodium current I_{Na-B}. The calcium currents $I_{Ca,L}$ and $I_{Ca,T}$, the sodium/potassium pump $I_{Na,K}$, and the sodium calcium exchanger $I_{Na,Ca}$ additionally may contribute to diastolic depolarization.

Variations in the duration and shape of the cardiac action potential exist depending on its location in the heart. Likewise, alterations of ion channel expression and activity in disease states contribute to prolongation of the action potential. The atrial action potential has a typical duration of 100 to 200 msec, whereas the ventricular action potential typically lasts 250 to 300 msec. Different layers of the ventricle exhibit marked changes in the action potential. Epicardial cells have a prominent phase 1 compared with endocardial cells, in which phase 1 is blunted. The phase 2 plateau is decreased in epicardial cells, leading to less activation of the delayed rectifier currents and a prolonged action potential in epicardial cells. M cells found in the midmyocardium have the longest action potential duration and may contribute to the U wave seen on the surface electrocardiogram (ECG). The J (Osborne) wave seen on the ECG in cases of hypothermia (Fig. 105–1) may be due to the increased prominence of I_{to} in the epicardial cells. Prolongation of the action potential is seen in cardiac hypertrophy or failure. At the molecular level, downregulation of the transient outward current I_{to} plays a prominent role in these disease states.

In a normal heart, the source of initial depolarizations occurs in the pacemaker cells of the sinus node. The sinoatrial (SA) node is found at the lateral border of the superior vena cava and right atrial junction in the sulcus terminalis. It is an ovoid structure measuring up to 2 cm long × 0.5 cm wide. The sinus node artery, branching from either the right coronary artery (55 to 60%) or the left coronary artery (40 to 45%), runs through the middle of the sinus node. Pacemaker cells, seen as spider-shaped and spindle-shaped cells in the node, spontaneously depolarize during diastole. The wave of depolarization spreads through the sinus node and into the surrounding myocardium. The sympathetic and parasympathetic nervous systems affect the sinus rate. Adrenergic stimulation increases the rate by increasing $I_{Ca,L}$ and I_f activity. Cholinergic stimulation decreases the rate by decreasing $I_{Ca,L}$ and I_f activity. Stretch mediators found in the node and coupled to chloride channels also may increase the atrial rate with increasing atrial pressure. The SA node is the predominant pacemaker in the heart owing to its rapid rates of depolarization and overdrive suppression of secondary pacemakers.

Depolarization occurs through the atria to the atrioventricular (AV) node and from the right atrium to the left atrium. Three intra-atrial pathways—anterior, middle, and posterior—connect the right and left atria. Three intranodal pathways—superior, middle, and inferior tracts—also may connect the SA node to the AV node, although various investigators have disputed their presence. The P wave on the ECG is formed by atrial depolarization. The AV node is found at the apex of the triangle of Koch, formed by the tendon of Todaro on one side and the tricuspid annulus on the other, on the right side of the heart and anterior to the os of the coronary sinus. The arterial supply of the AV node arises from the right coronary artery in 85 to 90% of cases. The AV node itself is complex and can be divided into three general regions, with further subdivisions possible. A transitional zone

contains multiple atrial inputs that extend to the compact AV node, which penetrates the central fibrous body and becomes the bundle of His. The compact AV node ranges from 5 to 7 mm × 2 to 5 mm in size. At least two distinct populations of AV node cells, rod-shaped and ovoid, have been described. These cells spontaneously depolarize because of a strong I_f current. Most ovoid cells lack I_{Na} and I_{to}, leading to slower depolarization. Conduction is relatively slow through the AV node compared with atrial and ventricular tissue, in part because of the decreased density of gap junction proteins, such as connexin43, which is 33 times less prevalent in the AV node compared with ventricular cells. This reduction in gap junctions and intercalated discs leads to slower depolarization of neighboring cells. On the surface ECG, most of the PR interval depends on this slow AV node conduction.

The bundle of His arises from the compact AV node as it enters the central fibrous body. Conduction through the His bundle is rapid, on the order of 35 to 55 msec to the ventricles, owing to the presence of rapidly acting sodium channels. The arterial supply of the bundle of His originates from the left anterior descending artery in 90% of cases, with 10% emanating from the right coronary artery. The right and left bundle branches originate from the bundle of His. The left bundle branch further subdivides into the left anterior fascicle and left posterior fascicle before supplying the ventricular endocardium with Purkinje fibers. The right bundle branch trifurcates distally into a network that supplies the anterolateral papillary muscle, the low right septum, and the parietal band. Activation of the His-Purkinje system can be seen as the later portion of the PR interval on the surface ECG.

Ventricular activation occurs first from the left to right septum, followed by the synchronized depolarization of both ventricles from apex to base and endocardium to epicardium. The rapid activation of myocardial cells is due in part to the strong presence of the gap junction protein connexin43. Knockout mice homozygous for connexin43 deletions die with conotruncus malformations early in life, whereas mice heterozygous for connexin43 deletion (Cx43+/−) have significant decreases in ventricular conduction in otherwise normal ventricles. Ventricular depolarization can be seen as the QRS complex on the surface ECG and is followed by repolarization seen as the ST, T, and U waves.

Normally the only connection between the atria and the ventricles is through the AV node and His bundle because the fibrous rings surrounding the tricuspid valve and mitral valve are electrically insulating (Fig. 57–3). In a small percentage of the population (0.15 to 0.25%), anomalous myocardial bypass tracts join atrium to ventricle (Kent bundle) or, less frequently, atrium to AV node (James fiber), atrium to His bundle (Brechenmacher fiber), or AV node or His to Purkinje fiber or ventricle (Mahaim fiber). The classic AV bypass tract involved in the Wolff-Parkinson-White syndrome is composed of fibers containing I_{Na} and conducts rapidly in a nondecremental manner similar to that seen in the atria, His-Purkinje, or ventricular tissue. A missense mutation in the γ2 regulatory subunit of adenosine monophosphate (AMP)–activated protein kinase gene *PRKAG2* can cause the Wolff-Parkinson-White syndrome, with a possible effect of interfering with muscle fiber regression during embryogenesis. The surface ECG often shows a δ wave (see Fig. 59–4), the hallmark of ventricular preexcitation, preceding the QRS complex.

The heart is innervated by the sympathetic and the parasympathetic nervous systems, with their influence on ion channels manifested as changes in the heart rate, refractoriness, and contractility. Sympathetic stimulation causes the release of norepinephrine at the postganglionic nerve terminal, leading to $β_1$-adrenergic and $β_2$-adrenergic receptor activation, followed by G protein–mediated adenylyl cyclase production, which increases production of cyclic AMP (cAMP), which leads to the activation of protein kinase A, ultimately resulting in the phosphorylation of ion channels, which alter their gating and function. Parasympathetic activity leads to release of acetylcholine at the nerve terminal, which stimulates muscarinic cholinergic receptors, followed by direct G protein–mediated activation of channels, or indirect G protein–mediated secondary messenger activation using cAMP. Multiple membrane currents are influenced by sympathetic or parasympathetic activity. The L-type calcium channel current $I_{Ca,L}$ is increased four times with β-adrenergic stimulation, leading to increased conduction of the SA and AV nodes. β-Adrenergic stimulation also leads to a cAMP-mediated change in the activation of I_f, with the result being increased activity of cardiac pacemaker cells and higher heart rates. Parasympathetic stimulation leads to

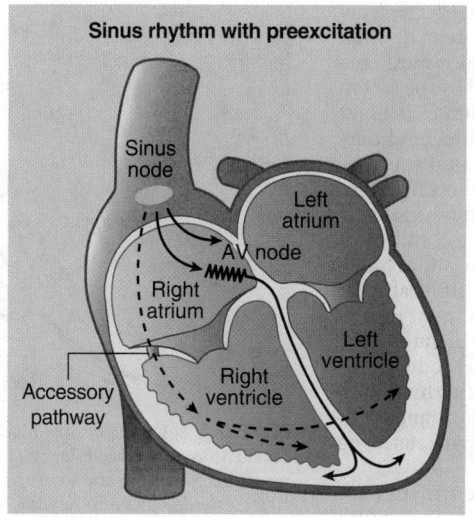
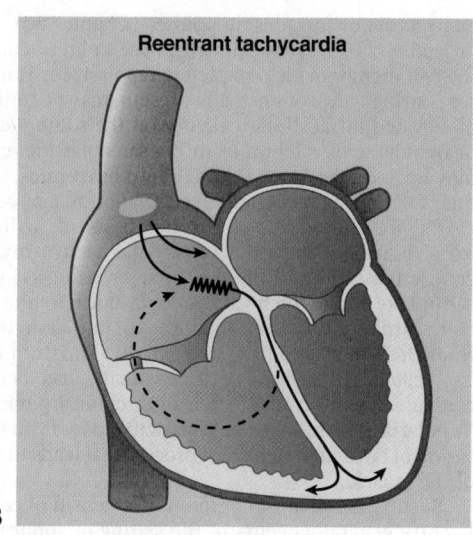

FIGURE 57–3 • Accessory pathway in sinus rhythm and in ortho-dromic reentrant tachycardia. (From Bassam CT: A molecular basis for Wolff-Parkinson-White syndrome. N Engl J Med 2001;344:1861. Copyright © 2001 Massachusetts Medical Society. All rights reserved.)

activation of the acetylcholine-activated potassium current I_{KACh}, which results in decreased pacemaker activity and slowing of conduction over the AV node. Purinergic receptors are a third family of G protein–coupled receptors that are activated by adenosine. Exposure to adenosine leads to activation of I_{KACh} and inhibition of $I_{Ca,L}$, resulting in slowing of the pacemaker activity for SA and AV nodes and conduction delay through the AV node.

Mechanisms of Cardiac Tachyarrhythmias

A cardiac arrhythmia is an abnormality in the timing or sequence of cardiac depolarization. There are two predominant types of cardiac arrhythmias: (1) tachyarrhythmia—an abnormally rapid cardiac rhythm (heart rate >100 beats per minute) and (2) bradyarrhythmia—a slow cardiac rhythm (heart rate <60 beats per minute) (Chapters 59 and 60).

The mechanism of cardiac tachyarrhythmias can be grouped into two general categories, abnormalities of impulse formation and reentry (Fig. 57–4). Abnormalities of impulse formation can be subdivided further into abnormal automaticity and triggered activity. In the normal heart, the sinus node is the predominant pacemaker, with secondary pacemakers located in the atria, AV node, and His-Purkinje system, which function in the event that normal initiation or propagation is affected by disease or drugs. Automaticity is the ability to initiate spontaneous impulses. Under normal circumstances, there is a

hierarchical sequence in the rate of firing of the heart cells that have the capacity for automaticity. Normally, spontaneous firing is fastest in the sinus node (70 to 80 beats per minute under resting conditions), and the sinus node is the predominant pacemaker. The AV node and His bundle fire at 50 to 60 beats per minute, and the Purkinje fibers fire at 30 to 40 beats per minute. The lower pacemaker may take over the pacemaking function of the heart if the faster pacemaker fails or slows. Variations in autonomic tone may have a major effect on normal automaticity. In general, activation of the sympathetic nervous system increases automaticity, whereas activation of the parasympathetic nervous system decreases automaticity. Under pathologic conditions that depolarize cells, myocardial cells outside the specialized conduction system also may acquire automaticity, a phenomenon termed *abnormal automaticity*.

Triggered activity is an uncommon mechanism of cardiac arrhythmias. Triggered activity occurs when a preceding depolarization does not repolarize completely before depolarizing again. *Early after-depolarizations* (EADs) occur during phase 2 and phase 3 of the action potential. The basis for EADs seems to involve the L-type calcium channel. EADs are facilitated by increased repolarization times, as seen in either congenital or acquired long QT syndromes. With drugs that prolong the QT interval, such as erythromycin, quinidine, sotalol, and procainamide, the block of potassium channels involved in repolarization leads to prolongation of the action potential. The ultimate effect of EADs may be in initiating polymorphic ventricular

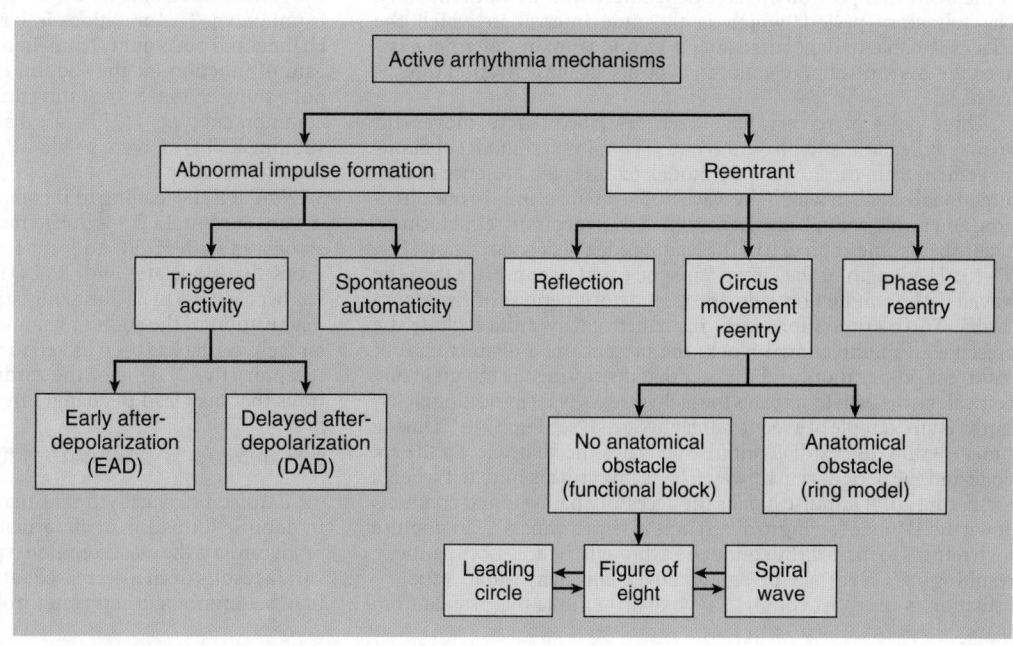

FIGURE 57–4 • Classification of cardiac arrhythmia mechanisms. (From Antzelevich C: Basic mechanisms of reentrant arrhythmias. Curr Opin Cardiol 2001;16:1–7.)

tachycardia or torsades de pointes (Chapter 60). *Delayed afterdepolarizations* (DADs) arise during phase 4 of the action potential, when the cell membrane is completely repolarized. Transient inward currents, which are not normally present, may be initiated by the action of elevated intracellular calcium on the sodium/calcium exchanger or by release of calcium from the sarcoplasmic reticulum, and they may form the basis for DADs. Rapid heart rates, increased extracellular calcium, and adrenergic stimulation all may contribute to DADs. DADs are thought to form the basis of arrhythmias resulting from digitalis, idiopathic ventricular tachyarrhythmias, and idioventricular rhythms, and they may be reduced by drugs that block the uptake of calcium by the sarcoplasmic reticulum. Multifocal atrial tachycardia is another example of an arrhythmia that results from DAD-mediated triggered activity. The third type of automaticity, *depolarization-induced automaticity,* has been reproduced in cardiac tissues but may not lead to clinically relevant arrhythmias. Depolarization-induced automaticity arises from the constant application of current to muscle, a process that leads to spontaneous firing of the muscle.

Reentry is the most common mechanism of cardiac arrhythmias. Reentry generally occurs in the setting of abnormalities in impulse conduction. The abnormalities in impulse conduction may result from an anomalous electrical connection in the heart (i.e., an accessory pathway) or from poor impulse propagation. The basis for poor propagation of the depolarizing wave front in the heart may be attributed to pathology, drugs, or hormonal modulation of the conduction system. Fibrosis or calcification of the AV node, His bundle, or right and left bundle branches may lead to AV block or right and left bundle-branch blocks. AV nodal block may be a result of high vagal tone, as seen during sleep or in a well-conditioned athlete, or may be due to agents that act on the AV node, such as digitalis, β-adrenergic blockers, or calcium channel blockers. Slowing of conduction in the atrium and ventricles also may be affected directly by hyperkalemia or ischemia.

The basis for poor propagation of the depolarizing wave front in the heart usually results from pathologic changes in patients with structural heart disease, including coronary artery disease, left ventricular hypertrophy, and heart failure. Fibrotic changes in the heart, with increases in collagen and intracellular matrix as seen in hypertrophy or infarction, can lead to areas of slow conduction and provide portals for reentry. Changes in the gap junction proteins have been noted in hypertrophy with increases of connexin43. These changes typically result from advanced age or the presence of structural heart disease, such as a prior myocardial infarction or a cardiomyopathy. In ischemia, the action potential is abbreviated owing to activation of I_{KACh}; in hypertrophy and failure, action potential prolongation from loss of I_{to} is found. Other influences on remodeling include catecholamines, free radicals, angiotensin-converting enzyme, angiotensin II, aldosterone, cytokines, and nitric oxide. Reentry occurs when there is continuation of a propagating wave front, which reactivates areas of the heart that previously have depolarized and are not refractory. The refractory period, which is the time interval in which the cells are unable to depolarize after a second stimulus, often persists until the transmembrane voltage is −60 mV at the activation threshold of I_{Na}.

Three types of reentry have been described: circus movement reentry, reflection, and phase 2 reentry. The simplest model of circus movement tachycardia, the ring model, requires the presence of unidirectional block, in which the wave front can travel only in one direction, and a long enough circuit, in which recovery from refractoriness occurs before the approach of the leading edge of depolarization (Fig. 57–5). The length of the circuit must be equal to or greater than the wavelength (conduction velocity × refractory period) of the tachycardia. Three criteria for circus movement tachycardia include the presence of unidirectional block, the presence of a distinct path of recurrent propagation, and the fact that disrupting the circuit at any point along the path terminates the tachycardia. AV reciprocating tachycardia is an example of a reentrant tachycardia (see Fig. 57–3). During sinus rhythm, the cardiac impulse activates the ventricle via the AV node and the accessory pathway. The tachycardia is initiated when a premature atrial impulse blocks the accessory pathway and conducts down the AV node (owing to differences in refractoriness). The impulse then returns to the atria by conduction through the accessory pathway, resulting in a reentrant or circus movement tachycardia. Atrial fibrillation is the most common type of arrhythmia that results from

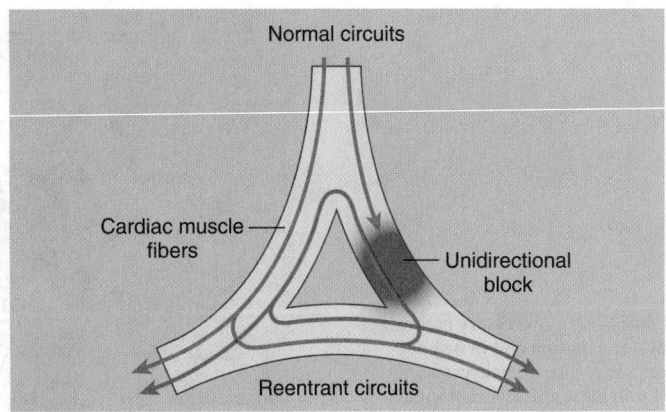

FIGURE 57–5 • Unidirectional block as a result of abnormal repolarization, conduction, or intracellular calcium homeostasis. Red arrows show normal conduction, and blue arrows show reentry through previously refractory tissue. (From Keating MT, Sanguinetti MC: Molecular and cellular mechanisms of cardiac arrhythmias. Cell 2001;104:569.)

reentry. In contrast to arrhythmias with an accessory pathway in which there is only a single fixed reentrant circuit, however, atrial fibrillation results from the presence of many functional reentrant wavelets that propagate throughout the atria simultaneously. It has been estimated that at least three reentrant wavelets must coexist for atrial fibrillation to be sustained. *Reentry resulting from reflection* occurs when an impulse proceeds back and forth over a functionally unexcitable pathway, depolarizing proximal tissue on each return cycle. *Phase 2 reentry* occurs when an action potential dome during phase 2 is propagated from normal myocytes to myocytes lacking the dome, followed by local reexcitation, extrasystolic beats, and circus movement reentry. Phase 2 reentry notably is found in Brugada's syndrome (Chapter 60). Brugada's syndrome is the result of a sodium channel mutation in the α subunit SCN5A. The hallmark of Brugada's syndrome is ST-segment elevation and a right bundle-branch pattern in V_1 to V_3 on the ECG. The ECG abnormalities can be explained by the loss of a phase 2 action potential dome in the epicardium but not in the endocardium owing to a failure of I_{Na} to reach a more positive voltage before phase 1. Endocardium-to-epicardium phase 2 reentry occurs, leading to the ventricular tachycardia or ventricular fibrillation that is seen in Brugada's syndrome.

Multiple intrinsic and extrinsic factors can affect the initiation and propagation of cardiac arrhythmias (Fig. 57–6). At the molecular level, multiple mutations contribute to the inherited long QT syndrome and to idiopathic ventricular fibrillation (Brugada's syndrome). Six different subtypes of long QT syndrome have been described with the genes responsible for LQT1–5 characterized. The gene for LQT6 is unknown. The mutations in long QT syndrome affect the sodium channel and potassium channels involved in repolarization with either gain of function for the sodium channel or loss of function for the potassium channels, resulting in a prolonged phase 2. The most common subtype, LQT1, is a disorder of the potassium channel α subunit KVLQT1 responsible in part for I_{Ks}. LQT2 is due to mutations in HERG, a component of I_{Kr}. LQT3 affects the sodium channel SCN5A at a site leading to incomplete inactivation and a continuing inward current. LQT4 is due to mutations in MiRP, the β subunit that associates with HERG to form I_{Kr}. LQT5 results from mutations in minK that associates with KVLQT1 to form I_{Ks}. Brugada's syndrome has been shown to be due to mutations in SCN5A, which causes faster inactivation of the sodium channel. Familial polymorphic ventricular tachycardia has been linked to mutations in the cardiac ryanodine receptor (RyR2) gene of the cardiac sarcoplasmic reticulum, mutations that may lead to changes in calcium-induced activation.

Mechanism of Bradyarrhythmias

Cardiac bradyarrhythmias may result from either abnormalities in impulse formation or abnormalities in impulse conduction. Sinus bradycardia is the most common type of bradyarrhythmia. Sinus bradycardia results from a decreased rate of firing of the sinus node, which may be physiologic and result from increased parasympathetic tone

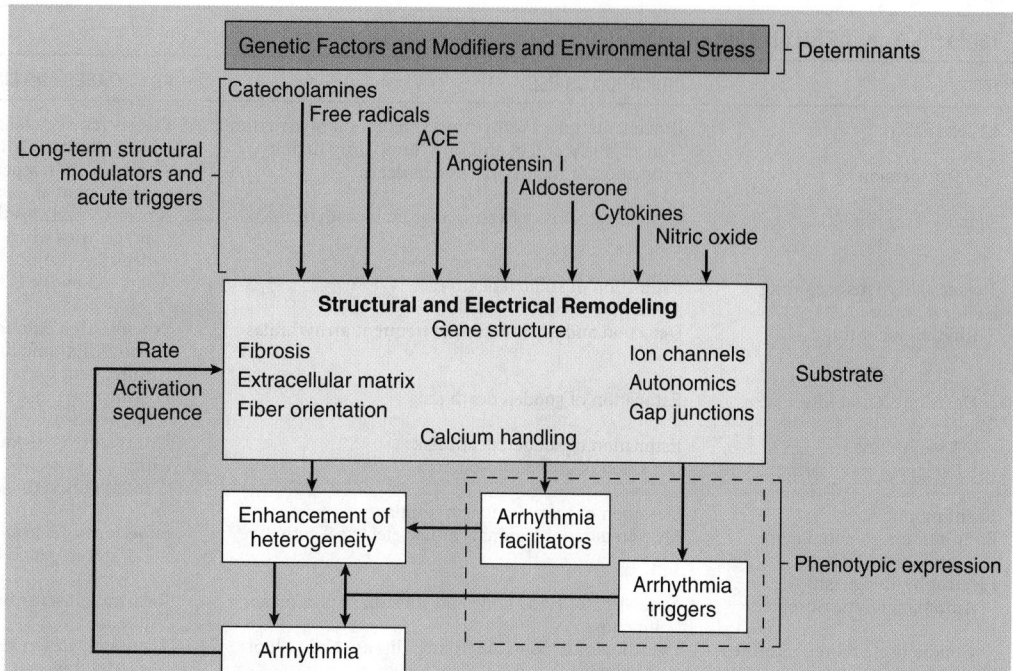

FIGURE 57–6 • Determinants of cardiac arrhythmias. (From Members of the Sicilian Gambit: New approaches to antiarrhythmic therapy: Emerging therapeutic applications of the cell biology of cardiac arrhythmias. Cardiovasc Res 2001;52:345, with permission.)

(i.e., during sleep) or pathologic and result from a fibrosis of the sinus node, such as occurs with aging. Bradyarrhythmias also occur when abnormalities of conduction interrupt the normal sequence of cardiac depolarization. Depending on the site of block, subsidiary pacemakers begin to fire, creating an "escape" rhythm. Conduction block usually is due to fibrosis or calcification of the AV node, His bundle, or right and left bundle branches. Conduction block also may result from increased parasympathetic tone, however, as seen during sleep or in a well-conditioned athlete, or may be due to agents that act on the AV node, such as digitalis, β-adrenergic blockers, or calcium channel blockers.

SUGGESTED READINGS

Antzelevich C: Basic mechanisms of reentrant arrhythmias. Curr Opin Cardiol 2001; 16:1–7. *In-depth explanation of the various models of reentry.*

Armoundas AA, Wu R, Juang G, et al: Electrical and structural remodeling of the failing ventricle. Pharmacol Ther 2001;92:213–230. *Review of the current state of knowledge on cardiac remodeling.*

Keating MT, Sanguinetti MC: Molecular and cellular mechanisms of cardiac arrhythmias. Cell 2001;104:569–580. *Excellent review of the known ion channel disorders and their effects on arrhythmias.*

Members of the Sicilian Gambit: New approaches to antiarrhythmic therapy: Emerging therapeutic applications of the cell biology of cardiac arrhythmias. Cardiovasc Res 2001;52:345–360. *State-of-the-art approaches to the pursuit of antiarrhythmic therapy are detailed.*

Wolbrette DL: Risk of proarrhythmia with class III antiarrhythmic agents: Sex-based differences and other issues. Am J Cardiol 2003;91(Suppl 1):39D–44D. *An updated review.*

58 ELECTROPHYSIOLOGIC DIAGNOSTIC PROCEDURES

Jay W. Mason

Clinical cardiac electrophysiology relies on a large and growing array of tests for diagnosis of cardiac arrhythmias and for estimation of risk for sudden death (Table 58–1).

Electrocardiography

The 12-lead electrocardiogram (ECG) provides powerful predictions of the site of atrioventricular block (Chapter 50), the location of accessory fibers in the Wolff-Parkinson-White syndrome (Chapter 59), the reentry mechanism in certain supraventricular

tachyarrhythmias (Chapter 59), and the site of origin and drug responsiveness of certain ventricular tachycardias (Chapter 60). The ECG often is used as a means of detecting incipient antiarrhythmic drug toxicity, as in the case of excessive QRS widening by class IC drugs or QT prolongation by class IA and III drugs (Chapter 62). The importance of recording a 12-lead ECG during symptoms of potential arrhythmic origin cannot be overemphasized because uncertainty regarding the true cause of symptoms persists when ECG documentation is lacking. Treadmill and other forms of exercise stress testing with ECG monitoring are useful to induce exercise-related arrhythmias for diagnosis, to evaluate the efficacy of drugs in suppressing arrhythmias, and to evaluate the propensity of class IC antiarrhythmic drugs, such as flecainide and propafenone (Chapter 62), to promote exercise-induced ventricular tachycardia.

QT dispersion correlates more powerfully with disease states than does the QT interval, an indirect ECG measurement of total cardiac repolarization time that has prognostic and therapeutic significance. Dispersion of the QT interval is measured in various ways, all of which estimate the difference between the longest and shortest QT intervals on a single 12-lead tracing. QT dispersion is generally less than 60 msec in normal persons, 60 to 80 msec in patients with previous myocardial infarction, 80 to 100 msec in patients with left ventricular hypertrophy, and 100 to 120 msec in patients with the long QT syndrome. QT dispersion, which likely reflects local disparities in repolarization, predisposes to ventricular fibrillation.

Fluctuations in the amplitude of the T wave also have been correlated with arrhythmia risk. A new measurement, microvolt T-wave alternans, has been approved by the U.S. Food and Drug Administration for detection of increased risk of sudden death in patients with preexisting disorders, such as coronary artery disease and heart failure, that predispose to ventricular arrhythmias. The technique measures beat-to-beat variation in the amplitude of the T wave during exercise, with sustained alternation of more than 2 μV at heart rates less than 110 beats per minute considered indicative of increased risk.

New molecular genetic knowledge of inherited cardiac arrhythmias allows clinicians to diagnose some of these conditions with gene specificity using the 12-lead ECG, allowing more definitive therapy. At present, there are many genetically distinct forms of the long QT syndrome (Chapter 60). LQT1, LQT2 and LQT3, the most thoroughly studied genetic forms of LQT, often are associated with characteristic ECG changes (broad, high-voltage T waves in LQT1; broad, notched T waves in LQT2; lengthened ST segments with narrow T waves in LQT3). Characteristic changes also occur in some cases of the inherited forms of Brugada's syndrome and arrhythmogenic right ventricular dysplasia (Chapter 60).

Table 58–1 • ARRHYTHMIA DIAGNOSTIC TESTS

TEST	INDICATION OR USE	ADVANTAGES AND LIMITATIONS
12-lead ECG	Documentation of arrhythmia, prediction of arrhythmia mechanism and of antiarrhythmic drug toxicity	ECG is readily available, but other tests may be required for definitive arrhythmia diagnosis
QT dispersion	Estimation of the risk of sudden death	Although an independent predictor, accuracy is insufficient as a basis for therapy
Signal-averaged ECG	Estimation of risk of ventricular tachyarrhythmia	A positive test tips the scale toward therapy or invasive procedures when available data are equivocal, but decisions cannot be based on this test alone
T-waves alternans recording	Estimation of sudden death risk	Approved by the U.S. FDA to assess risk of sudden death
Holter monitor		
Rhythm recording	Detection and quantitation of frequent arrhythmias	Provides rich data for diagnosis and assessment of antiarrhythmic therapy, but not useful for detection of infrequent events
Heart rate variability	Estimation of sudden death risk	Possibly the most accurate predictor of the risk of sudden death
QT variability	Estimation of sudden death risk	Utility not yet adequately studied
ST segment monitoring	Detection of coronary ischemia	Although proven to predict coronary events, efficacy of intervention unclear
Event monitor	Detection of infrequent arrhythmias	
Body surface potential map	Measurement of regional cardiac electrical activity	Superior to 12-lead ECG for localizing abnormalities, but not in general clinical use
Electrophysiologic study		
Automaticity measurement	Evaluation of sinus node and subsidiary pacemaker function	Relatively insensitive but specific marker of sinus node disease
Conduction and refractoriness measurement	Detection of conduction system disease and risk of AV block	Accurately describes existing refractoriness and conduction, but a relatively insensitive predictor of AV block
Tachycardia induction	Identification of the mechanism of tachyarrhythmia and of possible cause of syncope and other symptoms	Invaluable in management of tachyarrhythmias, but weakened by excessive false-positive responses
Pharmacologic study	Prediction of the efficacy of antiarrhythmic drugs	Useful but less important with advent of implanted cardioverter defibrillators
Device assessment	Evaluation of pacemaker and implanted cardioverter defibrillator function	Irreplaceable
Activation mapping	Identification of arrhythmia mechanisms and of targets for ablation and evaluation of myocardial viability	Critically important for invasive treatment of tachyarrhythmias, but less useful for ventricular tachycardia associated with coronary artery disease
Tilt test	Detection of cardioinhibitory and vasodepressor mechanisms of syncope	Most important new diagnostic tool for syncope; false-positive rate not adequately defined

ECG = electrocardiogram; FDA = Food and Drug Administration; AV = atrioventricular.

SIGNAL-AVERAGED ELECTROCARDIOGRAM

Typically a standard 12-lead ECG is recorded with amplifier filter settings that accept frequencies between 0.1 and 150 Hz. Most of the frequencies of the QRS complex are between 25 and 150 Hz, but muscle artifact and other noncardiac signals also reside in that range. Small, high-frequency myocardial signals that might contain useful information cannot be detected within the background noise by the standard ECG. Signal averaging can detect meaningful low-amplitude signals because they occur during each QRS complex, whereas the background noise occurs either randomly or independent of the cardiac rhythm. The signal-averaged ECG (SAECG) averages 100 or more QRS complexes to identify reproducible, low-amplitude cardiac signals, most importantly, low-amplitude potentials that are in the terminal portion of the QRS complex and are predictive of ventricular tachycardia in patients with previous myocardial infarction, independent of left ventricular function and other risk predictors. SAECG also has been proved helpful in identifying patients whose unexplained syncope may be caused by tachycardia. An abnormal SAECG predicts arrhythmic, cardiac, and total mortality in patients with coronary disease, left ventricular dysfunction, and unsustained ventricular tachycardia. SAECG does not identify risk in all arrhythmia-prone groups, however, and is not used routinely by all cardiac electrophysiologists. Signal averaging also can detect abnormalities of the P wave that are predictive of atrial fibrillation and other atrial arrhythmias and their response to drugs.

HOLTER MONITORING

The Holter monitor, developed in the early 1960s by Holter and colleagues as a long-term tape recording of the cardiac rhythm, has become an indispensable and highly refined tool for cardiac rhythm analysis and risk prediction. Present-day systems record 24 hours or more of rhythm data using three distinctly different technologies for data storage and analysis: tape recording for subsequent analysis, digital recording with real-time analysis, and digital storage for subsequent analysis. Recording to print 24 hours of cardiac rhythm is still used despite more advanced technology because real-time analysis systems are subject to errors owing to the lack of human interaction to eliminate artifact and correct misclassification of beats.

The original sole objective of Holter monitoring was to record the cardiac rhythm continuously so as to capture episodes of arrhythmia; but multifaceted analysis, including classification and quantification of normal and abnormal beats, characterization of tachyarrhythmias, identification and quantification of bradyarrhythmias and pauses, detection of ST-segment changes, and correlation of these events with symptoms, is now possible. These analyses are useful in determining the need for antiarrhythmic drug therapy, estimating antiarrhythmic drug effects, and identifying the need for cardiac pacing.

When cardiac rhythm data are digitized for analysis, every recorded R-R interval can be calculated. A variety of conditions, including heart failure and previous myocardial infarction, modify either the autonomic input to the heart or its ability to respond to the input and decrease the variability of the heart rate. Loss of heart rate variability in patients with diseases such as heart failure and prior myocardial infarction is probably the combined result of reduced vagal influence and increased sympathetic activity, which is known to promote ventricular fibrillation. Decreased heart rate variability predicts mortality in patients with ventricular ectopy after myocardial infarction independent of other factors, and it may help select patients who would benefit from interventions. Heart rate variability is largely a result of vagal activity, which is known to be protective against ventricular fibrillation.

The QT interval varies directly with heart rate and can be affected by cardiac disease. Some forms of the long QT syndrome result in enhanced prolongation of QT interval at slower heart rates. The QT interval also may be altered independent of heart rate, such as in patients after myocardial infarction, in whom the QT interval is abnormally long. Computer programs have been developed to automate measurement of the QT interval from Holter monitor recordings. Lengthening of the QT interval may be predictive of an adverse outcome, and altered variability of the QT interval may be a more specific indicator of risk.

Episodes of ST-segment depression not associated with symptoms on Holter monitor are predictive of the presence and severity of coronary artery disease and are presumed to be the result of silent ischemic episodes. Although false-positive and false-negative ST-segment shifts occur, and there is controversy over the interpretation and appropriate therapeutic response to Holter monitor–detected silent ischemia, it is clear that these episodes are independently predictive of ischemia-related adverse events.

EVENT MONITORING

Holter monitoring is limited to relatively short periods of continuous ECG recording. When the objective is to record the cardiac rhythm during symptomatic episodes that occur infrequently (less often than daily), event monitoring is the diagnostic procedure of choice.

Event monitors are designed for intermittent capture of the cardiac rhythm over long periods. A noninvasive system typically is provided to the patient for 1 month, during which time he or she can make heart rhythm recordings as often as symptoms occur. One variety of event monitor depends on semi-long-term lead placement. The patient is instructed in electrode removal and replacement and usually reattaches the leads one or more times each day. The system records the ECG into a loop buffer that continuously refreshes previous data. The duration of memory, varying from seconds to several minutes, is usually programmable. The patient records symptomatic events by pressing an event button. The recorder freezes a period of previously recorded data and continues to record the rhythm in real time according to previously programmed instructions. Other recorders are applied by the patient, often with wristbands or hand-held chest electrodes, during symptomatic episodes. These instruments are less complex and do not require continuous attachment of electrodes, but because they have no memory of the preceding cardiac rhythm and require time to be applied, they are useful only for patients whose spells last for a few minutes and who always can have the recorder nearby. Both varieties of recorders can transmit rhythm strips over the telephone to centralized receivers, where they can be analyzed and brought promptly to the physician's attention. Implantable devices can monitor the rhythm continuously without interruption for months or years, retain arrhythmic episodes in memory, and telemetrically transfer the stored information for review. These implantable loop recorders are more efficient than conventional noninvasive methods for diagnosing infrequent, unexplained syncope.

BODY SURFACE POTENTIAL MAPPING

Body surface potential mapping places 200 or more electrodes circumferentially around the entire surface of the thorax. Although the specialized equipment and data interpretation required for body surface potential mapping have limited its clinical utility, this modality is better than the 12-lead ECG to estimate regional heterogeneity of repolarization, to locate accessory pathways, and to localize and size regions of infarction. It is also superior to standard electrocardiography in detecting the origin of ventricular tachyarrhythmias.

Electrophysiologic Study

Electrophysiologic study involves use of temporary or permanent cardiac electrodes for direct recording and pacing of the heart for diagnostic and therapeutic purposes. The most common indications for electrophysiologic study are supraventricular tachycardia (Chapter 59), ventricular tachycardia (Chapter 60), and sudden death (Chapter 60). Other important indications include atrioventricular block, sinus node dysfunction, and syncope of unknown cause (Chapters 59 and 435).

PACING AND RECORDING TECHNIQUES

Catheters with 1 to 12 or more electrodes are inserted through veins and arteries and placed under fluoroscopic guidance into a variety of locations in the heart for recording and pacing. The primary measurement is the timing of each recorded signal to detect locally abnormal conduction times and sequences of activation. Other important measurements include local repolarization times, local tissue refractoriness, and spontaneous pacemaker activity.

During most electrophysiologic studies, a catheter is placed just across the tricuspid valve in the region of the bundle of His, where a sharp, high-frequency deflection is identified between the atrial and ventricular depolarizations during sinus rhythm. The presence and timing of this deflection determine sites of atrioventricular block and mechanisms of tachyarrhythmia.

Programmed electrical stimulation, or precisely timed pacing, is used to evaluate conduction over normal and abnormal pathways and to initiate tachyarrhythmias for detailed analysis. When supraventricular tachycardia is being studied, multiple atrial sites, including the coronary sinus, are paced and recorded to determine the mechanism of the tachycardia (Chapter 59), including potential sites for catheter ablation (Chapter 61). When ventricular tachycardia or sudden death is the indication for study, ventricular pacing and recording are emphasized. When syncope of uncertain cause is being evaluated, the study should assess the ability of the sinus node and atrioventricular conduction system to withstand pacing stress and the vulnerability of the heart to initiation of ventricular and supraventricular tachyarrhythmias.

PHARMACOLOGIC TESTING

Most supraventricular and ventricular tachyarrhythmias can be initiated by programmed stimulation during electrophysiologic study. Prevention of their initiation by an antiarrhythmic drug predicts long-term drug efficacy, so pharmacologic testing is a common indication for electrophysiologic study. Holter monitoring also predicts the efficacy of antiarrhythmic therapy, however, and a large, randomized trial found no difference in the accuracy of predictions made by electrophysiologic study and Holter monitoring. Because of demonstrations of superior efficacy of implanted cardioverter-defibrillator devices compared with antiarrhythmic drugs in patients with ventricular tachyarrhythmias (Chapters 60 and 61), pharmacologic electrophysiologic testing has been supplanted partially by device implantation.

DEVICE ASSESSMENT

With increased use of implanted devices for control of supraventricular and ventricular tachyarrhythmias, assessment of these devices has become a major component of electrophysiologic testing (Chapter 61). In patients with recurrent ventricular tachycardia, arrhythmia initiation and termination is performed to define effective sensing and pacing algorithms to be programmed in the implanted device's memory. In patients with ventricular fibrillation, the effectiveness of lead placement and of the delivery of the defibrillating shock is tested. Effective pacemaker settings are determined by electrophysiologic study. In patients with recurrent, persistent atrial fibrillation, atrial defibrillator devices are tested in much the same way as ventricular devices to ascertain the effectiveness of arrhythmia detection and termination.

Activation Sequence Mapping

In patients with reentrant supraventricular tachyarrhythmias unresponsive to medical therapy, ablation usually is performed by catheter delivery of an ablative agent, usually radiofrequency energy, to a specific myocardial site involved in arrhythmogenesis (Chapter 61). Most patients undergo a complex intracardiac electrophysiologic mapping procedure before the ablation to locate the appropriate target tissue.

Mapping of the sequence of electrical activation of the heart is a procedure of major importance in diagnosis and management of resistant cardiac arrhythmias. The objective of mapping is to determine the mechanism of the arrhythmia, such as delineation of a large reentrant pathway and segments within it that might be responsive to therapy. In other cases, a small focus of origin of a tachycardia may be identified for subsequent ablation. Mapping compares the time of electrical activation of the tissue in contact with an electrode with a fiducial time point, such as the onset of the QRS complex. The process is repeated until enough sites have been recorded to permit construction of an activation map showing the relative time of activation at each site, showing the direction and velocity of the activation wave front. Most mapping catheters bear multiple electrodes so that several sites can be recorded simultaneously. Newer mapping arrays deployed by intravascular catheters include noncontact probes with numerous closely spaced electrodes on their surfaces for recording endocardial signals from a distance and "basket" arrays that spring out to contact the chamber walls when advanced beyond the catheter lumen. Pathologic rhythms need to be sustained for only a few beats if many mapping sites are recorded simultaneously. Powerful data acquisition systems allow the clinician to see an immediate display of activation data. Useful mapping data can be obtained from all four cardiac chambers and from the pulmonary artery, the aortic root, the coronary sinus, the coronary veins, and the coronary arteries. Activation mapping also is performed during open-chest cardiac surgical procedures.

Viability mapping, a new application of multisite intracardiac electrical recording, can distinguish among myocardium that is permanently dysfunctional owing to scar, muscle that is stunned or hibernating but capable of regaining function, and normal myocardium. The accuracy of this technique has not yet been tested adequately against a gold standard.

Tilt Testing

When no cause for syncope is apparent, head-up tilt testing may reveal a neurocardiogenic origin. Most tilt protocols involve a 30-minute baseline measurement period followed by elevation of the table to 60 to 80 degrees for 60 minutes. Heart rate and the blood pressure are always monitored. In some laboratories, multiple ECG leads, intra-arterial pressure, an electroencephalogram, respirations, thoracic impedance (to estimate stroke volume), and cerebral blood flow velocity by transcranial Doppler ultrasound also are measured. Isoproterenol or nitroglycerin may be administered to increase the sensitivity of the test. The classic response in a patient with neurocardiogenic syncope is a sudden and precipitous fall in heart rate and blood pressure (Fig. 58–1). In some patients, the blood pressure drops without a fall in heart rate. Tilt testing is an important diagnostic modality in the evaluation of syncope, but it is best applied after other cardiac causes are excluded because false-positive tests are common. A study showed no difference in the subsequent incidence of bradyarrhythmic syncope as diagnosed by implanted loop recorders in patients with positive compared with negative tilt tests.

Neurocardiogenic syncope includes the well-known vasovagal faint. In all forms of neurocardiogenic syncope, autonomic reflexes inappropriately dilate arterial resistance vessels and may inhibit the activity of the sinus node and lower pacemakers. In some cases, initiation of the reflex results from excessive stimulation of cardiac mechanoreceptors caused by dehydration or venous blood pooling and leading to a compensatory increase in cardiac contractile force and to mechanoreceptor activation. Many other triggers of the inhibitory reflexes also are likely involved.

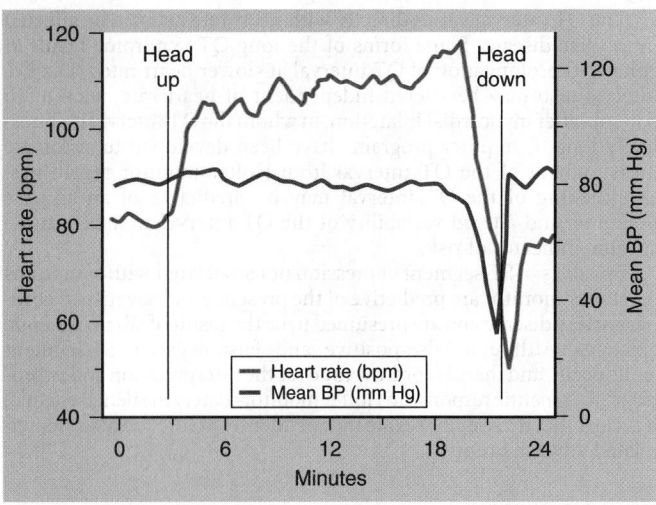

FIGURE 58–1 • Head-up tilt test performed on an 18-year-old woman with a history of syncope associated with pain, preceded by a prodrome of dizziness, graying vision, and diaphoresis. A similar prodrome preceded syncope during the test. Note the precipitous, nearly simultaneous, decline of heart rate and blood pressure (BP) after an initial rise in heart rate. Vital signs returned to normal rapidly after the head was lowered. (Courtesy of Robert F. Sprung, University of Utah.)

Diagnostic Approach to Palpitations, Dizziness, and Syncope

Palpitations, dizziness, and syncope are among the most common complaints (Table 58–2). In many cases, a specialist is not needed to diagnose and treat these symptoms.

PALPITATIONS

Palpitations often are described as a fluttering sensation or a "flip-flop" in the chest. They are usually due to atrial or ventricular extrasystoles and usually do not require further evaluation, especially if cardiac auscultation or palpation of the pulse are consistent with single premature beats. When presyncope accompanies the palpitations, evaluation is necessary. Most patients with benign palpitations do not require therapy. Antiarrhythmic drug therapy is inappropriate except for frequent and highly symptomatic ectopy or more advanced forms of arrhythmia (Chapters 59 and 60).

DIZZINESS

The term *dizziness* includes lightheadedness, disequilibrium, vertigo, and presyncope and has numerous potential causes. The history is paramount in determining the appropriate work-up for dizziness. Many patients, especially elderly individuals, experience postural hypotension associated with standing, especially after stooping or bending over. If the physical examination is normal, further evaluation of these patients is usually unnecessary. If the problem is loss of

Table 58–2 • **DIAGNOSTIC APPROACH TO PALPITATIONS, DIZZINESS, AND SYNCOPE**		
CONDITION	**MOST COMMON CAUSES**	**ORDER OF DIAGNOSTIC TESTING**
Palpitations	PACs, PVCs, SVT including AF, VT, AVB, psychiatric disorder	History and examination → Holter or external event monitor, depending on frequency of symptoms → Exercise stress test if exercise related → EPS if symptoms suggest sustained arrhythmia
Dizziness	Cardiac arrhythmia, medications, vestibular disorder, cerebellar disease, psychiatric disorder	History and examination → Holter or external event monitor, depending on frequency of symptoms → ENT or neurologic consultation → Tilt test → EPS if symptoms are severe and arrhythmia has not been excluded
Syncope	Cardiac arrhythmia, neurocardiogenic reflex, medications, psychiatric disorder	History and examination → external or implanted event monitor → Tilt test → SAECG → EPS if arrhythmia still suspected → Glucose tolerance test → Neurologic or psychiatric consultation

PACs = premature atrial contractions; PVCs = premature ventricular contractions, SVT = supraventricular tachycardia; AF = atrial fibrillation; VT = ventricular tachycardia; AVB = atrioventricular block; EPS = electrophysiologic study; ENT = ear, nose, and throat; SAECG = signal-averaged ECG.

Cardiovascular Disease

balance or vertigo (Chapters 435 and 470), a noncardiac cause should be sought. When presyncope, defined as near loss of consciousness, is not postural in origin, it deserves further evaluation similar to what is recommended for frank syncope.

SYNCOPE

The medical history is the most important tool in the evaluation of syncope (Chapter 435). A carefully documented history divulges the likely cause in many patients and always should be the principal determinant of further evaluation. If the syncopal spell was witnessed, it is essential to speak directly to the witness as part of a complete history.

Most syncopal spells have a cardiovascular cause. The most common cardiovascular causes are arrhythmia and neurocardiogenic syncope (in essence, an exaggerated vasovagal response). Bradyarrhythmic syncope usually is caused by sinoatrial nodal disease or atrioventricular conduction disease (Chapters 50 and 435). Patients with sinus node disease usually experience presyncope rather than syncope. When they experience true syncope, they usually have several seconds of warning symptoms before fainting. Drop attacks associated with His-Purkinje disease, or Morgagni-Stokes-Adams attacks, are usually more abrupt. Tachyarrhythmic syncope may occur with or without warning, depending on the rhythm. Supraventricular tachycardia and ventricular tachycardia usually are accompanied by a warning and usually abate spontaneously. The patient often is aware of rapid heart action before losing consciousness. Ventricular fibrillation causes abrupt syncope and rarely abates without cardioversion. Neurocardiogenic syncope usually is heralded by dizziness and other symptoms but may be abrupt. Often the event is preceded by a change in posture to sitting or standing, a prolonged period of standing with little movement, or an inciting incident such as venipuncture.

Psychogenic syncope is probably the second most common cause of fainting. The spells are usually recurrent, usually witnessed, and rarely associated with injury secondary to the fall. Although a psychogenic cause may be suspected at the initial interview, the diagnosis can be made only if cardiovascular and neurologic causes are excluded.

Neurologic causes of syncope are much less common (Chapter 435) and include epileptic seizures and transient ischemia involving the vertebrobasilar arterial bed. Epilepsy is suspected when seizure activity is noted or a typical postictal state follows the event. A seizure does not guarantee a neurologic cause because cardiovascular collapse rarely can cause a typical seizure complex. Seizure activity induced by hypotension is usually brief, however, and may not be associated with incontinence or a postictal state.

Event monitoring is the preferred diagnostic test. Holter monitoring has only a secondary role in the evaluation of syncope and is likely to be helpful only in patients with daily episodes. In a randomized trial of patients with unexplained syncope, an implantable loop recorder was better than the combination of an external loop recorder, tilt testing, and electrophysiologic studies for diagnosing an arrhythmic cause of syncope. **1**

℞ Treatment of Neurocardiogenic Syncope

Treatment of neurocardiogenic syncope is challenging. Support stockings prevent venous blood pooling, whereas fludrocortisone and increased salt intake expand blood volume. Randomized trials have shown that midodrine, a pure α-agonist that serves as a vasoconstrictor, and paroxetine, an antidepressant that is a selective serotonin reuptake inhibitor, can reduce markedly the recurrence rate of neurocardiogenic syncope. **2,3** β-Blockers, which have been recommended for the same reasons that isoproterenol provokes symptoms, have shown variable results but are generally better than placebo. **4** For recurrent, debilitating neurocardiogenic syncope associated with marked bradycardia on tilt testing, permanent pacing may protect against the inappropriate bradycardia and greatly reduce recurrences, **5** but a recent double-blind trial found no significant benefit in patients with more modest bradycardia. **6**

 1. Krahn AD, Klein GJ, Yee R, Skanes AC: Randomized assessment of syncope trial: Conventional diagnostic testing versus a prolonged monitoring strategy. Circulation 2001;104:46–51.

2. Di Girolamo E, Di Iorio C, Sabatini P, et al: Effects of paroxetine hydrochloride, a selective serotonin reuptake inhibitor, on refractory vasovagal syncope: A randomized, double-blind, placebo-controlled study. J Am Coll Cardiol 1999;33:1227–1230.
3. Ammirati F, Colivicchi F, Santini M, for the Syncope Diagnosis and Treatment Study Investigators: Permanent cardiac pacing versus medical treatment for the prevention of recurrent vasovagal syncope: A multicenter, randomized, controlled trial. Circulation 2001;104:52–57.
4. Ventura R, Maas R, Zeidlev D, et al: A randomized and controlled pilot trial of beta-blockers for the treatment of recurrent syncope in patients with positive or negative response to head-up till test. Pacing Clin Electrophysiol 2002;25:816–821.
5. Perez-Lugones A, Schweikert R, Pavia S, et al: Usefulness of midodrine in patients with severely symptomatic neurocardiogenic syncope: A randomized control study. J Cardiovasc Electrophysiol 2001;12:935–938.
6. Connolly SJ, Sheldon R, Thorpe KE, et al: Pacemaker therapy for prevention of syncope in patients with recurrent severe Vasovagal syncope: Second Vasovagal Pacemaker Study (VPS II): A randomized trial. JAMA 2003;289:2224–2229.

SUGGESTED READINGS

Brignole M, Alboni P, Benditt D, et al: Guidelines on management (diagnosis and treatment) of syncope. Eur Heart J 2001;22:1256–1306. *A comprehensive and authoritative recommendation on management of syncope authored by the European Society of Cardiology's Task Force on Syncope.*

Chen LY, Gersh BJ, Hodge DQ, et al: Prevalence and clinical outcomes of patients with multiple causes of syncope. Mayo Clin Proc 2003;78:414–420. *The 18% of patients with multiple causes do worse.*

Gold MR, Bloomfield DM: A comparison of T-wave alternans, signal averaged electrocardiography and programmed ventricular stimulation for arrhythmia risk stratification. J Am Coll Cardiol 2000;36:2247–2253. *This multicenter, prospective study found T-wave alternans to be as accurate as electrophysiologic testing for predicting spontaneous ventricular arrhythmias and death.*

Sarasin FP, Louis-Simonet M, Carballo D, et al: Prospective evaluation of patients with syncope: A population-based study. Am J Med 2001;111:177–184. *This Swiss study shows the effectiveness of a diagnostic strategy based on history, physical examination, and electrocardiography in an unselected population with syncope.*

59 CARDIAC ARRHYTHMIAS WITH SUPRAVENTRICULAR ORIGIN

Masood Akhtar

The atria and ventricles are electrically insulated from each other by fibrous tissue that is the anatomic atrioventricular (AV) junction. The fibrous structures in the AV junction are the annuli of the mitral and tricuspid valves and the fibrous portion of the interventricular septum. In the absence of an electrical bridge, the atrial impulses cannot cross this fibrous gap. Normally the AV node and the His-Purkinje system (HPS) provide the only electrical conduit. In some individuals, additional electrical bridges connect the atria with ventricles directly, bypassing these normal pathways and forming the basis for pre-excitation syndromes, such as Wolff-Parkinson-White (WPW) syndrome.

Any arrhythmia arising above the bifurcation of the His bundle into the right and left bundle branches is classified as supraventricular. The resultant QRS complex morphology either can be normal or may be wide owing to bundle-branch or fascicular block (aberrant conduction) or conduction over an accessory pathway (anomalous conduction or pre-excitation). Supraventricular cardiac arrhythmias can be categorized broadly into tachyarrhythmias or bradyarrhythmias.

TACHYARRHYTHMIAS

Supraventricular tachyarrhythmias can occur either as isolated premature complexes or in the form of nonsustained or sustained tachycardias. The most frequent definition of nonsustained tachycardias is an arrhythmia with a rate of more than 100 beats per minute lasting 3 beats or more but less than 30 seconds. Sustained tachycardia is a prolonged episode of tachycardia lasting 30 seconds or more or terminated earlier with an intervention, such as intravenous medication, overdrive pacing, or direct current electrical cardioversion.

Premature Atrial Complexes

Premature atrial complexes (PACs) can arise from any part of the right or left atrium or from the pulmonary veins. The P wave morphology depends on the origin but differs from sinus rhythm unless PACs arise near the upper right atrial junction with the superior vena cava, that is, close to the location of sinus node. The P wave always precedes the QRS complex (Fig. 59–1A); if it encounters the absolute

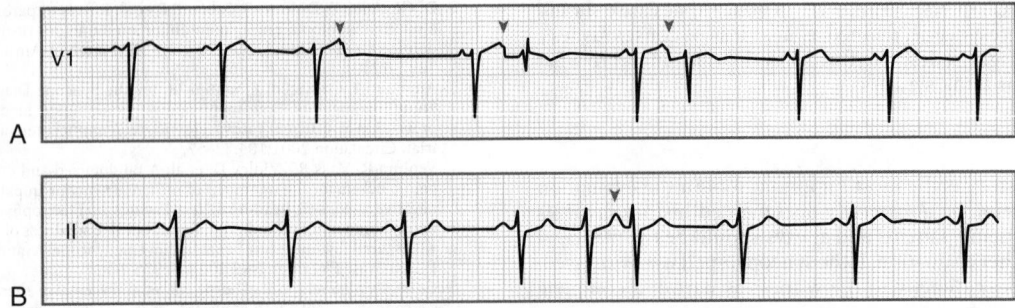

FIGURE 59–1 • Isolated premature complexes. *A*, Three premature atrial complexes (arrows). The first one blocks and the remaining two conduct to the ventricles with QRS morphology different from that of sinus complexes owing to encroachment of premature impulses on the refractory period of the His-Purkinje system (aberrant conduction). *B*, Premature junctional complex (fifth complex). Note the similarity of QRS complex between the sinus and premature beat that is not preceded by a P wave. The next sinus P wave (arrow) occurs on time and conducts to the ventricles. ECG leads are labeled. (Modified from Akhtar M: Examination of the heart: V. The electrogram. With permission from the American Heart Association, Dallas, Tx.)

refractory period of the AV node or the HPS, the P wave is blocked and is not followed by a QRS complex. A blocked PAC may be confused with second-degree AV block, unless its prematurity is recognized from the PP interval shortening or with sinus node dysfunction (SND) if it is inconspicuous. Distortion of the ST-T segment is often a clue to the presence of a P wave. When a premature QRS complex has the morphology of the underlying sinus rhythm but is not preceded by a P wave, it is labeled as *AV junctional* (Fig. 59–1B). When two or more morphologically distinct P waves result in a rate less than 100 beats per minute, the rhythm is termed *wandering atrial pacemaker*.

Premature complexes from the atria or AV junction usually maintain the same intraventricular conduction pattern seen during sinus complexes; that is, if the sinus rhythm shows a normal QRS complex or bundle-branch block pattern, the same configuration would be expected during the premature complexes (Fig. 59–2B). If the premature complexes are relatively early (i.e., closely coupled), however, they can encroach on the refractory period of the right or left bundle branches, resulting in aberrant conduction and producing a right or left bundle-branch or fascicular block pattern (see Fig. 59–1A) despite normal intraventricular conduction during sinus rhythm. Closely

coupled PACs also frequently initiate sustained or nonsustained supraventricular tachycardias.

Sustained Supraventricular Tachycardias

Supraventricular tachycardias can be categorized broadly into atrial and AV junctional (Table 5–1). Atrial tachycardias are independent of AV nodal conduction such that with effective vagal maneuvers (e.g., carotid sinus massage, Valsalva) AV block occurs, but the atrial process continues. Conversely, most AV junctional tachycardias require propagation through the AV node to continue so that AV junctional tachycardias generally terminate if vagal maneuvers induce AV nodal block.

ATRIAL TACHYCARDIAS

See also Figures 50–5 and 50–6.

SINUS TACHYCARDIA. Sinus tachycardia is usually due to an enhancement of normal automaticity seen in settings of increased adrenergic drive. Because sympathetic stimulation and vagal withdrawal also enhance AV nodal conduction, the PR interval does not prolong despite sinus rate acceleration. The P wave configuration is the same as with sinus rhythm—upright in leads II, III, and aVF (see Fig. 59–2B) and biphasic in V_1—because of the normal sequence with which the sinus node depolarizes the two atria. The atrial rate during sinus tachycardia seldom exceeds 200 beats per minute and is generally less than 150 beats per minute.

SINUS NODE RE-ENTRY. The P wave morphology is similar to sinus rhythm, but the underlying mechanism is re-entry in the region of the sinus node. In contrast to the physiologic form of sinus tachycardia, which has a gradual onset and termination, sinus node re-entry starts and ends abruptly. As with many other atrial re-entrant tachycardias, sinus node re-entry generally is triggered by a PAC. Sudden acceleration of the atrial rate prolongs the PR interval or even leads to AV nodal block owing to the expected physiologic delay in AV nodal conduction unless concomitant sympathetic stimulation facilitates AV nodal conduction. The atrial rates range between 150 and 250 beats per minute. Depending on the state of AV conduction, 1:1 AV conduction or a variable degree of AV block may be noted.

ATRIAL TACHYCARDIA. Any tachycardia arising above the AV junction that has a P wave configuration different than sinus rhythm is called *atrial tachycardia* (see Fig. 59–2C). In general, impulses arising in the superior portion of the right or left atrium produce a positive P wave in the inferior leads (i.e., leads II, III, and aVF), whereas impulses arising in the lower or inferior portions result in negative P waves in the same leads. Atrial tachycardias can result from enhanced normal automaticity, abnormal automaticity, triggered activity, and re-entry (Chapter 57). The re-entrant forms can be reproduced easily in the electrophysiology laboratory with electrical stimulation of the atria (Chapter 58). When the P wave configuration is uniform from beat to beat, the tachycardia is unifocal; the term *multifocal atrial tachycardia* implies several different P wave morphologies. Atrial rates range between 100 and 250 beats per minute, and the ventricular response depends on the status of AV conduction; a 1:1 P wave-to-QRS complex

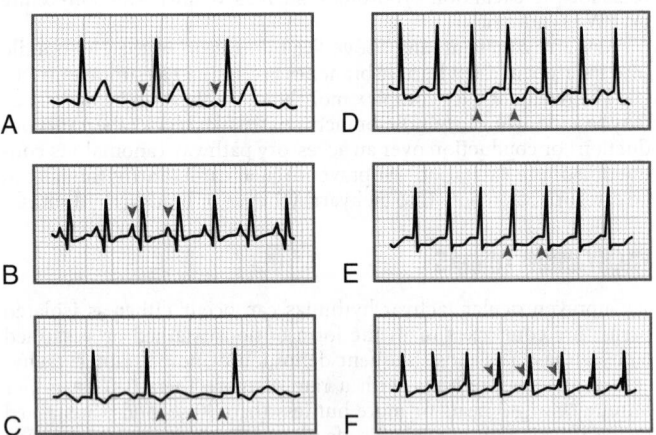

FIGURE 59–2 • P-QRS relationship in supraventricular tachycardia. Sinus rhythm (*A*), usual type of sinus tachycardia (*B*), and unifocal atrial tachycardia (*C*) are shown. Note the positive P wave and normal PR interval during sinus tachycardia. Atrial tachycardia (*C*) originates in the low atrium (negative P wave) and is accompanied by a variable degree of atrioventricular (AV) block. The P wave during AV junctional re-entry follows the QRS and is in the ST segment during AV re-entry (*D*) and buried in the QRS complex during common AV nodal re-entry (*E*). Nonparoxysmal junctional tachycardia in which the atria and ventricles are stimulated independently is shown (*F*). Resultant AV dissociation occurs because the junctional rate accelerates and competes with the sinus mechanism. Note the gradual march of P waves in and out of the QRS. Electrocardiogram lead II in all panels.

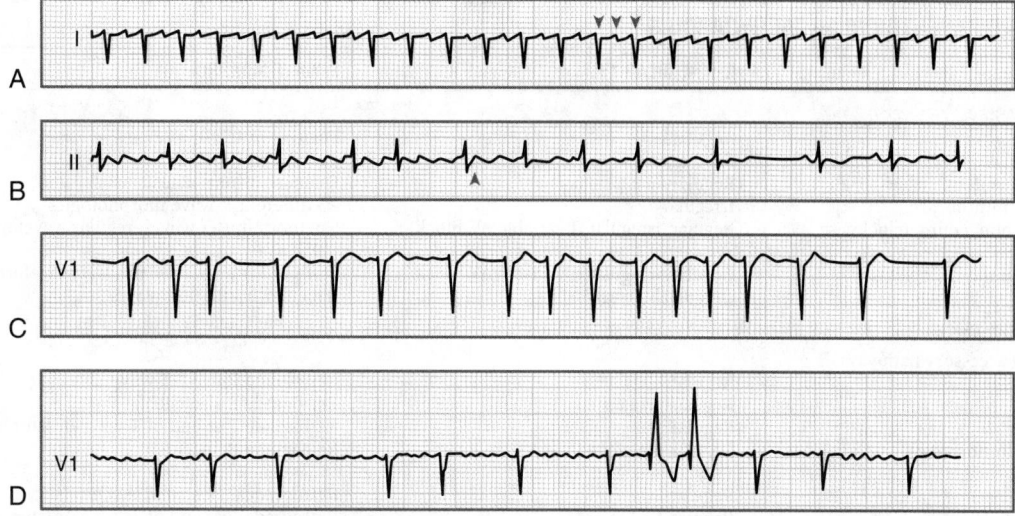

FIGURE 59–3 • Atrial flutter and atrial fibrillation. *A,* Regular narrow QRS tachycardia with ventricular rate of 150 beats per minute, most commonly seen in atrial flutter with 2:1 atrioventricular (AV) block. *B,* With a higher degree of AV block, the flutter waves can be seen more clearly, and in this case, the atrial flutter converted briefly to atrial fibrillation (at the arrow), then to sinus rhythm. *C* and *D,* Atrial fibrillation. The atrial activity is difficult to identify in *C,* but it is clear in *D;* in both tracings, the RR intervals are irregularly irregular. Two consecutive QRS complexes owing to aberrant conduction (right bundle-branch block) are noted in *D.* (Modified from Akhtar M: Examination of the heart: V. The electrogram. With permission from the American Heart Association, Dallas, Tx.)

ratio is common with rates less than 200 beats per minute, whereas at higher rates various degrees of block (e.g., 3:2, 2:1, 3:1) are common (see Fig. 59–2*C*). Atrial rates and AV conduction can be altered markedly by cardioactive drugs, particularly antiarrhythmic agents (Chapter 57).

ATRIAL FLUTTER. Atrial flutter causes regular atrial rates ranging from 250 to 350 beats per minute (300 being the most common) (Fig. 59–3*A, B*). Common atrial flutter, with a "sawtooth" appearance in leads II, III, and aVF, has a fairly uniform route of impulse propagation localized to the right atrium. The re-entrant impulse travels over the anterolateral right atrium, through a narrow isthmus in the posteroseptal area, then along the atrial septum toward the superior portion of the right atrium (counterclockwise). Incidental left atrial activation produces a negative sawtooth flutter wave in the inferior leads. A reverse of this direction in the circuit could cause a positive flutter wave in the same leads (uncommon or clockwise). Flutter waves with other configurations may have other origins, including the left atrium. The ventricular response is usually 2:1 or 4:1, representing ventricular rates of 150 beats per minute and 75 beats per minute. A 3:1 AV ratio is uncommon and fairly well tolerated. A 1:1 AV response is rare and can cause serious hemodynamic consequences.

ATRIAL FIBRILLATION. Atrial fibrillation (AF) is the most common sustained arrhythmia in adults: More than 2 million individuals in the United States have AF, with more than 160,000 new cases diagnosed every year. The incidence of AF increases with advancing age, affecting more than 6% of the population older than age 75. During AF, the atria have disorganized, rapid, irregular electrical activity exceeding 400 beats per minute (Fig. 59–3*C*). The ventricular response is also irregular and variable (irregularly irregular). The atria do not contract effectively so that intra-atrial clot formation is promoted. With subsequent resumption of atrial contraction, embolism can occur with devastating consequences. On the surface ECG, the AF waves may be coarse, fine, or difficult to discern (Fig. 59–3*C, D*), but the irregularity of the RR wave makes the diagnosis of AF relatively easy. Aberrant conduction may be noted if the impulses reach the bundle branches during their refractory period. In the absence of accessory pathways, the average ventricular response by the AV node—HPS is seldom more than 200 beats per minute and is generally less than 150 beats per minute. With a rapidly conducting accessory pathway, ventricular rates can exceed 300 beats per minute, however, and precipitate ventricular fibrillation.

ATRIOVENTRICULAR JUNCTIONAL TACHYCARDIA

Most AV junctional tachycardias (see Table 59–1) requiring long-term management are re-entrant. AV re-entry in the WPW syndrome

is the classic form and is usually (>90%) initiated by atrial and/or ventricular premature complexes.

WOLFF-PARKINSON-WHITE SYNDROME AND ASSOCIATED TACHYCARDIAS. A combination of a short PR interval and initial slurring of the QRS (Fig. 59–4*A*) is termed *ventricular pre-excitation,* which in association with a history of tachycardia constitutes the WPW syndrome. Normally the sinus impulse must travel through the AV node–HPS to reach the ventricles, resulting in a PR interval of 120 to 200 msec. When an accessory pathway (often called the *Kent bundle*) directly connects the atrium with the ventricle, it bypasses the AV nodal conduction delay, and the impulse reaches the ventricles sooner than expected, hence the term *pre-excitation* (Chapter 57). The length of the PR interval is a function of proximity of the accessory pathway to the origin of impulse and conduction time through it. When location or relatively slow conduction delays the accessory impulse, ventricular depolarization may occur through the normal pathway. In a typical case of WPW, however, the impulse reaches the ventricle first through the accessory pathway and starts the QRS earlier, resulting in a shorter PR interval (see Fig. 59–3*A*). Because the initial QRS activation is due to muscle-to-muscle conduction, as opposed to Purkinje-to-muscle activation during normal QRS, the beginning of the QRS is slurred and produces a so-called delta wave. Soon after, ventricular activation also starts through the normal pathway and is spread more rapidly through the ventricular myocardium, resulting in a fusion QRS activation with a rapid inscription after the delta wave. If the atrial or sinus impulse never reaches the ventricle through the accessory pathway because of either delayed arrival at or lack of antero-grade conduction over the accessory pathway, the abnormality is termed the *concealed WPW syndrome* because retrograde conduction through the accessory pathway may be intact and able to cause orthodromic tachycardia. The most common accessory pathway (>50%) is in the left ventricle free wall, that is, left atrium-to-left ventricle connection. Posteroseptal pathways (connecting the right atrium with left ventricle) are the next most common (30%). Right free wall and anteroseptal accessory pathways, both of which are right atrium-to-right ventricle connections, account for the remaining pathways.

The most common sustained arrhythmia in patients with WPW syndrome is orthodromic AV re-entry (see Figs. 59–2*D* and 59–4*B*), in which the impulse propagates to the ventricles by means of the normal pathway and in retrograde fashion to the atria through the accessory pathway; during the tachycardia, there is no evidence of ventricular pre-excitation (see Fig. 59–2*D*). In rare instances, the circuit of re-entry may be reversed (antidromic) so that the impulse reaches the ventricle through the accessory pathway and in retrograde conducts to the atria through the normal pathway and produces a pre-excited QRS complex (see Fig. 59–4*C*). The second most common

Table 59–1 • SUPRAVENTRICULAR TACHYCARDIAS

	R-R REGULARITY	P-WAVE MORPHOLOGY
ATRIAL TACHYCARDIAS		
Sinus tachycardia	Regular	Positive in II, III, aVF
Sinus node reentry	Regular	Positive in II, III, aVF
Atrial tachycardia, unifocal	Regular	P different from sinus
Atrial tachycardia, multifocal	Irregular	≥3 different P-wave morphologies
Atrial flutter, common, counterclockwise	Regular, irregular if variable AV block	Sawtooth flutter waves; regular waveform; negative in II, III, aVF
Atrial flutter, uncommon, clockwise	Regular, irregular if variable AV block	Upright flutter waves; positive waveform II, III, aVF
Atrial fibrillation	Irregularly irregular	Irregular fibrillation waves
AV JUNCTIONAL TACHYCARDIA		
AV re-entry (using accessory pathways)		
Orthodromic	Regular	Retrograde P in ST-T wave
Antidromic	Regular preexcited	Retrograde P, short RP
Slow conducting	Regular	Retrograde P at end of T wave or later (long RP)
Atriofascicular (antidromic)	Regular preexcited	Retrograde P, short RP
AV nodal re-entry		
Common (slow-fast)	Regular	Retrograde P obscured by QRS (short RP)
Uncommon (fast-slow)	Regular	Retrograde P at end of T wave or later (long RP)
Others (slow-slow)	Regular	PR-RP approximately equal
NONPAROXYSMAL JUNCTIONAL TACHYCARDIA*	Regular, slow rate	AV dissociation
AUTOMATIC JUNCTIONAL TACHYCARDIA*	Regular	AV dissociation

*Site of origin usually infranodal.
AV = atrioventricular.

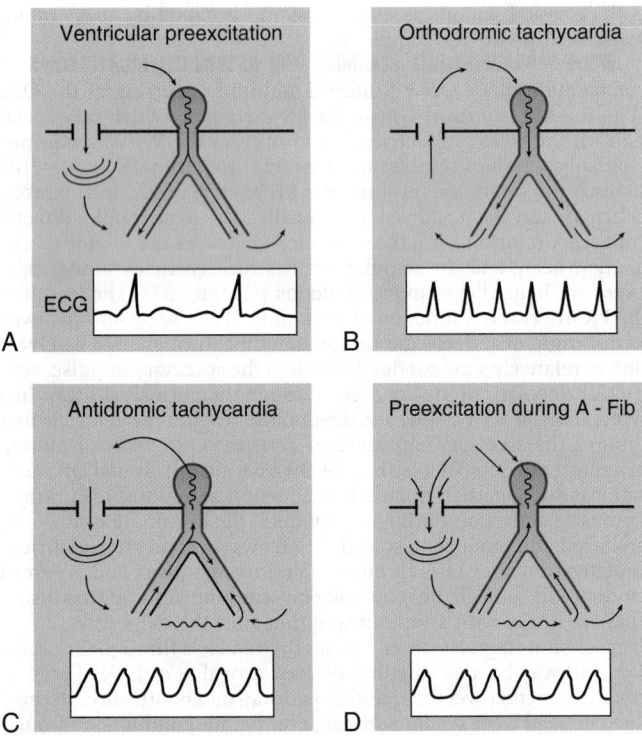

FIGURE 59–4 • Wolff-Parkinson-White syndrome. *A*, Ventricular pre-excitation (short PR and delta wave) owing to earlier ventricular activation via the accessory pathway. *B*, Narrow QRS tachycardia with anterograde conduction over the atrioventricular node–His-Purkinje system and retrograde propagation via the accessory pathway (orthodromic tachycardia). *C*, The reversal of this re-entrant circuit produces antidromic tachycardia with regular and pre-excited complexes. *D*, During atrial fibrillation, preferential conduction over the accessory pathway produces rapid irregular pre-excited complexes. (Modified from Akhtar M: Examination of the heart: V. The electrogram. With permission from the American Heart Association, Dallas, Tx.)

arrhythmia and frequently the most serious is AF (see Fig. 59–4*D*), which is experienced by 40% of patients with WPW syndrome. If the accessory pathway conducts rapidly during AF, a relatively fast ventricular rate may occur and cause severe hypotension and/or syncope and even precipitate ventricular fibrillation. Other accessory pathways implicated in clinical tachycardias are the atriofascicular fibers (previously referred to as *Mahaim fibers*) and slowly conducting retrograde pathways.

ATRIOVENTRICULAR NODAL RE-ENTRY. In the absence of ventricular pre-excitation, the most common AV junctional tachycardia is AV nodal re-entry (AVNR). The entire re-entry circuit is localized to the region of the AV node and results from differences of conduction and refractory periods in various portions of the AV node. Fast conducting fibers (fast pathway) are situated more anteriorly and have longer refractory periods, whereas slower conducting fibers are posterior and have a shorter refractory period. In the common type of AVNR, anterograde conduction is over the slow pathway, and retrograde conduction is through the fast pathway such that the conduction times of the impulse anterograde to the ventricles and retrograde to the atria are similar (see Fig. 59–2*E*), resulting in near-simultaneous P and QRS complexes. The retrograde P wave either is obscured by the QRS complex (see Fig. 59–2*E*) or alters the appearance of the terminal portion of the QRS and may be recognized in the early part of the ST segment. Less frequently, the direction of conduction through the re-entry circuit is reversed, with anterograde conduction to the ventricle over the fast pathway and retrograde conduction to the atria through the slow pathway; the result is a shorter PR interval. If the P wave follows the T wave, its retrograde morphology (i.e., negative in leads II, III, and aVF) is clearly recognizable. Sustained AVNR and AV re-entry together account for more than 75% of cases frequently labeled as *paroxysmal atrial tachycardia* (PAT).

NONPAROXYSMAL JUNCTIONAL TACHYCARDIA. Nonparoxysmal junctional tachycardia arises within the region of the His bundle and activates the ventricles with a QRS morphology similar to sinus beats (see Fig. 59–2*F*). Retrograde conduction through the AV node may or may not take place. If there is retrograde block, sinus rhythm remains uninterrupted, and the sinus P wave also blocks when the AV node is refractory because of retrograde AV nodal penetration of the junctional impulse; AV dissociation may result (see Fig. 59–2*F*). A 1:1 P wave/QRS complex relationship may occur, and if the P wave is negative, junctional origin is suggested. Ventricular rates seldom exceed 150 beats per minute, and when the rate is less than 100 beats per minute, the term *accelerated junctional rhythm* is applied. The underlying mechanism is enhanced normal automaticity.

AUTOMATIC JUNCTIONAL TACHYCARDIA. The main difference between automatic junctional tachycardia and nonparoxysmal junctional

Table 59–2 • SELECTION OF MEDICATIONS FOR SPECIFIC SUPRAVENTRICULAR ARRHYTHMIAS

ARRHYTHMIA	ACUTE INTRAVENOUS MANAGEMENT	LONG-TERM ORAL THERAPY	LONG-TERM ANTICOAGULATION
Atrial fibrillation	Verapamil, diltiazem, metoprolol, or digoxin for rate control; Ibutilide for cardioversion	No organic cardiac disease—classes IA or IC; Heart failure—amiodarone or dofetilide; Hypertension—sotalol or class IC	Yes
Atrial fibrillation with rapid rate owing to Wolff-Parkinson-White syndrome	Ibutilide or procainamide; avoid verapamil or digoxin	Amiodarone, sotalol, or class IA or IC	No
Atrial flutter	Verapamil, diltiazem, metoprolol, esmolol, or digoxin	Amiodarone, sotalol, classes IA or IC	Yes
Paroxysmal supraventricular tachycardia	Adenosine, verapamil, propranolol, esmolol, or metoprolol	β-Blockers, calcium channel blockers, classes IA or IC, or sotalol	No

Class IA = procainamide, quinidine, disopyramide.
Class IC = flecainide, propafenone.
Adapted from Scheinman MM, Kaushik V: Recognition and management of patients with tachyarrhythmias In Braunwald E, Goldman L (eds): Primary Care Cardiology, 2nd ed. Philadelphia, WB Saunders, 2003.

tachycardia on the surface electrocardiogram (ECG) is the rate. In the automatic variety, rates are faster (range, 130 to 200 beats per minute). This arrhythmia can be episodic or persistent. Because the rates are fairly comparable to paroxysmal AV junctional re-entrant tachycardia and the QRS complex morphology is similar to sinus beats, the presence of AV dissociation is the main distinction from re-entrant arrhythmias on the ECG. The underlying cause is abnormal automaticity in the AV junction.

Clinical Manifestations

The usual type of sinus tachycardia is caused by increased metabolic demands from high adrenergic states, such as fever, physical exertion, hypovolemia, heart failure, sympathomimetic or parasympatholytic medications, thyrotoxicosis, and pheochromocytoma. All other supraventricular tachycardias represent abnormalities of rhythm and commonly produce tachycardia-related symptoms, including palpitation, racing of the heart, dizziness, shortness of breath, chest discomfort, presyncope, and sometimes frank syncope. Incessant supraventricular tachycardia and uncontrolled ventricular rates in AF can cause tachycardia-related cardiomyopathy, which is reversible with control of these arrhythmias.

Atrial dilation, fibrosis, and acute or chronic inflammatory states involving atrial myocardium or pericardium may cause atrial tachycardias. Multifocal atrial tachycardia is relatively frequent in the presence of chronic pulmonary disease. AF often is associated with aging, hypertension, valvular and pulmonary diseases, acute and chronic coronary disease, hyperadrenergic states, and metabolic abnormalities such as thyrotoxicosis. AF also may be noted in the absence of any detectable cardiac pathology, in which case it is termed *lone AF*. The risk of thromboembolism in AF increases with age, diabetes mellitus, hypertension, previous embolic episodes, valvular disease, and heart failure. The lowest incidence (<1% annually) is in patients younger than age 65 years with lone AF.

Re-entrant tachycardias have an abrupt onset and an abrupt ending, particularly when terminated with vagal maneuvers or intravenous medications. Although a functioning accessory pathway is a congenital abnormality, its clinical manifestation can occur at any age. If no ECG is done, asymptomatic ventricular pre-excitation can go undetected for many years. When discovered, ventricular pre-excitation can mimic inferior or anteroseptal myocardial infarction, right ventricular hypertrophy, and right and left bundle-branch block. WPW syndrome is not clearly associated with mitral valve prolapse or hypertrophic cardiomyopathy, but single and multiple right-sided accessory pathways are more common with Ebstein's anomaly.

Nonparoxysmal AV junctional tachycardia is seen frequently with high adrenergic drive, that is, after myocardial infarction or cardiac surgery, with sympathomimetic and parasympatholytic agents, or with digitalis toxicity. Automatic junctional tachycardia is not known to be associated with any particular cardiovascular pathology.

 Treatment

See Tables 59–2 and 59–3. See also Chapters 61 and 62.

ACUTE THERAPY. Isolated premature beats seldom pose any significant risk, do not cause severe arrhythmic symptoms, and do not warrant aggressive therapy. Conversely, sustained or prolonged repeated episodes of nonsustained supraventricular tachycardias generally require effective therapy. Whenever rapid control of supraventricular tachycardia is desired (e.g., in patients with myocardial ischemia or hypotension), cardioversion is the best solution (Chapter 61). Atrial tachycardias, including atrial flutter or AF, may convert spontaneously or convert after treatment of an underlying cause, such as hypoxia or heart failure, or after cessation of precipitating medications.

An acute episode of junctional tachycardia from either AVNR or AV re-entry usually can be terminated with vagal maneuvers, such as carotid massage, which produce a marked sinus slowing and AV nodal block. In most atrial tachycardias, adenosine and/or vagal stimulation produces enough AV block to unmask the atrial origin of the tachycardia. Some atrial tachycardias, particularly those arising near the sinus node, also may terminate after adenosine administration, however. Intravenous β-blockers and calcium channel blockers also can be used for the same purpose. For sustained control of the ventricular rate during atrial tachycardia, intravenous esmolol and diltiazem are effective.

For acute AF without hypotension, rate control is crucial and can be accomplished with esmolol, metoprolol, verapamil, or diltiazem; digoxin is usually a third-line agent. All patients with new-onset AF should be anticoagulated acutely with heparin (Fig. 59–5; see also Chapter 33). If the patient is seen within 8 hours of the onset of AF, transesophageal echocardiography should be performed (Chapter 51); if no clot is detected in the left atrium, it is safe to proceed to cardioversion followed by warfarin anticoagulation. If transesophageal echocardiography detects clot, however, the patient should receive 3 weeks of oral anticoagulation before elective cardioversion. A variety of medications can be used to sustain sinus rhythm in patients with AF. Amiodarone is the most effective but should be used selectively because of its potential side effects.■ Data from randomized trials suggest that a strategy of controlling the heart rate in atrial fibrillation generally is as good as a strategy of trying to restore sinus rhythm if patients are treated with appropriate anticoagulation. ⬛ If ventricular response during AF is through a rapidly conducting accessory pathway, intravenous digitalis and calcium channel blockers are contraindicated, and procainamide is a better choice.

LONG-TERM MANAGEMENT. For symptomatic patients with sustained AV junctional reentry, control sometimes can be achieved with digitalis, β-blockers, and calcium channel blockers or with class I and class III drugs (Chapter 62). In patients with atrial tachycardia or atrial flutter, ventricular rate control is possible through AV nodal block with digitalis, β-blockers, and calcium channel blockers (see Table 59–3). Radiofrequency ablation is now the

Continued

Cardiovascular Disease

preferred choice, however, for most symptomatic sustained regular reentrant supraventricular tachycardias, including atrial tachycardia and atrial flutter, which now can be cured reliably with catheter ablation (Chapter 61). For termination or prevention of atrial tachyarrhythmias, class Ia, Ic, or III drugs usually are needed (Chapter 62). Amiodarone is the most effective drug for long-term control of AF and atrial flutter (see Table 59–2).

Long-term anticoagulation therapy with warfarin generally is recommended in all patients who are over 65 years of age, who have persistent AF, and who have no contraindications to anticoagulation. ▣ The international normalized ratio goal is 2.0 to 3.0, unless mitral stenosis is present, in which case the target is an international normalized ratio of 2.5 to 3.5. Aspirin may be better than no treatment for patients who cannot tolerate warfarin (Chapter 33).

BRADYARRHYTHMIAS

Bradyarrhythmias (Table 59–4) can be classified broadly into sinus node dysfunction (SND) and AV blocks.

Sinus Node Dysfunction

Among the various pacemaker cells distributed throughout the cardiac conduction system, the sinus node has the highest rate of automaticity, and it functions as the dominant pacemaker (Chapter 57). The usual sinus rate varies between 60 beats per minute and 100 beats per minute, determined by physiologic need and modulated through the autonomic nervous system. SND has several different manifestations, including sinus bradycardia, sinoatrial (SA) exit block, sinus arrest, and bradycardia-tachycardia syndrome.

SINUS BRADYCARDIA. Rates less than 60 beats per minute usually are described as bradycardia (Fig. 59–6A). In healthy persons, rates of 50 beats per minute are not unusual, however, and rates of 30 beats per minute may be recorded during sleep. Sinus bradycardia of clinical significance usually is defined as persistent rates less than 45 beats per minute while awake. SND also may be manifested by the failure to accelerate the sinus rate (lack of chronotropic response) in response to situations such as exercise, heart failure, fever, sympathomimetic drugs, or parasympatholytic drugs. It is important to determine that SND including sinus bradycardia in an individual is not secondary to cardioactive drugs such as β-blockers and calcium channel blockers.

Table 59–3 • DRUGS AND DOSES USED TO TREAT SUPRAVENTRICULAR TACHYCARDIAS

DRUG	INTRAVENOUS BOLUS	INTRAVENOUS INFUSION	ORAL DOSE
Digoxin	0.5–1.0 mg		0.125–0.5 mg/day
Adenosine	6–12 mg		
β-Blockers			
Esmolol	5 µg/kg/min	3 µg/kg/min	
Propranolol	1–3 mg		10–40 mg tid
Metoprolol	5 mg (can repeat ×2)		25–200 mg/day
Calcium channel blockers			
Verapamil	5–15 mg		120–480 mg/day
Diltiazem	15–25 mg	15 mg/kg	120–360 mg/day
Class IA			
Procainamide	10–15 mg/kg	5 mg/kg	750–1500 mg qid
Quinidine			300–600 mg qid
Disopyramide			100–200 mg tid
Class IC			
Flecainide			50–200 mg bid
Propafenone			150–300 mg tid
Class III			
Ibutilide	1–2 mg		
Sotalol			80–160 mg bid
Amiodarone	2–3 mg/kg	0.5–1 mg/min	600–1200 mg/day for 7- to 10-day loading dose, then 100–400 mg/day
Dofetilide			125–500 µg bid

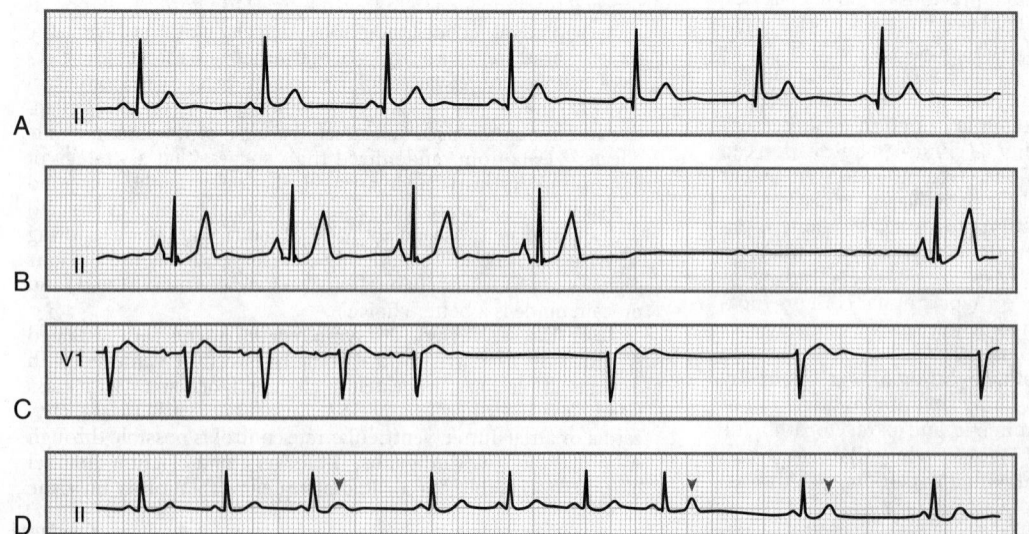

FIGURE 59–5 • Management of recent-onset atrial fibrillation. (From Falk RH: Atrial fibrillation. N Engl J Med 2001;344: 1067–1078.)

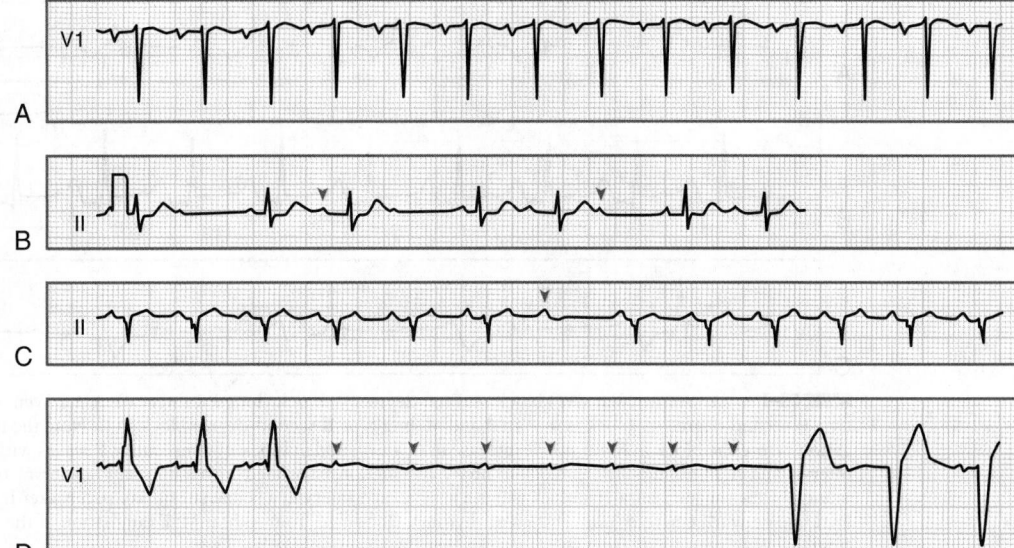

FIGURE 59–6 • Sinus node dysfunction. *A,* Sinus bradycardia, with sudden loss of sinus activity (no P waves) in *B* and *C*. Sinus rhythm resumes after a 4.5-second pause (*B*), whereas junctional rhythm emerges as a subsidiary mechanism in *C*. The exact cause (i.e., sino-atrial exit block versus sinus arrest) cannot be determined from the surface electrocardiogram in these examples. In *D*, blocked premature atrial complexes (note distortion of the T wave at arrows compared with sinus cycles) mimic sinus node dysfunction.

Table 59–4 • BRADYCARDIAS

SINUS NODE DYSFUNCTION
Sinus bradycardia <45/min
Sinoatrial exit block
    First degree
    Second degree
    Third degree
Sinus arrest
Bradycardia-tachycardia syndrome

ATRIOVENTRICULAR BLOCK
First degree
Second degree
    Mobitz type I (Wenckebach phenomenon)
    Mobitz type II
    Higher degree (e.g., 2:1, 3:1)
Third degree
    Atrioventricular node
    His-Purkinje system

SINOATRIAL EXIT BLOCK. The sinus node may fire, but the impulse to the atrium can be delayed or interrupted periodically with loss of P wave (Fig. 59–6B); this abnormality, termed *SA exit block,* has been confirmed by intracardiac recordings. Because sinus node activity is not recorded on the surface ECG, however, the diagnosis of SA exit block is made from analysis of PP intervals. First-degree SA exit block is difficult to determine from the surface ECG. Diagnosis of second-degree SA block (type I, II, and higher degrees) can be established more easily. In type I SA block (SA Wenckebach or Mobitz type I), the PP interval progressively shortens after a pause (reflecting the dropped P wave), then the cycle repeats. In Mobitz type II or type II second-degree SA block, a sudden absence of an expected P wave is noted, and the pause is a multiple of the dominant PP cycle. With a higher degree of block, two or more P waves may be missing. A subsidiary pacemaker from the AV nodal junction usually emerges during these circumstances. Third-degree SA block means complete absence of sinus P waves (Fig. 59–6C).

SINUS ARREST. Sudden disappearance of P waves could be due to either SA exit block or cessation of sinus node pacemaker function. The two are difficult to distinguish unless the resultant PP interval has a predictable periodicity or is a multiple of sinus PP cycle (see Fig. 59–6B). SA exit block and sinus arrest must be distinguished from blocked PACs (see Fig. 59–6D) and sinus arrhythmia. Blocked PACs are likely to distort the ST-T segment and reset the sinus node so that the PP cycle with a blocked atrial premature contraction is less than two PP intervals. Sinus arrhythmia, which is a physiologic variation of PP change, usually follows the respiratory cycle (phasic sinus arrhythmia). The nonphasic variety may result in an abrupt sinus pause and may be confused with SND.

BRADYCARDIA-TACHYCARDIA SYNDROME. Because SND often represents atrial disease processes (e.g., fibrosis, degeneration, inflammation), coexistence of atrial tachyarrhythmias with bradycardia is not surprising. When an atrial tachycardia such as AF is terminated, the underlying rhythm may reveal sinus bradycardia, SA exit block, or even complete atrial standstill with an escape rhythm from a lower pacemaker in the AV node, the HPS, or the ventricles.

Atrioventricular Blocks

In a resting state, the normal AV node is capable of conducting 200 impulses per minute. With facilitation of AV nodal conduction owing to adrenergic stimulation or vagal withdrawal, this rate can reach 250 impulses per minute and even 300 impulses per minute in exceptional cases. With rapid atrial tachycardia, atrial flutter, and AF, some degree of AV block (in the AV node) is expected. Abnormal AV block is defined when some impulses are delayed or do not reach the ventricle during normal sinus rhythm or sinus tachycardia.

ELECTROPHYSIOLOGIC AND ELECTROCARDIOGRAPHIC FEATURES

FIRST-DEGREE ATRIOVENTRICULAR BLOCK (PROLONGED ATRIOVENTRICULAR CONDUCTION OR PR INTERVAL WITH 1:1 P-QRS RELATIONSHIP). The normal PR interval is 120 to 200 msec. Because the PR interval incorporates intra-atrial, AV nodal, and HPS conduction, it could be prolonged because of conduction delay in any of these areas. The intra-atrial conduction time can be estimated from the onset of the P wave on surface ECG to the onset of atrial deflection on the His bundle electrogram. The AH interval represents conduction through the AV node and is normally 60 to 140 msec; the HPS time estimated by the HV interval is 35 to 55 msec. When the PR interval is prolonged, delay is usually in the AV node (Fig. 59–7A); intra-atrial conduction delays and abnormal HPS conduction time seldom prolong the PR interval more than 200 msec and are highly unlikely to prolong it to more than 300 msec. Block in the AV node or within the His bundle does not alter the QRS complex morphology compared with sinus rhythm; if a fascicular or bundle-branch block occurs, infra-His block is likely.

SECOND-DEGREE ATRIOVENTRICULAR BLOCK (INTERMITTENT ATRIOVENTRICULAR CONDUCTION). With second-degree AV block, some P waves fail to produce a QRS complex. In type I, also called *Mobitz type I* or *Wenckebach phenomenon,* there is a progressive increase in the PR interval, despite a constant PP rate, until a P wave blocks and the cycle is repeated (Fig. 59–7B). Any P-to-QRS ratio can be seen (e.g., 3:2, 4:3, 5:4). In a typical Wenckebach phenomenon, the PR interval after the block is the shortest. The largest increase in PR interval occurs after the second conducted beat; the RR interval after the pause, which contains the blocked P wave, progressively shortens until the next pause (see Fig. 59–7B). The Wenckebach phenomenon can be

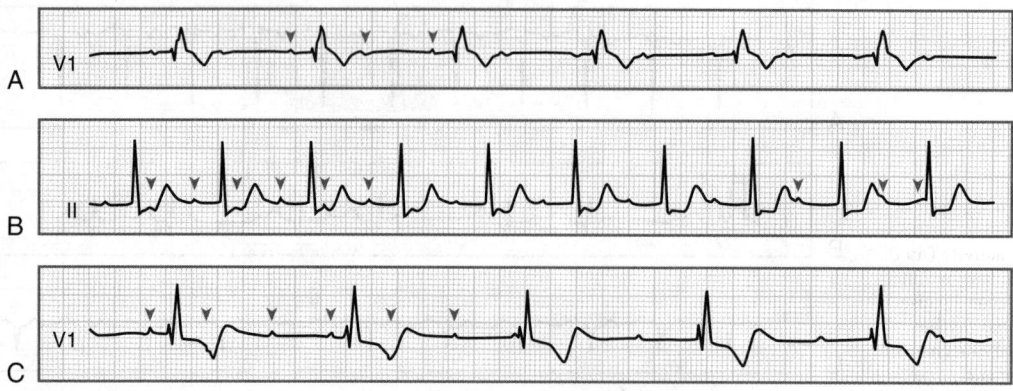

FIGURE 59-7 • Atrioventricular (AV) block. *A*, First-degree AV block (long PR interval). A 3:2 Wenckebach (Mobitz type I) second-degree AV block is seen in *B* and Mobitz type II second-degree block in *C*. Note the PR interval prolongation before the block in *B* but no PR increase in *C*. *D*, A sudden block of consecutive P waves with a normal PR interval and right bundle-branch block to no AV conduction associated with a normal PR interval and right bundle-branch block suggests infra-His block: After a long escape interval, a stable subsidiary pacemaker from the peripheral Purkinje network emerges (idioventricular rhythm). (Modified from Akhtar M: Examination of the heart: V. The electrogram. With permission from the American Heart Association, Dallas, Tx.)

found in all cardiac conducting tissues, but the magnitude of PR prolongation or shortening from beat to beat is maximum in the AV node and most noticeable. The AV node is the likely site of block when the PR interval increment with any subsequent PP cycle exceeds 100 msec, PR shortening is more than 100 msec after the block, or the absolute value of PR interval with any of the conducted beats is greater than or equal to 300 msec. Most but not all type I second-degree AV blocks are localized to the AV node.

Type II AV, or Mobitz type II, block causes a sudden, unexpected block of a P wave without a discernible change in the PR interval before the AV block (see Fig. 59–7*C*). AV block associated with marked prolongation of PR interval (>300 msec) is usually within the AV node, but type II AV block typically suggests disease in the HPS. When the QRS complex of the conducted beat is normal or narrow, the block is within the His bundle; an associated bundle-branch block or fascicular block suggests an infra-His site. With a normal or only slightly prolonged PR interval, HPS is a more likely location of block.

A 2:1, 3:1, or higher AV ratio of AV block may be noted with progression of Mobitz I or II to third-degree AV block. The site of block is more difficult to decipher, particularly when the PR interval of the conducted beat is normal. Documentation of progression from Mobitz type I or II is helpful in determining the site of block. In the presence of bundle-branch block and a normal PR interval, HPS block should be suspected (Fig. 59–8*A*). Conversely the AV node is the more likely site of block when the PR of the conducted beat is 300 msec or more because a junctional escape rhythm emerges from a relatively normal

HPS. When the HPS is the site of block, subsidiary pacemakers from a diseased HPS tend to be slower and permit several blocked P waves before an escape mechanism emerges. In the absence of marked vagal influences, a 3:1 or 4:1 ratio seldom is noted with AV nodal block during sinus rhythm so that HPS is the more likely site of block. Vagally mediated AV block is accompanied by concomitant slowing of sinus rate.

THIRD-DEGREE (COMPLETE) ATRIOVENTRICULAR BLOCK (NO ATRIOVENTRICULAR CONDUCTION). Complete failure of impulse propagation along the AV conduction system necessitates emergence of subsidiary pacemaker distal to the site of block. Normally the rate of resting pacemaker activity is highest in the sinus node (60 to 100 beats per minute), followed by the AV junction (40 to 60 beats per minute) and the bundle branch—Purkinje system (20 to 40 beats per minute). When the tissues expected to function as subsidiary pacemakers are abnormal, the rates may be even slower. During intact AV conduction, all of the subsidiary pacemakers remain suppressed (overdrive suppression). With abrupt cessation of AV conduction, the first subsidiary pacemaker response (often referred to as escape beat) is almost always slower than the subsequent rate from the same subsidiary foci; the rate of the emergent pacemaker below the site of block gradually accelerates (warm-up phenomenon) to its usual anticipated rate.

When the AV node is the site of third-degree AV block, the AV junctional pacemakers drive the ventricular rates (see Fig. 59–8*B*). The QRS complex morphology is similar to sinus beats and normally warms up to 40 to 60 beats per minute. With infra-His block, the

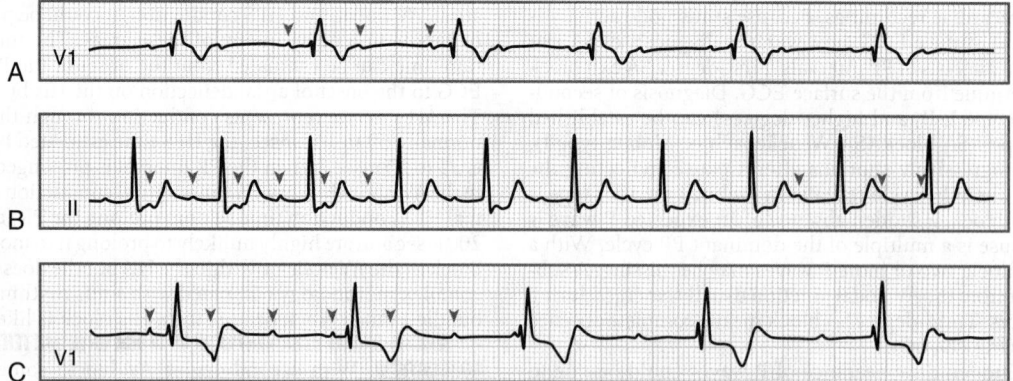

FIGURE 59-8 • A 2:1 and third-degree block. *A*, A 2:1 atrioventricular (AV) ratio, a slightly prolonged PR interval of conducted beats, and right bundle-branch block. The site of block is difficult to determine from the surface electrocardiogram (ECG). *B* and *C*, Third-degree block. The escape mechanism has a narrow QRS complex in *B* at a rate of 50 beats per minute and suggests intranodal block and a junctional subsidiary pacemaker. The escape mechanism in *C* is from the peripheral Purkinje network (idioventricular), as indicated by its slow rate (33 beats per minute) and wide complexes. In both panels, the atrial rates are constant and unrelated to ventricular rates, which also are constant but driven by a slower subsidiary pacemaker located distal to the sites of block (AV dissociation). The ECG leads are labeled. (Modified from Akhtar M: Examination of the heart: V. The electrogram. With permission from the American Heart Association, Dallas, Tx.)

escape rhythm shows a wide QRS complex, originates distally in the HPS (idioventricular), and has a relatively slow rate (see Fig. 59–8C). When the block is within the His bundle and the escape rhythm is also in the His bundle distal to the block, a narrow QRS complex appears at a slower than expected escape rate because of the disease process involving the junctional pacemakers.

AV dissociation occurs when the atria and ventricles are driven by different pacemakers. AV dissociation per se does not represent an arrhythmic entity and is due to AV or ventriculoatrial block. Complete AV block requires a subsidiary pacemaker to depolarize the ventricles; in this situation, the P wave is faster than the QRS complexes, and the two are unrelated (see Fig. 59–8B, C). AV dissociation also occurs when the rate of subsidiary pacemakers is faster than a normal sinus, such as nonparoxysmal junctional tachycardia (see Fig. 59–2F) or ventricular tachycardia; if there is retrograde (ventriculoatrial) block, the atria are driven by the SA node or other atrial pacemakers. *Isorhythmic AV dissociation* is the term used when atria and ventricles are driven independently but at similar rates.

Clinical Manifestations

Aside from medications such as digitalis and antiarrhythmic drugs and vagal influences, the exact cause for SND is frequently difficult to determine. The most common causes for SND are muscle degeneration, fibrosis with advanced age, and cardiac pathology such as coronary artery disease. Acute inferior wall myocardial ischemia or infarction associated with disease of the proximal right coronary artery may cause transient SND. Other, less common causes include acute or chronic inflammation from myocarditis or pericarditis and prior cardiac surgery with trauma to the sinus node. Congenital SND and complete atrial standstill with no detectable sinus node activity are seen rarely.

AV nodal blocks can be caused by digitalis, antiarrhythmic drugs, and vagal influences. Involvement of the AV junctional area with any inflammatory or other disease process can result in AV nodal block of varying degrees. The most common cause of chronic AV block in the HPS is progressive fibrosis and/or calcification in the HPS with aging or myocardial fibrosis from any cause. Because of the proximity of aortic and mitral valves to the distal His bundle and proximal bundle branches, annular calcification or valve surgery can cause acute or chronic intra-His and infra-His block. Myocardial infiltration by an infectious agent (i.e., Chagas' disease) is an important cause of chronic heart block in Latin American countries. Acute inferior wall ischemia and/or infarction can cause various degrees of AV nodal block because of ischemia in the nodal artery distributions. Involvement of HPS during acute anterior MI can lead to bundle-branch block and/or AV block.

Sinus bradycardia and various degrees of AV nodal blocks also are noted during sleep even in otherwise healthy people. Asymptomatic first-degree and second-degree AV block, particularly when partially or completely reversed by exercise, points toward a benign condition. Persistent second-degree and third-degree AV nodal block during the waking hours and during activity is abnormal and often is associated with symptoms of bradycardia, including dizziness, fatigue, exertional dyspnea, aggravation of heart failure, near-syncope, or syncope. Third-degree AV block with a good junctional escape mechanism that accelerates during exercise, as often noted in patients with congenital AV block, may remain asymptomatic. Patients with congenital heart block may not appreciate their potential for a more active lifestyle because of the lack of a reference point but feel much better when an appropriate heart rate acceleration can be achieved after pacemaker therapy.

Bradycardias of all types may be secondary to profound vagal influences, as seen with neurally mediated syndromes such as vasovagal episodes, vomiting, abdominal surgery, and upper and lower gastrointestinal invasive procedures. Periods of prolonged sinus arrest and AV nodal block with marked suppression of subsidiary pacemaker can occur and lead to symptomatic asystole. Vasovagal (neurocardiogenic) syndromes are a common cause of syncope in relatively healthy populations (Chapters 58 and 435); in most cases, vasodepression (hypotension) is the primary cause of syncope, and rate control alone does not relieve symptoms.

 Treatment

Asymptomatic SND or AV nodal block requires no therapy. Acute management of symptomatic SND and second-degree and third-degree AV block includes administration of intravenous atropine (1 mg) or isoproterenol (usually 1 to 2 µg/min infusion) to increase the heart rate. Temporary cardiac pacing may be needed. When SND or AV block is due to transient abnormalities, such as drug-induced or acute ischemic syndromes, temporary pacing is usually sufficient; however, when infra-His or intra-His block is suspected (e.g., exercise-induced AV block or asymptomatic Mobitz type II block) and the site can be documented with His bundle recording, permanent pacing is indicated. For all forms of persistent symptomatic SND or second-degree or third-degree AV block, permanent pacing is the therapy of choice (Chapter 61). Nevertheless, even prolonged paroxysmal asystole resulting from a neurocardiogenic mechanism is not an indication for permanent pacing; instead, pharmacologic therapy that relieves hypotension controls bradycardic symptoms as well. As a general rule, bradycardia in individuals younger than age 55 is vagal in origin and does not require permanent pacing unless proved otherwise.

Future Directions

Implantable devices, such as pacing, atrial tissue ablation, and atrial defibrillation therapy, are likely to be used more frequently because of technologic advances and patients' preferences, although it is conceivable that pharmacologic agents with more targeted effects and fewer side effects will be developed.

Grade A

1. Roy D, Talajic M, Dorian P, et al: Amiodarone to prevent recurrence of atrial fibrillation. N Engl J Med 2000;342:913–920.
2. Hohnloser SH, Kuck K-H, Lilienthal J: Rhythm or rate control in atrial fibrillation—Pharmacological Intervention in Atrial Fibrillation (PIAF): A randomized trial. Lancet 2000;356:1789–1794.
3. Wyse DG, Waldo AL, DiMarco JP, et al: A comparison of rate control and rhythm control in patients with atrial fibrillation. N Engl J Med 2002;347:1825–1833.
4. Van Gelder IC, Hagens VE, Bosker HA, et al: A comparison of rate control and rhythm control in patients with recurrent persistent atrial fibrillation. N Engl J Med 2002;347:1834–1840.
5. Taylor FC, Cohen H, Ebrahim S: Systematic review of long term anticoagulation or antiplatelet treatment in patients with non-rheumatic atrial fibrillation. BMJ 2001;322:321–326.

SUGGESTED READINGS

Fuster V, Ryden LE, Asinger RW, et al: ACC/AHA/ESC guidelines for the management of patients with atrial fibrillation: Executive summary. A Report of the American College of Cardiology/American Heart Association Task Force on Practice Guidelines and the European Society of Cardiology Committee for Practice Guidelines and Policy Conferences (Committee to Develop Guidelines for the Management of Patients With Atrial Fibrillation): Developed in Collaboration with the North American Society of Pacing and Electrophysiology. J Am Coll Cardiol 2001;38:1231–1266. *A consensus statement.*

Malouf JF, Ammash NM, Chandrasekaran K, et al: Critical appraisal of transesophageal echocardiography in cardioversion of atrial fibrillation. Am J Med 2002;113:587–595. *Review of the current standing of TEE-facilitated early cardioversion.*

Peters NS, Schilling RJ, Kanagaratnam P, Markides V: Atrial fibrillation: Strategies to control, combat, and cure. Lancet 2002;359:593–603. *A comprehensive review.*

Vidaillet H, Granada JF, Chyou PH, et al: A population-based study of mortality among patients with atrial fibrillation or flutter. Am J Med 2002;113:365–370. *In the general population, both atrial flutter and atrial fibrillation are independent predictors of increased late mortality.*

Wellens HJ: Contemporary management of atrial flutter. Circulation 2002;106:649–652. *Emphasizes roles of cardioversion and catheter ablation.*

60 VENTRICULAR ARRHYTHMIAS AND SUDDEN DEATH

Bruce B. Lerman

PREMATURE VENTRICULAR COMPLEXES

Electrocardiographic Features

Premature ventricular complexes (PVCs) are ubiquitous arrhythmias that are recognized on the surface electrocardiogram (ECG) by their wide (generally >120 msec) and bizarre QRS morphology,

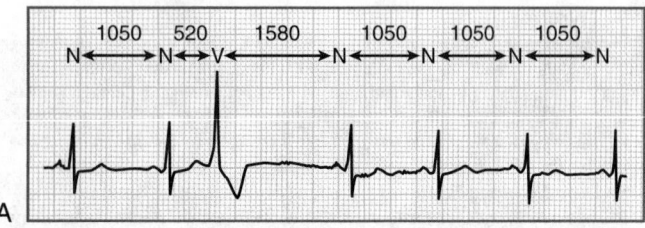

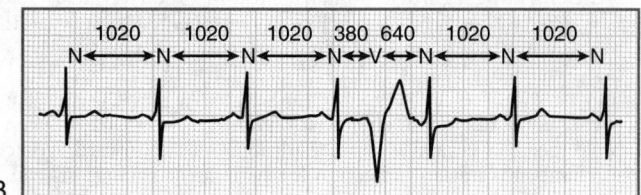

FIGURE 60–1 • Multiform premature ventricular contractions (PVCs). *A,* PVC followed by a compensatory pause. *B,* Recording from the same individual shows an interpolated PVC of a different morphology. Tracings are from lead I. N = normal sinus beat; V = ventricular premature beat. Intervals are given in milliseconds.

occurring independently of atrial activation (P waves). Late cycle PVCs may follow a P wave that occurs on time and are identified by a shorter than normal PR interval. PVCs may be due to enhanced automaticity, triggered activity, or re-entry.

Most PVCs are followed by a "compensatory pause" because the PVC fails to conduct retrogradely to the atria and cannot affect or reset the electrical activity of the sinus node. The interval between the first sinus beat and the PVC plus the interval between the PVC and the next sinus beat equals two normal sinus intervals (Fig. 60–1). Occasionally, PVCs may be interpolated between two sinus beats (i.e., produce no pause), and, rarely, PVCs may penetrate and reset the sinus node.

PVCs may be isolated or occur in groups. Two consecutive PVCs are termed a *couplet.* Three or more consecutive PVCs at a rate of 100 beats per minute or more are termed *ventricular tachycardia* (VT). Single PVCs may occur sporadically or as bigeminy (every other beat is a PVC), trigeminy (every third beat is a PVC), or higher order periodicities. A patient may manifest PVCs with two or more different morphologies, in which case the ectopy is termed *multiform.* Single PVCs, regardless of whether or not they occur sporadically or in a periodic pattern, sometimes are referred to as "simple" ventricular ectopy, whereas multiform PVCs, closely coupled PVCs (so-called R-on-T), ventricular couplets, and nonsustained VT are referred to as "complex" ventricular ectopy. Fusion beats result from simultaneous activation of the ventricle by a normally conducted supraventricular beat and a concurrent PVC and have a morphology with some similarities to the supraventricular and ventricular beats.

Epidemiology

Ventricular ectopy is exceedingly rare in infants but increases in frequency with age. PVCs occur in patients with and without structural heart disease. Holter monitoring (Chapter 58) reveals at least one PVC in 40 to 75% of normal adults and complex ventricular ectopy in 5 to 10% of normal adults. PVCs occur with greater frequency and complexity in patients with structural heart disease, especially ischemic and valvular heart disease and idiopathic cardiomyopathy. PVCs also may occur in the setting of drug toxicity (e.g., digitalis intoxication) or electrolyte disturbances (e.g., hypokalemia).

Prognosis

PVC frequency and complexity have no prognostic significance for patients without structural heart disease. Among patients with prior myocardial infarction (MI), frequent (>10 PVCs/hr) and complex ventricular ectopy are associated with an increased risk of death. This risk is strongly concentrated in patients with depressed left ventricular function, however. Likewise, among patients with valvular heart disease, sudden death is rare when ventricular

function is normal (e.g., uncomplicated mitral valve prolapse), but risk increases when complex ventricular ectopy is observed in depressed left ventricular function. R-on-T PVCs may be more likely to result in ventricular fibrillation (VF) or polymorphic VT than later coupled PVCs. This relationship is weak, however, and has limited prognostic utility.

Sustained re-entrant ventricular arrhythmias likely result from the interaction of a critically timed triggering event (PVC) with an appropriate substrate (myocardial scarring resulting in mechanical and electrical ventricular dysfunction). Owing to the high prevalence of ventricular ectopy in patients with structural heart disease, however, the predictive value for future events is low. Even among patients for whom PVCs indicate a poor prognosis, antiarrhythmic drug therapy aimed specifically at suppressing PVCs does not provide benefit. Suppression of PVCs with encainide, flecainide, or moricizine results in a significant increase in mortality in patients with frequent PVCs after MI.

Treatment

Because there is no evidence that treatment directed at suppressing PVCs improves overall mortality, the primary indication for treatment is to relieve symptoms. Although most PVCs are asymptomatic, in some patients they may result in troubling palpitations. Frequent PVCs also may cause a pounding sensation in the neck secondary to cannon a waves from atrioventricular dissociation. Because PVCs result in a reduced stroke volume, patients with frequent PVCs occasionally may have fatigue, exertional intolerance, dyspnea, and lightheadedness.

Most patients with symptomatic PVCs in the absence of structural heart disease can be managed with a β-blocker. Class I or class III antiarrhythmic drugs may be considered, but the potential for proarrhythmia and organ toxicity must be weighed (Chapter 62). An alternative to antiarrhythmic drug therapy for highly symptomatic patients, particularly for patients without structural heart disease whose PVCs originate from the right ventricular outflow tract, is radiofrequency catheter ablation of the arrhythmogenic focus (Chapter 61).

PARASYSTOLE

Ventricular parasystole results when an automatic focus arises from the ventricles and fires independently of supraventricular impulses conducted through the atrioventricular node. Classically a surrounding region of depressed conductivity protects the focus by creating complete entrance block that prevents supraventricular beats from resetting the focus. Independence of the parasystolic focus from the underlying rhythm is shown by variable coupling intervals between the ectopic beats and the preceding sinus beats and a fixed minimum time interval between PVCs, with any longer interectopic intervals being integer multiples of this minimum interval (reflecting exit block from the parasystolic focus) (Fig. 60–2).

The entrance block surrounding the parasystolic focus can be partial rather than complete, so conducted supraventricular beats may influence depolarization of the parasystolic focus and either delay or accelerate its next discharge. Clinically, parasystole may manifest as sporadic PVCs or as bigeminy or trigeminy. Although generally benign, parasystolic rhythms may result in PVCs at a critical point during repolarization (R-on-T) and precipitate VF.

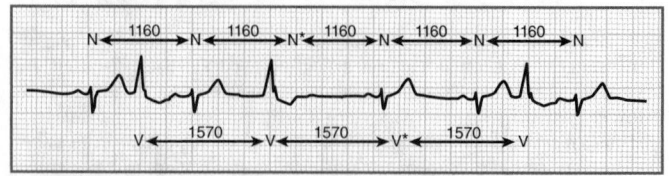

FIGURE 60–2 • Parasystole: Sinus rhythm with a competing ventricular parasystolic focus. N = normal sinus beat; V = ventricular parasystolic beat; N* = timing of normal sinus discharge (occurring during the ventricular refractory period); V* = timing of ventricular parasystolic discharge (occurring during the ventricular refractory period). Intervals are given in milliseconds.

ACCELERATED IDIOVENTRICULAR RHYTHM

Electrocardiographic Features

Accelerated idioventricular rhythm (AIVR) refers to an ectopic ventricular rhythm characterized by three or more consecutive PVCs occurring at a rate faster than the normal ventricular escape rate of 30 to 40 beats per minute but slower than VT. No single rate differentiates "fast" AIVR from "slow" VT, however. In general, the upper rate limit for AIVR is 100 to 120 beats/min. Because AIVR has different prognostic and therapeutic implications than VT, it is important to recognize AIVR's gradual onset, acceleration ("warm-up"), and deceleration before termination (consistent with an automatic mechanism) compared with the paroxysmal initiation and abrupt termination characteristic of re-entrant VT. AIVR is generally brief (<1 minute) and is suppressed when the sinus rate exceeds its rate.

Clinical Manifestations

AIVR occurs most often in acute MI, particularly after reperfusion, and usually resolves spontaneously. AIVR also is observed in patients with rheumatic heart disease, dilated cardiomyopathy, acute myocarditis, hypertensive heart disease, digitalis toxicity, and cocaine intoxication and in patients without structural heart disease. It is generally benign, and because most runs of AIVR are brief and asymptomatic, it requires no specific treatment. If patients with left ventricular dysfunction do not tolerate AIVR owing to the loss of atrioventricular synchrony, increasing the atrial rate with atropine or by pacing suppresses AIVR.

VENTRICULAR TACHYCARDIA

Definitions

VT, which originates below the bundle of His at a rate greater than 100 beats per minute, is a wide-complex rhythm that may be monomorphic (uniform) or polymorphic with beat-to-beat changes in the QRS configuration (Fig. 60–3). Sustained VT persists for 30 seconds or more or requires termination because of hemodynamic instability. Sustained polymorphic VT is usually unstable and often degenerates into VF. Sustained monomorphic VT may be stable for long periods or, with faster rates or myocardial ischemia, may degenerate into polymorphic VT or VF. Torsades de pointes (TdP), a particular form of polymorphic VT, has a characteristic morphology ("twisting around a point") and is associated with prolongation of the QT interval on the surface ECG.

Electrocardiographic Features

It is important to distinguish monomorphic VT from supraventricular tachycardia with aberrant conduction because both present as wide-complex tachycardias (Table 60–1). Features on the surface ECG permit differentiation of VT from supraventricular tachycardia with an overall accuracy that approaches 90%. Atrioventricular dissociation, which can be identified on the surface ECG in 25% of VTs, strongly suggests a ventricular origin. The presence of a one-to-one

Table 60–1 • ELECTROCARDIOGRAPHIC CHARACTERISTICS OF VENTRICULAR TACHYCARDIA
ATRIOVENTRICULAR RELATIONSHIP
Atrioventricular dissociation
Sinus capture beats
Fusion beats
QRS WIDTH
Left bundle-branch block: >160 msec
Right bundle-branch block: >140 msec
QRS AXIS
Extreme left axis (−90° to −180°)
Right-axis deviation in the presence of left bundle-branch block (+90° to +180°)
QRS MORPHOLOGY
Right bundle-branch block
Morphology in V_1
Monophasic R wave
Biphasic (qR or RS)
Triphasic with R > R′
Morphology in V_6
R/S ratio < 1
Left bundle-branch block
Morphology in V_1
Broad R wave (>30 msec)
Onset of R wave to nadir of S wave >60 msec
Notched downstroke in lead V_1
Morphology in V_6
QR or QS complex
Onset of R wave to nadir of S wave >100 msec in any precordial lead
Absence of RS wave in any precordial lead
Postitive or negative precordial concordance

atrioventricular relationship does not imply a supraventricular origin, however, because some patients with VT have one-to-one retrograde conduction from the ventricles to the atria during tachycardia. Capture and fusion beats also suggest VT but usually are seen only during slow VT. A capture beat represents activation of the ventricles by a supraventricular impulse that conducts via the His-Purkinje system. This beat prematurely "captures" both ventricles during VT and results in a single narrow QRS interposed between wide tachycardia complexes. Other features on the surface ECG that permit differentiation of VT from supraventricular tachycardia include QRS width, axis, and morphology. Although helpful in most situations, these morphologic criteria are not 100% specific. An irregular wide-complex rhythm with essentially a single QRS morphology raises the possibility of atrial fibrillation with ventricular pre-excitation (Chapter 59), particularly in patients without structural heart disease.

Other diagnostic measures include the response of the tachycardia to vagal maneuvers and adenosine. Most VT is insensitive to vagal maneuvers, such as carotid sinus massage and Valsalva, and to adenosine, whereas most forms of supraventricular tachycardia terminate or persist with transient high-grade atrioventricular block in response to these maneuvers. Idiopathic right ventricular outflow tract tachycardia in patients with normal hearts also may terminate with vagal maneuvers and adenosine, however.

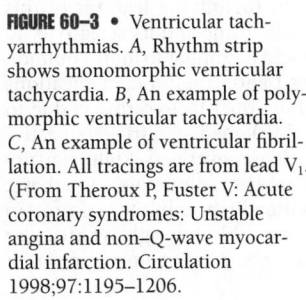

FIGURE 60–3 • Ventricular tachyarrhythmias. *A,* Rhythm strip shows monomorphic ventricular tachycardia. *B,* An example of polymorphic ventricular tachycardia. *C,* An example of ventricular fibrillation. All tracings are from lead V_1. (From Theroux P, Fuster V: Acute coronary syndromes: Unstable angina and non–Q-wave myocardial infarction. Circulation 1998;97:1195–1206.

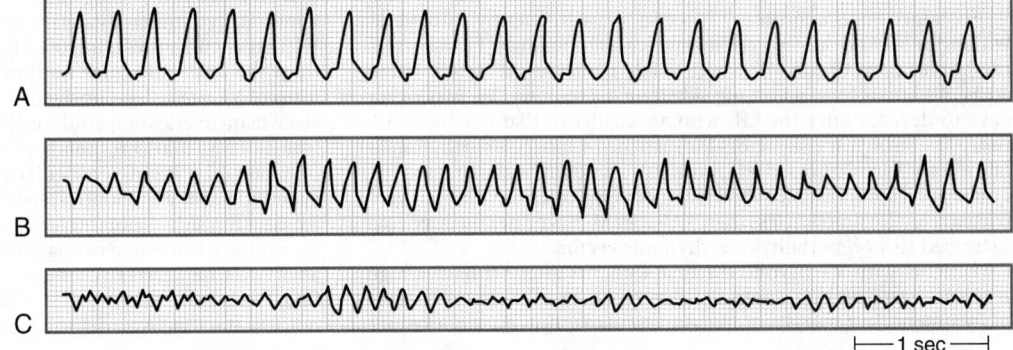

├── 1 sec ──┤

Clinical Manifestations and Acute Treatment

Patients with monomorphic VT may present with sudden cardiac death or symptoms of impaired consciousness, such as syncope or near-syncope. Associated symptoms may include chest pain, dyspnea, and palpitations. Occasionally, patients with VT and slow rates may be asymptomatic, and hemodynamic stability is unreliable in distinguishing VT from supraventricular tachycardia.

Physical examination during VT may reveal signs of cardiogenic shock, including pulselessness, apnea, cool extremities, and cyanosis. Physical examination may reveal hypotension or signs of heart failure, such as pulmonary rales or jugular venous distention. Characteristic features during VT include cannon a waves and variable intensity of S_1, both of which result from atrioventricular dissociation.

Acute therapy for VT depends on the degree of hemodynamic instability that accompanies the arrhythmia. For stable VT in patients with left ventricular dysfunction, pharmacologic therapy should be initiated with either intravenous amiodarone (150 mg over 10 minutes, followed by 1 mg/min over the next 6 hours, then 0.5 mg/min over 18 hours) or lidocaine (bolus dose of 0.5 to 0.75 mg/kg, followed by additional boluses of 0.5 to 0.75 mg/kg at 5- to 10-minute intervals, up to a maximal dose of 3 mg/kg and maintained with an infusion of 1 to 4 mg/min). If these drugs are ineffective, intravenous procainamide (maximal dose 17 mg/kg), at an infusion rate of 20 to 30 mg/min, can be considered (Chapter 62). If pharmacologic therapy is unsuccessful for hemodynamically stable VT, synchronized cardioversion with a direct-current shock may be required, beginning with 50 to 100 J and increasing to 360 J if necessary.

For patients with severe signs or symptoms during VT, such as chest pain or myocardial ischemia, heart failure or shortness of breath, decreased level of consciousness, or hypotension (systolic blood pressure <90 mm Hg), immediate synchronous cardioversion is indicated, with subsequent intravenous antiarrhythmic therapy to maintain sinus rhythm. After resuscitation from VT, the patient must be evaluated for a possible primary cause, such as electrolyte imbalance, acid-base disturbance, hypoxemia, drug toxicity, and myocardial ischemia.

Rx Diagnosis and Treatment

Invasive electrophysiologic testing (Chapter 58) can guide pharmacologic (Chapter 62) or device-based therapy (Chapter 61) in patients with sustained monomorphic VT and previous MI. In these patients, a sustained ventricular tachyarrhythmia can be induced with programmed stimulation in approximately 90%.

ISCHEMIC HEART DISEASE

VT during acute MI may be monomorphic or polymorphic. Sustained ventricular arrhythmias within the first 48 hours of an acute MI do not convey an increased risk of future spontaneous arrhythmias. Coronary revascularization or antianginal medical therapy may be sufficient to control arrhythmias resulting from acute ischemia. Antiarrhythmic medications, such as lidocaine, also are useful to control recurrent sustained arrhythmias in this setting. Polymorphic VT and VF also can result from coronary vasospasm, which may occur in diseased or normal coronary arteries.

Sustained monomorphic VT occurs most frequently in patients with prior MI and depressed left ventricular function. VT arises from the border zone of the MI, where viable myocytes scattered within areas of fibrosis form a chronic substrate for re-entry. VT may occur days to decades after the MI, with an incidence that declines with time. The strongest risk factors for sustained ventricular arrhythmias late after MI are depressed left ventricular function and increased frequency and complexity of ventricular ectopy. Patients with a left ventricular ejection fraction less than 30% after MI have a nearly three-fold increased risk of mortality or arrhythmic events.

Patients with VT beyond the first 48 hours after MI have a high recurrence rate, with an annual risk that approaches 30% in the absence of treatment. In general, coronary revascularization does not reduce the risk of recurrent VT arising from a chronic substrate after a remote MI, and definitive antiarrhythmic therapy is required. Randomized trials have shown the superiority of implantable cardioverter-defibrillators (ICDs) over antiarrhythmic medications in patients with sustained monomorphic VT. Catheter ablation may have an adjunctive role for controlling frequent ventricular arrhythmias.

CARDIOMYOPATHY

Monomorphic and polymorphic VT occur in patients with nonischemic dilated cardiomyopathy (Chapter 73). The signal-averaged ECG and invasive programmed stimulation (Chapter 58) have limited sensitivity and specificity for predicting future risk in these patients. VF, polymorphic VT, and, to a lesser extent, monomorphic VT occur in hypertrophic cardiomyopathy owing to myocyte disarray, fibrosis, or ischemia. ICDs are effective for primary and secondary prevention in patients with hypertrophic cardiomyopathy. ICDs implanted in high-risk patients, including patients with syncope, nonsustained VT, a family history of sudden death, or left ventricular wall thickness greater than or equal to 30 mm, have an appropriate yearly discharge rate of 5% (patients with documented VF have an 11% annual discharge rate), with most shocks occurring during sedentary periods. Other potential risk factors for sudden cardiac death (SCD) in these patients are a blunted exercise blood pressure response and the presence of myocardial bridging of the left anterior descending artery in children.

ARRHYTHMOGENIC RIGHT VENTRICULAR DYSPLASIA

Arrhythmogenic right ventricular dysplasia (ARVD) is a cardiomyopathy characterized by myocyte loss with fibroadipose replacement of the right ventricle. The condition is usually sporadic, but familial forms have been identified, and the condition has been linked to at least seven chromosomal loci and mutations in two genes: the cardiac ryanodine receptor gene (see later: catecholaminergic VT) and the gene for plakoglobin, a component of desmosomes (Naxos disease—ARVD, palmoplantar keratoderma, and wooly hair). ARVD causes SCD in adolescents and young adults. Patients develop re-entry involving diseased portions of the right ventricle.

The surface ECG of patients with ARVD may show a terminal notch on the QRS complex (ϵ wave) in lead V_1 and T-wave inversions in the anterior precordial leads. Echocardiography (Chapter 51) and right ventriculography show abnormalities of the right ventricle, including wall motion abnormalities and aneurysmal dilation. Electron-beam computed tomography and magnetic resonance imaging (Chapters 52 and 53) show fatty replacement of the right ventricle, thinning of the right ventricular wall, and wall motion abnormalities. Endomyocardial biopsy may show characteristic fatty replacement and fibrosis but has limited sensitivity owing to the patchy nature of the cardiomyopathy. During invasive electrophysiologic testing, multiple morphologies of monomorphic VT may be inducible, usually with a left bundle-branch block configuration.

Therapeutic modalities for treating arrhythmogenic right ventricular dysplasia include antiarrhythmic medication and an ICD. Catheter ablation, although rarely curative, may ameliorate frequent ventricular arrhythmias.

IDIOPATHIC VENTRICULAR TACHYCARDIA

The most common form of idiopathic monomorphic VT typically arises from the right ventricular outflow tract and has a left bundle-branch block morphology and inferior axis. It may present as a sustained arrhythmia facilitated by exercise or as repetitive nonsustained VT that occurs at rest. In 10% of patients, tachycardia may originate from the left ventricular outflow tract. Identifying features of this form of VT are its responsiveness to adenosine and its sensitivity to vagal maneuvers, verapamil, and β-blockers. Similar to more common forms of VT, it also responds to class I antiarrhythmic medications (Chapter 62). Right ventricular outflow tract tachycardia is due to cyclic adenosine monophosphate (cAMP)–mediated triggered activity, which results from intracellular calcium overload. Right ventricular outflow tract tachycardia can be cured by radiofrequency catheter ablation (Chapter 61). A somatic mutation in the inhibitory G protein ($G_{\alpha i2}$) has been identified and is responsible for right ventricular outflow tract tachycardia in some patients. A less common form of monomorphic VT that also occurs in patients without structural heart disease is *fascicular re-entrant tachycardia*. This arrhythmia usually originates in the left ventricular region of the left posterior fascicle and has a right bundle-branch block, left superior axis morphology. The tachycardia terminates in response to verapamil (but not to adenosine, vagal maneuvers, or β-blockers) and is readily treated by radiofrequency catheter ablation.

LONG QT SYNDROME

The *congenital* long QT syndromes (LQTS) are related to cardiac ion channel defects that affect cardiac repolarization, resulting in prolongation of the QT interval and TdP. In the United States, the estimated prevalence of LQTS is 1 in 7000. Traditionally, congenital LQTS was classified into two forms: the Romano-Ward syndrome (more common; autosomal dominant and associated with normal hearing); and the Jervell and Lange-Nielsen syndrome (autosomal recessive and associated with congenital sensorineural deafness).

Molecular genetics has identified at least five genes that account for five genotypic designations (representing 50% of patients with LQTS). The most common form, LQT1, accounts for approximately 45% of genotyped patients. The responsible gene, *KvLQT1* (also known as *KCNQ1*), is found on chromosome 11 and encodes a potassium channel pore-forming α subunit. Coexpression of *KvLQT1* with *KCNE1*, which encodes the non–pore-forming minK β subunit, forms I_{Ks}, the slowly activating component of the delayed rectifier potassium current. The next most common form is LQT2 (40%), which is related to the *HERG* (or *KCNH2*) gene located on chromosome 7. *HERG* encodes a potassium channel α subunit, and four *HERG* subunits assemble with *MiRP1* (*minK* related protein; β subunit), which is encoded by *KCNE2* to form I_{Kr}, the rapidly activating component of the delayed rectifier potassium current. Failure of these potassium channels to activate normally ("loss of function") prolongs the action potential duration and provokes early afterdepolarizations. Mutations in *MinK* and *MiRP1* also are linked to compromised potassium flux and inherited LQT5 and LQT6. LQT3 (10%) is due to a mutation in the gene *SCN5A*, which encodes the cardiac sodium channel and is located on chromosome 3. Failure of this channel to inactivate prolongs the action potential duration. Mutations in one allele (heterozygous condition) of any one of the five known genes responsible for the LQTS causes the Romano-Ward syndrome, whereas homozygous mutations in *KvLQT1* or *minK* or the compound heterozygous condition (simultaneous heterozygous mutations in the two genes) results in the Jervell and Lange-Nielsen syndrome, suggesting that a mutation of a single allele is sufficient to produce QT prolongation, whereas a mutation of both alleles is necessary to produce congenital deafness. The gene or ion channel involved in LQT4 (chromosome 4) is unknown.

The most common trigger for a cardiac event in patients with LQT1 is exercise (particularly swimming), followed by emotional stress (fear, anger, or startle response). More than 80% of patients have a first cardiac event by age 20, whereas the median age is higher in the LQT2 and LQT3. In LQT2 patients, the most frequent precipitant is emotional stress (auditory stimuli), followed by sleep or rest without arousal. Most events in LQT3 patients occur during sleep or rest, suggesting they are at higher risk at slow heart rates.

The corrected QT interval (QTc) in LQTS is usually greater than 0.46 in men and 0.47 in women (each associated with 100% specificity), although one third of affected individuals may have QTc intervals that fall within the normal or nondiagnostic range. A QTc interval less than or equal to 0.40 in men and less than or equal to 0.42 in women virtually excludes LQTS. The QT interval fails to shorten normally or may prolong with exercise in patients with LQT1 and to a lesser extent in patients with LQT2. Other diagnostic features on the surface ECG include ST-T wave patterns. In LQT1, the T wave may be broad-based or normal with late onset. Very young patients may have a juvenile ST-T wave pattern. LQT2 patients usually have bifid or notched T waves, whereas LQT3 patients have either late-onset peaked/biphasic T waves or asymmetrical peaked T waves. T-wave alternans also can be observed in LQTS.

A genotype-specific approach to therapy potentially may improve long-term outcome in patients with the congenital LQTS. Patients with LQT1 respond well to β-blockers and should refrain from strenuous physical activity. β-Blockers also are recommended for patients with LQT2 because of their risk to auditory stimuli. Although patients with LQT1 and LQT2 have higher rates of syncope, patients with LQT3 have the highest mortality rate, and ICDs should be strongly considered in these patients, along with ancillary measures, including left sympathectomy and cardiac pacing. β-Blockers may cause potential harm in these patients.

The *acquired* LQTS, which predisposes to TdP, occurs more frequently in women; usually is related to drugs that block the potassium channel I_{Kr}; and is potentiated by subclinical LQTS, hypokalemia, and bradycardia. Evidence suggests that there may be a genetic predisposition to these types of arrhythmias because sporadic mutations and single nucleotide polymorphisms in *MiRP1* have been identified in some patients. Offending agents may include tricyclic antidepressants, phenothiazines, nonsedating antihistamines such as terfenadine and astemizole (whose levels may be elevated by drugs that reduce hepatic metabolism by inhibiting cytochrome P450 3A4 enzymes, such as ketoconazole), antibiotics (including macrolide antibiotics, quinolone antibiotics, sulfamethoxazole, and pentamidine), the lipid-lowering drug probucol, and class IA and class III antiarrhythmic medications. A liquid protein diet, starvation, central nervous system disease, and electrolyte abnormalities such as hypokalemia and hypomagnesemia also may predispose to TdP. Therapy for the acquired LQTS is directed at reversing the metabolic abnormalities or withholding the offending medication. Infusion of magnesium and temporary pacing decrease the QT interval and prevent pause-dependent arrhythmias, whereas isoproterenol is a temporizing measure to increase the sinus rate. Class IB antiarrhythmic medications (Chapter 62), which tend to shorten the action potential duration and decrease the QT interval, also may be used.

BRUGADA SYNDROME

Brugada syndrome occurs in young people (mean age 30 to 40 years) without known structural heart disease and is thought to be responsible for the sudden and unexpected nocturnal death syndrome in Southeast Asian men. The syndrome is associated with malignant ventricular arrhythmias, including VF, and has an autosomal dominant inheritance with variable expression. The characteristic finding on ECG is right precordial ST-segment elevation that also may be associated with a right ventricular conduction delay. These ECG findings may be transient and can be provoked with sodium channel blockers, such as procainamide and flecainide (approximate positive predictive value 35%). The QT interval is normal. In some patients, mutations in the *SCN5A* gene, which results in diminished inward sodium current, is thought to result in the heterogeneous loss of the action potential dome in the right ventricular epicardium, giving rise to the ST-segment elevation and the electrophysiologic milieu that leads to VF. Right precordial ST-segment elevation also can be observed in normal subjects and in patients with other clinical conditions. In survivors of aborted SCD, the signal-averaged ECG is often positive, but induction of polymorphic VT or VF is variable during electrophysiologic studies (positive and negative predictive value about 50%). Magnetic resonance imaging, cardiac catheterization, and myocardial biopsy are normal. An ICD is the most effective treatment for symptomatic patients. Although asymptomatic Brugada patients have a more favorable prognosis than symptomatic patients, they are still at increased risk of sudden death compared with the general population.

CATECHOLAMINERGIC POLYMORPHIC VENTRICULAR TACHYCARDIA

Catecholaminergic polymorphic VT has been identified in children and young adults with normal hearts; sporadic and familial forms have been described. Patients may present with bidirectional VT, polymorphic VT, or idiopathic VF. The arrhythmias are precipitated by exercise, catecholamines, or emotional stress and usually are associated with syncope or SCD. Children may be misdiagnosed as having a seizure disorder. Patients often respond to β-blockers. Missense mutations in the myocardial ryanodine receptor gene, which controls calcium release from the sarcoplasmic reticulum during excitation-contraction coupling, have been identified in patients with this arrhythmia.

A less well-delineated form of idiopathic VF is known as *short-coupled TdP*. This entity occurs in patients at a mean age of 35 years who have no structural heart disease. The QT interval is normal, but the initiating ventricular extrasystole characteristically has a short coupling interval. Initiation of the arrhythmia with adrenergic stress is the exception, not the rule. Therapeutic data are sparse. Anecdotally, verapamil has had modest efficacy, but an ICD should be strongly considered.

POSTOPERATIVE TETRALOGY OF FALLOT

Patients who have undergone surgical repair of tetralogy of Fallot through right ventriculotomy are at an increased risk of sudden death and VT (Chapter 65). Tachycardia is due to re-entry around the right ventriculotomy scar in the infundibulum. Catheter or surgical ablation or resection is effective in preventing recurrent VT.

BUNDLE-BRANCH RE-ENTRY

Patients with dilated cardiomyopathy and disease in the His-Purkinje system are prone to develop a specific form of VT known as bundle-branch re-entry, in which the right and left bundle branches participate in a macro re-entrant tachycardia circuit, with one branch involved in the antegrade limb and the other in the retrograde limb. The tachycardia typically shows a left bundle-branch block morphology and often is associated with presyncope or syncope. The diagnosis is made with invasive electrophysiologic testing, and the tachycardia may be cured by catheter ablation of one of the bundle branches.

DIGITALIS TOXICITY

Ventricular arrhythmias seen in digitalis toxicity include single PVCs, nonsustained VT, and sustained polymorphic or monomorphic VT. Some digitalis-toxic rhythms are due to triggered activity from intracellular calcium overload that results from inhibition of the Na^+/K^+ ATPase. A characteristic digitalis-toxic rhythm is bidirectional VT, characterized by a right bundle-branch block configuration and alternating right-axis and left-axis deviations. Therapy for severe digitalis-toxic arrhythmias includes infusion of digoxin immune Fab fragments, which may be life-saving. Alternatives are class IB antiarrhythmic medications, such as lidocaine and phenytoin (Chapter 62).

VENTRICULAR FLUTTER AND FIBRILLATION

Definitions

VF is a malignant arrhythmia characterized by disorganized electrical activity resulting in a failure of sequential cardiac contraction and the inability to maintain cardiac output (see Fig. 60–3). If not promptly terminated, VF results in hypoxemia and eventually SCD. Ventricular flutter is an extremely rapid, hemodynamically unstable VT that typically progresses to VF. The evaluation and management of ventricular flutter should parallel that for VF.

Etiology

With rare exceptions, VF occurs in patients with underlying structural heart disease, especially ischemic heart disease with left ventricular systolic dysfunction. In patients resuscitated from an episode of VF, it is imperative to identify the cause of the arrhythmia (see Sudden Cardiac Death) and to search for evidence of an acute ischemic event. Patients who survive an episode of VF within 48 hours of an acute MI generally have a good prognosis, with a 2% recurrence rate at 1 year.

De novo VF can be caused by myocardial ischemia, which results in complex changes in the electrophysiologic properties of the ventricle, including delays in conduction and changes in refractoriness, that potentiate the multiple re-entrant wave fronts that characterize VF. Alternatively, PVCs during the vulnerable period of ventricular repolarization (R-on-T phenomenon) may initiate VF. Prolonged VT may result in hypotension and myocardial ischemia, causing degeneration of VT to VF.

Electrocardiographic Features

The ECG during ventricular flutter is characterized by a sinusoidal QRS complex, without a distinct ST segment or T wave, at a rate of 240 to 280 beats per minute. In contrast, VF is an irregular rhythm with an undulating low-amplitude baseline without organized QRS complexes or T waves.

Table 60–2 • CAUSES OF SUDDEN CARDIAC DEATH
STRUCTURAL HEART DISEASE
Coronary artery disease
Myocarditis
Cardiomyopathy
Hypertrophic
Infiltrative (e.g., amyloidosis, hemochromatosis, sarcoidosis)
Cardiac tumors
Valvular heart disease
Congenital heart disease
Anomalous origin of coronary arteries
Arrhythmogenic right ventricular dysplasia
WITHOUT STRUCTURAL HEART DISEASE
Long QT syndrome
Congenital
Acquired (e.g., drugs, electrolyte abnormalities)
Brugada syndrome
Catecholaminergic polymorphic ventricular tachycardia
Short-coupled torsades de pointes
Chest wall trauma (commotio cordis)
Wolff-Parkinson-White syndrome
Idiopathic ventricular fibrillation

SUDDEN CARDIAC DEATH

Definitions, Incidence, and Prevalence

Half of all cardiac deaths are sudden, accounting for approximately 300,000 deaths per year in the United States. SCD is death due to instantaneous, unanticipated circulatory collapse within 1 hour of initial symptoms and is often, but not always, due to a cardiac arrhythmia. More than 70% of all sudden natural deaths have a cardiac cause, and 80% of these are attributable to coronary artery disease (Table 60–2). Approximately 70% of SCDs occur in men. Compared with routine activities, vigorous exercise increases the immediate risk of SCD 17-fold. In more recent years, the incidence of SCD has declined in parallel with the decrease in coronary artery disease, likely secondary to a reduction in cardiac risk factors, more effective secondary preventive measures, improved resuscitative efforts, and expansion of emergency medical services. Similar to acute MI, SCD has a circadian pattern with a primary peak in the morning hours after awakening, from 6 AM to 12 noon. This peak may be due in part to a surge in sympathetic activity with its attendant arrhythmogenic effects and its effects on platelet aggregability and diurnal fluctuations in thrombogenic factors. β-Blockers attenuate the morning peak pattern. SCD also shows a seasonal predilection, with a higher incidence in December and January than in the summer months (in the Northern Hemisphere), a trend that is attributed to colder temperatures, holiday stress, and shorter daylight hours. Prodromal symptoms in the 2 weeks preceding collapse may include fatigue, dyspnea, and chest pain. Risk factors for SCD are identical to those for coronary artery disease and include age, male gender, hypertension, tobacco use, hypercholesterolemia, and left ventricular hypertrophy.

Holter monitor data indicate that approximately 85% of the rhythms leading to SCD are ventricular tachyarrhythmias, with the remaining 15% due to bradyarrhythmias. Among tachyarrhythmias, 75% are due to VT, either monomorphic (two thirds) or polymorphic (one third), and 25% are due to TdP and primary VF. When VT precedes VF, it usually persists for 30 seconds to 3 minutes before degenerating into VF. By 4 minutes after collapse, VF is identified in nearly 90% of SCD cases, whereas asystole is identified in 10%. As more time elapses, asystole and pulseless electrical activity are identified in more than 40% of victims, suggesting that these rhythms reflect prolonged hypoxemia. This prolonged hypoxia likely explains the lower long-term survival (1 to 4%) in SCD patients presenting with these arrhythmias, in contrast with the 34% rate of survival to hospital discharge in patients found to be in VF after a witnessed arrest.

Etiology

Most cardiac arrest survivors have structural heart disease, with nearly 75% having coronary artery disease. VF may be the first manifestation of coronary artery disease in 25% of patients with ischemic heart disease. Only 20% of patients have evidence for a new Q wave MI at the time of cardiac arrest, whereas a remote MI is present in 40 to 80% of victims. Acute coronary occlusion is found in 50% of survivors of out-of-hospital cardiac arrest.

Of SCD survivors, 10 to 15% have a dilated cardiomyopathy, which may be idiopathic or due to viral myocarditis, sarcoidosis, hemachromatosis, or amyloidosis (Chapter 73). In patients with dilated cardiomyopathy, the risk of SCD is related to symptomatic status. The annual mortality in patients who are New York Heart Association functional class II is estimated to be 5 to 15%, of which 50 to 80% is due to SCD. In patients who are functional class IV, the annual mortality is 30 to 70%, of which 5 to 30% are arrhythmogenic. Another cause of SCD is valvular heart disease. In younger patients, particularly those who arrest during physical activity, causes such as hypertrophic cardiomyopathy (with or without outflow obstruction), arrhythmogenic right ventricular dysplasia, LQTS, anomalous origin of the coronary arteries, and Wolff-Parkinson-White syndrome should be considered for patients who can conduct rapidly over the accessory pathway during atrial fibrillation. Other causes include acute myocarditis, cardiac tumors, and repair of congenital anomalies such as transposition of the great arteries and tetralogy of Fallot (Chapter 65). In a small subset of patients, no structural heart disease is detected. These patients include patients with Brugada syndrome, exercise-related polymorphic VT, LQTS (congenital and acquired), short coupled TdP, drug toxicity (including cocaine use), and electrolyte disturbances. More recently, it has been appreciated that a nonpenetrating blow to the chest caused by bodily collision or a projectile, such as a baseball or hockey puck (commotio cordis), can precipitate VF, presumably by occurring during the vulnerable phase of the T wave.

Pathogenesis

Although SCD is not usually associated with an acute Q wave MI, transient ischemia often precedes SCD. In patients with stable high-grade atherosclerotic plaques (>75% occlusion) but no previous MI or unstable ischemia, VF may be due to coronary vasospasm. The true prevalence and significance of ischemia in precipitating VF is unknown, especially because ischemic ST-segment changes are rarely present at the time of SCD. An acute coronary thrombus may be observed in 50% of patients with preexisting coronary artery disease, however. The electrophysiologic consequences of acute ischemia that ultimately result in VF are mediated through acidosis, potassium efflux from the cell with membrane depolarization, increased intracellular calcium, and an increase in adrenergic tone.

Risk Stratification

Because the incidence of SCD is 0.1 to 0.2% in the general population, preventive measures are meaningful and cost-effective only for patients who are identified as high risk. The relatively poor sensitivity, specificity, and predictive value of risk factors often diminish the utility of specific recommendations, however. Most data regarding risk stratification have been derived from post-MI patients, in whom the left ventricular dysfunction (particularly an ejection fraction <30%) is the strongest independent predictor of SCD. Frequent or complex ventricular ectopy, commonly defined as 10 or more PVCs per hour, is a usual comorbidity of myocardial dysfunction and an independent predictor of SCD. The risks of left ventricular dysfunction and ventricular ectopy are additive. The combination of an ejection fraction less than 30% and 10 or more PVCs per hour carries a far greater risk of SCD than either risk factor alone. As the Cardiac Arrhythmia Suppression Trial (CAST) showed (Table 60–3), however, suppression of ventricular ectopy does not improve prognosis. Despite this caveat, data from the Multicenter Automatic Defibrillator Implantation Trial (MADIT) and the Multicenter Unsustained Tachycardia Trial (MUSTT) indicate that surveillance Holter recordings should be obtained in patients with ischemic heart disease and an ejection fraction less than or equal to 40%. Patients with at least 3 beats per minute of nonsustained VT should undergo electrophysiologic testing for further risk stratification (Fig. 60–4). Late potentials on the signal-averaged ECG (Chapter 58), despite a low positive predictive value (<25%), also identify post-MI patients at risk of VT/VF, particularly in patients with an ejection fraction less than 40%. The negative predictive value of the test in this group of patients approaches 95%.

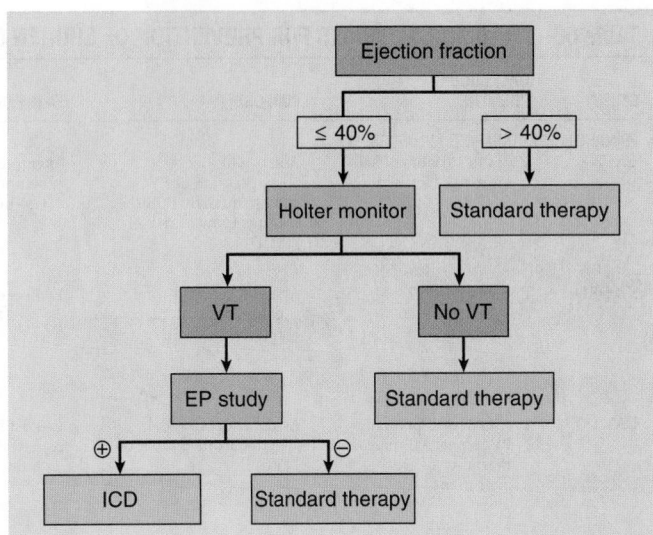

FIGURE 60–4 • Stratification of risk and need for antiarrhythmic therapy in post–myocardial infarction patients. Standard therapy may include aspirin, anti-ischemic therapy, lipid-lowering therapy, β-blocker, or angiotensin-converting enzyme inhibitor (Chapter 69). VT = ventricular tachycardia; EP = electrophysiology; ICD = implantable cardioverter defibrillator.

In general, reduced baroreceptor sensitivity and decreased heart rate variability, both reflections of diminished parasympathetic tone, are associated with increased arrhythmic events after MI. T-wave alternans, which measures surface ECG repolarization alternans at the microvolt level, is a promising technology for identifying high-risk patients. The predictive role of electrophysiologic testing in post-MI patients without sustained ventricular arrhythmias has evolved over time. Earlier studies showed little prognostic value, whereas more recent studies show a strong association between inducible sustained VT and future arrhythmic events (see Table 60–3).

Diagnosis

In assessing prognosis and planning a treatment strategy, it is useful to classify SCD as either primary (without a clear trigger) or secondary. A primary episode has a 10 to 30% 1-year recurrence rate, whereas most secondary episodes are associated with recurrence rates of less than 2%. Identifiable reversible precipitants of secondary VF include transient ischemia possibly related to vasospasm; hypokalemia resulting from diuretics; hyperkalemia secondary to renal failure, angiotensin-converting enzyme inhibitors, prostaglandin inhibitors, or potassium-sparing diuretics; proarrhythmia secondary to antiarrhythmics, tricyclics, and antihistamines; or substance abuse with drugs such as cocaine and amphetamines. Therapy is directed toward removing or treating the acute precipitant. SCD related to acute ischemia in the absence of prior MI often is associated with severe proximal occlusive disease, normal left ventricular function, normal signal-averaged ECG, and noninducibility (absence of VT) during electrophysiologic study.

Most patients should undergo comprehensive evaluation of myocardial function and coronary anatomy. Echocardiography is useful for excluding hypertrophic cardiomyopathy and valvular heart disease (Chapter 51); magnetic resonance imaging, for diagnosing arrhythmogenic right ventricular dysplasia (Chapter 53); and myocardial biopsy, for identifying infiltrative diseases such as myocarditis, amyloidosis, hemochromatosis, and sarcoidosis (Chapter 73). Coronary angiography should be performed to assess for the presence of coronary occlusive disease and to exclude coronary artery anomalies (Chapters 54 and 65). Myocardial perfusion scintigraphy provides complementary data for assessing ischemic burden (Chapter 52). Left ventricular function can be assessed by contrast ventriculography, radionuclide ventriculography, or echocardiography.

Evaluation of SCD survivors also includes Holter monitoring and/or electrophysiologic testing (Chapter 58). The Electrophysiological Study Versus Electrocardiographic Monitoring (ESVEM) trial showed, however, a 50% 2-year recurrence of ventricular tachyarrhythmias in

Cardiovascular Disease

Table 60–3 • CLINICAL TRIALS FOR PREVENTION OF SUDDEN CARDIAC DEATH

STUDY	BACKGROUND/ PREMISE	PURPOSE	ENTRY CRITERIA	DESIGN	OUTCOME
PRIMARY PREVENTION POST MI: DRUGS					
CAST	PVCs in survivors of MI are a risk factor for SCD	Assess whether suppression of PVCs with antiarrhythmic drugs reduces risk of SCD	Asymptomatic/ mildly symptomatic PVCs (≥6/hr) post MI	1. Primary prevention 2. Titration: encainide, flecainide or moricizine 3. Randomized: suppressive drug vs. placebo 4. End point: SCD	Antiarrhythmic drugs: 1. Increase overall mortality 2. Increase risk of SCD
SWORD	Patients post MI with ↓ EF have increased mortality	Assess whether d-sotalol compared with placebo reduces mortality	1. Recent MI 2. EF ≤40%	1. Primary prevention 2. Randomized: d-sotalol vs. placebo 3. End point: mortality	1. d-sotalol associated with increased mortality 2. Increased mortality presumed secondary to proarrhythmia
CAMIAT	Frequent or repetitive PVCs post MI increase mortality 1–2 yr after event	Assess effect of amiodarone on risk of VF	1. Post MI 2. ≥10 PVCs/hr or ≥ one 3 beat run	1. Primary prevention 2. Randomized: amiodarone vs. placebo 3. End point: resuscitated VF or arrhythmic death	1. Amiodarone reduces VF and arrhythmic death (relative risk reduction: 38%) 2. No difference between groups in overall mortality
EMIAT	Patients post MI with ↓ EF are at increased risk for SCD	Assess whether amiodarone reduces mortality in patients post MI with ↓ EF	1. Post MI 2. EF ≤40%	1. Primary prevention 2. Randomized: amiodarone vs. placebo	1. 35% risk reduction in arrhythmic deaths with amiodarone 2. No difference in mortality between amiodarone and placebo
PRIMARY PREVENTION POST MI/CAD: ICD					
MADIT	Patients with NSVT, post MI, and ↓ EF have 30% 2-yr mortality	Assess whether prophylactic ICD vs. conventional medical therapy improves survival	1. Prior MI 2. EF ≤35% 3. NSVT 4. Inducible but nonsuppressible VT with antiarrhythmic drug during EPS	1. Primary prevention 2. Randomized: ICD vs. conventional medical therapy 3. End point: mortality	1. Prophylactic ICD reduces mortality by 54% at 27 mo
MUSTT	Patients post MI with ↓ EF are at high risk for SCD	Assess whether EPS-guided antiarrhythmic therapy decreases risk of SCD	1. Prior MI/CAD 2. EF ≤40% 3. NSVT 4. Induced sustained VT	1. Primary prevention 2. Antiarrhythmic drugs or ICD vs. no antiarrhythmic therapy 3. End point: SCD	1. ICD results in a 27% reduction in risk of SCD at 5 yr
MADIT-II	Patients post MI with ↓EF are at high risk for SCD	Assess effect of ICD on survival	1. Prior MI 2. EF ≤30%	1. Primary prevention 2. Randomized ICD vs. conventional therapy 3. Endpoint: mortality	1. ICD associated with a 29% reduction in mortality at 20 mo
CABG Patch	Patients with CAD, ↓ EF, and (+) SAECG are at increased risk of SCD	Assess effect of prophylactic ICD at time of elective CABG surgery on survival	1. CAD 2. EF ≤35% 3. (+) SAECG	1. Primary prevention 2. Randomized: ICD vs. control 3. End point: mortality	1. No difference in mortality between ICD and control patients
SECONDARY PREVENTION SCD/HYPOTENSIVE VT: ICD					
AVID	Patients who survive VF or hypotensive VT are at increased risk for recurrence	Assess relative efficacy of ICD vs. amiodarone (majority) or sotalol on mortality	1. VF 2. VT and syncope/ presyncope (EF ≤40%)	1. Secondary prevention 2. Randomized: ICD vs. antiarrhythmic drugs 3. End point: mortality	1. ICD reduces mortality compared with amiodarone 2. Relative risk reduction 39 and 31% at 1 and 3 yr
CIDS	Patients who survive VF or hypotensive VT are at increased risk for recurrence	Assess relative efficacy of ICD vs. amiodarone on mortality	1. VF 2. VT and syncope/ presyncope 3. Syncope and spontaneous/ induced VT	1. Secondary prevention 2. Randomized: ICD vs. amiodarone 3. End point: mortality	1. ICD therapy results in 20% relative risk reduction in mortality (P = .14)
CASH	Survivors of SCD are at high risk for recurrent event	Assess relative efficacy class I, II, and III antiarrhythmic drugs and ICD	1. Survivor of SCD due to VF/VT	1. Secondary prevention 2. Randomized: propafenone vs. metoprolol vs. amiodarone vs. ICD 3. End point: mortality	1. ICD reduces mortality 42 and 28% (1 and 3 yr) compared with amiodarone/metoprolol (P = .08) 2. Propafenone arm aborted owing to increased mortality vs. ICD

AVID = Antiarrhythmics Verus Implantable Defibrillators; CABG = coronary artery bypass graft; CAD = coronary artery disease; CAMIAT = Canadian Amiodarone Myocardial Infarction Arrhythmia Trial; CASH = Cardiac Arrest Study Hamburg; CAST = Cardiac Arrhythmia Suppression Trial; CIDS = Canadian Implantable Defibrillator Study; EF = ejection fraction; EMIAT = European Myocardial Infarct Amiodarone Trial; EPS = electrophysiology study; ICD = implantable cardioverter defibrillator; MADIT = Multicenter Automatic Defibrillator Implantation Trial; MI = myocardial infarction; MUSTT = Multicenter Unsustained Tachycardia Trial; NSVT = nonsustained ventricular tachycardia; PVCs = premature ventricular contractions; SCD = sudden cardiac death; SAECG = signal averaged electrocardiogram; SWORD = Survival With Oral d-Sotalol; VF = ventricular fibrillation; VT = ventricular tachycardia.

patients in whom antiarrhythmic drugs successfully suppressed PVCs. These data suggest a dissociation between PVC suppression and recurrence of VT; PVCs may represent a marker of left ventricular dysfunction rather than a trigger of SCD, or the arrhythmogenic substrate may change over time.

In SCD survivors, sustained monomorphic VT is inducible by electrophysiologic testing (Chapter 58) in 40 to 50% and polymorphic VT in 10 to 20%; in 30 to 50%, no sustained arrhythmia is induced. In patients with ischemic heart disease and left ventricular dysfunction, inducibility of sustained VT carries a poor prognosis. A low ejection fraction is associated with a poor prognosis, however, regardless of whether sustained VT is inducible; patients with an ejection fraction of 30% or less and who are noninducible have a 25% arrhythmia recurrence rate at 1 year, whereas noninducible patients with an ejection fraction greater than 30% have a 10 to 15% recurrence rate. In patients with SCD and idiopathic dilated cardiomyopathy, sustained monomorphic VT is rarely induced. Neither the inability to induce VT nor the ability of drugs to suppress inducible polymorphic VT or VF is a predictor of a favorable outcome.

Therapy

ACUTE MANAGEMENT. A key element for success is bystander initiation of cardiopulmonary resuscitation (CPR). The most important factor that determines the outcome of cardiac arrest secondary to VF or pulseless VT is the time to defibrillation, however. Emerging data from newer defibrillators using biphasic waveforms that deliver 150 to 200 J suggest they are at least as effective as standard defibrillators that deliver 200 to 360 J. Optimal chances for survival occur when CPR is initiated within 4 minutes of the arrest, and advanced cardiac life support, including intubation, intravenous medications, and defibrillation, is implemented within 8 minutes. If VF or pulseless VT does not respond to defibrillation and intravenous epinephrine (1-mg push repeated every 3 to 5 minutes) or vasopressin (40 IU), a rapid intravenous bolus of amiodarone can be given (300 mg diluted in 20 to 30 mL of normal saline; if needed, additional doses of 150 mg).

Despite public education in bystander CPR and efforts to train emergency medical technicians, early in-hospital mortality is 50 to 60%, and only 4 to 34% of patients with out-of-hospital SCD survive to discharge from the hospital, underscoring the importance of primary and secondary prevention. One third of deaths are attributable to heart failure or cardiogenic shock; 90% who recover from coma with meaningful function do so by the third hospital day. Public access defibrillation with the automatic external defibrillator, which recognizes VF and delivers high-energy shocks, allows laypersons and nonmedical personnel to function as first responders and has the potential to have a positive impact on survival.

PRIMARY AND SECONDARY INTERVENTION. Primary preventive approaches to SCD prophylactically treat patients identified as being at high risk and generally include reduction or elimination of myocardial ischemia with antianginal agents and/or coronary revascularization (Fig. 60–5). Regardless of whether or not residual ischemia is present, initial therapy in all patients without contraindications should include a β-blocker, which reduces SCD and total mortality (25%) in survivors of MI. Results are similarly persuasive in patients with heart failure who can tolerate β-blockers. The beneficial effects of β-blockers in prevention of SCD occur independently of their limited effect on PVC suppression. Angiotensin-converting enzyme inhibitors also reduce SCD and overall mortality in survivors of MI with left ventricular ejection fraction less than or equal to 35% (Chapter 69).

In general, with the exception of amiodarone, antiarrhythmic drugs have proved to be proarrhythmic and often decrease survival (see Table 60–3), showing that suppression of PVCs is not an appropriate surrogate for prevention of SCD. In contrast, amiodarone reduces arrhythmic deaths in MI survivors who have an ejection fraction of 40% or less with either frequent PVCs or nonsustained VT, and amiodarone and β-blockers may be synergistic in their benefits. Amiodarone does not seem to improve overall mortality, however, and approximately 5% of patients discontinue the drug because of pulmonary toxicity.

In two randomized trials, ICDs have reduced mortality in MI survivors who have a low ejection fraction, nonsustained VT, and inducible sustained VT.[1,2] ICDs also reduce total mortality in patients who are risk-stratified solely on the basis of severely impaired left ventricular function (EF ≤30%).[3] In contrast, a primary prevention trial failed to show that ICDs decrease mortality in patients undergoing elective coronary revascularization who have reduced left ventricular function and a positive signal-averaged ECG. These discrepant results may be due to several factors, including the positive effects of revascularization on outcome and the relative limitations of the signal-averaged ECG to stratify risk (compared with an electrophysiologic study). Finally, although the ICD reduced arrhythmic death by 45% in this third study, overall mortality was not altered because approximately 70% of deaths were due to nonarrhythmic causes.

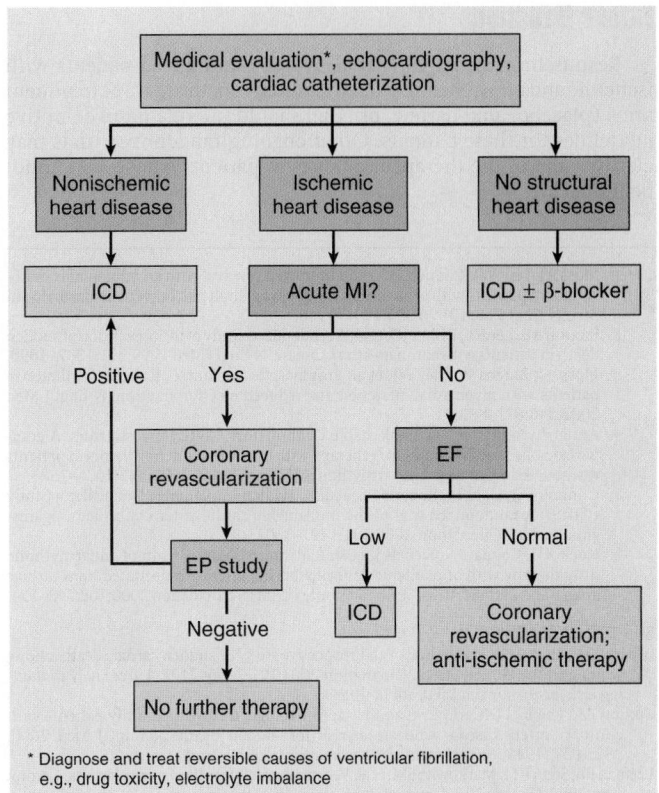

FIGURE 60–5 • Approach to the patient resuscitated from ventricular fibrillation. EF = ejection fraction; EP = electrophysiology; ICD = implantable cardioverter defibrillator; MI = myocardial infarction.

In patients with heart failure secondary to nonischemic cardiomyopathy, amiodarone seems to reduce total mortality, SCD, and deaths resulting from heart failure. It does not confer benefit, however, in patients with heart failure secondary to ischemic cardiomyopathy.

Patients with syncope and left ventricular dysfunction are known to have rates of SCD and total mortality similar to patients who survive cardiac arrest. Sustained VT is induced in greater than 40% of patients with syncope and impaired left ventricular function secondary to coronary artery disease. Despite receiving ICDs and having a high incidence of appropriate therapy, these patients have a considerably worse prognosis than patients who are noninducible. Likewise, syncope in patients with nonischemic dilated cardiomyopathy carries a poor prognosis.

Long-term outcome is poor in survivors of SCD, with a 50% mortality rate within 3 years. Coronary revascularization is the principal mode of secondary prevention in patients with significant coronary disease, in patients with normal ventricular function, and in patients in whom VT cannot be induced during electrophysiologic study (Chapter 71). Revascularization is not effective, however, in preventing VT in patients with sustained monomorphic VT owing to scar from a previous MI; treatment with catheter ablation may be effective in patients with hemodynamically tolerated VT. Data from the Antiarrhythmics Versus Implantable Defibrillators (AVID) trial suggest, however, that 3-year mortality rates in patients with stable VT are equivalent to rates in patients with unstable VT. An ICD should be strongly considered in these patients.

Secondary prevention trials for sudden death survivors secondary to VF/VT or patients with hemodynamically unstable VT in the aggregate show a 20 to 30% reduction in mortality at 3 years with ICD therapy compared with amiodarone.[4-6] Antiarrhythmic therapy is seldom considered a reliable means of secondary prevention, although some data suggest that amiodarone is as effective as ICD therapy in patients with relatively well-preserved left ventricular function (ejection fraction ≥35%) (see Table 60–3). Currently, it is reasonable to conclude, however, that in appropriately identified patients, the ICD has emerged as the most effective therapy for primary and secondary prevention of SCD.

Future Directions

Results from an ongoing trial, which randomized patients with ischemic and nonischemic dilated cardiomyopathy to three treatment arms (placebo, amiodarone, or ICD) should provide more definitive guidelines for these patients. Other ongoing randomized trials may clarify some of the therapeutic issues in patients whose VT cannot be induced.

1. Moss AJ, Hall WJ, Cannon DS, et al: Improved survival with an implantable defibrillator in patients with coronary artery disease at high risk for ventricular arrhythmia. N Engl J Med 1996;335:1933–1940.
2. Buxton AE, Lee KL, Fisher JD, et al: A randomized study of the prevention of sudden death in patients with coronary artery disease. N Engl J Med 1999;341:1882–1890.
3. Moss AJ, Zareba W, Hall WJ, et al: Prophylactic implantation of a defibrillator in patients with myocardial infarction and reduced ejection fraction. N Engl J Med 2002;346:877–883.
4. Antiarrhythmics versus Implantable Defibrillators (AVID) investigators: A comparison of antiarrhythmic-drug therapy with implantable defibrillators in patients resuscitated from near fatal arrhythmias. N Engl J Med 1997;337:1576–1583.
5. Connolly SJ, Gent M, Roberts RS, et al: Canadian Implantable Defibrillator Study (CIDS): A randomized trial of the implantable cardioverter defibrillator against amiodarone. Circulation 2000;101:1297–1302.
6. Kuck KH, Cappato R, Siebels J, et al: Randomized comparison of antiarrhythmic drug therapy with implantable defibrillators in patients resuscitated from cardiac arrest: The Cardiac Arrest Study Hamburg (CASH). Circulation 2000;102:748–754.

SUGGESTED READINGS

Albert CM, Chae CC, Grodstein F, et al: Prospective study of sudden cardiac death among women in the United States. Circulation 2003;107:2096–2101. *Large study evaluating risk factors for sudden death in women.*
Buxton AE, Lee KL, DiCarlo L, et al: Electrophysiologic testing to identify patients with coronary artery disease who are at risk for sudden death. N Engl J Med 2000; 342:1937–1945. *Pivotal multicenter primary prevention trial.*
Lerman BB, Stein KM, Markowitz SM, et al: Ventricular tachycardia in normal hearts. Cardiol Clin 2000;18:265–291. *Comprehensive review of idiopathic ventricular tachycardia.*
Raitt MH, Renfroe EG, Epstein AE, et al: "Stable" ventricular tachycardia is not a benign rhythm: Insights from the antiarrhythmics versus implantable defibrillators (AVID) registry. Circulation 2001;103:244–252. *Poor prognosis of well-tolerated sustained ventricular tachycardia.*
Vincent GM: Long QT syndrome. Cardiol Clin 2000;18:309–325. *Basic and clinical aspects of the long QT syndrome.*

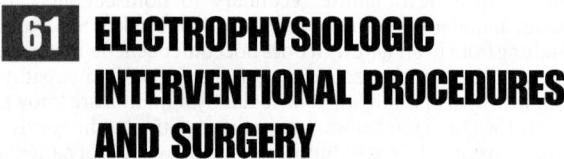

61 ELECTROPHYSIOLOGIC INTERVENTIONAL PROCEDURES AND SURGERY

Fred Morady

PACEMAKERS

Pacemaker Generators and Leads

Pacemaker batteries, which are lithium iodide cells that typically have a lifespan of 7 to 8 years, now often weigh less than 30 g. They usually are implanted subcutaneously in the infraclavicular area (Fig. 61–1). Programmability of many different variables has become standard, as has the ability of the pacemaker to provide diagnostic and telemetric data.

Pacemaker leads usually are bipolar, with the distal electrode serving as the cathode. Unipolar leads are less commonly used because of the potential for pacing chest wall muscles and for inhibition of pacing by skeletal muscle myopotentials. The leads are inserted into the heart either percutaneously through a subclavian vein or by cutdown into a cephalic vein. Atrial leads usually are positioned in the right atrial appendage, and ventricular leads are placed in the right ventricular apex. Fixation to the myocardium is achieved either passively with tines or actively with a screw mechanism. Newer electrode designs, such as porous carbon or steroid-eluting electrodes, have resulted in lower acute and chronic pacing thresholds.

Pacing Modes

The mode of pacing is described in shorthand fashion by a three- to five-letter code. The first letter designates the chamber being paced (A for atrium, V for ventricle, D for dual-chamber); the second letter

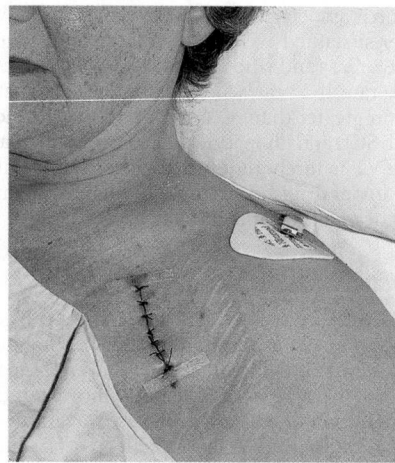

FIGURE 61–1 • The site of implantation of a permanent pacemaker or automatic implantable cardioverter defibrillator. The pacemaker is usually implanted in the left pectoral region, but it may be placed elsewhere if necessary. (From Forbes CD, Jackson WF: Color Atlas and Text of Clinical Medicine, 3rd ed. London, Mosby, 2003, with permission.)

designates the chamber being sensed (A, V, D, or O for no sensing); the third letter designates whether the pacemaker functions in an inhibited (I) or tracking mode (T), in both modes (D), or asynchronously (O); and the fourth letter indicates whether the pacemaker is capable of rate-modulation independent of atrial activity. An additional fifth letter may be used to designate the capability for anti-tachycardia pacing (P), delivery of shocks (S), or both (D). The most commonly employed pacing modes are VVI (pacing and sensing within the ventricle in inhibited fashion), VVIR (VVI plus rate-responsiveness), and DDD (pacing and sensing of atrium and ventricle, both in inhibited and tracking fashion).

The most appropriate pacing mode must always be determined on an individual basis, the goal being to meet the patient's physiologic needs with the simplest system possible. For example, in a patient with chronic atrial fibrillation who has symptomatic pauses but not chronotropic incompetence, a VVI pacemaker is sufficient. However, if the patient also has chronotropic incompetence, a VVIR pacemaker is necessary to restore a normal rate-response to exercise. In a patient with high-degree atrioventricular (AV) block and normal sinus node function, DDD pacing is optimal. However, if a patient with high-degree AV block also has sinus node dysfunction, the ideal pacing mode is DDDR.

In patients who have paroxysmal atrial fibrillation and high-degree AV block, no single pacing mode is optimal. DDD pacing is ideal when the patient is in sinus rhythm, but during atrial fibrillation DDD pacing may result in tracking of the atrium at the upper rate limit of the pacemaker. Conversely, VVIR pacing, which is ideal during atrial fibrillation, will not provide AV synchrony during periods of sinus rhythm. The development of mode-switching pacemakers has solved this dilemma. Mode-switching pacemakers are capable of pacing in the DDD mode during sinus rhythm and automatically switching to rate-responsive ventricular pacing during atrial fibrillation or other supraventricular arrhythmias (Fig. 61–2).

The choice between ventricular (VVIR) as compared with atrial (AAIR) or dual chamber (DDDR) pacing remains controversial. Although a randomized trial of 225 patients with sinus node dysfunction reported a significant reduction in cardiovascular death at 8 years with AAIR versus VVIR pacing, studies of nearly 5000 patients have shown no survival differences when patients were randomized to DDDR pacing compared with VVIR pacing. Dual chamber pacing, like atrial pacing, reduces the incidence of atrial fibrillation, and appears to result in slightly better quality of life (grade A). [1-3] In these randomized trials, 5 to 25% of patients who initially received VVIR pacemakers "crossed over" to DDDR pacing because of physician-diagnosed pacemaker syndrome (see Complications of Pacemakers).

Indications for a Permanent Pacemaker

(Tables 61–1 and 61–2)

In general, pacemakers are implanted either to alleviate symptoms caused by bradycardia or to prevent severe symptoms in patients who

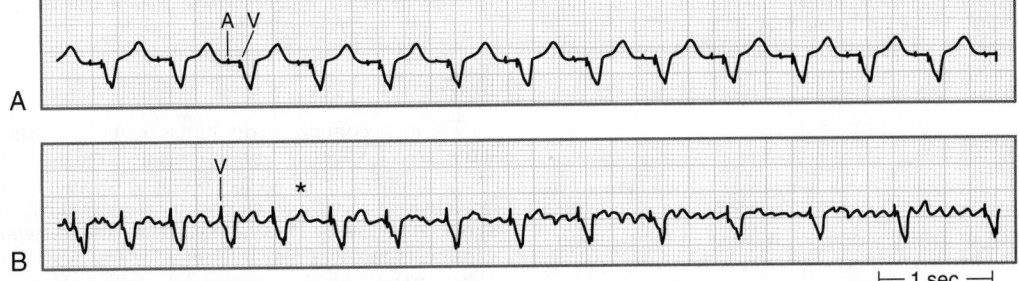

FIGURE 61–2 • Rhythm strips from a Holter monitor in a patient with complete atrioventricular block, sinus bradycardia, paroxysmal atrial fibrillation, and a rate-responsive dual-chamber pacemaker with mode-switching capability. A, When the patient is in sinus rhythm, the pacemaker functions in a DDDR mode, with synchronized atrial and ventricular pacing at 105 beats per minute while the patient is walking. B, At the onset of an episode of atrial fibrillation, there is tracking of the atrium that results in ventricular pacing at 140 beats per minute, which is the upper rate limit of the pacemaker. Within 2 seconds (asterisk), the mode-switch feature results in VVIR pacing, and the ventricular pacing rate gradually falls to 70 beats per minute, which is the lower rate limit of the pacemaker. A = atrial stimulus; V = ventricular stimulus.

Table 61–1 • CLASS I INDICATIONS* FOR IMPLANTATION OF A PERMANENT PACEMAKER

I. Atrioventricular block
   A. Third-degree atrioventricular block associated with symptoms
   B. Third-degree atrioventricular block with pauses >3 seconds or with an escape rate <40 beats per minute in awake patients
   C. Postoperative atrioventricular block that is not expected to resolve
   D. Second-degree atrioventricular block associated with symptoms
   E. Chronic bifascicular or trifascicular block with intermittent third-degree atrioventricular block or type II second-degree atrioventricular block
II. Atrioventricular block associated with myocardial infarction
   A. Second- or third-degree atrioventricular block in the His-Purkinje system
   B. Transient second- or third-degree infranodal atrioventricular block and associated bundle branch block
   C. Persistent, symptomatic second- or third-degree atrioventricular block
III. Sinus node dysfunction
   A. Symptomatic sinus bradycardia or sinus pauses
   B. Symptomatic chronotropic incompetence
IV. Carotid sinus syndrome: recurrent syncope or near-syncope due to carotid sinus syndrome

*Class I indications are conditions for which there is general agreement that a pacemaker is indicated.

Adapted from Cheitlin MD, Conill A, Epstein AE, et al: ACC/AHA guidelines for implantation of cardiac pacemakers and antiarrhythmia devices: A report of the American College of Cardiology/American Heart Association Task Force on Practice Guidelines (Committee on Pacemaker Implantation). J Am Coll Cardiol 1998;31:1175–1209.

Table 61–2 • CLASS II INDICATIONS* FOR IMPLANTATION OF A PERMANENT PACEMAKER

I. Atrioventricular block
   A. Asymptomatic third-degree atrioventricular block with an escape rate >40 beats per minute
   B. Asymptomatic Mobitz II second-degree atrioventricular block
   C. Asymptomatic Mobitz I second-degree atrioventricular block in the His-Purkinje system
   D. Bifascicular or trifascicular block and syncope without identifiable cause
   E. His-ventricular interval >100 msec
   F. Pacing-induced block in the His-Purkinje system
II. Atrioventricular block associated with myocardial infarction: persistent second- or third-degree atrioventricular block at the level of the atrioventricular node
III. Sinus node dysfunction: heart rate <40 beats per minute, without clear association between symptoms and bradycardia
IV. Neurocardiogenic syncope: recurrent neurocardiogenic syncope associated with significant bradycardia reproduced by tilt-table testing.

*Class II indications are conditions for which pacemakers are often used, without unanimous agreement among experts that a pacemaker is necessary.

Adapted from Cheitlin MD, Conill A, Epstein AE, et al: ACC/AHA guidelines for implantation of cardiac pacemakers and antiarrhythmia devices: A report of the American College of Cardiology/American Heart Association Task Force on Practice Guidelines (Committee on Pacemaker Implantation). J Am Coll Cardiol 1998;31:1175–1209.

are likely to develop symptomatic bradycardia. The most common bradycardia-induced symptoms are dizziness or lightheadedness, syncope or near-syncope (Chapter 58), exercise intolerance, or symptoms of heart failure. Because these symptoms are nonspecific, documentation of an association between symptoms and bradycardia should be obtained before pacemaker implantation. If the bradycardia is persistent, such as in a patient who presents with complete AV block, a simple electrocardiogram may be sufficient to document the need for a pacemaker. If the bradycardia is intermittent, other diagnostic testing, such as 24-hour ambulatory monitoring, a continuous loop recorder, an implantable event monitor, or an electrophysiology test (Chapter 58) may be needed to document a relationship between symptoms and bradycardia.

After a symptomatic bradycardia has been documented, a correctable cause for the bradycardia should be excluded before a pacemaker is implanted. Correctable causes for symptomatic bradycardias include hypothyroidism, an overdose with drugs such as digitalis, electrolyte disturbances, and several categories of medications, most commonly β-adrenergic blocking agents (administered either orally or in the form of eyedrops for glaucoma), calcium channel blocking agents, and antiarrhythmic medications (Chapter 62). At times, a pacemaker is necessary to allow continued treatment with a medication

that is responsible for the bradycardia, such as in a patient who develops symptomatic sinus bradycardia after initiation of therapy with a β-adrenergic blocking agent for paroxysmal atrial fibrillation associated with a rapid ventricular response.

Complications of Pacemakers

Complications related to the implantation procedure occur in less than 2% of patients and include pneumothorax, perforation of the atrium or ventricle, lead dislodgement, infection, and erosion of the pacemaker pocket. Thrombosis of the subclavian vein occurs in 10 to 20% of patients and is more likely in the presence of multiple leads; it rarely causes symptoms.

Pacemaker-mediated tachycardia is a possible complication of DDD pacing when the atrial lead senses retrograde depolarizations because of ventriculoatrial conduction. The resulting tachycardia often has a rate equal to the upper rate limit of the pacemaker. Pacemaker-mediated tachycardia can be eliminated by various reprogramming maneuvers, such as lengthening of the post-ventriculoatrial refractory period.

The pacemaker syndrome consists of symptoms of weakness, lightheadedness, exercise intolerance, or palpitations caused by the absence of AV synchrony during ventricular pacing. It is treated by restoring AV synchrony with DDD pacing or, if AV conduction is intact, AAI pacing. During long-term follow-up after pacemaker implantation, potential problems include failure to pace, failure to capture, and changes in pacing rate. These problems may be a manifestation of suboptimal programming, a lead fracture or insulation break, generator malfunction, or battery depletion.

Temporary Pacemakers

Temporary pacemaker leads generally are inserted percutaneously into an internal jugular or subclavian vein, or by cutdown into a brachial vein, then positioned under fluoroscopic guidance in the right ventricular apex and attached to an external generator. Temporary pacing is used to stabilize patients awaiting permanent pacemaker implantation, to correct a transient symptomatic bradycardia due to drug toxicity or a metabolic defect, or to suppress torsades de pointes by maintaining a rate of 85 to 100 beats per minute until the causative factor has been eliminated. Temporary pacing may also be used in a prophylactic fashion in patients at risk of symptomatic bradycardia during a surgical procedure or high-degree AV block in the setting of an acute myocardial infarction (MI). The most common complication of temporary pacemakers is infection; this risk is minimized by limiting the use of a pacemaker lead to 48 hours. In emergent situations, ventricular pacing can be instituted immediately by transcutaneous pacing using electrode pads applied to the chest wall.

TRANSTHORACIC CARDIOVERSION AND DEFIBRILLATION

Mechanism of Action

Direct-current defibrillators store an electrical charge and discharge it across two paddle electrodes in a damped, sinusoidal waveform. The shock terminates arrhythmias caused by reentry by simultaneously depolarizing large portions of the atria or ventricles, thereby causing reentry circuits to extinguish (Chapters 57, 59, and 60).

A nonsynchronized shock that is delivered coincident with the T wave during supraventricular tachycardia (SVT) or ventricular tachycardia (VT) may precipitate ventricular fibrillation (VF). *Cardioversion* refers to the termination of SVT or VT by delivery of a shock in synchrony with the QRS complex. When shocks are delivered to terminate VF, synchronization to the QRS complex is not necessary, and this process is referred to as *defibrillation*.

Technique

Whenever cardioversion or defibrillation is performed on an elective basis, the patient should be in a fasting state. Intravenous access to a peripheral vein should be established, and oxygen, suction, and equipment needed for airway management should be readily available. Transthoracic shocks are painful, and drugs commonly used for anesthesia or amnesia include short-acting barbiturates such as methohexital or a short-acting amnestic agent such as midazolam. In the anteroapical configuration, one electrode is positioned to the right of the sternum at the level of the second intercostal space, and the second electrode is positioned at the midaxillary line, lateral to the apical impulse. In the anteroposterior configuration, an electrode is placed to the left of the sternum at the fourth intercostal space, and the second electrode is positioned posteriorly, to the left of the spine, at the same level as the anterior electrode. These two electrode configurations result in similar success rates of cardioversion and defibrillation.

Important variables affecting the success of cardioversion or defibrillation are the shock waveform and the shock strength. Defibrillators that deliver biphasic shocks are now clinically available and have a significantly higher success rate than conventional defibrillators. Other technique-dependent variables that maximize energy delivery to the heart include firm paddle pressure, delivery of the shock during expiration, and repetitive shocks. Patient-related variables that may decrease the probability of successful cardioversion/defibrillation include metabolic disturbances, a long arrhythmia duration, some antiarrhythmic drugs such as amiodarone, and a body weight more than 80 kg.

Because cardioversion of atrial fibrillation (Chapter 59) may be complicated by thromboembolism, anticoagulation with warfarin is generally necessary for 3 weeks before cardioversion and for 1 month after cardioversion whenever atrial fibrillation has been present for 48 hours or more. The 3-week period of anticoagulation before cardioversion can be eliminated if no atrial thrombi are seen on a transesophageal echocardiogram, but anticoagulation for 1 month after

cardioversion still is necessary to prevent thrombus formation due to transient, postconversion atrial stunning.

Indications

The most common arrhythmias treated by cardioversion/defibrillation are VF, VT, atrial fibrillation, and atrial flutter (Chapters 58 and 59). Treatment of VF always is emergent, and a 200-J shock should be delivered as quickly as possible, followed by one or more 360-J shocks if necessary. Depending on the patient's hemodynamic status, cardioversion of VT may be elective or emergent; if elective, an initial shock strength of 50 J is appropriate, followed by higher energy levels if additional shocks are needed. An initial energy level of 50 J is appropriate for cardioversion of atrial flutter. In atrial fibrillation, in which cardioversion usually is performed on an elective basis, an initial shock of 100 to 200 J is appropriate, depending on the patient's body weight. Shocks of 300 to 360 J then are used if necessary. If atrial fibrillation must be treated on an urgent basis, for example, in a patient with the Wolff-Parkinson-White syndrome who has a very rapid ventricular rate and hemodynamic compromise, an initial shock of 200 J should be followed by 360-J shocks, as needed. Because the defibrillation energy requirement is a probability function and not a discrete value, subsequent shocks may be effective for cardioversion/defibrillation even when the first 360-J shock is ineffective.

Complications

Asynchronous shocks may precipitate VF. Rarely, VF may occur even when shocks are synchronized to the QRS complex. The risk of post-shock ventricular arrhythmias is increased in the presence of a supratherapeutic plasma concentration of digitalis, so cardioversion in the presence of digitalis toxicity should be avoided.

Transient ST-segment elevation may occur after cardioversion and usually is of no clinical consequence. Mild myocardial necrosis occasionally may occur if a total energy exceeding 425 J is delivered in a short period of time. Another rare complication of cardioversion is pulmonary edema, which may be due to transient left ventricular dysfunction.

Post-shock bradycardia or asystole may occur because of vagal discharge or an underlying sick sinus syndrome. At times, atropine or emergent transcutaneous pacing may be necessary. In patients who have a pacemaker or implantable cardioverter-defibrillator (ICD), the shocking electrodes should be positioned as far away from the generator as possible and the generator and pacing threshold should be checked afterward.

IMPLANTABLE CARDIOVERTER-DEFIBRILLATORS

ICD Pulse Generators and Leads

ICDs now weigh as little as 75 g, are multiprogrammable, have improved detection algorithms, are capable of antitachycardia and antibradycardia (including dual-chamber) pacing, can deliver biphasic shocks at strengths of less than 1 to 42 J, and provide a record of the electrograms recorded during arrhythmia episodes. An ICD that delivers shocks to terminate atrial fibrillation as well as VT and VF is now clinically available. With the development of pulse generators small enough to implant in the infraclavicular area and endocardial leads that are inserted transvenously, the implantation procedure has been greatly simplified and now is very similar to that for permanent pacemakers.

A single lead that contains a pacing-sensing electrode and two defibrillating coils can be used. If adequate defibrillation is not achieved with a single lead configuration, a subcutaneous patch electrode or subcutaneous array can be added. In another commonly used configuration, the pulse generator itself functions as an electrode, and a lead that has a pacing-sensing electrode at its tip and a distal defibrillating coil electrode is positioned at the right ventricular apex. Multiple other combinations of a chest wall patch electrode with defibrillating electrodes in the right ventricular apex, superior vena cava, or coronary sinus also can be used.

Indications

ICDs have become first-line therapy in patients who have survived an episode of VF not associated with acute MI or who have had an episode of hemodynamically significant, sustained VT ▣ (Chapter 60).

ICDs also are implanted in patients at high risk of cardiac arrest, including patients with idiopathic, dilated cardiomyopathy and unexplained syncope or patients with coronary artery disease (CAD), ejection fraction less than 35%, spontaneous episodes of nonsustained VT, and inducible sustained VT in the electrophysiology laboratory ▣ (Chapter 60). The results of several ongoing clinical trials may expand the indications for prophylactic use of ICDs.

Programming of ICDs

Testing is performed at the time of implantation to determine the energy requirement for defibrillation. A safety margin of at least 10 J should be present; for example, if the maximum output of the pulse generator is 32 J, successful defibrillation should be achieved with shocks of 22 J or less in strength. If the patient has had episodes of VT, antitachycardia pacing can be evaluated and programmed as needed to terminate the VT. Appropriate programming of the device is performed during predischarge testing.

With ICDs that are tiered-therapy devices, as many as two VT zones and one VF zone are available to provide individualized therapy for ventricular arrhythmias that have different rates. The rate threshold and various sequences of antitachycardia pacing and low- and/or high-energy shocks can be programmed for each of the two VT zones. The VF zone is a high-rate zone in which high-energy shocks are delivered. Optimal programming is important for many reasons, including minimizing patient discomfort, reducing the chance of syncope with an arrhythmia episode, maximizing the battery life of the pulse generator, and preventing inappropriate shocks.

Complications

Complications related to the implantation procedure include pneumothorax, myocardial perforation, and infection, all of which should have an incidence less than 1%. Complications associated with the subcutaneous or submuscular pocket into which the device is placed include hematoma formation and erosion of the pocket. The endocardial leads that are used in the ICD system occasionally become dislodged shortly after implantation, necessitating a second procedure to reposition the leads. Other lead complications include a fracture or insulation breakdown, either of which may result in a failure to defibrillate. A lead fracture also may result in artifact that mimics VF and triggers inappropriate shocks.

Patients who have an ICD do not require evaluation every time they experience a device discharge. However, urgent evaluation is necessary if the patient experiences flurries of discharges. Analysis of stored electrograms often reveals the underlying problem (Fig. 61–3). The frequent shocks may be appropriate shocks triggered by flurries of VT or VF; if a correctable cause such as a metabolic defect or proarrhythmic drug cannot be identified, antiarrhythmic drug therapy and/or catheter ablation should be used to eliminate these arrhythmia flurries. Flurries of shocks may be triggered by atrial fibrillation with a rapid ventricular response, in which case aggressive management of the atrial fibrillation is indicated. In addition, flurries of shocks may be a manifestation of a lead fracture, in which case lead replacement is necessary.

In patients who have a pacemaker and a separate ICD, precautions must be taken to avoid device interactions. Pacemaker stimuli that occur during an episode of VF may result in failure of the ICD to detect the VF. In addition, sensing of pacemaker stimuli by an ICD may result in inappropriate shocks. Interactions between pacemakers and ICDs can be avoided by the use of a single device that functions as both an ICD and pacemaker.

RADIOFREQUENCY CATHETER ABLATION
Tissue Effects of Radiofrequency Energy

Radiofrequency ablation is a percutaneous catheter technique that can permanently eliminate a variety of supraventricular and ventricular tachycardias that previously required either chronic pharmacologic treatment for suppression or surgery for cure. Radiofrequency energy is delivered through an electrode catheter whose tip is in contact with tissue that is critical to maintenance of the tachycardia. The radiofrequency energy results in resistive heating of the tissue and irreversible tissue destruction when the tissue temperature exceeds 50° C. The lesions that are created are 5 to 6 mm in diameter and 2 to 3 mm deep. Chronic lesions demonstrate coagulation necrosis and are well demarcated.

Procedural Aspects

Diagnostic electrophysiologic testing (Chapter 50) and radiofrequency ablation often are performed during the same procedure, commonly on an outpatient basis. Various pacing techniques and/or an infusion of isoproterenol are used to induce the patient's arrhythmia, allowing the specific mechanism of the tachycardia to be determined. Depending on the type of tachycardia, sites in the heart are targeted for ablation based on the results of mapping (Chapter 58) or as guided

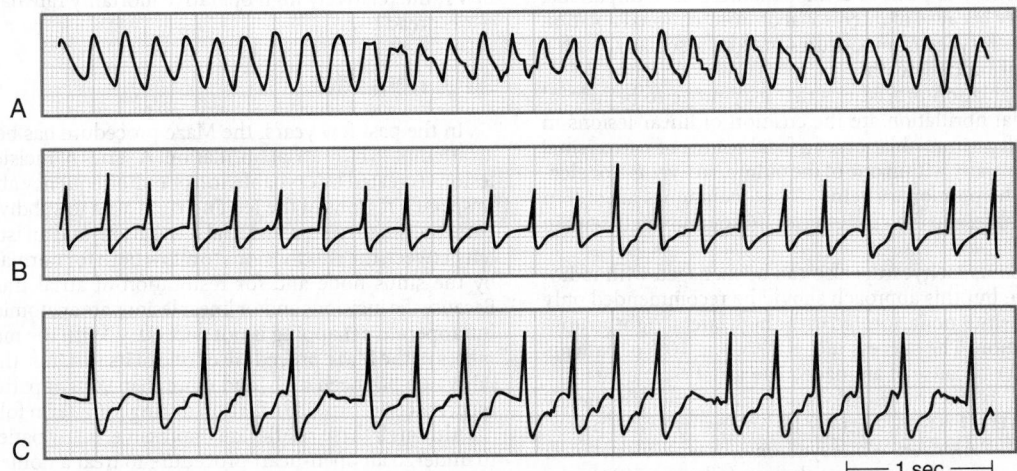

FIGURE 61–3 • Examples of stored electrograms obtained several hours after three different patients had experienced a flurry of shocks from an implantable cardioverter-defibrillator and showing the rhythm recorded by the device immediately before a shock was delivered. *A,* In this patient, the stored electrogram demonstrates ventricular tachycardia, rate 300 beats per minute, indicating that the shock was appropriate. He was treated with amiodarone to reduce the frequency of episodes of ventricular tachycardia. *B,* This patient received shocks because of paroxysmal supraventricular tachycardia at a rate of 206 beats per minute, which exceeded the programmed rate cutoff of 170 beats per minute. He underwent radiofrequency ablation of the paroxysmal supraventricular tachycardia and received no further inappropriate shocks. *C,* The stored electrograms in this patient indicate that the patient received inappropriate shocks that were triggered by atrial fibrillation, rate 180 beats per minute. The rate cutoff of the device in this patient was 150 beats per minute. This patient was treated with a β-blocker to keep the ventricular rate less than 150 beats per minute during atrial fibrillation.

by specific anatomic landmarks. Radiofrequency energy is delivered, typically in applications of 1 minute, at a power setting sufficient to result in adequate tissue heating of 60 to 70°C.

Radiofrequency Ablation of Supraventricular Arrhythmias

AV nodal reentrant tachycardia (Chapter 59), the most common type of paroxysmal SVT, is eliminated by radiofrequency ablation of either the "fast" or "slow" limb of the reentry circuit. For slow pathway ablation, which is the preferred technique, target sites for ablation are located in the posteroseptal right atrium, near the ostium of the coronary sinus. Slow pathway ablation has a success rate of 98 to 100% and is associated with a 0 to 1.3% risk of high-degree AV block.

Left-sided accessory pathways are ablated using either a retrograde aortic or transseptal approach, and those that are right-sided or septal are ablated using a venous approach. Detailed mapping of the accessory pathway is essential for identification of an appropriate ablation site, and the ablation catheter is positioned either on the atrial or ventricular aspect of the mitral or tricuspid annulus. The success rate of accessory pathway ablation is 90 to 98%, and the complication rate is 2 to 3%. A fatal complication occurs in less than 0.1% of patients. The most common nonfatal but serious complications are cardiac tamponade due to mechanical perforation of the heart by an electrode catheter and high-degree AV block in patients with a septal accessory pathway.

Detailed mapping also is needed to identify sites for ablation of atrial tachycardias (Chapter 59). Most atrial tachycardias arise in the right atrium and are mapped using a venous approach, but left atrial tachycardias are mapped using a transseptal approach. Assuming that the atrial tachycardia is arising only at one site, the success rate of ablation is approximately 90%, and complications are rare.

Type I atrial flutter (Chapter 59) arises in the right atrium and can be eliminated by radiofrequency ablation directed at a critical isthmus in the low right atrium, between the tricuspid annulus and the inferior vena cava. The success rate of this type of ablation is greater than 90%, and the risk of a serious complication is less than 1%.

In patients with drug-refractory atrial fibrillation (Chapter 59) associated with an uncontrolled ventricular rate, either radiofrequency ablation or modification of the AV node can improve symptoms, functional capacity, and left ventricular function. In AV node ablation, third-degree AV block is intentionally induced; the success rate is 100%, and all patients require a permanent pacemaker. In the AV node modification procedure, the intent is to slow the ventricular rate without creating the need for a pacemaker. The success rate of the modification procedure is 75%, and the remaining 25% of patients require a pacemaker because of intentional or unintentional ablation of the AV node. Both types of procedures may be associated with a late, 1 to 2% risk of sudden death.

Other catheter ablation procedures that may prove to be helpful in eliminating atrial fibrillation are the creation of linear lesions in the right and/or left atrium, ablation of a focal source of paroxysmal atrial fibrillation (usually within one of the pulmonary veins), or electrical isolation of the pulmonary veins. These techniques are still in a developmental phase, and their long-term efficacy and safety remain to be determined.

Inappropriate sinus tachycardia also can be managed with radiofrequency ablation, but this approach should be recommended only as a last resort. The sinus node, located in the high lateral right atrium, is targeted for ablation. The success rate is 80%, and 10% of patients require a pacemaker because of an inadequate atrial escape rate.

Because of a very favorable risk-benefit ratio, radiofrequency ablation is appropriate first-line therapy for any patient with paroxysmal SVT, the Wolff-Parkinson-White syndrome, or type I atrial flutter that is symptomatic enough to warrant therapy (Chapter 59). In the case of atrial flutter other than type I, atrial fibrillation, and inappropriate sinus tachycardia, an ablation procedure is appropriate only in patients with severe symptoms who are refractory to medication.

Radiofrequency Ablation of Ventricular Tachycardia

Radiofrequency ablation has been used as first-line treatment for idiopathic VT. The most common type of idiopathic VT arises in the outflow tract of the right ventricle and has a left bundle branch block configuration and superior axis. Another type of idiopathic VT has a

right bundle branch block configuration and a superior axis and arises in the inferoapical left ventricle (Chapter 60). The success rate of radiofrequency ablation of these types of VT has been 85 to 100%, and complications have been rare.

In patients with CAD, VT usually arises in diseased tissue adjacent to an area of prior infarction in the left ventricle. Because the disease process is diffuse instead of focal and because VT may originate at multiple sites, radiofrequency ablation of VT usually is not curative in patients with CAD. More often, radiofrequency ablation is used as adjunctive therapy with an ICD or with antiarrhythmic drug therapy. In the setting of CAD, the success rate of radiofrequency ablation of VT has been 65 to 95%, with a serious complication occurring in less than 2% of patients.

ARRHYTHMIA SURGERY

Wolff-Parkinson-White Syndrome

At present, surgical accessory pathway ablation may be indicated for the occasional patient with the Wolff-Parkinson-White syndrome who has potentially dangerous arrhythmias and in whom radiofrequency catheter ablation is unsuccessful. When performed by an experienced surgeon, the success rate of surgical accessory pathway ablation approaches 100% and the risk of a serious complication is low. Intraoperative mapping is necessary to establish the location of the accessory pathway, which then can be ablated either cryosurgically using an epicardial approach or by direct dissection using an endocardial approach.

Ventricular Tachycardia in Patients with Coronary Artery Disease

Subendocardial resection may be appropriate at the time of another surgical cardiac procedure in patients with CAD and recurrent, sustained, monomorphic VT. The substrate for monomorphic VT in patients with CAD usually lies within visually apparent scar tissue surrounding an area of prior MI (Chapter 60). Subendocardial resection has been successful in eliminating VT when performed either on a visual basis, with resection or cryoablation of all visually apparent scar tissue, or on a map-guided basis, with resection or cryoablation limited to the areas found to be participating in the generation of the VT. At centers experienced in this type of operation, the success rate of subendocardial resection has been 85 to 90%, and the operative mortality rate has been in the range of 5 to 10%. Although subendocardial resection has the potential advantage of preventing recurrences of VT, the relatively high operative mortality rate has discouraged its widespread use.

Atrial Fibrillation

In the past few years, the Maze procedure has been developed in an attempt to cure atrial fibrillation. A series of incisions and/or linear lesions (created by cryoablation or radiofrequency ablation) are made in specific regions of the left and right atria to subdivide the atria into parts too small to sustain atrial fibrillation, and an isthmus of tissue is left between the subdivisions to allow both for normal atrial activation by the sinus node and for restoration of atrial transport function. Because the incisions and/or linear lesions are anatomically determined, intraoperative mapping is not necessary. With the most recent refinements in the Maze procedure or one of its variants, the operative mortality rate has been <2%, and more than 90% of patients have had no recurrences of atrial fibrillation during long-term follow-up.

Although these results are impressive, many patients are reluctant to undergo an open-heart procedure to treat a nonlethal arrhythmia. The most appropriate role for the Maze procedure today may be as an adjunct to valve repair or replacement in patients with atrial fibrillation who require valve surgery.

Future Directions

An ongoing area of intensive research has been the development of catheter ablation techniques to cure atrial fibrillation. At present, the success rate is modest. It is anticipated that catheter ablation techniques that can reliably cure both paroxysmal and persistent atrial fibrillation will evolve over the next few years.

1. Lamas GA, Orav EJ, Stambler BS, et al: Quality of life and clinical outcomes in elderly patients treated with ventricular pacing as compared with dual-chamber pacing. Pacemaker Selection in the Elderly Investigators. N Engl J Med 1998;338:1097–1104.
2. Connelly SJ, Kerr CR, Gent M, et al: Effects of physiological pacing versus ventricular pacing on the risk of stroke and death due to cardiovascular causes. N Engl J Med 2000;342:1385–1391.
3. Lamas GA, Lee KL, Sweeney MO, et al: Ventricular pacing or dual-chamber pacing for sinus-node dysfunction. N Engl J Med 2002;346:1854–1862.
4. The Antiarrhythmics versus Implantable Defibrillators (AVID) Investigators: A comparison of antiarrhythmic-drug therapy with implantable defibrillators in patients resuscitated from near-fatal ventricular arrhythmias. N Engl J Med 1997;337:1576–1583.
5. Buxton AE, Lee KL, Fisher JD, et al: A randomized study of the prevention of sudden death in patients with coronary artery disease. Multicenter Unsustained Tachycardia Trial Investigators. N Engl J Med 1999;341:1882–1890.

SUGGESTED READINGS

Gregoratos G, Abrams J, Epstein AE, et al: ACC/AHA/NASPE 2002 guideline update for implantation of cardiac pacemakers and antiarrhythmia devices—summary article. J Am Coll Cardiol 2002;40:1703–1719. *A detailed description of the indications for implantation of permanent pacemakers and implantable cardioverter-defibrillators.*

Kusumoto F, Goldschager N: Device therapy for cardiac arrhythmias. JAMA 2002;287:1848–1852. *An excellent review.*

Scheinman MM, Morady F: Nonpharmacological approaches to atrial fibrillation. Circulation 2001;103:2120–2125. *An overview of ablation and pacemaker therapies.*

62 ANTIARRHYTHMIC DRUGS

Raymond L. Woosley

Antiarrhythmic drugs were developed with the expectation that they would extend and/or improve life for many patients with cardiovascular disease, especially patients with a history of life-threatening arrhythmias. Their usefulness has been limited, however, by toxicity and/or lack of efficacy. In mortality trials, benefit has not been seen, and worsened mortality has been observed with several drugs. Although most of the drugs can reduce symptomatic arrhythmias, care must be taken in deciding the mode of treatment or whether to treat with drugs at all.

Many antiarrhythmic agents are available today, but no agent is completely effective for all patients, and every agent has the potential for causing serious toxicity. Drug selection is often empirical, and known side effects may prohibit the use of certain classes of drugs for a specific patient.

Because of discouraging results with class I sodium channel–blocking drugs (e.g., quinidine, encainide, flecainide, moricizine) in CAST (Cardiac Arrhythmic Suppression Trial), class III drugs, which prolong the action potential duration (APD), have been developed. Amiodarone may improve mortality in some categories of patients, but the d-isomer of sotalol increases mortality after myocardial infarction (MI). A newer agent for prevention of atrial fibrillation, dofetilide, failed to improve mortality but provided reassuring results that mortality was not increased. Drugs used to control the rate of atrial fibrillation provide outcomes similar to those achieved by a strategy of cardioversion plus drugs to try to maintain sinus rhythm.

CLASSIFICATION OF ANTIARRHYTHMIC DRUGS

Antiarrhythmic drugs often are classified according to their electrophysiologic effects with approaches such as the Vaughan Williams classification (Fig. 62–1). Most antiarrhythmic drugs have multiple actions, however; their pharmacology is complex and may differ in different cardiac tissues. Many antiarrhythmic agents have pharmacologically active metabolites whose production varies extensively within the population and whose activity may be different from that of the parent compound. These factors limit the utility of any classification method.

CLASS I DRUGS. Drugs having class I action possess "local anesthetic" or "membrane-stabilizing" activity by blocking the fast inward sodium

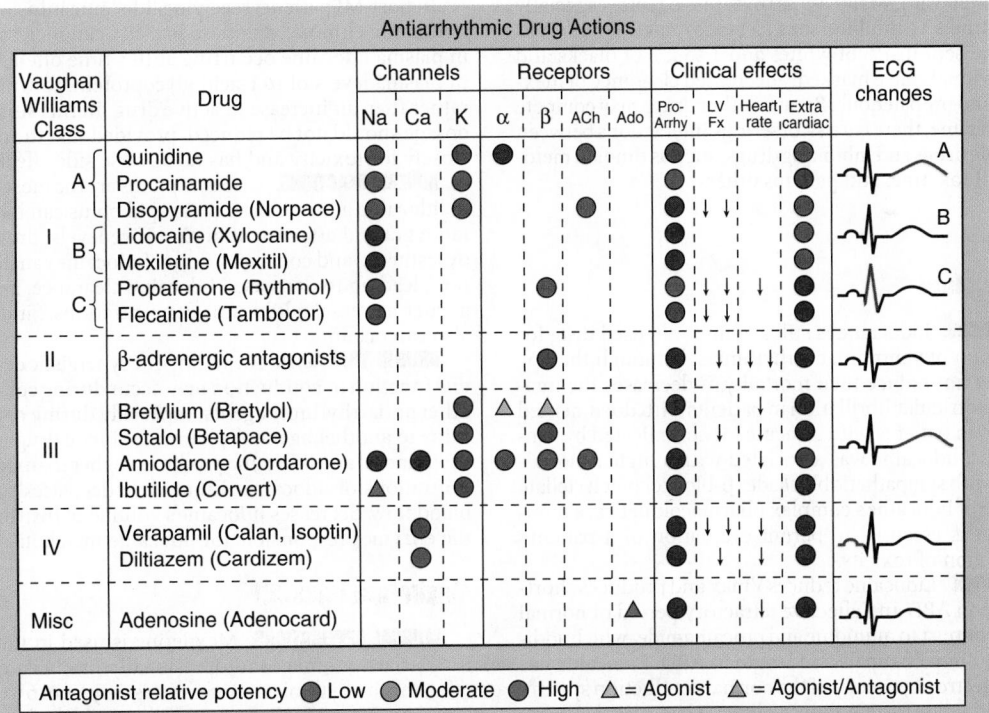

FIGURE 62–1 • A modification of the Sicilian Gambit drug classification system, including designation by the Vaughan Williams system. The sodium channel blockers are subdivided into the A, B, and C subgroups based on their relative potency. The targets of antiarrhythmic drugs, listed across the columns, are the ion channels (sodium, calcium, and potassium) and the receptors (α-adrenergic, β-adrenergic, cholinergic [ACh], and adenosinergic [Ado]). The next four columns compare the drugs' clinical actions. These include proarrhythmic potential (Proarrhy), effect on left ventricular function (LV Fx), effects on heart rate (Heart rate), and potential for extracardiac side effects (Extra cardiac). The electrocardiogram (ECG) tracings indicate the changes (in color) that are caused by usual dosages of the drug (i.e., PR interval, QRS interval, and QT interval). The drugs are listed in rows with brand names in parentheses. The symbols indicate the drugs' relative potency as agonists or antagonists. The yellow triangle indicates the biphasic effects of bretylium initially to release norepinephrine and act as an agonist and subsequently to block further release and act as an antagonist of adrenergic tone. The number of arrows and their direction indicate the magnitude and direction of effect of the drugs on heart rate and left ventricular function (i.e., inotropy).

channel to produce a decrease in the maximum depolarization rate, Vmax, of the action potential (phase 0) and slow intracardiac conduction (see Fig. 62–1). Class IA drugs, including quinidine, procainamide, and disopyramide, increase ventricular refractoriness and prolong the QT interval. Class IB drugs, including lidocaine, mexiletine, and tocainide, are modest sodium channel blockers that shorten the APD and refractoriness with little effect on PR, QRS, or QT intervals. Class IC drugs, including flecainide and propafenone, are potent sodium channel blockers that slow conduction velocity, have little effect on repolarization, and increase PR and QRS intervals but cause little change in the QT interval.

CLASS II DRUGS. Class II drugs are β-adrenergic antagonists, which are effective for supraventricular arrhythmias and tachyarrhythmias caused by excessive sympathetic activity but are of limited efficacy for severe, life-threatening ventricular arrhythmias. Although their exact mechanism is unknown, they are the only drugs found to be effective in preventing sudden cardiac death in survivors of prior MI.

CLASS III DRUGS. The predominant effect of class III drugs is to prolong the duration of the cardiac action potential and refractoriness. Examples include amiodarone, sotalol, bretylium, ibutilide, dofetilide, and N-acetyl-procainamide (NAPA), which is the major metabolite of procainamide.

CLASS IV DRUGS. Class IV drugs are calcium channel antagonists. Currently, only verapamil and diltiazem are used as antiarrhythmics.

Because of the many limitations of the Vaughan Williams classification, "The Sicilian Gambit" classification system has been developed based on the differential effects of antiarrhythmic drugs on channels, receptors, and transmembrane ion pumps (see Fig. 62–1). Quinidine, a class IA drug, is a sodium channel antagonist but also has the ability to block potassium channels and antagonize acetylcholine and catecholamines at cholinergic and α-adrenergic receptors. One would expect conduction slowing, increased APD (and refractoriness), and vasodilation to result from these three actions of quinidine.

POLYMORPHIC METABOLISM. Because antiarrhythmic drugs typically have a narrow therapeutic index, variable metabolism and clearance are often clinically relevant. Many antiarrhythmic agents, especially in class I, are substrates or inhibitors for a cytochrome P-450 (CYP) that is genetically absent in 7% of whites and 1 to 2% of blacks and Asians. These individuals have markedly decreased clearance of mexiletine, flecainide, and propafenone. Because other drugs may compete for or inhibit this enzyme, there is a risk of serious interactions between these antiarrhythmic drugs and inhibiting drugs, such as timolol, metoprolol, quinidine, fluoxetine, and perhaps others.

CLASS I DRUGS

Lidocaine (Xylocaine)

CLINICAL APPLICATIONS. Lidocaine is still a commonly used drug for the acute suppression of ventricular arrhythmias. Although therapy with lidocaine does not reduce total mortality, it decreases the incidence of primary ventricular fibrillation in patients with documented acute MI. However, in patients with an acute MI complicated by ventricular arrhythmias, lidocaine was associated with a higher mortality than was found with sympathetic blockade (β-blocker or left stellate blockade). Because of lidocaine's complex pharmacokinetics, a monitored environment is essential to permit evaluation of a patient's response and detection of toxicity.

MECHANISM OF ACTION. Lidocaine reduces Vmax and produces shortening or no change in APD and effective refractory period of normal Purkinje fibers, in contrast to quinidine and procainamide, which additionally block potassium channels and lengthen APD. Lidocaine has little effect on the electrophysiology of the normal conduction system; in patients with conduction system abnormalities, it has variable effects.

CLINICAL PHARMACOLOGY. The two desethyl metabolites of lidocaine that are excreted by the kidneys have less antiarrhythmic potency than the parent drug and may contribute to the production of central nervous system (CNS) side effects. Antiarrhythmic activity is correlated with lidocaine's concentration in the central compartment, and the half-life of distribution out of this compartment is rapid (8 minutes). The time required to reach steady-state conditions is 8 to 10 hours in normal individuals and 20 to 24 hours in some patients with heart failure and/or liver disease, whose elimination half-life is much longer than the 1.5 to 2 hours in normal subjects.

DOSAGE AND ADMINISTRATION. Lidocaine's primary use is for acute rapid suppression of ventricular arrhythmias. Single intravenous boluses

achieve only transient therapeutic effects because the drug is distributed rapidly out of the plasma and myocardium. For a stable patient, a total loading dose of lidocaine should be 3 to 4 mg/kg administered as a series of doses over 20 to 30 minutes. After injection of an initial dose of 1 mg/kg over 2 minutes, a series of three loading "boluses" can be administered slowly (50 mg each over 2 minutes) 8 to 10 minutes apart, while the patient is observed continuously for the development of side effects. At the time of initiation of the loading regimen, a maintenance infusion, designed to replace ongoing losses resulting from drug elimination, should be started, usually in a range of 20 to 60 µg/kg/min to achieve the desired plasma concentration of about 3 µg/mL.

Even in normal individuals, there is great variability in the peak plasma concentration. During loading, the patient's electrocardiogram (ECG), blood pressure, and mental status should be monitored; loading should be stopped at the first sign of lidocaine excess, usually transient CNS effects. When symptomatic arrhythmias persist in the presence of documented adequate dosage, defined by side effects or plasma concentration greater than 5 to 7 µg/mL, another agent should be used. Little therapeutic effect is evident at lidocaine plasma concentrations less than 1.5 µg/mL, whereas the risk of toxicity increases at concentrations greater than 5 µg/mL. When steady-state conditions have been achieved, terminating the lidocaine infusion gradually reduces plasma levels over the next 8 to 10 hours.

Initial loading regimens require no adjustment in patients with renal or liver disease; however, maintenance infusions must be decreased in these patients. With liver disease, there is little change in the volume of distribution, but the half-life of elimination is prolonged greatly to 5 hours; steady-state conditions are not achieved for 20 to 25 hours. During mechanical ventilation, there is low cardiac output and hepatic blood flow, so a decrease in lidocaine dosage is required. Patients with heart failure achieve lidocaine levels that are almost double the levels in normal individuals given the same dose, and clearance is approximately halved; loading doses and maintenance infusions should be reduced by 50%.

In post-MI patients receiving lidocaine infusions for more than 24 hours, the elimination phase half-life can increase 50%. An increase in plasma lidocaine occurring at this time often reflects an elevation in plasma levels of α-1-acid glycoprotein, to which lidocaine binds, rather than an increase in active drug. In this situation, the lidocaine dosage should not be reduced, provided that the patient is monitored closely for toxicity and has no adverse side effects.

ADVERSE REACTIONS. CNS symptoms are the most frequent side effects of lidocaine administration. A rapid bolus can induce seizures. With more gradual attainment of excessive levels, drowsiness, dysarthria, dysesthesia, and coma may occur. Lidocaine can depress cardiac function, leading to decreased lidocaine clearance, and produce an even greater increase in lidocaine concentrations. Sinus node dysfunction also can occur.

DRUG INTERACTIONS. An additive or synergistic depression of myocardial function or conduction may occur during combined therapy with other antiarrhythmic agents, especially during conversion from lidocaine to another agent. A pharmacokinetic drug interaction between propranolol and lidocaine produces higher than expected plasma concentrations of lidocaine. Cimetidine decreases splanchnic and liver blood flow, decreases lidocaine's volume of distribution, and inhibits the enzymes responsible for lidocaine metabolism.

Mexiletine (Mexitil)

CLINICAL APPLICATIONS. Mexiletine is used in the treatment of ventricular arrhythmias and occasionally has been effective in treating refractory arrhythmias. Success rates vary from 6 to 60% but are usually less than 20%. Mexiletine does not prolong the QT interval, and it can be useful in patients with a history of torsades de pointes (TdP) or long QT syndrome when quinidine, sotalol, procainamide, and disopyramide are contraindicated. It is often combined with drugs that prolong refractoriness for increased efficacy.

CLINICAL PHARMACOLOGY. Mexiletine has little first-pass metabolism but is eliminated primarily by hepatic metabolism with only 10 to 15% being excreted unchanged in the urine. Its half-life of elimination is 8 to 20 hours (9 to 12 hours for healthy subjects), with the time needed to reach steady state ranging from 1 to 3 days.

DOSAGE AND ADMINISTRATION. Mexiletine therapy should be initiated with a low dosage and increased at 2- to 3-day intervals until efficacy or intolerable side effects, such as tremor or other CNS symptoms, develop. With normal renal function, the recommended initial oral mexiletine dosage is 200 mg every 8 hours. As with most drugs having extensive liver metabolism, clearance is widely variable within the population. This is especially true for mexiletine because CYP2D6, responsible for its metabolism, is missing in 7% of the white population.

All patients with renal failure should be given low initial doses, especially because patients with hepatic CYP2D6 deficiency are dependent on renal excretion. Elimination half-life and clearance may be prolonged by overt heart failure and hepatic failure, and dosage reduction is required.

ADVERSE REACTIONS. Adverse reactions to mexiletine are most often dose related and include tremor, visual blurring, dizziness, dysphoria, and nausea. Thrombocytopenia and a positive antinuclear antibody test occur infrequently. Severe bradycardia may occur in patients with sinus node dysfunction, and worsening of heart block has been reported at high concentrations. Usual oral dosages of mexiletine do not depress ventricular function or induce increased heart failure.

DRUG INTERACTIONS. Mexiletine's hepatic metabolism can be increased by prior treatment with phenobarbital, phenytoin, or rifampicin, which increases clearance of mexiletine, possibly reducing an effective dose to an ineffective one. Mexiletine decreases clearance of theophylline. Quinidine inhibits the CYP2D6 enzyme that is partially responsible for mexiletine clearance.

Procainamide (Pronestyl-SR, Procan-SR)

CLINICAL APPLICATIONS. Procainamide, similar to quinidine, is effective against supraventricular and ventricular arrhythmias. Although the two drugs have similar electrophysiologic effects, they are clinically different, and one agent may be effective when the other is not. Procainamide is useful in acute management of patients with re-entrant supraventricular tachycardia and atrial fibrillation and flutter associated with Wolff-Parkinson-White syndrome.

Procainamide can be used intravenously to convert hemodynamically stable sustained ventricular tachycardia. Because it takes approximately 20 minutes to administer a loading dose of procainamide safely, its use is limited to clinical situations in which adequate time is available.

MECHANISM OF ACTION. Procainamide slows conduction and decreases automaticity and excitability of atrial and ventricular myocardium and Purkinje fibers. Because of its effect on potassium channels, it also prolongs APD and refractoriness. Compared with quinidine, procainamide has little vagolytic activity and causes less prolongation of the QT interval. Its major metabolite, N-acetyl-procainamide (acecainide, NAPA), has predominantly class III antiarrhythmic activity; it prolongs APD and refractoriness in atrial and ventricular myocardium and prolongs the QT interval.

CLINICAL PHARMACOLOGY. Procainamide is absorbed rapidly and 100% orally bioavailable. About 15% of procainamide is bound to serum proteins. Procainamide's short half-life of elimination of 2 to 4 hours in patients with normal renal function has led to the use of sustained-release preparations, which can be given every 3 to 6 hours.

Slightly more than half of the general population are phenotypic rapid acetylators of procainamide and quickly convert it to NAPA. The usually effective plasma concentrations are 4 to 8 µg/mL for procainamide and 7 to 15 µg/mL for NAPA. Plasma concentrations should be monitored to determine compliance and prevent toxicity.

DOSAGE AND ADMINISTRATION. When administered intravenously, procainamide can be given as a constant 25-minute loading infusion of 275 µg/min/kg or as a series of doses (100 mg delivered over 3 minutes) given every 5 minutes to a total dose of 1 g. If the loading infusion is well tolerated with no hypotension and less than 25% QRS or QT widening, the maintenance intravenous infusion is 20 to 60 µg/kg/min (depending on renal function).

With normal renal and cardiac function, the initial recommended oral maintenance dose is 50 mg/kg/day in the sustained-release form every 6 to 8 hours. Because the electrophysiologic effects of procainamide and NAPA are different, monitoring of patients receiving procainamide should include measurement of plasma concentrations of both agents to determine their relative concentrations. Patients with the rapid acetylator phenotype or impaired renal function may develop high plasma concentrations of NAPA and should be monitored to maintain NAPA levels less than 20 µg/mL. With renal dysfunction or a low cardiac output, procainamide and especially NAPA in usual doses may accumulate to potentially toxic levels.

ADVERSE REACTIONS. Of patients, 40% discontinue procainamide in the first 6 months because of adverse reaction. Arrhythmia may be aggravated, including the development of TdP most often secondary to NAPA; procainamide should not be used in patients with a long QT syndrome, a history of TdP, or hypokalemia. Of patients treated long-term, 15 to 20% develop a lupus-like syndrome that regresses with discontinuation of the drug. Procainamide can cause agranulocytosis, so a white blood cell count should be obtained every 2 weeks for the first 3 months.

DRUG INTERACTIONS. In contrast to quinidine, procainamide does not cause an increase in digoxin levels. Procainamide's clearance is reduced by 10 to 50% by cimetidine and ranitidine, which block its renal tubular secretion.

Disopyramide (Norpace)

CLINICAL APPLICATIONS. Disopyramide (class IA) is effective against a broad range of supraventricular and ventricular arrhythmias, with an antiarrhythmic profile similar to that of quinidine and procainamide. Its negative inotropic and anticholinergic actions frequently limit its usefulness.

DOSAGE AND ADMINISTRATION. A loading dose is not recommended with disopyramide because of the risk of heart failure or anticholinergic side effects. The usually effective dosage for disopyramide is 100 to 400 mg two to four times daily, to a maximal dose of 800 mg/day. Therapy should begin with low doses to allow ample time for steady-state equilibrium.

Unless a sustained-release preparation is used, rapid fluctuations in plasma concentration are difficult to avoid because of disopyramide's saturable protein binding. The generally accepted therapeutic range for total (free and bound) disopyramide is 2 to 5 µg/mL but should not be strictly relied on.

DRUG INTERACTIONS. Phenytoin, rifampicin, and phenobarbital induce hepatic metabolism of disopyramide, increase its elimination, and potentially reduce its antiarrhythmic effect. Significant depression of myocardial contractility may result from the combined administration of disopyramide with β-adrenergic or calcium channel antagonists; these combinations should be avoided in patients with impaired ventricular function.

Quinidine

CLINICAL APPLICATIONS. Quinidine (class IA) is used for a variety of supraventricular and ventricular arrhythmias, including conversion of atrial fibrillation, atrial flutter, or supraventricular tachycardia and suppression of ventricular extrasystoles and ventricular tachycardia. Small studies suggest that quinidine may prevent recurrent ventricular fibrillation in patients with the Brugada syndrome. Meta-analysis of six placebo-controlled trials in patients with atrial fibrillation showed a small but statistically significant increase in mortality in the patients treated with quinidine, however. Because of the similarity to the results in CAST, these results should be assumed to be valid until a definitive prospective study is available.

CLINICAL PHARMACOLOGY. Although quinidine sulfate usually is administered every 6 hours, its elimination half-life varies from 3 to 19 hours. Oral bioavailability is approximately 70%. Quinidine is inactivated or eliminated by hepatic metabolism (50 to 90%) and renal elimination (10 to 30%). Several active metabolites are variably present among individuals.

DOSAGE AND ADMINISTRATION. Quinidine is available as sulfate, gluconate, and polygalacturonate; the quinidine content varies among these at 83, 62, and 60%, respectively. The usually effective dosage of quinidine sulfate ranges from 800 to 2400 mg/day, with the maximum recommended single dose being 600 mg. Doses of other forms should be adjusted based on quinidine content. Elderly patients often require lower dosages of quinidine because of reduced clearance and volume of distribution. Because the half-life varies from 3 to 19 hours, doses should be adjusted only every 2 to 4 days to prevent unexpected drug accumulation. The range of therapeutic plasma concentrations measured using assays that differentiate quinidine from its metabolites is 0.7 to 5.5 µg/mL. Intravenous therapy with quinidine is potentially hazardous and rarely indicated.

No adjustment in initial dosage is needed for patients with renal or hepatic disease, but lower than usual total plasma concentrations can produce toxicity in patients with decreased protein binding caused by hepatic failure. Patients with rapid quinidine elimination, often resulting from induction of hepatic metabolism caused by other drugs, may require doses of 600 mg every 6 hours.

Patients with congenital long QT syndrome, hypokalemia, or a history of TdP should not be given quinidine because of their increased risk for TdP. For patients with heart failure, quinidine can cause proarrhythmia and precipitate digitalis toxicity; quinidine titration should begin at a lower dose. The dose of any concomitant cardiac glycoside should be reduced and monitored, and the potassium level should be maintained at greater than 4 mEq/L.

The direct negative inotropic effects of quinidine are usually offset by its vasodilatory effect so that oral quinidine is usually well tolerated hemodynamically in patients with reduced ventricular function or heart failure. The risk of quinidine-induced TdP is potentiated, however, in patients with heart failure in the setting of bradycardia and low serum magnesium or potassium levels.

ADVERSE REACTIONS. Marked prolongation of the QT interval can occur with usual or even low doses, and the risk of TdP is markedly increased. This arrhythmia may be responsible for quinidine syncope, which occurs in 5 to 10% of patients within the first days of quinidine treatment, and for quinidine-induced sudden death. For patients who develop TdP, treatment with pacing or isoproterenol is usually effective. Magnesium sulfate injection also has been recommended as initial therapy, but controlled trials are not currently available.

Because quinidine acts through α-adrenergic blockade to produce vasodilation, hypotension may occur, especially in patients concomitantly receiving nitrates or other vasodilators. Other adverse effects include diarrhea, vomiting, tinnitus, and rarely thrombocytopenia; conduction block can occur in patients with preexisting conduction system disease. In patients treated with quinidine for atrial flutter without prior atrioventricular nodal blockade by digitalis, sudden increases in atrioventricular conduction and rapid ventricular rates may develop owing to quinidine's anticholinergic effects.

DRUG INTERACTIONS. Quinidine metabolism is inhibited by cimetidine and induced by phenytoin, phenobarbital, and rifampicin. Clinical digoxin toxicity has been described in 20 to 40% of patients receiving concurrent quinidine and digoxin. Quinidine is a potent inhibitor of the hepatic cytochrome P-450 specific for debrisoquine metabolism (CYP2D6), although it is not metabolized by this specific P-450 isozyme.

Propafenone (Rythmol)

CLINICAL APPLICATIONS. Propafenone (class IC) is similar to other antiarrhythmic agents in overall efficacy and patient tolerance for many types of arrhythmias, including supraventricular arrhythmias, such as atrial fibrillation in patients without structural heart disease.

CLINICAL PHARMACOLOGY. Propafenone has a marked structural similarity to propranolol and can produce clinically significant β-adrenergic inhibition. As with mexiletine and flecainide, patients deficient in CYP2D6 have slow elimination of propafenone and develop significant β-receptor antagonism at low doses.

DOSAGE AND ADMINISTRATION. Effective dosages range from 300 to 900 mg/day in two to four divided doses. Propafenone dosage should not be changed more frequently than every 3 days because of slow elimination of the parent drug in poor metabolizers and slow accumulation of metabolites in extensive metabolizers. Drug interactions occur with many antidepressants and neuroleptics. Quinidine results in higher propafenone concentrations. Combination with β-blockers should be avoided. The dose should be reduced by 70 to 80% in patients with hepatic disease.

Flecainide (Tambocor)

CLINICAL APPLICATIONS. Flecainide (class IC) is effective in suppressing a variety of ventricular and supraventricular tachycardias. The finding of increased mortality in patients with ischemic heart disease generally has restricted its use to treat supraventricular arrhythmias in patients without known structural heart disease. Its negative inotropic actions restrict its use to patients having moderately well-preserved ventricular function.

CLINICAL PHARMACOLOGY. Most of flecainide is metabolized by CYP2D6 in the liver to compounds that are not pharmacologically active. Because flecainide also is eliminated by the kidneys to a considerable extent, the enzyme deficiency usually has little effect on its pharmacokinetics except in patients with renal insufficiency.

DOSAGE AND ADMINISTRATION. Patients with supraventricular tachycardia should receive 50 mg every 12 hours as a starting dose; after 3 to 4 days, the dose can be adjusted up to 100 to 150 mg every 12 hours based on clinical response. Because 7% of white patients with renal failure do not have the CYP2D6 enzyme and because flecainide usually is eliminated by metabolism and renal excretion, all patients with renal failure should be given low dosages and have the doses titrated carefully.

ADVERSE REACTIONS. Flecainide can induce proarrhythmic events even when prescribed as recommended, especially in patients with severe heart disease. Flecainide produces a measurable decrease in left ventricular function in most patients and can depress sinus node activity in patients with preexisting sinus node dysfunction; it also prolongs the QRS and PR intervals on the surface ECG. Flecainide increases pacing thresholds by 200% and must be used with caution in pacemaker-dependent patients. It also increases the threshold for electrical defibrillation in patients with defibrillators.

DRUG INTERACTIONS. Cimetidine reduces flecainide clearance and prolongs its half-life. Digoxin, propranolol, and amiodarone increase flecainide levels.

β-RECEPTOR ANTAGONISTS

β-Receptor antagonists (β-blockers) usually are considered as relatively equivalent members of a class of agents that block adrenergic agonists at the β-receptor. There are few comparative trials to evaluate their equivalence as antiarrhythmic agents and to determine the dosages at which they might have equivalence. They generally are considered to be effective for arrhythmias associated with excessive sympathetic stimulation (e.g., pheochromocytoma) or arrhythmias associated with exercise or acute MI. The antiarrhythmic efficacy of β-blockers is thought to be due to two actions: blockade of the postsynaptic cardiac receptor and membrane-stabilizing activity. The direct membrane effect produces shortening of the action potential in vitro but requires concentrations far higher than can be achieved clinically. For some drugs in this class, however, it is important to consider other ancillary actions that might augment or impede their efficacy. The class III action (potassium channel blockade) of sotalol augments its antiarrhythmic potency, whereas the intrinsic sympathomimetic activity of pindolol is thought to impede antiarrhythmic efficacy. β-Blockers such as propranolol, atenolol, and metoprolol generally are considered to be effective in supraventricular arrhythmias, such as atrioventricular nodal re-entry, atrial fibrillation, and atrial flutter. Esmolol, an ultra-short-acting β-blocker with a half-life of 9 minutes, is useful for slowing ventricular response to atrial fibrillation or flutter for short periods, such as after surgery. Long-term therapy with β-blockers is also effective in preventing life-threatening arrhythmias in many patients with the congenital long QT syndrome, especially patients whose symptoms are associated with adrenergic stimulation.

Although β-blockers generally are considered to be ineffective or contraindicated in patients with sustained ventricular tachycardia, they are often useful, especially when combined with other antiarrhythmic agents, for prevention of recurrent episodes of ventricular tachycardia. Although they are not usually effective in suppressing premature ventricular contractions, they often are able to reduce the troublesome symptoms of palpitations and, more importantly, in patients with prior MI, reduce the associated risk of sudden death.

The dosages of β-blockers required for treatment of arrhythmias are generally similar to dosages required for treatment of hypertension or angina. In some patients, higher dosages (equivalent to >320 mg/day of propranolol) are required to suppress ventricular arrhythmias, but these dosages also are associated with a higher incidence of fatigue and potentially serious depression.

Sotalol (Betapace)

CLINICAL APPLICATIONS AND PHARMACOLOGY. Sotalol blocks β-receptors and increases the QT interval and cardiac refractoriness. This unique combination of properties makes sotalol effective in suppressing a variety of supraventricular and ventricular arrhythmias; however, sotalol increases instability in patients with ventricular arrhythmias after an MI.

Peak plasma concentrations are seen 2.5 to 4 hours after a dose. Sotalol is eliminated by the kidneys unchanged with a half-life of approximately 12 hours.

DOSAGES AND ADMINISTRATION. The recommended initial dose of sotalol is 80 mg every 12 hours. In patients with relatively normal renal function, steady state occurs in 2 to 3 days. In patients who do not respond and have QT intervals less than 500 msec, the dosage may be increased to 160 mg twice daily and, if necessary, to 240 mg twice daily.

Because sotalol mainly is eliminated unchanged in the urine, the dosing interval should be 24 hours if the creatinine clearance is 30 to 60 mL/min and every 36 to 48 hours if it is 10 to 30 mL/min. Because of the increased risk of TdP and heart failure, patients with reduced cardiac output should be given lower doses and monitored carefully.

ADVERSE REACTIONS. A major concern with sotalol treatment is the occurrence of TdP, which occurs with an overall incidence of approximately 2%. It is more common in women, in patients with heart failure, and in patients with a history of sustained ventricular tachycardia (7%). The incidence of TdP should be minimized by careful screening for predisposing factors, such as bradycardia, baseline prolongation of the QT interval, and hypokalemia; by careful dose escalation beginning at 160 mg/day; and by limiting the maximum QT interval prolongation to less than 550 msec. The incidence of new or worsened heart failure is only about 3%. Other side effects typical of β-blockers are to be expected.

DRUG INTERACTIONS. Concomitant use of sotalol with agents that prolong repolarization has the potential to increase the likelihood of TdP. No pharmacokinetic interactions have been seen with sotalol.

Amiodarone (Cordarone)

CLINICAL APPLICATIONS. Amiodarone is approved by the Food and Drug Administration only for life-threatening ventricular arrhythmias refractory to other available forms of therapy. Nevertheless, numerous trials describe its efficacy in the conversion and slowing of atrial fibrillation, atrioventricular nodal re-entrant tachycardia, and tachycardias associated with Wolff-Parkinson-White syndrome. The reasons for amiodarone's restrictive labeling include its documented potentially lethal complications, the difficulties associated with its variable time for onset of action, and multiple dangerous drug interactions. Large clinical trials of oral amiodarone in patients with prior MI or heart failure have been negative or have shown a reduction in sudden death but not total mortality. In contrast to the class IC drugs, amiodarone does not increase mortality in these patients. Intravenous amiodarone can be used for recurrent life-threatening ventricular tachycardia or fibrillation; hypotension is the major side effect. In patients with out-of-hospital cardiac arrest, amiodarone increases survival to hospitalization but not to time of discharge.

CLINICAL PHARMACOLOGY. Amiodarone is absorbed slowly from the gastrointestinal tract, and bioavailability varies over a four-fold range. It is metabolized extensively to its desethyl metabolite (DEA), and little, if any, is excreted unchanged in the urine. Concentrations of DEA, which has antiarrhythmic potency equal to or greater than amiodarone, vary from 0.4 to 2.0 times that of amiodarone during long-term therapy. After intravenous administration, the measured half-life in plasma is 4.8 to 68.2 hours. Slow redistribution of drug out of adipose and muscle tissues leads to slow and extremely variable elimination from plasma, with half-lives ranging from 13 to 103 days in the steady state.

DOSAGE AND ADMINISTRATION. Without a loading dose, amiodarone requires several weeks to months before producing its antiarrhythmic action. Large intravenous dosages or oral loading dosages can hasten the onset of therapeutic effects. Large clinical trials have used an oral loading dose of 600 to 800 mg daily for 14 days. The usual maintenance dose varies from 200 to 600 mg/day, and because of the severity of adverse reactions, the lowest effective dosage should be prescribed. Patients with supraventricular arrhythmias may respond to lower dosages than patients with ventricular arrhythmias.

For intravenous administration, the manufacturer recommends a three-phase infusion over the first 24 hours: 150 mg over 10 minutes, followed by 360 mg over the next 6 hours, followed by 0.5 mg/min. The drug can be continued at this rate, but monitoring of plasma concentrations is recommended. An additional 150 mg can be infused over 10 minutes for patients who continue to have recurrent ventricular tachycardia or fibrillation or whose arrhythmia recurs during downward titration of the infusion. For pulseless ventricular tachycardia or ventricular fibrillation, a rapid bolus of 300 mg diluted in 20 to 30 mL of saline or dextrose in water is recommended, followed by an additional dose of 150 mg if necessary.

Amiodarone concentrations are usually between 1 and 2 μg/mL during effective oral therapy. Similar concentrations of DEA accumulate during therapy and, although unproven, are likely to contribute to antiarrhythmic efficacy. Monitoring of plasma concentrations is of limited value, but levels of amiodarone greater than 3 to 4 μg/mL for prolonged periods are associated with a higher incidence of adverse effects.

ADVERSE REACTIONS. Intravenous amiodarone at dosages greater than 5 mg/kg decreases contractility and peripheral vascular resistance, producing severe hypotension in some instances. This effect may be due to the effects of the diluent polysorbate 80, because oral administration at usual dosages improves myocardial contractility.

The safety of amiodarone is controversial. The early reports and some more recently completed trials found it to be well tolerated, but the only experience in the United States revealed a high incidence of intolerable, sometimes lethal reactions.

The most serious adverse reaction is lethal interstitial pneumonitis, which may be more common in patients with preexisting lung disease. Monitoring is essential because the pneumonitis is reversible if detected early. A chest radiograph every 3 months may be useful, but serial pulmonary function tests are of little value. Hyperthyroidism or hypothyroidism is seen in about 4% of patients. Accumulation of corneal microdeposits is almost uniform during long-term therapy and can progress to interfere with vision. Some white patients notice a slate-gray or bluish discoloration of sun-exposed areas of the skin. Of patients, 30% or more have abnormally elevated serum hepatic enzyme levels, and progression to jaundice and cirrhosis has been reported.

DRUG INTERACTIONS. Amiodarone interferes with the clearance of many drugs, such as digoxin, warfarin, quinidine, procainamide, disopyramide, mexiletine, and propafenone. The elimination of many other drugs may be impaired by amiodarone, and the lowest effective dosage should be sought.

Ibutilide (Corvert)

CLINICAL APPLICATIONS. Ibutilide is a class III drug for rapid conversion of recent-onset atrial fibrillation or flutter. It has not yet been tested in other arrhythmias or in patients with atrial fibrillation or flutter of long duration (>90 days). It should not be given to patients who have hypokalemia, hypomagnesemia, or a QTc more than 440 msec at baseline. In controlled studies, ibutilide has terminated the arrhythmia in 5 to 88 minutes in approximately 44% of patients treated with 1 mg followed by either 0.5 or 1 mg; approximately 20% of patients responded to the first infusion, and approximately 25% of patients not responding to the first infusion responded to the second infusion. It can also be used to improve the success of electrical cardioversion.

CLINICAL PHARMACOLOGY. Ibutilide is available currently only for intravenous administration. When given over 10 minutes, it distributes rapidly in a multiexponential fashion with the clinically relevant component having a half-life of 2 to 12 hours (mean 6 hours). The drug is eliminated mainly by oxidative hepatic metabolism, and systemic clearance is rapid. Because formal drug interaction studies have not been performed, it is not possible to anticipate which enzymes are likely responsible for its elimination.

DOSAGE AND ADMINISTRATION. The recommended dose for a patient weighing more than 60 kg is 1 mg; if the patient weighs less than 60 kg, 0.01 mg/kg should be given over 10 minutes. For patients whose arrhythmias have not converted by 10 minutes after completion of the first dose, a second dose of equal size can be administered.

ADVERSE REACTIONS. The most serious adverse reaction is TdP, which was seen in 1.7% of patients in premarketing experience. The risk of TdP is higher in patients who are female and/or who have reduced ventricular function or electrolyte disorders.

Dofetilide (Tikosyn)

CLINICAL APPLICATION. Oral dofetilide is of limited value for the reversion of atrial fibrillation, but it is more effective for reversion of atrial flutter. Dofetilide seems to have more utility for the maintenance of sinus rhythm after reversion.

CLINICAL PHARMACOLOGY. Dofetilide is absorbed completely after oral administration, and bioavailability ranges from 75 to 100%. Elimination is divided relatively evenly between renal and hepatic routes. The elimination half-life is approximately 8 to 10 hours after oral administration. Clearance is 12 to 18% lower in women.

Dofetilide is metabolized predominantly by the CYP3A4 family and interacts with drugs such as erythromycin or ketoconazole, resulting in higher, potentially toxic dofetilide levels. After intravenous infusion, there is an approximately 9-minute lag between peak concentrations and peak effect on the QT interval.

DOSAGE AND ADMINISTRATION. The prescription of dofetilide is restricted to physicians who can document that they have participated in an educational program. The recommended dosage of dofetilide is 500 µg twice a day. Lower doses are recommended for patients who develop excessive QTc prolongation greater than 500 msec or greater than 15% longer than baseline. The dosage should be reduced or the drug avoided in patients with renal disease.

ADVERSE REACTIONS. In clinical trials, TdP occurred in 3% of patients receiving dofetilide. In pooled analysis of 1346 patients receiving dofetilide and 677 treated with placebo in randomized trials of supraventricular arrhythmias, dofetilide was not associated with a significant increase in mortality (adjusted hazard ratio 1.1).

DRUG INTERACTIONS. Increased plasma concentrations are seen with coadministration of ketoconazole, verapamil, megestrol, cimetidine, prochlorperazine, and hydrochlorothiazide, especially in patients with reduced renal function.

CALCIUM CHANNEL BLOCKERS

Verapamil and diltiazem are useful in the management of supraventricular tachycardia, when they are administered to slow the ventricular rate in patients with atrial fibrillation or flutter and to treat and prevent atrioventricular nodal re-entrant tachycardia. Intravenous diltiazem is useful for the temporary control of rapid ventricular rate during atrial fibrillation and flutter. In controlled clinical trials, conversion to sinus rhythm is no more likely with diltiazem than with placebo. The usual dosages for calcium channel blockers for acute treatment are verapamil, 2.5 to 5 mg intravenously over 2 to 4 minutes, with another 5 to 10 mg if necessary 15 to 30 minutes later to a maximum total dose of 20 mg, or diltiazem, either an intravenous bolus of 0.25 mg/kg (about 20 mg) over 2 minutes, with a second dose of 0.35 mg/kg if necessary, or a continuous infusion at 5 to 10 mg/hr with maximum dose of 15 mg/hr and maximum duration of 24 hours.

Adenosine (Adenocard)

CLINICAL APPLICATIONS AND PHARMACOLOGY. By directly slowing atrioventricular nodal conduction, adenosine is effective for the acute conversion of paroxysmal supraventricular tachycardia caused by re-entry involving the atrioventricular node. Because of the fleeting and relatively selective action of adenosine on the atrioventricular node, it may be used as a diagnostic tool in patients with narrow- or wide-complex tachycardia. It is preferable, however, to make the correct diagnosis before giving any drugs because of the risk of adverse effects.

After rapid intravenous injection, the half-life of elimination has been estimated as 1.5 to 10 seconds. The drug is metabolized rapidly in the plasma and in cells to form inosine and adenosine monophosphate. Maximal pharmacologic effects are seen within 10 to 20 seconds when given into a central line.

DOSAGE AND ADMINISTRATION. Adenosine should be injected intravenously into a proximal tubing site and flushed quickly with saline. For adults, the initial dose is 6 mg injected over 1 to 2 seconds. If the arrhythmia persists, a 12-mg dose can be injected 1 to 2 minutes later. An alternative regimen is an initial dose of 50 µg/kg incremented every few minutes by 50 µg/kg until the paroxysmal supraventricular tachycardia is terminated, side effects become intolerable, or a maximum dose of 0.3 mg/kg is administered.

ADVERSE REACTIONS. Adenosine is contraindicated in patients with sick sinus syndrome or second-degree or third-degree heart block unless the patient has a functioning artificial pacemaker. Because of the rapid clearance of adenosine, side effects such as facial flushing, dyspnea, or chest pressure persist less than 60 seconds. Other less frequent side effects include nausea, lightheadedness, headache, sweating, palpitations, hypotension, and blurred vision.

DRUG INTERACTIONS. Dipyridamole pretreatment increases the potency of adenosine, probably because it blocks its cellular uptake; carbamazepine may potentiate the actions of adenosine. Caffeine and theophylline antagonize the actions of adenosine.

SUGGESTED READINGS

Chevalier P, Durand-Dubief A, Burri H, et al: Amiodarone versus placebo and classic drugs for cardioversion of recent-onset atrial fibrillation: A meta-analysis. J Am Coll Cardiol 2003;41:255–262. *Amiodarone is superior to placebo and similar to class Ic drugs for cardioversion of AF.*

Haverkamp W, Breithardt G, Camm AJ, et al: The potential for QT prolongation and proarrhythmia by non-anti-arrhythmic drugs: Clinical and regulatory implications. Report on a Policy Conference of the European Society of Cardiology. Cardiovasc Res 2000;47:219–233. *Overview of mechanisms, detection, clinical manifestations, and results and implications of post-marketing surveillance.*

Roden DM: Pharmacogenetics and drug-induced arrhythmias. Cardiovasc Res 2001;50:224–231. *Polymorphisms as a cause of drug-induced arrhythmias.*

Rodriguez I, Kilborn MJ, Liu XK, et al: Drug-induced QT prolongation in women during the menstrual cycle. JAMA 2001;285:1322–1326. *QTc prolongs during the first half of the menstrual cycle.*

63 ARTERIAL HYPERTENSION

Ronald Victor

Definition

In populations, blood pressures fit a normal distribution, but the attendant risks of heart disease and stroke increase curvilinearly with increasing levels of blood pressure, without any obvious breakpoint (Fig. 63–1). Thus, the separation of normal from high blood pressure is arbitrary, and the definition of hypertension has been a moving target. The first estimate was that systolic blood pressure should be 100 plus a person's age and that only higher values needed to be treated. This formula was predicated on the incorrect notion that the progressive increase in blood pressure with advancing age is essential to maintain blood flow through atherosclerotic arteries, hence the term *essential hypertension.* Later, *hypertension in adults* was redefined as a blood pressure of 160/95 mm Hg or greater, regardless of age, because this is the value above which the risk of stroke or myocardial infarction roughly doubles compared with the risk associated with pressures below 120/80 mm Hg. Now, however, based on the results of randomized clinical drug trials, *hypertension* is defined as a blood pressure of 140/90 mm Hg or greater because this is the

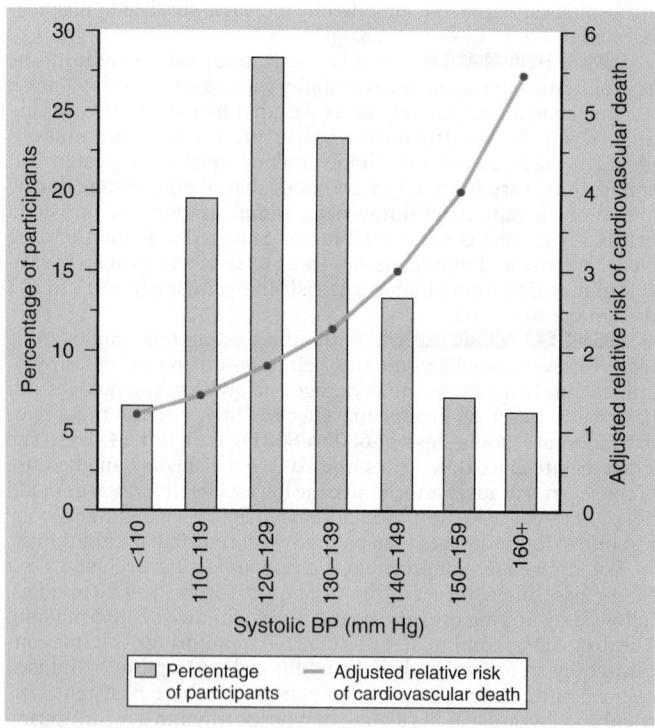

FIGURE 63–1 • Adjusted relative risk of cardiovascular mortality by systolic blood pressure (BP) levels in men screened for the Multiple Risk Factor Intervention Trial (MRFIT). (From the National High Blood Pressure Education Program Working Group. Arch Intern Med 1993;153:186–208.)

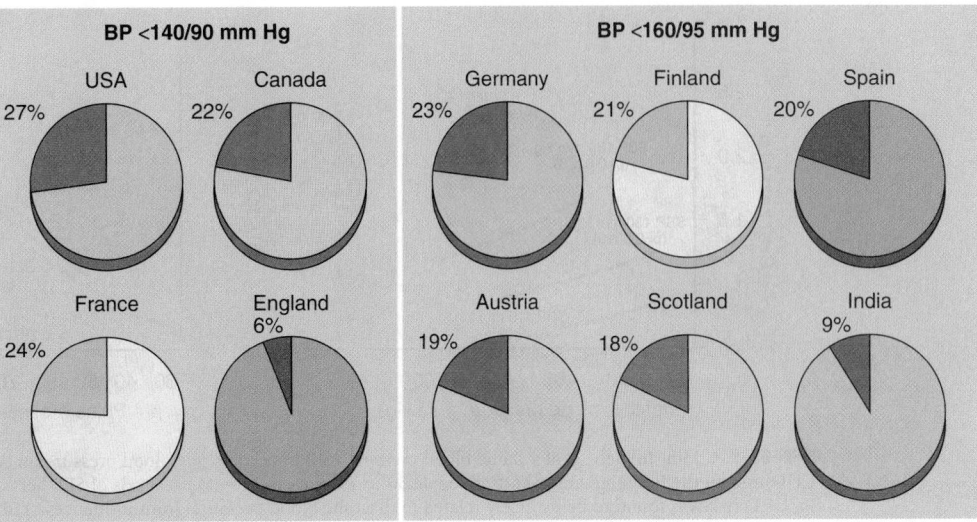

FIGURE 63–2 • Percentage of hypertensive patients whose blood pressures are both treated and controlled to either less than 140/90 mm Hg or less than 160/95 mm Hg in different countries. (From Laragh J: Laragh's lessons in pathophysiology and clinical pearls for treating hypertension. Am J Hypertens 2001;14:84-86. Redrawn with permission from Mancia G, Grassi G: Rationale for the use of a fixed dose combination in the treatment of hypertension. Eur Heart J 1999;1[suppl L]: L14–L19.)

value above which the benefits of treatment appear to outweigh the risks. *Prehypertension* is now defined as a blood pressure of 130–139/80–89 mm Hg. Individuals with blood pressure in this range are twice as likely to progress to hypertension compared with individuals with lower blood pressures.

Epidemiology

Affecting one fourth of the adult population (50 million in the United States and 1 billion people worldwide), arterial hypertension is the most common cause for a visit to a physician and the most widely recognized treatable risk factor for stroke (Chapters 439 and 440), myocardial infarction (Chapters 68 and 69), heart failure (Chapters 55 and 56), peripheral vascular disease (Chapter 78), aortic dissection (Chapter 75), and chronic renal failure (Chapter 117). Despite this knowledge and unequivocal scientific proof that treating hypertension dramatically reduces its attendant morbidity and mortality, hypertension remains untreated or poorly treated in the majority of affected individuals in all countries, including those with the most advanced health care (Fig. 63–2). Inadequate treatment of hypertension is a major factor contributing to some of the adverse secular trends in the last decade, including an increased incidence of stroke, heart failure, and renal failure plus a leveling off of the decline in coronary heart disease mortality.

AGING AND PULSE PRESSURE. Patients often ask what is more important: systolic or diastolic blood pressure? The answer depends on the age of the patient. In industrialized societies, systolic pressure rises progressively with age; if individuals live long enough, almost all develop systolic hypertension. This age-dependent rise in blood pressure is not an essential part of human biology, because in less industrialized societies, where the consumption of calories and salt is low, blood pressures remain low and do not rise with age. In industrialized societies, diastolic pressure rises until age 50 and decreases thereafter, producing a dramatic rise in pulse pressure (systolic pressure minus diastolic pressure) (Fig. 63–3).

Different hemodynamic faults underlie hypertension in younger and older individuals. The minority of patients who develop hypertension before the age of 50 typically have *combined systolic and diastolic hypertension*: systolic pressure greater than 140 mm Hg *and* diastolic pressure greater than 90 mm Hg. The risks of coronary heart disease and stroke increase curvilinearly with either systolic or diastolic blood pressure. The main hemodynamic fault is vasoconstriction at the level of the resistance arterioles. In contrast, the majority of patients who develop hypertension after the age of 50 have *isolated systolic hypertension*: systolic pressure greater than 140 mm Hg but diastolic pressure less than 90 mm Hg. In these older patients, cardiovascular risk increases curvilinearly with increasing systolic pressure but is inversely related to diastolic pressure. A blood pressure of 170/70 mm Hg carries twice the risk of coronary heart disease as a blood pressure of 170/110 mm Hg! (see Fig. 63–4.)

In isolated systolic hypertension, the main hemodynamic fault is decreased distensibility of the large conduit arteries. This problem is

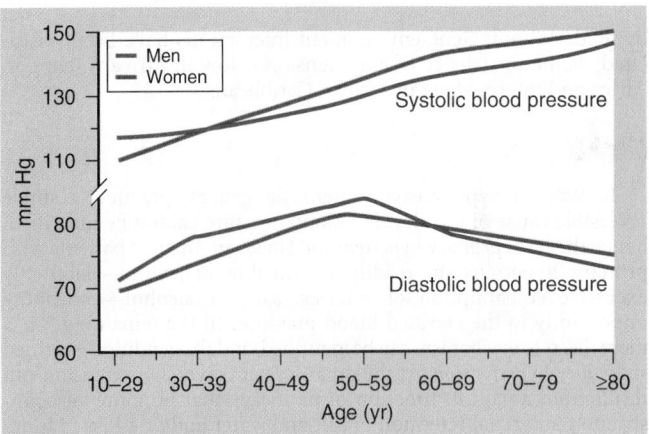

FIGURE 63–3 • Age-dependent changes in systolic and diastolic blood pressure in the United States. (From Burt V, Whelton P, Rocella EJ, et al: Prevalence of hypertension in the U.S. adult population. Results from the Third National Health and Nutrition Examination Survey, 1988-1991. Hypertension 1995;25:305–313.)

caused by the replacement of elastin by collagen and fibrous tissue in the elastic lamina of the aorta, an age-dependent process that is accelerated by atherosclerosis and hypertension. The cardiovascular risk associated with isolated systolic hypertension is related to pulsatility, the repetitive pounding of the blood vessels with each cardiac cycle and a more rapid return of the arterial pulse wave from the periphery, both begetting more systolic hypertension. The importance of these findings for patients and physicians is that the prior clinical emphasis on diastolic blood pressure was misplaced. In the United States, the majority of uncontrolled hypertension occurs in older patients with isolated systolic hypertension, a problem perpetuated by a persistent focus on lowering diastolic blood pressure, a fear of lowering blood pressure excessively in older patients, and an inherently greater difficulty in achieving systolic blood pressure goals with available medications.

GENDER AND ETHNICITY. Before age 50, the prevalence of hypertension is lower in women than in men, suggesting a protective effect of estrogen. After menopause, the prevalence of hypertension increases rapidly in women and exceeds that in men.

Within the United States, the prevalence of hypertension varies widely by ethnicity, being most prevalent in African Americans. Hypertension is present in one in three African American adults compared with one in four or five white or Mexican American adults. Compared with all other ethnic groups, hypertension in African Americans is not only more prevalent but also starts at a younger age and causes much more target organ damage, leading to excessive and premature disability and death. In the Bogalusa Heart Study, higher blood pressures in black than in white children were already evident

Cardiovascular Disease

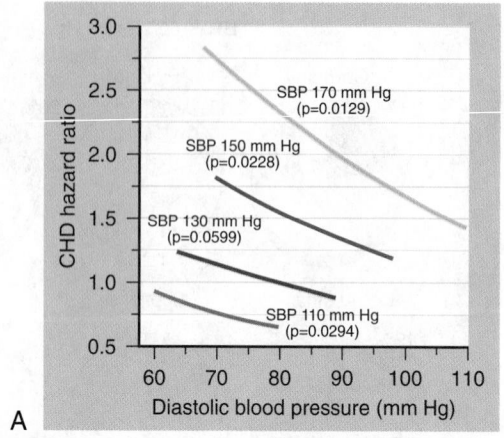
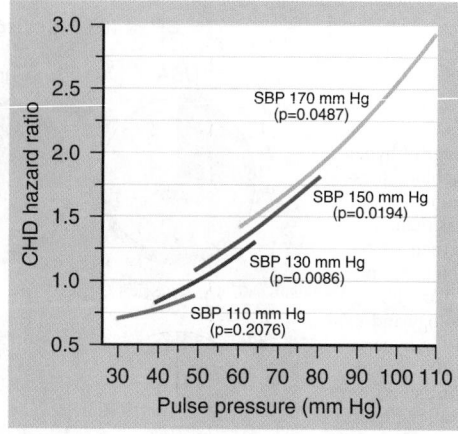

FIGURE 63-4 • Joint influences of systolic blood pressure (SBP) and diastolic blood pressure on coronary heart disease (CHD) risk in the Framingham cohort of people 50 to 79 years of age (*A*). At levels of SBP between 110 and 170 mm Hg, CHD risk was found to be inversely related to diastolic blood pressure. Joint influences of SBP and pulse pressure (*B*). At levels of SBP between 110 and 170 mm Hg, CHD risk increases with increasing pulse pressure (PP). (From Franklin S, Khan SA, Wong DH, Larson MG, Levy D. Is pulse pressure useful in predicting risk for coronary heart disease? Circulation 1999;100:354–360.)

by grade school. Gene-environment interactions have been postulated, as the prevalence of hypertension is low in Africans living in Africa and intermediate in African-Caribbeans.

Mechanisms of Hypertension

In 95% of hypertensive patients in general practice, a single reversible cause of the elevated blood pressure cannot be identified, hence the term *primary hypertension*. However, in most patients with primary hypertension, readily identifiable behaviors—habitually excessive consumption of calories, salt, or alcohol—contribute importantly to the elevated blood pressure. In the remaining 5%, a more discrete mechanism can be identified, and the condition is termed *secondary hypertension*. At the organ-system level, hypertension can result from a gain in function of pathways that promote vasoconstriction and renal retention of salt and water and/or a loss in function of pathways that promote vasodilatation and renal excretion of salt and water.

BEHAVIORAL DETERMINANTS OF HUMAN BLOOD PRESSURE VARIATION. The most important behavioral determinants of blood pressure are related to dietary consumption of calories and salt. In all populations studied, the prevalence of hypertension increases linearly with body mass index. With the rapidly growing incidence of obesity in industrialized societies, reaching epidemic proportions in the United States, increasing attention is being paid to the *metabolic syndrome* that often accompanies hypertension. The metabolic syndrome refers to the frequent clustering of hypertension with abdominal ("male-pattern") adiposity, insulin resistance, and a dyslipidemic pattern consisting typically of elevated plasma triglyceride and low high-density lipoprotein (HDL) cholesterol levels. Although the causal links remain to be elucidated, this constellation of metabolic abnormalities dramatically increases cardiovascular risk. In the Framingham Heart Study, obesity has been estimated to account for 50 to 60% of the new cases of hypertension. The underlying mechanisms by which weight gain leads to hypertension are incompletely understood, but there is mounting evidence for an expanded plasma volume plus sympathetic overactivity. The latter is thought to be a compensatory attempt to burn fat but at the expense of peripheral vasoconstriction, renal salt and water retention, and hypertension. In some obese individuals, sleep apnea (Chapter 96) is an important cause of hypertension. Repeated arterial desaturation sensitizes the carotid body chemoreceptors, causing sustained sympathetic overactivity.

Dietary sodium intake is another key behavioral determinant of human hypertension. The epidemiologic, clinical, and experimental support for this association is strong. In the Intersalt Study of 52 locations around the world, the risk of developing hypertension over three decades of adult life was linearly and very tightly related to dietary sodium intake. Dietary sodium reduction and diuretics have proved to be effective treatments for primary hypertension. However, both normotensive and hypertensive persons show tremendous interindividual variability in their blood pressure responses to dietary sodium

loading and sodium restriction. This variability, which has led to some questioning about the "salt hypothesis," indicates a strong genetic underpinning.

GENETIC DETERMINANTS OF HUMAN BLOOD PRESSURE VARIATION. The familial aggregation of hypertension documents an important genetic component. Concordance of blood pressures is greater within families than in unrelated individuals, greater between monozygotic than between dizygotic twins, and greater between biological than between adoptive siblings living in the same household. About 70% of the familial aggregation of blood pressure is attributed to shared genes rather than shared environment. Thus, hypertension can be viewed as a maladaptive interplay between the human genome and modern society. However, very little is known about the genetic determinants of blood pressure variation in the general population. The number of sequence variations, the specific loci, and their individual and combined effects remain conjectural.

In contrast, dazzling genetic research has elucidated the molecular mechanisms by which rare forms of human hypertension and hypotension are inherited as Mendelian traits. Mutations have been identified in eight genes that cause Mendelian forms of hypertension and in nine genes that cause Mendelian forms of hypotension. In every case, the mechanism involves the renal handling of salt and water and emphasizes the pivotal importance of the renin-angiotensin-aldosterone system in human blood pressure regulation. The Mendelian forms of hypertension altogether are responsible for a very small portion of the 50 million cases of hypertension in the United States. The Mendelian hypotensive and hypertensive traits represent the extremes of human blood pressure variation, and the key question is whether milder mutations in any of these 17 genes, alone or in combination, confer resistance against or sensitivity to the hypertensive effects of the common environmental exposures in the general population.

Clinical Manifestations

Hypertension has been termed the "silent killer," a chronic illness with a long asymptomatic phase that, if undetected and untreated, silently damages the heart, brain, and kidneys. Although headaches are common in patients with mild-to-moderate hypertension (Chapter 428), episodes of headaches do not correlate with fluctuations in ambulatory blood pressure but rather with a person's awareness of his or her diagnosis.

Initial Evaluation for Hypertension

The initial evaluation for hypertension should focus on three goals: (1) staging of the blood pressure, (2) assessment of the patient's overall cardiovascular risk, and (3) detection of clues indicating potential identifiable causes of hypertension that require further evaluation. *The initial clinical data needed to accomplish these goals are obtained through a thorough history and physical examination, routine blood and urine tests, and a resting 12-lead electrocardiogram.* In some patients, ambulatory blood pressure monitoring and an echocardiogram provide helpful additional data about the time-integral burden of blood pressure on the cardiovascular system.

GOAL 1: ACCURATE ASSESSMENT OF BLOOD PRESSURE

OFFICE BLOOD PRESSURE. Because blood pressure normally varies dramatically throughout a 24-hour period, multiple readings on more than one occasion are required to obtain a clear picture of a person's "usual" blood pressure. For this reason, *hypertension should never be diagnosed on the basis of a single elevated reading.*

To minimize variability in readings, blood pressure should be measured at least twice after 5 minutes of rest with the patient seated, the back supported, and the arm at heart level. The cuff should not be too small for the arm, and tobacco and caffeine should be avoided for at least 30 minutes. Most overweight adults require a large-adult cuff. To avoid underestimation of systolic pressure in older persons who may have an auscultatory gap, radial artery palpation should be performed to estimate systolic pressure; then the cuff should be inflated to a value 20 mm Hg higher than the level that obliterates the radial pulse and deflated at a rate of 3 to 5 mm Hg/sec. Blood pressure should be measured in both arms and after 5 minutes of standing, the latter to exclude a significant postural fall in blood pressure, particularly in older persons and in those with diabetes or other conditions (e.g., Parkinson's disease) that predispose to autonomic insufficiency.

BLOOD PRESSURE STAGE. Blood pressure is staged as normal, prehypertension, or hypertension based on the average of two or more readings taken at two or more office visits. When a person's systolic and diastolic pressures fall into different stages, the higher stage should apply (Table 63-1).

Table 63-1 • STAGING OF OFFICE BLOOD PRESSURE

BLOOD PRESSURE STAGE	SYSTOLIC BLOOD PRESSURE (mm Hg)	DIASTOLIC BLOOD PRESSURE (mm Hg)
Normal	<120	<80
Prehypertension	120–129	80–89
Stage 1 Hypertension	140–159	90–99
Stage 2 Hypertension	≥160	≥100

From Chobanian A, et al: The Seventh Report of the Joint National Committee on the Prevention, Evaluation, and Treatment of High Blood Pressure: The JNC 7 Report. JAMA 2003;289:2560–2572.

The designation of *prehypertension* has been added to reflect the increased risk of progression to hypertension associated with blood pressures in the 130–139/80–89 mm Hg range. The time interval for recommended followup depends on the degree of blood pressure elevation recorded at the initial examination. Patients with prehypertension should be followed at least annually, patients with stage 1 hypertension should be examined in two months, and patients with stage 2 hypertension should be seen in one month or sooner depending on the patient's overall clinical condition.

HOME AND AMBULATORY BLOOD PRESSURE MONITORING. Due to the anxiety of going to the physician, blood pressures often are higher in the physician's office than when measured at home. Self-monitoring of blood pressure at home actively engages a patient in his or her own health care and provides a better estimate of a person's usual blood pressure for diagnostic and therapeutic purposes. However, the devices need to be checked for accuracy in the office. Patients should be instructed to record their pressures both when relaxed and when stressed; even then, record-keeping may not be accurate.

Ambulatory blood pressure monitoring provides the best measure of the time-integral blood pressure burden on the cardiovascular system. As such, ambulatory blood pressures correlate better than office readings with target organ damage such as left ventricular hypertrophy (LVH). Recommended standards for normal ambulatory blood pressure values currently include daytime blood pressure less than 135/85 mm Hg, nighttime blood pressure less than 120/70 mm Hg, and 24-hour blood pressure less than 130/80 mm Hg.

Up to 30% of patients with elevated office blood pressures have normal home blood pressures. If the daytime ambulatory blood pressure is completely normal despite consistently elevated office readings, the patient has "office only," or "white coat," hypertension, presumably owing to an excessive adrenergic response to the measurement of blood pressure in the physician's office. In such individuals with rigorously defined white coat hypertension, the 5-year mortality rate was found in one study to be indistinguishable from that for those with normal office blood pressures. However, cross-sectional data suggest that white coat hypertension may not be so benign. For example, echocardiographic left ventricular mass is higher in patients with white coat hypertension than in patients with normal office blood pressures but not as high as in patients with persistent hypertension. For now, patients with white coat hypertension should be followed every 6 months for possible progression to persistent hypertension.

In up to 30% of treated patients with persistently elevated office blood pressures, ambulatory monitoring documents adequate or excessive control of their hypertension, eliminating overtreatment. In other patients, office blood pressures underestimate ambulatory blood pressures, presumably because of sympathetic overactivity in daily life owing to job or home stress, tobacco abuse, or other adrenergic stimulants that are discontinued before coming to the office. Such documentation prevents undertreatment of this masked hypertension.

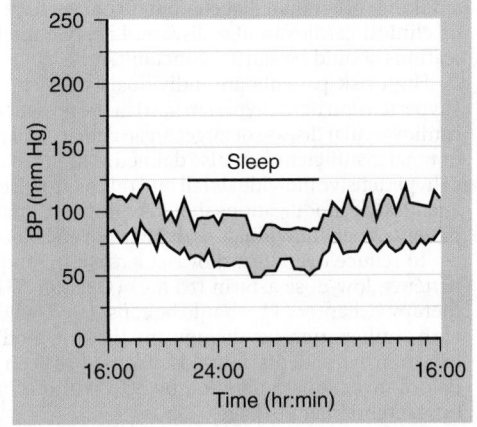
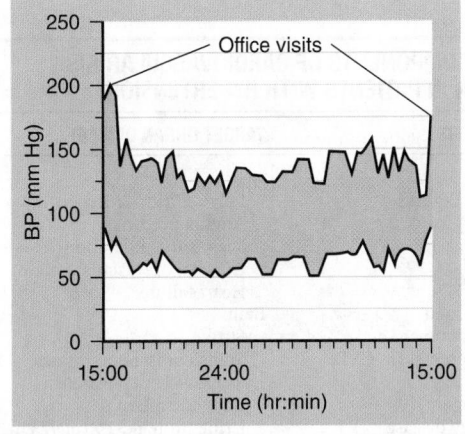

FIGURE 63-5 • Twenty-four-hour ambulatory blood pressure (BP) monitor tracings in two different patients. *A,* Optimal blood pressure in a healthy 37-year-old woman. Note the normal variability in blood pressure, the nocturnal dip in blood pressure during sleep, and the sharp increase in blood pressure on awakening. (Tracing courtesy of Meryem Tuncel, MD, Hypertension Division, Department of Internal Medicine, University of Texas Southwestern Medical Center, Dallas, Texas.) *B,* Pronounced white coat effect in an 80-year-old woman referred for evaluation of medically refractory hypertension. Documentation of the white coat effect prevented overtreatment of the patient's isolated systolic hypertension. (Tracing provided by Wanpen Vongpatanasin, MD, Hypertension Division, Department of Internal Medicine, University of Texas Southwestern Medical Center, Dallas, Texas.)

Table 63–2 • CURRENTLY RECOMMENDED INDICATIONS FOR AMBULATORY BLOOD PRESSURE MONITORING

- Evaluate suspected "white coat hypertension"*
- Exclude a "white coat" effect in a patient with medically refractory hypertension
- Prevent overtreatment of hypertension in older patients
- Evaluate suspected white coat normotension or nocturnal hypertension
- Evaluate efficacy of drug treatment over entire 24-hr period
- Aid in the diagnosis and treatment of hypotension (drug induced or due to autonomic failure)

*Currently in the U.S., Medicare reimburses for ambulatory monitoring only to confirm the diagnosis of white coat hypertension that is suspected on the basis of three normal home readings in patients with no evidence of target organ damage despite elevated office blood pressure readings.

Modified from O'Brien E, Coats A, Owens P, et al: Use and interpretation of ambulatory blood pressure monitoring: Recommendations of the British Hypertension Society. BMJ 2000;320:1128–1134.

Blood pressure normally dips during sleep at night and increases sharply when a person awakens and becomes active in the morning (Fig. 63–5). Persistent nocturnal hypertension increases the aggregate blood pressure burden on the cardiovascular system and increases the risk of target organ disease. The morning surge in blood pressure is strongly associated with the peak incidence of stroke, myocardial infarction, and sudden cardiac death. Thus, in high-risk individuals, medications ideally should be finely tuned to optimize the 24-hour blood pressure profile (Table 63–2).

GOAL 2: CARDIOVASCULAR RISK STRATIFICATION

It is important to emphasize that blood pressure is only one component of cardiovascular risk, and the approach to the hypertensive patient should be highly individualized based on a thorough assessment of the person's overall cardiovascular risk. The additive effects of multiple risk factors on atherosclerosis have been firmly established both in autopsy studies that directly measured subclinical atherosclerotic burden in young adults and in numerous longitudinal studies that evaluated clinical cardiovascular outcomes. There are three broad components to cardiovascular risk: (1) blood pressure level, (2) comorbidity, and (3) target organ damage (Table 63–3 and Fig. 63–6).

The low-risk group (mild risk) includes individuals who are free of clinical cardiovascular disease, target organ damage, or other associated risk factors. Only 2% of hypertensive patients fall into this low-risk category. Low-risk individuals with prehypertension or stage 1 hypertension may be treated with lifestyle modifications alone for up to 12 months. If blood pressure does not fall to the goal, lifestyle modifications should be supplemented, not replaced, by medications. For

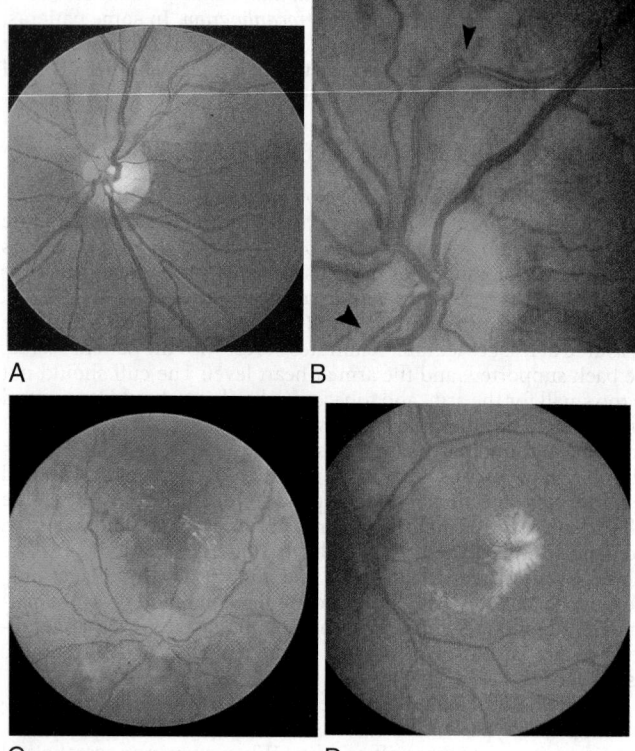

FIGURE 63–6 • Hypertensive retinopathy is traditionally divided into four grades. *A*, Grade 1 shows very early and minor changes in a young patient: increased tortuosity of a retinal vessel and increased reflectiveness (silver wiring) of a retinal artery are seen at 1 o'clock in this view. Otherwise, the fundus is completely normal. *B*, Grade 2 also shows increased tortuosity and silver wiring (arrowheads). In addition, there is "nipping" of the venules at arteriovenous crossings (arrow). *C*, Grade 3 shows the same changes as grade 2 plus flame-shaped retinal hemorrhages and soft "cotton wool" exudates. *D*, In grade 4, there is swelling of the optic disc (papilledema), retinal edema is present, and hard exudates may collect around the fovea, producing a typical "macular star." (From Forbes CD, Jackson WF: Color Atlas and Text of Clinical Medicine, 3rd ed. London, Mosby, 2003, with permission.)

low-risk patients with stage 2 hypertension, medications should be initiated without delay.

Moderate-risk patients, who represent by far the largest number of hypertensive patients (60%), include those who have one or more of the major cardiovascular risk factors (e.g., hyperlipidemia, smoking) other than diabetes but do not yet have target organ damage or clinical cardiovascular disease. Lifestyle modifications and medications should be started concomitantly.

High-risk patients are individuals with elevated blood pressure (hypertension or prehypertension) in the presence of clinically evident cardiovascular disease or target organ damage. All patients with diabetes or renal insufficiency are also defined as high risk. More than one third of hypertensive individuals fall into this high-risk category. Medications and lifestyle modifications should be initiated immediately in high-risk patients, even individuals with high-normal blood pressures.

To reduce overall cardiovascular risk in moderate- and high-risk patients, low-dose aspirin (81 mg) (Chapter 33) and lipid-lowering therapy (Chapter 211) should be considered, when appropriate, along with antihypertensive therapy and lifestyle modifications. In treated hypertensive patients, low-dose aspirin has been shown to reduce the risk of myocardial infarction by 36% without increasing the risk of intracerebral hemorrhage.

GOAL 3: IDENTIFICATION OF SECONDARY (IDENTIFIABLE) CAUSES OF HYPERTENSION

A thorough search for secondary causes is not cost-effective in most patients with hypertension but becomes critically important in two circumstances: (1) when there is a compelling finding on the initial evaluation, or (2) when the hypertensive process is so severe

Table 63–3 • COMPONENTS OF CARDIOVASCULAR RISK STRATIFICATION IN PATIENTS WITH HYPERTENSION

MAJOR RISK FACTORS	TARGET ORGAN DAMAGE
Cigarette smoking	Heart
Obesity* (BMI >30 kg/m²)	Left ventricular hypertrophy
Physical inactivity	Angina pectoris
Dyslipidemia*	Myocardial infarction
Diabetes mellitus*	Coronary revascularization
Age	Heart failure
Old than 55 for men	Brain
Old than 65 for women	Stroke
Family history of premature CVD	Transient ischemic attack
Men under age 55	Hypertensive nephrosclerosis
Women under age 65	GFR <60 mL/min
Any chronic kidney disease	Urine protein >150 mg/24 hr
GFR <60 mL/min	Retinopathy
Urine protein >150 mg/24rhr	Peripheral atherosclerosis

*Components of metabolic syndrome.
GFR = glomerular filtration rate.
Modified from Chobanian A, et al: The Seventh Report of the Joint National Committee on the Prevention, Evaluation, and Treatment of High Blood Pressure: The JNC 7 Report. JAMA 2003;289:2560–2572.

Table 63–4 • GUIDE TO EVALUATION OF SECONDARY HYPERTENSION

SUSPECTED DIAGNOSIS	CLINICAL FEATURES	DIAGNOSTIC TESTING
Renal parenchymal hypertension	Elevated serum creatinine or abnormal urinalysis	24-Hour urine creatinine and protein, renal ultrasound
Renovascular disease	New elevation in serum creatinine, marked elevation in serum creatinine with initiation of ACEI or ARB, refractory hypertension, flash pulmonary edema, abdominal bruit	Captopril renogram, duplex Doppler sonography, magnetic resonance or CT angiogram, invasive angiogram
Coarctation of the aorta	Arm pulses > leg pulses, arm BP > leg BP, chest bruits, rib notching on chest radiograph	MRI, aortogram
Primary aldosteronism	Hypokalemia, refractory hypertension	Plasma renin and aldosterone, 24-hour urine potassium, 24-hour urine aldosterone and potassium after salt loading, adrenal CT scan
Cushing's syndrome	Truncal obesity, purple striae, muscle weakness	Plasma cortisol, urine cortisol after dexamethasone, adrenal CT scan
Pheochromocytoma	Spells of tachycardia, headache, diaphoresis, pallor, and anxiety	Plasma metanephrine and normetanephrine, 24-hour urine catechols, adrenal CT scan
Obstructive sleep apnea	Loud snoring, daytime somnolence, obesity	Sleep study

ACEI = angiotensin-converting enzyme inhibitor; ARB = angiotensin receptor blocker; BP = blood pressure; CT = computed tomography.
Modified from Kaplan NM: Clinical Hypertension, 8th ed. Philadelphia, Williams & Wilkins, 2002.

that it either is refractory to intensive multiple drug therapy or requires hospitalization. Table 63–4 summarizes the major causes of secondary hypertension that should be suspected on the basis of a good history, physical, and routine laboratory tests.

RENAL PARENCHYMAL HYPERTENSION. Chronic renal failure is the most common cause of secondary hypertension (Chapter 117). Hypertension is present in more than 80% of patients with chronic renal failure and is a major factor causing their increased cardiovascular morbidity and mortality. The mechanisms causing the hypertension include an expanded plasma volume and peripheral vasoconstriction, with the latter caused by both activation of vasoconstrictor pathways (renin-angiotensin and sympathetic nervous systems) and inhibition of vasodilator pathways (nitric oxide). Renal insufficiency should be considered when there is proteinuria by dipstick or when the serum creatinine level is greater than 1.2 mg/dL in hypertensive women or greater than 1.4 mg/dL in hypertensive men. The diagnosis is confirmed either by a 24-hour urine collection showing a creatinine clearance of <60 mL/min or a total protein excretion of >150 mg or by a spot urine specimen showing microalbuminuria defined as a urine albumin-to-urine creatinine ratio between 30 and 300 mg/g. In patients with mild or moderate renal insufficiency, stringent blood pressure control is imperative to slow the progression to end-stage renal disease and reduce the excessive cardiovascular risk. Specific treatment recommendations are addressed later. In patients with far-advanced renal insufficiency, hypertension often becomes difficult to treat and may require either (1) intensive medical treatment with loop diuretics, potent vasodilators (e.g., minoxidil 2.5 to 100 mg daily), β-adrenergic blockers, and central sympatholytics or (2) initiation of chronic hemodialysis as the only effective way to reduce plasma volume. In chronic hemodialysis patients, the challenge is to control interdialytic hypertension intensively without exacerbating dialysis-induced hypotension. The gross annual mortality rate in the hemodialysis population is 25%, with half of this excessive mortality being caused by cardiovascular events that are related, at least in part, to suboptimal control of hypertension.

RENOVASCULAR HYPERTENSION. Unilateral or bilateral renal artery stenosis is present in less than 2% of hypertensive patients in a general medical practice but up to 30% in patients referred to a hypertension specialist for refractory hypertension. The main causes of renal artery stenosis are atherosclerosis (90% of cases), typically in older persons with other manifestations of atherosclerosis, and fibromuscular dysplasia (10% of cases), typically in women between the ages of 15 and 50 (Chapter 124). Unilateral renal artery stenosis leads to underperfusion of the juxtaglomerular cells, thereby producing renin-dependent hypertension even though the contralateral kidney is able to maintain normal blood volume. In contrast, bilateral renal artery stenosis (or unilateral stenosis with a solitary kidney) constitutes a potentially reversible cause of progressive renal failure and volume-dependent hypertension. The following clinical clues increase the suspicion of renovascular hypertension: any hospitalization for urgent or emergent hypertension, recurrent "flash" pulmonary edema, refractory hypertension, severe hypertension in a young adult or after

the age of 50, precipitous and progressive worsening of renal function in response to angiotensin-converting enzyme (ACE) inhibition, unilateral small kidney by any radiographic study, extensive peripheral arteriosclerosis, or a flank bruit.

The evaluation and treatment of fibromuscular dysplasia in a young women with recent-onset hypertension are straightforward. The diagnosis usually is readily supported by noninvasive testing with captopril renography, duplex Doppler ultrasonography, or magnetic resonance (MR) or spiral computed tomography (CT) angiography, the latter imaging studies showing the classic "string-of-beads" appearance of a renal artery (Chapter 124). Once the diagnosis is confirmed with invasive angiography, balloon angioplasty is the treatment of choice, with complete cure of hypertension in 40% of patients, improved blood pressure control in almost all patients, and restenosis rates of about 10%. Medical therapy with an ACE inhibitor also may be effective, but the risks of teratogenicity must be considered in women of childbearing age.

In contrast, the approach to the older patient with generalized atherosclerosis and renal artery stenosis (Fig. 63–7) is not straightforward and must be highly individualized. Primary and renovascular hypertension frequently coexist in older persons, and renal artery stenosis can be present without being an important cause of the hypertension. For this reason, revascularization leads to clinical

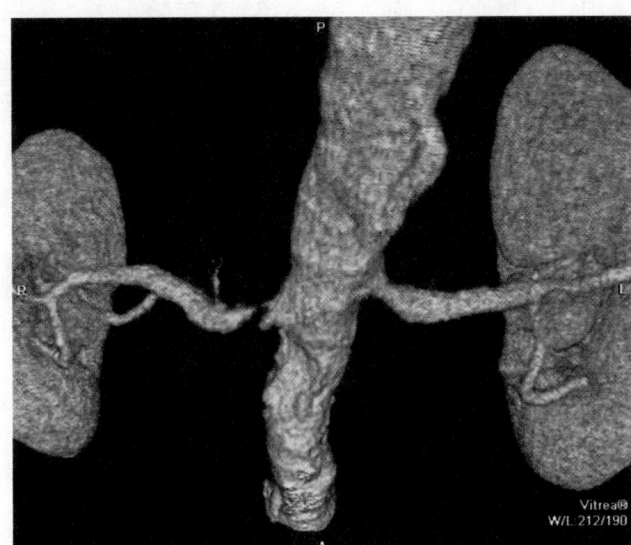

FIGURE 63–7 • Computed tomography angiogram with three-dimensional reconstruction, showing a severe proximal stenosis of the right renal artery and mild stenosis of the left renal artery. (Image courtesy of Bart Domatch, MD, Radiology Department, University of Texas Southwestern Medical Center, Dallas, Texas.)

improvement in hypertension in less than 30% of patients, and complete cures are rare.

With current surgical procedures, the perioperative mortality rate is 2 to 6%, late graft failure requiring a second procedure occurs in 5 to 15% of patients, and the 5-year survival rate is 65 to 81%. Randomized trials show a small but probably real benefit of balloon angioplasty. Nevertheless, in this group of patients, the first line of therapy should be intensive medical treatment of hypertension and associated cardiovascular risk factors, with concomitant lipid lowering, smoking cessation, and aspirin. Surgical revascularization or stenting should be considered for the following indications: (1) medically refractory or accelerating hypertension, (2) progressive renal failure on medical therapy, and (3) bilateral renal artery stenosis.

MINERALOCORTICOID-INDUCED HYPERTENSION DUE TO PRIMARY ALDOSTERONISM.
The most common causes of primary aldosteronism (Chapter 240) are (1) a unilateral aldosterone-producing adenoma in two thirds of cases and (2) bilateral adrenal hyperplasia in one third. Because aldosterone is the principal ligand for the mineralocorticoid receptor in the distal nephron, excessive aldosterone production causes excessive renal Na^+-K^+ exchange, resulting in hypokalemia. The initial clue to the diagnosis is either unprovoked hypokalemia (serum K^+ <3.5 mmol/L in the absence of diuretic therapy) or a tendency to develop excessive hypokalemia during diuretic therapy (serum K^+ <3.0 mmol/L) in a patient with hypertension. However, up to one third of patients do not have hypokalemia on initial presentation, and the diagnosis should be considered in any patient with severe refractory hypertension.

Mendelian Forms of Mineralocorticoid-Induced Hypertension.
Almost all of the mendelian forms of hypertension, although rare, are mineralocorticoid induced and involve excessive activation of the epithelial sodium channel (*ENaC*), the final common pathway for reabsorption of sodium from the distal nephron (Fig. 63–8). Thus, salt-dependent hypertension can be caused both by gain-of-function mutations of *ENaC* or the mineralocorticoid receptor or by increased production or decreased clearance of mineralocorticoid receptor ligands, which are aldosterone, deoxycorticosterone, or cortisol.

Glucocorticoid-Remediable Aldosteronism (GRA).
Fewer than 100 cases of GRA have been reported, but many additional cases likely go undetected or misdiagnosed as bilateral adrenal hyperplasia. Inherited as an autosomal dominant mutation, GRA mimics an aldosterone-producing adenoma by causing severe mineralocorticoid-induced hypertension with hypokalemia, elevated plasma aldosterone, and suppressed plasma renin activity (PRA). In the normal adrenal gland, angiotensin II (Ang II) acts on the enzyme aldosterone synthase in the zona glomerulosa to drive production of aldosterone, whereas ACTH causes transcriptional activation of the enzyme 11-β-hydroxylase in the zona fasciculata to drive production of cortisol. GRA is caused by a gene duplication arising by unequal crossing over between the genes encoding aldosterone synthase and 11-β-hydroxylase. The resulting chimeric gene encodes a hybrid protein that has aldosterone synthase activity, is expressed "ectopically" in the zona fasciculata, and is regulated entirely by ACTH rather than by Ang II. Thus, aldosterone production becomes inappropriately linked to cortisol production. In the attempt to maintain the appropriate production of normal cortisol, aldosterone is constantly produced, resulting in volume-dependent hypertension. Although the expanded plasma volume suppresses PRA, the reduced Ang II cannot downregulate aldosterone production. The clinical clue to the diagnosis is that the hypertension is familial and discovered before age 20. In contrast, primary aldosteronism is sporadic and usually discovered between ages 30 and 60. The diagnosis of GRA is confirmed by Southern blot analysis for the chimeric gene, a test available at no cost through the International Registry for GRA (www.bwh.partners.org/gra/clinhx.htm). By suppressing ACTH, and thus aldosterone secretion from the zona fasciculata, low-dose dexamethasone completely reverses the biochemical abnormalities in GRA and is the recommended antihypertensive therapy.

HYPERTENSION CAUSED BY DEOXYCORTICOSTERONE.
The rare but distinctive hypertensive syndromes caused by deoxycorticosterone include those due to congenital deficiency of either 11β-hydroxylase or 17α-hydroxylase. In both cases, decreased production of cortisol decreases feedback inhibition on ACTH, which drives overproduction of deoxycorticosterone (a potent mineralocorticoid). These patients typically present to the pediatrician with hypertension plus abnormal sexual development.

HYPERTENSION CAUSED BY CORTISOL.
Although cortisol is a glucocorticoid, surprisingly it is equipotent to aldosterone in activating the mineralocorticoid receptor. As a result, both excessive production of cortisol and defective cortisol metabolism cause hypertension plus hypokalemia. Cushing's syndrome (excessive cortisol production) is discussed in detail in Chapter 240.

Cortisol at the mineralocorticoid receptor normally is kept at a very low local concentration because the enzyme 11β-hydroxysteroid dehydrogenase type 2 (11β–HSD2) converts cortisol to cortisone, which cannot bind the mineralocorticoid receptor. The syndrome of apparent mineralocorticoid excess is an autosomal recessive disease due to a loss in function mutation of 11β-HSD2. Loss of protection of the mineralocorticoid receptor from an excessive local concentration of cortisol results in early-onset hypertension with hypokalemia accompanied by suppressed PRA and undetectable plasma aldosterone. Glycerrhetinic acid, a metabolite found in licorice, numerous herbal supplements, and chewing tobacco, is a potent inhibitor of 11β-HSD2. Thus, habitual ingestion of these substances by normal individuals causes a phenocopy of apparent mineralocorticoid excess. Biochemical confirmation consists of elevations in urinary free cortisol. The congenital syndrome is treated with spironolactone, whereas the phenocopy is treated with diet.

HYPERTENSION CAUSED BY PROGESTERONE.
A gain-in-function mutation in the mineralocorticoid receptor has been identified as a cause of autosomal dominant, early-onset hypertension that is markedly accelerated during pregnancy. Because of missense mutation in the ligand-binding domain of the mineralocorticoid receptor, steroids that bind but do not activate the normal receptor become potent agonists of the mutant receptor, causing mineralocorticoid receptor–induced hypertension with secondary suppression of plasma renin and aldosterone. These steroids include progesterone and spironolactone, which normally is a potent receptor antagonist. Because progesterone levels increase 100-fold during pregnancy, this mutation constitutes a rare but dramatic cause of accelerated hypertension during pregnancy. All the male carriers in one family developed hypertension before age 20. Amiloride is the suggested treatment of choice, and spironolactone is contraindicated.

LIDDLE'S SYNDROME.
Liddle's syndrome is a rare monogenic form of salt-dependent hypertension due to gain-in-function mutations in *ENaC*, resulting in an excessive number of channels on the

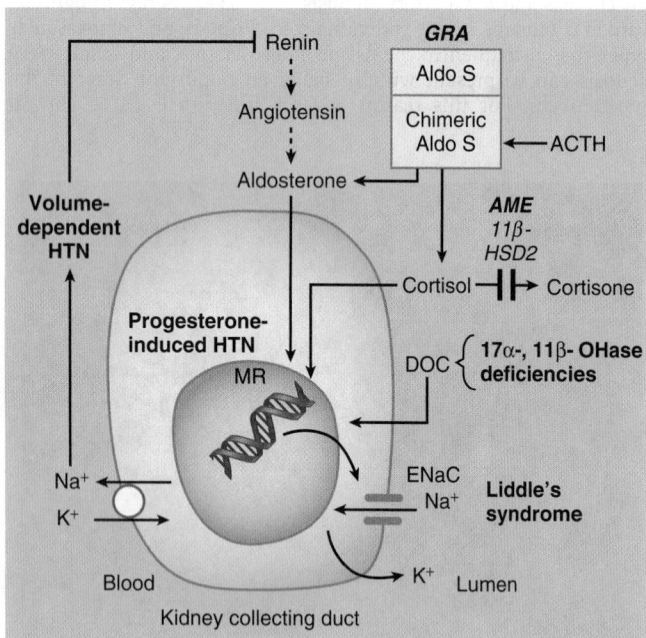

FIGURE 63–8 • Mendelian forms of hypertension that cause mineralocorticoid-induced hypertension. Aldo S = aldosterone synthase; AME = apparent mineralocorticoid excess; GRA = glucocorticoid-remediable aldosteronism; 11β-HSD2 = 11β-hydroxy steroid dehydrogenase type 2; DOC = deoxycorticosterone; ENaC = epithelial sodium channel; HTN = hypertension; MR = mineralocorticoid receptor. See text for explanation. (Adapted from Lifton RP, Gharavi AG, Geller DS: Molecular mechanisms of human hypertension. Cell 2001;104:545–556.)

epithelial surface of the distal renal tubule. Mutations that truncate large segments of the cytoplasmic C-terminus of the beta or gamma ENaC subunits disrupt the NEDD4 ubiquitin ligase binding site so that the channels cannot be internalized. Inherited as an autosomal dominant trait, these mutations cause severe salt-dependent hypertension beginning in young adulthood. Plasma renin activity and plasma aldosterone levels are suppressed secondarily. The diagnosis is confirmed by genetic testing for the mutant gene. Because the defect is downstream from the mineralocorticoid receptor, the hypertension is unresponsive to spironolactone but is best treated with thiazides plus amiloride or triamterene, which are potassium-sparing diuretics that block *ENaC*.

FAMILIAL BRACHYDACTYLY AND HYPERTENSION. Several large kindreds have been reported to have severe autosomal dominant hypertension associated with brachydactyly and short stature. The gene has been mapped to the short arm of chromosome 12, but the mechanism causing the hypertension is unknown. In contrast to the other mendelian forms of hypertension, plasma renin and aldosterone levels are normal, and this syndrome does not appear to represent volume-dependent hypertension.

PHEOCHROMOCYTOMAS. Pheochromocytomas are rare catecholamine-producing tumors of the adrenal (or sometimes extra-adrenal) chromaffin cells (Chapter 241). The diagnosis should be suspected when hypertension is accompanied by frequent or refractory headaches or by paroxysms of headache, palpitations, pallor, or diaphoresis. In some patients, pheochromocytoma may be misdiagnosed as panic disorder. A family history of early onset hypertension may suggest pheochromocytoma as part of the multiple endocrine neoplasia syndromes (Chapter 244). If the diagnosis is missed, outpouring of catecholamines from the tumor can cause unsuspected hypertensive crisis and death during unrelated surgical or radiologic procedures.

Other causes of neurogenic hypertension, which can be confused with pheochromocytoma, include sympathomimetic agents (cocaine, amphetamines; Chapter 30), baroreflex failure, and obstructive sleep apnea. Continuous positive airway pressure or corrective surgery can improve blood pressure control in some patients with sleep apnea (Chapter 96).

OTHER CAUSES OF SECONDARY HYPERTENSION. *Coarctation of the aorta* typically occurs just distal to the origin of the left subclavian artery, so the blood pressure is lower in the legs than in the arms (the opposite of the normal situation) (Chapter 65). The clue is that the pulses are weaker in the lower than upper extremities, indicating the need to measure blood pressure in the legs as well as in both arms. Intercostal collaterals can produce bruits on examination and rib notching on the chest radiograph. Coarctations can be cured with surgery or angioplasty.

Thyroid disease is another cause of secondary hypertension (Chapter 239). Hyperthyroidism tends to cause systolic hypertension with a wide pulse pressure, whereas hypothyroidism tends to cause mainly diastolic hypertension.

Cyclosporine has emerged as an important cause of secondary hypertension. The mechanism by which this immunosuppressive drug causes hypertension remains an enigma, but hypertension is a general property of immunosuppressive agents (e.g., tacrolimus) that inhibit calcineurin, the Ca^{2+}-dependent phosphatase that is expressed not only in lymphoid tissue but also in neural, vascular, and renal tissue. In the absence of outcomes data, nondihydropyridine calcium channel blockers (CCBs) have become the drugs of first choice even though they increase cyclosporine blood levels.

Rx Prevention and Treatment of Primary Hypertension

Because primary hypertension cannot be cured, it requires lifelong treatment. However, it can usually be controlled by a combination of lifestyle modifications and medications. The objective is to reduce the blood pressure and associated metabolic abnormalities sufficiently to reduce the risk of cardiovascular and renal target organ disease without compromising the patient's quality of life.

LIFESTYLE MODIFICATIONS

Every antihypertensive regimen should include lifestyle modifications. If implemented in childhood and sustained, these nondrug strategies would likely prevent millions of cases of hypertension. Once

hypertension is established, however, lifestyle modifications alone are rarely sufficient to obviate the need for medications. These modifications, however, can decrease medication requirements, affect associated cardiovascular risk factors, and emphasize the active role patients can play in controlling their blood pressure.

The most consistently effective lifestyle modification is weight loss for overweight hypertensives: losing only 10 to 12 pounds often lowers blood pressure by 10/5 mm Hg.[1] Moderate dietary sodium reduction on average lowers blood pressure by 5/2 mm Hg and should be part of every antihypertensive regimen (Chapters 12 and 233) despite the variable response from one patient to the next and the fact that the full benefits are not seen for 5 weeks. In addition to independent blood pressure–lowering effects, dietary sodium reduction can dramatically improve the efficacy of ACE inhibitors, angiotensin-receptor blockers (ARBs), and β-blockers, and it can permit a reduction in the dose of diuretic and the associated need for potassium supplementation. Most dietary sodium comes from processed foods rather than the salt shaker. Without draconian measures, daily salt consumption can be reduced from 10 to 6 g (6 g of NaCl = 2.4 g of Na^+ = 100 mmol of Na^+) by teaching patients to read food labels. The Dietary Approaches to Stop Hypertension (DASH) study showed that individuals with high normal blood pressure or stage 1 hypertension can lower their blood pressures even without decreased caloric or sodium intake if they adhere to a diet rich in fresh fruits and vegetables (for high potassium content) and use low-fat dairy products. The DASH diet (www.nhlbi.nih.gov/health/public/heart/hbp/dash/) is strongly recommended because the blood pressure–lowering effects can approach the magnitude of drug monotherapy, can be enhanced by dietary sodium reduction, and are seen in all ethnic groups, especially in African-Americans.[2] How to effect these dietary changes in free-living individuals remains a considerable challenge, but these impressive trial results document what could be achieved if dietary habits could be changed throughout the population.

Smokers should be counseled in the best methods to quit because smoking is such a potent cardiovascular risk factor, not only for coronary heart disease but also for progression of hypertensive nephrosclerosis (Chapter 14). Because blood pressure increases transiently by 10 to 15 mm Hg after each cigarette, smokers of more than 20 cigarettes per day often have higher blood pressures out of the office. Blood pressure increases similarly with the first morning cup of coffee, but the pressor response to caffeine habituates throughout the day. Thus, caffeine consumption need not be eliminated.

Excessive alcohol consumption is one of the most frequently overlooked reversible factors contributing to hypertension (Chapter 17). The relation between alcohol consumption and mortality is J-shaped. Cardiovascular death rates are 50% lower in moderate drinkers (one or two drinks a day) than in teetotalers. Red wine may be the most cardioprotective because of its high content of polyphenols, which decrease production of endothelin. However, individuals who drink more than two standard-sized drinks a day are at greatly increased risk of developing hypertension, possibly because large quantities of alcohol activate the sympathetic nervous system. In those who drink three or more standard portions of alcohol per day, reducing alcohol consumption can improve control of hypertension.[3]

In hypertensive individuals, regular aerobic exercise can exert modest reductions in blood pressure, averaging 5/2 mm Hg (Chapter 13). Although small in magnitude, these reductions can persist for up to 16 hours after a bout of aerobic exercise.[4] Relaxation techniques (e.g., meditation, biofeedback, hypnosis) can decrease blood pressure acutely but generally produce little effect on chronic hypertension. In some individuals, however, in whom overwhelming home or job strain is a major determinant of high blood pressure, as determined by ambulatory monitoring, stress management techniques or anxiolytics may be beneficial. Because patients often associate hypertension directly with life stress, patients should be counseled that stress management alone rarely is sufficient to control their hypertension.

PHARMACOLOGIC THERAPY

Historical Perspective

The current approach to the treatment of the hypertensive patient began in the 1960s, with the sequential development of effective antihypertensive medications. The memoirs of President Franklin Roosevelt's physician chronicle the frustrations of trying to manage severe hypertension with only bed rest and sedatives, which were the ineffective mainstays of antihypertensive therapy through the end of World War II. Shortly thereafter, Kempner demonstrated the blood pressure–lowering effects of treating overweight hypertensives with a rigorously low-sodium/low-calorie diet, the first effective lifestyle modification for hypertension. With the development of the first antihypertensive drugs in the late 1950s, the vanguard VA Cooperative Studies demonstrated that lowering blood pressure with medications prolongs life and reduces morbidity, not only in patients with very severe hypertension but also in those with moderate and even mild degrees of hypertension.

Probably no other field of clinical medicine enjoys a greater scientific base. Increasingly detailed understanding of the basic mechanisms involved in blood pressure regulation has fueled the identification of new drug targets and therapeutic agents. More than 70 antihypertensive medications are marketed. Randomized controlled trials have provided unequivocal proof that lowering blood pressure with medications dramatically reduces target organ damage and the resultant morbidity and mortality. There also is mounting but still incomplete evidence that certain classes of antihypertensive agents exert organoprotective effects above and beyond their ability to lower blood pressure. Thus, in certain circumstances, all antihypertensive medications are not equal, and the treatment of hypertension is no longer totally empiric.

The major challenges now are (1) to identify the key gene-environment interactions that cause hypertension and those that confer protection from it, thereby providing the conceptual framework for preventing or curing the disordered blood pressure regulation, and in the meantime, (2) to eliminate the patient and physician barriers that impede the control of hypertension with available measures. To improve the dissemination of the rapid advances in the field, practice guidelines are regularly updated (e.g., the Joint National Committee [JNC] 7 Report).

Target Blood Pressure Levels

Based on each patient's overall cardiovascular risk, a target level of blood pressure needs to be set, achieved, and sustained. For most patients, the goal is to intensify the medical regimen until blood pressure is lowered to systolic and diastolic values that are consistently below 140/90 mm Hg. For those with diabetes or chronic kidney disease, the high risk associated with these comorbid conditions requires that blood pressure be lowered further to values that are below 130/80 mm Hg. Unfortunately, in the United States, one third of all hypertensive individuals are unaware of their diagnosis, one half are not receiving treatment, and two thirds do not have their pressure controlled to a value less than 140/90 mm Hg. This worldwide problem (see Fig. 63–2) is not limited to underserved areas. In a survey of adults in Olmsted County, Minnesota, a well-educated community in proximity to the Mayo Clinic, 39% of the hypertensive participants were unaware of their diagnosis and only 17% of the affected individuals had their hypertension treated and controlled. A study from five Veterans Administration hospitals in the northeastern United States showed that, despite patients' having ample access to clinic care by attending physicians, antihypertensive therapy was intensified during only 7% of hypertension-related visits over a 2-year period, resulting in persistently poor rates of control; blood pressure remained greater than 160/90 mm Hg in 40% of the patients. Similarly disconcerting figures have been found in numerous practice settings.

In contrast, randomized clinical trials have demonstrated that teams of physicians and nurses who adhere to a forced titration schedule can achieve target blood pressures in up to two thirds of patients. With current regimens, diastolic pressures of less than 90 mm Hg can be achieved in more than 90% of hypertensive patients, whereas systolic pressures of less than 140 mm Hg can be achieved in more than 60%. New medications with greater efficacy for systolic blood pressure are under investigation.

To improve hypertension control rates in clinical practice, a number of principles can be borrowed from the successful conduct of multi-center trials. First, greater attention needs to be paid to titrating blood pressure medications to achieve target goals. Lowering blood pressure by the additional 10/5 mm Hg often needed to achieve, rather than almost achieve, current treatment goals has been proved repeatedly to confer a remarkable degree of added protection from adverse cardiovascular outcomes.[5] Almost is not good enough. Second, to achieve these goals, most patients require two or three

antihypertensive medications. To achieve the more stringent blood pressure goals indicated for diabetics and patients with chronic renal failure, three or four medications are usually needed. Third, to achieve and sustain patient compliance with multidrug regimens, greater attention needs to be paid to the patient's quality of life.

Compliance and Quality of Life

The importance of honest patient dialogue and patient education cannot be overemphasized. Despite decades of nationwide blood pressure education programs about the "silent killer," many patients perceive hypertension as being episodic and symptomatic. Because hypertension requires lifelong treatment and because medications can produce side effects, quality of life becomes a major issue that affects patients' compliance. Medication costs are considerable and beyond the means of some patients. For patients who must pay for some or all of their medications, costs can be cut drastically by prescribing generic drugs.

Men are often concerned about medication-induced sexual dysfunction. However, sexual dysfunction often precedes the initiation of antihypertensive therapy. In a double-blind, prospective, placebo-controlled trial, thiazide diuretics were the only one of the six major classes of antihypertensive drugs associated with more new cases of male sexual dysfunction over the next year than placebo. Thus, the incidence of medication-induced sexual dysfunction previously has been overstated. Much of the blame assigned to the drugs is caused by impaired endothelial function (impaired nitric oxide–mediated dilation of the corpus cavernosum) due to obesity-induced insulin resistance, cigarette smoking, hyperlipidemia, and uncontrolled hypertension. Indeed, patients generally rate their overall quality of life as significantly improved when their blood pressures are controlled with medical therapy compared with when uncontrolled on placebo. In addition to these considerations, several additional principles have been shown to facilitate patients' compliance: (1) titrating medical therapy based on home readings, which engages the patient's active participation; (2) using long-acting preparations with once-a-day dosing; (3) using low-dose combinations of medications from different drug classes to achieve synergistic effects on blood pressure while avoiding dose-dependent side effects; and (4) using fixed-dose combinations to reduce the overall number of pills.

Choice of Initial Drug Therapy

The choice of the initial antihypertensive medication is less important now than in the stepped-care era of the 1970s (which encouraged high-dose monotherapy) because most patients require multiple medications (Table 63–5). There is increasing movement toward initiating treatment with low-dose combination therapy. Based on the recent results of The Antihypertensive and Lipid Lowering Treatment to Prevent Heart Attack Trial (ALLHAT)[6] and other recent treatment trials, it takes at least two medications of different classes to treat most cases of mild hypertension and three or four different medications to treat the more difficult cases and to reach more stringent blood pressure goals in high-risk patients.[7] The JNC 7 Report recommends starting a two-drug combination regimen for patients with stage 2 hypertension. As a rule of thumb, an additional medication will be needed for each 10 mm Hg of systolic blood pressure above goal. The great majority of these multi-drug regimens should include a low-dose diuretic.

DIURETICS

Mechanism of Action. With initiation of diuretic therapy, contraction of blood volume explains the initial fall in blood pressure. With continued diuretic therapy, blood volume is partially restored, and vasodilator mechanisms (e.g., opening of ATP-sensitive potassium channels) sustain the antihypertensive action. Based on their sites of action in the kidney, there are three main classes of diuretics. Loop diuretics are the most potent because they block $Na^+/K^+/2Cl^-$ transport in the thick ascending loop of Henle, where a large portion of the filtered Na^+ is reabsorbed. Thiazide diuretics and the indoline derivative indapamide are less potent because they block Na^+/Cl^- cotransport in the distal convoluted tubule, where a small portion of the filtered sodium is reabsorbed. The potassium-sparing diuretics are the weakest because they act most distally in the collecting duct. Spironolactone prevents aldosterone from activating the mineralocorticoid receptor, thereby inhibiting activation of ENaC, the final common pathway for reabsorption of Na^+ from the distal nephron.

Table 63–5 • ORAL ANTIHYPERTENSIVE AGENTS

DRUG	DOSE RANGE, TOTAL mg/DAY (DOSES PER DAY)	DRUG	DOSE RANGE, TOTAL mg/DAY (DOSES PER DAY)
DIURETICS		**ACEIs**	
Thiazide Diuretics		Benazepril	10–80 (1–2)
HCTZ	6.25–25 (1)	Captopril	25–150 (2)
Chlorthalidone	6.25–25 (1)	Enalapril	2.5–40 (2)
Indapamide	1.25–5 (1)	Fosinopril	10–80 (1–2)
Metolazone	2.5–5 (1)	Lisinopril	5–80 (1)
		Moexipril	7.5–30 (1)
Loop Diuretics		Perindopril	4–16 (1)
Furosemide	20–160 (2)	Quinapril	5–80 (1–2)
Torsemide	2.5–20 (1–2)	Ramipril	2.5–20 (1)
Bumetanide	0.5–2 (2)	Trandolapril	1–8 (1)
Ethacrynic acid	25–100 (2)		
		ARBs	
Potassium Sparing		Candesartan	8–32 (1)
Amiloride	5–20 (1)	Eprosartan	400–800 (1–2)
Triamterene	25–100 (1)	Irbesartan	150–300 (1)
Spironolactone	12.5–200 (1–2)	Losartan	25–100 (2)
		Telmisartan	20–80 (1)
β-BLOCKERS		Valsartan	80–320 (1)
Acebutolol	200–800 (2)		
Atenolol	25–100 (1)	**α-BLOCKERS**	
Betaxolol	5–20 (1)	Prazosin	1–40 (2–3)
Bisoprolol	2.5–20 (1)	Doxazosin	1–16 (1)
Carteolol	2.5–10	Terazosin	1–20 (1)
Metoprolol	50–200 (2)	Phenoxybenzamine	20–120 (2) for
Metoprolol XL	50–200 (1)		pheochromocytoma
Nadolol	20–320 (1)		
Penbutolol	10–80 (1)	**SYMPATHOLYTICS**	
Pindolol	10–60 (2)	Clonidine	0.2–1.2 (2–3)
Propranolol	40–160 (2)	Clonidine patch	0.1–0.6 (weekly)
Propranolol LA	60–180 (1)	Guanabenz	2–32 (2)
Timolol	20–60 (2)	Guanfacine	1–3 (1)
		Methyldopa	250–1000 (2)
β-/α-BLOCKERS		Reserpine	0.05–0.25 (1)
Labetolol	200–1200 (2)		
Carvedilol	6.25–50 (2)	**DIRECT VASODILATORS**	
		Hydralazine	25–200 (2)
CCBs		Minoxidil	2.5–100 (1)
Dihydropyridines			
Amlodipine	2.5–10 (1)	**SELECTED COMBINATIONS**	
Felodipine	2.5–20 (1–2)	Triamterene/HCTZ	37.5/25 (½–1)
Isradipine CR	2.5–20 (2)	Spironolactone	25/25 (½–1)
Nicardipine SR	30–120 (2)	Bisoprolol/HCTZ	2.5–10/6.25 (1)
Nifedipine XL	30–120 (1)	Benazepril/HCTZ	5–20/6.25–25 (1)
Nisoldipine	10–40 (1)	Amlodipine/benazepril	2.5–5/10–20 (1)
		Trandolepril/verapamil	2–4/180–240 (1)
Nondihydropyridines		Candesartan/HCTZ	16–32/12.5–25 (1)
Diltiazem CD	120–540 (1)	Irbesartan/HCTZ	15–30/12.5–25 (1)
Verapamil HS	120–480 (1)	Losartan/HCTZ	50–100/12.5–25 (1)
		Valsartan/HCTZ	80–160/12.5–25 (1)

ACEI = angiotensin-converting enzyme inhibitor; ARB = angiotensin receptor blocker; CCB = calcium channel blocker; HCTZ = hydrochlorothiazide.

Triamterene and amiloride block ENaC directly. Because less Na^+ is presented to the Na^+,K^+-ATPase on the apical surface (i.e., vascular side) of the collecting duct cells, less K^+ is excreted in the urine.

Side Effects and Contraindications. Thiazides and prolonged exposure to loop diuretics cause renal potassium wasting because increased Na^+ is presented to the Na^+,K^+-ATPase. The hypokalemia is dose dependent and minimized by using lower doses the equivalent of 6.25 to 12.5 mg of hydrochlorothiazide (HCTZ). Hypokalemia predisposes to ventricular arrhythmias and negates the cardioprotective benefit of lowering blood pressure. Serum Na^+ also needs to be followed because thiazide diuretics occasionally cause hyponatremia, which in older patients can be severe. Although thiazides are said to elevate plasma LDL cholesterol, the effect is negligible with lower doses. Although thiazides can increase blood glucose, the effect is small with low doses, and thiazide-based therapy has been proved to reduce cardiovascular morbidity and mortality in diabetic hypertensives. They occasionally cause erectile dysfunction. Thiazide diuretics are relatively contraindicated in patients with hyperuricemia because they can precipitate gout. Potassium-sparing diuretics are contraindicated in patients who are prone to hyperkalemia, especially patients with renal failure and diabetics with hyporeninemic hypoaldosteronism. In high doses, spironolactone antagonizes the testosterone receptor,

thereby producing sexual dysfunction and painful gynecomastia in men. Except for ethacrynic acid, all diuretics contain a sulfur moiety, can cause photosensitivity, and should be avoided in patients with a history of allergic reaction to sulfa drugs. Furosemide can rarely cause interstitial nephritis.

Compelling Indications and Therapeutic Principles. Diuretics are the oldest, least expensive, and still among the best antihypertensive medications. With the marketing of new classes of antihypertensive agents since the 1970s, the number of prescriptions written for diuretics unfortunately has fallen steadily. Hopefully, this trend will change with publication of the ALLHAT, which documented that thiazide-type diuretics are at least as effective as (and in some instances more effective than) newer agents in lowering blood pressure and preventing the attendant cardiovascular morbidity and mortality. As first line therapy, the thiazide-type diuretic (chlorthalidone) was equally effective as the ACE inhibitor (lisinopril) or the dihydropyridine CCB (amlodipine) in preventing the primary endpoint of combined fatal coronary heart disease and nonfatal myocardial infarction. The effectiveness of the diuretic-based therapy was demonstrated in all patient subgroups including older persons, women, African Americans, and those with diabetes. When combined with other classes of antihypertensive medications, diuretics exert a synergistic effect on blood pressure. The most common cause of apparent drug-resistant hypertension is the failure to include a diuretic or dose it correctly in the therapeutic regimen. Thus, thiazides remain the first drug of choice for the majority of hypertensive patients. Thiazide diuretics exert a larger effect on systolic than diastolic blood pressure and, based on hard outcomes data, are the initial drugs of choice for isolated systolic hypertension.[8] Almost every antihypertensive regimen should include a low-dose diuretic or at least a low-sodium diet.

Because of their long half-lives, thiazide diuretics are much more effective than the short-acting loop diuretics in the long-term management of chronic hypertension. Very low doses of HCTZ (6.25 mg/day in combination or 12.5 mg/day alone) maintain much of the antihypertensive efficacy while greatly minimizing the adverse metabolic profile associated with the much larger doses (50 to 100 mg/day) used previously. Chlorthalidone, the thiazide-type diuretic used in the ALLHAT and many other landmark hypertension treatment trials, is more potent and has a much longer duration of action than HCTZ, which for decades has replaced chlorthalidone as the main thiazide-type diuretic used in clinical practice. According to some experts, 25 mg of chlorthalidone is roughly equivalent to 40 mg of HCTZ. Combinations of HCTZ with potassium-sparing diuretics reduce, but do not always eliminate, the need for potassium supplements; serum K+ levels must be followed after initiating therapy. Adherence to a moderately low-salt diet also reduces the need for potassium supplements in patients taking diuretics. Thiazide diuretics, except for metolazone, are ineffective when the glomerular filtration rate falls below 30 mL/min.

Loop diuretics are the diuretics of choice for treating hypertension in patients with chronic renal insufficiency or heart failure. Because the duration of action of furosemide is 6-8 hours, twice daily dosing is required for sustained lowering of blood pressure. Torsemide may be a better alternative because of its longer half-life. The addition of low-dose metolazone (2.5 mg/day) to a loop diuretic can sometimes restore blood pressure responsiveness in patients with resistant hypertension due to severe volume expansion in the setting of advanced chronic renal failure. However, metolazone and the potent loop diuretics are not appropriate treatment for the vast majority of patients with uncomplicated hypertension.

Spironolactone (50 to 200 mg/day) is the drug of choice for the medical treatment of primary aldosteronism. Low-dose spironolactone (12.5 to 25 mg/day) also can be effective in some patients with primary low-renin hypertension. Eplerenone, a more specific mineralocorticoid receptor antagonist that does not block the testosterone receptor, is in the final stages of clinical trials and could have broad implications for the treatment of primary hypertension. Amiloride is the drug of choice for treating primary aldosteronism in men and is the drug of choice for patients with Liddle's syndrome.

β-ADRENERGIC RECEPTOR BLOCKERS

Mechanism of Action. Interaction of epinephrine or norepinephrine with β_1-adrenoreceptors in the heart causes G protein–linked activation of adenylate cyclase, resulting in positive chronotropic and inotropic effects. Interaction of catecholamines with β_2-adrenoreceptors relaxes bronchiolar and arteriolar smooth muscle. With the initiation of β-blocker therapy, blood pressure at first is little affected because the fall in cardiac output is offset by a compensatory increase in peripheral resistance. Over several weeks, blood pressure falls progressively as the peripheral vasculature relaxes. Thus, the antihypertensive effect of β-blockade involves decreases in cardiac output (β_1-receptors), renin release (β_1-receptors), and norepinephrine release (prejunctional β_2-receptors).

All 11 β-blockers are antihypertensive. *First-generation* agents (e.g., propranolol) nonselectively block both β_1- and β_2-receptors. *Second-generation* agents (e.g., metoprolol, atenolol, acebutolol, bisoprolol) are *relatively* cardioselective. In low doses, they exert a greater inhibitory effect on β_1- than on β_2-receptors, but selectivity is lost at high doses. *Other* agents cause vasodilatation either by stimulating β_2-adrenoreceptors (i.e., *intrinsic sympathomimetic activity*) (e.g., pindolol) or by blocking α_1-adrenoreceptors (labetalol, carvedilol) on vascular smooth muscle.

Side Effects and Contraindications. β-Adrenergic receptor blockade can cause adverse side effects through (1) contraction of smooth muscle (bronchospasm, Raynaud's phenomenon), (2) exaggeration of therapeutic negative chronotropic and inotropic effects (heart failure, heart block), and (3) penetration of the central nervous system (CNS) (depression, nightmares). Contraindications to β-blockers include asthma and other forms of reactive airway disease, heart block, acutely

decompensated heart failure, Prinzmetal's angina, and depression. In brittle type I diabetes, β-blockers can mask the adrenergic signs of hypoglycemia, but this effect often can be avoided with a cardioselective β-blocker. Before starting β-blockers for hypertension, it should be appreciated that chronic β-blocker therapy has been associated with a 28% increased risk of developing type II diabetes. In patients with known or suspected coronary disease, β-blockers must be tapered slowly to avoid rebound angina.

Compelling Indications and Therapeutic Principles. For the treatment of hypertension, the long-acting (once-a-day) and cardioselective β-blockers are preferred, but all β-blockers are effective, particularly when combined with a diuretic. Although numerous clinical trials have demonstrated that treating hypertension with β-blockers reduces cardiovascular outcomes, in most cases the β-blocker has been combined with a thiazide diuretic. β-Blockers, which are very effective in reducing myocardial oxygen demands, are first-line therapy for hypertensive patients with coronary disease and should be prescribed in all patients who also have sustained a myocardial infarction and who can tolerate them. β-Blockers also can be very useful in hypertensive patients who have anxiety disorders.

CALCIUM CHANNEL BLOCKERS

Mechanism of Action. The CCBs block the opening of voltage-gated (L-type) Ca^{2+} channels, thereby preventing the entry of Ca^{2+} into cardiac myocytes and vascular smooth muscle cells. The resultant decrease in the cytosolic Ca^{2+} signal decreases heart rate and ventricular contractility and relaxes vascular smooth muscle. The major classes of CCBs are the dihydropyridines (e.g., nifedipine, felodipine, amlodipine) and the nondihydropyridines (verapamil and diltiazem). Dihydropyridines are more potent antihypertensive agents, but any directly negative chronotropic or inotropic effects are offset by reflex sympathetic activation. By comparison, the nondihydropyridines are weaker antihypertensive drugs because they cause less peripheral vasodilation, but they exert more pronounced negative chronotropic and inotropic effects (especially verapamil), thereby decreasing cardiac output.

Side Effects and Contraindications. The CCBs are generally very well tolerated. Because of their negative inotropic and negative chronotropic actions, the nondihydropyridine CCBs are contraindicated in patients with severe left ventricular dysfunction and those with impaired cardiac conduction because they can precipitate heart failure or heart block. Verapamil often causes considerable constipation by blocking contraction of smooth muscle in the gut. The most frequent annoying side effects of the dihydropyridines—headaches, flushing, and ankle edema—are all related to arterial vasodilation. In the absence of venodilation, arterial vasodilation increases capillary hydrostatic pressure, leading to dose-dependent ankle edema. *Short-acting dihydropyridines should not be used to treat hypertension.* By triggering an abrupt fall in blood pressure with reflex sympathetic activation, these rapidly acting vasodilators can precipitate myocardial ischemia, infarction, stroke, and death.

Compelling Indications and Therapeutic Principles. Controversy has arisen on the indications for long-acting dihydropyridine CCBs, which cause much less (but still some) reflex sympathetic activation. A meta-analysis suggests that, for the majority of patients with hypertension, cardiovascular outcomes with dihydropyridine CCBs are on balance equivalent to those seen with other classes of antihypertensive medications, with the caveat that they possibly provide less protection against myocardial infarction and heart failure but greater protection against stroke and dementia.[9] With the publication of ALLHAT, much of the conroversy around dihydropyridine CCBs has ended. After five years of treatment with a long-acting dihydroperidine CCB, the primary outcome of fatal coronary heart disease and nonfatal myocardial infarction was identical to that seen with the ACE inhibitor or the diuretic. For patients with proteinuric renal insufficiency, there is mounting evidence that dihydropyridine CCB–based therapy is less renoprotective than ARB or ACE inhibitor–based therapy.[10] However, in the vast majority of patients with renal disease, multiple classes of medications, *including dihydropyridines*, are required to achieve blood pressure goals. The key point is that a dihydropyridine should not be used as first-line therapy for hypertension in patients with proteinuric renal disease but may be used as adjunctive therapy once the dose of the ACE inhibitor or ARB has been maximized in combination with an appropriate diuretic. Dihydropyridine CCB–based therapy has been proved to improve cardiovascular outcomes, especially stroke, dramatically in older hypertensives and particularly in older hypertensive patients with diabetes.

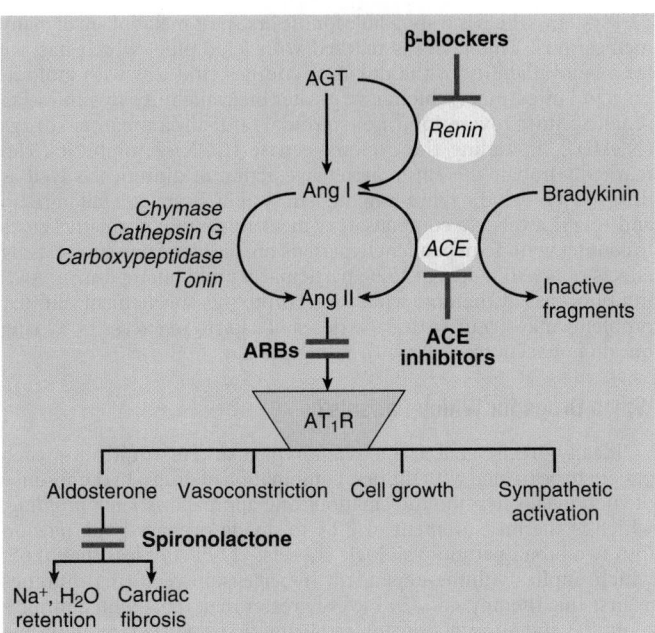

β-blockers

AGT

Renin

Chymase
Cathepsin G
Carboxypeptidase
Tonin

Ang I

Bradykinin

ACE

Ang II

Inactive
fragments

ARBs

**ACE
inhibitors**

AT₁R

Aldosterone   Vasoconstriction   Cell growth   Sympathetic
activation

Spironolactone

Na⁺, H₂O   Cardiac
retention   fibrosis

FIGURE 63–9 • The renin-angiotensin-aldosterone pathway as an antihypertensive drug target. ACE = angiotensin-converting enzyme; AGT = angiotensinogen; Ang = angiotensin; ARB = angiotensin II receptor blocker; AT₁R = angiotensin II receptor type 1.

ANGIOTENSIN-CONVERTING ENZYME INHIBITORS AND ANGIOTENSIN RECEPTOR BLOCKERS

Mechanism of Action. The renin-angiotensin system is one of the most important targets for antihypertensive drugs (Fig. 63–9). The interaction of Ang II with G protein–coupled receptors termed AT₁ receptors accelerates numerous cellular processes that contribute not only to hypertension but also to its end-organ damage, including (1) aldosterone secretion, which produces renal salt and water retention, as well as collagen deposition leading to cardiac fibrosis; (2) peripheral vasoconstriction; (3) growth of cardiac and vascular smooth muscle cells, leading to cardiac and vascular hypertrophy; (4) production of superoxide anions and other reactive oxygen species that inactivate nitric oxide, thereby inhibiting endothelium-dependent vasodilatation; and (5) augmentation of both central sympathetic outflow and prejunctional modulation of norepinephrine release from peripheral sympathetic nerve terminals, thereby leading to excessive stimulation of α adrenergic receptors. For these reasons, blockade of the renin-angiotensin-aldosterone system may exert organoprotective effects above and beyond the lowering of blood pressure. ACE inhibitors block the conversion of Ang I to Ang II, leading to a dramatic fall in plasma Ang II levels with the initiation of therapy. However, with continued treatment with an ACE inhibitor, plasma Ang II levels return to normal in part because ACE inhibitors do not block alternative pathways that generate Ang II. The sustained antihypertensive action of ACE inhibitors is explained in part by their ability to block the metabolism of bradykinin, a potent endothelial-dependent vasodilator, to inactive fragments. By comparison, ARBs lower blood pressure specifically by blocking the interaction of Ang II on the AT₁ receptors. Thus, ARBs do not increase bradykinin, which has been implicated in both the therapeutic and side effects of ACE inhibitors.

Side Effects and Contraindications. The ACE inhibitors are generally well tolerated, but the ARBs have the best side effect profile to date. The most common side effect of ACE inhibitors is a dry cough, which occurs in 3 to 39% of patients and resolves in a few days after the drug is discontinued. The incidence is higher in African Americans than whites and highest in Asians. Because the cough seems to be bradykinin mediated, this annoying side effect is avoided by switching to an ARB. The rare (1 : 2000) but most serious side effect of ACE inhibitors, angioedema (Chapter 269), also has been blamed on bradykinin, and thus is even rarer with ARBs. Angioedema, which can occur at any time during the course of treatment, is more common in African Americans and can be fatal. With either ACE inhibitors or

ARBs, hyperkalemia can result from reduced aldosterone secretion or impairment of renal function; however, even in the setting of significant renal disease, the risk of hyperkalemia requiring drug discontinuation is low (<2%) and is seen mainly when these drugs are administered to diabetics with hyporeninemic hypoaldosteronism or are mistakenly used in patients who are also taking potassium supplements, an error that should be avoided. ACE inhibitors and ARBs can precipitate acute renal failure in patients with bilateral renal artery stenosis or hypovolemia. After correction of hypovolemia, the ACE inhibitor or ARB usually can be restarted safely at a lower dose. These drugs are contraindicated in pregnancy because they are teratogenic.

Compelling Indications and Therapeutic Principles. Because of their low side effect profiles and ancillary benefits, ACE inhibitors and ARBs are gaining popularity for the general treatment of hypertension. At present, however, diabetic nephropathy, nondiabetic renal insufficiency, and heart failure are considered (by many authorities) to be the compelling indications for initiating hypertension treatment with an ACE inhibitor or ARB.[11-13] Randomized trials have dispelled the fear that ACE inhibitors and ARBs are contraindicated for patients with mild or moderate degrees of renal impairment by showing that the incidence of hyperkalemia or acute renal failure is very low and that renoprotection is provided. Although serum creatinine and potassium need to be monitored in all patients receiving an ACE inhibitor or ARB, small and typically transient increases at the onset of therapy are not an indication to discontinue these drugs.

All ARBs have approximately comparable antihypertensive efficacy. Losartan, the prototype, differs from the other ARBs in two ways: a shorter duration of action, requiring twice-daily dosing if used as monotherapy, and a uricosuric effect, which may be beneficial in patients with hyperuricemia.

α-ADRENERGIC BLOCKERS

Mechanism of Action. By blocking the interaction of norepinephrine on vascular α-adrenergic receptors, these drugs cause peripheral vasodilation, thereby lowering blood pressure. By increasing skeletal muscle blood flow, they increase insulin sensitivity. By dilating urethral smooth muscle, they improve symptoms of prostatism. Prazosin, doxazosin, and terazosin selectively block α₁-adrenoreceptors, whereas phenoxybenzamine blocks both α₁- and α₂-receptors.

Side Effects and Contraindications. The most troubling side effect is orthostatic hypotension, which is less often seen with the second-generation agents with a slower onset of action.

Compelling Indications and Therapeutic Principles. Phenoxybenzamine remains the drug of choice for preoperative management of pheochromocytoma; after α-blockade is achieved, a β-blocker should be added to block an otherwise excessive reflex tachycardia. The selective α₁-blockers are effective general antihypertensive agents and are particularly useful in older men with prostatism. It is important to emphasize that α-blockers should not be used as monotherapy because their propensity to cause fluid retention can lead to tachyphylaxis and unmask heart failure.[14] When prescribed correctly in combination with a diuretic, there is no evidence to contraindicate their use.

CENTRAL SYMPATHOLYTICS

Mechanism of Action. Stimulation of α₂-adrenergic receptors and imidazoline receptors in the CNS lowers central sympathetic outflow, whereas stimulation of presynaptic α₂-receptors causes feedback inhibition of norepinephrine release from peripheral sympathetic nerve terminals. The combined effect is reduced sympathetic drive to the heart and peripheral circulation, leading to decreased heart rate, cardiac output, and peripheral vascular resistance.

Side Effects and Contraindications. Although highly effective as antihypertensive agents, the clinical utility of these agents is limited by their side effects profile. The major CNS side effects are sedation, dry mouth, and depression. Depression is a contraindication to all available central sympatholytic agents. These side effects are lessened with more selective imidazoline receptor blockers that are available in Europe. Central sympatholytics should not be combined with a β-blocker because excessive bradycardia can ensue. Reserpine also depletes norepinephrine stores from sympathetic nerve terminals, causing dose-dependent orthostatic hypotension. α-Methyldopa can cause autoimmune hemolytic anemia and lupus erythematosus. Although clonidine does not cause these latter side effects, *rebound hypertension* is a major problem if oral clonidine is discontinued abruptly. Rebound hypertension is reduced by using longer acting preparations (guanfacine or transdermal clonidine).

Therapeutic Principles. Central sympatholytics can be effective as add-on therapy for patients with difficult-to-control hypertension. Aldomet remains the drug of choice for nonemergent hypertension in pregnancy (Chapter 253).

DIRECT VASODILATORS

Mechanism of Action. Minoxidil and hydralazine are potent hyperpolarizing arterial vasodilators that work by opening vascular ATP-sensitive potassium channels.

Side Effects and Contraindications. By causing selective arterial dilation, both drugs cause profound reflex sympathetic activation and tachycardia as well as peripheral edema. When hydralazine is administered parenterally, the magnitude of the blood pressure lowering is unpredictable and can result in extreme hypotension. Chronic treatment with high doses of oral hydralazine can cause a lupus-like syndrome. Minoxidil causes diffuse hirsutism.

Therapeutic Principles. Hydralazine has largely been replaced by the dihydropyridine CCBs because of side effect profiles. However, hydralazine remains the treatment of choice for acute severe hypertension in pregnancy (Chapter 253). Difficult-to-control hypertension in chronic renal failure (Chapter 117) is the main indication for minoxidil, which must be combined with a β–blocker, to prevent excessive reflex tachycardia, and with a loop diuretic, to prevent excessive fluid retention.

COMBINATION THERAPY. Some drug combinations are particularly effective for treating hypertension, and some should be avoided. Because higher doses of diuretics cause reflex activation of both the renin-angiotensin and sympathetic nervous systems, preventing such activation with the addition of an ACE inhibitor, an ARB, or a β-blocker produces synergistic effects on blood pressure. With fixed-dose combinations, the dose of HCTZ should be 12.5 mg or, even better, 6.25 mg. Unfortunately, many fixed-dose combinations contain 25 mg of HCTZ, which often is too high. Combining HCTZ with a potassium-sparing diuretic may obviate unpleasant potassium supplements, but again the dose of the HCTZ component often is too high, requiring that pills be cut in half.

Because dihydropyridine CCBs also produce reflex increases in plasma renin and sympathetic activity, the addition of an ACE inhibitor or ARB produces synergistic effects on blood pressure (and potentially on end-organ protection). In addition, high doses of dihydropyridine CCBs cause ankle edema because these drugs preferentially dilate arteries rather than veins, producing elevated hydrostatic pressure in the cutaneous circulation. This elevated hydrostatic pressure and the resulting ankle edema often can be relieved by the addition of an ACE inhibitor or ARB, which dilates veins as well as arteries. In contrast, the hydrostatic edema is not relieved by addition of a diuretic.

Furthermore, combining a dihydropyridine CCB with a diuretic produces less blood pressure synergy because of excessive reflex neurohormonal activation. This combination should be avoided in patients with ischemic heart disease unless a β-blocker also is used. β-Blockers generally should not be combined with nondihydropyridine CCBs or with clonidine or other central sympatholytics because these combinations can lead to excessive bradycardia and depression, particularly in older persons. Labetalol, although marketed for its α-blocking action, is primarily a β-blocker and should not be combined with other β-blockers.

Vasopeptidase inhibitors, a new class of agent under final stages of clinical investigation, inhibit both ACE and neutral endopeptidase (NEP), the enzyme that breaks down the endogenous natriuretic peptides. As a result, the natriuretic and vasodilatory actions of these peptides are enhanced. NEP inhibition alone has very little effect on blood pressure because of compensatory activation of the renin-angiotensin-aldosterone system. In contrast, simultaneous inhibition of NEP and ACE by this single molecule produces a powerful antihypertensive effect that may be particularly useful in treating systolic hypertension. However, clinical safety trials showed a greater incidence of life-threatening angioedema with the first vasopeptidase inhibitor than with a conventional ACE inhibitor. Whether serious angioedema is an unavoidable side-effect of this class of drugs remains to be determined. Studies also are under way to determine if combining an ACE inhibitor with an ARB provides more complete blockade of the renin-angiotensin system than maximal doses of either drug alone.

MAJOR DRUG INTERACTIONS THAT AFFECT BLOOD PRESSURE CONTROL. Grapefruit juice (even a single glass) increases the bioavailability of dihydropyridine CCBs by inhibiting the intestinal cytochrome P-450

3A4 system, which is responsible for the first-pass metabolism of many medications. This effect is marked with felodipine, which has the least bioavailability of the dihydropyridines, and less with amlodipine and nifedipine, which have greater bioavailability. By inhibiting renal sodium excretion, nonsteroidal anti-inflammatory drugs (NSAIDs), including the cyclooxygenase (COX)-2 inhibitors, can markedly impair the antihypertensive action of diuretics as well as drugs that block the renin-angiotensin system. Because a fall in renin and Ang II levels is a compensatory mechanism that normally serves to counter volume-dependent hypertension, the blood pressure–raising effects of NSAIDs appear to be particularly problematic during ACE inhibitor–based therapy, which interrupts this mechanism. Similar problems may occur with daily doses of aspirin in excess of 325 mg but do not seem to occur with 81 mg per day.

Which Drugs for Which Patients?

Ideally, precise genetic and phenotypic markers would allow each patient to be treated with the best combination of drugs. In the absence of such ideal scientific information, one approach is *renin profiling,* which is the measurement of PRA to divide primary hypertension into two broad pathophysiologic subsets: (1) PRA of less than 0.65, which implies volume-dependent hypertension requiring diuretics as first-line therapy, and (2) PRA of greater than 0.65, which implies renin-dependent hypertension requiring first-line therapy with one or more drugs that block the renin-angiotensin system, such as β-blockers, ACE inhibitors, or ARBs. In hypertensive populations, PRA shows a normal distribution, with the lowest values occurring in mineralocorticoid-induced hypertension, the highest values in renovascular hypertension, and a broad distribution of values in primary hypertension. However, because of feedback inhibition of renin release and progressive loss of nephrons, PRA can decrease secondarily with increasing severity and duration of chronic hypertension regardless of the etiology. Whether renin-guided therapy improves patient outcomes remains to be determined.

Pharmacogenetic profiling is another possible approach. A few single-nucleotide polymorphisms have been associated with greater blood pressure reductions with specific drugs. However, none of the reported effects have been large enough to make specific treatment recommendations.

For most patients, the current recommendation is to choose drugs based on comorbidities and the optimization of cardiovascular-renal protection (Table 63–6).

HYPERTENSION IN AFRICAN AMERICANS. The lower plasma renin levels common in African American hypertensives may suggest volume-dependent hypertension requiring diuretic therapy. Alternatively, lower plasma renin levels may be caused by a longer duration and greater severity of hypertension or by concomitant nephrosclerosis, with the latter being a compelling indication for ACE inhibitor–based therapy (see later). As monotherapy, an ACE inhibitor or a β-blocker yields a smaller decrease in blood pressure in older hypertensive African American men than in white men. The key point, however, is that when higher doses of an ACE inhibitor, an ARB, or a β-blocker are used in combination with a thiazide diuretic (or low-sodium diet), antihypertensive efficacy is amplified, and ethnic differences seem to disappear. Because combination therapy is required to reach blood pressure goals in most hypertensive patients, especially those with more severe hypertension and additional cardiovascular risk factors, the results achieved with monotherapy have less and less practical relevance to modern clinical practice.

HYPERTENSIVE PATIENTS WITH NEPHROSCLEROSIS. Hypertension is the second most common cause of chronic renal failure (Chapter 117), accounting for 25% of cases. Hypertensive nephrosclerosis is thought to result from severe constriction of the afferent renal arteriole, resulting in chronic glomerular ischemia. Typically, proteinuria is mild (<0.5 g/24 hr), and the diagnosis should be questioned in the presence of heavier degrees of proteinuria or in the absence of additional target organ damage (retinopathy, LVH). Mild-to-moderate non-diabetic renal insufficiency is now considered to be a compelling indication for ACE inhibitor–based antihypertensive therapy.[II] ACE inhibitors preferentially dilate the efferent renal arteriole, thereby minimizing intraglomerular hypertension. In contrast, arterial vasodilators such as dihydropyridine CCBs, when used without an ACE inhibitor or ARB, preferentially dilate the afferent arteriole, thereby promoting intraglomerular hypertension. This adverse effect on the renal microcirculation opposes the beneficial effect of lowering

Cardiovascular Disease

Table 63–6 • CONSIDERATIONS FOR INDIVIDUALIZING ANTIHYPERTENSIVE DRUG THERAPY

DRUG CLASS	COMPELLING INDICATIONS	MAJOR CONTRAINDICATIONS	SIDE EFFECTS
Diuretics	Most hypertension Isolated systolic hypertension CHF	Gout (relative)	Hypokalemia Hyponatremia Hypertriglyceridemia Hyperuricemia Erectile dysfunction Glucose intolerance, type 2 diabetes Interstitial nephritis (loop diuretics)
β-Blockers	Angina After MI CHF Tachyarrhythmias	Heart block Asthma and COPD Depression Peripheral vascular disease (relative) Athletes (relative)	Heart block CHF Bronchospasm Depression Type 2 diabetes Cold extremities Nightmares
ACE inhibitors	Diabetic nephropathy Hypertensive nephrosclerosis CHF After MI Left ventricular dysfunction	Pregnancy Bilateral renal artery stenosis Hyperkalemia	Cough Hyperkalemia Angioedema Leukopenia Fetal toxicity
ARBs	Diabetic (type 2) nephropathy CHF ACEI cough	Pregnancy Bilateral renal artery stenosis Hyperkalemia	Hyperkalemia Angioedema (very rare) Fetal toxicity
Dihydropyridine CCBs	Angina Isolated systolic hypertension (especially in diabetics)	As monotherapy in chronic renal disease	Headaches Flushing Ankle edema
Nondihydropyridine CCBs	Angina	Heart block CHF	Bradycardia First-degree atrioventricular block Constipation (often severe) Worsening of systolic function
α-Blockers	Prostatic hypertrophy Pheochromocytoma	As monotherapy for hypertension Orthostatic hypotension	Orthostatic hypotension Drug tolerance (in the absence of diuretic therapy) Ankle edema CHF

ACE = angiotensin-converting enzyme; ARB = angiotensin receptor blocker; CCB = calcium channel blocker; CHF = congestive heart failure; MI = myocardial infarction.

systemic blood pressure. In addition, dihydropyridine CCB monotherapy reflexively increases the activity of the sympathetic and renin-angiotensin systems, which could promote glomerular hypertrophy. In contrast, monotherapy with an ACE inhibitor decreases sympathetic activity in patients with nondiabetic renal insufficiency. In African Americans with moderate hypertensive nephrosclerosis and baseline proteinuria, an ACE inhibitor (ramipril)–based regimen is superior to a dihydropyridine CCB (amlodipine)–based regimen in slowing the progression to renal failure. The ACE inhibitor should be withdrawn only if the rise in serum creatinine exceeds 30% of the baseline value or the serum K$^+$ increases to greater than 5.6 mmol/L.

DIABETIC HYPERTENSIVE PATIENTS. Compared with its 25% prevalence in the general adult population, hypertension is present in 70% of diabetic patients and is a major factor contributing to excessive risk of myocardial infarction, stroke, heart failure, microvascular complications, and diabetic nephropathy progressing to end-stage renal disease (Chapter 242). To reduce these risks, three current principles should guide therapy. *First, in all diabetic patients, blood pressures should be lowered to less than 130/80 mm Hg.* [15] Compared with less intensive treatment, more intensive reduction of blood pressure has been proved repeatedly to reduce cardiovascular and microvascular end points dramatically in patients with diabetes. In one study, for example, lowering diastolic blood pressure to 81 versus 85 mm Hg led to a 60% decrease in coronary events, a 43% reduction in stroke, and an impressive 77% decrease in mortality. The cardiovascular benefits of tight blood pressure control in diabetic patients cannot be overemphasized because they exceed and are additive to those of tight glucose control. In addition, tight blood pressure control is the key to retarding the progression of diabetic nephropathy. In those with heavy proteinuria (>1 g/24 hr), additional renal protection may be obtained if blood pressure is lowered to less than 125/75 mm Hg.

Second, to achieve such stringent blood pressure goals typically requires three or four drugs. According to most authorities, the first drug should be an ACE inhibitor or ARB, the second drug a diuretic, and the third a dihydropyridine CCB and/or a β-blocker. The rationale is as follows.

The third therapeutic principle is that an ACE inhibitor or ARB should be the drug of first choice for the hypertensive diabetic because of mounting evidence that these agents provide special renoprotective and perhaps cardioprotective effects. [10,12,13] Type I diabetes with renal insufficiency is a compelling indication for ACE inhibitor–based antihypertensive therapy. Based on consistent results of three recent multicenter trials that examined renal outcomes, type II diabetes with renal insufficiency is now considered by some authorities to be a compelling indication for ARB-based antihypertensive therapy because similar data do not yet exist for ACE inhibitor–based regimens in type II diabetics. [10,13] However, an ACE inhibitor or ARB alone rarely achieves the stringent blood pressure goals in diabetic patients with renal insufficiency. A loop diuretic is usually needed to shrink the expanded plasma volume. A dihydropyridine CCB is usually needed for antihypertensive synergy. The dihydropyridine CCB should not be started until antihypertensive therapy has been initiated with an ACE inhibitor or ARB. A β-blocker should be added if the patient has coronary disease, which is prevalent in diabetes or heart failure.

HYPERTENSIVE PATIENTS WITH CORONARY ARTERY DISEASE. To lower myocardial oxygen demands in patients with coronary artery disease, the antihypertensive regimen should reduce blood pressure without causing reflex tachycardia. β-Blockers and CCBs are both antianginal and antihypertensive, but dihydropyridine CCBs should not be used without a β-blocker. β-Blockers are indicated for hypertensive patients who have sustained a myocardial infarction (Chapter 69) and, in low doses, for most patients with chronic heart failure. ACE inhibitors are indicated for almost all patients with left ventricular systolic dysfunction and may be considered for post–myocardial infarction patients even in the absence of ventricular dysfunction (Chapter 69). In patients with very high cardiovascular risk profiles but without known left ventricular dysfunction, the ACE inhibitor ramipril (10 mg/day) reduces cardiovascular outcomes, an effect that may or may not be beyond what can be explained by blood pressure reductions alone.

ISOLATED SYSTOLIC HYPERTENSION IN OLDER PERSONS. In older persons with isolated systolic hypertension, lowering systolic pressure from greater than 160 to less than 150 mm Hg has been unequivocally proved to reduce the risk of stroke by 30%, myocardial infarction by 23%, and overall cardiovascular mortality by 18%, and to slow the progression of dementia. [6,14]

Because of slower drug metabolism, slower postural autonomic reflexes, and more prevalent coronary artery disease in older persons, it is important to start with low doses of antihypertensive medications and titrate slowly (over months). Lifestyle modifications such as weight loss and moderate salt reduction reduce medication requirements. To prevent the development of orthostatic hypotension, medications should be titrated to standing blood pressure. For nondiabetic patients, low-dose thiazide diuretics (combined with a potassium-sparing diuretic) are the first-line drugs of choice because of their proved benefit in reducing risks of myocardial infarction and stroke as well as osteoporosis. HCTZ may need to be combined with an ACE inhibitor, an ARB, or a β-blocker. However, in older persons, β-blockers should be restricted to those with coronary disease and should be used with caution because they are more likely to precipitate heart block, impair exercise tolerance, or cause depression. For older hypertensive patients with diabetes, dihydropyridine CCBs are considered by many authorities to be the drugs of choice (in combination with an ACE inhibitor or ARB) because of even better cardiovascular outcomes than with thiazide-based therapy. [17] Trial data do not yet exist in older persons to determine whether the treatment of isolated elevations in systolic pressure between 140 and 160 mm Hg is beneficial; however, in the absence of such data, most authorities recommend treatment to prevent progression of systolic hypertension. To avoid precipitating myocardial ischemia, antihypertensive drugs may need to be reduced if diastolic (i.e., coronary perfusion) pressure falls below 65 mm Hg while attempting to lower systolic pressure below 140 mm Hg.

BLOOD PRESSURE LOWERING FOR SECONDARY PREVENTION OF STROKE.
Most authorities do not recommend blood pressure reduction during an acute stroke (Chapters 440 and 441). In middle-aged or older patients whose clinical condition was stable at least 2 weeks after a stroke or transient ischemic attack, lowering blood pressure by 12/5 mm Hg with a combination of the thiazide diuretic indapamide plus the ACE inhibitor perindopril was shown to reduce the risk of recurrent stroke by 43% in both hypertensive and normotensive patients. In such patients, therefore, a reasonable approach is to lower blood pressure slowly over several months beginning with a thiazide diuretic, adding an ACE inhibitor or additional drugs as needed. [18]

HYPERTENSIVE DISORDERS OF WOMEN

Hypertension Associated with Oral Contraceptives. Oral contraceptives, particularly current low-dose estrogen preparations, cause a small increase in blood pressure in most women but rarely cause a large increase into the hypertensive range. The mechanism is unknown, but women over 35 and those who smoke or are overweight appear to be at increased risk. If hypertension develops, oral contraceptive therapy should be discontinued in favor of other methods of contraception.

Hypertension in Pregnancy. Hypertension, the most common nonobstetric complication of pregnancy, is present in about 10% of all pregnancies (Chapter 253). Of these cases, one third are caused by chronic hypertension and two thirds are due to preeclampsia, which is defined as an increase in blood pressure to 140/90 mm Hg or greater after the twentieth week of gestation accompanied by proteinuria and pathologic edema, sometimes accompanied by renal and hepatic abnormalities, and a tendency toward seizures (eclampsia). Given the current trend of childbearing in women over age 35, the incidence of chronic hypertension in pregnancy is rising. α-Methyldopa remains the drug of choice for chronic hypertension in pregnancy, and hydralazine remains the drug of choice for preeclampsia. In the latter condition, magnesium sulfate is predictably effective in preventing seizures but, despite being a vasodilator, has inconsistent effects on blood pressure.

Hypertension after Menopause. In large clinical trials, oral estrogen replacement therapy has a neutral effect on blood pressure. In normotensive women, transdermal estrogen therapy has been shown to cause a small but consistent decrease in blood pressure. It is unclear whether routes of administration that bypass hepatic first-pass metabolism may unmask an antihypertensive effect of estrogen replacement therapy.

RESISTANT HYPERTENSION.
Defined as blood pressure that is not less than 140/90 mm Hg despite treatment with adequate doses of three different classes of medications, *resistant hypertension* is the most common reason for referral to a hypertension specialist. In practice, the problem usually falls into one of four categories: (1) pseudo-resistance, (2) an inadequate medical regimen, (3) noncompliance or ingestion of pressor substances, or (4) secondary hypertension. Pseudo-resistant hypertension is caused by either the white coat effect or panic attacks and is best diagnosed with ambulatory monitoring. The most common cause of apparent drug resistance is the absence of appropriate diuretic therapy: either no diuretic, inappropriate use of a loop diuretic in a patient with normal renal function, infrequent dosing with a short-acting loop diuretic (e.g., once-a-day furosemide), or a thiazide diuretic in a patient with impaired renal function. It is important to remember that significant impairment in renal function can be present with serum creatinine in the 1.2 to 1.4 mg/dL range or even lower. Other common shortcomings of the medical regimen include reliance on monotherapy and inadequate dosing. Several common causes of resistant hypertension are related to the patient's behavior: noncompliance with the medical regimen, noncompliance with lifestyle modifications (obesity, a high-salt diet, excessive alcohol intake), or habitual use of pressor substances such as sympathomimetics (tobacco, cocaine, amphetamines, phenylephrine-containing herbal remedies) or NSAIDs, with the latter causing renal sodium retention. Once these causes of resistant hypertension have been excluded, the search should begin for secondary causes of hypertension (see earlier).

ACUTE, SEVERE HYPERTENSION.
Twenty-five percent of all emergency department patients present with an elevated blood pressure. *Hypertensive emergencies* are acute, severe elevations in blood pressure that are accompanied by progressive target organ dysfunction such as myocardial or cerebral ischemia/infarction, pulmonary edema, or renal failure. *Hypertensive urgencies* are acute, severe elevations in blood pressure without evidence of progressive target organ dysfunction. Thus, the key distinction and approach to the patient depend on the clinical state of the patient and not the absolute level of blood pressure. Chronically elevated blood pressure, even when severe, does not necessitate urgent treatment. The full blown clinical picture of a hypertensive emergency is a critically ill patient who presents with a blood pressure greater than 220/140 mm Hg, headaches, confusion, blurred vision, nausea and vomiting, seizures, grade III or IV hypertensive retinopathy, heart failure, and oliguria. Hypertensive emergencies require immediate intensive care unit (ICU) admission for intravenous therapy and continuous blood pressure monitoring, whereas hypertensive urgencies often can be managed with oral medications and appropriate outpatient follow-up in 24 to 72 hours. The most common hypertensive cardiac emergencies include acute aortic dissection (Chapter 75), hypertension after coronary artery bypass graft surgery (Chapter 71), acute myocardial infarction (Chapter 69), and unstable angina (Chapter 68). Other hypertensive emergencies include eclampsia (Chapter 253), head trauma (Chapter 431), severe body burns (Chapter 108), postoperative bleeding from vascular suture lines, and epistaxis that cannot be controlled with anterior and posterior nasal packing. Neurologic emergencies—acute ischemic stroke, hemorrhagic stroke, subarachnoid hemorrhage, and hypertensive encephalopathy—can be difficult to distinguish from one another (Chapters 439 to 441). Hypertensive encephalopathy (Chapter 441) is characterized by severe hypertensive retinopathy (retinal hemorrhages and exudates, with or without papilledema) and a posterior leukoencephalopathy (affecting mainly the white matter of the parieto-occipital regions) seen on cerebral MR imaging or CT scanning. A new focal neurologic deficit suggests a stroke-in-evolution, which demands a much more conservative approach to the elevated blood pressure (Chapter 440).

In most other hypertensive emergencies, the goal of parenteral therapy is to achieve a controlled and gradual lowering of blood pressure. A good rule of thumb is to lower the initially elevated arterial pressure by 10% in the first hour and by an additional 15% over the next 3 to 12 hours to a target blood pressure of about 170/110 mm Hg. Blood pressure can be reduced to a more normal value over the next 48 hours. The principal exceptions to this rule are aortic dissection (Chapter 75) and postoperative bleeding from vascular suture lines, two situations that demand much more rapid normalization of blood pressure. In most other cases, unnecessarily rapid correction of the elevated blood pressure to completely normal values places the patient at high risk for worsening cerebral, cardiac, and renal ischemia. In chronic hypertension, cerebral autoregulation is reset to higher-than-normal blood pressures. This compensatory adjustment prevents tissue over-perfusion (increased intracranial pressure) at very high blood pressures, but it also predisposes to tissue underperfusion (cerebral ischemia) when an elevated blood pressure is lowered too quickly

Table 63–7 • PARENTERAL AGENTS FOR MANAGEMENT OF HYPERTENSIVE EMERGENCIES

AGENT	DOSE	ONSET OF ACTION	PRECAUTIONS
PARENTERAL VASODILATORS			
Sodium nitroprusside	0.25–10 µg/kg/min IV infusion	Immediate	Thiocyanate toxicity with prolonged use
Nitroglycerin	5–100 µg/min IV infusion	2–5 min	Headache, tachycardia, tolerance
Nicardipine	5–15 mg/h IV infusion	1–5 min	Protracted hypotension after prolonged use
Fenoldopam mesylate	0.1–0.3 µg/kg/min IV infusion	1–5 min	Headache, tachycardia, increased intraocular pressure
Hydralazine	5–10 mg as IV bolus or 10–40 mg IM repeat q4–6 h	10 min IV 20 min IM	Unpredictable and excessive falls in pressure; tachycardia; angina exacerbation
Enalaprilat	0.625–1.25 mg q6 h IV bolus	15–60 min	Unpredictable and excessive falls in pressure; acute renal failure in patients with bilateral renal artery stenosis
PARENTERAL ADRENERGIC INHIBITORS			
Labetolol	20–80 mg as slow IV injection q10 min, or 0.5–2 mg/min IV as infusion	5–10 min	Bronchospasm, heart block, orthostatic hypotension
Metoprolol	5 mg IV q10 min × 3 doses	5–10 min	Bronchospasm, heart block, heart failure, exacerbation of cocaine-induced myocardial ischemia
Esmolol	500 µg/kg IV over 3 min then 25–100 mg/kg/min as IV infusion	1–5 min	Bronchospasm, heart block, heart failure
Phentolamine	5–10 mg IV bolus q5–15 min	1–2 min	Tachycardia, orthostatic hypotension

(Chapter 440). In patients with coronary disease, overly rapid or excessive reduction in diastolic blood pressure in the ICU can precipitate myocardial ischemia or infarction.

After the blood pressure has been brought under acute control, oral labetalol and dihydropyridine CCBs are particularly useful agents in weaning patients from parenteral therapy so they can be transferred from the ICU. A few doses of intravenous furosemide are often needed to overcome drug resistance due to secondary volume expansion resulting from parenteral vasodilator therapy.

Secondary causes of hypertension should be considered in every patient admitted to the ICU with a hypertensive crisis. Normal 24-hour urinary catecholamines or a normal plasma normetanephrine and metanephrine collected when the blood pressure is the highest (first 24 hours in ICU) effectively rules out pheochromocytoma (Chapter 241). Renal artery stenosis and other secondary causes should be excluded after the patient has been transferred out of the ICU but before being discharged from the hospital (Chapter 124).

Parenteral Agents for Hypertensive Emergency. Sodium nitroprusside, a nitric oxide donor that causes both venous and arterial dilation, is the most popular agent because it can be titrated rapidly to control blood pressure (Tables 63–7 and 63–8). Intravenous nitroglycerin, another nitric oxide donor, is useful for reducing moderately elevated blood pressure in the setting of myocardial ischemia or infarction, but, compared with nitroprusside, the lowering of blood pressure is less predictable. Nicardipine is a parenteral dihydropyridine CCB that is particularly useful in the postoperative cardiac patient. Fenoldopam is a selective dopamine-1 receptor agonist that causes both systemic and renal vasodilation, as well as increased glomerular filtration, natriuresis, and diuresis. Intravenous labetalol is an effective treatment of hypertensive crisis particularly in the setting of myocardial ischemia with preserved ventricular function.

Oral Medications for Hypertensive Urgencies. Most patients who present to the emergency department with hypertensive urgencies either are noncompliant with their medical regimen or are being treated with an inadequate regimen. To expedite the necessary changes in medications, outpatient follow up should be arranged within 72 hours. To manage the patient during the short interim period, labetalol is effective in a dose of 200 to 300 mg, which can be repeated in 2 to 3 hours and then prescribed in twice-daily dosing. If a β-blocker is contraindicated, clonidine is effective in an initial dose of 0.1 or 0.2 mg followed by additional hourly doses of 0.1 mg. Patients can be discharged on 0.1 to 0.2 mg twice daily. Captopril, a short-acting ACE inhibitor, lowers blood pressure within 15 to 30 minutes of oral dosing. A small test dose of 6.25 mg should be used to avoid an excessive fall in blood pressure in hypovolemic patients; then, the full oral dose is 25 mg, which can be repeated in 1 to 2 hours and prescribed as 25–75 mg twice daily.

Table 63–8 • PARENTERAL TREATMENT OF SPECIFIC HYPERTENSIVE EMERGENCIES

TYPE OF CRISIS	SPECIFIC TREATMENT
CARDIAC	
Myocardial ischemia/ infarction	β-Blocker + nitroprusside (or nicardipine); titrate to eliminate ischemia
Heart failure	Furosemide + nitroprusside (or fenoldopam)
Aortic dissection	β-Blocker + nitroprusside to lower SBP to <120 mm Hg in 20 min
Postcardiac surgery hypertension	Nicardipine
VASCULAR	
Bleeding from suture lines	Nicardipine; titrate to stop the bleeding
Uncontrolled epistaxis	Nitroprusside + short-acting anxiolytic
NEUROLOGIC	
Hypertensive encephalopathy	Nitroprusside or nicardipine or fenoldopam
Acute stroke in evolution	No antihypertensive therapy (controversial)
Subarachnoid hemorrhage	Nimodipine
RENAL	
Hematuria or acute deterioration in renal function	Fenoldopam
CATECHOLAMINE EXCESS	
Pheochromocytoma	Phentolamine or nitroprusside + labetalol
Cocaine or amphetamines	Phentolamine or nitroprusside + labetalol
Clonidine withdrawal	Clonidine
PREGNANCY RELATED	
Preeclampsia/eclampsia	$MgSO_4$ for seizures and methyldopa + hydralazine to lower diastolic pressure below 90 mm Hg (oral nifedipine and oral labetolol are second-line drugs before cesarean section)

Modified from Calhoun DA: Hypertensive crisis. *In* Oparil S and Weber MA (eds): Hypertension: A Companion to Brenner and Rector's The Kidney. Philadelphia, WB Saunders, 2000, pp 715–718.

Prognosis

One of the most important prognostic factors in hypertension is electrocardiographic or echocardiographic LVH, with the latter already present in as many as 25% of patients with newly diagnosed hypertension. In a multicenter observational study of hypertensive patients with no prior history of cardiovascular or renal disease, echocardiographic LVH at baseline was accompanied by a 3-fold increase in the cumulative 4-year incidence of cardiovascular events (Fig. 63–10).

Because of the firmly established prognostic significance of LVH, numerous studies have examined the ability of antihypertensive therapy to cause regression of LVH. Meta-analyses, mostly of trials of monotherapy, estimate that left ventricular mass can be reduced by 11 to 12% with an ACE inhibitor or a CCB, by 8% with a thiazide diuretic, and by only 5% with a β-blocker. In contrast, in patients

undergoing valve replacement for aortic stenosis, near-complete surgical normalization of systolic load results in a rapid and dramatic 35% reduction in left ventricular mass. The comparatively disappointing effects of the antihypertensive drug trials are likely related to the incomplete normalization of systolic load with monotherapy, and there is no evidence that differentiated effects on LVH should be the dominant determinant in the choice among antihypertensive medications.

Randomized controlled trials have provided unequivocal evidence that intensive lowering of blood pressure with combination therapy greatly reduces the risks of fatal and nonfatal cardiovascular events associated with untreated or inadequately treated hypertension. Until further evidence is provided, most of the cardiovascular benefit is explained by lowering the blood pressure per se rather than by the specific types of antihypertensive medication selected[10] (Fig. 63–11).

Despite the impressive body of randomized clinical trial data, it remains to be determined whether even intensive antihypertensive therapy can completely normalize the excessive risks of cardiovascular and renal disease associated with untreated hypertension. In a large hypertensive referral clinic in Gothenburg, Sweden, treating hypertension in initially middle-aged men to a goal of 160/90 to 95 mm Hg with diuretics and β-blockers for 20 years did not completely normalize the risk of myocardial infarction. The persistently elevated risks in the treated patients were related to the existence of associated risk factors, such as cigarette smoking and elevated blood lipids, and emphasize the need for global risk reduction and more intensive reductions in blood pressure. Randomized trials have not yet established whether even lower blood pressure goals than those presently endorsed would produce further reductions in cardiovascular morbidity and mortality and in the risk of end stage renal disease. *Because of their relatively short duration (typically <5 years), randomized trials probably underestimate the protection against premature disability and death afforded by long-term antihypertensive therapy in clinical practice.* In the Framingham Heart Study, treating hypertension for 20 years in middle-aged adults reduced total cardiovascular mortality by 60%, which is considerably greater than the results of most randomized trials despite the less intense treatment guidelines when therapy was initiated in the 1950s–1970s.

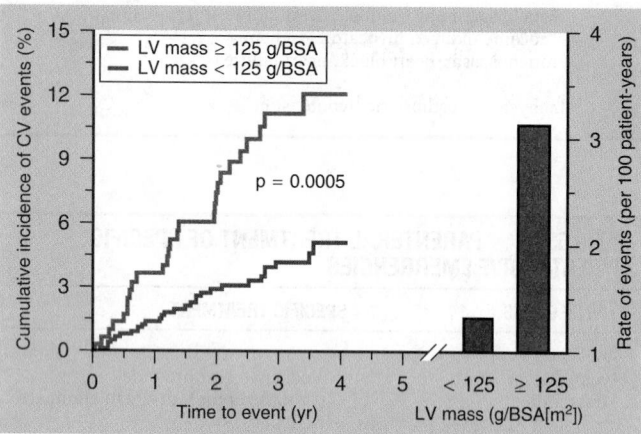

FIGURE 63–10 • Cumulative incidence (left) and crude rate (right) of cardiovascular (CV) events in hypertensive patients with and without echocardiographic left ventricular hypertrophy, defined as a left ventricular (LV) mass index of greater than 125 g per body surface area (BSA). (From Verdecchia P, Carini G, Circo A, et al: J Am Coll Cardiol 2001;38:1829–1835.)

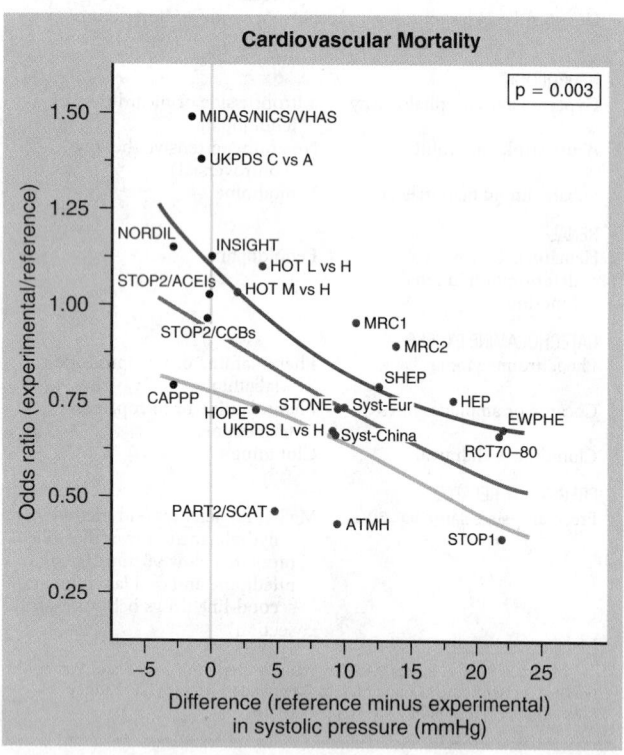

A

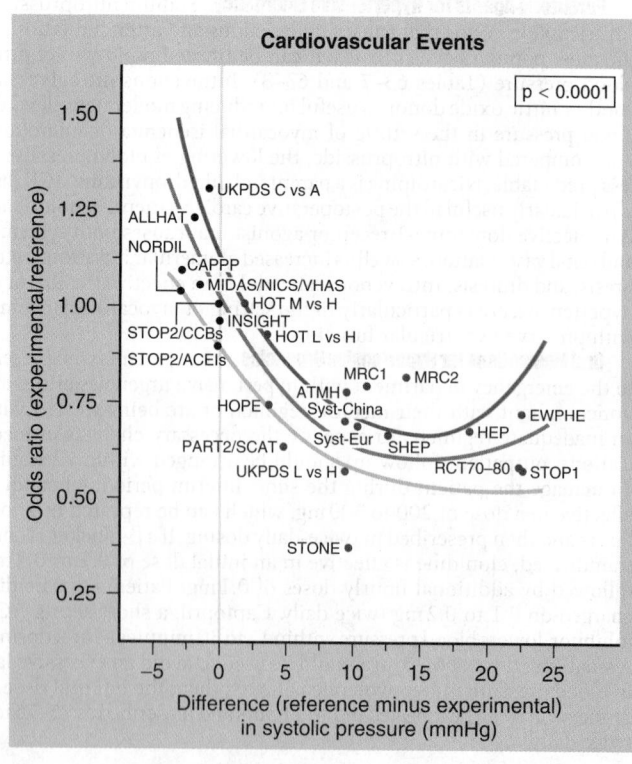

B

FIGURE 63–11 • Meta-analysis of randomized controlled intervention trials. The difference in systolic blood pressure between placebo and active treatment or between less intense and more intense treatment for hypertension is plotted against the relative risk of fatal or nonfatal cardiovascular events. Within the 95% confidence intervals used in this regression analysis, the reduction in cardiovascular mortality afforded by the various antihypertensive treatment regimens in these large numbers of trials is linearly related to the magnitude of blood pressure lowering. (From Staessen JA, Wang JG, Thijs L: Cardiovascular protection and blood pressure reduction: A meta-analysis. Lancet 2001;358:1305–1315.)

1. Whelton PK, Appel LJ, Espeland MA, et al: Sodium reduction and weight loss in the treatment of hypertension in older persons—A randomized controlled trial of nonpharmacologic interventions in the elderly (TONE). JAMA 1998;279:839–846.
2. Sacks FM, Svetkey LP, Vollmer WM, et al: Effects on blood pressure of reduced dietary sodium and the Dietary Approaches to Stop Hypertension (DASH) diet. DASH-Sodium Collaborative Research Group. N Engl J Med 2001;344:3–10.
3. Xin X, He J, Frontini MG, et al: Effects of alcohol reduction on blood pressure: A meta-analysis of randomized controlled trials. Hypertension 2001;38:1112–1117.
4. Taylor-Tolbert N, Dengel D, Brown M, et al: Ambulatory blood pressure after acute exercise in older men with essential hypertension. Am J Hypertens 2000;13:44–51.
5. Staessen JA, Wang JG, Thijs L: Cardiovascular protection and blood pressure reduction: A meta-analysis. Lancet 2001;358:1305–1315.
6. The ALLHAT Officers and Coordinators for the ALLHAT Collaborative Research Group: The major outcomes in high risk hypertensive patients randomized to angiotensin-converting enzyme Inhibitor or calcium channel blocker vs. diuretic: The Antihypertensive and Lipid-Lowering Treatment to Prevent Heart Attack Trial (ALLHAT). JAMA 2002;288:2981–2997.
7. Cushman WC, Ford CE, Cutler JA, et al: Success and predictors of blood pressure control in diverse North American settings: The Antihypertensive and Lipid-Lowering Treatment to Prevent Heart Attack Trial (ALLHAT). J Clin Hypertens 2002;4:393–404.
8. Staessen JA, Gasowski J, Wang JG, et al: Risks of untreated and treated isolated systolic hypertension in the elderly: Meta-analysis of outcome trials. Lancet 2000;355:865–872.
9. Blood Pressure Lowering Treatment Trialists' Collaboration: Effects of ACE inhibitors, calcium antagonists, and other blood-pressure-lowering drugs: Results of prospectively designed overviews of randomized trials. Lancet 2000;356:1955–1964.
10. Lewis EJ, Hunsicker LG, Clarke WR, et al: Renoprotective effect of the angiotensin-receptor antagonist irbesartan in patients with nephropathy due to type 2 diabetes. N Engl J Med 2001;345:851–860.
11. Wright JT Jr, Bakris G, Greene T, et al: Effect of blood pressure lowering and antihypertensive drug class on progression of hypertensive kidney disease. Results from the AASK trial. JAMA 2002;288:2421–2431.
12. Brenner BM, Cooper ME, de Zeeuw D, et al: Effects of losartan on renal and cardiovascular outcomes in patients with type 2 diabetes and nephropathy. N Engl J Med 2001;345:861–869.
13. Parving H-H, Lehnert H, Brochner-Mortensen J, et al: Effect of irbesartan on the development of diabetic nephropathy in patients with type 2 diabetes. N Engl J Med 2001;345:870–878.
14. ALLHAT Officers and Coordinators: Major cardiovascular events in hypertensive patients randomized to doxazosin vs chlorthalidone: The Antihypertensive and Lipid-Lowering Treatment to Prevent Heart Attack Trial (ALLHAT). JAMA 2000;283:1967–1975.
15. Adler AI, Stratton IM, Neil HA, et al: Association of systolic blood pressure with macrovascular and microvascular complications of type 2 diabetes (UKPDS 36): Prospective observational study. BMJ 2000;321:409–412.
16. Liu L, Wang JG, Gong L, et al: Comparison of active treatment and placebo for older patients with isolated systolic hypertension. J Hypertens 1998;16:1823–1829.
17. Tuomilehto J, Rastenyte D, Birkenhager WH, et al: Effects of calcium-channel blockade in older patients with diabetes and systolic hypertension. Systolic Hypertension in Europe Trial Investigators. N Engl J Med 1999;340:677–684.
18. PROGRESS Collaborative Group: Randomized trial of a perindopril-based blood-pressure-lowering regimen among 6105 individuals with previous stroke or transient ischaemic attack. Lancet 2001;358:1033–1041.

SUGGESTED READINGS

August P: Initial treatment of hypertension. N Engl J Med 2003;348:610–617. *A practical review.*

Chobanian A, Bakris G, Black H, et al: The Seventh Report of the Joint National Committee on Prevention, Detection, Evaluation, and Treatment of High Blood Pressure. The JNC 7 Report. JAMA 2003;289:2560–2572. *The latest consensus guidelines.*

Kaplan NM: Kaplan's Clinical Hypertension, 8th ed. Baltimore, Williams & Wilkins, 2002. *A lucid, updated text.*

Lifton RP, Gharavi AG, Geller DS: Molecular mechanisms of human hypertension. Cell 2001;164:545–556. *A review of the molecular genetics of human hypertension.*

Psaty BM, Lumley T, Furberg CD, et al: Health outcomes associated with various antihypertensive therapies used as first-line agents: A network meta-analysis. JAMA 2003;289:2534–2544. *Low-dose diuretics were the most effective first-line treatment.*

Wing LM, Reid CM, Ryan P, et al: A comparison of outcomes with angiotensin-converting–enzyme inhibitors and diuretics for hypertension in the elderly. N Engl J Med 2003;348:583–592. *ACE inhibitors were better than diuretics in the elderly.*

64 PULMONARY HYPERTENSION

Robyn J. Barst

Pulmonary hypertension is a common accompaniment of many cardiac and pulmonary disorders, for which the status of the pulmonary vascular bed is often the principal determinant of the clinical manifestations, course, and feasibility of surgical treatment. The prognosis varies greatly, depending on the cause of the pulmonary hypertension and its severity at the time of diagnosis. Although knowledge of the pulmonary circulation has advanced substantially, why one patient behaves differently from another with what appears to be the same degree of pulmonary hypertension remains unclear.

Table 64–1 • ADULT VALUES FOR NORMAL PULMONARY HEMODYNAMICS AT SEA LEVEL (REST AND MILD EXERCISE) AND AT ELEVATED ALTITUDE (REST)

	SEA LEVEL		ALTITUDE (~15,000 FT)
	Rest	**Mild Exercise**	**Rest**
Pulmonary arterial pressure, (mean) in mm Hg	20/10 (15)	30/13 (20)	38/14 (26)
Cardiac output, in L/min	6.0	12.0	6.0
Left atrial pressure (mean), mm Hg	5.0	9.0	5.0
Pulmonary vascular resistance, U	1.7	0.9	3.3

From Barst RJ: Proceedings of XXI ESC. Barcelona, August 28–September 1, 1999.

Definition

The pulmonary circulation is a low-resistance, highly distensible circulation. In normal individuals lying supine, systolic pressures are of the order of 15 to 25 mm Hg; corresponding diastolic pressures are 5 to 10 mm Hg (Table 64–1). The mean driving pressure (i.e., the difference between the mean blood pressure in the pulmonary artery and in the left atrium) is about 10 to 12 mm Hg, one eighth that in the systemic circulation. Because blood flow (cardiac output) is the same in both circulations in the absence of any systemic-to-pulmonary communications, the pulmonary vascular resistance is about one eighth of systemic vascular resistance. The large aggregate cross-sectional area of the pulmonary circulation is responsible for this low resistance, which is reflected in the sparsity of muscle in the pulmonary resistance vessels, the large runoff of blood from the pulmonary arterial tree during each systole, the large capacity and expansibility of the pulmonary arterial tree, and the large number of minute vessels that are held in reserve. During exercise, pulmonary blood flow increases. Accompanying this increase in blood flow is a decrease in pulmonary vascular resistance brought about by recruiting new parts of the pulmonary vascular bed and by widening the calibers of the vessels that already were open. As a result of these accommodations, a considerable increase in pulmonary blood flow elicits only a moderate increase in pulmonary arterial pressure. For an adult at sea level, pulmonary arterial hypertension is said to exist when the mean pulmonary arterial pressure is greater than 25 mm Hg at rest or greater than 30 mm Hg during exercise. This level, which would represent a modest increase for adults at sea level, is normal, however, for adults at high altitude.

Epidemiology

In adults, the most common cause of pulmonary hypertension is lung disease, especially chronic obstructive pulmonary disease (COPD). An estimated 30,000 persons die of COPD each year, many of whom have pulmonary hypertension and resulting right ventricular failure as a contributing cause of death (Chapter 85). Patients with interstitial lung disease (Chapter 88), cystic fibrosis (Chapter 86), sleep apnea syndrome (Chapter 96), and lung disorders caused by occupational and other exposures (Chapters 89 and 90) also commonly develop secondary pulmonary hypertension when they become chronically hypoxic. In the United States, about 200,000 patients die annually from acute pulmonary embolism (Chapter 94), often with acute right ventricular failure owing to acute and severe pulmonary hypertension. Pulmonary hypertension also is seen in patients with chronic or recurrent pulmonary embolism, regardless of the source of the embolic material.

Estimates of the incidence of primary pulmonary hypertension (PPH) range from 1 to 2 newly diagnosed cases per 1 million people per year in the general population. The prevalence of pulmonary vascular disease in patients with other illnesses is not known, but it seems that 1 to 2% of patients with portal hypertension (Chapter 156) or human immunodeficiency virus (HIV) infection (Chapter 415) have pulmonary arterial hypertension. The incidence of pulmonary arterial hypertension in patients with collagen vascular disease ranges from 2 to 35% in patients with systemic sclerosis (scleroderma, Chapter 281) and may reach 50% in patients with limited cutaneous systemic sclerosis. Pulmonary hypertension has been reported to occur in 23 to 53% of patients with mixed connective tissue diseases (Chapter 290) and in 1 to 14% of cases of systemic lupus erythematosus (Chapter 280), but it is rare in patients with rheumatoid arthritis (Chapter 278), Sjögren's syndrome (Chapter 282), or dermatomyositis (Chapter 283). PPH also has been associated with autoimmune phenomena, including Raynaud's syndrome, positive antinuclear antibodies, and autoimmune thyroid disorders. It also is estimated that the approximately 5% rate of increased pulmonary arterial reactivity in patients with mitral stenosis (Chapter 72) or left ventricular dysfunction (Chapter 55) may represent a genetic predisposition for pulmonary arterial hypertension.

Pulmonary hypertension probably reflects an interaction between a genetic predisposition and exposures. Risk factors can be categorized based on the strength of the association with pulmonary arterial hypertension and a possible causal role (Table 64–2). The risk of pulmonary arterial hypertension related to the use of appetite suppressants (e.g., fenfluramine or dexfenfluramine) increased concomitantly with longer exposure.

Pulmonary vascular obstructive disease related to congenital systemic-to-pulmonary shunts (i.e., Eisenmenger's syndrome; Chapter 65) develops after a period of decreased pulmonary vascular resistance and increased pulmonary flow. The high rates of pulmonary vascular obstructive disease in uncorrected congenital heart disease (Table 64–3) show that even if all other causes of death could be eliminated, approximately one third of these patients eventually would die of pulmonary vascular disease. Why some patients develop irreversible pulmonary vascular obstructive disease in the first year of life and other patients remain "operable" from a pulmonary vascular disease standpoint into the second or third decade of life or later with the

Table 64–2 • RISK FACTORS AND ASSOCIATED CONDITIONS FOR PULMONARY HYPERTENSION

DRUGS AND TOXINS
Definite
  Aminorex
  Fenfluramine
  Dexfenfluramine
  Toxic rapeseed oil
Very likely
  Amphetamines
  L-tryptophan
Possible
  Methamphetamines
  Cocaine
  Chemotherapeutic agents, such as mitomycin-C, carmustine, etoposide, cyclophosphamide, bleomycin
Unlikely
  Antidepressants
  Oral contraceptives
  Estrogen therapy
  Cigarette smoking

DEMOGRAPHIC AND MEDICAL CONDITIONS
Definite
  Gender
Possible
  Pregnancy
  Systemic hypertension
Unlikely
  Obesity

DISEASES
Definite
  HIV infection
Very likely
  Portal hypertension/liver disease
  Collagen vascular diseases
  Congenital systemic-pulmonary cardiac shunts
Possible
  Thyroid disorders

HIV = human immunodeficiency virus. From Barst RJ: Medical therapy of pulmonary hypertension: An overview of treatment and goals. *In* Rich S, McLaughlin V (eds): Clinics in Chest Medicine. Philadelphia, WB Saunders, September 2001.

Table 64–3 • RISK OF PULMONARY VASCULAR DISEASE IN PERSONS WITH CONGENITAL HEART DISEASE*

LESION	%	TOTAL NO.	NO. AT RISK
Ventricular septal defect	30	9000	3000
Patent ductus arteriosus	9	2700	900
Atrial septal defect	7	2100	700
Atrioventricular septal defect	3	900	800
Aortic stenosis	5	1500	0
Pulmonic stenosis	7	2100	0
Coarctation	6	1800	0
Tetralogy	5	1500	200
Transposition of the great arteries	5	1500	500
Truncus arteriosus	1	300	300
Hypoplastic right heart	2	600	50
Hypoplastic left heart	1	300	0
Double outlet right ventricle	0.2	60	60
Total anomalous pulmonary venous connection	1	300	300
Univentricular heart	0.3	90	90
Miscellaneous	17.5	5250	2625
Total	100.0	30,000	9525 (32%)

*Assumptions: 3 million live births per year; 1% incidence of congenital heart disease. From NHLBI Pediatric Cardiology Workshop: Frontiers in Pulmonary Hypertension. Bethesda, Maryland, Author, 1985.

same congenital cardiac defect remains unknown. The prevalence of Eisenmenger's syndrome among patients with a secundum atrial septal defect (Chapter 65) is 6 to 9% and is unrelated to the size of the defect. In contrast, a large ventricular septal defect or a large patent ductus arteriosus invariably leads to Eisenmenger's syndrome. Although secundum atrial septal defects are twice as common among females as among males, Eisenmenger's syndrome is still more prevalent among female patients with a secundum atrial septal defect (5:1 ratio in some series), a pattern reminiscent of what is observed with PPH (2:1). For other congenital heart defects, the risk of Eisenmenger's syndrome is not sex-related, raising the question of whether some Eisenmenger's syndrome patients with an atrial septal defect do have PPH.

Genetics

The prevalence of genetic or familial PPH is uncertain, but it represents at least 6% of all cases and perhaps considerably more. Familial PPH seems to be inherited as an autosomal dominant disorder with reduced or incomplete penetrance and genetic anticipation. It is estimated that individuals in a family with familial PPH have only a 5 to 10% lifetime risk of developing PPH.

The identification of bone morphogenetic protein receptor 2 mutations (Fig. 64–1) in patients with familial PPH indicates a crucial role for transforming growth factor–β superfamily ligand-receptor interactions in vascular homeostasis and in embryologic development. Studies are in progress to determine whether this gene is relevant to various forms of pulmonary arterial hypertension related to other disorders.

Pathology and Pathobiology

The pathology of pulmonary vascular disease first was classified in the 1950s by Heath and Edwards (Table 64–4). This pathologic classification does not correlate well with the pathogenesis or clinical and hemodynamic findings of pulmonary hypertension. The vascular endothelium is an important source of locally active mediators that contribute to the control of vasomotor tone. Imbalances in the production or metabolism of vasoactive mediators of pulmonary vascular tone include increased thromboxane and endothelin and decreased prostacyclin and nitric oxide (NO). Thromboxane and endothelin are vasoconstrictors and mitogens; in contrast, prostacyclin and NO are vasodilators with antiproliferative effects. Vasoconstrictors also may serve as factors or cofactors that stimulate growth of smooth muscle or elaboration of matrix. It seems likely that endothelial injury results in the release of chemotactic agents, leading to migration of smooth muscle cells into the vascular wall. This endothelial injury, coupled with excessive release of vasoactive

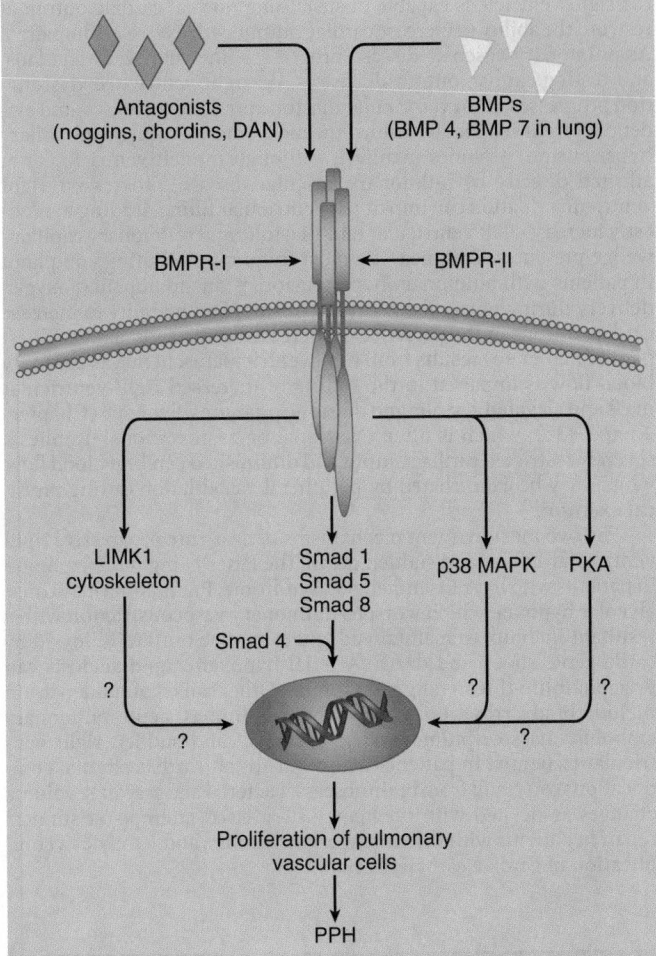

FIGURE 64–1 • Signaling pathways of the bone morphogenetic protein receptor type II (BMPR-II). In the extracellular space, the receptor ligand BMPs bind directly to the BMPR-II on the cell membrane. The bioavailability of BMPs is regulated by the presence of BMPR-II receptor antagonists such as noggins, chordins, and DAN (*d*ifferential screening-selected gene *a*berrative in *n*euroblastoma). The binding of ligands to BMPR-II leads to the recruitment of BMPR-I to form a heteromeric receptor complex at the cell surface. This complex results in the phosphorylation and activation of the kinase domain of BMPR-I. The activated BMPR-I subsequently phosphorylates and activates cytoplasmic signaling protein Smads (Smad 1, 5, and 8). Phosphorylated Smads bind to the common mediator Smad 4, and the resulting Smad complex moves from the cytoplasm into the nucleus and regulates gene transcription. Other downstream signaling pathways that can be activated after the engagement of BMPR-I and BMPR-II by BMPs include cell-type dependent activation of p38 mitogen activated protein kinase (p38 MAPK) and protein kinase A (PKA). In addition, the cytoplasmic tail of BMPR-II has been shown to interact with the LIM motif-containing protein kinase 1 (LIMK1) that is localized in the cytoskeleton. Germline mutations of the gene encoding BMPR-II underlie primary pulmonary hypertension (PPH), which is characterized by the abnormal proliferation of pulmonary vascular cells. The specific cytoplasmic proteins and nuclear transcription factors that are involved in the development of PPH have not been identified, however.

mediators locally, promotes a procoagulant state, leading to further vascular obstruction. The process is characterized by an inexorable cycle of endothelial dysfunction leading to the release of vasoconstrictive and vasoproliferative substances, ultimately progressing to vascular remodeling and progressive vascular obstruction and obliteration. Potassium channel down regulation in the pulmonary artery smooth muscle cells also may be involved in the initiation and/or progression of pulmonary hypertension.

PATHOPHYSIOLOGY. Whether the pulmonary hypertension is due to increased flow or increased resistance depends on its cause (Table 64–5). The pulmonary artery wedge pressure is elevated in patients with pulmonary venous hypertension but normal in other patients

Table 64–4 • HEATH-EDWARDS CLASSIFICATION: PULMONARY VASCULAR DISEASE

Grade 1 Medial hypertrophy in the small pulmonary arteries
Grade 2 Concentric or eccentric cellular intimal proliferation and thickening within the smaller pulmonary arteries and arterioles
Grade 3 Relatively acellular intimal fibrosis with accumulation of concentric or eccentric masses of fibrous tissue leading to widespread occlusion of the smaller pulmonary arteries and arterioles
Grade 4 Progressive, generalized dilation of the muscular arteries and the appearance of plexiform lesions, complex vascular structures composed of a network or plexus of proliferating endothelial tissue, frequently accompanied by thrombus, within a dilated thin-walled sac
Grade 5 Thinning and fibrosis of the media superimposed on the formation of numerous complex dilation lesions
Grade 6 Necrotizing arteritis within the media with surrounding areas of inflammatory reaction and granulation tissue

Table 64–5 • DIAGNOSTIC CLASSIFICATION OF PULMONARY HYPERTENSION

1. Pulmonary arterial hypertension
   1.1 Primary pulmonary hypertension
       (a) Sporadic
       (b) Familial
   1.2 Related to
       (a) Collagen vascular disease
       (b) Congenital systemic-to-pulmonary shunts
       (c) Portal hypertension
       (d) HIV infection
       (e) Drugs/toxins
           (1) Anorexigens
           (2) Other (see Table 64–2)
       (f) Persistent pulmonary hypertension of the newborn
       (g) Other
2. Pulmonary venous hypertension
   2.1 Left-sided atrial or ventricular heart disease
   2.2 Left-sided valvular heart disease
   2.3 Extrinsic compression of central pulmonary vein
       (a) Fibrosing mediastinitis
       (b) Adenopathy/tumors
   2.4 Pulmonary veno-occlusive disease
   2.5 Other
3. Pulmonary hypertension associated with disorders of the respiratory system and/or hypoxia
   3.1 Chronic obstructive pulmonary disease
   3.2 Interstitial lung disease
   3.3 Sleep-disordered breathing
   3.4 Alveolar hypoventilation disorders
   3.5 Chronic exposure to high altitudes
   3.6 Neonatal lung disease
   3.7 Alveolar-capillary dysplasia
4. Pulmonary hypertension owing to chronic thrombotic and/or embolic disease
   4.1 Thromboembolic obstruction of proximal pulmonary arteries
   4.2 Obstruction of distal pulmonary arteries
       (a) Pulmonary embolism (thrombus, ova and/or parasites, foreign material)
       (b) In situ thrombosis
       (c) Sickle cell disease
5. Pulmonary hypertension owing to disorders affecting the pulmonary vasculature
   5.1 Inflammatory
       (a) Schistosomiasis
       (b) Sarcoidosis
       (c) Other
   5.2 Pulmonary capillary hemangiomatosis

HIV = human immunodeficiency virus. From Barst RJ: Medical therapy of pulmonary hypertension: An overview of treatment and goals. In Rich S, McLaughlin V (eds): Clinics in Chest Medicine. Philadelphia, WB Saunders, September 2001.

with pulmonary hypertension unless there is incidental, coexisting left heart disease. PPH is defined by the absence of all secondary causes of pulmonary hypertension and related disorders and by the presence of a normal pulmonary artery wedge pressure. In patients with pulmonary venous hypertension (e.g., mitral stenosis or left ventricular dysfunction), the same elevation of pulmonary venous pressure may result in different pulmonary artery pressures because of individual differences in pulmonary arterial vasoreactivity.

Pulmonary hypertension can be classified according to the site of increased pulmonary vascular resistance. In patients with *precapillary pulmonary hypertension,* the abnormalities occur in the pulmonary arteries or arterioles. In *passive pulmonary hypertension,* the increase in pulmonary artery pressure is caused by an increase in pulmonary venous pressure, owing to disease of the pulmonary veins or, more commonly, increased left atrial pressures owing to diseases of the mitral valve, left ventricle, or aortic valve. In passive pulmonary hypertension, the increase in pulmonary arterial blood pressure is a direct reflection of the increase in pulmonary venous pressures. In *reactive pulmonary hypertension,* increased pulmonary venous pressure leads to reactive precapillary pulmonary artery abnormalities that raise the pulmonary arterial pressure more than would be expected based on the pulmonary venous hypertension alone. This mixed picture, which was seen commonly with long-standing mitral valve disease during the rheumatic fever era, is seen less often today.

The pulmonary hypertension related to collagen vascular disease, drugs, toxins, and PPH is precapillary. Similarly, in Eisenmenger's syndrome, high pulmonary arteriolar blood flows cause precapillary pulmonary hypertension, which then progresses independent of flow by a reactive phase.

The normal pulmonary vascular bed has a remarkable capacity to dilate and recruit unused vasculature to accommodate increases in blood flow. In pulmonary hypertension, this capacity is lost, however, leading to increases in pulmonary artery pressure at rest and further elevations in pulmonary artery pressure with exercise. In response to this increased afterload, the right ventricle hypertrophies. Initially the right ventricle is capable of sustaining normal cardiac output at rest, but the ability to increase cardiac output with exercise is impaired. As pulmonary vascular disease progresses, the right ventricle fails, and resting cardiac output decreases. As right ventricular dysfunction progresses, right ventricular diastolic pressure increases, and evidence of right ventricular failure, the most ominous sign of pulmonary hypertension, becomes manifest. Although the left ventricle is not affected directly by pulmonary vascular disease, progressive right ventricular dilation can impair left ventricular filling, leading to modestly increased left ventricular end-diastolic and pulmonary capillary wedge pressures. Dyspnea, the most frequent presenting complaint in patients with pulmonary hypertension, is due to impaired oxygen delivery during physical activity as a result of an inability to increase cardiac output in the presence of increased oxygen demands. Chest pain (Chapter 46) results from right ventricular ischemia as coronary blood flow is impaired in the setting of increased right ventricular mass and elevated systolic and diastolic pressures. Syncope (Chapters 46 and 435), which is often exertional or postexertional, implies a severely restricted cardiac output and diminished cerebral blood flow, which may be exacerbated by peripheral vasodilation during physical exertion.

The two most frequent mechanisms of death are progressive right ventricular failure and sudden death, the latter being more common in patients who have Eisenmenger's syndrome. Pneumonia may cause alveolar hypoxia, which worsens pulmonary vasoconstriction with a resultant inability to maintain adequate cardiac output, followed by cardiogenic shock and death. Arterial hypoxemia and acidosis can precipitate life-threatening arrhythmias. Other causes of sudden death include bradyarrhythmias and tachyarrhythmias, acute pulmonary embolus, massive pulmonary hemorrhage, and sudden right ventricular ischemia. In patients with right-to-left cardiac shunts, complications can result from brain abscess, bacterial endocarditis, volume changes associated with pregnancy, ill-advised attempts at surgical repair in patients with Eisenmenger's syndrome, and, rarely, as a complication of cardiac catheterization.

Clinical Manifestations

With mild pulmonary hypertension, the earliest complaints are often fatigue and vague chest discomfort. These symptoms often are ignored unless the patient has another underlying condition, such as COPD (Chapter 85), interstitial lung disease (Chapter 88), or alveolar hypoventilation (Chapter 83; Table 64–5). Nevertheless, the clinical picture still generally is dominated by any associated disorders until dyspnea and tachypnea are present.

When the pulmonary hypertension is advanced, the clinical manifestations include cyanosis, dyspnea on exertion, hemoptysis, atypical chest pain or angina pectoris, syncope, heart failure, arrhythmias, cerebrovascular accidents from paradoxical emboli, and gout. Dyspnea, the most common symptom of PPH, is also the most frequent symptom of Eisenmenger's syndrome. Syncope is an exceedingly rare symptom in unoperated patients with Eisenmenger's syndrome because of the ability to decompress the right heart through an open atrial septal defect, ventricular septal defect, or patent ductus arteriosus. In contrast, patients with PPH with an intact atrial septum (i.e., without a patent foramen ovale) and patients with elevated pulmonary vascular resistance after complete surgical repair of congenital shunts may present with syncope. Angina, a common symptom, results from right ventricular ischemia, which often is underappreciated. Edema is generally a reflection of right ventricular failure and is more likely to be associated with advanced pulmonary vascular disease.

PHYSICAL EXAMINATION. Each underlying or associated condition (see Table 64–5) affects the clinical presentation. COPD usually is associated with hyperinflation of the lungs, and this hyperinflation often shifts the position of the heart so that heart sounds are more difficult to hear. With interstitial lung disease, tachypnea invariably occurs. Nevertheless, certain physical findings (e.g., an increased intensity of P_2, a palpable P_2, a right-sided third heart sound (S_3), and, as pulmonary hypertension progresses, murmurs of pulmonary and tricuspid insufficiency) typically develop. Ultimately the neck veins are distended, and the liver is pulsatile, and the patient may develop peripheral edema, pleural effusions, and ascites. In patients with pulmonary venous hypertension, the presentation frequently is overshadowed by signs of left-sided heart disease (e.g., mitral stenosis, systemic hypertension, or heart failure; Chapters 55, 63, and 72).

In PPH, there is no evidence of underlying pulmonary or cardiac disease. The cardiac examination shows right ventricular overload as for any cause of pulmonary hypertension (see earlier).

Physical examination in a patient with Eisenmenger's syndrome shows central cyanosis, clubbing of the digits, right ventricular lift, palpable P_2, increased intensity of P_2 (frequently with a single loud S_2), a pulmonic ejection sound associated with a dilated pulmonary trunk, and a diastolic murmur of pulmonary insufficiency. In the presence of heart failure, patients develop edema, ascites, and hepatosplenomegaly. In patients who have undergone corrective surgery for congenital heart disease when the pulmonary vascular resistance already was elevated, the physical examination is similar to that seen with PPH (i.e., an increase in the pulmonic component of S_2, a right-sided S_4, and tricuspid regurgitation; a right ventricular S_3 and pulmonary insufficiency generally reflect advanced disease). Peripheral cyanosis and edema are common. Clubbing, which is common with Eisenmenger's syndrome, typically is not seen in PPH or in patients who have undergone repair of the congenital heart defects after pulmonary vascular resistance already was increased.

NATURAL HISTORY. PPH historically has exhibited a course of relentless deterioration and early death. Newer pharmacologic and surgical treatments have altered not only symptomatic status, but also the progression of the disease and duration of survival. Until the 1980s, the survival of patients with PPH who did not undergo heart-lung or lung transplantation was 68 to 77% at 1 year, 40 to 56% at 3 years, and 22 to 38% at 5 years; patients presenting with more advanced symptoms had a shorter subsequent survival, with a median survival of 59 months for patients in New York Heart Association class I or II compared with 32 months for class III and 6 months for class IV. Survival for several decades has been reported, as have rare cases of apparent regression of the disease.

Pulmonary arterial hypertension associated with HIV infection or anorectics has an overall survival comparable to PPH. In con-

Cardiovascular Disease

trast, patients with pulmonary arterial hypertension and coexisting portal hypertension have a substantially worse prognosis with a mean survival of 15 months.

The natural history of Eisenmenger's syndrome is markedly better than for PPH, with an overall 80% 5-year survival (Fig. 64–2). A natural history study reported a 54% survival at 20 years after diagnosis.

Similarly the natural history of patients who have only mild pulmonary hypertension owing to underlying pulmonary diseases, such as COPD, is much better than for PPH. In most cases, the natural history of the COPD determines the patient's ultimate prognosis. In patients with pulmonary venous hypertension, the picture often is mixed and varies depending on the severity of the pulmonary vasoreactivity (which determines the magnitude of the pulmonary arterial hypertension) and the degree of pulmonary venous hypertension with or without left-sided heart failure. When pulmonary arterial hypertension is the predominant abnormality, the natural history still can vary substantially owing to the wide range of biologic variability of progressive pulmonary vascular disease.

Diagnosis and Assessment

DETECTING PULMONARY HYPERTENSION. Using current medical technology, a correct diagnosis and assessment of the severity of the pulmonary hypertension in an individual patient can be made with a high level of confidence. When pulmonary hypertension is suspected, an electrocardiogram (ECG) and chest radiograph should be performed. Although the ECG may be unremarkable, it more frequently shows right-axis deviation and right ventricular hypertrophy with secondary T-wave changes; however, the ECG changes often do not parallel the severity of the pulmonary hypertension (see Fig. 50–6B). The chest radiograph shows a large right ventricle, dilated hilar pulmonary arteries, and variably oligemic peripheral lung fields depending on the amount of pulmonary blood flow (see Fig. 49–6).

If the ECG and chest radiograph are either nondiagnostic or consistent with pulmonary hypertension, the evaluation continues with an echocardiogram to exclude congenital heart disease, myocardial dysfunction, and valvular disease. The typical echocardiographic appearance of a patient with PPH shows right ventricular and right atrial enlargement with normal or reduced left ventricular size. Pulmonic insufficiency and tricuspid insufficiency also often are detected easily with Doppler interrogation. Right ventricular pressure overload in advanced disease reverses the normal interventricular septal curvature. Underfilling of the left ventricle, manifested by reduced dimensions, is a reflection of the severity of the pulmonary vascular disease. Doppler ultrasound is useful to estimate the pulmonary artery systolic pressure noninvasively as the sum of systemic venous pressure plus four times the tricuspid regurgitation velocity squared (Chapter 51). Transesophageal echocardiography can provide a more precise assessment of intracardiac defects, including the detection of a patent foramen ovale. Saline contrast echocardiography also can assess the integrity of the atrial septum.

SEARCHING FOR SECONDARY CAUSES. The echocardiogram is the key to detecting congenital or acquired heart disease as the cause of pulmonary hypertension. Pulmonary function tests and cardiopulmonary exercise tests help evaluate patients with uncertain causes of dyspnea. When a cardiac cause is not found, the evaluation should follow a systematic approach (Fig. 64–3). Based on the results of the sequentially performed tests, underlying causes and/or related conditions can be diagnosed (see Table 64–5).

SCREENING HIGH-RISK PATIENTS. Screening may lead to the early identification of pulmonary hypertension in asymptomatic or minimally symptomatic systemic sclerosis, who have a high prevalence of pulmonary hypertension compared with the much lower prevalence in patients with systemic lupus erythematosus, rheumatoid arthritis, and other connective tissue diseases. Screening also is recommended for first-degree relatives of patients with documented PPH. A transthoracic echocardiogram is performed in all patients with portal hypertension when they are evaluated for liver transplantation. There is no definitive recommendation regarding routine screening for pulmonary hypertension in patients with pulmonary disease such as COPD, unless there are also signs or symptoms suggestive of pulmonary hypertension.

Magnetic resonance imaging (Chapter 53) and computed tomography (Chapter 52) can help assess anatomy in patients with cardiac defects, and high-resolution computed tomography is useful for the evaluation of patients with suspected interstitial lung disease. Exercise testing is useful for the initial assessment of functional capacity before initiating treatment and serially to assess the response to therapy.

Ventilation-perfusion lung scanning and spiral computed tomography are useful screening tests for chronic thromboembolic disease, although pulmonary angiography remains the "gold standard" for this assessment (Chapter 94). In thromboembolic pulmonary hypertension, the clots are incorporated into the wall of the pulmonary arteries and become endothelialized; pulmonary angiography may underestimate the extent of the obstruction or be difficult to interpret. Angioscopy and/or magnetic resonance imaging may be useful in selected cases. It is crucial to diagnose chronic thromboembolic disease because thromboendarterectomy provides a clinical, hemodynamic, and survival benefit in patients with chronic thromboembolic pulmonary arterial hypertension.

ASSESSING THE SEVERITY OF PULMONARY HYPERTENSION. For all patients in whom pulmonary hypertension still is suspected after performing a chest radiograph, ECG, and echocardiogram, right heart cardiac catheterization is recommended to confirm the diagnosis and measure intracardiac, systemic, and pulmonic pressures and cardiac output. Acute testing with a short-acting vasodilator (at the time of right heart catheterization) to determine the degree of pulmonary vasoreactivity is recommended for patients who have documented pulmonary hypertension and who are being considered for medical therapy (Fig. 64–4). No hemodynamic or demographic variables predict whether a patient will respond to acute vasodilator testing. Testing with the following vasodilators is recommended: intravenous epoprostenol sodium (dose range, 2 to 12 ng/kg/min; half-life, 2 to 3 minutes), inhaled NO (dose range, 10 to 80 ppm; half-life 15 to 30 seconds), inhaled iloprost (aerosolized dose range, 14 to 17 µg; half-life, 20 to 30 minutes), or intravenous adenosine (dose range, 50 to 200 ng/kg/min; half-life, 5 to 10 seconds). Patients who respond, commonly defined as a clinically significant reduction in mean pulmonary artery pressure of at least 20% to a mean pulmonary artery pressure ≤35 mm Hg with no change or an increase in cardiac output, usually, although not always, have a favorable response to long-term treatment with oral calcium channel blockers. Patients who do not respond to acute vasodilator challenge are unlikely to have clinical benefit from oral calcium channel blockers and may deteriorate with them.

Abnormalities of pulmonary function testing may be present in patients with PPH or Eisenmenger's syndrome, particularly in more advanced stages of the disease, owing to derangements in either the mechanical or gas exchanging properties of the lung. Severe hypoxemia can occur in PPH owing to a patent foramen ovale and in Eisenmenger's syndrome owing to systemic-to-pulmonary communications.

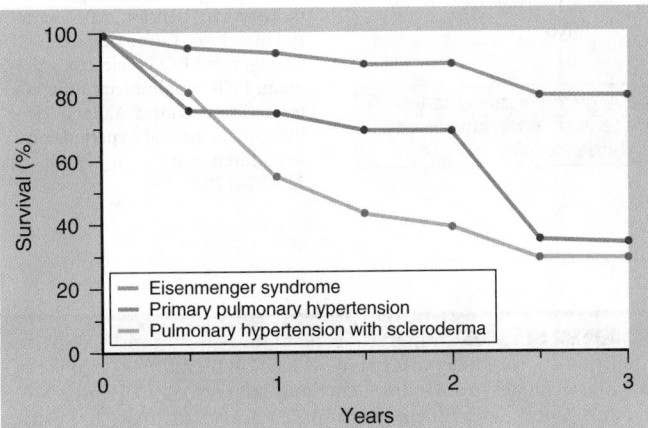

FIGURE 64–2 • Comparison of survival in primary pulmonary hypertension, Eisenmenger's syndrome, and pulmonary arterial hypertension associated with scleroderma in patients treated with conventional therapy only (e.g., without transplantation, epoprostenol, or other novel therapeutic agents).

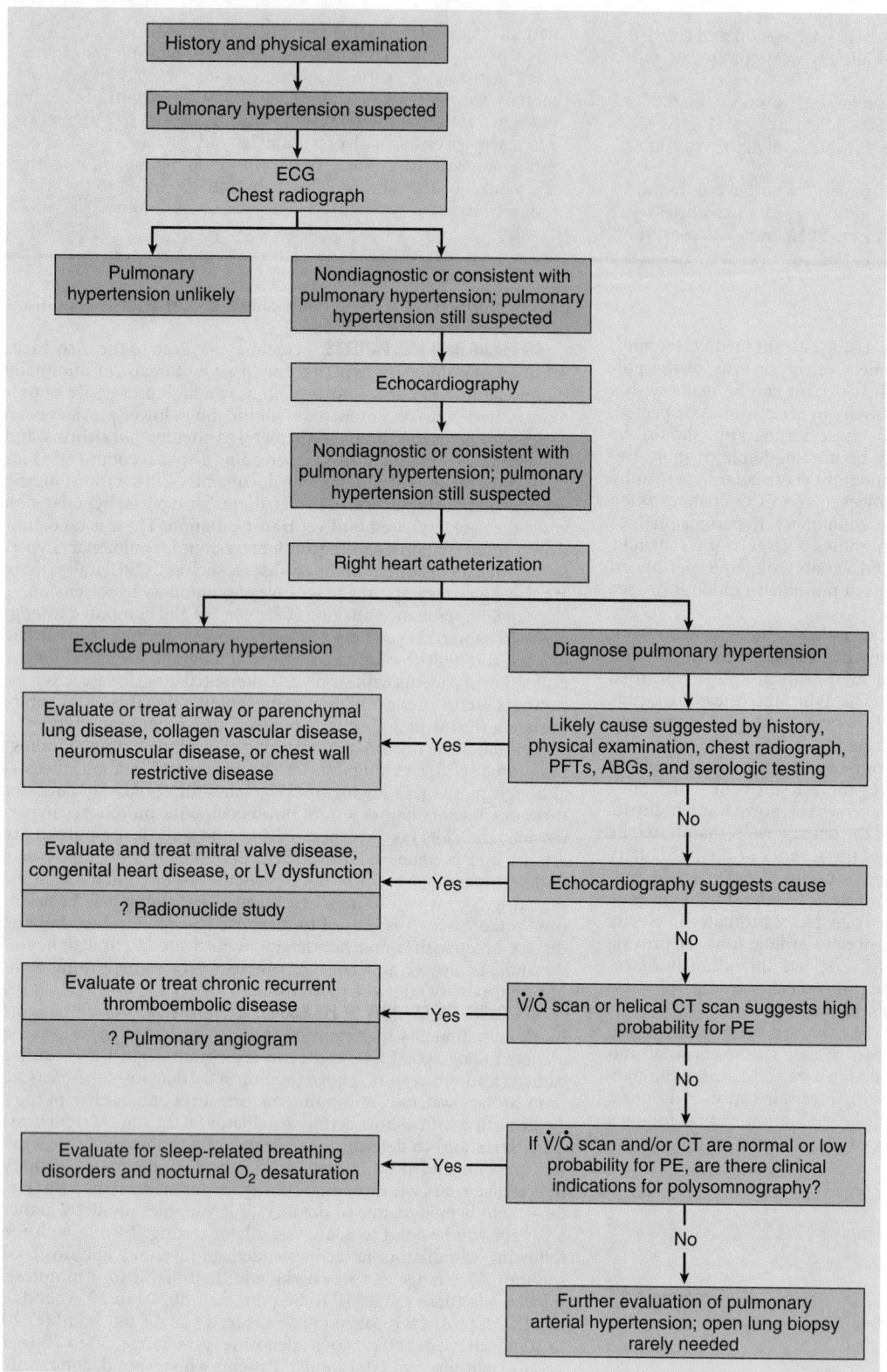

FIGURE 64–3 • An approach to determining the cause of pulmonary hypertension. ABG = arterial blood gas; CT = computed tomography; ECG = electrocardiogram; PFTs = pulmonary function tests. (From Widlitz A, Barst RJ: Pulmonary arterial hypertension in children. Eur Respir J 2003; 21:155–176.)

Rx Treatment

Treatment for pulmonary hypertension depends on an accurate assessment of the cause (see Fig. 64–3).

MEDICAL THERAPY

Although there is neither a cure nor a single therapeutic approach that is uniformly successful for pulmonary arterial hypertension, therapy has improved substantially (see Fig. 64–4).

GENERAL MEASURES. Important general measures for patients with all forms of pulmonary arterial hypertension include the avoidance of circumstances or substances that may aggravate the disease state. Exercise should be guided by symptoms, and exposure to high altitude may worsen pulmonary arterial hypertension by producing hypoxia-induced pulmonary vasoconstriction. Pregnancy, oral contraceptives, and appetite suppressants should be avoided. Phlebotomy with replacement of fluid (e.g., plasma or albumin) is helpful in

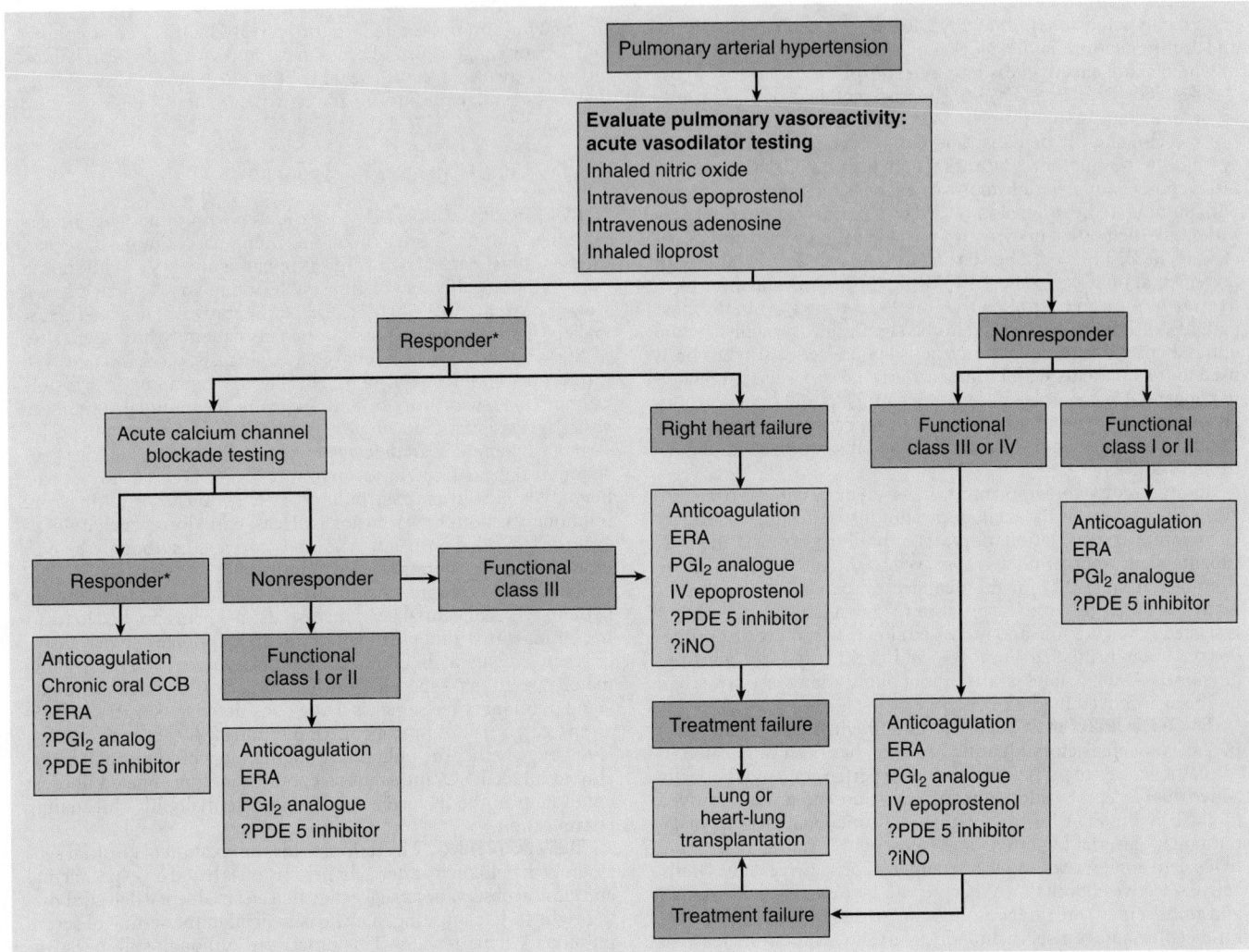

FIGURE 64–4 • Treatment algorithm for pulmonary arterial hypertension. Response to testing with inhaled nitric oxide (iNO), intravenous epoprostenol, intravenous adenosine, or inhaled iloprost is defined as a clinically significant decrease in mean pulmonary arterial pressure of equal to or greater than 20% to a mean pulmonary artery pressure less than or equal to 35 mm Hg without a fall in the cardiac output. CCB = calcium channel blockade; ERA = endothelin receptor antagonist; PDE 5 = phosphodiesterase type 5; PGI₂ = prostacyclin. (From Widlitz A, Barst RJ: Pulmonary arterial hypertension in children. Eur Respir J 2003;21:155–176.)

patients with pulmonary vascular disease and cyanotic congenital heart disease in whom severe hypoxemia has evoked substantial polycythemia. Phlebotomy is recommended for symptoms of polycythemia, such as headache or blurry vision, or if the hematocrit is greater than 65 to 70%. Caution is required to avoid depletion of iron stores and reduction in the circulating blood volume. Cerebrovascular events are related more often to iron-deficiency anemia; however, plasma exchange seems to relieve symptoms for patients with severe polycythemia.

Supplemental low-flow oxygen alleviates the arterial hypoxemia and attenuates the pulmonary hypertension in patients with chronic pulmonary parenchymal disease. In contrast, most patients with Eisenmenger's syndrome derive little hemodynamic benefit from supplemental oxygen, although patients with Eisenmenger's syndrome and patients with other forms of pulmonary arterial hypertension, including PPH, may benefit from supplemental ambulatory oxygen if they have oxygen desaturation with activity. Supplemental oxygen is often helpful for patients who have substantial right heart failure and who have a low cardiac output at rest.

TREATMENT OF UNDERLYING CONDITIONS. Before initiating treatment for a patient's pulmonary arterial hypertension, treatment should be started for any underlying or associated conditions. After these other disorders have been treated optimally, additional treatment for the pulmonary arterial hypertension should be considered (see Fig. 64–4).

ANTICOAGULATION. Histologic data show thrombotic lesions in small pulmonary arteries in a large percentage of patients with PPH, and limited clinical data support the long-term use of anticoagulation in PPH. Warfarin anticoagulation is recommended to achieve an international normalized ratio (INR) of 1.5 to 2; however, certain clinical circumstances may require a higher INR (Chapter 33), and a lower INR is often appropriate for patients at a higher risk for bleeding. Heparin subcutaneously (5000 to 10,000 U twice daily) or low-molecular-weight heparin (1 mg/kg subcutaneously twice daily) may be suitable alternatives in patients with adverse effects from warfarin. Patients with chronic thromboembolic disease are treated with higher doses of warfarin (i.e., to achieve an INR of 2.5 to 3.5). Whether long-term anticoagulation is useful in patients with other forms of pulmonary arterial hypertension is unknown.

CALCIUM CHANNEL BLOCKERS. Approximately 20% of adult patients with PPH seem to have a favorable response with acute vasodilator testing and (in uncontrolled studies) respond to long-term oral calcium channel blockade, as documented by an improvement in symptoms, exercise tolerance, hemodynamics, and survival. Although most studies have used calcium channel blockers at relatively high doses (e.g., long-acting nifedipine, 120 to 240 mg daily, or amlodipine, 20 to 40 mg daily), the optimal dosing for patients with PPH is uncertain. Patients with no evidence of an acute hemodynamic response to these drugs are unlikely to benefit from long-term therapy. Because of the frequent adverse effects, including

Continued

systemic hypotension, pulmonary edema, right ventricular failure, and death, calcium channel blockers should be used only in patients in whom acute effectiveness has been shown.

PROSTAGLANDINS. Prostacyclin (epoprostenol) or prostacyclin analogue treatment is supported by the imbalance of thromboxane to prostacyclin and the demonstration of a reduction in prostacyclin synthase in the pulmonary arteries of patients with PPH. Continuous intravenous epoprostenol improves exercise tolerance in patients with pulmonary hypertension caused by scleroderma and improves symptoms, hemodynamics, and survival in patients with functional class III or IV PPH. [1,2] The starting dose is 1 to 2 ng/kg/min with incremental increases, especially during the first several months of treatment. A mean dose after 1 year is 20 to 40 ng/kg/min for most patients, although there seems to be significant variability of the optimal dose. Continuous intravenous epoprostenol also has been used to treat patients with pulmonary arterial hypertension related to congenital systemic-to-pulmonary shunts, portal hypertension, HIV infection, drugs, and toxins, with reported improvement in exercise capacity, hemodynamics, and possibly survival, in uncontrolled studies.

In an attempt to avoid intravenous therapy, clinical trials are evaluating prostacyclin analogues administered subcutaneously (treprostinil), by inhalation (iloprost), or orally (beraprost). In 2002, subcutaneous treprostinil was approved by the U.S. Food and Drug Administration (FDA) for the treatment of patients with symptomatic pulmonary arterial hypertension. [3] Subcutaneous treprostinil is started at 1 ng/kg/min and increased slowly to achieve an optimal dose. Although inhaled iloprost [4] and oral beraprost [5] are used outside the United States, at the time of publication these drugs had not been approved by the FDA.

ENDOTHELIN RECEPTOR ANTAGONISTS. Endothelin-1, one of the most potent vasoconstrictors identified to date, has been implicated in the pathogenesis of pulmonary arterial hypertension, and the orally active dual receptor endothelin antagonist bosentan was approved in 2001 by the FDA for the treatment of functional class III or IV pulmonary arterial hypertension. [6] Bosentan is started at 62.5 mg twice daily for 4 weeks and titrated up to 125 mg twice daily. Orally active selective endothelin-A receptor antagonists (e.g., sitaxsentan and ambrisentan) are under evaluation. Adverse effects of endothelin receptor antagonists include liver toxicity, with an increase in hepatic transaminase levels.

NITRIC OXIDE. NO activates guanylate cyclase in pulmonary vascular smooth muscle cells, which increases cyclic guanosine monophosphate and decreases intracellular calcium concentration, leading to smooth muscle relaxation. When inhaled, the rapid combination of NO with hemoglobin inactivates any NO diffusing into the blood, preventing systemic vasodilation. NO is a potent and selective pulmonary vasodilator when administered by inhalation. Although there is considerable experience with the use of inhaled NO as a short-term treatment for pulmonary hypertension in a variety of clinical situations, the role of inhaled NO as a long-term therapy for pulmonary hypertension remains under clinical investigation. Additional investigation assessing NO potentiating compounds, such as type 5 phosphodiesterase inhibitors, also is being evaluated.

INOTROPIC AGENTS AND DIURETICS. The efficacy and toxicity of cardiac glycosides in pulmonary arterial hypertension remain unknown. Diuretics can reduce the increased intravascular volume and hepatic congestion that occur in patients with right heart failure, although great care should be taken to avoid excessive diuresis that decreases cardiac output in patients who are highly dependent on preload.

INTERVENTIONAL CARDIOLOGIC SURGERY

CONGENITAL HEART DISEASE. Most patients with pulmonary hypertension resulting from systemic-to-pulmonary shunts have had interventional cardiologic surgical repair as infants or children to prevent the development of irreversible pulmonary vascular disease. New approaches to evaluation and perioperative management now make surgical correction possible in many patients who present later in life with elevated pulmonary vascular resistance. Inhaled NO, intravenous epoprostenol, or inhaled iloprost can unmask reversible pulmonary vasoconstriction and determine the minimal pulmonary vascular resistance that can be achieved. Temporary balloon occlusion of congenital heart defects or a patent foramen ovale with subsequent remeasurement of pressures can predict post-repair hemodynamics. In contrast, pulmonary hypertension resulting from pulmonary venous hypertension is at least partially reversible whenever the left-sided obstructive lesion is corrected, although the pulmonary hypertension may take months to decrease.

These newer approaches to the evaluation of repairability in patients with congenital heart disease also are being applied to treating perioperative and postoperative acute pulmonary hypertensive crises in patients with pulmonary arterial hypertension undergoing major operations, especially cardiac surgery. If a patient with elevated pulmonary resistance is being considered for surgery, there is an increased risk of postoperative pulmonary hypertensive crises. Knowing whether the pulmonary circulation would respond favorably to inhaled NO, intravenous epoprostenol, or inhaled iloprost could help in the management of this potentially life-threatening complication.

ATRIAL SEPTOSTOMY. The rationale for the creation of an atrial septostomy in pulmonary arterial hypertension is based on experimental and clinical observations suggesting that an atrial septal defect, allowing right-to-left shunting, may be beneficial in the setting of severe pulmonary hypertension. This procedure, although still investigational, may help patients who have severe pulmonary hypertension, recurrent syncope, or right ventricular failure despite maximal medical therapy and who have an intact atrial septum or a restrictive patent foramen ovale. It also is used for temporary palliation as a bridge to transplantation, in which case the atrial septostomy can be closed at the time of transplantation.

TRANSPLANTATION. Since 1981, more than 1500 patients have undergone single-lung, double-lung, or heart-lung transplantation for progressive pulmonary hypertension worldwide (Chapters 80 and 97). The operative mortality ranges from 16 to 29% and is affected by the primary diagnosis. The 1-year survival is 70 to 75%, the 3-year survival is 55 to 60%, and the 5-year survival is 40 to 45%. Timing a referral for transplantation depends on the patient's prognosis with optimal medical therapy, the anticipated waiting time for transplantation in the region, and the expected survival after transplantation.

Future Directions

Future progress is likely to focus on attempts to discover any final common pathways for pulmonary hypertensive diseases, to identify genes that predispose to sporadic and familial PPH, to develop molecular and physiologic tests to monitor and diagnose pulmonary vascular disease, and to test currently available therapies and develop new ones based on established pathobiologic mechanisms.

1. Badesch DB, Tapson VF, McGoon MD, et al: Continuous intravenous epoprostenol for pulmonary hypertension due to the scleroderma spectrum of disease. Ann Intern Med 2000;132:425–434.
2. Barst RJ, Rubin LJ, Long WA, et al, for the Primary Pulmonary Hypertension Study Group: A comparison of continuous intravenous epoprostenol (prostacyclin) with conventional therapy in primary pulmonary hypertension. N Engl J Med 1996;334:296–302.
3. Simonneau G, Barst RJ, Galie N, et al: Continuous subcutaneous infusion of treprostinil, a prostacyclin analogue, in patients with pulmonary arterial hypertension: A double-blind randomized controlled trial. Am J Respir Crit Care Med 2002;165:800–804.
4. Olschewski H, Simonneau G, Galie N, et al: Inhaled iloprost for severe pulmonary hypertension. N Engl J Med 2002;347:322–329.
5. Galie N, Humbert M, Vachiery JL, et al: Effects of beraprost sodium, an oral prostacyclin analogue, in patients with pulmonary arterial hypertension: A randomized, double-blind, placebo-controlled trial. J Am Coll Cardiol 2002;39:1496–1502.
6. Rubin LJ, Badesch DB, Barst RJ, et al: Bosentan in patients with pulmonary arterial hypertension. N Engl J Med 2002;346:896–903.

SUGGESTED READINGS

Barst RJ (ed): Pulmonary Arterial Hypertension in Infants and Children. Prog Pediatr Cardiol 2001. *A monograph reviewing the pathology, pathobiology, genetics, diagnosis, and assessment of infants and children with pulmonary hypertension.*

Peacock AJ, Rubin LJ (eds): Pulmonary Circulation, 2nd ed. London, Edward Arnold, 2002. *A comprehensive reference for diseases of the pulmonary circulation and their treatments.*

Rich S, McLaughlin V (eds): Pulmonary Hypertension. Clin Chest Med 2001;22:3. *A monograph reviewing pulmonary arterial hypertension based on the consensus of participants in the 1998 World Health Organization International Symposium on Primary Pulmonary Hypertension.*

65 CONGENITAL HEART DISEASE IN ADULTS

Ariane J. Marelli

Over the past four decades, the convergence of major progress in medicine, pediatrics, and cardiovascular surgery has resulted in the survival to adulthood of an increasingly large number of patients with complex structural heart lesions. Adult physicians are becoming increasingly responsible for these patients, commonly in concert with a cardiologist and a tertiary care facility.

Definitions

Patients can be subdivided into three categories according to their surgical status: Patients may be unoperated or surgically palliated or may have undergone physiologic repair. Congenital heart lesions can be classified as *acyanotic* or *cyanotic. Cyanosis* refers to a blue discoloration of the mucous membranes resulting from an increased amount of reduced hemoglobin. Central cyanosis occurs when the circulation is mixed because of a right-to-left shunt.

A *native lesion* refers to an anatomic lesion present at birth. Acquired lesions, naturally occurring or as a result of surgery, are superimposed on the native anatomy. *Palliative* interventions are performed in patients with cyanotic lesions and are defined as operations that serve either to increase or decrease pulmonary blood flow while allowing a mixed circulation and cyanosis to persist (Table 65–1). *Physiologic* repair applies to procedures that provide total or nearly total anatomic and physiologic separation of the pulmonary and systemic circulations in complex cyanotic lesions and result in patients who are acyanotic.

Eisenmenger's complex refers to flow reversal across a ventricular septal defect (VSD) when pulmonary vascular resistance exceeds systemic levels. *Eisenmenger's physiology* is used to designate the physiologic response in a broader category of shunt lesions in which a right-to-left shunt occurs in response to an elevation in pulmonary vascular resistance. *Eisenmenger's syndrome* is a term applied to common clinical features shared by patients with Eisenmenger's physiology.

Each congenital lesion can influence the course of another. For example, the physiologic consequences of a VSD are different if it occurs in isolation or in combination with pulmonary stenosis. A *simple lesion* is defined as either a shunt lesion or an obstructive lesion of the right or left heart occurring in isolation. A *complex lesion* is a combination of two or more abnormalities.

Etiology

In 90% of patients, congenital heart disease is attributable to multifactorial inheritance; only 5 to 10% of malformations are due to primary genetic factors, either chromosomal or related to a single mutant gene. The most common defect observed in patients with *chromosomal aberrations* is a VSD, which occurs in 90% of patients with trisomy 13 and 18. Defects of the endocardial cushions and the ventricular septum are found in 50% of patients with Down syndrome

(trisomy 21). The most frequently observed defects in patients with Turner's syndrome (45,X) are aortic coarctation, aortic stenosis, and atrial septal defect (ASD). About 15% of patients with tetralogy of Fallot have a deletion on chromosome 22q11, with a higher prevalence in those with a right aortic arch. Abnormalities involving the chromosomal band 22q11 can also result in a group of syndromes, the most common of which is DiGeorge's syndrome. The shared phenotypic features are designated *CATCH-22 syndromes*, that is, a combination of cardiac defects, abnormal facies, thymic hypoplasia, cleft palate, and hypocalcemia. The recurrence risk for families with a child who carries a congenital cardiac malformation due to a chromosomal anomaly is related to the recurrence risk of the chromosomal anomaly itself.

Typically, *single mutant genes* are also associated with syndromes of cardiovascular malformations, although not every patient with the syndrome has the characteristic cardiac anomaly. Examples include osteogenesis imperfecta (autosomal recessive) associated with aortic valve disease, Jervell and Lange-Nielsen (autosomal recessive) and Romano-Ward (autosomal dominant) syndromes associated with a prolonged QT interval and sudden death, and Holt-Oram (autosomal dominant) syndrome, in which an ASD occurs with a range of other skeletal anomalies. Osler-Weber-Rendu telangiectasias are associated with pulmonary arteriovenous fistulas. William's syndrome occurs with supravalvar aortic stenosis in most cases. Noonan's syndrome is associated with pulmonary stenosis, ASD, and hypertrophic cardiomyopathy. Although autosomal dominant inheritance has been implicated for both, most cases are sporadic. Deletion at chromosome 7q11.23 has been identified in patients with William's syndrome, and a gene defect has been mapped to 12q22-qter in patients with Noonan's syndrome.

The *risk of recurrence* when the mother carries a sporadically occurring congenital lesion varies from 2.5 to 18%, depending on the lesion. Obstructive lesions of the left ventricular outflow tract have the highest recurrence rates in offspring. When the father carries the lesion, 1.5 to 3% of the offspring are affected. When a sibling has a congenital cardiac anomaly, the risk of recurrence in another sibling varies from 1 to 3%.

Incidence and Prevalence

Congenital cardiac malformations occur at a rate of 8 per 1000 live births, which corresponds to approximately 32,000 infants with newly diagnosed congenital heart disease each year in the United States. An estimated 20% die within the first year of life—a substantial decrease from the reported 40% in the late 1960s. Each year an estimated 20,000 surgical procedures are performed to correct circulatory defects in patients with congenital malformations. Approximately 80% of the first-year survivors live to reach adulthood. The estimated prevalence of adults with congenital heart disease in the United States is approximately 800,000.

Bicuspid aortic valve occurs in about 2% of the general population, is the most common congenital cardiac anomaly encountered in adult populations, and accounts for up to half of operated cases of aortic stenosis in adults (Chapter 72). ASDs constitute 30 to 40% of cases of congenital heart disease seen in adults, with ostium secundum ASD accounting for 7% of all congenital lesions. A solitary VSD accounts for 15 to 20% of all congenital lesions and is the most common congenital cardiac lesion observed in the pediatric population; its high spontaneous closure rates explain the lesser prevalence in adults. Patent ductus arteriosus (PDA) accounts for 5 to 10% of all congenital cardiac lesions in infants with a normal birthweight. Pulmonary stenosis and coarctation of the aorta account for 3 to 10% of all congenital lesions.

Tetralogy of Fallot is the most common cyanotic congenital anomaly observed in adults. Together with complete transposition of the great arteries (TGA), these lesions account for 5 to 12% of congenital heart disease in infants. More complex lesions such as tricuspid atresia, univentricular heart, congenitally corrected TGA, Ebstein's anomaly, and double-outlet right ventricle account for 2.5% or less of all congenital heart disease.

Approach to the Patient

Congenital heart disease is a lifelong condition during which the patient and the lesion evolve concurrently. A patient may have been

Table 65–1 • PALLIATIVE SURGICAL SHUNTS FOR CONGENITAL HEART LESIONS

PALLIATIVE SHUNT	ANASTOMOSIS
Systemic Arterial-to-Pulmonary Artery Shunts	
Classic Blalock-Taussig	Subclavian artery to PA
Modified Blalock-Taussig	Subclavian artery to PA (prosthetic graft)
Potts anastomosis	Descending aorta to left PA
Waterston shunt	Ascending aorta to right PA
Systemic Venous-to-PA Shunts	
Classic Glenn	SVC to right PA
Bidirectional Glenn	SVC to right and left PA
Bilateral Glenn	Right and left SVC to right and left PA

PA = pulmonary artery; SVC = superior vena cava.
From Marelli A, Mullen M: Palliative surgical shunts for congenital heart lesions. Clin Paediatr 1996;4:189.

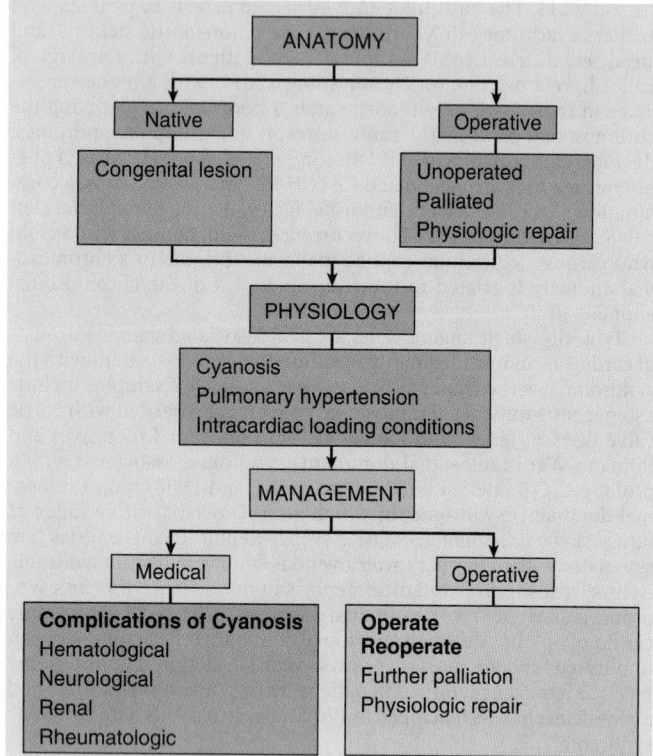

FIGURE 65–1 • The goals of complete clinical assessment in congenital heart disease are to define the anatomy and physiology to determine appropriate management.

monitored for many years because of an erroneous diagnosis made in infancy or childhood when diagnostic techniques were more limited. The differential diagnosis of native and surgical anatomy in the adult with an unknown diagnosis depends on whether the patient is cyanotic or acyanotic. On completion of the evaluation, the following questions should be answered (Fig. 65–1): What is the native anatomy? Has this patient undergone surgery for the condition? What is the physiology? What can and should be done for this patient both medically and surgically? And importantly, who should do it?

If the patient has not undergone surgery, the question is "why not?" If the patient is palliated, has the degree of cyanosis progressed as evidenced by a drop in systemic saturation or a rise in hemoglobin? If the patient has undergone a physiologic repair, what procedure was performed? Are residual lesions present and have new lesions developed as a consequence of surgery? The patient's *physiology* is determined by the presence or absence of cyanosis, pulmonary hypertension, adequate filling of the cardiac chambers, and any resulting medical complications.

A clinical assessment, 12-lead electrocardiogram (ECG), chest radiograph, and baseline oxygen saturation should be part of every initial assessment. Two-dimensional transthoracic echocardiography (Chapter 51), Doppler, and color flow imaging are used to establish the diagnosis and monitor the evolution of documented hemodynamic complications. *Transesophageal echocardiographic* (TEE) examination is particularly useful in adults and is increasingly important during interventional catheter-guided therapy and surgery. *Magnetic resonance imaging* (MRI) (Chapter 53) and computed tomography (Chapter 52) are useful adjuncts. *Cardiac catheterization* for congenital heart disease has shifted from pure diagnosis to include intervention. Coronary arteriography is recommended for adults older than 40 years in whom surgical intervention is contemplated.

PULMONARY HYPERTENSION

Pulmonary hypertension secondary to structural disease of the heart or circulation can occur with or without an increase in pulmonary vascular resistance. Pulmonary vascular obstructive disease occurs when pulmonary vascular resistance rises and becomes fixed and irreversible. In the most common congenital anomalies, pulmonary

hypertension occurs as a result of increased pulmonary blood flow because of a native left-to-right shunt. Examples include ASD, a moderately sized VSD, PDA, and a variety of complex lesions. The rate at which pulmonary hypertension progresses to become pulmonary vascular obstructive disease varies from one lesion to another and depends at least in part on the source of pulmonary blood flow. Pulmonary hypertension typically develops in patients with an ASD after the fourth decade, with Eisenmenger's syndrome being a late complication seen in only 5 to 10% of cases. In contrast, in patients with a large VSD or persistent PDA, progressive elevation in pulmonary vascular resistance occurs rapidly because the pulmonary vascular bed is exposed not only to the excess volume of the left-to-right shunt but also to systemic arterial pressures. As a result, Eisenmenger's complex develops in approximately 10% of patients with a large VSD during the first decade. Surgical pulmonary artery banding is a palliative measure aimed at decreasing pulmonary blood flow and protecting the pulmonary vascular bed against the development of early pulmonary vascular obstructive disease.

If forward flow from the right heart is insufficient, native collaterals and/or surgical shunts provide an alternative source of pulmonary blood flow (see Table 65–1). With large surgical shunts, however, direct exposure of the pulmonary vascular bed to the high pressures of the systemic circulation causes pulmonary vascular obstructive disease. As a result, systemic-to-pulmonary arterial shunts are currently less favored in neonates and infants, in whom systemic venous–to–pulmonary arterial shunts are now preferred.

EISENMENGER'S SYNDROME

The term *Eisenmenger's syndrome* should be reserved for patients in whom pulmonary vascular obstructive disease is present and pulmonary vascular resistance is fixed and irreversible. These findings in combination with the *absence of left-to-right shunting* render the patient inoperable.

The clinical manifestations of Eisenmenger's syndrome include dyspnea on exertion, syncope, chest pain, congestive heart failure, and symptoms related to erythrocytosis and hyperviscosity. On physical examination, central cyanosis and digital clubbing are hallmark findings. Systemic oxygen saturations typically vary between 75 and 85%. The pulse pressure narrows as the cardiac output falls. Examination of jugular venous pressure can reveal a dominant *a* wave reflecting a noncompliant right ventricle until tricuspid insufficiency is severe enough to generate a large *v* wave. A prominent right ventricular impulse is felt in the left parasternal border in end-expiration or in the subcostal area in end-inspiration. A palpable pulmonary artery is commonly felt. The pulmonary component of the second heart sound is increased and can be felt in most cases. Pulmonary ejection sounds are common when the pulmonary artery is dilated with a structurally normal valve. Right atrial gallop is heard more frequently when the *a* wave is dominant. A murmur of tricuspid insufficiency is common, but the inspiratory increase in the murmur (Carvallo's sign) disappears when right ventricular failure occurs. In diastole, a pulmonary insufficiency murmur is often heard. The 12-lead ECG shows evidence of right atrial enlargement, right ventricular hypertrophy, and right axis deviation. Chest radiographic findings include a dilated pulmonary artery segment, cardiac enlargement, and diminished pulmonary vascular markings. Echocardiography confirms the right-sided pressure overload and pulmonary artery enlargement, as well as the tricuspid and pulmonary insufficiency. Cardiac catheterization is indicated if doubt exists about the potential reversibility of the elevated pulmonary vascular resistance in a patient who might otherwise benefit from surgery.

SYSTEMIC COMPLICATIONS OF CYANOSIS

Cyanosis occurs when persistent venous-to-arterial mixing results in hypoxemia. Adaptive mechanisms to increase oxygen delivery include an increase in oxygen content, a rightward shift in the oxyhemoglobin dissociation curve, a higher hematocrit, and an increase in cardiac output. When cyanosis is not relieved, chronic hypoxemia and erythrocytosis result in hematologic, neurologic, renal, and rheumatic complications.

Hematologic complications of chronic hypoxemia include erythrocytosis, iron deficiency, and bleeding diathesis. Hemoglobin and hematocrit levels, as well as red blood cell indices, should be checked regularly and correlated with systemic oxygen saturation levels.

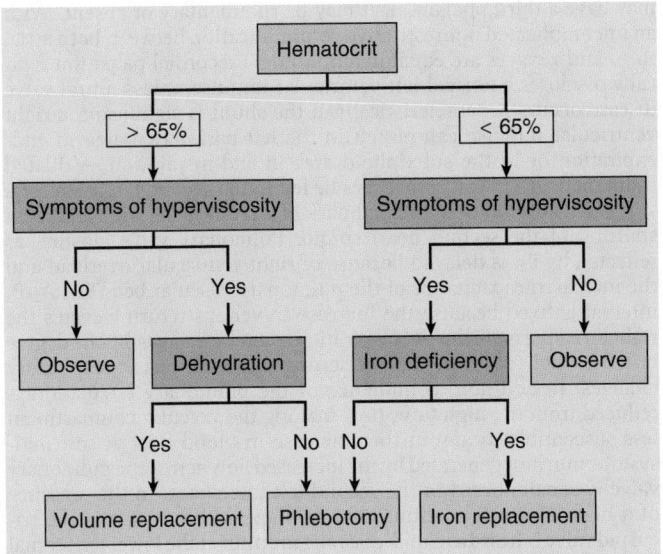

FIGURE 65–2 • Treatment algorithm for erythrocytosis of cyanotic congenital heart disease.

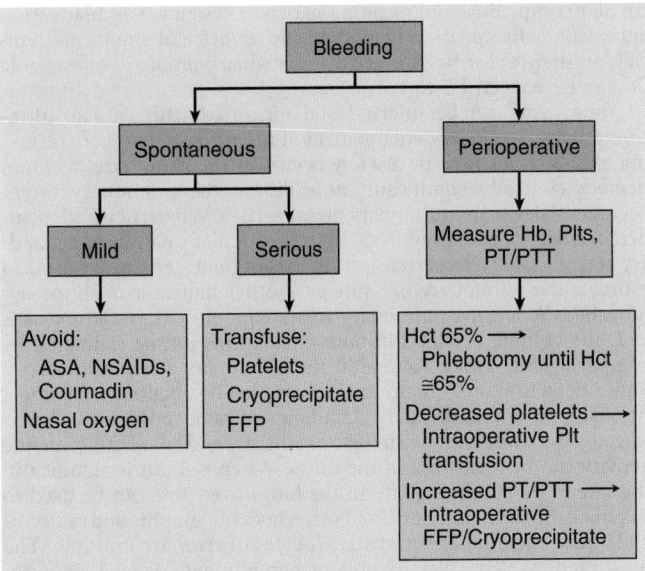

FIGURE 65–3 • Treatment algorithm for bleeding diathesis of cyanotic congenital heart disease. ASA = acetylsalicylic acid; FFP = fresh-frozen plasma; Hb = hemoglobin; Hct = hematocrit; NSAIDs, nonsteroidal anti-inflammatory drugs; Plts = platelets; PT = prothrombin time; PTT = partial thromboplastin time.

Symptoms of hyperviscosity include headaches, faintness, dizziness, fatigue, altered mentation, visual disturbances, paresthesias, tinnitus, and myalgia. Symptoms are classified as mild to moderate when they interfere with only some activities, or they can be marked to severe and interfere with most or all activities. Patients with *compensated erythrocytosis* establish an equilibrium hematocrit at higher levels in an iron-replete state with minimal symptoms. Patients with *decompensated erythrocytosis* manifest unstable, rising hematocrit levels and experience severe hyperviscosity symptoms.

In the iron-replete state, moderate to severe hyperviscosity symptoms typically occur when hematocrit levels exceed 65%. If no evidence of dehydration is present, removal of 500 mL of blood over a 30- to 45-minute period should be followed by quantitative volume replacement with normal saline or dextran (Fig. 65–2). The procedure may be repeated every 24 hours until symptomatic improvement occurs.

Hemostatic abnormalities can occur in up to 20% of cyanotic patients with erythrocytosis. Bleeding is usually mild and superficial and leads to easy bruising, skin petechiae, or mucosal bleeding, but epistaxis, hemoptysis, or even life-threatening postoperative bleeding can occur. A variety of clotting factor deficiencies and qualitative and quantitative platelet disorders have been described.

Treatment for spontaneous bleeding is dictated by its severity and the abnormal hemostatic parameters (Fig. 65–3). For severe bleeding, platelet transfusions, fresh-frozen plasma, vitamin K, cryoprecipitate, and desmopressin have been used. Reduction in erythrocyte mass also improves hemostasis, so cyanotic patients undergoing surgery should have prophylactic phlebotomy if the hematocrit is greater than 65%.

Iron deficiency is common in cyanotic adult patients because of excessive bleeding or phlebotomy. In contrast to normocytic erythrocytosis, which is rarely symptomatic at hematocrit levels less than 65%, iron deficiency may be manifested by hyperviscosity symptoms at hematocrit levels well below 65%. The treatment of choice is not phlebotomy but oral iron repletion until a rise in hematocrit is detected, typically within 1 week.

Neurologic complications, including cerebral hemorrhage, can be caused by hemostatic defects and are most often seen after inappropriate use of anticoagulant therapy. Patients with right-to-left shunts may be at risk for paradoxical cerebral emboli. Focal brain injury may provide a nidus for brain abscess if bacteremia supervenes. Attention should be paid to the use of air filters in peripheral intravenous lines to avoid paradoxical emboli through a right-to-left shunt.

Prophylactic phlebotomy has no place in the prevention of cerebral arterial thrombosis. Indications for phlebotomy are the occurrence of symptomatic hyperviscosity in an iron-repleted patient and prevention of excessive bleeding perioperatively.

Pulmonary complications include massive pulmonary hemorrhage and in situ arterial thrombosis. A rapid clinical deterioration associated with progressive hypoxemia often marks the terminal stage of disease . No clear benefits are observed with the use of anticoagulants (systemic or intrapulmonary) because of the risk of prolonged bleeding owing to the underlying coagulopathy. The chronic disease process and high mortality prohibit pulmonary endarterectomy.

Chronic oxygen therapy is unlikely to benefit hypoxemia secondary to right-to-left shunting in the setting of a fixed pulmonary vascular resistance. Chronic oxygen therapy results in mucosal dehydration with an increased incidence of epistaxis and is therefore not recommended.

Renal dysfunction can be manifested as proteinuria, hyperuricemia, or renal failure. Focal interstitial fibrosis, tubular atrophy, and hyalinization of afferent and efferent arterioles can be seen on renal biopsy. Increased blood viscosity and arteriolar vasoconstriction can lead to renal hypoperfusion with progressive glomerulosclerosis. Hyperuricemia is commonly seen in patients with cyanotic congenital heart disease and is thought to be due mainly to the decreased reabsorption of uric acid rather than overproduction from erythrocytosis. Asymptomatic hyperuricemia need not be treated because lowering uric acid levels has not been shown to prevent renal disease or gout.

Rheumatologic complications include gout and hypertrophic osteoarthropathy, which is thought to be responsible for the arthralgias affecting up to one third of patients with cyanotic congenital heart disease. In patients with right-to-left shunting, megakaryocytes released from the bone marrow bypass the lung and are entrapped in systemic arterioles and capillaries where they release platelet-derived growth factor, which promotes local cell proliferation. Digital clubbing and new osseous formation with periostitis occur and cause the symptoms of arthralgia. Symptomatic hyperuricemia and gouty arthritis can be treated as necessary with colchicine, probenecid, or allopurinol; nonsteroidal anti-inflammatory drugs are best avoided, given the baseline hemostatic anomalies in these patients.

SPECIFIC SIMPLE LESIONS

ISOLATED SHUNT LESIONS

Hemodynamic complications of significant shunts relate to volume overload and chamber dilation of the primary chamber receiving the excess left-to-right shunt and to secondary complications of valvar dysfunction and damage to the pulmonary vascular bed. The size and duration of the shunt determine the clinical course and therefore the indications for closure. The degree of shunting is a function of both the size of the communication and, depending on its location, biventricular compliance and/or pulmonary and systemic vascular resistance. Clinically apparent hemodynamic sequelae of shunts are typically apparent or can be expected to occur when pulmonary-to-systemic flow ratios exceed 1.5 to 1.

Shunt size can be inferred and measured with cardiac ultrasonography. Secondary enlargement of the cardiac chambers receiving excess shunt flow in diastole occurs as the shunt size becomes hemodynamically significant; in addition, the pulmonary artery becomes enlarged as pulmonary pressure rises. When tricuspid insufficiency occurs primarily from right ventricular dilation or secondary to pulmonary hypertension, the regurgitant jet can be used to estimate the pulmonary pressure as another indicator of shunt significance. When the pulmonary-to-systemic flow (Qp:Qs) exceeds 2:1, the volume of blood in both circulations can be estimated by comparing the stroke volume at the pulmonary and aortic valves. Shunt detection and quantification can also be obtained by using a first-pass radionuclide study. As a bolus of radioactive substance is injected into the systemic circulation, the rise and fall of radionuclide activity can be measured in the lungs. When a shunt is significant, the rate of persistent activity in the lungs over time can be used to calculate the shunt fraction. For both echocardiographic and radionuclide quantification of shunt size, sources of error are multiple. The most predictable results are obtained only in experienced laboratories. Uncertainty about the physiologic significance of a borderline shunt can be minimized by integrating serial determinations from multiple clinical and relevant diagnostic sources rather than basing management decisions on a single calculated shunt value.

ATRIAL SEPTAL DEFECT

Classification of ASDs is based on anatomic location. Most commonly, an *ostium secundum* ASD occurs in the central portion of the interatrial septum as a result of an enlarged foramen ovale or excessive resorption of the septum primum. The combination of a secundum ASD and acquired mitral stenosis is known as *Lutembacher's syndrome*, the pathophysiology of which is determined by the relative severity of each. Abnormal development of the embryologic endocardial cushions result in a variety of atrioventricular canal defects, the most common of which consists of a defect in the lower part of the atrial septum in the *ostium primum* location, typically accompanied by a cleft mitral valve and mitral regurgitation. The *sinus venosus* defect, which accounts for 2 to 3% of all interatrial communications, is located superiorly at the junction of the superior vena cava and right atrium and is generally associated with anomalous drainage of the right-sided pulmonary veins into the superior vena cava or right atrium. Less commonly, interatrial communications can be seen at the site of the coronary sinus, typically associated with an anomalous left superior vena cava.

The *pathophysiology* is determined by the effects of the shunt on the heart and pulmonary circulation. Right atrial and right ventricular dilation occurs as shunt size increases with pulmonary-to-systemic flow ratios greater than 1.5:1.0. Superimposed systemic hypertension and coronary artery disease modify left ventricular compliance and favor left-to-right shunting. Mitral valve disease can occur in up to 15% of patients older than 50 years. Right heart failure, atrial fibrillation, or atrial flutter can occur as a result of chronic right-sided volume overload and progressive ventricular and atrial dilation. Stroke can result from paradoxical emboli, atrial arrhythmias, or both. A rise in pulmonary pressure occurs because of the increased pulmonary blood flow. Pulmonary hypertension is unusual before 20 years of age but is seen in 50% of patients older than 40 years. The overall incidence of pulmonary vascular obstructive disease is 15 to 20% in patients with ASD. Eisenmenger's disease with reverse shunting, a late and rare complication of isolated secundum ASD, is reported in 5 to 10% of patients.

Diagnosis

Although most patients are minimally symptomatic in the first three decades, more than 70% become impaired by the fifth decade. Initial *symptoms* include exercise intolerance, dyspnea on exertion, and fatigue caused most commonly by right heart failure and pulmonary hypertension. Palpitations, syncope, and stroke can occur with the development of atrial arrhythmias.

On *physical examination* most adults have a normal general physical appearance. When Holt-Oram syndrome is present, the thumb

may have a third phalanx or it may be rudimentary or absent. With an uncomplicated nonrestrictive communication between both atria, the *a* and *v* waves are equal in amplitude. Precordial palpation typically discloses a normal left ventricular impulse unless mitral valve disease occurs. Characteristically, if the shunt is significant, a right ventricular impulse can be felt in the left parasternal area in end-expiration or in the subxiphoid area in end-inspiration. A dilated pulmonary artery can sometimes be felt in the second left intercostal space. On auscultation, the hallmark of an ASD is the wide and fixed splitting of the second heart sound. Pulmonary valve closure, as reflected by P_2, is delayed because of right ventricular overload and the increased capacitance of the pulmonary vascular bed. The A_2-P_2 interval is fixed because the increase in venous return elevates the right atrial pressure during inspiration, thereby decreasing the degree of left-to-right shunting and offsetting the usual phasic respiratory changes. In addition, compliance of the pulmonary circulation is reduced from the high flow, thus making the vascular compartment less susceptible to any further increase in blood flow. A soft mid-systolic murmur generated by the increased flow across the pulmonary valve is usually heard in the second left interspace. In the presence of a high left-to-right shunt volume, increased flow across the tricuspid valve is heard as a mid-diastolic murmur at the lower left sternal border. With advanced right heart failure, evidence of systemic venous congestion is present.

The ECG characteristically shows an incomplete right bundle branch pattern (Fig. 65–4). Right axis deviation and atrial abnormalities, including a prolonged PR interval, atrial fibrillation, and flutter, are also seen. Typically, the chest radiograph shows pulmonary vascular plethora with increased markings in both lung fields consistent with increased pulmonary blood flow (see Fig. 49–13). The main pulmonary artery and both its branches are dilated. Right atrial and right ventricular dilation can be seen. *Cardiac ultrasonography* is diagnostic and provides important prognostic information (Fig. 65–5).

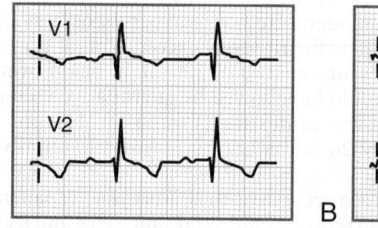
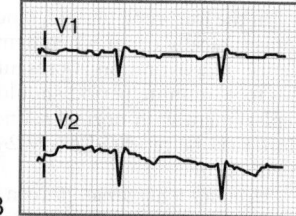

FIGURE 65–4 • Electrocardiographic hallmark in atrial septal defect. Right precordial leads V_1 and V_2 illustrate two variants of an incomplete right bundle branch block pattern: *A* shows the rSrT pattern and *B* shows the rsR′ pattern.

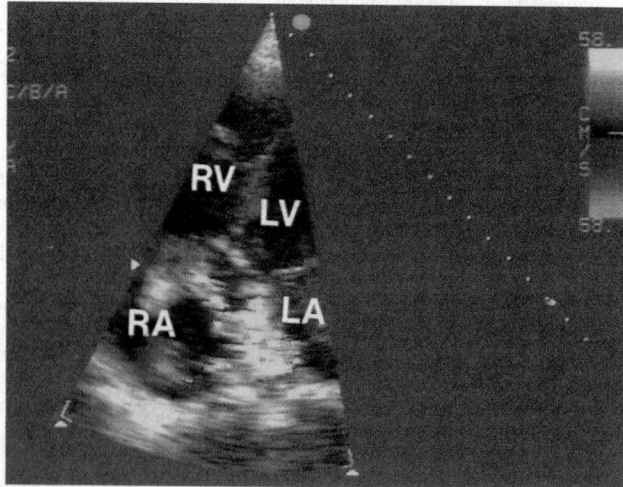

FIGURE 65–5 • Color flow Doppler apical four-chamber view showing blood flow from the left atrium (LA) to the right atrium (RA) through a moderately sized atrial septal defect. LV = left ventricle; RV = right ventricle. (From Forbes CD, Jackson WF: Color Atlas and Text of Clinical Medicine, 3rd ed. London, Mosby, 2003.)

Ostium primum and secundum ASDs are easily identifiable with transthoracic imaging, but a sinus venosus ASD can be missed unless specifically sought. For more accurate visualization of the superior interatrial septum and localization of the pulmonary veins, TEE is useful. With Doppler, pulmonary artery pressures can be quantified, and the $\dot{Q}p:\dot{Q}s$ can be measured.

 Treatment

The decision to close an ASD is based on the size of the shunt and the presence or absence of symptoms. In the presence of a significant shunt, closure of an ASD before 25 years of age without evidence of pulmonary hypertension results in a long-term outcome that is similar to that of age- and sex-matched controls. After age 40, closure is indicated in symptomatic patients with significant shunts because it results in improved survival, prevention of deterioration in functional capacity, and improvement in exercise capacity as compared with patients treated medically. Advanced age (>60 years) is not a contraindication to ASD closure in the presence of a significant shunt because a significant number of patients will show evidence of symptomatic improvement. Closure is also indicated in patients with systemic embolization in the presence of patent foramen ovale.

Uncomplicated secundum ASDs may be closed surgically in children and adults with minimal operative mortality, in the range of 1 to 3% or less. Preoperative pulmonary artery pressure and the presence or absence of pulmonary vascular disease are important predictors of successful surgical outcome.

Centrally located defects measuring up to 3.5 cm can be occluded using transcatheter techniques in a cardiac catheterization laboratory. Advantages of this approach include the avoidance of sternotomy and cardiopulmonary bypass. Complications, including device fracture with embolization and residual shunts, should decrease as newer devices are used.

VENTRICULAR SEPTAL DEFECT

For anatomic classification of VSDs, the interventricular septum can be divided into four regions. Defects of the membranous septum, or infracristal VSDs, are located in a small translucent area beneath the aortic valve and account for up to 80% of VSDs. These VSDs typically show a variable degree of extension into the inlet or outlet septum, hence their designation as "perimembranous." Infundibular defects or supracristal outlet VSDs occur in the conal septum above the crista supraventricularis and below the pulmonary valve. Inlet defects are identified at the crux of the heart between the tricuspid and mitral valves and are usually associated with other anomalies of the atrioventricular canal. Defects of the trabecular or muscular septum can be multiple and occur distal to the septal attachment of the tricuspid valve and toward the apex.

The pathophysiology and clinical course of VSDs depend on the size of the defect, the status of the pulmonary vascular bed, and the effects of shunt size on intracardiac hemodynamics. Unlike ASDs, the size of a VSD may decrease with time. Approximately half of all native VSDs are small, and more than half of them close spontaneously; moderate or even large VSDs may also close in 10% or fewer of cases. The highest closure rates are observed in the first decade of life; spontaneous closure in adult life is unusual.

Patients who have a small defect with trivial or mild shunts are defined as those with a $\dot{Q}p:\dot{Q}s$ of less than 1.5 and normal pulmonary artery pressure and vascular resistance. Patients with moderate defects have a $\dot{Q}p:\dot{Q}s$ ratio of greater than 1.2 and elevated pulmonary artery pressure but not elevated pulmonary vascular resistance. Patients with a large and severe defect have an elevated $\dot{Q}p:\dot{Q}s$ ratio with high pulmonary pressure and elevated pulmonary vascular resistance. Eisenmenger's complex develops in about 10% of patients with VSDs, usually when there is no resistance to flow at the level of the defect, which can be as large as the aorta. When a systolic pressure gradient is present between the ventricles, the physiologic severity may be trivial or mild but can also be moderate or severe.

Minimal or mild defects usually cause no significant hemodynamic or physiologic abnormality. A moderate or severe defect causes left atrial and ventricular dilation consistent with the degree of left-to-right shunting. Shunting across the ventricular septum occurs predominantly during systole when left ventricular pressure exceeds that

on the right; diastolic filling abnormalities occur in the left atrium. With moderate or severe defects, the right heart becomes affected as a function of the rise in pulmonary pressure and pulmonary blood flow.

Diagnosis

An adult with a VSD most commonly has a small restrictive lesion that either was small at birth or has undergone some degree of spontaneous closure. A second group of patients consists of those with unoperated large, nonrestrictive VSDs who have had Eisenmenger's complex for most of their lives. Patients with a moderately sized defect are typically symptomatic as children and are therefore more likely to have repair at a young age.

Patients with a trivial or mild shunt across a small, restrictive VSD are usually asymptomatic. Physical examination discloses no evidence of systemic or pulmonary venous congestion, and jugular venous pressure is normal. A thrill may be palpable at the left sternal border. Auscultation reveals a normal S_1 and S_2 without gallops. A grade 4 or louder, widely radiating, high-frequency, pansystolic murmur is heard maximally in the third or fourth intercostal space and reflects the high-pressure gradient between the left and right ventricles throughout systole. The striking contrast between a loud murmur and an otherwise normal cardiac examination is an important diagnostic clue. The ECG and chest radiograph are also normal in patients with small VSDs.

At the other end of the spectrum are patients with Eisenmenger's complex (see earlier). Between these two extremes are patients with a moderate defect, whose pathology reflects a combination of pulmonary hypertension and left-sided volume overload resulting from a significant left-to-right shunt. In adults, shortness of breath on exertion can be the result of both pulmonary venous congestion and elevated pulmonary pressure. On *physical examination,* a diffuse palpable left ventricular impulse occurs with a variable degree of right ventricular hypertrophy and an accentuated second heart sound. A systolic murmur persists as long as pulmonary vascular resistance is below systemic resistance. The ECG commonly shows left atrial enlargement and left ventricular hypertrophy. The *chest radiograph* shows shunt vascularity with an enlarged left atrium and ventricle. The degree of pulmonary hypertension determines the size of the pulmonary artery trunk.

Echocardiography can identify the defect and determine the significance of the shunt by assessing left atrial and ventricular size, pulmonary artery pressure, and the presence or absence of right ventricular hypertrophy. Cardiac catheterization is reserved for those in whom surgery is considered. Adults with a small defect of no physiologic significance need not be studied invasively. Those with Eisenmenger's complex have severe pulmonary vascular disease and are not surgical candidates. Patients who have a moderately sized shunt that appears hemodynamically significant and in whom pulmonary pressures are elevated are most likely to benefit from direct measurements of pulmonary vascular resistance and reactivity.

 Treatment

All patients with a VSD of any size require endocarditis prophylaxis (Chapter 310). Patients with Eisenmenger's complex have pulmonary vascular resistance that is prohibitive to surgery. For this group of patients, management centers on the medical complications of cyanosis (see earlier). In a few patients with small defects, complications can relate to progressive tricuspid insufficiency caused by septal aneurysm formation or to acquired aortic insufficiency when an aortic cusp becomes engaged in the high-velocity jet flow generated by the defect. The intermediate group of patients with a defect of moderate physiologic significance should have surgical closure unless contraindicated by high pulmonary vascular resistance.

Late results following operative closure of isolated VSDs include residual patency in up to 20% of patients, only about 5% of whom need a reoperation. Rhythm disturbances after surgical closure of VSDs include tachyarrhythmias and conduction disturbances. Right bundle branch block occurs in one third to two thirds of patients, whereas first-degree atrioventricular block and complete heart block occur in fewer than 10%. Sudden cardiac death following surgical repair of VSD occurs in 2% of patients.

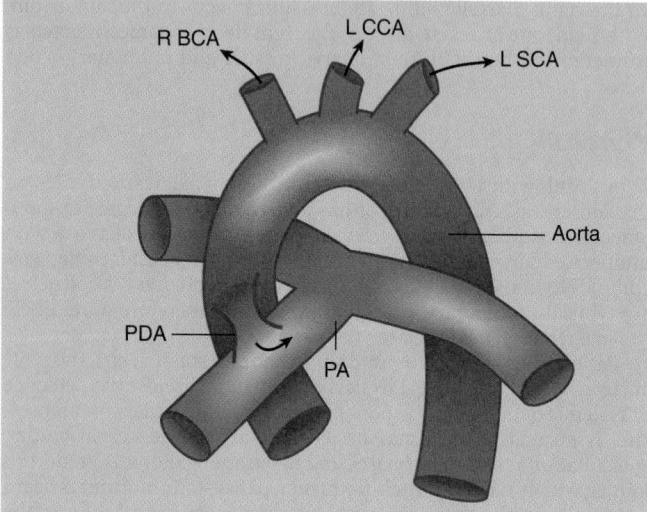

FIGURE 65–6 • The anatomy of a patent ductus arteriosus is shown. Note the relation between the position of the ductus and the right and left brachiocephalic vessels. BCA = brachiocephalic; CCA = common carotid artery; L = left; PA = pulmonary artery; PDA = patent ductus arteriosus; R = right; SCA = subclavian artery.

PATENT DUCTUS ARTERIOSUS

The ductus arteriosus connects the descending aorta to the main pulmonary trunk near the origin of the left subclavian artery (Fig. 65–6). Normal postnatal closure results in fibrosis and degenerative changes in the ductal lumen, leaving in its place the residual ligamentum arteriosum, which rarely can become part of an abnormal vascular ring. When the duct persists, significant calcification of the aortic ductal end is observed.

The physiologic consequences of a PDA are determined by its size and length, as well as by the ratio of pressure and resistance of the pulmonary and aortic circulations on either end of the duct. If systolic and diastolic pressure in the aorta exceeds that in the pulmonary artery, aortic blood flows continuously down a pressure gradient into the pulmonary artery and then returns to the left atrium. The left atrium and subsequently the left ventricle dilate, whereas the right heart becomes progressively affected as pulmonary hypertension develops.

A small PDA has continuous flow throughout the entire cardiac cycle without left heart dilation, pulmonary hypertension, or symptoms. Patients with a small PDA, although protected from hemodynamic complications of a significant left-to-right shunt, remain at risk for infectious endarteritis, which usually develops on the pulmonary side of the duct and occurs at a rate of about 0.45% per year after the second decade. Because endarteritis accounts for up to one third of the total mortality in patients with PDA, ductal closure should be considered even when the PDA is small.

A PDA is of moderate or large size but still restrictive when a left-to-right shunt occurs throughout systole and diastole is of variable duration. Left atrial and/or ventricular dilation and pulmonary hypertension will vary with the quantity of left-to-right shunting, as well as with the secondary effects on the pulmonary vascular bed. Symptoms generally increase by the second and third decades and include dyspnea, palpitations, and exercise intolerance. As heart failure, pulmonary hypertension, and/or endarteritis develops, mortality rises to 3 to 4% per year by the fourth decade, and two thirds of patients die by 60 years of age. Eisenmenger's physiology with systemic or suprasystemic pulmonary pressure and a right-to-left shunt develops in 5% of patients with an isolated PDA.

Diagnosis

In patients with Eisenmenger's physiology, a right-to-left shunt from the pulmonary artery to the descending aorta results in decreased oxygen saturation in the lower extremities as compared with the upper extremities; this difference in cyanosis and clubbing is most prominent in the toes, variably affects the left arm via the left subclavian artery, and typically spares the right arm. With a large left-to-right shunt, the pulse pressure widens as diastolic flow into the pulmonary artery lowers systemic diastolic pressure. The arterial pulse becomes bounding as a result of increased stroke volume. Precordial palpation discloses variable left and right ventricular impulses as determined by the relative degree of left-sided volume overload and pulmonary hypertension. In the presence of a continuous aortopulmonary gradient, the classic "machinery" murmur of a PDA can be heard at the first or second left intercostal space below the left clavicle. As the pulmonary pressure rises, the diastolic component of the murmur becomes progressively shorter. With the development of Eisenmenger's physiology and equalization of aortic and pulmonary pressure, the entire murmur may disappear and the clinical findings are dominated by pulmonary hypertension.

In adult patients with a significant left-to-right shunt, the *ECG* shows a bifid P wave in at least one limb lead consistent with left atrial enlargement and a variable degree of left ventricular hypertrophy. The PR interval is prolonged in about 20% of patients. In older patients, the *chest radiograph* shows calcification at the location of the PDA. Characteristically, the ascending aorta and pulmonary artery are dilated, and the left-sided chambers are enlarged. *Echocardiography* may not directly visualize the PDA but can accurately identify it by a Doppler signal that often parallels the length of the PDA. Left heart dilation and pulmonary hypertension can be quantified and monitored. Cardiac catheterization to assess pulmonary vascular resistance is commonly indicated before closure.

Rx Treatment

After ligation of a PDA in infancy or early childhood, bacterial endocarditis prophylaxis is not required, cardiac function is commonly normal, and no special follow-up is required. In patients with an audible PDA by auscultation but without Eisenmenger's disease, the combined risk of endarteritis, heart failure, and late mortality provides the rationale for shunt closure. If pulmonary artery pressure and/or pulmonary vascular resistance are substantially elevated, preoperative evaluation should assess the degree of reversibility. With Eisenmenger's disease, closure is contraindicated.

The PDA can be closed surgically or via transcatheter methods. Reported operative mortality rates vary from less than 1 to 8%, depending on the presence of calcification and the degree of pulmonary hypertension. Transcatheter or coil occlusion is an accepted procedure in adults. Residual shunt rates vary from 0.5 to 8%, depending on the device used. Small residual defects that are detected by echocardiography but are not associated with an audible murmur or hemodynamic findings do not appear to carry a significant risk for endarteritis.

AORTOPULMONARY WINDOW

An aortopulmonary window is typically a large defect across the adjacent segments of both great vessels above their respective valves and below the pulmonary artery bifurcation. The pathophysiology is similar to that of a PDA. The shunt is usually large, so pulmonary vascular resistance rises rapidly and abolishes the aortopulmonary gradient in diastole. The murmur is usually best heard at the third left intercostal space. With a right-to-left shunt, differential cyanosis never occurs because the shunt is proximal to the brachiocephalic vessels. Differentiation of an aortopulmonary window from a PDA can usually be confirmed with echocardiography; the left-to-right shunt is seen in the main pulmonary artery in the former as compared with the left pulmonary artery bifurcation in the latter. Cardiac catheterization confirms the diagnosis and hemodynamics. Surgical repair is necessary unless pulmonary vascular obstructive disease precludes closure.

PULMONARY ARTERIOVENOUS FISTULAS

Pulmonary arteriovenous fistulas can occur as isolated congenital disorders or as part of generalized hereditary hemorrhagic telangiectasia, or Osler-Weber-Rendu syndrome. These fistulas typically occur in the lower lobes or the right middle lobe and can be small or large, single or multiple. The arterial supply usually comes from a dilated, tortuous branch of the pulmonary artery.

The most common finding is that of abnormal opacity on a chest radiograph in a patient with buccal ruby patches or in an otherwise healthy adult who has mild cyanosis. Shunting between deoxygenated pulmonary arterial blood and the oxygenated pulmonary venous blood results in a physiologic right-to-left shunt. The degree of shunting is typically small and not significant enough to result in dilation of the left atrium and ventricle. Heart failure is unusual. Hemoptysis can result if a fistula ruptures into a bronchus. In patients with hereditary hemorrhagic telangiectasia, angiomas occur on the lips and mouth, as well as the gastrointestinal tract, and on pleural, liver, and vaginal surfaces. Epistaxis is most common, but cerebrovascular accidents can also occur. Patients with hereditary hemorrhagic telangiectasia can have symptoms that resemble those of a transient ischemic attack even in the absence of right-to-left shunting. On *physical examination,* cyanosis and clubbing can be notable or barely detectable. Auscultation can disclose soft systolic or continuous noncardiac murmurs on the chest wall adjacent to the fistula. The murmur typically increases with inspiration. The *ECG* is usually normal. The *chest radiograph* shows one or more densities, typically in the lower lobes or in the right middle lobe. An *echocardiogram* can confirm the presence of the fistula by showing early opacification of the left atrium in the absence of any other intracardiac communication when saline is injected into a peripheral vein. The absence of a hemodynamically significant shunt can be confirmed by documenting normal cardiac chamber size.

If the hypoxemia is progressive or if a neurologic complication is documented to have occurred because of paradoxical emboli, fistula closure should be considered. Options include percutaneous catheter techniques if the fistula is small and accessible or a pulmonary wedge resection or lobectomy if the fistula is large. Multiple or recurrent fistulas create a major therapeutic challenge.

ISOLATED OBSTRUCTIVE LESIONS OF THE RIGHT AND LEFT VENTRICULAR OUTFLOW TRACT

Complications of obstructive lesions of the outflow tract relate to the secondary effects of exposure to pressure overload in the chamber proximal to the obstruction. The inability to increase systemic or pulmonary blood flow in the face of a fixed obstruction can cause exercise intolerance, inadequate myocardial perfusion, ventricular arrhythmias, and sudden death.

RIGHT VENTRICULAR OUTFLOW TRACT OBSTRUCTION

Obstruction of the right ventricular outflow tract can occur at the level of the pulmonary valve (see later), above it in the main pulmonary artery or its branches, or below it in the right ventricle itself. *Supravalvar* and *branch pulmonary artery stenoses* are important and common complications of patients with the tetralogy of Fallot (see later). Residual supravalvar pulmonary stenosis is sometimes seen after palliative pulmonary artery banding to decrease pulmonary blood flow in patients with large left-to-right shunts. Congenital branch pulmonary artery stenosis can occur in isolation or with valvar pulmonary stenosis, shunt lesions, or a variety of syndromes. Patients with Noonan's syndrome have a characteristic phenotypic facial appearance, short stature, and webbed neck; cardiac lesions may include a dysplastic pulmonary valve, left ventricular hypertrophic cardiomyopathy, and peripheral pulmonary artery stenosis. Supravalvar pulmonary stenosis can be seen with supravalvar aortic stenosis in Williams (elfin facies) syndrome.

Pulmonary atresia refers to an absent, imperforate, or closed pulmonary valve, which typically occurs in conjunction with other malformations. Pulmonary atresia with a nonrestrictive VSD is a complex cyanotic malformation that is discussed later.

Primary *infundibular stenosis* with an intact ventricular septum can result from a fibrous band just below the infundibulum. In a *double-chambered right ventricle,* obstruction is caused by anomalous muscle bundles that divide the right ventricle into a high-pressure chamber below the hypertrophied muscle bundles and a low-pressure chamber above the bundles and below the valve. The clinical features vary depending on the presence or absence of other lesions such as pulmonary valvar stenosis or VSD.

VALVAR PULMONARY STENOSIS

Isolated congenital *valvar pulmonary stenosis* is a common lesion caused by a bicuspid valve in 20% of cases, a dysplastic valve caused by myxomatous changes and severe thickening in 10% of cases, and an abnormal trileaflet valve in most of the remaining cases. Fusion of the leaflets results in a variable degree of thickening and calcification in older patients.

Twenty-five-year survival of patients with valvar pulmonary stenosis is greater than 95% but is worse in those with severe stenosis and peak systolic gradients greater than 80 mm Hg. For patients with mild (<50-mm Hg gradients) and moderate (50- to 80-mm Hg gradients) pulmonary stenosis, bacterial endocarditis, complex ventricular arrhythmias, and progression of the stenosis are uncommon.

Diagnosis

A patient with moderate or even severe pulmonary stenosis may be asymptomatic. With severe stenosis, exercise intolerance can be associated with presyncope and ventricular arrhythmias. Progressive right heart failure is the most common cause of death. On *physical examination* of patients with significant pulmonary stenosis, jugular venous pressure has a dominant *a* wave, reflecting a noncompliant right ventricle. Palpation discloses a sustained parasternal lift of right ventricular hypertrophy. An expiratory systolic ejection click is characteristic if the leaflets are still mobile. In moderate or severe stenosis, a grade 3 or louder systolic murmur can be heard and felt in the second left interspace. The length of the murmur increases as it peaks progressively later in systole with an increasing degree of obstruction. If right heart failure occurs, tricuspid insufficiency and systemic venous congestion develop. The *ECG* can show right axis deviation and tall, peaked right atrial P waves in lead II. With more than mild stenosis, the R wave exceeds the S wave in lead V_1. On *chest radiography,* the main pulmonary artery can be dilated even if the stenosis is mild. Characteristically, the left pulmonary artery is more dilated than the right because of the leftward direction of the high-velocity jet. A variable degree of right ventricular hypertrophy is manifested as right-sided chamber enlargement. *Echocardiography* can establish the diagnosis and determine the severity by Doppler ultrasound.

Rx Treatment

For patients with valvar pulmonic stenosis and gradients less than 50 mm Hg, conservative management is usually indicated unless symptoms are present. For patients with gradients greater than 80 mm Hg by cardiac catheterization and for symptomatic patients with gradients greater than 50 mm Hg, intervention is recommended. Percutaneous pulmonary angioplasty is the procedure of choice for adults, who achieve persistently good results at 10-year follow-up. For patients with subvalvar stenosis (double-chambered right ventricle), surgical resection of right ventricular muscle bands can be performed.

LEFT VENTRICULAR OUTFLOW TRACT OBSTRUCTION

Stenosis of the left ventricular outflow tract can occur at, below, or above the aortic valve. Discrete *subaortic stenosis,* most commonly caused by a fibromuscular ring located just below the valve, accounts for 15 to 20% of all cases of congenital obstruction of the left ventricular outflow tract. Concomitant aortic insufficiency occurs in 50% of cases. Supravalvar aortic stenosis occurs as a result of thickened media and intima above the aortic sinuses; early coronary atherosclerosis or even ostial coronary obstruction can occur.

CONGENITAL VALVAR AORTIC STENOSIS

The normal aortic valve has three cusps and commissures. A unicuspid aortic valve accounts for most cases of severe aortic stenosis in infants (Chapter 72). A *bicuspid aortic valve,* which is the most common congenital cardiac malformation, functions normally at birth but often becomes gradually obstructed as calcific and fibrous changes occur; prolapse of one or both cusps can cause aortic insufficiency.

The pathophysiology of aortic stenosis depends not only on its severity but also on the age at diagnosis. When a functionally normal bicuspid aortic valve becomes stenotic in adulthood because of degenerative changes, criteria for diagnosis and intervention parallel those for other forms of acquired aortic stenosis (Chapter 63). When the valve is congenitally stenotic, myocardium with a lifelong exposure to pressure overload behaves differently than if the hemodynamic burden occurred later in life.

The estimated overall 25-year survival rate for patients with congenital valvar aortic stenosis diagnosed in childhood is 85%. Children with initial peak cardiac catheterization gradients less than 50 mm Hg have long-term survival rates of higher than 90%, as opposed to survival rates of 80% in those with gradients of 50 mm Hg or greater.

Diagnosis

Symptoms include angina, exertional dyspnea, presyncope, and syncope and may progress to heart failure. The auscultatory hallmark of a bicuspid aortic valve is an audible systolic ejection click that is typically of a higher pitch than the first heart sound and is best heard not at the cardiac base but at the apex. The sound is caused by sudden movement of the stenotic valve as it moves superiorly in systole and is followed by the typical aortic stenosis murmur (Chapter 72). When significant calcification of the valve results in reduced mobility, the ejection sound is no longer heard. The diagnosis is easily confirmed by two-dimensional echocardiography, with which the number and orientation of aortic cusps can readily be identified.

Rx Treatment

Conservative management is generally indicated for mild stenosis with a peak gradient of less than 25 mm Hg, but close supervision is required because 20% of these patients require an intervention during long-term follow-up. Unlimited athletic participation is allowed only for asymptomatic patients with peak gradients of less than 20 to 25 mm Hg, a normal ECG, and a normal exercise test. For children who are symptomatic or have gradients greater than 30 mm Hg but do not have significant aortic insufficiency, transcatheter aortic valvotomy is preferred. Aortic valvuloplasty can be considered in young adults, but calcification limits its success and valve replacement is usually required (Chapter 72). For adults, treatment decisions are similar to those for aortic stenosis from other causes. For patients with subvalvar aortic stenosis, surgical intervention is indicated in the presence of peak gradients above 50 mm Hg, symptoms, or progressive aortic insufficiency.

COARCTATION OF THE AORTA

Aortic coarctation typically occurs just distal to the left subclavian artery at the site of the aortic ductal attachment or its residual ligamentum arteriosum. Less commonly the coarctation ridge lies proximal to the left subclavian. A bicuspid aortic valve is the most common coexisting anomaly, but VSDs and PDAs are also seen. "Pseudocoarctation" refers to buckling or kinking of the aortic arch without the presence of a significant gradient.

The most common complications of aortic coarctation are systemic hypertension and secondary left ventricular hypertrophy with heart failure. Systemic hypertension is caused by decreased vascular compliance in the proximal aorta and activation of the renin-angiotensin system in response to renal artery hypoperfusion below the obstruction. Left ventricular hypertrophy occurs in response to chronic pressure overload. Congestive heart failure occurs most commonly in infants and then after 40 years of age. The high pressure proximal to the obstruction stimulates the growth of collateral vessels from the internal mammary, scapular, and superior intercostal arteries to the intercostals of the descending aorta. Collateral circulation increases with age and contributes to perfusion of the lower extremities and the spinal cord. This mechanism, although adaptive in a patient who has not undergone surgery, accounts for significant morbidity during surgery when the motor impairment results from inadequate protection of spinal perfusion. Aneurysms occur most notably in the ascending aorta and in the circle of Willis. Premature coronary disease is thought to be related to the resulting hypertension. Complications, including bacterial endarteritis at the coarctation site or, more commonly, endocarditis at the site of a bicuspid aortic valve, cerebrovascular complications, myocardial infarction,

heart failure, and aortic dissection, occur in 2 to 6% of patients, more frequently in those with advancing age who have not undergone surgery.

Diagnosis

Young adults may be asymptomatic with incidental systemic hypertension and decreased lower extremity pulses. Coarctation should always be considered in adolescents and young adult men with unexplained upper extremity hypertension. The pressure differential can cause epistaxis, headaches, leg fatigue, or claudication. Older patients have angina, symptoms of heart failure, and vascular complications.

On *physical examination*, the lower half of the body is typically slightly less developed than the upper half. The hips are narrow and the legs are short, in contrast to broad shoulders and long arms. Blood pressure measurements should be obtained in each arm and one leg; an abnormal measurement is a less than 10 mm Hg increase in popliteal systolic blood pressure as compared with arm systolic blood pressure. The diastolic pressure should be the same in the upper and lower extremities. A pressure differential of more than 30 mm Hg between the right and the left arms is consistent with compromised flow in the left subclavian artery. Right brachial palpation characteristically reveals a strong or even bounding pulse as compared with a slowly rising or absent femoral, popliteal, or pedal pulse. Examination of the eyegrounds can reveal tortuous or corkscrew retinal arteries. Precordial palpation is consistent with left ventricular pressure overload. On auscultation, a systolic ejection sound reflecting the presence of a bicuspid aortic valve should be sought. The coarctation itself generates a systolic murmur heard posteriorly, in the mid-thoracic region, the length of which correlates with the severity of the coarctation. Over the anterior of the chest, systolic murmurs reflecting increased collateral flow can be heard in the infraclavicular areas and the sternal edge or in the axillae.

In adult coarctation, the most common finding on the *ECG* is left ventricular hypertrophy. *Chest radiographic* findings are diagnostic. Location of the coarctation segment between the dilated left subclavian artery above and the leftward convexity of the descending aorta below results in the "3 sign" (Fig. 65–7). Bilateral

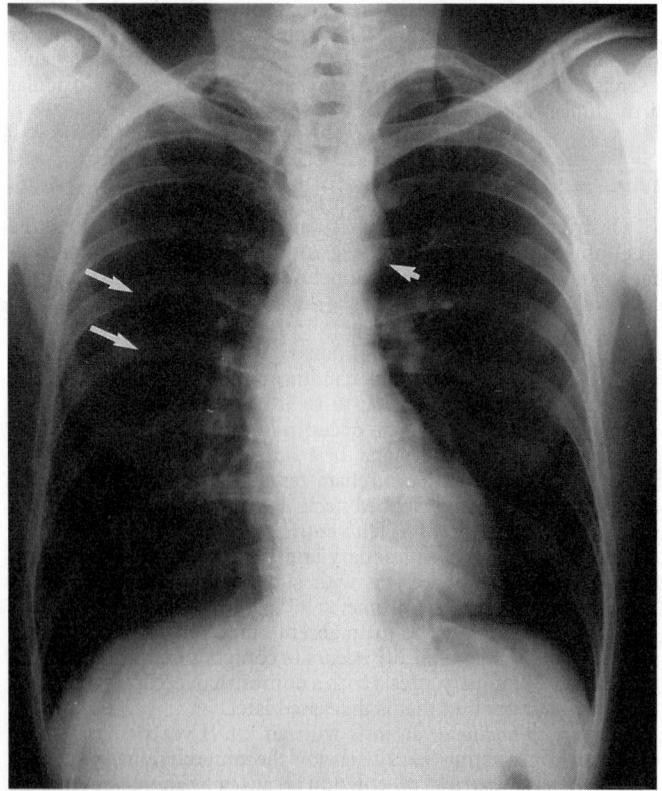

FIGURE 65–7 • Chest radiograph of a patient with coarctation of the aorta showing the radiographic "3" formed by the dilated subclavian artery above and the dilated aorta below (short arrow). Note the notching best seen at the level of the seventh and eighth ribs (long arrows). The dilated ascending aortic segment can also be seen.

rib notching as a result of dilation of the posterior intercostal arteries is seen on the posterior of the 3rd to 8th ribs when the coarctation is located below the left subclavian. Unilateral rib notching sparing the left ribs is observed when the coarctation occurs proximal to the left subclavian artery. Transthoracic *echocardiography* documents the gradient in the descending aorta and determines the presence of left ventricular hypertrophy. MRI (Chapter 53) is the best modality for visualizing the anatomy of the descending aorta. *Cardiac catheterization* should measure pressures and assess collaterals when surgery is contemplated.

 Treatment

Intervention is considered in patients with gradients greater than 30 mm Hg on cardiac catheterization. Fifty per cent of patients repaired when older than 40 years have residual hypertension, whereas those who have undergone surgery between the ages of 1 and 5 years have a less than 10% prevalence of hypertension on long-term follow-up. Balloon angioplasty is the treatment of choice for focal recoarctation in previously operated patients. The incidence of incomplete relief and restenosis is decreased in adults by endovascular stent placement. Focal complications include aortic aneurysms and, rarely, aortic rupture.

ANOMALIES OF THE SINUSES OF VALSALVA AND CORONARY ARTERIES

SINUS OF VALSALVA ANEURYSMS

At the base of the aortic root, the aortic valve cusps are attached to the aortic wall, above which three small pouches, or sinuses, are seated. The right coronary artery originates from one sinus and the left main coronary artery from a second; the third is called the *noncoronary sinus*. A weakness in the wall of the sinus can result in aneurysm formation with or without rupture. In more than 90% of cases the aneurysm involves the right or noncoronary cusp. Rupture typically occurs into the right heart at the right atrial or ventricular level with a resulting large left-to-right shunt driven by the high aortic pressure.

A previously asymptomatic young man typically has chest pain and rapidly progressing shortness of breath sometimes after physical strain. The *physical examination* is consistent with significant heart failure. Even if the communication is between the aorta and the right heart, biventricular failure is not unusual. The classic murmur is loud and continuous, often with a thrill. A murmur of aortic insufficiency secondary to damage to the adjacent aortic valve may be superimposed. The *chest radiograph* shows volume overload of both ventricles with evidence of shunt vascularity and pulmonary venous congestion. The *echocardiogram* is diagnostic. *Cardiac catheterization* can verify the integrity of the coronary artery adjacent to the ruptured aneurysm.

Even though symptoms may abate as the heart dilates, progressive cardiac decompensation typically results in death within 1 year of the rupture. A ruptured sinus of Valsalva aneurysm therefore requires urgent surgical repair.

CORONARY ARTERY FISTULAS

Fistulas arise from the right or left coronary arteries and in 90% of cases drain into the right ventricle, the right atrium, or the pulmonary artery in order of decreasing frequency. Typically, young patients are asymptomatic, but supraventricular arrhythmias are seen with progressive dilation of the intracardiac chambers. Angina can occur as the fistula creates a coronary steal by diverting blood away from the myocardium. Congestive heart failure is seen with large fistulas. A continuous murmur heard in a young, otherwise normal acyanotic, asymptomatic patient should raise suspicion of the diagnosis. Most fistulas are associated with a small shunt and hence the murmur is often less than grade 3 and is heard in the precordial area. Unless the shunt is large, the *ECG* is normal, as is the *chest radiograph*. The *echocardiogram*, especially the TEE, is diagnostic. Percutaneous transcatheter closure with coil embolization is preferred, but surgical ligation is also an alternative.

ANOMALOUS ORIGIN OF THE CORONARY ARTERIES

The left main coronary artery normally arises from the left sinus of Valsalva and courses leftward, posterior to the right ventricular outflow tract. The right coronary artery arises from the right sinus of Valsalva and courses rightward to the right ventricle. Isolated ectopic or anomalous origins of the coronary arteries (see Fig. 54–2) are seen in 0.6 to 1.5% of patients undergoing coronary angiography.

The most common anomaly is ectopic origin of the left circumflex artery from the right sinus of Valsalva, followed by anomalous origin of the right coronary artery from the left sinus and anomalous origin of the left main coronary artery from the right sinus. If the anomalous coronary artery does not course between the pulmonary artery and aorta, the prognosis is favorable. Risks of ischemia, myocardial infarction, and death are greatest when the left main coronary artery courses between both great vessels.

Coronary arteries can also originate from the pulmonary trunk. If both the right and left arteries originate from the pulmonary trunk, death usually occurs in the neonatal period. If only the left anterior descending coronary artery originates from the pulmonary trunk, the rate of survival to adulthood is approximately 10%, depending on the development of collateral retrograde flow to the anomalous artery from a normal coronary artery. This collateral flow may cause a continuous murmur along the left sternal border, congestive heart failure from the large shunt, and a coronary steal syndrome as blood is diverted away from the normal artery.

A single coronary ostium can provide a single coronary artery that branches into right and left coronary arteries, the left then giving rise to the circumflex and the anterior descending arteries. The ostium can originate from the right or left aortic sinus. The coronary circulation is functionally normal unless one of the branches passes between the aorta and the pulmonary artery.

Diagnostic procedures include angiography, MRI, and TEE. For an anomalous coronary artery that originates from the pulmonary artery, surgical reimplantation into the aorta is preferred. For an anomalous artery that courses between the pulmonary artery and aorta, a bypass graft to the distal vessel is preferred.

SPECIFIC COMPLEX LESIONS

TETRALOGY OF FALLOT

Tetralogy of Fallot, the most common cyanotic malformation, is characterized by superior and anterior displacement of the subpulmonary infundibular septum, which causes the tetrad of pulmonary stenosis, VSD, aortic override, and right ventricular hypertrophy. The VSD is perimembranous in 80% of cases. Additional cardiac anomalies include a right-sided aortic arch in up to 25% of patients. An anomalous left anterior descending artery originating from the right coronary cusp and crossing over the right ventricular outflow tract is seen in 10% of cases. Other associated anomalies include ASD, left superior vena cava, defects of the atrioventricular canal, and aortic insufficiency. With pulmonary atresia, pulmonary blood flow occurs via aortic-to-pulmonary collaterals. Life expectancy is limited unless staged reconstructive surgery is performed.

The physiology in unrepaired tetralogy of Fallot is determined by the severity and location of the pulmonic outflow obstruction and by the interaction of pulmonary and systemic vascular resistance across a nonrestrictive VSD. Because the pulmonary stenosis results in a relatively fixed pulmonary resistance, a drop in systemic vascular resistance as occurs with exercise is associated with increased right-to-left shunting and increasing cyanosis. A child who squats after running is attempting to reverse the process by increasing systemic vascular resistance by crouching with bent knees. Native pulmonary blood flow is typically insufficient. Unless a PDA has remained open, a cyanotic adult will typically have undergone a palliative procedure to increase pulmonary blood flow.

Examination of unrepaired patients reveals central cyanosis and clubbing. The right ventricular impulse is prominent. The second heart sound is single and represents the aortic closure sound with an absent or inconspicuous P_2. Typically, little or no systolic murmur is heard across the pulmonary valve because the more severe the obstruction, the more right-to-left shunting occurs and the less blood flows across a diminutive right ventricular outflow tract. A diastolic murmur of aortic insufficiency is often heard in adults. In the presence of a palliative systemic arterial–to–pulmonary artery shunt, the high-pressure gradient generates a loud continuous murmur. In a patient who has not undergone surgery, progressive infundibular stenosis and cyanosis occur. Before the advent of palliative surgery, mortality rates were 50% in the first few years of life and survival past the third decade was unusual.

Complete surgical repair consists of patch closure of the VSD and relief of the right ventricular outflow tract obstruction. Adequate pulmonary blood flow is ensured by reconstructing the distal pulmonary artery bed. Previous palliative shunts are usually taken down. Complete repair in childhood yields a 90 to 95% 10-year survival rate with good functional results, and 30-year survival rates may be as high as 85%. Total correction with low mortality and a favorable long-term follow-up is possible even in adulthood.

After repair, residual pulmonary stenosis, proximal or distal, with a right ventricular pressure greater than 50% of systemic occurs in up to 25% of patients. Some degree of pulmonary insufficiency is common, particularly if a patch has been inserted at the level of the pulmonary valve or if a pulmonary valvotomy has been performed. Residual VSDs can be found in up to 20% of patients. Patients may be asymptomatic or may have symptoms related to long-term complications following surgical repair. Symptoms can reflect residual right ventricular pressure or volume overload or arrhythmias at rest or with exercise. Angina can occur in a young patient if surgical repair has damaged an anomalous left anterior descending artery as it courses across the right ventricular outflow tract. In acyanotic adults, clubbing commonly regresses. A right ventricular impulse is often felt as a result of residual pulmonary insufficiency or stenosis. Typically, no functioning pulmonary valve is present and hence the second heart sound is still single. A systolic murmur can represent residual pulmonary stenosis, residual VSD, or tricuspid insufficiency. A diastolic murmur can reflect aortic or pulmonary insufficiency. Ventricular arrhythmias are common following repair, with an incidence of sudden death as high as 5%.

The *ECG* in unrepaired tetralogy of Fallot shows right axis deviation, right atrial enlargement, and dominant right ventricular forces over the precordial leads. The most common finding following repair is complete right bundle branch block, which is seen in 80 to 90% of patients. The *chest radiograph* typically shows an upturned apex with a concave pulmonary artery segment giving the classic appearance of a "boot-shaped" heart. Figure 65–8 demonstrates the findings in an adult following repair. The apex is persistently upturned, although the pulmonary artery segment is no longer concave. *Echocardiography* can confirm the diagnosis and document intracardiac complications in repaired and unrepaired patients. Shunt patency can be determined by Doppler. *MRI* can accurately document stenosis in the distal pulmonary artery bed. *Cardiac catheterization* is reserved for patients in whom operative or reoperative treatment is contemplated or in whom the integrity of the coronary circulation needs to be verified.

Patients with a change in exercise tolerance, angina, or evidence of heart failure, as well as those with symptomatic arrhythmias and/or syncope, should be referred for complete evaluation. Surgical *reintervention* is generally considered when right ventricular pressure is more than two thirds as high as systemic pressure because of residual right ventricular outflow tract obstruction, free pulmonary regurgitation occurs with right ventricular dysfunction and/or sustained arrhythmias, or a residual VSD causes a significant shunt.

COMPLETE TRANSPOSITION OF THE GREAT ARTERIES

Complete TGA is the second most common cyanotic lesion, and surgically corrected adults are increasingly common. In simple TGA, the atria and ventricles are in their normal positions but the aorta arises from the right ventricle and the pulmonary artery arises from the left ventricle. When the aorta is anterior and rightward with respect to the pulmonary artery, as is most common, D-transposition is present. The native anatomy has the pulmonary and systemic circulations in parallel, with deoxygenated blood recirculating between the right side of the heart and the systemic circulation, whereas oxygenated blood recirculates from the left side of the heart to the lungs. The condition is incompatible with life unless a VSD, PDA, or ASD is present or an ASD is created; a hemodynamically significant VSD is present in 15% of cases. Subpulmonary obstruction of the *left* ventricular outflow tract occurs in 10 to 25% of cases.

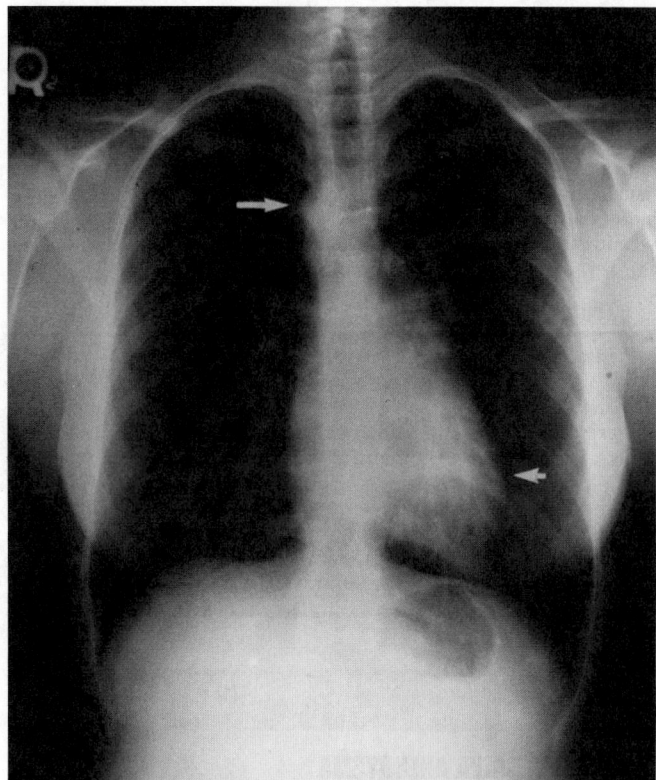

FIGURE 65–8 • Chest radiograph of an adult after tetralogy of Fallot repair. A right aortic arch with rightward indentation of the trachea (long arrow) can be seen. The right ventricular apex remains upturned (short arrow). Note the sternal wires consistent with intracardic repair, thus clarifying the fullness of the pulmonary artery segment often seen after extensive enlargement of the right ventricular outflow tract.

The *Senning* or *Mustard atrial baffle repairs*, which were the first corrective procedures, redirect oxygenated blood from the left atrium to the right ventricle so that it may be ejected into the aorta while deoxygenated blood detours the right atrium and heads for the left ventricle and into the pulmonary artery. Although this operation results in acyanotic physiology, the right ventricle assumes a permanent position under the aorta and pumps against systemic pressures, a lifelong task for which it was not designed. When the subpulmonary obstruction is significant, the *Rastelli* procedure reroutes blood at the ventricular level by tunneling the left ventricle to the *aorta* inside the heart through a VSD. A conduit is then inserted outside the heart between the left ventricle and aorta. More recently, the *arterial switch operation* transects the aorta and pulmonary artery above their respective valves and switches them to become realigned with their physiologic outflow tracts and appropriate ventricles. The proximal coronary arteries are translocated from the sinuses of the native aorta to the neoaorta (native pulmonary artery). In this operation, each ventricle reassumes the role that it was embryologically destined to fulfill.

If an adult patient is cyanotic and has a native intracardiac shunt or a palliative shunt, referral to an appropriate facility should be undertaken to explore the possibility of intracardiac repair. At present, adults with TGA most commonly have undergone an *atrial baffle repair*, with an expected 15-year survival rate of 75% and a 20-year survival rate of 70%. For patients with an atrial baffle procedure, symptoms include exercise intolerance, palpitations caused by bradyarrhythmias or atrial flutter, and right ventricular failure. Typically the patient is acyanotic unless a baffle leak exists. The clinical findings are determined by the presence or absence of systemic right ventricular failure. On auscultation, the second heart sound is classically single. The ECG reveals sinus bradycardia, but nodal rhythms and heart block occur as the patient ages. The chest radiograph shows a variable degree of right ventricular enlargement. Echocardiography can be used to confirm the diagnosis and explore related abnormalities. Cardiac catheterization is performed when an operation or reoperation is contemplated.

Reoperation is performed in approximately 20% of patients for baffle-related complications, progressive left ventricular outflow tract stenosis, or severe tricuspid regurgitation.

CONGENITALLY CORRECTED TRANSPOSITION OF THE GREAT ARTERIES

In congenitally corrected TGA, the great arteries are transposed, the ventricles are inverted, but the atria remain in their normal position. The systemic circulation (left atrium, morphologic right ventricle, and aorta) and pulmonary circulation (right atrium, morphologic left ventricle, and pulmonary artery) are in series. The patient is therefore acyanotic unless an intracardiac shunt is also present. The right ventricle is aligned with the aorta and performs lifelong systemic work, which accounts in part for its eventual failure. Associated lesions include a VSD, pulmonary stenosis, and Ebstein's malformation of the left-sided tricuspid valve. Complete heart block develops at a rate of 2% per year. Patients with congenitally corrected TGA and no other associated defects can remain free of symptoms until the sixth decade, at which time significant atrioventricular valve regurgitation, failure of the right (systemic) ventricle, supraventricular arrhythmias, and heart block occur.

RIGHT-SIDED EBSTEIN'S ANOMALY

The septal and posterior cusps of the tricuspid valve are largely derived from the right ventricle as it liberates a layer of muscle that skirts away from the cavity to become valve tissue. When this process occurs abnormally, the posterior and septal cusps of the tricuspid valve remain tethered to the muscle and adhere to the right ventricular surface—hence the diagnostic hallmark of Ebstein's anomaly, apical displacement of the septal tricuspid leaflet.

In right-sided Ebstein's anomaly of the tricuspid valve, the right heart consists of three anatomic components: right atrium proper, true right ventricle, and the atrialized portion of the right ventricle between the two. The displaced septal and posterior tricuspid leaflets lie between the atrialized right ventricle and the true right ventricle. In mild Ebstein's anomaly, the degree of tricuspid leaflet tethering is only mild, the anterior leaflet retains mobility, and the size of the true right ventricle is only mildly reduced. Severe Ebstein's anomaly is associated with severe tethering of the tricuspid leaflet tissue and a diminutive, hypocontractile true right ventricle. Functionally the valve is regurgitant because it is unable to appose its three leaflets during ventricular contraction. Valvar regurgitation and asynchronous, abnormal right ventricular function cause the dilation and right heart failure observed in the more severe forms of the lesion. The wide spectrum of severity of the anomaly is based on the degree of tricuspid leaflet tethering and the relative proportion of atrialized and true right ventricle. The most common associated cardiac defect, a secundum ASD or patent foramen ovale, is reported in more than 50% of patients. On physical examination, a clicking "sail sound" is heard as the second component of S_1 when tricuspid valve closure becomes loud and delayed.

The 12-lead ECG typically shows highly peaked P waves with a wide, often bizarre-looking QRS complex. Pre-excitation occurs in 20% of patients; supraventricular tachyarrhythmias, atrial fibrillation, and atrial flutter occur in 30 to 40% of patients and constitute the most common findings in adolescents and adults with right-sided Ebstein's anomaly.

When patients of all ages are taken together, the predicted mortality is approximately 50% by the fourth or fifth decade. Complications include atrial arrhythmias due to severe right atrial enlargement and cyanosis caused by a right-to-left atrial shunt as tricuspid insufficiency increases and the right ventricle fails. Atrial arrhythmias, cyanosis, and the presence of an intra-atrial communication also increase the risk of stroke.

Intervention is considered when functional status or cyanosis worsens, significant atrial arrhythmias are documented, and/or a cerebrovascular accident occurs. Surgical options include replacement or repair of the tricuspid valve and closure of the ASD. The feasibility of tricuspid valvuloplasty depends on the size and mobility of the anterior tricuspid leaflet, which is used to construct a unicuspid right-sided valve.

ATRIOVENTRICULAR CANAL DEFECT

Embryologic septation of the atrioventricular canal results in closure of the inferior portion of the interatrial septum and the superior portion of the interventricular septum. Septation is achieved with the growth of endocardial cushions, which also contribute to development of the mitral and tricuspid valves. Hence the nomenclature *atrioventricular canal defect* or *endocardial cushion defect* is used to designate this group of anomalies.

A *partial atrioventricular canal defect* refers to an ostium primum ASD with a cleft mitral valve. The anomaly is manifested as a hemodynamic combination of an ASD with a variable degree of mitral regurgitation. The 12-lead ECG shows the typical findings of left axis deviation with a Q wave in leads I and aVL and a prolonged PR interval. The echocardiogram shows a defect in the inferior portion of the interatrial septum and a cleft mitral valve.

A *complete atrioventricular canal defect* is an uncommon defect consisting of a primum ASD, an inlet VSD that usually extends to the membranous interventricular septum, and a common atrioventricular valve. Unoperated adults usually have Eisenmenger's syndrome unless concomitant pulmonary stenosis has protected the pulmonary vascular bed or the VSD has undergone spontaneous closure, in which case the physiologic consequences are similar to those of a partial atrioventricular canal.

Surgical repair of an atrioventricular defect consists of closing the interatrial and/or interventricular communication with reconstruction of the common atrioventricular valve or closure of the cleft in the mitral valve. An adult who has undergone repair may have significant residual regurgitation of the mitral or tricuspid valve. Even after surgery, acquired subaortic obstruction can occur in the long left ventricular outflow tract, which has a classic "gooseneck deformity" on cardiac angiography.

UNIVENTRICULAR HEART AND TRICUSPID ATRESIA

The terms *single ventricle*, *common ventricle*, and *univentricular heart* have been used interchangeably to describe the "double-inlet" ventricle, in which one ventricular chamber receives flow from both the tricuspid and mitral valves. In 75 to 90% of cases, the single ventricle is a morphologic left ventricle. Obstruction of one of the great arteries is common, and life expectancy is short without an operation. The patients most likely to survive to adulthood palliated or, rarely, unoperated have a single ventricle of the left morphologic type, with pulmonary stenosis protecting the pulmonary vascular bed.

In tricuspid atresia, no orifice is found between the right atrium and right ventricle, and an underdeveloped or hypoplastic right ventricle is present. The morphologic left ventricle is consistently normally developed and therefore becomes the single functional ventricle. Typically, blood flows into the right atrium then through an obligatory ASD and to the left atrium, where it then proceeds to the left ventricle. Variable features include a VSD, abnormal position of the great arteries, and the relative degree of pulmonary stenosis, all of which are used to classify tricuspid atresia. Unoperated, 50% of patients die in the first 6 months and 90% in the first decade.

Adult patients rarely are unoperated. They may be acyanotic after the Fontan operation; if cyanotic and palliated, the patient may benefit from further palliation or may be eligible for the Fontan operation. With the Glenn shunt or the Fontan operation, a direct anastomosis is created between the systemic venous and pulmonary circulations. Venous blood flows passively from the systemic veins to the pulmonary circulation and returns oxygenated to a left-sided atrium and into the single functional ventricle, which then pumps oxygenated blood into the systemic circulation. The Glenn anastomosis diverts part of the systemic venous return to the lungs, whereas the Fontan procedure makes the patient acyanotic by diverting the entire systemic venous circulation to the pulmonary vascular bed. For optimum results, a successful Fontan operation requires low pulmonary vascular resistance, preserved single ventricular function, and an unobstructed anastomosis between the systemic veins and the pulmonary arteries. At 5-year follow-up, 80% or more of Fontan survivors are in New York Heart Association functional class I or II, with successful pregnancy reported in a small number of patients. When patients of all ages are considered together, 10-year survival rates vary from 60 to 70%. Late deaths are due to reoperation, arrhythmia, ventricular failure, and protein-losing enteropathy.

VASCULAR MALFORMATIONS

AORTIC ARCH ANOMALIES

VASCULAR RINGS AND OTHER ARCH ANOMALIES. One of the most frequent developmental errors of the aortic arch is an aberrant right subclavian artery originating distal to the left subclavian and coursing rightward behind the esophagus at the level of the third thoracic vertebrae. Although the finding is frequent, symptoms are uncommon. When symptoms occur, the term *dysphagia lusoria* has been used in reference to swallowing difficulties that result from esophageal compression. Abnormal development of the brachial arches and dorsal aorta can result in a variety of anomalies that lead to the formation of *vascular rings* around the trachea and esophagus. The outcome is often benign, but symptoms of respiratory compromise or dysphagia warrant surgery. When the left pulmonary artery arises from the right and passes leftward between the trachea and esophagus, a *pulmonary artery sling* occurs. Symptoms of tracheal compression warrant correction.

A *right aortic arch* occurs when the aortic arch courses toward the right instead of the left. Mirror-image branching is the most common anatomic variant. In most cases, this anomaly coexists with other congenital lesions, notably tetralogy of Fallot.

ANOMALOUS VENOUS CONNECTIONS

ANOMALIES OF SYSTEMIC VENOUS RETURN. A *persistent left superior vena cava* can be fortuitously diagnosed on a chest radiograph or on echocardiography. Its clinical relevance depends on development of the coronary sinus. If the coronary sinus is normally formed, typically the left superior vena cava drains into the right atrium through the coronary sinus. If the coronary sinus is not normally developed, the persistent left superior vena cava drains into the left atrium and cyanosis results from the obligatory right-to-left shunt. The latter commonly occurs with an ASD or a complex cardiac anomaly. Venous return above the renal veins can be abnormal with *inferior vena cava interruption* and azygos or hemiazygos continuation. In the former, inferior vena cava flow above the renal veins continues into the azygos vein, which courses normally up the right of the spine to empty into the junction between the superior vena cava and right atrium. In a less common anatomic arrangement, the caval flow empties into a hemiazygos vein, which empties into a persistent left superior vena cava. The finding rarely occurs in isolation but can be seen in patients with associated simple or complex malformations.

ANOMALIES OF PULMONARY VENOUS RETURN. In *partial anomalous pulmonary venous return*, one or more but not all four pulmonary veins are not connected to the left atrium. The most common pattern has the right pulmonary veins connected to the superior vena cava, usually with a *sinus venosus* ASD. Anomalous connection of the right pulmonary veins to the inferior vena cava results in a chest radiographic shadow that resembles a Turkish sword, hence the designation *scimitar syndrome*. Associated anomalies include hypoplasia of the right lung, anomalies of the bronchial system, hypoplasia of the right pulmonary artery, and dextroposition of the heart. Partial anomalous pulmonary venous return results in a left-to-right shunt physiology similar to that of an ASD.

In *total anomalous pulmonary venous return,* all the pulmonary veins connect abnormally to either the right atrium or one of the systemic veins above or below the diaphragm. Concurrent obstruction of the pulmonary veins is present when drainage occurs below the diaphragm and variable when drainage occurs above it. An ASD is essential to sustain life. One third of cases occur with major complex cardiac malformations.

In *cor triatriatum,* the pulmonary veins drain into an accessory chamber that is usually connected to the left atrium through an opening of variable size. The hemodynamic consequences are determined by the size of this opening and are similar to those of mitral stenosis. If symptoms of pulmonary venous hypertension occur, surgical treatment is indicated.

CARDIAC MALPOSITIONS

The normal heart is left sided and hence the designation *levocardia.* Cardiac malpositions are defined in terms of the intrathoracic position of the heart in relation to the position of the viscera (visceral situs), which are usually concordant with the position of the atria. That is, when the liver is on the right and the stomach is on the left, the atrium receiving systemic venous blood (right atrium) is right sided and the atrium receiving pulmonary venous blood (left atrium) is left sided. Asplenia and polysplenia syndromes are associated with a variety of complex cardiovascular malformations.

DEXTROCARDIA AND MESOCARDIA. In *dextrocardia* the heart is on the right side of the thorax with or without situs inversus. When the heart is right sided with inverted atria, a right-sided stomach, and a left-sided liver, the combination is *dextrocardia with situs inversus.* In this arrangement, also called *mirror-image dextrocardia,* the ventricles are inverted, but so are the viscera and therefore the atria. The heart usually functions normally, and the diagnosis is often fortuitous. The heart sounds are louder on the right side of the chest and the liver is palpable on the left. The chest radiograph shows a right-sided cardiac apex with a lower left hemidiaphragm and a right-sided stomach bubble. The ECG shows an inverted P and T wave in lead I with a negative QRS deflection and a reverse pattern between aVR and aVL. A mirror-image progression is seen from V_1 to a right-sided V_6 lead. An echocardiogram should be performed to ensure that intracardiac anatomy is normal. When *dextrocardia with situs solitus* occurs, the ventricles are inverted but not the viscera and therefore not the atria. Associated severe cardiac malformations are typical. In mesocardia, the heart is centrally located in the chest with normal atrial and visceral anatomy. The apex is central or rightward-displaced on the chest radiograph. Typically, no associated cardiac malformations are present.

SPECIALIZED ISSUES

ENDOCARDITIS PROPHYLAXIS. Prolonged survival of patients with complex congenital heart disease has resulted in a population at increased risk for infective endocarditis (Chapter 310). Infection most commonly affects sites of turbulent blood flow on the low-pressure side of gradients. Such sites include restrictive VSDs; PDAs; a cleft mitral valve, aortic coarctation (most often at the site of an associated bicuspid aortic valve); and prosthetic shunts, valves, and conduits in a postoperative patient. The risk of endocarditis associated with isolated low-pressure lesions in the right heart is low.

Endocarditis should be suspected early and cultures obtained before antibiotic therapy is begun. Current recommendations for the prevention of bacterial endocarditis apply to most congenital heart lesions, with the exception of an isolated ASD and surgically repaired ASD, VSD, or PDA without residual shunting beyond 6 months after repair.

EXERCISE. The goal of exercise evaluation is to assess the functional results of therapeutic interventions and provide guidelines for exercise prescriptions. Patients with residual hemodynamic lesions or unrepaired congenital cardiac anomalies should be evaluated on an annual basis with physical examination, an ECG, and a cardiac ultrasonographic examination if indicated. Pertinent additional tests may include Holter monitoring and exercise testing. Attention should be directed to the detection of pulmonary hypertension, arrhythmias, myocardial dysfunction, and symptoms such as exercise-induced dizziness, syncope, dyspnea, or chest pain.

A series of exercise guidelines have been proposed for major groups of congenital heart defects (Table 65–2). Patients beyond 6 months after repair of a single shunt lesion without pulmonary hypertension, arrhythmias, or evidence of myocardial dysfunction can participate in all sports. In patients with residual shunts, if the peak pulmonary artery pressure is less than 40 mm Hg in the absence of ventricular dysfunction or significant arrhythmias, patients can enjoy a free range of activity. Patients with elevated pulmonary vascular resistance are at risk of sudden death during intense exercise; although most self-limit their activity, participation in competitive sports is contraindicated. Patients with aortic and pulmonary stenosis should be counseled as recommended earlier, according to gradient severity. For patients with uncomplicated aortic coarctation, athletic participation is permitted if the arm-leg blood pressure gradient is 20 mm Hg or less at rest and the peak systolic blood pressure during exercise is normal. For patients after tetralogy of Fallot repair, repair of TGA, and the Fontan operation, exercise recommendations vary according

Table 65–2 • EXERCISE RECOMMENDATIONS IN ADULTS WITH CONGENITAL HEART DISEASE

CONDITION	UNRESTRICTED	LOW/MODERATE INTENSITY*	PROHIBITED
ASD[†]	No PHT. No arrhythmia. Normal ventricular function	PA pressure > 40 mm Hg *with* normal ETT; no arrhythmia	Eisenmenger's
VSD[†]	Small. No PHT. No arrhythmia; normal ventricular function	Moderate VSD	Eisenmenger's
PDA[†]	Small. No PHT. No arrhythmia; normal ventricular function	PA pressure > 40 mm Hg *with* normal ETT; no arrhythmia	Eisenmenger's
Coarctation[‡]	Gradient ≤ 20 mm Hg arm to leg; normal BP at rest and exercise	Gradient ≥ 20 mm Hg arm to leg *with* normal BP and normal ETT	Gradient ≥ 50 mm Hg arm to leg *or* aortic aneurysm
PS	Gradient < 50 mm Hg. No arrhythmia; normal ventricular function	Gradient ≥ 50 mm Hg	Gradient ≥ 70 mm Hg *or* ventricular arrhythmia
AS	Gradient ≤ 20 mm Hg, normal ECG, normal ETT; asymptomatic	Gradient > 20 mm Hg *with* normal ECG, normal ETT; asymptomatic	Gradient ≥ 50 mm Hg *or* ventricular arrhythmia
TOF after repair	Normal RV pressure. No shunt. No arrhythmia	Increased RV pressure *or* moderate PR *or* SVT	RV pressure ≥ 65% systemic *or* ventricular; arrhythmia on ETT *or* severe PR
Mustard or Senning		No cardiomegaly, arrhythmia, or syncope. Normal ETT	Cardiomegaly *or* arrhythmia at rest or exercise
c-TGA unoperated	No cardiomegaly, Mild TR. No arrhythmia; normal ETT	Moderate RV dysfunction, moderate TR. No arrhythmia	Severe TR *or* uncontrolled arrhythmia
Ebstein's	Mild Ebstein's. No arrhythmia. Operated with mild TR	Moderate TR *with* no arrhythmia	Severe Ebstein's *or* uncontrolled arrhythmia
Fontan		Normal O₂ saturation *with* near-normal ETT and ventricular function	Moderate/severe MR/TR *or* uncontrolled arrhythmia

*Based on peak dynamic and static components of exercise during competition for individual sports (see credit line).
†Unoperated or 6 months after surgery.
‡Unoperated or 1 year after surgery.
AS = aortic stenosis; ASD = atrial septal defect; BP = blood pressure; c-TGA = corrected transposition of the great arteries; ECG = electrocardiogram; ETT = exercise toler-ance test; MR = mitral regurgitation; PA = pulmonary artery; PDA = patent ductus arteriosus; PHT = pulmonary hypertension; PR = pulmonary regurgitation; PS = pulmonary stenosis; RV = right ventricle; SVT = supraventricular tachyarrhythmia; TOF = tetralogy of Fallot; TR = tricuspid regurgitation; VSD = ventricular septal defect.
Based on guidelines recommended in Graham TP, Bricker TJ, James FW, et al: Task Force 1: Congenital Heart Disease, 26th Bethesda Conference. Eligibility for competi-tion in athletes with cardiovascular abnormalities. Reprinted with permission from the American College of Cardiology; *J Am Coll Cardiol* 1994;24:867.

to residual ventricular function and the presence or absence of arrhythmias.

1. Attie F, Rosas M, Granados N, et al: Surgical treatment for secundum atrial septal defects in patients >40 years old. A randomized clinical trial. J Am Coll Cardiol 2001;38:2035–2042.

SUGGESTED READINGS

Care of the Adult with Congenital Heart Disease. Paper presented at the 32nd Bethesda Conference, October 2–3, 2000, Bethesda, Maryland. J Am Coll Cardiol 2001;37:1161–1198. *The current consensus in terms of the changing profile, organiza-tion of care, and special needs of this patient population.*

Meier B, Lock JE: Contemporary management of patent foramen ovale. Circulation 2003;107:5–9. *A brief, practical review.*

Perloff JK, Child JS (eds): Congenital Heart Disease in Adults, 2nd ed. Philadelphia, WB Saunders, 1998. *Problem oriented rather than lesion oriented. Comprehensive coverage of all medical complications of congenital cardiac disease.*

Therrien J, Dore A, Gersony W, et al: CCS Consensus Conference 2001 update: Recommendations for the management of adults with congenital heart disease. I. Can J Cardiol 2001;17:940–959. II. Can J Cardiol 2001;17:1029–1050. *Updated prac-tical guidelines for the management of all the major congenital lesions seen in adults, with graded recommendations for intervention.*

66 ATHEROSCLEROSIS, THROMBOSIS, AND VASCULAR BIOLOGY

Valentin Fuster

Atherothrombotic cardiovascular disease is a diffuse condition involv-ing the heart (coronary arteries), brain (carotid, vertebral, cerebral arteries), aorta, and peripheral arteries. Most of the risk factors that apply to one arterial bed also apply to the others. The presence of one atherosclerotic cardiovascular disease increases the risk of developing others.

MORPHOLOGY OF CORONARY ATHEROSCLEROSIS-THROMBOSIS

Normal Artery

The normal artery consists essentially of a tube with an *intima* covered by a continuous layer of endothelial cells that maintains the circulating blood flow (antithrombotic), acts as a barrier to entry of circulating monocytes/macrophages (antiadhesion/migration) into the vessel wall, and regulates smooth muscle cell function (relaxation/anti-growth); the *media* of pure smooth muscle cells, which contract and maintain the tone of the artery wall, and of extracellular matrix or fibrils (elastin, collagen, and proteoglycans), which provide supportive structure; and the *adventitia* of loose connective tissue (fibroblasts, extracellular matrix, and vasa vasorum).

Atherosclerosis-Thrombosis

Atherosclerosis is the descriptive term for thickened and hardened lesions of the medium and large muscular and elastic arteries. This lesion is lipid-rich, in contrast to *arteriosclerosis*, which is the generic term for thickened and stiffened arteries of all sizes. In atherosclero-sis, lesions occur within the innermost layer of the artery (the intima), but the media and adventitia also may be involved. Lesions are gen-erally eccentric and, if they become complicated by mural or occlu-sive thrombosis, may cause ischemia with onset of clinical angina, or necrosis with the characteristic clinical sequelae of myocardial in-farction (MI) (Chapter 69), cerebral infarction (Chapter 439), or gan-grene of the extremities (Chapter 76); hence the term, *atherothrombosis*.

Classification and Phases of the Lesions of Coronary Atherosclerosis-Thrombosis

Progression of the atherosclerotic plaque in any arterial bed can be subdivided into six phases (Fig. 66–1). Phase 1 consists of a small lesion that commonly is found in persons younger than age 30 and that may progress over several years. Type I lesions consist of macrophage-derived foam cells that contain lipid droplets; type II lesions contain macrophages and smooth muscle cells with extra-cellular lipid deposits; and type III lesions contain smooth muscle cells surrounded by extracellular connective tissue, fibrils, and lipid deposits.

Phase 2 vulnerable lipid-rich plaques are prone to disruption because of their high lipid content. The lesion is categorized mor-phologically as one of two variants. Type IV plaques consist of con-fluent cellular lesions with a great deal of extracellular lipid intermixed with fibrous tissue, whereas type Va plaques possess an extracellular lipid core covered by a thin fibrous cap. Phase 2 can evolve into acute

Cardiovascular Disease

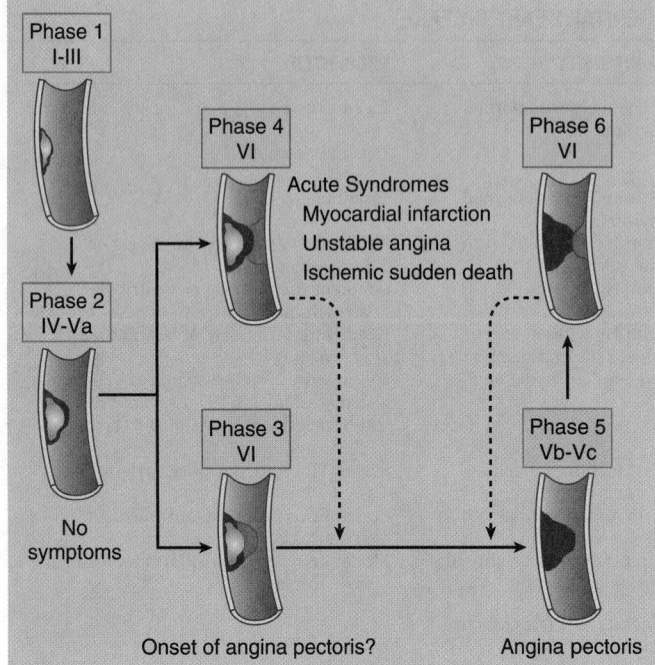

FIGURE 66–1 • Phases and morphology of the progression of coronary atherothrombosis according to clinical and gross pathology findings.

phase 3 with a mural thrombus, with or without the onset of clinical angina (Chapter 68), or phase 4, with an occlusive thrombus and an acute coronary syndrome (Chapters 68 and 69). Either phase 3 or phase 4 plaques can evolve into fibrotic plaques of phase 5, characterized by type Vb or Vc lesions, with or without predominant calcification. The significantly stenotic or occlusive and fibrotic types of Vb or Vc lesions of phase 5 may cause angina; however, because the preceding stenosis or occlusion with associated ischemia can give rise to a protective collateral circulation, these lesions may be silent clinically.

Approximately two thirds of the acute coronary syndromes relate to phase 4 or "complicated" type VI occlusive thrombosis and are the result of mild disruption of nonseverely stenotic lipid-rich plaques of phase 2. About one third relate to phase 6 or "complicated" type VI occlusive thrombus overlying a superficial erosion of a markedly stenotic and fibrotic plaque of phase 5.

VASCULAR BIOLOGY OF CORONARY ATHEROSCLEROSIS-THROMBOSIS

Early Dynamic Process of Lipoprotein Transport in Plaque Formation

Chronic minimal injury to the arterial endothelium is physiologic and is often the result of a disturbance in the pattern of blood flow at bending points and near bifurcations of the arterial tree. Local shear forces are probably enhanced in hypertension. In addition, chronic minimal endothelial injury or dysfunction, leading to accumulation of lipids and monocytes (macrophages), is produced by hypercholesterolemia, advanced glycation end products in diabetes, chemical irritants in tobacco smoke, circulating vasoactive amines, immune complexes, and infections (Fig. 66–2B).

Most lipids deposited in the atherosclerotic lesions are derived from plasma low-density lipoproteins (LDLs) that enter the vessel wall through the injured or dysfunctional endothelium. All major cell types within the vessel wall and atherosclerotic lesions can oxidize LDLs, but the endothelial cell is probably crucial in these early stages by mildly oxidizing LDLs. Mildly oxidized LDLs (or minimally modified LDLs) and regional low shear and turbulent flow may play an initial role in monocyte recruitment by inducing the endothelial expression of two cell adhesive molecules (CAM) or surface glycoproteins, intercellular adhesion molecule-1 (ICAM-1) and vascular cell adhesion molecule-1 (VCAM-1). After monocytes adhere to the surface

of the vessel wall, other specific molecules, such as monocyte chemotactic protein-1 (MCP-1) and macrophage colony-stimulating factor (M-CSF), may attract and modify monocytes within the subendothelial space. After entering the vessel wall, monocytes differentiate into macrophages, which may be responsible for converting mildly oxidized LDLs into highly oxidized LDLs, which bind to the scavenger receptors of macrophages and enter the cells, converting them into foam cells.

High-density lipoproteins (HDLs) may protect against excess lipid accumulation in the vessel wall by inhibiting the oxidation of LDLs or its subsequent effects. HDLs also may contribute to reverse cholesterol transport, which is active LDL removal from the vessel wall and from the macrophages or foam cells.

Macrophages or foam cells, after saturation with lipid and before or after their death, can liberate many products, including oxidized LDLs and free radicals, which cause further endothelial damage. Such early alteration of the endothelium from the lumen (shear forces and risk factors) and from the vessel wall (macrophages) may lead to local vasoconstriction. The endothelium can affect vascular tone profoundly by releasing relaxing factors, such as prostacyclin and nitric oxide, and contracting factors, such as endothelin-1. Under physiologic conditions, nitric oxide seems to predominate, but in early atherogenesis the endothelial damage may cause these cells to generate more mediators that enhance constriction and fewer mediators that enhance dilation. When the endothelium disappears as a result of the damage, the de-endothelialized surface is exposed to circulating platelets; the platelet-derived growth factors (released from platelets, macrophages, injured endothelial cells, and smooth muscle cells) cause intimal smooth muscle cell proliferation and synthesis of extracellular matrix. Cardiovascular risk factors known to affect the epicardial coronary arteries also affect coronary microcirculatory function, with a tendency for vasoconstriction that may contribute to anginal pain.

The earliest atherosclerotic lesion, the so-called fatty streak or type III lesion, represents a dynamic balance of the entry and exit of lipoproteins and the development of the extracellular matrix. A decrease in lipoprotein entry (e.g., by modifying risk factors and endothelial injury) is likely to result in a predominance of lipoprotein exit and final scarring. An increase of lipoprotein entry can predominate over the efflux and scarring, however, resulting in the vulnerable, lipid-rich type IV and Va plaques that are prone to disruption.

Vulnerable Lipid-Rich Plaque and Its Disruption

Type IV and Va plaques commonly are composed of an abundant crescentic mass of lipids, separated from the vessel lumen by a discrete component of extracellular matrix (see Fig. 66–1; Fig. 66–3). The relatively small coronary lesions by angiography may be associated with acute progression to severe stenosis or total occlusion and eventually may account for two thirds of the patients in whom unstable angina or other acute coronary syndromes develop. This unpredictable and episodic progression most likely is caused by disruption of type IV and V plaques with subsequent thrombus formation, which changes the plaque geometry and leads to acute or intermittent plaque growth and acute occlusive coronary syndromes.

Plaques that undergo disruption tend to be relatively small and soft; they have a high concentration of cholesterol esters, rather than of free cholesterol monohydrate crystals. This passive phenomenon of plaque disruption is related to physical forces and occurs most frequently between the lipid core and the lumen, where the fibrous cap is thinnest, most heavily infiltrated by foam cells, and weakest. This physical vulnerability to disruption depends on three factors:

1. Circumferential wall stress or cap "fatigue," which in part relates to a combination of the thickness and collagen content of the fibrous cap covering the core, the blood pressure, and the radius of the lumen; long-term repetitive cyclic stresses may weaken the plaque and increase its vulnerability to fracture, ultimately leading to sudden and unprovoked (i.e., untriggered) mechanical failure.
2. Location, size, and consistency of the atheromatous core.
3. Blood flow characteristics, particularly the impact of flow on the proximal aspect of the plaque (i.e., configuration and angulation of the plaque).

There is also an active phenomenon of plaque disruption related to macrophage activity. Macrophages can degrade extracellular

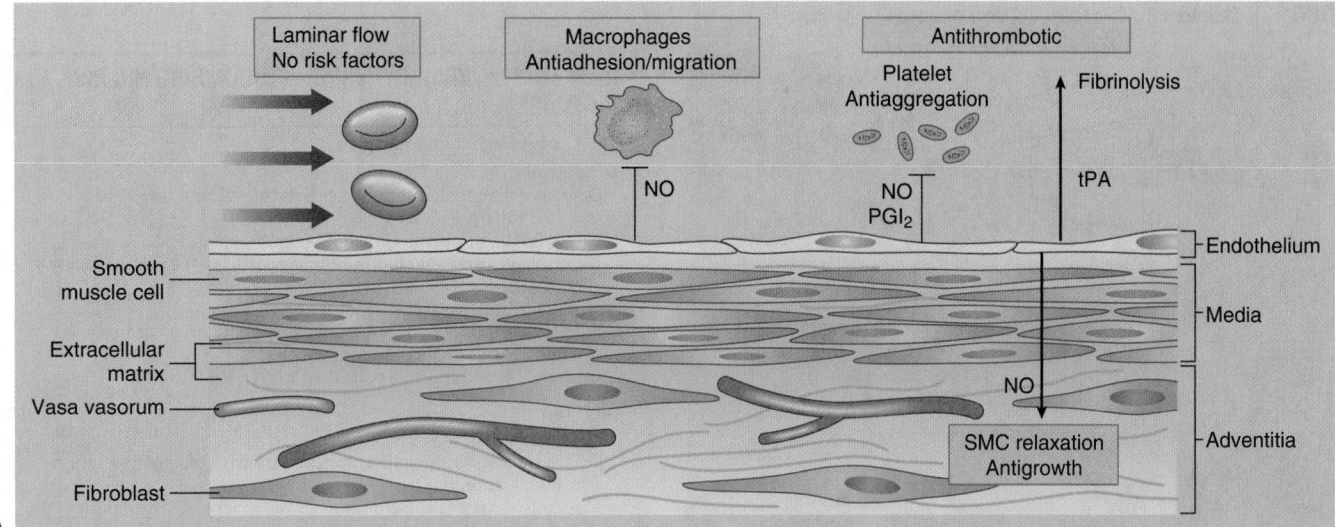

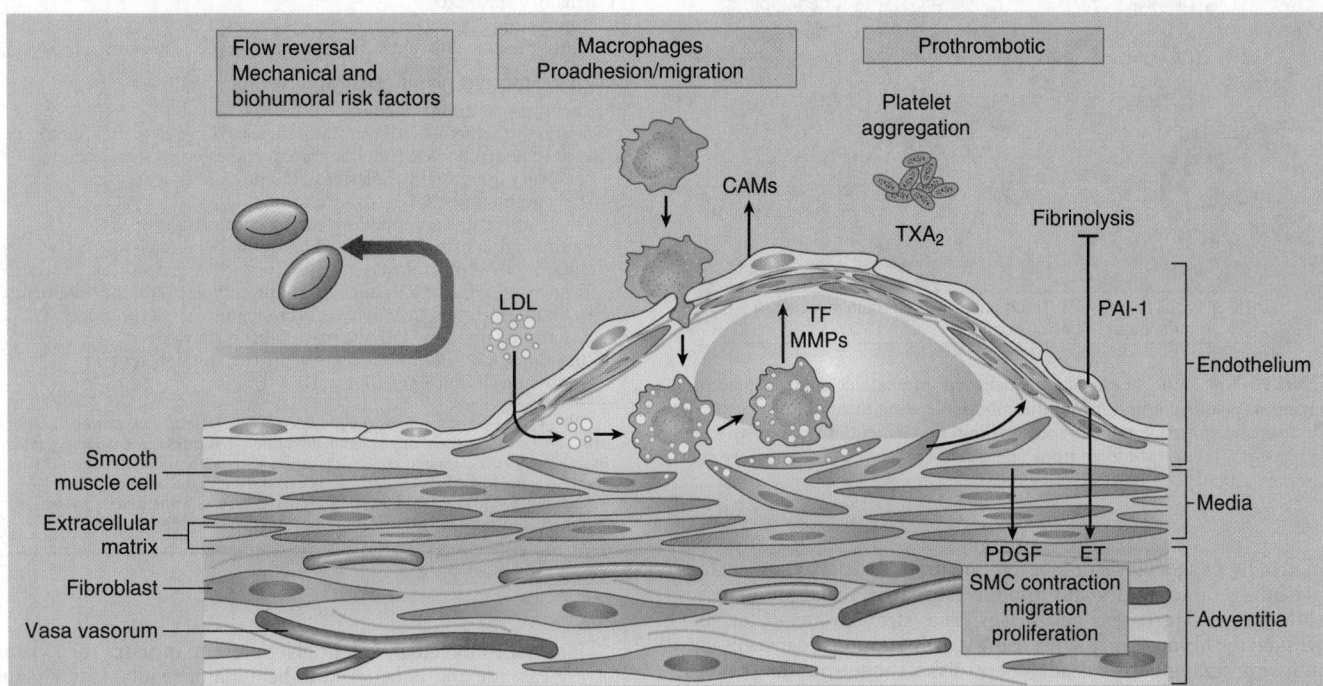

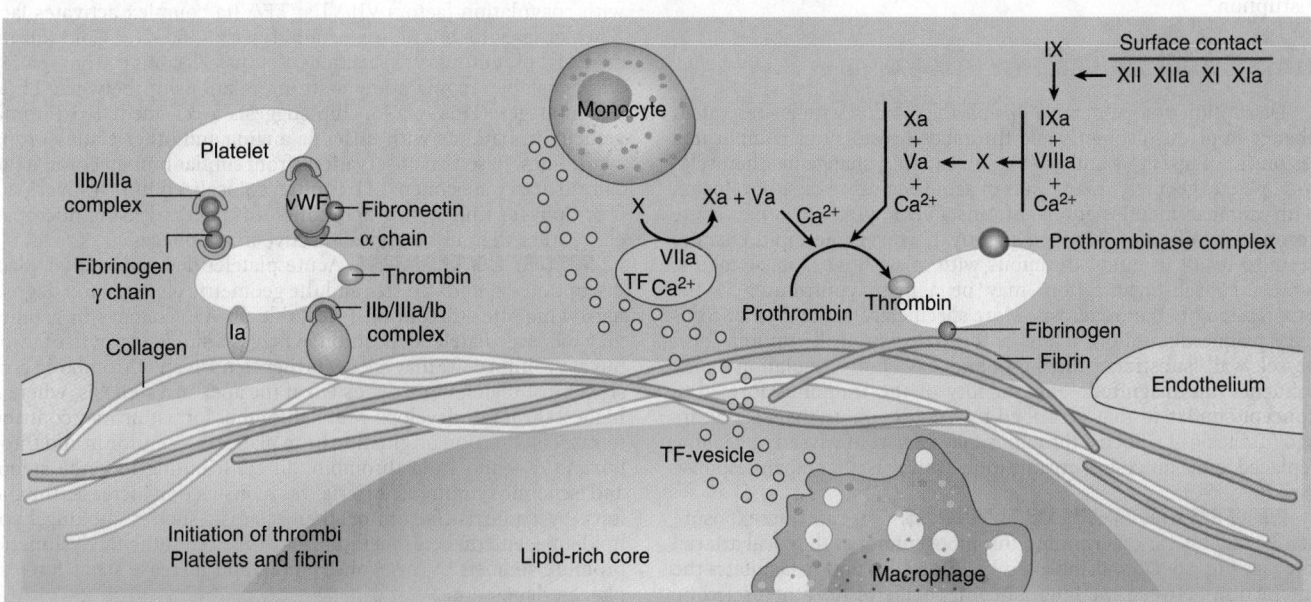

FIGURE 66–2 • Schematic representation of arterial wall biology and shear stress. *A*, Laminar shear stress and normal artery. *B*, Low shear stress/flow reversal and early events of atherosclerosis. *C*, Atherosclerotic plaque–dependent and hyperthrombogenic blood–dependent arterial thrombosis. Ca = calcium; CAMs = cell adhesive molecules; ET = endothelin; LDL = low-density lipoprotein; MMP = matrix metalloproteinases; NO = nitrous oxide; PAI = plasminogen activator inhibitor; PDGF = platelet-derived growth factor; PG = prostaglandin; SMC = smooth muscle cell; TF = tissue factor; tPA = tissue plasminogen activator; TX = thromboxane; vWF = von Willebrand factor.

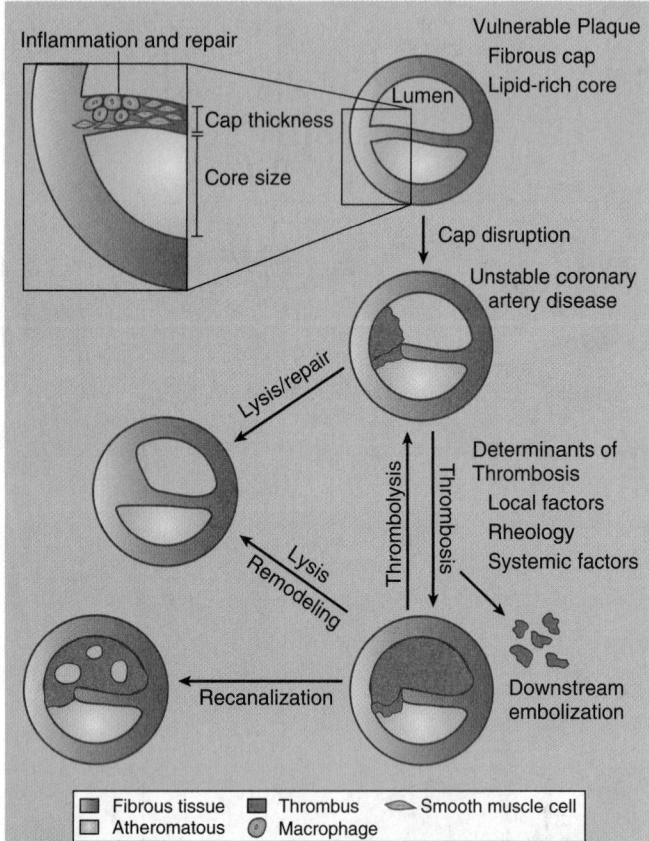

FIGURE 66–3 • Pathogenesis of a frequent type of unstable angina: anatomic changes (plaque disruption and thrombosis) leading to acute coronary syndromes and subsequent plaque remodeling. An element of vasoconstriction is usually present. (Modified from Théroux P, Fuster V: Acute coronary syndromes. Circulation 1998;97:1195.)

Table 66–1 • VIRCHOW TRIAD—THROMBOGENIC RISK FACTORS*

LOCAL VESSEL WALL SUBSTRATES
Atherosclerosis
   Degree of plaque disruption (i.e., erosion, ulceration)
Vessel wall inflammation
   Components of plaque (i.e., lipid core)
   Macrophages and generation of microparticles (i.e., tissue factor content)
Postinterventional vessel wall injury
   Plaque disruption after percutaneous transluminal coronary angioplasty, atherectomy, or stenting
   Injury of smooth muscle cells (i.e., rich in thrombin)

RHEOLOGY
High shear stress
   Severe stenosis (i.e., change in geometry with plaque disruption, residual thrombus)
   Vasoconstriction (i.e., serotonin, thromboxane A_2, thrombin, dysfunctional endothelium)
Oscillatory shear stress
   Bifurcation of arteries, plaque irregularities
Postintervention slow blood flow/local stasis (i.e., dissecting aneurysm)

SYSTEMIC FACTORS OF THE CIRCULATING BLOOD
Metabolic or hormonal factors
   Dyslipoproteinemia (triglycerides, increased low-density lipoprotein or oxidized low-density lipoprotein cholesterol, decreased high-density lipoprotein cholesterol, lipoprotein(a))
   Diabetes mellitus (i.e., glycosylation)
   Catecholamines (i.e., smoking, stress, cocaine use)
   Renin-angiotensin system (i.e., high-renin hypertension)
Plasma variables of hemostasis
   Tissue factor, factor VII, fibrinogen, thrombin generation (fragments 1 and 2), thrombin activity (fibrinopeptide A), plasminogen activator inhibitor-I, tissue plasminogen activator
   Infectious and cellular blood elements (i.e., monocytes and polymorphonuclear leukocytes)

*High risk—presumably by the presence of several local or systemic thrombogenic risk factors at the time of plaque disruption, indicates acute occlusive labile thrombus (unstable angina, non–ST-elevation acute myocardial infarction, ST-elevation acute myocardial infarction) versus fixed mural thrombus; low risk—presumably by the paucity of thrombogenic risk factors at the time of plaque disruption, indicates only mural thrombus (progressive atherogenesis).

matrix by phagocytosis or by secreting proteolytic enzymes such as plasminogen activators and a family of matrix metalloproteinases (MMPs)—collagenases, gelatinases, and stromelysins—that may weaken the fibrous cap, predisposing it to disruption. Foam cells may induce programmed cell death (apoptosis) of the surrounding smooth muscle cells and predispose to the active phenomenon of plaque disruption.

Acute Thrombosis, Occlusive or Mural

Disruption of a vulnerable or unstable plaque with a subsequent change in plaque geometry and thrombosis results in a complicated lesion (see Figs. 66–1 and 66–3). Such a rapid change in atherosclerotic plaque geometry may result in acute occlusion or subocclusion with clinical manifestations of unstable angina or other acute coronary syndromes. More frequently, however, the rapid changes seem to result in mural thrombus with or without clinical angina, which, by self-organization, may be a main contributor to the progression of atherosclerosis. More specifically, at the time of coronary plaque disruption, many factors—degree of disruption, local vessel wall substrate, rheology, and systemic circulation—may influence the magnitude and stability of the thrombus formed, a concept similar to that described by Virchow more than 100 years ago (Table 66–1). Such a thrombus may be partially lysed or become replaced in the process of organization by the vascular repair response (see Fig. 66–3).

PLAQUE TISSUE FACTOR–DEPENDENT THROMBOSIS. The substrate exposure is a key factor for determining thrombogenicity at the local arterial site (see Fig. 66–2C and Table 66–1). Plaque disruption facilitates the interaction between the internal components of the atherosclerotic lesions and the flowing blood. The lipid core, abundant in cholesterol ester, displays the highest thrombogenicity and the most intense tissue factor (TF) staining compared with other components; a mural thrombus in itself is also highly thrombogenic.

TF, a small-molecular-weight glycoprotein, initiates the extrinsic clotting cascade and is believed to be a major regulator of coagulation, hemostasis, and thrombosis. TF forms a high-affinity complex with coagulation factors VII/VIIa; TF/VIIa complex activates factor X, which leads to thrombin generation (see Fig. 66–2C). Colocalization analysis of coronary specimens (culprit lesions) from patients with unstable angina show a strong relationship between TF and macrophages. This relationship suggests a cell-mediated thrombogenicity in patients with unstable angina and other acute coronary syndromes. Based on observations from similar human coronary and carotid artery specimens, TF is often colocalized in LDL-overloaded macrophages undergoing apoptotic death and releasing microparticles, rather than in biologically active macrophages.

RHEOLOGY AND THROMBOSIS. Acute platelet deposition after plaque disruption depends on size and the geometric changes and degree of narrowing after disruption (see Table 66–1). Changes in geometry may increase platelet deposition, whereas a sudden growth of thrombus at the injury site may create further stenosis and thrombotic occlusion. Most platelets are deposited at the apex of a stenosis, where the highest shear rate develops. Mural thrombus formation may contribute to vasoconstriction originating from platelets—serotonin and thromboxane A_2—and from thrombin, all contributing to acute stenosis and ischemic symptoms. Arterial vasoconstriction increases the shear force. Systemic risk factors for atherosclerosis, such as smoking, hyperlipidemia, and diabetes mellitus, may cause endothelial dysfunction, promote stenosis by vasoconstriction, and increase shear force and platelet deposition.

BLOOD-DEPENDENT THROMBOGENICITY AND SYSTEMIC RISK FACTORS. In about one third of acute coronary syndromes, there is no disruption of a fairly small lipid-rich plaque but just a superficial erosion of a markedly stenotic and fibrotic plaque (see Fig. 66–1). Complicated thrombi in such cases may depend on a hyperthrombogenic state triggered by systemic factors. Systemic factors, including high LDL, cigarette smoking, hyperglycemia, hemostasis, and others, are associated with increased blood thrombogenicity (see Table 66–1). The hyperthrombogenic state associated with such risk factors may share a common biologic pathway: an activation of leukocyte-platelet interactions associated with release of TF microparticles and thrombin activation (see Fig. 66–2C).

Within the context of "proinflammatory" or "prothrombotic" effects on the circulating blood exerted by cardiovascular risk factors, such as high LDL cholesterol, cigarette smoking, and diabetes, there is evolving evidence that circulating monocytes and white blood cells may be involved in TF expression and thrombogenicity. It has been suggested that the predictive value for coronary events of high titers of C-reactive protein (CRP) may be a manifestation of such systemic phenomena. CRP, similar to fibrinogen, is a protein of the acute-phase response and a sensitive marker of low-grade inflammation. CRP is considered to be produced in the liver as a result of mediators such as interleukin-6 generated by circulating monocytes or by inflammation in the vessel wall. Increased levels of CRP independently predict acute coronary events even in persons whose blood lipid values fall below the median levels in the population. CRP seems to activate blood monocytes and vessel wall endothelial cells.

VASCULAR BIOLOGY OF RISK FACTORS

LIPOPROTEINS. Lipoproteins are high-molecular-weight complexes of lipid and protein that circulate in the blood plasma (Chapter 211). Their physiologic functions include transport of lipids to cells for energy, growth requirements, or storage. Lipoproteins are also metabolic precursors of biologic regulators, such as prostaglandins, thromboxanes, and leukotrienes. LDLs promote atherogenesis by affecting one or several of the processes of influx and efflux of the vessel wall. Elevated LDL levels also promote thrombosis formation, and reducing LDL levels pharmacologically with statins decreases thrombosis.

HDLs promote cholesterol efflux from atherosclerotic lesions. In addition, it seems that HDLs inhibit the oxidation and subsequent accumulation of LDL-cholesterol. Observational data and experiments in vitro and in transgenic mice suggest that HDLs containing apo A-I but not apo A-II are protective, whereas HDLs with both apolipoproteins are neutral. Apo A-I has been identified as a prostacyclin stabilizing factor, suggesting another possible mechanism of benefit.

Evidence is growing that triglyceride-rich lipoproteins are important contributors to the development of atherothrombotic disease. Mechanisms by which hypertriglyceridemia may contribute to atherothrombotic disease risk include increased thrombogenicity, "small dense" LDLs (see later section on diabetes), postprandial lipidemia with increased chylomicron and very-low-density lipoprotein (VLDL) remnant particles, decreased HDL levels, and insulin resistance (see later section on diabetes). An elevated lipoprotein (a) (Lp[a]) level in plasma may be a significant risk factor for atherothrombotic disease, particularly in the presence of elevated LDL levels, although this risk has not been well characterized, and the distribution of Lp(a) levels in some ethnic populations is highly skewed.

DIET. Serum cholesterol and LDL concentrations are associated strongly with dietary intakes of total fat, saturated fatty acids, and cholesterol. Saturated fat intake is associated with increased thrombogenicity. Salt intake is associated with elevated blood pressure in susceptible persons.

HYPERTENSION. In elevated blood pressure, endothelial dysfunction promotes atherogenesis by attenuating responses to endothelium-dependent vasodilators, increasing vascular permeability to macromolecules (including lipoproteins), and increasing endothelin production and leukocyte adherence (Chapter 63). Hypertension also may be associated with phenotypic changes that increase the proliferative potential of vascular smooth muscle cells and their response to growth factors.

SMOKING. Observational data suggest that smoking exerts its atherogenic effects by inducing catecholamine release, which may elevate blood fibrinogen levels, activate monocytes, and increase platelet reactivity (Chapter 14). These catecholamine effects may explain the increase in sudden cardiac death and acute cardiovascular events. Endothelial dysfunction, caused by catecholamines and/or nicotine, also increases in vascular tone. Smoking lowers HDL and promotes oxidation of LDL, presumably owing to the exposure of the latter to free radicals present in cigarette smoke.

DIABETES. Insulin resistance in patients with type II diabetes mellitus or in patients with poorly controlled type I diabetes is accompanied by hyperinsulinemia, which may elevate circulating insulin-related growth factors such as insulin growth factor-1 (Chapter 242). In chronic hyperglycemia, glycated proteins and various local growth factors can stimulate the proliferation of the fibromuscular component of the mature atherosclerotic plaque. Levels of lipoproteins such as LDL may not be abnormal in patients with diabetes mellitus; however, lipoproteins may be glycated, resulting in abnormal function. Hypertriglyceridemia with HDL depletion is the characteristic lipid profile of insulin resistance and poorly controlled diabetes. As an important consequence of hypertriglyceridemia, abnormalities in the metabolism of triglyceride-rich lipoproteins result in modifications of LDL structure, so as to produce a smaller, denser, so-called subclass B form of LDL, which has markedly enhanced atherogenicity. Abnormalities of Lp(a) levels also are widespread in patients with poorly controlled diabetes.

SYSTEMIC THROMBOGENIC RISK FACTORS. Thrombotic mechanisms contribute not only to acute events after plaque activation, but also to the growth of atheromas (see Table 66–1 and Fig. 66–2C). Aside from the thrombogenic effect of high levels of LDL cholesterol, a high catecholamine drive, such as from cigarette smoking, emotional stress, or cocaine, may enhance thrombogenicity, perhaps by inducing vasoconstriction, and directly trigger plaque disruption.

Several hemostatic determinants, including fibrinogen, von Willebrand factor, and factor VIIa, have been associated with an increased risk of cardiovascular disease; however, the association with fibrinogen is the most powerful and most consistent. Increased plasminogen activator inhibitor-1 and tissue-type plasminogen activator antigen (most likely a marker for endothelial dysfunction) are associated with an increased risk of cardiovascular events; elevated tissue-type plasminogen activator activity, by contrast, is associated with a decreased risk of events.

Systemic infections (e.g., with *Chlamydia pneumoniae*, cytomegalovirus, and *Helicobacter pylori*) may be linked to atherosclerotic disease and its thrombotic complications, although a true cause-and-effect relationship is still uncertain. Increased antibody titers have been associated in some studies with future adverse cardiovascular events. Infectious agents may activate circulating monocytes and lymphocytes and create a hypercoagulable state.

OBESITY AND PHYSICAL INACTIVITY. Obesity predisposes to hyperlipidemia, diabetes, and hypertension, but obesity itself is associated with only a small increase in the risk of coronary artery atherosclerosis, principally in youth. Physical activity favorably influences plasma lipoprotein profiles, adiposity, blood pressure, glucose tolerance, and cardiovascular and pulmonary functional capacity; individuals prone to become physically active also are prone to modify favorably their risk factors. Physical fitness, a condition that is measured more objectively than physical activity, also independently reduces the risk of coronary heart disease.

GENETIC FACTORS (FAMILY HISTORY). Single-gene mutations influence lipid metabolism. Complex polygenic disorders include hypertension, diabetes mellitus, and homocysteinemia and contribute to atherogenesis. Currently identifiable genetic abnormalities only partially account for the risk predicted by a positive family history for premature coronary artery disease, however.

PATHOBIOLOGY AND CLINICAL PRESENTATION

Atherothrombosis As a Systemic Disease: Clinical Impact

Atherothrombotic cardiovascular disease is a diffuse condition involving the heart (coronary arteries), brain (carotid arteries), aorta, and peripheral arteries. At the time of clinical presentation, about 3 to 8% of patients have symptomatic atherosclerotic disease in three main arterial districts, and 23 to 32% of patients have disease in two.

In patients with atherothrombotic disease, myocardial ischemia or MI causes 70% of deaths. Cerebrovascular disease (Chapter 439) causes approximately 10 to 17% of deaths, and another 10% are caused by ruptured thoracic or abdominal aortic aneurysms (see Chapter 75). Peripheral arterial disease (Chapter 76) does not directly cause

Cardiovascular Disease

mortality, but it is an ominous manifestation of underlying disseminated atherosclerosis and portends an increased mortality related to coronary disease and cerebrovascular disease.

Coronary Atherothrombotic Disease

Coronary atherothrombotic disease includes a wide spectrum of conditions, ranging from silent ischemia and exertion-induced angina (Chapter 67) to the acute coronary syndromes (Chapter 68). Stable angina (usually exertional) or stable silent ischemia (exertional or not) commonly results from increases in myocardial oxygen demand that outstrip the ability of stenosed coronary arteries to increase oxygen delivery. In contrast, acute coronary syndromes are characterized by an abrupt reduction in coronary flow, generally by a thrombotic occlusion related to local vessel wall substrates (i.e., plaque ulceration or erosion), rheology (i.e., high shear stress after plaque disruption/distortion, vasoconstriction) and systemic factors (i.e., blood hyperthrombogenicity) (see Table 66–1). Such factors also contribute in different degrees to the completeness and duration of the occlusion and, as a consequence, to whether the acute coronary syndrome is manifested clinically as unstable angina, non–ST-segment elevation acute MI, or ST-segment elevation acute MI.

Alterations in perfusion and myocardial oxygen supply probably account for two thirds of episodes of unstable angina; the remainder may be caused by transient increases in myocardial oxygen demand. A fairly small fissuring of a lipid-rich plaque may lead to an acute change in plaque structure and a reduction in coronary blood flow, resulting in exacerbation of angina. Transient episodes of thrombotic occlusion at the site of plaque damage, perhaps lasting only 10 to 20 minutes, may precipitate angina at rest. In addition, release of vasoactive substance (serotonin, thromboxane A_2) by platelets, the vasoconstrictive effect of thrombin, and vasoconstriction secondary to neighboring endothelial vasodilator dysfunction may contribute to a reduction in coronary flow.

In patients with non–ST-segment elevation acute MI, a more persistent thrombosis may cause occlusion for 2 hours; in about 25% of patients, an infarct-related vessel occlusion may persist for longer if the distal myocardial territory is supplied by collaterals. Spontaneous thrombolysis, resolution of vasoconstriction, and presence of collateral circulation are important in preventing the development of ST-segment elevation MI by limiting the duration of myocardial ischemia. In Q wave infarction, the formation of a fixed and persistent thrombus, which leads to an abrupt cessation of myocardial perfusion for more than 2 hours, results in transmural necrosis of the involved myocardium. Some cases of sudden coronary death probably involve a rapidly progressive coronary lesion in which plaque disruption or a superficial erosion, with resultant thrombosis, leads to ischemic and fatal ventricular arrhythmias in the absence of collateral flow. Platelet microemboli also may contribute to the development of sudden ischemic death.

Carotid Atherothrombotic Disease

About 20% of ischemic strokes (Chapter 440) occur when a significant stenotic atherosclerotic plaque of the extracranial carotid arteries is acutely complicated by disruption, which results in further obstruction or coexistent thrombosis and/or thromboemboli. In contrast with most high-risk coronary plaques, high-risk carotid plaques are significantly stenotic, and they are not lipid-rich but rather heterogeneous and fibrous-rich. Their disruption often represents an intramural hematoma or dissection that probably relates to the impact of blood during systole against the resistance of the stenotic lesion. Atherosclerotic stenosis of greater than 50% of the carotid lumen, usually close to the carotid bifurcation in the neck, causes about 20% of all ischemic strokes and transient ischemic attacks.

Atherothrombotic Disease of the Thoracic Aorta

Severe atherosclerosis of the ascending aorta (Chapter 75) is not only a significant marker for coronary disease, but also the most important morphologic indicator of an increased risk for cerebrovascular events. Atherosclerosis may be identified by transesophageal echocardiography (Chapter 51) identifying noncalcified aortic plaques greater than 4 mm in thickness or by magnetic resonance imaging (Chapter 53) disclosing the lipid-rich composition of the plaques. Atheroemboli originating from the atherosclerotic aorta are widely recognized complications of operations involving manipulations of the aorta (Chapter 124). It is likely that of the 30% of ischemic strokes commonly considered to be cryptogenic, a sizable proportion are caused when lipid-rich plaques of the thoracic aorta are complicated by disruption and thromboemboli.

Peripheral Arterial Atherothrombotic Disease

Atherothrombosis is the cause of most chronic peripheral arterial occlusive disease of the lower extremities (Chapter 76). The most frequently involved arteries are the femoropopliteal, tibial, and aortoiliacs. Epidemiologic studies have documented that 2 to 3% of men and 1 to 2% of women 60 years old and older have intermittent claudication. Acute occlusion may be embolic or thrombotic. Arterial embolism is a common cause of acute arterial occlusion, and, in approximately 85% of cases, the emboli arise from a cardiac source. In situ thrombotic occlusion of the arteries usually is associated with advanced disease. The pathology of peripheral vascular atherosclerotic disease seems to be similar to carotid disease because the plaques at high risk for acute ischemic syndromes of the lower extremities (i.e., sudden ischemic pain, gangrene) also appear to be stenotic and fibrous-rich. In contrast to carotid artery disease, however, acute ischemic syndromes of the lower extremities are mostly due to severe focal stenosis and thrombosis rather than to plaque disruption.

VASCULAR BIOLOGY OF PREVENTIVE APPROACHES

Lipid-Modifying Approaches to Prevention

Aggressive approaches to retard or reverse atherosclerosis can decrease significantly the progression of disease and improve prognosis (Chapter 47) but overall yield only minimal regression of atherosclerosis. The lack of substantial regression observed in the atherosclerotic lesions seen on arteriography is probably because these lesions already tend to be advanced, fibrotic, and less rich in lipids; they are less prone to reabsorption or to favorable remodeling. The substantial reduction in coronary events from lipid-lowering therapy probably relates to the marked reduction in LDL cholesterol, a reduction that stimulates the efflux of liquid or esterified cholesterol from the plaques (Chapter 211). Deposition of cholesterol crystals in the vessel wall predominates over the influx of LDL cholesterol, and the number and activity of the monocytes/macrophages are decreased. As a result, plaques become less soft and presumably less likely to be disrupted.

Antithrombotic Approaches to Prevention and Treatment

If atherosclerotic plaque disruption cannot be prevented, antiplatelet and anticoagulant agents still can be beneficial (Chapter 33). Aspirin, which is effective in unstable angina and acute MI and in primary and secondary coronary prevention, interferes with the thromboxane A_2–dependent pathway of platelet activation. The other three pathways, which are dependent on adenosine diphosphate (ADP) and serotonin, collagen, and thrombin, remain unaffected, as does the coagulation system. Combination therapy with two platelet inhibitors (e.g., aspirin and clopidogrel, which inhibits the ADP pathway) or a platelet inhibitor (aspirin) and an anticoagulant agent (intravenous heparin, subcutaneous low-molecular-weight heparin, or oral warfarin) has an additive effect. Newer antithrombotic approaches act either by blocking the late stage of receptor glycoprotein IIb/IIIa–related platelet activation (various intravenous agents) or by blocking the early stage of thrombin-related platelet activation (specific antithrombins). In acute unstable angina and non–ST-segment elevation acute MI, fibrinolytic agents are of no benefit but platelet glycoprotein IIb/IIIa inhibition is beneficial (Chapter 68), related to the predominance of platelet thrombus as an initiator of labile, short-term thrombotic occlusion. By contrast, in ST-segment elevation acute MI, fibrinolytic agents are of benefit (Chapter 69), presumably because of the predominance of fibrin deposition, which occurs as a result of stasis caused by the initial obstructive platelet thrombus and which leads to a more stable and persistent thrombotic occlusion.

SUGGESTED READINGS
Biondi-Zoccai GGL, Abbate A, Liuzzo G, et al: Atherothrombosis, inflammation, and diabetes. J Am Coll Cardiol 2003;41:1071–1077. *Overview of how diabetes contributes to atherosclerosis.*
Fuster V, Gotto AM: Risk reduction. Circulation 2000;102:IV94–IV102. *An overview of the pathogenesis of coronary artery disease (atherosclerosis and thrombosis) and the role of risk factors and risk factor modification.*
Libby P, Ridker PM, Maseri A: Inflammation and atherosclerosis. Circulation 2002;105:1135–1143. *A review of the role of inflammation (accumulation and activity of monocytes and lymphocytes) and the possible role of infectious agents in coronary artery disease.*
Witztum JL, Steinberg D: The oxidative modification hypothesis of atherosclerosis: Does it hold for humans? Trends Cardiovasc Med 2001;11:93–102. *An outline of how lipid oxidation and metabolism play a role in coronary artery disease.*

67 ANGINA PECTORIS

Pierre Théroux

There is a disorder of the breast marked with strong and peculiar symptoms and considerable for the kind of danger belonging to it. . . . The seat of it, and sense of strangling and anxiety with which it is attended, may make it not improperly be called Angina pectoris. Those who are afflicted with it, are seized, while they are walking, and more particularly when they walk soon after eating, with a painful most disagreeable sensation in the breast, which seems as if it would take their life away, if it were to increase or to continue: the moment they stand still, all this uneasiness vanishes. After it has continued some months, it will not cease so instantaneously upon standing still; and it will come on, not only when the persons are walking, but when they are lying down. . . .(Heberden)

The quote from a 1772 publication already contained the clinical elements for the recognition and classification of stable and unstable angina pectoris. Angina is one clinical expression of myocardial ischemia. Ischemia rapidly develops when myocardial oxygen needs exceed myocardial oxygen delivery. It typically is triggered by physical activity and relieved with rest. Ischemia may be clinically silent or associated with clinical manifestations other than pain. It may be stable for years or rapidly progress to become unstable and cause myocardial infarction (MI) or sudden death (Chapter 69).

Atherosclerosis, the most common cause of myocardial ischemia, may evolve for years without symptoms. Conversely, chest pain can result from a variety of nonischemic cardiac or noncardiac causes. In all instances, the diagnosis is first clinical and subsequently supported by further diagnostic investigation. It has been estimated that approximately half of the 13 million individuals with coronary artery disease (CAD) in North America experience angina pectoris, with 400,000 new cases emerging every year. An estimated 5.5 million patients present to emergency departments with chest pain each year, and there are about 1.5 million hospitalizations annually for unstable angina or non–ST segment elevation acute MI.

Definition

Angina is a symptom, which must be recognized by its clinical manifestations. The pain usually builds up rapidly within 30 seconds and disappears in decrescendo within 5 to 15 minutes, more promptly when nitroglycerin is used. The pain may have visceral, somatic, and cerebral components. It is variably described but typically presents as tightness, squeezing, or constriction; some patients describe an ache, a feeling of dull discomfort, indigestion, or burning pain (see Chapter 46). The discomfort is most commonly midsternal with radiation to the neck, left shoulder, and left arm. It also can be precordial or radiate to the jaw, teeth, right arm, back, and, more rarely, epigastrium. The clenching of the fist over the sternum while describing the pain (Levine's sign) is classic.

Angina may be defined by the stability or nonstability of its manifestation, its precipitating factors, or its pathophysiology. The clinical diagnosis of *stable angina* first is based on symptom recognition. Stable angina is usually reproducible in an individual patient and is consistent over time. In most patients, it is precipitated by effort, relieved by rest, and related to fixed stenoses of one or more epicardial coronary arteries. *Unstable angina* (Chapter 68) is

diagnosed clinically when a patient has new-onset angina (by definition, any patient with new-onset angina has a brief interval of instability), increasing angina (angina that is more frequent, more prolonged, or precipitated by less effort than before), or angina occurring at rest.

Angina most commonly is precipitated by increasing effort; in stable angina, this degree of effort is reasonably predictable from day to day in an individual patient. Some patients have angina during exercise, but then the discomfort disappears with continued exercise (*walk-through angina*). *Nocturnal angina* may develop soon after a patient lies down or several hours later. *Postprandial angina* develops during or soon after meals because of an increased oxygen demand in the splanchnic vascular bed.

The underlying pathophysiologic basis of angina may be due to fixed coronary obstruction, clot superimposed on a fixed coronary obstruction, or vasospasm on a coronary artery lesion of variable severity. In addition, angina can be caused by situations associated with excess myocardial oxygen demand, with a lower threshold for angina when high left ventricular diastolic pressures impede myocardial blood flow during diastole.

Etiology

Angina most commonly is caused by atherosclerotic narrowing of one or more epicardial coronary arteries. It also can occur when myocardial ischemia develops despite normal epicardial coronary arteries. Patients with aortic stenosis (Chapter 72) or hypertrophic cardiomyopathy (Chapter 73) have marked increases in myocardial oxygen demand because of myocardial hypertrophy. In syndrome X, patients with normal epicardial coronary arteries may develop true myocardial ischemia and angina because of the failure to have normal vasodilation of the resistance vessels with exercise or other stimuli.

The diagnosis of angina requires documentation of the presence of myocardial ischemia. Conversely, some patients can have substantial CAD and even demonstrable myocardial ischemia by diagnostic testing yet not experience angina.

A key diagnostic feature is the pattern of stability or instability (Fig. 67–1). Physician's expertise is needed to elicit more subtle features and to evaluate less typical symptoms in the perspective of the patient's other characteristics. Appropriate diagnostic measures subsequently are indicated to document the diagnosis, evaluate the immediate and long-term risk, and institute treatment and follow-up. A sound knowledge of the mechanisms of disease facilitates these processes.

Pathophysiology

Myocardial ischemia is caused by an imbalance between myocardial oxygen supply and oxygen demand. Ischemia releases active substances, such as adenosine and bradykinin, that stimulate cardiac chemosensitive and mechanosensitive receptors, whose afferent nerves connect in the upper fifth sympathetic ganglia and upper thoracic spinal cord and converge with other afferent somatic nerves and descending supraspinal signals to be transmitted to the thalamus and the cortex. These interconnections explain the various facets of anginal pain. Angina is a complex phenomenon, and its features are only partly explained. It can be considered conveniently as primary or secondary. The former denotes a reduction in oxygen supply typically present in patients with Prinzmetal's angina and MI, and the latter is a reflection of increased demand as typically present in effort angina. Often angina has a mixed presentation, however, with elements of supply and demand. Mental stress, emotions, nyctohemeral variations, the postprandial state, exposure to cold, and other personal circumstances may reduce coronary flow and increase myocardial oxygen consumption.

MYOCARDIAL ENERGETICS. Myocardial metabolism is essentially aerobic. Free fatty acids and protons accumulate within a few seconds after oxygen deprivation; ST segment changes ensue within minutes, followed by appearance of chest pain. The major determinants of myocardial oxygen consumption associated with heart contraction are, in decreasing order of importance, heart rate, wall tension generated during systole (afterload), the inotropic state of the myocardial cell (contractility), and end-diastolic volume (preload) (Chapter 48).

Cardiovascular Disease

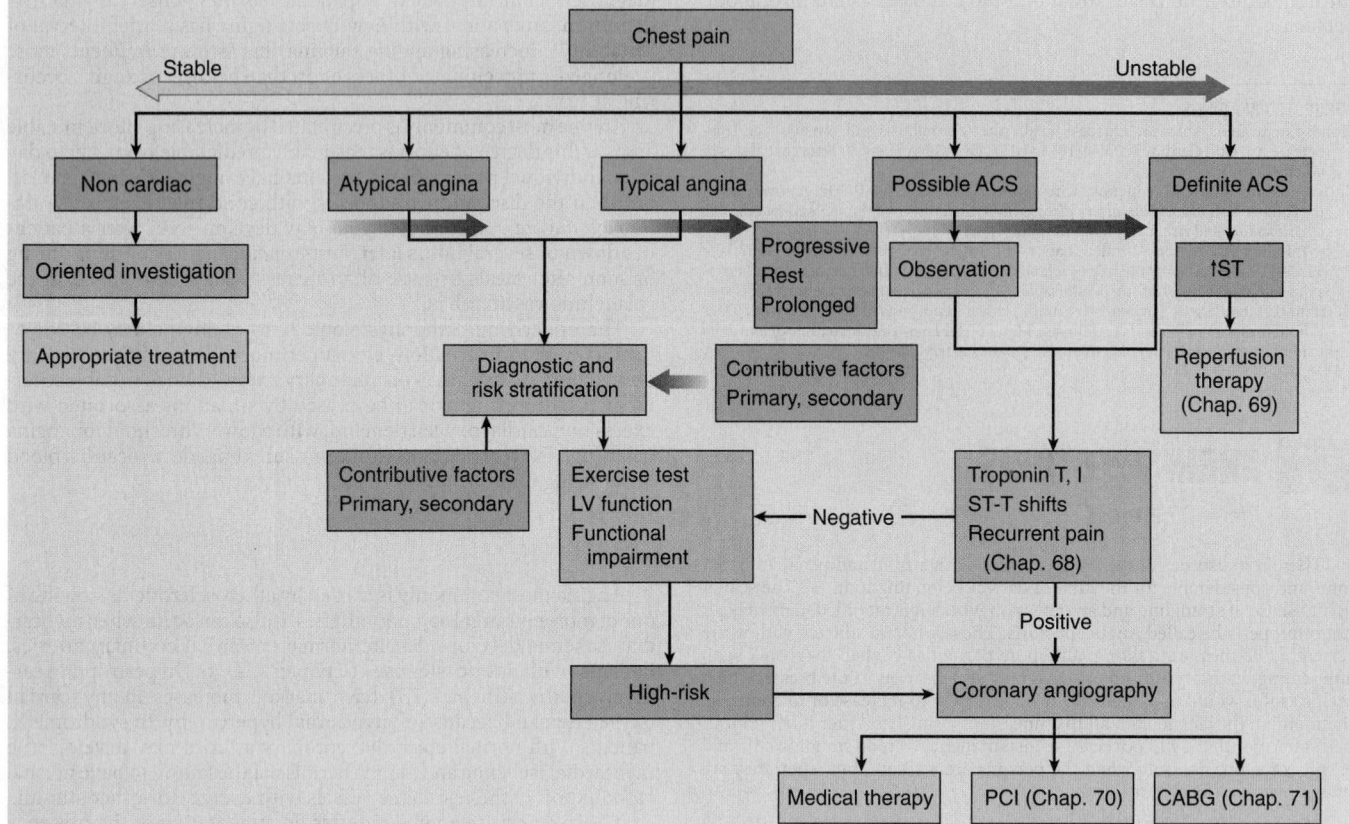

FIGURE 67–1 • Evaluation of chest pain. ACS = acute coronary syndrome; CABG = coronary artery bypass graft; LV = left ventricular; PCI = percutaneous coronary intervention.

CORONARY CIRCULATION. Myocardial oxygen extraction is high in the basal state (75% at rest, 90% during ischemia), and adaptation of the heart to increased demand is achieved mainly through vasodilation of coronary resistance vessels. Coronary blood flow can increase fivefold to sixfold during exercise from resting values of 0.8 mL/g/min by the ability of the coronary circulation to autoregulate in response to changes in perfusion pressure and oxygen demand. The autoregulation is modulated by sympathetic and parasympathetic influences; metabolic factors (primarily adenosine, a potent vasodilator produced by oxidative phosphorylation of adenosine nucleotides that are produced when adenosine triphosphate use exceeds production); and many important vasoactive substances, such as nitric oxide (NO) and endothelin produced by and acting through the endothelium. Coronary perfusion of the left ventricle is mainly diastolic when wall tension and coronary resistance are lowest. As per Laplace's law, an intramural gradient in tension exists, highest in the subendocardium and lowest in the subepicardium, rendering subendocardial areas more sensitive to ischemia. When more severe, ischemia progresses transmurally from the subendocardial to the subepicardial areas.

A gradient of pressure across the coronary obstruction builds up as the severity of luminal obstruction increases. The pressure drop through a stenosis is influenced mainly by the cross-sectional area of the stenosis (Δ pressure = 1/area^2 × length of stenosis × flow rate). The reduced distal pressure is associated with vasodilation, which limits the potential coronary reserve (i.e., the potential for any further increase in flow).

In the absence of adequate collateralization, stenoses of more than 75% of the cross-sectional area (corresponding to >50% lumen diameter by angiography) result in ischemia when the energy requirements are high, as during exercise in stable effort angina. The threshold to ischemia decreases as the severity of the obstruction increases. The extreme is chest pain at rest caused by severe stenoses with inadequate collateral circulation, by thrombus formation in acute coronary syndromes, or by inappropriate spasm in Prinzmetal's variant angina. An important contributor to ischemia in acute coronary syndromes is the shedding and distal embolization of plaque and thrombus material, which may occlude the microvasculature and result in cell necrosis and release of troponin.

ENDOTHELIUM. The endothelium is an extremely active surface that produces potent vasoactive, anticoagulant, procoagulant, and fibrinolytic substances and inflammatory mediators (Chapter 66). NO is the most potent modulator of endothelial function. NO increases the intracellular content of cyclic guanosine monophosphate and mediates the vasodilator response to shear rate and a variety of vasoactive products, such as acetylcholine, adenosine diphosphate (ADP), bradykinin, and serotonin. The NO system, although important, is fragile and becomes ineffective in atherosclerotic vessels and when the endothelium is rendered dysfunctional by the presence of risk factors such as smoking, hypercholesterolemia, hypertension, and diabetes mellitus. Prostacyclin derived from the metabolism of arachidonic acid relaxes smooth muscle cells and inhibits platelet aggregation through an increase in the intracellular concentration of cyclic adenosine monophosphate. Endothelin produced by the endothelium is a potent vasoconstrictor with prolonged effect.

ACTIVE PLAQUE. Atherosclerosis is a degenerative process of the vessel wall in response to injury such as oxidative stress and oxidized low-density lipoprotein (LDL) cholesterol. The early endothelial dysfunction is accompanied with expression of cell adhesion molecules, monocyte infiltration, foam cell formation, cytokine production, and proliferation and migration of smooth muscle cells (Chapter 66). In acute coronary syndromes, the culprit lesion is the site of exaggerated inflammatory reaction with dense infiltration of neutrophils, lymphocytes, and mast cells accompanied by degeneration of the matrix, rendering the plaque friable and prone to rupture under hemodynamic stress. Intravascular thrombus formation may follow (Chapters 68 and 69). Typically the thrombi associated with an acute coronary syndrome form on plaques of only moderate severity, with a preexisting luminal diameter redirection of only 40 to 60%. Fully occlusive thrombi result in transmural ischemia and ST segment elevation (Chapter 69). Partially occlusive thrombi are associated with intermittent ischemic episodes varying in duration in relation to the dynamics of the thrombus and the shedding of thrombotic material and plaque debris into the distal circulation (Chapter 68).

Clinical Manifestations

STABLE ANGINA. Typical angina is recognized by the quality of pain; location and duration of pain; and factors that trigger and relieve pain, including rest or nitroglycerin (see Fig. 67–1). Some specific patterns of stable angina include *first-effort, warm-up, second-wind,* or *walk-through* angina manifested on first but not subsequent efforts or pain disappearing with continued exercise. The mechanism likely is related to the phenomenon of ischemic preconditioning, which is reduced severity of ischemia after repeated short periods of occlusion. Nocturnal angina may occur soon after lying down in patients with subclinical heart failure that is manifested as venous return increases, in the early morning hours when the sympathetic tone is highest in patients with vasospastic disease, or any time in patients with sleep apnea. Postprandial angina develops during or soon after meals because of an increased oxygen demand in the splanchnic vascular bed. Approximately 80% of individuals with typical symptoms have demonstrable CAD (≥75% reduction in cross-sectional diameter of one or more of the large coronary arteries) and evidence of myocardial ischemia; however, 20% of patients, including a higher percentage of younger patients without risk factors, have no evidence of myocardial ischemia despite typical complaints. Even then, the probability of CAD varies by age range, gender, and characteristics of symptoms (Table 67–1). Although angina of any severity (see Table 46–4) can be stable by this definition, class IV angina and worsening or new-onset angina are usually termed *unstable angina*. The intensity of pain ranges from mild to severe discomfort. The characteristics and triggers are variable among patients but usually reproducible in a given patient.

Angina Equivalents. Some patients deny pain or discomfort and instead note shortness of breath, dizziness, fatigue, or gastrointestinal complaints. When these symptoms occur in response to exercise or other stress, patients must be evaluated for possible myocardial ischemia.

Atypical angina describes symptoms that meet two of the three criteria of typical angina. In these patients, the prevalence of underlying CAD and myocardial ischemia ranges from 20 to 50% and higher when many risk factors are present. In women and in the elderly, the symptoms may be more atypical, the initial manifestations more subtle, and the results of noninvasive testing less reliable. Although CAD occurs on average 10 years later in women than in men, the prognosis may be worse. *Noncoronary chest pain* is diagnosed when chest pain meets none or only one of the typical symptoms.

Symptoms allow classification of individuals into categories of high-risk, intermediate-risk, or low-risk probability of CAD, but they are not diagnostic. Numerous patients have had CAD incorrectly diagnosed for years until angiography showed no disease, whereas others have been treated symptomatically for various other diseases until angiography documented CAD.

VARIANT ANGINA (PRINZMETAL'S VARIANT ANGINA). Prinzmetal's variant angina is diagnosed when transient ST segment elevation is documented during an episode of chest pain. The chest pain occurs predominantly at rest, but it also occurs during exercise in approximately one third of patients. There is a predilection for the pain to wake the patient in the early morning hours when sympathetic activity is increasing. The syndrome may be cyclical with periods of exacerbation associated with repetitive episodes of chest pain that can persist only for seconds or be more prolonged and severe, alternating with periods with few or no symptoms. Syncope during an episode of chest pain is infrequent but strongly suggests an ischemic ventricular tachyarrhythmia. Prinzmetal's variant angina typically is caused by an occlusive spasm superimposed on a nonsevere coronary artery stenosis; however, at times, no underlying stenosis is present, and sometimes the underlying stenosis is severe. Because of these uncertainties, coronary angiography is recommended in all patients with vasospastic disease. Associated Raynaud's phenomenon and migraine headache have been described in some patients, suggesting that the syndrome may be part of a more generalized vasospastic disorder. A provocative test for spasm can be useful for the diagnosis and to assess the response to therapy in patients with normal or near-normal coronary angiograms in whom the diagnosis is unclear.

ANGINA WITH NORMAL CORONARY ANGIOGRAPHY (SYNDROME X, MICROVASCULAR ANGINA). Microvascular dysfunction without detectable lesions or spasm in the large coronary vessels is a frequent and often a disturbing cause of chest pain. The diagnosis requires objective documentation of ischemia with ST segment changes or a transient regional perfusion defect or of endothelial dysfunction with limited flow reserve with pharmacologic provocation. The chest pain occurs most frequently at rest, often in relation to emotional stress; periods of exacerbation commonly alternate with symptom-free periods. The exact causes of syndrome X are not known; several abnormalities have been described, including endothelial dysfunction, microvascular hyperresponsiveness, sympathetic vagal imbalance, altered adrenergic activity, and increased oxidative stress. An important component is altered perception of pain or hypersensitivity to certain stimuli. Treatment is difficult, but the prognosis is favorable and not different from a general age-matched population.

Diagnosis

DIFFERENTIAL DIAGNOSIS

It is crucial to evaluate if symptoms of possible angina are related to myocardial ischemia. Ischemia of cardiac origin usually is related to coronary atherosclerosis, but it also can be caused by other anatomic abnormalities interfering with epicardial flow (e.g., bridging and congenital abnormalities of the coronary circulation); conditions that increase the oxygen demands on the myocardium (e.g., aortic valve stenosis, hypertrophic cardiomyopathy, uncontrolled hypertension, and cocaine intoxication); and noncardiac conditions, such as anemia, thyrotoxicosis, and carbon monoxide intoxication (Table 67–2).

Nonischemic pain of extracardiac origin includes pulmonary, gastrointestinal, chest wall, and psychogenic causes (Chapter 46). In acute situations, it is important to exclude aortic dissection (Chapter 75), acute pericarditis (Chapter 74), pulmonary embolism (Chapter 94), and pneumothorax (Chapter 95). The clinical picture and differential diagnosis may be complicated by interactions of different mechanisms for chest pain. No historical evidence, physical examination findings, or tests are infallible for the diagnosis of angina.

PHYSICAL EXAMINATION

The cardiopulmonary physical examination may be totally normal in patients with stable angina. During ischemia, however, pulmonary rales, a transient S_4 or S_3 gallop, a sustained or dyskinetic left ventricular impulse, a transient mitral regurgitation murmur caused by papillary muscle dysfunction, or paradoxical splitting of S_2 (from transient left ventricular dysfunction or left bundle-branch block) may be appreciated. Presence of hypertension, xanthomata, xanthelasma, corneal arcus, or evidence of atherosclerosis in the peripheral circulation such as diminished pulses or vascular bruits raises the likelihood of coronary atherosclerosis and angina. The physical examination also may help identify other cardiac and noncardiac causes

Table 67–1 • PROBABILITY (%) OF CORONARY ARTERY DISEASE BY AGE, GENDER, AND SYMPTOMS

GENDER	AGE (YR)	DEFINITE ANGINA	ATYPICAL ANGINA	NONCARDIAC CHEST PAIN
Men	30–39	83	46	3
	40–49	88	57	12
	50–59	94	71	18
	60–69	95	78	31
	≥70	97	94	63
Women	30–39	—	20	4
	40–49	56	31	4
	50–59	68	30	6
	60–69	81	48	10
	≥70	96	56	—

From Chaitman BR, et al: Angiographic prevalence of high-risk coronary artery disease in patient subsets (CASS). Circulation 1981;64:360–367.

Table 67–2 • DIFFERENTIAL DIAGNOSIS OF CHEST PAIN

ISCHEMIC PAIN
Cardiac Origin
Decreased oxygen supply
  Coronary atherosclerosis
    Significant atherosclerosis
    Coronary thrombosis
  Coronary, nonatherosclerotic causes
    Aortic or coronary dissection
    Coronary spasm
    Microvascular spasm
    Cocaine-induced vasoconstriction
Increased oxygen demand
  Hypertrophic cardiomyopathy
  Aortic stenosis
  Dilated cardiomyopathy
  Increased preload (e.g., aortic or mitral valve regurgitation)
  Tachycardia
  Myocardial bridging
  Congenital abnormality of the coronary circulation

Noncardiac Origin
Decreased oxygen supply
  Anemia, sickle cell disease
  Hypoxemia (e.g., sleep apnea, pulmonary fibrosis, chronic lung
    disease, pulmonary embolism)
  Carbon monoxide intoxication
  Hyperviscosity (e.g., polycythemia, hypergammaglobulinemia)
Increased oxygen demand
  Hyperthyroidism
  Hyperthermia
  High inotropic state (e.g., adrenergic stimulation)

NONISCHEMIC PAIN
Cardiac Origin
Pericarditis
Aortic dissection

Noncardiac Origin
Gastrointestinal (e.g., esophageal [esophagitis, spasm, reflux, rupture,
  ulcer]; biliary [colic, cholecystitis]; gastric [peptic ulcer];
  pancreatitis)
Psychogenic (e.g., anxiety disorders [hyperventilation, panic];
  affective disorders [depression]; somatization; cardiac psychosis)
Pulmonary (e.g., pulmonary embolism, pneumothorax, pleuritis,
  pneumonia, pulmonary hypertension)
Neuromuscular (e.g., costochondritis, fibrositis, Tietze's syndrome,
  rib fracture, herpes zoster, thoracic outlet syndrome, sternoclavicular
  arthritis)

Table 67–3 • OTHER LABORATORY TESTS SUGGESTED IN PATIENTS WITH STABLE ANGINA

LDL and HDL cholesterol
Triglyceride level
Fasting glucose
Homocysteine level in patients with strong family history, especially if
  not explained by other risk factors
Hematocrit
Test of thyroid function (T_4 or TSH level)
Consider C-reactive protein and lipoprotein(a) [Lp(a)] levels

HDL = high-density lipoprotein; LDL = low-density lipoprotein; T_4 = thyroxine; TSH = thyroid-stimulating hormone. From Braunwald E, Goldman L (eds): Primary Care Cardiology, 2nd ed. Philadelphia, WB Saunders, 2003.

of chest discomfort, such as aortic stenosis, pericarditis, aortic dissection, costochondritis, and pulmonary disorders (see Table 46–2).

DIAGNOSTIC TESTS

LABORATORY EVALUATION. Routine blood tests cannot establish or exclude the diagnosis of angina but are important to assess abnormalities that may precipitate or worsen angina and to distinguish unstable angina from a non–Q wave MI (Table 67–3). The laboratory evaluation should include a complete blood cell count to exclude anemia, which may precipitate or worsen angina; thyroid function tests to exclude hyperthyroidism, which also may precipitate or worsen angina; and assessment of renal function to exclude renal insufficiency as a precipitating or aggravating cause. Patients routinely should be evaluated for coronary risk factors, including an evaluation for hyperlipidemia (Chapter 211), diabetes mellitus (Chapter 242), and homocysteine levels. Elevated levels of C-reactive protein may identify patients at higher risk for developing unstable angina or MI; many experts now recommend this test routinely. Enzyme markers (troponin T, troponin I, CK-MB) help distinguish unstable angina from a non–ST segment elevation MI (see Chapter 68) but are not needed to evaluate stable angina.

RESTING ELECTROCARDIOGRAM. A 12-lead electrocardiogram (ECG) obtained at times when the patient is pain-free may show arrhythmias, a previous MI, or left ventricular hypertrophy. When obtained during or shortly after an episode of chest pain, the ECG has high sensitivity for the diagnosis of ischemia and provides information on its extent and location. ST segment shift, most often depression, is the most specific finding, followed by T wave inversion. Transient ST segment elevation may indicate Prinzmetal's angina or a severely obstructive lesion with impending MI.

RADIOLOGY. A chest radiograph is recommended when intrathoracic disease is a possibility and in patients with suspected heart failure (Chapter 55). Electron beam computed tomography (CT) has improved the accuracy for the detection of coronary calcifications, which correlate with the presence and number of atherosclerotic plaques; however, the clinical yield of the test is not sufficiently documented to recommend routine clinical use (Chapter 52).

PROVOCATIVE TESTING. Provocative testing can confirm the presence of ischemia (Table 67–4). Ischemia is diagnosed by ST-T changes on the ECG, a perfusion defect on perfusion scintigraphy, or a regional wall motion abnormality on two-dimensional echocardiography. Some patients with angina pectoris and significant underlying CAD may have negative results on these various provocative tests, however. Conversely, a positive test can be a false positive. Patients with *silent ischemia* may have positive results in the absence of angina pectoris.

The *exercise ECG* significantly enhances the value of the ECG for detecting myocardial ischemia and making the presumptive diagnosis of ischemic heart disease. The exercise ECG is most likely to indicate ischemia when the ST segment changes are horizontal or downsloping, are more than 1 mV (Fig. 67–2), occur during the early stages of exercise or at a low workload, persist for several minutes after exercise, and are accompanied by symptoms consistent with angina. The appearance of a new mitral regurgitation murmur, a 10-mm Hg or greater drop in blood pressure, or typical anginal pain during exercise adds to the diagnostic value. False-positive results are most common in patients with underlying left ventricular hypertrophy or intraventricular conduction abnormalities on the resting ECG, a pre-excitation syndrome such as the Wolff-Parkinson-White syndrome, electrolyte abnormalities, or digitalis use. The risk associated with exercise testing is low (1 per 10,000 tests) if the test is avoided in patients with significant aortic stenosis, severe hypertension, or severe heart failure.

A variety of exercise test protocols (see Table 67–4) are used to measure exercise performance and, in patients with positive test results, the functional class (see Table 46–4). The sensitivity of exercise ECG for detecting CAD is about 70%, and its specificity for excluding CAD is about 75% (Table 67–5). The predictive value is influenced by the prior probability of ischemic heart disease (see Table 67–1). ST segment changes in patients with a lower clinical probability of angina pectoris are more likely to be a false-positive result than are the same changes in patients with higher clinical probability of the disease.

Perfusion scintigraphy using thallium-201 or technetium-99m sestamibi (Chapter 52) is performed commonly in conjunction with exercise or dipyridamole injection. Myocardial scintigraphy also can localize the site of active ischemia in patients with more than one-vessel disease and help plan an interventional procedure (Chapters 68 through 71). The sensitivity and specificity of perfusion scintigraphy using either the planar or the single-photon emission CT imaging techniques are generally better than for exercise ECG (see Table 67–5). A false-negative result can be encountered in patients with three-vessel disease and global left ventricular ischemia.

Echocardiography (Chapter 51) with exercise has a sensitivity and specificity at least equivalent to those of exercise ECG (see Table 67–5). When performed after the infusion of dobutamine, stress echocardiography has been associated with a sensitivity of 86 to 96% for diagnosing CAD and a specificity of 66 to 95% for excluding it.

Table 67–4 • COMMON EXERCISE TEST PROTOCOLS

PROTOCOL	STAGE	DURATION (MIN)	GRADE (%)	RATE (MPH)	METABOLIC EQUIVALENTS AT COMPLETION	FUNCTIONAL CLASS
Modified	1	3	0	1.7	2.5	III
Bruce protocol*	2	3	10	1.7	5	II
	3	3	12	2.5	7	I
	4	3	14	3.4	10	I
	5	3	16	4.2	13	I
Naughton protocol[†]	0	2	0	2	2	III
	1	2	3.5	2	3	III
	2	2	7	2	4	III
	3	2	10.5	2	5	II
	4	2	14	2	6	II
	5	2	17.5	2	7	I

*Commonly used in ambulatory patients.
[†]Commonly used in patients with recent myocardial infarction, unstable angina, or other conditions that are expected to limit exercise.
Adapted from Braunwald E, Goldman L (eds): Primary Cardiology, 2nd ed. Philadelphia, WB Saunders, 2003.

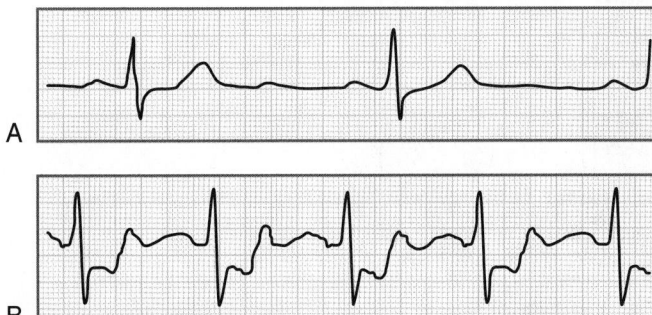

FIGURE 67–2 • Classic electrocardiographic ST segment depression of myocardial ischemia. *A,* Normal lead V_5 at rest. *B,* Lead V_5 with 2- to 3-mm ST segment depression during exercise.

revascularization. Rates of death or MI after 2 years of follow-up were 12.1, 8.8, and 4.7%.

In patients with angina and a previous MI or symptoms of heart failure, left ventricular function should be assessed quantitatively by echocardiography (Chapter 51) or nuclear techniques (Chapter 52). The combination of multivessel disease and poor left ventricular function is associated with a poor enough prognosis to consider a mechanical revascularization procedure (see later). Often, segmental dysfunction can be caused by stunned myocardium (transient dysfunction secondary to acute ischemia) or hibernating myocardium (poorly functioning myocardium secondary to chronic hypoperfusion). These conditions should be recognized because they can be reversible with appropriate treatment.

CHOOSING THE RIGHT TEST FOR AN INDIVIDUAL PATIENT. When selecting a diagnostic test (Table 67–6 and Fig. 67–3), it is important to realize that the predictive value of the test depends on the prevalence of the disease as determined by Bayes' theorem; the post-test likelihood of CAD is influenced by the pretest prevalence of the disease. In

Table 67–5 • APPROXIMATE SENSITIVITIES AND SPECIFICITIES OF COMMON TESTS TO DIAGNOSE CORONARY ARTERY DISEASE

	SENSITIVITY	SPECIFICITY
Exercise electrocardiography		
>1 mv ST depression	0.70	0.75
>2 mv ST depression	0.33	0.97
>3 mv ST depression	0.20	0.99
Perfusion scintigraphy		
Planar	0.83	0.88
SPECT	0.86–0.88	0.60–0.68
Echocardiography		
Exercise	0.83–0.87	0.74–0.80
Pharmacologic stress	0.86–0.96	0.66–0.95

SPECT = single-photon emission computed tomography.

Positron emission tomography can assess myocardial perfusion and metabolism and diagnose CAD with sensitivities and specificities that may approach 95%. This more expensive test is not widely available, however, and generally is not needed for the diagnosis (Chapter 52).

Continuous ECG monitoring allows detection of otherwise clinically silent ischemia. Many patients with symptomatic angina also have multiple additional episodes of asymptomatic ischemia with a total ischemic burden higher than suspected. Control of asymptomatic ischemia by approaches that reduce ischemic burden rather than focus on symptoms may improve prognosis in some patients with episodes of silent ischemia. The ACIP (Asymptomatic Cardiac Ischemia Pilot) trial randomized 558 patients with asymptomatic ischemia and a positive exercise test or ambulatory ECG monitoring to angina-guided therapy, ischemia-guided therapy, or routine

Table 67–6 • SUGGESTED NONINVASIVE TESTS IN DIFFERENT TYPES OF PATIENTS WITH STABLE ANGINA

Exertional angina, mixed angina, walk-through angina, postprandial angina with or without prior myocardial infarction:
  Normal resting ECG: *treadmill exercise ECG test*
  Abnormal uninterpretable resting ECG: *exercise myocardial perfusion scintigraphy (thallium-201, technetium-99m sestamibi) or exercise echocardiography*
  Unsuitable for exercise: *dipyridamole or adenosine myocardial perfusion scintigraphy, dobutamine stress echocardiography*
Atypical chest pain with normal or borderline abnormal resting ECG or with nondiagnostic stress ECG, particularly in women: *exercise myocardial perfusion scintigraphy, exercise echocardiography*
Vasospastic angina: *ECG during chest pain, ST segment ambulatory ECG, exercise test*
Dilated ischemic cardiomyopathy with typical angina or for assessment of hibernating or stunned myocardium: *regional and global ejection fraction by radionuclide ventriculography or two-dimensional echocardiography, radionuclide myocardial perfusion scintigraphy; in selected patients, flow and metabolic studies with positron emission tomography*
Syndrome X: *treadmill exercise stress ECG, coronary blood flow by positron emission tomography, Doppler probe*
Known severe aortic stenosis or severe hypertrophic cardiomyopathy with stable angina: *exercise stress tests contraindicated; dipyridamole or adenosine myocardial perfusion scintigraphy in selected patients. Coronary angiography preferred*
Mild aortic valvular disease or hypertrophic cardiomyopathy with typical exertional angina: *"prudent" treadmill myocardial perfusion scintigraphy, dipyridamole or adenosine myocardial perfusion scintigraphy*

ECG = 12-lead electrocardiogram.
Adapted from Braunwald E, Goldman L (eds): Primary Care Cardiology, 2nd ed. Philadelphia, WB Saunders, 2003.

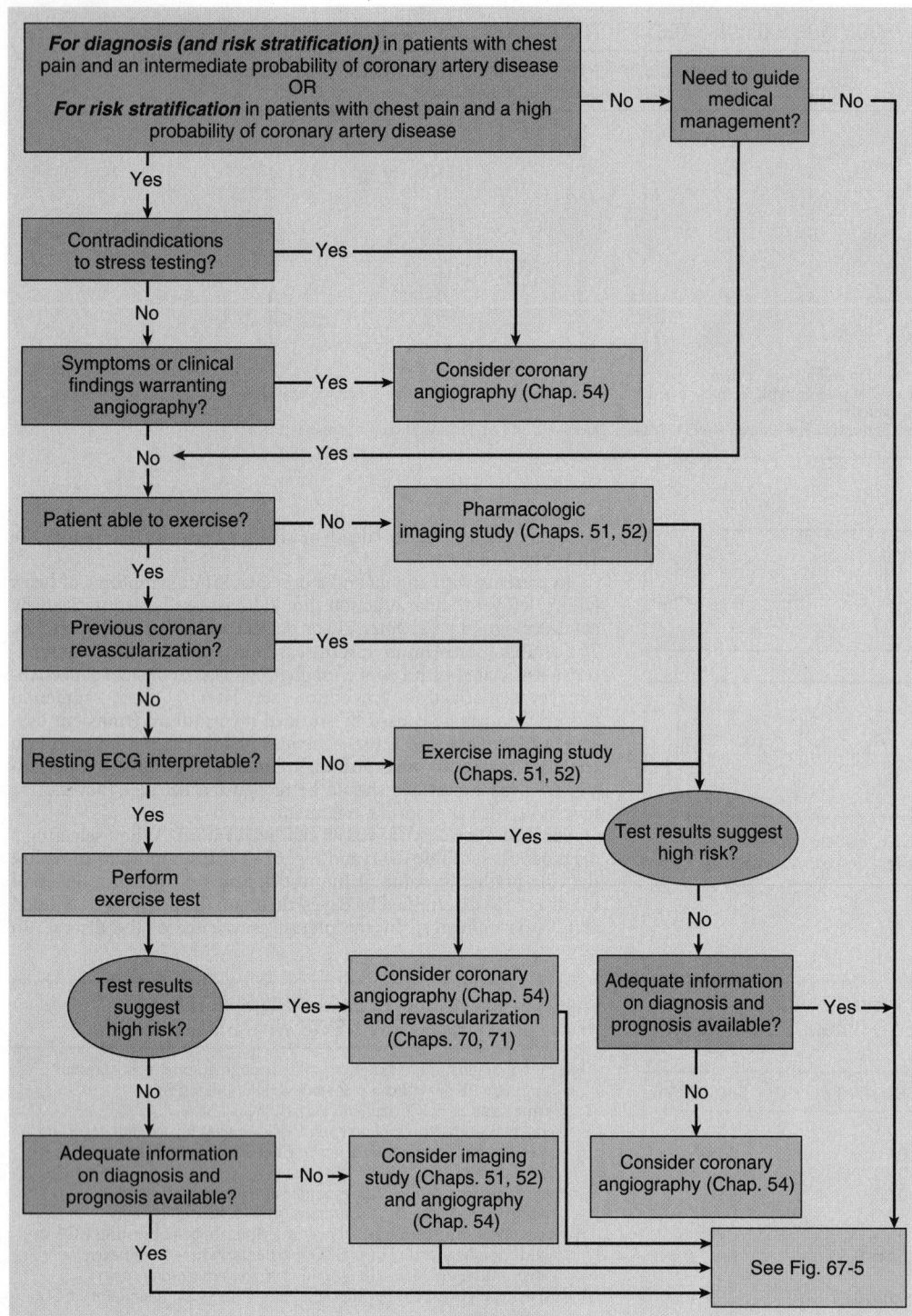

FIGURE 67–3 • Approach to the use of stress testing and angiography for the evaluation of chronic stable angina. ECG = electrocardiogram. (Adapted from American College of Cardiology/American Heart Association Task Force on Practice Guidelines: Management of patients with chronic stable angina. ACC/AHA/ACP-ASIM Pocket Guidelines, Elsevier Science, 2000, p 37.)

populations with low or high prevalence of CAD, the probability of disease is influenced little by the test's results; the diagnostic yield is maximal in patients with less typical presentations and intermediate probabilities. In addition to being informative on diagnosis, the exercise test provides information on the functional class and on prognosis. Exercise is combined with a perfusion scan or echocardiography in patients with baseline abnormal ST segment shifts as found in left ventricular hypertrophy, left bundle-branch block, pre-excitation syndrome, electrolyte abnormalities, or digitalis use. Perfusion scanning or echocardiography often is preferred in patients with previous coronary artery bypass graft (CABG) surgery or previous angioplasty. Pharmacologic agents are useful in patients who cannot exercise or have poor tolerance to exercise. Dipyridamole and adenosine are better suited for nuclear scintigraphy, and dobutamine is better suited for echocardiography.

Coronary angiography (Chapter 54) is required in some patients to exclude CAD with certainty. In some patients with otherwise unexplained symptoms, coronary angiography provides unique information on the extent of the disease, on prognosis, and on the best treatment modalities to offer (Table 67–7). Arteriography also can be useful to diagnose vasospastic angina by performing coronary angiography after injection of ergonovine or acetylcholine, which causes a focal vasospasm in patients with Prinzmetal's variant angina. The usual indication for coronary arteriography is to explore the possibility of a percutaneous coronary intervention (PCI), such as percutaneous transluminal angioplasty (Chapter 70), or CABG surgery (Chapter 71) to correct limiting symptoms, improve the quality of life, and improve prognosis. Spiral CT scan (Chapter 52) and magnetic resonance angiography (Chapter 53) are emerging as valid methods for noninvasive visualization of coronary arteries.

Table 67–7 • CORONARY ARTERY DISEASE PROGNOSTIC INDEX

EXTENT OF CORONARY ARTERY DISEASE	PROGNOSTIC WEIGHT (0–100)	5-YEAR MORTALITY RATE (%)*
1-vessel disease, 75%	23	7
>1-vessel disease, 50–74%	23	7
1-vessel disease, ≥95%	32	9
2-vessel disease	37	12
2-vessel disease, both ≥95%	42	14
1-vessel disease, ≥95% proximal LAD	48	17
2-vessel disease, ≥95% LAD	48	17
2-vessel disease, ≥95% proximal LAD	56	21
3-vessel disease	56	21
3-vessel disease, ≥95% in at least 1	63	27
3-vessel disease, 75% proximal LAD	67	33
3-vessel disease, ≥95% proximal LAD	74	41

*Assuming medical treatment only.
CAD = coronary artery disease; LAD = left anterior descending coronary artery.
From Califf RM, et al: Task Force 5: Stratification of patients into high, medium and low risk subgroups for purposes of risk factor management. J Am Coll Cardiol 1996;27:1007–1019.

Risk Stratification

Risk stratification guides the assessment of prognosis and the choices among therapies. This process requires information on the patient's demographics (e.g., age, gender), risk factors, stability or instability of the symptoms, extent and severity of coronary disease and systemic atherosclerosis, left ventricular function, comorbidities, and other related variables. Left ventricular function should be assessed by echocardiography. High-risk findings on an exercise test include equal to or greater than 2 mm ST segment depression, equal to or greater than 1 mm ST segment depression in the first stage of the Bruce protocol, sustained ST segment depression equal to or greater than 5 minutes after cessation of exercise, a blood pressure decrease of equal to or greater than 10 mm Hg, severe ventricular arrhythmias at a heart rate less than 120 beats/min, and inability to complete 6 minutes of the Bruce protocol. The Duke prognostic score incorporates clinical information into a risk scale that provides incremental prognostic information to that of clinical evaluation and angiography. The score is calculated as:

$$\text{(The duration of exercise in minutes)} - (5 \times \text{the number of mm of ST segment depression) and} - (4 \times \text{the angina score)}$$

where 0 = no angina, 1 = nonlimiting angina, and 2 = angina that causes discontinuation of activity. A score of equal to or greater than 5 predicts a 0.25% annual mortality; of −10 to +4, a 1.25% annual mortality; and of less than or equal to 10, a 5% annual mortality.

High-risk features on the nuclear scan are ischemia in greater than 15% of the left ventricle, multiple perfusion defects in more than one vascular bed, large and severe perfusion defects, left ventricular dilation, lung uptake with exercise, and postexercise left ventricular dilation. High-risk stress echocardiographic criteria are multiple reversible wall motion abnormalities and more severe and extensive abnormalities.

Coronary angiography with a view to coronary revascularization is performed in patients with high-risk criteria. The unique prognostic information provided by angiography (see Table 67–7) adds to the demographics, clinical history, comorbid conditions, physical examination, and ejection fraction in assessing risk. All of this information has been incorporated in a nomogram that permits accurate evaluation of the 5-year risk (Fig. 67–4). Beyond the number of vessels with significant stenoses, the total number of lesions, notwithstanding their severity, is a strong indicator of a worse prognosis.

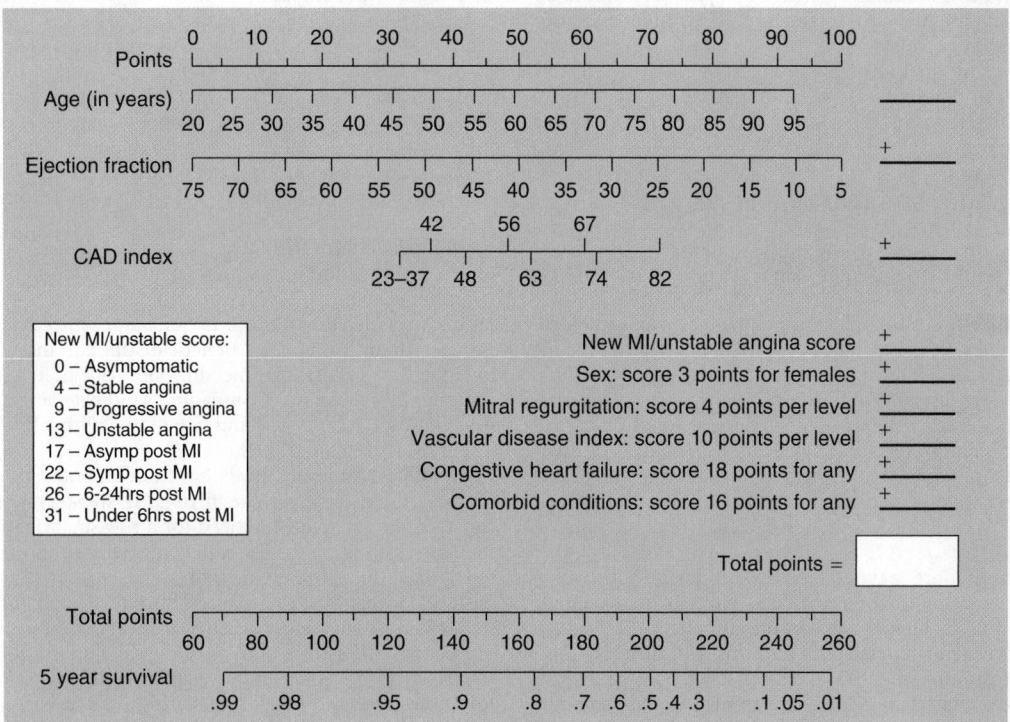

FIGURE 67–4 • Nomogram for prediction of 5-year survival from clinical, physical examination, and cardiac catheterization findings. How to read the nomogram: Score points for each of the nine factors on the far right, sum them up arithmetically, then refer to the 5-year survival chart to locate the probability of 5-year survival. For example, age = 45 years corresponds to 31 points; ejection fraction = 40, 50 points; extent of CAD = two-vessel disease corresponds to a prognostic weight of 37, 32 points (use Table 67–7 to score CAD index); new MI/unstable angina score = stable angina, 4 points; sex = female, 3 points; mitral regurgitation = level 4, 16 points; vascular disease index = level 2, 20 points; congestive heart failure = yes, 18 points; comorbid conditions = yes, 16 points. Total points: 31 + 50 + 32 + 4 + 3 + 16 + 20 + 18 + 16 = 190, which corresponds to a 5-year survival of 0.6. There is a probability of 60% that the patient in this example will survive 5 years. Asymp = asymptomatic; CAD = coronary artery disease; MI = myocardial infarction; Symp = symptomatic. (From Califf RM, et al: Task Force 5: Stratification of patients into high, medium and low risk subgroups for purposes of risk factor management. J Am Coll Cardiol 1996;27:1007–1019.)

Cardiovascular Disease

Table 67–8 • TREATMENT OF PATIENTS WITH STABLE ANGINA

GENERAL MEASURES
Smoking cessation (Chapter 14)
Control hypertension (Chapter 63)
Treat diabetes (Chapter 242)
Exercise prescription

REDUCE PROGRESSION TO ACUTE CORONARY SYNDROME, MYOCARDIAL INFARCTION, AND DEATH
Lipid management (Chapter 211)
Antiplatelet agents/anticoagulants (Chapter 33)
 Aspirin: 75–325 mg daily
 Clopidogrel: 75 mg daily if aspirin is not tolerated
 Warfarin: International normalized ratio 2.0–3.0 for postinfarction
  patients not able to take aspirin or clopidogrel

Vitamin therapy to lower homocysteine levels
β-Blockers
 Postinfarction patients (Chapters 68 and 69)
 Continue in patients with depressed left ventricular ejection fraction
  (but reduce dose if necessary)
Angiotensin-converting enzyme inhibitors
 Postinfarction patients with or without depressed left ventricular
  function and with or without heart failure (Chapters 56 and 69)
High-risk patients, especially diabetics, without clinical heart failure

CONTROL SYMPTOMS
β-Blockers
Nitrates, including pre-exercise prophylaxis
Calcium channel blocker

Adapted from Gibbons RJ, Chatterjee K, Daley J, et al: ACC/AHA/ACP-ASIM Guidelines for the management of patients with chronic stable angina: A report of the American College of Cardiology/American Heart Association Task Force on Practice Guidelines. J Am Coll Cardiol 1999;33:2143.

 Treatment

Management of angina is oriented to the improvement of quality of life and to the prevention of MI and death. The former is achieved by improving the ratio of myocardial oxygen supply and demand by drugs and the latter by interrupting the progression of the underlying atherosclerotic process and promoting its regression (Table 67–8 and Fig. 67–5). Correction of coronary risk factors improves prognosis in patients with CAD and may be associated with regression of the disease. An aggressive program for correction of risk factors is mandated. This program includes control of blood cholesterol, blood glucose, and hypertension; smoking cessation; and physical fitness. A statin also is indicated for the potential to alter plaque content and control plaque activation; it probably should be administered to all patients with documented CAD independently of the LDL cholesterol levels. Coronary revascularization can dramatically improve the quality of life and prolong life in selected patients. Teaching and individual counseling on CAD and its treatment with a positive focus on the control of risk factors are crucial at all steps of management.

PREVENTION OF DEATH AND MYOCARDIAL INFARCTION

Death and MI can be prevented by antithrombotic therapy, lipid-lowering agents, and angiotensin-converting enzyme (ACE) inhibitors.

ANTIPLATELET THERAPY. Antiplatelet therapy with aspirin is the cornerstone of treatment. It is indicated in all patients with CAD and other vascular disease.

Clopidogrel is at least as effective as aspirin in secondary prevention; in patients with an acute coronary syndrome, the benefits of a combination of clopidogrel and aspirin are additive. The general guidelines are to use aspirin as a first-line agent, clopidogrel as an alternative in patients intolerant to aspirin, and the combination of aspirin and clopidogrel in selected patients at high risk.

Aspirin's benefits are related to its inhibition of cyclo-oxygenase-1 in platelets (Chapter 33). This effect is dose-related, cumulative, and fully achieved with an initial bolus of 300 mg to inhibit the pretreatment platelet pool and doses of 80 to 160 mg daily thereafter to inhibit the 10% of the platelet pool generated every day. An anti-inflammatory mechanism may explain some of the benefit of aspirin. In the meta-analyses by the Antiplatelet Trialists' Collaboration that included more than 200,000 patients with cardiovascular disease, antiplatelet therapy, mainly aspirin, reduced the risk of MI, stroke, or vascular death by 22% (P < .00001); the risk of death by 15% (P < .00001); the risk of nonfatal MI by 35% (P < .00001); and the risk of nonfatal stroke by 25% (P < .00001).[1] The benefits were dose-independent.

Aspirin is also effective in primary prevention in patients without known CAD. A meta-analysis of more than 51,000 subjects

in four primary prevention trials showed significant risk reduction, reaching 32% for nonfatal MI and 13% for any important vascular events, with no increases in risk of vascular death and nonfatal stroke but a significant 1.7-fold increase in the risk of hemorrhagic stroke.[2]

Clopidogrel is a thienopyridine that partially and irreversibly inhibits the ADP PY12 receptor (Chapter 33). The CAPRIE (Clopidogrel versus Aspirin in Patients at Risk of Ischemic Events) trial in patients with a previous stroke, previous MI, or peripheral vascular disease showed a reduction of 8.7% in the risk of stroke, MI, and vascular death with clopidogrel, 75 mg/day, compared with aspirin, 325 mg/day (P = .04).[3] Clopidogrel was associated with fewer gastrointestinal side effects, slightly more cutaneous reactions, and no excess total bleeding. There was no excess leukopenia or thrombocytopenia with clopidogrel compared with aspirin. In the CURE (Clopidogrel in Unstable Angina to Prevent Recurrent Events) trial of patients with acute coronary syndromes, the combination aspirin plus clopidogrel reduced the risk of cardiovascular death, nonfatal MI, or stroke from 11.4% to 9.3% (relative risk 0.80; P = .00005), with no excess risk of thrombocytopenia or leukopenia.[4]

ANTICOAGULANT THERAPY. Warfarin is as effective as aspirin for secondary prevention but is associated with a higher risk of bleeding. Combination therapy with warfarin plus aspirin is superior to aspirin alone, provided that the international normalized ratio is maintained greater than 2.0, but the benefit of the combination needs to be weighed again a risk of bleeding in 1 out of 100 patient-years of treatment.[5] Warfarin (Coumadin) is indicated in patients with atrial fibrillation (Chapter 59) and in patients with left ventricular mural thrombosis (Chapter 69).

STATINS. Numerous trials have documented that statin therapy reduces the risk of death, recurrent MI, stroke, rehospitalization for unstable angina, and the need for a revascularization.[6] In selected patients, statins may be better than revascularization. In a randomized trial, fixed doses (40 mg/day) of simvastatin in patients at increased risk of coronary death because of prior MI, CAD or peripheral vascular disease, diabetes mellitus, treated hypertension, or age 40 to 80 years with a total cholesterol greater than 135 mg/dL reduced the risk of MI, stroke, and revascularization by one third regardless of cholesterol and LDL cholesterol levels at baseline, age, sex, or other treatments[6]

ANGIOTENSIN-CONVERTING ENZYME INHIBITORS. ACE inhibitors benefit patients with evidence of vascular disease or diabetes plus one other cardiovascular risk factor, even in the absence of low ejection fraction or heart failure. During a mean follow-up of 5 years, ramipril, 10 mg daily, reduced the composite end point of MI, stroke, or death from cardiovascular causes from 17.8% to 14% (relative risk 0.78; 95% confidence interval, 0.70 to 0.86; P < .001) in patients with no known left ventricular dysfunction. Based on these results,

Continued on page 398.

Cardiovascular Disease

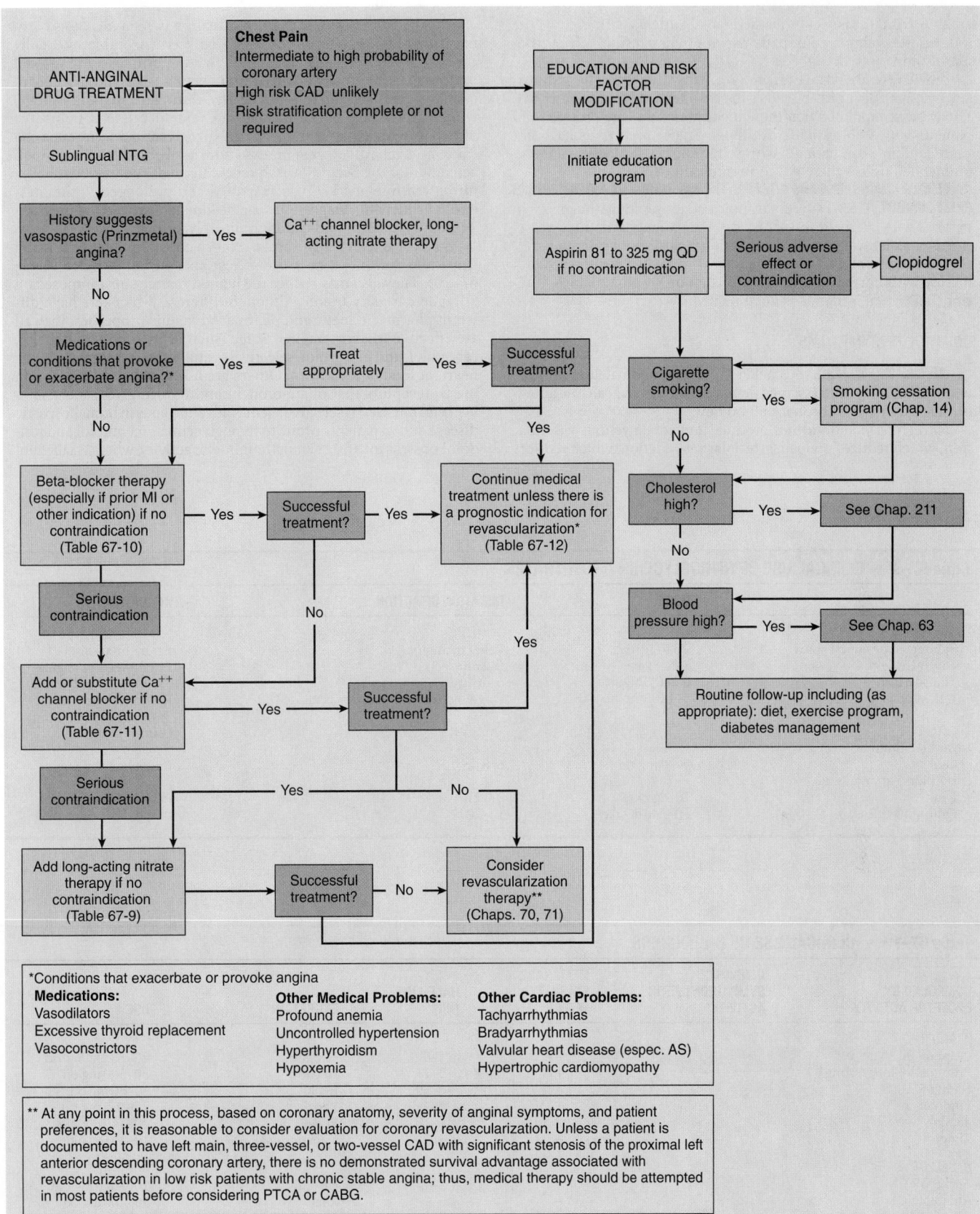

FIGURE 67–5 • Treatment of stable angina. AS = aortic stenosis; CABG = coronary artery bypass graft; CAD = coronary artery disease; JNC = Joint National Committee; MI = myocardial infarction; NCEP = National Cholesterol Education Program; NTG = nitroglycerin; PTCA = percutaneous transluminal coronary angioplasty. (Adapted from American College of Cardiology/American Heart Association Task Force on Practice Guidelines: Management of patients with chronic stable angina. ACC/AHA/ACP-ASIM Pocket Guidelines, Elsevier Science, 2000.)

an ACE inhibitor is recommended for all patients with CAD[7]; the indication is reinforced in patients with hypertension, left ventricular dysfunction, or diabetes.

β-BLOCKERS. Based on the results of many studies that have shown a protective effect of β-blockers in secondary prevention after MI, it may be extrapolated that these medications also are protective in patients with stable angina. Although randomized trials have not been conducted in patients with stable angina, β-blockers are recommended unless there are contraindications.

PERCUTANEOUS CORONARY INTERVENTION AND CORONARY ARTERY BYPASS GRAFT SURGERY. CABG surgery is indicated for prolongation of life in patients with left main vessel disease or in patients with three-vessel disease and left ventricular dysfunction regardless of symptoms.[8-10] CABG surgery or PCI also generally is indicated for three-vessel disease with normal ventricular function or for proximal left anterior CAD when ischemia is documented.[8-10]

CONTROL OF SYMPTOMS

MEDICAL MANAGEMENT. β-Blockers, nitrates, and calcium antagonists reduce myocardial oxygen demand. Nitrates and calcium antagonists also increase coronary blood flow.

Nitroglycerin and *nitrates* produce immediate venous vasodilation, which reduces preload; arteriolar vasodilation, which reduces afterload; and epicardial artery vasodilation, which increases coronary flow (Table 67–9). Sublingual nitroglycerin or oral spray equally can terminate an angina attack. Long-acting nitrates administered orally or transdermally are used to prevent angina and to improve exercise tolerance, and they can be used during the night in patients with nocturnal angina. To avoid nitrate tolerance, 8 to 12 hours free of exposure daily is recommended. Nitroglycerin and nitrates can cause headache, hypotension, and, more rarely, bradycardia through activation of the Bezold-Jarisch reflex. Because the vasodilation by nitroglycerin is markedly exaggerated and prolonged in the presence of sildenafil (Viagra), the use of sildenafil within the previous 24 hours is a contraindication to nitroglycerin.

β-Blockers reduce myocardial oxygen consumption by reducing heart rate and blood pressure at rest and during exercise (Table 67–10). They also may reduce the hemodynamic stress imposed on a fragile coronary lesion. Although different β-blockers have different pharmacokinetic and pharmacodynamic properties, they all are effective in effort angina. Some, such as metoprolol, atenolol, carvedilol, and bisoprolol, selectively inhibit the β_1-receptors in the heart, at least at low doses. Others are nonspecific, acting also on the β_2-receptors that dilate bronchi and induce glycogenolysis in liver and muscles. A selective agent is advantageous in bronchospastic disease and in patients prone to hypoglycemia. Acebutolol and pindolol possess intrinsic sympathomimetic activity, whereas labetalol

Table 67–9 • CLINICAL USE OF NITROGLYCERIN AND NITRATES

	DOSE	DURATION OF ACTION	INDICATION
Nitroglycerin			
Sublingual or buccal spray	0.15–1.5 mg	Relief of angina	Before or at onset of pain
Ointment	7.5–40 mg	8–12 hr	Prophylaxis of angina
Transdermal	0.2–0.8 mg/hr	8–16 hr	Prophylaxis of angina
Intravenous	5–1000 mg/hr	Ongoing; increasing doses as needed	Recurrent chest pain Systemic hypertension Left heart failure
Isosorbide dinitrate			
Oral	5–40 mg tid	6–8 hr	Prophylaxis of angina
Isosorbide-5-mononitrate			
Oral	20 mg bid	8–12 hr	Prophylaxis of angina
Oral, slow release	30–240 mg day	12–20 hr	Prophylaxis of angina

Table 67–10 • CLINICAL USE OF β-BLOCKERS

COMPOUND BY RECEPTOR ACTIVITY	INTRINSIC SYMPATHOMIMETIC ACTIVITY*	MEMBRANE STABILITY EFFECT	HALF-LIFE (HR)	EXCRETION	USE
β_1 AND β_2					
Propranolol	–	++	1–6	Hepatic	20–80 mg bid/tid
Propranolol long-acting	–	++	8–11	Hepatic	80–360 mg od
Nadolol	–	–	40–80	Renal	40–80 mg od
Pindolol	+	+	3–4	Renal	2.5–7.5 mg tid
Sotalol	–	–	7–18	Renal	40–160 mg bid
Timolol	–	–	4–5	Hepatic-renal	10–15 mg bid
β_1 SELECTIVE					
Acebutolol	+	+	3–4	Hepatic	200–600 mg bid
Atenolol	–	–	6–9	Renal	50–200 mg od
Bisoprolol	–	–	9–12	50% Renal	5–20 mg od
Metoprolol	–	–	3–7	Hepatic	50–200 mg bid
Metoprolol long-acting	–	–	14–25	Hepatic	100–400 mg
Esmolol	–	–	4.5 min	Esterases in red cells	Bolus 500 μg/kg 50–300 μg/kg/min IV
β_1, β_2, α_2					
Labetalol	+	–	6	Hepatic	200–600 mg bid
Carvedilol	–	+	6–10	Hepatic	200–600 mg bid

*Presence commonly associated with maintenance or increase in heart rate; absence associated with decrease in heart rate.

and carvedilol have α-adrenergic blocking effects. The former property is useful in patients with significant bradycardia at rest and can be advantageous in peripheral vasospasm and heart failure. Sotalol also possesses class 3 amiodarone-like antiarrhythmic activity (Chapter 62), which makes it useful in patients with arrhythmias. Lipid solubility tends to be associated with more central nervous system side effects, more rapid absorption, and liver metabolism. Agents with no intrinsic sympathetic activity can increase triglycerides levels and reduce high-density lipoprotein (HDL) cholesterol levels. Contraindications to β-blockers are significant bradyarrhythmias, acute heart failure, and active asthma. Relative contraindications are Raynaud's phenomenon, severe claudication, severe depression, and diabetes with labile blood glucose levels. Patients with Prinzmetal's angina may have an exacerbation with β-blockers. The most frequent side effects are fatigue, nightmares, and erectile dysfunction, the last-mentioned less frequently than often believed.

Calcium channel antagonists reduce calcium flux through the voltage-sensitive L-type calcium channels. All calcium channel antagonists are potent coronary vasodilators that can relieve coronary artery spasm. They also decrease myocardial oxygen needs by slowing heart rate and by reducing blood pressure and contractility. Significant differences exist between drugs in the in vivo expression of these properties (Table 67–11). The dihydropyridines are more potent vasodilators, resulting in reflex adrenergic stimulation that masks the negative chronotropic effects. Short-acting nifedipine and other dihydropyridines may be associated with poorer outcomes in unstable CAD and should be avoided unless the patient is also effectively treated with β-blockers. Verapamil has potent effects on cardiac conduction and contractility. The heart rate and vasodilator properties of diltiazem are intermediate between those of the dihydropyridines and verapamil, often resulting in a more favorable side-effect profile. The dihydropyridines are advantageous when a bradyarrhythmia is present, and the new dihydropyridines are a better choice in heart failure. Verapamil and diltiazem are contraindicated in sinus node disease, in atrioventricular nodal block, and in patients with left ventricular dysfunction after MI; they are better choices in patients with atrial tachyarrhythmias. Calcium antagonists are as effective as β-blockers for improving effort angina and are better in rest angina, particularly Prinzmetal's angina. Side effects related to vasodilation include hypotension, headache, and peripheral edema. Worsening of heart failure can occur with all drugs, whereas bradycardia and atrioventricular dissociation can occur with verapamil and diltiazem, particularly when combined with β-blockers. Constipation is common with verapamil.

OTHER INTERVENTIONS. Spinal cord stimulation may alleviate pain in patients who are poor candidates for revascularization procedures. Chelation therapy seems to be ineffective. External counterpulsation has shown promising results for refractory angina in small trials.

REVASCULARIZATION. PCI (Chapter 70) and CABG surgery (Chapter 71) result in an immediate relief of the obstruction to blood flow. The option of revascularization should be investigated by coronary angiography in patients with stable angina whenever the symptoms are not controlled in a satisfactory way or when they are unacceptable for the patient (Table 67–12). Angiography also should be performed in high-risk patients, including patients with left ventricular dysfunction, unless contraindicated. With PCI, symptomatic and angiographic improvement is expected in more than 90% of patients, with a complication rate less than 10%. Elective CABG surgery is associated with a mortality rate of 0.2%. The risk of CABG surgery is affected by many factors, including age, comorbid diseases, left ventricular function, and the extent of CAD. Internal mammary artery grafts are associated with a better short-term and long-term outcome. For single-vessel disease, PCI and CABG surgery can provide substantial symptomatic relief, but neither has been documented to improve survival.[8] In patients with multivessel disease, PCI and CABG surgery seem to have equivalent results in terms of death and MI, with PCI in general allowing patients to return to work sooner and CABG surgery being associated with fewer symptoms and better exercise tolerance.[8-10] CABG surgery is usually preferred to PCI in patients with diabetes mellitus.[11] The choice between CABG surgery and PCI is influenced mainly by the anatomy of coronary lesions and often by local expertise and by the preferences of the patient and physician. PCI and CABG surgery are in constant evolution with increasing expertise and improving technology. As mini-CABG surgery and beating heart surgery become more popular and as drug-eluting stents reduce restenosis, the success rates and safety of these two revascularization approaches are continuing to evolve.

Table 67–11 • PROPERTIES OF CALCIUM CHANNEL BLOCKING DRUGS IN CLINICAL USE

DRUGS*	USUAL DOSE	ELIMINATION HALF-LIFE (HRS)	HEMODYNAMIC EFFECT		SIDE EFFECTS
			HR	PVR	
DIHYDROPYRIDINES					
Nifedipine PA*	10–40 mg bid	10	↑↑	↓↓↓	Hypotension, dizziness, flushing, edema,
Nifedipine XL*	30–180 mg od	24	↑	↓↓	constipation
Amlodipine	2.5–10 mg od	30–50	=	↓↓↓	Headache, edema
Felodipine	2.5–10 mg od	11–16	↑	↓↓↓	Headache, dizziness
Isradipine	2.5–10 mg twice daily	8	=	↓↓↓	Headache, fatigue
Nicardipine	20–40 mg tid	2–4	↑	↓↓↓	Headache, dizziness, flushing, edema
Nicardipine SR*	30–60 mg bid	8–10	↑	↓↓	
Nisoldipine	10–40 mg od	7–12	=	↓↓↓	As nifedipine
Nitrendipine	20 mg od/bid	5–12	↑	↓↓↓	As nifedipine
OTHERS					
Bepridil	200–400 mg od	24–40	↓	↓	Arrhythmias, dizziness, nausea
Diltiazem	30–90 mg tid	4–6	↓	↓	Hypotension, dizziness, bradycardia, edema
Diltiazem CD*	120–440 mg od	—	↓	↓	
Verapamil	80–160 mg tid	3–8	↓	↓↓	Hypotension, heart failure, edema, bradycardia
Verapamil SR*	120–480 mg od	—	↓	↓↓	

*XL, CD, SR, PA: long-acting.
HR = heart rate; PVR = peripheral vascular resistance.

Cardiovascular Disease

Table 67–12 • CURRENT RECOMMENDATIONS FOR MYOCARDIAL REVASCULARIZATION IN PATIENTS WITH CHRONIC STABLE ANGINA

CABG SURGERY VERSUS MEDICAL THERAPY

1. Among patients with medically refractory angina pectoris, CABG surgery is indicated for symptom improvement[8,9]
2. Among patients with medically stable angina pectoris, CABG surgery is indicated to prolong life in left main coronary artery disease or three-vessel disease (regardless of left ventricular function)[8] but not to improve symptoms[12]
3. CABG surgery may be indicated for prolongation of life if the proximal left anterior descending coronary artery is involved (regardless of the number of diseased vessels)

PCI VERSUS MEDICAL THERAPY

1. Among patients with medically refractory angina pectoris, PCI is indicated for symptom improvement[9,10]
2. PCI may be indicated in the presence of severe myocardial ischemia, regardless of symptoms. It is unclear whether PCI improves survival compared with medical treatment among patients with one- or two-vessel disease[12]
3. In the absence of symptoms or myocardial ischemia, PCI is not indicated (merely for the presence of an anatomic stenosis)

PCI VERSUS CABG SURGERY

1. For single-vessel disease, PCI and CABG surgery provide excellent symptom relief, but repeat revascularization procedures are required more frequently after PCI. Intracoronary stenting is preferred to regular PCI, but direct comparison with CABG surgery is limited[8-11]
2. For treated diabetics with two- or three-vessel disease, CABG surgery is the treatment of choice[11]
3. For nondiabetics, multivessel PCI and CABG surgery are acceptable alternatives. The choice of PCI or CABG surgery for initial treatment depends primarily on local expertise and patient and physician preference[8-10]
   a. In general, PCI is preferred for patients at low risk and CABG surgery for patients at high risk
   b. Large differences in mortality are unlikely, but smaller, potentially important differences in mortality cannot be excluded by the available data
   c. CABG surgery is associated with more complete revascularization and superior early relief of angina, but these differences diminish after 3–5 years
   d. No significant differences in rates of myocardial infarction have been shown
   e. Repeat revascularization procedures are required significantly more often after PCI; this problem is reduced with drug-eluting stents
   f. Initial costs, quality of life, and return to work are initially more favorable with PCI than CABG surgery, but these outcomes roughly equalize over 3–5 years

CABG = coronary artery bypass graft; PCI = percutaneous coronary intervention.

Adapted from Rihal CS, Gersh BJ, Yusuf S: Chronic coronary artery disease: Coronary artery bypass surgery vs. percutaneous transluminal coronary angioplasty vs. reduced therapy. *In* Yusuf S, Cairns JA, Camm AJ, et al. (eds): Evidence-Based Cardiology. London, BMJ Books, 1999, pp 389–390.

Reproduced from Braunwald E, Goldman L (eds): Primary Care Cardiology, 2nd ed. Philadelphia, WB Saunders, 2003.

1. Collaborative meta-analysis of randomised trials of antiplatelet therapy for prevention of death, myocardial infarction, and stroke in high risk patients. BMJ 2002;324:71–86.
2. Aspirin for the primary prevention of cardiovascular events: Recommendation and rationale. Ann Intern Med 2002;136:157–160.
3. CAPRIE Steering Committee: A randomised, blinded, trial of clopidogrel versus aspirin in patients at risk of ischaemic events(CAPRIE). Lancet 1996;348:1329–1339.
4. The Clopidogrel in Unstable Angina to Prevent Recurrent Events trial investigators: Effects of clopidogrel in addition to aspirin in patients with acute coronary syndromes without ST-segment elevation. N Engl J Med 2001;345:494–502.
5. Verheugt FW: Warfarin for ischemic heart disease. Cardiol Rev 2001;9:325–328.
6. MRC/BHF Heart Protection Study of cholesterol lowering with simvastatin in 20,536 high-risk individuals: A randomized placebo-controlled trial. Lancet 2002;360:7–22.
7. Yusuf S, Sleight P, Pogue J, et al: Effects of an angiotensin-converting-enzyme inhibitor, ramipril, on cardiovascular events in high-risk patients. The Heart Outcomes Prevention Evaluation study investigators. N Engl J Med 2000;342:145–153.
8. Parisi AF: Clinical trials of coronary revascularization for chronic stable angina: Medical treatment versus coronary revascularization. Curr Opin Cardiol 2000;15:275–280.
9. Morrison DA, Sethi G, Sacks J, et al: Percutaneous coronary intervention versus coronary bypass graft surgery for patients with medically refractory myocardial ischemia and risk factors for adverse outcomes with bypass: The VA AWESOME multicenter registry: Comparison with the randomized clinical trial. J Am Coll Cardiol 2002;39:266–273.
10. Serruys PW, Unger F, Abbas MA, et al: Comparison of coronary artery bypass surgery and stenting for the treatment of multivessel disease. N Engl J Med 2001;344:1117–1124.
11. The Bypass Angioplasty Revascularization Investigation: Comparison of coronary bypass surgery with angioplasty in patients with multivessel disease. N Engl J Med 1996;335:217–225.
12. Pfister M, Buser P, Osswald S, et al: Outcome of elderly patients with chronic symptomatic coronary artery disease with an invasive vs. optimized medical treatment strategy. JAMA 2003;289:1117–1123.

SUGGESTED READINGS

Fihn SD, Williams SV, Daley J, Gibbons RJ: Guidelines for the management of patients with chronic stable angina: Treatment. Ann Intern Med 2001;135:616–632. *An evidence-based review.*

Gibbons RJ, Abrams J, Chatterjee K, et al: ACC/AHA 2002 guideline update for the management of patients with chronic stable angina—summary article: A report of the American College of Cardiology/American Heart Association Task Force on Practice Guidelines (Committee on Management of Patients with Chronic Stable Angina). Circulation 2003;107:149–158. *Executive guidelines and extensive review of diagnosis, risk stratification, and management of stable angina.*

Williams SV, Fihn SD, Gibbons RJ: Guidelines for the management of patients with chronic stable angina: Diagnosis and risk stratification. Ann Intern Med 2001; 135:530–547. *An analytic synthesis.*

68 ACUTE CORONARY SYNDROME: UNSTABLE ANGINA AND NON–ST SEGMENT ELEVATION MYOCARDIAL INFARCTION

David D. Waters

Definition and Epidemiology

Acute coronary syndrome (ACS) describes the continuum of myocardial ischemia that ranges from unstable angina at one end of the spectrum to non–ST segment elevation myocardial infarction (MI) at the other end. Unstable angina is distinguished from stable angina (Chapter 67) by the new onset or worsening of symptoms in the previous 60 days or by the development of post-MI angina 24 hours or more after the onset of MI. When the clinical picture of unstable angina is accompanied by elevated markers of myocardial injury, such as troponins or cardiac isoenzymes, non–ST segment elevation MI is diagnosed. The distinction between non–ST segment elevation MI and MI with ST segment elevation (Chapter 69) is clinically important because early recanalization therapy improves the outcome in ST elevation MI but not in non–ST segment elevation MI.

For ACS, whether defined clinically as unstable angina or as non–ST segment elevation MI, the pathophysiologic mechanisms are the same. Most ACS are caused by nonocclusive thrombosis occurring in a native vessel, a vessel that has been the previous site of a coronary angioplasty (Chapter 70), or a coronary artery bypass graft (Chapter 71). In other situations, ACS may be precipitated by coronary spasm or by an increase in myocardial oxygen demand superimposed on preexisting fixed coronary stenoses. From a clinical perspective, the presentation of patients with ACS ranges from that of typical unstable angina to a presentation indistinguishable from ST segment elevation MI. Regardless of the clinical presentation, however, the rapid clinical detection of ACS is key to the institution of appropriate therapy, which is different from that used for stable angina, on the one hand, or ST segment elevation MI, on the other hand.

Approximately 1.5 million patients are hospitalized annually in the United States with unstable angina or non–ST segment elevation MI. These conditions are more common in older people, in people with a history of coronary disease, and in people with atherosclerosis known to be present in other vascular beds or with multiple coronary risk factors.

Classification

Several systems have been proposed for classifying unstable angina. Distinguishing *primary* from *secondary* unstable angina is of clinical value. Acute worsening of a coronary stenosis causes primary unstable angina by limiting coronary blood flow. Secondary unstable angina arises as a consequence of increased myocardial oxygen demand superimposed on severe underlying coronary disease. The conditions with the potential to provoke secondary unstable angina include tachyarrhythmia, fever, hypoxia, anemia, hypertensive crisis, and thyrotoxicosis. Secondary unstable angina should resolve with successful treatment of the precipitating condition. Patients with non–ST segment elevation ACS should be categorized according to their level of short-term risk because patients at higher risk benefit from more aggressive treatment, whereas low-risk patients do not.

Various classifications have been proposed for primary unstable angina based on presenting symptoms. The most common approach (Table 68–1) includes three levels of severity and three clinical circumstances, to yield nine categories in all. This classification is used frequently to categorize patients for research purposes, but no system is used widely in clinical practice.

The recognition of three specific subtypes of primary unstable angina is worthwhile because their pathophysiology, prognosis, and management are different from those of typical unstable angina. *Variant* or *Prinzmetal's angina* is caused by coronary spasm and usually can be controlled by calcium channel blockers. *Unstable angina within 6 months after coronary angioplasty* (Chapter 70) almost invariably is caused by restenosis. Because the underlying mechanism is cellular proliferation instead of plaque rupture, antithrombotic drugs are not needed; intravenous nitroglycerin provides effective acute treatment, and repeat revascularization typically is required. *Unstable angina in a patient with previous coronary artery bypass graft (CABG) surgery* (Chapter 71) often involves advanced atherosclerosis of venous bypass grafts or progression of native vessel disease and portends a lower likelihood of long-term symptomatic relief compared with other patients with unstable angina. For each of these presentations,

unstable angina may progress to non–ST segment elevation MI if adequate treatment is not instituted promptly.

Pathobiology

With the exception of ACS caused by the systemic stresses listed previously, plaque rupture or erosion with overlying thrombosis is considered to be the initiating mechanism of ACS, including unstable angina and non–ST segment elevation MI (Chapter 66). Mechanical factors contribute to plaque disruption: A thin fibrous cap is more prone to rupture than a thick one, and plaque rupture occurs commonly where the plaque joins the adjacent vessel wall. Plaque erosion and plaque rupture can initiate an ACS. Erosion usually occurs centrally through a thinning cap rather than at the lateral edge of the plaque.

Inflammation also seems to play a key role in plaque disruption. Macrophages and T lymphocytes accumulate in atherosclerotic plaques because of the expression of adhesion molecules on monocytes, endothelial cells, and leukocytes. These cells release growth factors and chemotactic factors, which lead to local oxidation of low-density lipoprotein cholesterol, proliferation of smooth muscle cells, and production of foam cells.

Increased serum levels of C-reactive protein (CRP) are found in most patients with unstable angina and MI, but not in stable angina, and elevated CRP levels are a strong predictor of subsequent coronary events in patients with coronary disease. Similarly the cytokine interleukin-6, which is the main producer of CRP in the liver, is elevated in unstable angina but not in stable angina.

The stimulus that initiates the acute inflammatory process in ACS has not been identified. *Chlamydia pneumoniae*, cytomegalovirus, and *Helicobacter pylori* have been identified within human atherosclerotic lesions, and antibodies against *Chlamydia* heat-shock proteins can cross-react against heat-shock proteins produced by endothelium, resulting in endothelial damage and accelerated atherosclerosis. Antibodies to *Chlamydia*, cytomegalovirus, and *Helicobacter* are found more often in patients with atherosclerosis compared with controls. These associations do not prove causality, however, and clinical trials of antibiotic therapy in patients with ACS have shown no benefit.

Platelet deposition onto the exposed, thrombogenic surface of the ruptured plaque is an important step in the pathogenesis of ACS, yet only a small fraction of disrupted plaques culminate in symptoms. Patients with coronary or peripheral vascular disease have increased platelet reactivity compared with normal controls. Healthy endothelium releases nitric oxide, which inhibits platelet aggregation. This protective mechanism is attenuated in atherosclerosis.

In ACS, platelets are activated and generate thromboxane and prostaglandin metabolites. Severe or persistent unstable angina is associated with the highest thromboxane output, and stabilization of unstable angina is accompanied by a return to normal levels.

Activated platelets and leukocytes interact to stimulate the coagulation system. Monocytes release tissue factor, a small glycoprotein that initiates the extrinsic clotting cascade, leading to an increase in thrombin generation. Transient increases in thrombin-antithrombin III and prothrombin fragment 1 + 2 can be shown in the hour after an ischemic attack in most patients with ACS.

Tissue factor is also present in the lipid-rich core of atherosclerotic plaque and may be one of the major determinants of the thrombogenicity of plaques when they rupture. When tissue factor specifically is inhibited, the deposition of platelets and fibrin onto the ruptured plaque is reduced. Patients with ACS and high circulating levels of tissue factor have unfavorable outcomes.

Overactivity of other components of the coagulation system has been reported in unstable angina, including levels of factor XII, bradykinin precursor, and fibrinogen. Lower tissue-type plasminogen activator and plasminogen activator inhibitor-1 levels indicate that an impairment of the fibrinolytic system also is present.

Culprit lesions in unstable angina and non–ST segment elevation MI exhibit a heightened response to vasoconstrictor stimuli. This response is not present in other coronary segments and is not seen in culprit lesions of patients with stable angina. One explanation for this finding is that endothelin levels are higher in culprit lesions as a result of inflammation. Under experimental conditions, the degree of vasoconstriction varies, however, directly with the amount of platelet deposition. The process of platelet aggregation and thrombus formation releases potent vasoconstrictors, such as thromboxane A_2

Table 68–1 • BRAUNWALD CLASSIFICATION OF UNSTABLE ANGINA

SEVERITY

Class I   New-onset, severe or accelerated angina. (Angina of <2 mo duration, severe or occurring >3 times/day, or angina that is distinctly more frequent and precipitated by distinctly less exertion. No rest pain within 2 mo)

Class II   Angina at rest, subacute. (Angina at rest within the preceding month but not within the preceding 48 hr)

Class III   Angina at rest, acute. (Angina at rest within the preceding 48 hr)

CLINICAL CIRCUMSTANCES

Class A   Secondary unstable angina. (A clearly identified condition extrinsic to the coronary vascular bed that has intensified myocardial ischemia, e.g., anemia, hypotension, tachyarrhythmia)

Class B   Primary unstable angina

Class C   Postinfarction unstable angina. (Within 2 wk of a documented myocardial infarction)

INTENSITY OF TREATMENT

1. Absence of treatment or minimal treatment
2. Standard therapy for chronic stable angina. (Conventional doses of oral β-blockers, nitrates, and calcium channel blockers)
3. Maximal therapy. (Maximally tolerated doses of all three categories of oral therapy and intravenous nitroglycerin)

Adapted from Braunwald E: Unstable angina: A classification. Circulation 1989;80:410–414.

Cardiovascular Disease

and serotonin. Vasoconstriction, or the absence of appropriate vasodilation, probably contributes significantly to the development of ischemic episodes in ACS and is a potential target for therapy.

The angiographic aspects of the culprit lesion have been defined from before, to during, to after the episode of unstable angina or non–ST segment elevation MI. If a patient with ACS previously has had a coronary angiogram, the culprit lesion usually can be documented to have progressed markedly since that time. Lesions that progress to cause acute coronary events usually are not severely stenotic; two thirds cause less than a 50% reduction in diameter and would not be targets for revascularization. Angiographic features of a lesion that predict that it will precipitate an acute coronary event include greater asymmetry, greater length, and a steeper outflow angle.

At the time of an episode of unstable angina or a non–ST segment elevation MI, the culprit lesion is more likely to be asymmetrical or eccentric, with a narrow base or neck, compared with control lesions. These angiographic features reflect the underlying plaque disruption with thrombus. Obvious thrombus is visible at angiography in a few patients with unstable angina. Coronary angioscopy reveals plaque rupture with overlying thrombus in most culprit lesions, however.

During the months after an episode of unstable angina or non–ST segment elevation MI, the initial culprit lesion is far more likely to progress and to precipitate another coronary event than are other lesions in the same patient or lesions in stable patients. Lesions with irregular borders, overhanging edges, or obvious thrombus at angiography are more likely to precipitate another event in the ensuing months than are smooth lesions.

Clinical Manifestations

SYMPTOMS AND SIGNS. The patient with unstable angina or non–ST segment elevation MI seeks medical attention because he or she has recognized either that new symptoms have appeared or that a previously stable pattern of symptoms has become unstable. Patients with non–ST segment elevation MI also may present with a pattern of increasing anginal episodes at rest or at lower levels of activity, but these patients are more likely to experience a prolonged episode of discomfort at rest. In many patients, the clinical presentation is indistinguishable from acute ST segment elevation MI (Chapter 69), whereas other patients may have nonspecific symptoms (Chapter 46).

The sensation of myocardial ischemia usually is located in the retrosternal area but may be felt only in the epigastrium, back, arms, or jaw. The description may include adjectives such as *burning, squeezing, pressure-like,* and *heavy* and, less often, *sharp, jabbing,* and *knife-like.* The physician should be cautioned that atypical features do not exclude unstable angina (Chapter 46).

Nausea, sweating, or shortness of breath may accompany episodes of acute myocardial ischemia. In elderly or diabetic patients, these symptoms may be the only indication that myocardial ischemia is present. Women who present with ACS are more likely to have diabetes, hypertension, hyperlipidemia, and heart failure and to be older than men; they are less likely to be smokers and to have had a previous MI or a previous coronary revascularization.

On physical examination, transient signs of left ventricular dysfunction, such as basilar rales or a ventricular gallop, may accompany or follow shortly after an episode of unstable angina. More ominous signs of severe transient left ventricular dysfunction, such as hypotension or peripheral hypoperfusion, are not encountered commonly in the absence of myocardial necrosis. When ACS is manifested as a non–ST segment elevation MI, however, signs and symptoms may be similar to those of ST segment elevation MI (Chapter 69) depending on the size and location of the damage. Physical examination may reveal precipitating causes of or contributing factors to unstable angina, such as pneumonia or uncontrolled hypertension.

ELECTROCARDIOGRAM. The electrocardiogram (ECG) may be entirely normal or show only nonspecific abnormalities in patients with unstable angina or non–ST segment elevation MI. Transient ST segment depression of at least 1 mm that appears during chest pain and disappears with relief is objective evidence of transient myocardial ischemia. When ST segment depression is a persistent feature of ECGs recorded with or without chest pain, the finding commonly represents non–ST segment elevation MI. A common ECG pattern of patients with unstable angina or non–ST segment elevation MI is a persistently negative T wave, which usually indicates that a

severe stenosis is present in the corresponding coronary artery. Deeply negative T waves occasionally are seen across all of the precordial leads, a pattern that suggests a severe, proximal stenosis of the left anterior descending coronary artery as the culprit lesion (Chapter 54).

The ECG in ACS may show Q waves from an old MI or left bundle-branch block owing to extensive prior left ventricular damage. Patients with these findings are at increased risk because they are less likely than other patients to be able to tolerate an additional insult to the myocardium. ECG abnormalities may appear or evolve in the absence of new symptoms in patients with ACS. The development of significant Q waves may be the first indicator that the diagnosis is non–ST segment elevation MI, not unstable angina. T wave abnormalities may appear, worsen, or resolve. It is worthwhile to obtain serial ECGs during the first 48 hours and during episodes of chest pain.

Continuous 12-lead ECG monitoring can be performed using new, multiprocessor-controlled, programmable devices. The limited clinical experience with this technology suggests that it can detect episodes of ST segment depression when the presenting ECG is normal and that this information has prognostic and diagnostic value.

CARDIAC MARKERS. According to the traditional paradigm, elevated serum levels of cardiac enzymes or the MB isoenzyme of creatine kinase distinguished between unstable angina and acute MI. The diagnosis of unstable angina could be retained when minor elevations of CK or CK-MB were detected by serial sampling, but it was recognized that these elevations were an adverse prognostic sign. It now is recognized that one fifth to one quarter of patients who otherwise would be diagnosed with unstable angina have elevated levels of troponin T or troponin I on admission or soon thereafter, and most of them have normal levels of CK-MB. In 2000, a Joint European Society of Cardiology/American College of Cardiology committee recommended that these patients be classified as having acute MI, and this change has been widely adopted (Chapter 69). The rationale for this change is that several large studies have shown that elevations of troponin are independent predictors of adverse events.

Troponin measurements may be normal early after the onset of ACS and become positive later, usually by 6 and almost always by 12 hours. Myoglobin, a low-molecular-weight heme protein found in skeletal and cardiac muscle, may be detected 2 hours after the onset of symptoms but is not specific for myocardial damage. CK-MB subforms are usually positive within 6 hours, and troponin T or I is usually positive within 12 hours. Troponin levels remain elevated for 1 week and are useful in making a diagnosis when the patient presents late after a coronary event.

Diagnosis

Patients with suspected ACS must be evaluated rapidly and efficiently. A prompt and accurate diagnosis permits the timely initiation of appropriate therapy, which is important because complications are clustered in the early phases of ACS, and appropriate treatment reduces the rate of complications.

Patients with chest pain lasting longer than 20 minutes, hemodynamic instability, or recent syncope or presyncope should be referred

to a hospital emergency department. Other patients with suspected unstable angina may be seen initially either in an emergency department or in an outpatient facility where a 12-lead ECG can be obtained quickly.

An ECG must be obtained as soon as possible in the initial evaluation of any patient with suspected ACS. The diagnostic yield is enhanced greatly if a tracing also can be recorded during an episode of chest pain. A normal ECG during chest pain does not exclude unstable angina; however, it does indicate that an ischemic area, if

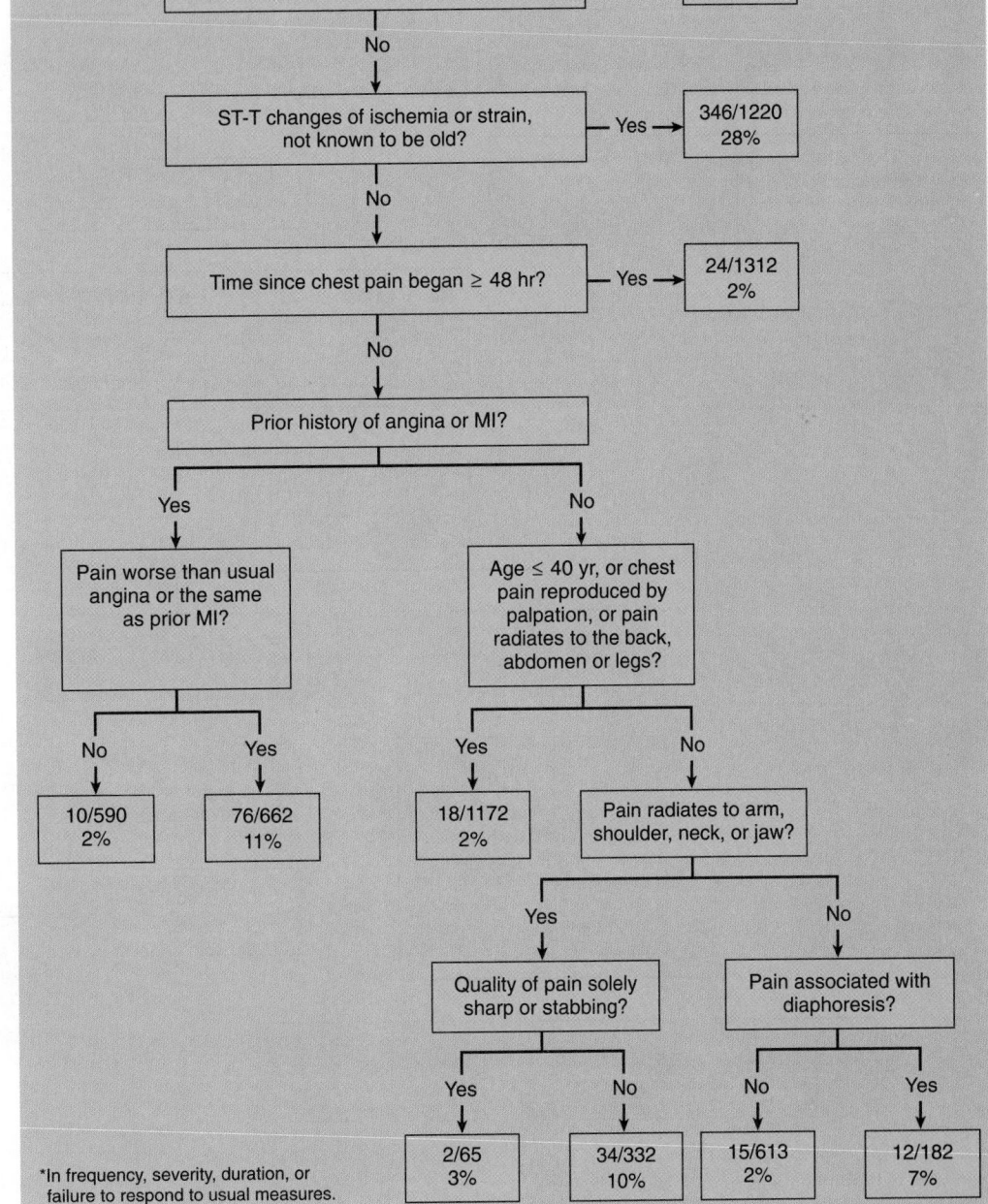

FIGURE 68–1 • Flow diagram for estimating the risk of acute myocardial infarction (MI) in emergency departments in patients with acute chest pain. For each clinical subset, the numerator is the number of patients with the set of presenting characteristics who developed an MI, whereas the denominator is the total number of patients presenting with that characteristic or set of characteristics. (Adapted from Pearson SD, Goldman L, Garcia TB, et al: Physician response to a prediction rule for the triage of emergency department patients with chest pain. J Gen Intern Med 1994;9:241–247.)

present, is not extensive or severe enough to induce ECG changes, and this finding is a favorable prognostic sign.

The initial assessment should be directed toward determining whether or not the symptoms are caused by myocardial ischemia and, if so, the level of risk. The probability of MI can be estimated from the history, physical examination, and ECG (Fig. 68–1). This information and the assessment of the patient's clinical features should indicate whether the probability that symptoms are due to myocardial ischemia is high, intermediate, or low (Table 68–2). Based on this information, the patient's initial triage and management should be determined (Fig. 68–2).

If chest pain and ST segment elevation greater than 1 mm in two contiguous leads are present, the diagnosis is ST segment elevation MI; reperfusion with thrombolytic therapy or primary angioplasty should be considered without delay (Chapter 69). In a patient known to have coronary disease, typical symptoms are highly likely to be caused by myocardial ischemia, particularly if the patient confirms that the symptoms are identical to previous episodes. Conversely, even if chest pain has some typical features, it is unlikely to be related to

myocardial ischemia in a young individual known not to have risk factors for coronary disease. In one prospective multicenter study, older age, male sex, and the presence of chest or left arm pain or pressure as the presenting symptom all increased the likelihood that the patient was experiencing acute myocardial ischemia.

When ACS is suspected in a patient younger than age 50 years, it is particularly important to ask about cocaine use, regardless of social class or ethnicity. Cocaine can cause coronary vasospasm and thrombosis in addition to its direct effects on heart rate and arterial pressure, and it has been implicated as a cause of unstable angina and MI (Chapter 30).

Unstable angina may be more difficult to diagnose than stable angina, owing to an absence of some of the distinguishing features. The characteristic relationship between stable angina and physical exertion or other stressful activities is a key diagnostic feature of stable angina that is lacking in unstable angina. ACS may be relieved poorly by nitroglycerin, whereas stable angina almost always responds. The duration of an episode of chest discomfort is usually longer and more variable in unstable angina than in stable angina.

Cardiovascular Disease

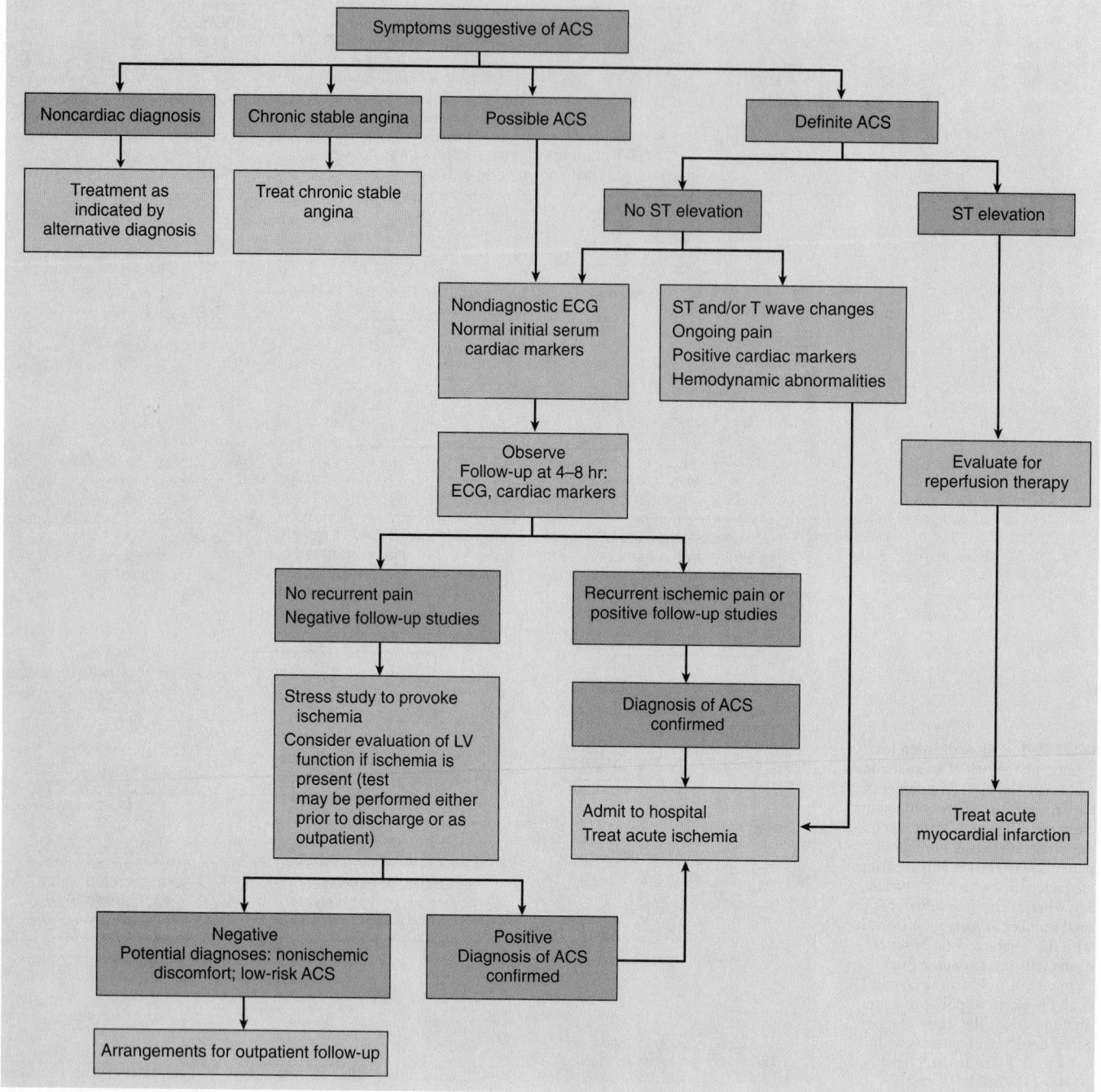

FIGURE 68–2 • Initial triage for patients with symptoms suggestive of an acute coronary syndrome (ACS). ACC/AHA/ACP = American College of Cardiology/American Heart Association/American College of Physicians; ECG = electrocardiogram. (Adapted from Braunwald E, Antman EM, Beasley JW, et al: ACC/AHA guidelines for the management of patients with unstable angina and non-ST-segment elevation myocardial infarction. J Am Coll Cardiol 2000;36:970–1062, with permission.)

RISK ASSESSMENT AND INITIAL TRIAGE

The evaluation of a patient with a possible ACS requires not only establishing the diagnosis, but also assessing the short-term risk of complications requiring intensive care (Fig. 68–3). This risk assessment determines the appropriate intensity of therapy. At the low end of the risk scale, a patient might be discharged home with aspirin and a β-blocker, to be followed as an outpatient. At the opposite end of the scale, a patient might be hospitalized in a coronary care unit, treated with multiple drugs, and undergo coronary arteriography urgently as a prelude to revascularization.

Troponin levels should be measured when the patient first is seen and again 6 to 12 hours later (Chapter 69). Myocardial perfusion imaging during or shortly after an episode of chest pain can aid in diagnosis and prognosis but is not indicated routinely (Chapter 52). The sensitivity of this test decreases as the interval between chest

pain and injection of the nuclear tracer lengthens. Large or multiple reversible perfusion defects indicate increased risk.

Patients with symptoms that suggest ACS can be categorized into low-risk, intermediate-risk, and high-risk groups, based on data available at the time of first assessment (Table 68–3). High-risk patients have ongoing chest pain lasting longer than 20 minutes, reversible ST segment changes of at least 1 mm, or signs of serious left ventricular dysfunction. Low-risk patients have worsening angina without rest pain, are not older than age 65 years, and have a normal or unchanged ECG, without evidence of a previous MI.

The risk assessment should be updated during hospitalization because patients frequently change. Continuing angina with ST segment changes despite medical therapy is an ominous sign that should precipitate urgent coronary arteriography with a view to revascularizations (Chapters 70 and 71) because the risk of progressing to MI is high (Fig. 68–4). Most episodes of recurrent myocardial

Table 68–2 • LIKELIHOOD THAT UNSTABLE ANGINA SYMPTOMS ARE CAUSED BY MYOCARDIAL ISCHEMIA

HIGH LIKELIHOOD
Any of the following features:
  Known coronary disease
  Definite angina in men ≥60 years old or women ≥70 years old
  Hemodynamic or ECG changes during pain
  Variant angina
  ST elevation or depression of at least 1 mm
  Marked symmetrical T-wave inversion in multiple precordial leads

INTERMEDIATE LIKELIHOOD
Absence of high-likelihood features and any of the following:
  Definite angina in men <60 years old or women <70 years old
  Probable angina in men ≥60 years old or women ≥70 years old
  Probably not angina in diabetics, or in nondiabetics with ≥2 other
    risk factors*
  Extracardiac vascular disease
  ST depression 0.05–1 mm
  T-wave inversion of at least 1 mm in leads with dominant R waves

LOW LIKELIHOOD
Absence of high- or intermediate-likelihood features, but may have:
  Chest pain, probably not angina
  One risk factor, but not diabetes
  T-waves flat or inverted <1 mm in leads with dominant R waves
  Normal ECG

────

*Risk factors include diabetes, smoking, hypertension, and hypercholesterolemia.
ECG = electrocardiogram.
Adapted from Braunwald E, et al: Diagnosing and managing unstable angina. Circulation 1994;90:613–622.

Table 68–3 • SHORT-TERM RISK OF DEATH OR MYOCARDIAL INFARCTION IN PATIENTS PRESENTING WITH SYMPTOMS SUGGESTING ACUTE CORONARY SYNDROME

HIGH RISK
At least one of the following features must be present:
  Prolonged, ongoing (>20 min) rest pain
  Pulmonary edema
  Angina with new or worsening mitral regurgitation murmurs
  Rest angina with dynamic ST changes of at least 1 mm
  Angina with S_3 or rales
  Angina with hypotension

INTERMEDIATE RISK
No high-risk features but must have any of the following:
  Rest angina now resolved but not low likelihood of coronary disease
  Rest angina (>20 min or relieved with rest or nitroglycerin)
  Angina with dynamic T-wave changes
  Nocturnal angina
  New-onset Canadian Cardiovascular Society class III or IV angina in
    past 2 weeks but not low likelihood of coronary disease
  Q waves or ST depression of at least 1 mm in multiple leads
  Age >65 years

LOW RISK
No high-risk or intermediate-risk feature but may have any of the
    following:
  Increased angina frequency, severity, or duration
  Angina provoked at a lower threshold
  New-onset angina within 2 wk to 2 mo
  Normal or unchanged ECG

────

Adapted from Braunwald E, et al: Diagnosing and managing unstable angina. Circulation 1994;90:613–622.

ischemia are silent, and some investigators have reported that ST segment depression as detected by Holter monitoring is a better predictor of an unfavorable outcome.

Troponin measurements should be used in the risk stratification of patients with ACS to supplement the assessment from clinical features and the ECG. Elevated troponin levels strongly predict coronary events over the short-term. A major advantage of troponin measurements is that they contribute to risk independently of most of the other major predictors. In one large study, elevated troponin T, age, hypertension, number of antianginal drugs, and ECG changes at baseline predicted cardiac death or MI. Higher troponin T levels predict higher risk, especially in patients with ST segment depression. Elevated levels of CRP, serum amyloid A, and interleukin-6 also are associated with a poorer prognosis in patients with unstable angina.

The widely used Thrombolysis in Myocardial Infarction (TIMI) risk score, which has been validated in clinical trials, includes seven factors: (1) age 65 years or older, (2) at least three of the standard risk factors for coronary disease, (3) a prior coronary stenosis of 50% or more, (4) ST segment deviation on the presenting ECG, (5) at least two anginal episodes in the previous 24 hours, (6) use of aspirin in the previous week, and (7) elevated serum cardiac markers. Among more than 7000 patients with unstable angina or non–ST segment elevation MI in two trials, the event rate over 14 days increased from 4.7% for patients with a score of 0 or 1 to 41% for patients with a score of 6 or 7.

Patients with suspected ACS but with low-risk features often undergo stress testing if the ECGs are nondiagnostic and troponin levels remain normal for 12 hours. The type of test can vary from exercise with ECG monitoring or nuclear imaging to dipyridamole, adenosine, or dobutamine stress with nuclear imaging or echocardiography (Chapters 46, 51, and 52).

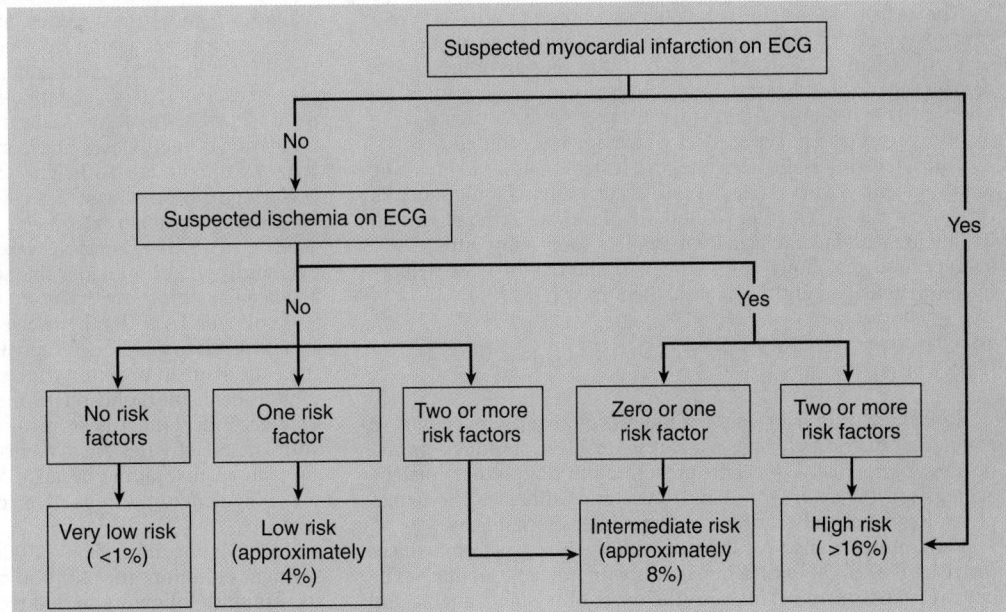

FIGURE 68–3 • Derivation and validation of four groups into which patients can be categorized according to risk of major cardiac events within 72 hours after admission for acute chest pain. ECG = electrocardiogram. (From Lee TH, Goldman L: Evaluation of the patient with acute chest pain. N Engl J Med 2000;342:1187–1195.)

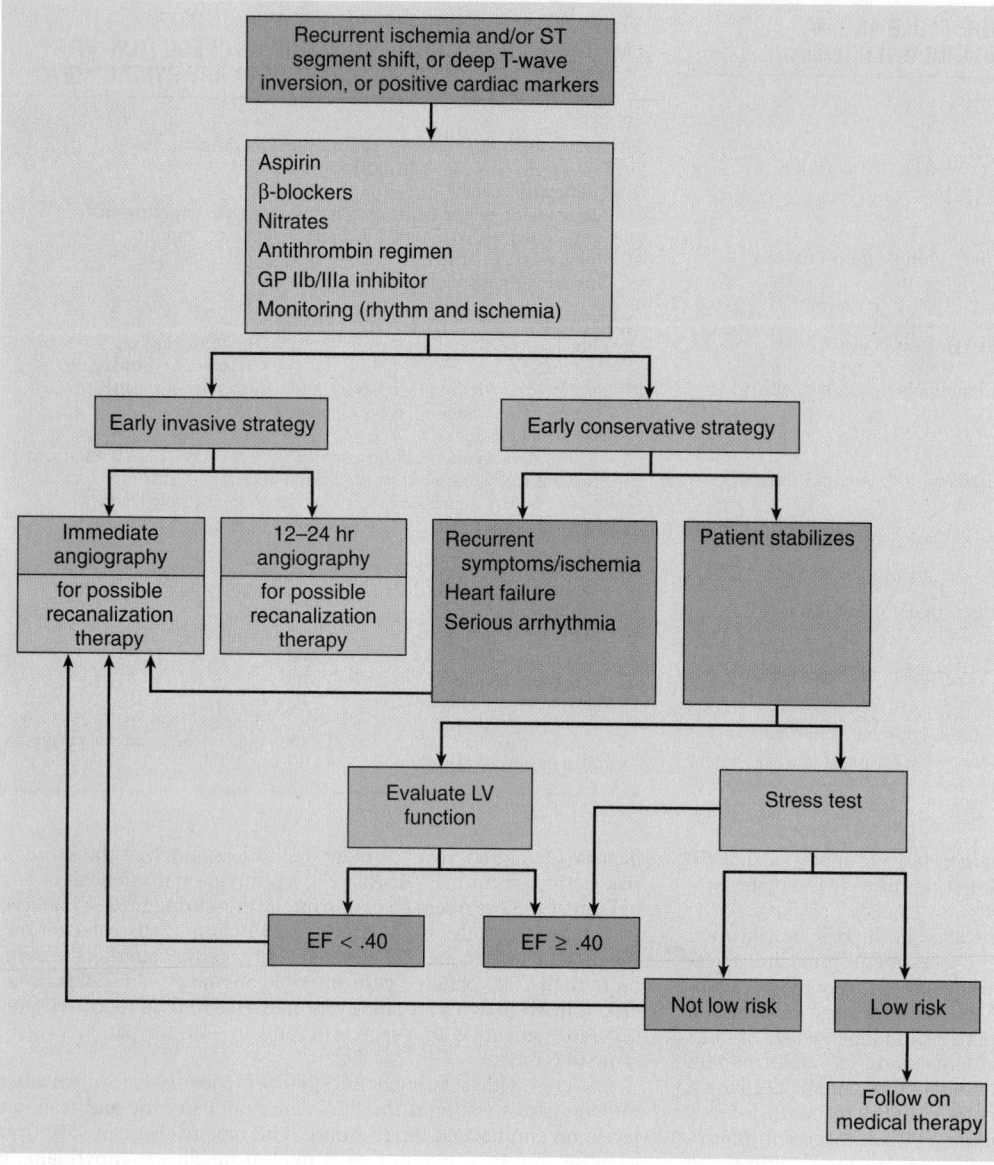

FIGURE 68–4 • Approach to the high-risk patient with an acute coronary syndrome. EF = ejection fraction; GP = glycoprotein. (Adapted from Braunwald E, Antman EM, Beasley JW, et al: ACC/AHA guidelines for the management of patients with unstable angina and non-ST-segment elevation myocardial infarction. J Am Coll Cardiol 2000;36:970–1062, with permission.)

Rx Prevention and Treatment

The goals of treatment in patients who present with ACS are to control symptoms and either to prevent progression to non–ST segment elevation MI or at least to limit the amount of myocardial damage. Rapid intervention is crucial because the severity of the initial presentation does not inalterably predict the ultimate severity of myocardial damage if effective therapy is instituted.

Nitroglycerin, β-blockers, and, to a lesser extent, calcium channel blockers reduce the risk of recurrent ischemic attacks. Revascularization (Chapters 70 and 71) eliminates ischemia entirely in patients with favorable anatomy, and, in some subgroups, CABG surgery has been shown to prolong life. The risk of MI is reduced by antiplatelet and antithrombotic therapy.

TREATMENTS TO REDUCE PROGRESSION TO OR SIZE OF MYOCARDIAL INFARCTION

ASPIRIN. Aspirin irreversibly inhibits cyclooxygenase activity in platelets. Consequently the platelet is unable to produce thromboxane A_2, the platelet-specific prostaglandin that induces platelet aggregation (Chapter 32). Aspirin also may influence the pathophysiology of unstable angina through other mechanisms.

Randomized trials have shown conclusively that aspirin reduces the risk of MI by 50 to 67% in patients with unstable angina.◼ The benefit from aspirin begins with the onset of unstable angina and

extends for more than 1 year. Because aspirin reduces the risk of MI in patients with stable coronary disease (Chapter 67), the drug should be continued for life after an episode of unstable angina. The dose of aspirin in trials of patients with unstable angina has ranged from 75 to 1300 mg/day. Gastrointestinal side effects increase with increasing dosage. Doses of 325 mg acutely and 81 mg during long-term treatment are sufficient to inhibit maximally the platelet cyclooxygenase pathway.

Although women have been underrepresented in the trials of aspirin, it seems reasonable to assume that the benefit of aspirin extends to women with unstable angina, particularly because aspirin has been shown to reduce coronary events across the broad spectrum of patients with atherosclerosis.

CLOPIDOGREL. Clopidogrel and ticlopidine are thienopyridines, and their mechanism of action differs from that of aspirin. Both drugs inhibit adenosine diphosphate–mediated platelet activation. Because they act independently from the arachidonic acid pathway, their antiplatelet activities are synergistic with aspirin. Clopidogrel has supplanted ticlopidine because of its more rapid onset of action, lower incidence of serious adverse events, and stronger clinical trial data.

In a trial of more than 12,000 patients with ACS without ST segment elevation, the addition of clopidogrel to aspirin over a 3- to 12-month follow-up period reduced the composite end point of cardiovascular death, nonfatal MI, or stroke by a relative 20%, representing a 2.1% reduction in absolute risk.[2] This benefit was obtained at the risk of a small increase in the incidence of bleeding. Clopidogrel increases the risk of bleeding during coronary bypass surgery, so this drug usually is not started if the patient is considered to be a surgical candidate.

PLATELET GLYCOPROTEIN IIb/IIIa RECEPTOR INHIBITORS. Platelet membranes contain glycoprotein (GP) receptors. The GP IIb/IIIa receptor changes from its resting to its active state when the platelet is activated by agonists or other platelets and serves as a receptor for fibrinogen and von Willebrand factor. Fibrinogen binding is central to platelet aggregation and thrombus formation in the arterial circulation. In contrast to aspirin or clopidogrel, which do not block thrombin-induced platelet aggregation, GP IIb/IIIa inhibitors block aggregation in response to all potential agonists.

Three GP IIb/IIIa blockers have been approved and are used widely clinically. Abciximab is the Fab fragment of a monoclonal antibody, eptifibatide is a peptide GP IIb/IIIa inhibitor, and tirofiban is a smaller molecule. These drugs must be administered by parenteral infusion; oral GP IIb/IIIa inhibitors failed to reduce events in large clinical trials and have not been approved for use.

Platelet GP IIb/IIIa inhibition at the time of angioplasty reduces ischemic complications in patients with ACS.[3] The benefit with respect to the primary end point of the trials was less with eptifibatide and tirofiban (15 to 20%) than with abciximab (30 to 60%). A trial directly comparing tirofiban and abciximab during angioplasty revealed a lower event rate in the abciximab group.[4]

In addition, five large trials have assessed the value of these drugs in the broader population of patients with unstable angina or non–Q wave MI. Although abciximab was the most successful drug in the angioplasty trials, eptifibatide and tirofiban predominate in the ACS trials.

The value of GP IIb/IIIa inhibitors in patients with unstable angina who are not undergoing intervention is not fully defined. GP IIb/IIIa inhibitors have not been compared with clopidogrel or with low-molecular-weight heparins or studied in patients taking these drugs as background therapy. The current high cost of these drugs makes it tempting to limit their use to high-risk patients. Patients with troponin elevations or other high-risk features seem to benefit from GP IIb/IIIa blockade, but low-risk patients may not benefit.

Current guidelines recommend that eptifibatide or tirofiban should be added to aspirin and heparin in the treatment of patients with high-risk features or with refractory ischemia. These drugs should be continued during coronary angioplasty (Chapter 70) and for 12 to 24 hours after the procedure for tirofiban and for 24 to 72 hours after the procedure for eptifibatide. Abciximab also can be used in patients with unstable angina in whom angioplasty is planned within the following 24 hours. When abciximab is administered before diagnostic coronary angiography, however, the prolonged platelet inhibition it induces may force a delay in the urgent CABG surgery that is needed for some patients. When aspirin and unfractionated heparin are used with GP IIb/IIIa inhibitors, the dose of heparin should be conservative during coronary procedures, and heparin should be discontinued after the procedure if it is uncomplicated.

HEPARIN. The principal inhibitory effect of heparin on coagulation is probably via the inhibition of thrombin-induced activation of factor V and factor VIII (Chapter 33). Platelets inhibit the anticoagulant effect of heparin by binding factor Xa and protecting it from inactivation.

The pharmacokinetics of heparin are complex, and the dose-response relationship is nonlinear. Heparin therapy is monitored to maintain the activated partial thromboplastin time ratio within 1.5 to 2.5 times normal. The anticoagulant response to a standard dose of heparin varies widely among patients, such that even when a weight-based nomogram is used in a clinical study, the activated partial thromboplastin time falls outside the therapeutic range more than one third of the time. Results in routine clinical practice are probably much worse. Pooled analyses of randomized trials reveal an average incidence of major bleeding of 6.8% in the continuous infusion groups and 14.2% in the intermittent infusion groups.

The addition of heparin to aspirin reduced the event rate in one trial of patients with unstable angina, and a meta-analysis including several smaller trials concluded that the event reduction conferred by heparin therapy was approximately one third.[5]

Discontinuation of heparin in patients with unstable angina can result in a reactivation of refractory ischemic episodes within hours. Aspirin or warfarin may block this phenomenon. Rebound has been described with other thrombin inhibitors, but the mechanism has not been defined. Mild thrombocytopenia occurs in 10 to 20% of patients treated with unfractionated heparin. In 2 to 10% of patients, a more severe form of thrombocytopenia develops. This antibody-mediated response occurs within 5 to 10 days after initiation of treatment and is associated with thromboembolic sequelae in 30 to 80% of cases. Other adverse effects of heparin include osteoporosis, skin necrosis, alopecia, hypersensitivity reactions, and hypoaldosteronism.

Low-molecular-weight heparins (LMWH) are fragments of unfractionated heparin produced by enzymatic or chemical depolymerization processes that yield chains with average molecular weights of approximately 5000. Compared with unfractionated heparin, LMWH produce a more predictable anticoagulant response because of their better bioavailability, longer half-life, and dose-independent clearance. The plasma half-life of LMWH after subcutaneous injection ranges from 3 to 6 hours so that once-daily or twice-daily administration is feasible. Monitoring is not required, and LMWH cause less bleeding. The main disadvantage of LMWH is that they currently are far more expensive than unfractionated heparin.

In patients with unstable angina or non–Q wave MI, enoxaparin is superior to unfractionated heparin for the first few days of therapy.[6,7] The early benefit of LMWH treatment seems to dissipate over the ensuing months, and continuing therapy was not beneficial in most trials. In one trial, treatment from 5 days to 3 months with dalteparin produced an impressive reduction in death or MI at 1 month, with gradual loss of this benefit thereafter.[8]

Heparin is recommended for the acute treatment of all patients with unstable angina except patients determined to be at low risk. Unfractionated heparin should be started with an intravenous bolus of 60 to 70 U/kg followed by a constant infusion of approximately 16 U/kg/hr, adjusted to maintain the activated partial thromboplastin time at 1.5 to 2.5 times control, or 50 to 70 seconds. Subcutaneous administration of enoxaparin or dalteparin may be used instead of unfractionated heparin. The dose of enoxaparin is 1 mg/kg twice daily, and the dose of dalteparin is 120 IU/kg (maximum 10,000 IU) twice daily. Either standard heparin or LMWH should be continued for 2 to 5 days, or until the patient has been stabilized for 24 hours, or until revascularization is performed. The dose of unfractionated heparin should be reduced during coronary angioplasty when aspirin and GP IIb/IIIa inhibitors are being administered concomitantly, and heparin should be discontinued after an uncomplicated procedure. Information is accumulating on the combined use of LMWH and GP IIb/IIIa inhibitors, particularly during coronary interventions; this combination is probably acceptable.

OTHER MEDICAL THERAPY. Thrombolytic therapy improves the outcome of patients with ST segment elevation MI (Chapter 69) but is of no benefit in unstable angina or non–ST segment elevation MI. The direct thrombin inhibitor bivalirudin has been recommended as an improvement over heparin during angioplasty and is the agent of choice in patients with heparin-induced thrombocytopenia. Long-term anticoagulation with warfarin is not recommended for patients with unstable angina or non–ST segment elevation MI.

In the only major trial to date that has tested the early effects of cholesterol lowering after ACS, high-dose atorvastatin for 16 weeks in patients with unstable angina for whom revascularization was not planned reduced the composite primary end point.[9] Several other trials showed long-term event reduction in patients with coronary disease; long-term compliance to this therapy is improved if it is begun in the hospital.

TREATMENTS FOR ISCHEMIC SIGNS AND SYMPTOMS

An oral β-blocker at a dose that reduces heart rate and an intravenous nitroglycerin infusion are reasonable treatments to control symptoms in high-risk or intermediate-risk patients with

Continued

ACS. Low-risk and some intermediate-risk patients can be treated with oral or transdermal nitrates and β-blockers. A patient who develops unstable angina while already taking two or three antianginal drugs should be treated with intravenous nitroglycerin, but symptoms are harder to control compared with a patient who previously took no antianginal drugs.

NITROGLYCERIN AND NITRATE THERAPY. In patients with unstable angina, sublingual nitroglycerin usually relieves attacks promptly, although it may be less efficacious than in stable angina. Nitroglycerin is a venodilator at low doses and an arteriolar dilator at higher doses; it reduces preload and afterload and myocardial oxygen consumption. The drug directly dilates coronary stenoses and increases oxygen delivery to the ischemic region. Nitroglycerin increases collateral flow and favorably redistributes regional coronary flow. Because of its preferential effect on capacitance as opposed to resistance vessels, it does not induce a coronary steal, in contrast to other vasodilators.

Nitroglycerin and longer acting nitrates act by releasing nitric oxide in vascular smooth muscle through an enzymatic process. Sulfhydryl-donating compounds are necessary for this activity, and their rapid depletion during long-term therapy with nitroglycerin or other nitrate preparations rapidly leads to tolerance to the hemodynamic effects of the drug. This phenomenon is a major problem when nitrates are used as long-term therapy but is less relevant to their use in ACS. Nitroglycerin inhibits platelet aggregation and, in experimental models, reduces platelet thrombus deposition. This effect seems to persist even after tolerance develops for the hemodynamic effects of the drug.

Patients with unstable angina often are treated with an infusion of intravenous nitroglycerin to prevent further attacks. A common starting dose is 10 μg/min. The dose can be increased by 10 μg/min increments until symptoms are controlled or unwanted side effects develop. The most common adverse effects are headache, nausea, dizziness, hypotension, and reflex tachycardia.

The evidence that intravenous nitroglycerin prevents ischemic attacks in unstable angina patients is based on small, uncontrolled studies. No studies of sufficient power have examined whether intravenous nitroglycerin or other nitrate preparations reduce the risk of MI in unstable angina.

Angina episodes usually disappear entirely when patients with unstable angina or non–ST segment elevation MI are hospitalized and given medical therapy. At that point, intravenous nitrates often are replaced with transdermal or oral nitrates.

β-BLOCKERS. Although it is accepted widely that β-blockers are useful to control ischemic episodes in patients with unstable angina or non–ST segment elevation MI, the data to support this claim are mainly inferential or derived from small trials without placebo-treated controls from the early 1980s, an era when patients were not treated routinely with aspirin and heparin. Taken together, these trials indicate that β-blockers effectively reduce symptoms in patients with unstable angina who are not already taking one of these drugs on admission. Whether or not a β-blocker also reduces the risk of MI is uncertain because the trials in unstable angina are underpowered to answer this question.

During long-term therapy, a long-acting β-blocker is preferable to a short-acting one because it can be given once daily. In the context of ACS, it is reasonable to try to achieve β-blockade within hours, however, and not days. β-Blockade sometimes is initiated with intravenous boluses titrated to reduce heart rate. Early heart rate control is particularly important in high-risk patients or in patients with tachycardia or a high arterial pressure on admission. A reasonable target heart rate is 50 to 60 beats per minute at rest.

The main contraindications to β-blockers in unstable angina are reactive airway disease, sinus node dysfunction or atrioventricular block, and severe heart failure. Most patients with chronic obstructive pulmonary disease tolerate a β-blocker; a β$_1$-selective agent (e.g., metoprolol or atenolol) is theoretically less likely to provoke bronchoconstriction. In some patients with conduction system disease, permanent pacing may be indicated in part so that long-term β-blocker therapy can be given. Mild heart failure that is stable is not a contraindication to β-blockers in unstable angina. Diltiazem or verapamil should be considered when a β-blocker cannot be used.

CALCIUM CHANNEL BLOCKERS. Calcium channel blockers increase coronary blood flow globally and to the ischemic zone. Diltiazem and verapamil slow heart rate, reduce afterload, and reduce myocardial contractility; they reduce myocardial oxygen demand and are useful to control ischemic symptoms. Diltiazem and verapamil have been compared with placebo or a β-blocker in several small clinical trials in unstable angina, and they seem to be more effective than placebo and equivalent to a β-blocker in preventing recurrent angina episodes.

Most dihydropyridine calcium channel blockers induce a reflex increase in heart rate in the absence of β-blockade, a feature that is likely to mitigate any benefit on myocardial ischemia. The rapid absorption and short half-life of the short-acting formulation of nifedipine produce frequent abrupt changes in arterial pressure and heart rate. The calcium channel blocker that has been used most often in the limited number of studies in unstable angina is this formulation of nifedipine. Taken together, these trials provide fairly strong evidence that nifedipine is harmful when used in patients with unstable angina not receiving β-blockers, but that it may be helpful in controlling angina in patients with an adequate level of β-blockade. Whether the poor results seen with nifedipine in trials of unstable angina and post-MI patients would have been different with a long-acting formulation or newer dihydropyridines such as amlodipine is open to debate because these drugs have not been evaluated under these conditions.

Diltiazem and verapamil are reasonable choices to treat unstable angina when β-blockers are contraindicated. The scant evidence suggests that both drugs reduce the frequency of attacks in unstable angina, but there is no evidence that they prevent MI. The combination of either diltiazem or verapamil with a β-blocker is not generally used in patients with unstable angina because the effect of these calcium channel blockers on heart rate and myocardial contractility are additive to the effects of β-blockers.

Diltiazem reduced the risk of reinfarction within 14 days in a placebo-controlled trial among patients with non–Q wave MI in the early 1980s. Diltiazem and β-blockers have not been compared in this situation, and the relevance of this trial to the current management of non–ST segment elevation MI is uncertain.

RECURRENT OR REFRACTORY UNSTABLE ANGINA. In most patients hospitalized with unstable angina, symptoms do not recur after institution of antianginal therapy. Patients with refractory unstable angina have a high risk of developing MI. Patients who are labeled as refractory often become asymptomatic when medical therapy is intensified.

Intra-aortic balloon counterpulsation prevents myocardial ischemia effectively in patients whose unstable angina is truly refractory. This mechanical approach improves myocardial blood flow and reduces myocardial oxygen demand by collapsing the resistance to left ventricular ejection in early systole. Intra-aortic balloon counterpulsation is needed for control of symptoms in less than 1% of patients with unstable angina, but it also is used in high-risk cases at the time of coronary angioplasty to provide a margin of safety. Intra-aortic balloon counterpulsation causes lower limb ischemia in approximately 10% of cases, but this complication almost always resolves with removal of the device.

CORONARY REVASCULARIZATION

CABG surgery (Chapter 71) and coronary angioplasty (Chapter 70) are performed frequently in patients with unstable angina; however, the precise indications for revascularization, the choice of procedure, and its timing are controversial. CABG surgery relieves angina completely in approximately 90% of patients who undergo the procedure, and symptoms usually do not recur for many years. In patients with lesions amenable to angioplasty, angina also almost always is relieved, but it usually recurs within 6 months in the 20 to 30% of patients who develop restenosis. Whether revascularization prolongs survival and prevents future coronary events in patients at different levels of risk has not been determined adequately from trials.

Randomized trials comparing revascularization with medical therapy in unstable angina first were performed more than 20 years ago. The results of all but the most recent trials are hardly applicable to current clinical decision making because major advances in medical and interventional practices have improved vastly the outcomes with both types of therapy.

An overview of the 10-year results from the clinical trials comparing CABG surgery with medical treatment for stable angina indicates that patients with left main coronary artery stenosis or three-vessel disease obtain the most benefit from surgery. In low-risk groups, such as patients with single-vessel involvement, no survival advantage can be shown with CABG surgery. These conclusions also may be relevant to patients with unstable angina.

Trials of coronary revascularization in unstable angina have compared an "aggressive" approach with a "conservative" approach. The aggressive approach involves early coronary angiography with revascularization by either coronary angioplasty or CABG surgery, depending on the coronary anatomy. Usually, patients with one or two severe stenoses are treated with angioplasty, and patients with more extensive disease undergo CABG surgery. The conservative approach usually limits coronary arteriography to patients who require revascularization to control persistent symptoms and to patients with high-risk features.

Although early trials suggested that the conservative approach was as good as or better than the aggressive approach in patients with ACS, a Scandinavian study of patients with unstable angina showed that the aggressively treated patients had a significantly lower rate of death or nonfatal MI at 6 months. [10] In a more recent study of patients with either unstable angina or non–ST segment elevation MI, the patients randomized to routine catheterization within 4 to 48 hours and revascularization "as appropriate" had a better outcome than patients for whom catheterization was limited to objective evidence of recurrent ischemia or an abnormal stress test. [11] The composite end point of death, nonfatal MI, or rehospitalization

for ACS within 6 months was reduced from 19.4 to 15.9%, a 22% relative risk reduction. The degree of benefit was large in high-risk patients (e.g., patients with elevated troponin levels) and marginal or nonexistent in low-risk subgroups.

OTHER COMPLICATIONS

Patients with non–ST segment elevation MI can develop all of the complications associated with ST segment elevation MI, including arrhythmias, heart failure, and mechanical complications (Chapter 69).

INTEGRATED APPROACH TO TREATMENT

The treatment of unstable angina should be individualized to consider the specific features of the disease and the particular circumstances of the patient. Nevertheless, algorithms provide a useful framework (see Fig. 68–1).

Unstable angina is an acute episode related to one active culprit lesion, but the patient has diffuse atherosclerosis. Coronary disease is a chronic condition that usually causes recurrent events spread out over many years. Smoking cessation (Chapter 14), cholesterol lowering (Chapter 211), control of hypertension (Chapter 63) and diabetes (Chapter 242), and other risk factor reductions (Chapters 67 and 69) may be at least as important long-term as are the specific treatment decisions related to the acute event. An episode of unstable angina may be viewed as an opportunity to improve the patient's profile with respect to secondary prevention.

Prognosis

Prognosis in unstable angina and non–ST segment elevation MI can be viewed as a composite of the expected prognosis based on the extent of coronary disease and left ventricular function, overlaid with the short-term risk associated with the culprit lesion and the unstable state. The short-term risk is related almost entirely to MI and its complications and to recurrences of unstable angina. Risk is highest in the hours, days, and first month after the onset of symptoms. The incremental risk associated with the unstable state dissipates completely by 1 year. Of unstable angina patients in one series, 11% experienced an MI between hospital discharge and 1 year, but the subsequent annual MI rate was less than 2%.

Published data on prognosis in unstable angina are influenced by patient selection and treatment and can be misleading. The inclusion and exclusion criteria for clinical trials may bias the prognosis by eliminating either low-risk or high-risk patients. If large numbers of younger patients with atypical symptoms and no objective evidence of myocardial ischemia are included, the prognosis of the cohort tends to be better. Conversely, if ECG changes or elevated troponin levels are required, the prognosis tends to be worse.

Prognosis has improved dramatically since the 1980s with the introduction of increasingly more sophisticated medical therapy and revascularization techniques. In a compilation of 10 representative series with a total of nearly 2000 patients with unstable angina, excluding patients with new-onset or post-MI angina, the mortality was 4% in-hospital and 10% at 1 year. Survival without MI was 89% at 1 month and 79% at 1 year. Among 4488 patients with unstable angina in another large study, the mortality rate was 2.4% at 30 days, 5% at 6 months, and 7% at 1 year; the MI rate was 4.8% at 30 days and 6.2% at 6 months. Recurrent ischemia has a major impact on these rates; the 30-day MI rate increases from 2.3 to 7.2 to 21.7% in patients with no ischemia, ischemia, and refractory ischemia. These outcomes represent what can be expected now with modern therapy.

myocardial infarction undergoing coronary angioplasty. Circulation 1997;96:1445–1453.

4. Topol EJ, Moliterno DJ, Herrmann HC, et al, for the TARGET Investigators: Comparison of two platelet glycoprotein IIb/IIIa inhibitors, tirofiban and abciximab, for the prevention of ischemic events with percutaneous coronary revascularization. N Engl J Med 2001;344:1888–1894.

5. Oler A, Whooley MA, Oler J, Grady D: Adding heparin to aspirin reduces the incidence of myocardial infarction and death in patients with unstable angina: A meta-analysis. JAMA 1996;276:811–815.

6. Wong GC, Giugliano RP, Antman EM: Use of low-molecular-weight heparins in the management of acute coronary artery syndromes and percutaneous coronary intervention. JAMA 2003;289:331–342.

7. Antman E, McCabe CH, Gurfinkel EP, et al: Enoxaparin prevents death and cardiac ischemic events in unstable angina/non-Q-wave myocardial infarction: Results of the Thrombolysis in Myocardial Infarction (TIMI) 11B study. Circulation 1999;100:1593–1601.

8. Fragmin and Fast Revascularisation during Instability in Coronary artery disease (FRISC II) Investigators: Long-term low-molecular-mass heparin in unstable coronary-artery disease: FRISC II prospective randomised multicentre study. Lancet 1999;354:701–707.

9. Schwartz GG, Olsson AG, Ezekowitz MD, et al: Effects of atorvastatin on early recurrent ischemic events in acute coronary syndromes. The MIRACL Study: A randomized controlled trial. JAMA 2001;265:1711–1718.

10. Lagerqvist B, Husted S, Kontny F, et al: A long-term perspective on the protective effects of an early invasive strategy in unstable coronary artery disease: Two-year follow-up of the FRISC-II invasive study. J Am Coll Cardiol 2002;40:1902–1914.

11. Cannon CP, Weintraub WS, Demopoulos LA, et al, for the TACTICS—Thrombolysis in myocardial Infarction 18 Investigators: Comparison of early invasive and conservative strategies in patients with unstable coronary syndromes treated with the glycoprotein IIb/IIIa inhibitor tirofiban. N Engl J Med 2001;344:1879–1887.

SUGGESTED READINGS

Boersma E, Harrington RA, Moliterno DJ, et al: Platelet glycoprotein IIb/IIIa inhibitors in acute coronary syndromes: A meta-analysis of all major randomised clinical trials. Lancet 2002;359:189–198. *Glycoprotein IIb/IIIa inhibitors reduce the occurrence of death or myocardial infarction in patients with acute coronary syndromes not routinely scheduled for early revascularisation.*

Braunwald E, Antman EM, Beasley JW, et al: ACC/AHA 2002 guideline update for the management of patients with unstable angina and non-ST-segment elevation myocardial infarction: Summary article. Circulation 2002;106:1893–1900. *A comprehensive, evidence-based summary of recommended management of non–ST segment elevation acute coronary syndromes.*

Fox KA, Poole-Wilson PA, Henderson RA, et al: Interventional versus conservative treatment for patients with unstable angina or non–ST-elevation myocardial infarction: The British Heart Foundation RITA 3 randomised trial. Randomized Intervention Trial of unstable Angina. Lancet 2002;360:743–751. *An interventional strategy is preferable mainly because of the halving of refractory or severe angina.*

Libby P: Current concepts of the pathogenesis of the acute coronary syndromes. Circulation 2001;104:365–372. *Excellent, well-referenced summary of current thinking regarding the pathogenesis of acute coronary syndromes.*

Mahoney EM, Jurkovitz CT, Chu H, et al: Cost and cost-effectiveness of an early invasive vs conservative strategy for the treatment of unstable angina and non–ST-segment elevation myocardial infarction. JAMA 2002;288:1851–1858. *Estimated cost per year of life gained for the invasive strategy was $13,000.*

1. RISC Group: Risk of myocardial infarction and death during treatment with low dose aspirin and intravenous heparin in men with unstable coronary disease. Lancet 1990;336:827–830.

2. Yusuf S, Mehta SR, Zhao F, et al, on behalf of the CURE (Clopidogrel in Unstable angina to prevent Recurrent Events) Trial Investigators: Early and late effects of clopidogrel in patients with acute coronary syndromes. Circulation 2003;107:966–972.

3. RESTORE Investigators: Effects of platelet glycoprotein IIb/IIIa blockade with tirofiban on adverse cardiac events in patients with unstable angina or acute

Cardiovascular Disease

69 ST-ELEVATION ACUTE MYOCARDIAL INFARCTION AND COMPLICATIONS OF MYOCARDIAL INFARCTION

Jeffrey L. Anderson

Definition

Conceptually, myocardial infarction (MI) is myocardial necrosis caused by ischemia. Practically, MI can be diagnosed and evaluated by clinical, electrocardiographic, biochemical, radiologic, and pathologic methods. Technologic advances in detecting much smaller amounts of myocardial necrosis than previously possible (e.g., by troponin determinations) have required a redefinition of MI. Given these developments, the term MI now should be qualified as to size, precipitating circumstance, and timing. This chapter focuses on acute MI associated with ST segment elevation on the electrocardiogram (ECG). This category of acute MI is characterized by profound ("transmural") acute myocardial ischemia affecting relatively large areas of myocardium. The underlying cause essentially always is *complete* interruption of regional myocardial blood flow (due to coronary occlusion, usually atherothrombotic) (Chapter 66). This clinical syndrome should be distinguished from the non–ST-elevation MI, in which the blockage of coronary flow is incomplete and for which different acute therapies are appropriate (Chapter 68).

Incidence and Impact

Cardiovascular disease is responsible for almost one half of all deaths in the United States and other developed countries and for one fourth of deaths in the developing world (Chapter 47). By 2020, cardiovascular disease will cause one of every three deaths worldwide. Cardiovascular disease causes about 1 million deaths in the United States each year, accounting for more than 40% of all deaths. Annually, an estimated 1,100,000 Americans suffer a fatal or nonfatal acute MI. Coronary heart disease, the leading cause of cardiovascular death, claims 460,000 lives. Half of coronary heart disease deaths (one quarter million per year) are directly related to acute MI, and at least half of these acute MI–related deaths occur within 1 hour of onset of symptoms and before patients reach a hospital emergency department.

More than 5 million people visit emergency departments in the United States each year for evaluation of chest pain and related symptoms, and almost 1.5 million are hospitalized for an acute coronary syndrome (Chapter 46). The presence of ST-elevation or new left bundle branch block (LBBB) distinguishes patients with acute MI who require consideration of immediate recanalization therapy from other patients with the acute coronary syndrome (non–ST-elevation MI/unstable angina; Chapter 68). Changing demographics, lifestyles, and medical therapies have led to a relative decrease in ST-elevation MI. In 1990, ST-elevation MI accounted for 55% of acute MIs, whereas in 1999, the rate had declined to 37%. ST-elevation MI is associated with greater in-hospital (but not post-hospital) mortality than non–ST-elevation MI and is an important contributor to total population mortality.

Pathophysiology and Pathology

Coronary occlusion as a precipitant of acute MI was suggested by the American physician James Herrick in 1912. Concurrently, Obrastzow and Straschesko published cases of "acute coronary thrombosis" in the Russian literature. Full understanding of thrombosis as the mechanism for acute MI did not meet with acceptance until the 1980s. In a seminal study, DeWood and colleagues performed coronary angiography in patients during the early hours of acute MI and found coronary occlusion to be present in 87% of patients studied within 4 hours of onset of symptoms. At emergency coronary bypass surgery, the nature of occlusion was shown to be thrombotic.

In a canine model of coronary occlusion and recanalization, myocardial cell death begins within 15 minutes of occlusion and proceeds rapidly in a wavefront from endocardium to epicardium. Partial myocardial salvage can be achieved by releasing the occlusion within 3 to 6 hours; the degree of salvage is inversely proportional to the duration of ischemia and occurs in a reverse wavefront from epicardium to endocardium. The extent of myocardial necrosis can also be altered by modification of metabolic demands and collateral blood supply. Extensive clinical research over the past two decades has confirmed the promise and defined the limitations of coronary recanalization for human acute MI. Recanalization therapy and advances in adjunctive medical therapy have been associated with progressive declines in 30-day mortality rates from ST-elevation acute MI (from about 30% to 5 to 10%).

Over the past 2 decades, pathologic, angiographic, and angioscopic observations have further refined the pathophysiologic basis of coronary thrombosis. Underlying plaque erosion, fissuring, or rupture of vulnerable atherosclerotic plaques has been determined to be the initiating mechanism of coronary thrombotic occlusion, precipitating intraplaque hemorrhage, coronary spasm, and occlusive luminal thrombosis (Chapter 66).

Further studies have shown that plaque erosion or rupture most frequently occurs in lipid-laden plaques with an endothelial cap weakened by internal collagenase (metalloproteinase) activity derived primarily from macrophages. These macrophages are recruited to the plaque from blood monocytes responding to inflammatory mediators and adhesion molecules.

With plaque rupture, elements of the bloodstream are exposed to the highly thrombogenic lipid-, tissue-factor-, and collagen-containing plaque core and matrix. Platelets adhere, become activated, and aggregate; vasoconstrictive and thrombogenic mediators are secreted; vasospasm occurs; thrombin is generated and fibrin formed; and a partially or totally occlusive platelet- and fibrin-rich thrombus is generated. When coronary flow is occluded, electrocardiographic ST-elevation occurs (ST-elevation acute MI). Partial occlusion, occlusion in the presence of adequate collateral circulation, and/or distal coronary embolization results in unstable angina or non–ST-elevation MI (Chapter 68). Ischemia from impaired myocardial perfusion causes myocardial cell injury or death, ventricular dysfunction, and cardiac arrhythmias.

Although the vast preponderance of MIs are caused by atherosclerosis, occasional patients may develop complete coronary occlusions owing to coronary emboli, in situ thrombosis, vasculitis, primary vasospasm, infiltrative or degenerative diseases, diseases of the aorta, congenital anomalies of a coronary artery, or trauma (Table 69–1).

Clinical Manifestations

Traditionally, the diagnosis of acute MI has rested on the triad of ischemic chest discomfort, ECG abnormalities, and elevated serum cardiac markers. Acute MI was considered present when at least two of the three were present. With their increasing sensitivity and specificity, serum cardiac markers (e.g., troponin I or T) have assumed a dominant role in confirming the diagnosis of acute MI in patients with suggestive clinical and/or ECG features.

HISTORY. Ischemic-type chest discomfort is the most prominent clinical symptom in the majority of patients with acute MI (see Table 46–1). The discomfort is characterized by its quality, location, duration, radiation, and precipitating and relieving factors. The discomfort associated with acute MI is qualitatively similar to that of angina pectoris but more severe. It often is perceived as heavy, pressure-like, crushing, squeezing, bandlike, viselike, strangling, constrict-

ing, aching, or burning; it is rarely perceived as sharp pain, and generally not as stabbing pain (Chapters 46 and 67).

The primary location of typical ischemic pain is most consistently retrosternal, but it also may present left parasternally, left precordially, or across the anterior chest (Chapter 46). Occasionally, discomfort is predominantly perceived in the anterior neck, jaw, arms, or epigastrium. It is generally somewhat diffuse; highly localized pain (finger-point) is rarely angina or acute MI. The most characteristic pattern of radiation is to the left arm, but the right or both arms may be involved. The shoulders, neck, jaw, teeth, epigastrium, and interscapular area also are sites of radiation. Discomfort above the jaws or below the umbilicus is not typical of acute MI. Associated symptoms often include nausea, vomiting, diaphoresis, weakness, dyspnea, restlessness, and apprehension.

The pain of the acute MI lasts longer (typically 20 minutes to several hours) than angina and is not reliably relieved by rest or nitroglycerin. The onset of acute MI usually is unrelated to exercise or other apparent precipitating factors. Nevertheless, acute MI begins during physical or emotional stress and within a few hours of arising more frequently than explained by chance.

It is estimated that at least 20% of acute MIs are painless ("silent") or atypical (unrecognized). Elderly patients and patients with diabetes are particularly prone to painless or atypical MI, which may occur in as many as one third to one half of such patients. Because the prognosis is worse in elderly and diabetic patients, diagnostic vigilance is required. In these patients, acute MI may present as sudden dyspnea (which may progress to pulmonary edema), weakness, light-headedness, nausea, and/or vomiting. Confusional states, sudden loss of consciousness, new rhythm disorders, or an unexplained fall in blood pressure are other, uncommon presentations. The differential diagnosis of ischemic chest pain also should include gastrointestinal disorders (e.g., reflux esophagitis; Chapter 136), musculoskeletal pain (e.g. costochondritis), anxiety or panic attacks, pleurisy or pulmonary embolism (Chapter 94), and acute aortic dissection (Chapter 75 and Table 46–2).

PHYSICAL EXAMINATION. There are no physical findings that are diagnostic or pathognomonic of acute MI. The physical examination may be entirely normal or reveal only nonspecific abnormalities. An S_4 gallop frequently is found if carefully sought. Blood pressure often is initially elevated, but it may be normal or low. Signs of sympathetic hyperactivity (tachycardia and/or hypertension) may accompany anterior wall MI, whereas parasympathetic hyperactivity (bradycardia and/or hypotension) is more common in inferior wall MI.

The examination is best focused on an overall assessment of cardiac function. Adequacy of vital signs and peripheral perfusion should be noted. Signs of cardiac failure, both left- and right-sided (e.g., S_3 gallop, pulmonary congestion, elevated neck veins) should be sought, and observation for arrhythmias and mechanical complications (e.g., new murmurs) is essential. If hypoperfusion is present, determination of its primary cause (e.g., hypovolemia, right heart failure, left heart failure) is critical to management.

Diagnostic Tests

ELECTROCARDIOGRAM

The initial ECG is neither perfectly specific nor perfectly sensitive for all patients who develop acute ST-elevation MI; nevertheless, it plays a critical role in initial stratification, triage, and management (Chapter 46; Fig. 69–1). In an appropriate clinical setting, a pattern of regional ECG ST segment elevation suggests coronary occlusion, causing marked myocardial ischemia; hospital admission is indicated, with triage to the coronary care unit (CCU). An emergent recanalization strategy (thrombolysis or primary angioplasty) should be used

Table 69–1 • CONDITIONS OTHER THAN CORONARY ATHEROSCLEROSIS THAT MAY CAUSE ACUTE MYOCARDIAL INFARCTION	
Coronary emboli	Causes include aortic or mitral valve lesions, left atrial or ventricular thrombi, prosthetic valves, fat emboli, intracardiac neoplasms, infective endocarditis, and paradoxical emboli
Thrombotic coronary artery disease	May occur with oral contraceptive use, sickle cell anemia and other hemoglobinopathies, polycythemia vera, thrombocytosis, thrombotic thrombocytopenic purpura, disseminated intravascular coagulation, antithrombin III deficiency and other hypercoagulable states, macroglobulinemia and other hyperviscosity states, multiple myeloma, leukemia, malaria, and fibrinolytic system shutdown secondary to impaired plasminogen activation or excessive inhibition
Coronary vasculitis	Seen with Takayasu's disease, Kawasaki's disease, polyarteritis nodosa, lupus erythematosus, scleroderma, rheumatoid arthritis, and immune-mediated vascular degeneration in cardiac allografts
Coronary vasospasm	May be associated with variant angina, nitrate withdrawal, cocaine or amphetamine abuse, and angina with "normal" coronary arteries
Infiltrative and degenerative coronary vascular disease	May result from amyloidosis, connective tissue disorders (such as pseudoxanthoma elasticum), lipid storage disorders and mucopolysaccharidoses, homocystinuria, diabetes mellitus, collagen vascular disease, muscular dystrophies, and Friedreich's ataxia
Coronary ostial occlusion	Associated with aortic dissection, luetic aortitis, aortic stenosis, and ankylosing spondylitis syndromes
Congenital coronary anomalies	Including Bland-White-Garland syndrome of anomalous origin of the left coronary artery from the pulmonary artery, left coronary artery origin from the anterior sinus of Valsalva, coronary arteriovenous fistula or aneurysms, and myocardial bridging with secondary vascular degeneration
Trauma	Associated with and responsible for coronary dissection, laceration, or thrombosis (with endothelial cell injury secondary to trauma such as angioplasty); radiation; and cardiac contusion
Augmented myocardial oxygen requirements exceeding oxyen delivery	Encountered with aortic stenosis, aortic insufficiency, hypertension with severe left ventricular hypertrophy, pheochromocytoma, thyrotoxicosis, methemoglobinemia, carbon monoxide poisoning, shock, and hyperviscosity syndromes

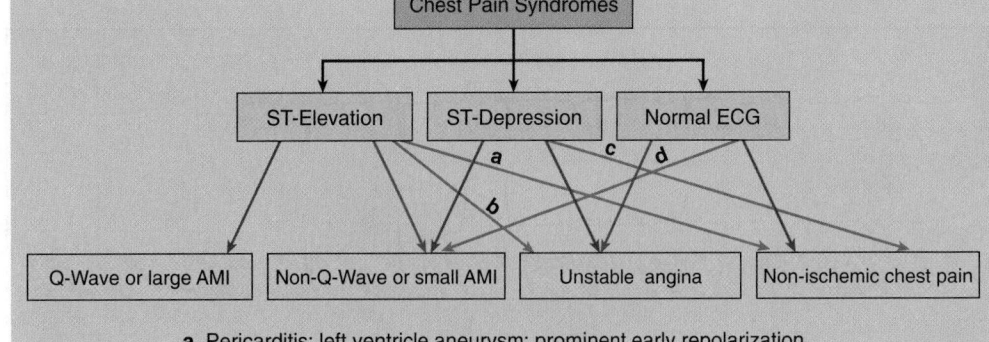

FIGURE 69–1 • Electrocardiographic stratification of chest pain. Size and color of arrow indicate relative frequency of final diagnosis (red = most frequent, blue = less common, green = least common). AMI = Acute myocardial infarction; ECG = electrocardiogram.

a. Pericarditis; left ventricle aneurysm; prominent early repolarization
b. Coronary spasm
c. Left ventricle hypertrophy with strain; digoxin
d. Posterior MI; very early (<10 minutes) or late presentation

unless contraindicated. Other ECG patterns (ST segment depression, T wave inversion, nonspecific changes, normal ECG) in association with ischemic chest discomfort are consistent with an acute coronary syndrome (non–ST-elevation MI or unstable angina) and are treated with different triage and initial management strategies (Chapter 68).

ECG EVOLUTION. Serial ECG tracings improve the sensitivity and specificity of the ECG for the diagnosis of acute MI and assist in assessing the outcomes of therapy. When typical ST elevation persists for hours and is followed within hours to days by T wave inversions and Q waves, the diagnosis of acute MI can be made with virtual certainty. The ECG changes in ST-elevation acute MI evolve through three overlapping phases: (1) hyperacute or early acute, (2) evolved acute, and (3) chronic (stabilized).

Early Acute Phase. This earliest phase begins within minutes, persists, and evolves over hours. T waves increase in amplitude and widen over the area of injury (hyperacute pattern). ST segments evolve from concave to a straightened to a convex upward pattern (acute pattern). When prominent, the acute injury pattern of blended ST-T waves may take on a "tombstone" appearance (Fig. 69–2). ST segment depressions that occur in leads opposite those with ST elevation are known as "reciprocal changes" and are associated with larger areas of injury and worse prognosis, but also with greater benefits from recanalization therapy.

Other causes of ST elevation must be considered and excluded. These conditions include pericarditis (Chapter 74), left ventricular (LV) hypertrophy with J point elevation, and normal variant early repolarization (Chapter 50). Pericarditis (or perimyocarditis) is of particular concern because it may mimic acute MI clinically, but thrombolytic therapy is *not* indicated and may be hazardous.

Evolved Acute Phase. During the second phase, ST elevation begins to regress, T waves in leads with ST elevation become inverted, and pathologic Q or QS waves become fully developed (>0.03 sec duration or >30% of R-wave amplitude).

Chronic Phase. Resolution of ST elevation is quite variable. It is usually complete within 2 weeks of inferior MI but may be more delayed after anterior MI. Persistent ST elevation, often seen with large anterior MI, is indicative of a large area of akinesis, dyskinesis, or ventricular aneurysm. Symmetric T wave inversions may resolve over weeks to months or persist for an indefinite period of time; hence, the age of an MI in the presence of T wave inversions is often termed "indeterminate." Q waves usually do not resolve after anterior MI but often disappear after inferior wall MI.

Early recanalization therapy accelerates the time course of ECG changes so that, upon coronary recanalization, the pattern may evolve from acute to chronic over minutes to hours instead of days to weeks. ST segments recede rapidly, T wave inversions and losses of R wave occur earlier, and Q waves may not develop or progress and occasionally may regress. Indeed, failure of ST elevation to resolve by more than 50 to 70% within 1 to 2 hours suggests failure of thrombolysis and may prompt urgent angiography for "rescue angioplasty."

TRUE POSTERIOR MI AND LEFT CIRCUMFLEX MI PATTERNS. "True posterior" MI presents a mirror-image pattern of ECG injury in leads V_1 to V_2–V_4. The acute phase is characterized by ST depression rather than ST elevation. The evolved and chronic phases show increased R wave amplitude and widening instead of Q waves. Recognition of a true posterior acute MI pattern may lead to an early recanalization strategy. Other

causes of prominent upright anteroseptal forces include RV hypertrophy, ventricular preexcitation variants (Wolff-Parkinson-White syndrome; Chapter 59), and normal variants with early R wave progression. New appearance of these changes and/or association with an acute or evolving inferior MI usually allows the diagnosis to be made.

Occlusion of the left circumflex artery, especially when it is nondominant, often is not associated with diagnostic ST elevation and is therefore more difficult to recognize and appropriately triage and manage. Extending the ECG to measure left posterior leads V_7–V_9 increases sensitivity for detecting left circumflex–related posterior wall injury patterns with excellent specificity (Chapter 50).

RIGHT VENTRICULAR INFARCTION. Proximal occlusion of the right coronary artery before the acute marginal branch may cause right ventricular (RV) as well as inferior acute MI in about 30% of cases. Because the prognosis and treatment of inferior acute MI differ in the presence of RV infarction, it is important to make this diagnosis. The diagnosis is assisted by obtaining right precordial ECG leads, which are routinely indicated for inferior acute MI (Chapter 50). Acute ST elevation of at least 1 mm (0.1 mV) in one or more of leads V_{4R} to V_{6R} is both sensitive and specific (>90%) for identifying acute RV injury, and Q or QS waves effectively identify RV infarction.

DIAGNOSIS IN PRESENCE OF BUNDLE BRANCH BLOCK. The presence of LBBB often obscures ST segment analysis in suspected acute MI. The presence of a new (or presumed new) LBBB in association with clinical (and laboratory) findings suggesting acute MI is associated with high mortality; these patients benefit substantially from recanalization therapy and should be triaged and treated in the same way as patients with ST-elevation MI. Certain ECG patterns, although relatively insensitive, suggest acute MI if present in the setting of LBBB: Q waves in two of leads I, aVL, V_5, V_6; R-wave regression from V_1 to V_4; ST elevation of 1 mm or more in leads with a positive QRS complex; ST depression of 1 mm or more in leads V_1, V_2, or V_3; and ST elevation of 5 mm or more with a negative QRS complex. The presence of right bundle branch block (RBBB) usually does not mask typical ST-T wave or Q-wave changes except for rare cases of isolated true posterior acute MI, which is characterized by tall right precordial R waves and ST depressions.

SERUM CARDIAC MARKERS

The increasing sensitivity and specificity of serum cardiac markers have made them the "gold standard" for detection of myocardial necrosis. However, because there is a delay of from 1 to 12 hours after onset of symptoms before markers become detectable or diagnostic, and given laboratory delays even when markers are positive, the decision to proceed with an urgent recanalization strategy (thrombolysis or primary angioplasty) must be based on the clinical history and initial ECG (Chapter 46; see Fig. 69–1).

Candidate serum cardiac markers of acute MI are macromolecules (proteins) released from myocytes undergoing necrosis. Clinically ideal markers are not present normally in serum, become rapidly and markedly elevated during acute MI, and are not released from other injured tissues. In recent years, troponins I and T have emerged as the best markers, although creatine kinase (CK) and its MB isoenzyme continue to be useful. Both myoglobin and CK isoforms have

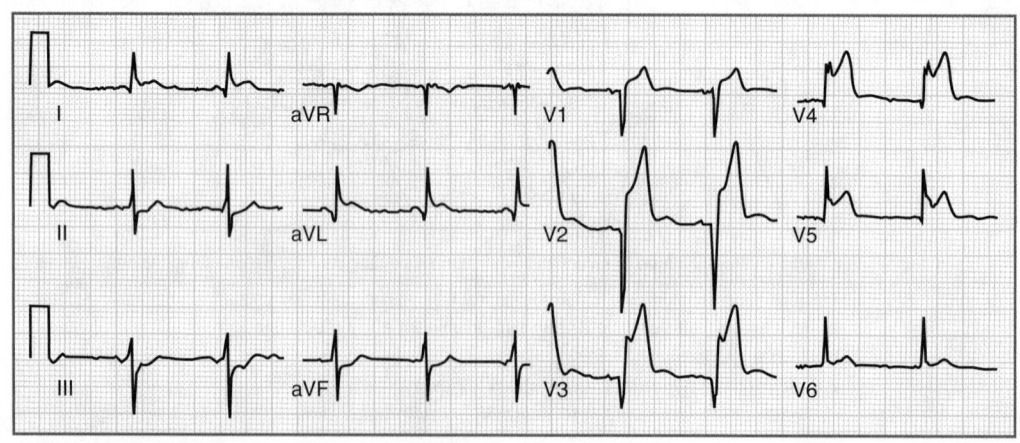

FIGURE 69–2 • Electrocardiographic tracing shows an acute anterior-lateral MI. Note ST elevation in leads I, L, and V_{1-6} with Q waves in V_{1-4}. (Courtesy of Dr. Thomas Evans.)

Table 69–2 • FEATURES OF SERUM MARKERS OF ACUTE MYOCARDIAL INFARCTION

MARKER	TIME TO APPEARANCE	DURATION OF ELEVATION	SENSITIVITY AT:		SPECIFICITY	COMMENTS
			6 hr	12 hr		
Troponin I	2–6 hr	5–10 d	~75%	90–100%	~98%	Generally regarded as a test of choice
Troponin T	2–6 hr	5–14 d	~80%	95–100%	~95%	A test of choice. Less specific than troponin I (elevated in renal insufficiency)
CK-MB	3–6 hr	2–4 d	~65%	~95%	~95%	Test of choice for recurrent angina once troponin elevated
MB2 Isoform	2–6 hr	1–2 d	~95%	~98–100%	~95%	Not widely available
Myoglobin	1–2 hr	<1 d	~85%	~90%	~80%	Slightly improved sensitivity early in AMI when added to troponin/CK-MB, but not widely used due to low specificity

Adapted from Martin E: ST-Elevation/Q-Wave Myocardial Infarction. *In* Best Practice of Medicine Praxis Press, 2001; Adams JE III, Abendschein DR, Jaffe AS: Biochemical markers of myocardial injury. Is MB creatine kinase the choice for the 1990s? Circulation 1993;88:750–763.

AMI = acute myocardial infarction; CK = creatine kinase.

a characteristic molecular weight; time of first and maximal detection, peak concentration, and circulatory persistence; and pattern of increase in acute MI (Table 69–2).

TROPONINS I AND T. Cardiac-derived troponin I (cTnI) and troponin T (cTnT), proteins of the sarcomere, have amino acid sequences distinct from their skeletal muscle isoforms. Cardiac TnI and TnT are not normally present in the blood. With even small acute MIs, troponins increase to 20-fold or more of the lower limits of the assay, and elevations persist for several days. Troponins have progressively replaced routine CK and CK-MB because they are more specific in the setting of injuries to skeletal muscle or other organs that release CK and (to a lesser extent) CK-MB, and they also are more sensitive in the setting of minimal myocardial injury.

The troponins generally are first detectable 2 to 4 hours after the onset of acute MI, are maximally sensitive at 8 to 12 hours, peak at 10 to 24 hours, and persist for 5 to 14 days. Their long persistence has allowed them to replace lactate dehydrogenase (LDH) and LDH isoenzymes for the diagnosis of acute MI in patients presenting late (>1 to 2 days) after symptoms. However, this persistence may obscure the diagnosis of recurrent MI, for which more rapidly cleared markers (i.e., CK-MB) are more useful. Clinically, cTnI and cTnT appear to be of approximately equivalent utility. However, renal failure is more likely to be associated with false-positive elevations of cTnT than cTnI. Although qualitative point-of-service troponin tests can speed the diagnosis of acute MI in the emergency department, serum cardiac markers are often negative within the first few hours after the onset of symptoms.

CK, CK-MB, AND CK ISOFORMS. CK and CK-MB served as the standard cardiac markers for many years, before the advent of cTnI and cTnT. The presence of CK in skeletal muscle and its elevation with even minor skeletal muscle trauma (e.g., intramuscular injections) limits its specificity for acute MI. The MB isoenzyme of CK, although present in lower concentrations than total CK, is much more specific (though not entirely so) for cardiac injury. An increased ratio of CK-MB mass to total CK activity substantially improves the specificity of the diagnosis of acute MI with only a modest reduction in sensitivity. A problem in using the ratio occurs when total CK is markedly elevated (in the presence of skeletal muscle damage, including prolonged cardiac resuscitation) and CK-MB is elevated by units but not ratio. Another clinical dilemma occurs when total CK is within the normal range but the ratio is elevated. Serial measurements of CK and CK-MB are more useful than single measurements in assessing diagnosis, timing, sizing, and success of therapy of acute MI. CK-MB increases within 3 to 4 hours after the onset of acute MI, is maximally sensitive within 8 to 12 hours, peaks at 12 to 24 hours, and returns to normal in 2 to 4 days.

The total quantity of CK/CK-MB protein released correlates with infarct size. Peak concentrations (e.g., for CK/CK-MB) correlate generally but less well with infarct size. Early reperfusion leads to higher and earlier peaks but similar or smaller integrated concentrations over time (consistent with myocardial salvage). The timing of the peak CK-MB may provide useful insight into the success (peak at 10 to 18 hours) or failure (peak at 18 to 30 hours) of recanalization therapy.

The myocardial form (MB-isoform) of CK-MB (designated CK-MB2) undergoes modification (terminal lysine cleavage) by carboxypeptidase to produce the circulating form of MB (CK-MB1). Acute MI disturbs the normal ratio of these two forms, relatively enriching CK-MB2. A ratio of CK-MB2:CK-MB1 of more than 1.5 can detect acute MI as early as 2 hours after the onset of the symptoms and is highly sensitive and specific for diagnosis by 4 to 6 hours. However, the electrophoretic assay is cumbersome, and the test has not been widely adopted because troponin assays are easier to perform.

It does not appear to be cost-effective to measure both a cardiac specific troponin and CK/CK-MB serially over time in every suspected case of acute MI. However, CK/CK-MB still is useful for certain applications, such as to confirm the diagnosis when the troponin level is elevated in a confusing clinical setting, to evaluate possible reinfarction in patients with recurrent chest pain, and, in specific settings, to assess the success of recanalization noninvasively (using time to peak).

MYOGLOBIN AND OTHER NONSPECIFIC MARKERS. Myoglobin is the most rapidly released and cleared serum cardiac marker. It may be detectable within 1 to 2 hours after the onset of acute MI. However, it also is abundant in skeletal muscle and suffers from a lack of specificity. For this reason, it is not commonly used clinically. LDH, aspartate serum transaminase (AST, formerly SGOT), and myosin light chain assays are not recommended because of lower specificity and sensitivity than cTnI, cTnT, and CK-MB.

OTHER LABORATORY TESTS

On admission, routine assessment of complete blood count and platelet count, standard blood chemistries, a lipid panel, and coagulation tests (prothrombin time, partial thromboplastin time) is useful. Results assist in assessing comorbid conditions and prognosis and in guiding therapy. Hematologic tests provide a useful baseline before initiation of antiplatelet, antithrombin, and thrombolytic therapy or coronary angiography/angioplasty. Myocardial injury precipitates a polymorphonuclear leukocytosis, commonly resulting in a white blood cell count of up to 12,000 to 15,000/μL that appears within a few hours and peaks at 2 to 4 days. The metabolic panel provides a useful check on electrolytes, glucose, and renal function. On admission or the next morning, a fasting lipid panel is recommended to assist in decision making for inpatient lipid lowering (i.e., statin therapy if low-density lipoprotein [LDL] is greater than 100 to 130 mg/dL; Chapter 211). Unless CO_2 retention is suspected, finger oximetry is adequate to titrate oxygen therapy. Systemic acute phase inflammatory markers (e.g., C-reactive protein, erythrocyte sedimentation rate) increase with acute MI, but their incremental value for routine testing remains to be shown.

IMAGING

A chest radiograph is the only imaging test *routinely* obtained on admission for acute MI. Although the chest radiograph is often normal, findings of pulmonary venous congestion, cardiomegaly, or widened mediastinum may contribute importantly to diagnosis and management decisions. For example, a history of severe, "tearing" chest and back pain in association with a widened mediastinum should raise the question of a dissecting aortic aneurysm (Chapter 75). In such cases, thrombolytic therapy must be withheld pending more definitive diagnostic imaging of the aorta. Other noninvasive imaging (e.g., echocardiography [Chapter 51], cardiac nuclear scans [Chapter 52], and other tests) is performed for evaluation of specific clinical issues, including suspected complications of acute MI. Coronary angiography (Chapter 54) is performed urgently as part of an interventional strategy for acute MI or later for risk-stratification in higher-risk patients managed medically.

ECHOCARDIOGRAPHY. Two-dimensional transthoracic echocardiography with color-flow Doppler imaging is the most generally useful noninvasive test obtained on admission or early in the hospital course (Chapter 51). Echocardiography efficiently assesses global and regional cardiac function and evaluates suspected complications of acute MI. The sensitivity and specificity of echocardiography for regional wall motion assessment are high (>90%), although the age of the abnormality (new versus old) must be distinguished clinically or by ECG. Echocardiography is helpful in determining the cause of circulatory failure with hypotension (relative hypovolemia, LV failure, RV failure, or mechanical complication of acute MI). Echocardiography also can differentiate pericarditis and perimyocarditis from acute MI.

Doppler echocardiography is indicated to evaluate a new murmur and other suspected mechanical complications of acute MI (papillary muscle dysfunction or rupture, acute ventricular septal defect, LV free wall rupture with tamponade or pseudoaneurysm). Later in the course of acute MI, echocardiography may be used to assess the degree of recovery of stunned myocardium after recanalization therapy, the degree of residual cardiac dysfunction and indications for angiotensin-converting enzyme (ACE) inhibitors and other therapies for heart failure, and the presence of LV aneurysm and mural thrombus (requiring oral anticoagulants).

NUCLEAR AND OTHER IMAGING STUDIES. Radionuclide techniques generally are too time consuming and cumbersome for routine use in the acute setting. More commonly, they are used in predischarge or postdischarge risk stratification to augment exercise or pharmacologic stress testing (Chapter 52). Thallium-201 and technetium-99m-sestamibi alone or together (dual isotope imaging) are currently the most frequently used "cold spot" tracers to assess myocardial perfusion and viability, and infarct size. Infarct avid tracers to identify, locate, and size recent myocardial necrosis are available but rarely required for ST-elevation MI. Computed tomography (Chapter 52) and magnetic resonance imaging (Chapter 53) may be useful to evaluate patients with a suspected dissecting aortic aneurysm and, together with positron-emission tomography, for research purposes and in highly selected clinical applications such as for assessment of myocardial viability.

 Treatment

ASSESSMENT AND MANAGEMENT

Prehospital Phase

More than one half of deaths related to acute MI occur within 1 hour of onset of symptoms and before the patient reaches a hospital emergency department. Most of these deaths are caused by ischemia-related ventricular fibrillation (VF) and can be reversed by defibrillation (Chapters 60 and 61). Rapid defibrillation may allow resuscitation in 60% of patients when delivered by a bystander using an on-site automatic external defibrillator or by a first-responding medical rescuer. Moreover, the first hour represents the best opportunity for myocardial salvage with recanalization therapy. Thus, the three goals of prehospital care are (1) to recognize symptoms promptly and seek medical attention, (2) to deploy an emergency medical system team capable of cardiac monitoring, defibrillation and resuscitation, and emergency medical therapy (e.g., nitroglycerin, lidocaine, atropine), and (3) to transport the patient expeditiously to a medical care facility staffed with personnel capable of providing expert coronary care, including recanalization therapy (thrombolysis or primary angioplasty).

The greatest time lag to recanalization therapy is the patient's delay in calling for help. Public education efforts have yielded mixed results, and innovative approaches are needed. The feasibility of initiating thrombolytic therapy by highly trained ambulance personnel in coordinated ambulance–emergency department systems has been shown. In coordinated systems and when transportation delays are substantial, initiation of thrombolytic or other antithrombotic therapy in the field may be considered, thereby shortening the time to recanalization.

Hospital Phases

EMERGENCY DEPARTMENT. The goals of emergency department care are to identify rapidly patients with acute myocardial ischemia, to stratify them into acute ST-elevation MI as compared with other acute coronary syndromes (see Figs. 68–1 and 69–1), to initiate a recanalization strategy and other appropriate medical care in qualifying patients with acute ST-elevation MI, and to triage rapidly to inpatient (CCU, step-down unit, observation unit) or outpatient care (patients without suspected ischemia) (see Table 68–3).

The evaluation of patients with chest pain and other suspected acute coronary syndromes begins with a 12-lead ECG even as the physician is beginning a focused history, including contraindications to thrombolysis, and a targeted physical examination. Continuous ECG monitoring should be started, an intravenous line

established, and admission blood tests should be drawn (including cardiac markers such as cTnI or cTnT). As rapidly as possible, the patient should be stratified as having a probable ST-elevation acute MI, non–ST-elevation acute MI, probable or possible unstable angina, or likely noncardiac chest pain.

In patients with presumed ST-elevation acute MI, a recanalization strategy must be selected: alternative choices are thrombolysis (begun immediately in the emergency department with a goal of door-to-needle time of less than 30 minutes) or primary percutaneous coronary intervention (PCI; patient is transferred directly to the cardiac catheterization laboratory with a goal of coronary door-to-angiography time of less than 60 to 90 minutes and door-to-balloon time of less than 90 to 120 minutes; Fig. 69–3).

Aspirin should be given to all patients unless contraindicated (Fig. 69–3). Intravenous heparin is appropriate in most patients. Patients with chest pain should be given sublingual nitroglycerin. Persistent ischemic pain may be treated with titrated doses of morphine. Initiation of β-blocker therapy is usually indicated, especially with hypertension, tachycardia, and ongoing pain. Oxygen should be used in doses sufficient to avoid hypoxemia (fingertip oximetry may be used to monitor). The ideal systolic blood pressure is 100 to 140 mm Hg. Excessive hypertension usually responds to titrated nitroglycerin, β-blocker therapy, and morphine (for pain). Relative hypotension may require discontinuation of these medications, fluid administration, or other measures as appropriate to the hemodynamic subset (see Table 69–3). Atropine should be available to treat symptomatic bradycardia and hypotension related to excessive vagotonia. Transfer to the CCU or catheterization laboratory should occur as expeditiously as possible.

EARLY HOSPITAL PHASE (CORONARY CARE). Coronary care for early hospital management of acute MI has reduced in-hospital mortality by more than 50%. The goals of CCU care include (1) continuous ECG monitoring and antiarrhythmic therapy for serious arrhythmias (i.e., rapid defibrillation of VF), (2) initiation or continuation of a coronary recanalization strategy to achieve myocardial reperfusion, (3) initiation or continuation of other acute medical therapies, (4) hemodynamic monitoring and appropriate medical interventions for different hemodynamic subsets of patients, and (5) diagnosis and treatment of mechanical and physiologic complications of acute MI. General care and comfort measures also are instituted. A sample of CCU admission orders is given in Table 69–4.

General care measures include attention to activity, diet, bowels, education, reassurance, and sedation. Bedrest is encouraged for the first 12 hours. In the absence of complications, dangling and bed-chair and self-care activities can begin within 24 hours. When stabilization has occurred, usually within 1 to 3 days, patients may be

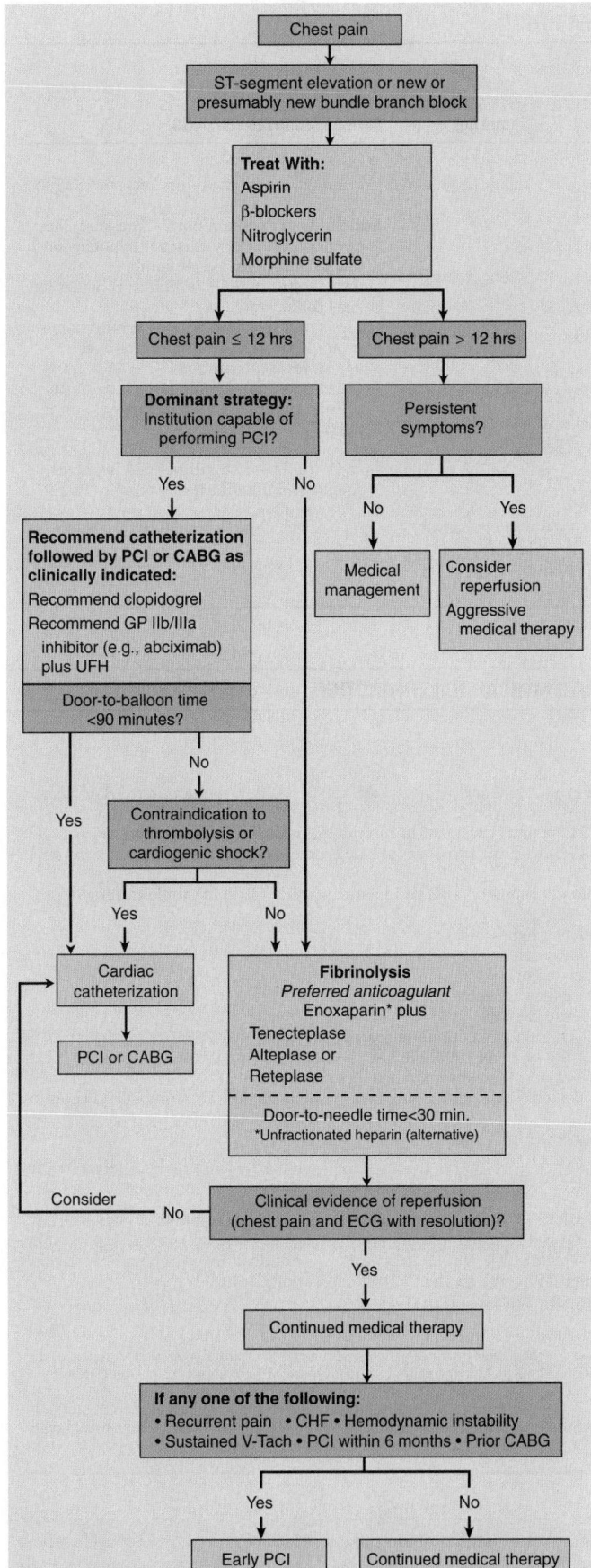

FIGURE 69–3 • Acute ST-elevation myocardial infarction: practical evidence-based guidelines for outcome-effective management. (Original guidelines developed by Kurt Kleinschmidt, M.D., FACEP, for Emergency Medicine Reports, November 2000. Final adaptation and revisions by the CTAP Panel. "Acute Coronary Syndrome [ACS] Pharmacotherapeutic Interventions for UA/NSTEMI—An Evidence-Based Review and Outcome-Optimizing Guidelines for ACS Patients with and without Procedural Coronary Intervention [PCI].")

transferred to a step-down unit where progressive reambulation occurs. The risk of emesis and aspiration or the anticipation of angiography or other procedures usually dictates nothing by mouth or clear liquids for the first 4 to 12 hours. Thereafter, a heart-healthy diet in small portions is recommended. In patients at high risk for bleeding gastric stress ulcers, a proton pump inhibitor or an H_2-antagonist is recommended for prophylaxis in patients on antithrombotic therapy. Many patients benefit from an analgesic (e.g., morphine sulfate in 2 to 4 mg increments) to relieve ongoing pain and an anxiolytic or sedative during the CCU phase. A benzodiazepine is frequently selected. Sedatives should not be substituted for education and reassurance from concerned caregivers to relieve emotional distress and improve behavior; routine use of anxiolytics is neither necessary nor recommended. Constipation often occurs with bedrest and narcotics; stool softeners and a bedside commode are advised.

The ECG should be monitored continuously in the CCU (and usually in the step-down unit) to detect serious arrhythmias and guide therapy. Measures to limit infarct size (i.e., coronary recanalization) and to optimize hemodynamics also stabilize the heart electrically. Routine antiarrhythmic prophylaxis (e.g., with lidocaine or amiodarone) is not indicated, but specific arrhythmias require treatment (see later text).

Hemodynamic evaluation is helpful in assessing prognosis and guiding therapy (see Table 69–3). Clinical and noninvasive evaluation of vital signs is adequate for normotensive patients without pulmonary congestion. Patients with pulmonary venous congestion alone can usually be managed conservatively. Invasive monitoring is appropriate when the cause of circulatory failure is uncertain and when titration of intravenous therapies depends on hemodynamic measurements (e.g., pulmonary capillary wedge pressure and cardiac output). Similarly, an arterial line is not necessary in all patients and may be associated with local bleeding after thrombolysis or potent antiplatelet and antithrombin therapy; arterial catheters are appropriate and useful in unstable, hypotensive patients who do not respond to intravenous fluids to replete or expand intravascular volume (see "Complications").

LATER HOSPITAL PHASE. Transfer from the CCU to the step-down unit usually occurs within 1 to 3 days, when the cardiac rhythm and hemodynamics are stable. The duration of this late phase of hospital care is usually an additional 2 to 3 days in uncomplicated cases. Activity levels should be increased progressively under continuous ECG monitoring. Medical therapy should progress from parenteral agents to oral medications appropriate for long-term outpatient use.

Risk stratification and functional evaluations are critical to assess prognosis and guide therapy as the time for discharge approaches. Functional evaluation also can be extended to the early postdischarge period. Education must be provided about diet, activity, smoking, and other risk factors (lipids, hypertension).

SPECIFIC THERAPEUTIC MEASURES

RECANALIZATION THERAPY. Early reperfusion of ischemic, infarcting myocardium represents the most important conceptual and practical advance for ST-elevation acute MI and is the primary therapeutic goal. Coronary recanalization is accomplished by using thrombolytic (fibrinolytic) therapy or a primary PCI with angioplasty and, commonly, stenting. Each has relative advantages and disadvantages as the primary recanalization strategy (see Tables 69–6 and 69–7). With broad application of recanalization therapy, 30-day mortality rates from ST-elevation acute MI have progressively declined over the past 3 decades (from 20 to 30% to 5 to 10%).

Thrombolytic Therapy. During the 1980s and early 1990s, studies demonstrating the ability of thrombolytics to recanalize occluded coronary arteries acutely were followed by controlled trials; an overview of the larger randomized studies, primarily of streptokinase and including a total of 58,600 patients, showed a highly significant 18% reduction in mortality (from 11.5% to 9.8%) at 5 weeks.[1] Patients with anterior ST-elevation benefited more (37 lives saved per 1000) than those with inferior ST-elevation only (8 lives saved per 1000), and younger patients benefited more than the elderly (>75 years). No benefit or a slight adverse trend was observed for patients presenting with normal ECGs or

Continued

Table 69–3 • HEMODYNAMIC SUBSETS OF ACUTE MYOCARDIAL INFARCTION

	BLOOD PRESSURE (RELATIVE)	TYPICAL PHYSICAL FINDINGS	CARDIAC INDEX (L/min/m²)	PA WEDGE PRESSURE (mm Hg)	SUGGESTED INTERVENTIONS
Normal	Normal	+/– S$_4$	>2.5	≤12	None required
Hyperdynamic	Normal or high	Anxious	>3	<12	Control pain, anxiety; β-blocker; treat SBP to <140 mm Hg
Hypovolemia	Low	Dry	≤2.7	≤9	Add fluids to maintain normal pressure. May develop pulmonary edema if hypotension due to unrecognized LV failure
Mild LV failure	Low to high	Rales, +/– S$_3$	2.0–2.5	>15	Diuresis; nitrates, ACE inhibitor; consider low-dose β-blocker
Severe LV failure	Low to normal	Above + S$_3$, +/– ↑ JVP, +/– edema	<2.0	>20	Diuresis; nitrates; low-dose ACE inhibitor; avoid β-blockers. Consider inotropes, urgent revascularization
Cardiogenic shock	Very low	Above + cool, clammy; ↓ mental, renal function	≤1.5	>25	Avoid hypotensive agents; place intra-aortic balloon pump; urgent revascularization if possible
RV infarct	Very low	↑ JVP with clear lungs	<2.5	≤12	Give IV fluids. Avoid nitrates and hypotensive agents. Dobutamine if refractory to fluids

Adapted from Forrester JS, Diamond G, Chatterjee K, Swan HJ: Medical therapy of acute myocardial infarction by application of hemodynamic subsets (second of two parts). N Engl J Med 1976;295:1404–1413.

ACE = angiotensin-converting enzyme; IV = intravenous; JVP = jugular venous pressure; LV = left ventricle; PA = pulmonary artery; RV = right ventricle; SBP = systolic blood pressure.

Table 69–4 • SAMPLE ADMISSION ORDERS FOR ST-ELEVATION ACUTE MYOCARDIAL INFARCTION

Diagnosis:	Acute ST-elevation myocardial infarction
Admit:	CCU with telemetry
Condition:	Serious
Vital signs:	q 1/2h until stable, then q 4h and prn. Pulse oximetry × 24 hr. Notify if heart rate <50 or >100; respiratory rate <8 or >20; SBP <90 or >150; O$_2$ saturation <90%.
Activity:	Bedrest × 12 hr with bedside commode. Oxygen at 2 L by nasal cannula 3 hr minimum; titrated to O$_2$ saturation >90%
Diet:	NPO until pain-free, then clear liquids progressing to heart-healthy diet as tolerated, unless on call for catheterization (or other test requiring NPO).
Laboratory*:	Troponin or CK/CK-MB q 8h × 3; comprehensive blood chemistry, CBC with platelets; PT, PTT; lipid profile (fasting in morning). Portable CXR.
IV:	D$_5$W or NS to keep vein open (increase fluids for relative hypovolemia)
Recanalization Therapy*:	Primary coronary angioplasty or thrombolysis (if appropriate)
	1. Primary angioplasty (preferred if available within 1–2 hr)
	2. Tenecteplase, alteplase, reteplase, or streptokinase (see Table 69–5 for dosing)
Medications:	1. Nasal O$_2$ at 2 L/min × 3 hr, then by order (per O$_2$ saturation)
	2. Aspirin 325 mg chewed on admission, then 162–325 mg PO qd (enteric coated)
	3. IV heparin 60 U/kg bolus (max 4000 U) and 12 U/kg/hr (max 1000 U/hr) or enoxaparin 30 mg IV then 1 mg/kg SQ q 12h (maximum SQ doses 100 mg on day 1)
	4. Metoprolol 5 mg IV q 5 min up to 3× then 25–50 mg bid or atenolol 5 mg IV q 10 min × 2 then 25–50 mg PO qd (hold for systolic BP <100, pulse <50, asthma, heart failure)
	5. Consider nitroglycerin drip × 24–48 hr (titrated to SBP 100–140)
	6. Morphine sulfate 2–4 mg IV prn for unrelieved pain
	7. Stool softener
	8. Anxioluytic or hypnotic if needed
	9. ACE inhibitor for hypertension, anterior acute MI, or LV dysfuction, in low oral dose (e.g., captopril 6.25 mg q 8h), begun within 24 hours or when stable (SBP >100) and adjusted upward.
	10. Consider: lipid-lowering (i.e., statin if LDL >100 mg/dL), GP IIb/IIIa inhibitor (e.g., eptifibatide or tirofiban) "upstream" for planned PCI, and clopidogrel 300 mg PO, then 75 mg PO qd after PCI (if CABG not planned).
	11. Specific treatments for hemodynamic subgroups (see Table 69–3).

*If not ordered in emergency department.

Adapted from Ryan TJ, Antman EM, Brooks NH, et al: 1999 update: ACC/AHA guidelines for the management of patients with acute myocardial infarction. A report of the American College of Cardiology/American Association Task Force on Practice Guidelines (Committee on Management of Acute Myocardial Infarction). J Am Coll Cardiol 1999;34:890–911.

ACE = angiotensin-converting enzyme; CABG = coronary artery bypass graft; CCU = coronary care unit; CK = creatine kinase; CBC = complete blood count; CXR = chest radiograph; GP = glycoprotein; IV = intravenous; LDL = low density lipoprotein; LV = left ventricle; MI = myocardial infarction; NPO = nothing by mouth; NS = normal saline; PCI = percutaneous coronary intervention; PT = prothrombin time; PTT = partial thromboplastin time; SBP = systemic blood pressure; SQ = subcutaneous.

ST-depression alone. Benefit was time-dependent, declining from about 40 lives saved per 1000 within the first hour, to 20 to 30 lives saved per 1000 for hours 2 to 12, to a nonsignificant 7 lives saved per 1000 for hours 13 to 24. Even greater relative and absolute benefit within the first 1 to 2 hours was demonstrated in another overview that also included smaller studies.[2]

The additional recanalization benefit of tissue plasminogen activator (tPA) compared with streptokinase was best shown in a ran-

domized international study of 41,021 patients with ST-elevation acute MI. Mortality at 30 days was significantly lower (by 14%) with an accelerated tPA regimen plus intravenous heparin (6.3%) than with streptokinase (7.3%).[3] In an angiographic substudy, the patency rate of the infarct-related artery at 90 minutes varied inversely with mortality, being higher for tPA (81%) than with the streptokinase regimens (53 to 60%). Differences in mortality were accounted for by differences in complete restoration of flow (54% versus 29 to

Table 69–5 • CHARACTERISTICS OF FDA-APPROVED INTRAVENOUS THROMBOLYTIC AGENTS

	SK (STREPTOKINASE)	APSAC (ANISTREPLASE)	tPA (ALTEPLASE)	rPA (RETEPLASE)	TNK-tPA (TENECTEPLASE)
Dose	1.5 MU in 30–60 min	30 U in 5 min	100 mg in 90 min*	10 U + 10 U, 30 min apart	30–50 mg[†] over 5 sec
Circulating half-life (min)	≅20	≅100	≅4	≅18	≅20
Antigenic	Yes	Yes	No	No	No
Allergic reactions	Yes	Yes	No	No	No
Systemic fibrinogen depletion	Severe	Severe	Mild–moderate	Moderate	Minimal
Intracerebral hemorrhage	≅0.4%	≅0.6%	≅0.7%	≅0.8%	≅0.7%
Patency (TIMI-2/3) rate, 90 min[†]	≅51%	≅70%	≅73–84%	≅83%	≅77–88%
Lives saved per 100 treated	≅3[‡]	≅3[§]	≅4[‖]	≅4	≅4
Cost per dose (approx U.S. dollars)	300	2100	1800	2200	2200

*Accelerated tPA given as follows: 15-mg bolus, then 0.75 mg/kg over 30 min (maximum, 50 mg), then 0.50 mg/kg over 60 min (maximum 35 mg).
[†]TNK-tPA is dosed by weight (supplied in 5 mg/mL vials): <60 kg = 6 mL; 61–70 kg = 7 mL; 71–80 kg = 8 mL; 81–90 kg = 9 mL; >90 kg = 10 mL.
[‡]Based on: Granger CB, Califf RM, Topol EJ: Thrombolytic therapy for acute myocardial infarction. A review. Drugs 1992;44:293–325; Bode C, Smalling RW, Berg G, et al: Randomized comparison of coronary thrombolysis achieved with double-bolus reteplase (recombinant plasminogen activator) and front-loaded, accelerated alteplase (recombinant tissue plasminogen activator) in patients with acute myocardial infarction. The RAPID II Investigators. Circulation 1996;94:891–898.
[§]Patients with ST elevation or bundle branch block, treated <6 hr.
[‖]Based on the finding from the GUSTO trial that tPA saves one more additional life per 100 treated than does SK. (From an international randomized trial comparing four thrombolytic strategies for acute myocardial infarction. The GUSTO investigators. N Engl J Med 1993;329:673–682; and Simes RJ, Topol EJ, Holmes DR Jr, et al: Link between the angiographic substudy and mortality outcomes in a large randomized trial of myocardial reperfusion. Importance of early and complete infarct artery reperfusion. GUSTO-I Investigators. Circulation 1995;91:1923–1928.)

Table 69–6 • INDICATIONS AND CONTRAINDICATIONS TO THROMBOLYTIC THERAPY

INDICATIONS
Ischemic-type chest discomfort or equivalent for 30 min to 12 hr with new or presumed new ST-segment elevation in two contiguous leads of ≥2 mm (≥0.2 mV) in leads V₁, V₂, or V₃ or ≥1 mm in other leads
New or presumed new left bundle branch block with symptoms consistent with myocardial infarction
Absence of contraindications

CONTRAINDICATIONS, ABSOLUTE
Active bleeding or bleeding diathesis (menses excluded)
Prior hemorrhagic stroke, other strokes within 1 year
Intracranial or spinal cord neoplasm
Suspected or known aortic dissection

CONTRAINDICATIONS, RELATIVE
Severe, uncontrolled hypertension (>180/110 mm Hg)
Anticoagulation with therapeutic or elevated INR (>2–3)
Old ischemic stroke; intracerebral pathology other than above
Recent major trauma/surgery (<2–4 wk)
Pregnancy
Recent noncompressible vascular punctures
Recent retinal laser therapy
Cardiogenic shock when revascularization is available

Adapted from Ryan TJ, Antman EM, Brooks NH, et al: 1999 update: ACC/AHA Guidelines for the management of patients with acute myocardial infarction. A report of the American College of Cardiology/American Association Task Force on Practice Guidelines (Committee on Management of Acute Myocardial Infarction). J Am Coll Cardiol 1999;34:890–911.
INR = international normalized ratio.

Table 69–7 • INDICATIONS FOR PRIMARY ANGIOPLASTY AND COMPARISON WITH THROMBOLYTIC THERAPY

INDICATIONS
Alternative recanalization strategy for ST-elevation or LBBB acute MI within 12 hr of symptom onset (or >12 hr if symptoms persist)
Cardiogenic shock developing within 36 hr of ST-elevation/Q-wave acute MI or LBBB acute MI in patients <75 years old who can be revascularized within 18 hr of shock onset
Recommended only at centers performing >200 PCI/yr with backup cardiac surgery and for operators performing >75 PCI/yr

ADVANTAGES OF PRIMARY PCI
Higher initial recanalization rates
Reduced risk of intracerebral hemorrhage
Less residual stenosis; less recurrent ischemia/infarction
Useful when thrombolysis contraindicated
Improves outcomes with cardiogenic shock

DISADVANTAGES OF PRIMARY PCI (C/W THROMBOLYTIC THERAPY)
Access, advantages restricted to high-volume centers, operators
Longer average time to treatment
Results more operator dependent
Higher system complexity, costs

Adapted from Ryan TJ, Antman EM, Brooks NH, et al: 1999 update: ACC/AHA Guidelines for the management of patients with acute myocardial infarction. A report of the American College of Cardiology/American Association Task Force on Practice Guidelines (Committee on Management of Acute Myocardial Infarction). J Am Coll Cardiol 1999;34:890–911.
LBBB = left bundle branch block; MI = myocardial infarction; PCI = percutaneous coronary intervention (includes balloon angioplasty, stenting).

33%). Longer-acting variants of tPA, given by single (tenecteplase) or double bolus (reteplase) injections, have been developed and approved for clinical use; these agents are more convenient to give but have not further improved survival.

The major risk of thrombolytic therapy is bleeding. Intracerebral hemorrhage is the most serious and frequently fatal complication; its incidence rate is 0.5 to 1% with currently approved regimens. Older age (>70 to 75 years), female gender, hypertension, and higher relative doses of tPA and heparin increase the risk of intracranial hemorrhage. The risk:benefit ratio should be assessed in each patient when thrombolysis is being considered and specific regimens are being selected.

The characteristics of currently approved intravenous thrombolytics are summarized in Table 69–5; current indications for and contraindications to thrombolytic therapy are summarized in Table 69–6. Patients with ST-elevation or new/presumed new LBBB presenting within 12 hours of the onset of symptoms and without contraindications are candidates for thrombolytic therapy.

Primary Percutaneous Coronary Intervention. PCI has emerged as an alternative, usually as the preferred, recanalization strategy (Table 69–7). PCI achieves mechanical recanalization by inflation of a catheter-based balloon centered within the thrombotic occlusion (Chapter 70). Percutaneous transluminal coronary angioplasty (PTCA) is generally augmented by placing a stent at the site of occlusion as a scaffold to enlarge the lumen and retain optimal postangioplasty expansion.

The relative benefits of primary PTCA or PCI over thrombolysis have been established through moderate-sized comparative studies, registry data, and indirect evidence. A meta-analysis of ten randomized trials found a significantly lower mortality rate (4.4%

Continued

vs. 6.5%, odds ratio [OR] 0.66) and lower rates of non-fatal reinfarction (2.9% vs. 5.3%, OR 0.53) and intracerebral hemorrhage with primary PTCA compared with thrombolysis.[1] In recent registry studies, PCI yielded better outcomes across all age groups than thrombolysis when performed within 1 to 2 hours of presentation.

Currently, a primary PCI strategy may begin with initiation of a GP IIb/IIIa inhibitor in the emergency department, together with aspirin and heparin, followed by rapid application of coronary angioplasty with stenting. Whether the addition of a reduced dose of a plasminogen activator to a GP IIb/IIIa therapy in the emergency department could further improve outcomes with early PCI without compromising safety is under investigation.

Operator and institutional experience is an issue more important to outcomes with primary PCI than thrombolysis and has been incorporated into current recommendations (Table 69–7). Primary PCI is feasible in community hospitals without surgical capability, but concerns about timing and safety remain, and this approach is not yet advocated in current guidelines.

Patients with ST-elevation or new/presumed new LBBB presenting within 12 hours are candidates for primary PCI. An additional important indication is cardiogenic shock occurring within 36 hours of the onset of acute MI and treated within 18 hours of the onset of shock. However, benefit was not established for patients older than 75 years of age, and benefit was greater with earlier PCI.[5]

Selecting a Recanalization Regimen.
Whether to use PCI or thrombolytic therapy depends on local resources and experience, as well as on patient factors. Outcomes appear to be determined more by the care with which a strategy is developed and implemented than whether thrombolytic therapy or primary PCI forms the preferred approach to recanalization. In general, in experienced facilities (>200 PCIs/center; surgical capability; >75 PCIs/operator annually; frequent *primary* PCI, e.g., >16/year/center; >4/operator/year) able to mobilize and treat quickly (<60 to 120 minutes to angiography and balloon inflation), primary PCI is generally considered the preferred strategy, with stenting preferred over balloon PTCA.[6] PCI is particularly preferred for patients at higher risk for mortality (including shock), for later presentations (>4 hours), and for patients with greater risk of intracerebral hemorrhage (age older than 70 years, female gender, therapy with hypertensives). Ancillary antithrombotic therapy with primary PCI includes aspirin, unfractionated heparin or a low-molecular-weight heparin, and a GP IIb/IIIa inhibitor (preferably initiated on admission before catheterization). Clopidogrel is begun directly after PCI and continued after discharge.

For other situations, thrombolytic therapy becomes the recommended recanalization strategy. The selection of a specific thrombolytic regimen is based on the risk of complications of the acute MI, the risk of intracerebral hemorrhage, and a consideration of economic constraints. Using these factors, longer-acting variants of tPA (i.e., tenecteplase and reteplase) have become dominant in the United States market; in Europe and elsewhere, less costly streptokinase is still widely used. A nonimmunogenic thrombolytic is preferred for patients with a history of prior streptokinase use. Streptokinase has a lower risk of intracerebral hemorrhage if excessive heparin is avoided. Tenecteplase combined with enoxaparin was more effective than tenecteplase with standard heparin or with a GP IIb/IIIa inhibitor (abciximab) plus heparin in a recent large trial.[7] Reteplase with abciximab also showed no mortality advantage when combined (in half-dose) with abciximab than with heparin alone; ischemic events decreased but intracerebral hemorrhage increased, especially in the elderly. In hospitals with long ambulance transport times (>60 to 90 minutes), a strategy for initiating prehospital thrombolysis may be considered.

Over the past decade, the application of recanalization therapy has remained relatively constant in the United States at 70 to 75% of "eligible" acute MI patients. Primary PCI use has increased (24% of eligible patients), although thrombolytic therapy continues to be more commonly applied (48% of eligible patients).

ANCILLARY AND OTHER THERAPIES

Antiplatelet Therapy

ASPIRIN. Platelets form a critical component of coronary thrombi. Aspirin inhibits platelet aggregation by irreversibly blocking cyclooxygenase-1 (COX-1) activity by selective acetylation of serine at position 530. COX-1 catalyzes the conversion of arachidonic acid to thromboxane-1, a potent platelet aggregator (Chapter 32).

Aspirin has been extensively tested to prevent coronary heart disease (Chapter 33). Aspirin trials in ST-elevation acute MI have been more limited but positive. The most important trial of aspirin in ST-elevation acute MI randomized over 17,000 patients with "suspected acute MI" (representing mostly but not entirely ST-elevation acute MI) to aspirin or control and to intravenous streptokinase or control. At 5 weeks, the relative risk of vascular death was reduced 21% by aspirin alone, 25% by streptokinase alone, and 40% by aspirin plus streptokinase.[8] Since that time, aspirin has been included as standard therapy in most ST-elevation acute MI treatment regimens.

Current guidelines strongly recommend aspirin (class I indication) on admission in a dose of 162 to 325 mg, preferably chewed. Aspirin is continued in the same dose throughout hospitalization and then indefinitely in a dose of 81 to 325 mg daily as an outpatient (enteric-coated forms are popular).

ADENOSINE DIPHOSPHATE RECEPTOR ANTAGONISTS. Clopidogrel and ticlopidine exert potent antiplatelet effects by blocking the platelet membrane adenosine diphosphate (ADP) receptor (Chapter 33). Because of its lower hematologic (neutropenic) toxic potential, clopidogrel has become the preferred agent in this class. For aspirin-allergic patients, clopidogrel has become the alternative of choice for acute and chronic therapy of ST-elevation acute MI. A loading dose of 300 mg/day followed by 75 mg/day provides effective antiplatelet activity.

The efficacy of clopidogrel has been demonstrated for secondary prevention, for post-PCI patients, and for non–ST-elevation acute coronary syndromes, but limited data are available for acute therapy of ST-elevation acute MI. Begun on admission for non–ST-elevation acute MI or unstable angina, clopidogrel added to aspirin reduced vascular events (by 22%) at 3 to 12 months compared with aspirin alone. Extrapolation has led to the recommendation that clopidogrel be used as an alternative antiplatelet for ST-elevation acute MI patients when aspirin is contraindicated and be considered routinely (in addition to aspirin) in patients after primary PCI. Therapy for longer than 1 month might specifically be considered for higher-risk patients with more vascular disease or with complications of PCI.

GP IIB/IIIA INHIBITORS. Inhibitors of the platelet membrane glycoprotein IIb/IIIa receptor, a fibrinogen receptor, have been shown to benefit high-risk patients with non–ST-elevation acute coronary syndrome (Chapters 33 and 68) on admission or after PCI. The benefit in ST-elevation MI is smaller when route stenting is used and if GP IIb/IIIa therapy is administered only in the catheterization laboratory. Earlier GP inhibition in the emergency department or pre-catheterization may be more effective to improve coronary patency at the time of angiography and event-free survival at 6 months. If early coronary artery bypass graft (CABG) surgery is a possibility after angiography, a shorter-acting inhibitor (eptifibatide, tirofiban) may impart a lower perioperative risk of bleeding than abciximab. For ST-elevation acute MI patients treated with thrombolysis, GP IIb/IIIa inhibitors added to reduced-dose tPA (e.g., half-dose tPA) improves early coronary patency. However, larger trials have not shown improved survival, and serious bleeding risks (including intracerebral hemorrhage) are increased. Whether such regimens are appropriate for specific subgroups, such as younger patients with large ST-elevation acute MIs scheduled with some delay for PCI remains to be determined.

Antithrombin Therapy

UNFRACTIONATED HEPARIN. Upon injection, heparin complexes with antithrombin (AT)-III. The heparin–AT-III complex inactivates circulating thrombin and, less effectively, factor X. Clot-bound thrombin is resistant. Evidence for the contribution of heparin to antithrombotic regimens is mostly observational, indirect, or inferential (Chapter 33).

Heparin is recommended with primary PCI and for patients receiving thrombolysis with tPA (see Fig. 69–3 and Table 69–4). It also is recommended intravenously with streptokinase or anistreplase for patients at high risk for systemic emboli (e.g., large or anterior acute MI with LV thrombus, atrial fibrillation [AF]). Low-dose subcutaneous heparin (7500 U twice daily) has been recommended for patients with acute MI to prevent deep vein thrombosis in the absence of intravenous heparin; however, current early reambulation after acute MI and routine use of aspirin may make routine subcutaneous heparin unnecessary.

Excessive bleeding when heparin is used in combination with antithrombotic regimens has led to reductions in heparin doses with improved safety. When given with a thrombolytic, intravenous heparin is begun concurrently and given for 48 hours. Currently recommended doses include a 60 U/kg bolus (maximum 4000 U) followed initially with a 12 U/kg per hour infusion (maximum 1000 U/hour) with adjustment after 3 hours based on aPTT (target of 50 to 70 seconds, 1.5 to 2 times control). Experimental regimens including a GP IIb/IIIa inhibitor and a thrombolytic have used even lower heparin doses. During primary PCI, high-dose heparin is used (Activated Clotting Time [ACT] 300 to 350 seconds). Given together with a GP IIb/IIIa inhibitor during PCI, heparin is dosed to a lower ACT range (150 to 300 seconds).

LOW-MOLECULAR-WEIGHT HEPARIN. Low-molecular-weight heparins (LMWHs) have enhanced inhibitory activity for factor Xa (Chapter 33). They also have more reliable bioavailability and longer durations of action, permitting once or twice daily subcutaneous administration in fixed (weight-adjusted) doses. LMWHs have been extensively tested for the non–ST-elevation acute coronary syndrome and for prophylaxis of deep vein thrombosis. The LMWH enoxaparin combined with tenecteplase was more effective than tenecteplase combined with standard heparin or with a GP IIb/IIIa inhibitor (abciximab) plus heparin in ST-elevation acute MI.[9]

DIRECT ANTITHROMBINS. Direct acting thrombins, such as hirudin and its analogues, do not require AT-III for activity; they inhibit clot-bound heparin and are not neutralized by plasma proteins (Chapter 33). Unlike heparin, hirudins do not induce thrombocytopenia. Early trials using surrogate end points were promising. However, bleeding can be problematic, and clinical trials to date have not shown a survival advantage.

Nitrates. Nitroglycerin and other organic nitrates (isosorbide dinitrate and isosorbide mononitrate) induce vascular smooth muscle relaxation by generating vascular endothelial nitric oxide. The resulting vasodilation of veins and peripheral and coronary arteries may beneficially reduce excessive cardiac preload and afterload, increase coronary caliber in responsive areas of stenosis, reverse distal small coronary arterial vasoconstriction, improve coronary collateral flow to ischemic myocardium, and inhibit platelet aggregation in acute MI (Chapter 67). The result is improved oxygen delivery and reduced oxygen consumption. Potential clinical benefits include relief of ischemia, limitation of infarct size, prevention of dilative remodeling, control of hypertension (afterload), and relief of congestion (preload).

In the pre-reperfusion era, nitrates appeared to confer a mortality benefit in acute MI. In the context of thrombolytic therapy and aspirin, however, mortality benefits are modest, with a relative mortality reduction of about four lives saved per 1000 treated.[9] Nitroglycerin is definitely recommended for the first 24 to 48 hours for patients with acute MI and heart failure, large anterior MI, persistent ischemia, or hypertension. For other patients without contraindications, nitrates are possibly useful.

When nitrates are clearly indicated early in acute MI, intravenous nitroglycerin is preferred. Intravenous nitroglycerin may begin with a bolus injection of 12.5 to 25 μg followed by an infusion of 10 to 20 μg/min. Infusion dose is increased by 5 to 10 μg every 5 to 10 minutes up to about 200 μg/min during hemodynamic monitoring until clinical symptoms are controlled or blood pressures targets are reached (decreased by 10% in normotensives, decreased by 30% in hypertensives, but not below 80 mm Hg mean or 90 mm Hg systolic).

β-Blocker Therapy. β-Adrenoceptor blockers reduce heart rate, blood pressure, and myocardial contractility, and they stabilize the heart electrically. These actions provide clinical benefit to most patients with acute MI by limiting myocardial oxygen consumption, relieving ischemia, reducing infarct size, and preventing serious arrhythmias.

In the prethrombolysis era, a meta-analysis of 28 randomized trials involving 27,500 patients found a modest early benefit on

mortality (14% odds reduction), cardiac arrest (16% reduction), and nonfatal reinfarction (19% reduction). In acute MI subjects receiving thrombolytic therapy, immediate (intravenous then oral) metoprolol reduced recurrent ischemic events and reinfarction compared with deferred oral therapy.[10] Experience has shown that moderate to severe heart failure should preclude early intravenous β-blocker use but not predischarge and outpatient oral therapy, initiated in small doses and carefully adjusted once stability is achieved.

Early β-blockade is generally recommended (class I) for acute MI patients without severe LV failure or other contraindications (asthma, hypotension, severe bradycardia) who can be treated within 12 hours, regardless of concomitant thrombolysis or PCI, in those with ongoing or recurrent ischemic pain, and in those with tachyarrhythmias. Long-term β-blocker therapy is recommended for all MI survivors without uncompensated heart failure, if not otherwise contraindicated. Therapy is begun within a few days (if not acutely) and continued indefinitely.

Angiotensin-Converting Enzyme Inhibitor Therapy. The renin-angiotensin system is activated in acute MI and heart failure. Inhibition of ACE has been shown to improve remodeling after acute MI (especially after large anterior acute MI). ACE inhibitors also have demonstrated efficacy in heart failure, wherein they prevent disease progression, hospitalization, and death (Chapter 56). A meta-analysis of three major trials and 11 smaller ones involving more than 100,000 patients showed an overall mortality reduction of 6.5%, representing about five lives saved per 1000 patients treated.[9] Benefit was concentrated in higher-risk patients with large or anterior acute MIs and with LV dysfunction or failure.

ACE inhibitor therapy should begin within the first 24 hours (in the absence of hypotension—systolic pressure less than 100 mm Hg—or other contraindications). Patients with anterior injury and clinical heart failure should be particularly targeted (class I indication), although other patients also are candidates (class IIa). Long-term therapy should be given to patients with depressed ejection fraction or clinical heart failure and probably to all patients who tolerate these drugs.[11]

ACE inhibitor therapy should begin with low oral doses and be progressively adjusted to full dose as tolerated. For example, the short-acting agent captopril may be started in a dose of 6.25 mg or less and adjusted over 1 to 2 days to 50 mg twice daily. Before discharge, therapy may be transitioned to longer-acting agents such as ramipril, lisinopril, zofenopril, enalapril, or quinapril.

Antiarrhythmics. Antiarrhythmic therapy is reserved for treatment of, or short-term prevention after, symptomatic or life-threatening ventricular arrhythmias, together with other appropriate measures (cardioversion, treatment of ischemia and metabolic disturbances). Patients with severe left ventricular dysfunction (ejection fraction less than 30%) with or without nonsustained ventricular tachycardia (VT) more than a few days after acute MI may be considered for an implantable cardioverter defibrillator (ICD) (Chapter 61).[12]

Inotropes. Digitalis and intravenous inotropes may increase oxygen demand, provoke serious arrhythmias, and extend infarction. Current recommendations support the use of digoxin in selected patients recovering from acute MI who develop supraventricular tachyarrhythmias (e.g., AF) or heart failure refractory to ACE inhibitors and diuretics. Intravenous inotropes (e.g., dobutamine, dopamine, milrinone, and norepinephrine) are reserved for temporary support of patients with hypotension and circulatory failure unresponsive to volume replacement (Chapters 56 and 103). Other treatment measures for these patients (e.g., intra-aortic balloon pump, early revascularization) are discussed herein.

Lipid-Lowering Therapy. Lipid lowering, particularly with HMG-CoA-reductase inhibitors (statins), has been progressively validated for secondary (and primary) prevention in large clinical trials over the past decade (Chapter 211). Statins also have been shown to have anti-inflammatory effects, and inflammation now is known to play a prominent role in progression and destabilization of atherosclerotic plaques, leading to acute MI. Studies on non–ST-elevation acute coronary syndromes show early benefits from lipid lowering begun during hospitalization (Chapter 68), and randomized studies are underway in patients with ST-elevation acute MI.

Continued

A fasting lipid profile should be obtained on admission. An LDL cholesterol greater than 100 mg/dL should lead to in-hospital initiation of lipid-lowering therapy, usually with a statin. Statin therapy also appears to benefit post-MI patients whose LDL is less than 100 mg/dL.

Other Medical Therapies

Calcium channel blockers, although anti-ischemic, also are negatively inotropic and have not been shown to reduce mortality after ST-elevation acute MI. With certain agents and patient groups, harm has been suggested. For example, short-acting nifedipine has been reported to cause reflex sympathetic activation, tachycardia, hypotension, and increased mortality. Verapamil or diltiazem (heart-rate slowing drugs) may be given to patients in whom β-blockers are ineffective or contraindicated for control of rapid ventricular response with AF or relief of ongoing ischemia *in the absence of heart failure, left ventricular dysfunction, or atrioventricular (AV) block.*

Magnesium is protective for myocytes against calcium overload under conditions of experimental ischemia and recanalization, but magnesium, given 1 hour after thrombolysis was of no benefit in a large randomized trial of patients with acute MI. Magnesium currently is not recommended in acute MI unless levels are below normal or for patients with torsades de pointes–type VT associated with a prolonged QT interval.

Glucose-insulin-potassium (GIK) infusion was proposed as a beneficial metabolic therapy for acute MI in 1962 and subsequently has been tested in several small- to moderate-sized trials. Although intriguing, GIK requires further testing in the context of contemporary therapy.

Complications and Their Treatment

RECURRENT CHEST PAIN

When chest pain recurs after acute MI, the diagnostic possibilities include postinfarct ischemia, pericarditis, infarct extension, and infarct expansion. Characterization of the pain, physical examination, ECG, echocardiography, and cardiac marker determinations assist in differential diagnosis. CK-MB often discriminates reinfarction better than cTnI or cTnT.

Postinfarction angina developing spontaneously during hospitalization for acute MI despite medical therapy usually merits coronary angiography. β-Blockers (intravenously, then orally) and nitroglycerin (intravenously then orally or topically) are recommended medical therapies. Pain with recurrent ST elevation or re-elevation of cardiac markers may be treated with (re)administration of a tPA or, possibly, a GP IIb/IIIa inhibitor, together with nitroglycerin, β-blockade, and heparin. Streptokinase, which induces neutralizing antibodies, generally should not be reutilized after the first few days. If facilities for angiography, PCI, and surgery are available, an invasive approach is recommended for discomfort occurring hours to days after acute MI and associated with objective signs of ischemia. Radionuclide testing (e.g., adenosine thallium) may be helpful in patients with discomfort that is transient or of uncertain ischemic etiology.

Infarct expansion implies circumferential slippage with thinning of the infarcted myocardium. Infarct expansion may be associated with chest pain but without re-elevation of cardiac markers. Expansive remodeling may lead to an LV aneurysm. The risk of remodeling is reduced with early recanalization therapy and administration of ACE inhibitors.

Acute pericarditis most commonly presents on days 2 to 4 in association with large, "transmural" infarctions causing pericardial inflammation. Occasionally, hemorrhagic effusion with tamponade develops; thus, overanticoagulation should be avoided. Pericarditis developing later (2 to 10 weeks) after acute MI may represent **Dressler's syndrome**, which is believed to be immune-mediated. The incidence of this post-MI syndrome has decreased dramatically in the modern era. Pericardial pain is treated with aspirin (preferred, especially in the acute setting) or other nonsteroidal agents (indomethacin); severe symptoms may require corticosteroids.

RHYTHM DISTURBANCES

Ventricular Arrhythmias (Chapter 60)

Acute MI is associated with a proarrhythmic environment that includes heterogeneous myocardial ischemia, heightened adrenergic tone, intracellular electrolyte disturbance, lipolysis and free fatty acid production, and oxygen free radical production on recanalization. Arrhythmias thus are common early during acute MI. Micro-reentry is likely the most common electrophysiologic mechanism of early phase arrhythmias, although enhanced automaticity and triggered activity also are observed in experimental models.

Primary VF is the most serious MI-related arrhythmia and contributes importantly to mortality within the first 24 hours. It occurs with an incidence of 3 to 5% during the first 4 hours and then declines rapidly over 24 to 48 hours. Polymorphic VT, and less commonly monomorphic VT, are associated life-threatening arrhythmias that may occur in this setting. Clinical features (including warning arrhythmias) are not adequately specific or sensitive to identify those at risk for sustained ventricular tachyarrhythmias, so all patients should be continuously monitored. Prophylactic lidocaine reduces primary VF but may increase mortality and is not recommended. Primary VF is associated with higher in-hospital mortality, but long-term prognosis is unaffected in survivors.

Accelerated idioventricular rhythm (AIVR) (60 to 100 beats/min) frequently occurs within the first 12 hours and is generally benign (i.e., is not a risk factor for VF). Indeed, AIVR frequently heralds recanalization after thrombolytic therapy. Antiarrhythmic therapy is not indicated except for sustained, hemodynamically compromising AIVR.

Late VF develops more than 48 hours after the onset of acute MI, often in patients with larger MIs or heart failure, portends a worse prognosis for survival, and may require aggressive measures (e.g., consideration of an ICD). Monomorphic VT resulting from reentry in the context of an MI or scar also may appear later after MI and require long-term therapy (e.g., ICD, antiarrhythmic medications).

Electrical cardioversion is required for VF and sustained polymorphic VT (synchronized shock) and sustained monomorphic VT that causes hemodynamic compromise (unsynchronized shock) (Chapters 60 and 61). Brief intravenous sedation is given to conscious, "stable" patients. For slower, stable VT and nonsustained VT requiring therapy, intravenous amiodarone, intravenous lidocaine, or intravenous procainamide are commonly recommended. After episodes of VT/VF, infusions of antiarrhythmic drugs may be given for 6 to 24 hours; the ongoing risk of arrhythmia then is reassessed. Electrolyte and acid-base imbalance and hypoxia should be corrected. β-Blockade is useful for frequently recurring polymorphic VT associated with adrenergic activation ("electrical storm"). Additional, aggressive measures should be considered to reduce cardiac ischemia (e.g., emergent PCI or CABG) and left ventricular dysfunction (intra-aortic balloon pump) in patients with recurrent polymorphic VT despite β-blockers and/or amiodarone.

Patients with sustained VT or VF occurring late in the hospital course should be considered for long-term prevention and therapy. An ICD provides greater survival benefit than antiarrhythmic drugs (i.e., amiodarone or sotalol) alone in patients with ventricular arrhythmias and can improve survival after acute MI for patients with an ejection fraction less than 30% regardless of their rhythm status. **12**

Atrial Fibrillation and Other Supraventricular Tachyarrhythmias (Chapter 59)

AF occurs in up to 10 to 15% of patients after an acute MI, usually appearing within the first 24 hours. The incidence of atrial flutter or another supraventricular tachycardia is much lower. The risk of AF increases with age, larger MIs, heart failure, pericarditis, atrial infarction, hypokalemia, hypomagnesemia, hypoxia, pulmonary disease, and hyperadrenergic states. The incidence of AF is reduced by effective early recanalization. Hemodynamic compromise with rapid rates and systemic embolism (in ≈2%) are adverse consequences of AF. Systemic embolism may occur on the first day, so prompt anticoagulation with heparin is indicated.

Recommendations for management of AF include electrical cardioversion for patients with severe hemodynamic compromise or ischemia; rate control with intravenous digitalis for patients with ventricular dysfunction (i.e., give 0.6 to 1.0 mg; one half initially and one half in 4 hours), with an intravenous β-blocker in those without clinical ventricular dysfunction, or with intravenous diltiazem or verapamil in compensated patients with a contraindication to β-blockers; and anticoagulation with heparin (or LMWH). Class I or III antiarrhythmic drugs are generally reserved for patients with or at high risk for recurrence and may be continued for 6 weeks if sinus rhythm is restored and maintained. Amiodarone is currently the most popular choice for this indication.

BRADYCARDIAS, CONDUCTION DELAYS, AND HEART BLOCK

Sinus and AV nodal dysfunction are common during acute MI. Sinus bradycardia, a result of increased parasympathetic tone often in association with inferior acute MI, occurs in 30 to 40% of patients. Sinus bradycardia is particularly common during the first hour of acute MI and with recanalization of the right coronary artery (Bezold-Jarisch reflex). Vagally mediated AV block also may occur in this setting. Anticholinergic therapy (atropine) is indicated for *symptomatic* sinus bradycardia (heart rate generally less than 50 beats/minute associated with hypotension, ischemia, or escape ventricular arrhythmia), including ventricular asystole, and *symptomatic* second-degree (Wenckebach) or third-degree block at the AV nodal level (narrow QRS complex escape rhythm). Atropine is not indicated and may worsen infranodal AV block (anterior MI, wide complex escape rhythm).

New-onset infranodal AV block and intraventricular conduction delays or bundle branch blocks (BBBs) predict substantially increased in-hospital mortality. Fortunately, their incidence has declined in the recanalization era (from 10 to 20% to about 4%). Mortality is more related to extensive myocardial damage than to heart block itself, so cardiac pacing only modestly improves survival. Prevention and treatment are accomplished by transcutaneous (standby or active) pacing, temporary intravenous pacing, and/or permanent pacing, applied in decreasing frequency.

Prophylactic placement of multifunctional patch electrodes in high-risk patients allows for immediate pacing (and defibrillation) if needed. Application is indicated for symptomatic sinus bradycardia refractory to drug therapy, infranodal second-degree (Mobitz II) or third-degree AV block, and new or indeterminate-age bifascicular (LBBB; RBBB with left anterior or left posterior fascicular block) or trifascicular block (bilateral or alternating BBB [any age], BBB with first-degree AV block). Transcutaneous pacing (Chapter 61) is uncomfortable and intended for prophylactic and temporary use only. In patients requiring pacing, a transvenous pacing electrode is inserted as soon as possible. Pacing electrode insertion also is indicated (prophylactically) in patients at very high risk (>30%) of requiring pacing, including patients with bilateral (alternating) BBB, with new/indeterminate age bifascicular block with first-degree AV block, and with infranodal second-degree AV block.

Indications for permanent pacing after acute MI depend on the prognosis of the AV block and not solely on symptoms. Class I indications include even transient second- or third-degree AV block in association with BBB, and symptomatic AV block at any level. Advanced block at the AV nodal level ("Wenckebach") rarely is persistent or symptomatic enough to warrant permanent pacing.

HEART FAILURE AND OTHER LOW-OUTPUT STATES

Cardiac pump failure is the leading cause of circulatory failure and in-hospital death from acute MI. Manifestations of circulatory failure may include a weak pulse, low blood pressure, cool extremities, a third heart sound, pulmonary congestion, oliguria, and obtundation. However, several distinct mechanisms, hemodynamic patterns, and clinical syndromes characterize the spectrum of circulatory failure in acute MI. Each requires a specific approach to diagnosis, monitoring, and therapy (see Table 69–3).

Left Ventricular Dysfunction

The degree of LV dysfunction correlates well with the extent of acute ischemia/infarction. Hemodynamic compromise becomes evident when impairment involves 20 to 25% of the left ventricle, and cardiogenic shock or death occurs with involvement of 40% or more (Chapter 103). Pulmonary congestion and S_3 and S_4 gallops are the most common physical findings. Early recanalization (via thrombolytics, PCI, or CABG) is the most effective therapy to reduce infarct size, ventricular dysfunction, and associated heart failure. Medical treatment of heart failure related to the ventricular dysfunction of acute MI is otherwise generally similar to that of heart failure in other settings (Chapter 56) and includes adequate oxygenation and diuresis (begun early, blood pressure permitting, and continued long-term if needed). Intravenous vasodilator therapy (for preload and afterload reduction), inotropic support, and intra-aortic balloon counterpulsation are indicated in cardiogenic shock (Chapter 103). Nitrates (nitroglycerin) reduce preload and effectively relieve congestive symptoms.

Volume Depletion

Relative or absolute hypovolemia is a frequent cause of hypotension and circulatory failure and is easily corrected if recognized and treated promptly. Poor hydration, vomiting, diuresis, and disease- or drug-induced peripheral vasodilation may contribute. Hypovolemia should be identified and corrected with intravenous fluids before more aggressive therapies are considered. An empirical fluid challenge may be tried in the appropriate clinical setting (e.g., hypotension in absence of congestion; inferior or RV infarction; hypervagotonia). If filling pressures are measured, cautious fluid administration to a pulmonary capillary wedge pressure of up to about 18 mm Hg may optimize cardiac output and blood pressure without impairing oxygenation.

Right Ventricular Infarction

RV ischemia and infarction occur with proximal occlusion of the right coronary artery (before the takeoff of the RV branches). Ten to 15% of inferior acute ST-elevation MIs show classic hemodynamic features, and these patients form the highest risk subgroup for morbidity and mortality (25 to 30% vs. <6% hospital mortality). Improvement in RV function commonly occurs over time, suggesting reversal of ischemic stunning and other favorable accommodations, if short-term management is successful.

Hypotension with clear lung fields and elevated jugular venous pressure in the setting of inferior or inferoposterior acute MI should raise the suspicion of RV infarction. Kussmaul's sign (distention of the jugular vein on inspiration) is relatively specific and sensitive in this setting. Right-sided ECG leads show ST-elevation, particularly in V_{4R}, in the first 24 hours of RV infarction. Echocardiography is helpful in confirming the diagnosis (RV dilation and dysfunction are observed). If right heart pressures are measured, a right atrial pressure of ≥10 mm Hg and ≥80% of the pulmonary capillary wedge pressure is relatively sensitive and specific for RV ischemic dysfunction.

Management of RV infarction consists of early maintenance of RV preload, reduction of RV afterload, early recanalization, short-term inotropic support if needed, and avoidance of vasodilators (e.g., nitrates) and diuretics used for left ventricular failure (which may cause marked hypotension). Volume loading with normal saline alone is often effective. If the cardiac output fails to improve after 0.5 to 1 liter of fluid, inotropic support with dobutamine is recommended. High-grade AV block is common, and restoration of AV synchrony with temporary AV sequential pacing may lead to substantial improvement in cardiac output. The onset of AF (in up to one third of RV infarcts) may cause severe hemodynamic compromise requiring prompt cardioversion. Early coronary recanalization with thrombolysis or PCI markedly improves outcomes.

Cardiogenic Shock

Cardiogenic shock (Chapter 103) is a form of severe LV failure characterized by marked hypotension (systolic pressures less than 80 mm Hg) and reductions in cardiac index (<1.8 L/min/m^2) despite high LV filling pressure (pulmonary capillary wedge pressure greater than 18 mm Hg). The cause is loss of a critical functional mass (>40%) of the left ventricle. Cardiogenic shock is associated with mortality rates of more than 70 to 80% despite aggressive medical therapy. Risk factors include age, large (usually anterior) acute MI, previous MI, and diabetes. In patients with suspected shock, hemodynamic monitoring and intra-aortic balloon counterpulsation (IABP) are indicated. Intubation often is necessary. With early application, urgent mechanical revascularization (PCI or CABG) affords the best chance for survival, especially in patients younger than 75 years old.

HEMODYNAMIC MONITORING. Invasive hemodynamic monitoring is not indicated routinely for acute MI but should be used selectively for high-risk patients. Indeed, routine use of balloon catheters in intensive care patients may cause net hazard. Hence, class I recommendations for balloon flotation right-heart catheter monitoring are limited to severe or progressive heart failure or pulmonary edema, progressive hypotension and cardiogenic shock, and suspected mechanical complications (e.g., papillary muscle rupture or acute ventricular septal defect). Intra-arterial pressure monitoring is recommended for patients with severe hypotension and/or cardiogenic shock, those receiving vasopressors and (class IIa) potent vasodilators (e.g., nitroprusside). Intravenous nitroglycerin and intravenous inotropes often can be safely given with noninvasive blood pressure monitoring.

INTRA-AORTIC BALLOON COUNTERPULSATION. Introduced more than 30 years ago, IABP has been frequently used for medically refractory unstable ischemic syndromes and cardiogenic shock. The deflated balloon catheter is introduced into the femoral artery and advanced to the aorta. Balloon inflation is triggered by the ECG during early diastole, augmenting coronary blood flow, and deflated in early systole, reducing LV afterload. Primary IABP therapy for cardiogenic shock associated with acute MI provides temporary stabilization, but it has not reduced in-hospital mortality (>80%). Its greatest utility has proved to be for temporary hemodynamic support in patients whose ventricular dysfunction is spontaneously or surgically reversible. IABP is currently recommended in the setting of acute MI as a stabilizing measure for patients undergoing angiography and subsequent PCI or surgery for (1) cardiogenic shock, (2) mechanical complications (acute mitral regurgitation, acute ventricular septal defect), (3) refractory post-MI ischemia, and (4) recurrent intractable VT or VF associated with hemodynamic instability. IABP is not useful in patients with significant aortic insufficiency or severe peripheral vascular disease.

MECHANICAL COMPLICATIONS

MI may result in mechanical complications associated with substantial morbidity and mortality. These occur usually within the first week and account for about 15% of acute MI-related deaths. Complications include acute mitral valve regurgitation, ventricular septal defect, free wall rupture, and LV aneurysm. Suspicion and investigation of a mechanical defect should be raised by a new murmur and/or sudden, progressive hemodynamic deterioration with pulmonary edema and/or a low output state. Transthoracic or transesophageal echocardiography/Doppler usually establishes the diagnosis. A balloon flotation catheter may be helpful in confirming the diagnosis and monitoring therapy. Arteriography to identify correctable coronary artery disease is warranted in most cases. Surgical consultation should be requested promptly, and urgent repair is usually indicated.

Acute mitral valve regurgitation (Chapter 72) results from infarct-related rupture or dysfunction of a papillary muscle. Total rupture leads to death in 75% of cases within 24 hours. Medical therapy is begun with nitroprusside to lower preload and improve peripheral perfusion. Emergent surgical repair (if possible) or replacement is then undertaken. Surgery is associated with high mortality (up to 25 to 50%) but leads to better functional and survival outcomes than medical therapy alone.

Postinfarction septal rupture with **ventricular septal defect**, which occurs with increased frequency in the elderly, in hypertensive patients, and possibly after thrombolysis, also warrants emergent surgical repair. Because a small ventricular septal defect may suddenly enlarge and cause rapid hemodynamic collapse, all septal perforations should be repaired. Upon diagnosis, an IABP should be inserted, a surgical consultation obtained, and surgical repair undertaken as soon as feasible.

LV free wall rupture usually causes acute tamponade with sudden death, but in a small percentage of cases, resealing or localized containment ("pseudoaneurysm") may allow medical stabilization, usually with inotropic support and/or IABP followed by emergent surgical repair.

A **left ventricular aneurysm** may develop after a large, usually anterior, acute MI. When refractory heart failure, VT, or systemic embolization occurs despite medical therapy, surgical repair is indicated. Current techniques better preserve LV integrity and geometry, with improved outcomes.

THROMBOEMBOLIC COMPLICATIONS

Thromboembolism has been described in about 10% of clinical series and 20% of autopsy series, suggesting a high rate of undiagnosed events. Thromboembolism contributes to 25% of hospital deaths from acute MI. The incidence appears to be declining in the "recanalization era" in association with greater use of antithrombotics, reductions of infarct size, and earlier ambulation. Systemic arterial emboli (including cerebrovascular emboli) arise typically from an LV mural thrombus, whereas pulmonary emboli commonly arise from thrombi in leg veins. Arterial embolism may cause dramatic clinical events, such as hemiparesis, loss of a pulse, ischemic bowel, or sudden hypertension, depending on the regional circulation involved.

Mural thrombosis with embolism typically occurs in the setting of large (especially anterior) ST-elevation acute MI and heart failure. The risk of embolism is particularly high when a mural thrombus is detected by echocardiography (up to one third of anterior ST-elevation acute MI patients). Thus, in anterior ST-elevation acute MI and other high-risk patients, echocardiography should be performed during hospitalization; if positive, anticoagulation should be started (with an antithrombin), if not already initiated, and continued (with warfarin) for 6 months.

Deep vein thrombosis may be prevented by lower extremity compression therapy, by limiting the duration of bedrest, and by subcutaneous unfractionated heparin or LMWH (in those not receiving intravenous heparin) until fully ambulatory (Chapter 78). Pulmonary embolism is treated with intravenous heparin, then oral anticoagulation for 6 months (Chapter 94).

Post-MI Risk Stratification

The goal of risk stratification before and early after discharge for acute MI is to assess ventricular and clinical function, latent ischemia, and arrhythmic risk, and to use this information for patient education and prognostic assessment and to guide therapeutic strategies.

CARDIAC CATHETERIZATION AND NONINVASIVE STRESS TESTING. Risk stratification generally involves functional assessment by one of three strategies: cardiac catheterization, submaximal exercise stress ECG before discharge (at 4 to 6 days), or symptom-limited stress testing at 2 to 6 weeks after discharge. Many patients with ST elevation–acute MI undergo invasive evaluation for primary PCI or after thrombolytic therapy. Catheterization generally is performed during hospitalization for patients at high risk. In others, predischarge submaximal exercise testing (to peak heart rate of 120 to 130 beats/min or 70% of the predicted maximum) appears safe when performed in patients who are ambulating without symptoms; it should be avoided within 2 to 3 days of acute MI and in patients with unstable post-MI angina, uncompensated heart failure, or serious cardiac arrhythmias. Alternatively or in addition, patients may undergo symptom-limited stress testing at 2 to 6 weeks before returning to work or other increased physical activities. Abnormal test results include not only ST-depression but also low functional capacity, exertional hypotension, and serious arrhythmias. Patients with positive tests are considered for coronary angiography.

The sensitivity of stress testing can be augmented with radionuclide perfusion imaging (thallium-201 and/or technetium-99m-sestamibi; Chapter 52) or echocardiography (Chapter 51). Supplemental imaging also can quantify the LV ejection fraction and size the area of infarct and/or ischemia. For patients on digoxin or with ST-segment changes that preclude accurate ECG interpretation (e.g., baseline LBBB or LV hypertrophy), an imaging study is recommended with initial stress testing. In others, an imaging study may be performed selectively for those in whom the exercise ECG test is positive or equivocal. For patients unable to exercise, pharmacologic stress testing can be performed using adenosine or dipyridamole scintigraphy or dobutamine echocardiography.

AMBULATORY ECG MONITORING. Routine 24- to 48-hour predischarge or postdischarge ambulatory ECG (Holter) monitoring is not currently recommended. Modern telemetry systems capture complete rhythm information during hospital observations and allow for identification of those with serious arrhythmias. Sustained VT or VF occurring late during hospitalization or provoked at electrophysiologic study in patients with nonsustained VT are candidates for an ICD (especially if ejection fraction is less than 40%) or antiarrhythmic drug therapy (amiodarone or, possibly, sotalol). The utility of other tests

Table 69–8 • DISCHARGE MEDICATION CHECKLIST AFTER MYOCARDIAL INFARCTION

MEDICATION	REASONS FOR NON-USE	COMMENTS
Aspirin (81–325 mg qd)	High bleeding risk	Reduces mortality, reinfarction, and stroke
Clopidogrel (75 mg qd)	High bleeding risk	Indicated after PCI for 1 mo-1 yr. Also, reduces vascular events when added to aspirin in non–ST-elevation acute MI (not yet tested for routine use after ST-elevation acute MI)
β-blocker	Asthma, bradycardia, severe CHF	Reduces mortality, reinfarction, sudden death, arrhythmia, hypertension, angina, atherosclerosis progression
ACE inhibitor	Hypotension, allergy, hyperkalemia	Reduces mortality, reinfarction, stroke, heart failure, diabetes, atherosclerosis progression
Lipid lowering (e.g., a statin)	Myopathy, rhabdomyolysis, hepatitis	Goal = LDL < 100 (Statins also may benefit patients with lower LDL.*) Consider addition of niacin or fibrate for high non-HDL cholesterol, low HDL
Nitroglycerin sublingual	Aortic stenosis; sildenafil (Viagra) use	Instruct on prn use and appropriate need for medical attention

Medications given at hospital discharge improve long-term compliance.
*Heart Protection Study, 2002 (Lancet 2002;360:7–22).
CHF = congestive heart failure; HDL = high-density lipoprotein; LDL = low-density lipoprotein; MI = myocardial infarction; PCI = percutaneous coronary intervention. See also Ryan TJ, Antman EM, Brooks NH, et al: 1999 update: ACC/AHA Guidelines for the management of patients with acute myocardial infarction. A report of the American College of Cardiology/American Association Task Force on Practice Guidelines (Committee on Management of Acute Myocardial Infarction). J Am Coll Cardiol 1999;34:890–911.

of arrhythmia vulnerability (signal-averaged ECG, heart rate variability, baroreflex sensitivity, T-wave alternans) has not yet been established (Chapter 58). Prophylactic ICD placement prevents sudden death after acute MI for patients with severely depressed function (ejection fraction less than 30%) regardless of rhythm status. [12]

SECONDARY PREVENTION, PATIENT EDUCATION, AND REHABILITATION

SECONDARY PREVENTION. Advances in secondary prevention have resulted in increasingly effective measures to reduce recurrent MI and cardiovascular death. Secondary prevention should be conscientiously applied after acute MI (Table 69–8).

A fasting **lipid profile** is recommended on admission, and **lipid lowering** (statin preferred) is begun in-hospital if LDL exceeds 100 mg/dL (Chapter 211). Recent data show statins are effective in *secondary* prevention regardless of age or baseline lipids levels, even when the LDL is less than 100[13]; thus, near universal application after acute MI may be recommended in the near future.

Continued smoking doubles subsequent mortality risk after acute MI, and **smoking cessation** reduces risk of reinfarction and death within 1 year. Because the risks of continued smoking or early relapse after quitting are high, smoking cessation measures should receive the highest priority (Chapter 14). An individualized cessation plan should be formulated including pharmacologic aids (nicotine gum and patches, bupropion).

Antiplatelet therapy (Chapter 33) should consist of aspirin, given long-term to all patients without contraindications (usual dose, 81 to 325 mg/day). Clopidogrel (75 mg/day) also is given after PCI and may be appropriate for others at higher risk for recurrent vascular events. Duration of therapy should be at least 1 month, but a study of patients with non–ST-elevation acute coronary syndrome supports a 3- to 12-month treatment course. **Anticoagulant therapy** (i.e., warfarin) is indicated after acute MI for patients unable to take antiplatelet therapy (aspirin or clopidogrel), those with persistent or paroxysmal AF, those with LV thrombus, and those who have suffered a systemic or pulmonary embolism. Anticoagulants also may be considered for patients with extensive wall motion abnormalities and markedly depressed ejection fraction with or without heart failure (class II indication). Data on the benefit of warfarin instead of or in addition to aspirin are inconclusive.

ACE inhibitor therapy may prevent adverse myocardial remodeling after acute MI and reduce heart failure and death; it is clearly indicated for long-term use in patients with anterior acute MI or LV ejection fraction less than 40%. There is increasing evidence that ACE inhibitors also may reduce atherosclerosis progression and acute MI recurrence regardless of ejection fraction. [9] These data provide adequate rationale to use ACE inhibitors routinely in patients without hypotension or other contraindications. Other physicians are awaiting the results of additional ongoing trials in lower risk

secondary prevention groups. At the very least, patients with other indications for therapy (hypertension, mild renal insufficiency, intermediate glucose tolerance) should be strongly considered for long-term therapy.

β-blockers are strongly recommended for long-term therapy in all post-MI patients without contraindications. Even those with moderately severe but compensated LV dysfunction may tolerate and benefit from β-blockers if begun in small, slowly adjusted doses. β-blockers are continued indefinitely if tolerated.

Nitroglycerin is prescribed routinely for sublingual or buccal administration for acute anginal attacks. Longer-acting oral (isosorbide mononitrate or dinitrate) or topical nitrates may be added to treatment regimens for angina or heart failure in selected patients. **Calcium channel blockers** are negatively inotropic and are *not* routinely given; however, they may be given to selected patients without LV dysfunction (ejection fraction greater than 40%) who are intolerant of β-blockers and require these drugs for antianginal therapy or control of heart rate in AF. Short-acting nifedipine should be avoided.

Hormone replacement therapy is not begun after an acute MI because it increases thromboembolic risk during the first year and does not prevent reinfarction. Continuing therapy in those already on hormone replacement is individualized.

Hypertension (Chapter 63) and diabetes mellitus (Chapter 242) must be assessed and controlled compulsively in patients after acute MI. ACE inhibitors or β-blockers as described earlier are usually the first choice therapies for hypertension, with angiotensin receptor blockers (ARBs) indicated when ACE inhibitors are not tolerated. ACE inhibitors and ARBs may also reduce the long-term complications of diabetes.

Despite theoretical rationale and promising early reports, **antioxidant supplementation** (e.g., vitamin E, vitamin C) has not been demonstrated to benefit patients after acute MI in large, controlled trials, and is *not* generally recommended. Folate therapy is recommended in patients with elevated homocysteine levels.

Antiarrhythmic drugs are *not* generally recommended after acute MI, and class I antiarrhythmics may increase the risk of sudden death. Class III drugs (amiodarone, sotalol, dofetilide) may be used as part of the management strategy for specific arrhythmias (e.g., AF, VT).

PATIENT EDUCATION AND REHABILITATION. The hospital stay provides an important opportunity to educate patients about their MI and its treatment, coronary risk factors, and behavioral modification. Education should begin on admission and continue after discharge. However, the time before discharge is particularly opportune. Many hospitals use case managers and prevention specialists to augment physicians and nurses, provide educational materials, review important concepts, assist in formulating and actualizing individual risk-reduction plans, and ensure proper and timely outpatient follow-up. The latter should include early return appointments with the patient's physician (within a few weeks). Instructions on activities also should be given

Cardiovascular Disease

before discharge. Many hospitals have cardiac rehabilitation programs that provide supervised, progressive exercise.

Grade
A

1. Indications for fibrinolytic therapy in suspected acute myocardial infarction: Collaborative overview of early mortality and major morbidity results from all randomised trials of more than 1000 patients. Fibrinolytic Therapy Trialists' (FTT) Collaborative Group. Lancet 1994;343:311–322.
2. Boersma E, Maas AC, Deckers JW, Simoons ML: Early thrombolytic treatment in acute myocardial infarction: Reappraisal of the golden hour. Lancet 1996;348:771–775.
3. An international randomized trial comparing four thrombolytic strategies for acute myocardial infarction. The GUSTO investigators. N Engl J Med 1993;329:673–682.
4. Keeley EC, Boura JA, Grines CL: Primary angioplasty versus intravenous thrombolytic therapy for acute myocardial infarction: A quantitative review of 23 randomised trials. Lancet 2003;361:13–20. *Primary PTCA is preferred for ST-elevation MI.*
5. Hochman JS, Sleeper LA, Webb JG, et al: Early revascularization in acute myocardial infarction complicated by cardiogenic shock. SHOCK Investigators. Should we emergently revascularize occluded coronaries for cardiogenic shock? N Engl J Med 1999;341:625–634.
6. Stone GW, Grines CL, Cox DA, et al: Comparison of angioplasty with stenting, with or without abciximab, in acute myocardial infarction. N Engl J Med 2002;346:957–966.
7. Efficacy and safety of tenecteplase in combination with enoxaparin, abciximab, or unfractionated heparin: The ASSENT-3 randomised trial in acute myocardial infarction. Lancet 2001;358:605–613.
8. Randomised trial of intravenous streptokinase, oral aspirin, both, or neither among 17,187 cases of suspected acute myocardial infarction: ISIS-2. ISIS-2 (Second International Study of Infarct Survival) Collaborative Group. Lancet 1988;2:349–360.
9. ISIS-4: A randomised factorial trial assessing early oral captopril, oral mononitrate, and intravenous magnesium sulphate in 58,050 patients with suspected acute myocardial infarction. ISIS-4 (Fourth International Study of Infarct Survival) Collaborative Group. Lancet 1995;345:669–685.
10. The TIMI Study Group: Comparison of invasive and conservative strategies after treatment with intravenous tissue plasminogen activator in acute myocardial infarction. Results of the thrombolysis in myocardial infarction (TIMI) phase II trial. N Engl J Med 1989;320:618–627.
11. Yusuf S, Sleight P, Pogue J, et al: Effects of an angiotensin-converting enzyme inhibitor, ramipril, on cardiovascular events in high-risk patients. The Heart Outcomes Prevention Evaluation Study Investigators. N Engl J Med 2000;342:145–153.
12. Moss AJ, Zareba W, Hall J, et al: Prophylactic implantation of a defibrillator in patients with myocardial infarction and reduced ejection fraction. N Engl J Med 2002;346:877–883.
13. Heart Protection Study Collaborative Group: MRC/BHF Heart Protection Study of cholesterol lowering with simvastatin in 20 536 high-risk individuals: A randomised placebo-controlled trial. Lancet 2002;360:7–22.

SUGGESTED READINGS

Armstrong PW, Collen D: Fibrinolysis for acute myocardial infarction: Current status and new horizons for pharmacological recanalization, part 1. Circulation 2001;103:2862–2866. *Excellent and comprehensive review on fibrinolysis and ancillary therapy for pharmacologic recanalization.*
Aversano T, Aversano LT, Passamani E, et al: Thrombolytic therapy vs primary percutaneous coronary intervention for myocardial infarction in patients presenting to hospitals without on-site cardiac surgery: A randomized controlled trial. JAMA 2002;287:1943–1951. *Primary PTCA is preferred even in the absence of backup cardiac surgery.*
Birnbaum Y, Fishbein MC, Blanche C, Siegel RJ: Ventricular septal rupture after acute myocardial infarction. N Engl J Med 2002;347:1426–1432. *A comprehensive overview of this potentially devastating complication.*
Braunwald E, Antman EM, Beasley JW, et al: ACC/AHA 2002 guideline update for the management of patients with unstable angina and non–ST-segment elevation myocardial infarction: Summary article: A report of the American College of Cardiology/American Heart Association Task Force on Practice Guidelines (Committee on the Management of Patients With Unstable Angina). Circulation 2002;106:1893–1900. *Consensus treatment guidelines and comprehensive background, rationale, and references for management of non–ST-elevation acute coronary syndromes.*
Canto JG, Every NR, Magid DJ, et al: The volume of primary angioplasty procedures and survival after acute myocardial infarction. National Registry of Myocardial Infarction 2 Investigators. N Engl J Med 2000;342:1573–1580. *This database, with others, provides the rationale for minimal volume requirements for primary angioplasty procedures to ensure optimal outcomes.*
Gheorghiade M, Goldstein S: Beta-blockers in the post–myocardial infarction patient. Circulation 2002;106:394–398. *A review emphasizing the benefit of this therapy in all post-MI patients.*
Mehta RH, Montoye CK, Gallogly M, et al: Improving quality of care for acute myocardial infarction: The Guidelines Applied in Practice (GAP) Initiative. JAMA 2002;287:1269–1276. *Use of guidelines can improve care.*
Ryan TJ, Antman EM, Brooks NH, et al: 1999 update: ACC/AHA guidelines for the management of patients with acute myocardial infarction. A report of the American College of Cardiology/American Heart Association Task Force on Practice Guidelines (Committee on Management of Acute Myocardial Infarction). http://www.acc.org/clinicalguidelines. *Consensus treatment guidelines and comprehensive background, rationale, and references for management of ST-elevation acute MI.*
Topol EJ: Reperfusion therapy for acute myocardial infarction with fibrinolytic therapy or combination reduced fibrinolytic therapy and platelet glycoprotein IIb/IIIa inhibition: the GUSTO V randomised trial. Lancet 2001;357:1905–1914. *This large, randomized trial showed that more aggressive recanalization therapy (combined glycoprotein IIb/IIIa inhibition and half dose fibrinolytic therapy) decreased ischemic complications but not mortality, and it caused excessive bleeding, particularly in the elderly.*

70 PERCUTANEOUS CORONARY INTERVENTIONS

Paul S. Teirstein

Percutaneous transluminal coronary angioplasty (PTCA), first performed by Gruntzig in 1977, initially was viewed as having limited application to a few patients with simple, discrete narrowings within a single coronary vessel. In the 1990s, however, advances in technology and pharmacology allowed widespread application of PTCA to most forms of coronary artery disease, including patients with multivessel pathology, total occlusions, saphenous vein graft disease, unstable angina (Chapter 68), and acute myocardial infarction (MI) (Chapter 69). An estimated 1.5 million coronary angioplasties are performed worldwide, making it one of the most widely used procedures. The popularity of PTCA is based largely on its simplicity, the need for only local anesthesia, a short (approximately 1 day) hospitalization, and negligible postprocedure recovery time. Continued rapid technologic advances are likely to create an even greater demand for PTCA in the near future.

Mechanisms and Technical Considerations

Coronary angioplasty (Greek *angeion* ["vessel"]; Greek *plastos* ["to form or shape"]) requires manipulation of the diseased coronary segment using tools that are operated percutaneously using fluoroscopic guidance. Under local anesthesia, a hollow-bore needle is inserted into a peripheral artery (usually the femoral or radial artery). A guidewire (approximately 0.038 inch) is placed through this needle and advanced into the aorta. The needle is removed, leaving the guidewire, over which a small-caliber (approximately 3 mm), specially shaped catheter (called a *guiding catheter*) is advanced into the ostium of the obstructed coronary artery. Using radiographic contrast injections that provide fluoroscopic visualization of the coronary artery lumen, a thin (approximately 0.014 inch), highly steerable guidewire is directed down the coronary artery and across the stenotic lesion. This guidewire becomes a "rail" over which therapeutic tools such as inflatable balloons, stents, and atherectomy catheters are passed to the diseased segment (Fig. 70–1).

Balloon catheters (Fig. 70–2) typically have two lumens, one to allow passage over the guidewire and another to carry a saline and radiographic contrast mixture used to inflate a balloon located at the distal catheter tip. Under fluoroscopy, the balloon is centered across the lesion and inflated to 3 to 20 atm of pressure. Balloon inflation widens the narrowed lumen by stretching the vessel and, in most cases, causing a tear (a therapeutic dissection) at the edges of the plaque, where the atheroma meets the nondiseased media. Atherectomy

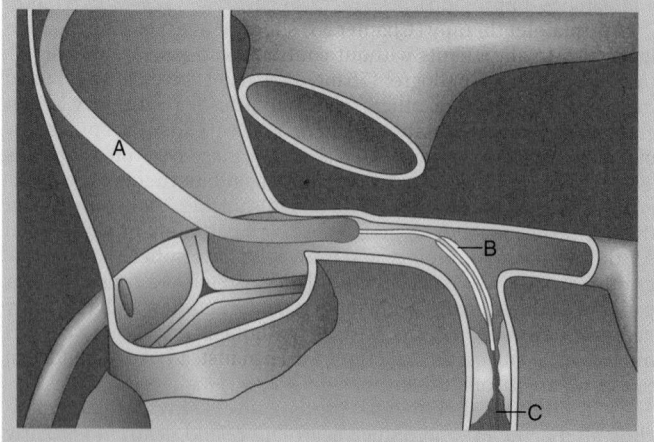

FIGURE 70–1 • Schematic view of coronary angioplasty technique. A guide catheter (*A*) is inserted into the orifice of the coronary artery (in this figure, the left main); a balloon catheter (*B*) is advanced over a thin guidewire (*C*) into the lesion. Balloon inflation dilates the stenotic region. (Adapted from Baim DS, Faxon DP: Coronary Angioplasty, from Grossman W [ed]: Cardiac Catheterization and Angiography, 3rd ed, Philadelphia, Lea & Febiger, 1986.)

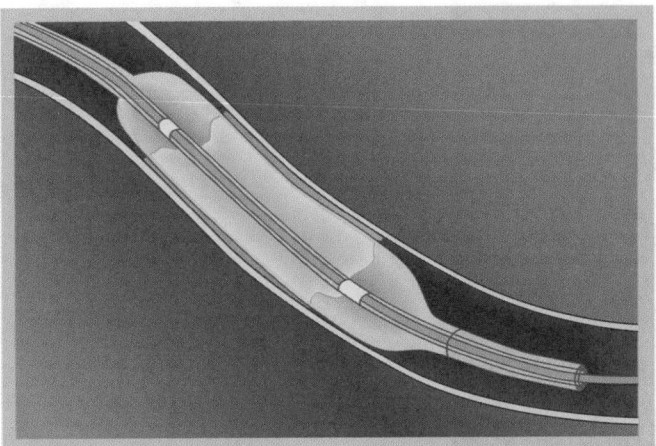

FIGURE 70–2 • Balloon angioplasty catheter. The catheter consists of two lumens, an inflation lumen and a guidewire lumen. Two radiopaque markers, indicating the lateral balloon margins, aid in positioning the balloon before inflation.

catheters, which also are passed over a guidewire to the diseased segment, remove plaque by a shaving, grinding, slicing, or suction mechanism. The Directional Atherectomy (Guidant Corp., Santa Clara, CA) device shaves plaque and stores it in the catheter nose cone; the Rotablator (Boston Scientific, Maple Grove, MN) pulverizes plaque into microparticles that pass through the coronary microcirculation; the Transluminal Extraction (Interventional Technologies, San Diego, CA) catheter slices, then extracts plaque into a vacuum bottle; and laser catheters use excimer or holmium laser energy to ablate plaque.

Coronary stents are metallic (usually 316 L stainless steel or nitinol) scaffolding devices that are crimped onto a deflated balloon catheter before insertion into the diseased vessel. During balloon inflation, the collapsed stent expands to support the vessel lumen (Fig. 70–3). While balloons and atherectomy devices create an adequate, albeit

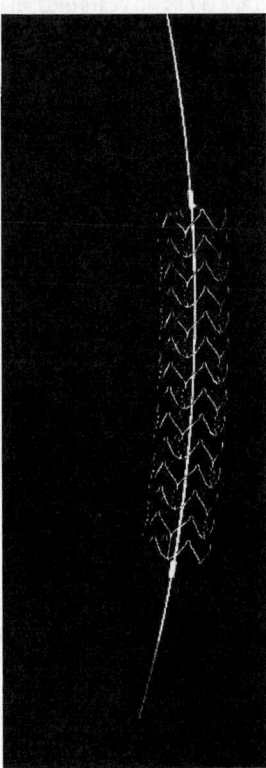

FIGURE 70–3 • Balloon expandable coronary stent. The stainless steel stent is crimped onto a balloon catheter to allow low-profile passage through the coronary artery. When positioned across the lesion, the balloon is inflated, expanding the stent. After balloon deflation and removal, the stent remains, providing a scaffold that supports the vessel lumen.

rough channel through diseased arteries, the supporting structure of the stent can widen the lumen to near its predisease dimensions. With a stent, tissue flaps are "pinned" against the wall, and recoil is limited. Most stents are designed so that the metallic struts comprise only about 20% of the surface area to allow a rapid endothelialization (over about 2 weeks) and reduced thrombosis risk.

During the procedure, the interventionalist is able to assess the target vessel fluoroscopically using contrast injections through the guiding catheter (Fig. 70–4). When the coronary artery has been opened successfully, all catheters are withdrawn, and the arterial access site is sealed by mechanical pressure, an absorbable plug, or a remote suturing device. Patients without comorbidity ambulate in 3 to 6 hours. Discharge from the hospital usually occurs on the morning after the procedure, after stability of the arterial access site, cardiac biomarkers, and electrocardiogram (ECG) is confirmed. Selected patients in some medical centers are treated as outpatients and released 6 to 12 hours after the procedure without an overnight stay.

Percutaneous Transluminal Coronary Angioplasty Success and Complications

Using modern techniques in appropriately selected patients, most PTCA procedures have a greater than 95% success rate. The single exception to this is the totally occluded vessel (100% obstruction of the lumen), in which the interventionalist's ability to negotiate a guidewire through the blockage is only about 50 to 70%. Procedural complications during and after PTCA have decreased dramatically with the increased use of coronary stents and adjunctive antiplatelet agents (thienopyridines and platelet glycoprotein IIb/IIIa inhibitors). Abrupt coronary artery closure, previously the most frequent and feared cause of morbidity and mortality during PTCA, now is encountered rarely. When PTCA is performed by an experienced interventionalist in appropriately selected patients, the risk of in-hospital death is less than 1%; MI (usually small, non–ST segment elevation MI) is approximately 5%; the need for urgent or emergent coronary artery bypass graft (CABG) surgery is less than 1%; the risk of stroke is less than 0.1%; the chance of coronary perforation is less than 1%; and morbidity at the arterial access site (i.e., hematoma, pseudoaneurysm, or arteriovenous fistula) occurs in less than 5%. Balloons and filters deployed within a coronary vessel beyond the target lesion to limit distal embolization of plaque, platelet aggregates, and other "debris" can reduce ischemic complications further in selected, high-risk patients.

Discharge planning after PTCA represents an important opportunity to emphasize evidence-based medical treatment of atherothrombotic disease and coronary risk factor modification. For patients receiving stents, a minimum 2-week course of aspirin and a thienopyridine is mandatory. Prolonged use of aspirin, thienopyridines, angiotensin-converting enzyme inhibitors, β-blockers, and lipid-lowering agents should be considered based on randomized trials showing improved long-term outcome, particularly in patients who present with unstable angina syndromes (Chapters 67, 68, and 69). Smoking cessation, stress management, exercise, weight loss, changes in dietary habits, and strict blood glucose control for diabetics also are important elements of the discharge plan.

Activity restrictions after PTCA are modest. If the femoral artery was instrumented, heavy lifting is discouraged for several days. Intense aerobic exercise usually is discouraged for 2 to 4 weeks (especially after stent implantation) because exercise can activate platelets and lead to thrombus formation at the angioplasty site. Patients may return to work 1 to 2 days after the procedure if their occupation does not include heavy lifting or excessive physical exercise.

Patient Selection

Any decision to perform PTCA must include a review of the coronary angiogram (Chapter 54) by an experienced interventionalist to assess the lesion's technical suitability for the procedure. The disease must narrow the coronary artery lumen by at least 60%, and the quantity of myocardium subtended by the vessel should not be trivial. High-risk lesion characteristics (Table 70–1), such as longer lesion length, vessel tortuosity, lesion calcification, or the presence of thrombus, must be taken into consideration. Subtle angiographic findings, such as the presence of collateral vessels that supply a different myocardial territory and that originate distal to the target, should

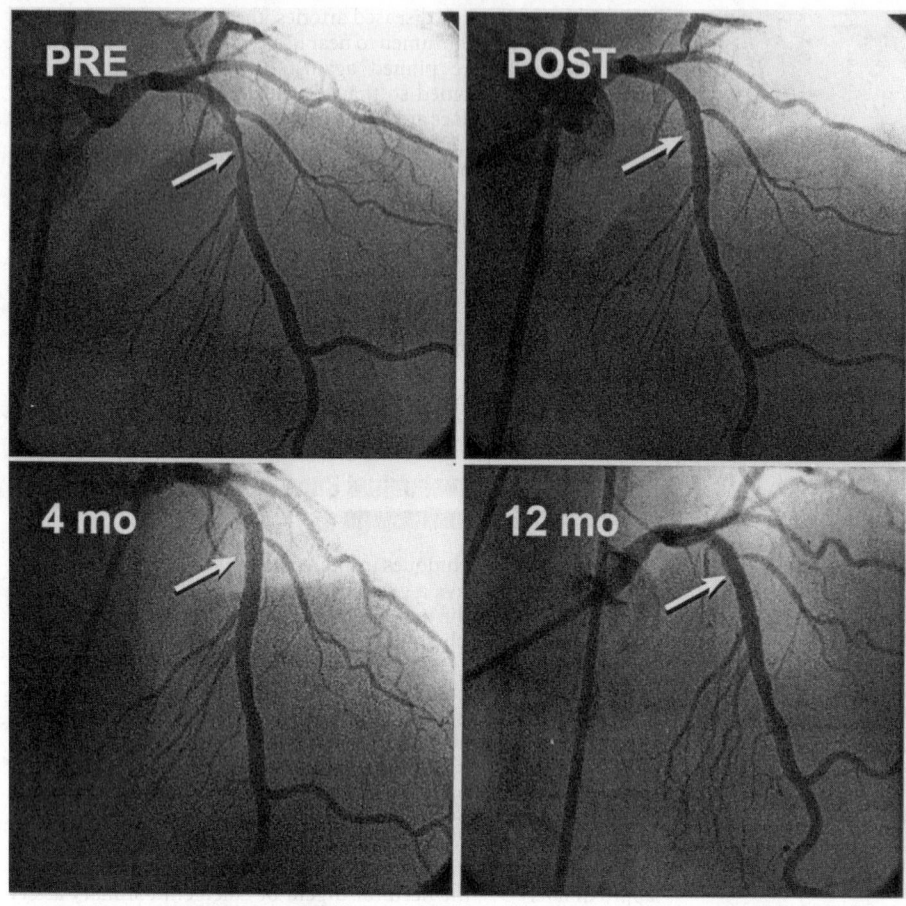

FIGURE 70–4 • Angiographic images before, after, and at late follow-up after placement of a sirolimus eluting stent. The left anterior descending artery contains a tight stenosis (arrow, upper left panel). After stent implantation (upper right panel), the stenosis is abolished (arrow). Follow-up at 4 and 12 months (bottom panels) reveals a completely open lumen, with no evidence of restenosis (arrows).

Table 70–1 • LESION CHARACTERISTICS ASSOCIATED WITH INCREASED CORONARY ANGIOPLASTY RISK

LOW RISK
Discrete (length <10 mm)
Concentric
Readily accessible
Nonangulated segment (<45°)
Smooth contour
Little or no calcification
Less than totally occlusive
Not ostial in location
No major side branch involvement
Absence of thrombus

MODERATE RISK
Tubular (length 10–20 mm)
Eccentric
Moderate tortuosity of proximal segment
Moderately angulated segment (>45°, <90°)
Irregular contour
Moderate or heavy calcification
Total occlusions <3 months old
Ostial in location
Bifurcation lesions requiring double guidewires
Some thrombus present

HIGH RISK
Diffuse (length >20 mm)
Excessive tortuosity of proximal segment
Excessive angulated segments (>90°)
Total occlusion >3 months old and/or bridging collaterals
Inability to protect major side branches
Degenerated vein grafts with friable lesions

From Smith SC Jr, Dove JT, Jacobs AK, et al: ACC/AHA guidelines for percutaneous coronary intervention: Executive summary and recommendations: A report of the American College of Cardiology/American Heart Association Task Force on Practice Guidelines (Committee to Revise the 1993 Guidelines for Percutaneous Transluminal Coronary Angioplasty). J Am Coll Cardiol 2001;37:2215–2238.

be appreciated. For each patient, the benefits of PTCA must be weighed against the procedural risk. Patient characteristics conveying increased risk include advanced age (i.e., >75 years old), diabetes, smaller vessels that are often found in women, prior MI, significant impairment of left ventricular function, and renal insufficiency.

CORONARY ANGIOPLASTY VERSUS MEDICAL THERAPY

Although coronary angioplasty reduces angina, reductions in death and MI have not been well documented. In a trial of 212 patients with single-vessel, symptomatic coronary disease randomized to PTCA or medical therapy, there was no difference in MI or death at 6-month follow-up, but patients randomized to PTCA had less angina, better treadmill exercise performance, and improved quality-of-life measurements.[1]

When PTCA is undertaken in truly asymptomatic patients, significant ischemia first should be documented by functional testing and/or a large quantity of myocardium should be subtended by the stenotic coronary artery. In a trial that randomized 558 patients with at least one episode of asymptomatic ischemia on a 48-hour ambulatory ECG and treadmill exercise test to one of three treatments (medication to suppress angina, medication to suppress angina and ambulatory ECG ischemia, or revascularization with either PTCA or CABG surgery), mortality at 1 year was 6.6% in the angina-guided group, 4.4% in the ischemia-guided group, and 1.1% in the revascularization group. Although this trial showed a mortality benefit for revascularization in patients with minimal anginal symptoms (with the greatest benefit found in patients treated with CABG surgery), its relatively small size has limited its impact on practice guidelines.

Patients experiencing acute MI comprise an important subgroup in whom PTCA has proved beneficial compared with medical therapy (Fig. 70–5). In this setting, when PTCA is compared with thrombolytic therapy, randomized trials consistently have reported a reduction in mortality, stroke, and subsequent MI and/or recurrent ischemia.[2] Coronary angioplasty for acute MI should be undertaken only in experienced medical centers, however, where a catheterization laboratory team can be mobilized rapidly to perform immediate PTCA (Chapter 69).

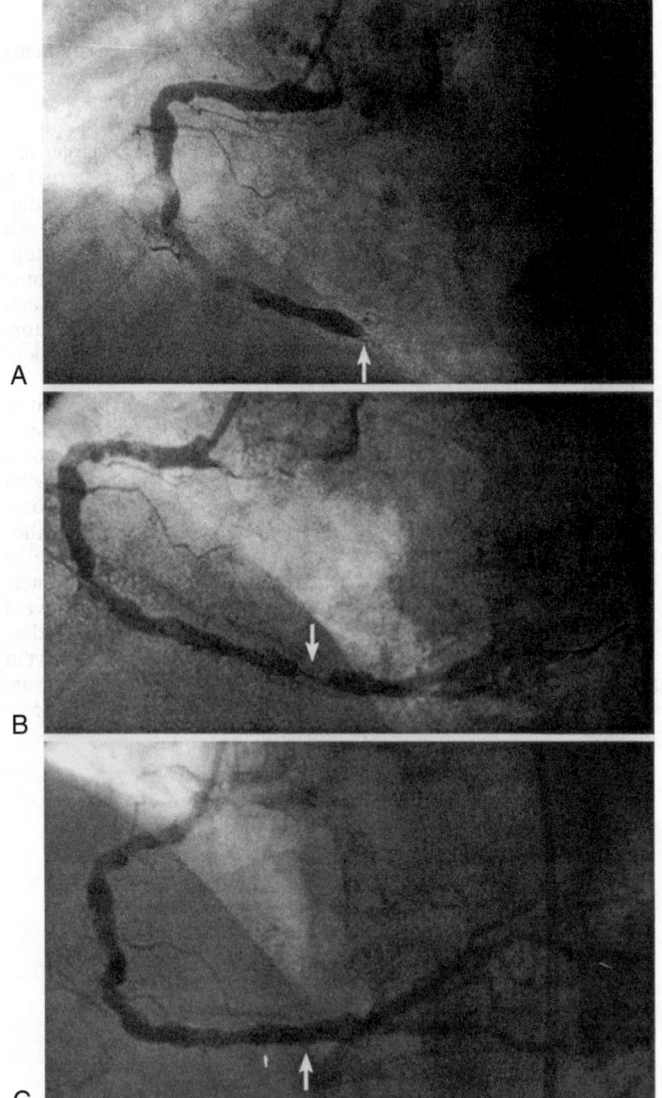

FIGURE 70–5 • Primary coronary angioplasty for acute myocardial infarction. This 50-year-old man presented at midnight with 70 minutes of crushing substernal chest pressure accompanied by inferior ST segment elevation. Emergency angiography performed 45 minutes after arrival found 100% occlusion of the right coronary artery (*A*, arrow). Within 10 minutes, a guidewire was negotiated through the obstruction (presumably caused by fresh thrombus), allowing perfusion into the distal vessel and uncovering a high-grade stenotic lesion (*B*, arrow). After deployment of a coronary stent (*C*, arrow), the stenosis was abolished and significant myocardial damage aborted.

For unstable angina, several early trials supported medical therapy, using coronary angiography and revascularization only if patients had evidence of recurrent ischemia, but subsequent data support an aggressive strategy of early coronary angiography with revascularization, if appropriate, to reduce the likelihood of death or MI significantly. For high-risk and intermediate-risk patients with unstable angina, current recommendations call for initial medical stabilization followed by early referral for cardiac catheterization and, if warranted, PTCA or CABG surgery as dictated by the coronary anatomy (Chapter 68). [3,4]

CORONARY ANGIOPLASTY VERSUS CORONARY ARTERY BYPASS GRAFT SURGERY

The decision between PTCA and CABG surgery (Chapter 71) largely is determined by anatomic features. Symptomatic patients with one or more total occlusions that cannot be revascularized using PTCA techniques will have better relief of angina with CABG surgery. Patients with several lesions in two or three coronary arteries often are referred for CABG surgery because the risk of restenosis is considered

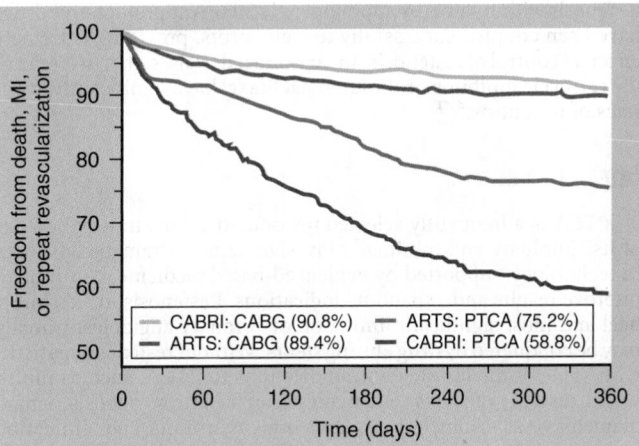

FIGURE 70–6 • The evolution of coronary stenting for multivessel disease over time. The CABRI trial, performed in 1995, found substantial differences in death, myocardial infarction (MI), or repeat revascularization in patients treated with coronary artery bypass surgery (CABG) surgery versus percutaneous transluminal coronary angioplasty (PTCA). In 2000, the ARTS trial found these differences to be less pronounced when CABG surgery was compared with stenting. (Adapted from CABRI Trial Participants: First-year results of CABRI [Coronary Angioplasty versus Bypass Revascularisation Investigation]. Lancet 1995;346:1179–1184; and Serruys PW, Unger F, Abbas MA, et al: Comparison of coronary artery bypass surgery and stenting for the treatment of multivessel disease. N Engl J Med 2001;344:1117–1124.)

unacceptably high. Left main and left main equivalent stenoses often are treated surgically because they are associated with a moderately increased procedural risk, and if restenosis of the left main occurs, it can manifest as sudden death.

Several large, randomized trials of PTCA versus CABG surgery in patients with multivessel disease generally show no differences in late (approximately 5 years) death and MI, although the need for repeat revascularization procedures is consistently higher in patients randomized to PTCA even in the era of stenting (Fig. 70–6). [5] For diabetic patients with multivessel coronary disease, data are controversial but suggest that bypass surgery may provide better outcomes, although these data precede the use of drug-eluting stents.

Restenosis

Restenosis is a renarrowing of an artery after a PTCA procedure, usually resulting from one of two general mechanisms. The first mechanism, unfavorable remodeling and elastic recoil, is a mechanical renarrowing caused by adventitial constriction and shrinkage of the vessel lumen. The second mechanism, neointimal hyperplasia, is due to the proliferation of smooth muscle cells and matrix in response to the injury caused by balloons, stents, or atherectomy devices. Restenosis occurs in 10 to 50% of PTCA patients, usually within the first 6 months after the procedure. Characteristics associated with higher risk of restenosis include longer lesions, small-diameter vessels, diabetes, and multivessel disease. Treatment with either balloon angioplasty or atherectomy devices results in similar rates of restenosis. Coronary stents provide a semirigid scaffolding within the lumen and reduce restenosis by eliminating the mechanical renarrowing caused by unfavorable remodeling and elastic recoil. In randomized trials, stents have reduced restenosis by about one third, from approximately 30 to 40% in patients randomized to balloon angioplasty to 20 to 30% in patients receiving stents.

Although stents reduce restenosis, they do not eliminate restenosis because the stent struts that embed into the vessel wall increase the intimal proliferative response to injury. With stents, the mechanical component of restenosis is eliminated, but the proliferative component is enhanced. Smooth muscle cell division and matrix formation migrate through the stent struts to renarrow the vessel lumen. Advances in technology have coupled antiproliferative agents to stents, providing inhibition of the mechanical and the proliferative restenosis mechanisms. Intravascular radiation therapy (brachytherapy) using gamma or beta radioactive emitters reduces the risk of recurrent restenosis within stents by approximately 50%. Antiproliferative drugs have been coupled successfully to stent struts, providing extremely effective control of restenosis. In randomized trials, stents that release the cell cycle inhibitor sirolimus or paclitaxel have significantly lower rates of restenosis. [6,7]

Future Directions

PTCA is a frequently selected revascularization strategy because of its simplicity and minimally invasive nature. Dramatic advances in technology, supported by evidenced-based medicine, continue to improve results and expand its indications. Restenosis, the Achilles' heel and most significant limitation of coronary angioplasty, finally may be conquered by drug eluting stents. Without restenosis, patients with some of the classic contraindications to PTCA, such as multivessel disease, diabetes, left main coronary artery stenosis, small-diameter vessels, long lesions, saphenous vein grafts, and bifurcation lesions, may become excellent candidates for this minimally invasive procedure. Freed from the constraint of restenosis, the number of PTCA procedures will likely grow, and the use of CABG surgery may diminish.

1. Parisi AF, Folland ED, Hartigan P: A comparison of angioplasty with medical therapy in the treatment of single-vessel coronary artery disease. N Engl J Med 1992;326:10–16.
2. Weaver WD, Simes RJ, Betriu A, et al: Comparison of primary coronary angioplasty and intravenous thrombolytic therapy for acute myocardial infarction: A quantitative review. JAMA 1997;278:2093–2098.
3. Cannon CP, Weintraub WS, Demopoulos LA, et al: Comparison of early invasive and conservative strategies in patients with unstable coronary syndromes treated with the glycoprotein IIb/IIIa inhibitor tirofiban. N Engl J Med 2001;344:1879–1887.
4. Wallentin L, Lagergvist B, Husted S, et al: Outcome at 1 year after an invasive compared with a non-invasive strategy in unstable coronary-artery disease: The FRISC II invasive randomised trial. FRISC II Investigators. Fast Revascularisation during Instability in Coronary artery disease. Lancet 2000;356:9–16.
5. Serruys PW, Unger F, Abbas MA, et al: Comparison of coronary artery bypass surgery and stenting for the treatment of multivessel disease. N Engl J Med 2001;344:1117–1124.
6. Morice M-C, Serruys PW, Sousa JE, et al: A randomized comparison of a sirolimus-eluting stent with a standard stent for coronary revascularization. N Engl J Med 2002;346:1773–1780.
7. Grube E, Silber S, Hauptman KE, et al: Six- and twelve-month results from a randomized, double-blind trial on a slow-release paclitaxel-eluting stent for de novo coronary lesions. Circulation 2003;107:38–42.

SUGGESTED READINGS

Casterella PJ, Teirstein PS: Prevention of coronary restenosis. Cardiol Rev 2001;7:219–231. *Concise description of the pathophysiology and treatment options for restenosis after coronary angioplasty.*

Fattori R, Piva T: Drug-eluting stents in vascular intervention. Lancet 2003;361:247–249. *Concise review of this rapidly evolving field.*

Grech ED, Ramsdale DR (eds): Practical Interventional Cardiology, 2nd ed. London, Martin Dunitz, 2002. *A well-written presentation of the latest coronary angioplasty techniques, including stenting, atherectomy, angioplasty for acute MI, restenosis, physiologic measurement of coronary blood flow, thrombectomy, and intravascular ultrasound imaging.*

Smith SC Jr, Dove JT, Jacobs AK, et al: ACC/AHA guidelines for percutaneous coronary intervention: Executive summary and recommendations. A report of the American College of Cardiology/American Heart Association Task Force on Practice Guidelines (Committee to Revise the 1993 Guidelines for Percutaneous Transluminal Coronary Angioplasty). J Am Coll Cardiol 2001;37:2215–2238. *A succinct discussion of coronary angioplasty case selections, outcomes, predictors of success and complications, and institutional operator competency.*

71 SURGICAL TREATMENT OF CORONARY ARTERY DISEASE

Bruce W. Lytle

Coronary artery bypass grafting (CABG) is based on the premise that the morbidity and mortality associated with coronary atherosclerosis is largely related to atherosclerotic coronary stenoses that can be demonstrated by coronary angiography (Chapter 54) and that if grafts are constructed that route blood flow around these stenoses, then myocardial blood supply can be improved or preserved, cardiac symptoms relieved, cardiac events diminished, and survival prolonged. Over time, the fundamentals of that concept have been shown to be correct.

Coronary Bypass Operation

The most common types of CABGs have been reversed segments of saphenous vein and the internal thoracic arteries. Saphenous vein grafts are anastomosed to the aorta (proximal anastomosis) and to the coronary artery distal to the major obstruction (Fig. 71–1). Saphenous vein grafts have the advantages of availability, a larger size than most coronary arteries, and favorable handling characteristics. However, with time, saphenous vein grafts may develop intrinsic pathologic changes, intimal fibroplasia, and vein graft atherosclerosis, each of which may lead to narrowing or occlusions. By 10 years postoperatively, approximately 30 to 50% of saphenous vein grafts become occluded, and 30 to 35% of the remaining exhibit angiographic evidence of vein graft atherosclerosis. Treatment with platelet inhibitors and HMG coenzyme A inhibitors (Chapter 211) decreases the risk of vein graft failure but does not eliminate it.

Internal thoracic artery grafts, on the other hand, are resistant to the development of late atherosclerosis. When used as an in situ (subclavian origin intact) graft to the left anterior descending (LAD) coronary artery, the left internal thoracic artery graft has a more than 90% patency rate up to 20 years after operation. Because the LAD coronary artery has a strong prognostic influence, the left internal thoracic artery to LAD graft is a clinically important part of myocardial revascularization. Patients who have received a left internal thoracic artery to LAD graft with or without saphenous vein grafts have a better long-term survival rate, fewer reoperations, and fewer cardiac events when compared with patients receiving only saphenous vein grafts. The right internal thoracic artery may also be used for revascularization as an in situ graft, as an aorta-to-coronary graft, or as a

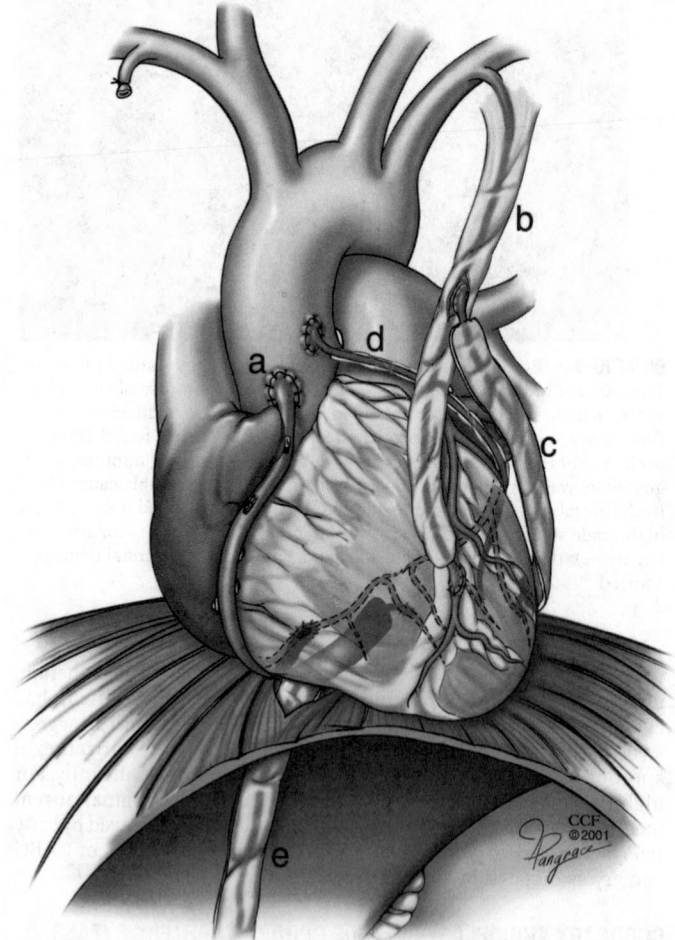

FIGURE 71–1 • Types of bypass grafts include reversed saphenous vein graft from aorta to right coronary artery (a), in situ left internal mammary artery graft to anterior descending coronary artery (b), Y-graft of right internal mammary artery from left internal mammary artery to circumflex coronary artery (c), radial artery graft from aorta to circumflex coronary artery (d), and in situ gastroepiploic graft to posterior descending branch of the right coronary artery (e).

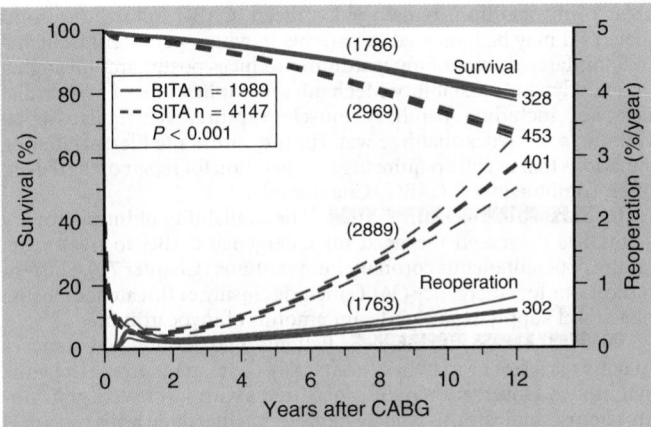

FIGURE 71–2 • Comparison of survival and rates of reoperation for patients undergoing single internal thoracic artery (SITA)($n = 4147$) compared with bilateral internal thoracic artery (BITA)($n = 1989$) coronary artery bypass grafting (CABG). Patients in the BITA group experienced better survival and a lower risk of reoperation (both $P < 0.0001$).

composite arterial graft from the left internal thoracic artery to a coronary artery. Recently, evidence has accumulated that supports using both internal thoracic arteries as grafts, which provides incremental benefit over a single internal thoracic artery graft strategy and produces an improved survival rate and a lower risk of reoperation (Fig. 71–2).

The success of internal thoracic artery grafts has led to the use of other arterial bypass grafts, including the radial arteries and gastroepiploic artery. The radial arteries may have improved patency rates relative to vein grafts and have become popular bypass conduits, but the long-term outcomes of these grafts are as yet unknown. Gastroepiploic artery in situ grafts have late patency rates that are superior to those for vein grafts, but these grafts are difficult to use and have not become standard practice.

Most CABG operations have been performed using a full median sternotomy incision with the aid of cardiopulmonary bypass, aortic cross clamping, and cardioplegic solution—techniques that allow exposure and arrest of the heart such that detailed microsurgical anastomoses can be constructed while effectively protecting myocardial function. Recently, strategies for performing operations through smaller incisions (minimally invasive surgery) and/or without the use of cardiopulmonary bypass (beating-heart or off-pump surgery) have been developed. To date, minimally invasive operations have had limited application for coronary revascularizations, but the prospect of robotics and newer technologies for performing vascular anastomoses may expand the field of small-incision surgery. Beating-heart surgery, on the other hand, has become a standard surgical option. For patients with severe and diffuse coronary disease, complex revascularization remains more difficult using beating-heart techniques. However, beating-heart surgery is clearly feasible, the spectrum of patients receiving effective surgery with off-pump techniques has increased, and, for patients with comorbidities such as aortic atherosclerosis, off-pump surgery offers some clear advantages.

Perioperative Risks

The risk of mortality associated with CABG correlates with ischemia at the time of operation, left ventricular function, the extent of coronary stenoses, noncardiac atherosclerosis, comorbid conditions, and the experience, skill, and judgment of the surgeon. Effective myocardial protection has diminished much of the incremental risk based on the severity of cardiac disease. For patients younger than 70 years of age without serious comorbid conditions, the mortality risk of primary CABG surgery is less than 1% in experienced hands regardless of the number of coronary arteries that are stenotic, and left ventricular dysfunction only slightly increases risk until it becomes severe (ejection fraction <20%). Nevertheless, CABG surgery in the presence of ongoing myocardial ischemia owing to acute myocardial infarction (MI), unstable angina, or vessel closure associated with percutaneous treatments is still associated with increased risk.

National U.S. data on primary CABG operations from the voluntary Society of Thoracic Surgeons Database show a 1.7% mortality rate for elective operations, a 2.6% risk for "urgent" operations, a 6% risk for "emergency" procedures, and a 23.3% risk for "salvage" operations. Noncardiac comorbid conditions (aortic atherosclerosis, renal function, chronic obstructive pulmonary disease, and coagulation system disorders) increase perioperative risk when these conditions are severe.

The most serious postoperative morbidity after CABG is stroke, often related to aortic or cerebrovascular atherosclerosis and atherosclerotic embolization. Heightened awareness of the importance of aortic and carotid atherosclerosis and improved management strategies, including off-pump surgery and ascending aortic replacement, appear to have decreased the risk of focal stroke for patients previously at high risk. Serious wound complications of median sternotomy are uncommon (1 to 2%). Obesity, diabetes, and bilateral internal thoracic artery grafting (particularly in combination with diabetes) are associated with higher rates of wound complications.

Late Outcomes

The late outcomes after CABG are related to age, the severity of cardiac disease before operation, noncardiac comorbid conditions, progression of atherosclerosis, and the operation itself. Many of these factors can be influenced by treatment choices. CABG tends to diminish but not eliminate long-term survival differences based on the number of diseased coronary vessels, left main stenosis, and different levels of left ventricular function. The achievement of complete revascularization (bypass grafts to all stenotic coronary vessels) and the use of internal thoracic artery grafts improve long-term survival and symptomatic status.

Patients often have prolonged survival after CABG, with more than 80% of patients being alive more than 10 years after operation. Over the long term, control of the progression of atherosclerosis by lifestyle modifications, pharmacologic treatment for hypertension (Chapter 63) and lipids (Chapter 211), and platelet inhibitors (Chapter 33) appears to extend the benefits of CABG.

Indications for Bypass Surgery (Table 71–1)

The goals of CABG are to relieve symptoms and prolong life expectancy. Based on randomized trials and the emergence of alternative medical and percutaneous treatments, the surgical population has evolved toward patients with complex conditions, often involving left main or triple-vessel disease, diffuse coronary stenoses, totally obstructed vessels, abnormal left ventricular function, and diabetes.[1] Surgically treated patients with single-vessel disease usually have LAD stenoses or have failed alternative treatments.

SYMPTOM RELIEF

If patients who experience angina have severe stenoses in graftable coronary arteries that supply areas of myocardium that are ischemic at rest or with stress, CABG will reliably relieve angina. Randomized trials have shown that the relief of angina after CABG is more consistent than that achieved with alternative treatments.■ When intermittent heart failure symptoms represent an "anginal equivalent" that is also caused by ischemia, such symptoms also respond well to relief of that ischemia by CABG. Patients with symptoms of heart failure at rest are more complex, but dobutamine echocardiography (Chapter 51) and positron emission tomography (Chapter 52) can identify segments of viable but hibernating myocardium (ischemic at rest) that may improve with bypass grafting, thus reducing symptoms of heart failure.

SURVIVAL

Randomized Trials

CHRONIC STABLE ANGINA. In randomized trials of patients with mild to moderate chronic stable angina, an improved survival rate has been documented for patients treated with initial CABG compared with initial medical treatment in the presence of a greater than 50% left main diameter stenosis, triple-vessel disease, double-vessel disease with a proximal LAD lesion, abnormal left ventricular function, and/

Cardiovascular Disease

Table 71–1 • INDICATIONS FOR CORONARY ARTERY BYPASS SURGERY

RANDOMIZED TRIALS AVAILABLE: INITIAL CABG VS. INITIAL MEDICAL TREATMENT	LEVEL OF EVIDENCE
Chronic stable angina (mild to moderate angina)	
To prolong survival	
Left main coronary stenosis (≥50% diameter)	A*†
Three-vessel disease (EF ≥50%)	A*†
Two-vessel disease with proximal LAD stenosis and either EF ≥50% or ischemia	A*†
Single proximal LAD stenosis with ischemia	A*†
To relieve symptoms	
Significant angina (with significant coronary stenoses and objective evidence of ischemia) despite alternative therapy	A*
Unstable angina	
To prolong life and relieve symptoms Multivessel disease (EF ≥50%)	A*

RANDOMIZED TRIALS NOT AVAILABLE: CABG VS. MEDICAL TREATMENT	LEVEL OF EVIDENCE
To prolong survival	
Severe angina, multivessel disease, normal LV function	B†
Previous CABG with late stenoses in multiple SVGs or SVG-LAD	B†
ST-elevation acute myocardial infarction not responsive to other therapy	C
Life-threatening ventricular arrhythmias	C
Failed PTCA with ongoing ischemia	C
CABG in conjunction with surgery for other cardiac conditions	C
To relieve symptoms	
Previous CABG with disabling angina despite medical management	B

*Individual randomized trials
†Meta-analysis of randomized trials
‡Comparative observational trials
CABG = coronary artery bypass graft; EF = ejection fraction; LAD = left anterior descending coronary artery; LV = left ventricular; PTCA = percutaneous transluminal coronary angioplasty; SVG = saphenous vein graft.

or a strongly positive exercise test (Chapter 67). Meta-analysis of these randomized trials also suggests there is a survival benefit of CABG for any patient with a proximal LAD lesion and myocardial ischemia.■ These are subgroups of patients for whom bypass surgery should be strongly considered even in the absence of severe symptoms. During these trials, patients with severe angina were not randomized but were included in observational studies that noted improved survival rates with CABG for patients with double- and triple-vessel disease and normal or abnormal left ventricular function. Medical, interventional, and surgical treatments have all advanced since these trials were completed.

UNSTABLE ANGINA/NON–ST ELEVATION MYOCARDIAL INFARCTION. During the early years of bypass surgery, emergency operation for patients with unstable angina was noted to carry increased risk of death and MI. As the evolution of treatment has allowed acute ischemic episodes to be controlled pharmacologically or with intra-aortic balloon counterpulsation, more elective operations can be performed. In hemodynamically stable patients, the risks of surgery are similar for stable and unstable angina. Current data suggest an aggressive strategy, including CABG when indicated, in patients with unstable angina or non–ST elevation acute MI (Chapters 68 and 70).■

Ischemic Syndromes without Randomized Trials

ACUTE MYOCARDIAL INFARCTION/FAILED PERCUTANEOUS INTERVENTION. For patients with ST segment elevation acute MI, the emergence of thrombolytic therapy, acute angiography, and primary percutaneous interventions has meant that CABG is rarely used as an emergency revascularization strategy. CABG may be indicated in the acute setting when thrombolytic therapy or primary percutaneous intervention reperfusion has not been effective, ischemia is ongoing, and large

areas of myocardium remain jeopardized. CABG following a completed MI may be indicated in patients in whom persistent ischemia in noninfarcted areas of myocardium produces postinfarction angina or hemodynamic instability. Mechanical complications of myocardial necrosis, including papillary muscle rupture, ventricular septal rupture, and myocardial free wall rupture, are acute life-threatening situations that usually require urgent operation for repair of the defect, often combined with CABG (Chapter 69).

FAILED PERCUTANEOUS INTERVENTION. The availability of intracoronary stents has decreased the need for emergency CABG to treat acute failure of percutaneous coronary interventions (Chapter 70). Current indications for emergency CABG include closure or threatened closure of a vessel supplying a significant amount of myocardium.

CORONARY BYPASS REOPERATIONS. Patients who develop new stenoses in native arteries or in bypass grafts may develop recurrent ischemic syndromes. Observational study of patients with severe vein graft atherosclerosis indicate this is an unstable lesion that often leads to serious cardiac events, particularly if the LAD or multiple vessels are jeopardized; reoperation appears to improve the survival rate of these patients. Reoperations are more difficult and dangerous than primary procedures, but the risk now approaches that for primary procedures in institutions performing a large number of reoperations. Percutaneous coronary intervention (angioplasty) has often been effective in the treatment of new native vessel stenoses but has been much less effective in the treatment of vein graft disease (Chapter 70).

Coexisting Cardiac Disease

During cardiac operations performed for valvular (Chapter 72) or aortic (Chapter 75) disease, the standard treatment is to perform bypass grafts to major coronary arteries with angiographic stenoses of greater than 50% of the luminal diameter. No randomized trials have addressed this issue, and these indications, although logical given the natural history of atherosclerosis, remain practice patterns based on consensus but not on definitive data.

Coronary Bypass Surgery versus Percutaneous Coronary Interventions

CABG and percutaneous coronary interventions (PCIs) are alternative anatomic treatments for coronary artery disease; each has different advantages and disadvantages. PCI produces less periprocedure morbidity, shorter hospital stays, and lower initial costs, but, for the majority of patients with multivessel disease, PCI is either not possible or produces less complete revascularization than CABG. When PCI is initially successful, early restenosis of treated vessels may compromise long-term outcomes, leading to recurrent symptoms, repeat revascularization, and increased costs. The disadvantages of CABG of increased initial morbidity, longer hospital stays, and higher costs are counterbalanced by the advantages of more complete, reliable, and longer-lasting revascularization.

Randomized trials comparing initial PCI and initial CABG have confirmed and quantified many of these observations.■■ For example, in the Bypass Surgery Angioplasty Revascularization Investigation (BARI), about 60% of the potentially randomizable patients with multivessel disease were excluded because of anatomic characteristics unfavorable for PCI. After 7 years of follow-up, the PCI patients experienced more angina and underwent significantly more repeat revascularization procedures (PCI 60% versus CABG 13%), and 34% of PCI patients had "crossed over" to CABG.

The survival rates for these selected patients in the BARI trial were equivalent for PCI and CABG except for patients with treated diabetes. Patients with treated diabetes had a significantly worse survival rate with PCI than with CABG. Since completion of BARI, advances have improved outcomes with both PCI and CABG. Thus, for some of the indications for CABG listed in Table 71–1, PCI may be used as an alternative treatment if there are favorable anatomic characteristics (Chapter 70).

1. Yusuf S, Zucker D, Peduzzi P, et al: Effect of coronary artery bypass graft surgery on survival: Overview of 10-year results from randomized trials by the Coronary Artery Bypass Graft Surgery Trialists Collaboration. Lancet 1994;344:563–570.
2. Cannon CP, Weintraub WS, Demopoulos LA, et al: Comparison of early invasive and conservative strategies in patients with unstable coronary syndromes treated with the glycoprotein IIb/IIIa inhibitor tirofiban. N Engl J Med 2001;344:1879–1887.

3. The BARI Investigators. Seven-year outcome in the bypass angioplasty revascularization investigation (BARI) by treatment and diabetic status. J Am Coll Cardiol 2000;35:1122–1129.
4. Diegler A, Thiele H, Falk V, et al: Comparison of stenting with minimally invasive bypass surgery for stenosis of the left anterior descending coronary artery. N Engl J Med 2002;347:561–566.

SUGGESTED READINGS
Charlson ME, Isom OW: Care after coronary-artery bypass surgery. N Engl J Med 2003;348:1456–1463. *Overview of postoperative issues with emphasis on their medical management.*
Eagle KA, Guyton RA, Davidoff R, et al: ACC/AHA guidelines for coronary artery bypass surgery. A report of the American College of Cardiology/American Heart Association Task Force on Practice Guidelines (Committee to Revise the 1991 Guidelines for Coronary Artery Bypass Graft Surgery). J Am Coll Cardiol 1999;34:1262–1347. *Guidelines for the indications for coronary bypass surgery in a variety of clinical situations.*
Gibbons RJ, Chatterjee K, Daley J, et al: ACC/AHA/ACP-ASIM guidelines for the management of patients with chronic stable angina. A report of the American College of Cardiology/American Heart Association Task Force on Practice Guidelines (Committee on Management of Patients with Chronic Stable Angina). J Am Coll Cardiol 1999;33:2092–2197. *Guidelines for the management of patients with chronic stable angina, the most common indication for bypass surgery.*
Lytle BW, Blackstone EH, Loop FD, et al: Two internal thoracic artery grafts are better than one. J Thorac Cardiovasc Surg 1999;117:855–872. *Largest study of the influence of internal thoracic artery grafting on long-term outcomes after bypass surgery.*

72 VALVULAR HEART DISEASE

Blase A. Carabello

The cardiac valves permit unobstructed forward blood flow through the heart when they are open, while preventing backward flow when they are closed. Most valvular heart diseases cause either valvular stenosis with obstruction to forward flow or valvular regurgitation with backward flow. Valvular stenosis imparts a pressure overload on the left or right ventricle because those chambers must generate higher than normal pressure to overcome the obstruction to pump blood forward. Valvular regurgitation imparts a volume overload on the heart, which now must pump additional volume to compensate for that which is regurgitated. When valve disease is severe, these hemodynamic burdens can lead to ventricular dysfunction, heart failure, and sudden death (Table 72–1). In almost every instance, the definitive therapy for severe valvular heart disease is mechanical restoration of valve function.

AORTIC STENOSIS

Etiology

BICUSPID AND OTHER CONGENITALLY ABNORMAL AORTIC VALVES. Approximately 1% of the population is born with a bicuspid aortic valve; there is a male predominance (Chapter 65). Although this abnormality usually does not cause a hemodynamic disturbance at birth, bicuspid aortic valves tend to deteriorate with age. Approximately one third of these valves become stenotic, another third become regurgitant, and the remainder cause only minor hemodynamic abnormalities. When stenosis develops, it usually occurs in the 40s, 50s, and 60s.

Sometimes congenital aortic stenosis from a unicuspid, bicuspid, or even abnormal tricuspid valve causes symptoms during childhood and requires correction by adolescence. Occasionally, these congenitally stenotic aortic valves escape detection until adulthood.

TRICUSPID AORTIC VALVE STENOSIS. Some patients born with apparently normal tricuspid aortic valves develop thickening and calcification similar to that which occurs in bicuspid valves. When aortic stenosis develops in previously normal tricuspid aortic valves, it usually does so in the 60s to 80s. Although stenosis and calcifications of bicuspid and tricuspid aortic valves formerly were considered to be degenerative processes, it is clear that this type of aortic stenosis arises from an active inflammatory process similar to that of coronary heart disease. This concept is supported by many pieces of evidence. First, the initial lesion of aortic stenosis is similar to the plaque of coronary disease. Second, both diseases have hypertension and hyperlipidemia as risk factors. Third, there is an excellent correlation between calcification of the aortic valve and calcification of the coronary arteries. Fourth, patients with the most severe aortic stenosis have the highest levels of C-reactive protein. Finally, "statin" drugs seem to retard the progression of aortic stenosis.

RHEUMATIC VALVULAR HEART DISEASE. Rheumatic valve disease is now a rare cause of aortic stenosis in developed countries. In virtually every case, the mitral valve also is detectably abnormal.

Pathophysiology and Its Relation to Symptoms

The presence or absence of the classic symptoms of aortic stenosis—angina, syncope, and the symptoms of heart failure—is the key to the natural history of the disease. Before the onset of symptoms, survival is similar to that for the normal population, and sudden death is rare. When the classic symptoms develop, however, survival declines precipitously. Approximately 35% of patients with aortic stenosis present with angina. Of these, 50% are dead in 5 years unless aortic valve replacement is performed. Approximately 15% present with syncope; of these, 50% are dead in only 3 years unless the aortic valve is replaced. Of the 50% who present with the symptoms of congestive heart failure, 50% are dead in 2 years without aortic valve replacement. In all, only 25% of patients with symptomatic aortic stenosis survive 3 years in the absence of valve replacement, and the annual risk of sudden death ranges from 10% in patients with angina to 15% with syncope to 25% with heart failure. Prompt recognition of symptoms and evaluation for possible severe aortic stenosis are crucial in managing the disease.

The normal aortic valve area is 3 to 4 cm^2, and little hemodynamic disturbance occurs until the orifice is reduced to about one third of normal, at which time a systolic gradient develops between the left ventricle and aorta. Left ventricular (LV) and aortic pressures normally are nearly equal during systole. In aortic stenosis, intercavitary LV pressure must increase above aortic pressure, however, to produce forward flow across the stenotic valve and to achieve an acceptable downstream pressure (see Fig. 54–1). There is a geometric progression in the magnitude of the gradient as the valve area narrows. Given a normal cardiac output, the gradient rises rapidly from 10 to 15 mm Hg at valve areas of 1.5 to 1.3 cm^2 to about 25 mm Hg at 1.0 cm^2, 50 mm Hg at 0.8 cm^2, 70 mm Hg at 0.6 cm^2, and 100 mm Hg at 0.5 cm^2. The rate of progression of aortic stenosis varies widely from patient to patient; it may remain stable for many years or increase 15 mm Hg per year.

A major compensatory response to the increased LV pressure of aortic stenosis is the development of concentric LV hypertrophy. The Laplace equation—stress (s) = pressure (p) × radius (r)/2 × thickness (th)—indicates that the force on any unit of LV myocardium (afterload) varies directly with ventricular pressure and radius and inversely with wall thickness. As pressure increases, it can be offset by increased LV wall thickness (concentric hypertrophy). The determinants of LV ejection fraction are contractility, preload, and afterload. By normalizing afterload, the development of concentric hypertrophy helps preserve ejection fraction and cardiac output despite the pressure overload. Although hypertrophy clearly serves a compensatory function, it also has a pathologic role and is in part responsible for the classic symptoms of aortic stenosis.

ANGINA. In general, angina occurs from myocardial ischemia when LV oxygen (and other nutrient) demand exceeds supply, which is predicated on coronary blood flow. In normal subjects, coronary blood flow can increase five-fold to eight-fold under maximum metabolic demand, but in aortic stenosis this reserve is limited. Reduced coronary blood flow reserve may be caused by a relative diminution of capillary ingrowth to serve the needs of the hypertrophied left ventricle or by a reduced transcoronary gradient for coronary blood flow because of the elevated LV end-diastolic pressure. Restricted coronary blood flow reserve appears to be responsible for angina in many patients who have aortic stenosis despite normal epicardial coronary arteries. In other patients, angina is due to increased oxygen demand when inadequate hypertrophy allows wall stress, a key determinant of myocardial oxygen consumption, to increase.

SYNCOPE. Syncope usually occurs because of inadequate cerebral perfusion. In aortic stenosis, syncope usually is related to exertion. It may result when exertion causes a fall in total peripheral resistance that cannot be compensated by increased cardiac output because output is limited by the obstruction to LV outflow; this combination reduces systemic blood pressure and cerebral perfusion. In addition, high LV pressures during exercise may trigger a systemic vasodepressor response that lowers blood pressure and produces syncope. Cardiac arrhythmias, possibly caused by exertional ischemia, also cause hypotension and syncope.

Table 72–1 • SUMMARY OF SEVERE VALVULAR HEART DISEASE

	AORTIC STENOSIS	MITRAL STENOSIS	MITRAL REGURGITATION	AORTIC REGURGITATION
ETIOLOGY	Idiopathic calcification of a bicuspid or tricuspid valve Congenital Rheumatic	Rheumatic fever Annular calcification	Mitral valve prolapse Ruptured chordae Endocarditis Ischemic papillary muscle dysfunction or rupture Collagen vascular diseases and syndromes Secondary to LV myocardial diseases	Annuloaortic ectasia Hypertension Endocarditis Marfan syndrome Ankylosing spondylitis Aortic dissection Syphilis Collagen vascular disease
PATHOPHYSIOLOGY	Pressure overload on the LV with compensation by LV hypertrophy As disease advances, reduced coronary flow reserve causes angina Hypertrophy and afterload excess lead to systolic and diastolic LV dysfunction	Obstruction to LV inflow increases left atrial pressure and limits cardiac output mimicking LV failure. Mitral valve obstruction increases the pressure work of the right ventricle Right ventricular pressure overload is augmented further when pulmonary hypertension develops	Places volume overload on the LV. Ventricle responds with eccentric hypertrophy and dilation, which allow for increased ventricular stroke volume Eventually, however, LV dysfunction develops if volume overload is uncorrected	*Chronic* Total stroke volume causes hyperdynamic circulation, induces systolic hypertension and causes pressure and volume overload. Compensation is by concentric and eccentric hypertrophy *Acute* Because cardiac dilation has not developed, hyperdynamic findings are absent. High diastolic LV pressure causes mitral valve preclosure and potentiates LV ischemia and failure
SYMPTOMS	Angina Syncope Heart failure	Dyspnea Orthopnea PND Hemoptysis Hoarseness Edema Ascites	Dyspnea Orthopnea PND	Dyspnea Orthopnea PND Angina Syncope
SIGNS	Systolic ejection murmur radiating to neck Delayed carotid upstroke S_4, soft or paradoxical S_2	Diastolic rumble following an opening snap Loud S_1 Right ventricular lift Loud P_2	Holosystolic apical murmur radiates to axilla, S_3 Displaced PMI	*Chronic* Diastolic blowing murmur Hyperdynamic circulation Displaced PMI Quincke pulse DeMusset's sign *Acute* Short diastolic blowing murmur Soft S_1
ECG	LAA LVH	LAA RVH	LAA LVH	LAA LVH
CHEST RADIOGRAPH	Boot-shaped heart Aortic valve calcification on lateral view	Straightening of left heart border Double density at right heart border Kerley B lines Enlarged pulmonary arteries	Cardiac enlargement	*Chronic* Cardiac enlargement Uncoiling of the aorta *Acute* Pulmonary congestion with normal heart size
ECHOCARDIOGRAPHIC FINDINGS	Concentric LVH Reduced aortic valve cusp separation Doppler shows mean gradient ≥50 mm Hg in most severe cases	Restricted mitral leaflet motion Valve area ≤1.0 cm² in most severe cases Tricuspid Doppler may reveal pulmonary hypertension	LV and left atrial enlargement in chronic severe disease Doppler: large regurgitant jet	*Chronic* LV enlargement Large Doppler jet PHT <400 msec *Acute* Small LV, mitral valve preclosure
CATHETERIZATION FINDINGS	Increased LVEDP Transaortic gradient 50 mm Hg AVA ≤0.7 in most severe cases	Elevated pulmonary capillary wedge pressure Transmitral gradient usually >10 mm Hg in severe cases MVA <1.0 cm²	Elevated pulmonary capillary wedge pressure Ventriculography shows regurgitation of dye into LV	Wide pulse pressure Aortography shows regurgitation of dye into LV Usually unnecessary
MEDICAL THERAPY	Avoid vasodilators Digitalis, diuretics, and nitroglycerin in inoperable cases	Diuretics for mild symptoms Anticoagulation in atrial fibrillation Digitalis, β-blockers, verapamil, or diltiazem for rate control	Vasodilators in acute disease No proven therapy in chronic disease (but vasodilators commonly used)	*Chronic* Vasodilators in chronic asymptomatic disease with normal left ventricular function *Acute* Vasodilators
INDICATIONS FOR SURGERY	Appearance of symptoms in patients with severe disease (see text)	Appearance of more than mild symptoms Development of pulmonary hypertension Appearance of persistent atrial fibrillation	Appearance of symptoms EF <0.60 ESD ≥45 mm	*Chronic* Appearance of symptoms EF <0.55 ESD ≥55 mm *Acute* Even mild heart failure Mitral valve preclosure

AVA = aortic valve area; EF = ejection fraction; ESD = end-systolic diameter; LAA = left atrial enlargement; LV = left ventricle; LVEDP = left ventricular end-diastolic pressure; LVH = left ventricular hypertrophy; MS = mitral stenosis; MVA = mitral valve area; PMI = point of maximal impulse; PND = paroxysmal nocturnal dyspnea; PHT = pressure half-time; RVH = right ventricular hypertrophy.

HEART FAILURE. In aortic stenosis, contractile dysfunction (systolic failure) and failure of normal relaxation (diastolic failure) occur and cause symptoms. The extent of ventricular contraction is governed by contractility and afterload. In aortic stenosis, contractility (the ability to generate force) often is reduced. The mechanisms of contractile dysfunction may include abnormal calcium handling, microtubular hyperpolymerization causing an internal viscous load on the myocyte, and myocardial ischemia. In some cases, contractile function is normal, but hypertrophy is inadequate to normalize wall stress and leads to excessive afterload. Excessive afterload inhibits ejection, reduces forward output, and leads to heart failure.

The increased wall thickness that helps to normalize stress increases diastolic stiffness. Even if muscle properties remain normal, higher filling pressure is required to distend a thicker ventricle. As aortic stenosis advances, collagen deposition also stiffens the myocardium and adds to the diastolic dysfunction.

Diagnosis

PHYSICAL EXAMINATION. The diagnosis of aortic stenosis usually is first suspected when the classic systolic ejection murmur is heard during physical examination. The murmur is loudest in the aortic area and radiates to the neck. In some cases, the murmur may disappear over the sternum and reappear over the LV apex, giving the false impression that the murmur of mitral regurgitation also is present (Gallivardan's phenomenon). The intensity of the murmur increases with cycle length because longer cycles are associated with greater aortic flow. In mild disease, the murmur peaks in intensity in early or mid systole. As stenosis severity worsens, the murmur peaks progressively later in systole. Perhaps the most helpful clue to the severity of aortic stenosis by physical examination is the characteristic delay in the carotid pulse with the diminution in its volume (see Fig. 46–2); in elderly patients, however, increasing carotid stiffness may pseudo-normalize the carotid upstrokes. The LV apical impulse in aortic stenosis is not displaced but is enlarged and forceful. The simultaneous palpation of a forceful LV apex beat and a delayed and weakened carotid pulse are persuasive clues that severe aortic stenosis is present. The S_1 in aortic stenosis is usually normal. In congenital aortic stenosis when the valve is not calcified, S_1 may be followed by a systolic ejection click. In calcific disease, S_2 may be single and soft when the aortic component is lost because the valve neither opens nor closes well. In some cases, delayed LV emptying secondary to LV dysfunction may create paradoxical splitting of S_2. An S_4 gallop is common. In advanced disease, pulmonary hypertension and signs of right-sided failure are common.

Because of the dire consequences of missing the diagnosis of aortic stenosis, the physician must have a low threshold for obtaining an echocardiogram whenever aortic stenosis cannot be excluded by physical examination. In asymptomatic patients with suspicious murmurs, early diagnosis allows the patient and the physician to be more vigilant regarding possible early signs and symptoms and to guide the use of prophylactic regimens to prevent bacterial endocarditis (see Chapter 310).

NONINVASIVE EVALUATION. The electrocardiogram (ECG) in aortic stenosis usually shows LV hypertrophy. In some cases of even severe aortic stenosis, LV hypertrophy is absent on the ECG, however, possibly owing to the lack of LV dilation. Left atrial abnormality is common because the stiff left ventricle increases left atrial afterload and causes the left atrium to dilate.

The chest radiograph in aortic stenosis is usually nondiagnostic. The cardiac silhouette is usually not enlarged but may assume a boot-shaped configuration. In advanced cases, there may be signs of cardiomegaly and pulmonary congestion; aortic valve calcification may be seen in the lateral view.

Echocardiography is indispensable to assess the extent of LV hypertrophy, systolic ejection performance, and aortic valve anatomy (Fig. 72–1). Doppler interrogation of the aortic valve makes use of the modified Bernoulli equation (gradient = $4 \times$ velocity^2) to assess the severity of the stenosis (see Chapter 51). As blood flows from the body of the left ventricle across the stenotic valve, the flow rate must accelerate for the volume to remain constant. Doppler interrogation of the valve detects this increase in velocity to estimate the valve gradient. The peak aortic flow velocity in patients with preserved LV systolic function is a useful clinical guide to prognosis. In patients with a flow velocity of less than or equal to 3.0 mL/sec, symptoms are unlikely to develop in the next 5 years; by comparison, in patients with a flow velocity of equal to or greater than 4 mL/sec, symptoms usually develop within 2 years.

EXERCISE TESTING. Although exercise testing is contraindicated in symptomatic patients with aortic stenosis because of the high risk of complications, cautious exercise testing is gaining favor in asymptomatic patients. This testing often reveals latent symptoms or hemodynamic instability that have gone unrecognized during the patient's normal daily activities. Exercise-induced hypotension or symptoms are indications for aortic valve replacement in patients with severe aortic stenosis; in patients with mild-to-moderate aortic stenosis, another source for exercise limitation should be sought.

CARDIAC CATHETERIZATION. When echocardiography shows severe aortic stenosis and the patient has one or more of the classic symptoms of the disease, aortic valve replacement should be performed.

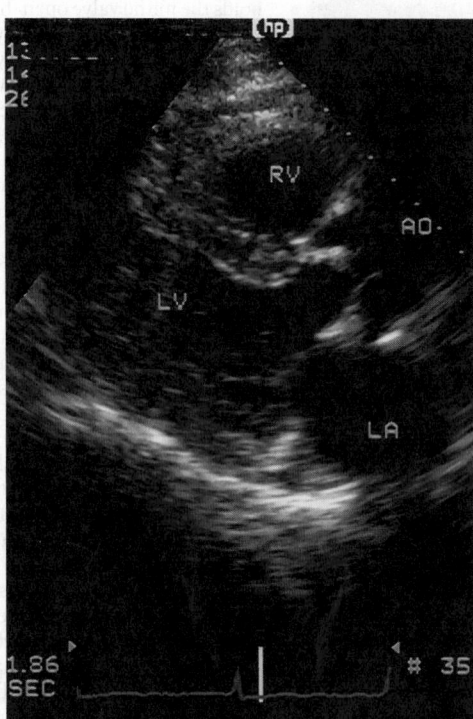
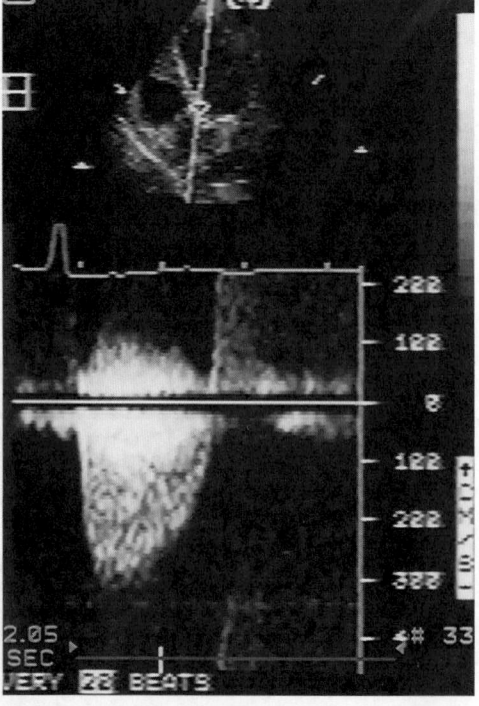

FIGURE 72–1 • Doppler echocardiogram obtained in a patient with aortic stenosis. The left panel shows thickened aortic valve leaflets that dome into the aorta with restricted opening in systole. The right panel shows a miniaturized apical four-chamber view at top with Doppler cursor through the aorta, whereas the bottom panel shows a continuous-wave spectral Doppler signal with a peak velocity of 3 m/sec. The peak valve gradient can be calculated as 4×3^2 or 36 mm Hg. (Courtesy Dr. Anthony DeMaria.)

Because most patients with aortic stenosis are of the age in which coronary disease is common, cardiac catheterization to perform coronary arteriography usually is accomplished before surgery. When the hemodynamic diagnosis is unclear, right-sided and left-sided heart catheterization should be performed to obtain a transaortic valvular pressure gradient and cardiac output, which are used to calculate the aortic valve area by the Gorlin formula:

$$A = \frac{CO/SEP \times HR}{44.3\sqrt{h}}$$

where CO is cardiac output (mL/min), SEP is systolic ejection period (sec), HR is heart rate, and h is mean gradient.

Rx Treatment

SURGERY. The only effective therapy for aortic stenosis is aortic valve replacement. As noted earlier, once the symptoms of aortic stenosis develop, the 3-year mortality is 75% without aortic valve replacement. When the valve is replaced, however, survival returns nearly to normal. Even octogenarians benefit from valve replacement unless other comorbid factors preclude surgery, so aortic valve replacement should not be denied simply on the basis of age. Valve replacement should not be denied because ejection fraction is reduced; the excess afterload imposed by the stenotic valve is relieved with valve replacement, and depressed ejection performance usually improves dramatically after surgery. The exception to this rule is severely reduced ejection fraction in the face of only a small aortic valve gradient in which the severity of the aortic stenosis may be overestimated because the failing left ventricle has difficulty opening a mildly to moderately stenotic valve. In these cases, LV muscle dysfunction either has another cause or is often so severe that it does not recover after valve replacement. Evidence indicates, however, that even some well-selected patients in this category may benefit from aortic valve replacement.

BALLOON AORTIC VALVOTOMY. In acquired calcific aortic stenosis, leaflet restriction results from heavy calcium deposition in the leaflets themselves and is not due to commissural fusion. Balloon aortic valvotomy is relatively ineffective in improving aortic stenosis, usually resulting in a residual gradient of 30 to 50 mm Hg and a valve area of $1.0\,cm^2$. Mortality after this procedure is similar to that of untreated patients. Balloon aortic valvotomy is used only palliatively in cases in which aortic valve replacement is impossible because of comorbidity or is impractical when immediate temporary relief is required because of the demands of other noncardiac conditions.

MEDICAL THERAPY. The only medical therapy indicated in aortic stenosis is antibiotic prophylaxis to prevent bacterial endocarditis (Chapter 310). Otherwise the patient either is asymptomatic and requires no therapy or is symptomatic and requires surgery. In patients with heart failure awaiting surgery, diuretics can be used cautiously to relieve pulmonary congestion. Nitrates also may be used cautiously to treat angina pectoris. Although vasodilators, especially angiotensin-converting enzyme inhibitors, have become a cornerstone of the therapy for heart failure, they are not recommended in aortic stenosis. With fixed valvular obstruction to outflow, vasodilation reduces pressure distal to the obstruction without increasing cardiac output and may cause syncope. When surgery and valvoplasty are unsuccessful or impossible, digitalis and diuretics can be used to improve symptoms with the understanding that they will not improve life expectancy.

MITRAL STENOSIS

Etiology

In almost all cases of acquired mitral stenosis, the cause is rheumatic heart disease. Occasionally, severe calcification of the mitral annulus can lead to mitral stenosis in the absence of rheumatic involvement. Mitral stenosis is three times more common in women and usually develops in the 40s and 50s. Although the disease has become rare in developed countries because of the waning incidence of rheumatic fever, mitral stenosis is still prevalent in developing nations, where rheumatic fever is common.

Pathophysiology

At the beginning of diastole, a transient gradient between the left atrium and left ventricle normally initiates LV filling. After early filling, left atrial and LV pressures equilibrate. In mitral stenosis, obstruction to LV filling increases left atrial pressure and produces a persistent gradient between the left atrium and the left ventricle (see Fig. 54–1). The combination of elevated left atrial pressure (and pulmonary venous pressure) and restriction of inflow into the left ventricle limits cardiac output. Although myocardial involvement from the rheumatic process occasionally affects LV muscle function, the muscle itself is normal in most patients with mitral stenosis. However, in approximately one third of patients with mitral stenosis, LV ejection performance is reduced despite normal muscle function, owing to reduced preload (from inflow obstruction) and increased afterload as a result of reflex vasoconstriction caused by reduced cardiac output.

Because the right ventricle generates most of the force that propels blood across the mitral valve, the right ventricle incurs the pressure overload of the transmitral gradient. In addition, secondary but reversible pulmonary vasoconstriction develops, further increasing pulmonary artery pressure and the burden on the right ventricle. As mitral stenosis worsens, right ventricular (RV) failure develops.

Diagnosis

HISTORY. Patients with mitral stenosis usually remain asymptomatic until the valve area is reduced to about one third its normal size of 4 to $5\,cm^2$. Then the symptoms typical of left-sided failure—dyspnea on exertion, orthopnea, and paroxysmal nocturnal dyspnea—develop. As the disease progresses and RV failure occurs, ascites and edema are common. Hemoptysis, which is common in mitral stenosis but uncommon in other causes of left atrial hypertension, develops when high left atrial pressure ruptures anastomoses of small bronchial veins. In some cases, a large left atrium may impinge on the left recurrent laryngeal nerve, causing hoarseness (Ortner's syndrome), or may impinge on the esophagus, causing dysphagia.

PHYSICAL EXAMINATION. Although mitral stenosis produces a typical and diagnostic physical examination, the diagnosis is missed frequently because the auscultatory findings may be subtle. Palpation of the precordium finds a quiet apical impulse. If pulmonary hypertension and RV hypertrophy have developed, the examiner notes a parasternal lift. S_1 is typically loud and may be the most prominent physical finding of the disease. A loud S_1 is present because the transmitral gradient holds the mitral valve open throughout diastole until ventricular systole closes the fully opened valve with a loud closing sound. In far-advanced disease, the mitral valve may be so damaged, however, that it neither opens nor closes well, so S_1 may become soft. S_2 is normally split; the pulmonic component is increased in intensity if pulmonary hypertension has developed. Left-sided S_3 and S_4 gallop sounds, which represent the ventricular and atrial components of rapid LV filling, are exceedingly rare in mitral stenosis because obstruction at the mitral valve prevents rapid filling. S_2 usually is followed by an opening snap. The distance between S_2 and the opening snap provides a reasonable estimation of left atrial pressure and an estimate of the severity of the mitral stenosis. The higher the left atrial pressure, the sooner the left atrial pressure and the falling LV pressure of early ventricular relaxation equilibrate. At this equilibration point, the mitral valve opens, and the opening snap occurs. When left atrial pressure is high, the opening snap closely (0.06 second) follows S_2. Conversely, when left atrial pressure is relatively normal, the snap occurs later (0.12 second) and may mimic the cadence of an S_3 gallop. The opening snap is followed by the classic low-pitched early diastolic mitral stenosis rumble, which increases in length as the mitral stenosis worsens. This murmur can be inaudible if the patient has a relatively low resting cardiac output. Modest exercise, such as isometric handgrip, may accentuate the murmur's intensity. If the patient is in sinus rhythm, atrial systole may produce a presystolic accentuation of the murmur. If pulmonary hypertension has developed, the pulmonic component of S_2 increases in intensity to become as loud or louder than the aortic component. With pulmonary hypertension, a diastolic blowing murmur of pulmonary insufficiency (Graham Steell's murmur) is often heard, although in many cases a coexistent murmur of mild aortic

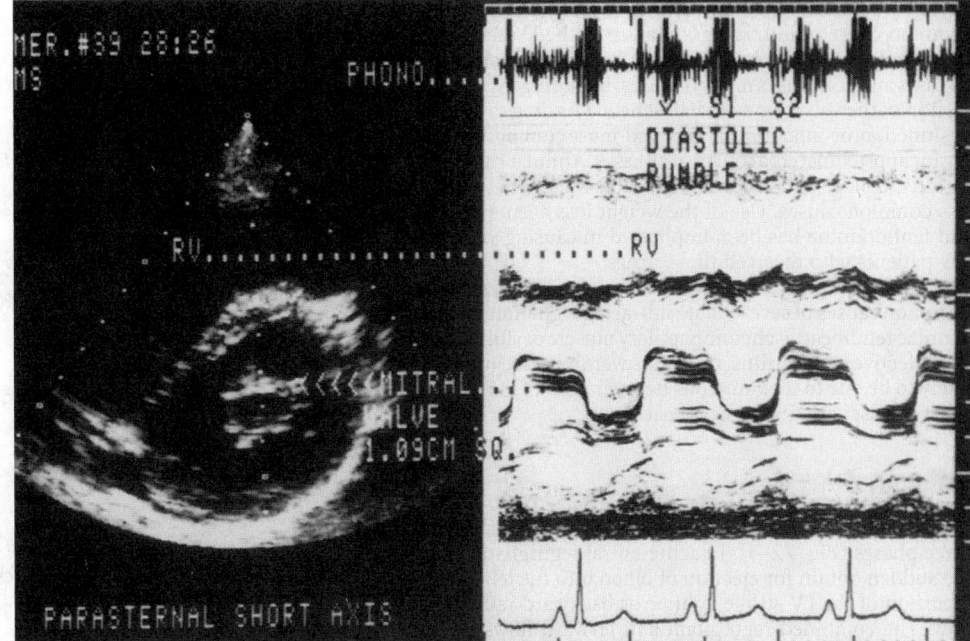

FIGURE 72–2 • An en fosse view of a stenotic mitral valve in the short-axis view of the left ventricle is shown on the left. Planimetry for the mitral valve orifice yielded an area of 1.09 cm². The M-mode echocardiogram on the right has been aligned with the appropriate structures on the left. It shows the restricted opening of the mitral valve in diastole associated with the classic diastolic rumbling murmur. (From Assey ME, Usher BW, Carabello BA: The patient with valvular heart disease. *In* Pepine CJ, Hill JA, Lambert CR [eds]: Diagnostic and Therapeutic Cardiac Catheterization, 2nd ed. Baltimore, Williams & Wilkins, 1994, p 709.)

insufficiency is mistaken for this murmur. Neck vein elevation, ascites, and edema are present if RV failure has developed.

NONINVASIVE EVALUATION. If the patient is in sinus rhythm, left atrial abnormality is usually present on the ECG. Atrial fibrillation is common, however. If pulmonary hypertension has developed, there is often evidence of RV hypertrophy.

On the chest radiograph, left atrial enlargement produces straightening of the left heart border and a double density at the right heart border owing to the combined silhouettes of the right atrium and left atrium. Pulmonary venous hypertension produces increased vascularity. Kerley B lines, which represent thickening of the pulmonary septa owing to chronic venous engorgement, also may be seen.

The echocardiogram produces excellent images of the mitral valve and is the most important diagnostic tool in confirming the diagnosis (Fig. 72–2). Transthoracic echocardiography or, if necessary, transesophageal echocardiography makes the diagnosis in nearly 100% of cases and accurately assesses severity. Mitral stenosis, similar to aortic stenosis, can be quantified by assessing the transvalvular gradient using the modified Bernoulli principle. The stenosis is considered mild when the calculated or planimetered valve area is more than 1.75 cm², moderate at 1.25 to 1.75 cm², moderately severe at 1.0 to 1.25 cm², and severe at less than 1.0 cm².

During echocardiography, the suitability of the valve for balloon valvotomy also can be assessed (see later). If even mild tricuspid regurgitation is present, the systolic gradient across the tricuspid valve can be used to gauge the pulmonary artery pressure, which is an important prognostic factor in mitral stenosis because prognosis worsens as pulmonary pressure increases.

CARDIAC CATHETERIZATION. Cardiac catheterization is usually unnecessary to assess the severity of mitral stenosis. Because many patients with mitral stenosis are of an age when coronary disease might be present, however, coronary arteriography usually is performed if cardiac surgery is anticipated or if the patient has coexistent angina. In these cases, it is common to perform left-sided and right-sided heart catheterizations to confirm the transmitral gradient and to calculate the valve area from the Gorlin formula (see earlier).

Rx Treatment

MEDICAL THERAPY. Asymptomatic patients with mitral stenosis and sinus rhythm require no therapy. Symptoms of mild dyspnea and orthopnea can be treated with diuretics alone. When symptoms worsen to more than mild or if pulmonary hypertension develops, mechanical correction of the stenosis is preferable to medical therapy because it improves longevity in severely symptomatic patients.

Patients with mitral stenosis who develop atrial fibrillation usually decompensate because the rapid heart rate reduces diastolic filling time and increases left atrial pressure and decreases cardiac output. The heart rate must be controlled promptly, preferably with an infusion of diltiazem or esmolol for acute atrial fibrillation or with oral digoxin, a β-blocker, or a calcium channel blocker in chronic atrial fibrillation. When rate is controlled, anticoagulation and conversion to sinus rhythm should be undertaken either pharmacologically or with direct-current countershock (Chapter 59). If sinus rhythm cannot be maintained, mechanical intervention usually is done with the hope that sinus rhythm can be restored after the obstruction to atrial outflow is corrected.

Because patients with concomitant mitral stenosis and atrial fibrillation have an extraordinarily high risk of systemic embolism, they are anticoagulated with warfarin, targeting an international normalized ratio (INR) of 2.5 to 3.5. Anticoagulation is warranted in all patients unless there is a serious contraindication to its use.

MECHANICAL THERAPY. When symptoms progress past early New York Heart Association class II, that is, symptoms with more than ordinary activity, or if pulmonary hypertension develops, prognosis is reduced unless the mitral stenosis is relieved. In most instances, an excellent result can be obtained from percutaneous balloon valvotomy. In contrast to aortic stenosis, in mitral stenosis there is fusion of the valve leaflets at the commissures. Balloon dilation produces a commissurotomy and a substantial increase in valve area that appears to persist for at least a decade and provides improvement comparable to that of closed or open commissurotomy in suitable patients. Suitability for balloon valvotomy is determined partially during echocardiography. Patients with pliable valves, little valvular calcification, little involvement of the subvalvular apparatus, and less than moderate mitral regurgitation are ideal candidates. Even when valve anatomy is not ideal, however, valvotomy may be attempted in cases of advanced age or in situations in which comorbid risk factors increase surgical risk. In otherwise healthy patients with unfavorable valve anatomy, surgery to perform an open commissurotomy or valve replacement is undertaken.

MITRAL REGURGITATION

Etiology

The mitral valve is composed of the mitral annulus, the leaflets, the chordae tendineae, and the papillary muscles. Abnormalities of any of these structures may lead to mitral regurgitation. The most common cause of mitral regurgitation in the United States is mitral valve prolapse, which is responsible for approximately two thirds of all cases and comprises many diseases, including myxomatous degeneration of the valve. Myocardial ischemia leading to papillary muscle dysfunction or infarction is the next most common cause, accounting for approximately a fourth of all cases. Annular calcification, endocarditis, collagen vascular disease, and rheumatic heart disease are less common causes. Use of the weight loss agents dexfenfluramine and fenfluramine has been implicated in causing valve damage in a few patients who received those drugs.

Mitral regurgitation can be subdivided on the basis of chronicity. Common causes of severe acute mitral regurgitation include ruptured chordae tendineae, ischemic papillary muscle dysfunction or rupture, and infective endocarditis. Chronic severe mitral regurgitation is more likely to be due to myxomatous degeneration of the valve, rheumatic heart disease, or annular calcification.

Pathophysiology

The pathophysiology of mitral regurgitation can be divided into three phases (Fig. 72–3). In acute mitral regurgitation of any cause, the sudden option for ejection of blood into the left atrium "wastes" a portion of the LV stroke volume as backward rather than forward flow. The combined regurgitant and forward flows cause a volume overload of the left ventricle, stretching existing sarcomeres toward their maximum length. Use of the Frank-Starling mechanism is maximized, and end-diastolic volume increases concomitantly. The regurgitant pathway unloads the left ventricle in systole because it allows ejection into the relatively low impedance left atrium, reducing end-systolic volume. Although increased end-diastolic volume and decreased end-systolic volume act in concert to increase total stroke volume, forward stroke volume is subnormal because a large portion of the total stroke volume is regurgitated into the left atrium. This regurgitant volume increases left atrial pressure, so the patient experiences heart failure with low cardiac output and pulmonary congestion despite normal LV contractile function.

In many cases, severe acute mitral regurgitation necessitates emergent surgical correction. Patients who can be managed through the acute phase may enter the phase of compensation. In this phase, eccentric LV hypertrophy and increased end-diastolic volume, combined with normal contractile function, allow for ejection of a sufficiently large total stroke volume to allow forward stroke volume to return toward normal. Left atrial enlargement allows for accommodation of the regurgitant volume at a lower filling pressure. In this phase, the patient may be relatively asymptomatic even during strenuous exercise.

Although severe mitral regurgitation may be tolerated for many years, the lesion eventually causes LV dysfunction. The now damaged ventricle has impaired ejection performance, and end-systolic volume increases. Greater LV residual volume at end-systole increases end-diastolic volume and end-diastolic pressure, and the symptoms of pulmonary congestion may reappear. Additional LV dilation may worsen the amount of regurgitation by causing further enlargement of the mitral annulus and malalignment of the papillary muscles. Although there is substantial contractile dysfunction, the increased preload and the presence of the regurgitant pathway, which tends to normalize afterload despite ventricular enlargement, augment ejection fraction and may maintain it in a relatively normal range.

The causes of LV contractile dysfunction in mitral regurgitation may relate to loss of contractile proteins and abnormalities in calcium handling. In at least some cases, contractile dysfunction is reversible by timely mitral valve replacement.

Diagnosis

The standard symptoms of left-sided congestive heart failure should be sought. An attempt to discover potential causes should be made by questioning for a prior history of a heart murmur or abnormal cardiac examination, rheumatic heart disease, endocarditis, myocardial infarction, or the use of anorexigenic drugs.

PHYSICAL EXAMINATION. Volume overload of the left ventricle displaces the apical impulse downward and to the left. S_1 may be reduced in intensity, whereas S_2 is usually physiologically split. In severe mitral

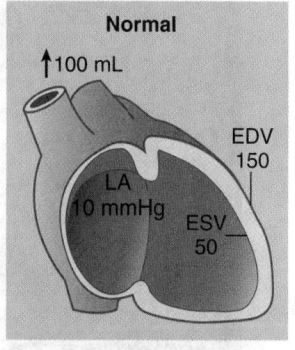

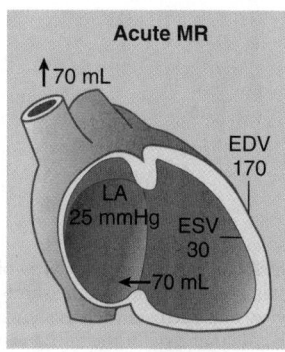

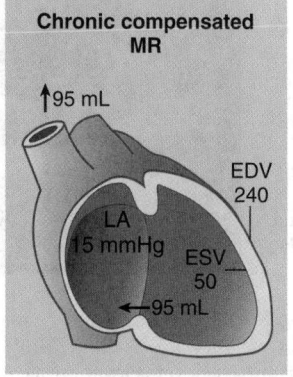

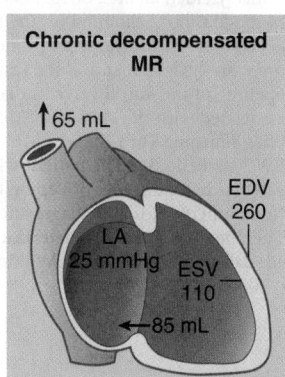

	Preload SL (μ)	Afterload ESS (Kdyne/cm²)	CF	EF	RF	FSV (mL)
N	2.07	90	N	.67	.0	100
AMR	2.25	60	N	.82	.50	70
CCMR	2.19	90	N	.79	.5	95
CDMR	2.19	120	↓	.58	.57	65

FIGURE 72–3 • *A* and *B*, Normal physiology (N) (*A*) is compared with physiology of acute mitral regurgitation (AMR) (*B*). Acutely the volume overload increases preload (sarcomere length [SL]) and end-diastolic volume (EDV) increases from 150 to 170 mL. Unloading of the left ventricle by the presence of the regurgitant pathway decreases afterload (end-systolic stress [ESS]), and end-systolic volume (ESV) falls from 50 to 30 mL. These changes result in an increase in ejection fraction (EF). Because 50% of the total left ventricular (LV) stroke volume (regurgitant fraction [RF]) is ejected into the left atrium (LA), however, forward stroke volume (FSV) falls from 100 to 70 mL. At this stage, contractile function (CF) is normal. *C*, Chronic compensated mitral regurgitation (CCMR). In CCMR, eccentric cardiac hypertrophy has developed, and EDV has increased substantially. Increased EDV combined with normal contractile function permits ejection of a larger total stroke volume and a larger forward stroke volume than in the acute phase. Left atrial enlargement permits lower left atrial pressure. Because the radius term in the Laplace equation has increased with increasing LV volume, afterload and ESV return to normal. *D*, Chronic decompensated mitral regurgitation (CDMR). In this stage, contractile dysfunction causes a large increase in ESV with a fall in total and forward stroke volume. Additional LV enlargement leads to worsening mitral regurgitation. The relatively favorable loading conditions in this phase still permit a normal EF, however, despite contractile dysfunction. (From Carabello BA: Mitral regurgitation: Basic pathophysiologic principles. Mod Concepts Cardiovasc Dis 1988;57:57.)

regurgitation, S_2 is followed by S_3, which does not indicate heart failure but reflects rapid filling of the left ventricle by the large volume of blood stored in the left atrium during systole. The typical murmur of mitral regurgitation is a holosystolic apical murmur that often radiates toward the axilla. There is a rough correlation between the intensity of the murmur and the severity of the disease, but this correlation is too weak to use in clinical decision making because the murmur may be soft when cardiac output is low. In contrast to aortic stenosis, the murmur intensity usually does not vary with the RR interval. In acute mitral regurgitation, the presence of a large v wave may produce rapid equilibration of left atrial and LV pressure, reducing the driving gradient and shortening the murmur. Pulmonary hypertension may develop and produce right-sided signs, including a RV lift, increased P_2, and, if RV dysfunction has developed, signs of right-sided heart failure.

NONINVASIVE EVALUATION. The ECG usually shows LV hypertrophy and left atrial abnormality. The chest radiograph usually shows cardiomegaly; the absence of cardiomegaly indicates either that the mitral regurgitation is mild or that it has not been chronic enough to allow cardiac dilation to occur.

Echocardiography shows the extent of left atrial and LV enlargement. Ultrasonic imaging of the mitral valve is excellent and offers clues to the mitral valve abnormalities responsible for the regurgitation. Color flow Doppler interrogation of the valve (Fig. 72–4) helps assess the severity of regurgitation, but because this technique images flow velocity rather than actual flow, it is subject to errors in interpretation. The Doppler technique is excellent for excluding the presence of mitral regurgitation and for distinguishing between mild and severe degrees. Although newer techniques may quantify regurgitation more precisely, they are not yet in widespread use, and standard color flow Doppler examination may not be sufficient for exact quantification of mitral regurgitation or to determine if the severity of the lesion is sufficient to cause eventual LV dysfunction. When the severity of mitral regurgitation is in doubt or if mitral valve surgery is contemplated, cardiac catheterization is helpful in resolving the severity of the lesion; it should include coronary arteriography in patients older than age 40 or with symptoms suggesting coronary disease (Chapter 67).

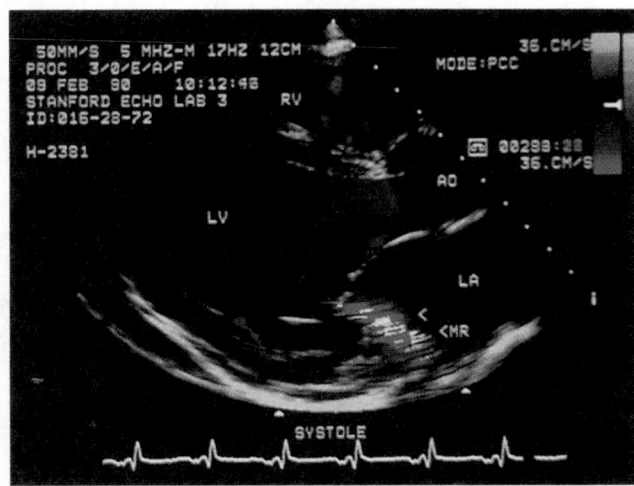

FIGURE 72–4 • A two-dimensional echocardiogram with Doppler flow mapping superimposed on a portion of the image. The color information is represented in the sector of the imaging plane extending from the apex of the triangular plane to the two small arrows at the bottom of the image plane. Mitral regurgitation (MR) is indicated (open arrows), extending from the mitral valve leaflets toward the posterior aspect of the left atrium (LA) during systole. The mosaic of colors representing the mitral regurgitant signal is typical of high-velocity turbulent flow. The low-intensity orange-brown signal represents flow directed away from the transducer on the chest wall, and the blue shades represent blood in the left ventricular outflow tract moving toward the transducer. AO = aorta; LV = left ventricle; RV = right ventricle.

 Treatment

MEDICAL THERAPY

SEVERE ACUTE MITRAL REGURGITATION. In severe acute mitral regurgitation, the patient is usually symptomatic with heart failure or even shock. The goal of medical therapy is to increase forward cardiac output, while concomitantly reducing regurgitant volume (Chapter 56). Arterial vasodilators reduce systemic resistance to flow and preferentially increase aortic outflow and simultaneously decrease the amount of mitral regurgitation and left atrial hypertension. If hypotension already exists, vasodilators such as nitroprusside lower blood pressure further and cannot be used. In these cases, intra-aortic balloon counterpulsation is preferred if the aortic valve is competent. Counterpulsation increases forward cardiac output by lowering ventricular afterload, while augmenting systemic diastolic pressure.

CHRONIC ASYMPTOMATIC MITRAL REGURGITATION. Vasodilator therapy is effective in the treatment of acute mitral regurgitation and in chronic aortic regurgitation (see later). Perhaps because afterload usually is not increased in chronic asymptomatic mitral regurgitation, vasodilators have had little effect in reducing LV volume or in improving normal exercise tolerance in mitral regurgitation.

In patients with *symptomatic* mitral regurgitation, angiotensin-converting enzyme inhibitors have been shown to reduce LV volumes and to improve symptoms. Mitral valve surgery rather than medical therapy usually is preferred, however, in most symptomatic patients with mitral regurgitation. When atrial fibrillation is present, long-term anticoagulation should achieve the same INR goal as for mitral stenosis.

SURGICAL THERAPY

The timing of mitral valve surgery must weigh the risks of the operation and of a prosthesis, if one is inserted, versus the risk of irreversible LV dysfunction if surgery is delayed unwisely. For most other types of valve disease, surgical correction usually requires placement of a prosthetic valve, but in mitral regurgitation the native valve often can be repaired. Because conservation of the native valve obviates the risks of a prosthesis, the option of mitral valve repair should influence the patient and physician toward earlier operation.

Types of Mitral Valve Surgery

STANDARD MITRAL VALVE REPLACEMENT. In the standard mitral valve replacement, the mitral valve leaflets and its apparatus are removed and a prosthetic valve is inserted. Although this operation almost guarantees mitral valve competence, destruction of the mitral valve apparatus is problematic. The mitral valve apparatus has a much wider physiologic function than simply to prevent mitral regurgitation. The apparatus is responsible for coordinating LV contraction and for helping to maintain the efficient prolate ellipsoid shape of the left ventricle. Destruction of the apparatus leads to a sudden fall in LV function and a decline in postoperative ejection fraction that is often permanent. This operation is used only in circumstances in which the native valve cannot be repaired, such as in severe rheumatic deformity or in ischemic mitral regurgitation.

MITRAL VALVE REPLACEMENT WITH APPARATUS PRESERVATION. In this procedure, a prosthetic valve is inserted, but the continuity between the native leaflets and the papillary muscles is maintained. This procedure has the advantage of ensuring mitral valve competence, while preserving the LV functional aspects of the mitral apparatus. Even if only the posterior leaflets and chordae are preserved, the patient benefits from improved postoperative ventricular function and better survival. In many cases, it is possible to preserve anterior and posterior chordal attachments, although anterior continuity can be associated with LV outflow tract obstruction. Although the patient benefits from restored mitral valve competence and maintenance of LV function, insertion of a prosthesis still carries all prosthesis-associated risks.

MITRAL VALVE REPAIR. When feasible, mitral valve repair is the preferred operation. Repair restores valve competence, maintains the functional aspects of the apparatus, and avoids insertion of a prosthesis. Repair is most applicable in cases of posterior chordal rupture; anterior involvement and rheumatic involvement make repair more difficult. In all cases, the feasibility of repair depends on the pathoanatomy that is causing the mitral regurgitation and on the skill and experience of the operating surgeon.

Timing of Surgery

SYMPTOMATIC PATIENTS. Most patients with the symptoms of dyspnea, orthopnea, or fatigue should undergo surgery regardless

Continued

of which operation is performed because they already have lifestyle limitations from their disease. The mere presence of symptoms may worsen prognosis despite relatively well-preserved LV function. The onset or worsening of symptoms is a summary of the patient's pathophysiology and may give a broader view of cardiovascular integrity than any single measurement of pressure or function.

ASYMPTOMATIC PATIENTS WITH NORMAL LEFT VENTRICULAR FUNCTION. Surgery has been considered increasingly in asymptomatic patients who have normal LV function but echocardiographic findings to indicate that valve *repair* is likely to be successful. Although these patients are at low risk without surgery, the risk of valve repair is less than 1%, and this approach avoids the risks of valve *replacement*, which may be required if the valvular disease progresses. Valve repair obviates the need for protracted, expensive follow-up and provides a durable correction of the lesion. This approach is sensible, however, only if it is certain that valve repair can be performed because insertion of a prosthesis carries unacceptable risk in this low-risk group.

ASYMPTOMATIC PATIENTS WITH LEFT VENTRICULAR DYSFUNCTION. The onset of LV dysfunction in mitral regurgitation may occur without causing symptoms. Early surgery is warranted to prevent muscle dysfunction from becoming severe or irreversible. Whether valve repair or replacement eventually is performed, survival is prolonged to or toward normal if surgery is performed before ejection fraction declines to less than 0.60 or before the left ventricle is unable to contract to an end-systolic dimension of 45 mm. Patients with severe mitral regurgitation should be followed yearly with a history, a physical examination, and an echocardiographic evaluation of LV function. When the patient reports symptoms or echocardiography shows the onset of LV dysfunction, surgery should be undertaken.

ASYMPTOMATIC ELDERLY PATIENTS. Patients older than age 75 years may have poor surgical results, especially if coronary disease is present or if mitral valve replacement rather than repair must be performed. Although elderly patients with symptoms refractory to medical therapy may benefit from surgery, there is little compelling reason to commit elderly *asymptomatic* patients to a mitral valve operation.

MITRAL VALVE PROLAPSE

Mitral valve prolapse occurs when one or both of the mitral valve leaflets prolapses into the left atrium superior to the mitral valve annular plane during systole. The importance of mitral valve prolapse varies from patient to patient. In some cases, prolapse is simply a consequence of normal LV physiology without significant medical impact, whereas in other cases there is severe valvular deformity associated with an increased risk of stroke, arrhythmia, endocarditis, and progression to severe mitral regurgitation. Examples of the former situation are those that produce a small left ventricle (i.e., the Valsalva maneuver or atrial septal defect), in which reduction of ventricular volume causes relative lengthening of the chordae tendineae and subsequent mitral valve prolapse. At the other end of the spectrum, severe redundancy and deformity of the valve, which occurs in myxomatous valve degeneration, increases the risk of the complications noted earlier.

Diagnosis

HISTORY. Most patients with mitral valve prolapse are asymptomatic. In some cases, mitral valve prolapse is associated with a symptom complex, however, including palpitation, syncope, and chest pain. The exact cause-and-effect relationship between the presence of mitral valve prolapse and these symptoms has been difficult to determine. In some cases, chest pain is associated with a positive thallium scintigram indicating the presence of true ischemia despite normal epicardial coronary arteries, perhaps because excessive tension on the papillary muscles increases oxygen consumption and causes ischemia. Palpitation, syncope, and presyncope, when present, are linked to autonomic dysfunction, which seems to be more prevalent in mitral valve prolapse.

PHYSICAL EXAMINATION. On physical examination, the mitral valve prolapse syndrome produces characteristic findings of a midsystolic click and a late systolic murmur. The click occurs when the chordae tendineae are stretched taut by the prolapsing mitral valve in midsystole. As this occurs, the mitral leaflets move past their coaptation point, permit mitral regurgitation, and cause the late systolic murmur. Maneuvers that make the left ventricle smaller, such as the Valsalva maneuver, cause the click to come earlier and the murmur to be more holosystolic and often louder. In some cases of echocardiographically proven mitral valve prolapse, neither the click nor the murmur is present; in other cases, only one of these findings is present.

NONINVASIVE EVALUATION. Echocardiography is useful to prove that prolapse is present, to image the amount of regurgitation and its physiologic effects, and to discern the pathoanatomy of the mitral valve. Although an echocardiogram is not necessary to diagnose prolapse in patients with the classic physical findings, the echocardiogram adds significant prognostic information because it can detect patients who have specifically abnormal valve morphology and in whom most of the complications of the disease occur.

In the 1990s, it became clear that the mitral annulus did not exist in a single plane but had a saddleback shape. Prolapse shown in the four-chamber echocardiographic view should be confirmed in the parasternal long-axis view. Echocardiographic diagnoses made before the understanding that the mitral valve plane was multidimensional (circa 1987) may have been made in error.

Clinical Course

Most patients with mitral valve prolapse have a benign clinical course; even for complication-prone patients with redundant and misshapen mitral leaflets, complications are relatively rare. Approximately 10% of patients with thickened leaflets experience infective endocarditis, stroke, progression to severe mitral regurgitation, or sudden death. The progression to severe mitral regurgitation varies with gender and age, and men are approximately twice as likely to progress as women. By age 50 years, only approximately 1 in 200 men requires surgery to correct mitral regurgitation. By age 70, the risk increases to approximately 3%.

(Rx) Treatment

Because most patients with mitral valve prolapse are asymptomatic, therapy is unnecessary. Patients with mitral valve prolapse and its characteristic murmur should observe standard endocarditis prophylaxis (Chapter 310). Patients with otherwise normal valve leaflets shown to prolapse during echocardiography with no heart murmur do not require endocarditis precautions. Patients with clearly abnormal valves but no murmur fall into a middle category of endocarditis risk in which a firm recommendation about prophylaxis cannot be made. In patients with palpitation and autonomic dysfunction, β-blockers are often effective in relieving symptoms. Low-dose aspirin therapy has been recommended for patients with redundant leaflets because these patients have a slightly increased risk of stroke. No data from large studies are available to support this contention, however. In patients developing severe mitral regurgitation, the therapy is the same as for other causes of mitral regurgitation.

AORTIC REGURGITATION

Etiology

Aortic regurgitation is caused either by abnormalities of the aortic leaflets or by abnormalities of the proximal aortic root. Leaflet abnormalities causing aortic regurgitation include bicuspid aortic valve, infective endocarditis, and rheumatic heart disease; anorexigenic drugs also are implicated. Common aortic root abnormalities that cause aortic regurgitation include Marfan syndrome (Chapter 276), hypertension-induced annuloaortic ectasia, aortic dissection (Chapter 75), syphilis (Chapter 349), ankylosing spondylitis (Chapter 279), and psoriatic arthritis (Chapter 279). Acute aortic regurgitation usually is caused by infectious endocarditis or aortic dissection.

Pathophysiology

As with mitral regurgitation, aortic regurgitation imparts a volume overload on the left ventricle because the left ventricle must pump the forward flow entering from the left atrium and the regurgitant volume returning through the incompetent aortic valve. As with mitral regurgitation, compensation for the volume overload occurs from the development of eccentric cardiac hypertrophy, which increases chamber size and allows the ventricle to pump a greater total stroke volume and a greater forward stroke volume. Ventricular enlargement also allows the left ventricle to accommodate the volume overload at a lower filling pressure. In contrast to mitral regurgitation, in aortic regurgitation the entire stroke volume is ejected into the aorta. Because pulse pressure is proportional to the stroke volume and the elastance of the aorta, the increased stroke volume increases systolic pressure. Systolic hypertension leads to afterload excess, which usually does not occur in mitral regurgitation. Ventricular geometry also differs between mitral and aortic regurgitation because the afterload excess in aortic regurgitation causes a modest element of concentric hypertrophy as well as severe eccentric hypertrophy.

In acute aortic insufficiency, such as might occur in infective endocarditis, severe volume overload of the previously unprepared left ventricle results in a sudden fall in forward output, while precipitously increasing LV filling pressure. It is probably this combination of pathophysiologic factors that leads to rapid decompensation, presumably because the gradient for coronary blood flow is severely diminished, causing ischemia and a progressive deterioration in LV function. In acute aortic insufficiency, reflex vasoconstriction increases peripheral vascular resistance. In compensated chronic aortic insufficiency, vasoconstriction is absent, and vascular resistance may be reduced and contribute to the hyperdynamic circulation observed in these patients.

Clinical Manifestations

The most common symptoms from chronic aortic regurgitation are those of left-sided heart failure, that is, dyspnea on exertion, orthopnea, and fatigue. In acute aortic regurgitation, cardiac output and shock may develop rapidly. The onset of symptoms in chronic aortic regurgitation usually heralds the onset of LV systolic dysfunction. Some patients with symptoms have apparently normal systolic function, however, and symptoms may be attributed to diastolic dysfunction. Other patients may have ventricular dysfunction yet remain asymptomatic.

Angina also may occur in patients with aortic insufficiency but less commonly than in aortic stenosis. The cause of angina in aortic regurgitation is probably multifactorial. Coronary blood flow reserve is reduced in some patients because diastolic runoff into the left ventricle lowers aortic diastolic pressure, while increasing LV diastolic pressure—these two influences lower the driving pressure gradient for flow across the coronary bed. When angina occurs in aortic regurgitation, it may be accompanied by flushing. Other symptoms include carotid artery pain and an unpleasant awareness of the heartbeat.

Diagnosis

PHYSICAL EXAMINATION. Aortic regurgitation produces a myriad of signs because a hyperdynamic, enlarged left ventricle ejects a large stroke volume at high pressure into the systemic circulation. Palpation of the precordium finds a hyperactive apical impulse displaced downward and to the left. S_1 and S_2 are usually normal. S_2 is followed by a diastolic blowing murmur heard best along the left sternal border with the patient sitting upright. In mild disease, the murmur may be short, heard only in the beginning of diastole when the gradient between the aorta and the left ventricle is highest. As the disease worsens, the murmur may persist throughout diastole. A second murmur, a mitral valve rumble, is heard at the LV apex in severe aortic insufficiency. Although the cause is still debated, this Austin Flint murmur is probably produced as the regurgitant jet impinges on the mitral valve and causes it to vibrate.

In chronic aortic regurgitation, the high stroke volume and reduced systemic arterial resistance result in a wide pulse pressure, which may generate a plethora of signs. These include Corrigan's pulse (sharp upstroke and rapid decline of the carotid pulse), de Musset's sign (head bobbing), Duroziez's sign (combined systolic and diastolic bruits created by compression of the femoral artery with the stethoscope), and Quincke's pulse (systolic plethora and diastolic blanching in the nail bed when gentle traction is placed on the nail). Perhaps the most reliable of physical signs indicating severe aortic regurgitation is Hill's sign, an increase in the femoral systolic pressure of 40 mm Hg or more compared with systolic pressure in the brachial artery.

In contrast to chronic aortic insufficiency with its myriad of clinical signs, acute aortic insufficiency may have a subtle presentation. The eccentric hypertrophy, which compensates chronic aortic insufficiency, has not yet had time to develop, and the large total stroke volume responsible for most of the signs of chronic aortic insufficiency is absent. The only clues to the presence of acute aortic insufficiency may be a short diastolic blowing murmur and reduced intensity of S_1. This latter sign occurs because high diastolic LV pressure closes the mitral valve early in diastole (mitral valve preclosure) so that when ventricular systole occurs, only the tricuspid component of S_1 is heard.

NONINVASIVE EVALUATION. The ECG in aortic insufficiency is nonspecific but almost always shows LV hypertrophy. The chest radiograph shows an enlarged heart, often with uncoiling and enlargement of the aortic root.

Echocardiography is the most important noninvasive tool for assessing the severity of aortic insufficiency and its impact on LV geometry and function (Fig. 72–5). During echocardiography, LV end-diastolic dimension, end-systolic dimension, and fractional shortening are determined. Aortic valve anatomy and aortic root anatomy can be assessed and the cause of the aortic regurgitation often can be determined. Color flow Doppler examination of the aortic valve helps quantify the severity of aortic regurgitation by assessing the depth and width to which the diastolic jet penetrates the left ventricle. Another way to assess the severity of aortic regurgitation is the pressure half-time method: Continuous-wave Doppler interrogation of the aortic valve displays the decay of the velocity of retrograde flow across the valve. In mild aortic insufficiency, the gradient across the valve is high throughout diastole, and its rate of decay is slow, producing a long Doppler half-time (the time it takes the velocity to decay from its peak to that value divided by the square root of 2). In severe aortic regurgitation, there is rapid equilibration between pressure in the aorta and pressure in the left ventricle, and the Doppler half-time is short. If mitral valve preclosure is detected in acute aortic insufficiency, urgent surgery is necessary. In cases in which the severity of aortic insufficiency is in doubt, catheterization to perform aortography is useful in resolving the issue.

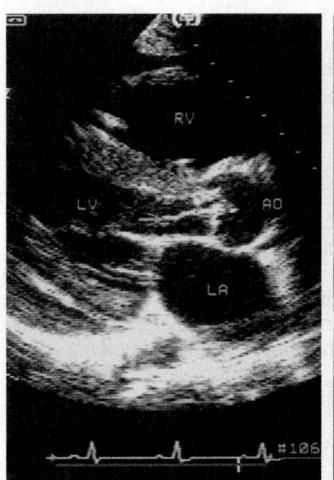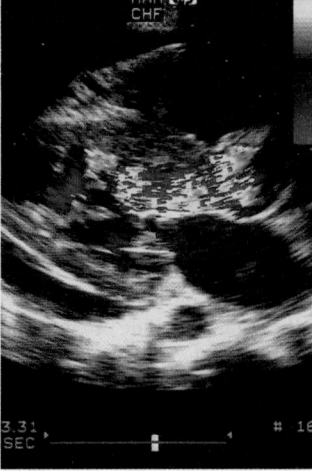

FIGURE 72–5 • Echocardiogram of a patient with aortic regurgitation caused by infectious endocarditis. The left panel shows a linear vegetation (arrow) prolapsing into the left ventricular outflow tract from the aortic valve leaflet in diastole. The right panel is a color flow Doppler exhibiting turbulent blood flow filling the left ventricular tract during diastole. (Courtesy Dr. Anthony DeMaria.)

Treatment

MEDICAL THERAPY

ASYMPTOMATIC PATIENTS WITH NORMAL LEFT VENTRICULAR FUNCTION.
Because aortic regurgitation increases LV afterload, which decreases cardiac efficiency, afterload-reducing drugs are efficacious in the treatment of the disease. Patients who are symptomatic or manifest LV dysfunction should undergo aortic valve surgery. For *asymptomatic* patients with normal LV function, afterload reduction is recommended because it delays or reduces the need for aortic valve surgery without any adverse effects when surgery finally is carried out. Currently the best prognostic data are for nifedipine, but other vasodilators, including angiotensin-converting enzyme inhibitors and hydralazine, also have shown hemodynamic improvement for aortic regurgitation and may prove to be at least equally beneficial.

ACUTE AORTIC REGURGITATION.
When any of the symptoms or signs of heart failure develop, even if mild, medical mortality is high, approaching 75%. Therapy with vasodilators, such as nitroprusside, may help improve the patient's condition before surgery but is not a substitute for surgery. In patients with acute aortic regurgitation caused by bacterial endocarditis (Chapter 310), surgery may be delayed to permit a full or partial course of antibiotics, but persistent, severe aortic regurgitation requires emergency valve replacement. Even when blood cultures have been positive recently and antibiotic therapy has been of brief duration, valve reinfection rate is low, 0 to 10%. Emergent surgery should not be withheld simply because the duration of antibiotic therapy has been brief.

SURGICAL THERAPY

Although some patients may be able to undergo successful aortic valve repair to restore aortic valve competence, most patients require insertion of an aortic valve prosthesis. Patients with advanced symptoms are at increased risk for a suboptimal surgical outcome whether or not they have evidence of LV dysfunction. Patients should undergo aortic valve replacement before symptoms impair lifestyle. Asymptomatic patients who manifest evidence of LV dysfunction benefit from surgery. Because loading conditions differ between aortic and mitral regurgitation, the objective markers for the presence of LV dysfunction also differ. In aortic regurgitation, when ejection fraction is less than 0.55 or end-systolic dimension is greater than 55 mm, postoperative outcome is impaired, presumably because these markers indicate that LV dysfunction has developed. Surgery should occur before these benchmarks are reached.

TRICUSPID REGURGITATION

Etiology

Tricuspid regurgitation is usually secondary to a hemodynamic load on the right ventricle rather than to a structural valve deformity. Diseases that cause pulmonary hypertension, such as chronic obstructive airway disease or intracardiac shunts, lead to RV dilation and subsequent tricuspid regurgitation. Because most of the force that is needed to fill the left ventricle is provided by the right ventricle, LV dysfunction leading to elevated LV filling pressure also places the right ventricle under a hemodynamic load and eventually can lead to RV failure and tricuspid regurgitation. In some instances, tricuspid regurgitation may be caused by pathology of the valve itself. The most common cause of primary tricuspid regurgitation is infective endocarditis, usually stemming from drug abuse and unsterile injections. Other causes include carcinoid syndrome, rheumatic involvement of the tricuspid valve, myxomatous degeneration, RV infarction, and mishaps during endomyocardial biopsy.

Diagnosis

The symptoms of tricuspid regurgitation are those of right-sided heart failure, including ascites, edema, and occasionally right upper quadrant pain. On physical examination, tricuspid regurgitation produces jugular venous distention accentuated by a large v wave as blood is regurgitated into the right atrium during systole. Regurgitation into the hepatic veins causes hepatic enlargement and liver pulsation. RV

enlargement is detected as a parasternal lift. Ascites and edema are common.

The definitive diagnosis of tricuspid regurgitation is made during echocardiography. Doppler interrogation of the tricuspid valve shows systolic disturbance of the right atrial blood pool. Echocardiography also can be used to determine the severity of pulmonary hypertension, to measure RV dilation, and to assess whether the valve itself is intrinsically normal or abnormal.

 Treatment

The therapy for secondary tricuspid regurgitation usually is aimed at the cause of the lesion. If LV failure has been responsible for RV failure and tricuspid regurgitation, the standard therapy for improving LV failure (Chapter 56) lowers LV filling pressure, reduces secondary pulmonary hypertension, relieves some of the hemodynamic burden of the right ventricle, and partially restores tricuspid valve competence. If pulmonary disease is the primary cause, therapy is directed toward improving lung function. Vasodilators, so useful in the treatment of left-sided heart failure, are often ineffective in treating pulmonary hypertension itself. Medical therapy directed at tricuspid regurgitation itself usually is limited to diuretic use.

Surgical intervention for the tricuspid valve is rarely entertained in isolation. However, if other cardiac surgery is planned in a patient with severe tricuspid regurgitation, ring annuloplasty or tricuspid valve repair often is attempted to ensure postoperative tricuspid competence. Tricuspid valve replacement is often not well tolerated and is performed rarely now except when severe deformity, as often seen in endocarditis or carcinoid disease, precludes valve repair.

PULMONIC STENOSIS

Pulmonic stenosis is a congenital disease resulting from fusion of the pulmonic valve cusps (Chapter 65). It usually is detected and corrected during childhood, but occasionally cases are diagnosed for the first time in adulthood. Symptoms of pulmonic stenosis include angina and syncope. Occasionally, patients develop symptoms of right-sided heart failure. During physical examination, the uncalcified valve in pulmonic stenosis produces an early systolic ejection click on opening. During inspiration, the click diminishes or disappears because increased flow into the right side of the heart during inspiration partially opens the pulmonic valve in diastole so that systole causes less of an opening sound. The click is followed by a systolic ejection murmur, which radiates to the base of the heart. If the transvalvular gradient is severe, RV hypertrophy develops and produces a parasternal lift.

The diagnosis of pulmonic stenosis is confirmed by echocardiography, which quantifies the transvalvular gradient and the degree of RV hypertrophy and dysfunction.

Treatment

In asymptomatic patients with a gradient of less than 25 mm Hg, no therapy is required. If symptoms develop or the gradient exceeds 50 mm Hg, balloon commissurotomy is effective in reducing the gradient and relieving symptoms.

POSTOPERATIVE CARE OF PATIENTS WITH SUBSTITUTE HEART VALVES

Different types of prosthetic valves (Fig. 72–6) have different advantages and disadvantages (Table 72–2). After a prosthetic valve has been inserted, a baseline echocardiogram should be obtained to provide a reference point in the event valve dysfunction is suspected at a later date. Echocardiography does not need to be repeated unless there is a change in clinical status or in physical findings. The major causes of valve dysfunction are infectious endocarditis, clot, and valve degeneration. Dysfunction is manifested most commonly by valvular regurgitation, but valvular stenosis also can occur with clot, vegetations, or degeneration, especially degeneration of a bioprosthesis.

Whenever a patient with a prosthetic heart valve develops a temperature greater than 100° F, endocarditis must be excluded by blood

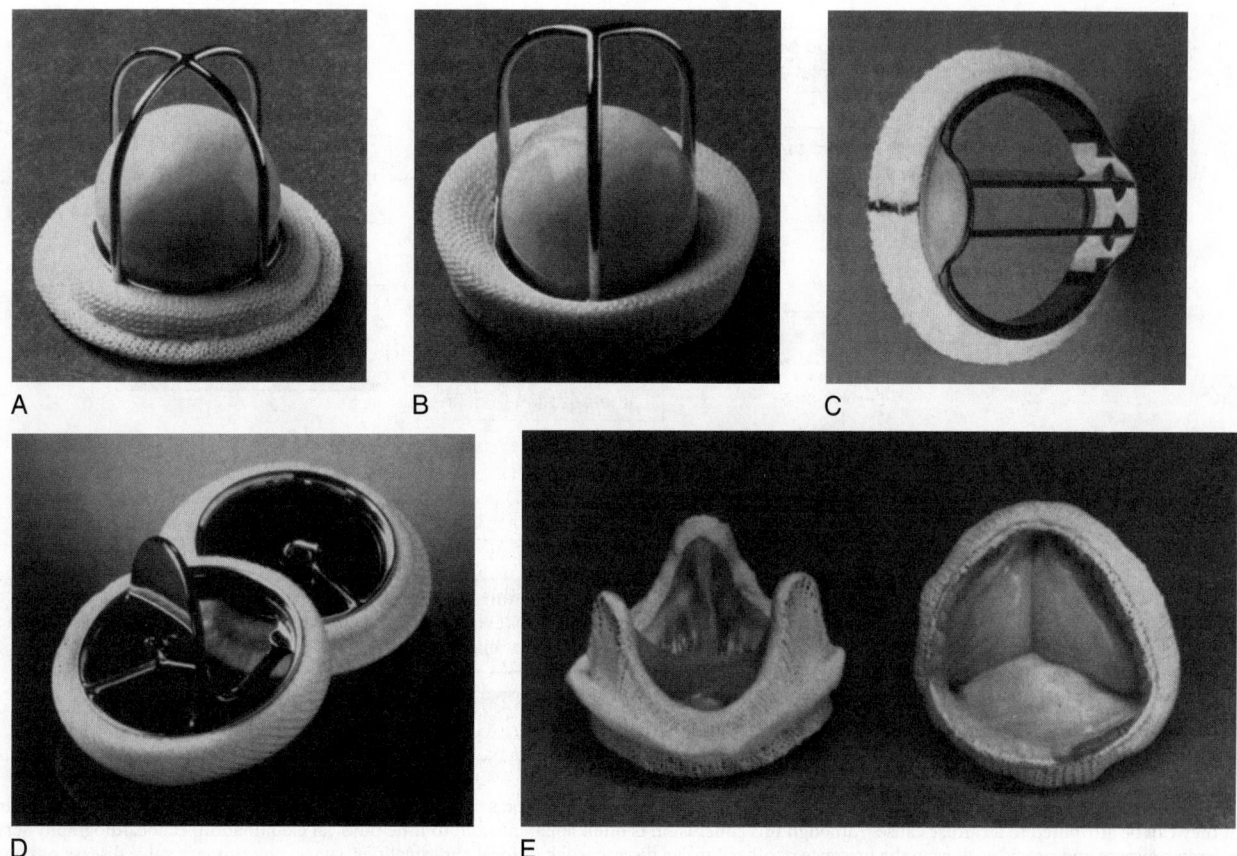

FIGURE 72–6 • Different types of commonly used prosthetic valves. *A,* Starr-Edwards caged ball mitral prosthesis. *B,* Starr-Edwards aortic prosthesis. *C,* St. Jude Medical bileaflet prosthesis. *D,* Medtronic-Hall tilting disc valve. *E,* Carpentier-Edwards bioprosthesis. (From Wernly JA, Crawford MH: Choosing a prosthetic heart valve. Cardiol Clin 1991;9:329–338.)

Table 72–2 • ADVANTAGES AND DISADVANTAGES OF SUBSTITUTE CARDIAC VALVES

TYPE OF VALVE	ADVANTAGES	DISADVANTAGES
Bioprosthesis (Carpentier-Edwards, Hancock)	Avoid anticoagulation in patients with sinus rhythm	Durability limited to 10–15 yr Relatively stenotic
Mechanical valves (St. Jude, Medtronic-Hall, Starr-Edwards)	Good flow characteristics in small sizes Durable	Require anticoagulation
Homografts and autografts	Anticoagulation not required Durability increased over that of bioprostheses	Surgical implantation technically demanding

culture; for fever with signs of sepsis, broad-spectrum antibiotics must be begun while awaiting culture results. For patients with bioprosthetic valves, mechanical prostheses, and homografts, endocarditis prophylaxis should be used at the time of procedures that have a high risk for bacteremia (Chapter 310). Whether prophylaxis is necessary for pulmonary autografts is currently unclear, but physicians usually prescribe prophylaxis for these patients.

By 15 years after surgery, a randomized trial showed no differences in mortality in patients with mechanical valves versus tissue valves in the mitral position. In the aortic position, all-cause mortality was worse for bioprostheses (79%) than for mechanical prostheses (66%), with much of the increased mortality related to a higher rate of bioprosthetic valve failure.

All patients with a mechanical heart valve require anticoagulation. Recommended INR values range from 2.0 for the young normotensive patient in sinus rhythm with an aortic valve prosthesis to 3.5 for the patient with atrial fibrillation and a mitral valve prosthesis. Aspirin, 325 mg, is recommended in addition to warfarin to reduce the risk of valve thrombosis in patients who have mechanical prosthetic valves that are at higher risk for thromboembolic complications.

Grade A

1. Ben Farhat M, Ayari M, Maatouk F, et al: Percutaneous balloon versus surgical closed and open mitral commissurotomy: Seven-year follow-up results of a randomized trial. Circulation 1998;97:245–250.
2. Hammermeister K, Sethi GK, Henderson WG, et al: Outcomes 15 years after valve replacement with a mechanical versus a bioprosthetic valve: Final report of the Veterans Affairs randomized trial. J Am Coll Cardiol 2000;36:1152–1158.

SUGGESTED READINGS

Babu AN, Kymes SM, Carpenter Fryer SM: Eponyms and the diagnosis of aortic regurgitation: What says the evidence? Ann Intern Med 2003;138:736–742. *Eponymous signs of aortic regurgitation are insensitive and nonspecific.*

Bonow RO, Carabello B, de Leon AC Jr, et al: Guidelines for the management of patients with valvular heart disease: Executive summary. A report of the American College of Cardiology/American Heart Association Task Force on Practice Guidelines (Committee on Management of Patients with Valvular Heart Disease). Circulation 1998;98:1949–1984. *Consensus guidelines that provide a useful approach to common valvular abnormalities.*

Carabello BA: Evaluation and management of patients with aortic stenosis. Circulation 2002;105:1746–1750. *A comprehensive overview.*

Otto CM: Clinical evaluation and management of chronic mitral regurgitation. N Engl J Med 2001;345:740–746. *An up-to-date review with practical recommendations.*

Rahimtoola SH: Choice of prosthetic heart valve for adult patients. J Am Coll Cardiol 2003;41:893–904. *Argues that bioprostheses generally are the preferred aortic valve in patients ≥60 to 65 years of age and mitral valve in patients ≥65 to 70 years of age, and that mechanical valves are generally preferred in younger patients.*

Rahimtoola SH, Durairaj A, Mehra A, et al: Current evaluation and management of patients with mitral stenosis. Circulation 2002;106:1183–1188. *A comprehensive review.*

73 DISEASES OF THE MYOCARDIUM

Lynne Warner Stevenson

Cardiomyopathy, which means heart muscle disease, is a term used to distinguish disorders originating in the myocardium from those in which myocardial dysfunction results from other cardiovascular disease. Less specifically, however, the term *ischemic cardiomyopathy*

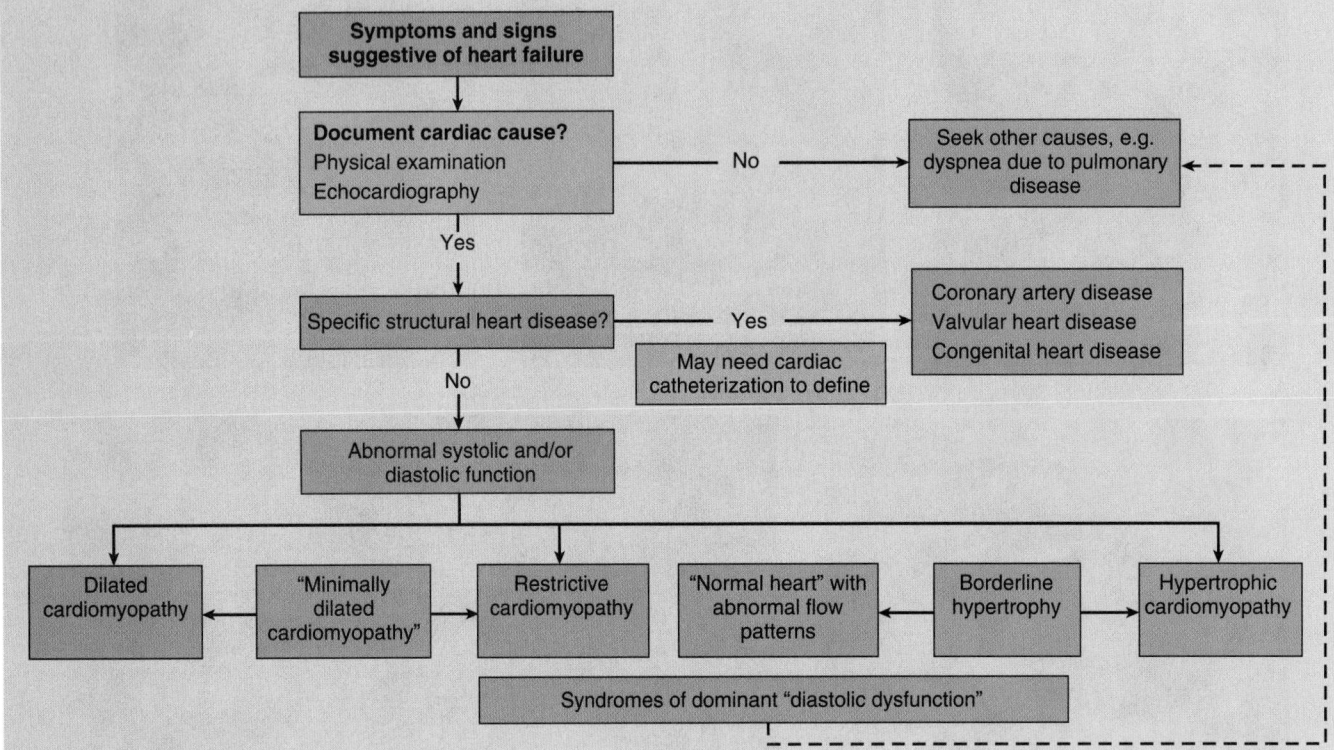

FIGURE 73–1 • Initial approach to classification of cardiomyopathy. The evaluation of symptoms or signs consistent with heart failure first includes confirmation that they can be attributed to a cardiac cause. Although this conclusion is often apparent from routine physical examination, echocardiography serves to confirm cardiac disease and provides clues to the presence of other cardiac disease, such as focal abnormalities, suggesting primary valve disease or congenital heart disease. Having excluded these conditions, cardiomyopathy is generally considered to be dilated, restrictive, or hypertrophic, as shown in Figure 73–2. Patients with apparently normal cardiac structure and contraction are occasionally found to demonstrate abnormal intracardiac flow patterns consistent with diastolic dysfunction but should also be evaluated carefully for other causes of their symptoms. Most patients with so-called diastolic dysfunction also demonstrate at least borderline criteria for left ventricular hypertrophy, frequently in the setting of chronic hypertension and diabetes. A moderately decreased ejection fraction without marked dilation or a pattern of restrictive cardiomyopathy is sometimes referred to as "minimally dilated cardiomyopathy," which may represent either a distinct entity or a transition between acute and chronic disease.

has been used to describe the diffuse dilation and hypocontractility that can result from severe coronary artery disease with or without antecedent clinical myocardial infarctions. The broad term *nonischemic cardiomyopathy* is a convenient descriptor for patients who have heart failure (Chapters 55 and 56) without coronary artery disease. This chapter is devoted to specific heart muscle disease, estimated to account for approximately 5 to 10% of the 4 million to 5 million patients in the United States diagnosed with heart failure. The types of cardiomyopathy are defined by ventricular dimensions and by systolic and diastolic function: dilated, restrictive, and hypertrophic (Fig. 73–1).

The distinct entity of arrhythmogenic right ventricular dysplasia (Chapter 60) can occur with or without concomitant left ventricular dysfunction. There is increasing recognition of the syndrome of heart failure with preserved systolic function in the elderly.

DILATED CARDIOMYOPATHY

Dilated cardiomyopathy is characterized by increased left ventricular or biventricular dimensions with decreased left ventricular ejection fraction (Table 73–1). Myocardial contractility is severely

Table 73–1 • PROFILES OF SYMPTOMATIC CARDIOMYOPATHY

	DILATED	RESTRICTIVE	HYPERTROPHIC
Ejection fraction (normal > 55%)	<30%	25–50%	>60%
Left ventricular diastolic dimension (normal < 55 mm)	≥60 mm	<60 mm	Often decreased
Left ventricular wall thickness	Decreased	Normal or increased	Markedly increased
Atrial size	Increased	Increased; may be massive	Increased
Valvular regurgitation	Mitral first during decompensation; tricuspid regurgitation in late stages	Frequent mitral and tricuspid regurgitation, rarely severe	Mitral regurgitation
Common first symptoms*	Exertional intolerance	Exertional intolerance, fluid retention	Exertional intolerance; may have chest pain
Congestive symptoms*	Left before right, except right prominent in young adults	Right often exceeds left	Primary exertional dyspnea
Risk for arrhythmia	Ventricular tachyarrhythmias; conduction block in Chagas' disease, giant cell myocarditis, and some families; atrial fibrillation	Ventricular tachyarrhythmias uncommon except in sarcoidosis; conduction block in sarcoidosis and amyloidosis; atrial fibrillation	Ventricular tachyarrhythmias, atrial fibrillation

*Left-sided symptoms of pulmonary congestion: dyspnea on exertion, orthopnea, paroxysmal nocturnal dyspnea. Right-sided symptoms of systemic venous congestion: discomfort on bending, hepatic and abdominal distention, peripheral edema.

impaired and labeled "systolic failure." Abnormalities in diastolic function often reflect excessive volume overload and are generally less marked than in restrictive or hypertrophic cardiomyopathy. At the time of diagnosis, half of the patients are younger than 65 years and as many as one fourth may have New York Heart Association class III or IV symptoms. Evidence from population screening suggests a higher frequency of asymptomatic disease than previously recognized.

Etiology

Dilated cardiomyopathy has many causes (Table 73–2). A brief primary injury such as toxic exposure may be fatal to some myocytes, after which the increased burden of pressure and volume stimulates hypertrophy in the surviving myocytes. This hypertrophy initially preserves global function but can eventually lead to progressive functional impairment. One mechanism leading to progressive deterioration late after an initial injury may be the triggering of programmed cell death, known as *apoptosis*. Some chronic exposures, such as to ethanol (Chapter 17), may reversibly impair global contractility without directly causing cell injury but cause irreversible dysfunction if continued chronically. Inflammatory myocarditis may combine

Table 73–2 • MAJOR CAUSES OF DILATED CARDIOMYOPATHY

Inflammatory
Infectious myocarditis
  Viral
  Rickettsial
  Bacterial
  Mycobacterial
  Spirochetal
  Parasitic
  Fungal
Noninfectious
  Collagen vascular disease
  Peripartum cardiomyopathy
  Hypersensitivity myocarditis
  Transplant rejection
Granulomatous inflammatory disease
  Sarcoidosis
  Giant cell myocarditis

Toxic
Alcohol
Chemotherapeutic agents: doxorubicin, cyclophosphamide, interferon
Antibiotics: emetine, chloroquine, antimony compounds
Heavy metals: lead, mercury
Occupational exposure: hydrocarbons, arsenicals
Catecholamines: amphetamines, cocaine

Metabolic
Nutritional deficiencies: thiamine, selenium, carnitine
Electrolyte deficiencies: calcium, phosphate, magnesium
Endocrinopathy: thyroid disease, diabetes, pheochromocytoma
Obesity

Familial
Skeletal myopathy with cardiac involvement
  Duchenne's dystrophy
  Becker's dystrophy
  Emery-Dreifuss dystrophy
  Limb-girdle dystrophy
Cardiomyopathy
  X-linked cardiomyopathy due to dystrophin promoter defect
  Lamin mutations
Mitrochondrial myopathy (e.g., Kearns-Sayre syndrome)
Arrhythmogenic right ventricular dysplasia
Associated with other systemic diseases
Susceptibility to immune-mediated myocarditis

Overlap with Restrictive Cardiomyopathy
Hemochromatosis
Amyloidosis
Sarcoidosis

Idiopathic
Primary left ventricular or biventricular cardiomyopathy
Arrhythmogenic right ventricular dysplasia

irreversible cell death with reversible depression from inflammatory mediators such as cytokines. Many injuries also affect the collagen scaffolding of the myocardium, influencing stiffness and the potential for ventricular dilation. Genetic abnormalities in the cytoskeletal proteins compromise cell membrane integrity and intercellular communication in many of the familial cardiomyopathies. Most cardiomyopathies reflect the sum of irrevocable myocyte loss plus functional impairment, some of which may be reversible, in the remaining myocardium that continues to survive under stress. For some patients, identification of a specific etiology determines details of diagnosis, therapy, and prognosis as described later, but the approach to most patients follows the principles for heart failure in general (Chapter 56).

MYOCARDITIS

Myocarditis is an inflammatory process involving the myocardium. The most common agents implicated are infectious organisms, which can cause myocardial injury through direct invasion, production of toxin, and induction of chronic inflammatory responses that are nonspecific or directed against specific myocardial proteins.

VIRAL MYOCARDITIS. Most of our conception of viral myocarditis derives from murine animal models in which initial viral replication can be exacerbated by exercise and immunosuppression. Subsequently, active replication ceases, although some viral DNA may still be detectable, and multiple cellular and antibody responses have been implicated in later myocardial dysfunction. Infected animals may die, recover, or develop dilated hearts with areas of fibrosis. Our understanding of the process in humans is limited by lack of unambiguous criteria for diagnosis. Viruses are frequently suspected but rarely isolated as the direct cause of myocarditis in humans. *Viral myocarditis* may be suspected from the clinical picture of recent febrile illness, often with prominent myalgias, followed by onset of cardiac symptoms. Elevated creatine kinase, with or without an elevated MB fraction, supports the diagnosis because many cardiotropic infections also affect skeletal muscle. Increasing viral titers confirm recent infection. Troponin levels also may be elevated. Patients may present with angina-type chest pain or arrhythmias. Although coxsackieviruses and echoviruses have often been invoked, more recent experience implicates adenoviruses and influenza viruses as well. The strict histologic definition of myocarditis requires extensive lymphocyte infiltration with adjacent myocyte necrosis, which is identified in fewer than 10 to 20% of patients who undergo biopsy within the first few weeks of typical symptoms. Biopsy specimens obtained from patients without recent onset of symptoms frequently show scattered lymphocytes but meet the criteria for myocarditis in fewer than 5% of cases. Some patients with strong clinical history for recent postviral myocarditis have extensive edema without lymphocytic infiltrates. The assumption that many cases of human cardiomyopathy represent sequelae of previous viral myocarditis has been strengthened by recent identification in cardiomyopathy specimens of increased frequency of coxsackievirus and adenovirus DNA (compared with control myocardial samples). These viruses share a common cell surface receptor on myocardial cells. Even with a history of recent viral symptoms, however, primary causation is difficult to demonstrate. Most systemic viral infections can further depress impaired myocardial function at least transiently, owing to induction of cytokines. Many cases of heart failure presumed to be acute may represent chronic occult left ventricular dysfunction exacerbated by acute viral illness.

The general prognosis of truly "new-onset" heart failure attributed to recent viral infection is major improvement in left ventricular function in up to half of patients, which can occur whether or not an initial biopsy met the criteria for myocarditis. In some patients, ejection fraction returns to normal with normal clinical function, whereas others may demonstrate residual diastolic dysfunction limiting cardiac reserve and exercise capacity. Treatment of biopsy-proven acute myocarditis, presumed to be postviral, has included azathioprine, prednisone, and cyclosporine, but there has been no proven benefit in controlled trials[1] and thus no mandate to perform endomyocardial biopsy to identify myocarditis. The rationale for immunosuppressive therapy in part reflects the dramatic response of transplant rejection, which has equivalent histology, and of anecdotal cases of postviral myocarditis that respond to immunosuppression, with later relapse. A common current approach to the patient with recent symptoms is to defer biopsy and observe the patient closely during treatment of heart failure. An exception would be the patient in whom

Cardiovascular Disease

tachyarrhythmias or conduction disturbances complicate newly diagnosed heart failure, raising the possibility of giant cell myocarditis or sarcoidosis, which might be diagnosed on biopsy (as described later). Activity is restricted severely for an arbitrary duration of about the first 3 months, with restriction of vigorous exercise for at least 6 months. If deterioration continues during the months after referral, the prognosis for recovery becomes poor and biopsy may then be considered, with the intent to treat a patient with positive findings with a brief trial of immunosuppression in the hopes of averting the need for cardiac transplantation.

Occasionally, acute viral myocarditis may present over a few days with a "fulminant" picture, characterized by fevers and often by compromise of hepatic and renal as well as cardiac function. Such patients are assumed to be undergoing active viral replication, during which immunosuppression would be deleterious. On rare occasions, it has been necessary to support the patient with mechanical ventricular assist devices in hopes of spontaneous resolution, which occurs frequently, or until cardiac transplantation (Chapter 80) if no recovery is apparent after several weeks. Biopsy, which could be complicated by the coagulopathy that frequently accompanies the acute syndrome, may show severe edema with or without dramatic lymphocyte infiltration but is generally deferred in fulminant myocarditis except as obtained at the time of assist device placement.

Cardiomyopathy defined by echocardiographic abnormalities occurs in 10 to 40% of patients clinically infected with human immunodeficiency virus (HIV) (Chapter 420). Lymphocytic myocarditis has been found in up to 50% of autopsied hearts. The causative role of HIV is difficult to isolate from the contribution of coinfecting organisms such as cytomegalovirus and related cytokine secretion. Antiviral therapy itself has also been implicated in depressed systolic function. The role of secondary factors is supported by the frequent improvement observed in impaired ventricular function. Detection of HIV particles in myocytes, however, supports a direct causation. Pericardial effusions as well as myocarditis may occur.

OTHER INFECTIONS CAUSING MYOCARDITIS. Numerous infectious agents have been associated with myocarditis (see Table 73–2). *Chagas' disease* (Chapter 394), due to infection with *Trypanosoma cruzi*, carried by the reduviid bug, affects up to 15% of the rural population in South America and is also common in Central America, occurring rarely elsewhere in emigrants or others exposed to emigrating reduviid bugs. The acute tissue-invasive phase can present as myocarditis but is usually silent. Subsequent progression of myocardial disease occurs over years, with a predilection to develop apical aneurysms, right bundle branch block, and other arrhythmias. Destruction of parasympathetic ganglia may contribute to cardiac dysfunction as well as to impaired gastrointestinal motility. The chronic process has been attributed to a triggered autoimmune reaction, but frequent eruption of a generalized trypanosomal infection during immunosuppression after transplantation for chronic Chagas' disease suggests continued infection. Serologic diagnosis is made by the complement-fixation (Machado-Guerreiro) test and by immunofluorescent and immunosorbent assays. Antiparasitic agents such as nifurtimox and benzimidazole reduce parasitemia, but benefit in late phase disease is not established. Implantable defibrillator-pacemakers may decrease the chance of sudden death from conduction block or tachyarrhythmias. Once patients have developed symptomatic heart failure, the 5-year survival rate is 20%.

Toxoplasmosis (Chapter 396) can cause myocarditis, with intermittent rupture of cysts in the myocardium leading to atypical chest pain, arrhythmias, pericarditis, and symptomatic heart failure. The endomyocardial biopsy may show focal lymphocytic infiltration and, rarely, a fortuitous cyst. Diagnosis is made from antibody titers. Therapy is with pyrimethamine and sulfadiazine, on which relapses are common.

Lyme carditis (Chapter 352) classically refers to presentation with conduction system abnormalities due to infection with *Borrelia burgdorferi*, diagnosed serologically. However, there have been isolated cases of heart failure attributed to this infection.

NONINFECTIOUS MYOCARDITIS. Myocardial inflammation may occur without preceding infection. It can be associated with systemic inflammatory disorders such as polymyositis (Chapter 283) or systemic lupus erythematosus (Chapter 280), although pericarditis and coronary artery vasculitis are more common. Hypersensitivity reactions, particularly to drugs, can cause myocarditis characterized by infiltration of eosinophils in addition to lymphocytes. Such hypersensitivity is frequently unsuspected and may complicate cardiomyopathy of other causes; it may be suspected from peripheral eosinophilia and confirmed by endomyocardial biopsy. Response to withdrawal of the offending agent and to corticosteroid therapy is often seen.

Rejection after cardiac transplantation is the paradigm for lymphocyte-mediated myocarditis (Chapter 80). Lessons derived from this "model" include (1) the frequent and rapid reversibility of myocardial depression during immunosuppression; (2) the potential importance of noncellular mediators such as antibodies and cytokines even when cellular infiltration is mild or absent; and (3) the association between chronic immune stimulation and coronary vascular disease. The average transplant recipient experiences one to two episodes of rejection requiring enhanced immunosuppression. Only 10% of rejection episodes cause clinical compromise, and 95% of all episodes resolve.

Heart failure developing during the last month of pregnancy and first 5 months postpartum is termed *peripartum cardiomyopathy* when there is no evidence of preexisting cardiac disease (Chapter 253). The frequency is between 1 in 3,000 and 1 in 15,000 deliveries, with increased risk for mothers with older age, increased parity, twins, malnutrition, tocolytic therapy, toxemia, or hypertension. Lymphocytic myocarditis has been found in 30 to 50% of biopsy specimens, suggesting an immune component postulated to be cross reactivity between uterine and cardiac myocyte proteins or an enhanced susceptibility to viral myocarditis. Presentation is usually with orthopnea and excessive dyspnea on minimal exertion, most often within the first weeks after delivery when excess volume of pregnancy would normally be mobilized. The major differential diagnosis is of preexisting cardiac disease aggravated by pregnancy. The prognosis of peripartum cardiomyopathy is for improvement to normal or near-normal ejection fraction during the next 6 months in more than half of patients. Diuretics should be used as needed to facilitate postpartum diuresis. Discontinuation of breast feeding, which requires vigorous hydration, is often recommended. It is not known whether therapy with angiotensin-converting enzyme inhibitors improves the likelihood of recovery.

GRANULOMATOUS DISEASE. Although considered to be distinct diseases, cardiac sarcoidosis and giant cell myocarditis are both characterized by granulomatous infiltration, ventricular arrhythmias, and conduction block. In addition, both infectious and noninfectious immune causes have been suggested for each.

Sarcoidosis is a multisystem granulomatous disease that often presents in young adults and is more common in African Americans (Chapter 91). Although cardiac involvement is found in up to half of autopsies, clinical cardiac involvement occurs in fewer than 10% of patients, who can present with ventricular tachyarrhythmias, or less often with heart failure and reduced left ventricular ejection fraction. There is often less initial ventricular dilation with sarcoidosis than with other dilated cardiomyopathy, so it may be present as either a dilated or restrictive cardiomyopathy. Biopsy diagnosis of sarcoidosis from extracardiac sites is often adequate for the diagnosis in a patient with typical cardiac abnormalities. Gallium scan may be useful to demonstrate cardiac inflammation. Cardiac biopsy may show granulomas (Fig. 73–2); however, because of the focal distribution of the lesions, the specimens obtained are frequently nondiagnostic.

Immunosuppression with corticosteroids has been associated with improvement of arrhythmias, although implantable defibrillators are generally indicated for significant ventricular arrhythmias. Additional immunosuppressive agents have occasionally been added. Moderate left ventricular dysfunction may also improve with immunosuppressive therapy, although severe heart failure due to sarcoidosis may worsen rapidly, regardless of therapy. Therapy leads granulomas to "resolve" into fibrosis, sometimes forming ventricular aneurysms that may be more common after corticosteroid therapy.

Giant cell myocarditis accounts for 10 to 20% of biopsy-positive cases of myocarditis. Onset is usually rapid, with chest pain, fever, and hemodynamic compromise. There is a higher incidence of ventricular tachycardia and atrioventricular block than in lymphocytic myocarditis. Giant cell myocarditis has been associated with thymomas, thyroiditis, pernicious anemia, and systemic lupus erythematosus. The rapid time course and diffuse histology of the disease suggest that it is distinct from sarcoidosis, although some believe that it may be related. Immunosuppression is frequently used but does not appear to improve the clinical course, which is usually one of rapid deterioration and death from failure and refractory ventricular tachyarrhythmias.

When ventricular tachyarrhythmias are a major feature of new-onset heart failure, particularly in a young person, endomyocardial

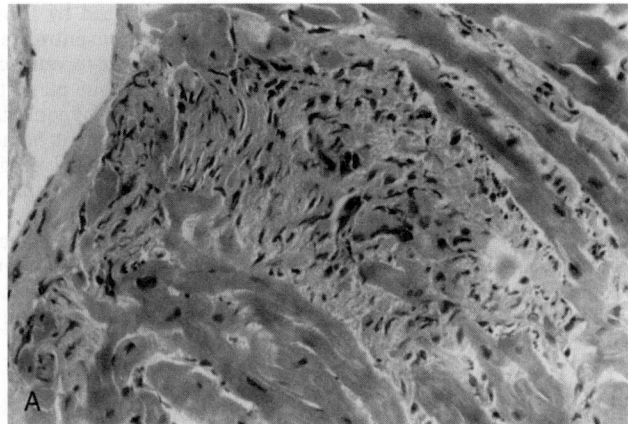
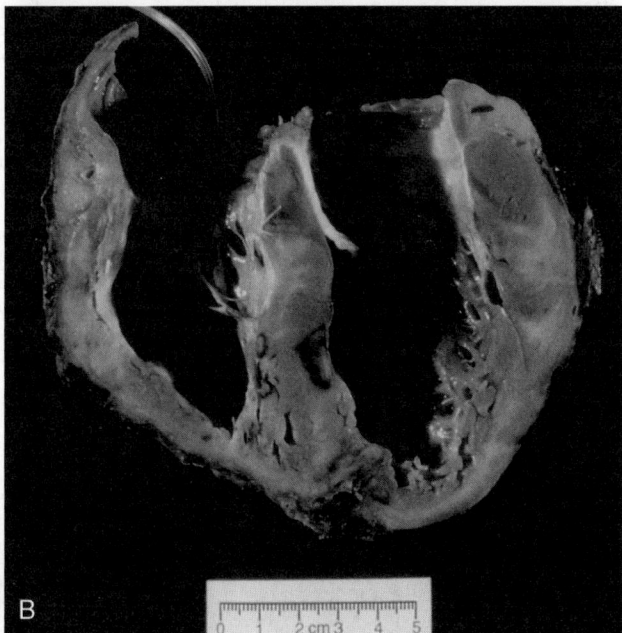

FIGURE 73-2 • *A,* Endomyocardial biopsy specimen from a patient with asymptomatic pulmonary sarcoidosis who presented with syncope and new heart failure. Shown is a large granuloma with slightly more active inflammation than the usual noncaseating sarcoid granuloma. *B,* Gross specimen from the same patient who had been treated with corticosteroid therapy for sarcoidosis, showing the heart removed 4 months later at the time of cardiac transplantation. Histologic examination revealed no further evidence of active inflammation, which was replaced by numerous areas of fibrosis (white areas on the gross specimen). The dark area on the septum is a site where radiofrequency ablation had been performed at one of the multiple foci of ventricular tachycardia. (*A* and *B,* Courtesy of Dr. Gayle Winters, Department of Pathology, Brigham and Women's Hospital, Boston, MA.)

biopsy is generally indicated to determine whether granulomatous inflammation is present, even though the more likely diagnosis will be a negative biopsy or lymphocytic myocarditis. If granulomatous inflammation is severe and accompanied by clinical decompensation and a left ventricular ejection fraction less than 20 to 25%, transplantation should be considered early in patients with otherwise good noncardiac function, whether the diagnosis appears to be sarcoidosis or giant cell myocarditis.

HYPERSENSITIVITY MYOCARDITIS. A variety of drug allergies may cause hypersensitivity myocarditis, characterized by myocardial infiltration of lymphocytes and mononuclear cells, of which a greater proportion are eosinophils than seen in other myocarditides. Peripheral eosinophilia is common. Most agents implicated are antibiotics, but anticonvulsants, thiazides, spironolactone, indomethacin, and methyldopa are also among the drugs cited. In patients undergoing cardiac transplantation after prolonged therapy with dobutamine, eosinophilic myocarditis has been seen in 10 to 15% of explanted hearts, perhaps contributing to late decompensation after transplant listing.

TOXIC CAUSES OF CARDIOMYOPATHY

Many substances have been reported to cause acute cardiac injury or chronic cardiomyopathy. In the United States, *excess alcohol consumption* (Chapter 17) contributes to more than 10% of cases of heart failure. Alcohol and its direct metabolite acetaldehyde are direct cardiotoxins acutely and chronically. Ethanol can contribute to heart failure with another primary cause, such as coronary artery disease. This myocardial depression is initially reversible but, if sustained, can lead to irreversible injury characterized histologically by vacuolization, mitochondrial abnormalities, and fibrosis. Even in chronic stages, however, the heart failure represents a sum of reversible and irreversible depression. The amount of alcohol necessary to produce symptomatic cardiomyopathy in susceptible individuals is not known but has been estimated to be six drinks (about 4 oz of pure ethanol) a day for 5 to 10 years. Frequent binging without heavy daily consumption may also be sufficient. Alcoholic cardiomyopathy can develop in patients without social evidence of an alcohol problem. It is crucial to convince them of the value of abstention, which leads to improvement in at least half of patients with severe symptoms, some of whom normalize left ventricular ejection fraction. Patients with other causes of heart failure should also limit alcohol consumption.

CHEMOTHERAPY AND CARDIOMYOPATHY

Doxorubicin (Adriamycin) cardiotoxicity (Chapter 191) causes characteristic histologic changes on endomyocardial biopsy, with vacuolar degeneration and myofibrillar loss. Potential mechanisms of cardiotoxicity include free radical formation, release of histamines and catecholamines, and effects on mitochondrial function and nucleic acid synthesis. Between 5 and 10% of patients receiving at least $450\,mg/m^2$ of body surface area develop overt heart failure, but more than half of patients receiving multiple courses have a 10% decline in resting ejection fraction. Patients with higher doses and lower baseline ejection fractions have a higher risk for clinical heart failure, which is more likely when doxorubicin is combined with radiation. Presentation with heart failure may occur several years after anthracycline exposure. Patients with a history of doxorubicin therapy may be particularly susceptible to a superimposed insult, such as cardiac ischemia, alcohol, or viral infection, and may improve if the new insult is relieved. Clinical status may also improve with supportive hemodynamic therapy to reduce filling pressures and systemic vascular resistance when elevated, even though the heart is often relatively nondilated. Patients who have received anthracyclines in the prepubertal period without apparent cardiotoxicity may develop cardiac failure in young adulthood, in which there appears to be chronic loss of myofibrils within the myocytes. The dysfunction may continue to progress, with 63% of pediatric patients who have received at least $500\,mg/m^2$ having some cardiac dysfunction detected after 10 years.

Cyclophosphamide (Chapter 191) has been associated with more acute cardiac dysfunction during therapy or the first few weeks, frequently with decreased electrocardiographic voltage. Pericarditis with effusion has been seen, and increased left ventricular mass has been attributed to hemorrhagic necrosis. Ifosfamide is a newer, similar compound that can cause acute severe heart failure and malignant ventricular arrhythmias. Death from cardiogenic shock and recovery of normal left ventricular function have both been reported. 5-Fluorouracil has been implicated rarely in coronary artery spasm and depressed left ventricular contractility. The new agent trastuzumab (Herceptin) has been associated with increased incidence of heart failure, particularly in patients who have received previous chemotherapy for breast cancer.

Interferon-α has been used to treat malignancies, HIV infection, and chronic hepatitis. Initial administration may be associated with hypotension and arrhythmias in up to 10% of patients. Heart failure has occurred occasionally and may be reversible after drug discontinuation. Another cytokine, interleukin-2, has been associated rarely with cardiotoxicity.

METABOLIC CAUSES

Cardiomyopathy has been associated with *catecholamine excess* (Chapter 241), which may injure the heart by compromising the coronary microcirculation but also through direct toxic effects on myocytes exposed to excessive stimulation and calcium loading. Pheochromocytoma can cause a reversible cardiomyopathy. *Cocaine*

(Chapter 30), which leads to increased synaptic concentrations of catecholamines through inhibition of re-uptake at nerve terminals, can cause chronic cardiomyopathy as well as acute coronary syndromes. Amphetamines have also been implicated.

Nutritional deficiencies (Chapter 231) are not commonly implicated in cardiomyopathy in developed Western countries. Thiamine deficiency can lead to beriberi heart disease, which is initially a vasodilated state with high cardiac output, later deteriorating to low output. Thiamine deficiency can result from poor nutrition or alcoholism but has also been reported in teenagers with diets dominated by processed foods. Abnormal regulation of carnitine can cause dilated or restrictive forms of cardiomyopathy, particularly in children. Calcium deficiency due to hypoparathyroidism, gastrointestinal abnormalities, or chelation directly compromises myocardial contractility, as does deficiency of phosphate, which is needed for high-energy compounds. Hypophosphatemia (Chapter 114) may occur in alcoholism, in diabetes, during recovery from malnutrition, and in hyperalimentation. Magnesium, a cofactor for thiamine-dependent reactions and for sodium-potassium adenosine triphosphatase, may be depleted by impaired absorption or increased renal excretion (Chapter 115).

Endocrinopathies have multiple systemic effects that may affect the heart. Hyperthyroidism (Chapter 239) may impair cardiac reserve, in part due to tachycardia and to enhanced adrenergic sensitivity in addition to direct affects of triiodothyronine. Hypothyroidism depresses contractility and conduction and may cause pericardial effusions. Diabetes (Chapter 242) has been associated with cardiomyopathy independently of the epicardial coronary atherosclerosis for which it is a risk factor. Particularly in combination with hypertension, cardiomyopathy with diabetes may present a picture in which diastolic function is more impaired than systolic function. In addition to aggravating heart failure by increasing demand, massive obesity (Chapter 233) is implicated as a cause of cardiomyopathy with increased ventricular mass and decreased contractility, which improve after weight loss.

FAMILIAL CARDIOMYOPATHY

Inherited genetic factors have been implicated in familial dilated cardiomyopathy, although with less frequency and more varied inheritance patterns than in hypertrophic cardiomyopathy. The frequency of familial involvement is now estimated at 20 to 30% for patients without other obvious etiology. Autosomal dominant inheritance is seen in approximately 75%, with most of the remaining cases X-linked. The best-characterized are those relating to dystrophin, abnormalities of which cause Duchenne's and Becker's X-linked skeletal muscle dystrophy with cardiac dysfunction, and an X-linked dilated cardiomyopathy without obvious skeletal involvement from an abnormal dystrophin promoter. At the inner face of the sarcolemmal membrane, dystrophin participates in the stabilization and support of the myocytes, in complexes with multiple cytoskeletal components, abnormalities of which cause other familial cardiomyopathies. Emery-Dreifuss muscular dystrophy with abnormalities of the anchoring protein emerin occurs in an X-linked pattern, whereas the same phenotype in an autosomal dominant pattern results from abnormalities of nuclear laminar proteins. Abnormalities in actin (missense mutations at 15q14) and other cytoskeletal proteins such as a desmin deletion and an alternative splicing of metavinculin have been identified in familial cardiomyopathies.

There have been five loci thus far identified for classic familial inheritance of dilated myocardiopathy. In addition to the dystrophies, families have been identified with dilated myocardiopathy associated with mitral valve prolapse (an abnormality on chromosome 10q21-23) and early-onset conduction system disease (abnormalities of the centromeric region of chromosome 1).

The contribution of inheritance becomes more complex when considering the interaction of genetic and environmental factors. A gene deletion in the angiotensin-converting enzyme influences the degree of hypertrophy in response to stimuli. Genetic traits may determine susceptibility to viral infection. A coxsackievirus protease was recently reported to cleave dystrophin with disruption of the cytoskeletal complex.

Mitochondrial myopathies are maternally transmitted, such as Kearns-Sayre syndrome of cardiomyopathy, ophthalmoplegia, retinopathy, and cerebellar ataxia. The mitochondrial abnormalities frequently cause skeletal as well as cardiac myopathic changes that can be rapidly progressive in young adulthood. Some kindreds have prominent ptosis.

Arrhythmic right ventricular dysplasia is characterized by focal fibrous-fatty replacement of the right ventricle. The right ventricular free wall and the atria are primarily involved, giving rise to ventricular and supraventricular arrhythmias, which are often the presenting symptom. Proposed pathology includes congenital hypoplasia of myocardial tissue and focal injury with fibrous replacement. Some patients present with left ventricular dysfunction, without initial recognition of the right ventricular abnormalities, which are often unappreciated on routine echocardiography. Currently, about one third of patients have evidence of familial involvement in an autosomal dominant pattern, with at least four genes currently identified on chromosomes 1 and 14. A well-known variant is Naxos syndrome originating from the Mediterranean area, in which the affected family members share strikingly curly hair and palmar hyperkeratosis.

OVERLAP WITH RESTRICTIVE CARDIOMYOPATHY

Diseases causing primarily restrictive cardiomyopathies (see later) can occasionally overlap to cause a picture consistent with dilated cardiomyopathy, particularly when the ventricle is not severely dilated. *Hemochromatosis* (Chapter 225) and *sarcoidosis* (Chapter 91) should be considered when evaluating all cardiomyopathy, although they are more often considered with the restrictive diseases. *Amyloidosis* (Chapter 290) is less commonly confused with dilated than with hypertrophic cardiomyopathy but should be considered for a thick-walled ventricle with moderately depressed contractile function.

Increasing understanding of processes leading to heart failure and particularly of the genetic contribution have reduced the number of cases with no known etiology. Even after careful evaluation, however, most cases of dilated cardiomyopathy are still considered to be *idiopathic*, of unknown cause.

EVALUATION OF DILATED CARDIOMYOPATHY

Clinical Manifestations and History

The history for a patient with dilated cardiomyopathy is gradual exertional intolerance and onset of congestive symptoms, occasionally including or preceded by chest pain, syncope or tachyarrhythmias, or clinical embolic events. An acute presentation may reflect a new problem, such as hyperthyroidism, superimposed on an unrecognized chronic cardiomyopathy of other origin. Rapid development over days to weeks, however, suggests postviral or giant cell myocarditis. Chest pain, typical of pericarditis or mimicking acute myocardial infarction, may result from acute myocarditis, as can ventricular arrhythmias in the absence of detectable left ventricular dysfunction. Chest pain occurs in almost one third of patients with chronic cardiomyopathy despite normal epicardial coronary arteries and may result from pulmonary hypertension, pericardial involvement, microvascular ischemia, or unknown factors. Adequate history regarding alcohol and cocaine use requires tactful diligence. Family history of possible cardiomyopathy should be specifically sought, with careful questioning about sudden deaths attributed to "massive heart attacks." Other specific clues such as toxic or occupational exposure, residence in rural South or Central America, or frequent exposure to raw meat products can suggest specific causes.

The history should also include careful questioning to elucidate symptoms indicative of the level of hemodynamic compensation, because most heart failure symptoms result from hemodynamic abnormalities of intracardiac filling pressures or systemic perfusion. Elevated filling pressures at rest can cause orthopnea, supine cough, and paroxysmal nocturnal dyspnea (Chapter 55). Dyspnea on minimal exertion such as dressing or walking to the bathroom usually is also indicative of elevated resting filling pressures, whereas dyspnea on moderate exertion such as two flights of stairs or two blocks generally indicates low cardiac output reserve. Anorexia, early satiety, and abdominal discomfort usually indicate elevated right-sided heart filling pressures, often with secondary tricuspid regurgitation. Edema generally indicates fluid retention but is frequently absent in young patients, despite severely elevated filling pressures, and may reflect local noncardiac factors in the elderly. These symptoms are common in all types of cardiomyopathy and in fact are common to all cardiac diseases when filling pressures become elevated. The term *congestive heart failure* describes this syndrome of elevated filling pressures but not the cause of heart failure or the type of cardiomyopathy.

The history for patients without evidence of resting congestion should quantify their activity as precisely as possible (Chapter 46). The history should also include specific elucidation of recent presyncope or syncope that could indicate dysrhythmic events and the need for specific electrophysiologic evaluation. In addition, patients should be asked specifically about symptoms that may indicate cerebral or peripheral embolic events.

General Cardiac Examination

Common components of the examination for all patients with suspected cardiac disease should address systemic circulatory compensation, evidence of intracardiac abnormalities, and any extracardiac clues to etiology. New guidelines for evaluation in heart failure place increased emphasis on regular assessment of circulating volume status. Elevated filling pressures at rest are diagnosed from elevated jugular venous pressures, abnormal hepatojugular reflux, hepatic distention and ascites, peripheral edema, and the presence of rales, the last three being perhaps the best-known but least sensitive signs of congestion in chronic heart failure. Because compensation of pulmonary lymphatics will maintain freedom from rales for most patients with chronically elevated filling pressures, the absence of rales should not be assumed to indicate normal volume status. Adequacy of perfusion is best assessed by pulse pressure (the difference between systolic and diastolic), which generally exceeds 25% of systolic when the cardiac index is adequate (>2.2 L/min/m²). Cool legs and arms often reflect severe hypoperfusion, but hands and feet can be cool in anyone who is anxious. Vague mental status, inattention, or lapses into sleep during conversation may indicate cerebral hypoperfusion. Pulsus alternans or periodic breathing may be detected in some patients with marked decompensation. If resting hemodynamics appear to be normal, functional cardiac reserve is assessed by a careful activity history and may be observed during a walk in the corridor or stairwell.

In dilated cardiomyopathy, the left ventricular impulse is often displaced laterally, although considerable posterior dilation can occur without detectable lateral displacement. The impulse is generally diffuse but not sustained. For restrictive cardiomyopathy, the impulse is less displaced and is often accompanied by a very prominent S_4. Any process leading to secondary right-sided heart failure may cause a separate right ventricular impulse to be felt along the left sternal border and beneath the xiphoid process during inspiration. S_3 gallops are often heard, with or without accompanying S_4 sounds, in any cardiomyopathy, with increasing prominence of the S_3 for a given patient frequently reflecting more ventricular volume overload. Absence of gallop rhythms does not mean that heart failure is absent, because many patients never manifest them. Mitral regurgitation is usually significant once hemodynamic decompensation has developed but is not always audible. This murmur, heard best in the axilla, may overlap with a sternal area murmur of tricuspid regurgitation, which generally develops later during decompensation. A short, medium-pitched murmur of pulmonic regurgitation may occur early in diastole in patients with marked pulmonary hypertension.

Diagnosis

Once a patient has been recognized to have symptoms or signs consistent with heart failure, the first aspect of the differential diagnosis is determination of cardiac contribution. For example, acute renal failure or intrinsic lung disease may cause some of the same symptoms and signs. Diagnosis can often be established on the basis of physical examination, but it is generally confirmed by echocardiography (see Fig. 73–1). Once the heart is implicated, it is important to identify surgical pericardial disease or primary valve disease, for which the echocardiogram provides major information. Although the classification (see Table 73–2) implies rigid distinctions, there is a blurring of the spectrum that extends from restrictive disease, to patients with normal ejection fraction and impaired ventricular filling, to borderline hypertrophy and classic hypertrophic cardiomyopathy. Although the myocardial pathology differs markedly, similar clinical manifestations of elevated filling pressures and fluid retention feature prominently throughout this spectrum.

Specific cardiac conditions such as coronary artery disease or valvar heart failure are often suggested by the history, physical examination, and echocardiogram but may require cardiac catheterization for confirmation and quantification. Evaluation should also determine whether heart failure results from excessive peripheral cardiac demand, such as in chronic severe anemia (generally requiring a hemoglobin level <8 mg/dL) or peripheral arteriovenous shunt (such as in Paget's bone disease or occasionally in patients with a large fistula for dialysis). Tachycardia-induced cardiomyopathy, most commonly observed in children and young adults, can result in adults from supraventricular or slow ventricular tachycardias when rates are chronically or frequently above 120 to 140 beats per minute and is completely reversible. If these other conditions are absent or inadequate to explain the cardiac dysfunction, the next task is to distinguish among dilated, restrictive, and hypertrophic cardiomyopathy by echocardiography.

LABORATORY ASSESSMENT (Table 73–3)

The chest radiograph (Chapter 49) usually shows cardiomegaly, although in some patients marked left ventricular dilation occurs posteriorly before the silhouette enlarges on the anteroposterior view. The degree of cardiomegaly on radiography often reflects more the degree of right than left ventricular dilation, which may explain its prognostic significance, because right ventricular failure carries a more ominous prognosis. Pulmonary vascular redistribution is variable and lags behind the clinical state, so it is not adequate for determination of volume status in patients with known heart failure.

A complete blood count should be sent; severe anemia can cause heart failure. Peripheral blood eosinophilia should stimulate a search for a systemic allergic reaction, which could be causing a hypersensitivity myocarditis, or for a parasitic disease, as well as consideration of endocardial restrictive disease (see later). Hyponatremia and evidence of renal and/or hepatic dysfunction usually reflect the degree of hemodynamic compromise rather than any specific cause. Severe hypocalcemia or hypophosphatemia, such as from malnutrition, can cause heart failure. Creatine kinase levels may be elevated in acute myocarditis, reflecting both cardiac and skeletal myositis, and they

---

Table 73–3 • LABORATORY EVALUATION OF CARDIOMYOPATHY

Clinical Evaluation
Thorough history and physical examination to identify cardiac and noncardiac disorders*
Assessment of ability to perform routine and desired activities*
Assessment of volume status*

Laboratory Evaluation
Electrocardiogram*
Chest radiograph*
Two-dimensional and Doppler echocardiogram*
Chemistry
   Serum sodium,* potassium,* glucose, creatinine,* blood urea nitrogen,* calcium,* magnesium*
   Albumin,* total protein,* liver function tests,* serum iron, ferritin
   Urinalysis
   Creatine kinase
   Thyroid-stimulating hormone*
Hematology
   Hemoglobin/hematocrit*
   White blood cell count with differential,* including eosinophils
   Erythrocyte sedimentation rate

Initial Evaluation in Selected Patients Only
Titers for suspected infection
   Acute viral (coxsackievirus, echovirus, influenza virus)
   Human immunodeficiency virus, Epstein-Barr virus
   Lyme disease, toxoplasmosis
   Chagas' disease
Catheterization with coronary angiography in patients with angina who are candidates for intervention*
Serologies for active rheumatologic disease
Endomyocardial biopsy

*Level I recommendations from ACC/AHA Practice Guidelines for Chronic Heart Failure in the Adult. (Hunt SA, Baker DW, Chin MH, et al: Executive summary. J Am Coll Cardiol 2001;38:2001–2013.)

may also be elevated in the chronic dystrophies. Serum assays for natriuretic peptides have been proposed both to diagnose and to guide therapy for heart failure. A level of brain natriuretic peptide less than 100 pg/mL generally excludes heart failure as a cause of dyspnea during initial evaluation in an urgent care setting (Chapter 56).

Serial viral titers may support a diagnosis of myocarditis, and titers for toxoplasmosis, Chagas' disease, or antistreptolysin may also be considered. HIV serology should be sent in patients at risk. Serology for toxoplasmosis and Lyme disease may be positive incidentally or as a cause of cardiomyopathy. In the presence of other suggestive signs or symptoms, tests should be done for a collagen vascular disease, which may cause cardiac involvement. Thyroid-stimulating hormone should be measured to exclude hyperthyroidism or hypothyroidism. Other endocrinologic diagnoses, particularly pheochromocytoma, should be entertained but do not all need to be excluded by extensive laboratory testing. Studies of iron and transferrin should exclude hemochromatosis (Chapter 225).

CARDIAC LABORATORY ASSESSMENT. In dilated cardiomyopathy, the electrocardiogram (Chapter 50) usually shows left ventricular dilation, with poor R wave progression and higher voltage in V_6 than in V_5. Marked decrease in voltage suggests amyloidosis or pericardial effusion. Left atrial abnormality is generally present. Atrial fibrillation may be present. Left bundle branch block occurs in approximately 20%, and many other patients have nonspecific QRS prolongation. Right bundle branch block is less common, except in Chagas' disease. Prolongation of the PR interval is common and has been associated with worse survival in some series. More profound conduction block may suggest giant cell myocarditis, sarcoidosis, or amyloidosis. Nonspecific T-wave abnormalities are usually present. Left ventricular hypertrophy without dilation is common in heart failure with preserved ejection fraction.

Echocardiography (Chapter 51) is the major initial cardiac laboratory examination in most patients, identifying left ventricular and often right ventricular dilation and hypocontractility and allowing distinction of dilated cardiomyopathy from other forms of cardiomyopathy (see Fig. 73–1). In addition, primary valve disease and septal defects can be detected if present. Primary mitral regurgitation may be difficult to distinguish from mitral regurgitation secondary to dilated heart failure but is more likely if the leaflets or chordae tendineae are abnormal. In general, congestive symptoms with severe mitral regurgitation and an ejection fraction greater than 30% are due to primary valve disease or restrictive cardiomyopathy, whereas mitral regurgitation secondary to ventricular dilation develops at lower ejection fractions. Focal wall motion abnormalities often result from coronary artery disease but are common in Chagas' disease and in sarcoidosis and may be seen in any cardiomyopathy. Disproportionate left ventricular hypertrophy may implicate previous hypertension or "burned out" hypertrophic cardiomyopathy as primary causes. Nuclear imaging (Chapter 52) may occasionally be useful to diagnose inflammatory conditions but has limited sensitivity for biopsy-proven myocarditis. Focal thallium defects make coronary disease more likely but are also found in nonischemic cardiomyopathy, particularly sarcoidosis. Coronary artery disease cannot be diagnosed or excluded on the basis of nuclear imaging in patients with severely depressed left ventricular ejection fraction, in whom perfusion abnormalities may be widespread, or missed due to lack of normal myocardium for reference.

Coronary arteriography (Chapter 54) should be performed in all patients with angina and heart failure in whom revascularization procedures could be considered. Coronary arteriography is also recommended in patients with chest pain in whom it is not known whether coronary artery disease is present. It is controversial whether or not patients should undergo catheterization or revascularization in the absence of symptoms of ischemia. Determining cardiac output and filling pressures with right-sided heart catheterization may be useful to confirm information from the clinical assessment and to guide subsequent therapy when hemodynamic decompensation is present.

Endomyocardial biopsy is not indicated for the routine evaluation of heart failure. It is routine in the surveillance for rejection after cardiac transplantation (Chapter 80); may help diagnose hemochromatosis, endocardial fibroelastosis, amyloidosis, sarcoidosis, eosinophilic myocarditis, and giant cell myocarditis; and has been used to assess the risk of continued anthracycline therapy. Most biopsies of nonspecific chronic cardiomyopathy show abnormalities of varying myocyte size, nuclear hypertrophy ("box-car" nuclei), and fibrosis; although considered "diagnostic" of cardiomyopathy, these findings do not have unique therapeutic implications.

Prognosis

Patients with recent-onset cardiomyopathy have almost a 50% chance of substantial recovery, which is lower in patients with the most severe compromise at presentation. For patients with chronic cardiomyopathy of unknown cause, the prognosis is determined by the stability or deterioration of their left ventricular function and hemodynamic compensation. In general, prognosis parallels the functional class at which they can be maintained, with a 1-year mortality of less than 10% for class I patients with dilated cardiomyopathy, 10 to 15% for class II patients, 20 to 25% for class III patients, and up to 50% for patients who remain class IV despite aggressive therapy to relieve congestion. Other major prognostic factors include left ventricular ejection fraction, the exact value of which becomes less predictive once it is below 25% and symptoms are severe. Larger left ventricular diastolic dimension is a robust predictor of worse outcome at every stage of heart failure. Decrease in left ventricular ejection fraction and/or increase in dimensions over time are ominous. Preservation of right ventricular function predicts better outcome. Serum sodium level and peak oxygen consumption with exercise are useful prognostic factors.

Rx Treatment

Patients considered to have a recent active process with some potential for improvement, such as postviral or peripartum cardiomyopathy, are often advised to avoid vigorous exercise for the next 3 to 6 months. This proscription is derived weakly from data that swimming enhanced mortality in the murine model of acute viral myocarditis and from anecdotal human experience. Patients should be advised, however, to remain mobile, continue regular walking, and avoid daytime bedrest, which leads to deconditioning, depression, and altered sleep patterns and may precipitate venous thrombosis.

When there is no cause or aggravating factor that dictates specific intervention, the therapy for cardiomyopathy is as described for various stages of heart failure (Chapter 56). Angiotensin-converting enzyme inhibition is prescribed for patients from asymptomatic to severe, unless contraindicated due to angioedema, intolerable cough, progressive renal dysfunction, or symptomatic hypotension. [2] β-Blocking agents are indicated for all patients with stable heart failure. [1] These agents must be titrated to higher doses over months during close observation for evidence of decompensation. When tolerated, they can improve ventricular function and decrease the progression of disease leading to hospitalization. β-blocking agents are not recommended in patients with active volume overload, symptomatic hypotension, or recent instability requiring need for intravenous therapy, [4] and in some patients may need to be discontinued because of unremitting fatigue or depression even in the absence of clinically worsening heart failure. Digoxin improves symptoms of heart failure and decreases hospitalizations without demonstrable impact on mortality. [5] Aldosterone blockade provides incremental benefit. [6] When symptoms of congestion or dyspnea on minimal exertion persist despite empiric therapy with angiotensin-converting enzyme inhibitors, diuretics, an aldosterone antagonist and digoxin, compensation can frequently be restored and maintained on a regimen tailored to approach near-normal filling pressures with a combination of vasodilators and diuretics. Cardiac resynchronization is beneficial in patients who do not respond to medical therapy and who have a prolonged QRS complex. [7] For patients who are truly refractory to medical therapy but have no other conditions that would compromise long-term survival, cardiac transplantation may be appropriate (Chapter 80). It should be recognized however, that fewer than 2500 donor hearts are available each year in the United States, compared with an estimated 50,000 to 100,000 patients with refractory systolic heart failure. Ventricular reduction surgery for nonischemic heart failure (Batista procedure) is no longer performed, although recognition of the importance of ventricular geometry has led to increased performance of anterior ventricular resection surgery for myocardial scar at the time of coronary artery bypass surgery. Left ventricular assist devices are commonly used as "bridges" for patients awaiting cardiac transplantation, and in the future they may be considered in highly selected patients as "destination" therapy.

Table 73-4 • CAUSES OF RESTRICTIVE CARDIOMYOPATHIES

Infiltrative
Amyloidosis
Sarcoidosis
Gaucher's disease: glucocerebroside-laden macrophages
Hurler's disease: mucopolysaccharide-laden macrophages

Storage
Hemochromatosis
Fabry's disease
Glycogen storage diseases

Fibrotic
Radiation
Scleroderma
Doxorubicin

Metabolic
Carnitine deficiency
Defects in fatty acid metabolism

Endomyocardial
Possibly related diseases
    Tropical endomyocardial fibrosis
    Hypereosinophilic syndrome (Löffler's endocarditis)
Carcinoid syndrome
Radiation
Drugs, e.g., serotonin, ergotamine

Dilated Cardiomyopathy Overlap
Early stage ("minimally dilated cardiomyopathy")
Partial recovery from dilated cardiomyopathy
Myocardial metabolic defects

Idiopathic

RESTRICTIVE CARDIOMYOPATHIES

The restrictive cardiomyopathies are the least common of the three major categories of cardiomyopathy. Although characterized primarily by decreased distensibility ("diastolic dysfunction"), the restrictive cardiomyopathies are frequently accompanied by some degree of depressed contractility and ejection fraction ("systolic dysfunction"). Hemodynamically, end-diastolic pressures and consequently atrial pressures are elevated initially, with relative preservation of cardiac output until disease is advanced. Although classically considered to be "nondilated" with normal ventricular dimensions, many restrictive cardiomyopathies are associated with some global or focal ventricular dilation, although less than for equivalent degrees of congestive symptoms in the primary dilated cardiomyopathies. The atria, however, frequently become greatly enlarged after chronic exposure to high filling pressures. Restrictive cardiomyopathies commonly result from deposition of abnormal substances in the myocardium (Table 73–4), which can be divided into "infiltrative" diseases, in which the abnormal substance is largely between the myocytes, and "storage" diseases, in which abnormal substances accumulate within myocytes. The restriction of endomyocardial fibrosis and eosinophilic cardiomyopathy results from intense fibrotic reaction, particularly at the endocardial and subendocardial layers. Fibrosis is more widespread with radiation and scleroderma and contributes also to the cardiomyopathy of doxorubicin. Restrictive disease can occur without obvious cause, sometimes in a familial pattern.

Diagnosis

The initial challenge is to distinguish restrictive cardiomyopathy from dilated cardiomyopathy or pericardial disease (Chapter 74). Restrictive disease is often characterized by earlier onset of right-sided symptoms than in most dilated cardiomyopathy. The cardiac impulse is less prominent. Abnormalities of filling, such as a pronounced S_4 and rapid Y descents in the jugular venous pulse are more obvious. Echocardiography in restrictive disease usually shows left ventricular diastolic dimension less than 6 to 6.5 cm and ejection fraction of more than 30%. Symptomatic congestion, the major clinical feature of *restrictive* cardiomyopathy, rarely occurs in primary *dilated* cardiomyopathy until after the ejection fraction is below 30%.

Echocardiographic profiles of abnormal relaxation and diastolic filling are helpful in confirming physiologic impairment in patients with near-normal ejection fraction but are less helpful in distinguishing restrictive from other cardiomyopathy, in which the degree of volume overload determines filling pattern. It can be difficult to distinguish between restrictive disease and pericardial disease, which often requires comparison of right and left ventricular filling during invasive hemodynamic measurement and pericardial imaging by computed tomography or magnetic resonance imaging. This distinction is particularly critical in patients with a history of mediastinal radiation, which can cause both myocardial and pericardial disease.

℞ Treatment

Because systolic function is relatively preserved, some patients with restrictive disease may be misdiagnosed for many years as hypochondriacal or deconditioned. Prolonged exposure to elevated filling pressures can cause irreversible pulmonary hypertension, analogous to that with mitral stenosis, and occasionally true cardiac cirrhosis before diagnosis. When congestive symptoms develop, they may be dominated by refractory pleural effusions, ascites, and sometimes dramatic cachexia. Therapy with diuretics is helpful but not curative. The theoretical rationale for calcium-channel blockers to improve diastolic relaxation has not been confirmed by clinical results; a reduction in venous return without a concomitant improvement in ventricular compliance can markedly reduce cardiac output. Occasional patients with radiation, familial, or idiopathic restrictive cardiomyopathy are candidates for transplantation due to persistent severe symptoms despite more preserved ejection fraction than in most transplant candidates. When possible, definitive therapy should be undertaken before severe inanition develops.

INFILTRATIVE RESTRICTIVE CARDIOMYOPATHY

Amyloidosis (Chapter 290) is the most common cause of restrictive cardiomyopathy. Clinically evident cardiac amyloidosis usually results from primary amyloidosis, caused by plasma cell production of immunoglobulin light chains commonly with multiple myeloma, or familial amyloidosis, in which the deposits contain an abnormal prealbumin (transthyretin) associated with different specific point mutations, many of which involve the kidney or liver without cardiac compromise. Secondary amyloidosis rarely involves the heart. Senile amyloidosis, involving normal transthyretin, occasionally causes clinical heart failure in the elderly but progresses quite slowly compared with primary amyloidosis. A point-mutation in transthyretin occurs commonly in African Americans and may contribute to age-related amyloidosis. Amyloid fibrils infiltrate into the interstitium, stiffening the ventricles and replacing some contractile elements (Fig. 73–3). Although amyloidosis is also found in the atria, it is not extensive enough to prevent atrial dilation. Deposits frequently affect the conduction system, leading to bradyarrhythmias. When amyloid also surrounds the arterioles, it may compromise the microcirculation, further impairing systolic and diastolic function and leading to anginal chest pain and even myocardial infarction in some patients.

Like other cardiomyopathies, the earliest symptom may be dyspnea with exertion. Congestion occurs earlier in the course than with dilated cardiomyopathy, frequently with disproportionate right-sided congestive symptoms of abdominal discomfort and peripheral edema. Syncope may reflect sinus or atrioventricular node involvement. Occasional angina may be due to small vessel ischemia. Some patients may present with orthostatic hypotension due to amyloid autonomic neuropathy. Evidence of involvement elsewhere such as macroglossia, carpal tunnel syndrome with hypothenar wasting, skin friability, nephrotic syndrome, or multiple myeloma may also suggest the diagnosis of amyloidosis.

The electrocardiogram characteristically shows markedly decreased voltage despite increased wall thickness on echocardiography. Specific diagnosis in some cases can be made from a characteristic sparkling refractile pattern on echocardiography. Up to 80% of patients have a monoclonal protein identified from either serum or urine. Biopsy of subcutaneous fat or the rectum frequently reveals amyloidosis. Endomyocardial biopsy, which carries a higher risk of perforation in the amyloid-infiltrated heart, reveals infiltration in the interstitium

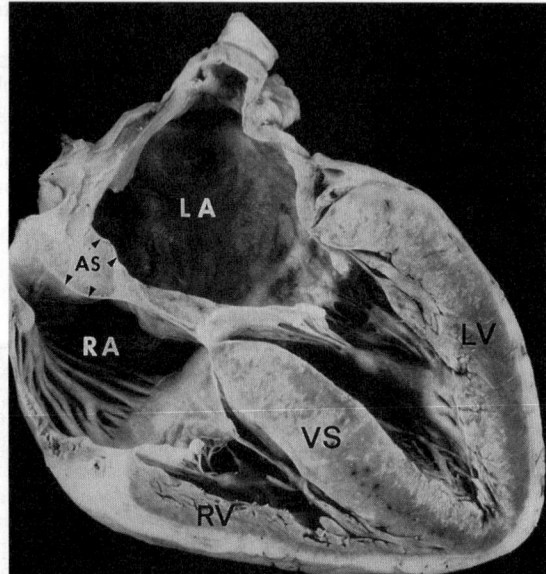

FIGURE 73–3 • A necropsy specimen of an amyloid heart demonstrating the thickened ventricular septum (VS), atrial septum (AS), and free walls of the left ventricle (LV) and right ventricle (RV), and the dilated left atrium (LA). (Courtesy of Dr. William Edwards, Mayo Clinic, Rochester, MN.)

and around the coronary vasculature with deposits that are pale pink on hematoxylin-eosin stain and are birefringent with the specific Congo red stain. Symptomatic patients generally have more than 25% of myocardial areas involved.

Once amyloidosis has been associated with heart failure, the median survival is less than 1 year, with less than 5% 5-year survival. Most deaths occur suddenly. Patients with familial amyloidosis have a slower course than those with a monoclonal gammopathy. Amyloidosis is usually a contraindication to cardiac transplantation because it recurs in the donor heart and can progress rapidly in other organs. Heart transplantation with subsequent autologous stem cell transplantation has been performed in a limited research protocol. Therapy with colchicine or the combination of melphalan and prednisone for patients with associated monoclonal gammopathy has yielded response rates of 20 to 30%.

Symptomatic therapy focuses on the congestive picture. Vasodilator therapy is less effective than in dilated cardiomyopathy, owing to less pronounced systolic dysfunction, greater reliance on high filling pressures, and the frequently accompanying autonomic neuropathy, which predisposes to postural hypotension. Digoxin has been anecdotally reported to have increased toxicity in amyloidosis, but this problem was not documented in a systematic review. Intracardiac thrombi are common, and anticoagulation may be recommended.

Gaucher's disease (Chapter 222) of glucocerebroside metabolism and *Hurler's disease* (Chapter 276) of mucopolysaccharide metabolism result in infiltration of the myocardium by cells filled with abnormal metabolites and are generally considered with the infiltrative cardiomyopathies. Hurler's disease can also affect cardiac valves and coronary arteries. *Sarcoidosis* (Chapter 91) of the heart causes interstitial inflammation and fibrosis that can initially affect diastolic function more than systolic function. More common presentation, however, is with reduced left ventricular ejection fraction with variable degrees of ventricular dilation, possibly with arrhythmias or chest pain syndromes. It can present as either restrictive or dilated cardiomyopathy (discussed earlier under Granulomatous Disease).

STORAGE DISEASES

Although amyloidosis and sarcoidosis are seen infiltrating the interstitium around myocytes, compromise from the storage diseases results primarily from intracellular accumulation. *Hemochromatosis* (Chapter 225) is the most common example in adults, frequently arising from an autosomal recessive disorder in the gene that regulates iron absorption. The estimated frequency of homozygosity for the mutant allele is 5 per 1000. In the absence of the genetic defect

in iron regulation, hemochromatosis can result from iron overload due to hemolytic anemia and transfusions. Iron is deposited primarily in the perinuclear areas of myocytes. Disrupted cellular architecture and mitochondrial function lead to cell death and replacement fibrosis. The atrioventricular node may be involved. The degree of left ventricular dilation is variable, leading to both dilated and restrictive pictures, with the restrictive aspects dominating earlier in the course. Dilation is generally to left ventricular diastolic dimensions of less than 60 mm, but ejection fractions in severe cases are often less than 30%, unlike the other restrictive diseases. The diagnosis is generally made from the clinical picture, an elevated serum iron level, and high transferrin saturation (>50%). Serum ferritin is elevated in hemochromatosis but is also elevated in other liver diseases and as a general acute-phase reactant. Genetic testing may be helpful. The diagnosis can be made from endomyocardial biopsy tissue stained for iron. Early diagnosis is important, because phlebotomy and iron chelation therapy with deferoxamine may improve cardiac function before cell injury becomes irreversible. Deaths from hemochromatosis result more from cirrhosis and liver carcinoma than from cardiac disease (Chapter 154).

Specific metabolic enzyme deficiencies can lead to abnormal metabolites accumulating in the myocardium, causing increased ventricular mass and restrictive cardiomyopathy. *Fabry's disease* (Chapter 222) results in intracellular glycolipid accumulation in myocardium and valves, vessel walls, skin, cornea, kidneys, gastrointestinal tract, and central nervous system. Mortality from this X-linked disorder in men results from multiple organ involvement in the fourth or fifth decade. Some heterozygous women have also developed cardiomyopathy. *Glycogen storage disease* (Chapter 213) results from enzyme deficiencies that lead to excessive deposition of normal glycogen in myocardium, skeletal muscle, and liver. The most common is type II, Pompe's disease, associated with dramatic thickening of ventricular septal and free walls, large QRS amplitude, short PR interval, and death usually within the first few years of life.

FIBROTIC RESTRICTIVE CARDIOMYOPATHY

Restrictive myocardial disease can occur with diffuse fibrotic changes in the absence of abnormal substance accumulation. Radiation for thoracic malignancy (Chapter 19) can produce restrictive cardiomyopathy, usually presenting within several years, although occasionally up to 15 years later. Patients treated with both doxorubicin and radiation are at higher risk. Doxorubicin itself causes a cardiomyopathy characterized by decreased systolic function in which fibrosis limits ventricular dilation (Chapter 191). Radiation causes both restrictive cardiomyopathy and constrictive pericarditis, the relative contributions of which are hard to distinguish.

Fibrosis in the scleroderma heart (Chapter 281) accumulates in the interstitium but may also result from small vessel ischemia with microinfarction. Left ventricular dilation is uncommon, and the congestive symptoms may be refractory to therapy.

ENDOMYOCARDIAL RESTRICTIVE CARDIOMYOPATHY

The picture of restrictive cardiomyopathy can be caused also by specific involvement of the endocardium with relative sparing of the remaining ventricular wall thickness. In equatorial Africa, endomyocardial fibrosis accounts for 15 to 25% of cardiac deaths, occurring most commonly in young patients of low socioeconomic status. It can involve either ventricle, most commonly both, with dense thickening of the ventricular inflow tracts and atrioventricular valves while sparing the underlying myocardium and systolic function. The atria may be very large, and pericardial effusions may be present.

Although endomyocardial fibrosis bears similarities to the hypereosinophilic syndrome (Chapter 184) occurring in more temperate climates, Löffler's endocarditis is characterized by older age, male predominance, and more aggressive course than endomyocardial fibrosis. Persistent eosinophilia of more than 1500 eosinophils per cubic millimeter without other cause leads to dysfunction of the heart, lungs, and other organs. The eosinophilic granules are thought to injure the endocardium, which is then the site of platelet thrombi and fibrosis. Varying degrees of eosinophilic myocarditis may also be present. The cardiac apices may be obliterated, creating small ventricular cavities with characteristic echocardiographic appearance. The mitral and tricuspid valves are affected, leading to prominent atrioventricular valve regurgitation. Cardiac catheterization reveals high ventricular filling pressures, often with evidence of valvar regurgitation. The thrombotic surface can be the origin of multiple systemic emboli. Renal and pulmonary involvement are common, and patients may have a rash, fever, and cough. Immunosuppressive therapy with corticosteroids and cytotoxic drugs can reduce the burden of eosinophils and the cardiac injury caused by the eosinophilic granules.

For both endomyocardial fibrosis and Löffler's endocarditis, diuretics and anticoagulation are important adjuncts to therapy. Extensive surgical resection has been performed for otherwise refractory disease, but the perioperative mortality rate is about 20%, and many patients suffer recurrent fibrosis and continued functional limitation.

Endocardial injury can also result from the 5-hydroxyindoleacetic acid and other substances released by carcinoid tumors (Chapter 245), which are inadequately cleared when hepatic metastases are present. The major sites affected are the tricuspid valve, the pulmonic valve, and the right ventricular endocardium, although occasionally the left-sided valves can be involved as well due to exposure to carcinoid secretions from a patent foramen ovale or pulmonary metastases.

IDIOPATHIC RESTRICTIVE CARDIOMYOPATHY

Restrictive cardiomyopathy may occasionally be diagnosed in the absence of any specific cause. Although isolated systolic function may be relatively normal, the ejection fraction is usually in the 30 to 45% range, in which cardiac output may become compromised from restricted filling and secondary valvar regurgitation. For a given patient with slightly reduced left ventricular ejection fraction and slightly elevated left ventricular volume, overt congestive symptoms and abnormal diastolic filling pattern suggest a restrictive cardiomyopathy, whereas a relative lack of symptoms is more consistent with a "minimally dilated" cardiomyopathy. Some patients who demonstrate marked improvement of left ventricular function after an obvious dilated cardiomyopathy attributed to viral infection or alcohol may be left with an ejection fraction greater than 40% but significant exertional dyspnea related to reduced compliance. In general, the course of idiopathic restrictive disease tends to be more prolonged than that for the same degree of symptomatic limitation with dilated cardiomyopathy. Families have been described with restrictive cardiomyopathy without other obvious cause. This syndrome can occur either with or without skeletal myopathy, and it has been seen in association with conduction system disease. A restrictive nonhypertrophic cardiomyopathy with autosomal dominant inheritance has been seen in Noonan's syndrome.

HYPERTROPHIC CARDIOMYOPATHY

CLASSIC

Etiology and Physiology

Hypertrophic cardiomyopathy is a common genetic abnormality that may occur in as many as 1 in 500 persons and results from any of more than 125 different mutations on at least eight genes, which code for the sarcomeric proteins β-myosin heavy chain, cardiac troponin T, α-tropomyosin, and myosin-binding C protein genes. Almost half of cases occur in an autosomal dominant pattern, with the majority of sporadic cases attributed to spontaneous mutation. The phenotypic expression of the disease varies markedly between and within families.

The cardinal features are marked left ventricular hypertrophy not due to other cardiac disease, frequently with asymmetrical involvement of the septum, accompanied by supranormal ejection fraction and decreased left ventricular systolic cavity dimension (Fig. 73–4). Pathologically, the myocytes show marked disarray in a characteristic whorled pattern and disorganization of the larger muscle bundles as well. The descriptor *obstructive* or *nonobstructive* refers to whether a pressure gradient that impedes left ventricular outflow can be detected. Previous names for this syndrome included *asymmetrical septal hypertrophy*, *hypertrophic obstructive cardiomyopathy*, and *idiopathic hypertrophic subaortic stenosis*, but these have been largely replaced by the term *hypertrophic cardiomyopathy*.

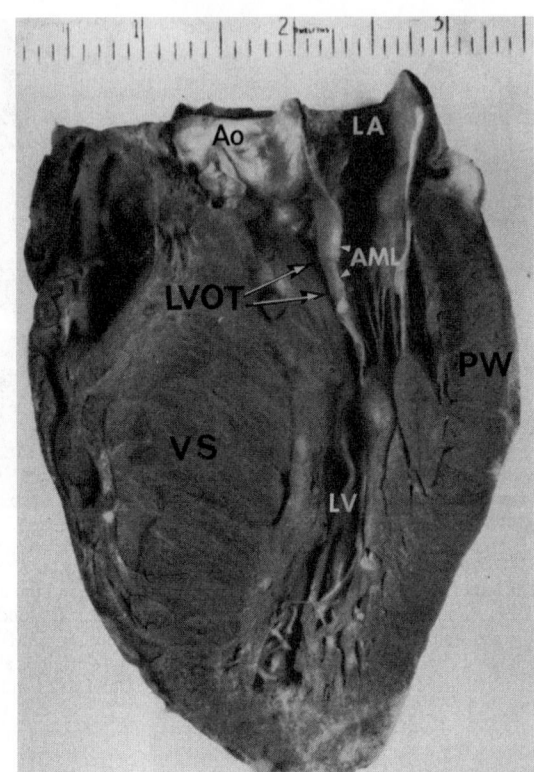

FIGURE 73–4 • A classic case of hypertrophic cardiomyopathy, demonstrating the marked hypertrophy of the ventricular septum (VS) in contact with the anterior mitral leaflet (AML), impinging on the left ventricular outflow tract (LVOT). The left ventricular (LV) cavity is severely reduced. Ao = aorta; LA = left atrium. (From Teare D: Asymmetric hypertrophy of the heart in young adults. Br Heart J 1958;20:1. Labels superimposed.)

The affected ventricle is hypercontractile with a supranormal ejection fraction, at times almost obliterating the left ventricular cavity. Diastolic distensibility is markedly limited, leading to elevated filling pressures that can cause shortness of breath. Filling pressures rise further and aggravate dyspnea when the heart rate accelerates during exercise or atrial fibrillation. Myocardial ischemia despite the absence of epicardial coronary artery disease can cause anginal-type chest pain owing to the increased oxygen demands and reduced oxygen delivery for the hypertrophied ventricle with high intracavitary pressures.

Outflow obstruction, present or inducible in about 25% of patients, is caused by apposition of the anterior mitral valve leaflet to the septum and can elevate filling pressures further and compromise forward output. When present, the midsystolic gradient can approach levels seen in severe aortic stenosis. The gradient may be elicited or enhanced by maneuvers that decrease left ventricular volume, such as vasodilation, the Valsalva maneuver, or standing after squatting (Chapter 46). Enhanced contractility also aggravates the gradient, as for the beat after a premature ventricular contraction (Brockenbrough phenomenon). Handgrip increases systemic resistance and decreases the gradient. Syncope can result from an increased gradient leading to decreased cardiac output, from elevated intraventricular pressures activating vagal reflexes, or from ventricular arrhythmias arising within the areas of abnormal myocyte organization.

When hypertrophic cardiomyopathy is detected on screening of family members or populations, almost 90% of patients are asymptomatic. Most symptoms present between ages 20 and 40 years, although occasional patients present after age 50. The most common presenting symptom is dyspnea on exertion. Chest pain is present in 75% of patients with symptoms. Palpitations are most commonly due to supraventricular arrhythmias. Presyncope and syncope occur most often during or shortly after heavy exertion. Cardiac examination in asymptomatic patients may be unrevealing except for a slightly prominent left ventricular impulse. Decreased compliance during atrial filling may lead to a palpable and audible S_4 gallop. When present, the murmur is usually best heard at the left lower sternal border and represents a sum of the outflow murmur and mitral regurgitation. It usually does

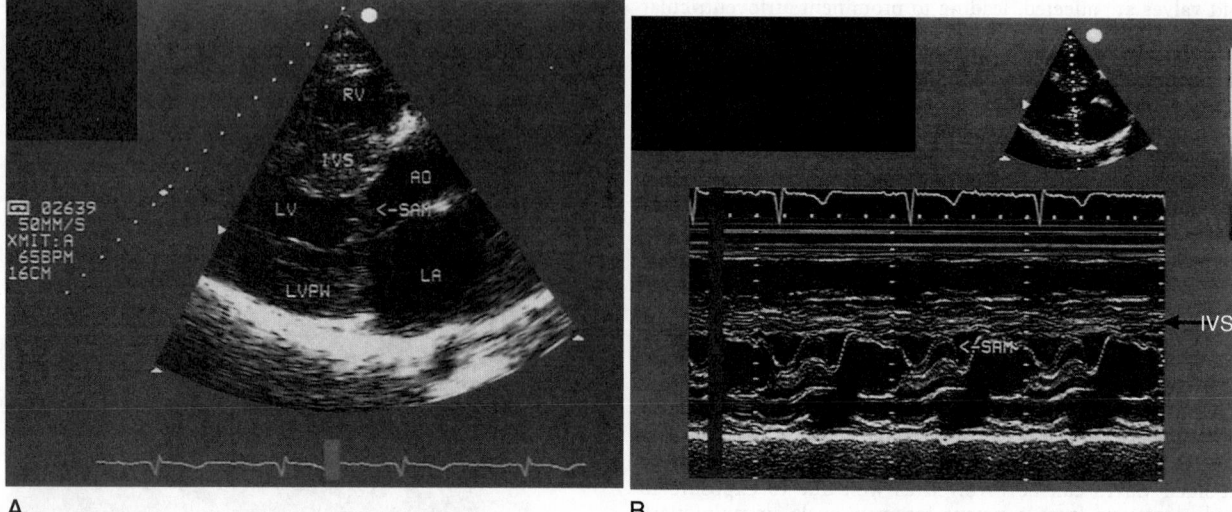

FIGURE 73–5 • Hypertrophic obstructive cardiomyopathy. *A,* The two-dimensional long-axis parasternal view shows the chambers of the heart. The left ventricle posterior wall (LVPW) is thickened, and the most striking abnormality is the hypertrophy of the interventricular septum (IVS). Another characteristic feature is a Venturi effect: as blood leaves the left ventricle (LV), it sucks the anterior leaflet of the mitral valve forward—a phenomenon called systolic anterior motion (SAM). This phenomenon is more clearly shown in the parasternal long-axis M-mode echocardiogram (*B*). The massive thickening of the septum is also obvious in the M-mode (IVS). AO = aorta; LA = left atrium; RV = right ventricle. (*A* and *B,* From Forbes CD, Jackson WF: Color Atlas and Text of Clinical Medicine, 3rd ed. London, Mosby, 2003.)

not radiate to the carotid arteries. It is typically harsh and increases in intensity with the maneuvers described earlier, which decrease ventricular size. When a gradient impedes ejection, the carotid impulse may transmit both an early and late systolic ("bifid") pulse. An enhanced wave in the jugular venous pulse usually reflects decreased right ventricular compliance because of the abnormal septum rather than right-sided heart failure.

Echocardiography establishes the diagnosis of hypertrophy (Fig. 73–5). Classic asymmetrical septal hypertrophy is defined as a septal–posterior wall thickness ratio of at least 1.5, but asymmetry is not necessary to diagnose hypertrophic cardiomyopathy. Doppler interrogation can identify resting gradients. Cardiac catheterization is often performed to quantify the gradient and in older patients to exclude coexistent coronary disease as a component of chest pain.

Electrocardiographic abnormalities most commonly include left ventricular hypertrophy and increased Q waves, which occasionally are misdiagnosed as myocardial infarction. Left atrial abnormality may be detected in the P waves, and a short PR interval with slurred QRS upstroke may be misdiagnosed as pre-excitation.

Considerable debate exists over appropriate screening for hypertrophic cardiomyopathy, which is the most common cause identified in sudden deaths occurring in athletes. It is unclear to what degree the increased recognition in athletes results from the addition of physiologic to pathologic ventricular hypertrophy, the superimposition of sudden autonomic surges predisposing to arrhythmias during competition, or their high public profile. Echocardiographic abnormalities are found in approximately 25% of first-degree relatives of affected patients.

Rx Treatment

TREATMENT OF SYMPTOMS. The controversy regarding therapy in asymptomatic patients is increasing as genetic screening reveals more asymptomatic young patients in whom preventive therapy could be beneficial but also more asymptomatic older patients who have already achieved normal longevity, suggesting a more benign course than previously recognized in some people. In the absence of data regarding benefits, therapy in asymptomatic patients is generally not encouraged except when accompanied by severe hypertrophy, such as ventricular wall thickness over the equivalent of 35 mm in adults, or by a marked outflow gradient (Fig. 73–6).

Once symptoms are present, therapy is directed to improve diastolic filling and perhaps reduce myocardial ischemia and to reduce sudden death. β-Adrenergic blocking drugs and verapamil are most commonly used to address symptoms. A major action of both is to improve diastolic filling by increasing the duration of diastole as heart rate decreases. Additional effects on reducing inotropic state may decrease myocardial oxygen consumption directly, thus decreasing any ischemia, and decrease generation of an outflow gradient. Although β-blocking agents are generally the initial treatment, patients who do not respond well to this therapy may respond well to verapamil and conversely. Because of its vasodilation, verapamil can aggravate a dynamic outflow gradient in some patients. On the other hand, verapamil is sometimes used initially when chest pain is the dominant symptom. Disopyramide decreases the inotropic state but can also increase atrioventricular conduction if atrial fibrillation occurs; therefore, if used, it is usually combined with a β-blocking agent. Clinical benefits from disopyramide may decrease over time, and it is less used than previously.

Patients with impaired diastolic function of any cause tend to develop fluid retention beyond the level of volume needed for optimal ventricular filling. Diuretics should be used to treat obvious fluid retention, but caution is needed to avoid excessive diuresis to a volume-depleted state that would compromise cardiac output and increase a "provokable" gradient.

Atrial fibrillation occurs commonly in hypertrophic cardiomyopathy, perhaps even more commonly than in other conditions associated with chronically elevated atrial pressures. Because of the deleterious effects of rapid ventricular rates and loss of the atrial kick on ventricular filling and symptoms of congestion, vigorous attempts to achieve and maintain sinus rhythm are warranted, most commonly with amiodarone (Chapters 59 and 62). When sinus rhythm cannot be maintained, amiodarone may also be useful for maintaining slow ventricular response, facilitated also by β-blockers or verapamil, which are often not in themselves sufficient. For refractory fast ventricular rates, it may be necessary to ablate the atrioventricular node and provide permanent dual-chamber pacing (Chapter 61). Anticoagulation is strongly indicated for patients with a history of atrial fibrillation, even if sinus rhythm has been restored, owing to the high risk of embolic events with recurrence (Chapter 59).

Symptoms truly refractory to medications are uncommon, occurring in only 5 to 10% of patients. They should be addressed according to whether systolic performance is preserved and whether or not there is outflow obstruction (resting gradient usually >50 mm Hg). It is estimated that fewer than 5% of patients with hypertrophic cardiomyopathy have refractory severe symptoms and major outflow obstruction. For those patients, dual-chamber pacing has often been tried, with variable results. Septal reduction procedures abolish or substantially reduce the gradient in more than 90% of cases, with persistent symptomatic improvement in 70%. Approaches include surgical myotomy-myectomy or alcohol injection into the septal coronary artery. Mitral valve replacement may also improve the gradient by reducing apposition of the valve leaflet to the septum and may also be considered when there are intrinsic abnormalities of the mitral valve contributing to mitral regurgitation, whether or not obstruction is present.

In perhaps 10% of symptomatic patients, hypertrophic cardiomyopathy may "burn out" into a condition more typical of dilated heart failure, with thinner walls and no outflow gradient but persistence of mitral regurgitation. Residual diastolic stiffness renders such patients less likely to have marked ventricular dilation and more likely to have symptoms of congestion at left ventricular ejection fractions that are not severely reduced (often in the range of 30 to 40%, as opposed to usual dilated cardiomyopathy in which severe symptoms are rare above an ejection fraction of 25%). Such patients should discontinue verapamil and disopyramide, continue β-blocking agents only at low doses with caution, and begin therapy with angiotensin-converting enzyme inhibitors, with diuretics as needed for fluid retention. Cardiac transplantation (Chapter 80) may be considered in these patients, in whom deterioration may occur rapidly.

PREVENTION OF SUDDEN DEATH. With hypertrophic cardiomyopathy, sudden death accounts for most of the annual mortality, which is reported as 3% in referral centers and 1% in less selected populations. There are multiple potential causes of syncope and sudden death in hypertrophic cardiomyopathy, with the most common being primary and secondary ventricular tachyarrhythmias. Highest risk is conferred by previous sustained ventricular tachycardia or sudden death; young age with either a family history of sudden death or, in some cases, a genetic mutation associated with high risk of sudden death; frequent, nonsustained ventricular tachycardia; recurrent syncope; and massive left ventricular hypertrophy. Patients in the highest risk category in general receive therapy with either amiodarone or an implantable cardioverter-defibrillator (Chapters 60 and 61). Patients with syncope should also be carefully evaluated for specific arrhythmic causes.

For patients not included in the high-risk groups just mentioned, risk stratification has been difficult. It does appear possible, however, to define a relatively low-risk group by the absence of any of these factors and the absence of exercise-induced hypotension on exercise testing. Although these low-risk patients may not need to be restricted from vigorous activity, it has been recommended that all patients with hypertrophic cardiomyopathy avoid intense training and competition.

APICAL GIANT T-WAVE HYPERTROPHY

A separate entity of apical hypertrophic cardiomyopathy has been recognized, predominantly in Japan, where it accounts for one fourth of hypertrophic cardiomyopathy. It is characterized by systolic apical obliteration that creates a "spade-like" cavity on angiography and frequently by giant negative T waves in the precordial electrocardiogram. There is no intraventricular gradient. Symptoms are usually mild. Malignant ventricular arrhythmias appear less commonly than in other forms of hypertrophic cardiomyopathy. Some patients, particularly elderly women, have marked symmetrical hypertrophy that is disproportionate to the degree of their hypertension.

SPECTRUM OF HEART FAILURE WITH PRESERVED LEFT VENTRICULAR EJECTION FRACTION

Many patients have moderate concentric hypertrophy without any characteristics of classic genetic hypertrophic cardiomyopathy or the apical hypertrophic cardiomyopathy. Although most of these cases reflect chronic hypertension (Chapter 63) and do not have any symptoms of cardiac disease, there is an increasing recognition that some of these patients develop typical symptoms of congestion, with elevated filling pressures, fluid retention, and pulmonary edema. The clinical syndrome overlaps that of restrictive disease with normal or mildly reduced left ventricular ejection fraction. Many patients have abnormal diastolic filling patterns, leading to the term *diastolic*

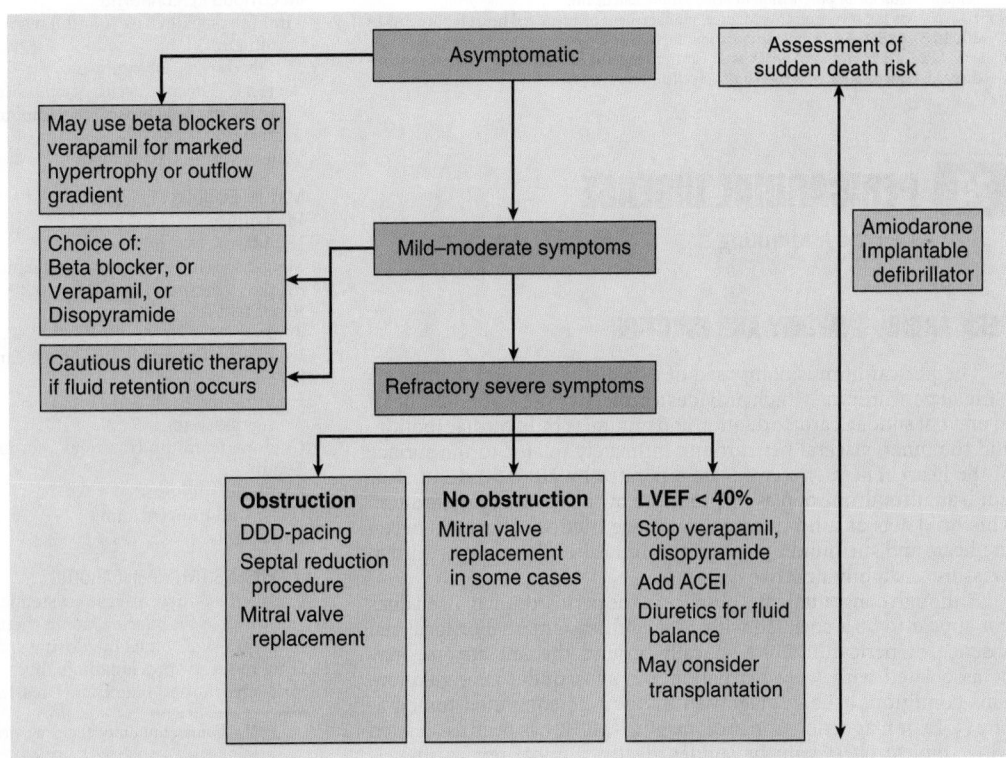

FIGURE 73–6 • Approach to therapy of hypertrophic cardiomyopathy according to the severity of symptoms. Risk for sudden death should be considered regardless of symptomatic status. ACEI = angiotensin-converting enzyme inhibitor; LVEF = left ventricular ejection fraction.

dysfunction. Increasingly, however, the term *heart failure with preserved ejection fraction* is preferred, because diastolic dysfunction cannot always be demonstrated objectively and systolic function may be abnormal despite a preserved ejection fraction (Chapters 55 and 56). This picture is particularly common in older patients with a history of hypertension and diabetes mellitus. The major focus of symptomatic therapy is control of hypertension and reduction of heart rate. Therapy with an angiotensin-converting enzyme inhibitor and a β-adrenergic blocking agent is often indicated to achieve these goals; their use otherwise has not been established for this type of heart failure. Diuretics should be used as needed to treat fluid retention. Atrial fibrillation often leads to clinical decompensation both because of increased rate and loss of the atrial contribution to ventricular filling. Although there is no controlled evidence that sinus rhythm confers more benefit than rate control and anticoagulation, sinus rhythm is generally maintained when possible.

1. Mason JW, O'Connell JB, Herskowitz A, et al: A clinical trial of immunosuppressive therapy for myocarditis. N Engl J Med 1995;333:269–275.
2. Garg R, Yusuf S: Overview of randomized trials of angiotensin-converting enzyme inhibitors on mortality and morbidity in patients with heart failure. Collaborative Group on ACE Inhibitor Trials. JAMA 1995;273:1450–1456.
3. Heidenrich PA, Lee TT, Massie BM: Effect of beta-blockade on mortality in patients with heart failure: A meta-analysis of randomized clinical trials. J Am Coll Cardiol 1997;30:27–34.
4. Packer M, Coats AJ, Fowler MB, et al: Effect of carvedilol on survival in chronic heart failure. N Engl J Med 2001;344:1651–1658.
5. Digitalis Investigators Group: The effect of digoxin on mortality and morbidity in patients with heart failure. N Engl J Med 1997;336:525–533.
6. Pitt B, Remme W, Zannad F, et al: Eplerenone, a selective aldosterone blocker, in patients with left ventricular dysfunction after myocardial infarction. N Engl J Med 2003;348:1309–1321.
7. Bradley DJ, Bradley EA, Baughman KL, et al: Cardiac resynchronization and death from progressive heart failure: A meta-analysis of randomized controlled trials. JAMA 2003;289:730–740.

SUGGESTED READINGS

ACC/AHA Guidelines for the Evaluation and Management of Chronic Heart Failure in the Adult. (Hunt SA, Baker DW, Chin MH, et al: Executive summary. J Am Coll Cardiol 2001;38:2001–2013.) *The complete text represents the diligent consensus of a large panel regarding diagnosis and therapy of all stages of heart failure, and is available at both www.acc.org and www.americanheart.org.*
Braunwald E, Seidman CE, Sigwart U: Contemporary evaluation and management of hypertrophic cardiomyopathy. Circulation 2002;106:1312–1316. *A case-based discussion.*
Maron BJ: Hypertrophic cardiomyopathy: A systematic review. JAMA 2002;287:1308–1320. *Although an important cause of death and disability, hypertrophic cardiomyopathy is compatible with normal longevity.*
Maron MS, Olivotto I, Betocchi S, et al: Effect of left ventricular outflow tract obstruction on clinical outcome in hypertrophic cardiomyopathy. N Engl J Med 2003;348:295–303. *Left ventricular outflow tract obstruction at rest is a strong, independent predictor of progression to heart failure and death.*
Nohria A, Lewis E, Stevenson LW: Medical management of advanced heart failure. JAMA 2002;287:628–640. *An update of current therapies.*
Shaw T, Elliott P, McKenna WJ: Dilated cardiomyopathy: A genetically heterogeneous disease. Lancet 2002;360:654–655. *Excellent brief overview.*

74 PERICARDIAL DISEASE

Warren J. Manning

PERICARDIAL ANATOMY AND FUNCTION

The pericardium is composed of two distinct layers: the fibrous parietal pericardium, which provides a protective sac around the heart to prevent sudden cardiac dilation and minimize bulk cardiac motion, and the inner, visceral pericardium intimately related to the surface of the heart. These two layers are separated by 10 to 50 mL of clear fluid, an ultrafiltrate of plasma produced by the visceral pericardium. This fluid acts as a lubricant to minimize frictional forces between the heart and surrounding structures. In health, the intrapericardial pressure is slightly negative.

Although congenital total absence of the pericardium in itself does not appear to be associated with clinical disease, partial or localized absence of pericardium, specifically around the left atrium, may be associated with focal herniation and subsequent strangulation. This condition, usually diagnosed by thoracic computed tomography (CT) or magnetic resonance imaging (MRI), has been associated with atypical chest pain or sudden death; surgical repair often is

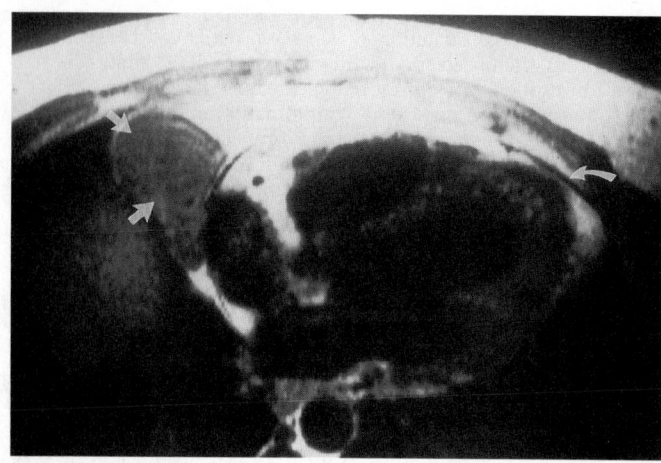

FIGURE 74–1 • Transverse (axial) magnetic resonance image. Note the anterior pericardial cyst (straight white arrows) and the normal pericardium (curved white arrow). (Courtesy of Robert R. Edelman, MD.)

recommended when a partial pericardial defect is confirmed. Benign pericardial cysts are rare and often seen as rounded or lobulated structures adjacent to the usual cardiac silhouette on the chest radiograph or adjacent to the right atrium on transthoracic echocardiography; thoracic CT and MRI (Fig. 74–1) are useful for the diagnosis of these cysts.

Acquired pericardial disease may have numerous causes, most of which produce responses that are pathophysiologically and clinically similar. These responses most frequently result in acute pericarditis, pericardial effusion, or constrictive pericarditis.

ACUTE PERICARDITIS

The most common clinical pathologic process involving the pericardium is acute pericarditis. Although multiple causes are possible (Table 74–1), the most common is viral infection. Classically, this

Table 74–1 • ETIOLOGY OF PERICARDITIS

INFECTIOUS PERICARDITIS
Viral (coxsackievirus A and B, echovirus, mumps, adenovirus, HIV, influenza)
Mycobacterium tuberculosis
Bacterial (*Pneumococcus, Streptococcus, Staphylococcus, Legionella*)
Fungal (histoplasmosis, coccidioidomycosis, candidiasis, blastomycosis)
Other (syphilis, parasites)

NON-INFECTIOUS PERICARDITIS
Idiopathic
Neoplasm
Metastatic (lung cancer, breast cancer, melanoma, lymphoma)
Primary (mesothelioma)
Renal failure
Trauma
Irradiation (especially for breast cancer, Hodgkin's disease)
Myocardial infarction
Hypothyroidism
Aortic dissection
Chylopericardium (thoracic duct injury)
Trauma
Postpericardiotomy
Chest wall injury/trauma
Pneumonia

HYPERSENSITIVITY PERICARDITIS
Collagen vascular disease (systemic lupus erythematosus, rheumatoid arthritis, scleroderma, acute rheumatic fever, Sjögren's syndrome, Reiter's syndrome, ankylosing spondylitis)
Drug induced (procainamide, hydralazine, isoniazid)
Post–myocardial infarction (Dressler's syndrome)

HIV = human immunodeficiency virus.

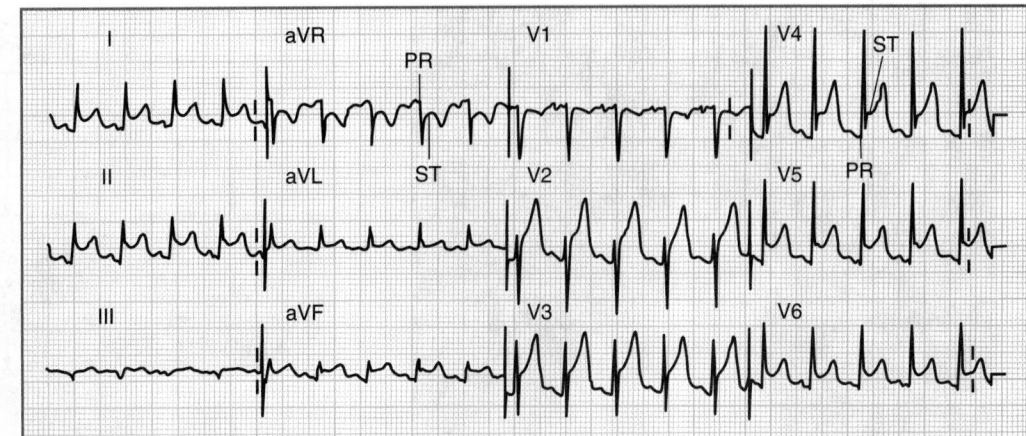

FIGURE 74–2 • A 12-lead electrocardiogram from a patient with acute pericarditis. Note the diffuse ST-T wave changes and PR elevation in lead aVR and PR segment depression in leads II and aVF and in the precordial leads. (Courtesy of Ary L. Goldberger, MD.)

disorder is characterized by chest pain, a pericardial friction rub, diffuse electrocardiographic (ECG) changes, and a pericardial effusion. The clinical syndrome is often relatively brief (days to weeks) in duration and uncomplicated, although vigilance for progression to tamponade is always prudent.

Clinical Manifestations

Chest pain of acute infectious (viral) pericarditis typically develops in young adults (18 to 30 years) 1 to 2 weeks after a "viral illness." The symptoms are sudden and severe in onset, characteristically with retrosternal and/or left precordial pain and referral to the back and trapezius ridge. Pain may be *preceded* by low-grade fever (in contrast to myocardial infarction [MI], in which the pain precedes the fever). Although radiation to the arms in a manner similar to myocardial ischemia also may occur, it is less common. The pain is often pleuritic (e.g., accentuated by inspiration or coughing) and may be aggravated (supine or left lateral decubitus posture) or relieved (upright posture) by changes in posture.

The physical examination in patients with acute pericarditis is most notable for a pericardial friction rub. Although classically described as triphasic, with systolic and early (passive ventricular filling) and late (atrial systole) diastolic components, more commonly a biphasic (systole and diastole) or a monophasic rub may be heard. The rub may be transient and positional, often best appreciated in the supine or left lateral decubitus posture. A low-grade fever, resting tachycardia, and atrial ectopy are common, but atrial fibrillation is unusual.

Diagnostic Tests

ECG changes (Fig. 74–2) are common, particularly with infectious etiologies because of associated inflammation of the superficial epicardium. During the initial few days, diffuse (limb leads and precordial leads) ST segment elevations occur in the absence of reciprocal ST segment depression. PR segment depression also is common and reflects atrial involvement. After several days, the ST segments normalize and then the T waves become inverted (in contrast to the ECG changes seen with MI, in which the temporal relationship of the T wave inversions is earlier and precedes normalization of the ST segment changes). In a large pericardial effusion, tachycardia, loss of R wave voltage (absolute R wave magnitude of ≤5 mm in all limb leads and ≤10 mm in all precordial leads), and electrical alternans (Fig. 74–3) also may be seen (see Pericardial Effusion).

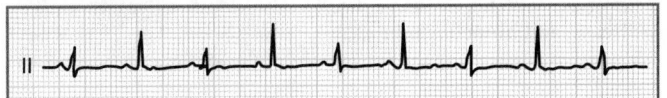

FIGURE 74–3 • Lead II rhythm strip taken from a patient with acute pericarditis complicated by a large pericardial effusion and tamponade physiology. Note the resting sinus tachycardia with relatively low voltage and electrical alternans. (Courtesy of Ary L. Goldberger, MD.)

If the pericardial effusion is minimal, the chest radiograph is often unrevealing, although a small left pleural effusion may be seen. With larger effusions (see Pericardial Effusion), there may be a loss of distinct cardiac contours and "water bottle" appearance to the cardiac silhouette. An elevated erythrocyte sedimentation rate and mild elevation of the white blood cell count also are common.

Rx Treatment

In the absence of significant pericardial effusion (see later), treatment is directed primarily at relieving the patient's symptoms. Nonsteroidal anti-inflammatory drugs, particularly indomethacin (25 to 50 mg three times daily), are generally effective, although aspirin (325 to 650 mg three times daily) also may be used. Glucocorticoids (prednisone, 20 to 60 mg/day) may be useful for resistant situations. Anti-inflammatory drugs should be continued at a constant dose until the patient is afebrile and asymptomatic for 1 week, followed by a gradual taper over the next several weeks. The use of warfarin and/or heparin should be avoided if possible to minimize the risk of hemopericardium, but anticoagulation may be required in atrial fibrillation or in the presence of a coexistent prosthetic valve. Avoidance of vigorous physical activity is recommended during the acute and early convalescent periods.

Viral and idiopathic pericarditis usually is self-limited. A quarter of patients may have recurrent symptoms, however. For this group, prolonged treatment with colchicine, 1 mg/day, or pericardiectomy should be considered. Patients with recurrent pericarditis are at increased risk for progression to constrictive pericarditis (see later).

PERICARDIAL EFFUSION

Excess fluid may develop in the pericardial space in all forms of pericardial disease. Most commonly, the fluid is exudative and reflects pericardial injury and/or inflammation. Serosanguineous effusions are typical of tuberculous and neoplastic disease but also may be seen in uremic and viral/idiopathic disease or in response to mediastinal irradiation. Hemopericardium is seen most commonly with trauma, myocardial rupture after MI, catheter-induced myocardial or epicardial coronary artery rupture, aortic dissection with rupture into the pericardial space, or primary hemorrhage in patients receiving anticoagulant therapy (often after cardiac valve surgery). Chylopericardium is rare and results from leakage or injury to the thoracic duct.

Although the presence of pericardial effusion indicates underlying pericardial disease, the clinical relevance of the pericardial effusion is associated most closely with the *rate* of fluid collection, intrapericardial pressure, and subsequent development of tamponade physiology. A rapidly accumulating effusion, as in hemopericardium caused by trauma, may result in tamponade physiology with collection of only 100 to 200 mL. By comparison, a more slowly developing effusion (hypothyroidism or chronic renal failure) may allow for gradual stretching of the pericardium, with effusions exceeding 1500 mL in the absence of hemodynamic embarrassment.

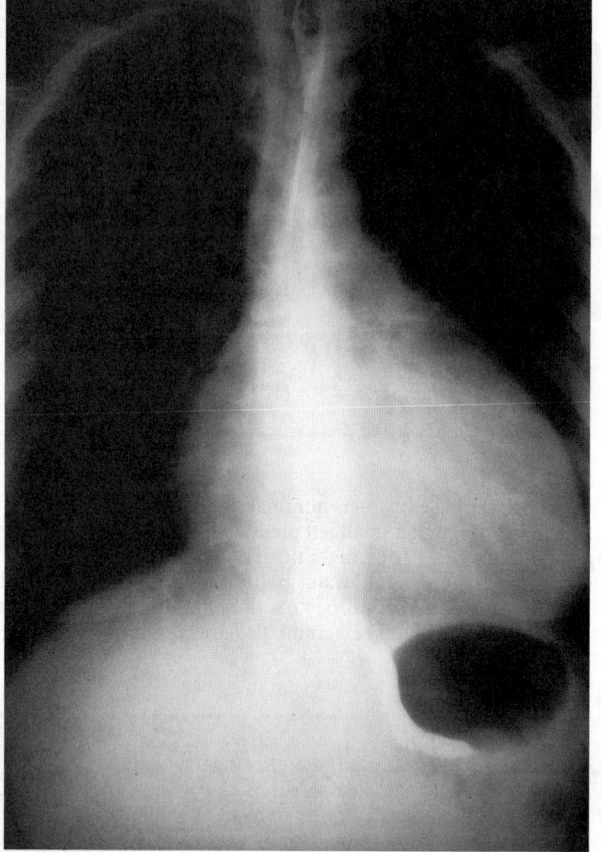

FIGURE 74–4 • Posteroanterior chest radiograph in a patient with a large pericardial effusion. Note the loss of customary heart borders and a "water bottle" configuration. (Courtesy of Sven Paulin, MD.)

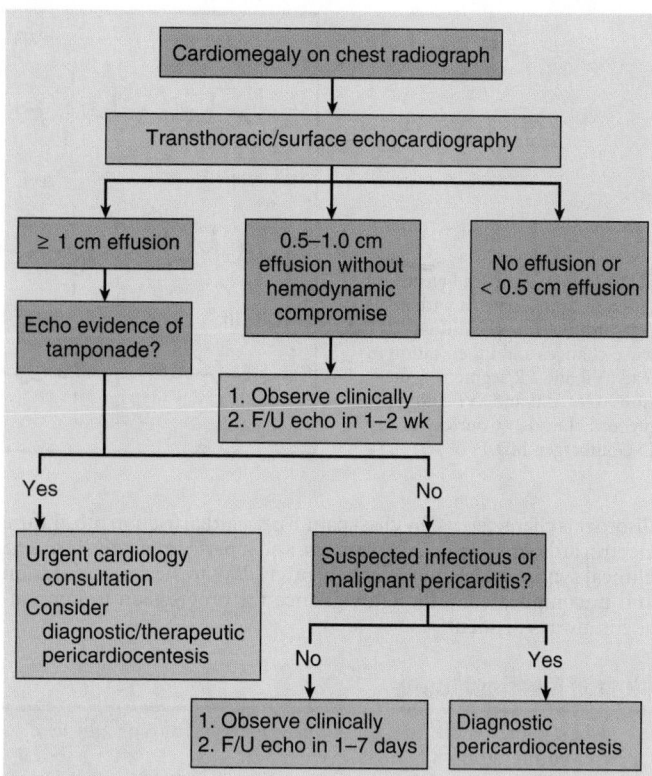

FIGURE 74–5 • Schematic for the clinical management of patients with cardiomegaly on chest radiograph and suspected pericardial effusion in patients with normal left ventricular systolic function and normal thyroid-stimulating hormone. (Adapted from Lorell BH: Pericardial disease. *In* Goldman L, Braunwald E [eds]: Primary Cardiology. Philadelphia, WB Saunders 1998, p 440.)

Diagnosis

Pericardial effusion often is suspected clinically when the patient has symptoms and signs of tamponade physiology (see later), but it also may be suggested first by unsuspected cardiomegaly on the chest radiograph, especially if loss of the customary cardiac borders and a water bottle configuration are noted (Fig. 74–4). Fluoroscopy, which may display minimal or absent motion of cardiac borders, is performed commonly when myocardial or epicardial coronary artery perforation is suspected during a diagnostic or interventional percutaneous procedure.

In most situations, two-dimensional transthoracic (surface) echocardiography is the diagnostic imaging procedure of choice for the evaluation and qualitative assessment of suspected pericardial effusion (Fig. 74–5). In emergency situations, it can be performed at the bedside, with the subcostal four-chamber view being the most informative imaging plane. This imaging plane is particularly relevant because it allows the size and location of the effusion to be assessed from an orientation that determines whether the effusion can be drained percutaneously. Transudative effusions typically appear relatively echolucent (Fig. 74–6A), whereas organized/exudative and hemorrhagic effusions have an echo-filled or a ground-glass appearance (Fig. 74–6B). Stranding, which may be appreciated in organized or chronic effusions, suggests an inability to drain the effusion fully by percutaneous approaches. In patients with large effusions, which are associated with electrical alternans, the heart may appear to swing freely within the pericardial sac.

CARDIAC TAMPONADE

Accumulation of fluid in the pericardium with a resultant increase in pericardial pressure and impairment of ventricular filling results in cardiac tamponade. This complication of pericarditis may be fatal if it is not recognized quickly and treated aggressively. The hallmarks of cardiac tamponade are increased intracardiac pressure and the resulting impaired ventricular filling and depressed cardiac output. In tamponade, ventricular filling is impaired throughout diastole; by

comparison, early diastolic filling is relatively normal with pericardial constriction. Invasive hemodynamic assessment reveals equalization of right and left atrial and right and left ventricular diastolic pressures. Tamponade may not be an "all-or-none" phenomenon; mild or "low-pressure" tamponade can be seen when intrapericardial pressures are only modestly elevated, with resultant equalization of atrial pressures but not diastolic ventricular pressures.

Clinical Manifestations

The clinical features of cardiac tamponade may mimic those of heart failure, with dyspnea on exertion, orthopnea, and hepatic engorgement. Many clinical features help distinguish cardiac tamponade from constrictive pericarditis and restrictive cardiomyopathy (Table 74–2). The typical physical examination with tamponade includes jugular venous distention with a prominent *x* descent (Fig. 74–7), sinus tachycardia with hypotension, a narrow pulse pressure, elevated (>10 mm Hg) pulsus paradoxus, and distant heart sounds. The pulsus paradoxus may be apparent with palpation, but more commonly it is measured with a sphygmomanometer during slow respiration; direct arterial monitoring is not generally necessary for quantification. A small (<10 mm Hg) pulsus is normal and is related to the ventricles being confined within the pericardium and sharing a common septum. With inspiration, right ventricular filling is enhanced, displacing the interventricular septum toward the left ventricle and exaggerating the reduction in left ventricular filling and resultant stroke volume. The exaggerated pulsus is not specific for tamponade; it also may be present with hypovolemic shock, chronic obstructive pulmonary disease, and bronchospasm.

Diagnosis

For patients in whom the history and/or physical examination suggest tamponade, emergency transthoracic echocardiography is imperative and generally diagnostic. Echocardiographic evidence of

Figure 74–5 flowchart

Cardiomegaly on chest radiograph
→ Transthoracic/surface echocardiography

- ≥ 1 cm effusion → Echo evidence of tamponade?
- 0.5–1.0 cm effusion without hemodynamic compromise → 1. Observe clinically 2. F/U echo in 1–2 wk
- No effusion or < 0.5 cm effusion

Echo evidence of tamponade?
- Yes → Urgent cardiology consultation / Consider diagnostic/therapeutic pericardiocentesis
- No → Suspected infectious or malignant pericarditis?
  - No → 1. Observe clinically 2. F/U echo in 1–7 days
  - Yes → Diagnostic pericardiocentesis

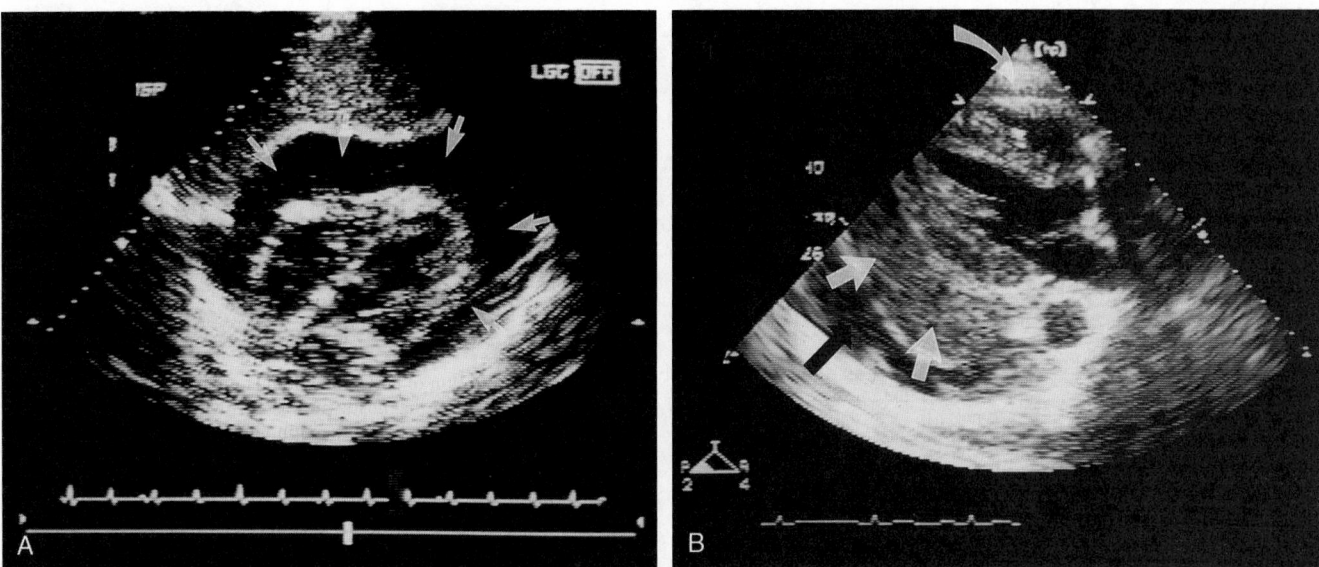

FIGURE 74–6 • *A*, Transthoracic echocardiogram from the subcostal approach. Note the large echolucent area/pericardial effusion (white arrows) surrounding the heart. The right ventricle is compressed. *B*, Transthoracic echocardiogram from the parasternal long-axis window in another patient. Note the large echo-filled pericardial effusion posterior (straight white arrows) to the left ventricle and anterior (curved white arrow) to the right ventricle. This patient had a hemorrhagic pericardial effusion that developed several weeks after aortic valve replacement and long-term warfarin treatment. A pleural effusion (black arrow) also is seen.

Table 74–2 • **COMPARISON OF PHYSICAL EXAMINATION AND DIAGNOSTIC TESTS FOR CARDIAC TAMPONADE, CONSTRICTIVE PERICARDITIS, AND RESTRICTIVE CARDIOMYOPATHY**

CHARACTERISTIC	CARDIAC TAMPONADE	CONSTRICTIVE PERICARDITIS	RESTRICTIVE CARDIOMYOPATHY
CLINICAL			
Pulsus paradoxus	+	+/–	–
Prominent *y* descent	–	+	–
Prominent *x* descent	+	+	–
Kussmaul's sign	–	+	–
S₃ or pericardial "knock"	–	+	+
S₄	–	–	+
ECG			
Low voltage	+	+	+
Abnormal P waves	–	+	+/–
Electrical alternans	+	–	+
CHEST RADIOGRAPHY			
Cardiomegaly	+	–	–
Pericardial calcification	–	+	–
ECHOCARDIOGRAPHY			
Pericardial effusion	+	–	–
Pericardial thickening	–	+	–
Small right ventricle	+	–	–
Thickened myocardium	–	–	+
Enhanced respiratory variation in E wave	+	+	–
CT/MRI			
Pericardial thickening	–	+	–
Pericardial calcification	–	+	–
CARDIAC CATHETERIZATION			
Equalization of pressures	+	+	–
Abnormal myocardial biopsy	–	–	+

CT = computed tomography; ECG = electrocardiography; MRI = magnetic resonance imaging.

tamponade physiology includes a compressed/small right ventricular chamber with late diastolic invagination of the right atrial and right ventricular free wall on two-dimensional imaging (Chapter 51). Because of the frequent coexistence of tachycardia, the latter sometimes is appreciated best with higher temporal resolution M-mode echocardiography. In addition to diastolic invagination, M-mode echocardiography also may show exaggerated inspiratory septal motion and variation in the duration of aortic valve opening. Localized right

atrial, left atrial, and left ventricular diastolic collapse also may be seen and are particularly relevant for loculated effusions, such as effusions after trauma and cardiac surgery. Pseudoprolapse of the mitral valve may be seen because of the compressed left ventricular cavity. When surface echocardiography is inadequate, as in a post-thoracotomy patient or a patient with chest wall trauma, transesophageal echocardiography may be helpful. Thoracic CT and MRI may be particularly valuable for delineation of loculated pericardial

Cardiovascular Disease

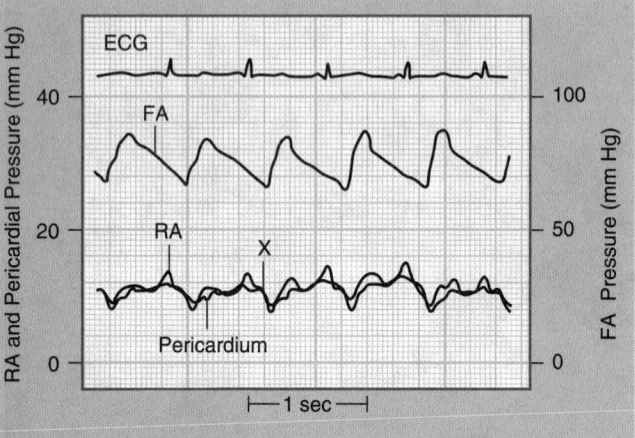

FIGURE 74-7 • Simultaneous right atrial (RA), intrapericardial, and femoral artery (FA) pressure recordings in a patient with cardiac tamponade. Note the elevated and equilibrated intrapericardial and RA pressures with a prominent x descent and blunted y descent suggestive of impaired right atrial emptying in early diastole. The arterial pulse pressure is narrowed. (From Lorell BH: Profiles in constriction, restriction and tamponade. In Baim DS, Grossman W [eds]: Cardiac Catheterization, Angiography, and Intervention, 6th ed. Philadelphia, Williams & Wilkins, 2000, p 840.)

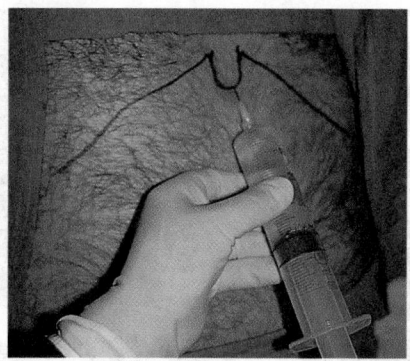

FIGURE 74-8 • Aspiration of pericardial fluid is indicated in cardiac tamponade or to obtain fluid for diagnostic purposes. A wide-bore needle is inserted in the epigastrium below the xiphoid process and advanced in the direction of the medial third of the right clavicle. The procedure is preferably performed in a catheterization laboratory under echocardiographic guidance, but it may need to be performed emergently for life-saving purposes in other settings. If the needle is connected to the V lead of an ECG monitor, ST elevation usually is seen if the needle touches the epicardium. This can be useful in distinguishing a bloody pericardial effusion from accidental puncture of the heart. Other complications of the procedure may include arrhythmias, vasovagal attack, and pneumothorax. (From Forbes CD, Jackson WF: Color Atlas and Text of Clinical Medicine, 3rd ed. London, Mosby, 2003, with permission.)

effusions. Finally, Doppler echocardiography may be used to assess transtricuspid and transmitral flow profiles, with an exaggerated peak E wave respiratory variation seen in tamponade. Many of these typical echocardiographic findings may be absent in patients with significant pulmonary artery hypertension.

Rx Treatment

When tamponade is suggested clinically and confirmed on echocardiography, immediate treatment may be life-saving (Fig. 74-8). When time allows, right heart catheterization should be performed to confirm elevated intrapericardial pressure and "equalization" of right atrial, left atrial, pulmonary capillary wedge, right ventricular diastolic, and left ventricular diastolic pressures. If echocardiography shows at least 1 cm of fluid anterior to the mid right ventricular free wall, percutaneous pericardiocentesis generally can be performed safely. During this procedure, a small catheter is advanced over a needle inserted into the pericardial cavity. Echocardiographic guidance is particularly useful for smaller effusions or if percutaneous pericardiocentesis is performed by less experienced operators. As much fluid as possible should be removed, with monitoring of filling pressures. Unless the cause already has been identified, pericardial fluid should be sent for evaluation (including cytology and cultures for bacteria, fungi, and tuberculosis). A flexible drainage catheter may be left in the pericardial space for several days to avoid early reaccumulation. Serial echocardiography should be performed to confirm that the fluid has not reaccumulated.

Hemodynamically significant effusions of less than 1 cm, organized or multiloculated effusions, or focal effusions confined to the posterior or lateral cardiac borders or around the atria should be approached surgically through a limited thoracotomy/mediastinoscopy and pericardial window. For all effusions related to a malignancy and for which aggressive chemotherapy is *not* being administered, reaccumulation in the ensuing weeks or months is the norm, and elective surgery (pericardial window) should be considered before hospital discharge. Hemorrhagic effusions related to cardiac trauma or aortic dissection also are managed best by emergency surgery (if available) or in combination with temporizing pericardiocentesis. If the patient is in extremis, emergency pericardiocentesis should be performed at the bedside.

APPROACH TO EFFUSION WITHOUT TAMPONADE

For patients with suspected pericardial effusion, transthoracic echocardiography is the initial test of choice and in most patients is

definitive in confirming the presence or absence of a significant pericardial effusion (loculated effusions may be identified better by CT or MRI). If a small (0.5 to 1 cm) echolucent or "organized" pericardial effusion is seen, the patient generally can be observed with a follow-up echocardiogram in 1 to 2 weeks (sooner if clinical deterioration is evident). If the follow-up study shows a smaller effusion, subsequent echocardiograms are not necessary (unless the patient's clinical condition changes). Assuming a clinical history of "viral" pericarditis, assessment of renal function and thyroid-stimulating hormone is reasonable, but the results probably will be normal. A tuberculin skin test should be performed routinely. One also should exclude a drug-induced etiology (e.g., cromolyn, hydralazine, isoniazid, phenytoin, procainamide, reserpine).

In a moderate (1 to 2 cm) or large (>2 cm) pericardial effusion, treatment and follow-up depend on the clinical scenario and echocardiographic findings. If the patient is clinically unstable and tamponade is suggested (see earlier), urgent cardiology consultation and diagnostic/therapeutic pericardiocentesis should be planned. If the patient is hemodynamically stable and tamponade is not suggested, the patient can be observed and a follow-up study performed in 1 to 7 days. The initial evaluation is the same as listed earlier for a small effusion. Follow-up echocardiographic studies should be continued until the size of the effusion has decreased, but they need not be repeated until complete resolution. If bacterial or malignant pericarditis is suspected, diagnostic pericardiocentesis should be performed even in the absence of clinical instability or suggestion of tamponade; tuberculous pericarditis is diagnosed best by pericardial biopsy. A complete blood count with differential, platelet count, and coagulation parameters also should be assessed. Anticoagulation with heparin or warfarin should be discontinued unless the patient has a mechanical heart valve or atrial fibrillation. Blood cultures are indicated if an infectious cause is suspected. Complement, antinuclear antibodies, and the sedimentation rate may be helpful if systemic lupus erythematosus is being considered, although isolated pericardial effusion is unlikely to be the first manifestation of this disorder. Pericarditis after MI (Dressler's syndrome) is now unusual; given experimental laboratory evidence that some of the nonsteroidal drugs promote left ventricular aneurysm formation in this setting, aspirin is the preferred agent to relieve pain in Dressler's syndrome. The presence of an echo-filled effusion should raise concern for hemorrhagic or organized pericarditis, which may progress to constriction.

CHRONIC PERICARDIAL EFFUSIONS

Tuberculous pericarditis is the most common cause of a chronic pericardial effusion. Frequently, pericardial calcification develops and can be appreciated by thoracic CT. Symptoms are those of a chronic systemic illness and include weight loss, fatigue, and dyspnea on exertion (Chapter 341). Chest radiograph to obtain evidence of pulmonary tuberculosis, analysis of gastric aspirates, and tuberculin skin tests should be performed. Pericardial biopsy is more commonly diagnostic of tuberculous pericarditis than is pericardial fluid staining or culture.

Hypothyroidism/myxedema is another common cause of large pericardial effusions, especially in the elderly (Chapter 239). The effusion commonly is identified first on a chest radiograph and often is seen in the absence of resting tachycardia. Measurement of thyroid-stimulating hormone is diagnostic. The effusion and coexistent cardiomyopathy respond to hormone replacement. In the absence of hemodynamic compromise, pericardiocentesis often is not needed in this situation. Uremic pericardial effusions also are common and often respond to initiation of or more intensive dialysis (Chapter 117).

CONSTRICTIVE PERICARDITIS

Constrictive pericarditis is an uncommon condition with impairment of mid and late ventricular filling from a thickened/noncompliant pericardium. In the classic form, fibrous scarring and adhesions of both pericardial layers lead to obliteration of the pericardial cavity. Early ventricular filling is unimpeded, but diastolic filling subsequently is reduced abruptly as a result of the inability of the ventricles to fill because of physical constraints imposed by a rigid, thickened, and sometimes calcified pericardium. In less developed countries, tuberculosis is the most common cause of chronic constrictive pericarditis, whereas in the United States, tuberculosis is infrequently the culprit. Constriction may be associated with malignancy (lung cancer, breast cancer, lymphoma), histoplasmosis, mediastinal irradiation, purulent or recurrent viral pericarditis, rheumatoid arthritis, uremia, chest trauma or hemopericardium, and cardiac surgery. Constriction may follow cardiac surgery by several weeks to months and may occur decades after chest wall irradiation. The "cause" may not be identified in many patients.

Pathophysiology

The normal pericardium is 3 mm or less thick. With chronic constriction, especially from tuberculosis, the pericardium may thicken to 10 mm or greater, calcify, and intimately involve the epicardium. In subacute constriction, calcification is less prominent, and the pericardium may be only minimally thickened. As with cardiac tamponade, the pathophysiology of constriction includes impaired diastolic ventricular filling, which leads to elevated venous pressure. Tamponade and constriction have many important differences (see Table 74–2), however. With constriction, the impairment in ventricular filling is minimal in early diastole, and a prominent y descent is present.

Subsequently, diastolic pressure rises abruptly when cardiac volume reaches the anatomic limit set by the noncompliant pericardium; by comparison, in tamponade, ventricular filling is impaired throughout diastole. Diastolic pressure remains elevated until the onset of systole. This prominent y descent with an elevated plateau of ventricular pressure has been termed the *dip and plateau* or *square root sign* (Fig. 74–9); by comparison, in tamponade, the y descent is absent. Stroke volume and cardiac output are reduced because of impaired filling, whereas intrinsic systolic function of the ventricles may be normal or only minimally impaired.

Clinical Manifestations

In constriction, the most prominent physical finding is an abnormal jugular venous pulse. Central venous pressure is elevated and displays prominent x and y descents. For patients in sinus rhythm, the x descent is coincident with the carotid pulse. The y descent, which is absent or diminished in tamponade, is most prominent and abbreviated because of a rapid rise in pressure in mid-diastole. A diagnosis of constriction always should be suspected in patients with a prominent y descent with dyspnea, weakness, anorexia, peripheral edema, hepatomegaly, splenomegaly, and ascites. The pulse pressure is often narrowed, but pulsus paradoxus is usually absent. Pleural effusions are common. The clinical picture may mimic hepatic cirrhosis, but with distended neck veins. Venous pressure often fails to fall with inspiration (Kussmaul's sign), and arterial pulse pressure is normal or reduced. The apical pulse is often poorly defined, and heart sounds may be distant. A loud S_3, the *pericardial knock,* may be audible early after aortic valve closure because of the sudden deceleration in ventricular filling.

Diagnostic Tests

The ECG of patients with constriction is often abnormal and displays low QRS voltage, especially in the limb leads; P mitrale; and nonspecific ST-T wave changes. Atrial fibrillation may be present in one third of patients. The chest radiograph may show pericardial calcification in tuberculous constriction, but the finding of pericardial calcification is not diagnostic for constriction. Cardiac size may be small, normal, or enlarged. Transthoracic echocardiography is less helpful than with cardiac tamponade, but it may display pericardial thickening/calcification, abrupt posterior deflection of the interventricular septum at end-diastole, and M-mode posterior wall "flat tiring." Enhanced transmitral and transtricuspid Doppler E wave variation with respiration may be particularly helpful in establishing the diagnosis. The inferior vena cava and hepatic veins often are markedly dilated with blunted respiratory variability in caval diameter.

Increased pericardial thickness is diagnosed most reliably by CT or MRI (Fig. 74–10). CT is more helpful for the identification of

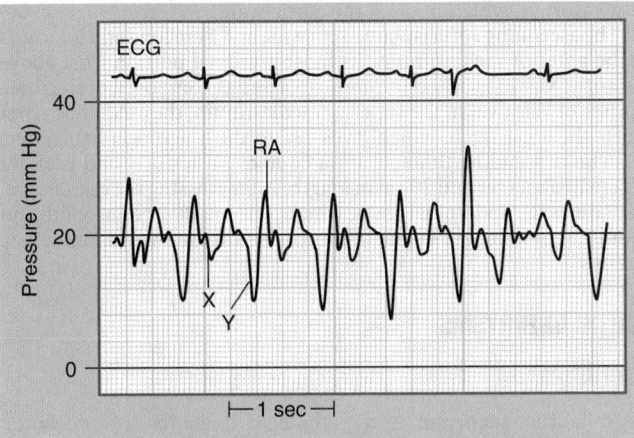

FIGURE 74–9 • Right atrial (RA) pressure recording from a patient with constrictive pericarditis. Note the elevation in pressure and prominent y descent corresponding to rapid early diastolic right atrial emptying. (From Lorell BH: Profiles in constriction, restriction and tamponade. *In* Baim DS, Grossman W [eds]: Cardiac Catheterization, Angiography, and Intervention, 6th ed. Philadelphia, Williams & Wilkins, 2000, p 832.)

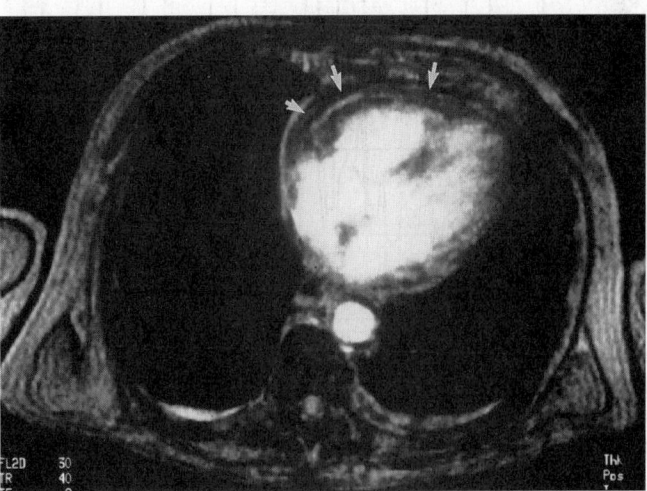

FIGURE 74–10 • Transverse magnetic resonance image. Note the markedly thickened pericardium (white arrows) in this 35-year-old man who had received radiation therapy for Hodgkin's disease 20 years earlier and was seeking medical attention for progressive dyspnea on exertion.

pericardial calcification. Right atrial, inferior vena cava, and hepatic vein distention also are seen commonly with CT and MRI. As with the chest radiograph, CT and MRI do not indicate the physiologic significance of these anatomic findings and need to be interpreted in the context of the clinical findings.

At cardiac catheterization, patients with chronic constrictive pericarditis usually have elevation (>15 mm Hg) and equalization (within 5 mm Hg) of right atrial, right ventricular diastolic, pulmonary capillary wedge, and left ventricular diastolic pressures. Right ventricular end-diastolic pressure is often one third of systolic pressure, and pulmonary artery hypertension is mild. Cardiac output usually is depressed. Right atrial pressure is characterized by a preserved *x* descent with a prominent early diastolic *y* descent. The right atrial pressure fails to decrease appropriately or may rise during inspiration. Right and left ventricular diastolic pressures display an early diastolic dip followed by a plateau (Fig. 74–11), although this finding may be difficult to appreciate if the patient is tachycardic or in atrial fibrillation.

Rx Treatment

Constrictive pericarditis occasionally may reverse spontaneously when it develops in acute pericarditis. More commonly, the natural history of this disease is one of progression with declining cardiac output and progressive renal and hepatic failure. Surgical stripping/removal of both layers of the adherent pericardium is the definitive therapy. The benefits of pericardial stripping may be modest initially but continue to be manifested over the ensuing months. Operative mortality is generally low but may exceed 5 to 15% in the most advanced cases. The surgical risk is related to the extent of myocardial involvement and the severity of secondary hepatic and/or renal dysfunction. For patients with suspected tuberculous constriction, antituberculous therapy should be administered before and after pericardial surgery.

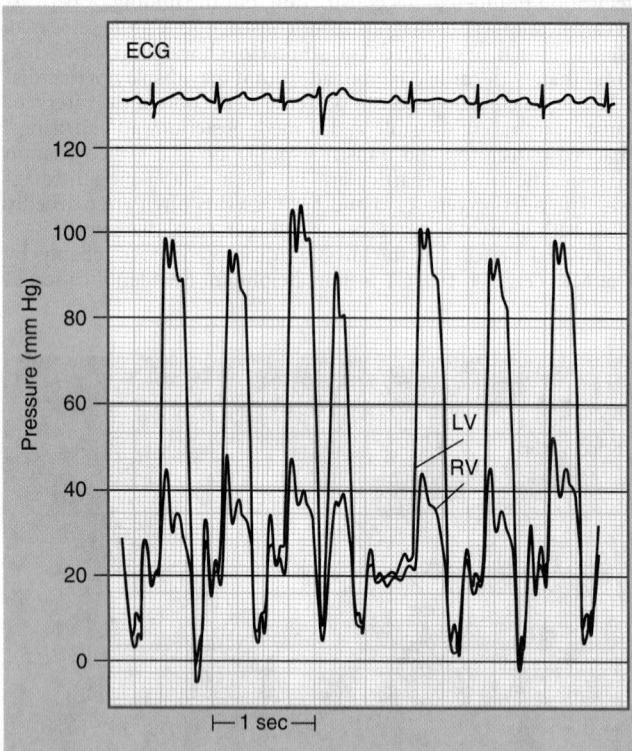

FIGURE 74–11 • Simultaneous left (LV) and right (RV) ventricular pressure recordings in a patient with constrictive pericarditis. Note the equilibration of LV and RV diastolic pressures and the "dip and plateau" most apparent with the prolonged diastole. (From Lorell BH: Profiles in constriction, restriction and tamponade. In Baim DS, Grossman W [eds]: Grossman's Cardiac Catheterization, Angiography, and Intervention, 6th ed. Philadelphia, Lippincott Williams & Wilkins, 2000, p 832.)

EFFUSIVE-CONSTRICTIVE PERICARDITIS

Effusive-constrictive pericarditis is characterized by the combination of a tense pericardial effusion in the presence of visceral pericardial constriction and may represent an intermediate stage in the development of constrictive pericarditis. Causes of effusive-constrictive pericarditis are the same as those associated with constriction, and the clinical features resemble those of tamponade and constriction. Physical examination shows pulsus paradoxus and a prominent *x* descent in the absence of a *y* descent. The cardiac silhouette is generally enlarged because of the associated pericardial effusion, whereas the ECG displays low QRS voltage and nonspecific ST-T wave changes. Surface echocardiography may show an echo-filled pericardial effusion with thickened pericardium and fibrinous pericardial bands. Although this echocardiographic appearance should heighten suspicion, the diagnosis generally is made after successful pericardiocentesis. Rather than normalizing after pericardiocentesis, intracardiac pressures remain elevated with a square root sign in the ventricular tracings and development of a prominent *y* descent in the atrial and jugular venous pressure pulses. Kussmaul's sign also may be evident. Treatment by excision of visceral and parietal pericardium is usually effective.

Future Directions

Access to the pericardial space may provide a new means to deliver novel gene or pharmacologic therapies to treat myocardial (angiogenesis, antiarrhythmics) and/or pericardial disease.

SUGGESTED READINGS

Adler Y, Finkelstein Y, Guindo J, et al: Colchicine treatment for recurrent pericarditis. A decade of experience. Circulation 1998;97:2183–2185. *Colchicine is often effective.*

Hoit BD: Management of effusive and constrictive pericardial heart disease. Circulation 2002;105:2939–2942. *A case-based review.*

Spodick DH: Acute pericarditis: Current concepts and practice. JAMA 2003;289:1150–1153. *A brief review.*

Tsang TS, Enriquez-Sarano M, Freeman WK, et al: Consecutive 1127 therapeutic echocardiographically guided pericardiocenteses: Clinical profile, practice patterns, and outcomes spanning 21 years. Mayo Clin Proc 2002;77:429–436. *Emphasizes the increasing prevalence of postprocedure effusions and the current role of catheter drainage.*

75 DISEASES OF THE AORTA

Eric M. Isselbacher

The aorta is composed of three tissue layers. The intima is a thin inner layer lined with endothelial cells. The middle layer, or media, is the thickest layer of the aortic wall and is composed of sheets of elastic tissue that give the aorta tremendous tensile strength. The outermost layer, or adventitia, is composed mostly of collagen and carries the vasa vasorum, which nourish the aortic wall.

The ascending aorta is about 3 cm wide and 5 cm long and is located in the anterior mediastinum. Its most proximal portion (just above the aortic valve) is called the *aortic root* and is composed of the three sinuses of Valsalva. In the superior mediastinum, the ascending aorta meets the aortic arch, which gives rise to the brachiocephalic arteries. The descending thoracic aorta courses posteriorly and is about 2.5 cm in diameter and 20 cm in length. After crossing the diaphragm, it becomes the abdominal aorta, which is normally 2 cm in width and about 15 cm in length before it bifurcates into the two common iliac arteries.

AORTIC ANEURYSMS

Definition

An aortic aneurysm is a pathologic dilatation of the aorta. Aneurysms are described in terms of their location, size, shape, and etiology. The shape of an aneurysm is *fusiform* when there is symmetrical dilatation of the aorta and *saccular* when the dilatation involves mainly one wall. In addition, there may be a *false aneurysm* or *pseudoaneurysm* when the aorta is enlarged as a consequence of dilatation of only the outer layers of the vessel wall, such as occurs with a contained rupture of the aortic wall.

Aneurysms may involve any part of the aorta, but abdominal aortic aneurysms are much more common than thoracic aneurysms. Abdominal aortic aneurysms are four to five times more common in men than in women and have a prevalence of at least 3% in persons older than age 50. Among thoracic aortic aneurysms, aneurysms of the descending aorta are most common, followed by aneurysms involving the ascending aorta; aneurysms of the aortic arch are uncommon. Descending thoracic aortic aneurysms may extend distally and involve the abdominal aorta, creating a thoracoabdominal aortic aneurysm.

Etiology

Atherosclerosis is the major underlying cause of abdominal aortic aneurysms. The infrarenal aorta tends to be affected most severely by the atherosclerotic process and is accordingly the common site for aortic aneurysm formation. The mechanism by which atherosclerosis leads to the growth of aneurysms is uncertain. Evidence suggests that the atherosclerotic thickening of the aortic intima reduces diffusion of oxygen and nutrients from the aortic lumen to the media, in turn causing degeneration of the elastic elements of the media and a weakening of the aortic wall. As the wall begins to dilate, tension on the wall increases according to Laplace's law (tension is proportional to the product of the pressure and the radius), promoting further expansion of the aneurysm. In addition to atherosclerotic factors, there seems to be a genetic predisposition to the development of abdominal aortic aneurysms: 28% of first-degree relatives of patients with abdominal aortic aneurysms may be affected.

Although atherosclerosis is also a common cause of aneurysms of the descending thoracic aorta, the most important cause of aneurysms of the ascending thoracic aorta is degeneration of the elastin and collagen within the media of the aortic wall. When this process is severe, it is known as *cystic medial necrosis*, which histologically appears as smooth muscle cell necrosis and degeneration of elastic layers within the media. Cystic medial necrosis is found in almost all patients with Marfan syndrome (Chapter 276), placing these patients at high risk for aortic aneurysm formation. Among patients without overt evidence of connective tissue disease, it is unclear what specifically predisposes to the development of medial degeneration. A history of hypertension is a common risk factor, however. Syphilis was a common cause of thoracic aortic aneurysms, with degeneration of the aortic media during the secondary phase of the disease producing a weakening of aortic wall; however, syphilis now has become a rare cause. Other rare causes of thoracic aortic aneurysms include infectious aortitis, great vessel arteritis, aortic trauma, and aortic dissection.

Clinical Manifestations

Most abdominal and thoracic aortic aneurysms are asymptomatic when they are discovered incidentally on a routine physical examination or imaging study. When patients with abdominal aortic aneurysms experience symptoms, pain in the hypogastrium or lower back is the most frequent complaint. The pain tends to have a steady gnawing quality that may last hours or days. Aneurysm expansion or impending rupture may be heralded by new or worsening pain, often of sudden onset. With rupture, the pain often is associated with hypotension and the presence of a pulsatile abdominal mass.

Patients with thoracic aortic aneurysms may have chest pain or, less often, back pain. Vascular complications include aortic insufficiency (sometimes with secondary heart failure), hemoptysis, and thromboembolism. An enlarging aneurysm may produce local mass effects owing to compression of adjacent mediastinal structures, producing symptoms such as coughing, wheezing, dyspnea, hoarseness, recurrent pneumonia, or dysphagia.

Diagnosis

Abdominal aortic aneurysms may be palpable on physical examination, although obesity may obscure even large aneurysms. Typically, abdominal aortic aneurysms are hard to size accurately by physical examination alone because adjacent structures often make an aneurysm feel larger than it really is. Thoracic aortic aneurysms usually cannot be palpated at all.

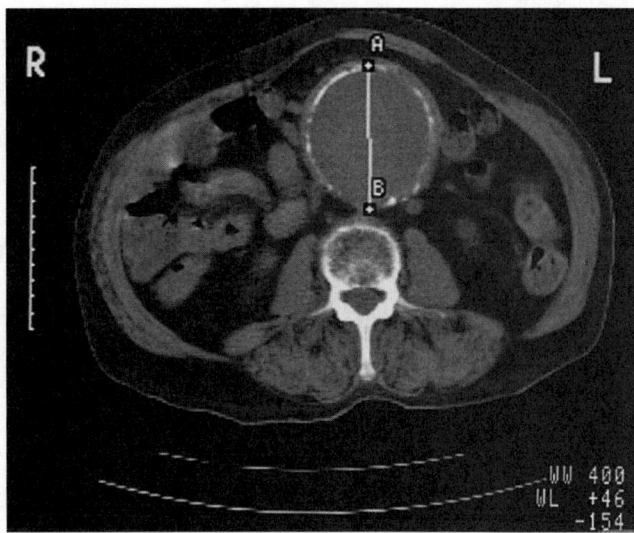

FIGURE 75–1 • Abdominal aortic aneurysm on CT scan. This is a sensitive imaging method that allows precise measurement of size (point A to point B) and demonstrates the thickened wall of the aneurysm. (From Forbes CD, Jackson WF: Color Atlas and Text of Clinical Medicine, 3rd ed. London, Mosby, 2003, with permission.)

The definitive diagnosis of an aortic aneurysm is made by radiographic examination. Abdominal aortic aneurysms can be detected and sized by either abdominal ultrasonography or computed tomography (CT). Ultrasound is extremely sensitive and is the most practical method to use in screening for aortic aneurysms. CT is even more accurate (Fig. 75–1) and can size an aneurysm to within a diameter of ± 2 mm. Although CT is less practical than ultrasound as a screening tool, when the diagnosis has been made, it is the preferred modality for following the serial changes in aneurysm size over time.

Thoracic aortic aneurysms frequently are recognized on chest radiographs, often producing widening of the mediastinal silhouette, enlargement of the aortic knob, or displacement of the trachea from midline. CT is an excellent modality for detecting and sizing thoracic aneurysms and is particularly useful for following aneurysm size over time. Transthoracic echocardiography, which generally visualizes the aortic root and ascending aorta well, is useful for screening patients with Marfan syndrome because this group is at particular risk for aneurysms involving this portion of the aorta.

Prognosis

The chief concern in managing an aortic aneurysm is its tendency to rupture. Most aneurysms expand over time, and the risk of rupture increases with aneurysm size. Abdominal aortic aneurysms of less than 4 cm have only a 0 to 2% risk of rupture, whereas aneurysms larger than 5 cm have a 22% risk of rupture within 2 years. The overall mortality in patients who rupture an abdominal aortic aneurysm is 80%, including a mortality of 50% even for patients who reach the hospital. Thoracic aneurysms smaller than 5 cm typically expand slowly and rarely rupture, but the rate of growth and risk of rupture increase significantly when aneurysms are 6 cm or larger. Similar to what is seen with abdominal aneurysms, the rupture of thoracic aneurysms has a high early mortality of 76% at 24 hours.

Rx Treatment

The goal of medical therapy for patients with aortic aneurysms is to attempt to reduce the risk of aneurysm expansion and rupture. β-Blockers are the mainstay because they are effective in reducing aortic pressure and the abrupt rise in pressure during systole so as to reduce the force of the blood striking the aortic wall. Aneurysms should be followed closely with serial imaging studies (e.g., CT) to detect any progressive enlargement over time that may indicate the need for surgical repair.

Continued

Aortic aneurysms that produce symptoms secondary to aneurysm expansion, vascular complications, or compression of adjacent structures should be repaired. Size is the major indicator for repair of asymptomatic aortic aneurysms. Abdominal aortic aneurysms larger than 5.5 cm should be repaired,[1,2] as should aneurysms larger than 5 cm in good operative candidates. Abdominal aneurysms larger than 4 cm should be monitored every 6 months. Descending thoracic aortic aneurysms larger than 6 cm should undergo surgical repair. Aneurysms of the ascending thoracic aorta should be repaired at 5.5 to 6 cm or larger, whereas patients with Marfan syndrome should undergo repair when the aneurysm is 5 to 5.5 cm or larger because of the high risk of rupture in these patients.

Surgical repair consists of insertion of a synthetic prosthetic tube graft. When aneurysms involve branch vessels, such as renal or mesenteric arteries, these must be reimplanted into the graft. Similarly, when a dilated aortic root must be replaced in the repair of an ascending thoracic aortic aneurysm, the coronary arteries must be reimplanted. In some centers, an alternative approach for repair of abdominal aortic aneurysms (and some descending thoracic aneurysms) is the percutaneous placement of an expandable endovascular stent graft inside the aneurysm; however, this technique usually is reserved for high-risk patients.

AORTIC DISSECTION

Definition

Aortic dissection is a rare but life-threatening condition with an early mortality of 1% per hour. Survival is significantly improved, however, if the diagnosis is made promptly and appropriate medical and/or surgical therapy is instituted. Aortic dissection classically begins with a tear in the aortic intima that exposes a diseased medial layer to the systemic pressure of intraluminal blood. The blood penetrates into the media, cleaving it into two layers longitudinally and producing a blood-filled false lumen within the aortic wall. This false lumen propagates distally (or sometimes retrograde) a variable distance along the aorta from the site of intimal tear.

The location of an aortic dissection may be described according to one of several classification systems (Fig. 75–2). Two thirds of aortic dissections are type A (proximal) and the other one third is type B (distal). The classification schemes all serve the same purpose, which is to distinguish dissections that involve the ascending aorta from dissections that do not. Involvement of the ascending aorta carries a high risk of early rupture and death from cardiac tamponade, so prognosis and management differ according to the extent of aortic involvement. Dissections also are classified according to their duration, with dissections present for less than 2 weeks considered acute and dissections present for 2 weeks or more considered chronic.

Etiology

Disease of the aortic media, with degeneration of the medial collagen and elastin, is the most common predisposing factor for aortic dissection. Patients with Marfan syndrome have classic cystic medial degeneration and are at particularly high risk of aortic dissection at a relatively young age. The peak incidence of aortic dissection in patients without Marfan syndrome is in the 60s and 70s, and men are affected twice as often as women. A history of hypertension is present in most cases, whereas a bicuspid aortic valve or known preexisting thoracic aortic aneurysm is less common. Rarely, aortic dissection may occur in a young woman during the peripartum period. Iatrogenic trauma from intra-aortic catheterization procedures or cardiac surgery also may cause aortic dissection.

Clinical Manifestations

Pain, occurring in 96% of cases and typically severe, is the most common presenting symptom of aortic dissection. The pain may be retrosternal, in the neck or throat, interscapular, in the lower back, abdominal, or in the lower extremities depending on the location of the aortic dissection. The pain may migrate as the dissection propagates distally. Thoracic pain is often of sudden onset and at its most severe at the start. It sometimes is described as "tearing," "sharp," or "stabbing." Patients also may present with acute aortic insufficiency, right coronary artery occlusion, hemopericardium, syncope, a cerebrovascular accident, or ischemic peripheral neuropathy.

Hypertension is a common finding on physical examination and is present in 70% of patients with distal aortic dissection. Hypotension also may occur, particularly among patients with proximal dissections, and is usually due to rupture into the pericardium or severe aortic insufficiency. Lastly, *pseudohypotension* may be present, in which there is a falsely low measure of upper extremity blood pressure owing to involvement of a subclavian artery by the dissection. Similarly, pulse deficits are a common finding on physical examination, particularly among patients with proximal aortic dissections, when there is involvement of the subclavian, carotid, or femoral arteries. Aortic insufficiency is another important physical finding that occurs in more than one third of patients with a proximal dissection. Paradoxically, when acute aortic insufficiency is severe, the murmur may not be appreciable, so a widened pulse pressure and congestive heart failure should raise suspicion of its presence.

Vascular complications from aortic dissection include compromise of a coronary artery causing myocardial ischemia or infarction. Involvement of the brachiocephalic arteries may produce a stroke or coma, whereas compromise of the spinal arteries may produce paraplegia. When a dissection extends into the abdominal aorta, there may be compromise of flow to one or both renal arteries, producing acute renal failure that may exacerbate hypertension. Mesenteric ischemia or frank infarction may present as abdominal pain. Finally, the dissection may extend distally to the aortic bifurcation and compromise or occlude one of the common iliac arteries, producing a femoral pulse deficit and lower extremity ischemia.

An abnormality on a chest radiograph often first raises the suspicion of aortic dissection. The findings on chest radiography are nonspecific, however, and rarely diagnostic. An enlarged mediastinal silhouette is the most common finding, present in 81 to 90% of cases. A left pleural effusion is seen commonly in patients with involvement of the descending thoracic aorta and, when small, typically represents a transudate from the inflamed aortic wall. A normal chest radiograph does not exclude the diagnosis of aortic dissection. Electrocardiogram findings in aortic dissection are nonspecific.

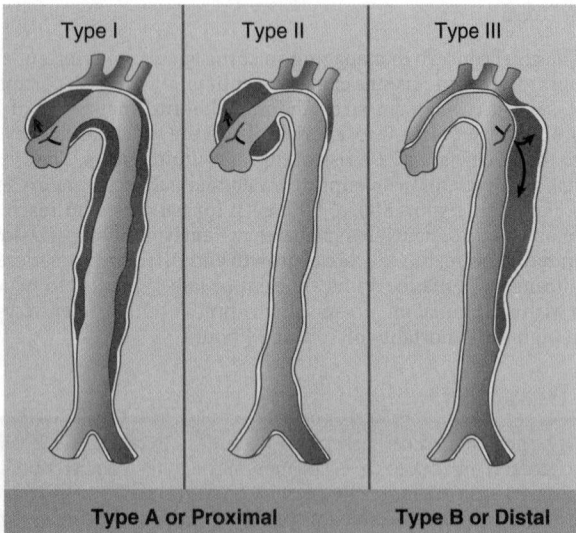

| Type I | Type II | Type III |

Type A or Proximal   **Type B or Distal**

FIGURE 75–2 • Classification systems for aortic dissection. (From Isselbacher EM: Diseases of the aorta. *In* Braunwald E, Zipes DP, Libby P [eds]: Heart Disease: A Textbook of Cardiovascular Medicine, 6th ed. Philadelphia, WB Saunders, 2001, p 1432.)

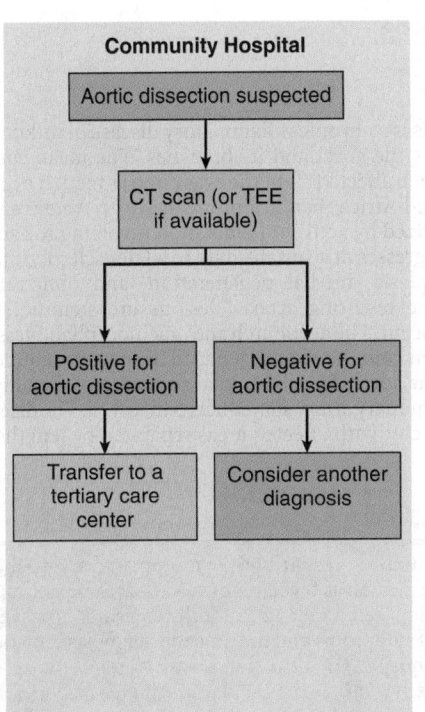

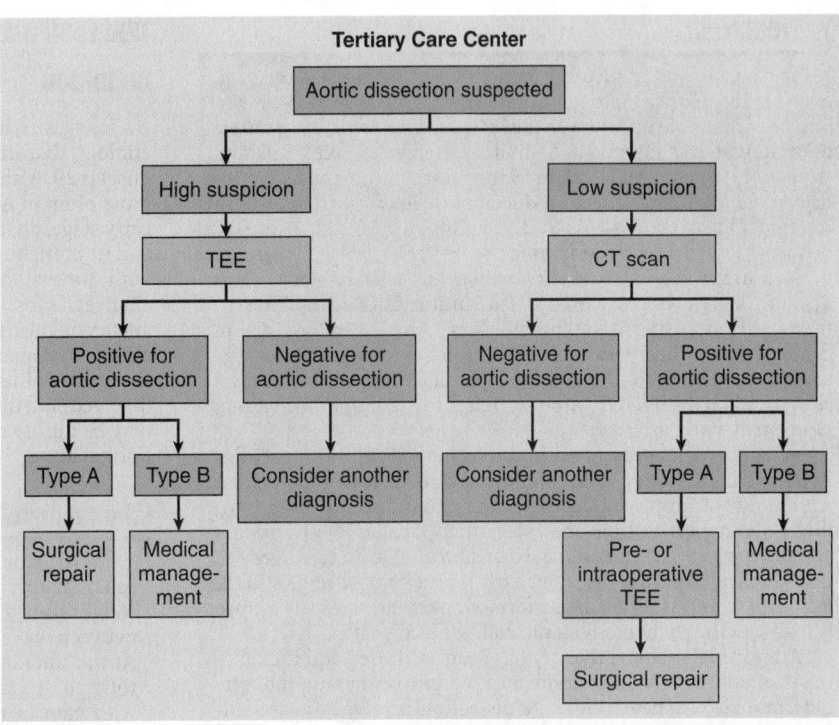

FIGURE 75–3 • Suggested algorithms for the evaluation of suspected acute aortic dissection. *A*, Approach used in many community hospitals where cardiac surgery is not performed. *B*, Approach used in many tertiary care centers where transesophageal echocardiography (TEE) and cardiac surgery are available. CT = computed tomography.

Diagnosis

When there is clinical suspicion of aortic dissection, it is essential to confirm or exclude the diagnosis promptly with an imaging study (Fig. 75–3). Several imaging modalities can diagnose the presence of aortic dissection accurately, including aortography, CT (Chapter 52), magnetic resonance imaging (Chapter 53), and transesophageal echocardiography (TEE) (Chapter 51). Each institution must determine which of these modalities is most appropriate as an initial diagnostic approach based on the availability of each and the skill and experience of the clinicians who perform and interpret the diagnostic studies.

Nevertheless, when suspicion of aortic dissection is high, TEE (Fig. 75–4) is the most rapid way to provide sufficient detail to enable the surgeon to take the patient directly to the operating room. When clinical suspicion is low (i.e., when one wants to rule out aortic dissection) contrast medium–enhanced CT (Fig. 75–5) is preferred because it is entirely noninvasive. If TEE is not readily available, contrast medium–enhanced CT is the test of choice in high-probability and low-probability patients.

FIGURE 75–4 • A transesophageal echocardiogram of the ascending aorta in long axis in a patient with a type A aortic dissection. The aortic valve (AV) is on the left, and the ascending aorta extends to the right. Within the aorta is an intimal flap (I) that originates at the level of the sinotubular junction. The true (T) and the false (F) lumens are separated by the intimal flap. LA = left atrium. (From Isselbacher EM: Diseases of the aorta. *In* Braunwald E, Zipes DP, Libby P [eds]: Heart Disease: A Textbook of Cardiovascular Medicine, 6th ed. Philadelphia, WB Saunders, 2001, plate 24.)

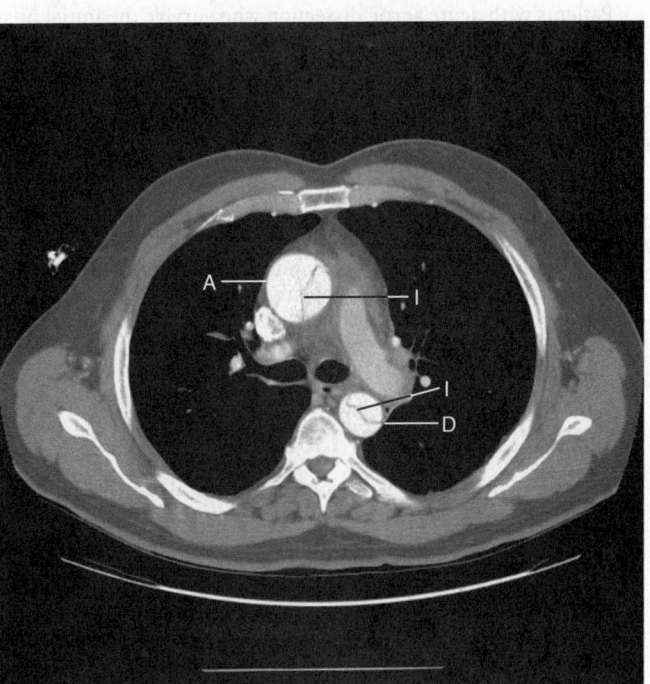

FIGURE 75–5 • A contrast medium–enhanced computed tomography scan of the chest at the level of the pulmonary artery shows an intimal flap (I) separating the two lumens of the ascending (A) and descending (D) thoracic aorta in a type A aortic dissection.

Treatment

The goal of initial medical therapy for acute aortic dissection is to halt any further progression of the aortic dissection and to reduce the risk of rupture. Whenever there is a suspicion of aortic dissection, therapy should be instituted immediately while imaging studies are ordered, rather than waiting until the diagnosis is confirmed. The initial goal is to reduce the force of ventricular contraction and reduce systolic blood pressure to 100 to 120 mm Hg or to the lowest level that maintains cerebral, cardiac, and renal perfusion. Intravenous labetalol, which acts as an α-blocker and a β-blocker, may be particularly useful in aortic dissection for controlling hypertension and contractile force. After labetalol or a pure β-blocker has been administered, intravenous nitroprusside should be added to titrate blood pressure minute by minute as needed. If β-blockers are contraindicated, calcium channel blockers may be useful.

When patients present with significant hypotension, pseudo-hypotension first should be carefully excluded. True hypotension may be due to rupture of the dissection into the pericardium, producing hemopericardium and cardiac tamponade. These patients should be treated with volume expansion and taken to surgery as quickly as possible because their early mortality is extremely high. Pericardiocentesis should be performed only as a last resort because it may precipitate hemodynamic collapse and death.

After initial medical therapy has been instituted and the diagnosis of aortic dissection confirmed, definitive therapy must be determined. Whenever an acute dissection involves the ascending aorta, surgical repair is indicated to minimize the risk of life-threatening complications, such as rupture, cardiac tamponade, severe aortic insufficiency, or stroke. Patients with acute dissections confined to the descending aorta are at much lower risk of these complications and tend to fare as well with medical therapy as with surgical repair. When a type B dissection is associated with a serious complication, however, such as end-organ ischemia, surgery is indicated. Patients with chronic type A dissections can be managed medically because they already have survived the early period of high mortality associated with acute proximal dissections.

Prognosis

Patients with acute aortic dissection who survive the initial hospitalization generally do well thereafter, whether treated medically or surgically. Late complications, such as aortic insufficiency, recurrent dissection, aneurysm formation, and aneurysm rupture, can occur, however. Medications to control hypertension and reduce ventricular contractility can reduce dramatically the incidence of late complications and should be continued indefinitely. β-Blockers are the drug of choice in this setting, but typically a second or third agent needs to be added to achieve the goal of a systolic blood pressure less than 120 mm Hg.

Patients are at highest risk of complications during the first 2 years after aortic dissection. Progressive aneurysm expansion typically occurs without symptoms, so patients must be observed closely with serial aortic imaging at 6-month intervals for the first 2 years and annually thereafter, provided that the anatomy is stable.

INTRAMURAL HEMATOMA OF THE AORTA

Intramural hematoma of the aorta is an atypical form of aortic dissection. It is believed to occur when there is rupture of the vasa vasorum within the aortic media that results in a contained hemorrhage within the medial layer. This hematoma may propagate longitudinally along a variable length of the aorta; because the intimal layer remains intact, however, the hematoma does not communicate with the aortic lumen. It initially was termed *aortic dissection without intimal rupture*. Although intramural hematoma of the aorta is clinically indistinguishable from aortic dissection, on cross-sectional imaging it appears as a crescentic thickening around the aortic wall rather than as a true and false lumen separated by an intimal flap. The presence of an intramural hematoma may be missed on aortography. The prognosis and management of intramural hematoma is essentially the same as described earlier for classic aortic dissection.

TAKAYASU'S ARTERITIS

Definition

Takayasu's arteritis is a chronic inflammatory disease of unknown etiology that involves the aorta and its branches. The mean age at onset is 29, with women affected eight times as often as men. It occurs more often in Asia and Africa than in Europe or North America. An early stage, characterized by active inflammation involving the aorta and its branches, progresses at a variable rate to a later sclerotic stage with intimal hyperplasia, medial degeneration, and obliterative changes. Most of the resulting arterial lesions are stenotic, but aneurysms also may occur. The aortic arch and brachiocephalic vessels are affected most often, and the disease tends to be most pronounced at branch points in the aorta. The abdominal aorta also commonly is involved, and the pulmonary artery sometimes is involved. The disease may be diffuse or patchy, with affected areas separated by lengths of normal aorta.

Clinical Manifestations

Most patients initially present with symptoms of a systemic inflammatory process, such as fever, night sweats, arthralgias, and weight loss. There is often a delay of months to years, however, between the onset of symptoms and the time the diagnosis is made. At the time of diagnosis, 90% of patients have entered the sclerotic phase and have symptoms of vascular insufficiency, typically with pain in the upper (or less often lower) extremities. There often are absent pulses and diminished blood pressures in the upper extremities, and the condition has earned the name *pulseless disease*. There may be bruits over affected arteries. Significant hypertension (owing to renal artery involvement) occurs in more than half of patients, but its presence may be difficult to recognize, owing to the diminished pulses. Aortic insufficiency may result from proximal aortic involvement. Heart failure may result from either hypertension or aortic insufficiency. Involvement of the ostia of the coronary arteries may cause angina or myocardial infarction. Carotid artery involvement may cause cerebral ischemia or stroke. Abdominal angina may result from mesenteric artery compromise.

The overall 15-year survival for patients diagnosed with Takayasu's arteritis is 83%, with most deaths caused by stroke, myocardial infarction, or heart failure. The survival rate for patients with major complications of the disease is 66%; the survival rate for patients without a major complication is 96%.

Diagnosis

Laboratory abnormalities during the acute phase include an elevated erythrocyte sedimentation rate, a mild leukocytosis, anemia, and elevated immunoglobulin levels. The diagnosis is best made by aortography, which reveals stenosis of the aorta and stenosis or occlusion of its branch vessels, often with poststenotic dilation or associated aneurysms.

 Treatment

Corticosteroids are the primary therapy for the acute inflammatory stage and may be effective in improving constitutional symptoms, lowering the erythrocyte sedimentation rate, and slowing disease progression. Cyclophosphamide or methotrexate may be used when corticosteroid therapy alone is ineffective. It is unknown whether medical therapy reduces the risk of major complications or prolongs life.

Balloon angioplasty can dilate stenotic lesions of the aorta and renal arteries. Surgery may be necessary to bypass or reconstruct key segments, such as the coronary, carotid, or renal arteries, or to treat aortic insufficiency. Ideally, when possible, surgery should not be performed during the inflammatory phase.

GIANT CELL ARTERITIS

Giant cell arteritis (Chapter 285) is more common than Takayasu's arteritis. Its cause is also unclear, but it tends to occur in an older population, with a mean age of 67. It typically affects medium-sized arteries, but in 15% of cases it involves the aorta and branches of the aortic arch. Narrowing of the aorta is rare, but weakening of the ascending aortic wall may lead to localized thoracic aortic aneurysms and secondary aortic insufficiency. Narrowing of the branches of the aortic arch produces symptoms similar to those seen in Takayasu's arteritis. Because the temporal artery is commonly involved, the diagnosis usually is made with a temporal artery biopsy. Management involves the use of high-dose corticosteroid therapy, to which the disease is usually responsive.

1. United Kingdom Small Aneurysm Trial Participants. Long-term outcomes of immediate repair compared with surveillance of small abdominal aortic aneurysms. N Engl J Med 2002;346:1445–1452.
2. Ashton HA, Buxton MJ, Day NE, et al: The Multicentre Aneurysm Screening Study (MASS) into the effect of abdominal aortic aneurysm screening on mortality in men: A randomised controlled trial. Lancet 2002;360:1531–1539.

SUGGESTED READINGS

Davies RR, Goldstein LJ, Coady MA, et al: Yearly rupture or dissection rates for thoracic aortic aneurysms: Simple prediction based on size. Ann Thorac Surg 2002;7:17–27. *An important retrospective study on a series of 304 patients with thoracic aortic aneurysms showing the correlation of size with risk of rupture or dissection.*
Hagan PG, Nienaber CA, Isselbacher EM, et al: International Registry of Acute Aortic Dissection (IRAD)—new insights into an old disease. JAMA 2000;283:897–903. *This study summarizes the findings of the world's largest series of patients with acute aortic dissection, emphasizing risk factors, signs and symptoms, diagnostic imaging, and outcomes.*
Klompas M: Does this patient have an acute thoracic aortic dissection? JAMA 2002;287:2262–2272. *A good pooled analysis that shows the inadequacy of the clinical history and physical examination to exclude the presence of acute aortic dissection.*
Powell JT, Greenhalgh RM: Clinical practice. Small abdominal aortic aneurysms. N Engl J Med 2003;348:1895–1901. *A case-based review.*

76 ATHEROSCLEROTIC PERIPHERAL ARTERIAL DISEASE

William R. Hiatt

Definition

Peripheral arterial disease (PAD) due to atherosclerotic occlusion of the arterial circulation to the lower extremities is part of a systemic disorder of atherosclerosis affecting other major circulations. The disease may initially be asymptomatic, then become manifested by intermittent claudication or severe critical leg ischemia. These clinical manifestations are related to the severity of the hemodynamic obstruction and reduced perfusion to skeletal muscle and skin of the lower extremity.

Epidemiology

The incidence of intermittent claudication in men ranges from 6/10,000 at 30 to 44 years of age to 61/10,000 at 65 to 74 years of age. In women, the incidence ranges from 3/10,000 at 30 to 44 years of age to 54/10,000 at 65 to 74 years of age. The prevalence of PAD based on ankle-brachial blood pressure ratios is approximately 3% in persons younger than 60 years and increases to 20% in those older than 70 years. In these same studies, the prevalence of symptomatic claudication was less than half the prevalence of PAD. Severe critical leg ischemia affects fewer than 1 million adults in the United States. A recent screening program conducted in primary care offices identified a 29% prevalence of PAD in patients who were 50 to 69 years of age with diabetes or smoking or who were older than 70 years.

When patients with PAD are assessed by history alone, the physician recognizes the presence of significant coronary disease only 20 to 40% of the time. However, when these patients are evaluated with noninvasive testing such as dipyridamole-stress thallium, the preva-

lence of coexistent significant coronary disease is 60%; when evaluated by angiography, the prevalence is as high as 90%. The prevalence of critical cerebrovascular disease is also markedly increased in patients with PAD.

Pathobiology

PAD is caused by atherosclerosis and has an etiology and pathogenesis similar to that of atherosclerosis in other circulations (Chapter 66). In contrast to coronary heart disease, women have the same risk of development of PAD as men. Patients with type II diabetes mellitus have a four-fold increased risk of PAD as compared with a two-fold increased risk of myocardial infarction (MI) or stroke. However, the severity of PAD is not directly correlated with glycemic control but rather with the coexistence of cardiovascular risk factors in addition to diabetes. The risk of PAD increases 10% with a 10-mg/dL increase in total cholesterol. Whereas an elevated low-density lipoprotein (LDL) cholesterol level is highly associated with the development of coronary disease, reduced high-density lipoprotein (HDL) cholesterol and increased triglyceride levels are more often associated with PAD. Cigarette smoking is associated with a three- to four-fold increased risk for PAD and is synergistic with other risk factors; the prevalence of cigarette smoking in the PAD population is approximately twice that of the general population. As with coronary heart disease, risk of PAD is doubled in hypertensive patients. Elevated homocysteine levels promote PAD as well as coronary heart disease. Patients with hypercoagulable states more commonly have venous thrombosis and thromboembolism, but they may also have peripheral arterial thrombosis, particularly younger patients.

HEMODYNAMICS. The hemodynamic significance of arterial stenosis is a function of not only the percent of stenosis but also flow velocity across the lesion. For example, resting blood flow velocity in the femoral artery may be as low as 20 cm/second; at this velocity a stenosis does not become hemodynamically significant until it is 90% occlusive, after which flow and pressure rapidly decrease across the stenosis with increasing obstruction. With exercise in a normal extremity, flow velocity may increase to as high as 150 cm/second. At these higher flow velocities, about a 50% stenosis becomes hemodynamically significant in a patient with PAD. Thus, patients with claudication have normal flow to skeletal muscle at rest but markedly impaired flow to meet metabolic demand with exercise.

The hemodynamic significance of arterial occlusive disease can be assessed easily by measuring the systolic blood pressure in the ankle and forming a ratio of that pressure to the systolic blood pressure in the arm (the ankle-brachial index, or ABI, Fig. 76–1). In a normal extremity, with exercise ankle blood pressure increases in proportion to the increase in arm blood pressure. With PAD, however, ankle blood pressure becomes markedly reduced following exercise.

Patients with PAD often have numerous arterial segments involved. When blood flow in the extremity is reduced at *rest*, symptoms of severe critical leg ischemia develop. In contrast to claudication (in which the supply-demand mismatch involves skeletal muscle with exercise), severe leg ischemia affects the most distal portion of the extremity with ischemia to the skin and subcutaneous tissues of the forefoot. These patients have ischemic rest pain, distal ulceration, and gangrene.

METABOLIC AND NEUROLOGIC ABNORMALITIES. In patients *with claudication*, the ABI is not well correlated with exercise performance on a treadmill or the severity of symptoms in the community setting. The pathogenesis of PAD is initiated by atherosclerotic occlusion of the major conduit vessels in the lower extremity, but over time the disease affects the neurologic and metabolic function of skeletal muscle, leading to further impairment in muscle performance and functional status. Key factors include deconditioning and skeletal muscle injury, which is characterized as distal axonal denervation leading to loss of muscle fibers and mild atrophy of the affected muscle. Oxidative metabolism is severely impaired in patients with PAD beyond what can be explained simply by the reduction in blood flow. Patients with PAD have impaired resynthesis of phosphocreatine and abnormally high levels of adenosine diphosphate; they may also accumulate intermediates of oxidation such as acylcarnitines. Treatment should focus not only on improving the hemodynamic state of the patient but also on modifying factors such as alterations in skeletal muscle metabolism and function.

Cardiovascular Disease

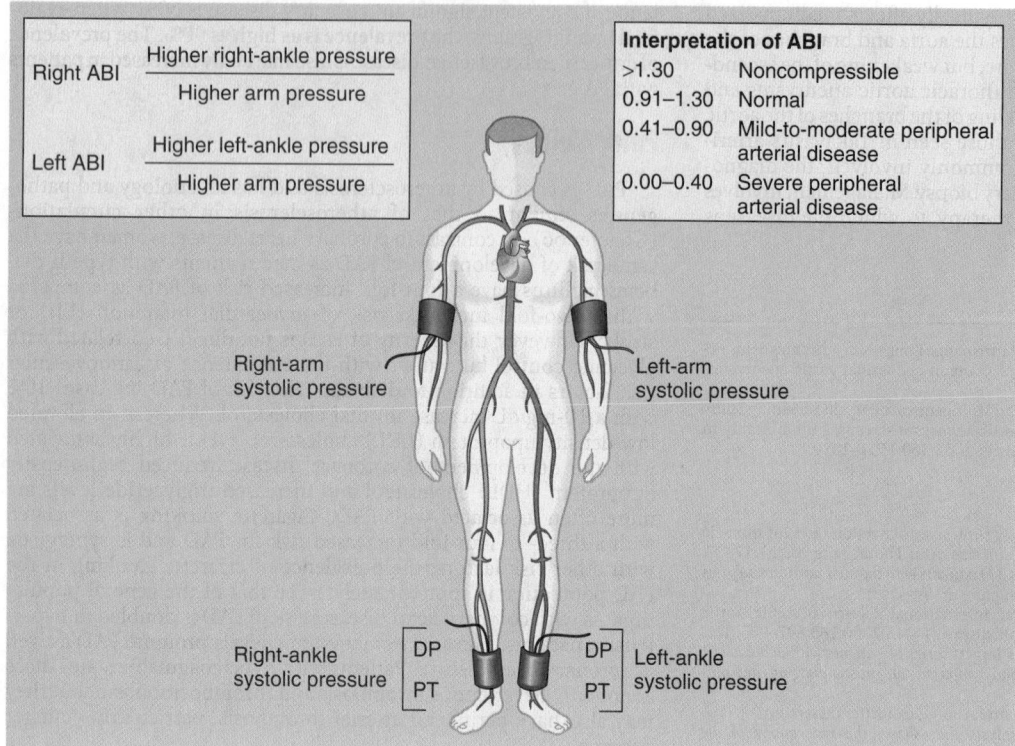

Right ABI	$\dfrac{\text{Higher right-ankle pressure}}{\text{Higher arm pressure}}$
Left ABI	$\dfrac{\text{Higher left-ankle pressure}}{\text{Higher arm pressure}}$

Interpretation of ABI

>1.30	Noncompressible
0.91–1.30	Normal
0.41–0.90	Mild-to-moderate peripheral arterial disease
0.00–0.40	Severe peripheral arterial disease

Right-arm systolic pressure

Left-arm systolic pressure

Right-ankle systolic pressure

DP
PT

DP
PT

Left-ankle systolic pressure

FIGURE 76–1 • Measurement and interpretation of the ankle-brachial index (ABI). (From Hiatt WR: Medical treatment of peripheral arterial disease and claudication. N Engl J Med 2001;344:1608–1621, with permission.)

Clinical Manifestations

Chronic arterial insufficiency of the lower extremity causes two characteristic types of pain, intermittent claudication and ischemic rest pain, often with ulceration or gangrene. Claudication is derived from the Latin word meaning to limp, which accurately describes the gait pattern of the patient at the onset of symptoms. Depending on the level and extent of the PAD, the patient may have claudication affecting the buttock and thigh (iliac occlusive disease), calf (most commonly), or foot (rarely).

Claudication is caused by reversible muscle ischemia and is characterized by cramping and aching in the affected muscle. The discomfort develops only during exercise and steadily increases with walking until the patient has to stop because of intolerable pain. The discomfort is quickly relieved by rest without change of position. Claudication may occur in one leg only (40% of the time) or affect both legs (60% of the time). The physician should ascertain severity by the distance that the patient can walk before experiencing discomfort (initial claudication distance) and before being forced to stop (absolute or maximal claudication distance). Any recent change should be determined.

Foot claudication is rare and is usually seen in thromboangiitis obliterans (Chapter 77) rather than atherosclerotic PAD. The complaint is usually of a painful ache or cramp in the forefoot associated only with walking. Patients also complain of a persistently cold foot at night.

Ischemic (or nocturnal) rest pain is a severe form of pain that diffusely involves the foot distal to the tarsal bones, although it may be localized to the vicinity of an ischemic ulcer or gangrenous toe. The progression from claudication to rest pain reflects severe arterial occlusive disease with inadequate blood flow to the distal end of the extremity at rest. The pain typically occurs at night when the patient assumes the horizontal position without gravity to help arterial flow. The pain may become so severe that it is not relieved even by substantial doses of narcotics.

DIAGNOSIS

An approach to the diagnostic evaluation of the patient with PAD is suggested in Figure 76–2.

RISK FACTOR EVALUATION. All patients should have a smoking history to define current smoking status and previous pack-years. Diabetes can be evaluated by a fasting and postprandial glucose and/or hemoglobin A_{1C} level. A complete lipid profile should be obtained, including measurements of LDL and HDL cholesterol and triglycerides. Blood pressure should be routinely measured. Screening for elevated homocysteine levels should be considered in patients with an early age of onset or a history of thrombotic events.

PHYSICAL EXAMINATION. A complete physical examination should be performed to evaluate the patient for systemic hypertension, cardiac murmurs or arrhythmias, carotid bruits, or an abdominal aortic aneurysm. The skin of the legs, especially the foot, should be inspected for color changes, ulceration, infection, or trauma from poorly fitting shoes.

All arterial pulses should be palpated, including the brachial, femoral, and pedal arteries. Absence of a femoral pulse indicates inflow disease of the iliac arteries. Patients with a palpable femoral pulse but absent pedal pulses have disease confined to the femoropopliteal or infrapopliteal arteries. Bruits of the aorta or femoral vessels reflect turbulent flow and are markers of systemic atherosclerosis. Any patient with a femoral bruit or absent pedal pulses should be suspected of having PAD and should have ankle blood pressure measured.

With severe claudication or ischemic rest pain, calf muscles atrophy, hair is lost over the dorsum of the toes and foot, and toenails thicken. More advanced ischemic atrophy results in a shiny, "skeletonized" appearance. Severely affected limbs also display pallor on elevation because of inadequate arterial pressure and flow; rubor on dependency occurs with very restricted arterial inflow and chronic dilatation of the peripheral vascular bed.

Severe critical leg ischemia (Fig. 76–3) can cause ulceration initially affecting the most distal aspect of the toes. These ulcers are painful, do not bleed when manipulated, and often have a dark necrotic base (Fig. 76–4). The foot may be edematous from being continually kept in the dependent position in an attempt to relieve the ischemic pain. Gangrene usually begins with the toes and forefoot and may occur separately from ulceration.

LABORATORY EVALUATION. An electrocardiographic study should be done for all patients with suspected PAD. Elevations in the hematocrit and/or platelet count can result in hyperviscosity with an associated decrease in peripheral perfusion. Significant anemia reduces

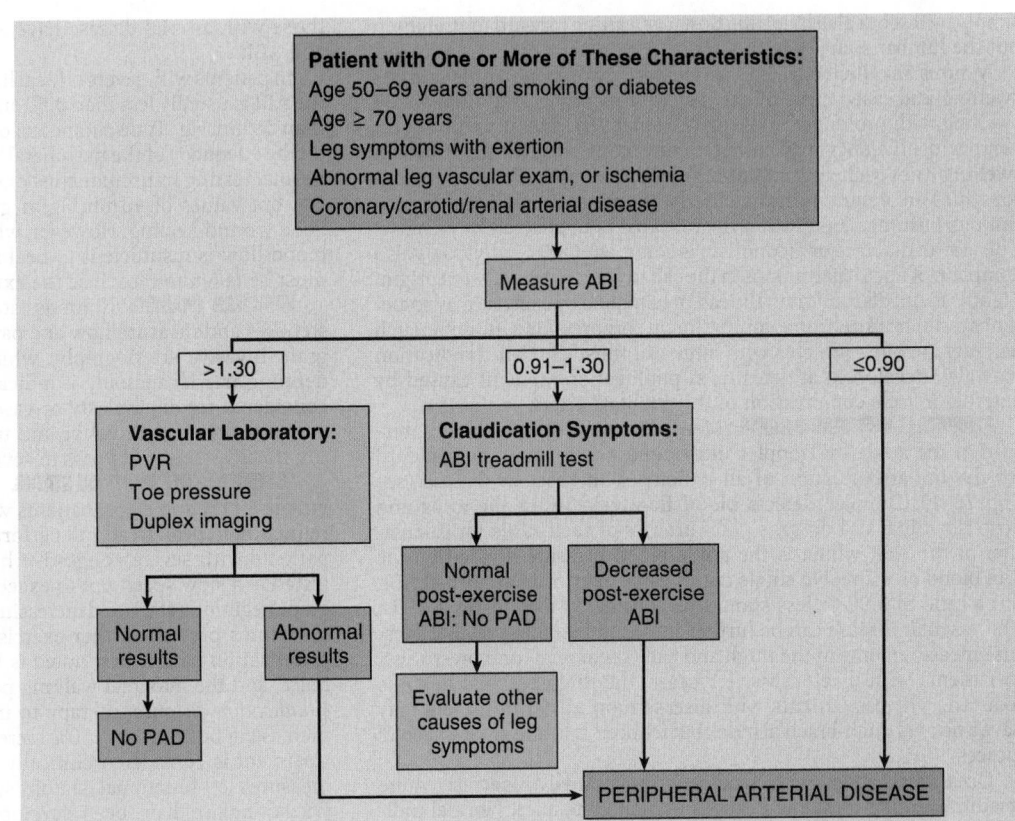

FIGURE 76–2 • Diagnosis of peripheral arterial disease. ABI = ankle-brachial index; PAD = peripheral arterial disease. (Modified from Hiatt WR: Medical treatment of peripheral arterial disease and claudication. N Engl J Med 2001;344:1608–1621, with permission.)

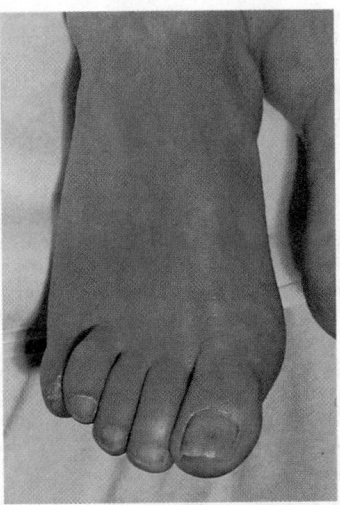

FIGURE 76–3 • "Critical" ischemia of the foot. The patient had a sudden onset of discomfort, with coldness and loss of sensation in the toes and the dorsum of the foot. He had previously suffered from intermittent claudication and has evidence of chronic ischemia, including absence of hair and thinness of the skin. Arteriography is necessary to define the nature of the lesion. (From Forbes CD, Jackson WF: Color Atlas and Text of Clinical Medicine, 3rd ed. London, Mosby, 2003, with permission.)

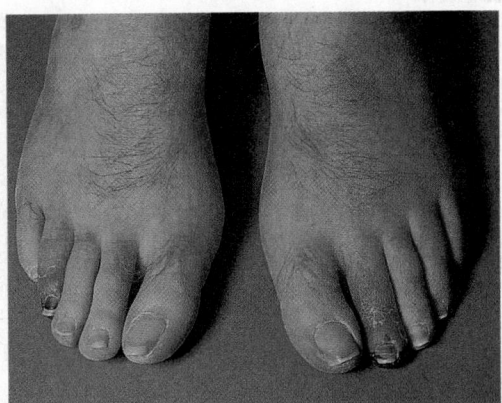

FIGURE 76–4 • Typical dry gangrene of two toes in a patient with diffuse atheroma. The patient had a history of intermittent claudication. Note the chronic nail changes that are also seen (resembling onycholysis). The residual hair on the dorsum of the feet is unusual in chronic ischemia; usually the hair is lost. (From Forbes CD, Jackson WF: Color Atlas and Text of Clinical Medicine, 3rd ed. London, Mosby, 2003, with permission.)

the oxygen content and decreases oxygen delivery. An elevated erythrocyte sedimentation rate suggests inflammatory causes of vascular disease, including vasculitis (Chapter 284). In patients with significant lung disease, arterial saturation should be measured to determine whether a low saturation could exacerbate peripheral oxygen delivery. Renal function should be evaluated because chronic renal failure is a significant risk factor for PAD and patients with PAD are at risk for renovascular hypertension and renal insufficiency.

An occasional patient with PAD has acute thrombotic occlusion of a peripheral vessel from in situ thrombosis or an embolus from a more proximal site. These patients may need a coagulation screen consisting of (but not limited to) factor V Leiden, protein S, protein C, antithrombin III, and other tests of coagulation.

DIFFERENTIAL DIAGNOSIS. Pain from arthritis of the hip or knee is often present at rest and exacerbated by exercise. With cessation of exercise, the pain may not improve unless the patient rests and unloads the joint. Claudication-like symptoms may also arise from spinal stenosis, which is due to osteophytic narrowing of the lumbar neurospinal canal (Chapter 429). These symptoms are usually lower extremity numbness and weakness produced by standing or increasing lumbar lordosis rather than just ambulation. The symptoms are relieved not simply by rest but also by sitting down or leaning forward to straighten out the lumbar spine.

Venous insufficiency (the sequela of thrombophlebitis) causes swelling and discomfort in the calf with standing and often worse swelling with prolonged walking (Chapter 78). Patients with severe venous insufficiency may complain of venous claudication from calf swelling (not ischemic cramping) with exercise. Peripheral neuropathies are common in the elderly but are associated with a continuous burning sensation in the foot that is unaffected by exercise; a history of diabetes or alcoholism is common. Older individuals also complain of nocturnal cramps in the calf that are not vascular in origin. Tightness and discomfort in the calf precipitated by exercise may sometimes result from a chronic compartment compression syndrome; such patients are often athletes with large calf muscles. Calf claudication may also develop in athletes from popliteal entrapment caused by external muscle compression of the popliteal artery.

PERIPHERAL VASCULAR STUDIES. Measurement of systolic blood pressure in the ankle by Doppler ultrasound has become the standard for the initial evaluation of all patients with vascular disease (see Fig. 76–1). Doppler detects blood flow velocity in the arms and posterior tibial and dorsalis pedis arteries of each ankle for calculation of the ABI, which is the ankle blood pressure divided by the arm blood pressure. No single cutoff value defines an abnormal ABI, but a ratio of 0.90 or less should be considered diagnostic of PAD. The vascular disease can be further localized by taking several pressure measurements in the thigh and calf (segmental limb pressures). In patients with iliac occlusive disease, the thigh-brachial index is reduced, whereas patients with disease more distal in the leg may have a normal thigh-brachial index but reduced calf- and ankle-brachial indices.

Occasional patients with claudication but normal ABIs at rest require treadmill testing to define changes in hemodynamics. Normal individuals increase their ankle blood pressure with exercise, whereas those with arterial disease have a decrease in ankle blood pressure and ABI.

In patients with severe critical limb ischemia and nonhealing ulcers, the ABI is usually less than 0.50 and the ankle systolic pressure is less than 50 mm Hg. Transcutaneous oximetry also provides information on the adequacy of the peripheral circulation for wound healing. The normal resting transcutaneous oxygen tension is greater than 60 mm Hg, but values of 40 mm Hg or greater are usually associated with good wound healing. However, when values are less than 20 mm Hg, blood flow is insufficient to heal a wound and additional measures must be taken to reperfuse the extremity.

VASCULAR IMAGING. Color-assisted duplex ultrasound can detect stenoses and measure flow at a particular arterial segment or bypass graft. Invasive arteriography, which is the most accurate means of defining arterial anatomy, is indicated only when the patient is being considered for angioplasty or vascular surgery. Magnetic resonance angiography is noninvasive and useful in selected patients to identify tibial vessels for bypass in severe PAD.

ASSESSMENT OF FUNCTIONAL STATUS. When compared with healthy individuals of the same age, patients with claudication have a 50 to 60% reduction in peak treadmill performance, a severity similar to that of patients with severe congestive heart failure. Patients are typically tested at a slow speed not to exceed 2 miles/hour, with the treadmill grade beginning at 0% and increasing 2% every 2 minutes until maximal symptoms prevent further exercise. The time or distance at which claudication pain is first noted is termed the *initial claudication distance*, and the maximal walking performance is termed the *absolute claudication distance*; therapy to improve claudication results in an increase in both. A 25 to 50% increase in treadmill performance after treatment is considered clinically significant. Several questionnaire measures of functional status, such as the Walking Impairment Questionnaire, have been developed and validated in patients with PAD and are useful adjuncts to treadmill testing.

Rx Treatment

MEDICAL THERAPY

Medical therapy in patients with PAD should be designed to reduce cardiovascular morbidity and mortality by treating systemic atherosclerosis and to improve functional status and limb preservation by relieving claudication and severe leg ischemia (Fig. 76–5). Smoking cessation is critical to delay the progression of PAD and reduce cardiovascular morbidity and mortality. Several large clinical trials have shown the benefit of lowering cholesterol levels in patients with coronary atherosclerosis; although similar studies have not been performed in patients with PAD, the current aggressive recommendations for lipid therapy are similar to those for secondary prevention in persons with coronary artery disease (Chapters 67, 69, and 211). Aggressive control of blood glucose has not been shown to modify the natural history of PAD, but normalization of blood glucose is an important goal to mitigate against the complications of this disease in other circulations. Although clinical trials have not assessed the benefits of lowering blood pressure on the peripheral circulation, the goals for lowering blood pressure should be similar in patients with PAD as in other forms of cardiovascular disease (Chapter 63). Recent well-designed studies have not found any adverse effects on claudication with β-blocker use. However in the HOPE study, the use of the angiotensin-converting enzyme (ACE) inhibitor ramipril was shown to prevent MI, stroke, and vascular death in patients with PAD.[1] Aggressive blood pressure reduction with any medication reduces perfusion pressure into the limb and may result in a slight worsening of claudication, but this side effect should not alter the blood pressure goal. Homocysteine elevation is a well-described risk factor for PAD, but the benefits of lowering homocysteine levels have not yet been demonstrated. Nevertheless, vitamin therapy with folic acid is often recommended for elevated levels (Chapter 231).

Antiplatelet therapy in patients with PAD reduces the risk of MI, stroke, and vascular death by 23%.[2] Clopidogrel, an antagonist of adenosine diphosphate–induced platelet aggregation, provides a 24% relative risk reduction in the incidence of vascular death, MI, and stroke when compared with aspirin in patients with PAD.[3] In terms of symptomatic relief, an established agent is cilostazol, which has antiplatelet and vasodilating properties and has been shown by questionnaire to improve treadmill performance and functional status.[4] Propionyl-L-carnitine is a naturally occurring compound that improves skeletal muscle metabolism and is also effective in treating the symptoms of claudication. Pentoxifylline lowers blood viscosity and may improve flow in the microcirculation; however, most patients perceive no benefit. Treatments such as vascular endothelial growth factor or fibroblast growth factor have shown promise in selected patients under experimental conditions, but large randomized, blinded studies are needed to prove efficacy.

For severe critical leg ischemia, medical treatments are limited. Prostaglandin drugs may help heal ischemic ulcers and reduce the risk of amputation, but these benefits are not fully established. Analgesics may also be needed, and spinal cord stimulation may reduce ischemic pain. Topical antibiotics, growth factors, and débriding agents have not been effective in treating ulcerated lesions of the lower extremity. Patients in whom cellulitis develops around an ischemic ulceration should be treated with systemic antibiotics. Chelation therapy has no benefit.

EXERCISE THERAPY

Supervised exercise training is a well-documented treatment to relieve claudication and improve exercise performance.[5] Typically, the initial workload on the treadmill is set at the speed and grade that precipitated claudication during the evaluation treadmill test. For training purposes, patients should be able to walk between 3 and 5 minutes at this workload until they achieve a moderately severe level of claudication pain. The patient steps off the treadmill and rests until the pain subsides and then repeats this activity for approximately 40 to 60 minutes per training session. The speed and grade of the treadmill are increased on a regular basis to induce a training effect. Results of this program are typically a 100 to 200% increase in peak exercise performance, an improvement comparable to that achieved with surgery or angioplasty without the side effects of pharmacologic therapy and without the morbidity and mortality of interventional procedures. However, the training benefit is maintained only if patients continue with their exercise program. Home-based exercise and simple recommendations to exercise are much less effective than supervised programs. There are few supervised training programs across the country, and third-party payers often do not reimburse for exercise training.

INVASIVE THERAPIES

INDICATIONS FOR SURGERY OR ANGIOPLASTY. Invasive therapies should be limited to claudicating patients who fail initial medical treatment, have severe disability as defined by validated questionnaires or treadmill testing, and have an appropriate anatomic lesion for bypass or angioplasty (see Figs. 76–5 and 76–6). In contrast, patients with critical leg ischemia should be considered for vascular surgery and/or angioplasty, which is necessary to heal ischemic lesions, relieve ischemic rest pain, and prevent amputation.

Angioplasty guidelines emphasize that more proximal lesions have better patency rates and durability than do more distal lesions (Table 76–1). Below the inguinal ligament, the initial success and long-term patency rates have been less well studied but are not as good as for more proximal lesions.

SURGERY. Surgery is principally used to treat severe critical leg ischemia rather than claudication because of the associated morbidity and mortality of surgery, the relatively benign natural history of claudication, and the efficacy of medical (particularly exercise) therapies. In aortoiliac disease, prosthetic materials are usually implanted. Aortoiliac surgery is associated with an average mortality of 3% and morbidity of 8%. In patients with femoropopliteal disease, the best conduit is saphenous vein. Femoropopliteal surgery with vein bypass is associated with a mortality of 2%, morbidity of 5 to 10%, and a 5-year patency rate of 70 to 80%. The use of prosthetic material (required if a vein is not available)

reduces 5-year patency rates to 50%. Distal femorotibial operations for limb salvage have a similar morbidity and mortality as femoropopliteal surgery but slightly lower 5-year patency rates of 50 to 60%.

Additional cardiac evaluation should be considered in patients undergoing peripheral vascular or aortic surgery because the risk of cardiovascular morbidity and mortality can be as high as 30%. Several clinical decision rules have been proposed to separate patients into low- and high-risk groups. For example, patients with PAD and three or more of the following factors are at high risk for surgery: Q waves on the electrocardiogram (or a history of prior MI), congestive heart failure, angina, diabetes, and age older than 70 years. Additional risk stratification can be obtained by using dipyridamole thallium scintigraphy (Chapter 52) or stress echocardiography with dipyridamole or dobutamine (Chapter 51). An abnormal result presumably leads to coronary revascularization before the planned peripheral vascular intervention. However, the wisdom of this approach has not been validated. At present, patients who need vascular surgery (e.g., to prevent limb loss) but are believed to be high risk on clinical grounds should have aggressive intraoperative monitoring of central and peripheral hemodynamics and modulation of their sympathetic responses during anesthesia. β-Adrenergic blocking drugs have been shown to reduce the operative risks of vascular surgery. Only patients with extensive symptomatic coronary artery disease in whom the coronary disease is more severe or life-threatening than the PAD should undergo additional evaluation for cardiac revascularization. This approach results in exposing the patient to two invasive procedures with the attendant increased risk.

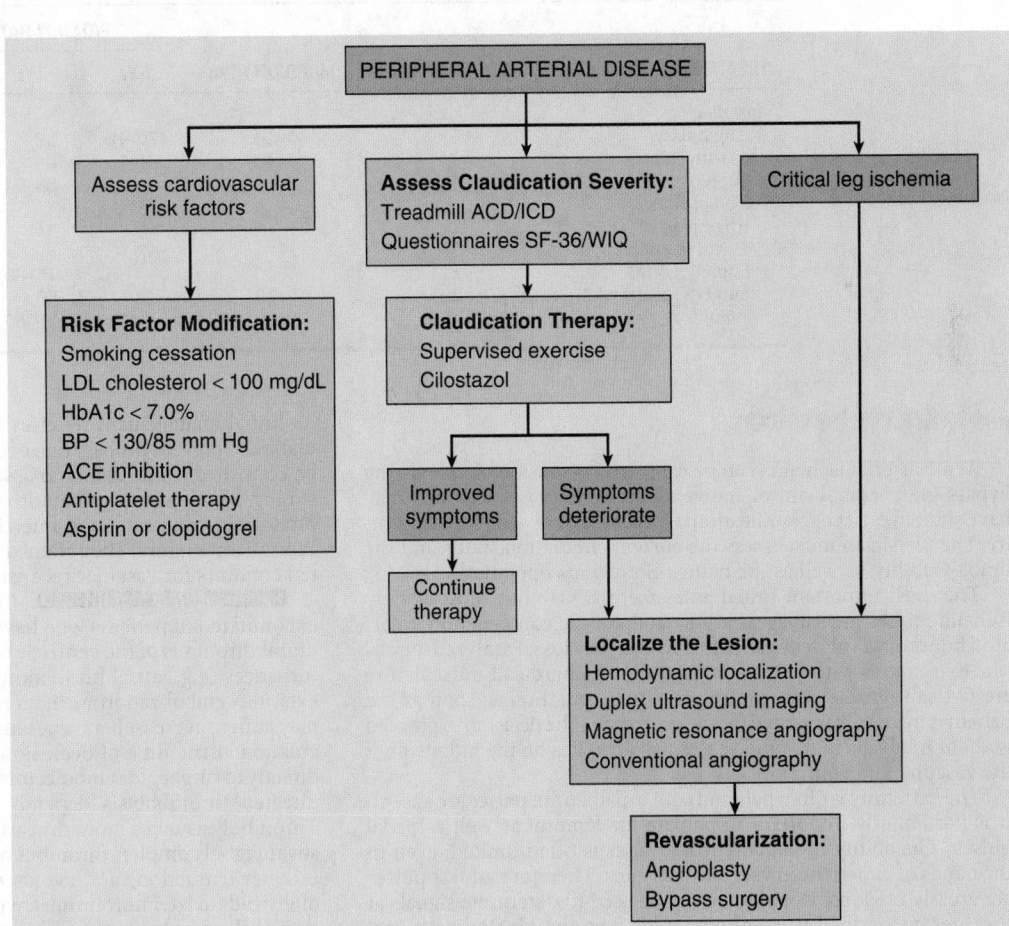

FIGURE 76–5 • Therapy for peripheral arterial disease. (Modified from Hiatt WR: Medical treatment of peripheral arterial disease and claudication. N Engl J Med 2001;344:1608–1621, with permission.)

Cardiovascular Disease

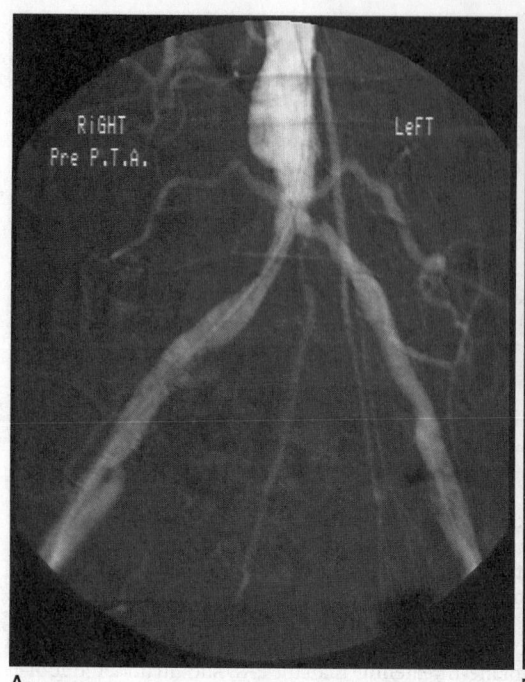

A

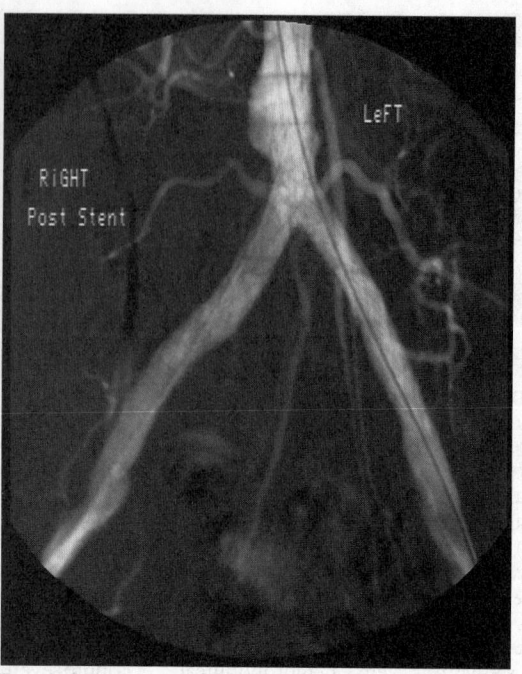

B

FIGURE 76–6 • Percutaneous transluminal angioplasty (PTA) may be used in peripheral vascular disease. *A,* Significant narrowing of the aortic bifurcation and both common iliac arteries. The narrowing in both common iliacs was successfully treated by angioplasty, and bilateral stents were inserted to maintain patency (*B*). The patient had presented with bilateral calf claudication, which was relieved by this procedure. (From Forbes CD, Jackson WF: Color Atlas and Text of Clinical Medicine, 3rd ed. London, Mosby, 2003, with permission.)

Table 76–1 • RESULTS OF ANGIOPLASTY AND SURGERY FOR PERIPHERAL ARTERIAL DISEASE

TREATMENT	MORTALITY (%)	MORBIDITY (%)	PATENCY RATES (%)		
			3 Yr	5 Yr	10 Yr
Aortoiliac					
Angioplasty	<1	5–14	70–78	58	—
with stent	<1	3–13	81	—	—
Surgery	3	8	—	88–91	82–87
Femoropopliteal					
Angioplasty	<1	7	56	51	—
with stent	<1	2	67	—	—
Surgery (vein)	2	5–10	—	70–80	—
Surgery (prosthetic)	2	5–10	—	50	—
Femorotibial	3–5	10–20	—	50–60	—

Acute Arterial Ischemia

Acute arterial ischemia can be caused by occlusion of an existing bypass graft, embolism, or native vessel thrombosis. Patients may have sudden onset of claudication, rest pain, or a cool or cold extremity. The physician must assess the current circulation status and the limb's viability, as well as the nature of previous operations.

The most important initial assessment is viability. Most acutely ischemic limbs are salvageable; skeletal muscle can generally tolerate 6 hours of warm ischemia before irreversible loss. Paralyzed, insensate extremities with fixed skin mottling and hard calf musculature are not salvageable and require primary amputation as soon as the patient is medically prepared for the procedure. The decision to proceed with limb salvage in marginal cases usually relies on the judgment of the vascular surgeon.

The extremity is often pale and cool to palpation; pulses are absent. It is particularly important to palpate the femoral as well as pedal pulses. The ability to palpate pedal pulses is often limited, even in the hands of experienced vascular surgeons. Therefore, unless pulses are grossly obvious, Doppler should be used to determine signals at the three major tibial arteries in the ankle. Any audible Doppler signal should prompt measurement of ankle pressure at that site to calculate an ABI.

GRAFT OCCLUSION. The most common cause of acute arterial ischemia is occlusion of an existing bypass graft. Patients have either rest pain or increasing claudication, depending on the degree of acute change in ischemia.

Initial management requires rapid therapeutic heparin anticoagulation to prevent propagation of thrombus. A vascular surgeon should be consulted immediately to assess the timing of arteriography and surgery. Management of comorbid diseases such as heart failure, respiratory insufficiency, and infection should be initiated, and central venous access should be obtained while preserving arm veins as potential conduits for vascular reconstruction.

EMBOLISM (CARDIAC/ARTERIAL). Cardiac embolism is most commonly encountered in patients who have preexisting valvular heart disease, mural thrombus of the ventricle or atrium, or underlying rhythm disturbances (e.g., atrial fibrillation). The most frequent sites of lower extremity embolization are the aortic and femoral bifurcations. Patients may suffer severe ischemia because of a lack of existing collateral circulation at the time of occlusion. The decision whether to proceed directly to surgery for embolectomy versus angiography with catheter-directed thrombolysis depends on the severity of the ischemia. Thrombolysis takes more time to relieve the occlusion but offers the advantage of complete thrombus removal (often incomplete with blind catheter extraction) and avoids endothelial balloon trauma, which often leads to later fibrointimal hyperplasia and branch stenosis/occlusion of the involved arteries.

Arterial-arterial embolization (atheroembolism) may be spontaneous or iatrogenic. Patients with spontaneous atheroembolism have painful, cyanotic digits of acute onset. If embolization is ipsilateral, iliac or femoral artery sources are more likely; bilateral findings indicate an aortic source. Aneurysms of the aorta and femoral and popliteal arteries are also causes. The patient has a normal or only slightly diminished ABI because the circulation from the digital arteries to the embolic source must be relatively uninterrupted. Cases of iatrogenic atheroembolism occur after aortic catheterization procedures. The clinical picture of limb atheroembolism in this setting can vary from mild livedo reticularis to severe limb pain/cyanosis and eventual tissue loss with concurrent elevated plasma muscle enzymes and myoglobinuria (Chapter 124). The diagnosis of cholesterol emboli can be confirmed by skin biopsy of peripheral lesions demonstrating cholesterol crystals in the capillaries. Elevated creatinine, oliguria, and urine eosinophils are present in patients with renal atheroemboli. Arteries that are occluded by atheroembolic material usually cannot be reopened surgically because of the small particle/vessel size. Similarly, most patients with catheter-induced atheroembolism have diffuse aortic disease not amenable to surgical treatment. An exception occurs when catheter-induced atheroembolism calls attention to an arterial aneurysm as the suspected source of the embolic material.

NATIVE ARTERY THROMBOSIS. Native artery thrombosis occurs in two common scenarios: (1) A native artery becomes acutely occluded in a patient with a known or unknown hypercoagulable state (frequently with previous subclinical thromboses of small arteries) and (2) acute thrombosis in the iliac artery secondary to catheter trauma from coronary angiography develops in a patient with severe aortoiliac occlusive disease (as a result of either dissection of the iliac artery from the catheter or overzealous compression and occlusion of the groin after catheterization). The primary goals in this setting are to make the diagnosis (baseline ABI before cardiac catheterization is critical), determine the level of ischemia, determine the viability of the distal end of the limb, achieve rapid therapeutic heparin anticoagulation, and make appropriate plans for diagnostic angiography (usual) or urgent surgical exploration (unusual).

Prognosis

In patients with PAD, all-cause mortality is increased in both men and women, and cardiovascular mortality is six-fold higher than in age-matched control patients. This mortality risk is almost exclusively due to death from MI and stroke. In one study of persons with an average age of 66 years, healthy individuals had an approximate 80% 10-year survival rate, patients with asymptomatic PAD (defined as an ABI less than 0.95) had an approximate 55% 10-year survival rate, patients with intermittent claudication resulting from peripheral atherosclerosis had a 40% 10-year survival rate, and those with severe symptoms had only a 25% 10-year survival rate. In addition, the severity of PAD in the legs is closely associated with the risk of MI, ischemic stroke, and vascular death. The lower the ABI, the greater the risk of cardiovascular events.

In contrast to the marked increased risk of mortality, patients with claudication have very little risk of limb loss. The risk of amputation over 5 years is estimated at 4%. In addition, most patients with claudication have stable symptoms over 5 years and do not require a revascularization procedure. In contrast, patients with critical leg ischemia have a 20% annual mortality risk and a 35% annual risk of amputation.

1. Yusuf S, Sleight P, Pogue J, et al: Effects of an angiotensin-converting-enzyme inhibitor, ramipril, on cardiovascular events in high-risk patients. The Heart Outcomes Prevention Evaluation Study Investigators. N Engl J Med 2000; 342:145–153.
2. Collaborative meta-analysis of randomised trials of antiplatelet therapy for prevention of death, myocardial infarction, and stroke in high-risk patients. Antithrombotic Trialists' Collaboration. BMJ 2002;324:71–86.
3. CAPRIE Steering Committee: A randomized, blinded trial of clopidogrel versus aspirin in patients at risk of ischaemic events (CAPRIE). Lancet 1996;348: 1329–1339.
4. Dawson DL, Cutler BS, Hiatt WR, et al: A comparison of cilostazol and pentoxifylline for treating intermittent claudication. Am J Med 2000;109:523–530.
5. Gardner AW, Poehlman ET: Exercise rehabilitation programs for the treatment of claudication pain. A meta-analysis. JAMA 1995;274:975–980.

SUGGESTED READINGS
Hiatt WR: Medical treatment of peripheral arterial disease and claudication. N Engl J Med 2001;344:1608-1621. *A recent review of medical therapy for PAD.*

Hirsch AT, Criqui MH, Treat-Jacobson D, et al: Peripheral arterial disease detection, awareness, and treatment in primary care. JAMA 2001;286:1317–1324. *Defines the prevalence of PAD in the primary care setting.*

McDermott MM, Guralnik JM, Greenland P, et al: Statin use and leg functioning in patients with and without lower-extremity peripheral arterial disease. Circulation 2003;107:757–761. *Statin use improves leg symptoms in patients with peripheral arterial disease.*

Stewart KJ, Hiatt WR, Regensteiner JG, et al: Exercise training for claudication. N Engl J Med 2002;347:1941–1951. *Exercise training is beneficial.*

77 OTHER PERIPHERAL ARTERIAL DISEASES
Jeffrey W. Olin

LIVEDO RETICULARIS

Livedo reticularis is characterized by a reticular, fishnet, or lacy pattern on the skin of the lower extremities and other parts of the body. This pattern is red or blue and caused by deoxygenated blood in the surrounding horizontally arranged venous plexus.

Primary or benign livedo reticularis occurs most commonly in young women between the ages of 20 and 40 years. Ulceration generally does not occur with this form of the disease, which may be due to vasomotor instability or hyperreactivity of the dermal blood vessels. It is intensified by cold exposure and relieved by rewarming, and it may occur in association with Raynaud's phenomenon.

Secondary livedo reticularis occurs in association with atheromatous embolization (see later), polyarteritis nodosa, systemic lupus erythematosus, leukocytoclastic vasculitis, other connective tissue diseases, therapy with amantadine, and various neurologic or endocrine diseases and in patients receiving large doses of vasopressors such as epinephrine, norepinephrine, and dopamine. Livedo reticularis is also one of the many skin manifestations of the antiphospholipid antibody syndrome. In Sneddon's syndrome, there is the combination of livedo racemosa (a variant of livedo reticularis) and small vessel ischemic disease of the brain, producing transient ischemic attack or stroke. Approximately 50% of patients with Sneddon's syndrome have elevated levels of anticardiolipin antibodies.

In livedoid vasculopathy or livedoid vasculitis, extensive livedo reticularis surrounds a painful, ischemic-appearing ulceration located on the anterior or posterior portion of the lower leg. Pathologically, there is thrombosis of the microvasculature with little or no active inflammatory component. Small doses of tissue plasminogen activator (10 mg intravenously daily for 14 days) may be effective in treating the ulcerations. Atrophe blanche is a variant of livedoid vasculopathy. These ulcerations generally occur around the ankle or foot. They have a white or yellowish base with poor granulation tissue and are exquisitely painful and difficult to heal.

The benign variety of livedo reticularis often needs no treatment other than measures to keep the body part as warm as possible. In patients with secondary livedo reticularis, therapy should be directed at the underlying cause.

ATHEROMATOUS EMBOLIZATION

Atheromatous embolization (cholesterol embolization) refers to the embolization of cholesterol crystals or platelet fibrin aggregates to the extremities or one or more organs. Atheromatous emboli usually originate from ulcerated or stenotic atherosclerotic plaques or aneurysms that are primarily in the thoracic or abdominal aorta, iliac artery, or carotid artery.

Atheromatous embolization of the kidneys is a common histologic finding and may occur in 15 to 30% of patients with severe aortic atherosclerosis or aneurysm of the abdominal aorta. Increasing aortic plaque thickness, protruding aortic atheroma, and mobile aortic atheroma are associated with a high likelihood for atheromatous embolization. Atheromatous embolization may be spontaneous, but it occurs more often after cardiac catheterization, percutaneous transluminal coronary angioplasty, peripheral or cerebrovascular arteriography, or peripheral angioplasty. Recent reports have described fatal diffuse atheromatous embolization following endovascular grafting for an abdominal aortic aneurysm. Pathologically, arterioles are filled with biconvex cholesterol crystals, which produce a foreign body reaction in which polymorphonuclear leukocytes, macrophages, and multinucleated giant cells appear several days to several weeks after the inciting event.

Table 77–1 • CLINICAL MANIFESTATIONS OF ATHEROMATOUS EMBOLIZATION

Skin	**Gastrointestinal**
Purple or blue toes	Abdominal pain
Gangrenous digits	Gastrointestinal bleeding
Livedo reticularis	Ischemic bowel
Nodules	Acute pancreatitis
Kidney	**Constitutional symptoms**
Uncontrolled hypertension	Fever
Renal failure	Weight loss
Neurologic	Malaise
Transient ischemic attack	Anorexia
Amaurosis fugax	
Stroke	
Hollenhorst plaque	
Cardiac	
Myocardial infarction or ischemia	

From Bartholomew JR, Olin JW: Atheromatous embolization. *In* Young JR, Olin JW, Bartholomew JR, eds: Peripheral Vascular Diseases, 2nd ed. St. Louis, CV Mosby, 1996.

Clinical Manifestations

The most common clinical manifestations (Table 77–1) are skin changes, which occur in more than one third of patients and are generally found in the lower extremities but may be seen in the trunk, over the buttocks, and rarely in the upper extremities. These manifestations include livedo reticularis (embolization to the dermal blood vessels), purple or blue toes, splinter hemorrhages, gangrenous digits or ulcerations, and nodules in the presence of palpable foot pulses.

Atheroembolic renal disease is a small vessel occlusive disease leading to uncontrolled hypertension and advanced or end-stage renal disease (Chapter 124). Atheromatous embolization may also involve the gastrointestinal tract and produce ischemic bowel with generalized abdominal pain, nausea, vomiting, melena, or hematochezia. Cholesterol emboli to the gallbladder may produce acute gangrenous cholecystitis, whereas emboli to the pancreas can cause acute pancreatitis.

Cardiac manifestations of atheroemboli include angina pectoris and myocardial infarction. Patients may develop amaurosis fugax or blindness caused by retinal artery occlusion. A Hollenhorst plaque (yellow, highly refractile atheromatous material) may be present at the bifurcation of retinal blood vessels. Stroke, headache, confusion, organic brain syndrome, dizziness, and spinal cord infarction can occur. Constitutional signs and symptoms such as fever, weight loss, anorexia, fatigue, myalgias, headache, nausea, vomiting, or diarrhea may suggest a necrotizing vasculitis, infection, or malignancy.

Diagnosis

Atheromatous embolization is frequently overlooked or misdiagnosed. No single laboratory test is diagnostic. Nonspecific findings such as elevation in the erythrocyte sedimentation rate, leukocytosis, or anemia may be present. Increased levels of serum amylase, hepatic transaminases, blood urea nitrogen, or serum creatinine may be noted if the pancreas, liver, or kidney is involved. The urine sediment may be abnormal but is nonspecific. Eosinophilia and eosinophiluria may be present early in the course, and hypocomplementemia has been reported in a small number of series. Biopsy remains the most specific way to make the diagnosis, but it is often not required because the clinical findings may be highly suggestive of atheromatous embolization.

On arteriography, a markedly irregular and shaggy aorta may be demonstrated. Transesophageal echocardiography may detect mobile, protruding atheroma, which are associated with a very high risk for future embolization.

Atheromatous embolization may mimic a vasculitis, such as polyarteritis nodosa or leukocytoclastic vasculitis, or suggest an underlying malignancy, nonbacterial thrombotic endocarditis, subacute bacterial endocarditis, multiple myeloma, the antiphospholipid antibody syndrome, or atrial myxoma. A cardiac source of emboli should always be excluded.

 Treatment

The treatment of atheromatous embolization should be directed toward three goals: (1) removal of the source of atheromatous material (by surgical exclusion and bypass, percutaneous transluminal angioplasty, stent implantation or stent graft); (2) symptomatic care of the end organs where the emboli are located; and (3) risk factor modification to prevent the progression of atherosclerosis.

Local care of ischemic ulcers is important, and chemical or surgical sympathectomy may be helpful. Intravenous prostaglandin analogues (iloprost or PGE_1) may be useful in the healing of ischemic ulcerations secondary to atheromatous embolization. Patients should be placed on antiplatelet therapy with aspirin and clopidogrel. Use of anticoagulants such as heparin or warfarin should be avoided unless there is a compelling reason to use this class of drugs. If a vasospastic component is present, a dihydropyridine calcium channel blocker may be effective in relieving some of the symptoms.

In the past, surgical bypass therapy was the standard for treating patients with atheromatous embolization of the thoracic and abdominal aorta, whereas patients who were poor surgical risks often underwent ligation of the common femoral arteries followed by an extra-anatomic bypass such as an axillobifemoral bypass. Now, however, covered stents or stent grafts, which can be inserted in the thoracic or abdominal aorta for aneurysms or occlusive disease, represent a new technique with a relatively low morbidity and mortality.

Patients with atheromatous embolization generally have advanced atherosclerosis and poor prognosis. All patients should receive aggressive risk factor modification to slow the progression of atherosclerosis and improve overall cardiac and cerebrovascular morbidity and mortality.

THROMBOANGIITIS OBLITERANS (BUERGER'S DISEASE)

Thromboangiitis obliterans (Buerger's disease) is a nonatherosclerotic segmental, inflammatory disease that most commonly affects the small and medium-sized arteries and veins in the upper and lower extremities. The etiology of Buerger's disease is unknown, but there is an extremely strong association with heavy tobacco use, and progression of disease is closely linked to continued use.

Patients with Buerger's disease may be hypercoagulable, and some have antiendothelial cell antibodies, anticollagen antibodies, circulating immune complexes, and/or impaired endothelial-dependent vasorelaxation. There is also an increase in cellular sensitivity to type I and III collagen (normal constituents of human arteries) in patients with thromboangiitis obliterans.

Incidence and Prevalence

Buerger's disease has a worldwide distribution, but it is more prevalent in the Middle East, Near East, and Far East than in North America and Western Europe. The prevalence of Buerger's disease among patients with peripheral arterial disease varies from a low of 0.5 to 5.6% in Western Europe to a high of 60 to 89% in India, Korea, and Japan and in Ashkenazi Jews in Israel.

Pathology

In the acute phase of thromboangiitis obliterans, a highly inflammatory thrombus may affect both the arteries and veins. The lesion is characterized by acute inflammation involving all coats of the vessel wall in association with occlusive inflammatory cellular thrombosis. Around the periphery of the thrombus, there are often polymorphonuclear leukocytes with karyorrhexis, the so-called microabscess in which one or more multinucleated giant cells may be present. The acute phase lesion is followed by an intermediate phase in which there is progressive organization of the acute occlusive thrombus in the arteries and veins; there may be persistence of a prominent, inflammatory cellular infiltrate within the thrombus. The chronic phase or end-stage lesion is characterized by complete organization of the occlusive thrombus with extensive recanalization, prominent vascularization of the media and adventitia, and perivascular fibrosis.

Clinical Manifestations

Classically, Buerger's disease occurs in a young male smoker with the onset of symptoms before the age of 40 to 45 years, but 20 to 30% of patients with Buerger's disease may be women. Buerger's disease usually begins with ischemia of the toes, feet, fingers, and hands (Fig. 77–1). As the disease progresses, it may involve more proximal arteries, but involvement of large arteries is unusual.

Patients may present with claudication of the foot, legs, and occasionally the arms and hands. Foot or arch claudication may be the presenting manifestation and is often mistaken for an orthopedic problem. Seventy-five to 80% present with ischemic rest pain and/or ulcerations. Two or more limbs are almost always involved, and angiographic abnormalities are consistently found in limbs that are not yet clinically involved. Superficial thrombophlebitis and Raynaud's phenomenon each occur in approximately 40% of patients.

A positive Allen test indicates the distal nature of thromboangiitis obliterans and its involvement of the lower and upper extremities to help differentiate it from atherosclerosis. In this test, the physician simultaneously occludes both the radial and ulnar arteries. When pressure is released from either artery, there should be prompt filling from that artery with the return of color to the hand. A positive test result is indicated when color does not return to the blanched hand.

Diagnosis

No specific laboratory tests aid in the diagnosis of Buerger's disease, but tests should exclude vasculitis, hypercoagulable states, antiphospholipid antibodies, and a proximal source of emboli. On arteriography, the proximal arteries are normal, and the disease is most often infrapopliteal in the lower extremities and distal to the brachial artery in the upper extremities. There may be multiple vascular occlusions with collateralization around the obstruction (corkscrew collaterals), similar to what may be seen in other small vessel occlusive diseases such as CREST syndrome or scleroderma, but the arteriographic appearance of Buerger's disease may also be identical to that seen in patients with systemic lupus erythematosus, rheumatoid vasculitis, mixed connective tissue diseases, and antiphospholipid antibody syndrome. However, these other diseases can usually be established or excluded by other tests. Patients with Takayasu's arteritis or giant cell arteritis present with proximal vascular involvement and can readily be distinguished from Buerger's disease.

Rx Treatment

The cornerstone of therapy for thromboangiitis obliterans is the complete discontinuation of cigarette smoking or the use of tobacco in any form. Quitters almost always avoid amputations, whereas 40% or more of patients who continue tobacco use progress to one or more amputations.

All other forms of therapy (calcium channel blockers, antibiotics, anticoagulants, sympathectomy) are palliative. In a prospective, randomized trial, intravenous iloprost was superior to aspirin at 28 days in relieving rest pain and healing all ischemic ulcerations. At 6 months, 88% of patients receiving iloprost responded to therapy, compared with 21% in the aspirin group, and only 6% underwent amputation in the iloprost group, compared with 18% in the aspirin group. In a recently reported double-blind, placebo-controlled, randomized trial, oral iloprost was slightly more effective than placebo in relieving rest pain but not in healing ischemic ulcerations.

Surgical bypass is not a viable option in most patients because there may not be a distal target vessel with which to bypass. Sympathectomy and implantable spinal cord stimulators may help some patients. Vascular endothelial growth factor has helped in the healing of ischemic ulcers and the prevention of amputation in patients with Buerger's disease.

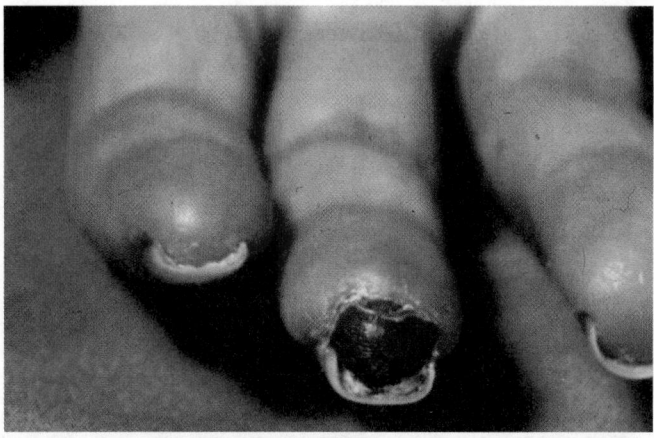

A

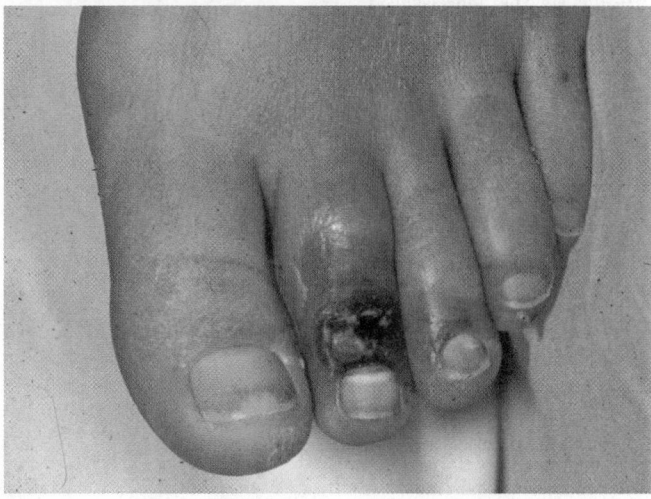

B

FIGURE 77–1 • Ischemic finger of a young male (*A*) and ischemic toe of a 28-year-old woman (*B*) with Buerger's disease.

VASOSPASTIC DISEASES AND VASCULAR DISEASES ASSOCIATED WITH CHANGES IN ENVIRONMENTAL TEMPERATURES

RAYNAUD'S PHENOMENON

Raynaud's phenomenon is the abrupt onset of a triphasic color response: well-demarcated pallor of the digits progressing to cyanosis with pain and often numbness followed by reactive hyperemia on rewarming. This vasospastic phenomenon is often precipitated by cold exposure or stress. Primary Raynaud's phenomenon (formerly known as Raynaud's disease) denotes patients who have no underlying cause, whereas secondary Raynaud's phenomenon (formerly known as Raynaud's syndrome) is associated with or caused by some other systemic illness or disease process (Table 77–2).

Raynaud's phenomenon is common in patients with connective tissue diseases. Approximately 90% of patients with scleroderma (Chapter 281) experience Raynaud's phenomenon and it may be a presenting manifestation in many patients with scleroderma. Raynaud's phenomenon is also a component of the CREST (*c*alcinosis, *R*aynaud's phenomenon, *e*sophageal dysmotility, *s*clerodactyly, *t*elangiectasias) syndrome. These patients have small vessel occlusive disease that may lead to digital pitting or ulceration and eventual amputation.

The β-adrenergic receptor antagonists are the most common drugs associated with Raynaud's phenomenon because they block the vasodilatory β receptors and thus leave the vasoconstrictive α receptors unopposed. Ergotamine preparations, polyvinyl chloride, and several cancer chemotherapeutic agents can also cause Raynaud's phenomenon.

Raynaud's phenomenon is common in individuals who use vibratory tools such as pneumatic hammers, chain saws, sanders, and grinders. This syndrome has been termed the *hand-arm vibration*

Cardiovascular Disease

Table 77–2 • CONDITIONS ASSOCIATED WITH SECONDARY RAYNAUD'S PHENOMENON

CONNECTIVE TISSUE DISEASES
Scleroderma of CREST syndrome
Systemic lupus erythematosus
Rheumatoid arthritis
Mixed connective tissue disease
Polymyositis, dermatomyositis
Sjögren's syndrome

ARTERIAL OCCLUSIVE DISEASES
Vasculitis: Takayasu's arteritis, giant cell arteritis, and necrotizing vasculitidies
Thromboangiitis obliterans (Buerger's disease)
Thromboembolism
Thoracic outlet syndrome
Atherosclerosis of the innominant and subclavian arteries

DRUGS AND TOXINS
β-adrenergic blocking agents
Ergotamine preparations
Methysergide
Vinblastine
Bleomycin
Cisplatin
Polyvinyl chloride
Heavy metals
Interferon alpha and beta
Tegafur

TRAUMA
Vibratory tools, grinders, sanders
Thermal injury
Electric shock injury
Percussive injury
Hypothenar hammer syndrome

HEMATOLOGIC ABNORMALITIES
Cryoglobulinemia and cryofibrinogenemia
Cold agglutinin disease
Myeloproliferative diseases
Hyperviscosity syndrome

NEUROLOGIC DISORDERS
Carpal tunnel syndrome
Reflex sympathetic dystrophy
Stroke
Intervertebral disk disease
Poliomyelitis
Syringomyelia

OTHER
Hypothyroidism
Pulmonary hypertension
Arteriovenous fistula
Neoplasms
Renal failure
Migraine or vascular headaches
Carcinoid syndrome
Pheochromocytoma
Parvovirus B19
Helicobacter pylori

syndrome, and the prevalence of Raynaud's phenomenon may exceed 90% at 10 years in individuals with heavy exposure. Continued use of vibratory tools can lead to a chronic occlusive small vessel vascular disease. The syndrome has also been described in typists, pianists, meat cutters, and sewing machine operators.

Trauma to the distal ulnar artery (several centimeters distal to the wrist) may occur with activities such as pounding with the palm of the hand, karate, or other activities that traumatize the hypothenar eminence and lead to an aneurysm or pseudoaneurysm of the distal ulnar artery (hypothenar hammer syndrome). Thrombus within the aneurysm may then embolize to the fingers, or the distal ulnar artery may thrombose.

Pathogenesis

The initial manifestation of Raynaud's phenomenon occurs when the digits turn white as a result of the intense vasoconstriction or spasm of the digital arteries. At this point there is total cessation of blood flow and the digits are often numb. As the arterial vasoconstriction becomes less severe, postcapillary venule constriction causes the blood in the capillaries and veins to become deoxygenated, thus producing the cyanotic appearance. When rewarming occurs, there is a markedly increased blood flow producing reactive hyperemia to the digits (red color). Factors that may be involved in precipitating vasospasm include aberrant endothelium-dependent vasoregulation, low levels of calcitonin gene-related peptide, abnormal sympathetic nervous system activity specifically at the level of the postsynaptic α_2 receptors, and abnormal platelet activation.

Clinical Manifestations

The symptoms of Raynaud's phenomenon may include pallor (Fig. 77–2), cyanosis, and reactive hyperemia. The triphasic color response occurs in 4 to 65% of patients. Exposure to the cold is the typical precipitating factor, but emotional lability may also cause or exacerbate attacks in some patients. Vasospastic attacks usually occur only in the fingers, but vasospasm can occur in the toes, nose, ears, lips, and other body parts.

In primary Raynaud's disease, the physical examination is normal between attacks. However, in patients with secondary Raynaud's phenomenon, pits or ulcerations on the fingertips may be present in patients with scleroderma, CREST syndrome, or thromboangiitis obliterans. An abnormal result of the Allen test on physical examination indicates fixed arterial obstruction.

Diagnosis

The diagnosis of Raynaud's phenomenon is not difficult when based on the patient's description of the attacks. Patients with persistent cyanosis or persistent hyperemia generally have some condition other than Raynaud's phenomenon. In primary Raynaud's, vasospastic attacks are precipitated by exposure to the cold or emotional stimuli, there is bilateral involvement of the extremities without gangrene, and, after a careful search, there is no evidence of underlying systemic diseases that could be responsible for the vasospastic attacks (Table 77–3).

To evaluate systemic illnesses, a serologic evaluation should include a complete blood cell count, multiphasic serologic analysis, urinalysis, Westergren sedimentation rate, C-reactive protein, antinuclear antibody, extractable nuclear antigen (anti-Smith and ribonuclear protein), anti-DNA, cryoglobulins, complement, anticentromere antibodies, and SCL70 scleroderma antibodies. In addition, nailfold capillaroscopy can be performed to help confirm a diagnosis of CREST syndrome or scleroderma in patients in whom the symptoms are not clear. An abnormal nailfold capillaroscopy indicates the patient does not have primary Raynaud's.

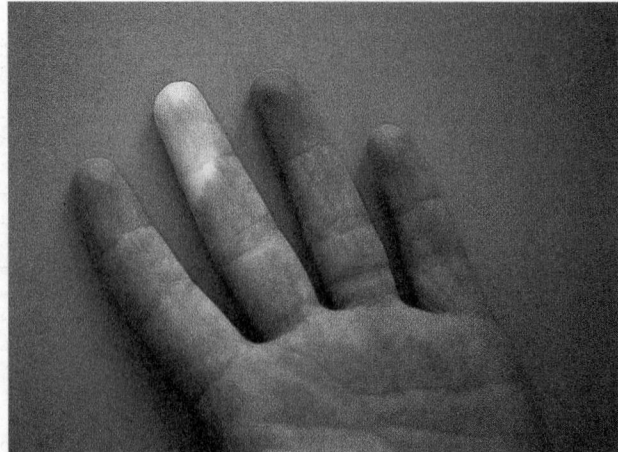

FIGURE 77–2 • Raynaud's phenomenon in the acute phase, with severe blanching of the tip of one finger. (From Forbes CD, Jackson WF: Color Atlas and Text of Clinical Medicine, 3rd ed. London, Mosby, 2003, with permission.)

Table 77–3 • DIFFERENTIATING PRIMARY FROM SECONDARY RAYNAUD'S PHENOMENON

CHARACTERISTICS	PRIMARY	SECONDARY
Associated diseases	No	Yes
Age at onset	Younger (<30 yr)	Older (>30 yr)
Nailfold capillaries	Normal	Large, tortuous with "drop out"
Autoantibodies	Negative or low titers	Frequent
Endothelial cell activation	Yes	Yes
Endothelial damage	No	Frequent
Structural occlusion	No	Yes
Digital gangrene	Rare; only superficial	Common
α_2-adrenergic activity	High	High
Calcitonin gene-related peptide	Low	Low

From Block JA, Sequeira W: Raynaud's phenomenon. Lancet 2001;357:2042–2048.

The noninvasive vascular laboratory (pulse volume recordings) is useful in identifying the degree of digital arterial occlusive disease (fixed ischemia) and predicting whether ischemic ulcerations on the digits will heal. Arteriography is not routinely performed.

Rx Treatment

In patients with mild vasospastic attacks, reassurance about the benign nature of the disease and instructions on how to prevent attacks are often all that is needed. Patients should limit the amount of exposure to the cold and should dress warmly and protect not only their extremities but also their entire body. Smoking should be avoided because nicotine causes intense vasoconstriction. β-Blocking agents may exaggerate the symptoms of Raynaud's phenomenon. Mittens are better than gloves for keeping the hands warm. Patients need to be especially careful when handling cold objects. Hand and foot warming devices (battery operated or chemical) may be helpful. Conditioning techniques or biofeedback is sometimes helpful in controlling vasospastic episodes.

The dihydropyridine calcium channel blocking agents are the most effective pharmacotherapy for Raynaud's phenomenon. Patients who have infrequent attacks may benefit from a short-acting calcium channel blocker such as nifedipine, 10 to 20 mg, given 30 minutes to 1 hour before cold exposure. When vasospasm occurs more frequently, the extended-release preparations of nifedipine (30 to 90 mg daily) or amlodipine (2.5 to 10 mg daily) should be used. The α_1-adrenergic receptor antagonists such as prazosin or terazosin can also decrease the severity, frequency, and duration of vasospastic attacks in patients.

Nitroglycerin can be used topically, whereas prostacyclin can be given intravenously. The ACE inhibitors and the angiotensin receptor antagonists have shown some benefit in uncontrolled trials, but other vasodilators such as niacin and papaverine are not beneficial. Several reports have suggested a beneficial effect from selective serotonin reuptake inhibitors such as fluoxetine. There are also a few case reports suggesting that cilostazol may improve ulcer healing in patients with secondary Raynaud's phenomenon.

Although sympathectomy may be beneficial in the short term, with about a 50% improvement rate, the vasospastic attacks may recur after 6 months to 2 years. Some patients with severe disease have had success with digital sympathectomy.

Prognosis

The prognosis in patients with primary Raynaud's is excellent. There is no mortality associated with this condition. In a long-term study involving 307 patients with primary Raynaud's disease, 38% had stable disease, 36% improved, 16% worsened, and the syndrome disappeared in 10%. The prognosis associated with secondary Raynaud's phenomenon depends on the underlying condition that caused it.

PERNIO (CHILBLAINS)

Pernio (a Latin word that literally means frostbite; however, its synonym chilblains is an Anglo-Saxon term that means cold sore) is a localized inflammatory lesion of the skin as a result of abnormal response to the cold. Up to 50% of women developed pernio in wartime conditions in northern Europe. Pernio is now less common but is still seen in the temperate, humid climates of northwestern Europe and in the northern United States.

Pernio develops in susceptible individuals who are exposed to non-freezing cold. The pathologic changes include edema of the papillo-dermis, vasculitis characterized by perivascular infiltration (with lymphocytes) of the arterioles and venules of the dermis, thickening and edema of the blood vessel walls, fat necrosis, and chronic inflammatory reaction with giant cell formation.

Pernio most commonly occurs in young women between the ages of 15 and 30 years but may occur in older individuals or in children. Acute pernio may develop 12 to 24 hours after exposure to the cold. Single or multiple erythematous, purplish, edematous lesions appear accompanied by intense itching or burning. These lesions may have a yellowish or brownish discoloration and may be associated with some flaking. They tend to affect the toes and dorsum of the proximal phalanges. The lesions of acute pernio are usually self-limited, although they may lead to recurrent disease. The arterial circulation is normal on physical examination and in the noninvasive vascular laboratory. Chronic pernio occurs when repeated exposure to the cold results in the persistence of lesions with subsequent scarring and atrophy. Characteristically, the lesions begin in the fall or winter and disappear in the spring or early summer. In advanced cases, the seasonal variation may disappear and chronic occlusive vascular disease may develop.

In the typical form, the patient develops violet or yellow-brown blisters and shallow ulcers on the toes that burn and itch. The lesions first appear in the fall or winter and disappear each spring. The differential diagnosis of pernio includes recurrent, erythematous, nodular, and ulcerative lesions such as erythema induratum, nodular vasculitis, erythema nodosum, and cold panniculitis. The skin lesions of pernio may look similar to atheromatous embolization (see earlier), and an arteriogram may sometimes be required.

Prevention is the best form of therapy. Cold exposure should be minimized as much as possible. In a randomized trial, nifedipine reduced the pain and facilitated the healing process. The severe itching may be treated with local application of an antipruritic agent.

ACROCYANOSIS

Acrocyanosis, which is a persistent blue or cyanotic discoloration of the digits, occurs most commonly in the hands and may worsen with exposure to cold and improve with rewarming. The primary form is a benign cosmetic condition, but it may also be seen in patients with connective tissue diseases, thromboangiitis obliterans, and diseases associated with central cyanosis. The exact pathophysiologic abnormality is not clear but may be vasospasm in the cutaneous arteries and arterioles with compensatory dilatation in the postcapillary venules.

Ulceration or tissue loss is unusual, and the overall prognosis is excellent. Patients should be advised to keep their extremities warm. Drugs such as α-adrenergic blocking agents or calcium channel blockers may be helpful.

FROSTBITE

Frostbite is freezing of tissues resulting from exposure to cold. It may occur in above-freezing temperatures under circumstances such as wetness, strong wind, or high altitude.

A person's response to cold is aimed at conserving the core (internal body) temperature as well as the viability of the extremity. Heat loss is reduced by peripheral vasoconstriction caused by sympathetic stimulation and catecholamine release. Maintenance or augmentation of body heat is accomplished by muscular activity such as shivering. However, the heat production from shivering cannot be sustained for more than a few hours because of the depletion of glycogen, which is the source of heat during shivering. The extremities are also protected by the "hunting reaction," which consists of irregular

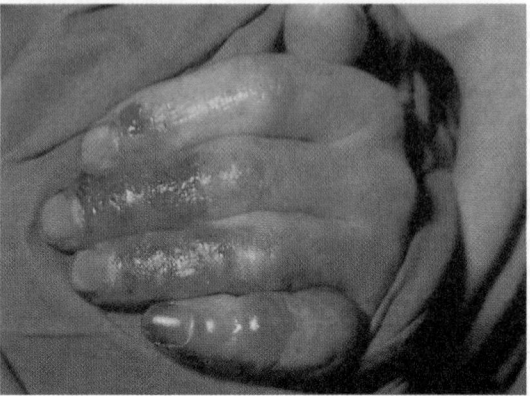

FIGURE 77–3 • Frostbite of the hand in a mountaineer. On rewarming, the hand became painful, red, and edematous, with signs of probably gangrene in the fifth finger. (From Forbes CD, Jackson WF: Color Atlas and Text of Clinical Medicine, 3rd ed. London, Mosby, 2003, with permission.)

5- to 10-minute cycles of alternating periods of vasoconstriction and vasodilatation that protect the extremities against excessive sustained vasoconstriction at minimal loss of internal body temperature. However, when the body is exposed to cold of a magnitude or duration so as to threaten the internal body temperature, this mechanism fails. Because the disruption of core temperature is more deleterious to the body than peripheral vasoconstriction, conservation of core temperature takes precedence over rewarming of the extremities, and the hunting response is replaced by continuous and more intense vasoconstriction that promotes frostbite by means of ice crystal formation, cellular dehydration, and thrombosis of the microvasculature.

Soon after exposure to the cold, pain develops and gradually progresses to numbness; the frozen part turns white because of intense vasoconstriction (Fig. 77–3). With rewarming or thawing, the circulation is restored and the affected parts become hyperemic. Edema may first occur within hours of thawing and remains for days or weeks. Blisters appear within the first 24 hours and are reabsorbed within 1 to 2 weeks, after which a black eschar may persist (Fig. 77–4). Overactivity of the sympathetic nervous system is manifested by hyperhidrosis or a burning sensation.

Seventy percent of victims develop chronic sequelae including cold sensitivity, pain, and sensory disturbances, often resembling reflex sympathetic dystrophy. Frostbite arthritis may occur in particularly severe cases.

It is important to establish the depth of the frostbite and determine whether the tissue is viable, which may not be obvious on initial clinical examination but is usually determined weeks or months after the cold injury when the demarcation zone appears and the dead tissue is sloughed.

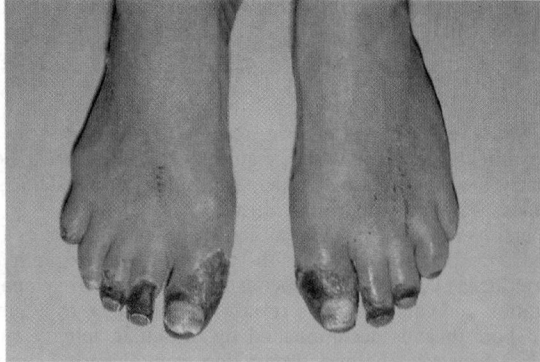

FIGURE 77–4 • Gangrene after frostbite. (From Forbes CD, Jackson WF: Color Atlas and Text of Clinical Medicine, 3rd ed. London, Mosby, 2003, with permission.)

Rx Treatment

In mild cases of frostbite, the only necessary treatment may be daily whirlpool baths with bedrest. However, treatment of deep frostbite should be considered a medical emergency because the early institution of medical therapy may reduce the amount of subsequent tissue loss. Thawing, the mainstay of therapy, should not be implemented if the patient may be re-exposed to cold because refreezing of thawed tissue promotes further tissue damage. Walking on a frozen limb produces substantially less damage than walking on a thawed limb.

After transfer to a medical facility, frozen tissue should be rapidly rewarmed in a water bath of 40 to 42° C (104–108° F) for 15 to 30 minutes until complete thawing has occurred. After thawing, reappearance of normal color signifies the reestablishment of blood flow. Thawing is often a painful process and may require the administration of narcotics.

After thawing, the extremity should be cleansed twice daily in a whirlpool bath with an aseptic solution at 35 to 37° C (95–99° F). Care should be taken to prevent and treat secondary infections. Tetanus prophylaxis should be administered. A frostbite protocol consisting of débridement of clear blisters with a topical application of aloe vera, oral ibuprofen, and daily hydrotherapy is highly effective. An important principle is to avoid early débridement or amputation, which is indicated only when infected gangrene or generalized sepsis occurs.

ERYTHROMELALGIA

Erythromelalgia literally means red, painful extremities. It may be classified as the primary or idiopathic category, which may be nonfamilial or familial. The secondary category is associated with other diseases, the most common being myeloproliferative disorders such as polycythemia vera and essential thrombocythemia. Other diseases associated with secondary erythromelalgia include hypertension, diabetes, rheumatoid arthritis, gout, spinal cord disease, multiple sclerosis, systemic lupus erythematosus, cutaneous vasculitis, and viral infection; it also may result from therapy with various drugs (e.g., nifedipine, nicardipine, verapamil, bromocriptine, and pergolide). The histology varies from normal to arterial occlusion with thrombus formation.

Erythromelalgia is characterized by the clinical triad of erythema, burning pain, and increased temperature usually of the extremities. The feet, especially the soles, are more commonly involved than the hands. The peripheral pulses are generally normal in the primary type and variable in secondary erythromelalgia. The symptoms may occur in "attacks" that last for minutes to hours and occasionally days and are precipitated by a warm environment. Exercise and dependency tend to exacerbate symptoms. Patients seek relief by exposing the affected extremity to a cooler environment, such as placing the extremity in cold water, walking on a cold floor barefoot, or running the air conditioner even in the winter.

Other causes of painful erythematous extremities include reflex sympathetic dystrophy, atherosclerotic peripheral arterial disease (Chapter 76), and thromboangiitis obliterans (Buerger's disease). Erythromelalgia may precede the clinical appearance of a myeloproliferative disorder by several years, so patients older than age 30 years should be monitored periodically with blood cell counts.

The treatment of erythromelalgia is often difficult and frustrating. In secondary erythromelalgia, treatment of the underlying disease (phlebotomy in patients with polycythemia vera and normalization of the platelet count in patients with thrombocythemia) may relieve the symptoms. Aspirin is the most effective treatment available, particularly for patients with erythromelalgia secondary to myeloproliferative disorders. Other therapies with variable success include methysergide, ephedrine, nonsteroidal anti-inflammatory drugs, phenoxybenzamine, nitroglycerin, sodium nitroprusside, corticosteroids, and surgical sympathectomy.

POPLITEAL ARTERY ENTRAPMENT SYNDROME

In the popliteal artery entrapment syndrome, there is compression of the popliteal artery due to a congenital anatomic abnormality or an abnormal muscle or fibrous band. The most frequent abnormality is when the medial head of the gastrocnemius muscle compresses the popliteal artery, causing medial deviation of the popliteal artery.

The clinical presentation is in a healthy, "athletic type" male complaining of typical claudication symptoms in the absence of premature atherosclerosis. Disappearance of the pulse with passive dorsiflexion of the foot or active plantar foot flexion against resistance may suggest the diagnosis. Duplex ultrasound may help, and computed tomography (CT) or magnetic resonance imaging (MRI) can confirm the diagnosis; on arteriography, the characteristic finding is a medial deviation of the popliteal artery with poststenotic dilatation. Other diseases that can cause midpopliteal occlusion include cystic adventitial disease, thrombosed popliteal artery aneurysm, and atherosclerosis of the superficial femoral and popliteal arteries. The primary treatment of popliteal artery entrapment syndrome is surgical.

CYSTIC ADVENTITIAL DISEASE

In cystic adventitial disease, gelatinous fluid accumulates in an arterial wall cyst and then the cyst encroaches on the vessel lumen, resulting in stenosis or occlusion. The cyst arises in the outer portion of the media or subadventitial layer, most commonly in the popliteal artery. Cystic adventitial disease is an isolated lesion not associated with a systemic process, and the precise pathophysiologic mechanism is unknown.

The disease predominates in men with an approximate ratio of 5 : 1, and the mean age at diagnosis is about 45 years. Claudication is the most frequent symptom. The pulses may disappear on flexion of the knee (Ishikawa's sign). However, if the artery is occluded, no pulses are palpable.

Pulse volume recordings may show the characteristic decrease in blood pressure and change in waveform configuration in the affected limb. A perivascular cystic structure may be visualized on duplex ultrasound. CT or MRI can show the anatomy in the popliteal region. CT-guided needle aspiration can partially but usually not completely remove the high viscosity and gelatinous fluid. If arterial occlusion has occurred, catheter-directed thrombolytic therapy and/or surgical resection is indicated.

FIBROMUSCULAR DYSPLASIA OF THE EXTREMITIES

Although fibromuscular dysplasia (in particular, medial fibroplasia) is most common in the renal and carotid arteries (Chapter 124), it may also occur in peripheral arteries of the extremity (iliac, superficial femoral, popliteal, tibial, subclavian, axillary, radial, and ulnar). These lesions may be asymptomatic or may produce a difference in blood pressure between the two limbs with paresthesias, claudication, or critical limb ischemia.

The typical arteriographic appearance of "a string of beads" is virtually pathognomonic of medial fibroplasia. Long, smooth areas of narrowing are characteristic of intimal fibroplasia but may also be seen with Takayasu's arteritis (Chapter 75) and giant cell arteritis (Chapters 75 and 285).

Therapy should be reserved for symptomatic disease. Under most circumstances, percutaneous balloon dilatation is the treatment of choice.

SUGGESTED READINGS

Begelman SM, Olin JW: Fibromuscular dysplasia. Curr Opin Rheum 2000;12:41–47. *Classification, clinical manifestations and treatment options in patients with fibromuscular dysplasia of the renal, carotid, and peripheral arteries.*

Davis JD, O'Fallon WM, Rogers RS 3rd, Rooke TW: Natural history of erythromelalgia: Presentation and outcome in 168 patients. Arch Dermatol 2000;136:406–409. *The largest published series of patients with erythromelalgia describing the clinical presentation as well as the natural history of the disease.*

Olin JW: Thromboangiitis obliterans (Buerger's Disease). N Engl J Med 2000;343:864–869. *A contemporary review of the clinical manifestations, pathogenesis, and treatment of thromboangiitis obliterans.*

Wigley FM: Clinical practice. Raynaud's Phenomenon. N Engl J Med 2002;347:1001–1008. *A case-based review.*

78 PERIPHERAL VENOUS DISEASE

Russell D. Hull

Deep vein thrombosis (DVT) usually begins in the deep veins of the calf muscles. When confined to the calf veins, DVT carries a low risk

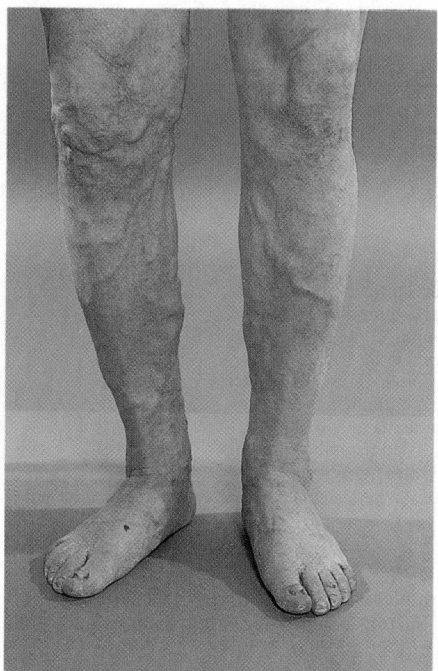

FIGURE 78–1 • Varicose veins are a risk factor for deep vein thrombosis and may result from it. (From Forbes CD, Jackson WF: Color Atlas and Text of Clinical Medicine, 3rd ed. London, Mosby, 2003, with permission.)

of clinically important pulmonary emboli, but the DVT may propagate into the proximal venous system, where it becomes a serious and potentially life-threatening disorder. Although most clinically important pulmonary emboli (Chapter 94) arise from thrombi in the popliteal or proximal deep veins of the leg, they may also arise from the iliac or deep pelvic veins, renal veins, inferior vena cava (IVC), or the right side of the heart. Less commonly, thrombosis may involve the axillary and subclavian venous systems; upper extremity DVT can also cause pulmonary emboli.

Superficial thrombophlebitis involves the superficial veins of the lower or sometimes the upper extremity, is commonly associated with the presence of varicose veins (Fig. 78–1) or pregnancy, and may be precipitated by trauma. Superficial thrombophlebitis may be associated with DVT, particularly when the more proximal superficial veins in the thigh are involved. Indeed, if any doubt exists, objective tests for DVT should be performed.

With the exception of thrombolytic therapy for some pulmonary emboli, management of DVT and pulmonary embolism is basically the same. The diagnostic approach to patients with venous thromboembolism (VTE) may involve the lungs or the legs, and prevention of pulmonary embolism is essentially the prevention of DVT.

Etiology and Pathogenesis

VTE often complicates the course of sick, hospitalized patients but may also affect ambulant and otherwise apparently healthy individuals. Pulmonary embolism remains the most common preventable cause of hospital death and is responsible for approximately 150,000 to 200,000 deaths per year in the United States. Most patients who die of pulmonary embolism succumb suddenly or within 2 hours of the acute event, before therapy can be initiated or can take effect. Effective prophylaxis against VTE is now available for most high-risk patients.

Venous thrombi are composed predominantly of fibrin and red cells and have a variable platelet and leukocyte component. The factors that predispose to the development of VTE are venous stasis, activation of blood coagulation, and vascular damage. Protective mechanisms that counteract these thrombogenic stimuli include (1) inactivation of activated coagulation factors by circulating inhibitors (e.g., antithrombin III [ATIII], α_2-macroglobulin, α_1-antitrypsin, and activated protein C), (2) clearance of activated coagulation factors and soluble fibrin polymer complexes by the reticuloendothelial system and by the liver, and (3) dissolution of fibrin by fibrinolytic enzymes

Table 78–1 • FACTORS PREDISPOSING TO VENOUS THROMBOEMBOLISM

Surgical and nonsurgical trauma
Previous venous thromboembolism
Immobilization
Malignant disease
Heart failure
Leg paralysis
Age (>40 yr)
Obesity
Estrogens and oral contraceptives
Inherited or acquired disorders
   Antithrombin III deficiency
Protein C or S deficiency
Activated protein C resistance (factor V Leiden)
Prothrombin mutant
Homocysteinemia
Heparin-induced thrombocytopenia
Antiphospholipid syndrome

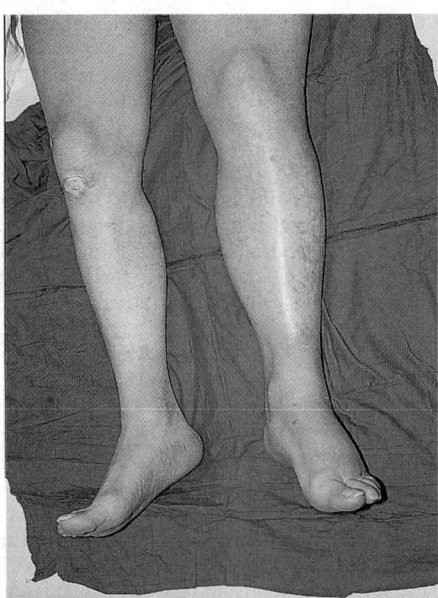

FIGURE 78–2 • Deep vein thrombosis, presenting as an acutely swollen left leg. Note the dilatation of the superficial veins. The leg was hot to the touch, and palpation along the line of the left popliteal and femoral veins caused pain. Less than 50% of DVTs present in this way, and other conditions may mimic DVT, so further investigation is always indicated. Note the coincidental psoriatic lesion below the patient's right knee. (From Forbes CD, Jackson WF: Color Atlas and Text of Clinical Medicine, 3rd ed. London, Mosby, 2003, with permission.)

derived from plasma and endothelial cells and digestion of fibrin by leukocytes. Various coagulation abnormalities and other risk factors predispose to VTE (Table 78–1).

Clinical Manifestations

The clinical features of venous thrombosis (Fig. 78–2) include leg pain, tenderness, swelling, a palpable cord, discoloration, venous distention, prominence of the superficial veins, and cyanosis. In most patients who have clinically suspected DVT, the symptoms and signs are nonspecific; in more than 50% of these patients, the clinical suspicion of DVT is not confirmed by objective testing. Conversely, patients with relatively minor symptoms and signs may have extensive venous thrombosis.

Upper extremity DVT involving the subclavian, axillary, and brachial veins is often caused by strenuous exercise and is more common in males than females. Other risk factors include central venous catheters and previous venous thrombosis, but limited studies have shown little relationship to the presence of hypercoagulable states. Unilateral swelling, distention of superficial veins, cyanosis, and a palpable cord in the axillary vein are common clinical manifestations. The diagnosis is best confirmed by compression ultrasonography or ascending contrast venography.

Pulmonary emboli originate from thrombi in the proximal deep veins of the leg in 90% or more of patients (Chapter 94). Other less common sources of pulmonary emboli include the deep pelvic veins, the renal veins, the IVC, the right ventricle, and the axillary veins. Pulmonary embolism occurs in 50% of patients with objectively documented proximal leg vein thrombosis; many of the emboli are asymptomatic. Usually, only part of the thrombus embolizes, and 50 to 70% of patients with angiographically documented pulmonary emboli have detectable DVT of the legs at the time of initial evaluation. The clinical significance of pulmonary embolism depends on the size of the embolus and the cardiorespiratory reserve of the patient.

Differential Diagnosis

A number of conditions can mimic venous thrombosis (Table 78–2), but without objective testing it is often impossible to exclude venous thrombosis. The cause of symptoms can often be determined by careful follow-up after a diagnosis of venous thrombosis has been excluded by objective testing. In some patients, however, the cause of pain, tenderness, and swelling remains uncertain.

OBJECTIVE DIAGNOSTIC TESTS. Objective tests used in the diagnosis of venous thrombosis include B-mode ultrasonography (commonly with color flow Doppler), and ascending venography. The only laboratory test of proven value in the diagnosis and management of DVT is the D-dimer test.

Real-time *B-mode ultrasound,* preferably with *Doppler assessment,* has become the standard technique for the evaluation of patients with clinically suspected DVT. Prospective studies have shown that the

Table 78–2 • ALTERNATIVE DIAGNOSES IN 87 CONSECUTIVE PATIENTS WITH CLINICALLY SUSPECTED VENOUS THROMBOSIS AND NEGATIVE VENOGRAMS*

DIAGNOSIS	PATIENTS (%)
Muscle strain	24
Direct twisting injury to the leg	10
Leg swelling in paralyzed limb	9
Lymphangitis, lymphatic obstruction	7
Venous reflux	7
Muscle tear	6
Baker's cyst	5
Cellulitis	3
Internal abnormality of the knee	2
Unknown	26

*The diagnosis was made once venous thrombosis was excluded by venography.

single criterion of vein compressibility is highly sensitive and specific for the detection of *proximal* DVT (sensitivity and specificity, both >95%). Other ultrasound criteria are insensitive, nonspecific, or both. Doppler ultrasonography is still not sufficiently sensitive for the detection of isolated calf vein thrombosis; serial testing is required to detect proximal extension. Serial ultrasound, based on the now confirmed concept that calf vein thrombi are clinically important only when they extend into the proximal veins and are reliably detected by ultrasound, is a useful clinical approach. A positive result is highly predictive of acute proximal DVT and warrants anticoagulation, whereas anticoagulant therapy can be safely withheld in symptomatic patients who have negative results by serial ultrasound (Fig. 78–3).

Doppler ultrasonography (or even real-time B-mode ultrasonography without Doppler) has become the most popular noninvasive test for the detection of venous thrombosis. However, Doppler ultrasonography lacks sensitivity and specificity for the detection of asymptomatic venous thrombosis in patients who have undergone surgery.

Venography, the "gold standard" objective method for the diagnosis of DVT, requires considerable experience to execute and interpret accurately. The most reliable criterion for DVT is an intraluminal filling

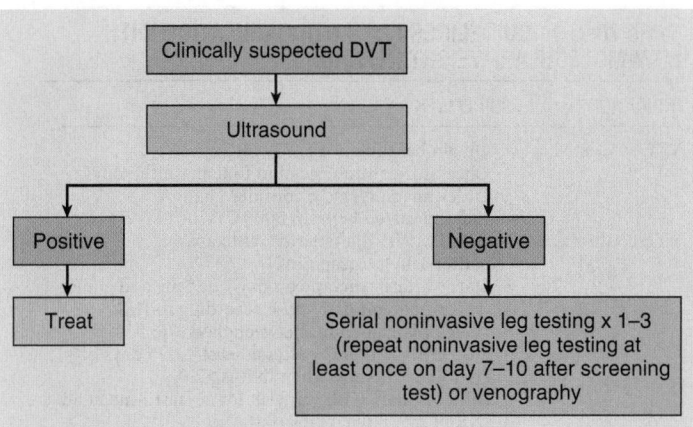

FIGURE 78-3 • Algorithm for the diagnosis of deep vein thrombosis (DVT) in patients with no evidence of pulmonary embolism.

defect that is constant in all films and is seen in numerous projections. Other abnormalities such as nonfilling of a segment of the deep venous system or nonfilling of the entire deep venous system above the knee may be caused by technical artifacts. Even in the best of circumstances, it may be impossible to cannulate a vein on the dorsum of the foot, thus making ascending venography impossible. Venography is also associated with pain in the foot while dye is being injected or 1 to 2 days after injection. The procedure may be complicated by superficial phlebitis and even DVT in 1 to 2% of patients with normal results on venography. Other less common complications include dye hypersensitivity or aggravation of renal insufficiency. The risks of venography must be carefully weighed against its benefits, and ultrasonography has largely replaced contrast venography in symptomatic patients because of its widespread availability.

D-dimer, which can be measured rapidly by a number of enzyme-linked immunosorbent assays or less reliably by latex agglutination, has a high negative predictive value for excluding suspected VTE. The combination of a negative D-dimer and a low clinical probability of DVT, or the combination of a normal D-dimer and normal ultrasound or impedance plethysmography (IPG) may sufficiently exclude DVT so that further diagnostic testing can be safely limited and anticoagulation avoided.

However, the main limitation of D-dimer testing is that patients with suspected venous thrombosis frequently have significant comorbid disease or are elderly; the majority of these patients have abnormal D-dimer assays. The findings in two clinical trials that a single repeat venous ultrasound at 1 week could safely exclude the diagnosis of DVT has made the use of clinical probabilities and D-dimer testing less relevant.

For patients with suspected DVT, screening compression ultrasound should be the first test; patients who are positive should be treated. Patients with a negative screening ultrasound should undergo serial noninvasive leg testing one to three times (minimum of one test at 1 week). If a diagnosis is urgently required, venography may be used. In centers using a D-dimer assay of proven validity, patients with a negative ultrasound and low clinical probability require no further testing or treatment if the D-dimer test is negative. Because patients with a high or intermediate clinical probability still require serial noninvasive leg tests or venography despite a negative ultrasound and negative D-dimer, D-dimer assay adds little to the evaluation of such patients.

The diagnosis of upper extremity DVT can be made by compression ultrasonography, with or without color flow Doppler imaging, or by venography. Many patients with suspected upper extremity venous thrombosis have negative objective studies that exclude the diagnosis. Pulmonary embolism frequently complicates upper extremity DVT and may be the initial manifestation; objective testing for pulmonary emboli is required if the diagnosis will alter management. In patients with superficial thrombophlebitis, objective testing should be performed whenever DVT is suspected, particularly in patients with extensive phlebitis.

Prevention of Venous Thromboembolism

Without prophylaxis, the frequency of DVT ranges from less than 10% in low-risk patients to 40 to 80% in high-risk patients, and the frequency of fatal pulmonary embolism ranges from 0.1 to 0.8% in patients undergoing elective general surgery, 2 to 3% in patients undergoing elective hip replacement, and 4 to 7% in patients undergoing surgery for a fractured hip (Table 78-3). Factors increasing the risk of postoperative venous thrombosis include advanced age, malignancy, previous VTE, obesity, heart failure, and paralysis.

Two approaches can be taken to prevent DVT and the resulting risk of fatal pulmonary embolism: (1) secondary prevention involves the early detection and treatment of subclinical DVT by screening postoperative patients with sensitive, objective tests, and (2) primary prophylaxis against DVT involves either drugs or physical methods. Primary prophylaxis is preferred in most clinical circumstances, and prevention of DVT and pulmonary embolism is more cost-effective than treatment of complications when they occur. Secondary prevention by case-finding studies should be reserved for patients in whom primary prophylaxis is either contraindicated or relatively ineffective.

The primary prophylactic measures most commonly used are low-dose, low-molecular-weight heparin (LMWH), oral anticoagulants (to an international normalized ratio [INR] of 2.0 to 3.0), and intermittent pneumatic leg compression (Table 78-4). More recently, specific antithrombin agents, such as hirudin and pentasaccharide agents, have become available, and data suggest that the pentasaccharide agents are more efficacious than LMWHs to prevent DVT in patients undergoing hip and knee surgery.▪ Other less common measures include aspirin. Combined modalities such as graduated compression stockings or intermittent pneumatic leg compression along with pharmacologic agents may have an additive effect. Despite the convincing evidence for the efficacy and safety of prophylactic regimens, prophylaxis tends to be underused, even in high-risk patients.

Table 78-3 • RISK OF VENOUS THROMBOEMBOLISM ASSESSED BY OBJECTIVE TESTING

RISK CATEGORY	CALF VEIN THROMBOSIS	PROXIMAL VEIN THROMBOSIS	FATAL PULMONARY EMBOLISM
HIGH RISK Major orthopedic surgery on the lower limbs General urologic surgery in patients older than 40 yr with a recent history of DVT or PE Extensive pelvic or abdominal surgery for malignant disease	40–80%	10–30%	1–5%
MODERATE RISK General surgery in patients older than 40 yr that lasts 30 min or more, in patients younger than 40 yr taking oral contraceptives, and in women older than 35 yr having emergency cesarean section	10–40%	2–10%	0.1–0.8%
LOW RISK Minor surgery, i.e., <30 min in patients older than 40 yr without additional risk factors Uncomplicated surgery in patients younger than 40 yr without additional risk factors	<10%	<1%	<0.01%

DVT = deep vein thrombosis; PE = pulmonary embolism.
Modified with permission from Clagett GP, Anderson FA, Heit J, et al; Prevention of venous thromboembolism. Chest 1995;108:312S–334S.

Cardiovascular Disease

Table 78–4 • SPECIFIC RECOMMENDATIONS FOR PROPHYLAXIS FOR VARIOUS CLINICAL RISK CATEGORIES

PATIENT CATEGORY RECOMMENDATION	PROPHYLAXIS*
MODERATE RISK	
General abdominal, thoracic, gynecologic, or urologic surgery; medical patients	Low-dose unfractionated heparin or LMWH, IPC in patients at high risk of bleeding
Pregnancy with previous DVT	Low-dose heparin or adjusted-dose heparin
MODERATE TO HIGH RISK	
Neurosurgery	IPC
HIGH RISK	
Elective hip replacement	LMWH, warfarin, IPC
Elective knee replacement	LMWH, IPC
Hip fracture	LMWH, warfarin
Spinal cord injury with paralysis	LMWH, IPC

*See Tables 33–3 and 78–5 for dose recommendations for various LMWH preparations.

LMWH = low-molecular-weight heparin; IPC = intermittent pneumatic leg compression; DVT = deep vein thrombosis.

Table 78–5 • GUIDELINES FOR ANTICOAGULATION WITH LOW-MOLECULAR-WEIGHT HEPARIN

INDICATIONS	GUIDELINES
VTE suspected	• Obtain baseline aPTT, PT, CBC
	• Check for contraindication to heparin therapy
	• Order imaging study, consider giving unfractionated heparin 5000 U IV or LMWH
VTE confirmed	• Give LMWH (dalteparin*, enoxaparin†, nadroparin‡, tinzaparin§)
	• Start warfarin therapy on day 1 at 5 mg and adjust the subsequent daily dose according to INR
	• Check platelet count between days 3 to 5
	• Stop LMWH therapy after at least 4 to 5 days of combined therapy when INR is >2.0
	• Anticoagulate with warfarin for at least 3 mo at an INR of 2.5, range of 2.0–3.0

*Dalteparin sodium 200 anti-Xa IU/kg/day subcutaneously. Single dose should not exceed 18,000 IU. (Approved in Canada.)

†Enoxaparin sodium 1 mg/kg q12h subcutaneously or enoxaparin sodium 1.5 mg/kg/day subcutaneously. Single daily dose should not exceed 180 mg. (Approved in both the United States and Canada.)

‡Nadroparin calcium 86 anti-Xa IU/kg two times a day subcutaneously for 10 days (approved in Canada) or nadroparin calcium 171 anti-Xa IU/kg subcutaneously daily. Single dose should not exceed 17,100 IU.

§Tinzaparin sodium 175 anti-Xa IU kg/day subcutaneously daily. (Approved in Canada and the United States.)

VTE = venous thromboembolism; aPTT = activated partial thromboplastin time; PT = prothrombin time; CBC = complete blood count; IV = intravenous; LMWH = low-molecular-weight heparin; INR = international normalized ratio; VTE = venous thromboembolism

Adapted from Hyers TM, Agnelli G, Hull RD, et al: Antithrombotic therapy for venous thromboembolic disease. Chest 2001;119:176S–193S.

Rx Treatment

The objectives of treatment in patients with VTE are to prevent death from pulmonary embolism, prevent recurring VTE, and prevent the post-phlebitic syndrome. Anticoagulant drugs, especially heparin, LMWH, and warfarin, constitute the cornerstone of treatment of DVT. For selected patients, thrombolysis, thrombectomy, and IVC filters are appropriate.

HEPARIN THERAPY. The anticoagulant activity of unfractionated heparin depends on a unique pentasaccharide that binds to ATIII and potentiates the inhibition of thrombin and activated factor X (Xa) by ATIII (Chapter 33). About one third of all heparin molecules contain the unique pentasaccharide sequence regardless of whether they are low- or high-molecular-weight fractions. It is the pentasaccharide sequence that confers the molecular high affinity for ATIII. In addition, heparin catalyzes the inactivation of thrombin by cofactor II, which acts independently of ATIII.

Heparin also increases the release of tissue factor pathway inhibitor; binds to numerous plasma and platelet proteins, to endothelial cells, and to leukocytes; and increases vascular permeability. The anticoagulant response to a standard dose of heparin varies widely among patients, so the anticoagulant response to heparin should be monitored by using either the activated partial thromboplastin time (aPTT) or heparin levels to titrate the dose in an individual patient.

Low-Molecular-Weight Heparin. Standard heparin is polydispersed, with a mean molecular weight ranging from 10 to 16 kD. LMWH, by comparison, has a mean molecular weight of 4 to 5 kD (Chapter 33).

The LMWHs commercially available are made by different processes (such as nitrous acid, alkaline, or enzymatic depolymerization), and they differ chemically and pharmacokinetically. The clinical significance of these differences, however, is unclear. The doses of each of the different LMWHs have been established empirically.

When compared with unfractionated heparin, LMWHs have greater bioavailability when given by subcutaneous injection and a longer duration of anticoagulant effect (permitting once- or twice-daily administration), and because the anticoagulant response (anti-Xa activity) to LMWH is highly correlated with body weight, a fixed dose can be administered. Laboratory monitoring is not necessary with LMWH; in fact, little correlation is seen between anti-Xa activity and either bleeding or recurrent thrombosis. Three LMWHs and one heparinoid have been approved for use in the United States, and four LMWHs are approved for clinical use in Canada.

Recommended Regimens. In pooled data from a number of clinical trials, subcutaneous unmonitored LMWH results in a

reduction in major bleeding and mortality when compared with unfractionated heparin for the treatment of proximal DVT.[2] Furthermore, LMWH used predominantly out of hospital is as effective and safe as intravenous unfractionated heparin given in the hospital.[2] Oral warfarin therapy can be started simultaneously. Subcutaneous LMWH treatment is continued for 5 to 6 days and discontinued subsequently when the INR is therapeutic (INR above 2.0) on 2 consecutive days (Table 78–5).

Another approach to anticoagulant therapy for VTE is a combination of continuous intravenous heparin and oral warfarin, with both started simultaneously. The suggested duration of the initial intravenous heparin therapy is 5 days. Exceptions include patients who require immediate medical or surgical intervention, such as thrombolysis or insertion of an IVC filter, or patients at very high risk of bleeding. Heparin is continued until the INR has been within the therapeutic range (2 to 3) for 2 consecutive days.

The efficacy of heparin therapy depends on achieving a critical therapeutic level of heparin within the first 24 hours of treatment. The critical therapeutic level is an aPTT 1.5 times the mean of the control value or the upper limit of the normal aPTT range within the first 24 hours of treatment. This aPTT corresponds to a heparin blood level of 0.2 to 0.4 U/mL by the protamine sulfate titration assay or 0.3 to 0.6 IU/mL by amidolytic assay. Because of the wide variability in the aPTT and in heparin blood levels with different reagents and even with different batches of the same reagent, each laboratory must establish its own minimal therapeutic level. Although subtherapeutic aPTT values are strongly correlated with recurrent thromboembolism, the relationship between supratherapeutic aPTT and bleeding (aPTT ratio of 2.5 or more) is less definite. Indeed, bleeding during heparin therapy is more closely related to underlying clinical risk factors than to aPTT elevation above the therapeutic range. To avoid underdosing or overdosing with heparin, standardized nomograms based on a patient's weight are recommended (Table 78–6).

Complications of Heparin Therapy. The main adverse effects of heparin therapy include bleeding, thrombocytopenia, and osteoporosis. Patients at particular risk are those who have had recent surgery or trauma or those who have other clinical factors that predispose to bleeding while taking heparin, such as peptic ulcer,

Table 78–6 • WEIGHT-BASED NOMOGRAM FOR INITIAL INTRAVENOUS HEPARIN THERAPY

aPTT	DOSE (IU/KG)
Initial dose	80 bolus, then 18/hr
<35 sec (<1.2×)*	80 bolus, then 4/hr
35–45 sec (1.2–1.5×)	40 bolus, then 2/hr
46–70 sec (1.5–2.3×)	No change
71–90 sec (2.3–3.0×)	Decrease infusion rate by 2/hr
>90 sec (>3.0×)	Hold infusion 1 hr, then decrease infusion rate by 3/hr

*Figures in parentheses show comparison with control.
aPTT = activated partial thromboplastin time.
Adapted from Raschke RA, Reilly BM, Guidry JR, et al: The weight-based heparin dosing nomogram compared with a "standard care" nomogram. A randomized controlled trial. Ann Intern Med 1993;119:874–881.

occult malignancy, liver disease, other hemostatic defects, age older than 65 years, and female gender.

Management of bleeding while undergoing heparin therapy will depend on the location and severity of bleeding, the risk of recurrent VTE, and the aPTT. Heparin therapy should be discontinued temporarily or permanently. Patients with recent VTE may be candidates for insertion of an IVC filter. If urgent reversal of heparin effect is required, protamine sulfate can be administered.

Heparin-induced thrombocytopenia is a well-recognized complication of heparin therapy that usually occurs within 5 to 10 days after heparin treatment has started. Approximately 1 to 2% of patients receiving unfractionated heparin will experience a decrease in the platelet count to less than the normal range or a 50% decrease in the platelet count within the normal range. Heparin-induced thrombocytopenia occurs considerably less frequently in patients receiving LMWH, with this complication occurring in only 1 or 2 per 1000 patients. In most cases, this mild to moderate thrombocytopenia appears to be a direct effect of heparin on platelets and is of no consequence. However, an immune thrombocytopenia mediated by IgG antibody directed against a complex of PF4 and heparin develops in approximately 0.1 to 0.2% of patients receiving heparin. The development of thrombocytopenia may be accompanied by arterial or venous thrombosis, which may lead to serious consequences such as death or limb amputation. The diagnosis of heparin-induced thrombocytopenia, with or without thrombosis, must be made on clinical grounds because the assays with the highest sensitivity and specificity are not readily available. When the diagnosis of heparin-induced thrombocytopenia is made, administration of heparin in all forms must be stopped immediately. In patients requiring ongoing anticoagulation, the heparinoid danaparoid or hirudin may be used. Warfarin is another alternative, but it should probably not be started until one of the aforementioned agents has been used for 3 or 4 days to suppress thrombin generation. The defibrinogenating snake venom Arvin has been used extensively in the past but, like plasmapheresis or intravenous gamma globulin infusion, will probably be replaced by other agents. Insertion of an IVC filter is often indicated.

Osteoporosis has been reported in patients receiving unfractionated heparin in dosages of 20,000 U/day (or more) for more than 6 months. Demineralization can progress to fracture of vertebral bodies or long bones, and the defect may not be entirely reversible.

Protamine sulfate has been shown to reduce clinical bleeding in patients experiencing bleeding while receiving heparin or LMWHs, presumably by neutralizing the high-molecular-weight fractions of heparin that are thought to be most responsible for bleeding.

THROMBOLYTIC THERAPY. Thrombolytic therapy may benefit selected patients with acute massive venous thrombosis, such as those with phlegmasia cerulea dolens. In most patients with acute DVT, however, the indication for thrombolytic therapy remains controversial, and most patients do well with unfrac-

tionated heparin or LMWH. Currently, randomized clinical trials have yielded no definitive evidence that thrombolytic therapy is associated with improved benefit by prevention of the post-phlebitic syndrome.

THROMBECTOMY. Thrombectomy has been recommended in patients with massive iliofemoral thrombosis, particularly patients with vascular insufficiency and in whom thrombolytic therapy is contraindicated. These patients tend to have recurrent thrombosis after thrombectomy, and the procedure has fallen into disrepute in most centers. The finding of a free-floating thrombus on ultrasound has been another indication for urgent thrombectomy. However, a recent clinical trial reported no difference in outcomes for patients with free-floating thrombi and patients with proximal venous thromboses that were not free floating. Adequate anticoagulation is therefore the most important aspect of management.

INFERIOR VENA CAVA INTERRUPTION. The main indications for the insertion of an IVC filter for DVT are acute VTE and an absolute contraindication to anticoagulant therapy and the very rare instance of objectively documented recurrent VTE during adequate anticoagulant therapy. Prophylactic placement may be considered in very high-risk patients, including those with cor pulmonale or a previous history of thromboembolism who are in high-risk situations because of acetabular fracture or who have cancer. Patients who have had pulmonary embolectomy either surgically or via percutaneous catheters should have IVC filters inserted.

In a recent treatment trial of patients randomized to receive or not receive an IVC filter, the mortality and rate of major bleeding were not different at 2 years in the two groups, thus suggesting that interruption of the IVC may be unnecessary in patients who can receive adequate anticoagulant therapy. Because IVC filters were associated with an increased rate of recurrent DVT, patients receiving filters may require long-term anticoagulation.

TREATMENT OF UPPER EXTREMITY DEEP VEIN THROMBOSIS. Treatment of upper extremity DVT is the same as for proximal venous thrombosis, that is, LMWH or heparin and then warfarin for at least 3 months. Patients with recent-onset upper extremity DVT have been treated with thrombolytic agents, but clinical trials have not demonstrated that the use of thrombolytic agents decreases long-term sequelae. The rare patient with thoracic outlet obstruction may benefit from surgery.

TREATMENT OF SUPERFICIAL THROMBOPHLEBITIS. In the absence of associated DVT, treatment of superficial thrombophlebitis is usually confined to symptomatic relief with analgesia and rest of the affected limb. The exception is in patients with superficial thrombophlebitis involving a large segment of the long saphenous vein, particularly when it occurs above the knee. These patients should be treated with either LMWH or heparin, with or without oral anticoagulant therapy, or by superficial venous ligation. The presence of associated DVT requires the usual treatment with heparin and warfarin for at least 3 months.

ORAL ANTICOAGULANT THERAPY. Coumarin derivatives (primarily warfarin), the oral anticoagulants of choice, exert their anticoagulant effect by inhibition of the vitamin K–dependent γ-carboxylation of coagulation factors II, VII, IX, and X; the result is the synthesis of immunologically detectable but biologically inactive forms of these coagulation proteins. Warfarin also inhibits the vitamin K–dependent γ-carboxylation of proteins C and S. Therefore, vitamin K antagonists such as warfarin create a biochemical paradox by producing an anticoagulant effect caused by the inhibition of procoagulants (factors II, VII, IX, and X) and a potentially thrombogenic effect by impairing the synthesis of naturally occurring inhibitors of coagulation (proteins C and S). Heparin and warfarin treatment should overlap by 4 to 5 days when warfarin treatment is initiated in patients with thrombotic disease.

The anticoagulant effect of warfarin is delayed until the normal clotting factors are cleared from the circulation, and the peak effect does not occur until 36 to 72 hours after drug administration. During the first few days of warfarin therapy, the prothrombin time mainly reflects the depression of factor VII, which has a half-life of 5 to 7 hours. Equilibrium levels of factors II, IX, and X are not reached until about 1 week after the initiation of therapy. The

Continued

Cardiovascular Disease

Table 78–7 • **DURATION OF ANTI-THROMBOTIC THERAPY***

3 to 6 months	• First event with reversible† or time-limited risk factor (patient may have underlying factor V Leiden or prothrombin 20210)
≥6 months	• Idiopathic VTE, first event

12 months to lifetime	• First event‡ with
	  ▪ Cancer, until resolved
	  ▪ Anticardiolipin antibody
	  ▪ Antithrombin deficiency
	• Recurrent event, idiopathic or with thrombophilia

*All recommendations are subject to modification by individual characteristics including patient preference, age, comorbidity, and likelihood of recurrence.
†Reversible or time-limited risk factors: surgery, trauma, immobilization, estrogen use.
‡Proper duration of therapy is unclear in first event with homozygous factor V Leiden, homocystinemia, deficiency of protein C or S, or multiple thrombophilias, and in recurrent events with reversible risk factors.
VTE = venous thromboembolism.
Adapted from Hyers TM, Agnelli G, Hull RD, et al: Antithrombotic therapy for venous thromboembolic disease. Chest 2001;119:176S–193S.

use of small initial daily doses (e.g., 5.0 to 10 mg) is the preferred approach for initiating warfarin treatment.

The dose-response relationship to warfarin therapy varies widely among individuals; therefore, the dose must be carefully monitored to prevent overdosing or underdosing. A number of drugs interact with warfarin, and patients must be warned against taking any new drugs without their physician's knowledge.

Laboratory Monitoring and Therapeutic Range. The laboratory test most commonly used to measure the effects of warfarin is the one-stage prothrombin time. The prothrombin time is sensitive to reduced activity of factors II, VII, and X, but it is insensitive to reduced activity of factor IX. The INR is the prothrombin time ratio obtained by testing a given sample against the World Health Organization reference thromboplastin.

Warfarin is administered in an initial dosage of 5 to 10 mg/day for the first 2 days. The daily dose is then adjusted according to the INR. Heparin therapy is discontinued on the fourth or fifth day after initiation of warfarin therapy, provided that the INR is prolonged into the recommended therapeutic range (INR of 2.0 to 3.0). Because some individuals are either fast or slow metabolizers of the drug, selection of the correct dosage of warfarin must be individualized by making frequent INR determinations. Once the anticoagulant effect and patient's warfarin dose requirements are stable, the INR should be monitored at regular intervals (every 2 to 4 weeks) throughout the course of warfarin therapy for VTE. However, with factors that may produce an unpredictable response to warfarin (e.g., concomitant drug therapy), the INR should be monitored frequently to minimize the risk of complications caused by poor anticoagulant control.

LONG-TERM TREATMENT

Patients with established DVT or pulmonary embolism require long-term anticoagulant therapy to prevent recurrent disease. Warfarin therapy is highly effective and is preferred in most patients. In patients with proximal vein thrombosis (popliteal, femoral, or iliac vein thrombosis), long-term therapy with warfarin reduces the frequency of objectively documented recurrent VTE from 47 to 2%.[3] A warfarin regimen with an INR of 2.0 to 3.0 markedly reduces the risk of bleeding (from 20 to 4%) without loss of effectiveness in comparison with more intense doses.[3]

All patients with a first episode of VTE should receive warfarin therapy for 3 to 6 months because shorter durations have resulted in higher rates of recurrent VTE.[3] In patients with a continuing risk factor that is potentially reversible (e.g., prolonged bed rest), therapy should be continued for at least 3 months or until the risk factor is reversed. Warfarin treatment for more than 6 months is indicated for patients with recurrent VTE or in patients who have a continuing risk factor for VTE. The optimum duration of therapy

in patients with recurrent VTE is the subject of ongoing clinical trials, but the current recommendation is to continue oral anticoagulant therapy for at least 12 months in patients with a first recurrence and indefinitely for those who have more than one recurrence (Table 78–7).

Patients with idiopathic DVT confront the clinician with a challenging management problem. The clinical benefit of long-term oral anticoagulant therapy is not maintained after therapy is discontinued. Inadequate therapy comes with the risk of bleeding and trials are underway evaluating oral thrombotic regimens that may be safer.

Recurrent Venous Thrombosis

The diagnosis of recurrent DVT is problematic, particularly if previous studies are not available for review. Abnormalities persist on ultrasound for more than 12 months in most patients, and IPG remains abnormal at 3 months in approximately 30% of patients. If these tests have reverted to negative and then become positive with a symptomatic recurrence or if a new defect is detected in the same or the contralateral leg, the diagnosis is evident. Similarly, a new intraluminal filling defect on repeat venography is diagnostic, and a new defect on ventilation-perfusion lung scanning is helpful in making the diagnosis of pulmonary embolism. A normal D-dimer assay may exclude recurrent venous thrombosis.

1. Turpie AG, Bauer KA, Eriksson BI, et al: Fondaparinux vs. enoxaparin for the prevention of venous thromboembolism in major orthopedic surgery: A meta-analysis of randomized double-blind studies. Arch Intern Med 2002;162:1833–1840.
2. Hyers TM, Agnelli G, Hull RD, et al: Antithrombotic therapy for venous thromboembolic disease. Chest 2001;119:176S–193S.
3. Geerts WH, Heit JA, Clagett GP, et al: Prevention of venous thromboembolism. Chest 2001;119:132S–175S.

SUGGESTED READINGS
Joffe HV, Goldhaber SZ. Upper extremity deep vein thrombosis. Circulation 2002;106:1874–1880. *A comprehensive review of a diagnosis that is often missed or delayed.*
The diagnostic approach to acute venous thromboembolism. Official statement of the American Thoracic Society. Am J Respir Crit Care Med 1999;160:1043–1066. *Consensus report for the use of diagnostic tests in venous thromboembolism.*

79 MISCELLANEOUS CONDITIONS OF THE HEART: TUMOR, TRAUMA, AND SYSTEMIC DISEASE

Joshua Wynne

CARDIAC TUMORS

Although the heart is resistant to the development of primary malignancies, it is a frequent site of secondary involvement by metastatic tumors. Most primary cardiac tumors are benign, whereas all secondary tumors are malignant (Fig. 79–1). Primary tumors of the heart are noted in 1 per 2000 to 4000 unselected autopsies, whereas metastatic involvement may be found in up to 20% of cancer patients. Recognition of cardiac involvement by tumor is often delayed because of a low index of suspicion or absence of symptoms, yet it is usually detectable by standard noninvasive techniques (echocardiography, computed tomography, and magnetic resonance imaging). The clinical features of a patient with a cardiac tumor are determined less by the histology of the tumor than by its location and size. Conversely, the tumor type most directly determines management and prognosis. Intracavity tumors typically involve a cardiac valve and may produce obstruction and/or regurgitation. Intramyocardial tumors may be clinically silent or may lead to arrhythmia or heart block. Intrapericardial tumors generally become apparent when they compress the heart chambers, usually by tamponade from an effusion but occasionally by constriction.

The most common primary tumor in adults is the myxoma, whereas rhabdomyomas predominate in children (often in association with

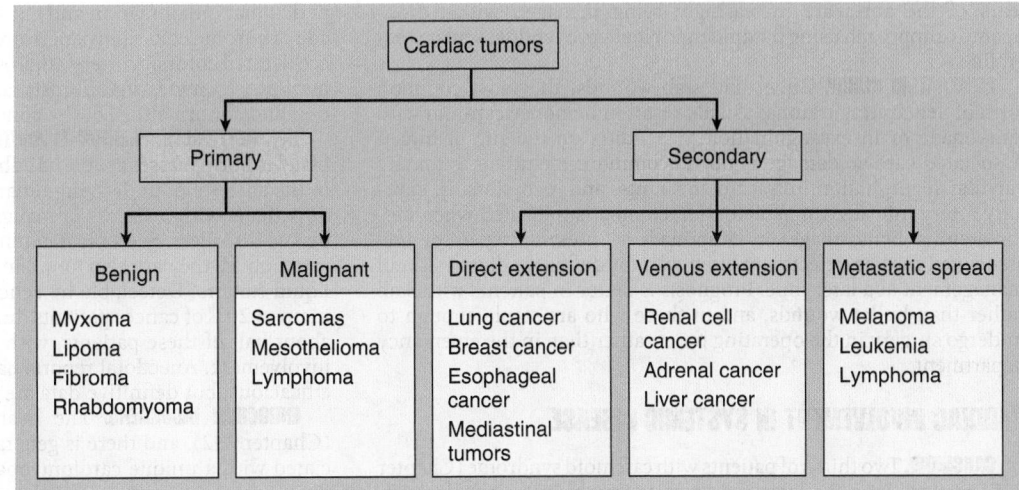

FIGURE 79-1 • Classification of the most common primary and secondary tumors. (Adapted from Salcedo EE, Cohen GI, White RD, Davison MC: Cardiac tumors: Diagnosis and management. Curr Probl Cardiol 1992;17:73–137.)

tuberous sclerosis). Other tumors include fibromas, lipomas, and fibroelastomas. Only an occasional malignant primary tumor is encountered, usually a sarcoma. Secondary tumor involvement of the heart is much more common than a primary neoplasm and is dominated by cancers of the lung and breast, which is a reflection of their relative frequency overall. Together they account for more than half of all cases of cardiac tumors. Cardiac involvement by lymphomas, leukemia, and melanoma is also common, and usually results from hematogenous or lymphatic spread.

INTRAPERICARDIAL TUMORS. Tumor involvement of the heart most commonly occurs by contiguous spread and direct extension of neoplasms involving the chest cavity, usually with invasion of the pericardium. Lung and breast cancers typically invade the heart in this manner and produce attendant pericardial effusion and cardiac tamponade. Because tumor invasion often extends beyond the pericardial space to involve the myocardium as well, expectations of long-term therapeutic success are often very low. Nevertheless, pericardiocentesis (often guided by echocardiography), balloon pericardiotomy, or surgical drainage and limited pericardiectomy ("pericardial window") are often life-saving short- and intermediate-term palliative procedures. Even very debilitated patients may benefit from a subxiphoid pericardiectomy, a quick and low-morbidity procedure that may provide brief palliation.

INTRACAVITY TUMORS. The most common intracavity tumor is the *myxoma,* a benign polypoid neoplasm of endocardial origin that is usually located within the left atrium and attached to the interatrial septum. Sometimes it is also seen in the right atrium and rarely in the ventricles. Myxomas are found most commonly in women between 30 and 60 years of age and are usually an isolated finding. On occasion they are familial (found most commonly in a young man), or occur in association with other systemic abnormalities (such as pigmented skin lesions and noncardiac tumors). Although they may not be clinically apparent when small, myxomas usually produce findings secondary to tumor embolization, mitral valve obstruction, and constitutional symptoms such as fever, malaise, and arthralgias. During diastole, a left atrial myxoma may be drawn into the mitral orifice and produce obstruction to blood flow from the left atrium to the left ventricle, thus simulating rheumatic mitral stenosis. Even the physical examination may be misleading, with a tumor "plop" simulating an opening snap and a diastolic rumble similar to the murmur found with rheumatic involvement.

If the diagnosis is suspected, echocardiography (often using the transesophageal approach) provides the definitive diagnosis; most myxomas are discovered when embolization or valve dysfunction leads to an echocardiographic study (Chapter 51). Once diagnosed, the tumor is removed surgically, which is usually a low-risk procedure that results in cure. Myxomas can be multiple or recur in about 5% of cases, so even after successful removal, continued surveillance is indicated.

Other intracavity tumors are uncommon. Papillary fibroelastomas are frondlike excrescences that typically arise from a cardiac valve (often the mitral) and are usually detected incidentally during echocardiography. They may produce symptoms by virtue of systemic or coronary embolization and are usually amenable to surgical excision. Angiosarcomas occur in men more frequently than women and have a predilection for the pericardium and right atrium, where they may cause obstruction and attendant right-sided congestive heart failure. A unique type of cardiac involvement that occurs most commonly with renal cell carcinoma (and occasionally with adrenal and hepatic neoplasms) consists of extension of the tumor via the inferior vena cava, with resultant tumor involvement of the right atrial cavity.

INTRAMYOCARDIAL TUMORS. The least common location for cardiac tumors is within the myocardium, where the tumors may be clinically silent, produce arrhythmias, or protrude into a cardiac chamber with attendant obstructive features. Lipomas are encapsulated benign primary cardiac tumors that are often clinically silent. Sarcomas (angiosarcomas, rhabdomyosarcomas, fibrosarcomas) often demonstrate widespread cardiac involvement, with protrusion into the cardiac chambers and extension into the pericardial space. No good therapy is available for these tumors, although a small number of patients have undergone cardiac transplantation.

CARDIAC TRAUMA

Cardiac damage may result from trauma as a consequence of either penetrating or nonpenetrating injury. The usual cause of penetrating trauma is a bullet or stab wound, whereas deceleration injuries as a consequence of automobile accidents are the most common cause of nonpenetrating injury. Either type often results in death before the patient comes to medical attention, usually from hemopericardium and attendant tamponade or massive hemorrhage.

NONPENETRATING INJURY. The most common manifestation of blunt trauma is myocardial contusion, often the result of impact of the chest wall against the steering wheel. Although the diagnosis of contusion is straightforward when new electrocardiographic changes or arrhythmias are noted, the diagnosis is more difficult in the typical chest trauma patient. In such cases, demonstration of new regional left ventricular wall motion abnormalities on echocardiography or radionuclide ventriculography helps secure the diagnosis. Measurement of myocardial biomarkers, including troponin I, has been disappointing in assessing the diagnosis or prognosis of presumed myocardial contusion, although normal biomarker levels and a normal electrocardiogram are predictive of a low risk of cardiac damage or complications. The prognosis is generally excellent if the patient is otherwise clinically stable after myocardial contusion. Other less common manifestations of blunt trauma include traumatic ventricular septal defect, myocardial rupture and/or pseudoaneurysm formation, coronary artery trauma with myocardial infarction, valvular regurgitation, and pulmonary artery rupture.

The most feared complication of blunt trauma is traumatic transection of the descending aorta, which occurs just distal to the ligamentum arteriosum. It results from the shear forces that occur during deceleration injury as the more mobile aortic arch continues to move anteriorly while the descending aorta remains fixed because of its attachment to the posterior mediastinum. It is usually fatal if not rapidly repaired surgically. Patients with more limited intimal tears of the aorta are increasingly being managed with a non-operative approach using β-adrenergic blockers or endovascular stent grafts.

PENETRATING INJURY. Bullet and stab wounds, the most common form of penetrating trauma, usually result in hemopericardium with tamponade or in exsanguination, depending on the site of injury. Associated cardiac damage is not uncommon, including traumatic valvular regurgitation, intracardiac shunts, and, occasionally, coronary artery injuries. Immediate thoracotomy is indicated when life-threatening hemorrhage or tamponade is present; repair of any associated cardiac defects can often wait for definitive diagnosis and management at a later time. Prognosis is better in patients with stab rather than bullet wounds, and in those who are stable enough to undergo surgery in the operating room rather than in the emergency department.

CARDIAC INVOLVEMENT IN SYSTEMIC DISEASE

CARCINOID. Two thirds of patients with carcinoid syndrome (Chapter 245) metastatic to the liver have cardiac involvement, usually consisting of thickening and scarring of the endocardium and the tricuspid and/or pulmonary valves (often both) and producing both stenosis and regurgitation. Left-sided valvular involvement may be found in the presence of an intracardiac shunt (patent foramen ovale) or as a late manifestation of advanced cardiac involvement. Myocardial metastases and pericardial effusions occur on occasion. These valvular and endocardial changes may be produced by serotonin and other vasoactive substances released by the tumor. Morphologically similar valvular abnormalities have been seen with the anorectic agents fenfluramine and phentermine. Dyspnea is a common finding, and right heart failure may contribute to the death of one third of these patients. Systemic symptoms and survival can be improved with the use of a somatostatin analogue. In selected patients, valve replacement (often with a bioprosthesis) has resulted in significant symptomatic improvement, but operative mortality rate may be 25% or greater and is especially high in older patients.

CARDIOTOXICITY OF CANCER THERAPY. Cardiotoxicity following chemotherapy (Chapter 191) is most common with doxorubicin (Adriamycin) and consists of dose-related systolic (and diastolic) dysfunction that may produce clinical congestive heart failure months to years after treatment. Although less common with current dosing schemes that use more frequent but lower doses than prior regimens, doxorubicin cardiotoxicity continues to be associated with a poor prognosis and significant mortality. Detection of early or subclinical cardiotoxicity is difficult but best accomplished by monitoring for a decrease in resting or exercise left ventricular ejection fraction with radionuclide ventriculography or echocardiography. Periodic percutaneous right ventricular endomyocardial biopsy may be more predictive but is not widely used. Concomitant use of the iron chelator dexrazoxane in selected patients appears to offer some degree of protection from the toxic cardiac effects of the anthracyclines. Cardiotoxicity appears to be potentiated in the setting of mediastinal irradiation, preexisting cardiac disease, young or advanced age, and concomitant administration of other chemotherapeutic drugs, especially paclitaxel and trastuzumab, a monoclonal antibody against the HER2 growth factor receptor that is useful in metastatic breast cancer (Chapter 204). The best treatment for cardiotoxicity is discontinuation of doxorubicin treatment, after which improvement sometimes results. Once congestive heart failure appears, the use of digitalis, diuretics, and vasodilators usually results in significant symptomatic improvement.

Cardiotoxicity may also be seen with cyclophosphamide, which occasionally produces fatal hemorrhagic myocardial necrosis. Myocardial ischemia and infarction can occur during 5-fluorouracil infusions, and some patients appear to respond to nitrates. Paclitaxel usually produces cardiotoxicity only when used in combination with other chemotherapeutic agents, but has, on rare occasion, been associated with a variety of often asymptomatic arrhythmias and abnormalities of the cardiac conduction system when used alone. Arsenic trioxide, used to treat relapsed or refractory promyelocytic leukemia, may prolong the QT interval and result in ventricular arrhythmias.

Cardiotoxicity as a consequence of radiation therapy has declined in frequency with better shielding of the heart, use of improved dosing schedules, and use of multiple radiation portals (Chapter 19). Nevertheless, cardiac damage occurring months and years after radiation therapy continues to be seen, most commonly consisting of

pericardial inflammation and effusion that may progress to tamponade or chronic constrictive pericarditis. Other manifestations include accelerated coronary artery atherosclerosis (often involving the coronary ostia), myocardial fibrosis, and occasionally valvular dysfunction and abnormalities of the conducting system.

NONBACTERIAL THROMBOTIC (MARANTIC) ENDOCARDITIS. Sterile verruciform platelet-fibrin masses are found adherent to the mitral and aortic valves in the absence of underlying inflammation in about 1% of autopsies in patients with a variety of malignant tumors and various nonneoplastic disorders. Seen most commonly in mucin-producing adenocarcinomas, they are also found in malignant melanoma and various liquid tumors. Detectable by echocardiography, they may be found in up to 20% of cancer patients during life. Systemic emboli occur in about half of these patients, with the brain being a frequent site of involvement. Anecdotal reports have suggested that heparin may be efficacious, but definitive data are lacking.

ENDOCRINE DISORDERS. The heart is often involved in diabetes (Chapter 242), and there is general agreement that diabetes is associated with a unique cardiomyopathy independent of the effects of the coronary artery disease and hypertension that so frequently accompany diabetes. Hyperthyroidism (Chapter 239) commonly results in a hyperkinetic cardiovascular state manifested by a decrease in systemic vascular resistance, an increase in cardiac output, and enhanced left ventricular emptying. Other effects include atrial fibrillation and, especially with preexisting heart disease, congestive heart failure. Patients with coronary artery disease often experience an exacerbation of angina pectoris. Hypothyroidism may be associated with hypertension, bradycardia, and a pericardial effusion that rarely progresses to cardiac tamponade. Because myocardial ischemia is often exacerbated in myxedematous patients with preexisting coronary artery disease as therapy is begun, thyroid hormone replacement should be started with very low doses that are increased slowly. Pheochromocytomas (Chapter 241) are associated with histologic evidence of catecholamine-induced myocardial damage in about 50% of patients. Focal myocardial contraction band necrosis, inflammation, and fibrosis are seen histologically but only occasionally result in clinical congestive heart failure. Treatment with adrenergic receptor blockers (initially α and then β) is usually effective in treating both the hypertension and the cardiotoxicity before surgery to remove the tumor.

INFILTRATIVE DISEASES. Amyloidosis (Chapter 290), hemochromatosis (Chapter 225), and sarcoidosis (Chapter 91) can cause infiltrative myocardial diseases leading to cardiomyopathy (Chapter 73). Treatment focuses on the systemic disease process.

NEUROMUSCULAR DISEASES. Cardiac involvement is common in Friedreich's ataxia, with symmetric or asymmetric left ventricular hypertrophy often grossly resembling hypertrophic cardiomyopathy. Associated ST segment and T wave abnormalities of the electrocardiogram are common. Duchenne's muscular dystrophy (Chapter 463) is due to mutations in the dystrophin gene and is associated with a peculiar form of myocardial necrosis that principally involves the posterobasal portion of the left ventricle and the adjacent papillary muscle. The echocardiogram is often distinctive, as is the electrocardiogram, which demonstrates tall R waves in the right precordial leads and deep Q waves in the limb and lateral precordial leads. Myotonic dystrophy is an autosomal dominant multisystem disorder that produces a variety of electrocardiographic abnormalities, especially abnormalities of atrioventricular conduction with the attendant risk of syncope and sudden death. Cardiac muscle involvement is uncommon.

COLLAGEN VASCULAR DISEASES. Although demonstrable cardiac involvement is common in rheumatoid arthritis, major clinical manifestations are rare (Chapter 278). The endocardium, myocardium, or pericardium may be involved, but the most common manifestation is pericarditis, with a variable amount of pericardial effusion. Symptomatic pericardial involvement is seen in one fourth of the patients. Cardiac valvular involvement occurs in more than 50% of patients with systemic lupus erythematosus (Chapter 280) and in one third of patients with the antiphospholipid syndrome in the absence of lupus. Valvular abnormalities include thickening and sterile vegetations that may be evanescent but produce valve regurgitation in one fourth of patients. Although usually asymptomatic and clinically quiescent, over time the valvular abnormalities may result in significant cardiovascular morbidity and mortality from embolism, infective endocarditis, and heart failure, and may require surgical valve replacement.

In progressive systemic sclerosis (Chapter 281), focal myocardial necrosis and fibrosis may occur and culminate in a dilated cardiomyopathy. Ankylosing spondylitis and the associated seronegative arthropathies (Reiter's syndrome, psoriatic arthritis) may involve the proximal aortic root and produce clinically important aortic regurgitation.

SUGGESTED READINGS

Kulke MH, Mayer RJ: Carcinoid tumors. N Engl J Med 1999;340:858–868. *A definitive summary of carcinoid tumors, including their effect on the heart.*

Moder KG, Miller TD, Tazelaar HD: Cardiac involvement in systemic lupus erythematosus. Mayo Clin Proc 1999;74:275–284. *A complete summary of the cardiac manifestations of lupus.*

Moller JE, Connolly HM, Ruin J, et al: Factors associated with progression of carcinoid heart disease. N Engl J Med 2003;348:1005–1015. *Details the relationship among serotonin levels, progression of cardiac disease, and effect of therapy on patients with carcinoid heart disease.*

Pinede L, Duhaut P, Loire R: Clinical presentation of left atrial cardiac myxoma. A series of 112 consecutive cases. Medicine (Baltimore) 2001;80:159–172. *The largest single institution experience available, with a review of the clinical and surgical data from a consecutive series of 112 patients seen over a 40-year period.*

Salim A, Velmahos GC, Jindal A, et al: Clinically significant blunt cardiac trauma: Role of serum troponin levels combined with electrocardiographic findings. J Trauma 2001;50:237–243. *A clinical series of 115 consecutive patients with blunt thoracic trauma and suspected cardiac damage.*

80 CARDIAC TRANSPLANTATION

Robert C. Bourge

Cardiac transplantation, once considered an experimental procedure, has emerged as the therapy of choice for appropriately selected patients with life-threatening, irremediable heart disease. The procedure and its postoperative medical regimen result in significant morbidity and mortality, and they are warranted only if the prognosis of the underlying cardiac disease is sufficiently grave.

The incidence of congestive heart failure increases with age and affects more than 500,000 people in the United States every year (Chapter 55); transplantation is a therapeutic option for many of these patients. As survival after cardiac transplantation has markedly improved, the population of long-term survivors has grown. Primary care physicians, as well as cardiologists not based at cardiac transplantation centers, often assist in the care of these patients, most often in consultation with cardiac transplantation physicians. In addition, a physician may be called upon to assist in the management and evaluation of a potential cardiac donor.

THE CARDIAC TRANSPLANT RECIPIENT

Indications for Cardiac Transplantation (Table 80–1)

Patients who are dependent on intravenous inotropic support or mechanical cardiac support or who have undergone mechanical cardiac replacement are at the highest priority for cardiac transplantation. Other indications include class IV heart failure and symptoms at rest despite optimal medication therapy (1-year survival of <50%) or class III heart failure despite maximal medical therapy (1-year survival of 30 to 70%) (Chapters 55 and 56). Patients with class II symptoms may benefit from evaluation and subsequent transplantation if concomitant cardiac conditions, such as uncontrollable ventricular arrhythmias, adversely affect predicted survival. Patients with sustained ventricular tachycardia that is refractory to all forms of therapy, including the placement of an implantable cardioverter-defibrillator (Chapter 61), should also be considered for cardiac transplantation.

In the United States, the most common underlying cause of heart failure leading to cardiac transplantation is ischemic coronary heart disease. Most large studies have shown that patients with heart failure secondary to coronary heart disease have a higher mortality than those with nonischemic causes.

The second most common disease leading to cardiac transplantation is idiopathic dilated cardiomyopathy (Chapter 73). Factors that correlate with a high mortality and hence suggest potential benefit from cardiac transplantation, include (1) a peak oxygen consumption on an exercise gas exchange stress test of less than 11 to 14 mL/kg/minute; (2) a low plasma sodium level, especially after

Table 80–1 • INDICATIONS FOR CONSIDERATION FOR CARDIAC TRANSPLANTATION (CONSIDER REFERRAL TO CARDIAC TRANSPLANT CENTER)

Irremediable cardiac disease with estimated mortality of more than 25–30% at 1 yr; survival without transplantation is estimated from heart disease etiology, disease duration, hemodynamics, functional capacity, and presence or absence of cardiac arrhythmias
Unacceptable quality of life primarily due to cardiac disease limitations
Acceptable social and financial support
Acceptable neurocognitive function
Absence of significant psychological or pathologic disorders or substance abuse
Transplantation surgical risk acceptable from a technical standpoint
Absence of comorbid conditions that would significantly limit posttransplantation survival or significantly worsen posttransplantation quality of life, including advanced physiologic age, coexistent systemic illness with poor prognosis, irreversible pulmonary hypertension, acute pulmonary thromboembolism, severe peripheral and/or cerebrovascular disease, irreversible renal or liver disease, active peptic ulcer, active diverticulitis, diabetes mellitus with significant end-organ disease, severe obesity, severe osteoporosis, and active severe infection

Adapted from Costanzo MR, Augustine SA, Bourge R, et al. Selection and treatment of candidates for heart transplantation (Tables 1 and 2). Circulation 1995;92:3593–3612.

intensive medical management; (3) high right ventricular and/or left ventricular filling pressures (a very high right atrial or jugular venous pressure and/or pulmonary capillary wedge pressure), especially after intensive medical management; (4) a very low ejection fraction (<15 to 20%; not predictive alone, however); (5) uncontrolled complex ventricular arrhythmias; (6) a very large left ventricular cavity (end-diastolic maximal dimension >70 to 75 mm); and (7) the need for recurrent hospitalization to treat worsening symptoms despite maximum medical therapy. Other less common cardiac diseases that may be treated with cardiac transplantation include sarcoidosis (especially if limited to the heart), restrictive cardiomyopathy, hypertrophic cardiomyopathy, congenital heart disease (not amenable to surgical palliation or correction; Chapter 65), valvular heart disease (when the risk of cardiac surgery is prohibitively high; Chapter 72), and, occasionally, inoperable nonmalignant cardiac tumors.

Evaluation for Cardiac Transplantation

EVALUATION OF UNDERLYING DISEASE AND ESTIMATION OF RISK OF MORTALITY. The evaluation for cardiac transplantation, which should generally be performed at an experienced cardiac transplantation center, typically involves identifying the underlying cardiac disease (if not already established), considering other acceptable (or preferable) treatment options, evaluating the patient for comorbid conditions that may limit survival or increase morbidity after transplantation, and educating the patient (and family) regarding the rigors of the posttransplant medical regimen. The complete history and physical examination help to direct further tests.

The transplantation evaluation includes an assessment of the immunologic state of the potential recipient. Typically, a panel (or percentage) reactive antibody (PRA) study by cytotoxic methods or flow cytometry is performed to assess for the presence or absence of preexisting antibodies to other (non-"self") human leukocyte antigens. A high PRA predicts a higher likelihood of posttransplant rejection and death. Patients with a high PRA require a negative crossmatch between their sera and a potential donor's lymphocytes before transplantation; a very high PRA may preclude transplantation.

EVALUATION FOR COMORBID CONDITIONS AND OTHER ISSUES. Any major co-existing medical condition that would not be reversible with better cardiac function is a relative contraindication to transplantation, but active severe infection and neoplasm are the two near-absolute contraindications. Because posttransplant compliance is so critical, psychological instability and substance abuse are strong relative contraindications. When in doubt, a transplant physician should be consulted to determine potential eligibility.

An evaluation of social and financial resources is very important during the transplantation evaluation. The charges for the initial cardiac transplantation hospitalization and for follow-up procedures are formidable, even if no posttransplant complications occur; medications alone can cost $6000 to $20,000 for the first year after transplantation. Most insurance carriers and Medicare help defray some of the costs, but the patient's portion may be significant. An assessment of an individual patient's need for financial support after transplantation should be performed before transplantation, especially because noncompliance due to inability to pay for medications is life-threatening.

PATIENT AND FAMILY EDUCATION. The decision by an institution to offer cardiac transplantation includes a responsibility to assist in the ongoing medical care of the patient. The prospective organ recipient should understand the individualized risks involved with the decision to proceed with transplantation, including the possible complications that may occur.

Recipient Medical Care: "The Waiting List"

Occasionally, a patient is deemed to be too well to be listed for transplantation (i.e., when the estimated risk of transplantation is higher than the risk of continued medical care or a surgical intervention). Most patients should be reevaluated at intervals of 3 to 6 months until either (1) the underlying cardiac problem improves or resolves, which occasionally occurs; or (2) worsening symptoms or risk factors for death develop and prompt the decision to proceed with transplantation.

In the United States, the responsibility for cadaveric donor organ procurement and distribution is contracted to the United Network for Organ Sharing (UNOS) and its regional organ procurement organizations (OPOs). Patients are "listed" for transplantation by being placed on a national computerized list maintained by UNOS. Donor organs are distributed by location of the donor (within an OPO), ABO blood type, body size, and, occasionally, the need for specialized immunologic testing. Organ distribution is also based on the amount of time that a patient has been listed and a status system that varies slightly within different regions. Patients are typically listed as follows:

UNOS Status 1a: Inpatient on mechanical ventricular assist for less than 30 days or with a complication from the device, total artificial heart, intra-aortic balloon, extracorporeal membrane oxygenator, mechanical ventilation, high-dose inotropic agents and continuous hemodynamic monitoring, or expected to live less than 7 days (these patients have highest priority).
UNOS Status 1b: Patient with mechanical assist implanted for more than 30 days, non–high-dose continuous inotropic agent infusion (inpatient or outpatient).
UNOS Status 2: All others active on transplant list.
UNOS Status 7: Temporarily inactive.

About 2500 patients receive transplants annually, but of about 3500 to 4000 patients newly listed annually for heart transplantation, almost 85% will still be awaiting cardiac transplantation at the end of the year (depending on status, location, and blood type). As a result, 10 to 30% of listed patients die before an appropriate donor is located. Once the decision is made to list the patient, the goal of ongoing medical care is to improve and maintain the patient's functional class and quality of life and to avoid medical complications that could delay or prevent transplantation.

THE CARDIAC DONOR

In general, any brain-dead patient younger than 55 to 60 years who has adequate heart function is a potential cardiac donor. Even with the Uniform Anatomical Gift Act, it is estimated that only 10 to 20% of potential cardiac donors are procured in the United States. This is in part owing to the failure of medical professionals optimally to consider pursuing organ donation with a brain-dead patient's family, preferably by contacting a local OPO. Physicians should consult the local or regional OPO regarding potential donors so that appropriate measures can be instituted to optimize the likelihood of successful donations. Physicians should also encourage their patients to become donors, and donor status is stated on the driver's license in many states.

THE TRANSPLANT PROCEDURE

The cardiac transplantation admission begins with an urgent evaluation for occult infection or other medical problems not previously recognized. The patient is placed on cardiopulmonary bypass, which is timed to minimize the period of bypass for the recipient and the period of ischemia (during which the allograft is not perfused) for the donor heart. The recipient's heart is then replaced with the donor heart, with suture lines placed (and "connections" therefore made) in the ascending aorta, pulmonary artery, and either the right atrium or, more recently favored by many centers, the superior and inferior venae cavae. Allograft electrical activity and contraction usually begin spontaneously as oxygenated blood is supplied, or they do so after direct current is applied. In the modern era, in the absence of significant preoperative debilitation or comorbid problems, postoperative care is usually routine, with discharge to local housing possible at about 5 to 7 days after surgery. Before discharge, the recipient is instructed about posttransplant medical care and precautions.

MEDICAL CARE AFTER TRANSPLANTATION (Table 80–2)

Routine Posttransplant Follow-Up

The maximum mortality from two of the most common causes of death following transplant—allograft rejection and infection—occurs during the first days to 6 to 8 weeks after transplantation. Endomyocardial biopsies are typically performed once per week for the first 4 to 8 weeks, and then at gradually longer intervals.

ROUTINE IMMUNOSUPPRESSION

Immunosuppression begins with the preoperative administration of azathioprine and often cyclosporine. Intraoperative corticosteroids are often given and continued intravenously in the immediate postoperative period. Cyclosporine and azathioprine or mycophenolate are started soon after surgery and may be given intravenously until oral medications are tolerated. In some centers, polyclonal or monoclonal antibodies toward lymphocytes (ATG, ATGAM, OKT3) are used as "induction therapy" to delay the onset of rejection, but these agents may increase the risk of infection, especially cytomegalovirus infections, and, especially if used repeatedly, may increase the risk of malignancy. The use of humanized monoclonal antibodies to the interleukin-2 receptor (basiliximab and daclizumab) is growing due to evidence of a decrease in rejection with few side effects.

Routine chronic immunosuppression for most patients consists of triple-drug therapy, which usually includes steroids (prednisone), an antiproliferative agent (azathioprine or mycophenolate), and a calcineurin inhibitor (cyclosporine or tacrolimus). Mycophenolate mofetil, which may be superior to azathioprine to prevent rejection and cardiac allograft vasculopathy, is preferred in many centers despite a significantly higher cost than azathioprine.∎ Because higher dosages of cyclosporine may induce renal insufficiency, relatively high initial doses are subsequently tapered over 1 to 3 months to target cyclosporine levels. Tacrolimus is occasionally substituted for cyclosporine in patients with persistent or recurrent rejection and is also occasionally used in women and children to avoid the hirsutism associated with cyclosporine. A few institutions routinely use tacrolimus as part of the initial immunosuppressive regimen.

Prednisone doses are tapered and, in some centers, discontinued if no significant rejection occurs during tapering. In general, the azathioprine dose is lowered if the white blood cell count consistently falls below 4000 to 5000 cells/mL.

PROPHYLACTIC DRUG ADMINISTRATION/IMMUNIZATIONS

Immunosuppressed patients should not receive certain live viral vaccines (Chapter 16), and Sabin oral polio vaccine should not be given to close contacts of transplant recipients because viral shedding occurs. Routine use of influenza vaccine, although controversial, is of little risk and may offer some protection.

The 3-hydroxy-3-methylglutaryl coenzyme A (HMG CoA) reductase inhibitors (usually pravastatin or simvastatin, based on available data) reduce the allograft vasculopathy, lower the incidence of cardiac rejection, and may improve posttransplant survival. Diltiazem is also routinely used at many transplant centers, as it may also lower the risk of cardiac allograft vasculopathy; diltiazem also increases cyclosporine levels, resulting in reduced cyclosporine dosing and an overall savings in drug costs.

Table 80–2 • MEDICAL CARE AFTER TRANSPLANTATION

DURING FIRST 6 TO 8 WEEKS AFTER OPERATION

Recipient resides within a reasonable distance from the center, usually with a family member or friend for support and observation

Discharge goal is 5 to 7 days after operation

Patient seen twice weekly as an outpatient with directed history and physical to assess for signs or symptoms of infection, rejection, or allograft dysfunction

Routine studies (weekly during first 6 to 8 wk)

    Chest radiograph to screen for infection

    ECG to evaluate allograft conduction system

    Echocardiogram with Doppler to assess left and right ventricular function and valve function

    Blood work to evaluate liver or kidney dysfunction

    Serum or whole blood cyclosporine (or tacrolimus) levels to guide dosing

    White blood cell and platelet counts and hematocrit to assess response to azathioprine (or mycophenolate) and screen for excessive effect

Encourage establishment of long-term exercise program and proper nutrition (low fat, low sodium)

Counsel regarding expected lifestyle changes and stress

2–24 MO AFTER OPERATION

Visit every 3 mo with examination and routine studies noted above

>24 MO AFTER OPERATION

Twice yearly as above, plus coronary angiography, with or without intracoronary ultrasound study, or stress echocardiography

PROPHYLACTIC DRUG ADMINISTRATION/IMMUNIZATIONS

PROPHYLAXIS AGAINST	DRUG
Oropharyngeal *Candida* infections (thrush)	Oral daily clotrimazole or nystatin until steroid dose is minimized
Herpes zoster (shingles)	Varicella-zoster immunization if negative serology before transplantation; oral acyclovir for 1 yr post-transplantation for all patients
Cytomegalovirus (primarily in seronegative recipient of heart from seropositive donor)	Ganciclovir (Cytovene), IV for 2–4 wk, then oral valganciclovir for 8–10 wk
Pneumocystis carinii (especially in endemic areas)	Oral trimethoprim-sulfamethoxazole (Bactrim), 3 times per week for 1 yr
Toxoplasma gondii (therapy in seronegative recipients of heart from seropositive donor)	Pyrimethamine and sulfadiazine (or clindamycin in sulfa-allergic patients) for 6 mo
Cardiac allograft vasculopathy (allograft coronary artery disease)	Pravastatin, 10–40 mg at bedtime, indefinitely, as tolerated; use with caution initially due to increased risk of rhabdomyolysis; diltiazem 180 mg/day indefinitely (may also increase cyclosporine and tacrolimus levels, lowering overall medication cost).

ECG = electrocardiogram.

Posttransplant Medical Problems

ALLOGRAFT REJECTION

INCIDENCE. Cardiac rejection may be cell mediated (cellular rejection), the most common form, and/or antibody mediated (humoral rejection). Hyperacute humoral rejection in the immediate postoperative period is due to preformed antibodies to the HLA type of the donor heart and results in sudden severe allograft dysfunction and often death. Cellular rejection, which leads to substantive or chronic rejection, is characterized initially by a mononuclear infiltrate. Higher grades of rejection are classified according to the presence and extent

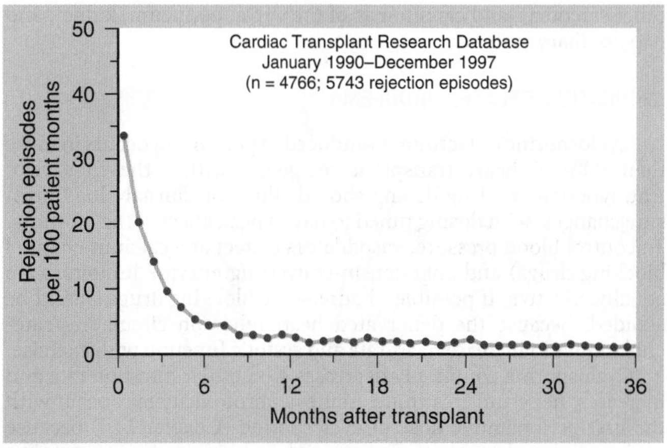

FIGURE 80–1 • Rejection incidence over time following initial cardiac transplantation for 4766 patients with follow-up of at least 12 months. The incidence of rejection episodes, calculated as the number per 100 patients occurring each month after transplant, is highest in the first month following transplantation (34 rejections per 100 patient-months) and then rapidly declines over time. The average rejection rate after the first year following transplantation is 1.07 rejections per 100 patient-months. (Data from the Cardiac Transplant Research Database and includes information about the population who received cardiac transplants from January 1990 through December 1997 at 42 major U.S. transplantation centers.) (The author would like to thank David C. Naftel, Ph.D., University of Alabama at Birmingham, Birmingham, AL, for his assistance with data analysis and preparation of the figure.)

of myocyte infiltration, myocyte necrosis, hemorrhage, and/or vasculitis. The incidence of cardiac rejection is highest early after transplantation and subsequently decreases to a low but constant rate (Fig. 80–1).

DETECTION. Symptoms and signs associated with rejection may be nonspecific and include malaise, lethargy, fatigue, low-grade fever, and mood changes, or they may be cardiac-specific, such as dyspnea, lower blood pressure, jugular venous distention, a new S_3 or S_4 gallop, or a new supraventricular arrhythmia.

Depressed cardiac function after cardiac transplantation, with or without hemodynamic changes, is usually caused by acute rejection. Surveillance endomyocardial biopsies, especially within the first 6 months after transplantation, remain the standard for detecting early signs of rejection.

THERAPY. The therapy of cardiac rejection, which may include bolus oral or intravenous administration of steroids, antilymphocyte therapy, plasmapheresis, and augmentation of the patient's existing immunosuppressive drug regimen, should be administered under the supervision of an experienced transplant physician, preferably at the patient's transplant center.

INFECTION

About one third of patients develop a serious infection (defined as requiring intravenous antibiotics and/or considered to be life-threatening) during the first year after transplantation, and infection remains the most common cause of death in the first year. Lung and blood-borne infections are most common, accounting for 50% of serious infections. The risk of a bacterial infection is highest in the early postoperative period. The risk of a viral infection is highest at 1 to 1.5 months, fungal infection within the first month, and protozoal infection from 2 to 5 months after transplantation.

MALIGNANCY

Immunosuppressed transplant recipients of any organ have an estimated risk of developing a malignancy of 1 to 2% per year. The overall risk is 6%, approximately 100 times that of the age-controlled population of persons not receiving transplants, and is most notable for squamous cell carcinoma of the skin, lymphoma, Kaposi's sarcoma, other sarcomas, and carcinomas of the vulva, perineum, kidney, and hepatobiliary system.

MEDICATION-RELATED PROBLEMS

Cyclosporine or tacrolimus-induced hypertension occurs in more than 90% of heart transplant recipients within the first year. Antihypertensive drug dosing should allow for diurnal blood pressure changes, with dosing timed to have a peak effect in the morning. To control blood pressure, vasodilators (direct and calcium-channel blocking drugs) and angiotensin-converting enzyme inhibitors are equally effective. If possible, β-adrenergic blocking drugs should be avoided, because the denervated heart relies on circulating catecholamines to increase heart rate and systolic function with exercise.

Cyclosporine commonly decreases glomerular filtration rate and increases the serum creatinine. Acute nephrotoxicity may occur with the first perioperative dose of cyclosporine (Chapter 118) because of drug-induced renal afferent arteriolar vasoconstriction superimposed on chronic renal hypoperfusion from a low cardiac output. Cyclosporine also appears to have dose-dependent toxic effects on the renal tubules and can cause renal tubular acidosis. Tacrolimus has perhaps a higher incidence of associated diabetes, neuropathy, and alopecia.

Hepatic dysfunction, which occurs in up to 10% of patients following transplantation, may be the result of many causes, including intraoperative or perioperative hepatic hypoperfusion, a response to cyclosporine or azathioprine, or viral hepatitis. Cyclosporine-induced hepatotoxicity is dose-dependent and usually occurs when serum levels are extremely high.

Cyclosporine decreases urate clearance by the kidney; hyperuricemia and gout commonly occur. Allopurinol is associated with a decrease in azathioprine metabolism, and azathioprine dosing must therefore be adjusted accordingly. Nonsteroidal anti-inflammatory drugs should be avoided, if possible, because of their nephrotoxic effects. Short-term colchicine may be useful, but long-term use can increase immunosuppression and cause bone marrow toxicity.

Cyclosporine and tacrolimus are metabolized by the cytochrome P-450 enzyme pathway and therefore interact with numerous medications and substances that are metabolized by or that influence that enzyme system (including alcoholic beverages). Many drugs, including certain antibiotics, may directly worsen the renal toxicity of these drugs. Physicians should not prescribe *any* medication without first determining its compatibility with cyclosporine or tacrolimus. Corticosteroid use after transplantation may result in or worsen glucose intolerance and hyperlipidemia and may precipitate osteoporosis and its complications (Chapter 31). The most common adverse effect associated with azathioprine is bone marrow toxicity, most commonly leukopenia and less commonly thrombocytopenia, megaloblastic anemia, red cell aplasia, and reticulocytopenia, which usually appears 7 to 14 days after initial dosing or elevations in dosing. The most common side effect from mycophenolate is gastrointestinal problems, which may be severe and preclude its use.

DRUG EFFECTS ON THE CARDIAC ALLOGRAFT

Although postganglionic parasympathetic neurons remain in the donor heart, transplanted hearts are effectively denervated because conduction does not traverse the atrial anastomotic suture lines. Any drug that affects the heart via either a change in vagal tone or a direct increase in sympathetic nerve activity has little effect on the transplanted heart. However, systemic effects still occur. Thus, for example, atropine, which increases heart rate primarily by a vagolytic effect, does not increase the heart rate in cardiac allograft recipients. However, it still has noncardiac effects such as dry mouth, mydriasis, cycloplegia, constipation, and urinary retention.

The denervated heart is, however, more sensitive to both β-adrenergic agonists (e.g., isoproterenol) and β-adrenergic antagonists. Ocular β-blockers can occasionally cause profound bradycardia. Isoproterenol, by virtue of its chronotropic effect, is used routinely to stimulate heart rate in cases of sinus node dysfunction early after transplantation. The denervated heart is hypersensitive to adenosine; if adenosine is administered to convert supraventricular tachycardia, it should be given at 25% of the usual dose.

CARDIAC ALLOGRAFT VASCULOPATHY

Cardiac allograft vasculopathy affects all vessels in the transplanted heart (including veins) and leads to vessel lumen obliteration. It is a leading cause of death after the first year of transplantation.[2] Depending on the means used to detect it, the incidence of the disease ranges from 10 to 50% at 1 year to 50 to 90% at 5 years after transplantation. Histologically, the disease manifests as hyperplasia of smooth muscle cells, intimal proliferation, mononuclear cell infiltration of the intima, and the presence of lipid-laden macrophages in all areas of the vessel wall. The process is thought to be multifactorial in origin, but it probably stems from an initial and/or ongoing immunologically mediated or infection-induced (e.g., cytomegalovirus) injury to the vascular endothelium. The therapy of the disease involves coronary angioplasty, the placement of intracoronary stents, and consideration of retransplantation.

SOCIAL AND PSYCHOLOGICAL PROBLEMS

Adapting to life after cardiac transplantation involves an interplay of many variables, including the patient's pretransplant condition, the duration of illness, and the patient's personality, intelligence, social support, and financial support. End-stage cardiac patients often become depressed; after transplantation, early exhilaration followed by mild to moderate depression is common, possibly as a result of corticosteroid use. Constant vigilance for symptoms suggestive of more significant or longer-term depression is required.

POSTTRANSPLANT LIFE

Cardiac Function and Quality of Life

In major North American cardiac transplant centers from 1990 to 1999, survival for 7283 recipients of their first allograft was 85% at 1 year, 78% at 3 years, and 72% at 5 years after transplantation. About 80 to 85% of patients become physically active after cardiac transplantation, but only 33 to 50% of patients return to work. Barriers to employment include employers' fears regarding the patient's health and the costs of health care.

Cardiac transplantation, in most cases, markedly improves the cardiovascular hemodynamics of the transplant recipient. However, the transplant recipient is often left with a slightly diminished maximal cardiac output owing to denervation (neural decentralization), limited atrial function, decreased myocardial compliance, and donor-recipient size mismatch. Because parasympathetic influences that normally lower the heart rate in normal hearts are absent after cardiac transplantation, the resting heart rate is typically 95 to 115 beats per minute. Furthermore, the loss of sympathetic innervation blunts the normal increases in heart rate and contractility that occur with exercise, with low cardiac filling pressures, and after vasodilation. The cardiac allograft increases cardiac output primarily by an increase in filling pressure and secondarily in response to circulating catecholamines. In transplant recipients, the native and donor atria do not contract in unison, further decreasing the atrial component of ventricular filling.

Immediately after transplantation, the cardiac allograft exhibits compliance abnormalities as evidenced by a restrictive hemodynamic pattern. This pattern usually gradually improves over a few days to weeks, but 10 to 15% of recipients develop a chronic restrictive hemodynamic pattern (Chapter 73).

HEART-LUNG TRANSPLANTATION (Chapter 97)

The heart and lung can be transplanted en bloc from a donor to an appropriate recipient in a single operation, but fewer than 20% of heart donors are potential heart-lung donors. The primary indications for transplant are congenital cardiac abnormalities and severe pulmonary hypertension (Eisenmenger's complex), irremediable primary lung disease and associated severe secondary right ventricular failure, and primary end-stage cardiac disease and secondary irreversible pulmonary arterial hypertension, which would preclude isolated cardiac transplantation.

1. Kobashigawa J, Miller L, Renlund D, et al: A randomized active-controlled trial of mycophenolate mofetil in heart transplant recipients. Transplantation 1998;66:507–515.
2. Costanzo MR, Naftel DC, Pritzker MR, et al: Heart transplant coronary artery disease detected by coronary angiography. A multi-institutional study of preoperative donor and recipient risk factors. J Heart Lung Transplant 1998;17:744–753.

SUGGESTED READINGS

Deng MC: Cardiac transplantation. Heart 2002;87:177–184. *A well-referenced overview of the history, physiology, and current status of heart transplantation directed to the nontransplant physician.*

Kirklin JK, Young JB, McGiffin DC: Heart Transplantation. New York, Churchhill Livingstone, 2002. *An extensive, authoritative, well-referenced, and up-to-date textbook outlining all aspects of heart transplantation.*

Stevenson LW, Kormos RL, Bourge RC, et al: Mechanical cardiac support 2000: Current applications and future trial design. June 15–16, 2000 Bethesda, Maryland. J Am Coll Cardiol 2001;37:340–370. *An extensive review of use of currently available and experimental devices as a bridge to cardiac transplantation. Offers an excellent scheme to select patients for devices.*

Cardiovascular Disease

part IX

Respiratory Diseases

81 APPROACH TO THE PATIENT WITH RESPIRATORY DISEASE

Gerard M. Turino

The process of respiration includes many structural and functional components (Chapter 82) in addition to the lungs, such as the nose, pharynx, sinuses, chest cage and musculature, pleura, diaphragm, extrathoracic airways, cerebral regulatory respiratory centers, and cardiovascular system. In addressing the patient with pulmonary disease, the physician must maintain a circumspect approach to possible pathogenic factors. Pulmonary infiltrates on the chest film may be a manifestation of a pulmonary infection or primary lung tumor, but they may also be the result of metastatic cancer from extrapulmonary sites. Pulmonary densities of various types on chest film may be caused by generalized systemic diseases such as lupus erythematosus (Chapter 280), scleroderma (Chapter 281), rheumatoid arthritis (Chapter 278), or embolic disease (Chapter 94). Abnormal blood gas analysis findings may result from defective regulation of ventilation rather than from intrinsic lung disease.

The lungs contribute to the vital processes of all other organ systems. Pulmonary oxygen and carbon dioxide exchange is necessary for metabolism and acid-base homeostasis. The pulmonary circulation is subject to hemodynamic disturbances originating in the cardiac chambers, but it may be affected by primary pulmonary hypertension (Chapter 64). The lungs are the interface between gases and particulate matter in the external atmosphere and the body, so lung function must be considered in terms of exposure to atmospheric toxins. Also, lung cells not only are responsible for normal respiratory and circulatory functions of the lung but also contribute to extrapulmonary processes, such as blood pressure control by the action of angiotensin-converting enzyme, which resides on pulmonary endothelium.

Respiratory failure from the acute respiratory distress syndrome (Chapter 99) is a dire complication of a variety of initiating factors such as gastric aspiration, trauma, fractures, and circulatory shock, as well as pulmonary and extrapulmonary sepsis. It usually requires ventilatory support in the setting of intensive care (Chapter 101).

History

A detailed account of the patient's primary symptoms is essential, but other critical information includes the amount of exposure to tobacco smoke (including passive exposure); atmospheric pollutants, such as nitrogen dioxide, beryllium, asbestos, coal, and silica dust (Chapters 18 and 89); fumes from industrial processes; and animal danders. If the patient is exposed to a potentially toxic industrial process, precise historical details on the place and duration of occupational exposure are necessary. The family history of lung disease with respect to asthma (Chapter 84), allergies, cystic fibrosis (CF) (Chapter 86), lung cancer (Chapter 198), and emphysema (Chapter 85) is also important. A family history of emphysema may be present in cases of serum α_1-antitrypsin deficiency. Living in certain regions of the country may predispose the patient to histoplasmosis (Chapter 379) or coccidioidomycosis (Chapter 380). Infections such as *Pneumocystis carinii* pneumonia (Chapter 387), chronic sinusitis (Chapter 468), pneumococcal pneumonia (Chapter 303), and tuberculosis or other mycobacteria (Chapters 341 and 342) are recognized common complications of human immunodeficiency virus (HIV) infection, so the history should explore the possibility of exposure to HIV infection (Chapter 415).

A history of the medications taken previously and currently is necessary to evaluate certain pulmonary infiltrative lesions, such as interstitial pulmonary fibrosis as a complication of therapy with bleomycin, cyclophosphamide, methotrexate, or nitrofurantoin (Chapter 191). Bronchospasm may be initiated or exacerbated by β-adrenergic–blocking drugs. Cough and angioedema are occasional complications of angiotensin-converting enzyme inhibitor drugs.

Physical Examination

Obesity can affect the mechanics of breathing and can predispose a patient to obstructive sleep apnea (Chapter 96). An increased thoracic anteroposterior diameter may be evidence of obstructive lung disease and pulmonary hyperinflation, whereas shortening and deformation of the thorax, as occur in kyphoscoliosis of the spine, may cause a restrictive breathing pattern. Lagging of one side of the chest may be evidence of unilateral fibrothorax or atelectasis. Accessory muscles of ventilation are frequently used in severe airway obstruction (Table 81–1).

If there is audible wheezing on ventilation, airway obstruction in the tracheobronchial tree must be distinguished from obstruction in the larynx and pharynx. Extrathoracic airway obstruction in the upper airway is frequently more marked during the inspiratory phase, whereas lower airway obstruction is more marked in the expiratory phase. The presence of nasal voice and/or tenderness over sinus regions of the face may be a manifestation of acute or chronic sinus disease. Full inspection of the nose and pharynx is essential to detect polyps or septal deviations, which can cause obstruction or postnasal secretions.

Râles and crackles are a manifestation of an increase in luminal fluid in alveoli and small airways, through which inspired and expired air pass. Rales and crackles may be audible in both lungs, as in pulmonary edema from circulatory or noncirculatory causes, or patchy, from a localized inflammatory reaction, as in bronchopneumonia.

A loud pulmonary second sound, a right ventricular heave, jugular venous distention, and peripheral edema may be manifestations of primary or secondary pulmonary hypertension (Chapter 64), whereas systemic hypertension, left ventricular enlargement, or gallop sounds may be manifestations of poor left ventricular function and may suggest heart failure (Chapters 55 and 56) as a cause of pulmonary symptoms. Clubbing of the fingers may be a manifestation of carcinoma of the lung (Chapter 198), but it is frequently present in cystic fibrosis with hypoxemia and in severe bronchiectasis as well as in hypoxemia associated with congenital heart disease (Chapters 65, 86, and 87).

Table 81–1 • PHYSICAL SIGNS OF PULMONARY DISEASE

PATHOGENIC PROCESS	CHEST WALL MOTION AND CONFIGURATION	BREATH SOUNDS	PERCUSSION	FREMITUS
Asthmatic and bronchitic airway obstruction	Increased anteroposterior diameter, use of accessory muscles of ventilation	May be decreased; prolonged expiration; inspiratory and expiratory wheezes and rhonchi	Hyperresonant	Decreased
Airway obstruction of emphysema	Increased anteroposterior diameter, reduced chest wall musculature with general weight loss, use of accessory muscles of ventilation	Markedly diminished; prolonged expiratory phase; may be rhonchi	Hyperresonant	Decreased
Atelectasis	Inspiratory lag on affected side	Absent over affected area	Dullness	Decreased
Consolidation of acute pneumonia	Splinting of chest wall on affected side	Bronchial breath sounds, whispered pectoriloquy, rales and/or rhonchi	Dullness	Increased
Pleural effusion	Lag on affected side	Absent or decreased	Flatness	Absent
Pneumothorax	Lag on affected side, tracheal deviation away from affected side	Absent	Hyperresonant	Absent
Diffuse alveolitis or fibrosis	Restricted inspiratory and expiratory excursion	May be increased with diffuse fine rales	Decreased resonance or normal	Increased or normal

Evaluating Blood Gas Composition and Pulmonary Function Testing

In many patients, an arterial blood gas measurement is essential to establish or exclude significant hypoxemia and/or hypercapnia. Unless the patient is severely hypoxemic with polycythemia and visible cyanosis, significant degrees of hypoxemia can be undetected clinically unless blood gas composition is measured. Similarly, significant degrees of hypercapnia may be present without symptoms of somnolence or headache.

Pulmonary function testing, including blood gas measurements during rest and exercise, can characterize and quantify pulmonary dysfunction. Simple spirometry can quantify airway obstruction and determine the response to bronchodilator therapy. Lung volume measurements can establish whether the air-containing volume of the lung is reduced and a restrictive pattern of lung disease (as occurs in interstitial alveolitis, sarcoidosis, or fibrosis) is present. The pulmonary diffusing capacity is a sensitive measurement of parenchymal disease of the lung, such as alveolitis or interstitial fibrosis (Chapter 88), in which the surface area of the pulmonary capillary membrane is reduced and the thickness of the alveolar capillary membrane is increased. In obstructive airways disease, diffusing capacity can determine the presence of pulmonary emphysema (Chapter 85). A low diffusing capacity indicates alveolar destruction and the presence of emphysema as a primary process or in association with chronic bronchitis or asthma.

Detection of pulmonary hypertension and estimates of pulmonary artery pressure can be provided by echocardiography (Chapter 51). For more thorough evaluation of the hemodynamics of the pulmonary circulation, measurements of pulmonary artery pressure and pulmonary vascular resistance should be obtained by right heart catheterization (Chapter 54). When indicated, a pulmonary angiogram can be obtained if pulmonary embolism is suspected clinically and a ventilation-perfusion scan or helical computed tomography (CT) scan is not definitive.

Radiologic Techniques for the Diagnosis of Pulmonary Lesions

CHEST FILMS. The standard posteroanterior and lateral chest roentgenograms can indicate diaphragmatic and rib cage abnormalities as well as the air-containing volumes of each lung. They also define the presence of opacities, cavitary lesions, pneumothoraces, atelectasis, pleural fluid or pleural thickening, cardiac size and chamber contours, pulmonary congestion, pulmonary edema, and enlargement of the pulmonary arteries.

COMPUTED TOMOGRAPHY. CT scans can easily measure relative tissue density, homogeneity, the relationship of parenchymal opacities to bronchi and adjacent vascular structures, and the location and extent of lymphadenopathy. Unlike conventional CT, which requires the patient to take discrete breathholds for each slice acquired, helical (spiral) CT allows volumetric data acquisition with a single breathhold and hence provides better detection of small lung lesions and pulmonary nodules, faster imaging for dynamic vascular studies, and the ability to perform three-dimensional reconstruction.

The rapidity of helical CT saves time, reduces the risk of performing the procedure in critically ill patients, and permits use of a smaller bolus of contrast for detailed studies of vascular anomalies, aneurysms, or pulmonary emboli. Sections as precise as 1 mm apart can be obtained for a pulmonary nodule without respiratory motion artifacts. Helical CT also provides a more accurate assessment of mediastinal and hilar lymph nodes as well as direct extension of lung neoplasms to the mediastinum, pleura, or chest wall. Helical CT is essential for the assessment of focal lung disease and often can distinguish between a granuloma and primary bronchogenic carcinoma.

High-resolution CT detects and quantifies the lung parenchymal destruction of pulmonary emphysema from reductions in lung tissue density. In this regard, high-resolution CT is a most useful technique to diagnose and follow patients with emphysema and chronic obstructive pulmonary disease.

POSITRON EMISSION TOMOGRAPHIC (PET) SCANNING. By PET scan, a high uptake of labeled glucose characterizes most lung cancers. In single pulmonary nodules for which no previous radiographic examinations are available to assess a change in size, the normal uptake of glucose by PET scan may allow for continued observation, whereas increased uptake of labeled glucose would be a reason to consider immediate resection.

MAGNETIC RESONANCE IMAGING (MRI). MRI has limited value in the chest and is best used in studying the heart, vascular anatomy, and masses or lymph nodes of the mediastinum (Chapter 49). It can be helpful when the use of iodinated contrast agents is contraindicated.

INTERVENTIONAL RADIOGRAPHIC TECHNIQUES. Radiographic CT or ultrasound guidance has added greatly to the accuracy and reliability of needle biopsies of intraparenchymal and mediastinal masses. Similarly, pleural collections and lung abscesses can be drained using guided catheter techniques.

Invasive Techniques in Pulmonary Diagnosis

To evaluate suspected pulmonary neoplasm or to investigate hemoptysis, fiberoptic bronchoscopy is essential and may include sampling of bronchial cells by brushing or bronchial biopsy or, when indicated, bronchoalveolar lavage to determine the cell composition in alveoli.

If pleural disease is detected, pleural fluid analysis and pleural biopsy are helpful diagnostically. Thoracoscopy is an effective technique to evaluate lesions on the pleura or periphery of the lung by biopsy or local resection.

Clinical Symptomatic Manifestations of Pulmonary Disease

Although a wide array of pathologic factors can produce respiratory symptoms and signs, the five common manifestations of pulmonary disease that require evaluation are (1) cough, (2) shortness of breath or dyspnea, (3) chest pain, (4) hemoptysis, and (5) a solitary pulmonary nodule.

COUGH WITH AND WITHOUT SPUTUM. Cough results from transmission of nervous impulses to the integrative cough centers in the brain from sensory stimuli in the tracheobronchial tree. Cough may be a transient or persistent symptom. Common causes of transient cough are inflammatory reactions on the surface of the trachea or bronchial branches, usually from bacterial or viral infections. Occasionally, noxious vapors in the atmosphere can induce cough (e.g., tobacco smoke, volatile chemical compounds, and vehicular exhaust). For persistent cough, one of the most prominent causes is an allergic inflammatory reaction of the bronchi associated with asthma; cough may be the earliest presenting manifestation, preceding complaints of shortness of breath or wheezing.

Another common cause of tracheobronchial irritation is regurgitation of acidic gastric contents into the tracheobronchial tree during sleep. Such regurgitation and aspiration result from failure of gastric emptying due to gastric outlet obstruction or an incompetent gastroesophageal junction (Chapter 136). Many individuals regurgitate gastric and esophageal contents during sleep and are totally unaware of this phenomenon.

An important cause of persistent cough is a tumor in the tracheobronchial tree that leads to distortions of the bronchial wall and increases stimuli to the cough center. In any patient with persistent cough, and particularly in smokers, the possibility of a bronchial carcinoma or adenoma must be considered. Extrabronchial lesions that cause cough include a mediastinal or esophageal tumor, an aortic aneurysm that compresses a bronchus, or an enlarged left atrium compressing the left main bronchus. Sinusitis with persistent nasal secretions into the pharynx and upper airway is a frequent cause of therapy-resistant chronic cough.

Diagnostic investigations of cough include chest radiography and, if necessary, sinus radiography and CT of the thorax. When indicated, bronchoscopy and laryngoscopy should be performed. The presence, type, and amount of sputum can be useful in differential diagnosis. Acute onset of sputum with cough suggests acute pulmonary infection or sinusitis. Long-standing sputum production, usually in the morning, is characteristic of chronic bronchitis from smoking. Large volumes of sputum throughout the day are characteristic of bronchiectasis or lung abscess. Foul-smelling sputum suggests anaerobic infection associated with lung abscess. Yellow or green sputum, due to the release of myeloperoxidase by leukocytes, is a common sign of infection. In asthma, sputum may be yellow or even green without concomitant infection; evaluations by microscopy or culture is required.

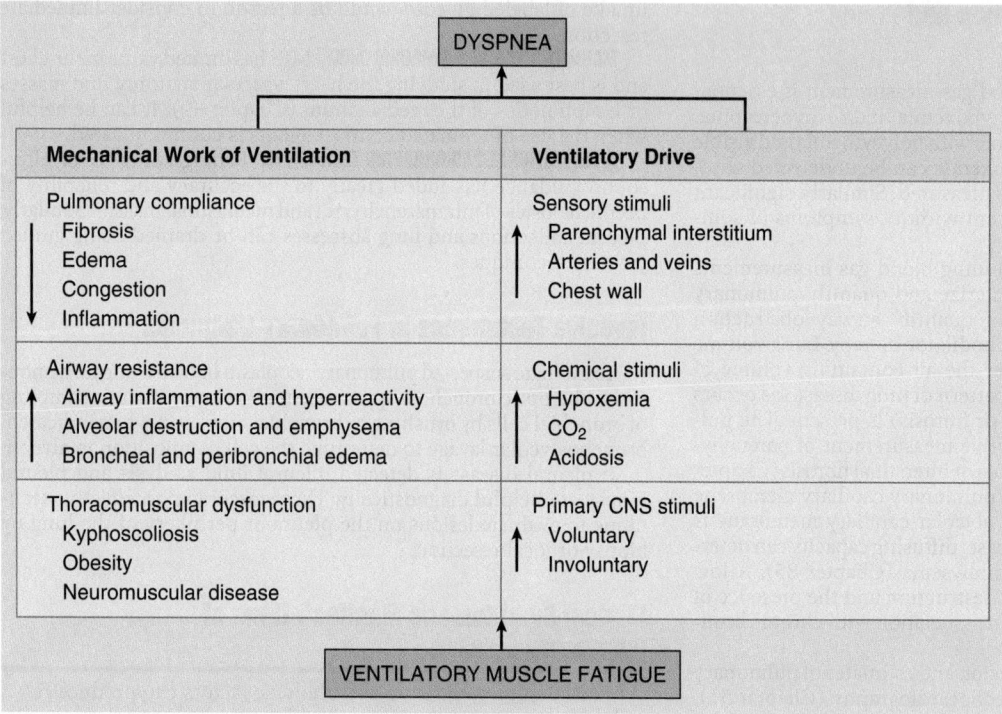

Mechanical Work of Ventilation	Ventilatory Drive

Pulmonary compliance
↓   Fibrosis
  Edema
  Congestion
  Inflammation
	Sensory stimuli
	↑ Parenchymal interstitium
	  Arteries and veins
	  Chest wall

Airway resistance
↑   Airway inflammation and hyperreactivity
  Alveolar destruction and emphysema
  Broncheal and peribronchial edema
	Chemical stimuli
	↑ Hypoxemia
	  CO_2
	  Acidosis

Thoracomuscular dysfunction
  Kyphoscoliosis
  Obesity
  Neuromuscular disease
	Primary CNS stimuli
	↑ Voluntary
	  Involuntary

DYSPNEA

VENTILATORY MUSCLE FATIGUE

Figure 81–1 • The symptom of dyspnea can best be related to increases in the mechanical work of breathing and/or increases in ventilatory drive as a result of the effect of different pathogenic factors on ventilatory mechanics and increased ventilatory stimuli. Ventilatory muscle fatigue is an added factor (see text).

SHORTNESS OF BREATH. "Shortness of breath," "a feeling of not being able to get enough air," and "labored breathing" are all terms used by patients to describe the symptom of dyspnea. The cause of dyspnea may be pulmonary disease, circulatory disease, or both. It is the physician's responsibility to define the causative mechanisms of shortness of breath so that diagnostic techniques and therapies can be directed appropriately. The most consistent correlate of the symptom of dyspnea is increased mechanical work of breathing, usually brought on by increased airway resistance as occurs in asthma, chronic bronchitis, and emphysema, or decreased distensibility of the lungs as occurs in interstitial fibrotic reactions (Fig. 81–1). In the latter diseases, increased effort is required to produce a higher negative pressure in the pleural space to inflate the lungs. The increased mechanical work done on the lungs to overcome obstruction to airflow or decreased distensibility is perceived as an increased effort to breathe and produces the symptom of dyspnea.

An increased drive to ventilate may also cause dyspnea. Such stimuli include hypoxia, usually when arterial oxygen tensions are less than 60 mm Hg, and stimuli from inflamed lung parenchyma, as occur in bacterial pneumonia or alveolitis and that drive the respiratory centers of the brain. These stimuli often lower the resting carbon dioxide pressure (P_{CO_2}) to less than the normal level of 40 mm Hg and cause dyspnea, especially on mild exertion.

Patients with pulmonary emboli (Chapter 94) may present with shortness of breath and a normal chest roentgenogram. However, the inefficiency of the embolized lung for gas exchange, characterized by an enlarged deadspace, requires abnormally high ventilatory rates to maintain a normal arterial P_{CO_2}. Unless this particular presentation of pulmonary embolism is appreciated, embolic disease goes unrecognized in many patients until they suddenly die or are extremely incapacitated by pulmonary hypertension and right ventricular failure.

Because of the high prevalence of heart disease and heart failure in the general population, many patients with dyspnea have cardiac abnormalities. The basis of the dyspnea is usually a high filling pressure of the left ventricle, which causes high left atrial pressures and high pulmonary capillary and pulmonary arterial pressures, which in turn increase the pulmonary blood volume and reduce lung compliance. If the pulmonary capillary wedge pressure is in the range of 25 mm Hg, capillary fluid transudates into the pulmonary matrix, thereby reducing lung compliance, increasing the work of breathing, and causing dyspnea (Chapter 55). Echocardiography (Chapter 51) is usually diagnostic of abnormal ventricular or valvular function and

should be performed in any patient in whom the cause of dyspnea is not readily apparent.

CHEST PAIN. Chest pain is also a common presenting symptom of lung disease. Pleuritic pain is sharp and severe, magnified by breathing, and may be associated with a pleural friction rub. Pericarditis (Chapter 74) causes chest pain that may not be related to breathing and often is relieved by leaning forward; pericardial friction rubs may be audible in synchrony with the heartbeat. Pleuropericardial friction rubs may induce pain related to breathing and be heard in relation to both breathing and cardiac contraction.

The chest pain of myocardial ischemia from coronary artery disease should be discernible on the basis of its relation to physical exertion and its characteristic radiation to the left shoulder or arm, neck, and jaw (Chapter 46). The chest pain of pulmonary embolism may also be characterized by a feeling of anterior chest pressure, which may persist for hours and be related to pulmonary hypertension (Chapter 94).

HEMOPTYSIS. The most common cause of hemoptysis (Fig. 81–2) is pneumonia or pulmonary infection, including bronchiectasis (Chapter 87). Bloody streaking of purulent sputum occurs during pneumonia or severe bronchitis and subsides as the infection is treated.

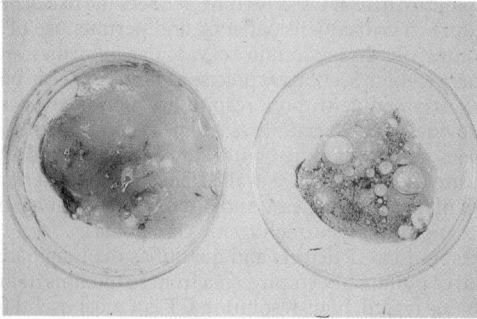

Figure 81–2 • Rusty-red sputum (left) compared with fresh hemoptysis (right) in two sputum samples. The rusty-red sputum comes from a patient with pneumococcal pneumonia, whereas the hemoptysis occurred in a patient with small-cell lung cancer. (From Forbes CD, Jackson WF: Color Atlas and Text of Clinical Medicine, 3rd ed. London, Mosby, 2003, with permission.)

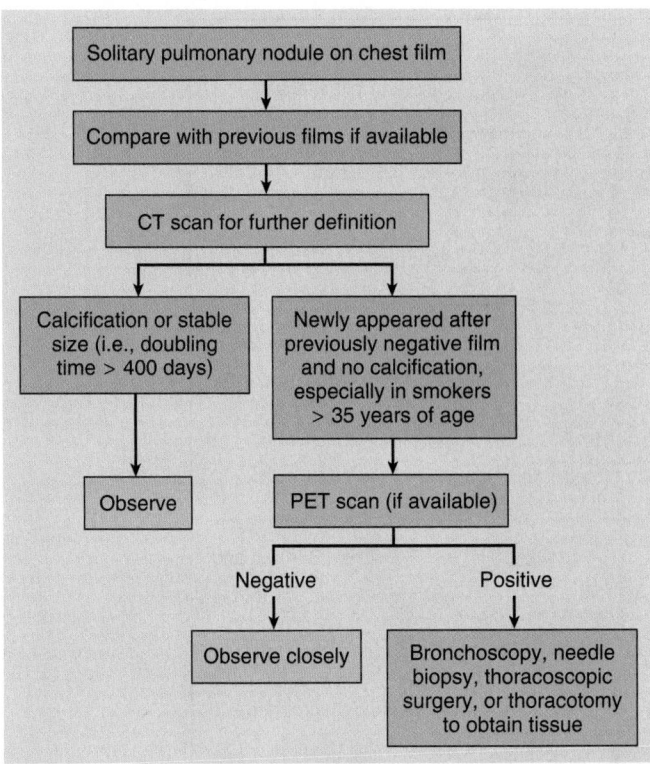

Figure 81–3 • Steps in the evaluation of the solitary pulmonary nodule.

The sudden appearance of hemoptysis without other cause must be considered a possible manifestation of lung tumor, either benign or malignant (Chapter 198). Such hemoptysis necessitates full investigation with a chest radiograph, CT scan, and bronchoscopy. A pulmonary embolism that leads to pulmonary infarction almost always results in hemoptysis (Chapter 94); it is usually associated with a pulmonary infiltration as a manifestation of infarction, which occasionally leads to a cavity in the lung parenchyma. Pulmonary tuberculosis (Chapter 341), especially with cavity formation, is a prominent cause of hemoptysis, especially in patients with HIV infection. Hemoptysis is not uncommon in cystic fibrosis (Chapter 86) of the lung and can be severe and even life threatening. A certain proportion of patients have sudden and usually mild hemoptysis for which no cause can be found; such episodes may result from a ruptured blood vessel or varix in the bronchial mucosa, and clotting parameters should be checked. Mild hemoptysis also results from coughing stimulated by blood from the oropharynx; comprehensive oropharyngeal evaluation is diagnostic (Chapter 468). Bronchopulmonary aspergillosis or an aspergilloma (Chapter 386) can cause persistent hemoptysis, whereas an arteriovenous malformation can cause sudden, life-threatening hemoptysis.

SOLITARY PULMONARY NODULE (Chapter 198). A solitary pulmonary nodule on a chest radiograph, especially if it is new, poses the possibility of a malignancy and requires immediate diagnostic evaluation (Fig. 81–3). The presence of calcification in at least 10 to 20% of the nodule near its center is the most reliable indicator of a benign lesion. However, calcification of a solitary nodule is not specific for benign disease, because a cancer can develop within a scar or granuloma.

SUGGESTED READINGS
Blum J, Handmaker H, Lister-James J, et al: A multicenter trial with a somatostatin analog 99-M Tc depreotide in the evaluation of solitary pulmonary nodules. Chest 2000;117:1232–1237. *A multicenter study by the NeoTech Solitary Pulmonary Nodule Study Group of the use of a more accessible nuclear radiographic technique for the detection of malignant neoplasms in solitary pulmonary nodules.*
Gould MK, Sanders GD, Barnett PG, et al: Cost-effectiveness of alternative management strategies for patients with solitary pulmonary nodules. Ann Intern Med 2003;138:724–735. *Computed tomography (CT) is usually preferred, but PET scanning is useful when the clinical probability and CT result are discordant or the patient is at high operative risk.*

82 RESPIRATORY STRUCTURE AND FUNCTION

Herbert Y. Reynolds

The lungs are designed for gaseous exchange (oxygen uptake and carbon dioxide elimination) through the process of ventilation and molecular diffusion. To maintain health, purified air must be presented to the alveolar epithelial surface to aerate pulmonary capillary blood. Ambient air, which contains environmental debris, microbes, and possibly solubilized toxins and which is admixed at times with aspirated oropharyngeal secretions, must be cleansed. Inspired ambient air encounters a system of host defenses that usually removes these contaminants mechanically (by sneezing, rhinorrhea, coughing, and mucociliary clearance), through innate (natural) immunity mechanisms, or immunologically through adaptive (acquired) immunity. This nonventilatory function can be missing (primary host defects) or can be compromised by systemic illness or the side effects of other medical therapy. Because ventilation and nonventilatory function are so intertwined, both are described together; then methods for assessing clinical function follow.

Respiratory Tract Structure

Although the respiratory tract is a continuum of branching tubes leading to the air exchange–alveolar surface, it functionally has four distinct anatomic segments: the naso-oropharynx or upper airways, conducting airways (larynx, trachea, and bronchi that branch to terminal bronchioles), respiratory bronchioles, and alveolar ducts/alveoli. Vascular and neural structures are integral to each segment; lymphatic channels begin at the level of respiratory bronchioles and flow upward or cephalad into the hilar nodes.

Embryologically the airways and their accompanying blood supply develop from an evagination of the foregut and primitive esophagus. The conducting airways form a continuum of approximately 14 generations of branches, which are extended by another 10 or so branches within the acinar airways, finally ending as alveolar sacs. This anatomic structure has been described as a tree with irregular, dichotomously branching tubes. Later developments in the fetus initiate progressive thinning down of the mucosal epithelial layer in distal bronchi and then the respiratory bronchioles to a single cellular surface, which defines the beginning of the gas exchange unit within the acinar/alveolar structures. Because this mucosal surface that lines the airways down to the respiratory bronchioles is in breath-to-breath contact with the external environment, mechanisms to cleanse inspired air are dispersed along the entire tract.

The *naso-oropharynx* includes the upper airways and associated sinuses (Chapter 468). It begins at the nares and lips, extends back through richly vascular, undulant mucosal covering of the nasal passage and through the glottis into the extrathoracic trachea. Nasal hairs and turbinates filter out large particles (>10 μm diameter) as turbulent air passes over the surface; also, air is humidified and warmed as necessary. These climatologic adjustments occur as air passes through the nose and over the soft palate and are completed before air reaches the posterior pharynx. Sinus and posterior nasal secretions can collect in the posterior pharynx, where salivary fluids stimulated by mastication also accumulate. Deglutition and respiration are coordinated exquisitely by the epiglottis and laryngeal musculature to direct fluids and food into the esophagus and air into the subglottic trachea. Control is not perfect, however, and aspiration can occur in normal persons during sleep; also, esophageal reflux causing cough and asthma symptoms is common (Chapters 84 and 136). The nasal mucosal surface is similar to that in the lower conducting airways with respect to ciliary function and immunologic components. Mucociliary clearance declines with age, explaining in part the more frequent occurrence of respiratory infections in the elderly.

The *conducting airways* begin with the trachea, a flexible tube held open by cartilaginous, horseshoe-shaped rings with a posterior muscular face that abuts the esophagus. The trachea is oval, is about 10 cm in length, and contains about 15 rings. At the carina, it divides into two major bronchi, and thereafter multiple smaller bronchial branches diverge through many generations of smaller divisions. In aggregate, however, the branching creates a much greater overall cross-

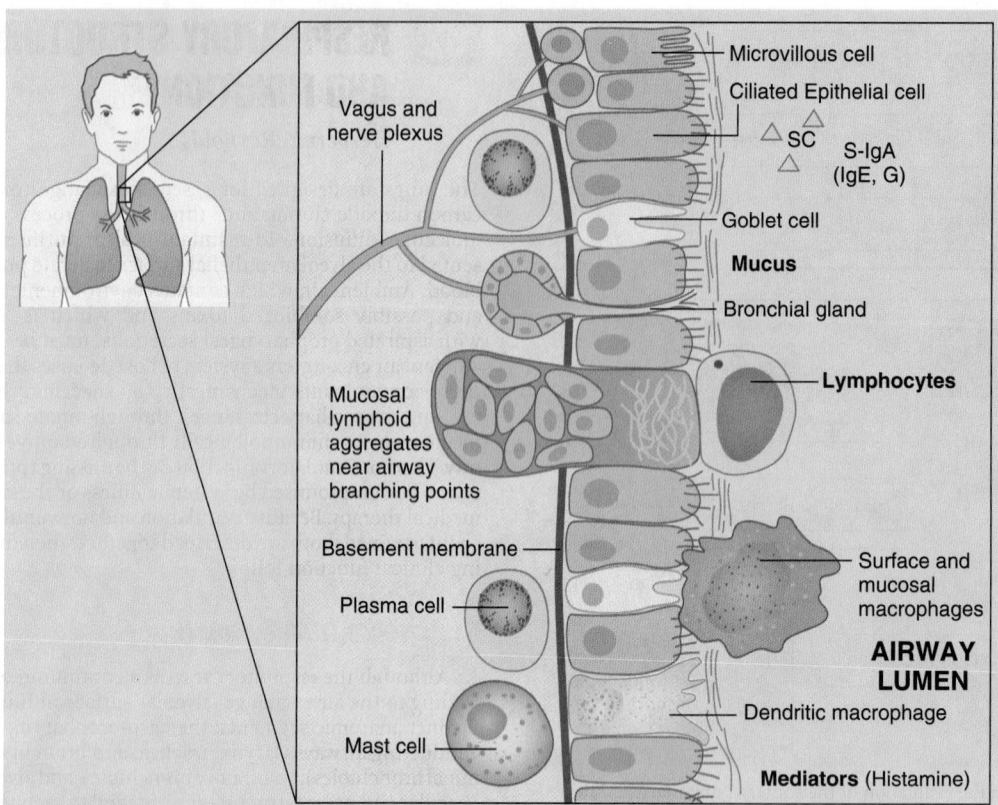

FIGURE 82-1 • A portion of the bronchial airway surface depicts the mucosa and its submucosal structures. The pseudostratified ciliated epithelium has a covering layer of mucus (produced by goblet cells and bronchial glands) and film of fluid that contains various proteins, including immunoglobulins and free secretory component (SC). A few surface cells may be present, such as lymphocytes (from bronchial-associated lymphoid aggregates) and macrophages. Among the epithelial cells are absorptive microvillous cells and dendritic cells, whose cellular processes interdigitate with the mucosal surface. The epithelial cells can produce inflammatory cytokines that affect mucosal swelling and permeability. In the submucosa below the basement membrane, mast cells and plasma cells reside that secrete mediators (e.g., histamine) and local immunoglobulins (e.g., IgA). Interacting with all of these glandular and cellular networks are nerves, exerting their control through neuropeptides and by adrenergic and cholinergic nerve fibers. A rich bronchial arterial vascular supply exists also. (Modified from Reynolds HY: Pulmonary host defenses. Chest 1989;95:223S–230S.)

sectional area that not only reduces resistance to airflow, but also decelerates the velocity of air molecules as they prepare to enter the acinar ducts and alveolar sacs. Although airflow is laminar, the slower movement further cleanses the air by allowing for the settling out of any 0.5- to 3-µm size particulates that still are present and would impact at branching points. This action seems especially important in the respiratory bronchioles, which serve as the transition segment between the conducting airways and alveoli, where several adaptations facilitate further removal of particulates or antigens. Throughout the conducting airways (Fig. 82–1), the mucosal surface provides a barrier function because of the tight apical junctions between epithelial cells. About half of the epithelial cells are ciliated; a fluid film and mucus cover the beating cilia, creating the mucociliary apparatus. The thickness of the mucosal surface attenuates as the pseudostratified cell layer flattens down to become a single cellular layer in the terminal bronchioles. Here the less-protected surface may become more vulnerable to injury from inhaled toxins and microbes and more susceptible to ravages of chronic inflammation (bronchiolitis).

The *respiratory bronchioles*, which are positioned between the distal conducting airways and the alveolized air exchange surface, functionally separate the upper and lower respiratory tracts. This segment is a bottleneck for airflow and a last surface to capture small particulates and microbial or antigenic debris before the alveolar space; immune responses can be initiated here. The respiratory bronchioles can be the site for airway obstruction, however, owing to inflammation typical of bronchiolitis obliterans (Chapter 88) and associated with several lung diseases, such as chronic graft rejection after lung transplantation (Chapter 97) and lung involvement by collagen-vascular diseases (Chapter 88). In this transition segment, several changes occur: The single-layer cuboidal epithelial surface further differentiates into alveolar type I cells that cover the alveolar lining surface; mucus-secreting cells disappear, although globlet cells can develop in cigarette smokers; and another secretory cell type emerges,

the Clara cells. Also, many dendritic macrophage-like cells, which may constitute 1% of the cells, are present to capture antigens. Surface host defenses change from a focus on mucociliary clearance to an emphasis on featuring macrophage phagocytes, inflammatory cells (neutrophils or eosinophils), and opsonins. Lymphatic channels form to collect the lymphatic fluid squeezed up from the interalveolar interstitial spaces into lymphatic capillaries that course along pulmonary capillaries and venules in the alveolar walls. Finally, the changeover is made from the bronchial arterial blood supply for the conducting airways to the pulmonary artery/pulmonary capillary blood that courses around the alveoli for aeration.

The *air exchange* compartment, or the alveolar space, is composed of several hundred million alveoli supported by a fibrous scaffolding and intertwined with a meshwork of pulmonary artery capillaries that permit air-blood contact. Oxygen uptake and carbon dioxide elimination occur across a thin tissue layer of type I epithelial cells and capillary endothelium that, in aggregate, creates a large surface area of approximately 130 square feet. To increase the likelihood that respiratory function will support a healthy human life span despite pollutants, infections, or systemic diseases that affect the lungs, an intricate system of host defenses has evolved. The system specialized for the alveoli is different than the system described in the proximal airways. Although an alveolus is reasonably protected from airborne debris by aerodynamic filtration that occurs in the upper respiratory tract, small particles (<0.5 µm) can remain suspended in air or toxic gases can gain access to the alveoli directly.

Respiratory host defenses balance two mechanisms that eliminate or detoxify microbes and other antigens that enter the airways. First is an innate or quick response reaction that produces inflammation as an end point (bronchitis or pneumonitis) with subsequent apoptosis of neutrophils and suppression of inflammation to limit the reaction. Second is a more deliberate approach that stimulates lymphocytic pathways, creating a versatile and adaptive response

FIGURE 82–2 • In bronchial airways, dendritic macrophage cells, embedded in the mucosa or residing on its surface, can direct the major protective immune pathways, innate and adaptive immunity, to confront microbes and foreign antigens that have evaded upper airway defense mechanisms and threaten the airway lumen, potentially disrupting normal respiration. A choice of the inflammatory reaction for quick removal or a more deliberate cellular immune elimination is made and proceeds by the major lymphocytic pathways, Th1 or Th2, and other cell-mediated processes that are described in the text. CD = cluster of differentiation; GNR-LPS = gram-negative rods–lipopolysaccharide; IFN = interferon; Ig = immunoglobulin; IL = interleukin; TLR = Toll-like receptor; TNF = tumor necrosis factor. (From Reynolds HY: Modulating airway defenses against microbes. Curr Opin Pulm Med 2002;8:154–165.)

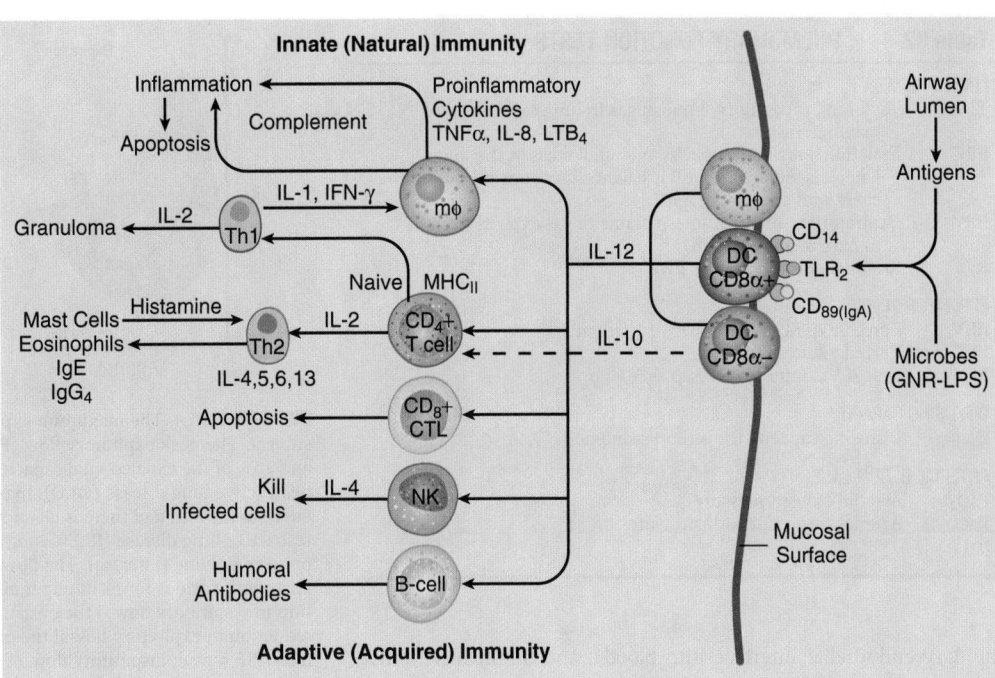

involving specific T-cell activity and/or production of immunoglobulins (antibodies).

Microbes can be contained in aspirated fluid or carried intravascularly to the parenchyma (septicemia). A microbe entering an alveolus may encounter several opsonins in the epithelial lining fluid, including IgG antibodies (IgG1 and IgG3 subtypes) and nonimmune substances (type II cell–secreted surfactant protein A, fibrinogen, and complement fragments [C3b]). These opsonins coat the epithelial lining and promote receptor-mediated uptake by macrophages as part of the innate immune response. Alveolar T lymphocytes can stimulate the macrophage with cytokines that enhance its bactericidal activity, or, if microbes are too numerous or too virulent, can create an inflammatory response quickly. Chemokines derived from macrophages or epithelial cells can attract neutrophils and other inflammatory products from adjacent capillaries into the alveolus (Fig. 82–2). If inflammation, or pneumonitis, is successful in eradicating infection, neutrophils undergo apoptosis, the inflammation resolves, and normal lung tissue function is restored. If the inflammatory process is prolonged, a smoldering, chronic inflammatory response can persist and lead to tissue injury that causes fibrosis and scarring or, depending on the antigen-particle or microbe involved, a granulomatous reaction. If this wound-type healing occurs after substantial injury, respiratory function can be lost permanently.

Cellular Structure

The airway layer of pseudostratified epithelial cells creates a physical barrier by forming tight apical junctions that control premeability and promote pericellular ion and fluid flux in addition to the usual transepithelial uptake and secretion. About half of the epithelial cells have cilia that propel a covering layer of fluid and admixed mucus that can collect airway debris and eliminate it by mucociliary clearance. These epithelial cells have dynamic cellular turnover and continuous self-renewal, but the normal replication rate may vary at different locations along the airways. If airway injury has destroyed epithelial cells and denuded the surface, regeneration begins quickly from reservoirs of self-renewing stem cells found in niches located in the ducts of submucosal glands in the trachea or bronchi and within the surface epithelium of more distal airways.

Epithelial cells have about the same repertoire of proinflammatory chemokines as alveolar macrophages, including interleukin (IL)-8, leukotriene B4 (LTB4), transforming growth factor (TGF)-β, monocyte chemotactic protein (MCP)-1, and RANTES. They also can inhibit or downregulate inflammation. This dual capability to help initiate inflammation and then suppress it makes the epithelium crucial for the pathogenesis of diseases such as asthma (Chapter 84),

bronchitis, and emphysema (Chapter 85). Chronic inflammatory changes can cause bronchiectasis (Chapter 87) or cell atypia that leads to endobronchial cancer (Chapter 198).

Dendritic cells or surface macrophages process antigens and present them to major histocompatibility complex (MHC)–compatible but naive CD4+ lymphocytes, a process facilitated with the stimulatory cytokine IL-12. IL-2 produced by CD4+ T cells subsequently can direct Th1 lymphocytes to develop and proliferate. Th1 cells can produce IL-1 and interferon-γ, which can stimulate macrophages for heightened activity (phagocytic uptake) in the inflammatory pathway. Also, IL-2 can induce clonal expansion of CD4+ lymphocytes that contributes to creating granulomas for containment of certain microbes, such as mycobacteria, or particles (silica or beryllium).

Another subset of dendritic cells (or macrophages) can produce IL-10, an inhibitory cytokine that promotes the Th1 response preferentially in normal subjects and suppresses the Th2 cellular pathway. Th2 lymphocytes stimulate mast cells, eosinophils, and the production of reaginic antibodies (IgE, IgG4). The host usually needs to suppress this response so that every inhaled, environmental antigen entering the airways does not elicit an allergic response.

Dendritic cells or macrophages also interact with other lymphocytes to create a delayed or more protracted cellular immune response (adaptive). Stimulation of CD8+ suppressor lymphocytes creates cytotoxic functioning cells or natural killer cells that can destroy aberrant cells, can destroy cells containing intracellular microbes, or can program another cell's death. Finally, antigens can be presented to B lymphocytes that become plasma cells.

Assessment of Pulmonary Function

Documenting the working capacity and condition of the overall respiratory tract, or some of its individual components, requires lung function tests, arterial blood gases, imaging studies, or measurements of secretions from specific sites.

PULMONARY FUNCTION TESTS

Lung function tests (Table 82–1) are essential to measure a person's objective ability to move the ventilatory apparatus in comparison with normal subjects, adjusted for sex, height, ethnicity, and age. Basic tests for preliminary assessment and for monitoring disease progression include spirometry, which is a record of exhaled volume versus time during a forced exhalation (with or without determining the response to an inhaled bronchodilator for possible reversible airflow), diffusion capacity (DL_{CO}) (the transfer of carbon monoxide to indicate how well inspired gases cross the alveolar-interstitial-

Table 82–1 • PULMONARY FUNCTION TESTS

LUNG VOLUME

TLC	Total lung capacity (volume of gas in lungs at the end of maximal inspiration)
FRC	Functional residual capacity (volume of gas in the lungs when elastic inward pull is balanced by outward pull of the chest wall and diaphragm)
ERV	Expiratory reserve volume (volume of gas expired from FRC to maximal expiration)
RV	Residual volume (FRC – ERV)

EXPIRATORY FLOW

FEV_1	Forced expiratory volume (in 1 second)
FVC	Forced vital capacity
FEV_1 %	FEV_1/FVC ratio (expressed as %)

DIFFUSING CAPACITY

DL_{CO}	Diffusing capacity for carbon monoxide

ARTERIAL BLOOD GASES

PaO_2	Arterial oxygen pressure
$PaCO_2$	Arterial carbon dioxide pressure
pH	

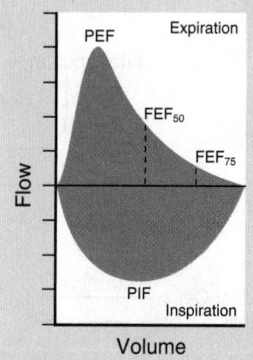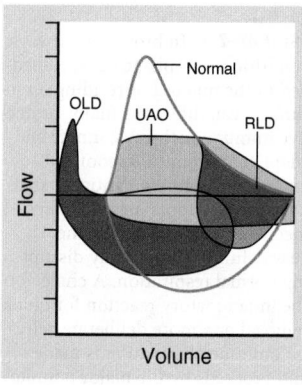

FIGURE 82–3 • *A,* The maximum expired flow/volume curve in a normal subject. The peak expiratory flow (PEF) and forced expiratory flows at 50% and 75% of the exhaled vital capacity (FEF_{50} and FEF_{75}) are indicated. *B,* In obstructive lung disease (OLD), hyperinflation pushes the position of the curve to the left, and there is characteristic scalloping on expiration. In restrictive lung disease (RLD), lung volumes are reduced, but flow for any point in volume is normal. The flow/volume curve displays different patterns with various forms of upper airway obstruction (UAO), with reduction in respiratory flow if the obstruction is outside the thoracic cavity and reduction in expiratory flow if the obstruction is caused by a fixed deformity. PIF = peak inspiratory flow. (From Diagnostic techniques and their indications. *In* Andreoli T, et al [eds]: Cecil Essentials of Medicine, 5th ed. Philadelphia, WB Saunders, 2001, p 183.)

capillary endothelial interface into blood), and noninvasive pulse oximetry (for oxygen saturation measured at rest or during ambulation). More specialized tests include body plethysmography for determining total lung volumes and airway resistance, as well as cardiopulmonary exercise testing to assess cardiac function and oxygen uptake/consumption.

SPIROMETRY. Spirometry is used to document baseline lung function, to make a preliminary diagnostic assessment, or to monitor patients as lung or cardiac disease evolves and responds to treatment. Spirometry requires considerable physical effort and attentiveness to perform well. Patients, especially during hospitalization, after procedures, or if still deconditioned, often cannot give maximum effort or cooperate/coordinate well, and test results are not optimal. Too often, patients who are responding to therapy for an exacerbation of chronic obstructive pulmonary disease (COPD) or asthma but who are not yet back to preillness status are sent prematurely for lung function tests in an attempt to reestablish a baseline for future reference. Recent prior nebulizer or metered-dose inhaler treatment with a bronchodilator also may confuse results. Reproducibility of several test attempts (at least three) is important and is a criterion for valid test interpretation. Other medical problems that can confuse spirometric testing include pulmonary congestion, thyroid dysfunction, poor nutrition, and corticosteroid-associated muscle weakness.

Spirometry is recorded by having a seated subject breathe calmly several times at tidal volume, then draw a maximum inhalation followed by a forced exhalation that is continued for at least 6 seconds or more with sustained vigorous effort (forced vital capacity [FVC]) and completed by a vigorous full inspiration (inspiratory vital capacity). These maneuvers are represented as a volume-time loop or as a flow-volume loop (plotting flow against FVC and inspiratory vital capacity). Flow-volume loops are scrutinized for special patterns that can indicate various clinical or anatomic conditions (Fig. 82–3).

Among the most helpful spirometric values are FVC (liters), forced expiratory volume in the first second of exhalation (FEV_1) (liters), ratio of FEV_1 to FVC (percentage), and forced expiratory flow in the middle of expiration ($FEF_{25-75\%}$) (liters/sec). Residual volume (RV) (liters) cannot be determined by spirometry and often is measured by helium dilution or plethysmographic methods. RV is necessary to compute total lung capacity (TLC) (liters), which is a measure of the air capacity of the maximally inflated lung. FEV_1, although recorded as a volume, is equated with a measure of airflow and is effort dependent. Because FEV_1 represents the most effective portion of the breathing volume, it usually correlates well with the amount of physical activity a patient can sustain. For patients with significant airway obstruction, a slow expiratory vital capacity is obtained. Peak flow measured with portable devices is used often for outpatient monitoring of lung function in subjects with asthma, COPD, or interstitial lung diseases. Although a healthy young person can produce a peak flow of 500 to 600 L/min, many people with COPD are unable

to achieve a peak flow greater than 200 to 350 L/min and experience significant exertional dyspnea when peak flow decreases to less than 200 L/min. Patients whose peak flow is around 150 L/min are usually sedentary.

From analysis of measured values for FEV_1, FVC (and their ratio), and TLC, the main categories of ventilatory lung disease—obstructive or restrictive—can be defined (Fig. 82–4). A reduced FEV_1 and low FEV_1/FVC ratio combined with a large TLC indicate obstructive disease of large airways and bronchi, a pattern typically observed in patients with COPD and asthma. FVC is preserved, but the time of exhalation is prolonged. After bronchodilators, the FEV_1 and FVC may increase by 10 to 15%, especially in asthma, indicating reversibility of airway obstruction. A lesser degree of improvement often is

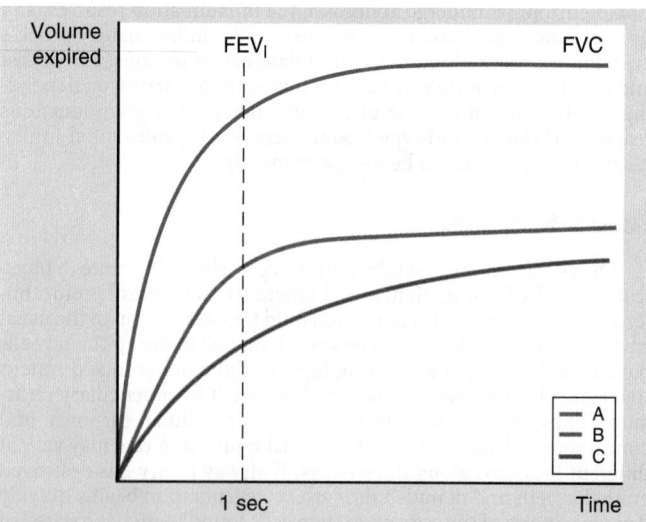

FIGURE 82–4 • Typical results of spirometry in a normal patient (A), a patient with a restrictive defect (B), and a patient with an obstructive defect (C). In a patient with a restrictive defect, the FEV_1/FVC ratio is preserved at the normal level, but both absolute values are reduced. In a patient with an obstructive defect, both absolute values are again reduced, but the FEV_1/FVC ratio is considerably reduced, as the forced expiratory time required to reach the FVC is greatly prolonged. (Redrawn from Forbes CD, Jackson WF: Color Atlas and Text of Clinical Medicine, 3rd ed. London, Mosby, 2003, with permission.)

Table 82–2 • BRONCHOALVEOLAR LAVAGE CELL AND FLUID FINDINGS

STATUS OR ILLNESS	CELLULAR PROFILE	NONCELLULAR COMPONENTS	OTHER ILLNESSES IN THE DIFFERENTIAL DIAGNOSIS WITH OVERLAPPING FINDINGS
Normal nonsmokers	Differential cell count (mean %): AM 85%, lymphocytes 7–12%, PMN 1–2%, Eos/Baso <1%, ciliated cells 1–5% Lymphocyte subsets: CD4 helper 50%, CD8 suppressor or cytotoxic 30%, CD4/CD8 ratio 1.5 B-lymphocytes (plasma) 5%	95% as IgA (40% as IgA2), almost no IgM, IgG (IgG1–3/albumin ratios similar to serum), increased IgG4; low concentrations of cytokines (IL-6, IL-8) Adhesion molecules detectable Histamine Surfactant	
Healthy moderate smokers	3-fold increase of total cells, 95% AM, 3–5 fold increased AM; PMN approximately 3%; lymphocytes 3% in differential cell count	Increased IgG as IgG/albumin ratio with serum, increased IgG3 and IgG4, decreased FSC, less surfactant recovered (lipid component profile same as nonsmoker); decreased A_1AT elastase inhibitory activity; may find increased ACE (in AM)	
DIFFUSE INTERSTITIAL LUNG DISEASES			
Sarcoidosis	Lymphocytes >20% total cells, increased CD4 cells, increased CD4/CD8 ratio, AM-lymphocytes (T-cell) form spontaneous rosettes	Increased IL-2, IL-6, IL-8; can have increased ACE level; increased adhesion molecule ICAM-1; increased fibronectin	Extrathoracic granulomatous diseases (e.g., Crohn's disease), primary biliary cirrhosis, extrinsic allergic alveolitis, idiopathic pulmonary fibrosis, collagen vascular disease
Extrinsic allergic alveolitis (hypersensitivity pneumonitis)	Increased lymphocytes to >40–60% of total cells, often increased CD8; foamy cytoplasm of AM; increased plasma cells, sometimes increased mast cells or Baso	Increased IgM and IgG, IgG fraction may have specific precipitating antibody activity against etiologic antigens (thermophilic microbes)	Drug-induced hypersensitivity
Idiopathic pulmonary fibrosis	Increased PMN, approximately 15–20% of cells Increased Eos, approximately 4–6% Increased lymphocytes, 20% in some cases	Increased IgG, increased monomeric IgA Increased IL-6, IL-8 Increased collagenase and histamine levels Increased fibronectin	Usually diagnosis of exclusion (occupational, environmental)
Langerhans' cell histiocytosis	Cell profile similar to smokers: Increased CD1+ cells (>4% AM), cytoplasmic x-body or Birbeck granule on EM		Most patients are smokers
Alveolar lipoproteinosis	Foamy cytoplasm of AM	Milky, turbid fluid with altered phospholipid proportions; increased surfactant protein A	Extrinsic allergic alveolitis, lipoid pneumonia, drug-induced hypersensitivity (e.g., amiodarone), silicosis
Eosinophilic pneumonia	Increased Eos % to 40% of cells		Churg-Strauss, allergic bronchopulmonary aspergillosis, drug-induced hypersensitivity
Alveolar hemorrhage (Goodpasture's, Wegener's)	Hemosiderin-laden AM		
Inhalation exposure (asbestosis, fiber, silica)	Asbestos bodies or fiber in AM		Subclinical exposure must be considered in asymptomatic subjects

A_1AT = α_1-antitrypsin protease; ACE = angiotensin-converting enzyme; AM = alveolar macrophages; Baso = basophils; CD4 = T-helper lymphocyte subset; CD8 = T-suppressor lymphocyte; EM = electron microscopy; Eos = eosinophils; FSC = free secretory component; ICAM-1 = intercellular adhesion molecule-1; PMN = polymorphonuclear neutrophils.

found, however, in patients who are already using inhaled bronchodilators regularly. A decrease in the $FEF_{25-75\%}$ typically is found in patients with obstruction of small airways. In patients with restrictive lung disease, the FEV_1 and FVC are reduced, as is TLC, but the FEV_1/FVC ratio is usually normal or increased. Causes of restrictive interstitial lung disease include fibrosis of the lung parenchyma caused by many toxic and inhalation exposures and toxic drug reactions (Chapters 89 and 90) and idiopathic interstitial lung diseases (Chapter 88). Restrictive physiology with a normal or low FEV_1 may reflect the chest wall habitus, chest wall muscle weakness or deformity, and pleural thickening (Chapters 83 and 89).

DIFFUSION CAPACITY (DL_{CO}). DL_{CO} measurement assesses how well gas in inspired air can cross the two tissue layers and one tissue space that make up the alveolar-capillary exchange surface (i.e., the alveolar type I epithelial cells, the interstitial space [not continuously present], and the vascular endothelial cells). The test measures the absorption of a low concentration of carbon monoxide in inhaled air by hemoglobin in red blood cells that circulate through pulmonary capillaries. Results must be corrected for reduced lung volumes, anemia, increased carbon monoxide levels in cigarette smokers, and high altitude. The DL_{CO} provides a general assessment of the air-blood interface; reduced values are obtained when interstitial fibrosis is extensive or when the capillary surface is compromised by vascular obstruction or nonperfusion (e.g., pulmonary embolism; Chapter 94) or destroyed as in emphysema (Chapter 85).

SITE-SPECIFIC SAMPLING, INCLUDING BRONCHOALVEOLAR LAVAGE

Pulmonary function tests measure the effectiveness of breathing and air exchange but not the health of the respiratory tract's structure or cells or the metabolic and immunologic activity of inflammatory cells that accumulate in airways. Noninvasive methods can assess in situ airway inflammation by measuring breath pH and endogenously produced markers of oxidative stress (i.e., reactive oxygen and nitrogen species) in exhaled air and breath condensate and by assaying mediators in sputum (e.g., IL-8, LTB$_4$, myeloperoxidase, IL-6, and elastase products). For example, as COPD worsens, sputum specimens show neutrophilic inflammation with higher concentrations of exhaled nitric oxide and more LTB$_4$.

Site-specific sampling to detach cells by washing or abrading the mucosal surface coupled with endobronchial or transbronchial biopsy can provide contiguous samples containing viable cells, noncellular secretions, and adjacent tissue. Multiple sites can be sampled; mucosal cell function can be compared between the nose and lower airways to assess allergic diseases. Bronchoalveolar lavage retrieves cells and secretions from the distal airways and the alveolar space surface. In combination with a thorough clinical evaluation and lung imaging studies, distinctive cellular patterns sometimes can obviate the need for lung biopsy (Table 82–2). Biopsy tissue and recovered cells can be prepared for microarray analysis, using gene chips created specifically for gene expression patterns that may prove helpful for diagnosis and to monitor clinical activity.

SUGGESTED READINGS

Davies DE, Wicks J, Powell RM, et al: Airway remodeling in asthma: New insights. J Allergy Clin Immunol 2003;111:215–225. *Current concepts of airway repair.*

Ho JC, Chan KN, Hu WH, et al: The effect of aging on nasal mucociliary clearance, beat frequency, and ultrastructure of respiratory cilia. Am J Respir Crit Care Med 2001;163:983–988. *These respiratory protective mechanisms decline with normal aging.*

Reynolds HY: Modulating airway defenses against microbes. Curr Opin Pulm Med 2002;8:154–165. *Review of host defenses in the nasopharynx, conducting airways, and alveoli.*

Silkoff PE, Martin D, Pak J, et al: Exhaled nitric oxide correlated with induced sputum findings in COPD. Chest 2001;119:1049–1055. *As pulmonary function worsens, the fractional concentration of exhaled nitric oxide increases.*

83 DISORDERS OF VENTILATORY CONTROL

Steven A. Shea
David P. White

Normal Ventilatory Control System

The human ventilatory control system (Fig. 83–1) determines the neural output to the respiratory muscles, thereby dictating the quantity and pattern of ventilation in an attempt to maintain arterial blood gas values within fairly tight constraints despite substantial alterations in metabolic rate (exercise), the work of breathing (underlying cardiopulmonary or chest wall disease), or disease of the respiratory muscles. Although the respiratory rhythm emerges primarily from neurons in the medulla and pons, these neurons receive afferent input from a number of sources that provide constant information about blood gases (e.g., arterial oxygen partial pressure [Pao$_2$], arterial carbon dioxide partial pressure [Paco$_2$]), lung/chest wall inflation, and respiratory muscle function. The principal sources of this afferent input include the carotid bodies (responsive to changes in Pao$_2$, Paco$_2$, and pH), the medullary chemoreceptor (Paco$_2$ and pH), muscle spindles and Golgi tendon organs (responsive to respiratory muscle activity and chest wall inflation), and receptors located in the airways and lungs (responsive to temperature, stretch, and pressure). During wakefulness, ventilation is also substantially influenced by behavioral activities such as speech, swallowing, and anxiety. The principal focus of this chapter is disorders of the chemoreceptor mechanisms (Pao$_2$, Paco$_2$), because these are more common and clinically important.

AWAKE

In awake resting individuals, Paco$_2$ is generally stable, varying by less than 2 to 4 mm Hg (slightly more in premenopausal adult women, because progesterone stimulates breathing during the luteal phase of the menstrual cycle). Ventilation increases briskly if Paco$_2$ is acutely elevated above this resting level but does not decline significantly if

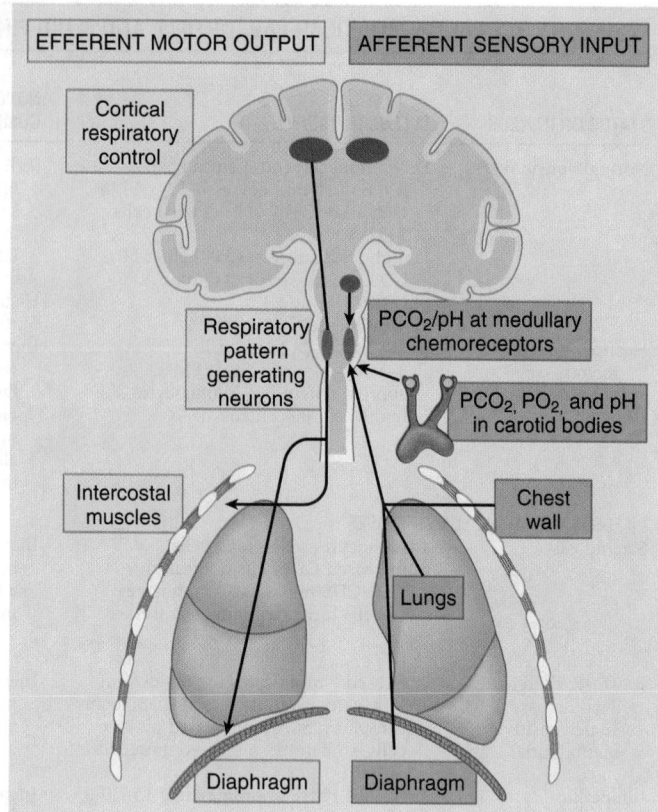

FIGURE 83–1 • A simplified diagram of the principal efferent (*left*) and afferent (*right*) respiratory control pathways. A section through the brain, brain stem, and spinal cord is shown (with pertinent respiratory areas indicated by shading), as are the central nervous system links with the respiratory apparatus.

Paco$_2$ decreases. This "dog-leg" appearance of the awake hypercapnic ventilatory response (Fig. 83–2) has led to the concept of a "wakefulness drive to breathe" that persists in the absence of chemoreceptive (Paco$_2$, Pao$_2$) stimulation of breathing. Similarly, decreases in Pao$_2$ from 500 mm Hg to approximately 65 mm Hg have a negligible effect on breathing; at less than 65 mm Hg, a hyperbolic relationship occurs between decreasing Pao$_2$ and increasing ventilation (yielding a roughly linear relationship between decreasing arterial oxyhemoglobin saturation and increasing ventilation). Within the normal physiologic

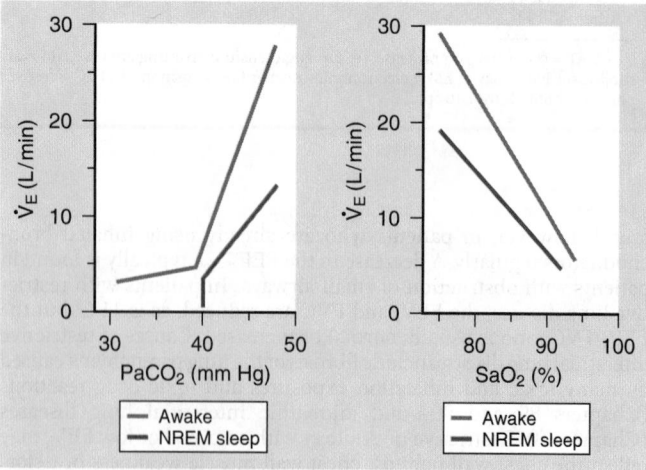

FIGURE 83–2 • Typical ventilatory responses to hypercapnia (*left*) and hypoxia (*right*). Compared with wakefulness, the ventilatory responses decline during non–rapid eye movement (NREM) sleep and decline even further during REM sleep (not shown). V̇E = expired minute ventilation.

range, the fairly weak chemical control system permits relatively unfettered behavioral control of breathing. However, if the $PaCO_2$ increases to greater than about 42 mm Hg or the PaO_2 decreases to less than about 65 mm Hg, then ventilation increases rapidly. Because of the shapes of the ventilatory response curves relative to those of normal blood gases, hypercapnia rather than hypoxia elicits the greater response to hypoventilation and thereby normalizes blood gases. Nonetheless, in clinical situations in which $PaCO_2$ and PaO_2 change simultaneously, hypoxia does accentuate the ventilatory response to hypercapnia in a synergistic fashion.

During mild exercise, ventilation normally increases in direct proportion to CO_2 production, such that $PaCO_2$ does not change. Surprisingly, the chemoreceptive feedback system seems unlikely to be responsible for such tight $PaCO_2$ control, in that no detectable change in $PaCO_2$ or PaO_2 is generally noted during mild exercise. Other proposed mechanisms that may contribute to hyperpnea during exercise include stimulation of breathing via afferents in the moving limbs, afferents from receptors detecting CO_2 flow to the lungs, mixed venous chemoreceptors, and conditioned responses. However, ventilatory control during exercise remains poorly understood.

ASLEEP

Numerous important changes occur in respiratory control on falling asleep. During non–rapid eye movement (NREM) sleep, both wakeful and behavioral influences on respiration are largely lost, leaving the chemoreceptive (primarily $PaCO_2$) metabolic system to control breathing. Despite its importance during sleep, the responsiveness to changes in $PaCO_2$ is altered in several ways. First, the entire ventilation-$PaCO_2$ curve is shifted to the right, such that higher $PaCO_2$ levels are required to stimulate breathing, allowing $PaCO_2$ to elevate during sleep. Second, if $PaCO_2$ goes below a certain level, ventilation is substantially inhibited, so that apnea commonly occurs at $PaCO_2$ values near the waking level (as may occur at altitude where hypoxia leads to hyperventilation and hypocapnia). Finally, the slope of the ventilatory response to $PaCO_2$ is also mildly reduced. In addition, during NREM sleep, the resistance to airflow through the upper airway commonly increases as a result of decreasing pharyngeal dilator muscle activity (Chapter 96). This increase is likely important because, unlike during wakefulness, the respiratory control system during sleep does not compensate well for increased resistive work. As a result, ventilation generally decreases in response to this increased upper airway resistance. During REM sleep, a further decrement is seen in ventilatory responsiveness to $PaCO_2$ but behavioral influences on breathing return. Breathing may become quite erratic during REM sleep. These changes in ventilatory control during sleep are important clinically. Because there is less robust ventilatory control during sleep, many disorders that ultimately lead to clinically important hypoventilation manifest themselves during sleep well before they can be detected during wakefulness.

Disorders of Ventilatory Control

RELATIONSHIP TO RESPIRATORY FAILURE

Ventilatory control disorders that cause respiratory failure are more commonly hypercapnic than hypoxic. First, the development of hypercapnic respiratory failure generally reflects an interaction between ventilatory control (often quantified by the slope of the hypoxic and hypercapnic ventilatory responses; Fig. 83–2) and the work of breathing (increments in work of breathing are usually a product of parenchymal lung disease or chest wall disease, including obesity). When chemoresponsiveness is markedly diminished or absent, hypercapnia may develop in an individual with a normal respiratory apparatus and normal work of breathing. Conversely, when the work of breathing is extraordinarily high (as might occur with severe chronic obstructive pulmonary disease [COPD]; Chapter 85), respiratory failure may develop despite normal or robust ventilatory control. Therefore, although low or diminished chemoresponsiveness may predispose an individual to hypercapnia, the work required to maintain ventilation often determines when hypercapnia actually occurs. Second, individual variability in chemoresponsiveness is substantial, with slopes varying seven-fold from one individual to another because of genetic differences, previous neurologic disease (e.g., encephalitis, meningitis), prolonged exposure to hypoxia and hypercapnia, and other poorly understood influences. Studies are beginning to

identify the numerous genes underlying this chemosensitivity and may eventually explain the differences in ventilatory chemosensitivity and disease vulnerability among individuals. Regardless of the cause, low chemoresponsiveness in combination with increased work of breathing contribute to the development of hypercapnic respiratory failure. Finally, the speed of development of respiratory failure (Chapter 99) is variable. Acute changes in blood gas values (over hours), such as occur with a respiratory infection, can generally be detected quickly by a patient (e.g., by sensing shortness of breath) and lead to effective early treatment. Conversely, with diminished ventilatory control, hypercapnia and hypoxia may develop slowly, with little sensation of dyspnea, making the early detection of respiratory failure difficult.

HYPOVENTILATION ASSOCIATED WITH "PURE" CONTROL OF BREATHING ABNORMALITIES (WITHOUT CARDIOPULMONARY DISEASE)

Hypoventilation can develop in an individual with quite normal lungs and respiratory muscle function but with a markedly diminished ability to respond to hypoxia or hypercapnia. The most common such disorder in adults is acquired central alveolar hypoventilation, which is defined by markedly diminished ventilatory chemoresponsiveness, normal respiratory apparatus (normal pulmonary function), and an absence of obesity or chest wall disease. Due to their decreased chemoresponsiveness, these patients have arterial blood gas values that are quite labile when awake and that worsen substantially with sleep. Ventilation also may deteriorate during respiratory infections, even if the work of breathing increases only minimally. Therefore, most of these individuals are chronically hypoxic and hypercapnic, often with cor pulmonale. Despite these severe blood gas abnormalities, patients rarely complain of dyspnea or respiratory discomfort and can often correct the hypercapnia with voluntary hyperventilation. Some patients with acquired central hypoventilation have previously documented neurologic disease as the explanation for their diminished chemoresponsiveness.

HYPOVENTILATION WITH INCREASED WORK OF BREATHING

Hypercapnia may also develop in patients with increased work of breathing in whom chemoresponsiveness may be diminished but is not necessarily absent; the most common example is COPD (Chapter 85). As airflow obstruction worsens (increasing work of breathing), the incidence of respiratory failure increases, although the relationship between pulmonary function and increasing $PaCO_2$ is certainly not linear. Such patients are sometimes classified as either "pink puffers" (high chemoresponsiveness and a general maintenance of blood gas homeostasis) or "blue bloaters" (low chemoresponsiveness and frequent respiratory failure), implying an important role for individual variability in chemosensitivity. However, overlap between groups is considerable, and hypercapnia in COPD has a multifactorial etiology.

The obesity hypoventilation ("Pickwickian") syndrome is characterized by morbid obesity, diminished to absent ventilatory chemoresponsiveness during wakefulness, hypoxia and hypercapnia during wakefulness, absence (generally) of parenchymal lung disease, and severe obstructive sleep apnea (Chapter 96). Although the diminished responsiveness to hypoxia and hypercapnia almost certainly contributes to the blood gas abnormalities when the patient is awake and asleep, the cause of this abnormal ventilatory control is controversial. Some argue that genetically diminished chemoresponsiveness leads to the entire syndrome, whereas others contend that the obstructive apnea desensitizes the chemoreceptors and ultimately culminates in waking hypercapnia.

HYPOVENTILATION WITH NEUROMUSCULAR DISEASE

Hypoventilation is also commonly observed in patients with neuromuscular weakness (e.g., motor neuron disease, muscular dystrophy, myasthenia gravis, poliomyelitis, Guillain-Barré syndrome, and quadriplegia). In these patients, the neural output from the brain stem respiratory center cannot always fully compensate for the defects in neuromuscular function, particularly during REM sleep, when chemoreceptor responsiveness is substantially reduced and a general loss of accessory respiratory muscle activity occurs (skeletal hypotonia characterizes this stage of sleep). Therefore, REM sleep becomes a potentially vulnerable time for patients with diaphragmatic

Table 83-1 • APPROACHES TO THERAPY OF THE MOST COMMON DISORDERS OF VENTILATORY CONTROL

DIAGNOSIS	APPROACH	SPECIFIC THERAPY	TIME UNTIL RESPONSE
COPD "blue bloaters"	Reduce work of breathing	Bronchodilators	Hours to days
		Nocturnal ventilation	Days to weeks
	Improve oxygenation	O₂ supplementation	Immediate
	Ventilatory stimulants*	Rarely used	
Central alveolar hypoventilation	Improve oxygenation	O₂ supplementation	Immediate
	Nocturnal ventilation	Nasal ventilator	Days to weeks
		Diaphragmatic pacers	Days to weeks
	Ventilatory stimulants*	Progesterone (20 mg tid)	~1 wk
		Acetazolamide (250 mg qid: 500 mg bid)	~1 wk
Obesity hypoventilation	Reduce work of breathing	Weight loss	Months
		Nasal CPAP	Days to weeks
		Nocturnal ventilation	Days to weeks
	Improve oxygenation	O₂ supplementation	Immediate
	Ventilatory stimulants*	Progesterone (20 mg tid)	~1 wk
		Acetazolamide (250 mg qid; 500 mg bid)	~1 wk

*Ventilatory stimulants, although used occasionally in the disorders listed, are generally of limited efficacy, particularly when compared to nocturnal ventilation. COPD = Chronic obstructive pulmonary disease; tid = three times a day; qid = four times a day; bid = two times a day.

dysfunction. Other rare neurologic disorders that influence ventilatory control include *Ondine's curse* (patients lack the ability to breathe automatically but are able to breathe voluntarily) and the *locked-in syndrome* (patients lack the ability to breathe voluntarily but are able to breathe automatically).

 Treatment (Table 83-1)

Treatments for ventilatory control disorders include (1) reducing the work of breathing (e.g., with bronchodilators or weight loss), (2) using ventilatory stimulants, such as acetazolamide or progesterone, (3) providing supplemental oxygen, and (4) using assisted ventilation. There is no "Grade A" evidence from randomized controlled trials addressing any of these therapeutic approaches. Nonetheless, reducing the work of breathing is always advisable (although not always possible). Ventilatory stimulants are often of only limited effectiveness, particularly in patients with central neural defects. Supplemental oxygen may improve oxygenation but rarely corrects hypercapnia; in some situations, oxygen may actually worsen hypercapnia. Assisted ventilation is most often the treatment of choice, particularly for patients with central neural defects and neuromuscular disease. Positive-pressure assisted ventilation is usually applied noninvasively via a nose mask, but it may be administered via tracheotomy, depending on the clinical situation. Currently, positive-pressure ventilation is predominantly administered during sleep, so the patient can have a more normal waking existence; however, improved nocturnal ventilation also often leads to diminished daytime hypercapnia, which suggests a role for nocturnal hypoventilation in the development of waking hypercapnia.

SUGGESTED READINGS

Carroll JL: Developmental plasticity in respiratory control. J Appl Physiol 2003;94:375–389. *Early-life experiences and genes influence ventilatory responses in adults.*

Spengler CM, Gozal D, Shea SA: Chemoreceptive mechanisms elucidated by functional and pathological studies of Congenital Central Hypoventilation Syndrome. Respir Physiol 2001;129:247–255. *A review of genetic influences and congenital defects in chemoreceptive control of breathing.*

 **ASTHMA**

Jeffrey M. Drazen

Definition

Asthma is a clinical syndrome of unknown etiology characterized by three distinct components: (1) recurrent episodes of airway obstruction that resolve spontaneously or as a result of treatment; (2) an exaggerated bronchoconstrictor response to stimuli that have little or no effect in nonasthmatic subjects, a phenomenon known as *airway hyperresponsiveness;* and (3) inflammation of the airways as defined by a variety of criteria. Although reversible, it is currently thought that, in some settings, changes in the asthmatic airway may be irreversible.

Epidemiology and Statistics

Asthma is an extremely common disorder affecting boys more commonly than girls and after puberty, women slightly more commonly than men; approximately 7% of the adult population of the United States has signs and symptoms consistent with a diagnosis of asthma. Although most cases begin before the age of 25 years, asthma may develop at any time throughout life.

The worldwide prevalence of asthma has increased more than 40% since the late 1970s. The greatest increases in asthma prevalence have occurred in countries that have recently adopted an "industrialized" lifestyle. The reasons for the overall increase in asthma prevalence are not known but are thought to relate to the lack of exposure, during early childhood, to infectious agents, tending to skew the immune system toward a T_H1 phenotype (Chapter 41).

Asthma is among the most common reasons to seek medical treatment; in the United States, asthma is responsible for about 15 million annual outpatient visits to physicians and for nearly 2 million annual inpatient hospital days of treatment. The yearly direct and indirect costs of asthma care are more than $8 billion dollars, with more than 80% of these costs attributable to direct expenditures on medical care encounters or asthma medications.

Pathology and Pathogenesis

GENETICS OF ASTHMA

In twin studies, asthma has about 60% heritability, indicating that both genetic and environmental factors are important in its etiology. Worldwide, more than half a dozen family-based linkage studies have been carried out in asthma. Through linkage analysis and case-control association studies, two "asthma genes," *ADAM 33* on Human Cr 20 and *PhF11* on Human Cr 13, have been identified. Since asthma is a complex disease, many genes, each accounting for a portion of the phenotypic variability, are likely to be identified.

PATHOLOGY OF ASTHMA

The pathology of mild asthma, as delineated by bronchoscopic and biopsy studies, is characterized by edema and hyperemia of the mucosa and by infiltration of the mucosa with lymphocytes bearing the T_H2 phenotype, mast cells, and eosinophils. These cells produce interleukin (IL)-3, IL-4, and IL-5, and thereby create a microenvironment that promotes the synthesis of immunoglobulin E (IgE), an important allergic effector molecule. Chemokines, such as eotaxin, RANTES, MIP1a, and IL-8, produced by epithelial and inflammatory cells, and the loss of the T-cell signaling molecule T-bet, serve to amplify and perpetuate the inflammatory events within the airway. As a result of these inflammatory stimuli coupled with the mechanical deformation of the epithelium from airway smooth muscle constriction, the airway wall is thickened by the deposition of type III and type V collagen below the true basement membrane. In addition, in severe chronic asthma there is hypertrophy and hyperplasia of airway glands and secretory cells, as well as hyperplasia of airway smooth muscle. Morphometric studies of airways from asthmatic subjects have demonstrated airway wall thickening of sufficient magnitude to increase airflow resistance and enhance airway responsiveness. During a severe asthmatic event, the airway wall is thickened markedly; in addition, patchy airway occlusion occurs by a mixture of hyperviscous mucus and clusters of shed airway epithelial cells.

The episodic airway narrowing that constitutes an asthma attack results from obstruction of the airway lumen to airflow. Although it is now well established that asthma is associated with infiltration of the airway by inflammatory cells, the links between these cells and the pathobiologic processes that account for asthmatic airway obstruction have not been clearly delineated. Three possible, but not mutually exclusive, links have been postulated: (1) constriction of airway smooth muscle, (2) thickening of the airway epithelium, and (3) the presence of liquids within the confines of the airway lumen. Among these mechanisms, the constriction of airway smooth muscle due to the local release of bioactive mediators or neurotransmitters is the most widely accepted explanation for the acute reversible airway obstruction in asthma attacks. Several bronchoactive mediators are thought to be the agents causing airway obstruction in the asthmatic patient.

MEDIATORS OF THE ACUTE ASTHMATIC RESPONSE

ACETYLCHOLINE. Acetylcholine released from intrapulmonary motor nerves causes constriction of airway smooth muscle through direct stimulation of muscarinic receptors of the M_3 subtype. The potential role for acetylcholine in the bronchoconstriction of asthma primarily derives from the observation that atropine and its congeners have some bronchodilator action, albeit less than β-agonists, when administered by inhalation for the treatment of asthma.

HISTAMINE. Histamine, or β-imidazolylethylamine, was identified as a potent endogenous bronchoactive agent nearly 100 years ago. Mast cells, which are prominent in airway tissues obtained from patients with asthma, constitute the major pulmonary source of histamine. Clinical trials with novel potent antihistamines indicate a minor role for histamine as a mediator of airway obstruction in asthma.

KININS. Bradykinin and related molecules are cleaved from plasma precursors by the actions of enzymes known as *kallikreins;* at least one type of kallikrein is released from activated mast cells. Bradykinin is a potent bronchoconstrictor mediator when administered exogenously. It is also unique among asthmatic mediators in that the sensation of dyspnea evoked by exogenous administration of bradykinin has been shown to mimic the subjective sensations reported by patients during spontaneously occurring asthmatic episodes.

LEUKOTRIENES AND LIPOXINS. The cysteinyl leukotrienes—namely LTC_4, LTD_4, and LTE_4, as well as the dihydroxy leukotriene, LTB_4—are derived by the lipoxygenation of arachidonic acid released from target cell membrane phospholipids during cellular activation. 5-Lipoxygenase, the 5-lipoxygenase-activating protein, and LTC_4 synthase make up the cellular protein/enzyme content needed to produce the cysteinyl leukotrienes. The production of LTB_4 requires 5-lipoxygenase, the 5-lipoxygenase-activating protein, and LTA_4 epoxide hydrolase. Mast cells, eosinophils, and alveolar macrophages have the enzymatic capability to produce cysteinyl leukotrienes from their membrane phospholipids, whereas polymorphonuclear leukocytes produce exclusively LTB_4, which is predominantly a chemoattractant molecule; LTC_4 and LTD_4 are potent contractile agonists on airway smooth muscle. Clinical trials with leukotriene receptor antagonists or synthesis inhibitors have shown significant clinical efficacy in the treatment of chronic persistent asthma, leading to the conclusion that the leukotrienes are important, but not exclusive, mediators of the asthmatic response. Lipoxins are double lipoxygenase products of arachidonic acid metabolism and are thought to be endogenous downregulators of the inflammatory response. Their role in human asthma remains inferential.

NEUROPEPTIDES. Neuropeptides are small peptides found in pulmonary nerves. Two peptides, substance P and neurokinin A (substance K), are found in the terminal axon dendrites of certain sensory nerves. When these nerves are stimulated by appropriate sensory stimuli, their peptides are released into the airway microenvironment. The released peptides transduce signals through binding at NK_1 and NK_2 receptors, thereby causing constriction of airway smooth muscle and bronchovascular leak. Although these molecules have the potential to mediate asthmatic airway narrowing, specific antagonists of their action have not shown therapeutic efficacy in asthma.

NITRIC OXIDE. Nitric oxide (NO·) is produced enzymatically by airway epithelial cells and by inflammatory cells found in the asthmatic lung. Free NO· has a half-life on the order of seconds in the airway and is stabilized by conjugation to thiols to form RS-NO. Both NO· and RS-NO have bronchodilator actions and may play a homeostatic role in the airway. Paradoxically, high levels of NO·, when co-available with superoxide anion, may form toxic oxidation products, such as peroxynitrite (OONO⁻), which could damage the airway. Patients with asthma have higher than normal levels of NO· in their expired air, and these levels decrease after treatment with corticosteroids. Thus, the primary role of NO· in asthma may be as a proinflammatory molecule, and levels of exhaled NO· are a marker of asthma.

PLATELET-ACTIVATING FACTOR. Platelet-activating factor (PAF), a phospholipid with an ether-linked fatty acid (C_{16}-C_{20}) in the *sn-1* position, an acetyl moiety in the *sn-2* position, and phosphatidylcholine in the *sn-3* position, is derived from lyso-PAF by the action of specific acetyltransferases and is produced by a variety of inflammatory cells, including mast cells and eosinophils. PAF transduces its effects through action at a well-characterized receptor and has a potential role in asthma as an inducer of airway hyperresponsiveness and inflammation. In Japan, a disproportionate number of asthmatics with severe, as compared with mild, asthma are known to harbor a functionally important mutation in the gene encoding the enzyme that degrades PAF. Because individuals with the dysfunctional gene probably have higher levels of PAF in the airway microenvironment and have more severe asthma, it has been inferred that the presence of PAF contributes to the severity of asthma.

PHYSIOLOGIC CHANGES IN ASTHMA

An increased resistance to airflow is the consequence of the airway obstruction induced by smooth muscle constriction, thickening of the airway epithelium, or free liquid within the airway lumen. Resistance to airflow is manifested by increased airway resistance (Raw) and decreased flow rates throughout the vital capacity. At the onset of an asthma attack, obstruction occurs at all airway levels; as the attack resolves, these changes reverse—first in the large airways (i.e., mainstem, lobar, segmental, and subsegmental bronchi) and then in the more peripheral airways. This anatomic sequence of onset and reversal is reflected in the physiologic changes observed during resolution of an asthmatic episode (Fig. 84–1). Specifically, as an asthma attack resolves, flow rates first normalize at a high point in the vital capacity, and only later at a low point in the vital capacity. Because asthma is an airway disease, no primary changes occur in the static pressure-volume curve of the lungs. However, during an acute attack of asthma, airway narrowing may be so severe as to result in airway closure, with individual lung units closing at a volume that is near their maximal volume. This closure results in a change of the pressure-volume curve such that, for a given contained gas volume within the thorax, elastic recoil is decreased, which in turn further depresses expiratory flow rates.

Additional factors influence the mechanical behavior of the lungs during an acute attack of asthma. During inspiration in an asthma attack, the pleural pressure becomes more negative than the 4 to 6 cm H_2O subatmospheric pressure usually required for tidal airflow. The expiratory phase of respiration also becomes active as the patient tries to force air from the lungs. As a consequence, peak pleural pressures during expiration, which normally are, at most, only a few centimeters of water above atmospheric pressure, may be as high as 20 to 30 cm H_2O above atmospheric pressure. The low pleural pressures during inspiration tend to dilate airways, whereas the high pleural pressures during expiration tend to narrow airways. During an asthma attack, the wide pressure swings coupled with alterations in the mechanical properties of the airway wall lead to a much higher resistance to expiratory airflow than to inspiratory airflow.

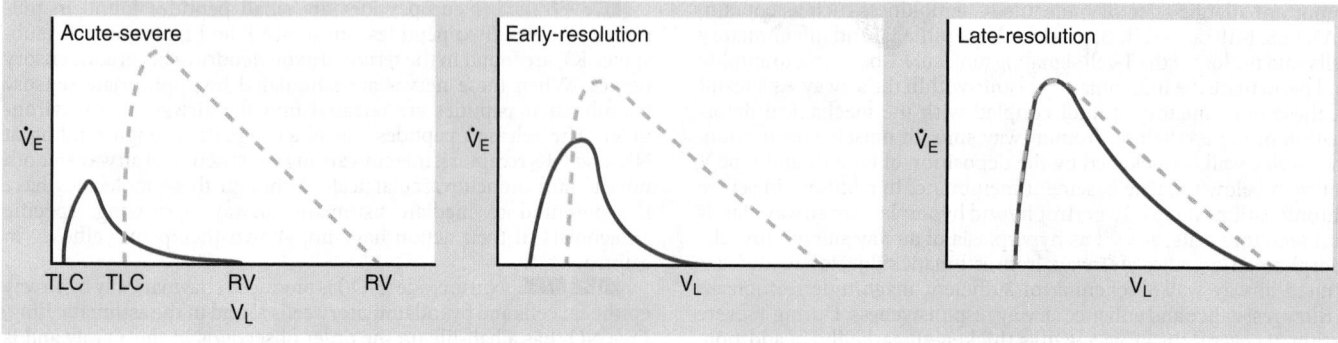

FIGURE 84–1 • Schematic flow-volume curves in various stages of asthma; in each figure the dashed line depicts the normal flow-volume curve. Predicted and observed total lung capacity (TLC) and residual volume (RV) are shown at the extremes of each curve. $\dot{V}_E$ = expiratory flow rate; V_L = lung volume.

Table 84–1 • **COMMON OCCUPATIONAL CAUSES OF ASTHMA**

HIGH-MOLECULAR-WEIGHT COMPOUNDS*			LOW-MOLECULAR-WEIGHT COMPOUNDS†		
Agent	**Occupation**	**Prevalence‡**	**Agent**	**Occupation**	**Prevalence‡**
ANIMALS			METALS		
Laboratory animals (rats, mice, rabbits, guinea pigs)	Laboratory workers, veterinarians	Moderate	Platinum	Platinum refining	High
			Vanadium	Hard metal industry	High
Chicken	Poultry workers		OTHER		
Crab	Crab processing	Moderate	Trimetallic anhydride	Epoxy resin, plastics	High
Prawns	Prawn processing	High	Toluene diisocyanate	Polyurethane industries, varnishing, plastics	Moderate
Hoya	Oyster farmers	High			
River fly	Contact with riverside power plants	Low	Western red cedar	Carpenters, cabinet makers, sawmill workers	Low-moderate
Screw worm fly	Flight crews	High	Azidocarbonamide	Plastic and rubber workers	Moderate
Bee moth	Fish bait breeders	Moderate	Formalin	Hospital workers	
			Urea formaldehyde	Insulation workers, affected homeowners	
PLANTS/VEGETABLES					
Grain dust	Grain handlers				
Wheat/rye flour	Bakers, millers				
Gum acacia	Printers	High			
BIOLOGIC ENZYMES					
Bacillus subtilis	Detergent industry	High			
Trypsin	Plastics, pharmaceutical	High			
Papain	Packing	High			

*High-molecular-weight compounds are usually considered to induce occupational asthma via an allergic mechanism.
†Asthma induced by low-molecular-weight compounds that act as haptens; other mechanisms also exist but are not clearly elucidated.
‡Prevalence is indicated by low (i.e., <3% of exposed individuals); moderate (i.e., 3 to 20% of exposed individuals); or high (i.e., >20% of exposed individuals).
Adapted from Chan-Yeung M: Occupational asthma. Chest 1990;98:148S–161S.

The respiratory rate is usually rapid during an acute asthmatic attack. This tachypnea is driven not by abnormalities in arterial blood gas composition, but rather by stimulation of intrapulmonary receptors with subsequent effects on central respiratory centers. One consequence of the combination of airway narrowing and rapid airflow rates is a heightened mechanical load on the ventilatory pump. During a severe attack, the load can increase the work of breathing by a factor of 10 or more and can predispose to fatigue of the ventilatory muscles.

The patchy nature of asthmatic airway narrowing results in a maldistribution of ventilation (V) relative to pulmonary perfusion (Q). A shift occurs from the normal preponderance of V/Q units, with a ratio of near unity, to a distribution with a large number of alveolar-capillary units, with a V/Q ratio of less than unity. The net effect is to induce arterial hypoxemia. In addition, the hyperpnea of asthma is reflected as hyperventilation with a low arterial P_{CO_2}.

Clinical Presentation

HISTORY

During an acute asthma attack, patients seek medical attention for shortness of breath accompanied by cough, wheezing, and anxiety. The degree of breathlessness experienced by the patient is not closely related to the degree of airflow obstruction but is often influenced by the acuteness of the attack. Dyspnea may occur only with exercise (exercise-induced asthma), after aspirin ingestion (aspirin-induced asthma), after exposure to a specific known allergen (extrinsic asthma), or for no identifiable reason (intrinsic asthma). Variants of asthma exist in which cough, hoarseness, or an inability to sleep through the night is the only symptom. Identification of a provoking stimulus through careful questioning helps to establish the diagnosis of asthma and may be therapeutically useful if the

stimulus can be avoided. Most patients with asthma complain of shortness of breath when exposed to rapid changes in the temperature and humidity of inspired air. For example, during the winter months in less temperate climates, patients commonly become short of breath when leaving a heated house; in warm humid climates, patients may complain of shortness of breath when entering a cold dry room, such as an air-conditioned theater. An important factor to consider when taking a history from a patient with asthma is the potential for occupational exposures leading to the asthmatic diathesis (Table 84–1). In such cases, preexisting asthma may be exacerbated or asthma may occur de novo after workplace exposure; it is this clue that eventually leads to the diagnosis of *occupational asthma*. However, one cannot depend on a reversal of asthmatic symptoms when the patient is removed from the offending environment.

PHYSICAL EXAMINATION

VITAL SIGNS. Common features noted during an acute attack of asthma include a rapid respiratory rate (often 25 to 40 breaths per minute), tachycardia, and pulsus paradoxus (an exaggerated inspiratory decrease in the systolic pressure). The magnitude of the pulsus is related to the severity of the attack. Pulse oximetry, with the patient respiring ambient air, commonly reveals an oxygen saturation near 90%.

THORACIC EXAMINATION. Inspection may reveal that patients experiencing acute attacks of asthma are using their accessory muscles of ventilation; if so, the skin over the thorax may be retracted into the intercostal spaces during inspiration. The chest is usually hyper-inflated, and the expiratory phase is prolonged relative to the inspiratory phase. Percussion of the thorax demonstrates hyper-resonance, with loss of the normal variation in dullness due to diaphragmatic movement. Auscultation reveals wheezing, which is the cardinal physical finding in asthma but does not establish the diagnosis (Table 84–2). Wheezing, commonly louder during expiration but heard during inspiration as well, is characterized as polyphonic in that more than one pitch may be heard simultaneously. Accompanying adventitious sounds may include rhonchi, which are suggestive of free secretions in the airway lumen, or rales, which are indicative of localized infection or heart failure. The loss of intensity or the absence of breath sounds in a patient with asthma is an indication of severe airflow obstruction.

Diagnosis

LABORATORY FINDINGS

PULMONARY FUNCTION FINDINGS. A decrease in airflow rates throughout the vital capacity is the cardinal pulmonary function abnormality during an asthmatic episode. The peak expiratory flow rate (PEFR), the forced expiratory volume in the first second (FEV_1), and the maximal midexpiratory flow rate (MMEFR) are all decreased in asthma. In severe asthma, dyspnea may be so severe as to prevent the patient from performing a complete spirogram. In this case, if 2 seconds of forced expiration can be recorded, useful values for PEFR and FEV_1 can be obtained. It cannot be overemphasized that gradation of attack severity (Table 84–3) *must* be assessed by objective measures of airflow; no other methods yield accurate and reproducible results. As the attack resolves, the PEFR and the FEV_1 increase toward normal in concert while the MMEFR remains substantially depressed; as the attack resolves further, the FEV_1 and the PEFR may normalize while the MMEFR remains depressed (see Table 84–3). Even when the attack has resolved clinically, residual depression of the MMEFR is not uncommon; this depression may resolve over a prolonged course of treatment. If the patient is able to cooperate such that more complete measurements of lung function can be made, lung volume measurements demonstrate an increase in both total lung capacity (TLC) and residual volume (RV); the changes in TLC and RV resolve with treatment.

ARTERIAL BLOOD GASES. Blood gas analysis need not be undertaken in individuals with mild asthma. If the asthma is of sufficient severity to merit prolonged observation, however, blood gas analysis is indicated; in such cases, hypoxemia and hypocarbia are the rule. With the subject breathing room air, the PaO_2 is usually between 55 and 70 mm Hg and the $PaCO_2$ between 25 and 35 mm Hg. At the onset of the attack, an appropriate pure respiratory alkalemia is usually evident; with attacks of prolonged duration, the pH normalizes as a result of a compensatory metabolic acidemia. A normal $PaCO_2$ in a patient with moderate to severe airflow obstruction is reason for concern, because it may indicate that the mechanical load on the respiratory system is greater than can be sustained by the ventilatory muscles and that respiratory failure is imminent. When the $PaCO_2$ increases in such settings, the pH decreases quickly, because the bicarbonate stores have become depleted as a result of renal compensation for the prolonged preceding respiratory alkalemia. Because this chain of events can take place rapidly, close observation is indicated for asthmatic patients with "normal" $PaCO_2$ levels and moderate to severe airflow obstruction.

OTHER BLOOD FINDINGS. Asthmatic subjects are frequently atopic; thus, blood eosinophilia is common. In addition, elevated serum levels of IgE are often documented; epidemiologic studies indicate that asthma is unusual in subjects with low IgE levels. If indicated by the patient's history, specific radioallergosorbent tests (RASTs), which measure IgE directed against specific offending antigens, can be conducted. In rare instances during severe asthma attacks, serum concentrations of aminotransferases, lactate dehydrogenase, muscle creatine kinase, ornithine transcarbamylase, and antidiuretic hormone may be elevated.

RADIOGRAPHIC FINDINGS. The chest radiograph of a subject with asthma is often normal. Severe asthma is associated with hyperinflation, as indicated by depression of the diaphragm and abnormally lucent lung fields. Complications of severe asthma, including pneumomediastinum or pneumothorax, may be detected radiographically. In mild to moderate asthma without adventitious sounds other than wheezing, a chest radiograph need not be obtained; if the asthma is of sufficient severity to merit hospital admission, a chest radiograph is advised.

ELECTROCARDIOGRAPHIC FINDINGS. The electrocardiogram, except for sinus tachycardia, is usually normal in acute asthma. However, right axis deviation, right bundle branch block, "P pulmonale," or even ST-T wave abnormalities may arise during severe asthma and resolve as the attack resolves.

SPUTUM FINDINGS. The sputum of the asthmatic patient may be either clear or opaque with a green or yellow tinge. The presence of color does not invariably indicate infection, and examination of a Gram-stained and Wright-stained sputum smear is indicated. Often the sputum contains eosinophils, Charcot-Leyden crystals (crystallized eosinophil lysophospholipase), Curschmann's spirals (bronchiolar casts composed of mucus and cells), or Creola bodies

---

Table 84–2 • DIFFERENTIAL DIAGNOSIS OF WHEEZING OTHER THAN ASTHMA

COMMON
Acute bronchiolitis (infectious, chemical)
Aspiration (foreign body)
Bronchial stenosis
Cardiac failure
Chronic bronchitis
Cystic fibrosis
Eosinophilic pneumonia

UNCOMMON
Airway obstruction due to masses
  External compression
    Central thoracic tumors, superior vena cava syndrome, substernal thyroid
  Intrinsic airway
    Primary lung cancer, metastatic breast cancer
Carcinoid syndrome
Endobronchial sarcoid
Pulmonary emboli
Systemic mastocytosis
Systemic vasculitis (polyarteritis nodosa; Churg-Strauss syndrome)

Table 84–3 • RELATIVE SEVERITY OF AN ASTHMATIC ATTACK AS INDICATED BY PEFR, FEV_1, AND MMEFR

TEST	% OF PREDICTED VALUE	ASTHMA SEVERITY
PEFR	>80%	
FEV_1	>80%	No spirometric abnormalities
MMEFR	>80%	
PEFR	>80%	
FEV_1	>70%	Mild asthma
MMEFR	55–75%	
PEFR	>60%	
FEV_1	45–70%	Moderate asthma
MMEFR	30–50%	
PEFR	<50%	
FEV_1	<50%	Severe asthma
MMEFR	10–30%	

FEV_1 = forced expiratory volume in the first second; MMEFR = maximal midexpiratory flow rate; PEFR = peak expiratory flow rate.

(clusters of airway epithelial cells with identifiable cilia), which can affect color without the presence of infection.

DIFFERENTIAL DIAGNOSIS

Asthma is easy to recognize in a young patient without comorbid medical conditions who has exacerbating and remitting airway obstruction accompanied by blood eosinophilia. A rapid response to bronchodilator treatment is usually all that is needed to establish the diagnosis. However, in the patient with cryptic episodic shortness of breath, airway challenge testing by a laboratory familiar with this procedure is indicated. Challenge testing, performed during minimal airway obstruction, determines the presence and magnitude of airway hyperresponsiveness. In such tests, subjects are exposed to increasing amounts of inhaled bronchoconstrictor agonists or breathe graded levels of cold dry air. Subjects with asthma usually require smaller amounts of a stimulus to reach a given end point in airway response than do nonasthmatic subjects. Airway hyperresponsiveness strongly suggests asthma, whereas its absence does not exclude asthma as a possibility. However, in the absence of airway hyperresponsiveness, other causes of wheezing (see Table 84–2) should be investigated.

Rx Prevention and Treatment

There is currently no way to prevent a patient from developing an asthmatic diathesis. Once a patient has such a diathesis, if there is an allergic component, avoidance of allergens can reduce the frequency of asthma attacks.

The treatment of asthma is directed at airway obstruction and inflammation; resolution of obstruction should be documented by objective measures such as FEV_1 or PEFR. Inexpensive and easy-to-use peak flowmeters make the latter measurement feasible in virtually all cases. Asthma treatment has two components. The first is the use of acute reliever (rescue) agents (i.e., bronchodilators) for acute asthmatic airway obstruction. The second is the use of controller treatments, which modify the asthmatic airway environment such that acute airway narrowing, requiring rescue treatments, occurs much less frequently.

In a given individual, the intensity of asthma treatment depends on the severity of disease (Table 84–4). It is now well established that asthma is a chronic disease that should, in all but its mildest forms, be treated long term. The scheme outlined herein is based on, but is not a precise copy of, the U.S. National Asthma Education and Prevention Program Guidelines for Asthma Treatment.

CLASSIFICATION OF ASTHMA SEVERITY

Asthma is classified by the severity of its presentation into one of four categories. *Mild intermittent asthma* is the term used to describe the condition in the largest group of patients with asthma. Patients in this diagnostic classification have normal or near normal lung function, infrequent asthma symptoms, usually sleep through the night without difficulty, and need to use asthma rescue medications infrequently. The only treatment needed for such patients is an inhaled medium-acting bronchodilator. Indeed, if a patient is able to maintain a normal functional status and airway function using no more than eight 200-actuation metered-dose inhalers a year, no further long-term treatment is required. Patients with *mild persistent asthma* have normal or near normal lung function on most occasions but have asthma symptoms daily, have difficulty sleeping one or two nights a week, and use their asthma rescue medications so frequently that a single 200-actuation canister is inadequate to provide 6 to 7 weeks' treatment. Such patients require a controller agent, such as an inhaled corticosteroid, an antileukotriene agent, or cromolyn sodium, in addition to their rescue treatment. Despite therapy with a single controller agent, patients with *moderate or severe persistent asthma* have chronically abnormal lung function, have asthma symptoms more than once daily, and have difficulty sleeping many nights a week. These patients require multiple asthma medications to achieve adequate disease control, and their care is best directed by an asthma care specialist.

RELIEVER TREATMENTS

β-ADRENERGIC AGENTS. β-Adrenergic agents given by inhalation are the mainstay of bronchodilator treatment for asthma. Constricted airway smooth muscle relaxes in response to stimulation of β_2-adrenergic receptors. β-Adrenergic agonists with varying degrees of β_2-selectivity are available for use in inhaled (by nebulizer or metered-dose inhaler; Fig. 84–2), oral, or parenteral preparations. Patients with mild intermittent asthma should be treated with a moderate-duration β_2-selective inhaler on an as-needed basis. This treatment should consist of two "puffs" from the inhaler, with the first and second puffs separated by a 3- to 5-minute interval, which is thought to allow enough time for the first "puff" to dilate narrowed airways, thus giving the agent better access to affected areas of the lung. Patients should be instructed to exhale to a comfortable volume, to breathe in very slowly (such as they would when sipping hot soup), and to actuate the inhaler as they inspire. Inspiration to near TLC is followed by holding the breath for 5 seconds to allow the deposition of smaller aerosol particles in more peripheral airways. Patients should receive specific instructions for correct inhaler use. Aerosol "spacers" (Fig.

Table 84–4 • MANAGEMENT OF AMBULATORY ASTHMA

	DETERMINE SEVERITY		
	Mild Intermittent	**Mild Persistent**	**Moderate-Severe Persistent**
Asthma symptoms*	<2× per week	>2× but <5× per week	>5× per week
Nocturnal awakening	<2× per month	>2× but <6× per month	>6× per month
Peak flow variability[†]	<20%	>20%	>20%
FEV_1	Normal for age, sex, and height	≥70% of predicted	<70% of predicted

MILD INTERMITTENT	**MILD PERSISTENT**	**MODERATE-SEVERE PERSISTENT**
Inhaled medium acting β_2-agonist only as needed. Choose from • Albuterol • Terbutaline • Dibuterol • Metaproterenol	One controller medication Inhaled corticosteroid *or* Antileukotriene *or* Nedocromil inhaler *or* Theophylline PLUS Inhaled β-agonist as needed	Multiple controller medications. Choose from: • Inhaled corticosteroid • Long-acting inhaled β-agonist • Antileukotriene • Theophylline Give enough of above so that asthma symptoms require 6 or fewer puffs of inhaled medium-acting β-agonist per day.

*Days per week with symptoms of dyspnea that limit activity.
† $\frac{\text{PM peak flow} - \text{AM peak flow}}{\text{PM peak flow}}$

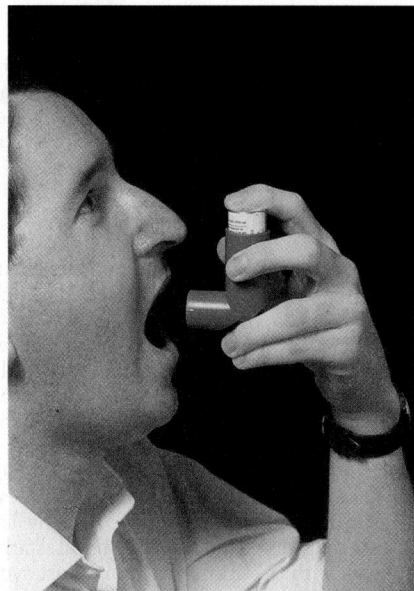

FIGURE 84–3 • Large-volume "spacer" or extension chamber added to a pressurized metered-dose inhaler. Spacers allow the aerosol cloud to slow down and overcome problems of patient coordination. They may increase lung deposition and reduce oral impaction, a potentially useful feature with high-dose inhaled steroid therapy. They may also be used in acute attacks of asthma to deliver repeat aerosol doses of bronchodilator every few minutes. (From Forbes CD, Jackson WF: Color Atlas and Text of Clinical Medicine, 3rd ed. London, Mosby, 2003, with permission.)

FIGURE 84–2 • A pressurized metered-dose inhaler. All commonly used inhaled therapy for asthma is available in this form. Although convenient and portable, the metered-dose inhaler requires good coordination between actuation and inhalation by the patient. (From Forbes CD, Jackson WF: Color Atlas and Text of Clinical Medicine, 3rd ed. London, Mosby, 2003, with permission.)

84–3) are available from many manufacturers for patients who have difficulty coordinating inspiration and inhaler actuation. In addition, novel devices improve inhaler coordination by actuating the inhaler only when the inspiratory flow pattern is within certain well-defined limitations. There is definitive evidence from prospective, randomized, placebo-controlled trials that the regularly scheduled use of prophylactic inhaled β-agonists overall has no deleterious effects; however, these trials also showed no beneficial effects compared with as-needed treatments.[1,2] Although there are no prospective studies, current evidence indicates that about one of six patients who are homozygous for the arginine 16 allele of the β_2-adrenergic receptor may experience a deleterious effect from the regularly scheduled use of medium-acting β_2-agonists.

ANTICHOLINERGICS. For more than a century, atropine has been known to be useful in the treatment of asthma. Its mechanism of action is thought to be inhibition of the effects of acetylcholine released from the intrapulmonary motor nerves that run in the vagus and innervate airway smooth muscle. The adverse central nervous system effects of atropine, which limited its utility in the past, have been overcome with the development of ipratropium bromide, available for use in a metered-dose inhaler. Although ipratropium bromide has

a salutary effect on cough in asthma and is useful as an adjunct to inhaled β_2-agonists in chronic stable asthma, it is not as effective as inhaled β_2-agonists for the treatment of acute asthmatic bronchospasm.

CONTROLLER TREATMENTS

INHALED CORTICOSTEROIDS. Inhaled corticosteroids, which have less systemic impact for a given level of therapeutic effect than systemic steroids, are effective controller treatments for patients with persistent asthma; there is clear evidence from multiple well designed and executed trials, in both children and adults, demonstrating the therapeutic efficacy of these agents.[3] When given to patients with established asthma, inhaled corticosteroids do not modify the progression of the disease and thus are only symptomatic relief. A wide variety of inhaled corticosteroid products are on the market in the United States (Table 84–5), with little solid data to guide the physician in choosing among them. All available products have been shown to be effective treatments for persistent asthma; the major unresolved controversy is the potential for systemic effects, including growth retardation in children, loss of bone mineralization, cataracts, and glaucoma. An adverse effect common to all inhaled corticosteroids, at recommended doses, is oral thrush and hoarseness of voice (from myopathy of the laryngeal muscles); the risk and severity of this complication can be reduced by means of aerosol spacers and good oropharyngeal hygiene (i.e., rinsing out the mouth by gargling after dosing).

Table 84–5 • **INHALED CORTICOSTEROIDS AVAILABLE FOR ASTHMA TREATMENT IN THE UNITED STATES***

STEROID NAME		DOSAGE		
Generic	Trade	µg/Actuation	Starting Dose	COMMENTS
Beclomethasone	Beclovent	42	2 puffs bid	Available in 2 strengths; prescription must indicate strength
	Vanceril	84		
Budesonide	Pulmicort	200	2 puffs bid	Available only in dry powder Turbuhaler
Flunisolide	AeroBid	250	2 puffs bid	
Fluticasone	Flovent	44, 110, or 220	2 puffs bid (44 µg/puff)	Available in 3 strengths; prescription must indicate dose level; available in pressurized metered-dose inhaler or as dry powder
Triamcinolone	Azmacort	100	2 puffs bid	

*Products marketed as of May 2003. Agents are listed in alphabetical order by generic name.

ANTILEUKOTRIENES. Agents with the capacity to inhibit the synthesis (zileuton [Zyflo]) or action (montelukast [Singulair], pranlukast [Onon or Ultair], zafirlukast [Accolate]) of the leukotrienes are effective controller medications for the patient with mild or moderate persistent asthma. These treatments can be used on their own for mild persistent asthma or in combination with inhaled steroids for more severe asthma.

LONG-ACTING β-AGONISTS. In contrast to medium-acting β-agonists, long-acting β-agonists currently available in the United States (salmeterol [Serevent]) have a duration of action of nearly 12 hours; they are considered a controller rather than a bronchodilator agent. Randomized controlled trials demonstrate that long-acting β-agonists should not be used as a sole controller agent.[4] Long-acting β-agonists have, however, been shown to provide effective asthma control in patients with mild intermittent asthma when given in concert with inhaled corticosteroids.[5] Although fixed dose-combination products with both inhaled steroids and long-acting β-agonists are available, their use should be avoided, because they make it difficult to lower the dose of inhaled steroids to the lowest possible effective dose.

THEOPHYLLINE. Theophylline and aminophylline are bronchodilators of moderate potency that are useful in both inpatient and outpatient management of asthma. Theophylline is sold in a large number of formulations that allow therapy to proceed with daily or twice-daily dosing. The mechanism by which theophylline exerts its effects has not been established with certainty but is probably related to the inhibition of certain forms of phosphodiesterase. The utility of theophylline is limited by its toxicity and by wide variations in the rate of its metabolism, both in a single individual over time and among individuals in a population. As a result of this variability, monitoring of plasma theophylline levels is indicated to ensure that patients are treated appropriately. Acceptable plasma levels for therapeutic effects are between 10 and 20 μg/mL; higher levels are associated with gastrointestinal, cardiac, and central nervous system toxicity, including anxiety, headache, nausea, vomiting, diarrhea, cardiac arrhythmias, and seizures. These last catastrophic complications may occur without antecedent mild side effects when plasma levels exceed 20 μg/mL. Because of these potentially life-threatening complications of treatment, plasma levels need to be measured with great frequency in hospitalized patients receiving intravenous aminophylline and less frequently in stable outpatients receiving one of the long-acting theophylline preparations. Most asthma care providers use dosing amounts and intervals to achieve steady-state theophylline levels of 10 to 14 μg/mL, thereby avoiding the toxicity associated with decrements in metabolism. Treatment with theophylline is recommended only for patients with moderate or severe persistent asthma who are receiving controller medications, such as inhaled steroids or antileukotrienes, but whose asthma is not adequately controlled.

SYSTEMIC CORTICOSTEROIDS. Systemic corticosteroids are effective for the treatment of moderate to severe persistent asthma as well as occasional severe exacerbations of asthma that occur in a patient with otherwise mild asthma. The mechanism of their therapeutic effect in asthma has not been established.

No consensus has been reached on the specific type, dose, or duration of corticosteroid to be used in the treatment of asthma. In nonhospitalized patients with asthma refractory to standard therapy, a steroid "pulse" with initial doses of prednisone on the order of 40 to 60 mg/day, tapered to zero over 7 to 14 days, is recommended. For patients who cannot stop taking steroids without having recurrent uncontrolled bronchospasm despite the addition of multiple other controller treatments, alternate-day administration of oral steroids is preferable to daily treatment. For patients whose asthma requires in-hospital treatment but is not considered life-threatening, an initial intravenous bolus of 2 mg/kg of hydrocortisone, followed by continuous infusion of 0.5 mg/kg/hour, has been shown to be beneficial within 12 hours. In attacks of asthma that are considered life-threatening, the use of intravenous methylprednisolone (125 mg every 6 hours) has been advocated. In each case, as the patient improves, oral steroids are substituted for intravenous steroids, and the oral dose is tapered over 1 to 3 weeks; addition of inhaled steroids to the regimen is strongly recommended when oral steroids are started.

OTHER CONTROLLER DRUGS. Cromolyn sodium and nedocromil sodium are nonsteroid inhaled treatments that have proved beneficial[5] in the management of mild to moderate persistent asthma. They appear to be most useful in pediatric populations or when an identifiable stimulus (such as exercise or allergen exposure) elicits an asthmatic response. Anti-IgE antibodies can reduce exacerbations and improve quality of life in severe allergic asthma,[6] but their place in treatment schema has not been established.

The use of systemic gold (as in rheumatoid arthritis), methotrexate, or cyclosporine has been suggested as adjunctive treatment for patients with severe chronic asthma who cannot otherwise discontinue high-dose corticosteroid treatment. However, these agents are experimental, and their routine use is not advocated.

SPECIFIC TREATMENT SCENARIOS

CONCURRENT PULMONARY INFECTION. In some patients, acute exacerbations of asthma may be due to concurrent infection, which requires targeted therapy (Chapters 85, 87, and 92).

ASPIRIN-INDUCED ASTHMA. Approximately 5% of patients with moderate to severe persistent asthma develop asthma when they ingest agents that inhibit cyclooxygenase, such as aspirin and other nonsteroidal anti-inflammatory drugs (Chapter 32). Such patients quite often have difficult-to-manage asthma, with nasal polyposis and chronic sinusitis even in the absence of exposure to agents that inhibit cyclooxygenase. Although the physiologic manifestations of laboratory-based aspirin challenge can be blocked by leukotriene pathway inhibitors, these agents do not prevent clinical aspirin-induced asthma. Thus, patients with this form of asthma must avoid aspirin and other nonsteroidal anti-inflammatory drugs.

ASTHMA IN THE EMERGENCY DEPARTMENT. When a patient with asthma presents for acute emergency care, objective measures of the severity of the attack, including quantification of pulsus paradoxus and measurement of airflow rates (PEFR or FEV_1), should be evaluated in addition to the usual vital signs. If the attack has been prolonged and failed to respond to treatment with bronchodilators and high-dose inhaled steroids before arrival at the emergency department, intravenous steroids (40 to 60 mg of methylprednisolone or its equivalent) should be administered. Treatment with inhaled β-agonists should be repeated at 20- to 30-minute intervals until the PEFR or FEV_1 increases to greater than 40% of the predicted values. If this point is not reached within 2 hours, admission to the hospital for further treatment is strongly advocated.

When patients have PEFR and FEV_1 values that are greater than 60% of their predicted value on arrival in the emergency department, treatment with inhaled β_2-agonists alone is likely to result in an objective improvement in airflow rates. If significant improvement takes place in the emergency department, such patients can usually be treated as outpatients with inhaled β_2-agonists and an additional controller agent.

For patients whose PEFR and FEV_1 values are between 40% and 60% of the values predicted at the time of initial evaluation in the emergency care setting, a plan of treatment varying in intensity between the two cited above is indicated. Failure to respond to treatment by objective criteria (PEFR or FEV_1) within 2 hours of arriving at the emergency department is an indication for more intense therapy.

STATUS ASTHMATICUS. The asthmatic subject whose PEFR or FEV_1 does not increase to greater than 40% of the predicted value with treatment, whose $PaCO_2$ increases without improvement of indices of airflow obstruction, or who develops major complications such as pneumothorax or pneumomediastinum should be admitted to the hospital for close monitoring. Frequent treatments with inhaled β-agonists, intravenous aminophylline (at doses yielding maximal acceptable plasma levels), and high-dose intravenous steroids are indicated. Oxygen should be administered by face mask or nasal cannula in amounts sufficient to achieve SaO_2 values between 92% and 94%; a higher FIO_2 promotes absorption atelectasis and provides no therapeutic benefit. If objective evidence of an infection is present, appropriate treatment for that infection should be given. If no improvement is seen with treatment and respiratory failure appears imminent, bronchodilator treatment should be intensified to the maximum tolerated by the patient. If indicated, intubation of the trachea and mechanical ventilation can be instituted; in this case, the goal should be to provide a level of ventilation just adequate to sustain life but *not sufficient to normalize arterial blood gases*. For example, a $PaCO_2$ of 60 to 70 mm Hg, or even higher, is acceptable for a patient in status asthmaticus.

ASTHMA IN PREGNANCY. Asthma may be exacerbated, remain unchanged, or remit during pregnancy (Chapter 253). There need not be substantial departures from the ordinary management of asthma during pregnancy. However, no unnecessary medications should be administered; systemic steroids should be used sparingly to avert fetal complications, and certain drugs should be avoided, including tetracycline (as a treatment for intercurrent infection), atropine and atropine-like drugs (which may cause fetal tachycardia), terbutaline (which is contraindicated during active labor because of its tocolytic effects), and iodine-containing mucolytics (such as saturated solution of potassium iodide). Moreover, use of prostaglandin $F_{2\alpha}$ as an abortifacient should be avoided in asthmatic patients.

Prognosis

Asthma is a chronic relapsing disorder. Most patients have recurrent attacks without a major loss in lung function. A minority of patients experience a significant irreversible loss in lung function over and above the normal pulmonary senescence.

1. Drazen JM, Israel E, Boushey HA, et al: Comparison of regularly scheduled with as-needed use of albuterol in mild asthma. N Engl J Med 1996;335:841–847.
2. Dennis SM, Sharp SJ, Vickers MR, et al: Regular inhaled salbutamol and asthma control: The TRUST randomised trial. Therapy Working Group of the National Asthma Task Force and the MRC General Practice Research Framework. Lancet 2000;355:1675–1679.
3. Pauwels RA, Pedersen S, Busse WW, et al: Early intervention with budesonide in mild persistent asthma: A randomised, double-blind trial. Lancet 2003;361:1071–1076.
4. Lemanske RF Jr, Sorkness CA, Mauger EA, et al: Asthma Clinical Research Network for the National Heart, Lung and Blood Institute. Inhaled corticosteroid reduction and elimination in patients with persistent asthma receiving salmeterol: A randomized controlled trial. JAMA 2001;285:2594–2603.
5. Lazarus SC, Boushey HA, Fahy JV, et al: Asthma Clinical Research Network for the National Heart, Lung and Blood Institute. Long-acting beta2-agonist monotherapy vs continued therapy with inhaled corticosteroids in patients with persistent asthma: A randomized controlled trial. JAMA 2001;285:2583–2593.
6. Finn A, Gross G, van Bavel J, et al: Omalizumab improves asthma-related quality of life in patients with severe allergic asthma. J Allergy Clin Immunol 2003;111:278–284.

SUGGESTED READINGS
Ball TM, Castro-Rodriguez JA, Griffith KA, et al: Siblings, day-care attendance, and the risk of asthma and wheezing during childhood. N Engl J Med 2000;343:538–543. *A study showing that exposure of children during the first year of life to multiple infections, as found in daycare, appears to protect the child from developing asthma.*
Naureckas ET, Solway J: Mild asthma. N Engl J Med 2001;345:1257–1262. *A review.*
Van Eerdewegh P, Little RD, Dupuis J, et al: Association of the ADAM33 gene with asthma and bronchial hyperresponsiveness. Nature 2002;418:426–430. *Convincing evidence for an asthma-susceptibility gene.*

85 | CHRONIC OBSTRUCTIVE PULMONARY DISEASE

Nicholas Anthonisen

Definitions

Chronic obstructive pulmonary disease (COPD) is the term used to describe slowly progressive airways obstruction, usually associated with smoking, that is not reversible and is not due to another specific cause. Patients with COPD have varying degrees of three pathologic processes, each associated with smoking: chronic bronchitis, small airways obstruction, and emphysema. Whereas chronic bronchitis can be defined clinically, small airways obstruction and emphysema cannot be reliably diagnosed during life. COPD results in airways obstruction, which is easily measured, and current therapy is largely aimed at reducing obstruction. Physicians, therefore, can commonly focus on the COPD syndrome and not its specific pathologic causes.

Although patients with COPD may improve with treatment, especially when an acute infection or exposure precipitates decompensation, COPD by definition implies some degree of fixed, irreversible disease. By comparison, patients with pure asthma (Chapter 84) have intermittent airway obstruction that may revert to normal after treatment and in between exacerbations.

Epidemiology

COPD is common, affecting about 16 million Americans. It is the fourth most common cause of death in the United States, and

mortality from COPD is increasing. The economic burden of COPD is enormous, although extremely difficult to assess accurately and inclusively.

The prevalence of COPD reflects societal smoking habits, increasing steadily in men in the United States until about 10 years ago and then leveling off. In women, COPD was previously uncommon, but the prevalence has increased and is still rising owing to increased smoking rates in women. It is unusual for a person to develop clinically apparent COPD without a history of smoking for at least 20 pack-years, and most patients have at least 40 pack-years of exposure. A pack-year is the equivalent of 20 cigarettes per day for a year (Chapter 14).

Figure 85–1 shows a well-validated model of the development of COPD in terms of the most commonly used index of airways obstruction, which is the forced expiratory volume in 1 second, or FEV_1 (Chapter 82). In normal nonsmoking men, FEV_1 declines by about 30 mL per year after the age of 30 years, and disability due to dyspnea does not occur. In the "average" smoker, FEV_1 declines at a rate that is approximately twice as fast but still slow enough so that disability due to dyspnea is unlikely until quite late in life. About 15 to 20% of smokers, however, have more rapid declines of up to 100 mL/year, and it is these patients in whom symptomatic COPD develops in middle age. These individuals are in some way "sensitive" to tobacco products and constitute a high-risk group. A variety of additional risk factors have been identified, but all have relatively weak effects, and no currently known combination of factors satisfactorily explains why some smokers fare so much worse than others (Chapter 14).

Quitting smoking alters the subsequent loss of lung function to the same rate as in nonsmokers. Thus, smoking cessation early enough in life can prevent the onset of clinical disease in middle age. However, severe COPD may progress even in patients who stop smoking.

Pathogenesis

CHRONIC BRONCHITIS

Chronic bronchitis is a clinical diagnosis, defined as the presence of chronic cough and sputum production for at least 3 months of the year for at least two consecutive years in the absence of any other disease. At least one third of smokers ages 35 to 59 years have chronic bronchitis, and its prevalence increases with age.

The anatomic basis of chronic bronchitis is hypertrophy and hyperplasia of the mucus-secreting glands normally found in the epithelium of larger airways. These cells increase in size and are found in smaller airways than in nonsmokers. This expansion of mucus-secreting cells is accompanied by low-grade neutrophilic inflammation and increased airway smooth muscle. Chronic bronchitis is not necessarily associated with airways obstruction, and smokers can develop severe COPD in the absence of bronchitis. However, chronic bronchitis is associated with an increased tendency to develop

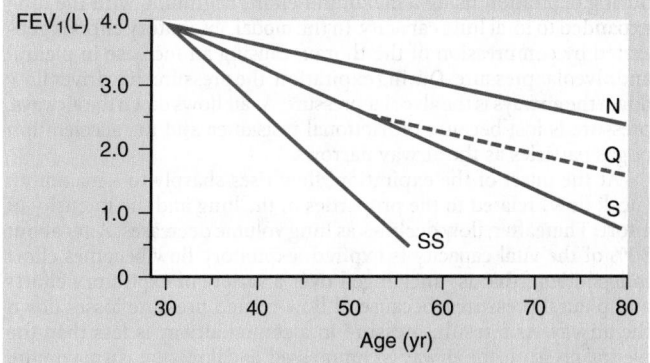

FIGURE 85–1 • Course of lung function decline through adulthood. The vertical axis is forced expiratory volume in 1 second (FEV_1), the horizontal axis is age. The course of decline is shown in a normal nonsmoker (N), in an average smoker (S), in a smoker who is sensitive to tobacco smoke (SS), and in an individual who quits smoking (Q, dashed line). Dyspnea first occurs when the FEV_1 is less than 2 L (50% of the normal value) and becomes severe when the FEV_1 is about 1 L.

repetitive episodes of acute bronchitis, which may contribute to the progression of airways obstruction.

PERIPHERAL AIRWAY DISEASE

In COPD, the most striking increase in the resistance to airflow occurs in peripheral airways or bronchioles. Smokers have increased bronchiolar smooth muscle, inflammation, and fibrosis that narrow the airway lumens and thicken their walls. The degree of abnormality in these airways is correlated with lung function. The mechanisms involved in these changes are unknown.

EMPHYSEMA

Emphysema is defined as the enlargement of air spaces distal to the conducting airways, that is, respiratory bronchioles and alveoli, due to destruction of the walls of these air spaces. There are two important types of emphysema: centrilobular and panacinar. Centrilobular emphysema primarily involves the respiratory bronchioles, often with normal distal alveoli; however, in severe disease, distal alveoli may also be damaged and incorporated into the central air space. Centrilobular emphysema is seen almost exclusively in smokers, in whom it tends to occur in the upper lung lobes. Panacinar emphysema involves the entire distal lung unit, distorting and destroying alveoli and respiratory bronchioles alike; it can occur throughout the lung but may involve chiefly the lower lobes.

Some families develop early onset, severe panacinar emphysema associated with α_1-antitrypsin (AAT) deficiency. AAT is an acute phase serum protein that is secreted by the liver and that binds to and neutralizes neutrophil elastase; it is the most abundant antiprotease in the lung periphery. Smoking causes an inflammatory process by which activated neutrophils are recruited into the lung; elastase released by neutrophils digests lung tissue in the absence of AAT. The elastase-antielastase imbalance present in patients with AAT deficiency might also occur in people without the deficiency under the proper conditions, such as oxidation of AAT, but it is not clear that this is the case.

There are a number of abnormal alleles of the gene *AAT*, the most common and important of which is termed "Z." Patients homozygous for the Z allele (ZZ), a rare condition, have very low serum AAT levels and develop severe panacinar emphysema early in life if they smoke. Patients who do not smoke may not develop significant lung disease. Heterozygotes (AZ) are more common, representing about 2 to 3% of North European populations, and have serum levels of AAT that are intermediate between normals and homozygotes. It is currently unclear whether these individuals are predisposed to emphysema.

REDUCTION IN MAXIMUM EXPIRATORY FLOW

Reduced expiratory flow is the hallmark of COPD (Chapter 82). Figure 85–2 shows a maximum expiratory flow-volume curve and a diagrammatic representation of the lungs and airways inside the thorax. In the former, flow from the lungs is plotted against lung volume during expiration using a maximum effort, beginning with the lung expanded to total lung capacity. In the model, expiratory effort is generated by compression of the thorax, causing an increase in pleural and alveolar pressure. During expiration, the pressure that drives flow down the airways is the alveolar pressure. As air flows down the airways, pressure is lost because of frictional resistance and the acceleration of gas particles as the airway narrows.

At the onset of the expiration, flow rises sharply to a maximum (peak flow) related to the properties of the lung and the intensity of effort. Thereafter, flow declines as lung volume decreases. After about 30% of the vital capacity is expired, expiratory flow becomes effort independent, that is, unchanged over a variety of expiratory efforts and pleural pressures, because of flow-related pressure losses down the airway. As a result, pressure in a central airway is less than the pleural pressure, the airway is compressed, and flow attains a maximum value after which further increases in pleural pressure compress the airway further. These so-called flow-limiting segments are initially found only in large central airways, but such segments exist in intrapulmonary airways at low lung volumes. Under the condition of flow limitation, the maximum flow attained depends on the upstream, or alveolar, pressure, the resistance of the airways, and the properties of the compressed, flow-limiting segment. If the lung's elastic recoil is

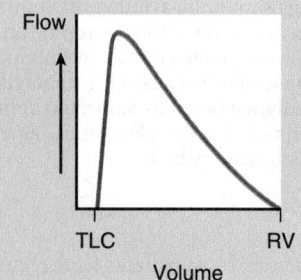
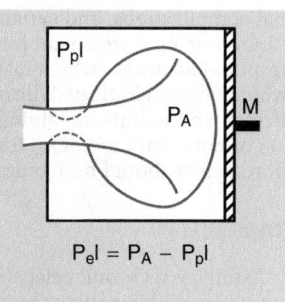

FIGURE 85–2 • Maximum expiratory flow-volume curve (*left*) with an explanatory model (*right*). The left panel shows flow as a function of expired volume during forced expiration at maximum effort, from the total lung capacity (TLC) before expiration to the residual volume (RV) after expiration in a normal individual. Flow rises to a maximum and then declines as lung volume decreases. Flow over much of the declining limb is independent of expiratory effort, provided that a threshold effort is achieved. In the right-hand model, the thorax is represented by a box and the expiratory muscles by a piston (M). The lung is a balloon inside the box, and the airways are represented as a tube that branches as it goes from outside the lung to the inside. The expiratory muscles compress the thoracic contents and raise pleural pressure (Ppl). Alveolar pressure (P_A) in the lung increases by the same amount, because it is related to the pleural pressure by the elastic recoil of the lung (Pel). Because of the increase in Ppl and P_A, gas flows out of the lung, reaching a peak (peak flow) and declining thereafter. The pressure driving flow is P_A, and the flow achieved is related to the resistance of the airways (R). As lung volume decreases, Pel decreases, so P_A decreases in relation to Ppl. Also, as lung volume decreases, R increases. Because of the reduced P_A and increased R, as lung volume decreases, the pressure in a major airway becomes less than Ppl, and the airway is compressed (dashed lines), thereby limiting flow. Further increases in effort (Ppl) simply further compress the airway and do not increase flow. Flow limitation occurs after about 30% of the vital capacity is expired. When this limitation occurs, maximum expiratory flow is dependent on lung elastic recoil (Pel), which determines P_A, the resistance of the airways upstream from the flow-limiting segment, and the mechanical properties of the flow-limiting segment.

reduced, alveolar pressures are reduced relative to pleural pressure, and so is maximum expiratory flow. Increases in airways resistance increase pressure losses down the airway and decrease maximum expiratory flow. Finally, abnormally "floppy" segments of airway, a rare phenomenon, undergo premature collapse and cause abnormal limitation of flow.

In normal lungs, flow decreases as lung volume decreases because the lung's elastic recoil decreases and resistance increases. In COPD, the lung's elastic recoil is reduced by emphysema, and airways resistance is increased. Maximum expiratory flow is reduced, and even less effort than normal causes limitation of flow. Tests of maximum expiratory flow such as the flow-volume curve and the FEV$_1$ are of clinical value because they reflect major pathologic processes in COPD and because they are relatively insensitive to a patient's effort and cooperation.

Clinical Manifestations

LUNG FUNCTION

The decrease in maximum expiratory flow that characterizes COPD is most easily identified in terms of a reduction in FEV$_1$ that is larger than the reduction in vital capacity, measured in the same forced expiratory maneuver and termed the *forced vital capacity* (FVC) (Chapter 82). Both FEV$_1$ and FVC decline with normal aging (see Fig. 85–1), but their ratio, FEV$_1$/FVC, normally exceeds 0.7; lower ratios indicate airways obstruction. Both the FEV$_1$ and the FVC may increase after treatment with an inhaled bronchodilator, but the FEV$_1$ does not attain normal values in COPD, whereas it can return to normal in patients with asthma (Chapter 84).

Hyperinflation of the lungs is characteristic of COPD and reflects loss of lung recoil and limitation of expiratory flow. Residual volume, the lung volume after a maximum expiration, often is increased even in mild cases of COPD. Functional residual capacity, the lung volume at the end of a normal expiration, is routinely increased in moderate and severe COPD. Total lung capacity, the maximum lung volume, is commonly increased in severe COPD because of reduced lung recoil.

The diffusing capacity for carbon monoxide (CO), which measures the alveolar uptake of trace amounts of CO, is reduced in emphysema because of loss of alveolar surface area. It is the most reliable physiologic method for assessing the presence of emphysema.

Arterial hypoxemia with or without carbon dioxide (CO_2) retention is common in severe COPD. Hypoxemia generally precedes CO_2 retention, rarely occurs in patients with an FEV_1 in excess of 40% of the predicted normal value, and is common when the FEV_1 is less than 30% of the predicted value. Gas exchange abnormalities in COPD are due to abnormally large differences in ventilation-perfusion ratios among units in the lung.

DYSPNEA

Dyspnea is the major cause of disability in COPD. It arises from a sense of increased muscular effort to breathe in relation to the level of ventilation achieved (Chapter 81). Normal subjects, even at the most strenuous levels of exercise, use only 60 to 70% of their maximum voluntary ventilation and never experience dyspnea comparable to that of diseased patients.

Patients with obstructive airways disease usually characterize dyspnea as difficulty in inspiring because airways obstruction especially disadvantages inspiratory muscles. Expiratory flow limitation does not permit adequate expiration at normal lung volumes, so patients breathe at increased lung volumes. This hyperinflation renders inspiratory muscles relatively ineffective, so that greater inspiratory effort is required to achieve the needed ventilation, as illustrated in Figure 85–3, which shows flow-volume plots in a patient with COPD during resting breathing and forced expiration after full inspiration. At the same lung volume, expiratory flows during resting breathing are similar to flows during a maximum effort. The only way this patient can increase expiratory flow, and therefore ventilation, is to breathe at higher lung volumes than at rest.

The degree of dyspnea in patients with COPD generally correlates inversely with the FEV_1, but patients with similar degrees of airways obstruction may complain of quite different degrees of dyspnea. Careful assessment of dyspnea is a useful way to follow the progress of patients with COPD.

Diagnosis

HISTORY

COPD is insidious. Although the diagnosis can be made in any smoker with airways obstruction, most people are first seen only when they experience dyspnea. Dyspnea typically does not occur until the FEV_1 is about 50% of normal, when the disease has usually been present for decades.

COPD patients often have a history of chronic bronchitis that has antedated the onset of dyspnea. Dyspnea usually is first experienced during episodes of acute bronchitis. Eventually, dyspnea becomes consistent, and, over approximately 10 to 15 years, dyspnea progresses from occurring only with extreme exertion, to being present with any effort, and finally to being present at rest. Wheezing is also common in COPD, usually with exertion, but may occur at rest in severe disease.

Patients with COPD have periodic exacerbations, marked by increased dyspnea, wheezing, cough, and sputum production. The sputum often changes in color from the usual white (mucoid) to yellow or green, sometimes with blood streaking. Exacerbations usually occur in the winter, often with upper respiratory infections, and are more common in patients with symptomatic chronic bronchitis and in those with severe obstruction. The causes vary from patient to patient and from time to time, but many are associated with bacterial infection of the airways. Exacerbations of COPD are the most common cause of hospitalization and result in substantial morbidity.

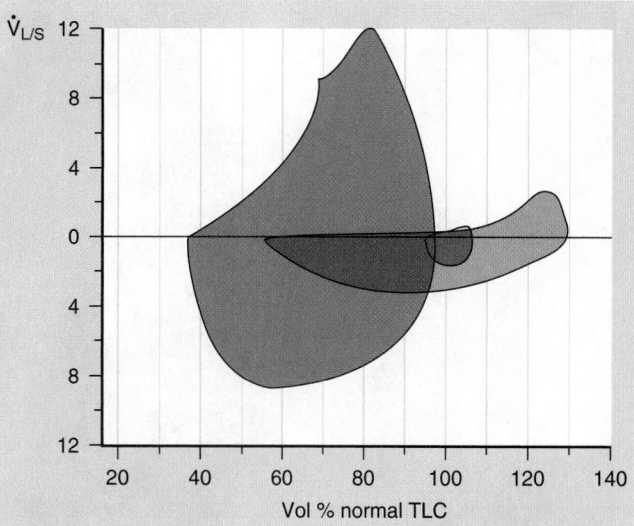

FIGURE 85–3 • Flow-volume relationships during quiet resting breathing (small inner loop) and maximum forced expiration in a patient with severe COPD. The vertical axis is flow in liters per second; the horizontal axis is lung volume, expressed as a percentage of the normal total lung capacity (TLC). The shaded area shows normal maximal inspiration and expiration. The patient has substantial increases in the maximum lung volume (TLC) and the minimum lung volume attained (residual volume). Expiratory flow during maximal expiration is grossly reduced and is similar to the flow used during resting breathing. With exercise, the only way for this patient to increase expiratory flow and thereby increase ventilation is to breathe at higher lung volumes than at rest.

Some patients with COPD lose weight and muscle mass especially in the presence of severe emphysema. Weight loss is an ominous prognostic sign in COPD.

PHYSICAL EXAMINATION

In mild to moderate COPD, the physical examination is usually normal. In severe disease, signs are often apparent but are not specific. The breathing rate is increased, often to greater than 20/min at rest in patients with hypoxia and/or CO_2 retention. Physical signs related to hyperinflation include the appearance of a barrel chest with increased anteroposterior diameter, relatively low-lying diaphragms, and faint heart sounds. Patients with severe disease use the strap muscles of the neck during inspiration. Breath sounds are often diminished, and both crackles and wheezes may be heard. Hypoxemic patients may be cyanotic.

In advanced disease, secondary pulmonary hypertension (Chapter 64) leads to right heart failure, which commonly is termed *cor pulmonale*. Signs of cor pulmonale include an increased pulmonic second sound, jugular venous distention, hepatic congestion, and ankle edema.

SPIROMETRY

Spirometry, the measurement of the FEV_1 and FVC, is the gold standard for diagnosing COPD and is easy to perform in the office setting (Chapter 82). Airways obstruction (FEV_1/FVC < 0.70) in a person with at least 20 pack-years of tobacco exposure is a presumptive diagnosis of COPD.

RADIOLOGIC STUDIES

Routine chest radiographs are insensitive for detecting COPD. In advanced cases, patients develop hyperinflation with flattened diaphragms, increased retrosternal airspace, and an apparently small, vertical heart (Fig. 85–4). Increased or decreased lung markings and thin-walled bullae may be seen. Signs of pulmonary hypertension, including fullness of the main pulmonary arteries, are occasionally observed. The chief value of the chest radiograph is to assess other causes of airways obstruction and to look for evidence of lung cancer (Chapter 198).

Computed tomographic (CT) scans are of considerable value in assessing the distribution and extent of emphysema. Emphysematous

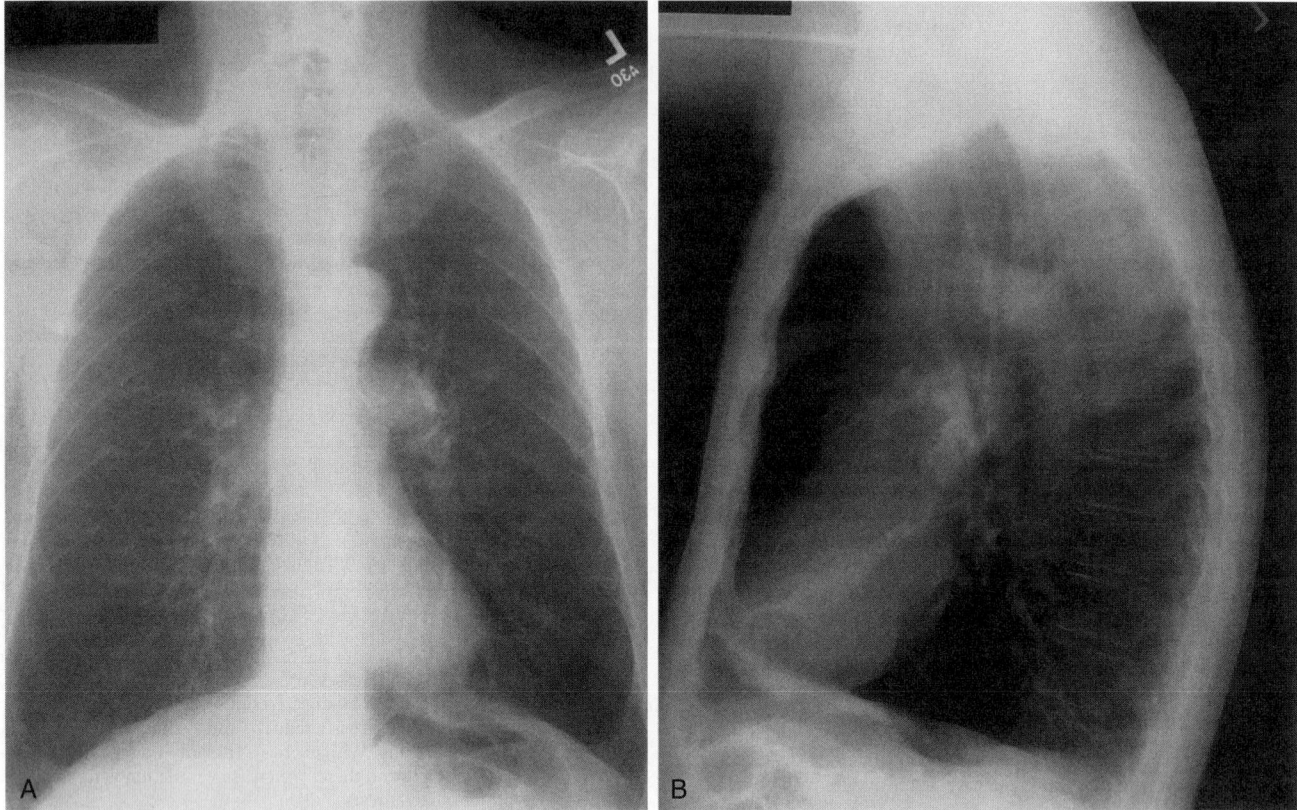

FIGURE 85–4 • Posteroanterior (PA) and lateral roentgenograms of the thorax in a patient with emphysema. The most obvious abnormalities are those associated with increased lung volume. The lungs appear dark because of their increased air relative to tissue. The diaphragms are caudal to their normal position and appear flatter than normal. The heart is oriented more vertically than normal because of caudal displacement of the diaphragm and the transverse diameter of the rib cage is increased; as a result, the width of the heart relative to the rib cage on the PA view is decreased. The space between the sternum and heart and great vessels is increased on the lateral view.

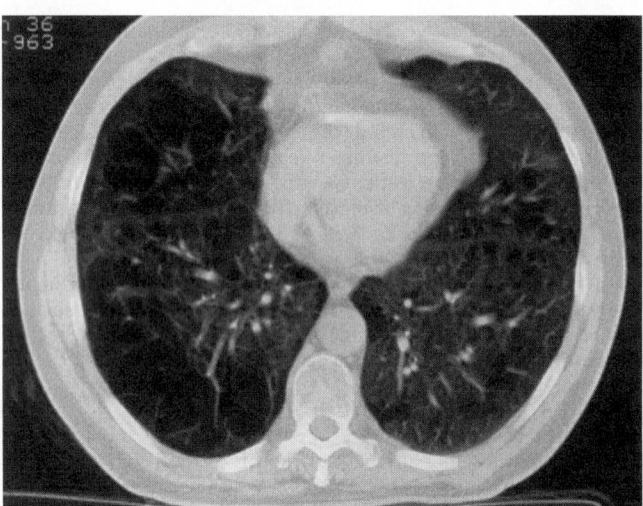

FIGURE 85–5 • High-resolution axial CT scan of a 1-mm section of the thorax of a patient with emphysema. The emphysema is evident in the form of multiple dark holes in the lung surrounded by more normal lung. The superior segments of the lower lobes are located posterior on each side. The right lung (left in the figure) is more severely affected.

spaces are seen as "holes" in the lung (Fig. 85–5). CT methods to quantify emphysema are under development.

Differential Diagnosis

The most difficult disease to differentiate from COPD is asthma (Chapter 84), although in most cases the distinction can be made based on history alone. Asthma typically begins early in life with episodes of dyspnea and wheezing of rapid onset and that reverse

rapidly and completely. However, patients with asthma can develop chronic airways obstruction that reverses little with therapy, and some smokers with chronic airways obstruction demonstrate substantial reversibility with therapy. In these instances, the difference between asthma and COPD can become a matter of semantics. Fortunately, the therapy of asthma and COPD are similar enough so that diagnostic uncertainties between these two entities should have little impact on patient management.

Several other diseases cause chronic airways obstruction, but differ from COPD in important ways. Cystic fibrosis (Chapter 86) and bronchiectasis (Chapter 87) occur at an earlier age and are normally accompanied by specific radiologic abnormalities. Eosinophilic granuloma (Chapter 235), which is associated with cigarette smoking, and lymphangioleiomyomatosis (Chapter 88) cause airways obstruction, but both present with abnormal chest radiographs and have characteristic abnormalities on CT scan. Bronchiolitis obliterans (Chapter 88) also causes airways obstruction; however, bronchiolitis obliterans usually occurs in a different setting from COPD, and it may be accompanied by more radiographic changes than COPD.

It is important to differentiate upper or central airways obstruction from COPD. Extrathoracic airways obstruction (Chapters 96 and 468) is accompanied by stridor and compromised inspiratory flow. Intrathoracic tracheal obstruction produces characteristic changes in the maximum expiratory flow-volume curve.

Clinical Evaluation

Patients thought to have COPD should undergo full pulmonary function testing at least once (Chapter 82). Testing should also include repeat spirometry at yearly intervals and when the patient is acutely ill. If the FEV_1 is less than 40% of the predicted normal value, arterial blood gas analysis is advisable (Chapter 100). Annual chest radiographs should be performed only if the patient is a candidate for cancer surgery. Finally, the degree of dyspnea should be documented carefully, as should dietary intake, weight loss, and occurrence of exacerbations.

Rx Treatment

STABLE COPD

Smoking cessation is the only treatment that has been shown to alter the course of COPD.[1] Smoking cessation when the FEV_1 exceeds 50% of the predicted normal value either averts or greatly delays the onset of symptomatic disease. It is probably never too late for patients with COPD to stop smoking.

Inhaled bronchodilators afford symptomatic relief in COPD and should be prescribed for all patients who find them helpful. There are a number of effective agents with few side effects. Short-acting B_2 agonists have rapid onset of action and are useful as rescue agents, used on a discretionary basis. Albuterol is the prototypical short-acting B_2 agonist, the normal dose being 200 μg (two puffs from a metered-dose inhaler). Ipratropium bromide is an inhaled anticholinergic drug that is as effective as B_2-agonists in COPD. Because it has a slower onset of action, it is usually given on a schedule of 3 to 4 times a day at a dose of 36 μg (two puffs from a metered-dose inhaler). Higher doses of these drugs are of benefit in some patients, and many use both; a combination inhaler is available. Longer acting bronchodilators, such as salmeterol (50 μg) and formoterol (12 μg), have durations of action up to 12 hours. A very long-acting (once a day) inhaled anticholinergic drug, tiotropium, is likely to be available soon. Long-acting bronchodilators are unquestionably effective, but whether they produce better results than frequent use of short-acting agents has not been critically addressed. Metered-dose and powdered formulations of these drugs are less expensive than those used in wet nebulizers but are equally effective.

Theophylline is an orally administered bronchodilator that is less effective than inhaled drugs. Some patients receive symptomatic benefit from theophylline when it is added to inhaled agents, and a trial of theophylline is reasonable in patients with severe dyspnea. Theophylline has a relatively narrow dosage range in which it is effective and nontoxic, and many drugs and conditions influence theophylline metabolism. Serum levels should be measured, and a target of about 10 μg/mL is usually achieved with a dose of approximately 300 mg twice a day.

Inhaled steroids do not change the long-term rate of decline in lung function in COPD, but inhaled steroid therapy may produce a small (about 200 mL) one-time increase in FEV_1. Of greater importance is evidence that inhaled steroids reduce the frequency and severity of exacerbations. Patients with severe disease and multiple exacerbations should be given inhaled steroids in relatively high doses, such as 500 to 1000 μg of fluticasone per day. The combined use of a long-acting β-agonist with an inhaled steroid produces better control of symptoms without increased side effects compared with either used alone.[2] Inhalers that combine a steroid with a long-acting bronchodilator have recently become available.

Many older COPD guidelines recommend trials of high-dose oral steroids in patients who are not doing well. The evidence cited earlier has largely superseded these recommendations, and at present there is not convincing evidence for the use of oral steroids in stable COPD, although many current guidelines recommend trials of oral steroids.

COPD patients benefit from pulmonary rehabilitation.[3] The major component of rehabilitation programs is exercise training. Regular exercise improves exercise tolerance and quality of life in patients with COPD. In addition, rehabilitation programs teach coping skills and self-reliance, and they tend to reduce anxiety and depression.

In hypoxemic COPD, home oxygen therapy prolongs life, and home oxygen should be prescribed for stable patients with arterial PO_2 <60 mm Hg.[4] Acceptable blood gases (PO_2 65 to 80 mm Hg) can usually be achieved with oxygen flows of 2 L/minute delivered by nasal cannula. There is no good evidence that oxygen therapy benefits COPD patients who do not have continuous hypoxemia. However, some patients who are not hypoxemic during the day exhibit hypoxemia while asleep, and many patients with severe COPD develop significant hypoxemia with exercise. As a result, oxygen therapy may be considered in such patients during sleep or exercise. Oxygen delivery systems vary greatly in terms of mobility and cost, and the choice among systems should be individualized.

Surgical approaches to COPD include lung transplantation and lung volume reduction surgery (Chapter 97). The former is falling out of favor, because it is not clear that it prolongs useful life. Lung volume reduction surgery involves removal of substantial amounts of emphysematous lung, usually from the upper lobes. It has produced striking improvement in lung function and quality of life in some patients, but carries considerable risk and is expensive; clear selection criteria have not been developed.

Influenza vaccine should be administered annually to all patients with COPD[5] to prevent exacerbations. Pneumococcal vaccination is also recommended because pneumococcal pneumonia is devastating in these patients (Chapters 16 and 303).

EXACERBATIONS OF COPD

Exacerbations of COPD are associated with transient decreases in lung function, which account for the increased dyspnea. Increased bronchodilator therapy is rational and recommended (Table 85–1). When exacerbations are accompanied by increases in sputum volume and/or purulence, antibiotic therapy is associated with measurable benefit[6] (Table 85–2). Sputum smear and culture are not usually helpful, and empirical treatment is the rule. In low-risk patients, inexpensive antibiotics such as amoxicillin (see Table 85–1) or trimethoprim-sulfamethoxazole may be used for 10 days, but bacterial resistance to these agents is common. In high-risk patients, newer antibiotics, such as the newer macrolides (e.g., azithromycin 500 mg on day 1, 250 mg on days 2 to 5) or fluoroquinolones (e.g., levofloxacin, 500 mg per day for 7 to 10 days) may be advisable. In severe exacerbations, systemic steroid therapy has been shown to result in a relatively rapid recovery,[7] and the equivalent of 40 mg of prednisone per day for 10 to 14 days is justifiable. It is reasonable to give compliant patients with COPD a supply of antibiotics and steroids so they self-treat exacerbations.

In severe exacerbations seen in the hospital or emergency department, other diagnoses must be considered. Exacerbations of COPD must be distinguished from pneumonia (Chapter 92), pneumothorax (Chapter 95), and pulmonary embolism (Chapter 94). The first two of these usually can be diagnosed using the chest radiograph. In patients with signs and symptoms typical for pneumonia, especially substantial fevers or elevated white blood cell counts, empirical treatment for pneumonia is appropriate until it can be excluded. Pulmonary embolism can be difficult to diagnose in patients with COPD, and spiral CT angiography should be used if embolic disease is suspected (Chapter 94).

Exacerbations of COPD may be difficult to distinguish from acute heart failure (Chapters 55 and 56), and many elderly smokers may have both conditions concurrently. The distinction can be especially difficult in patients with right heart failure, in whom the cause may be cor pulmonale from advanced COPD or worsening right heart failure caused by worsening left heart failure. The chest radiograph and the electrocardiogram are the best tools for differentiation here. A careful physical examination may reveal left-sided murmurs or a left-sided S_3 gallop typical of left heart failure. An electrocardiogram is occasionally helpful, whereas a chest radiograph may provide diagnostic information. An echocardiogram can detect left ventricular systolic dysfunction, valvular heart disease, and sometimes diastolic dysfunction causing heart failure (Chapter 51). Most recently, brain natriuretic peptide levels have been shown to be a reliable way to distinguish an exacerbation of heart failure (elevated levels) from a worsening of COPD or other conditions (Chapter 55).

Exacerbations of COPD are often accompanied by hypoxia, which can precipitate heart failure (Chapters 55 and 56), angina (Chapter 67), an acute coronary syndrome (Chapter 68), or hypoxic death in susceptible individuals. Hypoxia may also cause an acute worsening of pulmonary hypertension (Chapter 64) or systemic hypertension (Chapter 63). The key is to measure the arterial PO_2 and treat hypoxemia with oxygen.

Severe exacerbations of COPD require hospitalization and should be treated with bronchodilator therapy, intravenous antibiotics, and steroids. Arterial blood gases should be measured, and oxygen therapy instituted. In COPD, uncontrolled high-flow oxygen carries the risk of precipitating CO_2 narcosis, and the initial goals should be to maintain arterial PO_2 at levels of about 60 mm Hg (Chapters 98 to 101). In patients who can be discharged from the emergency department, a 10-day course of 40 mg of prednisone per day improves symptoms and reduces the relapse rate.[8]

Table 85–1 • COMMONLY USED MEDICATIONS FOR ACUTE EXACERBATIONS OF CHRONIC OBSTRUCTIVE PULMONARY DISEASE

DRUG	MODE OF DELIVERY	DOSE	FREQUENCY
Bronchodilators			
β-adrenergic agonist			
Albuterol	Metered-dose inhaler	100–200 µg	4 times daily
	Nebulizer	0.5–2.0 mg	4 times daily
Fenoterol	Metered-dose inhaler	12–24 µg	Twice daily
Metaproterenol	Nebulizer	0.1–0.2 mg	4 times daily
Terbutaline	Metered-dose inhaler	400 µg	4 times daily
Anticholinergic agent			
Ipratropium bromide*	Metered-dose inhaler	18–36 µg	4 times daily
	Nebulizer	0.5 mg	4 times daily
Methylxanthines			
Aminophylline†	Intravenous	0.9 mg/kg of body weight/hr	Infusion
Theophylline	Pill (sustained-release preparations)	150–450 mg‡	Twice daily
Corticosteroids			
Methylprednisolone succinate	Infusion, then	125 mg	Every 6 hours for 3 days, then
	Pill	60 mg	Daily for 4 days
		40 mg	Daily for 4 days
		20 mg	Daily for 5 days
Prednisone (for outpatients)	Pill	30–60 mg	Daily for 5 to 10 days
Limited-spectrum antibiotics			
Trimethoprim-sulfamethoxazole	Pill	160 mg and 800 mg	Twice daily for 5 to 10 days
Amoxicillin	Pill	250 mg	4 times daily for 5 to 10 days
Doxycycline	Pill	100 mg	2 tablets first day, then 1 tablet/day for 5 to 10 days

*Quaternary ammonium anticholinergic agents (e.g., ipratropium, glycopyrrolate) are preferred to tertiary ammonium compounds (e.g., atropine) because they have fewer side effects.

†Aminophylline is sometimes administered after a loading dose; the dose should be determined on the basis of serum levels of theophylline.

‡The dose varies among and within patients.

From Stoller JK: Acute exacerbations of chronic obstructive pulmonary disease. N Engl J Med 2002;346:988–994.

Table 85–2 • RECOMMENDATIONS BY PROFESSIONAL SOCIETIES REGARDING THE MANAGEMENT OF ACUTE EXACERBATIONS OF CHRONIC OBSTRUCTIVE PULMONARY DISEASE

VARIABLE	BRITISH THORACIC SOCIETY	AMERICAN COLLEGE OF CHEST PHYSICIANS AND AMERICAN COLLEGE OF PHYSICIANS–AMERICAN SOCIETY OF INTERNAL MEDICINE	EUROPEAN RESPIRATORY SOCIETY	AMERICAN THORACIC SOCIETY	GOLD
Date of statement	1997	2001	1995	1995	2001
Type of statement	Consensus	Evidence-based systematic review	Consensus	Consensus	Evidence-based review
Diagnostic testing	Recommended for patients being admitted: chest radiography, arterial blood gases, complete blood count, electrolytes, blood urea nitrogen, electrocardiography, and FEV₁, peak flow, or both; sputum culture and sensitivity	Recommended for patients admitted from emergency department: chest radiography Not recommended: spirometry	Recommended for hospitalized patients: FEV₁, arterial blood gases, chest radiography, complete blood count, sputum Gram stain and culture, electrolytes, electrocardiography	Recommended: determine the cause of exacerbation; sputum culture in severe exacerbations, if condition has worsened despite use of antibiotics, or for residents of a nursing home	Recommended: chest radiography, electrocardiography, arterial blood gases, sputum culture and sensitivity testing (if no response to initial antibiotics), electrolytes, hematocrit
Bronchodilator therapy	Recommended: For outpatients: β-adrenergic agonists, anticholinergic agents, or both For inpatients: β-adrenergic agonists and anticholinergic agents; add IV aminophylline if no response	Recommended: anticholinergic agent in maximal dose as first-line agent; then add β-adrenergic agonist Not recommended: methylxanthines	Recommended: β-adrenergic agonists, anticholinergic agents, or both in increased dose or frequency; consider IV aminophylline in severe exacerbations	Recommended: β-adrenergic agonist as first-line agent, possibly in combination with anticholinergic agent; IV aminophylline if aerosol therapy cannot be given or proves inadequate	Recommended: β-adrenergic agonist as first-line agent; add anticholinergic agent if prompt response not evident; consider oral or IV methylxanthine in severe exacerbation
Bronchodilator delivery	For outpatients: metered-dose inhaler (with instruction) For inpatients: nebulizer	Insufficient evidence for a preferred delivery device	Metered-dose inhaler can generally achieve good response; some patients prefer nebulizer during exacerbations	No preference	Not discussed
Antibiotics	Recommended for moderate or severe exacerbations: oral route; "common" antibiotic (e.g., tetracycline, amoxicillin) as first-line agent; broader spectrum cephalosporin or macrolide if no response	Optimal duration of therapy unclear	Recommended: 7–14 day course of inexpensive antibiotic (e.g., amoxicillin or tetracycline)	Recommended for abnormal mucus: "simple" antibiotic (e.g., doxycycline or amoxicillin) unless severe exacerbation, in which case consider extended-spectrum penicillin or cephalosporin	Recommended with increased sputum volume and purulence: choice should reflect local sensitivity for Streptococcus pneumoniae, Haemophilus influenzae, and Moraxella catarrhalis
Corticosteroids	Not recommended for outpatients unless already receiving, known response, or failure to achieve response to increased bronchodilator dose Recommended for inpatients: e.g., 30 mg of prednisone daily for 7–14 days	Recommended for patients not receiving long-term oral corticosteroids: systemic corticosteroids for up to 2 wk	Recommended: 0.4–0.6 mg/kg/day of oral corticosteroids for outpatients; IV for severe exacerbation in hospitalized patients	Recommended: reassess use after 1–2 wk	Recommended: 30–40 mg of oral or IV prednisolone per day for 10–14 days
Supplemental oxygen	Recommended: to achieve PaO₂ ≥50 mm Hg without pH <7.26; initial treatment with face mask with FIO₂ ≤0.28	Recommended	Recommended: to raise PaO₂ ≥60 mm Hg without raising PaCO₂ by ≥10 mm Hg	Recommended: to raise PaO₂ just above 60 mm Hg	Recommended: target PaO₂ >60 mm Hg or SaO₂ >90%; measure arterial blood gases 30 min after the initiation of oxygen
Chest physiotherapy and clearance of secretions	Not recommended	Not recommended	Recommended: coughing to clear sputum; physiotherapy at home	Recommended for hospitalized patients with ≥25 ml of sputum/day	Manual or mechanical chest percussion and postural drainage possibly beneficial for patients with lobar atelectasis or >25 mL of sputum/day; facilitate sputum clearance by stimulating coughing

Adapted from Stoller JK: Acute exacerbations of chronic obstructive pulmonary disease. N Engl J Med 2002;346:988–994.

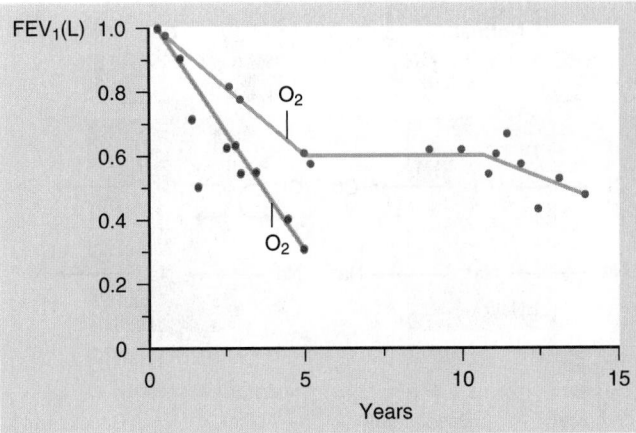

FIGURE 85–6 • Time course of forced expiratory volume in 1 second (FEV₁) decline of two patients from the author's practice. Both were initially seen when their FEV₁ was about 1.0 L, or 30% of the predicted normal value. One had a relentless further decline to death in respiratory failure. The other, after some decline, stabilized for years before experiencing a slight further decline. He died of pneumonia complicated by empyema.

Prognosis

Even though the average patient with COPD suffers relentless progression of the disease, the course may be quite variable in different individuals (Fig. 85–6). The two most important predictors of the course of COPD are age and the severity of airways obstruction as evidenced by FEV₁. Other key prognostic factors include weight loss and poor quality of life.

The need for hospital admission for an exacerbation, especially if intensive care is required, is an ominous prognostic sign in COPD; at least half such patients do not survive a year after admission. In patients with severe COPD, the issue of intensive care and artificial ventilation should be raised to ascertain the patient's attitudes with regard to these interventions and end of life care, and the results of these discussions must be documented (Chapters 3 and 98).

1. Anthonisen NR, Connett JC, Kiley JP, et al: Effects of smoking intervention and the use of an inhaled anticholinergic bronchodilator on the rate of decline of FEV1: The Lung Health Study. JAMA 1994;272:1497–1505.
2. Calverley P, Pauwels R, Vestbo J, et al: Combined salmeterol and fluticasone in the treatment of chronic obstructive pulmonary disease: A randomised controlled trial. Lancet 2003;361:449–456.
3. Goldstein RS, Gort EH, Stubbing D, et al: Randomised controlled clinical trial of respiratory rehabilitation. Lancet 1994;344:1394–1397.
4. Nocturnal Oxygen Therapy Trial Group: Continuous or nocturnal oxygen therapy in hypoxemic chronic obstructive pulmonary disease. Ann Intern Med 1980;93:391–398.
5. Nichol KL, Margolis KL, Wuorenma J, Von Sternberg T: The efficacy and cost-effectiveness of vaccination against influenza among elderly patients living in the community. N Engl J Med 1994;331:778–784.
6. Anthonisen NR, Manfreda J, Warren CP, et al: Antibiotic therapy in exacerbations of chronic obstructive pulmonary disease. Ann Intern Med 1987;106:196–204.
7. Niewoehner DE, Erbland ML, Deupree RH, et al: Effect of systemic glucocorticoids on exacerbations of chronic obstructive pulmonary disease. Department of Veterans Affairs Cooperative Study Group. N Engl J Med 1999;340:1941–1947.
8. Aaron SD, Vandemheen KL, Hebert P, et al: Outpatient oral prednisone after emergency treatment of chronic obstructive pulmonary disease. N Engl J Med 2003;348:2618–2625.

SUGGESTED READINGS

Bach PB, Brown C, Gelfand SE, McCrory DC: Position paper: Management of acute exacerbations of chronic obstructive pulmonary disease: A summary and appraisal of published evidence. Ann Intern Med 2001;134:600–620. *Lengthy and detailed review with explicit methods.*

Pauwels RA, Buist S, Calverly PM, et al: Global strategy for the diagnosis, management and prevention of chronic obstructive pulmonary disease. Am J Respir Crit Care Med 2001;163:1256–1276. *Summary of recommendations by an international panel jointly sponsored by NIH and WHO, which are well referenced.*

Sethi S, Evans N, Grant BJ: New strains of bacteria and exacerbations of chronic obstructive pulmonary disease. N Engl J Med 2002;347:465–471. *Support for the causative role of bacteria in exacerbations of chronic obstructive pulmonary disease.*

Stoller JK: Acute exacerbations of chronic obstructive pulmonary disease. N Engl J Med 2002;346:988–994. *A thoughtful, balanced review.*

86 CYSTIC FIBROSIS

Michael J. Welsh

Definition

Cystic fibrosis is an autosomal recessive genetic disease caused by mutations in the gene encoding the cystic fibrosis transmembrane conductance regulator (CFTR). It is relatively common, with an incidence of 1 in 2000 to 3000 whites; approximately 30,000 persons in the United States are affected. About 1 in 20 to 25 whites carry mutations in the CFTR gene; carriers are completely asymptomatic. The disease affects several different organs, but most current morbidity and 90 to 95% of mortality result from chronic pulmonary infections. Pancreatic insufficiency is also a common cause of morbidity.

Historical Perspective

The first known reference to cystic fibrosis is an adage from northern European folklore: "Woe to that child which when kissed on the forehead tastes salty. He is bewitched and soon must die." That saying describes the salty sweat that is the basis of an important diagnostic test and the early mortality. The first pathologic and clinical description came in 1938, when the disease was called cystic fibrosis of the pancreas. The severity and frequency of lung disease was soon appreciated. Since then, marked improvements have occurred in diagnosis, clinical management, understanding, and treatment of the disease. As a result, the current median survival is approximately 30 years.

In addition to its importance as a clinical disease, the study of cystic fibrosis is important because it provides an instructive example of the pathway of discovery in the investigation of a genetic disease. Because it was one of the earliest diseases identified by positional cloning, a review of the advances, problems, and opportunities that physicians and scientists have encountered since discovery of the CFTR gene may presage events that will be repeated and varied as an increasing number of disease-associated genes are discovered.

Pathogenesis and Pathology

The gene for CFTR was positionally cloned in 1989. The gene encodes a 1480 amino acid protein that belongs to a family of proteins called *a*denosine triphosphate (ATP) *b*inding *c*assette (ABC) transporters. Several members of this family are clinically important including the multidrug resistance protein (MDR), the sulfonylurea receptor (SUR), lipid transport proteins that are defective in sitosterolemia (ABCG8 and ABCG5) and Tangier disease (ABC1), and the Stargardt macular dystrophy protein (ABCR). Although most ABC transporters form membrane pumps, CFTR forms a Cl⁻ permeable ion channel that is regulated by phosphorylation. It contains five domains: two membrane-spanning domains, each composed of six membrane spanning sequences, that contribute to the formation of the Cl⁻ conducting pore; two nucleotide-binding domains that bind and hydrolyze ATP to gate the channel; and a regulatory (R) domain that stimulates channel opening when it is phosphorylated by cyclic adenosine monophosphate (cAMP) dependent protein kinase. CFTR is located in the apical (lumen-facing) membrane of epithelium in the pulmonary airways, pancreatic duct, intestine, biliary ducts, and in the apical and basolateral membranes of the sweat gland duct (Fig. 86–1).

The most common cystic fibrosis mutation is a 3 base pair deletion that causes the loss of a phenylalanine at position 508 (ΔF508). The ΔF508 mutation occurs on about 70% of cystic fibrosis chromosomes; the percentage is somewhat higher in persons of northern European descent. More than 700 other mutations and variations have been discovered in the gene, with only a handful accounting for more than 1% of mutations. CFTR protein with the ΔF508 mutation is made in the endoplasmic reticulum but it is misfolded. As a result, it is recognized by the cellular quality control system, which prevents its traffic to the Golgi complex and then the apical membrane, instead targeting it for degradation by the proteosome. Although it is not normally delivered to the cell membrane, the ΔF508 protein retains significant Cl⁻ channel activity. Thus, correction of the defective processing could provide a novel approach to treatment. It is now appreciated that there are four general classes of mutation. Class I

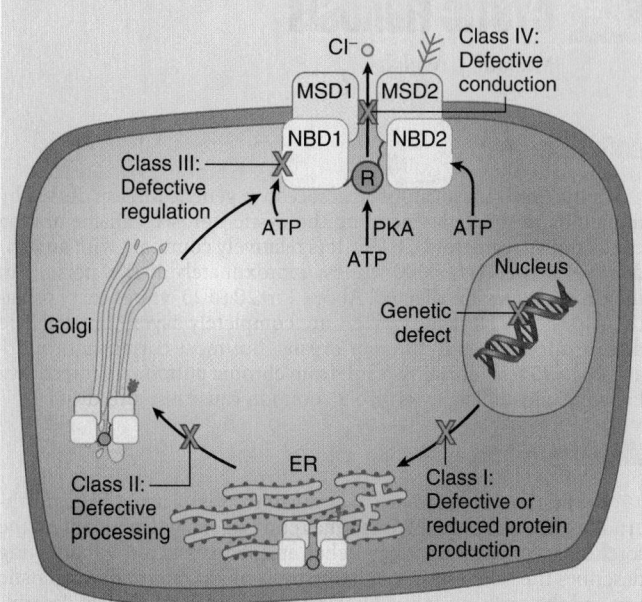

FIGURE 86–1 • Biosynthesis and function of CFTR in an epithelial cell. Glycosylation is indicated by the orange branched structure. Domains of CFTR are labeled as MSD, membrane-spanning domains; NBD, nucleotide-binding domains; and R, regulatory domain. Loss of CFTR function can result from four different classes of mutation. The ΔF505 mutation is a class II defect. (From Welsh MJ, Smith AE: Molecular mechanisms of CFTR chloride channel dysfunction in cystic fibrosis. Cell 1993;73:1251–1254.)

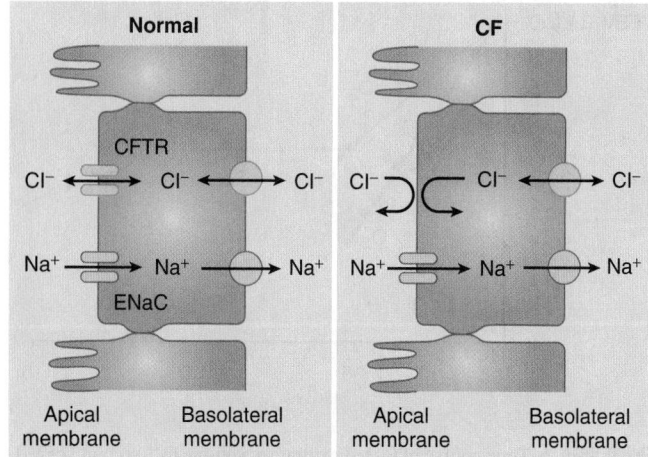

FIGURE 86–2 • Model of electrolyte transport by normal and cystic fibrosis airway epithelia. The apical membrane of normal epithelia contains CFTR Cl⁻ channels and ENaC Na⁺ channels. The paracellular pathway between the cells through the tight junctions also shows some permeability to ions.

mutations in the CFTR gene cause the loss or reduction of CFTR Cl⁻ channel activity by generating an incomplete messenger RNA (mRNA) due to premature stop signals, frame shifts, and abnormal splice sites or reduced amounts of CFTR mRNA. Class II mutations, such as ΔF508, cause misfolding. Class III and IV mutations generate correctly localized proteins, which either do not open appropriately or which form pores that do not allow the normal passage of Cl⁻, respectively. Much of the variability in the clinical disease can be explained by variations in the severity of specific CFTR gene mutations. Nevertheless, other genes and environmental factors also modify the clinical course. A search is underway to identify modifier genes because they might suggest novel therapeutic strategies. At present, counseling patients about prognosis based on genotype is unreliable.

Knowledge that CFTR is an epithelial Cl⁻ channel combined with an appreciation of the epithelial physiology of organs affected by the disease has provided some insight into the pathogenesis and manifestations of the disease (Fig. 86–2). The water-impermeable sweat gland duct absorbs NaCl through Na⁺ channels and CFTR Cl⁻ channels as sweat flows from the secretory coil to the surface of the skin. In cystic fibrosis, loss of CFTR prevents absorption of Cl⁻ and, because of the requirements for electroneutrality, absorption of Na⁺. As a result, sweat emerges onto the skin with high Cl⁻ and Na⁺ concentrations. In pancreatic ducts, CFTR Cl⁻ channels are important for alkalinization and hydration of the pancreatic secretions as they flow from the pancreatic acinar cells to the intestine. In cystic fibrosis, loss of CFTR prevents this process and causes obstruction of the small pancreatic ducts, thereby blocking the output of pancreatic enzymes. Ultimately, the organ atrophies. A similar scenario appears to apply in the liver; loss of CFTR Cl⁻ channels disrupts normal salt and water balance in the small biliary ducts, causing their obstruction. It seems likely, although it has not been shown, that obstruction of the small ducts in the male genital tract also leads to the atrophy, fibrosis, or absence of the vas deferens, tail and body of the epididymis, and seminal vesicles. In the ileum, CFTR Cl⁻ channels play a central role in salt and water secretion. Disruption of this process is thought to produce dehydrated intestinal contents that obstruct the ileum in the newborn, causing meconium ileus and producing distal intestinal obstruction syndrome later in life.

Persistent bacterial airway infection, especially with *Pseudomonas aeruginosa*, is the hallmark of lung disease in cystic fibrosis. Intractable infections appear to develop in a two-step process. First, cystic fibrosis impairs pulmonary defenses, predisposing to infection. Then, the microorganisms develop altered growth characteristics, and the host develops a chronic inflammatory state.

Cystic fibrosis causes a host defense defect restricted to the lung; patients are not predisposed to infection elsewhere, and normal lungs transplanted into a cystic fibrosis patient do not develop the same infections. Normal lungs are protected from inhaled and aspirated bacteria by a multicomponent defense system involving mucociliary clearance, phagocytic cells (macrophages and neutrophils), and the innate immune system. The latter includes lysozyme, lactoferrin, β-defensins, and other antimicrobial proteins contained in the thin layer of liquid covering the airways. Several hypotheses might explain the pulmonary host defense defect. One hypothesis suggests that loss of CFTR Cl⁻ channels leads to increased NaCl concentrations in airway surface liquid, and this high concentration impairs the activity of salt-sensitive antimicrobial factors. Another hypothesis suggests that loss of CFTR increases Na⁺ and liquid absorption, reducing airway surface liquid volume and impairing mucociliary clearance. Other hypotheses suggest increased binding of bacteria to airway epithelia, defective bacterial phagocytosis, or impaired secretion from submucosal glands. These defects might give inhaled bacteria a survival advantage, predisposing to infection.

After recurrent infections, cystic fibrosis lungs become permanently colonized, most often with *P. aeruginosa*. The strain first colonizing the airway usually persists, perhaps for the life of the patient. In the lung, *P. aeruginosa* organisms live as biofilms, community structures in which bacteria are encased in a self-produced polymeric matrix. This specialized growth mode allows the bacteria to persist in a hostile environment. *P. aeruginosa* biofilms are extremely resistant to antibiotics, thereby explaining the failure of even prolonged, intensive antibiotic treatment to eradicate *P. aeruginosa*.

Chronic infection is associated with an intense neutrophil-dominated inflammatory response, and there is some suggestion that cystic fibrosis lungs may have an abnormally profuse inflammatory response compared with normal lungs. The inflammatory stimulus remodels the airways, causes submucosal gland hypertrophy, and increases mucus output. The combination of increased mucus, abundant neutrophils, and inflammatory debris that includes DNA, actin, and other macromolecules produces thick, purulent sputum that obstructs airways. The resulting damage leads to bronchitis, progressive bronchiectasis, and respiratory failure.

Clinical Manifestations

Patients with cystic fibrosis can present at several ages with a variety of clinical manifestations. For example, they may present as newborns with meconium ileus, as infants or children with failure to thrive, or from childhood to adulthood with recurrent respiratory tract infections. These and other symptoms can mimic those found in a variety of other diseases.

LUNG DISEASE

CLINICAL PRESENTATION. Cough is usually the earliest manifestation. At first it is intermittent, occurring with what appear to be acute respiratory illnesses. Coughing is worse at night and on awakening. The cough is sometimes accompanied by wheezing, particularly in infants and young children. Episodes of cough tend to persist longer than expected for an acute respiratory illness and, with time, occur more and more frequently. As the disease progresses, the cough becomes productive of thick, purulent, often green sputum. Patients may have symptoms of bronchitis for several years or even a decade or two. Eventually, however, exacerbations of cough and sputum production are accompanied by dyspnea, reduced appetite, and weight loss. Exercise tolerance decreases as the disease progresses. Acute exacerbations improve with intensive therapy but tend to increase in frequency and severity until the patient develops symptoms of bronchiectasis (Chapter 87). Physical findings depend on the stage of the disease. At first crackles are intermittent, occurring with exacerbations. Lung sounds may be decreased due to pulmonary hyperinflation. As the disease progresses, rales and rhonchi are common and continuous.

LABORATORY EVALUATION

Sputum Culture. Early in the disease, cystic fibrosis airways become colonized with bacteria, which are virtually impossible to eliminate. *Staphylococcus aureus* and *Haemophilus influenzae* are often found initially. With time, however, *P. aeruginosa* becomes common, often as a mucoid species. Although mucoid *P. aeruginosa* is occasionally cultured from patients with other lung diseases, its presence in sputum should immediately alert the physician to the possibility of cystic fibrosis. Infection with *Burkholderia cepacia* is also common, especially later in the course of the disease.

Radiologic Evaluation. With standard chest radiographs, hyperinflation may be the first finding, followed by peribronchial cuffing, which creates linear opacities. Impaction of mucus and changes consistent with bronchiectasis are observed as the disease progresses. For unknown reasons, the right upper lobe is often the first and most severely involved. High-resolution chest computed tomography (CT) reveals early changes of bronchiectasis that may be widespread before conventional radiographs show any change. Hilar adenopathy is uncommon. Changes of pulmonary hypertension become obvious late in the disease.

Pulmonary Function. The first changes are of airways obstruction, particularly of the small airways. Spirometry shows reduced airflow rates, including a decreased forced expiratory volume in 1 second (FEV_1), FEV_1/forced vital capacity (FVC) ratio, and maximal midexpiratory flow (MMEF). The ratio of residual volume to total lung capacity is often increased. Changes consistent with airway obstruction may even be present in infants. Evidence of airway hyperreactivity is common. The arterial Po_2 tends to decrease with time due to ventilation-perfusion mismatching. Only in late-stage disease is the Pco_2 increased and chronic respiratory acidosis apparent. The course of the disease and the response to therapy are often followed by serial measurement of spirometry, lung volumes, and oxygenation.

COMPLICATIONS. Pneumothorax (Chapter 95) is a well-recognized complication, and the incidence increases with age. Although it is occasionally an incidental finding on the chest radiograph, it is often associated with chest pain, dyspnea, and hemoptysis. Indications for chest tube placement are the same as for pneumothorax from other causes. The rate of recurrence is high; pleural sclerosis may be required to prevent recurrences.

Hemoptysis becomes common as bronchiectasis develops (Chapters 81 and 87). Blood-streaked sputum is the most frequent finding. Massive hemoptysis occurs in approximately 1% of patients and is usually associated with an exacerbation of the chronic respiratory infection. Treatment is usually directed at the underlying pulmonary disease, but when hemoptysis is life-threatening, bronchial artery embolization or surgery may be required.

Digital clubbing, which occurs in nearly all patients with cystic fibrosis, is often discovered when the lung disease becomes symptomatic. Hypertrophic pulmonary osteoarthropathy may occur in up to 15% of patients, especially adolescents and adults; its symptoms may correlate with exacerbations of the pulmonary disease.

Loss of CFTR function also affects the upper airway epithelium, and chronic rhinitis is common. The sinuses are almost universally involved, as evidenced by opacification on plain radiography or magnetic resonance imaging (MRI), but acute or chronic sinusitis is not common. Nasal polyps occur in 15 to 20% of patients and occasionally require resection to prevent nasal obstruction. Of note, epithelial cells isolated from resected nasal polyps are critical in producing model systems used in research on pathogenesis and novel therapies. When surgery is scheduled to resect nasal polyps, a cystic fibrosis research center should be contacted, because the polyps are a valuable research resource.

Although more than 50% of patients have antibodies to *Aspergillus fumigatus*, only a small number develop allergic bronchopulmonary aspergillosis (Chapters 84 and 386). Expectoration of rusty brown sputum plugs is suggestive of this condition. Late in the disease, untreated hypoxemia and progressive loss of functional lung may produce pulmonary artery hypertension and right ventricular failure (Chapter 64). Respiratory failure (Chapter 99) becomes increasingly difficult to manage as the disease worsens. Because patients with cystic fibrosis rely on cough to clear their airways, they often respond poorly to mechanical ventilation, which is generally instituted only if there is an acute or reversible precipitating event.

PANCREATIC DISEASE

Failure of the exocrine pancreas (Chapter 145) occurs in approximately 85% of patients. It is almost universal in patients homozygous for the ΔF508 mutation. Some mutations appear to produce CFTR with sufficient residual function to prevent complete pancreatic failure, although the pancreas is usually not normal. Obstruction of ducts, loss of acinar cells, and pancreatic enzyme deficiency lead to malabsorption of protein, fat, and fat-soluble vitamins. Bulky, foul-smelling stools are often difficult to flush. If left untreated, patients with pancreatic insufficiency may show a failure to thrive, weight loss, and growth inhibition. Weight loss can also be associated with severe respiratory disease and increased work of breathing.

Symptoms of pancreatitis (Chapter 145) occur in a small percentage of adolescents and adults, particularly patients who have retained some pancreatic function. Although the islets of Langerhans are relatively spared, destruction of the pancreas can cause endocrine pancreatic dysfunction in approximately 7% of all patients and is more common in adults. The presentation of symptomatic hyperglycemia is similar for patients with cystic fibrosis and type 1 diabetes. If diabetes occurs, insulin therapy should be initiated because oral agents are ineffective. Interestingly, the frequency of pancreatic disease in cystic fibrosis led to the discovery that patients with idiopathic and chronic pancreatitis have a higher than expected frequency of one or two abnormal copies of the CFTR gene; in patients with two mutations, additional investigation revealed laboratory or clinical findings consistent with mild cystic fibrosis.

GASTROINTESTINAL DISEASE

Symptoms of gastrointestinal disease are common in cystic fibrosis, although they are rarely life-threatening if properly managed. Meconium ileus, which occurs in approximately 18% of cystic fibrosis newborns, is virtually diagnostic. Small bowel obstruction, "distal intestinal obstruction syndrome," occurs in approximately 3% of patients, and intermittent abdominal pain, perhaps from partial obstruction, is much more common. Another cause of abdominal pain is intussusception, which usually requires surgical intervention. Rectal prolapse occurs occasionally in children but infrequently in adults.

GENITOURINARY DISEASE

More than 95% of males are sterile because of atrophy of wolffian duct structures. Spermatogenesis is intact, and retrieval of sperm has been used for in vitro fertilization. Interestingly, male patients with infertility due to congenital bilateral absence of the vas deferens, but no other symptoms of cystic fibrosis, also have an increased prevalence of mild mutations in the CFTR gene and/or sequence variations that decrease the number of functional transcripts. It may be that the vas deferens is the tissue most sensitive to a decrease in functional CFTR, followed by the lung and then the pancreas. Female patients with cystic fibrosis also have a reduced fertility, due to poor nutrition, chronic lung infections, and/or the presence of a thick plug of mucus at the cervical os. Women with severely compromised pulmonary and nutritional status may show an accelerated deterioration during pregnancy.

HEPATOBILIARY DISEASE

Focal biliary cirrhosis appears to be increasing as patients live longer (Chapter 156). The severity varies widely, with evidence in many patients limited to an elevated alkaline phosphatase level. Obstructive biliary tract disease occurs in approximately 4% of patients. In severe cases, hepatosplenomegaly, jaundice, ascites, and edema develop. Hematemesis from esophageal varices is a severe complication that may require endoscopy and sclerosis of affected vessels. Hepatic insufficiency may require liver transplantation.

OTHER ABNORMALITIES

The increased salt loss in cystic fibrosis sweat can lead to salt depletion, especially with heat stress. Volume depletion and metabolic alkalosis are uncommon but serious complications. Enlarged submandibular, sublingual, and submucosal glands are commonly observed on physical examination. The parotid glands are not enlarged. Adult patients may develop osteoporosis owing to poor nutrition or vitamin deficiency. Psychosocial issues in dealing with a lethal disease need to be recognized and treated appropriately.

Diagnosis

Meconium ileus, pancreatic insufficiency, typical pulmonary manifestations, and/or a history of cystic fibrosis in the immediate family should prompt the consideration of cystic fibrosis. One or two of these abnormalities combined with a positive sweat Cl^- test make the diagnosis almost certain. DNA testing and measurement of the voltage across the nasal epithelium are helpful in establishing the diagnosis, especially when other findings are equivocal.

SWEAT Cl^- TEST. An increased concentration of Na^+ and Cl^- in sweat is one of the most consistent findings in cystic fibrosis. The sweat Cl^- should be measured by an experienced laboratory using pilocarpine iontophoresis, and it should always be repeated. A sweat Cl^- greater than 60 mEq/L, when accompanied by the major clinical manifestations, is sufficient to make the diagnosis. Only 2% of cystic fibrosis patients have a normal sweat Cl^- level.

GENETIC TESTING. If the diagnosis is strongly suspected, DNA testing may provide definitive evidence of cystic fibrosis. DNA testing, which is readily available from a few commercial and university laboratories, is also of value for detection of carriers, genetic counseling, and prenatal screening. Standard tests that can be performed from buccal swab specimens report on >80 of the most common mutations, which yields a detection rate of approximately 90% for northern European whites.

In the absence of a positive sweat test or the detection of cystic fibrosis mutations on both chromosomes, evidence for the diagnosis has been established in some research laboratories by measurement of the voltage across the nasal epithelium. This test evaluates the function of CFTR Cl^- channels in airway epithelia.

Course of Disease

The course is punctuated by exacerbations of lung disease followed by improvement with intensive therapy. Exacerbations are characterized by an increased frequency and severity of cough, increased sputum production, a change in the color or appearance of the sputum, increased dyspnea (especially with exertion), reduced appetite, and a feeling of chest congestion. These findings are accompanied by an increased respiratory rate, use of accessory muscles of respiration, and increased rales, rhonchi, and wheezes. Laboratory evaluation may show worsening pulmonary function, new infiltrates on chest radiograph, and leukocytosis.

The lung disease is progressive. Patients with an FEV_1 less than 30% predicted, an arterial PO_2 less than 55 mm Hg, or an arterial PCO_2 greater than 50 mm Hg have 2-year mortality rates greater than 50%. Among patients with the same FEV_1, there is a greater relative risk for female and younger patients.

Rx Treatment

Current therapy for cystic fibrosis is targeted at prevention and treatment of the various organ dysfunctions and symptoms. The aggressive care of these patients has substantially increased the length and quality of their lives. In part, this increase has been owing to a network of Cystic Fibrosis Foundation-accredited care centers that provide multidisciplinary care for these complicated patients. These centers have been critical to obtaining information about the course of the disease, identifying complications, validating therapies, and education.

ANTIBIOTICS. Exacerbations of lung disease usually require an intensive course of parenteral antibiotics for 2 to 3 weeks. The choice of antibiotics is based on sputum cultures to identify and test the susceptibility of organisms. *P. aeruginosa* is a particularly common pathogen, and therefore the combination of an aminoglycoside and a β-lactam antibiotic are commonly used. Emergence of antibiotic-resistant organisms is a serious problem, especially with *P. aeruginosa* and *B. cepacia*.

Although *P. aeruginosa* is rarely eradicated, an important benefit is gained by decreasing the net bacterial load with intensive intravenous antibiotics. As the number of organisms decreases, airway inflammation is reduced, thereby decreasing airway destruction and the accompanying systemic symptoms. The response to therapy is assessed by improvement of symptoms, of pulmonary function, and, in some cases, of quantitative bacterial counts in sputum. During therapy, serum concentrations of aminoglycosides must be measured frequently, because cystic fibrosis patients usually require higher-than-normal antibiotic doses due to increased clearance rates and increased volumes of distribution.

Use of quinolone antibiotics has been appealing because they can be administered orally. However, resistant strains of *P. aeruginosa* and *S. aureus* have become common. Delivery of long-term maintenance antibiotics or quarterly administration of antibiotics in an attempt to suppress chronic infection and the development of bronchiectasis is being studied. A potential risk of such strategies is more rapid development of highly resistant strains of bacteria.

Administration of antibiotics by inhalation is attractive because high concentrations can be attained at the airway surface and in the mucus. Moreover, systemic toxicity can be minimized. Using optimal nebulizers, aerosolized high-dose tobramycin can reduce the density of *P. aeruginosa* and improve FEV_1. [1]

CHEST PHYSIOTHERAPY. Chest percussion and postural drainage are mainstays of treatment designed to clear purulent secretions. Other recent approaches to physiotherapy, as well as high-frequency chest compression with an inflatable vest and airway oscillation with a flutter valve, are of benefit for some patients.

BRONCHODILATORS. Beneficial effects of β-adrenergic agonists and anticholinergic agents (Chapter 84) have been demonstrated in short-term studies. Bronchodilator therapy should be considered during exacerbations and in hospitalized patients. However, the benefit of long-term bronchodilator therapy remains controversial.

DEOXYRIBONUCLEASE. DNA released from neutrophils forms long fibrils that contribute to the viscosity of cystic fibrosis sputum. By cleaving the DNA, inhaled, recombinant human deoxyribonuclease I can increase the cough clearance of sputum and decrease the frequency of respiratory exacerbations that require intravenous antibiotics. [2] It is sometimes prescribed for patients with purulent sputum and airway obstruction.

ANTI-INFLAMMATORY AGENTS. Glucocorticoids have improved lung function in some studies, but adverse effects have tempered enthusiasm for their use. [3] Very high doses of ibuprofen have been reported to slow the rate of decline in FEV_1, but frequent monitoring of serum concentrations is required, and long-term safety data are not available.

PANCREATIC ENZYMES AND NUTRITION. The frequency of pancreatic dysfunction means that pancreatic enzymes are critical for nutrition. Enzymes are administered at mealtimes as enteric-coated capsules. The number of capsules is adjusted based on weight gain or loss, abdominal cramping, and the character of stools. High doses of delayed-release pancreatic enzymes have been associated with colonic strictures. The fat-soluble vitamins A, D, and E are administered routinely, and vitamin K may be given sporadically for bleeding or to correct a prolonged prothrombin time. Patients are encouraged to eat a balanced diet, and an increase in total calories is encouraged. For some children and for patients with anorexia, supplemental feedings through percutaneous gastrostomy or duodenostomy is recommended. In general, the better the nutritional state, the slower the decline in pulmonary function.

OTHER CONSIDERATIONS. Attention should be paid to adequate salt intake during hot weather. Exercise is encouraged for its effects on the cardiovascular system, physical conditioning, and the promotion of cough. Adequate immunizations, including influenza, are mandatory. Supplemental oxygen should be given to patients with hypoxemia. Cigarette smoke, including passive smoke, should be avoided. Other air pollutants can have adverse effects, although their role in pulmonary deterioration is not certain. Lung transplantation (Chapter 97) should be considered for patients with an FEV_1 less than 30% predicted.

NOVEL TREATMENTS. Conceptually, the simplest approach to treating this disease would be to transfer a normal CFTR gene or cDNA into the affected cells. Correction of approximately 5 to 10% of airway epithelial cells could correct the electrolyte transport defect, and the airway epithelium is accessible to local inhalant delivery. Studies using recombinant viral and nonviral vectors in animals and humans indicate that gene transfer is possible, but at present it is not efficient enough. Additional problems include limited persistence of expression and development of an immune response to some vectors. Progress in this area of research has been substantial, and it is hoped that successful gene therapy will become a reality. Other experimental approaches include attempts to modulate ion transport of the airway epithelium by compensating for the loss of CFTR Cl⁻ channels. Although amiloride has been evaluated to inhibit Na⁺ transport, in multicenter trials the rate of decline in pulmonary function was not different in control and amiloride groups. Attempts to retarget CFTR containing the ΔF508 mutation to the cell surface (class II mutations), to suppress stop mutations (class I), and to increase the opening of channels present at the cell surface (class III) are under investigation.

Prognosis

Therapeutic regimens for cystic fibrosis have continued to improve. Nearly half of patients with cystic fibrosis are now adults. The dramatic improvement in the length and quality of life have been the result of aggressive treatment, attention to the details of treating a complex disease that affects numerous organs, and vigilant monitoring and treatment of early lung disease.

1. Ramsey BW, Pepe MS, Quan JM, et al: Intermittent administration of inhaled tobramycin in patients with cystic fibrosis. N Engl J Med 1999;340:23–30.
2. Fuchs HJ, Borowitz DS, Christiansen DH, et al: Effect of aerosolized recombinant human DNase on exacerbations of respiratory symptoms and on pulmonary function in patients with cystic fibrosis. N Engl J Med 1994;331:637–642.
3. Eigen H, Rosenstein BJ, FitzSimmons S, Schidlow DV: A multicenter study of alternate-day prednisone therapy in patients with cystic fibrosis. J Pediatr 1995;126:515–523.

SUGGESTED READINGS
Davies JC, Geddes DM, Alton EWFW: Gene therapy for cystic fibrosis. J Gene Med 2001;3:409–417. *Discussion of the prospects for and barriers to gene therapy of cystic fibrosis and other diseases.*
McKone EF, Emerson SS, Edwards KL, et al: Effect of genotype on phenotype and mortality in cystic fibrosis: A retrospective cohort study. Lancet 2003;361:1671–1676. *Patients homozygous for the Δ508 mutation generally had a worse prognosis than did compound heterozygous patients.*
Ratjen F, Doring G: Cystic fibrosis. Lancet 2003;361:681–689. *Summary of the disease, with emphasis on the pulmonary manifestations.*
Singh PK, Schaefer AL, Parsek MR, et al: Quorum sensing signals indicate that cystic fibrosis lungs are infected with bacterial biofilms. Nature 2000;407:762–764. *Evidence that P. aeruginosa infections in cystic fibrosis are biofilm infections and the implications.*

87 BRONCHIECTASIS AND LOCALIZED AIRWAY/PARENCHYMAL DISORDERS

Alan F. Barker

BRONCHIECTASIS

Pathophysiology and Etiology

Bronchiectasis is an acquired disorder of the major bronchi and bronchioles; it is characterized by permanent abnormal dilation and destruction of bronchial walls. The affected areas show a variety of changes including transmural inflammation, mucosal edema (cylindrical bronchiectasis), cratering and ulceration (cystic bronchiectasis) with bronchial arteriole neovascularization, and distortion due to scarring or obstruction from repeated infection (varicose bronchiectasis). The obstruction often leads to postobstructive pneumonitis that may temporarily or permanently damage the lung parenchyma. The induction of bronchiectasis requires two factors: (1) an infectious insult and (2) impairment of drainage, airway obstruction, and/or a defect in host defense.

AIRWAY OBSTRUCTION DUE TO FOREIGN BODY ASPIRATION. Examples of airway obstruction causing bronchiectasis include previous foreign body aspiration or encroaching lymph nodes (middle lobe syndrome). Bronchiectasis as a sequela of foreign body aspiration generally occurs in the right lung and in the lower lobes or the posterior segments of the upper lobes. It is important to identify the presence of airway obstruction (as with foreign body aspiration) because surgical resection often produces a cure. Although witnessed or recognized aspiration is uncommon, an episode of choking and coughing or unexplained wheezing or hemoptysis should raise the suspicion of a foreign body.

Particulate aspiration is typically associated with an altered state of consciousness due to stroke, seizures, inebriation, or emergent general anesthesia. The foreign body is often unchewed food or part of a tooth or crown. Delayed or ineffective therapy and poor nutrition may contribute to prolonged pneumonitis with resultant focal bronchiectasis.

HUMORAL IMMUNODEFICIENCY. Patients with hypogammaglobulinemia usually present in childhood with repeated sinopulmonary infections. In adults, the history may include frequent episodes of "sinusitis" and "bronchitis." Establishing the diagnosis of humoral immunodeficiency is important, because γ-globulin replacement can diminish or even prevent further respiratory tract infections and lung damage. Intravenous immunoglobulin (Ig) augmentation should be administered when levels of IgG, IgA, and IgM are less than 5 to 10% of normal values. In patients with isolated IgG subclass deficiency, tests of humoral competency, such as an antibody response to *Haemophilus influenzae* or pneumococcal vaccine, help decide whether low levels are functional.

CYSTIC FIBROSIS (Chapter 86). Major respiratory diseases in cystic fibrosis (CF) are sinusitis and bronchiectasis; the latter may be the sole feature of CF in adults. Clues suggesting the presence of this disorder are upper lobe radiographic involvement and sputum cultures showing mucoid *Pseudomonas aeruginosa* or *Staphyloccus aureus*.

YOUNG'S SYNDROME. Patients with Young's syndrome exhibit clinical features similar to CF including bronchiectasis, sinusitis, and obstructive azoospermia. They are often middle-aged men identified during evaluation for infertility. They do not have increased sweat chloride values, pancreatic insufficiency, or genetic abnormalities. No cause has been identified.

RHEUMATIC DISEASES. Rheumatoid arthritis and Sjögren's syndrome can be complicated by bronchiectasis (Chapters 278 and 282). Although most patients have obvious rheumatic features when the bronchiectasis is discovered, some patients have only mild arthropathy. The presence of bronchiectasis increases mortality rate associated with respiratory infections.

DYSKINETIC CILIA. Although immotile cilia were originally described in the respiratory tract and sperm of patients with Kartagener's syndrome (dextrocardia, sinusitis, bronchiectasis), other patients have dyskinetic cilia leading to poor mucociliary clearance, repeated respiratory infections, and subsequent bronchiectasis. Several candidate genes responsible for the abnormal protein involved in the modified motility of cilia have been identified.

Table 87–1 • BRONCHIECTASIS: DIAGNOSTIC FEATURES OF ASSOCIATED CONDITIONS

CONDITION	DIAGNOSTIC TEST	ABNORMAL RESULT
Immunodeficiency	Quantitative IgG, IgA, IgM	All low; rarely, isolated subclass G is low
Ciliary dyskinesia	Respiratory mucosa biopsy (examine by electron microscopy)	Ciliary struts or spokes broken or missing
Bronchopulmonary aspergillosis	IgE	High, often >1000
	Types I and III skin tests; precipitins	Positive
	Fungal sputum cultures	Positive about 50% of time
Mycobacterium avium-intracellulare	Mycobacterial sputum culture/DNA probe	Positive in about two thirds of patients
Cystic fibrosis	Sweat chloride	>55–60 mEq/L
	Sputum culture	*Pseudomonas aeruginosa*
	Genetic testing	ΔF508 most frequent
Foreign body aspiration	Bronchoscopy	Lobar or segmental obstruction

Ig = immunoglobulin.

PULMONARY INFECTIONS. Pulmonary infections have been associated with the development of bronchiectasis. Some individuals with presumed viral or *Mycoplasma* infection develop repeated respiratory infections and bronchiectasis. In addition to direct tissue injury, a sequela of virulent infections (tuberculosis) may include enlarged and caseous lymph nodes around bronchi or damaged airways that predispose to bacterial colonization (Chapter 341). The recognition of bronchiectasis in acquired immunodeficiency syndrome (AIDS; Chapter 415) illustrates the accelerated destructive interaction between repeated infections and impaired host defense. Childhood whooping cough (pertussis; Chapter 316) is now of mostly historical interest in the pathogenesis of bronchiectasis. It is unclear whether many of these children had secondary bacterial pneumonia. *Mycobacterium avium-intracellulare* (MAI) has traditionally been considered a secondary pathogen in an abnormal host (AIDS) or in already damaged lung (bullous emphysema). However, presumed normal hosts have developed bronchiectasis with primary MAI infections (Chapter 342). The syndrome has been recognized in white women older than age 55 years with chronic cough and middle lobe or lingual involvement.

ALLERGIC BRONCHOPULMONARY ASPERGILLOSIS. *Aspergillus* may also be associated with bronchiectasis (Chapter 386). This disorder should be suspected in patients with a long history of asthma that is resistant to bronchodilator therapy and is associated with a cough productive of sputum plugs or mucopurulence. Allergic bronchopulmonary aspergillosis probably represents a hyperimmune reaction to the presence of the *Aspergillus* organism, airway damage due to mycotoxins and inflammatory mediators, and even direct infection.

CIGARETTE SMOKING. A causal role for cigarette smoking in bronchiectasis has not been shown. However, smoking and repeated infections may worsen pulmonary function and accelerate the progression of already present disease.

Clinical Manifestations

Patients often report frequent bouts of "bronchitis" requiring therapy with repeated courses of antibiotics (Chapter 360). Symptoms in most patients include daily cough productive of mucopurulent phlegm, intermittent hemoptysis, pleurisy, and shortness of breath. In bronchiectasis, bleeding can be brisk; it is often associated with acute infective episodes and is produced by injury to superficial mucosal neovascular bronchial arterioles. Physical findings on chest examination include crackles, rhonchi, and/or wheezing. Digital clubbing is rare.

Diagnostic Evaluation

The diagnostic evaluation is designed to confirm the diagnosis of bronchiectasis, to identify potentially *treatable* underlying causes, and to provide functional assessment (Table 87–1). However, a defined etiology is found in fewer than 50% of patients with suspected bronchiectasis. Imaging of the chest is always necessary to confirm the diagnosis.

CHEST RADIOGRAPHY. The chest radiograph is abnormal in most patients with bronchiectasis, and this, in combination with the clinical findings, may be sufficient to establish the diagnosis. Suspicious but not diagnostic radiographic findings include platelike atelectasis, dilated and thickened airways (tram or parallel lines; ring shadows on cross section), and irregular peripheral opacities that may represent mucopurulent plugs. The distribution of changes also may be helpful. A central (perihilar) distribution of the abnormal shadowing is suggestive of allergic bronchopulmonary aspergillosis, whereas predominant upper lobe distribution is suggestive of CF.

HIGH-RESOLUTION COMPUTED TOMOGRAPHY. High-resolution computed tomography (HRCT) of the chest is the defining modality for diagnosis of bronchiectasis. The major features of bronchiectasis on HRCT include airway dilatation, lack of airway tapering toward the periphery, varicose constrictions or ballooned cysts off the end of a bronchus, and bronchial wall thickening (Fig. 87–1). HRCT is indicated in the following settings: a patient with suspicious clinical findings but a relatively normal chest radiograph; a patient whose chest radiograph is abnormal (e.g., pneumonic infiltrate) and underlying bronchiectasis is strongly suspected; a patient for whom management decisions, such as surgical resection of the abnormal areas of lung, depend on the extent of bronchiectasis; and patients in whom the presence or absence of other confounding diseases, such as chronic obstructive lung disease or interstitial lung disease, needs to be defined. The HRCT may also demonstrate other findings, such as consolidation of a segment or lobe (from pneumonia), which can be seen in bronchiectasis but is not diagnostic as an isolated finding; enlarged lymph nodes, which may be indicative of reaction to infection; or areas of low attenuation and vascular disruption, probably due to the

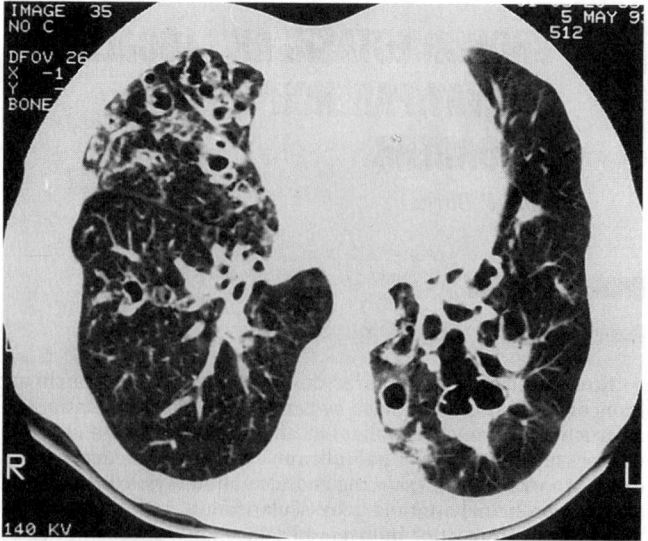

FIGURE 87–1 • High-resolution chest CT of a patient with bronchiectasis shows dilated and thickened airways in both lungs. Airways on the left have grapelike clusters of saccular bronchiectasis.

distorting effect of inflammatory small airways and suggestive of emphysema.

BRONCHOSCOPY. Bronchoscopy is an important diagnostic tool in focal (segmental or lobar) bronchiectasis to examine for obstruction by a foreign body, tumor, structural deformity, or extrinsic compression from lymph nodes. Bronchoscopic lavage may help identify or confirm pathogens such as MAI, and biopsy can be examined by electron microscopy for the ultrastructural features of ciliary dyskinesia. Bronchoscopy plays a key role in patients with hemoptysis to help localize the bleeding to a lobe so that appropriate intervention can be performed.

PULMONARY FUNCTION TESTS. Pulmonary function testing allows a functional assessment of the impairment induced by bronchiectasis. Spirometry before and after the administration of a bronchodilator is adequate in most patients. Obstructive impairment (reduced or normal forced vital capacity [FVC], low forced expiratory volume in 1 second [FEV_1], and/or FEV_1/FVC ratio) is the most frequent finding, but a very low FVC is also seen in advanced disease in which much of the lung has been destroyed.

Table 87–2 • ANTIBIOTIC STRATEGIES TO SUPPRESS BACTERIAL INFECTIONS IN PATIENTS WITH BRONCHIECTASIS

STRATEGY	EFFECTIVENESS	ISSUES/PROBLEMS
Daily antibiotic	Moderately effective	Resistance develops; oral and vaginal yeast
7–14 days of antibiotic alternating with 7–14 days of no antibiotic	Well tolerated	Resistance develops after several cycles
Aerosol antibiotic (tobramycin)	Effective for virulent gram-negative organisms	Requires nebulizer and bronchodilator
Intermittent intravenous antibiotics	Effective; reserve for severe bronchitis and/or resistant organisms	Maybe only rescue therapy; most expensive

 Treatment

Antibiotics are used to treat an acute exacerbation and to prevent recurrent infection by suppression or eradication of pathogens.

ACUTE EXACERBATION. The diagnosis of an acute exacerbation depends on symptomatic changes rather than any specific laboratory feature. Acute bacterial infections are usually heralded by increased sputum production with enhanced viscidity, shortness of breath, and pleuritic chest pain and are often accompanied by lassitude. Systemic complaints such as fever and chills are generally absent, and the chest radiograph rarely shows new infiltrates. The bacterial flora includes *Haemophilus influenzae* and *Pseudomonas aeruginosa,* often different than in patients with chronic bronchitis. Initial treatment should include a fluoroquinolone such as levofloxacin or ciprofloxacin. The duration of therapy is not well defined, but a minimum of 7 to 10 days has become frequent practice. Sputum culture and sensitivity to help define antibiotic selection and resistance patterns are indicated in patients who fail to respond to the initial antibiotic or who have repeated symptomatic attacks in a short interval.

PREVENTION. Less clear is the role of suppressive antibiotic regimens (Table 87–2). Three organisms that contribute to symptomatic episodes and are particularly problematic and difficult to eradicate include *Pseudomonas aeruginosa,* MAI, and *Aspergillus* species. *P. aeruginosa* is almost impossible to eradicate in patients with bronchiectasis; ciprofloxacin is currently the only effective oral agent against this organism, but resistance often develops after one to two treatment cycles. Aerosolized tobramycin or intravenous antibiotics are often needed when *Pseudomonas* causes repeated symptomatic episodes. Studies have shown that aerosolized tobramycin and gentamicin reduce the load of *Pseudomonas* and improve symptoms.[1,2] MAI and *Aspergillus* species are often harbored in damaged lung tissue and bronchiectatic airways. Guidelines to help decide infectivity with MAI or *Aspergillus* include (1) symptomatic episodes not responding to antibacterial agents, (2) two or more independent positive sputum cultures, (3) new infiltrates on chest radiograph with sputum culture growing either organism, and (4) HRCT showing diffuse nodular opacities with MAI infection. For the treatment of MAI infection, a four-drug regimen is recommended by the American Thoracic Society, including the following: clarithromycin, 500 mg twice daily, or azithromycin, 250 mg/day; rifampin, 600 mg/day; ethambutol, 15 mg/kg/day; and streptomycin, 15 mg/kg two to three times a week for the first 8 weeks as tolerated. Therapy is continued until the patient is culture-negative for 12 months. For patients with *Aspergillus* infection or allergic bronchopulmonary aspergillosis, a prolonged course of itraconazole (400 mg/day) reduces the sputum load, allows reduced steroid dosing, and improves clinical outcome in some patients.[3]

BRONCHIAL HYGIENE. Bronchiectasis is the prototypical disease for which secretion loosening or thinning, combined with enhanced removal techniques, should be salutary. This approach is particu-

larly important in patients in whom tenacious secretions are not reduced with appropriate antibiotic administration. Potential therapies include hydration, nebulization with saline solutions and mucolytic agents, mechanical techniques, bronchodilators, and corticosteroids.

HYDRATION AND NEBULIZATION. General hydration with oral liquids and nebulization with saline solutions or mucolytic agents are important considerations in the management of bronchiectasis. The mucolytic agent acetylcysteine is beneficial in some patients when delivered by nebulization. Although effective in CF, rhDNase in bronchiectasis neither reduces pulmonary exacerbations nor improves pulmonary function in bronchiectasis.[4]

PHYSIOTHERAPY. Mechanical techniques to loosen viscid secretions followed by gravitational positioning should be effective if followed assiduously. Chest percussion techniques include hand clapping of the chest by an assistant or application of a mechanical vibrator to the chest wall. Because bronchiectasis most often follows a middle or lower lobe distribution, reclining prone on a bed with the head over the edge is needed for postural drainage but may be difficult or uncomfortable for many patients. When physiotherapy is performed regularly, three to four times daily, enhanced sputum mobilization occurs in many patients. However, patients often do not take the time (15 to 30 minutes per session), do not have assistance to do vibratory techniques, or cannot tolerate proper positioning to get maximal benefit. Despite decades of enthusiasm for physiotherapy, a systemic review found little justification for these techniques.[5] Alternatives for patients who cannot perform chest physiotherapy include handheld positive expiratory pressure devices or flutter valves, which facilitate secretion drainage by maintaining airway patency; good evidence for the efficacy of these approaches does not exist.

BRONCHODILATORS. Airway reactivity, presumably due to transmural inflammation, is often present in patients with bronchiectasis. Aerosol bronchodilator therapy, as used in chronic bronchitis (Chapter 85), may be appropriate but has not been studied in patients with bronchiectasis.

ANTI-INFLAMMATORY MEDICATION. Because inflammation plays a major role in bronchiectasis, corticosteroid therapy might theoretically be beneficial. However, systemic steroids can further depress host immunity and promote increased bacterial and fungal colonization and even perpetuation of infection. One practical approach involves oral systemic prednisone therapy (20 to 30 mg/day for 2 days, tapering completely over 10 to 14 days) along with antibacterial therapy at the time of acute exacerbations. Regular inhaled steroids could be considered at other times. Pilot studies of aerosol beclomethasone and fluticasone show reduced sputum inflammatory mediators and improved pulmonary function.[6]

HEMOPTYSIS. Bleeding in bronchiectasis can be brisk and life-threatening. It is often associated with acute infective episodes and

Continued

is produced by injury to superficial mucosal neovascular bronchial arterioles. HRCT and bronchoscopy may help localize the bleeding to a lobe or segment. If an interventional radiology service is available, selective bronchial arterial embolization becomes the treatment of choice, because it preserves lung tissue. Thoracotomy and resection may still be necessary if bleeding persists.

SURGERY. The combination of impaired defense mechanisms and recurrent infection often results in bronchiectasis becoming a diffuse lung disease with little opportunity for surgical cure. Nevertheless, surgery may help some patients, even if it does not cure or eliminate all areas of bronchiectasis (Chapter 97).

The major indications and goals for surgery in bronchiectasis include removal of destroyed lung partially obstructed by a tumor or the residue of a foreign body; reduction in acute infective episodes occurring in the same pulmonary segment; reduction in overwhelming purulent and viscid sputum production from a specific lung segment; elimination of bronchiectatic airways causing poorly controlled hemorrhage; or removal of an area suspected of harboring resistant organisms, such as MAI or *Aspergillus*. Surgical intervention is often combined with an aggressive antibiotic and bronchodilator regimen to reduce bacterial infection and allow better drainage.

The immediate goal of surgical extirpation includes removal of the most involved segments or lobes with preservation of non-suppurative or nonbleeding areas. Middle and lower lobe resections are most often performed. Surgical mortality is less than 10%, depending on patient selection. Complications include empyema, hemorrhage, prolonged air leak, and poorly expanding remaining lung due to persistent atelectasis or suppuration.

LUNG TRANSPLANTATION. Patients with suppurative lung disease were initially considered poor candidates for lung transplantation due to the potential persistence of infection that might worsen during prolonged immunosuppression (Chapter 97). More than 2000 patients with CF have received bilateral lung or heart-lung transplantation with a survival of 75% at one year and 45% at 5 years. Other patients with non-CF bronchiectasis have undergone bilateral lung or heart-lung transplantation; no survival data are available. Timing and selection for lung transplantation in patients with bronchiectasis are similar to the guidelines for individuals with CF (Chapter 86).

CONGENITAL CYSTIC DISEASES OF THE LUNG

Lung cysts involve abnormal foregut branching or development. The cyst lining contains airway or alveolar epithelium. Cysts communicate poorly with normal airway or lung tissue. Cysts are usually clinically apparent in childhood but occasionally remain unrecognized until later in life. Presentations include an abnormal chest radiograph with a localized cyst, irregular focal infiltrate, pneumonia that resolves slowly or recurs in the same location, compression of normal lung or mediastinal structure, or hemoptysis. Although the chest radiograph may show a focal abnormality or even a well-developed cyst, CT of the chest with contrast or MRI is needed to define the location (lung, mediastinum, or abdomen), vascular supply, and degree of compression of other structures.

Of these rare disorders, the two that may present in adults are bronchogenic cysts and pulmonary sequestration. Bronchogenic cysts rarely produce symptoms. Commonly, an asymptomatic mass is noted at the cardiophrenic angle or along the heart border on a chest radiograph. CT of the chest usually distinguishes a bronchogenic cyst from a pericardial or esophageal cyst, diaphragmatic hernia, or tumor. Unless the cyst is infected or compresses other structures, no intervention is required.

Pulmonary sequestration is characterized by nonfunctioning pulmonary parenchyma that has no connection to the tracheobronchial airways. The blood supply is from a systemic artery, usually the aorta. Pulmonary sequestrations may be intralobar (75% of all sequestrations), in which the abnormal lung is within a normal lobe and does not have a separate visceral pleura, or extralobar (25% of all sequestrations), in which the abnormal lung is separate from a normal lobe and surrounded by its own visceral pleura. Extralobar sequestrations may be seen at or below the diaphragm. Repeated pneumonia in the same lobe or segment is a feature. The lower lobes (left posterior segments more often than right) are the most affected areas. The chest radiograph shows an infiltrate, atelectasis, and sometimes a cystic mass accompanied by a tubular extension to the mediastinum suspicious for a feeding vessel. Aortography, CT with contrast, or MRI confirms the diagnosis (aberrant blood supply) and defines the anatomy. Surgical resection with attention to the systemic feeding vessel is the treatment of choice and is usually curative.

HYPERLUCENT LUNG. Areas of lung with reduced markings on a chest radiograph are considered hyperlucent. At one extreme is a pneumothorax (Chapter 95), with complete absence of markings due to air in the pleural space that causes collapse of lung tissue; patients with pneumothorax are almost always symptomatic and have chest pain and shortness of breath. At the other extreme are lung parenchymal collections of air and sometimes fluid; patients are commonly asymptomatic and the disorder is usually noted on a routine chest radiograph. These collections, which may compress surrounding lung or airways and lead to infection, respiratory impairment, rupture, and pneumothorax may be due to a variety of causes. *Developmental cysts* are lined by respiratory epithelium and contain air and fluid; *congenital lobar hyperinflation* or *emphysema* is a localized anomaly that almost always presents in infancy with respiratory distress due to compression of an airway or normal lung. Occasionally an older individual presents with a chest radiograph showing focal hyperlucency. Lobar emphysema usually has areas of vasculature, whereas a pneumothorax has complete absence of markings. Surgical resection of the lobe is indicated in individuals with respiratory impairment from compressed lung or mediastinal shift. *Blebs* develop after barotrauma during mechanical ventilation; *pneumatoceles* are noted after staphylococcal or *Pneumocystis* pneumonia and are similar to blebs; *bullae* are due to alveolar destruction in severe emphysema and are sometimes amenable to surgical decompression (Chapter 97).

Hyperlucency of an entire lung (Swyer-James or Macleod's syndrome) is unilateral bronchiolitis obliterans. Histopathologic specimens show fibrosis in and around small airways. The genesis is presumed to be remote virulent respiratory viral or atypical bacterial infection or toxic fume inhalation. Exertional dyspnea and cough are occasional symptoms. Inspiratory and expiratory chest CT imaging studies demonstrate complete unilateral hyperlucency and air trapping of the affected lung with normal appearance of the contralateral lung. No specific intervention is required.

ATELECTASIS. Atelectasis, or collapse, is associated with hypoventilation of the lung (Fig. 87–2). Atelectasis may include the whole lung due to an intrinsic mainstem mass or extrinsic compression from lymph node enlargement. Lobar, segmental, or subsegmental regions may be involved. The decreased ventilation and sustained blood flow lead to ventilation-perfusion mismatch and hypoxemia.

Platelike or discoid atelectasis refers to the appearance on chest radiograph of horizontal or curvilinear lines. This type of atelectasis is seen after surgery or lengthy recumbency with conditions such as stroke or head or spinal injuries. Sustained chest pain of any etiology may also lead to splinting and platelike atelectasis.

Patchy atelectasis occurs in any air-space filling disease such as pulmonary hemorrhage, pulmonary edema, or respiratory distress syndrome. Fluid-filled alveoli and loss of surfactant contribute to patchy areas of infiltrate.

Passive, relaxation, or compression atelectasis occurs when the lung recoils to a smaller volume due to a process in the adjacent pleural space such as pneumothorax or pleural effusion. Obstructive atelectasis can be caused by an obstructed bronchus due to an intrinsic process, such as a tumor or mucus plug, or an extrinsic process, such as enlargement of peribronchial lymph nodes (middle lobe syndrome).

Rounded atelectasis is a round masslike density abutting the pleura. It is caused by pleural scar that invaginates and contracts lung tissue. Rounded atelectasis is almost always seen in the setting of asbestos pleural disease.

Rx Diagnosis and Treatment

The chest radiograph is a key diagnostic tool. Volume loss is almost always present and involves displacement of a lobar fissure, the mediastinum, or diaphragm to the affected area or side. Diagnosis and management of segmental or lobar obstructive atelectasis includes bronchoscopy. An intrinsic mass can be visualized

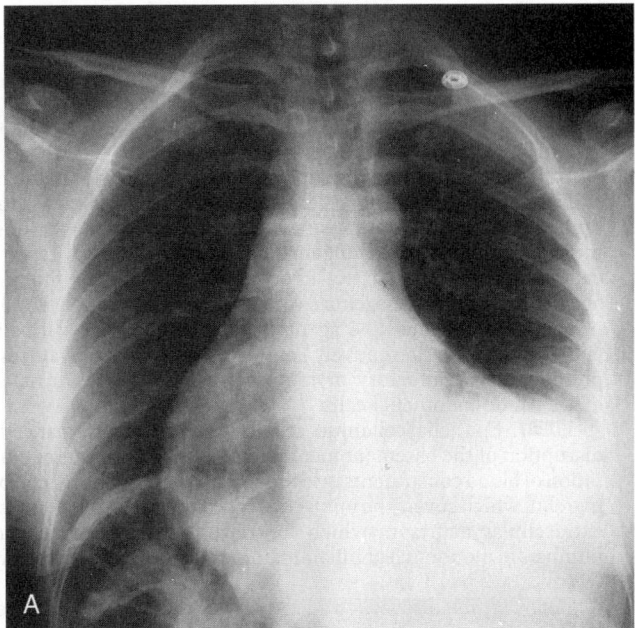
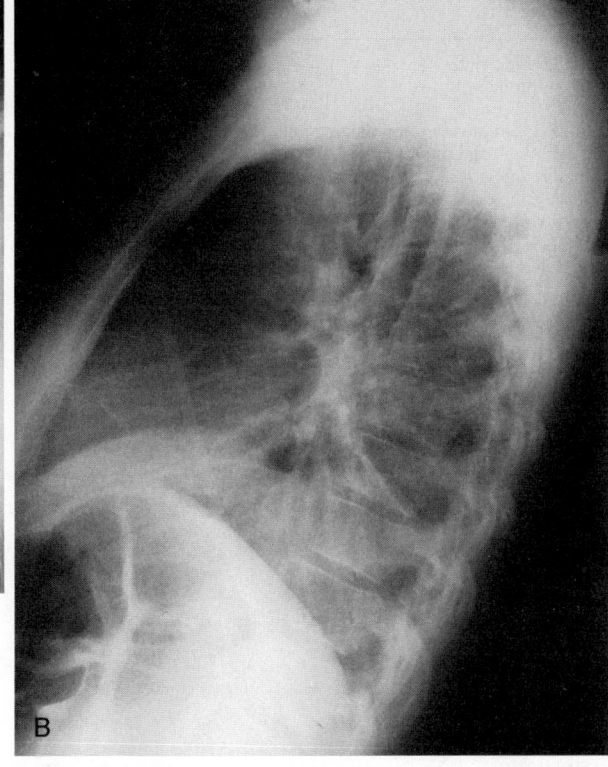

FIGURE 87–2 • Chest films of a patient with left lower lobe atelectasis. *A*, The posteroanterior film shows on the left opacity over the heart, loss of the diaphragmatic contour, and diagonal line of the major fissure. *B*, The lateral projection shows an elevated left diaphragm.

and biopsied for cytologic analysis. Mucus plugs can be removed by lavage and suctioning.

Rounded atelectasis must be distinguished from a tumor mass; CT scan may confirm the pleural thickening and the invaginating lung tissue. For patients at bedrest or with other risks for developing platelike atelectasis, attention to deep breathing, mobilization, analgesic medication for chest pain, and bronchial hygiene will improve gas exchange and prevent pneumonia. For patchy atelectasis, treatment is directed at the underlying disease and to the types of measures that also enhance lung volume in platelike atelectasis. Passive atelectasis requires attention to the pleural space process, such as evacuation of a pneumothorax or drainage of a pleural effusion.

1. Lin HC, Cheng HF, Wang CH, et al: Inhaled gentamicin reduces airway neutrophil activity and mucus secretion in bronchiectasis. Am J Respir Crit Care Med 1997;155:2024–2025.
2. Barker AF, Couch L, Fiel SB, et al: Tobramycin solution for inhalation reduces sputum *Pseudomonas aeruginosa* density in bronchiectasis. Am J Respir Crit Care Med 2000;162:481–485.
3. Stevens DA, Schwartz HJ, Lee JY, et al: A randomized trial of itraconazole in allergic bronchopulmonary aspergillosis. N Engl J Med 2000;342:756–762.
4. O'Donnell AE, Barker AF, Ilowite JS, Fick RB, for the rhDNase Study Group: Treatment of idiopathic bronchiectasis with aerosolized recombinant human DNase I. Chest 1998;113:1329–1334.
5. Jones A, Rowe BH: Bronchopulmonary hygiene physical therapy in bronchiectasis and chronic obstructive pulmonary disease: A systemic review. Heart Lung 2000;29:125–135.
6. Tsang KW, Ho PL, Lam WK, et al: Inhaled fluticasone reduces sputum inflammatory indices in severe bronchiectasis. Am J Respir Crit Care Med 1998;158: 723–727.

SUGGESTED READINGS

Barker AF: Bronchiectasis. N Engl J Med 2002;346:1383–1393. *An updated review.*
Cohen M, Sahn SA: Bronchiectasis in systemic diseases. Chest 1999;116:1063–1074. *Thorough discussion of unusual causes of bronchiectasis.*
Evans DJ, Greenstone M: Long-term antibiotics in the management of non-CF bronchiectasis—do they improve outcome? Respir Med 2003;97:851–858. *Weighs evidence, which is not conclusive.*
Patel SR, Meeker DP, Biscotti CV, et al: Presentation and management of bronchogenic cysts in the adult. Chest 1994;106:79–85. *Seventeen-year review at one institution of 18 patients; 65 references.*

88 INTERSTITIAL LUNG DISEASE

Galen B. Toews

General Description

The interstitial lung diseases (ILDs) represent a large and heterogeneous group of lower respiratory tract disorders that are considered together because of shared clinical, radiographic, and physiologic presentations (Table 88–1). They also share certain pathogenic mechanisms and histopathologic features. The target structure in ILD is the alveolar wall, which includes the alveolar epithelium, the capillary endothelium, and the connective tissues surrounding blood vessels, lymphatic vessels, and airways. Although distinctive pathologic changes are present, the common denominator among ILDs is that they are all characterized by widespread disruption of alveolar walls with loss of functional alveolar capillary units and accumulation of collagenous scar tissue.

The array of conditions that lead to ILD is broad and includes many rare disorders. A clinician must appreciate the value and limitations inherent in each step of a diagnostic evaluation. Virtually all ILDs may involve breathlessness, exercise intolerance, progressive respiratory insufficiency, and diffuse parenchymal abnormalities on chest radiograph. Therefore, the key element of the history is careful identification of the exposures to exogenous agents and symptoms of associated systemic illnesses that point to specific conditions. The physical examination may suggest the presence of ILD, but occasionally, ancillary findings (such as evidence of a pleural effusion or a systemic rheumatic disease) also suggest or discount specific diagnoses. The radiographic features of ILD may be entirely nonspecific or may be tremendously valuable in narrowing the diagnostic possibilities. Pulmonary function testing is most useful for demonstrating physiologic abnormalities consistent with ILD and for managing patients and assessing responses to therapy. Only occasionally does physiologic testing help narrow the differential diagnosis. The clinician is often left with only a presumptive diagnosis, and accordingly must decide when to obtain tissue for histopathologic examination, knowing that lung biopsy findings may be nonspecific.

Table 88–1 • CLINICAL CLASSIFICATION OF INTERSTITIAL LUNG DISEASE

PRIMARY LUNG DISEASES
Idiopathic pulmonary fibrosis*
Sarcoidosis*
Bronchiolitis obliterans with organizing pneumonia*
Nonspecific interstitial pneumonia
Desquamative interstitial pneumonia
Respiratory bronchiolitis-associated interstitial lung disease
Lymphocytic interstitial pneumonia
Histiocytosis X
Lymphangioleiomyomatosis

ILD ASSOCIATED WITH SYSTEMIC RHEUMATIC DISORDER
Rheumatoid arthritis*
Systemic lupus erythematosus*
Scleroderma*
Polymyositis-dermatomyositis*
Sjögren's syndrome
Mixed connective tissue disease*
Ankylosing spondylitis

ILD ASSOCIATED WITH DRUGS OR TREATMENTS
Antibiotics*
Anti-inflammatory agents
Cardiovascular drugs*
Antineoplastic agents*
Illicit drugs
Dietary supplements
Oxygen
Radiation
Paraquat

ENVIRONMENT/OCCUPATION–ASSOCIATED ILD
Organic dusts/hypersensitivity pneumonitis (>40 known agents)
Farmer's lung*
Air conditioner lung*
Bird breeder's lung*
Bagassosis
Inorganic dusts
Silicosis*
Asbestosis*
Coal worker's pneumoconiosis*
Berylliosis
Gases/fumes/vapors
Oxides of nitrogen
Sulfur dioxide
Toluene diisocyanate
Oxides of metals
Hydrocarbons
Thermosetting resins

ALVEOLAR FILLING DISORDERS
Diffuse alveolar hemorrhage
Goodpasture's syndrome
Idiopathic pulmonary hemosiderosis
Pulmonary alveolar proteinosis
Chronic eosinophilic pneumonia*

ILD ASSOCIATED WITH PULMONARY VASCULITIS
Wegener's granulomatosis
Churg-Strauss syndrome
Hypersensitivity vasculitis
Necrotizing sarcoid granulomatosis

INHERITED DISORDERS
Familial idiopathic pulmonary fibrosis
Neurofibromatosis
Tuberous sclerosis
Gaucher's disease
Niemann-Pick disease
Hermansky-Pudlak syndrome

*Disorders that are the most common causes of ILD or less common conditions in which ILD is a prominent manifestation of disease.
ILD = interstitial lung disease.

Epidemiology

The prevalence of ILD is estimated to be 20 to 40 per 100,000 of the population. ILD accounts for 100,000 hospital admissions yearly. The increased use of pneumotoxic drugs to treat malignant and cardiovascular disease and given for organ transplantation, and the increased identification of occupationally induced ILD are likely to contribute to an increased incidence.

Pathobiology

ILDs are the result of the superimposed processes of tissue injury and attempted repair (Fig. 88–1). If the events associated with a self-limited inflammatory response are altered, the result may be ongoing injury and structural derangement rather than normal repair. The causes of most ILDs are not known. Bacteria, viruses, fungi, toxic agents, environmental agents and genetic abnormalities have all been implicated. The causative agents may directly injure epithelial or endothelial cells. Alternatively, causative agents may activate resident pulmonary inflammatory or immune cells, which, in turn, injure epithelial or endothelial cells.

INJURY. Epithelial cell injury results in the loss of alveolar cells and disruption of the basement membrane. Tissue injury causes extravasation of blood constituents into the area of injury. A fibrin-rich exudative clot, which covers the injured alveolar surface, forms a provisional extracellular matrix in which the repair process begins. Variable numbers of mononuclear inflammatory cells are present in the injured alveoli.

INTRA-ALVEOLAR FIBROSIS/REPAIR. Whether the repair process results in fibrosis or in a return to normal lung anatomy depends on the success in clearing the intra-alveolar exudate and on the rapid re-epithelialization of the denuded alveolar surface by means of epithelial cell migration, proliferation, and differentiation. The forming alveolar exudate contains a group of cytokines and mediators not normally present in the alveolar spaces. These cytokines result in (1) fibroblast migration, (2) fibroblast proliferation, and (3) differentiation into myofibroblasts, which produce abundant extracellular matrix components. This process results in the formation of fibroblastic foci in areas of injured lung. Imbalances in eicosanoids and metalloproteinases and their inhibitors likely contribute to progressive deposition of matrix. Angiogenic factors such as C-X-C chemokines induce formation of new blood vessels in the organizing provisional matrix. Alveolar re-epithelialization is impaired; hyperplastic type II alveolar epithelial cells eventually resurface the organizing intra-alveolar exudate. Alveolar surface area is lost as a result of intraluminal fibrosis and also as a result of alveolar collapse.

Diagnosis

HISTORY. Breathlessness is the most prevalent complaint. Initially, dyspnea develops only on exertion. This symptom is often attributed to other causes (out of shape, overweight, viral infection). As the disease progresses, dyspnea occurs even at rest. Nonproductive cough and fatigue are also prominent complaints. Cough is a frequent complaint in patients with bronchiolitis obliterans organizing pneumonia (BOOP), eosinophilic pneumonia, and idiopathic pulmonary fibrosis. Pleuritic chest pain may occur with ILDs associated with systemic rheumatic disease and some drug-induced disorders. Pleuritic chest pain and sudden worsening of dyspnea suggest a spontaneous pneumothorax, a characteristic finding in lymphangioleiomyomatosis, neurofibromatosis, tuberous sclerosis, and pulmonary histiocytosis X. Hemoptysis may be the presenting complaint of patients who have diffuse alveolar hemorrhage syndromes or in lymphangioleiomyomatosis, but it is infrequent in other ILDs. Hemoptysis should prompt a search for complications such as pulmonary embolus, superimposed infection, or malignancy. Substernal chest discomfort may be noted late in the disease as a result of pulmonary hypertension.

A specific diagnosis is most often made because of information gathered during the history. A detailed, lifelong occupational history must be obtained; ILDs have long latency periods between occupational exposure and onset of symptoms and radiographic abnormalities (Chapter 89). Exposure to agents that cause ILDs may also occur as a result of hobbies or recreational activities (bird breeder's lung, wood dust worker's lung, farmer's lung, sauna taker's disease). Specific questions relating to medications that induce ILDs must be asked. The agents to which the patient has been exposed and the circumstances, intensity, and duration of exposure must be determined. Fever and chills, common symptoms in hypersensitivity pneumonitis, are often temporally related to the workplace or to hobbies. Symptoms may diminish or disappear after a weekend, vacation, or an absence

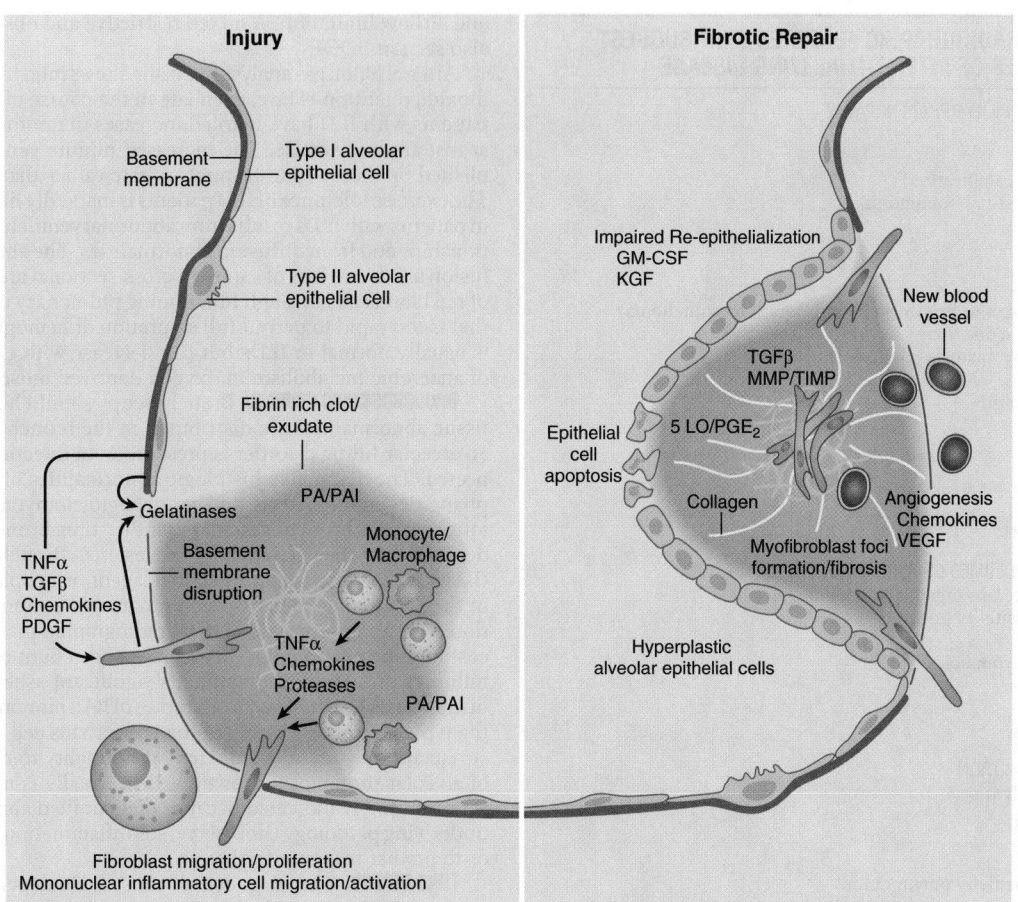

FIGURE 88–1 • Multiple localized injuries damage alveolar epithelial cells and alter alveolar-capillary wall permeability. A fibrin rich clot forms a provisional matrix. Repair of the damaged alveolar surface requires removal of the provisional matrix, regulated angiogenesis, and replacement of lost epithelial cells. Plasminogen activator (uPA) generates plasmin, which participates in matrix remodeling. If the provisional matrix is not cleared, fibroblasts migrate into the alveolar spaces, proliferate, and differentiate into myofibroblasts. The fibroproliferative response is regulated by cytokines, growth factors, and arachidonic acid metabolites. Both intra-alveolar and interstitial fibroblasts secrete extracellular matrix proteins, mainly collagens. The balance of angiogenic and angiostatic factors regulate the formation of new vessels. An imbalance between metalloproteinases and their inhibitors may favor deposition of extracellular matrix. Re-epithelialization of denuded basement membrane involves a balance between epithelial cell migration/proliferation and cell death. 5-LO = 5-lipoxygenase; GM-CSF = granulocyte-macrophage colony stimulating factor; KGF = keratinocyte growth factor; MMP = membrane metalloproteinase; PA = plasminogen activator; PAI = plasminogen activator inhibitor; PDGF = platelet-derived growth factor; PGE_2 = prostaglandin E_2; TGFβ = transforming growth factor beta; TIMP = tissue inhibitors of metalloproteinases; TNF = tumor necrosis factor; TNFα = tumor necrosis factor alpha; VEGF = vascular endothelial growth factor.

from the workplace for several days, only to reappear on return. Patients with idiopathic pulmonary fibrosis or BOOP may date the onset of their symptoms to a preceding upper respiratory tract infection.

A smoking history should be obtained. Ninety percent of patients with histiocytosis X are active smokers. The pulmonary component of Goodpasture's syndrome occurs in only 20% of affected individuals who are nonsmokers, but it occurs in 100% of affected individuals who are smokers. Hypersensitivity pneumonitis is infrequent in patients who are active smokers.

A family history should be sought. An autosomal dominant inheritance pattern has been described for familial idiopathic pulmonary fibrosis, tuberous sclerosis, and neurofibromatosis, and an autosomal recessive pattern of inheritance is found in Gaucher's disease, Niemann-Pick disease, and Hermansky-Pudlak syndrome (Chapter 222).

PHYSICAL EXAMINATION. The physical examination may reveal typical findings of underlying causes, such as systemic rheumatic disorders or inherited diseases. In other patients, the findings are commonly restricted to the cardiopulmonary system. Bilateral, basilar, crepitant Velcro-like rales are found in most patients with ILD. Wheezing, rhonchi, and coarse rales are occasionally heard. The lung examination may be normal. With advanced disease, patients may have tachypnea and tachycardia, even at rest. Clubbing of the fingers and toes is a common but nonspecific finding in many fibrotic lung disorders; it is most often seen in patients with idiopathic pulmonary fibrosis and is unusual in sarcoidosis. The syndrome of hypertrophic pulmonary

osteoarthropathy is rare. The new appearance of digital clubbing in a patient with known ILD should prompt a search for a complicating lung malignancy. The heart examination is normal early in the course of the disease. Later, with the onset of pulmonary hypertension and cor pulmonale, an accentuated P_2, tricuspid insufficiency, a right ventricular heave, and peripheral edema may be noted. Physical findings characteristic of associated diseases (e.g., rash of systemic lupus erythematosus [SLE], skin changes of scleroderma) may be noted.

LABORATORY STUDIES. Laboratory tests can either confirm or suggest a diagnosis in ILD, but these studies are seldom diagnostic. Rheumatoid factor and antinuclear antibodies are occasionally present in patients with ILD, but their presence does not necessarily indicate an underlying collagen vascular disorder. If hypersensitivity pneumonitis is suspected, serum-precipitating antibodies to a limited number of inhaled organic antigens may be measured. Tests for antineutrophil cytoplasmic antibodies (ANCA) should be obtained if Wegener's granulomatosis (Chapter 284) is suspected. Tests for anti–basement membrane antibodies should be obtained when Goodpasture's syndrome (Chapter 119) is suspected. The electrocardiogram (ECG) is usually normal in ILD. With progressive loss of alveolar capillary units, the ECG may demonstrate a pattern of right atrial and ventricular strain.

CHEST RADIOGRAPHY. The chest radiograph plays a major role in establishing the presence of ILD and may suggest a specific diagnosis (Table 88–2). The majority of ILDs cause infiltrates in the lower lung zones. A diffuse ground-glass pattern is seen early in the disease. More

Table 88–2 • RADIOGRAPHIC FEATURES THAT SUGGEST SPECIFIC CAUSES OF INTERSTITIAL LUNG DISEASE

HILAR OR MEDIASTINAL LYMPHADENOPATHY
Sarcoidosis
Berylliosis
Silicosis (eggshell calcification)
Lymphocytic interstitial pneumonia
Amyloidosis
Gaucher's disease

PLEURAL DISEASE
Asbestosis (pleural effusion, thickening, plaques, mesothelioma)
Systemic rheumatic disorders
Lymphangioleiomyomatosis (chylous effusion)
Nitrofurantoin
Radiation pneumonitis

PNEUMOTHORAX
Histiocytosis X
Lymphangioleiomyomatosis
Neurofibromatosis
Tuberous sclerosis

PRESERVED LUNG VOLUMES OR HYPERINFLATION
Bronchiolitis obliterans organizing pneumonia
Chronic hypersensitivity pneumonitis
Histiocytosis X
Lymphangioleiomyomatosis
Neurofibromatosis
Sarcoidosis
Tuberous sclerosis

UPPER LOBE DISTRIBUTION
Ankylosing spondylitis
Berylliosis
Histiocytosis X
Silicosis
Chronic hypersensitivity pneumonitis
Necrobiotic nodules of rheumatoid arthritis

typically, a chest radiograph demonstrates nodules, linear (reticular) infiltrates, or a combination of the two (reticulonodular infiltrates). On chest radiography, alveolar filling disorders produce a diffuse abnormality, characterized by ill-defined alveolar nodules (acinar rosettes); air bronchograms may be noted in these patients. As the disease progresses, the infiltrates become coarser and lung volume is lost. Cystic areas (honeycomb pattern) appear late in the course of ILD. In 5 to 10% of patients with biopsy-proven disease, results of a chest radiograph are normal.

HIGH-RESOLUTION COMPUTED TOMOGRAPHY. High-resolution computed tomography (HRCT) allows a detailed evaluation of the lung parenchyma by using 1- to 2-mm sections with a reconstruction algorithm that maximize spatial resolution. HRCT allows earlier diagnosis of ILD, helps narrow the differential diagnosis based on the CT pattern, and increases the level of diagnostic confidence for idiopathic pulmonary fibrosis. HRCT can detect ILD despite normal chest radiographs in patients with asbestosis, silicosis, sarcoidosis, and scleroderma. HRCT abnormalities may be present before pulmonary function tests are abnormal. Conversely, a normal HRCT cannot be used to exclude ILD. Patients with predominant reticular opacities or honeycombing on HRCT usually progress despite treatment. HRCT is also valuable for identifying a suitable site for transbronchial or open lung biopsy.

PULMONARY FUNCTION TESTS. Physiologic testing can document the physiologic abnormalities associated with ILD, determine the severity, and determine the course and response to treating ILD. The classic physiologic alterations in ILD include reduced lung volumes (vital capacity, total lung capacity [TLC]), reduced diffusing capacity (DL_{CO}), and a normal or supernormal ratio of forced expiratory volume in 1 second (FEV_1) to forced vital capacity (FVC). Static lung compliance is decreased (decreased lung volume for any given transpulmonary pressure), and maximal transpulmonary pressure is increased (a very high negative pressure must be generated to open the fibrotic alveoli). Exceptions to this classic presentation are histiocytosis X, lymphangioleiomyomatosis, neurofibromatosis, sarcoidosis, and tuberous sclerosis, in which primary airway disease results in an increase in TLC

and airflow limitation. A mixed restrictive and obstructive pattern is also seen in BOOP.

Arterial blood gas analysis typically shows mild hypoxemia. Carbon dioxide retention is rare, even late in the course of the disease. Most patients with ILD have marked increases in minute ventilation both at rest and at exercise. The increased minute ventilation is accomplished by increases in respiratory rate rather than in tidal volume. The exercise tolerance of ILD patients is markedly limited. Hypoxemia in patients with ILDs results from abnormal ventilation-perfusion relationships and from diffusion abnormalities. The abnormalities in diffusion are due to loss of capillary cross-sectional area and the passage of red blood cells through functioning pulmonary capillaries at a rate that is too rapid to permit full saturation of hemoglobin. Arterial pH is usually normal in ILDs but can decrease with exercise as a result of anaerobic metabolism in oxygen-deprived muscles.

BRONCHOSCOPIC STUDIES. Bronchoscopy should be performed when tissue abnormalities are distributed in the bronchovascular bundle, an alveolar filling disorder is present, or an infectious disease is suspected. The distinctive histologic abnormalities of sarcoidosis, lymphangitic carcinomatosis, and lymphangioleiomyomatosis are usually found in the bronchovascular bundle; transbronchial biopsy may demonstrate their characteristic lesions. Bronchoalveolar lavage (BAL) is diagnostic if an infectious agent or neoplastic cell is noted in the lavage specimen. A predominance of eosinophils in conjunction with an appropriate clinical/radiographic picture can diagnose eosinophilic pneumonia. An asbestos body count of more than 1 per milliliter of BAL fluid documents significant asbestos exposure. In histiocytosis X, ultrastructural studies of BAL mononuclear cells reveal the typical Birbeck granule of the Langerhans cell. Special stains for surfactant may reveal a sufficient abnormality to enable a diagnosis of alveolar proteinosis. However, BAL usually is nonspecific, and it is not routinely indicated because of its limited ability to predict the underlying pathology (fibrosis versus inflammation), to stage disease, or to predict response to therapy.

LUNG BIOPSY. The diagnosis of most ILDs depends on histologic studies of lung parenchyma. Transbronchial biopsy should be performed if sarcoidosis or alveolar filling diseases are likely. An open lung or thoracoscopic biopsy is required to secure a specific diagnosis and accurately stage most cases of ILD in patients who do not have systemic rheumatic disease or drug-induced injury. Open or thoracoscopic biopsy is performed if the diagnosis remains questionable after reviewing the clinical, radiographic, BAL, and transbronchial biopsy data, and if the patient is not at high risk for this procedure because of age or other serious medical disease. The mortality rate for open lung biopsy is less than 1%, and the morbidity is less than 3%. A specific diagnosis is established in 90% of cases.

PRIMARY LUNG DISEASE

IDIOPATHIC PULMONARY FIBROSIS. Idiopathic pulmonary fibrosis is one of several idiopathic interstitial pneumonias. The prevalence of idiopathic pulmonary fibrosis is estimated to be 20 cases per 100,000 for males and 13 per 100,000 for females. Typically, idiopathic pulmonary fibrosis is diagnosed in patients between ages 40 and 60 years. No geographic, racial, or seasonal predilections have been noted. Patients present with the insidious onset of breathlessness with exercise and a dry, nonproductive cough. Constitutional symptoms including fever, fatigue, weight loss, myalgia, and arthralgia are present in some patients. Chest examination reveals late inspiratory fine (Velcro) rales at the lung bases. A right-sided heave, an augmented P_2, and an S_3 gallop are present in late stages of disease. Chest radiographs typically show a reticular or reticulonodular infiltrate that is most prominent in the lower lung zones. Multiple cystic or honeycombed areas with translucencies measuring 0.5 to 1 cm in diameter are seen late in the course of the disease and indicate a poor prognosis. Spontaneous pneumothorax may occur secondary to rupture of honeycomb cysts. HRCT shows patchy, predominantly peripheral, subpleural bibasilar reticular abnormalities. A variable amount of ground-glass opacity may be present (Fig. 88–2). Traction bronchiectasis and bronchiolectasis and/or subpleural honeycombing is seen in areas of severe involvement (Fig. 88–3). Physiologic testing reveals a restrictive impairment with normal airflow parameters. The DL_{CO} frequently is reduced; this reduction may precede the restrictive abnormalities. Arterial blood gases may be normal or reveal hypoxemia (secondary to ventilation-perfusion mismatch) and respiratory alkalosis.

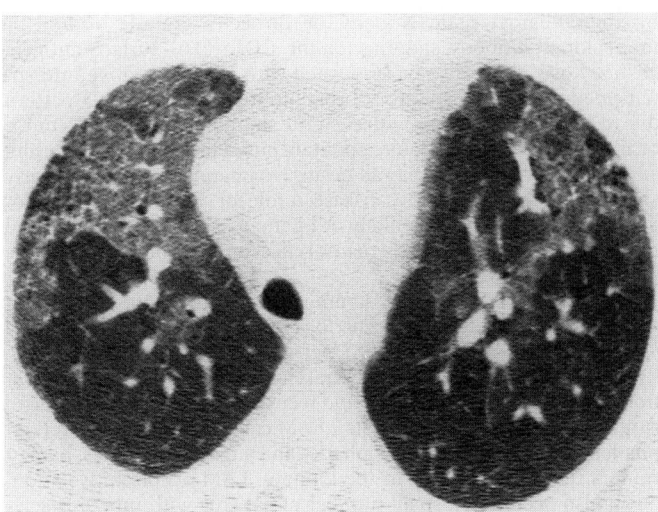

FIGURE 88–2 • Idiopathic pulmonary fibrosis. High-resolution computed tomographic scan from a patient with biopsy-proven idiopathic pulmonary fibrosis shows patchy, peripheral ground-glass opacification and small honeycomb cysts.

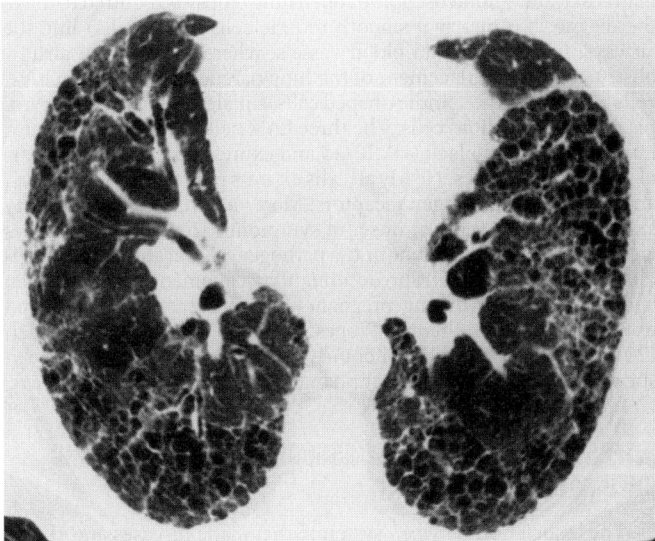

FIGURE 88–3 • Idiopathic pulmonary fibrosis. High-resolution computed tomographic scan from a patient with biopsy-proven idiopathic pulmonary fibrosis shows numerous large cystic radiolucencies (honeycombing) involving both lungs. Although most of the lung parenchyma of the lower lobes is involved, the cystic process is more prominent in the subpleural regions.

Lung tissue obtained by thoracoscopic or open lung biopsy is required to establish the diagnosis. Usual interstitial pneumonia is the pathologic abnormality that identifies idiopathic pulmonary fibrosis. Usual interstitial pneumonia is a heterogenous disease with alternating areas of normal lung, interstitial inflammation, fibrosis, and honeycomb changes. The peripheral, subpleural parenchyma is most seriously affected. The interstitial inflammation is patchy; an alveolar septal infiltrate of macrophages and lymphocytes is associated with hyperplasia of alveolar type II pneumocytes. Fibrotic areas contain dense collections of collagen; scattered foci of proliferating fibroblasts termed "fibroblastic foci" are a consistent finding. Cystic fibrotic air spaces that are lined by bronchiolar epithelium and filled with mucin (honeycombing) are noted. Both usual interstitial pneumonia and nonspecific interstitial pneumonia patterns may be seen in multiple biopsy specimens from the same patient.

The mean survival after diagnosis of idiopathic pulmonary fibrosis is 5 to 7 years. No treatment has been shown to improve survival or the quality of life for patients with idiopathic pulmonary fibrosis.

Although a trial of corticosteroid treatment has been advocated for all patients with idiopathic pulmonary fibrosis in the past, the potential benefits of treatment may be outweighed by increased risk for treatment-related complications, particularly for patients older than 70 years of age, those with end-stage honeycomb lung on HRCT, and those with concomitant major illness (diabetes mellitus, cardiac disease, extreme obesity, osteoporosis). Response rates may be higher when treatment is initiated early in the course of the disease before irreversible fibrosis has developed. If therapy is offered, it should be started at the first identification of clinical, radiographic, or physiologic evidence of impairment or documentation of a decline in lung function. Combined therapy with corticosteroids and azathioprine is the recommended therapy. Prednisone at a dose of 0.5 mg/kg/day orally should be given for 4 weeks, followed by 0.25 mg/kg/day for 8 weeks. Prednisone should then be tapered to 0.125 mg/kg/day. Azathioprine at a dose of 2 to 3 mg/kg/day orally to a maximum dose of 150 mg/day orally is administered concomitantly. Combined therapy should be continued for at least 6 months. If the patient is improved or stable, therapy should be continued. If the patient is worse, therapy should be stopped or changed. A different cytotoxic agent (cyclophosphamide) or lung transplantation should be considered. A small study reported improved lung function in patients treated with interferon-γ1b in addition to prednisolone. A large multicenter study to evaluate this agent is ongoing.

Supplemental oxygen is recommended for patients who have an arterial oxygen tension of less than 55 mm Hg at rest or with exercise. Patients with cor pulmonale and right ventricular failure or those with significant erythrocytosis should also receive oxygen therapy. Respiratory tract infections should be treated promptly. Influenza and pneumococcal vaccines should be given.

Lung transplantation is an accepted therapy for patients with end-stage ILD that is refractory to medical therapy (Table 88–3; Chapter 97). Single-lung transplantation is the preferred therapy for most patients. Two-year survival ranges from 60 to 80%, with most deaths being due to infections that complicate immunosuppressive therapy or to chronic allograft rejection.

SARCOIDOSIS. Sarcoidosis (Chapter 91) is a multisystem granulomatous disease characterized by noncaseating granulomas and derangement of normal tissue architecture. It often presents as ILD.

BRONCHIOLITIS OBLITERANS ORGANIZING PNEUMONIA. BOOP is a clinical entity that shares certain features of idiopathic pulmonary fibrosis and bronchiolitis obliterans. The onset of a flulike illness with a nonproductive cough is the most common presentation. Fever, malaise, weight loss, and fatigue are usually present for 2 months before the onset of dyspnea. Patients often have been unsuccessfully treated with multiple courses of antibiotics. Rales are common, but wheezing is rare. A restrictive defect with a reduction in DL_{CO} is present in most patients. An obstructive defect is present in 20% of patients, most of whom are current or past smokers. Chest radiography reveals bilateral diffuse alveolar opacities with normal lung volumes. Infiltrates may be peripheral, as seen in chronic eosinophilic pneumonia, or migratory. Reticulonodular infiltrates and honeycombing are rare. The diagnosis can be made by transbronchial biopsy, but thoracoscopic or open lung biopsy is usually required to confirm this diagnosis. Key

Table 88–3 • GUIDELINES FOR LUNG TRANSPLANTATION IN PATIENTS WITH INTERSTITIAL LUNG DISEASE

RECIPIENT SELECTION GUIDELINES
Untreatable, end-stage interstitial lung disease
Substantial limitation of daily activities
Limited life expectancy (<12 to 18 mo)
No other significant medical disease
Ambulatory, good rehabilitation potential
Acceptable nutritional status
Acceptable psychosocial profile and support system

RELATIVE CONTRAINDICATIONS
Presence of active systemic disease
Significant disease of other organ systems
Significant psychosocial problems, substance abuse, or history of noncompliance
Poor nutritional status
Poor rehabilitation potential

histologic features are excessive proliferation of granulation tissue within the small airways and the alveolar ducts as well as chronic inflammation in the surrounding alveoli. The intraluminal buds of granulation tissue are composed of loose collagen and myofibroblasts and often extend from one alveolus to an adjacent one via pores of Kohn. Honeycombing and diffuse alveolar wall fibrosis are not features of BOOP. Corticosteroid therapy is the most common treatment and results in recovery in two thirds of patients. Clinical improvement is rapid (days to a few weeks) in some individuals, but relapse may occur when steroids are withdrawn; retreatment is often successful.

NONSPECIFIC INTERSTITIAL PNEUMONIA. Nonspecific interstitial pneumonia is a comparatively new term used to describe a histologic pattern of idiopathic interstitial pneumonia. The clinical presentation is similar to idiopathic pulmonary fibrosis. HRCT shows bilateral symmetrical ground-glass opacities or bilateral air space consolidation. The main histologic feature of nonspecific interstitial pneumonia is the homogeneous appearance of the inflammation and/or fibrosis. Most cases of nonspecific interstitial pneumonia are of unknown etiology, although connective tissue diseases, drug-induced ILD, and chronic hypersensitivity pneumonias may be associated features. Most patients with nonspecific interstitial pneumonia have a good prognosis; most show improvement after treatment with corticosteroids. Five-year mortality is estimated to be 15 to 20%.

DESQUAMATIVE INTERSTITIAL PNEUMONIA. Desquamative interstitial pneumonia is a rare entity (<3% of all ILDs) that affects cigarette smokers in their fourth and fifth decades of life. HRCT shows diffuse ground-glass opacity in the middle and lower lung zones. Lung biopsy reveals a uniform, diffuse intra-alveolar macrophage accumulation. There is little fibrosis. Overall survival is 70% after 10 years.

RESPIRATORY BRONCHIOLITIS-ASSOCIATED INTERSTITIAL LUNG DISEASE. Respiratory bronchiolitis-associated ILD is found in current or former cigarette smokers. Chest radiographs and HRCT reveal diffuse fine reticular or nodular opacities associated with hazy opacities. A mixed obstructive/restrictive pattern is noted on spirometry. Lung biopsy reveals pigmented macrophages within the lumens of respiratory bronchioles and peribronchiolar fibrosis that extends to contiguous alveolar septa, which are lined with hyperplastic alveolar type II cells. Smoking cessation is important in the resolution of these lesions. The prognosis appears substantially better than for idiopathic pulmonary fibrosis.

LYMPHOCYTIC INTERSTITIAL PNEUMONIA. Lymphocytic interstitial pneumonia is an uncommon cause of ILD. It must be differentiated from other lymphocytic infiltrations of the lung, including primary lymphomas and lymphomatoid granulomatosis. This disorder is sometimes idiopathic but is frequently associated with other conditions such as hypogammaglobulinemic or hypergammaglobulinemic states, acquired immunodeficiency syndrome (AIDS), systemic rheumatic disorders, and bone marrow transplantation. Infectious complications occur in patients with AIDS and hypogammaglobulinemia. Corticosteroid therapy is successful in approximately 50% of patients, although some patients progress to end-stage lung disease or lymphoma.

HISTIOCYTOSIS X. Histiocytosis X is a term that encompasses three systemic diseases (eosinophilic granuloma, Letterer-Siwe disease, and Hand-Schüller-Christian disease) that have in common an abnormal infiltration of tissues by a mononuclear cell, the Langerhans cell. *Langerhans cell granulomatosis* has been proposed as an alternative term to histiocytosis X. Most patients are 20 to 40 years old, with an equal gender distribution. A history of cigarette smoking is obtained in more than 90% of patients. Patients present with nonproductive cough and exertional dyspnea. Hemoptysis, fever, weight loss, and wheezing are occasionally noted. Pleuritic chest pain and acute dyspnea secondary to spontaneous pneumothorax occur in 25% of patients. Cystic bone lesions (skull, ribs, pelvis) accompany the pulmonary disease in 10% of cases. Diabetes insipidus complicates 10% of cases and indicates a poor prognosis. The combination of ill-defined or stellate nodules (2 to 10 mm), upper lung zone cysts or honeycombing, preservation of lung volumes, and costophrenic angle sparing on HRCT is virtually diagnostic of histiocytosis X. Pulmonary function studies demonstrate a mixed obstructive and restrictive pattern. DL_{CO} is reduced, and hypoxemia is present at rest or with exercise.

Definitive diagnosis requires a thoracoscopic or open lung biopsy. An interstitial lesion characterized by the presence of centrally scarred stellate nodules is noted. Diagnosis of histiocytosis X is predicated on recognition of Langerhans cells. Langerhans cells may be detected by their characteristic X body or Birbeck's granule and/or by monoclonal antibody staining for the CD1a (T6) surface antigen. Histiocytosis X can also be associated with a desquamative interstitial pneumonia or respiratory bronchiolitis-associated ILD pattern due to strong associations with cigarette smoking. The clinical course of histiocytosis X is variable; spontaneous remission, stabilization, and disease progression may all occur. No treatment has been clearly shown to be beneficial in this disease. A role for smoking in the pathogenesis of this disorder is likely. All patients should be encouraged to stop smoking, although a beneficial effect on the evolution of disease has not been proven.

LYMPHANGIOLEIOMYOMATOSIS. Lymphangioleiomyomatosis (LAM) is a rare, nongenetic, disorder occurring only in women of child-bearing age. The prevalence of LAM is 1 per million. Patients present with dyspnea, hemoptysis, chylous pleural effusions (secondary to obstruction of the pleural lymphatics), and recurrent pneumothorax (due to rupture of emphysematous cysts). LAM can be associated with lymphadenopathy of the axial lymphatics and angiomyolipomas, benign tumors that occur chiefly in the kidneys. LAM occurs in isolation, but it also occurs in a small number of patients with tuberous sclerosis. Coarse reticular infiltrates with areas of cystic dilation are noted on chest radiography. HRCT reveals numerous thin-walled cysts (2 to 20 mm in diameter) distributed diffusely without a predilection for specific regions or lobes. The main radiologic differential is histiocytosis X, which has a more nodular appearance, spares the costophrenic angle, and shows more variation in cyst size. Pleural effusions or recurrent pneumothoraces may be the sole radiographic manifestation. Thoracoscopic or open lung biopsy is required to make the diagnosis. Abnormal smooth muscle cells (LAM cells) line the airways, lymphatics, and blood vessels, where they lead to airflow obstruction and replacement of the lung parenchyma by cysts. LAM cells appear as large spindle-shaped cells, smaller cells with little cytoplasm and epithelioid cells. The three LAM cells differ in staining for human melanoma black (HMB)-45 and express differential amounts of metalloproteinases. Nearly all cells express progesterone receptors, and 80% express estrogen receptors. Most patients die of respiratory failure within 10 years of onset of symptoms. Hormonal influences are thought to be important in the pathogenesis because lymphangioleiomyomatosis occurs predominantly in premenopausal women and is accelerated during pregnancy, the postpartum period, and exogenous estrogen therapy. Progesterone (10 mg/day) or tamoxifen (20 mg/day) are the drugs of choice. Lung transplantation has been successful in patients with lymphangioleiomyomatosis.

INTERSTITIAL LUNG DISEASE ASSOCIATED WITH SYSTEMIC RHEUMATIC DISORDERS

The association between systemic rheumatic diseases and ILD is well established. All systemic rheumatic disorders are associated with ILD (Table 88–4). The airways, alveoli, vascular system, and pleura are all variably affected. ILD associated with systemic rheumatic diseases accounts for 1600 deaths/year, which constitutes 25% of all mortality associated with ILD and 2% of all respiratory deaths.

RHEUMATOID ARTHRITIS (Chapter 278). Although rheumatoid arthritis is more common in women (female-to-male ratio, 2:1 to 4:1), rheumatoid arthritis associated with ILD is more common in men (male-to-female ratio, 3:1) and occurs in patients with late-onset rheumatoid arthritis. Most cases occur between ages 50 and 60 years. Symptoms are similar to those seen with idiopathic pulmonary fibrosis. Tachypnea and bibasilar rales are common. Associated pleural rubs may be heard, and clubbing occurs in as many as 75% of cases. Pulmonary symptoms most often follow the onset of arthritis. In one fifth of cases, ILD precedes joint manifestations. Pleural disease accompanies ILD in 20% of patients. The physiologic abnormalities of rheumatoid ILD are identical to those of other fibrosing lung diseases. Open lung biopsy early in the course of the disease reveals interstitial pneumonitis with perivascular, peribronchiolar, and interstitial infiltration by lymphocytes, plasma cells, and macrophages. This prominent lymphocytic infiltrate, which may contain germinal follicles adjacent to vessels and airways, is useful in differentiating rheumatoid ILD from idiopathic pulmonary fibrosis. The presence of rheumatoid nodules, pleural fibrosis, and adhesions is also helpful diagnostically. Rheumatoid ILD appears to be more indolent and less severe than idiopathic pulmonary fibrosis; prolonged periods of symptomatic and clinical stability may occur. Gold salts and methotrex-

Table 88–4 • PULMONARY MANIFESTATIONS OF SYSTEMIC RHEUMATIC DISORDERS

RHEUMATOID ARTHRITIS
Interstitial lung disease (ILD)
Pleural disease (pleuritis with or without effusion, empyema, pyopneumothorax)
Bronchiolitis obliterans with or without organizing pneumonia
Caplan's syndrome
Pulmonary vascular disease
Apical fibrobullous disease
Central airway obstruction secondary to cricoarytenoid arthritis

SYSTEMIC LUPUS ERYTHEMATOSUS
Pulmonary infection
ILD-acute, chronic
Pleuritis with or without effusion
Pulmonary hemorrhage
Pulmonary vascular disease, thromboembolic disease
Bronchiolitis obliterans
Diaphragmatic dysfunction
Central airway obstruction

SYSTEMIC SCLEROSIS (SCLERODERMA)
ILD
Pulmonary hypertension
Aspiration pneumonia (gastroesophageal reflux)
Bronchogenic carcinoma (scar carcinoma)

POLYMYOSITIS/DERMATOMYOSITIS
Aspiration pneumonia (pharyngeal/esophageal disorder)
ILD
Bronchiolitis obliterans organizing pneumonia (BOOP)
Respiratory muscle dysfunction (pneumonia, atelectasis, hypoventilation, respiratory failure)
Malignancy (primary, metastatic)

SJÖGREN'S SYNDROME
ILD
Lymphocytic interstitial pneumonitis
BOOP
Lymphoma
Chronic bronchitis
Recurrent pneumonia

MIXED CONNECTIVE TISSUE DISEASE
ILD
Pleuritis with or without effusion
Pulmonary hypertension
Aspiration pneumonia (esophageal disorder)

ANKYLOSING SPONDYLITIS
Upper lobe fibrobullous disease
Pleural disease (pleural thickening, pneumothorax)
Mycobacterial infections (tuberculous and nontuberculous)
Aspergillomas
Abnormal chest wall mobility
Bronchogenic carcinoma (scar carcinoma)

ate, common therapies for rheumatoid arthritis, can also induce ILD. It is difficult to distinguish between drug-induced and rheumatoid-induced ILD, except that the drug-induced disease may reverse when the drug is discontinued.

Progressive bronchiolitis obliterans also is associated with rheumatoid arthritis. Clinical manifestations include the abrupt onset of dyspnea and dry cough associated with rales and midinspiratory squeaks, occurring particularly in middle-aged women with seropositive rheumatoid arthritis. Pulmonary function studies reveal airflow obstruction, arterial hypoxemia, and respiratory alkalosis. The predominant lesion is bronchiolitis with lymphoplasmacytic infiltration of the small airway walls and obliteration of the bronchiolar airspace with granulation tissue. The prognosis is poor because treatment is ineffective. BOOP, which has also been described in patients with rheumatoid arthritis, has a more favorable prognosis than obliterative bronchiolitis alone.

SYSTEMIC LUPUS ERYTHEMATOSUS (Chapter 280). Acute lupus pneumonitis is characterized by the acute or subacute onset of tachypnea, tachycardia, dyspnea, cough, and cyanosis. Fever is common, hemoptysis is infrequent, and clubbing is absent. In 50% of patients with acute lupus pneumonitis, the acute pneumonitis is the presenting manifestation of SLE. An evolution from acute to chronic interstitial lung disease likely occurs in some individuals because persistent disease can occur after an acute onset. Clubbing is seen in some of these patients, but less frequently than in rheumatoid interstitial lung disease. The overall impact of interstitial lung disease on mortality in SLE appears small; acute and chronic interstitial lung disease causes death in 2.5% of cases of SLE. Strong consideration should be given to the possibility of pulmonary infections in patients with acute infiltrates in SLE, because infections outnumber SLE pneumonitis by a ratio of more than 30:1. High doses of corticosteroids are indicated in severely ill patients with acute pneumonitis; azathioprine can be added for refractory cases.

SYSTEMIC SCLEROSIS (Chapter 281). Interstitial lung disease is the most common pulmonary manifestation of scleroderma. Morphologic changes are found in 90% of patients at autopsy, and radiographic evidence of interstitial lung disease has been noted in 14 to 67% of cases. Clinical manifestations include dyspnea, initially with exertion and later at rest, but this symptom may be denied because of marked limitation of physical activity. Cough is usually present. Primary pulmonary hypertension may occur in the absence of pulmonary fibrosis and is often the cause of cor pulmonale. In general, correlation between the severity of pulmonary and cutaneous manifestations in scleroderma is poor. Pulmonary symptoms may antedate either cutaneous changes or Raynaud's phenomenon by intervals as long as 14 years. Reticulonodular densities may be noted on chest radiographs in both CREST syndrome (calcinosis, Raynaud's phenomenon, esophageal involvement, sclerodactyly, and telangiectasia) and diffuse scleroderma, but ILD is much less common in the former. A strikingly high incidence of calcified pulmonary granulomas (65%) has been noted in the CREST syndrome. A restrictive ventilatory defect with impaired DL_{CO} is found on pulmonary function testing. Bronchoalveolar studies of scleroderma have demonstrated an alveolitis in a significant proportion of patients, with or without ILD. Pulmonary function abnormalities have significant prognostic implications: patients with normal function have a greater than 90% 5-year survival, whereas those with restrictive spirometry have a 58% 5-year survival. Patients with a DL_{CO} of less than 40% predicted have a dismal 9% 5-year survival rate. No consistently effective treatment exists for scleroderma ILD. No data support a favorable long-term effect of corticosteroid therapy. D-Penicillamine may diminish the rate of visceral disease, but no data show improvement in lung function.

A significant association exists between the development of bronchogenic carcinoma and chronic pulmonary fibrosis in scleroderma. The majority of bronchogenic carcinomas are either bronchoalveolar cell or adenocarcinoma.

POLYMYOSITIS/DERMATOMYOSITIS (Chapter 283). The clinical presentation includes progressive dyspnea on exertion, nonproductive cough, and basilar rales, but a rapidly progressive syndrome (Hamman-Rich) may occur. Lung disease may precede muscle complaints by months to years or be superimposed on established muscular disease. No correlation exists between the severity or duration of the muscular disease and the ILD. Interstitial pneumonitis and BOOP are the most common histologic patterns identified in patients with polymyositis/dermatomyositis. Active inflammation on lung biopsy, especially BOOP, predicts a good therapeutic response. Corticosteroids have stabilized and improved symptoms and physiologic abnormalities in up to 40% of patients. Methotrexate and azathioprine have been used as therapies; both can cause ILD.

SJÖGREN'S SYNDROME (Chapter 282). Diffuse ILD is the most common lung abnormality identified in patients with primary Sjögren's syndrome. Malignant lymphomas may occur in primary Sjögren's syndrome and are usually fatal. Corticosteroids and immunosuppressive drugs are used in patients with extraglandular involvement. Lymphocytic interstitial pneumonia or BOOP may be present and often responds well to corticosteroid or immunosuppressive therapy.

MIXED CONNECTIVE TISSUE DISEASE (Chapter 281). Evidence of pulmonary dysfunction has been reported in as many as 80% of patients with mixed connective tissue disease. A proliferative vasculopathy with initial thickening and medial muscular hypertrophy affects pulmonary arteries and arterioles and is usually more prominent than the associated interstitial fibrosis. Although early detection and treatment of the ILD with corticosteroid therapy and/or immunosuppressive therapy has been advocated, prevention of irreversible pulmonary fibrosis has not been documented.

ANKYLOSING SPONDYLITIS (Chapter 279). Upper lobe fibrobullous disease, the most common pulmonary manifestation of ankylosing spondylitis, is found in patients with advanced disease. The disease is usually bilateral, and the chest radiograph commonly shows diffuse reticulonodular infiltrates in the upper lung zones with cyst formation as a result of parenchymal destruction. Patients with ankylosing spondylitis appear to be predisposed to typical and atypical tuberculosis. Additionally, aspergillomas are a late complication of colonization of the apical fibrobullous cavities. No therapy is available for the apical fibrobullous disease.

DRUG-INDUCED INTERSTITIAL LUNG DISEASE

More than 100 drugs are known to alter the structure or function of the lower respiratory tract (Table 88–5). Most drug-induced ILD is reversible if it is recognized early and the responsible drug is discontinued. Drugs can cause acute, subacute, or chronic ILD. Acute and subacute forms of drug-induced ILD usually present with fever and cough and may be mistakenly treated as bacterial pneumonia. Rales, tachypnea, tachycardia, and, occasionally, cyanosis are noted. A diffuse reticulonodular infiltrate, perhaps accompanied by a pleural effusion, is noted on the chest radiograph. Blood eosinophilia is frequent. Pulmonary function studies reveal a restrictive defect, and arterial blood gas analysis reveals hypoxemia and hypocarbia. The chronic form of drug-induced ILD is more difficult to associate with a specific causative agent because of the insidious nature of this disease. Mild, nonproductive cough is the most common symptom. Fever and eosinophilia are less common. The pathogenesis of most drug-induced reactions is poorly understood.

ANTIBIOTICS. Nitrofurantoin-induced ILD is one of the most commonly reported drug-induced pulmonary diseases. Both acute and chronic ILD occur. The mechanisms of acute and chronic ILD secondary to nitrofurantoin appear to be different, and chronic reactions can occur without previous acute ILD. The acute ILD begins 2 hours to 10 days after the onset of therapy and does not appear to be dose related. A reticulonodular or alveolar infiltrate, most prominent at the bases, is noted. The infiltrate may be asymmetrical; a pleural effusion (usually unilateral) is present in one third of patients. Discontinuing the drug is the only treatment required. Chronic nitrofurantoin-induced ILD mimics idiopathic pulmonary fibrosis. Dyspnea and nonproductive cough begin 6 months to several years after initiating therapy. In these cases, fever, eosinophilia, and pleural effusion are unusual. A diffuse interstitial process with lower zone predominance is noted on chest radiograph. A restrictive pattern is present on pulmonary function testing. Discontinuation of the drug is important, but function can be permanently lost. Corticosteroid therapy can be used if no improvement occurs after 2 months, but data regarding its use are scanty. Chronic nitrofurantoin-induced ILD is fatal in approximately 8% of cases.

ANTI-INFLAMMATORY DRUGS. Methotrexate causes granulomatous pneumonitis in 5% of patients on low-dose methotrexate for rheumatoid arthritis or other chronic inflammatory conditions. Most patients present with dyspnea, fever, rales, and hypoxemia. Hilar lymphadenopathy is seen in 10 to 15% of patients, and pleural effusion is present in 10%. When methotrexate is used in low doses, granulomatous pneumonitis is usually noted after administration of approximately 10 mg/week for an average of 80 weeks. BAL reveals a marked lymphocytosis. Most patients respond favorably to discontinuing methotrexate; corticosteroids may also be helpful, but deaths have been associated with this pneumonitis.

CARDIOVASCULAR DRUGS. Amiodarone, an antiarrhythmic drug used predominantly for treating refractory ventricular dysrhythmias (Chapter 62), causes ILD in 5 to 10% of patients. Risk factors include maintenance doses greater than 400 mg/day and previous pulmonary disease. The combination of amiodarone with general anesthesia, cardiopulmonary bypass, or pulmonary angiography is synergistic for development of acute lung injury.

Two clinical patterns exist. The most common presentation includes the insidious development of dyspnea, cough, fever, and malaise accompanied by weight loss. Pleuritic chest pain occurs in 10 to 20% of patients. Histologic findings include phospholipid-laden lamellar inclusions within lung parenchymal cells. These distinctive histologic findings may be seen in any patient receiving amiodarone and do not prove a drug-induced lung injury. Diffuse reticulonodular infiltrates are present on chest roentgenograph. Other patients may present with a more abrupt onset of an acute illness characterized by fever and localized alveolar infiltrates. This clinical presentation may strongly mimic infectious pneumonia or, in severe cases, adult respiratory distress syndrome. Multiple, nodular pulmonary infiltrates with necrotizing pneumonia and cavities have also been reported. Amiodarone-induced ILD is unlikely in the absence of a 15% decline in DL_{CO}. If reasonable alternative therapy is available (Chapters 59 through 62), amiodarone should be withdrawn if ILD is present. The same is true for patients with ventricular arrhythmias. If no alternative is available but to continue the drug, a trial of corticosteroid therapy is reasonable.

ANTINEOPLASTIC AGENTS (Chapter 191). Chemotherapeutic drug-induced ILD is a major cause of morbidity and mortality in immunocompromised patients and patients with malignancies. In these patients, drug toxicity may be the cause of 20% of diffuse pulmonary infiltrates. The diagnosis of chemotherapeutic drug-induced ILD is one of exclusion. Dyspnea occurs within the first few weeks of treatment, followed by cough and intermittent fever. Auscultation reveals dry rales; clubbing has not been reported. Symptoms frequently precede chest radiographic findings. An asymmetrical infiltrate limited to a single lobe may be the initial radiographic presentation, but the infiltrate generally becomes diffuse and uniform in distribution. Pulmonary function studies invariably show a restrictive pattern with a reduction in DL_{CO}.

Table 88–5 • DRUG-INDUCED INTERSTITIAL LUNG DISEASE

ANTIBIOTICS
Nitrofurantoin
Cephalosporins
Sulfonamides
Penicillin
Isoniazid

ANTI-INFLAMMATORY AGENTS
Methotrexate
Gold
Penicillamine
Phenylbutazone
Nonsteroidal anti-inflammatory agents

CARDIOVASCULAR DRUGS
Amiodarone
Tocainide
β-blockers (propranolol, practolol, pindolol, acebutolol)
Hydralazine
Procainamide
Hydrochlorothiazide

ANTINEOPLASTIC AGENTS
Bleomycin
Busulfan
Cyclophosphamide
Methotrexate
Nitrosoureas (BCNU, CCNU, methyl-CCNU, DCNU)
Melphalan
Chlorambucil
Mercaptopurine
Mitomycin
Procarbazine

CENTRAL NERVOUS SYSTEM DRUGS
Phenytoin
Carbamazepine
Chlorpromazine
Imipramine

ORAL HYPOGLYCEMIC AGENTS
Tolbutamide
Tolazamide
Chlorpropamide

ILLICIT DRUGS
Heroin
Propoxyphene
Methadone

OXYGEN

RADIATION

Bleomycin-induced lung disease is common. Parenchymal lung disease develops in 10% of patients; the mortality rate approaches 50%. The incidence of pulmonary reactions to bleomycin increases in the presence of risk factors such as age (older than 70 years), oxygen therapy, radiation therapy, multidrug regimens, and a cumulative dose of more than 450 units. Busulfan-induced ILD occurs in 2 to 3% of patients and frequently develops a year after onset of therapy; the process usually does not respond to withdrawal of the drug or to administration of corticosteroids. Cyclophosphamide-induced lung disease, which can begin a few weeks to 6 years after initiating therapy, has a variable course; both steroid-responsive and nonresponsive disease has been reported. Nitrosourea (BCNU and methyl-CCNU) induced ILD has been reported in as many as 50% of patients who have received doses of more than 1500 mg/m^2. These agents may have a synergistic effect with cyclophosphamide. Procarbazine causes acute ILD with peripheral and pulmonary eosinophilia and pleural effusions.

ENVIRONMENTAL/OCCUPATIONAL-ASSOCIATED INTERSTITIAL LUNG DISEASE (Chapters 89 and 90)

Alveolar Filling Disorders

Alveolar filling diseases occur when air spaces distal to the terminal bronchiole are filled with blood, lipid, protein, water, or inflammatory cells. An acinar infiltrate characterized roentgenographically by small nodular densities with ill-defined margins is noted. Virtually all of the alveolar filling disorders can ultimately result in ILD.

GOODPASTURE'S SYNDROME (Chapter 119). Goodpasture's syndrome is characterized by diffuse pulmonary hemorrhage, progressive glomerulonephritis, circulating antiglomerular basement membrane (anti-GBM) antibodies, anti-alveolar basement membrane (anti-ABM) antibodies, and ILD. Goodpasture's syndrome occurs primarily in young men between ages 18 and 35 years. The most common presenting symptoms are hemoptysis, dyspnea, cough, and fatigue. Hemoptysis may be modest, but it can be massive and life-threatening. Gross hematuria, nausea, and vomiting are present in 50% of patients. Fever and weight loss are noted in approximately one fourth of patients. Hypochromic, microcytic anemia is characteristic of Goodpasture's syndrome. Bilateral symmetrical alveolar or acinar infiltrates are present on chest radiographs. When active bleeding stops, the alveolar infiltrates fade within 48 hours, leaving residual reticulonodular infiltrates. The DL$_{CO}$ increases during intrapulmonary bleeding due to CO uptake by the intra-alveolar erythrocytes. An increase in DL$_{CO}$ (>30%) is highly suggestive of diffuse hemorrhage. The differential diagnosis of Goodpasture's syndrome includes SLE, Wegener's granulomatosis, Henoch-Schönlein syndrome, polyarteritis nodosa, and cryoglobulinemia. Serologic assays for anti-GBM antibodies are positive in 95% of patients. The diagnosis is confirmed by immunofluorescent studies of renal tissue in some patients; lung biopsy is seldom necessary.

Spontaneous remissions can occur but are rare. The severity of the renal involvement best predicts the outcome. Therapy consists of corticosteroids and cytotoxic drugs together with plasmapheresis until circulating anti-GBM antibodies have been removed.

IDIOPATHIC PULMONARY HEMOSIDEROSIS. Idiopathic pulmonary hemosiderosis is a rare disorder characterized by intermittent, diffuse alveolar hemorrhage without evidence of vasculitis, inflammation, granulomas, necrosis, circulating anti-GBM antibodies, elevated pulmonary venous pressure, or systemic disease. Iron deficiency anemia and ILD frequently accompany this disorder. Although predominantly a disease of children, about 20% of patients with idiopathic pulmonary hemosiderosis are adults, usually younger than age 30 years. There is a 2:1 male predominance in adults. Respiratory symptoms include cough, fatigue, substernal chest pain, and malaise due to anemia. Tachycardia, tachypnea, fever, and hepatosplenomegaly (20%) may be found. Roentgenographic examination usually reveals diffuse, bilateral, acinar infiltrates. Following repeated episodes, a chronic interstitial infiltrate, infrequently associated with hilar and mediastinal adenopathy, remains. Systemic corticosteroids appear to be beneficial in improving the immediate outcome of acute exacerbations, but a long-term beneficial effect has not been demonstrated.

PULMONARY ALVEOLAR PROTEINOSIS. Pulmonary alveolar proteinosis is a rare disorder characterized by alveolar filling with an acellular, periodic acid-Schiff–positive, lipoproteinaceous material. The prevalence of pulmonary alveolar proteinosis is 3.7 per million. Pulmonary alveolar proteinosis encompasses three distinct classes of disease with a similar spectrum of histologic findings: acquired, congenital, and secondary. Acquired pulmonary alveolar proteinosis, which accounts for more than 90% of cases, presents as progressive dyspnea of gradual onset associated with productive cough, fatigue, weight loss, and fever. Most patients are men (male:female ratio = 2.65:1.0). Most patients (72%) are smokers, although smoking varies according to gender (85% for males and 39% for females). Spirometry reveals a restrictive defect with a disproportionate reduction in diffusing capacity. HRCT has a characteristic appearance of geographic air space ground-glass opacities with thickening of interlobular septa resulting in a "crazy paving" pattern. A diagnosis of pulmonary alveolar proteinosis can be established in 75% of clinically suspected cases by the findings of a "milky" effluent from BAL. Because mice lacking either GM-CSF or the βc chain of the GM-CSF receptor develop a condition that resembles human pulmonary alveolar proteinosis, studies of pathogenesis have focused on GM-CSF. GM-CSF neutralizing autoantibody has been identified in the serum and BAL fluid of patients with acquired pulmonary alveolar proteinosis but not in patients with congenital or secondary pulmonary alveolar proteinosis. It is likely the anti–GM-CSF antibody is pathogenic, with its ability to inhibit endogenous GM-CSF leading to functional GM-CSF deficiency and impaired surfactant clearance by alveolar macrophages and perhaps type II alveolar epithelial cells.

The treatment of choice is therapeutic whole lung lavage using 40 to 60 L of fluid via a double lumen endotracheal tube while the patient is under general anesthesia. Treatment with GM-CSF has been evaluated in several small studies, and approximately 50% of patients appear to benefit. The clinical course is highly variable and may include a progressive disease with superimposed infections despite frequent repeated lavages. Secondary opportunistic infections are found in 15% of patients and include *Nocardia* (most common), *Cryptococcus*, *Aspergillus*, *Histoplasma*, *Mycobacteria*, *Pneumocystis*, and cytomegalovirus. Pulmonary alveolar proteinosis may be a stable, recurrent disease requiring repeated lavage (every 6 to 24 months), improve without relapse, or progress to a severe ILD. Survival rates at 2, 5, and 10 years are 70%, 75%, and 68%, respectively.

Congenital pulmonary alveolar proteinosis is transmitted in an autosomal recessive manner. It is most often caused by homozygosity for a frame shift mutation (121 in 2) in the surfactant protein B (SP-B) gene, which leads to unstable SP-B mRNA, reduced protein levels, and secondary disturbances of surfactant protein C (SP-C) processing. Homozygotes develop severe respiratory distress shortly after birth, usually with progression to death despite extracorporeal life support, lung lavage, or surfactant replacement. Heterozygotes for this mutation appear to have normal respiratory function into their fourth decade of life, but murine models suggest that heterozygotes are at risk for reduced lung compliance and gas trapping with aging and could be at increased risk for hyperoxic lung injury.

Secondary pulmonary alveolar proteinosis is associated with exposure to dust or solvents, including silica, asbestos, tin, cadmium, molybdenum, titanium dioxide, aluminum dust, and cement dust. Alveolar proteinosis also develops rarely as a complication of immunodeficiency disorders such as thymic alymphoplasia, severe combined immunodeficiency, or IgA deficiency. Pulmonary alveolar proteinosis also has been associated with hematologic abnormalities, including myeloid leukemias and myelodysplastic syndromes.

CHRONIC EOSINOPHILIC PNEUMONIA. A wide spectrum of clinical illness may be seen at presentation, ranging from no symptoms to respiratory failure. Cough, fever (temperature as high as 40°C), dyspnea, weight loss, malaise, and night sweats are the most common symptoms. Wheezing is part of the syndrome in one third to one half of patients, but some patients never wheeze. Peripheral blood eosinophilia is present in 85% of patients during the course of chronic eosinophilic pneumonia, but it may be absent at initial presentation in as many as one third of patients. The proportion of eosinophils in peripheral blood may be as high as 65%, although it is more commonly 10 to 40%. BAL eosinophils may be greater than 40% during exacerbations. The abnormalities on chest roentgenograms are variable, but a classic, almost pathognomonic, group of findings occurs in about 25% of cases: peripheral, nonsegmental alveolar infiltrates that resolve within 2 to 4 days after treatment with corticosteroids but recur in the same distribution with clinical relapses. The dense peripheral infiltrates have been characterized as the "photographic negative of pulmonary edema." Dense apical or axillary peripheral infiltrates, lobar consolidation, patchy perihilar infiltrates, nodules with cavities, and bilateral reticulonodular infiltrates also have been described. Although the diagnosis of chronic eosinophilic pneumonia often can be made with enough certainty to justify a therapeutic trial of corticosteroids, transbronchial biopsy and BAL should be performed unless contraindications exist. Open lung biopsy is rarely required. Administration of corticosteroids almost universally leads to rapid improvement in chronic eosinophilic pneumonia; failure to improve with corticosteroids should raise doubts about the accuracy of the diagnosis. Improvement often occurs within hours, and chest roentgenograms usually clear in 2 to 4 days. Prolonged therapy is often required (6 to 12 months), and the rate of relapse is high, even after a year of corticosteroid therapy.

INTERSTITIAL LUNG DISEASE ASSOCIATED WITH PULMONARY VASCULITIS

The pulmonary vasculitic syndromes are a diverse, rare group of diseases with overlapping clinical and pathologic manifestations. Although ILD is not a common presenting feature of the pulmonary vasculitides, most patients ultimately develop significant pulmonary fibrosis.

WEGENER'S GRANULOMATOSIS (Chapter 284). Wegener's granulomatosis is a systemic disease in which granulomatous, necrotizing vasculitis involves the upper and lower respiratory tracts and kidneys. All patients have respiratory tract involvement, but certain patients with a limited form of the disease have no apparent renal disease. Chest radiographs usually reveal multiple nodular or cavitary infiltrates, but single nodules may be found. Patients in whom Wegener's granulomatosis is expected should be tested for antineutrophil cytoplasmic antibody (ANCA), but a negative ANCA does not exclude Wegener's granulomatosis. An open lung biopsy is the procedure of choice for establishing the diagnosis. Cyclophosphamide (1 to 2 mg/kg/day orally) in conjunction with oral corticosteroids (prednisone 60 mg/day) is the standard initial therapy for Wegener's granulomatosis. After clinical manifestations have subsided, the prednisone dose can be decreased. Initial remission occurs in more than 90% of patients. Relapses occur in 25 to 30% of patients after a successful course of therapy or during the period of corticosteroid dose reduction. Trimethoprim-sulfamethoxazole (one double-strength tablet twice a day) can be used to treat early, predominantly granulomatous disease if systemic vasculitis is absent. Patients with disease confined to the upper respiratory tract or lungs or both may respond to as little as 10 days of therapy with trimethoprim-sulfamethoxazole, but 8 weeks of treatment is often required. If this therapy fails, conventional therapy as outlined earlier should be given. The serum C-ANCA is a useful monitor of disease activity.

CHURG-STRAUSS SYNDROME (ALLERGIC ANGIITIS AND GRANULOMATOSIS) (Chapter 284). This systemic necrotizing vasculitis affects the upper and lower respiratory tracts and is almost invariably preceded by allergic manifestations such as asthma, allergic rhinitis, or a drug reaction. Chest radiographs reveal bilateral patchy, fleeting infiltrates, diffuse nodular infiltrates without cavitation, or diffuse reticulonodular disease. Open lung biopsy provides definitive histologic evidence of Churg-Strauss syndrome.

INHERITED DISORDERS

ILD may result from a group of rare inherited disorders, both autosomal dominant and recessive.

FAMILIAL IDIOPATHIC PULMONARY FIBROSIS. This is an autosomal dominant disease with clinical, roentgenographic, physiologic, and morphologic features that are indistinguishable from nonfamilial idiopathic pulmonary fibrosis. Mutations in the SP-C gene cause dominantly inherited familial interstitial pneumonia in extended sibships. Heterozygous individuals bearing a wild type and a mutant gene in which exon 5+ 128T →A transversion results in a nonconservative substitution of a leucine by glutamine in the C-terminal domain of propeptide SP-C suffer from idiopathic lung disease with variable histopathologic patterns, including desquamative interstitial pneumonitis, nonspecific interstitial pneumonitis, and usual interstitial pneumonitis. The variability may be secondary to modification of the genetic defect by age, environmental, genetic, or infectious factors. The region of the mutation is critical for proper folding and processing

of Pro-SP-C. Another defect has been reported in which expression of Pro-SP-C and active SP-C protein was undetectable.

NEUROFIBROMATOSES (Chapter 459). ILD occurs in 20% of patients with neurofibromatosis, usually between ages 35 and 60 years. Dyspnea is the predominant symptom. The ILD has histologic features similar to those of idiopathic pulmonary fibrosis. There is no known therapy.

TUBEROUS SCLEROSIS (Chapter 459). Tuberous sclerosis is an autosomal dominant condition with equal gender incidence and variable expression. A linkage has been found with a locus on the long arm of chromosome 9 (9q34) and with a locus on the short arm of chromosome 16 (16p13). The classic triad includes dermal angiofibromas (adenoma sebaceum), epilepsy, and mental retardation. Only 1% of patients present with symptomatic pulmonary disease, and all are female. The radiographic changes may be cystic and reticular. Histologic changes are identical to LAM.

AUTOSOMAL RECESSIVE DISEASES. ILD has been described in several autosomal recessive diseases, including Gaucher's disease, Niemann-Pick disease (Chapter 222), and Hermansky Pudlak syndrome (partial oculocutaneous albinism, a hemorrhagic defect due to platelet dysfunction, and accumulation of ceroid in the reticuloendothelial system).

SUGGESTED READINGS

American Thoracic Society and European Respiratory Society: International multidisciplinary consensus classification of idiopathic interstitial pneumonia: General principles and recommendation. Am J Respir Crit Care Med 2002;165:277–304. *A consensus statement to standardize the classification of idiopathic interstitial pneumonias and to establish a uniform set of definitions and criteria for diagnosis of idiopathic interstitial pneumonias.*

American Thoracic Society: Pulmonary fibrosis: Diagnosis and treatment international consensus statement Am J Respir Crit Care Med 2000;161:646–664. *A consensus statement for diagnosis and management of idiopathic pulmonary fibrosis.*

Collard HR, King TE Jr, Bartelson BB, et al: Changes in clinical and physiologic variables predict survival in idiopathic pulmonary fibrosis. Am J Respir Crit Care Med 2003 [Epub ahead of print]. *Changes over a six month period add to baseline characteristics in predicting outcomes.*

Selman M, King TE Jr, Pardo A: Idiopathic pulmonary fibrosis: Prevailing and evolving hypothesis about its pathogenesis and implication for therapy. Ann Intern Med 2001;134:136–151. *A review of evolving concepts regarding the pathogenesis of idiopathic pulmonary fibrosis.*

Thomas AP, Lane K, Phillips J III, et al: Heterozygosity for a surfactant protein C gene mutation associated with usual interstitial pneumonias and cellular non-specific interstitial pneumonitis in one kindred. Am J Respir Crit Care Med 2002;165:1322–1328. *A report of a large kindred which demonstrates mutations in surfactant protein C are associated with familial idiopathic interstitial pneumonias.*

Wells AU: Lung disease in association with connective tissue diseases. Eur Respir Mon 2000;14:137–164. *Reviews the clinical presentation, radiographic findings, and treatment of lung disease associated with connective tissue diseases.*

89 OCCUPATIONAL PULMONARY DISORDERS

Jonathan M. Samet

Interstitial lung diseases (ILDs) damage the pulmonary interstitium by disrupting alveolar structures and the small airways. Occupational diseases affecting the pulmonary interstitium include primarily the pneumoconioses, or dust diseases of the lung (Table 89–1), and hypersensitivity pneumonitis. The principal pneumoconiosis—asbestosis, coal workers' pneumoconiosis, and silicosis—typically occur after sustained exposures to dust concentrations that are no longer legally permissible in many developed countries, including the United States.

Table 89–1 • PRINCIPAL PNEUMOCONIOSES CAUSED BY MINERAL DUSTS

AGENT	DISEASE	RADIOGRAPHIC APPEARANCE
Asbestos	Asbestosis	Reticular, basilar predominance
Coal dust	Coal workers' pneumoconiosis	Nodular, upper lobe predominance
Cobalt	Hard metal disease	Reticular, basilar predominance
Silica	Silicosis	Nodular, upper lobe predominance
Talc	Talcosis	Rounded, irregular, or both

Although these diseases are declining, cases still occur in locales where industries have been historically associated with high dust exposures and as "sentinel" cases, signaling unsuspected and uncontrolled occupational exposures. In many developed countries, these diseases remain common. Beryllium, originally linked to lung disease in workers making fluorescent lamps, now has widespread usage in high-technology applications and the nuclear weapons industry. New agents introduced into the workplace may also cause unanticipated diseases, as in the recent example of workers in a nylon flocking plant. People with occupational ILD may present to health care providers through diverse paths. Physicians may evaluate previously undiagnosed patients with occupational ILD who present with dyspnea or unexplained radiographic infiltrates or previously diagnosed patients who present for assessment of the extent of associated physiologic impairment, often in the context of a legal proceeding or a claim for disability. Current or former workers exposed to agents causing lung disease may also present for screening for adverse effects.

The occupational ILDs result from inhaling and retaining dusts that induce inflammation and fibrosis. Dust particles in the respirable size range are generated in workplaces by diverse processes; power-driven equipment, such as drills and grinders, place their operators at risk for diseases caused by dust, and nearby workers, even if not working directly with the materials, may be secondarily exposed. The lung is defended against dust particles by a system that includes the physical barrier posed by the upper airway that filters out larger particles, the mucociliary escalator that removes inhaled particles, and the alveolar macrophages that scavenge inhaled and deposited particles in the small airways and alveoli. Particle size determines the likelihood and site of deposition in the respiratory tract. During quiet breathing, most particles larger than $10\,\mu m$ in aerodynamic diameter are deposited in the upper respiratory tract, although some particles in this size range may enter the lung during exertion. Particles between approximately 3 and $10\,\mu m$ tend to deposit in the larger airways of the lung, whereas smaller particles down to about $0.1\,\mu m$ are preferentially deposited in the small airways and alveoli.

Inflammation and subsequent fibrosis are central in the pathogenesis of the occupational ILDs, although the mechanisms underlying the distinctive pathologic responses found in the different pneumoconioses are still not characterized. Present concepts of pathogenetic mechanisms for the pneumoconioses emphasize the roles of alveolar macrophages in the initial response to dust inhalation, of cytokine release, and of interactions among macrophages, lymphocytes, neutrophils, and fibroblasts. Hypersensitivity pneumonitis reflects cell-mediated immune responses to inhaled antigens. As for idiopathic pulmonary fibrosis, genetic susceptibility has been postulated as a determinant of the response to inhaled occupational agents. To date, however, a genetic linkage has been found for only one agent and disease—beryllium and chronic beryllium disease.

Preventing these diseases rests largely on controlling exposures in the workplace through regulations that limit exposures to levels considered to be safe and that specify respiratory protection. Medical screening for early evidence of disease represents a complementary but secondary control approach. In the United States, the standard-setting agencies are the Occupational Safety and Health Administration (OSHA) and the Mine Safety and Health Administration (MSHA). Physicians who make a diagnosis indicating a failure of control measures should follow through by contacting relevant agencies, and with permission and possibly preservation of confidentiality, the employer or the union, as appropriate. The burden of respiratory morbidity and mortality in workers at risk for occupational lung disease can also be reduced by preventing and stopping smoking (Chapter 14). For the nonmalignant occupational lung diseases, the adverse effects of cigarette smoking on lung function appear additive to those of the occupational agents, whereas for lung cancer, synergism with smoking has been found for most occupational carcinogens. New genetic approaches may eventually provide strategies for identifying workers with the greatest susceptibility; however, prevention continues to be based on workplace controls for the foreseeable future.

For patients with clinically significant impairment, supportive treatment, as for other chronic lung diseases, is warranted. Patients should receive pneumococcal and influenza vaccines and oxygen therapy, as needed. Physical activity should be encouraged, and a comprehensive pulmonary rehabilitation program may benefit some patients. As for other patients with advanced chronic lung diseases, lung transplantation may be a consideration (Chapter 97). Adequate

controlled clinical trials to test agents that might retard or reverse the loss of function that occurs in these diseases have not been performed.

EVALUATING THE PATIENT WITH SUSPECTED OCCUPATIONAL INTERSTITIAL LUNG DISEASE

GENERAL APPROACH. Diagnosis of an occupational ILD is based on an appropriate clinical picture and documentation of exposure, related in a temporarily appropriate fashion to the occurrence of the disease. In addition to the exposure history, chest radiography, lung function testing, and high-resolution computed tomography (HRCT) are the key components of the diagnostic evaluation (Fig. 89–1). As indicated, evaluation may also be needed to exclude other disorders associated with a comparable clinical picture. For example, in an elderly man with a history of underground mining and of cigarette smoking, a lung nodule might represent complicated silicosis or a primary cancer of the lung. The clinical history should cover the cardinal respiratory symptoms—cough, phlegm production, dyspnea, and wheezing; emphasis should be placed on quantifying the degree of dyspnea. Graded questions should be used for this purpose that inquire, for example, about having dyspnea while hurrying on the level ground or walking up a slight hill, about walking slower on level ground than same-age peers, about stopping for breath after walking about 100 yards, and about having dyspnea during such routine activities as dressing and bathing. On physical examination, the physician should look for finger clubbing or cyanosis, indicative of advanced disease. On examining the chest, the physician should note the quality of the breath sounds and the timing (early or late) and the type (fine or coarse) of any crackles (Chapter 81).

HISTORY. A comprehensive occupational history should be taken from all patients with suspected occupational disease. The history needs to cover each job systematically, describing the industry in which the patient worked, the specific occupation and job duties, materials handled, required and actual use of respiratory protective equipment, and occurrence of disease in fellow workers. Seasonal, part-time, and temporary jobs should not be omitted, as such jobs may have a greater likelihood of hazardous exposure. The dates of specific jobs may also be relevant because exposures for many agents were higher during past decades. Although the frequency of the more common pneumoconioses is now declining, some exposures (e.g., beryllium) are still widespread, and newer exposures may cause ILD. The history

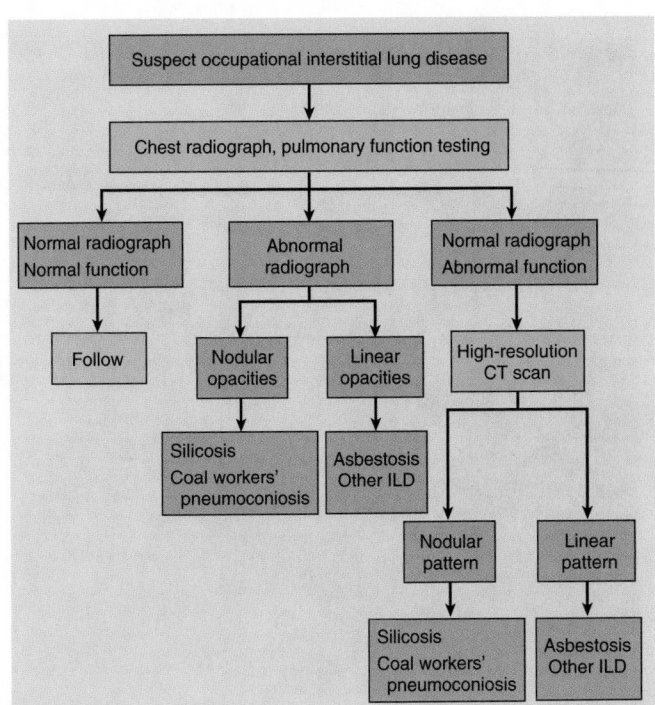

FIGURE 89–1 • Diagnostic approach to occupational interstitial lung disease (ILD). CT = computed tomography.

Respiratory Diseases

should inquire about specific materials (e.g., asbestos) and about exposure through hobbies and the jobs of family members. A temporal association between entering the workplace and symptoms may indicate an exposure that triggers hypersensitivity pneumonitis.

The history should also cover cigarette smoking and other tobacco use (Chapter 14). Chronic bronchitis and chronic airflow obstruction associated with smoking may explain cough and dyspnea or complicate the diagnosis of a distinct occupational lung disease.

IMAGING OF THE CHEST. In addition to a comprehensive occupational history, the diagnostic evaluation of patients with suspected occupational ILD also includes imaging of the lungs to establish the presence of disease and the characteristics of any infiltrates. All patients suspected of having an occupational ILD need to have standard posteroanterior (PA) and lateral radiographs. Most patients with a pneumoconiosis have an abnormal chest radiograph, but 10 to 20% do not. The type of infiltrates, nodular or reticular, and the distribution provide an indication of the underlying disease (see Table 89–1). The International Labour Organization has developed a standardized system for classifying the abnormalities found on the PA radiograph in pneumoconioses. Although intended for use in epidemiologic research, the scheme is now widely applied clinically and for legal and compensation purposes. In this system, small parenchymal opacities are classified by shape (irregular or rounded), size, distribution, and profusion or concentration. The profusion, scored on a 12-point scale, is indicative of the degree of histopathologic derangement. The pneumoconiosis is termed "simple" if all opacities are less than 1 cm in diameter and "complicated" if opacities of 1 cm or greater are present.

HRCT is increasingly used to evaluate patients with ILD, including occupational diseases. The narrow slice thickness of 1 to 2 mm provides visualization of fine parenchymal detail and detects interstitial changes and emphysema. For example, in berylliosis, the chest radiograph shows hilar adenopathy and extensive infiltrates, whereas the HRCT documents extensive air-space destruction and infiltration (Fig. 89–2). In silicosis, the typical nodular opacities are evident in the chest radiograph, whereas the HRCT shows the nodules as well as air space enlargement (Fig. 89–3). Although the role of HRCT is still evolving, it should be considered for patients who have a normal chest radiograph but are suspected of having an occupational ILD. HRCT may also prove valuable for quantifying the degree of abnormality and the extent of coexisting emphysema, but it cannot be recommended for these purposes at present.

PULMONARY FUNCTION TESTING. Spirometry should be performed on all patients at risk for an occupational ILD and the results compared with predicted values based on gender, race, age, and height (Chapter 82). If the results are within the limits of normal, further testing is not indicated except for patients complaining of dyspnea or having roentgenographic abnormalities indicative of pneumoconiosis. Those patients, as well as patients with abnormal spirometry, should have measurements of the single breath diffusing capacity for carbon monoxide and lung volumes (total lung capacity [TLC] and residual volume). Exercise testing with measurement of blood gases and gas exchange parameters may be needed to evaluate dyspnea and to quantitate exercise impairment.

INVASIVE DIAGNOSTIC MEASURES. Invasive procedures are rarely indicated to establish the diagnosis of an occupational ILD, although biopsy may be warranted on clinical grounds to exclude alternative diagnoses. Bronchoalveolar lavage, the least invasive approach, provides fluid that can be analyzed for dusts and fibers and for cell populations; it is primarily a research tool. Transbronchial lung biopsy specimens obtained via the fiberoptic bronchoscope may yield a specific diagnosis, and the specimens can be analyzed for dusts and fibers, as can those obtained by open lung biopsy. Polarized light microscopy, which is routinely available, can detect crystals, and ferruginous bodies—ferritin-coated fibers—can be identified with routine optical microscopy. More sophisticated techniques can be used to quantify and identify particles in lung tissue if needed for medicolegal purposes.

PNEUMOCONIOSES

ASBESTOSIS

Definition

Asbestosis refers to fibrosis of the lung parenchyma and not to the pleural fibrosis and plaques that are frequently found in asbestos-exposed workers. Asbestos exposure is also associated with mesothelioma of the pleura and peritoneum, lung cancer, laryngeal cancer, and, possibly, gastrointestinal cancers.

Etiology

Asbestos refers to several fibrous silicate minerals having unique physical-chemical properties that make them effective for insulation, reinforcing materials, friction products, and other purposes. All types of asbestos fibers are associated with asbestosis, pleural disease, and

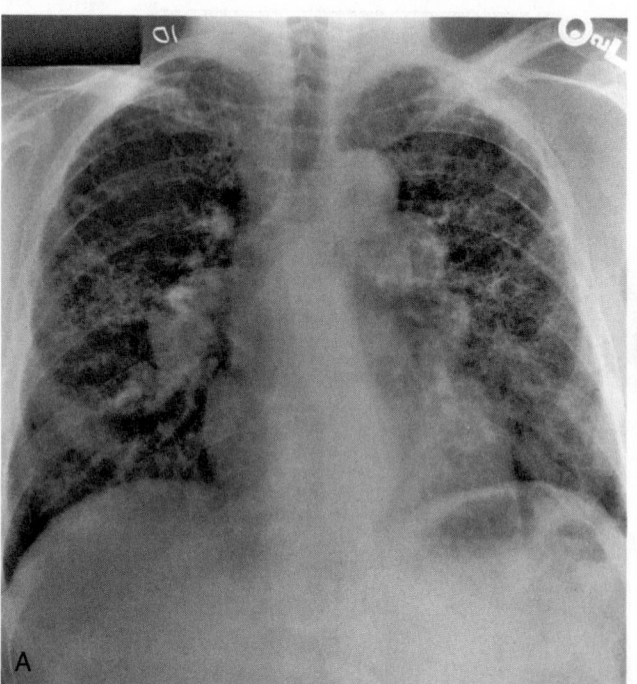
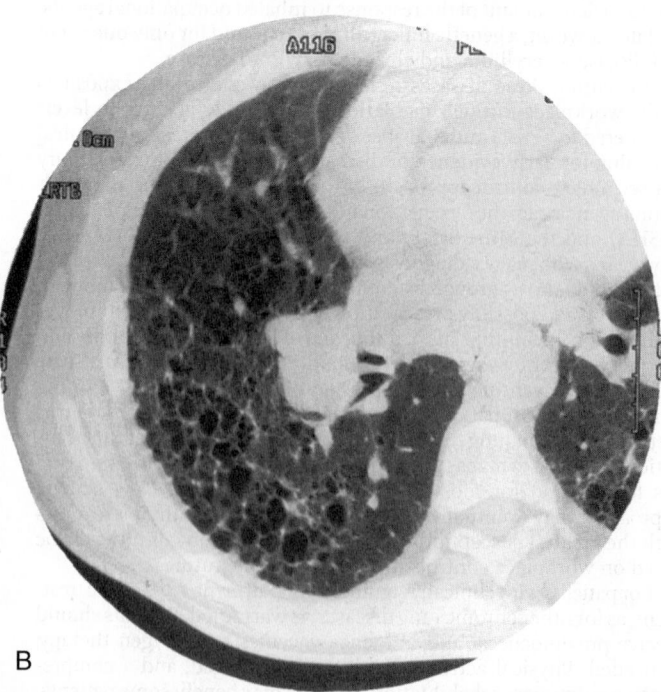

FIGURE 89–2 • Posteroanterior chest radiograph (*A*) and high-resolution computed tomography (HRCT) scan (*B*) from a patient with berylliosis. The chest radiograph demonstrates hilar adenopathy and extensive infiltrates, and the HRCT shows extensive air-space destruction and infiltrates.

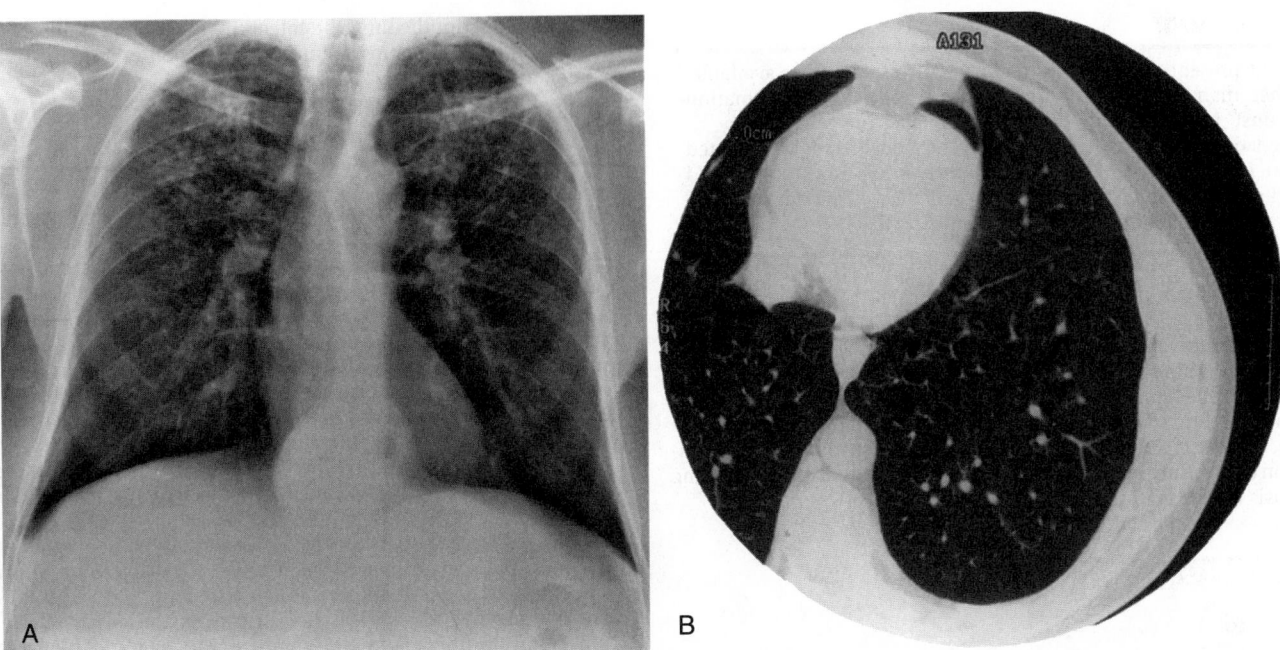

FIGURE 89–3 • Posteroanterior chest radiograph (*A*) and high-resolution computed tomography (HRCT) scan (*B*) from a patient with silicosis. The chest radiograph demonstrates the typical nodular opacities, and the HRCT shows the nodules as well as air-space enlargement.

lung cancer. Chrysotile, the type principally used in the United States, is a serpentine mineral that undergoes gradual physical and chemical dissolution in tissues. Crocidolite, anthophyllite, and amosite, the other principal asbestos types used, are in the amphibole mineral group and are more needle-like than the curly chrysotile fibers and not as prone to dissolution. Chrysotile asbestos appears to be a weaker cause of mesothelioma than the amphiboles.

Epidemiology

Asbestos fibers have been widely used during the 20th century, and large numbers of workers directly handling asbestos have been exposed, along with indirectly exposed nearby workers and even family members exposed to fibers brought home on clothing. The exposed worker groups include asbestos miners and millers, workers manufacturing asbestos products such as textiles and brake linings, and workers using asbestos products such as insulators and other construction trades. With a large number of buildings now having asbestos-containing materials, custodial and maintenance workers may also be exposed, as may workers involved in removing asbestos and demolishing buildings. Exposures for general building occupants are quite low and in a range not associated with asbestosis. The risk of asbestosis increases with cumulative exposure to asbestos fibers; with the exception of extraordinarily high exposures, manifestations of disease are not usually present until 15 to 20 years have elapsed since first exposure. With the widespread recognition of the disease risks associated with asbestos, exposures have been lowered and substitutes introduced in many developed countries, including the United States. The cohort of workers at greatest risk for asbestosis was exposed through the early 1970s, after which asbestos use was sharply reduced and the incidence of asbestosis should diminish as these workers age.

Pathology

In experimental models of asbestosis, the earliest lesions are found in the alveolar ducts and peribronchiolar regions, where deposited asbestos fibers attract alveolar macrophages. The lungs of asbestos-exposed workers show an inflammatory and fibrotic lesion of the small airways, termed *mineral dust–induced small airways disease*. As disease progresses, the fibrotic process becomes more extensive and may ultimately involve the entire lung. In advanced cases, extensive fibrosis may destroy the normal architecture of the lung to cause honeycombing, cystic spaces bounded by fibrosis. In advanced disease,

the lungs are small and stiff with macroscopically visible fibrosis and honeycombing. Asbestos bodies are typically visible with conventional microscopy.

Clinical Manifestations

Patients with asbestosis present with the same clinical picture found in other interstitial lung diseases: cough and exertional dyspnea. Some cases of asbestosis may also be detected by screening exposed worker populations. Bibasilar fine crackles are heard on auscultation of the chest in most patients, and clubbing may be present in advanced cases. The chest radiograph shows irregular opacities that are typically most prominent in the lung bases; pleural disease, particularly in the form of localized and often calcified plaques, is often present as well. The degree of physiologic impairment on lung function testing varies with the severity of the asbestosis. The small airways lesions produce airflow obstruction, manifest by changes in the shape of the expiratory flow-volume curve, with corresponding reduction of flow rates at lower lung volumes. Airflow obstruction cannot be readily attributed to asbestos exposure in individual patients who have smoked cigarettes. In patients with clinically significant dyspnea, spirometry typically shows a reduced forced vital capacity (FVC) with preservation of the ratio of the forced expiratory volume in 1 second (FEV$_1$) to FVC, and reduced TLC and diffusing capacity; however, this typical physiologic profile is not invariably observed, and obstruction secondary to smoking may complicate interpretation of pulmonary function findings. Progressive exercise testing shows pulmonary limitation of exercise capacity and desaturation in many patients with asbestosis.

Diagnosis

Asbestosis can be diagnosed with confidence if there is a history of significant exposure to asbestos; radiographic, clinical, and physiologic evidence of ILD compatible with asbestosis; and no indication of another disease process associated with a comparable clinical picture of interstitial lung disease, such as scleroderma (Chapter 281). At typical levels, the exposure should have started at least 15 years before the disease developed. Pleural plaques provide a strong indication of past asbestos exposure. In patients with biopsy-proven ILD without a firm history of exposure, the presence of asbestos bodies should increase suspicion for asbestosis. More formal counting of asbestos bodies or of fibers may be warranted.

Respiratory Diseases

 Treatment

At present, no effective treatment for asbestosis is available, other than appropriate supportive care, including vaccination against influenza and pneumococci, and oxygen therapy as needed. Lung transplantation may be considered for selected patients. Because of the increased risk of asbestos-exposed individuals for lung cancer, perhaps particularly those with asbestosis, smoking cessation should be emphasized.

Prognosis

The course of radiographically identified asbestosis is variable, with some cases showing progression, whereas others remain static. Factors influencing progression are not well established but appear to include the cumulative exposure to asbestos, the duration of exposure, and the type of asbestos exposure. Early identification and cessation of exposure may improve prognosis. The extent of radiographic fibrosis is a strong predictor of mortality.

COAL WORKERS' PNEUMOCONIOSIS

Definition

Coal workers' pneumoconiosis is the parenchymal lung disease caused by inhaling coal mine dust. The disease is termed *simple* if all radiographic opacities are less than 1 cm in diameter. Progressive massive fibrosis complicates simple coal workers' pneumoconiosis if any nodular opacities of 1 or greater cm are present on the chest radiograph. Exposure to coal mine dust is also associated with industrial bronchitis and loss of lung function at a rate beyond that associated with aging; these consequences of such exposure are not considered coal workers' pneumoconiosis, although they do contribute to the respiratory morbidity experienced by coal miners. The group of lung diseases caused by coal mine dust are commonly referred to as *black lung*.

Etiology

Coal refers to a group of carbonaceous materials characterized by the hardness or "rank," ranging from peat, the softest, to anthracite, the hardest. Inhaling coal dust causes coal workers' pneumoconiosis, but inhaling more pure carbon materials—lamp-black and carbon black—has also been associated with a comparable lung disease. Silica in the coal dust may also contribute to the development of coal workers' pneumoconiosis. Determinants of progression from simple coal workers' pneumoconiosis to progressive massive fibrosis, other than coal rank and coal mine dust exposure, have not been identified.

Epidemiology

Extensive epidemiologic information shows that the risk of coal workers' pneumoconiosis increases with dust level in the mine and cumulative exposure to coal mine dust. Risk also increases with the rank of the coal, being greatest for the harder coals. In studies of the mortality of underground coal miners, progressive massive fibrosis increases risk of death, whereas simple coal workers' pneumoconiosis has a lesser adverse effect. Reduced exposures for U.S. miners since the passage of the Coal Mine Health and Safety Act of 1969 should reduce risks for those recently starting to mine.

Pathology

The characteristic lesion of coal workers' pneumoconiosis is the coal macule, an inflammatory lesion consisting of focal collections of coal mine dust–laden macrophages surrounding respiratory bronchioles. The coal macule may extend to the alveoli and be accompanied by fibrosis of the small airways and alveoli and by focal emphysema. Larger "coal nodules," which are grossly firm and contain dust-filled macrophages in collagen and reticulin, may develop. Progressive massive fibrosis is diagnosed pathologically if nodules reach at least 2 cm, although the radiographic definition is based on opacities of at least 1 cm. These lesions are also collagen-containing

and tend to disrupt the lung's architecture. In Caplan's syndrome, or rheumatoid pneumoconiosis, multiple lung nodules, ranging from 1 to 5 cm, are present, typically in the periphery.

Clinical Manifestations

Coal mine dust–exposed miners may present with cough and sputum production reflecting industrial bronchitis and dyspnea associated with pulmonary function impairment, whether secondary to progressive massive fibrosis involving the parenchyma or accelerated loss of ventilatory function related to dust-induced airways disease. Other than characteristic radiographic findings, there are no specific clinical manifestations of simple coal workers' pneumoconiosis; despite widespread radiographic abnormalities, many miners are asymptomatic or have only mild adverse changes in lung function, whereas some may have significant impairment with little or no radiographic abnormality. In simple disease, the chest radiograph typically shows small nodules that tend to predominate in the upper lung zones. Reticular opacities may also be present, more often in cigarette smokers.

Progressive massive fibrosis is associated with progressive dyspnea, pulmonary hypertension, and even respiratory failure. The chest radiograph shows the characteristic nodules of progressive massive fibrosis, often with contraction of the affected lung, typically upper lobes, and compensatory hyperinflation, typically lower lobes. The nodules may cavitate and produce melanoptysis. In progressive massive fibrosis, lung function is typically impaired, particularly if larger nodules are present. Both airflow obstruction (reduced FEV_1 and FEV_1/FVC ratio) and lung restriction (reduced TLC) can occur. The single-breath diffusing capacity for carbon monoxide is also reduced, and resting hypoxemia or desaturation with exercise may be present. Caplan's syndrome should be considered in miners with multiple peripheral nodules; this uncommon syndrome may develop in miners with rheumatoid arthritis or with circulating rheumatoid factor without arthritis (Chapter 286).

Diagnosis

Coal workers' pneumoconiosis is diagnosed on the basis of an appropriate history of exposure and characteristic radiographic abnormalities. In patients with probable progressive massive fibrosis, consideration should be given to alternative causes of lung masses, including lung cancer.

 Treatment

No effective treatment is currently available for coal workers' pneumoconiosis. Appropriate supportive care and rehabilitation should be provided for those with impaired lung function, *as for asbestosis*.

Prognosis

Total coal mine dust exposure and increasing severity of simple pneumoconiosis predict the development of progressive massive fibrosis, which is associated with more severe morbidity and increased overall mortality. Simple pneumoconiosis alone does not increase mortality.

SILICOSIS

Definition

Silicosis refers to the parenchymal lung diseases associated with crystalline silica exposure, including acute, accelerated, and chronic or classic silicosis. These entities are distinguished by their clinical pictures and time course in relation to silica exposure. In acute silicosis, an alveolar filling process follows heavy exposure within a few years. Accelerated silicosis occurs within 5 to 10 years of exposure and has a clinical picture comparable to that of chronic silicosis, which develops after a longer latent period.

Table 89–2 • PRINCIPAL OCCUPATIONS ASSOCIATED WITH SILICON EXPOSURE

Abrasives workers	Silica flour workers
Foundry workers	Silica millers
Glass makers	Stone workers
Pottery workers	Surface mine drillers
Quarriers	Underground miners
Sandblasters	

Etiology

Crystalline silicon dioxide, the causal agent, is abundant and ubiquitous in the earth's crust and is used in a variety of industrial applications. Quartz is the most common form. Consequently, large numbers of workers, probably millions in the United States, are still exposed (Table 89–2).

Epidemiology

As for the other pneumoconioses, the risk of developing disease increases with the level and duration of exposure. Although the hazard posed by silica exposure has long been recognized and exposure standards have been promulgated, new cases continue to occur, even of acute silicosis, which has been recently reported in sandblasters, ground silica workers, and rock drillers.

Pathology

Like coal workers' pneumoconiosis, chronic silicosis occurs in a simple form and as progressive massive fibrosis. The earliest lesions are collections of dust-laden macrophages in the peribronchiolar and paraseptal or subpleural areas. The silicotic nodule has an acellular core composed of collagen surrounded by a cellular capsule with macrophages, lymphocytes, and fibroblasts. Silicotic nodules may also involve the hilar lymph nodes. Silicotic nodules coalesce to form the lesions of progressive massive fibrosis, masses of dense hyalinized connective tissue with little inflammation. Accelerated silicosis progresses rapidly to progressive massive fibrosis, whereas acute silicosis has a distinct pattern with few or no nodules and alveolar filling with proteinaceous material. Polarized light microscopy may show birefringent particles indicative of silica in the lungs of silica-exposed persons, including those with silicosis.

Clinical Manifestations

Chronic silicosis without progressive massive fibrosis is associated with little physiologic impairment. Cough and sputum production may reflect underlying bronchitis related to dust exposure or cigarette smoking. As in coal workers' pneumoconiosis, progressive massive fibrosis can be associated with significant impairment on lung function testing and clinically significant dyspnea. Both airflow obstruction and lung restriction may be present. Acute silicosis presents with rapidly progressive dyspnea. Persons with silicosis are at increased risk for mycobacterial infection (Chapter 341), and they may present with manifestations of infection such as fever and weight loss.

In chronic silicosis, the chest radiograph shows small nodules that tend to predominate in the upper lobes (Fig. 89–3). Calcification of the nodules is rare, as is so-called eggshell calcification of enlarged hilar nodes. In progressive massive fibrosis, the mass lesions are typically in the upper lobes and are often associated with compensatory hyperinflation of the lower lobes. Widespread consolidation is present on the chest radiograph in acute silicosis. Caplan's syndrome may also occur in silica-exposed workers, but it is rare.

Diagnosis

The diagnosis of chronic silicosis is made on the basis of characteristic radiographic findings and history of employment in a job associated with exposure to silica-containing dust. Before accepting a diagnosis of progressive massive fibrosis in a silica-exposed worker, other causes of lung masses should be considered, including, specifically, lung cancer and mycobacterial infection. Acute silicosis should be considered in heavily exposed individuals with a diffuse consolidating process. Unless the epidemiologic features of the case make the diagnosis of acute silicosis certain, lung biopsy may be indicated to establish the diagnosis and to exclude other diseases.

Rx Treatment

As in any chronic lung disease, supportive therapy, oxygen, and rehabilitation may be indicated. One report suggested possible short-term benefits of corticosteroid therapy, but steroid therapy cannot be recommended at present. Because of the increased risk of mycobacterial diseases, particularly *Mycobacterium tuberculosis*, all persons with silicosis should receive yearly tuberculin skin tests and evaluation for active tuberculosis if the test is positive. Isoniazid prophylaxis is recommended if the test is positive and active disease is not present. Some studies indicate that prolonged antituberculous therapy may be indicated in patients with silicosis and active tuberculosis (Chapter 341).

Prognosis

The prognosis of accelerated and acute silicosis is poor; both are associated with progressive loss of function, and acute silicosis may be rapidly fatal. Progressive massive fibrosis has a more variable course, which may also lead to progressive impairment and respiratory failure. Factors determining progression from chronic silicosis to progressive massive fibrosis are uncertain.

OTHER PNEUMOCONIOSES

Inhaling other minerals and metals may also cause pneumoconioses (see Table 89–1). Silicates other than asbestos have been linked to interstitial lung disease, including talc, kaolinite, mica, and vermiculite. Benign pneumoconioses are associated with inhaling forms of barium (baritosis) and tin (stannosis). Hard-metal disease occurs in workers exposed to cobalt in applications involving its use in alloys and abrasives. This diffuse interstitial disease, which can be associated with clinically significant impairment, should be considered in workers in foundries and in industries involving grinding of metals, gems, and other materials. Some workers exposed to man-made fibers develop small opacities, but a distinct pneumoconiosis has not yet been identified from exposure to these newer fibers. *Mixed-dust pneumoconiosis* is a nonspecific label often used for the presence of both rounded and irregular opacities on the chest radiograph of a worker with exposure to several types of dust. Typically, there is exposure to silica and to an additional mineral.

BERYLLIUM DISEASE

Beryllium disease is a granulomatous lung disease that results from inhaling beryllium, a rare metal now widely used in high-technology applications (Table 89–3). The typical cases currently observed present with gradual onset and are referred to as *chronic beryllium disease*; a more acute form was reported with past higher levels of exposure. When first recognized, the disease was found in workers who extracted and produced beryllium and in workers making fluorescent lamps containing a beryllium phosphor. Cases have been reported in bystanders not working directly with the metal and in persons

Table 89–3 • CURRENT INDUSTRIES USING BERYLLIUM

Aerospace	Nuclear reactors
Beryllium extraction, fabrication, smelting	Nuclear weapons
Ceramics	Plating
Dental alloys and prostheses	Telecommunications
Electronics	Tool and die
Foundries	

residing in the vicinity of beryllium processing plants. More contemporary industries place a large number of workers at risk. In a study of nuclear weapons workers, about 5% of exposed workers were shown to be sensitized to beryllium. Cases of chronic beryllium disease continue to be identified, even though an exposure standard promulgated by OSHA is in place.

Advances in understanding of the pathogenesis of beryllium disease are providing insights into the immunologic basis of the disease and the genetic basis of susceptibility. Beryllium, a metal, acts as an antigen or hapten, sensitizing T cells when presented in the context of a major histocompatibility complex class II molecule (Chapter 42). A specific genetic marker, HLA-DP B1 Glu69, has been linked to increased susceptibility for chronic beryllium disease; this marker may affect binding to receptors in the T cells of the lung. This marker may eventually prove useful to identify workers at greatest risk. Sensitization to beryllium can be shown using the beryllium lymphocyte transformation test. In this in vitro assay, blood lymphocytes or lung lymphocytes obtained by bronchoalveolar lavage are exposed to beryllium salts; cells from sensitized individuals show proliferation. This test can identify workers who are sensitized but without evidence of chronic beryllium disease as well as those having disease.

The lymphocyte transformation test can confirm beryllium exposure, but the metal can also be measured in tissue specimens and urine. Patients with beryllium disease may have both respiratory and systemic symptoms and chest radiograph findings ranging from normal to diffuse interstitial infiltrates and hilar adenopathy. Corticosteroid therapy may be beneficial, but life-long treatment is needed.

HYPERSENSITIVITY PNEUMONITIS

Hypersensitivity pneumonitis, typically a granulomatous ILD, results from inhaling diverse environmental antigens and chemicals. Although interstitial fibrosis is classically considered to be a granulomatous disorder, some patients may have interstitial fibrosis without granulomas. If granulomas are present in lung or other tissue specimens, the differential diagnosis includes sarcoidosis and hypersensitivity pneumonitis. Hypersensitivity pneumonitis may present as an acute illness, but it may also present in a chronic form with pulmonary fibrosis. The workplace is often a site of exposure to antigens generated by microbial contaminants of heating, ventilating, and air conditioning systems or other moist devices or materials. Chemical agents associated with hypersensitivity pneumonitis include isocyanates and trimellitic anhydride. The diagnosis is made on the basis of the clinical picture, exposure history, and demonstration of precipitating antibodies to antigens. Researchers are exploring polymorphisms in immune response genes for hypersensitivity pneumonitis.

SUGGESTED READINGS

Balmes J, Becklake M, Blanc P, et al: Environmental and Occupational Health Assembly, American Thoracic Society. American Thoracic Society Statement: Occupational contribution to the burden of airway disease. Am J Respir Crit Care Med 2003;167: 787–797. *A comprehensive review.*

Eschenbacher WL, Kreiss K, Lougheed D, et al: Nylon flock-associated interstitial lung disease. Am J Respir Crit Care Med 1999;159:2003–2008. *Describes features of a new form of occupational interstitial lung disease.*

Saltini C, Amicosante M: Beryllium disease. Am J Med Sci 2001;321:89–98. *A review of emerging understanding of the pathogenesis of beryllium disease.*

90 PHYSICAL, CHEMICAL, AND ASPIRATION INJURIES OF THE LUNG

Claude A. Piantadosi

PHYSICAL AND CHEMICAL INJURIES OF THE LUNG

The lung's large and delicate surface area is protected from toxic substances in the environment by extensive defense mechanisms. Normally, inspired gas is fully humidified and warmed to body temperature, and all large particulate substances are cleared by the upper airways (Chapter 82). These normal defenses are not adequate to handle exposure to many physical and chemical substances that cause

Table 90–1 • TOXIC BY-PRODUCTS OF SMOKE IMPLICATED IN RESPIRATORY INJURY

SOURCE	BY-PRODUCTS
Cotton, paper, wood	Acrolein, CO, acetaldehyde
Petroleum products	Acrolein, CO, benzene
Polyvinyl chloride (PVC)	Hydrocyanic acid, CO, chlorine, phosgene
Nylon, silk, wool	Hydrocyanic acid, ammonia
Nitrocellulose	Oxides of nitrogen
Sulfur compounds	Sulfur dioxide

CO = carbon monoxide.

lung injury, so lung disorders may be initiated by inhalation or aspiration of injurious chemicals or by exposure to potentially harmful physical environments.

THERMAL INJURIES AND SMOKE INHALATION

Etiology

After major burns (Chapter 108), about one third of patients have pulmonary complications; as burn treatment has improved, inhalation injury has emerged as an increasingly important factor for many patients, who often die of pneumonia or multiple-organ failure. Smoke inhalation sufficient to cause respiratory injury may also occur without external burns. Thermal injury to the lung is associated with four types of complications: (1) *immediate reaction*—direct thermal injury to upper airways leading to upper airway obstruction; (2) *carbon monoxide and cyanide poisoning*; (3) *acute respiratory distress syndrome* (ARDS) developing 24 to 48 hours after the thermal injury (Chapter 108); and (4) *late-onset pulmonary complications*, which include pneumonia, atelectasis, thromboembolism, and, in case of thoracic burns, chest wall restriction.

The constituents of smoke are by-products of pyrolysis and incomplete combustion. Many of these products are potent mucosal irritants and bronchoconstrictors and contribute to both upper and lower lung injury. Certain constituents of smoke have been identified consistently as contributors to respiratory injury (Table 90–1). Smoke inhalation rarely causes thermal injury to the lung parenchyma; the large capacity of the upper airways to humidify and modify the temperatures of inhaled air protects the alveolar tissue from heat. Exceptions are steam burns and explosions in an enclosed space.

Clinical Manifestations

The initial signs and symptoms of smoke inhalation are tachypnea, cough, dyspnea, wheezing, cyanosis, hoarseness, and stridor (an ominous sign). Facial burns are associated with a high incidence of smoke inhalation and thermal injury to the larynx and conducting airways. During the 12 to 48 hours after the injury, increasing hypoxemia may manifest, and lung compliance may decrease owing to noncardiogenic pulmonary edema. Roentgenograms of the chest may reveal a pattern of diffuse, patchy infiltrates. A major complication is infection, often caused by *Pseudomonas aeruginosa* or *Staphylococcus aureus*. The lung defenses against infection are compromised by thermal and chemical injury to the airway epithelium as well as by the presence of an endotracheal or tracheostomy tube. The pathway for infection is either by inhaling airborne organisms or by hematogenous spread from cutaneous burns.

ARDS may develop 24 to 48 hours after the initial injury. The causes of ARDS are controversial in burn patients, but possibilities include chemical injury from constituents of smoke, a circulating burn toxin, microembolism and disseminated intravascular coagulation, and a poorly regulated systemic inflammatory response. The extent of surface thermal injury does not correlate with the degree of respiratory distress that occurs subsequently.

Rx Treatment and Prognosis

The most immediate life-threatening complications in patients with major burns or with a history of smoke inhalation are upper airway obstruction and carbon monoxide (CO) poisoning. The patient should be closely observed for evidence of these complications. Laryngeal and tracheobronchial edema, friability, and epithelial denudation may be detected by fiberoptic bronchoscopy. Arterial blood gases should be measured; prompt intubation or tracheostomy should be performed if there is evidence of significant airway obstruction. Corticosteroids may help treat edema of the upper airways, but they must be used with caution, because infection is a major concern for managing both skin and pulmonary injuries. Prophylactic antibiotics are of no value in preventing pneumonia and may predispose to infection with resistant organisms. Careful pulmonary toilet, humidification, and sterile suctioning should be used to reduce the risk of pneumonia. Serial bronchoscopy may be necessary to remove mucus plugs and thereby prevent segmental atelectasis and postobstructive infection. Late-onset pulmonary burn complications include atelectasis (Chapter 87), thromboembolism (Chapter 94), and pneumonia (Chapter 92).

CARBON MONOXIDE POISONING

Etiology

Smoke inhalation is invariably accompanied by CO uptake by the body. In some fires, CO exposure is complicated by cyanide poisoning from the combustion of plastic compounds. CO poisoning also is encountered frequently after exposure to automobile exhaust and, in the winter, when victims are exposed to fumes from faulty furnaces. As a result, CO is the leading cause of accidental poisoning in the United States.

CO poisoning is caused by tissue hypoxia created by the displacement of oxygen from hemoglobin. CO competes with oxygen for binding at the heme centers of hemoglobin. These centers bind CO reversibly, but with an affinity more than 200 times greater than that for oxygen. The affinity for oxygen of heme not occupied by CO is also increased by carboxyhemoglobin (HbCO) formation. This HbCO-related increase in oxygen affinity shifts the oxyhemoglobin dissociation curve to the left and impairs the release of oxygen to the tissues. These two effects of CO on hemoglobin decrease the partial pressure of oxygen in the tissues. Tissue hypoxia has serious functional consequences for organ systems that require a continuous supply of oxygen, such as the brain and the heart. In addition, when tissue partial pressure of oxygen (Po_2) is low, CO binds to intracellular hemoproteins, such as myoglobin and cytochrome c oxidase, inhibiting their functions.

Clinical Manifestations

The clinical features of acute CO poisoning are diverse but are most often related to the central nervous system. In normal nonsmoking individuals, symptoms may appear when HbCO levels reach 10%. Patients with chronic obstructive pulmonary disease (COPD) and coronary artery disease are more sensitive to the effects of HbCO. Smokers often maintain HbCO levels of 3 to 10%, and they may tolerate slightly higher levels without symptoms. Common symptoms of CO poisoning include headache, nausea, vomiting, confusion, and visual disturbances. More severe CO poisoning can produce seizures, transient unconsciousness, coma, and death. Metabolic acidosis, pulmonary edema, and rhabdomyolysis (Chapter 109) may also accompany serious CO poisoning. The "classic" clinical findings of cherry red lips and nail beds are rare. Approximately 10% of patients suffer a delayed neurologic syndrome characterized most often by problems with memory, concentration, and personality; it appears 2 to 30 days after the initial poisoning and is slow to resolve. Major risk factors for the delayed syndrome include older age, prolonged exposure, and loss of consciousness.

Diagnosis

The diagnosis is based on the history of exposure and an elevated HbCO level in the blood. The differential diagnosis includes drug overdoses, other poisonings (e.g., cyanide), and cerebrovascular accidents. The clinical diagnosis is confirmed by an elevated blood HbCO level measured by CO oximetry. The severity of the clinical illness, however, correlates better with the duration and extent of the exposure than with HbCO level.

Rx Treatment and Prognosis

Symptoms of mild CO poisoning generally subside within minutes to a few hours after removing the patient from the noxious environment. Patients with serious CO poisoning are improved by breathing 100% oxygen, which hastens the removal of CO from hemoglobin. In obtunded or other seriously poisoned patients, 100% oxygen should be administered via endotracheal tube for a minimum of 6 to 12 hours. Oxygen reduces the half-time for eliminating HbCO from the body from approximately 240 minutes to 60 minutes. Use of hyperbaric oxygen at 2.5 atmospheres absolute (ATA) reduces the HbCO half-life to approximately 20 minutes. Hyperbaric oxygen is recommended for patients with loss of consciousness or other neurologic impairment, cardiac symptoms or signs, or evidence of a heavy CO burden, such as HbCO levels of 20 to 25%.[1] During hyperbaric oxygen therapy, oxygen dissolved in plasma circumvents problems with oxyhemoglobin dissociation and hastens removal of CO from tissue binding sites such as myoglobin and cytochrome oxidase. Hyperbaric oxygen has been effective in averting neurologic injury, including the delayed neurologic syndrome, in several randomized controlled trials, as long as adequate therapy was instituted promptly, usually within 6 hours.[1,2] Adjunctive therapies, such as hyperventilation, hypothermia, or administration of corticosteroids or mannitol, are unproven modalities for treatment of severe CO poisoning.

Neurologic recovery in patients with mild CO poisoning is good. The prognosis after more severe CO poisoning is variable and correlates with the extent and duration of the insult. Short-term memory impairment, depression, and syndromes related to lesions of the basal ganglia are well described. The delayed neurologic syndrome usually improves gradually over 6 to 12 months.

OTHER TOXIC INHALED GASES

A large number of gases and chemicals, to which exposures most frequently occur in an industrial setting, can acutely and sometimes chronically injure the respiratory system. A few agents cause an "asthma-like" reaction with cough, chest pain, and wheezing. Toluene diisocyanate and other isocyanates (liberated as a gas in making polyurethane foams), aluminum soldering flux, and platinum salts are typical examples. Reaginic and precipitating antibodies against platinum salts and soldering flux have been found in symptomatic individuals, suggesting an immunologic basis for the reaction. An allergic basis has not been demonstrated for the reaction to toluene diisocyanate. The symptoms usually subside after removal from exposure; however, chronic lung injury may occur if the exposure is prolonged.

Etiology

A number of highly irritating gases cause *acute chemical pneumonitis*. Such gases include chlorine (used in the chemical and plastics industries and to disinfect water), ammonia (used in refrigeration), sulfur dioxide (used in making paper and smelting sulfide-containing ores), ozone (generated in welding and in photochemical smog), nitrogen dioxide (released from decomposed corn silage), and phosgene (used in producing aniline dyes).

Different mechanisms are involved in the injury caused by irritant gases. Most of them cause injury by acting as a strong acid, a strong base, or an oxidant. Gases of chemicals that are strong acids or bases in water solution, such as hydrogen chloride, sulfuric acid, sulfur dioxide, and ammonia, tend to react more in the upper airways.

The clinical response caused by irritant gases varies but appears to be related closely to the degree of acute irritation and to the water solubility of the gas. The less irritating gases, such as ozone and the oxides of nitrogen, phosgene, mercury, and nickel carbonyl, can be inhaled for prolonged periods and thereby cause injury throughout the respiratory system. Highly irritating and soluble gases, such as ammonia and hydrochloric acid, are less likely to be inhaled deeply and tend to result in immediate injury to the upper airways and have potential for obstruction secondary to mucosal edema. Less-soluble substances, such as chlorine, cadmium, zinc chloride, osmium tetroxide, and vanadium, can cause injury to the entire tracheo-bronchial tree and generally do not produce upper airway obstruction as the initial presentation. Bronchiolitis and pulmonary edema are common, ultimately leading to bronchiolitis obliterans. Long-term consequences vary with the gas. Cadmium, for example, can cause diffuse emphysema and severe airway obstruction but only minimal fibrosis.

Clinical Manifestations

A typical syndrome occurs in silo-filler's disease (nitrogen dioxide). During the exposure, no symptoms may be present, tracheobronchitis with cough and shortness of breath may be noted, or immediate acute pulmonary edema may occur. Signs of ocular and oropharyngeal mucous membrane irritation may be present. The symptoms can progress rapidly, but commonly the initial symptoms resolve and are followed by a period of minimal symptoms (cough) lasting up to 48 hours. Fever, myalgias, dyspnea, and progressive hypoxemia then occur, and the radiographic picture is that of pulmonary edema. These severe symptoms can resolve, only to recur 2 to 5 weeks later and lead to progressive bronchiolitis obliterans.

Rx Treatment and Prognosis

The initial step of removing the victim from the noxious environment is usually sufficient to treat mild exposures. The prognosis for more severe toxic gas exposures varies with duration and extent of exposure. Bronchodilators and supplemental oxygen may be necessary. In silo-filler's disease, treatment with corticosteroids (prednisone, 1 mg/kg/day) for 4 to 6 weeks can dramatically improve the acute illness. Because improvement after the initial exposure may be temporary, close observation for 48 hours after the exposure is advisable.

PULMONARY OXYGEN TOXICITY

Etiology and Pathogenesis

Oxygen is toxic to the lungs when used in high concentrations for prolonged periods. This toxicity occurs clinically in patients in intensive care units who are on mechanical ventilators. The toxic effects of hyperoxia are believed to result from excessive generation of superoxide, an unstable free radical produced by the single electron reduction of oxygen. Superoxide is produced as a normal by-product of oxidative metabolism and scavenged by the protective superoxide dismutase enzymes, which catalyze its dismutation to hydrogen peroxide (Fig. 90–1). If it is not scavenged, superoxide anion can donate an electron to hydrogen peroxide in the presence of transition metals (e.g., iron) to form hydroxyl radical (OH·). Hydroxyl radical is highly reactive and can initiate lipid peroxidation and oxidize protein and nucleic acids.

In the adult, the major sites of oxygen injury are the alveolar epithelium and the capillary endothelium. Pathologically, the lungs are atelectatic, congested, and edematous. Hyaline membranes are often present. Oxidant injury attracts inflammatory cells to the lung, including neutrophils. Advanced injury destroys the capillary bed with result-

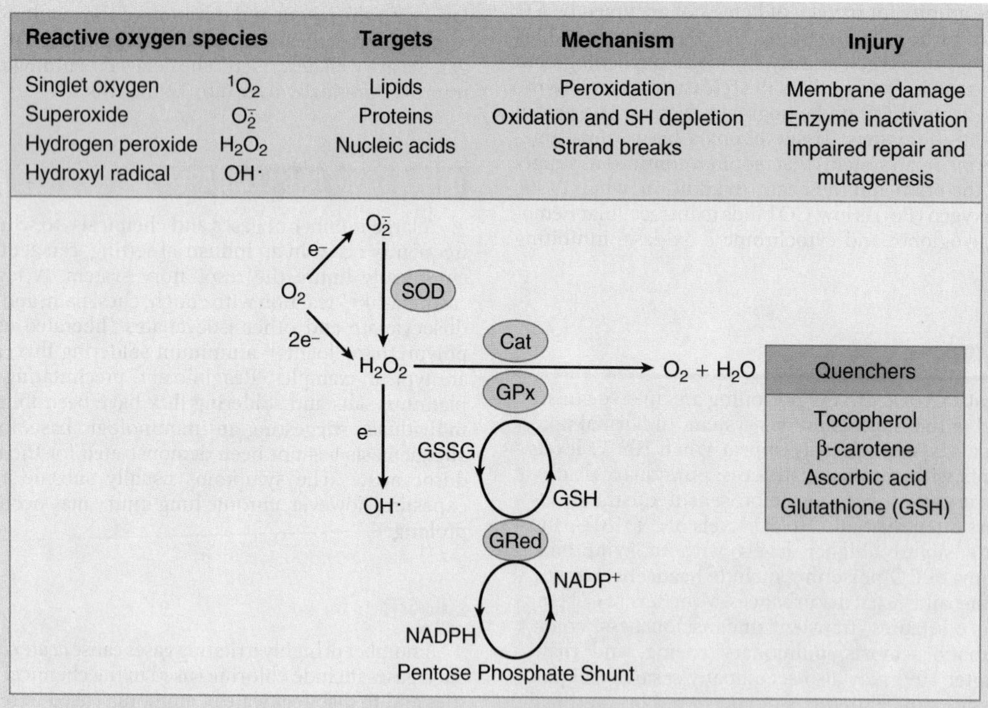

Reactive oxygen species		Targets	Mechanism	Injury
Singlet oxygen	$^1O_2$	Lipids	Peroxidation	Membrane damage
Superoxide	O_2^-	Proteins	Oxidation and SH depletion	Enzyme inactivation
Hydrogen peroxide	H_2O_2	Nucleic acids	Strand breaks	Impaired repair and
Hydroxyl radical	OH·			mutagenesis

FIGURE 90–1 • Reactive oxygen species and antioxidant defenses. When oxygen (O_2) is reduced incompletely, reactive oxygen species are formed such as singlet oxygen ($^1O_2$), superoxide anion ($\cdot O_2^-$), and hydrogen peroxide (H_2O_2). H_2O_2 in the presence of iron (Fe^{2+}) or other reduced transition metals can generate highly reactive hydroxyl radical (OH·). Reactive oxygen species can oxidize lipids (lipid peroxidation), proteins, and nucleic acid (DNA strand breaks). Quenchers react with reactive oxygen species or with oxidized cellular molecules to prevent further oxidation. The enzymatic antioxidant defenses consist of the superoxide dismutases (SOD), catalase (Cat), and the glutathione peroxidase-reductase system (GPx and GRed). These enzymes detoxify O_2 and H_2O_2 to prevent undesirable biologic oxidations. NADPH is required both for reduction of glutathione and for pathways for repair of oxidant damage. Glucose-6-phosphate dehydrogenase determines availability of NADPH because it is the rate-limiting step in the pentose phosphate shunt.

ant interstitial and alveolar edema, hypoxemia, and sometimes death. Other pathologic changes include hyperplasia of type II cells, and histologic changes have been found in the ciliated epithelium and Clara cells of the small airways.

Clinical Manifestations

Oxygen toxicity usually occurs in acutely ill patients who are receiving mechanical ventilation (Chapter 101) and oxygen at concentrations above 50% for lung injuries that obscure the onset of pulmonary toxicity. Lung compliance progressively falls; the alveolar-arterial oxygen gradient gradually widens, and increasing concentrations of oxygen are needed to maintain adequate oxygenation of arterial blood. This cycle progresses to pulmonary edema, respiratory failure, and death.

The earliest symptoms of oxygen toxicity are those of acute tracheobronchitis. A dry, hacking cough and substernal pain may occur after 6 to 12 hours of breathing pure oxygen. Vital capacity decreases, and respiratory rate increases. The flow of tracheal mucus decreases after short exposures to excess oxygen, probably reflecting functional injury of airway epithelium. These patients are therefore more susceptible to mucus impaction and to infection caused by failure to clear inhaled pathogens adequately.

 ## Treatment and Prognosis

The only proven therapy is to prevent the insult by judicious use of high oxygen concentrations. The physician often faces a dilemma in that increasing concentrations of oxygen are needed to save the patient immediately but can eventually kill the patient. Alternative methods to improve arterial oxygen content should be used whenever possible; these methods include a number of maneuvers related to optimizing mechanical ventilation (Chapter 101) and transfusion of packed red cells when appropriate. Cardiac output should be maintained and accompanied by measures to decrease the tissue oxygen demand by reducing fever or agitation.

The safe maximal concentration of oxygen is not known. Little or no injury occurs in normal animals or human volunteers breathing oxygen concentrations of 40 to 50% for prolonged periods. Injured or diseased lungs, however, may be more susceptible to oxygen injury. A rational therapy is to use only enough oxygen to provide adequate arterial blood saturation, (e.g., an SaO_2 of 90%). Corticosteroids have no benefit and may actually worsen the lung injury caused by hyperoxia. Chemotherapeutic drugs that produce oxidant-based lung toxicity, such as bleomycin, potentiate lung injury from oxygen. If the patient survives oxygen toxicity, some residual damage to the lung parenchyma may remain, with septal fibrosis replacing areas where the pulmonary capillary bed was destroyed by the hyperoxia.

RADIATION LUNG INJURY (Chapter 19)

Etiology and Pathogenesis

Ionizing radiation produces oxidant lung injury related to the degree of the radiation exposure. Occurrence of radiation pneumonitis is determined by total radiation dose, number of fractions, and the period over which the radiation is given. Chemotherapeutic drugs, such as bleomycin, may also potentiate lung injury from radiation. A total lung dose of less than 2000 cGy generally is not associated with significant radiation pneumonitis, whereas a total dose in excess of 4000 cGy, even if distributed over as many as 30 fractions, has virtually a 100% risk of radiation pneumonitis.

The reaction of the lung to radiation injury can be divided into three phases. (1) An *acute phase,* occurring 1 to 2 months after radiation exposure, is characterized by vascular damage, congestion, edema, and mononuclear cell infiltration. Alveolar type II cells and alveolar macrophages are increased in number. (2) A *subacute phase* occurs 2 to 9 months later. The alveolar walls become infiltrated with mononuclear inflammatory cells and fibroblasts. (3) The *chronic* or *fibrotic phase* generally occurs more than 9 months after irradiation. Alveolar fibrosis and capillary sclerosis are its predominant histologic features.

Clinical Manifestations

Signs of bronchial irritation (e.g., cough) may appear immediately after radiation therapy, followed shortly thereafter by esophagitis. Some patients may have no symptoms for 6 to 12 weeks. If large volumes of lung have been irradiated, or if high radiation doses have been given over short periods, the patient can develop dyspnea, tachypnea, and fever. These symptoms can either progress to severe dyspnea and death or gradually subside, leaving varying degrees of respiratory impairment due to lung fibrosis. Permanent fibrosis takes 6 to 24 months to evolve, and it then usually remains stable if no further exposure occurs. Auscultation of the chest is usually normal, although rales, signs of consolidation, and pleural rubs may be found. Clubbing does not develop after radiation injury. Laboratory findings include a mild leukocytosis and an increased erythrocyte sedimentation rate. If the irradiated area is extensive, arterial hypoxemia may develop. Radiographic changes generally appear 1 to 3 months after treatment. The affected areas are generally demarcated by a "straight edge" defining the margins of the radiation portal, and they have a "ground-glass appearance"—a hazy increase in density with indistinct pulmonary markings. In the later phases of the radiation injury, fibrosis and contraction of the irradiated region are the predominant radiographic findings. Pulmonary function tests rarely change without symptoms, and then pulmonary restriction may be noted. Capillary sclerosis is associated with a decrease in blood flow to the affected region and a decrease in diffusing capacity.

Diagnosis

The diagnosis of acute radiation pneumonitis may be difficult to establish because of coincidental disease. The clinical picture is often complicated by immunocompromise in the patients, resulting in increased risk of bacterial or opportunistic pneumonias or by the signs and symptoms of the original neoplasm. Radiation pneumonitis in parts of the lung outside the radiation portal has been suspected in a few patients on the basis of typical clinical and radiographic features. Complications of radiation pneumonitis include small pleural effusions and, occasionally, spontaneous pneumothorax.

 ## Treatment and Prognosis

The patient in whom radiation pneumonitis develops requires supportive care, including cough suppression, antipyretics, and supplemental oxygen for hypoxemia. Corticosteroids (prednisone, 1 mg/kg/day of body weight) have been advocated for treating severe cases of radiation pneumonitis, and even though randomized controlled trials are not available, the response to steroids is often quite dramatic with complete resolution of symptoms within 24 hours. No evidence supports the prophylactic use of corticosteroids, but initiating therapy at the very onset of pneumonitis appears to be more effective than later therapy. Corticosteroids should be tapered carefully after achieving maximal clinical benefit. Recurrent pneumonitis has been reported occasionally after withdrawal of steroids. No other effective therapeutic strategies are known. Antibiotic therapy should be reserved for patients in whom the clinical findings suggest infection. Because the lesion involves occlusion and thrombosis of many small blood vessels, anticoagulation has been tried, but no evidence of its effectiveness has been compiled.

ASPIRATION-RELATED INJURIES

Etiology

Injury to the respiratory system by aspiration can be categorized by the nature of the aspirate as (1) *infectious material* (Chapter 92), (2) *chemical* or *inflammatory substances,* and (3) *inert material.* Aspirating gastric acid is the most common example of chemical aspiration in adults; hydrocarbon aspiration occurs predominantly in children and occasionally in adults. Both of these injuries can cause fulminant illness. By contrast, lipids (mineral oil, vegetable and animal fats) most often provoke a chronic inflammatory reaction. Aspirating inert material, such as water, causes injury (e.g., drowning), predominantly by asphyxia. Food particles can cause a fibrotic, granulomatous lesion or, if large enough to occlude the larynx or trachea, sudden death by asphyxiation ("café coronary").

ASPIRATION PNEUMONITIS

Aspiration pneumonitis refers to pulmonary injury caused by acid gastric contents. This condition is different than but may be accompanied by "aspiration pneumonia," which is an infectious process caused by aspiration of oropharyngeal flora into the tracheobronchial tree (Chapter 306). Aspiration of gastric acid can occur during vomiting or regurgitation, and in the latter instance the event may go unnoted (i.e., "silent aspiration"). The normal protective mechanisms of the upper airway include epiglottic closure during deglutition, glottic closure on contact with solids or fluids, the cough reflex, and esophageal sphincters. Altered states of consciousness, anesthesia and surgery, neuromuscular disease, gastrointestinal disease, and medical devices (nasogastric tubes or tracheostomy tubes) impair these defenses. Protecting the airway is a major concern in these high-risk situations. Using low-pressure, high-volume cuffs on endotracheal tubes reduces the extent of aspiration of gastric contents in patients at risk.

Etiology and Pathogenesis

The main factors determining the extent of illness caused by gastric acid aspiration are as follows:

1. *The pH of the aspirate.* The acidity of the material is the single most important contributor to lung injury. A pH of 2.5 or less has been proposed as a critical value for inducing severe pneumonitis from acid aspiration.
2. *The presence of food particles.* Aspiration of gastric particulates even at normal pH causes a severe pneumonitis and peribronchial inflammatory reaction.
3. *Volume of the aspirate.* Aspirating as little as 30 mL of gastric acid is sufficient to cause pneumonitis in the adult.
4. *Distribution of the aspirate.* Many patients who aspirate immediately begin to cough, which may partially protect the lung from injury or may enhance dispersion of the acid over a greater area and create a diffuse injury.

Acid in the trachea is rapidly distributed in the lungs and can reach the pleura in 12 to 18 seconds. It is neutralized by bronchial secretions; in less than 30 minutes, the pH at the bronchial surface returns to normal. Acid causes chemical burns of the bronchi, bronchioles, and alveolar walls, with subsequent exudation of fluid into the lungs. Plasma volume may decrease by as much as 35% in severe injury without fluid replacement, and cardiac output and systemic arterial blood pressure may fall. Pulmonary capillary wedge pressure is normal or low, indicating a nonhydrostatic cause of the pulmonary edema. The characteristics of phospholipids in the alveolar lining fluid layer (surfactant) are altered, increasing surface forces and promoting early alveolar collapse. Lung compliance decreases secondary to the increase in interstitial fluids and altered surface forces. These disturbances of airways, alveoli, and vascular elements profoundly unbalance the normal ventilation-perfusion relationships. Increased intrapulmonary shunting is also common. As a result, hypoxemia is invariably present and is usually severe.

Clinical Manifestations

Some patients aspirate a large volume of gastric acid and almost immediately become apneic and hypotensive and die. More often, the patient survives the initial crisis but later develops a fulminant illness marked by dyspnea, cough, and frothy sputum. Alternatively, aspiration may not be accompanied by immediate coughing and agitation. After such silent aspiration, the patient may develop acute respiratory failure without an obvious reason for a precipitous deterioration in gas exchange. Within 1 to 5 hours after aspiration of gastric acid, tachypnea, rales, and rhonchi occur, and wheezing, cyanosis, cough, and hypotension may be present. Fever occurs in the first 36 hours in about 50% of patients.

Laboratory tests are nonspecific. Moderate leukocytosis with left shift develops early. Arterial blood gases show hypoxemia, and

the arterial oxygen tension does not reach predicted levels after the patient has been breathing 100% oxygen for several minutes, indicating increased intrapulmonary shunting of blood. The arterial P_{CO_2} may be slightly elevated, normal, or mildly reduced. Abnormalities on chest roentgenograms are extremely variable, and no characteristic pattern is present. Radiographic abnormalities do not correlate with clinical outcome, although about 50% of patients have changes consistent with pneumonitis. The acid is sometimes distributed preferentially to dependent areas, but usually the radiographic abnormalities are diffuse, presumably from enhanced dispersion of the acid during coughing. Pleural effusions and cavitation of infiltrates are not seen in uncomplicated cases. Bronchoscopic findings are diagnostic if food particles or other gastric contents are seen in the trachea or bronchi.

The diagnosis of aspiration pneumonitis begins with a high index of suspicion in patients with abrupt respiratory deterioration, especially patients with conditions that predispose to gastric acid aspiration. The differential diagnosis includes cardiogenic pulmonary edema, pulmonary embolism, bacterial pneumonia, and many of the causes of ARDS, such as sepsis and hypotension.

Rx Treatment

Treatment of the individual whose aspiration was witnessed begins with promptly establishing an adequate airway. The airway should be suctioned to remove any particulate matter. Supplemental oxygen is given to maintain a PaO_2 of more than 60 mm Hg. Aerosolized bronchodilators may be helpful. Associated pulmonary edema is noncardiogenic in origin and is usually associated with intravascular volume depletion. General supportive measures include judicious replacement of fluids.

The prophylactic use of antibiotics for acid aspiration is not indicated because they do not reduce morbidity or mortality and may increase the risk of subsequent infection with a resistant organism. The acid-damaged respiratory tract is more susceptible to bacterial infection, and one third of patients with significant aspiration develop bacterial pneumonia. Such patients undergo new deterioration after 2 or 3 days, with increasing fever, leukocytosis, production of purulent sputum, worsening hypoxemia, and new infiltrates on the chest radiograph. Systemic corticosteroids should not be used routinely in aspiration pneumonitis. As for other forms of ARDS, use of corticosteroids is controversial and may increase the rate of infection.

Positive-pressure ventilation (Chapter 101) is helpful after severe cases of aspiration to improve arterial oxygen tension. Other measures useful to treat ARDS, such as low tidal volume ventilation and maintaining a normal pulmonary capillary wedge pressure, are beneficial after aspiration injury of the lung. Positive-end expiratory pressure (PEEP) is commonly used to improve oxygenation in patients with gastric acid aspiration. Caution should be used in applying PEEP because it can markedly increase in extravascular water content in the acid-injured lung.

Because aspiration pneumonitis carries a high mortality rate and occurs largely in a defined population at increased risk, efforts should be made at prevention. Elevating the head of the bed retards regurgitation. In intubated patients, a nasogastric tube should be considered to keep the stomach decompressed. Aspiration may occur even in the presence of a cuffed endotracheal tube. Elective general anesthesia should be given with the stomach empty, after at least a 12-hour fast. Preoperatively, the pH of gastric contents can be raised by an H_2-receptor blocker given 2 hours before surgery or proton pump inhibitors given the day before surgery.

Prognosis

Mortality from aspiration pneumonitis ranges from 30 to 50%. Factors associated with high mortality are age older than 50 years, the early development of shock or apnea, severe and prolonged hypoxemia, very low pH of gastric contents at the time of aspiration, and the development of secondary bacterial pneumonia. Most patients survive the early moments but deteriorate over 12 to 24 hours. Some then show steady improvement, with radiographic resolution within a week. Others have a second episode of deterioration, an event that should suggest a new problem, such as bacterial infection, pulmonary embolism, heart failure, or another aspiration. Still others pursue a relentlessly worsening course to death. Few data exist regarding long-term clinical follow-up, but pulmonary fibrosis of varying degrees may occur in some of the survivors.

HYDROCARBON PNEUMONITIS

Etiology

Hydrocarbon pneumonitis results from the direct toxic effects of volatile hydrocarbons on the respiratory epithelium and vasculature. It occurs in individuals who, having ingested the hydrocarbons, aspirate them into the respiratory tract. It is uncommon in adults, occurring in industrial accidents, in siphoning of gasoline, in alcoholics seeking an ethanol substitute, in individuals inhaling gasoline for its euphoric effects, and in patients attempting suicide.

The lower the viscosity or the larger the volume of the hydrocarbons, the worse the injury. As lipid solvents, these compounds are directly toxic to respiratory tissues. The lungs of children dying of hydrocarbon pneumonitis demonstrate hemorrhage, pulmonary edema, atelectasis, hyaline membrane formation, and necrosis of airway epithelium and alveolar septa. These compounds also have systemic toxicity, and in fatal cases, degenerative changes are often seen in the liver and kidneys.

Clinical Manifestations

Aspiration usually occurs when hydrocarbons are ingested, and a history of vomiting after ingestion is obtained in fewer than half the patients. Dyspnea, tachypnea, tachycardia, and high fever quickly ensue. Sputum may be bloody. Lethargy is common, but more severe disturbances of consciousness also occur, such as confusion, coma, and seizures. Auscultation is frequently normal, but rales and rhonchi may be present.

Laboratory tests give nonspecific results. Moderate leukocytosis with left shift is common. Arterial hypoxemia of various degrees develops owing to shunting and to ventilation-perfusion mismatching. The chest radiograph is particularly helpful, because infiltrates may occur within 20 to 30 minutes after aspirating some types of hydrocarbons. The multiple, fluffy, ill-defined infiltrates favor dependent areas of the lungs. Some patients present a picture of bilateral perihilar infiltrates, a pulmonary edema pattern. Pleural effusions, pneumothorax, and pneumomediastinum are uncommon. Pneumatoceles can form later, especially in children.

Diagnosis

The differential diagnosis is that of sudden respiratory distress. Frequently, the patient has an impaired sensorium at presentation. The adult patient is often an alcoholic. Gastric acid aspiration, cardiogenic pulmonary edema, pulmonary embolism, and acute bacterial pneumonia can all manifest similarly. The correct diagnosis requires the history of hydrocarbon ingestion or aspiration. The diagnosis is also suggested by the odor of the patient's breath and by extensive radiographic abnormalities in a patient with a clear chest on auscultation.

 ### Treatment

Emesis to remove residual hydrocarbons is contraindicated. Gastric lavage by nasogastric tube may cause vomiting in the patient who has recently ingested a large volume of hydrocarbons and should be performed only after placing a cuffed endotracheal tube. Supplemental oxygen should be given to maintain a PaO_2 of 60 mm Hg. Mechanical ventilation and PEEP may be necessary. No data support the routine use of antibiotics. Benefit of systemic corticosteroids (prednisone, 1 mg/kg/day) during the acute illness has been suggested in anecdotal reports.

Prognosis

Hydrocarbon pneumonitis in adults is rare, so that estimates of morbidity and mortality are not available. In children, death occurs in about 10% of cases, but most children have a prompt clinical recovery. Bronchiectasis, recurrent bronchitis, and/or pulmonary fibrosis develop in an unknown portion of cases. After recovery, children frequently have normal chest examinations and radiographs, although pulmonary function abnormalities suggestive of small airway (<2 mm in diameter) disease have been found in asymptomatic patients as late as 8 to 14 years after hydrocarbon pneumonitis.

LIPOID PNEUMONIA

Lipoid pneumonia is a chronic inflammatory reaction of the lungs to the presence of lipid substances. Exogenous lipoid pneumonia results from the aspiration of vegetable, animal, or (most commonly) mineral oils. This material differs greatly from the excessive accumulation of endogenous lipids in the lungs occurring in fat embolism, cholesterol pneumonitis, pulmonary alveolar proteinosis, and the lipid storage diseases (endogenous lipoid pneumonia).

Etiology

The most frequently implicated agent is mineral oil used as a laxative and to reduce dysphagia, either in clear liquid form or as petroleum jelly. Mineral oil is bland and, when introduced into the pharynx, can enter the bronchial tree without eliciting the cough reflex. It also mechanically impedes the ciliary action of the airway epithelium. The risk of mineral oil aspiration is increased in debilitated or senile patients, in those with neurologic disease that interferes with deglutition, and in patients with esophageal disease. Mineral oil taken as nose drops to relieve nasal dryness has caused lipoid pneumonia and was a frequent cause of the illness years ago. Inhalation of mineral oil mist by airplane and automobile mechanics has also been implicated as a cause of the problem.

Mineral oils, which cannot be hydrolyzed in the body, provoke a chronic inflammatory reaction that may not become clinically overt until years later. In the alveolar spaces, macrophages accumulate and phagocytize the emulsified oil. Some macrophages disintegrate, releasing their lysosomal enzymes and oil. The alveolar septa become thickened and edematous, containing lymphocytes and lipid-laden macrophages. Oil droplets are seen in the pulmonary lymphatics and hilar nodes. Later, fibrosis develops, and the normal lung architecture is effaced. It is usual in a single specimen to find both the early inflammatory and the later fibrotic picture, in keeping with repetitive aspirations over many months or years. If nodular, the lesion may grossly resemble tumor and is called a *paraffinoma*.

Clinical Manifestations

Most patients are asymptomatic, coming to the physician's attention because of an abnormal chest radiograph. When patients are symptomatic, cough and exertional dyspnea are the most frequent complaints. Chest pain (sometimes pleuritic), hemoptysis, fever (usually low grade), chills, night sweats, and weight loss may occur. The physical examination may be completely normal, or fever, tachypnea, dullness on percussion of the chest, bronchial or bronchovesicular breath sounds, rales, and rhonchi may be found. Clubbing and cor pulmonale are rare.

In mild lipoid pneumonia, arterial blood gas values may be normal with the patient at rest but may show hypoxemia after exercise. In more severe disease, resting hypoxemia, hypocapnia, and mild respiratory alkalosis develop. Pulmonary function testing reveals a restrictive ventilatory defect; lung compliance is decreased. The only specific laboratory finding is the presence in sputum of macrophages with clusters of vacuoles 5 to 50 μm in diameter that stain deep orange with Sudan IV and of extracellular droplets that stain similarly.

Radiographically, the earliest abnormalities are air space infiltrates; these infiltrates may be unilateral or bilateral, localized or diffuse, but most often occur in the dependent portions of the lung. Air bronchograms may be seen. Hilar adenopathy and pleural reaction are rare. As fibrosis develops, volume loss occurs and linear and nodular infiltrates appear. A solid lesion that closely resembles bronchogenic carcinoma may develop. High-resolution computed tomography (HRCT) usually shows consolidated areas of low attenuation and "crazy paving."

Diagnosis

The differential diagnosis is extensive, particularly in the late phase, when multiple other causes of pulmonary fibrosis must be considered. The key to the correct diagnosis before biopsy is the history of chronic oral or intranasal use of an oil- or a lipid-based product, or an occupational exposure to oil mists. The presence of lipid-laden macrophages in sputum or bronchoalveolar lavage fluid also can be used to confirm the diagnosis, particularly in conjunction with the HRCT findings noted earlier.

Treatment and Prognosis

Once the diagnosis has been made and the aspiration stopped, the subsequent course is variable. Because the only way the lung can dispose of mineral oil is by expectoration, the patient should be instructed in coughing exercises to be performed many times each day for months. Expectorants have not been shown to help. Systemic corticosteroids have been recommended on the basis of improvement seen in a few uncontrolled reports. Because of the well-recognized side effects of systemic corticosteroids, their use for lipoid pneumonia should be limited to patients who have significant symptoms, and then for as brief a period as possible.

SUBMERSION INCIDENTS (NEAR-DROWNING)

Drowning is one of the three leading causes of accidental death in children and young adults. In adults, alcohol consumption and shallow water blackout during breath-hold diving are common aggravating factors. An appreciable number of drowning incidents, particularly in cold water, have no identifiable explanation. In these cases, sudden cardiac arrhythmias, particularly those associated with the long-QT syndrome, have been implicated. Compared with other physical activities, swimming is particularly arrhythmogenic in these patients. Pathophysiologically, drowning can be of two types: (1) "wet" drowning, or initial laryngospasm but early relaxation and subsequent aspiration of copious amounts of fluid; and (2) "dry" drowning, or asphyxiation secondary to intense glottic spasm that persists beyond the point of apnea, so that when the muscles relax, little or no water is aspirated; this latter type accounts for 10 to 20% of drowning. The immediate cause of death in many victims of drowning is cardiac arrhythmia. Victims who survive the submersion incident or "near-drowning" frequently develop ARDS a few hours to a few days after the event (secondary drowning).

Pathogenesis

The most important consequence of prolonged submersion is asphyxia, which results in severe hypoxemia, hypercarbia, and metabolic acidosis. The metabolic consequences of drowning in fresh water or salt water differ little except for drowning in water with very high mineral content (e.g., the Dead Sea). In both cases, hypoxemia is caused by the occlusion of airways with water and particulate debris, by changes in surfactant activity, by direct injury to the alveolar septa, and by bronchospasm. Right-to-left shunting is markedly increased, and physiologic dead space is increased. Life-threatening electrolyte disturbances caused by water aspiration in humans are rare. Cardiac arrhythmias, hypoxic encephalopathy, and renal insufficiency often occur after near-drowning. Global brain anoxia, if it is of sufficient duration and magnitude, leads to diffuse cerebral edema.

Autopsies of drowned persons demonstrate wet, heavy lungs with varying amounts of hemorrhage and edema and some disruption of alveolar walls. In about 70% of victims, vomitus, sand, mud, and aquatic vegetation are aspirated. Specimens from victims dying of secondary drowning show desquamation of alveolar epithelial cells, hemorrhage, hyaline membrane formation, acute inflammatory infiltrates, and foreign body reactions to particulate matter. Cerebral edema and diffuse neuronal injury are seen. Acute tubular necrosis is common in the kidneys.

Clinical Manifestations

The initial appearance of the patient can vary widely, from coma to agitated alertness. Cyanosis, coughing, and the production of frothy pink sputum are common. Tachypnea, tachycardia, and a low-grade fever in the first few hours are seen if the patient did not become hypothermic during submersion. Rales, rhonchi, and, less often, wheezes are heard. Neurologic signs vary and can fluctuate in any given patient, but they usually derive from diffuse cerebral dysfunction. Signs of associated trauma to the head and neck should be sought.

Laboratory studies reveal mild hypokalemia, hypernatremia, and hyperchloremia. Moderate leukocytosis may be present. Hematocrit and hemoglobin usually are normal at first measurement; in fresh water aspiration, the hematocrit may fall slightly in the first 24 hours owing to hemolysis. An isolated increase in free hemoglobin without a change in hematocrit is more common. Occasionally, the clinical picture of disseminated intravascular coagulation occurs in near-drowning. Arterial blood gas values, usually obtained after preliminary resuscitation, show severe hypoxemia and metabolic acidosis. Common electrocardiography changes are sinus tachycardia and nonspecific ST-segment and T-wave changes, which revert to normal within hours; however, other more ominous abnormalities may occur, such as ventricular arrhythmias, complete heart block, or myocardial infarction. The chest radiograph may be normal initially despite severe respiratory disturbances; however, it often shows patchy infiltrates, and sometimes a classic pattern of pulmonary edema is seen.

Treatment

Treatment of the near-drowning victim begins with establishing an adequate airway and, if necessary, emergency cardiopulmonary resuscitation. Oxygen in high concentrations is necessary, because hypoxemia is present in essentially all victims. Even the patient who quickly becomes apparently normal should be hospitalized for 24 hours to watch for a subsequent clinical picture of ARDS. Supplemental oxygen should be continued and precautions taken for potential head and neck injuries and other serious trauma.

In the hospital, therapy is dictated largely by the arterial blood gas values and the degree of respiratory failure. Continuous positive airway pressure or PEEP is particularly helpful for managing hypoxemia (Chapter 101). Bronchospasm should be treated with aerosolized β-agonists. Patients with persistent localized atelectasis or localized wheezing should undergo bronchoscopy to exclude a foreign body as the cause. Prophylactic antibiotics have not been shown to be beneficial, although many victims of near-drowning develop pneumonia, which may be caused by unusual microorganisms. No controlled human studies are available to support the use of corticosteroids for the pulmonary lesions of near-drowning; animal models and retrospective studies in humans have failed to demonstrate benefit.

The therapeutic approach to brain resuscitation after near-drowning is controversial. If cerebral edema develops, intracranial pressure (ICP) monitoring may be used to guide therapy; however, elevated ICP is usually a manifestation of irreversible cellular injury and not the cause of the damage. In the event of cerebral edema, PEEP should be minimized because it may increase ICP. Hyperventilation to maintain a $PaCO_2$ of 25 to 30 mm Hg decreases ICP at expense to cerebral blood flow. Mannitol may decrease cerebral edema; it should be used to maintain the serum osmolarity near 300 mOsm/L. Corticosteroids are used widely (e.g., dexamethasone), but they are of no proven benefit for the brain injury. Seizures should be treated with anticonvulsants. Shivering or random, purposeless movements can increase ICP and should be controlled. Hypothermia and barbiturate coma for 24 to 48 hours recommended by some are highly controversial, difficult to control, and unlikely to benefit the patient.

Prognosis

Outcome in near-drowning is best judged by the neurologic status (i.e., the presence or absence of coma). The initial clinical presenta-

Table 90–2 • FACTORS ASSOCIATED WITH DEATH AFTER SUBMERSION INCIDENTS

GRADE	FINDINGS	ESTIMATED MORTALITY (%)
1	Normal lung examination	0
2	Abnormal lung examination	<1
3	Acute pulmonary edema	5
4	Pulmonary edema + hypotension	20
5	Respiratory arrest	40–50
6	Cardiorespiratory arrest	>90%

Table 90–3 • HIGH-ALTITUDE SYNDROMES

SYNDROME	CLINICAL DESCRIPTION
Acute mountain sickness (AMS)	Common, self-limited; characterized by headache, anorexia, and malaise after ascent to altitudes >8,000 ft; "normal puna"
High-altitude pulmonary edema (HAPE)	Noncardiac pulmonary edema recognized by dyspnea and tachypnea at rest, cough, and bibasilar crackles; usually at altitudes >9,500 ft; "pulmonary puna"
High-altitude cerebral edema (HACE)	Uncommon, severe central nervous system dysfunction following AMS, characterized by severe headache, memory loss, ataxia, hallucinations, and confusion; may progress to coma and death; "nervous puna"
High-altitude retinal hemorrhages (HARH)	Dilated retinal vessels and peripheral flame-shaped or dot hemorrhages, which occasionally cause visual symptoms
Chronic mountain sickness (Monge's disease)	Cor pulmonale with minimal lung disease in long-term residents of high altitude

tion provides a rough indication of prognosis for recovery (Table 90–2). The absence of spontaneous respiration after resuscitation from near-drowning is an ominous sign associated with severe neurologic sequelae. Permanent neurologic sequelae persist in about 20% of comatose victims. Common problems include minimal brain dysfunction, spastic quadriplegia, extrapyramidal syndromes, optic and cerebral atrophy, and peripheral neuromuscular damage. Survival without neurologic damage is best in children who are hypothermic when recovered and may occur even after more than 60 minutes of submersion. Similar reports of survival after prolonged immersion in adults are rare.

DISORDERS CAUSED BY ALTERED BAROMETRIC PRESSURE

Changes in environmental pressure are encountered in humans during ascent to altitude and during underwater diving. As altitude increases, barometric pressure decreases from approximately 760 mm Hg at sea level to 380 mm Hg (0.5 ATA) at 18,000 feet. In sea water, the pressure of the water column increases by an amount equal to the barometric pressure for every 33 feet of depth. Hence, at 33 feet of seawater, the absolute pressure is doubled (2 ATA). As a result, participants in activities such as mountaineering and scuba diving are often exposed to extremes of environmental pressure. Rapid pressure changes produce notable physiologic effects related to the behavior of atmospheric gases in the lungs and body tissues.

DISEASES OF HIGH ALTITUDES

Physiologic changes, characterized primarily by hyperventilation, appear at 8000 to 10,000 feet. At altitudes above 10,000 feet, the physiologic responses become more pronounced owing to the shape of the oxygen-hemoglobin dissociation curve, which has a steep slope downward below a P_{O_2} of approximately 60 mm Hg. A small decrease in P_{O_2} below this level results in a relatively large decrease in arterial saturation. At 10,000 feet (3048 m), the alveolar P_{O_2} is approximately 60 mm Hg, and some individuals manifest impairment of memory, judgment, and the ability to perform complex calculations. At 18,000 feet (5486 meters), the alveolar P_{O_2} is 40 mm Hg, and unacclimatized individuals may develop serious neurologic signs and symptoms.

Exposure to high altitude occurs most commonly in commercial aviation. Commercial jet aircraft are pressurized to maintain a cabin altitude of 6000 to 8000 feet, so that supplemental oxygen is not required. Some patients with reduced cardiac reserve or with COPD, however, may not tolerate even a small decrease in arterial oxygen saturation and may require oxygen during flights. Aircraft regulations require that the flight crew receive supplemental oxygen when cabin pressure drops below 10,000 feet, and that passengers receive supplemental oxygen should the cabin pressure drop below 15,000 feet.

ACUTE MOUNTAIN SICKNESS. High altitude produces a spectrum of illness that depends on the rate of ascent, final altitude, sleeping altitude, duration of stay, and other individual factors (Table 90–3). The acute syndromes probably reflect a common pathophysiology initiated by a relatively abrupt lack of oxygen, although the precise mechanisms remain uncertain. The ventilatory response to hypoxia and poor physical conditioning may play a role in susceptible individuals. The most common malady is acute mountain sickness (AMS), and self-limited symptoms of headache, anorexia, malaise, and disturbed sleep may appear within a few hours of arriving at altitudes above 7000 feet. The incidence of AMS in unacclimatized individuals is approximately 20% after routine ascent to 7000 to 9000 feet, 40% at 10,000 to 14,000 feet and more than 50% above 14,000 feet. Symptoms may become worse with exercise owing in part to further oxygen desaturation of arterial blood. At altitudes above 9500 feet, AMS may become severe and accompanied by high-altitude pulmonary edema (HAPE) and high-altitude cerebral edema (HACE), which may coexist. High-altitude retinal hemorrhages (HARH) are prevalent above 14,000 feet and probably share a similar pathophysiology with cerebral edema. Retinal hemorrhages are not significant unless they produce visual symptoms; the latter circumstance usually indicates involvement of the macula and mandates immediate descent.

HIGH-ALTITUDE PULMONARY EDEMA. Acute pulmonary edema is a potentially fatal complication of rapid ascent to altitudes above 9500 feet. HAPE occurs by noncardiogenic mechanisms, although pulmonary hypertension is involved in its pathogenesis. Symptoms begin after 6 to 36 hours at high altitude and may follow an episode of AMS. Dyspnea at rest, tachypnea, and crackles are characteristic features of HAPE. Cyanosis, orthopnea, and hemoptysis commonly develop in more advanced cases.

At autopsy, the lungs are typically heavy, congested, and edematous and have hyaline membranes in small airways and alveoli. Hemodynamic studies have shown elevated pulmonary artery pressure with normal pulmonary venous pressure. Pulmonary edema may be due to capillary stress failure from an increase in pressure in local regions of the pulmonary vascular bed leading to plasma leakage and inflammation in the alveolar capillary region.

HIGH-ALTITUDE CEREBRAL EDEMA. HACE is relatively uncommon, occurring in perhaps 1.5% of individuals affected by AMS. Hypoxemia produces cerebral vasodilation and increased cerebral blood flow, which may lead to mild brain edema and produce the symptoms of AMS. By factors yet to be defined, the brain edema may progress and become life-threatening. Signs and symptoms of HACE include severe, progressive headache, ataxia, confusion, anxiety, hallucinations, and coma. Papilledema and meningeal signs occur. Examining the cerebrospinal fluid reveals high opening pressures and perhaps hemorrhage or leukocytosis. Pathologically, the pattern of cerebral edema appears to be heterogeneous, and focal areas of capillary damage, red cell sludging, and platelet aggregation are seen.

Rx **Treatment**

The simple approach for dealing with acute altitude illness is to ascend to altitude gradually and to descend when troubling symptoms appear. Gradual ascent allows time for the body to adapt. If possible, the rate of ascent should be limited to approximately 1000 feet/day between altitudes of 8000 and 10,000 feet. Slower ascent (500 feet/day) is recommended for altitudes above 10,000 feet. If slow ascent is impractical, prophylactic treatment with acetazolamide is effective in preventing AMS. Acetazolamide increases renal bicarbonate excretion and lessens the degree of respiratory

Continued

Respiratory Diseases

alkalosis. The drug is administered (250 mg) every 12 hours the day before, during, and for 1 day after the ascent. The use of twice-daily acetazolamide minimizes dehydration and potassium depletion over the 3 days. Other diuretics have not proved to be effective, and, in practice, liberal water intake hastens bicarbonate excretion and prevents hemoconcentration. Prophylactic inhaled salmeterol can reduce the risk of HAPE by two thirds in patients who are known to be susceptible to this syndrome. Dexamethasone also reduces the incidence and early symptoms of AMS; however, its prophylactic use is not recommended because of potential side effects.

AMS is usually managed conservatively with rest, mild analgesics, alcohol avoidance, and hydration. The symptoms usually abate within a few days. Further ascent with symptoms of AMS may precipitate more severe forms of altitude illness. Definitive treatment for HAPE, HACE, and severe HARH is oxygen administration and descent to lower altitude. High-altitude pulmonary edema may improve dramatically with a descent of only a few thousand feet. If the descent is delayed, the combination of oxygen with PEEP or continuous positive airway pressure, or placing the victim in a pressurized bag or chamber, is effective. Nifedipine and dexamethasone also ameliorate serious symptoms when descent is not feasible.

CHRONIC MOUNTAIN SICKNESS. Chronic mountain sickness occurs in people living at high altitudes, usually over 14,000 feet, for many years. These "highlanders" have a blunted respiratory drive in response to hypoxia and have less ventilation at altitude than those who reside normally at low altitude. Chronic mountain sickness is characterized by an exaggerated response to hypoxia, which leads to cor pulmonale. Physiologic responses include erythrocytosis with hemoglobin levels as high as 25 g/dL, decreased ventilation with elevated P_{CO_2}, hypoxemia, and impaired sensitivity of the respiratory center to hypoxia. Clinical manifestations are similar to those of polycythemia rubra vera and include cyanosis, dyspnea, cough, palpitations, headache, giddiness, muscular weakness, pain in the extremities, sensory and motor changes, and episodic stupor. The only therapy is to move the patient to a lower altitude. Subacute forms of this illness, in which cyanosis and alveolar hypoventilation are absent, also occur.

DECOMPRESSION ILLNESS

Rapid ascent to a high altitude or from underwater toward the surface can cause decompression illness (DCI). Ambient pressure changes outside the body must be reflected across the lungs by proportional changes in the partial pressures of various gases dissolved in the tissues of the body. This condition is a consequence of the physical behavior of gases and their interactions in solution. Because the quantity of gas dissolved in tissue varies directly with atmospheric pressure, changes in gas concentrations in the body are most pronounced during diving with compressed air, when, in order for divers to expand their lungs, the pressure of the breathing gas must be increased in proportion to the column of water around them. Nitrogen uptake is most important in this respect because it comprises 80% of the atmosphere and, unlike oxygen, it is inert (not metabolized). Inert gases like nitrogen must be eliminated from the body after a decrease in ambient pressure, e.g., return from a compressed air dive or rapid ascent to high altitude. The process of eliminating inert gas is called *decompression.*

During decompression, inert gas dissolved in the tissues may come out of physical solution if environmental pressure falls too rapidly. Bubbles of inert gas form within the tissues and venous blood and produce pain (sometimes also called *Caisson's disease* or *bends*) or other manifestations of DCI. The pathophysiology of DCI, however, is not entirely explained by gas bubbles in blood and tissue, and not all bubbles cause symptoms. Bubbles produce a number of secondary manifestations attributed to surface activity at the interface between the bubble and the blood or tissue. These secondary effects, such as activation of complement, platelet aggregation, and release of vasoactive mediators, may lead to ischemia and manifestations of DCI.

Clinical Manifestations

DCI can occur during decompression after diving to more than 20 feet of seawater (1.6 ATA) or during rapid ascent from sea level to 18,000 feet (0.5 ATA). DCI is most commonly encountered in compressed air (or gas) divers after prolonged or repetitive dives or after severe exercise and in divers with excessive body fat, poor physical conditioning, and increasing age. The signs and symptoms of DCI usually appear within a few minutes to 24 hours after the end of the dive. Historically, DCI has been classified as either mild (type 1) or serious (type 2) (Table 90–4). This distinction is somewhat arbitrary, because both mild and serious manifestations of DCI occur simultaneously in about one third of patients. Type 2 DCI usually involves the nervous system, most notably the spinal cord. Vascular endothelial injury is common and often leads to hemoconcentration. In overwhelming DCI, abnormal gas exchange and hemodynamic compromise occur, which is known as "chokes."

Rx: Treatment and Prognosis

The first step in treating DCI is the administration of supplemental oxygen. For altitude DCI, oxygen breathing and return to sea level usually alleviates the symptoms. In divers, administration of oral or intravenous fluids and recompression in a hyperbaric chamber with 100% oxygen usually relieves symptoms effectively. If recompression therapy is delayed for more than a few hours, the illness is more refractory to treatment. The rationale for oxygen recompression is based on (1) enhancing the dissolution of gas bubbles by compression, (2) lowering the concentration of inert gas in venous blood with oxygen, thus increasing the rate of nitrogen removal from body tissues and bubbles, and (3) the high incidence of incomplete resolution and relapse with air recompression. With prompt treatment, complete recovery is achieved in more than 95% of the cases. If recompression is delayed for more than 24 hours, particularly when neurologic symptoms are present, the outcome is less certain. However, many patients, even those with spinal cord paralysis, respond to recompression after delays of 1 or more days.

PULMONARY BAROTRAUMA AND ARTERIAL GAS EMBOLISM

Pulmonary barotrauma and arterial gas embolism may occur in compressed air divers when they ascend to the surface, particularly with failure to exhale normally. They are also encountered during explosive decompression at high altitude and in blast injury of the thorax. Under these circumstances, ambient hydrostatic or barometric pressure decreases rapidly, and gas within the lungs expands reciprocally according to Boyle's law. Under water near the surface, small

Table 90–4 • CLASSIFICATION OF DECOMPRESSION ILLNESS

ORGAN SYSTEM	SIGNS AND SYMPTOMS
MILD DCI (TYPE 1)	
Skin	Pruritus, mottling, urticaria
Musculoskeletal	Pain (bends), usually in the joints; numbness; edema
SERIOUS DCI (TYPE 2)	
Central nervous system	
Cerebral	Loss of consciousness, ataxia, vertigo, aphasia, hemiparesis
Audiovestibular	Vertigo, nystagmus, auditory symptoms
Spinal cord	Back pain, paraparesis, bladder and bowel dysfunction
Cardiopulmonary	Cough, substernal pain, tachypnea, asphyxia (chokes)
Systemic	Extreme fatigue, hypovolemic shock

DCI = decompression illness.

decreases in depth result in large increases in gas volume. If the expanding gas is not allowed to escape, it may create a pressure gradient that exceeds the compliance of lung tissue. This positive-pressure gradient between alveolar gas and pulmonary interstitium may lead to barotrauma, that is, alveolar disruption and pulmonary interstitial emphysema, then to soft tissue or mediastinal emphysema, pneumothorax, or pneumopericardium. Free gas may also enter pulmonary venous blood and travel through the left side of the heart to the systemic circulation. Air can circulate throughout the arterial system and obstruct cerebral, coronary, and renal arteries. Venous gas bubbles formed during rapid ascent in divers who do not have barotrauma can enter the arterial circulation in persons with intracardiac shunts, including a previously undetected patent foramen ovale, which is present in about 15% of the normal population.

Clinical Manifestations

The clinical manifestations of gas embolism usually occur within minutes after the diver surfaces. Signs and symptoms that suggest distribution of gas to the carotid arteries frequently develop. This condition leads to acute cerebral dysfunction characterized by severe headache, blindness, loss of consciousness, seizures, or paralysis. Depending on the amount of pulmonary barotrauma, the quantity of embolized gas may be very large. This serious complication of ascent can occur in compressed air diving after very brief exposures or at very shallow depths, when DCI is not a diagnostic concern.

 ## Treatment and Prognosis

Cerebral gas embolism is a true medical emergency. Severe central nervous system deficits from gas embolism are more likely to be permanently disabling or lethal in the absence of adequate treatment than is DCI. Recompression therapy should commence within minutes if complete neurologic recovery is to be expected. The management of gas embolism is similar to that of DCI, but greater pressure, and longer and more treatment sessions may be necessary. If treatment is delayed more than 12 to 24 hours, benefit from recompression therapy is likely to be small.

 1. Thom SR, Taber RL, Mendiguren II, et al: Delayed neuropsychologic sequelae after carbon monoxide poisoning: Prevention by treatment with hyperbaric oxygen. Ann Emerg Med 1995;25:474–480.
2. Weaver LK, Hopkins RO, Chan KJ, et al: Hyperbaric oxygen for acute carbon monoxide poisoning. N Engl J Med 2002;347:1057–1067.
3. Sartori C, Allemann Y, Duplain H, et al: Salmeterol for the prevention of high-altitude pulmonary edema. N Engl J Med 2002;346:1631–1636.

SUGGESTED READINGS

Anonymous: Advanced challenges in resuscitation. Submersion or near drowning. Resuscitation 2000;46:273–277. *Review of treatment and prognosis of victims of submersion incidents.*

Basnyat B, Murdoch DR: High-altitude illness. Lancet 2003;361:1967–1974. *A comprehensive overview.*

Hampson NB, Mathieu D, Piantadosi CA, et al: Carbon monoxide poisoning: Interpretation of randomized clinical trials and unresolved treatment issues. Undersea Hyperb Med 2001;28:157–164. *Analysis of findings of six controlled trials of hyperbaric oxygen for CO poisoning.*

Marik PE: Aspiration pneumonitis and aspiration pneumonia. N Engl J Med 2001;344:665–671. *Practical synopsis of aspiration pneumonitis and pneumonia.*

 # 91 SARCOIDOSIS

Steven E. Weinberger

Definition

Sarcoidosis is a disease of unknown cause that is characterized by the presence of noncaseating granulomas in multiple organ systems. Although the lungs and the lymph nodes in the mediastinum and hilar regions are the most common sites of involvement, the disorder is considered a systemic disease, and a variety of other organ systems

or tissues may be the source of either primary or concomitant clinical manifestations and morbidity. The clinical course is variable, ranging from asymptomatic disease with spontaneous resolution to progressive disease with organ system failure and even death.

Epidemiology

Although sarcoidosis has a worldwide distribution, its reported incidence and prevalence vary considerably in different geographic areas and among disparate population subgroups. However, the accuracy and the comparability of available data are suspect, based on a high frequency of asymptomatic cases and widely differing methods of case identification.

Sarcoidosis appears to be relatively common in northern Europe (especially Scandinavia, Ireland, and Great Britain), North America, and Japan, whereas countries with a reportedly low incidence include China, Africa, India, and Russia. Even in these presumed low-incidence countries, it is likely that more cases of sarcoidosis have been present but have been misdiagnosed, especially as tuberculosis or leprosy. In a number of countries, such as Italy and Japan, the incidence of the disease is significantly greater in the northern than the southern part of the country, raising the possibility that climate affects the likelihood of the disease.

The peak age incidence of sarcoidosis is in the 20s and 30s, and women are affected slightly more often than men. Approximately 50% of patients are younger than age 30 at the time of presentation, and approximately 75% are younger than age 40. In some countries, such as Sweden and Japan, a second peak in incidence has been noted in middle age, especially in women.

In the United States, sarcoidosis is more frequent in blacks than in whites, with age-adjusted annual incidences reported as 35.5 and 10.9 per 100,000, respectively. Worldwide, however, nearly 80% of affected patients are white.

There are also geographic, ethnic, and racial differences in the mode of presentation and the clinical manifestations of sarcoidosis. Erythema nodosum is common in Scandinavian and British patients with sarcoidosis but is rare in African Americans and Japanese. Cardiac and ocular involvement are particularly prevalent in Japan, where cardiac involvement is the most common cause of death from sarcoidosis.

Pathobiology

The cause of sarcoidosis is unknown. A substantial body of information has suggested that immune mechanisms are important in disease pathogenesis, and it has been presumed that one or more causal antigens trigger a cascade of immunologic events. Genetic factors may also contribute in determining susceptibility.

Several observations have suggested that an exogenous agent may be responsible for sarcoidosis:

1. Identification of case clusters of sarcoidosis (e.g., in nurses and firefighters, and in specific geographic regions) supports the possibility of either person-to-person transmission of an infectious agent or shared exposure to an environmental agent.
2. The disease berylliosis, which is due to exposure to beryllium, produces a histologic pattern and a clinical presentation that are quite similar to those seen with sarcoidosis.
3. Recurrence of disease can occur in the transplanted lung of patients who receive a transplant for end-stage sarcoidosis. In addition, sarcoidosis has been reported to develop in the transplant recipient of tissue from a donor with sarcoidosis.

A variety of exogenous agents, both infectious and noninfectious, have been hypothesized as possible causes of sarcoidosis. Proposed infectious causes include mycobacteria (both *Mycobacterium tuberculosis* and nontuberculous mycobacteria), cell wall–deficient mycobacteria (called *L-forms*), *Propionibacterium acnes*, *Borrelia burgdorferi*, viruses, fungi, spirochetes, and the agent associated with Whipple's disease. Although the diagnosis of sarcoidosis depends on the absence of organisms that are known to be associated with granuloma formation (e.g., mycobacteria and fungi on stain or culture), the possibility remains that sarcoidosis may represent a variant host response to an infectious agent and that the organism may not be readily identifiable or recoverable at the time of disease presentation. For example, a number of studies have used the polymerase chain reaction to identify mycobacterial DNA from biologic specimens obtained from patients with sarcoidosis, but the results are inconclusive.

Environmental or occupational exposure to noninfectious agents has been an important alternative theory of the etiology of sarcoidosis. Based on the model provided by berylliosis, it has been suggested that an exogenous agent induces immunologic sensitization, perhaps by acting as a "hapten" that binds to peptides or alters major histocompatibility complex molecules. Noninfectious agents proposed to be causally related to sarcoidosis have included beryllium and other metals, organic antigens (e.g., pine pollen, peanut dust), and inorganic dusts (e.g., clay). However, the weight of evidence does not adequately support any of these agents as a primary cause of sarcoidosis.

It is believed, although not proved, that genetic factors may influence the development of sarcoidosis by affecting the nature of the cellular and immune response to the exogenous agents. Familial sarcoidosis, in which an individual with sarcoidosis is found to have a first- or second-degree relative with the disease, has been noted in up to 15% of patients and appears to be more common in blacks than in whites. However, the relative role of genetics versus shared environmental exposure in explaining these findings has not yet been defined, and studies of human leukocyte antigen associations in sarcoidosis have not been conclusive.

Despite the lack of definitive evidence about intrinsic and extrinsic factors that initiate sarcoidosis, a substantial body of information has been accumulated about the intermediate pathogenesis of the disease (i.e., the role played by cellular responses, immune mechanisms, and elaboration of cytokines). Antigen processing by macrophages is believed to trigger an oligoclonal expansion of CD4 (helper-inducer) lymphocytes of the T_H1 phenotype, with production of interleukin (IL)-2 and interferon-γ. IL-2 causes the proliferation of more CD4 cells, which elaborate cytokines that recruit macrophages into the granuloma. A variety of cytokines, adhesion molecules, and growth factors are released from both lymphocytes and macrophages, with amplification of the inflammatory response and the potential to induce fibrosis. Tumor necrosis factor-α (TNF-α), released from alveolar macrophages involved in the inflammatory process, is believed to be a particularly important cytokine mediator involved in the formation of granulomas.

Although B lymphocytes do not appear to play a primary role in the disease, their function is altered secondarily by mediators released from activated T lymphocytes. Polyclonal hyperglobulinemia results, with formation of antibodies reactive against a variety of microbial agents and self-antigens.

Clinical Manifestations

Sarcoidosis is notable for its protean manifestations and variable course. Not only can almost any organ system be affected, but the clinical presentation and natural history of disease affecting a particular organ system are also quite variable. The respiratory system is most commonly affected, with approximately 90% of patients demonstrating intrathoracic involvement on a chest radiograph. Patients can develop extrathoracic disease either with or without concomitant intrathoracic involvement. Extrathoracic disease can be the predominant component of the clinical picture or alternatively can be either subclinical or less problematic than intrathoracic disease.

As many as 30 to 60% of patients have no symptoms at the time of presentation, and the disease is identified because of abnormalities on a chest radiograph. Alternatively, patients commonly present with respiratory symptoms, such as dyspnea and cough; nonspecific retrosternal chest discomfort is sometimes present. Approximately one third of patients may have constitutional symptoms, including fever, weight loss, malaise, and fatigue. As many as 10 to 20% of patients present with a syndrome of bilateral hilar adenopathy and erythema nodosum, a constellation of findings that is called *Löfgren's syndrome*; fever and/or arthralgias may also accompany this form of presentation. Presentations related primarily to extrathoracic involvement are less common; specific signs and symptoms depend on the particular organ systems involved.

RESPIRATORY SYSTEM DISEASE. Intrathoracic nodal involvement and parenchymal lung disease are the two most common ways in which

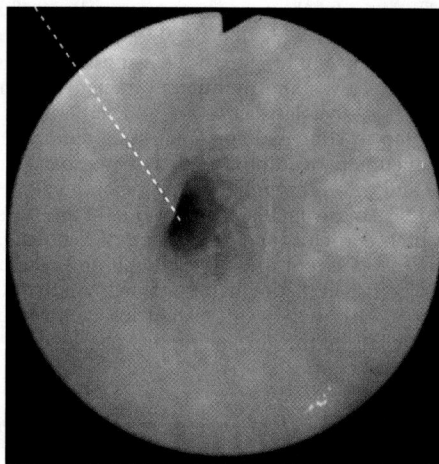

FIGURE 91–1 • Bronchoscopic findings in a patient with infiltrative sarcoidosis. The lumen of the left main bronchus (indicated by tip of dotted line) is so narrowed that a fiberoptic bronchoscope can hardly pass through it. There are dilated mucosal vessels, and multiple sarcoid nodules in the mucosa. (From Forbes CD, Jackson WF: Color Atlas and Text of Clinical Medicine, 3rd ed. London, Mosby, 2003, with permission.)

sarcoidosis affects the respiratory system. Both hilar and mediastinal lymph nodes may be affected; involvement of the hilar nodes is usually bilateral and relatively symmetrical. The pulmonary parenchyma demonstrates well-defined, noncaseating granulomas within the pulmonary interstitium, typically in a pattern that preferentially follows bronchovascular bundles. Upper lobes of the lung tend to be more involved than the lower lobes. The granulomatous inflammation is often accompanied by nonspecific mononuclear cell infiltration; in severe disease, parenchymal involvement may progress to irreversible fibrosis and honeycombing. Cystic lesions may be complicated by colonization with *Aspergillus* and the development of intracavitary aspergillomas.

Granulomatous involvement of the airways (i.e., endobronchial sarcoidosis) is common and may lead to bronchostenosis (Fig. 91–1) in a small proportion of cases. The upper respiratory tract may be affected by sarcoidosis, with involvement taking the form of nasal mucosal, nasal bone, or laryngeal disease. Pleural disease is relatively infrequent, with effusions occurring in fewer than 5% of patients.

Dyspnea and cough, typically nonproductive, are the primary symptoms that accompany either pulmonary parenchymal or endobronchial sarcoidosis. Examination of the chest can reveal crackles resulting from parenchymal lung involvement, although the examination is often notable for the paucity or even absence of findings despite the extent of radiographic changes. Wheezing may be present in a small proportion of cases, resulting either from endobronchial involvement or airway distortion as a consequence of end-stage fibrotic disease.

Pulmonary function tests (Chapter 82) in the presence of parenchymal lung disease often demonstrate a pattern of restrictive disease, with a relatively symmetrical decrease in lung volumes, although they can remain normal despite parenchymal changes on chest radiograph. Obstructive changes may also be seen in some patients as a result of airway involvement. The diffusing capacity of the lung for carbon monoxide may be either normal or abnormal and does not necessarily follow the presence or absence of abnormal lung volumes.

SKIN DISEASE. Cutaneous manifestations of sarcoidosis resulting from granulomatous involvement of the skin affect 15 to 25% of patients. A variety of lesions can be seen, including papules, plaques, nodules, infiltration of old scars, and lupus pernio (Fig. 91–2). Old scars or tattoos often become infiltrated with granulomas, so that previously atrophic scars develop an appearance of keloid formation. *Lupus pernio* is a chronic, violaceous, often disfiguring lesion primarily affecting the nose, cheeks, and ears. It tends to affect women older than 40 years of age, especially African Americans and individuals from the West Indies.

Erythema nodosum commonly occurs in combination with bilateral hilar adenopathy as part of Löfgren's syndrome. These raised, red, tender, nodular lesions, generally but not exclusively on the anterior

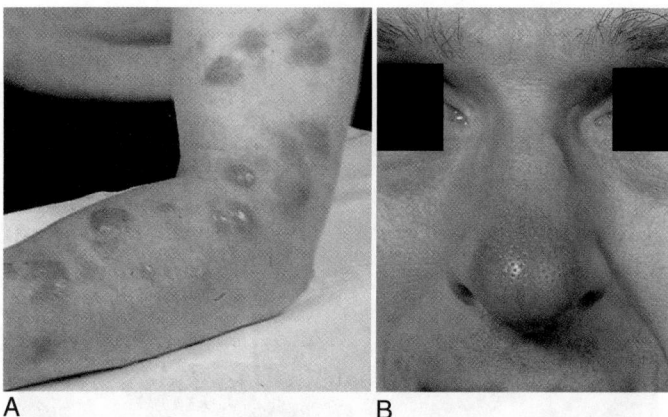

FIGURE 91–2 • Skin lesions of sarcoidosis. *A,* Sarcoid lesions may occur at any site, and they may take nodular, papular, or plaque forms. Biopsy is often necessary for diagnosis. *B,* Lupus pernio is the term used to describe a dusky-purple infiltration of the skin of the nose, cheeks, or ears in chronic sarcoidosis. (From Forbes CD, Jackson WF: Color Atlas and Text of Clinical Medicine, 3rd ed. London, Mosby, 2003, with permission.)

surface of the lower leg, do not represent granulomatous involvement of the skin. Rather, the histopathology is primarily that of a panniculitis, with cellular inflammation and edema of the deep dermis and subcutaneous tissue, especially involving connective tissue septa of adipose tissue.

EYE DISEASE. Ocular sarcoidosis can take a number of forms, including anterior or posterior uveitis, conjunctival involvement, and papilledema. Overall, 15 to 25% of patients have some form of ocular involvement. Anterior uveitis (Fig. 91–3), the most common form of ocular sarcoidosis, is often associated with the relatively acute onset of a red eye, photophobia, and ocular discomfort. *Heerfordt's syndrome,* or uveoparotid fever, is a form of sarcoidosis in which anterior uveitis is accompanied by parotid gland enlargement and often fever and facial palsy. Posterior uveitis, which may be obscured on examination by anterior chamber involvement, can present with vitreous infiltrates, choroidal nodules, periphlebitis, retinal hemorrhage, and papilledema. Conjunctival involvement can produce small, pale yellow nodules that demonstrate granulomatous inflammation on biopsy.

CARDIAC DISEASE. The frequency of cardiac sarcoidosis is difficult to ascertain, but 5 to 10% of patients have significant cardiac involvement (Chapter 73). Potential clinical consequences of such involvement include conduction defects (e.g., first-, second-, or third-degree heart block or a bundle branch block), ventricular or supraventricular arrhythmias, and heart failure.

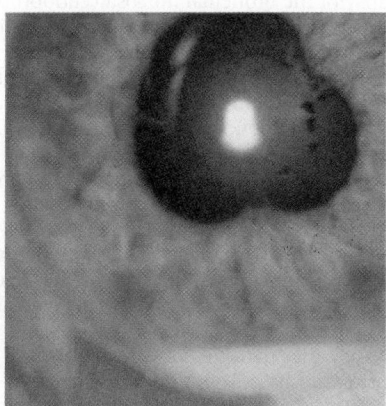

FIGURE 91–3 • Acute anterior uveitis occurs in up to 25% of patients with sarcoidosis. Note the fluid level of pus in the anterior chamber (hypopyon) and the distortion of the pupil caused by the development of posterior synechiae. Prompt treatment is necessary to prevent formation of a cataract. (From Forbes CD, Jackson WF: Color Atlas and Text of Clinical Medicine, 3rd edition. London, Mosby, 2003, with permission.)

NEUROLOGIC DISEASE. Five to 10% of patients with sarcoidosis develop neurologic complications of their disease. Although involvement of the base of the brain is particularly common, virtually any part of the nervous system can be involved, including cranial nerves, peripheral nerves, meninges, cerebrum, spinal cord, and the hypothalamic-pituitary axis. The most common form of clinically apparent neurologic involvement is unilateral facial nerve palsy, but other clinical consequences include seizures, meningitis, peripheral neuropathy, and psychiatric symptoms. Involvement of the hypothalamic-pituitary axis can cause hyperprolactinemia and diabetes insipidus.

OTHER EXTRATHORACIC DISEASE. Although granulomas are commonly found on histologic examination of the liver in patients with sarcoidosis, symptoms related to hepatic involvement are uncommon, and clinical evidence is usually limited to abnormalities in one or more hepatic enzymes. In addition to intrathoracic lymph node involvement, peripheral lymph nodes may be enlarged because of granulomatous infiltration, but they rarely produce important clinical consequences. Parotid gland enlargement, lacrimal gland infiltration, bone lesions, splenomegaly, and myopathy due to granulomas within muscle tissue may also be seen.

Biochemical Changes

Biochemical changes noted in many patients with sarcoidosis include alterations in calcium metabolism and elevations in the level of angiotensin-converting enzyme (ACE). Hypercalcemia, a potentially important complication of sarcoidosis, occurs in fewer than 10% of patients and is due to elevated levels of 1,25-dihydroxyvitamin D (calcitriol), produced by macrophages within the granulomas. As a result, calcium absorption from the intestine is increased, leading to hypercalciuria with or without hypercalcemia.

ACE, which catalyzes breakdown of the decapeptide angiotensin I to the octapeptide angiotensin II, is normally found in the lung. Elevated levels of ACE occur relatively frequently in sarcoidosis, with estimates varying widely but usually in the range of 40 to 90%. This elevation in ACE is believed to be due to production of the enzyme by epithelioid cells and macrophages within the granulomas. Although it was initially proposed that measurement of serum ACE might be a useful diagnostic and prognostic test in sarcoidosis, subsequent experience has shown its lack of diagnostic specificity and poor prognostic value in identifying patients with progressive disease.

Diagnosis

The initial consideration of sarcoidosis is usually based on the clinical and/or chest radiographic findings. When intrathoracic disease is the primary mode of presentation, the differential diagnosis generally depends on the radiographic presentation. Hilar and/or mediastinal adenopathy, either with or without associated parenchymal lung disease, can also be produced by lymphoma, mycobacterial or fungal infection, and selected pneumoconioses, such as berylliosis and silicosis. When interstitial lung disease is present in the absence of intrathoracic lymphadenopathy, a much broader differential diagnosis is raised, including idiopathic pulmonary fibrosis, pulmonary fibrosis associated with systemic rheumatic disease (e.g., scleroderma, rheumatoid arthritis, polymyositis), and disease due to a broad range of inorganic dusts (i.e., pneumoconiosis), organic antigens (i.e., hypersensitivity pneumonitis), and drugs (e.g., cancer chemotherapeutic agents).

The diagnosis of sarcoidosis is confirmed by the finding of well-formed noncaseating granulomas in one or more affected organ systems or tissues, with appropriate additional studies to exclude other causes of granulomas. Special stains and cultures must be performed for mycobacteria and fungi, and specimens should be examined under polarized light to identify foreign, potentially granulomagenic material. In patients with symmetrical bilateral hilar lymphadenopathy, either in association with erythema nodosum (Löfgren's syndrome) or in the absence of any symptoms, physical findings, or screening laboratory data that might indicate another cause, many clinicians believe that a clinical diagnosis of sarcoidosis can be made without needing histologic confirmation. Estimates of the likelihood of finding a diagnosis other than sarcoidosis in the patient with asymptomatic bilateral hilar lymphadenopathy suggest that the risk and cost of an invasive procedure outweigh its benefit.

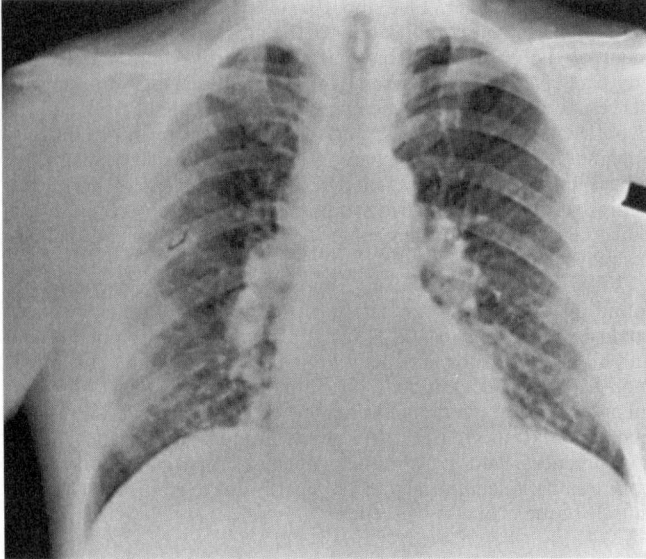

FIGURE 91–4 • Chest radiograph shows characteristic features of stage II sarcoidosis: bilateral hilar adenopathy and diffuse interstitial lung disease. In stage I sarcoidosis (not shown), patients have hilar adenopathy without interstitial lung disease, whereas in stage III sarcoidosis (not shown), patients have diffuse interstitial lung disease without hilar adenopathy. (From Weinberger SE: Principles of Pulmonary Medicine. Philadelphia, WB Saunders, 2003, p 164.)

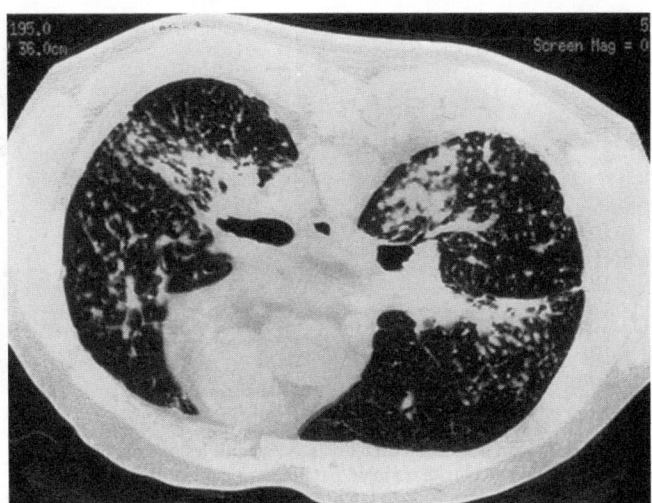

FIGURE 91–5 • High-resolution chest CT scan in a patient with pulmonary parenchymal involvement by sarcoidosis. There are numerous small nodules in a predominantly bronchovascular distribution. (Courtesy of Dr. David Levin.)

CHEST RADIOGRAPHY AND OTHER IMAGING PROCEDURES. The plain chest radiograph is an important component of the diagnostic evaluation of patients with sarcoidosis; the diagnosis is frequently suspected initially based on the radiographic abnormalities, either in the presence or absence of symptomatic disease. The major abnormalities seen on the chest radiograph include lymphadenopathy, usually involving both hila in a relatively symmetrical fashion as well as the right paratracheal region, and involvement of the pulmonary parenchyma (Fig. 91–4). Although the pattern of parenchymal involvement is typically described as interstitial, alveolar and nodular patterns may also be seen. A commonly used radiographic staging system considers the pattern of involvement seen on the chest radiograph (Table 91–1).

CT of the chest is not generally indicated in the evaluation of suspected sarcoidosis, especially when typical findings are seen on plain chest radiography. However, when the findings are atypical or if there is a need for better definition of mediastinal lymph node involvement, CT may be beneficial. In addition to bilateral hilar lymphadenopathy, the chest CT scan commonly shows much more mediastinal involvement than was suspected on the chest radiograph, especially involving right paratracheal, subcarinal, and aortopulmonary lymph nodes. High-resolution CT commonly demonstrates that pulmonary parenchymal involvement is localized around bronchovascular structures, producing an appearance resembling budding branches on a tree (Fig. 91–5).

Scanning with gallium citrate-67 may demonstrate uptake of this isotope in regions involved with granulomatous inflammation, probably reflecting a combination of increased capillary permeability as well as uptake of tracer by activated macrophages. However, because tracer uptake is nonspecific and because the correlation with other indices of disease activity or involvement is not particularly good, gallium scanning is not generally recommended as part of the routine evaluation of patients with suspected sarcoidosis.

TISSUE BIOPSY. Noncaseating granulomas found on biopsy of an affected organ or tissue are generally well formed, consisting of a localized collection of epithelioid histiocytes surrounded by a rim of variable numbers of lymphocytes. Multinucleated giant cells are typically present within the granulomas. Additional findings of a mononuclear cell alveolitis and variable amounts of fibrosis are diagnostically nonspecific. Although noncaseating granulomas may also be seen in hypersensitivity pneumonitis, the granulomas are generally less discrete and well formed than in sarcoidosis.

The pulmonary parenchyma, intrathoracic lymph nodes, and skin are the most common sites of diagnostic biopsy in sarcoidosis. Flexible bronchoscopy with transbronchial biopsy of the lung parenchyma is particularly useful, with a yield of 60 to 95%, depending on the radiographic stage of the disease and the number of biopsy specimens. Interestingly, even when pulmonary parenchymal involvement is not grossly visible on plain chest radiography (e.g., in radiographic stage I disease), transbronchial lung biopsy is positive in more than 60% of patients. Biopsy of the bronchial mucosa (endobronchial biopsy) may also demonstrate noncaseating granulomas, particularly when mucosal nodularity is seen upon visualization of the airways through the bronchoscope. Bronchoalveolar lavage, which samples the inflammatory cell population within the lung, characteristically shows an increased proportion of lymphocytes, with the ratio of CD4+ to CD8+ cells typically elevated to greater than 3.5:1.

Mediastinoscopy is sometimes performed in the presence of isolated mediastinal adenopathy without parenchymal lung disease, when another diagnosis such as lymphoma is being strongly considered. Thoracoscopic lung biopsy is sometimes used when a broader differential diagnosis of parenchymal lung disease has been raised, and more tissue is believed to be necessary than can be obtained by transbronchial lung biopsy.

Biopsy of tissue other than the lung or mediastinal lymph nodes is performed primarily based on clinical evidence of involvement. Skin biopsy, a relatively noninvasive procedure, is useful when findings suggestive of cutaneous sarcoidosis are present and when the overall clinical picture is compatible with sarcoidosis. Similarly, biopsy of peripheral lymph nodes, conjunctiva, parotid glands, skeletal muscle, and myocardium can be performed in selected cases. Liver biopsy is generally thought to be less useful because of the nonspecificity of granulomatous liver disease.

Table 91–1 • **RADIOGRAPHIC STAGING OF INTRATHORACIC SARCOIDOSIS**

STAGE	HILAR ADENOPATHY	PARENCHYMAL DISEASE	PERCENT AT ONSET	PERCENT WITH RESOLUTION
0	No	No	<10	NA
1	Yes	No	50	65 (<10% progress to parenchymal disease)
2	Yes	Yes	30	20–50
3 or 4	No	Yes (with fibrosis in stage 4)	10–15	<20

NA = not applicable.

Rx Treatment

Because sarcoidosis follows a variable natural history, with many patients experiencing spontaneous resolution, it is often difficult to decide whether and when to institute therapy. Consequently, serial evaluation of physical and physiologic findings is often useful before beginning treatment to characterize the course of the disease, provided that severe disease does not obligate immediate therapy. Whenever there is significant ocular, myocardial, or neurologic involvement, treatment is generally instituted promptly. For pulmonary disease, intrathoracic nodal involvement is not an indication for treatment, but parenchymal lung disease is a potential indication, depending on its effects on pulmonary function and symptoms, rather than on the severity of radiographic involvement alone. Presentation with Löfgren's syndrome does not warrant therapy, except as needed for symptoms (e.g., nonsteroidal anti-inflammatory drugs for associated joint symptoms).

Although corticosteroids acutely suppress the manifestations of the disease, it has never been clearly demonstrated that they alter its long-term natural history. Typically, prednisone is started at a dose of 0.5 mg/kg/day, although occasionally at up to 1.0 mg/kg/day, and continued at that dose for several weeks in an attempt to suppress the disease acutely. The dose can then be tapered, with the goal of using the lowest possible dose that keeps the disease under adequate control. Many clinicians taper to 10 to 30 mg every other day. Patients requiring systemic corticosteroid therapy for hypercalcemia can often be treated with relatively low doses of prednisone even initially, such as 10 to 20 mg/day.

The optimal overall duration of therapy is unknown and needs to be customized for each patient depending on the response to therapy and the effect of drug tapering. Treatment durations of 6 to 12 months are typical, and premature discontinuation of therapy may lead to recurrence of symptomatic and functional disease. Patients must be advised about and monitored for the myriad potential side effects observed with systemic corticosteroids (Chapter 31).

Alternative agents when systemic corticosteroids are ineffective or not tolerated include methotrexate, generally at a dose of 10 to 15 mg/week, or other immunosuppressive or cytotoxic agents, especially azathioprine. Although methotrexate has been used mostly as a corticosteroid-sparing agent, it can be used as the sole agent, particularly for musculoskeletal or cutaneous sarcoidosis. Hydroxychloroquine has been used for serious and disfiguring cutaneous sarcoidosis. Topical corticosteroid preparations are used for anterior uveitis, but refractory disease may require treatment with systemic corticosteroids. Clinical experience with cyclosporine has been disappointing. In patients with severe, end-stage pulmonary disease refractory to therapy, lung transplantation is an important option (Chapter 97), but the disease may recur in the allograft.

Natural History and Prognosis

The natural history of sarcoidosis is variable, ranging from spontaneous resolution to either smoldering or progressive disease. The prognosis is good for the majority of patients, with approximately two thirds of patients experiencing resolution of their disease, whereas 10 to 30% have chronic or progressive course. Resolution typically occurs within 2 years of disease onset, so that persistence of disease beyond that time often predicts a more chronic course.

Patients who present with Löfgren's syndrome tend to have a good prognosis characterized by spontaneous resolution of disease. The chest radiographic stage of disease is also a useful prognostic indicator, as patients with radiographic stage I disease are much more likely to experience spontaneous resolution than are patients in higher radiographic stages (see Table 91–1).

Assessment of functional involvement of an organ and its course over time provides the general framework for monitoring the natural history of disease. For pulmonary disease, monitoring includes symptoms, pulmonary function tests, and chest radiographs; conversely, gallium scanning, bronchoalveolar lavage (using lavage lymphocytosis as a marker of alveolitis), and measurement of serum ACE level are not recommended.

Progressive disease can lead to significant organ system involvement and to disability, particularly respiratory failure from severe interstitial lung disease. Fewer than 5% of patients die of sarcoidosis, with pulmonary, neurologic, and cardiac involvement being the major reasons for disease-related mortality.

Future Directions

Investigators continue their attempts to elucidate the underlying etiology of sarcoidosis, focusing on the identification of genetic factors that may predispose to the disease, as well as exogenous agents that may trigger the disease. A multicenter study has recruited more than 700 patients with a new diagnosis of sarcoidosis and an equal number of matched controls, with the intent of furthering knowledge about the etiology and the natural history of the disease. Other studies are focusing on identifying new agents, particularly drugs that antagonize the effect of TNF-α, that may alter the course of the disease.

SUGGESTED READINGS

American Thoracic Society: Statement on sarcoidosis. Am J Respir Crit Care Med 1999;160:736–755. *A comprehensive review of sarcoidosis, including recommendations regarding diagnosis and treatment, that represents a consensus statement of the American Thoracic Society, the European Respiratory Society, and the World Association of Sarcoidosis and Other Granulomatous Disorders.*

Baughman RP, Lower EE, du Bois RM: Sarcoidosis. Lancet 2003;361:1111–1118. *A practical review.*

Costabel U: Sarcoidosis: Clinical update. Eur Respir J 2001;(Suppl. 32):56S–68S. *A concise, excellent review of all aspects of sarcoidosis.*

Paramothayan S, Jones PW: Corticosteroid therapy in pulmonary sarcoidosis: A systematic review. JAMA 2002;287:1301–1307. *Usefulness and limitations of this common treatment for sarcoidosis.*

92 OVERVIEW OF PNEUMONIA

Andrew H. Limper

In excess of five million cases of infectious pneumonia are estimated to occur annually in the United States, resulting in more than one million hospitalizations. Pneumonia is the sixth leading cause of death and the most common lethal infectious disease. The mortality of community-acquired pneumonia ranges from less than 5% in mildly ill outpatients to somewhat greater than 12% overall in patients who are admitted to a hospital. Mortality is even greater in patients who have severe invasive disease, which often is associated bacteremia, and in elderly nursing home patients. Mortality from pneumonia can exceed 40% in patients who require management in the intensive care unit.

This chapter discusses the common clinical features, diagnosis, prevention, and initial management of infectious pneumonia. The term pneumonia itself, however, includes other causes of inflammation of the lower respiratory air spaces, particularly the alveoli, such as acute or chronic eosinophilic pneumonia, bronchiolitis obliterans with organizing pneumonia, and usual interstitial pneumonia, all of which are presented in more detail elsewhere (Chapter 88).

Mechanisms of Infection

The most common mechanism by which the lung is inoculated with pathogenic organisms is through microaspiration of oropharyngeal contents, a process that occurs in otherwise healthy individuals during sleep (Chapter 82). Colonization of the oral pharynx with pathogenic organisms, such as *Streptococcus pneumoniae* (Chapter 303), can thereby lead to delivery of sufficient quantities of organisms to infect the lung. In contrast, gross aspiration normally occurs only in individuals with an altered sensorium, depressed consciousness, abnormalities of protective cough or gag reflexes, or substantial gastroesophageal reflux. Gross aspiration, which also can deliver large numbers of anaerobic bacteria to the lower respiratory tract, is a major contributing factor to anaerobic lung infection and abscess formation (Chapter 93).

The second most frequent mechanism of lung infection is the inhalation of small, suspended aerosolized droplets, which range in size from 0.5 to 1 micron and which may contain microorganisms. In view of the limited number of organisms delivered in such a manner, only relatively aggressive pathogenic organisms such as *Mycobacterium tuberculosis* (Chapter 341), *Legionella pneumophila* (Chapter 307), *Yersinia pestis* (plague; Chapter 331), *Bacillus anthracis* (anthrax; Chapter 333), and some viral infections can be transmitted in this manner.

Less commonly, the lung may become infected as a consequence of a bloodstream infection. Blood-borne pneumonia is seen especially in staphylococcal sepsis (Chapter 311) or right-sided endocarditis (Chapter 310), which are more common in intravenous drug users (Chapter 30), and in gram-negative bacteremias, particularly in the immunocompromised host. The lung also may be rarely inoculated directly by penetrating chest trauma or by local spread from a nearby infected organ (paragonimiasis or amebic liver abscess; Chapters 403 and 399) or a contiguous soft tissue infection.

Fortunately, the lung is well equipped to defend against inoculation with most microbes. When large droplets of infected material reach the airways, they are removed by the mucociliary escalator, which sweeps entrapped contents up to the oropharynx, where they are swallowed or expectorated. Smaller particles, in the range of 0.5 to 2.0 microns, are deposited in the alveoli, where alveolar macrophages phagocytize and destroy most pathogens. These macrophages are further activated to release potent cytokines and chemokines, including tumor necrosis factor-α, interleukin-8, and leukotriene B_4, which help recruit neutrophils from the bloodstream into the alveolar spaces, where they participate in the uptake and degradation of microorganisms. For many microorganisms, such as *S. pneumoniae* (Chapter 303), clearance of infection is greatly facilitated by the development of specific immunoglobulin (Ig) G, which binds the surface of the organisms or its polysaccharide capsule. These specific antibodies, which act as immune opsonins, greatly augment the ability of neutrophils and macrophages to phagocytize and destroy the bacteria. In addition, pattern recognition receptors and other nonimmune opsonins, including surfactant proteins A and D, fibronectin, and vitronectin, also bind to specific epitopes on the surface of organisms that reach the lower respiratory tract and assist in their recognition and elimination. Only when organisms overwhelm or evade these multiple host defense systems does inoculation of the lung result in clinically significant pneumonia.

Clinical Manifestations

The possibility of pneumonia should be considered in any patient who has new respiratory symptoms including cough, sputum, or dyspnea, particularly when these symptoms are accompanied by fever or abnormalities on physical examination of the chest, such as rhonchi and rales. The initial presentation can be more subtle in patients who are elderly or have an altered immunologic status; in such patients, nonspecific symptoms, including loss of appetite, confusion, dehydration, worsening of symptoms or signs of other chronic illnesses, or failure to thrive may be the initial manifestation of pneumonia. Pneumonia also is increasingly prevalent in patients with specific comorbid diseases, including smoking, chronic obstructive pulmonary disease (COPD), diabetes mellitus, malignancy, heart failure, neurologic diseases, narcotic and alcohol use, and chronic liver disease.

The presenting symptoms and signs are often variable from patient to patient and cannot be reliably used to establish a specific (microbiologic) diagnosis. Classic physical findings of lobar pneumonia include evidence of consolidation with altered transmission of breath sounds, egophony, crackles, and changes in tactile fremitus. However, in many patients, the physical findings are more subtle and may be limited to scattered rhonchi. A thorough physical examination, posteroanterior and lateral chest radiographs, and blood leukocyte count with differential cell count should be performed when pneumonia is suspected. An assessment of gas exchange (oximetry or arterial blood gas determination) should be obtained for all patients who are admitted to the hospital. The clinician needs to be mindful of competing diagnoses that can mimic the presentation of pneumonia such as pulmonary embolism (Chapter 94), bronchogenic and bronchoalveolar carcinoma (Chapter 198), drug-induced lung diseases (Chapter 90), and idiopathic interstitial lung diseases (Chapter 88).

Diagnosis

MICROBIOLOGY OF PNEUMONIA. Even with intensive laboratory investigation, the specific microbiologic cause can be established with certainty only in approximately 50% of patients with pneumonia. The likely predominant organism varies based on the host's epidemiologic factors, the severity of illness, and which laboratory approach is used to establish the diagnosis. *S. pneumoniae* (Chapter 303) is the organism most frequently detected by culture of the sputum or blood. In contrast, *Mycoplasma pneumoniae* (Chapter 304) is frequently detected with serologic tests. Additional bacterial agents include *Haemophilus influenzae* (Chapter 314), *Staphylococcus aureus* (Chapter 311), enteric gram-negative bacilli (Chapter 305), and *L. pneumophila* (Chapter 307). Chlamydia and respiratory viruses have also been implicated in up to 10% of cases (Chapters 354 and 360). The so-called atypical pathogens, including *M. pneumoniae*, *Chlamydia pneumoniae*, and *Legionella* species, are being increasingly recognized as important and prevalent causes of pneumonia. In addition, mixed infections particularly related to co-infection with these "atypical" pathogens, have been reported in up to one third of patients with lower respiratory tract infection. Specific host factors also influence the relative risk for infection with specific microorganisms (Table 92–1). For instance, smokers and those with COPD are at increased risk for invasive *S. pneumoniae*, as well as *H. influenzae*, *M. catarrhalis*,

Table 92–1 • HOST FACTORS ASSOCIATED WITH SPECIFIC PATHOGENIC CAUSES OF PNEUMONIA

UNDERLYING CONDITION	ASSOCIATED MICROORGANISM
Active smoking/chronic obstructive lung disease	*Streptococcus pneumoniae, Haemophilus influenzae, Legionella pneumophila*
Nursing home residents	*S. pneumoniae*, gram-negative bacilli, *H. influenzae, Staphylococcus aureus, Chlamydia pneumoniae*, anaerobes, tuberculosis
Alcoholism	*S. pneumoniae* (including drug-resistant strains), gram-negative bacilli, anaerobes, and tuberculosis
Gross aspiration/poor dentition	Anaerobes
Travel to southwestern United States	*Coccidioides immitis*
Exposure to bats	*Histoplasma capsulatum*
Exposure to birds	*Cryptococcus neoformans, Chlamydia psittaci, H. capsulatum*
Exposure to rabbits	*Francisella tularensis*
Exposure to farm animals	*Coxiella burnetii* (Q fever)
Viral influenza	Influenza, *S. aureus, S. pneumoniae, H. influenzae*
Bronchiectasis, cystic fibrosis	*Pseudomonas aeruginosa, P. cepacia, S. aureus, Aspergillus* species, *Mycobacterium avium complex*
Intravenous drug use	*S. aureus*, anaerobes, tuberculosis, *Pneumocystis carinii*
Endobronchial obstruction	Anaerobes
Recent antibiotic therapy	Drug-resistant *S. pneumoniae, P. aeruginosa*

Adapted from American Thoracic Society: Guidelines for management of adults with community-acquired pneumonia: Diagnosis, assessment of severity, initial antimicrobial therapy, and prevention. Am J Respir Crit Care Med 2001:163:1730–1754.

and *Legionella*. Alcoholism is associated with increased risk for drug-resistant *S. pneumoniae*, anaerobic lung infection, and tuberculosis. The clinician also should solicit information about household and workplace exposures, such as to other ill persons, as well as travel to specific geographic regions, such as the central United States, where histoplasmosis is common, or the Southwest, where coccidioidomycosis is found, or environmental exposures such as to birds (psittacosis), bats (histoplasmosis), rabbits (tularemia), and farm animals (Q fever).

Although most attention focuses on bacterial causes of severe community-acquired pneumonia, viruses can also cause serious lower respiratory tract infections. Recently, *severe acute respiratory syndrome* (SARS), which is caused by the SARS-associated coronavirus (SARS-CoV), has been identified as the cause of rapidly progressive respiratory insufficiency with a case fatality rate of 4 to 15%, depending on the age and geographic location of the patient. SARS should be considered in any patient who, within the past ten days, has traveled (including transit in an airport) to an area with documented or suspected SARS or had close contact with a person known or suspected to have SARS. Signs and symptoms of SARS include: temperature >100.4° F (>38° C) and one or more clinical findings of respiratory illness (e.g., cough, shortness of breath, difficulty breathing, or hypoxia), particularly if there is radiographic evidence of pneumonia or clinical evidence of the respiratory distress syndrome without another identifiable cause. The Centers for Disease Control and Prevention (CDC) maintains updated lists of regions with community transmission of SARS and management of SARS through their website (www.cdc.gov).

SARS is highly contagious, and lethal transmission to health care workers has been documented. Isolation procedures and equipment appropriate for SARS include standard, contact, and airborne isolation precautions such as scrupulous hand hygiene, gowning, disposable gloves, the use of N95 respirators, and eye protection to prevent transmission in health care settings. Suspected cases of SARS require notification of local public health departments and the CDC. The CDC has access to appropriate testing for case confirmation, including detection of antibody to SARS-CoV, detection of SARS-CoV RNA by RT-PCR, and the ability to isolate SARS-CoV from specimens.

In addition to SARS, other respiratory viruses that can cause severe pneumonia include influenza and respiratory syncytial virus (RSV). Both influenza virus and RSV can be detected in respiratory secretions, which should be obtained in suspected cases. It is estimated that influenza infections are responsible for between 25,000 to 50,000 deaths annually in the United States, predominantly in elderly patients and in patients with underlying cardiopulmonary or metabolic diseases. Influenza-associated pneumonia should be considered in the differential diagnosis of respiratory infections in high-risk patients with underlying disease and in residents of nursing homes or other chronic care facilities during the season of October through May, especially in patients who have not received appropriate vaccination. It is also being increasingly appreciated that RSV, though formerly considered mainly an infection in pediatric populations, can lead to serious lower respiratory tract infections in adults during the winter season. Host immunity to RSV infection in childhood is incomplete, and recurrent infections can occur in both immune-competent and immune-impaired adults, particularly in the elderly. An effective vaccine for RSV is not currently available.

RADIOGRAPHIC AND LABORATORY INVESTIGATION. Clinical suspicion of pneumonia should prompt standard posteroanterior and lateral chest radiography. Although the pattern of infiltration can rarely establish a specific microbiologic etiology, the chest films are most useful for providing essential information on the distribution and extent of involvement, as well as potential pneumonic complications. Many bacterial pneumonias result in localized alveolar infiltrates and consolidation. Even though pneumococcal pneumonia is classically described as having a lobar distribution, the pattern can be multilobar (Fig. 92–1) or bilateral. The "bulging" fissure sign, which represents lobar filling and consolidation, has traditionally been attributed to *Klebsiella pneumoniae*, but this finding is not specific and can be observed with *S. pneumoniae* and other bacteria, and even with bronchoalveolar carcinoma. Diffuse interstitial and alveolar infiltrates should suggest viral infections (cytomegalovirus, influenza, or respiratory syncytial virus), *L. pneumophila*, or enteric gram-negative pneumonia, particularly in neutropenic patients. These diffuse

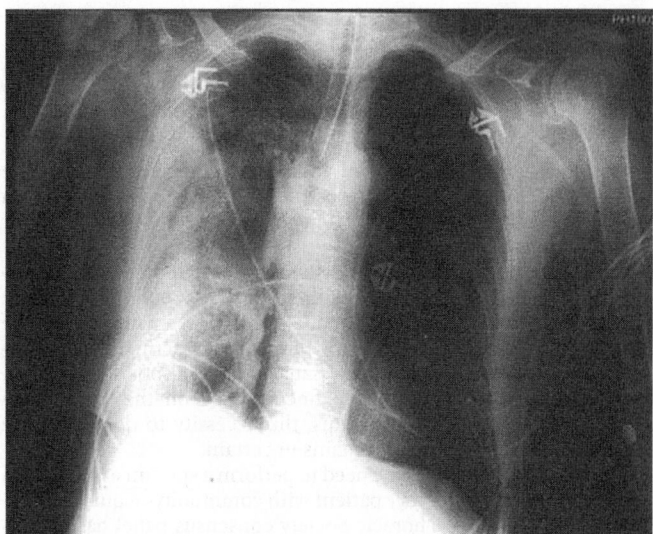

FIGURE 92–1 • Standard posteroanterior radiograph of a 70-year-old woman with chronic obstructive pulmonary disease complicated by right multilobar *Streptococcus pneumoniae* pneumonia and empyema.

pulmonary infiltrations can be indistinguishable from other causes of the adult respiratory distress syndrome. Diffuse alveolar and interstitial infiltration can also be observed in patients with *Pneumocystis carinii* pneumonia (Chapter 387) related to immune suppression, such as in AIDS. Cavitary lesions often indicate a necrotizing infection related to *S. aureus, M. tuberculosis* (Fig. 92–2), and certain endemic fungi, such as *Coccidioides immitis, Aspergillus* infection in the immunocompromised patient, or anaerobic lung infection with abscess formation.

The chest radiograph provides further important information about potential infectious complications of pneumonia. Pleural effusions, which occur in a variety of respiratory infections, are best documented with lateral decubitus views. The discovery of any pleural effusion of

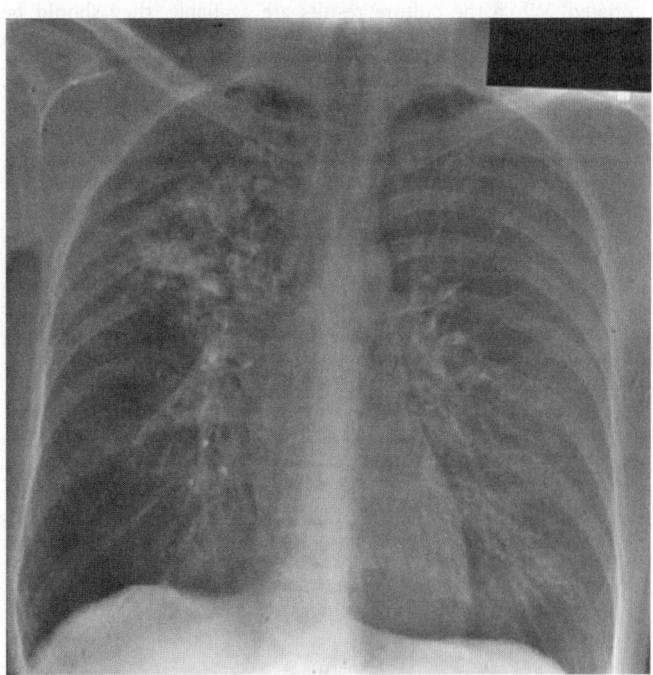

FIGURE 92–2 • Posteroanterior radiograph of a 54-year-old man with cough, fever, and a right upper lobe cavitary process due to *Mycobacterium tuberculosis* infection.

greater than 10-mm thickness on a lateral decubitus film or of any loculated effusion should prompt thoracentesis to aid in the identification of a complicated parapneumonic effusion or empyema, which may require definitive drainage (Chapter 95). Enlargement of mediastinal and hilar lymph nodes, which is rare in acute bacterial infection, suggests fungal or mycobacterial infection, or an underlying lung cancer. Loss of volume of a lung segment or lobe should raise suspicion of postobstructive pneumonia distal to an endobronchial lesion caused by a neoplasm, occult foreign body, or broncholithiasis.

Considerable controversy exists over the appropriate microbiologic evaluation of patients with suspected pneumonia. Despite intensive microbiologic evaluation, a specific organism may not be discovered in half of patients with pneumonia. Furthermore, the majority of patients with pneumonia satisfactorily respond to simple, relatively nontoxic antibiotic regimens based on the most likely organisms causing infection. Thus, the necessity to document the precise cause of the process remains uncertain.

Debate continues over the need to perform a sputum examination with Gram staining in every patient with community-acquired pneumonia. An American Thoracic Society consensus panel has recommended that a sputum Gram stain and culture be obtained primarily if an organism that is resistant to the usual empirical treatment regimens is suspected. To be useful, sputum should contain fewer than 10 squamous cells and more than 25 leukocytes per low-power field; a well-performed Gram stain may reveal a single, predominant organism such as encapsulated gram-positive cocci (pneumococci) or small pleomorphic gram-negative coccobacilli (*Haemophilus*). However, current data have not clearly correlated Gram stain findings with the results of cultures of alveolar materials in large numbers of patients with community-acquired pneumonia. Nevertheless, sputum examination can strongly support the diagnosis of certain specific infections, including *M. tuberculosis* (acid-fast stain), endemic fungi (KOH preparations), *P. carinii* (methenamine silver or fluorescent antibody stain), or *Legionella* species (direct fluorescent antibody staining). In most cases of community-acquired pneumonia, the general intent of sputum Gram stain examination, if it is performed, should be to detect additional or unusual pathogens, and hence to expand rather than to narrow the initial antibiotic therapy. All too often, an adequate sputum specimen cannot be obtained, and the Gram stain interpretation may be equivocal. Therefore, an initial therapeutic plan must be formulated based on the most likely pathogens responsible for the pneumonia.

If unusual or drug-resistant pathogens are suspected, sputum specimens should be sent for culture before antibiotic therapy is initiated. When the culture results are available, they should be compared with the predominant organisms observed on the Gram stain. Unfortunately, the sensitivity and specificity of sputum culture are not optimal, each being roughly 50%. Antibiotic susceptibility information on an isolated pathogenic organism can, however, be useful both for epidemiologic surveillance and for management of patients who do not respond to initial empirical therapy. Cultures of normally sterile body fluids such as blood, pleural fluid, or occasionally cerebrospinal fluid (CSF) are highly specific when positive. Approximately one fourth of patients with bacterial pneumonia have demonstrable bacteremia. Blood cultures should be obtained before antibiotic administration in patients with serious illness due to pneumonia, and diagnostic thoracentesis should be performed if an effusion is large enough to be aspirated safely. CSF examination is usually reserved for patients with additional signs and symptoms of meningeal irritation (Chapter 312) or abnormalities on the neurologic examination.

Invasive sampling of respiratory secretions is usually not necessary in patients with community-acquired pneumonia. Flexible fiberoptic bronchoscopy with a protected catheter brush and bronchoalveolar lavage sampling has largely supplanted transtracheal and transthoracic needle aspiration. Bronchoscopy is indicated in selected clinical situations in which a delay in accurate diagnosis may have serious consequences, such as in immunocompromised hosts or patients whose conditions have worsened despite initial antimicrobial therapy. Other indications for bronchoscopy in the setting of apparent community-acquired pneumonia include either lung abscess detected on the chest radiograph (Chapter 93) or evidence of volume loss and distal consolidation suggesting an endobronchial obstruction.

Immunologic techniques, such as immunofluorescence, enzyme-linked immunosorbent assay, antigen detection, polymerase chain reaction, and DNA hybridization, may be considered when specific organisms are strongly suspected on clinical grounds, but these tests are not routinely indicated in most cases of community-acquired pneumonia. For example, *Legionella* urinary antigen screening and acute and convalescent serologies may be helpful when *L. pneumophila* pneumonia is suspected (Chapter 307). Furthermore, the judicious use of fungal serologies can detect endemic mycoses, particularly histoplasmosis and coccidioidomycosis (Chapters 379 and 380). Bronchoscopy with lavage for immunostaining may, in selected circumstances, provide enhanced sensitivity, such as in the diagnosis of *P. carinii* pneumonia (Chapter 387).

Prevention of Pneumonia

In light of the significant morbidity and potential mortality of pneumonia, appropriate measures should be instituted to reduce the possibility of lung infection. Important but often neglected interventions include smoking cessation (Chapter 14) and avoidance of illicit drugs (Chapter 30) or excess alcohol (Chapter 17), which may impair consciousness. Optimizing the patient's nutritional status is also important, in that markedly underweight or obese patients are at increased risk. Finally, the appropriate and consistent use of vaccines can strongly reduce the risk of pneumonia in appropriate patient populations (Chapter 16). The current pneumococcal vaccine contains 23 purified capsular polysaccharides from the serotypes of *S. pneumoniae* that are responsible for more than 85% of invasive pneumococcal infections. Overall, this vaccine is approximately 50 to 80% effective in preventing death from invasive infection. Accordingly, current recommendations are that it should be administered to all patients older than 65 years of age and to patients younger than age 65 who have chronic pulmonary diseases, heart disease, diabetes mellitus, alcoholism, chronic liver disease, cerebrospinal fluid leaks, or asplenia, and to patients who live in certain settings, including Alaskan natives, high-risk native American populations, and patients in long-term care facilities. Current pneumococcal vaccines have little toxicity, limited mainly to local site irritation. Individuals generally receive one dose of vaccine, but a single revaccination should be considered 5 years later in those who received their vaccination before age 65 years or who are at increased risk for severe pneumonia.

Vaccination should also be considered for viral influenza (Chapter 16). Although usually manifest as an upper respiratory tract infection, influenza can itself cause pneumonia in both immune competent and immunosuppressed individuals. More commonly, influenza may precipitate a subsequent bacterial infection, often due to *S. aureus*. Influenza vaccines are developed annually against the current influenza strains, so annual revaccination is necessary (Chapter 16). Influenza vaccines are estimated to be roughly 80% effective in preventing mortality related to influenza. The vaccine should be considered in all patients older than age 65 years, residents of nursing homes and chronic care facilities, persons with chronic pulmonary, cardiac, or other chronic diseases requiring ongoing medical care, and pregnant women in the second or third trimester during influenza season. Contraindications to influenza vaccine include allergy to raw eggs or thimerosal. Side effects are generally self-limited and include injection site soreness, myalgias, mild fever, and malaise. The vaccine does not contain live virus and therefore cannot cause influenza. The vaccine should be administered in the fall of the year, but it can also be administered during local epidemics.

Table 92–2 • COMMON MICROBIOLOGIC ETIOLOGIES OF COMMUNITY-ACQUIRED PNEUMONIA IN APPROXIMATE ORDER OF FREQUENCY

OUTPATIENTS	HOSPITALIZED PATIENTS	SEVERE PNEUMONIA/ICU
Streptococcus pneumoniae	*S. pneumoniae*	*S. pneumoniae*
Mycoplasma pneumoniae	*H. influenzae*	*Legionella* spp
Chlamydia pneumoniae	*M. pneumoniae*	*H. influenzae*
Haemophilus influenzae	*C. pneumoniae*	*M. pneumoniae*
Respiratory viruses	Mixed infections	Enteric gram-negative organisms
Miscellaneous, including	Enteric gram-negative organisms	*Pseudomonas aeruginosa*
Legionella spp and endemic	Aspiration (anaerobes)	*Mycoplasma pneumoniae*
fungi	Respiratory viruses	Respiratory viruses
	Legionella spp	Miscellaneous, including
	Miscellaneous, including	*C. pneumoniae, M. tuberculosis*
	M. tuberculosis, P. carinii,	and endemic fungi
	and endemic fungi	

Adapted from American Thoracic Society: Guidelines for management of adults with community-acquired pneumonia: Diagnosis, assessment of severity, initial antimicrobial therapy, and prevention. Am J Respir Crit Care Med 2001;163:1730–1754.

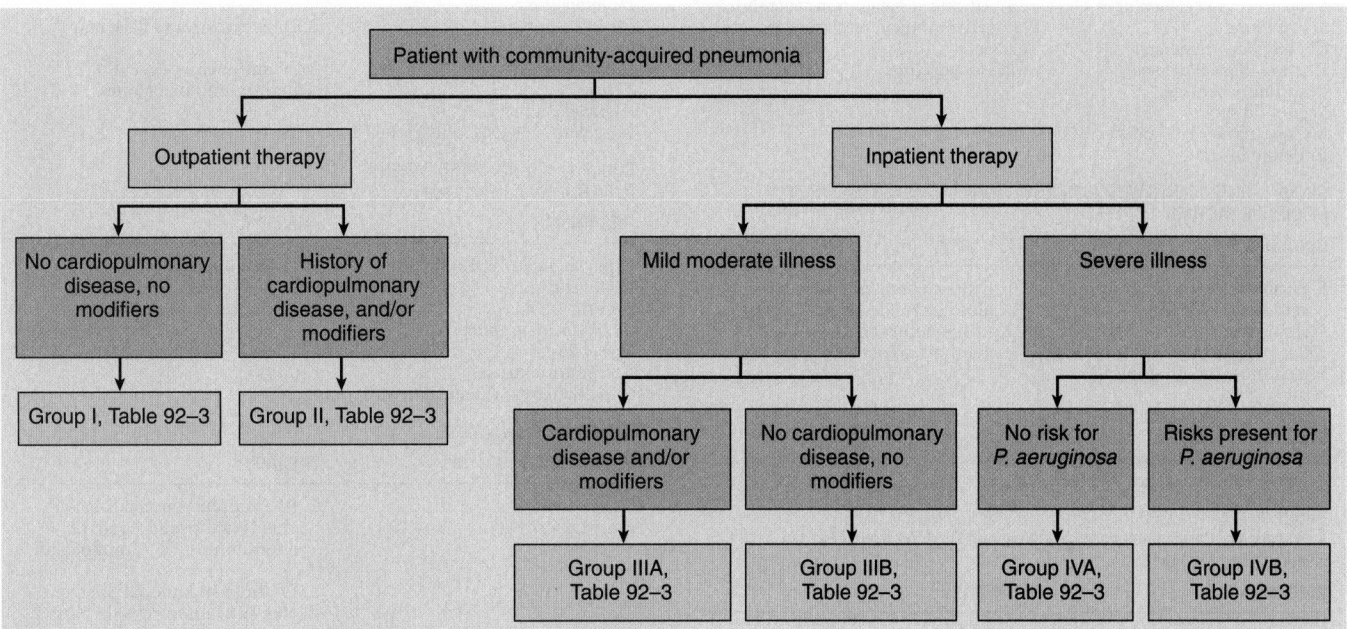

FIGURE 92–3 • Initial empirical therapy for community-acquired pneumonia based on severity of illness, underlying cardiopulmonary disease and location of treatment, as recommended in the American Thoracic Society: Guidelines for management of adults with community-acquired pneumonia: Diagnosis, assessment of severity, and antimicrobial therapy and prevention. Am J Respir Crit Care Med 2001;163:1730–1754.

Rx Treatment

INITIAL EMPIRICAL THERAPY. Because the microbiologic etiology of community-acquired pneumonia is determined in only approximately 50% of cases and because this diagnosis may take a day or two, the clinician must institute appropriate empirical therapy based on the most likely agents contributing to the lung infection (Table 92–2). When possible, empirical therapy should be initiated within 8 hours of diagnosis, an interval that appears to reduce the 30-day mortality. Empirical antimicrobial therapy is based on the severity of illness (inpatient or outpatient settings) and should broadly cover the most likely organisms (Fig. 92–3). Therapy can be narrowed later based on any relevant culture information.

Effective guidelines for initial empirical therapy of community-acquired pneumonia target the most common pathogens and lead to better clinical outcomes compared with therapies not based on such guidelines (Table 92–3). The most common bacterial pathogens are *S. pneumoniae* and *H. influenzae*; however, the so-called atypical pathogens, including *M. pneumoniae, C. pneumoniae,* and

Legionella species, can be the primary or co-infecting agents in up to 40% of community-acquired pneumonia and must be covered in empirical antibiotic regimens.

Under current guidelines, patients are stratified with respect to where treatment is initiated (outpatient, inpatient, or intensive care unit [ICU] setting), the presence of underlying cardiopulmonary disease, and other modifying factors, such as whether the patient is likely to be infected with drug-resistant *S. pneumoniae*, gram-negative enteric bacilli, or *P. aeruginosa*. In general, outpatients who are mildly ill and without underlying cardiopulmonary disease or other modifying factors are usually infected with *S. pneumoniae, M. pneumoniae, C. pneumoniae, H. influenzae,* respiratory viruses, or *Legionella* species. These uncomplicated outpatient cases can be managed with an advanced generation macrolide, such as azithromycin or clarithromycin, which are better tolerated and have better coverage of *Haemophilus* than does erythromycin. **2** Alternatively, doxycycline can be used in patients who are intolerant of macrolides, although this is less optimal because increasing

Continued on page 557.

Table 92–3 • EMPIRICAL TREATMENT GUIDELINES FOR COMMUNITY-ACQUIRED PNEUMONIA

GROUP I: OUTPATIENTS WITHOUT CARDIOPULMONARY DISEASE OR MODIFYING FACTORS

ORGANISMS	THERAPY
Streptococcus pneumoniae *Mycoplasma* *Chlamydia pneumoniae* *Haemophilus influenzae* Respiratory viruses *Legionella* spp *Mycobacterium tuberculosis* (MTb) Endemic fungi	1. Advanced generation macrolide: (azithromycin or clarithromycin) or 2. Doxycycline

GROUP II: OUTPATIENTS WITH CARDIOPULMONARY DISEASE OR OTHER MODIFYING FACTORS

ORGANISMS	THERAPY
S. pneumoniae (consider drug resistance—DRSP) *Mycoplasma* *Chlamydia* Mixed infection (± atypical) *H. influenzae* Gram-negative organisms Respiratory viruses Miscellaneous (*Moraxella, Legionella* spp, aspiration, anaerobes, MTb, fungi)	1. Oral or parenteral β-lactam plus macrolide or doxycycline or 2. Antipneumococcal fluoroquinolone

GROUP III: HOSPITALIZED INPATIENTS NOT REQUIRING ICU CARE
A. Presence of Cardiopulmonary Disease and/or Other Modifying Factors (Including Nursing Home)

ORGANISMS	THERAPY
S. pneumoniae (including DRSP) *H. influenzae* *Mycoplasma* *Chlamydia* Mixed infection Enteric gram-negative organisms Aspiration (anaerobes) Viruses *Legionella* spp Miscellaneous (Mtb, fungi, PCP)	1. IV β-lactam plus a macrolide or doxycycline or 2. IV antipneumococcal fluoroquinolone alone

B. No Cardiopulmonary Disease and/or Modifying Factors

ORGANISMS	THERAPY
S. pneumoniae *Haemophilus* *Mycoplasma* *Chlamydia* Mixed infection Viruses *Legionella* spp Miscellaneous (Mtb, fungi, PCP)	1. IV azithromycin alone or 2. Doxycycline and β-lactam or 3. IV antipneumococcal fluoroquinolone alone

GROUP IV: ICU-ADMITTED PATIENTS
A. No Risk for *P. aeruginosa*

ORGANISMS	THERAPY
S. pneumoniae (±DRSP) *Legionella* spp Enteric GNRs *Staphylococcus aureus* *Mycoplasma* Respiratory viruses Miscellaneous (*Chlamydia*, Mtb, fungi, PCP)	IV β-lactam plus a. IV macrolide or b. IV fluoroquinolone

B. Risks for *P. aeruginosa*

ORGANISMS	THERAPY
Same as above *P. aeruginosa*	1. IV antipseudomonal β-lactam plus IV antipseudomonal fluoroquinolone (ciprofloxacin) or 2. IV antipseudomonal β-lactam plus IV aminoglycoside plus a. IV macrolide or b. IV fluoroquinolone

Adapted from American Thoracic Society: Guidelines for management of adults with community-acquired pneumonia: Diagnosis, assessment of severity, initial antimicrobial therapy, and prevention. Am J Respir Crit Care Med 2001;163:1730–1754.

DRSP = drug-resistant *Streptococcus pneumoniae*; GNR = gram-negative rod; ICU = intensive care unit; Mtb = myobacteria tuberculosis; PCP = *Pneumocystis carinii* pneumonia.

levels of tetracycline resistance are being observed in *S. pneumoniae* isolates. Patients who also have underlying cardiopulmonary illnesses or modifying factors are more likely to be infected with drug-resistant *S. pneumoniae* or *M. catarrhalis*; such patients should be managed initially not only with a macrolide or doxycycline but also either with an extended spectrum oral β-lactam (such as cefpodoxime, cefuroxime, high-dose amoxicillin, amoxicillin-clavulanate) or with parenteral ceftriaxone followed by oral cefpodoxime. Alternatively, single agent treatment can be instituted with an antipneumococcal fluoroquinolone, such as levofloxacin, gatifloxacin, or ciprofloxacin.

The decision to admit a patient to the hospital must be made on clinical grounds. Patients can be effectively and safely managed as outpatients if they are mildly ill, are younger than age 50 years, and do not have coexisting cardiopulmonary disease, malignancy, immune compromise, or renal, liver, or other significant systemic diseases.[2] Features such as a respiratory rate greater than 30 breaths/minute, a diastolic blood pressure less than 60 mm Hg, evidence of poor perfusion or end-organ dysfunction (e.g., confusion or an elevated blood urea nitrogen or creatinine level), multilobar disease on the chest radiograph, or hypoxemia predict a more severe course and generally require inpatient management. Inpatients who do not require intensive care but who have underlying cardiopulmonary disease or are elderly are at risk for infection with enteric gram-negative bacteria. Such patients should be managed initially with intravenous β-lactams (i.e., cefotaxime, ceftriaxone, ampicillin/sulbactam) plus either an intravenous macrolide or doxycycline to cover atypical organisms.[3] Alternatively, an intravenous antipneumococcal fluoroquinolone may be used alone.[4] Patients who require hospitalization but not intensive care may be treated initially with intravenous azithromycin alone or may be started on doxycycline plus a β-lactam if they cannot tolerate macrolides. Alternatively, such patients can again be managed empirically with intravenous antipneumococcal fluoroquinolone monotherapy.

Patients who have respiratory insufficiency, septicemia, or significant multiorgan dysfunction require management in an ICU and evaluation to exclude infection with *P. aeruginosa*. High-risk patients include those with structural lung disease (particularly bronchiectasis), greater than 10 mg/day of previous corticosteroid therapy, neutropenia, malnutrition, or prior broad-spectrum antibiotics for more than 7 days in the last month. ICU patients who are not considered at risk for *P. aeruginosa* infection can be treated initially with an intravenous β-lactam (such as cefotaxime or ceftriaxone) combined with either an intravenous macrolide (azithromycin) or an intravenous fluoroquinolone.

Fluoroquinolone monotherapy is not considered appropriate in the setting of severe community-acquired pneumonia. In the ICU patient population considered to be at risk for *P. aeruginosa* infection, combination antipseudomonal therapy should be used, including intravenous antipseudomonal β-lactams (e.g., cefepime, imipenem, meropenem, piperacillin/tazobactam) plus an intravenous antipseudomonal fluoroquinolone (e.g., ciprofloxacin). Alternatively, an intravenous antipseudomonal β-lactam can be administered along with an aminoglycoside plus either an intravenous macrolide (azithromycin) or an intravenous nonpseudomonal fluoroquinolone.

Treatment for SARS is largely supportive, with oxygen and ventilator therapy as necessary. Specific antiviral therapies for SARS have not yet been well studied, although aerosolized ribavirin has been used empirically.

RESPONSE TO THERAPY AND FURTHER STUDIES. Most patients respond to empirical antibiotic regimens over the first 3 days of therapy. In general, it is not advisable to alter the antibiotic program in the first 72 hours, unless the patient is deteriorating or culture results indicate alternative therapy. Patients initially begun on parenteral therapy may be changed to an oral regimen when they are afebrile (temperature less than 100° F on two occasions 8 hours apart) and demonstrate improvement in cough, dyspnea, and leukocytosis. For the minority of patients who do not respond to initial empirical coverage, an aggressive search should be undertaken to detect unusual pathogens, alternative diagnoses, such as pulmonary embolism, or complications of pneumonia, such as a complicated pleural effusion, empyema, or lung abscess. Additional diagnostic testing may include computed tomography (CT) of the chest, sampling of pleural fluid, and/or bronchoscopy with collection of respiratory secretions, brushings, and bronchoalveolar lavage for microbiologic analysis. Even when the patient appears to respond to the initial antibiotic regimen, the chest radiograph signs resolve more slowly (over 6 to 8 weeks) than other clinical signs and symptoms. The physician must document that abnormalities on the chest radiograph have resolved completely or, in some cases, led to the formation of a fibrotic scar. Usual practice includes obtaining repeat radiography 6 to 8 weeks after completion of the antibiotic regimen. Persistence of abnormalities on the chest radiograph or the development of recurrent pneumonia in a similar distribution should prompt a careful search for an underlying endobronchial obstruction such as an occult neoplasm, foreign body, bronchostenosis, or broncholithiasis. Follow-up CT scanning is usually the prelude to formal pulmonary consultation for consideration of bronchoscopy and other further diagnostic tests.

1. Bridges CB, Fukuda K, Uyeki TM, et al: Centers for Disease Control and Prevention, Advisory Committee on Immunization Practices. Prevention and control of influenza. Recommendations of the Advisory Committee on Immunization Practices (ACIP). MMWR 2002;51(RR-3):1–31.
2. Atlas SJ, Benzer TI, Borowsky LH, et al: Safely increasing the proportion of patients with community-acquired pneumonia treated as outpatients: An interventional trial. Arch Intern Med 1998;158:1350–1356.
3. Vergis EN, Indorf A, File TM Jr, et al: Azithromycin vs. cefuroxime plus erythromycin for empirical treatment of community-acquired pneumonia in hospitalized patients: A prospective, randomized, multicenter trial. Arch Intern Med 2000;160:1294–1300.
4. Marrie TJ, Lau CY, Wheeler SL, et al: A controlled trial of a critical pathway for treatment of community-acquired pneumonia. CAPITAL Study Investigators. Community-Acquired Pneumonia Intervention Trial Assessing Levofloxacin. JAMA 2000;283:749–755.

SUGGESTED READINGS

American Thoracic Society: Guidelines for the management of adults with community-acquired pneumonia: Diagnosis, assessment of severity, and antimicrobial therapy and prevention. Am J Respir Crit Care Med 2001;163:1730–1754. *A comprehensive guide to diagnosis and initial therapy of patients with community-acquired pneumonia based on treatment setting, underlying diseases, and modifying factors, including risk for resistant organisms.*

Bartlett JG, Dowell SF, Mandell LA, et al: Practice guidelines for the management of community-acquired pneumonia in adults. Clin Infect Dis 2001;31:347–382. *A comprehensive clinical review on relevant organisms causing community-acquired pneumonia.*

Centers for Disease Control and Prevention: Severe acute respiratory syndrome (SARS). http://www.cdc.gov/ncidod/sars/ *A regularly updated source of information about this newly recognized syndrome.*

Halm EA, Teirstein AS: Management of community-acquired pneumonia. N Engl J Med 2002;347:2039–2045. *A brief practical review.*

Holmes KV: SARS-associated coronavirus. N Engl J Med 2003;348:1948–1951. *Overview of the causative virus.*

Whitney CG, Farley MM, Hadler J, et al: Increasing prevalence of multidrug-resistant *Streptococcus pneumoniae* in the United States. N Engl J Med 2000;343:1917–1924. *Documentation of this emerging problem, with an emphasis on the role for vaccination.*

93 LUNG ABSCESS

Sydney M. Finegold

Definition

Lung abscess is a cavity containing pus and necrotic debris. Although mycobacterial, fungal, and parasitic infections can cause cavitary lesions, the term *lung abscess* is usually reserved for other bacterial infections and is distinguished from empyema (Chapter 95), which is a collection of pus within the pleural space rather than the lung parenchyma. Many different microorganisms may produce lung abscess, and a number of conditions may simulate it radiographically (Table 93–1). Lung abscess formation usually reflects infection with an unusual microbial burden (e.g., acute aspiration), an especially virulent organism (e.g., *Staphylococcus aureus*), and/or a failure in microbial clearance mechanisms (e.g., bronchial obstruction).

Epidemiology

Most lung abscesses involve the indigenous flora of the oropharynx. Abscesses involving *S. aureus* or gram-negative bacilli are most often nosocomial (Chapter 299). *Nocardia* and *Rhodococcus* are found almost exclusively in immunocompromised hosts (Chapter 298). Septic pulmonary emboli are usually due to *S. aureus*, primarily in intravenous drug abusers with tricuspid valve endocarditis (Chapter 310). Lung abscesses due to infection with *Paragonimus westermani* and melioidosis are usually acquired in the Far East or Indonesia.

Table 93–1 • ORGANISMS AND CONDITIONS WITH THE RADIOGRAPHIC APPEARANCE OF LUNG ABSCESS

INFECTIOUS
Bacterial Aspiration/Pneumonia
Anaerobes: pigmented and nonpigmented *Prevotella, Fusobacterium, Peptostreptococcus* (now divided into five additional genera— *Anaerococcus, Finegoldia, Gallicola, Micromonas,* and *Peptoniphilus*), *Bacteroides fragilis,* and *Clostridium perfringens*
Aerobes: streptococci, *Staphylococcus aureus,* Enterobacteriaceae, *Pseudomonas aeruginosa, Klebsiella pneumoniae, Legionella* spp., *Nocardia asteroides, Haemophilus influenzae, Eikenella corrodens, Salmonella* spp., *Burkholderia pseudomallei, B. mallei, Rhodococcus equi*

Bacterial Embolic
S. aureus, P. aeruginosa, F. necrophorum

Mycobacteria (often multifocal)
Mycobacterium tuberculosis, Mycobacterium-avium complex, *Mycobacterium kansasii,* other mycobacteria

Fungi
Aspergillus spp., Mucoraceae, *Histoplasma capsulatum, Pneumocystis carinii, Coccidioides immitis, Blastomyces dermatitidis, Cryptococcus neoformans*

Parasites
Entamoeba histolytica, Paragonimus westermani, Stronglyoides stercoralis (postobstructive)
Empyema (with air-fluid level)
Septic embolism (endocarditis)

PREDISPOSING CONDITIONS
Fluid-filled cysts or bullae
Infarction without infection
Pulmonary embolism
Vasculitis
    Goodpasture's syndrome
    Wegener's granulomatosis
    Polyarteritis nodosa
Bronchiectasis
Postobstructive pneumonia (neoplasm, foreign body)
Pulmonary sequestration
Pulmonary contusion
Neoplasm

Etiology

Conditions that predispose to lung abscess include any cause of aspiration or reduced ciliary action, such as reduced levels of consciousness, alcoholism, seizure disorders, general anesthesia, cerebrovascular accidents, drug addiction, dysphagia, esophageal reflux, and mechanical interference with the cardiac sphincter, such as is caused by nasogastric tubes and endotracheal intubation (Chapters 92 and 306). Periodontal disease, gingivitis, sinus infection, and bronchiectasis provide a source for anaerobic infection and are other important background factors. Another cause of lung abscess is septic pulmonary embolism, most commonly with *S. aureus* and most commonly in intravenous drug users. Unlike lung abscesses related to aspiration, which are usually solitary, the lung abscesses seen with septic pulmonary emboli are commonly multiple or are associated with other septic embolic lesions in various stages of development. Any necrotizing pneumonia can also present with areas of abscess, which are commonly small and multiple and less likely to be defined clearly as abscesses by chest radiograph than by pathologic specimen. When bronchial obstruction develops distal to a pulmonary neoplasm (Chapter 198), drainage is difficult and abscess formation is common. For all causes of abscess, however, diabetes, malignancy, and other immunocompromising conditions are common predisposing factors.

A total of 90% of cases involve anaerobic bacteria; half include aerobes as well. The principal anaerobes are pigmented and nonpigmented *Prevotella, Fusobacterium,* and *Peptostreptococcus. Bacteroides fragilis* group strains are found in 7% of cases. Among the aerobes, streptococci, staphylococci, and gram-negative bacilli are prominent.

Incidence and Prevalence

The incidence of lung abscess has decreased since the advent of antimicrobial therapy, but larger hospitals see 10 to 25 cases per year.

Pathogenesis

Small numbers of oropharyngeal bacteria are commonly aspirated during sleep but are readily cleared by host defense mechanisms (Chapters 82, 92, and 306). Defense mechanisms are not as efficient in handling larger numbers of aspirated bacteria.

Counts of anaerobes in oral flora are lower than usual in edentulous subjects and higher in patients with periodontal disease. Alcoholics and patients who are acutely or chronically ill (especially if hospitalized) often demonstrate oropharyngeal colonization with aerobic or facultative gram-negative bacilli and *S. aureus*. Among the anaerobes, organisms more likely to cause infection as sole agents are *Fusobacterium nucleatum, F. necrophorum, B. fragilis,* and *Clostridium perfringens*. Both the size of the bacterial inoculum and the role of associated organisms and host defenses are important. Organisms such as *S. aureus* and *Klebsiella pneumoniae*, which produce extracellular toxins or enzymes, often produce abscesses.

The various types of aspiration-related pleuropulmonary infections—pneumonitis (the initial stage), necrotizing pneumonia (multiple excavations <2 cm in diameter), lung abscess (one or more cavities >2 cm in diameter communicating with a bronchus), and empyema—should be considered as one process with a continuum of changes. A predilection for infection in dependent segments is seen, particularly the posterior segments of the upper lobes and the superior segments of the lower lobes, but the location of the abscess depends on gravity and the position of the subject (Fig. 93–1). Normally, the

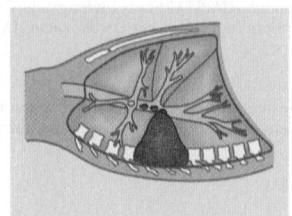 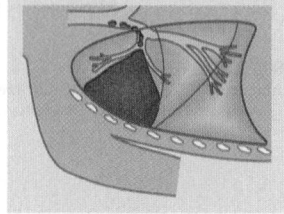

A   B

FIGURE 93–1 • Relationship between posture and location of lung abscess. With patient lying on back (*A*), aspiration occurs into the superior segment of the lower lobe. With patient lying on side (*B*), aspiration occurs into the posterior segment of the lower lobe. (From Brock RC: Lung abscess. Oxford, Blackwell, 1952.)

aspirated material is handled effectively by ciliary action, cough, and alveolar macrophages (Chapters 82 and 92). Endotracheal tubes impair coughing, impede pulmonary clearance mechanisms, and allow leakage of oropharyngeal secretions into the tracheobronchial tree. Thick or particulate matter and foreign bodies are not easily removed and can produce bronchial obstruction and atelectasis. In pneumonia following aspiration of gastric contents, gastric acid and enzymes are the primary offending agents (Chapter 306). Subdiaphragmatic infection may extend to the lung by way of lymphatic vessels, directly through the diaphragm, or by way of the blood stream.

Clinical Manifestations

A relatively insidious onset of infection is seen in many patients; additional clues are involvement of dependent segments of lung, predisposition to aspiration, and, often, periodontal disease. After 1 to 2 weeks, tissue necrosis, with abscess formation or empyema, occurs. Following cavitation, putrid sputum is noted in 50% or more of patients, and hemoptysis may be seen. Weeks to months of malaise and low-grade fever may be associated with cough, weight loss, and anemia. Neoplasia is a serious diagnostic consideration in such patients. On occasion, the picture is acute, with fever, malaise, cough, and pleurisy. Patients with lung abscess due to infection with *S. aureus* or gram-negative bacilli and those with secondary lung abscess due to septic pulmonary emboli may have a more fulminant course. In edentulous persons with intact oropharyngeal function, lung abscesses are uncommon and suggest the presence of an obstructing lesion of the bronchus (carcinoma or other) or pulmonary embolus.

Diagnosis

The classic radiographic appearance of lung abscess is a cavity with an air-fluid level, with or without surrounding infiltrate (Fig. 93–2); in some patients, however, repeat chest radiographs or computed tomographic (CT) scanning may be needed to detect the cavity. A similar radiographic appearance can be seen with a variety of conditions other than bacterial lung abscess (Table 93–1), so definitive bacterial confirmation is required. Radiography occasionally reveals mediastinal lymphadenopathy, making the differential diagnosis include tuberculosis, fungal infection, and lung cancer. Infected cysts or bullae and pulmonary sequestration are often evident with radiography. CT can readily distinguish between lung abscess and an air-fluid level in an empyema cavity.

The spectrum of organisms causing lung abscess has widened as patients present with more complex medical and surgical conditions. Antibiotic resistance has emerged and the number of immunocompromised persons has increased. Thus, microbiologic studies are increasingly desirable to guide therapy. Expectorated sputum cannot be used for anaerobic culture because large numbers of anaerobes are present in the indigenous flora. Even for infection with *S. aureus* and gram-negative bacilli, use of expectorated sputum is a problem because of frequent oropharyngeal colonization with such organisms in institutionalized patients. Bacteremia is uncommon in aspiration pneumonia, and all organisms involved in the lung abscess may not be recovered in blood cultures. Empyema fluid constitutes an excellent source for anaerobic (and aerobic) culture. Transtracheal aspiration bypasses the normal flora of the upper respiratory tract, but contamination with indigenous flora can be a problem, and the procedure is now seldom performed. Two approaches that are preferable to transtracheal aspiration are the use of a protected specimen brush and the use of bronchoalveolar lavage. The protected specimen brush procedure involves sampling with a bronchial brush protected within a telescoping plugged double-catheter via a fiberoptic bronchoscope. It is essential that the technique be used exactly as described and that cultures be done quantitatively. For the protected specimen brush procedure, 10^3 to 10^4 or more colony-forming units per milliliter is significant. The small volume of material obtained and the difficulty in anaerobic transport are concerns. Quantitative culture of fluid obtained by bronchoalveolar lavage, during or without bronchoscopy, also provides reliable results. Counts of 10^4 or more organisms per milliliter are considered significant. Demonstration of bacteria intracellularly in at least 3 to 5% of cells in bronchoalveolar lavage fluid is good evidence of pneumonia, and the morphology of those bacteria is extremely useful in directing therapy. Specimens must be placed under anaerobic conditions immediately after being obtained. Bronchoscopy also is often important to exclude cavitating or obstructing malignancy or presence of a foreign body.

Rx Treatment

Antimicrobial therapy and drainage are the keystones of treatment; identification and treatment of underlying or primary processes is also important. Prolonged therapy is important to prevent relapse; the actual duration of treatment must be individualized, but periods of 1 to 3 months or more may be required. The approach to a specific patient is based on the clinical status of the patient as well as the microbiologic features of the infection. The initial choice of antimicrobial agents is empirical but should be guided by the Gram stain and the likely bacteriologic source of the infection, and then it should be adjusted as culture and susceptibility data become available. A small to moderate-sized abscess in an otherwise healthy person may respond to conservative management with antimicrobial therapy and postural drainage. A rapidly expanding pulmonary abscess in an immunocompromised host (e.g., due to one of the Mucoraceae) requires urgent lung resection in addition to antimicrobial therapy. Secondary lung abscesses may require more intensive antimicrobial therapy.

Therapy for infections due to aerobic bacteria (Chapter 92), mycobacteria (Chapter 341), fungi (Chapter 327), and parasites (Chapter 391) is based on their susceptibilities to specific agents. Anaerobic agents, which include *Prevotella* and *Bacteroides* species, fusobacteria, anaerobic cocci, clostridia, and *B. fragilis*, and which predominate in bacterial lung abscesses, produce β-lactamases and demonstrate resistance to penicillin G in up to 40% of cases. Clindamycin, given initially at a dose of 600 mg every 6 hours intravenously, then when the patient is afebrile and improved, 300 mg orally every 6 hours, is more effective than penicillin. When penicillin is used, it should be used in high doses (12 million units/day intravenously in average-sized adults with normal renal

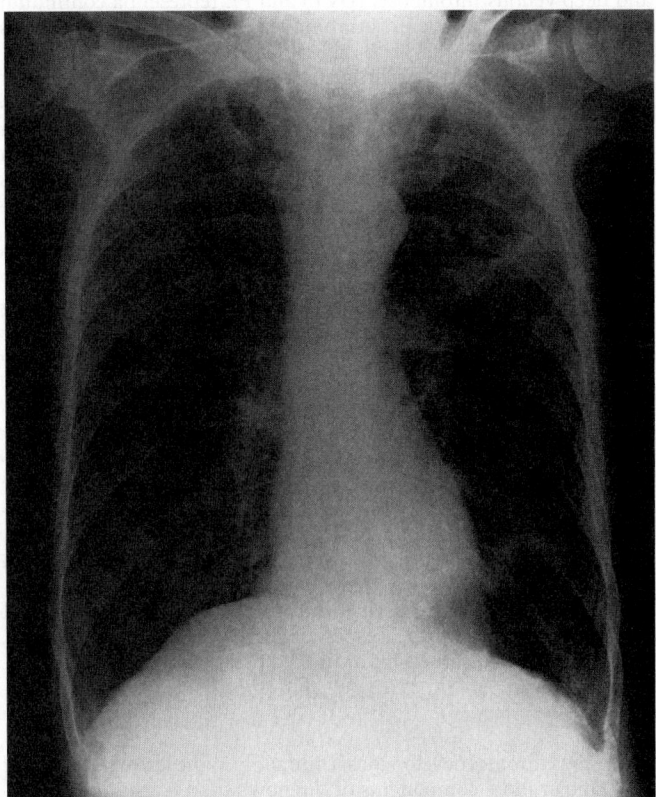

FIGURE 93–2 • Left upper lobe lung abscess distal to a bronchogenic carcinoma in the left hilum. Note the loss of volume in the left upper lung and the air-fluid level.

Continued

function) and in combination with clindamycin or metronidazole (2 g/day intravenously in four divided doses). Metronidazole alone may be ineffective because of resistance of aerobic bacteria, *Actinomyces*, and some anaerobic streptococci. After improvement, one option is to give ampicillin or amoxicillin plus metronidazole orally, each in a dose of 500 mg every 6 to 8 hours. Imipenem or meropenem and β-lactam/β-lactamase inhibitor combinations such as ticarcillin and clavulanic acid are active against essentially all anaerobes and many of the aerobes important in nosocomial aspiration pneumonia. If a specific anaerobe or set of anaerobes is identified in the lung abscess, antibiotic therapy can be targeted on the basis of general susceptibility characteristics (Table 93–2) while awaiting local susceptibility testing results.

Postural drainage is important in therapy of lung abscess. Bronchoscopy may help in effecting good drainage, removal of foreign bodies, and diagnosis of tumor. Experience dictates caution with the bronchoscopic drainage of closed cavities; spillage of cavity contents into other lung segments may occur and be catastrophic.

Persistence of bacteremia or high-grade fever after 72 hours, or the absence of change in sputum production or character or in radiographic images during a period of 7 to 10 days, suggests undiagnosed obstruction, empyema, or resistant organisms. Progression of pulmonary infiltrates may occur after the initiation of appropriate therapy, reflecting poorly ventilated and underperfused infected lung tissue. Surgical resection of necrotic lung may occasionally be needed if the response to antibiotics is poor or if airway obstruction limits drainage. In patients who are poor surgical risks, percutaneous or CT-guided drainage via catheters may be useful. Bronchoscopic balloon dilatation and stent placement may be useful in malignant disease with poststenotic abscess.

Prevention

Precautions should be taken to minimize aspiration, particularly in feeding feeble or confused patients and patients with swallowing difficulties. In the case of gross aspiration, immediate clearing of the airway by postural drainage and suctioning, preferably by bronchoscopy, is important. Proper treatment of periodontal disease and gingivitis and early treatment of pneumonia minimize the risk of bacterial lung abscess.

Prognosis

Mortality is 5 to 10%. Patients with large abscesses (>6 cm), progressive pulmonary necrosis, obstructing lesions, aerobic bacterial

---

Table 93–2 • DRUGS OF CHOICE FOR ANAEROBES INVOLVED IN LUNG ABSCESS*

PRINCIPAL PATHOGENS
Prevotella: Metronidazole, clindamycin, β-lactam/β-lactamase inhibitor combinations, carbapenems
Fusobacterium: As for *Prevotella*
Peptostreptococcus (see Table 93–1): β-lactam/β-lactamase inhibitor combinations, carbapenems, penicillin (high dosage)
Streptococcus (anaerobic, microaerophilic strains): penicillin (high dosage), β-lactam/β-lactamase inhibitor combinations, carbapenems

LESS COMMON PATHOGENS
Bacteroides: Metronidazole, β-lactam/β-lactamase inhibitor combinations, carbapenems
Clostridium: Metronidazole, β-lactam/β-lactamase inhibitor combinations, carbapenems, penicillin
Actinomyces: Penicillin (high dosage), clindamycin
Eikenella corrodens (microaerophilic): Penicillin, β-lactam/β-lactamase inhibitor combinations, carbapenems

UNKNOWN BACTERIOLOGY
Metronidazole plus penicillin, β-lactam/β-lactamase inhibitor combinations, carbapenems

*Drugs listed for each group of organisms are roughly comparable in activity and are the drugs that are most active. Other drugs (e.g., cefoxitin or clindamycin, alone or with penicillin) may be useful in patients with abscess of unknown bacteriologic origin who are only mildly to moderately ill.

---

infection, immune compromise, old age, and systemic debility, and those in whom major delays have occurred in seeking medical attention have a higher mortality and a higher incidence of complications. The most common complication is empyema, with or without bronchopleural fistula. Spillover of pus from a large lung abscess sometimes leads to spread of infection and even to asphyxiation. Other complications, which are rare, include brain or other distal abscesses, generalized infection, severe hemorrhage, and pulmonary gangrene. Superinfection by other bacteria or by fungi can occur in relation to antimicrobial therapy. In chronic lung abscess, chronic bronchitis, localized emphysema, or bronchiectasis may be present, with subsequent recurrences of acute pneumonitis in the involved area.

SUGGESTED READINGS

Fernandez-Sabé N, Carratalà J, Dorca J, et al: Efficacy and safety of sequential amoxicillin-clavulanate in the treatment of anaerobic lung infections. Eur J Clin Microbiol Infect Dis 2003;22:185–187. *A good study of 40 consecutive anaerobic pulmonary infections, 25 with lung abscess, with an excellent response to amoxicillin-clavulanate.*
Mansharamani N, Balachandran D, Delaney D, et al: Lung abscess in adults: clinical comparison of immunocompromised to non-immunocompromised patients. Respir Med 2002;96:178–185. *Nonimmunocompromised patients have mostly anaerobes in their infecting flora, whereas immunocompromised patients have mostly aerobic or facultative bacteria, often with multiple isolates.*
Rolston KV: The spectrum of pulmonary infections in cancer patients. Curr Opin Oncol 2001;13:218–223. *A good review of lung abscess and other pulmonary infections in cancer patients.*

---

94 PULMONARY EMBOLISM

Victor Tapson

Definitions

Pulmonary embolism (PE) refers to exogenous or endogenous material traveling to the lungs and causing a potential spectrum of consequences, including dyspnea, chest pain, hypoxemia, and sometimes death. Thrombus from the deep veins of the lower extremities (Chapter 78) is the most common material embolizing to the lungs, and deep venous thrombosis (DVT) and PE represent a continuum of one disease entity (venous thromboembolism). Other substances such as neoplastic cells, air bubbles (Chapter 90), carbon dioxide, intravenous catheters, fat droplets, and talc in intravenous drug abusers (Chapter 30) are also potential sources of emboli. In this chapter, "pulmonary embolism" refers to thromboemboli arising from the deep leg veins or, less frequently, from the axillary-subclavian system. Subsequently, embolism of nonthrombotic substances is discussed.

Incidence

Both DVT and PE are frequently clinically unsuspected, leading to significant diagnostic and therapeutic delays and accounting for substantial morbidity and mortality. Even though venous thromboembolism is diagnosed and treated in as many as 260,000 patients in the United States each year, more than half of the cases that actually occur are never diagnosed, and as many as 600,000 cases may therefore occur. Many patients dying of acute PE have coexisting terminal illnesses, but this disease entity appears to be responsible for the deaths of at least 100,000 to 200,000 patients who have an otherwise good prognosis and whose deaths are otherwise preventable. Autopsy studies have repeatedly documented the high frequency with which PE has gone unsuspected and undetected; furthermore, prophylaxis continues to be dramatically underused. The incidence of venous thromboembolism is especially high in hospitalized patients, whether on a medical service or in the postoperative setting.

Pathophysiology

Venous thrombi develop most commonly in the leg veins (Chapter 78). One or more components of Virchow's triad (stasis, hypercoagulability, and intimal injury) is present in nearly all patients. The risk increases with age. More than 95% of pulmonary emboli arise from the proximal deep veins of the lower extremities (including and above the popliteal veins). However, calf vein thrombi can propagate into the proximal veins and even occasionally embolize to the lung. Patients with central vein catheters, particularly those with malignancies, may develop emboli from axillary-subclavian vein thrombosis. Individuals with effort-induced upper extremity thrombosis (Paget-Schroetter syndrome) may develop pulmonary emboli as well.

GAS EXCHANGE AND HEMODYNAMIC ALTERATIONS. In acute PE, minute ventilation acutely increases with resulting tachypnea; in most patients, hypoxemia develops. When no concomitant cardiopulmonary disease is present, the obstruction of blood flow creates alveolar dead space with regions of high ventilation-perfusion ratios as well as shunting due to perfusion of atelectatic areas. This imbalance appears to be the principal explanation for hypoxemia in acute PE.

When emboli obstruct a substantial portion of the pulmonary arterial bed, profound hemodynamic alterations occur. The impact of the embolic event depends on the extent of reduction of the cross-sectional area of the pulmonary vasculature as well as on the presence or absence of underlying cardiopulmonary disease. Submassive emboli in normal individuals may actually augment cardiac output. Hypoxemia stimulates an increase in sympathetic tone, with resulting systemic vasoconstriction, increased venous return, and an increase in stroke volume. With massive emboli, cardiac output is diminished but may be sustained as the mean right atrial pressure increases. The increase in pulmonary vascular resistance impedes right ventricular outflow and reduces left ventricular preload. In the absence of underlying cardiopulmonary disease, occlusion of 25 to 30% of the vascular bed by emboli is associated with a significant increase in pulmonary artery pressure. With increasing vascular obstruction, hypoxemia worsens, stimulating vasoconstriction and a further increase in pulmonary artery pressure. More than 50% obstruction of the pulmonary arterial bed is usually present before there is substantial elevation of the mean pulmonary artery pressure. When the extent of obstruction of the pulmonary circulation approaches 75%, the right ventricle must generate a systolic pressure in excess of 50 mm Hg and a mean pulmonary artery pressure of greater than 40 mm Hg to preserve pulmonary perfusion. A normal right ventricle is rarely able to achieve this and, hence, fails. Patients with underlying cardiopulmonary disease often experience a more substantial deterioration in cardiac output than normal individuals in the setting of massive PE. A depressed cardiac output *without* elevation of the right atrial pressure suggests cardiac dysfunction superimposed upon PE. Although supportive measures may sustain a patient with massive embolism, any additional increment in embolic burden may be fatal.

Pathology

The pathologic findings of PE vary depending on the age and extent of the emboli. In most cases, both lungs are affected, and the lower lobes are involved more often than the upper lobes. An embolus generally has blunt, nontapering ends and may be folded over on itself. When unfolded, emboli may be "Y" shaped from branch points of the veins from which they formed and may have imprints of venous valve cusps. In cases of massive embolism with rapid deterioration and death, the autopsy may reveal large emboli obstructing the main pulmonary artery or the pulmonary artery bifurcation. Smaller, more peripheral emboli of various ages and in various stages of organization usually indicate emboli predating the terminal event. Pulmonary infarction, which may be evident in areas of the peripheral lung supplied by smaller vessels, is characterized histologically by intra-alveolar hemorrhage and necrosis of alveolar walls. However, the dual pulmonary circulation from both the pulmonary and bronchial arteries and veins prevents most emboli from causing infarction.

Clinical Manifestations

The history and physical examination are notoriously insensitive and nonspecific for both DVT and PE. Patients with lower extremity venous thrombosis often do not exhibit erythema, warmth, pain, swelling, or tenderness (Chapter 78). When these signs are present, they are nonspecific but still merit further evaluation. Pain with dorsiflexion of the foot (Homans' sign) may be present in the setting of venous thrombosis, but this finding is neither sensitive nor specific. The most common symptom of acute PE is dyspnea, which is often sudden in onset. Pleuritic chest pain and hemoptysis occur more commonly with pulmonary *infarction*

due to smaller, peripheral emboli. Palpitations, cough, anxiety, and lightheadedness are all symptoms of acute PE but may also result from a number of other entities, thereby contributing to difficulty in making the diagnosis. Syncope and/or sudden death may occur with massive PE. PE should always be considered whenever unexplained dyspnea, syncope, hypotension, or hypoxemia is present. Tachypnea and tachycardia are the most common signs of PE but are also nonspecific. Other physical findings may include fever, wheezing, rales, a pleural rub, a loud pulmonic component of the second heart sound, a right-sided third or fourth heart sound, and a right ventricular lift. Both the cardiac and pulmonary physical examinations are nonspecific in patients with PE. Findings such as dyspnea, tachypnea, and hypoxemia in patients with concomitant cardiopulmonary disease (such as heart failure, pneumonia, or chronic obstructive pulmonary disease) may be caused by the underlying disease or be superimposed acute PE. Symptoms and signs consistent with PE (Table 94–1) should be particularly heeded in the setting of risk factors for venous thromboembolism, such as concomitant malignancy, immobility, or the postoperative state.

Diagnosis

The differential diagnosis for acute PE (Table 94–2) depends on the clinical presentation and the presence of concomitant disease (Fig.

Table 94–1 • SYMPTOMS AND SIGNS IN 117 PATIENTS WITH ACUTE PULMONARY EMBOLISM WITHOUT PREEXISTING CARDIAC OR PULMONARY DISEASE

SYMPTOMS	% OF PATIENTS	SIGNS	% OF PATIENTS
Dyspnea	73	Tachypnea (≥20/min)	70
Pleuritic pain	66	Rales (crackles)	51
Cough	37	Tachycardia (>100/min)	30
Leg swelling	28	Fourth heart sound	24
Leg pain	26	Increased pulmonary component of second sound	23
Hemoptysis	13		
Palpitations	10	Deep venous thrombosis	11
Wheezing	9	Diaphoresis	11
Angina-like pain	4	Temperature >38.5°C	7
		Wheezes	5
		Homans' sign	4
		Right ventricular lift	4
		Pleural friction rub	3
		Third heart sound	3
		Cyanosis	1

Adapted from Stein PD, Terrin ML, Hales CA, et al: Clinical, laboratory, roentgenographic and electrocardiographic findings in patients with acute pulmonary embolism and no pre-existing cardiac or pulmonary disease. Chest 1991;100:598–603.

Table 94–2 • DIFFERENTIAL DIAGNOSIS OF ACUTE PULMONARY EMBOLISM

Myocardial infarction
Pericarditis
Congestive heart failure
Pneumonia
Asthma
Chronic obstructive pulmonary disease
Pneumothorax
Pleurodynia
Pleuritis from collagen vascular disease
Thoracic herpes zoster ("shingles")
Rib fracture
Musculoskeletal pain
Primary or metastatic intrathoracic cancer
Infradiaphragmatic processes (e.g., acute cholecystitis, splenic infarction)
Hyperventilation syndrome

Respiratory Diseases

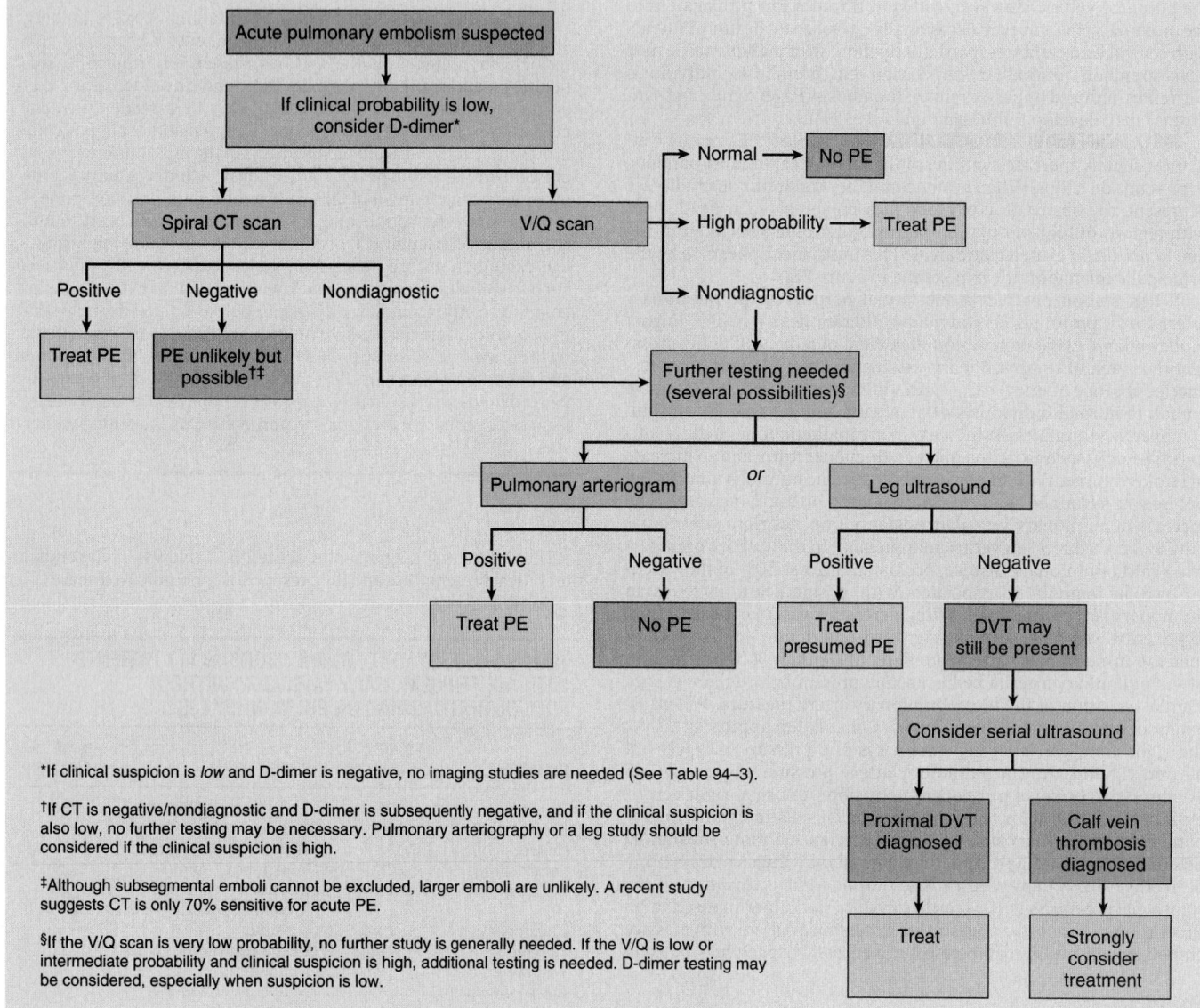

FIGURE 94-1 • An algorithm for the diagnostic approach to suspected acute pulmonary embolism. CT = computed tomography; ELISA = enzyme linked immunoabsorbent assay; PE = pulmonary embolism; VQ = ventilation-perfusion.

94–1). When patients present with dyspnea (Chapter 81) and/or chest pain (Chapters 46 and 68), the differential diagnosis includes pneumonia (Chapter 92), a flare of asthma or chronic obstructive lung disease (Chapters 84 and 85), anxiety with hyperventilation, pneumothorax (Chapter 95), heart failure (Chapter 55), angina or myocardial infarction (Chapters 67, 68, and 69), musculoskeletal pain, pericarditis (Chapter 74), pleuritis from collagen vascular disease, herpes zoster, rib fracture, intrathoracic cancer, and, occasionally, intra-abdominal processes such as acute cholecystitis (Chapter 158). Acute PE can be superimposed on another underlying cardiopulmonary disease, upon which new or worsening symptoms are sometimes blamed.

BLOOD TESTS. Hypoxemia is common in acute PE. Some individuals, particularly young patients without underlying lung disease, may have a normal arterial oxygen tension (PaO_2) and, rarely, a normal alveolar-arterial difference. A sudden decrease in the PaO_2 or in the oxygen saturation in a patient unable to communicate an accurate history (e.g., a mechanically ventilated patient) may be evidence of acute PE.

The diagnostic utility of plasma measurements of circulating D-dimer (a specific derivative of cross-linked fibrin) has been extensively evaluated in patients with PE. A normal enzyme-linked immunosorbent assay appears sensitive for detecting PE. For example, when the D-dimer level is 500 μg/L or greater, the sensitivity for PE may be as high as 96 to 98%, but the specificity is much lower. In a

recent prospective study, only one of 437 patients with a negative D-dimer test and low clinical probability developed PE during follow-up; thus, the negative predictive value for this strategy was 99.5% (Table 94–3). Careful use of such approaches may reduce the need for diagnostic imaging. A number of D-dimer assays are available, and the sensitivity and specificity of these assays vary. A positive D-dimer test means that DVT or PE is possible, but it is by no means proof of venous thromboembolism. Similarly, although a negative D-dimer may strongly suggest that venous thromboembolism is absent, a high clinical suspicion should not be ignored.

Several studies have suggested that troponin levels may be elevated in acute PE. Troponin elevation is specific for cardiac myocyte damage, and the right ventricle appears to be the source of the enzyme elevation in acute PE. Both cardiac troponin T and troponin I levels have been found to be elevated in acute PE, especially in more massive embolism when myocyte injury owing to right ventricular strain might be expected. Troponin levels cannot, however, be used like D-dimer testing; that is, they are not sensitive enough to exclude PE, even when the clinical suspicion is relatively low, without additional diagnostic testing.

ELECTROCARDIOGRAPHY. Electrocardiographic findings, which are present in the majority of patients with acute PE, include ST-segment abnormalities, T-wave changes, and left or right axis deviation. Only one third of patients with massive or submassive emboli have manifestations of acute cor pulmonale such as the S1-Q3-T3 pattern, right

Table 94–3 • DETERMINING THE PRETEST PROBABILITY OF ACUTE PULMONARY EMBOLISM BASED ON POINT SYSTEM AND D-DIMER RESULT

VARIABLE	POINTS
DVT symptoms/signs*	3.0
PE as or more likely†	3.0
HR > 100 beats/min	1.5
Immobilization/surgery‡	1.5
Previous DVT or PE	1.5
Hemoptysis	1.0
Malignancy	1.0

TOTAL SCORE	PRETEST PROBABILITY§
<2.0	Low
2.0 to 6.0	Moderate
>6.0	High

*Including objectively measured leg swelling and pain with palpation in the deep vein region.
†PE as likely or more likely than an alternative diagnosis. Physicians were told to use clinical information, along with chest radiography, electrocardiography, and laboratory tests.
‡If in previous 4 weeks.
§Of the 437 patients with a negative D-dimer result (by the SimpliRED assay) and low clinical probability, only one developed PE during follow-up; thus, the negative predictive value for the combined strategy of using the clinical model with D-dimer testing in these patients was 99.5%.
DVT = deep venous thrombosis, PE = pulmonary embolism, HR = heart rate.
From Wells PS, Anderson DR, Rodger M, et al: Excluding pulmonary embolism at the bedside without diagnostic imaging: Management of patients with suspected pulmonary embolism presenting to the emergency department by using a simple clinical model and D-dimer. Ann Intern Med 2001;135:98.

bundle branch block, P-wave pulmonale, or right axis deviation. All of these findings are also nonspecific. The utility of electrocardiography in suspected acute PE is derived more from its ability to establish or exclude alternative diagnoses, such as acute myocardial infarction, rather than diagnosing or excluding PE.

CHEST RADIOGRAPHY. The chest radiograph is often abnormal in patients with acute PE, but it is nearly always nonspecific. Common radiographic findings include pleural effusion, atelectasis, pulmonary infiltrates, and mild elevation of a hemidiaphragm. Classic findings of pulmonary infarction, such as Hampton's hump or decreased vascularity (Westermark's sign), are suggestive of the diagnosis, but they are infrequent. A normal chest radiograph in the setting of dyspnea and hypoxemia without evidence of bronchospasm or anatomic cardiac shunt is strongly suggestive of PE. Under most circumstances, however, the chest radiograph cannot be used for conclusive diagnosis or exclusion. Although the radiograph may exclude other processes, such as

pneumonia, pneumothorax, or rib fracture, which may cause symptoms similar to acute PE, PE may frequently coexist with other underlying heart or lung diseases. Symptoms, signs, radiographic findings, electrocardiography, and the plasma D-dimer measurement cannot be considered diagnostic of PE or DVT. When these entities are suspected, further evaluation with noninvasive or invasive testing is necessary.

VENTILATION-PERFUSION SCANNING. Although the ventilation-perfusion scan has historically been the most common diagnostic test used when PE is suspected, spiral (helical) computed tomography (CT) scanning (see later text) has essentially replaced it at many centers. Normal and high probability scans are considered diagnostic (Fig. 94–2). A normal perfusion scan excludes the diagnosis with a high enough degree of certainty that further diagnostic evaluation is almost never necessary; although large, central nonocclusive emboli might transiently permit tracer to perfuse the lungs normally, this phenomenon is exceedingly unusual and should be pursued only when the clinical suspicion is exceptionally high. Matching areas of decreased ventilation and perfusion in the presence of a normal chest radiograph generally represent a process other than PE. However, low or intermediate probability (nondiagnostic) scans are commonly found with PE, and in such situations further evaluation with pulmonary arteriography is often appropriate. In the Prospective Investigation of Pulmonary Embolism Diagnosis (PIOPED), the specificity of high probability scans was 97%, but the sensitivity was only 41%. Of note, 33% of patients with intermediate probability scans and 12% of patients with low probability scans were diagnosed definitively with PE by pulmonary arteriography. When the clinical suspicion of PE was considered very high, PE was found to be present in 96% of patients with high probability scans, 66% of patients with intermediate scans, and 40% of patients with low probability scans. Thus, the diagnosis of PE should be rigorously pursued even when the lung scan is of low or intermediate probability if the clinical setting suggests the diagnosis. Therefore, although the ventilation-perfusion scan either may be diagnostic of PE in higher risk patients or may exclude the possibility with sufficient certainty in low-risk patients, it is often nondiagnostic. Even in the latter circumstance, however, it may serve as a guide for the interventional radiologist, by directing selective dye injection to minimize the contrast load and limit the duration of pulmonary arteriography.

Stable patients with suspected acute PE, nondiagnostic lung scans, and adequate cardiopulmonary reserve (absence of hypotension or severe hypoxemia) may undergo noninvasive lower extremity testing in an attempt to diagnose DVT (Chapter 78). A positive compression ultrasound or impedance plethysmogram presents the opportunity to treat without further testing. If the lower extremity test is negative, pulmonary angiography is an appropriate option. *Serial* noninvasive lower extremity testing in the setting of suspected PE should be performed only in centers where follow-up is guaranteed and validated protocols are used. Impedance plethysmography has been essentially entirely replaced by ultrasonography at nearly all medical centers.

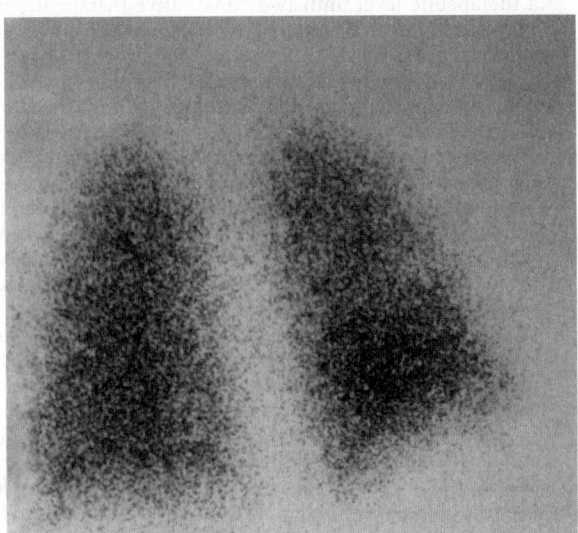
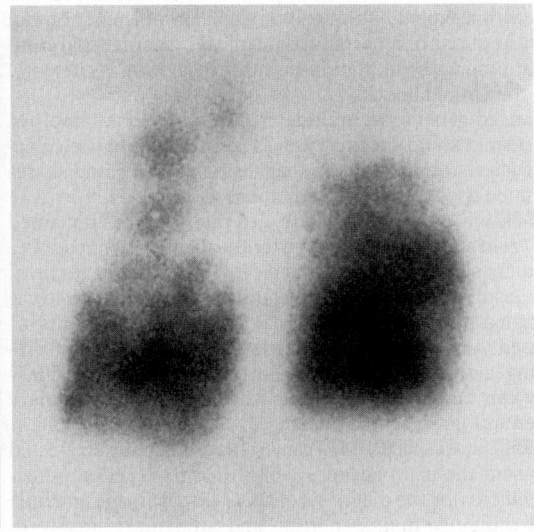

FIGURE 94–2 • High probability ventilation-perfusion scan.

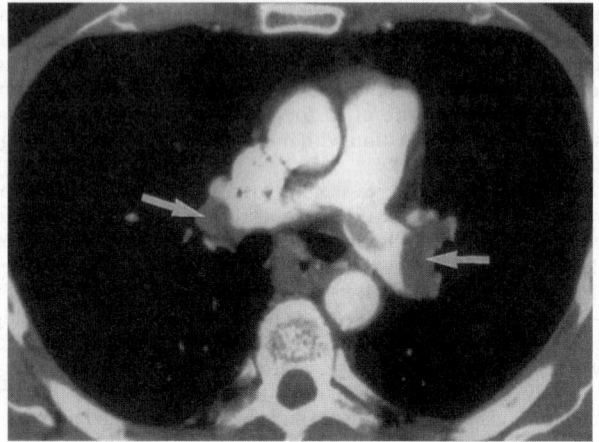

FIGURE 94–3 • Spiral computed tomography image of acute pulmonary emboli in both main pulmonary arteries in a postoperative patient with the sudden onset of dyspnea, hypoxemia, and hypotension.

Magnetic resonance imaging (MRI) of the lower extremities may also be useful after a nondiagnostic lung scan if the medical facility has experience with this technique.

SPIRAL (HELICAL) COMPUTED TOMOGRAPHY. Spiral CT scanning can be used for diagnosing both acute and chronic PE and is replacing ventilation-perfusion scanning at many centers (Fig. 94–3). Spiral CT involves continuous movement of the patient through the CT scanner and allows concurrent scanning by a constantly rotating gantry and detector system. This technique enables rapid scanning with continuous acquisitions obtained during a single breath. Retrospective reconstructions can be performed. A contrast bolus is required for imaging the pulmonary vasculature.

In at least one clinical trial, spiral CT had both sensitivity and specificity greater than 95%. However, a large, prospective Swiss study reported a sensitivity of only 70%, suggesting that a negative CT scan does not exclude smaller emboli. Spiral CT is most sensitive for detecting emboli in the main, lobar, or segmental pulmonary arteries; its specificity for clot in these vessels is also excellent. For subsegmental emboli, spiral CT appears to be less accurate, but the importance of emboli of this size has been questioned.

An advantage of spiral CT over ventilation-perfusion scanning and arteriography is the ability of CT to define nonvascular conditions such as lymphadenopathy, lung tumors, emphysema, and other parenchymal abnormalities as well as pleural and pericardial disease. A second advantage of spiral CT over other diagnostic methods is the rapidity (10 to 15 minutes) with which the scan can be performed. Third, several preliminary studies suggest that CT scanning may also be used to evaluate the proximal leg veins for venous thrombosis. Conversely, disadvantages of CT include its poor sensitivity for detecting clots in small vessels, the fact that it is not portable at present, and the problem that patients with significant renal insufficiency cannot be scanned without risk of renal failure. A large multicenter trial comparing CT scanning with ventilation-perfusion scanning is currently underway in the United States.

More advanced generation multidetector scanners may improve the current sensitivity and specificity of CT. Contrast-enhanced electron beam CT also appears useful in diagnosing acute PE and shares many of the same advantages and limitations as spiral CT.

PULMONARY ARTERIOGRAPHY. Pulmonary arteriography has remained the accepted "gold standard" technique for the diagnosis of acute PE. It is an extremely sensitive, specific, and safe test. Complications of pulmonary arteriography among 1111 patients suspected of PE in the PIOPED included death in 0.5% and major nonfatal complications in 1%. It is used when PE must be diagnosed or excluded, but preliminary testing has been nondiagnostic. In some centers, pulmonary arteriography can be performed at the bedside using a pulmonary artery catheter and fluoroscopic guidance.

MAGNETIC RESONANCE IMAGING. MRI can evaluate clinically suspected PE, but at present the main advantage of MRI is its excellent sensitivity and specificity for the diagnosis of DVT. Disadvantages include the potential difficulty in transporting and studying critically ill patients.

ECHOCARDIOGRAPHY. Echocardiography (Chapter 51), which can often be obtained more rapidly than either lung scanning or pulmonary arteriography, may reveal abnormalities of right ventricular size or function that strongly support the diagnosis of hemodynamically significant PE. However, because these patients often have underlying cardiopulmonary disease such as chronic obstructive lung disease, neither right ventricular dilation nor hypokinesis can be reliably used even as indirect evidence of PE. In the setting of documented PE, echocardiographic evidence of right ventricular dysfunction can identify patients who may benefit from thrombolytic therapy (see Treatment). Transesophageal echocardiography, although less convenient, may be a better approach than the transthoracic approach. Intravascular ultrasound imaging can detect large emboli and may be performed at the bedside; this technique may become clinically useful in the future.

 Treatment

Options for treatment of acute PE include anticoagulation with heparin or low-molecular-weight heparin (LMWH), thrombolytic therapy, and inferior vena cava (IVC) filter placement. Massive PE may occasionally be treated with surgical embolectomy. Each approach has specific indications as well as advantages and disadvantages.

HEPARIN, LOW-MOLECULAR-WEIGHT HEPARIN, AND WARFARIN

The primary anticoagulants used to treat acute venous thrombosis and/or PE include unfractionated heparin and LMWH (Chapter 78). By accelerating the action of antithrombin III, these substances exert a prompt antithrombotic effect that prevents the extension of thrombus (Chapter 33). Although heparins do not directly dissolve thrombus or emboli, they allow the fibrinolytic system to proceed unopposed and more readily reduce the size of the thromboembolic burden. Whereas the growth of thrombus can be prevented, early recurrence can sometimes develop, even in the setting of therapeutic anticoagulation.

Anticoagulation has been proven to reduce mortality in acute PE. When DVT or PE is diagnosed, anticoagulation should be instituted immediately unless contraindications are present. It is appropriate to initiate therapy in patients with a high index of suspicion for acute PE even while diagnostic testing is underway, as long as the risk of anticoagulation is not excessive.

If possible, warfarin therapy should be initiated within the first 24 hours, but premature initiation of warfarin without a heparin preparation may intensify hypercoagulability and increase the clot burden due to the short half-life of anticoagulation factors that are dissipated by warfarin. Factor VII, which is the primary clotting factor affecting the prothrombin time, has a half-life of about 6 hours. Definitive anticoagulation requires the depletion of factor II (thrombin), a process that takes approximately 5 days. Thus, at least 5 days of intravenous heparin is generally recommended. Heparin should be maintained at a therapeutic level until two consecutive therapeutic international normalized ratio values of 2.0 to 3.0 have been documented at least 24 hours apart.

The LMWH preparations have tremendous advantages over unfractionated heparin and have dramatically changed the treatment of thromboembolic disease (see Tables 78–5 and 78–6). Among the differences between standard, unfractionated heparin and LMWH is the greater bioavailability of the LMWHs (Tables 94–4 and 94–5). The dosing of these drugs is thus more predictable. They can be administered once or twice per day subcutaneously even at therapeutic doses and do not require monitoring of the activated partial thromboplastin time (aPTT). In addition, LMWHs have a more profound effect in inhibiting clotting factor Xa relative to factor IIa (thrombin). A number of clinical trials have strongly suggested the efficacy and safety of LMWH for treatment of established acute proximal DVT using recurrent symptomatic venous thromboembolism as the primary outcome measure,[1,2] and efficacy has been demonstrated for acute PE as well.[3] The incidence of recurrent DVT or PE and bleeding in these trials indicates that LMWH preparations are at least as effective and as safe as unfractionated heparin; for example, the risk of heparin-induced thrombocytopenia is much lower with LMWH than with standard heparin (Chapter 33). Two recent meta-analyses have also concluded that the mortality rate is lower in

Table 94–4 • A COMPARISON OF LOW-MOLECULAR-WEIGHT HEPARIN WITH UNFRACTIONATED HEPARIN

CHARACTERISTIC	UNFRACTIONATED HEPARIN	LMWH
Mean molecular weight	12,000–15,000	4000–6000
Protein binding	Substantial	Minimal
Platelet inhibition	Substantial	Minimal
Anti-Xa activity	Substantial	Substantial
Anti-IIa activity	Substantial	Minimal
Vascular permeability	Moderate	None
Microvascular permeability	Substantial	Minimal

Heparin-induced thrombocytopenia is less common than with unfractionated heparin, but it can occur.
LMWH = Low-molecular-weight heparin.

Table 94–5 • POTENTIAL ADVANTAGES OF LOW-MOLECULAR-WEIGHT HEPARINS OVER UNFRACTIONATED HEPARIN

Similar or superior efficacy
Similar or superior safety
Superior bioavailability
Once or twice daily dosing
No laboratory monitoring*
Less phlebotomy
Subcutaneous administration†
Earlier ambulation
Home therapy in certain patient subsets

*No monitoring needed for either prophylaxis or treatment. In a few specific settings (renal insufficiency, body weight less than 40 kg, and obesity with weight greater than 120 kg), measuring anti-factor Xa levels are recommended to aid in dosing.
†For either prophylaxis or treatment.

patients receiving LMWH than in those receiving unfractionated heparin.

Anti-factor Xa levels may be used to monitor LMWH in certain settings, such as in morbidly obese patients, very small patients (<40 kg), pregnant patients, and patients with renal insufficiency; it is unnecessary to monitor other patients with anti-factor Xa levels. Because LMWHs are renally metabolized, they should be used with caution when the creatinine clearance is less than 30 mL per minute. There is not clear agreement on a creatinine clearance below which LMWH should be avoided entirely or on a weight limit above which these drugs should not be used. Some believe that an upper limit of approximately 120 to 150 kg is reasonable, with intravenous standard heparin being used in larger patients. In a number of large randomized trials, therapy with LMWH has been safely initiated at home or continued at home after a brief hospitalization. [4]

In the United States, two LMWH preparations are currently approved by the Food and Drug Administration (FDA) for treatment of patients with DVT with or without acute PE. Enoxaparin is approved for both inpatient and outpatient use at a dose of 1 mg/kg subcutaneously every 12 hours or as 1.5 mg/kg once daily for inpatient use; both doses are as effective and safe as unfractionated heparin. [1] The second preparation, tinzaparin, is administered as 175 units once daily, with the FDA-approval being based on therapy of inpatients with DVT.

When standard, unfractionated continuous intravenous heparin is initiated, the aPTT should be followed at 6-hour intervals until it is consistently in the therapeutic range of 1.5 to 2.0 times control values. This range corresponds to a heparin level of 0.2 to 0.4 U/mL as measured by protamine sulfate titration. Achieving a therapeutic aPTT within 24 hours after PE has been documented to reduce recurrences. Heparin should be administered as an intravenous bolus of 5000 units followed by a maintenance dose of at least 30,000 to 40,000 units per 24 hours by continuous infusion. The lower dose is administered if the patient is considered at high risk for bleeding. This aggressive approach decreases the risk of subtherapeutic anticoagulation. An alternative regimen consisting of a bolus of 80 U/kg followed by

18 U/kg/hr has been recommended. Further adjustment of the heparin dose should also be based on weight.

Proximal lower extremity thrombosis is more likely to result in PE, whereas calf thrombi should either be followed for proximal extension over 10 to 14 days with noninvasive leg testing or treated with anticoagulation (Chapters 33 and 78). Documented proximal DVT or PE should be treated for 3 to 6 months. Treatment over a more extended interval is appropriate when significant risk factors persist, when thromboembolism is idiopathic, or when previous episodes of venous thromboembolism have been documented. For idiopathic VTE, low intensity warfarin (INR goal 1.5–2.0) probably should be continued indefinitely. [5]

Newer antithrombotic agents are being investigated. Heparin and LMWH work indirectly, requiring antithrombin III as a cofactor; by comparison, hirudin is a direct thrombin inhibitor that has several advantages over heparin, including efficacy against fibrin clot-bound thrombin (Chapter 33). This drug, derived from the saliva of the medicinal leach (*Hirudo medicinalis*), does not require cofactors and is not inactivated by platelet factor 4 or plasma proteins. More data are available for hirudin and related agents in acute coronary syndromes than in venous thromboembolism. As with heparin, these direct thrombin inhibitors have very narrow therapeutic indices. Currently, ximelagatran, an oral direct thrombin inhibitor, is being studied extensively in hopes of simplifying the treatment of acute venous thromboembolism. A disadvantage of the direct thrombin inhibitors is lack of reversibility.

Bleeding is the major complication of anticoagulation. The rates of major bleeding in recent trials are less than 5% using heparin by continuous infusion or high-dose subcutaneous injection. Heparin-induced thrombocytopenia (defined as a decrease in the platelet count to less than 30 to 50% of the baseline level or to less than 150,000/mm³) typically develops 5 or more days after the initiation of heparin therapy (Chapter 33). Either venous or arterial thrombosis may occur. The syndrome is caused by heparin-dependent IgG antibodies that activate platelets via their Fc receptors. If a patient is placed on heparin for venous thromboembolism and the platelet count progressively decreases to 100,000/mm³ or less, all heparin therapy should be discontinued.

Both argatroban and lepirudin have been FDA-approved for use in the setting of venous thromboembolism with heparin-induced thrombocytopenia (Chapter 33). Argatroban is an arginine derivative that interacts only with the active site of thrombin. It is metabolized in the liver, which generates at least three active intermediates. The half-life of argatroban is 45 minutes, but it is prolonged in patients with hepatic dysfunction. Lepirudin is excreted by the kidneys, so the dosage must be reduced in renal insufficiency; patients on dialysis should receive lepirudin with caution and at a reduced dose. The circulating half-life is only 1.3 hours in patients with normal renal function but may be as long as 2 days in patients with advanced renal failure. Although there is no antidote for lepirudin at present, the short half-life in patients with normal renal function allows for rapid correction of a prolonged aPTT.

Bleeding related to warfarin increases with the intensity and duration of therapy. Warfarin-induced skin necrosis is a rare but serious complication mandating immediate cessation of the drug. It is related, at least in some patients, to protein C or S deficiency. Warfarin crosses the placenta and may cause fetal malformations if used during pregnancy.

VENA CAVA INTERRUPTION

If a patient cannot be anticoagulated, IVC filter placement can prevent lower extremity thrombi from embolizing to the lungs. The primary indications for IVC filter placement include contraindications to anticoagulation, recurrent embolism while on adequate therapy, and significant bleeding complications during anticoagulation. IVC filters are sometimes placed in the setting of massive PE when it is believed that any further emboli might be lethal, particularly if thrombolytic therapy is contraindicated. A number of filter designs exist but the Greenfield filter has been most widely used. Filters can be inserted via the jugular or femoral vein. These devices are effective, and complications including insertion-related problems and migration of the filter are unusual. More recently, temporary filters have been used in patients in whom the risk of bleeding appears to be short term; such devices can be removed up to 2 weeks later.

THROMBOLYTIC THERAPY

Thrombolytic agents activate plasminogen to form plasmin, which then results in fibrinolysis as well as fibrinogenolysis (Chapter 33). Because anticoagulants do not actively lyse emboli, thrombolytic agents are considered in certain settings to hasten the reduction in thromboembolic burden. The use of thrombolytic therapy is recommended in patients with hemodynamic instability (hypotension) and/or severely compromised oxygenation. An argument can also be made for thrombolytic therapy when the embolic burden approaches the equivalent of one half of the pulmonary vascular bed, even without clear hemodynamic stability, or when extensive DVT accompanies submassive embolism. Currently approved drugs for the treatment of massive PE, a situation in which thrombolysis appears to result in more rapid resolution of abnormal right ventricular function, include streptokinase, urokinase, and recombinant tissue-type plasminogen activator (t-PA) (Table 94–6). A recent, randomized, trial suggested that patients with echocardiographic right ventricular dysfunction without hypotension or severe hypoxemia had a lower mortality with thrombolytic therapy (alteplase) compared with heparin alone.[6] There are no clear data proving that one thrombolytic agent is superior to the others. Catheter-directed administration of intraembolic thrombolytic therapy remains experimental.

Coagulation assays are unnecessary during thrombolysis because the approved regimens are administered as fixed doses. Heparin should be withheld until the thrombolytic infusion is completed. The aPTT is then determined, and heparin is initiated without a loading dose if this value is less than twice the upper limit of normal. If the aPTT exceeds this value, the test is repeated every 4 hours until it is safe to proceed with heparin.

Hemorrhage is the primary adverse effect associated with thrombolytic therapy, and this therapy is contraindicated in patients at high risk for bleeding (Table 94–7). Both lysis of hemostatic fibrin plugs and fibrinogenolysis can lead to bleeding complications, which commonly occur at sites of invasive procedures such as pulmonary arteriography or arterial line placement. If possible, invasive procedures should be minimized. The most devastating complication associated with this form of treatment is intracranial hemorrhage, which occurs in less than 1% of patients. Retroperitoneal hemorrhage may result

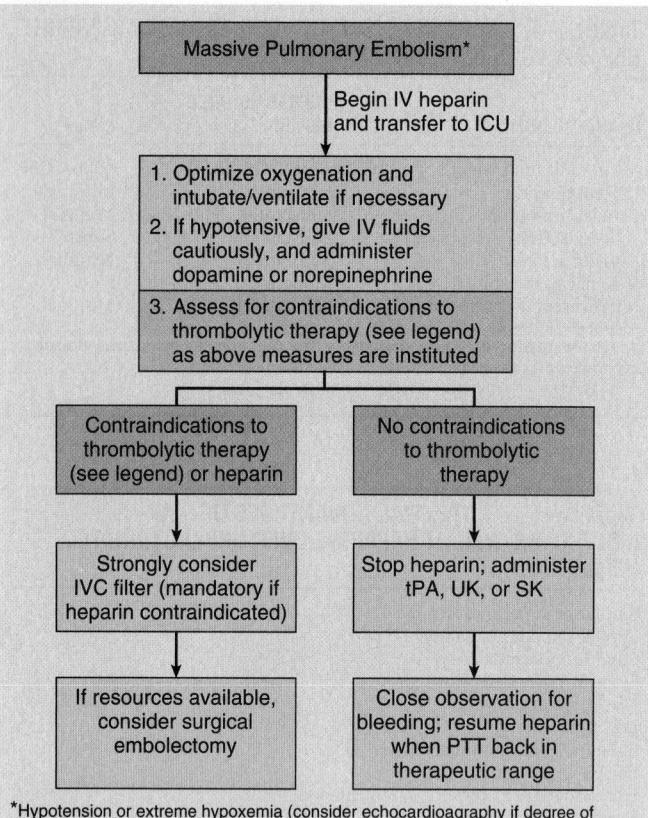

*Hypotension or extreme hypoxemia (consider echocardioagraphy if degree of stability unclear). In patients with right ventricular dysfunction by echocardiography, thrombolytic therapy should be *considered* even in the absence of other indications.

FIGURE 94–4 • An algorithm for the approach to the patient with massive acute pulmonary embolism. Contraindications to thrombolytic therapy include intracranial abnormality, gastrointestinal or other bleeding, bleeding diathesis, surgery within previous 10 days, and pregnancy (see text). ICU = intensive care unit; IV = intravenous; IVC = inferior vena cava; PTT = partial thromboplastin time; SK = streptokinase; tPA = tissue-type plasminogen activator; UK = urokinase.

from a vascular puncture above the inguinal ligament and may be life-threatening.

HEMODYNAMIC MANAGEMENT OF MASSIVE PULMONARY EMBOLISM

Massive PE should always be suspected in the setting of the sudden onset of hypotension, extreme hypoxemia, electromechanical dissociation, or cardiac arrest. Once massive PE associated with hypotension and/or severe hypoxemia is suspected, supportive treatment is immediately initiated (Fig. 94–4). Intravenous saline should be infused rapidly but cautiously because right ventricular function is often markedly compromised. Dopamine or norepinephrine appears appropriate in massive PE and should be administered if the blood pressure is not rapidly restored. Because death in this setting results from right ventricular failure, dobutamine has been recommended to augment right ventricular output; however, dobutamine may also worsen hypotension. Oxygen therapy is administered, and thrombolytic therapy is considered as described above. Intubation and mechanical ventilation are instituted to support respiratory failure. Pulmonary embolectomy may be appropriate in patients who have massive embolism and cannot receive thrombolytic therapy.

Chronic Thromboembolic Pulmonary Hypertension

Although most cases of acute PE resolve with therapy, occasionally a substantial residual thromboembolic burden persists or develops over time. If the obstruction becomes extensive, pulmonary hypertension develops (Chapter 64). This syndrome most commonly occurs in patients 40 to 70 years of age, but can occur at any age. Fatigue and dyspnea with exertion are the most common complaints.

Table 94–6 • THROMBOLYTIC THERAPY FOR ACUTE PULMONARY EMBOLISM: REGIMENS APPROVED FOR USE IN THE UNITED STATES

Streptokinase: 250,000 U IV (loading dose over 30 min); then 100,000 U/hr for 24 hr*
Urokinase: 2000 U/lb IV (loading dose over 10 min); then 2000 U/lb/hr for 12 to 24 hr†
Tissue-type plasminogen activator: 100 mg IV over 2 hr

*Streptokinase administered over 24 to 72 hr (at this loading dose and rate) has also been approved for use in patients with extensive DVT.
†Urokinase not currently available.

Table 94–7 • CONTRAINDICATIONS TO THROMBOLYTIC THERAPY IN PULMONARY EMBOLISM*

ABSOLUTE
Intracranial surgery or pathology
Active or recent internal bleeding

RELATIVE
Bleeding diathesis/thrombocytopenia
Uncontrolled severe hypertension
Cardiopulmonary resuscitation
Surgery within the previous 10 days
Pregnancy

*The use of thrombolytic therapy depends on the severity of pulmonary embolism; resultant hypotension is the clearest indication. There should be a lower threshold to administer thrombolytic therapy in the setting of a contraindication when a patient is extremely unstable from life-threatening pulmonary embolism.

The nonspecific nature of these findings may substantially delay the correct diagnosis. At least 50% of patients who develop chronic thromboembolic pulmonary hypertension have no documented history of previous thromboembolic disease. The physical examination generally reveals a right ventricular heave, a loud P2, and tricuspid regurgitation consistent with pulmonary hypertension. In 20% of patients, one or more murmurs may be auscultated over the lung fields. The chest radiograph usually shows right ventricular enlargement and enlarged main pulmonary arteries. The electrocardiogram often has changes consistent with pulmonary hypertension (Chapter 50). Arterial blood gases generally reveal hypoxemia with a widened alveolar-arterial difference, although some patients may demonstrate hypoxemia only with exercise. Echocardiography documents pulmonary hypertension and enlargement of the right ventricle. Spiral CT scanning may reveal evidence of chronic thrombi or other rare causes of pulmonary hypertension, such as mediastinal fibrosis. The ventilation-perfusion scan is usually high probability for PE but occasionally is less impressive. Right heart catheterization and pulmonary arteriography should be performed, both to establish the diagnosis with certainty and to determine operability. Pulmonary angioscopy frequently has proven complementary to arteriography in assessing these patients.

When chronic thromboembolic pulmonary hypertension is diagnosed, anticoagulation should be instituted and an IVC filter should be placed. Pulmonary thromboendarterectomy should be performed via median sternotomy on cardiopulmonary bypass; the overall mortality rate is less than 5%. Lung transplantation can be performed in patients in whom thrombi are too distal to extract if they meet appropriate criteria (Chapter 97).

Prognosis

In the International Cooperative Pulmonary Embolism Registry, the 3-month mortality rate was 17.5% and PE was the principal cause of death among 2454 consecutive patients with PE. In the PIOPED, the mortality rate was approximately 15%, but only 10% of deaths during the first year of follow-up were attributed to PE. Mean 1-month mortality rates of treated and untreated PE have been estimated at 8% and 30%, respectively.

Although a small percentage of patients with acute PE ultimately develop chronic dyspnea and hypoxemia due to chronic thromboembolic pulmonary hypertension, most patients who survive the acute episode have no long-term pulmonary sequelae. However, chronic leg pain and swelling from DVT (postphlebitic syndrome) may result in significant morbidity.

Prevention

A substantial reduction in the incidence of DVT can be achieved when patients at risk receive appropriate prophylaxis (see Table 78–4). Such preventive measures appear to be grossly underused. For example, the risk of DVT after total hip or knee replacement is 50% or greater without prophylaxis. The efficacy of LMWH has been clearly demonstrated in these settings. In general medical patients at risk for venous thrombosis, either LMWH (enoxaparin 40 mg subcutaneously once daily) or subcutaneous heparin (5000 units every 8 hours) is usually adequate. Although 5000 units of heparin every 12 hours has been commonly used, there are less data to support this regimen. Intermittent pneumatic compression devices should be used when prophylactic doses of LMWH or heparin are contraindicated. Both methods combined would be reasonable in patients deemed to be at exceptionally high risk, but an additional reduction in risk in such patients has not been substantiated.

Three LMWH preparations (enoxaparin, dalteparin, and ardeparin) are available for specific prophylactic indications (Chapter 33). At present, enoxaparin has the most prophylaxis indications, including patients undergoing total hip replacement, total knee replacement, and general abdominal surgery, as well as general medical patients. In addition, fondaparinux, a pentasaccharide (very small LMWH), has recently been approved for several orthopedic prophylactic settings including total hip and knee replacement and hip fracture surgery; it is a pure anti-factor Xa inhibitor with a longer half-life than other larger LMWH preparations. It appears quite effective, but at present there is not a way to reverse this drug in the setting of bleeding. Other LMWHs are approximately 70% reversible with protamine sulfate.

Every hospitalized patient should be assessed for the need for such prophylactic measures, and all hospitals should strongly consider formulating their own written guidelines for each particular clinical setting based on the available medical literature.

Nonthrombotic Pulmonary Emboli

Because of the venous blood return to the lungs, the pulmonary vascular bed is exposed to a wide variety of potentially obstructing and detrimental substances. These substances, which may be exogenous or endogenous in origin, may result in a number of consequences, including dyspnea, chest pain, hypoxemia, and sometimes death.

FAT EMBOLISM. Fat embolism generally occurs in the setting of traumatic fracture of long bones (Chapter 108) and is usually a more impressive clinical syndrome when larger bones and multiple fractures are involved. However, orthopedic procedures and trauma to other fat-rich tissues such as the liver or subcutaneous tissue can occasionally result in similar consequences. After the traumatic event, there is generally a delay of 24 to 48 hours before symptoms develop. As neutral fat enters the vascular system, a characteristic syndrome of dyspnea, petechiae, and mental confusion often develops. It is not clear why the syndrome develops in some patients and not in others, even when the extent of injury is comparable, but it is possible that the presence of a patent foramen ovale could render patients more susceptible.

The pathophysiologic consequences of fat embolism derive from both obstruction of multiple vessels by neutral fat particles and from the deleterious effects of free fatty acids released from neutral fat by lipases. These free fatty acids cause diffuse vasculitis with capillary leakage from cerebral, pulmonary, and other vascular beds.

The diagnosis is made from the clinical and radiographic findings in the setting of risk factors such as surgery or trauma. Although fat droplets (by oil red O stain) in bronchoalveolar lavage fluid may be suggestive of fat embolism, this finding does not appear to be sensitive or specific. The diagnosis of fat embolism syndrome remains a diagnosis of exclusion and is based on clinical criteria. Although clinically apparent fat embolism syndrome is uncommon, it also may be masked by the effects of concomitant injuries in more severely injured patients (Chapter 108).

Treatment is supportive, including oxygen and mechanical ventilation, and the prognosis is generally good. Corticosteroid therapy remains controversial.

AMNIOTIC FLUID EMBOLISM. Although uncommon, amniotic fluid embolism represents one of the leading causes of maternal death in the United States. This syndrome occurs during or after delivery when amniotic fluid gains access to uterine venous channels and then to the pulmonary and general circulations. The delivery may be either spontaneous or by cesarean section and usually has been without complication. There are no identifiable risk factors in either the mother or the baby. The syndrome is heralded by the sudden onset of severe respiratory distress; hypotension and death frequently result. The primary mechanism of injury appears to involve the thromboplastic activity of amniotic fluid, which leads to extensive fibrin deposition in the pulmonary vasculature and sometimes in other organs. A severe consumptive coagulopathy ensues, with marked hypofibrinogenemia. After the acute event, an enhanced fibrinolytic state often develops. Left ventricular dysfunction may occur, possibly due to the myocardial depressant effect of amniotic fluid. The resulting pulmonary edema may be both hydrostatic and noncardiogenic. The differential diagnosis includes pulmonary thromboembolism, septic and hemorrhagic shock, venous air embolism, aspiration pneumonia, heart failure (from acute myocardial infarction or other causes), placentae abruptio, and ruptured uterus. The diagnosis may be suspected based on the clinical picture. Examination of the pulmonary arterial blood may or may not reveal the amorphous fragments of vernix caseosa, squamous cells, or mucin. Although administration of heparin, antifibrinolytic agents such as α-aminocaproic acid, and cryoprecipitate have been suggested, the primary treatment is supportive, with oxygen, mechanical ventilation, and any necessary hemodynamic support.

AIR EMBOLISM. The consequences of venous air embolism range from none to death. The incidence of this entity reflects the variety of invasive surgical and medical procedures now available, the frequent use of indwelling venous and arterial catheters, and the frequency of thoracic and other forms of trauma. With venous embolism in the setting of a patent foramen ovale, embolization to the coronary or cerebral circulation is of most concern. In the absence of a patent foramen ovale, the lungs can filter modest amounts of air, but large single or continuous episodes of air embolism can still gain access to the systemic arterial circulation. Symptoms and signs are dependent upon the severity of the episode. Air in the systemic circulation may be difficult to recognize because only small quantities may cause significant symptoms, yet intravascular air clears quickly. Dyspnea, wheezing, chest pain, cough, agitation, confusion, tachycardia, and hypotension may be evident. A "mill wheel murmur" (air in the right ventricle) may sometimes be auscultated. Hypoxemia and hypercapnia are present in severe cases, and the chest radiograph may reveal pulmonary edema or air fluid levels. The treatment of venous air embolism includes immediate placement of the patient in the Trendelenburg/left lateral decubitus position and administration of 100% oxygen. If a central venous catheter is in place near the right atrium, air aspiration should be attempted. Occasionally, hyperbaric oxygen is indicated. Anticonvulsants are administered in the presence of seizures.

SCHISTOSOMIASIS. Schistosomiasis (Chapter 402) causes severe pulmonary vascular obstruction and pulmonary hypertension from both anatomic obstruction by the organism itself and an inflammatory vasculitic response. In endemic areas (e.g., Egypt), schistosomal disease is a common cause of cor pulmonale. The liver is always involved, usually quite extensively, before pulmonary involvement occurs. The disease is refractory to treatment unless it is detected before extensive hepatic and pulmonary inflammation occurs.

SEPTIC EMBOLISM. Septic embolism was first noted as a complication of septic pelvic thrombophlebitis owing to septic abortion or postpartum uterine infection (Chapter 253). Now, however, intravenous drug abuse and infections caused by indwelling intravenous catheters are the most common causes (Chapter 30).

OTHER EMBOLI. A variety of other substances can also embolize to the lungs. Cancer cells may enter and adhere to pulmonary vessels, occasionally mimicking PE (Chapter 188). Brain tissue has been discovered in the lungs after head trauma, and liver cells have been found after abdominal trauma. Bone marrow has been reported in lung tissue after cardiopulmonary resuscitation.

Noninfectious vasculitic-thrombotic complications also occur in intravenous drug users. Materials such as talc, used to "cut" heroin or cocaine and occasionally the drugs themselves may provoke vascular inflammation and secondary thrombosis (Chapter 30). Perfusion scans occasionally demonstrate segmental or smaller defects. Distinguishing these from venous thromboemboli can be difficult.

Grade Ⓐ

1. Merli G, Spiro T, Olsson C-G, et al: Subcutaneous enoxaparin once or twice daily compared with intravenous unfractionated heparin for treatment of venous thromboembolic disease. Ann Intern Med 2001;134:191–202.
2. Hull RD, Raskob GE, Pineo GF, et al: Subcutaneous low-molecular-weight heparin compared with continuous intravenous heparin in the treatment of proximal-vein thrombosis. N Engl J Med 1992;326:975–982.
3. Simonneau G, Sors H, Charbonnier B, et al: A comparison of low-molecular-weight heparin with unfractionated heparin for acute pulmonary embolism. N Engl J Med 1997;337;663–669.
4. Levine M, Gent M, Hirsh J, et al: A comparison of low molecular-weight-heparin administered primarily at home with unfractionated heparin administered in the hospital for proximal deep vein thrombosis. N Engl J Med 1996;334:677–681.
5. Ridker PM, Goldhaber SZ, Danielson E, et al: Long-term, low-intensity warfarin therapy for the prevention of recurrent venous thromboembolism. N Engl J Med 2003;348:1478–1480.
6. Konstantinides S, Geibel A, Heusel G, et al: Heparin plus alteplase compared with heparin alone in patients with submassive pulmonary embolism. N Engl J Med 2002;347:1143–1150.

SUGGESTED READINGS
Dalen JE, Hirsh J, Guyatt GH (eds): Sixth American College of Chest Physicians Consensus Conference on Antithrombotic Therapy. Chest 2001;119:1S–370S. *Guidelines for prophylaxis and treatment of venous thromboembolism using an evidence-based approach.*
Dolovich L, Ginsberg J, Douketis J, et al: A meta-analysis comparing low-molecular-weight heparins with unfractionated heparin in the treatment of venous thromboembolism: Examining some unanswered questions regarding location of treatment, product type, and dosing frequency. Arch Intern Med 2000;160:181–188. *Low-molecular-weight heparins are at least as effective as standard heparin in preventing recurrent venous thromboembolism. Interestingly, use of low-molecular-weight heparins was associated with a statistically significant decrease in total mortality, although not reduction in fatal pulmonary embolism.*
Musset D, Parent F, Meyer G, et al: Diagnostic strategy for patients with suspected pulmonary embolism: a prospective multicentre outcome study. Lancet 2002;360:1914–1920. *If the clinical probability of PE is low or intermediate and if a spinal CT and venous ultrasound are negative, anticoagulant therapy can be safely withheld.*
Perrier A, Howarth N, Didier D, et al: Performance of helical computed tomography in unselected outpatients with suspected pulmonary embolism. Ann Intern Med

2001;135:88–97. *These investigators found a sensitivity of 70% for helical (spiral) CT in patients presenting with suspected pulmonary embolism.*
Wells PS, Anderson DR, Rodger M, et al: Excluding pulmonary embolism at the bedside without diagnostic imaging: Management of patients with suspected pulmonary embolism presenting to the emergency department by using a simple clinical model and D-dimer. Ann Intern Med 2001;135:98–107. *Using a pretest probability model, a low clinical suspicion for pulmonary embolism combined with a negative SimpliRed D-dimer assay, eliminated the need for imaging studies.*

95 DISEASES OF THE DIAPHRAGM, CHEST WALL, PLEURA, AND MEDIASTINUM

Bartolome R. Celli

THE DIAPHRAGM

The diaphragm, the most important muscle of respiration, is shaped like a thin dome and separates the thoracic and abdominal cavities. It has two components—the central noncontractile tendon and the muscle fibers that arise from it and radiate down and outward to insert distally in the circumferential caudal limits of the rib cage. There is a hiatus for the structures that pass from thorax to abdomen. The diaphragm is neurologically controlled by the phrenic nerve, the motor neurons of which arise in the cervical spinal cord at levels C3 to C5. The anatomic arrangement of the diaphragm and its coupling to the rib cage and abdomen explain its mechanical action. Diaphragmatic contraction displaces the abdominal contents downward and raises the ribs outward, resulting in the negative intrapleural inspiratory pressure. Like the heart, the diaphragm and, to a lesser degree, the other respiratory muscles must intermittently contract throughout a person's life. Unlike the heart, it has no intrinsic contractile mechanism, and the respiratory cycle is regulated by a complex set of centrally organized neurons and several peripheral feedback mechanisms that synchronize the diaphragm with many other muscles. The diaphragm serves other nonrespiratory functions such as speech, defecation, and parturition. The blood supply to the diaphragm is rich and is arranged to minimize interruption during contraction. Nevertheless, the muscle itself is highly oxygen dependent.

DYSFUNCTION AND FATIGUE. Diaphragmatic dysfunction is most frequently caused by lung hyperinflation—acute as in asthma or chronic as in chronic obstructive pulmonary disease (COPD). Hyperinflation shortens the diaphragm and changes its shape to a flatter one in which the horizontal fibers do not generate the normal expanding action on the thorax but rather an inward retraction of the lower rib cage (i.e., Hoover's sign in COPD). These changes, coupled with increased airways resistance and decreased lung and chest wall compliance, result in increased work of breathing. If the increased energy demand outstrips the energy supply, the muscle fatigues and ventilation may fail.

Diaphragmatic fatigue can be determined by using pressure measurements across the diaphragm (transdiaphragmatic pressure) or by the more elaborate power spectrum analysis of electromyographic signals. Both correlate well with the simpler clinical sign of rapid and shallow breathing. As fatigue progresses, ventilation is maintained by intermittent expansions of rib cage and abdomen (respiratory alternans) and then paradoxical inward abdominal motion during inspiration (abdominal paradox). A number of strategies can improve diaphragmatic function in impending fatigue (Table 95–1); if fatigue results in hypercapnia and acidosis, the respiratory muscles must be rested with noninvasive or invasive mechanical ventilation.∎

DISORDERS OF DIAPHRAGMATIC MOTION. Unilateral diaphragmatic paralysis is usually secondary to phrenic nerve involvement by a tumor, with bronchogenic carcinoma being the most frequent. Paralysis may result from neurologic diseases such as myelitis, encephalitis, poliomyelitis, and herpes zoster; from trauma to the thorax or cervical spine; or from compression by benign processes such as a substernal thyroid, aortic aneurysm, and infectious collections. With the advent of cardiac surgery, paralysis secondary to phrenic nerve cooling has increased. Occasionally, the paralysis may be idiopathic. The diagnosis is suspected when, on the chest radiograph, the diaphragmatic leaflet is elevated and is confirmed fluoroscopically by observing

Table 95-1 • THERAPEUTIC MODALITIES TO IMPROVE DIAPHRAGMATIC FUNCTION

REDUCE MECHANICAL LOAD
1. Decrease airways resistance (administer bronchodilators, treat infection, decrease inflammation).
2. Reduce hyperinflation.
3. Decrease ventilatory requirement (administer oxygen, control fever, avoid caloric loads).

IMPROVE RESPIRATORY MUSCLE CONTRACTILITY AND ENDURANCE
1. Administer oxygen therapy.
2. Improve nutrition.
3. Improve cardiovascular performance.
4. Correct electrolytes (sodium, potassium, calcium, phosphorus).
5. Administer drugs that improve contractility (β_2-agonist, caffeine).
6. Check for hypothyroidism or drugs that impair contractility (aminoglycosides).
7. Give ventilatory muscle training.

IMPROVE RESPIRATORY MUSCLE COORDINATION AND ENERGY CONSERVATION

REHABILITATION

RESPIRATORY MUSCLE RESTING

---

paradoxical diaphragmatic motion on sniff and cough. In patients with normal lungs, unilateral paralysis is usually asymptomatic and rarely requires treatment. Irreversible symptomatic unilateral paralysis may be treated with surgical plication of the affected hemidiaphragm. Bilateral paralysis usually results from high cervical trauma (C3 to C5), neuropathies, or myopathies. The myopathy may be generalized (muscular dystrophy, polymyositis, hypothyroidism) or limited, primarily affecting the diaphragm (acid maltase deficiency, collagen vascular disorders). In many cases, the cause remains unknown. Patients become symptomatic early. The dyspnea is characteristically worsened by the supine position because abdominal contents displace the diaphragm into the thorax, resulting in a significant (>500 mL) decrease in the vital capacity and in oxygen saturation. Fluoroscopy is not reliable because the flaccid diaphragm may lag behind the rib cage expansion when accessory muscles contract, thus giving the impression of diaphragmatic contraction. The diagnosis is suspected by the presence of inspiratory abdominal paradoxical retraction. It is confirmed by measuring transdiaphragmatic pressure with and without electromyographic recording. Phrenic nerve conduction establishes the diagnosis of neuropathy. Treatment of ventilatory failure secondary to bilateral paralysis consists of intermittent mechanical ventilation. In some cases, such as cardiac surgery, the paralysis recovers, and ventilation may be discontinued. In permanent paralysis with intact muscle function (e.g., high quadriplegic), diaphragmatic pacing has been life-saving.

Hiccup (singultus) is a disorder produced by spasm of the diaphragm followed by closure of the glottis during an inspiratory effort. Hiccups are usually self-limited but may persist for days or weeks. In most patients a cause is never found, but hiccups may occasionally be a sign of serious disease such as a central nervous system disorder (encephalitis, stroke, tumor), uremia, herpes zoster, and pleural or abdominal processes that irritate the diaphragm. Prolonged hiccups are sometimes psychogenic. In general, hiccups subside spontaneously or when the initiating disease improves. When hiccups are chronic or debilitating, local anesthesia or phrenic nerve crushing may be required (permanent paralysis may occur with the latter). Diaphragmatic flutter is a rare disorder in which rhythmic contractions of the diaphragm occur at a rate of 1 to 8 per second; the cause and treatment are similar to those of hiccups.

Diaphragmatic hernias occur through congenitally weak or incompletely fused areas of the diaphragm, through the esophageal hiatus (>70% of all hernias), or because of traumatic rupture of the muscle. Anterior hernias occur through the foramina of Morgagni, are rare, and tend to occur in obese patients; they usually show as a rounded density in the right cardiophrenic angle. Posterior hernias through the foramina of Bochdalek are more common, especially in infants; they occur more frequently on the left. Traumatic diaphragmatic hernias may result from penetrating injuries or abdominal compression. Diaphragmatic hernias usually contain omentum but may also contain stomach, bowel, or liver anteriorly or kidney and spleen posteriorly.

Symptom severity depends on the extension of abdominal contents into the thorax and the presence of strangulation. Hernias may be asymptomatic for several years before respiratory and abdominal symptoms occur.

Eventration may resemble a hernia but consists of a localized elevation of the diaphragm resulting from impaired muscle development or weakness. Eventration is more frequent in the right anteromedial portion and tends to occur in middle-aged obese persons; once differentiated from neoplasm, it rarely requires surgical treatment.

A diaphragmatic hernia is suspected on chest radiography and in some cases when there is borborygmus over the chest. Computed tomographic (CT) scans, gastrointestinal contrast films, radioisotope scan of the liver, and induction of a pneumoperitoneum with a follow-up film help establish the diagnosis. In infants, large hernias may compromise ventilation, requiring immediate surgical correction. In the asymptomatic adult with previous evidence of a hernia, observation is indicated. Surgery may be needed for diagnosis or to relieve strangulation of sac contents.

THE CHEST WALL

The chest wall, an integral part of the ventilatory pump, consists of the bony thoracic cage (ribs, sternum, and vertebrae) and the various muscles of respiration. Besides the diaphragm, the intercostal and scalene muscles are active even during quiet breathing in normal persons. Other muscles such as the sternocleidomastoid, pectoralis minor and major, serratus anterior, latissimus dorsi, and trapezius partake in respiration during increased ventilatory demand. Even the abdominal muscles can participate in ventilation by contracting during exhalation. The thoracic cage is a major determinant of ventilation and of static and dynamic lung volumes. Diseases that disrupt the system alter the ventilation and ventilation-perfusion relationship, thus causing hypoxemia or hypercapnia. Primary disorders of the chest wall may occur from impairments of the neuromuscular apparatus or the bony thoracic cage. Alterations in the neuromuscular apparatus are discussed elsewhere in the text; primary alterations of the bony thoracic cage are discussed in this section.

Diseases of the bony thoracic cage (Table 95–2) are all linked by a similar pathophysiologic process: (1) changes in chest wall compliance, (2) variable lung compression, (3) ventilation-perfusion imbalance, (4) alveolar hypoventilation, and (5) pulmonary hypertension and cor pulmonale. Clinical symptoms include dyspnea without significant cough, sputum, or pain. Physical examination usually establishes the diagnosis and helps determine the presence of cor pulmonale.

KYPHOSCOLIOSIS. Deformities of the dorsolumbar spine are the most common causes of symptomatic derangements of the chest wall. Scoliosis consists of lateral angulation and rotation of the spine and is categorized as right (most frequent) or left according to the direction of the convexity of the curvature. Kyphosis is less important and consists of anteroposterior angulation of the spine.

The severity of scoliosis is quantified by measuring the angle (Cobb's angle) between the upper and lower portions of the spinal curve on a radiograph. Only when this angle exceeds 70 degrees is any abnormality of respiratory function detectable. When the angle is more than 120 degrees, dyspnea and respiratory failure are expected. The ribs over the convex side are separated and rotated posteriorly, giving rise to the kyphoscoliotic hump. On the concave side, the ribs are crowded, displaced anteriorly, and combined with decreased thoracic height. These abnormalities produce forward bulging of the anterior wall.

Table 95-2 • MOST IMPORTANT RIB CAGE DERANGEMENTS

SPINE
Scoliosis (idiopathic, congenital, paralytic)
Kyphosis
Ankylosing spondylitis

STERNUM, RIBS, OR PLEURA
Pectus excavatum
Thoracoplasty
Fibrothorax

Kyphoscoliosis is usually idiopathic and begins in childhood. Ventilatory failure may result in death in the fourth to sixth decade. If the scoliosis is not severe and progressive, life expectancy may be normal. Static lung volumes, chest wall, and, to a lesser degree, lung compliance are also decreased. Ventilation-perfusion imbalances result in hypoxemia. When the mechanical load, caused by progressive scoliosis or superimposed infection, is such that the muscles fail, the hypoxemia may be associated with hypercapnia. Blood gases may worsen during sleep and cause the frequent worsening of some patients with otherwise stable kyphoscoliosis.

Several therapeutic approaches are available. Surgical correction includes traction, plasters, and rods; the effects are mostly cosmetic, and improvement in pulmonary function is usually minimal. In hypoxemic patients, oxygen is beneficial. Intermittent positive-pressure ventilation increases tidal volume, temporarily improving compliance and lung volumes. In chronic ventilatory failure, nighttime ventilatory assistance is beneficial. Efforts must be made to induce the patient to stop smoking. Bronchospasm and respiratory infections must be treated aggressively. If obese, the patient should lose weight.

ANKYLOSING SPONDYLITIS. This inflammatory disease results in fusion of costotransverse and vertebral joints but may also involve sternomanubrial and clavicular joints (Chapter 279). With relative fixation of the rib cage in an inspiratory position, most of the ventilatory movement is performed by the diaphragm-abdomen, which is already placed in a mechanical disadvantage because of a normal or increased functional residual capacity. In contrast to kyphoscoliosis, cor pulmonale and ventilatory failure are rare. Some patients may develop upper lobe fibrosis with minimal alterations in gas exchange.

PECTUS EXCAVATUM. This congenital deformity of the lower portion of the sternum produces symmetrical bowing of the anterior ribs. In infants it tends to occur with multiple abnormalities and is associated with high mortality. It may also be associated with mitral valve prolapse. With severe deformity, the heart and mediastinal structures are laterally displaced. Although some patients may fail to increase cardiac output normally during exercise, functional impairment is usually mild. Surgical correction is mainly cosmetic.

THORACOPLASTY. Surgical procedures used from 1940 to 1950 to treat tuberculosis included resection of several ribs with collapse of the underlying lung. This procedure results in paradoxical retraction of that portion of the chest wall. Thoracoplasty was originally thought to have minimal physiologic consequences, but the incidence of cardiorespiratory failure is increased in these patients.

FIBROTHORAX. Resulting from pleural diseases such as hemothorax or asbestosis, fibrothorax is also considered a primary disease of chest wall because the lung itself may not be affected. It may result in ventilatory and cardiac failure. The treatment is similar to that for kyphoscoliosis. Pleurectomy may help patients with fibrothorax secondary to pleural fibrosis.

FLAIL CHEST. Flail chest is produced by double fractures of three or more adjacent ribs or by combined sternal and rib fractures. The flail segment paradoxically moves inward during inspiration. The inefficient ventilation increases the work of breathing, which may worsen ventilation owing to the frequent association with neuromuscular impairment. Flail chest occurs most frequently with accidental chest trauma and/or after cardiopulmonary resuscitation. Ventilation-perfusion mismatch and lung contusion cause hypoxemia. In most cases, supportive care with attention to oxygenation, clear airways, and infection prevention is the preferred therapy. Artificial ventilation should be reserved for patients with ventilatory failure. When the flail segment is large, chest fixation may be considered.

THE PLEURA

Anatomy and Physiology

The pleura consists of a layer of mesothelial cells with a smooth semitransparent appearance. The pleura is supported by a network of connective and fibroelastic tissue, lymphatics, and vessels. The mesothelial cells are rich in microvilli, and their most important function is to deliver glycoproteins rich in hyaluronic acid to decrease friction between lung and chest wall. The parietal pleura covers the surface of the chest wall, diaphragm, and mediastinum; it is supplied with blood from the systemic circulation and contains sensory nerves. The visceral pleura covers the surface of the lungs, including the interlobar fissures; its blood supply arises from the low-pressure pulmonary

---

Table 95–3 • MECHANISMS THAT LEAD TO ACCUMULATION OF PLEURAL FLUID

1. Increased hydrostatic pressure in microvascular circulation (heart failure)
2. Decreased oncotic pressure in microvascular circulation (severe hypoalbuminemia)
3. Decreased pressure in the pleural space (lung collapse)
4. Increased permeability of the microvascular circulation (pneumonia)
5. Impaired lymphatic drainage from the pleural space (malignant effusion)
6. Movement of fluid from peritoneal space (ascites)

---

circulation and has no sensory nerves. The two layers are separated by a virtual cavity, which is lubricated by 5 to 10 mL of fluid, facilitates lung expansion, and helps maintain lung inflation by coupling it with the chest wall.

Pleural fluid has a low protein concentration (<2 g/dL) with a pH and glucose value similar to that of blood. Pleural fluid is formed primarily from the parietal pleura, and part of its turnover depends on the same Starling forces that govern vascular and interstitial fluid exchange. The parietal pleura has a hydrostatic pressure similar to that of the systemic circulation (30 cm H$_2$O), whereas that of the visceral pleura depends on the pulmonary circulation (10 cm H$_2$O). Oncotic pressure is similar in both (25 cm H$_2$O), but the pressure within the pleural cavity is affected by the gravity gradient. Thus, the pleural space is heterogeneous with a nondependent portion in which Starling forces favor outpouring of fluid to the cavity and into parenchymal capillaries. The stomas, or "lacunae," which are present over the parietal surface of the low mediastinum, low chest wall, and diaphragm, seem to empty into lymphatics. These subpleural lymphatics represent the major pathway for liquid and solute drainage. Alterations of this formation-resorption mechanism frequently result in the accumulation of pleural fluid. Increases in hydrostatic forces or decreases in oncotic pressures result in low-protein "transudates." Increased outpouring by capillaries or cells and/or blocking of lymphatics results in high-protein "exudates" (Table 95–3).

Diagnosis

HISTORY AND PHYSICAL EXAMINATION. Although suggestive, a patient's history of pain, dyspnea, or cough is neither sensitive nor specific. These symptoms may be absent in some large effusions and in critically ill patients. When present, the pain is usually unilateral and sharp and worsens with inspiration or cough. It may radiate to the shoulder, neck, or abdomen. Dyspnea may result from compression of lung tissue and from mechanical alterations in the respiratory muscles as the fluid changes their length-tension relationship. The degree of dyspnea relates to fluid volume and intrathoracic pressure and their effect on mechanics and gas exchange. Pleural effusions in patients with minimal lung compromise are well tolerated, whereas similar effusions in patients with lung disease may cause ventilatory failure. The physical examination reveals decreased breath sounds and excursions in the affected hemithorax (splinting). Percussion reveals dullness with absent tactile fremitus over the area. Frequently there are E to A changes (egobronchophony) at the upper fluid border where underlying lung parenchyma is compressed.

RADIOLOGIC EXAMINATION. An effusion is suspected when there is blunting and medial displacement of the sharp costophrenic angle. Fluid accumulation between the lung and the diaphragm (subpulmonic effusion) is suspected when there is apparent elevation of the hemidiaphragm or widening of the shadow between the gas-containing stomach and the lower left lung margin. Up to 300 mL of fluid may fail to be seen in a posteroanterior chest radiograph, whereas as little as 150 mL may be seen in a lateral decubitus view. A supine film (frequent in patients in intensive care units) may obscure the diagnosis because the fluid layers posteriorly. A pseudotumor occurs when fluid loculates in an interlobar fissure, most commonly in the minor fissure, and gives the radiologic appearance of a tumor; a clue to the diagnosis is the presence of pleural fluid elsewhere and a biconvex lenticular configuration of the mass. A collection of pleural air and fluid (hydropneumothorax) usually produces horizontal and not concave margins. A pneumothorax is identified by the contrast between the

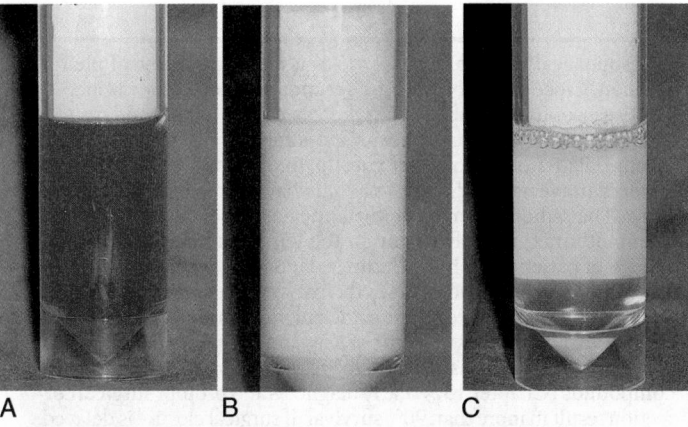

A   B   C

FIGURE 95-1 • *A*, Blood-stained pleural aspirate. This patient had pleural metastases from carcinoma of the breast. *B*, Chylous pleural effusion. This patient had bronchial carcinoma, which had invaded and obstructed the thoracic duct. *C*, Pleural transudate. This pale effusion is typically found in patients with heart failure or other causes of generalized edema. (From Forbes CD, Jackson WF: Color Atlas and Text of Clinical Medicine, 3rd ed. London, Mosby, 2003, with permission.)

water density of the visceral pleura centrally and the gas lucency without vascular markings laterally. Small pneumothoraces may be harder to diagnose, but an expiratory film may help outline them. Pleural plaques may be seen when calcified or may be detected when viewed tangentially but not en face. Ultrasonography and CT scans may provide better definition of pleural and parenchymal abnormalities.

THORACENTESIS AND PLEURAL FLUID ANALYSIS. Thoracentesis may be performed for diagnosis or therapy. A thoracentesis is diagnostic in approximately 75% of patients; even when not diagnostic, it helps exclude other important diagnoses, such as empyema. Diagnostic thoracentesis (Fig. 95-1) requires a relatively small amount of material (30 to 50 mL). As a rule, newly discovered effusions should be tapped. Although there are no absolute contraindications to a diagnostic thoracentesis, relative contraindications include a bleeding diathesis, anticoagulation, a small volume, mechanical ventilation, and low benefit-to-risk ratio. Therapeutic thoracentesis involves removing larger amounts of fluid (no more than 1000 to 1500 mL at one time because edema may occur in the re-expanded underlying lung, especially in cases of tension effusions).

Although the classification of "transudate" or "exudate" is not absolute, the distinction is helpful in suggesting further evaluation and possible diagnoses. To differentiate transudates and exudates, it is cost-effective to obtain total protein, lactate dehydrogenase (LDH), white blood cell count with differential, and either glucose or pH (Table 95-4). *Transudates* are due to imbalances in hydrostatic and oncotic pressures such as is seen in heart failure or hypoalbuminemia; they may result from movement of fluid from the peritoneum to the pleural space. *Exudates* (Table 95-5) are defined by the presence of at least one of the following criteria: (1) pleural fluid/serum protein ratio greater than 0.5; (2) pleural fluid/serum LDH ratio of more than 0.6; and (3) pleural fluid LDH greater than 200 IU/L. A fluid cholesterol level greater than 45 mg/dL may also be helpful.

Table 95-4 • CHARACTERISTICS OF PLEURAL FLUID TRANSUDATES

	ABSOLUTE VALUE	PLEURAL FLUID/ SERUM VALUE
Protein	<3 g/dL	<0.5
Lactate dehydrogenase	<200 IU/L	<0.6
Glucose	>60 mg/dL	1.0
White blood cell count	<1000/mm³	—
Cholesterol	<45 mg/dL	

Table 95-5 • CORRELATION OF PLEURAL FLUID EXUDATE FINDINGS AND CAUSATIVE DISEASE

TESTS	DISEASE(S)
pH <7.2	Empyema, malignancy, esophageal rupture; rheumatoid, lupus, and tuberculous pleuritis
Glucose (<60 mg/dL)	Infection, rheumatoid pleurisy, tuberculous and lupus effusions, esophageal rupture
Amylase (>200 µg/dL)	Pancreatic disease, esophageal rupture, malignancy, ruptured ectopic pregnancy
Rheumatoid factor, antinuclear antibody, LE cells	Collagen vascular disease
Complement (decreased)	Lupus erythematosus, rheumatoid arthritis
Red blood cells (>5000/µL)	Trauma, malignancy, pulmonary embolus
Chylous effusion (triglycerides >110 mg/dL)	Tuberculosis, violation of thoracic duct (trauma, malignancy)
Biopsy (+)	Malignancy
Adenosine deaminase (>40 µg/L)	Tuberculosis

The diagnoses that can be established by thoracentesis include malignancy, empyema (pus), tuberculosis (positive acid-fast bacillus in smear or cultures; Chapter 341), fungal infection (positive potassium hydroxide stains or culture), lupus pleuritis (LE cells; Chapter 280), chylothorax (high triglycerides or presence of chylomicrons), urinothorax (pleural fluid/serum creatinine ratio > 1), and esophageal rupture (increased pleural fluid amylase and pH around 6.0). Because many diagnoses produce overlapping values, acid-fast and Gram stains, aerobic and anaerobic cultures, cell count and differential, and cytologic analysis should be included in the study of these effusions. A predominance of polymorphonuclear leukocytes (PMNs) is most compatible with bacterial infection, whereas lymphocytes (particularly with paucity of mesothelial cells) suggest tuberculosis. Lymphocytes are also seen in lymphoma and leukemic effusions. Eosinophils are nonspecific and suggest long-standing fluid or air, sometimes even in small amounts, as from a prior thoracentesis. A bloody effusion not due to trauma is most likely due to malignancy or pulmonary infarction (Chapters 94 and 198). A white effusion suggests chyle, cholesterol, or lymphoma. Black fluid suggests aspergillosis (Chapter 386). A yellow-green color may be seen in rheumatoid pleurisy (Chapter 278). A putrid odor is diagnostic of anaerobic empyema, whereas an ammonia odor suggests urinothorax. The value of other diagnostic markers is uncertain, except for adenosine deaminase, which is useful for tuberculosis (see later text). β₂-microglobulin, pleural/serum cholinesterase, and lysozyme remain to be determined. The complications of thoracentesis include pain, bleeding (local, pleural, or abdominal), pneumothorax, infection, and spleen or liver puncture. With therapeutic thoracentesis, up to 50% of patients experience a temporary decrease in PaO₂ of as much as 20 mm Hg.

PERCUTANEOUS PLEURAL BIOPSY. Biopsy is indicated to evaluate patients with undiagnosed exudative effusion (particularly those with lymphocytic predominance) because the most frequently diagnosed disease is malignancy or tuberculosis. The procedure is performed under local anesthesia using a hook-type needle (Cope or Abrams). The contraindications are a small or loculated pleural effusion, an uncooperative patient, and anticoagulation or bleeding diathesis including azotemia with abnormal bleeding time. Because pleural seeding may not be uniform, multiple samples are needed. The overall diagnostic yield is about 60% for malignancy and 75% for tuberculosis.

EXPLORATION OF THE PLEURA. In most of the 5 to 10% of patients with undiagnosed effusion, the effusion itself disappears spontaneously or the cause becomes evident. When it is considered necessary to make a diagnosis, a biopsy specimen can be obtained through thoracoscopy (usually video-assisted thoracoscopy, VAT; Chapter 97). Thoracoscopy may be performed under local anesthesia and has a high yield (>85%). In some cases, it is necessary to perform an open pleural biopsy under general anesthesia. The main advantage is the possibility of obtaining larger specimens and concomitant lung tissue.

Clinical Manifestations

TRANSUDATIVE EFFUSION

Heart failure (Chapters 55 and 56) that results in biventricular failure with venous hypertension is the most common cause of a transudative effusion. Effusions are often bilateral, usually larger on the right, and on the chest radiograph are associated with vascular congestion and cardiomegaly (Chapter 49). In chronic heart failure (months) or as the effusion is in the process of resolving as the heart failure is treated, the total protein may be more than 3 g/dL. Thoracentesis is indicated if the patient is febrile, the effusion is large and unilateral, or there is pain or unexplained hypoxemia. Transudates occur in 5 to 10% of patients with liver cirrhosis (Chapter 156), secondary to movement of ascitic fluid through diaphragmatic defects or lymphatic channels; the effusion is more frequent on the right (70%). If in doubt, radioactive tracer injected in the ascitic fluid appears in the chest. The effusion often improves with improvement of the ascites (Chapter 146). Occasionally, chemical pleurodesis has effectively relieved symptomatic, recurrent effusions. A transudate is seen in up to 20% of patients with nephrotic syndrome (Chapter 119) due to decreased oncotic pressure (hypoalbuminemia) and increased hydrostatic forces; frequently bilateral, it improves by correcting the protein-losing nephropathy. Peritoneal dialysis (Chapter 118) and atelectasis may also cause transudative effusions. Urinothorax is a rare ipsilateral pleural transudate that occurs with urinary system obstruction; the effusion has the characteristic odor of urine, and relief of the obstruction promptly resolves the effusion.

EXUDATIVE EFFUSIONS

INFECTIONS. Parapneumonic effusion (pleural fluid associated with pneumonia or lung abscess; Chapters 92 and 93) is the most common cause of exudates. They may be uncomplicated and resolve spontaneously with antibiotics or may be complicated and require drainage. Complicated effusions are rich in white blood cells (empyema) and/or have positive Gram stains or cultures. Uncomplicated effusions are usually small and contain moderate amounts of PMNs, a glucose value similar to that of blood, a pH greater than 7.30, and an LDH level less than 500 U/L. In contrast, complicated effusions have large numbers of PMNs, often more than 100,000/mm³, pH less than 7.20, glucose value less than 40 g/dL, and LDH greater than 1000 U/L. If the effusion is also purulent and has bacteria, immediate drainage is necessary and is best achieved with a chest tube. If a fever persists for more than 48 to 72 hours in patients with complicated effusions, either the drainage is inadequate (such as when fluid becomes loculated), the antibiotic is inappropriate, or the diagnosis is wrong. If drainage is not effective because of loculation, inserting an additional tube or instilling intrapleural streptokinase may be effective. Poorly treated empyemas may result in communications with the bronchial tree (bronchopleural fistula) or skin (bronchopleurocutaneous fistula) and require open drainage with rib resection, decortication, and extensive reconstruction. In some patients with uncontrolled pleural sepsis, a thoracotomy with drainage and decortication may be life-saving. Pleural involvement by nonbacterial, nontuberculous infection is uncommon and, when present, is usually small. Fungal diseases rarely affect the pleura except for coccidioidomycosis, which may cause a hypersensitivity pleuritis.

OTHER INFECTIVE-INFLAMMATORY DISORDERS. Exudative effusions may result from subdiaphragmatic processes such as upper abdominal abscess, of which a subphrenic site is the most common location. Frequently postoperative in origin, subphrenic abscesses may result from hepatic diseases and gastrointestinal perforations. Patients are usually febrile and dyspneic and manifest an elevated hemidiaphragm with ipsilateral splinting. Abscesses may also arise in the liver or spleen. Antibiotics alone may not be sufficient; drainage may be necessary.

Pancreatitis and pancreatic pseudocyst (Chapter 145) can cause pleural effusions, more often on the left or bilaterally. The amylase level is higher than that in the serum, and the exudates may be blood tinged; the exudate tends to resolve as the pancreatic problem improves.

Esophageal rupture (Chapter 136) is an urgent cause of pleural effusion. Close to half of cases are secondary to endoscopy (Chapter 132) or esophageal dilatation, whereas others are secondary to a foreign body or trauma or occur spontaneously (Boerhaave's syndrome). Patients complain of chest pain, dyspnea, and dysphagia. Fever is universal, and half of patients have subcutaneous emphysema. The radiograph may confirm the emphysema and may show pneumothorax, more frequent on the left. Pleural effusion occurs in 75% of patients, with the findings depending on the time of thoracentesis. Early in the course, the exudate has abundant PMNs, followed by high concentrations of salivary amylase. Later, anaerobic mouth organisms seed the space, and the pH approaches 6.0. The diagnosis is established by using barium sulfate or water-soluble compounds (Chapter 136). Early diagnosis and prompt surgical correction result in more than 90% survival. If surgical closure is delayed, antibiotics for anaerobes, parenteral nutrition, and mediastinal and pleural drainage are necessary.

TUBERCULOSIS. (Chapter 341.) Pleural effusion occurs in most cases of pulmonary tuberculosis but is frequently inapparent. The effusion may accompany the primary infection, in which case it is an exudate, is commonly unilateral, and results from a hypersensitivity phenomenon. These patients, who usually are febrile, may recover without treatment, but close to two-thirds develop active tuberculosis within 5 years. A second form occurs when a subpleural focus of *Mycobacterium tuberculosis* ruptures into the pleural space. The clinical presentation simulates an acute pneumonia (60% of cases) with fever, nonproductive cough (80%), chest pain (75%), or a subacute or chronic fever. Chest radiography shows small to moderate effusion (4% are large), with parenchymal disease seen in one third of cases. Intermediate-strength purified protein derivative (PPD) testing is positive in 70% of patients, and, if repeated after 6 to 8 weeks, it may become positive in those with a prior negative test. The fluid is usually rich in protein (>4 g/dL), with a leukocyte count about 5000 cells/mm³ (90 to 95% lymphocytes). A PMN predominance may occur the first few days after the bacillus reaches the pleural space. The glucose level may be low, but rarely lower than 20 mg/dL. The pH ranges between 7.00 and 7.30, with pH more than 7.40 virtually excluding tuberculosis. The fluid is characteristically free of mesothelial cells. Recently, the presence of adenosine deaminase greater than 40 μg/L and lysozyme has been found to correlate with tuberculosis. An enzyme-linked immunosorbent assay or polymerase chain reaction to demonstrate mycobacterial antigen may be helpful diagnostically and may provide more rapid diagnosis in the more than 90% of cases in which acid-fast bacilli are not seen on smear. Multiple samples from a closed pleural biopsy are positive in 50 to 80% of cases, whereas positive cultures range from 30 to 70%. With all methods combined, the yield is close to 95%. The fever usually resolves within 2 weeks after instituting treatment but may persist for 6 or 8 weeks. The effusion usually resolves by 6 weeks but may persist for 3 to 4 months. Very ill patients may be helped by short-term corticosteroid treatment. Rarely, surgical drainage or decortication may be necessary.

OTHER INFECTIOUS EFFUSIONS. Actinomycosis (Chapter 337) caused by the anaerobic organism *Actinomyces israelii* may cause purulent effusions that may bulge the thoracic wall and drain through the chest. Sulfur granules (whitish yellow or brown interwoven filaments) can be identified in the fluid. Pleural effusions are also common in *Nocardia* infection (Chapter 338); the effusion is usually purulent with abundant PMNs, and sulfonamides are the treatment of choice. Aspergillosis (Chapter 386) of the pleura is uncommon, but an inflammatory, thickened pleura is frequently seen in progressive invasive aspergillosis. Pleural effusions due to parasitic diseases are uncommon but increasing among immigrants from developing countries. Paragonimiasis (Chapter 403) causes pleural thickening or effusion in up to 48% of patients; the effusion has a triad of low glucose (<10 g/dL), high LDH (>1000 U/L), and low pH (<7.10); complement-fixation antibodies greater than 1:64 are diagnostic. Amebiasis and echinococcosis are rare causes of pleural effusions.

HEMOTHORAX. Frank blood in the pleural space (hematocrit > 20%) is usually the result of trauma, hematologic disorders, pulmonary infarction, or pleural malignancies. Left-sided pneumothorax, particularly with a widened mediastinum, may indicate rupture of the aorta. Pleural blood often does not clot and can be readily removed by lymphatics if the volume is small. Larger effusions require tube drainage. Persistent bleeding requires surgical correction.

CHYLOTHORAX. Leakage of the lymph (chyle) from the thoracic duct most commonly results from mediastinal malignancy (50%), especially lymphoma. Chylothorax may also result from thoracic surgery (20%) or trauma (5%). The triad of slow-growing yellow nails, lymphedema, and pleural effusion (yellow-nail syndrome) is due to hypoplastic or dilated lymphatics. Because chyle collects within the posterior mediastinum, the chylothorax may not appear for days, until the mediastinal pleura ruptures. The usual milky appearance of the effusion may be confused with a cholesterol effusion or an effusion with many leukocytes. The best diagnostic criterion for chylothorax is the presence of a triglyceride concentration greater than 110 mg/dL, with rare instances of values between 50 and 110 mg/dL. The major complications are malnutrition and immunologic compromise, because fat, protein, and lymphocytes are depleted with repeated thoracentesis or chest tube drainage. Treatment should include drainage of the pleural space and attempts to decrease chyle formation by intravenous hyperalimentation, decreased oral fat intake, and intake of medium-chain triglycerides, which are absorbed directly into the portal circulation. For traumatic effusions, thoracic duct ligation should be considered; when due to tumor, treatment should focus on the primary cause.

IMMUNOLOGIC CAUSES OF PLEURAL EFFUSIONS. Clinical pleurisy occurs in close to 5% of patients with *rheumatoid arthritis* (Chapter 278), even though autopsy studies suggest up to 50% involvement. It has a male predominance and appears within 5 years after onset of the disease; nevertheless, effusions have occurred up to 20 years before the onset of articular disease. The fluid is an exudate with low glucose (<30 mg/dL), low pH, and high LDH. The complement level is usually low, with high titers of rheumatoid factor. The patient may complain of pleuritic pain or dyspnea. Fever is not common, in contrast to lupus pleuritis. The effusion does not resolve quickly but rather over months and occasionally persists over years. The major complication is fibrosis with lung trapping. Anti-inflammatory agents and corticosteroids are the recommended therapy. Pleuritic pain or effusion can be the presenting manifestation in 5% of patients with *systemic lupus erythematosus* (Chapter 280) and occurs at some point in the course in up to 50% of patients. Pain (86%), cough (64%), dyspnea (50%), pleural friction rub (71%), and fever (57%) are common. The effusions are exudates that in the majority of cases have normal pH and glucose. Hemolytic complement, especially C3 and C4 components, is low, and classic LE cells may be present. Lupus pleuritis is likely if the antinuclear antibody ratio in the fluid is more than 1:160. Spontaneous resolution of lupus pleuritis is uncommon, but it usually disappears within 2 weeks after beginning therapy with corticosteroids. Sarcoidosis (Chapter 91), Wegener's granulomatosis (Chapter 284), Sjögren's syndrome (Chapter 282), and immunoblastic lymphadenopathy are rare causes of pleural effusions.

OTHER CONDITIONS. Asbestosis (Chapter 88) is frequently associated with pleural disease; the effusion is often unilateral, small, and serosanguineous. The cell count is less than 6000 cells/mm^3, with either PMNs or mononuclear predominance. Eosinophilia up to 50% of the white blood cell count has been described. The diagnosis is suspected with known exposure. Exclusion of malignant mesothelioma in the presence of pleural plaques may be difficult and requires follow-up. The effusion tends to resolve in 1 month to 1 year, leaving a blunted costophrenic angle in more than 90% of patients and diffuse pleural thickening in about 50%. Calcification of the plaques occurs late (20 to 40 years after exposure). About 5% of patients may have underlying pulmonary parenchymal asbestosis.

Meigs' syndrome is the triad of benign fibroma or other ovarian tumors with ascites and large pleural effusions (usually on the right side). Most commonly seen after menopause, the symptoms are malaise, chest pain, and increased abdominal girth. Fluid moves from the abdomen through small diaphragmatic defects or lymphatics. The fluid is usually an exudate with a paucity of mononuclear cells. When suspected, the pelvic examination or abdominal-pelvic CT scan documents the ovarian tumor. Removal of the tumor resolves the effusion within 2 to 3 weeks.

Uremia (Chapter 117) causes a polyserositis and usually a bloody pleural exudate that resolves with treatment of the uremia. The diagnosis must be distinguished from a urinothorax or a hydrothorax caused by the nephrotic syndrome. Repeated thoracentesis may be needed if the patient is symptomatic (dyspnea, cough, chest pain).

Other causes of inflammatory effusions include radiation therapy, esophageal sclerotherapy, enteral feeding misplacement, and drug-induced pleural disease from medications such as nitrofurantoin, dantrolene, methysergide, methotrexate, procarbazine, amiodarone, mitomycin, bleomycin, and minoxidil. Pleuritis with a lupus-like syndrome has been associated with procainamide, hydralazine, isoniazid, and quinidine; signs and symptoms usually resolve after discontinuing the medicine but may occasionally require corticosteroids.

MALIGNANCY. Malignant effusions probably are the most common cause of exudate in patients older than age 60 years. Invasion by lung cancer is the most frequent (Chapter 198), whereas spread from liver metastasis or chest wall lymphatic invasion is the most frequent mechanism in breast cancer (Chapter 204). Ovarian (Chapter 205) and gastric cancer (Chapter 199) represent close to 5% of cases, whereas 7% may have an unknown primary lesion at time of diagnosis. Patients may be asymptomatic or develop cough, pain, and dyspnea. The effusion is an exudate with abundant red cells (30,000 to 50,000/mL) and mononuclear cells (lymphocytes > 50%). Occasionally, they are transudative (5 to 10%), and about one-third may have pH less than 7.3 or glucose value less than 60 mg/dL. Cytology is positive in close to 60% of cases, but biopsy increases the yield only to 70%. Thoracentesis should be repeated if the diagnosis is still suspected. Malignant pleural effusion carries a very poor prognosis, with the exception of breast and small cell carcinoma of the lung, both of which may respond temporarily to therapy. The best method, short of pleurectomy or pleural abrasion, to control recurrent malignant effusion is to instill tetracycline, talc, or medroxyprogesterone intrapleurally after chest tube drainage.

Lymphomas, especially non-Hodgkin's lymphoma (Chapter 195), may cause exudative effusions because of tumor spread to the pleura. Mediastinal invasion with lymphatic blockage and effusion is more common with Hodgkin's lymphoma (Chapter 194). Although the prognosis is unsure when lymphoma causes pleural effusion, patients frequently respond to chemotherapy.

MALIGNANT MESOTHELIOMA. Asbestos exposure precedes 80 to 90% of malignant mesotheliomas. Patients may present with dyspnea, cough, weight loss, and pain. Smoking is not a risk factor. The tumors often encase the underlying lung. The effusion may be massive and is often bloody; in 70% of cases, the pH is less than 7.30. Cytology is controversial because even when positive it may be difficult to differentiate mesothelioma from metastatic carcinoma. Elevated levels of hyaluronic acid and special stains and electron microscopy of biopsy tissue may help in the diagnosis. Median survival is 8 to 12 months after diagnosis. Malignant mesotheliomas may be confused with benign mesothelioma, which has the histology of a fibroma. Benign mesotheliomas may reach a large size and be pedunculated (migrating with position changes); they are often associated with hypertrophic pulmonary osteoarthropathy and clubbing. Treatment of mesothelioma involves surgical removal and, in malignant cases, chemotherapy.

PNEUMOTHORAX. Pneumothorax is defined as an accumulation of gas in the pleural space. It may be caused by (1) perforation of the visceral pleura and entry of gas from the lung; (2) penetration of the chest wall, diaphragm, mediastinum, or esophagus; or (3) gas generated by microorganisms in an empyema. When gas originates in the lung, the rupture may occur in the absence of known disease (simple pneumothorax) or as a result of parenchymal disease (secondary pneumothorax).

Simple spontaneous pneumothorax occurs most commonly in previously healthy men between 20 and 40 years of age and is due to spontaneous rupture of subpleural blebs at the apex of the lungs. The right lung is more frequently involved, and recurrence is frequent (30% ipsilateral, 10% contralateral). Patients usually present with acute pain, dyspnea (related to size of pneumothorax), and cough. Physical examination shows decreased breath sounds and tactile fremitus with ipsilateral hyperresonance. The chest radiograph classically shows the visceral pleural line, but small

Continued

pneumothoraces may become evident only with an expiratory or lateral decubitus film. Small amounts of fluid (sometimes blood) are present in 25% of patients. *Tension pneumothorax* (caused by increased positive pressure through a "ball-valve" air leak) can cause mediastinal shift and compromise circulation. For a small pneumothorax (<20% of the hemithorax) in an asymptomatic patient, observation may suffice because the air may reabsorb in 7 to 14 days. Larger pneumothoraces can be treated with air aspiration. A chest tube, which can be connected to suction or placed under water seal, is required for a pneumothorax that occupies more than 50% of the hemithorax, for symptomatic patients, or for a tension pneumothorax. The tube should be left in until the leak seals. Because of frequent recurrences, chemical pleurodesis or surgical correction usually by VAT may be necessary.

Secondary or complicated pneumothorax results from trauma or pulmonary diseases. Widespread emphysema (Chapter 85) is the most common cause, but rupture of an abscess with spillage of pus into the pleural space can cause a pyopneumothorax. Less frequent underlying conditions are asthma (Chapter 84), certain interstitial lung diseases (idiopathic fibrosis, eosinophilic granu-lomatosis, sarcoidosis, tuberous sclerosis; Chapters 88 and 91), neoplasms (sarcoma, bronchogenic carcinoma; Chapter 198), some rare diseases such as Marfan and Ehlers-Danlos syndromes (Chapter 276), and endometriosis (catamenial pneumothorax). Iatrogenic injuries (e.g., insertion of central lines) and barotrauma (Chapter 101) are frequent causes in the intensive care unit. The patient should be hospitalized and a chest tube inserted because spontaneous expansion is rare and the decreased reserve result-ing from the pneumothorax may cause ventilatory compromise. Surgery must not be taken lightly because the rate of complica-tions is high, but it may be lifesaving in some patients. In patients on ventilatory support, a pneumothorax is always under tension and requires immediate insertion of a chest tube. If a bronchopleural fistula persists, a portion of the minute ventila-tion exits through it; hence, it is necessary to increase ventilation to compensate for this loss. For severe leak, high-frequency low-pressure ventilation or synchronized chest tube occlusion may be helpful. Frequent complications of chest tube insertion include re-expansion pulmonary edema, lung trauma or infarction, sub-cutaneous emphysema, bleeding, and infection.

MEDIASTINUM

The mediastinum is the anatomic space that lies in the midtho-rax and separates the two pleural cavities. It is limited by the diaphragm below and the suprasternal thoracic outlet above. The mediastinum contains several vital structures in a small space, so mediastinal abnor-malities can produce important symptoms. For clinical purposes, it is convenient to divide the mediastinum into anterior, middle, and posterior compartments (Fig. 95–2). The anterior compartment con-tains the thymus, substernal extensions of the thyroid and parathy-roid glands, blood vessels, pericardium, and lymph nodes. The middle compartment contains the heart, great vessels, trachea, main bronchi, lymph nodes, and phrenic and vagus nerves. The posterior com-partment contains the vertebrae, descending aorta, esophagus, tho-racic duct, azygous and hemizygous veins, lower portion of the vagus, sympathetic chains, and posterior mediastinal nodes.

Signs and Symptoms

Most patients with mediastinal masses are asymptomatic, and the finding is incidental on a chest radiograph obtained for another reason. The most common symptoms are chest pain, cough, hoarse-ness, and dyspnea, whereas stridor, dysphagia, and Horner's syn-drome are less frequent. Occasionally, some syndromes are associated with a primary mediastinal lesion. Myasthenia gravis (Chapter 463) is seen in nearly 50% of patients with thymoma. Hypoglycemia has been seen in patients with mesotheliomas, fibrosarcomas, and teratomas. Parathyroid tumors (Chapter 260) may induce hypercalcemia, whereas neurogenic tumors may cause neurologic symptoms. The physical examination is usually non-specific. The mass may produce superior vena caval obstruction with facial edema, dilated veins, and arm edema. The masses may erode the trachea, esophagus, and great vessels with life-threatening consequences.

Diagnosis

Most mediastinal masses are detected on a plain chest radiograph (Figs. 95–3 and 95–4). Chest CT is the initial procedure of choice (Fig. 95–5) because it provides good definition of mediastinal struc-tures. If the patient is asymptomatic and the noninvasive informa-tion obtained by CT, with and without contrast medium enhancement, suggests a benign process, careful follow-up is justified. The radio-logic evaluation may include angiography and an esophagogram. The role of magnetic resonance imaging is being investigated, specifically for evaluating vessels and blood flow without the need for contrast medium enhancement. In some patients it may be necessary to obtain tissue for histologic diagnosis. Classically, anterior and middle com-partment lesions are reached through mediastinoscopy or medi-astinotomy. Thoracotomy may be needed for middle and posterior compartment lesions or when surgery is the treatment of choice for the suspected lesion (i.e., lung cancer). Direct sampling using CT-

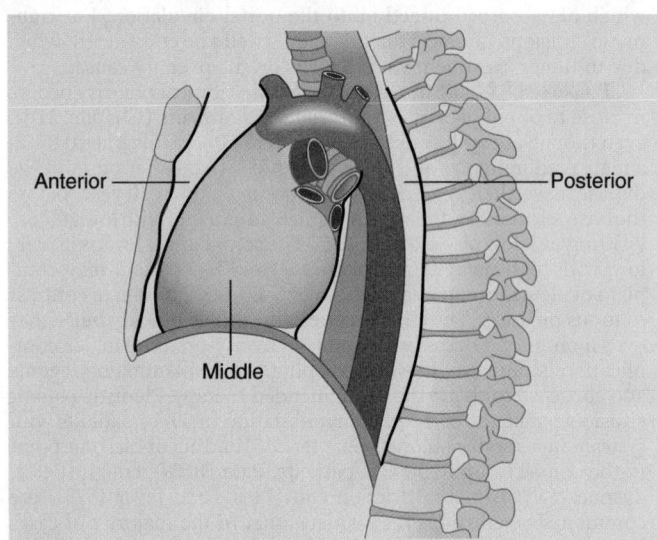

FIGURE 95–2 • Anatomic compartments of the mediastinum. The anterior compartment is bound posteriorly by the pericardium, ascending aorta, and brachiocephalic vessels and anteriorly by the sternum. The middle com-partment extends from the posterior limits of the anterior compartment to the posterior pericardial line. The posterior compartment extends from the pericardial line to the dorsal chest wall.

Table 95–6 • MOST FREQUENT CAUSES OF MEDIASTINAL MASSES

ANTERIOR	MIDDLE	POSTERIOR
Thymoma	Lymphoma	Neurogenic tumors
Lymphoma	Cancer	Enteric cysts
Teratogenic tumors	Cysts	Esophageal lesions
Thyroid aneurysms	Aneurysms	Diaphragmatic hernias
Parathyroid aneurysms	Hernia (Morgagni)	(Bochdalek)

guided needle aspiration has become the procedure of choice in many centers.

Specific Diseases

TUMORS (Table 95–6). The most common cause of a mediastinal mass in older patients is a metastatic carcinoma (most commonly bronchogenic carcinoma). In young adults, primary mediastinal pathol-ogy is more frequent.

In the posterior mediastinum, neurogenic tumors are most common (20%). Nonspecific chest pain and nonproductive cough

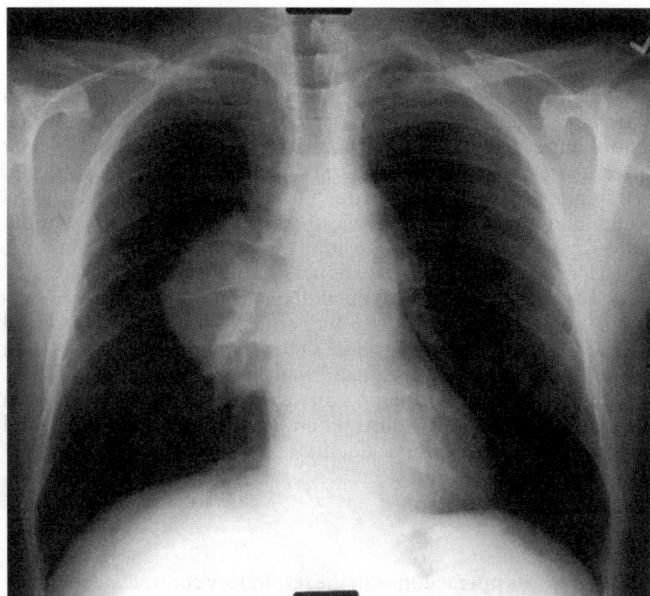

FIGURE 95–3 • Posteroanterior radiograph of a patient with a mass in the anterior mediastinum.

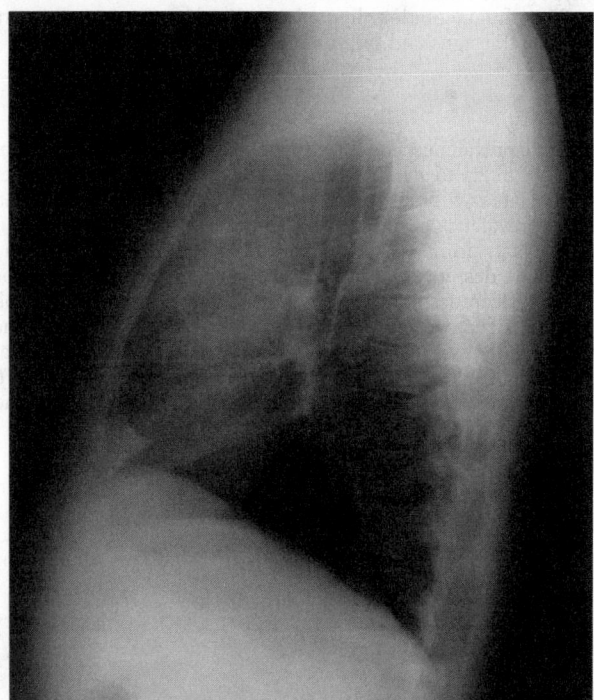

FIGURE 95–4 • Lateral chest radiograph of the patient in Figure 95–3.

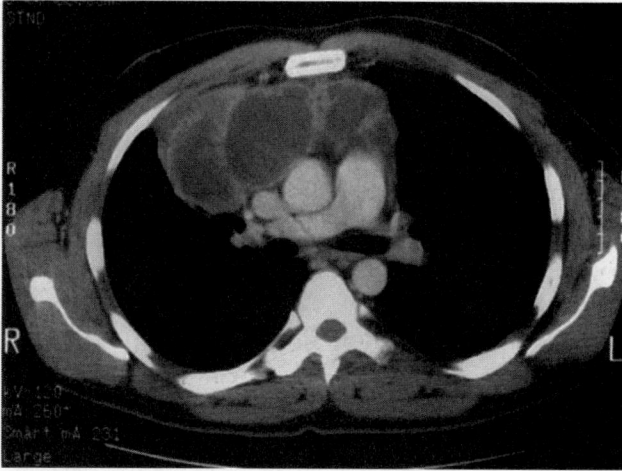

FIGURE 95–5 • Computed tomography scan of the patient in Figures 95–3 and 95–4. The mass proved to be a dermoid cyst. (Courtesy Paul Palefsky, MD, and Barbara Balkin, MD, Department of Radiology, St. Elizabeth's Medical Center, Boston, MA.)

with occasional compression of intercostal nerves, trachea, and bronchi are the most frequent symptoms. Most tumors are benign, originating in the nerve sheath (neurilemoma, neurofibroma) or sympathetic ganglion cells (ganglioneuroma). Neuroblastoma (malignant tumor of sympathetic ganglion cells) has a better prognosis than the same tumor occurring in the adrenals. Neurofibromas may occur in association with von Recklinghausen's disease (Chapter 459). Ganglioneuromas and neuroblastomas may secrete hormones that cause flushing, diarrhea, and hypertension. Pheochromocytomas (Chapter 241) may occasionally arise in the mediastinum. Neurogenic tumors should be resected; neuroblastomas require postoperative radiation.

Lymphoreticular. Thymomas (Chapter 463) account for 20% of mediastinal tumors and are located in the superior portion of the anterior mediastinum. Two thirds of them are malignant. Myasthenia gravis is seen in 40% of cases, and other paraneoplastic syndromes such as

Cushing's syndrome, refractory anemia, and hypogammaglobulinemia have been reported. All thymomas should be regarded as malignant, and surgical resection should be followed with radiation. Lymphatic tumors (17%) also arise in the anterior mediastinum. Hodgkin's lymphoma (Chapter 194) is the most frequent and carries the best prognosis. Non-Hodgkin's lymphoma (Chapter 195), plasmacytomas (Chapter 196), and angiomatous lymphoid hamartomas with similar clinical presentation carry a worse prognosis. Teratomatous tumors, also located in the anterior compartment, comprise 10% of mediastinal tumors, and one third of them are malignant. They are embryologically and histologically linked to the thymus. Cystic teratomas are more frequent and may contain squamous cells, hair follicles, sweat glands, cartilage, and linear calcifications. Intrathoracic goiter (10%) is usually a benign nodular or follicular enlargement of the thyroid gland (Chapter 239). Three fourths of patients present with stridor, cough, and dyspnea. Most frequently located in the anterior mediastinum, intrathoracic goiters occasionally cause superior vena cava syndrome. Benign cysts are usually asymptomatic and occur as an incidental radiographic finding. Bronchogenic cysts develop around the paratracheal area or carina and are seen in the middle and posterior compartments; they are filled with liquid and are lined with respiratory epithelium and cartilage but do not communicate with the tracheobronchial tree. Pericardial cysts (Chapter 74) occur in the anterior compartment and cardiophrenic angle; they contain clear liquid and flattened endothelial or mesothelial lining with a bland fibrous wall. Enteric cysts are located in the posterior mediastinum and are lined by gastric or intestinal epithelium. All cysts may become infected, bleed, or rupture into the mediastinum or pleural cavity.

Vascular tumors may originate primarily in the mediastinum. The vascular hamartomas, lymphangiomas, and hemangiomas are benign tumors, whereas hemangiopericytomas are malignant. Mesenchymal benign (lipoma) or malignant (liposarcoma, mesothelioma, rhabdomyosarcoma, and mesenchymoma) tumors rarely cause mediastinal masses.

Hernias through the diaphragm may also present as mediastinal masses. They may be retrosternal through the foramen of Morgagni, posterolateral through the foramen of Bochdalek, or most commonly through the esophageal hiatus. When gas is contained in the herniated organ, the presumptive diagnosis is easily made.

PNEUMOMEDIASTINUM. Air may enter the mediastinum through a tear in the esophagus or tracheobronchial tree or as dissecting air from ruptured alveoli. Tears in the esophagus and tracheobronchial tree commonly have a traumatic origin, whereas alveolar rupture may occur spontaneously or as a complication of artificial ventilation. Air may track to the neck and the body, producing subcutaneous emphysema and/or pneumothorax. The patient complains of retrosternal pain and dyspnea. Subcutaneous emphysema may cause classic crepitus. Auscultation may reveal a crunching sound synchronous with the heartbeat (Hamman's sign). Rarely, cardiac function is compromised. A lateral chest radiograph is usually diagnostic. Simple spontaneous pneumomediastinum usually resolves without treatment. When severe

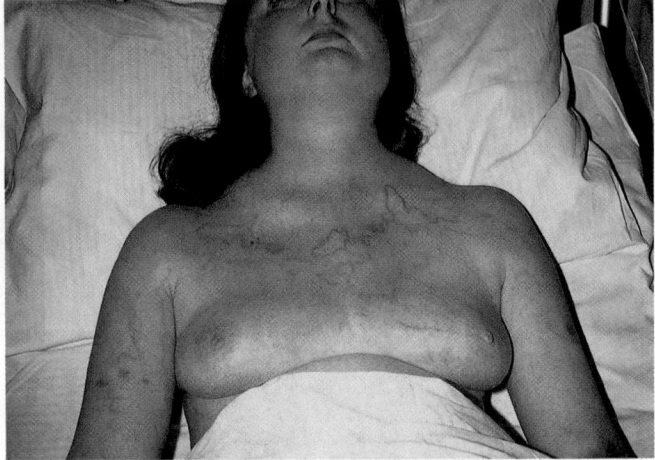

FIGURE 95–6 • Superior vena caval obstruction in bronchial carcinoma. Note the swelling of the face and neck and the development of a collateral circulation in the veins of the chest wall. (From Forbes CD, Jackson WF: Color Atlas and Text of Clinical Medicine, 3rd ed. London, Mosby, 2003, with permission.)

or resulting from organ rupture, surgical drainage and repair are required.

SUPERIOR VENA CAVA SYNDROME. Obstruction of blood flow through the superior vena cava causes dilatation of collateral veins of the upper thorax and neck and edema and congestion of the face (Fig. 95–6); patients may have headache, dyspnea, dysphagia, and wheezes. Malignancy is the most frequent cause of this syndrome, with bronchogenic carcinoma responsible for more than 70% of cases and lymphoma a distant second. Fibrosing mediastinitis after granulomatous diseases such as histoplasmosis (Chapter 379) or tuberculosis (Chapter 341) or associated with methysergide ingestion can also be seen. Aortic aneurysm (Chapter 75) and retrosternal thyroid (Chapter 239) are relatively benign causes of superior vena cava syndrome. Because of vessel dilatation, invasive procedures are contraindicated. When the obstruction is thought to be caused by tumor, an effort must be made to obtain tissue elsewhere. Irradiation, chemotherapy, or stent placement should be begun before attempts are made to obtain mediastinal tissue.

1. Plant PK, Owen JL, Elliott MW: Early use of non-invasive ventilation for acute exacerbations of chronic obstructive pulmonary disease on general respiratory wards: A multicentre randomised controlled trial. Lancet 2000;355:1931–1935.
2. Rowell NP, Gleeson FV: Steroids, radiotherapy, chemotherapy and stent for superior vena caval obstruction in carcinoma of the bronchus. Cochrane Database Syst Rev 2001;4:CD001316.

SUGGESTED READINGS
Celli BR: Respiratory management of diaphragm paralysis. Semin Respir Crit Care Med 2002;2:275–281. *Review that addresses the cause and treatment of unilateral and bilateral diaphragmatic paralysis.*
Khalil MY, Mapa M, Shin HJ, et al: Advances in the management of malignant mesothelioma. Curr Oncol Rep 2003;5:334–341. *An up-to-date overview.*
Light RW: Pleural effusion. N Engl J Med 2002;346:1971–1977. *Outlines the clinical approach to pleural effusion.*
Management of Spontaneous Pneumothorax: An American College of Chest Physicians Delphi Consensus Statement. Chest 2001;119:590–602. *Expert opinion consensus on the management of pneumothorax.*
Maskell NA, Butland RJ: BTS guidelines for the investigation of a unilateral pleural effusion in adults. Thorax 2003;58 (Suppl 2):II8–II17. *A consensus overview.*

96 OBSTRUCTIVE SLEEP APNEA-HYPOPNEA SYNDROME

Kingman P. Strohl

Definitions

Obstructive sleep apnea-hypopnea syndrome is a sleep disorder characterized by a constellation of neurobehavioral symptoms associated with recurrent episodes of partial and/or complete closure of the upper

airway during sleep. The disorder resolves when the sleep-induced upper airway instability is eliminated.

During *obstructive apnea,* respiratory efforts persist, but airflow is absent at the nose and mouth. *Central* or *nonobstructive apnea* occurs when both airflow and respiratory efforts are absent. Obstructive and central apnea are not necessarily unrelated. Many adult patients exhibit *mixed apnea,* in which both central and obstructive patterns occur. In a single apneic episode, a period may be noted in which no efforts occur, followed by the appearance of respiratory efforts, also without airflow. In addition, patients can have a mix of greater than 10 second, central, mixed, and obstructive apneas in the same night.

Hypopnea is a 50 to 80% reduction of airflow and arises by mechanisms similar to those that produce apnea. It can lead to increased arterial CO_2 and decreased arterial O_2 levels as well as arousals from sleep. Like apnea, hypopnea may result from either a reduction in respiratory efforts or partial upper airway obstruction. Snoring, which is a form of partial airway obstruction, results in flow limitation and increased respiratory efforts and, like apneas, produces hypoventilation and/or arousals from sleep.

Etiology

Sleep and its interaction with the respiratory control system destabilize the ability of the upper airway to conduct air to and from the lungs. Partial or complete obstruction of the nasopharynx, oropharynx, or both occurs during sleep (Fig. 96–1). Obstruction causes large swings in inspiratory efforts and a reduction in gas exchange; apneas and hypopneas often end with microarousals or changes in the sleep state. Sleep fragmentation, hypoxia, and/or hypercapnia all interact to produce the signs and symptoms of this disorder.

Incidence and Prevalence

Overall prevalence is approximately 2 to 4% with a male predominance of 2:1 to 4:1. The prevalence of excessive daytime sleepiness associated with sleep apnea (2 to 4%) is very high compared with the prevalence of narcolepsy (0.02 to 0.16%).

Surveys in primary care offices find low rates of recognition by practitioners despite a very high rate (>30%) of chronic symptoms of snoring, sleepiness, and obesity, and therefore high pretest probability for obstructive sleep apnea-hypopnea syndrome. Sleep apnea-hypopnea is also associated with hypertension, stroke, diabetes, and heart disease (see later text), and there is a higher prevalence of the obstructive sleep apnea-hypopnea syndrome in patients with these disorders.

Epidemiology

Healthy volunteers exhibit obstructive apnea at sleep onset or during periods of sleep. Apneic episodes are usually less than 10 to 15

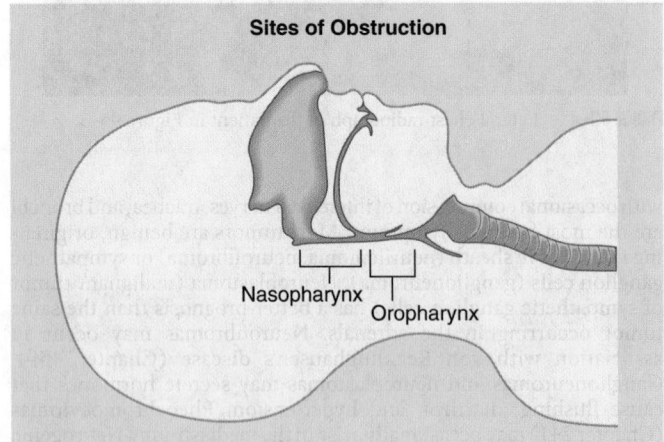

Sites of Obstruction

Nasopharynx
Oropharynx

FIGURE 96–1 • Potential sites for airway closure during sleep are indicated. Patients with a normal examination of the upper airway during wakefulness exhibit functional narrowing (heavy snoring or obstructive hypopnea) or complete closure (obstructive apnea) of the nasopharynx or oropharynx, or both. Relief of airway closure comes with activation of muscles, often accompanied by arousal from sleep.

seconds in duration and are not repetitive. Occasionally, longer periods of apnea last up to 30 seconds, particularly during rapid-eye-movement (REM) sleep. These episodes are not usually accompanied by arousal or sleep-state changes. No gender differences are seen in the appearance of brief episodes of sleep apnea in healthy subjects.

In one U.S. study, 9% of women and 27% of men had an apnea-hypopnea index (AHI) greater than 5 (see Sleep Monitoring), a number often quoted as a "threshold value" for normality; however, many people with an AHI greater than 5 have no symptoms or apparent illness. Community-based studies, however, suggest that subjects with an AHI greater than 5 *and* with symptoms (about 2% of women and 4% of men) have higher rates of motor vehicle crashes, disability, and high blood pressure.

Snoring is a predisposing feature in the development of obstructive sleep apnea-hypopnea syndrome. Snoring increases markedly with age, so that 45% of men and 30% of women older than 65 years snore. Hypertension and diabetes are twice as common among persons who snore, even after age and obesity are taken into account. A history of heavy snoring is reported in 80 to 85% of adult patients with obstructive sleep apnea-hypopnea syndrome, and is associated with a seven-fold increase in the likelihood of having an AHI greater than 5.

Mechanisms and Pathogenesis

The rhythmic cycle of a breath depends on interactions among groups of neurons located in the brain stem. Efferent activity of the cranial nerves that supply upper airway muscles is adjusted by nucleus ambigualis activity and the neural discharge to the chest-wall muscles by dorsal nuclei of the medulla. The activity of these medullary groups of respiratory neurons can be altered by descending pathways from pontine and suprapontine areas and are influenced by the sleep-wake cycle.

Sleep changes the sensitivity of upper airway muscles to chemical and nonchemical reflex activation even more than the diaphragm.

An essential feature of obstructive sleep apnea-hypopnea syndrome is the presence of recurrent apneic episodes during sleep. Causes for an apneic event include reduced excitatory stimulation; active suppression of breathing from inhibitory reflexes arising from the cardiovascular system, the lungs, and the chest wall or via other somatic and visceral afferents; and loss of reflexes that normally ensure the maintenance of ventilation and do not depend on chemical drive. Recurrent apnea results from instability in the feedback control of breathing, which causes ventilation to cycle rather than to maintain a constant level. Upper airway instability occurs in response to the cyclic changes in drive or if the mechanical outputs of chest-wall muscles and upper airway muscles are not identical either in phase or in amplitude.

The mechanical features of a small lumen for airflow and a collapsible airway wall are essential in the pathogenesis of obstructive apnea. Inspiratory efforts against an obstruction produce large, episodic increases in cardiac output, cerebral blood flow, and blood pressure.

No genes causative of obstructive sleep apnea-hypopnea syndrome have been identified, but work in this area is in progress. Symptoms relating to apnea and the number of apneas per hour of sleep are present with two to six times greater frequency in family members of affected patients than in age-, sex-, and socioeconomically matched control families. Craniofacial structures (mandibular length and head form) track with the occurrence of apnea in African-American families; in contrast, the effects of obesity are more apparent in white families. In an adult community sample, there was a report of an association between sleep-disordered breathing and the apolipoprotein E epsilon4 polymorphism, a genetic risk marker for Alzheimer's disease and cardiovascular risk. Animal models not only indicate inheritance of craniofacial risk, but also suggest that genes operate to produce variations in ventilatory drive, periodic breathing (the cyclic waxing and waning of ventilation), and the sleep-wake cycle. Orexin knockout mice show loss of regulation of sleep-wake cycles and vigilance, suggesting that the reaction to sleep fragmentation might vary among individuals according to genetic factors. In animal models of genetic obesity, ventilatory control is more dependent on genetic background than on fat accumulation and distribution. Recent studies of familial risk report only a 17% overlap between obesity and the expression of obstructive sleep apnea. Therefore, the clinical associations among obesity and the obstructive sleep apnea-hypopnea syndrome seen in clinical populations may not result just from weight

---

Table 96–1 • DEFINITION OF OBSTRUCTIVE SLEEP APNEA-HYPOPNEA SYNDROME

Episodes of upper airway obstruction during sleep result in recurrent arousals associated with excessive daytime sleepiness, unexplained by other factors, and two or more of the following:

Loud disruptive snoring
Nocturnal choking/gasping/snorting
Recurrent nocturnal awakening
Unrefreshing sleep
Daytime fatigue
Impaired concentration

AND
Overnight sleep monitoring documenting >5 episodes of hypopnea and apnea per hour

---

Table 96–2 • EPWORTH SLEEPINESS SCALE

How likely are you to doze off or fall asleep in the following situations, in contrast to just feeling tired? This refers to your usual way of life in recent time. Even if you have not done some of these things recently, try to work out how they would have affected you. Use the following scale to choose the **most appropriate number** for each situation.

0 = would **never** doze
1 = **slight** chance of dozing
2 = **moderate** chance of dozing
3 = **high** chance of dozing

SITUATION	CHANCE OF DOZING
Sitting and reading	
Watching TV	
Sitting and inactive in a public place (theater or meeting)	
As a passenger in a car for an hour without a break	
Lying down to rest in the afternoon when circumstances permit	
Sitting and talking to someone	
Sitting quietly after lunch (without alcohol)	
In a car, while stopped for a few minutes in the traffic	
TOTAL	

From Johns MW: A new method for measuring daytime sleepiness: The Epworth Sleepiness Scale. Sleep 1991;14:540–545.

---

gain or fat deposition, but may reflect an underlying genetic predisposition to both.

Clinical Manifestations

The essential features of the obstructive sleep apnea-hypopnea syndrome are loud disruptive snoring, nocturnal choking or gasping, daytime fatigue or sleepiness, and impaired concentration (Table 96–1). One eight-item patient-based measure, the Epworth Sleepiness Scale (ESS: 0-24), is commonly used to follow the extent to which sleep, or dozing, intrudes into periods of inactivity (Table 96–2). Excessive daytime sleepiness is subdivided into the following three categories:

MILD. Sleep episodes are present only during times of rest or when little attention is required. Examples include sleepiness that occurs while lying down in a quiet room, watching television, reading, or traveling as a passenger. Symptoms produce little or no impairment of social or occupational function. The ESS is usually less than 12.

MODERATE. Sleep episodes occur during activities that require some attention. Examples include sleep episodes that often occur while attending activities such as concerts, meetings, or presentations. Symptoms produce impairment of social or occupational function, to the extent that people take efforts to avoid situations where sleep is likely to occur and cause embarrassment. The ESS for this category is between 12 and 17.

Continued

SEVERE. Sleep episodes are present during activities that require at least moderate attention. Examples include uncontrollable sleepiness while eating or during conversation, walking, or driving. Symptoms produce marked impairment in social or occupational function. Families are highly aware, perhaps more aware than the person, of adverse consequences of this level of sleepiness. The ESS is greater than 17.

In the obstructive sleep apnea-hypopnea syndrome, the frequency of sleep complaints (snoring, apneas, and restless sleep) and degree of daytime sleepiness are roughly related to the number and length of nocturnal arousals. Most of the time, the chronicity and alarming nature of these symptoms are such that the patient can report them accurately. Women commonly report fatigue or decreased alertness, whereas men more frequently report being sleepy. Sleepiness symptoms should be elicited by direct questioning and be distinguished from fatigue. Inquiry into the sleep habits of the patient is necessary to distinguish sleepiness due to sleep restriction or medications from other causes.

A number of associated features should suggest the diagnosis of obstructive sleep apnea-hypopnea syndrome (Table 96–3). The suspicion that the syndrome is present should not be limited to the obese patient or to those with characteristics previously called the pickwickian syndrome.

Diagnosis

Routine laboratory examinations are generally not helpful. Likewise, pulmonary function tests reveal no abnormality except those caused by associated obesity (somewhat diminished lung capacities, with greater reduction in the expiratory reserve volume). In the patient without upper airway or respiratory complaints, the flow-volume loop is not useful. The routine measurement of thyroid function is unhelpful. Certain tests, such as arterial blood gas analyses, thyroid function testing, echocardiogram, and chest roentgenogram, are electively indicated if there is new onset peripheral edema in an adult.

Patients with heart disease are prone to sleep disordered breathing. In larger series, approximately 25% have obstructive sleep apnea and an equal proportion recurrent central apneas, or Cheyne-Stokes respiration. In patients with chronic obstructive pulmonary disease (Chapter 85), the obstructive sleep apnea-hypopnea syndrome should be considered when hypercapnia is disproportionate to abnormalities in the mechanical function of the lungs. Hypercapnia rarely occurs with obstructive lung disease unless the forced expiratory volume in 1 second is reduced to less than 50% of predicted. Patients with unexplained right-sided heart failure or pulmonary hypertension (Chapter 64) should be questioned for the presence of sleep-disordered breathing. Finally, some patients with the syndrome may be mistakenly treated for primary heart disease because cardiac arrhythmias have been detected during sleep, whereas the respiratory disturbances have not.

SLEEP MONITORING

The definitive test is the monitoring of the patient during sleep with continuous measurements of breathing and gas exchange. Sleep staging requires monitoring of the electroencephalogram (EEG) (usually with two or three leads), the chin electromyogram (activity decreases in REM), and the electro-oculogram to detect REM. It is also useful to record the electrocardiogram to determine whether arrhythmias occur with the apneic episodes.

Other variables recorded may include pulse oximetry (looking for decreases of more than 3% from baseline values), muscle activity from the limbs (looking for nonrespiratory causes for arousal), and body

Table 96–3 • FEATURES COMMONLY ASSOCIATED WITH OBSTRUCTIVE SLEEP APNEA-HYPOPNEA SYNDROME

Obesity
Mandibular/maxillary hypoplasia
Systemic hypertension
Pulmonary hypertension
Tonsillar hypertrophy
Sleep fragmentation
Sleep-related arrhythmias
Nocturnal angina
Gastroesophageal reflux
Impaired quality of life

Table 96–4 • THERAPY FOR OBSTRUCTIVE SLEEP APNEA-HYPOPNEA SYNDROME

Electromechanical: Nasal continuous positive airway pressure (CPAP), orthodontic devices, nasal splints, electrical simulation
Surgical: Tracheostomy, uvulopalatopharyngoplasty, hyoplasty, linguoplasty, mandibular advancement, plastic remodeling of the uvula (laser-assisted or radiofrequency ablation)
Medical: Vasoconstrictive anti-inflammatory nasal sprays,* weight-loss medications,* oxygen, and miscellaneous agents (e.g., progesterone, serotonin receptor blockade, acetazolamide, methylxanthines*)

*Not formally approved for obstructive sleep apnea-hypopnea syndrome.

position (looking for expression of apneas only in the supine position). In some instances, it may be necessary to measure esophageal pressure to identify transient episodes of inspiratory flow limitation leading to arousals or producing a decrease in oxygen saturation of more than 3%.

A common summary measure used to describe respiratory disturbances during sleep is the AHI, the total number of episodes of apnea and hypopnea during sleep divided by the hours of sleep time. AHI values can be computed for the different stages of sleep. Another term used is the respiratory disturbance index (RDI), which most often refers to the number of times per hour that oxygen saturation decreases more than 3%. If EEG measures are performed, an arousal index (AI) is computed. The number of arousals per hour of sleep may be correlated with AHI or RDI; however, some episodes (approximately 20%) of apnea or hypopnea are not accompanied by arousals and/or other causes for arousals are present. The number of arousals during sleep or respiratory disturbances per se is not a good indicator of disease; however, symptoms of sleepiness are better predictors of treatment success.

Differential Diagnosis

The most common factor producing mild and moderate degrees of sleepiness is sleep restriction (a reduction in nocturnal sleep length) as a result of lifestyle issues. Narcolepsy (Chapter 438) and restless leg syndrome (Chapters 438 and 445) are two less common disorders of moderate and severe sleepiness; each has a set of signature symptoms. Cardiovascular, respiratory, or metabolic disturbances or their therapy (e.g., diuretics, insulin) may predispose the patient to restless sleep. Drug addiction or depression may masquerade as sleep apnea. In the elderly, in whom reports of snoring are high and a higher number of episodes of apnea during sleep may be considered "normal," sleepiness can be secondary to a lifestyle or medication effect. A sleep history is the key to recognizing sleep apnea as well as these other diseases.

℞ Treatment

Therapy is directed at sleep fragmentation and prevention of hypoxemia. Initially, a review should be undertaken for the presence of anatomic (e.g., nasal obstruction or tonsillar hypertrophy) or medical conditions (e.g., hypothyroidism) whose reversal would ameliorate or eliminate breathing disturbances during sleep. Because respiratory depressants and sleep loss seem to increase the likelihood of respiratory disturbances during sleep, withdrawal of res-

piratory depressants (major tranquilizers, antihistamines, or alcohol) is indicated, and a trial of sleep extension advocated.

Treatment should be tailored to the individual patient and to the degree to which he or she is functionally impaired (Table 96–4). Thyroid hormone replacement reverses the sleep apnea and clinical symptoms in myxedema (Chapter 239). Treatment of hypertension in obstructive sleep apnea-hypopnea syndrome with angiotensin converting enzyme inhibitors modestly decreases apneic activity. Patients with sleep apnea and cardiac or respiratory disease, such as heart failure (Chapter 56) or asthma (Chapter 84), should be placed on maximal therapy for the concomitant disease, because decreased circulation time and/or increased oxygenation may decrease the incidence or severity of respiratory disturbances during sleep. In the patient with recent stroke (Chapters 440 and 441), time may be all that is needed before respiratory stability is restored. Nasal (vasoconstrictive and anti-inflammatory) decongestants are warranted when nasal obstruction is present (Chapter 468).

ELECTROMECHANICAL DEVICES

Nasal continuous positive airway pressure (CPAP) is effective in the long-term treatment of obstructive sleep apnea and in the prevention of snoring. The effect is dependent on the level of positive pressure applied to the upper airway, and the optimal levels of pressure differ among patients. In general, at lower levels of pressure (3 to 6 cm H_2O), apneic episodes are eliminated, but episodes of partial upper airway obstruction (snoring) persist. At higher levels of pressure (5 to 20 cm H_2O), regular breathing tends to be restored. Positive pressures must be present over the entire respiratory cycle for nasal CPAP to be effective.

If CPAP is withdrawn, symptoms recur gradually over several days, so short interruptions of therapy for surgery or acute medical illnesses are usually well tolerated. Late failures of nasal CPAP occur occasionally: some are due to poor condition or fitting of the mask, so that pressure is lost; some are due to too low a pressure; and some are due to an increase in the pressure required to prevent apnea. Factors such as alcohol use, hypothyroidism, and obesity may worsen airway stability.

Bilevel ventilation for obstructive apnea is the application of an inspiratory pressure assist over and above the expiratory pressure required to keep the pharyngeal airway open. One indication for this approach is a concomitant finding of chronic hypoventilation in addition to obstructive apnea.

Studies comparing CPAP to sham therapy indicate that in the sleepy patient, regardless of AHI, prescription of CPAP reduces neurocognitive impairments and hypertension. [1,2] In patients who deny subjective sleepiness, there is little benefit. Compared to behavioral interventions such as recommendations for weight loss, CPAP also has an effect.

Absolute contraindications to nasal CPAP therapy are complete nasal obstruction and a communicating fracture of the base of the skull. Patients generally accept CPAP therapy fairly well, but most large series indicate that some patients (approximately 30%) do not. Side effects of therapy include feelings of suffocation, nasal drying or rhinitis, ear pain, and conjunctivitis. Inner ear and eye problems may resolve spontaneously and do not recur with continued CPAP therapy. Pulmonary function does not deteriorate with nasal CPAP, and patients with lung disease apparently have no adverse effects.

Intraoral appliances improve symptoms, quality of life, and apnea/hypopnea frequency, [1,2] and are gaining wider acceptance in the treatment of both snoring and obstructive apnea. Some devices are designed to tug the tongue forward; others protrude the mandible or, at the very least, prevent the mandible from retruding with sleep. The main advantages of oral devices are the relative simplicity of the treatment, its reversibility, and its use as an alternative treatment in patients who are unable to tolerate nasal CPAP or who are poor surgical risks. Side effects of jaw and tooth pain occur in a significant proportion of patients. Comparisons of oral appliances with CPAP suggest equal efficacy, but specific indications and cost-effectiveness comparisons are not yet determined.

SURGICAL INTERVENTIONS

Tracheostomy bypasses the site of obstruction during sleep and is the most effective therapeutic maneuver for obstructive apnea. The tracheostomy may be technically difficult owing to morphologic features such as obesity, a short neck, or a short mandible.

Problems with infection and granulation tissue often occur, and it may take a year or more before the stoma is well healed.

Surgical correction directed at a specific pathologic narrowing of the upper airway caused by enlarged tonsils, nasal polyps, macroglossia, or micrognathia has improved signs and symptoms of sleep apnea. In prospective studies in which tonsillectomy has been performed for sleep apnea, obstructive apnea may persist, but the frequency is greatly diminished; there are no randomized trials.

Extensive excision of soft tissue in the oropharynx, termed *uvulopalatopharyngoplasty,* may improve pharyngeal function during sleep. The procedure involves a submucosal resection of redundant tissue from the tonsillar pillars to the arytenoepiglottic folds. The indications for the procedure are the same as for a tracheostomy. In one series, the success rate was approximately 60%, but success has varied considerably from center to center. In one study in which CPAP was given as a bridge to surgical treatment, there was equivalent success with surgery or CPAP; however, there are no formal head-to-head trials of surgical versus medical management that permit estimates of relative clinical utility. Patients with massive obesity or with anatomic narrowing of the airway may not show success with uvulopalatopharyngoplasty. Experience does matter; temporary complications of the procedure include speech and nasal regurgitation of food. Some patients may have an increased number of respiratory disturbances during sleep after the procedure, but recognition of the disturbances is obscured because snoring is absent. These "silent obstructions" may be as severe as apneic episodes before surgical intervention.

Newer procedures, such as laser-assisted uvuloplasty and radiofrequency tissue ablation, are designed and promoted as outpatient treatments for loud snoring. Outcome studies show some short-term (70 to 80% at 2 to 6 months) reductions in snoring loudness; however, long-term success rates rapidly decline after 1 to 2 years. Nonobstructive sleep apnea syndrome should be excluded before either procedure is contemplated, because apnea may increase after these procedures and because use of these procedures may delay more definitive treatment.

The two-stage surgical management of obstructive sleep apnea is based on the fact that a uvulopalatopharyngoplasty (stage I) is often not curative, as defined by a resolution of symptoms along with a reduction in AHI below some threshold (usually 10). An adjunctive procedure is a midline glossectomy. The second procedure (stage II) is mandibulomaxillary advancement. Success is reported, but studies across centers in unselected patients are not available.

MEDICAL TREATMENT

Even a 5 to 10% decrease in body weight can be accompanied by clinical and objective remission of sleep apnea syndrome in obese subjects. Few investigators, however, are enthusiastic about the long-term efficacy of dietary strategies, perhaps because adherence to dietary restrictions is difficult in the sleepy patient. Better treatments for obesity would have an immediate and major impact on the management and prevention of sleep apnea.

A beneficial effect of oxygen on upper airway obstruction during sleep cannot be found in every patient. Indeed, in some patients with obstructive sleep apnea syndrome, oxygen administration provokes respiratory acidosis. At present, it is not possible to predict which patients will respond to oxygen therapy.

Various drugs have been used in an attempt to stimulate upper airway muscles, to increase respiratory neural drive, or to increase both upper airway and chest-wall muscle activation. Although this kind of therapy would seem optimal, it has not yet shown much success.

PSYCHOLOGICAL FACTORS

Sleepiness compromises the patient's ability to solve problems at work or at home or to perform even simple tasks. Unrecognized and untreated sleep apnea is a factor in automobile crashes, and risk

Continued

is reduced by effective therapy. Family members may also suffer injury from automobile accidents caused by the patient's falling asleep while driving. Family conflicts may result in personal and financial losses before a diagnosis is sought or made.

If the patient and family feel reasonably informed of therapeutic intent and alternatives, they will be better able to cope with a treatment strategy, including tracheostomy in cases refractory to other treatment. Support groups are effective in delivering information and reinforcing treatment regimens.

After effective treatment, changes in family dynamics may occur as the patient becomes a more active person. With successful treatment, the patient can return to full employment and duties, and the level of risk for a sleep-induced automobile accident decreases to that found in the general population. Commercial drivers, pilots, and persons employed in situations in which others are at more risk by a sleep-induced mishap may be requested to undergo closer clinical follow-up and monitoring of adherence to treatment.

Prognosis

In longitudinal studies of community-based populations, apneas increase in number with advancing age and weight gain. After about age 65 years, the effect of sleep apnea on morbidity and mortality is uncertain.

Death and sleep apnea are associated, but the nature and strength of causality have not been satisfactorily explained. Accidents, crashes, and errors related to excessive daytime sleepiness may have a greater impact on morbidity and mortality than cardiovascular complications or other nonaccidental sudden death. Perioperative morbidity and death in patients with suspected or known obstructive sleep apnea-hypopnea are reported to result from preoperative and postoperative medications, inattention, and spinal anesthesia. The magnitude of risk in regard to conscious sedation remains to be defined.

Prevention

Obstructive sleep apnea-hypopnea syndrome is a relatively common chronic disease. Modifiable risk factors include obesity, use of sedatives and respiratory depressants, inadequate sleep, and, possibly, hypertension.

The perioperative period in elective or emergent surgery is a time of risk for lethal respiratory disturbances. The patient should be advised to inform the anesthesiologist of his or her diagnosis before undergoing any elective surgical procedure and be permitted to use CPAP during the hospitalization. In addition, the excessively sleepy untreated patient should not operate a motor vehicle or engage in activities during which sleep attacks would be hazardous. The risk of serious injury or death from accidents is reduced by behavioral measures and by direct treatment of obstructive events during sleep.

1. Monasterio C, Vidal S, Duran J, et al: Effectiveness of continuous positive airway pressure in mild sleep apnea-hypopnea syndrome. Am J Respir Crit Care Med 2001;164:939–943.
2. Montserrat JM, Ferrer M, Hernandez L, et al: Effectiveness of CPAP treatment in daytime function in sleep apnea syndrome: A randomized controlled study with an optimized placebo. Am J Respir Crit Care Med 2001;164:608–613.
3. Mehta A, Qian J, Petocz P, et al: A randomized, controlled study of a mandibular advancement splint for obstructive sleep apnea. Am J Respir Crit Care Med 2001;163:1457–1461.

SUGGESTED READINGS
Buxbaum SG, Elston RC, Tishler PV, Redline S: Genetics of the apnea hypopnea index in Caucasians and African Americans: I. Segregation analysis. Genet Epidemiol 2002;22:243–253. *These results provide strong support for an underlying genetic basis for obstructive sleep apnea that, in African Americans, is independent of the body mass index.*
Flemons WW: Obstructive sleep apnea. N Engl J Med 2002;347:498–503. *An excellent clinical review.*
George CF: Reduction in motor vehicle collisions following treatment of sleep apnoea with nasal CPAP. Thorax 2001;56:508–512. *Evidence is presented that the recognized and treated patient has a lower risk of automobile accidents.*
Heitman SJ, Flemons WW: Evidence-based medicine and sleep apnea. Respir Care 2001;46:1418–1432. *This review grades the treatment literature in general on CPAP, oral appliances, and surgery.*
Kaneko Y, Floras JS, Usui K: Cardiovascular effects of continuous positive airway pressure in patients with heart failure and obstructive sleep apnea. N Engl J Med 2003;348:1233–1241. *Treatment reduced systolic blood pressure and improved left ventricular function.*
Vilaseca I, Morello A, Montserrat JM, et al: Usefulness of uvulopalatopharyngoplasty with genioglossus and hyoid advancement in the treatment of obstructive sleep apnea. Arch Otolaryngol Head Neck Surg 2002;128:435–440. *Patients with mild and moderate obstructive sleep apnea and multilevel obstruction in the upper airway may benefit from uvulopalatopharyngoplasty plus genioglossus and hyoid advancement.*

97 SURGICAL APPROACH TO LUNG DISEASE

John J. Reilly, Jr.
Steven J. Mentzer

The role of surgery in the diagnosis and therapy of lung disease has expanded greatly as lung transplantation has gained acceptance as a therapeutic option for selected patients with advanced lung disease. In addition, the concept of surgery to reduce lung volume in patients with emphysema has been reintroduced and is an area of active clinical investigation. Minimally invasive thoracic surgery has also created new options for lung biopsy and pulmonary resection.

LUNG TRANSPLANTATION

Human lung transplantation was first attempted in the 1960s but little success was achieved until the availability of more effective immunosuppressive drugs (cyclosporine) and improved surgical techniques in the early 1980s. The annual number of lung transplant procedures increased steadily from 1982 through 1995, but it has remained relatively constant at 1300 to 1400 patients annually since 1996 because of limited donor availability.

Transplant Types

Currently, four types of lung transplantation procedures are performed. *Single lung transplantation* is typically performed through a posterolateral thoracotomy incision and requires three anastomoses: mainstem bronchus, pulmonary artery, and pulmonary veins/left atrium. The contralateral lung is not removed, so single lung transplantation is not performed in patients with bilaterally infected lungs (e.g., patients with cystic fibrosis).

Bilateral lung transplantation was initially performed as an en bloc procedure but is currently performed in a sequential fashion that is functionally equivalent to two single lung transplantations done during a single operation, most commonly through a transverse sternotomy ("clamshell") incision. It requires six anastomoses: both mainstem bronchi, both pulmonary arteries, and both sets of pulmonary veins. It is the procedure of choice for patients with bilaterally infected lungs and is also performed in certain patients with emphysema, primary pulmonary hypertension, and other diseases.

Heart-lung transplantation was initially the most common type of lung transplant procedure but is now performed infrequently (approximately 100 cases in the United States in the year 2000). It is an en bloc procedure, with right atrial, aortic, and distal tracheal anastomoses. It is performed in patients with advanced lung disease and coexistent cardiac disease, such as those with Eisenmenger's syndrome (Chapter 65) who have uncorrectable intracardiac defects, end-stage lung disease, and irreversible cor pulmonale, or patients who have advanced lung disease and left ventricular dysfunction due to coronary artery disease.

The most recently introduced lung transplant procedure is *living donor lobar transplantation*. This procedure involves the removal of a lower lobe from each of two living donors, with the implantation of one in each hemithorax of the recipient in a manner similar to bilateral lung transplantation.

Indications

The most common indications for transplantation are diseases or conditions that share the following common features: they produce

Table 97–1 • INDICATIONS FOR LUNG TRANSPLANTATION

SINGLE LUNG TRANSPLANT	% OF PATIENTS	DOUBLE LUNG TRANSPLANT	% OF PATIENTS
COPD	47	Cystic fibrosis	33
Idiopathic pulmonary fibrosis	21	Emphysema	20
α₁-Antitrypsin deficiency	11	α₁-Antitrypsin deficiency	10
Primary pulmonary hypertension	4	Primary pulmonary hypertension	9
Other	17	Other	28

COPD: Chronic obstructive pulmonary disease.
From the Registry of the International Society for Heart and Lung Transplantation. See Figure 97–1.

extreme disability in affected patients, they are unresponsive to medical therapy, and they are responsible for limited life expectancy in affected patients (Table 97–1). With the exception of a small number of cases of sarcoidosis and lymphangioleiomyomatosis, the original lung disease does not recur after lung transplantation.

Evaluation of Potential Transplant Recipients

The ideal candidate for lung transplantation has lung disease unresponsive to medical therapy but is in otherwise good health. In contrast to cardiac transplantation (Chapter 80), patients who are critically ill are usually not appropriate candidates for lung transplantation. Patients who experience critical illness due to lung disease often have poor nutritional status, coexistent major organ dysfunction, refractory infection, or other contraindications to transplantation (Table 97–2). Older patients have a higher mortality after transplantation, leading to the current recommendations that single lung transplant recipients should be younger than 65 years and bilateral transplant recipients should be younger than 60 years; nevertheless, policies concerning age limits vary between programs. The specific recommendations for referral for transplant evaluation vary depending on the underlying disease (Table 97–3). As waiting times for transplantation lengthen because of the expansion of the potential number of recipients, patients will likely need to be referred earlier to have a reasonable chance of surviving until transplantation. The most recent statistics from the United Network for Organ Sharing show that waiting list mortality for lung transplantation is 16%.

Post-transplant Issues

Most of the medical issues that patients and physicians face after lung transplantation are the consequence of the transplant and post-transplant medication, rather than the underlying disease for which the transplantation was performed. Examples include immunosuppression, infections and their prophylaxis, acute allograft rejection, chronic allograft rejection, and nonpulmonary complications of transplantation.

Table 97–2 • CONTRAINDICATIONS TO LUNG TRANSPLANTATION

ABSOLUTE CONTRAINDICATIONS
Major organ dysfunction (other than lung)
Recent active malignancy
Infection with human immunodeficiency virus
Hepatitis B antigen positivity
Hepatitis C with histologic evidence of active liver disease
Active substance abuse (including cigarettes)
Severe musculoskeletal disease affecting the thorax

RELATIVE CONTRAINDICATIONS
Poor nutritional status (<70% or >130% ideal body weight)
Symptomatic osteoporosis
Colonization with fungi, atypical mycobacteria, or pan-resistant bacteria
Requirement for invasive ventilation
Psychosocial problems likely to affect outcome adversely
High-dose (>20 mg of prednisone daily) corticosteroid use

From Joint Statement of American Society of Transplant Physicians/American Thoracic Society/International Society of Heart and Lung Transplantation: International guidelines for the selection of lung transplant candidates. Am J Respir Crit Care Med 1998;158:335–339.

IMMUNOSUPPRESSION. The standard chemotherapeutic regimen for immunosuppression after lung transplantation consists of cyclosporine or tacrolimus, azathioprine or mycophenolate mofetil, and corticosteroids. Conclusive data demonstrating the superiority of the newer agents over cyclosporine or azathioprine are not available. Some centers add an antilymphocyte antibody preparation in the first days after transplantation, but the effect of this practice on rates of acute and chronic rejection are unknown. Experience with rapamycin is limited, and its role remains to be defined.

INFECTIONS AND PROPHYLAXIS AFTER LUNG TRANSPLANTATION. Lung transplant recipients are at high risk for bacterial, viral, fungal, and protozoal infections; infections are the leading causes of death during the early post-transplant period. Predisposing factors include the susceptibility of the allograft after ventilator-induced damage, the severing of the lymphatic drainage at the time of the procedure,

Table 97–3 • GUIDELINES FOR LUNG TRANSPLANT REFERRAL

DISEASE	PULMONARY FUNCTION	ARTERIAL BLOOD GAS VALUES	NYHA CLASS	OTHER CONSIDERATIONS
Chronic obstructive lung disease	FEV₁ <25% predicted	PCO₂ >55 mm Hg		Pulmonary hypertension, progressive deterioration
Cystic fibrosis	FEV₁ <30% predicted or rapid decline	PCO₂ >50 mm or PO₂ <55 mm Hg		Increasing admissions or rapid deterioration
Idiopathic pulmonary fibrosis	VC <60% predicted or D_LCO <50% predicted	Exertional desaturation		Lack of response to therapy
Pulmonary hypertension			Functional class III or IV despite vasodilator therapy	CI, <2 L/min/m², RAP, >15 mm Hg; mean PAP, >55 mm Hg
Eisenmenger's syndrome			Functional class III or IV	

CI = cardiac index; FEV₁ = forced expiratory volume in 1 second; NYHA = New York Heart Association; PAP = pulmonary artery pressure; RAP = right atrial pressure; VC = vital capacity.
Adapted from Joint Statement of American Society of Transplant Physicians/American Thoracic Society/International Society of Heart and Lung Transplantation: International guidelines for the selection of lung transplant candidates. Am J Respir Crit Care Med 1998;158:335–339.

and ischemia and/or reperfusion injury. Additionally, patients are pharmacologically immunosuppressed, are in a catabolic state, have impaired defenses as a result of endotracheal intubation, and have arterial and central venous catheters, chest tubes, and a large surgical incision.

In the first 3 months after transplantation, bacterial infections are responsible for most deaths. In approximately one third of patients, pneumonia is diagnosed in the first weeks after transplantation, with gram-negative organisms being the etiology in 75% of cases. Patients with chronic rejection often develop colonization and recurrent infections, usually with *Pseudomonas* species.

Among potential viral pathogens, *cytomegalovirus* (CMV) is the most important in lung transplant recipients. Seronegative patients who receive an allograft from a seropositive donor are at particularly high risk for the development of a clinically significant CMV infection. Seronegative patients who have a seronegative donor are at low risk for infection, as long as they are treated with seronegative blood products. The CMV syndrome includes fever, bone marrow suppression, hepatitis, enteritis, and pneumonitis. Most programs use prophylactic ganciclovir or valganciclovir in patients at risk, although the optimal dosing regimen and duration of treatment are as yet undetermined.

Epstein-Barr virus (EBV) has been associated with the development of post-transplant lymphoproliferative disorder. *Herpes simplex* infections are relatively unusual, in part because of the standard use of prophylactic antiviral medication (ganciclovir or acyclovir). There are reports of *paramyxovirus* and *respiratory syncytial virus* infections after lung transplantation.

Aspergillus species are the most common cause of invasive fungal infection. Predisposing factors for such infection include preoperative colonization with *Aspergillus*, stenotic airways, or the presence of an airway stent.

Because of the nature of the immunosuppressive chemotherapeutic regimen used, patients are at high risk for infection by the protozoan *Pneumocystis carinii*. The use of trimethoprim-sulfamethoxazole prophylaxis has virtually eliminated *Pneumocystis* pneumonia.

ACUTE REJECTION. Histologically, the initial manifestation of acute rejection is a lymphocyte-predominant inflammatory response, usually centered around blood vessels and/or airways. The vascular inflammation is accompanied by endothelial inflammation, and the lymphocyte infiltration can progress to involve alveolar walls. By convention, acute rejection is graded from 0 (normal) to 4 (severe), with subclasses defined by the presence or absence of airway inflammation.

The risk of acute allograft rejection is highest in the early months after transplantation and declines with time. Multiple episodes of acute rejection are the major risk factor for the subsequent development of chronic rejection. Because up to 25% of surveillance bronchoscopies reveal asymptomatic rejection, some programs perform surveillance biopsies at regular intervals with the goal of reducing the incidence of chronic rejection; however, the efficacy of this approach has not been established.

Clinically, patients may present with fever, cough, and exertional dyspnea. Evaluation may demonstrate rales or rhonchi on chest examination, a decline in pulmonary function by spirometry, leukocytosis, opacities on chest radiography, and exertional desaturation. The clinical presentation is often indistinguishable from infectious pneumonia, and the clinical impression is accurate in only 50% of cases. Bronchoscopy with bronchoalveolar lavage and/or transbronchial biopsy is commonly needed to clarify the diagnosis.

Treatment of acute rejection most often consists of high-dose corticosteroids administered intravenously for 3 days. In patients with persistent or recurrent acute rejection, therapeutic strategies include antilymphocyte antibodies, changing maintenance immunosuppressive drugs, and other attempts to augment immunosuppression.

CHRONIC REJECTION. The bronchiolitis obliterans syndrome (Chapter 88) is thought to be a manifestation of chronic rejection. Risk factors for the development of the syndrome include the number of acute rejection episodes and, in some series, prior symptomatic CMV infection. Evidence supporting the conclusion that it is a manifestation of chronic rejection includes the association with the number of acute rejection episodes, the association with donor and/or recipient HLA locus mismatch, the similarity to the syndrome seen after bone marrow transplantation (graft versus host disease), and laboratory evidence of donor-specific alloreactivity in certain allograft recipients.

Pathologically, "early" lesions demonstrate inflammation and disruption of the epithelium of small airways followed by growth of granulation tissue into the airway lumen, resulting in complete or partial obstruction. The granulation tissue then organizes in a stereotypical pattern with resultant fibrosis that obliterates the lumen of the airway.

Clinically, bronchiolitis obliterans presents with nonspecific symptoms. Patients typically develop progressive exertional breathlessness, and pulmonary function testing usually demonstrates evidence of progressive airflow obstruction. Bronchiolitis obliterans is classified according to the forced expiratory volume in 1 second (FEV_1): 0 (no significant abnormality) if FEV_1 is greater than 80% of baseline; 1 (mild) if FEV_1 is 65 to 80% of baseline; 2 (moderate) if FEV_1 is 50 to 65% of baseline; 3 (severe) if FEV_1 is 50% or less of baseline. In early stages, chest radiography is notable only for hyperinflation, but it may show bronchiectasis as the syndrome progresses. Later stages of bronchiolitis obliterans may include a syndrome of bronchiectasis with chronic productive cough and airway colonization with *Pseudomonas* species.

The diagnosis of bronchiolitis obliterans is made on both clinical and pathologic grounds. Transbronchial biopsy has a low yield for demonstrating histologic evidence of bronchiolitis obliterans; but when such evidence is seen, it is diagnostic. In patients with a compatible clinical syndrome, the exclusion of anastomotic stenosis and occult pulmonary infection is sufficient to establish the diagnosis.

A variety of types of therapy have been tried, including pulse corticosteroids, antilymphocyte antibodies, total lymphoid irradiation, photopheresis, and nebulized cyclosporine, but none has been clearly established as effective. Most patients with bronchiolitis obliterans experience a progressive decline in pulmonary function despite augmentation of immunosuppression. Bronchiolitis obliterans is the leading cause of late mortality after lung transplantation.

NONPULMONARY MEDICAL COMPLICATIONS OF LUNG TRANSPLANTATION. Most of the nonpulmonary medical complications that arise in patients after lung transplantation are the result of immunosuppressive therapy. Virtually all lung transplant recipients develop one or more of these complications.

Osteoporosis is common owing to the long-term use of corticosteroids and cyclosporine. Bone density should be monitored periodically, and pharmacologic therapy should be instituted if excessive bone loss is identified (Chapter 258).

Chronic renal insufficiency is common and is the result of therapy with cyclosporine or tacrolimus, both of which affect afferent vascular tone in the kidneys and result in an average 50% drop in the glomerular filtration rate in the 12 months after lung transplantation. Hypertension is also common and is caused by corticosteroids and cyclosporine. Calcium-channel blockers, which are often used to treat hypertension, raise serum cyclosporine levels; appropriate monitoring and dose adjustment are needed when starting such therapy. Both corticosteroids and tacrolimus contribute to the development of diabetes mellitus and hyperlipidemia.

Organ transplantation is associated with an increased incidence of malignancy, thought to be due to pharmacologic immunosuppression and alteration in immune surveillance. Patients are at increased risk for lymphoproliferative malignancies and other types of cancer. *Post-transplant lymphoproliferative disorders* occur in about 4% of patients after organ transplantation; most are associated with EBV. These syndromes can be polyclonal or monoclonal. Reduction in immunosuppression is sometimes therapeutic in those with polyclonal disease. The prognosis in patients with monoclonal disease is poor, with little response to modification of immunosuppression or antineoplastic chemotherapy. Patients are also at increased risk for skin, cervical, anogenital, and hepatobiliary malignancy after solid organ transplantation.

Outcomes After Lung Transplantation

A comparison of survival data in lung transplantations done before 1990 with those done between 1991 and 1993 shows that 1-year survival rates improved significantly (64.2% versus 70.5%), but little subsequent change was noted in 1994 through 2000 (73.6%). The subsequent rate of decline in survival (approximately 8 to 10% annually) has not changed and largely reflects the effects of bronchiolitis obliterans on patient survival. Median survival after lung transplantation is approximately 4 years (Fig. 97–1).

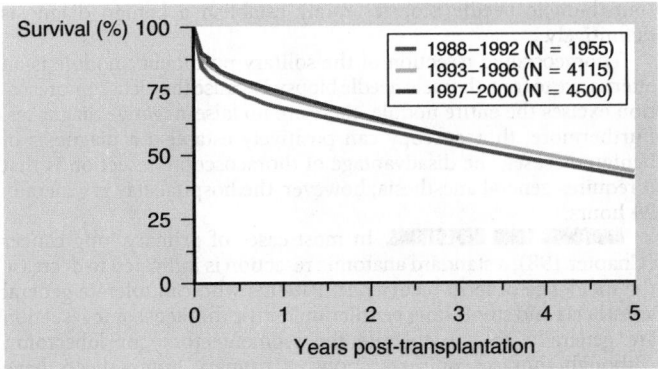

FIGURE 97–1 • Survival after lung transplantation. (Data from International Society of Heart and Lung Transplantation, 18th Annual Data Report. [*http://www.ishlt.org/regist_slides_2001/Registry%202001.ppt*].)

LUNG VOLUME REDUCTION SURGERY

Lung volume reduction surgery was first proposed by Dr. Otto Brantigan in the early 1950s, and there has been a resurgence of interest since the mid-1990s. Initial reports demonstrated the technical feasibility of the procedure and marked variability in surgical outcome. Current concepts of the operation are that physiologic benefit results from increasing lung elastic recoil and a resizing of the lung in relationship to the chest wall.

Types of Lung Volume Reduction Surgery

A variety of approaches may be taken in the common goal of reducing lung volume by about 30%. In the absence of a specific contraindication, bilateral lung volume reduction surgery is currently the procedure of choice. Currently favored techniques include stapled resection of peripheral lung tissue, with or without the use of exogenous material to buttress the suture lines, and plication, in which the lung is rolled on itself and stapled without resection.

Evaluation of Potential Candidates for Lung Volume Reduction Surgery

The evaluation of candidates for lung volume reduction surgery can be viewed as both an assessment of risk and an attempt to identify those most likely to benefit from the procedure. Few of the criteria used to select or exclude patients have been subject to prospective validation.

In general terms, the principles of evaluation are similar to those before lung transplantation. In addition, pulmonary hypertension and marked deconditioning are contraindications to lung volume reduction surgery. The ideal candidate has severe airflow obstruction due to emphysema but is otherwise in good health. Patients undergo computed tomographic (CT) scanning, pulmonary function testing (with lung volumes by plethysmography), echocardiography to assess pulmonary artery pressure, and some form of noninvasive screening for significant coronary artery disease. If a candidate appears suitable for lung volume reduction surgery, most programs require completion of a 6- to 10-week course of pulmonary rehabilitation before surgery.

The ideal candidate for this experimental procedure has anatomic evidence of emphysema; severe obstruction not reversed by bronchodilators on spirometry; no significant cardiac, hepatic, or renal disease; a pulmonary artery systolic pressure less than 45 mm Hg; does not smoke cigarettes; has completed pulmonary rehabilitation; and has no significant pleural disease or prior thoracic surgery. Contraindications include severe deconditioning (6-minute walk <150 m), use of parenteral corticosteroids (e.g., prednisone >20 mg/day), clinically significant bronchiectasis, a pulmonary artery systolic pressure greater than 45 mm Hg, or a need for invasive mechanical ventilation. Hypercarbia, age greater than 75 years, marked anatomic deformity of the thorax, or marked pleural scarring are relative contraindications.

Outcomes of Lung Volume Reduction Surgery

The National Emphysema Treatment Trial demonstrated a 16% 30-day mortality in patients with an FEV_1 of less than or equal to 20% predicted and a diffusing capacity less than or equal to 20% predicted and/or homogenously distributed emphysema on CT scan undergoing lung volume reduction surgery, as compared to no deaths in comparable patients randomized to medical therapy.[1] Based on these findings, such patients should not be considered candidates for lung volume reduction surgery.

In other randomized patients with severe emphysema, lung-volume-reduction surgery improved exercise capacity but not survival compared with medical therapy.[2] In the subgroup of patients with both predominantly upper-lobe emphysema and low baseline exercise capacity, survival was better with surgery. Patients in other subgroups had no substantive functional benefit and a higher mortality with surgery. Operative mortality rates are 5 to 10%.

THORACOSCOPY AND VIDEO-ASSISTED THORACIC SURGERY

Thoracoscopy was originally limited to pleural biopsies and the drainage of empyemas or pleural effusions (Chapter 95). The recent improvement in light sources and video-optic instrumentation has led to the integration of the thoracoscope into most thoracic surgical procedures. The coincident development of advanced endoscopic surgical instrumentation has facilitated the performance of these operations through "minimally invasive" thoracic incisions. The widespread application of the thoracoscope in thoracic surgery has led to the more inclusive term of *video-assisted thoracic surgery*.

Video-Assisted Thoracic Surgery Procedures

Video-assisted thoracic surgery generally involves at least three small incisions or "access ports" placed in any intercostal space: one port for the video-thoracoscope and two ports for endoscopic instrumentation. Although the access ports are small, the rigid instruments result in trauma to the intercostal nerves and rib periosteum that can result in regional postoperative discomfort.

The size of video-assisted surgery incisions depends on the goals of the procedure and the anatomic findings at the time of exploration. Unexpected pleural symphysis or incomplete lobar fissures may require extension of the incision to facilitate visualization. In patients undergoing anatomic resection, such as segmentectomy or lobectomy, at least one of the incisions is extended to permit extraction of the resected lung from the hemithorax. For most video-assisted thoracic procedures, the operation requires single lung ventilation. The requirement for selective ventilation excludes many patients with severe pulmonary hypertension or acute respiratory failure. In contrast, many patients with chronic respiratory insufficiency and preserved ventilation-perfusion matching tolerate periods of selective lung ventilation. The ability of many patients with severe emphysema to tolerate selective ventilation has led to the application of thoracoscopy for lung volume reduction surgery. Obliteration of the pleural space, either from infection or previous surgery, is a relative contraindication for thoracoscopic surgery.

Indications

BENIGN LUNG DISEASE. A variety of benign lung diseases present as focal parenchymal lesions that require a tissue biopsy for diagnosis. The traditional approach to lung biopsy has been a limited thoracotomy and wedge resection. As an alternative to limited thoracotomies, thoracoscopy has proven to be an effective approach to the diagnosis of localized disorders of the lung. Thoracoscopy can provide a more complete view of the ipsilateral hemithorax, including the visceral, parietal, and mediastinal pleura. Additional subpleural nodules that were not visualized by preoperative radiography can be examined, and representative biopsies can be obtained.

Diffuse lung diseases can often be diagnosed clinically on the basis of history, characteristic chest radiographs, physical findings, and pulmonary function testing. In cases that require histopathologic confirmation, lung tissue can be obtained by transbronchial biopsy. Thoracoscopy plays a limited role in diffuse lung disease but may be helpful when a large tissue sample is required.

BULLOUS LUNG DISEASE. Most patients with chronic obstructive pulmonary disease (COPD) (Chapter 85) have diffuse parenchymal disease. A small number of patients with COPD can develop heterogeneous disease with dominant bullae and relatively preserved lung parenchyma. In some cases, the rapid expansion of these bullae can be associated with a substantial increase in dyspnea and a decrease in expiratory airflow. Chest radiographs of patients with an expanding bulla frequently demonstrate compression of surrounding lung tissue. Patients with bullous lung disease may also present with an infected bulla that requires drainage before definitive surgery.

The indications for thorascopic bullectomy are similar to lung volume reduction surgery for emphysema. Patients who benefit most from surgery are those who have rapidly progressive symptoms associated with the expansion of a single bullous lesion and radiographic demonstration of compression of the surrounding lung parenchyma. Either excision or plication can remove the bullous lesion.

RECURRENT SPONTANEOUS PNEUMOTHORAX. Primary spontaneous pneumothorax (Chapter 95) is caused by rupture of subpleural blebs of the lung. In more than 95% of cases, the blebs are located at the apex of the lung. In approximately 5% of cases, associated subpleural blebs are found at the margin of the lower lobe, usually in the superior segment. In an otherwise healthy patient with less than a 20% pneumothorax, the uncomplicated pneumothorax can be observed without intervention. In patients with larger pneumothoraces, a tube may be necessary to evacuate the pleural air and re-expand the lung. Most cases of primary spontaneous pneumothorax heal from the inflammation associated with pleural rupture and are free of ongoing air leak after re-expansion of the lung.

Although most spontaneous pneumothoraces are uncomplicated, 3 to 20% of patients with pneumothoraces develop complications such as tension pneumothorax, persistent air leaks, or recurrent pneumothoraces. Patients who develop a second pneumothorax have a 70 to 80% chance of a third recurrence within 2 years. The surgical approach to the treatment of recurrent pneumothoraces has been the removal of subpleural blebs. These blebs can be effectively removed using a thoracoscopic approach or through a more traditional axillary incision.

SOLITARY PULMONARY NODULES. Solitary pulmonary nodules or "coin lesions" are defined as spherical lesions, less than 3 cm in diameter, present in the outer one third of the lung (Chapter 81). Although most solitary pulmonary nodules do not represent cancer (Chapter 198), the diagnosis must be considered in all patients, especially those with a smoking history.

Transthoracic needle biopsy has a low morbidity: fewer than 10% of normal patients and a slightly higher percentage of patients with emphysema develop a postprocedure pneumothorax. However, a small but tangible false-negative rate occurs with transthoracic needle biopsies. Furthermore, in the absence of a malignant diagnosis, transthoracic needle biopsies rarely establish a benign diagnosis definitively.

Thoracoscopic resection of the solitary pulmonary nodule is an alternative to transthoracic needle biopsy. Because thoracoscopic resection excises the entire nodule, there are no false-negative diagnoses. Furthermore, thoracoscopy can positively establish a diagnosis of benign disease. The disadvantage of thoracoscopic resection is that it requires general anesthesia; however, the hospital stay is generally 24 hours.

ANATOMIC LUNG RESECTIONS. In most cases of primary lung cancer (Chapter 198), a standard anatomic resection is indicated to decrease the incidence of local recurrence. Patients who can tolerate general anesthesia and single lung ventilation for the thoracoscopic resection are generally able to tolerate the segmentectomy or lobectomy. Although thoracoscopic resections of primary lung cancers have not been studied in a randomized setting, the available evidence indicates that a parenchymal margin within 2 cm results in a 20% incidence of local recurrence. In addition, a recent Lung Cancer Study Group report demonstrated a 2.5-fold increase in local recurrence rates with limited resection. Another disadvantage to limited parenchymal wedge resection is that the peripheral wedge resection does not provide segmental or lobar lymph node staging. In patients with isolated regional metastases, this staging information could provide important information to guide possible adjuvant therapy.

Anatomic resections can be performed with a variety of techniques, including video-assisted surgical techniques. The difference between standard lobectomy and a thoracoscopic lobectomy has become less distinct in recent years. Thoracoscopic instruments have become commonplace in the resection of a lobe of the lung, even when performed through a standard thoracotomy. The improved visualization and smaller instruments have resulted in smaller incisions and less morbidity.

1. NETT Research Group: Patients at high risk of death after lung-volume-reduction surgery. N Engl J Med 2001;345:1075–1083.
2. Fishman A, Martinez F, Naunheim K, et al: A randomized trial comparing lung-volume-reduction surgery with medical therapy for severe emphysema. N Engl J Med 2003;348:2059–2073.

SUGGESTED READINGS

McKenna RJ Jr: Thoracoscopic evaluation and treatment of pulmonary disease. Surg Clin North Am 2000;80:1543–1553. *An overview of this increasingly useful approach.*

Ramsey SD, Berry K, Etzioni R, et al: Cost effectiveness of lung-volume-reduction surgery for patients with severe emphysema. N Engl J Med 2003;348:2092–2102. *Lung-volume-reduction surgery is costly relative to medical therapy but may be cost effective if its benefits can be maintained over time.*

Steinman TI, Becker BN, Frost AE, et al: Guidelines for the referral and management of patients eligible for solid organ transplantation. Transplantation 2001;71:1189–1204. *Consensus statement concerning guidelines for evaluation and listing of patients considered for transplantation.*

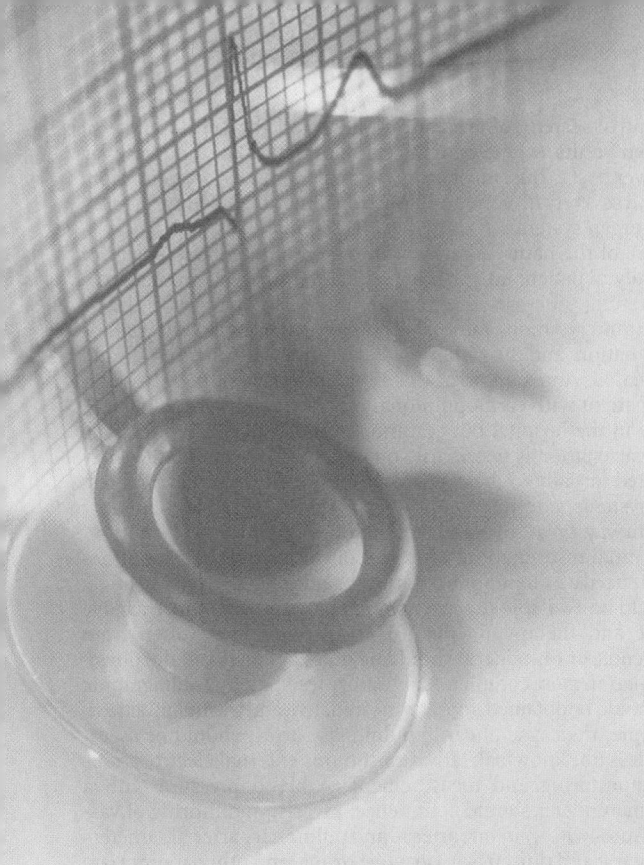

part X

Critical Care Medicine

98 APPROACH TO THE PATIENT IN A CRITICAL CARE SETTING

John M. Luce

Characteristics of Critical Care Medicine

Many kinds of patients require critical care, mostly because of dysfunction or failure of one or more organ systems. Circulatory and respiratory failures are most common, and patients who manifest dysfunction or failure of two or more organ systems are said to have multiple organ dysfunction syndrome (MODS).

The parent boards of internal medicine, anesthesiology, surgery, and pediatrics provide certification of special competence in critical care medicine, and many hospitals require such certification of physicians who direct or practice in critical care units. The Joint Commission on Accreditation of Healthcare Organizations has mandated that critical care units have medical directors to ensure that quality is improved and proper utilization is maintained.

Although physicians usually manage the care of critically ill patients, critical care medicine is a team approach that involves nurses, respiratory care practitioners, nutritionists, biomedical technologists, and other health care professionals. Also essential are mental health experts, clergy, social workers, and other persons who serve as counselors to patients and families and sources of support for the critical care team.

Attributes of Critical Care Units

Critical care units were first developed in the 1950s for patients who required mechanical ventilation because they had poliomyelitis or were recovering from anesthesia. Currently, critical care units are defined by their ability to provide the environment, facilities, and personnel for the care of severely ill patients (Table 98–1).

Critical care units may have a general orientation, treating all kinds of severely ill patients, or be more specialized, accepting only specific categories of patients as defined by the type of illness (e.g., burn units; Chapter 108), organ system involved (e.g., coronary and acute neurologic care units), specialty service designation (e.g., medical and surgical units), or the patient's age (e.g., neonatal and pediatric units). Specialized units provide medical personnel specifically skilled in the unit's areas of care and have available particular forms of technology.

Because of the severity of the illness of their patients, critical care units require clear delineation of administrative and medical lines of authority and responsibility. Critical care units must also have general guidelines for admission and discharge, specifically described roles for nurses and respiratory therapists, standing orders, critical pathways and clinical guidelines for management of common disorders, and programs of continuing staff education and quality assurance. Such policies and guidelines reduce the apparent ambiguity often inherent in the difficult environment of a critical care unit and enable prompt decision making by health care professionals.

Approach to the Critically Ill Patient

Patients are admitted to critical care units from a variety of settings, including the emergency department, medical or surgical service, or operating room. Although a few patients may be admitted for simple monitoring purposes, such as the online measurement of pulse and blood pressure, these admissions have become less prevalent because of the relative scarcity of critical care beds and the development of "step-down" units, where patients can be monitored noninvasively and at lower cost. Thus, most critical care patients are, by definition, acutely and severely ill, commonly with dysfunction or failure of more than one organ system.

Because of the nature of critical illness, the initial assessment of the critically ill patient must be rapid and focus on real or potentially life-threatening processes that require immediate diagnostic and/or therapeutic intervention (Table 98–2). As a result, history taking, physical examination, and the gathering of laboratory information should be abbreviated. An example of this rapid approach is the resuscitation of a patient with cardiopulmonary arrest, which may take place elsewhere in the hospital but continue in the critical care unit. The pace of resuscitation is necessarily quick; physical examination may be restricted initially to the central nervous, cardiovascular, and respiratory systems, and interventions may be limited to the essential ABCs of *a*irway, *b*reathing, and *c*irculation.

After initial resuscitation, or in lieu of this step if the patient has not experienced cardiopulmonary arrest or another major catastrophe, time should be available to form a broader and more comprehensive diagnostic and therapeutic plan. The history taking (often from family, friends, or onlookers) should be more detailed and the physical examination more complete. Laboratory tests, such as radiographic studies, should be obtained, monitoring initiated, and treatment started. For example, the cause of cardiopulmonary arrest should be ascertained, if it is not known already. Continuous external electrocardiographic monitoring and measurement of blood pressure with a sphygmomanometer should commence; invasive monitoring of vascular pressures with systemic arterial and pulmonary arterial catheters may be useful; and diuretics, vasoactive drugs, and other appropriate agents should be administered if the cause is heart failure.

Management of the critically ill patient should be based primarily on an understanding of physiology and pathophysiology. Although the contributions of cell and molecular biology to critical care medicine are substantial, the critical care unit resembles somewhat a physiology laboratory, wherein variables such as heart rate and blood pressure are measured in an online fashion, and the effects of interventions such as vasoactive drugs can be directly observed. Although the benefit of the critical care unit is related to the availability of these physiologic data, practitioners must exercise clinical judgment and avoid the temptation to collect data for their own sake.

Consistent with this pathophysiologic approach, the interdependence of organ systems must be kept in sharp focus in critical care practice. Limited attention to one component of an illness, even if it is predominant, frequently yields a therapeutic approach that is detrimental to the patient as a whole. For example, treatment directed toward reducing intravascular volume in a patient with MODS to improve respiratory function may adversely affect renal and central nervous system function. Conversely, increasing intravascular volume to raise cardiac output in a patient with left ventricular infarction may result in noncardiogenic pulmonary edema if preexistent parenchymal lung injury is present. One of the major challenges of critical care is that physicians caring for severely ill patients must synthesize an overall management strategy that supports several organ systems and often incorporates the view of numerous consultants.

Finally, the management should be directed and dynamic. Diagnostic studies should be performed for good reasons, not just because the results are intellectually interesting, and treatments should be initiated with specific end points in mind. Although many such treatments constitute therapeutic trials, both their potential benefits and adverse effects should be appreciated. Practitioners also should appreciate that critically ill patients frequently (and often swiftly) change, and that such change must be explained and addressed. Thus, although standing orders may be appropriate in many circumstances,

---

Table 98–1 • FEATURES OF CRITICAL CARE UNITS
High nurse-to-patient ratio
Ready accessibility of physicians
Ability to provide invasive cardiovascular and respiratory monitoring
Availability of respiratory support techniques
Ability to provide supervised continuous infusion of pharmacologic agents
Ability to provide humane end-of-life care

Table 98–2 • APPROACH TO THE CRITICALLY ILL PATIENT
Rapid initial assessment and intervention
Formulation of a broader and more comprehensive diagnostic and treatment plan
Management based on understanding of physiology and pathophysiology
Appreciation of organ–system interdependence
Directed and dynamic management approach

other orders should be revised regularly. Similarly, while making rounds, critical care physicians should review not only the patient's overall course, but also the functioning of all organ systems, preferably several times a day.

Prognosis of Critically Ill Patients

Critical care units have been used in more or less their present form since approximately the late 1960s, yet their contribution to health care has not been well quantified. For example, the outcome of patients with bacteremic pneumococcal pneumonia has not been appreciably improved by critical care. Cardiopulmonary resuscitation (CPR), when performed on hospitalized patients or persons older than 70 years out of the hospital, may be successful less than 10% of the time. The survival rate of patients with three or more organ failures after 5 days in a critical care unit approached zero in one large investigation. Also, the mortality rate of patients with cardiogenic shock (Chapter 103) in the absence of coronary revascularization remains approximately 75% despite pulmonary artery catheterization, a finding that has led to questions regarding the value of this monitoring technique. Indeed, in a recent observational study of a wide variety of critically ill patients, after adjustment for treatment selection bias, pulmonary artery catheterization was associated with increased mortality as well as increased cost. In response to this study, investigations of the benefits of pulmonary artery catheterization in patients with disorders such as the acute respiratory distress syndrome (ARDS; Chapters 102 and 104) and heart failure are underway.

Data such as these imply that critical care is of little or no value in several categories of illness. Yet patients in the postoperative period and patients with cardiac arrhythmias, narcotic and sedative drug overdose, reversible neuromuscular disease, hypovolemic shock, and asthma and chronic obstructive pulmonary disease clearly benefit from critical care. Furthermore, the prognoses in certain diseases seem to be improving. For example, 90% of patients with ARDS died in a series from the 1970s compared with only 40% of patients with ARDS receiving traditional high tidal volume ventilation in a trial conducted from 1996 through 1999. Given the lack of therapeutic breakthroughs, other than low tidal volume ventilation in the treatment of ARDS since the 1970s, the most likely explanation for the better outcome of patients with this disorder over time is improved supportive care.

Establishing prognosis is difficult in critically ill patients because such patients are heterogeneous and their prognosis changes over time. In recent years, a number of prognostic scoring systems based on the findings from large groups of patients have been developed to help quantify the severity of illness and determine whether individual patients will survive to hospital discharge. For example, the Acute Physiology and Chronic Health Evaluation (APACHE) III system uses major medical and surgical disease categories, acute physiologic abnormalities, age, preexisting functional limitations, major comorbidities, and treatment location before critical care admission for these purposes. Mortality estimated by APACHE III is comparable to that estimated by physicians in most circumstances, and this and other systems are increasingly used as adjuncts to clinical judgment in critical care medicine.

Ethical Issues in Critical Care Medicine

Despite their potential usefulness, prognostic scoring systems such as APACHE are rarely used to restrict admission to critical care units because most clinicians who treat severely ill patients hope that the patient may survive; they therefore request critical care almost regardless of the likely prognosis. One reason for this clinical approach is that statistical prediction is difficult in individual patients despite data derived from groups. Another is that patients and their families usually desire critical care if it will prolong life, assuming that self-awareness and social interaction are maintained. A third reason is that physicians may respond to what has been called the technologic imperative: the desire to do everything possible despite the ratio of benefit to cost.

Critical care is extraordinarily expensive. The issue of who should be admitted to critical care units and how aggressively they should be treated is a social, as well as medical, concern. This concern is likely to increase as society grapples with limited medical resources and adopts approaches such as managed care to reduce health care costs. Nevertheless, although marginally beneficial critical care can

be theoretically restricted on the basis of high cost relative to benefit, decisions to limit care should be made only by explicit institutional policies that reflect a social consensus in support of such limitations (Chapter 3). Furthermore, patients and the public should be informed of any potential financial incentives for physicians or health care institutions to limit care (Chapter 2).

Until this issue of allocation of critical care resources is resolved at a societal level, physicians should base decisions regarding critical care primarily on the wishes of well-informed, mentally capable patients or their surrogates (Chapter 2). Certainly physicians are not obligated to provide care they consider nonbeneficial, but patients and surrogates who request critical care should receive it if they can benefit and if space in the unit permits. Conversely, the wishes of mentally capable patients who choose against therapies, such as endotracheal intubation and mechanical ventilation, should be respected, as should the wishes of the surrogates who speak for them.

Orders not to initiate CPR, which are also called "do-not-attempt-resuscitation" or "DNAR" orders (Chapter 3), may be written at the request of patients or surrogates or may be initiated by physicians when, to the best of their knowledge, CPR will not be successful in the restoring of life. In most instances, such decisions should be discussed with the patient and, when appropriate, with his or her family. The order should then be written in standard fashion on the order sheet, and a note describing the basis for the order and the decisions that took place should be included in the chart. Such orders clarify the ambiguity that surrounds the decisions concerning critical care for patients with irreversible illnesses, and they relieve nurses or uninvolved physicians from the responsibility of deciding not to initiate CPR.

Some patients with preexisting DNAR orders may still benefit from critical care. Treatment of airway obstruction, metabolic abnormalities, or arrhythmias may at least temporarily improve the patient's condition and make the existence of prior DNAR orders moot. Nevertheless, when written in a critical care unit, DNAR orders usually represent the start of a pattern of withholding or withdrawing of life support. Most patients who die in critical care units do so during the forgoing of life-sustaining therapy, which allows death to result from the patient's underlying disease. The withholding and withdrawal of life support at the request of patients or surrogates is supported by numerous state court decisions and by decisions of the U.S. Supreme Court. The Supreme Court also has sanctioned generally the administration of sedatives and analgesics to reduce pain and suffering, which might be called intensive palliative care (Chapter 2). The ability to provide humane end-of-life care to patients who are unlikely to recover is as important a feature of critical care units as is the ability to provide potentially life-saving monitoring and medical interventions to patients who are likely to live.

SUGGESTED READINGS

The Acute Respiratory Distress Syndrome Network: Ventilation with lower tidal volumes as compared with traditional tidal volumes for acute lung injury and the acute respiratory distress syndrome. N Engl J Med 2000;342:1301–1308. *Patients who received high tidal volume ventilation similar to that used since ARDS was first described had a 40% mortality in this study.*

Curtis JR, Rubenfeld GO, eds: Managing death in the intensive care unit: the transition from cure to comfort. Oxford: Oxford University Press, 2001. *The first book to describe the legal, ethical, and clinical aspects of managing death in the ICU.*

Herridge MS, Cheung AM, Tansey CM, et al: One-year outcomes in survivors of the acute respiratory distress syndrome. N Engl J Med 2003;348:683–693. *Most patients had persistent functional disability at one year.*

Luce JM, Alpers A: Legal aspects of withholding and withdrawing life support from critically ill patients in the United States and providing palliative care to them. Am J Respir Crit Care Med 2000;162:2029–2032. *A discussion of the court decisions that sanction the forgoing of life-sustaining treatment and the administration of palliative care.*

99 ACUTE RESPIRATORY FAILURE

Leonard D. Hudson
Arthur S. Slutsky

Definition

Acute respiratory failure occurs when dysfunction of the respiratory system results in abnormal gas exchange that is potentially life-threatening. Each element of this definition is important to understand. The term *acute* implies a relatively sudden onset (from hours to days) and a substantial change from the patient's baseline condition. Dysfunction of the respiratory system indicates that the abnormal gas exchange may be caused by abnormalities in any element of the respiratory system (e.g., a central nervous system abnormality affecting regulation of breathing or a musculoskeletal thoracic abnormality affecting ventilation; Chapter 83) in addition to abnormalities of the lung itself. The term *respiration* in its broad sense refers to the delivery of oxygen (O_2) (Table 99–1) to metabolically active tissues for energy usage and the removal of carbon dioxide (CO_2) from these tissues. Respiratory failure is a failure of the process of delivering oxygen to the tissues and/or removing CO_2 from the tissues. Abnormalities in the periphery (e.g., cyanide poisoning, pathologic distribution of organ blood flow in sepsis) also can lead to tissue hypoxia; although these conditions represent forms of respiratory failure in the broadest terms, this chapter focuses on respiratory failure resulting from dysfunction of the lungs, chest wall, and control of respiration.

Abnormal gas exchange is the physiologic hallmark of acute respiratory failure. Although gas exchange can be abnormal either for oxygenation or for CO_2 removal, significant hypoxemia is nearly always present in patients with acute respiratory failure. If CO_2 retention is present at a level that is potentially life-threatening, it usually is accompanied by significant hypoxemia (see later). The *life-threatening* aspect of the definition places the degree of abnormal gas exchange in a clinical context and calls for urgent treatment.

The diagnosis of acute respiratory failure requires a significant change from baseline. Many patients with chronic respiratory problems can function with blood gas tensions that might be alarming in a normal individual. Over time, these patients with so-called chronic respiratory failure or chronic respiratory insufficiency have developed mechanisms to compensate for inadequate gas exchange. Conversely the chronic condition makes them vulnerable to insults that could be tolerated easily by a previously healthy individual.

In acute respiratory failure, the O_2 content in the blood (available for tissue use) is reduced to a level at which the possibility of end-organ dysfunction increases markedly. The value of the partial pressure of O_2 in the arterial blood (PaO_2) that demarcates this vulnerable zone is the point of the oxyhemoglobin dissociation relationship where any further decrease in the PaO_2 results in sharp decreases in the amount of hemoglobin that is saturated with O_2 (SaO_2) and in the arterial blood O_2 content (CaO_2). Although arbitrary, acute respiratory failure often is defined in practice as occurring when the PaO_2 is less than 55 mm Hg (Fig. 99–1). In general, the patient's position on the curve at the location where O_2 is being unloaded to the tissues is the most important determinant of how much O_2 is available for the cells and their mitochondria. Usually the ability to unload O_2 at the tissue level more than compensates for small decreases in the amount of O_2 that is picked up in the lungs when the oxyhemoglobin dissociation curve is shifted rightward. With a leftward shift in the curve, O_2 is bound more tightly to hemoglobin so that less O_2 is available for tissue delivery.

These clinical considerations imply that any definition of acute respiratory failure based on an absolute level of PaO_2 is arbitrary. A healthy, young, conditioned individual climbing at high altitude might have a PaO_2 of less than 50 mm Hg because of the reduction in inspired O_2 pressure. This individual is not in acute respiratory failure even though the PaO_2 might be in the low 40s. A patient who has chronic obstructive pulmonary disease (COPD) and whose usual range of PaO_2 is 50 to 55 mm Hg would not be considered to be in acute respiratory failure if the PaO_2 is now 50 mm Hg. If a patient's usual PaO_2

Table 99–1 • ABBREVIATIONS COMMONLY USED IN ACUTE RESPIRATORY FUNCTION

ABG	Arterial blood gas or arterial blood gas analysis
ALI	Acute lung injury
ARDS	Acute respiratory distress syndrome
ARF	Acute respiratory failure
cm H_2O	Centimeters of water
CaO_2	Content of oxygen in the arterial blood
CcO_2	Content of oxygen in the end-capillary blood
CO_2	Carbon dioxide
COPD	Chronic obstructive pulmonary disease
CPAP	Continuous positive airway pressure (used when positive pressure during exhalation is applied with spontaneous ventilation)
CvO_2	Content of oxygen in the mixed venous blood
FIO_2	Fraction of inspired oxygen
g/dL	Grams per deciliter
HbO_2	Saturation of hemoglobin by oxygen
L/min	Liters per minute
mL/kg	Milliliters per kilogram
mL/min	Milliliters per minute
mm Hg	Millimeters of mercury
NIPPV	Noninvasive positive-pressure ventilation
O_2	Oxygen
$P(A-a)O_2$	Difference of the partial pressure of oxygen between the alveolar gas and the arterial blood (alveolar-to-arterial oxygen difference)
$PACO_2$	Partial pressure of carbon dioxide in the alveolar gas
$PaCO_2$	Partial pressure of carbon dioxide in the arterial blood
PAO_2	Partial pressure of oxygen in the alveolar gas
PaO_2	Partial pressure of oxygen in the arterial blood
PaO_2/FIO_2	Ratio of partial pressure of oxygen in the arterial blood to the fraction of inspired oxygen
PBW	Predicted body weight
$PcCO_2$	Partial pressure of carbon dioxide in the end-capillary blood
PcO_2	Partial pressure of oxygen in the end-capillary blood
PEEP	Positive end-expiratory pressure (used when positive pressure during exhalation is applied with mechanical ventilation)
P/F	PaO_2/FIO_2 ratio
PIO_2	Partial pressure of oxygen in the inspired gas
PO_2	Partial pressure of oxygen
$PvCO_2$	Partial pressure of carbon dioxide in the mixed venous blood
PvO_2	Partial pressure of oxygen in the mixed venous blood
Q	Blood flow or perfusion
RR	Respiratory rate
SaO_2	% saturation of hemoglobin by oxygen in the arterial blood
V̇	Ventilation
V̇/Q̇	Ventilation-to-perfusion ratio
VT	Tidal volume

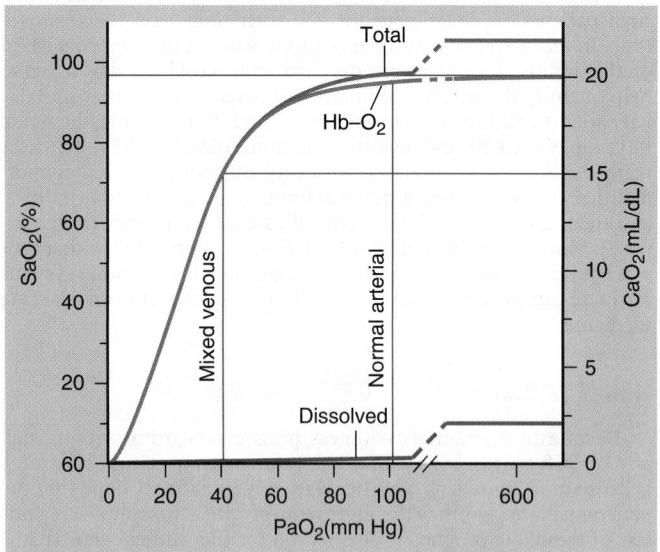

FIGURE 99–1 • The oxyhemoglobin association-dissociation curve. The axis for oxygen saturation (SaO_2) is on the left, and the axis for arterial content of oxygen (CaO_2) is on the right. CaO_2 is the sum of the oxygen dissolved in plasma (denoted as "Dissolved" in the figure) plus the oxygen bound to hemoglobin (Hb-O_2). Note that at a normal hemoglobin, most of the oxygen is carried in combination with hemoglobin (Hb-O_2), with only a relatively small amount of oxygen dissolved in plasma. When the value of PaO_2 is on the "flat" portion of the curve (PaO_2 of ≥60 to 65 mm Hg, normal PCO_2, and normal pH), raising the PaO_2 further has relatively little effect on total oxygen content. Increases in temperature, PCO_2, hydrogen ion concentration, or 2,3-diphosphoglycerate cause a rightward shift in the oxyhemoglobin association-dissociation curve. SaO_2, % saturation of hemoglobin by oxygen in the arterial blood.

was 60 to 70 mm Hg, however, a PaO_2 of 50 mm Hg would be associated with a substantial risk for a further life-threatening reduction in oxygenation; this patient should be considered to have acute respiratory failure.

The level of arterial CO_2 partial pressure ($PaCO_2$) that defines acute respiratory failure traditionally has been 50 mm Hg or greater if accompanied by an arterial acidosis with pH of 7.30 or less. The $PaCO_2$ is linked to pH in the definition because it generally is thought that the acidosis leads to tissue dysfunction and symptoms. Patients with severe COPD may have chronic CO_2 retention, but their compensated respiratory acidosis protects them against abnormalities related to the elevation in CO_2. A further acute rise in $PaCO_2$ can precipitate symptoms and other organ dysfunction, however. By comparison, respiratory acidosis (even as severe as a pH of 7.1) seems to be well tolerated in most previously healthy individuals if arterial and tissue oxygenation is adequate.

Pathophysiology of Hypoxemia

Five pathophysiologic mechanisms can lead to a reduction in PaO_2: (1) decreased inspired partial pressure of oxygen (PIO_2) (e.g., at high altitude or when breathing a reduced percent O_2 mixture); (2) hypoventilation; (3) ventilation-perfusion ($\dot{V}/\dot{Q}$) mismatch; (4) a shunting of blood from the pulmonary to systemic circulation, bypassing the alveoli anatomically or functionally; and (5) abnormal diffusion of O_2 from the alveoli into the capillary blood. In essence, a shunt is an extreme $\dot{V}/\dot{Q}$ mismatch in which blood perfuses alveoli with *no* ventilation; it is differentiated clinically from other $\dot{V}/\dot{Q}$ mismatching by the response to breathing supplemental O_2 (see later).

For clinical purposes, diffusion abnormalities are not an important cause of hypoxemia at sea level because there is sufficient time for adequate diffusion during the transit of a red blood cell through the pulmonary capillary bed, even in the presence of severe lung disease. Even when diffusion abnormalities are present and contribute to hypoxemia, $\dot{V}/\dot{Q}$ mismatch or shunting nearly always coexist and are quantitatively more important causes of hypoxemia. Except at high altitude or when a subject is breathing a gas mixture low in O_2, hypoventilation, $\dot{V}/\dot{Q}$ mismatch, and shunting are the dominant causes of acute respiratory failure.

If only hypoventilation is present, the resulting hypoxemia is associated with a normal difference between the alveolar and arterial oxygenation levels ($P(A-a)O_2$). In this setting, an elevated $PaCO_2$ suggests disease processes that affect nonpulmonary respiratory function (e.g., central respiratory depression resulting from drug overdose, neuromuscular diseases such as Guillain-Barré syndrome, or chest wall disease such as flail chest; Chapter 83). In contrast, $\dot{V}/\dot{Q}$ mismatch and shunting are associated with an elevated $P(A-a)O_2$, which may or may not coexist with hypoventilation.

When $\dot{V}/\dot{Q}$ mismatch or shunting is the cause of hypoxemia, some alveolar regions have increased $PACO_2$ and reduced PAO_2; the blood in the vessels perfusing these alveoli reflects these abnormal gas tensions. The increased $PACO_2$ usually can be reversed by increasing overall ventilation, but hyperventilation does not correct the decreased PaO_2 (Chapter 100).

$\dot{V}/\dot{Q}$ mismatch is distinguished from shunting by assessing the PaO_2 response to enhanced O_2 administration. Hypoxemia caused by $\dot{V}/\dot{Q}$ mismatch can be corrected to a nearly complete O_2 saturation of the hemoglobin in most patients by a relatively small increase in the fraction of inspired oxygen (FIO_2), such as an increase in FIO_2 from 0.21 to 0.24 to 0.28 or 1 to 2 L/min O_2 (by nasal prongs) in patients with acute exacerbations of COPD. If the airways to poorly ventilated alveoli remain open and the enriched O_2 mixture is administered for an adequate length of time (ranging from a few minutes to 20 minutes, depending on the degree of $\dot{V}/\dot{Q}$ inequality), the increased PIO_2 is reflected by an increased PAO_2 and an increased PaO_2. When a shunt is present (no ventilation but continued perfusion), a relatively small increase in the FIO_2 has little or no effect on the PaO_2, and even large increases in FIO_2 up to 1.0 result in only modest increases in PaO_2 (Fig. 99-2).

APPROACH TO ACUTE RESPIRATORY FAILURE

Acute respiratory failure can be classified in several ways (Table 99-2).

Diagnosis

As part of the diagnosis of acute respiratory failure, the physician should address three objectives: (1) confirm the clinical suspicion that acute respiratory failure is present; (2) classify the type of acute respiratory failure (e.g., hypoxemia caused by hypoventilation versus hypoxemia caused by $\dot{V}/\dot{Q}$ mismatch); and (3) determine the specific cause (e.g., acute lung injury secondary to sepsis or decompensated COPD because of acute bronchitis). Defining the type of acute respiratory failure and the specific cause are prerequisites to optimal management.

The initial approach to diagnosis consists of consideration of information from four sources: (1) the clinical history and physical examination; (2) the physiologic abnormalities, particularly the arterial blood gas derangements, which help establish the pathophysiologic mechanisms of hypoxemia; (3) the chest radiographic findings; and (4) other tests aimed at elucidating specific causes. In many cases, the clinical picture from the history is so clear that the presumptive type of acute respiratory failure (and sometimes the cause) is obvious, so treatment can be started while confirmatory laboratory studies are ordered. In other cases, the clinician may be asked to see the patient because of an abnormal chest radiograph or abnormal arterial blood gases that were ordered by someone else and may elicit the pertinent history based on these clues. When the degree of hypoxemia is life-threatening, therapeutic decisions must be made quickly, even if data are limited. The clinician must obtain updated information continually and view most therapeutic decisions as therapeutic trials, with careful monitoring to assess desired benefits and possible detrimental effects.

HISTORY AND PHYSICAL EXAMINATION. The presentation often reflects one of three clinical scenarios: (1) the effects of hypoxemia and/or respiratory acidosis; (2) the effects of primary (e.g., pneumonia) or secondary (e.g., heart failure) diseases involving the lungs; and (3) the nonpulmonary effects of the underlying disease process. The clinical effects of hypoxemia and/or respiratory acidosis are manifest mainly in the central nervous system (e.g., irritability, agitation, changes in personality, a depressed level of consciousness, or coma) and the cardiovascular system (e.g., arrhythmias, hypotension, or hypertension) (Table 99-3). In patients with underlying COPD with gradual onset of acute respiratory failure, central nervous system abnormalities may be the major presenting findings. Cyanosis, which requires at least 5 g/dL of unsaturated hemoglobin to be detectable, may not be seen before serious tissue hypoxia develops, especially in patients with underlying anemia.

Pulmonary symptoms and signs often reflect the respiratory disease that is causing the acute respiratory failure. Examples include cough and sputum with pneumonia (Chapter 92) or chest pain from pulmonary thromboembolism with infarction (Chapter 94). Conversely, dyspnea and respiratory distress are nonspecific reflections of increased demands on the respiratory system from pulmonary and nonpulmonary diseases.

Physical findings may be associated with a particular pathologic lung process, such as pneumonia causing bronchial breathing and crackles on auscultation or the rales of cardiogenic pulmonary edema (Chapter 55). Physical findings may be minimal or absent with acute lung injury or pulmonary thromboembolism.

In some patients, the clinical picture is dominated by the underlying disease process, particularly with diseases that cause acute lung injury, such as sepsis (Chapter 104), severe pneumonia, aspiration of gastric contents (Chapter 90), or trauma. In these conditions, the physical examination is often nonspecific, without obvious clues except fever and hypotension.

ASSESSMENT OF PHYSIOLOGIC ABNORMALITIES. The clinical suspicion of acute respiratory failure must be addressed by arterial blood gas analysis to answer several questions. (1) *Is hypoxemia present?* The answer is largely based on the value of the PaO_2 or SaO_2, and the degree of the hypoxemia not only confirms the diagnosis of acute respiratory failure, but also helps define its severity. (2) *Is hypoventilation present?* If the $PaCO_2$ is elevated, alveolar hypoventilation is present. (3) *Does the degree of hypoventilation explain the hypoxemia?* If the $P(A-a)O_2$ is normal, hypoventilation explains the presence and degree of hypoxemia. In this circumstance, the most likely causes of acute respiratory failure are central nervous system abnormalities or a chest wall abnormality. If the $P(A-a)O_2$ is increased, hypoventilation does not explain all of the hypoxemia, and another condition must be present: Common diagnoses include COPD, severe asthma, and

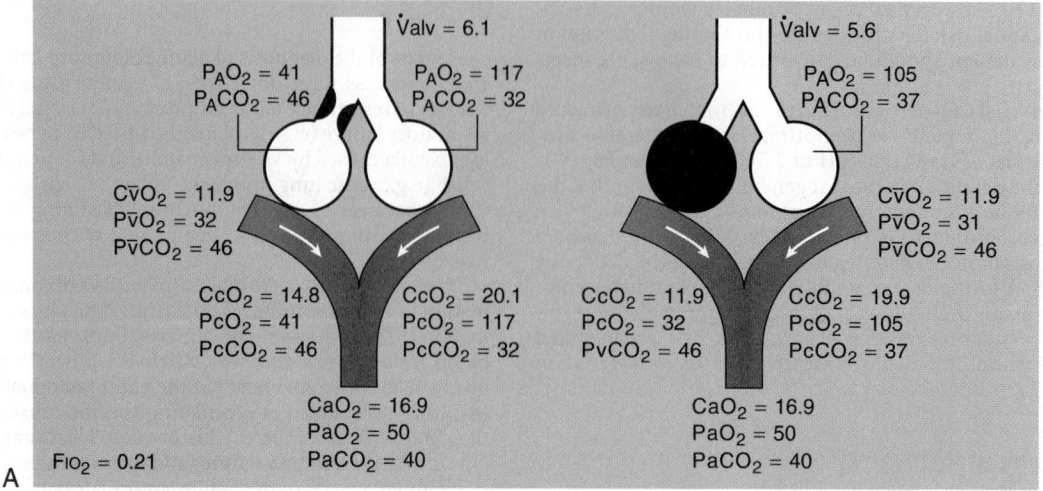

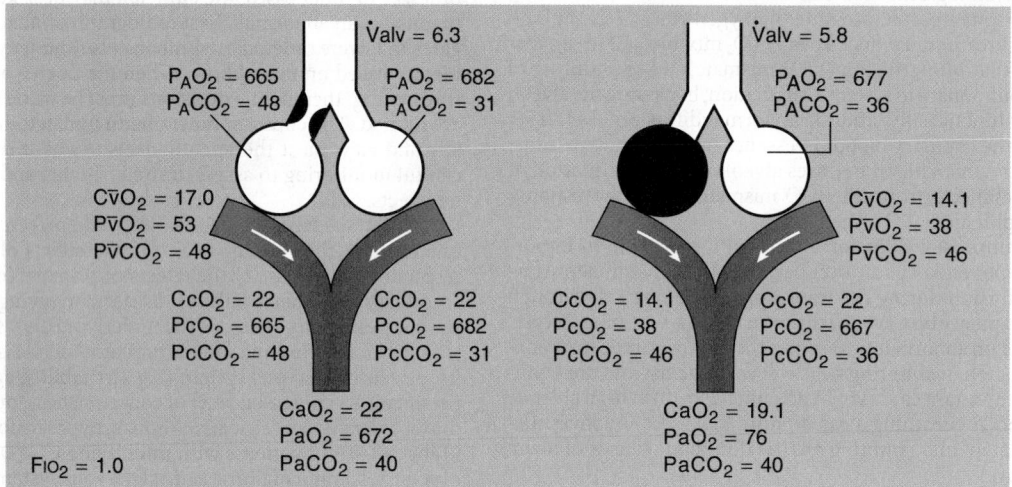

FIGURE 99–2 • The difference in the effect on arterial oxygenation of increasing fraction of inspired oxygen (F_{IO_2}) from breathing room air ($F_{IO_2} = 0.21$) (*A*) compared with breathing 100% oxygen ($F_{IO_2} = 1.0$) (*B*) between low ventilation-to-perfusion ratio ($\dot{V}/\dot{Q}$) (*left*) and shunt (*right*), using a two-compartment lung model. Shunt and decreased $\dot{V}/\dot{Q}$ can lead to identical arterial blood gases (partial pressure of oxygen in the arterial blood [Pa_{O_2}] = 50 mm Hg; partial pressure of carbon dioxide in the arterial blood [Pa_{CO_2}] = 40 mm Hg); the response to supplemental oxygen administration is markedly different. Hypoxemia is only partially corrected by breathing 100% oxygen when a shunt is present because arterial oxygenation represents an average of the end-capillary oxygen contents (Cc_{O_2}) from various parts of the lung, not an average of the partial pressures of oxygen (partial pressure of carbon dioxide in the end-capillary blood [Pc_{CO_2}]). When the Cc_{O_2} values are mixed, the Pa_{O_2} is determined from the resultant content of oxygen in the arterial blood (Ca_{O_2}) by the oxyhemoglobin association-dissociation relationship (see Fig. 99–1). With low $\dot{V}/\dot{Q}$ (as is often the case in patients with chronic obstructive pulmonary disease), an increase in F_{IO_2} increases the alveolar P_{O_2} of the low $\dot{V}/\dot{Q}$ unit and leads to a marked increase in arterial P_{O_2}. The values in this figure were generated from modeling so as to result in the same Pa_{CO_2} ($Pa_{CO_2} = 40$ mm Hg) for all four situations shown, and this is the reason for slight changes in alveolar ventilation ($\dot{V}_{alv}$) for some of the conditions. Several assumptions are made: (1) No diffusion limitation is present; (2) oxygen consumption = 300 mL/min and CO_2 production = 240 mL/min; (3) cardiac output = 6.0 L/min; (4) the low $\dot{V}/\dot{Q}$ region in the left panels represents 60% of the cardiac output perfusing alveoli with $\dot{V}/\dot{Q}$ of 25% of normal; and (5) the shunt in the right panels represents a 37% shunt (i.e., 37% of the cardiac output is perfusing alveoli with no ventilation). F_{IO_2} = fraction of inspired oxygen; $\dot{V}/\dot{Q}$ = ventilation to perfusion ratio; Pa_{CO_2} = partial pressure of carbon dioxide in the arterial blood; Cc_{O_2} = content of oxygen in the end-capillary blood; Pc_{CO_2} = partial pressure of carbon dioxide in the end-capillary blood; Ca_{O_2} = content of oxygen in the arterial blood; P_{O_2} = partial pressure of oxygen; $\dot{V}_{alv}$ = alveolar ventilation; ml/min = milliliters per minute; L/min = liters per minute.

early-stage acute respiratory distress syndrome (ARDS). (4) If hypoxemia exists without hypoventilation, an elevated P(A-a)O₂ should be confirmed, and the response to breathing an enhanced O₂ mixture would answer the question: *Is the increase in P(A-a)O₂ due to a $\dot{V}/\dot{Q}$ abnormality or to shunting?* If hypoxemia is primarily due to a $\dot{V}/\dot{Q}$ abnormality, the likely cause is an airway disease, either COPD or acute severe asthma, or a vascular disease, such as pulmonary thromboembolism. If shunting is the major explanation for the hypoxemia, processes that fill the airspaces (e.g., cardiogenic pulmonary edema, noncardiogenic pulmonary edema in early acute lung injury or ARDS, or purulent pulmonary secretions in acute pneumonia) or, less commonly, an intracardiac or anatomic intrapulmonary shunt are the likely causes. Conditions that fill air spaces should be confirmed by an abnormal chest radiograph; if the radiograph is normal, an intracardiac shunt should be considered by echocardiography.

CHEST RADIOGRAPH. The chest radiograph in acute respiratory failure is likely to show one of three patterns (Fig. 99–3): (1) normal (or relatively normal), (2) localized alveolar-filling opacities, and (3) diffuse alveolar-filling opacities. Diffuse interstitial opacities are also possible, but diseases that cause this pattern are usually of more gradual onset and are associated with chronic respiratory failure. If the chest radiograph is normal (i.e., it is clear or relatively clear), airway diseases, such as COPD and asthma, or pulmonary vascular diseases,

Table 99–2 • SYSTEMS TO CLASSIFY ACUTE RESPIRATORY FAILURE

HYPOXIC ARF VERSUS HYPERCAPNIC-HYPOXIC ARF

Causes of hypoxic ARF
Acute lung injury/ARDS
Pneumonia
Pulmonary thromboembolism
Acute lobar atelectasis
Cardiogenic pulmonary edema
Lung contusion
Acute collagen-vascular disease (Goodpasture's syndrome, systemic
lupus erythematosus)
Causes of hypercapnic-hypoxic ARF
Pulmonary disease
COPD
Asthma—advanced acute severe asthma
Drugs causing respiratory depression
Neuromuscular
Guillain-Barré syndrome
Acute myasthenia gravis
Spinal cord tumors
Metabolic derangements causing weakness (including
hypophosphatemia, hypomagnesemia)
Musculoskeletal
Kyphoscoliosis
Ankylosing spondylitis
Obesity hypoventilation syndrome (often with acute superimposed
additional abnormality as cause of ARF)

ETIOLOGIC MECHANISMS OF HYPOXEMIA

Normal $P(A-a)O_2$*
↓ PIO_2
High altitude; inadvertent administration of low FIO_2 gas mixture
hypoventilation
See causes of hypercapnic-hypoxic ARF above
Increased $P(A-a)O_2$*
Ventilation-perfusion ($\dot{V}/\dot{Q}$) mismatch
Airway disease
Vascular disease including pulmonary thromboembolism
Shunt
Acute lung injury/ARDS
Pneumonia
Parenchymal lung disease
Cardiogenic pulmonary edema
Pulmonary infarction
Diffusion limitation†

ARF: WITH AND WITHOUT CHRONIC LUNG DISEASE

With chronic lung disease
COPD
Asthma
Parenchymal lung diseases
Restrictive lung/chest wall diseases
Without lung disease (these also can be superimposed on chronic
disease)
Acute lung injury/ARDS
Pneumonia
Pulmonary thromboembolism

ARF BY ORGAN SYSTEM INVOLVED

Respiratory (lungs and thorax)
Airways/airflow obstruction
COPD
Asthma
Pulmonary parenchyma
Pneumonia
Acute lung injury/ARDS
Acute flair of chronic collagen-vascular disease (e.g., Goodpasture's
syndrome or systemic lupus erythematosus)
Central nervous system
Respiratory depression
Increased sedatives, tranquilizers with respiratory effect, opiates,
alcohol
Brainstem and spinal cord involvement
Tumors, trauma, vascular accidents
Neuromuscular
Guillain-Barré syndrome
Myasthenia gravis
Cardiovascular
Cardiogenic pulmonary edema
Pulmonary thromboembolism
Renal/endocrine
Volume overload
Metabolic abnormalities

*Calculated using the alveolar-air equation; see text for description.
†See text for discussion.
ARDS = acute respiratory distress syndrome; ARF = acute respiratory failure; COPD = chronic obstructive pulmonary disease; FIO_2 = fraction of inspired oxygen;
$P(A-a)O_2$ = alveolar-to-arterial oxygen difference; PIO_2 = partial pressure of inspired oxygen; $\dot{V}/\dot{Q}$ = ventilation-to-perfusion ratio.

Table 99–3 • CLINICAL MANIFESTATIONS OF HYPOXEMIA AND HYPERCAPNIA

HYPOXEMIA	HYPERCAPNIA
Tachycardia	Somnolence
Tachypnea	Lethargy
Anxiety	Restlessness
Diaphoresis	Tremor
Altered mental status	Slurred speech
Confusion	Headache
Cyanosis	Asterixis
Hypertension	Papilledema
Hypotension	Coma
Bradycardia	Diaphoresis
Seizures	
Coma	
Lactic acidosis*	

*Usually requires additional reduction in oxygen delivery because of inadequate cardiac output, severe anemia, or redistribution of blood flow.

such as thromboembolism, are more likely. If a localized alveolar-filling abnormality is present, pneumonia is the major consideration, but pulmonary embolism and infarction also should be considered. When diffuse (bilateral) alveolar-filling abnormalities are present, cardiogenic pulmonary edema, acute lung injury (such as is seen with sepsis, trauma, or aspiration of gastric contents; see Table 99–4), and a diffuse pneumonia are the major considerations. The combination of the chest radiograph with the arterial blood gas interpretation can be helpful. The finding of a significant shunt may suggest acute lung injury in a patient in whom this diagnosis was not otherwise clinically obvious; the chest radiograph should help confirm that possibility.

OTHER DIAGNOSTIC TESTING. All patients with acute respiratory failure should have a complete blood count, including a platelet count, routine blood chemistry tests, a prothrombin time, and a urinalysis to screen for possible underlying causes and comorbid conditions. Other blood tests should be guided by the clinical picture. Examples include a serum amylase level if pancreatitis is a possible cause of ARDS and thyroid indices if severe hypothyroidism is a possible cause of hypoventilation. Blood cultures are recommended whenever sepsis is suspected.

Any abnormal fluid collections, especially pleural effusion (Chapter 95), should be aspirated for diagnostic purposes. Sputum culture is indicated when pneumonia is suspected.

Other specific tests should be directed by the history, physical examinations, arterial blood gas levels, and chest radiograph. An abdominal computed tomography (CT) scan may be indicated to search for the source of infection in a patient with sepsis and acute lung injury. A chest CT scan may help define pulmonary pathology if the chest radiograph is not definitive. A head CT scan may be indicated if a stroke involving the respiratory center is suspected. Routine blood chemistries can detect diabetic ketoacidosis or renal failure as contributing causes.

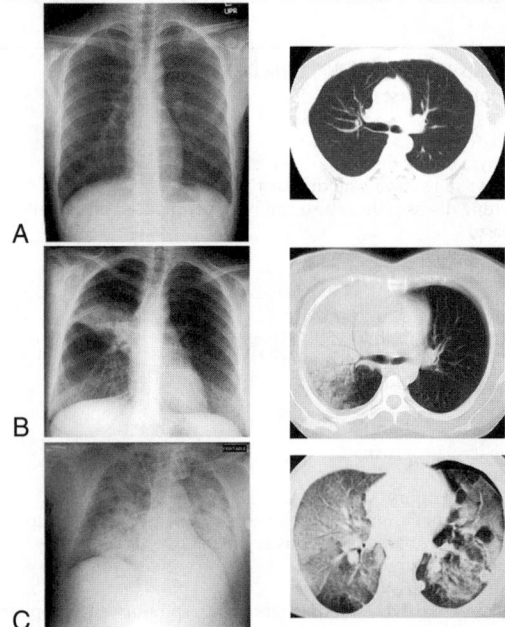

FIGURE 99–3 • Chest radiographs and computed tomography (CT) scans of the three most common findings in diseases causing acute respiratory failure. *A*, A relatively clear chest, consistent with airway disease with an acute exacerbation (i.e., asthma and chronic obstructive pulmonary disease) or a central nervous system or neuromuscular disease cause of acute respiratory failure. *B*, A localized alveolar-filling opacity, most commonly seen with acute pneumonia. *C*, Diffuse bilateral alveolar-filling opacities consistent with acute lung injury and acute respiratory distress syndrome. The CT scan in *C* shows a small left pneumothorax and cavities or cysts that are not apparent on the anteroposterior chest radiograph.

Rx Treatment

GENERAL PRINCIPLES. The management of acute respiratory failure depends on its cause, its clinical manifestations, and the patient's underlying status. Certain goals apply to all patients: (1) improvement in the hypoxemia to eliminate or reduce markedly the acute threat to life, (2) improvement of the acidosis if it is considered to be life-threatening, (3) maintenance of cardiac output or improvement if the cardiac output is compromised, (4) treatment of the underlying disease process, and (5) avoiding predictable complications.

The precise methods for improving hypoxemia depend on the cause of the acute respiratory failure. An increase in the inspired O_2 concentration is a cornerstone of treatment for nearly all patients, however.

The level of acidosis that requires treatment other than for the underlying disease process is not clear. Although normalization of the arterial pH has been suggested in the past, respiratory acidosis and combined respiratory and metabolic acidosis are apparently well tolerated in many patients with severe ARDS so that a pH of 7.15 may not require bicarbonate therapy. If the acidemia coexists with clinical complications, such as cardiac arrhythmias or a decreased level of consciousness, that have no other obvious cause, the acidosis should be treated. The therapeutic goal is alleviation or reduction of the accompanying complications by improving the level of acidosis; it usually is not necessary to normalize the pH (Chapter 113).

The maintenance of cardiac output is crucial for O_2 delivery in acute respiratory failure, especially because mechanical ventilation and positive end-expiratory pressure (PEEP) may compromise cardiac output. Pulmonary artery catheterization can measure cardiac output and fluid status, but patients who have these catheters seem to do no better and perhaps do worse than similar patients managed without them; ongoing trials currently are addressing the role for pulmonary artery catheters in this setting.

Many therapeutic interventions that improve short-term physiologic variables may worsen long-term, clinically important outcomes. Transfusing all patients to maintain a hemoglobin greater than 10 g/dL increases mortality in noncardiac patients, even though the O_2-carrying capacity of the blood is acutely increased[1]; use of a relatively large tidal volume (i.e., 10 mL/kg) increases mortality in patients with ARDS, even though it acutely improves PaO_2 better than a lower tidal volume does.[2]

Improvements in oxygenation, acid-base status, and cardiac output are of no more than temporary benefit, unless the underlying disease process is diagnosed and treated properly. In patients with acute lung injury, sepsis may worsen the injuries to the lung and other organs despite optimal supportive care. Similarly, if the precipitating cause of acute respiratory failure in the patient with COPD is not identified and treated, supportive care is likely to be futile. Complications may arise from the physiologic effects of the acute respiratory failure and whatever disease process is causing it, from being critically ill with its associated treatment settings (e.g., sleep deprivation), or from iatrogenic complications associated with therapy.

MEASURES TO IMPROVE OXYGENATION. A PaO_2 of greater than 60 mm Hg is usually adequate to produce an SaO_2 in the low to mid 90s. The PaO_2 can be increased by administration of supplemental O_2, by pharmacologic manipulations, by continuous positive airway pressure (CPAP), by mechanical ventilation with or without maneuvers such as PEEP, and by use of the prone position. PEEP, pharmacologic manipulations, and positioning are used primarily in patients with acute lung injury (see later).

The initial choice of the concentration and amount of supplemental O_2 likely to be needed is based on the severity of the hypoxemia, the clinical diagnosis, the likely pathophysiologic mechanism causing the hypoxemia, and the O_2 delivery systems available. For the tracheal FIO_2 to be the same as the delivered FIO_2, the O_2 delivery system must deliver a flow that is able to match the patient's peak inspiratory flow rate with gas of a known FIO_2. High-flow O_2 blenders can achieve this goal by delivering gas at equal to or greater than 80 L/min or with any FIO_2 to a nonintubated patient. These systems require a large flow of O_2 (from a wall unit or tank), however, and are not universally available. Other systems for nonintubated patients (including nasal prongs, simple facemasks, and nonrebreather and partial-rebreather masks) use a simple regulator that mixes room air with O_2 at 12 L/min from a wall unit or tank, resulting in flows that frequently are not able to match the patient's peak inspiratory flow rate. The patient entrains more air from the environment, and the resulting tracheal FIO_2 or PIO_2 is unknown. The amount of air entrained depends on the patient's inspiratory pattern and minute ventilation. Although the resulting FIO_2 is unknown, these systems are satisfactory if the delivery is constant and if they result in adequate arterial O_2 saturation, as monitored by arterial blood gases or oximetry. Nasal prongs are able to deliver a tracheal FIO_2 of approximately 0.50, and nonrebreather masks can deliver 50 to 100% O_2, in both cases depending on the inspiratory pattern and flow rate. If only hypoventilation or $\dot{V}/\dot{Q}$ mismatch is present, only a small increment in FIO_2 (e.g., an FIO_2 of 0.24 or 0.28 delivered by a Venturi principle facemask or 1 to 2 L/min O_2 delivered by nasal prongs [or mechanical ventilation]) is likely to be required. By comparison, if marked shunting is the cause of hypoxemia, a considerably higher FIO_2 (e.g., >0.7) is required; a common practice when a significant shunt is suspected is to give an FIO_2 of 1.0, then to adjust the FIO_2 downward as guided by the resulting PaO_2.

The concentration of O_2 that is toxic to the lungs in critically ill patients is not known, but prior injury may provide tolerance to O_2 toxicity, whereas other conditioning agents, such as bleomycin, may enhance oxidative injury. An FIO_2 of equal to or greater than 0.8 generally is considered to be injurious to the human lung, at least the normal human lung. Because it is unknown what lower concentration is safe, however, patients should be given the lowest FIO_2 that provides an adequate O_2 saturation ($SaO_2 \geq 90\%$). If an FIO_2 of equal to or greater than 0.5 to 0.7 is required for adequate oxygenation, other measures described subsequently, especially PEEP or CPAP, should be considered. Even a lower FIO_2 of about 0.5 may be associated with impaired ciliary action in the airways and impaired bacterial killing by alveolar macrophages, but the clinical importance of these effects is not known.

A low concentration of supplemental O_2 can be administered by nasal prongs or nasal cannula, which are generally well tolerated and allow the patient to cough, speak, eat, and drink while receiving O_2. If the nasal passages are open, the PIO_2 does not depend greatly on whether the patient breathes through the nose or mouth because O_2 is entrained from the posterior nasal pharynx during a breath taken through the mouth. The level of O_2 can be adjusted by the flow rate to the nasal prongs. In patients with COPD, flows as low as 0.5 to 2 L/min are usually adequate, unless an intrapulmonary shunt is contributing to the hypoxemia, as usually occurs in acute pneumonia. At flows of greater than approximately 6 L/min, only a small further augmentation in the PIO_2 can be achieved. Because gas flow through the nose has a drying and irritating effect, a facemask should be considered at high flow rates. Oxygen facemasks using the Venturi principle allow regulation of the FIO_2 and can be particularly useful when COPD is suspected and it is important to avoid the CO_2 retention that can be associated with the unregulated administration of O_2. A higher FIO_2 of 0.5 to nearly 1.0 can be administered through a nonrebreathing facemask with an O_2 reservoir. If an FIO_2 of equal to or greater than 0.70 is required for more than several hours, particularly in an unstable patient, endotracheal intubation should be considered so that O_2 can be administered by a closed system with reliable maintenance of the patient's SaO_2. Indications for placing an artificial airway in the patient with acute respiratory failure include airway protection against massive aspiration of gastric contents, delivery of an increased FIO_2, facilitation of prolonged mechanical ventilation, and aid in the control of respiratory secretions (Chapter 101).

Ventilatory maneuvers that may increase arterial oxygenation include mechanical ventilation itself and the administration of PEEP or CPAP, all of which allow ventilation of areas of lung that previously were poorly ventilated or unventilated. Although large tidal volumes with mechanical ventilation may open areas of atelectasis and improve oxygenation initially, these higher tidal volumes can cause lung injury, particularly if the lung is already injured. Because the mechanism of injury is related to overdistention, which is related to the distending pressure, the plateau pressure (the pressure measured at end-inspiration during a period of no flow with any given tidal volume) can serve as a surrogate for the possibility of injury. If a tidal volume is associated with a plateau pressure of greater than 25 to 30 cm H_2O, overdistention may be occurring. Conditions other than an overdistending tidal volume, such as abdominal distention, pleural effusion, or pneumothorax, also may contribute to increases in plateau pressure.

CPAP refers to the maintenance of positive pressure during the expiratory cycle with spontaneous breathing. *PEEP* refers to the maintenance of positive pressure throughout the expiratory cycle when applied together with mechanical ventilation (Chapter 101). CPAP and PEEP can result in recruitment of microatelectatic regions of the lung that are perfused but were not previously ventilated. CPAP and PEEP have the theoretical advantage of keeping some of these regions open during exhalation, preventing cyclical closure and reopening of lung units, which can result in alveolar wall stress and injury. The optimal tradeoff between the use and level of CPAP/PEEP compared with the risk of O_2 toxicity from the administration of a higher FIO_2 is not known. PEEP results in an increased intrathoracic pressure, which can diminish venous return to the heart and decrease cardiac output. PEEP should be titrated to a level that allows adequate O_2 saturation at a nontoxic FIO_2 without impairing cardiac output.

SPECIFIC ACUTE RESPIRATORY FAILURE SYNDROMES
CHRONIC OBSTRUCTIVE PULMONARY DISEASE

Acute respiratory failure in patients with severe COPD is associated with an in-hospital mortality of 6 to 20% (Chapter 85). The severity of the underlying disease and the severity of the acute precipitating illness are important determinants of hospital survival. Hospital mortality is higher if the respiratory failure is associated with a pH less than 7.25. The pH, the $PaCO_2$, and other clinical characteristics cannot be used, however, to predict reliably a particular patient's chances of survival. It is unclear whether an episode of acute respiratory failure changes the long-term prognosis if the patient survives the acute episode.

Diagnosis

When COPD causes acute respiratory failure, patients commonly have a history of increasing dyspnea and sputum production. Acute respiratory failure may present in more cryptic ways, however, such as changes in mental status, arrhythmias, or other cardiovascular abnormalities. Acute respiratory failure must be considered whenever patients with COPD have significant nonspecific clinical changes; the diagnosis can be confirmed or excluded by arterial blood gas analysis. The pH is helpful in assessing whether the hypoventilation is partly or exclusively acute: The pH drops by approximately 0.08 for each 10 mm Hg rise in the $PaCO_2$ in acute respiratory acidosis without renal compensation. By comparison, in chronic respiratory acidosis with normal renal compensation, the pH drop is only about approximately 0.03 for each 10 mm Hg rise in the $PaCO_2$.

Treatment

As soon as acute respiratory failure is confirmed in a patient with COPD, attention must focus on detecting any precipitating events (Table 99–4). Examples include decreased ventilatory drive, commonly because of oversedation; decreased muscle strength or function, often related to electrolyte abnormalities including hypophosphatemia and hypomagnesemia; decreased chest wall elasticity, possibly related to rib fracture, pleural effusion, ileus, or ascites; decreased lung capacity for gas exchange, related to atelectasis, pneumonia, or pulmonary edema; increased airway resistance, caused by bronchospasm or increased secretion; or increased metabolic O_2 requirements, such as with systemic infection. Many of these abnormalities can impair the cough mechanism, diminish the clearance of airway secretions, and precipitate acute respiratory failure.

The most common specific precipitating event is airway infection, especially acute bronchitis. The role played by viral agents, *Mycoplasma pneumoniae*, chronic contaminants of the lower airway such as *Haemophilus influenzae* and *Streptococcus pneumoniae*, and other acute pathogens is difficult to determine on a clinical or even microbiologic basis. Acute exacerbations of COPD commonly result from new infections rather than re-emergence of an infection from preexisting colonization. Antibiotics modestly shorten the duration of the exacerbation without a significant increase in toxicity compared with placebo[3]; the impact of antibiotics on the subsequent emergence of resistant organisms is not known. It is standard practice, however, to use antibiotics to treat the COPD patient who has an exacerbation severe enough to cause acute respiratory failure and who has evidence consistent with acute tracheobronchitis (Chapter 85). Pneumonia may account for 20% of cases of acute respiratory failure in patients with COPD. Compared with the normal population, COPD patients with community-acquired pneumonia are more likely to have gram-negative enteric bacteria or *Legionella* infections and are more likely to have antibiotic-resistant organisms.

Other common precipitating causes of acute respiratory failure include heart failure and worsening of the underlying COPD, often related to noncompliance with medications. Less common and often difficult to diagnose in this setting is pulmonary thromboembolism. The severe acute respiratory syndrome (SARS) requires supportive care; no specific anti-viral therapies are currently available (Chapters 92 and 299).

Many patients with COPD and acute respiratory failure can be managed on a general medical floor rather than in an intensive care unit if the precipitating cause for acute respiratory failure has been diagnosed and is potentially responsive to appropriate therapy, if any blood gas abnormalities respond to O_2 therapy and are not life-threatening, if the patient can cooperate with the treatment, and if appropriate nursing and respiratory care can be provided (Chapter 85). An unstable patient who requires closer observation and monitoring should be admitted to an intensive care unit.

The decision to use mechanical ventilation in patients with COPD and acute respiratory failure must be made on clinical

Continued

grounds and is not dictated by any particular arterial blood gas values. In general, if the patient is alert and able to cooperate with treatment, mechanical ventilation is unlikely to be necessary. If ventilatory support is required, the decision is whether to use non-invasive therapy or endotracheal intubation. Many studies have shown that noninvasive ventilatory support (without endotracheal intubation) is particularly beneficial for patients with COPD and can decrease mortality if applied in appropriate patients without factors that are likely to lead to complications. ◪ Patients must be able to tolerate the nasal or facial mask, must be cooperative and hemodynamically stable, and must have intact upper airway reflexes to prevent aspiration. Noninvasive ventilation is usually more comfortable for the patient, and it reduces the need for sedation. The correction of blood gases is slower with noninvasive ventilation, and gastric distention can occur. Patients must be monitored carefully, and endotracheal intubation is required if the patient deteriorates or cannot tolerate the facemask.

Auto-PEEP or intrinsic PEEP with air trapping is a common and dangerous complication of ventilation in the patient with COPD. For any given increase in alveolar pressure, patients with significant emphysema and increased lung compliance have a greater increase in lung volume and a greater increase in pleural pressure. The result is a greater risk of decreasing venous return and impairing of cardiac output. This complication must be considered and looked for when mechanical ventilation is used in the patient with COPD.

ACUTE LUNG INJURY/ACUTE RESPIRATORY DISTRESS SYNDROME

Definition

ARDS first was described in 1967 as the abrupt onset of diffuse lung injury characterized by severe hypoxemia (shunting) and generalized pulmonary infiltrates on the chest radiograph in the absence of overt cardiac failure. In the early 1990s, the term *acute lung injury* officially was introduced to include traditional ARDS and less severe forms of lung injury. The definitions of acute lung injury and ARDS require bilateral pulmonary infiltrates compatible with pulmonary edema in the absence of clinical heart failure (usually as determined by no evidence of elevated left atrial pressures), but the two are differentiated by the degree of abnormal oxygenation: Patients are defined as having acute lung injury if the PaO_2 divided by the FIO_2 is less than or equal to 300; when the PaO_2 divided by the FIO_2 is less than or equal to 200, the patient meets criteria for ARDS.

Epidemiology

Current data suggest an annual incidence of acute lung injury of 40 to 75 cases per 100,000 population/year. These incidence figures taken together with the associated case-fatality rates, which currently are 30 to 50% but are highly dependent on the severity of disease, make acute lung injury and ARDS major public health problems and major causes of death.

Acute lung injury should be considered as a clinical syndrome that is secondary to some other cause (Table 99–5). This underlying clinical disorder may affect and injure the lungs directly, such as with diffuse pneumonia or aspiration of gastric contents, or may affect the lungs indirectly, such as in severe sepsis (Chapter 104) or severe non-thoracic trauma (Chapter 108). Severe sepsis is the most common precipitating cause of acute lung injury worldwide. The organisms vary widely, ranging from gram-negative and gram-positive bacteria and viruses, to leptospiral infections, or to malaria. It may be difficult to determine whether pneumonia is diffuse, with endo-bronchial spread involving most of the lungs, or whether a localized pneumonia has precipitated a sepsis syndrome with secondary injury to other parts of the lung.

Pathology

Despite the variety of underlying disease processes leading to acute lung injury, the response to these insults in the lung is monotonously characteristic, manifest by similar clinical findings, physiologic

---

Table 99–4 • KEY PRINCIPLES IN THE MANAGEMENT OF CHRONIC OBSTRUCTIVE PULMONARY DISEASE PATIENTS WITH ACUTE RESPIRATORY FAILURE

1. Monitor and treat life-threatening hypoxemia (these measures should be preformed virtually simultaneously)
   a. Assess patient clinically, and measure oxygenation by arterial blood gases and/or oximetry
      (1) If the patient is hypoxemic, initiate supplemental oxygen therapy with nasal prongs (low flows [0.5–2.0 L/min] are usually sufficient) or by Venturi face mask
      (2) If patient needs ventilatory support, consider noninvasive ventilation
      (3) Determine whether the patient needs to be intubated; this is almost always a clinical decision—immediate action is required if the patient is comatose or severely obtunded
   b. A reasonable goal in most patients is PaO_2 of 55–60 mm Hg or an oxygen saturation (SaO_2) of 88–90%
   c. After changes in FIO_2, check blood gases and check regularly for signs of carbon dioxide retention
2. Start to correct life-threatening acidosis
   a. Most effective approach is to correct underlying cause of ARF (e.g., bronchospasm, infection, heart failure)
   b. Consider ventilatory support, based largely on clinical considerations
   c. With severe acidosis, the use of bicarbonate can be considered, but it is often ineffective, and little evidence exists for clinical benefit
3. If ventilatory support is required, consider noninvasive mechanical ventilation
   a. Patient must have intact upper airway reflexes and be alert, cooperative, and hemodynamically stable
   b. Careful monitoring is required—if patient does not tolerate mask, becomes hemodynamically unstable, or has deteriorating mental status, consider intubation
4. Treat airway obstruction and underlying disease process that triggered episode of ARF
   a. Treat airway obstruction with pharmacologic agents: systemic corticosteroids and bronchodilators (ipratropium and/or β-adrenergic agents)
   b. Improve secretion clearance: encourage patient to cough, chest physiotherapy if cough is impaired and a trial appears effective
   c. Treat underlying disease process (e.g., antibiotics, diuretics)
5. Prevent complications of disease process and minimize iatrogenic complications
   a. Pulmonary thromboembolism prophylaxis: subcutaneous heparin if no contraindications
   b. Gastrointestinal complications: prophylaxis of gastrointestinal bleeding
   c. Hemodynamics: if patient is ventilated, monitor and minimize auto-PEEP
      (1) Treat underlying obstruction
      (2) Minimize minute ventilation; use controlled hypoventilation
      (3) Use small tidal volumes; increase inspiratory flow rate to decrease inspiratory time and lengthen expiratory time
   d. Cardiac arrhythmias: maintain oxygenation, normalize electrolytes

ARF = acute respiratory failure; FIO_2 = fraction of inspired oxygen; PEEP = positive end-expiratory pressure.

---

changes, and morphologic abnormalities. The pathologic abnormalities in acute lung injury and ARDS are nonspecific and are described as *diffuse alveolar damage* by pathologists. Abnormalities of epithelial cells, particularly type 1 alveolar cells, and pulmonary vascular endothelial cells are seen. The initial process is inflammatory in nature, with neutrophils usually predominating in the alveolar fluid. Hyaline membranes, similar to those seen in premature infants with infant respiratory distress syndrome, develop, presumably related to the presence of large-molecular-weight proteins that have leaked into the alveolar space. Alveolar flooding leads to impairment of surfactant, which is abnormal in quantity and quality. The result is microatelectasis, which may be associated with an impairment of immune function. Cytokines and other inflammatory mediators usually are markedly elevated, although with different patterns over time in the bronchoalveolar lavage and the systemic blood. Lung repair also is disturbed; there is early evidence of profibrotic processes manifest by the appearance of breakdown products of procollagen in the bronchoalveolar lavage fluid, followed by subsequent scarring. The

Table 99-5 • DISORDERS ASSOCIATED WITH ACUTE LUNG INJURY AND ACUTE RESPIRATORY DISTRESS SYNDROME

COMMON
Sepsis (gram-positive or gram-negative bacterial, viral, fungal, or parasitic)
Diffuse pneumonia (bacterial, viral, or fungal)
Aspiration of gastric contents
Trauma (usually severe)

LESS COMMON
Near-drowning (fresh or salt water)
Drug overdoses
    Acetylsalicylic acid
    Heroin and other narcotic drugs
Massive blood transfusion (likely a marker of severe trauma but also seen with severe gastrointestinal bleeding, especially in patients with severe liver disease)
Leukoagglutination reactions
Inhalation of smoke or corrosive gases (usually requires high concentrations)
Pancreatitis
Fat embolism

UNCOMMON
Miliary tuberculosis
Aspiration of paraquat
Central nervous system injury or anoxia (neurogenic pulmonary edema)
Cardiopulmonary bypass
Severe acute respiratory syndrome (SARS)

Table 99-6 • FEATURES ASSOCIATED WITH NONCARDIOGENIC AND CARDIOGENIC PULMONARY EDEMA*

NONCARDIOGENIC (ARDS)	CARDIOGENIC/VOLUME OVERLOAD
PRIOR HISTORY	
Younger	Older
No history of heart disease	Prior history of heart disease
Appropriate fluid balance (difficult to assess after resuscitation from shock or trauma)	Hypertension, chest pain, new-onset palpitations; positive fluid balance
PHYSICAL EXAMINATION	
Flat neck veins	Elevated neck veins
Hyperdynamic pulses	Left ventricular enlargement, lift, heave, dyskinesis
Physiologic gallop	S_3 and S_4; murmurs
Absence of edema	Edema: flank, presacral, legs
ELECTROCARDIOGRAM	
Sinus tachycardia, nonspecific ST-T wave changes	Evidence of prior or ongoing ischemia, supraventricular tachycardia, left ventricular hypertrophy
CHEST RADIOGRAPH	
Normal heart size	Cardiomegaly
Peripheral distribution of infiltrates	Central or basilar infiltrates; peribronchial and vascular congestion
Air bronchogram common (80%)	Septal lines (Kerley lines), air bronchograms (25%), pleural effusion
HEMODYNAMIC MEASUREMENTS	
Pulmonary artery wedge pressure <15 mm Hg, cardiac index >3.5 L/min/m²	Pulmonary capillary wedge pressure >18 mm Hg, cardiac index <3.5 L/min/m² with ischemia, may be >3.5 with volume overload

*These features generally are neither highly sensitive nor specific. Although the findings more commonly are associated with the types of pulmonary edema as listed, they have not been shown to have high positive or negative predictive values.

pulmonary fibrosis observed on lung biopsy or at autopsy is identical to that seen in patients with idiopathic pulmonary fibrosis (Chapter 88). Because lung function improves over time in survivors of ARDS, however, it has been assumed that this scarring is potentially reversible.

Pathophysiology

The physiologic abnormalities are dominated by severe hypoxemia with shunting, decreased lung compliance, decreased functional residual capacity, and increased work of breathing. Initially the $PaCO_2$ is low or normal, usually associated with increased alveolar ventilation. The initial abnormalities in oxygenation are thought to be related to alveolar flooding and collapse. As the disease progresses, especially in patients who require continued ventilatory support, fibroproliferation develops; the lungs (including alveoli, blood vessels, and small airways) remodel and scar, with a loss of microvasculature. These changes may lead to pulmonary hypertension and increased dead space; marked elevations in minute ventilation are required to achieve a normal $PaCO_2$ even as oxygenation abnormalities are improving.

Diagnosis

Most cases of acute lung injury have an onset that either coincides with the recognition of the underlying disease process or occurs within 72 hours of its onset; the mean time from onset of the underlying cause to onset of acute lung injury is 12 to 24 hours. The presenting picture is dominated by respiratory distress and the accompanying laboratory findings of severe hypoxemia and generalized infiltrates or opacities on the chest radiograph, or it is dominated by the manifestations of the underlying disease process, such as severe sepsis with hypotension and other manifestations of systemic infection. The key is to distinguish ARDS from cardiogenic pulmonary edema (Table 99-6).

There is no specific biochemical test to define ARDS. Certain blood or bronchoalveolar lavage (Chapter 82) abnormalities are frequent but are not sufficiently specific to be useful clinically.

Rx Treatment

Treatment for acute lung injury and ARDS consists predominantly of respiratory support and treatment of the underlying disease (Fig. 99-4). Current recommendations for mechanical ventilation via endotracheal intubation (Table 99-7) emphasize lower tidal volumes based on a patient's predicted body weight (Chapter 101).[2] PEEP remains a mainstay in the ventilatory strategy for acute lung injury, although the method for determining the optimal level of PEEP has not been established. PEEP may allow a lower FIO_2 to provide adequate oxygenation, avoiding O_2 toxicity. It also may prevent the cyclical collapse and reopening of lung units, a process that is thought to be a major cause of ventilator-induced lung injury, even when adequate oxygenation can be obtained at relatively low levels of FIO_2.

Inhaled nitric oxide is a potent vasodilator and bronchodilator that can enhance arterial oxygenation. It has not been shown to improve outcome in clinical trials, however,[3] so its routine use cannot be recommended in adults with acute respiratory failure. To date, no therapy manipulating or targeting elements of inflammation has been successful, but activated protein C can improve outcome in patients with sepsis (Chapter 104), in whom ARDS is often one of the manifestations.

Changing from the supine to the prone position improves arterial oxygenation in many patients with acute lung injury, apparently by reducing shunting. At the same time, new areas of airless collapsed lungs occur in the ventral (now dependent) lung regions. Complications of prone positioning include potential dislodgement of lines and tubes, some difficulty in performing certain nursing procedures, and facial swelling and skin complications. With careful nursing care, most of these can be avoided or managed adequately. A single large randomized clinical trial failed to show an outcome survival advantage in patients randomized to prone position despite a persistent improvement in oxygenation.[6] Nevertheless, the prone position should be considered in patients who have severe oxygenation abnormalities that require high FIO_2 and PEEP.

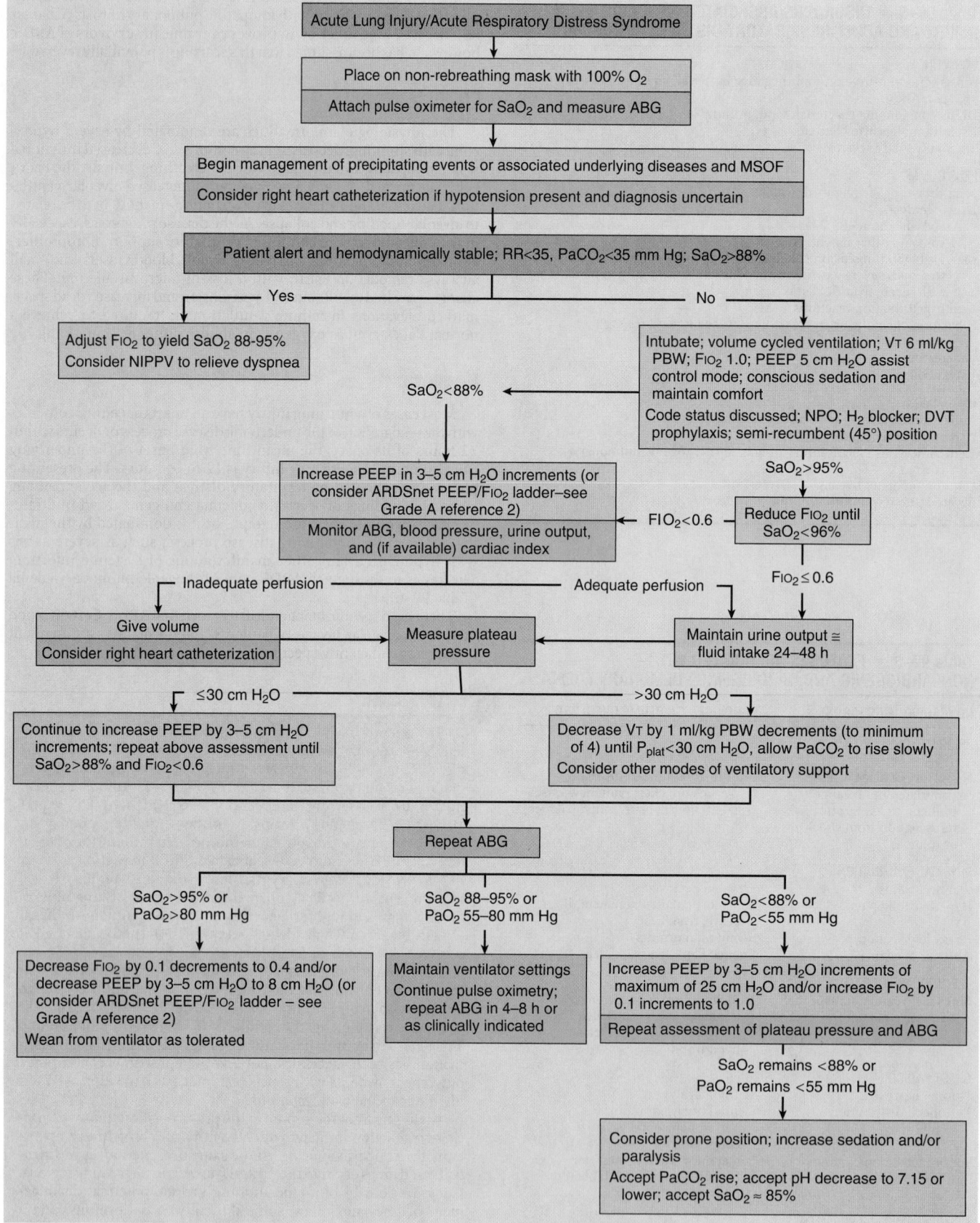

FIGURE 99-4 • An algorithm for the initial management of acute respiratory distress syndrome. ABG = arterial blood gas analysis; CO_2 = carbon dioxide; DVT = deep venous thrombosis; FIO_2 = inspired oxygen concentration; MSOF = multisystem organ failure; NIPPV = noninvasive intermittent positive-pressure ventilation; O_2 = oxygen; $PaCO_2$ = arterial partial pressure of carbon dioxide; PaO_2 = arterial partial pressure of oxygen; PBW = predicted body weight; PEEP = positive end-expiratory pressure; P_{plat} = plateau pressure; RR = respiratory rate; SaO_2 = arterial oxygen saturation; V_T = tidal volume.

Table 99–7 • ARDSNETWORK VENTILATORY MANAGEMENT PROTOCOL FOR TIDAL VOLUME (V$_T$) AND PLATEAU PRESSURE (P$_{plat}$)*

Calculate PBW
  Male PBW: 50 + 2.3 (height in inches −60)†
  Female PBW: 45.5 + 2.3 (height in inches −60)†
Select assist-control mode
Set initial V$_T$ at 8 mL/kg PBW
Reduce V$_T$ by 1 mL/kg at intervals <2 hr until V$_T$ = 6 mL/kg PBW
Set initial RR to approximate baseline minute ventilation (maximum RR = 35/min)
Set inspiratory flow rate above patient's demand (usually >80 L/min)
Adjust V$_T$ and RR further to achieve P$_{plat}$ and pH goals
  If P$_{plat}$ >30 cm H$_2$O: decrease V$_T$ by 1 mL/kg PBW (minimum = 4 mL/kg PBW)
  If 7.15 ≤pH ≤7.30, increase RR (maximum = 35)
  If pH <7.15, increase RR to 35; consider NaHCO$_3$ administration or increase V$_T$

*See ARDSNet website (http://www.ardsnet.org) for further details of the protocol, including the approach for setting PEEP and FIO$_2$.
†See text for PBW formula by height in centimeters.
FIO$_2$ = fraction of inspired oxygen; NaHCO$_3$ = sodium bicarbonate; PBW = predicted body weight; PEEP = positive end-expiratory pressure; P$_{plat}$ = plateau pressure (airway pressure at the end of delivery of a tidal volume breath during a condition of no airflow); RR = respiratory rate; V$_T$ = tidal volume.

ACUTE RESPIRATORY FAILURE WITHOUT LUNG DISEASE

Acute respiratory failure without pulmonary abnormalities (see Table 99–2) is seen in patients with depressed ventilatory drive secondary to central nervous system dysfunction and in patients with severe neuromuscular disease. The prototypical patient with suppressed ventilatory drive is a patient who has taken an overdose of a sedative or tranquilizing medication. The prototypical patient with neuromuscular disease is the patient with Guillain-Barré syndrome. The treatment for both of these types of patients is supportive. In the patient with a sedative overdose, there should be a low threshold for intubation with mechanical ventilatory support because this temporary condition should be quickly reversible when the responsible drug is eliminated. The patient with a sedative overdose may require intubation for airway protection against aspiration of gastric contents.

Patients with Guillain-Barré syndrome or other forms of progressive neuromuscular disease should be monitored with serial measurements of vital capacity. In general, when the vital capacity decreases to less than 10 to 15 mL/kg body weight, intubation and mechanical ventilatory support should be considered.

GENERAL SUPPORTIVE MEASURES IN PATIENTS WITH ACUTE RESPIRATORY FAILURE

Every patient with acute respiratory failure is at risk for deep venous thrombosis, pulmonary thromboembolism, and gastric stress ulceration. Prophylactic anticoagulation generally is recommended in patients who are not at high risk of bleeding complications; sequential leg compression therapy may be preferred for patients who are at high risk (Chapter 33).

The best means of preventing stress ulceration is not known; current evidence indicates that the use of an H$_2$ blocker is superior to gastric administration of sucralfate [7] based on a large randomized controlled trial that found a higher incidence of significant bleeding in patients receiving sucralfate than in patients receiving ranitidine. There is little firm evidence to guide nutritional management in patients with acute respiratory failure (Chapters 227 and 230).

Current evidence supports maintaining the head of the bed in the critically ill patient at a 45-degree angle to reduce aspiration. Attempts should be made to ensure a normal day/night sleep pattern, including minimizing activity and reducing direct lighting at night. The patient should change position frequently, including sitting in a chair and walking short distances if possible, even while still receiving mechanical ventilatory support. Mobilization can enhance the removal of secretions, help maintain musculoskeletal function, reduce the risk of deep venous thrombosis, and provide psychological benefits.

 1. Hebert PC, Wells G, Blajchman MA, et al: A multicenter, randomized, controlled clinical trial of transfusion requirements in critical care. Transfusion Requirements in Critical Care Investigators, Canadian Critical Care Trials Group. N Engl J Med 1999;340:409–417.
2. Ventilation with lower tidal volumes as compared with traditional tidal volumes for acute lung injury and the acute respiratory distress syndrome. The Acute Respiratory Distress Syndrome Network. N Engl J Med 2000;342:1301–1308.
3. Anthonisen NR, Manfreda J, Warren CPW, et al: Antibiotic therapy in exacerbations of chronic obstructive pulmonary disease. Ann Intern Med 1987;106:196–204.
4. Evans TW: International Consensus Conference in Intensive Care Medicine: Noninvasive positive pressure ventilation in acute respiratory failure. Intensive Care Med 2001;27:166–178.
5. Sokol J, Jacobs SE, Bohn D: Inhaled nitric oxide for acute hypoxemic respiratory failure in children and adults. Cochrane Database Syst Rev 2000;4:CD002787.
6. Gattinoni L, Tognoni G, Pesenti A, et al: Effect of prone positioning on the survival of patients with acute respiratory failure. N Engl J Med 2001;345:568–573.
7. Cook D, Guyatt G, Marshall J, et al: A comparison of sucralfate and ranitidine for the prevention of upper gastrointestinal bleeding in patients requiring mechanical ventilation. Canadian Critical Care Trials Group. N Engl J Med 1998;338:791–797.

SUGGESTED READINGS

Dakin J, Griffiths M: The pulmonary physician in critical care: 1. Pulmonary investigations for acute respiratory failure. Thorax 2002;57:79–85. *An approach to the evaluation of patients with acute respiratory failure.*
Ram FS, Lightowler JV, Wedzicha JA: Non-invasive positive pressure ventilation for treatment of respiratory failure due to exacerbations of chronic obstructive pulmonary disease. Cochrane Database Syst Rev 2003;(1):CD004104. *Randomized trials suggest NPPV should be first-line therapy early in respiratory failure.*
Vincent JL, Sakr Y, Ranieri VM: Epidemiology and outcome of acute respiratory failure in intensive care unit patients. Crit Care Med 2003;31(4 Suppl):S296–S299. *Only about 20% of deaths are primarily respiratory.*
Ware LB, Matthay MA: The acute respiratory distress syndrome. N Engl J Med 2000;342: 1334–1349. *A review of the pathophysiology, epidemiology, and management of ARDS.*

100 RESPIRATORY MONITORING IN CRITICAL CARE

John M. Luce

RESPIRATION

The word *respiration* describes the exchange of oxygen (O$_2$) and carbon dioxide (CO$_2$) between humans (or other animals) and the environment. Human respiration may be divided into the following four processes: (1) *ventilation*, in which O$_2$ is inhaled and CO$_2$ is excreted into the atmosphere; (2) *arterial oxygenation*, in which O$_2$ is transferred from the alveoli into mixed venous blood in the pulmonary capillaries in exchange for CO$_2$; (3) *oxygen transport* or *delivery*, in which O$_2$ is carried in systemic arterial blood to the tissues; and (4) *oxygen extraction* and *utilization*, in which the tissues take up O$_2$ from the blood and give up CO$_2$, which is transported in venous blood to the lungs.

ASSESSMENT OF VENTILATION

Physical Examination

Ventilation requires the rhythmic use of the respiratory muscles to pump gases in and out of the lungs. Measurement of the respiratory rate is particularly important in assessing the adequacy of ventilation. The respiratory rate at rest usually ranges from 12 to 22 breaths/min; a respiratory rate substantially less than 12 breaths/min suggests that ventilation is inadequate to meet metabolic needs, whereas a respiratory rate substantially greater than 22 breaths/min may reflect incipient ventilatory failure. In fact, patients may require mechanical ventilation if their respiratory rate exceeds 35 breaths/min over a prolonged period.

Whereas respiratory rate can be easily measured by direct observation, tidal volume, which is the amount of gas that enters and leaves the lungs with each breath (Chapter 82), can only be approximated. Such approximation may be useful, for example, when the respiratory rate and tidal volume are so low or high that ventilation must be impaired and medical intervention is necessary. Nevertheless, clinicians should avoid using words such as hypoventilation and hyperventilation for patients whose respiratory rates and tidal volumes appear low or high because these words refer to specific abnormalities in the

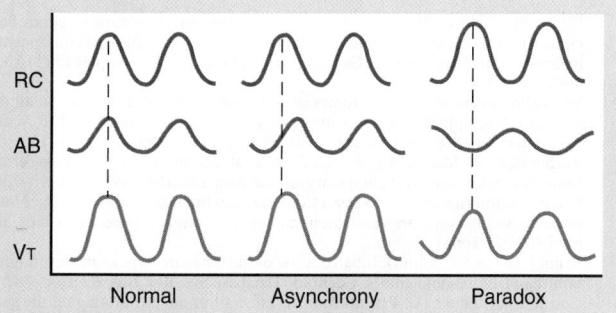

FIGURE 100–1 • Tracings of the movements of the rib cage (RC), the abdomen (AB), and their sum (VT) recorded by inductance plethysmography. The dashed lines are drawn at the time of maximum inspiratory volume. (From Dantzker DR, Tobin MJ: Monitoring respiratory muscle function. Respir Care 1985;30:422–428.)

systemic arterial CO_2 tension ($PaCO_2$) that can be diagnosed only by blood gas analysis.

In the presence of increased airway resistance or decreased lung or chest wall compliance, patients must expend more respiratory muscle work to achieve adequate ventilation (Chapter 83). The work of breathing in such patients is the product of the tidal volume and the pressure required to generate that tidal volume. This pressure, the transpulmonary pressure, is the difference between airway and pleural pressure. Transpulmonary pressure cannot be measured on physical examination. Recession of the suprasternal and intercostal spaces during inspiration suggests a greater than normal negative swing in pleural pressure and hence an increase in the work of breathing. Another manifestation of increased breathing effort is the forceful contraction of the sternocleidomastoid muscles.

Finally, a marked increase in the work of breathing, along with probable ventilatory inadequacy, may be suggested by certain abnormal breathing patterns. The first, an asynchrony between the peak excursions of the chest wall and abdomen, is called respiratory muscle asynchrony (Fig. 100–1). The second, respiratory muscle paradox, is seen when the abdomen moves inward rather than outward during inspiration, indicating that the chest wall muscles are being recruited more than the diaphragm.

Systemic Arterial Blood Gas Analysis

Samples of systemic arterial blood may be obtained by repeated percutaneous arterial punctures or from indwelling arterial catheters for measurement of $PaCO_2$, pH, arterial O_2 tension (PaO_2), and bicarbonate (HCO_3^-) concentration. Miniature intra-arterial sensors may also be placed through the catheters for continuous analysis of blood gases, although this technology is not sufficiently accurate for clinical use.

The $PaCO_2$ is used to assess the adequacy of ventilation and to diagnose hypercapnic respiratory failure, also called failure of ventilation. At sea level, the $PaCO_2$ normally ranges from 35 to 45 mm Hg. Hyperventilation and respiratory alkalosis are said to be present if the $PaCO_2$ is less than 35 mm Hg. Hypoventilation, hypercapnia, and respiratory acidosis are present if the $PaCO_2$ is greater than 45 mm Hg, and ventilatory failure exists when the $PaCO_2$ exceeds 50 mm Hg.

The pH and HCO_3^- concentration measurements can be used to determine whether hypercapnia and hypocapnia and respiratory acidosis and respiratory alkalosis are acute or chronic. Such determination is based on the Henderson-Hasselbalch equation for the HCO_3^- buffer system:

$$pH = 6.1 + \log [HCO_3^-]/0.003\ PaCO_2 \qquad (1)$$

In keeping with this equation, acute increases or decreases in $PaCO_2$ cause the pH to fall or rise until the kidneys gradually retain or release HCO_3^- to buffer the fall or rise in pH (Chapter 113).

The pH normally ranges from 7.35 to 7.45. An acute increase in $PaCO_2$ causes the pH to fall below 7.35, a condition called acute respiratory acidosis. If the $PaCO_2$ is increased, the pH is below normal,

and the HCO_3^- concentration is increased, the patient has either a chronic respiratory acidosis with a compensatory metabolic alkalosis or a respiratory acidosis of unknown duration with a concurrent but not compensatory metabolic alkalosis.

Conversely, an acute decrease in $PaCO_2$ causes the pH to rise above 7.45, creating an acute respiratory alkalosis. If the $PaCO_2$ is decreased, the pH is above normal, and the HCO_3^- concentration is decreased, the patient has either a chronic respiratory alkalosis with a compensatory metabolic acidosis or a respiratory alkalosis of unknown duration with a concurrent metabolic acidosis.

Measurement of Transcutaneous Carbon Dioxide Tensions

The $PaCO_2$ can be estimated by measuring the transcutaneous CO_2 tension through an electrode placed on the skin. Because the electrode is heated, this value is generally higher than the $PaCO_2$, although the transcutaneous CO_2 tension can be adjusted to obtain a close approximation of the $PaCO_2$. In contrast to transcutaneous O_2 values, the transcutaneous CO_2 tension is relatively insensitive to alterations in skin perfusion and does not change significantly with age. Transcutaneous monitoring of the CO_2 tension is performed most commonly in neonates, in whom percutaneous arterial punctures and arterial catheters are impractical.

Measurement of End-Tidal Carbon Dioxide Tensions

In intubated patients of all ages, the $PaCO_2$ may be approximated by measuring the end-tidal CO_2 tension in expired gas. The end-tidal CO_2 tension can be measured either by a capnometer, which displays its value breath by breath, or by a capnograph, which also displays its wave form.

The capnogram (Fig. 100–2A) reflects the sequential measurement of CO_2 tensions from several dead space compartments that do not participate in CO_2 exchange—apparatus, anatomic, and alveolar—in addition to the CO_2 tension in alveolar gas that is in equilibrium with end-capillary blood. When a plateau is reached, indicating the presence of CO_2 in alveolar gas and minimal amounts of gas from areas of dead space, the end-tidal CO_2 tension should be similar to the $PaCO_2$, albeit usually 1 to 5 mm Hg less. If the CO_2 tensions in samples of systemic arterial blood and end-tidal gas obtained simultaneously are measured, the correlation of CO_2 tensions can be known.

When alveolar ventilation decreases compared with perfusion, as might occur in a patient with chronic obstructive pulmonary disease (COPD; Chapter 85), there may not be a plateau on the capnogram and the gradient between the end-tidal CO_2 tension and the $PaCO_2$ may decrease (Fig. 100–2B). Conversely, when perfusion decreases compared with ventilation, as might occur in a patient with pulmonary embolism or another dead space–producing disease, the end-tidal CO_2 may be considerably less than the $PaCO_2$.

Measurement of Dead Space

Dead space is usually expressed as a fraction of tidal volume. The ratio of dead space to tidal volume (VD/VT) per breath can be calculated in patients whose $PaCO_2$ and mean expired PCO_2 ($PECO_2$) are known, using the modified Bohr equation:

$$VD/VT = (PaCO_2 - PECO_2)/PaCO_2 \qquad (2)$$

The ratio of dead space to tidal volume is usually 0.30 to 0.40 in healthy persons breathing spontaneously. In patients with normal lungs being ventilated mechanically, it approaches 0.50 because gas is stored transiently in compressible portions of the ventilator circuit. The ratio of dead space to tidal volume may rise to values of 0.7 or more in patients with significant respiratory disease.

Measurement of Ventilatory Variables

Ventilatory variables such as respiratory rate and tidal volume may be measured by respiratory inductance plethysmography, which uses wire coils embedded in bands that fit around the chest and abdomen

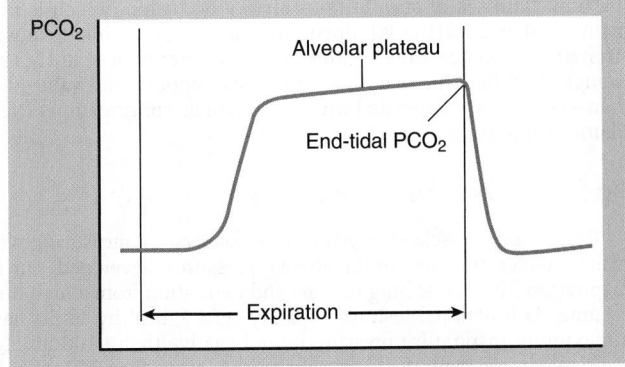

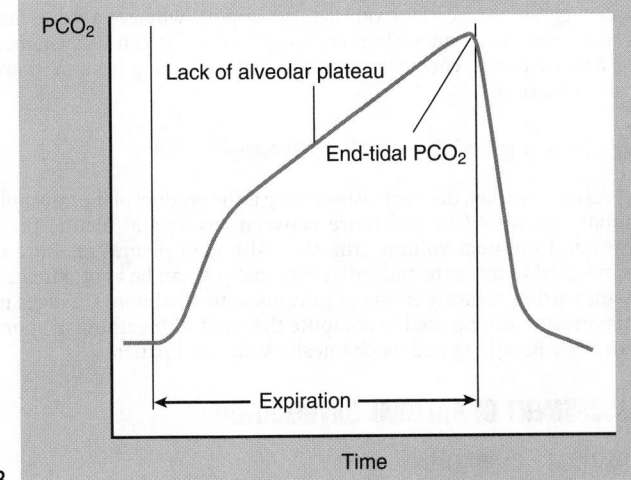

FIGURE 100–2 • *A*, Illustration of a normal capnogram, in which the carbon dioxide tension (PCO_2) rises as dead-space gas from the apparatus, the airways, and the alveoli is supplanted by alveolar gas with a high concentration of CO_2. The high point of this "alveolar plateau" represents the end-tidal PCO_2. *B*, Capnogram of patient with chronic obstructive pulmonary disease in whom end-tidal PCO_2 does not reach a plateau because of delayed CO_2 excretion. See text for further discussion.

to detect movements in these areas. These variables may also be measured with a pneumotachograph or other types of spirometers in patients who are breathing through endotracheal tubes. In healthy persons, tidal volume is approximately 400 mL. A patient with a tidal volume of less than 300 mL or 5 mL/kg during spontaneous breathing is unlikely to be weaned from mechanical ventilation.

The product of respiratory rate and tidal volume is the minute ventilation. Minute ventilation ($\dot{V}E$) is approximately 6 L/min in normal adults (at rest) and is usually increased in critically ill patients because of increases in CO_2 production, increases in the ratio of dead space to tidal volume, or both. Values in excess of 10 L/min are difficult to maintain without mechanical ventilatory support.

The ratio of respiratory rate to tidal volume increases as patients breathe rapidly and shallowly. This breathing pattern is inefficient in excreting CO_2 when the ratio of dead space to tidal volume is normal and is associated with CO_2 retention when this ratio is increased. Studies have demonstrated that weaning from mechanical ventilation is unlikely in patients whose ratio of respiratory rate to tidal volume exceeds 105 breaths/min/L (Chapter 101).

Measurement of Carbon Dioxide Production

The body's CO_2 production can be measured in patients breathing spontaneously or receiving mechanical ventilation by closed systems that compare the difference in CO_2 in inspired (with virtually no CO_2) and expired gases. Newer systems such as indirect calorimeters allow rapid calculation of CO_2 production at the bedside. The CO_2 production of a healthy adult is approximately 200 mL/min, and it varies with body temperature and metabolism.

Use of the Alveolar Ventilation Equation

Although measurement or approximation of the $PaCO_2$ helps determine the adequacy of ventilation, the explanation of why ventilation is inadequate in a given patient can be derived only by using the alveolar ventilation equation:

$$PaCO_2 = (K)\ \dot{V}CO_2/\dot{V}A \qquad (3)$$

where K is a constant, $\dot{V}CO_2$ is the body's CO_2 production, and $\dot{V}A$, the alveolar ventilation, is equal to the minute ventilation minus the dead space. From Equation 3 it follows that hypercapnia and ventilatory failure can occur if the body's CO_2 production increases and alveolar ventilation does not, if alveolar ventilation decreases and CO_2 production does not, or if dead space increases out of proportion to the minute ventilation.

An example of the first situation might be a patient who becomes septic and thereby increases CO_2 production but cannot increase minute ventilation (and alveolar ventilation) because of respiratory muscle weakness. Patients with severe asthma (Chapter 84) and COPD (Chapter 85) may have ventilatory failure because alveolar ventilation is reduced by airway obstruction, especially when CO_2 production is increased. A primary reduction in alveolar ventilation is seen in cases of narcotic or sedative drug overdose. Diseases such as the acute respiratory distress syndrome (ARDS; Chapters 102 and 104) and pulmonary embolism (Chapter 94), in which dead space may increase because of vascular obstruction in the lungs, can cause ventilatory failure if patients cannot increase alveolar ventilation, for example, because of oversedation.

Measurement of Respiratory Mechanics

Vital capacity (VC) is the greatest amount of gas that can be exhaled after a maximum inspiration. The normal VC is approximately 70 mL/kg. VC is reduced in most obstructive and restrictive respiratory diseases (Chapter 82), and a VC less than 10 mL/kg is generally associated with inadequate ventilation. VC can be measured by a variety of spirometers in intubated or nonintubated patients.

The volume change per unit of pressure change across the lungs and chest cavity is termed the compliance of the respiratory system. When determined in a patient who is being mechanically ventilated, effective respiratory system compliance (CEFF) is tidal volume divided by the maximum or peak airway pressure (PMAX) required to deliver a given tidal volume (VT) minus the amount of positive end-expiratory pressure (PEEP) the patient is receiving. Thus,

$$C_{EFF} = V_T/(P_{MAX} - PEEP) \qquad (4)$$

Because it is a dynamic measurement made when gas is flowing, CEFF includes the resistance to gas flow in the airways and ventilator tubing as well as the volume and pressure characteristics of the lungs and chest wall. Normal CEFF is 50 to 80 mL/cm H_2O; it is decreased by airway obstruction, secretions, and a small-diameter endotracheal tube.

Static respiratory system compliance (CSTAT) is a measure of the airway pressure required to distend the lungs and chest wall and maintain the increase in volume after a VT has been delivered and gas is not flowing in or out of the lungs. This pressure is called the plateau pressure or static recoil pressure (PSTAT) and is measured while temporarily occluding the expiratory port of a mechanical ventilator for approximately 2 seconds (Fig. 100–3). The amount of PEEP should be subtracted from the PSTAT. Thus,

$$C_{STAT} = V_T/(P_{STAT} - PEEP) \qquad (5)$$

Because it is a static measurement, CSTAT reflects the compliance of the lungs and chest wall and is not affected by resistance to gas flow. It is decreased (normal level is 60 to 100 mL/cm H_2O) by conditions, such as ARDS, that decrease lung volume. Weaning from mechanical ventilation is difficult if CSTAT is less than 25 mL/cm H_2O.

Intrinsic or auto-PEEP occurs in patients with airway obstruction and other disorders who fail to complete expiration during either spontaneous breathing or mechanical ventilation. The result is air

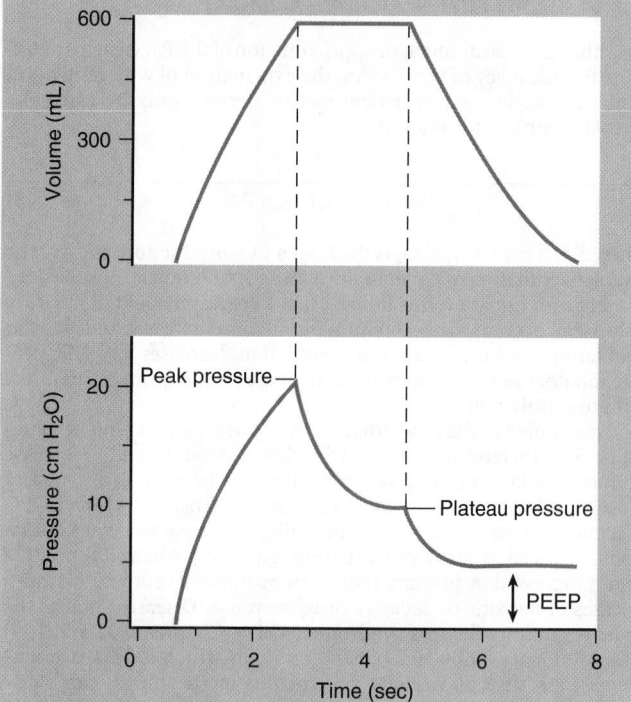

FIGURE 100–3 • Relationship between tidal volume and airway pressure in a mechanically ventilated patient. The peak pressure is used to calculate effective respiratory system compliance, whereas the plateau pressure is used to calculate static compliance. PEEP = positive end-expiratory pressure. (From Tobin MJ: Respiratory monitoring in the intensive care unit. Am Rev Respir Dis 1988;138:1625–1642.)

trapping that produces positive pressure at end expiration. The positive pressure in turn can decrease cardiac filling and increase vascular pressures in the chest, as intentional PEEP can. Auto-PEEP can be measured in mechanically ventilated patients by stopping airflow at end expiration just before the next breath, allowing pressure in the airways and the ventilator tubing to equilibrate, and reading the pressure from the ventilator manometer or airway pressure tracing (Fig. 100–4). Auto-PEEP should be taken into account in calculating effective respiratory system compliance and CSTAT.

Measurement of Ventilatory Drive

The drive to breathe is responsible in large part for the sensation of dyspnea and determines how avidly patients attempt to achieve adequate ventilation. Ventilatory drive can be estimated in intubated patients by measuring the inspiratory pressure developed in the first 100 msec of surreptitious airway occlusion. This measurement provides only an estimate because the inspiratory pressure developed in

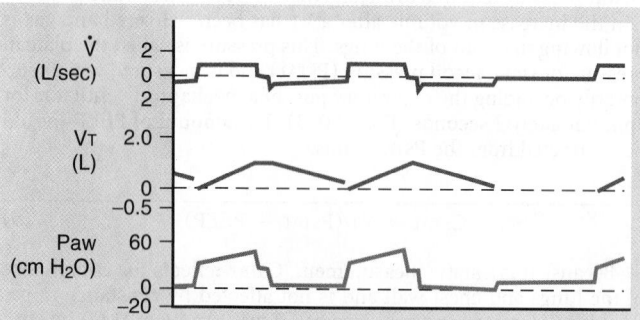

FIGURE 100–4 • As airflow ($\dot{V}$) is stopped at end expiration after a tidal volume (VT) is given and pressures in the airways and ventilator tubing equilibrate, auto-PEEP can be measured as an increase in airway pressure (Paw). PEEP = positive end-expiratory pressure. See text for further discussion.

the first 100 msec of surreptitious airway occlusion, which is normally less than 2 cm H_2O, is influenced somewhat by respiratory muscle strength and, hence, lung volume. Values greater than 4 cm H_2O are thought to reflect the need for ventilatory support, and values less than 4 cm H_2O are associated with successful discontinuation of ventilatory support.

Measurement of Respiratory Muscle Strength

Respiratory muscle strength can be assessed by measuring with a manometer the maximum airway pressures developed during inspiration from a low lung volume and expiration from a high lung volume. At functional residual capacity (FRC), healthy adults have a maximum inspiratory pressure more negative than −100 cm H_2O and a maximum expiratory pressure more positive than 150 cm H_2O. A maximum inspiratory pressure that is less negative than −30 cm H_2O suggests the need for ventilatory support, whereas a value that is more negative than −30 cm H_2O, especially if it can be sustained for 3 to 5 seconds, correlates with successful weaning from mechanical ventilation.

Measurement of the Work of Breathing

As noted earlier, the work of breathing is the product of the transpulmonary pressure (the difference between airway and pleural pressure) and the tidal volume (the VT). Although pleural pressure is impractical to measure and varies regionally, it can be approximated by measuring pressure in the esophagus with a balloon. Changes in this pressure can be used to compute the work of breathing in spontaneously breathing and mechanically ventilated patients.

ASSESSMENT OF ARTERIAL OXYGENATION
Physical Examination

Cyanosis of the tongue and oral mucosa, which is called central cyanosis, provides a crude estimation of the adequacy of arterial oxygenation. Central cyanosis reflects the presence of 3 g/dL or more of reduced, that is, deoxygenated, hemoglobin. However, the blue discoloration of tissues caused by deoxygenated hemoglobin may also be caused by dyshemoglobins such as sulfhemoglobin. Furthermore, clinicians vary in their ability to detect cyanosis when it actually occurs.

Arterial Blood Gas Analysis

The systemic arterial O_2 tension (PaO_2) obtained by arterial blood gas analysis is the standard for assessing the adequacy of arterial oxygenation. The normal PaO_2 at sea level is approximately 100 mm Hg (Fig. 100–5). However, the PaO_2 is inversely correlated with age, as expressed in the following equation:

$$\text{Normal } PaO_2 = 100 \, \text{mm Hg} - (0.3) \, \text{age in years} \qquad (6)$$

However, Equation 6 does not correct for the effects of barometric pressure.

Measurement of Transcutaneous Oxygen Tensions

As with CO_2, the transcutaneous tension of O_2 can be measured by a heated electrode on the skin. However, the correlation between PaO_2 and transcutaneous tension of O_2 is affected by both age and perfusion status, which is not the case with the correlation between $PaCO_2$ and transcutaneous CO_2 tension.

Use of the Alveolar Gas Equation

Although the alveolar O_2 tension (PAO_2) cannot be measured directly, it can be calculated from the alveolar gas equation:

$$PAO_2 = FIO_2(PB - 47) - PaCO_2/R \qquad (7)$$

where FIO_2 is the fraction of inspired O_2 (0.21 when breathing ambient air), PB is barometric pressure, 47 is the vapor pressure of water at

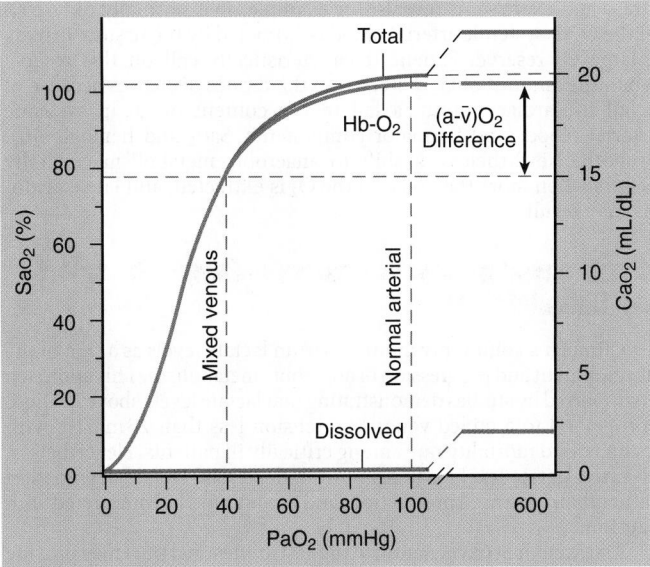

FIGURE 100–5 • Normal oxyhemoglobin dissociation curve showing the relationship between the systemic arterial O_2 saturation (SaO_2), tension (PaO_2), and content (CaO_2). See text for further discussion.

37°C, and R is the respiratory exchange ratio, which represents the ratio of CO_2 production to O_2 consumption (usually assumed to be 0.8). Normally, a difference or gradient of 10 mm Hg or less exists between the PAO_2 and PaO_2. This difference, the $P(A - a)O_2$, increases to 30 mm Hg with age and increases further with respiratory disease.

The word hypoxemia is used to describe a PaO_2 of less than normal; hypoxemic respiratory failure, also called failure of arterial oxygenation, exists when the PaO_2 is below 50 to 60 mm Hg. As indicated by the alveolar gas equation and the relationship between PaO_2 and PAO_2, hypoxemia can be caused by a decrease in FIO_2, as might result from breathing air in a fire in which O_2 has been consumed; a decrease in barometric pressure, as occurs at altitude; an increase in $PaCO_2$, as might happen during a drug overdose; or an increase in the alveolar-arterial gradient of oxygen as caused, for example, by a mismatch of ventilation and perfusion in the lungs.

Even if the PaO_2 of a patient with hypoxemic respiratory failure is normalized by the administration of supplemental O_2, O_2 exchange in the lungs may remain abnormal. In this situation, the inadequacy of O_2 exchange is reflected by an increased alveolar-arterial gradient of oxygen, which remains a helpful indicator of respiratory function at all but the highest levels of FIO_2, where it may change unpredictably.

Other Indicators of Arterial Oxygenation

The arterial-to-alveolar PO_2 ratio (PaO_2/PAO_2) can be calculated using the alveolar gas equation. The PaO_2/PAO_2 is relatively stable with changing levels of FIO_2 and can be used to predict the expected PaO_2 when the FIO_2 is altered. The normal PaO_2/PAO_2 is 0.9. The PaO_2-to-FIO_2 ratio (PaO_2/FIO_2) is easier to calculate because it does not require use of the alveolar gas equation. The normal PaO_2/FIO_2 is 460. Although the PaO_2/FIO_2 does not account for changes in $PaCO_2$, this limitation is not important at high levels of FIO_2.

Measurement of Venous Admixture and Shunt Fraction

Venous admixture ($\dot{Q}VA/\dot{Q}T$) is the fraction of mixed venous blood that does not become oxygenated as it courses through the lungs. It can be calculated with the equation:

$$\dot{Q}VA/\dot{Q}T = (C'cO_2 - CaO_2)/(C'cO_2 - C\bar{v}O_2) \qquad (8)$$

where $\dot{Q}T$ is the cardiac output and $C'cO_2$, CaO_2, and $C\bar{v}O_2$ are the O_2 contents of end-capillary, arterial, and mixed venous blood, respectively. Although end-capillary blood cannot be sampled routinely, the end-capillary O_2 content can be calculated by assuming that the tension of end-capillary blood is the same as PAO_2.

The normal $\dot{Q}VA/\dot{Q}T$ is less than 0.07; increases in $\dot{Q}VA/\dot{Q}T$ are caused by ventilation-perfusion mismatching or right-to-left intrapulmonary shunting ($\dot{Q}s/\dot{Q}T$). Equation 8 can be used to calculate $\dot{Q}s/\dot{Q}T$ in patients receiving an FIO_2 of 1.0 because this FIO_2 eliminates areas of ventilation-perfusion mismatch in the lungs. A simpler but less precise way of estimating $\dot{Q}s/\dot{Q}T$ is to divide the $P(A - a)O_2$ by 20. The PaO_2 can rarely be improved by increasing FIO_2 if $\dot{Q}s/\dot{Q}T$ exceeds 0.25.

Measurement of Systemic Arterial Saturation

The saturation of hemoglobin by O_2 in systemic arterial blood (SaO_2) is related to the PaO_2 by the O_2 hemoglobin dissociation curve. Hemoglobin is almost 100% saturated at a PaO_2 of 100 mm Hg, and its saturation cannot be significantly increased by increasing the PaO_2 (see Fig. 100–5). The SaO_2 increases somewhat, signifying that less O_2 is available to the tissues at a given PaO_2, if the O_2 hemoglobin dissociation curve is shifted to the left by alkalosis or hypothermia. Conversely, the SaO_2 decreases, signifying *more* O_2 release to the tissues, if the curve is shifted to the right by acidosis and hyperthermia.

In many arterial blood gas analyses, the SaO_2 is estimated from the PaO_2 using an ideal, unshifted O_2 hemoglobin dissociation curve. Nevertheless, the SaO_2 can also be measured with co-oximeters that record the absorbency of light passing through a dilute solution of hemoglobin. Co-oximeters use several wavelengths of light and can determine not only the percentages of oxygenated hemoglobin and reduced hemoglobin but also the percentages of carboxyhemoglobin, methemoglobin, and sulfhemoglobin. Co-oximetry is especially important in diagnosing carbon monoxide poisoning.

The pulse oximeter records the absorbency of light passing through a pulsatile tissue bed such as a fingertip. The absorption characteristics of oxygenated hemoglobin and reduced hemoglobin are different at the two wavelengths of light used. Pulse oximetry accurately measures SaO_2 values above 80% in persons with adequate peripheral arterial flow. This technique is particularly helpful in patients who are hemodynamically stable and in whom a nonshifted O_2 hemoglobin dissociation curve allows good correlation between SaO_2 and PaO_2. The SaO_2 measured by pulse oximetry does not account for hemoglobin that is saturated by substances other than O_2, such as carbon monoxide; because of this, the SaO_2 is falsely elevated in patients with carbon monoxide poisoning. In addition, the SaO_2 provides no information about $PaCO_2$ or pH. Nevertheless, the accuracy, ease, and low expense of pulse oximetry make it a useful substitute for analysis of PaO_2 in many situations.

ASSESSMENT OF OXYGEN DELIVERY AND UTILIZATION

Physical Examination

The adequacy of O_2 delivery and utilization may be appreciated by examination of the skin. For example, the presence of normal skin color and warmth suggest an adequate peripheral flow of oxygenated blood in some circumstances. Such adequacy is also suggested by normal capillary refill, in which skin color returns to baseline 2 to 3 seconds after the skin is blanched. Nevertheless, although these findings may help exclude significant hypovolemia or impairment of cardiac output, which are associated with increased systemic vascular resistance, they do not exclude sepsis and other processes in which systemic vascular resistance is decreased.

When skin findings are unreliable, O_2 delivery and utilization may be assessed in other organs where blood supply is maintained despite hypoperfusion elsewhere. In this regard, the onset of confusion or obtundation in a previously healthy patient may signify a significant decrease in cerebral oxygenation. Similarly, a decrease in urine output below 0.5 mL/kg/hr may result from a reduction in renal blood flow from sepsis and other causes.

Measurement of Oxygen Delivery

The amount of O_2 delivered to the tissues ($\dot{D}O_2$) is the product of cardiac output ($\dot{Q}T$) and the content of O_2 in systemic arterial blood (CaO_2). Thus,

$$\dot{D}O_2 = (\dot{Q}T)(CaO_2) \qquad (9)$$

The CaO_2 (mL O_2/dL blood) can be calculated from the following equation:

$$CaO_2 = (1.39)(Hb)\frac{(SaO_2)}{100} + (0.003)(PaO_2) \qquad (10)$$

where 1.39 is the oxygen-carrying capacity of hemoglobin in mL O_2/g and 0.003 is the solubility coefficient of O_2 in plasma. Most of the O_2 in blood is bound to hemoglobin (see Fig. 100–5), although additional O_2 can be dissolved in blood if the PaO_2 is raised to supranormal levels. At a normal SaO_2 of approximately 100%, a PaO_2 of 100 mm Hg, and a hemoglobin concentration of 14 g/dL, the CaO_2 is 20 mL O_2/dL of blood.

Cardiac output can be measured with the thermodilution technique using a pulmonary artery catheter. With this technique, a bolus of cold liquid, usually dextrose in water, is rapidly injected into the right atrium through the proximal catheter port, causing the negative heat to be diluted by mixing with blood as it passes into the pulmonary artery. A thermistor senses the temperature of blood on passing the distal catheter port, and the temperature change is used to compute cardiac output, which averages 5 L/min in healthy persons. If arterial O_2 content is normal, the amount of O_2 delivered to the tissues normally averages 1000 mL O_2/min.

Measurement of Mixed Venous Oxygen Saturation

Placement of a pulmonary artery catheter allows the collection of samples for determination of the O_2 tension, saturation, and content of mixed venous blood. The saturation can also be measured continuously with an oximetric pulmonary artery catheter containing fiberoptic bundles that transmit and receive light from the catheter tip.

Normal persons have a mixed venous O_2 saturation of approximately 75%, which corresponds to a mixed venous O_2 tension of 40 mm Hg on an unshifted O_2 hemoglobin dissociation curve. Reductions in mixed venous O_2 saturation to below 60%, corresponding to mixed venous O_2 tension values less than 28 mm Hg, are associated with a severely impaired amount of O_2 delivered to the tissues. Indeed, anaerobic metabolism commonly develops when the mixed venous O_2 saturation falls below 50%.

Although a low mixed venous O_2 saturation may be clinically alarming, inadequate O_2 transport and utilization may exist in the presence of normal or supranormal values. For example, a mixed venous O_2 saturation greater than 80% may be seen in sepsis, when the tissues either cannot extract O_2 from the blood or perform aerobic metabolism or when blood is redistributed to metabolically inactive organs such as the skin.

Measurement of Oxygen Consumption

Total body O_2 consumption, which reflects the amount of O_2 utilized during aerobic metabolism, can be measured in closed systems by comparing the difference in O_2 in inspired and expired gases, which is difficult to accomplish in patients with a high minute ventilation and FIO_2. Alternatively, total body O_2 consumption can be measured by indirect calorimetry and calculated using Fick's equation.

Use of Fick's Equation

Fick's equation holds that total body O_2 consumption ($\dot{V}O_2$) is equal to the product of cardiac output ($\dot{Q}T$) and the amount of O_2 extracted by the tissues, which is the difference in O_2 contents in systemic arterial (CaO_2) and mixed venous ($C\bar{v}O_2$) blood. Thus,

$$\dot{V}O_2 = (\dot{Q}T)(CaO_2 - C\bar{v}O_2) \qquad (11)$$

The mixed venous O_2 content is normally 15 mL O_2/dL of blood. Because the mixed arterial content is usually 20 mL/dL, the normal difference is 5 mL O_2/mL blood. With this value and a cardiac output of 5 L/min, total body O_2 consumption averages 250 mL O_2/min in healthy persons.

In addition to allowing calculation of total body O_2 consumption, Fick's equation provides insights into physiologic function during stress and exercise. It reveals, for example, that normally only 25% of the O_2 in systemic arterial blood is extracted by the tissues, leaving a large O_2 reserve. Patients characteristically call on this reserve when the amount of O_2 delivered to the tissues decreases because of a fall in cardiac output, a fall in the content of O_2 in systemic arterial blood (and its major components, SaO_2 and hemoglobin), or both. Nevertheless, a shift to anaerobic metabolism generally occurs when more than 50% of the O_2 is extracted, and lactic acidosis may result.

Measurement of Other Indicators of Oxygen Transport and Utilization

Clinicians commonly monitor serum lactate levels as a sign of the development and progression of anaerobic metabolism. This approach is supported by studies demonstrating that lactate levels above 2 mEq/L correspond to a mixed venous O_2 tension less than 28 mm Hg with an increased mortality rate among critically ill patients. Nevertheless, elevated lactate levels may result from decreased lactate degradation rather than increased production, and they should be interpreted with caution.

Assessment of oxygenation of the gastrointestinal tract may provide an early indication of inadequate tissue perfusion in the critically ill. Such assessment can be derived from measurement of gastric intramucosal pH using a saline-filled balloon passed into the lumen of the stomach. After approximately 30 minutes, the gastric CO_2 tension equilibrates with the CO_2 tension in the balloon; the equilibrated CO_2 tension can then be combined with the HCO_3^- concentration in blood to calculate intramucosal gastric pH using the Henderson-Hasselbalch equation.

Studies have suggested that a gastric intramucosal pH lower than the normal level of 7.35 correlates with a high mortality rate in patients admitted to a critical care unit and that such mortality can be reduced by therapy designed to restore intraluminal pH to normal. Nevertheless, this approach has not been verified in large groups of patients. In fact, it is not clear whether any method of assessing O_2 delivery and utilization is superior to monitoring urine output and changes in the physical examination.

SUGGESTED READINGS
Gomersall CD, Joynt GM, Freebairn RC, et al: Resuscitation of critically ill patients based on the results of gastric tonometry: A prospective, randomized, controlled trial. Crit Care Med 2000;28:607–614. *The largest major trial of therapy aimed at correcting low gastric intramucosal pH yielded negative results.*
Nuckton TJ, Alonso JA, Kallet RH, et al: Pulmonary dead-space fraction as a risk factor for death in the acute respiratory distress syndrome. N Engl J Med 2002;346:1281–1286. *Dead space was the most powerful predictor of death.*

101 VENTILATOR MANAGEMENT IN THE INTENSIVE CARE UNIT

John M. Luce

MECHANICAL VENTILATION

Indications for Mechanical Ventilation

The term *mechanical ventilation* is used to describe the artificial support of ventilation in which oxygen (O_2) is inhaled and carbon dioxide (CO_2) is excreted. Mechanical ventilation may be necessary for patients who have inadequate ventilation as reflected in a high systemic arterial CO_2 tension ($PaCO_2$), inadequate arterial oxygenation as reflected in a low arterial O_2 tension (PaO_2), or both (Table 101–1). Furthermore, severe airway obstruction caused by asthma (Chapter 84) and chronic obstructive pulmonary disease (COPD; Chapter 85) or parenchymal disease caused by disorders such as the acute respiratory distress syndrome (ARDS; Chapters 88 and 104) may increase the work of breathing to levels that cannot be maintained by spontaneous breathing. Finally, mechanical ventilation may be required for clinically unstable patients such as those in shock (Chapters 102, 103, and 104) and for patients who require

Table 101–1 • INDICATIONS FOR MECHANICAL VENTILATION

Acute increase in $PaCO_2$ to > 50 mm Hg with a decrease in pH to < 7.30
Respiratory rate > 35 breaths/min for prolonged period
Tidal volume < 5 mL/kg body weight
Ratio of respiratory rate (breaths/min) to tidal volume (L) > 105
Minute ventilation > 10 L/min
Vital capacity < 10 mL/kg body weight
Maximum inspiratory pressure between 0 and −20 cm H_2O
Dead space to tidal volume fraction 0.60 or more
Acute hypoxemia (PaO_2 < 60 mm Hg or SaO_2 < 90%, especially if
    inspired oxygen fraction is 0.4 or more, or $P(A - a)O_2$ > 300 mm Hg
    on inspired FIO_2 of 1.0)
Clinical instability
Need for hyperventilation therapy

$PaCO_2$ = systemic arterial carbon dioxide tension; PaO_2 = systemic arterial oxygen tension; SaO_2 = systemic arterial oxygen saturation; $P(A - a)O_2$ = alveolar to arterial oxygen pressure difference; FIO_2 = fraction of inspired oxygen.

hyperventilation to decrease cerebral blood flow and intracranial pressure (Chapter 431).

Ventilatory support supplied through endotracheal intubation is called *invasive mechanical ventilation*. *Noninvasive ventilation* can be provided by devices that apply intermittent negative extrathoracic pressure or furnish intermittent positive pressure through a tight-fitting nasal or face mask without an artificial airway in place. Both types of ventilation can create a closed system for delivering O_2 at a high inspired fraction (FIO_2) and for furnishing positive end-expiratory pressure (PEEP).

Noninvasive positive-pressure ventilation (NPPV) is generally used in or outside of intensive care units to provide partial ventilatory support while other therapies, such as bronchodilators and diuretics, are given time to work. By not requiring endotracheal intubation, NPPV may increase patient comfort, decrease upper airway trauma, and reduce the incidence of sinusitis and pneumonia, especially in immunocompromised patients. Suitable candidates for NPPV are the minority of critically ill patients who are conscious, cooperative, hemodynamically stable, and not in need of airway protection. They should have acute respiratory failure that is not severe and is likely to be reversible within hours or days. Such patients include those with exacerbations of COPD and those with ARDS who have declined endotracheal intubation or are reluctant to undergo it. In patients who are willing to be intubated, NPPV should be regarded as a trial that will be superseded by endotracheal intubation if it is unsuccessful.

Kinds of Mechanical Ventilation

NEGATIVE-PRESSURE VENTILATION

Ventilation can be supported by devices that generate a negative pressure around the chest during inspiration to substitute for the negative pleural and airway pressures normally created by contraction of the respiratory muscles. Negative-pressure ventilation can be achieved by including the entire body except the head in an iron lung, by encompassing the thorax in a garment or poncho wrap, or by fitting a cuirass to the anterior chest. Negative-pressure ventilators are best suited for stable patients with neuromuscular diseases whose lungs are normal and who do not require O_2 at a high FIO_2.

POSITIVE-PRESSURE VENTILATION

Because of the limitations of negative-pressure ventilation, positive-pressure ventilation is the kind of mechanical ventilation most widely used for both invasive and noninvasive ventilation. With positive-pressure ventilation, gas is delivered under positive pressure into the airways and the lungs. In contrast to negative-pressure ventilation, positive-pressure ventilation produces a positive airway pressure during inspiration. This pressure overcomes the impedance to gas flow and the elastance (reciprocal of the compliance, which is the change in volume with a given change in pressure) of the respiratory system and thereby inflates the alveoli, providing both ventilation and arterial oxygenation while reducing the work of breathing.

Most positive-pressure ventilators regulate gas delivery to maintain a constant pressure (pressure limited) or volume (volume limited) during inspiration. The first approach allows set limits on the peak and plateau pressures used for lung inflation but allows tidal volume, and hence minute ventilation, to vary, depending on the impedance of the respiratory system. Alternatively, the ventilators may deliver a preset tidal volume at whatever pressure is required to inflate the lungs, which guarantees minute ventilation but may increase peak and plateau pressures. Maintenance of airway pressure and lung volume is usually achieved by ventilator manipulation of gas flow.

When positive-pressure ventilation was first introduced, clinicians generally hoped to achieve a tidal volume in the range of 10 to 15 mL/kg of ideal body weight at whatever peak and plateau pressures were required or resulted, yielding a normal $PaCO_2$ in patients unless hyperventilation was desired. However, increasing concerns about barotrauma and ventilator-induced lung injury, as discussed later, have led clinicians to seek a lower tidal volume (6 to 8 mL/kg) and low plateau pressure (less than 35 cm H_2O) in many patients. Because this approach may lead to an increase in $PaCO_2$, the strategy is called *permissive hypercapnia* or *intentional hypoventilation*.

Permissive hypercapnia with low tidal volumes and plateau pressures was first used to reduce barotrauma in patients with status asthmaticus. More recently, clinicians have applied the same strategy to patients with ARDS to reduce ventilator-induced lung injury. Following a number of small and inconclusive studies, investigators of the ARDS network randomized 861 patients to receive traditional positive-pressure ventilation with tidal volumes of 12 mL/kg and plateau pressures of 50 cm H_2O or less or ventilation with tidal volumes of 6 mL/kg and plateau pressures of 30 cm H_2O or less. Because their respiratory rates were allowed to reach 35 breaths/minute, the patients receiving low tidal volume ventilation had a normal $PaCO_2$ during the study and did not receive permissive hypercapnia. Nevertheless, their mortality rate was 31% compared with 40% in the patients receiving larger tidal volumes and higher airway pressures. This landmark study suggests that patients with ARDS should be ventilated with low tidal volumes and plateau pressures, an approach that is being widely adopted. The implications of the study for patients with other kinds of respiratory failure are unclear.

With most modes of positive-pressure ventilation, an inspiratory-to-expiratory ratio of 1:3 or less is generally used to achieve an inspiratory time of 0.8 to 1.0 second and allow adequate time for expiration. This helps avoid air trapping, which may cause intrinsic or auto-PEEP. Auto-PEEP is most common in patients with COPD and other causes of airway obstruction. In addition, inspiratory flow rates of about 60 L/min are usually selected unless a higher flow rate is used to achieve a more rapid inflation and hence more time for exhalation, as might be desirable in patients with COPD. Flow can be delivered either with a square wave (constant flow) or a decelerating pattern; the latter may allow for a more uniform transpulmonary pressure throughout inspiration, which may be desirable in patients with ARDS.

MODES OF POSITIVE-PRESSURE VENTILATION. Perhaps the simplest mode of positive-pressure ventilation is *controlled mechanical ventilation*, in which the ventilator delivers gas at a preset respiratory rate and inspiratory time and either a preset peak pressure or tidal volume (Fig. 101–1 and Table 101–2). A square wave flow pattern is customarily used with controlled mechanical ventilation. In volume-limited controlled mechanical ventilation, the ventilator adjusts inspiratory flow over time to ensure stable tidal volume delivery. For example, as impedance increases during a breath, the resulting decreases in flow output are detected, and the ventilator's inspiratory valve opens wider to increase flow and maintain a constant tidal volume. Volume-limited controlled mechanical ventilation is most often used for patients who are unconscious as a result of illness or drugs, who are being intentionally hyperventilated, or who are recovering from anesthesia. Because patients receiving controlled mechanical ventilation cannot increase their minute ventilation voluntarily, their ventilatory status must be followed closely. Thus, the advantage of controlled mechanical ventilation—complete control of ventilatory function—is also its major limitation, and this mode is rarely used today.

Assisted mechanical ventilation is a positive-pressure ventilation mode in which the patient triggers the ventilator to deliver a preset tidal volume. As with controlled mechanical ventilation, the ventilator monitors and adjusts inspiratory flow to ensure stable tidal volume delivery. Triggering is accomplished by generating an airway pressure less than that in the ventilator and tubing. This pressure is usually

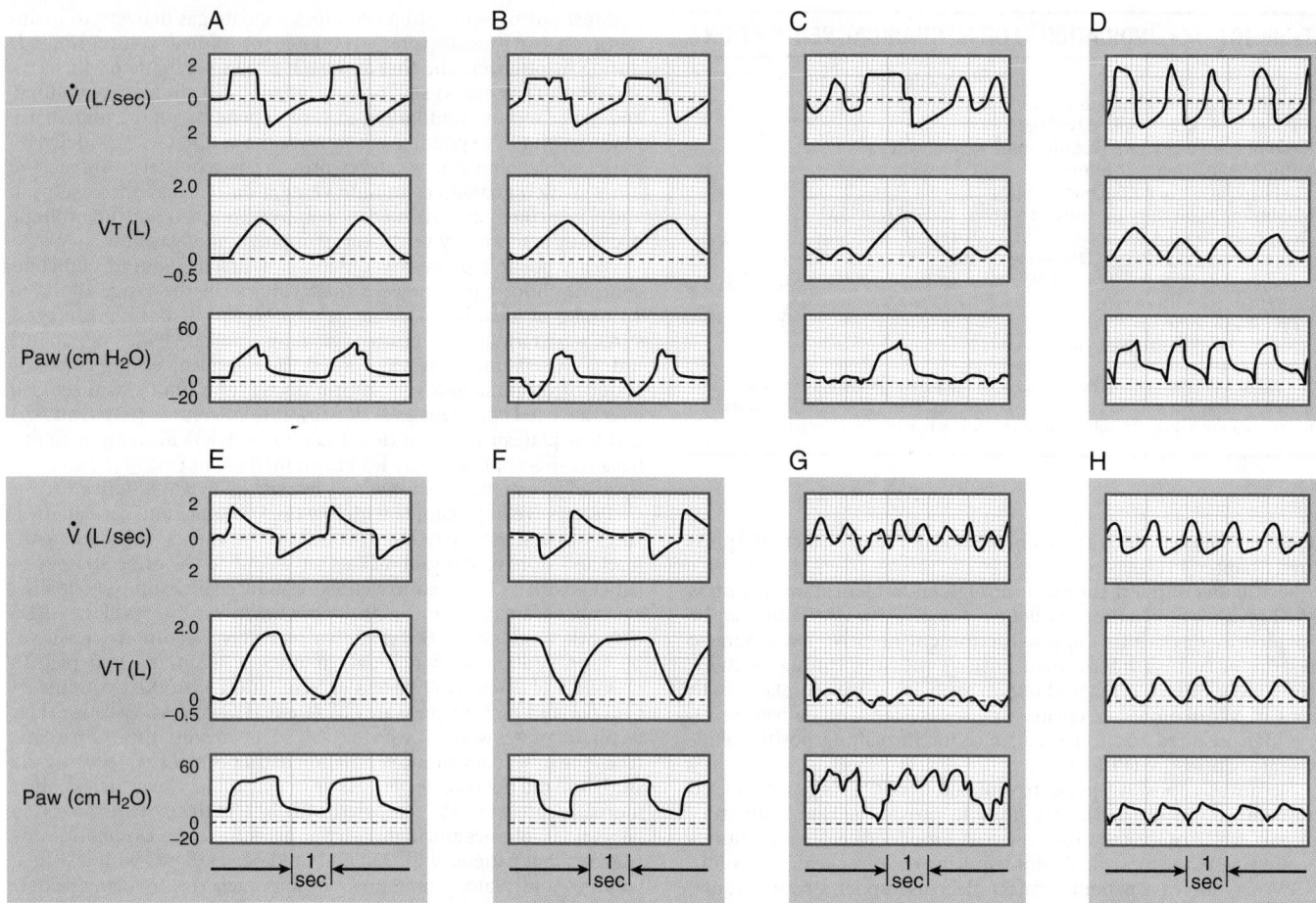

FIGURE 101–1 • Tracings drawn from a lung model illustrating gas flow ($\dot{V}$ in L/sec), tidal volume (V_T in L), and airway pressure (Paw in cm H_2O) during controlled mechanical ventilation (*A*), assisted volume-limited mechanical ventilation (*B*), synchronized intermittent mandatory ventilation (*C*), pressure support ventilation (*D*), pressure control ventilation (*E*), pressure control ventilation with inverse ratio ventilation (*F*), airway pressure release ventilation (*G*), and continuous positive airway pressure (*H*). Positive end-expiratory pressure is applied during all modes so that Paw does not return to 0 at end-expiration.

Table 101–2 • MODES OF POSITIVE PRESSURE VENTILATION

MODE	DESCRIPTION	ADVANTAGES/DISADVANTAGES
Controlled mechanical ventilation (CMV)	Ventilator f, inspiratory time, V_T (and thus $\dot{V}E$), preset	May be used with sedation or paralysis; ventilator cannot respond to ventilatory needs
Assisted mechanical ventilation (AMV) or assist/control	Ventilator V_T and inspiratory time preset but patient can increase f (and thus $\dot{V}E$)	Ventilator may respond to ventilatory needs; ventilator may under- or over-trigger, depending on sensitivity
Intermittent mandatory ventilation (IMV)	Ventilator delivers preset V_T, f, and inspiratory time, but patient also may breathe spontaneously	May decrease asynchronous breathing and sedation requirements; ventilator cannot respond to ventilatory needs
Synchronized intermittent mandatory ventilation (SIMV)	Same as IMV, but ventilator breaths delivered only after patient finishes inspiration	Same as IMV, and patient not overinflated by receiving spontaneous and ventilator breaths at same time
High-frequency ventilation (HFV)	Ventilator f is increased and V_T may be smaller than $\dot{V}D$	May reduce peak airway pressure; may cause auto-PEEP
Pressure-support ventilation (PSV)	Patient breathes at own f; V_T determined by inspiratory pressure and CRS	Increased comfort and decreased work of breathing; ventilator cannot respond to ventilatory needs
Pressure-control ventilation (PCV)	Ventilator peak pressure, f, and respiratory time preset	Peak inspiratory pressures may be decreased; hypoventilation may occur
Inverse ratio ventilation (IRV)	Inspiratory time exceeds expiratory time to facilitate inspiration	May improve gas exchange by increasing time spent in inspiration; may cause auto-PEEP
Airway pressure release ventilation (APRV)	Patient receives CPAP at high and low levels to simulate V_T	May improve oxygenation at lower airway pressure; hypoventilation may occur.
Proportional assist ventilation (PAV)	Patient determines own, f, V_T, pressures, and flows	May amplify spontaneous breathing; depends entirely on patient's respiratory drive.

f = respiratory rate; V_T = tidal volume; $\dot{V}D$ = dead space; $\dot{V}E$ = minute ventilation; PEEP = positive end-expiratory pressure; CPAP = continuous positive airway pressure; CRS = respiratory system compliance.

set at 1 to 2 cm H_2O below the ambient pressure or PEEP level. If the ventilator is sensitive to this pressure, it increases the respiratory rate and thereby minute ventilation in response to patient demands. The machine does not trigger if it is insensitive, however, and if it is unduly sensitive, it triggers in response to small fluctuations in airway pressure in addition to actual attempts to breathe. The latter problem, which is called *auto-cycling*, may be circumvented by establishing a proper sensitivity or, if this is not possible, by sedating the patient. Because sedation or neurologic changes may prevent patients from adjusting minute ventilation, an obligatory backup (or controlled mechanical ventilation) rate that provides the minimum allowable minute ventilation should be used with assisted mechanical ventilation. The combination of assisted mechanical ventilation and controlled mechanical ventilation, called the *assist/control mode*, offers the great advantage of responding to changes in a patient's status without the close monitoring needed with controlled mechanical ventilation. Traditionally, assisted mechanical ventilation and controlled mechanical ventilation have been referred to as intermittent positive-pressure ventilation (IPPV).

In *intermittent mandatory ventilation*, the ventilator delivers a preset tidal volume at specific intervals while also providing a flow of gas for spontaneous breathing. The form of intermittent mandatory ventilation most often used is synchronized intermittent mandatory ventilation, in which the ventilator is synchronized to deliver a mandatory breath in phase with the next spontaneous effort. This synchronization prevents patients from being hyperinflated by receiving a machine-delivered breath either in the middle or the end of a spontaneous inspiration ("breath stacking"). With synchronized intermittent mandatory ventilation, the ventilator respiratory rate may be set high enough to provide most, if not all, of the patient's minute ventilation initially; respiratory rate then may be lowered as the patient improves. Maintaining tidal volume delivery during mandatory breaths is accomplished in the same manner with synchronized intermittent mandatory ventilation as with controlled mechanical and assisted mechanical ventilation. However, during spontaneous breaths, flow from the inspiratory valve is regulated to maintain a constant target airway pressure rather than a constant volume. Thus, if a patient inspires vigorously, which causes a decrease in pressure in the ventilator circuit, the inspiratory valve opens wider and boosts flow to bring airway pressure back to the target level. Conversely, when the lungs fill and pressure begins to rise above the target level, the ventilator cycles into expiration. The potential benefits of synchronized intermittent mandatory ventilation include less asynchronous breathing and lower sedation requirements, reducing mean airway pressure by combining spontaneous and machine breaths, and improved respiratory muscle function by allowing patients to breathe spontaneously. Disadvantages include (1) the lack of a backup to guarantee minute ventilation in unstable patients if the ventilator respiratory rate is low and (2) the possibility of causing respiratory muscle fatigue in patients who receive synchronized intermittent mandatory ventilation at a low ventilator respiratory rate.

High-frequency ventilation delivers gas to the lungs by means of a conventional ventilator with very high internal compressibility, a high-pressure jet source, or an oscillator that entrains ambient air. The ventilator respiratory rate with high-frequency ventilation is greater than 60 per minute, the inspiratory-to-expiratory ratio is very high, and the tidal volume is either greater than the patient's anatomic dead space (in convective flow high-frequency ventilation) or less than the dead space (in nonconvective flow high-frequency ventilation). Measuring gas flow and tidal volume delivery is difficult during high-frequency ventilation, so ventilator parameters are usually based on airway pressure measurement, chest-wall expansion, and arterial blood gas analysis. Although adequate ventilation with a dead space/tidal volume in excess of 1.0 seems to be physiologically impossible, nonconvective flow high-frequency ventilation can adequately eliminate CO_2 in some patients, probably by enhancing diffusion in the lung. Both convective and nonconvective flow high-frequency ventilation commonly produce peak and plateau pressures that are less than those with other modes of positive-pressure ventilation, although the high inspiratory-to-expiratory ratio usually produces auto-PEEP. The lower peak and plateau pressures favor high-frequency ventilation to treat patients with bronchopleural fistulas and conditions such as ARDS. However, ventilation and arterial oxygenation may be inadequate with high-frequency ventilation.

Pressure-support ventilation augments spontaneous ventilatory efforts with a level of positive airway pressure that is preset to achieve a desired tidal volume. With pressure-support ventilation, the ventilator senses when the patient initiates a breath, and inspiratory flow is regulated to maintain a constant airway pressure. As impedance increases during a breath, the resulting increases in airway pressure are sensed, and the inspiratory valve narrows to decrease flow and thereby achieve the desired pressure. The ventilator then terminates the flow and pressure when it detects a decrease in the inspiratory flow rate to approximately 25% of the peak flow achieved during that breath. The initial pressure-support ventilation level is set to the plateau pressure level needed to achieve the tidal volume used during assisted mechanical ventilation or synchronized intermittent mandatory ventilation, or the pressure-support ventilation level is arbitrarily set around 25 cm H_2O. Pressure-support ventilation allows patients to set their own respiratory rate, timing of breaths, and peak flow, which may be more comfortable than other modes of positive-pressure ventilation. Pressure-support ventilation is also useful in overcoming the work of breathing through an endotracheal tube. Inasmuch as patients must initiate breaths with pressure-support ventilation, it should not be used in unstable patients and is most applicable during discontinuation of mechanical ventilation.

With *pressure-control ventilation*, gas is not delivered at a constant tidal volume. Instead, inspiratory flow is regulated to maintain a constant peak pressure during inspiration, and the patient's minute ventilation is determined by the preset peak pressure, ventilator rate, and inspiratory time. Monitoring and control of ventilator function is the same with pressure-control ventilation as with pressure-support ventilation, except that pressure-control ventilation is time-cycled rather than flow-cycled to expiration. As with pressure-support ventilation, peak pressure is usually set at the plateau pressure needed to achieve the tidal volume used during assisted mechanical ventilation or synchronized intermittent mandatory ventilation, or it can be set to the level considered safe in patients with ARDS (less than 35 cm H_2O). Advocates of pressure-control ventilation believe that barotrauma is reduced because peak pressure and plateau pressure are reduced. Nevertheless, the theoretical benefits of pressure-control ventilation in reducing barotrauma have not been documented conclusively. In addition, pressure-control ventilation may not provide a minute ventilation that is sufficient to prevent hypoventilation, assuming that hypoventilation is not desired.

In *inverse ratio ventilation*, the inspiratory-to-expiratory ratio is increased above the normal level of 1:3 or less to 1:1 or more. The rationale for this approach is that the longer duration of inspiratory positive-pressure opens stiff or fluid-filled alveoli, and the shorter expiratory time does not allow these alveoli to collapse. Peak pressure also may be lower than with other modes of positive-pressure ventilation, although the increase in inspiratory-to-expiratory time probably increases auto-PEEP. It has been argued that inverse ratio ventilation improves oxygenation primarily by such an increase in auto-PEEP. Inverse ratio ventilation is usually used in conjunction with pressure-control ventilation to allow a limited peak pressure. One drawback to inverse ratio ventilation is that it is often uncomfortable and usually requires sedation or paralysis of the patient. The discomfort stems in part from the long inspiratory time with inverse ratio ventilation; if patients try to exhale during this period, they perform Valsalva's maneuver because the expiratory valve on the ventilator remains closed.

With *airway pressure release ventilation*, a high level of continuous positive airway pressure (CPAP; 12 to 20 cm H_2O) is maintained for 2 to 4 seconds. The pressure is then released to a lower level of CPAP (2 to 5 cm H_2O) for 0.5 to 1.5 seconds. With the release of pressure, lung volume decreases and CO_2 is excreted. The number of cycles per minute to the lower pressure levels is titrated to the desired $PaCO_2$ and generally does not exceed 20 cycles/minute As the patient's spontaneous breathing ability improves, the number of cycles is decreased; as the patient's oxygenation improves, the high level of CPAP is decreased. As with pressure-support ventilation and pressure-control ventilation, inspiratory flow is regulated with airway pressure release ventilation to maintain a constant airway pressure. In addition, the ventilator may contain an "open circuit" whereby both the inspiratory and expiratory valves are potentially open during all phases of a breath and even when a patient is coughing. As a result of this feature, pressure overshoot during inspiration is attenuated because excess flow is vented through the expiratory valve. Airway pressure release ventilation has the potential advantage of maintaining oxygenation at lower airway pressures, but it has not been fully investigated in large clinical trials.

Proportional assist ventilation is a new mode in which the positive pressure delivered to the airways increases in direct proportion to the patient's instantaneous effort. Respiratory system resistance and elastance are calculated from a passive ventilator breath, and the ventilator tidal volume and flow are set to achieve 80% of these values. Proportional assist ventilation is described by its proponents as providing greater patient comfort, lower airway pressure, less need for sedation and paralysis, and less likelihood for overventilation. However, these attributes have not been widely demonstrated, and rapid changes in resistance and elastance may cause ventilator "runaway" with large tidal volumes. In addition, initiation of gas flow during proportional assist ventilation is entirely dependent on a patient's drive to breathe.

COMPLICATIONS OF POSITIVE-PRESSURE VENTILATION. One possible result of positive-pressure ventilation is that inflating lungs at high pressure may damage them. Such damage has been described traditionally as *barotrauma*, implying that it is the consequence of pressure changes. However, because alveolar distention occurs as a result of changes in pressure and because such distention is probably responsible for lung damage, "volutrauma" may be a more accurate term. Pneumothorax is a common kind of barotrauma, but subcutaneous and mediastinal emphysema, parenchymal lung cysts, and systemic air embolism may also occur. Recent studies suggest that positive-pressure ventilation at high pressures and volumes also cause bronchopulmonary dysplasia and diffuse alveolar damage that is identical to ARDS; this damage is termed *ventilator-induced lung injury*.

In addition to these respiratory effects, positive-pressure ventilation may also compromise the cardiovascular system, because the positive airway pressure during inspiration reduces venous return to the chest and may depress cardiac output. This effect may be increased if PEEP is intentionally added to positive-pressure ventilation or if auto-PEEP is unintentionally produced. Conversely, this effect may be decreased if adequate time is allowed for airway and alveolar pressure to return to or close to ambient levels during exhalation.

DISCONTINUING POSITIVE-PRESSURE VENTILATION. Mechanical ventilatory support can generally be discontinued when there is complete or near-complete resolution of the patient's disease process, whether or not it involves the lungs. Such resolution should be reflected in clinical stability and a return of $PaCO_2$ to less than 50 mm Hg, a respiratory rate to less than 35 breaths/minute, tidal volume to greater than 5 mL/kg, respiratory rate/tidal volume to less than 105 (breaths/minute/L), peak pressure to more negative than -20 cm H_2O, dead space/tidal volume to less than 0.6, PaO_2 to greater than 60 mm Hg on an FIO_2 of 0.4, and alveolar-arterial gradient of oxygen to less than 300 mm Hg on an FIO_2 of 1.0.

Discontinuing assisted mechanical ventilation and other modes of positive-pressure ventilation may be accomplished by connecting the endotracheal tube to a piece of tubing (T-piece), which is connected to a source of O_2 that is diluted with air to create the desired FIO_2. The patients then may breathe spontaneously through the T-piece at their own respiratory rate and tidal volume until they meet some or all of the weaning criteria just described. Otherwise healthy persons recovering from anesthesia or drug overdoses may be put on a T-piece when they wake up and may be extubated after a brief (15 to 30 minutes) period. Long-term ventilation patients may be put on a T-piece for a few minutes each hour or a few hours each day; 2-hour trials have been used in most clinical studies. When their respiratory muscles are less fatigued and patients can tolerate longer periods on a T-piece, discontinuation of the ventilator may be appropriate.

To discontinue synchronized intermittent mandatory ventilation, it is recommended that the ventilator respiratory rate be reduced until the patient can maintain an adequate minute ventilation by breathing spontaneously; reduction rates of 2 to 4 breaths/minute, two or more times daily, have been used in clinical studies. Synchronized intermittent mandatory ventilation can usually be discontinued if patients tolerate a ventilator rate of less than four per minute for 2 hours. In discontinuing pressure-support ventilation, the pressure-support ventilation level may be reduced in increments of 2 to 5 cm H_2O every 2 to 4 hours or so until patients tolerate a level of 5 cm H_2O for 2 hours.

Large studies have shown that mechanical ventilation can be discontinued more rapidly in patients using T-piece trials and pressure-support ventilation than in patients using synchronized intermittent mandatory ventilation.[2] These studies differed somewhat in how the three techniques were used, and all three techniques can be effective if used aggressively. One approach is to subject stable patients to daily testing to determine whether the indications for mechanical ventilation are no longer present. Patients who perform satisfactorily on these tests should then undergo 2-hour trials on either a T-piece with or without 5 cm H_2O of CPAP or 5 cm H_2O of pressure-support ventilation. When patients pass such trials and their physicians are aware of these results, there may be a striking reduction in the duration of positive-pressure ventilation and in its complications. Similar results may be obtainable with shorter trials.

EXTRACORPOREAL VENTILATION

Mechanical ventilation can also be extracorporeal, in that gas exchange takes place entirely, or in part, outside the body. With extracorporeal membrane oxygenation (ECMO), venous blood is circulated through a CO_2 scrubber and membrane oxygenator and returned to the body as arterial blood with the desired $PaCO_2$ and PaO_2. Low-frequency positive-pressure ventilation with extracorporeal CO_2 removal also uses an extracorporeal circuit to remove CO_2 from venous blood, but oxygenation is achieved by insufflating O_2 into the lungs at high flow rates while the lungs are inflated with positive-pressure ventilation at a low rate and held open with small amounts of PEEP to recruit alveoli. Both ECMO and extracorporeal CO_2 removal are used only occasionally, primarily in neonates and occasionally in patients with severe ARDS. In a randomized trial of patients with ARDS, extracorporeal CO_2 removal was not superior to more conventional forms of positive-pressure ventilation.[3]

POSITIVE END-EXPIRATORY PRESSURE

Indications for Positive End-Expiratory Pressure

PEEP improves arterial oxygenation by recruiting alveoli for gas exchange. PEEP does not improve ventilation; in fact, the $PaCO_2$ may increase because PEEP increases dead space/tidal volume by distending the airways and alveoli in normal lung units. PEEP also does not reduce extravascular lung water. Rather, PEEP either opens alveoli that would otherwise remain collapsed at end expiration or acts as a counterforce mechanism that prevents or reverses compression atelectasis caused by extravascular fluid in the lungs.

One indication for PEEP is to prevent or reverse atelectasis (Table 101–3). For example, low levels such as 5 cm H_2O of PEEP commonly are given to intubated patients who are supine in bed. Some investigators believe that low levels of PEEP facilitate weaning from mechanical ventilation by maintaining higher lung volumes while patients breathe through an endotracheal tube; these investigators, therefore, continue PEEP during T-piece trials and when patients are receiving synchronized intermittent mandatory ventilation at a low ventilator respiratory rate or pressure-support ventilation.

Another major indication for PEEP is to improve arterial oxygenation in patients with diffuse parenchymal lung disorders such as ARDS. Because their hypoxemia is primarily due to intrapulmonary shunt, such patients often cannot be oxygenated adequately even at an FIO_2 of 1.0. Administered in levels in excess of 5 cm H_2O, PEEP usually improves the PaO_2 of these patients. It also allows the FIO_2 to be reduced to levels of 0.6 or less, thereby minimizing the risk of O_2 toxicity.

Finally, PEEP (usually in levels of less than 10 cm H_2O) may be used to decrease the work of breathing related to triggering the ventilator in patients on assisted mechanical ventilation, synchronized intermittent mandatory ventilation, or pressure-support ventilation who have significant amounts of auto-PEEP. In this setting, the patients have to reduce airway pressure from a positive pressure to below 0 to trigger the ventilator. However, if PEEP is added intentionally, only a small downward reduction in pressure from the auto-PEEP level is necessary to provide inspiratory flow.

Table 101–3 • INDICATIONS FOR POSITIVE END-EXPIRATORY PRESSURE

To prevent or reverse atelectasis
To facilitate weaning from mechanical ventilation
To improve arterial oxygenation at a low inspired oxygen fraction
To reduce trigger-related work of breathing in patients with auto-PEEP

PEEP = positive end-expiratory pressure.

Modes of Positive End-Expiratory Pressure

PEEP may be administered to spontaneously breathing patients through either a tight-fitting face mask or an endotracheal tube, in which case it is called CPAP. PEEP may also be combined with intermittent positive mechanical ventilation to create continuous positive-pressure ventilation (CPPV). The improvement in oxygenation that may be produced by these two modes of PEEP depends on the increase in mean airway pressure. The increase in mean airway pressure is generally greater with CPPV than with CPAP; hence, patients who have merely atelectasis often may be managed solely with CPAP. However, because they also have pulmonary edema and because their ventilatory needs are greater, patients with diffuse parenchymal lung disease generally receive CPPV or bilevel CPAP in the form of airway pressure release ventilation.

Complications of Positive End-Expiratory Pressure

As with its benefits, the complications of PEEP are related to lung volume and airway pressure. Delivering gas at high pressure to achieve an increase in lung volume throughout the ventilatory cycle is more likely to cause barotrauma or "volutrauma" than is delivering pressurized gas solely during inspiration. It also is more likely to decrease venous return to the chest and thereby depress blood pressure and cardiac output. Although the incidence of complications due to PEEP has not been well studied, these complications appear to be significant if levels higher than 12 cm H_2O are used.

Discontinuing Positive End-Expiratory Pressure

Patients who receive low levels of PEEP for atelectasis can usually be discontinued from PEEP without difficulty. However, premature withdrawal or reduction of PEEP from patients with diffuse parenchymal lung disorders can worsen oxygenation and cause clinical deterioration that requires hours or days of therapy to reverse. For this reason, PEEP should be withdrawn slowly, in small (2 to 5 cm H_2O) increments, with close monitoring of PaO_2 or systemic arterial saturation (SaO_2) in such patients. Prematurely reduced PEEP can be avoided if the disease process for which PEEP was initiated has resolved or is substantially improved, if the PaO_2 is greater than 80 mm Hg on an FIO_2 less than 0.4, and if these conditions have been present for several hours.

ENDOTRACHEAL INTUBATION

Indications for Intubation

Humidified O_2 at an FIO_2 greater than 0.40 is most reliably delivered through the closed system provided by an endotracheal tube. Although intubation (Table 101–4) often precedes mechanical ventilation, the indications for these two therapies and their timing are not necessarily the same. For example, some patients who are intubated to prevent aspiration of gastric contents never require mechanical ventilation.

Kinds of Intubation

Endotracheal intubation may be performed either via the translaryngeal route through the nose or mouth or via a tracheotomy. Tracheotomy tubes once were used routinely in patients requiring intubation for longer than 1 or 2 days. However, the development of low-pressure, high-compliance cuffs that limit tracheal damage from nasal or oral tubes demonstrates that such tubes can be left in place for weeks and even months without severe sequelae, and documentation of complications after tracheotomy has led to a preference for

nasotracheal or orotracheal intubation over tracheotomy in all but a few patients. Such patients include those with laryngeal fractures and those who will require intubation for longer than 3 weeks. Tracheotomy tubes generally are more comfortable than translaryngeal tubes; they also are easier to suction through, and talking may be made possible by fitting the tubes with a device that directs a stream of air retrograde through the larynx above the cuff site.

Nasal intubation provides good support for the endotracheal tube and may allow patients to swallow their secretions better than when the tube passes orally. Oral intubation usually permits passage of a tube with a larger diameter than the nostril will accommodate and is the preferred route during emergency intubations. Small endotracheal tubes have the potential disadvantage of increasing airway resistance during spontaneous breathing, especially when minute ventilation is high. Although smaller tubes may decrease pressure on posterior laryngeal structures, they may require higher cuff pressures to achieve a snug airway seal for positive-pressure ventilation. Larger tubes, on the other hand, may create a better seal and facilitate access to the trachea for suctioning and bronchoscopy, but they apply greater pressure to the posterior larynx. To balance these considerations, endotracheal tubes with a 7.0 mm or 7.5 mm internal diameter generally are used in women, and tubes with an 8.0 mm or 8.5 mm internal diameter are used in men.

Whatever size tube is used, its diameter should be sufficient to seal the airway without cuff pressures in excess of 25 mm Hg, which is capillary pressure in the trachea. Cuff pressure should be monitored regularly. Tube position should be determined by chest radiograph or bronchoscopy immediately following insertion and on a regular basis thereafter. Intubation of the right mainstem bronchus, which extends from the trachea at less of an angle than the left mainstream bronchus, must be avoided. Because the lungs are the only source of CO_2, detection of expired CO_2 with a capnometer or with portable devices that change color when exposed to the gas is useful in demonstrating that a tube is in an airway and not in the esophagus, especially following emergency intubations.

Complications of Intubation

Some patients receiving endotracheal intubation suffer adverse consequences. Excessive cuff pressure requirements (>25 mm Hg), self-extubation, and inability to seal the airway are the most common complications with nasotracheal and orotracheal tubes. Problems associated with tracheotomy include stomal hemorrhage, excessive cuff pressure requirements, and subcutaneous emphysema. Follow-up studies of patients receiving intubation and mechanical ventilation reveal a higher incidence of tracheal stenosis after tracheotomy as compared with translaryngeal intubation, although laryngeal complications are more common with nasal and oral tubes.

Discontinuing Intubation

In general, endotracheal tubes may be removed when the original indications for their insertion are no longer present. For example, extubation frequently follows the return of consciousness and an adequate gag reflex in previously comatose patients or restored adequate ventilation and arterial oxygenation in patients with acute respiratory failure. If an endotracheal tube has been in place only briefly, it may be removed after secretions have been suctioned from above the cuff site and the patient has been seated upright. However, patients with previous neck surgery, laryngeal trauma, vocal cord paralysis, or infections of the neck or mouth may be at risk for upper airway obstruction following extubation. Obstruction at the tracheal level is unlikely if less than 10 cm H_2O of positive airway pressure is required to cause a leak of air around the endotracheal tube when the tube cuff is deflated. Obstruction is also unlikely if the patient can breathe around the tube when the cuff is deflated and the proximal end of the tube is blocked. Direct or indirect laryngoscopy may be helpful in evaluating potential obstruction at the pharyngeal level.

Table 101–4 • INDICATIONS FOR ENDOTRACHEAL INTUBATION

To provide a closed system for mechanical ventilation or oxygen delivery, especially at a high fraction of inspired oxygen
To prevent or reverse upper airway obstruction
To protect against aspiration of gastric contents
To facilitate tracheobronchial toilet

---

1. The Acute Respiratory Distress Syndrome Network: Ventilation with lower tidal volumes as compared with traditional tidal volumes for acute lung injury and the acute respiratory distress syndrome. N Engl J Med 2000;342:1301–1308.
2. Esteban A, Frutos F, Tobin MJ, et al: A comparison of four methods of weaning patients from mechanical ventilation. N Engl J Med 1995;332:345–350.
3. Morris AH, Wallace CJ, Menlove RL, et al: Randomized clinical trial of pressure-controlled inverse ratio ventilation and extracorporeal CO_2 removal for adult respiratory distress syndrome. Am J Respir Crit Care Med 1994;149:295–305.

SUGGESTED READINGS

Mehta S, Hill NS: Noninvasive ventilation. Am J Respir Crit Care Med 2001;163:540–577. *A review of noninvasive positive-pressure ventilation.*

Pinho L, Whitehead T, Evans T, et al: Ventilator-associated lung injury. Lancet 2003;361:332–340. *Mechanisms of injury and potential ways to prevent it.*

Tobin MJ: Advances in mechanical ventilation. N Engl J Med 2001;344:1986–1996. *Summarizes several topics, including ventilator-induced lung injury, low tidal volume ventilation, and weaning.*

102 APPROACH TO THE PATIENT WITH SHOCK

Joseph E. Parrillo

Shock is a very serious medical condition that results from a profound and widespread reduction in effective tissue perfusion leading to cellular dysfunction and organ failure. Unless it is promptly corrected, this circulatory insufficiency will become irreversible. The most common clinical manifestations of shock are hypotension and evidence of inadequate tissue perfusion. A number of diseases can result in shock, and the specific clinical characteristics of these diseases usually accompany the shock syndrome.

To understand the definition of shock, it is important to comprehend the meaning of *effective* tissue perfusion (Table 102–1). Certain forms of shock result from a global reduction in systemic perfusion (low cardiac output), whereas other forms produce shock as a result of a maldistribution of blood flow or a defect of substrate utilization at the subcellular level. These latter forms of shock have normal or high global flow to tissues, but this perfusion is not effective because of abnormalities at the microvascular or subcellular levels.

Classification

It is valuable to classify different forms of shock according to etiology and cardiovascular physiology (Fig. 102–1 and Table 102–2) because such a classification results in appropriate patient management. *Hypovolemic shock* results from blood and/or fluid loss and is due to a decreased circulating blood volume leading to reduced diastolic filling pressures and volumes. The result is inadequate cardiac output, hypotension, and shock. *Cardiogenic shock* (Chapter 103) is caused by a severe reduction in cardiac function resulting from direct myocardial damage or a mechanical abnormality of the heart; the cardiac output and blood pressure are reduced. *Extracardiac obstructive shock* results from obstruction to flow in the cardiovascular circuit, leading to inadequate diastolic filling or decreased systolic function due to increased afterload; this form of shock results in inadequate cardiac output and hypotension. The cardiovascular abnormality of *distributive shock* is more complex than the other shock categories. Distributive shock is characterized by vasodilatation: the venodilatation leads to a decrease in preload, which can be corrected with fluid administration, and the arterial vasodilatation leads to hypotension with a normal or elevated cardiac output. Myocardial depression frequently accompanies distributive shock. The most characteristic pattern is decreased vascular resistance, normal or elevated cardiac output, and hypotension. Distributive shock, which results from mediator effects at the microvascular and cellular levels, may produce inadequate blood pressure and multiple organ system dysfunction without a decrease in cardiac output.

Although many patients develop pure forms of shock as classified herein, others may manifest characteristics of several forms of shock, termed *mixed shock*. For example, septic shock (Chapter 104) is considered to be a distributive form of shock; however, before resuscitation with fluids, a substantial hypovolemic component may exist as a result of venodilatation. Also, septic shock patients have a cardiogenic component caused by myocardial depression. Patients with severe hemorrhage, classified as hypovolemic shock, may manifest significant myocardial depression. Thus, although these four categories are valuable for classifying the hemodynamics of shock, patients may manifest combinations of these categories.

Pathogenesis and Pathophysiology

Adequate, effective tissue perfusion of organs must be maintained for survival. Perfusion is dependent on a number of variables that are carefully regulated by the body's compensatory mechanisms (see Table 102–1).

CONTROL OF ARTERIAL PRESSURE. One excellent physiologic and clinical measure of perfusion is arterial pressure, which is determined

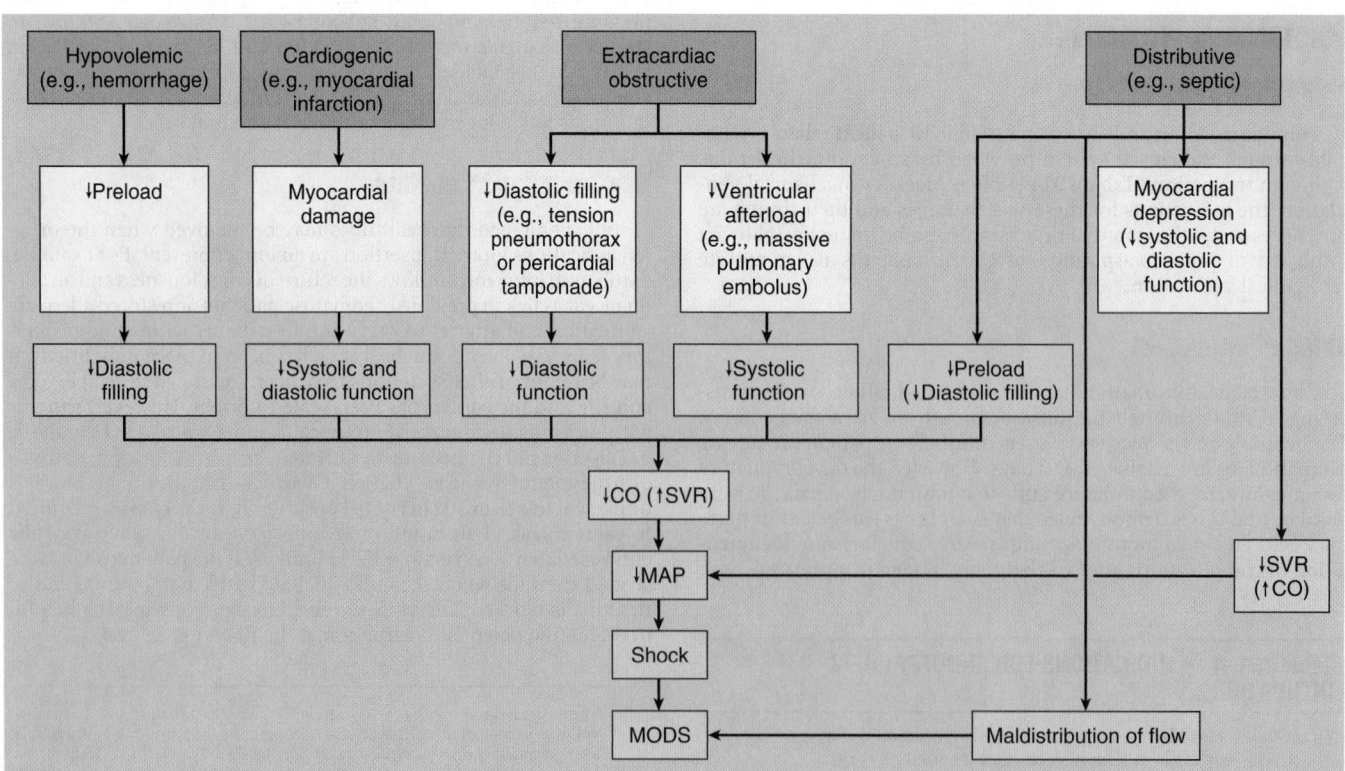

FIGURE 102–1 • A classification of shock showing interrelationships among the different forms of shock. CO = cardiac output; MAP = mean arterial pressure; MODS = multiple organ dysfunction syndrome; SVR = systemic vascular resistance.

Table 102–1 • DETERMINANTS OF EFFECTIVE TISSUE PERFUSION

ARTERIAL PRESSURE CARDIAC PERFORMANCE
Cardiac function
  Preload
  Afterload
  Contractility
  Heart rate
Venous return

VASCULAR PERFORMANCE
Distribution of cardiac output
  Extrinsic regulatory systems
    Sympathetic nervous system
    Adrenal hormone release
  Intrinsic regulatory systems
  Anatomic vascular disease
  Exogenous vasoactive agents
Microvascular function
  Pre- and post-capillary sphincter function
  Capillary endothelial integrity
  Microvascular obstruction

CELLULAR FUNCTION
Oxygen unloading and diffusion
  RBC 2, 3 DPG
  Blood pH
  Temperature
Cellular energy generation/substrate utilization
  Citric acid (Krebs) cycle
  Oxidative phosphorylation
  Other energy metabolism pathways

Table 102–2 • CLASSIFICATION OF SHOCK

HYPOVOLEMIC
Hemorrhagic
  Trauma
  Gastrointestinal
  Retroperitoneal
Fluid depletion (nonhemorrhagic)
  External fluid loss
    Dehydration
    Vomiting
    Diarrhea
    Polyurea
  Interstitial fluid redistribution
    Thermal injury
    Trauma
    Anaphylaxis
Increased vascular capacitance (venodilatation)
  Sepsis
  Anaphylaxis
  Toxins/drug

CARDIOGENIC
Myopathic
  Myocardial infarction
    Left ventricle
    Right ventricle
  Myocardial contusion (trauma)
  Myocarditis
  Cardiomyopathy
  Postischemic myocardial stunning
  Septic myocardial depression
  Pharmacologic
    Anthracycline cardiotoxicity
    Calcium channel blockers
Mechanical
  Valvular failure (stenotic or regurgitant)
  Hypertrophic cardiomyopathy
  Ventricular septal defect
Arrhythmic
  Bradycardia
  Tachycardia

EXTRACARDIAC OBSTRUCTIVE
Impaired diastolic filling (decreased ventricular preload)
  Direct venous obstruction (vena cava)
    Intrathoracic obstructive tumors
  Increased intrathoracic-pressure
    Tension pneumothorax
    Mechanical ventilation (with excessive pressure or volume
      depletion)
    Asthma
  Decreased cardiac compliance
    Constrictive pericarditis
    Cardiac tamponade
Impaired systolic contraction (increased ventricular afterload)
  Right ventricle
    Pulmonary embolus (massive)
    Acute pulmonary hypertension
  Left ventricle
    Aortic dissection

DISTRIBUTIVE
Septic (bacterial, fungal, viral, rickettsial)
Toxic shock syndrome
Anaphylactic, anaphylactoid
Neurogenic (spinal shock)
Endocrinologic
  Adrenal crisis
  Thyroid storm
Toxic (e.g., nitroprusside, bretylium)

by cardiac output and vascular resistance and can be defined by the following equation:

$$MAP - CVP = CO \times SVR$$

where MAP is mean arterial pressure, CVP is central venous pressure, CO is cardiac output, and SVR is systemic vascular resistance.

The MAP and cardiac output can be measured directly, these two variables are frequently used to describe tissue perfusion. SVR can be calculated as a ratio of MAP minus central venous pressure divided by cardiac output.

The arterial pressure is regulated by changes in cardiac output and/or SVR. These regulatory mechanisms consist of neural and hormonal reflexes and local factors. Blood flow to the heart and brain is carefully regulated and maintained over a wide range of blood pressures (from an MAP of 50 to 150 mm Hg); this autoregulation results from reflexes in the local vasculature and ensures the perfusion of these especially vital organs. Failure to maintain the minimal arterial pressure required for autoregulation during shock indicates a severe abnormality that may produce inadequate coronary perfusion and a further reduction in cardiac function as a result of myocardial ischemia.

CARDIAC PERFORMANCE. Cardiac output is a product of heart rate and stroke volume. The stroke volume is determined by preload, afterload, and contractility, whereas preload is dependent upon adequate venous return (Chapter 48).

VASCULAR PERFORMANCE. Effective perfusion requires appropriate resistance to blood flow to maintain arterial pressure. Resistance to flow of blood in a vessel is proportional to the length of the vessel and the viscosity of blood and is inversely proportional to the radius of the vessel raised to the fourth power. Therefore, the cross-sectional area of a vessel is by far the most important determinant of resistance to flow. In the systemic vasculature, the major (>80%) site of resistance is at the arteriolar sphincter, and regulation of this arteriolar tone constitutes the major determinant of vascular resistance.

Arteriolar smooth muscle tone is regulated by extrinsic and intrinsic factors (Fig. 102–2). The extrinsic factors consist of sympathetic nervous system innervation of arterioles, which are largely regulated by arterial and cardiopulmonary baroreceptors. Circulating epinephrine and norepinephrine are released into the circulation by stimulation of the adrenal medulla. The intrinsic mechanisms include a vascular smooth muscle (myogenic) response in which blood vessels relax or constrict in response to changes in transmural vessel

pressure to maintain vessel blood flow at a constant level despite changes in perfusion pressure. Other intrinsic mechanisms are a metabolic response that result from release of vasodilators in response to increased metabolic activity and an oxygen tension response that results in vasodilatation with low oxygen tensions. Vasodilators released locally and systemically include nitric oxide, prostacyclin, eicosanoids, kinins, and adenosine. Vasoconstrictor molecules include endothelin-1, renin, angiotensin II, thromboxane, vasopressin, and oxygen-free radicals.

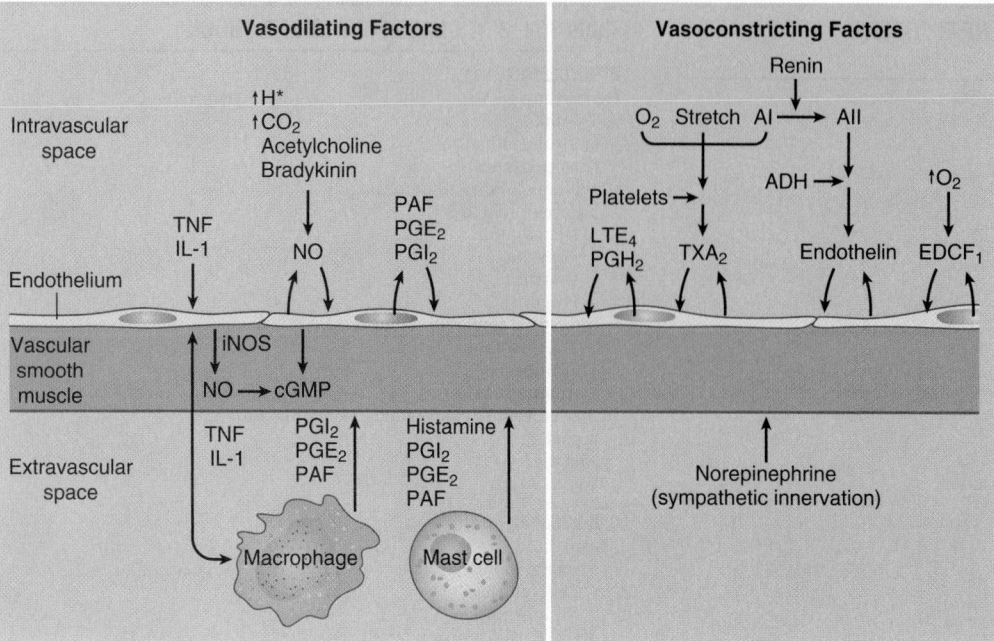

FIGURE 102–2 • The blood vessel in shock: physiologic and pathophysiologic vasoactive factors. ADH = antidiuretic hormone (vasopressin); AI = angiotensin I; AII = angiotensin II; cGMP = cyclic GMP; EDCF$_1$ = endothelium-derived contracting factor; IL-1β = interleukin-1β; iNOS = inducible nitric oxide synthetase; LTE$_4$ = leukotriene E$_4$; NO = nitric oxide; O$_2^-$ = superoxide anion; PAF = platelet-activating factor; PGE$_2$ = prostaglandin E$_2$; PGH$_2$ = prostaglandin H$_2$; prostacyclin; TNF-α = tumor necrosis factor α; TXA$_2$ = thromboxane A$_2$. (Adapted from Parrillo JE, Dellinger RP [eds]: Critical Care Medicine: Principles of Diagnosis and Management in the Adult, 2nd ed. St. Louis, Mosby, 2001, p 386.)

In addition to vascular tone, the microvasculature also affects perfusion by obstruction to microvascular flow. In shock, this obstruction can be caused by adhesion of leukocytes or platelets to the endothelium, with sludging and occlusion of microvessels. Leukocyte adhesion and rolling are mediated by integrins and selectins on the surface of activated neutrophils and endothelial cells. Activation of the coagulation system with fibrin deposition and microthrombi may contribute to this process. Shunting around these occluded vessels may occur. Decreased red or white cell deformability may also aggravate this microvascular dysfunction. Recent therapeutic success using activated protein C, an anticoagulant, emphasizes the importance of the coagulation cascade in the pathogenesis of septic shock (Chapter 104).∎

Microvascular permeability to fluids or other substances may also be altered by vasoactive mediators, activated leukocytes, and damaged endothelial cells. Because intravascular and extravascular fluid is determined by a balance between hydrostatic pressure and colloid osmotic pressure, damage to the endothelium may cause increased extravasation of fluid into the interstitial space and result in tissue edema. This fluid accumulation may further worsen organ dysfunction.

CELLULAR FUNCTION. At the cellular level, a number of factors regulate the unloading of oxygen and other substrates to cells. Shock produces cellular dysfunction through three major mechanisms: cellular ischemia, inflammatory mediators, and free radical injury. Cellular ischemia is probably the major cause of cell damage in shock with a low cardiac output. In hypovolemic shock, inadequate perfusion and the resultant lack of oxygen lead to increasing dependence on anaerobic glycolysis, which produces only two adenosine triphosphate (ATP) molecules during breakdown of one glucose molecule as opposed to 36 ATP molecules produced by aerobic metabolism through the citric acid (Krebs) cycle; the result is depletion of ATP and intracellular energy reserves. Intracellular acidosis occurs, and anaerobic glycolysis leads to accumulation of lactate. Lack of adequate energy leads to failure of energy-dependent ion transport pumps and the inability to maintain normal transmembrane gradients of potassium, chloride, and calcium; the result is mitochondrial dysfunction, abnormal carbohydrate metabolism, and failure of many energy-dependent enzyme reactions. Ultrastructural changes in mitochondria ensue, and the cell dies.

One important but controversial hypothesis regarding cellular ischemia in shock is the degree of dependence on oxygen supply. In normal humans, oxygen delivery to tissues (CO × O$_2$ content of arterial blood) is maintained at a high level so that tissue oxygen consumption [CO × (O$_2$ content of arterial blood − O$_2$ content of mixed venous blood)] is not altered or dependent on changes in oxygen delivery. However, if systemic flow drops below a critical value of oxygen delivery, tissues must switch from aerobic metabolism to the less efficient anaerobic metabolism. This deficiency of energy production may lead to multiple organ system dysfunction and death. Below this critical value (estimated at 8 to 10 mL of oxygen/min/kg in anesthetized humans), oxygen consumption is dependent on oxygen delivery (or supply), a relationship termed *physiologic oxygen supply dependency*. This process is believed to be an important mechanism of cellular damage in forms of shock that are characterized by low oxygen delivery caused by inadequate cardiac output, low oxygen saturation, or decreased hemoglobin concentration. The controversy regarding this mechanism stems from the hypothesis that a *pathologic oxygen supply dependency* exists in patients with sepsis, trauma, or adult respiratory distress syndrome (ARDS). These patients have oxygen delivery in the normal or elevated range but manifest lactate production and organ dysfunction. Some animal and human studies suggest the presence of a pathologic oxygen supply dependency because they demonstrate an increase in oxygen consumption with increases in oxygen delivery even at elevated levels of oxygen delivery. This finding suggests dependency of consumption on delivery over a wide range of delivery values. Proponents argue that inadequate oxygen delivery is occurring in these forms of shock because of microvascular and cellular abnormalities. This hypothesis has led to the argument that the management of sepsis, trauma, and ARDS should include methods to maximize cardiac output and oxygen delivery. In general, these studies have been inconclusive, and the hypothesis of pathologic oxygen supply dependency remains controversial.

Inflammatory mediators are a major cause of cell injury in shock due to sepsis and trauma and may play a significant role in other forms of shock. These mediators may exert their influence on the vasculature to produce inadequate perfusion, or they may produce direct injury to cells in a number of organs. The cytokines, especially tumor necrosis factor (TNF) and interleukin-1 (IL-1), can produce dysfunction of transmembrane ion gradients similar to that described with cellular ischemia. Administration of TNF to animals produces a cardiovascular state indistinguishable from septic shock. TNF can also stimulate release of many other mediators, including other cytokines, platelet-activating factor, leukotrienes, prostaglandins, and thromboxane.

The inflammatory response is a physiologic, homeostatic mechanism designed to respond to injury or infection. Release of inflammatory mediators usually provides beneficial effects such as activating host defense systems and enhancing blood flow to damaged tissues. With a self-limited insult, the inflammatory reaction is carefully controlled by counter-regulatory, anti-inflammatory mechanisms. In shock, the inflammatory response becomes excessive and unregulated, and it contributes to cell injury and tissue damage.

Free radicals are highly reactive oxygen intermediates that can occur after ischemia with subsequent reperfusion. Cellular ischemia and intracellular calcium accumulation can result in formation of xanthine oxidase, which can oxidize purines with the formation of the highly toxic superoxide radical. These oxygen products can inactivate proteins, damage DNA, induce lipid peroxidation of cell membranes, and lead to cell lysis and tissue injury.

Altered gene expression may also play a role in the cellular dysfunction during shock. For example, generation of cytokines, adhesion proteins, and inducible nitric oxide synthase enzymes represents upregulation of gene expression. The heat shock proteins may be an especially important genetic response in shock. These proteins are involved in the genetic program of cell death known as *apoptosis,* a physiologic mechanism that normally functions to remove senescent cells. During shock, the induction of heat shock proteins may interfere with cell synthetic pathways and may initiate a heightened activation of programmed cell death. Inappropriate initiation of this mechanism may be an important contributor to cell demise in shock. Recent genetic studies in septic shock have documented an association between the presence of the TNF2 allele, a polymorphism promoter in TNF-α, and a very high relative risk for septic shock and a high mortality from this disease. This finding demonstrates the potential predictive ability of genetic studies in shock.

Compensatory Mechanisms

With the onset of hemodynamic dysfunction in shock, homeostatic compensatory mechanisms attempt to maintain effective tissue perfusion, and many of the manifestations of shock represent the body's attempt to correct abnormalities. Most compensatory mechanisms are dependent on various sensing mechanisms designed to recognize hemodynamic or metabolic dyshomeostasis. The sensing mechanisms consist of pressure receptors located in the cardiovascular system (right atrium, pulmonary artery, aortic arch, carotid, and splanchnic baroreceptors) and the kidney (juxtaglomerular apparatus) as well as chemoreceptors sensitive to concentrations of carbon dioxide or oxygen and located in the central nervous system (mostly in the medulla).

The compensatory responses in shock maintain mean circulatory pressure, maximize cardiac performance, redistribute perfusion to the most vital organs, and optimize the unloading of oxygen to tissues. These effects are produced by stimulation of the sympathetic nervous system, release of hormones (angiotensin II, vasopressin, epinephrine, and norepinephrine), and creation of a local tissue environment that enhances the unloading of oxygen to tissues due to acidosis, pyrexia, and increased red blood cell 2,3-diphosphoglycerate. The magnitude of these compensatory mechanisms is dependent on the severity of hemodynamic or metabolic derangements. Compensation is effective at restoring tissue perfusion for a period during shock; however, if the initiating process is not reversed during this period, shock becomes irreversible as a result of widespread cellular damage.

Multiple Organ Dysfunction Syndrome

The clinical presentation of shock is variable and depends on the initiating cause and the response of multiple organs (Table 102–3). Different organs may be affected minimally, mildly, moderately, or severely. This leads to multiple organ dysfunction syndrome (MODS) (see Fig. 102–1), which is one of the major causes of death in shock.

CENTRAL NERVOUS SYSTEM. The most frequent findings in shock are alterations in the level of consciousness ranging from confusion to coma. Autoregulation protects the ischemia-sensitive neurons by maintaining adequate blood flow down to an MAP of approximately 50 to 60 mm Hg. Below this level, however, tissue ischemia ensues. Acid-base and electrolyte abnormalities also contribute to neuronal damage. Sepsis-related central nervous system dysfunction may occur at a higher MAP as a result of the effects of inflammatory mediators.

HEART. Many of the clinically apparent manifestations of cardiac involvement in shock result from sympathoadrenal stimulation, with tachycardia being the most sensitive indicator that shock is present. As in the brain, autoregulation ensures good coronary perfusion down to an MAP of approximately 50 mm Hg. In low cardiac output forms of shock, myocardial ischemia is prominent and produces a vicious cycle in which ischemia produces further reduction in cardiac output, which further aggravates ischemia. This cycle is believed to be

Table 102–3 • ORGAN SYSTEM DYSFUNCTION IN SHOCK

ORGAN SYSTEM	MANIFESTATIONS
Central nervous system	Encephalopathy (ischemic or septic)
	Cortical necrosis
Heart	Tachycardia, bradycardia
	Supraventricular tachycardia
	Ventricular ectopy
	Myocardial ischemia
	Myocardial depression
Pulmonary	Acute respiratory failure
	Adult respiratory distress syndrome
Kidney	Prerenal failure
	Acute tubular necrosis
Gastrointestinal	Ileus
	Erosive gastritis
	Pancreatitis
	Acalculous cholecystitis
	Colonic submucosal hemorrhage
	Transluminal translocation of bacteria/endotoxin
Liver	Ischemic hepatitis
	"Shock" liver
	Intrahepatic cholestasis
Hematologic	Disseminated intravascular coagulation
	Dilutional thrombocytopenia
Metabolic	Hyperglycemia
	Glycogenolysis
	Gluconeogenesis
	Hypoglycemia (late)
	Hypertriglyceridemia
Immune system	Gut barrier function depression
	Cellular immune depression
	Humoral immune depression

important in producing the high mortality (70 to 90%) rate of cardiogenic shock (Chapter 103).

Shock produces complex effects on myocardial contractility. Although sympathoadrenal stimulation should lead to increases in contractility due to adrenoreceptor stimulation, there is strong evidence for myocardial depression (decreased ejection fraction) and compliance abnormalities, especially in septic and hypovolemic shock. Septic myocardial dysfunction has been linked to cytokine-induced (specifically, TNF and IL-1) depression of myocardial contraction; this cytokine mechanism produces much of its effect via nitric oxide and cyclic guanosine monophosphate. In addition, there is evidence of decreased β-receptor function. Similar depressant mechanisms may also contribute to myocardial dysfunction in hypovolemic and cardiogenic shock.

LUNGS. Acute lung injury causes impaired gas exchange, decreased compliance, and shunting of blood through underventilated areas. The pathologic findings are fibrin-neutrophil aggregates within the pulmonary microvasculature, inflammatory damage to the interstitium and alveoli, and exudation of proteinaceous fluid into the alveolar space; the result is severe hypoxemia with bilateral pulmonary infiltrates, a condition termed *adult respiratory distress syndrome* (Chapter 99). The work of breathing is increased, and respiratory muscle fatigue and ventilatory failure ensue, often requiring mechanical ventilation.

KIDNEY. Acute renal failure (Chapter 116) is a major complication of shock and is associated with a high mortality rate. Hypoperfusion of the renal vasculature occurs frequently in shock, in part as a result of preferential direction of blood flow to the brain and heart. Initially, vasoconstriction may maintain glomerular perfusion, but when this compensatory mechanism fails, acute tubular necrosis and renal insufficiency occur. An important clinical challenge is to differentiate between acute tubular necrosis and hypovolemia, because both present with oliguria.

GASTROINTESTINAL TRACT AND LIVER. Typical clinical manifestations of gut involvement during shock include ileus, erosive gastritis, pancreatitis, acalculous cholecystitis, and submucosal hemorrhage. Some studies suggest that gut barrier integrity may be compromised, leading to translocation of bacteria and their toxins into the blood stream.

The most common manifestation of liver involvement in shock is mild increase in aminotransferases and lactate dehydrogenase

(Chapter 149). With severe hypoperfusion, shock liver may be manifested by massive aminotransferase elevations and extensive hepatocellular damage. With an acute insult that resolves, these transaminase elevations peak in 1 to 3 days and resolve by 10 days. Decreased levels of clotting factors and albumin may occur and reflect decreased synthetic function. In septic shock, significant elevations of bilirubin may be seen with only modest elevations in aminotransferases because of dysfunction of bile canaliculi caused by inflammatory mediators or bacterial toxins.

HEMATOLOGIC. Thrombocytopenia may result from dilution during volume repletion or from immunologic platelet destruction, which is especially common during septic shock. Activation of the coagulation cascade can lead to disseminated intravascular coagulation (Chapter 179), which results in thrombocytopenia, decreased fibrinogen, elevated fibrin split products, and microangiopathic hemolytic anemia.

IMMUNE SYSTEM. Widespread dysfunction of the immune system has been described especially during hypovolemic and traumatic shock. Abnormalities of function in macrophages, T and B lymphocytes, and neutrophils have been described. These abnormalities are not thought to produce immediate effects but may contribute significantly to late mortality, which is frequently due to complicating infection.

METABOLIC. Early in shock, hyperglycemia usually occurs as a result of glycogenolysis and gluconeogenesis mediated by increases in adrenocorticotropic hormone, glucocorticoids, glucagon, and catecholamines as well as decreases in insulin. Hypertriglyceridemia may also occur. Recent clinical trials in critically ill surgical patients have demonstrated a reduced morbidity and mortality associated with insulin administration, which was designed to lower the blood glucose toward a normal range.[2] This study emphasizes the importance of glucose, insulin, and cell metabolism in shock. Later in shock, hypoglycemia may occur due to glycogen depletion or failure of glucose synthesis in the liver. Also, protein catabolism ensues, resulting in negative nitrogen balance; this catabolism may be an important determinant of late mortality in shock, and some studies suggest nutritional supplementation (Chapter 230) is important in shock therapy.

Specific Forms of Shock (Chapter 104)

Inadequate tissue perfusion results from a low cardiac output in hypovolemic, cardiogenic, and extracardiac obstructive forms of shock. In distributive shock, although a low cardiac output may occur infrequently as a result of inadequate preload or myocardial depression, most commonly a low SVR and maldistribution of blood flow lead to low blood pressure and shock despite normal or increased cardiac output.

HYPOVOLEMIC SHOCK

This form of shock is characterized by a decrease in ventricular preload, resulting in decreased ventricular diastolic pressures and volumes, decreased stroke volume and cardiac output, and reduced blood pressure. Patients manifest pale, cool, clammy skin; tachycardia; decreased jugular venous pulse; decreased urine output; and altered mental status. The severity of hypovolemic shock is clearly associated with both the magnitude and the rate of fluid loss. Acute loss of 10% of circulating blood volume results in tachycardia and increased SVR with maintenance of blood pressure. Compensatory mechanisms begin to fail with a 20 to 25% volume loss: mild to moderate hypotension and decreased cardiac output occur, SVR is markedly increased, and lactate production may begin. With loss of 40% of circulating blood volume, severe hypotension develops with signs of shock; cardiac output and tissue perfusion are severely decreased. If this shock state persists for more than 2 hours, sufficient tissue damage occurs so that adequate fluid repletion is no longer effective in reversing shock; that is, the shock is irreversible.

If the volume loss is produced at a slower rate, the compensatory mechanisms are more effective, and similar amounts of volume depletion are better tolerated. Furthermore, a patient's underlying disease, especially a limited cardiac reserve, also influences the response to a hypovolemic insult.

CARDIOGENIC SHOCK

Cardiogenic shock results from failure of the heart as a pump as a result of myocardial, valvular, or structural abnormalities.

Hemodynamically, ventricular filling pressures and volumes are increased; cardiac output, stroke volume, and MAP are reduced. Patients manifest signs of peripheral hypoperfusion coupled with evidence of ventricular failure (Chapters 55 and 103).

EXTRACARDIAC OBSTRUCTIVE SHOCK

This form of shock results from an obstruction to flow in the cardiovascular circuit. Pericardial tamponade and constrictive pericarditis (Chapter 74) impair diastolic filling of the right ventricle. Massive pulmonary emboli (Chapter 94) may result in shock as a result of a severe increase in afterload. The hemodynamic pattern is similar to other low output shock states with decreased cardiac output, stroke volume, and MAP. Other hemodynamic variables depend on the site of the obstruction. With pericardial tamponade, patients usually develop increased and equalized right and left heart ventricular diastolic pressures. Constrictive pericarditis may produce a similar pattern. Acute pulmonary embolism results in right heart failure with elevated pulmonary artery and right heart pressures and low or normal left heart filling pressures.

The tempo of the disease process influences the clinical manifestations. With pericardial tamponade due to myocardial rupture following myocardial infarction (Chapter 69), for example, immediate tamponade and shock can occur within minutes with as little as 150 mL of blood in the pericardium. Survival requires immediate drainage and surgery. In patients with malignant or inflammatory causes of pericardial tamponade, fluid accumulates more slowly, and 1 or 2 L of fluid may be necessary to produce shock.

DISTRIBUTIVE SHOCK

The major feature of distributive shock is decreased peripheral resistance. Although anaphylaxis (Chapter 270), drug overdose, neurogenic insults, and addisonian crisis can produce this form of shock, the most important and prevalent cause is septic shock (Chapter 104). In this form of shock, tissue hypoperfusion results from either microvascular abnormalities (maldistribution or shunting of blood flow) or a mediator-induced metabolic block that prevents cells from adequately using oxygen and other nutrients delivered through the vasculature.

Early in distributive shock, venodilation and leakage of fluid from the microvasculature leads to an inadequate intravascular volume and reduced preload. Volume resuscitation corrects this preload abnormality and produces the usual hemodynamic pattern of distributive shock: a normal or elevated cardiac output, normal stroke volume, tachycardia, decreased SVR, and decreased MAP. Left and right heart filling pressures are variable and depend on the amount of fluid resuscitation.

In addition, most patients with distributive shock also manifest myocardial depression, which is characterized by a decreased stroke work response to volume loading, biventricular reduction in ejection fraction, and ventricular dilatation. The dilatation allows patients to compensate for a depressed ejection fraction and maintain stroke volume, which combined with a high heart rate leads to an elevated cardiac output. In approximately 10 to 15% of septic shock patients, the myocardial dysfunction is dominant and severe, and it results in a hypodynamic low cardiac output form of shock (see Fig. 102–1).

Clinical Approach to Shock

Shock is a life-threatening emergency. Diagnosis, evaluation, and management most often occur simultaneously, and speed in the evaluation is important to a good outcome. The clinical approach must balance two important goals: (1) the need to initiate therapy before shock causes irreversible damage to organs and (2) the need to perform a diagnostic evaluation to determine the cause of shock (Fig. 102–3). A reasonable approach is to make a rapid clinical evaluation initially based on a directed history and physical examination and to initiate diagnostic tests aimed at determining cause. In severe shock, therapy should be initiated based on the initial clinical impression. Certain symptoms and signs are similar to all forms of shock. Most patients have hypotension, tachycardia, cool extremities, oliguria, and a clouded sensorium. In general, an MAP less than 60 mm Hg in an adult is considered hypotension. However, blood pressure must be evaluated in terms of previous chronic blood pressures. A patient with chronic hypertension may experience shock pathophysiology

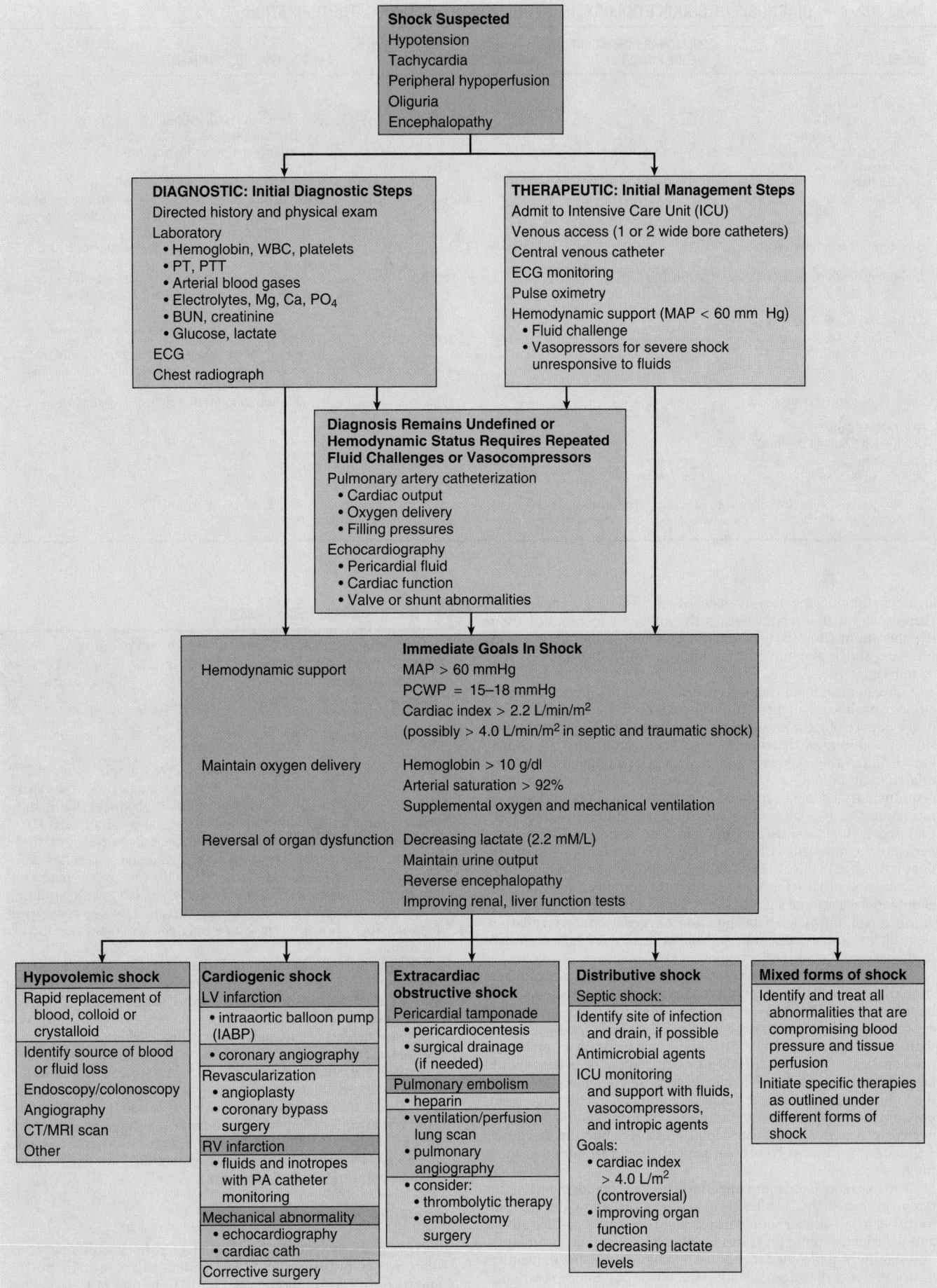

FIGURE 102–3 • An approach to the diagnosis and treatment of shock. MAP = mean arterial pressure; PCWP = pulmonary capillary wedge pressure.

Table 102–4 • DIAGNOSIS OF SHOCK ETIOLOGY USING PULMONARY ARTERY CATHETERIZATION

DIAGNOSIS	PULMONARY CAPILLARY WEDGE PRESSURE	CARDIAC OUTPUT (CO)	MISCELLANEOUS COMMENTS
CARDIOGENIC SHOCK			
Cardiogenic shock due to myocardial dysfunction	↑↑	↓↓	Usually occurs with evidence of extensive myocardial infarction (40% of LV infarcted), severe cardiomyopathy, or myocarditis.
Cardiogenic shock due to a mechanical defect			
Acute ventricular septal defect	↑	LVCO ↓↓ and RVCO > LVCO	Predominant shunt is left to right, pulmonary blood flow is greater than systemic blood flow: oxygen "step-up" occurs at RV level.
Acute mitral regurgitation	↑↑	Forward CO ↓↓	V waves in pulmonary capillary wedge pressure tracing.
Right ventricular infarction	Normal or ↓	↓↓	Elevated RA and RV filling pressures with low or normal pulmonary capillary wedge pressures.
EXTRACARDIAC OBSTRUCTIVE FORMS OF SHOCK			
Pericardial tamponade	↑	↓ or ↓↓	RA mean, RV end-diastolic, pulmonary capillary wedge mean pressures are elevated and within 5 mm Hg of one another.
Massive pulmonary embolism	Normal or ↓	↓↓	Usual finding is elevated right-sided pressures.
HYPOVOLEMIC SHOCK DISTRIBUTIVE FORMS OF SHOCK	↓↓	↓↓	
Septic shock	↓ or normal	↑ or normal, rarely ↓	
Anaphylactic shock	↓ or normal	↑ or normal	

LV = left ventricular; RV = right ventricular; RA = right atrial.
Adapted from JE Parrillo, SM Ayres (eds): Major Issues in Critical Care Medicine. Baltimore, Williams & Wilkins, 1984.

at higher blood pressures. A decrease of 50 mm Hg or more from chronic elevated levels is frequently sufficient to produce tissue hypoperfusion. Conversely, in some patients with chronically low blood pressure, shock may not develop until the MAP drops to less than 50 mm Hg.

Other clinical manifestations may be useful in differentiating the etiology of shock. Patients with hypovolemic shock frequently manifest evidence of gastrointestinal hemorrhage, bleeding from another site, or vomiting or diarrhea. Patients with cardiogenic shock may have manifestations of heart disease with prior angina or myocardial infarction and often have elevated filling pressures, cardiac gallops, or pulmonary edema (Chapter 55). Cardiac murmurs may suggest mechanical causes of cardiogenic shock (Chapters 69 and 103). Elevated jugular venous pressure and a quiet precordium suggest pericardial tamponade (Chapter 74). A site of infection with prominent fever should raise the possibility of septic shock (Chapter 104).

Even though a brief history and physical examination are directed at potential causes and signs of shock, blood should be drawn to evaluate hemoglobin, platelets, coagulation, oxygenation and ventilation, electrolytes, kidney function, and blood lactate levels. An electrocardiogram and chest radiograph should be taken.

Simultaneously, venous access with one or two large-bore catheters should be established, and central venous and arterial catheters should be inserted (see Fig. 102–3). Electrocardiographic monitoring and continuous pulse oximetry are usually valuable. If the MAP is less than 60 mm Hg or evidence of tissue hypoperfusion is present, a fluid challenge with 500 to 1000 mL of crystalloid or colloid should be given intravenously (if hemorrhage is likely, blood should be the volume replacement). If the patient remains hypotensive, vasopressors such as dopamine and/or norepinephrine should be administered to restore an adequate blood pressure while the diagnostic evaluation continues. The shock patient should be admitted to an intensive care unit.

If the diagnosis remains undefined or the hemodynamic status requires repeated fluid challenges or vasopressors, a flow-directed pulmonary artery catheter should be placed to determine cardiac output and ventricular filling pressures (Table 102–4), and echocardiography should be performed. Echocardiography is valuable in identifying the presence of pericardial fluid, tamponade physiology, ventricular function, valvular heart disease, and intracardiac shunts (Chapter 51). Based on these data, patients can usually be classified and managed according to the specific form of shock.

 Management and Therapy

In all forms of shock, restoration of blood pressure and tissue perfusion are critical goals and commonly require fluids, vasopressors, inotropic agents (Table 102–5), mechanical ventilation, and repeated monitoring.

HYPOVOLEMIC SHOCK

The major goal is to infuse adequate volume to restore perfusion before the onset of irreversible tissue damage without raising cardiac filling pressures to a level that produces hydrostatic pulmonary edema, which usually begins at a pulmonary artery occlusion (capillary wedge) pressure greater than 18 mm Hg. In hemorrhagic shock, restoration of oxygen delivery is achieved by transfusion of packed red blood cells with the goal of maintaining hemoglobin concentration greater than 10 g/dL. Restoration of intravascular volume must be accompanied by aggressive evaluation to identify a bleeding source and treatment to prevent further bleeding.

In other forms of hypovolemic shock, crystalloid solutions such as normal saline or Ringer's lactate are conventionally used. Some authors advocate use of colloid solutions, such as albumin or hetastarch, because they may produce faster restoration of intravascular volume, especially in traumatic shock where volume losses can be large. However, no convincing evidence demonstrates clear superiority of colloids over crystalloids in restoring volume depletion. Because colloids are more expensive, most physicians favor crystalloids unless the serum albumin is low and requires repletion. Hypertonic saline, which can provide volume repletion with small volumes of fluid, may be therapeutically useful in burns (Chapter 108) and head trauma (Chapter 431), in which limitation of free water is often important.

CARDIOGENIC SHOCK

In hypotensive patients with cardiogenic shock, pulmonary capillary wedge pressure should be maintained at 14 to 18 mm Hg, and medications should be used to try to restore MAP to greater than 60 mm Hg and the cardiac index (cardiac output divided by body surface area in meters squared) to more than 2.2 L/min/m²

Table 102–5 • RELATIVE POTENCY OF VASOPRESSORS AND INOTROPIC AGENTS IN SHOCK

AGENT	DOSE	CARDIAC		PERIPHERAL VASCULAR*		
		Heart Rate	Contractility	Vasoconstriction	Vasodilatation	Dopaminergic
Dopamine	1–4 μg/kg/min	1+	1+	0	1+	4+
	4–20 μg/kg/min	2+	2–3+	2–3+	0	2+
Norepinephrine	2–20 μg/min	1+	2+	4+	0	0
Dobutamine	2.5–15 μg/kg/min	1–2+	3–4+	0	2+	0
Isoproterenol	1–5 μg/min	4+	4+	0	4+	0
Epinephrine	1–20 μg/min	4+	4+	4+	3+	0
Phenylephrine	20–200 μg/min	0	0	3+	0	0
Amrinone	0.75 mg/kg bolus; then 5–15 μg/kg/min	1+	3+	0	2+	0
Milrinone	37.5–75 μg/kg bolus; then 0.375–0.75 μg/kg/min	1+	3+	0	2+	0
Vasopressin	0.1 U/min	0	0	4+	0	0

*The 1 to 4+ scoring system is an arbitrary system to allow a judgment of comparative potency among these vasopressor agents.
Adapted from JE Parrillo, SM Ayres (eds): Major Issues in Critical Care Medicine. Baltimore, Williams & Wilkins, 1984.

(Chapters 56 and 103). Appropriate patients benefit from an intra-aortic balloon pump or from surgical correction of valvular abnormalities or septal defects. In patients with acute myocardial infarction and cardiogenic shock due to myocardial damage, emergent coronary revascularization has been shown to be superior to medical therapy.[3]

EXTRACARDIAC OBSTRUCTIVE SHOCK

In pericardial tamponade, blood pressure can be maintained using fluids and vasopressors in a fashion similar to the method employed in cardiogenic shock. However, these are only temporizing measures, and one should move quickly to drain pericardial fluid using needle pericardiocentesis or surgery (Chapter 74).

In severe pulmonary embolism (Chapter 94) producing right ventricular failure and shock, thrombolytic therapy should be considered in addition to conventional anticoagulation with heparin and warfarin. If thrombolysis is contraindicated, emergency surgical pulmonary embolectomy can sometimes produce a successful outcome.

DISTRIBUTIVE SHOCK

For septic shock (Chapter 104), principles of management include eliminating the nidus of infection with surgical drainage and antimicrobial therapy, early restoration of blood pressure using fluids and vasopressor agents, and maintaining adequate tissue perfusion using fluids, inotropic agents, and other supportive measures. Recent trials demonstrate that early, aggressive therapy with fluids, blood transfusions, and inotropic agents results in a significantly lower mortality in severe sepsis and septic shock.[4] Arginine vasopressin appears to be useful in catecholamine-resistant vasodilatory shock.[5]

1. Bernard GR, Vincent JL, Laterre PF, et al: Efficacy and safety of recombinant human activated protein C for severe sepsis. N Engl J Med 2001;344:699–709.
2. Van den Berghe G, Wouters P, Weekers F, et al: Intensive insulin therapy in critically ill patients. N Engl J Med 2001;345:1359–1367.
3. Hochman JS, Sleeper LA, Webb JG, et al: Early revascularization in acute myocardial infarction complicated by cardiogenic shock. SHOCK Investigators. Should we emergently revascularize occluded coronaries for cardiogenic shock? N Engl J Med 1999;341:625–634.
4. Rivers E, Nguyen B, Havstad S, et al: Early goal-directed therapy in the treatment of severe sepsis and septic shock. N Engl J Med 2001;345:1368–1377.
5. Dünser MW, Mayr AJ, Ulmer H, et al: Arginine vasopressin in advanced vasodilatory shock: A prospective, randomized controlled study. Circulation 2003;107:2313–2319.

SUGGESTED READINGS

Kumar A, Parrillo JE: Shock: Classification, pathophysiology, and approach to management. In Parrillo JE, Dellinger RP (eds): Critical Care Medicine: Principles, Diagnosis and Management in the Adult, 2nd ed. St. Louis, Mosby, 2001, pp 371–400. *Provides a detailed review of pathogenesis and management of different forms of shock.*
Proctor RA: New drugs for the treatment of septic shock. Crit Care Med 2001;29:1650–1651. *A brief summary of the new medications recently developed for severe sepsis.*

103 CARDIOGENIC SHOCK

David R. Holmes

Definition

Cardiogenic shock describes tissue hypoperfusion as a result of an acute myocardial infarction (MI) or end-stage heart failure from any cause. Cardiogenic shock can be defined by clinical parameters alone (Chapter 102), including the manifestations of a low cardiac output state with peripheral hypoperfusion and cool, clammy extremities, cyanosis, oliguria, and altered central nervous system function. An obligate requirement is the presence of hypotension. The degree of hypotension required to fulfill the criteria of shock has varied but is usually a systolic blood pressure less than 90 mm Hg; an alternative definition is a systolic blood pressure more than 30 mm Hg *below* the patient's basal level. Although clinical manifestations of hypoperfusion and a systolic blood pressure less than 90 mm Hg are the hallmarks of shock, other important hemodynamic manifestations include elevated left ventricular (LV) filling pressures greater than 15 mm Hg and a reduction in cardiac index to less than approximately 2.2 L/minute/m². Also, many patients with end-stage heart failure, especially if treated with afterload-reducing agents (Chapter 56), may have blood pressures chronically less than 90 mm Hg but not be in shock.

Etiology

ACUTE CARDIOGENIC SHOCK. In the acute setting, cardiogenic causes of shock must be distinguished from septic shock and other causes of shock (Fig. 102–3). Even in cardiac patients, shock can be due to noncardiogenic causes, including hypotension caused by medications, such as nitrates, angiotensin-converting enzyme inhibitors, other vasodilators, or streptokinase; hemorrhage from anticoagulant or thrombolytic drugs; pulmonary embolism (Chapter 94); or hypovolemia. The causes of cardiogenic shock are diverse (Table 103–1). The classic etiology is pump failure secondary to extensive LV damage, but right ventricular infarction also may lead to cardiogenic shock if associated posterior LV infarction is present (Chapter 69). The differential diagnosis of *acute* cardiogenic shock also includes the mechanical causes of mitral regurgitation from papillary muscle rupture or dysfunction, rupture of the LV free wall, and ventricular septal defect (VSD). In a large registry, acute shock was due to predominant LV failure in 74.5% of patients but was related to acute severe mitral regurgitation in 8.3%, ventricular septal rupture in 4.6%, and isolated right ventricular shock in 3.4%. Cardiogenic shock also may result from other cardiac conditions, such as aortic stenosis (Chapter 72) or pericardial tamponade (Chapter 74), the latter of which may be the result of an ascending aortic dissection (Chapter 75) that propagates in a retrograde fashion, shearing off the right coronary artery, then creating a rupture into the pericardium. Cardiac arrhythmias, such as atrial fibrillation with a rapid ventricular response (Chapter

Table 103–1 • CARDIOGENIC SHOCK

Acute
  Acute myocardial infarction
    Pump failure
    Mechanical complication
      Ventricular septal defect
      Mitral regurgitation
      Ventricular rupture
  Tachyarrhythmia
  Valvular heart disease
    Acute mitral regurgitation
    Acute aortic regurgitation
    Aortic or mitral stenosis and acute comorbid condition, e.g.,
      infection, anemia, tachyarrhythmia
    Prosthetic valve dysfunction
  Traumatic cardiac injury—penetrating or blunt
  Myocarditis
  Orthotopic transplant rejection
  Peripartum cardiomyopathy
  Pericardial disease with effusion
End-stage low-output heart failure

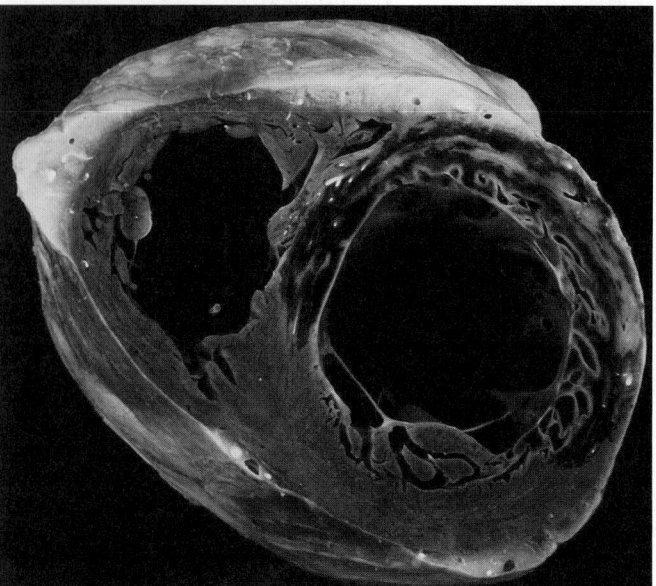

FIGURE 103–1 • Postmortem autopsy specimen from a patient who died of cardiogenic shock from acute myocardial infarction. Extensive necrosis is evident. (Courtesy William D. Edwards.)

59) or ventricular tachycardia (Chapter 60), may contribute to hypotension. Myocarditis (Chapter 73) also may result in shock.

The clinical circumstances and time course of shock often provide important clues to specific causes. Given the diverse number of disease states that may cause shock (Chapter 102), identifying the specific etiology is important because it may mandate a different treatment strategy and may affect prognosis.

REFRACTORY CHRONIC HEART FAILURE. Patients with end-stage refractory heart failure (Chapters 55 and 69) also may present with severe hypoperfusion. In general, shock develops more slowly than in patients with acute MI. In patients with chronic heart failure, the blood pressure may be less than 90 mm Hg in the absence of shock, especially when patients are receiving aggressive afterload reduction therapy; in these individuals, fluid overload may precipitate cardiogenic shock.

Incidence and Epidemiology

ACUTE CARDIOGENIC SHOCK. The incidence of cardiogenic shock after an acute MI has varied from 5 to 19%. The incidence may be underestimated because some reports may exclude patients with shock on admission or may not represent the full spectrum of the patient population with both ST segment elevation and non–ST segment elevation MIs. Compared with patients with ST segment elevation, patients with ST segment depression have approximately half the incidence of cardiogenic shock. The incidence of cardiogenic shock also has varied over time; earlier recognition of the symptoms of MI, earlier presentation for medical care, and the administration of thrombolytic therapy may have reduced the incidence. Typically, only a few patients with shock (approximately 10 to 15%) have it on admission. Shock develops in most patients within the next 48 hours. In a multicenter, country-wide survey from Denmark, 59% of patients developed shock within 48 hours, but 30% developed shock more than 4 days after the MI. When cardiogenic shock develops in patients without ST segment elevation, it usually develops relatively later, commonly secondary to reinfarction. As might be expected, prior MI; older age; diabetes mellitus; female gender; and a history of angina pectoris, stroke, or peripheral vascular disease have been associated with increased incidence of cardiogenic shock, but the predictive power of these factors in an individual patient is limited. Patients with pre-existing LV dysfunction also are at higher risk. Patients with severe myocarditis, especially postpartum cardiomyopathy, occasionally may develop cardiogenic shock.

REFRACTORY CHRONIC HEART FAILURE. Many of the chronic causes of refractory heart failure result in sudden death as often as or more often than they cause hospitalization or home treatment for refractory low-output heart failure. Essentially every cause of heart failure (Chapter 55) can result in a refractory low-output state, however, with congestion and systemic hypoperfusion.

Pathogenesis

ACUTE CARDIOGENIC SHOCK. Acute cardiogenic shock is typically the result of an extensive MI associated with damage to 40% or more of

Table 103–2 • RISK FACTORS FOR CARDIOGENIC SHOCK COMPLICATING ACUTE MYOCARDIAL INFARCTION

FACTORS ASSOCIATED WITH DEVELOPMENT OF SHOCK	FACTORS ASSOCIATED WITH INCREASED MORTALITY FROM SHOCK
Older age	Older age
Diabetes mellitus	Prior infarction
History of prior MI, stroke, or peripheral vascular disease	Altered sensorium
Female gender	Peripheral vasoconstriction
Reinfarction	Baseline systolic blood pressure
Initial EF <35%	Lower cardiac output
Lack of compensatory hyperkinesis in remote segments	Higher heart rate

EF = ejection fraction; MI = myocardial infarction.

the LV myocardium (Fig. 103–1). It does not seem to matter whether this loss of LV myocardium is the result of a single ischemic insult, with occlusion of a single artery that supplies a large region of myocardium, or a series of multiple prior MIs. The sequence of ischemic insults (i.e., a single catastrophic event or a series of multiple prior infarctions) may affect the time course of the shock, however. A single catastrophic event may result either in early shock or in sudden death, compared with patients with multiple smaller prior infarctions, who may present with shock after hospital admission. Multiple clinical factors have been associated with the development or outcome of shock (Tables 103–2 and 103–3). Autopsy and angiographic studies have documented that multivessel disease is almost universally present, particularly involving the left main and the left anterior descending coronary artery.

Infarct extension or reinfarction is common in patients with shock and is often the mechanism responsible for shock. Among the multiple factors that may be involved in infarct extension or expansion are impaired collateral flow, increased myocardial oxygen consumption, thrombus propagation or embolization, and passive collapse or vasoconstriction at a second site within the coronary circulation owing to low coronary perfusion pressure during diastole. In patients with hypertensive cardiovascular disease and LV hypertrophy or aortic stenosis, the hypotension and elevated LV end-diastolic pressure may cause or aggravate diffuse subendocardial ischemia. Other important factors that can aggravate shock include anemia and poor oxygenation.

The mechanical complications of mitral regurgitation, VSD, or rupture of the LV myocardium account for 15 to 25% of cases of

Table 103–3 • PREDICTING 30-DAY MORTALITY RATES FROM CARDIOGENIC SHOCK COMPLICATING ACUTE MYOCARDIAL INFARCTION

1. FIND POINTS FOR EACH PREDICTIVE FACTOR

AGE		MEAN ARTERIAL PRESSURE DURING SHOCK		HEART RATE DURING SHOCK		LOWEST CARDIAC OUTPUT		HIGHEST PULMONARY CAPILLARY WEDGE PRESSURE	
Yr	Points	mm Hg	Points	bpm	Points	L/min	Points	mm Hg	Points
20	0	20	20	20	5	2	42	10	31
30	11	40	38	40	11	4	13	20	0
40	22	60	35	60	16	6	0	30	24
50	33	80	17	80	22	8	7	40	26
60	44	100	19	100	27	10	13	50	25
70	56	120	25	120	33	12	20	60	24
80	67	140	32	140	38	14	27		
90	78	160	38	160	43	16	33		
100	89	180	44	180	49	18	40		

MISCELLANEOUS RISK FACTORS

Factor	Points	Factor	Points
Killip class		Prior infarction	15
I	7	Altered sensorium	15
II	26	Cold, clammy skin	15
III	25	Oliguria	23
IV		Ventricular septal defect	38

2. SUM POINTS FOR ALL PREDICTIVE FACTORS

3. LOOK UP RISK CORRESPONDING TO TOTAL POINTS

POINTS	PROBABILITY OF 30-DAY MORTALITY (%)
138	10
160	20
175	30
188	40
199	50
210	60
223	70
238	80
260	90

From Hasdai D, Holmes DR Jr, Califf RM, et al, for the GUSTO investigators: Cardiogenic shock complicating acute myocardial infarction: Predictors of mortality. Am Heart J 1999;138:21–31.

acute cardiogenic shock. The underlying MI may be only small or moderate in size but may involve crucial structures, such as the interventricular septum or papillary muscle. Free wall rupture accounts for 10% of all deaths from MI and typically is associated with an ST segment elevation anterior MI. In this setting, shock may develop abruptly and be followed by circulatory collapse with electromechanical dissociation. Rupture of the interventricular septum may result in a single direct perforation or many complex serpentine tracts; this defect also is seen with ST segment elevation anterior MI. Partial or complete rupture of one of the papillary muscles may result in severe mitral regurgitation; the posteromedial papillary muscle is involved more frequently than the anterolateral papillary muscle because the former usually receives its blood supply from just one source, the posterior descending coronary artery. Cardiogenic shock is a distinct and well-recognized complication of a right ventricular MI, which is always associated with posterobasal infarction of the left ventricle. With occlusion of the proximal right coronary artery, right ventricular pump function decreases, and the right ventricle dilates, leading to a decrease in LV preload and subsequent hypotension.

REFRACTORY CHRONIC HEART FAILURE. End-stage refractory heart failure can be the final stage of any of the diseases that cause chronic heart failure (Chapter 68). In these patients, key issues include evaluation of the underlying disease process, the development of new comorbid conditions, compliance with medication, and the adequacy of long-term therapy (Table 103–4).

Table 103–4 • HEART FAILURE DECOMPENSATION

Development of new comorbidities
  Infection/sepsis
  Renal insufficiency
  Uncontrolled diabetes
  Anemia
  Pulmonary embolus
  Hypothyroidism/hyperthyroidism
  Cardiac rhythm disorders—atrial fibrillation, bradycardia
Progression of underlying disease
  Myocardial ischemia
  Chronic renal insufficiency
  Uncontrolled hypertension
Patient compliance
  Poor compliance with drug therapy regimen
  Dietary indiscretion
  Alcohol
Drug therapy
  Inadequate doses of beneficial drugs
  Failure to prescribe beneficial drugs
  Over-diuresis or under-diuresis
  Sudden alteration in drug therapy
  Drug interactions
  Cardiotoxic medications

Clinical Manifestations and Assessment

Cardiogenic shock is manifest as tissue hypoperfusion. Hypotension usually is defined as systolic blood pressure less than 90 mm Hg or a decrease in systolic blood pressure from baseline by more than 30 mm Hg, although the latter criterion includes a larger group of patients who may not have shock or who have a milder form of shock. The term *preshock* has been used to define some of these patients. The prognosis of these patients with preshock may be substantially better than patients with full-blown shock. Hypoperfusion is recognized by altered sensorium, cyanosis, oliguria, and cool, clammy extremities. Attendant dyspnea and ongoing ischemic chest pain may be present.

This constellation of findings may be noted at the initial presentation with acute MI, but it more frequently develops later, 48 hours after the onset of MI. Either bradycardia, usually a manifestation of the Bezold-Jarisch reflex, or tachycardia may be present. Acute myocarditis with shock also presents with hypoperfusion; marked fluid retention may be prominent if the myocarditis has been present for several days to weeks. When accompanied by low blood pressure and systemic hypoperfusion, the clinical manifestations of refractory heart failure may be indistinguishable from acute cardiogenic shock.

PHYSICAL EXAMINATION. The physical examination should be focused on identification of hypoperfusion, volume status, and secondary causes of shock. Typically the venous pressure is elevated. The finding of a low venous pressure identifies a group of patients who usually have hypovolemia rather than cardiogenic shock as a predominant cause; correction by fluid administration may lead to improved outcome (Chapter 69). Concomitant pulmonary edema (Chapter 56) may be present, which in the hypotensive patient establishes the diagnosis of cardiogenic shock. In patients with a mechanical complication resulting in shock, the physical findings may not be typical of the underlying cause. Patients with acute mitral regurgitation may not have a systolic murmur because of equalization of the pressures between the left ventricle and left atrium (Chapter 72); in these patients, a high index of suspicion is required so that appropriate tests (e.g., LV angiography or echocardiography) can be performed to make the definitive diagnosis. In patients with a VSD, the systolic murmur may be at the lower left sternal border without a thrill. Patients with a free wall rupture commonly present with electromechanical dissociation, which is almost uniformly fatal. In patients with myocarditis, a pericardial rub or a pleuropericardial rub may be present.

ELECTROCARDIOGRAM. In patients with circulatory collapse, an initial electrocardiogram (ECG) is essential. In acute cardiogenic shock caused by acute MI, ST segment elevation is the most common finding, although cardiogenic shock can occur without it. ST segment depression or nonspecific ST segment changes may occur in approximately 25% of patients. The ECG also provides information on prior MI and rhythm disorders. Isolated elevation in aVR in a patient with acute MI and shock suggests the possibility of left main coronary artery involvement. In patients in whom a right ventricular MI is suspected, modified right precordial leads are helpful (Chapter 50). In acute myocarditis, ECG abnormalities are usually diffuse. Tachyarrhythmias, especially sinus tachycardia or atrial fibrillation, are common; in some patients, new intraventricular conduction defects may be seen. When cardiogenic shock complicates end-stage heart failure, the ECG may reflect extensive prior MI, interventricular conduction defects, or bundle-branch blocks.

ECHOCARDIOGRAPHY. Echocardiography is extremely useful in the evaluation of the patient with shock (Fig. 103–2). It can make the diagnosis of a mechanical complication, such as a ruptured papillary muscle or a VSD (Chapter 51). In addition, echocardiography can assess overall LV function, including compensatory hyperkinesis of noninfarcted segments. Patients with cardiogenic shock from a large MI can be expected to have severe regional wall motion abnormalities. Severe diffuse hypokinesis may suggest cardiomyopathy as the cause of shock, whereas a flail mitral leaflet would suggest acute mitral regurgitation (Chapter 72). In patients in whom rupture is suspected, echocardiography can document a pericardial effusion (Chapter 74). Although echocardiography is a vital tool, it must be performed expeditiously, particularly in the setting of an acute ischemic event. Other procedures, most importantly urgent cardiac catheterization in patients with acute MI (Chapter 54), should not be delayed excessively while echocardiography is being considered or performed. LV angiography can yield extremely important data on ventricular and valvular function.

PULMONARY ARTERY CATHETERIZATION. Despite concerns about the hazards of pulmonary artery catheterization, right-sided heart catheterization with flow-directed catheters can aid in diagnosis (e.g., by documenting low LV filling pressures in hypovolemic shock or right ventricular infarction, giant v waves in patients with unsuspected severe mitral regurgitation, or an oxygen saturation gradient in a patient with a VSD). Monitoring of left-sided heart pressures with periodic wedge recordings can help optimize filling pressures during the initial attempts at stabilization. Hemodynamic monitoring is also extremely useful for guiding aggressive afterload reduction. Nevertheless, the duration of pulmonary artery catheterization should be minimal; in some patients, the relationship between central venous pressure and pulmonary capillary wedge pressure may be sufficiently consistent to allow the physician to follow only the central venous pressure. Urine output also should be monitored.

Although findings such as altered sensorium and peripheral vasoconstriction are important predictors of prognosis, cardiac output and wedge pressure measurements add important independent information regarding prognosis and increase the ability to identify patients at greatest risk of dying with cardiogenic shock. Using clinical, laboratory, and the initial right-sided heart catheterization data, mortality for cardiogenic shock from acute MI can be predicted (see Table 103–3).

Rx Treatment

MEDICAL TREATMENT

The prognosis of patients with cardiogenic shock is poor. Supportive measures, such as maintenance of adequate oxygenation and treatment of arrhythmias, are essential, and documentation of volume status is important. Attempts to improve blood pressure are crucial to break the vicious cycle of progressive hypotension, which leads to further myocardial ischemia. If LV filling pressures are elevated as assessed by either hemodynamic monitoring or the presence of pulmonary edema, further volume expansion is not beneficial and may be harmful. If volume status is uncertain, a trial of volume expansion is warranted with careful monitoring. Right ventricular pressure measurement improves the assessment of filling pressures, especially when the clinical assessment is uncertain. In patients with acute MI, aspirin and heparin are important and serve as baseline treatments.

Vasopressor therapy (see Table 102–5) is usually essential to improve cardiac performance and stabilize the patient; its risks include aggravation of arrhythmias and, even more importantly, an increase in myocardial oxygen demand. Dopamine, which is usually the initial drug given, can increase systemic pressure and cardiac output. Dobutamine may be used in combination with dopamine to augment cardiac output, but it does not usually increase arterial pressure further. Levosimendan, a calcium sensitizer, may be better than dobutamine in low output heart failure.■ In patients who have severe hypotension or resistant hypotension, norepinephrine is usually used and may be effective. In general, myocardial oxygen demand can be minimized by titrating vasopressive agents to the lowest dose required to optimize blood pressure and maintain adequate cardiac output. Vasodilators, such as intravenous nitroglycerin or nitroprusside, are usually not used initially because they can aggravate hypotension; however, they may be used later in combination with vasopressors and inotropic agents. The effectiveness of all inotropic agents may diminish over time, so these drugs usually are not definitive therapies. Milrinone, a second-generation phosphodiesterase inhibitor, should not be used because of its substantial vasodilatory properties.

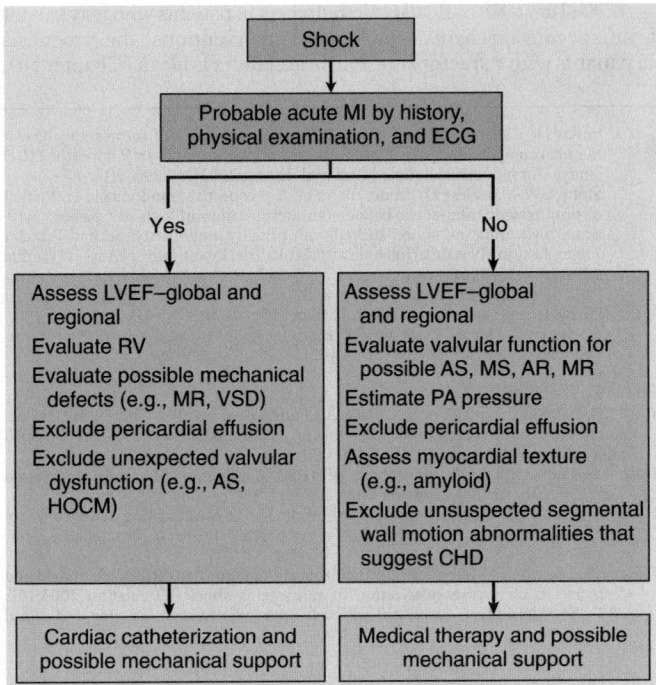

FIGURE 103–2 • Role of echocardiography for assessing the cause of cardiogenic shock. AR = aortic regurgitation; AS = aortic stenosis; CHD = coronary heart disease; ECG = electrocardiogram; HOCM = hypertrophic obstructive cardiomyopathy; LVEF = left ventricular ejection fraction; MI = myocardial infarction; MR = mitral regurgitation; MS = mitral stenosis; PA = pulmonary artery; RV = right ventricle; VSD = ventricular septal defect.

Thrombolytic drugs have been used widely for acute MI, but most trials have not included patients with preexisting cardiogenic shock. The benefit of thrombolysis has been equivocal, with some trials showing no benefit and others showing a small benefit. This equivocal benefit may be related to multiple factors, including (1) poor delivery or penetrance of lytic agents to the thrombus because of the hypotension and (2) impaired transformation of plasminogen to plasmin because of acidosis. To negate the effect of these factors as much as possible, thrombolytic therapy in patients with shock or preshock should be accompanied by vigorous attempts to augment blood pressure and treat acidosis. Thrombolysis may reduce the subsequent development of shock, perhaps owing to a decrease in reinfarction or to a limitation of the size of the initial infarct.

Other pharmacologic approaches aimed at altering myocardial metabolism include L-carnitine, adenosine, glucose-insulin-potassium infusions, and the nitrous oxide synthetase inhibitor L-NMMA. Despite favorable results in small series, none of these agents currently is recommended for clinical use.

MECHANICAL SUPPORT

Insertion of an intra-aortic balloon pump (IABP) for counterpulsation increases diastolic coronary artery perfusion pressure, decreases LV afterload, improves cardiac output, and decreases myocardial oxygen demand. An IABP can stabilize hemodynamics and improve survival at 30 days and 1 year[2] in acute cardiogenic shock complicating acute MI. A variety of percutaneous partial cardiopulmonary bypass techniques can be used in the acute or chronic setting, but these devices are used only in specialized centers because of the need for special equipment. Partial LV-assist devices decrease myocardial oxygen demand while maintaining or augmenting perfusion and may provide an important adjunct to myocardial salvage. In one randomized trial of patients with end-stage heart failure, an implantable LV-assist device improved survival and quality of life.[3] Clinical trials also are under way to test whether devices that lower the body temperature to approximately 33° C can improve outcome.

REVASCULARIZATION

Urgent percutaneous intervention (PCI) (Chapter 70) has been advocated for cardiogenic shock in the setting of an acute MI based on nonrandomized data and subset analyses of large randomized trials. In the one randomized trial that focused exclusively on cardiogenic shock in acute MI, a strategy of early coronary revascularization within 6 hours was compared with a strategy of medical stabilization and IABP followed by delayed coronary revascularization. The primary end point, 30-day mortality, was not significantly different in the two groups (46.7% in the early revascularization group compared with 56.0% in the initial medical stabilization group). At 6 months, however, the mortality in the revascularization group was significantly lower (50.3 versus 63.1%, P = .027), and the benefit was greatest in patients who were younger than age 75 years.[4]

In the clinical trials and in clinical practice, PCI generally is combined with other adjunctive therapies, such as IABP, which typically is placed before treatment. Historically, only the infarct-related artery was treated at the initial PCI, unless the patient had multivessel disease with other critical lesions and PCI of the infarct-related artery did not improve the clinical situation. With the advent of coronary stents (Chapter 61), it may be possible to treat all significant stenoses and provide more complete revascularization. Adjunctive therapy with glycoprotein IIb/IIIa inhibitors may be helpful, although these drugs may complicate the situation by increasing the potential for bleeding in patients in whom surgery subsequently is required.

Coronary stents provide improved angiographic success for PCI, and this higher angiographic success rate has been associated with improved 30-day survival. The additional benefit, if any, of newer adjunctive pharmacologic agents and new devices that prevent distal embolization is unknown, but they are being tested currently.

Coronary artery bypass graft (CABG) surgery (Chapter 71) has potential advantages, including the ability to achieve complete revascularization and the opportunity to vent the ventricle and cool the heart with cardioplegia to limit ongoing ischemia and reduce myocardial oxygen consumption. There currently are no randomized studies, however, to compare CABG surgery with PCI or medical therapy.

OTHER SURGICAL PROCEDURES

In patients with mechanical complications, surgery often provides the only therapeutic approach. If possible, these patients should be stabilized before surgery, often with an IABP. In patients with a VSD or severe mitral regurgitation, surgery can improve outcome dramatically despite high operative mortality rates. Free wall rupture commonly presents with electromechanical dissociation and is almost always fatal. Subacute rupture with false aneurysm formation is rare, but it can be treated surgically with suture or patch closure when it is diagnosed in time. In patients with shock from mechanical causes not related to acute MI, such as ruptured chordae or severe acute aortic regurgitation, surgical approaches are required. In some patients (e.g., patients with ruptured chordae), placement of an IABP may improve cardiac performance substantially and reduce the risk of surgery.

RECOMMENDED CURRENT APPROACH

ACUTE MYOCARDIAL INFARCTION. At present, an aggressive approach seems to have the most potential to improve outcome (Fig. 103–3). Management requires rapid evaluation of the multiple potential causes of shock in parallel with supportive therapy designed to improve perfusion and optimize right ventricular and LV pressures. An IABP and right-sided heart catheterization are helpful for stabilization management and diagnosis. Catheterization can detect an increase in oxygen saturation in the right ventricle as found in a post-MI VSD (Chapters 65 and 69). Revascularization with either emergent PTCA or CABG surgery seems to confer early and longer term survival benefits in eligible patients, although the problem of selection bias and its effect on outcome must be kept in mind.

ACUTE MYOCARDIAL DISEASE. General supportive measures (Chapter 56) are the cornerstone of therapy for severe heart failure. If the

Continued

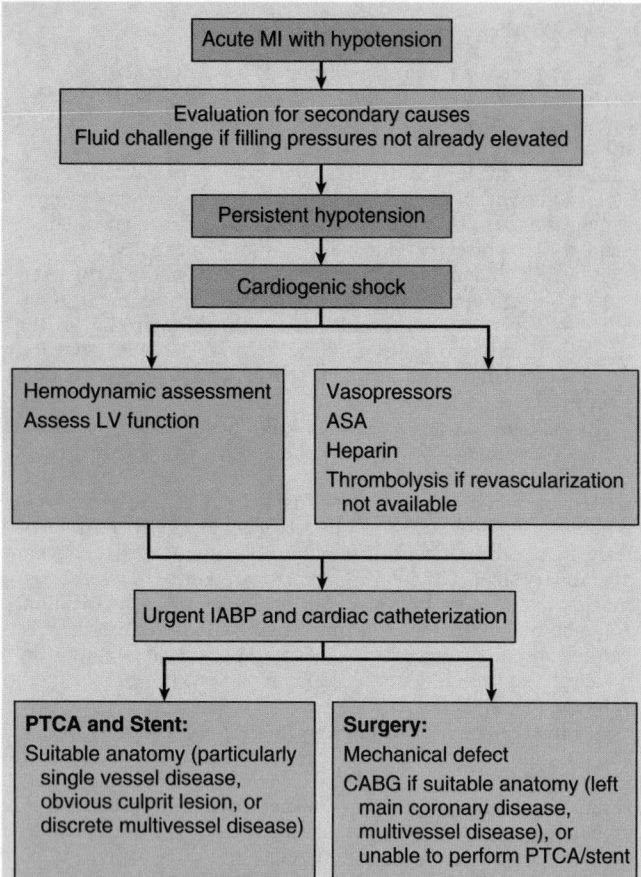

FIGURE 103–3 • Acute myocardial infarction with hypotension: An aggressive approach. ASA = acetylsalicylic acid (aspirin); CABG = coronary artery bypass graft; IABP = intra-aortic balloon pump; LV = left ventricular; PTCA = percutaneous transluminal coronary angioplasty.

patient is in shock despite supportive measures, circulatory support either with an IABP or with LV- or biventricular-assist devices should be considered. Some patients may have spontaneous recovery of ventricular function; alternatively, circulatory support may be used as a bridge to heart transplant (Chapter 80). Specific therapies, such as steroids and cyclosporine or azathioprine, may be helpful in specific patient groups (e.g., patients with idiopathic giant cell myocarditis or sarcoidosis), but not in patients with nonspecific myocarditis (Chapter 73).

REFRACTORY CHRONIC HEART FAILURE. In patients with refractory chronic heart failure, medical therapy is generally similar to therapy for acute cardiogenic shock. Mechanical and surgical interventions, including cardiac transplantation (Chapter 80), can benefit selected patients (Chapter 56).

Prognosis

ACUTE CARDIOGENIC SHOCK. Cardiogenic shock now accounts for most deaths related to acute MI. Before the era of reperfusion, mortality from cardiogenic shock approximated 80%. In the larger thrombolytic trials, mortality rates remain at 51 to 70%. In selected series of shock patients, an aggressive strategy with placement of an IABP followed by revascularization, either with PCI or with CABG surgery, may reduce 30-day mortality to 30 to 40%. The outlook in patients who survive for 1 month is good; among 1-month survivors, 85 to 90% are alive at 1 year. This survival rate is affected by coronary revascularization favorably, compared with the rate in patients who did not undergo revascularization.

The prognosis in myocarditis with shock is variable and depends on the underlying cause (Chapter 73). Some patients can be supported by a mechanical circulatory device until spontaneous recovery occurs or heart transplantation is available.

REFRACTORY CHRONIC HEART FAILURE. Except in patients who may benefit from specific mechanical or surgical interventions, the prognosis of patients with refractory chronic heart failure is bleak (Chapter 56).

1. Follath F, Cleland JGF, Just H, et al: Efficacy and safety of intravenous levosimendan compared with dobutamine in severe low-output heart failure (the LIDO study): A randomised double-blind trial. Lancet 2002;360:196–202.
2. Stone GW, Marsalese D, Brodie BR, et al: A prospective, randomized evaluation of prophylactic intra-aortic balloon counterpulsation in high-risk patients with acute myocardial infarction treated with primary angioplasty: Second Primary Angioplasty in Myocardial Infarction (PAMI-II) Trial Investigators. J Am Coll Cardiol 1997;29:1459–1467.
3. Rose EA, Gelijns AC, Moskowitz AJ, et al: Long-term use of a left ventricular assist device for end-stage heart failure. N Engl J Med 2001;345:1435–1443.
4. Hochman JS, Sleeper LA, White HD, et al: One-year survival following early revascularization for cardiogenic shock. JAMA 2001;285:190–192.

SUGGESTED READINGS

Cotter G, Kaluski E, Blatt A, et al: L-NMMA (a nitric oxide synthase inhibitor) is effective in the treatment of cardiogenic shock. Circulation 2000;101:1358–1136. *A small pilot study showing substantial benefits.*
Hasdai D, Berger PB, Battler A, Holmes DR (eds): Cardiogenic Shock: Diagnosis and Treatment. Totowa, NJ, Humana Press, 2002. *A detailed, current text.*
Hasdai D, Topol EJ, Califf RM, et al: Cardiogenic shock complicating acute coronary syndromes. Lancet 2000;356:749–756. *A systematic approach to the treatment of this syndrome.*
Picard MH, Davidoff R, Sleeper LA, et al: Echocardiographic predictors of survival and response to early revascularization in cardiogenic shock. Circulation 2003;107: 279–284. *Mortality is associated with left ventricular systolic function and mitral regurgitation.*

104 SHOCK SYNDROMES RELATED TO SEPSIS

Joseph E. Parrillo

Sepsis refers to the systemic response to serious infection. Patients with sepsis usually manifest fever, tachycardia, tachypnea, leukocytosis, and a localized site of infection. Microbiologic cultures from blood or the infection site are frequently, although not invariably, positive. When this syndrome results in hypotension or multiple organ system failure, the condition is called *septic shock*.

Incidence and Epidemiology

The incidence of sepsis and septic shock has been increasing since the 1930s, and all recent evidence suggests that this increase will continue. The reasons for this increasing incidence include (1) increased use of invasive devices such as intravascular catheters, (2) widespread use of cytotoxic and immunosuppressive drug therapies for cancer and transplantation, (3) increased lifespan of patients with cancer and diabetes who are prone to sepsis development, and (4) increase in infections due to antibiotic-resistant organisms. Septic shock is the most common cause of death in noncardiac intensive care units (ICUs). Recent population data suggest that 750,000 cases of sepsis or septic shock occur in the United States annually, and this syndrome is responsible for as many deaths as acute myocardial infarction (215,000 or 9.3% of all deaths). Because elderly patients are more likely to develop sepsis and septic shock, the numbers are projected to increase substantially in the next several decades. The present annual inpatient cost of the disease is estimated at $17 billion annually.

Etiology

Gram-negative and gram-positive organisms as well as fungi can cause sepsis and septic shock. Certain viruses and rickettsiae can produce a similar syndrome. Compared with gram-positive organisms, gram-negative bacteria are somewhat more likely to produce septic shock. Culture-positive gram-negative bacteremia produces shock in approximately 50% of infections, whereas gram-positive bacteremia produces shock in about 25% of infections.

Any site of infection can result in sepsis or septic shock. Frequent causes of sepsis are pyelonephritis (Chapter 344), pneumonia (Chapter 92), peritonitis (Chapter 146), cholangitis (Chapter 158), cellulitis, meningitis (Chapter 312), or abscess formation at any site. Many of these infections are nosocomial and occur in patients hospitalized for other medical problems. In patients with normal host defenses, a site of infection is usually identified. In neutropenic patients with sepsis, however, a clinical site of infection is found in less than 50%, probably because small, clinically inapparent infections in skin or bowel can lead to blood stream invasion in patients with inadequate circulating neutrophils (Chapter 298).

Definitions

Considerable effort has been directed toward identifying septic patients early in their clinical course, when therapies are most likely to be effective. Definitions have incorporated manifestations of the systemic response to infection (fever, tachycardia, tachypnea, and leukocytosis) as well as evidence of organ system dysfunction (cardiovascular, respiratory, renal, hepatic, central nervous system, hematologic, or metabolic abnormalities). The most recent definitions (Table 104–1) use the term *systemic inflammatory response syndrome* to emphasize that sepsis is one example of the body's inflammatory responses that can be triggered not only by infections but also by noninfectious disorders, such as trauma and pancreatitis.

Sepsis is severe and has a poorer prognosis when it is associated with organ dysfunction, hypoperfusion (lactic acidosis, oliguria, or altered mental status), or hypotension (septic shock). Septic shock is defined as sepsis-induced hypotension that persists despite adequate fluid resuscitation and is associated with hypoperfusion abnormalities or organ dysfunction. In clinical practice, many patients with these signs and symptoms are receiving vasopressor and/or inotropic agents and are no longer hypotensive when they manifest hypoperfusion abnormalities or organ dysfunction, but they still are considered to be experiencing septic shock.

Pathogenesis

Microorganisms proliferate at a nidus of infection; they may invade the blood stream, resulting in positive blood cultures, or they may grow locally and release their structural components, such as teichoic acid antigens from staphylococci, endotoxins from gram-negative organisms, or exotoxins (e.g., toxic shock syndrome toxin-1 [TSST-1]) synthesized and released by the microorganisms (Fig. 104–1). These organism-derived products can stimulate the release of a large number of endogenous host-derived mediators from plasma protein precursors or cells (e.g., monocytes-macrophages, endothelial cells, and neutrophils).

The endogenous mediators can produce profound physiologic effects on the vasculature and organ systems. When released in small amounts, these mediators result in beneficial effects such as regulating immune function, killing bacteria, and detoxifying bacterial products. However, an exaggerated response can result in harmful effects. Some of these effects stem from direct mediator-induced injury to end organs. However, a portion of the organ dysfunction is probably due to mediator-induced abnormalities in vasculature, resulting in abnormalities of systemic and regional blood flow. Although certain mediators are undoubtedly more important than others in producing sepsis, probably dozens of organism- and host-derived mediators interacting, accelerating, and inhibiting one another are responsible for the pathogenesis of septic shock.

Approximately 40 to 70% of patients who have hypotension secondary to sepsis and who are admitted to an ICU survive; the other 30 to 60% develop refractory hypotension or multiple organ system failure and die of progressive septic shock. Early and throughout the course of most of these patients, cardiovascular evaluation reveals a low systemic vascular resistance (SVR) and a high cardiac output—the hyperdynamic response to sepsis. Despite this elevated cardiac output, cardiac performance is abnormal, with a decreased ventricular ejection fraction and a dilated ventricle. In approximately 10% of patients, progressively diminished cardiac performance results in an abnormally low cardiac output. In nonsurvivors, organ system dysfunction progresses to multiple organ system failure, manifested by further myocardial dysfunction, acute respiratory distress syndrome (ARDS; Chapter 99), acute renal failure (Chapter 116), hepatic failure (Chapter 157), and disseminated intravascular coagulation (DIC; Chapter 179). Death results from progressive hypotension or complete failure of one or more organ systems.

MICROORGANISM-DERIVED MEDIATORS. A number of molecules can initiate the pathway leading to septic shock. Certain microorganisms synthesize and release exotoxins that can activate the cascade. Examples include toxin A produced by *Pseudomonas aeruginosa* and TSST-1 produced by staphylococci. More frequently, the structural components of the microorganism initiate the sequence. The polysaccharide surface of *Candida albicans,* the teichoic acid antigens of staphylococci, and the polysaccharide capsule of *Streptococcus pneumoniae* can all initiate the sepsis pathway.

However, endotoxins—the distinctive lipopolysaccharide (LPS) associated with the cell membrane of gram-negative organisms—represent the classic example of an initiator of the septic shock pathogenetic cascade. The endotoxin molecule consists of an outer core with a series of oligosaccharides that are antigenically and structurally diverse, an inner oligosaccharide core that has similarities among common gram-negative bacteria, and a core lipid A that is highly conserved across bacterial species. The lipid A, which is responsible for many of the toxic properties of endotoxin, has been the focus of attempts to synthesize nonactive analogues or develop inhibitors to interfere with the septic process.

Administering endotoxin to a variety of animals results in a cardiovascular response similar to that of human septic shock. Administering a very small dose of purified endotoxin to normal humans results in fever, mild constitutional symptoms, and a cardiovascular pattern qualitatively similar to that of spontaneous sepsis: tachycardia, decreased SVR, and depressed ventricular ejection fraction. In septic patients, detectable plasma levels of endotoxin are correlated with positive blood cultures, decreased SVR, depressed ventricular ejection fraction, and lactic acidemia. In patients with positive blood cultures and septic shock, detectable plasma endotoxin is associated with increased mortality (39% versus 7% for those without endotoxemia). Thus, endotoxin is an important mediator in many septic shock patients; however, routine measurement of circulating plasma endotoxin is not prognostically reliable enough to be used clinically.

CYTOKINES. The monocyte-macrophage plays an important role in the body's response to infection or endotoxin. Endotoxin can stimulate monocytes to produce tumor necrosis factor (TNF),

---

Table 104–1 • DEFINITIONS OF SEPSIS

Infection: A microbial phenomenon characterized by an inflammatory response to the presence of microorganisms or the invasion of normally sterile host tissue by those organisms.

Bacteremia: The presence of viable bacteria in the blood.

Systemic inflammatory response syndrome: The systemic inflammatory response to a variety of severe clinical insults. The response is manifested by two or more of the following conditions:
Temperature: >38°C or <36°C
Heart rate: >90 beats/min
Respiratory rate: >20 breaths/min or $PaCO_2$ < 32 mm Hg (<4.3 kPa)
White blood cell count: >12,000 cells/mm³, <4000 cells/mm³, or >10% immature (band) forms

Sepsis: The systemic response to infection. This systemic response is manifested by two or more of the following conditions as a result of infection:
Temperature: >38°C or <36°C
Heart rate: >90 beats/min
Respiratory rate: >20 breaths/min or $PaCO_2$ < 32 mm Hg (<4.3 kPa)
White blood cell count: >12,000 cells/mm³, 4000 cells/mm³, or >10% immature (band) forms

Severe sepsis: Sepsis associated with organ dsyfunction, hypoperfusion, or hypotension, Hypoperfusion and perfusion abnormalities may include, but are not limited to, lactic acidosis, oliguria, or an acute alteration in mental status.

Septic shock: Sepsis with hypotension, despite adequate fluid resuscitation, along with the presence of perfusion abnormalities that may include, but are not limited to, lactic acidosis, oliguria, or an acute alteration in mental status. Patients who are on inotropic or vasopressor agents may not be hypotensive at the time that perfusion abnormalities are measured.

Hypotension: A systolic blood pressure < 90 mm Hg or a reduction > 40 mm Hg from baseline in the absence of other causes for hypotension.

Multiple organ system failure: Presence of altered organ function in an acutely ill patient such that homeostasis cannot be maintained without intervention.

Adapted from American College of Chest Physicians Society of Critical Care Medicine Consensus Conference: Definitions for sepsis and organ failure and guidelines for the use of innovative therapies in sepsis. Crit Care Med 1992;20:864-874.

Critical Care Medicine

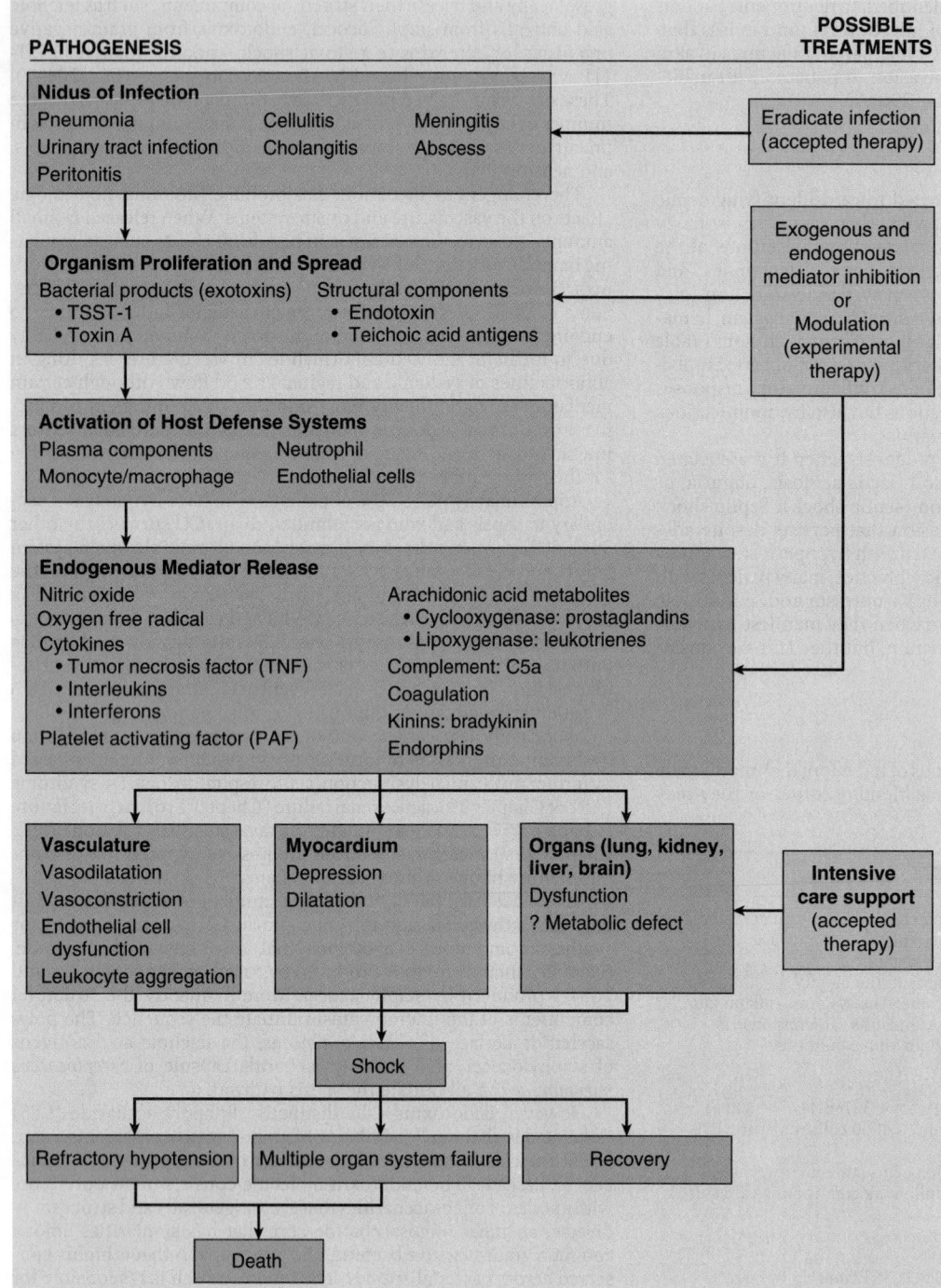

FIGURE 104–1 • Pathogenesis and possible treatment strategies in sepsis and septic shock. TSST-1 = toxic shock syndrome toxin-1.

interleukin-1 (IL-1), and other cytokines. Serum contains a protein, the LPS-binding protein, that can bind the lipid A portion of endotoxin. When complexed with this protein, LPS can bind the CD14 receptor and stimulate the monocyte to produce cytokines at concentrations far less than those required for stimulation by LPS alone.

Cytokines are 15- to 30-kD polypeptides that have profound immune regulatory and physiologic effects. Considerable evidence suggests that cytokines not only enhance host defense mechanisms (e.g., stimulating lymphocyte progenitor cells, enhancing neutrophil oxidative burst) but also produce harmful effects. In animal models, administering TNF results in a cardiovascular pattern of shock that is very similar to clinical sepsis. Anti-TNF antibodies have prevented shock and death from endotoxin and live organism challenge in animals. TNF produces vascular dilation and myocardial cell depression in biologic models, suggesting its involvement in these sepsis-associated physiologic abnormalities. Although TNF probably has a central role in mediating sepsis-induced injury, it most likely does not work alone. TNF and IL-1 have been shown to work synergisti-

cally to produce hypotension in animals, and additive or synergistic actions among a number of cytokines probably account for many sepsis-associated abnormalities.

Genetic factors influence the response to sepsis. Patients with the allele for TNF2, a TNF-α promoter polymorphism, have a much higher risk of septic shock development, and when shock develops, they have a much higher chance of dying of septic shock. The presence of this promoter probably results in greater TNF production and more toxicity. Identification of such genetic factors will provide important clinical prognostic information to improve patient management.

MYOCARDIAL DEPRESSION. A number of animal models suggest the presence of a circulating myocardial depressant as the cause of ventricular dysfunction during sepsis. Human studies have documented the presence of circulating myocardial depressant activity that correlates temporally with the reduced ventricular ejection fraction (Table 104–2). Recent data suggest that this depression results from a synergistic effect of TNF and IL-1 on myocardial cell contraction.

Table 104–2 • CARDIOVASCULAR RESPONSE TO SEPTIC SHOCK: A REPRESENTATIVE EXAMPLE

	ACUTE PHASE (HYPOTENSION AND REDUCED SYSTEMIC VASCULAR RESISTANCE)	RECOVERY PHASE (NORMOTENSION)
Mean arterial pressure (mm Hg)	40	75
Central venous pressure (mm Hg)	2	5
Cardiac output (L/min)	11.25	5.25
Heart rate (bpm)	150	70
Stroke volume (mL)	75	75
Systemic vascular resistance (dyne·sec·cm^{-5})	270	1067
Left ventricular volumes (mL):		
Diastole	225	125
Systole	150	50
Ejection fraction (%)	$\dfrac{225\,mL - 150\,mL}{225\,mL} = 33\%$	$\dfrac{125\,mL - 50\,mL}{125\,mL} = 60\%$

ENDOTHELIAL CELLS AND NEUTROPHILS. A number of mediators, including LPS and TNF, can cause endothelial cells to express adhesion receptors (selectins) and can activate neutrophils to express ligands for these receptors. Neutrophils must stick to the endothelial cell surface for their adherence, margination, and migration into foci of inflammatory tissue. Blockage of the adhesion process with monoclonal antibodies prevents tissue injury and improves survival in certain animal models of septic shock.

NITRIC OXIDE. In response to LPS, TNF, and other mediators, endothelial cells and macrophages can release nitric oxide, which causes smooth muscle cell relaxation and potent vasodilation. Inhibition of nitric oxide production with competitive inhibitors of nitric oxide synthase increases blood pressure in animals with endotoxin shock, suggesting that nitric oxide is partially responsible for the hypotension associated with sepsis. Although inhibition of nitric oxide restores blood pressure, such inhibition may also reduce tissue blood flow.

COMPLEMENT, KININ, AND THE COAGULATION SYSTEM. Endotoxin can activate the complement cascade, usually via the alternative pathway, and result in the release of the anaphylotoxins C3a and C5a, which can induce vasodilation, increased vascular permeability, platelet aggregation, and activation and aggregation of neutrophils. These complement-derived mediators may be responsible in part for the microvascular abnormalities associated with septic shock. Endotoxin can also result in the release of bradykinin via the activation of factor XII (Hageman factor), kallikrein, and kininogen. Bradykinin is a potent vasodilator and hypotensive agent. LPS activation of factor XII also leads to intrinsic and (through macrophage and endothelial cell release of tissue factor) extrinsic coagulation pathway activation, which may result in consumption of coagulation factors and DIC. TNF also activates the extrinsic pathway and may contribute to these coagulation abnormalities. Recent clinical trials have documented a survival advantage when patients with severe sepsis are treated with activated protein C, an anticoagulant that probably favorably modulates the coagulation and inflammatory pathways in sepsis.

ARACHIDONIC ACID METABOLITES. Different metabolites of the arachidonic acid cascade are known to cause vasodilation (prostacyclins), vasoconstriction (thromboxanes), platelet aggregation, or neutrophil activation. In experimental animals, inhibition of cyclooxygenase or thromboxane synthase has protected against endotoxin shock. Elevated levels of thromboxane B$_2$ (TBX$_2$) and 6-ketoprostaglandin F$_{1a}$ (the end product of prostacyclin metabolism) are present in patients with sepsis. A number of cytokines can cause release of these arachidonic acid metabolites from endothelial cells or leukocytes. In addition to nitric oxide, some arachidonic acid products are partially responsible for the vasodilation that is characteristic of septic shock.

OPIOID PEPTIDES. In certain animal models of endotoxin challenge, administering an endogenous opioid antagonist, such as naloxone, can reverse hypotension. The role of endogenous opioids in clinical septic shock is unclear.

Cardiovascular Dysfunction

Shock is classically defined as inadequate perfusion of tissues that results in cell dysfunction and, if prolonged, cell death. This definition adequately describes shock due to the hypovolemic, cardiogenic, and vascular obstructive mechanisms (Chapter 102) that result in reduced cardiac output and poor tissue perfusion. In these forms of shock, SVR is elevated as a compensatory mechanism to maintain blood pressure, and pulmonary artery oxygenation is reduced, reflecting enhanced extraction of oxygen from erythrocytes by hypoperfused peripheral tissues.

However, sepsis results in a much more complex form of shock. The onset of sepsis is frequently accompanied by hypovolemia as a result of both leakage of plasma (capillary leak) into the intravascular space and arterial and venous vasodilation. Correcting this hypovolemia by aggressive volume replacement results in a decreased SVR, increased or normal cardiac output, tachycardia, and elevated oxygen content in the pulmonary artery blood—the hyperdynamic shock syndrome. This hemodynamic pattern has been termed *distributive shock* (Chapter 102) to indicate the presumed maldistribution of systemic blood flow leading to the high blood oxygen content returning to the right side of the heart. Before volume resuscitation, patients with septic shock may manifest features of both hypovolemic and distributive shock, that is, a mixed form of shock.

Despite the elevated or normal cardiac output in volume-resuscitated septic shock, ventricular function is abnormal, as reflected by decreases in ventricular ejection fraction and stroke work and increases in end-diastolic and end-systolic volumes. In survivors, this cardiovascular dysfunction is reversible and returns to normal 5 to 10 days after septic shock. Certain hemodynamic patterns have prognostic implications. At disease onset, a lower heart rate predicts survival, probably reflecting less severe disease. Serial hemodynamic measurements demonstrate that normalization (within 24 hours) of either the elevated cardiac index or tachycardia is associated with survival, whereas persistence of the hyperdynamic state correlates with nonsurvival.

Vascular dysfunction is one of the most prominent physiologic and pathologic findings in septic shock. Patients usually manifest an overall decrease in SVR, reflecting widespread systemic vasodilation; however, some localized vascular beds are constricted. The decreased extraction of oxygen in the systemic circulation suggests that oxygen is not reaching or is not being used by cells. One hypothesis argues that vascular abnormalities (vasodilation, vasoconstriction, leukocyte aggregation, and endothelial cell dysfunction induced by complex interactions among the mediators summarized previously) result in decreased tissue perfusion. A second hypothesis argues that a direct mediator-induced cellular metabolic abnormality causes the failure of oxygen uptake. A central question in the pathogenesis of sepsis is whether decreased perfusion due to microvascular dysregulation is a primary cause or only an associated event in sepsis-induced organ failure.

Another method of judging whether a vascular perfusion abnormality is important in septic shock is to evaluate the relationship between oxygen delivery and oxygen consumption. In patients with cardiogenic or hypovolemic shock, in whom tissue hypoperfusion clearly occurs, increases in oxygen delivery result in increased consumption until hypoperfusion is reversed and oxygen consumption plateaus. Some investigators have argued that septic shock (especially with ARDS) is characterized by a pathologic delivery-consumption relationship in which consumption continues to increase (and not plateau) with increased delivery, suggesting the presence of a perfusion abnormality that can be overcome by increasing delivery to a supranormal range. This observation is controversial, and animal experiments have yielded conflicting results. Although some initial clinical studies reported improved outcomes when oxygen delivery was increased, subsequent larger clinical trials comparing conventional strategies with strategies designed to increase oxygen delivery to a supranormal range have failed to demonstrate a survival advantage for the supranormal approach. Some studies suggest that pretreatment of critically ill surgical patients with supranormal oxygen delivery may provide some benefit. A recent trial found that aggressive, goal-directed (protocol driven) therapy with fluids, blood transfusions, and inotropic agents initiated early in septic patients is associated with improved hospital survival. This study provides strong evidence favoring the importance of oxygen delivery in patients with severe sepsis (see Treatment).

Clinical Manifestations and Diagnostic Evaluation

Sepsis and septic shock produce three categories of clinical manifestations (Fig. 104–2). First, the patient usually manifests symptoms and signs related to the primary focus of infection. If it is pneumonia, the patient usually has cough, dyspnea, and productive sputum (Chapter 92); if a urinary tract infection is the focus, flank pain and dysuria are expected (Chapter 344). A careful history, physical examination, and directed imaging and laboratory studies reveal the probable infectious focus in most patients. However, elderly, debilitated, and immunosuppressed patients may not exhibit the usual localizing clinical signs (Chapter 298). In some patients, especially those with severe neutropenia, no site is identified. Second, patients usually manifest one or more signs of the systemic inflammatory response. Fever is the most characteristic and is frequently accompanied by shaking chills. A significant proportion of patients (perhaps 15%) are hypothermic (temperature <36.5°C [97.6°F]) or normothermic, especially the elderly, debilitated, or immunosuppressed. Elderly patients may present with tachypnea-induced respiratory alkalosis and mental status changes as the only signs of sepsis. Third, evidence of shock (e.g., hypotension, lactic acidemia, and progressive organ system dysfunction) may develop in septic patients.

The diagnosis of sepsis is confirmed by culturing pathogenic organisms from blood or from the likely site of infection. Blood cultures are positive in only 40 to 60% of patients with clinical manifestations of septic shock, probably owing to the intermittent nature of the bacteremia and the high incidence of prior antibiotic administration. A Gram stain from an abscess, empyema, or other usually sterile site can provide invaluable early diagnostic information.

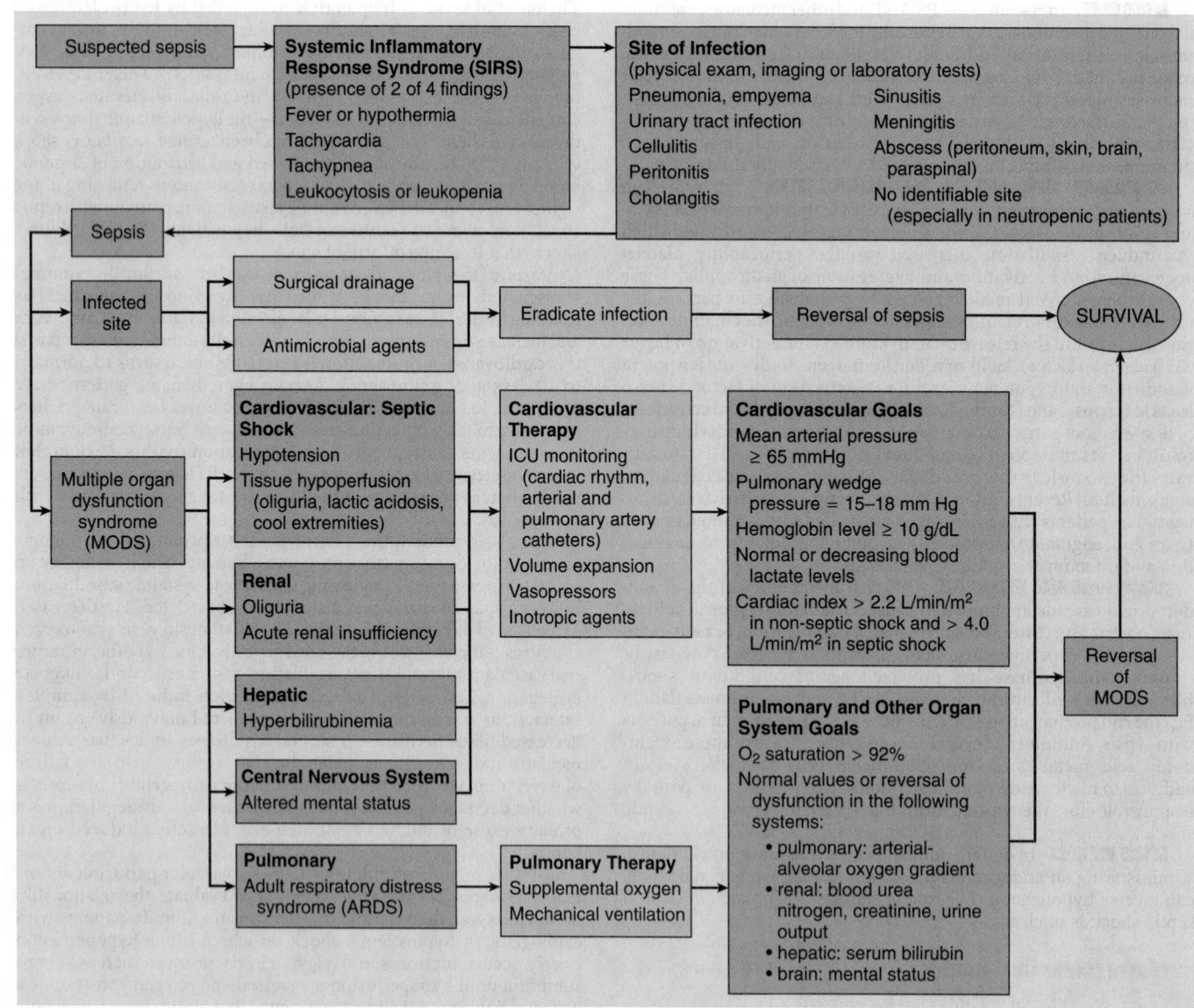

FIGURE 104–2 • Algorithm for diagnostic evaluation and management of sepsis and septic shock.

Rx Treatment

Septic shock can be managed effectively at three points along the pathogenetic sequence. First, the infection site can be eradicated with antimicrobials, surgical drainage, or both. Second, the serious disturbances in cardiovascular, respiratory, and other organ system physiology can be reversed in an ICU. Third, the toxic mediators of sepsis can be inhibited or modulated.

ANTIMICROBIAL THERAPY. Shock secondary to sepsis is a very major disease that should be treated aggressively. When the diagnosis is seriously entertained, blood cultures (usually three) and cultures of relevant body fluids and exudates should be obtained rapidly. Several large retrospective trials have provided convincing evidence that early appropriate antimicrobial therapy (i.e., the pathogen has in vitro sensitivity to the chosen antibiotic regimen) is associated with significantly improved patient survival. Once a specific pathogen is isolated, the antimicrobial spectrum can be narrowed.

A broad-spectrum regimen with activity against gram-positive and gram-negative organisms should be chosen. Generally, drugs should be administered intravenously at maximum recommended dosages, and bactericidal agents are preferred over bacteriostatic agents. Knowledge of the most likely organisms to infect a given site and the local institution's bacteriologic sensitivity and resistance patterns is important in choosing the best initial antimicrobial regimen. Many physicians favor using at least two effective antimicrobial agents in neutropenic patients with gram-negative pneumonia and a two-drug synergistic combination when treating serious enterococcal infection (Chapter 308). Anaerobes are likely pathogens in intra-abdominal infections, aspiration pneumonia, and abscesses. Intravascular catheter infection should raise the possibility of methicillin-resistant staphylococcal infection and the need for vancomycin therapy. In up to one third of patients, especially those who are neutropenic, no organism or source is identified. Such patients require a broad-spectrum regimen effective against gram-positive, gram-negative, and anaerobic organisms such as (1) vancomycin, gentamicin, and metronidazole or (2) ceftazidime and gentamicin. Early antifungal therapy with amphotericin B should be considered in neutropenic, immunosuppressed patients and in those unresponsive to antibacterial regimens.

THERAPY FOR SHOCK. Before the general availability of ICUs, gram-negative bacteremic shock had a higher than 90% mortality. Currently, about 50% of such patients survive, largely because of treatment in ICUs, in which cardiac rhythm, blood pressure, cardiac performance, oxygen delivery, and metabolic derangements can be monitored and abnormalities corrected. Adequate oxygenation and ventilatory support are critical goals of therapy and can be achieved with supplemental oxygen and, if necessary, mechanical ventilation and positive end-expiratory pressure. Although no prospective trial has evaluated outcomes with and without ICU support, two retrospective studies have reported a significantly reduced mortality in septic shock when patients were managed with aggressive hemodynamic support by critical care personnel. A controlled, prospective trial of ICU support has been conducted in dogs with gram-negative sepsis; survival was increased only in the animals that received both antibiotic therapy and cardiovascular support.

Patients with septic shock who remain hypotensive after a 1- or 2-L volume resuscitation should have arterial and pulmonary artery catheters placed to allow serial evaluations of blood pressure, ventricular filling pressures, cardiac output, and oxygen delivery. The pulmonary artery catheter is especially useful for initial assessment and titration of fluid status but should be removed as soon as the patient's hemodynamic stability can be maintained without it in the pulmonary artery. Initial emphasis should be placed on restoring mean blood pressure to greater than 65 mm Hg. Aggressive volume resuscitation using blood (if hemoglobin is less than 7 g/100 mL in noncardiac patients or less than 10 g/100 mL in patients with ischemic heart disease), colloid (if serum albumin is less than 2 g/100 mL), or crystalloid (in all other patients) should be instituted to raise the pulmonary artery mean wedge pressure to 15 to 18 mm Hg. If hypotension persists, dopamine (initially low-dose, then, if necessary, higher doses up to 20 µg/kg/minute) should be administered. In patients who are unresponsive to dopamine, norepinephrine

should be infused to raise mean blood pressure to higher than 65 mm Hg. Patients who require high doses of norepinephrine may benefit from concomitantly administered low-dose dopamine to enhance renal blood flow, although this latter point is controversial.

Once blood pressure is adequate, attention should be turned to cardiac output and oxygen delivery. Although the role of achieving very high levels of oxygen delivery and consumption is controversial, most investigators favor inotropic support (with dobutamine, if necessary) to offset the myocardial depression of sepsis and to maintain a cardiac index in the high normal range (higher than 4.0 L/minute/m²). Serial measures of lactate, urine output, and organ function can provide good measures of patient prognosis. A recent clinical trial in severe sepsis and septic shock found that aggressive, early resuscitation with fluids, blood transfusions, and inotropic therapy, instituted for 6 hours in the emergency department before ICU admission (goal-directed therapy), resulted in a substantial improvement in hospital mortality.[1] The study used arterial and central venous catheters to monitor blood pressure and cardiac filling pressures to guide a protocol that resulted in aggressive administration of fluids, blood, vasopressors, inotropic agents, and vasodilators. The authors argue that goal-directed therapy balanced oxygen delivery and oxygen demand resulting in improved perfusion, better organ function, and increased survival. If confirmed, these findings argue for early, aggressive support of hemodynamics and perfusion in severe sepsis.

MEDIATOR INHIBITORS. The pathogenesis of septic shock is complex and highly interdependent; many of the components represent the body's appropriate compensatory response to sepsis and therefore have salutary effects. Depending on the profile of inhibition, a mediator antagonist may produce a beneficial or harmful outcome. A recent trial administered recombinant activated protein C (APC; drotrecogin), a modulator of the coagulation and inflammatory cascade, to patients with severe sepsis. The study demonstrated an improved survival (Fig. 104–3), although there was a higher incidence of bleeding with APC, thus precluding its use in postsurgical patients. APC is the first biologic modulatory agent that has shown success in improving survival in sepsis.[2] Most experts recommend use of APC (drotrecogin alpha, 24 µg/kg/hour for 96 hours intravenously) in patients who have severe sepsis and who do not have contraindications to the drug. A number of other modulator/inhibitors of the inflammatory or coagulation cascade are being developed and tested.

High-dose corticosteroids can inhibit mediator release and improve survival in some animal models of endotoxemia. However, three prospective, randomized clinical trials conducted in the 1980s demonstrated convincingly that corticosteroids did not improve survival in human septic shock. More recently, two small trials have suggested that replacement doses of hydrocortisone may result in improved outcomes[3] in patients with septic shock that is refractory to vasopressor therapy. Another clinical study administered hydrocortisone to septic shock patients with relative adrenal insufficiency, as defined by inadequate hydrocortisone response to adrenocorticotropic hormone challenge; this study found improved survival with hydrocortisone therapy in the subpopulation with low adrenal reserve.[4] Thus, some groups of septic patients may respond favorably to corticosteroids, although further studies are needed to clarify the appropriate groups.

Another therapeutic approach has been to inhibit endotoxin. However, clinical trials of antiendotoxin antibodies have not shown improved outcomes. Recently, endotoxin binding by lipid products, especially high-density lipoprotein, has shown efficacy in animal models of sepsis. These endotoxin binding lipids show great promise, and clinical trials are underway.

Monoclonal antibodies to TNF, TNF receptor blockers, an IL-1 receptor antagonist, bradykinin antagonists, and platelet activating factor inhibitors have been evaluated in clinical trials and all have failed to demonstrate efficacy in sepsis. Several mediator inhibitors, including a nonselective nitric oxide synthase inhibitor (N-methyl arginine) and a specific TNF receptor antagonist, actually increased mortality, probably because these mediator inhibitors impaired some of the beneficial effects of the inflammatory cascade.

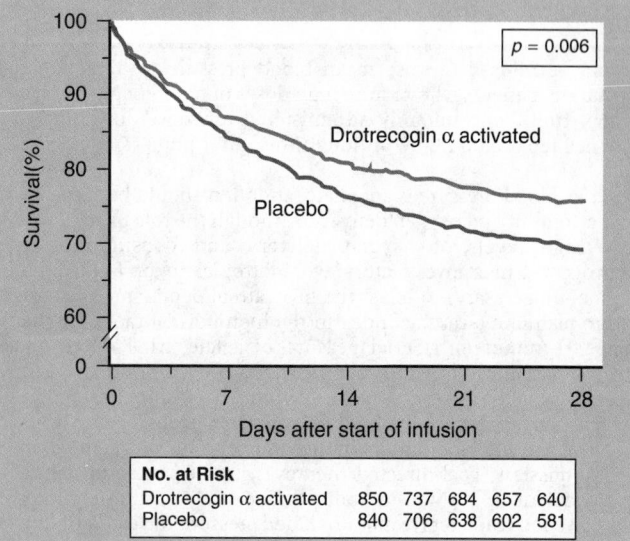

FIGURE 104–3 • Kaplan-Meier survival curves show improved survival in septic shock patients treated with activated protein C (drotrecogin alpha). (Adapted from Bernard GR, Vincent JL, Laterre PF, et al: Efficacy and safety of recombinant human activated protein C for severe sepsis. N Engl J Med 2001;344:699–709.)

1. Rivers E, Nguyen B, Havstad S, et al: Early goal-directed therapy in the treatment of severe sepsis and septic shock. N Engl J Med 2001;345:1368–1377.
2. Bernard GR, Vincent JL, Laterre PF, et al: Efficacy and safety of recombinant human activated protein C for severe sepsis. N Engl J Med 2001;344:699–709.
3. Bollaert PE, Charpentier C, Levy B, et al: Reversal of late septic shock with supraphysiologic doses of hydrocortisone. Crit Care Med 1998;26:645–650.
4. Annane D, Sebille V, Charpentier C, et al: Effect of treatment with low doses of hydrocortisone and fludrocortisone on mortality in patients with septic shock. JAMA 2002;288:862–871.

SUGGESTED READINGS

Hotchkiss RS, Karl IE: The pathophysiology and treatment of sepsis. N Engl J Med 2003;348:138–150. *Evolving concepts of sepsis, including new and potential therapies.*
MacKenzie IM: The hemodynamics of human septic shock. Anaesthesia 2001;56:130–144. *A concise review of septic shock hemodynamics.*
Manns BJ, Lee H, Doig CJ, et al: An economic evaluation of activated protein C treatment for severe sepsis. N Engl J Med 2002;347:993–1000. *The treatment is relatively cost-effective when targeted to high-risk patients with a reasonable life expectancy.*
Martin GS, Mannino DM, Eaton S, et al: The epidemiology of sepsis in the United States from 1979 through 2000. N Engl J Med 2003;348:1546–1554. *Sepsis and the number of sepsis-related deaths are increasing, but the mortality rate among patients with sepsis is declining.*

105 DISORDERS DUE TO HEAT AND COLD

Ernest Yoder

TEMPERATURE HOMEOSTASIS

As homeothermic organisms, humans depend on a highly integrated neuroendocrine system to maintain their thermal homeostasis. Equilibrium between heat gained and lost must be maintained to prevent the organism from becoming either hyperthermic or hypothermic. Thus, body temperature is normally maintained at 36.5 ± 0.7° C (97.7 ± 1.3° F). Mechanisms of heat transfer to the environment, largely dependent on a temperature gradient between the body and its milieu, are radiation, conduction, convection, and evaporation.

Information from peripheral and central receptors is integrated by the hypothalamus, which effects changes in autonomic tone and endocrinologic function to maintain stable body temperature. Voluntary responses, also important in preventing hypothermia and hyperthermia, include moving to a cooler or warmer environment, removing or adding clothing, decreasing or increasing activity level, and increasing or decreasing exposed skin areas.

HYPERTHERMIC SYNDROMES

Hyperthermia is present when core body temperature is higher than 37.2° C. Heat injury syndromes may result in body temperatures higher than 40° C (104° F) (Table 105–1). When temperatures are above 41° C, enzymes are denatured, mitochondrial function is disturbed, cell membranes are destabilized, and oxygen-dependent metabolic pathways are disrupted. Multisystem failure regularly occurs concomitantly with heat injury syndromes, along with significant associated morbidity and mortality. Patients with these syndromes usually require admission to the intensive care unit.

Painful spasm of major muscle groups is the hallmark of *heat cramps* and *heat tetany* (includes carpal-pedal spasm). Typically seen in young, unacclimatized athletes or laborers who exert themselves excessively in a hot climate, heat cramps are related to excessive losses of sodium, chloride, and water. Patients complain of nausea, vomiting, and fatigue in addition to muscle cramps, with the onset of symptoms typically occurring several hours after ceasing strenuous activity.

Heat exhaustion, the most common heat injury syndrome seen in athletes, may be preceded by heat cramps and is due to severe dehydration and electrolyte loss. In the young, heat exhaustion usually occurs after strenuous activity by unacclimatized individuals in a hot, humid environment. In the elderly, the problem is usually related to inadequate cardiovascular response to heat with disruption of normal compensatory mechanisms. Patients frequently complain of cramps, headache, fatigue, nausea, and vomiting. They appear listless, with pallor of the skin and profuse sweating. Other clinical findings include orthostatic hypotension, core temperatures of 37.5° to 39° C (99.5° to 102.2° F), altered mental status, incoordination, and diffuse weakness. Syncope may also occur.

Heatstroke, classified as *exertional* or *nonexertional*, is a syndrome due to acute disruption of thermoregulatory mechanisms that is manifested by central nervous system depression, hypohidrosis, core temperatures of 41° C or higher, and severe physiologic and biochemical abnormalities. Exertional heatstroke occurs in people working or exercising in a warm environment with an overwhelmed but unimpaired central thermoregulatory center. Nonexertional heat stroke occurs most frequently in elderly, debilitated, schizophrenic, intoxicated, or paralyzed individuals. These people have impaired central and/or peripheral thermoregulatory mechanisms (physiologic or drug-induced autonomic impairment), impaired awareness of or inability to leave a hot environment, poor acclimatization, and inadequate ability to increase cardiac output in response to heat.

Severe hypothermia associated with rhabdomyolysis, consumption coagulopathy, and acute renal failure may be related to ingestion of amphetamines, amphetamine cogeners (ecstasy), and cocaine. Presentation of such patients may mimic heat stroke. *Neuroleptic malignant syndrome* is a complex of extrapyramidal muscular rigidity (Chapters 442 to 445), high core temperature, altered level of consciousness, and elevated creatine kinase levels occurring as an acute or subacute reaction to therapy with neuroleptic medications.

Malignant hyperthermia (Chapter 463) is a hypermetabolic, myopathic syndrome that is chemically or stress induced and is manifested by an abrupt rise in core temperature, vigorous muscle contractions, metabolic and respiratory acidosis, and ventricular arrhythmias. It usually occurs when inducing anesthesia.

Consequences of heat-induced cell damage are rhabdomyolysis, heart failure, cardiac arrhythmias, vasodilation, cytotoxic cerebral edema, hypotension, acute renal failure, acute respiratory distress syndrome (Chapter 99), gastrointestinal hemorrhage, and acute hepatic failure (Chapter 157). Concomitant laboratory abnormalities include hyperkalemia, hypocalcemia, hyperphosphatemia or hypophosphatemia, rising creatinine, hemoconcentration, stress leukocytosis, thrombocytopenia, consumptive coagulopathy, lactic acidosis, hypoglycemia, proteinuria, and an active urinary sediment. Arterial blood gas values should be corrected for hyperthermia. PaO_2 values are incorrectly low and should be increased by 6% for each degree centigrade above 37; $PaCO_2$ is also lower and should be increased by 4.4% for each degree centigrade above 37; and pH is high and should be reduced by 0.015 unit for each degree centigrade above 37. These corrections are approximate, and nomograms provide the most precise

Table 105–1 • FACTORS PREDISPOSING TO HYPERTHERMIA

PATIENT FACTORS	MEDICAL CONDITIONS	DRUGS	ENVIRONMENTAL FACTORS
Lack of acclimatization	Alcoholism	Amphetamines	High ambient temperature
Dehydration	Neurologic lesions/events	Anticholinergics	High humidity
Exercising when poorly trained	Cardiovascular disease	Antidepressants	Lack of wind
Fever/infection	Obesity/high body mass index	Antihistamines	
Skin/sweat gland diseases	Diabetes mellitus	Anti-Parkinson's drugs	
Fatigue/exhaustion	Thyrotoxicosis	Barbiturates	
Excessive clothing	Hypokalemia	β-Blockers	
Advanced age	Chronic obstructive pulmonary disease	Butyrophenones	
Living/working on upper floors of buildings	Psychiatric illness	Diuretics	
		Ethanol	
		Hallucinogens	
		Phenothiazines	

Table 105–2 • INITIAL DIAGNOSTIC STUDIES: HYPERTHERMIC AND HYPOTHERMIC STATES

Electrocardiogram
Chest radiograph
Complete blood count with differential
Platelet count
Urinalysis

SERUM STUDIES
Lactate dehydrogenase
Transaminases
Alkaline phosphatase
Bilirubin
Creatine kinase
Blood urea nitrogen
Creatinine
Phosphate
Calcium
Glucose
Electrolytes
Uric acid
Lactate*
Cortisol*
Thyroid-stimulating hormone, T_3, T_4*
Prothrombin time and partial thromboplastin time
Fibrin split products
Fibrinogen
Arterial blood gases
Toxicology screen

*Necessary only in hypothermic states.

Table 105–3 • MANAGEMENT OF HYPERTHERMIA

1. Protect the airway
2. Insert at least two large-bore intravenous lines
3. Monitor core temperature
   a. Pulmonary artery
   b. Rectal probe
   c. Esophageal probe
4. Actively cool the skin until core temperature reaches 39° C
   a. Exposure to cool environment
   b. Wetting with water (avoid alcohol rubs)
   c. Continuous fanning
   d. Ice baths/immersion (22° C)
   e. Axillary/perineal ice packs
   f. Infusion of room-temperature saline
   g. Gastric/colonic iced saline lavage
   h. Peritoneal lavage with cool saline
5. If shivering occurs, administer chlorpromazine, 10 to 25 mg intramuscularly
6. Monitor for seizures
7. Monitor electrocardiogram for dysrhythmia
8. Obtain serial diagnostic studies (see Table 105–2)

corrections. The expected abnormalities guide the recommended laboratory evaluation of patients with pathologic states of altered core temperature (Table 105–2).

Rx Treatment

The primary goal of therapy is rapid cooling. Three initial steps include removal from the hot environment, inhibition of thermogenesis, and active cooling (Table 105–3). The severity of the patient's clinical condition dictates the aggressiveness of cooling techniques.

Heat cramps and heat exhaustion rarely result in permanent sequelae. Mild to moderate neurologic, hepatic, and renal dysfunction seen in heatstroke usually resolves after return to normothermia. Muscle weakness may persist for several months when rhabdomyolysis has been severe. The greater the severity of injury, the greater is the likelihood of permanent sequelae. Heatstroke mortality may approach 50% and is usually associated with advanced age and severe organ failure.

HYPOTHERMIC SYNDROMES

Hypothermia, defined as a core body temperature of lower than 35° C (95° F), is classified as *accidental* (primary) or *secondary.* The accidental form is defined as a spontaneous decrease of core temperature to lower than 35° C, usually in a cold environment, often but not necessarily associated with an acute medical problem, and without a primary disturbance of the temperature-regulating center.

Secondary hypothermia is characterized by dysfunction of hypothalamic thermoregulation. An underlying illness or drug is often the predisposing factor (Table 105–4).

Hypothermia affects virtually every body system owing to generalized slowing of enzymatic activity, peripheral vasoconstriction, and uncoupling of oxygen-dependent metabolism. Alterations in cardiovascular physiology include an early catecholamine-mediated increase in heart rate, cardiac output, and mean arterial pressure. Later, negative inotropic and chronotropic effects of hypothermia and decreased effective blood volume cause diminished cardiac output and tissue perfusion.

Patients may present with tachypnea, but as hypothermia becomes pronounced, there is depression of the respiratory center. Shivering increases oxygen consumption. Because alveolar ventilation is decreased, PaO_2 may decline to subnormal levels. Hypoxemia also may result from aspiration pneumonia, pulmonary edema, or adult respiratory distress syndrome. Arterial blood gas values should be corrected for hypothermia. PaO_2 values are incorrectly high and should be decreased by 4.4% for each degree centigrade below 37; $PaCO_2$ is also higher and should be decreased by 3.5% for each degree centigrade below 37; and pH is lower and should be increased by 0.015 unit for each degree centigrade below 37. These corrections are approximate, and nomograms provide the most precise corrections.

The electrocardiogram may demonstrate sinus bradycardia and slowing of conduction with atrioventricular block, prolonged QT interval, widened QRS complex, and T-wave inversion. P waves may be absent. When core temperature declines to 32° C, the classic Osborne (or J) wave appears (Fig. 105–1). The cold heart is highly irritable, and any physical stimulation may lead to ventricular fibrillation.

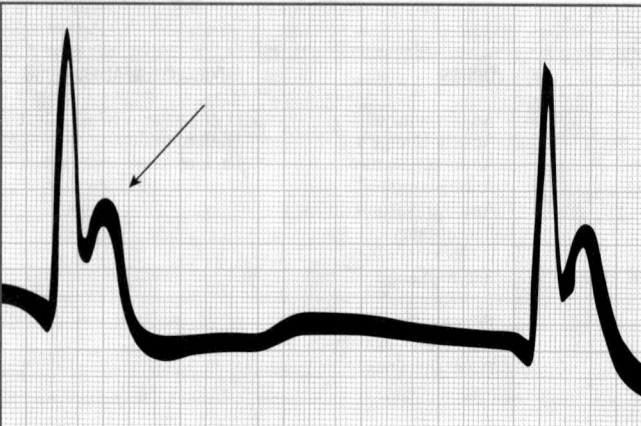

FIGURE 105–1 • J (Osborne) wave.

Table 105–4 • FACTORS PREDISPOSING TO HYPOTHERMIA

PATIENT FACTORS	MEDICAL CONDITIONS	DRUGS
Inadequate clothing	Alcoholism	Alcohol
Extremes of age	Burns, severe	Anesthetics (general)
Mental impairment	Cancer chemotherapy	Antidepressants
Immobility	Cardiac failure	Antithyroid agents
Atered level of	Central nervous system	Cannabis
consciousness	lesions/events	Hypoglycemic agents
Debility and	Dementia	Major tranquilizers
exhaustion	Encephalopathy	Narcotics
Wet clothing	Diabetes	Paralyzing agents
	Hypoadrenalism	Sedative/hypnotics
	Hypoglycemia	
	Hypopituitarism	
	Malnutrition	
	Myxedema	
	Prolonged	
	cardiopulmonary	
	resuscitation	
	Prolonged surgery	
	Sepsis	
	Shock	
	Uremia	

Table 105–5 • MANAGEMENT OF HYPOTHERMIA

MILD HYPOTHERMIA (34° TO 36° C)
1. Remove from cold environment, replace wet clothing, cover with blankets or equivalent, use gentle passive rewarming techniques.
2. Give warm oxygen through a mask or an endotracheal tube.
3. Give warm dextrose/saline intravenous fluids.
4. Warm the environment (thermostat, overhead lights).
5. Monitor electrocardiogram, respiratory status, core temperature.
6. Obtain initial diagnostic studies (see Table 105–2).

MODERATE TO SEVERE HYPOTHERMIA (<33° C)
1. Admit to intensive care unit.
2. Peripheral active rewarming: heating blankets, heating pads, hot-water bottles, warming lights, warm water immersion.
3. Actively warm central core: inhale heated, humidified oxygen, gastric lavage, colonic irrigation, and warmed intravenous fluids.
4. Consider special beds, and protect against pressure necrosis.
5. If core temperature is not rising 0.5° to 1.0° C per hour, consider peritoneal dialysis, bladder lavage, hemodialysis, or bypass.
6. Anticipate multiorgan dysfunction and secondary infection.

Owing to enzyme damage, renal concentrating ability is lost, resulting in very dilute (cold diuresis) urine and systemic hyperosmolarity. Later, with decreased perfusion, acute tubular necrosis may develop. Laboratory abnormalities include metabolic acidosis, hyperkalemia, hyponatremia, hyperglycemia, and hyperphosphatemia. Complications of hypothermia also include rhabdomyolysis, gastric

dilation, ileus, upper gastrointestinal bleeding, acute pancreatitis, and severe hepatic dysfunction. Hematologic alterations include hemoconcentration, increased blood viscosity, thrombocytopenia, granulocytopenia, and consumptive coagulopathy. Infection is a frequent sequela of hypothermia.

Hypothermia should be considered in the differential diagnosis of any hypotensive, comatose patient. Initial evaluation (see Table 105–2) should be directed toward identifying predisposing conditions (see Table 105–4).

Rx Treatment

The goals of management, although dependent on the severity of hypothermia, are to prevent further heat loss, increase core temperature, and anticipate and prevent complications (Table 105–5). If the person is without vital signs, cardiopulmonary resuscitation should be initiated and continued until the patient is normothermic.

Because of liver impairment and cardiac irritability, all drugs must be used with caution. Digitalis should be avoided. If myxedema or panhypopituitarism is suspected, proper hormonal replacement therapy should be initiated. Dysrhythmias can be treated safely with lidocaine, propranolol, and bretylium. Electrocardioversion is rarely successful. Vasoactive agents may be required for severe hypotension. Intravenous sodium bicarbonate should be used only in severe acidosis (pH < 7.1) and with extreme caution.

SUGGESTED READINGS
Bouchama A, Knochel JP: Heat stroke. N Engl J Med 2002;346:1978–1988. *Detailed discussion of pathophysiology, diagnosis, and treatment.*
Eddy VA, Morris JA, Cullinane DC: Hypothermia, coagulopathy, and acidosis. Surg Clin North Am 2000;80:845–854. *An excellent discussion of the acid-base and hematologic complications of hypothermia.*
Giesbrecht GG: Cold stress, near drowning, and accidental hypothermia: A review. Aviat Space Environ Med 2000;71:733–752. *A critical review of diagnosis and treatment, including analysis of the research literature.*
Sessler DI: Complications and treatment of mild hypothermia. Anesthesiology 2001;95:531–543. *A detailed review of complications of hypothermia and an update on methods of patient management.*

106 ACUTE POISONING

Marsha D. Ford

Each year, more than 2 million poisoning cases are reported to the Toxic Exposure Surveillance System of the American Association of Poison Control Centers, and about 40,000 deaths are attributed to the legal and illicit use of drugs and alcohol. Almost all patients who reach the hospital survive with appropriate care; inpatient mortality rates of 0.2 to 0.5% have been reported. The incidence of recurrent, purposeful self-poisoning is 12 to 18%, with most occurring within 3 months of the original attempt. These facts emphasize the need for aggressive treatment of poisoned patients, including early psychiatric intervention for suicidal behavior, to reduce fatalities and repeat attempts (Chapter 426).

Diagnosis and management of poisoned patients require knowledge and skill in five areas to identify and treat the factors that contribute to the risk of death or long-term disability: (1) history taking; (2) physical examination, with recognition of specific toxic syndromes, or *toxidromes*; (3) appropriate use of diagnostic tests; (4) treatment, including initial stabilization and critical care, decontamination, and administration of antidotes for specific poisonings; and (5) use of methods to enhance the elimination of specific toxins.

History

Details elicited about toxic exposures should include the involved drugs and toxins and their estimated or known amounts, the time and routes of exposure, the patient's symptoms and signs, and any treatment already administered. Intoxication may result from acute, chronic, or acute-on-chronic exposure. Determination of the chronicity is important because signs and symptoms of chronic intoxication can differ from those of acute and acute-on-chronic intoxication. A history of available medications (e.g., medications of patient, spouse, relative, or friend); use of nonprescription medications, herbal/dietary supplements, or ethnic remedies; and occupational and avocational activities should be obtained. Occupational and avocational histories should include present and all past jobs and hobbies, focusing on chemicals, metals, and gases. Known medical conditions may suggest classes of medications available to the patient. The history, which may be incomplete if the patient is confused or suicidal, should be correlated with the clinical presentation and course. Further history from relatives and friends and findings from the scene as reported by the transporting emergency medical services personnel may be relevant.

Physical Examination

The physical examination should focus on vital signs; the eye, ear, nose, and throat examination; and the neurologic, cardiopulmonary, gastrointestinal, and dermatologic systems. Findings can suggest certain toxins by recognition of toxidromes, which are clusters of signs and symptoms typical of poisoning with adrenergic, cholinomimetic, anticholinergic, opioid, and sedative-hypnotic agents (Table 106–1). Patients may present with some or all of these signs and symptoms; an incomplete clinical picture does not exclude a particular toxidrome but still can assist the clinician in identifying the correct category of toxin involved.

VITAL SIGNS. *Tachycardia* can occur with numerous toxins and with anxiety and other nontoxicologic conditions and is not a helpful finding. The limited differential diagnosis for toxin-induced *bradycardia* includes β-adrenergic receptor antagonists, L-type calcium channel antagonists (diltiazem or verapamil), cardiac glycosides, α-adrenergic receptor agonists (e.g., phenylpropanolamine, whose effects are mediated by baroreceptor reflexes), γ-hydroxybutyric acid, opioids, sedative-hypnotics, central α$_2$-agonists, organophosphates, carbamates, muscarine-containing mushrooms (*Clitocybe, Inocybe* species), therapeutic cholinesterase inhibitors (e.g., physostigmine), cyclic antidepressants (bradycardia is a preterminal sign), and some antiarrhythmic drugs (e.g., procainamide, flecainide, and other class IA and IC drugs) (Chapter 62).

Many toxins cause *hypotension.* The primary pathophysiologic mechanisms are decreased peripheral vascular resistance, decreased myocardial contractility, hypovolemia secondary to vomiting or loss of intravascular volume, and, occasionally, arrhythmias. Common causes of *hypertension* include amphetamines, cocaine, ephedrine and similar agents, ergots, phencyclidine, nicotine, phenylpropanolamine, thyroid hormones, and chronic lead toxicity. Blood pressure can rise early in poisoning with cyclic antidepressants, central α$_2$-adrenergic agonists, and monoamine oxidase inhibitors.

Hyperthermia occurs with toxins that cause agitation or excessive motor activity (e.g., cocaine, phencyclidine, monoamine oxidase inhibitors, strychnine), uncouple oxidative phosphorylation (e.g., salicylates, dinitrophenol), increase metabolic rate (thyroid hormones), impair sweating (e.g., antihistamines, anticholinergics, cocaine, phenothiazines, zonisamide), cause vasoconstriction (e.g., amphetamines, ephedrine), or impair vasodilation and alter perception of heat (cocaine). Other toxin-induced states associated with hyperthermia include malignant hyperthermia, neuroleptic malignant syndrome, serotonin syndrome, metal fume fever, and hydrocarbon aspiration. Toxin-induced *hypothermia* is typically due to sedative-hypnotics; opioids; barbiturates; ethanol; phenothiazines; or hypoglycemic agents such as insulin, sulfonylureas, meglitinides, or unripe Akee fruit. *Pulse oximetry* decreases with true hypoxemia or methemoglobinemia (Chapter 172) but remains normal or may be increased in carbon monoxide poisoning (Chapter 90).

EYES, EARS, NOSE, AND THROAT. Toxin-induced bilateral miosis has a limited differential diagnosis that includes central α$_2$-agonists; olanzapine; opioids; organophosphates/carbamates; phencyclidine; therapeutic cholinesterase inhibitors (e.g., physostigmine); topical miotic ophthalmic drugs (e.g., pilocarpine); and, variably, phencyclidine, phenothiazines, ethanol, and some sedative-hypnotics (Chapter 466). Pontine hemorrhage is the major nontoxicologic diagnosis to consider in a comatose patient with miotic pupils (Chapter 441). Mydriasis is a nonspecific finding. A unilateral dilated pupil may be due to topical ocular application of sympathomimetics (e.g., phenylephrine), antihistamines, or anticholinergic agents (e.g., dust or sap from *Datura* species) and can be caused by a postauricular scopolamine patch. Failure of topical 4% pilocarpine ophthalmic drops to constrict the pupil supports the diagnosis of pupillary dilation owing to a topical mydriatic agent. Visual disturbances, including partial or total blindness as a result of systemic toxicity, have been reported with anticholinergic agents, carbon monoxide, digitalis, ethambutol, methanol, methyl bromide, quinine, and agents that are associated with pseudotumor cerebri, including antimicrobials (e.g., ampicillin,

Table 106–1 • TOXIDROMES AND ASSOCIATED DRUGS AND TOXINS

TOXIDROME	SYNDROME FEATURES		DRUGS/TOXINS
	Vital Signs	**End-Organ**	
Adrenergic	Hypertension, hyperthermia, tachycardia, tachypnea	Agitation, arrhythmias, diaphoresis, mydriasis, seizures	Amphetamines, caffeine, cocaine, ephedrine/pseudoephedrine/ *Ephedra* spp., phenylpropanolamine,* theophylline
Anticholinergic	Hyperthermia, tachycardia	Agitation/delirium, decreased/ absent bowel sounds, dry flushed skin/mucous membranes, mydriasis/ blurred vision, seizures, urinary retention	First-generation H$_1$-receptor antagonists (e.g., classic antihistamines), belladonna alkaloids (e.g., scopolamine, hyoscyamine) from plants (e.g., *Datura* spp.—deadly nightshade, henbane), benztropine, cyclic antidepressants, dicyclomine, muscle relaxants, (e.g., orphenadrine, cyclobenzaprine), trihexyphenidyl
Cholinomimetic	Tachycardia/bradycardia†	Agitation/delirium/coma, bronchorrhea, bronchospasm, diaphoresis, fasciculations, lacrimation, miosis, urination, diarrhea/ vomiting, seizures (uncommon)	Carbamates, cholinesterase inhibitors (e.g., physostigmine, neostigmine, edrophonium), *Inocybe* or *Clitocybe* mushroom spp., nerve gases (e.g., soman, sarin), organophosphates
Opiate/opioid	Bradycardia, bradypnea/apnea, hypotension (rare), hypothermia	CNS depression, hypotonia, miosis, mydriasis (dextromethorphan, meperidine, pentazocine)	Codeine, fentanyl/designer fentanyls, heroin, opioids (e.g., hydrocodone, oxycodone, meperidine, morphine), propoxyphene, central α$_2$-agonists (e.g., clonidine, imidazolines)
Sedative-hypnotic	Bradypnea/apnea, hyporeflexia, hypotension, hypothermia	Ataxia, CNS depression, hyporeflexia, slurred speech, stupor/coma	Barbiturates, benzodiazepines, bromides, chloral hydrate, ethanol, ethchlorvinol, etomidate, glutethimide, meprobamate, methaqualone, methyprylon, propofol, zolpidem

*Reflex bradycardia owing to a pure α-adrenergic agonist effect.
†Tachycarida can occur early owing to a preganglionic nicotinic effect; as toxicity progresses, postganglionic muscarinic effects predominate, and bradycardia develops.
CNS = central nervous system.

metronidazole, nalidixic acid, nitrofurantoin, sulfa drugs, and tetracycline), glucocorticosteroids, lead, lithium, oral contraceptives, phenothiazines, phenytoin, and vitamin A.

Acute hearing loss (Chapter 470) can occur as a toxic effect of aminoglycosides, chloroquine, high-dose loop diuretics, quinine, and salicylates. Nasal septal erosions and perforations may be due to chronic exposure to intranasal cocaine (Chapter 30) or inhalation of fumes from chromium and nickel (Chapters 89 and 90).

NEUROLOGIC SIGNS. Many toxins affect the central nervous system (CNS) and can produce agitated delirium, depression, or seizures (Table 106–2). Distinguishing features of various toxins may assist in making the correct diagnosis. Patients withdrawing from opioids are alert and oriented, whereas patients withdrawing from alcohol, barbiturates, benzodiazepines, and other sedative-hypnotics can be disoriented. Initial CNS depression also can develop with large ingestions of acetaminophen or ibuprofen. Isoniazid and theophylline are noted for producing seizures refractory to usual doses of benzodiazepines and barbiturates. Pyridoxine treats isoniazid-induced seizures by increasing CNS γ-aminobutyric acid; phenytoin is relatively ineffective for theophylline-induced seizures. Plant or mushroom ingestions also can produce CNS depression (e.g., species of *Rhododendron, Solanum* [bittersweet], *Taxus* [yew] *Sophora* [mescal bean]), CNS stimulation (e.g., *Catha edulis* [khat], *Strychnos nux vomica* [contains strychnine], species of *Cicuta* [water hemlock] and *Ephedra* [Mormon tea]), atropine-like effects (e.g., *Atropa belladonna* [deadly nightshade], species of *Datura* [jimson weed]), and cholinomimetic effects (e.g., *Nicotiana* genus [tobacco], *Conium maculatum* [poison hemlock], and *Inocybe* and *Clitocybe* mushrooms). Seizures also can occur with many of these plants and with mushrooms that contain gyromitrins (e.g., *Gyrometra* species) and muscimol (e.g., *Amanita muscaria, Amanita pantherina*).

Distal axonopathy, a primary degeneration of peripheral nervous system axons with secondary degeneration of the myelin sheath, is the predominant type of toxin-induced peripheral neuropathy. Causative agents include acrylamide monomer, allyl chloride, arsenic (inorganic), capsaicin, carbon disulfide, chloramphenicol, cisplatin, colchicine, cyanate, dapsone, ddC, ddI, disulfiram, ethambutol, ethanol, ethylene oxide, gold salts, hexachlorophene, *n*-hexane, hydralazine, isoniazid, lead, mercury, methyl bromide, methyl *n*-butyl ketone, metronidazole, nitrofurantoin, nitrous oxide, some organophosphates, phenol, podophyllotoxin, polychlorinated biphenyls, pyridoxine, tacrolimus, taxoids, thalidomide, thallium, vidarabine, vinca alkaloids, and vinyl chloride. Amiodarone and arsenic can produce a demyelinating neuropathy, whereas pyrodoxine can produce a sensory neuronopathy.

Neuronal transmission can be altered by aminoglycosides; the venoms of *Latrodectus* species (widow spiders), scorpions (only the bark scorpion, *Centruroides exilicauda,* in the United States), and crotaline (e.g., rattlesnakes) and elapid snakes; brevetoxin (shellfish) and ciguatoxin (various fish); neuromuscular blocking drugs; nicotine and related alkaloids; saxitoxin (shellfish); organophosphates and carbamates; tetrodotoxin (pufferfish [fugu], blue-ringed octopus, salamanders, newts, and others); and veratridine (e.g., false hellebore). Cranial nerves can be affected by carbon disulfide, domoic acid (shellfish), elapid venom, ethylene glycol metabolites, bark scorpion, saxitoxin, tetrodotoxin, thallium, and trichloroethylene. Mononeuropathies and vasculitic neuropathies are unlikely to be toxin-induced.

CARDIOPULMONARY EFFECTS. The examination should focus on the blood pressure, heart rate, electrocardiographic abnormalities (e.g., rhythm, conduction, depolarization, and repolarization), and pulmonary findings, including pulse oximetry. Drugs and toxins that commonly cause other arrhythmias or conduction abnormalities include β-adrenergic receptor antagonists, L-type calcium channel antagonists, cardiac glycosides (e.g., digoxin, bufadienolides found in toxic toad venom and illicit "love" potions, and cardenolides found in plants such as oleander and lily of the valley), chloral hydrate, chloroquine, cocaine, cyclic antidepressants, ethanol, halogenated hydrocarbons (e.g., halothane, trichloroethylene), magnesium, potassium, propoxyphene, thioridazine/mesoridazine, and antiarrhythmics and other agents that affect the myocardial voltage-gated sodium channels (e.g., bupivacaine, chloroquine, cocaine, cyclic antidepressants,

Table 106–2 • CENTRAL NERVOUS SYSTEM (CNS) EFFECTS OF TOXINS

TOXIN CATEGORIES/AGENTS	Agitated Delirium	Decreased Level of Consciousness	Seizures
CATEGORIES			
Anticholinergic agents	X	X	X
Adrenergic agonists	X		X
Anticonvulsants		X	X (paradoxical with some agents)
Antipsychotic drugs	X	X	X
β-Adrenergic receptor antagonists		X	X
Hallucinogenic agents	X		X
Monoamine oxidase inhibitors	X	X	X
Opioids	X (propoxyphene, normeperidine, tramadol)	X	X (propoxyphene, normeperidine, tramadol)
Sedative-hypnotics		X	X (rare)
Serotonin agonists	X	X	X
AGENTS			
Amphetamines, cocaine	X	X	X
Antihistamines (first-generation, e.g., diphenhydramine)	X	X	X
Barbiturates		X	
Benzodiazepines		X	
Cyclic antidepressants	X	X	X
Cytochrome oxidase inhibitors (e.g., carbon monoxide, cyanide, hydrogen sulfide, and azides)		X	X
γ-Hydroxybutyrate (GHB) and precursors		X	X (rare)
Lithium	X	X	X
Organophosphates/carbamates (e.g., diazinon, malathion, fenthion/carbaryl)		X	X
Salicylates	X	X	X
Withdrawal from alcohol, barbiturates, benzodiazepines, and other sedative-hypnotics	X	X	X
Withdrawal from opioids			X (reported only in neonates)

flecainide, mexilitine, quinidine, procainamide, propafenone) and potassium channels (e.g., astemizole, cisapride, erythromycin, quinidine, sotalol, terfenadine). Bedside echocardiography may reveal depressed myocardial contractility owing to agents that block the myocardial voltage-gated sodium channel, β-adrenergic receptor antagonists, calcium channel antagonists, cyclic antidepressants, magnesium, arsenic, ciguatoxin, cyanide, ethanol, iron, scorpion venom, and tetrodotoxin.

Toxins can produce myriad pulmonary effects, including parenchymal, pleural, and vascular diseases, and airway irritation and barotrauma. Immediate life-threatening toxic effects include cardiogenic and noncardiogenic pulmonary edema, acute respiratory distress syndrome (ARDS), and rapidly developing pulmonary fibrosis or bronchiolitis obliterans. Typical syndromes and etiologic agents include cardiogenic pulmonary edema (β-adrenergic receptor antagonists, calcium channel antagonists, antiarrhythmics, daunorubicin, and doxorubicin), noncardiogenic pulmonary edema/ARDS (amphetamines, cadmium, chlorine, cocaine, etchlorvynol, methotrexate, opioids/heroin, paraquat, salicylates, and inhalation of smoke, zinc chloride, methyl bromide, and methyl chloride), and rapidly developing pulmonary fibrosis/bronchiolitis obliterans (nitrogen dioxide and paraquat).

GASTROINTESTINAL EFFECTS. Findings of nausea, vomiting, diarrhea, and abdominal pain are nonspecific and must be interpreted in the context of other findings. Agents that produce severe or life-threatening toxicity with early gastrointestinal findings include acid or large alkali ingestions; cardiac glycosides, colchicines, and other microtubular toxins; iron; metals such as arsenic, acute high-level lead, mercury salts, or thallium; mushrooms containing amanitin (*Amanita phalloides, Amanita virosa, Amanita verna, Lepiota chlorophyllum*), gyromitrins (*Gyromitra esculenta*), orellanines (*Cortinarius orellanus*), or allenic norleucine (*Amanita smithiana*); nicotine; organophosphates; and theophylline. Severe abdominal pain and rigidity can occur with envenomation by *Latrodectus* species (widow spiders). Right upper quadrant tenderness develops with toxic hepatitis. Hepatotoxicity can occur as an adverse effect of the therapeutic use of many drugs; in the United States, acetaminophen and ethanol are the most common causes of toxin-induced hepatotoxicity (Chapters 150 and 156). Other notable hepatotoxins include aflatoxins (in foods contaminated with *Aspergillus flavus*), arsenicals, carbon tetrachloride, copper sulfate, cyclopeptide mushrooms (e.g., *Amanita phalloides*), *Ephedra* species (e.g., ma huang), iron, methamphetamine, pennyroyal oil, pyrrolizidine alkaloids (various plant species used in herbal teas), and vitamin A in chronic excessive doses.

DERMATOLOGIC SIGNS. The skin, hair, nails, and mucous membranes should be examined for evidence of intravenous drug use, the presence or absence of skin and mucous membrane moisture, abnormal skin coloration including erythema and cyanosis, alopecia, and nail abnormalities. Bullous skin lesions have been reported with chronic barbiturate use, glutethimide, carbon monoxide, meprobamate, methadone, and valproic acid. Cyanosis may reflect hypoxia or methemoglobinemia. Commonly used agents that can cause methemoglobinemia include aniline dyes, benzocaine and other amide anesthetics, dapsone, naphthalene, nitrates, nitrites, phenazopyridine, rifampin, and sulfonamides (Chapter 172). Skin erythema or flushing occurs with anticholinergic agents, boric acid ingestion, monosodium glutamate, niacin, scombroid toxicity owing to ingestion of inadequately refrigerated fish with high histidine content (e.g., tuna, mahi-mahi, amberjack), vancomycin, and interactions between ethanol and numerous agents that produce disulfiram or disulfiram-like reactions (e.g., carbon disulfide, some cephalosporins, *Coprinus atramentarius* mushroom, disulfiram, griseofulvin, metronidazole, thiuram herbicides, and trichloroethylene).

Specific Toxins

Some common toxins can be suspected based on their characteristic presentations (Table 106–3). These suspicions should guide specific diagnostic and therapeutic strategies that complement general decontamination and supportive treatments.

Diagnostic Tests

Drug testing should be guided by the history and physical examination, with emphasis on tests that can influence management. Rapid qualitative urine drug screening tests are readily available in most hospitals, but their clinical value is limited by the number of drugs that can be tested and the reliability of the tests themselves. A positive test result may be unrelated to the patient's condition because drug analytes may be detectable within hours to more than 30 days after drug use, depending on the drug, dose, and frequency of use. False-positive and false-negative results occur (Table 106–4), and the screening result must be verified with a second method, such as gas chromatography–mass spectrometry. Varying drug use in a population should be considered when determining the drugs to be screened, to decrease the incidence of false-positive results. A test with a 99% specificity for a drug with a prevalence of 0.1% in a population would produce 10 false-positive results for every true-positive result. Clinically irrelevant true-positive findings also occur, such as when poppy seeds produce a positive opiate test. Failure to consider these limitations of drug screens can result in misdiagnosis.

For a limited number of drugs and toxins, levels in blood or urine are useful for diagnosis, therapy, or monitoring (Table 106–5). Threshold levels of certain toxins indicate the need for specific therapies: acetaminophen (*N*-acetylcysteine), ethylene glycol (fomepizole or ethanol and hemodialysis), iron (deferoxamine), methanol (fomepizole or ethanol and hemodialysis), methemoglobin (methylene blue), salicylates (urine alkalinization and hemodialysis), and theophylline (hemoperfusion/hemodialysis). In chronic poisoning with some drugs, such as salicylates or theophylline, these therapies may be indicated at lower drug levels. In general, end-organ toxicity that is evident or anticipated (based on the toxin, amount ingested, and time required to produce toxic effects) is more important than a specific level in determining the need for treatment.

Occult acetaminophen ingestion with toxic serum levels occurs in 0.3 to 1.9% of intentional ingestions. Given that these patients may be asymptomatic until hepatotoxicity develops and that administration of an antidote can prevent this hepatotoxicity, the current recommendation is to test all patients with intentional ingestions.

OTHER BLOOD TESTS. Anion gap metabolic acidosis resulting from a primary lactic acidosis can be caused by cyanide, hydrogen sulfide, iron, isoniazid, metformin, phenformin, sodium azide, and, rarely, acetaminophen with high serum levels. Anion gap metabolic acidoses not related to lactic acidosis occur with diethylene glycol, ethylene glycol, nonsteroidal anti-inflammatory drugs (NSAIDs), methanol, salicylates, and toluene. In poisonings resulting from ethylene glycol, ibuprofen, methanol, and salicylates, lactic acid also can be produced, but the level is insufficient to account for the anion gap.

Elevated serum creatinine and blood urea nitrogen levels indicative of declining renal function may be seen with numerous toxins and drugs. Direct toxicity occurs with acetaminophen, aminoglycosides, cadmium, Chinese weight-loss botanicals (containing *Stephania tetrandra* or *Magnolia officinalis*), chromium, diethylene glycol, diquat, ethylene glycol, fluorinated anesthetics, gold, heroin, lithium (diabetes insipidus), mercury salts, mushrooms (*Amanita smithiana* and *Cortinarius* species), paraquat, radiocontrast agents, solvents (e.g., carbon tetrachloride, trichloroethylene and tetrachloroethylene, toluene), and sulfonamides. Agents that decrease glomerular perfusion by reducing renal blood flow include amphotericin, angiotensin-converting enzyme inhibitors, angiotensin receptor blockers, cocaine, cyclosporine, mannitol (excessive chronic doses), methotrexate, and NSAIDs.

RADIOGRAPHIC STUDIES. A head computed tomographic scan can detect life-threatening cerebral edema owing to toxin-induced hepatic failure, ethylene glycol, and methanol. It also detects intracranial bleeding caused by anticoagulant drugs and rodenticides, scorpion venom, and sympathomimetics (e.g., amphetamines, cocaine, phenylpropanolamine). An abdominal radiograph can reveal radiopaque ferrous sulfate tablets or metals, such as arsenic, lead, mercury, and thallium.

Text continued on p. 635

Table 106–3 • PATHOPHYSIOLOGY, CLINICAL EFFECTS, AND MANAGEMENT OF SPECIFIC DRUGS AND TOXINS

DRUG OR TOXIN	PATHOPHYSIOLOGY	CLINICAL EFFECTS	LABORATORY	SPECIFIC THERAPY
Acetaminophen	*NAPQI (toxic metabolite)* binds hepatic and renal tubular cells; acetaminophen itself induces transient decrease in functional factor VII	*Initial:* nausea/vomiting, coma, lactic acidosis in severe cases *Days 1–3:* elevated INR, aminotransferase, and bilirubin levels; RUQ tenderness; increased creatinine level in severe cases *Days 4–14:* gradual recovery or continued increase in INR and creatinine, lactic acidosis, coma, cerebral edema, death	Potentially toxic level ≥150 µg/mL at 4 hr postingestion* INR may be transiently elevated in first 24 hr due to decrease in functional factor VII; further increases indicate hepatic necrosis; elevated aminotransferase and bilirubin levels not predictive of hepatic failure Creatinine elevated in severe cases	*N-acetylcysteine:* loading dose 140 mL/kg; then 70 mL/kg for 17 maintenance doses†; if hepatic failure, continue until patient recovers and INR is <2.0
Amphetamines	Increase release of presynaptic norepinephrine and dopamine Increase serotonin release (especially MDMA, PMA, DOB, other synthetic amphetamines)	*Mild:* euphoria, decreased appetite, repetitive behaviors *Moderate:* vomiting, agitation, hypertension, tachycardia, mydriasis, bruxism, diaphoresis *Severe:* hypertension/hypotension, arrhythmias, hyperthermia, seizures, coma, hepatotoxicity, rhabdomyolysis, DIC, hyponatremia (SIADH), renal failure, cerebral infarction/hemorrhage	Not helpful, many false-positives and false-negatives on screening tests (see Table 106–4)	IV crystalloids External cooling Benzodiazepines or barbiturates to control agitation/seizures Benzodiazepines or nitroprusside for hypertension Consider cyproheptadine 4–8 mg PO q1–4 h to a maximum of 32 mg/day for serotonin syndrome (disorientation, agitation, delirium, stupor, coma, seizures, hyperthermia, hypertension, tachycardia, diaphoresis, myoclonus, hyperreflexia, and muscle rigidity)
β-Adrenergic receptor antagonists	Block catecholamines from β-adrenergic receptors α-Adrenergic receptor antagonism: carvedilol, labetalol Delayed rectifier potassium channel blockade: sotalol	Bradyarrhythmias; decreased myocardial contractility; hypotension; respiratory depression; decreased consciousness with seizures, coma (liphophilic agents, e.g., propranolol); prolonged QT interval (sotalol)	ECG No specific tests	Glucagon 3.5–5 mg IV over 1 min. If no increase in BP or HR, can repeat up to 10 mg; if effective, immediately start continuous infusion at 1–7 mg/hr If still unstable, options include: (1) regular insulin 1.0 U/kg IV bolus, followed by 1.0 U/kg/hr, plus dextrose to maintain euglycemia; (2) norepinephrine or dobutamine infusion titrated to desirable BP and HR; (3) milrinone 50 µg/kg IV over 10 min, then 0.375–0.75 µg/kg/min Electrical pacing and IABP in refractory cases
L-type calcium channel antagonists	Block L-type voltage-sensitive calcium channels, decreasing calcium entry into myocardial and vascular smooth muscle cells Decrease pancreatic insulin release and increase insulin resistance	Bradyarrhythmias (verapamil and diltiazem) Hypotension Hyperglycemia	ECG No specific tests	10% calcium chloride 10–20 mg/kg (0.1–0.2 mL/kg) IV; can repeat once. If BP improves, continuous infusion 0.2–0.5 mL/kg/hr (20–50 mg/kg/hr). Ionized Ca²⁺ levels should not exceed 2× normal Glucagon, high-dose insulin and dextrose, catecholamines, and milrinone (as for β-adrenergic antagonists)
Cardiac glycosides, including digoxin, bufadienolides (toxic toad venom), or cardenolides (e.g., oleander, lily of the valley, dogbane)	Inhibits Na⁺,K⁺-ATPase Decreased CNS sympathetic output Decreased baroreceptor sensitivity Increased vagal acetylcholine discharge	Bradyarrhythmias including second-degree and third-degree AV block and asystole Ventricular ectopy, tachycardia, and fibrillation Junctional tachycardia, paroxysmal atrial tachycardia with block Weakness, visual disturbances, nausea, vomiting	Serum digoxin level Serum potassium (hyperkalemia occurs in acute poisoning; hypokalemia may be present in chronic poisoning), magnesium, and creatinine levels	Correct hypokalemia and hypomagnesemia; do not give calcium Digoxin-specific antibody fragments (Fab) indicated if patient has hemodynamically significant arrhythmias, serum potassium ≥5.0 mg/L, Mobitz II or third-degree AV block, ingestion of bufadienolide- or cardenolide-containing agents, or renal insufficiency (1) *Empirical* Chronic: 2–5 vials Acute: 10–20 vials

DRUG OR TOXIN	PATHOPHYSIOLOGY	CLINICAL EFFECTS	LABORATORY	SPECIFIC THERAPY
				(2) Calculated Chronic: number of vials = $2 \times$ serum digoxin level (ng/mL) $\times 5.6 \times$ weight (kg)/1000 Acute: number of vials = $2 \times$ oral digoxin dose (mg) $\times 0.8$
Cyclic antidepressants	Myocardial sodium and potassium channel blockade Blockade of α-adrenergic and cholinergic muscarinic receptors Inhibition of norepinephrine reuptake	Decreased level of consciousness (can develop rapidly), myoclonus, seizures, coma Anticholinergic toxidrome (see Table 106–1) Sinus tachycardia, ventricular conduction delays, ventricular arrhythmias, asystole Hypotension	Serum levels not helpful in management	Intermittent IV boluses of NaHCO₃ (1 mEq/kg) to maintain arterial pH at 7.5 because acidemia can worsen cardiovascular complications Intubation and vecuronium may be useful to ameliorate acidemia from muscular hyperactivity while seizures are being treated Contraindicated drugs: types IA and IC antiarrhythmic agents, physostigmine, flumazenil
Ethylene glycol/ methanol (e.g., antifreeze, window cleaners, camping stove fuels)	*Ethylene glycol*—toxic metabolites produce cytotoxicity in CNS, kidneys, lungs, heart, liver, muscles; metabolic acidosis is due to glycolate accumulation; oxalate complexes with calcium, so hypocalcemia can develop *Methanol*—metabolized to formic acid, which is responsible for the metabolic acidosis and inhibition of cytochrome aa_3; target organs include retina, optic nerve, CNS	*Ethylene glycol* CNS depression, cerebral edema, seizures Anion gap metabolic acidosis Renal failure with acute tubular necrosis Pulmonary edema Myositis *Methanol* Nausea, vomiting Cerebral edema, hemorrhage, infarcts Anion gap metabolic acidosis Visual disturbances, papilledema, hyperemic optic disc, nonreactive pupils	Serum ethylene glycol and methanol levels. Levels may be low or undetectable if significant metabolism has occurred *Ethylene glycol*—Serum calcium, creatinine, and BUN levels; examine urine for calcium oxalate crystals	*Both* Fomepizole (which inhibits alcohol dehydrogenase and blocks formation of toxic metabolites): 15 mg/kg IV loading dose, then 10 mg/kg IV for 4 doses, then 15 mg/kg for subsequent doses; dosing is q12 h (q4 h during hemodialysis with dosing adjustments at start and finish); continue until ethylene glycol or methanol is no longer detectable Hemodialysis: Initiate if level ≥50 mg/dL or metabolic acidosis with end-organ toxicity; continue until acidosis resolves and serum level of ethylene glycol or methanol is undetectable Monitor for cerebral edema with possible herniation *Ethylene glycol* IV calcium for symptomatic hypocalcemia *Methanol* Folinic acid 50 mg IV q4 h until methanol not detectable and acidosis cleared
γ-Hydroxybutyrate (GHB) and its precursors (γ butyrolactone and 1,4-butanediol) (1,4-BD)	Agonist effect on CNS GHB receptors; indirect action with opioid receptors (may increase proenkephalins); metabolized to GABA, interacts with GABA_B receptors Decreases dopamine release	CNS: rapid loss of consciousness, with recovery typical within 2–4 hr; myoclonus (possible seizures) Respiratory depression Bradycardia Nausea, vomiting	No specific tests	Supportive care, including respiratory support as needed
Lithium	Decreases brain inositol Alters CNS serotonin, dopamine, and norepinephrine Inhibits adenylate cyclases, including those that mediate vasopressin-induced renal concentration and thyroid function	*Chronic toxicity* usually more severe than acute toxicity: Tremor, hyperreflexia, drowsiness, incoordination, clonus, confusion, ataxia, and, in severe cases, seizures, coma, death; recovery may take weeks, and persistent defects may occur Sinus node dysfunction, QT prolongation, T wave abnormalities, U waves Nephrogenic diabetes insipidus, hypothyroidism and hyperthyroidism, hypercalcemia, pseudotumor cerebri *Acute toxicity*: nausea, vomiting, diarrhea, and milder neurologic findings	Peak serum levels: *Normal dose* 2–3 hr; up to 5 hr for sustained-release lithium *Acute overdose* Peak may be delayed ≥ 4–12 hr	Replete intravascular volume, maintain urinary output at 1–2 mL/kg/hr Consider GI decontamination with oral polyethylene glycol electrolyte solution within 1–2 hr after acute overdose Hemodialysis† in patients with altered mental status, ataxia, seizures, or coma or in patients with mild symptoms in the setting of acute overdose or renal insufficiency Ineffective or contraindicated therapies include oral activated charcoal, diuretics, and aminophylline

Continued

Critical Care Medicine

Table 106–3 • PATHOPHYSIOLOGY, CLINICAL EFFECTS, AND MANAGEMENT OF SPECIFIC DRUGS AND TOXINS—cont'd

DRUG OR TOXIN	PATHOPHYSIOLOGY	CLINICAL EFFECTS	LABORATORY	SPECIFIC THERAPY
Opioids (e.g., heroin, morphine, fentanyl)	Agonist effect at CNS μ, κ, and δ opioid receptors; result is cell hyperpolarization and decreased neurotransmitter release	CNS depression Respiratory depression Miosis (see Table 106–1) Dextromethorphan increases CNS serotonin and inhibits NMDA receptors, causing hallucinations Propoxyphene and its metabolite norpropoxyphene block sodium channels and can cause seizures and wide-complex arrhythmias similar to cyclic antidepressants; NaHCO₃ treats arrhythmias Seizure risk with tramadol, meperidine, propoxyphene	Rapid urine drug screens detect morphine and codeine but may not detect semisynthetic and synthetic opioids; some interferents/ irrelevants (see Table 106–4)	*Naloxone* 0.4–2.0 mg IV; can repeat up to 10 mg if no response Continuous infusion for recurrent symptoms or sustained-release opioid ingestions; give 50% of the dose that produces desired effect 15 min after initial effect is obtained, then infuse two thirds of this dose every hour; infusion rate can be increased or decreased to maintain normal respiration and avoid withdrawal symptoms *Contraindicated therapies* Nalmefene and naltrexone should not be used for acute opioid reversal
Organophosphates and carbamates (e.g., diazinon, mevinphos, fenthion, aldicarb)	Inhibit acetylcholinesterase, resulting in excessive acetylcholine stimulation of nicotinic and muscarinic receptors in the autonomic and somatic motor nervous systems and CNS	*Nicotinic-mediated effects:* tachycardia, mydriasis, hypertension, delirium, coma, seizures, muscle weakness, fasciculations *Muscarinic-mediated effects:* salivation, lacrimation, urination, vomiting, defecation, miosis, bronchorrhea, bronchospasm, bradycardia	Serum (butyrylcholinesterase) or RBC (acetylcholinesterase) activity <50% of normal (see Table 106–6) Clinical recovery occurs before serum cholinesterase levels normalize	*Atropine* 1–2 mg IV every 5 min; can increase to 5 mg every 2 min until drying of bronchial secretions and adequate oxygenation; continuous infusion 0.02–0.08 mg/kg/hr if needed *Pralidoxime* 1–2 g IV bolus over 30–60 min, then 500 mg/hr continuous infusion; administer soon after poisoning, before irreversible binding; wean after 24–48 h if patient improved
Salicylates	Inhibit cyclooxygenase; decrease formation of prostaglandins and thromboxane A₂ Stimulate CNS medullary respiratory receptor and chemoreceptor trigger zone Impair platelet function Disrupt carbohydrate metabolism Uncouple oxidative phosphorylation Increase vascular permeability	*Acute toxicity* *Mild:* nausea, vomiting, diaphoresis, tinnitus, decreased hearing, hyperpnea, tachypnea *Moderate/severe:* confusion, delirium, coma, seizures, hyperthermia, noncardiogenic pulmonary edema; death can occur within hours of an overdose *Chronic toxicity* Same as acute but may not have diaphoresis or vomiting Consider diagnosis in patients with new-onset confusion, anion gap metabolic acidosis, or noncardiogenic pulmonary edema	Serum salicylate level: toxic ≥30 mg/dL; level ≥100 md/dL indicates life-threatening toxicity with possible sudden, rapid clinical deterioration; in chronic toxicity, levels may be minimally elevated (>30 mg/dL), and clinical evaluation is more reliable for gauging the degree of toxicity Arterial blood gases: respiratory alkalosis with metabolic acidosis Anion gap metabolic acidosis Prolonged PT and PTT, ketonuria, ketonemia	Multidose activated charcoal q2–3 h in acute overdose with progressive symptoms or rising salicylate level Urinary alkalinization to increase renal elimination if level >40 mg/dL (except if noncardiogenic pulmonary edema, cerebral edema, or renal failure) NaHCO₃ 1–2 mEq/kg IV bolus, followed by infusion of 132–150 mEq in 850 mL of 5% D₅W at 1.5–2.0 × maintenance rate (see Table 106–6); adjust rate to maintain urine pH >7.5 while avoiding plasma pH >7.55 Replace potassium Avoid respiratory depression; hypercarbia can worsen acidemia Frequent monitoring of clinical status and salicylate levels is essential to gauge the progression of toxicity and need for hemodialysis Hemodialysis if level ≥100 mg/dL regardless of clinical condition, or if severe end-organ toxicity (e.g., CNS dysfunction, seizures, noncardiogenic pulmonary edema, renal failure, severe and ongoing acid-base disorder)

*Rumack BH, Matthew H: Acetaminophen poisoning and toxicity. Pediatrics 1975; 55:871–876. Provides a nomogram to evaluate potential toxicity of levels drawn more than 4 hours postingestion. The nomogram is valid only for levels drawn after a single acute ingestion.

†N-acetylcysteine can be discontinued in patients with uncomplicated disease after a loading dose plus six maintenance doses if hepatic aminotransferase levels and the INR are normal; otherwise, the full regimen should be administered.

‡Continue hemodialysis until the serum lithium level is <1 mEq/L. Recheck the level 8 hours after dialysis, and restart hemodialysis if the level is >1 mEq/L. Repeat this cycle until the serum lithium level remains <1 mEq/L.

AV = atrioventricular; BP = blood pressure; BUN = blood urea nitrogen; CNS = central nervous system; DIC = disseminated intravascular coagulation; DOB = 4-bromo-2, 5-dimethoxyamphetamine; ECG = electrocardiogram; GABA = γ-aminobutyric acid; GI = gastrointestinal; HR = heart rate; IABP = intra-aortic balloon counterpulsation; INR = international normalized ratio; MDMA = 3,4-methylenedioxymethamphetamine; Na⁺,K⁺-ATPase = sodium, potassium adenosine triphosphatase; NAPQI = N-acetyl-p-benzoquinoneimine; NMDA = N-methyl-D-aspartate; PMA = para-methoxyamphetamine; RBBB = right bundle-branch block; REM = rapid eye movement; RUQ = right upper quadrant (abdomen); SIADH = syndrome of inappropriate antidiuretic secretion.

Table 106–4 • QUALITATIVE URINE DRUG SCREENS: CAUSES OF ERRONEOUS RESULTS

DRUG/TOXIN	INTERFERENTS/IRRELEVANTS*	COMMENTS
Amphetamines	Chlorpromazine, ephedrine/pseudoephedrine, desoxyephedrine, *Ephedra* spp., mexilitine, phenylephrine, phenylpropanolamine, selegiline	Vicks nasal inhaler (desoxyephedrine) and selegiline also cause positive GC-MS; chiral confirmation is required. Interferents in older assays include labetalol and ranitidine
Benzodiazepines	Oxaprozin—false-negative result	Poor detection of parent drugs with absent or low concentration of oxazepam metabolite, e.g., alprazolam, lorazepam, triazolam
Cocaine	Coca leaf teas	Most reliable urine screen
Opiates/opioids	Poppy seeds; ofloxacin; rifampin	Does not detect semisynthetic or designer opioids (e.g., fentanyls, meperidine, methadone, propoxyphene)
Phencyclidine	Dextromethorphan, diphenhydramine, ketamine; thioridazine	
Tetrahydrocannabinol	Dronabinol, hemp consumables	Positive result is seldom clinically relevant
Tricyclic antidepressants	Cyclobenzaprine, diphenhydramine, phenothiazines	

*Irrelevants are agents causing true positive but clinically irrelevant results. GC-MS = gas chromatography–mass spectrometry; LDH = lactate dehydrogenase.

Table 106–5 • CLINICALLY IMPORTANT QUANTITATIVE DRUG LEVELS

DRUG OR TOXIN	LEVELS	
	Therapeutic	Toxic
SOURCE: BLOOD/SERUM		
Acetaminophen	10–30 µg/mL	≥150 µg/mL at 4 hr postingestion*
Carbamazepine	4–12 µg/mL	>15 µg/mL
Carboxyhemoglobin	Nonsmoker: 0.5–1.5% Smoker: 4–9%	>20%†
Cholinesterase†		
Serum (butyrylcholinesterase)	3100–6500 U/L	<50% of normal value
RBC (acetylcholinesterase)	26.7–49.2 U/g of hemoglobin	<50% of normal value
Digoxin (≥12 hr postdose for long-term therapy)	0.8–2.0 ng/mL	>2.0 ng/mL§
Ethanol	None measured	>80–100 mg/dL
Ethylene glycol	None measured	>25 mg/dL
Iron	50–175 µg/dL	>350 µg/dL
Lead	<10 µg/dL	>25 µg/dL
Lithium	0.6–1.2 mEq/L	>1.2 mEq/L‖
Methanol	None measured	>25 mg/dL
Methemoglobin	1–2% hemoglobin	>15% hemoglobin
Phenobarbital	15–40 µg/mL	>40 µg/mL
Phenytoin	10–20 µg/mL	>20 µg/mL
Salicylates	≤30 mg/dL	>30 mg/dL
Theophylline	8–20 µg/mL	>20 µg/mL
Valproic acid	50–100 µg/mL	>100 µg/mL
SOURCE: URINE		
Arsenic	<50 µg/24 hr urine‖	>100 µg/24 hr urine‖
Mercury	<20 µg/L	>20 µg/L
Thallium	<5 µg/L	>200 µg/L‖

*Levels drawn more than 4 hours after ingestion should be plotted on the nomogram provided in Rumack and Matthew (Rumack BH, Matthew H: Acetaminophen poisoning and toxicity. Pediatrics 1975;55:871–876) to assess the potential for toxicity.

†Lower levels may be toxic in pregnant patients and in patients exposed to carbon monoxide for a prolonged time.

‡Consult reference laboratory for normal values; results are assay-dependent. Therapeutic values listed are from Mayo Medical Laboratories, 2002.

§Some patients may require levels above the therapeutic range to control symptoms.

‖Lower values may indicate toxicity if appropriate clinical findings are present.

 Treatment

Figure 106–1 is an algorithm for management of acute poisoning.

INITIAL STABILIZATION

INTUBATION AND RESPIRATORY SUPPORT. Appropriate airway management should be instituted to correct hypoxemia and respiratory acidosis and to protect against pulmonary aspiration; intubation should be considered if the patient has depressed consciousness and a decreased gag reflex. Rapid-sequence intubation facilitates airway management. Anatomic difficulties should be anticipated in patients with caustic ingestions (hypopharyngeal burns that may perforate), angioedema caused by angiotensin-converting enzyme inhibitor therapy or envenomation by canebrake rattlesnakes (*Crotalus horridus atricaudatus*), and swelling secondary to direct tissue injury (e.g., huffing freon, snake bite to tongue) or secondary to anaphylactoid and anaphylactic reactions. Endotracheal intubation via flexible fiberoptic nasopharyngoscopy may be indicated in these cases. Hypoxemia can occur with any toxin that produces CNS depression, such as antidepressants, barbiturates, sedative-hypnotics, and central α₂-adrenergic receptor agonists (clonidine), or agents causing peripheral neuromuscular impairment, such as nicotine;

organophosphates; strychnine; tetrodotoxin (puffer fish, blue-ringed octopus); botulinum; or envenomation from elapids (coral snake), Mojave rattlesnake, or certain coelenterates (box jellyfish, Portuguese man-of-war).

Respiratory acidosis can worsen rapidly the toxicities of cyclic antidepressants and salicylates; sedation of these patients should be accompanied immediately by airway support. Intoxicated patients may have increased risk of pulmonary aspiration owing to concomitant CNS depression, attenuated airway reflexes, full stomachs, and delayed gastric emptying.

Succinylcholine can cause prolonged paralysis in patients with organophosphate poisoning and can exacerbate hyperkalemia from cardiac glycosides, hydrofluoric acid, or rhabdomyolysis. Rhabdomyolysis has been reported with adrenergic agents; doxylamine; phencyclidine; heroin; *Tricholoma equestre* spp. mushrooms; and envenomations from crotaline snakes, scorpions, or widow spiders (*Lactrodectus* species); short-acting nondepolarizing agents, such as vecuronium and rocuronium, are preferable in these cases.

CARDIAC RHYTHM AND RATE. Standard emergency cardiovascular care algorithms (Chapters 59 and 60) must be modified for effects caused by specific poisons. Atropine often does not reverse bradycardia secondary to β-adrenergic receptor antagonists, L-type calcium channel

Continued on page 637

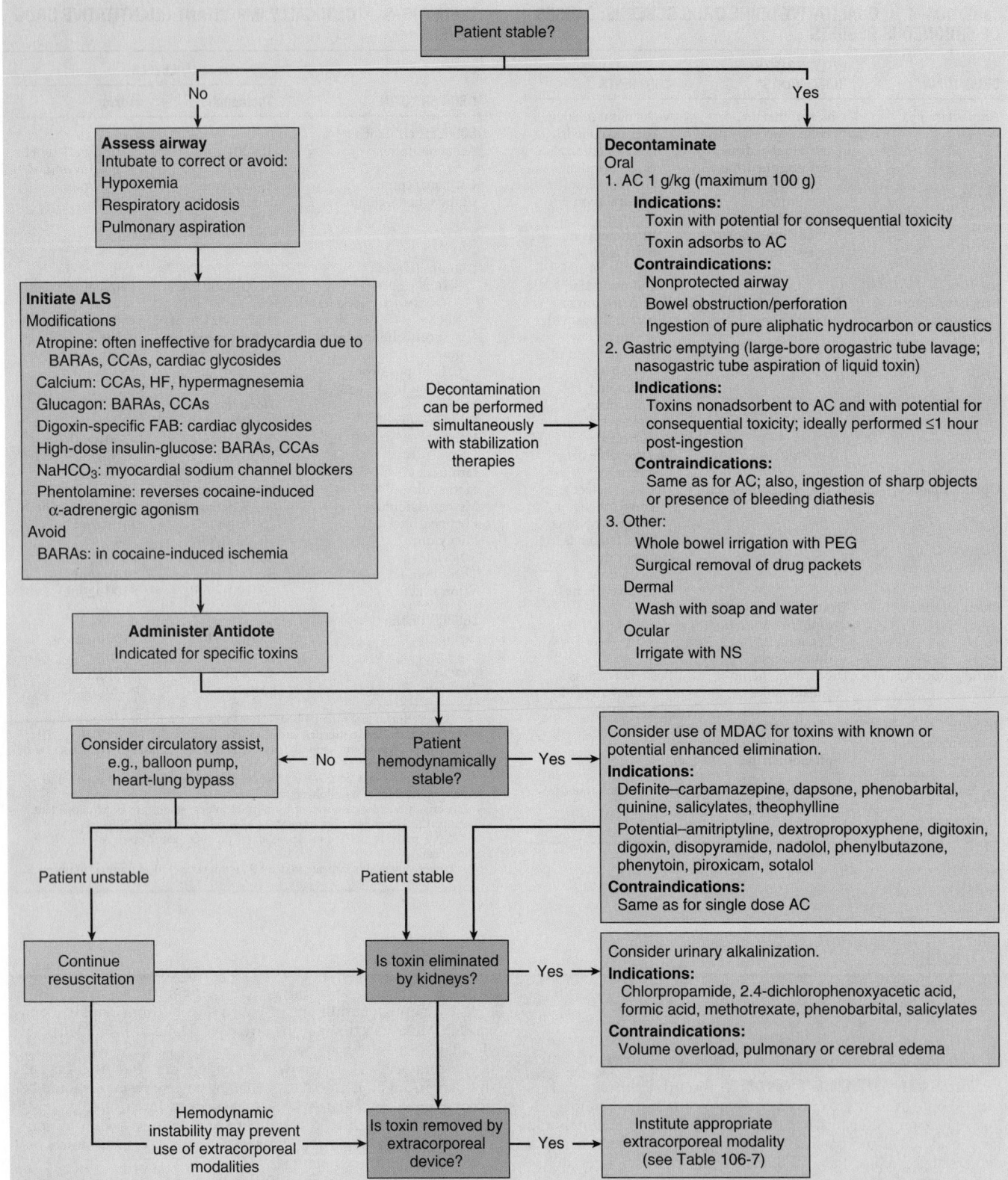

FIGURE 106–1 • Algorithm for the management of acute poisoning. AC = activated charcoal; BARAs = beta-adrenergic receptor antagonists; CCAs = L-type calcum channel antagonists; HF = hydrofluoric acid; MDAC = multidose activated charcoal; NS = 0.9% saline solution; PEG = nonabsorbable polyethylene glycol solution.

antagonists, or cardiac glycosides. In these cases, more specific therapies with intravenous calcium (calcium channel antagonists), high doses of glucagon (β-adrenergic receptor antagonists, calcium channel antagonists), or digoxin-specific Fab antibody (cardiac glycosides) are indicated. High-dose insulin-glucose therapy successfully can reverse myocardial depression and conduction abnormalities in humans poisoned with β-adrenergic receptor antagonists and calcium channel antagonists. Intravenous sodium bicarbonate may reverse cardiac conduction delays caused by antiarrhythmic drugs with sodium channel blockade recovery rates of greater than 1 second (Vaughn-Williams classification IA and IC), cocaine, cyclic antidepressants, diphenhydramine, propoxyphene, and quinine. β-Adrenergic receptor antagonists are contraindicated in patients with cocaine-induced myocardial syndromes, but phentolamine can reverse the agonistic effects of cocaine on α-adrenergic receptors. Calcium also may be life-saving in systemic hydrofluoric acid poisoning and severe hypermagnesemia, and it is indicated for symptomatic hypocalcemia caused by ethylene glycol toxicity. In patients with toxin-induced circulatory collapse refractory to therapy, circulatory assist devices may support the patient until sufficient toxin is eliminated.

DECONTAMINATION

Single-dose activated charcoal without prior gastric emptying is the preferred method for ingestions of substances that have the potential to cause moderate to life-threatening toxicity and that are known to adsorb to activated charcoal. The absence of clinical signs and symptoms does not preclude administering activated charcoal because drug absorption and toxicity can be delayed. Activated charcoal also can be administered when the ingested toxin cannot be identified but significant toxicity is a concern. Activated charcoal consists of pyrolysis products that have been specially cleaned to produce an internal pore structure to which substances can reversibly adsorb, preventing their absorption by the gastrointestinal tract. Activated charcoal can be administered with antiemetic drugs or given through a nasogastric tube, when necessary. The oral dose is 1 g per kilogram body weight, with a maximum single dose of 100 g. Efficacy in preventing toxin absorption declines with time, and activated charcoal should be given as soon as possible after ingestion: 50 g or more of activated charcoal administered within 30 minutes of ingestion reduces drug absorption by nearly 90%, whereas administration at 60 minutes diminishes absorption by only about 37%. Activated charcoal should not be used in patients with CNS depression until the airway is secure to prevent aspiration. Activated charcoal is contraindicated in patients with a perforated bowel, functional/mechanical bowel obstruction, ingestion of a pure aliphatic hydrocarbon such as gasoline or kerosene (no benefit and increased risk of aspiration), and ingestions of caustic acid and alkali (no benefit and obscures endoscopy). Certain agents, such as lithium, iron, metals, and ethanol, do not adsorb significantly to activated charcoal but also do not preclude its use if the patient has concomitantly ingested toxins that do adsorb to activated charcoal. Pulmonary aspiration and bowel obstruction from inspissated activated charcoal are the most common complications; both occur more frequently when multidose activated charcoal is administered but can be avoided by withholding treatment in patients who have suboptimal bowel function or decreased fecal elimination.

Two methods for gastric emptying, syrup of ipecac and orogastric lavage via a large-bore tube, no longer are routinely used. In most patients, these methods provide little benefit but potentially increase the risk of aspiration. One prospective study of gastric emptying showed clinical benefit in a few overdose patients who presented obtunded and who underwent lavage within 1 hour of ingestion, but other studies have shown no benefit of gastric emptying, either by lavage or by syrup of ipecac, compared with the use of activated charcoal alone. Gastric emptying via lavage or rarely by syrup of ipecac may be of benefit and should be performed in patients who have ingested toxins that do not adsorb to activated charcoal, that are known to produce significant morbidity, or for which aggressive decontamination may offer the best chance for survival (e.g., colchicine, sodium azide, sodium fluoroacetate). Removal of a liquid toxin, such as ethylene glycol, may be accomplished by aspiration of gastric contents via a nasogastric tube. Contraindications to gastric

emptying include those for activated charcoal, a bleeding diathesis, and the ingestion of sharp objects. Placement of an endotracheal tube before gastric lavage may be necessary to protect the airway in patients who have a decreased level of consciousness and impaired gag reflex; major complications of gastric emptying include pulmonary aspiration, esophageal tears and perforations, and laryngospasm (with lavage).

Whole bowel irrigation with a nonabsorbable polyethylene glycol solution has been recommended for sustained-release medications, for agents not adsorbed to activated charcoal, and for body packers (smugglers who swallow packets of illicit drugs). The most common complication is vomiting. An initial dose of 500 mL/hour given orally or via nasogastric tube, with titration to 2000 mL/hour as tolerated, is recommended; treatment continues until rectal content clears. Rarely, surgery may be necessary to remove packets in smugglers who develop symptoms of drug toxicity; endoscopic removal of these packets should never be attempted owing to the risk of packet rupture.

ANTIDOTES

Few toxins have specific therapies (Table 106–6). Although antidotes may be essential in treating certain toxins, their use does not preclude the need for ongoing supportive care and, in some cases, extracorporeal elimination.

ENHANCED ELIMINATION

Three methods are used to accelerate elimination of toxins or drugs from the body: (1) multiple doses of oral activated charcoal, (2) urinary alkalinization, and (3) extracorporeal removal. A fourth method using the oral ion exchange resins sodium polystyrene sulfonate and cholestyramine experimentally has enhanced the elimination of lithium, digoxin, digitoxin, and organochlorines but has limited clinical usefulness.

The rationale for administering multiple doses of oral activated charcoal includes the adsorption of any toxic agent remaining in the gastrointestinal tract (e.g., sustained-release drugs, drugs that retard their absorption); interfering with enterohepatic and enteroenteric recirculation of toxins; and enhancing the elimination of drugs with a long half-life, a volume of distribution less than 1.0 L/kg body weight, and low protein binding. The existing evidence shows enhanced elimination of carbamazepine, dapsone, phenobarbital, quinine, salicylates, and theophylline, but multiple doses of activated charcoal also may be effective for amitriptyline, dextropropoxyphene, digitoxin, digoxin, disopyramide, nadolol, phenylbutazone, phenytoin, piroxicam, and sotalol. Whether enhanced elimination translates into decreased morbidity and mortality has not been examined in controlled clinical trials. Usual recommendations are an average dose of 12.5 g of activated charcoal (after the initial dose), administered every 1, 2, or 4 to 6 hours after the previous dose. The contraindications for single-dose activated charcoal also apply to multidose activated charcoal. Reported complications include pulmonary aspiration, bowel obstruction, and fluid and electrolyte imbalances from multiple doses of a simultaneously administered cathartic.

Alkalinization of the urine increases the renal elimination of weak acids, such as chlorpropamide, 2,4-dichlorophenoxyacetic acid, formic acid, methotrexate, phenobarbital, and salicylates. In alkaline urine, weak acids exist predominantly in the ionized state. Nonionized acids in the peritubular fluid seek equilibrium by diffusing into the tubule (Fick's principle). The constant flow of urine through the tubule prevents equilibrium from occurring, promoting further diffusion of the weak acid from the peritubular fluid into the tubular lumen, increasing renal elimination. Urinary alkalinization is accomplished by an intravenous bolus of 1 to 2 mEq of sodium bicarbonate per kilogram body weight, followed by three ampules (150 mL) of sodium bicarbonate (44 mEq/50 mL) in 850 mL of 5% dextrose in water, infused at two to three times the normal maintenance fluid rate. Urinary pH should be checked hourly, and the infusion should be adjusted to maintain a pH of 7.5 to 8.0. Potassium should be administered simultaneously to avoid hypokalemia, which would result in urinary acidification as the distal tubule excretes hydrogen ion in exchange for potassium (Chapter 113). Serum pH should be monitored to avoid excessive alkalemia.

Continued on page 640

Table 106–6 • ANTIDOTES AND INDICATIONS FOR USE

ANTIDOTE	INDICATION FOR USE	COMMENTS
Antivenom (equine)		
Crotalid (Crotalidae polyvalent antivenin)	Crotalines: Rattlesnakes (*Crotalus* spp and *Sistrurus* spp), cottonmouth (*Agkistrodon* spp), copperhead (*Agkistrodon* spp)	Dosing based on severity of envenomation. Treatment end points: resolving coagulopathies and systemic effects, stabilization of tissue swelling. Adverse effects: urticaria, bronchospasm, hypotension, serum sickness (delayed)
Elapid	Eastern (*Micrurus fulvius fulvius*) and Texas (*Micrurus fulvius tenere*) coral snakes	Decision to administer in asymptomatic patient based on bite history. Same adverse effects as Crotalidae polyvalent antivenin
Antivenom (Fab)*	Crotalines	Better safety profile than equine-derived antivenom; same treatment end points. Earlier administration may minimize soft tissue injury. Repetitive dosing indicated for recurrent symptoms, coagulopathy
Antivenom, latrodectus (equine)	Black widow spider (*Latrodectus* spp)	Indications include severe pain unresponsive to opioids and severe hypertension
Antivenom, scorpion (goat)	Scorpions (*Centruroides* spp)	Available only in Arizona
Atropine	Carbamates Nerve agents Organophosphates	Cessation of excessive oral and pulmonary secretions is best indication of atropinization
Calcium	Calcium channel antagonists Hydrofluoric acid Hyperkalemia (except cardiac glycosides) Hypermagnesemia Hypocalcemia, e.g., ethylene glycol	*Calcium channel antagonists:* May be ineffective in severe toxicity *Hydrofluoric acid:* Can give intra-arterially or IV with a Bier block for extremity exposure *Cardiac glycosides:* May precipitate ventricular arrhythmias *Ethylene glycol:* Correct symptomatic hypocalcemia; avoid excessive administration that may increase production of calcium oxalate crystals
Calcium disodium edetate	Lead	Need for antidotal therapy depends on blood lead levels and clinical symptoms; hydrate patient before starting therapy
Cyanide antidote kit: Amyl nitrite Sodium nitrite Sodium thiosulfate	Cyanide	Coordinate amyl nitrite with continued oxygenation and give only until sodium nitrite infusion is begun; nitrites may produce hypotension and excess methemoglobinemia; sodium nitrite dose must be adjusted if patient has hemoglobin <12 g/dL
Deferoxamine	Iron	Indications: Symptomatic patients with lethargy, severe abdominal pain, hypovolemia, acidosis, shock; any symptomatic patient with peak serum iron level >350 µg/dL; prolonged therapy can cause pulmonary toxicity. Continue therapy until patient stable. Initial therapy of 15 mg/kg/h IV should not exceed 24 hr. If further deferoxamine required, 12-hr drug-free intervals should be alternated with 12-hr infusions of deferoxamine.
Digoxin-specific antibody fragments (Fab)	Digoxin Digitalis Other cardiac glycosides, e.g. bufodienalides (*Bufo* toads), oleander	Monitor ECG and potassium levels
Dimercaprol (BAL)	Arsenic Lead Mercury	Adverse effects: painful injections, fever, diaphoresis, agitation, headache, salivation, nausea/vomiting, hemolysis in G-6-PD–deficient patients, essential metal chelation
Ethanol	Diethylene glycol Ethylene glycol Methanol Experimental: sodium monofluoroacetate	Start immediately if toxic alcohol suspected without waiting for confirmatory levels; adjust infusion dose during hemodialysis
Flumazenil	Benzodiazepines Venlafaxine	Limit use to reversal of inadequate respiration in benzodiazepine-toxic patients; increases intracranial pressure and risk of seizures in presence of underlying seizure disorder or ingestion of seizure-producing toxins
Folic acid/tetrahydrofolic acid (leucovorin)	Methanol Methotrexate	Essential treatment for both toxins
Fomepizole	Ethylene glycol Methanol	Start immediately if toxic alcohol suspected without waiting for confirmatory levels; adjust dosing frequency during hemodialysis
Glucagon	β-adrenergic receptor antagonists Calcium channel antagonists	Can precipitate vomiting; be prepared to protect airway
Insulin-glucose	Calcium channel antagonists β-adrenergic receptor antagonists	Beneficial in case series; hypoglycemia can develop during recovery
Hyberbaric oxygen	Carbon monoxide Experimental: carbon tetrachloride, cyanide, hydrogen sulfide	Indicated in presence of coma, neurologic symptoms/signs, chest pain, arrhythmias, hypotension, pregnancy, or acidosis, regardless of carboxyhemoglobin level
Methylene blue	Methemoglobin-producing agents	Use if patient is symptomatic (i.e., dyspneic, altered mental status). Initial dose of 1–2 mg/kg body weight (0.1–0.2 mL/kg) of 1% methylene blue is administered over 5 min; repeat doses can be given for recurrent

Table 106–6 • ANTIDOTES AND INDICATIONS FOR USE—cont'd

ANTIDOTE	INDICATION FOR USE	COMMENTS
		symptoms or signs. Maximum dose should not exceed 7 mg/kg (0.7 mL/kg) Can cause hemolysis in G6-PD–deficient patients
N-acetylcysteine	Acetaminophen Experimental: carbon tetrachloride, chloroform, pennyroyal oil	Most effective if initiated within 8 hr after ingestion; may be started at any time after ingestion and is beneficial in severe hepatotoxic states
Naloxone, nalmefene, naltrexone	Opioids	Some opioids (e.g., propoxyphene, pentazocine, fentanyls) may require larger doses of naloxone; use continuous infusion for prolonged/recurrent symptoms
Octreotide	Sulfonylureas	Maintain dextrose infusion as needed
Physostigmine	Anticholinergic agents, e.g., diphenhydramine, jimsonweed (Datura spp), scopolamine	Adverse effects include seizures and bradyarrhythmias; contraindicated in cyclic antidepressant toxicity
Pralidoxime	Organophosphates Nerve agents—Sarin, VX	Can give initial dose over 2 min for life-threatening signs
Pyridoxine	Ethylene glycol (theoretical efficacy) Isoniazid Monomethylhydrazine mushrooms	Pyridoxine may stop seizures, but patient can remain comatose (isoniazid, mushrooms); benzodiazepines and phenobarbital also can be used to manage seizures
Sodium bicarbonate	Myocardial sodium channel blockers, e.g., cyclic antidepressants, cocaine, propoxyphene, sodium channel–blocking antiarrhythmics with $\tau_{recovery} > 1$ sec, piperidine phenothiazines (thioridazine, mesoridazine)	Bolus therapy (see text); monitor blood pH (optimal pH approximately 7.50); avoid pH > 7.55
	Altered tissue distribution/enhanced elimination: chlorophenoxy herbicides, chlorpropamide, formic acid, methotrexate, phenobarbital, salicylates	Bolus plus constant infusion (see text); maintain urine pH 7.5–8.0 (avoid blood pH >7.55); monitor ABGs
Succimer (DMSA)	Arsenic Lead Mercury	Oral chelator; adverse effects include rash, transient AST and alkaline phosphatase elevations, and gastrointestinal distress; minimal essential metal chelation
Vitamin K	Anticoagulants, e.g., warfarin, long-acting anticoagulant rodenticides	Anaphylactoid reaction can occur with IV administration

ABG = arterial blood gas; AST = aspartate aminotransferase; BAL = British antilewisite; DMSA = 2,3-dimercaptosuccinic acid; G6-PD = glucose 6-phosphate dehydrogenase; $\tau_{recovery}$ = drug blockade recovery rate.

Table 106–7 • COMMON TOXICANTS REMOVED BY HEMODIALYSIS/HEMOPERFUSION

TOXICANT	INDICATIONS	TECHNIQUE	COMMENTS
Ethylene glycol	Serum level ≥50 mL/dL, or lower levels with concomitant metabolic acidosis and evidence of end-organ toxicity	HD	May not be required in patient with normal creatinine clearance and acid-base status who is receiving fomepizole
Lithium*	Clinical indications	HD	Clinical indication is CNS toxicity (e.g., decreased mental status, ataxia, coma, seizures)
Methanol	Serum level ≥50 mL/dL, or lower levels with concomitant metabolic acidosis and evidence of end-organ toxicity	HD	Usually required owing to slow elimination half-life in presence of fomepizole or ethanol (30.3 to 54.4 hr), even in patients with no metabolic acidosis or evidence of end-organ toxicity
Phenobarbital	Clinical indications	HP/HD	Rarely necessary except when the patient is hemodynamically unstable despite aggressive support; clearance rates are better with HD than HP
Salicylates	Acute toxicity: serum level ≥100 mL/dL or <100 mg/dL in the presence of a clinical indication Chronic toxicity: any clinical indication	HD	Serum protein binding decreases with increasing toxic levels, increasing amount of free salicylate available for HD removal; clinical indications are one or more of the following: altered mental status, seizures, pulmonary edema, intractable acidosis, renal failure
Theophylline	Acute toxicity: serum level ≥90 µg/mL or <90 µg/mL plus any clinical indication Chronic toxicity: serum level ≥40 µg/dL and not declining despite MDAC; any clinical indication	HP/HD	Clinical indications: seizures, hypotension, ventricular arrhythmias; clearance rates better with HD than HP

*Hemodiafiltration removes lithium; clinical benefit with this technique is unknown. CNS = central nervous system; HD = hemodialysis; HP = hemoperfusion; MDAC = multidose activated charcoal.

Contraindications to this therapy include volume overload and cerebral or pulmonary edema. Urinary acidification no longer is recommended to enhance the elimination of weak bases, such as amphetamines, owing to the danger of precipitating tubular myoglobin in patients with rhabdomyolysis.

Extracorporeal techniques enhance elimination of a few drugs and toxins that exhibit single-compartment kinetics, a volume of distribution less than 1 L/kg, and an endogenous clearance of less than 4 mL/minute/kg (Table 106–7). For hemodialysis, the toxin must be water soluble, have a molecular weight less than 500 D, and exhibit low protein binding. For hemoperfusion, the toxin must adsorb to activated charcoal. For hemofiltration, the toxin must have a molecular weight less than 10,000 or 40,000 D (filter dependent). Rarely, extracorporeal removal has been used for aminoglycosides, atenolol, bromide, carbamazepine, diethylene glycol, isopropanolol, magnesium, metformin, methotrexate, phenobarbital, procainamide, N-acetylprocainamide, sotalol, valproic acid, and trichloroethanol (chloral hydrate).

SUGGESTED READINGS

Bernal W, Donaldson N, Wyncoll D, et al: Blood lactate as an early predictor of outcome in paracetamol-induced acute liver failure: A cohort study. Lancet 2002;359:558–563. *Lactate concentration is perhaps the best predictor of survival.*

Ford MD, Delaney KA, Ling LJ, Erickson T (eds): Clinical Toxicology. Philadelphia, WB Saunders, 2001. *A comprehensive textbook presenting the pathophysiology, clinical presentation, and management of commonly encountered toxins in a concise format.*

Lange RA, Hillis LD: Cardiovascular complications of cocaine use. N Engl J Med 2001;345:351–358. *Outline of the pathophysiology and management of adverse effects of cocaine and complications associated with β-adrenergic receptor antagonist therapy.*

Weber JE, Shofer FS, Larkin GL, et al: Validation of a brief observation period for patients with cocaine-associated chest pain. N Engl J Med 2003;348:510–517. *A 9 to 12 hour evaluation protocol is adequate for patients with normal troponin I, no new ischemic electrocardiographic changes, no arrhythmias, and no recurrent symptoms.*

107 ELECTRIC INJURY

Basil A. Pruitt, Jr.

Epidemiology

Electric injury, which is the tissue damage and necrosis caused by electric current, ranges from a transient increase in cell membrane permeability to immediate coagulation necrosis of large volumes of tissue. The clinical consequences include disturbances of physiologic electrical conduction systems, a process that may cause cardiopulmonary arrest; tetanic muscle contractions, with resulting compression fractures of vertebrae; and delayed tissue damage, such as cataract formation. As the use of electricity has increased worldwide, the number of electric injuries has increased. The precise incidence of electric injury is unknown, but the National Centers for Health/Centers for Disease Control has estimated that 52,000 trauma admissions each year are electric injuries. About 3.5% of the admissions to the U.S. Army Burn Center currently are related to high-voltage electric injury; at other burn centers, the percentage of admissions related to electric injury has ranged from 0.04 to 6.7%. In addition, an estimated 300 to 350 persons are struck by lightning each year, and about 30% of these patients die.

Pathobiology

Environmental conditions, duration of contact, pathway of the current, type of current (and if alternating current, the frequency of the current), and voltage all influence the effects of electricity on tissue. Voltage greater than 40 is potentially dangerous, and the likelihood of sudden death and remote tissue injury increase as voltage increases to 1000. Voltages greater than 1000 are considered to be high tension and are associated with immediate severe tissue damage. Alternating current is more dangerous than direct current because of its likelihood of producing cardiac arrest or cessation of respiration and its tetanic effect, which may prevent the patient from breaking contact with the source of electricity. As the frequency of alternating current increases to greater than 60 cycles per second, tissue injury decreases.

The path of the current through the body between the points of contact is important in determining tissue damage; a course through the heart or the respiratory center of the brain is especially dangerous. Ventricular fibrillation can be produced by current flow of only 100 mA from a hand to the feet. Rapid separation of a patient from the source of electricity is crucial because tissue damage increases in proportion to the duration of contact. Resistance to current flow at the point of contact is influenced by environmental conditions; dry and thickened palmar or plantar skin is more resistant to the passage of current than is skin that is moistened by perspiration or other liquid.

Heat is the principal mediator of tissue damage in electric injury, the severity of which is related to voltage and duration of contact. Tissue-specific differences in resistance to the flow of current (neural tissue least; blood vessels, muscle, and skin intermediate; and bone greatest) may explain differences in tissue injury caused by low-voltage current. Because all body tissues and fluids are conductive, the soft tissues between bone and skin can be viewed as a volume conductor. Heat is produced in tissues as a function of voltage drop and current flow per unit of cross-sectional area (i.e., density of current). The inverse relationship between the density of current and the tissue cross-sectional area accounts for the frequency of severe injury to the digits and extremities and the rarity of major injury to the trunk in patients with high-tension electric injury (Fig. 107–1). Contact with less than 1000 volts causes injuries that are self-limiting because at contact points, where the density of current is greatest, the skin is severely injured and chars, resulting in a rapid increase in resistance and reduction of passage of current. When the source is greater than 1000 volts, arcing is so intense that tissue destruction is increased markedly as relatively constant levels of current are maintained. Arcing, which may occur across flexor surfaces of joints, can char the skin in these areas and can ignite the patient's clothing. After cessation of the flow of current, the heated tissue acts like a volume radiator and cools unevenly, with the superficial portions cooling more rapidly than the deeper portions; deeper tissues are more prone to severe injury.

Tissue damage also can be caused by low-voltage direct current (i.e., contact with automobile battery terminals or with defective or inappropriately used medical equipment, such as electrosurgical devices, external pacing devices, or defibrillators). Direct current injuries have been reported to be particularly common during laparoscopy with high-voltage coagulation.

Clinical Manifestations and Diagnosis

Cardiopulmonary arrest can be caused by low-voltage electric injury but is more common with high-voltage electric injury. Extensive tissue necrosis also may liberate enough potassium to cause cardiac dysfunction. Because cardiac arrhythmias may recur after resuscitation or develop 24 to 48 hours after injury, all patients who have sustained high-voltage electric injury should undergo continuous electrocardiogram (ECG) monitoring for at least 48 hours after the last ECG-documented arrhythmia. Renal failure may occur in patients with high-voltage electric injury if inapparent deep tissue injury with accompanying occult edema results in an underestimation of fluid requirements, inadequate resuscitation, and oliguria. Additionally, the destruction of muscle and red blood cells liberates hemochromes that may precipitate in the renal tubules unless adequate urinary output is maintained (Chapter 109).

High-voltage electric injury commonly causes edema beneath the investing fascia of the involved muscle compartments, compromising nutrient blood flow to muscles within the compartments and to distal unburned tissue. The clinical indications for the surgical release of intracompartmental pressure by fasciotomy and surgical exploration of a limb include impaired capillary refilling of distal unburned skin or nails, cyanosis of distal unburned skin, stony hardness of a muscle compartment to palpation, and diminished or absent pulsatile flow in distal arteries as assessed by Doppler ultrasound. Pressures equal to or greater than 30 mm Hg, as measured by a catheter placed in the compartment, indicate the need for immediate decompression. If clinical signs are consistent with deep tissue injury but large vessel pulses are intact, arteriography can determine the need for operative intervention, including amputation of the affected limb. "Pruning" of the arterial tree, with a decrease in the density of nutrient branches in the muscles of an involved limb, identifies the level of amputation needed to remove muscle that has been irreversibly damaged. Muscle blood flow of 1 mL per minute per 100 g of tissue, as determined by xenon-133 "washout," has been proposed as the minimum level required for ultimate tissue viability.

On admission and at scheduled intervals thereafter, a detailed neurologic examination must be performed on all patients with high-voltage electric injury; all nerve deficits should be documented fully. Central nervous system or peripheral nerve dysfunction may be apparent immediately after electric injury or may appear later. Recovery of function after direct electrical nerve damage is rare. Conversely, spontaneous resolution of immediate and early functional deficits of nerves not injured directly (motor nerves are more sensitive to nondestructive injury than sensory nerves) is common. A polyneuritic syndrome of relatively late onset can induce deficits in the function of peri-pheral nerves far removed from the points of electric contact. Direct nerve damage of the spinal cord causes immediate deficits, which are more often transient than are deficits of later onset. Delayed-onset spinal cord deficits can present as quadriplegia, hemiplegia, localized nerve deficits with signs of ascending paralysis, transverse myelitis, and even an amyotrophic lateral sclerosis–like syndrome. The cause of delayed paresthesias and nerve dysfunction after electric injury is unknown, but an increase of permeability of the cell membrane and associated loss of cell contents induced by exposure to a millivoltage electric field (electroporation) has been implicated.

REMOTE ORGAN INJURY. Direct liver injury, focal pancreatic and gallbladder necrosis, and intestinal perforation have been reported after electric injury, but all are uncommon. Delayed hemorrhage from moderate to large size blood vessels has been ascribed to an arteritis caused by the electric injury, but this hemorrhage seems most closely related to inadequate débridement of injured tissue or to vascular wall necrosis owing to dessication as a consequence of exposure after débridement.

Compression fractures of vertebral bodies may be produced by the tetanic contractions of the paraspinous muscles. Long bone and skull fractures may be caused by falls after the electric shock.

DELAYED ORGAN DAMAGE. High-voltage electric injury has been associated with the subsequent formation of cataracts, most frequently in patients in whom the contact site was on the head or neck. Cataracts may form rapidly, but they more commonly form 3 or more years after the injury. Rarely, exfoliative debris may be evident in the anterior chamber of the eye immediately after injury. Cholelithiasis and gastrointestinal dysfunction have been reported after high-voltage injury, but most centers have not noted an increased rate of either of these problems.

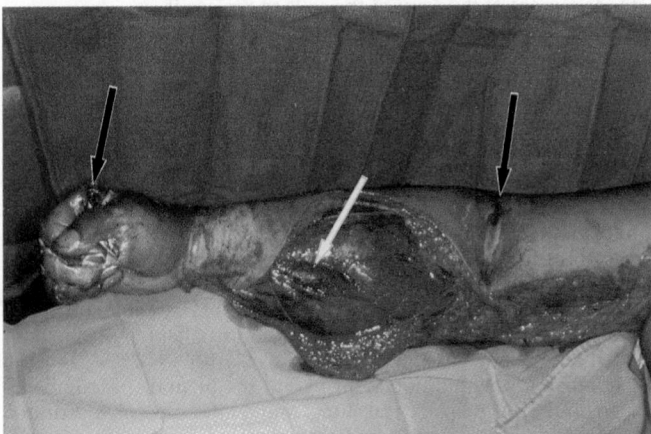

FIGURE 107–1 • Charring at the contact site in the first web space and at the site of arcing in the antecubital space (black arrows) of a victim of electric injury. The fixed flexion deformity of the thumb and other digits is characteristic of severe high-voltage injury of the hand and forearm. The severity of injury is indexed by the marked edema of the forearm muscles bulging above the cut edges of the fasciotomy incision and by the patchy dark discoloration of the muscles of the arm and the forearm, particularly the deeper muscle exposed in the central portion of the forearm incision (white arrow).

Treatment

Cardiopulmonary arrest must be treated by immediate institution of cardiopulmonary resuscitation (Chapters 60 and 61). In patients with high urinary hemochrome concentrations, a urinary output of 75 to 100 mL per hour should be maintained (Chapter 109). If the hemochromes do not clear promptly or the patient remains oliguric despite the administration of resuscitation fluids at more than twice the required rate as estimated on the basis of extent of burn and the patient's weight (Chapter 108), 25 g of mannitol should be given as an intravenous bolus and 12.5 g of mannitol should be added to each liter of intravenous fluid until the pigment has cleared from the urine. Hyperkalemia is treated as in any other patient (Chapter 112).

If the electric injury is limited to the skin and subcutaneous tissue, an antibacterial cream such as Sulfamylon burn cream should be applied twice daily to the burned tissue until débridement is performed. The antimicrobial (mafenide acetate) in Sulfamylon readily diffuses into the nonviable tissue to limit microbial proliferation. As soon as resuscitation has restored hemodynamic stability, severely damaged limbs or other areas of tissue necrosis should be surgically explored. The viability of vital structures and the extent of deep tissue damage are assessed to determine the need for amputation. If amputation is not required, all necrotic tissue should be débrided to eliminate the source of hyperkalemia and reduce the risk of infection. It is imperative to examine the periosseous muscles, which may be necrotic because of delayed heat dissipation yet be overlain by more superficial viable muscles. After débridement or amputation, the operative wound should be dressed but not surgically closed, and the patient should be scheduled for re-exploration of the wound 24 to 72 hours later. At that time, residual necrotic tissue is débrided, and the wound is closed by skin grafts, tissue transfer, or the use of biologic dressings depending on the condition, extent, and site of the wound.

Lightning Injury

The duration of a lightning bolt is 1/100th to 1/1000th of a second, but it may have a voltage of approximately 1 billion volts and induce currents ranging from 12,000 to 200,000 A. The temperature in a lightning bolt, which may be 30,000° K, dissipates in a few microseconds.

Cardiopulmonary arrest, which can be secondary to either asystole or ventricular fibrillation, is common in patients struck by lightning. Cardiopulmonary resuscitation must be instituted immediately; recovery has been reported in some patients who were apparently without life signs for 15 minutes or more. Although signs of acute myocardial damage may become evident later, persistent or recurrent ECG abnormalities are uncommon. Coma is common immediately after injury and typically resolves in a few hours. Keraunoparalysis (lightning paralysis), which is characterized by paresthesias and paralysis, usually involves the lower limbs, often develops over several days after lightning injury, typically is associated with vasomotor disorders, and is usually transient. Myoglobinuria is uncommon; when present, it is treated as described earlier for other electric injuries. Tympanic membrane rupture and hearing loss also may be caused by lightning injury. Cutaneous burns of the trunk and proximal limbs caused by lightning injury typically have a "splashed on" arborescent and spidery appearance and are generally superficial. Small, circular, full-thickness burns of the tips of the toes also are common and have been termed the *tiptoe sign*. Mottling of the skin and other signs of vasoconstriction previously considered to be specific to lightning injury typically resolve with adequate resuscitation. Current treatment, which emphasizes immediate cardiopulmonary resuscitation, has decreased mortality significantly to the point at which two thirds of lightning-injured patients now survive. Persistent nerve deficits and long-term problems are relatively uncommon in survivors.

Prognosis

Cardiopulmonary and fluid resuscitation combined with the monitoring of limb tissue pressure and wound care have maximized tissue salvage, reduced renal failure, and increased survival of patients with lightning and high-voltage electric injuries. In a 10-year period, only 28 (22%) of 127 patients admitted to the U.S. Army Burn Center with high-voltage electric injury had permanent neurologic deficits at discharge.

SUGGESTED READINGS

Duman H, Ergin ER, Turegün M, et al: Bilateral free myocutaneous latissimus dorsi flap repair of the upper limb amputation stumps due to electrical injury. Burns 2003;29:87–91. *Concise description of current diagnosis and treatment of tissue destructive high voltage injuries.*

Muehlberger T, Vogt PM, Munster AM: The long-term consequences of lighting injuries. Burns 2001;27:829–823. *Long-term follow-up documents an overall favorable outcome with few if any deficits or long-term problems related to the original lightning injury.*

Thaventhiran J, O'Leary MJ, Coakley JH, et al: Pathogenesis and recovery of tetraplegia after electrical injury. J Neurol Neurosurg Psychiatry 2001;71:535–537. *Extensive long-term recovery of nerve function supports the concept of nonthermal mechanisms, such as electroporation, as the cause of generalized polyneuropathy in patients with electric injury.*

108 MEDICAL ASPECTS OF TRAUMA AND BURN CARE

Robert H. Demling
Jonathan D. Gates

MEDICAL ASPECTS OF TRAUMA

Epidemiology

Trauma is the third leading cause of death among all ages in the United States (Chapter 15); it is surpassed only by cancer and atherosclerosis. Trauma is the leading cause of death among children, adolescents, and young adults age 1 to 44 years.

More than 140,000 deaths and twice as many permanent disabilities occur annually in the United States from injuries. Fatal injuries have a trimodal distribution. Half of all fatalities occur within minutes of the injury from massive hemorrhage from the heart, lacerations of large blood vessels, or catastrophic neurologic injury. In these cases, there is insufficient time for medical intervention to alter the outcome; the only method to reduce this category of trauma-related morbidity and mortality is by prevention and education programs (Chapter 15). Of fatalities, 30% occur within a few hours after injury from airway obstruction, shock, or neurologic dysfunction. This interval represents an opportunity during which appropriate and timely medical or surgical intervention is most likely to influence outcome. Fatalities within this second peak occur from epidural and subdural hematomas, chest injuries, liver lacerations, splenic ruptures, pelvic fractures, or the accumulation of multiple injuries resulting in significant blood loss. The third peak of trauma fatalities occurs from multisystem organ dysfunction or overwhelming infection weeks later. This delayed systemic response is related to the degree of the initial insult, the individual response to the injury, and the cumulative effect of any additional complications that arise after injury.

Motor vehicle crashes, firearms, and falls are major contributors to injury in the United States. Annually 4 million injuries from motor vehicle crashes occur, resulting in 500,000 admissions to the hospital and approximately 42,000 fatalities. About 50% of all traffic deaths among 15- to 34-year-olds are alcohol related (Chapter 17). About 35,000 gun-related deaths, unintentional and intentional, occur annually (Chapter 15). Of all injury deaths, 8% are related to falls, and fall from a height is responsible for one third of all injury-related hospitalizations.

Mechanism of Injury

Trauma is a structural or physiologic alteration in the individual resulting from an external force, whether it be mechanical, chemical, electrical, or thermal energy. The force that initiated the motion of an object must be absorbed or dissipated in an effort to decelerate that object. When an automobile traveling at a given speed strikes an immobile object, a tremendous amount of energy in the moving vehicle is transmitted to the immobile object and the structure of the vehicle, deforming both until the automobile stops. These same forces are imparted to the occupants of the vehicle with potentially dire consequences. In a head-on impact, the driver continues to move forward until impeded by objects inside the automobile or until the energy is dissipated by the restraint of a seat belt or air bag. Deceleration forces are imparted to individual organs. These same physical principles apply to injury after a fall from a height. Compression, shear, and overpressure from these and other forces injure internal organs.

Penetrating injuries, which are described as either low velocity or high velocity, result from the kinetic energy of the missile. In the case of a bullet discharged from a gun, the tissue immediately contacted by the bullet is crushed to create a permanent cavity. The transfer of energy further away from the bullet path creates a temporary cavity beyond the boundary of the permanent tract, resulting in so-called blast effect. The simple stab wound from a knife or sharp object is considered a low-velocity injury in which the wound is confined to the tract itself. Virtually no temporary cavity is created, but the consequences may be just as devastating as a high-velocity injury if a vital structure is affected.

Pathophysiology of Injury

Physiologic shock (Chapter 102) is an abnormality of the circulatory system that results in inadequate organ perfusion and subsequent failure to deliver sufficient oxygen to maintain aerobic metabolism. Poor peripheral perfusion results in cellular hypoxia and slowing of oxidative phosphorylation with the accumulation of H^+ ion in the extracellular fluid resulting in a metabolic acidosis. The initial step in managing shock in trauma is to recognize inadequate organ perfusion. The second step is to identify and treat the probable cause. The four general categories of shock in trauma are hemorrhagic, compressive, neurogenic, and cardiogenic; however, most shock is hypovolemic in nature. Adrenal insufficiency (Chapter 240), anaphylaxis (Chapter 270), and septic shock (Chapter 104) are less common but may occur during the recovery period. The goal of treatment is restoration of cellular and organ perfusion with adequately oxygenated blood volume.

HEMORRHAGIC SHOCK. Hemorrhagic shock results from a decline in cardiac filling pressures as blood is lost (Chapter 102). Cardiac output is preserved through compensatory mechanisms when the loss of blood is about 10% of blood volume. Endogenous neurogenic and endocrine responses result in peripheral vasoconstriction and shunting of blood from the nonessential areas of skin, muscle, and abdominal viscera to maintain perfusion to the heart and brain. Cardiac output decreases with a blood volume loss of 20 to 40%, with a resultant decrease in systolic blood pressure. Additional compensatory mechanisms to maintain perfusion pressure in the face of a sudden decrease in intravascular volume result in a shift of proteins and fluids from the extracellular space to the intravascular compartment. The relative decrease in volume and increase in osmolarity of the extracellular space stimulate movement of fluid out of the cells to replace it.

It is imperative to identify a patient in shock or compensated shock. A normal systemic arterial blood pressure or absence of a tachycardia may lead the inexperienced physician to believe the patient is hemodynamically stable, when the patient may be in the precarious situation of partially compensated shock. A high index of suspicion and early aggressive diagnostic evaluation and treatment minimize the possibility that occult blood loss may be mined and lead to appropriate volume resuscitation and possible surgical correction.

COMPRESSIVE SHOCK. Compressive shock arises when external compression of the lungs or heart from air, fluid, or blood either compromises the diastolic filling of the right ventricle or prevents adequate ventilation and oxygenation. The two most notable forms of compressive shock are tension pneumothorax (Chapter 95) and pericardial tamponade (Chapter 74).

In tension pneumothorax, air within the pleural space impedes expansion of the ipsilateral lung and shifts the mediastinum. Compression of the inferior and superior vena cavae leads to inadequate filling of the right atrium and ventricle, which decreases cardiac output. The identification of the injury is paramount: Typical findings include absence of breath sounds in the ipsilateral chest, jugular venous distention, and tracheal deviation to the ipsilateral side. Appropriate intervention involves release of air under tension in the hemothorax by means of needle or tube thoracentesis.

Cardiac tamponade occurs because of extrinsic compression of the chambers of the heart from blood in the pericardial space, which normally is a potential space filled with less than 50 mL of

Table 108-1 • CATEGORIZATION AND INITIAL TREATMENT OF HEMORRHAGIC SHOCK*

	CLASS I	CLASS II	CLASS III	CLASS IV
Blood loss (mL)	≤750	750–1500	1500–2000	≥2000
Blood loss (% of blood volume)	≤15%	15–30%	30–40%	≥40%
Pulse rate	<100	>100	>120	≥140
Blood pressure	Normal	Normal	Decreased	Decreased
Capillary refill test	Normal	Positive	Positive	Positive
Respiratory rate	14–20	20–30	30–40	>35
Urine output (mL/hr)	≥30	20–30	5–15	Negligible
Mental status	Slightly anxious	Mildly anxious	Anxious and confused	Confused and lethargic
Fluid replacement (3:1 rule)	Crystalloid	Crystalloid	Crystalloid + blood	Crystalloid + blood

*Based on a 70-kg adult.

pericardial fluid (Chapter 74). An external chest wound that penetrates the pericardium and the heart may create a rent in the pericardium too small to vent the accumulated blood; blood collects in the noncompliant pericardial sac, and the pressure is directed inward into the hollow chambers of the heart. The external compression inhibits diastolic filling of the chambers and reduces stroke volume. Pericardial tamponade should be suspected in patients who have wounds in the vicinity of the precordium and epigastrium, hypotension, tachycardia, jugular venous distention, and muffled heart sounds. Treatment is immediate evacuation of the pericardial space by needle pericardiocentesis, followed by sternotomy or left thoracotomy.

NEUROGENIC SHOCK. The patient with complete injury to the cervical or upper thoracic spinal cord may develop sympathetic denervation manifested as loss of vasomotor tone in the periphery (Chapter 430). Neurogenic shock should be considered in any trauma patient who is hypotensive but not actively bleeding. Only about 20% of patients with a complete high spinal cord injury have neurogenic shock, however, and patients with incomplete motor and/or sensory deficits rarely have hypotension directly caused by neurologic injury.

CARDIOGENIC SHOCK. Cardiogenic shock (Chapter 103) implies inadequate peripheral perfusion as a result of pump failure. It may be caused by arrhythmias, valvular dysfunction, or failing myocardial contraction. The latter may be seen with cardiac contusion or ischemic dysfunction of a previously damaged myocardium with marginal reserve.

The initial management of the trauma patient requires immediate intravenous access for volume resuscitation. The type and rapidity of solution delivered are determined by hemodynamic stability as a reflection of the degree of intravascular depletion or blood loss. Four classes of hemorrhage are widely accepted (Table 108–1). Intravenous access also allows administration of analgesics, sedatives, and antibiotics. The rapidity of volume resuscitation using isotonic crystalloid and blood products is determined by the initial degree or class of shock. The guidelines are based on the "three-to-one" rule, which derives from the empirical observation that most patients in hemorrhagic shock require 300 mL of electrolyte solution for each 100 mL of blood loss because crystalloid equilibrates in the entire extracellular space.

 Evaluation and Treatment

An organized approach to the trauma patient is mandatory to avoid confusion or missing life-threatening injury. The standardized response is divided into the primary survey for rapid diagnosis and treatment of life-threatening injuries and the secondary survey for a more complete, in-depth evaluation of the whole patient for definitive therapy.

PRIMARY SURVEY

The primary survey (airway, breathing, circulation) is the same whether the mechanism of injury was blunt, penetrating, or thermal. Evaluation of the airway is paramount. Supplemental oxygen is given to all trauma patients to maximize delivery of oxygen to the periphery. If the patient is hemodynamically unstable or is unable to maintain a patent airway because of mental status changes or airway debris, endotracheal intubation should be performed. There is little role for the use of oral airways or nasal trumpets in the trauma patient. Care must be taken to avoid movement of the cervical spine during intubation so as to avoid exacerbating an undiagnosed cervical spine fracture or ligamentous disruption. Inability to perform endotracheal intubation in a trauma patient should lead to rapid surgical control of the airway by cricothyroidotomy. Tracheostomy is a poor second choice because it is more time-consuming and potentially bloody, especially if the landmarks are obscured by trauma.

The primary survey should observe the symmetry of chest wall movement; determine whether breath sounds are equal bilaterally and adequate; and assess the chest wall for crepitus, instability, or tenderness. If a tension pneumothorax or massive hemothorax is suspected (and the findings are not caused by intubation of the right main stem bronchus), a large-bore chest tube is placed in the ipsilateral anterolateral fifth intercostal space. Chest tube insertion is diagnostic and therapeutic. The return of greater than 1500 mL

of blood suggests a significant injury within the ipsilateral hemothorax; this magnitude of initial output or an ongoing hourly blood loss through the chest tube of 200 to 250 mL may warrant thoracic surgical exploration.

Adequacy of circulation is determined clinically by noting the presence of carotid, radial, and femoral pulses. Brisk capillary refill, as elicited with transient compression of the nail bed, and a warm, well-perfused patient suggest good peripheral perfusion. The patient in extremis may have a barely palpable carotid pulse; mental status changes; and mottled, cold, clammy skin. During this evaluation, simultaneous insertion of short, large-caliber intravenous catheters in the antecubital veins is recommended for the initial administration of normal saline or Ringer's lactate.

The primary survey should include an evaluation of neurologic function. The Glasgow Coma Scale (Chapter 431) grades the patient's eye movement, best motor response, and best verbal response on a scale from 1 to 5; the score is the sum of the individual results.

The patient should be assessed for all evidence of traumatic injury. This assessment should include an examination of the back with the patient log-rolled using cervical spine precautions.

SECONDARY SURVEY

The secondary survey is the head-to-toe physical examination of the patient to evaluate the airway, reassess the adequacy of breathing and circulation, and look for any injuries or underlying conditions that were not immediately apparent during the primary survey. At this stage, pertinent radiographs, blood tests, and other tests (e.g., an electrocardiogram) are obtained, and a Foley catheter is inserted.

HEAD AND NECK. Evaluation of neurologic function should determine whether there is evidence for closed head injury (Chapter 431). Physical examination should assess for skull and facial fractures and

Continued

eye and ear injuries. The physician should have a low threshold for obtaining a computed tomographic (CT) scan of the head.

Management of penetrating wounds to the anterior neck is controversial. The neck is divided anatomically into three zones corresponding to ease of surgical access. Zone I is from the clavicles downward to the thoracic outlet. In the stable patient, injuries in this area require an arteriogram to define the injury and plan the surgical approach; hemodynamically unstable patients should undergo immediate surgical exploration. Zone III is from the angle of the mandible to the base of the skull. Most patients with injuries in this region are hemodynamically stable. Arteriography, bronchoscopy, esophagoscopy, and sometimes direct laryngoscopy should be performed to evaluate the type and extent of injury. Zone II is located between the other zones from the cricoid cartilage to the angle of the mandible. Any stab wound to the neck must be evaluated locally to determine if there has been penetration of the platysma muscle; if so, operative exploration is performed. It is controversial whether patients with penetrating wounds deep to the platysma should undergo mandatory neck exploration or should have a nonoperative evaluation with arteriography and diagnostic upper endoscopy and bronchoscopy, with operative intervention reserved for when the evaluation reveals pathology. Spiral CT scan with intravenous contrast material can help define arterial injuries, but angiography remains the gold standard. Hemodynamically unstable patients should be resuscitated and explored surgically without further testing.

CHEST. Life-threatening injuries of the chest include tension pneumothorax, massive hemothorax, cardiac tamponade (see earlier), flail chest, open pneumothorax, and disruption of the thoracic aortic. Flail chest implies an unstable segment of the chest wall as a result of multiple rib fractures. The negative pleural pressure required for inspiration pulls the unstable segment of chest wall inward, while the remainder of the chest moves in the opposite direction. An open pneumothorax implies air entering the pleural space through an external chest wound. The wound should be covered with a partially occlusive dressing, and a chest tube should be inserted to prevent the accumulation of air and the development of a tension pneumothorax. Large open chest wounds require endotracheal intubation, operative débridement, chest tube drainage, chest wall stabilization, and closure. Although not usually considered life-threatening, there are a myriad of chest injuries, including simple pneumothorax, pulmonary contusions (Fig. 108–1), rib fractures, and minor-to-moderate hemothoraces, that may play a major role in the duration of lung dysfunction and/or need for ventilatory support.

All trauma patients should have a supine chest radiograph to examine the lung fields, the mediastinal contour, and the chest wall. Thoracic aortic injury, which is a feared complication of severe acceleration-deceleration injury, results in the immediate death of 90% of persons with this injury. Survivors who reach medical care often have a contained mediastinal hematoma that appears as a widened superior mediastinum and/or loss of the aortic contour on the chest radiograph (Fig. 108–2). These patients historically have been evaluated by arteriography (Fig. 108–3), but now chest CT scan is used to screen for this injury. A contained mediastinal hematoma is an unstable condition that demands timely evaluation and possible operative intervention.

MYOCARDIAL CONTUSION. Myocardial contusion results from transmission of force to the myocardium in the form of compression, blast, or sudden deceleration. The true incidence is difficult to define given the absence of a consensus as to a reliable test to identify myocardial contusion. A high degree of suspicion is needed because there are no specific clinical signs of myocardial injury. Sternal fracture, anterior rib fractures, and aortic injuries all are examples of trauma that may suggest underlying cardiac contusion. Life-threatening myocardial contusion (5%) presents within the first 6 to 12 hours after injury as malignant arrhythmias or, if enough of the left ventricle is damaged, cardiogenic shock. Myocardial rupture is uncommon and typically involves the right ventricle owing to the thin muscular wall and close proximity to the sternum. More commonly, arrhythmias or conduction disturbances may occur with elevation of cardiac biomarkers. Electrocardiogram findings include ST-T wave anomalies, supraventricular and ventricular arrhythmias, and atrioventricular nodal dysfunction. The echocardiogram may show left ventricular wall motion abnormalities,

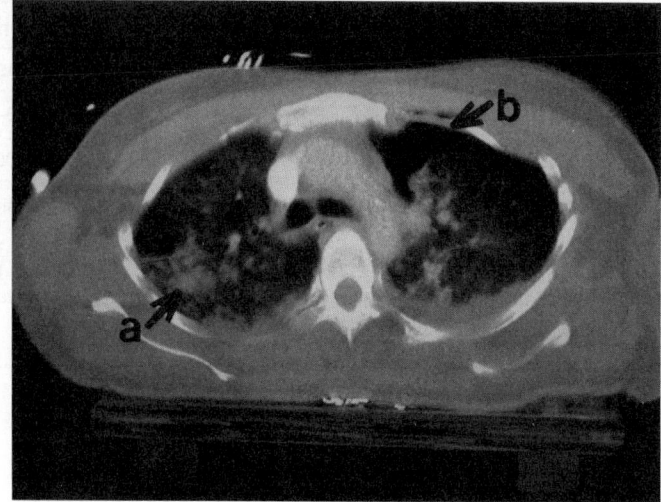

FIGURE 108–1 • Chest computed tomographic scan shows bilateral pulmonary contusions (arrow a) and effusions, with a small pneumothorax on the left (arrow b).

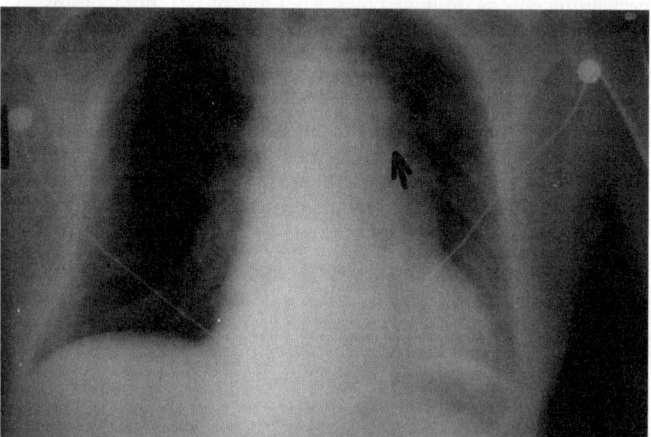

FIGURE 108–2 • Widened superior mediastinum on an upright chest radiograph. Note the loss of normal contour to the aortic knob (arrow).

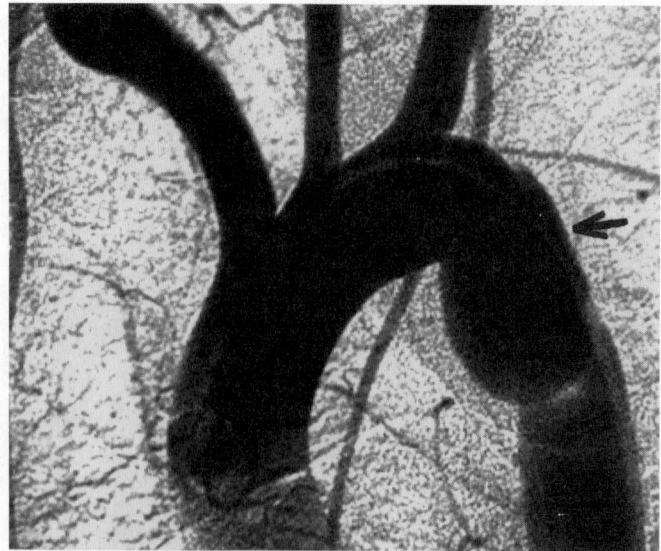

FIGURE 108–3 • Arteriogram shows thoracic aortic disruption (arrow) beyond the left subclavian artery from the patient depicted in Figure 108–2.

valvular dysfunction, or pericardial effusion. There is no evidence to support prophylactic treatment of arrhythmias, and emergent surgery for other injuries does not seem to carry a risk of increased morbidity or mortality in the presence of minor abnormalities.

Injuries to the coronary arteries are uncommon. Potential vascular injuries include laceration, intimal disruption with dissection, and vasospasm. The sequelae and treatment are similar to that of myocardial ischemia from atherosclerotic occlusion.

BACK. Palpation of the thoracic and lumbar spine combined with a thorough history is sufficient to exclude thoracolumbar spine fracture in the alert patient. Ongoing back discomfort or a mechanism suggestive of the possibility of injury should lead to radiographic examination of the spine.

ABDOMEN. The abdominal contents may be injured by blunt or penetrating mechanisms. The ability to identify intra-abdominal injury is limited on physical examinations. If the patient is hemodynamically stable, has a normal abdominal examination, and has no other injuries that warrant operative repair, serial abdominal examination, a complete blood count, and amylase/lipase levels suffice. If there is any question as to the normality of the abdominal examination or the ability to follow the patient reliably, further evaluation is warranted.

The abdominal CT scan has proved to be a reliable determinant of intra-abdominal injury in the stable patient (Fig. 108–4). CT scan identifies intraperitoneal and retroperitoneal injury (Fig. 108–5). CT evaluation can identify sources of blood loss and help decide whether the problem requires operative exploration.

The most frequently injured intra-abdominal organ is the spleen. Left-sided rib fractures, left upper quadrant pain or tenderness, and pain referred to the left shoulder owing to diaphragmatic irritation are suggestive of splenic injury. CT scan allows definition of the grade of splenic injury and the presence of free intraperitoneal blood. Hemodynamic instability, ongoing blood loss, and CT findings of a high-grade injury to the spleen all are indications for splenectomy or, preferably, splenorrhaphy for salvage of the damaged spleen with preservation of splenic function.

Blunt injury to the liver often presents with right-sided rib fractures and right upper quadrant tenderness with or without peritonitis. An abdominal CT scan with intravenous contrast material allows classification of the liver injury according to the location, depth, and extent of the hematoma or laceration. Currently, most (85%) blunt liver injuries are managed successfully nonoperatively if other intra-abdominal injuries do not require surgery.

Focused abdominal sonography in trauma (FAST) has become a popular method to identify intra-abdominal bleeding. FAST has a sensitivity of 95% for detecting free blood in the abdomen. It also enables evaluation of the pericardium for blood and tamponade physiology. FAST is limited in its ability to identify the source of bleeding or the retroperitoneal structures. It is effective in the pregnant trauma patient and allows an evaluation of the fetus.

An alternative to FAST is diagnostic peritoneal lavage. In this approach, a small midline infraumbilical incision is made in the peritoneum to allow sampling of the fluid in the peritoneal cavity. If blood is found, a laparotomy is necessary to identify and correct the source.

Penetrating wounds to the anterior abdomen are divided further into low-velocity stab wounds and gunshot wounds, each of which has a different management algorithm. Because mandatory laparotomy for stab wounds results in a high number of negative explorations, many institutions have adopted a selective approach. The unstable victim of an abdominal stab wound should be explored immediately in the operating room. In contrast, a stable patient can undergo local exploration of the wound to determine the depth of penetration. If the wound is superficial, it is irrigated, and the patient is observed; if the wound extends beneath the fascia, the patient should undergo exploratory laparotomy to exclude intra-abdominal injury. All gunshot wounds to the anterior abdomen are explored routinely except cases with tangential trajectories.

In an unstable patient or a patient with clinical signs of peritonitis, penetrating wounds to the flanks and posterior abdomen require exploratory laparotomy. In a stable patient without peritoneal signs, a CT scan with oral, intravenous, and occasionally rectal contrast material may help to identify injury to retroperitoneal structures, the ascending and descending colon, the duodenum, the pancreas, and the kidneys.

PELVIS, PERINEUM, AND BUTTOCKS. Clinical evaluation of the pelvis is done through compression of the lateral and anterior pelvis to elicit tenderness or bony instability. Rectal examination is essential to exclude bony fragments or blood. Bladder catheterization can identify hematuria and follow urinary output as a reflection of intravascular volume. Scrotal hematoma, meatal blood, or a high-riding boggy prostate indicates potential urethral injury and requires a urethrogram before insertion of a Foley catheter. All patients with major trauma require an anteroposterior plain film of the pelvis to exclude pelvic or hip fractures. A wound in the perineum in the presence of a pelvic fracture represents an open fracture until proved otherwise.

Penetrating wounds of the buttocks should not be overlooked or underestimated. The likelihood of concomitant peritoneal penetration is 25%, with a mortality of 5%. The structures at risk include the retroperitoneal rectum, bladder, ureters, and major arterial and venous structures within the pelvis.

Continued

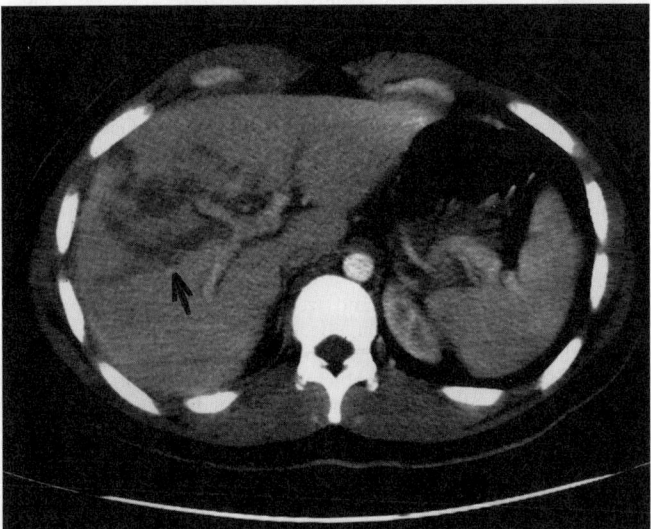

FIGURE 108–4 • Abdominal computed tomographic scan shows an injury to the right lobe of the liver (arrow).

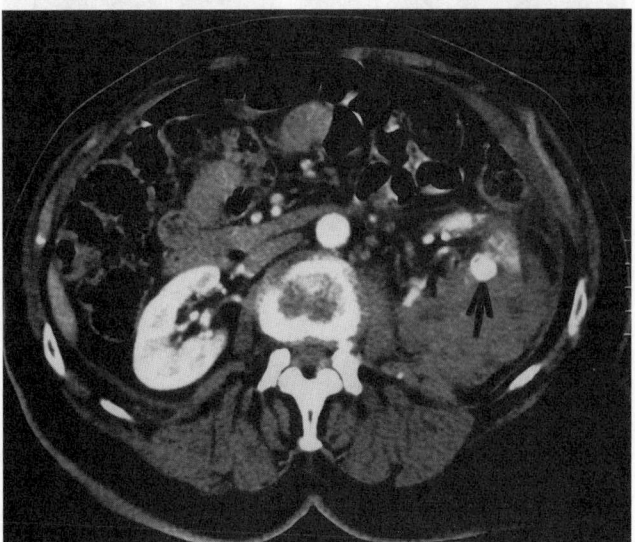

FIGURE 108–5 • Abdominal computed tomographic scan shows blood in the retroperitoneum surrounding a shattered left kidney, with pooling of contrast (arrow) in the kidney parenchyma. These findings are consistent with a pseudoaneurysm of a branch of the left renal artery.

EXTREMITIES. Palpation of the long bones is performed to determine if there is any tenderness or deformity. Range of motion should be assessed in all joints of upper and lower extremities. Areas of concern on examination should be evaluated radiographically. If there is any suspicion of vascular injury, angiographic examination should be performed.

The compartments of the lower leg are most prone to intra-compartmental swelling from direct trauma, long bone fracture, or arterial injury with ischemia or bleeding. Palpation of rigid compartments suggests elevated compartment pressures, which may be measured directly; if pressures are elevated, four-compartment fasciotomies should be performed.

Penetrating wounds to an extremity require operative exploration if they are associated with an enlarging hematoma, active arterial bleeding, or absent arterial pulses. Penetrating wounds resulting in diminished or fluctuating pulses require arteriography to document arterial injury (Fig. 108–6). Otherwise, extremity wounds in proximity to major arterial structures do not require an arteriogram, but the vascular territory should be observed for 24 hours.

MEDICAL ASPECTS OF BURNS

Epidemiology

Each year, about 1% of the population of the United States has a burn injury. More than 2 million burns occur annually, of which one fourth require medical care and produce significant disability.

Approximately 100,000 burn patients require hospital admission, and more than 10,000 persons die of burn-related causes annually in the United States. The most common age groups involved are toddlers (2 to 4 years), for whom scalds are the most common cause, and young adults (17 to 25 years), usually male, for whom the most common cause is a flammable liquid. Structural fires account for less than 5% of hospital admissions but are responsible for more than 45% of burn-related deaths. The National Fire Prevention and Control Administration estimates that there are 2.6 million reported fires annually.

Burns can be categorized as scalds, contact burns, and flame burns. Scald burns are the predominant injury in children, whereas contact and flame burns are most common in adults. The major cause of the injury to the skin is the exposure to high temperature, which destroys surface tissue. Flames result in temperatures of several thousand degrees, especially in a closed space. Because water can conduct heat 1000 times better than air, a much lower temperature (120°F to 130°F) is required to produce a deep burn from hot liquid.

Chemical and electrical burns (Chapter 107), although often severe, account for less than 5% of burn admissions. The mechanism of a chemical burn is protein coagulation of skin caused by the acids or alkali. The injury progresses until the chemical is removed by aggressive water lavage. An electrical burn produces tissue coagulation along the course of the passage of the current. This deeper injury is hidden from view and must be anticipated to make an early diagnosis and initiate effective treatment.

Anatomy and Function of Skin

The skin is the largest organ of the body, ranging from $0.25\,m^2$ in the newborn to more than $2\,m^2$ in the adult (Chapter 471). The outermost layer of the epidermis is composed of dead, cornified cells that act as a tough protective barrier against the environment. The second, thicker layer, the corneum (0.06 to 0.12 mm), is composed chiefly of fibrous connective tissue. The dermis contains the blood vessels and nerves to the skin and the epithelial appendages of specialized function. The nerve endings that mediate pain are found in the dermis. Partial-thickness injuries are extremely painful because the nerve endings are exposed. Full-thickness burns are usually anesthetic owing to destruction of the nerves.

The skin is also the barrier that prevents loss of body heat and fluids by evaporation. Sweat glands help maintain body temperature by controlling the amount of heat lost by evaporation. Increased loss of water and heat through burned skin is a major problem early after a burn. In addition, the skin is the primary protective barrier against invasive infection. The skin also detects the sensations of touch, pressure, pain, cold, and heat; loss of this function leads to long-term impairment.

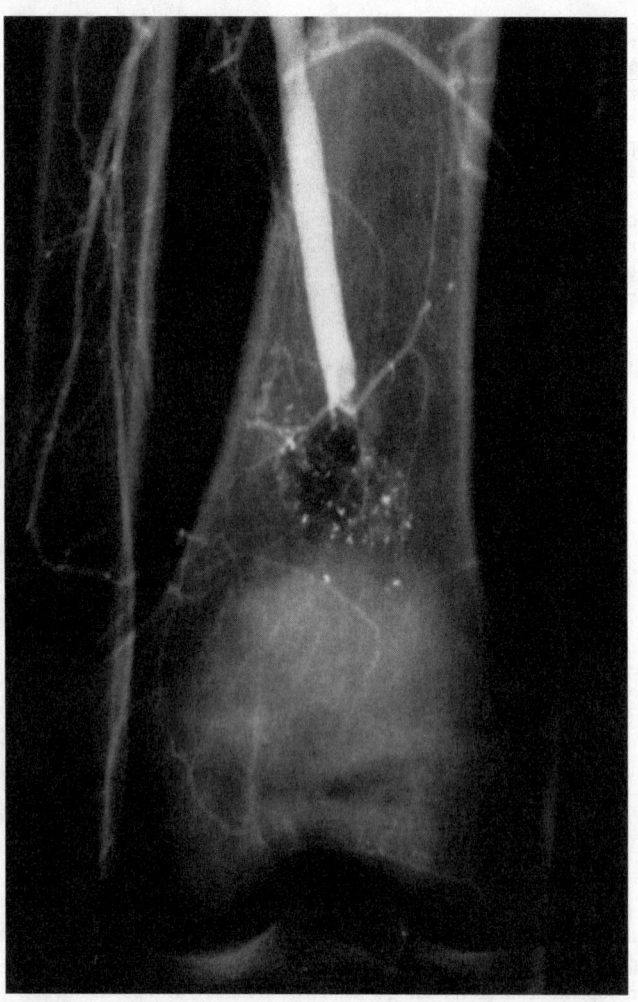

FIGURE 108–6 • Single gunshot wound of the first part of the popliteal artery, with absent blood flow below the knee. Note the femoral fracture.

Rx Treatment

The burn patient undergoes many dramatic physiologic and metabolic changes over the course of the injury. These changes are so marked that the physician may have the feeling of treating a different patient every several days as the process evolves. The burn injury is divided into four phases, each of which has many different physiologic and metabolic characteristics: (1) resuscitation phase (0 to 36 hours), (2) postresuscitation phase (2 to 6 days), (3) inflammation and infection phase (7 days to wound closure), and (4) rehabilitation and wound remodeling phase (admission to 1 year afterward).

RESUSCITATION PHASE (0 TO 36 HOURS)

Life-threatening airway and breathing problems are of major immediate concern, with the effects of smoke inhalation injury being the most concerning problem (Chapter 90). The initial phase also is characterized by hypovolemia as plasma volume is lost into the burn tissue. The burn itself is of less immediate concern except for initial assessment as to severity and depth and the selected need for escharotomy. Wound management becomes a higher priority in later phases. The adequacy of initial treatment of pulmonary and circulatory abnormalities sets the stage for subsequent management.

SMOKE INHALATION INJURY. The first priority in managing the burn victim is recognition and treatment of smoke exposure. Inhalation injury can be divided into three components based on onset of symptoms and pathophysiology (Table 108–2).

Table 108–2 • SMOKE INHALATION COMPLEX

Carbon monoxide (cyanide) toxicity
    Onset of peak symptoms is immediate
    Symptoms are systemic
Supraglottic injury
    Onset of peak symptoms is delayed (hours)
    Problem is upper airways edema
Infraglottic injury
    Onset of peak symptoms is delayed (days)
    Problem is lower airways mucosal

Carbon Monoxide Toxicity. Carbon monoxide and sometimes cyanide toxicity is evident immediately, with peak symptoms at the scene of the inhalation (Chapter 90). Carbon monoxide rapidly displaces oxygen from hemoglobin, producing carboxyhemoglobin that impairs oxygen delivery to tissues. The peak level of carboxyhemoglobin is at the scene of the burn; its half-life is about 20 minutes. The treatment is 100% oxygen. Symptoms range from confusion to coma, which resolve with oxygen therapy unless the patient also had severe anoxic injury.

Cyanide, which is present in smoke, is absorbed rapidly through the lung and causes systemic toxicity. Cyanide levels are difficult to obtain, but an unexplained base deficit can be assumed to be due to cyanide mitochondrial toxicity; treatment is oxygen along with sodium thiosulfate and hydroxycobalamin.

Supraglottic Injury. Smoke injures the mucosa above the glottis because of the combination of superheated air and the toxins in smoke. Mucosal edema, which usually develops over several hours, impedes and potentially obstructs the upper airway. Early endotracheal intubation is indicated if significant edema is evident on direct laryngoscopy, especially if the edema is increasing on subsequent examinations. Upper airway edema usually resolves in 3 to 4 days.

Infraglottic Injury. Toxins in the inhaled air or coating the inhaled soot particles damage the tracheobronchial mucosa, but heat does not usually reach this level (Chapter 90). The extent of damage depends on the toxicity of the chemicals and the time of exposure. Symptoms vary from transient bronchospasm to sloughing of the airway mucosa, which results in plugging and infection. Bronchoscopic evidence of erythema and edema indicates that an injury has occurred but does not predict the degree of injury or time course to recovery.

Endotracheal intubation and positive pressure ventilation are indicated if symptoms increase, especially if there is an early and progressive impairment in gas exchange. Aggressive pulmonary toilet is necessary to avoid respiratory failure. The time course to resolution may be days or weeks.

BURN SHOCK AND RESUSCITATION. Adequate volume resuscitation is crucial to the survival of the victim of a major body burn. Hypovolemia also can lead rapidly to conversion of viable burn tissue to a nonviable, full-thickness burn, further increasing mortality. With modern treatment in burn centers, the failure rate for initial volume restoration is less than 5% even for large burns involving greater than 85% of the total body skin surface.

Two processes lead to the postburn hypovolemia: an increase in the microvascular permeability in the burn wound or an increase in the osmolarity of surface burn tissue. A large intravascular-to-extravascular plasma shift occurs. The phase of rapid loss of intravascular fluid persists for about 24 to 36 hours.

Isotonic crystalloid, preferably lactated Ringer's solution, is used in the first 24 hours. Normal saline in large amounts predictably leads to a hyperchloremic metabolic acidosis. A volume of 4 mL/kg for each percent of body surface burned is given, with 50% given in the first 8 hours and 50% in the subsequent 16 hours. Isotonic crystalloid is used for the first 24 hours in view of the change in skin capillary permeability for protein. Albumin can be added to the resuscitation fluid to maintain a serum albumin level greater than 2.5 g/dL. After the acute injury, the major fluid loss is water from the injured skin surface, which is no longer able to act as a barrier for the evaporation of water.

BURN WOUND. The initial management of the burn wound is based on a knowledge of the anatomy of the skin and the functional

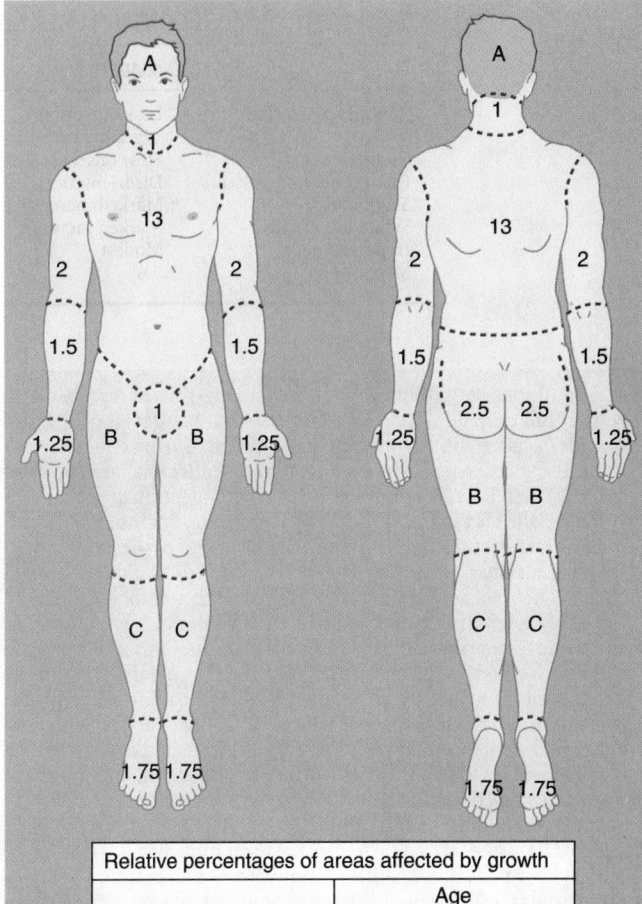

FIGURE 108–7 • Assessment tool for assessing burn size as percent of total body surface.

Relative percentages of areas affected by growth			
		Age	
Area	10	15	Adult
A = half of head	5.5	4.5	3.5
B = half of one thigh	4.25	4.5	4.75
C = half of one leg	3	3.25	3.5

losses with injury. The major objectives are to decrease the potential of further local damage and the systemic abnormalities that can be produced by the loss of the barrier function. The early treatment focuses on neutralizing the source of burn injury, avoiding excess heat loss, determining the extent of the injury, cleaning and débriding the wound, infection control with topical antibiotics, and maintaining tissue perfusion.

Assessment of Burn Depth and Size. Burns are categorized into partial thickness and full thickness. A partial-thickness burn is defined by destruction of the epidermis and a portion of the dermis; superficial partial-thickness burn is confined to the upper third of the dermis, mid partial-thickness burn involves the middle third, and deep partial-thickness burn leaves only a portion of the dermis viable. For management purposes, a deep partial-thickness burn is managed similar to a full-thickness burn: Wound excision and skin grafting are required. The approach to superficial partial-thickness burns is to provide for optimal healing, which is initiated by the remaining viable epidermal cells in the hair follicles. Burn size in older children and adults is determined by the percent of total skin surface area that is involved by the burn (Fig. 108–7).

POSTRESUSCITATION PHASE (2 TO 6 DAYS)

The early postresuscitation phase is a period of transition from the shock phase to the hypermetabolic phase. In general,

Continued

Table 108–3 • MOST COMMON ORGANISMS IN BURN INFECTIONS

	S. AUREUS	P. AERUGINOSA	C. ALBICANS
Wound appearance	Loss of wound granulation	Surface necrosis, patchy black	Minimal exudates
Course	Slow onset, 2–5 days	Rapid onset, 12–36 hr	Slow onset, days
Central nervous system	Disorientation	Modest changes	Often no change
Temperature	Marked increase	High or low	Modest changes
White blood cells	Marked increase	High or low	Modest changes
Hypotension	Modest	Often severe	Minimal change
Mortality	5%	20–30%	30–50%

cardiopulmonary stability is optimal during this period because wound inflammation and infection have not yet developed. Early wound excision and grafting are initiated during this period. Operative risks, especially blood loss and septicemia, are substantially less than later, when inflammation and infection are common.

PULMONARY SUPPORT. Continued upper airway maintenance with an endotracheal tube may be required. Placement of the patient with the head elevated to 30 to 45 degrees allows faster resolution of edema. The decision about when to extubate is difficult, and the degree of lower airway injury dictates the timing. Laryngoscopy to determine the presence of cord edema is helpful. Extubation should not be performed unless reintubation is feasible. Lower airway injury is managed by aggressive pulmonary toilet for increased sputum production and microbial overgrowth. Progressive tracheobronchitis and bronchopneumonia are common. The predicted extravascular-to-intravascular fluid shift results in an increased risk of pulmonary edema. Increased levels of antidiuretic stress hormones can prevent an appropriate diuresis.

HEMODYNAMIC STABILITY. The postresuscitation period is characterized by major fluid shifts mainly from the extravascular-to-intravascular fluid space. Edema in burned tissue is maximum between 24 and 30 hours after injury in well-controlled fluid resuscitation. Red blood cell mass continues to decrease. Electrolyte and acid-base changes are prominent.

Evaporation from the surface of the burn is a major source of water loss that persists until the wound is closed. The loss is measured in terms of water vapor pressure at the surface. In normal skin, the vapor pressure is 2 to 3 mm Hg, whereas the pressure is about 32 mm Hg on a full-thickness burn in which the eschar is soft and hydrated. The rate of loss is increased with increasing surface blood flow. A reasonable estimate of an average loss per hour can be obtained from the following formula: Evaporative water loss mL/hr = (25 + % total body surface burn) × (m² body surface area).

BURN WOUND. The wound undergoes dramatic changes during the next several days as inflammation develops. Of particular importance is the potential for change in the zone of injured but still viable tissue. Changes in local wound microcirculatory blood flow, as a result of vasoactive inflammatory agents or local infection, can convert this zone of ischemia to a zone of necrosis.

HYPERMETABOLIC-SEPSIS PHASE (7 DAYS TO RECOVERY)

The generalized inflammation of the final phase alters organ function and magnifies any preexisting organ dysfunction. The burn wound now is colonized with bacteria, so wound sepsis is of prominent concern. Infection, whether lung or wound, becomes increasingly difficult to diagnose owing to the continued presence of a noninfection-induced hyperdynamic state. Multisystem organ failure, if it is to occur, is seen during this period.

BURN WOUND INFECTION. Burn wounds are never sterile even in the presence of topical agents or systemic antibiotics. The presence of bacteria just on the wound surface is termed *colonization*. Colonization may be with a single type of organism or with multiple organism types. Infection of the wound (Table 108–3) indicates invasion of the underlying viable tissue; this process is diagnosed by eschar biopsy and a quantitative culture with greater than 10^5 organisms per gram of tissue. With progression, the viable tissue and its blood vessels are invaded, and septicemia develops. Wound infections require systemic antibiotics. Because all patients have a hyperdynamic state with an elevated temperature and

leukocytosis, it is difficult to make a diagnosis of infection based on systemic symptoms. Optimally, most of the eschar should be removed in the first week to avoid burn wound sepsis. *Staphylococcus aureus* is the most common organism isolated from the burn, especially during the first week.

HYPERMETABOLIC STATE. Beginning at day 5 or 6, there is a gradual increase in metabolic rate from a normal of 35 to 40 cal/m²/hr (25 cal/kg/day) to levels twice this value at about 10 days. The increase in metabolic rate after burns is far in excess of that seen after any other severe injury, including sepsis. The magnitude of the increase is related to the size of the burn. The hypermetabolic state is characterized by increased oxygen consumption, increased heat production, increased body temperature, and increased protein catabolism. Body temperature increases from normal to 100°F to 101°F (38°C to 38.5°C) owing to a resetting of the hypothalamic temperature center resulting from the altered hormonal environment (see Chapter 296).

Marked and sustained increases in circulatory catecholamines lead to hypermetabolism, and treatment with β-blockers may be protective. Sustained increases in glucagon and glucocorticoids result in excessive gluconeogenesis and an insulin-resistant state. Increased glucocorticoids also lead to a severe catabolic state, especially because anabolic hormones (growth hormone and testosterone) are decreased after a burn injury.

Optimal nutritional support is essential and can decrease net catabolism by about 50%. Decreasing stress by wound closure and control of pain, heat loss, and hypovolemia further controls the hypermetabolism. Caloric requirements can be measured using indirect calorimetric techniques. Because more than 95% of generated energy requires oxygen, there is a direct relationship between oxygen consumption and the metabolic rate. Caloric needs can be estimated by the formula whereby energy requirements = (basal metabolic rate) × (1.25) × (stress factor); the stress factor is 1.2 for a 10% burn, 1.5 for a 20% burn, 1.7 for a 30% burn, 1.8 for a 40% burn, and 2.0 for a greater than or equal to 50% burn. If the activity level is increased markedly or additional stress (e.g., severe pain) is present, metabolic rate can be increased further.

Nutrients Required. Carbohydrate is the preferred fuel for most tissues, but there is a limit to the amount that is used, especially in the hypermetabolic or septic patient (Chapters 227, 229, and 230). Current recommendations are that carbohydrate infusions not exceed 5 to 7 mg/kg/min, or approximately 1800 to 2200 carbohydrate calories per day. Excess carbohydrate results in the formation of fat, which requires energy rather than produces energy. Approximately 50% of estimated calorie requirements usually is given as glucose to spare nitrogen. Fat is used as a calorie source, but fat should comprise no more than 30% of total calories. Protein comprises 20% to 25% of infused calories. A standard estimate of 1.5 to 2 g of protein per kg body weight can be used for all major burns. Data in burn patients indicate that a 100:1 ratio of calories to nitrogen is preferable. By comparison, noninjured adults normally consume a diet with a ratio of about 250:1.

Necessary Vitamins and Trace Elements. Vitamin A should be given in a daily dose of 10,000 to 25,000 U, and vitamin C should be given in a daily dose of about 1 g. Zinc, a trace element required for healing, also is lost and should be replaced as 220 mg ZnSO₄ twice daily orally or 45 mg once daily parenterally. The vitamin B complex is also essential, with doses for burn patients being 5 to 10 times the recommended daily allowance. The specific added needs for the other trace minerals are not well defined.

Route of Administration of Nutrition. Nutritional support is managed best during this period by the enteral route, usually through a combination of a balanced tube feeding and voluntary intake (Chapter 229). Parenteral hyperalimentation (Chapter 230) through a central vein occasionally is required if, for some reason, the gastrointestinal tract is not functioning adequately, as sometimes occurs with a patient on a ventilator or a patient with sepsis.

SUGGESTED READINGS

Herndon D (ed): Total Burn Care. Philadelphia, WB Saunders, 2001. *A comprehensive text.*

Herndon DN, Hart DW, Wolf SE, et al: Reversal of catabolism by beta-blockade after severe burns. N Engl J Med 2001;345:1223–1229. *Propranolol can reverse muscle-protein catabolism after burns.*

Houshian S, Larsen MS, Holm C: Missed injuries in a level I trauma center. J Trauma 2002;52:715–719. *In about 8% of patients, serious injuries were missed on the original evaluations.*

Kirkpatrick AW, Simons RK, Brown R, et al: The hand-held FAST: Experience with hand-held trauma sonography in a level-I urban trauma center. Injury 2002;33:303–308. *Handheld portable ultrasound examinations facilitate rapid evaluation of victims of abdominal trauma.*

MacKenzie EJ, Hoyt DB, Sacra JC, et al: National inventory of trauma centers. JAMA 2003;289:1515–1522. *Overview of trauma centers and what they can accomplish.*

Resources for optimal care of patients with burn injury. *In*: Resources for Optimal Care of the Injured Patient. Chicago, IL, American College of Surgeons, 2000. *A detailed chapter.*

Table 109–1 • CLASSIFICATION OF RHABDOMYOLYSIS

Pure exertional rhabdomyolysis
Genetically transmitted defect leading to rhabdomyolysis
Nonhereditary, nonexertional rhabdomyolysis

Table 109–2 • PRECIPITATING FACTORS LEADING TO NONHEREDITARY, NONEXERTIONAL RHABDOMYOLYSIS

Alcoholism
Phosphate deficiency
Potassium deficiency
Various bacterial and viral infections
Drugs (e.g., cocaine, amphetamines, neuroleptics, statins, protein inhibitors, fibrates)
Toxins (e.g., tetanus, snake venom, toluene, *Tricholoma equestre* mushrooms)
Direct injury (e.g., crush, electric shock, burns)
Ischemic injury (compression, sickle cell disease*)

*Listed as nonhereditary because the mechanism of injury is not related to a genetic defect in the synthesis of adenosine triphosphate.

109 RHABDOMYOLYSIS

Juha P. Kokko

Rhabdomyolysis is a syndrome that results from destruction of skeletal muscle. It usually is diagnosed from laboratory findings that are characteristic of myonecrosis. Previously thought to be rare, rhabdomyolysis now is recognized with increased frequency, in part as a consequence of increased awareness of its potential presence in clinical settings that may predispose to muscle necrosis (e.g., exercise, hypophosphatemia, hypokalemia, alcoholism, sepsis, drug overdoses) and in part because of increased availability of routine tests for measurement of creatine kinase (CK) and myoglobin. In a 3-month period at one hospital serving predominantly economically disadvantaged individuals, 498 patients had nontraumatic elevations of CK to greater than 1000 IU/L, and 46 patients had CK levels greater than 10,000 IU/L. Although there are no standard CK values that establish the diagnosis of rhabdomyolysis, elevations greater 10,000 IU/L usually indicate clinically significant rhabdomyolysis; by comparison, with exercise to near exhaustion and its associated morphologic changes of muscle injury, CK increases only to about 1000 IU/L. Studies also have shown, however, that there is a poor correlation between CK elevations and the morphologic degree of muscle damage.

Clinical Manifestations

A careful history is crucial in evaluating patients with rhabdomyolysis. Although the approach to patients in the acute phase of rhabdomyolysis may be similar except in the extreme cases of malignant hyperthermia and neuroleptic malignant syndrome, the long-term preventive approach to these patients varies depending on the underlying reason and classification of rhabdomyolysis (Table 109–1). A functionally useful approach is to classify patients into three broad categories: (1) patients who have pure exertional rhabdomyolysis, (2) patients who have exertional precipitation of rhabdomyolysis in a setting of genetic defect in the synthesis of adenosine triphosphate (ATP), and (3) patients who have a precipitating cause that may or may not be associated with exercise (Table 109–2).

The most common clinical symptoms of rhabdomyolysis are muscle weakness, pain, swelling, and cramps. Some patients may be entirely asymptomatic, however, and the diagnosis may be established only from a laboratory profile. In patients who present with muscular signs and symptoms, the most commonly affected muscles are those that were involved with exercise. Some patients, especially patients without a history of exercise, may present with diffuse weakness and pain in all of their striated muscles. Usually the symptoms of rhabdomyolysis are self-limited because the muscle has a remarkable ability to repair itself completely. In the most severe cases of rhabdomyolysis, however, the muscle may swell sufficiently to cause compression of vessels and nerves and result in irreversible necrosis unless surgical decompression and fasciotomy are performed. The most common extramuscular complications are metabolic abnormalities and acute renal failure.

Striated muscle fibers are generally of two principal types. Type I are myoglobin-rich "red" muscles that use aerobic mechanisms to generate ATP, and type II are "white" muscles that use anaerobic (glycolytic) pathways to form ATP. The former muscles, which are better developed for endurance and are fatigue-resistant, are found, for example, in ducks; the latter, which are commonly used for intermediate sources of strength and are easily fatigable, are found, for example, in chickens. Humans have both types of muscle fibers, and individuals who are conditioned for endurance exercise have a higher percentage of red muscle fibers. Each of these fibers has similar intracellular constituents, however, and interruption of the sarcolemmal membrane causes these constituents to leak into the plasma, which produces the expected abnormalities of rhabdomyolysis (Fig. 109–1). Necrosis of only 100 g of muscle is roughly equivalent to the acute infusion of 10 to 15 mEq of potassium into the circulation. Whether this influx of potassium or other intracellular constituents can be measured as a metabolic abnormality depends on circulatory and renal status.

PURE EXERTIONAL RHABDOMYOLYSIS. Relatively heavy exercise to 80% of maximum for only three periods of 15 minutes each on an exercise bicycle is associated consistently with a rise in CK values and light microscopic evidence of muscle fiber damage, especially in untrained and older individuals. It is not surprising to see patients who have no presumptive inciting factors for rhabdomyolysis other than exercise. Most of these patients have no major laboratory findings except for CK elevations and marked myoglobinuria. Because myoglobin has a low molecular weight of roughly 17,800, it is filtered into urine rapidly and can be detected with only a urine dipstick 6 hours after muscle injury. Conversely, CK has a much higher molecular weight of more than 80,000 and takes several days to several weeks to return to normal levels. In the absence of volume contraction or renal failure, however, individuals with rhabdomyolysis from exercise usually do not develop the full laboratory picture of severe rhabdomyolysis.

Continued

GENETICALLY TRANSMITTED DEFECTS LEADING TO RHABDOMYOLYSIS. ATP is the intracellular currency of life; it is used for muscular contractions, to maintain the integrity of the cell membrane, and for many other vital functions. ATP is generated by two primary mechanisms: oxidative fatty acid oxidation and anaerobic glycolysis (Fig. 109–2). Failure in either of these pathways can lead to ATP depletion and can lead to muscle necrosis. The integrity of each of these pathways depends on many different enzymes, and defects in these enzymes can cause rhabdomyolysis that is associated with depletion of ATP during exercise (Table 109–3). Of these defects, carnitine palmitoyltransferase deficiency is the most common hereditary aerobic disorder causing rhabdomyolysis, and myophosphorylase deficiency (McArdle's disease) is the most common anaerobic disorder causing rhabdomyolysis.

Many patients who previously were thought to have "idiopathic" rhabdomyolysis instead have an inherited enzyme defect in ATP synthesis. The clinical suspicion for an enzymatic defect should be heightened if the patient has more than one episode of rhabdomyolysis or a positive family history of rhabdomyolysis. About 25 to 50% of patients with recurrent rhabdomyolysis have a metabolic inability to generate ATP rapidly enough to keep up with the demands. If patients develop symptoms of rhabdomyolysis after some duration of strenuous exercise, a defect in fatty acid metabolism should be suspected; by comparison, an abnormality in the glycolytic pathways usually becomes apparent in the earlier phases of exercise. It is important to differentiate between these pathways because alteration of dietary habits can be palliative.

NONHEREDITARY CAUSES OF RHABDOMYOLYSIS. Acquired rhabdomyolysis may occur in response to many precipitating factors, including drugs, toxins, or infections. Each of these factors may be the only precipitating cause, but often they are associated with exercise. Among the most common causes of rhabdomyolysis is exercise in patients who are alcoholics (especially if they have an associated potassium and phosphate deficiency) or patients who have ingested cocaine. Many patients who have drug-induced rhabdomyolysis have a prolonged recovery phase that may lead to death if the offending agent is not discontinued immediately (Table 109–4; see Table 109–3).

The HMG-CoA reductase inhibitors (statins) have become one of the more common precipitants of rhabdomyolysis. Statins are used widely for treatment of hypercholesterolemia, and their cardiovascular benefits have been well documented (Chapter 211). One of these drugs has been taken off the market, however, because of increased incidence of rhabdomyolysis leading to death, and cases of rhabdomyolysis have been reported with most of the other statins. Statins may be classified broadly as lipophilic or hydrophilic. The lipophilic statins cross cell membranes by passive diffusion, whereas hydrophilic statins require specific membrane interactive transport mechanisms to gain access to the hepatocyte. It has been argued that increased lipophilicity is the basis for gaining increased access to the muscle and is associated with increased incidence of rhabdomyolysis.

Millions of patients have taken statins for their antiatherosclerotic effects. The incidence of rhabdomyolysis with statins is relatively rare, but it is higher in patients concomitantly using drugs that are cytochrome P-450 3A4 inhibitors. It is prudent for the physician to avoid drugs that also are metabolized by the CYP P450 3A4 system if the patient is taking statins that are metabolized by the same cytochrome subfamily (see Table 109–4). Rhabdomyolysis is increased when statins are used in combination with gemfibrozil, which is not a known inhibitor of CYP 3A4. These drugs should be discontinued, and the patient with generalized muscle weakness and/or tenderness should be evaluated carefully.

Patients with nonhereditary rhabdomyolysis are most likely to develop the laboratory abnormalities of the syndrome (see Fig. 109–1), including hyperuricemia, hyperkalemia, and hypocalcemia. These findings are especially more frequent in the setting of myoglobinuric acute renal failure.

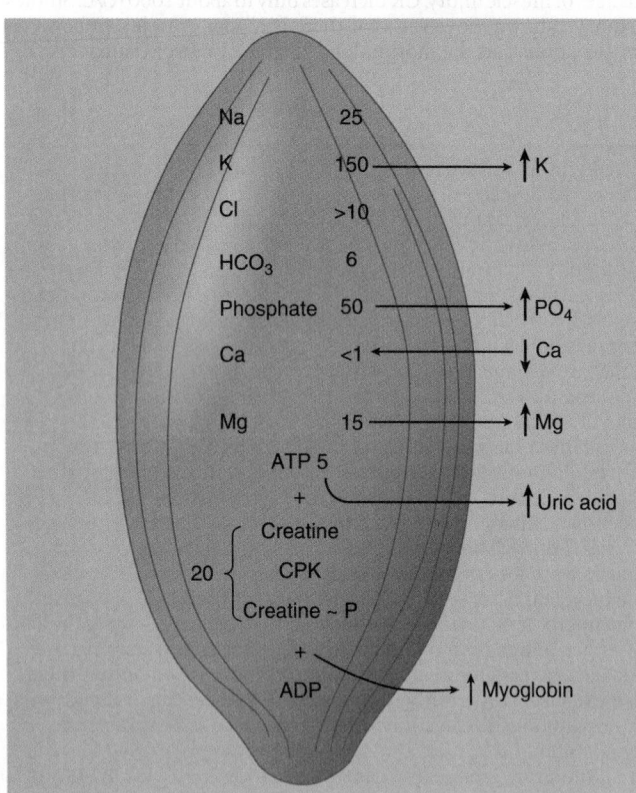

FIGURE 109–1 • Values within the depicted striated muscle cell reflect concentration (in mm/L of water) of various intracellular constituents. The values outside of the cell reflect increases (↑) or decreases (↓) that are characteristic of rhabdomyolysis, whereby intracellular constituents leak into the plasma through injured muscle membranes.

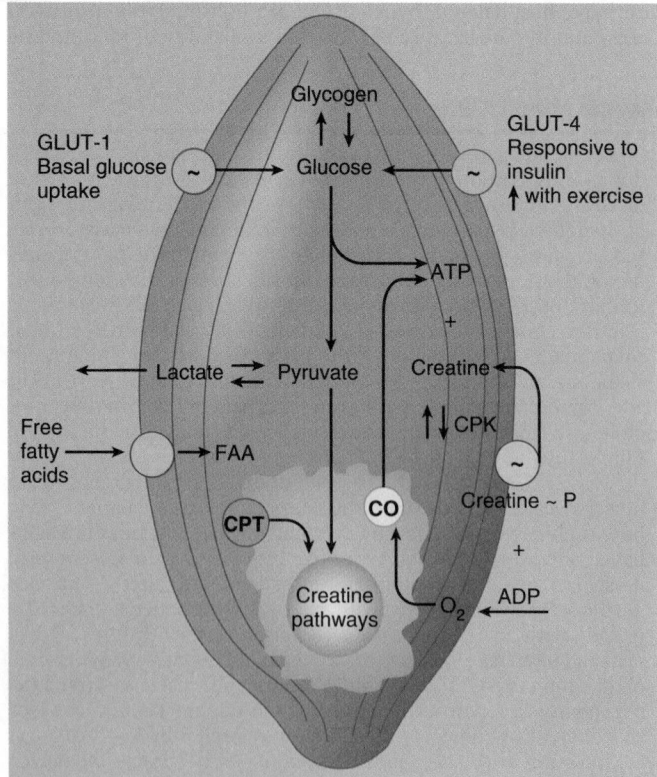

FIGURE 109–2 • ATP is the major energy for muscle. It is generated by the anaerobic metabolism of glycogen or the oxidative metabolism of fatty acids. Glucose uptake comes across two primary pumps: GLUT-1, which reflects basal glucose uptake, and GLUT-4, which can be increased with exercise and in response to insulin. The upregulation of GLUT-4 protein formulates the basis of why exercise improves glucose metabolism in diabetes and increases glycogen formation in well-conditioned humans.

Rx **Treatment**

Treatment of the acute phase of rhabdomyolysis must be highly individualized depending on the patient's presentation. If a patient complains of myalgias after strenuous exercise, if that exercise has occurred without nephrotoxic cofactors, if the urinary sediment is reasonably clear, and if the metabolic profile is otherwise normal, the patient can be treated on an outpatient basis, despite a significant CK elevation. These patients should be instructed to take ample oral fluids at home and should be seen again in follow-up within 2 days. If any of the classic metabolic findings of rhabdomyolysis are present (see Fig. 109–1), the patient should be admitted and treated aggressively (Table 109–5).

One of the most feared complications of rhabdomyolysis is the development of myoglobinuric acute renal failure. Although no large-scale prospective studies exist, the general consensus is that aggressive and early intravenous fluid therapy is the cornerstone for preventing acute renal failure. If the cardiovascular status permits (and most patients with rhabdomyolysis are in the younger age group), it is not unreasonable to administer 6 to 12 L of intravenous fluids in the acute phase of myoglobinuria while monitoring the urine output so that the rate of infusion can be individualized as dictated by the clinical circumstances. The aggressive infusion rate dilutes the various intraluminal constituents that otherwise might precipitate within the nephron, especially myoglobin, hemoglobin, and uric acid. Because all of these compounds have progressively increased solubility as the pH of the urine is increased, some authorities have suggested alkalinizing the urine by adding sodium bicarbonate to intravenous fluids; however, this approach can increase precipitation of calcium into soft tissues. A possible alternative if the plasma bicarbonate concentration is greater than 13 to 15 mEq/L is to use carbonic anhydrase inhibitors (e.g., acetazolamide [Diamox], 250 mg orally three times a day) to increase the alkalinity of the urine without inducing systemic alkalosis.

The duration of treatment also must be individualized because of the great variability among patients. Although no well-controlled studies exist to guide hospital length of stay, patients often are discharged from the hospital with an elevated CK, provided that the CK has shown a steady decrease for the previous 48 hours; there are no significant metabolic abnormalities; and the patient feels quite well, is compliant, and will return for an outpatient follow-up visit within 1 week. Myoglobinuric acute renal failure generally is self-limiting and starts to improve within 10 to 14 days of treatment if the release of myoglobin into the circulation has ceased.

Correction of the other metabolic abnormalities in rhabdomyolysis is no different from correction of these same abnormalities when they occur in other settings. Management of hypocalcemia, which is common in rhabdomyolysis, especially in association with acute renal failure, requires special consideration, however, because of deposition of calcium phosphate in muscle and other soft tissues early in the course of rhabdomyolysis. The greater the muscle damage, the greater the ectopic calcification. The hypocalcemia often coexists with hyperphosphatemia that is due in part to phosphate leak from injured muscle and in part to diminished phosphaturia in acute renal failure. It is imperative that *intravenous calcium generally should not be given to patients with rhabdomyolysis and hypocalcemia* because it could worsen ectopic calcification. The only indications for intravenous calcium in patients with rhabdomyolysis are severe symptoms of hypocalcemia or severe hyperkalemia.

Patients with ectopic calcifications are at increased risk of developing hypercalcemia during the diuretic phase of recovery. Many hypotheses for the cause of hypercalcemia have been advanced; the most important of these is dissolution of previous ectopic calcification. The rise in serum calcium can be high, but it is usually self-limited. The treatment is aggressive volume repletion (to the degree that the recovering renal failure allows) coupled with administration of a loop diuretic, such as furosemide or bumetanide (see Table 109–5).

Table 109–3 • ENZYME DEFECTS IDENTIFIED* AS A CAUSE OF MYOGLOBINURIA

Carnitine palmitoyltransferase
  Myophosphorylase
  Phosphofructokinase
  Phosphorylase kinase
  Phosphoglycerate kinase
  Phosphoglycerate mutase
  Lactate dehydrogenase
  Myoadenylate deaminase

*Other defects most likely will be identified in the future.

Table 109–4 • SOME COMMONLY USED DRUGS THAT ARE INHIBITORS OF CYTOCHROME P450 3A4 AND THAT MAY INCREASE THE INCIDENCE OF RHABDOMYOLYSIS BY STATINS* THAT ARE METABOLIZED BY THE SAME CYTOCHROME SUBFAMILY[†]

Triazo antifungal agents
Cyclosporine
Many selective serotonin reuptake inhibitors
Many protease inhibitors
Numerous macrolide antibiotics

*Statins known to be metabolized by CYP 3A4 include atorvastatin, lovastatin, and simvastatin.
[†]It is recommended that the physician be aware of the potential increased risk of concomitant use of specific drugs that are strong inhibitors of CYP 3A4 (not all drugs within a given family are metabolized by the same mechanism).

Table 109–5 • TREATMENT OF RHABDOMYOLYSIS

Fluid replacement—be aggressive but aware of renal function
Urine alkalinization—controversial. *Benefit*: Increased solubility of uric acid, myoglobulin. *Harmful*: HCO₃ could promote calcium deposition
Correct hyperkalemia
Management of hypocalcemia—avoid intravenous calcium unless tetany is present
Management of hypercalcemia—prevention is key. Intravenous fluid, furosemide
Correction of hypoalbuminemia—usually not necessary
Disseminated intravascular coagulation—usually resolves spontaneously
Dialysis—if necessary
Hyperphosphatemia—oral binders, dialysis
Fasciotomy—relief of compartment syndromes

SUGGESTED READINGS
De Meijer AR, Fikkers BG, De Keijzer MH, et al: Serum creatine kinase as predictor of clinical course in rhabdomyolysis: A 5-year intensive care survey. Intensive Care Med 2003;29:1121–1125. *Higher levels generally predict a higher risk of acute renal failure, which predicts a higher rate of death.*
Gruer PJK, Vega JM, Mercuri MF, et al: Concomitant use of cytochrome P450 3A4 inhibitors and simvastatin. Am J Cardiol 1999;84:811–815. *Excellent review of the long-term safety profile of statins and an up-to-date, in-depth analysis of data of compounds that increase the risk of myopathy when used concomitantly.*
Löfberg M, Jänkälä H, Paetau A, et al: Metabolic causes of recurrent rhabdomyolysis. Acta Neurol Scand 1998;98:268–275. *A clinical study using a specific ethnic and genetic group of patients showed that 23% of patients with recurrent rhabdomyolysis in Finland have identifiable enzyme defects.*
Vanholder R, Sükrü Sever M, Erek E, Lameire N: Rhabdomyolysis. J Am Soc Nephrol 2000;11:1553–1561. *Review of the history, pathophysiology, clinical presentation, and treatment of rhabdomyolysis.*

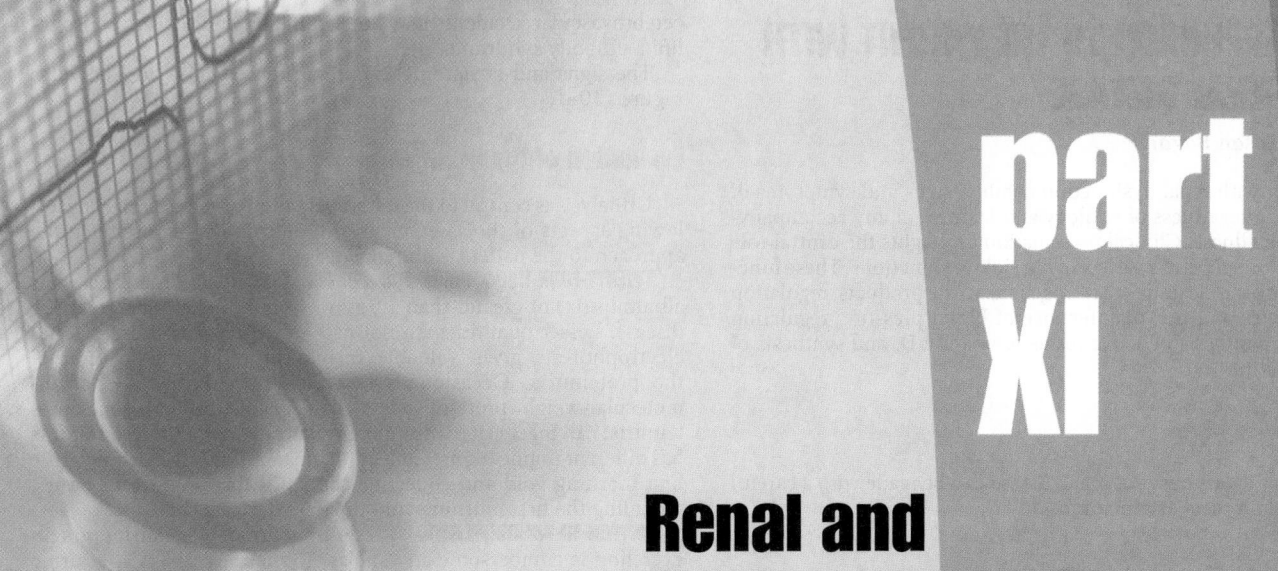

part XI

Renal and Genitourinary Diseases

110 APPROACH TO THE PATIENT WITH RENAL DISEASE

Hasan Bazari

The patient with renal dysfunction exhibits signs and symptoms of renal disease regardless of etiology and features of any accompanying systemic illness. Clinical presentation highlights the central role that the kidney plays in a variety of physiologic functions. These functions include the clearance of nitrogenous waste products, regulation of electrolytes and pH, maintenance of blood pressure, regulation of volume, synthesis of active forms of vitamin D, and synthesis of erythropoietin.

Clinical Evaluation

Most of the diagnoses of renal disease can be made with a careful history and physical examination.

HISTORY

The history reviews potential factors that contribute to the development of renal disease and identifies the systemic features of diseases that may affect the kidney. These factors include:

- Medication use
- Family history of renal disease
- The onset of symptoms of renal dysfunction
- Changes in bladder function, including nocturia, polyuria, and hesitancy
- Fatigue and weakness
- Dyspnea on exertion, a manifestation of fluid overload or acidosis

A systemic vasculitis may present in a variety of ways with skin manifestations including petechial rash, purpura, digital gangrene, and splinter hemorrhages. Otitis, sinusitis, epistaxis, hemoptysis, and nasal septal ulcers are common manifestations of Wegener's granulomatosis. Pulmonary hemorrhage can be a catastrophic manifestation of Goodpasture's syndrome or anti–glomerular basement membrane (GBM) disease. Abdominal distention may be seen with nephrotic syndrome and ascites and in autosomal polycystic kidney disease. Abdominal pain and tenderness may be seen in Henoch-Schönlein purpura and classic polyarteritis nodosa. Lower extremity edema is common in cirrhosis, congestive heart failure, and nephrotic syndrome. Neurologic symptoms may be a manifestation of vasculitis, such as microscopic polyangiitis and cryoglobulinemia.

PHYSICAL EXAMINATION

VITAL SIGNS. The vital signs are crucial. A patient with a "normal blood pressure" may be relatively hypotensive in the setting of renovascular disease. Pulsus paradoxus may reflect cardiac tamponade.
EYES. The eyes may exhibit conjunctivitis, episcleritis, or uveitis.
CARDIOVASCULAR. Assessment of the jugular venous pressure plays a crucial role in the bedside evaluation of volume status and, perhaps more than any other part of the examination, should be assessed daily. The presence of a pericardial friction rub can be seen in the serositis associated with systemic lupus erythematosus (SLE) or the pericarditis associated with uremia. Infiltrative diseases, such as amyloidosis and sarcoidosis, can lead to restrictive cardiomyopathy with associated congestive heart failure. The presence of S_4 may be a sign of cardiac hypertrophy, and S_3 may be a sign of congestive heart failure. Vascular bruits may reflect generalized atherosclerosis, and the presence of an abdominal bruit may be an important clue to the presence of renovascular disease.
ABDOMEN. Edema of the lower extremities is seen in cirrhosis, nephrosis, congestive heart failure, and severe renal insufficiency. Hepatomegaly is seen in passive congestion and amyloidosis. Splenomegaly may be seen in amyloidosis, endocarditis, and lymphoma. Kidney and liver enlargement may be seen in autosomal dominant polycystic kidney disease.
NEUROLOGIC. Peripheral neuropathy may be seen in vasculitis with involvement of the nerves as mononeuritis multiplex. Frank

cerebrovascular accidents may be seen in SLE and the antiphospholipid antibody syndrome.

The signs and symptoms of chronic renal failure are shown in Figure 110–1.

Evaluation of the Urine

Urinalysis is central to the renal evaluation of the patient. The following aspects of the assessment of the urine are important in the approach to the patient with renal disease.

TWENTY-FOUR-HOUR URINE FOR PROTEIN EXCRETION. Proteinuria (as albuminuria) of greater than 3.5 g in 24 hours indicates glomerular disease. Lesser quantities do not preclude glomerular disease, and electrophoresis gives valuable insight into the composition of the proteinuria. Occasionally, overflow proteinuria of a small-molecular-weight protein, such as light chains in Bence Jones proteinuria, can meet criteria for glomerular range proteinuria, but this has different implications. Collection must be done by discarding the first morning void and collecting the voids for the next 24 hours, including the first morning void the next day.

PROTEIN-TO-CREATININE RATIO. The 24-hour urine collection for protein excretion is cumbersome and subject to inaccuracies. A spot urine for protein and creatinine can be used to estimate the amount of protein excreted. A protein-to-creatinine ratio of 3 estimates that the 24-hour protein excretion is about 3 g. The ratio may be inaccurate in patients with orthostatic proteinuria.

URINE FOR MICROALBUMIN. The excretion of abnormal quantities of albumin below the level detectable by the urine dipstick is called *microalbuminuria*. Normal albumin excretion is less than 30 mg/day. This is detected by radioimmunoassay or enzyme immunoassay. Microalbuminuria is the earliest clinically detectable stage of diabetic nephropathy.

FRACTIONAL EXCRETION OF SODIUM. The excretion of sodium in the setting of oliguria and acute renal failure often gives insight into the appropriateness of tubular function in the setting of oliguria. The fractional excretion of sodium (FeNa) is calculated as follows:

$$FeNa = (urine\ Na/plasma\ Na)/(urine\ Cr/plasma\ Cr) \times 100$$

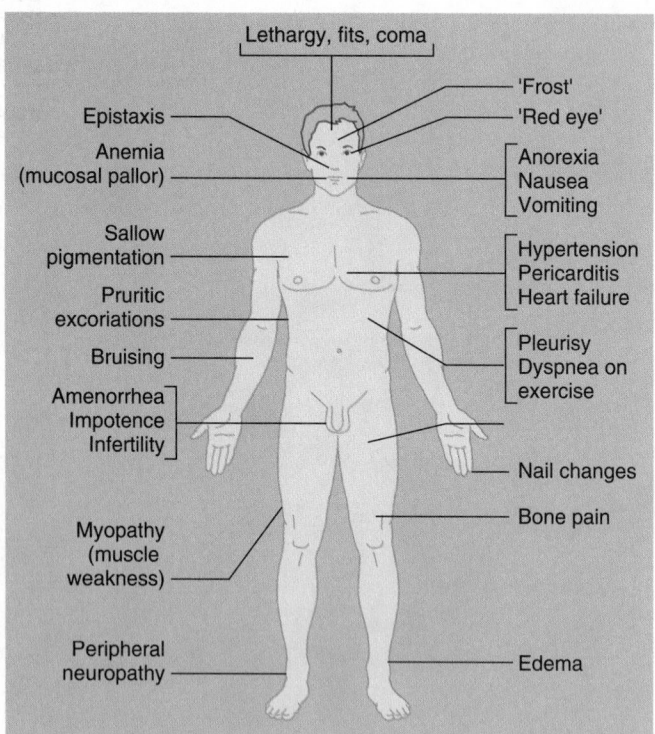

FIGURE 110–1 • Common symptoms and signs of chronic renal failure. (Redrawn from Forbes CD, Jackson WF: Color Atlas and Text of Clinical Medicine, 3rd ed. London, Mosby, 2003, with permission.)

where *Na* is sodium, and *Cr* is creatinine. An FeNa of less than 1% often denotes prerenal azotemia, whereas an FeNa of greater than 1% denotes intrinsic renal failure. Although generally useful, there are instances when an FeNa of less than 1% may be seen in cases without a prerenal component, including contrast nephropathy, hepatorenal syndrome, obstructive uropathy, interstitial nephritis, glomerulonephritis, and rhabdomyolysis. Conversely a high FeNa can be seen in cases in which there is a prerenal component, including diuretic use, adrenal insufficiency, cerebral salt wasting, and salt-wasting nephropathy. The FeNa has to be used in the context of the clinical situation. Ultimately, volume assessment is done best at the bedside assessing the patient and cannot be deduced from a measurement of electrolytes.

FRACTIONAL EXCRETION OF UREA. When diuretics are used, the FeNa is unreliable, and the fractional excretion of urea can be used as a surrogate for the assessment of volume status. Urea reabsorption varies with the volume status, decreasing in the setting of volume depletion. A fractional excretion of less than 30% indicates a state of decreased effective circulating volume. Calculation of the fractional excretion of urea is identical to that of FeNa.

TWENTY-FOUR-HOUR URINE FOR CALCIUM, URIC ACID, OXALATE, CITRATE, SODIUM, AND CREATININE. These studies are done in the evaluation of the patient with recurrent kidney stones. Depending on the laboratory, the calcium measurement may have to be done in a different collection than the others. These measurements should be conducted with the patient on a normal diet and with normal activity and should not be done during a hospitalization. Often these tests need to repeated before making therapeutic decisions. A 24-hour urine sodium and creatinine excretion should be included with each measurement to ensure adequacy of collection.

URINE POTASSIUM EXCRETION AND THE TRANSTUBULAR POTASSIUM GRADIENT. Potassium is handled differently than sodium. It is completely reabsorbed and excreted in a flow-dependent manner. Potassium excretion depends on adequate distal sodium delivery and reabsorption to provide an adequate electrochemical gradient for tubular potassium excretion. Failure to excrete potassium is seen in volume depletion. The excretion of less than 15 mmol of potassium a day in the face of hyperkalemia suggests an inadequate renal response. The transtubular potassium gradient (TTKG) is the approximation of the gradient of potassium before the effect of antidiuretic hormone on the concentration of potassium in the urine. The formula for the measurement of the TTKG is as follows:

$$TTKG = (urine\ K/plasma\ K)/(urine\ Osm/plasma\ Osm)$$

where *K* is potassium, and *Osm* is osmolality. A TTKG of less than 4 in the setting of hyperkalemia implies either inadequate distal sodium delivery or inadequacy of the distal potassium excretion system. A TTKG of greater than 10 in the setting of hypokalemia supports the presence of renal potassium wasting, and further elucidation of the exact stimulus for potassium loss is warranted.

URINE NET CHARGE. Urine net charge measures the ability of the kidney to synthesize ammonia (NH_4^+) and excrete acid in non–anion gap metabolic acidosis. The difference between the urine cations (Na^+ and K^+) and urine anions (mainly Cl^-) represents the urine net charge:

$$Urine\ net\ charge = (urine\ Na^+\ urine\ K^+) - (urine\ Cl^-)$$

A negative urine net charge indicates NH_4^+ in the urine. This formula does not apply when there is an anion gap metabolic acidosis. The unmeasured anion complicates the measurement of ammonium in the urine by the use of the urine net charge.

Urinalysis

The analysis of the urine sample involves simple observation and separate measurements using specific tools or commercially available dipsticks.

APPEARANCE AND COLOR. The normal color of the urine is derived from urochromes, which are pigments excreted in the urine. The abnormal color or appearance of the urine may be explained by many conditions, as listed in Table 110–1.

SPECIFIC GRAVITY. The specific gravity of the urine can be raised by the presence of an increased number of solutes or by molecules with a high molecular weight, such as glucose and contrast dye. There is

Table 110–1 • MACROSCOPIC APPEARANCE OF URINE

APPEARANCE	CAUSE
Milky	Acid urine: urate crystals
	Alkaline urine: insoluble phosphates
	Infection: pus
	Spermatozoa
	Chyluria
Smoky pink	Hematuria (>0.54 mL blood/L urine)
Foamy	Proteinuria
Blue or green	*Pseudomonas* urinary tract infection
	Bilirubin
	Methylene blue
Pink or red	Aniline dyes in sweets
	Porphyrins (on standing)
	Blood, hemoglobin, myoglobin
	Drugs: phenindione, phenolphthalein
	Anthocyaninuria (beetroot—"beeturia")
Orange	Drugs: anthraquinones (laxatives), rifampicin
	Urobilinogenuria
Yellow	Mepacrine
	Conjugated bilirubin
	Phenacetin
	Riboflavin
Brown or black	Melanin (on standing)
	Myoglobin (on standing)
	Alkaptonuria
Green or black	Phenol
	Lysol
Brown	Drugs: phenazopyridine, furazolidone, L-dopa, niridazole
	Hemoglobin and myoglobin (on standing)
	Bilirubin

From Forbes CD, Jackson WF: Color Atlas and Text of Clinical Medicine, 3rd ed. London, Mosby, 2003.

a linear relationship between specific gravity and osmolality, unless there is glycosuria or excretion of contrast media, in which case the specific gravity is higher. A fixed specific gravity of 1.010 is characteristic of chronic kidney disease.

pH. Urine pH is often 5 as a result of daily net acid excretion. An alkaline pH often is noted after meals, when an "alkaline tide" associated with gastric acid excretion causes a high urine pH. A high urine pH also is seen on a vegetarian diet or when there is an infection with a urea splitting organism, such as *Proteus*. An inappropriately high urine pH in the setting of systemic non–anion gap metabolic acidosis may be seen when there are certain forms of renal tubular acidosis (RTA). In a proximal RTA, the urine pH is high until the tubular threshold for bicarbonate, which is reset, is reached. At this point, the urine pH decreases to 5. In distal RTA, there is usually an inability to create a sufficient gradient for H^+ excretion, and the urine pH is always higher than 5.5. The urine net charge gives complementary and confirmatory information. In type 4 RTA, the urine pH is often 5, and the urine net charge is often positive, confirming the absence of significant amounts of ammonium in the urine, a defect that is exacerbated by the accompanying hyperkalemia.

GLUCOSE. Glucose in the urine is detected by an assay using dipsticks impregnated with the enzyme glucose oxidase. Glycosuria is seen in diabetes mellitus, when pregnancy causes the tubular threshold for glucose reabsorption to change, and in tubular diseases that affect the proximal convoluted tubule and cause tubular glycosuria. Evidence for pan-proximal tubular dysfunction (e.g., glycosuria, aminoaciduria, phosphaturia) indicates that Fanconi's syndrome is present.

PROTEIN. The dipstick for protein is a sensitive assay based on color change induced by the presence of proteins at a given pH. It is most sensitive to the presence of albumin and is much less sensitive to other proteins, such as the light chains seen with Bence Jones protein. The presence of 1+ protein correlates with about 30 mg/dL of albuminuria, and 3+ protein correlates with greater than 500 mg/dL of proteinuria. Because the dipstick is not a quantitative measurement, small amounts of proteinuria in an oliguric patient may give the false appearance of high-grade proteinuria.

HEME. The dipstick uses the peroxidase-like activity of the hemoglobin and myoglobin molecule to detect the presence of heme pigment.

The reaction occurs on exposure to hemoglobin, myoglobin, or intact red blood cells (RBCs). The presence of myoglobin or hemoglobin is suspected when the heme reaction is intensely positive and there is a paucity of cellular elements in the sediment.

LEUKOCYTES. The detection of leukocytes depends on the presence of leukocyte esterase in leukocytes. They can be seen usually in infections and in inflammatory conditions.

URINE SEDIMENT. The urine sediment is the most crucial step in the evaluation of renal disease. The sediment gives an insight through the cellular elements resulting from activity within the kidney. The cells that may be seen include RBCs, white blood cells (WBCs), tubular cells, transitional cells, and squamous epithelial cells. Casts are formed in tubules and may contain cells or be acellular.

RBCs may originate from intrarenal vessels, glomeruli, tubules, or anywhere in the urogenital tract. Dysmorphic RBCs are cells that have been deformed by transit through glomeruli (Figs. 110–2 and 110–3). The cells are often lysed and less refractile than nonglomerular RBCs. They often fragment with poikilocytosis and with blebs, forming so-called Mickey Mouse RBCs. Phase contrast microscopy aids in the identification of dysmorphic RBCs. The presence of a majority of dysmorphic RBCs in a urine sediment points to a glomerular origin for the hematuria. The presence of RBC casts is often conclusive

evidence for the presence of glomerulonephritis. WBCs are seen most commonly in urinary tract infections. They also can be seen in acute interstitial nephritis, with *Legionella* and *Leptospira* infections, chronic infections such as tuberculosis, allergic interstitial nephritis, atheroembolic diseases, and granulomatous diseases such as sarcoidosis and tubulointerstitial nephritis syndrome. Mononuclear cells often appear with transplant rejection. Tubular cells are seen in many conditions involving tubulointerstitial diseases. They also are seen in ischemic and nephrotoxic injury, such as with myeloma kidney or cast nephropathy. Eosinophils require special stains, with the Giemsa stain being much less sensitive than the Hansel stain. Urine eosinophils are seen in a variety of conditions. Classically associated with allergic interstitial nephritis, they also have been documented in atheroembolic disease, prostatitis, and vasculitis.

Other elements that may be seen in the urine sediment are bacteria. A spun urine sediment may show rods or cocci in chains, but these are identified best by a Gram stain done on the urine sediment. In the sediment, one may see budding yeast forms, which are highly refractile, and spermatozoa.

Casts. Casts are formed in tubules and are characterized by the arrangement of the cells in a clearly formed matrix composed of Tamm-Horsfall protein. Because casts are formed in the renal parenchyma, they may give a clue to the origin of accompanying cellular elements.

Hyaline casts are casts of Tamm-Horsfall proteins formed normally and are seen in increased numbers after exercise (Fig. 110–4). *Granular casts* are degenerated tubular cell casts that are seen in the setting of tubular injury (Fig. 110–5). *Pigmented granular casts* are seen in

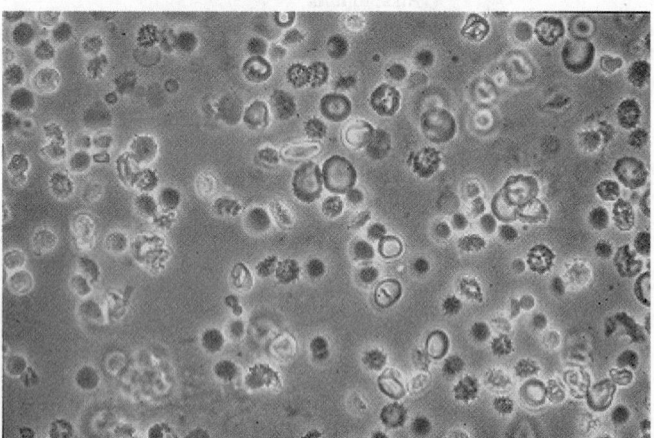

FIGURE 110–2 • Dysmorphic erythrocytes. These dysmorphic erythrocytes vary in size, shape, and hemoglobin content and reflect glomerular bleeding. (From Johnson RJ, Feehally J: Comprehensive Clinical Nephrology. London, Mosby, 2000, with permission.)

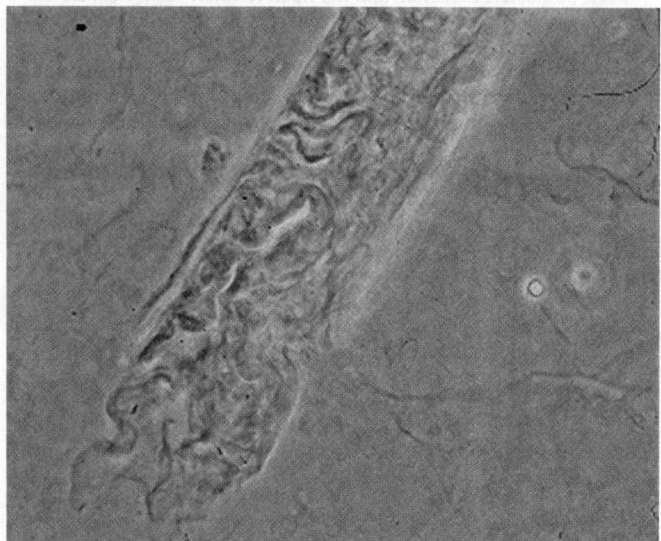

FIGURE 110–4 • Hyaline cast of the type seen in small numbers in normal urine. (From Johnson RJ, Feehally J: Comprehensive Clinical Nephrology. London, Mosby, 2000, with permission.)

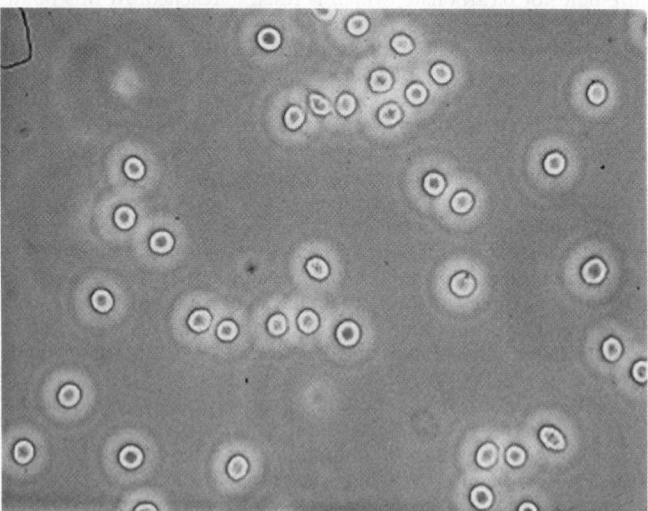

FIGURE 110–3 • Isomorphic erythrocytes. These erythrocytes are similar in size, shape, and hemoglobin content. Isomorphic cells reflect nonglomerular bleeding from lesions such as calculi or papillomas or hemorrhage from cysts in polycystic renal disease. (From Johnson RJ, Feehally J: Comprehensive Clinical Nephrology. London, Mosby, 2000, with permission.)

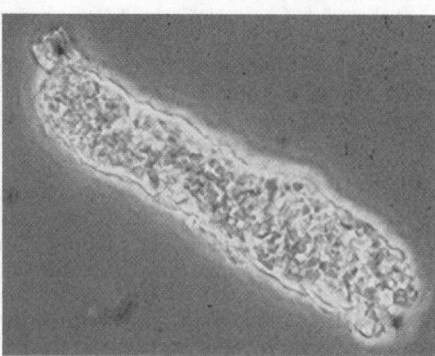

FIGURE 110–5 • Number and type of granules and their density in the cast vary in different casts. The presence of erythrocytes in this cast may mean that the granules are derived partly from disrupted erythrocytes. (From Johnson RJ, Feehally J: Comprehensive Clinical Nephrology. London, Mosby, 2000, with permission.)

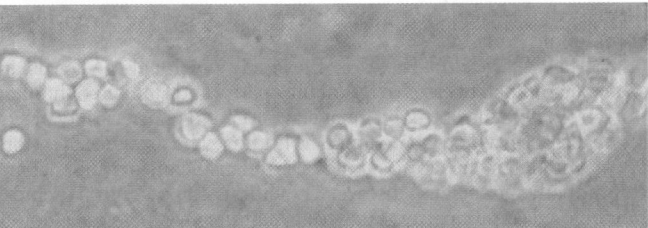

FIGURE 110–6 • A cast composed entirely of erythrocytes reflects heavy hematuria and active glomerular disease. Crescentic nephritis is likely to be present if erythrocyte casts are greater than 100/mL. (From Johnson RJ, Feehally J: Comprehensive Clinical Nephrology. London, Mosby, 2000, with permission.)

rhabdomyolysis with myoglobinuria and rarely hemoglobinuria. *RBC casts* are diagnostic of glomerulonephritis (Fig. 110–6). Although they have been reported in allergic interstitial nephritis and diabetic nephropathy, they almost always are seen in acute glomerulonephritis. The presence of RBC casts in a patient with microscopic hematuria can narrow the focus of the work-up to a glomerular lesion. *WBC casts* are seen commonly in pyelonephritis and in acute and chronic nonbacterial infections. They also are seen in other conditions in which WBCs are associated with parenchymal renal processes, such as allergic interstitial nephritis, atheroembolic diseases, and granulomatous diseases such as sarcoidosis. Rarely, they can be a dominant feature of many diseases, which traditionally are thought of as glomerular diseases, such as SLE and Wegener's granulomatosis. *Tubular cell casts* are seen with any acute tubular injury and are the dominant cellular casts in ischemic acute tubular necrosis. They also can be seen with nephrotoxic injury, such as with aminoglycosides and cisplatin. Casts may have leukocytes and tubular cells or be difficult to distinguish.

Crystals. Crystals often can be a normal finding in the urine or serve as clues to pathophysiologic processes. Certain crystals, such as the hexagonal crystals seen with cystinuria, are always abnormal (Fig. 110–7). Others, such as calcium oxalate crystals (Fig. 110–8), may be a normal finding or may be evidence for ethylene glycol intoxication in a patient with anion gap metabolic acidosis, acute renal failure, or hypocalcemia and mental status change. Triple phosphate crystals are composed of ammonium magnesium phosphate and are coffin shaped (Fig. 110–9). These are seen in urinary tract infections with urea splitting organisms. Uric acid crystals, sodium urate crystals (Fig. 110–10), and calcium phosphate amorphous crystals all are common and do not denote any pathologic significance.

Measurement of Renal Function

In clinical practice, renal function is measured by serum creatinine. It is normally a relatively fixed value in a given patient. Creatine is released as a waste product from myocytes and converted to creatinine in the liver. The normal range of serum creatinine is 0.6 to 1.5 mg/dL. About 10% of the daily creatinine is excreted through tubular secretion. Mild elevations of the plasma creatinine can occur during the use of cimetidine and trimethoprim, both of which

FIGURE 110–7 • Typical hexagonal cystine crystal; a single crystal provides a definitive diagnosis of cystinuria. (From Johnson RJ, Feehally J: Comprehensive Clinical Nephrology. London, Mosby, 2000, with permission.)

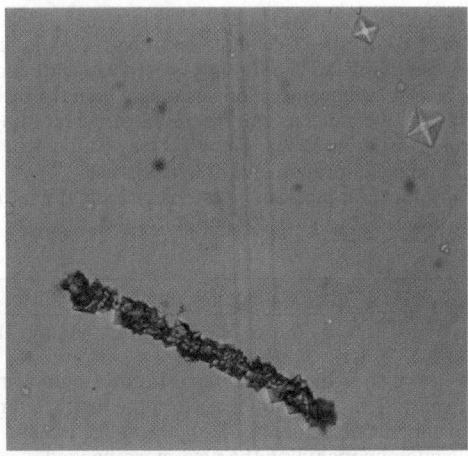

FIGURE 110–8 • Oxalate crystals. A pseudocast of calcium oxalate crystals accompanied by crystals of calcium oxalate dehydrate. (From Johnson RJ, Feehally J: Comprehensive Clinical Nephrology. London, Mosby, 2000, with permission.)

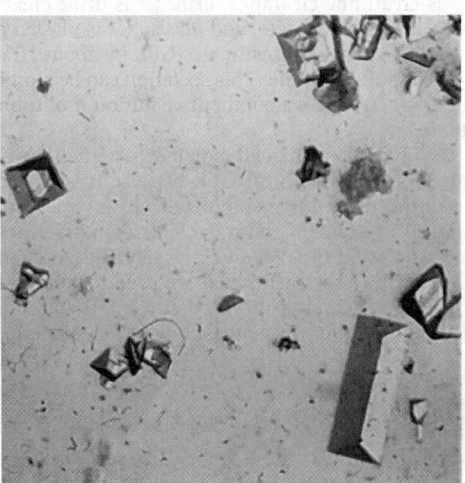

FIGURE 110–9 • Coffin lid crystals of magnesium ammonium phosphate (struvite). (From Johnson RJ, Feehally J: Comprehensive Clinical Nephrology. London, Mosby, 2000, with permission.)

FIGURE 110–10 • Urate crystals. Complex crystals suggestive of acute urate nephropathy or urate nephrolithiasis. (From Johnson RJ, Feehally J: Comprehensive Clinical Nephrology. London, Mosby, 2000, with permission.)

interfere with the tubular secretion of creatinine. These elevations are unlikely to cause significant elevations of the plasma creatinine. Ketoacids cause an artifactual increase in the plasma creatinine by interfering with the creatinine assay. The relationship between the glomerular filtration rate (GFR) and serum creatinine is such that there can be substantial loss of renal function while the serum creatinine remains in the normal range. The blood urea nitrogen (BUN), which is a product of protein catabolism, is about 10-fold higher, and the BUN-to-creatinine ratio commonly is used as a marker of volume status. There are circumstances, however, in which the BUN may be inappropriately high, such as with gastrointestinal bleeding and the use of steroids or tetracyclines. The BUN may be low when there is poor dietary intake of protein and in liver disease.

The creatinine clearance can be estimated from the serum creatinine by the use of the Cockcroft-Gault formula:

$$\text{Creatine Clearance} = \frac{(140 - \text{age})(\text{weight in kg})(0.85 \text{ for women})}{72 \times \text{serum creatine (mg/dL)}}$$

Creatinine clearance is calculated often using a 24-hour urine for creatinine concentration. The patient needs to be instructed to discard the first morning urine before initiating the collection and concluding the collection by including the next morning void.

The formula for calculating creatinine clearance is as follows:

$$CCr = \text{urine Cr} \times V/\text{plasma Cr}$$

where *CCr* is creatinine clearance, *urine Cr* is urine creatinine concentration, *V* is urine flow rate, and *plasma Cr* is plasma creatinine. The creatinine clearance overestimates GFR by about 10% owing to tubular secretion of creatinine. This secretion can be modified by the use of cimetidine, which is a competitive inhibitor of tubular creatinine secretion.

Inulin, a 5200 D uncharged polymer of fructose, is an ideal marker for the measurement of GFR because it is not reabsorbed, secreted, synthesized, or metabolized. It is not available for routine clinical assessment, however. Iothalamate clearance is an accurate measurement of GFR and is available as a diagnostic tool in clinical studies. Other agents that are used for the measurement of GFR include technetium-99m diethylenetriaminepentaacetic acid (DPTA) and sodium chromate Cr 51 ethylenediaminetetraacetic acid.

Serology and Urine Tests for the Evaluation of Renal Disease

The evaluation of renal dysfunction has to follow a stepwise progression from noninvasive serologic evaluation to a definitive or confirmatory diagnostic evaluation, such as a renal biopsy. Sometimes an expeditious diagnosis is needed, and a biopsy may be done relatively early in the evaluation. The advent of improved serologic diagnostic markers for certain diseases such as Wegener's granulomatosis has made the role of biopsy less mandatory than in the past. The following serologic tests are used commonly in the evaluation of renal insufficiency.

ANTINUCLEAR ANTIBODY. The antinuclear antibody (ANA) is one of the most commonly used tests in the evaluation of acute renal failure and chronic kidney disease, when there is the presumption of a glomerular disease, and in the evaluation of the cause of idiopathic nephrotic syndrome. Although a high titer, especially when accompanied by more specific serology such as anti–double-stranded DNA antibody or anti-Smith antibody, can be highly specific for the diagnosis of SLE, the usual titers are lower and have less specificity. The diagnosis of SLE still hinges on classic clinical criteria and often requires a renal biopsy, although there have been arguments in the literature regarding the utility of renal biopsy in the therapeutic decision making.

RHEUMATOID FACTOR. The role of rheumatoid factor (RF) is even less clear than ANA. Vasculitis in rheumatoid arthritis is a relatively late and rare event. RF can be detected in cases of cryoglobulinemia in which the IgM has RF activity in type II and type III cryoglobulinemia. RF can be seen as a nonspecific finding in diseases such as endocarditis and systemic vasculitis.

COMPLEMENT. The levels of C3, C4, and CH 50 usually are measured in the evaluation of suspected rapidly progressive glomerulonephritis. Complement levels are usually low in active SLE, poststreptococcal glomerulonephritis, endocarditis, membranoproliferative glomerulonephritis, cryoglobulinemia, shunt nephritis, and glomerulonephritis associated with visceral abscesses. A particularly

depressed C4 compared with C3 should raise the suspicion of cryoglobulinemia.

SERUM IMMUNOELECTROPHORESIS. Elevated polyclonal IgA levels are seen in about half of cases of IgA nephropathy and Henoch-Schönlein purpura. There may be polyclonal elevation of IgG in a variety of systemic diseases, which is a nonspecific finding. The presence of a monoclonal protein in the serum should raise the suspicion for a monoclonal gammopathy–associated disease. The differential diagnosis includes monoclonal gammopathy of uncertain significance, myeloma kidney, lymphomas, amyloidosis, light chain deposition disease, heavy chain deposition disease, immunotactoid glomerulonephritis, and cryoglobulinemia. The concentration of the monoclonal protein is higher when the diagnosis of multiple myeloma is made, but even small quantities of Bence Jones proteins in the serum can have clinical significance. Because a substantial fraction of multiple myelomas can have no heavy chain excretion, and small quantities of light chains may be hard to detect in a serum immunoelectrophoresis, a urine immunoelectrophoresis always must be sent with a serum immunoelectrophoresis to ensure a complete evaluation.

URINE FOR BENCE JONES PROTEIN. This test complements the serum immunoelectrophoresis and may reveal Bence Jones protein even in the absence of an M-component in the serum immunoelectrophoresis. Bence Jones proteinuria may be present in myeloma kidney, amyloidosis, light chain deposition disease, lymphoma, or occasionally monoclonal gammopathy of uncertain significance. One has to be cautious not to use these tests to exclude completely a diagnosis of amyloidosis because many patients with systemic amyloidosis may have a normal serum immunoelectrophoresis and no Bence Jones proteinuria.

ANTINEUTROPHIL CYTOPLASMIC ANTIBODY. The antineutrophil cytoplasmic antibody (ANCA) has allowed for earlier and more definitive recognition of one of the most common causes of rapidly progressive glomerulonephritis (RPGN). The ANCA test, when confirmed by enzyme-linked immunosorbent assay, is highly sensitive and specific for a group of vasculitides. The antibodies are present in the serum of the affected patient and cause two different patterns of staining—perinuclear (p-ANCA) and cytoplasmic staining (c-ANCA). Both antigens have cytoplasmic distribution, and the former pattern is an artifact of the fixation method. The antigen for p-ANCA is myeloperoxidase, and the antigen for c-ANCA is proteinase-3. The former often is associated with positive staining in the clinical setting of microscopic polyangiitis, idiopathic crescentic glomerulonephritis, or Churg-Strauss syndrome. The c-ANCA serology often correlates with the classic disease of Wegener's granulomatosis, but the relationship is not definitive. No cases have been reported with antibodies to both antigens. Immunofluorescence, although highly sensitive, is not specific, but it gains specificity when used with enzyme-linked immunosorbent assay and Western blotting and precludes the need for renal biopsy in the appropriate clinical setting. Anti-GBM antibody staining also may occur in the presence of a positive ANCA, the significance of which is unclear. It is speculated that exposure of the Goodpasture antigen, as a result of the glomerular injury, leads to the anti-GBM antibody formation as a secondary process.

ANTI–GLOMERULAR BASEMENT MEMBRANE ANTIBODY. The identification of the presence of autoantibodies to the Goodpasture antigen, which resides in a domain of the α chain of type 4 collagen, was an important step in elucidating the mechanism of renal injury in Goodpasture's syndrome. The availability of this test provides early and accurate diagnosis of a disease that when left untreated can lead to irreversible renal failure. Recovery is rare when renal failure is advanced to the point of requiring dialysis at the time of presentation. The initial diagnosis can be made by immunofluorescence and confirmed by Western blot analysis.

CRYOGLOBULINS. Cryoglobulins are thermolabile immunoglobulins of single monoclonal type (type I cryoglobulinemia) or a mixture of immunoglobulins in type II and type III cryoglobulinemia, in which one of the components has RF activity against IgG. The identification of cryoglobulins does not prove their role in a disease process, unless the clinical and pathologic features are characteristic. Type I and type II cryoglobulins are more likely to be associated with clinical disease, especially at higher titers. In type II cryoglobulinemia, the monoclonal component has the RF activity and is often an IgM κ M-component. Type III cryoglobulinemia is often of less clinical significance. Type I cryoglobulinemia is seen with Waldenström's macroglobulinemia and multiple myeloma; type II, with hepatitis C infection, Sjögren's syndrome, lymphomas, and SLE; and type III, with hepatitis C, chronic infections, and inflammatory conditions. In cryo-globulinemia that is associated with hepatitis C, the hepatitis C viral (HCV) RNA is concentrated in the cryoprecipitate. This may warrant an assay for HCV RNA in the cryoprecipitate to rule out hepatitis C as the offending agent. The sample must be transported warm (37°C) to the laboratory to avoid precipitation of the cryoglobulins at room temperature. The samples are handled warm in the laboratory before cryoprecipitate is allowed to form at 4°C. The precipitate is identi-fied by immunofixation and double diffusion in agar.

HEPATITIS B SEROLOGY. Membranous nephropathy is associated with hepatitis B infection and always denotes chronic infection with hep-atitis B surface antigenemia. Classic polyarteritis nodosa occasionally has been seen in the setting of hepatitis B infection with often surface antigenemia and hepatitis B e antigenemia.

HEPATITIS C SEROLOGY. This is associated with a variety of renal entities, including cryoglobulinemia, membranoproliferative glo-merulonephritis, and membranous nephropathy. The evaluation may include the antibody test and an assay for HCV RNA. Occasionally the HCV RNA analysis may have to be conducted on the cryopre-cipitate as discussed previously to verify that hepatitis C is the cause of the cryoglobulinemia.

HUMAN IMMUNODEFICIENCY VIRUS SEROLOGY. Human immunodeficiency virus (HIV)–associated nephropathy is associated with nephrotic syndrome and acute renal failure. In the appropriate clinical setting, HIV serology and viral titers are appropriate tests for both clinical syndromes.

ANTI-DNASE B OR ANTISTREPTOLYSIN O. Streptococcal infection is deter-mined in the evaluation of poststreptococcal glomerulonephritis. Acute and convalescent serologies are sent to confirm recent infection.

ERYTHROCYTE SEDIMENTATION RATE. The erythrocyte sedimentation rate (ESR) is a relatively nonspecific test in the evaluation of renal disease. High ESRs often point to systemic vasculitis, multiple myeloma, and malignancy as the underlying cause, however. One must use caution in pursuing an elevated ESR as the only finding in the setting of renal failure. The ESR often is elevated in nephrotic syndrome, including in diabetic nephropathy.

Imaging Studies of the Genitourinary Tract

A variety of renal imaging techniques have been developed to assist in the evaluation of diseases of the kidney.

PLAIN RADIOGRAPH OF KIDNEY, URETER, AND BLADDER. This study was used in the past for the estimation of renal size and the evaluation of calcium stones. It has been largely replaced by other studies.

INTRAVENOUS PYELOGRAM. Intravenous pyelogram has been largely replaced by computed tomography (CT) scanning for the evaluation of renal size and the detection of stones and masses.

RENAL ULTRASOUND. Renal ultrasound has become the most com-monly used imaging study (Fig. 110–11). It is expedient; is nonin-vasive; and gives reliable information regarding obstruction, renal size, and the presence of masses and renal echotexture. The study has only 90% sensitivity for the detection of hydronephrosis, however,

and should not be relied on to rule out hydronephrosis with certainty. Additionally, it cannot detect stones in the ureters and bladder and has limited utility in the evaluation for kidney stones. Doppler imaging permits evaluation of the renal vessels and resistive index.

COMPUTED TOMOGRAPHY SCAN OF KIDNEYS. A stone protocol CT scan of the kidneys, ureter, and bladder has become the study of choice for the detection of kidney stones because of its ability to detect stones of all kinds, including uric acid stones and the nonobstructing stones in the ureters (Fig. 110–12). Masses in the kidney can be evaluated using either contrast CT or a renal ultrasound.

COMPUTED TOMOGRAPHY ANGIOGRAPHY. CT angiography is used for the study of renal artery stenosis and is emerging rapidly as a useful study. Although it is comparable to magnetic resonance angiography as a noninvasive tool, it requires the use of iodinated contrast material, which may cause renal dysfunction in patients with chronic kidney disease.

MAGNETIC RESONANCE IMAGING WITH MAGNETIC RESONANCE ANGIOGRAPHY. The use of magnetic resonance imaging with magnetic resonance angiography has revolutionized the evaluation of renovascular disease (Fig. 110–13). The test is highly sensitive but tends to overestimate

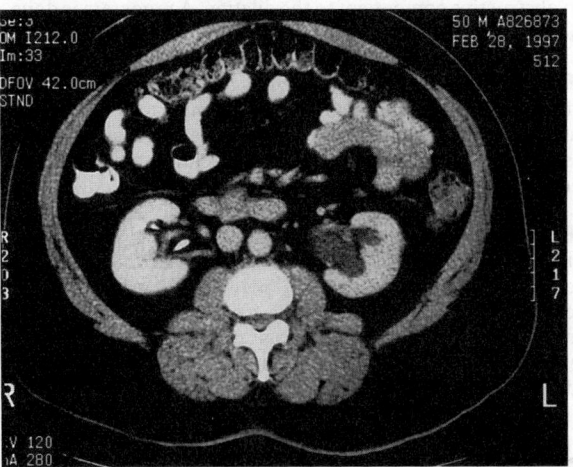

FIGURE 110–12 • Delayed excretion in the left kidney secondary to a distal calculus. Contrast-enhanced computed tomography scan shows dilated left renal pelvis (arrow). (From Johnson RJ, Feehally J: Comprehensive Clinical Nephrology. London, Mosby, 2000, with permission.)

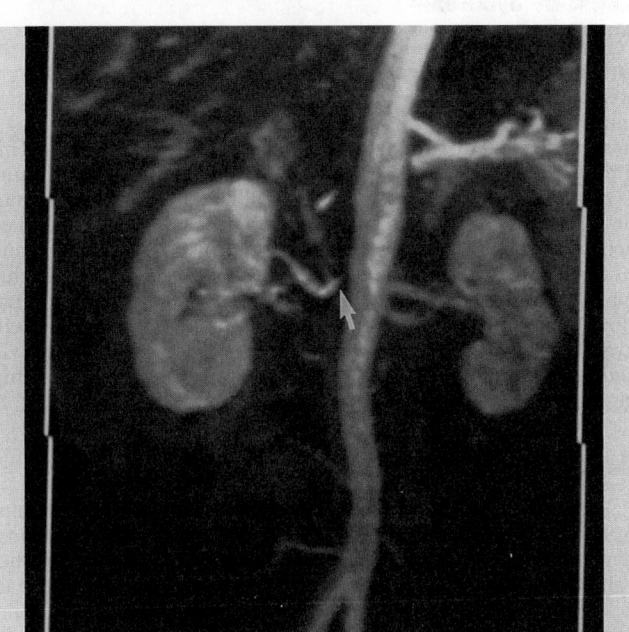

FIGURE 110–13 • Magnetic resonance angiography. Coronal three-dimensional image shows right renal artery stenosis (arrow). (From Johnson RJ, Feehally J: Comprehensive Clinical Nephrology. London, Mosby, 2000, with permission.)

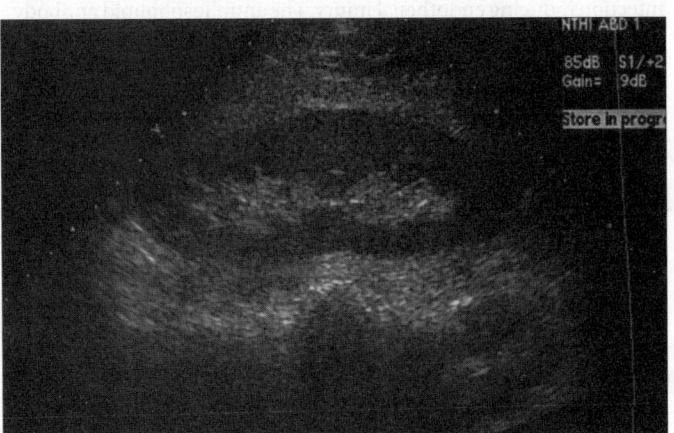

FIGURE 110–11 • Normal sagittal renal ultrasound. The cortex is hypoechoic compared with the echogenic fat containing the renal sinus. (From Johnson RJ, Feehally J: Comprehensive Clinical Nephrology. London, Mosby, 2000, with permission.)

the degree of stenosis. Its accuracy in detecting fibromuscular dysplasia causing renal artery stenosis has not been well validated. Magnetic resonance imaging also can be used to evaluate renal masses. Its main advantages are that it is a noninvasive test and does not require iodinated contrast material. Claustrophobic patients may not tolerate this study.

RENOGRAM. The uptake by the kidneys of technetium 99m–labeled DPTA and mercaptoacetyl triglycine, the former as a marker of GFR and the latter as a marker of renal blood flow, has been used to evaluate for the screening for renovascular disease. The first component reflects perfusion, whereas the second component evaluates renal function by the assessment of radiotracer uptake and excretion by the kidneys. The rate of uptake of the radioisotope often is decreased and delayed when there is renal artery stenosis, and the excretion is markedly delayed when captopril is administered before the study. There is also a decrease in the GFR of the affected kidney after the administration of captopril. Although useful for the evaluation of unilateral renal artery stenosis, it is of limited use in the evaluation of bilateral renal artery stenosis or in the setting of significant renal dysfunction.

FUROSEMIDE RENOGRAM. When there is dilation of the collecting system, furosemide renography is used to investigate whether there is an obstructive component to the dilation. A renogram is done, after which furosemide is administered intravenously. Rapid washout of the isotope suggests that there is no anatomic obstruction.

RENAL VEIN RENINS. Renal vein renins are predominantly of historical interest. The measurement of renins from each of the renal veins is used to determine whether the presence of renal artery stenosis causes a physiologic response of higher renin secretion on the ipsilateral side. A ratio of 1.5 on the affected side compared with the contralateral side gives support to a physiologically important stenosis.

RENAL ANGIOGRAPHY. Renal arteriography is the gold standard in the evaluation of renal artery stenosis. It also is used for the evaluation of arteriovenous malformations, polyarteritis nodosa, and other vascular lesions of the kidneys. The study is invasive, uses iodinated contrast material, and incurs a small risk of atheroembolic disease. Therapeutic angioplasty and stenting can be done at the time of the angiogram.

MAJOR RENAL SYNDROMES

Renal disease can be divided logically into major overlapping categories, which are used to characterize the most common renal syndromes.

Nephritic Syndrome

Acute nephritic syndrome is an uncommon but dramatic presentation of an acute glomerulonephritis. Some of the diseases that present with acute nephritic syndrome cause necrotizing crescentic glomerulonephritis with rapid and irreversible renal dysfunction, creating a narrow therapeutic window, whereas others are more forgiving. This group contains all of the causes of RPGN. The hallmark of acute nephritic syndrome is the presence of RBC casts, but their absence does not rule out the syndrome. Dysmorphic RBCs can be identified accurately by the trained eye under phase contrast microscopy and can be characterized to be of glomerular origin. The diseases that make up this group are detailed subsequently in the description of the RPGN group. This group warrants urgent and usually inpatient evaluation. The nephritic syndrome often is accompanied by avid sodium and water retention, leading to occasional diagnosis of congestive heart failure.

Nephrotic Syndrome

Nephrotic syndrome is characterized by the presence of proteinuria of greater than $3.5\,g/day/1.73\,m^2$, with accompanying edema, hypertension, and hyperlipidemia. It leads to a multitude of other consequences, such as predisposition to infection and hypercoagulability. In general, the diseases associated with nephrotic syndrome cause chronic kidney dysfunction, but rarely they can cause acute renal failure. Acute renal failure may be seen with minimal change disease, HIV-associated nephropathy, and bilateral renal vein thrombosis. The cause of nephrotic syndrome can be divided into primary and secondary causes. The latter include diabetic nephropathy,

amyloidosis, and SLE with membranous nephropathy. Of these, diabetic nephropathy is the most prevalent cause of end-stage renal disease in the United States. The causes of idiopathic nephrotic syndrome in decreasing order of prevalence are focal and segmental glomerulosclerosis, membranous nephropathy, minimal change disease, and membranoproliferative glomerulonephritis. In the 1990s, focal and segmental glomerulosclerosis emerged as the leading cause of idiopathic nephrotic syndrome in the United States, replacing membranous nephropathy.

Tubulointerstitial Diseases

Tubulointerstitial diseases vary in presentation from acute renal failure to chronic kidney dysfunction that presents as asymptotic mild renal insufficiency. It is more challenging to diagnose the cause of a mild chronic kidney disease than it is to determine the cause of RPGN. Because specific therapeutic options are much more limited for chronic kidney disease, it is less likely to be evaluated. The urine sediment often contains small-to-moderate amounts of proteinuria, usually less than 1 g/day. The sediment often contains tubular cells, WBCs, RBCs, and casts. Casts are composed of tubular cells, WBCs, granular casts, and waxy casts, the last-mentioned being seen in chronic kidney disease. RBC casts are rare in acute interstitial nephritis and are more characteristic of glomerular disease. The major causes of tubulointerstitial disease are listed in Table 110–2.

Vascular Diseases of the Kidney

Vascular diseases of the kidney can be divided into large vessel obstruction and medium-to-small vessel diseases. Renovascular disease is a common cause of hypertension, congestive heart failure, and renal insufficiency. The most common cause of renal artery stenosis is atherosclerotic renal artery stenosis. Fibromuscular dysplasia is much less prevalent, causing only about 10% of renal artery stenosis. The latter is more common in women who are 20 to 50 years old. Variants of fibromuscular dysplasia affect men and women and are associated with renal artery dissections and infarcts. Small vessel diseases, although they have similar effects on the kidney, vary greatly in terms of pathophysiology and etiology. One is classic polyarteritis nodosa, which is seen in patients with hepatitis B, HIV infection, and rarely hepatitis C. The symptoms include abdominal pain, hypertension, and mild renal insufficiency, often with a benign sediment. The diagnostic findings include demonstration of microaneurysms at the bifurcation of medium-sized arteries in the visceral organs by arteriography. Other diseases involving small vessels include atheroembolic disease, which is seen either spontaneously or after arteriography or surgery. This syndrome affects the kidneys, gastrointestinal tract, and lower extremities. Central nervous system involvement is seen when angiography or surgery affects the aortic arch. The thrombotic microangiopathies include hemolytic-uremic syndrome (HUS) and thrombotic thrombocytopenic purpura (TTP). TTP is associated with an acquired inhibitor to, or the congenital inherited absence of, a protease, which cleaves large-molecular-weight von Willebrand multimers. HUS is caused by Shiga's toxin from *Escherichia coli* 057:H7 infection inducing endothelial injury. The antiphospholipid antibody

---

Table 110–2 • MAJOR CAUSES OF TUBULOINTERSTITIAL DISEASE

Ischemic and toxic acute tubular necrosis.
Allergic interstitial nephritis
Interstitial nephritis secondary to immune complex–related collagen vascular disease, such as Sjögren's disease and SLE
Granulomatous diseases: sarcoidosis, tubulointerstitial nephritis with uveitis
Pigment-related tubular injury: myoglobulinuria, hemaglobinuria
Hypercalcemia with nephrocalcinosis
Tubular obstruction: drugs such as indinavir, uric acid in tumor lysis syndrome
Myeloma kidney or cast nephropathy
Infection-related interstitial nephritis: *Legionella, Leptospira*
Infiltrative diseases, such as lymphoma

SLE = systemic lupus erythematosus.

syndrome can affect the kidney in many ways. There can be large vessel thrombosis and stenosis and a thrombotic microangiopathy, with proteinuria, hypertension, and renal insufficiency. Scleroderma renal crisis is a manifestation of systemic sclerosis, with often an inexorable progression to end-stage renal insufficiency if untreated.

Acute Renal Failure

Acute renal failure is a syndrome in which there is a decline in glomerular filtration over a period of days. Most cases of acute renal failure in the hospital have hemodynamic or toxic etiologies. Other causes include obstruction, tubulointerstitial diseases such as myeloma kidney, vascular diseases such as HUS and TTP, scleroderma kidney, atheroembolic diseases, antiphospholipid antibody syndrome, and the glomerular diseases that cause RPGN. The patient with acute renal failure is approached best by evaluation for prerenal, renal, and postrenal causes. The careful and systematic evaluation of the patient should start with a careful history and physical examination. This should be followed by selected laboratory and radiographic tests. The urinalysis is often a key element in the evaluation of the cause.

Rapidly Progressive Glomerulonephritis

RPGN usually presents with dramatic acute renal failure often associated with the systemic features of vasculitis, a nephritic sediment, and a rapid decrement of GFR. There are four major groups of diseases in this category.

ANTI–GLOMERULAR BASEMENT MEMBRANE DISEASE. Anti-GBM disease may present with or without pulmonary hemorrhage. Anti-GBM disease is the most dramatic of the causes of RPGN. An acquired autoantibody to an epitope in type IV collagen leads to a necrotizing crescentic glomerulonephritis and rapid deterioration in renal function. Because recovery is unlikely if the creatinine is greater than 6.8 mg/dL or if the patient is anuric, diagnosis and treatment cannot be delayed. Serologic diagnosis is sensitive and specific, and occasionally a positive serology may obviate the need for tissue diagnosis.

ANTINEUTROPHIL CYTOPLASMIC ANTIBODY–ASSOCIATED VASCULITIS. The ANCA-associated vasculitides include Wegener's granulomatosis, microscopic polyangiitis, Churg-Strauss syndrome, and idiopathic pauci-immune crescentic glomerulonephritis. Wegener's granulomatosis is a necrotizing granulomatous vasculitis affecting the upper airways, sinuses, lungs, and kidneys. The lung lesions classically are cavitating nodules. The renal pathology is common to all ANCA-associated glomerulonephritis and shows pauci-immune necrotizing and crescentic glomerulonephritis. Microscopic polyangiitis is associated with skin lesions, mononeuritis multiplex, and pulmonary hemorrhage, which can be life-threatening. Churg-Strauss syndrome has the unique feature of eosinophilia and asthma. Idiopathic pauci-immune crescentic glomerulonephritis has the renal features of the disease, is ANCA positive, but does not have the extrarenal manifestations of the systemic vasculitides.

HYPOCOMPLEMENTEMIC IMMUNE COMPLEX GLOMERULONEPHRITIS. These are a group of diseases associated with low complements and an immune complex glomerulonephritis. They include SLE, poststreptococcal glomerulonephritis, infective endocarditis, shunt nephritis, membranoproliferative glomerulonephritis, cryoglobulinemia, and glomerulonephritis associated with visceral abscesses.

IMMUNE COMPLEX GLOMERULONEPHRITIS ASSOCIATED WITH NORMAL COMPLEMENT. This category includes IgA nephropathy and Henoch-Schönlein purpura. IgA nephropathy is the most common glomerulonephritis and is associated with mesangial deposits, predominantly of IgA. The disease is variable in severity and encompasses incidental asymptomatic hematuria to cases of RPGN from crescentic IgA nephropathy. Henoch-Schönlein purpura is often self-limited and associated with gastrointestinal involvement and palpable purpura of the extensor surfaces of the lower extremities.

Chronic Kidney Disease

The National Kidney Foundation has defined the stages of chronic kidney disease (Table 110–3). Chronic kidney disease is defined as either kidney damage or a GFR less than 60 mL/min/1.73 m² for more than 3 months. Kidney damage is defined as pathologic abnormalities or markers of kidney damage, including abnormalities in the composition of blood or urine or abnormalities in the imaging tests. The

Table 110–3 • STAGES OF CHRONIC KIDNEY DISEASE*

STAGE	DESCRIPTION	GFR (mL/min/1.73 m²)
1	Kidney damage with normal or ↑ GFR	≥90
2	Kidney damage with mild or ↓ GFR	60–89
3	Moderate ↓ GFR	30–59
4	Severe ↓ GFR	15–29
5	Kidney failure	<15 (or dialysis)

*Chronic kidney disease is defined as either kidney damage or GFR < 60 mL/min/1.73 m² for ≥ months. Kidney damage is defined as pathologic abnormalities or markers of damage, including abnormalities in blood or urine tests or image studies.
GFR = glomerular filtration rate.
From www.kidney.org/professionals/doqi/kdoqi/Gif_File/kck_t10.gif.

excretion of 30 to 300 mg of albumin in a 24-hour period defines microalbuminuria. It is estimated that 11.7% of the adult U.S. population have abnormal albumin excretion in the urine, increasing in frequency with age. Kidney failure is defined as either a GFR less than 15 mL/min/1.73 m², which is accompanied by signs and symptoms of uremia, or a need for initiation of kidney replacement therapy for treatment of complications of decreased GFR. End-stage renal disease includes patients treated by dialysis or transplantation regardless of the level of GFR.

Patients with chronic kidney disease warrant referral to a nephrologist. Care of these patients should focus on efforts to slow disease progression, optimize medical management, and make a seamless transition to renal replacement therapy. The care should include optimal blood pressure control, use of angiotensin-converting enzyme inhibitors and angiotensin receptor blockers where indicated, dietary counseling, careful management of calcium and phosphorus levels, monitoring of parathyroid hormone level, and the management of anemia with the use of erythropoietin and iron supplements. Early access placement and initiation of transplant evaluation are important components of the care of patients with chronic kidney disease. The quality of life can be well maintained, and the transition to renal replacement therapy can be made smooth with well-timed nephrology care.

RENAL BIOPSY IN EVALUATION OF RENAL DISEASE

Renal biopsy is an invaluable tool in the evaluation of renal disease. The use of renal biopsy has identified new entities, such as the collapsing variant of focal and segmental sclerosis and immunotactoid glomerulonephritis. Most biopsies are done percutaneously with realtime ultrasound guidance or with CT-guided localization. More recently, the transjugular approach is being used in patients in whom the risks of bleeding are high. The current indications for renal biopsy include the following:

1. RPGN without a serologic diagnosis. Although some use serology alone for ANCA-related vasculitis, others still seek pathologic confirmation. For many other entities, such as cryoglobulinemia and SLE, the biopsy is invaluable in stratifying patients before therapy and for follow-up on therapy.
2. Nephrotic syndrome without an obvious cause. In childhood nephrotic syndrome, empirical steroid therapy is used routinely because of the high prevalence of steroid-responsive minimal change disease. In adults, the approach is often to proceed with a biopsy followed by initiation of appropriate therapy based on the pathology (Fig. 110–14).
3. SLE with renal involvement, in which more proliferative glomerulonephritis, such as World Health Organization class IV SLE nephritis (Fig. 110–15), may be treated more aggressively with immunosuppression.
4. Unexplained renal failure of any cause. Although it is uncommon to perform a biopsy in patients with hospital-acquired renal failure, the biopsy can be useful, especially when steroid therapy is contemplated, such as in allergic interstitial nephritis.
5. Renal transplants with acute and chronic renal failure, in which the biopsy information can be crucial in guiding diagnosis and treatment.

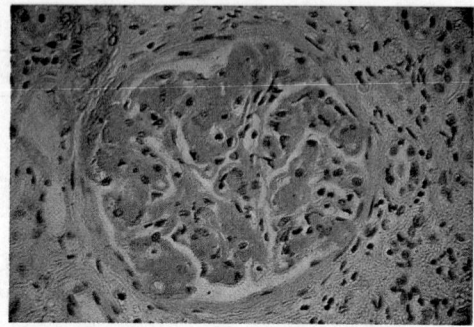

FIGURE 110–14 • Renal amyloidosis. The glomerulus shows amyloid deposition, stained by Congo red, in the glomerular capillaries (× 330). (From Johnson RJ, Feehally J: Comprehensive Clinical Nephrology. London, Mosby, 2000, with permission.)

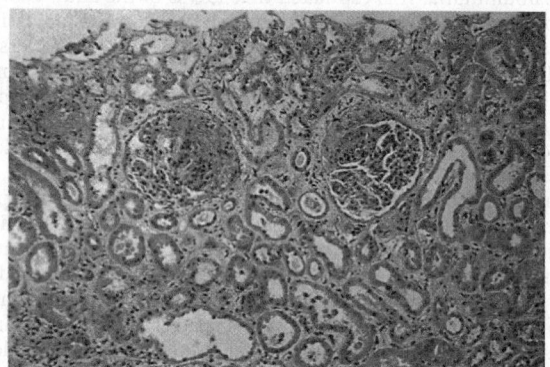

FIGURE 110–15 • Systemic lupus erythematosus. This renal biopsy specimen shows proliferative change and crescent formation in both glomeruli (H&E × 110). (From Johnson RJ, Feehally J: Comprehensive Clinical Nephrology. London, Mosby, 2000, with permission.)

6. Proteinuria, below the nephrotic range, is less established as an indication for renal biopsy. Here other factors, such as the presence of hypertension, renal insufficiency, and the age and preference of the patient, are included in the decision to pursue a renal biopsy.

A renal biopsy is generally a safe procedure in the hands of an experienced operator using real-time ultrasound guidance. The bleeding risk is 1% to 2% in patients without coagulopathy.

SUGGESTED READINGS
Kidney Foundation DOQI Guidelines: Available at http://www.kidney.org/professionals/doqi/index.cfm. *A periodically updated source of consensus guidelines for the management of chronic kidney disease.*
Massry S, Glasscock R (eds): Massry and Glasscock's Textbook of Nephrology. Philadelphia, Lippincott Williams & Wilkins, 2001. *A comprehensive text.*

111 STRUCTURE AND FUNCTION OF THE KIDNEYS

C. Craig Tisher

The complex multicellular composition of the kidney reflects the complicated nature of its functional properties. This organ is responsible for maintaining the volume and the ionic composition of the body fluids; excreting fixed or nonvolatile metabolic waste products, such as creatinine, urea, and uric acid; and eliminating exogenous drugs and toxins. The kidney is a major endocrine organ because it produces renin, erythropoietin, 1,25-dihydroxycholecalciferol, prostaglandins, and kinins; it also serves as a target organ for many hormones. The kidney also catabolizes small-molecular-weight proteins and is responsible for a host of metabolic functions (e.g., ammoniagenesis and gluconeogenesis).

Development

The kidney originates from two sources: (1) the ureteral bud, which gives rise to the ureter, pelvis, calyces, and collecting ducts, and (2) the metanephric blastema, which gives rise to the glomerulus and tubules. During embryogenesis, three successive sets of excretory organs develop: the pronephros, mesonephros, and metanephros. The permanent kidney evolves from the metanephros. Cellular and molecular mechanisms that underlie renal morphogenesis include cell proliferation, expression of nuclear proto-oncogenes and homeobox genes, actions of peptide growth factors, and alterations in cell adhesion and the composition of the extracellular matrix.

Gross Anatomy

The kidneys are located in the retroperitoneal space and extend from the 12th thoracic vertebra to the third lumbar vertebra. The right organ usually is more caudad, whereas the left organ tends to be slightly larger. Each adult human kidney weighs 115 to 170 g; measures approximately 11 × 6 × 2.5 cm; and is surrounded by a tough, fibroelastic capsule.

The cut surface of a bisected kidney reveals a darker inner region, the medulla, and a pale outer region approximately 1 cm in thickness, the cortex. The human kidney has a multipapillary configuration in which the medulla is divided into 8 to 18 striated conical masses called *pyramids* (Fig. 111–1). The base of each pyramid is positioned at the corticomedullary junction, and the apex extends toward the renal pelvis, forming a papilla. On the tip of each papilla, there are numerous small openings that represent the distal ends of the collecting ducts (of Bellini). Extending downward between the pyramids are portions of cortex, the septa of Bertin. Close examination of the cut surface reveals fine longitudinal striations, the medullary rays (of Ferrein), which extend into the cortex. Despite their name, the medullary rays represent part of the cortex and are formed by the straight segments of the proximal tubule, the thick ascending limbs, and the collecting ducts.

The renal pelvis is the saclike dilation of the upper ureter. Two or three major calyces extend from the pelvis and divide into the minor calyces that surround individual papillae.

Nephron

Each human kidney contains about 0.8 to 1.2 × 10⁶ nephrons—the functional units of the kidney. A nephron consists of the glomerulus or renal corpuscle, the proximal tubule, the thin limbs of Henle,

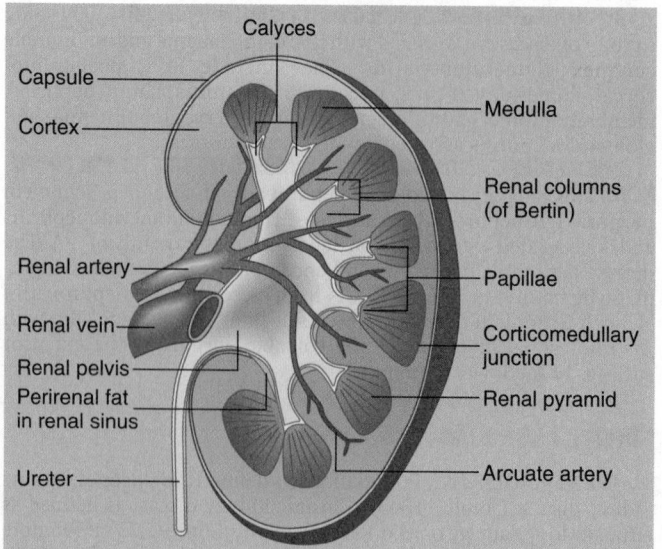

FIGURE 111–1 • Sagittal section of human kidney illustrating gross anatomic features.

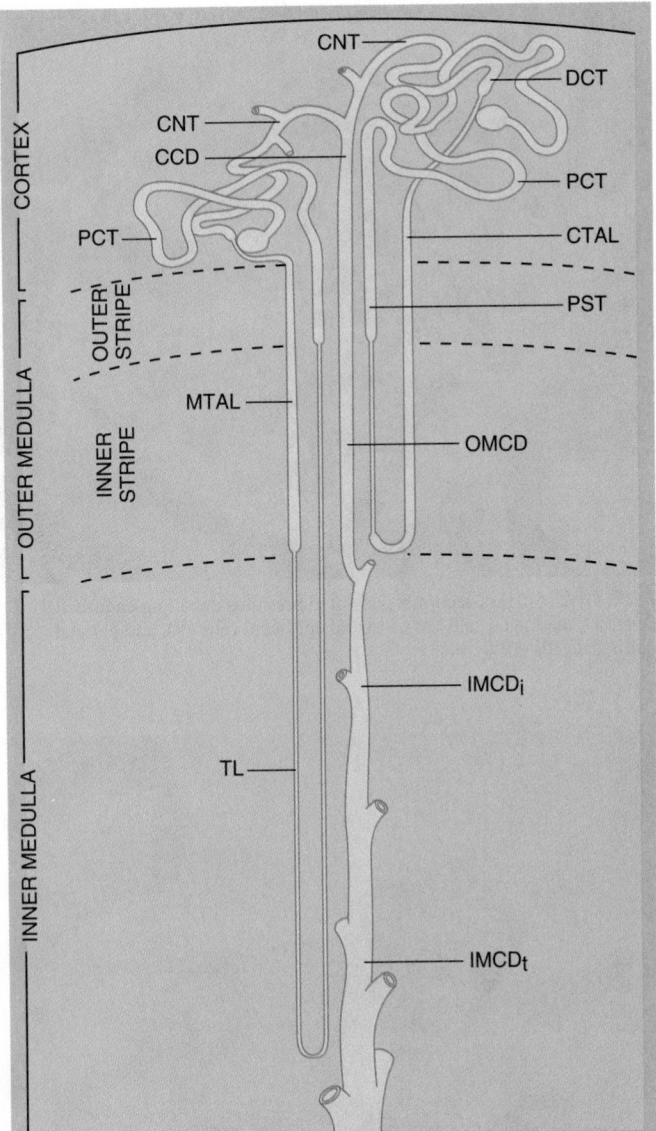

the latter subdivided into an inner and an outer stripe (see Fig. 111–2). In the outer stripe of the outer medulla are the terminal portions of the proximal straight tubules, the thick ascending limbs, and the collecting ducts. The thicker inner stripe of the outer medulla contains thin descending limbs, thick ascending limbs, and collecting ducts. The thin descending and thin ascending limbs of long loops and the collecting ducts are located in the inner medulla. This intricate arrangement of the parenchyma in the cortex and medulla provides an anatomic basis for integration of many of the complex functions of the kidney.

Vasculature

STRUCTURE. The kidney has an extensive vasculature that accommodates 20 to 25% of the cardiac output. The main renal artery branches to form anterior and posterior divisions, which divide into five segmental arteries. The *segmental arteries* traverse the renal sinus to divide into the *interlobar arteries*. The latter pierce the parenchyma and course toward the cortex along the septa of Bertin between adjacent renal pyramids (see Fig. 111–1). At the corticomedullary junction, the interlobar arteries branch into the *arcuate arteries,* which follow a gently curved course along the base of the pyramids. The arcuate arteries give rise to the *interlobular arteries* that ascend in the cortex toward the renal surface.

Afferent arterioles are branches of the interlobular arteries, and each supplies a single glomerulus (renal corpuscle) (Fig. 111–3). The *efferent arterioles* exit the glomeruli and divide to form an intricate peritubular microcirculation. The capillary networks formed by the efferent arterioles of superficial and midcortical glomeruli supply the cortical labyrinth and medullary rays, whereas the efferent arterioles of the juxtamedullary glomeruli are responsible for the entire medullary blood supply. In the outer stripe of the outer medulla, these vessels divide to form the *descending vasa recta,* which are located in vascular bundles. At various levels in the medulla, the descending vasa recta exit the bundles to form capillary networks. The *ascending vasa recta* drain the medulla.

FIGURE 111–2 • Diagram illustrating superficial and juxtamedullary nephrons. PCT = proximal convoluting tubule; PST = proximal straight tubule; TL = thin limb of Henle's loop; MTAL = medullary thick ascending limb; CTAL = cortical thick ascending limb; DCT = distal convoluted tubule; CNT = connecting segment; CCD = cortical collecting duct; OMCD = outer medullary collecting duct; IMCD$_i$ = initial inner medullary collecting duct; and IMCD$_t$ = terminal inner medullary collecting duct. (Modified from Madsen KM, Tisher CC: Structural-functional relationships along the distal nephron. Am J Physiol 1986;250:F1–F15.)

and the distal tubule, all of which originate from the metanephric blastema (Fig. 111–2). The connecting tubule, a transitional segment also believed to be derived from the metanephric blastema, joins the nephron to the collecting duct system.

Architecture

In the renal cortex, two architectural regions can be distinguished, the *cortical labyrinth* and the *medullary rays* (see Fig. 111–1). The cortical labyrinth is a continuous zone of parenchyma that surrounds the medullary rays. Glomeruli, proximal and distal convoluted tubules, connecting tubules, initial collecting tubules, interlobular veins, and a rich capillary network are located in the cortical labyrinth. Ascending connecting tubules of juxtamedullary nephrons fuse to form arcades within the cortical labyrinth. The medullary rays contain the proximal and distal straight tubules and collecting ducts that all enter the medulla.

In the medulla, specific nephron segments are found at precise levels and divide the medulla into an inner and an outer zone, with

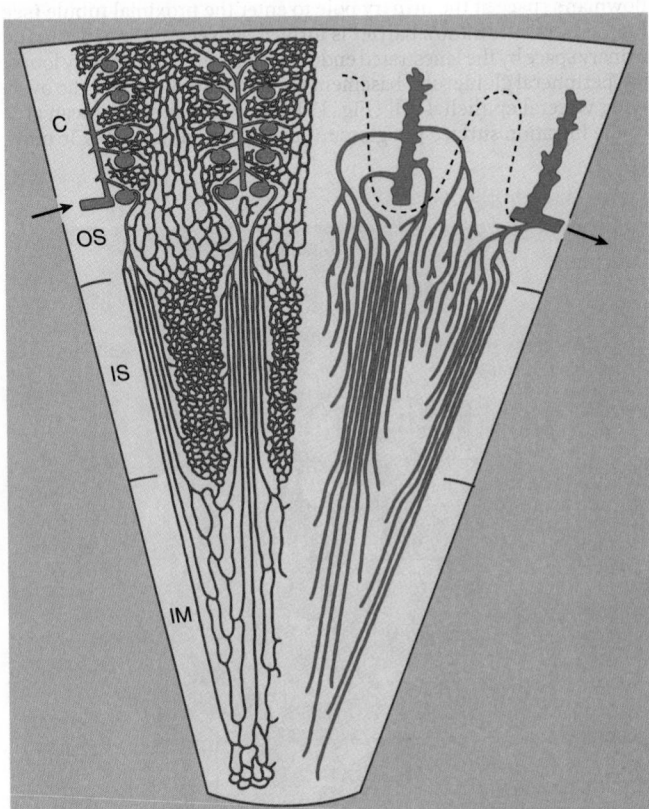

FIGURE 111–3 • Diagram illustrating the vascular arrangement in the renal cortex and medulla. (Reproduced with permission from Kriz W, Kaissling B: Structural organization of the mammalian kidney. *In* Seldin DW, Giebisch G [eds]: The Kidney: Physiology and Pathophysiology, 2nd ed. New York, Raven Press, 1992, p 709.)

FUNCTION. In a 70-kg person, renal blood flow (RBF) amounts to one fourth to one fifth of the resting cardiac output, or 1.2 L/min. The renal cortex receives 85 to 90% of this flow compared with 10% for the outer medulla and 1% to 2% for the inner medulla including the papilla. With one kidney removed, blood flow to the remaining kidney nearly doubles within a few weeks.

RBF and glomerular filtration rate (GFR) remain relatively constant over a wide range of perfusion pressures, a process that is termed *autoregulation.* An intrinsic property of smooth muscle cells in the renal vasculature—the myogenic reflex—permits instantaneous alterations in the tone of the vessel wall to maintain RBF and GFR constant over a pressure range of 80 to 180 mm Hg.

There are a host of hormonal and neural factors that can alter RBF. Renal vasoconstrictors that reduce RBF include endothelin, angiotensin II, thromboxane, stimulation of the α-adrenergic system, vasopressin, and catecholamines. Vasodilating agents include prostaglandins I_2 and E_2, atrial peptides, bradykinin, and endothelial-derived relaxing factor or nitric oxide.

Glomerulus

STRUCTURE. The anatomically correct name for the glomerulus is the *renal corpuscle.* Because of common usage, however, this structure usually is called the *glomerulus.* The glomerulus includes the glomerular tuft and Bowman's capsule (Fig. 111–4). The glomerular tuft contains three specialized cells, a basement membrane, and a supporting framework, the mesangium. The specialized cells include the *endothelial cells* that line the lumens of the capillaries, the *mesangial cells* located in the centrilobular region of the glomerular tuft, and the *visceral epithelial cells* that are situated on the outer surfaces of the capillaries (Fig. 111–5). A fourth cell type, the *parietal epithelial cell,* lines Bowman's capsule. At the vascular pole where the afferent and efferent arterioles enter and exit the glomerulus, the visceral epithelium is continuous with the parietal epithelium. The glomerulus resembles an epithelial-lined sac invaginated by a tuft of capillaries. Bowman's space, also called the *urinary space,* is the area between the visceral epithelial cells and the parietal epithelial layer lining Bowman's capsule. It receives the glomerular filtrate, which exits Bowman's space at the urinary pole to enter the proximal tubule (see Fig. 111–4). A filtration barrier is formed between the blood and the urinary space by the fenestrated endothelium lining the capillary loops, the peripheral glomerular basement membrane (GBM), and the overlying visceral epithelial cell (Fig. 111–6). In humans, the mean area of the filtration surface per glomerulus is approximately 0.136 mm².

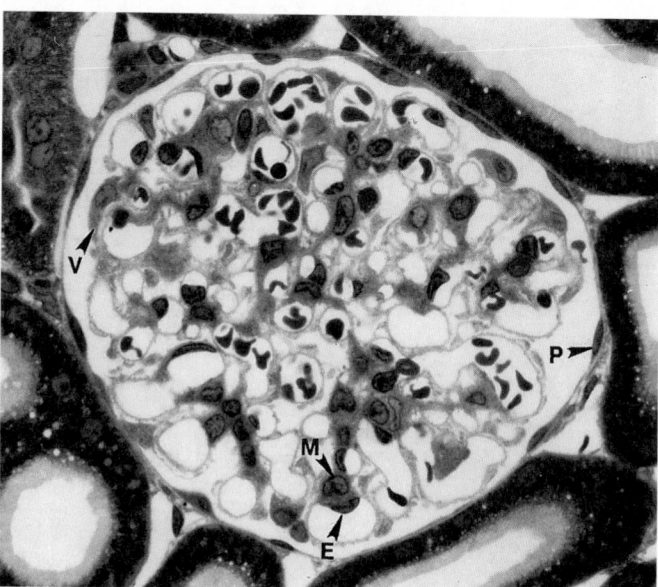

FIGURE 111–5 • Cross-sectional view of glomerulus depicting endothelial cells (E), mesangial cells (M), visceral epithelial cells (V), and parietal epithelial cells (P) (× 480).

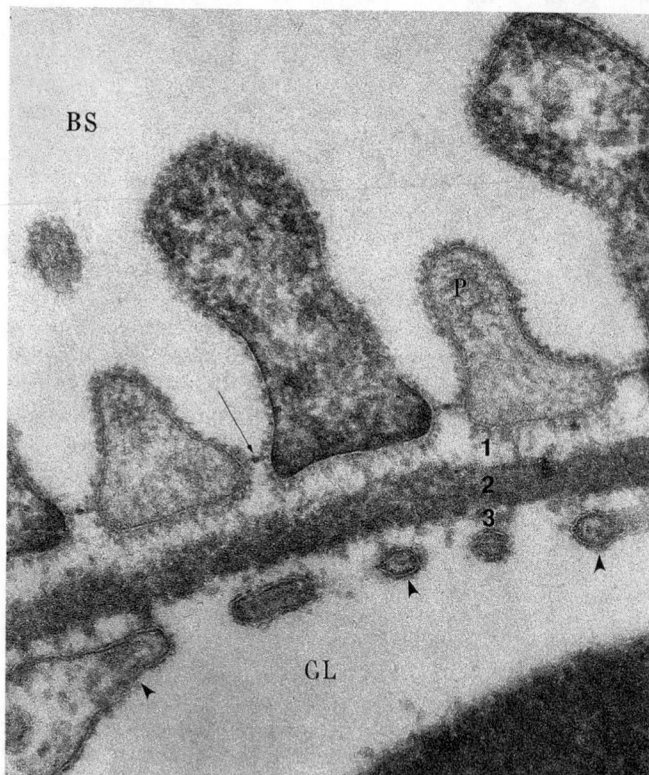

FIGURE 111–6 • Cross section of glomerular capillary wall illustrating the pedicels (P) of the visceral epithelial cells, the fenestrated endothelium (arrowheads), and the three layers of the glomerular basement membrane that include the lamina rara externa (1), the lamina densa (2), and the lamina rara interna (3). BS = Bowman's space; CL = capillary lumen; arrow = filtration slit diaphragm (× 120,000). (From Tisher CC, Madsen KM: Anatomy of the kidney. *In* Brenner BM, Rector FC Jr [eds]: The Kidney, 4th ed. Philadelphia, WB Saunders, 1991, p 14.)

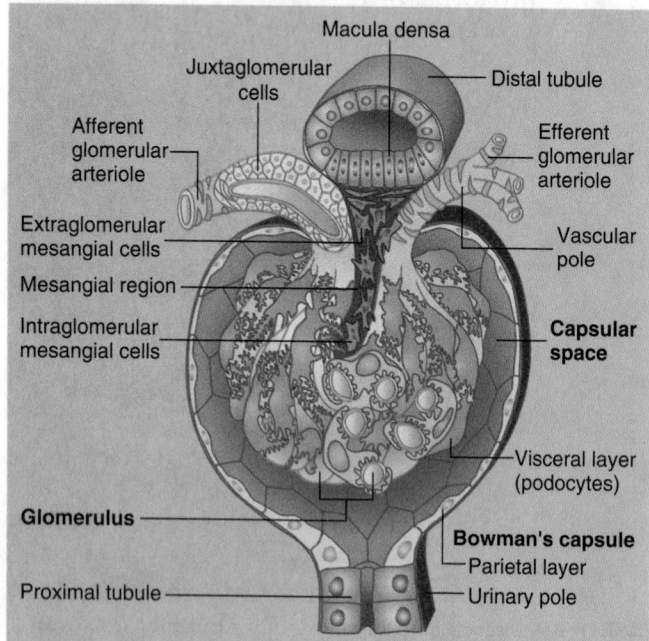

FIGURE 111–4 • Schematic three-dimensional depiction of the glomerulus. (From Bargmann W: Histologie und Mikronscopische Anatomie des Menschen. Stuttgart, Georg Thieme Verlag, 1977, p 86.)

FUNCTION. In a 70-kg person, the kidney forms approximately 180 L of glomerular filtrate each day through a process termed *ultrafiltration.* This is the initial step in urine formation. The driving force to move fluid from the glomerular capillaries across the glomerular capillary wall to the urinary space (Bowman's space) is derived from the hydraulic pressure that is generated by the pumping action of the heart. Each glomerulus has a filtration rate (single nephron glomerular filtration rate [SNGFR]) of 60 nL/min, which is much higher per unit surface area than in other capillary beds in the body. The rate of filtration is proportional to the net ultrafiltration pressure (P_{UF}) that is present across the glomerular capillary wall and is determined by the balance of hydraulic (P) and oncotic (Π) pressures (Starling forces) that are operative between the glomerular capillary lumen and Bowman's space. The intrinsic water permeability of the capillary wall (k) and the surface area (A), which together define the ultrafiltration coefficient (K_f), are also important determinants of ultrafiltration. Thus:

$$\begin{aligned} SNGFR &= K_f \cdot \overline{P}_{UF} \\ &= K_f \cdot [(\overline{P}_{GC} - P_T) - (\Pi_{GC} - \Pi_T)] \\ &= k \cdot A(\overline{\Delta P} - \overline{\Delta \Pi}) \end{aligned}$$

where *GC* and *T* refer to glomerular capillary and Bowman's space, and the overbar denotes mean values.

Because under normal circumstances there is virtually no protein in the ultrafiltrate, the oncotic pressure in the urinary space (Π_T) approaches 0 and does not affect ultrafiltration. Increasing the oncotic pressure in the glomerular capillary (as in multiple myeloma with its characteristic hyperproteinemia), increasing the hydraulic pressure in Bowman's space (via ureteral obstruction), and lowering glomerular capillary hydraulic pressure (as in hypotension) all reduce SNGFR.

Glomerular Basement Membrane

STRUCTURE. The GBM is a hydrated gel containing cross-linked molecules that form a complex, three-dimensional lattice-like network (see Fig. 111–6). The GBM is both synthesized and maintained by podocytes and endothelial cells. Biochemical and immunocytochemical studies revealed that the GBM is composed of type IV and type V collagen, laminin, heparan sulfate proteoglycans, and entactin as well as other components. Type IV collagen is the main component in the *lamina densa,* whereas in the *laminae rarae* proteoglycans predominate. The polyanionic character of the heparan sulfate proteoglycans is largely responsible for the net negative charge of the GBM.

FUNCTION. Physiologic and ultrastructural studies established that the GBM is a *size-selective* and a *charge-selective* barrier to the passage of macromolecules. The GBM, along with the endothelium, serves as the principal functional barrier to the passage of circulating polyanions across the glomerular capillary wall. The size-selective properties of the GBM allow molecules such as inulin, with a radius of about 1.4 nm, to pass freely from the capillary lumen to the urinary space. Because the concentration of inulin in the plasma water and the fluid in the urinary space is identical, the fractional clearance of inulin is equal to 1. As the radii of macromolecules increase to greater than 2.0 nm, their passage is restricted across the GBM, and molecules with a radius greater than 4.2 nm are completely restricted. Their fractional clearance approaches 0 under normal circumstances.

In addition to size, the charge of a molecule can affect its ability to cross the glomerular capillary wall. The size-selective and charge-selective properties of the GBM are summarized in Figure 111–7.

Juxtaglomerular Apparatus

STRUCTURE. The juxtaglomerular apparatus is located at the vascular pole of the glomerulus and is formed by four structures that include the macula densa, the afferent and efferent arterioles, and the extraglomerular mesangium (see Fig. 111–4). In the wall of the afferent arteriole, there are modified smooth muscle cells, the so-called granular cells, which secrete renin.

The macula densa is a plaquelike configuration of specialized cells within the cortical thick ascending limb of Henle that is in contact with the extraglomerular mesangium (see Fig. 111–4).

FUNCTION. The juxtaglomerular apparatus is believed to be responsible for *tubuloglomerular feedback,* in which the composition of tubular fluid delivered to the macula densa changes the filtration rate of the associated glomerulus, presumably by altering renin secretion, which ultimately regulates glomerular hemodynamics.

Proximal Tubule

STRUCTURE. The proximal tubule includes an initial convoluted portion, the *pars convoluta,* located in the cortical labyrinth, and a straight portion, the *pars recta,* located in the medullary ray. Proximal tubule cells are tall and possess a prominent brush border that markedly increases the surface area of the luminal membrane. The cells contain a well-developed endocytic-lysosomal apparatus that has an important role in the absorption and degradation of macromolecules, such as albumin from the glomerular filtrate.

The basolateral plasma membranes are markedly amplified owing to extensive interdigitations of basal and lateral cytoplasmic processes between adjacent cells. The localization of Na^+,K^+-ATPase (the sodium pump) to the basolateral membranes explains the active transport of sodium characteristic of this tubule segment. Numerous elongated mitochondria are located close to the interdigitating basolateral membrane processes, providing a source for the cellular energy required for active transport. There is an excellent correlation along the length of the proximal tubule between the elaborate basolateral membrane expressed as surface area, the high Na^+,K^+-ATPase activity localized to this membrane, and the capacity to transport sodium and other ions. The intrinsic rates at which solutes and fluid are transported decrease along the length of the proximal tubule.

FUNCTION. The proximal tubule is the first component of the nephron that modifies the volume and ionic composition of the glomerular ultrafiltrate. Through iso-osmotic fluid reabsorption, fluid volume is reduced by 60% or more under normal conditions. The principal driving force for the reabsorption of solutes is Na^+,K^+-ATPase located along the basolateral plasma membrane. By maintaining a low intracellular sodium concentration, there is passive entry of sodium into the cell across the luminal plasma membrane and down its electrochemical gradient. In the early proximal tubule, this leads to a small electrical potential difference that is lumen negative. Sodium is pumped out of the cell actively at the basolateral surface via Na^+,K^+-ATPase. This process also creates a slight osmotic gradient that facilitates the reabsorption of fluid. The balance between osmotic and hydraulic pressures (Starling forces) in the peritubular capillaries and the surrounding interstitium determines the extent of the backleak of sodium

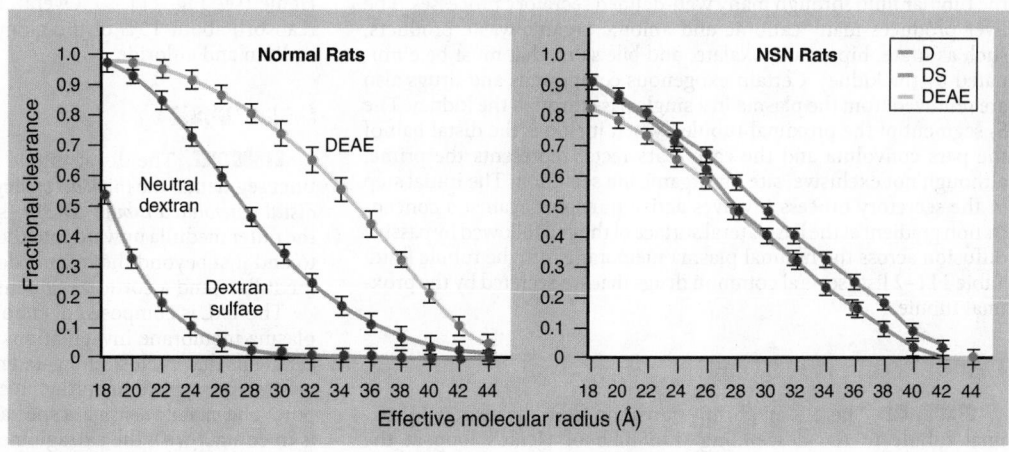

FIGURE 111–7 • Fractional clearances of diethylaminoethyl (DEAE) dextran (positively charged molecule), neutral dextran (D) (neutral charge), and dextran sulfate (DS) (negatively charged molecule), plotted as a function of effective molecular radius in normal rats (left) and in rats with nephrotoxic serum nephritis (NSN, right). Values are expressed as means ±1 SEM. (From Bohrer MP, Baylis C, Humes HD, et al: Permselectivity of the glomerular capillary wall: Facilitated filtration of circulating polycations. J Clin Invest 1978; 61:72–78, by copyright permission of the American Society for Clinical Investigation.)

Table 111–1 • TRANSPORT OF IONS IN THE PROXIMAL TUBULE

ION	PRINCIPAL SITE OF TRANSPORT	PROCESS
Potassium	Early proximal tubule	Freely filtered by the glomerulus; 70% reabsorbed by a passive process that parallels sodium and water and is regulated in part by the transepithelial potential difference
Bicarbonate	Early proximal tubule	Filtered by the glomerulus; 90% of the 4500 mEq filtered each day is reabsorbed secondary to proton secretion
Hydrogen	Proximal convoluted tubule	Approximately 65% secreted via Na^+/H^+ antiporter; 35% secreted by an electrogenic sodium-independent H^+-ATPase
Chloride	S_2 segment of proximal tubule	Coupled to active transport of sodium; passive transport driven by favorable lumen-to-peritubular concentration gradient for Cl^-
Calcium	Entire proximal tubule	Can exit tubule lumen through paracellular pathway via passive voltage-dependent diffusion; active transport via a Na^+-Ca^{2+} exchange and Ca^{2+}-ATPase

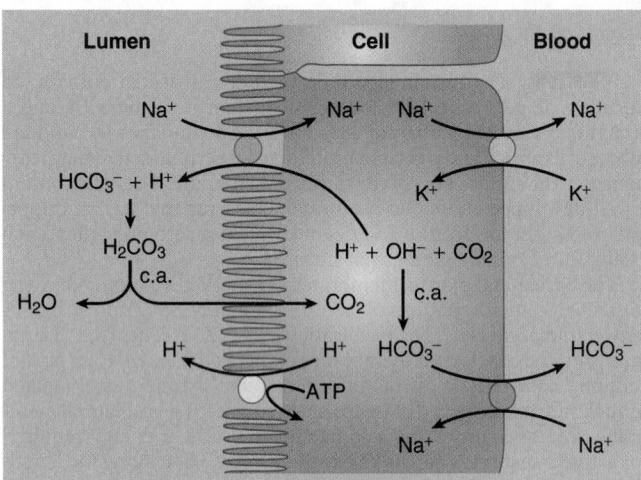

FIGURE 111–8 • Diagram depicting the major mechanism for bicarbonate reclamation in the proximal convoluted tubule. c.a. = carbonic anhydrase.

Table 111–2 • COMMON DRUGS SECRETED BY THE PROXIMAL TUBULE

CATIONIC	ANIONIC
Cimetidine	Penicillin
Paraquat	Furosemide
Quinine	Probenecid
Morphine	Salicylates
Trimethoprim	Acetazolamide
Atropine	Chlorothiazides
Epinephrine	Cephalothin
	Ethacrynic acid

and water to the tubule lumen via the intercellular space through the nonoccluding tight junction and the net reabsorption of sodium and water and other solutes. Water permeability of the proximal tubule is due largely to the presence of a transmembrane protein, aquaporin 1, that functions as a molecular water channel and is located in the luminal and basolateral membranes.

Reabsorption of glucose, amino acids, citrate, lactate, acetate, and phosphate also occurs early in the proximal tubule by sodium-coupled active transport processes. Other transported ions are listed in Table 111–1. The crucial elements of bicarbonate reabsorption are depicted in Figure 111–8.

The proximal tubule is also an important site for *ammoniagenesis,* in which glutamine serves as the substrate. Ammonia combines with protons, forming the ammonium ion (NH_4^+), which is secreted into the tubule lumen. This process is enhanced in metabolic acidosis and hypokalemia.

SECRETION. The proximal tubule also modifies the composition of the tubular fluid through many well-defined secretory processes. The liver produces many cationic and anionic organic waste products, such as urate, hippurate, oxalate, and bile salts, that must be eliminated by the kidney. Certain exogenous compounds and drugs also are removed from the plasma in a single pass through the kidney. The S_2 segment of the proximal tubule, which includes the distal half of the pars convoluta and the early pars recta, represents the prime, although not exclusive, site for organic ion secretion. The initial step in the secretory process involves active transport against a concentration gradient at the basolateral surface of the cell followed by passive diffusion across the luminal plasma membrane into the tubule fluid. Table 111–2 lists several common drugs that are secreted by the proximal tubule.

Thin Limbs of Henle's Loop

STRUCTURE. There is an abrupt transition from the terminal proximal tubule to the descending thin limb of Henle's loop at the junction between the outer and inner stripes of the outer medulla (see Fig. 111–2). Short-looped nephrons have a short descending thin limb that continues into the thick ascending limb near the bend in the loop. Long-looped nephrons have a long descending thin limb that enters the inner medulla, forms a bend, and returns as a long ascending thin limb. The thin limbs are lined with a low-lying simple epithelium.

FUNCTION. The thin limbs of Henle's loop play an important role in urine concentration and dilution. The thin descending limb in the inner medulla has a high osmotic water permeability (L_p) owing to the presence of the transmembrane protein aquaporin 1 but a low permeability to solutes (P_s). This facilitates transfer of water from the tubule lumen to the surrounding hypertonic medullary interstitium and raises the concentration of NaCl and urea in the tubule fluid (Fig. 111–9). In humans, the tonicity of the tubule fluid can reach 1200 mOsm/kg H_2O with severe water restriction.

The thin ascending limb of Henle has a low osmotic water permeability, a moderate permeability for urea, and a high permeability for NaCl. The surrounding interstitium has a NaCl concentration that is lower and a urea concentration that is higher than the tubule fluid at the hairpin turn. These characteristics favor formation of a dilute tubule fluid because the passive movement of NaCl out of the tubule exceeds the passive entry of urea into the tubule. At any given level in the inner medulla, the tonicity of the surrounding interstitial fluid is greater than that of the tubule fluid in the thin ascending limb of Henle (see Fig. 111–9). Overall the thin limbs of the loop of Henle reabsorb about 15% of the glomerular ultrafiltrate and 25% of the sodium and chloride.

Distal Tubule

STRUCTURE. The distal tubule includes two morphologically distinct segments: the *thick ascending limb* (TAL) of Henle's loop and the *distal convoluted tubule* (DCT) (see Fig. 111–2). The TAL traverses the outer medulla upward into the cortex near its glomerulus of origin to end just beyond the macula densa. The TAL can be divided into a medullary and a cortical segment.

The TAL is composed of cuboidal cells with extensive basolateral plasma membrane invaginations and interdigitations between adjacent cells that enclose elongated mitochondria. These ultrastructural features are typical of epithelial cells involved in active solute transport. The *macula densa* is a specialized region of the cortical TAL that is in contact with the extraglomerular mesangium (see Fig. 111–4).

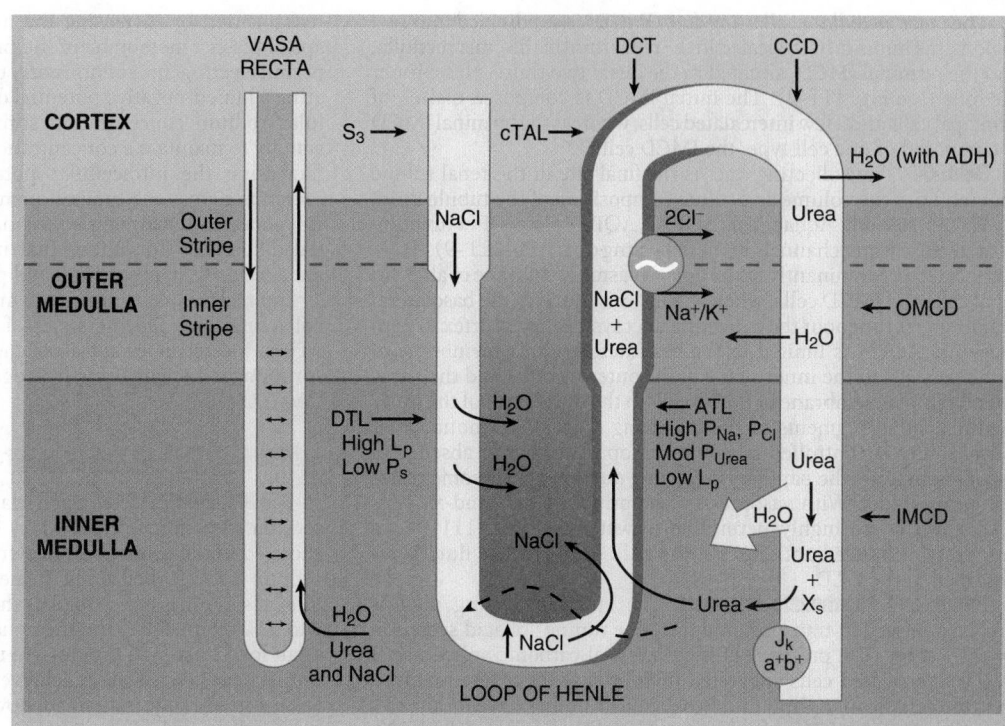

FIGURE 111–9 • Diagram illustrating the essential components of the countercurrent multiplication and exchange systems in the kidney (see text for explanation). The heavy black line indicates water-impermeable segments of the nephron, and shading denotes progressive increase in tonicity of the medullary interstitium. S_3 = third segment of proximal tubule; ADH = antidiuretic hormone; DTL = descending thin limb; ATL = ascending thin limb; cTAL = cortical thick ascending limb; DCT = distal convoluted tubule; CCD = cortical collecting duct; OMCD = outer medullary collecting duct; IMCD = inner medullary collecting duct; L_p = osmotic water permeability; P_S, P_{Na}, P_{Cl}, P_{ure} = permeability to solutes, Na^+, Cl^-, and urea; X_S = nonreabsorbable solutes; and $J_K a^+ b^+$ = Kidd antigen and urea transporter. (Modified from Brenner BM, Coe FL, Rector FC Jr [eds]: Renal Physiology in Health and Disease. Philadelphia, WB Saunders, 1987, pp 53 and 160.)

The DCT is the terminal part of the distal tubule and begins at a variable distance beyond the macula densa. The cells of the DCT resemble those of the TAL.

FUNCTION. The TAL actively reabsorbs NaCl, which is mediated by a Na^+-K^+-$2Cl^-$ cotransport mechanism in the apical plasma membrane (see Fig. 111–9). The energy for this process is provided by the Na^+,K^+-ATPase localized on the basolateral plasma membrane. A major function of the medullary TAL is to generate and maintain a hypertonic medullary interstitium that permits a maximally concentrated urine to form, while the cortical segment continues to dilute the tubule fluid, permitting the formation of a maximally dilute urine. The tubule fluid that exits the cortical TAL has an osmolality of less than 150 mOsm/kg H_2O. At this point, the total volume of the original glomerular ultrafiltrate in the nephron has been reduced by 85%.

The TAL also reabsorbs *calcium* from the tubular fluid. Throughout the TAL, a significant component of calcium transport is passive and driven by the transepithelial potential difference (PD_t). Active transport has been identified in the cortical TAL, which is independent of Ca^{2+}-ATPase activity, sodium transport, and anaerobic metabolism. Calcium transport is enhanced in the cortical TAL by parathyroid hormone (PTH) and cyclic adenosine monophosphate (AMP) and in the medullary TAL by calcitonin and cyclic AMP.

Bicarbonate transport is present along the entire TAL through a sodium-coupled HCO_3^- transport mechanism located on the basolateral plasma membrane. Active and passive transport of NH_4^+ out of the lumen and into the interstitium for subsequent transport in the form of NH_3 into the lumen of the collecting duct also occurs in the TAL. This region of the nephron also plays a role in acidification of the tubule fluid.

The cortical TAL is a major site for reabsorbing *magnesium*. The passive component of magnesium transport is facilitated by the Na^+-K^+-$2Cl^-$ cotransport mechanism that establishes a favorable lumen-positive electrochemical gradient, whereas the active magnesium transport mechanism is incompletely understood.

In the DCT, *sodium chloride* continues to be reabsorbed through a ouabain-sensitive Na^+,K^+-ATPase-driven active transport process. Because the DCT is also impermeable to water, there is further dilution of the tubule fluid to an osmolality of approximately 100 mOsm/kg H_2O. This segment is also a site for *calcium* reabsorption stimulated by calcitonin and PTH. The distal tubule is the principal target for the action of several commonly prescribed diuretic drugs. The so-called loop diuretics such as furosemide, bumetanide, and ethacrynic acid, block sodium chloride reabsorption in the TAL. Thiazide diuretics, including hydrochlorothiazide, chlorthalidone, and metalazone, act on the DCT.

Connecting Tubule

STRUCTURE. The connecting tubule or connecting segment joins the DCT with the collecting duct system (see Fig. 111–2). Representing a transitional segment in the human kidney, the connecting tubule is composed of four specific cell types resulting from an intermixing of cells from the adjacent DCT and the initial collecting tubule. The most characteristic cell type is the connecting tubule cell, which is intermediate in appearance between the DCT cell and the principal cell of the collecting duct. Intercalated cells involved in proton and bicarbonate transport vary considerably in structure in the connecting tubule.

FUNCTION. PTH affects *calcium* transport in this segment, whereas vasopressin (antidiuretic hormone) has no effect on adenylate cyclase activity or water permeability. This segment is responsible for reabsorbing *sodium* and secreting *potassium*. The latter is believed to be controlled at least partially by mineralocorticoids. The connecting segment also is involved in *proton* and *bicarbonate* transport and is a major site for kallikrein production and secretion in the kidney.

Collecting Duct

STRUCTURE. The collecting duct begins in the cortex and descends through the medulla to the tip of the papilla. It can be divided into cortical, outer medullary, and inner medullary segments (see Fig. 111–2). There is remarkable cellular heterogeneity along the collecting duct.

The *cortical collecting duct* (CCD) can be subdivided into the initial collecting tubule and the medullary ray portion. The CCD is composed of principal cells and intercalated cells. The principal cells, which represent approximately two thirds of the total cell population, have a light-staining cytoplasm and relatively few organelles but prominent infoldings of the basal plasma membrane. The intercalated or "dark" cells comprise approximately one third of the cells in the CCD.

There is evidence for the presence of two distinct configurations of intercalated cells, type A and type B, in the CCD. Type A cells have prominent microprojections on the apical plasma membrane and extensive tubulovesicular structures in the apical cytoplasm. Type B cells have a denser cytoplasm, more mitochondria, more spherical vesicular structures in the cytoplasm, and a larger basolateral membrane surface area. The type B cell is localized to the CCD.

The *outer medullary collecting duct* (OMCD) is lined by principal cells and intercalated cells. The latter comprise one third of the cells in the OMCD and resemble the type A cells in the CCD.

The *inner medullary collecting duct* (IMCD) is subdivided into two regions: the initial IMCD, located in the outer third of the inner medulla, and the terminal IMCD, situated in the distal two thirds of the inner medulla (see Fig. 111–2). The initial IMCD is composed mainly of principal cells and a few intercalated cells, whereas the terminal IMCD is composed of one cell type, the IMCD cell.

FUNCTION. The collecting duct is the final site in the renal tubule that modifies the volume and solute composition of the tubule fluid.

Water Transport. Aquaporin (AQP)-2, AQP-3, and AQP-4 function as molecular water channels in the collecting duct (Fig. 111–9). AQP-2 is located predominantly in the apical plasma membrane of all principal cells and IMCD cells, whereas AQP-3 is found in the basolateral membrane throughout the collecting duct system from cortex to papillary tip. AQP-4 is limited to the basolateral plasma membrane of principal cells in the inner stripe of the outer medulla and the basolateral plasma membrane of IMCD cells in the outer third of the inner medulla. In all segments of the collecting duct, the osmotic water permeability is controlled largely by vasopressin. In the absence of vasopressin, only the papillary collecting duct manifests some residual permeability. With vasopressin, the principal cells and all cells in the IMCD are highly permeable to water (see Fig. 111–9). In vasopressin-induced antidiuresis, the bulk of the tubule fluid is reabsorbed in the CCD.

Proton and Bicarbonate Transport. The entire collecting duct is involved in proton transport and the "fine tuning" of acid secretion by the kidney. The presence of high levels of carbonic anhydrase II in the intercalated cells suggested initially that they were involved in urine acidification. Immunocytochemical studies have localized a vacuolar type H^+-ATPase in the apical membrane and a Cl^-/HCO_3^- exchanger in the basolateral membrane of type A intercalated cells (Fig. 111–10A). These findings implicate the type A cell in proton or hydrogen ion secretion in the CCD. The immunolocalization of H^+-ATPase to the basolateral membrane of type B cells and the functional evidence for an apical Cl^-/HCO_3^- exchanger in these cells provide evidence that type B intercalated cells are involved in bicarbonate secretion (see Fig. 111–10B). Recent immunolocalization of a Cl^-/HCO_3^- exchanger in the apical membrane of type B cells confirms the functional evidence for Cl^-/HCO_3^- exchange.

The intercalated cells in the OMCD are responsible for hydrogen ion secretion, which is an active mineralocorticoid-stimulated, sodium-independent process driven in part by H^+-ATPase. The IMCD also is involved in urine acidification. Acid-secreting intercalated cells are present in the initial IMCD. Microcatheterization studies have documented a decrease in luminal pH along the IMCD.

Urea Transport. The cortical and outer medullary segments of the collecting duct are largely impermeable to urea in the presence and absence of vasopressin. In the terminal IMCD, urea reabsorption occurs by means of a vasopressin-sensitive, phloretin-inhibitable, facilitated transport pathway that helps to maintain a high urea concentration in the deep inner medulla to facilitate urea recycling, which is important for maximum urine concentration (see Fig. 111–9).

Sodium and Potassium Transport. Virtually all sodium transport and much of the potassium transport in the collecting duct are controlled by aldosterone. Although it is this region of the renal tubule that "fine tunes" sodium excretion, it is estimated that less than 10% of the filtered load of sodium is controlled by aldosterone. The target cell for aldosterone is the principal cell. Aldosterone increases sodium

reabsorption by increasing the number of sodium channels in the apical plasma membrane of the principal cell. The sodium channels permit electrogenic sodium entry down a concentration gradient, creating a lumen-negative potential difference. The increase in intracellular sodium concentration stimulates basolateral Na^+,K^+-ATPase activity to maintain a concentration gradient for sodium entry, while increasing the intracellular potassium concentration. Potassium secretion across the luminal membrane through aldosterone-sensitive potassium channels also is enhanced by the lumen-negative potential difference. Conditions that increase plasma aldosterone levels enhance sodium absorption and potassium secretion.

Intercalated cells also help maintain potassium balance by the collecting duct. During states of potassium deprivation, an H^+,K^+-ATPase located in the apical cell membrane facilitates potassium reabsorption in exchange for hydrogen ions throughout the CCD and OMCD.

Integration of Normal Nephron Function

SODIUM HOMEOSTASIS. Each day, approximately 25,000 mEq of sodium (140 mEq/L × 180 L) is filtered, whereas less than 1% is excreted in the urine by a euvolemic individual. The bulk of filtered sodium is reabsorbed along the nephron. Normally, about 65% of the filtered sodium is reabsorbed by the proximal tubule, 20% by the TAL, 7 to 10% by the DCT, and the remainder by the collecting duct. With a salt load, there is a progressive increase in urine sodium excretion until a new steady state is achieved in which output matches intake. Until a steady state is attained, however, the individual goes into positive sodium balance, retains water, and gains weight. Restricting sodium intake produces the opposite effect until the kidney fully compensates over a 3- to 5-day period.

Several factors influence normal sodium balance. The kidney is extremely sensitive to changes in effective arterial blood volume. Dehydration or acute volume depletion secondary to blood loss leads to a fall in RBF and GFR secondary to a decrease in cardiac output, activation of the renin-angiotensin-aldosterone system, and an increase in renal sympathetic nerve activity. As the filtered load of sodium decreases, the proximal tubule increases sodium reabsorption. Because the vasoconstrictive effect of angiotensin II affects the efferent glomerular arteriole to a greater degree than the afferent arteriole, the filtration fraction is increased, increasing the oncotic pressure in the peritubular capillaries. This enhances proximal tubule sodium and fluid reabsorption. An increase in the plasma level of aldosterone from activation of the renin-angiotensin-aldosterone system stimulates sodium reabsorption in the collecting duct. Expansion of the effective arterial blood volume, as occurs with excessive sodium intake or administering intravenous saline, has the opposite effect.

Other factors also control renal sodium excretion. Several hormones lead to retention of sodium by acting at the tubular level (e.g., growth hormone, cortisol, insulin, and estrogen). PTH, progesterone, and glycogen inhibit the tubular reabsorption of sodium. Atrial natriuretic peptide—a 28-amino acid peptide produced in the atria of the heart and released in the circulation in response to atrial stretch from, for example, expansion of the central blood volume—also enhances sodium excretion, in part by inhibiting sodium reabsorption by the collecting duct.

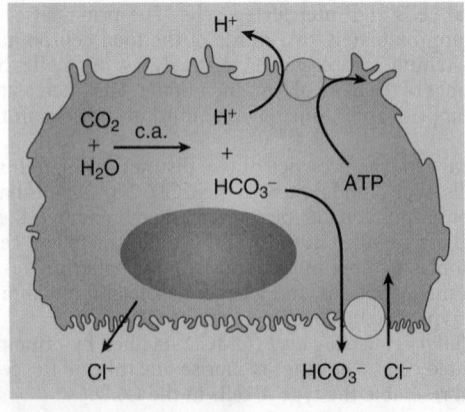

A

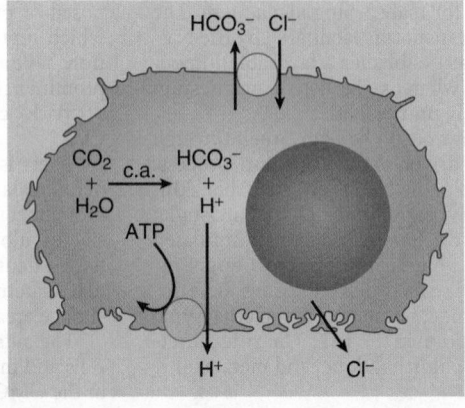

B

FIGURE 111–10 • Diagrams illustrating transport characteristics of type A (left) and type B (right) intercalated cells of the cortical collecting duct. c.a. = carbonic anhydrase (Used with permission from Madsen KM, Verlander JW, Kim J, Tisher CC: Morphological adaptation of the collecting duct to acid-base disturbances. Kidney Int 1991;33:S57–S63.)

POTASSIUM HOMEOSTASIS. The kidney is chiefly responsible for maintaining potassium homeostasis. The total body potassium content of a 70-kg individual is estimated at approximately 3500 mEq, 98% to 99% of which resides in the intracellular compartment at a concentration of 125 mEq/L. The concentration of potassium in the extracellular fluid ranges from 3.5 to 4.5 mEq/L. Each day, approximately 720 mEq of potassium (4.0 mEq/L × 180 L) is filtered, whereas only 10 to 15% is excreted in the urine by an individual with normal body potassium stores. In general, potassium excretion equals potassium ingestion. With a normal potassium intake of approximately 100 mEq/day, the kidney excretes all but about 10 mEq. Approximately 70% of the filtered load of potassium is reabsorbed in the proximal tubule, and another 15 to 20% is reabsorbed in the loop of Henle. The kidney can respond quickly to increase potassium excretion 10-fold when potassium intake is increased. With potassium deprivation, however, it takes 14 days to reach a new steady state, a period of time sufficient to develop a considerable potassium deficit.

It is the collecting duct that is responsible for fine tuning potassium excretion. In general, the principal cells secrete potassium under the control of mineralocorticoids, whereas intercalated cells reabsorb potassium. Most of the potassium that appears in the urine is secreted by the collecting duct. Several factors influence renal potassium secretion, including the rate of distal tubule fluid flow, acid-base balance, aldosterone, and the electronegativity of the distal tubule. The flow dependence of potassium secretion in the collecting duct is well documented. With an increase in flow (such as that induced by diuretics), there is a parallel increase in sodium delivery to the collecting duct, which facilitates sodium reabsorption and potassium secretion. With metabolic acidosis, and to a lesser extent with respiratory acidosis, potassium secretion is suppressed. An opposite effect is observed in metabolic alkalosis. With an increase in the circulating aldosterone level (such as that induced by hyperkalemia), there is a parallel increase in the exchange of sodium for potassium by the principal cells, leading to enhanced potassium secretion. Finally, an increase in the lumen-negative potential, a decrease in the luminal potassium concentration, an increase in the intracellular potassium concentration, and an increase in the luminal membrane permeability to potassium all favor potassium secretion by the principal cell.

The kidney also can protect against hypokalemia. The presence of H^+,K^+-ATPase has been documented in the intercalated cell of the collecting duct, and data suggest that with potassium deprivation there is enhanced reabsorption of potassium in exchange for protons in these cells.

ACID-BASE BALANCE. See Chapter 112.

CALCIUM, PHOSPHORUS, AND MAGNESIUM HOMEOSTASIS. See Chapters 257 and 262.

URINE CONCENTRATION AND DILUTION. See Chapter 112.

SUGGESTED READINGS
Alpern RJ: Renal acidification mechanisms. *In* Brenner BM (ed): The Kidney, 6th ed. Philadelphia, WB Saunders, 2000, p 455. *A detailed and up-to-date review of acidification in the kidney.*
Pallone TL, Zhang Z, Rhinehart K: Physiology of the renal medullary microcirculation. Am J Physiol Renal Physiol 2003;284:253–266. *Emphasizes the role of the renal medulla in salt and water balance.*
Schrier RW, Cadnapaphornchai MA: Renal aquaporin water channels: From molecules to human disease. Prog Biophys Mol Biol 2003;81:117–131. *A practical overview of aquaporins in water-losing and water-retaining states.*
Tisher CC, Madsen KM: Anatomy of the kidney. *In* Brenner BM (ed): The Kidney, 6th ed. Philadelphia, WB Saunders, 2000, p 3. *A detailed and lucid review of kidney structure.*

112 FLUIDS AND ELECTROLYTES

Juha P. Kokko

Volume Disorders

PHYSIOLOGIC CONSIDERATIONS

Considering that total body water is distributed into distinct compartments, the volumes of these compartments can be measured relatively accurately. To understand fluid homeostasis, however, one must recognize the significance of the term *effective arterial blood volume*. This term is discussed in Chapter 111, but in its broadest sense it refers to the volume of blood delivered to the volume-sensitive organs, predominantly brain and kidney.

Body Fluid Compartments

In healthy adults, body water constitutes about 60% of body weight and exists in two compartments: The intracellular fluid (ICF) contains two thirds of body water, or 40% of body weight; the extracellular fluid (ECF) contains the remaining one third of total body water; and total circulatory blood volume (CBV) (i.e., plasma plus formed elements) constitutes one third of the total ECF volume. This "rule of thirds" for the body fluid compartments is useful in assessing most clinically encountered fluid and electrolyte disorders. In a healthy 70-kg man, total body water is about 40 L, of which 25 L is intracellular. The functional ECF volume is 15 L, 5 L of which is blood. While blood is composed of cells with intracellular water and plasma that is extracellular, it is convenient to remember the various distributions of total body water by the "rule of thirds." It is for this reason that Figure 112–1 shows 5 L of blood. Since the normal hematocrit is 40 to 45%, total plasma volume is 2.75 to 3.0 L (Fig. 112–1). These values are clearly estimates and vary from individual to individual, but they are useful to guide the clinician's therapeutic approach and are usually accurate to within ±10%.

More than 95% of total body sodium is extracellular, and sodium and its associated anions, primarily chloride and bicarbonate, constitute the principal solutes of the ECF. Albumin and other macromolecules present in plasma are restricted to the vascular bed and constitute 5% of plasma volume so that plasma is about 95% water. Because capillaries are freely permeable to water and small solutes, interstitial fluid is a protein-poor, but not entirely protein-free, ultrafiltrate of plasma.

Principal anions of ICF vary while principal cations are relatively the same among different cells. Figure 112–1 summarizes the approximate concentrations of various intracellular and extracellular cation and anion concentrations.

REGULATION OF FLUID TRANSFER AMONG COMPARTMENTS

The transfer of fluid between vascular and interstitial compartments occurs at the capillary level and is governed by the balance between hydrostatic pressure gradients and plasma oncotic pressure gradients. This relationship may be stated by the familiar Starling equation:

$$J_v = K_f(\Delta P - \Delta\pi)$$

Intracellular Water (2/3)		Extracellular Water (1/3)	
		Interstitial (2/3)	Blood (1/3)
± 25	Na	140	
± 150	K	4.5	
± 15	Mg	1.2	
± 0.01	Ca	2.4	
± 2	Cl	100	
± 6	HCO₃	25	
± 50	Phos	1.2	

FIGURE 112–1 • Relative volumes of various body fluid compartments. In a normally built individual, the total body water content is roughly 60% of body weight. Because adipose tissue has a low concentration of water, the relative water-to-total body weight ratio is lower in obese individuals. The intracellular electrolyte concentrations are in millimoles per liter and are typical values obtained from muscle.

where J_v is the rate of fluid transfer between vascular and interstitial compartments, K_f is the water permeability of the capillary bed, ΔP is the hydrostatic pressure difference between capillary and interstitium, and $\Delta\pi$ is the oncotic pressure difference between capillary and interstitial fluids. Under normal circumstances, the colloid oncotic pressure of plasma is roughly 24 to 26 mm Hg, whereas that of interstitial fluid is about 12 mm Hg, creating a transcapillary gradient favoring entry of fluid from interstitium to circulation. The capillary hydrostatic pressure favors movement of fluid out of the circulation. Although the previous statements seem straightforward, and the validity of Starling's equation has withstood the test of time, at the clinical level the movement of fluid across the capillary wall is not easy to quantitate. First, the intracapillary driving forces change; at the arteriolar end of the capillary, the hydrostatic forces exceed oncotic forces and favor movement of fluid out, whereas at the venular end of the capillary the higher oncotic forces favor inward movement of fluid. Second, in some clinical circumstances, which have been studied best in nephrotic syndrome, there is close to a parallel decrease in interstitial oncotic pressure as the plasma oncotic pressure falls. The interstitial oncotic pressure is unknown to the clinician. Teleologically the decrease in interstitial oncotic force protects the volume of circulation as to minimize the oncotic gradients favoring efflux of fluid from the circulatory volume. There are limits to these protective mechanisms, and ultimately edema formation ensues.

What are these protein values that cause edema? The best studies are in nephrotic syndrome and are only partially extendable to other conditions. It has been shown that at a plasma oncotic pressure of 16.5 mm Hg (equates to an albumin concentration roughly 3 g/dL, assuming normal globulin concentration), the oncotic forces become such that there is enough movement of fluid to the interstitium to cause dependent edema around the ankles. At albumin concentrations less than 2 g/dL, generalized edema appears, and at albumin concentrations less than 1.5 g/dL, the circulatory volume no longer can be maintained at normal levels. These clinical guidelines should be considered only as rough indices.

PROTECTION OF FLUID BALANCE

As noted earlier, protection of the circulatory volume is the most fundamental characteristic of body fluid homeostasis. This primacy is underscored by the fact that in circumstances in which multiple physiologic variables are threatened simultaneously, the homeostatic response invariably protects CBV even at the expense of aggravating another electrolyte disorder. A volume-contracted patient replenished with water, and not sodium, retains water and becomes hyponatremic in an attempt to avoid circulatory collapse. Likewise, maintaining metabolic alkalosis in patients who have vomited and are not repleted with salt depends in part on an elevated renal absorptive capacity for sodium bicarbonate. The latter maintains fluid balance at the expense of pH homeostasis.

Two cardinal mechanisms protect CBV: (1) alterations in systemic hemodynamic variables and (2) alterations in external sodium and water balance. Both mechanisms maintain filling of the arterial tree and consequently are activated by external fluid losses, by inability to transfer fluid from the interstitium to the venous system (e.g., in ascites), or by impaired fluid transfer from venous to arterial systems (e.g., in congestive heart failure, pericardial tamponade, or constrictive pericarditis).

The combination of alterations in systemic hemodynamic variables and alterations in external water and solute balance has been termed the *integrated volume response* (Table 112–1). Increases in pulse rate and blood pressure are modulated not only by antidiuretic hormone (ADH), catecholamines, and angiotensin II, but also by a series of factors derived from vascular endothelial cells. These factors include endothelin-1, a 21-residue peptide with potent vasoconstrictor properties, and thromboxane A_2 and prostaglandin H_2, both derived from the cyclooxygenase pathway in vascular endothelial cells. The major inactivators of these systemic hemodynamic changes include prostaglandin E_2 and atriopeptin (both discussed later) and nitric oxide, an endogenous vasodilator released by vascular endothelial cells.

There are differences in the two response systems (see Table 112–1). Tachycardia, peripheral arteriolar vasoconstriction, and peripheral venoconstriction occur within minutes of external fluid losses, whereas renal salt and water conservation lags behind by 12 to 24 hours. The sensitivities of the two limbs also differ. A 2 to 3% decrease in ECF volume, which amounts to the loss of 40 to 60 mEq of sodium, results

Table 112–1 • INTEGRATED VOLUME RESPONSE

	SYSTEMIC HEMODYNAMIC CHANGES	EXTERNAL SALT AND WATER BALANCE
Response	Tachycardia ↑ Peripheral resistance ↓ Venous capacitance	Thirst Renal Na^+, water retention
Onset	Minutes	Hours

Major activators	Catecholamines
	ADH
	Angiotensin II
	Endothelin-1
	    Prostaglandin H_2
	    Thromboxane A_2
		Catecholamines
		Aldosterone
		ADH

Major inactivators	Prostaglandin E_2 Atriopeptin Nitric acid	Prostaglandin E_2 Atriopeptin

ADH = antidiuretic hormone.

in the virtual elimination of sodium from the urine, but produces negligible changes in systemic hemodynamic factors, such as heart rate, blood pressure, or systemic vascular resistance. Because there is 2500 to 3000 mEq of exchangeable sodium in the ECF, the system for conserving renal sodium is remarkably sensitive.

Total Body Water Regulation

A healthy human maintains the total body water at a remarkably constant value. This balanced state is achieved by equality of total fluid intake (including water formation as an end product of metabolism) and output (urinary output plus insensible nonrenal water losses).

A normal 2000 kcal/day diet contains approximately 250 to 440 mL of water with an additional 260 mL of water that is generated as a byproduct of carbohydrate, fat, and protein metabolism. These values vary with relative amounts of carbohydrates, fat, and protein in the diet and with the total caloric intake. It can be concluded that approximately 0.5 to 0.75 L of water is added to the "intake" side of the balance by consumption of an "average" diet. The remainder of the necessary fluid intake is regulated primarily by the thirst sensory mechanism (although habitual modifications, such as drinking soft drinks or coffee, may influence the total intake of fluid). The two primary regulators of thirst are effective plasma osmolality and effective circulating volume. Only a few percent increase in plasma osmolality and a decrease in circulatory volume are potent stimuli for thirst. Weaker stimuli for thirst include increased concentration of angiotensin II and hypokalemia. These factors are discussed more in depth later in the section on Water Balance.

The regulation of volume output is primarily the responsibility of the kidney through insensible water losses (breathing, sweating, and stools), which equal roughly 1 L/day at normal activity during normal atmospheric, temperature, and humidity conditions. The minimum amount of urine that a person must make is roughly 1 L/day because a normal diet produces about 1000 mOsm of solute for renal excretion; the most concentrated urine humans can generate is in the range of 1200 mOsm/L. A normal human under normal conditions must have a net intake of about 2 L of fluid per day to remain in balance. The kidney can regulate volume status, however, under wide varying intakes of fluid of 2 to 15 L/day.

The renal regulation of salt and water balance has fascinated renal physiologists and nephrologists for decades. It is beyond the scope of this book to review the inextricably complicated and redundant mechanisms that are responsible for fluid and electrolyte homeostasis. In summary, however, there are sensing (extrarenal baroreceptors) and effector (humoral mechanisms, such as angiotensin, catecholamines, ADH, aldosterone, prostaglandins, atriopeptides, and nitric oxide) mechanisms that strongly influence renal reabsorption of salt and water. Many of these mechanisms to protect CBV are redundant.

Angiotensin II release, catecholamine release, and ADH release all produce overlapping results. The magnitude of the volume repletion reaction varies depending on the degree of volume contraction. In modestly volume-contracted states, peripheral vasoconstriction and renal sodium conservation occur, but renal blood flow, glomerular filtration rate (GFR), and osmoregulation are unaffected. When volume contraction becomes advanced, nonosmotic ADH release, angiotensin II–mediated thirst, and reductions in the rate of salt delivery to the loop of Henle act in concert to produce hyponatremia. When catecholamine release and angiotensin II release become sufficiently great that renal blood flow is compromised beyond autoregulatory limits, prerenal azotemia ensues.

VOLUME DEPLETION

Definition

A true hypovolemic state is one in which there is reduced total body water; it occurs when the rate of salt and water intake is less than the combined rates of renal plus extrarenal volume losses. In chronic volume-contracted states, input and output may be equal.

Etiology and Pathogenesis

True volume contraction occurs as a consequence of decreased intake of fluid or increased loss of fluid. Increased loss conveniently may be considered as renal (as a result of either altered hormones or defective renal mechanisms) or extrarenal (Table 112–2).

HORMONAL DEFICIT. Volume contraction can occur whenever there is loss of ADH or aldosterone. Untreated pituitary or nephrogenic *diabetes insipidus* produces profound volume contraction and hypertonic encephalopathy in patients denied free access to water. The obligatory loss of solute-free water in diabetes insipidus may be 10 to 18 L daily. Both forms of diabetes insipidus are discussed in Chapter 238.

Addison's disease may impair aldosterone production and lead to renal sodium wasting. A second major cause of aldosterone lack occurs in *hyporeninemic hypoaldosteronism,* which may accompany interstitial renal disease. Disorders that damage the renal interstitium, such as hypertension, diabetes mellitus, gout, sickle cell disease, chronic ingestion of lead-containing illicit alcohol, and analgesic abuse, can suppress the ability of the juxtaglomerular apparatus to produce renin. The low rate of renin secretion results in low rates of aldosterone secretion. Hyporeninemic hypoaldosteronism is a disorder in which impaired aldosterone production results in renal salt wasting, hyperkalemia, and metabolic acidosis. It is not yet known why hyperkalemia, which is a potent stimulus to aldosterone secretion, fails to enhance rates of aldosterone secretion in patients with hyporeninemic hypoaldosteronism.

RENAL DEFICITS. Many disorders impairing renal tubular sodium or water conservation can lead to volume contraction. For convenience, these derangements may be grouped into different classes. First, various tubular nephropathies are characterized by specific deficits in salt or water absorption. As mentioned earlier, nephrogenic diabetes insipidus

and interstitial renal disease may produce water wasting and sodium wasting. Because interstitial renal disease often results in hyperchloremic, hyperkalemic metabolic acidosis, the term *renal tubular acidosis, type IV,* often is applied to this disorder. The general term *renal tubular acidosis* also includes other sodium-wasting disorders, however, accompanied by hyperchloremic acidosis, such as proximal tubular acidosis, a specific proximal defect in bicarbonate reabsorption, and gradient-limited distal renal tubular acidosis, a specific defect in distal tubular sodium bicarbonate regeneration (Chapter 120). Gitelman's syndrome has a similar clinical presentation to Bartter's syndrome, but in Gitelman's syndrome the main tubular defect is in the thiazide-sensitive sodium chloride cotransporter in the distal convoluted tubule. These two syndromes often can be differentiated by the urinary calcium excretion rate, however, which is high in Bartter's syndrome and low in Gitelman's syndrome.

Alternatively, Bartter's syndrome is a specific tubular nephropathy that results in failure of sodium chloride absorption by the thick ascending limb of the nephron; the disorder is accompanied by excessive production of prostaglandins by the renal medullary interstitium and is characterized by sodium chloride wasting, juxtaglomerular hyperplasia, high renin levels, and secondary hyperaldosteronism; the last-named results in hypokalemic metabolic alkalosis.

Inhibition of tubular sodium absorptive processes resulting from *chronic diuretic abuse* also may lead to salt wasting, volume contraction, and specific metabolic acid-base abnormalities. These abnormalities are discussed later.

Profound but reversible defects in tubular salt and water absorption may occur during *postobstructive diuresis* (i.e., shortly after relief of partial or complete urinary tract obstruction). Salt and water losses also may occur in the *diuretic phase* of acute tubular necrosis. Profound salt and water losses associated with the diuretic phase of acute tubular necrosis are seen uncommonly, however, if CBV is controlled carefully during oliguric acute tubular necrosis.

Second, glomerular filtration of large amounts of nonelectrolytes may produce volume deficits by overwhelming renal tubular reabsorptive capacity for salt and water; in this instance, water losses predominate so that hypernatremia generally occurs. This phenomenon, called *osmotic diuresis* or *solute diuresis,* occurs in diabetic ketoacidosis, hyperglycemic hyperosmolar coma, or hyperalimentation with large glucose loads in chronically debilitated patients; in patients with burns, in whom there are abnormally high rates of urea production; and during mannitol or glycerol administration to patients with central nervous system (CNS) disorders requiring reductions of intracranial pressure.

EXTRARENAL LOSSES. In addition to hemorrhage, two other classes of extrarenal losses account for volume contraction. Simple dehydration may result from increased insensible water loss in *excessive sweating* owing to high ambient temperatures or to fever. Because sweat usually contains less than 50 mEq/L of sodium, the ICF and the ECF share the water loss, and body water osmolality rises, whereas ECF volume loss is modest. *Burns* allow the loss of large amounts of plasma and interstitial fluid through affected areas and can lead rapidly to profound ECF losses.

Finally, gastrointestinal volume losses occur when portions of the 8 to 10 L of normal gastrointestinal secretions are lost, particularly in secretory diarrheas. Volume depletion is most commonly the consequence of vomiting, gastric drainage, or diarrhea but may occur with any type of bowel fistula. Loss of hydrochloric acid from the stomach may produce metabolic alkalosis, whereas loss of sodium bicarbonate from pancreatic secretions lost through the lower gastrointestinal tract, as in diarrhea, may produce hyperchloremic metabolic acidosis.

Clinical Manifestations

The clinical findings in states of true volume contraction are due to underfilling of the arterial tree and to the subsequent renal and hemodynamic responses. In mild or partially compensated volume contraction, particularly when the latter has occurred gradually, the patient may exhibit nothing more than mild postural giddiness, postural tachycardia, and weakness, whereas in severe volume contraction, life-threatening circulatory collapse may occur. The lack of physical findings does not exclude the presence of mild-to-moderate volume contraction in a given patient. In the

---

Table 112–2 • MAJOR CAUSES OF VOLUME DEPLETION

RENAL LOSSES	EXTRARENAL LOSSES
Hormonal deficit	Hemorrhage
Pituitary diabetes insipidus	Cutaneous losses
Aldosterone insufficiency	Sweating
Addison's disease	Burns
Hyporeninemic hypoaldosteronism	Gastrointestinal losses
Renal deficits	Vomiting
Specific tubular nephropathies:	Diarrheal disorders
Renal tubular acidosis	Gastrointestinal fistulas
Proximal	Tube drainage
Distal, gradient-limited	
Bartter's syndrome	
Nephrogenic diabetes insipidus	
Diuretic abuse	
Postobstructive diuresis	
Excessive filtration of nonelectrolytes:	
Osmotic diuresis	
Generalized renal disease:	
Chronic renal failure	
Interstitial nephritis	

Continued

postoperative period, 7 to 10% of blood volume losses in patients often are accompanied by normal vital signs and by only slight decreases in the central venous pressure or the pulmonary capillary wedge pressure. Skin turgor and the moistness of mucous membranes are valuable indices to the volume of body water in infants but are unreliable in adults. In young adults, reductions in skin turgor do not occur unless profound volume contraction is present, and normal loss of skin elasticity makes skin turgor difficult to assess in older patients. Similarly, mouth breathing and other factors affect the oral mucosa independently of external volume balances.

The signs and symptoms of volume contraction, regardless of cause, are referable to a reduction in ECF volume. Consequently the clinical findings in volume contraction depend primarily on the interplay among four major factors: (1) the magnitude of the volume loss, (2) the rate of volume loss, (3) the nature of the fluid loss (i.e., whether the fluid loss is primarily water, a combined sodium plus water loss, or a blood loss), and (4) the responsiveness of the vasculature to volume reduction. Some simple considerations illustrate these relationships.

The clinical manifestations of volume contraction are related intimately to the volume and rate of fluid loss. An acute gastrointestinal hemorrhage of 1 L of blood can result in oliguria, coupled with the signs and symptoms of circulatory collapse, while the hematocrit remains constant. The hemorrhage is sufficiently acute that fluid flux from the interstitial to the vascular bed makes a negligible contribution to expanding the vascular bed. The same amount of gastrointestinal blood loss occurring more slowly (e.g., over 1 day) permits a partial transfer of fluid from the interstitium to the vascular bed, however, and consequently produces a fall in hematocrit; because the CBV is restored at least partially by this fluid shift, the volume of urine flow and the hemodynamic response to volume contraction may be minimally affected.

Second, the kind of fluid loss significantly affects the clinical findings in volume contraction. Consider a 1-L loss of different kinds of body fluids in a 70-kg man with a total body water of 40 L and a hematocrit of 45%. The acute loss of 1 L of predominantly solute-free water, as in diabetes insipidus, reduces the blood volume by 2.5%; urine flow and systemic hemodynamics are minimally affected. The acute loss of 1 L of predominantly ECF reduces blood volume by 6.6% because sodium is confined to the ECF; in this circumstance, modest oliguria and tachycardia while the patient is recumbent ensue. Lastly, the acute loss of 1 L of blood by hemorrhage reduces blood volume by 20%, resulting in profound oliguria and near circulatory collapse.

Finally, peripheral vasoconstriction and tachycardia are important physiologic responses to volume losses. Consequently, even modest signs and symptoms of volume contraction are amplified appreciably in patients with diminished myocardial reserve or reduced sympathetic nervous system function. The former occurs commonly in cardiomyopathies of any cause or in pericardial tamponade or pericardial constriction. The latter occurs commonly in patients on prolonged bed rest, in diabetic patients with autonomic neuropathy, and as a consequence of therapy with certain antihypertensive drugs.

Diagnosis

The pulse, blood pressure, and changes of these variables with position, together with a clinical estimate of the venous pressure and skin temperature, provide an initial assessment of circulatory dynamics. Wide variations exist in blood pressure and pulse changes to orthostatic measurements. A decrease in orthostatic diastolic blood pressure of 10 mm Hg is considered to be the most reliable indicator of significant volume depletion. Even then, a physician cannot be certain, and it is useful to consider a fluid challenge to evaluate patients in whom a volume deficit is thought to contribute to a reduced cardiac output. A convenient way of achieving this goal is to administer 500 mL of normal saline over 1 to 3 hours.

In patients with a normal cardiac reserve, the effect of a fluid challenge may be monitored safely by evaluating the pulse, blood pressure, and urine flow. In patients with impaired cardiac function, using a flow-directed Swan-Ganz catheter to measure the pulmonary capillary wedge pressure or cardiac output, as estimated by thermal

dilution, provides a more precise indicator to early volume overload secondary to a fluid challenge. Because volume contraction is associated with vasoconstriction in the venous and the arterial circuits, transient changes in the pulmonary capillary wedge pressure may not reflect volume status accurately. During volume expansion, the wedge pressure rises and subsequently falls. The initial pressure elevation is due to fluid infusion into a vasoconstricted, low-capacity vascular bed and should not be misinterpreted to indicate adequacy of volume repletion. The subsequent reduction in wedge pressure coincides with decreases in arterial resistance coupled with increases in venous capacitance. Finally, central venous pressure measurements provide unreliable estimates of pulmonary vascular volume.

Rx Treatment

The major goal of treating volume contraction is to expand the CBV by replacing fluid deficits. The type of fluid, the route and rate of fluid administration, and the total amount of fluid to be given vary with the particular circumstance. A mild, nonpersisting upper gastrointestinal hemorrhage may be treated appropriately by infusing normal saline, whereas a major, persisting upper gastrointestinal hemorrhage generally requires replacement with whole blood.

The degree to which a given volume of crystalloid solution expands the CBV depends on solution composition. If glucose metabolism is normal, infusing 5% dextrose in water (D_5W) is equivalent to administering solute-free water, which distributes uniformly in total body water. Because less than 10% of total body water is in the intravascular compartment, infusing 1 L of D_5W expands the intravascular volume by 75 to 100 mL (i.e., by about 2%). Expansion of CBV by D_5W cannot be suggested except when used principally in hypertonic volume-contracted states, such as diabetes insipidus and excessive sweating.

Solutions containing sodium as the principal solute preferentially expand the ECF volume. Infusing 1 L of a normal saline solution increases blood volume by about 300 mL, or about 6%; the remaining portion is distributed in the interstitial compartment. Hypotonic sodium–containing salt solutions expand intravascular volume in a manner intermediate between that of D_5W and normal saline. Sodium-containing crystalloid solutions are indicated primarily in volume-contracted states secondary to renal or gastrointestinal sodium losses (see Table 112–2). They are also useful adjuncts to therapy in burns and in hemorrhage.

Colloid-containing solutions, such as iso-oncotic albumin solutions and plasma, preferentially expand the intravascular compartment because large molecules such as albumin are restricted mainly to the intravascular space. This kind of fluid replacement is most helpful in burns, in which cutaneous protein losses are appreciable, and in circulatory collapse, in which rapid intravascular expansion is crucial. In most other instances of volume contraction, using colloid-containing solutions is difficult to justify because the half-life of infused albumin in ill patients is relatively short, only 4 to 6 hours, and the cost of colloid solutions such as iso-oncotic albumin is more than 50 times greater than that of an equal volume of crystalloid solution.

Finally, blood—which contains formed elements—is the most potent expander of the intravascular space. A unit of packed red blood cells (RBCs) remains entirely in the vascular bed. In most hemorrhagic situations, the combination of packed RBCs with either normal saline solutions or colloid solutions is adequate for volume replacement. Few circumstances occur in modern practice, with the possible exception of massive hemorrhagic shock, in which whole blood therapy for volume expansion is used.

CIRCULATORY COMPROMISE WITHOUT EXTERNAL FLUID LOSSES

Definition

In the preceding section, we considered disorders characterized by inadequate filling of the arterial tree that occurred because of true volume deficits. The cardinal signs and symptoms of these disorders are referable to responses accompanying the integrated volume repletion reaction (Fig. 112–2). There are also disorders in which

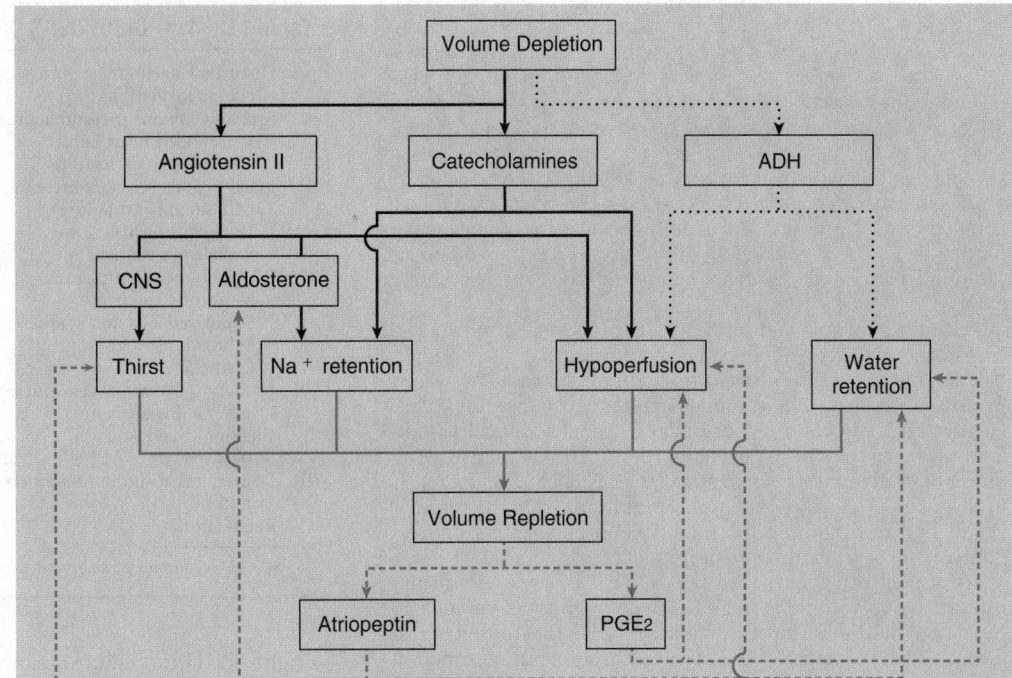

FIGURE 112–2 • The volume repletion reaction. The solid and dotted lines originating from *volume depletion* indicate positive mechanisms activated when volume depletion is either modest or severe. The dashed lines originating from *volume repletion* indicate negative feedback mechanisms. ADH = antidiuretic hormone; CNS = central nervous system; PGE_2 = prostaglandin E_2.

inadequate arterial filling occurs in the absence of external fluid losses and which often are associated with increased total body water. The signs and symptoms of these disorders mimic closely those that characterize true volume contraction, however.

Etiology and Pathogenesis

Table 112–3 lists three commonly encountered classes of derangements that may manifest clinically with tachycardia, acute hypotension, oliguria, azotemia, and a reduced fractional excretion of sodium.

IMPAIRED CARDIAC OUTPUT. A profound collapse of cardiac output, owing to acute myocardial infarction with pump failure (cardiogenic shock) or to acute pericardial tamponade, may result in circulatory collapse. In this instance, failure to fill the arterial tree and to maintain an effective arterial blood volume occurs because the heart fails to translocate blood adequately from venous to arterial beds.

INCREASED VASCULAR CAPACITANCE. Circulatory collapse with its attendant signs and symptoms occurs when there is a sudden increase in the capacitance of the vascular bed, most notably in the venous part of the circulation. This kind of increase in ratio of vascular capacitance to vascular volume occurs most commonly in sepsis and cirrhosis with increased arteriovenous shunts and decreased systemic vascular resistance. Increased vascular capacitance also may be seen

in circumstances in which peripheral vasodilators, particularly those having a postarteriolar locus of action, are administered injudiciously.

VASCULAR-INTERSTITIAL FLUID SHIFTS. Profound hypotension, tachycardia, progressive oliguria, and azotemia also are encountered when there is a translocation of fluid from vascular to interstitial compartments, presumably because of a sudden, profound increase in the permeability characteristics of peripheral capillaries or when there is decreased circulatory oncotic pressure, such as in any disease process with hypoalbuminemia. Some common causes of increased translocation of vascular fluid without hypoalbuminemia having an etiologic role include infarction of the small or large intestine, extensive tissue trauma, acute pancreatitis, and rhabdomyolysis. An analogous mechanism—a marked increase in the permeability of pulmonary capillaries—also is presumed to account for the formation of noncardiogenic pulmonary edema in adult respiratory distress syndrome.

Rx Diagnosis and Treatment

The diagnosis and therapy of acute myocardial infarction with circulatory collapse and of acute pericardial tamponade are considered in detail in Part VIII. Certain factors particularly germane to managing fluid therapy in these patients are cited, however. In individuals affected either by right ventricular infarction or by pericardial tamponade, maintaining adequate filling of the systemic arterial tree depends critically on providing a relatively high venous preload to the right side of the heart. Attempts at volume contraction in patients with right ventricular infarcts or pericardial tamponade may exacerbate systemic hypotension. Treating these disorders generally requires concomitant hemodynamic monitoring with a flow-directed Swan-Ganz catheter to avoid excessive preload to the left side of the heart.

In patients with left ventricular infarction and systemic hypotension, particular attention should be directed toward excluding the possibility that antecedent true volume depletion (e.g., with prolonged diuretic therapy and salt restriction before the myocardial infarction) may be a significant contributor to what otherwise might be mistaken for true cardiogenic shock. The combined findings of acute left ventricular infarction, systemic arterial hypotension, absence of pulmonary edema on the chest radiograph, reduced pulmonary capillary wedge pressure, and antecedent history of prolonged diuretic therapy, when taken together, indicate that improved systemic hemodynamics may be achieved by cautious attempts to expand volume, while also measuring—serially—the cardiac output and the pulmonary capillary wedge pressure.

Table 112–3 • CIRCULATORY COMPROMISE WITHOUT EXTERNAL FLUID LOSSES

I. Impaired cardiac output
  Acute myocardial infarction
  Pericardial tamponade
II. Increased vascular capacitance
  Septic shock
  Cirrhosis
III. Vascular → interstitial fluid shifts
  A. Hypoalbuminemia
    Nephrotic syndrome
    Liver failure
    Malnutrition
    Cytokine-mediated
  B. Normal plasma albumin
    Acute pancreatitis
    Bowel infarction
    Rhabdomyolysis
    Noncardiogenic pulmonary edema

Continued

The distinction between hypotension as being due to true volume contraction or to an increase in the capacitance-to-volume ratio of the vascular bed, as occurs in sepsis, is often difficult. This distinction is particularly difficult in patients who have been in intensive care units for prolonged periods and in patients at high risk for developing sepsis, such as cancer patients treated with potent chemotherapeutic agents. A useful clue to the presence of septic circulatory collapse is the occurrence of warm extremities coupled with hypotension and oliguria because true hypovolemia, particularly when advanced, ordinarily is accompanied by profound peripheral vasoconstriction and cool, often cyanotic extremities.

True hypovolemia and sepsis also may coexist. In such a circumstance, invasive hemodynamic monitoring may be helpful. In true hypovolemia and in sepsis, the pulmonary capillary wedge pressure is reduced, but in septic circulatory collapse, the calculated systemic vascular resistance falls because of peripheral vasodilation, whereas in true hypovolemia, peripheral vasoconstriction ordinarily raises the systemic vascular resistance. The diagnosis of disorders producing rapid transfer of fluids from the vascular bed to the interstitium, such as trauma, acute pancreatitis, or rhabdomyolysis, is generally evident from clinical appraisal.

Treatment of patients with sepsis and an increased vascular capacitance-to-volume ratio and patients with rapid vascular to interstitial fluid shifts has as a mainstay the administration of sufficient sodium-containing fluids, generally isotonic saline, to permit adequate filling of the arterial tree. This therapy necessarily expands total body water, particularly in the vascular and interstitial compartments. Consequently, during recovery from the underlying disorder, care must be taken to avoid unnecessary expansion of the vascular bed and consequently the risk of volume-mediated cardiac decompensation.

VOLUME EXCESS

Definition

Volume-expanded states are characterized by an increase in total body water, which usually is accompanied by an increase in total body sodium. Total body salt and water may be increased while the CBV is decreased. Certain volume-expanded states are characterized by dissociation between total body salt and water and the CBV.

Etiology and Pathogenesis

Volume expansion occurs whenever the rate of salt or water intake exceeds the rate of renal plus extrarenal losses; in chronic volume expansion, the external salt and water balance may be normal. A convenient way of considering volume-expanded states is to view them in the context of three different classes of physiologic explanations (Table 112–4).

DISTURBANCES IN STARLING FORCES. The most common diseases encountered in which volume expansion and edema occur are those in which derangements in the Starling forces regulating fluid transfer between capillaries and interstitium tend to expand the interstitial compartment. Consequently, renal sodium retention may increase to the point to maintain CBV, but these patients have edema. By definition, this group of disorders is characterized by increases in capillary hydrostatic pressure, by decreases in capillary oncotic pressure gradient between plasma and interstitium, or by a combination of these two factors.

Four groups include most edematous states characterized by abnormal Starling forces (see Table 112–4). First, the systemic venous pressure may be increased because of primary cardiac disorders, such

Table 112–4 • DISORDERS OF VOLUME EXCESS

I. Disturbed starling forces (reduced effective circulating volume; edema formation)
   Systemic venous pressure increases
     Right-sided heart failure
     Constrictive pericarditis
   Local venous pressure increases
     Left-sided heart failure
     Vena cava obstruction
     Portal vein obstruction
   Reduced oncotic pressure
     Nephrotic syndrome
     Decreased albumin synthesis
   Combined disorders
     Cirrhosis
II. Primary hormone excess (increased effective circulating volume)
   Primary aldosteronism
   Cushing's syndrome
   SIADH
III. Primary renal sodium retention (increased effective circulating volume)
   Renal failure

SIADH = syndrome of inappropriate antidiuretic hormone production.

as right-sided heart failure or constrictive pericarditis. Second, local elevations in pulmonary or systemic venous pressure may occur, as in left-sided heart failure, vena caval obstruction, or portal vein obstruction. Third, a reduction in plasma oncotic pressure and consequently a net increase in the tendency for fluid to transudate from capillaries to interstitium account plausibly for edema formation in the nephrotic syndrome. Finally, a combination of these factors may be responsible for edema. Hypoalbuminemia and portal hypertension are major contributory factors to developing ascites in hepatic cirrhosis.

Plasma renin activity and aldosterone concentrations in these disorders tend to be elevated, although the results also tend to be variable. In advanced cases of disorders characterized by increases in local or systemic venous pressure, most notably in severe congestive heart failure and in cirrhosis, hyponatremia may occur; this finding is an ominous prognostic sign. Finally, edema formation secondary to these derangements of Starling forces may result in the "third space" phenomenon—large volumes of interstitial fluid sequestered in regions such as the pleural or peritoneal cavities.

PRIMARY HORMONAL EXCESS. These disorders include disturbances with unregulated production of mineralocorticoids or ADH. The volume expansion that occurs in states of mineralocorticoid excess, such as primary hyperaldosteronism, is due to sodium retention and is accompanied by a primary, preferential expansion of the ECF and consequently by hypertension. The serum sodium level is generally normal. In the syndrome of inappropriate ADH production (SIADH), primary water retention occurs. Consequently the volume expansion involves the ICF and the ECF; dilutional hyponatremia is the hallmark of SIADH, whereas hypertension is uncommon. Edema is not characteristic in either of these two disorders. Instead, patients with primary aldosteronism or SIADH reach a volume-expanded steady state in which output equals input.

PRIMARY RENAL SODIUM RETENTION. The kidneys also may retain sodium abnormally when the ECF volume is normal and there is no effector excess. In acute glomerulonephritis, unidentified renal mechanisms are primarily responsible for edema. Patients with acute glomerulonephritis retain salt and water and become hypertensive without reductions in the GFR or in ECF volume. Sodium retention and edema may develop when intake exceeds renal capacity for excretion with a decrease in GFR of any cause.

℞ Diagnosis and Treatment

The recognition and management of volume-expanded states depend on proper identification and treatment of the underlying disorder. The cornerstones of therapy in volume-expanded states characterized by sodium excess include salt restriction and diuretics. Table 112–5 summarizes some of the major diuretics used commonly and certain of their properties; Figure 112–3 summarizes the sites of action of the various families of diuretics. For convenience, these drugs have been classified according to their sites of action in the nephron.

PROXIMAL TUBULE DIURETICS. The cardinal example of a proximal tubule diuretic is acetazolamide, a carbonic anhydrase inhibitor that blocks proximal reabsorption of sodium bicarbonate. Consequently,

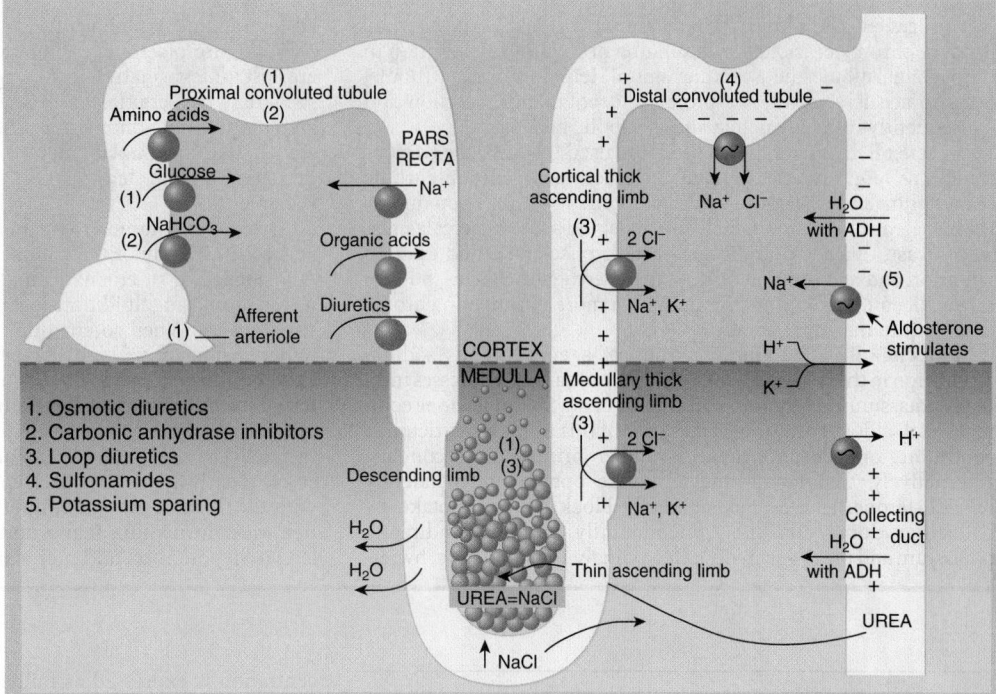

FIGURE 112–3 • Major transport processes along the nephron segment and the primary sites of action of the diuretics. The numbers next to diuretics in the insert refer to sites of action along the nephron. ADH = antidiuretic hormone. (From Kokko JP: Diuretics. *In* Alexander RW, Schlant RC, Fuster V [eds]: The Heart, 9th ed. New York, McGraw-Hill, 1998, with permission of The McGraw-Hill Companies.)

1. Osmotic diuretics
2. Carbonic anhydrase inhibitors
3. Loop diuretics
4. Sulfonamides
5. Potassium sparing

Table 112–5 • CHARACTERISTICS OF COMMONLY USED DIURETICS

DIURETIC	PRIMARY EFFECT	SECONDARY EFFECT	COMPLICATIONS
I. Proximal diuretics			
Acetazolamide	$\downarrow$ Na$^+$/H$^+$ exchange	$\uparrow$ K$^+$ loss, $\uparrow$ HCO$_3^-$ loss	Hypokalemic, hyperchloremic acidosis
Metolazone	$\downarrow$ Na$^+$ absorption	$\uparrow$ K$^+$ loss, $\uparrow$ Cl$^-$ loss	Hypokalemic alkalosis
II. Loop diuretics			
Furosemide			
Bumetanide	$\downarrow$ Na$^+$:K$^+$: 2Cl$^-$ absorption	$\uparrow$ K$^+$ loss, $\uparrow$ H$^+$ secretion	Hypokalemic alkalosis
Ethacrynic acid			Hearing deficits, hypomagnesemia
III. Early distal diuretics			
Thiazide	$\downarrow$ NaCl absorption	$\uparrow$ K$^+$ loss, $\uparrow$ H$^+$ secretion	Hypokalemic alkalosis
Metolazone			Hyperglycemia, hyperuricemia
IV. Late distal diuretics			
Aldosterone antagonists			
Spironolactone			
Nonaldosterone antagonists	$\downarrow$ Na$^+$ absorption	$\downarrow$ K$^+$ loss, $\downarrow$ H$^+$ secretion	Hyperkalemic acidosis
Triamterene			
Amiloride			

prolonged use of acetazolamide may lead to hyperchloremic acidosis, in contrast to all other diuretics, which act at loci before the late distal nephron. Metolazone, a congener of the thiazide class of diuretics, blocks sodium chloride absorption in two nephron sites by unknown mechanisms. Specifically, in addition to an action on the early distal tubule, metolazone also inhibits proximal tubular sodium chloride absorption. Because the major locus for phosphate absorption is in the proximal nephron, the phosphaturia accompanying metolazone administration exceeds considerably that observed with other thiazide class diuretics.

Proximal tubule diuretics rarely are used as primary diuretic therapy in modern practice. More commonly, these diuretics, particularly metolazone, are used as supplements to loop diuretics in instances in which loop diuretics alone are ineffective in producing diuresis.

Mannitol also inhibits proximal tubule reabsorption. It is used mainly to decrease the incidence of acute tubular necrosis.

LOOP DIURETICS. Loop diuretics, such as furosemide, bumetanide, and ethacrynic acid, produce diuresis by inhibiting the coupled entry on Na$^+$, Cl$^-$, and K$^+$ across apical plasma membranes in the thick ascending limb of Henle. The latter is responsible for the reabsorption of approximately 25% of filtered sodium. The natriuretic dose-response characteristics of these diuretic agents are considerably more linear than those of all other currently used diuretics, and data support an equivalent diuresis for bio-equivalent doses of forsemide and furosemide, two of the commonly used agents.[1] For practical purposes, these are the most potent diuretics and commonly are referred to as *high-ceiling diuretics*.

DISTAL TUBULE DIURETICS. Distal tubule diuretics, such as thiazide and metolazone, interfere primarily with sodium chloride absorption in the earliest segments of the distal convoluted tubule. The thiazide diuretics seem to exert their effect by blocking the sodium chloride cotransport mechanism across apical plasma membranes.

With the exception of acetazolamide (which impairs bicarbonate absorption), hypokalemia and metabolic alkalosis may complicate the administration of proximal diuretics, loop diuretics, and distal tubular diuretics. This occurs because the rate of sodium delivery to the collecting duct, in which a significant fraction of potassium and proton secretion occurs, is a major factor promoting these

Continued

two processes. Consequently, increase in salt delivery to the late distal nephron, occasioned by inhibition of sodium reabsorption in the proximal tubule, the ascending limb of Henle, or the distal tubule, leads to accelerated rates of proton and potassium secretion and consequently to hypokalemia and metabolic alkalosis.

In general, distal tubule diuretics are used for the same circumstances as loop diuretics. The major exception occurs in chronic renal failure and in disorders of calcium metabolism. Loop diuretics are calciuric and are valuable for managing acute hypercalcemia. In contrast, thiazide diuretics promote hypocalciuria and calcium retention and are useful in managing hypercalciuric states, but not hypercalcemia. Loop diuretics are much more effective in chronic renal failure than are thiazide diuretics.

COLLECTING DUCT DIURETICS. A group of agents inhibits sodium absorption in the collecting duct and concomitantly suppresses indirectly potassium secretion and proton secretion. Spironolactone competes with aldosterone; the primary use of this agent is restricted to conditions of aldosterone excess, either primary or secondary. Alternatively, triamterene and amiloride operate independently of aldosterone. These agents directly block sodium uptake by collecting duct cells and concomitantly suppress indirectly potassium and proton secretion. Accordingly, hyperkalemic, hyper-

chloremic metabolic acidosis may complicate the injudicious use of spironolactone, triamterene, or amiloride. These diuretics are useful especially in managing disorders characterized by secondary hyperaldosteronism, such as cirrhosis with ascites, and in promoting diuresis in hypokalemic patients. It also has been shown that spironolactone[2] or eplerenone[3] improves survival of patients with left ventricular dysfunction or heart failure (Chapter 56).

One factor common to treatment of disorders with reduced CBV and with expanded ECF volumes merits particular consideration. A major factor in edema formation is an increase in the Starling forces promoting fluid translocation from the vascular to the interstitial spaces. When potent diuretics are given to patients with portal hypertension or with severe hypoalbuminemia, urinary sodium excretion may exceed the rate at which salt and water are transferred from the interstitium to the vascular bed. As a result, vigorous diuretic therapy may result in further CBV contraction, reduced salt delivery to diluting segments, nonosmotic ADH release, and consequently hyponatremia. Hyponatremia occurs most commonly with the thiazide group of diuretics because these diuretics inhibit free water formation. Inappropriately aggressive diuretic use may lead to hypotension and prerenal azotemia.

---

1. Vasavada N, Saha C, Agarwal R: A double-blind randomized crossover trial of two loop diuretics in chronic kidney disease. Kidney Int 2003;64:632–640.
2. Pitt B, Zannad F, Remme WJ, et al, for the Randomized Aldactone Evaluation Study Investigators: The effect of spironolactone on morbidity and mortality in patients with severe heart failure. N Engl J Med 1999;341:709–717.
3. Pitt B, Remme W, Zannad F, et al: Eplerenone, a selective aldosterone blocker, in patients with left ventricular dysfunction after myocardial infarction. N Engl J Med 2003;348:1309–1321.

SUGGESTED READINGS
Costello-Boerrigter LC, Boerrigter G, Burnett JC Jr: Revisiting salt and water retention: New diuretics, aquaretics, and natriuretics. Med Clin North Am 2003;87:475–491. *Update on diuretics and natriuretic peptides, which, unlike diuretics, do not activate the renin-angiotensin system and may improve the glomerular filtration rate.*
Shankar SS, Brater DC: Loop diuretics: From the Na-K-2Cl transporter to clinical use. Am J Physiol Renal Physiol 2003;284:F11–F21. *How the altered expression or activity of the sodium-potassium-chloride transporter in the loop of Henle may account for the diuretic response to these agents.*
Verbalis JG: Diabetes insipidus. Rev Endocr Metab Disord 2003;4:177–185. *A comprehensive review of diagnosis and management of spontaneous and post-surgical disease.*

Osmolality Disturbances

PHYSIOLOGIC CONSIDERATIONS

In normal individuals, the serum osmolality as determined by freezing-point depression is virtually constant from day to day. It is useful to define *effective ECF osmolality* because the osmoregulatory mechanisms that adjust water balance in normal individuals are determined primarily by changes in cell volume that result from variations in effective ECF osmolality. Effective ECF osmolality is osmolality that is "sensed" across a specific membrane. In dilutional states, the measured and effective ECF osmolalities are approximately equal because ECF dilution also produces ICF dilution and, at least acutely, cell swelling. Osmoregulatory mechanisms are activated when ECF hypertonicity is due to a solute that is excluded from cells and produces, at least acutely, cell shrinkage; in this case, the measured and effective ECF osmolalities are approximately equal. If the ECF osmolality is increased by solutes, such as urea, which penetrate cell membranes, acute cell shrinkage does not occur to the degree predicted from freezing-point osmolality, and osmoregulatory mechanisms are not fully activated. In this case, the measured ECF osmolality is greater than the effective ECF osmolality.

The freezing-point serum osmolality can be approximated from the following formula:

$$\text{Osmolality} = 2[Na^+] + \{\{glucose//18\}\} + \{\{BUN//2.8\}\}$$

where the glucose and blood urea nitrogen (BUN) concentrations are expressed as milligrams per deciliter, and the serum sodium con-

centration is expressed as milliequivalents per liter. In normal circumstances, glucose contributes 5.5 mOsm/kg H_2O to the serum osmolality. When hyperglycemia occurs, the effective ECF osmolality increases because glucose entry into cells is limited.

Cell Volume Regulation

Starling forces regulate fluid transfer between the ICF and the ECF. Because plasma membranes cannot tolerate even small hydrostatic gradients, the operational Starling forces between ICF and ECF are almost entirely osmotic. Significant changes in cell volume, particularly in the CNS, are by themselves potentially lethal. The goals of fluid transport between the ECF and ICF are to maintain constancy of cell volume and to maintain a negligible hydrostatic pressure gradient between cells and the ECF. Because most cell membranes are freely permeable to water, these two goals are achieved when the ECF osmolality is normal, and intracellular and extracellular osmolalities are identical.

Because cell membranes are partially permeable to sodium and potassium, there is a tendency for sodium to leak into cells and for potassium to leak out of cells. Because impermeant macromolecules account for a large fraction of intracellular anions, passive sodium and potassium movements tend toward a Donnan distribution, in which total intracellular cations would exceed total interstitial cations, in precise analogy to the way in which total plasma water cations exceed total interstitial cations. If these passive cation movements across cell membranes were unopposed, osmotic water movement into cells would tend to produce cell lysis. Consequently, active transport mechanisms are required to balance intracellular and interstitial cation concentrations.

Specifically, sodium leakage from the ECF into cells and potassium leakage out of cells into the ECF are counterbalanced exactly by active outward sodium transport coupled to active inward potassium transport. These active transport events maintain the intracellular cation (and osmolar) content equal to that of ECF and maintain the predominant extracellular and intracellular distributions of sodium and potassium. Because cellular cation pumps balance cellular cation leaks, cells are *operationally* impermeable to sodium and to potassium. Active sodium efflux coupled to active potassium influx is mediated by membrane-bound Na^+, K^+-ATPase, and the activity of these cellular cation pumps accounts for more than 50% of the basal calorie consumption.

Cation transport mediated by Na^+, K^+-ATPase is the major factor regulating cell volume when the effective ECF osmolality is normal. When the effective ECF osmolality is increased or decreased, additional processes are required to maintain the constancy of cell volume. These auxiliary mechanisms are particularly important in minimizing potentially lethal changes in brain volume because of osmotic water shifts into or out of brain cells.

In chronic hypotonic disorders, cell swelling is offset by the loss of potassium chloride from cells. This potassium chloride efflux mechanism seems to be activated by small increases in cell volume produced by ECF dilution. In chronic hypernatremia, brain shrinkage is minimized by the accumulation of additional solutes within brain cells. These latter solutes, often called *idiogenic osmoles,* include amino acids and other solutes, including *myo*-inositol, sorbitol, inositol, betaine, and urea. As is discussed in the section on treatment, these auxiliary transport processes affect significantly the therapeutic approach to patients with osmoregulatory failure.

Water Balance

The key elements regulating water balance are summarized in Figure 112–4. The osmoreceptors for ADH release and for thirst respond to small changes in effective ECF osmolality, whereas baroreceptors respond to changes in CBV. A 2% increase in effective ECF osmolality shrinks osmoreceptor cells and stimulates ADH release from the posterior pituitary and thirst. A second way of stimulating ADH release and thirst involves volume-mediated stimuli that can operate independently of changes in plasma osmolality. When the CBV is reduced by approximately 10%, these volume-dependent mechanisms stimulate ADH release.

SENSORS AND EFFECTORS. Three kinds of *sensor* elements adjust water balance. Two of these, osmoreceptors and the thirst center, respond to small changes in effective ECF osmolality, whereas baroreceptors respond to changes in CBV. The osmoreceptors are situated in the supraoptic and paraventricular nuclei of the hypothalamus, whereas the thirst center is in the organum vasculosum of the anterior hypothalamus. A 2% increase in effective ECF osmolality produced by solutes such as sodium chloride, but not urea, shrinks osmoreceptor cells and thirst center cells. The osmoreceptors stimulate the release of the *effector* hormone ADH from storage sites in the posterior pituitary gland. The stimulation of thirst by the thirst centers depends on centrally produced angiotensin II.

Endothelin-1 also is released from the posterior pituitary in response to water deprivation. Administered endothelin-1 increases plasma ADH levels. Endothelin-1 may have a central role in modulating ADH release.

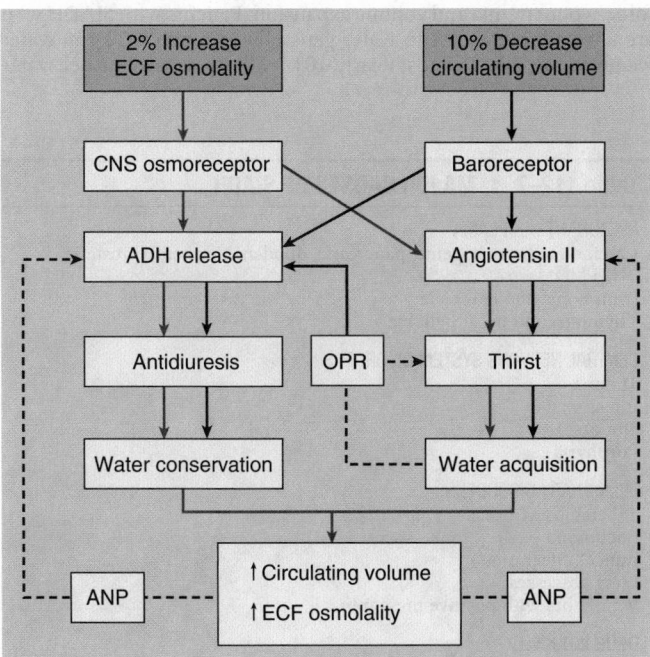

FIGURE 112–4 • The water repletion reaction. The blue lines are positive water conservation processes activated by osmolality. The black lines are water conservation processes that are volume activated. The dashed lines indicate negative feedback. ADH = antidiuretic hormone; ANP = atrial natriuretic peptide; CNS = central nervous system; ECF = extracellular fluid; OPR = oropharyngeal reflex. (From Reeves WB, Andreoli TE: The posterior pituitary and water metabolism. *In* Wilson JD, Foster DW [eds]: Williams Textbook of Endocrinology, 8th ed. Philadelphia, WB Saunders, 1992.)

When the CBV is reduced by more than 10%, volume-dependent blood produces afferent signals, carried by the ninth and tenth cranial nerves, which result in nonsmotic ADH release. Volume contraction also acts as a potent stimulus to thirst by means of angiotensin II.

ANTIDIURETIC RESPONSE. The cardinal characteristics of the antidiuretic response depend primarily on the integrated activity of two nephron regions: the medullary thick ascending limb of Henle, which concentrates the medullary interstitium, and the collecting duct, which, with ADH present, allows water reabsorption from this segment. The medullary thick ascending limb absorbs much (possibly 25%) of the filtered load of sodium. Some of this reabsorbed sodium is trapped in the renal medullary interstitium, accounting largely for the hypertonicity of the renal medullary interstitium. The medullary thick limb of Henle is also impermeable to water, however. Consequently, salt abstraction from the thick limb of Henle accounts simultaneously for the development of medullary hypertonicity, permitting—in the presence of ADH—maximal antidiuresis, and the appearance of maximally dilute urine in early distal convolutions, permitting—in the absence of ADH—maximal water diuresis.

In normal individuals, approximately 18 L/d of tubular fluid reaches the early distal tubule; the osmolality of this fluid is dilute, approximately 50 mOsm/kg H_2O. In the total absence of ADH and volume contraction, maximal rates of water diuresis include a urinary volume of 18 L/d having an osmolality of 50 mOsm/kg H_2O. During antidiuresis, ADH increases the water permeability of collecting ducts (Chapter 238). Tubular fluid equilibrates osmotically with the hypertonic medullary interstitium, reducing urinary volume, concentrating the urine, and conserving body water. When ADH is absent, the water permeability of collecting ducts is low, and absorption of tubular fluid is reduced so that it escapes unchanged as hypotonic urine. Because collecting ducts are partially permeable to water in the absence of ADH, a reduced volume of hypotonic fluid reaching collecting ducts equilibrates partially with the medullary interstitium, limiting the ability to dilute urine maximally.

NEGATIVE FEEDBACK. Water repletion activates a negative feedback of water conservation by at least two systems, atriopeptin and the oropharyngeal reflex. Immunoreactive atriopeptin is released within the CNS and by secretory granules in cardiac atria. The centrally released atriopeptin can suppress ADH release and thirst. Oropharyngeal stimulation by water suppresses ADH release and thirst before absorbing water or producing a fall in plasma osmolality. This oropharyngeal reflex probably depends on neural traffic between the oropharynx and the CNS.

Intrarenal prostaglandin E_2 suppresses the effects of ADH on nephron segments. Prostaglandin E_2 is produced by renal interstitial cells in response to increases in medullary osmolality. Prostaglandin E_2 impairs water conservation by inhibiting the actions of ADH on nephron segments involved in the antidiuretic response—the medullary thick ascending limb and the collecting duct.

HYPOTONIC DISORDERS

Definition

In a hypotonic disorder, the ratio of solutes to water in body fluids is reduced, and the serum osmolality and serum sodium are reduced in parallel. True hypotonicity must be distinguished from disorders in which the *measured* serum sodium is low, while the measured serum osmolality is either normal or increased.

The distinction among these disorders is presented in Table 112–6. The measured serum sodium concentration can be reduced either because there is an increased concentration of small, nonsodium solutes restricted to the ECF or because of a laboratory artifact. In hyperglycemia or excessive mannitol administration, these solutes, which are restricted to the ECF, draw water from the cellular compartment. The serum sodium level is reduced, even though the serum osmolality may be increased. When a small, nonsodium solute is distributed in total body water, as in ethanol intoxication or in azotemia, the serum osmolality rises, but the serum sodium concentration remains normal, resulting in an "osmolar gap." The latter is a useful diagnostic aid in intoxication with the different alcohols shown in Table 112–6. Instances of spurious hyponatremia caused by hyperlipemia or hyperproteinemia are becoming less common as more laboratories use ion-selective electrodes to measure the serum sodium concentration.

Table 112-6 • DISTINCTION BETWEEN APPARENT AND REAL HYPOTONICITY

CONDITION	MEASURED SERUM (NA)	MEASURED SERUM OSMOLALITY
True hypotonicity	↓	↓
Increased nonsodium ECF solutes		
Hyperglycemia	↓	↑
Mannitol administration	↓	↑
Increased nonsodium ECF and ICF solutes		
Ethanol	Normal	↑
Ethylene glycol	Normal	↑
Methanol	Normal	↑
Isopropyl alcohol	Normal	↑
Laboratory artifact		
Hyperlipemia	↓	Normal
Hyperproteinemia	↓	Normal

ECF = extracellular fluid; ICF = intracellular fluid.

Etiology and Pathogenesis

Hyponatremia and simultaneous body water hypotonicity develop whenever water intake exceeds the sum of renal plus extrarenal water losses; in chronic hyponatremia, the net water intake and net water output may be equal. Hyponatremia and body fluid hypotonicity occur when there is a primary increase in water ingestion, when the ability of the kidney to dilute urine maximally is limited, or when a combination of these factors is operative.

The kidney regulates serum sodium concentration by increasing or decreasing free water excretion. The term *free water* refers to the amount of solute-free water that has to be added or subtracted from urine to leave it isosmolar to blood. Adding free water to blood, either by failure to generate free water or by increased reabsorption of free water, decreases serum sodium concentration. Free water is generated by the kidney across the diluting segments by absorbing salt without water. Free water is formed and excreted. Failure to generate free water occurs in clinical circumstances in which less salt is delivered to the diluting segments or under circumstances in which diuretics block sodium chloride reabsorption across the diluting segment, most commonly seen with thiazide diuretics.

Free water is absorbed in the collecting duct. The rate of free water reabsorption is regulated in large part by ADH. The higher the ADH concentration, the greater is the rate of free water reabsorption, assuming that other driving forces for water reabsorption remain constant. Conditions with increased ADH concentrations generally are associated with hyponatremia. The collecting duct can maintain large osmotic gradients; however, this capacity is limited, and the minimal osmolality of the urine is approximately 50 mOsm/kg H_2O. If more dilute fluid is delivered to the collecting duct, this water is reabsorbed even in the absence of ADH, as occurs in psychogenic polydipsia and in beer potomania. These conditions are described next.

REDUCED SOLUTE DELIVERY TO DISTAL NEPHRON SEGMENTS

Reduced solute delivery disorders may occur because of decreased sodium delivery to the diluting segment or decreased solute delivery to the collecting duct. Decreased sodium delivery generally occurs in a setting of decreased effective arterial blood volume (e.g., congestive heart failure, hypoalbuminemic states, and decreases in systemic vascular resistance), as in sepsis and cirrhosis. These conditions often also are associated with ADH increases.

An example of decreased solute delivery to the collecting duct is *beer potomania*. Without beer, a normal individual on a normal diet produces roughly 1000 mOsm of solute for urinary excretion. Because maximally dilute urine is 50 mOsm/kg, each 50 mOsm of solute can capture no more than 1 L of free water. On a normal diet, an individual can consume 20 L of fluid without becoming hyponatremic. Beer has a low concentration of salts and other solutes except it has a relatively high carbohydrate content that prevents metabolic generation of solutes by preventing protein catabolism. It has been estimated that total urinary osmolal clearance is no more than 200 mOsm. Beer drinkers who get most of their calories from beer cannot drink

more than 4 L of free water (most of which is consumed as beer) without becoming hyponatremic.

Hyponatremia due to reduced solute intake is not restricted to individuals with beer potomania but may occur during starvation, when intake may be reduced dramatically without parallel reductions in water intake. This form of hyponatremia occurs with increasing frequency in elderly patients in nursing homes who are inadequately supervised.

PRIMARY EFFECTOR ANTIDIURETIC HORMONE EXCESS

SYNDROME OF INAPPROPRIATE ANTIDIURETIC HORMONE PRODUCTION. In SIADH, hyponatremia occurs as a result of sustained endogenous production and release of ADH or ADH-like substances; the ECF volume is normal or increased, and there are no other physiologic or pharmacologic stimuli to ADH release. Table 112–7 lists the major causes of SIADH. A similar process may account in part for the hyponatremia seen in myxedema.

ADH, or a peptide having comparable biologic activity, is produced by tumors. Increased ADH levels, estimated by either bioassay or radioimmunoassay, also have been noted in patients with cranial disorders, such as skull fractures, subdural hematomas, subarachnoid hemorrhage, and brain tumors; in acute intermittent porphyria; and possibly in myxedema. Four different patterns of plasma ADH concentrations have been described in patients with SIADH. Figure 112–5 illustrates three of these patterns; the yellow area in the figure illustrates the normal relationship between plasma ADH levels and serum osmolality. The pattern denoted "erratic ADH release" in Figure 112–5 accounts for about 37% of patients with SIADH; the hormone is released completely independently of osmotic control. About one third of patients with SIADH have a "reset osmostat"; there is an abnormally low threshold for ADH secretion, but if sufficiently hyponatremic, these patients with SIADH can produce a maximally dilute urine. About 16% of patients with SIADH exhibit the "ADH leak" pattern—sustained ADH production below the osmotic threshold and normal increases in serum ADH levels with osmotic challenge (see Fig. 112–4). About 14% of patients with SIADH have no detectable abnormality in ADH levels; they fail, for reasons not yet understood, to dilute urine maximally.

The typical features of SIADH are listed in Table 112–8. The cardinal results of the sustained water conservation in SIADH are twofold: hyponatremia and volume expansion. Patients with SIADH who are allowed free access to water generally gain about 3 kg in water weight or, in other words, nearly 10% of body water. Further water

Table 112-7 • MAJOR CAUSES OF SIADH

MALIGNANT NEOPLASIA
Carcinoma: bronchogenic, pancreatic, duodenal, ureteral, prostatic, bladder
Lymphoma and leukemia
Thymoma and mesothelioma

CENTRAL NERVOUS SYSTEM DISORDERS
Trauma
Infection
Tumors
Porphyria

PULMONARY DISORDERS
Tuberculosis
Pneumonia
Fungal infections
Lung abscesses
Ventilators with positive pressure

DRUG INDUCED
Desmopressin
Oxytocin
Vincristine
Chlorpropamide
Nicotine
Cyclophosphamide
Morphine
Amitriptyline
Selective serotonin reuptake inhibitors

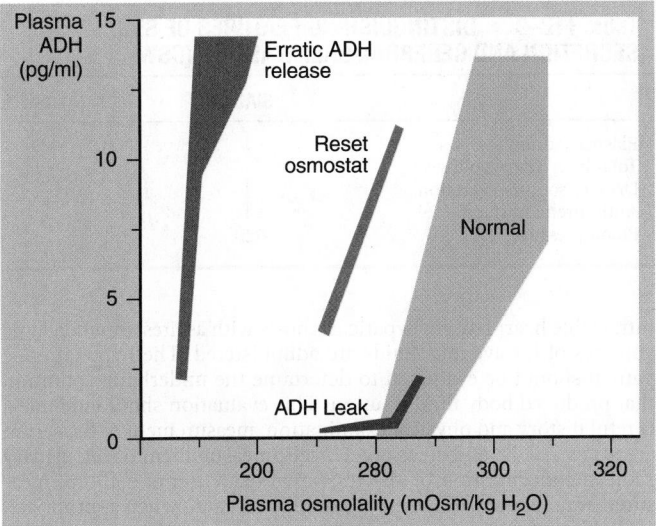

FIGURE 112–5 • The patterns of serum antidiuretic hormone (ADH) abnormalities in the syndrome of inappropriate secretion of antidiuretic hormone (SIADH). The shaded areas indicate the normal relationship between increases in effective extracellular osmolality and ADH levels; the normal osmotic threshold is lower than the normal serum osmolality. The three shaded areas indicate ADH patterns in SIADH. (Adapted from Zerbe R, Strope L, Robertson G: Vasopressin function in the syndrome of inappropriate diuresis. Annu Rev Med 1980;31:315–327.)

Table 112–8 • MAJOR CHARACTERISTICS OF SIADH
Hyponatremia
Volume expansion without edema
Natriuresis
Hypouricemia
Normal or reduced serum creatinine level
Normal thyroid and adrenal function

gain is partially prevented as the result of decreased expression of aquaporin-2, which is the ADH sensitive water channel in the collecting duct. In that respect, patients with SIADH differ from patients with hyponatremia secondary to salt depletion, Addison's disease, or diuretic excess because patients with the latter disorders are volume contracted. Patients with SIADH, although volume expanded, do not develop edema, however, and differ in that respect from patients with congestive heart failure or cirrhosis.

When total body water is expanded by about 10% by water conservation in SIADH, a natriuresis occurs even with hyponatremia. The patient with SIADH reaches a steady state when body water is expanded by water retention and when natriuresis, even with hyponatremia, prevents edema formation.

The causes for the natriuresis that is characteristic of SIADH are multiple. First, volume expansion results in enhanced release of atriopeptin, which enhances urinary sodium wasting by enhancing glomerular filtration and by suppressing tubular sodium absorption. Second, the volume expansion of SIADH also reduces the rate of proximal tubular sodium absorption and the rate of proximal uric acid absorption.

SIADH is a disorder in which hormone-stimulated water conservation results in hyponatremia; volume expansion; and consequently an increased GFR, tubular sodium wasting, and reduced net tubular absorption of creatinine and uric acid, but no edema formation. These characteristics are summarized in Table 112–8. As indicated in connection with Figure 112–5, the urinary osmolality in patients with SIADH may be either inappropriately high for the level of serum osmolality or maximally dilute.

OTHER CAUSES OF EXCESSIVE ANTIDIURETIC HORMONE PRODUCTION AND/OR RELEASE. There are other circumstances in which an increased level of ADH is the primary factor responsible for hyponatremia. Many commonly used drugs stimulate ADH release, including vincristine,

cyclophosphamide, carbamazepine, phenothiazines, morphine, barbiturates, chlorpropamide, amitriptyline, thiothixene, and clofibrate. Chlorpropamide also potentiates the effect of ADH on the water permeability of collecting ducts. The posterior pituitary peptide oxytocin (Pitocin) also has an antidiuretic action, although oxytocin is a much less potent antidiuretic agent than is vasopressin. Intravenous hypotonic solutions containing oxytocin given to induce labor may result in profound hyponatremia. Trauma or surgical stress also stimulates ADH release. Increasing numbers of patients, especially the elderly, who have been placed on selective serotonin reuptake inhibitors have been noted to develop hyponatremia with findings compatible with SIADH.

Ordinarily, diuretic-induced hyponatremia is related to volume contraction; this kind of body fluid dilution is discussed later. Chronic severe potassium depletion induced by diuretics also can result in ADH release, although the mechanisms by which potassium depletion stimulates ADH release are unknown.

MIXED DISORDERS

Hyponatremia occurs commonly in true volume contraction and in edematous states when filling of the arterial tree is impaired. The former disorders include patients in whom ECF and total body water are reduced; the latter group comprises patients with deranged Starling forces, notably local or systemic increases in venous pressure, which result in inadequate filling of the arterial tree. In both sets of disorders, two factors contribute, individually or in unison, to the pathogenesis of hyponatremia: nonosmotic, volume-mediated ADH release and reductions in the rate of sodium delivery to the diluting segment.

Volume contraction is a potent nonosmotic stimulus to ADH release. Figure 112–6 shows the relationships between osmotic and

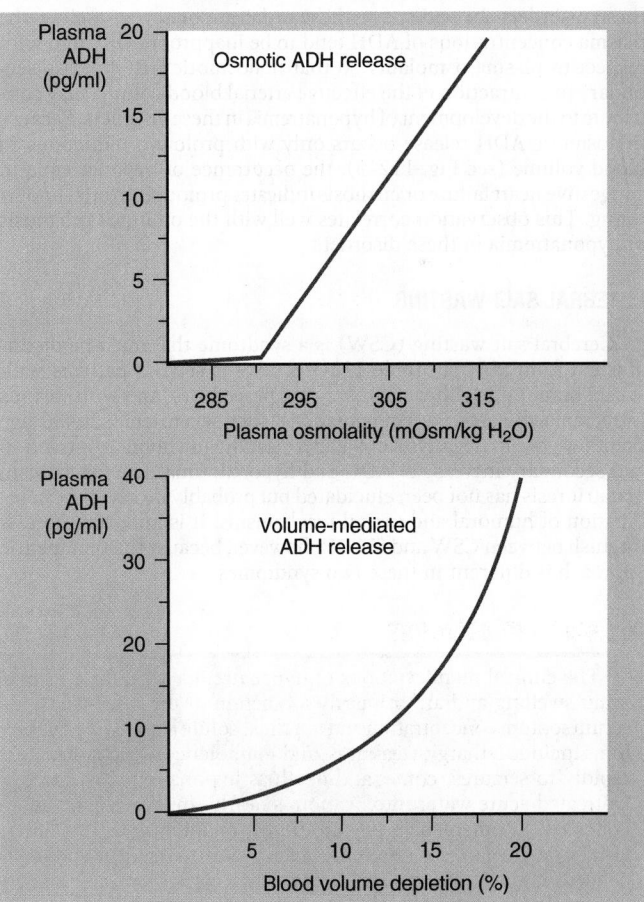

FIGURE 112–6 • Relationship between plasma antidiuretic hormone (ADH) concentrations and either effective extracellular fluid osmolality (upper plot) or the percentage of blood volume depletion (lower plot). (Adapted from Dunn FL, Brennan TJ, Nelson AE, et al: The role of blood osmolality and volume in regulating vasopressin secretion in the rat. J Clin Invest 1973;52:3212, with permission. Copyright American Society for Clinical Investigation.)

nonosmotic, volume-mediated stimuli and plasma ADH levels in experimental animals; comparable responses occur in humans. Increases in plasma osmolality are related linearly to increases in plasma ADH levels. The relationship between blood volume depletion and plasma ADH levels is nonlinear. With depletion of more than 7 to 10% blood volume, however, plasma ADH levels rise sharply and produce an antidiuretic effect even when the plasma osmolality is reduced below normal. Volume-mediated, nonosmotic ADH release occurs primarily when circulatory dynamics are moderately to severely advanced; in that circumstance, volume-mediated stimuli override osmotically mediated ADH release, and hyponatremia ensues.

A second factor that accounts for hyponatremia in volume-contracted states is an inability to dilute urine maximally because the rate of sodium delivery to diluting segments in the thick ascending limb and distal convoluted tubule is reduced. This situation occurs because increased rates of proximal tubular sodium absorption are stimulated by reduced sodium intake or by inadequate filling of the arterial tree in conditions with combined ECF volume expansion and reduced arterial tree filling.

Hyponatremia is a common feature of untreated Addison's disease and occurs because of a combination of circumstances. In mineralocorticoid deficiency, ECF volume contraction, glomerular filtration reduction, enhanced proximal tubular salt absorption, and volume-mediated, nonosmotic ADH release seem to be the major factors responsible for an inability to excrete water loads. Glucocorticoid deficiency also impairs the ability to excrete water loads. One of the factors responsible for water retention in Addison's disease is nonosmotic ADH release, which results from impaired cardiac function.

Hyponatremia occurs commonly in advanced stages of disorders characterized by edema formation and a reduced effective arterial blood volume, particularly in intractable heart failure and advanced hepatic cirrhosis with ascites. Reduced rates of salt delivery to diluting segments of the renal tubule contribute to impaired water excretion in these disorders. In patients with heart failure or severe ascites, the plasma concentrations of ADH tend to be inappropriately high with respect to plasma osmolality so that nonosmotic ADH release secondary to contraction of the effective arterial blood volume may contribute to the development of hyponatremia in these disorders. Because nonosmotic ADH release occurs only with profound reductions in blood volume (see Fig. 112–5), the occurrence of hyponatremia in congestive heart failure or cirrhosis indicates profound arterial underfilling. This observation correlates well with the ominous prognosis of hyponatremia in these disorders.

CEREBRAL SALT WASTING

Cerebral salt wasting (CSW) is a syndrome that must be distinguished from SIADH (Table 112–9). CSW is seen in patients with severe brain injury, after neurosurgical procedures, and with various intracranial diseases. Patients experience such severe renal salt wastage that they go into negative salt balance, leading to volume contraction and secondary increase in ADH and hyponatremia. The mechanism of natriuresis has not been elucidated but probably involves the combination of humoral and neural mechanisms. It is important to distinguish between CSW and SIADH, however, because the therapeutic approach is different in these two syndromes.

Clinical Manifestations

The clinical manifestations of hyponatremia are produced by brain swelling and are primarily a function of the rate of fall of serum sodium concentration and not the absolute level. Early symptoms include lethargy, weakness, and somnolence, which proceed rapidly to seizures, coma, and death as hyponatremia worsens. Untreated acute water intoxication is nearly uniformly fatal and is a medical emergency. In chronic hyponatremia, CNS manifestations are far less common, even when the serum sodium concentration is 100 mEq/L, because the loss of brain solutes, principally potassium chloride, minimizes brain cell swelling for a given reduction in body water osmolality.

Diagnosis

Hyponatremia should be considered whenever there is a sudden deterioration in CNS function, particularly in circumstances such as

Table 112–9 • DISTINGUISHING FEATURES OF SIADH SECRETION AND CEREBRAL SALT WASTING (CSW)

	SIADH	CSW
Plasma sodium	↓	↓
Total body water volume	↑	↓
Urinary sodium excretion	↑	↑
Antidiuretic hormone	↑	↑
Blood pressure	±↑	±↓

intractable heart failure, hepatic cirrhosis with ascites, or when large volumes of intravenous fluids are administered. The hyponatremic patient should be evaluated to determine the underlying condition that produced body fluid dilution. This evaluation should include a careful history and physical examination; measurement of the serum creatinine, BUN, and electrolyte levels; measurement of the urinary sodium concentration or the fractional excretion of sodium; measurement of serum and urinary osmolalities; and, when appropriate, evaluation of thyroid and adrenal function.

The history and physical examination are generally adequate for recognizing disorders such as beer potomania or compulsive water ingestion or for noting the ingestion of drugs that stimulate ADH release or enhance ADH action. The presence of edema is characteristic of individuals in whom hyponatremia occurs because of a reduced effective arterial blood volume combined with ECF volume expansion. In myxedema or Addison's disease, the typical clinical or laboratory findings of these disorders are generally present (Chapters 239 and 240).

The most difficult differential diagnosis among hyponatremic disorders involves the distinction between patients who are modestly volume contracted and patients who have SIADH. In both circumstances, the serum sodium and the serum osmolality are reduced, whereas the urinary osmolality is inappropriately high with respect to the reduced serum osmolality. Nonosmotic water conservation in SIADH and in volume contraction is recognized by the presence of a urinary osmolality greater than 120 to 150 mOsm/kg H_2O in association with a reduced serum osmolality. The distinction between the two disorders depends on a clinical and laboratory assessment of effective arterial blood volume.

Patients who are volume contracted may provide a history of volume losses or of diuretic ingestion and may exhibit the signs of ECF volume contraction discussed previously in the section on volume depletion. When the volume losses are due to extrarenal causes, the urinary sodium concentration is less than 10 to 15 mEq/L, and the fractional excretion of sodium is generally less than 1%. Uric acid concentration is influenced by volume status of the patient. In volume expansion, there is increased urinary excretion of uric acid and a tendency toward hypouricemia. Conversely the presence of hyperuricemia suggests effective arterial volume contraction. Prerenal azotemia may occur if the volume contraction is severe. Patients with SIADH are generally normovolemic or slightly volume expanded and exhibit none of the signs of volume contraction. The serum BUN and creatinine levels are normal, and the serum uric acid level is generally reduced. The urinary sodium concentration is usually greater than 30 mEq/L, and the fractional excretion of sodium is greater than 1%. Tests of adrenal function yield normal results (Table 112–10).

The previous studies usually discriminate between SIADH and extrarenal volume contraction. When ECF volume contraction is due to renal salt wasting, urinary sodium losses generally persist, unless volume contraction is profound. As noted previously (see Volume Depletion), the blood pressure and pulse may be normal in states of

Table 112–10 • DISTINGUISHING FEATURES OF APPROPRIATELY VERSUS INAPPROPRIATELY INCREASED ADH CONCENTRATIONS

APPROPRIATE		INAPPROPRIATE
↓	Plasma sodium	↓
↑	Urine osmolality	↑
↓	Urine sodium	↑
↑	Plasma uric acid	↓

modest volume contraction. A useful diagnostic and therapeutic maneuver in this situation is to observe the results of water restriction. This approach can be taken only in absence of neurologic findings and in absence of hypoxia. When water intake is restricted to 600 to 800 mL/day, patients with SIADH exhibit a highly characteristic response: A 2- to 3-kg weight loss is accompanied by correction of hyponatremia and cessation of salt wasting, usually over 2 to 3 days. If weight loss fails to correct hyponatremia and urinary sodium wasting simultaneously, the diagnosis of SIADH is doubtful. Renal sodium wasting with ECF volume contraction, secondary to Addison's disease or the other renal salt-losing disorders listed in Table 112–2, is the more probable diagnosis.

 Treatment

Neurologic symptoms secondary to osmotic swelling of the brain are much more common when hyponatremia develops rapidly in menstruant women and prepubescent children (i.e., age, gender, and hormonal status of patients are important factors in predisposing to symptoms of hyponatremia), but neurologic complications of acute treatment of hyponatremia are more common if existing hyponatremia is long-standing and developed chronically. Patients with CNS manifestations of hyponatremia require immediate therapy to prevent death, whereas too-rapid hyponatremia correction rarely has been associated with osmotic demyelination syndrome, which is the result of the selective loss of myelin (with sparing of neurons and axial cylinders). These histologic findings may occur in any part of the brain but are more common in the central areas of the pons. The symptoms of osmotic demyelinating syndrome often occur several days after too-rapid hyponatremia correction and include behavioral disturbances, fluctuating levels of consciousness, ataxia, pseudobulbar palsy, difficulty in speaking, and other varying features. In nonfatal cases, the recovery is slow, often taking weeks, and recovery may not be complete with residual sequelae. It cannot be stated strongly enough, however, that most of the complications in treatment of symptomatic hyponatremia have occurred in patients whose sodium concentration was corrected too slowly. Symptomatic hyponatremia is a medical emergency with high morbidity and mortality. Water restriction without hypertonic intravenous sodium chloride is not appropriate in a symptomatic hyponatremic patient. Differing opinions exist as to the ideal rate for correcting hyponatremia. The rate and magnitude of this correction can be considered conveniently as a two-step process: (1) acute correction of symptomatic hyponatremia and (2) long-term correction of asymptomatic or residual hyponatremia.

ACUTE CORRECTION OF HYPONATREMIA. Acute hyponatremia associated with a serum sodium concentration less than 120 mEq/L and with CNS manifestations requires immediate therapy. In volume-contracted states, the treatment of choice is to increase the serum sodium concentration by 10 mEq/L or to levels of 120 to 125 mEq/L over 6 hours by administering hypertonic 3 to 5% saline. As was discussed, elevating serum sodium too quickly to values greater than 125 mEq/L may be hazardous. Because the desired effect is to correct total body water osmolality, the amount of sodium administered must be sufficient to raise total body water osmolality to approximately 250 mOsm/kg H_2O (i.e., to approximately twice the desired serum sodium concentration). A convenient formula for calculating this sodium requirement is as follows:

$$[125 - \text{measured serum Na}^+] \times 0.6 \text{ body weight} = \text{required mEq of Na}^+$$

The serum sodium level is in milliequivalents per liter, and the body weight is in kilograms. Because 60% of body weight is water, the formula allows an estimate of the amount of sodium required to increase total body water osmolality to 250 mOsm/kg H_2O. If one cannot remember this formula, a useful practice is to administer 250 mL of either 3 or 5% saline over 4 to 6 hours. This usually increases the serum sodium concentration by 10 to 15 mEq/L and reduces the neurologic symptoms. When the acute corrective phase of hyponatremia is complete, one can initiate long-term correction of hyponatremia.

LONG-TERM CORRECTION OF HYPONATREMIA. The most important aspect in managing asymptomatic, non–volume-depleted hyponatremia is to restrict electrolyte-free water intake. If water intake is restricted to less than 1 L/day, the serum sodium concentration rises regardless of its cause. Fluid intake restriction should be coupled with high dietary salt intake. Because this approach is clinically unacceptably slow in certain patients, an alternative is to use normal saline in combination with a loop diuretic. The diuretic induces urinary salt loss and reduces the risk of ECF volume expansion. Isotonic saline infusion without a loop diuretic may lower the serum sodium concentration in patients with SIADH. One must use a loop diuretic with intravenous saline if this approach is taken.

Use of a vasopressin receptor antagonist (VPA-985) at about 100 mg per day can correct hyponatremia in patients with cirrhosis and perhaps in patients with heart failure.[12] Another approach to correcting chronic hyponatremia in SIADH is to use lithium carbonate or demeclocycline. These two compounds block the effect of ADH at the level of the collecting duct and increase the excretion of free water. Both of these drugs may have complications, however, and should be used only if the patient cannot comply adequately with water restriction and high dietary salt intake.

HYPERTONIC DISORDERS

Definition

A hypertonic disorder is one in which the ratio of solutes to water in total body water is increased. All hypernatremic states are hypertonic. In some hypertonic disorders, such as uncontrolled hyperglycemia, the increase in effective ECF osmolality is due to nonsodium solutes.

Etiology and Pathogenesis

Hypernatremia develops whenever water intake is less than the sum of renal and extrarenal water losses; in chronic hypertonic states, net water balance may be zero. The most common causes of clinically significant hypernatremia occur as a consequence of three pathogenic mechanisms: impaired thirst, solute or osmotic diuresis, excessive losses of water, either through the kidneys or extrarenally, and combinations of these derangements. These disorders are grouped in Table 112–11 according to the primary pathogenic mechanism. There is also a group of miscellaneous disorders, such as hypokalemia, hypercalcemia, interstitial renal disease, and chronic renal failure, which either partially impair renal urinary concentrating ability or partially blunt the responsiveness of collecting ducts to ADH. These disorders rarely cause significant hypernatremia and are not discussed further.

INADEQUATE INTAKE OF WATER. This problem occurs in patients who are comatose or who are otherwise unable to communicate thirst. Because of the exquisite sensitivity of thirst mechanisms to

Table 112–11 • MAJOR CAUSES OF HYPERNATREMIA

I.	Impaired thirst
	Coma
	Essential hypernatremia
II.	Solute diuresis
	Osmotic diuresis: diabetic ketoacidosis, non-ketotic hyperosmolar coma, mannitol administration
III.	Excessive water losses
	Renal
	Pituitary diabetes insipidus
	Nephrogenic diabetes insipidus
	Extrarenal
	Sweating
IV.	Combined disorders
	Coma plus hypertonic nasogastric feeding

changes in effective body water osmolality, hypernatremia owing to inadequate water intake is rare in conscious patients allowed free access to water. Rarely, patients have a primary thirst deficiency. Patients with Cushing's syndrome or primary hyperaldosteronism commonly have slight elevations in the serum sodium level for unknown reasons.

"Essential hypernatremia" is characterized by a slightly elevated serum sodium level that occurs in the conscious state. The defect in patients with essential hypernatremia seems to be an insensitivity of thirst centers and osmoreceptors to osmotic stimuli. Thirst and anti-diuresis occur, however, when these patients are volume contracted. Consequently, it has been inferred that volume-mediated stimuli to thirst and ADH release are intact in patients with essential hypernatremia. This disorder may be either congenital or acquired, sometimes in association with histiocytic infiltration of the CNS.

OSMOTIC DIURESIS. This is another mechanism for producing renal water losses in excess of sodium losses and hypertonicity. Osmotic diuresis occurs commonly in uncontrolled glycosuria and may occur when mannitol is given. Because these solutes are restricted to the ECF, the serum sodium level generally is reduced in the early stages of osmotic diuresis, and the effective ECF osmolality is increased primarily by the impermeant nonsodium solute. In prolonged osmotic diuresis, net water losses may be sufficiently great that hypernatremia develops. In this circumstance, the increase in effective ECF osmolality is due to the combined effects of hypernatremia and the nonsodium solute. Hypernatremia resulting from an osmotic urea diuresis can occur if large amounts of protein and amino acids are administered by nasogastric tube or if tissue catabolism is great, as in burns. In this circumstance, hypernatremia is responsible for the increased effective ECF osmolality.

Hypernatremia also may complicate use of normal saline solutions when the endogenous osmolar solute load is high and renal concentrating ability is limited. Patients with diabetic ketoacidosis, who are generally young, have sufficient urinary concentrating ability that hypernatremia does not occur when normal saline solutions are used to treat ketoacidosis. In contrast, the nonketotic hyperglycemic syndrome generally occurs in elderly patients, who can have partial impairment of urinary concentrating power. In this setting, hypernatremia can occur during therapy with normal saline solutions.

EXCESSIVE WATER LOSSES. Impairment of ADH production, release, or action, as occurs in pituitary or nephrogenic diabetes insipidus can lead to profound water deficits and to hypernatremia. In such circumstances, the urine volumes are large, the urinary osmolality is low, and the net rate of solute excretion is low, in contrast to individuals undergoing osmotic diuresis, in whom rates of urinary solute excretion are elevated.

Striking water losses also may occur with excessive sweating, particularly during rigorous physical activity by untrained individuals exercising in high humidity. This phenomenon plays a major role in the evolution of heatstroke.

COMBINED DISORDERS. Hypertonic dehydration may occur as a combination of these events. A common example in modern clinical practice involves injudiciously administering large amounts of carbohydrate or amino acids by nasogastric tube, coupled with limited amounts of water, to stroke patients unable to communicate thirst.

Clinical Manifestations and Diagnosis

Because two thirds of body water is intracellular, primary water losses tend to have modest effects on circulating volume unless fluid losses are profound. Rather the clinical manifestations are produced by brain shrinkage that results from increases in effective ECF osmolality. The symptoms of hypertonicity produced either by hypernatremia or by impermeant nonsodium solutes such as glucose are referable to the CNS and range from somnolence and confusion to coma, respiratory paralysis, and death. The degree of symptoms varies with the degree of hypertonicity and with the rate at which hypertonicity develops. In acute hypertonicity, symptoms generally appear when the effective ECF osmolality exceeds 320 to 330 mOsm/kg H_2O, and coma and respiratory arrest may occur when the ECF osmolality exceeds 360 to 380 mOsm/kg H_2O. Chronic hypertonicity generally produces fewer CNS manifestations because brain cells accumulate idiogenic osmoles, which minimize the tendency for brain shrinkage.

 Treatment

To treat acute hypernatremia, normal saline solutions initially are given intravenously. These factors should be considered when treating acute hypernatremia. In the highly volume-contracted patient with severe hypernatremia, administering isotonic saline solutions has two advantages. It provides fluid resuscitation in impending cardiovascular collapse. The isotonic salt solution, which is hypotonic with respect to the hypertonic patient, avoids an unnecessary rapid fall in the serum sodium level.

Rapid correction of hypertonicity to a normal serum osmolality is hazardous. Because accumulation of idiogenic osmoles by brain cells is a compensatory mechanism for preserving brain volume in hypertonic disorders, a normal serum osmolality may be relatively hypotonic to brain cells that have accumulated idiogenic solutes. If the serum osmolality is reduced rapidly, CNS damage secondary to brain swelling may occur. A useful guide to circumventing this difficulty is to reduce the serum sodium level by no more than 1 mEq/L during every 2 hours of the first 2 days of treatment.

1. Gerbes AL, Gulberg V, Gines P, et al, for the VPA Study Group: Therapy of hyponatremia in cirrhosis with a vasopressin receptor antagonist: A randomized double-blind multicenter trial. Gastroenterology 2003;124:933–939.
2. Wong F, Blei AT, Blendis LM, et al: A vasopressin receptor antagonist (VPA-985) improves serum sodium concentration in patients with hyponatremia: A multi-center, randomized, placebo-controlled trial. Hepatology 2003;37:182–191.

SUGGESTED READINGS

Adrogue HJ, Madias NE: Hyponatremia. Prim Care 2000;342:1581–1589. *Easy-to-read but comprehensive review of hyponatremia.*

Ayus JC, Arieff AI: Chronic hyponatremic encephalopathy in postmenopausal women. JAMA 1999;281:2299–2304. *This is a well-conducted study in 53 postmenopausal women with encephalopathic symptoms of hyponatremia that showed that rapid treatment with hypertonic saline decreased the tragic events seen in patients treated with simple water deprivation.*

Decaux G, Soupart A: Treatment of symptomatic hyponatremia. Am J Med Sci 2003;326:25–30. *Approach to the treatment of acute and chronic hyponatremia.*

Diederich S, Franzen NF, Bahr V, et al: Severe hyponatremia due to hypopituitarism with adrenal insufficiency: Report on 28 cases. Eur J Endocrinol 2003;148:609–617. *Hypopituitarism including secondary adrenal insufficiency is a frequently overlooked cause of severe hyponatremia.*

Fraser CL, Arieff AI: Epidemiology, pathophysiology, and management of hyponatremic encephalopathy. Am J Med 1997;112:67–77. *Review of pathogenesis of hyponatremia and hyponatremic encephalopathy. An easy-to-understand therapeutic approach is given to asymptomatic and symptomatic hyponatremia.*

Han DS, Cho BS: Therapeutic approach to hyponatremia. Nephron 2002;92(Suppl 1):9–13. *Review of consensus guidelines for treating hyponatremic patients.*

Harrigan MR: Endocrine and metabolic dysfunction syndromes in the critically ill. Crit Care Clin 2001;17:125–138. *An outstanding review that solidifies the existence of CSW and clearly differentiates it from SIADH.*

Kahn T: Reset osmostat and salt and water retention in the course of severe hyponatremia. Medicine (Baltimore) 2003;82:170–176. *Some patients may develop acute severe hyponatremia superimposed on chronic hyponatremia because of a reset osmostat.*

Oh MS: Pathogenesis and diagnosis of hyponatremia. Nephron 2002;92(Suppl 1):2–8. *Laboratory parameters are much more reliable in determining effective vascular volume than is careful physical examination.*

Palmer BF: Hyponatremia in patients with central nervous system disease: SIADH versus CSW. Trends Endocrinol Metab 2003;14:182–187. *In cerebral salt wasting, the low effective blood volume from renal losses is distinguished from the expanded blood volume in SIADH.*

Disturbances in Potassium Balance

PHYSIOLOGIC CONSIDERATIONS

Hypokalemia ($K^+ < 3.5$ mEq/L) and hyperkalemia ($K^+ > 5.5$ mEq/L) are common in medical practice. Although the plasma potassium concentration is influenced by total body potassium stores, factors influencing the distribution of potassium between extracellular and intracellular spaces are important determinants of plasma potassium concentration.

Transfer Between Intracellular Fluid and Extracellular Fluid

The intracellular compartment acts as a large potassium reservoir in series with the small ECF potassium pool. In potassium-depleted states with normal acid-base status, a 1 mEq/L decrease in the serum potassium level reflects the loss of about 300 mEq of potassium; the bulk of external potassium loss comes from the cellular compartment. Conversely, if large amounts of potassium are administered acutely, the rise in serum potassium level is less than would be expected if the administered potassium were distributed solely in the ECF. In this situation, cellular uptake of potassium occurs and prevents greater increases in the serum potassium concentration. This ability of cells to accumulate potassium can be enhanced strikingly by long-term administration of high-potassium diets.

Many *effector* mechanisms regulate the partition of potassium between the ICF and ECF. These include active and passive ionic transcellular transport processes.

ACTIVE TRANSPORT PROCESSES. The cardinal transport process regulating K^+ distribution between the ICF and ECF is cell membrane–bound Na^+, K^+-ATPase, which actively transports potassium into cells and counterbalances the passive leak of potassium from cells into interstitial fluid. Insulin is a second effector that promotes potassium transfer from ECF to ICF. This hormone promotes cellular uptake of potassium independently of cellular glucose uptake by increasing Na^+, K^+-ATPase activity. Insulin also reduces sodium permeability; the resultant cellular hyperpolarization of cells produces a passive driving force for potassium accumulation within cells. Hyperkalemia augments insulin release. Hyperkalemia may be the sensor that stimulates release of insulin, which then serves as an effector for potassium entry into cells. β-Adrenergic agents, particularly β₂-agonists such as terbutaline, also promote cellular potassium uptake by enhancing Na^+, K^+-ATPase activity; it is not yet known whether hyperkalemia can provoke β-agonist release, as it does for insulin release. Mineralocorticoids such as aldosterone, in addition to enhancing renal potassium excretion (see later), enhance cellular potassium uptake; the mode of aldosterone action in the latter instance is not understood.

PASSIVE TRANSPORT PROCESSES. Many passive effector mechanisms also regulate the partition of potassium between the ICF and the ECF. First, alterations in the pH of ECF reproducibly shift potassium between the ICF and the ECF. Systemic acidosis, whether metabolic or respiratory, promotes potassium efflux from cells, whereas systemic alkalosis, either metabolic or respiratory, promotes cellular potassium uptake. As a general rule, a reduction in plasma pH of 0.1 in metabolic acidosis increases the serum potassium level by 0.6 mEq/L, whereas a plasma pH increase of 0.1 produces a similar reduction in serum potassium. The magnitude of transcellular potassium shifts is not as great in response to acid-base balance changes secondary to respiratory causes as it is in changes secondary to metabolic causes.

Second, cellular shrinkage produced by increases in effective ECF osmolality increases the intracellular potassium concentration and increases the driving force for passive potassium leakage from the ICF to the ECF. This leakage may result in hyperkalemia when large glucose loads are administered to insulin-deficient diabetic patients who also have hyporeninemic hypoaldosteronism; the insulin lack limits cellular re-entry of potassium, and the aldosterone deficiency limits renal potassium excretion. Increases in cellular potassium concentrations produced by cellular shrinkage also contribute significantly to the hyperkalemia of diabetic ketoacidosis because hyperglycemia increases cellular potassium levels by cell shrinkage, and insulin lack prevents accelerated potassium re-entry into cells.

Finally, brain cells and renal tubular cells lose potassium when exposed to chronic ECF hypotonicity. Muscle cells, which are the largest component of ICF potassium, do not appear to participate in this process, however. Consequently, hypotonic disorders by themselves have little effect on the serum potassium level or on external potassium balance.

Renal Handling of Potassium

The kidney is responsible for the excretion of approximately 90% of dietary potassium. Although the stool potassium concentration is high (75 to 90 mEq/L of stool water) under normal circumstances, only roughly 10% of dietary potassium is excreted by the gastrointestinal tract. Factors that cause an increase in renal excretion of potassium are important (Table 112–12).

Almost all the potassium excreted in urine gains access to the urinary space by secretory mechanisms that are located across distal

Table 112–12 • FACTORS CAUSING INCREASED URINARY LOSS OF POTASSIUM

Increased mineralocorticoids
Increased delivery of Na^+ to collecting duct
Increased fluid flow to distal tubule
Metabolic and respiratory alkalosis
Increased excretion of nonreabsorbable solutes

convoluted and collecting duct segments. These transport processes are described in Chapter 111, but for the purposes of this chapter, it is important to identify these factors in clinical situations that cause increased excretion of potassium. Of the factors listed in Table 112–12, increased plasma aldosterone is most important, with a higher resultant kaliuresis occurring by the other factors if they are superimposed on a baseline of higher aldosterone concentration. The rate of urinary potassium excretion in any given clinical circumstance depends on the interplay between these factors.

The rate of renal tubular adaptation to factors regulating urinary excretion of potassium is relatively slow. The renal adaptation to excess loads occurs over 24 to 36 hours, however, and hyperkalemia from the ingestion of large oral potassium loads is uncommon in normal individuals. The renal response to dietary potassium restriction is more sluggish and requires 7 to 10 days for full development. Even under the latter circumstances, urinary potassium losses are rarely less than 20 mEq/day.

HYPOKALEMIA AND POTASSIUM DEPLETION

Definition

Chronic hypokalemia generally reflects a reduction in total body potassium. A 1-mEq reduction in serum potassium level generally implies the net loss of 300 mEq of potassium from the body. In extreme body potassium depletion, the serum potassium level may be 1.5 to 2.0 mEq/L. Acute reductions in serum potassium level without parallel reductions in total body potassium occur when potassium is shifted from the ECF to the ICF.

Etiology and Pathogenesis

Hypokalemia and simultaneous potassium depletion occur whenever renal plus extrarenal potassium losses exceed potassium intake. In advanced body potassium depletion, intake and output of potassium may be equal. The four major causes for hypokalemia are given in Table 112–13.

EXCESSIVE RENAL LOSSES. Many of the causes for renal potassium wasting can be analyzed in terms of factors that modulate the common

Table 112–13 • MAJOR CAUSES OF HYPOKALEMIA

I. Excess renal loss	II. Gastrointestinal losses
Mineralocorticoid excess	Vomiting
Bartter's syndrome	Diarrhea, particularly secretory
Diuresis	diarrheas
Diuretics with a pre-late	III. ECF → ICF shifts
distal locus	Acute alkalosis
Osmotic diuresis	Hypokalemic periodic paralysis
Chronic metabolic alkalosis	Barium ingestion
Antibiotics	Insulin therapy
Carbenicillin	Vitamin B_{12} therapy
Gentamicin	Thyrotoxicosis (rarely)
Amphotericin B	IV. Inadequate intake
Renal tubular acidosis	
Distal, gradient-limited	
Proximal	
Liddle's syndrome	
Gitelman's syndrome	
Acute leukemia	
Ureterosigmoidostomy	

ECF = extracellular fluid; ICF = intracellular fluid.

effector system for potassium secretion. *Mineralocorticoid excess* accelerates distal tubular potassium secretion. Consequently, hypokalemia occurs regularly in primary hyperaldosteronism, in Cushing's syndrome, and in secondary hyperaldosteronism. *Chronic European licorice ingestion* produces a syndrome that mimics primary hyperaldosteronism because glycyrrhizic acid, a component of licorice extract, has physiologic properties similar to those of aldosterone.

The primary pathophysiologic defect in Bartter's syndrome is incomplete reabsorption of sodium chloride by the thick ascending limb of Henle, whereas in Gitelman's syndrome, the primary defect is decreased sodium chloride reabsorption by the distal convoluted tubule. These defects cause increased delivery of Na^+ to the collecting duct and net salt wastage. The resulting volume contraction causes increased renin and aldosterone concentrations. These hormonal changes, together with increased delivery of Na^+ to the collecting duct, cause increased excretion of potassium.

Most diuretics having a locus of action before the late distal tubule (see Fig. 112–3) increase urinary potassium losses. Enhanced sodium delivery to distal nephron segments is the major factor responsible for the kaliuresis produced by these diuretics, and sodium restriction or volume depletion tends to minimize diuretic-induced potassium losses. Carbonic anhydrase inhibitors, such as acetazolamide, inhibit proximal bicarbonate absorption and accentuate potassium losses. Distal tubular segments are relatively impermeable to bicarbonate; consequently, increased delivery of bicarbonate to distal nephron regions has an impermeant anion effect that increases luminal electronegativity in these nephron regions.

Osmotic diuresis commonly is associated with increased renal potassium losses because increased tubular flow rates enhance net potassium secretion. In diabetic ketoacidosis, renal potassium losses are common. Yet patients with diabetic ketoacidosis and a reduced total body potassium concentration commonly present with hyperkalemia because metabolic acidosis tends to promote potassium shifts from the ICF to the ECF. Consequently, profound hypokalemia may develop if body potassium is not replenished concomitantly with insulin therapy and ECF volume expansion (Chapter 242).

Potassium depletion is seen frequently in *chronic metabolic alkalosis*. When the alkalosis is associated with volume contraction, secondary hyperaldosteronism results in renal potassium losses. Potassium depletion in chronic metabolic alkalosis also is enhanced if bicarbonaturia is present because of the impermeant anion effect produced by bicarbonate delivery to collecting duct segments. The hypokalemia associated with upper gastrointestinal fluid losses, as in vomiting or nasogastric suction, is primarily the result of the renal potassium losses produced by secondary hyperaldosteronism and/or bicarbonaturia. The potassium losses from the upper gastrointestinal tract are small because upper gastrointestinal tract fluid contains only about 10 mEq of potassium per liter.

Hypokalemia may develop during therapy with certain *antibiotics*. Carbenicillin or other penicillin-like antibiotics exist as sodium or potassium salts of impermeant anions and promote kaliuresis because they increase net sodium excretion and because of an impermeant anion effect. Amphotericin B increases the permeability of luminal membranes to potassium and promotes potassium secretion. Gentamicin produces potassium losses by unknown mechanisms.

Hypokalemia and potassium depletion are common findings in type II proximal tubular acidosis and type I *distal, gradient-limited renal tubular acidosis* (Chapter 120). Increased distal sodium delivery and the impermeant anion effect produced by bicarbonate wasting account for most of the potassium losses seen in proximal renal tubular acidosis. Consequently, salt restriction, which enhances the rate of proximal sodium bicarbonate absorption in this disorder, also tends to correct potassium depletion. In gradient-limited distal renal tubular acidosis, hypokalemia may be accentuated by volume losses and secondary hyperaldosteronism. Other factors, not yet understood, also contribute to hypokalemia in this disorder. Hyperkalemia, rather than hypokalemia, commonly accompanies the hyperchloremic acidosis of interstitial disease (type IV acidosis) or of voltage-dependent renal tubular acidosis (see later).

Liddle's syndrome is a rare inherited tubular disorder characterized by hypokalemia, metabolic alkalosis, hypertension, and subnormal aldosterone secretion rates. Therapy with triamterene or amiloride, but not with aldosterone antagonists such as spironolactone, ameliorates the disorder. These findings suggest that collecting duct sodium avidity and potassium secretion independent of aldosterone are major factors in the pathogenesis of Liddle's syndrome. Studies have shown that collecting duct sodium channels are mutated in such a manner as to be "open" even with subnormal aldosterone concentrations (aldosterone normally opens sodium channels in the collecting duct to increase sodium absorption). In operational terms, Liddle's syndrome may be described as distal nephron hyperfunction, in regard to Na^+ absorption and H^+ and K^+ secretion.

GASTROINTESTINAL LOSSES. Gastrointestinal losses provide the major route for potassium depletion, other than the kidney. As indicated earlier, potassium depletion associated with vomiting is referable primarily to renal potassium losses. Diarrhea produces significant potassium losses because normal stool water potassium concentration is 70 to 90 mEq/L, and voluminous diarrheal fluid contains 30 mEq/L of potassium. The most striking diarrheal potassium losses occur in secretory diarrheas, such as with non-β islet cell tumors of the pancreas, which produce vasoactive intestinal polypeptide, and in laxative abuse. In secretory diarrheas and chronic laxative abuse, hypokalemia probably is caused by increased rates of K^+ secretion through apical membrane K^+ channels. Villous adenomas of the colon produce potassium depletion because of excessive colonic K^+ secretion from the adenoma. Hypokalemia uncommonly is seen in inflammatory bowel disease.

EXTRACELLULAR FLUID–INTRACELLULAR FLUID SHIFTS. Acute hypokalemia with a normal total body potassium may occur because of *potassium shifts* from the ECF to the ICF. In *hypokalemic periodic paralysis*, acute shifts of potassium from the ECF to the ICF produce limb and trunk paralysis. The periodic attacks often are precipitated by high-carbohydrate meals. Patients with the disorder often can abort attacks by exercising affected muscles. The long-term use of acetazolamide can prevent attacks. A condition resembling hypokalemic periodic paralysis occurs with the ingestion of *barium salts* and is endemic in China, where the disorder is called *Pa-Ping*. Barium seems to produce hypokalemia by blocking K^+ channels in skeletal muscle and blocking efflux of potassium from the ICF to the ECF. *Insulin* therapy and *vitamin B_{12}* therapy also promote potassium shifts from the ECF to the ICF. Hypokalemia also can result rarely from thyrotoxicosis, especially in Asian males, for reasons that are unclear.

INADEQUATE INTAKE. Reduced potassium intake may result in potassium depletion and hypokalemia because maximal renal conservation of potassium requires, as indicated previously, 7 to 10 days. During this interval, the net renal potassium loss may be 150 to 200 mEq.

Clinical Manifestations

The clinical effects of potassium deficiency are manifest in one or more organ systems, including skeletal muscle, heart, kidneys, and gastrointestinal tract. The most serious disturbances are those affecting the neuromuscular system. At serum potassium concentrations of 2.0 to 2.5 mEq/L, muscular weakness is likely to occur; with more severe hypokalemia, the patient may develop areflexic paralysis, in which case respiratory insufficiency is an immediate threat to survival. The severity of the neuromuscular disturbance tends to be proportional to the speed with which the potassium level has declined. Losses of large amounts of potassium from skeletal muscle may contribute to the development of rhabdomyolysis and myoglobinuria.

The electrocardiogram (ECG) abnormalities of potassium depletion, shown in Figure 112–7, affect primarily repolarization segments of the ECG, in keeping with the effects of hypokalemia on the action potential. The common ECG manifestations of hypokalemia include sagging of the ST segment, depression of the T wave, and elevation of the U wave. With marked hypokalemia, the T wave becomes progressively smaller, and the U waves show increasing amplitude. In some cases, the merging of a flat or positive T wave with a positive U wave may be interpreted erroneously as a prolonged QT interval. Ordinarily, there are no serious clinical consequences from the abnormalities in cardiac excitation. In patients treated with digitalis, hypokalemia may precipitate serious arrhythmias.

Long-standing potassium depletion may produce renal tubular damage, called *hypokalemic nephropathy*. Potassium deficiency also affects smooth muscle of the gastrointestinal tract and can result in paralytic ileus.

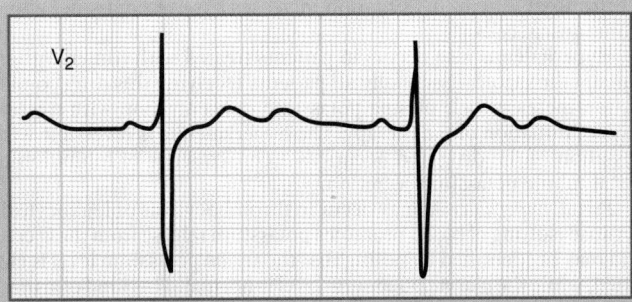

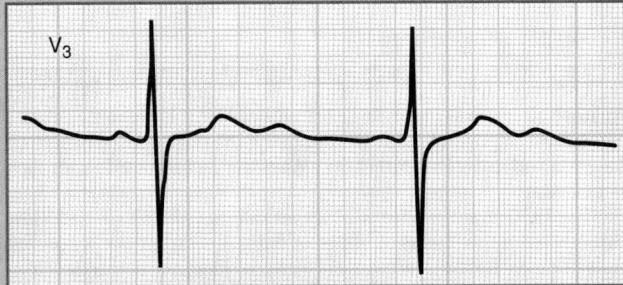

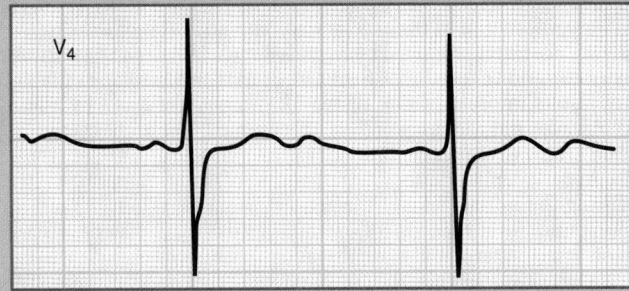

FIGURE 112–7 • The electrocardiographic manifestations of hypokalemia. The serum potassium was 2.2 mEq/L. The ST segment is prolonged, primarily because of a U wave following the T wave, and the T wave is flattened.

Rx Treatment

The treatment of potassium depletion involves replacement therapy with potassium salts and attempts to correct the underlying disorder. A decrease in plasma potassium concentration of 1 mEq/L with normal acid-base balance is roughly equivalent to 300 mEq of total body potassium deficiency.

Except in extreme circumstances, oral rather than parenteral potassium replacement is preferable. When gastrointestinal function is impaired or when neuromuscular manifestations of hypokalemia are present, however, parenteral therapy with potassium may be advisable. Because potassium deficits involve the ICF and the ECF, their correction requires the transfer of administered potassium from the ECF into the ICF. The major problem in parenteral therapy is to avoid intravenous administration of potassium at rates sufficiently great to produce hyperkalemia. A prudent protocol to follow is to add potassium chloride to intravenous solutions at a final concentration of 40 to 60 mEq/L and to administer no more than 10 to 20 mEq of potassium per hour. Except in unusual circumstances, the total amount of potassium administered daily should not exceed 200 mEq. The serum potassium level should be monitored at appropriate intervals; the frequency of monitoring should be determined by the patient's clinical condition, by the initial serum potassium, by the rate at which the serum potassium changes in a given patient, and by the patient's renal function. Because the ECG manifestations of hypokalemia are subtle, the ECG should not be used as a guide to replacement therapy.

Many potassium salts are available for intravenous replacement. The nature of associated anion deficiency can be used as a guide to choose the appropriate salt for potassium repletion. Potassium chloride is appropriate in contraction alkalosis with potassium deficiency (often seen in vomiting); potassium phosphate is indicated in patients with phosphate deficiency (common in alcoholics and patients with diabetic ketoacidosis); potassium bicarbonate may be given in metabolic acidosis with potassium deficiency (as seen in severe diarrhea). If potassium repletion is given by oral routes, potassium may be administered conveniently in the form of organic salts, such as gluconate or citrate. This form of therapy is not effective, however, in hypokalemic metabolic alkalosis with hypochloremia. In this circumstance, chloride supplementation is required with potassium replacement and is achieved most easily by administering sodium chloride supplementation. Enteric-coated potassium chloride tablets should be avoided because they may produce small bowel ulcerations. If the physician has difficulty in correcting potassium deficiency, he or she should evaluate the patient for coexisting magnesium deficiency because this could lead to refractory potassium depletion.

Although potassium depletion is a common electrolyte abnormality, data suggest that approximately 25 to 33% of hospitalized patients receive inadequate treatment. Often repeat serum potassium concentrations are not measured, and frequently potassium-depleting medications are used without regard to potassium supplementation. Failure to treat potassium deficiency leads to increased morbidity and mortality. Strategies to prevent potassium depletion should include potassium-rich diets, decreasing the dose of kaliuretic diuretics, prescription of potassium chloride supplements, and judicial use of potassium-sparing diuretics if the patient is not compliant with oral potassium supplements.

HYPERKALEMIA AND POTASSIUM EXCESS

Definition

Chronic hyperkalemia (>5.5 mEq/L) can occur with little or no increase in total body potassium. Acute increases in serum potassium concentrations, produced by potassium shifts from the ICF to the ECF, can occur, however, even when total body potassium is normal or reduced.

Etiology and Pathogenesis

Hyperkalemia develops whenever the rate of potassium intake or the rate of potassium efflux from ICF to ECF exceeds the sum of renal plus extrarenal potassium losses. The renal mechanisms for potassium excretion adapt efficiently to increase the rate of potassium excretion, particularly from dietary sources. Acute or chronic hyperkalemia secondary to exogenous potassium intake is uncommon, unless renal mechanisms for potassium excretion are compromised, such as in renal failure or when taking medications that decrease renal potassium secretion (Table 112–14).

In the latter setting, injudicious potassium administration may result in hyperkalemia. This occurs most commonly when intravenous potassium chloride is administered too rapidly, when potassium salts of antibiotics such as pencillin are administered, when transfusions

Table 112–14 • MAJOR CAUSES OF HYPERKALEMIA

I. Diminished renal excretion	II. Transcellular shifts
Reduced glomerular filtration rate	Acidosis
	β-Adrenergic blockade
Acute oliguric renal failure	Cell destruction
Chronic renal failure	Trauma, burns
Reduced tubular secretion	Rhabdomyolysis
Addison's disease	Hemolysis
Hyporeninemic hypoaldosteronism	Tumor lysis
	Hyperkalemic periodic paralysis
Potassium-sparing diuretics	Diabetic hyperglycemia
Voltage-dependent renal tubular acidosis	Insulin dependence plus aldosterone lack
Trimethoprim-sulfamethoxazole	Depolarizing muscle paralysis
	Succinylcholine
Angiotensin-converting enzyme inhibitors	

are given with blood that has been stored for long periods, or when salt substitutes containing potassium are used.

Acute or chronic hyperkalemia occurs most commonly either because of diminished *renal excretion* or because there is a sudden *transcellular shift* of potassium from the ICF to the ECF. The major causes for hyperkalemia listed in Table 112–14 follow this format.

DIMINISHED RENAL EXCRETION. Hyperkalemia may occur in *acute oliguric renal failure* of any cause. In *chronic renal failure,* hyperkalemia generally does not occur until the GFR has reached markedly low levels, usually not until the GFR is less than 15 mL/min. Hyperkalemia may be precipitated in chronic renal failure, however, by the development of acidosis or, as indicated earlier, by the injudicious administration of potassium salts. Hyperkalemia also occurs with little or modest reduction in the GFR, if there is impairment of potassium secretion by collecting duct segments. This occurs in *Addison's disease;* in *hyporeninemic hypoaldosteronism;* and with injudiciously administering *potassium-sparing diuretics,* such as triamterene, amiloride, or spironolactone. Hyperkalemia also may be seen with nonsteroidal anti-inflammatory drugs, ACE inhibitors, and ARBs. ACE inhibitors and ARBs decrease aldosterone blood levels and urinary excretion rates to nearly similar degrees, but it is not certain whether the degree of hyperkalemia seen with these two groups of drugs is similar.

Although mild hyperkalemia is relatively common, occurring in approximately 10% of patients taking ACE inhibitors or ARBS, severe hyperkalemia is rare in patients with normal renal function. The physician should be cautious and be aware of potential hyperkalemia in high-risk patients, such as patients with diabetic nephropathy or patients with otherwise elevated serum creatinine levels.

Hyperkalemia also characterizes *voltage-dependent renal tubular acidosis.* This is a specific defect in sodium transport of distal nephron segments. This blockade of distal sodium absorption reduces luminal electronegativity and consequently impairs proton secretion and potassium secretion. Voltage-dependent renal tubular acidosis, similar to hyporeninemic hypoaldosteronism, is characterized by sodium wasting and hyperkalemia. In hyporeninemic hypoaldosteronism, the urine is acidic, and plasma levels of aldosterone are reduced even during volume contraction, whereas in voltage-dependent renal tubular acidosis, there is impaired urinary acidification but a normal plasma aldosterone response to volume contraction.

In each of the disorders characterized by diminished renal potassium excretion, hyperkalemia can be aggravated by ECF volume contraction, which reduces sodium delivery to collecting duct segments, or by acidosis, which promotes cellular potassium efflux.

TRANSCELLULAR SHIFTS. The second class of disorders causing acute hyperkalemia includes situations when there is an abrupt shift of potassium from the ICF to the ECF. This shift occurs in acidosis or in circumstances that result in *cell destruction;* in the former, the serum potassium level increases by 0.6 mEq/L with a metabolic decrease in plasma pH of 0.1, whereas the latter occurs commonly with tissue trauma, burns, rhabdomyolysis, or hemolysis and with lysis of large masses of tumor cells.

Hyperkalemic periodic paralysis is an autosomal dominant disorder in which sudden increases in the serum potassium level result in muscle paralysis. The hyperkalemia often is provoked by excessive dietary potassium intake or by exercise. Myotonia occurs commonly in the disorder and appears either between attacks or immediately preceding attacks. The pathogenesis of the disorder is not understood but may be due in part to abnormalities in sodium channels. The acute paralytic attack can be treated by intravenous administration of calcium gluconate or glucose and insulin. Long-term treatment with diuretics, such as acetazolamide, minimizes the frequency of attacks.

Paradoxical hyperkalemia occurs when *sudden hyperglycemia* develops in insulin-dependent diabetics who also have interstitial renal disease and associated hyporeninemic hypoaldosteronism. The sudden increase in ECF osmolality draws water from cells, raises intracellular potassium concentrations, and promotes passive potassium efflux from cells. The insulin lack minimizes cellular re-entry of potassium, and the aldosterone deficiency blunts renal potassium excretion. Insulin therapy promptly corrects the hyperkalemia. Also, therapy with β-adrenergic blockers can increase plasma concentration. The increase in plasma potassium concentration can be 1 mEq/L in dialysis patients but usually is 0.1 to 0.2 mEq/L in patients with normal renal function. Finally, anesthetic agents or other drugs that cause a *depolarizing muscle paralysis,* such as succinylcholine, promote potassium efflux from muscle cells. The loss of cell

electronegativity in this situation increases passive potassium efflux from muscle cells.

Hyperkalemia also occurs in patients treated with trimethoprim-sulfamethoxazole. Essentially all patients receiving this drug combination increase their plasma potassium concentration within a few days of initiation of the therapy. The hyperkalemia is reversible with cessation of the drug and occurs as a consequence of inhibition of distal tubule potassium secretion.

Pseudohyperkalemia may occur in thrombocytosis or leukocytosis because clotting of blood promotes potassium release from these cells and may be identified by noting that the *serum* potassium level is elevated, while the *plasma* potassium level is normal. This kind of artifact occurs most commonly in patients with myeloproliferative disorders.

Clinical Manifestations

The most important clinical manifestations of hyperkalemia relate to alterations in cardiac excitability. For this reason, the ECG is the most important guide in appraising the threat posed by hyperkalemia and in determining how aggressive a therapeutic approach is necessary.

The ECG manifestations of hyperkalemia (Fig. 112–8) follow directly from the effects of hyperkalemia on cardiac action potentials. The earliest manifestation of hyperkalemia is the development of peaked T waves, which become evident when the serum potassium level exceeds 6.5 mEq/L. This peaking of the T waves is a manifestation of the accelerated repolarization of the cardiac action potential produced by hyperkalemia. When the potassium concentration exceeds 7 to 8 mEq/L, diminished cardiac excitability results in prolongation of the PR interval, followed by a loss of P waves and widening of the QRS complex. These changes indicate progressive inexcitability of cardiac muscle and are referable to hyperkalemia-induced inactivation of sodium permeability during the initial spike of the action potential. When the serum potassium level exceeds 8 to 10 mEq/L, the ECG may develop a sine wave pattern, and cardiac standstill can occur.

The correlation between serum potassium concentrations and ECG abnormalities is approximate at best; in a given patient, progression from peaked T waves to a sine wave pattern may occur rapidly, particularly if the serum potassium concentration increases rapidly. The development of peaked T waves in conjunction with hyperkalemia should be viewed as a serious disorder; more advanced ECG manifestations of hyperkalemia should be treated as life-threatening medical emergencies.

Rx Treatment

Treatment of hyperkalemia can be accomplished rapidly in a hospital setting. It is difficult to formulate specific guidelines, however, as to when to hospitalize a hyperkalemic patient. Part of the problem is that there are no large-scale studies to examine this issue, and part of the difficulty is that hyperkalemia often is discovered incidentally. Patients who have life-threatening hyperkalemia generally have no distinguishing symptoms from patients that have hyperkalemia that can be treated on an outpatient basis. In each of these groups of patients, the drugs that promote hyperkalemia often have not been discontinued (see Table 112–14). Hospitalizations for hyperkalemia generally are not necessary if the ECG is normal; renal function has not deteriorated recently; there are no other metabolic abnormalities such as hypocalcemia, hyponatremia, or acidosis; and serum potassium is less than 6.5 mmol/L. It is safest to admit all patients with serum potassium greater than 8 mmol/L. Three kinds of maneuvers are used to treat hyperkalemia: (1) agents such as glucose plus insulin, sodium bicarbonate, or β-agonists, which promote the transfer of potassium from the ECF to the ICF; (2) maneuvers that enhance potassium elimination from the body, such as diuretics, exchange resins, or dialysis; and (3) the use of calcium, which does not alter serum potassium concentrations but counteracts the effects of hyperkalemia on cardiac excitability.

Insulin and sodium bicarbonate promote potassium entry into cells. Administering 25 g of glucose, together with 10 U of regular insulin, is an effective way of reducing the serum potassium level rapidly. The glucose should be administered over 30 minutes

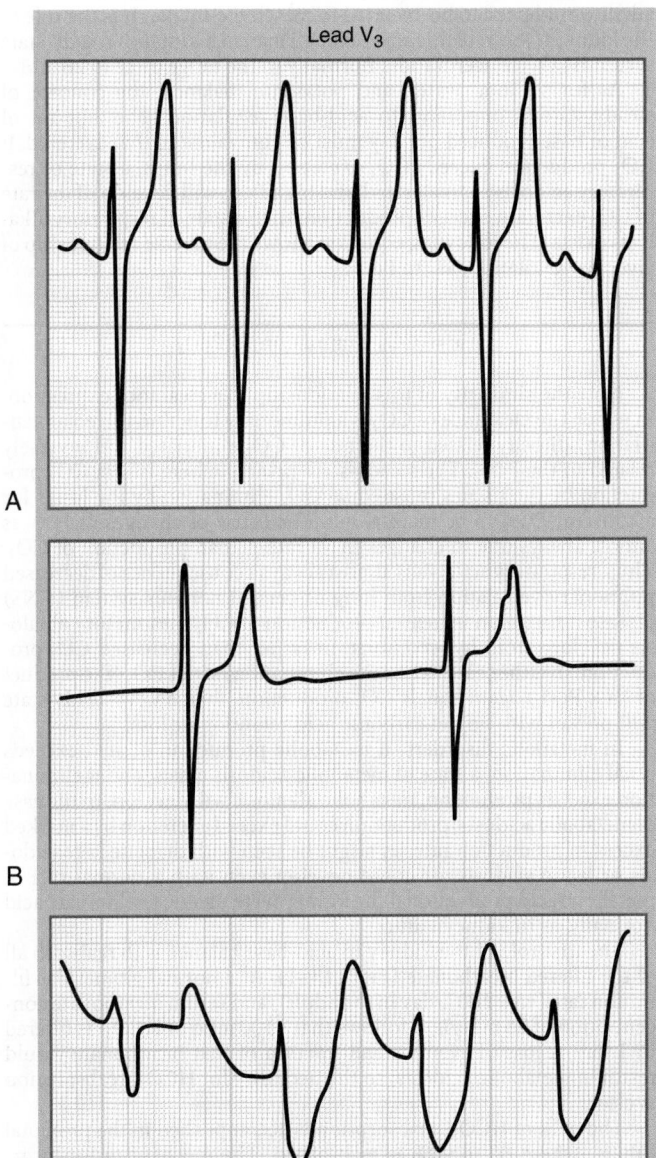

Lead V₃

A

B

C

FIGURE 112–8 • The effects of progressive hyperkalemia on the electrocardiogram. All of the illustrations are from lead V₃. A, Serum K⁺ = 6.8 mEq/L; note the peaked T waves together with normal sinus rhythm. B, Serum K⁺ = 8.9 mEq/L; note the peaked T waves and absent P waves. C, Serum K⁺ > 8.9 mEq/L; note the classic sine wave with absent P waves, marked prolongation of the QRS complex, and peaked T waves.

as a 10% solution. Using a 50% glucose solution may worsen the hyperkalemia transiently if given rapidly. Insulin promotes potassium entry into cells, and glucose is administered to prevent hypoglycemia. In insulin-dependent diabetic patients in whom sudden hyperglycemia has precipitated the hyperkalemia, insulin administration alone suffices to reduce the serum potassium concentration.

Administering 40 to 150 mEq of sodium bicarbonate intravenously over 30 to 60 minutes also promotes potassium entry into cells, particularly if acidosis is present. This maneuver should be used with caution in patients with compromised renal function because of the risks of hypernatremia and of ECF volume overload.

Potassium shifts from ECF to ICF may be enhanced by using aerosolized specific β_2-agonists; albuterol is a commonly used agent of this kind. Agents such as albuterol are most helpful in managing mild hyperkalemia in chronic disorders, such as chronic renal failure and hyperkalemic periodic paralysis.

In settings of extreme hyperkalemic cardiotoxicity, when P waves are absent and the QRS complexes are widened, calcium gluconate, 10 to 30 mL of a 10% solution given over 10 to 20 minutes, may be life-saving. This approach should be undertaken with constant ECG monitoring and should be used with extreme caution in patients who have received digitalis. In the latter circumstance, calcium administration may unmask digitalis intoxication, especially if other agents are used simultaneously to reduce the serum potassium level. Calcium salts should not be added to bottles of intravenous fluids containing bicarbonate because water-insoluble calcium salts form.

The influence of calcium salts in minimizing the cardiotoxic effects of hyperkalemia may be understood by noting that depolarization of excitable tissues by elevating serum K⁺ concentrations inactivates sodium channels and that the ECF sides of these sodium channels are electronegative. Divalent cations such as calcium provide a remarkably effective way of screening these electronegative sites. Calcium salts increase the voltage gradient across sodium channels by screening electronegative surface charges of these channels on their ECF sides and consequently restoring the voltage-dependent excitability of these channels.

None of the maneuvers described removes potassium from the body. Gastrointestinal potassium losses may be produced by the use of cation exchange resins in the sodium cycle, such as sodium polystyrene sulfonate (Kayexalate), or by agents that induce secretory diarrhea. Each 1 g of the resin contains approximately 1 mEq of sodium and exchanges for about 1 mEq of potassium. This stoichiometry is not precise because the sodium form of the resin also exchanges for other cations in gastrointestinal secretions, including calcium. In chronic hyperkalemia, 20 g of Kayexalate may be given three or four times a day in a 70% solution of sorbitol. The sorbitol creates an osmotic diarrhea and enhances resin passage through the gastrointestinal tract. Use of resin-cathartic therapy is unpleasant for the patient. Kayexalate also may be administered by enema, generally as 100 g of resin suspended in 200 g/mL of 20% sorbitol. The effect of single-dose Kayexalate on fecal potassium output is minimal compared with noncation exchange agents that induce secretory diarrhea; however, Kayexalate may be of benefit in management of hyperkalemia when given over the long-term. The use of long-term Kayexalate therapy in patients with chronic renal failure carries the risk of sodium overload.

Acute hemodialysis or peritoneal dialysis provides another mechanism for potassium removal from the body. This approach is particularly advantageous in acute renal failure, when patients are volume expanded, and sodium administration may produce congestive heart failure, or when there is a continued efflux of large amounts of potassium from the ICF to the ECF, as in burns or rhabdomyolysis.

SUGGESTED READINGS

Charytan D, Goldfarb DS: Indications for hospitalization of patients with hyperkalemia. Arch Intern Med 2000;160:1605–1611. *This thoughtful article discusses the indications for hospitalization of hyperkalemic patients.*

Choate KA, Kahle KT, Wilson FH, et al: WNK1, a kinase mutated in inherited hypertension with hyperkalemia, localizes to diverse Cl⁻-transporting epithelia. Proc Natl Acad Sci USA 2003;100:663–668. *This gene may be a potential target of new approaches to regulating potassium balance.*

Cohn JN, Kowey PR, Whelton PK, Prisant LM: New guidelines for potassium replacement in clinical practice: A contemporary review by the national council on potassium in clinical practice. Arch Intern Med 2000;160:2429–2436. *Summary and guidelines that have been developed for replacement of potassium deficiency by an expert multidisciplinary group who composed the National Council on Potassium in Clinical Practice.*

Gheno G, Cinetto L, Savarino C, et al: Variations of serum potassium level and risk of hyperkalemia in inpatients receiving low-molecular-weight heparin. Eur J Clin Pharmacol 2003;[Epub ahead of print]. *Short-term treatment with low-molecular-weight heparin induces a significant increase in serum potassium level. Although the risk of clinical events is low, routine monitoring of serum potassium levels should be considered.*

Paltiel O, Gordon L, Berg D, et al: Effect of a computerized alert on the management of hypokalemia in hospitalized patients. Arch Intern Med 2003;163:200–204. *A computerized alert system improved the management of hypokalemia in a tertiary care hospital.*

Perazella MA: Drug-induced hyperkalemia: Old culprits and new offenders. Am J Med 2000;109:307–314. *Review of drugs that decrease renal excretion of potassium.*

Reardon LC, Macpherson DS: Hyperkalemia in outpatients using angiotensin-converting enzyme inhibitors. Arch Intern Med 1998;158:26–32. *Reviews 1818 patients using ACE inhibitors and shows mild hyperkalemia is common; however, severe hyperkalemia is uncommon, unless patients are elderly and/or have significant decrease in renal function.*

113 ACID-BASE DISORDERS

Julian L. Seifter

Normal Acid-Base Physiology

Many of the body's metabolic and physiologic functions are pH-dependent or -sensitive. The range of normal arterial pH is 7.38 to 7.42. Venous pH is approximately 0.05 units more acid because of the appearance of carbonic acid and thus CO_2 entering from the cells for transport to the lungs. Intracellular pH is lower than extracellular pH because cells are electronegative to the extracellular fluid, and metabolically produced acids are constantly transported to the extracellular fluid for eventual elimination from the body. In severe disease states, the arterial pH may fall as low as 6.8 and rise as high as 7.8. However, even in normal healthy individuals, strenuous exercise with the metabolic production of lactate may transiently lower pH severely.

The pH is equal to minus the log of the hydrogen ion concentration. At a pH of 7.40, the hydrogen ion concentration is 40 nanoequivalents (nEq) per liter, a very small concentration compared to that for serum sodium, at 140 milliequivalents (mEq) per liter. The hydrogen ion concentration of body fluids is in equilibrium with each of multiple buffers, such as proteins, phosphate, and hemoglobin, but acid-base equilibria in the body are often analyzed using the CO_2/bicarbonate system and the relationship of the proton concentration (thus pH) to the ratio of bicarbonate to CO_2. The Henderson-Hasselbalch equation is a logarithmic expression of the relationship.

$$CO_2 + H_2O \leftrightarrow H_2CO_3 \leftrightarrow H^+ + HCO_3^-$$

$$pH = pK + \log [HCO_3]/0.03(P_{CO_2})$$

In this equation, the pK, or dissociation constant, is 6.1, and 0.03 (mM/mm Hg) is the solubility factor for CO_2 in solution. The product of $(0.03) \times P_{CO_2}$ represents the carbonic acid concentration, and the total CO_2 in plasma is the sum of HCO_3^-, normally about 25 mM, and $(0.03) \times P_{CO_2}$, normally about 1.2 mM. It is important to see that the pH is a function of the *ratio* of bicarbonate to P_{CO_2}. The bicarbonate concentration in the numerator is regulated by the kidney, and P_{CO_2} is regulated by the lung.

An increased bicarbonate concentration does not necessarily imply a more alkaline pH, since pH is related to the ratio of HCO_3^- over P_{CO_2}. A common confusion is to interpret an elevated bicarbonate concentration in the blood as being indicative of an alkaline pH, or a decreased HCO_3^- concentration as evidence for an acid pH. An example in which this is not true is the normal finding that venous blood has a higher bicarbonate concentration than arterial blood but a lower pH because the P_{CO_2} is proportionally higher.

The major organ systems involved in acid-base balance are the lungs and the kidneys. *Volatile acid* is the term used for carbon dioxide produced by metabolic processes in all tissues, an amount that approximates 20,000 mmol/day, and this CO_2 is carried to the lung, where it is eliminated by alveolar ventilation. The steady-state P_{CO_2} is normally 38 to 42 mm Hg.

Nonvolatile acid is a term used to describe acids other than carbonic acid that are formed primarily from protein metabolism. The usual amount of formation is approximately 1 to 2 mEq of H^+ per kilogram of body weight per day. Most diets that contain animal protein have a net positive quantity of nonvolatile acids, primarily due to sulfur-containing amino acids cysteine and methionine; phosphate from phosphoproteins, phospholipids, phosphonucleotides, and inorganic sources; and chloride salts of lysine, arginine, and histidine. The addition of protons to the body fluids by these acid end-products can be seen as consuming bicarbonate, which then needs to be replenished by the kidney as it eliminates the proton. The oxidation of carbohydrates and fats results in the production of water and CO_2 and not nonvolatile acids. High-protein diets increase the metabolic acid load. Under pathologic conditions, other acids are produced in the body such as ketoacids in diabetes and lactic acid in states of increased anaerobic metabolism.

In most humans, particularly those who eat animal protein, or an acid-ash diet, the requirement for net acid excretion dominates. However, vegetarians could have an overall alkaline-ash diet, meaning that to maintain a steady-state normal serum HCO_3^- concentration, net

alkali would need to be excreted to match the intake. It is the role of the kidney to excrete this acid or alkali load to maintain a steady-state serum HCO_3^- concentration, normally in the range of 22 to 28 mM.

As for sodium, water, and potassium balance, the concept of steady-state is important to acid-base regulation. The amount of acid or base produced per day must be equivalent to that excreted. If CO_2 production exceeds CO_2 excretion by the lungs, a state of respiratory acidosis characterized by a high P_{CO_2} will develop. If the rate of CO_2 excretion exceeds production, then a state of respiratory alkalosis exists. The following equation shows the inverse relationship of alveolar ventilation, $\dot{V}a$, to P_{CO_2}:

$$\dot{V}a = CO_2 \text{ elimination} \div P_{CO_2}$$

Note the similarity of this relationship to a clearance expression, in which the clearance of CO_2 is a pulmonary function (alveolar ventilation) directly related to the rate of CO_2 eliminated and inversely related to the P_{CO_2}. The steady-state principle here is that CO_2 production by the tissues must equal CO_2 elimination by the lungs for a constant P_{CO_2} to be maintained. The cause of changes in P_{CO_2} is almost always due to changes in $\dot{V}a$ rather than production of CO_2. Thus, respiratory acidosis is almost always a consequence of decreased pulmonary ventilation from lung or central nervous system (CNS) disease rather than increased production of CO_2. Respiratory alkalosis develops from hyperventilation rather than decreased CO_2 production. In either case, when the elimination rate of CO_2 (the product of $\dot{V}a \times P_{CO_2}$) again equals CO_2 production, then a new steady state will prevail with no net carbonic acid retention or loss.

In metabolic disorders, if metabolic production of acid exceeds renal elimination, a state of metabolic acidosis exists; and if elimination exceeds production, metabolic alkalosis will develop. In the case of metabolic acidosis, production could exceed excretion by a marked excess in production rate, as might be seen with diabetic ketoacidosis or lactic acidosis, or could develop even with a normal rate of metabolic acid production if the kidney were unable to eliminate acid normally, as in kidney failure.

The first role of the kidney in acid-base balance is to reabsorb all of the filtered bicarbonate (Fig. 113–1). At a normal glomerular filtration rate (e.g., 180 L/day in the adult), and serum bicarbonate concentration of 25 mEq/L, it follows that 4500 mEq of HCO_3^- is filtered in 1 day. A loss of even a small fraction of that bicarbonate would result in metabolic acidosis, so the necessity for HCO_3^- reabsorption is clear.

The bulk of HCO_3^- reabsorption is accomplished in the proximal tubule, where 80 to 90% is reabsorbed. The mechanism for bicarbonate reabsorption is a proton secretory process that works as follows. The brush border membranes of the proximal tubule cell contain transporters known as Na/H exchangers (NHE3 is the abundant isoform). Through the normal function of basolateral membrane Na/K ATPases, cell Na^+ is kept at low concentration so that filtered Na^+ in the lumen will be favored to enter the cell in exchange for H^+ secreted into the lumen. This H^+ will combine with a filtered HCO_3^- to rapidly form HCO_3^-, which then will dehydrate in the lumen to form CO_2 and H_2O. This process is greatly facilitated by luminal carbonic anhydrase. The CO_2 then enters the proximal cell, where it reforms HCO_3^-, also helped by intracellular carbonic anhydrase. The HCO_3^- then is transported back to the blood by a cotransporter coupling Na and $3HCO_3^-$ (NBC), accomplishing net HCO_3^- reabsorption. Note that the entire process requires a source of adenosine triphosphate (ATP) (mitochondrial) for the Na/K pump, intact NHE3 and NBC, and carbonic anhydrase. A disturbance at any of these sites may disrupt proximal HCO_3^- reabsorption enough to cause loss of the HCO_3^- in urine. There is continued bicarbonate reabsorption in the thick limb of Henle via a similar mechanism of Na/H exchange on the luminal membrane.

The cortical collecting duct continues to reabsorb bicarbonate, about 5 to 10% of the filtered load, by the following mechanism. In principal cells, Na^+ is reabsorbed by the epithelial Na^+ channel driven by secondary active transport (due to lowering of cell Na^+ level by the ATP-dependent active transport of Na^+ by the Na/K ATPases at the blood side). The lumen becomes electronegative, favoring the secretion of both K^+, through K^+ channels, and H^+, through H^+ ATPases on the luminal surface of the intercalated cells, which are the acid-secreting cells (Type A intercalated cells). The secreted H^+ will combine with the remaining HCO_3^- in the lumen, generating CO_2 and leading

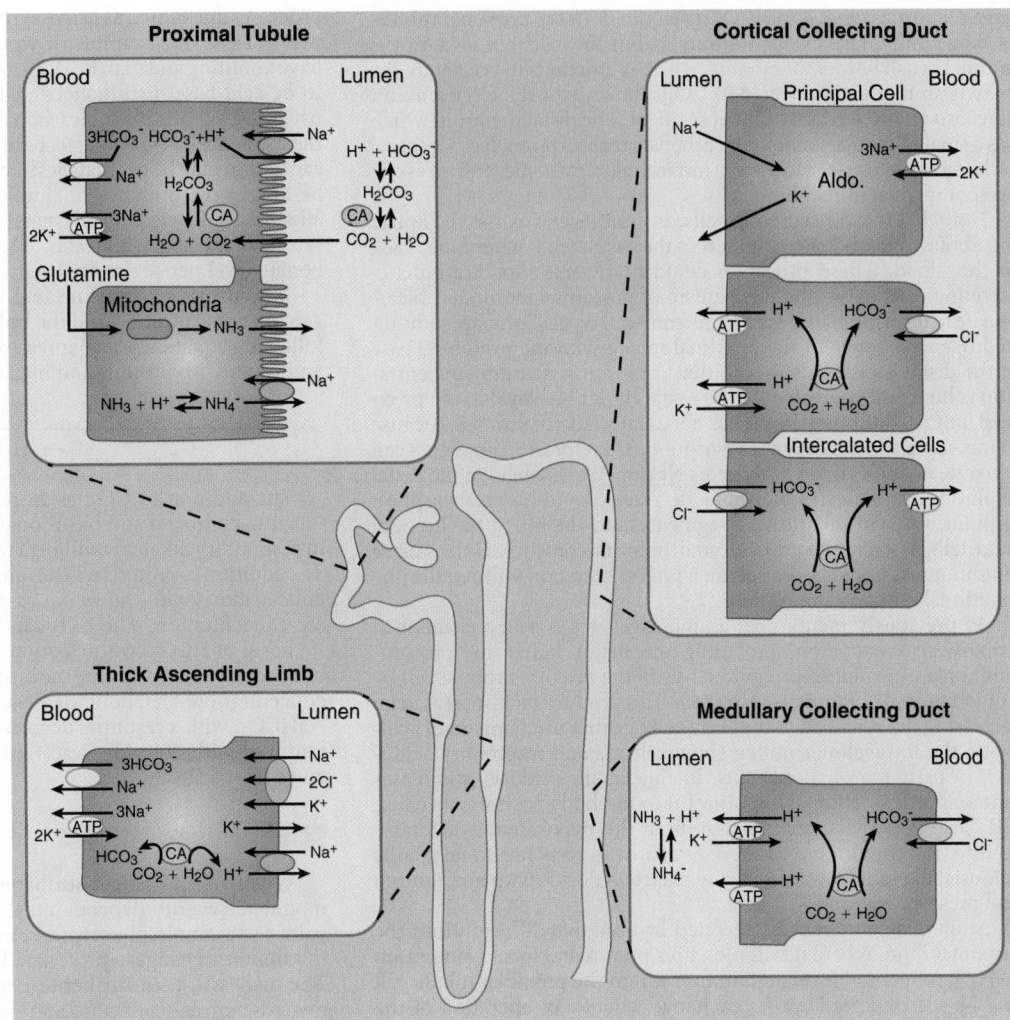

FIGURE 113–1 • Renal acidification mechanisms. See text for details.

to CO_2 reabsorption, reformation of cellular HCO_3^- with the help of cellular carbonic anhydrase, and then exchange of the HCO_3^- from cell to blood and entry of Cl^-, via Cl/HCO_3 exchangers. These exchangers belong to the family of proteins that includes the red blood cell, band 3, Cl/HCO_3 exchanger. It is at this distal site that the tubular fluid pH starts to fall to levels below pH 6.0.

There are some collecting duct cells that have reverse polarity such that they secrete HCO_3^- into the lumen in exchange for Cl^- entry into the cell, and the H^+ ATPase faces the blood side of the cell (Type B intercalated cells). These cells may be important when a net amount of HCO_3^- needs to be excreted, as with an alkaline-ash diet. An elevated extracellular HCO_3^- concentration will increase HCO_3^- secretion by these cells, in contrast to an inhibitory effect on HCO_3^- reabsorption in both proximal and type A cortical collecting duct cells.

The medullary collecting duct continues to secrete protons into the luminal fluid, where the pH reaches its lowest values of close to 5.0. The mechanism is due to continued function of H^+ ATPases with an additional role of an ATP-dependent K/H exchanger, a member of the family of K/H ATPases found in stomach and colon.

Once the filtered HCO_3^- is fully reabsorbed, the kidney is still required to eliminate an additional net amount of acid equivalent to that produced in metabolism. The majority of this net acid excretion is in the form of ammonium, NH_4^+, derived from the renal synthesis of ammonia from glutamine in the proximal tubule, and the titration of filtered phosphate to acid phosphate (titratable acidity).

$$NH_3 + H^+ \leftrightarrow NH_4^+ \text{ pK } 9.1, \text{ and}$$
$$HPO_4^{2-} + H^+ \leftrightarrow H_2PO_4^- \text{ pK } 6.8$$

As the collecting duct cells continue to secrete H^+ with diminishing luminal HCO_3^- concentration and a lowering of pH, the H^+ is captured by the urinary buffers. The resulting alkalinization of the cells after H^+ leaves results in HCO_3^- formation ready for transport into the blood. This is considered "new" HCO_3^- generation because it is not a result of filtered HCO_3^- reabsorption. The amount of new HCO_3^- matches the amount of net acid eliminated and results in a return to normal acid-base equilibrium.

The ability of the kidney to lower urinary pH to values as low as 5.0 enables the buffers to capture a proton. Net acid excretion in the urine is accomplished not simply by a decrease in urine pH, but also by the titration of these important urinary buffers. For example, a liter of urine at pH 5.0 contains only 10^{-5} molar hydrogen ion or 0.01 mmol/L. Note how this compares to the need to excrete 70 mmol of hydrogen ion daily in an average person. In fact, it is the failure to produce enough ammonium in chronic renal failure that leads to a poorly buffered, though acid, urine and an inability to excrete enough net acid to stay in normal balance.

Renal mechanisms of urinary acidification are adaptable. The transport processes such as H^+ ATPases, Na/H exchange, and Cl/HCO_3 exchange can increase or decrease their capacity to handle acid-base equivalents, depending on the challenge presented, and the renal ammoniagenic mechanisms are also critically regulated to serve the acid-base needs of the individual. Metabolic acidosis and respiratory acidosis increase the capacity to reabsorb HCO_3^- including increased expression of the transporters involved in acidifying the urine. At the same time, increased ammonia production enables increased acid excretion and new HCO_3^- generation. Metabolic and respiratory alkalosis have the opposite effects.

In the end, net acid production must equal net acid excretion. When the diet calls for excretion of acids, the urine pH will fall and become nominally free of bicarbonate. When there is an alkaline load, the kidney will reject the excess filtered HCO_3^- and the urine pH may approach a maximum value of 8.0 to 8.5.

Carbonic anhydrase is important in acid-secreting epithelia, as well as other cells such as red blood cells, in which conversion of large quantities of CO_2 to HCO_3^- is required. In the proximal tubule, carbonic anhydrase exists not only within the cells but also on the luminal brush border membrane, where it functions to accelerate the dehydration of carbonic acid to CO_2, allowing for the large amount of reabsorption necessary in that segment. The distal nephron, which has a smaller requirement for bicarbonate reabsorption, lacks luminal carbonic anhydrase. However, intracellular carbonic anhydrase is present in all acid-handling cells.

Note that in acid-secreting cells, as protons exit across the apical membrane, bicarbonate exits across the basolateral membrane, back to the blood. These processes could be reversed in bicarbonate-secreting cells. Also, the mechanism of proton secretion and bicarbonate reabsorption may vary in different cell types. Compare sodium-hydrogen exchange in the proximal tubule with the proton ATPase of the distal tubule. Also recall that the luminal sodium concentration is high and equivalent to the extracellular Na^+ level in the proximal luminal fluid, and the pH has not usually fallen below 6.8, because of incomplete bicarbonate reabsorption. Therefore, the gradients can generate enough energy to support Na^+ for H^+ exchange. In the distal nephron, Na^+ concentration may decrease due to Na^+ reabsorption without water in the diluting segments, and the pH of the luminal fluid falls as bicarbonate is cleared from its contents. Under these conditions, it is likely that further proton secretion will require the additional energy of an ATPase.

As previously mentioned, ammoniagenesis is a key element of urinary acid excretion, providing the major buffer for protons. Ammonia is produced predominantly in the proximal tubule cell by mitochondrial glutaminase enzymes. This production is increased by increasing the acid load to the body and by other mechanisms of acidifying the intracellular milieu (hypokalemia and respiratory acidosis). In particular, hypokalemia, like metabolic acidosis, stimulates ammonium excretion. This is useful to the body economy because NH_4^+ can preserve scarce potassium in the hypokalemic state as a counter-ion for anion excretion. Similarly, in response to metabolic acidosis, the kidney would ideally excrete chloride with ammonium and preserve Na^+ and K^+.

Ammonia can either be secreted by nonionic diffusion into the proximal fluid, where it will pick up a proton and form ammonium (NH_4^+), or it could form ammonium within the proximal tubule cell and be secreted via Na/NH_4 exchange, a mode of operation of the Na/H exchanger. Ammonium may be reabsorbed by the thick ascending limb of Henle on the $Na/K/2Cl$ transporter, where it can substitute for K^+. By countercurrent multiplication, the medullary interstitial fluid will contain large concentrations of NH_4^+. Less ammonium will therefore reach the highly perfused renal cortex, where it could otherwise dissipate into the renal venous blood; the countercurrent mechanism also allows for ammonia to diffuse into the lumen of the collecting duct, where it will be trapped as ammonium in the acid tubular fluid.

Regulation is accomplished at a number of levels. Hormones such as angiotensin II and catecholamines stimulate Na^+ reabsorption in the proximal tubule by increasing Na/H exchange. Aldosterone increases the proton ATPase in the distal collecting duct cell and stimulates Na^+ reabsorption, with the result of increasing proton secretion. A low extracellular fluid volume increases proximal HCO_3^- reabsorption, as does hypokalemia and high P_{CO_2}. These factors also stimulate distal proton secretion.

Hyperkalemia may limit urinary acidification by several mechanisms, including decreased ammonia synthesis, decreased NH_3 entering the countercurrent multiplier in the loop of Henle, and decreased H^+ secretion by ATPases in the collecting duct as the need to secrete K^+ predominates.

Definitions of Acid-Base Disorders

Assessment of clinical acid-base disturbances usually begins with the measurement of arterial blood gases. In some situations, venous blood can be used as an alternative to the more invasive arterial puncture, recalling that normal venous pH is approximately 0.05 pH units more acid than arterial, and the P_{CO_2} is 5 to 6 mm Hg higher than that of arterial blood. Except in conditions of low cardiac output, these assumptions are reasonable.

If the arterial pH is below normal, acidemia is said to exist. If the pH is greater than normal, an alkalemia exists. This does not exclude the possibility of many processes simultaneously present that would drive the pH in an upward or downward direction. The individual

processes are known as *acidoses* or *alkaloses*. Since multiple processes may coexist (for example, it would not be unusual for a patient to have vomiting and diarrhea), an abnormal pH is not required for there to be acid-base disturbances. A common mistake is that the more usual testing of serum bicarbonate leads one to a conclusion about the existence or type of acid-base disturbance. The bicarbonate concentration may be normal, despite an acidemia or alkalemia; or it may be low, in the presence of simple metabolic acidosis or respiratory alkalosis. Likewise, bicarbonate concentration may be high, in the setting of metabolic alkalosis or respiratory acidosis. Thus, the bicarbonate level per se does not indicate the nature of the disturbance.

It is customary to define acid-base balance in terms of the hydrogen ion concentration and the buffer pair bicarbonate and P_{CO_2}. The following equation is an expression of the overall equilibrium of CO_2 and water with protons and bicarbonate.

$$CO_2 + H_2O \leftrightarrow H_2CO_3 \leftrightarrow H + HCO_3^-$$

The addition of CO_2, as in respiratory acidosis, can be seen to increase hydrogen and bicarbonate concentrations. Removal of CO_2 in respiratory alkalosis will decrease CO_2, protons, and bicarbonate. The addition of protons with an anion other than bicarbonate in metabolic acidosis will lead to increased proton and decreased bicarbonate concentration. The CO_2 can be rapidly removed by the lungs. Removal of HCO_3^- with a cation such as Na^+, also a cause of metabolic acidosis, will increase the proton concentration and lower HCO_3^- concentration. Metabolic alkalosis might be caused by an addition of $NaHCO_3^-$ with a resulting decrease in proton concentration or by H^+ removed with chloride, leading to decreased proton concentration and a raised HCO_3^-.

Compensatory Changes

When an acid-base disturbance develops, the initial response to modulate severity depends on the titration of various body buffer pairs. For example, phosphate, hemoglobin, and other proteins, including albumin, change in protonated and unprotonated concentrations. The body will then further attempt to correct the extracellular pH towards normal (but not too normal). For metabolic disturbances due to increased or decreased nonvolatile acid, the response is respiratory, and for primary respiratory acidosis and alkalosis, the compensation is renal. The degree of this compensation cannot be calculated without the input of empirically obtained data indicating normal human responses (Table 113–1). Note that the direction of change of HCO_3^- and P_{CO_2} is the same when the primary disturbance is compensated; the ratio of HCO_3^- to P_{CO_2} and thus pH becomes more normal. In Table 113–1, also note that these compensations tend to take time to develop to their fullest, and therefore acid-base disturbances, particularly the respiratory conditions, are classified as acute or chronic (lasting longer than 24 to 48 hours).

In cases of metabolic acidosis resulting in acidemia, the CNS, through chemoreceptors, will stimulate ventilation with a subsequent

Table 113–1 • EXPECTED DEGREES OF COMPENSATION IN ACID-BASE DISORDERS

DISORDER	EXPECTED COMPENSATION
Metabolic acidosis	Steady state in 12–36 hours
	Expected P_{CO_2} = 1.5 (measured HCO_3) + 8 ± 2
Metabolic alkalosis	Less predictable
	Expected P_{CO_2} increases 0.5 mg Hg per 1 mEq/L increase in HCO_3
Respiratory acidosis	
Acute	Expected 1 mEq/L increase in HCO_3 per 10 mm Hg rise in P_{CO_2}
Chronic, 24–36 hours	Expected 3–5 mEq/L increase in HCO_3 per 10 mm Hg rise in P_{CO_2}
Respiratory alkalosis	
Acute	Expected 1–2 mEq/L fall in HCO_3 per 10 mm Hg fall in P_{CO_2}
Chronic, after 24–36 hours	Expected 5 mEq/L fall in HCO_3 per 10 mm Hg fall in P_{CO_2}

fall in P_{CO_2}. When the bicarbonate concentration increases as a result of metabolic alkalosis, there will be a hypoventilatory response, raising P_{CO_2}. Clinically, one should not equate respiratory rate with ventilation rate, as the typical Kussmaul respirations in metabolic acidosis, a sign of the respiratory compensation, are due to an increased minute ventilation rather than increased respiration frequency. Rapid breathing may not be associated with an increased minute ventilation or decreased P_{CO_2}.

The acute stimulus of hypercapnia to increase renal acid excretion disappears in chronic respiratory acidosis when, at the elevated P_{CO_2}, carbonic acid production and elimination are again equal. However, the hypochloremia and elevated serum HCO_3^- maintained by the high P_{CO_2} remains. In respiratory alkalosis, the primary event is a fall in P_{CO_2} due to increased $\dot{V}a$. In the transition from an acute to chronic respiratory alkalosis, the compensatory mechanisms that initially helped maintain a more normal systemic pH are no longer required when CO_2 production and elimination become equal. Thus, initial decreased renal acid excretion in compensation for respiratory alkalosis ceases, but the maintenance of low serum HCO_3^- and high serum Cl^- concentrations remain.

In identifying whether an acid-base disturbance is simple, that is, a single disturbance with its compensation, or complex, it is useful to compare the expected compensation to the observed parameters of the blood gases (Table 113–2). For example, if in a metabolic acidosis the P_{CO_2} is lower than would be predicted for the simple disorder, an additional process must be present, which, since it drives the P_{CO_2} down, must be a respiratory alkalosis. If the P_{CO_2} were higher than what would be predicted for a low bicarbonate level in a case of metabolic acidosis, then there would be coexistence of a respiratory acidosis.

Since there is no reason that multiple acid-base disturbances should not coexist, one should be able to expect a specific process by eliciting a proper history. For example, hypochloremic alkalosis would be suggested by a history of vomiting or the use of thiazide or loop diuretics. The process of metabolic acidosis might be anticipated in hypotensive shock, sepsis, diarrhea, and renal failure. A history of chronic lung disease could be associated with respiratory acidosis, whereas fever, infection, stroke, or acute pulmonary disease may be a cause of acute respiratory alkalosis. It is important to follow up on the history and physical examination with laboratory clues to detect the presence of these independent disturbances. Also, abnormal acid-base balance should always alert the clinician to the possible presence of an underlying condition rather than be considered an isolated problem.

Adaptations

In addition to the above-mentioned compensations, which usually involve the lung for metabolic disturbances and renal excretion for respiratory disturbances, it should be pointed out that the kidney will also compensate for metabolic disturbances, that is, help modify the pH toward normal. Furthermore, structural and functional changes in the kidney may occur over time, altered in an adaptive way to the disturbed environment. In cases of metabolic acidosis of extrarenal origin, the renal response will be to increase net acid excretion by increasing ammoniagenesis. Bicarbonate reabsorptive processes under the influence of hormones such as glucocorticoids, angiotensin II, and aldosterone will increase, thereby maximizing net acid excretion. In fact, at the membrane transport level, metabolic acidosis itself may result in an increased number of transporters, such as sodium-hydrogen exchange or proton ATPases, to maximize bicarbonate reabsorption. Limitation of the effectiveness of bicarbonate reabsorption is due to already low serum levels and therefore filtered bicarbonate and the near-complete clearance of bicarbonate from the urine. In metabolic alkalosis, the kidney may modulate the degree of alkalemia by enhancing urinary bicarbonate loss. As will be discussed, these responses may be limited by mitigating factors such as extracellular volume depletion and hypokalemia.

METABOLIC ACIDOSIS

In metabolic acidosis, the primary change is a fall in serum bicarbonate. The compensatory response is increased ventilation with fall in P_{CO_2}. Worsening acidosis elicits increasing alveolar ventilation.

Primary metabolic acidosis results from the imbalance between net acid production (NAP) and net acid excretion (NAE) in the form of urinary ammonium and acid phosphate. Consider the following relationship, where U_x represents urinary concentration and $\dot{V}$ urinary flow rate:

$$NAE = (U_{NH_4^+}\dot{V}) + (U_{phos}\dot{V}) - (U_{bicarb}\dot{V})$$

In a normal steady-state condition, the rate of excretion of net acid must be equal to the production rate. The normal production rate depends on diet. Metabolic acidosis can develop if there is an inequality in the relationship between NAP and NAE. Thus, if NAP were normal, metabolic acidosis could occur with either a failure of bicarbonate reabsorption leading to high bicarbonate excretion rates or a failure to elaborate enough urinary buffers, as in the case in renal failure and renal tubular acidosis. In contrast, an inequality could develop if NAP were excessive or if large extrarenal bicarbonate losses were unable to be matched by maximal adaptive increases in NAE. Endogenous sources of acid include ketoacidosis and lactic acidosis, whereas some exogenous sources are metabolic products of ingested ethylene glycol or methanol. On occasion, strong inorganic acids may be ingested. When net acid is retained in the body fluids, the serum bicarbonate concentration falls. However, the maintenance of a constant serum HCO_3^- concentration does not guarantee that there is a new steady state in which NAP is equal to NAE, since body buffers such as carbonate salts of bone may become depleted by relentless acid retention. Such is the case in renal failure and distal renal tubular acidosis.

Clinical Manifestations

The effects of metabolic acidosis depend on the rapidity of onset and severity. Patients are often tired and develop dyspnea, particularly on exertion. Nausea and vomiting are common. On examination, deep respirations, often labored with use of accessory muscles, may be detected in acute states, but patients with long-standing metabolic acidemia may be noted to have the signs of hyperventilation only with careful inspection of the respiratory pattern. Altered hemodynamics may accompany metabolic acidemia with vasodilation associated with tachycardia and hypotension. Acidemia may exert a negative inotropic effect on the heart. The stress of either an underlying illness or an increase in adrenergic and corticosteroid activity associated with acidemia may elevate the peripheral white blood cell count and may cause hyperglycemia. Other laboratory findings include variable degrees of hyperkalemia, hyperphosphatemia, and hyperuricemia (in lactic acidosis), as well as hypocalcemia due to decreased renal 1,25OH vitamin D synthesis.

Table 113–2 • LABORATORY STEPS IN IDENTIFYING ACID-BASE DISORDERS

EVALUATE PH:	Acidemic	Alkalemic
Elevated P_{CO_2}	Respiratory acidosis	Metabolic alkalosis
Elevated HCO_3	Respiratory acidosis	Metabolic alkalosis
Decreased P_{CO_2}	Metabolic acidosis	Respiratory alkalosis
Decreased HCO_3	Metabolic acidosis	Respiratory alkalosis

EVALUATE FOR EXPECTED COMPENSATION

Meets expectation: Simple disorder with compensation or could be offsetting metabolic alkalosis and acidosis.

Does not meet expectation: Complex disorder but pH indicates whether acidosis or alkalosis is dominant.

If a metabolic disorder is dominant, then a P_{CO_2} greater than predicted indicates additional respiratory acidosis. A P_{CO_2} less than predicted indicates an additional respiratory alkalosis.

If a respiratory disorder is dominant, then a HCO_3 greater than predicted indicates additional metabolic alkalosis. A HCO_3 less than predicted indicates an additional metabolic acidosis.

ASSESS ANION GAP

Elevated: Metabolic acidosis is present whether acidemic or alkalemic. If alkalemic, an additional metabolic or respiratory alkalosis is present.

If gap is greater than fall in HCO_3, then consider additional metabolic alkalosis or respiratory acidosis.

If gap is less than fall in HCO_3, then consider additional non-gap acidosis or respiratory alkalosis.

Causes

The causes of metabolic acidosis are usually categorized according to the presence of either a normal or an elevated serum anion gap. The serum anion gap is the net charge difference when the sum of chloride and bicarbonate is subtracted from the serum sodium concentration.

$$Anion\ Gap\ =\ Na^+ - (Cl^- + HCO_3^-)$$

The normal anion gap is due to the unmeasured anionic charge associated predominantly with albumin. When acidemia is present, the albumin is in a more protonated form, lowering the normal gap. In alkalemia, the effect of pH is to increase the gap attributed to albumin. Each 1 g/dL of albumin contributes approximately 2.8 mEq/L to the normal anion gap. The anion gap may be low with hypoalbuminemia, or with an increase in an unmeasured cation such as IgG myeloma proteins, calcium, lithium or magnesium. When the anion gap is increased above the normal value of approximately 10 to 12 mEq/L, an anion gap metabolic acidosis is said to exist. The anion gap reflects the presence of a nonchloride acid anion. The accompanying proton is responsible for lowering the serum bicarbonate concentration. The degree of increase in the anion gap, sometimes referred to as the *gap delta*, may be estimated by the difference between the observed gap and a normal value of 12 mEq/L. A similar calculation for a change in serum bicarbonate can be made by subtracting the observed HCO_3^- from a normal value of 25 mEq/L. Comparisons of the two values may help identify more complicated acid-base disorders. Much larger increases in the anion gap compared to decreases in serum HCO_3^- may indicate coexisting metabolic alkalosis, and larger decreases in the serum HCO_3^- compared to increases in the anion gap may signify the existence of an additional hyperchloremic acidosis or respiratory alkalosis.

It is important to consider the individual causes of anion gap acidosis; some common examples will be discussed (Table 113-3). Other substances may be detectable by screening for other organic anions; in such a way, rare metabolic disturbances, such as methylmalonic aciduria or oxoprolinuria, may be detected.

ANION GAP METABOLIC ACIDOSES

Uremic Acidosis

The metabolic acidosis of kidney failure may be due to tubular leak of bicarbonate but is often present when inadequate ammonia production is unable to facilitate the excretion of the normal metabolic acid load. Many patients with renal failure can acidify the urine, but due to the lack of buffering capacity, net acid excretion is diminished. Many organic and inorganic anions, such as phosphate and sulfates, are retained at glomerular filtration rates of less than 25 mL/min and constitute an increased anion gap in association with the metabolic acidosis. The magnitude of the gap is usually less than 20 mEq/L.

The systemic acid-base disturbance in renal failure is attributable to the kidney's inability to excrete hydrogen and generate and reabsorb bicarbonate. It is particularly pronounced in oliguric acute renal failure and is exacerbated by hypercatabolic states such as infection. Treatment of metabolic acidosis of chronic renal failure is directed at maintaining plasma bicarbonate concentration and potassium balance.

Table 113-3 • CAUSES OF INCREASED ANION AND OSMOLAL GAPS

ANION GAP METABOLIC ACIDOSIS	OSMOLAL GAP
Uremia	No
Lactic acidosis	Variable/no
D-Lactic acidosis	No
Diabetic ketoacidosis	No
Starvation ketoacidosis	No
Alcoholic ketoacidosis	If ethanol is present
Ethylene glycol	Yes
Methanol	Yes
Salicylates	No

It includes oral bicarbonate administration and furosemide if fluid overload and hyperkalemia are present.

Overproduction of Endogenous Acids

LACTIC ACIDOSIS. Lactic acidosis is caused by an imbalance in the rates of lactate production and clearance from the circulation. When production exceeds utilization of lactate, primarily in the liver, the anion gap increases and a state of lactic acidosis exists. Lactic acidosis is most often due to circulatory failure, hypoxia, and mitochondrial dysfunction resulting in decreased tissue ATP (type A lactic acidosis). The result is increased anaerobic glycolysis and rate of reaction of pyruvate to lactate. Other causes are thiamine deficiency, hypophosphatemia, isoniazid toxicity, and hypoglycemic states. Metformin may cause lactic acidosis, particularly in elderly patients with cardiac, hepatic, or renal dysfunction, and nucleoside antivirals including zidovudine may cause lactic acidosis and abnormal liver function due to toxic mitochondrial effects. Abnormal mitochondrial function is also a feature of toxicity with hypoglycin from ingestion of the unripe akee fruit and of aspirin.

Type B lactic acidosis is associated with overproduction, which might be caused by severe exertion and malignancies, particularly those with large tumor burden such as lymphomas and widely metastatic cancer. Lactic acidosis may accompany hepatic failure

Lactate, the final product in the anaerobic pathway of glucose metabolism, is produced from pyruvate by the following reaction catalyzed by lactate dehydrogenase:

$$NADH\ +\ pyruvate\ +\ H^+ \leftrightarrow lactate\ +\ NAD$$

A high NADH/NAD ratio will favor lactate formation. The conversions of ethanol to acetaldehyde and the ketoacid β-OH butyrate to acetoacetate each utilize NAD and produce NADH. Alcohol metabolism may be associated with excessive β-OH butyrate and lactic acidosis.

Sepsis is associated with elevated lactate related to poor clearance and impaired gluconeogenesis. The level of lactate is predictive of mortality in patients with acquired lactic acidosis. Symptoms are those of metabolic acidosis in addition to those of the underlying cause.

Lactic acidosis can result from seizure activity when lactate is released from muscle cells that have undergone a period of anaerobic metabolism. The lactate is quickly metabolized to bicarbonate by the liver and kidneys, and the acidosis often resolves within 60 minutes with an increase in HCO_3 as lactate is metabolized. Therefore, administration of bicarbonate is usually unnecessary and may in fact precipitate an overshoot metabolic alkalosis, a development of particular concern in a patient with seizures, because it lowers the seizure threshold. Seizures have also been associated with cerebral lactic acidosis.

Controversy exists regarding the treatment of lactic acidosis with $NaHCO_3$. Arguments against its use are concerned with potential for hypertonicity, volume expansion, worsened hemodynamics, lactic acidosis and intracellular acidosis due to increased CO_2 production. It has been argued, however, that severe systemic acidosis carries greater risk for cardiac function and hemodynamics and that intracellular acidosis is less likely when adequate ventilation is provided. A trial of $NaHCO_3$ versus NaCl use in lactic acidosis in an intensive care unit found that the acidemia could be decreased by $NaHCO_3$ although no difference in hemodynamics was demonstrated. Treatment of lactic acidosis is aimed at correcting the underlying cause. Tissue perfusion and ventilation should be restored if possible. Bicarbonate therapy should be considered when arterial pH is below 7.1 or 7.2.

Patients who have intestinal bacterial overgrowth may develop a syndrome of disorientation, ataxia, and anion gap metabolic acidosis following a carbohydrate meal, due to bacterial production of D-lactate. This isomer of the mammalian L-lactate can only be measured by a specific D-lactate assay. This condition is treated with oral antibiotics and appropriate diet.

DIABETIC KETOACIDOSIS. Diabetic ketoacidosis (DKA) is defined as hyperglycemia with metabolic acidosis resulting from generation of the ketones β-hydroxybutyrate and acetoacetate in response to insulin deficiency and elevated counter-regulatory hormones such as glucagon. Glucagon has an additional effect of increasing hepatic ketogenesis.

It is most commonly seen in cases of type I diabetes mellitus. Symptoms include nausea and vomiting, anorexia, polydipsia and polyuria, and occasionally abdominal pain. Patients often present with Kussmaul respirations and volume depletion. Neurologic symptoms include fatigue and lethargy with depression of the sensorium.

In this state, insulin lack leads to increased lipolysis in adipose tissue, with the transport of free fatty acids to the liver, where hepatic mitochondria produce ketone bodies from acetyl CoA with formation of acetoacetate. In the presence of high NADH/NAD, the more reduced form β-hydroxybutyrate is produced. The brain may use ketoacids as a fuel in this condition. Acetoacetate may also form the nonketoacid acetone. Direct measurements of β-hydroxybutyrate and acetoacetate are available, but tests such as the urinary dipstick that depend on a nitroprusside test may underestimate the degree of ketosis if the predominant form is β-hydroxybutyrate, which goes undetected by this test. In fact, the ketone test may become more positive with treatment, as the β-OHB is metabolized to acetoacetate. Unusually, in some cases of type II diabetes mellitus with severe infection or stress, the counter-regulatory hormones epinephrine and glucagon may be increased so as to enhance lipolysis even without complete insulin deficiency, leading to ketoacidosis. In addition to ketoacids increasing the anion gap, diabetic patients are more prone to lactic acidosis, due to an increase in NADH favoring formation of lactate from pyruvate, inhibition of pyruvate dehydrogenase in the absence of insulin, and increased pyruvate from alanine. Of note, some of the ketoacids will spill into the urine, with cations including sodium and potassium contributing to volume depletion and potassium depletion. The loss of the ketoacids in the urine with sodium will lead to a relative chloride retention, giving the appearance of a mixed anion gap and hyperchloremic acidosis. The "delta HCO_3^-" will exceed the "delta anion gap." This is more likely to be true when the glomerular filtration rate and therefore filtered load of ketoacids is high. The serum anion gap in general will be greatest when renal failure is present, because the additional anions cannot be cleared from the extracellular fluid.

Ketoacidosis is also observed in cases of starvation, in which it is generally mild and not associated with hyperglycemia.

Treatment of DKA may precipitate acid-base disturbances in the CNS with potentially devastating results. The administration of bicarbonate to these patients occasionally results in cerebral edema significant enough to lead to loss of consciousness and even death. This intracellular acidosis may be related to decreased oxygen delivery to brain tissue resulting from the withdrawal of the compensatory effect of acidemia on hemoglobin's affinity for oxygen. Hemoglobin's affinity for oxygen is generally in the normal range in metabolic acidosis despite systemic phosphate depletion and the resultant decrease in 2,3-DPG activity, since acidemia counteracts this effect. With the removal of acidemia, oxygen delivery to tissues decreases.

Treatment of DKA consists of volume repletion, insulin administration with dextrose if necessary to avoid hypoglycemia, and potassium replacement. Bicarbonate administration should be considered only if DKA is accompanied by shock or coma, or if the arterial pH is less than 7.1 or 7.2, and bolus infusion should be avoided.

The cerebrospinal fluid (CSF) exhibits a change in acid-base status with treatment of DKA. Even without bicarbonate administration, the CSF pH falls as a result of the ventilatory response to correction of acidosis and sudden rise in PCO_2. However, no correlation of decreased CSF pH and depression of sensorium has been established in DKA.

ALCOHOLIC KETOACIDOSIS. Alcoholic ketoacidosis usually follows binge drinking and may be associated with withdrawal symptoms and the associated hyperadrenergic state.

Alcoholic ketoacidosis is associated with abdominal pain, vomiting, starvation, and volume depletion. In contrast to DKA, coma is rare in these patients. Alcohol inhibits the conversion of lactate to glucose in the liver. Blood glucose levels are generally low or normal, and insulin is frequently low, with elevated glucagon and cortisol levels. Some patients have hyperglycemia due to the increased catecholamine response. Blood alcohol levels may be absent or elevated on presentation.

The pathophysiology of this disorder is thought to be overproduction of β-hydroxybutyrate and, to a lesser extent, acetoacetate secondary to increased free fatty acids produced in the altered hormonal milieu. The increase in the ratio of β-hydroxybutyrate to acetoacetate is believed to result from the oxidation of ethanol, which increases the ratio of NADH to NAD$^+$ and favors β-hydroxybutyrate

production. Damage to mitochondria by alcohol could further elevate this ratio by preventing reoxidation of NADH.

Treatment of alcoholic metabolic acidosis consists of volume repletion and thiamine and glucose administration with correction of hypophosphatemia, hypokalemia, and hypomagnesemia if present. The acid-base disturbance usually resolves after several hours. Hypophosphatemia may manifest 12 to 24 hours after initiation of treatment in the undernourished patient and is exacerbated by glucose administration.

Patients consuming alcohol typically present with a high osmolal gap (defined as the difference between the measured and the calculated serum osmolality).

$$\text{Calculated osmolality} = 2(Na^+) + (\text{glucose, mg/dL} \div 18) + (\text{BUN, mg/dL} \div 2.8)$$

This gap should be equal to the ethanol concentration in milligrams per decaliter divided by 4.6; if it is not, ingestion of another alcohol such as methanol, isopropanol, or ethylene glycol should be suspected (see Table 113–3). This population is at increased risk for ingestion of these alcohol substitutes. A clue to the diagnosis of a toxic alcohol ingestion is the simultaneous presence of an anion gap metabolic acidosis and an osmolal gap. The serum osmolality should be measured by a freezing point depression technique and compared to the calculated osmolality. The direct measurement of ethanol, ethylene glycol, and methanol should be performed when possible. Metabolic acidosis is associated with the ingestion of these other alcohols.

ETHYLENE GLYCOL INTOXICATION. Ethylene glycol is commonly found in antifreeze and is used as an industrial solvent. It has a sweet taste and is occasionally seen clinically after ingestion as a substitute for ethanol. Intoxication is characterized by profound CNS symptoms, including seizures and coma, severe metabolic acidosis, and cardiac, pulmonary, and renal failure.

Although ethylene glycol itself does not appear to be particularly damaging, its metabolites are highly toxic and include glyoxylate and glycolate, as well as oxalic acid and ketoaldehydes. The increased anion gap seen in ethylene glycol intoxication is attributable to ethylene glycol metabolites. A high osmolal gap will also be present due to the uncharged alcohol. Glycolic acid appears to be primarily responsible for the metabolic acidosis observed in this condition. The ketoaldehyde metabolites appear to be responsible for the CNS dysfunction by inhibiting oxidative phosphorylation. Lactic acid production is also increased with the inhibition of the Krebs cycle. Calcium oxalate crystals may be seen in the urine and may be responsible for intratubular obstruction and acute renal failure. Patients often present with dehydration due to the osmotic diuresis of the renal alcohol excretion. Treatment is aimed at rehydration and competitive inhibition of alcohol dehydrogenase by use of ethanol or fomepizole and hemodialysis.

Ethanol decreases the production of toxic metabolites and has been a mainstay of treatment, but its use is characterized by difficulty in controlling plasma levels and monitoring mental status. Fomepizole has recently been shown to be a safe and effective antidote to ethylene glycol intoxication.

METHANOL INGESTION. Methanol, a component of wood alcohol and windshield wiper fluid, is highly toxic to the CNS after metabolism to formaldehyde and formic acid. Optic papillitis may cause blindness. Treatment includes competitive inhibitors for alcohol dehydrogenase, including ethanol or fomepizole, which will reduce the formation of acid anions and the anion gap while maintaining a higher level of methanol in the blood. Hemodialysis may be necessary to increase elimination.

A toxic ingestion with isopropyl alcohol, as in rubbing alcohol, does not cause an increased anion gap or ketoacidosis since the metabolite is acetone, but tests for ketones are positive and a high osmolal gap will be present.

Occasionally, patients in the intensive care unit setting are given high doses of intravenous benzodiazepines, such as lorazepam. They may develop a high osmolal gap due to the diluent propylene glycol and develop a clinical picture of sedation, failure to wean from the respirator, and increased lactate, a metabolite of propylene glycol.

SALICYLATE INTOXICATION. Salicylate intoxication produces a complex acid-base picture. The most common manifestation is a combined metabolic acidosis and respiratory alkalosis, although the condition can manifest as either one or the other, or as a combined respiratory and metabolic acidosis. It is most often seen as a result of accidental overdose, therapeutic overdose, or suicide attempt. Manifestations of intoxication include hemorrhage, fever, nausea and vomiting, hyperventilation, diaphoresis, tinnitus, and occasionally polyuria followed by oliguria. Noncardiogenic pulmonary edema is sometimes seen in adults. An anion-gap metabolic acidosis may develop and in severe cases has led to seizures, respiratory depression, and coma.

The effects of salicylate are age-dependent. However, certain characteristics of salicylate intoxication are seen in all age groups. The first of these results in a respiratory alkalosis and is the result of a direct stimulatory effect of salicylate on the medullary respiratory control center.

The second characteristic of salicylate intoxication affecting patients of all ages is an increase in metabolic rate. Salicylate functions as an uncoupler of oxidative phosphorylation resulting in increased oxygen consumption and CO_2 production. However, the increase in alveolar ventilation resulting from stimulation of central chemoreceptors overcomes this increase in CO_2. Children often present with metabolic acidosis, whereas adults often present with respiratory alkalosis.

Treatment of salicylate intoxication is aimed at correcting the metabolic acidosis and removing salicylate. Bicarbonate should be administered if metabolic acidosis predominates. Salicylates are removed by an alkaline diuresis. In cases of severe intoxication, other methods include gastric lavage, osmotic diuresis, and dialysis. Urinary alkalinization with acetazolamide is controversial, since it may impair tissue to blood CO_2 transport and in theory worsen acidosis in the respiratory center.

NORMAL ANION GAP OR HYPERCHLOREMIC ACIDOSIS

HYPERCHLOREMIC METABOLIC ACIDOSIS OF NONRENAL ORIGIN ASSOCIATED WITH NORMAL OR INCREASED POTASSIUM. These acidoses can develop by the addition of chloride salts such as NaCl, KCl, $CaCl_2$, NH_4Cl, arginine, and lysine hydrochlorides or HCl itself (Table 113–4). If the quantity of Cl^- introduced exceeds the ability for the kidney to eliminate the Cl^- salts in the urine, hyperchloremia will develop. Electroneutrality is maintained by a decrease in the serum HCO_3^- concentration, and a hyperchloremic acidosis ensues. Renal production of NH_3 will increase in an attempt to improve HCl excretion. Hyperkalemia can occur in this situation, as the acidemia favors the exit of K^+ from cells. Hyperchloremic acidosis has a greater effect in causing cellular K efflux than the organic acidoses and respiratory acidosis. Another mechanism for hyperkalemia may be an inhibitory effect of intracellular acidity on K^+ secretion in the collecting duct cell.

HYPERCHLOREMIC METABOLIC ACIDOSIS OF NONRENAL ORIGIN ASSOCIATED WITH HYPOKALEMIA. Hypokalemic, hyperchloremic acidosis may result from loss of a body fluid that is low in Cl^- concentration relative to Na and K^+ concentrations, when compared to the Na^+ to Cl^- ratio in the extracellular fluid. For example, losses in the stool of Na^+ and K^+ with bicarbonate in small bowel diarrhea or organic acid anions from bacterial origin with colonic diarrheas lead to hyperchloremic acidosis. Pancreatic secretions or heavy losses from ileostomy sites may lead to loss of bicarbonate-containing fluids. Urinary diversions such as ureterosigmoidostomies and ileal loops may result in increased chloride absorption in exchange for bicarbonate in the intestinal segment, leading to hyperchloremic acidosis. As will be discussed next, renal

tubular acidosis causes the cations Na^+ and K^+ to be lost in the urine with HCO_3^-, rather than Cl^-, leading to hyperchloremia.

HYPERCHLOREMIC METABOLIC ACIDOSIS OF RENAL ORIGIN ASSOCIATED WITH HYPOKALEMIA. Proximal renal tubular acidosis (type II), is characterized by a decreased threshold for bicarbonate reabsorption, in which case there is initial bicarbonate wasting until a new low level of serum bicarbonate develops. At that point, the filtered bicarbonate is reduced, and the renal tubule can completely reabsorb the filtered load so that the new steady state allows for a normally acid urine pH. In proximal renal tubular acidosis, the urine pH is usually less than 5.3, the acidosis is not severe, and there is not relentless acid retention, since at this new steady state, acid excretion may balance acid production. In children, however, the acidosis may have effects on growth and may need to be treated with bicarbonate supplements. It is characteristic of proximal renal tubular acidosis that large quantities of HCO_3^- need be administered to correct the acidosis, since attempts to give alkali are associated with prompt renal excretion and an alkaline urine. Another characteristic related to the alkaline urine is the hypokalemia brought out by bicarbonate replacement.

Isolated proximal renal tubular acidosis may result from mutations of specific transporters of the proximal tubule such as the Na-HCO_3 cotransporter, or could be due to hereditary deficiency of carbonic anhydrase. The latter would resemble the effects of carbonic anhydrase inhibitors such as acetazolamide.

More commonly, proximal renal tubular acidosis is associated with generalized proximal tubule dysfunction: the Fanconi syndrome. Glycosuria, phosphaturia, aminoaciduria, and uricosuria may be present. Causes include genetic diseases such as the glycogen storage disease glucose-6-phosphatase deficiency, cystinosis, hereditary fructose intolerance, and Wilson's disease. Multiple myeloma and Sjögren's syndrome should be considered in the adult patient. Primary hyperparathyoidism results in proximal renal tubular acidosis and hypophosphatemia due to inhibition of Na/H exchange and Na-phosphate cotransport in the proximal tubule. Drug toxicity with aminoglycosides, cisplatin, and ifosfamide may cause proximal tubule dysfunction.

Distal renal tubular acidosis (type 1) is generally a more severe metabolic disorder and may be accompanied by hypercalciuria, nephrocalcinosis, kidney stones, and bone disease, in contrast to proximal renal tubular acidosis. The degree of acidemia is often more severe and the urine pH usually exceeds 5.3. This observation is the basis of the NH_4Cl loading test in which plasma bicarbonate is lowered by an acid challenge. If urine pH remains above 5.3, a distal abnormality is suspected. This test is rarely indicated to distinguish between proximal and distal acidosis.

In distal renal tubular acidosis, there is a failure to produce ammonia and therefore an inability to adequately excrete net acid, leading to the continuous retention of acid in the body. This disorder must be treated but usually can be managed with small amounts of bicarbonate or citrate salts amounting to daily production of acid in the amount of 1 to 2 mEq/kg/day. Hypokalemia often accompanies distal renal tubular acidosis and may improve with treatment.

Kindreds have been described with mutations in genes for the distal H^+ ATPase causing an autosomal recessive distal renal tubular acidosis with deafness, and mutations in the Cl/HCO_3 exchanger have been linked to an autosomal dominant form of distal renal tubular acidosis.

Distal renal tubular acidosis is also associated with autoimmune disorders, including systemic lupus erythematosus and Sjögren's syndrome, genetic diseases including sickle cell anemia, Wilson's disease, Fabry's disease, cystic kidney diseases, and hereditary elliptocytosis. Hypercalciuria and hyperoxaluria may cause distal renal tubular acidosis, and nephrocalcinosis may be present. Amyloidosis may manifest with severe acidemia and other tubular dysfunction, including nephrogenic diabetes insipidus. Tubulointerstitial disease of the kidney, including reflux nephropathy and urinary obstruction, may result in renal tubular acidosis with hypo- or hyperkalemia. Drugs such as amphotericin B cause hypokalemic distal renal tubular acidosis.

HYPERCHLOREMIC METABOLIC ACIDOSIS OF RENAL ORIGIN ASSOCIATED WITH HYPERKALEMIA. Hyperkalemic, hyperchloremic acidosis (type 4) suggests dysfunction of the cortical collecting duct where acidification of the urine and disorders in K secretion may occur. Some patients with high blood potassium and hyperchloremic acidosis can lower the urinary pH below 5.5, whereas others appear to have defects in both potassium balance and urinary acidification. Causes include

Table 113–4 • CAUSES OF HYPERCHLOREMIC ACIDOSIS

TYPE	CAUSES
Renal with hypokalemia	Proximal RTA, type 2
	Distal RTA, type 1
	Some anion gap acidoses with high anion clearance
Renal with hyperkalemia	Type 4 RTA; hyporenin–hypoaldosteronism
Nonrenal with hypokalemia	Diarrhea
	Urinary diversions
Nonrenal with hyperkalemia	NaCl, KCl, NH4Cl, CaCl2, ArgHCl, LysHCl

RTA = renal tubular acidosis.

hyporenin-hypoaldosteronism seen in diabetic renal disease, other tubulointerstitial diseases, usually with some renal impairment, sickle cell anemia, or use of drugs such as β-blockers and nonsteroidal anti-inflammatory drugs. Low renin and aldosterone levels can also be found in cases of volume expansion with hypertension. Cyclosporine may increase distal Cl⁻ reabsorption as Na⁺ is reabsorbed, leading to decreased electrical driving forces for K⁺ and H⁺ secretion. Increases in Na⁺ and Cl⁻ reabsorption lead to hypertension, hyperkalemic acidosis, volume expansion, and consequently low renin and aldosterone in the autosomal dominant condition known as Gordon's syndrome. Increased activity of the distal thiazide-sensitive NaCl transporter is suspected. Hyperkalemic acidosis with elevated renin and low aldosterone is found in cases of adrenal insufficiency, isolated hypoaldosteronism and with the use of angiotensin-converting enzyme inhibitors or angiotensin II receptor blockers. High renin and aldosterone levels are anticipated when the renal collecting duct cell is insensitive to aldosterone, as in urinary tract obstruction, sickle cell anemia, amyloidosis, and systemic lupus. Inhibition of aldosterone action with spironolactone will cause a hyperkalemic acidosis, as would inhibition of the epithelial Na⁺ channel by amiloride and triamterene. Pseudohypoaldosteronism is due to inactivating mutations of the Na⁺ channel.

Hyperkalemia itself may worsen metabolic acidosis by decreasing NH_3 accumulation by countercurrent multiplication in the medullary interstitium. Often, treatment of hyperkalemia improves urinary acidification without use of bicarbonate salts.

THE URINARY ANION GAP IN HYPERCHLOREMIC ACIDOSIS

An important means of distinguishing between renal tubular acidosis and extrarenal bicarbonate loss, for example from diarrhea, is to look at the urinary anion gap. Since the normal renal response to metabolic acidosis is an increase in ammoniagenesis, the urine in the case of diarrhea should normally contain large amounts of NH_4Cl while the kidney retains sodium and potassium. The urinary anion gap, which is $(Na^+ + K^+) - Cl^-$, should then be strongly negative because of the unmeasured NH_4^+. This test is superior to measurement of urine pH, since decreased Na^+ delivery to the distal nephron in the Na^+ avid state of diarrhea may impair urinary acidification and pH will not be maximally acid. In renal diseases in which there is either a failure of ammoniagenesis or the excretion of sodium plus potassium with bicarbonate, the urinary anion gap will be zero or positive. That is characteristic of distal renal tubular acidosis.

When other unmeasured anions such as ketoacids and lactate are present in the urine, a positive urinary anion gap does not indicate renal tubular acidosis. These situations are usually associated with an elevated serum anion gap but on occasion prompt renal excretion of organic anions with sodium and potassium may minimize an increase in the serum gap. This is particularly possible in cases of DKA and D-lactic acidosis, as D-lactate is not absorbed by the renal tubule. In the metabolic acidosis of glue-sniffers, hippurate, a product of toluene, is excreted, giving the appearance of a non-gap metabolic acidosis with positive urinary anion gap.

Rx Treatment

If possible, treatment of metabolic acidosis should focus on correcting the underlying cause and permitting the body's homeostatic mechanisms to correct the acid-base disturbance. It is often recommended to consider treatment of patients whose pH is less than 7.2 with alkali infusion. Sodium bicarbonate is most frequently used. However, rapid correction of arterial pH can lead to complications, including a paradoxical CSF acidosis and continued hyperventilation, hypokalemia, and hypocalcemia. Formulas have been developed that allow the physician to estimate roughly the base deficit in milliequivalents based on the serum HCO_3^- concentration in milliequivalents per liter:

$$\text{Amount of } HCO_3^- = (25 - [HCO_3^-]) \times wt \ (kg)/2$$

In general, only partial correction of the deficit should be attempted prior to recalculations using this formula. Also, this equation represents an estimate of deficit only, so ongoing losses need to be considered.

METABOLIC ALKALOSIS

In metabolic alkalosis, the primary event is an elevation of the plasma bicarbonate concentration. In response to increased systemic pH, alveolar ventilation is decreased in order to increase PCO_2 and thereby decrease pH. However, compensation is generally believed to be less effective in cases of metabolic alkalosis than in cases of metabolic acidosis. Contributing factors may include the fact that hypoventilation also decreases PO_2, a potent stimulus for the peripheral chemoreceptors to increase alveolar ventilation. A second mechanism that may blunt respiratory compensation is intracellular acidosis in the brain in the setting of hypokalemia. In acute metabolic alkalosis, there is an initial paradoxical acidotic shift in CSF pH secondary to a sudden increase in PCO_2, similar to the alkaline shift in CSF pH in acute metabolic acidosis. This may contribute to the unpredictable respiratory response to metabolic alkalosis by activating central chemoreceptors and increasing ventilatory drive in the face of peripheral stimulation to decrease alveolar ventilation. In chronic metabolic alkalosis, the CSF pH may return to normal values such that respiratory drive derives entirely from the peripheral chemoreceptors. Whatever the causes, the result is that the ventilatory response to metabolic alkalosis is highly varied. Many patients with metabolic alkalosis maintain near-normal PCO_2 levels, and the level rarely rises above 60 mm Hg.

Clinical Manifestations

Metabolic alkalosis has a profound effect on the CNS and is frequently associated with metabolic encephalopathy. This is the result of the alkalosis itself and of compensatory hypoventilation that leads to changes in blood flow and oxygenation. Significant cerebral tissue hypoxia is a result of cerebral vasoconstriction and increased hemoglobin affinity for oxygen. Symptoms include confusion, obtundation, delirium, and coma. The seizure threshold is lowered, and tetany, paresthesias, muscular cramping, and other symptoms reflecting low free calcium levels are observed. Neurologic manifestations are generally seen when the pH exceeds 7.55, although patients with hypocalcemia may exhibit signs at lower pH values. Other findings include cardiac arrhythmias and hypotension. Lactate production increases, reflecting increased anaerobic glycolysis.

Causes

Metabolic alkalosis requires a generation phase, in which new HCO_3^- is added to the extracellular fluid, and a maintenance phase, by which the new elevated serum HCO_3^- concentration is sustained. Without the latter phase, the kidney with normal filtration and tubular function has a high capacity to excrete bicarbonate, thereby preventing alkalosis. Maintenance of a high bicarbonate concentration is usually because of volume depletion, a reduced glomerular filtration rate, hypokalemia, or low chloride levels.

We will consider first how metabolic alkalosis can be generated. Metabolic alkalosis is generally divided into two categories based on its responsiveness to chloride (Table 113–5). Chloride-responsive metabolic alkalosis is associated with extracellular fluid and chloride

Table 113–5 • CAUSES OF METABOLIC ALKALOSIS

TYPE	CAUSES
Renal, hypochloremic alkalosis: Cl responsive with urine Cl >20	Loop and distal tubule diuretics Bartter's syndrome Gittelman's syndrome Posthypercapnic
Nonrenal, hypochloremic alkalosis: Cl responsive with urine Cl <20	Vomiting/nasogastric suction Chloridorrhea
Renal, alkalosis with extracellular expansion: Cl unresponsive with urine Cl >20	Hyperaldosteronism, primary and secondary Liddle's syndrome
Nonrenal alkalosis, Cl unresponsive	NaHCO₃, acetate, citrate, lactate
Other causes of metabolic alkalosis	Excessive non-reabsorbable anion excretion Hypoproteinemia

depletion and is seen in cases of gastric fluid loss and diuretic use. A diagnostic clue comes from the serum electrolytes. The bicarbonate is increased with a corresponding fall in serum chloride (hypochloremic alkalosis). Chloride-unresponsive metabolic alkalosis is seen in patients with extracellular fluid expansion in cases such as primary aldosteronism and hypokalemia.

Entry of hydrogen ions into cells can also lead to metabolic alkalosis, as seen in hypokalemia.

The discussion that follows addresses alkalosis of renal and extrarenal origin, according to the presence (chloride-responsive) or absence (chloride-unresponsive) of associated volume depletion.

METABOLIC ALKALOSIS OF RENAL ORIGIN ASSOCIATED WITH VOLUME DEPLETION

Metabolic alkalosis of renal origin may be the result of excessive urinary chloride excretion. The most common causes are diuretics that inhibit reabsorption of Cl^- proportionately more than Na^+. Most often, it is due to potent diuretics, such as furosemide and bumetanide, which inhibit the Na-K-2Cl cotransporter in the thick ascending limb, or thiazides that inhibit the Na-Cl cotransporter in the distal tubule and metolazone. In each case, the urine is found to be rich in Cl^- relative to Na^+ when one compares the concentrations to the starting point in the extracellular fluid of roughly 140 Na^+ to 100 Cl^-. The Cl^- loss results in hypochloremia and plasma HCO_3^- increases, maintaining electroneutrality. Extracellular volume depletion results in stimulation of the renin-angiotensin-aldosterone pathway, and high aldosterone superimposed on increased distal urinary flow rates results in increased K^+ excretion and hypokalemia. The volume depletion and hypokalemia enhance proximal HCO_3^- reabsorption, maintaining the alkalosis, and the prerenal fall in glomerular flow rate limits HCO_3^- filtration. Correction of this type of metabolic alkalosis requires replacement with NaCl and KCl solutions. Replacing with saline alone is potentially dangerous, since the consequent increased glomerular filtration and decreased proximal reabsorption will allow large quantities of alkaline urine to present to the aldosterone-sensitive distal sites, worsening hypokalemia.

Several important but rare genetic syndromes with urinary chloride wasting have been described. Bartter's syndrome is an autosomal recessive salt-losing state associated with extracellular volume depletion and excessive urinary chloride loss resulting in hypokalemia and hypochloremic metabolic alkalosis. There are secondary increased levels of plasma renin and aldosterone. The syndrome is reminiscent of effects of the diuretic furosemide on the thick ascending limb of Henle. Gene mutations associated with Bartter's syndrome have been described for the Na-K2-Cl cotransporter, K^+ channel, and Cl^- channels that take part in loop of Henle Cl^- transport. Since calcium reabsorption occurs in this segment, Bartter's syndrome, like furosemide, causes hypercalciuria. Polyuria is present due to the important role of the thick ascending limb of Henle in urinary concentration. Indomethacin has been used to treat Bartter's syndrome by interfering with prostaglandin E_2, allowing for greater Na-Cl reabsorption in the thick ascending limb.

Like Bartter's syndrome, Gitelman's syndrome is an autosomal recessive cause of extracellular volume depletion, urinary chloride wasting, and hypokalemic metabolic alkalosis. It is due to an inactivating gene mutation in the thiazide-sensitive NaCl cotransporter of the renal distal tubule. In contrast to Bartter's syndrome, but similar to the thiazide diuretics, urinary concentration is spared and patients are hypocalciuric, since decreased NaCl reabsorption in this segment is associated with a decrease in calcium excretion. Hypomagnesemia may also be severe.

Posthypercapnic alkalosis is a condition in which patients who are chronically hypercapnic experience a sudden decrease in PCO_2, leading to metabolic alkalosis. This scenario is commonly seen in patients with chronic pulmonary disease who acutely require mechanical ventilation because of respiratory failure. The renal adaptation to chronic respiratory acidosis results in high systemic bicarbonate levels, and when PCO_2 is quickly lowered, patients can become acutely and severely alkalemic. These patients are also commonly on low-chloride diets or diuretics, and this condition may persist as the kidney continues to reabsorb bicarbonate as a result of low chloride levels. This development can have severe consequences, resulting in arrhythmias, seizures, coma, and even death in some patients. To avoid this condition, PCO_2 should be allowed to rise as slowly as is possible to avoid hypoxemia, and chloride stores should be repleted if necessary.

METABOLIC ALKALOSIS OF NONRENAL ORIGIN, WITH EXTRACELLULAR VOLUME DEPLETION

Metabolic alkalosis may develop as a result of Cl^- losses in gastrointestinal secretions. In such cases, extracellular volume is usually contracted, hypochloremia develops, and, because the loss of Cl^- is nonrenal, the urinary chloride level is low, usually less than 20 mEq/L.

The most common disorder in this category is gastric alkalosis due to vomiting or nasogastric suctioning. Gastric juice is higher in Cl^- than Na^+, the reverse state of the extracellular fluids.

It is not uncommon for secretory diarrheas to lead to disproportionate Cl^- losses compared to Na^+. Infectious gastroenteritis, congenital chloridorrhea, and villous adenomas are causes of this syndrome. Diarrhea should not be equated with the development of metabolic acidosis. Alkalosis is most likely to develop when the stool electrolytes $[(Na^+ + K^+) - Cl^-]$ are less than plasma HCO_3^-.

In gastric alkalosis, the initiating event is loss of HCl. In acid-secreting epithelia, when protons are secreted into the lumen, a bicarbonate is transported back to the blood. Thus, in gastric alkalosis, the secretion of HCl into the stomach lumen by the parietal cell is coupled to the absorption of bicarbonate in exchange for chloride at the basolateral membrane. Normally, when gastric acid is secreted, a mild increase in serum bicarbonate occurs, and this spills into the urine, causing an "alkaline tide." With vomiting, a net loss of HCl is removed from the body, generating the alkalosis.

Initially, the increased HCO_3^- is filtered by the glomeruli, and since the proximal tubule is not yet poised to increase reabsorption, the HCO_3^- flows distally and is excreted in the urine. The accompanying cations are Na^+ and K^+ and the urine pH is alkaline. At this stage, the kidney appears to be protecting the body from alkalosis, but at the expense of Na^+ and K^+ losses. The presence of Na^+ in the HCO_3^- containing urine belies the volume depletion that begins to develop. Clinically, a low urinary Cl^- is more indicative of the volume depletion than is the urinary Na^+. As vomiting continues, extracellular volume depletion worsens and renal responses begin to change. Glomerular filtration falls, limiting HCO_3^- filtration. Volume depletion increases the renin–angiotension II–aldosterone system and as a consequence proximal volume and HCO_3^- reabsorption increase. Distal Na^+ reabsorption increases under the influence of aldosterone and greater H^+ secretion enhances HCO_3^- reabsorption. These effects begin to prevent renal Na^+ losses but at the expense of maintaining metabolic alkalosis; it becomes harder to excrete the HCO_3^-. Significant K^+ losses occur as a result of the bicarbonaturia and hyperaldosteronism leading to hypokalemia. The K^+ depletion associated with vomiting is actually due to renal not gastrointestinal losses. The loss of K^+ is a consequence of mechanisms to maintain extracellular volume. The hypokalemia further increases proximal $NaHCO_3$ reabsorption and distal H^+ secretion, effects that also maintain the alkalosis. Hypokalemia leads to increased K^+ reabsorption, probably through increased K/H ATPase activity in the collecting duct. Note that the mechanisms for conserving K^+ at this stage do so at the expense of further reabsorption of HCO_3^-. At the new steady state after vomiting or nasogastric suctioning stops, the urine has low levels of Na^+, K^+, and Cl^- and is acid, owing to complete HCO_3^- reabsorption. At this stage, the paradoxical aciduria of metabolic alkalosis is noted. In the end, the patient may be hypovolemic, hypokalemic, and alkalemic, but because Na^+, K^+, and acid-base balance are intrinsically linked, life-threatening volume depletion, K^+ depletion, and alkalemia are usually avoided. The overlap of Na^+, K^+, and acid-base balance is obvious at both the clinical level and the cellular level, where transporters such as Na/H exchange, K/H ATPase, and Cl/HCO_3 exchange are at work. Additionally, there is overlap in the hormonal regulation, with angiotensin II influencing Na/H exchange and aldosterone exerting effects on Na^+, K^+, and H^+ transport.

From the standpoint of the renal tubule, similarities exist in the initial bicarbonaturia leading to K^+ wasting in gastric alkalosis and in the development of proximal tubular acidosis; the difference is in the source of HCO_3^-. The source is a high filtered load in the alkalemic patient and a decreased reabsorptive component in the patient with proximal renal tubular acidosis.

METABOLIC ALKALOSIS OF RENAL ORIGIN WITH VOLUME EXPANSION AND HYPERTENSION

The renal conditions that cause metabolic alkalosis and volume expansion are due to the primary increase in Na^+ reabsorption above that required to maintain a steady state of Na⁺ balance, rather than a primary loss of the Cl⁻ anion. The reabsorption of Na⁺ is proportionately greater than that for Cl⁻. As Na⁺ is reabsorbed, electroneutrality is maintained by an increase in plasma HCO_3^-. The plasma Na⁺ concentration may be increased and Cl⁻ balance is normal; Cl⁻ appears in the urine and hypochloremia is not present. In the kidney, the loss of net acid as NH_4Cl in excess of produced acid would generate metabolic alkalosis, where again the new bicarbonate generated is due to the proton secretion by the distal nephron through H⁺ ATPases. The H⁺ then combines with NH_3 to form NH_4^+ in the urine.

The site in the nephron where Na⁺ is reabsorbed independently of Cl⁻ is the cortical collecting duct (CCD) through the aldosterone-sensitive cells containing the epithelial Na⁺ channel. When Na⁺ is reabsorbed by the principal cells of the CCD, the tubule lumen becomes electronegative. This will stimulate both K⁺ secretion and H⁺ secretion by the electrogenic H⁺ ATPases. To the extent that HCO_3^- remains in the lumen, the secreted protons will complete HCO_3^- reabsorption. Additional secreted protons will combine with NH_3 and phosphates, leading to net acid excretion. If there is an increase in the distal H⁺ secretory mechanism caused by disease, then more urinary net acid will be produced, more "new" HCO_3^- will be generated and returned to the now expanded extracellular fluid, and metabolic alkalosis will develop. The increased plasma HCO_3^- will be filtered, but in the absence of a stimulus to increase proximal HCO_3^- reabsorption, the HCO_3^- will flow distally to be reabsorbed by the increased H⁺ secretion of the collecting duct. At first the alkalosis in such a case is mild. However, increased CCD Na⁺ reabsorption will also lead to increased K⁺ secretion, and hypokalemia will develop. Hypokalemia will increase the capacity for proximal HCO_3^- reabsorption, opposing the effect of volume expansion, so that distal delivery of HCO_3^- decreases. That allows the higher than normal distal H⁺ secretion to titrate urinary buffers rather than complete HCO_3^- reabsorption, so further "new" HCO_3^- is formed and the alkalosis worsens. This is the process by which hypermineralocorticoid syndromes cause and sustain alkalosis; there is an important role for hypokalemia in the process. Patients with suspected hyperaldosteronism will develop hypokalemia when given a salt load because of increased Na⁺ delivery to distal sites and more K⁺ loss. Metabolic alkalosis can be lessened in hyperaldosteronism by potassium replacement or by blocking Na⁺ reabsorption with aldosterone antagonists or amiloride.

Specific causes of this type of renal alkalosis can be classified according to levels of renin and aldosterone. Primary increases in renin resulting in high aldosterone can be seen in patients with unilateral renal artery stenosis, renin-secreting tumors of the kidney, and malignant hypertension. A low renin and elevated aldosterone level is characteristic of primary hyperaldosteronism from adrenal adenoma or hyperplasia. Hypertension and hypokalemic alkalosis could result from increased function of the aldosterone receptor in the CCD driving greater Na⁺ reabsorption even without increased aldosterone levels. Since cortisol can also stimulate the receptor, patients with hypercortisolism or adrenocorticotropic hormone–secreting tumors develop the syndrome, with suppression of renin and aldosterone by the volume expansion. Inhibition of the intracellular enzyme 11-β OH steroid dehydrogenase, which normally inactivates cortisol to form cortisone in the CCD, will also result in low renin levels, low aldosterone levels, and hypokalemic alkalosis. Such is the effect of a substance found in licorice when taken in excess. Another cause of hypertension with hypokalemic alkalosis but with low renin and aldosterone levels is Liddle's syndrome, in which an activating mutation in the CCD Na⁺ channel leads to increased Na⁺ reabsorption.

Metabolic alkalosis may also develop without volume expansion when a non-reabsorbable anion is presented to the CCD lumen. Nitrates, sulfates, and certain antibiotics such as carbenicillin may obligate K⁺ and H⁺ secretion as Na⁺ is reabsorbed. Topical administration of silver nitrate to burn victims may result in alkalosis.

METABOLIC ALKALOSIS OF NONRENAL ORIGIN ASSOCIATED WITH NORMAL OR EXPANDED VOLUME

Sometimes inspection of the serum electrolytes fails to reveal hypochloremia. To maintain electroneutrality, there must either be an alternative anion that is depleted, or an excessive concentration of a cation. An example of metabolic alkalosis associated with depletion of a nonchloride anion is hypoproteinemic alkalosis, recognized by hypoalbuminemia and a small anion gap. Chloride balance is normal and chloride appears in the urine.

Alkalosis may be the result of addition of alkali salts of non-Cl⁻ organic anions. The normal response to the ingestion of $NaHCO_3$ is rapid urinary alkalinization because there is an unaltered threshold for HCO_3^- reabsorption. However, marked excesses of HCO_3^- may be administered such that volume expansion and alkalemia will result. It is more likely to occur in a patient with volume depletion or low glomerular filtration, since the low filtered load prevents HCO_3^- excretion. Practically, this is important whenever an effort is made to alkalinize a patient's urine, as for example in tumor lysis syndrome or myoglobinuria. When the glomerular filtration rate is low, such alkalinization may not occur until the patient develops severely elevated plasma bicarbonate concentrations. Milk-alkali syndrome is a form of alkalosis seen in renal failure patients associated with ingestion of milk and calcium antacids. The result is hypercalcemia and alkalemia with normal Cl⁻.

Other situations in which intake of alkali salts results in metabolic alkalosis include infusion of large quantities of sodium salts of metabolizable organic compounds such as acetate, citrate, lactate, or bicarbonate. Hyperalimentation with acetate salts, chronic peritoneal dialysis with acetate or lactate dialysate, or excessive transfusions or plasmapheresis, in which large quantities of citrate, used as an anticoagulant, are delivered, may all result in this type of metabolic alkalosis.

 Treatment

In treating metabolic alkalosis, it is important to distinguish whether the condition is chloride-responsive or chloride-unresponsive, as discussed earlier.

In chloride-responsive patients, treatment is directed at increasing urinary excretion of bicarbonate. In patients with mild to moderate alkalosis, administration of NaCl and KCl is effective in suppressing renal acid excretion and increasing renal HCO_3^- excretion. Unless KCl is also replenished, the improvement in filtration and proximal reabsorption will result in severe K⁺ wasting as bicarbonaturia develops and aldosterone's effects remain. In addition, complete resolution of alkalosis will not occur until K⁺ is normalized. In the patient with renal failure and vomiting, HCO_3^- elevation may be more severe because of poor HCO_3^- filtration. In cases of volume expansion and alkalosis, acetazolamide may be attempted with care, given the potential for losing K⁺. If that fails to work, dilute solutions of HCl may be cautiously administered.

In patients with more severe alkalemia with volume expansion, mineral acids (e.g., HCl or arginine monohydrochloride) may be necessary. In the absence of renal failure, acetazolamide may be effective but may greatly increase K⁺ losses.

Chloride-unresponsive patients include patients with mineralocorticoid excess. The hypokalemia and hyperaldosteronism lead to increased hydrogen secretion and bicarbonate reabsorption in the kidney. These patients respond to potassium replacement, which reverses the intracellular shift of hydrogen ions and increases bicarbonate excretion, and to agents that reduce aldosterone activity such as spironolactone and amiloride.

RESPIRATORY ACIDOSIS

Respiratory acid-base disturbances have a profound effect on the CNS. This phenomenon stems from the fact that the CNS must respond to changes in systemic PCO_2, reflected immediately in the CNS as a result of the permeability of the blood-brain barrier to CO_2, as well as to changes in the peripheral concentration of hydrogen ions as reflected in the bicarbonate concentration. Despite these changes, however, the CNS is able to maintain a remarkably constant pH in the face of even significant respiratory acid-base disturbances.

Respiratory acidosis is characterized by a primary elevation in PCO_2 reflected in reduced arterial pH with variable elevation in bicarbonate concentration. It is most frequently caused by a decrease in alveolar ventilation.

Respiratory acidosis is most frequently seen clinically in cases of pulmonary insufficiency and can be the result of pulmonary disease, respiratory muscle fatigue, or abnormalities of ventilatory control. Disorders include central effects of drugs, stroke, and infection; airway obstruction; primary parenchymal processes such as chronic obstructive pulmonary disease and acute respiratory distress syndrome; and neuromuscular diseases such as myasthenia gravis or muscular dystrophies. Recently, permissive hypercapnia has been utilized clinically in patients with acute respiratory distress syndrome to limit pulmonary damage secondary to mechanical ventilation. To maintain normal P_{CO_2} levels in patients with acute respiratory distress syndrome, it is necessary to deliver tidal volumes and pressures that can result in overdistention and damage of alveoli, potentially leading to rupture. By decreasing tidal volume and pressures, pulmonary injury is limited. This technique has been associated with improved survival in patients with acute respiratory distress syndrome and improved outcomes in patients with status epilepticus.

Clinically significant respiratory acidosis can result from elevations in P_{CO_2} using this approach, however. Effects are most commonly seen when the P_{CO_2} is allowed to rise precipitously and include increased intracranial pressure, increased cardiac output, and increased organ perfusion in some studies. The dangers of this technique rest in the fact that many patients have significant comorbidities that make the complications of respiratory acidosis particularly dangerous. By controlling peripheral pH with bicarbonate infusions, many of these potentially lethal effects can be lessened.

Clinical Manifestations

Clinical findings in respiratory acidosis are related to the degree and the duration of the respiratory acidosis and whether or not hypoxemia is present. Neurologic symptoms figure prominently in this disorder. A precipitous rise in P_{CO_2} can lead to confusion, anxiety, psychosis, asterixis, seizures, and myoclonic jerks, with progressive depression of the sensorium to coma at an arterial P_{CO_2} greater than 60 mm Hg (CO_2 narcosis). Hypercapnia has been shown to increase cerebral blood flow and volume. As a result, hypercapnia can lead to symptoms and signs reflecting elevated intracranial pressure, including headaches and papilledema. Other findings in acute respiratory acidosis include signs of catecholamine release, including skin flushing, diaphoresis, and increased cardiac contractility and output.

Symptoms of chronic hypercapnia include fatigue, lethargy, and confusion in addition to the findings seen in acute hypercapnia.

It can be difficult to distinguish the signs of hypercapnia from those of hypoxemia clinically, as the two often appear together. In many patients, however, the correction of hypoxemia does not improve the clinical picture: as a result, it can be surmised that hypercapnia is responsible for many of the findings seen.

Causes

The effect of acute respiratory acidosis on the CSF pH and the intracellular pH of brain cells is almost instantaneous, reflecting the ability of P_{CO_2} to cross the blood-brain barrier. However, the initial acidosis caused by elevated P_{CO_2} levels is compensated for more quickly in the CNS than in the periphery. The concentration of bicarbonate in the CSF rises within 1 hour, before the peripheral bicarbonate has changed significantly. It has been shown that within 1 day of sustained hypercarbia, the CSF pH returns to normal, with a bicarbonate level of 35 mmol/L, whereas the arterial pH remains acidotic. Both CSF and brain cells return to a normal pH significantly before systemic compensation is evident.

The primary mechanism by which the brain and CSF compensate for acute hypercapnia rests in an increase in bicarbonate concentration. It is now commonly believed that two mechanisms are largely responsible for this increase, called the *dual contribution theory*. The first is an increase in carbonic anhydrase activity in the cells of the choroid plexus, producing bicarbonate, which is then transported into the CSF. Second, it is believed that bicarbonate diffuses into the CSF from plasma as a result of the positive electrochemical gradient existing between the CSF and capillary blood. In hypercapnic states, the increase in cerebral blood flow secondary to the CO_2 vasodilatory effects would tend to decrease the production of lactic acid. In addition, intracellular bicarbonate could be released into the extracellular environment by a chloride shift into neurons similar to that occurring in red blood cells. And finally, increased ammonia production via the glutamine-α-ketoglutarate pathway during acute respiratory acidosis could buffer hydrogen ions via the creation of ammonium.

Possibilities for the intracellular increase in bicarbonate are carboxylation reactions producing CO_2, including those involving glucose metabolism and the conversion of glutamic acid to GABA. In addition, certain steps in glucose metabolism are pH-dependent, and CO_2-producing steps may be favored in intracellularly acidotic states.

Chronic hypercapnia is generally seen in patients as the result of chronic disease due to any of the causes discussed previously. These patients show a decreased ventilatory response to increased P_{CO_2}, decreased P_{O_2}, and increased hydrogen ion concentration. The slow time course of many of these diseases allows the kidney to compensate adequately as the disease progresses, increasing its excretion of hydrogen ion as ammonium and the generation and reabsorption of bicarbonate to restore systemic pH toward normal values. This process has been shown to take 3 days to take effect and is not maximal until 5 days after the onset of respiratory acidosis.

In acute respiratory acidosis, the peripheral and central chemoreceptors work in concert, both responding to increases in hydrogen ion concentrations to increase ventilation. However, with the rapid restoration of CSF pH to normal values, the stimulus for ventilation becomes entirely dependent on the peripheral chemoreceptors, which will sustain an increase in ventilation until renal compensation is complete.

Rx Treatment

Treatment of both chronic and acute respiratory acidosis is aimed primarily at correcting the underlying cause and ensuring adequate ventilation. Acute respiratory acidosis can be very dangerous, and measures to relieve severe hypoxemia and acidemia should be instituted immediately, including intubation and assisted mechanical ventilation if necessary.

Two complications can be seen in chronic respiratory acidosis patients as a result of renal compensation. In patients breathing spontaneously, oxygen should be carefully titrated; ventilation may be driven by hypoxemia, and correction of the hypoxemia can result in suppression of respiratory drive.

In patients with compensated chronic respiratory acidosis, rapid and complete correction of hypercapnia can also result in posthypercapnic alkalosis. Patients recovering from an acute-on-chronic respiratory acidosis should be monitored carefully to correct for hypokalemia, hypochloremia, and hypovolemia so that adequate renal excretion of bicarbonate can occur.

Bicarbonate therapy should not be considered for respiratory acidosis unless the pH falls below 7.1 and the patient is about to be intubated; in these cases, it can be used transiently until the patient is ventilated. There is also a role for bicarbonate therapy in patients with renal failure, in whom adequate compensatory acid excretion cannot take place.

RESPIRATORY ALKALOSIS

Respiratory alkalosis is characterized by a primary decrease in P_{CO_2} reflected in an increased arterial pH and variably decreased plasma bicarbonate concentration. It is most commonly the result of alveolar hyperventilation rather than underproduction of CO_2.

Alveolar hyperventilation leading to respiratory alkalosis may have multiple causes, including those secondary to hypoxemia, such as pulmonary disease, congestive heart failure, and high altitude living, or anemia. Direct stimulation of the medullary respiratory center can also result in hyperventilation, as seen in cortical hyperventilation resulting from anxiety or pain, as well as systemic conditions including endotoxemia, hepatic cirrhosis, salicylate intoxication, correction of metabolic acidosis, hyperthermia, and pregnancy. Mechanical ventilation is also a common cause of respiratory alkalosis.

Primary neurologic diseases have also been shown to stimulate alveolar hyperventilation. The causes include acute stroke, infection, trauma, and tumors. Two patterns of respiration are seen: central hyperventilation and Cheyne-Stokes respiration. Central hyperventilation associated with lesions at the pontine-midbrain level is regular but with increased rate and tidal volume, whereas Cheyne-Stokes breathing is characterized by periods of hyperventilation alternating with apnea in patients with bilateral cortical and upper pontine lesions and may be related to increased sensitivity of the respiratory center to P_{CO_2}.

This mechanism may contribute to the central sleep apnea associated with congestive heart failure and may respond to application of positive airway pressure.

Clinical Manifestations

The clinical manifestations of respiratory alkalosis depend on the degree and duration of the condition but are primarily those of the underlying disorder. Symptoms of acute hypocapnia are largely attributable to the alkalemia and include dizziness, perioral or extremity paresthesias, confusion, asterixis, hypotension, seizures, and coma. Most symptoms are manifested only when the PCO_2 has fallen below 25 or 30 mmHg and can be related to decreased cerebral blood flow or to reduced free calcium (since alkalosis increases calcium's protein-bound fraction). Some symptoms frequently seen in the hyperventilation syndrome secondary to pain or anxiety do not appear to be related to hypocapnia and include shortness of breath and chest wall pain. Chronic hypocapnia does not appear to be associated with significant clinical symptoms.

Cerebral blood flow is significantly decreased by hypocapnia, which is a potent vasoconstrictor. This phenomenon is used clinically to decrease intracranial pressure by hyperventilating patients with cerebral edema. Renal compensation over 36 to 72 hours returns systemic pH to normal values and restores cerebral blood flow to normal.

As in respiratory acidosis, the CNS is immediately affected by decreases in systemic PCO_2 because of the blood-brain barrier's permeability to CO_2. And as in respiratory acidosis, the CSF and intracellular pH show an initial short-lived response that parallels the systemic increase in pH.

Acute hypocapnia results in an initial increase in the pH of both the CSF and the brain's intracellular environment. However, this increase is quickly offset by a decrease in bicarbonate levels. In acute respiratory alkalosis, one of the primary mechanisms of this fall in bicarbonate appears to be the generation of lactate. The mechanism of this increase in lactate both in the CSF and intracellularly is thought to arise from tissue hypoxia secondary to cerebral vasoconstriction and increased hemoglobin affinity for oxygen. Alkalosis produces a transient left shift in the hemoglobin-oxygen dissociation curve via its effects on 2,3-DPG in red blood cells, decreasing delivery of oxygen to brain cells. Increased phosphofructokinase activity in brain cells may also contribute to increased lactate production. The combination of increased oxygen demand and decreased oxygen delivery may contribute to adverse clinical outcomes in hypocapnic alkalosis.

Chronic respiratory alkalosis can be seen in patients with chronic conditions due to any of these causes. As previously discussed, CNS compensation for this alkalosis occurs within hours. Chronic respiratory alkalosis does not appear to have a distinct symptomatology.

Renal compensation for sustained hypocapnia is complete in 36 to 72 hours. The mechanism rests primarily in the kidney's net reduction of hydrogen ion excretion, which it accomplishes largely by decreasing ammonium and titratable acid excretion. The threshold for bicarbonate excretion is also lowered, resulting in bicarbonaturia. As a result, systemic bicarbonate levels decrease, and arterial pH returns toward normal values.

Causes

Because of the many possible causes of respiratory alkalosis, the effects of this condition on the responses of the central and peripheral chemoreceptors are variable. Primary stimulation of the central chemoreceptor is a common cause of respiratory alkalosis, as seen in cortical hyperventilation, endotoxemia, and pregnancy. In these cases, the signals from central and peripheral chemoreceptors will be in opposition to each other, with central signals overriding peripheral input until the primary stimulus is removed. However, in cases in which the primary stimulus is the result of systemic conditions such as hypoxia secondary to pulmonary disease or anemia, the peripheral and central chemoreceptors initially receive similar signals to reduce ventilation from an increase in both peripheral and CSF pH. However, the CSF pH returns quickly to normal values, at which point the stimulus is derived solely from the peripheral

chemoreceptors, which will act to reduce hyperventilation until renal compensation is complete.

Adaptation to High Altitude

The respiratory response to high altitude is complex. Acute exposure to high altitude results in hypoxia-induced hyperventilation. Compensation requires at least several days to take effect and is characterized by a gradual increase in hyperventilation. The result of this continuing increased hyperventilation is a steadily decreasing PCO_2 and increasing PO_2 over this period. It is thought that this phenomenon may be the result of conflicting signals from peripheral and central chemoreceptors. The effect of the hypoxic stimulus to ventilate is initially modulated by the effects of alkalosis, both peripherally and centrally. However, as bicarbonate in the CSF falls, inhibition of the central stimulus to ventilate decreases. Therefore, the changing balance between hypoxemia, alkalosis, and CSF pH in adaptation to high altitude may be responsible for this gradual increase in hyperventilation over time. Once a steady state is achieved, the drive to ventilate is determined by the effects of hypoxemia and alkalemia on the peripheral chemoreceptors.

 Treatment

Treatment of respiratory alkalosis must address the underlying cause of the disturbance. Hyperventilation syndrome is a diagnosis of exclusion, but patients who exhibit symptoms, such as tetany and syncope, and do not have more serious causes of hyperventilation, can be treated with a rebreathing mask. Hypophosphatemia can be seen in these patients, but it usually improves with treatment of the alkalosis. Patients with respiratory alkalosis associated with mountain sickness can be pretreated with acetazolamide to induce a metabolic acidosis, thereby preventing extreme elevation of pH.

SUGGESTED READINGS

Calabrese AT, Coley KC, DaPos SV, et al: Evaluation of prescribing practices: Risk of lactic acidosis with metformin therapy. Arch Intern Med 2002;162:434–437. *Renal insufficiency and the concomitant administration of cationic agents were risk factors for lactic acidosis.*

Claessens YE, Chiche JD, Mira JP, et al: Bench-to-bedside review: Severe lactic acidosis in HIV patients treated with nucleoside analogue reverse transcriptase inhibitors. Crit Care 2003;7:226–232. *NRTIs can induce mitochondrial impairment that leads to a number of adverse events, including symptomatic lactic acidosis.*

De Backer D: Lactic acidosis. Intensive Care Med 2003;29:699–702. *An updated reiew.*

Galla JH: Metabolic Alkalosis. *In* DuBose TD Jr, Hamm LL (eds): Acid-Base and Electrolyte Disorders: A Companion to Brenner and Rector's The Kidney. Philadelphia, Saunders, 2002, pp 109–128. *A detailed chapter.*

Gauthier PM, Szerlip HM: Metabolic acidosis in the intensive care unit. Crit Care Clin 2002;18:289–308. *An approach to diagnosis and therapy.*

Hayes JB, Seifter JL: Acid-Base Disorders and the CNS. *In* Noseworthy JH (ed): Neurological Therapeutics: Principles and Practice. London, Martin Dunitz, 2003. *A comprehensive overview.*

Laffey JG, Kavanagh BP: Medical progress: Hypocapnia. N Engl J Med 2002;347:43–53. *A practical review of pathogenesis, diagnosis, and therapy.*

Moviat M, van Haren F, van der Hoeven H: Conventional or physicochemical approach in intensive care unit patients with metabolic acidosis. Crit Care 2003;7:R41–R45. *There was an excellent relation between the strong ion gap and the albumin-corrected and lactate-corrected anion gap, so calculation of the more time-consuming strong ion gap according to Stewart was unnecessary.*

Rodriguez Soriano J: Renal tubular acidosis: The clinical entity. J Am Soc Nephrol 2002;13:2160–2170. *A practical overview.*

114 PHOSPHORUS DEFICIENCY AND HYPOPHOSPHATEMIA

Wadi N. Suki

Phosphorus is an integral constituent of all body tissues. It is a component of hydroxyapatite, the main crystalline structure of bone, and a component of the phospholipids in all cell membranes. It is a constituent of nucleotides and furnishes the backbone of DNA. It is also a component of the second messengers cyclic adenosine monophosphate and cyclic guanosine monophosphate. Enzymes are activated after phosphorylation by kinases. As a component of 2,3-diphosphoglycerate, phosphorus facilitates the release of oxygen to tissues from oxyhemoglobin. In adenosine triphosphate (ATP) and creatine phosphate, it serves as an energy store. In the urine, phosphate is an important buffer to facilitate the excretion of urinary acid.

NORMAL PHOSPHORUS METABOLISM

More than 700 g (22 mol) of phosphorus is present in an average-sized adult: 80% of the total phosphorus is present in bone; 10% is present in skeletal muscle. In muscle cells and in other cells, phosphate in the form of phospholipids, phosphoproteins, and phosphosugars represents the major intracellular anion and is present in a concentration of approximately 100 mmol/L of cell water.

In the extracellular fluid, phosphorus is present in a concentration of 4.0 to 7.0 mg/dL in children and 2.7 to 4.5 mg/dL in adults. Phosphate in blood is mostly free (10% is protein bound) and is present in two ionic forms, dibasic (HPO_4^{2-}) and monobasic ($H_2PO_4^{-}$), the relative amounts of which vary with the blood pH, being present in a ratio of 4:1 at pH 7.4. The phosphate concentration in blood must be expressed in millimoles (0.9 to 1.5 mmol/L in adults and 1.4 to 2.2 mmol/L in children) rather than in milliequivalents (which would vary with blood pH).

Depending on the composition of the diet, the average adult in the United States consumes 800 to 1500 mg of phosphorus daily, derived primarily from dairy products and meat. Most ingested phosphorus is absorbed, and except in growing children, most is excreted in the urine. Urinary excretion depends on glomerular filtration and tubular reabsorption, with only 12% of the filtered load being excreted in the urine. Intestinal absorption of phosphate is augmented by the active metabolites of vitamin D, whereas renal tubular absorption is inhibited by parathyroid hormone and by the newly discovered phosphatonins.

HYPOPHOSPHATEMIA

Moderate or severe hypophosphatemia is seen in approximately 2% of hospitalized patients.

Etiology

Hypophosphatemia may result from a shift of phosphorus into cells, in which case body phosphorus stores are normal. Alternatively, hypophosphatemia may be associated with depleted total body stores resulting from poor dietary intake, reduced gastrointestinal absorption, or increased renal losses (Table 114–1).

Hypophosphatemia may be sustained or may be transient. Transient hypophosphatemia is seen after the ingestion of carbohydrates and is caused by the phosphorylation of sugars before they enter the body cells, or it is seen in respiratory alkalosis, wherein alkalinization of the cytosol activates phosphofructokinase and intracellular glycolysis and increases the formation of phosphorylated sugars. Decreased serum phosphorus without depleted total body stores also is seen after parathyroidectomy (hungry bone syndrome) wherein phosphorus, with calcium, is deposited in bone.

MODERATE HYPOPHOSPHATEMIA. Carbohydrate administration and respiratory alkalosis cause moderate hypophosphatemja (serum phosphorus, 1 to 2.5 mg/dL). Other disorders that result in moderate hypophosphatemia may be classified into disorders that increase renal losses of phosphate, decrease intestinal absorption of phosphate, or increase extracorporeal loss of phosphate, such as in hemodialysis against a phosphate-free dialysate. Renal losses of phosphate are increased when tubular absorption is depressed, as seen in hyperparathyroidism (Chapter 260), oncogenic hypophosphatemic osteomalacia, expansion of the extracellular fluid volume, administration of alkali or glucocorticoids, hypomagnesemia and magnesium depletion, and renal tubular defects such as Fanconi's syndrome (Chapter 122), or familial hypophosphatemic rickets (Chapter 259). Reduced intestinal absorption may be caused by drastically reduced intake, malabsorption, vitamin D deficiency, and use of phosphate-binding antacids. Moderate hypophosphatemia only causes osteomalacia.

SEVERE HYPOPHOSPHATEMIA. Severe hypophosphatemia (serum phosphorus, <1 mg/dL) causes serious systemic manifestations that

Table 114–1 • CLASSIFICATION OF HYPOPHOSPHATEMIA

TRANSIENT HYPOPHOSPHATEMIA WITH NORMAL BODY STORES
Ingestion of carbohydrates
Respiratory alkalosis
Hungry bone syndrome

SUSTAINED HYPOPHOSPHATEMIA WITH REDUCED BODY STORES
Moderate hypophosphatemia
  Depressed tubular absorption
  Hyperparathyroidism
  Expanded ECF volume
  Alkali administration
  Glucocorticoids
  Magnesium depletion
  Fanconi's syndrome
  Oncogenic hypophosphatemic osteomalacia
  Familial hypophosphatemic rickets
  Reduced intestinal absorption
  Reduced intake
  Malabsorption
  Vitamin D deficiency
  Phosphate-binding antacids
  Extracorporeal losses—dialysis
Severe hypophosphatemia
  Prolonged use of phosphate-binding antacids
  Parenteral alimentation
  Nutritional recovery syndrome
  Recovery phase of severe burns
  Severe respiratory alkalosis
  Poorly controlled diabetes mellitus
  Alcoholism and alcohol withdrawal

ECF = extracellular fluid.

demand prompt attention and correction. The most common causes of this disorder are prolonged use of phosphate-binding antacids, hyperalimentation, nutritional recovery syndrome, recovery from severe burns, severe respiratory alkalosis, poorly controlled diabetes mellitus, and alcoholism and alcohol withdrawal syndrome. Phosphate-binding compounds, such as aluminum and magnesium oxides, bind phosphate in the intestinal lumen and impair its absorption. Excess use of these compounds by patients with peptic ulcer disease or by patients with chronic renal failure who are treated with these compounds to prevent hyperphosphatemia results in phosphate depletion. Enteral and parenteral alimentation, if not supplemented with phosphate, also can result in phosphate depletion. The administered glucose and amino acids increase urinary phosphate excretion and when taken up by tissue cells consume phosphate.

Overzealous refeeding of severely malnourished subjects also may result in phosphate deficiency and deficiency of thiamine and of potassium. In the case of severely burned subjects, healing results in reabsorption of the edema fluid and consequent diuresis, which may be responsible for substantial renal phosphate loss. As new tissue is rebuilt, phosphate is taken up by the newly formed cells, aggravating the depletion of body phosphate stores. In contrast to metabolic alkalosis, which may result in a modest decrease in serum phosphorus, prolonged vigorous hyperventilation and respiratory alkalosis can result in profound hypophosphatemia. Urinary phosphate excretion in respiratory alkalosis is extremely low, whereas phosphate excretion in metabolic alkalosis is increased. In poorly controlled diabetes mellitus, the glucosuria and resulting osmotic diuresis increase urinary phosphate loss. Acetoacetate and β-hydroxybutyrate also increase urinary phosphate loss. Finally, the acidosis per se increases urinary phosphate loss. Serum phosphorus is not generally depressed when poorly controlled diabetics are evaluated initially, however, probably because phosphate shifts to the extracellular compartment from the intracellular space. The hypophosphatemia is manifested only after starting therapy with insulin and intravenous fluids.

In alcoholics, hypophosphatemia and phosphate depletion are caused by multiple factors: the phosphaturic effects of ethanol and magnesium depletion, poor dietary intake, and ketoacidosis. Other contributing factors include vomiting, diarrhea, and the use of phosphate-binding antacids.

Table 114–2 • MANIFESTATIONS OF HYPOPHOSPHATEMIA

SYMPTOMS AND SIGNS	COMMENTS
CENTRAL NERVOUS SYSTEM	
Symptoms and signs of metabolic encephalopathy	Irritability, malaise, ataxia, seizures, coma
NEUROMUSCULAR	
Generalized muscle weakness or paralysis	Ventilatory insufficency, respiratory failure
Rhabdomyolysis	Increased creatine kinase. Large muscle tenderness; may mask underlying hypophosphatemia
Cardiac muscle dysfunction	Congestive cardiomyopathy
HEMATOLOGIC	
Altered red blood cell function	Depleted 2,3-DPG shifts oxyhemoglobin dissociation curve to the left and impairs tissue oxygen delivery. Depleted ATP increases intracellular calcium, causing hemolysis
Impaired leukocyte function	Impaired leukotaxis, phagocytosis, and bactericidal activity, susceptibility to infection
Impaired platelet aggregation	Bleeding tendency affecting lips and oral mucosa
BONE	
Bone resorption, osteomalacia, increased 1α-hydroxylation of vitamin D	Increased calcium absorption, mild increase in serum calcium, depressed PTH secretion, marked renal hypercalciuria
RENAL	
Impaired tubular function	Increased urine calcium and magnesium, renal glucosuria, decreased ammoniagenesis, metabolic acidosis
LIVER	
Transient hyperbilirubinemia	
METABOLISM	
Hypoglycemia	

2,3D-PG = 2,3-diphosphoglycerate; ATP = adenosine triphosphate; PTH = parathyroid hormone.

Clinical Manifestations

Severe hypophosphatemia alters cell membrane composition and function, depletes intracellular phosphorylated compounds such as ATP and 2,3-diphosphoglycerate, and increases intracellular calcium (Table 114–2). This constellation of disorders results in disturbed function of multiple body systems.

Rx Treatment

When total body phosphorus stores are normal, phosphate supplementation is unnecessary (Table 114–3). When body phosphate stores are reduced, urinary losses need to be minimized, gastrointestinal absorption needs to be enhanced, and phosphate supplements may be necessary. To replete body phosphorus stores, 1000 to 2000 mg of phosphorus may need to be supplemented daily for 2 weeks. Whenever phosphate replacement is given, serum calcium, magnesium, phosphorus, and electrolytes should be monitored closely. Complications of administering phosphate include diarrhea (after oral administration), hypocalcemia, metastatic calcification, hypotension, hyperkalemia and/or hypernatremia, and metabolic acidosis.

SUGGESTED READINGS

Kumar R: New insights into phosphate homeostasis: Fibroblast growth factor and frizzled-related protein-4 are phosphaturic factors derived from tumors associated with osteomalacia. Curr Opin Nephrol Hypertens 2002;11:547–553. *The study of oncogenic osteomalacia has led to the discovery of a new class of regulators of renal tubular phosphate handling.*

Subramanian R, Khardori R: Severe hypophosphatemia: Pathophysiologic implications, clinical presentations, and treatment. Medicine (Baltimore) 2000;79:1–8. *A well-referenced review of the clinical disorders of phosphate and their pathophysiology, manifestations, and treatment.*

Weisbord SD, Chaudhuri A, Blauth K, et al: Monoclonal gammopathy and spurious hypophosphatemia. Am J Med Sci 2003;325:98–100. *Unusually low plasma phosphate concentrations in patients without symptoms or clinically apparent causes of hypophosphatemia suggest a monoclonal gammopathy.*

Table 114–3 • MANAGEMENT OF HYPOPHOSPHATEMIA

STATUS	TREATMENT	DOSE
NORMAL BODY PHOSPHORUS STORES		
Transient hypophosphatemia	Treat underlying disorder	No phosphate replacement
REDUCED BODY PHOSPHORUS STORES		
Moderate hypophosphatemia	Minimze urinary losses, reduce sodium diuresis, enhance gastrointestinal absorption, discontinue phosphate binders	
	If patient capable of oral intake: high-phosphate foods (e.g., skimmed cow's milk [contains 1 mg phosphorus/mL])	
	Oral supplements: Sodium salt	
	Potassium salt (potassium not contraindicated or desirable)	Phospho-Soda, 750 mg phosphorus/5 mL
		Neutra-Phos, 250 mg phosphorus/capsule with 7 mEq of potassium: Neutra-Phos K, 250 mg; phosphorus/capsule with 14 mEq of potassium: K-Phos, 150 mg; phosphorus/tablet with 3.65 mEq potassium, or K-Phos Neutral, 250 mg phosphorus with 2 mEq potassium
Severe hypophosphatemia		
Patient incapable of oral/enteral intake or with organ manifestations of phosphorus depletion	Parenteral	Phosphorus 2.5–5 mg/kg body weight (0.08–0.16 mmol/kg) infused over 6 hr repeated every 6 hr until serum phosphorus is 2.0–25 mg/dL
Hypocalcemic patient, renal failure patient		Lower dose than above

115 DISORDERS OF MAGNESIUM METABOLISM

Wadi N. Suki

Magnesium is the second most prevalent intracellular cation after potassium and the fourth most abundant in the human body after calcium, potassium, and sodium. As an integral part of reactions involving adenosine triphosphate (ATP), magnesium plays a crucial role in many enzymatic reactions and transport processes and in the synthesis of protein, DNA, and RNA.

NORMAL MAGNESIUM METABOLISM

Most of the body's 2000 mEq of magnesium is present in the skeleton and in soft tissue, with only 1% present in extracellular fluid. In plasma, magnesium concentration is maintained between 1.6 and 2.0 mEq/L by a balance between absorption from the intestine (primarily the small intestine) and renal excretion. The average American diet provides 250 to 350 mg of magnesium daily (mostly from grains, nuts, milk, and green leafy vegetables), of which 25 to 60% is absorbed. The kidneys filter 70 to 80% of plasma magnesium (fraction not bound to protein) but excrete only 2% to 3% of the filtered load (100 mg/day); the rest is reabsorbed primarily in the thick ascending limb of Henle's loop and to a lesser extent in the proximal and distal convoluted tubules. The kidneys are able to conserve magnesium greatly when magnesium intake or intestinal absorption is reduced.

MAGNESIUM DEPLETION

Magnesium deficiency usually is manifested by hypomagnesemia, but a deficiency state may exist with a normal serum magnesium level. Hypomagnesemia has been reported in 10% of patients admitted to a general hospital and in 60% of patients in the intensive care unit.

Etiology

Magnesium depletion results from decreased intestinal absorption or increased fecal losses, increased renal losses, or losses in other body fluids (Table 115–1). Increased loss of magnesium-containing gastrointestinal secretions can result in magnesium depletion, as would be seen with nasogastric suction, in severe diarrhea, or in intestinal or biliary fistulas. Magnesium losses are particularly severe in conditions associated with steatorrhea wherein the stool losses may exceed the intake of magnesium as a result of the formation of insoluble magnesium salts of fatty acids. In these disorders, the incidence of hypomagnesemia may be 30 to 40%. Markedly decreased intake, as in protein-calorie malnutrition, or decreased absorption secondary to small bowel resection or to an inborn error of metabolism also may cause magnesium depletion. Increased renal losses of magnesium are seen in conditions characterized by vigorous diuresis as after renal transplantation or relief of urinary tract obstruction or in the diuretic phase of acute tubular necrosis. Specific tubular defects resulting in magnesium wasting are seen occasionally, most often heredofamilial. The best known of these are Bartter's syndrome (seen mostly in infancy and childhood), which is caused by a defect in the thick ascending limb of Henle, and Gitelman's syndrome (seen in children and in adults), which is caused by a defect in the distal convoluted tubule. Defects in the apical Na,K,2Cl transporter or potassium channel, the basilar chloride channel, or the paracellular tight junction protein, paracellin-1, of the thick ascending limb have been identified in patients with hypomagnesemia, hypokalemia, and hypercalciuria, generally referred to as *Bartter's syndrome.* Defects in the thiazide-sensitive sodium-chloride cotransporter or in the gamma subunit of Na^+,K^+-ATPase in the distal convoluted tubule have been identified in patients with hypomagnesemia and hypokalemia but with hypocalciuria, generally referred to as *Gitelman's syndrome.*

Extrinsic factors causing renal wasting of magnesium include volume expansion, hypercalcemia, and diabetic ketoacidosis. Most important are drugs, such as the thick ascending limb–inhibiting and the distal convoluted tubule–inhibiting diuretics (e.g., furosemide and hydrochlorothiazide). Other drugs causing excessive renal magnesium loss are the antimicrobials pentamidine and amphotericin B, the aminoglycosides, the immunosuppressants cyclosporine and tacrolimus, and the oncolytic agent cisplatin and, to a lesser extent, its analogue carboplatin.

Other causes of magnesium loss are lactation and losses from burned skin surfaces. Alcoholism causes renal tubular wasting of magnesium, which when coupled with decreased dietary intake, loss in diarrheic stools, and sequestration in the pancreatic bed in cases of pancreatitis results in hypomagnesemia that is seen in 30% of hospitalized alcoholics. Redistribution of magnesium to tissues in hyperthyroidism or to bone in the hungry bone state that follows parathyroidectomy causes hypomagnesemia but without total body deficit.

Clinical Manifestations

The symptoms of hypomagnesemia, when they occur, consist of weakness, anorexia, cardiac arrhythmias, tetany, and seizures. The Chvostek and Trousseau signs may be present. These manifestations are also those of hypokalemia and of hypocalcemia, which frequently accompany hypomagnesemia. Hypokalemia occurs in 40 to 60% of patients and is thought to result from the opening of the luminal potassium channels in the cells of the distal nephron and the secretion of potassium into the tubular fluid. These channels normally are inhibited by ATP, and in the presence of deficient intracellular magnesium, ATP is less effective. Hypocalcemia results from three main causes. Moderate hypomagnesemia (<1 mEq/L or 1.2 mg/dL) results in resistance to the osteolytic action of parathyroid hormone (PTH). More severe hypomagnesemia suppresses PTH secretion so that in the face of hypocalcemia PTH level is low or normal instead of being elevated. The infusion of magnesium in these patients results in a sharp rise in PTH levels (whereas in normal individuals magnesium would lower PTH level similar to calcium). The last factor contributing to the hypocalcemia is a low level of calcitriol, the active form of vitamin D.

Rx Diagnosis and Treatment

In the presence of hypomagnesemia, it is safe to assume the presence of magnesium depletion. Magnesium excretion of less than 30 mg or a fractional excretion of less than 2% of the filtered magnesium (only 70 to 80% of the plasma magnesium is filterable) indicates extrarenal losses. Magnesium excretion in excess of these values indicates renal wasting. All measures must be taken to correct the underlying disorder. Asymptomatic patients may be treated with diet or with oral supplements of magnesium oxide, magnesium chloride, or magnesium lactate. Patients who are symptomatic or exhibit hypocalcemia or hypokalemia must be treated

Table 115–1 • CAUSES OF HYPOMAGNESEMIA

Gastrointestinal	
Increased losses	Malabsorption syndromes with steatorrhea
	Severe diarrhea and purgation
	Intestinal and biliary fistulas
Decreased absorption	Primary intestinal hypomagnesemia (neonatal)
	Small bowel resection
Decreased intake	Protein-calorie malnutrition
Renal	
Intrinsic	Gitelman's syndrome
	Bartter's syndrome
	Post-transplantation diuresis
	Postobstructive diuresis
	Diuretic phase of acute renal failure
Extrinsic	Volume expansion
	Hypercalcemia
	Diabetic ketoacidosis
	Diuretics
	Therapeutic agents
Body fluid losses	Lactation
	Burns
Miscellaneous	Alcoholism
	Thyrotoxicosis
	Postparathyroidectomy (hungry bone)

with parenteral (intramuscular or intravenous) 50% MgSO$_4$·7H$_2$O, which provides 1 g or 8 mEq in every 2 mL. A dose of 32 to 64 mEq over a 24-hour period is recommended. In patients experiencing a cardiac arrhythmia, tetany, or seizure, the rate of administration of magnesium may be accelerated so that half the total dose is given over 4 to 6 hours. Because the sudden increase in the serum magnesium concentration inhibits renal absorption of magnesium, half the administered dose is excreted in the urine. Consequently the dose of magnesium that is administered must be repeated over 2 to 3 days to replete fully the body deficit. Even patients with unexplained hypocalcemia or hypokalemia but without hypomagnesemia should be given a trial of parenteral magnesium therapy. The administration of magnesium to patients having an acute myocardial infarction has been shown in a large clinical trial to be without benefit, however.

HYPERMAGNESEMIA

Because elevation of the serum magnesium efficiently inhibits the reabsorption of magnesium in the thick ascending limb, hypermagnesemia is encountered almost exclusively in patients with renal insufficiency or patients who have received large doses of magnesium orally (Epsom salt), intravenously (e.g., in the treatment of preeclampsia), or per rectum (magnesium sulfate enema). In patients with impaired renal function, the use of magnesium-containing antacids or cathartics is contraindicated. Mild hypermagnesemia is encountered in other disorders such as hypothyroidism, adrenal insufficiency, acromegaly, tumor lysis syndrome, and familial hypocalciuric hypercalcemia.

Clinical Manifestations

Symptoms and signs of hypermagnesemia begin at a level of 4 mEq/L when deep tendon reflexes begin to be depressed, and they disappear at 6 mEq/L. At levels of 10 to 15 mEq/L, narcosis, respiratory muscle paralysis, quadriplegia, hypotension, and cardiac conduction defects are seen. Besides the hypermagnesemia, laboratory tests show hypocalcemia.

Rx Treatment

To antagonize the neuromuscular toxicity of hypermagnesemia, calcium chloride or calcium gluconate in a dose of 100 to 200 mg of elemental calcium may be given intravenously. In patients with adequate renal function, the intravenous infusion of isotonic saline solutions with loop-acting diuretics accelerates the renal elimination of magnesium. The most efficient treatment in critically ill patients, especially if renal function is impaired, is hemodialysis with a magnesium-free dialysate.

SUGGESTED READINGS
Cole DE, Quamme GA: Inherited disorders of renal magnesium handling. J Am Soc Nephrol 2000;11:1937–1947. *A current and authoritative review of a field in which much progress has been made in recent years.*
Dacey MJ: Hypomagnesemic disorders. Crit Care Clin 2001;17:155–173. *This article discusses magnesium deficit from the critical care perspective.*
Topf JM, Murray PT: Hypomagnesemia and hypermagnesemia. Rev Endocr Metab Disord 2003;4:195–206. *A practical review.*

116 ACUTE RENAL FAILURE

William E. Mitch

Acute renal failure (ARF) is defined as the deterioration of renal function occurring over a period of hours to days. Unfortunately, there is no uniformly accepted description of ARF, and this has to be considered when evaluating articles and clinical trials. Some use an increase of serum creatinine concentration by more than 50% or greater than 0.5 mg/dL above baseline, whereas others define it as a need for dialysis. In addition, terms such as *acute tubular necrosis* may be used to define ARF even when there is no pathologic diagnosis of tubular necrosis.

The serious clinical problems associated with an acute loss of kidney function arise from the patient's limited capacity to achieve a balance between the intake and excretion of water and minerals and the accumulation of metabolic byproducts (chiefly from protein) leading to the symptoms of uremia. Some of the complications of ARF include pulmonary edema, hyponatremia, hyperkalemia, acidosis, hyperphosphatemia, anorexia, nausea, vomiting, and other uremic symptoms. The severity of these complications depends on how much function is lost and on how successfully the treatment plan keeps a patient close to a zero balance between intake and excretion. When compared with chronic renal failure (CRF) (Chapter 117), the consequences of ARF are invariably more severe because patients with ARF have not had time to activate adaptive mechanisms that act to blunt the consequences of water and electrolyte imbalance and the accumulation of waste products.

Scope of the Problem

Some degree of ARF can be found in 2 to 5% of hospitalized patients, usually as a complication of other illnesses, surgery, or both; the incidence rises to 4 to 15% after cardiopulmonary bypass. How serious is ARF? It is associated with a 35 to 65% mortality, but this mainly depends on the presence of other diseases causing or associated with ARF and the complications of these diseases. Kidney failure has a lower impact because dialysis can substitute for kidney function. In fact, despite the almost universal availability of dialysis, only in obstetric patients with ARF has a sharp decline in mortality to about 1.2% been achieved. The reasons for a persistently high mortality is unknown, but it cannot be blamed on loss of kidney function alone. Undoubtedly, the serious illnesses associated with ARF (e.g., sepsis) and especially the degree of hypercatabolism occurring in ARF patients are important factors; mortality rates are higher in older patients and in those with more severe renal damage or serious underlying disorders (e.g., infection, cancer).

A Systematic Approach to Understanding the Cause of ARF

Understanding why a patient develops an acute decline in kidney function is crucial because some conditions are remediable (Table 116–1). First, it must be remembered that patients with ARF have impaired function of *both* kidneys (unless the patient initially has only one functioning kidney). This concept is emphasized because few or no clinical signs of renal insufficiency are seen in subjects with only one kidney or those who have donated a kidney for transplantation.

The steps in a systematic approach are shown in Table 116–2. A systematic approach yields information allowing the genesis of ARF to be classified into one of three categories: prerenal hemodynamic abnormalities, postrenal obstruction, or intrarenal intrinsic damage. Understanding the pathophysiology of each cause helps establish the diagnosis. The key is a careful examination of the urine sediment to identify signs of intrinsic damage to kidney cells. For this reason, the first step is to collect a urine sample to evaluate renal function. Subsequently, a bladder catheter should be placed to exclude obstructing lesions in the urethra or bladder (the urine is obtained first to avoid diagnostic problems caused by catheter-induced urethral or bladder trauma, such as hematuria).

PRERENAL ACUTE RENAL FAILURE

A frequent cause of ARF in hospitalized patients is related to decreased perfusion of the kidney leading to an accumulation of water and minerals (i.e., a positive balance) because of a reduced glomerular filtration rate (GFR) but normally functioning tubule cells. Prerenal ARF is not associated with histologic damage to the kidney and is often referred to as *prerenal azotemia* (azotemia means the accumulation of nitrogen-containing waste products). Prerenal azotemia can occur in several disorders (see Table 116–1). Because the GFR is low, the clearance of creatinine and urea is reduced, leading to higher serum values of creatinine and urea nitrogen (SUN). The pathophysiology depends on the function of undamaged kidney tubules that reabsorb filtered minerals, ions, and water leading to a lower urine flow rate and a reduced clearance of urea and other nitrogen-containing products that can be reabsorbed by the tubules. The crucial and therapeutically important point is that prerenal ARF is potentially reversible

Table 116–1 • CAUSES OF ACUTE RENAL FAILURE

PRIMARY DISORDER	CLINICAL EXAMPLES
Prerenal	
Hypovolemia	Hemorrhage, skin losses (burns, sweating), gastrointestinal losses (diarrhea, vomiting), renal losses (diuretics, glycosuria), extravascular pooling (peritonitis, burns)
Ineffective arterial volume	Congestive heart failure, cardiac arrhythmias, sepsis, anaphylaxis, liver failure
Arterial occlusion	Bilateral arterial thromboembolism, thromboembolism of a solitary kidney, aortic or renal artery aneurysm
Postrenal	
Ureteral obstruction	Bilateral or in a solitary kidney (calculi, neoplasm, clot, retroperitoneal fibrosis, iatrogenic)
Urethral obstruction	Prostatitis, clot, calculus, neoplasm, foreign object
Venous occlusion	Bilateral or a solitary kidney (renal vein thrombosis, neoplasm, iatrogenic)
Intrarenal/Intrinsic	
Vascular	Vasculitis, microangiopathy, malignant hypertension, vasopressors, eclampsia, hyperviscosity states, hypercalcemia, iodinated radiocontrast agents
Glomerulars	Acute glomerulonephritis
Tubular injury	
Ischemia	Profound hypotension, postrenal transplant, vasopressors, microvascular constriction, sepsis
Endogenous proteins	Hemoglobinuria, myoglobinuria, light chain myeloma
Intratubular crystals	Uric acid, oxalate, sulfonamides, phenazopyridine
Tubulointerstitial inflammation	Interstitial nephritis caused by drugs, infection, radiation
Nephrotoxins	Antibiotics (aminoglycosides, cephaloridine, amphotericin B); metals (mercury, bismuth, uranium, arsenic, silver, cadmium, iron, antimony); solvents (carbon tetrachloride, ethylene glycol, tetrachloroethylene); iodinated contrast agents; antineoplastic agents (bleomycin, cisplatin)

Table 116–2 • SYSTEMATIC APPROACH TO DIAGNOSING THE CAUSE OF ACUTE RENAL FAILURE

1. Medical history: clinical setting, medications
2. Physical examination: postural changes in blood pressure and evaluation of hemodynamic status, skin rash, signs of systemic diseases
3. Urinalysis with evaluation of sediment
4. Chemical analysis of blood and urine: serum bicarbonate, potassium, uric acid, calcium, phosphorus, urine osmolality, urine and serum urea, creatinine, sodium
5. Bladder catheterization
6. Fluid-diuretic challenge
7. Radiologic studies to exclude obstruction: ultrasonography, CT scan, or retrograde pyelography
8. Renal biopsy

because no histologic kidney damage has occurred. Fortunately, it is unusual for prerenal ARF to progress to intrinsic kidney damage if perfusion of the kidney is restored. The avoidance of intrinsic damage is due in large part to autoregulation, a response that preserves renal blood flow despite systolic blood pressure as low as 70 to 80 mm Hg. Although autoregulation depends on relaxation of the preglomerular arterioles, the mechanism of this phenomenon is still debated.

A particularly confusing term used to describe the genesis of prerenal ARF is a response to an "ineffective arterial volume." It is confusing because the obvious response is to expand extracellular volume, yet virtually all of these patients already have an expanded extracellular volume along with ARF. Specifically, in conditions such

as heart or liver failure, the patients usually have edema, ascites, or both, indicating expansion of the extracellular fluid volume, and consequently, additional expansion will not correct the underlying problem. A more appropriate term would be "ineffective kidney perfusion" because the kidneys are responding as though the blood and extracellular volumes were inadequate: glomerular filtration decreases and the tubules avidly reabsorb ions and minerals that are filtered, leading to expansion of the extracellular fluid volume. Because there is no evidence of histopathologic damage to kidneys of patients with ineffective arterial volume, the condition must involve a response to hormones or to physiologic factors, but no common mechanism has been identified to explain the findings in disorders shown in Table 116–1. Evidence of the normal functional capacity of these kidneys is the demonstration that kidneys obtained from patients with terminal ARF from liver failure can function normally when they are transplanted into patients with chronic kidney failure. Even though these observations are reassuring, there are certain prerenal conditions such as sepsis or anaphylaxis that can progress to cause histologic kidney damage. In addition, bilateral renal artery occlusion from emboli originating in the heart or from atheromas in the aorta (especially after difficult surgical procedures) can cause prerenal ARF, and if these lesions decrease blood flow to the kidneys sufficiently, sudden histologic damage to the kidney can occur because of ischemia.

To establish the presence of a prerenal disorder, the urine sediment examination is critical. Because there is no histologic damage to the tubules in prerenal ARF, no erythrocytes, inflammatory cells, or granular casts are present in the urine. Although a strict definition of prerenal ARF excludes patients with evidence of damage to the renal tubules, patients with established renal disease can develop heart failure or other calamities that decrease perfusion of the kidneys leading to a further loss of function. In this case, the diagnosis would be "acute-on-chronic" renal failure.

There are other tip-offs to the presence of prerenal ARF. One is the ratio of the blood urea nitrogen (BUN) to serum creatinine; the ratio in normal adults or in patients with uncomplicated CRF is approximately 10:1. When this ratio exceeds 10 to 1, there may be prerenal ARF. In this case, the BUN is excessively high (in relation to serum creatinine) because tubular function is unimpaired. The disorders in Table 116–1 promote avid reabsorption of filtered sodium and water to create a high concentration of urea in tubular fluid, thereby providing a concentration gradient to reabsorb urea and hence reduce its clearance. The reabsorption of water decreases urine flow, leading to the association between a low urine flow and decreased urea clearance (Fig. 116–1). It is critical to remember, however, that there are other causes of a high BUN-to-serum creatinine ratio, including gastrointestinal bleeding or consumption of excessive dietary protein by patients with renal insufficiency. (Note that in CRF patients as in normal adults, the ratio is usually 10 to 1.) Thus, the finding of a high BUN-to-serum creatinine ratio does not establish a diagnosis of prerenal ARF but should stimulate a vigorous search for other causes of a high ratio.

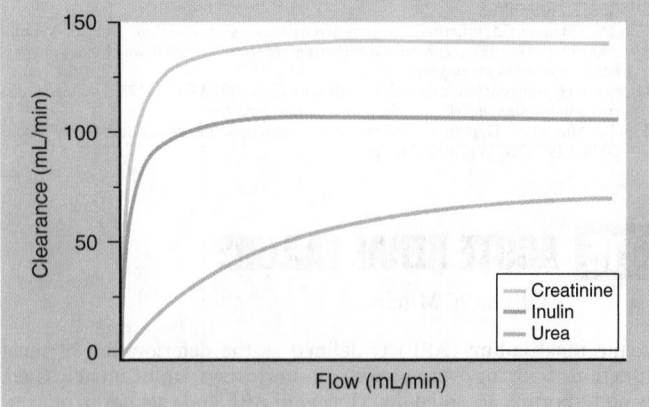

FIGURE 116–1 • The relationships between urine flow and renal clearance of creatinine, inulin (glomerular filtration rate), and urea are depicted schematically. The clearances of creatinine or inulin do not change when urine flow varies over a wide range, but the clearance of urea is lower when urine flow is low.

Table 116–3 • URINARY INDICES IN ACUTE RENAL FAILURE

LABORATORY TEST	PRERENAL	ACUTE TUBULAR INJURY
Urinary osmolality (mOsm/kg H_2O)	>500	<350
Urinary sodium (mEq/L)	<20	>40
Urinary/plasma creatinine ratio	>40	<20
Fractional sodium excretion*	<1	>1

$$*\frac{\text{Urine [Na]/serum [Na]}}{\text{Urine [creatinine]/serum [creatinine]}} \times 100.$$

Table 116–4 • CONDITIONS ASSOCIATED WITH FRACTIONAL SODIUM EXCRETION LESS THAN 1% DESPITE INTRINSIC RENAL DAMAGE

Intense Intrarenal Vasoconstriction
Liver disease
Congestive heart failure
Norepinephrine administration
Severe burns, sepsis
Nonsteroidal anti-inflammatory drugs
Acute bilateral ureteral obstruction
Iodinated radiocontrast agents

Vascular Inflammation
Acute glomerulonephritis
Acute vasculitis
Renal transplant rejection

Another tip-off to the presence of prerenal ARF is found in the "urine indices," or the urine osmolality, the sodium concentration in urine, and the fractional excretion of sodium (Table 116–4). The pathophysiology of prerenal azotemia includes reduced perfusion of the kidney, with high plasma levels of renin, aldosterone, and antidiuretic hormone resulting in avid tubular reabsorption of water and ions. The urine becomes concentrated (urine osmolality and creatinine concentration rise sharply) and contains small amounts of sodium (a urine sodium <10 mEq/L). The latter finding has been refined by correcting sodium excretion for the amount of functioning renal tissue (i.e., the fraction of filtered sodium that is excreted [FE_{Na}]). Because tubular function is intact, FE_{Na} is low (<1%) (Table 116–3). Like the BUN-to-serum creatinine ratio, however, a low FE_{Na} does not prove that a patient has prerenal ARF because a low FE_{Na} can be found in patients with heart failure and kidney damage or following toxic damage to the kidney (e.g., radiocontrast media).

POSTRENAL OBSTRUCTION

Bilateral ureteral obstruction can be caused by blood clots, calculi, or necrotic papillae (e.g., a complication of diabetes or analgesic nephropathy); neoplasms closing both ureters (e.g., retroperitoneal lymphoma); and iatrogenic factors affecting both of the ureters and/or the urethra. In obstructive nephropathy, it is possible that urine flow decreases rapidly or ceases, but the more usual occurrence is little or no abnormality in urine flow for the following reasons: (1) if only one kidney is obstructed, the other kidney will compensate for the loss; and (2) even if a solitary kidney is obstructed (or both kidneys are obstructed simultaneously), filtration continues and tubular pressure can rise to overcome the obstruction and restore urine flow.

The causes of postrenal ARF are listed in Table 116–1. In hospitalized patients with indwelling urinary catheters, the catheter must be checked for correct placement and its patency. Acute postrenal obstruction (like prerenal ARF) does not make the urine sediment abnormal unless a coexisting infection produces pyuria and bacteria. Because obstruction has no characteristic features, it should be excluded in all patients with ARF by ultrasonography (Chapter 121).

INTRARENAL HISTOLOGIC DAMAGE

The different types of acute vasculitis and glomerulonephritis fall in this category of ARF, as do scleroderma, malignant hypertension, eclampsia, and microangiopathies. Vascular damage in these disorders leads to infarction and/or ischemic damage to glomeruli. Glomerular inflammation (i.e., acute glomerulonephritis) (Chapter 119) also can cause ARF by sharply reducing blood flow to glomeruli, yielding reduced glomerular filtration. Finally, ischemic glomerular damage can result from the infusion of adrenergic agonists (e.g., norepinephrine) or the use of nonsteroidal anti-inflammatory drugs (NSAIDs) or iodinated radiocontrast agents (especially in patients with preexisting renal vasoconstriction associated with hypovolemia or diabetes).

Whenever glomerular damage occurs, it is reflected by abnormalities in clinical functioning of the kidney and in the urine. Since the kidney tubule cells are not damaged (or less severely damaged than glomeruli in disorders causing vasculitis), clinical abnormalities in renal function include a high BUN-to-creatinine ratio and a concentrated urine that contains very little sodium. Thus, these diseases also can cause a low FE_{Na} even though they are associated with kidney damage. Urinalysis reveals proteinuria, generally with hematuria; in classic cases, red blood cell casts are seen. Proteinuria and hematuria result from loss of the barrier function of the glomerular basement membrane. Urinary erythrocytes may appear to be irregular or crenated because their membranes are damaged, and hemoglobin is lost as erythrocytes pass through the inflamed glomerular capillaries.

Casts in the urine result from an aggregation of Tamm-Horsfall protein, which is exclusively secreted by cells of the ascending limb of the loop of Henle (plus protein filtered through the damaged glomerulus). Normal subjects constantly excrete Tamm-Horsfall protein, but when prerenal azotemia and a low urine flow coexist, Tamm-Horsfall proteins aggregate to form a cast of the tubule lumen and are excreted as hyaline casts. Thus, normal subjects with a low urine flow can form hyaline casts, and these do not signify histologic damage to the kidney. With ischemic glomerular damage from vasculitis involving smaller arteries, arterioles, or capillaries (Chapters 119 and 124) or with glomerulonephritis, erythrocytes passing through the damaged glomerulus are trapped in the aggregating Tamm-Horsfall protein. This produces red blood cell casts that are excreted when tubular fluid flow increases to flush them into the urine. Obviously, these casts signify histologic damage to the kidney.

The most common form of kidney damage causing ARF is damage to the renal tubules, often designated as *acute tubular necrosis* (ATN). Clinically, urine flow slows dramatically, and casts containing damaged tubular cells are formed. Although these tubular cell casts can be excreted, more commonly, blood flow in the kidney is sufficiently erratic that the tubular cell casts are not "flushed out" by erratic urine production and they remain in the kidney. Over time, the cells in these casts release enzymes that partially degrade the cells to form "coarsely granular casts" (Fig. 116–2). When these casts appear in the urine, they are often large and pigmented with a brownish color; this establishes the diagnosis. Note that if coarsely granular casts remain in the tubule for a prolonged period, the cellular debris continues to be degraded to form finely granular casts. Finally, if the injury is severe in ATN, red blood cells and inflammatory cells can be present in the urine.

Ischemic injury to the kidney can occur with hypotension during sepsis or surgery (especially in elderly patients), leading to tubular cell damage, and if ischemia is sufficiently severe, there may even be irreversible necrosis of the kidney cortex. Cells in the loop of Henle appear to be especially prone to ischemic damage because blood flow to this region of the kidney is low and if the high adenosine triphosphate (ATP) requirement of these cells is not met, they become necrotic. Other causes of ischemic damage include powerful vasoconstrictors (e.g., norepinephrine) and sepsis. Results from animal models of ATN suggest that tubule cell damage results not only from inadequate ATP production but also from the excessive production of reactive oxygen metabolites or "free radicals" released during oxidative processes. Free radicals are implicated because they can damage cell membranes directly. Free radical damage can be potentiated by enhanced expression of adhesion molecules (e.g., selectins and integrins) that stimulate the infiltration of leukocytes.

In view of the number of patients who experience hypotension from heart disease or during surgery, it is interesting that ATN does not occur more frequently. Presumably, the autoregulatory response protects the kidney. Alternative explanations are that tubular cell damage occurs but does not cause clinically significant abnormalities because the reserve capacity of the kidneys is sufficient to achieve water and mineral balance and excrete waste products (i.e., there is no increase in serum creatinine). It is also possible that hypovolemia

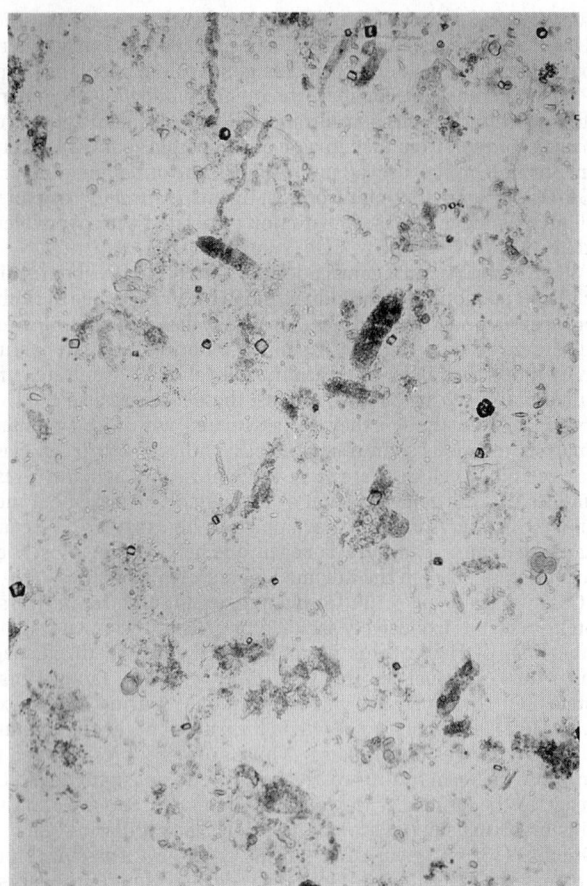

FIGURE 116–2 • The urine sediment of a patient with acute intrinsic renal failure from sepsis. Pigmented coarsely and finely granular casts of different size plus erythrocytes and clumps of cells are seen. The larger cells are probably renal tubular cells, and the crystals are talc from gloves worn to protect the examiner.

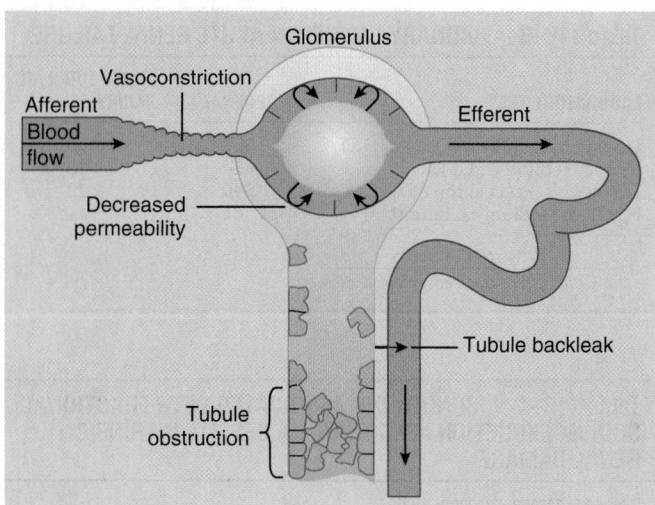

FIGURE 116–3 • Potential mechanisms causing oliguria in patients with acute renal failure.

and/or hypotension by itself is not sufficient to cause kidney damage unless one or more vasoactive agents (e.g., endothelin-1) that depress renal blood flow profoundly are released concomitantly. The need for a "second insult" is consistent with the widely held notion that acute tubular injury is usually clinically insignificant except in susceptible patients (e.g., the elderly or patients with infection or other serious illnesses). These considerations point out why there is no agreement about the pathophysiology of ATN.

Besides ischemia, renal tubular cells are susceptible to injury from nephrotoxic drugs, chemicals, and high levels of endogenous proteins that are filtered after hemolysis or muscle damage (i.e., hemoglobinuria and myoglobinuria, respectively) or certain proteins produced by multiple myeloma (i.e., the κ and γ light chains). Damage to renal tubules can also occur following occlusion of tubules by uric acid, oxalate, sulfonamide, or phenazopyridine hydrochloride (Pyridium) crystals. As a general rule, the kidney damage caused by filtration of toxic proteins or endogenous compounds is more severe in patients who are hypotensive or hypovolemic. Clinical manifestations are similar to ATN.

One reason that different types of chemicals, proteins, and other toxins cause damage to the kidney is that the nephrotoxic compound is concentrated in tubular fluid when water is reabsorbed. This establishes a concentration gradient to reabsorb the toxins by a passive process; there also can be transport mechanisms yielding reabsorption of a toxin into tubule cells. Once reabsorbed, the toxin impairs metabolic functions of the tubular cells and ultimately leads to their necrosis. Exogenous nephrotoxic agents include heavy metals (e.g., lead), certain antibiotics (e.g., aminoglycosides, cephaloridine, amphotericin), and chemotherapeutic drugs (e.g., cisplatin). Generally, nephrotoxicity occurs only when the blood level is high (from a high dose or with a "usual dose" in a patient with impaired drug clearance). The high blood level augments filtration of the toxin and,

ultimately, its reabsorption. There also are combinations of drugs (e.g., aminoglycosides and certain cephalothins, cisplatin plus an aminoglycoside) that can cause damage even with lower blood levels, presumably because of synergistic metabolic effects of the drugs on tubule cells. Nephrotoxic damage is more frequent in hypotensive or hypovolemic patients and in patients with impaired kidney function from other diseases. For example, radiocontrast agents are more likely to damage the kidneys of patients with diabetic nephropathy, systemic lupus erythematosus, or multiple myeloma.

Disorders causing interstitial nephritis also fall into the intrarenal damage classification. In these conditions, inflammatory cells (lymphocytes, mononuclear cells, and/or eosinophils) are present in the kidney interstitium when ARF results from immunologic or allergic damage. Whenever clinical findings suggest a hypersensitivity reaction (e.g., ARF associated with a rash following treatment with methicillin or allopurinol) or kidney infection, acute interstitial nephritis is likely to be present. Acute interstitial nephritis can cause a urinary sediment similar to that in Figure 116–2; more commonly, abundant polymorphonuclear leukocytes and especially eosinophils are found in the urine. Whenever acute interstitial nephritis is suspected, it has been suggested that a Hansel's stain rather than a Wright's stain of the urine sediment be made because it detects eosinophils more easily.

Clinical Manifestations

After there is damage to the kidney as in ATN, four factors depress renal function (Fig. 116–3): vasoconstriction, decreased glomerular permeability, tubular obstruction, and "backleak" of filtered fluid. Clinical evidence of recovery may not be observed for days or weeks (average, 10 to 14 days). The frequency of full recovery of function is most likely in younger individuals who have no serious complicating disease.

The most common problems in all cases of ARF are positive sodium and water balance causing weight gain and edema plus the problems associated with the accumulation of unexcreted waste products (i.e., uremia). Kidney pain is uncommon (except with acute pyelonephritis, urolithiasis, or tumors). In the early stages, serum creatinine and the SUN rise steadily, but their ratio should remain at 10:1 unless prerenal ARF is present or the patient has gastrointestinal bleeding, hypercatabolism, and/or excessive protein intake (or an excess of amino acids infused with hyperalimentation regimens). If renal function is stable, these possibilities can be resolved after an examination of the urine sediment and the collection of a 24-hour urine specimen. In the urine of patients in the prerenal classification, inflammatory cells, erythrocytes, or casts should not be present (Table 116–5). The 24-hour urine is used to measure urea and creatinine clearance (see Fig. 116–1). The ratio of the clearances of urea and creatinine should be about 0.6; patients in the prerenal category have a ratio of 0.3 or less. The 24-hour excretion of urea nitrogen is also used to assess why the SUN is high. If urea nitrogen excretion is greater than nitrogen intake, the extra nitrogen must have come from gastrointestinal bleeding or hypercatabolism. In short, a high SUN-to-serum creatinine ratio should always prompt a search for other causes inasmuch as the diagnosis of prerenal ARF is made only by excluding other causes.

It is often said that the serum creatinine should rise at a rate of about 1.0 to 2.0 mg/dL/day in ARF and that a more rapid rise means that the patient has myoglobinuric ARF. It is not wise to accept this guideline. The proposed standard rate of rise of 1 to 2 mg/dL/day was based on observations of injuries to Vietnam war soldiers who had varying degrees of kidney damage. In fact, the rise in serum creatinine depends on both the creatinine clearance and the rate of creatinine production. If renal failure is stable (i.e., body weight and serum creatinine are relatively constant), the 24-hour production rate of creatinine can be estimated from urinary creatinine excretion and compared with average values for patients of the same age and gender: in males, creatinine production per kilogram of ideal body weight is $28 - (0.2 \times$ age in years), whereas in females the value is $23.8 - (0.17 \times$ age in years). The maximal rate of rise in serum creatinine in a patient with no ability to clear creatinine can then be calculated as creatinine production divided by total body water ([0.6 ideal body weight] + weight from edema). If the rise in serum creatinine is higher than this value, myoglobinuria may be present.

Clinical problems caused by ARF include hyperkalemia and metabolic acidosis from impaired renal excretion of potassium and hydrogen ions, respectively. If no attention is given to maintaining water and sodium balances, hyponatremia will occur in ARF patients given too much water by mouth or as 5% dextrose in water intravenously, whereas excessive sodium intake will cause edema. In patients with more severe kidney damage, hyperphosphatemia, hypocalcemia, hyperuricemia, and anemia usually develop after several days, or more rapidly in patients with rhabdomyolysis or hemolysis. Hypercalcemia can occur in some patients recovering from myoglobinuric ARF for unclear reasons. Hypercalcemia associated with other diseases can cause ARF through a direct depression of glomerular function. Finally, the accumulation of unexcreted waste products can cause the uremic syndrome, which affects the normal function of virtually every organ. Manifestations include progressive anorexia, nausea, vomiting, nervous irritability, hyper-reflexia, asterixis, seizures, and coma. Disorders of coagulation can cause ecchymoses and gastric hemorrhage.

Table 116–5 • DIAGNOSTIC CLUES TO THE CAUSE OF ACUTE RENAL FAILURE

PRIMARY DISORDER	URINALYSIS	CLINICAL FINDINGS
Prerenal		
Hypovolemia	Hyaline casts, no RBC, or WBC, low FE_{Na}	Rapid weight loss, postural hypotension
Ineffective arterial volume	Hyaline casts, no RBC, or WBC, low Fe_{Na}	Weight gain, edema, normal or low blood pressure
Arterial occlusion	Hyaline casts, rare to many RBCs	Occasional flank or low back pain
Postrenal		
Ureteral obstruction	WBCs if infected, crystals or RBCs	Flank pain radiating into the groin
Urethral	WBCs and RBCs	Urethral pain
Venous occlusion	Proteinuria, hematuria	Occasional flank pain
Renal		
Vascular	Granular casts, proteinuria, RBCs and WBCs	Systemic illness suggesting vasculitis, hypertension
Glomerular	RBC casts, granular casts, RBCs, WBCs, proteinuria	Systemic illness, hypertension
Tubular	Granular casts, tubular cells, RBCs, WBCs	Hypotension, sepsis

FE_{Na} = fractional sodium excretion; RBC = red blood cell; WBC = white blood cell.

Table 116–6 • GUIDELINES FOR TREATING ACUTE RENAL FAILURE

General	Avoid drugs that reduce renal blood flow (e.g., NSAIDs) and/or are nephrotoxic (e.g., radiocontrast agent, certain antibiotics)
Prerenal	Restore blood pressure and intravascular volume
Postrenal	Urologic evaluation
Intrinsic	Prevent hypotension and try to convert oliguria to nonoliguria; if edematous, try 80–100 mg furosemide, but if nonedematous, try 250–500 mL saline intravenously

NSAID = nonsteroidal anti-inflammatory drug.

Treatment

Treatment of ARF includes correction of reversible causes, prevention of additional injury, use of metabolic support during the maintenance and recovery phases of the syndrome, and attempts to convert oliguric to nonoliguric renal failure (Table 116–6).

CORRECTION OF REVERSIBLE CAUSES. In all ARF patients, administration of drugs that interfere with renal perfusion or function or potential nephrotoxins should be stopped (e.g., radiocontrast agents should be avoided). Since the kidney is involved in the clearance of so many drugs, the dosage of all drugs should be adjusted according to guidelines for the degree of renal insufficiency: in patients with serum creatinine rising at rates of 1 to 2 mg/dL/day, it should be assumed that kidney function is virtually zero when adjusting the dosage. If there is any doubt, plasma drug levels should be monitored because the dosing guidelines for patients with renal insufficiency provide only average dosing recommendations. For hypovolemic, hypotensive patients in the prerenal classification, blood pressure should be restored by discontinuing the use of antihypertensive drugs and administering blood (if bleeding or anemia is present) or isotonic saline to expand the extracellular volume (unless the patient has

edema or ascites). In edematous patients, blood transfusions are the preferred means of increasing blood pressure. Finally, appropriate blood pressure guidelines should be used. For elderly patients with long-standing hypertension, a blood pressure of 100/70 mm Hg may in fact be inadequate to maintain the GFR. If doubt exists about the adequacy of the plasma volume, a rapid intravenous challenge of isotonic saline (250 to 500 mL) is warranted but only when the response of the blood pressure and edema are carefully documented. As noted, saline should not be given to patients with edema and/or ascites because in these cases the low perfusion of the kidney is due to hormonal- or neural-induced, intrarenal vasoconstriction and this is not counteracted by intravenous fluids. The presence of edema and ascites means that the patient is in positive sodium balance, and the infused saline merely increases the degree of edema and/or ascites. Obstructed patients require urologic consultation plus careful attention to maintenance of zero fluid balance.

Not all patients with intrinsic kidney damage and ARF are oliguric, even though the clearance function of their kidneys is low. The physiologic basis for nonoliguric ARF is not understood; it may

Continued

represent a milder form of tubular damage. These patients do not necessarily regain renal function more rapidly, but it is worthwhile to attempt to convert oliguric patients to the nonoliguric state of ARF because fluid balance in nonoliguric patients is more easily managed. In conditions associated with low FE_{Na} and no edema (see Table 116–4), a challenge with 500 mL of saline combined with 40 to 80 mg of intravenous furosemide may reverse an oliguric to a nonoliguric state and, in some cases, even prevent progressive tubular damage. Alternatively, a trial of 80 to 100 mg of furosemide can be used in edematous patients to attempt conversion of oliguric to nonoliguric renal failure. If urine flow does increase to exceed 20 to 30 mL/hour, furosemide should be used to achieve fluid balance. Although popular, there is no benefit to the infusion of low doses (1 to 3 µg/kg/minute) of dopamine; it does not hasten the recovery of renal function and can cause cardiac arrhythmias. If urine flow increases within hours of beginning furosemide (or another loop diuretic), the drug can be continued. If not, its administration should not be continued to prevent complications.

GENERAL SUPPORT. Indwelling urinary catheters should be avoided in uncomplicated cases; intermittent catheterization using sterile technique usually suffices even in oliguric, obtunded patients and reduces the risk of infection. In all patients, maintaining fluid balance is crucial. The simplest and most accurate estimate of fluid balance is a compulsively measured daily weight; fluid intake and output records are more cumbersome and generally less accurate. Initially, the required fluid intake can be approximated by giving the patient fluids (e.g., water, tea) equal to 500 mL plus the amount of urine excreted in the preceding 24 hours. The outcome should be no gain of extracellular volume, measured as an increase in weight. In febrile patients this limit can be increased as long as there is no increase in weight.

Extra sodium, potassium, and chloride besides that in food should not be given to patients with ARF. As long as the serum sodium concentration is normal, water restriction is unnecessary, but if weight increases, sodium should be restricted. If the serum sodium level does decrease, water should be restricted. Dietary protein should be limited to 0.8 g/kg of body weight per day unless the patient is hypercatabolic. Energy intake (carbohydrates plus fats) should supply 35 kcal/kg/day. In patients who cannot eat, an intravenous infusion of essential amino acids and glucose may be necessary, but oral or enteral feeding is always preferable. Besides the beneficial effects of enteral feeding on gastrointestinal tract function, intravenous feeding entails considerable fluid intake and may lead to the need for dialysis.

In addition to daily weight, serial determinations of blood pressure (supine and upright), serum electrolytes, creatinine, SUN, and hematocrit are needed. Hyperkalemia exceeding 6 mEq/L is potentially serious and can be treated by ingesting sodium polystyrene sulfonate exchange resin (20 to 30 g) in a solution containing sorbitol to ensure excretion of potassium polystyrene resin. Electrocardiographic abnormalities such as widened QRS complexes or atrioventricular dissociation demand immediate treatment with intravenous calcium gluconate or calcium chloride; this type of therapy is the most rapidly acting method of correcting the cardiac conduction abnormality. Glucose and insulin (0.5 U/kg/hour of regular insulin with 3 mL/kg/hour of 20% glucose) or hypertonic sodium bicarbonate (for acidotic patients) can reduce the serum potassium concentration within 30 to 60 minutes. However, none of these measures removes excess potassium, and dialysis is generally required (see Chapter 112 for a discussion of hyperkalemia).

Unfortunately, strategies based on intensive hemodialysis regimens have not improved the prognosis of patients with ARF and catabolic conditions.[1] However, hemodialysis is critical for treating some of the complications of ARF. It should be considered for hyperkalemia that is unresponsive to polystyrene exchange resins or if electrocardiographic abnormalities are present. Note that hemodialysis invariably requires several hours to reduce serum potassium effectively and should never be considered adequate treatment for acute effects of hyperkalemia. Hemodialysis is also required for severe metabolic acidosis that cannot be managed by sodium bicarbonate; it also is used to treat pulmonary edema, progressive azotemia (SUN values >100 mg/dL), encephalopathy, seizures, bleeding, pericarditis, and/or uremic enteropathy. Peritoneal dialysis may be the most suitable method of treatment for patients with severe heart failure because it avoids the rapid shifts in blood volume and blood components that occur with hemodialysis. This type of dialysis is not suitable if the patient requires rapid removal of potassium or waste products. The other benefit of peritoneal dialysis is that anticoagulants are not needed.

RECOVERY OF RENAL FUNCTION. ARF secondary to prerenal causes is potentially reversible if the underlying disease is treated. In postrenal, obstructive ARF, renal function may be expected to stabilize or improve significantly after the obstruction is relieved. The amount of function regained decreases sharply if the obstruction is severe and present for several days. Intrarenal, intrinsic ARF has a variable outcome. Glomerulonephritis and vasculitis may respond to immunosuppressive therapy with complete recovery of renal function. Renal tubular injury from ischemia or toxins is usually reversible; recovery to nearly normal renal function seems to be more likely in nonoliguric than in oliguric patients. Although a major improvement in renal function usually appears in the second week, mild defects in renal function can persist for months or years after acute tubular injury.

Prevention

Every effort should be made to prevent ARF. Patients should be given intravenous saline to improve hemodynamic function and urine flow before receiving iodinated radiocontrast material and or other toxins (to prevent hyperconcentration of any toxin in the kidney) and before surgical procedures, especially patients with poor kidney function or those in whom renal blood flow will be interrupted (e.g., repair of abdominal aortic aneurysm). Intravenous saline is also given with cisplatin or other nephrotoxic drugs. Pretreatment with allopurinol can decrease uric acid production when leukemia or massive tumors are being treated. Patients with renal disease should not be given NSAIDs, and nephrotoxic antibiotics should be avoided or carefully monitored in patients with ARF.

Grade A
1. Mehta RL, McDonald B, Gabbai FB, et al: A randomized clinical trial of continuous versus intermittent dialysis for acute renal failure. Kidney Int 2001;60:1154–1163.

SUGGESTED READINGS
Avasthi G, Sandhu JS, Mohindra K: Acute renal failure in medical and surgical intensive care units—a one year prospective study. Ren Fail 2003;25:105–113. *These patients have a 62% mortality rate.*
De Vriese AS: Prevention and treatment of acute renal failure in sepsis. J Am Soc Nephrol 2003;14:792–805. *A comprehensive review.*

Druml W: Nutritional support in acute renal failure. *In* Mitch WE, Klahr S (eds): Handbook of Nutrition and the Kidney, 4th ed. Philadelphia, JB Lippincott, 2002, pp 191–273. *A review of metabolic abnormalities associated with ARF that affect nutritional therapy. Guidelines for providing adequate nutrition are presented.*
Prakash J, Sen D, Kumar NS, et al: Acute renal failure due to intrinsic renal diseases: Review of 1122 cases. Ren Fail 2003;25:225–233. *In India, 80% were due to acute tubular necrosis, with post-infectious glomerulonephritis, acute interstitial nephritis, and renal cortical necrosis accounting for most of the remainder.*
Sheridan AM, Bonventre JV: Cell biology and molecular mechanisms of injury in ischemic acute renal failure. Curr Opin Nephrol Hypertens 2000;9:427–434. *The complex cellular responses of the kidney to experimental injury involve both metabolic defects and the induction of signaling pathways leading to apoptosis.*
Singri N, Ahya SN, Levin ML: Acute renal failure. JAMA 2003;289:747–751. *Overview emphasizing symptoms, diagnosis, treatment, and prevention, as well as the 20–70% mortality rate.*

117 CHRONIC RENAL FAILURE

Robert G. Luke

Definition and Epidemiology

Chronic renal failure (CRF) is associated with a falling glomerular filtration rate (GFR) and is a progressive disease characterized by an increasing inability of the kidney to maintain normal low levels of the products of protein metabolism (e.g., urea), normal blood pressure and hematocrit, and sodium, water, potassium, and acid-base balance. Renal function is clinically monitored by measurement of serum creatinine and blood urea nitrogen (BUN) urinalysis and by serial quantification of urinary protein excretion. Once serum creatinine in an adult reaches about 3 mg/dL and no factors in the pathogenesis of the renal disease are reversible, the renal disease is likely to progress to end-stage renal disease (ESRD) over a very variable period (from a few years to as many as 20 to 25 years). This progression can be very substantially slowed or even halted by appropriate therapy.[1] Unless contraindications are present such as terminal irreversible disease in another organ system(s) or the patient does not wish it, almost all patients reaching ESRD in industrialized nations receive renal replacement therapy (RRT). These modalities of treatment—dialysis and transplantation—are discussed in Chapter 118.

It is useful for the physician to regard CRF and RRT as a continuum of the same disease process. Chronic hemodialysis is equivalent, for example, to only about 10 to 15% of normal renal function. Preserving endogenous renal function as long as possible above that level is better for the patient than hemodialysis and, in slowly progressive renal disease, especially in an older patient, may avoid hemodialysis. The median age of patients now entering RRT is 63 years, and the major cause of death in patients receiving RRT is cardiovascular. Patients with progressive renal disease, including but not limited to patients with diabetes mellitus, must be regarded as "vasculopaths" and cardiovascular risk factors must be sought and treated vigorously. The treatment of such risk factors as hypertension, hyperlipidemia, and hyperhomocystinuria must begin early in the treatment of CRF to prevent long-term morbidity and mortality. In patients with an elevated serum creatinine level (1.5 to 3.0 mg/dL), the term *chronic renal insufficiency* is useful and implies that progression to CRF and ESRD is not inevitable.

In the United States, about 270,000 patients are presently undergoing dialysis and an additional 100,000 are living with a functioning renal transplant. In addition, it is estimated that about 11 million people have an elevated serum creatinine. Furthermore, such patients and those with proteinuria or microalbuminuria* have a markedly enhanced risk of adverse cardiovascular events.[2] Because of the progressive nature of chronic renal disease and our increasing ability to slow this progression, the association with worsening hypertension, and the predilection of these patients for cardiovascular disease, we should recognize and carefully monitor such patients.

Etiology

The causes of ESRD are well known, but because of varying rates of progression, the prevalence and relative frequency of the different types of chronic renal disease are less certain. Systemic diseases frequently involve and potentially destroy the kidneys (Table 117-1). Two thirds of incident cases are due to diabetes or hypertension.

There is good evidence that essential hypertension is caused by renal genetic mechanisms and that the propensity for the development of renal disease in response to renal injury may also, and separately, be in part genetically determined. For almost all causes except polycystic kidney disease, progressive renal disease is more common in African American than in white individuals by a factor of about 2 to 3:1. Indeed, in the 30- to 40-year-old group, the prevalence of hypertensive nephrosclerosis as a cause of ESRD is 25 times that in the white population.

Although most of the diseases that cause CRF are discussed in detail elsewhere, the relationship to progressive renal disease is emphasized here. CRF develops in about 30% of type I and type II diabetics, with a peak incidence at about 15 years after the development of diabetes mellitus. Predictors of the development of diabetic glomerulosclerosis are hypertension, poor glycemic control, microalbuminuria, and the development of proliferative retinal vascular disease. The drug of choice for diabetic patients with hypertension and/or microalbuminuria or fixed proteinuria is an angiotensin-converting enzyme (ACE) inhibitor or an angiotensin II receptor blocker (ARB).[3,4] If treatment commences at the stage of microalbuminuria and before fixed albuminuria (300 mg/24 hr) develops, especially if combined with improved glycemic control, progression to diabetic glomerulosclerosis may be prevented. Even after fixed albuminuria has developed, ACE inhibitors can markedly delay progression of the decline in the GFR to about 2 mL/min/yr. Untreated, the GFR in diabetic glomerulosclerosis progresses downward at a rate of about 10 to 12 mL/min/yr.

About 50 million Americans have hypertension, but each year ESRD develops in only 20,000 of them because of hypertensive nephrosclerosis. Evidence is increasing that microalbuminuria is a harbinger of hypertensive nephrosclerosis and that progression to overt proteinuria may be diminished by some, but not all, antihypertensive drugs. Microalbuminuria is certainly well documented as a cardiovascular risk factor, and that alone justifies intensifying antihypertensive treatment in such patients. ACE inhibitors have been shown to slow progression to ESRD compared with dihydropyridine calcium blockers in African-American patients with established renal impairment due to hypertensive nephrosclerosis.[5] This benefit occurred even though urine protein excretion was less than 1 g/24 hr; similar results have been obtained in other primary renal diseases with similar degrees of proteinuria.[6]

The primary care physician has a vital role in the prevention of ESRD, especially for patients with diabetes mellitus and hypertension. Without a fall in the present 5% annual rate of growth in patients with ESRD, at least 600,000 patients in the United States will be undergoing RRT by 2010.

Very large cysts, association with the *PKD-1* gene, onset of the disease at an early age, and hypertension are associated with progression in polycystic kidney disease, and intense study is ongoing to determine how to stop progression in that disease. The relevant causative genes are known, but how the defective protein product of these genes contributes to progressive renal cyst formation and loss of renal function has not yet been elucidated. Treatment of hypertension is best initiated with an ACE inhibitor.

Focal glomerulosclerosis and membranoproliferative glomerulonephritis are the most likely chronic glomerulonephritides to progress quickly in adults. Specific therapy for the progressive glomerulonephritides is discussed in Chapter 119.

A considerable decrease has been noted in the proportion of patients with lupus nephritis progressing to ESRD because of improved treatment. Scleroderma, Wegener's granulomatosis, and other vasculitides also now less often progress to ESRD, especially if the condition is detected and the patient is treated before severe renal impairment has developed.

Just as patients with coronary artery disease have benefited from coronary artery bypass graft surgery and coronary angioplasty with stenting, bilateral renal arterial stenoses or unilateral disease in a single functioning kidney can sometimes prevent the patient from progressing to ESRD by similar techniques applied to the renal arteries. The frequency of renovascular renal failure as a cause of ESRD has not yet been established, but some believe that it is a significant and preventable cause of ESRD, especially in elderly white men who smoke and have diffuse atherosclerotic vascular disease and no other overt

Table 117-1 • CAUSES OF CHRONIC RENAL FAILURE

Diabetic glomerulosclerosis*
Hypertensive nephrosclerosis
Glomerular disease
   Glomerulonephritis
   Amyloidosis, light chain disease*
   SLE, Wegener's granulomatosis*
Tubulointerstitial disease
   Reflux nephropathy (chronic pyelonephritis)
   Analgesic nephropathy
   Obstructive nephropathy (stones, BPH)
   Myeloma kidney*
Vascular disease
   Scleroderma*
   Vasculitis*
   Renovascular renal failure (ischemic nephropathy)
   Atheroembolic renal disease*
Cystic diseases
   Autosomal dominant polycystic kidney disease
   Medullary cystic kidney disease

*Systemic disease involving the kidney.
BPH = benign prostatic hypertrophy; SLE = systemic lupus erythematosus.

*Microalbuminuria is not detected by the "stix" tests used for routine analysis and is defined as an albumin of 30–300 mg/24 hrs.

cause of CRF; flash pulmonary edema and acute renal failure or deterioration in renal function on an ACE inhibitor or an ARB are also possible clinical clues to this condition.

The listed tubulointerstitial diseases offer a chance for amelioration or normalization of renal function if, for example, obstruction can be relieved before too much renal function has been lost. Cessation of analgesic abuse is likewise potentially beneficial, especially if the patient is still in the stage of chronic renal insufficiency.

Clinical Manifestations

Patients are often not seen until late in the course of the disease, when much of their kidney function has already been lost (Table 117–2). All CRF patients, except those with medullary cystic kidney disease (Chapter 127) and some in the earlier stages of hypertensive nephrosclerosis, have significant proteinuria (>200 mg/24 hr). Because many transient and benign causes of proteinuria are possible, population screening is not justified at the present. However, routine testing for microalbuminuria or proteinuria in patients with diabetes mellitus or hypertension is very important for determination of therapy.

The syndrome may also come to attention because of an elevated BUN or serum creatinine concentration in laboratory testing that was performed for a variety of reasons. It is unusual for CRF to initially manifest by urinary tract symptoms, and most patients with such symptoms as dysuria, frequency, and polyuria do not have CRF. Occasionally, patients with primary tubulointerstitial disease may have polyuria and nocturia because impaired renal concentrating ability is an early feature secondary to predominant damage to the renal medulla.

Patients with progressive primary glomerular disease may have nephrotic syndrome (e.g., membranous glomerulopathy), recurrent nephritic syndrome (e.g., membranoproliferative or mesangioproliferative glomerulonephritis), or recurrent gross hematuria (e.g., IgA nephropathy). Patients with systemic disease potentially involving the kidney must be checked regularly for proteinuria and abnormal urinary findings on microscopy. Examples include diabetes mellitus, hypertension, Wegener's granulomatosis, and systemic lupus erythematosus.

Screening for hypertension is cost-effective, and all patients with hypertension should undergo urinalysis. If a patient with what is believed to be essential hypertension is, or becomes, resistant to therapy and requires multiple drugs to control blood pressure, underlying renal or renovascular disease is the probable cause. In 95% of patients with CRF, hypertension develops before ESRD, and 5% of all hypertensive patients have an elevated blood pressure secondary to CRF or an underlying kidney disease before the development of azotemia. (*Azotemia* means an elevation of BUN above normal, but *uremia* implies the presence of symptoms secondary to renal nitrogen retention.) Examples of parenchymal renal diseases in which hypertension is commonly present before azotemia include polycystic kidney disease, type II diabetes mellitus, and focal glomerulosclerosis.

Initial presentation of patients who already have features of CRF such as uremic symptoms (see Table 117–2) is common because the remaining nephrons of the kidney adapt so well to progressive loss of nephrons and can maintain constancy of the internal environment until about 75% of renal function has been lost. Patients with uremic manifestations, the pathophysiology of which is discussed later, can have a myriad of different complaints referable to almost any organ system. Initial misdiagnosis is common, especially for anemic, gastrointestinal, and cardiovascular manifestations. In some specific renal diseases, other symptoms may call the causative disease into question. Polycystic kidney disease can be characterized by recurrent acute pain in renal cysts and/or gross hematuria. Patients with reflux nephropathy may come to medical attention with recurrent pyelonephritis or persistent hypertension after what is believed to have been preeclamptic toxemia of pregnancy.

Pathophysiology of Chronic Renal Failure

Regardless of the primary cause of nephron loss, some usually survive or are less severely damaged (Fig. 117–1). These nephrons

Table 117–2 • FEATURES OF CHRONIC RENAL FAILURE

Early
  Hypertension
  Proteinuria; elevated BUN or SCr
  Nephrotic syndrome
  Recurrent nephritic syndrome
  Gross hematuria
Late (GFR <15 mL/min, BUN >60 mg/dL) ("uremia")
  Cardiac failure
  Anemia
  Serositis
  Confusion, coma
  Anorexia
  Vomiting
  Peripheral neuropathy
  Hyperkalemia
  Metabolic acidosis

BUN = blood urea nitrogen; GFR = glomerular filtration rate; SCr = serum creatinine.

then adapt and enlarge, and clearance per nephron markedly increases. If the initiating process is diffuse, sudden, and severe, such as in some patients with rapidly progressive glomerulonephritis (crescentic glomerulonephritis), acute or subacute renal failure may ensue with the rapid development of ESRD. In most patients, however, disease progression is more gradual and nephron adaptation is possible. This process has been studied extensively in animal models, especially in rats with bilateral segmental renal infarction or a $1\frac{2}{3}$ nephrectomy. Glomerular hypertrophy, a marked increase in glomerular plasma flow and single-nephron GFR, and increased capillary pressure are noted. Focal glomerulosclerosis develops in these glomeruli, and they eventually become nonfunctional. At the same time that focal glomerulosclerosis develops, proteinuria markedly increases and systemic hypertension worsens. Some antihypertensive drugs, especially ACE inhibitors, slow this process and diminish proteinuria; even at the same level of blood pressure control, other drugs such as β–blockers, hydralazine, and dihydropyridine calcium channel blockers do not. Similar pathophysiology occurs in humans and ACE inhibitors and ARBs are also protective by mechanisms that include both a reduction in systemic blood pressure and a fall in intraglomerular pressure.

Other mechanisms of progression that are probably important in the sclerosis of adapted glomeruli include glomerular coagulation, hyperlipidemic effects, and mesangial cell proliferation. The pathophysiology of focal glomerulosclerosis has been compared with that of atherosclerosis. It is likely that tubulointerstitial fibrosis and interstitial inflammation contribute to nephron failure in the process of nephron adaptation. This result is in part secondary to the potential of proteinuria to cause proximal tubule atrophy (enhanced apoptosis); the release of transforming growth factor β, endothelin, and angiotensin II secondary to tubular injury; and nephron ischemia secondary to arteriosclerosis.

This process of nephron adaptation has been termed the "final common path." The ability of nephrons to adapt by enlarging and increasing function has beneficial effects in maintaining whole-kidney GFR, as well as rates of sodium potassium, phosphate, acid, and solute excretion, especially the end products of protein metabolism that cause the uremic syndrome. Adapted nephrons enhance the ability of the kidney to postpone uremia, but ultimately the adaptation process leads to the demise of these nephrons. Much of the present experimental work is aimed at maintaining adaptation but without deleterious effects on the nephron by blocking the release and effects of angiotensin II and aldosterone, endothelin, and transforming growth factor β, which promote mesangial proliferation, fibrogenesis, and vasculopathic changes.

If these processes are, initially at least, important in postponing ESRD, it is clear that monitoring renal function only by changes in serum creatinine is, at the least, insensitive to nephron dropout because whole-kidney GFR can be maintained by increasing single-nephron GFR in surviving adapted nephrons. Quantitation of urinary protein excretion, the use of urinary microscopy, and, perhaps in the future, measurement of potentially harmful urinary and blood cytokines may all be important. Whenever possible, primary continuing injury must

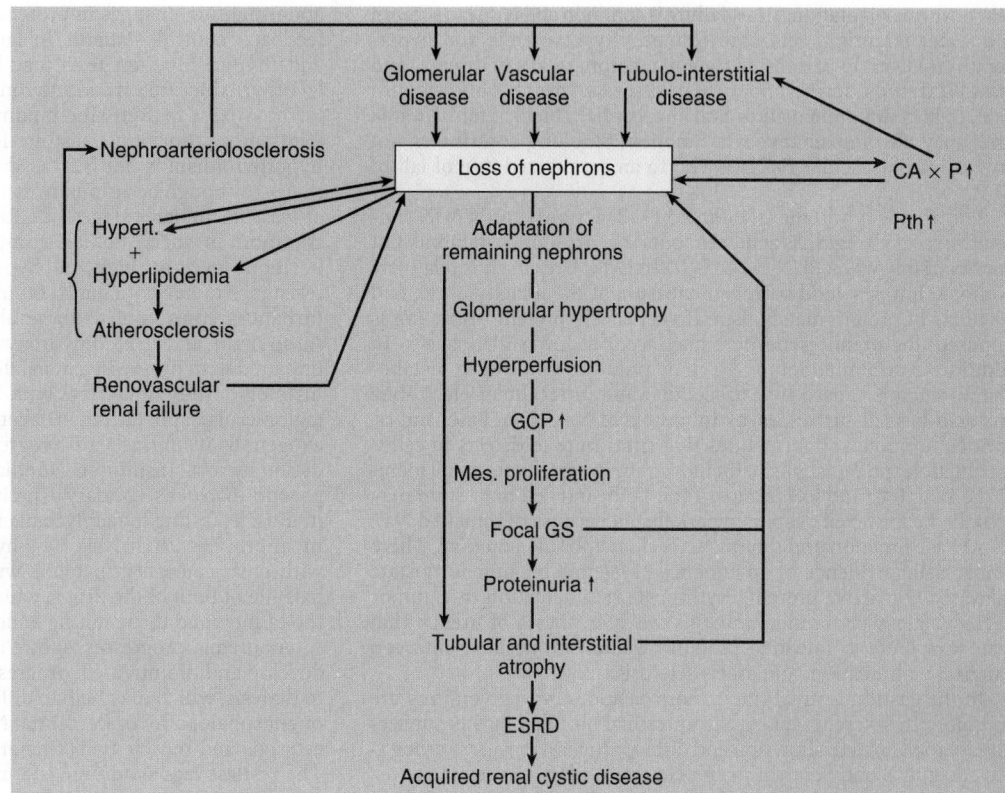

FIGURE 117-1 • Pathogenesis of the "final common path" in patients with chronic renal failure. It is assumed that all primary etiologies have been appropriately treated. The best-documented intermediate agents for these deleterious processes are angiotensin II, endothelin, and transforming growth factor. At least experimentally, blockers of these hormones/cytokines have slowed or prevented the further loss of nephrons. In humans, the value of the use of angiotensin-converting enzyme inhibitors is well documented. ESRD = end-stage renal disease; GCP = glomerular capillary pressure.

also be treated, as in immunosuppressive therapy for lupus nephritis, reduction of blood pressure in hypertensive nephrosclerosis, and control of blood sugar and the use of ACE inhibitors or ARBs in diabetic glomerulopathy.

Two other important concepts in understanding progression of CRF are the *intact-nephron hypothesis* and the *trade-off hypothesis*. The first states that in general, adapted nephrons behave like normal nephrons. Some of the failure to regulate sodium and water relates to increased solute excretion per nephron—in effect, an osmotic diuresis of the remaining nephrons that impairs sodium and water conservation, especially in states of extracellular fluid volume depletion. Thus, renal concentrating ability is lost, as well as the ability of the remaining nephrons to adjust to low and high intake of sodium, water, potassium, and other dietary solutes, because these nephrons are functioning at maximum capacity even with normal intake of these substances. For example, in a patient with an intake of 200 mEq of sodium and 100 mEq of potassium, serum Na of 140 mEq/L, K of 4 mEq/L, and a GFR of 5 mL/min (compared with a normal subject with a GFR of 100 mL/min on the same intake), to maintain balance the patient must excrete 20% of the filtered sodium load and 360% of the potassium load compared with 1% and 18%, respectively, in the normal subject. If the maximum concentrating ability is 300 mOsm and daily urinary solute excretion is 600 mOsm/kg, 2 L of urine is required to maintain excretion, whereas only 500 mL is needed in normal subjects with a renal concentrating ability of 1200 mOsm/kg.

Renal handling of solute is influenced by hormonal effects. For example, as serum phosphate levels rise secondary to a fall in GFR, plasma calcium levels decrease and serum parathormone levels increase, thereby decreasing tubular reabsorption of phosphate, and serum phosphate returns to normal. Elevation of serum parathormone level occurs relatively early in progressive renal disease and contributes to the pathogenesis of renal osteodystrophy. The "trade-off" is increased renal excretion of phosphate with serum levels maintained but at the expense of elevated parathormone levels. Similarly, normal serum potassium levels can be maintained at the expense of elevated aldosterone secretion.

The progressive drop in GFR, osmotic diuresis of the remaining nephrons, and elevated hormone levels all contribute to restrict the flexibility of the kidney to adapt to low and high intake of various solutes. CRF is thus associated with progressive loss of the ability of the kidney to maintain a constant internal environment in the face of substantial changes in solute intake. Adapted nephrons have not

only an enhanced GFR but also enhanced tubular functions in terms of, for example, potassium and proton secretion. If an ion is normally controlled by varying reabsorption, as with sodium, reabsorption is minimized, and if it is controlled by secretion, as with potassium, secretion is maximized and may lead to excretion that exceeds the filtered load.

Finally, it is likely that the growth factors responsible for hypertrophy of nephrons also eventually lead, after chronic dialysis for some years, to acquired renal cyst formation; these cysts are believed to be premalignant.

Pathophysiology of the Uremic Syndrome

The mechanisms of sodium and potassium retention and how the failing kidney adapts to loss of nephrons by increased excretion of these ions per remaining functional nephron have already been discussed. Progressive metabolic acidosis develops with CRF. The major cause of the failure to excrete enough acid is diminished renal ammonia production and excretion. High serum parathormone levels and extracellular fluid volume lead to proximal tubular acidosis and partially account for the early hyperchloremic metabolic acidosis of CRF. Patients who have hyperkalemic distal (type 4) renal tubular acidosis (e.g., in hyporeninemic hypoaldosteronism, common in diabetic patients) because of tubulointerstitial disease have more severe hyperkalemia and non–anion gap metabolic acidosis relative to the stage of progression of CRF.

Hypertension complicating CRF is due to retention of NaCl, inappropriately high renin levels for the status of expended extracellular fluid volume, sympathetic stimulation via afferent renal reflexes, and impaired renal endothelial function with deficient nitric oxide and enhanced endothelin production. If untreated, this type of hypertension is much more likely to enter the malignant phase than is essential hypertension.

Other cardiovascular risk factors include high parathormone levels, vascular (including coronary) and myocardial calcification, left ventricular hypertrophy, hyperlipidemia (characterized by hypertriglyceridemia and elevated lipoprotein[a] [Lp(a)] levels), hyperhomocystinemia, increased insulin resistance (even in nondiabetic patients), and smoking. All these factors must be vigorously managed as soon as possible. Acute cardiovascular events, especially stroke and myocardial infarction, account for about half of the deaths occurring in dialysis patients as well as deaths after the first year posttransplantation. Heart failure is common and is due to sodium and water retention, acid-base changes, hypocalcemia and hyperparathyroidism, hypertension, anemia, coronary artery disease, and diastolic dysfunction secondary to increased myocardial fibrosis with oxalate and urate deposition and myocardial calcification. Uremia itself may also impair myocyte function. Smoking contributes not only to cardiovascular risk but also to an accelerated rate of fall of GFR.

The uremic syndrome (see Table 117–2) is rare before a BUN concentration of 60 mg/dL is achieved, but it occurs more commonly but not invariably when BUN exceeds 100 mg/dL. Urea itself is relatively nontoxic but is a good surrogate measure of the toxicity of the end products of protein metabolism. If very severe protein restriction is imposed, the uremic syndrome may occur at lower BUN levels. In addition to accumulation of the toxic products of nitrogen metabolism, uremia is caused by extracellular and intracellular electrolyte and acid-base disturbances, by inhibitors of Na^+, K^+-ATPase, and by various hormonal abnormalities that contribute to defects in cellular function and metabolism, including energy production, cell membrane function, and ion pumps. Total body and cell potassium may actually be low even despite hyperkalemia because of impaired Na^+, K^+-ATPase function and diminished cell membrane potential. There is increasing evidence of an enhanced systemic inflammatory state (elevated C-reactive protein, erythrocyte sedimentation rate, tumor necrosis factor α, interleukin-6) in the later phases of uremia that may contribute to impaired protein metabolism, negative nitrogen balance, malnutrition, and atherosclerosis.

In the gastrointestinal tract, anorexia and morning vomiting are common. In severe uremia, gastrointestinal bleeding may occur secondary to platelet dysfunction and diffuse mucosal erosions throughout the gut. Bloody diarrhea can occur secondary to uremic colitis. Diverticular disease is more frequent in polycystic kidney disease; cysts in the liver may cause hepatic pain, more often after renal transplantation.

Uremic serositis is a syndrome of pericarditis, pleural effusion, and sometimes ascites in any combination. These fluid accumulations in serous cavities are secondary to defects in capillary permeability; other causes of exudative effusions such as infection and malignancy must also be considered. Pericarditis is fibrinous, hemorrhagic, and usually associated with a mild fever and may cause pericardial tamponade. Treatment by dialysis leads to improvement. Pruritus is a common and troublesome complication of uremia that is only partially explained by hyperparathyroidism and a high Ca × P product with increased microscopic calcification of subcutaneous tissues. In some patients, pruritus remains troublesome even after chronic hemodialysis is instituted.

Renal osteodystrophy (Chapter 262) is characterized by secondary hyperparathyroidism, which is due to hyperphosphatemia, hypocalcemia, marked parathyroid hypertrophy, and bony resistance to the action of parathormone; by inadequate formation of 1,25-dihydroxyvitamin D in the kidney resulting in osteomalacia in adults and rickets in children; and, for as yet obscure reasons, by areas of osteosclerosis. Tertiary hyperparathyroidism is said to exist when high parathormone levels persist despite normal or high levels of serum calcium. This condition is secondary to the marked increase in parathyroid mass with abnormal and inadequate suppression of parathormone secretion. Metabolic acidosis also contributes to the bone disease by titration of protons for calcium in bone matrix. High parathormone levels and high cytosol calcium concentrations probably contribute to uremic encephalopathy, myocyte dysfunction, and an impaired bone marrow response to erythropoietin. Severe syndromes termed "calciphylaxis" (or uremic calcific arteriolopathy with subcutaneous necrosis) include metastatic calcification in small blood vessels and ischemic necrosis of fatty subcutaneous tissues such as in the breast and abdomen of obese women; calcified ectopic masses can also occur in other soft tissues and occasionally diffusely in the lungs. Adynamic renal bone disease, which is associated with much-diminished bone turnover, is now being seen and requires bone biopsy for diagnosis. It may reflect skeletal resistance to the action of parathormone and has led to the recommendation to maintain serum parathormone levels at 2 to 3 times normal. Other joint diseases include secondary gout and pseudo-gout, which may be associated with chondrocalcinosis.

Endocrine function is diffusely abnormal in patients with uremia and CRF secondary to diminished renal degradation of polypeptides, receptor dysfunction, post–receptor signal transduction abnormalities, changes in protein binding, and abnormal endocrine feedback control. Patients in late CRF often appear hypothyroid and thyroid function tests may be abnormal, despite normal free levothyroxine; free triiodothyronine levels are low, and binding of levothyroxine to thyroxine-binding globulin is diminished. Thyroid-stimulating hormone testing is useful, and the incidence of hypothyroidism is not increased in CRF. Most women are amenorrheic—although occasionally menorrhagia can occur—and infertile, at least in the later stages of CRF. Impotence and oligospermia are common in men. Follicle-stimulating hormone and luteinizing hormone levels are high, and hyperprolactinemia is present; gonadal resistance to hormones and complicated hypothalamic-pituitary disturbances contribute to these abnormalities. Although renal erythropoietin and 1,25-dihydroxyvitamin D production is severely impaired with progressive renal disease, renin secretion is enhanced; histologic study of kidneys with ESRD often shows prominent juxtaglomerular apparatuses. Diabetic patients commonly require less exogenous insulin as CRF progresses because of diminished degradation by renal insulinase. Nondiabetic patients demonstrate uremic pseudo-diabetes secondary to peripheral insulin resistance, especially in muscle; fasting hyperglycemia is rarely severe, and this abnormality improves with dialysis. Oral hypoglycemic agents should be used with great caution in patients with CRF because of the prolonged half-life of both of the drugs, which are in whole or part excreted by the kidney, and the resulting endogenous insulin produced.

As uremia progresses, subtle mental and cognitive dysfunctions develop and, if untreated, progress to coma. These changes respond to dialysis, which may help to differentiate uremia from other causes of encephalopathy or dementia. Neuromuscular abnormalities with asterixis and muscle twitching are common, as are muscle cramps. The restless legs syndrome is a manifestation of sensory peripheral neuropathy. Motor neuropathy is a very late phenomenon in uremia and may not respond to RRT.

Progressively more severe normochromic, normocytic anemia develops as the GFR and renal erythropoietin secretion decrease. In most patients, the hematocrit reaches about 20 to 25% by the time that ESRD develops. Uremic coagulopathy is secondary to a defect in platelet function, as well as abnormal factor VIII function. It is characterized by a prolonged bleeding time but usually normal prothrombin and partial thromboplastin times, platelet count, and clotting time. The platelet dysfunction responds to dialysis and to infusion of desmopressin. Epistaxis, menorrhagia, bruising, and purpura, as well as gut bleeding, may all occur.

Uremic patients should be regarded as immunocompromised, and infection is an important cause of death in CRF and dialysis patients. The leukocyte count, but not polymorphonuclear function, is commonly normal with a normal differential, as are total immunoglobulin and complement levels. Cellular immune function is depressed, however. Antibody responses to hepatitis B and influenza immunization, for example, are less than those in normal subjects, but protection is still indicated and feasible.

Differential Diagnosis

It is sometimes difficult to differentiate between acute and chronic renal failure when a patient with azotemia and an elevated serum creatinine concentration is recognized for the first time. A diagnosis of CRF is supported by a history of nephrotic or nephritic syndrome, long-standing nocturia, findings of renal osteodystrophy, very severe renal anemia in the absence of blood loss, and the presence of bilaterally small kidneys with increased echogenicity on renal ultrasonography. Evidence of long-standing hypertensive disease in the cardiovascular system is supportive but not diagnostic of chronicity. Acute-on-chronic renal failure is a common circumstance, and reversible factors should always be sought when a diagnosis of CRF is made or when a patient with CRF shows unexpectedly rapid deterioration in renal function. A list of such reversible factors is shown in Table 117–3. A hypercatabolic state as in trauma, extensive surgical procedures, sepsis, or severe gastrointestinal bleeding can precipitate uremia even if the GFR is stable.

Because of the limited ability of a chronically damaged kidney to either conserve or excrete sodium in response to dietary changes or in response to gastrointestinal losses of salt and water, prerenal failure is a common reversible factor in patients with CRF. Cardiac failure responds to the usual therapy, and nonsteroidal anti-inflammatory drugs and ACE inhibitors can cause (hemodynamic) prerenal failure

Table 117–3 • POTENTIALLY REVERSIBLE FACTORS IN CHRONIC RENAL FALIURE

Prerenal failure
    ECF volume depletion
    Cardiac failure
Hemodynamic prerenal
    NSAIDs, ACE inhibitors, *cyclosporine*
Postrenal failure
    Obstructive uropathy
Intrinsic renal failure
    Severe hypertension
    Acute pyelonephritis
    Drug nephrotoxicity (ATN, AIN, vasculitis)
    Acute interstitial nephritis
    Radiocontrast agents (ATN)
    Hypercalcemia
Vascular
    Renovascular
    Renal vein thrombosis*
    Atheroembolism
Miscellaneous
    Hypoadrenalism
    Hypothyroidism

*In nephrotic syndrome.
ACE = angiotensin-converting enzyme; AIN = acute interstitial nephritis; ATN = acute tubular necrosis; ECF = extracellular fluid; NSAIDs = nonsteroidal anti-inflammatory drugs.

in such patients, as well as in CRF patients with normal renal function. Renal stones and benign prostatic hypertrophy are the most common causes of superimposed obstruction.

A careful review of all ingested drugs is mandatory. Renally excreted drugs may either accumulate and reach nephrotoxic levels (aminoglycosides) or cause superimposed acute interstitial nephritis (penicillins). Vascular diagnostic procedures can cause radiocontrast agent–induced renal failure or cholesterol emboli in the kidney as well as elsewhere, including the skin. Unilateral or bilateral renal artery stenosis can complicate CRF and lead to deteriorating renal function and worsening hypertension. Renal vein thrombosis can cause increased proteinuria and a falling GFR in patients with nephrotic syndrome. Hypercalcemia is commonly caused by the combination of 1,25-dihydroxyvitamin D and calcium carbonate, which is used to treat or prevent renal osteodystrophy.

Diagnosis

A history of nephrotic syndrome suggests previous glomerular disease as a cause of the CRF. Recurrent gross hematuria may accompany IgA nephropathy or membranoproliferative glomerulonephritis. A careful personal and family history for hypertension and diabetes mellitus should be obtained, including information on any family members in whom ESRD developed. Families may have a genetic predisposition not only for essential hypertension and diabetes mellitus but also for the development of renal disease secondary to these systemic diseases. A history of recurrent renal stones or obstructive

uropathy, including prostatism, or excessive mixed analgesic intake may suggest primarily tubulointerstitial disease. The family history is also very helpful in the diagnosis of autosomal dominant polycystic kidney disease—although in about 30% a spontaneous mutation occurs: familial glomerulonephritis (Alport's syndrome), IgA nephropathy, and medullary cystic kidney disease.

On physical examination, signs of hypertensive (left ventricular hypertrophy and hypertensive retinopathy) or diabetic disease (peripheral neuropathy, diabetic retinopathy) are important. Knobby, bilaterally enlarged kidneys support a diagnosis of polycystic kidney disease, and a palpable bladder or large prostate suggests obstructive uropathy and is an indication for measurement of residual urinary volume after voiding. Gouty tophi and a history of gout may be relevant. Signs and symptoms of polyarteritis nodosa, systemic lupus erythematosus, Wegener's granulomatosis, scleroderma, and essential mixed cryoglobulinemia should be sought because these systemic diseases often involve the kidney. Hepatosplenomegaly and macroglossia suggests renal amyloidosis.

Laboratory studies should include measurement of serum electrolytes, calcium, phosphorus, alkaline phosphatase, and albumin. Careful urinalysis and urinary microscopy should be performed, as well as measurement of 24-hour urine protein excretion or of urine protein/creatinine ratio in a "spot" urine sample. Marked proteinuria with an abundance of red blood cells, white blood cells, and granular casts suggests a proliferative type of glomerulonephritis, whereas membranous glomerulopathy and focal glomerulosclerosis are associated with less active findings on urinary microscopy. Predominant pyuria occurs in analgesic abuse nephropathy, polycystic kidney disease, and renal tuberculosis, even without superimposed bacterial urinary tract infection.

Urinary protein excretion of more than 3 g/24 hr suggests primary glomerular disease. Serum complement and antinuclear antibodies should then be measured because of the association of hypocomplementemia with membranoproliferative glomerulonephritis and lupus nephritis. Serologic screens for hepatitis B and C virus infection are important because of their respective associations with membranous and membranoproliferative glomerulonephritis. Human immunodeficiency virus–associated glomerulopathy is an important cause of focal glomerulosclerosis. Antineutrophil cytoplasmic antibodies are often positive in Wegener's granulomatosis.

Renal ultrasonography is a useful noninvasive test that can demonstrate cortical scarring (consistent with reflux nephropathy or segmental infarction), renal stones, hydronephrosis, ureteric obstruction, or polycystic kidney disease. Medical kidney disease may be associated with symmetrically diminished size and increased echogenicity; these findings are otherwise nonspecific. Asymmetry of renal size raises a question of renovascular renal failure or previous obstruction from a stricture or stone. Computed tomography without contrast may show papillary necrosis or papillary calcifications suggestive of analgesic abuse nephropathy. A more severe degree of anemia than would be anticipated for the degree of renal failure suggests myeloma kidney; serum and urine immunoelectrophoresis should be performed to detect, respectively, monoclonal antibodies, and/or lambda or kappa light chains. If a monoclonal antibody is found, bone marrow examination is usually necessary to confirm the diagnosis.

If the diagnosis remains obscure and kidney size is normal or only slightly reduced, renal biopsy should be considered for diagnosis after control of blood pressure and, if necessary, dialysis.

 TREATMENT

Once it is determined that a patient has CRF, careful and regular follow-up is mandatory (Fig. 117–2). It is best if the primary care physician and the nephrologist cooperate closely in the management of such patients. Blood pressure, status of extracellular fluid volume, and a careful history and examination for early signs and symptoms of the complications of CRF and the uremic syndrome (e.g., peripheral neuropathy) are essential. Serum electrolytes, BUN and serum creatinine, calcium, phosphorus, hematocrit and mean corpuscular volume, 24-hour urinary protein excretion, serum parathormone, and, in some patients, urinary microscopy are obtained at regular intervals. In the later stages of CRF and in all patients with nephrotic syndrome, serum albumin is also measured to help to assess nutritional status. The patient should

be advised to consult about any intake of over-the-counter or prescribed medications and should avoid nonsteroidal anti-inflammatory drugs and minimize the use of acetaminophen.

The treatment of hypertension is the most important measure to slow the progression of CRF and to reduce cardiovascular morbidity and mortality. Unlike essential hypertension, hypertension secondary to CRF usually progresses and causes a vicious circle of worsening hypertension and renal function (see Fig. 117–1), so any chronic elevation in blood pressure above normal should usually be treated. Patients with CRF commonly require multiple drug therapy for treatment of hypertension. Blood pressure should be reduced to or less than a mean of 95 mm Hg (125/75) unless relative contraindications such as significant coronary artery disease,

Continued

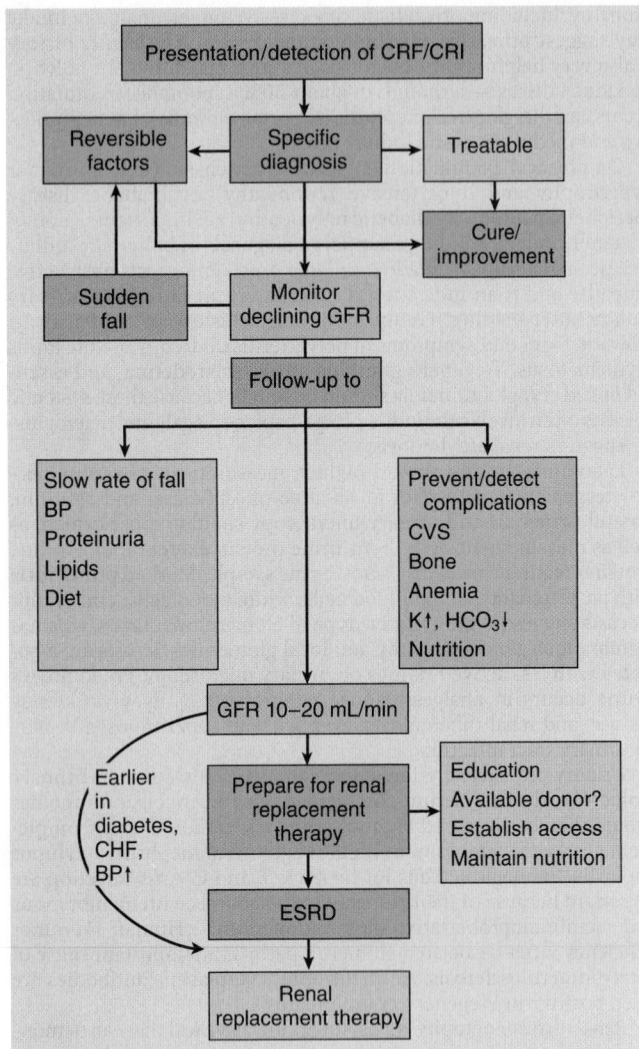

FIGURE 117–2 • Outline of management of patients in the various stages of chronic renal failure (CRF). BP = blood pressure; CHF = congestive heart failure; CRI = chronic renal insufficiency; CVS = cardiovascular system; ESRD = end-stage renal disease; GFR = glomerular filtration rate.

Measure urinary protein/creatinine ratio on morning urine at each visit

↓

Treat specific disease, e.g., SLE or MG

↓

Control mean BP to ≤ 92 mm Hg (ACE inhibitor or ARB* preferred ± loop diuretic for BP control)

↓

Increase dose of ACE inhibitor or ARB* as BP allows, and even if BP control good

↓

If needed to control BP or to reduce proteinuria further, use both ACE inhibitor and ARB*

↓

2 g sodium, 0.8 g/kg protein diet; HMG-CoA reductase inhibitor to reduce LDL to < 100 mg/dL

↓

Add non-DHP CCB

↓

Add spironolactone 25–50 mg daily

*Monitor serum potassium and renal function

FIGURE 117–3 • Downtitration of proteinuria in a patient with chronic renal failure. The goal is maximum possible reduction of proteinuria or less than 300 mg/24 hr. ACE = angiotensin-converting enzyme; ARB = angiotensin II receptor blocker; BP = blood pressure; DHP CCB = dihydropyridine calcium channel blocker; LDL = low-density lipoprotein; MG = membranous glomerulopathy; SLE = systemic lupus erythematosus.

cerebral vascular disease, or diabetic postural hypotension are present. ACE inhibitors or ARBs are the initial drugs of choice. Such treatment requires surveillance for hyperkalemia and hemodynamic prerenal failure. Virtually all patients with CRF require a loop diuretic as part of their antihypertensive treatment. Hyperkalemia develops in only about 5 to 10% of patients while taking ACE inhibitors until very late in the course of CRF. The presence of type 4 hyperkalemic renal tubular acidosis, which is common in diabetic glomerulosclerosis, may prevent their use. The most common side effect associated with ACE inhibitors is chronic cough; an ARB can then be substituted.

Long-acting calcium channel blockers are usually the next antihypertensive to be added, and they have synergistic effects with ACE inhibitors[10] and loop diuretics. Centrally acting α₂-blockers such as clonidine or peripheral α-blockers such as prazosin are good next choices. Minoxidil may also be required, and usually this drug mandates an increased diuretic dose and a β-blocker if reflex tachycardia occurs; both of these side effects occur in response to the profound vasodilatation produced by minoxidil. β–Blockers are used in patients who have had myocardial infarction. Other cardiovascular risk factors such as hyperlipidemia and hyperhomocystinuria should be treated appropriately.

Higher baseline proteinuria and serially increasing proteinuria are associated with more rapid decreases in GFR, and reduction in proteinuria is associated with a slower rate of progression of renal disease.[9] Titration of proteinuria downward by therapy should

now be part of the routine management of patients with CRF (Fig. 117–3). Measurement of serial urine protein/creatinine ratios in the morning urine specimen is a useful mechanism to follow these changes. ACE inhibitors and ARBs appear to have additive effects to reduce urine protein excretion without necessarily further dropping blood pressure.[11] The effective dose for controlling hypertension and that for diminishing urinary protein excretion may differ.

When hypertension or edema develops, sodium intake should be reduced to 2 g (5 g NaCl). Potassium restriction is not usually needed until late in the course of CRF, although the use of ACE inhibitors or β-blockers for hypertension may necessitate restriction sooner. Care should be exercised to avoid high potassium intake, as with potassium-containing salt substitutes. Modest dietary phosphate restriction is also indicated but is difficult to implement because of its presence in so many foods. Magnesium-containing antacids and laxatives should be avoided because of the dangers of hypermagnesemia.

Protein restriction should be instituted to reduce or forestall symptoms of uremia, which are secondary to accumulating products of protein metabolism at any given low GFR, and to reduce the rate of fall in GFR, even in nephrotic syndrome, caused by progressive glomerular disease. Protein restriction must always be accompanied by adequate caloric intake (35 kcal/kg) to avoid catabolism of endogenous protein. A high-protein diet accelerates the rate of loss of GFR and actually increases proteinuria. Protein restriction to 0.7

to 0.8 g/kg body weight per day is indicated. If proteinuria is greater than 5 g/24 hr, that amount should be added to the protein intake. Dietary protein restriction also has the advantage of reducing potassium and phosphate intake and proton production from sulfur- and phosphorus-containing amino acids. The metabolism of each gram of protein yields $\frac{1}{3}$ g urea and 1 mmol/L of hydrogen ion. Nitrogen balance can be maintained by a protein intake of 0.6 g/kg body weight/day, but a margin of safety is preferred. Patients who enter RRT in negative nitrogen balance have diminished survival and an increased complication rate. Uremia itself induces reduced intake of nitrogenous foods, and a vicious circle can ensue and must be terminated by initiating RRT. Protein catabolism in nephrotic syndrome is much greater than suggested by the loss of protein in urine—many times more protein is catabolized in the proximal tubule after passing through the glomerular capillaries. This process is now thought to also invoke tubular atrophy and tubulointerstitial fibrosis (see Fig. 117–1). Measurement of the BUN/serum creatinine ratio helps monitor the patient's dietary compliance with protein restriction. The ratio should be less than 10 in a stable patient with CRF who is ingesting 0.7 to 0.8 g/kg protein/day. The latter can also be estimated more accurately by periodically measuring 24-hour urinary urea nitrogen. Dietary protein intake (grams) = 6.25 (urinary urea nitrogen + 0.031 × body weight in kilograms) + urinary protein (if ≥5 g/24 hr). The 0.031 factor accounts for other sources of nitrogen loss in feces, skin, etc. A multivitamin preparation is usually given, and hyperhomocystinemia is treated by oral folic acid and vitamin B_{12} and B_6 tablets.

Metabolic acidosis leads to increased protein catabolism via the ubiquitin degradation pathway and should be treated by maintaining serum bicarbonate at normal levels with small doses of sodium bicarbonate (0.6 g three times daily gives 22 mmol/L bicarbonate). Metabolic acidosis should also be avoided because it contributes to renal bone disease; excess protons are buffered in the apatite of bone, with release of calcium. Oral calcium carbonate or acetate used as a phosphate binder also provides a base intake to counteract metabolic acidosis. It is obviously difficult to manage the dietary changes just mentioned without good patient compliance and expert dietetic help.

To avoid renal osteodystrophy, calcium carbonate is taken with meals to reduce dietary phosphate absorption as soon as serum phosphate rises to the upper limit of normal. If serum calcium levels remain low despite calcium carbonate or if renal bone disease is already detectable, small doses of 1,25-dihydroxyvitamin D (0.25 to 1 μg) are added with continued monitoring of serum calcium and phosphate to avoid hypercalcemia. Serum parathormone should also be monitored and is best maintained at twice normal because some resistance to its effect on bone is noted in patients with CRF. Patients who are initially seen late in the course of uremia may already have renal osteodystrophy as manifested by bone pain, pathologic fractures, elevated alkaline phosphatase levels, hypocalcemic hyperphosphatemia, radiologic evidence of hyperparathyroidism (e.g., erosion of the margins of the proximal phalanges and the outer third of the clavicle), and soft tissue and vascular calcification. To avoid the latter, the product of calcium × phosphate, with both measured in milligrams per deciliter (the "solubility product"), should be less than 65. Aluminum hydroxide is now best avoided as a phosphate blocker because of the danger of aluminum toxicity, especially in brain and bone. A new effective phosphate binder is sevelemer hydrochloride, a polymer with an organic cation that avoids the potential toxicity of increased calcium or aluminum absorption. This drug is valuable especially in patients in whom hypercalcemia or a high calcium-phosphate solubility product restricts the use of calcium carbonate on acetate.[12] Subtotal parathyroidectomy is still sometimes required for severe hyperparathryoidism and for calciphylaxis syndromes.

Anemia can be treated by the administration of subcutaneous erythropoietin (80 to 120 U/kg given weekly). The dose is carefully titrated against the hematocrit. Some of the so-called uremic symptoms are in fact caused by anemia. The hematocrit should be maintained at around 33% and 36% and not increased to normal levels. Erythropoietin often causes an increase in blood pressure, which should be treated in the same way as discussed earlier. Avoiding a low hematocrit appears to also help prevent left ventricular hypertrophy, an independent risk factor for cardiovascular morbidity.

Failure to respond to erythropoietin indicates a search for deficiencies of iron, folic acid, or vitamin B_{12} or the presence of an inflammatory or immunologic process.

When the serum creatinine reaches 4 to 6 mg/dL in women and 6 to 8 mg/dL in men, planning for RRT should begin. If 24-hour creatinine clearance is being monitored, it must be remembered that as the GFR falls, creatinine clearance progressively overestimates the true GFR because of increasing secretion of creatinine. The goal of the primary care physician and nephrologist must be to initiate RRT at the ideal time, just before or at the very onset of uremic symptomatology, which requires a combination of good clinical judgment and monitoring of the parameters already noted. Any suggestion of declining appetite and commencing negative nitrogen balance should be taken as an indication to proceed to RRT. If the patient has a willing and acceptable live donor, transplantation can sometimes be initiated without prior hemodialysis or peritoneal dialysis. All of the modalities discussed in Chapter 118 must be carefully explained to the patient, and it is very helpful for the patient to meet other patients who have experienced the various RRT modalities. The relative indications for hemodialysis, peritoneal dialysis, and renal transplantation are discussed in Chapter 118. Although there is not universal agreement, most nephrologists initiate RRT somewhat earlier in patients with diabetes, especially if evidence of other diabetic complications is present. Diabetic and uremic peripheral neuropathy and retinopathy tend to compound the effects of one another.

In some patients, hypertension, congestive heart failure, or anemia may indicate initiation of RRT sooner than otherwise would be expected. In patients who have continued to work, an inability to do so may be an indication for RRT. The uremic syndrome is variable in onset and in character in different patients, but subtle signs of anorexia, cognitive impairment, and sensory peripheral neuropathy must be searched for carefully. The development of pericarditis, acute pulmonary edema, or motor peripheral neuropathy, for example, is a clear indication that RRT has been delayed too long. It is now evident that if RRT is delayed too long, its initiation is associated with a longer hospital stay, increased cost, and increased morbidity. When performed appropriately, RRT can be initiated on an outpatient basis.

Vascular or peritoneal access should usually be established about 2 months before the probable requirement for hemodialysis. This practice gives the best chance of creating a viable arteriovenous (often radiocephalic) fistula in the nondominant forearm. Venipuncture should be avoided in that arm before and after fistula formation. Fistula survival is much greater than the survival of synthetic grafts, which are, however, still the most commonly used. Placement of a fistula too early in the course of CRF, however, can lead to thrombosis, whereas late CRF is associated with a hypocoagulable state. When patients are initially seen with frank uremia and no reversible factors are present, emergency dialysis may be required. As in acute renal failure, access can be obtained quickly via the internal jugular vein. In general, the subclavian vein is now avoided because of the development of subclavian stenosis and subsequent venous hypertension in the arm, which complicates the formation of a forearm fistula. Femoral vein access can also be used, but a semipermanent catheter is much more difficult to maintain and much more likely to become infected at that site. If the BUN is very high (>120 mg/dL), the initial hemodialysis should be done only for a short period and at relatively low blood flow rates to avoid the dialysis disequilibrium syndrome (discussed in Chapter 105). Great care must be taken with anticoagulation for hemodialysis if pericarditis is present; if possible, heparin administration should be avoided.

Patients with CRF are at increased risk for atherosclerosis. LDL reduction with statins is useful for secondary prevention of coronary events,[13] and it is increasingly recommended for primary prevention. The physician must be alert to neuropsychiatric and other complications of CRF that may be prematurely diagnosed as uremia secondary to ESRD. These complications include hyponatremia secondary to the much-diminished free water clearance as the GFR falls and to excess fluid intake, which is sometimes unfortunately iatrogenic. Hypernatremia may result from obligatory polyuria if free water intake is not maintained, as during surgery. Hypoxia associated with heart failure or pneumonia may cause confusion,

Continued

especially in elderly patients with CRF. Symptoms may be caused by the retention of drugs, the dosage of which has not been modified appropriately as the GFR falls, especially sedatives and tranquilizers excreted in whole or part via renal mechanisms. Digoxin toxicity may cause nausea, vomiting, and arrhythmias. It is most unwise to perform dialysis on a patient who is uremic because of superimposed prerenal failure; hypovolemic patients tolerate hemodialysis very poorly, and extracellular fluid volume must be repleted before initiation of hemodialysis. Often, if prerenal factors are corrected, dialysis can be postponed. Hyperkalemia is an unusual single cause for the initiation of hemodialysis and can usually be managed by potassium restriction, restoration of urinary flow rates by correction of prerenal failure, sodium polystyrene sulfonate (Kayexalate) retention enemas, intravenous glucose and insulin, and treatment of severe metabolic acidosis with sodium bicarbonate.

Grade A

1. Ruggenenti P, Perna A, Benini R, et al: Chronic nephropathies prolonged ACE inhibition can induce remission: Dynamics of time-dependent changes in GFR. J Am Soc Nephrol 1999;10:997–1006.
2. Mann JFE, Gerstein HC, Pogue J, et al: Renal insufficiency as a predictor of cardiovascular outcomes and the impact of ramipril: The HOPE randomized trial. Ann Intern Med 2001;134:629–636.
3. Lewis EJ, Hunsicker LG, Bain RP, et al: The effect of angiotensin-converting-enzyme inhibition on diabetic nephropathy. N Engl J Med 1999;329:1456–1462.
4. The GISEN Group: Randomized placebo-controlled trial of effect of ramipril on decline in glomerular filtration rate and risk of terminal renal failure in proteinuric, non-diabetic nephropathy. Lancet 1997;349:1857–1863.
5. Agodoa LY, Appel L, Bakris GL, et al: Effect of ramipril vs amlodipine on renal outcomes in hypertensive nephrosclerosis. JAMA 2001;285:2719–2728.
6. Cinotti GA, Zucchelli PC: Effect of lisinopril on the progression of renal insufficiency in mild proteinuric non-diabetic nephropathies. Nephrol Dial Trans 2001; 16:961–966.
7. Klahr S, Levey AS, Beck GJ, et al: The effects of dietary protein restriction and blood pressure control on the progression of chronic renal disease. Modification of Diet in Renal Disease Study Group. N Engl J Med 1994;330:877–884.
8. Kaplan NM: Management of hypertension in patients with type 2 diabetes mellitus: Guidelines based on current evidence. Ann Intern Med 2001;135:1079–1083.
9. Kidney Foundation DOQI Guidelines: Available at http://www.kidney.org/professionals/doqi/index.cfm.
10. Herlitz H, Harris K, Risler T, et al: The effects of an ACE inhibitor and a calcium antagonist on the progression of renal disease: The Nephros Study. Nephrol Dial Trans 2001;16:2158–2165.
11. Ruilope LM, Aldigier JC, Ponticelli C, et al: Safety of the combination of valsartan and benazepril in patients with chronic renal disease. European Group for the Investigation of Valsartan in Chronic Renal Disease. J Hypertens 2000;18:89–95.
12. Bleyer AJ, Burke SK, Dillon M, et al: A comparison of the calcium-free phosphate binder sevelamer hydrochloride with calcium acetate in the treatment of hyperphosphatemia in hemodialysis patients. Am J Kidney Dis 1999;33:694–701.
13. Tonelli M, Moye L, Sacks FM, et al, for the Cholesterol and Recurrent Events (CARE) Trial Investigators: Pravastatin for secondary prevention of cardiovascular events in persons with mild chronic renal insufficiency. Ann Intern Med 2003;138:98–104.

SUGGESTED READINGS

Bardin T: Musculoskeletal manifestations of chronic renal failure. Curr Opin Rheumatol 2003;15:48–54. *Overview including nephrogenic fibrosing dermopathy.*
Hostetter TH: Prevention of end-stage renal disease due to type 2 diabetes. N Engl J Med 2001;345:910–911. *This editorial summarizes the findings of three controlled trials (in the same issue), which demonstrate a renoprotective effect of angiotensin receptor blockers, independent of their hypotensive action, in patients with type II diabetes mellitus and microalbuminuria or proteinuria.*
Kurtzman NA (ed), Keane WF (guest ed): Progression of renal disease. Semin Nephrol 2001;21:533–602. *Journal issue devoted to review of the important role of the intrarenal renin-angiotensin-aldosterone axis in contributing to progressive renal disease after the initial injury; the genetic basis of the varying responses in that system is discussed.*
Pereira BJG: Optimization of pre-ESRD care: The key to improved dialysis outcomes. Kidney Int 2000;57:351–365. *A comprehensive review of primary prevention of ESRD and secondary prevention of its complications especially cardiovascular morbidity and mortality; comorbid disease is all too common—but preventable—in patients reaching ESRD.*
Trivedi HS, Brooks BJ: Erythropoietin therapy in pre-dialysis patients with chronic renal failure: Lack of need for parenteral iron. Am J Nephrol 2003;23:78–85. *Pre-dialysis erythropoietin was successful for treating anemia without parenteral iron.*
Yu HT: Progression of chronic renal failure. Arch Intern Med 2003;163:1417–1429. *Reviews the roles of antihypertensive agents, statins, and protein restriction.*

118 TREATMENT OF IRREVERSIBLE RENAL FAILURE

Nina Tolkoff-Rubin
Nelson Goes

Unlike other forms of end-stage organ failure, renal failure is unique in having three modalities of therapy: (1) hemodialysis, (2) peritoneal dialysis, and (3) renal transplantation. Each form of renal replacement therapy (RRT) has its unique risks and benefits.

Kolff first employed hemodialysis in the late 1940s for the treatment of acute renal failure. The development of vascular access by Scribner in the early 1960s enabled the use of hemodialysis as a chronic therapy. However, it was not until 1973, when the U.S. Congress approved Medicare funding for hemodialysis patients, recognizing end-stage renal disease (ESRD) as a "catastrophic illness," that hemodialysis achieved widespread availability. Currently there are approximately 250,000 patients on dialysis in the United States, and the ESRD population is projected to grow about 8% per year.

All three modalities of RRT have evolved significantly over the last four decades. The selection of a particular form of RRT is made according to the clinical setting and patient preference. It is important for the physician and the patient to recognize that each of these modalities should be viewed as alternative and complementary therapies, allowing flexibility of care under different clinical circumstances. The key is to identify patients with progressive renal failure early so as to enable them to make an educated choice that fits their lifestyle and medical situation. Planning and establishing access early decrease emergency hospitalizations and complications and significantly reduce cost. Early evaluation also enables identification of potential living donors so that preemptive transplantation can be performed.

HEMODIALYSIS

Dialysis substitutes two major renal functions: *solute removal* and *fluid removal*. In hemodialysis, solute removal occurs predominantly by diffusion, which is the movement of solutes from the blood compartment to the dialysate compartment across a semipermeable membrane. The key determinants of clearance of a particular substance are the following:

1. Molecular size—clearance is size dependent and is higher for smaller molecules
2. The concentration gradient between the blood and the dialysis solution of a particular substance—the greater the concentration gradient, the more rapidly diffusion occurs
3. Membrane surface area—the net transfer of solute increases as membrane surface area increases
4. Membrane permeability—this is determined by the specific characteristics of the membrane such as pore size, charge, and quaternary conformation
5. Blood and dialysate flow rates—higher flow rates allow greater solute removal, especially if the flow of dialysate is countercurrent to blood flow, which permits maximal gradient across the membrane

Solute removal can also occur by the process of convection, the movement of solutes by bulk flow in association with fluid removal (solvent drag). Although the convective mass transfer of solutes may not play a dominant role in conventional hemodialysis, convection does play a significant role in high flux dialysis and in continuous venovenous hemofiltration (CVVH).

Fluid removal in hemodialysis occurs by the process of ultrafiltration. The ultrafiltration rate is determined by the hydrostatic pressure gradient across the dialysis membrane—called the *transmembrane pressure*. Ultrafiltration increases when positive pressure is applied to the blood compartment or if negative pressure is applied to the dialysate side of the dialysis membrane. During dialysis the ultrafiltration rate is adjusted to obtain the desired fluid loss.

The hemodialysis machine has three main components: (1) the dialyzer (i.e., the dialysis membrane); (2) a pump that regulates blood flow; and (3) a dialysate solution delivery system. In addition, the

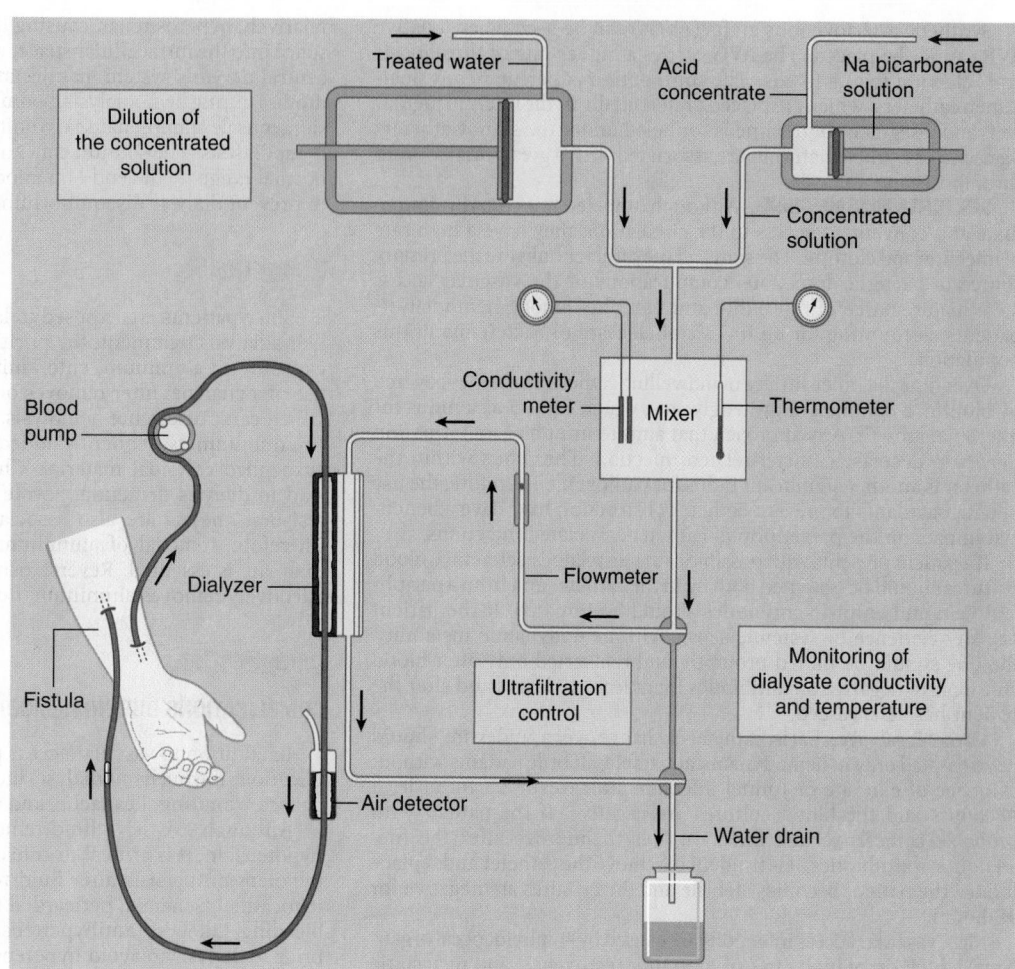

FIGURE 118–1 • Hemodialysis: Treated water is mixed with concentrated dialysate. The dialysate solution flows around the fibers of the hollow-fiber dialyzer countercurrent to the blood flow through the dialyzer. A computerized ultrafiltration control device regulates fluid removal.

machine has many safety devices to monitor arterial and venous pressures, concentration of ions and temperature in the dialysate, as well as air and blood leaks (Fig. 118–1).

Under most circumstances, solute removal and fluid removal occur simultaneously. However, if vigorous ultrafiltration is attempted during conventional hemodialysis, patients frequently complain of muscle cramping, nausea, and vomiting. Moreover, during aggressive fluid removal there may be a decrease in systemic vascular resistance, leading to a drop in blood pressure. Separating ultrafiltration from dialysis enables efficient fluid removal with greater hemodynamic stability. If osmotic changes are minimized with isolated ultrafiltration (i.e., blood is filtered in the absence of dialysate solution), vascular resistance is well maintained, and consequently less hypotension occurs in association with large fluid shifts.

Hemodialyzers

The hollow-fiber dialyzer is composed of thousands of parallel capillary tubes. Blood flows through the capillary tubes and dialysate flows through the canister, bathing the outside of the capillary tubes (see Fig. 118–1).

The dialysis membrane is an essential component of the dialyzer. The initial membranes were made of cuprophane, a derivative of cellulose, which has excellent clearance of small molecules but very poor clearance of middle-sized molecules. The contact of blood with these membranes leads to activation of inflammatory and clotting cascades. The alternative pathway of complement is also activated by contact with the dialysis membrane, leading to activation of granulocytes. Platelet-activating factor production is also increased in complement-activating membranes.

The activation of inflammatory and coagulation pathways leads to significant clinical events. Acutely, patients may develop chest pain, back pain, and shortness of breath, especially with cellulosic membranes. Chronic activation of inflammation may also lead to accumulation of β_2-microglobulin and a form of amyloidosis

described only in long-term hemodialysis patients. Dialysis-related amyloidosis is associated with carpal tunnel syndrome, diffuse arthropathy, lytic bone lesions, and pathologic fractures. The synthetic membranes made of polycarbonate, polysulfones, polyacrylonitrile, or polymethylmethacrylate are less proinflammatory and also have higher diffusive clearances for larger molecules and higher ultrafiltration rates.

The survival of patients with acute renal failure appears to be impacted by the type of membrane employed. Studies comparing cuprophane with synthetic membranes showed not only improved patient survival and more rapid recovery of kidney function after acute renal failure but a decrease in the incidence of death from sepsis in the patients dialyzed with a synthetic membrane.

Access

To perform hemodialysis on a repetitive basis, access to the circulation is essential. The arteriovenous fistula (AVF) is the "gold standard" hemodialysis access and involves the anastomosis of the radial artery to the cephalic vein, with subsequent "arterialization" of the superficial forearm veins to enable blood flow rates up to 400 mL/min. The most frequent problem associated with AVFs is failure to mature, particularly in patients with peripheral vascular disease and diabetes. Thus, it is important to spare the nondominant arm in all patients with chronic kidney disease (CKD) from venipuncture and to plan the placement of AVFs long in advance of the patient's approach to hemodialysis because the fistula generally takes 6 to 8 weeks to mature. Less than one half of patients initiating hemodialysis in the United States have a permanent vascular access in place. Elective placement of a permanent access before dialysis initiation reduces morbidity, mortality, and cost. The National Kidney Foundation/Disease Outcomes Quality Initiative (NKF/DOQI) guidelines recommend placement of an AVF when the serum creatinine exceeds 4 mg/dL, creatinine clearance falls below 25 mL/min, or hemodialysis initiation is anticipated within 1 year.

Synthetic arteriovenous grafts (AVGs) can be used when a native AVF cannot be placed. The AVG carries a higher rate of thrombosis and infection than a fistula. The third option is percutaneous dual-lumen catheters, which are placed preferentially in the internal jugular vein and a segment of the line is tunneled under the skin. Catheters placed in the subclavian vein are associated with a greater risk of vein thrombosis and stenosis.

VASCULAR ACCESS INFECTIONS. Although tunneled lines provide immediate and convenient access to the circulation, they have a high rate of infection and clotting. The skin and the catheter hubs are the primary source of bacteria. Infectious complications of the vascular access are a major source of morbidity and mortality among hemodialysis patients, accounting for up to 73% of all cases of bacteremia in this population.

Over time the inner surface of indwelling catheters becomes covered by biofilm, a complex of proteoglycans, which can act as a nidus for microbial growth. Any approach that aims to limit biofilm formation may help decrease catheter-related infection. Thrombus within the catheter is another significant nidus for pathogens. Therefore, the use of anticoagulants to prevent catheter obstruction may have a beneficial impact on the prevention of catheter-associated infections.

If a patient presents with possible catheter-related bacteremia, blood cultures should be obtained both from the catheter and from a peripheral vein and empiric antibiotics should be initiated. If the patient has any evidence of systemic sepsis with hemodynamic instability, the line should be pulled promptly and reinserted only after blood cultures are negative on antibiotics for at least 48 hours and after the patient has defervesced.

Catheter salvage, that is, catheter exchange over a guidewire, should be attempted only in hemodynamically stable, afebrile patients without evidence of exit site or tunnel infection after treatment for at least 48 hours and the blood cultures are negative. If the patient with probable catheter-related infection fails to improve after the first 24 hours of antibiotics, it is prudent to remove the catheter and replace it once the patient becomes afebrile and the cultures are negative for 48 hours.

Most vascular access infections are caused by staphylococcal organisms, which carry high rates of mortality, recurrence, and metastatic complications. Vancomycin is generally employed in institutions with an increased incidence of methicillin-resistant staphylococci. However, the indiscriminate and prolonged use of vancomycin should be avoided to prevent the emergence of vancomycin-resistant *Staphylococcus aureus* and *Enterococcus*.

In patients with a prompt response to antibiotic therapy, antimicrobials should be administered for at least 2 to 3 weeks. A prolonged course of antibiotic therapy (4 to 8 weeks) should be employed if there is persistent bacteremia or fungemia after catheter removal or if there is evidence of endocarditis, septic arthritis, osteomyelitis, epidural abscess, or other metastatic infection.

Anticoagulation

The contact of patient's blood with the dialysis membrane and the tubing leads to activation of the coagulation cascade. Heparin is generally required to prevent clotting of the hemodialysis circuit. Several complications may occur as a result of heparin use, including bleeding or the development of heparin-induced thrombocytopenia.

In patients at high risk of bleeding, hemodialysis can be performed without anticoagulation. Heparin-free dialysis requires a high blood flow rate and frequent flushing of the system with normal saline. Many patients may also develop a procoagulant state caused by the development of anticardiolipin and lupus anticoagulant antibodies or high homocysteine levels, which may contribute to the tendency to clot the dialyzer and vascular access.

Dialysate Solution

The dialysate is a balanced solution of sodium, potassium, calcium, magnesium, chloride, and dextrose using bicarbonate as buffer. During dialysis the sodium concentration is usually maintained at 135 to 140 mEq/L. The sodium concentration can be increased during part of the hemodialysis session to counterbalance the intracellular hyperosmolarity caused by the rapid fall in urea concentration—defined as sodium modeling. Because urea is cleared at a faster rate from the extracellular space, the intracellular space becomes relatively hyperosmolar, causing fluid to shift from the extracellular space into the intracellular space, which may lead to hypotension and central nervous system manifestations (dialysis disequilibrium syndrome) during hemodialysis. Sodium modeling helps prevent hypotension, muscle cramps, nausea, vomiting, headaches, and seizures during hemodialysis. The sodium concentration is programmed to return to normal range by the end of hemodialysis. Mannitol can also be used to prevent dialysis disequilibrium syndrome.

Water Quality

Since patients are exposed to large volumes of water during each hemodialysis treatment, the purity of the water is essential to avoid exposure to aluminum, chloramines, endotoxin, and bacteria. The use of a charcoal filter removes organic toxins such as chloramines, which can cause acute hemolysis.

Aluminum is frequently added to the water supply to precipitate suspended colloidal material. Chronic exposure to aluminum can lead to dialysis dementia. Severe bone disease and erythropoietin-resistant anemia are also associated with aluminum intoxication. Therefore, removal of aluminum from the water used to prepare dialysate is essential. Reverse osmosis or deionization of the water effectively removes aluminum, fluoride, and copper.

Complications

COMPLICATIONS DURING HEMODIALYSIS

In addition to vascular access problems, the most common complications during hemodialysis include hypotension, muscle cramps, nausea, vomiting, headache, and chest pain.

Although excessive fluid removal is the most frequent cause of hypotension, it is critical to rule out other potential etiologies if the hypotension persists after fluid replacement. These include sepsis, myocardial ischemia, pericardial tamponade, arrhythmias, or active bleeding. Likewise, antihypertensive agents may need to be withheld prior to dialysis to avoid hypotension.

Air embolus is the most dreaded technical complication of the hemodialysis procedure. Despite the presence of air detectors in the dialysis machine, there remains the risk of an air embolus with repeated disconnections of catheters. The patients may develop agitation, cough, dyspnea, and chest pain. As soon as the diagnosis is suspected, the patient should be positioned with the left side down in an attempt to trap air in the right ventricle and 100% oxygen should be administered.

LONG-TERM COMPLICATIONS IN HEMODIALYSIS

ANEMIA. The development of anemia parallels the progression of CKD. CKD-related anemia is usually normochromic and normocytic. Nearly two thirds of patients starting dialysis have hematocrit levels below 30%. The target hemoglobin range established by the NKF/DOQI is between 11 to 12 g/dL. Untreated anemia contributes to cardiovascular morbidity and mortality and has been associated with impaired cognition, exercise capacity, and ability to perform simple tasks. Decreased erythropoietin production is the major factor contributing to anemia among patients with CKD. Numerous other factors contribute to anemia, such as shortened life span of red blood cells, uremic inhibitors of erythropoiesis, iron deficiency due to poor iron absorption, gastrointestinal bleeding, loss of blood with frequent blood sampling, and losses during hemodialysis. Folic acid is removed by dialysis, making folate replacement necessary. Infection, inflammation, malignancy, and a high parathyroid hormone level can also inhibit red blood cell maturation. Aluminum toxicity, either from aluminum contamination of the water supply or through the use of aluminum-containing phosphate binders, has been associated with microcytic anemia in long-term dialysis patients with normal iron stores.

Anemia Therapy. The administration of erythropoietin, together with repletion of iron stores, folic acid supplementation, and treatment of concomitant infection, is effective in correcting the anemia of chronic renal disease. Failure to provide an adequate supply of iron is the most common cause of erythropoietin treatment failure in addition to the presence of ongoing inflammation and infection. The best way to replenish the iron stores is the administration of iron intravenously.

Some iron preparations have been associated with severe allergic reactions, including anaphylaxis, due to the presence of dextran. The newer iron preparations, containing sucrose instead of dextran, appear to be associated with fewer side effects. A transferrin saturation level (serum iron/total iron-binding capacity × 100%) below 20% is considered the point to initiate intravenous iron therapy.

A number of adverse effects have been described with erythropoietin therapy, including accelerated hypertension. Erythropoietin therapy has also been associated with seizures and thrombosis of vascular access. Hypertension and thrombosis appear to be directly related to the level of hematocrit and to how rapidly the increase in hematocrit was achieved. A lower dose of erythropoietin is needed to achieve similar hematocrit levels when the drug is administered subcutaneously.

MALNUTRITION. Hypoalbuminemia is associated with an increased mortality on dialysis. An albumin level below 3.0 g/dL has a 2-year mortality rate up to 40% in comparison with the expected mortality rate of 20%. Marked catabolism, anorexia, and severe diet limitations during the predialysis period lead to loss of lean weight. After the initiation of dialysis, patients generally have an improved appetite and the protein intake recommended should be at least 1.2 g/kg per day with a total caloric intake of 35 cal/kg. Water-soluble vitamins, including folic acid, need to be replaced because they are depleted during dialysis.

CHRONIC KIDNEY DISEASE AND CARDIOVASCULAR DISEASE. Cardiovascular disease is the most important cause of death among patients with CKD. CVD accounts for approximately 50% of the mortality among patients on dialysis and recipients of renal allografts. Two thirds of patients with CKD have diabetes mellitus or hypertension, but the rates of CVD and mortality are also elevated among patients with primary renal diseases such as glomerulonephritis. The relative hazard is greatest among patients younger than 45 years of age. In this age group, cardiac mortality is 100 times greater than in the general population.

In patients initiating dialysis, the main cardiac abnormality is left ventricular hypertrophy. Ventricular dilation, arterial stiffening (especially aortic), and coronary atherosclerosis with prominent calcification often accompany left ventricular hypertrophy. Although some of the risk factors for CVD in dialysis patients are similar to the general population, they also have unique risk factors, specific to the uremic state, including anemia, hypervolemia, pericardial disease, oxidative stress, hyperhomocysteinemia, and increased inflammatory markers such as C-reactive protein.

Disorders of mineral metabolism have also been proposed to play a crucial role in the cardiovascular abnormalities of CKD patients. A number of studies have shown a direct correlation between an elevated serum phosphorus (>5.5 mg/dL), a calcium-phosphorus product (Ca × P) greater than 56, and mortality in hemodialysis patients. A striking degree of coronary and aortic calcification has been demonstrated in young adults with ESRD using electron-beam tomography. This has been correlated with an elevated calcium-phosphorus product as well as the dose of calcium ingested. These striking findings have raised new questions about the therapy of hyperphosphatemia and the use of calcium- versus non-calcium-containing phosphate binders.

Indications for Renal Replacement Therapy

The decision as to when to institute dialysis depends on the patient's signs and symptoms rather than an absolute level of blood urea nitrogen (BUN) or serum creatinine. The current opinion is that patients who begin dialysis at a relatively higher level of residual renal function have less morbidity and mortality. The benefits of early initiation include the avoidance of malnutrition, fluid overload, and the deleterious effects of prolonged exposure to the accumulation of phosphorus, β_2-microglobulin, and other uremic toxins.

There is no question that hyperkalemia (unresponsive to diuretics, ion exchange resins, and dietary restriction), in the face of electrocardiographic changes, is an absolute indication for dialysis to avoid life-threatening arrhythmias such as ventricular tachycardia, ventricular fibrillation, or asystole. Likewise, volume overload refractory to intravenous diuretics is an indication to start dialysis. Increasing lethargy, difficulty concentrating, nausea, and anorexia all may reflect advancing renal failure and may be manifestations of the uremic syndrome requiring dialytic therapy. One wants to intervene prior to the progression of uremic encephalopathy, seizures, and coma or the development of pericarditis or pericardial tamponade. Emergent hemodialysis is more costly since these patients generally lack vascular access and are sicker, often requiring prolonged hospitalizations.

Dialysis Dose

Even though initiation of dialysis acutely prevents death from uremic complications, mortality of chronic dialysis patients remains high in the United States (~20% per year). Certainly age, comorbid conditions such as diabetes and CVD, and nutritional status as well as infection all contribute significantly to the high mortality in this population. However, it is also well established that patient outcome on dialysis is related to the dose and adequacy of dialysis.

The National Cooperative Dialysis Study (NCDS) was a landmark prospective, randomized study that demonstrated that the time-averaged concentration of urea and the nutritional status, determined by protein catabolic rate, were important determinants of morbidity and mortality in hemodialysis. It is better for patients to be dialyzed longer and be well nourished than to have a low BUN and be dialyzed for shorter periods. Thus, the main lesson is that quantifying and providing an adequate dose of dialysis impacts patient outcome. However, there appears not to be a significant benefit from increasing the dose beyond thrice weekly.∎

The prescription of hemodialysis is tailored to the patient's size and protein intake. Urea is used as surrogate marker for clearance because it reflects the efficiency of removal of small uremic toxins. Various methods have been proposed to quantify hemodialysis adequacy. The most frequently used methods are the urea reduction ratio (URR) and urea kinetic modeling (Kt/V). The URR (100 × [1 − postdialysis BUN/predialysis BUN]) has the advantage of simplicity but it does not account for the fact that urea is removed by ultrafiltration and that urea cannot be used to assess nutritional status. The Kt/V takes into account both of these variables and is the preferred method for determining adequacy for stable chronic dialysis patients.

Kt/V is a dimensionless formula that determines the fractional urea clearance per treatment normalized to the volume of urea distribution. K is the dialyzer clearance, t is the time of dialysis therapy, and V is the volume of distribution of urea, which is approximately equal to the total body water. When supplied with simple clinical information (predialysis and postdialysis weights, ultrafiltration volume, hematocrit, and predialysis and postdialysis BUN as well as the dialyzer clearance), computer software programs will perform the calculation. The NKF/DOQI recommends a Kt/V greater than 1.2 and URR greater than 65% to minimize uremic complications and hospitalizations.

Continuous Renal Replacement Therapy

Critically ill patients with renal failure are frequently hemodynamically unstable and hypercatabolic (e.g., sepsis, severe burns, brain injury, liver failure, trauma) and require large amounts of fluids (e.g., nutrition, antibiotics). Standard hemodialysis may be attempted to treat patients in the intensive care unit. However, hypotension, due in part to rapid fluid and solute removal, is usually an impediment to conventional dialysis. Moreover, patients with liver failure, traumatic brain injury, or coma do not tolerate the rapid osmolarity changes produced by hemodialysis, which can cause severe brain edema and herniation. In contrast, during continuous renal replacement therapy, the rate of fluid removal is slow, and solute clearance relies on convection (solvent drag) rather than diffusion, which does not cause osmolarity changes.

CVVH is the most commonly performed method of continuous RRT. This pump-based system requires central venous access (double-lumen catheter) and blood flows between 150 and 200 mL/min. Blood under pressure passes down one side of a highly permeable membrane, allowing both water and solutes up to a molecular weight of about 40 kD to pass across the membrane. During hemofiltration, in contrast to hemodialysis, urea, creatinine, and phosphate are cleared at similar rates (convective clearance). The filtrate is discarded and the fluid lost is partially replaced with a solution containing the major crystalloid components of the plasma at physiologic levels into either the inflow or outflow blood line (predilution vs. postdilution mode). However, if further clearance is needed in highly catabolic patients, diffusive dialysis can be added by passing dialysis solution through the dialysate compartment.

Anticoagulation is generally required to maintain the patency of the CVVH circuit. Although protocols using heparin can be employed, many patients are at high risk of bleeding, which precludes the use of heparin. One effective method of anticoagulation is the use of a calcium-free citrate replacement fluid administered prefilter. Calcium is infused in a separate central line and monitored to avoid hypocalcemia. Citrate chelates calcium in the blood, preventing clotting of the hemofilter. Citrate is metabolized to bicarbonate by the liver. If the patient cannot metabolize citrate, an anion gap metabolic acidosis will develop. Dissociation between ionized calcium (low) and total calcium (high) will also be observed. The calcium dissociation occurs because the measurement of total calcium includes calcium bound to citrate. Citrate toxicity may occur in patients with severe liver failure. Many of these patients with low platelets and coagulopathy may tolerate CVVH without anticoagulation using bicarbonate-containing replacement solution.

Presently there is no evidence from randomized studies demonstrating that CVVH offers a survival advantage to intermittent hemodialysis in patients with acute renal failure despite the advantages of CVVH in enabling the removal of large amounts of fluid with improved hemodynamic stability and excellent metabolic and acid-base control. However, what is emerging is that the dose of CVVH (ultrafiltration rates >35 mL/kg/hr) appears to correlate with improved survival in critically ill patients with acute renal failure, both in the chronic as well as acute setting.[2]

Future Directions

Nocturnal or daily hemodialysis is associated with marked benefits, including improved solute clearance with excellent control of serum phosphate and medium-sized molecules. It also provides excellent blood pressure control with a reduction in medication requirements. Nocturnal hemodialysis can be performed six or seven nights a week at home for a variable amount of time based on the length of sleep desired (usually 6 to 12 hours in total). A family member can perform it or the patient may be monitored at a central station through closed-circuit television. It remains to be determined whether increasing the dose of dialysis improves patient outcomes.

PERITONEAL DIALYSIS

More than 20% of ESRD patients in the United States and more than 50% in the United Kingdom are receiving continuous ambulatory peritoneal dialysis (CAPD). Several studies suggest that CAPD has survival rates comparable to hemodialysis, when adjusted for patient age and comorbid conditions. CAPD offers a number of potential advantages. Peritoneal dialysis obviates the need for vascular access, a major challenge in diabetic patients, young children, and patients with severe vascular disease. Moreover, peritoneal dialysis can be performed without anticoagulation, decreasing the possible risk for bleeding. Since peritoneal dialysis is a slow, continuous process, it avoids the marked hemodynamic and osmotic shifts associated with hemodialysis. Moreover, CAPD offers a number of quality-of-life advantages. Patients can be taught to do this at home, giving them a sense of control and independence. Also, peritoneal dialysis enables greater liberalization of diet with respect to salt, potassium, protein, and fluid. Clearly, peritoneal dialysis, when feasible, is the treatment modality of choice in children, avoiding frequent needle sticks, and most important, allowing them to grow.

Peritoneal dialysis uses the patient's own peritoneal membrane for the removal of waste products and removal of fluid (Fig. 118–2). During peritoneal dialysis in an adult, generally 2 to 3 L of dialysate solution containing electrolytes in physiologic concentrations to correct acid-base and electrolytes disturbances and varying concentrations of glucose are infused into the peritoneal cavity via a peritoneal catheter. After a specified dwell time varying between 3 and 6 hours per exchange, the fluid is drained and the process is repeated. The removal of solute from the body depends on the development of a concentration gradient between the blood and peritoneal fluid and occurs by diffusion across the peritoneal membrane. Osmotic ultrafiltration is achieved by the addition of increasing concentrations of glucose to the dialysate solution. The osmotic pressure generated by the glucose draws water from the extracellular fluid and the tissues into the peritoneal fluid. However, the net ultrafiltration rate decreases during the exchange secondary to glucose absorption during the exchange.

Unlike hemodialysis, where the characteristics of the dialyzer are specified by the manufacturer, in peritoneal dialysis, membrane characteristics vary from one individual to another. To appropriately determine a peritoneal dialysis prescription, it is critical to determine the peritoneal membrane characteristics of an individual patient. The peritoneal equilibration test (PET) is the semiquantitative clinical test commonly used to characterize the transport functions of the peritoneal membrane. The standardized PET procedure consists of a 4-hour dwell using 2 L of 2.5% solution; equilibration ratios are then determined between plasma and dialysate for creatinine at 0, 2, and 4 hours. The PET also enables measurement of net fluid removal by examining the ratio of dialysate glucose at 4 hours to dialysate glucose

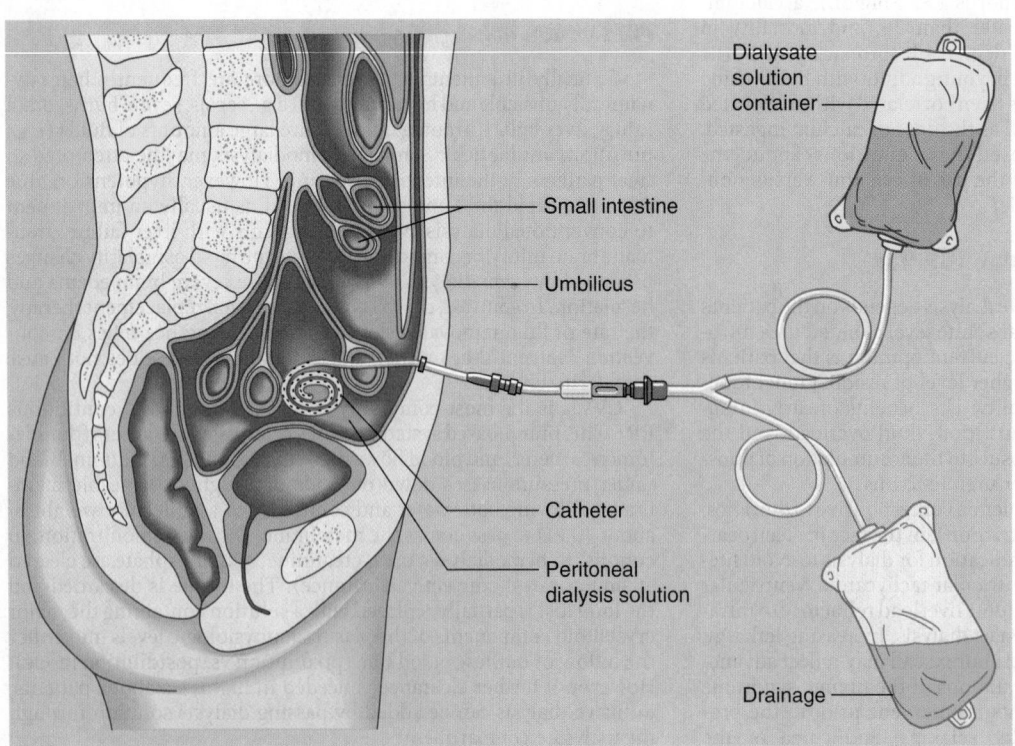

Small intestine

Umbilicus

Catheter

Peritoneal dialysis solution

Dialysate solution container

Drainage

FIGURE 118–2 • Peritoneal dialysis schematic picture.

at time zero. Patients are generally classified on the basis of their dialysate-to-plasma creatinine ratio into the following types:

1. *High transporters:* These patients have a high dialysis/plasma creatinine ratio and achieve rapid equilibration of creatinine and urea across the peritoneal membrane. However, because of their rapid absorption of glucose from the dialysate solution they also tend to lose their osmotic gradient for fluid removal. Thus high or rapid transporters tend to have excellent solute clearance but have difficulty with ultrafiltration. They tend to de well with frequent exchanges and short dwell times that can be achieved with the automated cycler machine. These exchanges can be performed at night while the patient sleeps.

2. *Low transporters:* In contrast, these patients have a low D/P for creatinine and urea, reflecting slower solute equilibration across the peritoneal membrane. They tend to do best with long dwells and high volumes of dialysate to maximize diffusion. However, these patients generally have excellent ultrafiltration and excellent fluid removal. Patients who are found to be average transporters can do well with either form of peritoneal dialysis—CAPD or automated cycler therapy.

Peritoneal Dialysis Dose

It has been well established by a number of studies that small solute clearance is a key predictor of survival in peritoneal dialysis patients. These results have led to the NKF/DOQI guidelines on peritoneal adequacy that advocate a target Kt/V for urea of 2 per week and a target creatinine clearance of 60 L/wk per 1.73 m^2 body surface area. However, what is emerging is the observation that this relationship between small solute clearance and patient outcome in large part is accounted for by residual renal clearance. A number of investigations have failed to demonstrate an independent effect of peritoneal clearance on outcome at least within the dose range commonly used in a clinical practice week (Kt/V of 1.8). Consequently, there may be a need to revisit target clearances. Certainly, what is emerging is the fact that residual and peritoneal clearances do not have equivalent physiologic significance in prolonging patient survival and that every effort should be made to maintain residual renal function as long as possible by avoiding nephrotoxins such as nonsteroidal anti-inflammatory drugs, iodinated contrast agents, and aminoglycosides.

Complications

INFECTION. Despite improvements in the technology of peritoneal dialysis, infection remains the most common problem plaguing CAPD patients and represents the most frequent cause for catheter removal and discontinuation of therapy. Infection can occur (1) at the exit site, with purulent or bloody drainage, erythema, tenderness, or induration; (2) around the subcutaneous tunnel of the catheter with redness, swelling, or tenderness; or (3) in the peritoneal cavity (peritonitis). The diagnosis of peritonitis should be entertained when a patient presents with abdominal pain and cloudy dialysate. The patients frequently have fever, nausea, and vomiting. Abdominal tenderness, often with rebound, is frequently found on physical examination. The major diagnostic criterion is the cell count in the peritoneal fluid. Patients with peritonitis generally show a white blood cell count greater than 100/mm^3 with a predominance of neutrophils. Lymphocytes may predominate with fungal or mycobacterial infections. Prompt recognition and treatment of these infections are critical to avoid relapsing or refractory infections that require catheter removal.

S. *aureus* is the organism responsible for the majority of exit site and tunnel infections. In contrast, *Staphylococcus epidermidis*, a frequent cause of peritonitis, is a less frequent cause of exit site and tunnel infection. Initial empiric therapy therefore should cover grampositive organisms. Oral penicillinase-resistant penicillins, fluoroquinolones, trimethoprim-sulfamethoxazole, or cephalosporins are recommended. Vancomycin should be avoided as first-line therapy except for methicillin-resistant S. *aureus*.

S. *aureus* nasal carriage is a recognized risk factor for exit site and tunnel infections. Mupirocin nasal ointment used twice daily for 5 days every 4 weeks, or mupirocin ointment applied to the exit site, has significantly reduced the incidence of S. *aureus* exit site infections.

S. *epidermidis* has been the most common organism causing bacterial peritonitis in CAPD patients and generally is the result of contamination, such as in the introduction of skin bacteria due to breaks in sterile technique. The recent introduction of disconnect systems has led to a reduction in overall peritonitis rates particularly due to S. *epidermidis*. *Pseudomonas* accounts for 5 to 8% of the episodes of CAPD peritonitis, which are often difficult to eradicate because of the development of a biofilm on the catheter and are frequently associated with catheter loss. Efforts to prevent the formation of biofilm may be an important future strategy in treating *Pseudomonas* as well as fungal infection. Likewise, fungal infections are extremely difficult to eradicate despite appropriate antifungal therapy. Consequently, many institutions have made a policy of removing the peritoneal dialysis catheter as soon as the diagnosis of fungal peritonitis is made.

The third major source of peritonitis is intra-abdominal pathology that can occur due to processes such as a perforated diverticulum, ruptured appendix, ischemic bowel, incarcerated hernia, pancreatitis, or gynecologic pathology. The major diagnostic clue is the presence of polymicrobial enteric organisms on culture, particularly the presence of anaerobic organisms in the dialysate. An abdominal computed tomographic (CT) scan may help in identifying the anatomic site of the lesion. Although free air may be seen in asymptomatic patients on peritoneal dialysis, the presence of free air should raise the possibility of a perforated viscus. The key is establishing the diagnosis rapidly and, where appropriate, moving directly to surgery.

A number of antibiotic regimens have been found effective in the treatment of CAPD peritonitis. The current guideline recommends a first-generation cephalosporin together with a third-generation cephalosporin with antipseudomonal activity (e.g. ceftazidime) intraperitoneally as initial empirical therapy. This strategy preserves vancomycin for true methicillin-resistant organisms and avoids aminoglycosides to preserve residual renal function. However, a number of clinicians have advocated that initial therapy continue to be vancomycin awaiting cultures and sensitivities owing to failures or relapses with first-generation cephalosporins.

OTHER COMPLICATIONS. Mechanical problems may occur, including catheter malfunction due to omental wraps and blood or fibrin clots in the catheter lumen; catheter migration; or abdominal hernias due to increased intra-abdominal pressure with large volumes of dialysate. A number of metabolic complications may also occur, including hyperglycemia and hypertriglyceridemia from high glucose loads; weight gain; and protein loss, especially during an episode of peritonitis. Because peritoneal dialysis requires daily multiple exchanges, it is essential to assess for compliance on an ongoing basis and to ensure that the patient has an adequate support system to avoid "burn-out."

Future Directions

One of the major advantages of peritoneal dialysis is the biocompatibility of the peritoneal membrane. In contrast, however, the dialysate solutions are bioincompatible in that they are acidic and hyperosmolar. Moreover, the high-glucose concentration has been shown not only to contribute to metabolic abnormalities but also to inhibit the function of leukocytes and impact the long-term function of the peritoneal membrane through the production of advanced glycosylation end products. A dialysate containing 7.5% icodextrin has been approved as a safe and effective substitute for hypertonic glucose as an osmotic agent. This new glucose polymer, which is metabolized to maltose and is not rapidly absorbed, has been particularly effective in patients with ultrafiltration failure (high transporters). The use of glucose alternatives may decrease some metabolic consequences of long-term glucose use as well as preserve peritoneal membrane function. Amino acid–containing solutions are under investigation as a possible source of nutrition as well as an effective osmotic agent.

RENAL TRANSPLANTATION

Successful renal transplantation offers patients the best quality of life. They are liberated from potassium and fluid restrictions, are free to travel and work, and achieve correction of metabolic abnormalities and anemia with restoration of normal renal function. Moreover, in comparison to hemodialysis, renal transplantation also improves long-term survival in both diabetic and nondiabetic patients.

Since 1975 the 1-year cadaver allograft survival rate has dramatically improved from approximately 50% to that of 90% in 2000. The 1-year allograft survival for kidneys from living donors has increased from 88 to 93%. The half-life for grafts from living donors has steadily increased from 13 to 21 years, and that for cadaver allografts has increased from 8 to 14 years. These data were obtained in the prednisone, cyclosporine, and azathioprine era before the routine use of newer agents such as tacrolimus, mycophenolate or sirolimus, and so it remains to be determined what additional effects these agents may have.

Many factors have contributed to the extraordinary advances in transplantation over the last 25 years, including the widespread improvement in organ preservation and surgical technique, advances in tissue typing and crossmatching, and better immunosuppressive agents, as well as the recognition that rejection and infection are closely linked and that one needs a concomitant anti-infective prescription to make the immunosuppressive regimen safe (Chapter 298).

Since renal transplantation offers patients the best chance for quality as well as quantity of life, it is essential to evaluate candidates early—especially diabetics—and, where possible, proceed directly to preemptive transplantation if a living donor can be identified. The ideal form of RRT for patients with type I diabetes mellitus and nephropathy is renal transplantation from a living related donor followed by pancreas or islet cell transplantation from a cadaver donor. If a living donor is unavailable, then simultaneous pancreas and kidney transplantation should be pursued from a cadaver donor. Although a successful pancreas transplant does not reverse the established macrovascular and microvascular complications of long-standing diabetes mellitus, it improves blood glucose control and quality of life and may prevent the progression of retinopathy and autonomic neuropathy. Islet cell transplantation after renal transplantation is presently under investigation.

Pretransplant Recipient Evaluation

The potential renal transplant recipient must have irreversible end-stage renal failure and no evidence of active infection or malignancy. In addition to a careful history and physical examination, the evaluation must address the likelihood of compliance and rule out unmanageable patients with psychosis, substance abuse, or alcohol abuse.

Cardiovascular complications have become the main cause of morbidity and mortality in renal transplant patients. The high incidence of CVD reflects the combination of pretransplant factors (e.g., diabetes, hypertension) with post-transplant factors (e.g., metabolic complications of immunosuppressive agents). A careful cardiovascular work-up is critical, including stress testing with imaging and a coronary angiogram if any evidence of ischemia is demonstrated. This is of particular importance in diabetic patients. In view of the increasing recognition of calcific aortic stenosis and hypertension in patients with CKD, an echocardiogram should be obtained to assess valve area as well as systolic and diastolic function.

Likewise, a careful evaluation of carotid and peripheral vessels should be undertaken, because the new kidney is anastomosed to the iliac vessels. The new kidney's ureter can be implanted into the recipient's bladder or the patient's own ureter may be used. Further urologic testing may be needed if a neurogenic bladder is suspected or if there is history of obstructive uropathy. Bilateral nephrectomies are required only if there is persistent, smoldering infection unresponsive to chronic suppressive antimicrobial therapy.

It is important to know the underlying cause of the renal failure to help guide the timing of the transplant and inform the patient as to the risk of recurrence in the new kidney. It is recommended that patients with Goodpasture's syndrome, systemic lupus erythematosus, and antineutrophil cytoplasmic antibody–positive vasculitis disease become clinically and serologically quiescent before transplantation. A number of primary glomerular diseases have been shown to recur in the renal allograft, including focal segmental glomerulosclerosis, membranous glomerulonephritis, membranoproliferative glomerulonephritis, as well as IgA nephropathy. Diabetic nephropathy also may recur after transplantation and can be prevented by combined kidney/pancreas transplantation. A combined kidney/liver transplant can cure oxalosis.

As part of the recipient evaluation, a number of infectious disease issues must be addressed. Human immunodeficiency virus (HIV) and hepatitis B and C serologies should be obtained. In this era of highly active antiretroviral therapy, HIV positivity is no longer an absolute contraindication to transplantation. However, transplantation in this setting should be performed only under an experimental protocol, because it is unclear as to the long-term impact of the immunosuppression on HIV, and dialysis offers a viable alternative. Although patients with hepatitis C do better with renal transplant than on dialysis, with time liver failure is the major cause of morbidity and mortality. It is therefore critical to stage patients with hepatitis C prior to transplant, with liver biopsy, viral load, α-fetoprotein, and a CT scan looking for hepatocellular carcinoma and portal hypertension. The possibility of a combined kidney and liver transplant needs to be explored. Combined therapy with pegylated interferon and ribavirin may be indicated post-transplant but requires cautious monitoring and is usually not well tolerated. Post-transplant interferon therapy may trigger allograft rejection, possibly by upregulation of MHC and various cytokine genes. Severe hemolytic anemia may occur with ribavirin administration.

All patients waiting for renal transplant should be vaccinated against hepatitis B, although the response rate appears to be less than 50%. If a patient is hepatitis B surface antigen positive, a DNA viral load and liver biopsy should be obtained for staging. Lamivudine therapy can be initiated either pretransplant or post-transplant. Once again, if there is significant cirrhosis, consideration should be given to combined kidney/liver transplantation.

Patients with a newly positive purified protein derivative (PPD) skin test should ideally be treated prior to transplant. A patient with positive PPD and negative chest radiograph prior to transplant can be closely followed. If the patient has a positive PPD and history of previous disease or positive chest radiograph, treatment with isoniazid would be indicated starting 1 to 2 months post-transplant.

Likewise, patients should be evaluated for previous exposure to varicella. If the varicella titer is negative pretransplant, an attempt at vaccination can be undertaken. If the patient remains varicella antibody negative or has not been vaccinated, the patient should be earmarked for varicella zoster immune globulin on exposure to patients with chickenpox or herpes zoster, because the immunosuppressed host is at risk for fulminant varicella with pulmonary infiltrates, pancreatitis, and liver disease.

Special attention needs to be directed to patients from tropical areas, where *Strongyloides stercoralis* is endemic. A *Strongyloides* titer should be obtained and, if positive, treated prior to immunosuppression, because fulminant disease can occur post-transplant. Likewise if a patient comes from an area where schistosomiasis is endemic, diagnosis and treatment should be initiated prior to transplantation.

LIVING DONORS. There are potentially two ways to obtain a renal transplant: from a living donor or from a cadaveric donor. The demand for cadaveric donors far exceeds the supply of organs, and the waiting list for cadaver renal transplant now is between 3 to 4 years in all blood groups throughout most of the United States. This is a major impetus for the increase in living donors. Living organ donation accounts for more than 50% of the transplants now being performed. First and foremost, living donation is generally safe although not without potential morbidity. Moreover, both short- and long-term outlooks are better with a living donor. Third, data from living but not genetically related donors suggest that the results from a living unrelated donor transplant are equivalent to a one haplotype parental match, with 1-year graft survival of 92%. This suggests that the quality of the organ is as important or more important than the closeness of the genetic "match." In living unrelated donors, as in all living donors, it is critical that not only a complete medical but a psychological evaluation be carefully performed by physicians and psychiatrists independent of the recipient, to ascertain the voluntary, altruistic nature of the donor's decision, that is, to ensure no coercion.

The donor must recognize both the short- and long-term risks of donating a kidney. These include the immediate risks of surgery, with a mortality rate of 0.05%, as well as pain, time out of work, and the possibility of phlebitis or pulmonary embolus, urinary tract infection, wound infection, or pneumonia. The long-term risks of having one kidney include the slightly increased risk of proteinuria, chance of trauma, or development of cancer to the one remaining kidney. Although isolated cases of chronic renal failure have been reported after donation, for the most part long-term mortality is not affected by kidney donation.

One impetus for the increase in the living donor pool is the potential for laparoscopic donor nephrectomy in carefully selected patients. This procedure offers the possibility of decreased time in the hospital, potential for faster recovery, and more rapid return to work. However, not all donors are candidates for this procedure because of anatomic variants. All donors must be carefully evaluated and closely followed long term.

TISSUE TYPING. A key element in the transplant evaluation is tissue typing. The recipient must receive a transplant from a blood group–compatible donor to avoid hyperacute rejection and immediate irreversible graft loss on the operating table. The donor and recipient need not share the same Rh factor.

The genes that code for major histocompatibility complex (MHC) proteins are some of the most polymorphic known (Chapter 42). That is, within a species, there is an extraordinary large number of alleles (alternative forms of the same gene). Because each individual has at least 12 genes encoding MHC proteins, it is rare for two unrelated individuals to have an identical set of MHC proteins. Inheritance of these MHC genes is codominant (i.e., each parent transmits one set of MHC genes, a haplotype, to his or her child). These antigens appear to be pivotal in the rejection process.

HLA typing is performed on all potential recipients and donors. Although generally this is done by serology, increasingly DNA-based typing techniques are being employed. It is critical to determine the recipient's sensitization (i.e., the level of preformed HLA antibodies in the serum of the recipient). These antibodies generally result from previous transplants, pregnancies, or blood transfusions. The critical test prior to renal transplantation is the final crossmatch, a complement-dependent cytotoxicity assay performed using the cells of the donor and serum of the recipient. If the crossmatch is positive, the transplant should not be performed to avoid hyperacute rejection caused by the presence of preformed antibodies.

Rejection

Rejection remains the Achilles heel of transplantation, and acute rejection is the most important predictor of chronic rejection. The introduction of cyclosporine in the early 1980s and mycophenolate mofetil in the 1990s significantly reduced the incidence of rejection, producing a significant increase in the allograft survival.

Allograft rejection is initiated by the recipient's recognition of donor MHC antigens leading to activation of humoral and cellular immunity. The immune system of the recipient has the following two mechanisms to recognize the donor MHC antigens:

1. Direct recognition, in which recipient T cells recognize intact MHC molecules on the surface of donor cells
2. Indirect recognition, in which the recipient's antigen-presenting cells (APCs) process donor MHC molecules and present the peptides in the groove of MHC class II molecules (indirect recognition)

T-cell activation is central in the development of acute cellular rejection. At least two signals are required for T-cell activation: Signal 1 is provided by the MHC molecule with its antigenic peptide, and signal 2 is delivered by costimulatory molecules on the surface of the APCs. Antigen recognition in the absence of costimulation makes the T cell anergic. In addition, APCs express adhesion molecules, which enable the APC to bind to the T cell long enough for activation of T cells. Once the T-cell receptor (TCR) recognizes its target antigen, the signal is transduced to the nucleus leading to cell activation, cytokine synthesis, and clonal proliferation. Interleukin-2 (IL-2) is an important T-cell growth factor mediating T-cell proliferation through an autocrine pathway. Once activated, cytotoxic T cells release a pore-forming protein called perforin, which polymerizes in the target cell membrane to form transmembrane channels. The secretory vesicles that store perforin also contain serine proteases that are thought to enter the target cell through the perforin channels. One of these serine proteases, granzyme B, activates the caspase cascade leading to apoptosis. Cytotoxic T cells have another killing strategy: They express the Fas ligand surface protein, which activates *Fas* on the target cell. The activation of *Fas* also leads to the activation of caspases, producing apoptosis. Cytokines produced by helper T cells act on T cells and on other cell types, including B cells, macrophages, granulocytes, and endothelial cells. Antigen-activated helper T cells crosstalk with B cells by engagement of CD40 ligand, with CD40 leading to activation of B cells and production of alloantibodies.

The hallmark of acute cellular rejection is the presence of tubulitis, which is characterized by the invasion of the tubular epithelium by lymphocytes (Fig. 118–3). Interstitial inflammation is usually present but not pathognomonic of acute cellular rejection because it can also be associated with infection or acute interstitial nephritis due to drugs. In severe forms of acute cellular rejection the endothelium of small blood vessels is also involved. The clinical manifestations of acute cellular rejection may be minimal with the use of

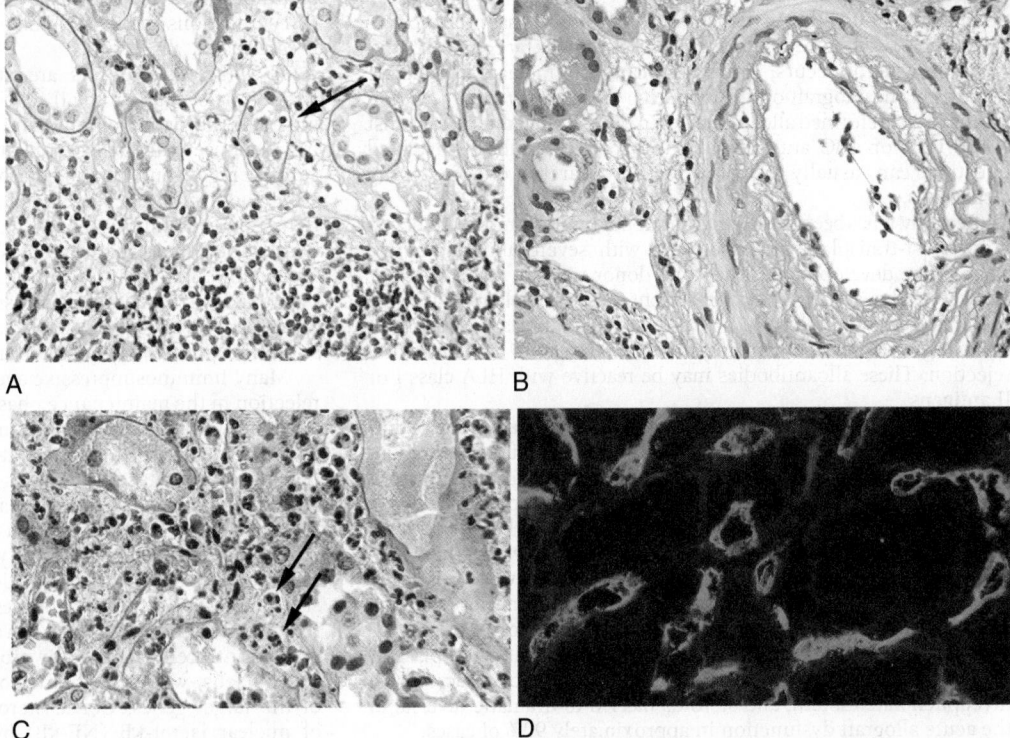

FIGURE 118–3 • Histology showing renal allograft with acute cellular rejection (*A* and *B*) and acute humoral rejection (*C* and *D*). *A,* Interstitial mononuclear infiltrate. The arrow points to an area with tubulitis. *B,* Arteritis. Note the accumulation of inflammatory cells beneath the intima, which is characteristic of acute cellular rejection type 2 (Banff classification). *C,* Acute humoral rejection. The peritubular space is occupied by an inflammatory infiltrate with the presence of polymorphonuclear neutrophils (arrows). *D,* Positive C4d staining in the peritubular capillaries by immunofluorescence, a hallmark of humoral rejection.

Table 118–1 • DIFFERENTIAL DIAGNOSIS OF RENAL ALLOGRAFT DYSFUNCTION

Immediate/Delayed Graft Function (1-3 days)
Acute tubular necrosis
Hyperacute humoral rejection
Urinary leak or obstruction
Renal artery or vein thrombosis
Recurrence of disease (e.g., FSGS)

Early Post-transplantation (first month)
Acute cellular rejection
Acute humoral rejection
Calcineurin inhibitor toxicity
Urinary tract obstruction
Volume depletion
Recurrence of disease

Late Acute Dysfunction
Acute rejection
Cyclosporine or tacrolimus toxicity
Recurrence of primary disease
Tubulointerstitial nephritis, drug induced
Renal artery stenosis
Infection (bacterial UTI, CMV, BK virus)
Hemodynamic (volume, use of ACEI, AIIRB)

Chronic Dysfunction
Chronic rejection
Cyclosporine or tacrolimus toxicity
Recurrent renal disease
De novo renal disease
Urinary tract obstruction
Bacterial UTI
Hypertensive nephrosclerosis

AIIRB = angiotensin II receptor blocker; ACEI = angiotensin-converting enzyme inhibitor; CMV = cytomegalovirus; FSGS = focal segmental glomerulosclerosis; UTI = urinary tract infection.

newer immunosuppressives but may include fever, allograft swelling and tenderness, or oliguria. The BUN and creatinine are usually elevated. A Doppler ultrasound should be performed to rule out obstruction and vascular thrombosis. The diagnosis of acute rejection can be reliably made only with an allograft biopsy. All other potential causes of acute allograft dysfunction should be considered (Table 118–1).

The role of antibodies in the acute rejection process has been increasingly appreciated. Hyperacute humoral rejection is a rare clinical event; however, when it occurs, it generally causes immediate irreversible necrosis of the allograft on the operating table. Hyperacute rejection is caused by preformed alloantibodies in the recipient directed against donor HLA or ABO antigens, and this form of antibody-mediated rejection can usually be prevented by careful crossmatching techniques.

Recently, it has been shown that antidonor humoral responses developing post-transplant are associated with severe allograft injury. That is, the development of de novo donor reactive cytotoxic antibodies in the serum of the recipient post-transplant that were not present preoperatively (i.e., positive post-transplant crossmatch but a negative pretransplant crossmatch) can lead to acute humoral rejection. These alloantibodies may be reactive with HLA class I or II antigens.

Acute humoral rejection has been found to have a unique pathologic picture characterized by the presence of neutrophils in peritubular capillaries and glomeruli and the presence of C4d staining, a byproduct of antibody-mediated complement activation deposited strongly in the peritubular capillary region (see Fig. 118–3). In the past, patients with this clinicopathologic picture would uniformly lose their allografts. However, early detection and treatment have dramatically changed the prognosis of acute humoral rejection. In those patients with a negative pretransplant crossmatch but de novo donor-specific antibodies demonstrated post-transplant, treatment with plasmapheresis and pooled human immune globulin in addition to tacrolimus, mycophenolate mofetil, and steroids has led to dramatic reversal of the acute allograft dysfunction in approximately 90% of cases.

Immunosuppression

The goal of immunosuppression therapy is to prevent allograft rejection but still allow the immune system to fight infection and malignancy. The multiagent strategy allows for a synergistic effect and reduction of specific drug toxicity. Immunosuppression is initiated at high doses during the initial period (induction) after transplantation when the risk of rejection is highest and reduced over time (maintenance immunosuppression). In recipients with a high risk of rejection (children, retransplant recipients, delayed graft function, multiparous women, and multitransfused patients), induction immunosuppression is often employed. Induction therapy consists of a course of either polyclonal antilymphocyte–antithymocyte globulin (ATG) or antilymphocyte globulin, monoclonal anti-CD3 antibodies (OKT3), or anti-IL-2 receptor monoclonal antibodies (basiliximab and daclizumab). Appropriate antiviral prophylaxis is essential to reduce the risk of severe cytomegalovirus (CMV) infection and Epstein-Barr virus (EBV)-associated post-transplant lymphoproliferative disease (PTLD).

Polyclonal antibodies are raised in different animals (rabbits, goats, horses) using different antigenic preparations (thymocytes, lymphocytes). Many different preparations of polyclonal antibodies are available, varying in degree of efficacy, purity, and side effects. Thymoglobulin is prepared by immunizing rabbits with human T thymocytes. The polyclonal antilymphocyte antibodies are used for induction therapy in high-risk recipients (high panel reactive antibodies (PRA), retransplant) at the onset of transplantation, for treatment of steroid-resistant acute cellular rejection, and as a calcineurin inhibitor–sparing agent in recipients with delayed graft function. The polyclonal antibodies can cause serum sickness, bone marrow suppressions, and hemolysis. The use of polyclonals may also trigger a potent cytokine response. Most side effects are related either to the degree of purity of the antigenic preparation used to immunize the animals or the purification of the serum. Serum sickness and anaphylactic reactions are related to previous exposure to the animal species used to raise the antibody.

OKT3 is a mouse monoclonal antibody directed against the CD3 antigen. The CD3 complex sits at the cytoplasmatic tail of the TCR transducing signals from the TCR to the cytoplasm. OKT3 interferes with T-cell function through modulation of the TCR and clearance of T cells. OKT3 is used for treatment of steroid-resistant acute cellular rejection and as an induction agent. OKT3 may cause a myriad of side effects, including fever, rigors, nausea, vomiting, diarrhea, hypotension, chest pain, dyspnea, wheezing, and occasionally pulmonary edema. These symptoms are secondary to massive cytokine release after OKT3 engages the TCR. OKT3 may also cause aseptic meningitis, and its use is associated with a higher incidence of severe CMV infections and PTLD. Therefore, appropriate CMV prophylaxis is essential.

IL-2 receptor blockers are engineered monoclonal antibodies against the α-chain of the IL-2 receptor. Daclizumab is a humanized molecule consisting of a human IgG1 with antigen-binding regions from a mouse antibody. Basiliximab is a chimeric construct with murine variable region and human constant regions. The impetus of humanizing these molecules included functional considerations beyond reduction in immunogenicity. Thus, unlike the original mouse antibodies, the humanized antibodies can activate antibody-directed cell-mediated cytotoxicity without activating complement-mediated cytotoxicity. Daclizumab and basiliximab are used only as induction agents to prevent rather than treat rejection. They both have a safe side effect profile largely due to human origin.

Many immunosuppressive agents are available for prevention of rejection in the maintenance phase. Common regimens include low-dose steroids, mycophenolate mofetil, or azathioprine and a calcineurin–nuclear factor of activated T lymphocyte (NFAT) inhibitor (cyclosporine or tacrolimus).

Corticosteroids have nonspecific immunosuppressive and anti-inflammatory actions. They are used for induction therapy, for maintenance immunosuppression, as well as in high doses (pulse) for the treatment of acute cellular rejection. Corticosteroids inhibit synthesis of almost all known cytokines and of several surface molecules required for immune function. On crossing the cell membrane, steroids bind to intracellular receptor proteins, which are transferred to the cell nucleus, where they bind to corticosteroid response elements of the target genes. Corticosteroids also inhibit the translocation of nuclear factor-κB (NF-κB) by induction of I κβ α-inhibitory protein, which traps activated NF-κβ in inactive cytoplasmic complexes. This action prevents activation of key cytokine genes, including tumor necrosis factor-α (TNF-α) and IL-1. Corticosteroids cause many metabolic changes, including diabetes, hypercholesterolemia, osteoporosis, increase the risk of cardiovascular events, obesity, and hypertension and can cause significant mood swings, irritability, and depression.

The *calcineurin inhibitors* cyclosporine and tacrolimus inhibit the translocation of NFAT from the cytoplasm to the nucleus. Both cyclosporine and tacrolimus bind to a cyclophilin in the cytoplasm; this complex then binds to calcineurin, inhibiting its capacity to dephosphorylate NFAT, thereby preventing NFAT translocation to the nucleus (Table 118–2). NFAT is essential in the activation of the IL-2, interferon-γ, IL-4, TNF-α, and granulocyte-macrophage colony-stimulating factor as well as the gene for CD40 ligand. Cyclosporine and tacrolimus levels must be closely monitored to avoid toxicity as well as rejection. The most important nonimmune toxicity of the calcineurin inhibitors is nephrotoxicity.

The following three distinct patterns of renal dysfunction may be observed with calcineurin inhibitors:

1. An acute hemodynamic effect secondary to afferent arteriolar constriction, which may exacerbate ischemic injury and delayed graft function. This produces a reversible decrease in glomerular filtration rate, which improves when the dose of the drug is adjusted.
2. Subacute to chronic nephrotoxicity, which may be evidenced by tubular lesions (vacuolization), hyalinosis of small arterioles, or striped fibrosis in the more chronic phase.
3. Thrombotic microangiopathy, which can present a picture similar to the hemolytic uremic syndrome with intimal proliferation, fibrin deposition, and thrombotic occlusion of the arcuate and intralobular arteries. The peripheral smear may show evidence of schistocytes. Thrombocytopenia may or may not be present. Switching the patient from cyclosporine to tacrolimus or vice versa may sometimes be beneficial.

Other side effects of the calcineurin inhibitors include neurotoxicity (tremors, mental status changes, irritability, and seizures), hypertension, hyperglycemia, hyperkalemia, hyperuricemia, gout, and an increased incidence of EBV-related B cell lymphomas (PTLD). Both cyclosporine and tacrolimus are metabolized by the cytochrome P450

system and are excreted by the liver. Therefore, administration of drugs that interact with the P450 system affects the levels of calcineurin inhibitors. Prescribing physicians need to be aware that inhibitors of the P450 system, such as macrolide antibiotics, the calcium-channel blocker diltiazem, imidazole, and triazole antifungals among many other drugs, may raise the levels of calcineurin inhibitors. In contrast, agents such as rifampin, phenobarbital, and phenytoin that induce cytochrome P450 enzymes increase the catabolism of calcineurin inhibitors. Many other significant interactions need to be recognized, including the risk of rhabdomyolysis with statins and interaction with most nephrotoxic agents.

Azathioprine was a cornerstone of transplant immunosuppression until the introduction of mycophenolate mofetil. Azathioprine inhibits DNA synthesis; its main side effect is bone marrow suppression (see Table 118–2). Azathioprine has also been associated with malignancies, especially skin cancers and increased frequency of warts (papillomavirus infection). Azathioprine is metabolized by xanthine oxidase. Concomitant administration of allopurinol, a xanthine oxidase inhibitor, should be avoided because significant toxicity may occur.

Mycophenolate mofetil selectively inhibits lymphocyte proliferation. This is a targeted action on the de novo pathway for purine synthesis, on which lymphocytes, unlike other cell types, are particularly dependent (see Table 118–2). The efficacy of mycophenolate mofetil has been demonstrated in large randomized, multicenter, blinded trials, which have shown a 50% reduction in the incidence of acute cellular rejection and a significant reduction in the use of OKT3/ATG. Gastrointestinal symptoms (e.g., nausea, epigastric discomfort, diarrhea) are the main side effects, which generally can be improved by dose reduction. The effect of mycophenolate mofetil on the prevention of chronic rejection is currently under study.

Sirolimus binds to the same immunophilin as tacrolimus (FK-binding protein-12 [FKBP-12]) but sirolimus-FKBP complex does not affect calcineurin activity (see Table 118–2). Rather, this complex binds to and inhibits the activation of a kinase called the mammalian target of rapamycin (mTOR). Inhibition of mTOR by sirolimus suppresses alloantigen and cytokine-driven T-cell proliferation, inhibiting the cell cycle. Regimens employing sirolimus have been shown to significantly reduce the incidence of acute cellular rejection. Sirolimus causes hyperlipidemia and is also associated with thrombocytopenia. Of note, sirolimus interacts with calcineurin inhibitors and may cause an increase in calcineurin inhibitor toxicity.

Future Directions

A number of strategies have been devised to improve long-term outcomes of renal transplant by preventing chronic rejection and chronic allograft loss, thereby improving long-term survival and life expectancy of renal transplant recipients. These include steroid- and/or calcineurin-inhibitor–sparing protocols, using more powerful immunosuppressive agents such as tacrolimus with mycophenolate mofetil, or sirolimus.

Patients may also benefit from aggressive control of coronary risk factors, since coronary disease is a major cause of death in these patients. For example, a statin can reduce nonfatal myocardial infarction and cardiac death in transplant patients.[■]

The Holy Grail of transplantation is tolerance—unresponsiveness to donor antigens while maintaining the ability to respond to third-party antigens in the absence of ongoing immunosuppression. Although tolerance has been demonstrated in a number of different small animal models, it has been difficult to achieve in large animal models and in humans. In 1990 it was reported that patients who had previously undergone an allogeneic bone marrow transplant for treatment of hematologic disease, and subsequently required a kidney transplant from the same donor, demonstrated immunologic nonresponsiveness; that is, the kidney was accepted without need for immunosuppression. Unfortunately, the morbidity associated with the full myeloablative-conditioning regimen required for successful complete bone marrow transplant, as well as graft-versus-host disease, precludes the routine use of this approach to induce tolerance in solid organ transplantation. However, the induction of mixed hemopoietic chimerism, using nonmyeloablative conditioning (i.e., a "kinder, gentler" approach), is a more clinically applicable strategy that has been successfully accomplished in rodents, miniature swine, and nonhuman primates.

These observations have now been extended to patients with multiple myeloma and end-stage renal failure. Two patients received

Table 118–2 • IMMUNOSUPPRESSIVE AGENTS

AGENT	MECHANISM OF ACTION	SIDE EFFECTS
Corticosteroids	Multiple anti-inflammatory actions, blockade of IL-1, IL-6, TNF-α	Infection, hypertension, glucose resistance, osteoporosis, hyperlipidemia, glaucoma, adrenal suppression
Azathioprine	Blockade of purine synthesis, which affects DNA and RNA synthesis	Bone marrow suppression
Cyclosporine	Binds to cyclophilin, causing calcineurin inhibition, which prevents NFAT activity on IL-2 gene; stimulates TGF-β production	Hypertension, glucose intolerance, nephrotoxicity, hirsutism, gingival hyperplasia
Tacrolimus	Binds to FKBP-12, causing calcineurin inhibition, which prevents NFAT activity on IL-2 gene	Neurotoxicity, increases the incidence of DM (≅20%)
Mycophenolate mofetil	Blocks de novo pathway of purine synthesis by inhibition of IMPDH, selective for lymphocytes	GI symptoms (diarrhea), leukopenia
Sirolimus	Binds to FKBP-12 and TOR, blocking cell cycle progression	Hyperlipidemia, leukopenia, thrombocytopenia

DM = diabetes mellitus; FKBP-12 = FK-binding protein 12; GI = gastrointestinal; IL-1 = interleukin-1; IMPDH = inosine monophosphate dehydrogenase; NFAT = nuclear factor of activated T lymphocyte; TGF-β = transforming growth factor-β; TNF = tumor necrosis factor; TOR = target of rapamycin.

simultaneous bone marrow and kidney transplants from HLA-matched donors using a nonmyeloablative protocol. These patients are now up to 4 years post-transplant with normal renal function, off immunosuppression, and show no evidence of myeloma.

Clearly there are other promising approaches to tolerance induction presently being investigated, with the hope that we can avoid chronic rejection as well as long-term immunosuppression and its multiple sequelae: drug toxicity, infection, and the risk of malignancy.

1. Eknoyan G, Beck GJ, Cheung AK, et al: Effect of dialysis dose and membrane flux in maintenance hemodialysis. N Engl J Med 2002;347:2010–2019.
2. Ronco C, Brendolan A, Lupi A, et al: Effects of different doses in continuous venovenous haemofiltration on outcomes of acute renal failure: A prospective randomised trial. Lancet 2000;356:26–30.
3. Paniagua R, Amato D, Vonesh E, et al: The Mexican Nephrology Collaborative Study Group. Effects of increased peritoneal clearances on mortality rates in peritoneal dialysis: ADEMEX, a prospective, randomized, controlled trial. Am Soc Nephrol 2002;13:1307–1320.
4. Holdaas H, Fellstrom B, Jardine AG, et al: Effect of fluvastatin on cardiac outcomes in renal transplant recipients: A multicentre, randomised, placebo-controlled trial. Lancet 2003;361:2024–2031.

SUGGESTED READINGS

Buhler LH, Spitzer TR, Sykes M, et al: Induction of kidney allograft tolerance after transient lymphohematopoietic chimerism in patients with multiple myeloma and end-stage renal disease. Transplantation 2002;74:1405–1409. *A non-myeloablative regimen followed by combined matched bone marrow and renal transplantation was successful in two patients.*
Goodman WG, Goldin J, Kuizon BD, et al: Coronary artery calcification in young adults with end-stage renal disease who are undergoing dialysis. N Engl J Med 2000;342:1478–1483. *Coronary calcification is common and progressive.*
Hariharan S, Johnson CP, Bresnahan BA, et al: Improved graft survival after renal transplantation in the United States, 1988 to 1996. N Engl J Med 2000;342:605–612. *The half-life for living-related grafts increased from 12.7 to 21.6 years and for cadaveric grafts from 7.9 to 13.8 years.*
Nassar GM, Ayus JC: Infectious complications of the hemodialysis access. Kidney Int 2001;60:1–13. *A comprehensive review.*
Pascual M, Theruvath T, Kawai T, et al: Strategies to improve long-term outcomes after renal transplantation. N Engl J Med 2002;346:580–590. *A comprehensive review.*

119 GLOMERULAR DISORDERS

Gerald B. Appel

More than 11 million persons in the United States have renal dysfunction, and glomerular diseases, including diabetes, are the major causes of this dysfunction. By 2000 in the United States more than 350,000 persons were in end-stage renal disease (ESRD) programs, largely as a result of renal involvement by glomerular diseases. Diabetic renal damage alone affects millions of persons and is the major cause of ESRD in the United States, with an annual cost to the government of billions of dollars. Worldwide, glomerular diseases associated with infectious agents such as malaria and schistosomiasis are major health problems. In both the United States and elsewhere, the emergence of glomerular diseases linked to viral causes, such as human immunodeficiency virus (HIV) and hepatitis B and C viruses, has focused new attention on the patterns and mechanisms of glomerular injury. The manifestations of glomerular injury range from asymptomatic microhematuria and albuminuria to abrupt oliguric renal failure. Some patients develop massive fluid retention with peripheral and periorbital edema as presenting symptoms and signs of glomerular damage, whereas others present with only the slow insidious signs and symptoms of chronic renal failure.

Although the mechanisms of the glomerular injury vary, certain common mechanisms may underlie common findings such as hematuria and proteinuria (e.g., loss of the glomerular charge barrier). The nature of the processes initiating this damage differs. In some glomerular disorders, such as diabetes and amyloidosis, there are structural and biochemical alterations of the glomerular capillary wall. In others, there is immune-mediated renal injury, whether through deposition of circulating immune complexes, through localization of anti–glomerular basement membrane (GBM) antibodies, or via other mechanisms.

Histopathologic Terms

Each *glomerulus*, the basic filtering unit of the kidney, consists of a tuft of anastomosing capillaries formed by the branchings of the afferent arteriole. Approximately 1 million glomeruli comprise about 5% of the kidney weight and provide almost 2 m² of glomerular capillary filtering surface. The GBM provides both a size- and charge-selective barrier to the passage of circulating macromolecules. Renal processes involving all glomeruli are called *diffuse* or *generalized;* if only some glomeruli are involved, the process is called *focal*. When dealing with the individual glomerulus, a process is *global* if the whole glomerular tuft is involved and *segmental* if only part of the glomerulus is involved. The modifying terms *proliferative, sclerosing,* and *necrotizing* are often used (e.g., focal and segmental glomerulosclerosis; diffuse global proliferative lupus nephritis). Extracapillary proliferation or crescent formation is caused by the accumulations of macrophages, fibroblasts, proliferating epithelial cells, and fibrin within Bowman's space. In general, crescent formation in any form of glomerular damage conveys a serious prognosis. Scarring of the tissue between the tubules and glomeruli, interstitial fibrosis, is also a poor prognostic sign in every glomerular disease.

Clinical Manifestations of Glomerular Diseases

Findings that indicate the presence of a glomerular origin of renal disease include erythrocyte casts and/or dysmorphic erythrocytes in the urinary sediment and the presence of large amounts of albuminuria. Urinary excretion of more than 500 to 1000 erythrocytes per milliliter is abnormal, and dysmorphic erythrocytes deformed in passage through the glomerular capillary wall and tubules indicate glomerular damage. Red blood cell casts, formed when erythrocytes pass the glomerular capillary barrier and become enmeshed in a proteinaceous matrix in the lumen of the tubules, are indicative of glomerular disease.

In a normal person, the urinary excretion of albumin is less than 50 mg/day. Although increases in urinary protein excretion may come from the filtration of abnormal circulating proteins (e.g., light chains in multiple myeloma) or from the deficient proximal tubular reabsorption of normal filtered small-molecular-weight proteins (e.g., β_2-microglobulin), the most common cause of proteinuria, and specifically albuminuria, is glomerular injury. Proteinuria associated with glomerular disease may range from several hundred milligrams to more than 30 g daily. In some diseases, such as minimal change nephrotic syndrome, albumin is the predominant protein found in the urine. In others, such as focal sclerosing glomerulonephritis and diabetes, the proteinuria, although still largely composed of albumin, contains many larger molecular weight proteins as well.

THE NEPHROTIC SYNDROME

The nephrotic syndrome is classically defined by albuminuria in amounts of more than 3 to 3.5 g/day accompanied by hypoalbuminemia, edema, and hyperlipidemia. In practice, many clinicians refer to "nephrotic range" proteinuria regardless of whether their patients have the other manifestations of the full syndrome because the latter are consequences of the proteinuria.

Hypoalbuminemia is in part a consequence of urinary protein loss. It is also due to the catabolism of filtered albumin by the proximal tubule as well as to redistribution of albumin within the body. This in part accounts for the inexact relationship between urinary protein loss, the level of the serum albumin, and other secondary consequences of heavy albuminuria.

The salt and volume retention in the nephrotic syndrome may occur through at least two different major mechanisms. In the classic theory, proteinuria leads to hypoalbuminemia, a low plasma oncotic pressure, and intravascular volume depletion. Subsequent underperfusion of the kidney stimulates the priming of sodium-retentive hormonal systems such as the renin-angiotensin-aldosterone axis, causing increased renal sodium and volume retention. In the peripheral capillaries with normal hydrostatic pressures and decreased oncotic pressure, the Starling forces lead to transcapillary fluid leakage and edema. In some patients, however, the intravascular volume has been measured and found to be increased along with suppression of the renin-angiotensin-aldosterone axis. An animal model of unilateral proteinuria shows evidence for primary renal sodium retention at a distal nephron site, perhaps due to altered responsiveness to hormones such as atrial natriuretic factor. Here only the proteinuric kidney retains sodium and volume and at a time when the animal is not yet hypoalbuminemic. Thus, local factors within the kidney may account for the volume retention of the nephrotic patient as well.

Epidemiologic studies clearly define an increased risk of atherosclerotic complications in the nephrotic syndrome. Most nephrotic patients have elevated levels of total and low-density lipoprotein (LDL) cholesterol with low or normal high-density lipoprotein (HDL) cholesterol. Lipoprotein(a) [Lp(a)] levels are elevated as well and return to normal with remission of the nephrotic syndrome. Nephrotic patients often have a hypercoagulable state and are predisposed to deep vein thrombophlebitis, pulmonary emboli, and renal vein thrombosis.

Initial evaluation of the nephrotic patient includes laboratory tests to define whether the patient has primary, idiopathic nephrotic syndrome or a secondary cause related to a systemic disease. Common screening tests include the fasting blood sugar and glycosylated hemoglobin tests for diabetes, an antinuclear antibody test for collagen vascular disease, and the serum complement, which screens for many immune complex-mediated diseases (Table 119–1). In selected patients, cryoglobulins, hepatitis B and C serology, anti-neutrophil cytoplasmic antibodies (ANCAs), anti-GBM antibodies, and other tests may be useful. Once secondary causes have been excluded, treating the adult nephrotic patient often requires a renal biopsy to define the pattern of glomerular involvement. In adults, the nephrotic syndrome is a common condition leading to renal biopsy. In many studies, patients with heavy proteinuria and the nephrotic syndrome have been a group highly likely to benefit from renal biopsy in terms of a change in specific diagnosis, prognosis, and therapy. Selected adult nephrotic patients such as the elderly have a slightly different spectrum of disease, but again the renal biopsy is the best guide to treatment and prognosis (Tables 119–2 and 119–3).

Idiopathic Nephrotic Syndrome

MINIMAL CHANGE DISEASE. Minimal change disease, also known as *nil disease* and *lipoid nephrosis,* is the most common pattern of nephrotic syndrome in children and comprises from 5 to 10% of idiopathic nephrotic syndrome in adults. A similar histologic pattern may be seen as an adverse reaction to certain medications (nonsteroidal anti-inflammatory drugs [NSAIDs], lithium) and associated with certain tumors (Hodgkin's disease and leukemias). Patients typically present

Table 119–1 • SERUM COMPLEMENT LEVELS IN GLOMERULAR DISEASES

DISEASES WITH A REDUCED COMPLEMENT LEVEL
Poststreptococcal glomerulonephritis
Subacute bacterial endocarditis/visceral abscess/shunt nephritis
Systemic lupus erythematosus
Cryoglobulinemia
Idiopathic membranoproliferative glomerulonephritis

DISEASES ASSOCIATED WITH A NORMAL SERUM COMPLEMENT
Minimal change nephrotic syndrome
Focal segmental glomerulosclerosis
Membranous nephropathy
IgA nephropathy
Henoch-Schönlein purpura
Anti-GBM disease
Pauci-immune rapidly progressive glomerulonephritis
Polyarteritis nodosa
Wegener's granulomatosis

Table 119–2 • CAUSES OF THE NEPHROTIC SYNDROME

IDIOPATHIC OR PRIMARY NEPHROTIC SYNDROME	INCIDENCE (%)
Minimal change disease	5–10
Focal segmental glomerulosclerosis	20–25
Membranous nephropathy	25–30
Membranoproliferative glomerulonephritis	5
Other proliferative and sclerosing glomerulonephritides	15–30

Table 119–3 • NEPHROTIC SYNDROME ASSOCIATED WITH SPECIFIC CAUSES ("SECONDARY" NEPHROTIC SYNDROME)

SYSTEMIC DISEASES
Diabetes mellitus
Systemic lupus erythematosus and other collagen diseases
Amyloidosis (amyloid AL or AA associated)
Vasculitic-immunologic disease (mixed cryoglobulinemia, Wegener's granulomatosis, rapidly progressive glomerulonephritis, polyarteritis, Henoch-Schönlein purpura, sarcoidosis, Goodpasture's syndrome)

INFECTIONS
Bacterial (poststreptococcal, congenital and secondary syphilis, subacute bacterial endocarditis, shunt nephritis)
Viral (hepatitis B, hepatitis C, HIV infection, infectious mononucleosis, cytomegalovirus infection)
Parasitic (malaria, toxoplasmosis, schistosomiasis, filariasis)

MEDICATION RELATED
Gold, mercury, and the heavy metals
Penicillamine
Nonsteroidal anti-inflammatory drugs
Lithium
Paramethadione, trimethadione
Captopril
"Street" heroin
Others—probenecid, chlorpropamide, rifampin, tolbutamide, phenindione

ALLERGENS, VENOMS, AND IMMUNIZATIONS

ASSOCIATED WITH NEOPLASMS
Hodgkin's lymphoma and leukemia-lymphomas (with minimal change lesion)
Solid tumors (with membranous nephropathy)

HEREDITARY AND METABOLIC DISEASE
Alport's syndrome
Fabry's disease
Sickle cell disease
Congenital (Finnish type) nephrotic syndrome
Familial nephrotic syndrome
Nail-patella syndrome
Partial lipodystrophy

OTHER
Pregnancy related (includes preeclampsia)
Transplant rejection
Serum sickness
Accelerated hypertensive nephrosclerosis
Unilateral renal artery stenosis
Massive obesity–sleep apnea
Reflux nephropathy

with periorbital and peripheral edema related to the proteinuria, which is usually well into the nephrotic range. Additional findings in adults are hypertension and microscopic hematuria, each in about 30% of patients. However, active urinary sediment with erythrocyte casts is not found. Many adult patients have mild to moderate azotemia, which may be related to hypoalbuminemia and intravascular volume depletion. Complement levels and serologic test results are normal.

In true minimal change disease, histopathology typically reveals no glomerular abnormalities on light microscopy (LM). The tubules may show lipid droplet accumulation from absorbed lipoproteins (hence the older term *lipoid nephrosis*). Immunofluorescence staining (IF) and electron microscopy (EM) (Fig. 119–1) show no immune-type deposits. By EM the GBM is normal, and effacement or "fusion," of the visceral epithelial foot processes is noted along virtually the entire distribution of every capillary loop.

The course of minimal change nephrotic syndrome is often one of remissions and relapses and responses to additional treatment. When treated with corticosteroids for 8 weeks, 90 to 95% of children experience a remission of the nephrotic syndrome. In adults, the response rate is somewhat lower, with 75 to 85% of patients responding to regimens of daily (60 mg) or alternate-day (120 mg) prednisone therapy, tapered after 2 months of treatment. The time to clinical response is slower in adults, and they are not considered steroid resistant until they have failed to respond to 16 weeks of treatment. Tapering of the steroid dose after remission should be gradual over 1 to 2 months.

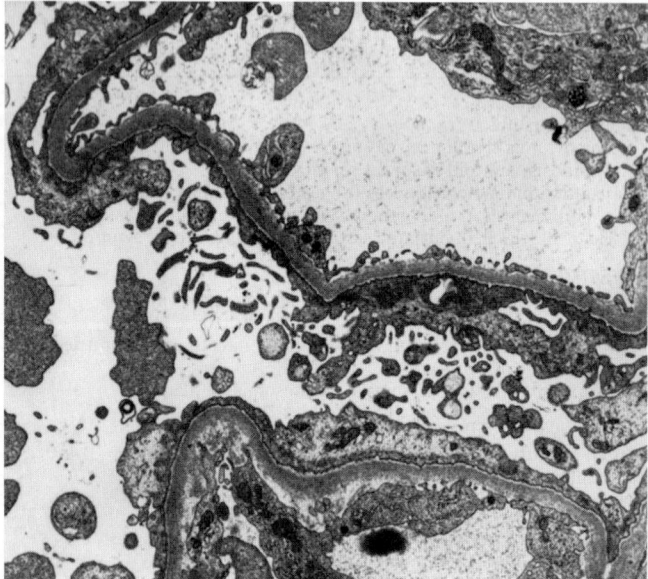

FIGURE 119-1 • Minimal change disease. Electron micrograph shows widespread effacement of foot processes with microvillous transformation of the visceral epithelium. No electron-dense deposits are present (uranyl acetate, lead citrate stain; original magnification × 6000).

Both children and adults are likely to have a relapse of their minimal change disease once corticosteroids have been discontinued. Approximately 30% of adults experience relapse by 1 year, and in 50% it occurs by 5 years. Most clinicians treat the first relapse similarly to the initial episode of nephrotic syndrome. Patients who relapse a third time or who become corticosteroid dependent (unable to decrease the prednisone dose without proteinuria recurring) may be treated with a 2-month course of an alkylating agent. Cyclophosphamide at a dose of up to 2 mg/kg/day has been used successfully, as has the use of chlorambucil. Up to 50% of these patients have a prolonged remission of the nephrotic syndrome (at least 5 years). The response rate is lower in corticosteroid-dependent patients. An alternative to an alkylating agent is low-dose cyclosporine (4 to 6 mg/kg/day for 4 months), but this carries some risk of nephrotoxicity and a higher relapse rate.

FOCAL SEGMENTAL GLOMERULOSCLEROSIS. From 20 to 25% of adults with idiopathic nephrotic syndrome are found on biopsy to have focal segmental glomerulosclerosis (FSGS). The incidence of FSGS is increasing, and it is the most common form of idiopathic nephrotic syndrome in blacks. FSGS may be either idiopathic or secondary to a number of different causes (e.g., heroin abuse, HIV infection, sickle cell disease, obesity, reflux of urine from the bladder to the kidneys, and lesions associated with single or remnant kidneys).

Patients with idiopathic FSGS typically present with either asymptomatic proteinuria or edema. Although the nephrotic syndrome is present in two thirds of patients at presentation, proteinuria may vary from less than 1 to 30 g/day. Hypertension is found in 30 to 50%, and microscopic hematuria occurs in about one half of these patients. The glomerular filtration rate (GFR) is decreased at presentation in 20 to 30% of patients. Complement levels and other serologic test results are normal.

By LM, initially only some glomeruli have areas of segmental scarring. As renal function declines, repeat biopsy specimens show more glomeruli with segmental sclerosing lesions and increased numbers of globally sclerotic glomeruli. By IF staining, IgM and C3 are commonly trapped in the areas of glomerular sclerosis. EM shows no deposits and only visceral epithelial cell foot process effacement.

The course of untreated FSGS is usually one of progressive proteinuria and declining GFR. Only a minority of patients experience a spontaneous remission of proteinuria, and eventually most untreated patients develop ESRD in 5 to 20 years from presentation.

Although there have been few randomized, controlled trials in FSGS, in general, patients with a sustained remission of their nephrotic syndrome are unlikely to progress to ESRD, whereas those with unremitting nephrotic syndrome are likely to progress. Studies using more intensive and more prolonged immunosuppressive regimens

(6 to 12 months) with corticosteroids and cytotoxic agents have achieved up to a 40 to 60% remission rate of the nephrotic syndrome with preservation of long-term renal function. Cyclosporine, 4 mg/kg/day for 4 to 6 months, has given greater remissions of the nephrotic syndrome and less long-term renal failure in a randomized controlled blinded trial in patients who have been steroid and often cytotoxic resistant. Focal sclerosis recurs in the transplanted kidney in up to 30% of cases, usually in association with elevated levels of a circulating permeability factor.

MEMBRANOUS NEPHROPATHY. Membranous nephropathy is the most common pattern of idiopathic nephrotic syndrome in white Americans. It may also be associated with infections (lues, hepatitis B and C), with systemic lupus erythematosus (SLE), with certain medications (gold salts), and with certain tumors (solid tumors and lymphomas). It typically presents as proteinuria and edema. Hypertension and microhematuria are not infrequent findings, but renal function and GFR are usually normal at presentation. Despite the finding of complement in the glomerular immune deposits, serum complement levels are normal. Membranous nephropathy is the most common pattern of the nephrotic syndrome to be associated with a hypercoagulable state and renal vein thrombosis. The presence of sudden flank pain, deterioration of renal function, or symptoms of pulmonary disease in a patient with membranous nephropathy should prompt an investigation for renal vein thrombosis and pulmonary emboli.

On LM, the glomerular capillary loops often appear rigid or thickened, but there is no cellular proliferation. IF and EM shows subepithelial immune dense deposits all along the glomerular capillary loops (Fig. 119-2).

In most large series, renal survival is more than 75% at 10 years. There is also a spontaneous remission rate of 20 to 30%. Both the slow progression and spontaneous remission rate have confounded clinical treatment trials. A number of studies using corticosteroids to treat membranous nephropathy have given conflicting results. Controlled trials of alternating monthly corticosteroids and monthly oral cytotoxic agents (either cyclophosphamide or chlorambucil) over 6 months have given greater numbers of total remissions and better preservation of renal function. Meta-analyses have confirmed beneficial results from the use of cytotoxic agents in idiopathic membranous nephropathy. In a randomized controlled trial, cyclosporine has been shown to lead to increased remissions of the nephrotic syndrome.∎

Membranoproliferative Glomerulonephritis

Membranoproliferative or mesangiocapillary glomerulonephritis (MPGN) is an uncommon glomerular disease that comprises only a

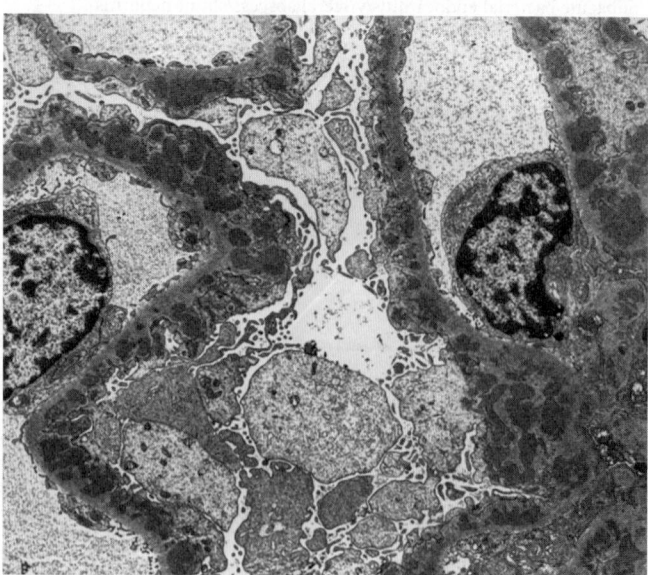

FIGURE 119-2 • Membranous glomerulopathy. On ultrastructural examination, there are numerous, closely apposed epimembranous electron-dense deposits separated by basement membrane spikes (uranyl acetate, lead citrate stain; original magnification × 2500).

small percentage of renal biopsies. By LM, similar patterns of glomerular damage have been seen in association with certain infectious agents (hepatitis C), autoimmune disease (SLE), and diseases of intraglomerular coagulation. All of these stimuli have been proposed to incite the glomerular mesangial cells to grow out along the capillary wall and split the GBM. Type II MPGN, dense deposit disease, has been called an autoimmune disorder with an autoantibody (an IgG, C3 nephrotic factor) directed against C3bBb, the alternate pathway C3 convertase. By preventing degradation of the enzyme, there is increased activation and consumption of complement noted in dense deposit disease.

Most adults with MPGN present with proteinuria or the nephrotic syndrome. A low serum complement level is found intermittently in type I MPGN, whereas the C3 level is always reduced in type II MPGN. Most studies have found a similar course and prognosis for the various patterns of MPGN. Attempts to treat MPGN have included using corticosteroids and other immunosuppressive medications as well as anticoagulants and antiplatelet agents. No therapy has proved to be effective in a controlled randomized trial in adults with MPGN.

ACUTE GLOMERULONEPHRITIS

Pathophysiology

Known inciting causes of acute glomerulonephritis include infectious agents such as streptococci and bacteria causing endocarditis, as well as the deposition of immune complexes in autoimmune diseases such as SLE, or the damaging effect of circulating antibodies directed against the GBM as in Goodpasture's syndrome. Regardless of the inciting cause, acute glomerulonephritis is characterized on LM by hypercellularity of the glomerulus. This may be secondary to infiltrating inflammatory cells, proliferation of resident glomerular cells, or both. Both invading inflammatory neutrophils and monocytes, as well as resident cells, can damage the glomerulus through a number of mediators, including a host of oxidants, chemoattractant agents, proteases, cytokines, and growth factors. Some factors, such as transforming growth factor-β, have been related to eventual glomerulosclerosis and chronic glomerular damage.

Patients with acute glomerulonephritis often present with a nephritic picture characterized by a decreased GFR and azotemia, oliguria, hypertension, and an active urinary sediment. The hypertension is caused by intravascular volume expansion, although renin levels may not be appropriately suppressed for the degree of volume expansion. Patients may note dark, smoky, or cola-colored urine in association with the active urinary sediment. This sediment is composed of erythrocytes, leukocytes, and a variety of casts, including erythrocyte casts. Although many patients with acute glomerulonephritis have proteinuria, sometimes even in the nephrotic range, most patients have lesser degrees of albumin leakage into the urine, especially when the GFR is markedly reduced.

IgA Nephropathy

IgA nephropathy was originally thought to be an uncommon and benign form of glomerulopathy (Berger's disease). It is now recognized as the most frequent form of idiopathic glomerulonephritis worldwide (comprising 15 to 40% of primary glomerulonephritides in parts of Europe and Asia) and clearly can progress to ESRD. In geographic areas where renal biopsies are commonly performed for milder urinary findings, a higher incidence of IgA has been noted. In the United States, some centers report this diagnosis in up to 20% of all primary glomerulopathies. Males outnumber females, and the peak occurrence is in the second to third decades of life.

The diagnosis of IgA nephropathy is established by finding glomerular IgA deposits either as the dominant or co-dominant immunoglobulin on IF microscopy. Deposits of C3 and IgG are also often found. The LM picture varies from mild mesangial proliferation to crescentic glomerulonephritis. The most common picture is mesangial hypercellularity. By EM, immune-type dense deposits are typically found in the mesangial and paramesangial areas. In IgA nephropathy, the predominant antibody is composed of polymeric IgA1 originating in the secretory-mucosal system, but the antigen—whether infectious dietary or other—to which it is directed is unknown in the vast majority of cases.

IgA nephropathy often presents either as asymptomatic microscopic hematuria and/or proteinuria (most common in adults) or as episodic gross hematuria following upper respiratory tract infection or exercise (most common in children). The course of IgA nephropathy is variable, with some patients showing no decline in GFR over decades and others developing the nephrotic syndrome, hypertension, and renal failure. Hypertension is present in 20 to 50% of all patients. Increased serum IgA levels, noted in one third to one half of cases, do not correlate with the course of the disease.

Factors predictive of a poor outcome in IgA nephropathy have included (1) older age at onset, (2) absence of gross hematuria, (3) hypertension, (4) persistent and severe proteinuria, (5) being male, (6) an elevated serum creatinine level, and (7) the histologic features of severe proliferation and sclerosis and/or tubulointerstitial damage and crescent formation. Renal survival is estimated at 80 to 90% at 10 years and 70 to 80% at 20 years. A significant percentage of patients transplanted have a morphologic recurrence in the allograft, but graft loss due to the disease is uncommon.

Because the pathogenesis of IgA nephropathy is thought to involve abnormal antigenic stimulation of mucosal IgA production and subsequent immune complex deposition in the glomeruli, treatment has been directed at these sites. Efforts to treat the disease by preventing antigenic stimulation, including broad-spectrum antibiotics (e.g., doxycycline), tonsillectomy, and dietary manipulations (e.g., gluten elimination), have been generally unsuccessful. Most physicians choose to treat only those patients at highest risk for progression to renal failure. The benefit of immunosuppressive agents is far from clear. However, controlled studies suggest glucocorticoids can decrease proteinuria and progressive renal failure for some patients. For patients with crescentic IgA nephropathy cytotoxic agents have been used. Although trials using fish oils to decrease proteinuria and slow progressive disease have given conflicting results, the largest trial to date showed benefits in the prevention of renal failure using 12 g of omega 3 fish oils daily.

Henoch-Schönlein Purpura

Henoch-Schönlein purpura (HSP) is characterized by a small-vessel vasculitis with arthralgias, skin purpura, and abdominal symptoms along with a proliferative acute glomerulonephritis that has similar histopathologic features to IgA nephropathy. HSP is predominantly a disease of childhood, although cases do occur in adults. Despite the finding of circulating IgA-containing immune complexes, no infectious agent or allergen has been defined as causative.

The renal histopathology of HSP is similar to that of IgA nephropathy. In the skin there is a small vessel vasculitis, a leukocytoclastic angiitis with immune deposition of IgA. The clinical manifestations of HSP (Chapter 284) include dermatologic, gastrointestinal, rheumatologic, and renal findings. Skin involvement typically starts with a macular rash on the ankles that extends to the legs and occasionally the arms and buttocks. The macules darken and coalesce into purpuric lesions that are often palpable. Gastrointestinal symptoms include cramps, diarrhea, and, less frequently, nausea and vomiting. Melena and bloody diarrhea are present in the most severely involved cases. Although arthralgias of the knees, wrists, and ankles are common, true arthritis is uncommon. Symptoms of different organ system involvement may occur concurrently or separately, and recurrent episodes during the first year are not uncommon.

Like IgA nephropathy, HSP has no proven therapy. Episodes of rash, arthralgias, and abdominal symptoms usually resolve spontaneously. Some patients with severe abdominal findings have been treated with short courses of high doses of corticosteroids. Patients with severe glomerular involvement may benefit by modalities used to treat patients with severe IgA nephropathy. Although most patients with HSP recover fully, patients with a more severe nephritic or nephrotic presentation and more severe glomerular damage on renal biopsy have an unfavorable long-term prognosis.

Poststreptococcal Glomerulonephritis

Acute poststreptococcal glomerulonephritis (PSGN) may present as an acute nephritic syndrome or with isolated hematuria and proteinuria. It may occur in either an epidemic form or as sporadic cases. PSGN is largely a disease of childhood, but well-documented cases of severe disease do occur in adults. The disease is most common in winter after episodes of pharyngitis, but it can occur after streptococcal infections at any site, and subclinical cases greatly outnumber clinical cases.

PSGN is an acute immune complex disease characterized by the formation of antibodies against streptococci with the localization of immune complexes with complement in the kidney. PSGN occurs only after infection with certain nephritogenic strains of group A β-hemolytic streptococci.

On LM, glomeruli are markedly enlarged and often fill Bowman's space. They exhibit hypercellularity due to an infiltration of monocytes and polymorphonuclear cells during the early weeks of the disease and a proliferation of the glomerular cellular elements. The capillary lumina are often compressed by the glomerular hypercellularity. Some cases demonstrate extracapillary proliferation with crescent formation. By IF microscopy, there is coarse granular deposition of IgG, IgM, and complement, especially C3, along the capillary wall. EM shows the classic dome-shaped, electron-dense subepithelial deposits resembling the humps of a camel at isolated intervals along the GBM.

Most cases are diagnosed by detecting hematuria, proteinuria, and hypertension, and only some of the findings of the nephritic syndrome after a latency period of 10 days to several weeks after a streptococcal pharyngitis or a longer interval after a streptococcal skin infection. Throat cultures and skin cultures of suspected sites of streptococcal involvement may often not be positive for group A β-hemolytic streptococci. A variety of antibodies (e.g., anti-streptolysin O [ASLO]), anti-hyaluronidase [AHT]) and a streptozyme panel of antibodies against streptococcal antigens (which includes ASLO, AHT, anti-streptokinase, and anti-DNase) often show high titers, but a change in titer over time is more indicative of a recent streptococcal infection. More than 95% of patients with PSGN secondary to pharyngitis and 85% of patients with streptococcal skin infections have positive antibody titers. The serum total hemolytic complement levels and C3 levels are decreased in more than 90% of patients during the episode of acute glomerulonephritis.

In the classic case of an acute nephritic episode after a latency period after a streptococcal infection and associated with both a change in streptococcal antibody titer and a depressed serum complement level, a renal biopsy adds little to the diagnosis. In other cases, a biopsy may prove necessary to confirm or refute the diagnosis. In most patients, PSGN is a self-limited disease, with recovery of renal function and disappearance of hypertension in several weeks. Proteinuria and hematuria may resolve more slowly over months. Therapy is symptomatic and directed at controlling the hypertension and fluid retention with antihypertensive agents and diuretics.

Glomerulonephritis with Endocarditis and Visceral Abscesses

Various glomerular lesions have been found in patients with acute and chronic bacterial endocarditis (Chapter 310). Although embolic phenomena can lead to glomerular ischemia and infarcts, a common finding is an immune complex pattern of glomerular damage. In the preantibiotic era with most cases of endocarditis due to *Streptococcus viridans,* both focal and diffuse proliferative glomerulonephritides were seen in some patients. More recently, with an increased incidence of *Staphylococcus aureus* endocarditis, 40 to 80% of these patients have clinical evidence of an immune complex proliferative glomerulonephritis. Glomerulonephritis is now more common with acute rather than subacute bacterial endocarditis, and the duration of illness is not an important determinant of the renal disease.

Patients often have hematuria and erythrocyte casts in urinary sediment, proteinuria ranging from less than 1 g/day to nephrotic levels, and progressive renal failure. Serum total complement and C3 levels are usually reduced. Renal insufficiency may be mild and reversible with appropriate antibiotic therapy or progressive, leading to dialysis and irreversible renal failure.

A proliferative immune complex glomerulonephritis has also been noted in patients with deep visceral bacterial abscesses and infections such as empyema of the lung and osteomyelitis. With appropriate antibiotic therapy, most patients' glomerular lesions heal and they recover renal function. Immune complex forms of acute glomerulonephritis have also been noted in patients with pneumonias associated with many bacterial organisms as well as *Mycoplasma.* Patients with chronically infected cerebral ventriculoatrial shunts for hydrocephalus may have similar glomerular pathology. Many have nephrotic-range proteinuria and only mild renal dysfunction.

Rapidly Progressive Glomerulonephritis

Rapidly progressive glomerulonephritis (RPGN) comprises a group of glomerulonephritides that have in common progression to renal failure in a matter of weeks to months and the presence of extensive extracapillary proliferation (i.e., crescent formation). RPGN thus includes renal diseases with different causes, pathogeneses, and clinical presentations (Table 119–4). Patients with primary RPGN have been divided into three patterns defined by immunologic pathogenesis: type I, with anti-GBM disease (e.g., Goodpasture's syndrome); type II, with immune complex deposition (e.g., SLE, poststreptococcal); and type III, without immune deposits or anti-GBM antibodies, so-called pauci-immune. Most of the last group fall into the category of ANCA-positive RPGN. In the past, with the exception of postinfectious RPGN, prognosis was generally poor for most patients regardless of pathogenesis. This prognosis has dramatically changed for some patterns of RPGN.

Anti–Glomerular Basement Membrane Disease

Anti-GBM disease (Table 119–5) is caused by circulating antibodies directed against the noncollagenous domain of type 4 collagen that damages the GBM. This leads to an inflammatory response, breaks in the GBM, and the formation of a proliferative and often crescentic glomerulonephritis. If the anti-GBM antibodies cross-react with and damage the basement membrane of pulmonary capillaries, the patient develops pulmonary hemorrhage and hemoptysis, an association called *Goodpasture's syndrome.* The disease occurs at all decades and can affect males and females. The patients present with a nephritic picture. Renal function may deteriorate from normal to dialysis-requiring levels in a matter of days to weeks. Patients with pulmonary involvement may have life-threatening hemoptysis. The course of the disease, once it has progressed to dialysis levels, is usually one of permanent renal dysfunction. If treatment is started before severe renal failure, most patients regain considerable kidney function.

The pathology of anti-GBM disease shows a proliferative glomerulonephritis, often with severe crescentic proliferation in Bowman's

---

Table 119–4 • CLASSIFICATION OF RAPIDLY PROGRESSIVE ("CRESCENTIC") GLOMERULONEPHRITIS

PRIMARY
Type I: Anti–glomerular basement membrane antibody disease (with pulmonary disease—Goodpasture's syndrome)
Type II: Immune complex mediated
Type III: Pauci-immune (usually antineutrophil cytoplasmic antibody-positive)

SECONDARY
Membranoproliferative glomerulonephritis
IgA nephropathy—Henoch-Schönlein purpura
Poststreptococcal glomerulonephritis
Systemic lupus erythematosus
Polyarteritis nodosa, hypersensitivity angiitis

Table 119–5 • COMMON RENAL DISEASES WITH ASSOCIATED PULMONARY DISEASES

DISEASE	MARKER
Goodpasture's syndrome	+ Anti–glomerular basement membrane antibodies
Wegener's granulomatosis, polyarteritis	+ Anti–neutrophil cytoplasmic antibodies
Systemic lupus erythematosus	+ Anti-DNA antibodies, low complement
Nephrotic syndrome, renal vein thrombosis, pulmonary embolus	+ Lung scan
Pneumonia with immune complex glomerulonephritis	− Low complement, circulating immune complexes
Uremic lung	− Elevated blood urea nitrogen and creatinine levels

space. There is linear deposition of immunoglobulin along the GBM by IF, but EM does not show any electron-dense deposits.

Although the treatment of this rare disease has not been studied in large controlled trials, standard therapy is intensive therapy to reduce the production of anti-GBM antibodies (immunosuppressive agents cyclophosphamide and corticosteroids) combined with daily plasmapheresis to remove circulating anti-GBM antibodies. Rapid treatment is necessary to prevent irreversible renal damage. For patients with pulmonary hemorrhage, high-dose oral or intravenous corticosteroids along with plasmapheresis have successfully halted the pulmonary bleeding.

Immune Complex Rapidly Progressive Glomerulonephritis

Type II RPGN is associated with immune complex–mediated damage to the glomeruli and may occur with idiopathic glomerulopathies such as IgA nephropathy and MPGN or diseases of known origin such as postinfectious glomerulonephritis and SLE. The therapy for IgA nephropathy and MPGN was discussed previously. Most cases of crescentic postinfectious glomerulonephritis resolve with successful treatment of the underlying infection. The treatment of severe SLE is considered later.

Pauci-immune and Vasculitis-Associated Rapidly Progressive Glomerulonephritis

Pauci-immune type III RPGN includes patients with and without evidence of systemic vasculitis. A large retrospective analysis found no difference in prognosis between the patients with or without small artery or medium-sized renal artery vasculitis along with crescentic and focal segmental necrotizing glomerulonephritis. Patients often present with progressive renal failure and a nephritic picture. Many patients have circulating antibodies directed against components of neutrophil primary granules, ANCA. Patients who are P-ANCA positive (antibodies usually directed against granulocyte myeloperoxidase) more often have a clinical picture akin to that of microscopic polyarteritis with arthritis, skin involvement with leukocytoclastic angiitis, and constitutional and systemic signs. Patients who are C-ANCA positive (antibodies usually directed against a granulocyte serine proteinase) more often have granulomatous disease associated with their glomerulonephritis as in Wegener's granulomatosis. There is considerable overlap between these groups. As in all forms of RPGN, renal function may deteriorate rapidly. Oral cyclophosphamide in addition to corticosteroids has led to markedly improved patient and renal survival rates in patients with Wegener's granulomatosis and polyarteritis nodosa. For example, in a series of 158 patients with Wegener's granulomatosis, more than 90% experienced marked improvement and 75% experienced a complete remission. These excellent results include patients with true crescentic glomerulonephritis. The use of steroids plus cytotoxic agents has produced successful results in both oliguric and dialysis-dependent patients. Intravenous treatment of ANCA-positive RPGN with cyclophosphamide leads to fewer complications but a higher relapse rate than oral cyclophosphamide.

ASYMPTOMATIC URINARY ABNORMALITIES

Some patients have the asymptomatic urinary abnormalities of microhematuria and/or proteinuria discovered through routine evaluations. Microscopic hematuria associated with deformed erythrocytes and/or erythrocyte casts is likely to be glomerular in origin. Levels of proteinuria less than the nephrotic range may be due to orthostatic proteinuria, hypertension, and tubular disease as well as glomerular damage.

In patients with a glomerular cause for their asymptomatic urinary abnormality, the underlying glomerular lesion is either the early phase of one of the progressive glomerular diseases (discussed in other sections) or due to a benign, nonprogressive glomerular lesion. Most such patients have a lesion with mild proliferation limited to the mesangial areas of the glomeruli. Some patients have mesangial IgA immune deposits and hence IgA nephropathy, whereas others have deposition of IgM or complement only. Some patients, often with a history of similar findings in siblings and other relatives, have

a hereditary nephritis. One form of hereditary nephritis is associated with areas of focal thinning of the GBM, so-called thin basement membrane disease. Another hereditary form of glomerulonephritis that often presents as asymptomatic urinary findings is Alport's syndrome, an X-linked condition associated with high-pitched hearing loss and abnormalities of the lens of the eye. In males, this disease often leads to progressive glomerulosclerosis and ESRD. In general, for patients with less than 1 g of proteinuria daily and/or glomerular microhematuria, if the GFR (as measured by the creatinine clearance) is normal, most clinicians would not proceed to a renal biopsy to establish a diagnosis. Because the vast majority of these patients need no therapy, they prefer to follow the patient closely and perform biopsy only on patients with progressive increasing proteinuria or evidence of a decreasing GFR.

GLOMERULAR INVOLVEMENT IN SYSTEMIC DISEASES

Systemic Lupus Erythematosus

Renal involvement may greatly influence the course and therapy of SLE (Chapter 280). The incidence of clinically detectable renal disease varies from 15 to 75%. Histologic evidence of renal involvement by immune deposits is found in the vast majority of biopsy specimens, even in the absence of clinical renal disease.

The World Health Organization (WHO) classification of lupus nephritis has been widely used for both clinical and research activities (Table 119–6). It has the advantages of using LM, IF, and EM to classify each biopsy; of separating the milder mesangial disease from true proliferative lupus nephritis; and of using well-defined criteria allowing different groups to compare results. The WHO classes correlate well with the clinical picture and subsequent course of patients with SLE.

In general, all patients with class IV lesions on biopsy deserve vigorous therapy for their lupus nephritis. Many class III patients (especially those with active necrotizing lesions and large amounts of subendothelial deposits) (Fig. 119–3) also benefit from such therapy. The optimal therapy for class V patients is less clear; some clinicians treat all membranous lupus nephritis patients vigorously, whereas others reserve such therapy for those with serologic activity or more severe nephrotic syndrome. Vigorous lupus nephritis therapy has included corticosteroids, plasmapheresis, azathioprine, or cyclophosphamide, as well as newer immunosuppressive medications such as cyclosporine, gamma globulin, and mycophenolate mofetil. Plasmapheresis, reported to be successful anecdotally, has proved to be unsuccessful in improving renal or patient survival in a major

---

Table 119–6 • WORLD HEALTH ORGANIZATION CLASSIFICATION OF LUPUS NEPHRITIS

CLASS	CLINICAL FEATURES
I. Normal glomeruli (LM, IF, EM)	No renal findings
II. (a) Mesangial disease normal by LM with mesangial deposits by IF and/or EM (b) Mesangial hypercellularity with mesangial deposits	Mild clinical renal disease; minimally active urinary sediment; mild to moderate proteinuria (never nephrotic) but may have active serology.
III. Focal proliferative glomerulonephritis	More active sediment changes; often active serology; increased proteinuria (about 25% nephrotic); hypertension may be present; some evolve into class IV pattern.
IV. Diffuse proliferative glomerulonephritis	Most severe renal involvement with active sediment, hypertension, heavy proteinuria (frequent nephrotic syndrome), often reduced glomerular filtration rate; serology very active.
V. Membranous glomerulonephritis	Significant proteinuria (often nephrotic) with less active lupus serology.

EM = electron microscopy; IF = immunofluorescence; LM = light microscopy.

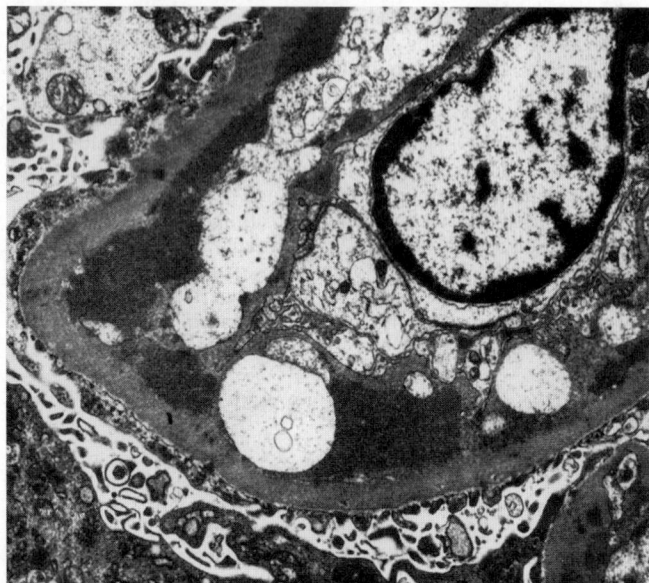

FIGURE 119–3 • Lupus nephritis. At the ultrastructural level, wire-loop deposits correspond to large subendothelial electron-dense deposits (uranyl acetate, lead citrate stain; original magnification × 5000).

clinical controlled trial. A series of well-performed randomized studies of patients with lupus nephritis at the National Institutes of Health found patients treated with cytotoxic agents had less renal failure at 10 years than those who had corticosteroid treatment. Extended follow-up at 20 years showed the azathioprine group to be no different from the prednisone groups. Intravenous cyclophosphamide appeared to be an effective therapy with fewer side effects than oral cyclophosphamide. Studies document the superiority of regimens with monthly high-dose intravenous cyclophosphamide therapy (0.5 to 1 g/m²) for 6 months over monthly pulse methylprednisolone in preventing renal progression and flares of disease. A controlled trial proved that combination therapy with monthly cyclophosphamide along with methylprednisolone was more effective in preventing renal failure than either drug regimen alone, with no increased long-term side effects. Daily oral mycophenolate mofetil appears to be equally effective in short studies of 6 to 12 months in diffuse proliferative lupus nephritis. At the present, for severe lupus nephritis most clinicians still use a regimen of monthly pulses of intravenous cyclophosphamide with low doses of corticosteroids given for 6 months followed by every-third-month pulses of the cytotoxic agent for up to 2 years. Whether daily azathioprine or mycophenolate can be substituted for the every third monthly cyclophosphamide is being studied.

Many patients with lupus nephritis (40 to 50%) produce autoantibodies against certain phospholipids, including anti-cardiolipin antibodies. Some of these patients have coagulation in the glomeruli and arterioles and require treatment with anticoagulation and/or antiplatelet agents as well as immunosuppressive medications.

Diabetes Mellitus

Diabetic nephropathy is the most common form of glomerular damage seen in developed countries. In 2003, more than 50% of all new patients with ESRD in the United States had diabetes (Chapter 123) as their primary etiology. From 20 to 30% of all patients with type I or type II diabetes develop nephropathy, with a much higher percentage of those with type I disease progressing to ESRD. However, because of the much greater prevalence of type II disease, the majority of the diabetics starting dialysis have this form of the disease.

The histopathologic changes in the kidneys of diabetics involve all components of the kidney, including the glomeruli, vessels, tubules, and interstitium. In the glomeruli there are thickening of the GBM, mesangial sclerosis, nodular intercapillary glomerulosclerosis (the so-called Kimmelstiel-Wilson [KW] nodules), lesions due to insudation of plasma proteins along the glomerular capillary walls, and microaneurysms of the glomerular capillaries.

A current goal of treatment in diabetics is to prevent diabetic renal failure by controlling hyperglycemia and blood pressure and reducing intracapillary glomerular pressures, and preventing the deleterious effects of growth factors and angiotensin II on the kidney. The superiority of angiotensin-converting enzyme (ACE) inhibitors over other antihypertensive agents in preventing the progression of renal disease and renal morbidity and mortality in type I diabetics has been documented in controlled trials. In type II diabetics with microalbuminuria, ACE inhibitors and angiotensin II receptor blockers also prevent the appearance of clinical proteinuria and progression of renal dysfunction. Studies have documented the efficacy of angiotensin II receptor antagonists in the prevention of renal disease progression in type II diabetics. In controlled, randomized, double-blind trials, proteinuria is reduced, doubling of the creatinine is reduced, and progression to ESRD reduced by the use of angiotensin II receptor blockers in addition to conventional blood pressure therapy versus conventional therapy alone.[2,3] Although survival is improving for the diabetic patient on dialysis, it is still inferior to that of the nondiabetic ESRD patient. Survival in diabetics with living-related donor renal transplantation may approach that of the nondiabetic population.

Amyloidosis

Renal amyloid deposits—whether due to AL or to AA amyloid—are predominantly found within the glomeruli, often appearing as amorphous eosinophilic extracellular nodules (Chapter 290). They stain positively with Congo red stain and, under polarized light, display apple-green birefringence. Under EM, amyloid appears as nonbranching rigid fibrils 8 to 10 nm in diameter.

Although almost 80% of patients with AL amyloid have renal disease, amyloidosis is a disease with multisystemic involvement, and hence patients may present with symptoms referable to cardiac or neural involvement as well as with renal symptoms. Diagnosis may be made from organ biopsy other than the kidney (e.g., gingival biopsy, rectal biopsy, or fat pad biopsy). Common renal manifestations are albuminuria and renal insufficiency found in almost one half of patients. Approximately 25% of patients with AL amyloid present with the nephrotic syndrome, and this is eventually found in up to one half of patients. Amyloid is rarely found in association with light chain cast nephropathy. Treatment strategies for renal amyloidosis have focused on combined therapy with melphalan, prednisone, and colchicines. Studies with stem cell or bone marrow transplantation and ablative therapy to destroy the clone of abnormal plasma cells leading to the amyloid production have given promising results in select patients.

Light Chain Deposition Disease

Light chain deposition disease (LCDD), like AL amyloidosis, is a systemic disease caused by the overproduction and extracellular deposition of a monoclonal immunoglobulin light chain (Chapter 196). However, the deposits do not form β-pleated sheets, do not stain with Congo red, and are granular rather than fibrillar. Most patients with LCDD have a lymphoplasmacytic B-cell disease similar to multiple myeloma. On LM, most glomeruli have eosinophilic mesangial glomerular nodules. Others are either normal or have sclerosing or proliferative features. By IF, a single class of immunoglobulin light chain (kappa in 80% of cases) stains in a diffuse linear pattern along the GBMs, in the nodules, and along the tubular basement membranes with little or no staining for complement components.

Moderate albuminuria is common, and the nephrotic syndrome is found in one half at presentation, often accompanied by hypertension and renal insufficiency. The treatment for most patients with LCDD is chemotherapy similar to that for myeloma, which has led to significant renal and patient survival, although marrow and stem cell transplantation is being tried in select cases.

Fibrillary Glomerulopathy-Immunotactoid Glomerulopathy

Some patients with renal disease have glomerular lesions with deposits of nonamyloid fibrillar proteins ranging in size from 12 to

49 nm. In the past, these lesions were called fibrillary glomerulopathy, immunotactoid glomerulopathy, amyloid-like glomerulopathy, Congo red–negative amyloid-like glomerulonephritis, and nonamyloiditic fibrillary glomerulopathy. Patients with these lesions have been divided into two groups: those with fibrillary glomerulonephritis with fibrils of 20 nm in diameter and those with immunotactoid glomerulonephritis, a rare disease in which the fibrils are much larger (30 to 50 nm). Proteinuria is found in almost all patients, and hematuria, the nephrotic syndrome, and renal insufficiency are eventually found in the majority. There is no proven therapy for fibrillary glomerulopathy at this time.

Human Immunodeficiency Virus Nephropathy

Infection with human immunodeficiency virus (HIV) has been associated with a number of patterns of renal disease, including acute renal failure and a unique form of glomerulopathy now called HIV-associated nephropathy.

Although histologic patterns of glomerulopathy seen in HIV-infected patients have included minimal change pattern, mesangial hyperplasia, with immune complex deposition and/or IgA deposition, by far the most common is HIV-associated nephropathy. HIV-associated nephropathy is characterized by heavy proteinuria and rapid progression to renal failure. The use of ACE inhibitors and highly active antiretroviral therapy (HAART) may slow this progression to renal failure and decrease proteinuria. Studies show corticosteroid use in selected patients with HIV-associated nephropathy may be beneficial.

Both clinical and histologic data suggest that HIV nephropathy differs from the older entity of heroin nephropathy. The latter is a form of FSGS, occurring in intravenous heroin users associated with proteinuria and often the nephrotic syndrome and renal insufficiency. HIV-associated nephropathy may occur in nonaddicted patients and has a more fulminant course to renal failure than heroin nephropathy. The pathology of HIV-associated nephropathy also shows distinct features from classic FSGS including, on LM, diffuse global glomerular collapse, severe tubulointerstitial changes with interstitial inflammation, edema, microcystic dilatation of tubules, and severe tubular degenerative changes and, on EM, tubuloreticular inclusions in the glomerular endothelium.

Mixed Cryoglobulinemia

Cryoglobulinemia is caused by the production of circulating immunoglobulins that precipitate on cooling and resolubilize on warming. Cryoglobulinemia may be found associated with many types of diseases, including infections, collagen-vascular disease, and lymphoproliferative diseases such as multiple myeloma and Waldenström's macroglobulinemia (Chapter 196). Many patients with what was originally described as glomerulonephritis due to essential mixed cryoglobulinemia have been found to have hepatitis C–associated renal disease. Some patients develop an acute nephritic picture with acute renal insufficiency. Most patients have proteinuria, and about 20% present with the nephrotic syndrome. The majority with renal disease have a slow, indolent renal course characterized by proteinuria, hypertension, hematuria, and renal insufficiency. Hypocomplementemia, especially of the early components Clq–C4, is a characteristic and often helpful finding in cryoglobulinemic glomerulonephritis.

Thrombotic Microangiopathies

A number of systemic diseases, including hemolytic-uremic syndrome, thrombotic thrombocytopenic purpura, and the antiphospholipid syndrome (Chapter 177), as well as microangiopathy associated with drugs such as mitomycin and cyclosporine, are characterized by microthromboses of the glomerular capillaries and small arterioles. The renal findings may be dominant or only part of a more generalized picture of microangiopathy.

The histologic findings in all of the microangiopathies resemble each other. Glomerular capillary thromboses are noted in some glomeruli, whereas others downstream from thrombosed arterioles may show only ischemic damage. Arterioles and small arteries show intimal proliferation with luminal narrowing by thrombus. The renal manifestations of the thrombotic microangiopathies may include gross or microscopic hematuria, proteinuria that is typically less than 2 g/day but may reach nephrotic levels, and renal insufficiency. Patients may have oliguric or nonoliguric acute renal failure. Treatment of the thrombotic microangiopathies includes correcting hypovolemia, controlling hypertension, and use of dialytic support for those with severe renal failure. In TTP and some other cases, infusion of fresh plasma with or without plasmapheresis has been beneficial. In the antiphospholipid syndrome, anticoagulation with heparin and then warfarin (Coumadin) has been useful.

Renal Vasculitis-Polyarteritis, Wegener's Granulomatosis, Hypersensitivity Angiitis

A number of systemic vasculitic disease processes can involve the kidney. In many cases of polyarteritis nodosa, hypersensitivity angiitis, and Wegener's granulomatosis (Chapters 293 and 294), renal involvement is predominant and overshadows other manifestations of the systemic vasculitis. The renal lesions of these disorders typically range from focal and segmental necrotizing glomerulonephritis to severe necrotizing crescentic glomerulonephritis. Therapy for the microscopic form of polyarteritis and Wegener's granulomatosis is discussed under the therapy for RPGN.

1. Cattran DC, Appel GB, Hebert L, et al: Cyclosporine in patients with steroid-resistant membranous nephropathy: A randomized trial. Kidney Int 2001;59:1484–1490.
2. Brenner BM, Cooper ME, de Zeeuw D, et al: Effects of losartan on renal and cardiovascular outcomes in patients with type 2 diabetes and nephropathy. N Engl J Med 2001;345:861–869.
3. Lewis EJ, Hunsicker LG, Clarke WR, et al: Renoprotective effect of the angiotensin-receptor antagonist irbesartan in patients with nephropathy due to type 2 diabetes. N Engl J Med 2001;345:851–860.

SUGGESTED READINGS

Chan TM, Li FK, Tang CSO, et al: Efficacy of mycophenolate mofetil in patients with diffuse proliferative lupus nephritis. N Engl J Med 2000;343:1156–1162. *Controlled randomized trial of mycophenolate versus oral cyclophosphamide followed by azathioprine showing similar short-term efficacy and low toxicity with mycophenolate.*

Contreras G, Roth D, Pando V, et al: Lupus nephritis: a clinical review for the practicing nephrologist. Clin Nephrology 2002;57:95–107. *A review of the histologic classes of lupus nephritis and their treatment.*

Couser WG: Complement inhibitors and glomerulonephritis: Are we there yet? J Am Soc Nephrol 2003;14:815–818. *A thoughtful review.*

Dember L, Sanchorawala V, Seldin DC, et al: Effect of dose-intensive melphalan and autologous blood stem-cell transplantation on AL—Amyloidosis-associated renal disease. Ann Intern Med 2001;134:746–753. *Prospective cohort study of 65 AL amyloid patients undergoing stem cell transplantation showing risks and benefits in individual patient subgroups.*

Donadia JV, Grande JP: IGA Nephropathy. N Engl J Med 2002;347:738–748. *A review of the pathogenesis, clinical features, course, and treatment of IgA nephropathy.*

Eustace JA, Neurmberger E, Choi M, et al: Cohort study of the treatment of severe HIV-associated nephropathy with corticosteroids. Kidney Int 2000;58:1253–1260. *Retrospective cohort study showing benefits of steroids in reducing proteinuria and renal progression in a very select group of patients with HIV-associated nephropathy.*

Illei GG, Austin HA III, Crane M, et al: Combination therapy with pulse cyclophosphamide plus pulse methylprednisolone improves long-term renal outcome without adding toxicity in patients with lupus nephritis. Ann Intern Med 2001;135:248–257. *The combination provided benefit without increasing adverse events.*

Jennette JC: Rapidly progressive crescentic glomerulonephritis. Kidney Intl 2003;63:1164–1177. *A review of the disease spectrum of RPGN.*

Korbet S: Treatment of primary focal and segmental glomerulosclerosis. Kidney Int 2002;62:2301–2310. *A review of the therapy of this important cause of the nephrotic syndrome.*

Kyle RA, Gertz MA, Greipp PR, et al: A trial of three regimens for primary amyloidosis: Colchicine alone, melphalan and prednisone, and melphalan, prednisone, and colchicine. N Engl J Med 1997;336:1202–1207. *An analysis of clinical features and response to therapeutic regimens of 220 patients with primary amyloidosis.*

Levy JB, Turner N, Rees AJ, et al: Long-term outcome of antiglomerular basement membrane antibody disease treated with plasma exchange and immunosuppression. Ann Intern Med 2001;134:1033–1042. *A relatively large experience with this uncommon form of rapidly progressive glomerulonephritis showing benefits of therapy.*

Rosenstack JL, Valeri AM, Appel GB, et al: Fibrillary glomerulonephritis: Definition of the disease spectrum. Kidney Int 2003;63:1450–1462. *A large single-center experience with the presentation, clinical histologic correlates, and course of the disease.*

Ross MJ, Klotman PE: Recent progress in HIV-associated nephropathy. J Am Soc Nephrol 2002;13:2997–3004. *A review of pathogenesis, clinical features, and treatment of the disease.*

120 TUBULOINTERSTITIAL DISEASES AND TOXIC NEPHROPATHIES

Garabed Eknoyan

TUBULOINTERSTITIAL NEPHROPATHY

At their onset, diseases of the kidney primarily affect the glomeruli, the vasculature, or the other two components of the renal parenchyma: the tubules and the interstitium. The tubules and interstitium of the kidney are separate structural and functional compartments that are intimately related, and any injury initially involving either of them inevitably is associated with damage to the other, hence the term *tubulointerstitial diseases*. A constant histologic feature of these diseases is an inflammatory cell infiltrate. The clinicopathologic syndrome that results from these disorders is commonly termed *tubulointerstitial nephropathy*. The abbreviation TIN is used in this chapter to refer synonymously to tubulointerstitial nephritis and tubulointerstitial nephropathy.

As a rule, TIN is categorized as being *primary* or *secondary* in origin. *Primary* TIN is defined as injury that affects the tubules and interstitium without significant involvement of the glomeruli or renal vasculature, at least in the early stages of the disease. *Secondary* TIN is defined as tubulointerstitial injury caused by diseases that initially affect the glomeruli or renal vasculature, with the subsequent superimposition of TIN. The presence of secondary TIN has come to be identified as an important determinant of reduced kidney function and its progression to kidney failure, both of which correlate better with the extent of secondary TIN than they do with the severity of the glomerular or vascular lesions that were the cause of the original kidney disease.

Clinically, TIN pursues an *acute* (ATIN) or *chronic* (CTIN) course. Primary ATIN accounts for some 15 to 20% of patients with acute renal failure, and primary CTIN, for 20 to 30% of those with chronic kidney disease who progress to end-stage renal disease (ESRD). The clinical and social implications of the primary forms of TIN are

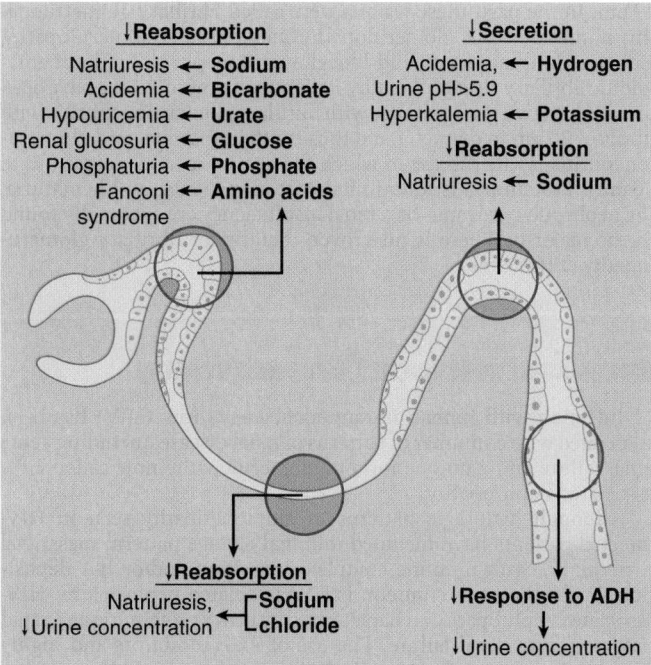

FIGURE 120–1 • Schematic presentation of the principal sites of injury and patterns of tubular dysfunction in tubulointerstitial diseases. Bold lettering indicates a functional abnormality, and lighter lettering, its consequent clinical manifestation. Arrows indicate the directional change of the abnormality. ADH = antidiuretic hormone.

especially important since more than half of these cases are the result of a toxic nephropathy produced by a drug or an environmental toxin. As such, potentially they are either preventable or treatable if recognized early, before the onset of irreversible loss of kidney function.

More broadly defined and inclusive of both its primary and secondary forms, TIN is a component of all cases of acute and chronic renal failure. The World Health Organization classification of the pathology of diseases of the kidney lists acute tubular necrosis (ATN) as a form of ATIN. Both are associated with tubulointerstitial injury; however, necrosis is more prominent in ATN, whereas interstitial inflammatory cellular infiltrates and edema are more prominent in ATIN (Table 120–1). In fact, their pathologic features may overlap sufficiently to make differentiation of ATN and ATIN difficult on morphologic examination of kidney tissue. Clinically, both result in acute renal failure and must be considered in the differential diagnosis of acute deterioration in kidney function. By the same token, most forms of primary glomerular or vascular kidney diseases that become chronic and progress to ESRD are associated with secondary CTIN. As such, apart from its importance as a primary cause of kidney disease, CTIN is the common pathway of all forms of progressive chronic renal failure.

Clinical Manifestations

In all cases of primary ATIN and in most cases of primary CTIN, loss of kidney function occurs in conjunction with or subsequent to the tubulointerstitial injury, and the earliest manifestations of the disease are usually those of tubular dysfunction. Whenever such dysfunction is detected clinically, removal of the toxic cause of injury or correction of the underlying disease can result in reversal of injury or preservation of kidney function.

The pattern of tubular dysfunction encountered clinically depends on the site of the lesions of TIN (Fig. 120–1), and their severity depends on the extent of interstitial infiltrates and tubular injury. Essentially, TIN affects either the cortex or the medulla of the kidney. Cortical lesions affect either the proximal or the distal tubule. Proximal tubular lesions result in bicarbonaturia (plasma CO_2 content, <20 mEq/L), glucosuria (with normal blood glucose), uricosuria (normal or low serum urate levels, particularly relative to the level of azotemia), and β_2-microalbuminuria and aminoaciduria (Fanconi's syndrome). Distal tubular lesions result

Table 120–1 • MORPHOLOGIC FEATURES OF ACUTE AND CHRONIC TUBULOINTERSTITIAL NEPHRITIS

MORPHOLOGY	ATN	ATIN	CTIN
Gross Features			
Size	Enlarged	Enlarged	Small
Surface	Normal	Normal	Scarred
Echogenicity	Normal	Normal	Increased
Microscopic Features			
Interstitium			
Edema	$+ \rightarrow ++$	$+ \rightarrow ++++$	$\pm \rightarrow ++$
Fibrosis	None	Unusual	Severe
Cell infiltrates	Few	Prominent	Modest
Tubules			
Cells	Necrotic	Injured	Atrophy/hypertrophy
Basement membrane	$\pm \rightarrow ++$	$+ \rightarrow +++$	Thickened
Shape	Preserved	Preserved	Atrophy/dilation
Glomeruli			
Capillaries	Normal	Normal $\rightarrow$ MCD	Sclerosis
Capsule	Normal	Normal	Thickened/fibrosed
Vasculature			
Endothelium	Normal $\rightarrow$ swollen	Normal	Normal
Wall	Normal	Normal	Variable sclerosis

ATN = acute tubular necrosis; ATIN = acute tubulointerstitial nephritis; CTIN = chronic tubulointerstitial nephritis; MCD = minimal change disease; + indicates presence, and the greater the number of + symbols, the more severe the morphologic feature.

in reduced hydrogen secretion or distal tubular acidosis (urine pH, >5.9; plasma CO_2 content, <20 mEq/L), either without or with coexistent impairment of distal tubular potassium secretion (hyperkalemia, type IV renal tubular acidosis). Medullary lesions result in a reduced ability to achieve the hypertonicity essential for concentrating urine and in impaired responsiveness of the distal tubule to antidiuretic hormone (nephrogenic diabetes insipidus), effects manifested clinically by polyuria and nocturia. On occasion, concomitant injury to several tubular segments may occur, and in fact, as the disease progresses, this pattern becomes the norm in most forms of primary TIN, in which case simultaneous cortical and medullary tubular dysfunction is present in the same patient.

Because epithelial cell sodium transport is a principal function of the entire tubule, some degree of reduced sodium reabsorption occurs independent of the tubular segment affected by TIN (see Fig. 120–1). This phenomenon accounts for the absence of the clinical features of sodium retention (hypertension, edema) in primary CTIN, an extremely useful clinical feature in the differential diagnosis of primary CTIN from its secondary forms caused by glomerular or vascular diseases, in which hypertension and edema are almost always present when kidney function is reduced.

Pathogenesis

The mechanism by which TIN is mediated remains to be elucidated. Tubular epithelial cell injury appears to be pivotal in initiation of the process. The initial injury may be direct cytotoxicity (drugs, environmental toxins) or indirect damage secondary to an inflammatory reaction (systemic diseases, autoimmune disorders). Studies in experimental models and humans provide compelling evidence for a role of immune mechanisms in subsequent progression of the process, which for purposes of clarification has been arbitrarily classified into three phases: antigen expression or recognition, integrative or regulatory, and effector or mediator.

In the first phase, either the injured tubular epithelial cells or the stimulated interstitial dendritic cells, both of which express the class II major histocompatibility complex, function as antigen-presenting cells. The second, or integrative or regulatory, phase determines the subsequent course of kidney involvement. In this intricate and poorly deciphered phase, the recruited infiltrating cells and antigenically activated T lymphocytes play a central role. In the final, or effector or mediator, phase, humoral factors released by the infiltrating cells and by the injured epithelial cells cause further recruitment of inflammatory cells and macrophages and the initiation of fibrogenesis. Cytokines, which have chemoattractant, proinflammatory, and cytotoxic properties and are actually operative in all three phases, assume a greater role in the perpetuation of this final phase.

Each of the individual phases of this immune response is usually part of a recuperative process to repair injury. It is the apparent loss of their regulatory mechanisms or continuous exposure to the causative injury that accounts for progressive damage.

Pathology

Although the clinical history and laboratory evidence of tubular dysfunction will strongly suggest the possibility of tubulointerstitial disease, a diagnosis of TIN can be established only from morphologic examination of kidney tissue (see Table 120–1). As a rule, it is the extent of the lesions of TIN, whether focal or diffuse, that correlates with the degree of impairment of kidney function.

Interstitial cellular infiltrates are present in all forms of TIN but are a more prominent feature of ATIN. They are composed mostly of activated lymphocytes and macrophages, but other types of inflammatory cells (polymorphonuclear leukocytes, fibroblasts, histiocytes) and even granulomatous reactions may be present. In all cases, the cortical tubules, which are normally quite closely approximated, are separated by an expanded interstitium as a result of edema in ATIN and fibrosis in CTIN. Consequently, the edematous kidneys of patients with ATIN are enlarged, whereas the fibrosclerotic kidneys of those with CTIN are small, contracted, and scarred. The shape of the tubules is well preserved in ATIN, but focal loss of tubular basement membrane and epithelial cell injury by infiltrating mononuclear cells may be present. By contrast, a principal feature of CTIN is epithelial cell

apoptosis and tubular atrophy and dilation. These changes are patchy in distribution, with areas of atrophic, chronically damaged tubules adjacent to dilated tubules displaying compensatory hypertrophy. In general, the glomeruli are normal in ATIN and in the early stages of CTIN, but they ultimately become sclerosed in CTIN and severe periglomerular fibrosis develops. The vasculature is normal in ATIN and early CTIN, but in progressive CTIN the vasculature demonstrates arteriosclerotic changes, even in the absence of elevated blood pressure. Immunofluorescent studies for immune deposits are unrevealing and in general are negative. In the few instances in which they are positive, no definite diagnostic pattern is evident, except in the rare instance of TIN caused by antitubular basement membrane antibodies, in which case the characteristic linear immunofluorescence of the tubular basement membrane is diagnostic.

ACUTE TUBULOINTERSTITIAL DISEASES

Drugs

Drugs have emerged as the most common cause of ATIN (Table 120–2).

Drug-induced ATIN is a hypersensitivity reaction that is not dose related, appears anywhere between 2 to 40 days after the initiation of treatment, and can occur in the absence of any systemic manifestations of hypersensitivity. Also termed *acute allergic interstitial nephritis*, ATIN is actually a rare complication of drugs. It is the increased frequency with which drugs are used that accounts for their emergence as a major cause of ATIN. The absence of previous reactions to an incriminated drug does not preclude the development of ATIN, although a previous systemic reaction to a drug should always suggest its causative role in the diagnosis. Recurrent episodes, often more severe and sudden in onset, can occur on re-exposure to the same drug or one of its structural analogues (Chapter 27).

Systemic manifestations indicative of a hypersensitivity reaction are more common with antibiotics. They are transient and may be mild enough to go undetected. In antibiotic-induced ATIN, fever occurs in the majority (60 to 100%); a fleeting skin rash of erythematous, pruritic, maculopapular lesions develops in 30 to 50% of cases; and eosinophilia is present in 30 to 60%. Elevated serum levels of IgE are detected in up to half of these patients. A history of nonspecific arthralgias (15 to 20%) and flank pain (variable) secondary to the distended renal capsule of the edematous kidney may be elicited. Hematuria, proteinuria, and pyuria are present in over 80% of cases. The hematuria, which is microscopic in 90% of cases, can be gross and be the initial symptom in some. The proteinuria is tubular in origin and generally mild (<2 g/day). The pyuria is nonspecific, except when eosinophils constitute 5% of the urinary white blood cells. Although the presence of eosinophiluria supports a diagnosis of ATIN, it does not establish it, just as its absence does not exclude it.

Sudden onset of renal insufficiency is generally the first evidence of ATIN. The impairment in kidney function is variable and occurs with or without oliguria. The increments in blood urea nitrogen and serum creatinine develop at a time when the patient is nonoliguric or even polyuric because of the tubular defect in concentrating ability.

Table 120–2 • PRINCIPAL CONDITIONS ASSOCIATED WITH ACUTE TUBULOINTERSTITIAL DISEASE

Drugs
Antibiotics: penicillins, cephalosporins, rifampin
Sulfonamides: cotrimoxazole, sulfamethoxazole
Nonsteroidal anti-inflammatory drugs: propionic acid derivatives
Miscellaneous: phenytoin, thiazides, allopurinol, cimetidine, ifosfamide

Infections
Invasion of renal parenchyma
Reaction to systemic infections: streptococcal, diphtheria, Hantavirus

Systemic Diseases
Immune mediated: lupus, transplanted kidney, cryoglobulinemias
Metabolic: urate, oxalate
Neoplastic: lymphoproliferative diseases

Idiopathic

Oliguria develops if the tubular dysfunction and mild azotemia go undetected and exposure to the drug is continued. Kidney failure is more severe in those in whom oliguria develops and more common in older individuals.

A renal ultrasonographic examination showing enlarged kidneys, indicative of interstitial edema, and a positive gallium scan, indicative of interstitial inflammatory cell infiltrates, are only suggestive of ATIN. The diagnosis can be established only by kidney biopsy.

 Treatment

The cornerstones of therapy are early diagnosis, identification of the responsible drug, and discontinuation of its use. Each of these steps is equally important because early diagnosis is essential if severe loss of kidney function is to be avoided, recognition of the responsible drug is important because patients are often taking several drugs that can cause ATIN, and discontinuation of therapy with the incriminated drug is crucial because this measure can result in complete recovery of kidney function. Those in whom severe loss of kidney function develops will require supportive therapy and, if oliguric, dialysis.

In cases of severe renal failure or in those with progressive loss of kidney function after discontinuation of therapy with the drug, a kidney biopsy is indicated to establish the diagnosis and rule out the ATN that occurs in the same prevailing clinical conditions of acutely ill hospitalized patients. It is in such cases that a short course of steroids (60 mg of prednisone per day for 10 to 14 days or 1 g of methylprednisolone per day intravenously for 3 days) can expedite recovery. The duration of steroid therapy should be guided by the response noted and should never exceed 2 to 4 weeks.

Nonsteroidal Anti-inflammatory Drugs

ATIN associated with nonsteroidal anti-inflammatory drugs (NSAIDs) is unique because of the accompanying massive proteinuria and the absence of evidence of a hypersensitivity reaction (fever, skin rash, eosinophilia). The proteinuria is insidious in onset and often precedes the onset of renal failure. In some cases, either nephrotic-range proteinuria (10%) or renal failure (15%) may be the only initial feature. Although ATIN has been reported to occur with most NSAIDs, including the selective cyclooxygenase-2 (COX-2) inhibitors, the propionic acid derivatives (ibuprofen, naproxen, fenoprofen) account for most cases encountered clinically.

Unlike the situation with other drugs, usually the patient has a long history of exposure to NSAIDs (weeks to months) before the onset of ATIN, and recovery is slow (months to a year) after withdrawal of the inciting agent. Steroids do not seem to hasten the course of recovery from NSAID-induced ATIN and probably should not be used. Permanent loss of kidney function can occur in about a third of these cases.

Other Causes

ATIN may complicate the course of several systemic diseases and infections (see Table 120–2). In about 15 to 20% of cases of ATIN, no etiology can be identified. Prominent among these are cases associated with an idiopathic bone marrow granulomatous reaction and cases with associated uveitis. In the latter, which is more common in adolescence, ocular symptoms may precede, accompany, or develop subsequent to clinical evidence of ATIN. Both the renal and ocular changes show a favorable and rapid response to a short course of steroid therapy, but recovery can be spontaneous in some and the disease recurrent in others.

CHRONIC TUBULOINTERSTITIAL DISEASES

CTIN is the unifying feature of an assorted group of diverse diseases (Table 120–3). By definition, *chronic kidney disease* is insidious in onset in these cases, and in most goes undetected unless specifically sought. Documentation requires testing for tubular dysfunction (see Fig. 120–1) and, if necessary, confirmation by kidney biopsy (see Table 120–1). The more common causes of primary CTIN are potentially treatable or preventable. In some 10% of cases of primary CTIN,

Table 120–3 • CONDITIONS ASSOCIATED WITH CHRONIC TUBULOINTERSTITIAL DISEASE

Drugs: Analgesics, nonsteroidal anti-inflammatory drugs, cisplatin, cyclosporine, lithium, 5-aminosalicylic acid, aristolochic acid
Heavy metals: lead, cadmium
Vascular diseases: hypertension, vasculitis, embolic disorders, radiation nephritis
Urinary tract obstruction: vesicoureteral reflux, mechanical
Metabolic disorders: urate, oxalate, cystinosis
Immune diseases: systemic lupus erythematosus, allograft rejection, Goodpasture's syndrome, amyloidosis
Granulomatous diseases: sarcoidosis, Wegener's granulomatosis
Infections: bacterial, mycobacterial, viral, fungal
Hematologic diseases: plasma cell dyscrasias, sickle hemoglobinopathies, lymphomas
Endemic: Balkan nephropathy
Hereditary: cystic diseases, Alport's syndrome
Idiopathic

the lesions are idiopathic and not associated with any of the conditions listed in Table 120–3. Epstein-Barr virus infection of the proximal tubular epithelial cells has been implicated in evoking the cellular immune response that results in the tubulointerstitial lesions of idiopathic CTIN.

Analgesic Nephropathy

The weight of the available clinical evidence indicates that lesions of analgesic nephropathy develop in those who use analgesic combinations (aspirin and acetaminophen, with or without caffeine) regularly and over extended periods. The extent of injury is related to the quantity of analgesic ingested chronically over the years. In those with severe loss of kidney function, the average dose consumed has been estimated to be about 10 kg over a mean period of 13 years. The minimum amount of drug consumption that is associated with detectable renal impairment is unknown. It has been estimated to be a cumulative dose of 3 kg, or the daily ingestion of 1 g of the index agent for 3 years or longer.

The intrarenal distribution and metabolism of analgesics provide a basis for the location of the kidney lesions and their mechanism of injury. Both acetaminophen and aspirin attain significant concentrations in the medulla and papilla of the kidneys. In experimental studies it has been shown that the state of hydration determines the intrarenal concentrations attained and that intrarenal concentrations can be abolished by forced diuresis, which actually results in protection from injury. The intrarenal oxidation of acetaminophen results in the generation of toxic reactive metabolites that are normally reduced by substances such as glutathione. Aspirin uncouples oxidative phosphorylation and reduces the ability of epithelial cells to generate reducing substances. Thus, these agents attain sufficient renal medullary concentration to exert a local detrimental effect on their own but tend to magnify the degree of kidney injury when they are used together.

The initial site of injury is the papilla, where analgesics attain their highest concentration, and patchy necrosis is the first sign of injury. With continued exposure, lesions extend to the outer medulla, increase in severity and extent, and begin to calcify as larger necrotic foci develop. Ultimately, the entire papilla becomes necrotic and may slough or remain in situ, where it shrinks and calcifies. Cortical atrophic scars develop over the necrotic medullary segments, with adjacent areas of compensatory hypertrophy imparting a characteristic cortical nodularity. Visualization of these configurational changes (reduced size, nodularity, calcification) by computed tomography can be extremely useful in the diagnosis of analgesic nephropathy (Fig. 120–2). A decrease in kidney size combined with bumpy contours of both kidneys provides a diagnostic sensitivity of 90% and a specificity of 95%. The additional finding of evidence of papillary necrosis increases the specificity to 97%, with a positive predictive value of 92%.

The lesions of analgesic nephropathy are patchy and slowly progressive, remain asymptomatic, and usually go undetected until the onset of azotemia. They should be considered in anyone with sterile

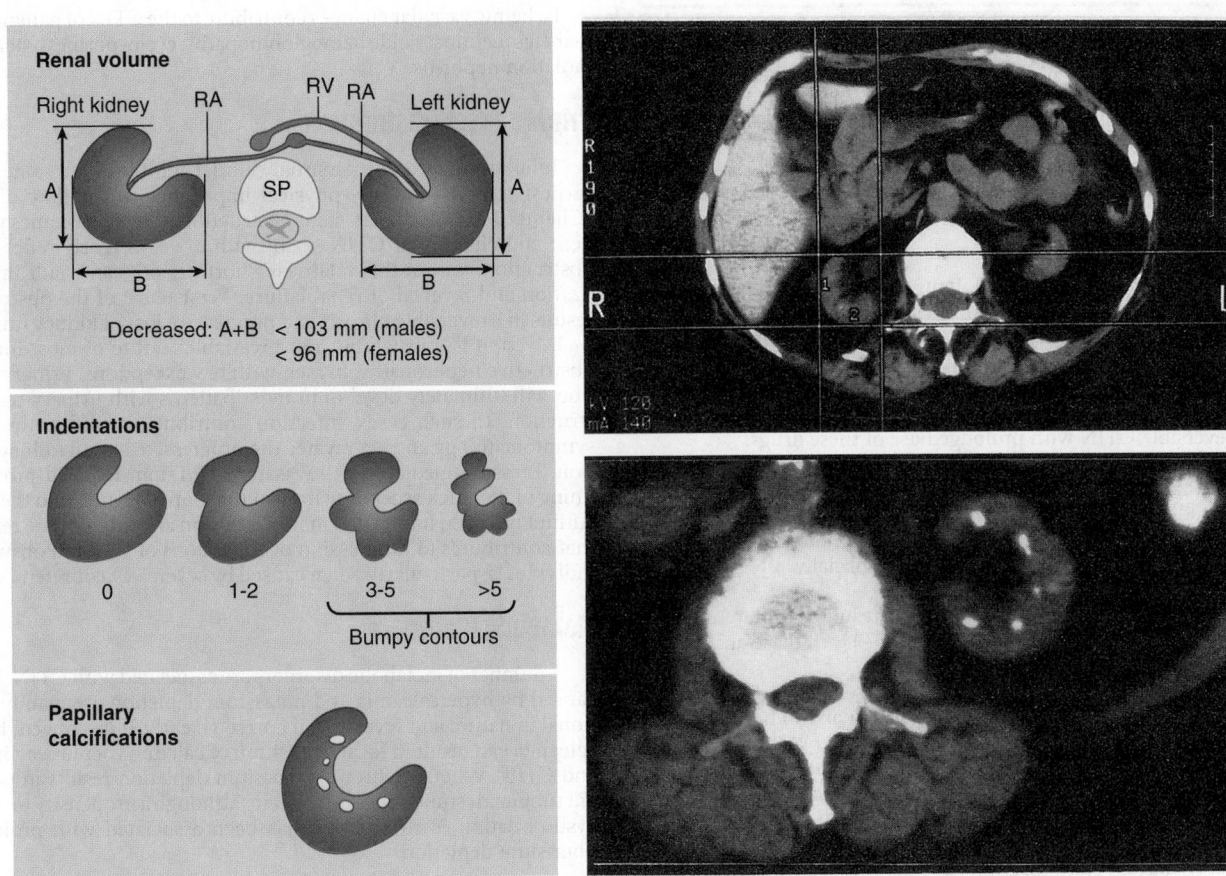

FIGURE 120–2 • Configurational changes (reduced volume, nodularity, calcification) observed on CT scanning of the kidney in analgesic nephropathy. RA = right artery; RV = right vein; SP = spinal vertebra. (From Elseviers MM, De Schepper A, Corthouts R, et al: High diagnostic performance of CT scan for analgesic nephropathy in patients with incipient to severe renal failure. Kidney Int 1995;48:1316, with permission.)

pyuria, reduced concentrating ability, and a distal tubular acidifying defect, effects that are evident at levels of mild renal insufficiency and gradually become more pronounced and clinically evident as kidney function deteriorates. Proximal tubular function is preserved in those with mild renal insufficiency, but it becomes abnormal with advanced renal failure. A tendency toward impaired sodium conservation is common. The presence of any tubular dysfunction, even with normal blood urea nitrogen and serum creatinine levels, should always lead to careful questioning about analgesic use and possible urinary screening for analgesic metabolites.

Analgesic nephropathy is more common in women, in those who are 30 to 50 years old, and in regions where over-the-counter sale of analgesic mixtures is high. Certain personality features (dependency, moodiness) and clinical complaints (headache, musculoskeletal pain, arthralgias) characterize individuals prone to analgesic use. Anemia and peptic ulcer symptoms caused by the gastrointestinal effects of analgesics are common findings and may be the initial complaint in some.

Rx Treatment

The primary goal of therapy should be discontinuation of analgesic use. In most of those who do, kidney function stabilizes or even improves. Those who do not discontinue analgesic use should be encouraged to increase fluid intake, which reduces the intramedullary concentration of analgesics, and to avoid dehydration or the use of diuretics and laxatives, which increases their medullary concentration. Psychological support and guidance can be useful in discontinuing analgesic use. Monitoring for uroepithelial malignancies is important, even after analgesic discontinuation, because chronic analgesic users are prone to this otherwise rare form of cancer.

Although discontinuation of chronic analgesic use is important, avoidance of their use in combination is by far more essential. In countries in which over-the-counter sale of analgesic

mixtures has been banned, a reduced incidence of analgesic nephropathy has been noted. Aspirin alone in therapeutic doses does not impair renal function in patients with normal kidney function. Most studies fail to demonstrate an increased risk of ESRD associated with the habitual use of aspirin as a single agent in therapeutic doses. However, aspirin overdosage may impair kidney function, especially in those with chronic kidney disease. Clinical evidence suggesting that the habitual use of acetaminophen alone causes the clinical entity of classic analgesic nephropathy is negligible. Acetaminophen has been preferentially recommended to patients with kidney disease because of the bleeding complications associated with aspirin in these individuals. As such, its reported association with kidney failure may well be an epiphenomenon rather than one of causal association. There is no evidence that the occasional use of acetaminophen causes renal injury or is detrimental to those with chronic kidney disease.

Other Drugs

Drugs that have been associated with CTIN include a number of therapeutic medications, antineoplastic agents, and immunosuppressive drugs (see Table 120–3). A rapidly progressive CTIN occurs with the use of alternative therapy with herbal medicines. Inappropriately termed "Chinese herbal nephropathy," this form of CTIN is due to aristolochic acid, present in the *Aristolochia* plant constituent of some herbal mixtures.

LITHIUM. The most common side effect of lithium is vasopressin-resistant nephrogenic diabetes insipidus, which is often accompanied by additional evidence of distal tubular dysfunction, such as a mild form of distal renal tubular acidosis and sodium wasting. CTIN develops in some of these cases, especially in patients with a history of prolonged exposure and recurrent episodes of lithium overdose.

IMMUNOSUPPRESSIVE DRUGS. Of the immunosuppressive drugs, the calcineurin inhibitors, cyclosporine and tacrolimus, should always

---

Table 120–4 • HEAVY METAL NEPHROTOXICITY

Chronic tubulointerstitial disease: bismuth, cadmium, chromium, copper, iron, lead, lithium, mercury, platinum, silicon, uranium
Acute renal failure: arsenic, bismuth, cadmium, chromium, copper, gold, iron, lead, mercury, silver, uranium
Nephrotic syndrome: bismuth, gold, mercury, nickel

---

be considered as a cause of CTIN. Drug-induced vasoconstriction of the microvasculature accounts for a characteristic occlusive arteriolopathy and subsequent tubular epithelial cell injury, which is difficult to distinguish from chronic allograft rejection. The lesions are characteristically patchy in their early stage and reversible after cessation of therapy, but they can result in more diffuse involvement and irreversible CTIN with prolonged use of these drugs.

ANTINEOPLASTIC AGENTS. A principal side effect of antineoplastic agents is direct tubular toxicity with the clinical features of acute renal failure. An invariable concern in all such cases is the prolonged half-life of the agents administered and their increased tendency to systemic toxicity. CTIN results in some patients, especially after cisplatin, nitrosourea compounds, and methotrexate.

HEAVY METALS. Exposure to heavy metals results in different forms of renal toxicity, including CTIN (Table 120–4). Of these agents, the more common and clinically relevant is lead.

Major sources of lead exposure are lead-based paints, lead leached into food during storage or processing, particularly in home-brewed illegal alcoholic beverages (moonshine), and increasingly, environmental exposure (gasoline, industrial fumes). This insidious accumulation of lead has been implicated in the etiology of a syndrome of hyperuricemia, hypertension, and progressive loss of kidney function. Gout occurs in over half of these cases. Blood levels of lead are usually normal. The diagnosis is established by demonstrating increased levels of urinary lead after infusion of the chelating agent calcium disodium ethylenediaminetetraacetic acid (EDTA). EDTA has also been used in the treatment of such cases but appears to be of limited value in mobilizing the total body load of lead or in reversing kidney failure.

The renal lesions of lead nephropathy are those of CTIN. Patients examined early, before the onset of ESRD, show primarily focal tubular epithelial cell accumulation of lead with relatively little interstitial cellular infiltrates. In more advanced cases, the kidneys are fibrotic and shrunken and on microscopy show diffuse lesions of CTIN. As might be expected from its association with elevated blood pressure, hypertensive vascular changes are a prominent feature of the kidney in these cases.

Acute lead intoxication is rare but may be encountered after accidental ingestion, usually by children. Its principal manifestations are abdominal colic, hemolytic anemia, and encephalopathy. Acute renal failure secondary to ATIN has been described but is rare.

Of the other heavy metals associated with CTIN (see Table 120–4), cadmium is a relatively more common source of renal toxicity. Exposure to cadmium results in the preferential accumulation of cadmium in the proximal tubule, where it is retained with a rather long biologic half-life of at least 10 years. Its local toxic effect results in CTIN whose principal manifestations are those of proximal tubular dysfunction: aminoaciduria, glucosuria, uricosuria, bicarbonaturia, and hypercalciuria. Urinary calculi occur in one fourth of these cases.

The other heavy metals are rarely a cause of CTIN, and their features mimic those of cadmium. Enough experimental data and some weak epidemiologic evidence suggest a possible role of organic solvents as a cause of CTIN.

Vascular Disease

Tubular degeneration, interstitial fibrosis, and mononuclear cell infiltration are central components of injury to the kidney by vascular diseases that affect the intrarenal circulation. In rare instances in which the onset of the vascular disease is sudden and severe, such as fulminant vasculitis, the kidney lesions are those of infarction and are associated with acute renal failure. More commonly, they are slow to develop and go undetected until renal insufficiency supervenes. It is this chronic form of TIN (nephrosclerosis) that accounts for the loss of kidney function of hypertensive individuals.

Ischemic vascular changes contribute to the CTIN of patients with diabetes mellitus, sickle hemoglobinopathy, cyclosporine toxicity, and radiation nephritis.

Urinary Tract Obstruction

Tubular injury and interstitial cellular infiltrates are some of the earliest responses to any physical impedance to the flow of urine (Chapter 121). With persistent obstruction, fibrosis becomes prominent and changes of CTIN set in within weeks. Early relief of the obstruction, within this relatively short period, can result in stabilization and reversal of renal failure. Persistence of the obstruction results in irreversible fibrosis and progressive loss of kidney function.

Infection is a usual, but not invariable feature of most forms of obstructive nephropathy. In fact, with few exceptions, urinary infection will ultimately develop in most patients with urinary tract obstruction. In such cases, infection contributes significantly to the symptomatology and aggravates the progressive loss of kidney function. Pressure-mediated extravasation of Tamm-Horsfall protein, a lining of the thick ascending limb of the loop of Henle, into the interstitium has been implicated in mediating an altered immune reaction that contributes to progression of the lesions of CTIN in obstructed individuals, particularly when caused by severe vesicoureteral reflux.

Metabolic Disorders

A number of metabolic disorders are associated with CTIN. Those caused by hypercalcemia and potassium depletion are mainly functional in nature and reversible if corrected early. If prolonged, hypercalcemia can result in focal deposition of calcium (nephrocalcinosis) and CTIN. Whether chronic potassium depletion results in persistent tubular dysfunction is not certain, although a propensity to microcystic dilation of the tubules has been associated with prolonged potassium depletion.

Uric Acid

The kidneys are the major organs of urate excretion and a principal target of its abnormal metabolism. The renal lesions result either from the intratubular crystallization of uric acid in the low pH of the distal tubules (acute urate nephropathy, uric acid nephrolithiasis) or from the deposition of amorphous tophi of sodium urate in the renal parenchyma (chronic urate nephropathy).

Acute urate nephropathy develops when nucleoprotein release following massive cell injury (tumor lysis syndrome, rhabdomyolysis) in a setting of volume depletion causes a sudden overproduction of urate that results in an acute, progressive deterioration of kidney function and oliguria. The serum urate concentration is usually greater than 20 mg/dL, and the ratio of the concentration of uric acid to that of creatinine is greater than 1 in a spot urine sample. Hyperphosphatemia, hyperkalemia, and hypocalcemia are common in these patients. The hyperphosphatemia and hyperkalemia are the result of the cell necrosis that also accounts for the hyperuricemia. The hypocalcemia is consequent to the precipitation of calcium at sites of injury where in situ concentrations of the released intracellular phosphate are high. Treatment consists of volume replacement sufficient to maintain a high urine flow rate, which washes out urate precipitates and reduces the urinary concentration of urate; alkalinization of the urine, which increases the solubility of uric acid; and reduction of the excreted urate load by blocking its production with allopurinol.

Chronic urate nephropathy results in CTIN from the deposition of urate microtophi in the renal parenchyma or the precipitation of uric acid in the collecting ducts. The latter form is more common in overproducers of uric acid and in those who have a defect in their ability to increase ammonia production in response to an acid load. *Uric acid nephrolithiasis* is common in these individuals, whose urinary excretion of uric acid is elevated even in the presence of normal blood levels. Intratubular uric acid precipitates can be a nidus for calcium oxalate stones, which are also common in these individuals. This propensity for nephrolithiasis, with its consequent obstructive effect and susceptibility to urinary tract infections, accounts for the CTIN that ultimately sets in.

Kidney failure as a result of intrarenal gouty tophi is rare but can occur in those with chronically elevated serum urate levels of more than 10 mg/dL in women and 13 mg/dL in men.

OXALATE. Increased renal excretion of the metabolic end product oxalate results in its intratubular precipitation as calcium oxalate. The hyperoxaluria may be primary or acquired. The former is a rare recessive disorder. Acquired forms of hyperoxaluria are secondary to ingestion or exposure to oxalate precursors (ethylene glycol, methoxyflurane anesthesia, ascorbic acid, pyridoxine deficiency) or increased intestinal absorption of oxalate (regional enteritis, small bowel resection).

Sudden, massive hyperoxaluria, such as after ethylene glycol poisoning or prolonged methoxyflurane anesthesia, manifests as acute renal failure. The more common chronic forms of hyperoxaluria result in CTIN, with a propensity for recurrent calcium oxalate nephrolithiasis.

IMMUNE DISEASES. CTIN is a feature of several immune disorders, such as Sjögren's syndrome, systemic lupus erythematosus, amyloidosis, mixed cryoglobulinemia, chronic allograft rejection, and Goodpasture's syndrome. Linear deposits of antitubular basement membrane antibodies are characteristic of Goodpasture's syndrome.

Granulomatous Diseases

Interstitial granulomatous reactions are a rare but characteristic hallmark of certain forms of CTIN such as tuberculosis, Wegener's granulomatosis, berylliosis, and other chronic inflammatory diseases. By far, the most common of these diseases is *sarcoidosis*. Granulomatous infiltrates of varying extent are present in as many as 40% of patients with sarcoidosis. Renal insufficiency is rare, except when the lesions are extensive, but distal tubular dysfunction (inability to acidify and concentrate the urine) is common. Almost invariably, the renal lesions of sarcoidosis are exquisitely responsive to a limited course of steroid therapy.

TOXIC NEPHROPATHIES

Most forms of toxic nephropathy are due to drugs, whose increased availability and use have been associated with a host of undesirable side effects, and to environmental toxins, whose increased risk has been brought about by industrial exposure and urban development. The kidneys, as the main excretory organs of the body, are especially exposed to the toxicity of these therapeutic agents and environmental hazards.

Several factors contribute to the increased susceptibility of the kidney to toxicity, specifically, the high renal blood flow, which increases the delivery of potential toxins to the kidney; the tubular epithelial cell transport and metabolism of most agents, which increases their intracellular concentration relative to that in the blood; the urinary concentration in the medulla, which increases the intratubular concentration of agents that have been filtered in the glomerulus or secreted in the proximal tubule; and the distal tubular acidification of the urine, which facilitates intratubular precipitation of some substances and nonionic back-diffusion of other substances.

The course of the resultant toxic nephropathy may be either *acute* or *chronic*. In its *acute* form, it manifests as a sudden onset of acute renal failure in which the renal lesions are those of potentially reversible ATN or ATIN (see Table 120–1). In its *chronic* form, the onset of renal failure is insidious, persistent, and often progressive, and its principal lesions are those of CTIN. In some instances, the mechanism of kidney injury may be secondary to vasculitis or an immune-mediated injury to the glomerular capillaries (Fig. 120–3).

The principal toxic nephropathies that result in ATIN and CTIN have been discussed in this chapter, and those that result in ATN are covered in the chapter on acute renal failure (Chapter 116) and are not reconsidered. One mechanism of injury illustrated in Figure 120–3 deserves special comment—that of drug-induced, intrarenal hemodynamic changes, with a potential to cause ischemic tubular injury. Prominent among those are NSAIDs, angiotensin-converting enzyme (ACE) inhibitors, and angiotensin II receptor blockers.

The ability of NSAIDs, including the selective COX-2 inhibitors, to inhibit prostaglandin synthesis results in an acute reduction in renal perfusion, which is of negligible import in normal individuals but, in subjects who are volume depleted, results in acute renal failure. The renal failure is often reversible with early drug withdrawal, but it can progress to ATN and necessitate dialysis with continued exposure. ACE inhibitors exert their effect by inhibiting the angiotensin-mediated efferent vasoconstriction necessary to maintain the glomerular intracapillary pressure essential for filtration. This mechanism, which comes into play in conditions of volume depletion, renders such individuals particularly susceptible to the inhibition of angiotensin. Each of these two broad category of agents, NSAIDs and ACE inhibitors, has been estimated to account for some 15 to 20% of cases of acute renal failure in hospitalized patients, and they are a leading cause of overt acute renal failure, equal in prevalence to the acute renal failure from aminoglycoside nephrotoxicity. Proper evaluation for evidence of intravascular volume (blood pressure and pulse changes in response to tilting) is essential before their use in any hospitalized, acutely ill patient, particularly the elderly and those taking potent diuretics for congestive heart failure, cirrhosis of the liver, or the nephrotic syndrome.

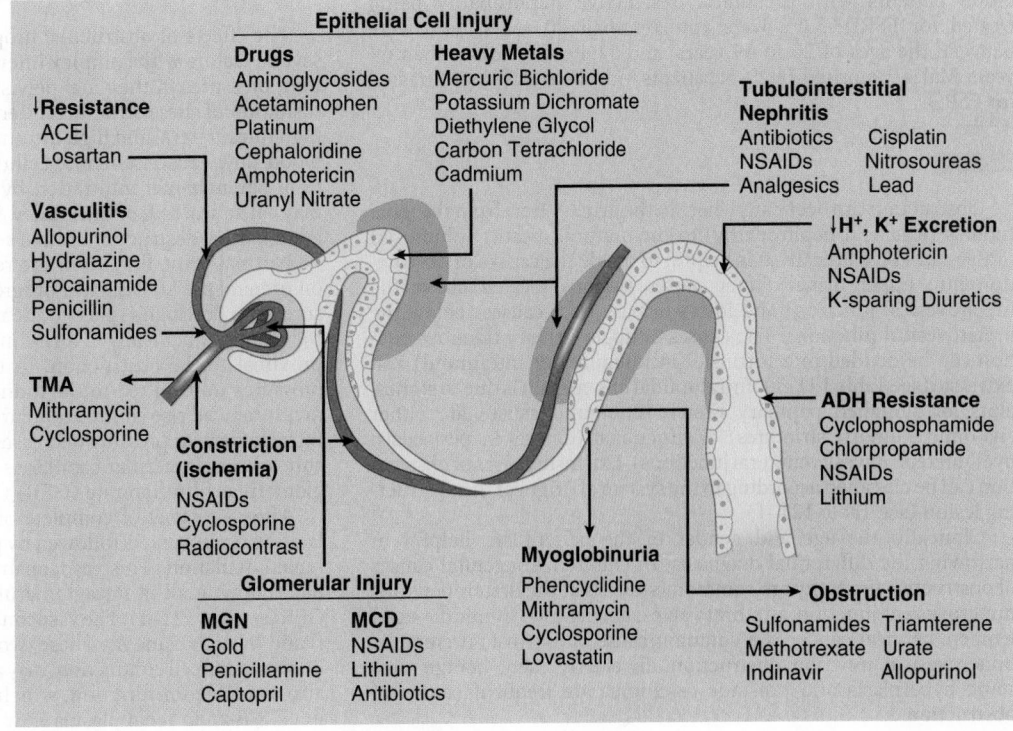

FIGURE 120–3 • Schematic presentation of the nephronal sites and mechanism of injury of the principal nephrotoxic agents. The heavy-set arrows indicate the directional changes observed. ACEI = angiotensin-converting enzyme inhibitor; ADH = antidiuretic hormone; MCD = minimal-change disease; MGN = membranous glomerulopathy; NSAIDs = nonsteroidal anti-inflammatory drugs; TMA = thrombotic microangiopathy.

SUGGESTED READINGS

Eknoyan G: Acute tubulointerstitial nephritis (Chapter 48); Chronic tubulointerstitial nephropathies (Chapter 72). *In* Schrier RW (ed): Diseases of the Kidney and Urinary Tract, 7th ed. Philadelphia, Lippincott Williams & Wilkins, 2001, pp 1273–1298, 2045–2082. *In-depth review of the subject matter of this chapter for the specialist; extensively referenced.*

Guo X, Nzerue C: How to prevent, recognize, and treat drug-induced nephrotoxicity. Cleve Clin J Med 2002;69:289–290, 293–294, 296–297 passim. *Patients who develop renal injury after drug exposure have risk factors that may be modifiable or may preclude the use of these drugs.*

Nasr SH, Koscica J, Markowitz GS, et al: Granulomatous interstitial nephritis. Am J Kidney Dis 2003;41:714–719. *A comprehensive review.*

Wali RK, Henrich WL: Recent developments in toxic nephropathy. Curr Opin Nephrol Hypertens 2002;11:155–163. *Approach to diagnosis and decisions regarding change in dose or discontinuation of the possible causative agent.*

121 OBSTRUCTIVE UROPATHY

Saulo Klahr

Obstructive uropathy refers to the structural or functional changes in the urinary tract that impede the normal flow of urine. It occurs in a variety of settings and is a relatively common cause of impaired renal function (*obstructive nephropathy*). Obstructive uropathy may also cause dilation of the urinary tract (hydronephrosis). Because the consequences of obstructive uropathy are potentially reversible, prompt diagnosis and appropriate treatment are important to prevent permanent loss of renal function, which is directly related to the degree and duration of the obstruction.

Incidence and Prevalence

A relatively common disorder, obstructive uropathy is seen in all age groups. Hydronephrosis has been found at autopsy in 3.5 to 3.8% of adults and in 2% of children. Urolithiasis occurs predominantly in young adults (25 to 45 years old) and is three times more common in men than women. In patients older than 60 years, obstructive uropathy is seen more frequently in men than in women owing to benign prostatic hyperplasia and prostatic carcinoma. Each year in the United States, approximately 166 patients per 100,000 population are hospitalized with a presumptive diagnosis of obstruction, and about 387 patient visits per 100,000 population are related to obstructive uropathy.

From 1996 to 1999, a 3-year span, 6,006 patients with the suspected diagnosis of obstructive nephropathy began treatment for end-stage renal disease (ESRD) in the United States. Among the 6,006 patients with presumed obstructive nephropathy being treated for ESRD, 3.6% were younger than 20 years, 44% were between the ages of 20 to 64 years, and 52.4% were older than 64 years. Males comprised 74.2% of patients with obstructive being treated for ESRD.

Etiology

Obstruction can occur anywhere in the urinary tract from the renal tubules (uric acid nephropathy) to the urethral meatus (phimosis) (Table 121–1). Clinically, it is helpful to divide the causes of obstruction into upper urinary tract causes (lesions located above the ureterovesical junction) and lower urinary tract causes (below the ureterovesical junction). The causes of upper urinary tract obstruction can be divided into intrinsic (intraluminal or intramural) and extrinsic (see Table 121–1). Intraluminal obstruction is due to stones, clots, or sloughed papillary tissue. Intramural causes are either anatomic (tumors, strictures) or functional (defects in peristalsis: pyeloureteral or vesicoureteral junctions). Extrinsic causes of obstruction can be classified according to the system of origin of the obstructing lesion (see Table 121–1).

Clinically, the age and gender of the patient are helpful in narrowing the differential diagnosis. In children, congenital causes of obstructive uropathy are common (stenosis at the ureteropelvic or ureterovesical junction, urethral valves, and so on). In middle-aged women, cervical cancer is a common cause of extrinsic ureteral or ureterovesical junction obstruction. In elderly men, benign prostatic hyperplasia and prostatic carcinoma are frequent causes of obstruction.

Table 121–1 • CAUSES OF URINARY TRACT OBSTRUCTION

UPPER URINARY TRACT	LOWER URINARY TRACT
INTRINSIC CAUSES 1. Intraluminal 　a. Intratubular deposition of crystals (uric acid, acyclovir) 　b. Ureter: stones, clots, renal papillae 2. Intramural 　a. Ureteropelvic or ureterovesical junction dysfunction 　b. Ureteral valve, polyp, stricture, or tumor **EXTRINSIC CAUSES** 1. Vascular system 　a. Aneurysm: abdominal aorta, iliac vessels 　b. Aberrant vessels: ureteropelvic junction 　c. Venous: retrocaval ureter 2. Reproductive system 　a. Uterus: pregnancy, prolapse, tumors endometriosis 　b. Ovary: abscess, tumors, ovarian remnants 　c. Gartner's duct cyst, tubo-ovarian abscess 3. Gastrointestinal tract: Crohn's disease; diverticulitis; appendiceal abscess; tumors; pancreatic tumor, abscess, or cyst 4. Retroperitoneal disease 　a. Retroperitoneal fibrosis (idiopathic, radiation, drugs) 　b. Inflammatory: tuberculosis, sarcoidosis 　c. Hematomas 　d. Primary tumors (lymphoma, sarcoma, etc.) 　e. Metastatic tumors (cervix, bladder, colon, prostate) 　f. Lymphocele 　g. Pelvic lipomatosis	1. Phimosis, meatal stenosis, paraphimosis 2. Urethra: strictures, stones, diverticulum, posterior or anterior urethral valves, periurethral abscess, urethral surgery 3. Prostate: benign hyperplasia, abscess, carcinoma 4. Bladder 　a. Neurogenic bladder; spinal cord defect or trauma, diabetes multiple sclerosis, cerebrovascular accidents, Parkinson's disease 　b. Bladder neck dysfunction 　c. Bladder calculus 　d. Bladder cancer 5. Trauma 　a. Straddle injury 　b. Pelvic fracture 6. Drugs: spinal anesthesia, anticholinergics, smooth muscle depressants

Pathology and Pathophysiology

The effects of obstructive uropathy on renal function are due to several factors with complex interactions. After the onset of obstruction, pressures in the renal pelvis and tubules increase and result in dilatation of these structures. Renal damage is probably initiated by high intraureteral and high intratubular pressures. Decreases in renal blood flow cause ischemia, cellular atrophy, and necrosis. In addition, parenchymal infiltration by macrophages and T lymphocytes may cause scarring of the kidney. Superimposed infection may accelerate kidney destruction in this setting.

Normal urine flow from the renal pelvis to the bladder depends on ureteral peristalsis and a progressive decrease in hydrostatic pressure from Bowman's space to the renal pelvis. Impaired urine flow in the urinary tract leads to a rise in the pressure and volume of urine proximal to the obstruction. In this setting, the high intraureteral pressures transmitted to the kidney result in increased intratubular pressure. The rise in intratubular pressure without a similar rise in intraglomerular pressure decreases the net hydrostatic filtration pressure across glomerular capillaries and thereby results in a fall in the glomerular filtration rate (GFR) (Fig. 121–1).

After the onset of complete obstruction, transient renal vasodilatation occurs and is followed by progressive vasoconstriction of the renal circulation. This vasoconstriction leads to a decrease in renal blood flow, a fall in intraglomerular pressure, and a decrease in the GFR (see Fig. 121–1). The vasoconstriction is mediated by angiotensin II and thromboxane A_2. These two compounds, through their effects on mesangial cell contraction, may also decrease the glomerular surface area available for filtration, which may explain the greater decrease in GFR than in renal plasma flow observed in obstruction.

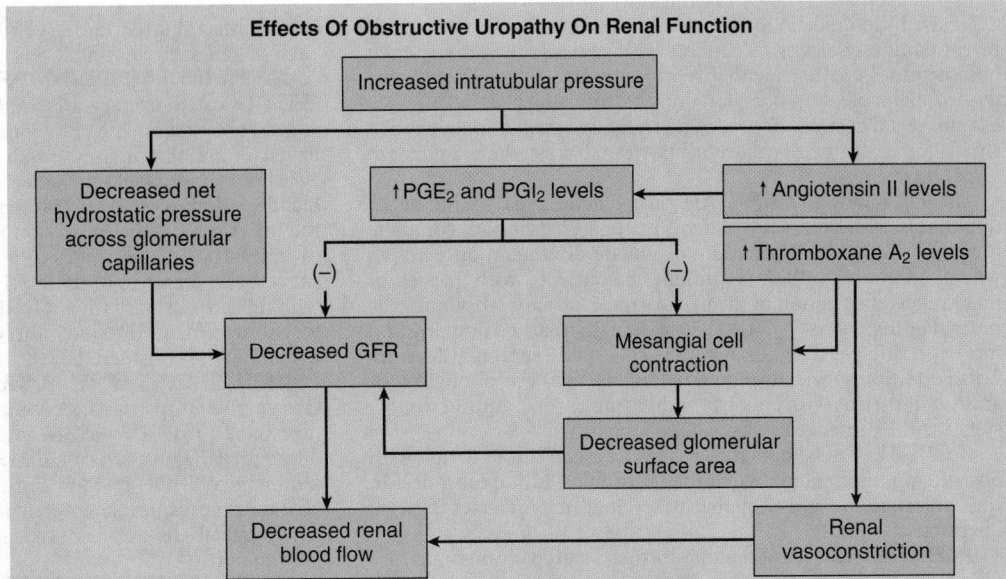

Effects Of Obstructive Uropathy On Renal Function

FIGURE 121–1 • Increased levels of prostaglandin E$_2$ (PGE$_2$) and prostacyclin (PGI$_2$) tend to antagonize (–) the effects of angiotensin II and thromboxane A$_2$ on mesangial cell contraction and renal vasoconstriction. Hence they tend to prevent the glomerular filtration rate (GFR) from decreasing further.

Because of increased intrarenal levels of angiotensin II, the synthesis of prostaglandin E$_2$ and prostacyclin is augmented. These eicosanoids are vasodilatory substances that also antagonize the effects of angiotensin II on mesangial cell contraction. Hence, in the setting of obstruction, the increased synthesis of both prostaglandin E$_2$ and prostacyclin tends to prevent the GFR and renal blood flow from decreasing further. In experimental animals after the obstruction is released, administration of inhibitors of prostaglandin synthesis, such as nonsteroidal anti-inflammatory agents or inhibitors of nitric oxide, decreases the GFR and renal blood flow.

Partial obstruction of the urinary tract may also decrease renal blood flow and the GFR. In addition, functional tubular defects are prominent. An inability to concentrate the urine and decreased excretion of hydrogen ions and potassium are noted. The concentrating defect is due in part to decreased osmolality of the renal medulla, probably related to decreased sodium reabsorption in the thick ascending limb of Henle's loop, and to the removal of medullary solutes (sodium, urea) as a consequence of the initial increase in medullary blood flow seen in obstruction. A decrease in the expression of aquaporins 1, 2, and 3 occurs after ureteral obstruction, suggesting that dysregulation of aquaporins located at the proximal tubule, thin descending limb of the loop of Henle, and the collecting duct may contribute to prolongation of the polyuria and impaired urinary concentrating capacity associated with obstructive nephropathy. The decreased excretion of hydrogen and potassium ions is due to impaired secretion of these ions in the distal segments of the nephron, presumably as a consequence of diminished response to the action of aldosterone.

Table 121–2 • CLINICAL MANIFESTATIONS AND LABORATORY FINDINGS IN URINARY TRACT OBSTRUCTION

1. No symptoms (chronic hydronephrosis)
2. Intermittent pain (chronic hydronephrosis)
3. Elevated levels of blood urea nitrogen and serum creatinine with no other symptoms (chronic hydronephrosis)
4. Renal colic (usually due to utereral stones or papillary necrosis)
5. Changes in urinary output
   a. Anuria or oliguria (acute renal failure)
   b. Polyuria (incomplete or partial obstruction)
   c. Fluctuating urinary output
6. Hematuria
7. Palpable masses
   a. Flank (hydronephrotic kidney, usually in infants)
   b. Suprapubic (distended bladder)
8. Hypertension
   a. Flank (hydronephrotic kidney, usually in infants)
   b. Suprapubic (distended bladder)
9. Hypertension
   a. Volume dependent (usually due to chronic bilateral obstruction)
   b. Renin dependent (usually due to acute unilateral obstruction)
10. Repeated urinary tract infections or infection that is refractory to treatment
11. Hyperkalemic, hyperchloremic acidosis (usually due to defective tubular secretion of hydrogen and potassium)
12. Hypernatremia (seen in infants with partial obstruction and polyuria)
13. Polycythemia (increased renal production of erythropoietin)
14. Lower urinary tract symptoms: hesistancy, urgency, incontinence, postvoid dribbling, decreased force and caliber of urinary stream, nocturia

Clinical Manifestations

The clinical manifestations of obstructive uropathy depend on the location (upper or lower urinary tract), degree (complete or partial), and duration (acute or chronic) of the obstruction (Table 121–2).

The symptoms of upper and lower urinary tract obstruction differ. Patients with acute complete obstruction may have acute renal failure. Patients with chronic partial obstruction (chronic hydronephrosis) may be asymptomatic, may have intermittent pain, or may have symptoms and laboratory findings of impaired renal function, including an inability to concentrate the urine manifested as nocturia and/or polyuria, with or without elevated levels of blood urea nitrogen and serum creatinine.

PAIN AND RENAL COLIC. Pain caused by distention of the bladder or stretching of the collecting system or the renal capsule is a common initial symptom in obstructive uropathy, particularly in patients with ureteral calculi. Classic "renal colic" is a steadily increasing severe pain located in the flank (in the case of stones lodged in the upper third of the ureter) or radiating to the labia, testicles, or groin (stones in the lower two thirds of the ureter) and may be associated with sweating and vomiting. The acute attack may last less than 30 minutes or as long as 1 day. Pain radiating into the flank during micturition is said to be pathognomonic of vesicoureteral reflux. Chronic partial obstruction may cause intermittent flank pain. Pain may be elicited in some of these patients by the administration of diuretics and/or

Continued

excessive fluid intake. Physical examination may be normal or may reveal flank tenderness in patients with acute upper urinary tract obstruction. In patients with lower urinary tract obstruction, a distended, palpable, and occasionally painful bladder may be found. Careful rectal examination in men or pelvic examination in women should be performed because it may reveal prostatic enlargement or pelvic masses.

CHANGES IN URINARY OUTPUT. Anuria and acute renal failure occur in patients with complete bilateral ureteral obstruction, complete lower urinary tract obstruction, or unilateral ureteral obstruction when a solitary kidney is present. In patients with partial or incomplete obstruction of the urinary tract, urinary output may be normal or increased (polyuria). Occasionally, marked polyuria and increased thirst (a diabetes insipidus–like syndrome) may develop. This condition may cause hypernatremia. A pattern of oliguria or anuria alternating with polyuria or the acute onset of anuria strongly suggests the presence of obstructive uropathy.

HEMATURIA. Gross hematuria may be seen in patients with obstruction, particularly when the obstruction is due to stones. In the presence of gross hematuria, clots may cause ureteral obstruction.

PALPABLE MASSES. Long-standing obstructive uropathy may increase kidney size. Such patients may have increased abdominal girth or a palpable flank mass. Hydronephrosis is a common cause of a palpable abdominal mass in children. In patients with lower urinary tract obstruction, particularly obstruction secondary to benign prostatic hyperplasia, a suprapubic mass may be caused by a distended bladder. This part of the physical examination should not be neglected in patients with anuria and suspected obstructive uropathy. This type of obstruction is readily reversed by placing a catheter in the bladder.

HYPERTENSION. Hypertension is commonly associated with renal disease of diverse causes. Patients with obstructive uropathy may have hypertension from (1) fluid retention and expansion of the extracellular fluid volume, (2) increased renin secretion, and (3) possibly decreased synthesis of medullary vasodepressor substances. In some patients with obstructive uropathy, hypertension may be coincidental and occurs in about one third of patients with acute unilateral obstruction and is usually, but not always, renin dependent. Release of the acute obstruction should alleviate the hypertension when the two are causally related.

In patients with chronic bilateral obstruction, the hypertension is usually due to impaired sodium excretion and expansion of the extracellular fluid volume (volume-dependent hyper-tension). In such patients, circulating levels of renin are usually suppressed.

URINARY TRACT INFECTIONS OR INFECTION THAT IS REFRACTORY TO TREATMENT. Repeated urinary tract infections without apparent cause suggest obstruction. Infection is more common in patients with lower urinary tract obstruction, possibly because of decreased bacterial "washout" and increased bacterial adherence to the mucosa of the bladder. Moreover, in the presence of obstruction, eradication of the infection is difficult. In noninstrumented patients, the finding of unusual organisms (*Proteus, Pseudomonas*) in urine cultures should suggest the presence of underlying obstruction. Thus, in patients with repeated urinary tract infections or persistent infection refractory to treatment, the possibility of underlying obstructive uropathy should be considered.

INCREASED LEVELS OF BLOOD UREA NITROGEN AND SERUM CREATININE. Obstructive uropathy is a potential cause of impaired renal function and end-stage renal disease and should be considered in the differential diagnosis, particularly in patients with a normal urinary sediment and no previous history of renal disease. Obstruction of the urinary tract may occur in patients with established renal parenchymal disease and cause an acceleration in the rate of progression.

HYPERKALEMIC, HYPERCHLOREMIC METABOLIC ACIDOSIS. A hyperkalemic, hyperchloremic (nonanion gap) metabolic acidosis may be present in patients with obstructive uropathy. It is seen more frequently in elderly individuals. The abnormality is due to decreased hydrogen ion and potassium secretion by distal segments of the nephron and may be caused by decreased aldosterone production and/or refractoriness of the distal tubule to the actions of this mineralocorticoid. Hyperchloremic metabolic acidosis may occur in the absence of hyperkalemia and results from a selective defect in hydrogen ion secretion.

POLYCYTHEMIA. Polycythemia that subsides after obstruction is relieved is a rare manifestation of urinary tract obstruction. Increased renal production of erythropoietin, presumably due to ischemia, may account for the development of polycythemia.

LOWER URINARY TRACT SYMPTOMS. Symptoms such as decreased force and caliber of the urine stream, intermittency, incontinence, postvoid dribbling, hesitancy, and urgency may develop in patients with obstruction of the lower urinary tract. Alterations in the process of micturition because of neurogenic bladder disease may also result in urgency, frequent urination, and urinary incontinence (overflow incontinence).

Differential Diagnosis

The differential diagnosis varies depending on the clinical signs and symptoms. Patients with anuria and acute renal failure should be evaluated for other potential causes of acute renal failure (Chapter 116). Partial obstruction and polyuria may mimic the entity of nephrogenic diabetes insipidus. Patients with obstruction manifested as hyperchloremic, hyperkalemic metabolic acidosis should be distinguished from patients who have the same syndrome on the basis of low levels of renin and aldosterone secretion. Gastrointestinal pathology may mimic flank pain from renal stones. In children, manifestations of obstructive uropathy can include gastrointestinal symptoms such as nausea, vomiting, and abdominal pain.

Diagnostic Approach

The presence of obstructive uropathy may not be obvious. Definitive tests are needed to exclude this diagnosis in suspected cases. Early diagnosis and prompt treatment are essential because the degree of renal impairment resulting from obstructive uropathy is related to its severity and duration. The diagnostic approach to obstructive uropathy depends on the symptoms and the clinical findings of patients with asymptomatic renal insufficiency, renal colic, or acute renal failure and anuria (Fig. 121–2).

When obstruction is suspected, the history may be of value: previous urinary tract infections, drugs ingested, and the presence of lower urinary tract symptoms (see earlier). In the hospital setting, the pattern of urinary output can be ascertained from input and output records. The physical examination may yield some clues: tenderness in the costovertebral angle, a mass in the flank area, and muscle rigidity over the kidney area. Abdominal distention and diminished peristalsis accompany acute renal colic. A suprapubic mass may be due to bladder outlet obstruction. Urinalysis may yield important clues: hematuria, bacteriuria, or a urinary pH greater than 7.5 is indicative of stones and/or infection with urea-splitting organisms. The urinary sediment should be examined carefully for the presence of crystals (uric acid, cystine, and so forth). Laboratory studies should include an assessment of renal function (blood urea nitrogen, serum creatinine).

Tests used to diagnose obstructive uropathy are summarized in Table 121–3. Ultrasonography is a noninvasive diagnostic test used as the initial procedure in suspected obstruction. The main finding, detected with ultrasonography, is dilation of the urinary tract. In a few instances, ultrasonography may give false-negative results because dilation does not occur as a consequence of dehydration or too recent an onset of obstruction (see Fig. 121–2). *Plain films of the abdomen (kidneys, ureter, bladder)* are particularly useful in patients with renal colic because ureteral calculi may be visualized (see Fig. 121–2). They also provide information on renal and bladder morphology, such as size differences between the two kidneys or an enlarged bladder, that suggests outlet obstruction. The *intravenous pyelogram* is used to investigate acute renal colic (see Fig. 121–2). Excretion of contrast medium may be delayed in patients with a low GFR because of a decrease in the filtered load of dye. In such patients, the procedure should be extended until the collecting system and the site of obstruction are identified. This identification may require delayed films. Intravenous

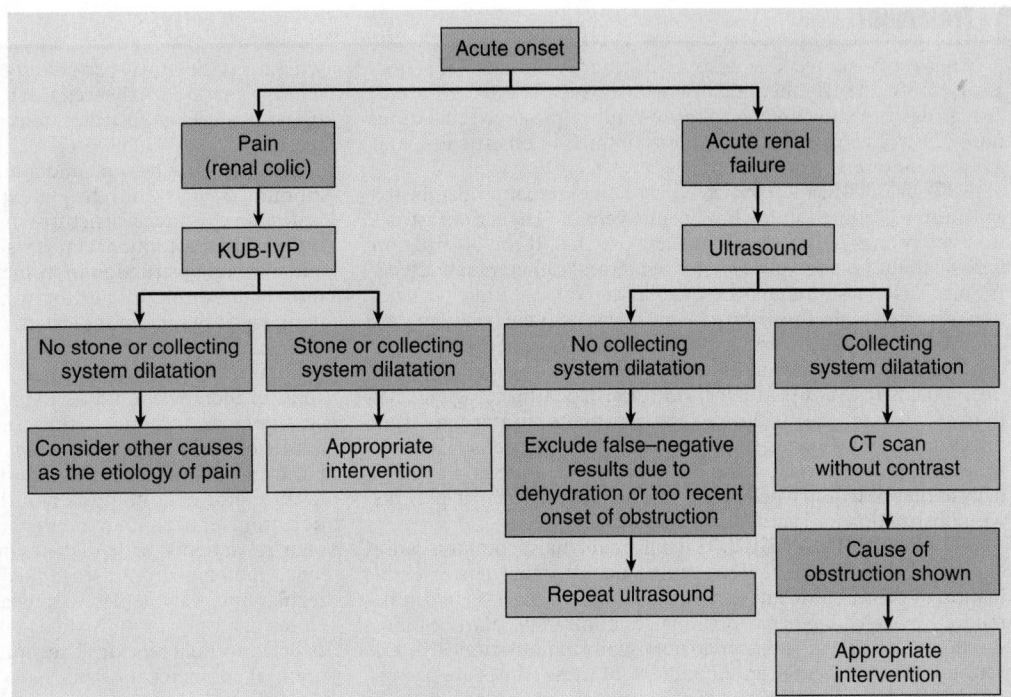

FIGURE 121–2 • Scheme of a diagnostic approach to urinary tract obstruction. CT, computed tomography; IVP, intravenous pyelography; KUB, kidney, ureter, bladder (a flat film of the abdomen without contrast medium).

Table 121–3 • DIAGNOSTIC TESTS USED IN OBSTRUCTIVE UROPATHY

UPPER URINARY TRACT OBSTRUCTION
Sonography (ultrasound)
Plain films of the abdomen (KUB)
Excretory or intravenous pyelography
Retrograde pyelography
Isotopic renography
Computed tomography
Magnetic resonance imaging
Pressure flow studies (the Whitaker test)

LOWER URINARY TRACT OBSTRUCTION
Some of the tests listed above
Cystoscopy
Voiding cystourethrogram
Retrograde urethrography
Urodynamic tests
    Debimetry
    Cystometrography
    Electromyography
    Urethral pressure profile

KUB = Kidneys, ureter, bladder.
From Klahr S: Obstructive uropathy. *In* Jacobson HR, Striker GE, Klahr S (eds): The Principles and Practice of Nephrology. Toronto, BC Decker, 1991, pp 432–441, Reproduced by permission of Mosby–Year Book.

of the obstruction. Isotopic renography can be used to diagnose upper urinary tract obstruction. It requires the intravenous injection of a radionuclide and subsequent imaging with a gamma scintillation camera. This imaging can be combined with intravenous furosemide administered 20 to 30 minutes after the isotope is injected. Other diagnostic procedures for obstructive uropathy include computed tomography and magnetic resonance imaging. *Computed tomography* is particularly useful for *diagnosing causes of obstruction.* Occasionally, upper urinary tract obstruction is difficult to diagnose with the techniques described above, and *pressure-flow studies* (the Whitaker test) may be required. This test consists of measuring pressure differences between the renal pelvis and the bladder during the infusion of fluid at a known rate into the renal pelvis.

A number of tests are useful in diagnosing lower urinary tract obstruction, including *voiding cystourethrography,* which is used to investigate the presence of vesicoureteral reflux as a cause of dilation of the urinary tract. *Cystoscopy* allows visual inspection of the entire urethra and bladder during the same procedure. However, this test requires the use of anesthesia in children and young adults. The anterior urethra can be assessed by *retrograde urethrography,* which is performed by occluding the urethral meatus with a syringe or catheter and injecting contrast medium. However, a retrograde urethrogram is not adequate to evaluate the posterior urethra. This anatomic area is best examined by *an excretory or retrograde cystogram.* The two tests combined usually provide a complete study of the urethra. *Urodynamic tests* with measurement of the urine flow rate per unit time are useful for evaluating bladder outlet obstruction. Measurement of the *urine flow rate (debimetry)* is a noninvasive test that examines the interplay between the expulsive force of the detrusor muscle and urethral resistance. *Cystometrography* can be used to assess the force of the detrusor muscle in the bladder, and it quantifies the pressure-volume relationships of this organ. "Dyssynergy" of the bladder sphincter refers to the inability of the sphincter to relax during contraction of the detrusor muscle and is seen in patients with neurologic disorders. This type of resistance is better analyzed by *electromyography* and *urethral pressure profiles.* About 25% of children with spina bifida have detrusor sphincter dyssynergia at birth.

pyelography is not useful in patients with compromised renal function, particularly those with serum creatinine levels greater than 3 to 4 mg/dL. It also has the risk of potential nephrotoxicity. *Retrograde pyelography* requires the retrograde injection of radiocontrast medium and is used to visualize the ureter and collecting system when intravenous pyelography cannot be performed or is not justified because of a history of allergic reaction to contrast medium or other contraindications. This procedure can identify both the site and the cause

Rx Treatment

After establishing a diagnosis of obstructive uropathy, it is necessary to decide whether surgery or instrumentation is required. The goals of therapy are to (1) restore and/or preserve renal function, (2) relieve pain and/or other symptoms of obstruction, and (3) prevent or eradicate infection.

ACUTE OBSTRUCTION (COMPLETE). Obstructive uropathy manifested as acute renal failure requires prompt intervention. The site of obstruction determines the approach in these patients. If the obstruction is distal to the bladder, placement of a urethral catheter may suffice. In some cases, a suprapubic cystostomy is required. If the obstruction is located in the upper urinary tract, placement of percutaneous nephrostomy tubes or passage of a retrograde ureteral catheter may be necessary. Nephrostomy tubes not only provide drainage of the urine but also can be used for local infusion of pharmacologic agents to treat infection, calculi, and so on. In patients with urinary tract infection and generalized sepsis, prompt relief of the obstruction is necessary, and appropriate antibiotic therapy is indicated. Sometimes dialysis may be required before instrumentation or surgery in patients with obstruction and acute renal failure.

ACUTE OBSTRUCTION (PARTIAL). Calculi are the most common cause of ureteral obstruction. Their treatment includes relief of pain, elimination of obstruction, and treatment of the infection. Pain can be relieved by injecting a narcotic analgesic intramuscularly. Stones smaller than 5 mm in diameter do not usually require surgical intervention or instrumentation. About 90% of these stones are passed spontaneously. If the stones are 5 to 7 mm, however, only about half will pass, and stones larger than 7 mm are not usually passed spontaneously. High fluid intake to increase the urinary volume to at least 2 L/day may help mobilize the stone. The urine must be strained through a gauze sponge to recover the calculi for analysis. If the stone completely occludes the ureter and does not move, surgical treatment is necessary. *Endourology* refers to the closed, controlled manipulation of the entire urinary tract. Endourologic methods can be used to successfully treat stones obstructing the ureter in about 98% of patients. In addition, this approach shortens the hospital stay to 2 to 3 days and the convalescence period to only 4 to 7 days. Extracorporeal shock wave or ultrasound lithotripsy involves the focusing of electrohydraulic or ultrasonically generated shock waves to disintegrate the stone. The method is effective for ureteral calculi of 7 to 15 mm that lie above the pelvic brim. The stone is disintegrated in 90% of patients, and all particulate matter passes within a 3-month period. Morbidity is low. However, all patients should be monitored for stone recurrence and should be given preventive therapy. In addition, posttreatment hypertension may occur and requires follow-up. In selected individuals, the procedure can be done on an outpatient basis, and most patients are back at work 2 to 3 days after shock wave therapy. Calculi located distal to the pelvic brim can be approached from below. Antibiotics are useful when infections complicate renal calculi, with the choice of antibiotic depending on appropriate urine cultures and sensitivity studies.

CHRONIC PARTIAL OBSTRUCTION. Surgical intervention can sometimes be delayed for weeks or even months in patients with low-grade obstruction or partial chronic obstruction. However, prompt relief of partial obstruction is indicated when (1) repeated episodes of urinary tract infection occur, (2) the patient has significant symptoms (dysuria, voiding dysfunction, flank pain), (3) urinary retention exists, or (4) evidence of recurrent or progressive renal damage is present.

LOWER URINARY TRACT OBSTRUCTION. Urethral and bladder neck obstruction requires surgery in patients with recurrent infections who are ambulatory, particularly when reflux, renal parenchymal damage, marked urinary retention, repeated bleeding, or other symptoms are present. Obstruction secondary to benign prostatic hyperplasia is not always progressive. Therefore, patients with minimal symptoms, no infection, and a normal upper urinary tract may be monitored safely until the patient and physician agree that surgery is desirable. Urethral strictures in men can be treated by dilation or internal urethrotomy via direct vision. The incidence of bladder neck and urethral obstruction in women is low. Hence, urethral dilation, internal urethrotomy, meatotomy, and revision of the bladder neck in women are seldom indicated.

When obstruction is the result of neuropathic bladder function, dynamic studies are essential to determine therapy. The main goals of therapy should be to (1) establish the bladder as a urine storage organ without causing renal injury and (2) provide a mechanism for bladder emptying that is acceptable to the patient. Patients fall into two categories: those with atonic bladders secondary to lower motor neuron injury and those with unstable bladder function from upper motor neuron disease. The neurogenic bladder seen in patients with diabetes mellitus is usually the result of lower motor neuron disease. Requesting these patients to void at regular intervals achieves satisfactory emptying of the bladder. Occasionally, these individuals respond to cholinergic agents such as bethanechol chloride (Urecholine). α-Adrenergic blockers relax urethral sphincter tone but have only limited success because of side effects. The best treatment for patients with significant residual urine and recurrent urosepsis is to establish clean, intermittent, regular self-catheterization. The goal is to catheterize four or five times per day so that the amount of urine drained from the bladder does not exceed 400 mL. This technique may be successful but requires patient acceptance and adequate training. In patients with a hypertonic bladder, the major goal is to improve its storage function. Anticholinergic agents may be indicated. Occasionally, long-term, clean, intermittent self-catheterization is necessary. In all patients with neurogenic bladder, long-term use of indwelling catheters should be avoided if possible because of the risk of infection and other complications.

POSTOBSTRUCTIVE DIURESIS. *Postobstructive diuresis* refers to the marked natriuresis and diuresis that occasionally follow the relief of obstruction. This diuresis is characterized by the excretion of large amounts of sodium, potassium, magnesium, and other solutes. Although usually self-limited, the losses of solutes and water may result in hypokalemia, hyponatremia or hypernatremia, hypomagnesemia, and marked volume depletion. In many patients, a brisk diuresis after relief of obstruction may represent a physiologic response to the expansion in extracellular fluid volume that occurred during the period of obstruction. This postobstructive diuresis is appropriate and does not compromise the volume status of the patient. Postobstructive diuresis in this setting can be prolonged by overzealous replacement of salt and water after the relief of obstruction.

Fluid replacement is justified only when excessive losses of sodium and water are inappropriate for the volume status of the patient and are presumably due to an intrinsic tubular defect in sodium and water reabsorption. Fluid replacement in these patients is guided in large part by what is excreted. Intravenous fluid administration may be necessary, but urinary losses should be replaced only to the extent necessary to prevent extracellular fluid volume contraction or electrolyte imbalance.

Prognosis

The return of renal function after relieving obstruction is variable and influenced by the severity and duration of the obstruction. Other events that condition the degree of recovery of renal function include the presence of infection, stones, preexisting renal disease, and/or the underlying cause of the obstruction. Renal cortical thickness is a prognostic indicator of residual renal function in patients with chronic hydronephrosis. Patients with a very thin cortex have lost considerable renal function.

SUGGESTED READINGS

Klahr S: Obstructive nephropathy: Pathophysiology and management. *In* Schrier RW (ed): Renal and Electrolyte Disorders, 6th ed. Philadelphia, Lippincott Williams & Wilkins, 2003, pp 498–538. *A chapter with major emphasis on the pathophysiology of obstructive nephropathy.*

Klahr S: Urinary tract obstruction. *In* Kurtzman N (ed): Milestones in nephrology in the last 20 years. Semin Nephrol 2001;21:133–145. *Discusses the therapeutic approach to patients with obstructive uropathy.*

Li C, Wang W, Knepper MA, et al: Downregulation of renal aquaporins in response to unilateral ureteral obstruction. Am J Physiol Renal Physiol 2003;284:F1066–F1079. *These changes help explain the physiology of impaired concentrating capacity during obstruction followed by the compensatory diuresis after relief of obstruction.*

122 SPECIFIC RENAL TUBULAR DISORDERS

Russell W. Chesney

Renal tubular disorders are a group of conditions in which the renal tubular reabsorption of either ions or organic solutes is diminished, resulting in excessive amounts of either substance in the urine. The defect can be characterized by the nephron segment affected. The functions of each segment influence the type of substance lost and the rate of loss. As noted in Chapter 111, the proximal nephron is responsible for reclaiming most of the filtered glucose, amino acids, uric acid, phosphate, bicarbonate, and low-molecular-weight proteins. Henle's loop reabsorbs more than half the filtered sodium chloride and divalent cations. The distal nephron (including the cortical and medullary collecting ducts), under the influence of aldosterone, reabsorbs the final amount of sodium and secretes hydrogen and potassium ions. The terminal collecting ducts are influenced by antidiuretic hormone to permit water reabsorption and lead to urinary concentration.

Many tubular disorders are inherited and seem to involve the loss or formation of a defective transport protein (*carrier*) and represent an inborn error of transport. Because the genes for many of these transporter proteins and channels have been cloned, the precise genetic defect of many of these conditions can be understood. These mutations result in diminished transport activity. Acquired conditions also can perturb transport function (Table 122–1). These conditions include (1) a single selective transport defect; (2) a class-specific defect (e.g., dibasic amino acids in cystinuria); and (3) solutes whose transport is influenced by a specific hormone, which can arise from hormone deficiency or resistance (e.g., in hypoaldosteronism or diabetes insipidus). Perturbation of tubular energy production or direct structural alteration is more likely to result in a global disorder, such as the generalized tubular dysfunction found in Fanconi syndrome. Luminal, intracellular, or peritubular components of the net transport process can be affected in each situation. Several of the more usual transport defects of individual nephron segments are described here.

DISORDERS OF PROXIMAL TUBULE FUNCTION

The proximal tubule is the site of reabsorption of 80 to 99% of filtered solutes, including glucose, amino acids, and phosphates. Urinary wastage of bulk quantities of these solutes implies a disorder of proximal tubular function.

RENAL GLYCOSURIAS

The renal glycosurias are caused by inherited or acquired defects in proximal tubule glucose reabsorption such that glycosuria is evident at normal serum glucose concentrations.

Pathophysiology

D-Glucose is actively reabsorbed across the luminal surface of the proximal tubule by a stereospecific carrier that requires sodium. The quantity of reabsorbed glucose changes, depending on the filtered glucose load, until a maximal reabsorptive capacity, or T_m, is achieved. Before saturation, glucose reabsorption is incomplete, and a "splay" is evident. The initial point in the splay is the filtered glucose concentration (the "threshold") at which reabsorption no longer equals filtration, and glucose appears in the urine. Normally the threshold concentration, 200 to 240 mg/dL, is far above the plasma values; scant glucose (<125 mg/day) appears in the urine. The kinetics of D-glucose reabsorption has been compared with classic enzyme kinetics. The T_m is likened to the V_{max}, whereas the degree of splay represents the K_m. In the two main forms of renal glucosuria, either the capacity (type A, V_{max}, or K_m mutation) or the affinity (type B, K_m, or extent-of-splay mutation) of glucose reabsorption is affected. Consistent with this view, the genes encoding high affinity (*SGLT1*) and low affinity (*SGLT2*) are found on different chromosomes: *SGLT1* is on chromosome 22q13.1, and *SGLT2* is on chromosome 16. *SGLT1* alone also transports galactose and is present in the intestine. A defect in *SGLT1* has been found in families with glucose-galactose malabsorption. Mutations in *SGLT2* account for familial glucosuria. In either form,

the threshold is influenced so that glucose is lost in the urine at a normal plasma glucose concentration. Glucosuria becomes marked after intravenous infusion of D-glucose.

Etiology

Renal glucosuria is uncommon, with a prevalence of 0.2 to 0.6%. Inheritance is autosomal recessive, and heterozygotes have more marked glucosuria. Usually, but not always, V_{max} and K_m variants are inherited separately, as would be anticipated with two separate genes. Renal biopsy samples reveal no consistent pathologic features. In contrast to the aminoacidurias, no intestinal transport defects are found. Renal glucosuria is completely asymptomatic.

Intermittent glucosuria is common during the third trimester of pregnancy (Chapters 123 and 253) and in terminal chronic renal insufficiency. In each instance, the functional change in glucose transport kinetics relates to an increase in tubular flow rate from an increase in total single-nephron glomerular filtration rate (GFR). In a rare disorder in children, markedly decreased *SGLT1* results in gut and renal malabsorption of glucose and galactose, which results in diarrhea and melituria.

Diagnosis

Diagnosis should be based on finding glucosuria of more than 500 mg/24 hours (on a diet containing 50% carbohydrate) without hyperglycemia (serum glucose <140 mg/dL). To confirm the excreted sugar as glucose, the glucose oxidase method should be used; this excludes other melituric conditions (pentosuria, fructosuria, sucrosuria, maltosuria, galactosuria, and lactosuria). Appropriate tests should be performed to exclude coexistent tubular transport defects (of amino acids, bicarbonate, phosphorus, and uric acid), such as Fanconi syndrome, and diabetes. If desired, differentiation of the V_{max} or K_m variants can be made by glucose loading. This condition is completely benign, and therapy is unnecessary.

RENAL AMINOACIDURIAS

The renal aminoacidurias are inborn errors of renal tubular transport in which a single amino acid or group of amino acids is hyperexcreted and often is accompanied by intestinal malabsorption of the same amino acids (see Table 122–1).

General Characteristics

The 20 L-amino acids are predominantly reabsorbed by the proximal tubule at a rate of reabsorption greater than 95 to 98% of the filtered load. Stereospecific amino acid transport occurs across the luminal membrane of the proximal tubule, accompanied by sodium and driven by the lumen-to-cell sodium concentration gradient. Reabsorptive kinetics are similar to those of D-glucose. Amino acid transport systems for at least five groups or classes of amino acids have been described: (1) *basic*—lysine, arginine, ornithine, and cystine; (2) *acidic*—aspartic and glutamic acid; (3) *neutral amino group*—glycine, proline, hydroxyproline, and sarcosine; (4) *neutral (Hartnup) group*—alanine, serine, threonine, valine, leucine, isoleucine, phenylalanine, glutamine, histidine, asparagine, tyrosine, tryptophan, and citrulline; and (5) β-*amino acids*—taurine, β-alanine, and β-aminoisobutyrate. Inherited dysfunction of a carrier results in urinary loss of the entire amino acid group: cystinuria (basic aminoaciduria), dicarboxylic aminoaciduria, Hartnup disease (neutral aminoaciduria), and iminoglycinuria. There are at least 25 selective amino acid carriers that transport a single amino acid or a few of a given amino acid group. Human disorders of these carriers result in even more selective aminoaciduria: hypercystinuria, histidinuria, and lysinuria.

Many proximal nephron amino acid carriers also are expressed within the luminal (brush border) membrane of gastrointestinal epithelial cells. Defective gut absorption occurs concomitantly with renal hyperexcretion of the amino acids in question. Dipeptides and tripeptides can be absorbed normally by the gut; nutritional problems arising from amino acid malabsorption are unusual.

To diagnose a renal aminoaciduria, an elevated plasma level of the amino acids must be excluded. Whenever the filtered load of an amino acid exceeds the transport capacity of the renal tubule, an "overload"

Table 122–1 • CLINICAL SYNDROMES ASSOCIATED WITH NEPHRON TRANSPORT DEFECTS

PROXIMAL NEPHRON

I. *Selective Transport Defects*
   A. Renal glycosurias
      1. Primary
      2. Combined
         a. Glucose/galactose malabsorption
         b. Glucoglycinuria
   B. Renal aminoacidurias
      1. Basic aminoacidurias
         a. General: cystinuria (cystine, lysine, arginine, ornithine)
         b. Specific: hypercystinuria, dibasic aminoaciduria (lysine, arginine, ornithine), lysinuria
      2. Neutral aminoacidurias
         a. General: Hartnup disease
         b. Specific: methioninuria, tryptophanuria, histidinuria
      3. Iminoglycinuria
         a. General (proline, hydroxyproline, glycine)
         b. Specific: glycinuria
      4. Dicarboxylic aminoaciduria
         a. General (glutamic, aspartic acids)
   C. Proximal renal tubular acidosis
      1. Primary: idiopathic or genetic
      2. Transient (infants)
      3. Carbonic anhydrase deficiency, inhibition, alteration
         a. Drugs: acetazolamide, sulfanilamide, mafenide acetate
         b. Idiopathic?
   D. Renal uric acid disorders (Chapter 113)
   E. Phosphate and calcium disorders (Chapter 257)
II. *Nonselective Transport Defects: Fanconi Syndrome*
   A. Primary: idiopathic or genetic
   B. Genetically transmitted systemic diseases
      1. Cystinosis
      2. Lowe's syndrome
      3. Wilson's disease
      4. Tyrosinemia
      5. Hereditary carboxylase deficiency
      6. Pyruvate carboxylase deficiency
   C. Dysproteinemic states
      1. Multiple myeloma
      2. Monoclonal gammopathy
   D. Secondary hyperparathyroidism with chronic hypocalcemia
      1. Vitamin D deficiency or resistance
      2. Vitamin D dependency
   E. Drugs and toxins
      1. Outdated tetracycline
      2. Methyl-3-chromone
      3. Streptozotocin
      4. Glue
      5. Gentamicin
      6. Ifosfamide
   F. Heavy metals
      1. Lead
      2. Cadmium
      3. Mercury
   G. Tubulointerstitial diseases
      1. Sjögren's syndrome
      2. Medullary cystic disease
      3. Renal transplantation
   H. Other diseases
      1. Nephrotic syndrome
      2. Amyloidosis
      3. Osteopetrosis
      4. Paroxysmal nocturnal hemoglobinuria

LOOP OF HENLE

I. *Bartter Syndrome*
II. *Drugs*
   A. Furosemide
   B. Bumetanide
   C. Ethacrynic acid

DISTAL NEPHRON

I. *Selective Transport Defects*
   A. Classic distal renal tubular acidosis
      1. Primary: genetic or idiopathic
      2. Genetically transmitted systemic diseases
         a. Ehlers-Danlos syndrome
         b. Hematologic disorders: hereditary elliptocytosis, sickle cell anemia, carbonic anhydrase I deficiency or alteration
         c. Medullary cystic disease
         d. With nerve deafness
         e. Glycogenosis type III
      3. Autoimmune diseases
         a. Hypergammaglobulinemia: hyperglobulinemic purpura, cryoglobulinemia, familial
         b. Sjögren's syndrome
         c. Thyroiditis
         d. Pulmonary fibrosis
         e. Chronic active hepatitis
         f. Primary biliary cirrhosis
         g. Systemic lupus erythematosis
      4. Diseases associated with nephrocalcinosis
         a. Primary hyperparathyroidism
         b. Vitamin D intoxication
         c. Hyperthyroidism
         d. Hypercalciuria: idiopathic or genetic
         e. Hereditary fructose intolerance
         f. Medullary sponge kidney
         g. Fabry's disease
         h. Wilson's disease
      5. Drug or toxic nephropathies
         a. Amphotericin B
         b. Toluene
         c. Glue
         d. Analgesics
         e. Cyclamate
      6. Tubulointerstitial diseases
         a. Chronic pyelonephritis secondary to urolithiasis
         b. Obstructive uropathy
         c. Renal transplantation
         d. Leprosy
         e. Hyperoxaluria
      7. Miscellaneous
   B. Renal tubular acidosis of glomerular insufficiency
   C. Hypermineralocorticoid and other potassium secretory disorders (Chapter 240)
II. *Nonselective Transport Defects: Generalized Distal Renal Tubular Acidosis, Hyperkalemia, and Renal Salt Wasting*
   A. Primary mineralocorticoid deficiency (Chapter 240)
   B. Hypoangiotensinemia
      1. Converting-enzyme inhibitors: captopril, enalapril
      2. Angiotensin receptor blockers
   C. Hyporeninemic hypoaldosteronism
      1. Diabetic nephropathy
      2. Tubulointerstitial nephropathies
      3. Nephrosclerosis
      4. Nonsteroidal anti-inflammatory drugs
      5. Acquired immunodeficiency syndrome
   D. Mineralocorticoid-resistant hyperkalemia
      1. Without salt wasting: genetic
      2. With salt wasting
         a. Childhood forms
         b. Tubulointerstitial nephropathies: methicillin, obstructive nephropathy, transplantation, sickle cell disease, cyclosporine
         c. Other drugs: spironolactone, amiloride, triamterene

LOOP AND MEDULLARY COLLECTING DUCTS

I. *Diabetes Insipidus* (Chapter 238)
II. *Syndrome of Inappropriate Secretion of Antidiuretic Hormone* (Chapter 112)
III. *Other Concentrating and Diluting Disorders*

or "prerenal" aminoaciduria can occur. Most inborn errors of amino acid metabolism exhibit this type of aminoaciduria because the plasma concentration of individual amino acids that are poorly metabolized rises sharply. By contrast, the renal aminoacidurias are associated with low or normal levels of plasma amino acid concentrations because the aminoaciduria is due to an inborn error of proximal tubule transport.

Cystinuria

Cystinuria is the term used to designate a group of renal transport disorders that have in common the excessive excretion of the highly insoluble amino acid cystine and the formation of urinary calculi. An autosomal recessive disease, it is estimated to affect 1 in 7000 individuals (between 1 in 1000 and 1 in 20,000, depending on the population examined). Urinary losses of lysine, arginine, and ornithine are asymptomatic. The gene defect in types II and III cystinuria involves single point or deletion mutations of *SLC7A9*, the luminal dibasic amino acid transporter. In classic cystinuria (type I), another transporter is coded by *SLC3A1*, and its transporter protein is known as *rBAT*. The gene is found on chromosome 2. Cystine loss leads to cystine urolithiasis, which accounts for 1 to 2% of all urinary calculi. Stone formation usually becomes evident during the second and third decades of life, although presentation may occur from infancy to the ninth decade, and males are more severely affected. Cystine stones are radiopaque, can create staghorn calculi, and often form a nidus for calcium oxalate stone formation. Symptoms include renal colic, which may be associated with obstruction and/or infection. Evidence associating cystinuria with central nervous system disorders has been tenuous. A more general discussion of nephrolithiasis can be found in Chapter 126.

The diagnosis of cystinuria should be considered in any patient with renal calculus, even if the stone is composed primarily of calcium oxalate. Typical hexagonal crystals may be recognized by urinalysis, particularly in a concentrated, acidic, early-morning specimen. A useful screening test is the cyanide-nitroprusside test, which detects a cystine concentration of more than 75 to 150 mg/L. Because of false-positive test results, a definitive diagnosis requires thin-layer or ion-exchange chromatography. Excretion ratios in an adult of more than 18 mg of cystine per gram of creatinine confirm the diagnosis. Homozygous individuals usually excrete more than 250 mg of cystine per gram of creatinine.

Medical therapy for cystinuria is aimed at reducing the urinary concentration below the solubility limit of 300 mg of cystine per liter. The production of a high-volume alkaline urine (pH >7.5) increases the solubility of cystine to this level. Because cystine excretion may be 1 g/24 hours, a total of 4 L of water should be ingested. The most effective means of converting cystine to a more soluble compound follows the therapeutic administration of D-penicillamine, which by way of a disulfide exchange reaction produces cysteine-penicillamine. Pyridoxine also should be given because penicillamine can deplete this cofactor. The compound α-mercaptopropionylglycine has proved to be more efficacious because it is more effective in disulfide exchange reactions, and its side effects seem to be fewer than those of D-penicillamine.

Hartnup Disease

Hartnup disease, a neutral aminoaciduria, is a rare autosomal recessive disorder (1 in 26,000 births) in which the clinical presentation is dominated by nicotinamide deficiency. Because 50% of nicotinamide normally is supplied by metabolism of tryptophan, malabsorption and renal loss of tryptophan contribute to nicotinamide deficiency, especially when dietary nicotinamide is insufficient. This disorder shows the importance of the intestinal and renal transport defects. Clinical evidence of nicotinamide deficiency is intermittent and often worse in children and includes pellagra in sun-exposed areas, cerebellar ataxia, and sometimes psychiatric disturbances.

Hartnup disease should be suspected in a patient with pellagra or cerebellar symptoms without a history of niacin deficiency. The diagnosis can be confirmed by chromatography of the urine. Siblings of an affected individual should be examined for heterozygosity. Supplemental nicotinamide (40 to 250 mg/day) prevents pellagra and neurologic problems.

Other Aminoacidurias

Less common aminoacidurias that are asymptomatic include iminoglycinuria, isolated hypercystinuria (without hyperexcretion of other basic amino acids), isolated glycinuria, and dicarboxylic aminoaciduria. Mental retardation predominates in the rare disorders of hyperdibasic aminoaciduria, isolated lysinuria, histidinuria, and methioninuria.

PROXIMAL RENAL TUBULAR ACIDOSIS

Proximal (type II) renal tubular acidosis (RTA) is a hyperchloremic, hypokalemic metabolic acidosis caused by a selective defect in

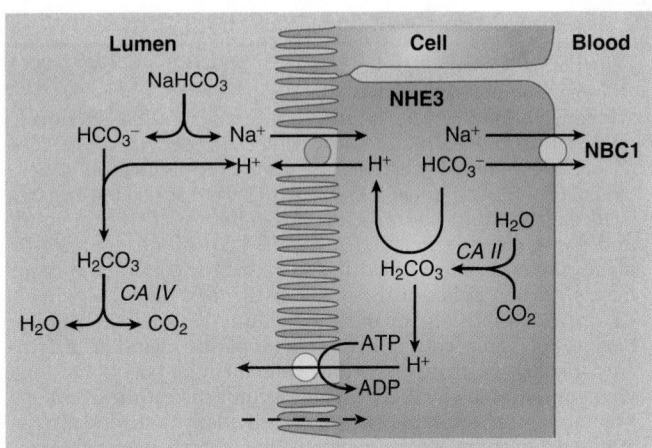

FIGURE 122-1 • Proximal tubule cell processes for the secretion of protons into the urine and for the reabsorption of bicarbonate. H^+ and HCO_3^- are formed by carbonic anhydrase II (CA II) action. H^+ exits across the luminal membrane by the apical NA^+/H^+ exchanger (NHE3) and the H^+-ATPase pump. The basolateral (blood surface) transfer of HCO_3^- occurs by the basolateral Na^+/HCO_3^- cotransporter (NBC1).

proximal acidification and defined by a normally acidic urine during acidosis but marked bicarbonate wasting after normalization of plasma bicarbonate concentrations.

Pathophysiology

Of the filtered bicarbonate load, 85 to 90% occurs in the proximal nephron, mainly by Na^+/H^+ exchange and the degradation of H_2CO to CO_2 plus H_2O by carbonic anhydrase (Fig. 122-1). The defective transport protein in autosomal recessive proximal RTA is the basolateral membrane Na^-HCO_3 cotransporter termed NBC1. Interference with a normal Na^+/H^+ exchange (NHE_3) or carbonic anhydrase activity also can result in excessive delivery of bicarbonate to the distal nephron. No human defect in NHE_3 has been found, but autosomal recessive mutations in carbonic anhydrase II have been detected along with osteopetrosis and cerebral calcifications.

Because of limited bicarbonate reabsorptive capacity, excessive bicarbonate is wasted into the urine. The loss of 15% or more of filtered bicarbonate at a normal plasma bicarbonate concentration is pathognomonic of proximal RTA. Excess delivery of bicarbonate to the distal nephron also results in accelerated potassium secretion and hypokalemia with defective proximal bicarbonate reabsorption. The plasma bicarbonate concentration and filtered load decrease, and absolute bicarbonate delivery to the distal nephron decreases progressively. After a certain time, usually when plasma bicarbonate is between 15 and 18 mM, the distal nephron can cope with excessive delivery from the proximal nephron. At this point, bicarbonaturia ceases, urinary pH can be lowered normally, and net acid excretion equals endogenous acid production. Acid-base homeostasis is reestablished at the expense of metabolic acidosis.

Clinical Manifestations

Clinical features of proximal RTA are related to acidemia (growth failure, anorexia and malnutrition, volume depletion); hypokalemia and potassium depletion (muscular weakness, polyuria, nocturia, polydipsia); and disordered mineral, parathyroid, and vitamin D metabolism (osteomalacia and rickets). Proximal RTA is rare; it usually is found in association with the complete Fanconi syndrome (see Table 122-1). Patients with *NBC1* mutations have cataracts, glaucoma, and band keratopathy. Patients with carbonic anhydrase II deficiency have osteopetrosis.

Rx Diagnosis and Treatment

Laboratory evidence of proximal RTA consists of a hyperchloremic, hypokalemic metabolic acidosis. When the patient is acidemic, the urine is acidic, and net acid excretion equals endogenous acid production. If bicarbonate is infused to normalize plasma bicarbonate concentrations, massive bicarbonaturia ensues (>15% of the filtered load). Proximal RTA is not usually an isolated diagnosis but part of Fanconi syndrome. Therapy for the underlying disease should be undertaken if possible (e.g., multiple myeloma) or offending drugs or toxins removed (e.g., heavy metals). When either of these options is not feasible, proximal RTA is treated with large quantities of sodium and potassium bicarbonate. Potassium wasting is enhanced as plasma bicarbonate rises after therapy, which increases the requirement for potassium supplements because bicarbonate alone cannot correct the disorder. Volume contraction using diuretics (particularly thiazides) also is attempted to stimulate fractional proximal bicarbonate reabsorption. Therapy with vitamin D analogues is indicated when clinically relevant.

GENERALIZED PROXIMAL TUBULE DYSFUNCTIONS: FANCONI SYNDROME

In Fanconi syndrome, the entire panoply of proximal tubule transport functions is impaired, resulting in glucosuria, generalized aminoaciduria, proximal RTA phosphaturia, and uricosuria. The lumen-to-cell sodium gradient provides the driving force in the proximal tubular epithelium for the reabsorption of these respective compounds. Collapse of the sodium gradient could arise by several mechanisms: a primary disturbance of the Na^+,K^+-ATPase, increased permeability of the cell to sodium, or reduced metabolic energy resulting from an abnormality in the redox potential or in the intracellular phosphate supply. Fanconi syndrome has been associated with a deletion in mitochondrial DNA, particularly in a mitochondrial myopathy associated with generalized renal tubulopathy. The gene responsible for Lowe's syndrome, *OCRL1*, also has been identified, and mutations have been detected in many patients. This gene normally codes for inositol polyphosphate-5 phosphatase, an enzyme that removes 5-phosphate from inositol (1,4,5)-triphosphate.

In addition to the solutes previously described, there exist impaired reabsorption and frequently reduced serum concentrations of calcium, magnesium, citrate, and low-molecular-weight (<50 kD) proteins. Because the proximal tubular mitochondria is the site of conversion of 25(OH) vitamin D to 1,25(OH)$_2$ vitamin D, the circulating value of this latter compound also may be reduced.

Clinical Manifestations

As a result of the complex disorders of mineral and vitamin D metabolism, the most frequent clinical finding is metabolic bone disease, either rickets in children or osteomalacia in adults (Chapter 259). Nausea, episodic vomiting, anorexia, and marked growth failure are common in children. Other features include polyuria and muscle weakness secondary to potassium depletion.

Etiology

The causes of Fanconi syndrome are listed in Table 122–1. The most common is the inherited disease cystinosis, in which cystine accumulates in cells, specifically in lysosomes of the kidney, liver, gut, lymphoid tissue, conjunctivae, thyroid gland, cornea, and bone marrow. Cystinosis may be present as Fanconi syndrome after the first birthday or with renal failure in childhood (infantile nephropathic form) or during adolescence. An adult form, which is generally benign, may involve corneal and conjunctival cystine crystal deposition. The defect represents a failure in the lysosomal cystine efflux process from a deletion or mutation in cystinosin, the lysomal cystine efflux transporter. A form of Fanconi syndrome that can be induced by diet is hereditary fructose intolerance secondary to a deficiency of fructose aldolase B (Chapter 214). Ingestion of fructose by affected patients causes acute symptoms, including nausea, vomiting, abdominal pain, and neurologic dysfunction, and profound

hypophosphatemia. Mutations in *GLUT4*, the gene for the facilitative diffusion liver-type glucose transporter, are found in patients with Fanconi-Bickel syndrome. Patients with this variant of Fanconi syndrome also have hepatorenal glycogen storage and impaired metabolism of glucose and galactose. In adults, acquired Fanconi syndrome is most often due to dysproteinemias, heavy metal exposure (especially chronic cadmium or acute lead), and immunologic disorders (see Table 122–1). An older adult presenting with Fanconi syndrome should be assumed to have multiple myeloma unless proved otherwise.

An X-linked form of nephrocalcinosis with hypercalciuria and low-molecular-weight proteinuria, termed *Dent's disease,* also shows other tubule abnormalities, including aminoaciduria, phosphaturia, and glycosuria with metabolic bone disease and progressive renal failure. This disorder is caused by a mutation in the voltage-gated chloride channel 5 (ClC5), particularly in the S$_3$ segment of the proximal tubule. Deletion of the gene for ClC5 in a knockout mouse model results in a murine homologue of Dent's disease.

The process of degradative endocytosis of filtered proteins occurs within the endosome of the renal proximal tubule, requiring the action of an H^+-ATPase at the endosome. With a mutation of ClC5, this process of endosome acidification is blocked, which diminishes the endosomal uptake of low-molecular-weight proteins.

Diagnosis

Diagnosis is established by finding evidence for global tubular dysfunction. Underlying causes of Fanconi syndrome should be sought. Serum and urine electrophoresis are indicated in adults.

Rx Treatment

Therapy includes sodium and potassium supplements (10 to 15 mEq/kg/day) and potassium, phosphate, magnesium, and vitamin D analogues. Therapy for the underlying disorder is also important. Efficacy has been shown for cysteamine in cystinosis, D-penicillamine in Wilson's disease (Chapter 224), fructose restriction in hereditary fructose intolerance, and removal of heavy metals by environmental changes or chelation (for lead).

DISORDERS OF FUNCTION OF THE ASCENDING LIMB OF THE LOOP OF HENLE

The thick ascending limb of the loop of Henle reabsorbs sodium chloride by means of a luminal $Na^+-K^+-2Cl^-$ system. A lumen-positive potential difference and parallel transport system affect potassium, calcium, and magnesium reabsorption. Defective reabsorption by the thick ascending limb of Henle occurs during diuretic therapy or in Bartter syndrome (Fig. 122–2).

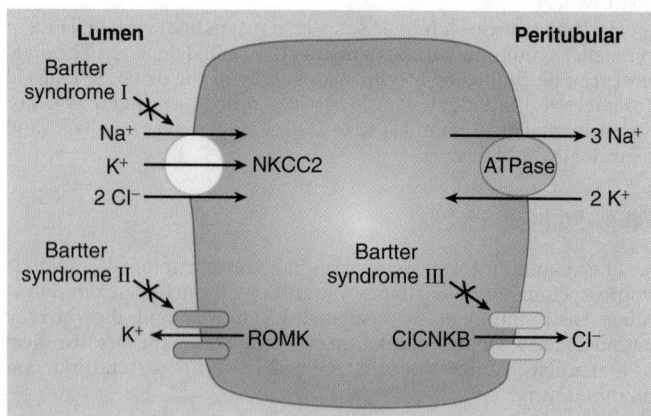

FIGURE 122–2 • Pathways in the thick ascending loop of Henle. The Na^+-K^+-2Cl$^-$ cotransporter (NKCC2) is responsible for Cl$^-$ reabsorption. This cotransporter is energized by the basolateral Na^+-K^+-ATPase and ClC-Kb. ROMK recycles K^+ back into the lumen and enhances NKCC2 activity. The defects for the three forms of Bartter syndrome are indicated.

BARTTER SYNDROME

Bartter syndrome includes hypokalemia, metabolic alkalosis, and hyperreninemic hyperaldosteronism. Hypertension and edema are absent.

Pathophysiology

Advances in research have elucidated at least three gene defects responsible for Bartter syndrome: (1) type I, a loss of function mutations of the gene encoding the bumetanide-sensitive Na^+-K^+-$2Cl^-$ cotransporter of the luminal membrane medullary thick ascending limb of Henle's loop; (2) type II, a defect in the gene for the inwardly rectifying potassium channel ROMK1 in the neonatal form; and (3) type III, a defect in the basolateral chloride channel ClCKB. Mild extracellular volume depletion causes hyperreninemic hyperaldosteronism and the juxtaglomerular hyperplasia evident in renal biopsy specimens. Enhanced sodium chloride delivery to the collecting duct stimulates potassium secretion (exacerbated by concurrent hyperaldosteronism), resulting in marked hypokalemia.

Clinical Manifestations

Bartter syndrome usually presents during childhood. Inheritance is autosomal recessive with males affected more often. Adult cases are described. Presenting features relate mainly to hypokalemia, including growth failure, muscle weakness, and vasopressin-resistant polyuria consisting of polyuria, nocturia, and enuresis. Divalent cation (calcium and magnesium), wasting, and metabolic alkalosis may result in hypocalcemia with Trousseau's and Chvostek's signs. These electrolyte abnormalities also can present as paralytic ileus or growth failure in children.

Diagnosis

Other conditions associated with hypokalemia, metabolic alkalosis, and secondary hyperreninemic hyperaldosteronism must be excluded before making the diagnosis of Bartter syndrome. Surreptitious vomiting, chronic diarrheal states, or surreptitious diuretic or laxative abuse can cause symptoms and laboratory findings indistinguishable from those of Bartter syndrome. The diagnosis must be preceded by determination that urinary chloride concentration is greater than 20 mmol/L and by negative screening test results for diuretics in the urine and for laxatives in the stool (phenolphthalein test). In general, other states of primary hyperreninism or hypermineralocorticoidism can be readily excluded because they normally are associated with hypertension.

 Treatment

Therapy involves amelioration of hypokalemia by disrupting the renin-angiotensin-aldosterone and the kinin-prostaglandin axes. Potassium supplementation, magnesium repletion, propranolol, spironolactone, prostaglandin inhibition (in the form of aspirin or indomethacin), and captopril all have been used.

DISORDERS OF DISTAL NEPHRON FUNCTION

Distal nephron, including the distal convoluted tubule and collection ducts, absorbs the final quantity of sodium in the tubular fluid and is the site for potassium and hydrogen ion secretion. Inherited and acquired defects exist for selected and combined disorders of sodium, potassium, and acid-base regulation.

GITELMAN'S VARIANT OF BARTTER SYNDROME

The hypocalciuric-hypomagnesemic variant described by Gitelman is due to a gene defect in the distal convoluted tubule, thiazide-sensitive Na^+-Cl^- cotransporter and is a distal tubule disorder. It consists of hypermagnesuria and hypocalciuria. The clinical features, in general, are less severe than the neonatal variant or adult Bartter syndrome. Nonetheless, patients may develop muscle cramps and fatigue. These patients require oral magnesium therapy around the clock.

CLASSIC DISTAL RENAL TUBULAR ACIDOSIS

Classic distal (type I) RTA is a hypokalemic, hyperchloremic metabolic acidosis related to a selective defect in distal acidification.

Pathophysiology

The distal nephron (especially the cortical and medullary collecting ducts) usually can lower the urinary pH 2 to 3 pH units below that of blood to hydrate the filtered buffers (mainly phosphate) to form titratable acids and endogenously produced ammonia to form ammonium. If the distal nephron is incapable of lowering the luminal pH to less than 5.5 after challenge by metabolic acidosis, classic distal RTA is present. As a result of the inappropriately high urinary pH, net acid excretion (titratable acid plus ammonium minus bicarbonate) is reduced and is less than total acid production by the body. Enhanced potassium secretion occurs, presumably because there is reduced competition by proton secretion for the electrochemical driving forces in the distal nephron. The acidification defect may result from an insufficient number of proton-secreting pumps in the distal nephron. Alternately a back leak of acid across the luminal membrane may exist so that establishment of a pH gradient is prevented even when proton secretion is normal.

A gene defect resulting in an abnormal AE-1, the chloride-bicarbonate anion exchanger, is a cause of autosomal dominant distal RTA, type I. A defect in the B1 subunit of the H^+-ATPase is found in patients with autosomal recessive distal RTA with deafness. An autosomal recessive form without deafness has been described resulting from a defect in an accessory subunit of H^+-ATPase.

Clinical Manifestations

Distal RTA is evident in infants, children, and adults; symptoms are those of acidosis or hypokalemia, as noted earlier. Nephrocalcinosis and nephrolithiasis are common, either as a cause or as a result of classic distal RTA. Bone disease is not as frequent as in proximal RTA, however. Classic distal RTA also may be genetic (usually autosomal dominant) or due to autoimmune diseases, drugs and toxins, and various tubulointerstitial diseases (see Table 122–1).

Diagnosis

The findings of hyperchloremic, hypokalemic metabolic acidosis with an inappropriately high urine pH (>5.5) and diminished net acid excretion confirm the diagnosis. Diagnosis is facilitated by measuring the urinary anion gap (defined as urinary sodium plus potassium minus chloride, which is proportionate to the negative value of urinary ammonium [NH_4^+]). Diarrhea causes a large, negative urinary anion gap and a high urinary ammonium concentration (accounting for the high urinary pH), whereas classic distal RTA has a zero or positive anion gap and a low urinary ammonium concentration as a result of impaired renal tubular acidification. In subjects with a normal plasma bicarbonate concentration, the failure to lower urinary pH to less than 5.5 after an acute acid challenge with NH_4Cl defines the syndrome of incomplete classic distal RTA.

 Treatment

Treatment with alkali is generally effective. The daily dose of alkali in adults is 1 to 3 mEq/kg, to compensate for the normal acid production by the body plus a small amount of urinary bicarbonate wastage. In contrast to proximal RTA, urinary potassium wasting is ameliorated with alkali therapy.

RENAL TUBULAR ACIDOSIS OF GLOMERULAR INSUFFICIENCY

Moderate renal insufficiency may be associated with a normokalemic, hyperchloremic metabolic acidosis (GFR of 20 to 30 mL/min) resulting from insufficient ammonia delivery. It is characterized by an appropriately low urine pH but subnormal urinary net acid (ammonium) excretion.

Table 122–2 • RENAL TUBULAR ACIDOSES

TYPE	RENAL DEFECT	GFR	PLASMA [K⁺]	PROXIMAL ACIDIFICATION HCO₃⁻ Reabsorption (During HCO₃⁻ Loading)	DISTAL ACIDIFICATION Minimal Urinary pH (During Acidosis)	DISTAL ACIDIFICATION UAG ≈ – Urine [NH₄⁺] (During Acidosis)
Proximal (type II)	⇓ Proximal acidification	N	⇓	⇓	<5.5	0 or +
Classic distal (type I)	⇓ Distal pH gradient	N	⇓	N	>5.5	0 or +
Glomerular insufficiency	⇓ NH₃ production	⇓	N	N	<5.5	0 or +
Generalized distal (type IV)	⇓ Aldosterone action	⇓	⇑	N	<5.5	0 or +

N = normal; UAG = urinary anion gap = $[Na^+] + [K^+] - [Cl^-] \approx -[NH_4^+]$; GFR = glomerular filtration rate.

NONSELECTIVE DISTAL NEPHRON DYSFUNCTION: GENERALIZED DISTAL RENAL TUBULAR ACIDOSIS, HYPERKALEMIA, AND RENAL SALT WASTING

Disorders of nonselective distal nephron dysfunction derive from global dysfunction of the distal nephron owing to aldosterone deficiency or antagonism and are typified by hyperkalemic, hyperchloremic (type IV) metabolic acidosis caused by subnormal net acid excretion and often by salt wasting.

Pathophysiology

Aldosterone influences distal sodium reabsorption to the extent that urinary sodium is less than 10 mEq/L. Sodium reabsorption creates a lumen negative potential difference that favors secretion of potassium and hydrogen ions. Disruption of sodium reabsorption and of potassium and hydrogen ion secretion may be ascribed to a defect in the integrity of the distal nephron cell, reduced aldosterone production or action, diminished sodium reabsorption, or blunting of the lumen negative potential by enhanced chloride reabsorption. Any of these processes can diminish total hydrogen and potassium excretion, resulting in hyperkalemic metabolic acidosis. This hyperkalemia also depresses renal ammoniagenesis independently, which enhances the defect in renal acidification. The ability of the distal nephron to lower urine pH remains intact.

℞ Treatment

Generalized distal RTA is unique among the hyperchloremic metabolic acidoses in being a hyperkalemic disorder (Table 122–2). The GFR invariably is reduced in hyporeninemic or tubulointerstitial nephropathy but may be at levels (>30 mL/min) greater than those typically found in the RTA of glomerular insufficiency. Treatment of the hyperkalemia and generalized distal RTA is with 9-fluorohydrocortisone, 0.1 mg/day, when mineralocorticoid is deficient. When hyporeninemia is the cause, high doses of the synthetic mineralocorticoid are necessary (0.5 mg/day) because of associated mineralocorticoid resistance. Hypertension can be precipitated with this treatment. A loop diuretic (furosemide or ethacrynic acid) is also useful, especially when hypertension precludes administration of mineralocorticoid, because it augments urinary potassium excretion even when endogenous aldosterone is reduced. Useful adjuncts to diuretic therapy include dietary potassium restriction (<50 mEq/dL), alkali therapy to compensate for daily acid generation (sodium bicarbonate, 1 to 3 mEq/kg/day), and sometimes short-term use of cation-exchange resin.

SUGGESTED READINGS

Igarashi T, Sekine T, Watanabe H: Molecular basis of proximal renal tubular acidosis. J Nephrol 2002;15(Suppl 5):S135–S141. *A general overview.*

Kalatzis V, Antignac C: New aspects of the pathogenesis of cystinosis. Pediatr Nephrol 2003;18:207–215. *Overview of the most common inherited cause of the renal Fanconi syndrome.*

Karet FE, Finberg KE, Nelson RD, et al: Mutations in the gene encoding B1 subunit of H⁺-ATPase cause renal tubular acidosis with sensorineural deafness. Nat Genet 1999;21:84–90. *An important article describing the mutation in one form of distal RTA.*

Scriver CR, Beaudet AL, Valle D, et al (eds): The Metabolic and Molecular Basis of Inherited Disease, 8th ed. New York, McGraw Hill, 2001, pp 4891–5240. *The chapters relating to membrane transport systems present the progress made in the understanding of renal proximal tubular disorders.*

Wills N, Fong P: C1C chloride channels in epithelia: Recent progress and remaining puzzles. News Physiol Sci 2001;16:161–166. *An overview of normal physiology and pathophysiology.*

Zelikovic I: Molecular pathophysiology of tubular transport disorders. Pediatr Nephrol 2001;16:919–935. *A comprehensive review of mutations responsible for tubular disorders.*

123 DIABETES AND THE KIDNEY

Raymond C. Harris

Epidemiology of Diabetic Nephropathy

In the industrialized world, diabetes mellitus represents the leading cause of end-stage renal disease (ESRD). Both the incidence and prevalence of ESRD secondary to diabetes continue to rise. In the United States, more than 30% of patients receiving either dialytic therapy or renal transplantation have ESRD as a result of diabetic nephropathy, and 40% of the new (incident) cases of ESRD are attributable to diabetes.

In the United States, Europe, and Japan, approximately 92% of diabetes represents type II rather than type I (insulinopenic). Correspondingly, more than 80% of the ESRD secondary to diabetes is seen in patients with type II diabetes. Although it was previously supposed that ESRD secondary to type II diabetes was less common than with type I diabetes, in fact when cohorts of patients with type I and type II diabetes are followed for an extended period, the incidence of renal disease is equivalent. The demographics for ESRD due to type II diabetes mirror the prevalence of type II diabetes in the U.S. population, with a higher incidence in females and in African Americans, Hispanic Americans, Native Americans, and Asian Americans, and with a peak incidence in the fifth to seventh decade.

Pathobiology of Diabetic Nephropathy

HYPERGLYCEMIA

Increasing evidence implicates the metabolic sequelae of hyperglycemia as the most important causative factor in the development of diabetic nephropathy. The Stockholm Diabetes Intervention Study and the Diabetes Control and Complications Trial (DCCT) both clearly demonstrated that aggressive control of blood sugar decreased the development of nephropathy, as well as other microvascular complications, in type I diabetes.■ Furthermore, after long-term (10 years) pancreas transplantation, the renal lesions of diabetic nephropathy have been demonstrated to reverse. Increased intracellular glucose metabolism, activation of the polyol pathway, which can lead to de novo synthesis of diacylglycerol and increased protein kinase C activity, and nonenzymatic protein glycation (advanced glycation end-products [AGEs]) have all been implicated in the development of diabetic nephropathy, as well as other diabetic microvasculopathies.

Although chronic hyperglycemia is undoubtedly the underlying abnormality that produces diabetic nephropathy, other genetic, hemodynamic, or metabolic factors must also be involved, because only a subset of diabetic patients develop the condition.

GENETIC FACTORS

There is evidence for familial clustering of both type I and type II diabetes. Type I diabetics with siblings with diabetic nephropathy have a greater than 70% lifetime risk of themselves developing diabetic nephropathy. There also appears to be an hereditary predisposition for the development of diabetic nephropathy in patients with type II diabetes. Modifier genes have been proposed to be important for the development of diabetic nephropathy, the rate of progression of the injury (from microalbuminuria to ESRD), or both. Diabetic nephropathy is likely to be a polygenic disease. A number of proposed candidate genes may modify and/or predispose to the development of diabetic renal disease, and a number of candidate genes have been suggested based on experimental models and/or gene linkage analysis. Of the identified candidate genes, there has been extensive interest in angiotensin-converting enzyme (*ACE*) gene polymorphisms. The preponderance of evidence suggests that the *ACE* gene insertion/deletion (I/D) polymorphism does not itself predispose to the development of diabetic nephropathy but may predict the rate of progression in both type I and type II diabetes. Some, but not all, linkage studies have also suggested involvement of angiotensinogen polymorphisms and type I angiotensin II receptor polymorphisms in the development of diabetic nephropathy. Endothelial dysfunction is present in diabetes and is associated with impaired vascular nitric oxide (NO) synthesis. Linkage studies have suggested an association of polymorphisms in endothelial nitric oxide synthase (eNOS) with nephropathy, which has been reported in Pima Indians with type II diabetes. It has also been suggested that genetic abnormalities in lipid metabolism may underlie a predisposition to development of diabetic nephropathy, and in this regard, polymorphisms in apolipoprotein E (apoE) have also been linked to a predisposition to development of diabetic nephropathy. Genes relating to extracellular matrix production (transforming growth factor-β [TGF-β], matrix metalloproteinase-

9) have also been linked in some, but not all, studies. Suffice it to say, the identity of the predisposing genes continues to be the subject of intensive current research, and our understanding of the involved genetic interactions will very likely increase dramatically in the next few years.

HEMODYNAMICS

Patients with type I and, to a lesser extent, type II diabetes exhibit increased glomerular filtration rate (GFR), so-called *hyperfiltration*, which has been suggested to be mediated by proportionately greater relaxation of the afferent arteriole than the efferent arteriole, leading to increased glomerular blood flow and elevated glomerular capillary pressure. There also is glomerular hypertrophy, with an increased glomerular capillary surface area. It has been suggested that these intraglomerular hemodynamic alterations may contribute to the development and/or progression of diabetic renal injury. Because ACE inhibitors and decreased dietary protein reduce this increased intraglomerular capillary pressure in experimental animals, the hyperfiltration hypothesis provides one rationale for the success of these interventions in the progression of diabetic nephropathy (see later).

HORMONES AND CYTOKINES

Studies in experimental animals have implicated a number of cytokines, hormones, and intracellular signaling pathways in either the development or progression of diabetic nephropathy, notably TGF-β, angiotensin II, endothelin, prostaglandins, NO, and protein kinase C. Because these factors have also been implicated in a variety of nondiabetic kidney diseases, it is likely that they will not prove to be specific for diabetic nephropathy.

Clinical Manifestations

Although a minority of patients presenting with diabetic nephropathy have type I diabetes, the natural history of the disease is best exemplified in this population because the onset of diabetes is more clearly definable and patients with type I diabetes usually do not present initially with the comorbid conditions often associated with type II diabetes (including essential hypertension, atherosclerotic cardiovascular disease, and obesity) that may independently produce chronic renal injury. Furthermore, the relatively advanced age of onset of type II diabetes and the increased cardiovascular mortality in this population may preclude the development of all manifestations of diabetic nephropathy. In this regard, definitive descriptions of diabetic nephropathy in type II diabetes have been obtained in studies of Pima Indians, who exhibit a strong genetic predisposition to development of type II diabetes around the fourth decade of life and who develop diabetic nephropathy that progresses in a similar pattern as is seen in type I diabetic patients.

In type I diabetes, it is possible to characterize the progression of diabetic nephropathy as occurring in four relatively distinct stages. In stage I, which commences soon after the overt manifestations of diabetes, the kidney undergoes hypertrophy compared with age- and weight-matched normal control subjects. Both the glomeruli and tubules are hypertrophied. In addition, there is an up to 50% increase in renal blood flow and GFR in the initial phase of diabetic nephropathy. There is no detectable macroalbuminuria, but transient microalbuminuria (measurable by radioimmunoassay [RIA], enzyme-linked immunosorbent assay [ELISA], or special dipsticks) is occasionally evident, especially when induced by stress, physical exertion, concurrent illness, or poor glycemic control. In type I diabetes, hypertension is usually absent in the early stages of the disease but is often present in type II diabetes at the time of presentation.

Approximately 30% of type I diabetic patients progress to stage II, characterized by fixed microalbuminuria of at least 30 mg/24 hr. The median duration of diabetes for progression to this clinically silent stage is 10 years. Although GFR either remains elevated or is within the normal range, abnormal renal histology is present, characterized by glomerular and tubular basement membrane thickening and inception of mesangial matrix expansion. The risk of developing microalbuminuria is greatly increased if other micro-

vascular insults coexist, and, in particular, the presence of proliferative retinopathy increases the likelihood that detected microalbuminuria reflects the presence of diabetic nephropathy. In this regard, the predictive value of microalbuminuria for diabetic nephropathy is greater in type I than in type II diabetics because of the high incidence in the latter population of hypertension, which may itself lead to microalbuminuria.

The great majority of patients who present with fixed microalbuminuria progress to overt nephropathy (stage III) within 5 to 7 years. In this stage, patients manifest overt proteinuria (>500 mg of total protein/24 hr) and macroalbuminuria (>200 mg/24 hr) (which is detectable with a routine urinary protein dipstick). Blood pressure begins to rise in type I patients with stage III nephropathy, and in type II patients, who frequently have preexistent hypertension, blood pressure control becomes more problematic.

Renal biopsy reveals diffuse or nodular (Kimmelstiel-Wilson) glomerulosclerosis. Although the Kimmelstiel-Wilson lesion is considered pathognomonic for advanced diabetic nephropathy, only approximately 25% of patients manifest this lesion. A nodular pattern of glomerulopathy mimicking Kimmelstiel-Wilson lesions may also be seen in light chain nephropathy. Older descriptions of "diabetic nephropathy without overt hyperglycemia" that were based solely on light microscopic analysis may have actually represented light chain disease. Nodular glomerular lesions can also be observed in amyloidosis and membranoproliferative glomerulonephritis type II.

An additional pathognomonic finding of diabetic nephropathy is the finding of both afferent and efferent arteriolar hyalinosis, unlike the arteriolar lesion of essential hypertension, which is restricted to the afferent arteriole. In overt diabetic nephropathy, there is also progressive tubulointerstitial fibrosis, which correlates most closely with the decline in renal function in a number of progressive renal diseases, including diabetic nephropathy. The GFR begins to decline from the normal range, but serum creatinine may remain in the normal range.

In stage IV, or advanced diabetic nephropathy, there is a relentless decline in renal function to end-stage disease. The patients have nephrotic range proteinuria (>3.5 g/24 hr) and systemic hypertension but no evidence of inflammatory glomerular (red blood cell casts) or tubulointerstitial (white blood cells, white blood cell

Continued

casts) lesions. The kidneys may be inappropriately large for the observed degree of renal insufficiency.

Although patients with type II diabetes also tend to have elevated GFR during their early presentation, the GFR increases are usually not as pronounced as are seen with insulin-dependent diabetes mellitus. In addition, there is a greater incidence of hypertension and microalbuminuria present at the time of detection of diabetes, with as many as 10 to 25% of patients presenting with these abnormalities. It is still unclear whether this difference in presentation represents a fundamental difference in the pathophysiology of the two conditions or, more likely, is due to the fact that type II patients may have unrecognized diabetes for many years because they are not ketosis prone and may have other associated conditions predisposing to renal abnormalities.

Other Renal Complications

In addition to the clinical presentation of diabetic nephropathy described earlier, there are other kidney and genitourinary abnormalities that can ensue in the diabetic patient. Type IV (hyporeninemic, hypoaldosteronemic) metabolic acidosis with hyperkalemia is commonly encountered in patients with diabetes and mild to moderate renal insufficiency. These patients should be carefully monitored for development of severe hyperkalemia in response to volume depletion or after inception of drugs that interfere with the renin-angiotensin system, such as ACE inhibitors, angiotensin type 1 (AT1) receptor blockers, β-adrenergic blockers, nonsteroidal anti-inflammatory agents, or heparin, or of potassium-sparing diuretics.

Patients with diabetes have an increased incidence of bacterial and fungal infections of the genitourinary tract. In addition to lower urinary tract infections, there is an increased risk of pyelonephritis and intrarenal and perinephric abscess formation.

Unilateral or bilateral renal artery stenosis is more frequent in the type II diabetic population than in aged-matched nondiabetic individuals and should be considered if a diabetic patient manifests intractable hypertension or a rapidly rising serum creatinine immediately after initiation of therapy with an ACE inhibitor or AT1 receptor blocker. Other causes of acute deterioration of renal function include papillary necrosis, with ureteral obstruction secondary to sloughing a papilla, obstructive uropathy due to bladder dysfunction resulting from autonomic neuropathy, and contrast media–induced acute tubular necrosis. In addition, diabetic patients may develop prerenal azotemia or acute tubular necrosis as a result of congestive heart failure or of volume depletion secondary to vomiting induced by gastroparesis or diarrhea due to autonomic neuropathy.

Prevention of Diabetic Nephropathy

As mentioned, studies have convincingly demonstrated that tight glycemic control significantly lessens but does not completely eliminate the incidence of diabetic nephropathy. Furthermore, in the DCCT, the incidence of clinically significant hypoglycemic episodes was increased 3-fold in the patients receiving intensive insulin therapy. Although the role of systemic hypertension as a pathogenic factor in development of diabetic nephropathy remains unresolved (see earlier), it is well established to be the most important single risk factor in its progression, and blood pressure levels should be lowered to levels below what is considered to be the upper levels of normal pressure in the nondiabetic population.[2] There also is evidence that smoking and elevated cholesterol may be predisposing factors in development of diabetic nephropathy in type II diabetic patients.

℞ Treatment of Latent (Stage II) and Overt (Stage III) Diabetic Nephropathy

Although the Stockholm Diabetes Intervention Study and the DCCT demonstrated that strict glycemic control was effective in preventing the development of fixed microalbuminuria, subgroup analysis of the DCCT patients who initially presented with microalbuminuria, as well as a subsequent study by the Microalbuminuria Collaborative Study Group, has determined that tight control of type I patients may not prevent progression to macroalbuminuria, although it does prevent other microvascular complications, such as retinopathy and peripheral neuropathy. There is increasing evidence that better glycemic control will slow the progression of nephropathy in type II diabetic patients as well as in type I diabetic patients (Chapter 242).

It is clear that optimal blood pressure control will retard progression of diabetic nephropathy.[1-5] Studies have determined that interfering with the renin-angiotensin system by administration of either ACE inhibitors or AT1 receptor blockers has additional benefit beyond lowering systemic blood pressure to retard progression in both type I and type II patients. Conversely, there is evidence that dihydropyridine calcium channel blockers may be less effective or even detrimental in preventing progression of diabetic nephropathy. The underlying pathophysiologic explanation relates to the ability of ACE inhibitors and AT1 receptor blockers to lower intraglomerular capillary pressure by decreasing efferent arteriolar pressure, while dihydropyridine calcium channel blockers increase intraglomerular capillary pressure by inducing selective afferent arteriolar vasodilatation.

When administering ACE inhibitors or AT1 receptor blockers to patients with diabetic nephropathy, serum potassium and creatinine should be monitored closely in the first week after initiation because of the associated comorbid conditions of type IV renal tubular acidosis and renal artery stenosis. If blood pressure control is not achieved with these agents, diuretics and other antihypertensive agents, including cardioselective β-blockers, α-blockers, and non-dihydropyridine calcium channel blockers, can be added. Smoking cessation and antihyperlipidemic medication to patients with documented lipid abnormalities should be encouraged. Judicial restriction of dietary protein (to 0.8 g/kg of ideal body weight/day) is recommended by the American Diabetes Association. Although there are some data suggesting that further dietary protein restriction may retard the progression of diabetic nephropathy, such an intervention must also take into account individual nutritional carbohydrate and lipid requirements of the patient.

Efficacy of treatment can be determined by monitoring albuminuria and/or total proteinuria. For patients with deterioration of renal function, GFR determined by creatinine clearance and/or plots of the reciprocal of serum creatinine vs. time (1/sCr) are effective indicators of whether interventions are affecting the rate of progression of the nephropathy.

RENAL REPLACEMENT THERAPY

More than 80% of the patients with end-stage diabetic nephropathy receive dialysis as their modality of renal replacement therapy, with 5.7 times as many of these patients receiving hemodialysis compared with peritoneal dialysis. Because of the associated macrovascular complications (cardiovascular, cerebrovascular, peripheral vascular) and the increased risk of infection, the survival of diabetic patients who receive either type of dialysis is lower than that of the nondiabetic dialysis population, with a mortality that is 1.5 to 2.0 times that of nondiabetic patients, and a 5-year survival rate of diabetic patients on maintenance dialysis of less than 20%. The survival of diabetic patients is slightly worse with peritoneal dialysis than with hemodialysis. It is not established whether this difference is a consequence of the therapy itself (dialytic adequacy may not be as easily obtained in larger patients and systemic absorption of the high glucose solutions used in peritoneal dialysis may lead to poorer glycemic control and accelerate microvascular and/or macrovascular complications) or is a reflection of the patients who may be more likely to be initiated on peritoneal dialysis (i.e., those patients whose associated vascular complications preclude hemodialysis). In general, the management of a diabetic patient nearing ESRD is similar to that of the nondiabetic patient. The patient should be under the care of a nephrologist, and planning should be initiated for the modality of dialysis. Although dialysis is usually initiated when GFR declines to approximately 10 to 15 mL/min, in diabetic patients, early initiation of dialysis is sometimes necessary when either volume-dependent hypertension or hyperkalemia is not manageable by nondialytic therapy or when uremia, combined with gastroparesis, leads to anorexia and malnutrition and/or uncontrollable recurrent emesis.

Approximately 25% of the renal transplant recipients in the United States are diabetic patients. The vast majority (>90%) are type I diabetic patients, due to their younger age and decreased associated macrovascular comorbidity compared with type II patients. The long-term survival and quality of life after transplantation are generally superior to those seen with dialytic therapy. However, the other microvascular complications (retinopathy, neuropathy) are not improved by renal transplantation alone. The advent of pancreas and combined kidney-pancreas transplantation has been shown to improve significantly the quality of life of patients with diabetic nephropathy, by improving autonomic neuropathy, either retarding or possibly correcting retinopathy, and avoiding the potential complications of insulin administration. However, all transplantation options remain limited by organ availability.

1. The Diabetes Control and Complications Trial Research Group: The effect of intensive treatment of diabetes on the development and progression of long-term complications in insulin-dependent diabetes mellitus. N Engl J Med 1993;329:977–986.
2. Kaplan NM: Management of hypertension in patients with type 2 diabetes mellitus: Guidelines based on current evidence. Ann Intern Med 2001;18:1079–1083.
3. Lewis EJ, Hunsicker LG, Bain RP, et al: The effect of angiotensin-converting-enzyme inhibition on diabetic nephropathy N Engl J Med 1993;329:1456–1462.
4. Lewis EJ, Hunsicker LG, Clarke WR, et al, Collaborative Study Group: Renoprotective effect of the angiotensin-receptor antagonist irbesartan in patients with nephropathy due to type 2 diabetes. N Engl J Med 2001;345:851–868.
5. Brenner BM, Cooper ME, de Zeeuw D, et al, RENAAL Study Investigators: Effects of losartan on renal and cardiovascular outcomes in patients with type 2 diabetes and nephropathy. N Engl J Med 2001;345:861–869.

SUGGESTED READINGS

Bakris GL, Williams M, Dworkin L, et al: Preserving renal function in adults with hypertension and diabetes: A consensus approach. National Kidney Foundation Hypertension and Diabetes Executive Committees Working Group. Am J Kidney Dis 2000;36:646–661. *This report provides the most recent consensus recommendations with a focus on level of blood pressure control, proteinuria reduction, and therapeutic approaches to achieve these goals.*
Keane WF, Lyle PA: Recent advances in management of type 2 diabetes and nephropathy: Lessons from the RENAAL study. Am J Kidney Dis 2003;41:S22–S25. *Proteinuria was shown to be the single most powerful predictor of the development of ESRD in patients with type 2 diabetes and nephropathy. The routine availability of the urinary albumin-creatinine ratio as a validated diagnostic test allows assessment of interventions to improve the prognosis of individuals with type 2 diabetes and nephropathy.*
Knoll GA, Nichol G: Dialysis, kidney transplantation, or pancreas transplantation for patients with diabetes mellitus and renal failure: A decision analysis of treatment options. J Am Soc Nephrol 2003;14:500–515. *Decision analysis suggesting that living kidney transplant is preferred but simultaneous pancreas-kidney transplantation is associated with the greatest life expectancy for patients without a living donor.*
Singh R, Barden A, Mori T, et al: Advanced glycation end-products: A review. Diabetologia 2001;44:129–146. *A comprehensive review of the potential pathophysiologic roles of AGEs in diabetic complications.*

124 VASCULAR DISORDERS OF THE KIDNEY

Thomas D. DuBose, Jr.

The fact that the kidneys depend on systemic blood pressure to maintain normal renal blood flow, glomerular filtration rate (GFR), and tubular function underscores the vulnerability of the kidneys to diseases involving the renal vasculature. Thrombosis, emboli, atherosclerosis, inflammation, or hypertension may involve renal vessels. Renal vascular disease can be classified according to anatomic location: arteries, arterioles and microvasculature, and renal veins.

ARTERIES

THROMBOEMBOLIC OCCLUSION OF THE RENAL ARTERIES

Definition and Etiology

Thrombosis of the renal arteries and segmental branches may arise as a result of intrinsic pathology of the renal arteries or as a complication of embolization of thrombi arising in distant vessels. In situ thrombosis occurs as a complication of progressive atherosclerosis in elderly patients and may be an important cause of progressive renal insufficiency in this population. In patients younger than age 60 years, traumatic thrombosis is the most common cause. Blunt trauma and

deceleration injuries may cause acute thrombosis. Trauma to the renal pedicle may result in an intimal tear with thrombosis in the middle third of the renal artery. Thrombosis may arise in the setting of dissection of the renal artery or as a complication of renal arteriography, angioplasty, or stent placement. Finally, thrombosis may occur as a consequence of inflammatory disorders that involve the large arteries (Takayasu's arteritis, syphilis, systemic vasculitides, and thromboangiitis obliterans) and structural lesions of the renal arteries, such as fibromuscular dysplasia or renal artery aneurysm. Embolization is a more common cause of renal artery occlusion than in situ thrombosis and is usually unilateral (bilateral in 15 to 30%). Total infarction of the kidney is much less common than is segmental infarction or ischemia. Approximately 90% of thromboemboli to the renal arteries originate in the heart, and a common cause is left atrial thrombi in patients with atrial fibrillation. Valvular heart disease, bacterial endocarditis, nonbacterial (aseptic) endocarditis, and atrial myxomas are other sources of emboli originating in the heart. The diverse causes of occlusion of the renal artery or its segmental branches are summarized in Table 124–1.

Clinical Manifestations

The manifestations of thromboembolic occlusion of the renal arteries depend on the extent and time course of the occlusive event and the preexisting status of the renal circulation. Occlusion of a primary or secondary branch of the renal artery in a patient with preexisting disease and established collateral circulation, such as long-standing renal artery stenosis, may produce little or no infarction and minimal symptoms. Acute thrombosis and infarction may result in sudden onset of flank pain (which resembles renal colic), fever, nausea, vomiting, and, occasionally, hematuria. Pain may be localized to the abdomen, back, or chest, but in more than half of cases, pain is absent. If infarction occurs, leukocytosis usually develops, and serum enzyme levels may be elevated (aspartate aminotransferase, lactate dehydrogenase, and alkaline phosphatase); urinary lactate dehydrogenase and alkaline phosphatase also may increase. Urinalysis usually reveals microscopic hematuria. The blood urea nitrogen and creatinine levels typically increase transiently with unilateral infarction, but more severe and protracted renal dysfunction may follow bilateral renal infarction or infarction of a solitary kidney. Hypertension, which usually occurs with infarction, is the result of release of renin from the ischemic renal parenchyma.

Table 124–1 • CAUSES OF RENAL ARTERY OCCLUSION

THROMBOSIS
Progressive atherosclerosis
Trauma, blunt
Aortic or renal artery aneurysm
Aortic or renal artery dissection
Aortic or renal artery angiography
Superimposed on inflammatory disorders
    Vasculitis
    Thromboangiitis obliterans
    Syphilis
Superimposed on structural lesions
    Fibromuscular dysplasia

THROMBOEMBOLISM
Atrial fibrillation
Mitral stenosis
Mural thrombus
Atrial myxoma
Prosthetic valve
Septic or aseptic valvular vegetations
Paradoxical emboli
Tumor emboli
Fat emboli

ATHEROEMBOLI (CHOLESTEROL EMBOLIZATION)
Elderly patients with advanced atherosclerosis
Abdominal aortic surgery
Trauma, blunt
Angiographic catheters
Angioplasty or stent placement
Excessive anticoagulation

Diagnosis

The diagnosis of renal artery occlusion is established most reliably by renal arteriography. The advantage of conventional arteriography is that the anatomy, even of subsegmental occlusion, can be established most reliably. Computed tomography (CT), especially spiral acquired-volume CT scans, magnetic resonance angiography (MRA), renal scintigraphy, and duplex ultrasound scanning can be used reliably as screening tests for the diagnosis of acute arterial thrombosis. MRA is superior to CT and duplex ultrasound. In embolic renal artery occlusion, the presence of an intracardiac thrombus must be sought by echocardiography.

Rx Treatment

Managing acute arterial thrombosis usually includes surgical revascularization, control of hypertension, adequate hydration, anticoagulation, and acute renal replacement therapy when needed. Alternative approaches, such as intra-arterial thrombolytic therapy, are being used more frequently, especially for iatrogenic occlusion of the renal artery as a result of angiographic manipulations or angioplasty. Newer distal balloon occlusion devices offer promise to limit thromboemboli and renal infarction. Atheroemboli should not be treated by fibrinolysis. Surgery is also the treatment of choice for traumatic renal artery thrombosis, which is associated with poor salvage of renal function unless surgery is done immediately. The warm ischemia time beyond which recovery of renal function would not be anticipated is several hours.

Prognosis

Mortality is high in these conditions, particularly because of the severity of underlying and associated conditions. The mortality rate of patients undergoing surgical revascularization for complete acute renal artery occlusion is 11 to 25%. Hypertension may develop as a late sequela of renal artery occlusion and may be treated by angiotensin-converting enzyme (ACE) inhibitors, angiotensin receptor blockers (ARBs), or nondihydropyridine calcium channel blockers or, if refractory, by balloon angioplasty. Long-term renal replacement therapy may be necessary.

RENAL ARTERY STENOSIS AND ISCHEMIC RENAL DISEASE

Definition and Etiology

The prevalence of renal artery stenosis as the cause of hypertension in the general population is only 2 to 4%. Nevertheless, renovascular hypertension is the most common curable form of hypertension. In selected subgroups of patients (accelerated hypertension with renal insufficiency), the prevalence increases to 30 to 40%. Atherosclerosis causes approximately 60 to 70% of cases of hypertension in middle-aged and elderly patients. A striking association has been noted between the number of peripheral vessels involved (more than five) with peripheral vascular disease and the presence of renal artery stenosis. Renal artery stenosis secondary to atherosclerosis is more prevalent among heavy smokers and individuals with high cholesterol levels. In younger women between the ages of 15 and 50 years, renal artery stenosis is usually the result of fibromuscular dysplasia. This disorder is a collection of vascular diseases that affects the intima, media, and adventitia. More than 90% of cases involve the media. The distribution of disease, as seen on selective renal arteriography as a beaded aneurysmal display, involves the distal two thirds of the renal artery and its branches. Medial fibromuscular dysplasia progresses in many patients and is not associated with dissection or thrombosis. In contrast, intimal and periarterial fibromuscular dysplasia commonly is associated with progressive dissection and thrombosis. Although the cause is unknown, there may be a genetic predisposition. Other factors include smoking and hormonal effects. Atherosclerosis accounts for 90% of cases of renal stenosis and usually involves the ostium and proximal third of the main renal artery (Fig. 124–1C). The prevalence increases with advancing age, especially in patients with diabetes, coronary artery disease, or hypertension. Atherosclerosis of one or both renal arteries is being recognized more frequently among the elderly, in whom it may or may not be associated with hypertension (Fig. 124–2C). It often is associated with generalized atherosclerotic peripheral vascular disease and may progress to cause progressive loss of renal function. This entity has been referred to as *ischemic* renal disease. The clinical characteristics of ischemic renal disease include advanced age, male gender, elevated serum creatinine, peripheral arteriopathy (68%), ischemic heart disease (45%), congestive heart failure (33%), and history of stroke (28%). Many patients have evidence of arteriosclerosis in both renal arteries.

Clinical Manifestations

Renal artery stenosis should be suspected when hypertension develops in a previously normotensive patient older than age 55 or younger than age 30 or when accelerated hypertension develops in a patient with previously established, controlled hypertension. Additional features that suggest renal artery stenosis include persistent hypokalemia and metabolic alkalosis in the absence of diuretic therapy, symptoms or signs of peripheral vascular disease, unexplained progression of renal insufficiency, recurrent pulmonary edema, disparate renal size, and presence of an epigastric bruit on physical examination. Ischemic nephropathy should be considered in all patients older than age 60 years with unexplained progression of renal insufficiency, with or without hypertension. Deterioration of renal function after initiation of ACE inhibitor or ARB therapy suggests bilateral renal artery stenosis or stenosis in a single functioning kidney. Similarly, deterioration of renal function in a patient after successful kidney transplantation when ACE inhibitor or ARB therapy is initiated suggests stenosis in the transplanted renal artery. ACE inhibitor–induced renal failure is augmented by volume depletion and preexisting renal insufficiency and occurs within 1 to 14 days. Nevertheless, cessation of therapy most often is associated with reversal.

Diagnosis

The captopril renal scintigram (scan) is an excellent noninvasive function test for screening patients with suspected renal artery stenosis. Captopril renography has been most useful in patients with unilateral renal artery stenosis associated with hypertension and relative preservation of renal function (serum creatinine <2.0 mg/dL). This test is based on the assumption that angiotensin II–dependent constriction of the efferent arteriole is a physiologic prerequisite for maintaining GFR and renal blood flow in significant renal artery stenosis (see Fig. 124–1A, B). ACE inhibition usually is associated with decreased uptake of the nuclide, prolonged retention, or a longer time to peak on the affected side (see Fig. 124–1B) but may not be helpful in bilateral renal artery disease. Three-dimensional phase-contrast MRA compares favorably with conventional arteriography (sensitivity and specificity of 94% and 98% for stenoses >50%) and offers significant advantages over the captopril renal scintigram in the face of renal insufficiency (see Fig. 124–2C). Duplex scanning or color Doppler flowmetry relies on combined techniques to localize the renal arteries and estimate blood flow, but it is less sensitive and is highly sonographer dependent. Intravenous urography and split renal function testing no longer play a role in the investigation of hypertension or chronic renal failure. Although no single screening test is sufficiently sensitive and specific, in patients in whom stenosis is suspected, renal arteriography may be required to confirm the diagnosis and define the vascular anatomy before surgical or nonsurgical intervention and is considered the gold standard diagnostic test (see Fig. 124–1C).

The risk for contrast nephropathy and the risks of catheterization must be considered, especially in older patients with renal insufficiency. The renal sonogram is helpful in patients with ischemic renal disease and/or bilateral renal artery stenosis to establish renal size and cortical thickness, avoiding unnecessary intervention in far advanced disease. A major advantage of MRA is that there is not a risk for contrast nephropathy. Quality and interpretation vary widely among centers, however. Selective renal artery carbon dioxide or gadolinium angiography may be employed when the risk of renal failure is prohibitive. Low-osmolar contrast is recommended, as is intravenous saline administration in all patients at risk for contrast nephropathy. Acetylcysteine has been shown to decrease the incidence of contrast nephropathy in patients at risk (creatinine

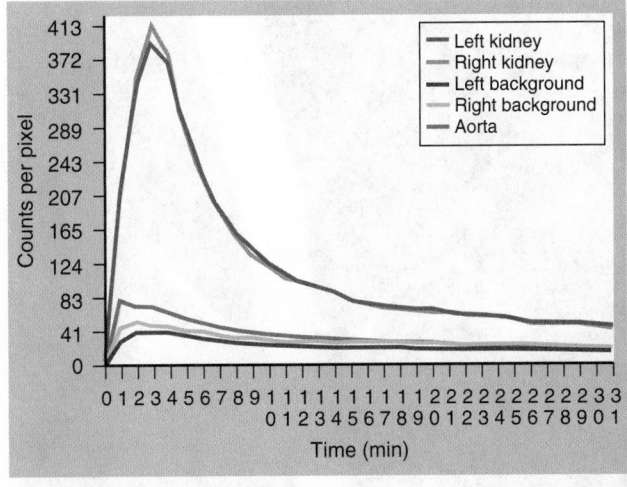

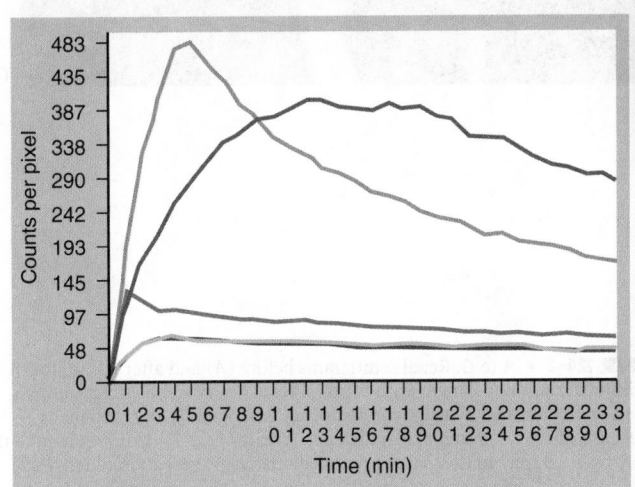

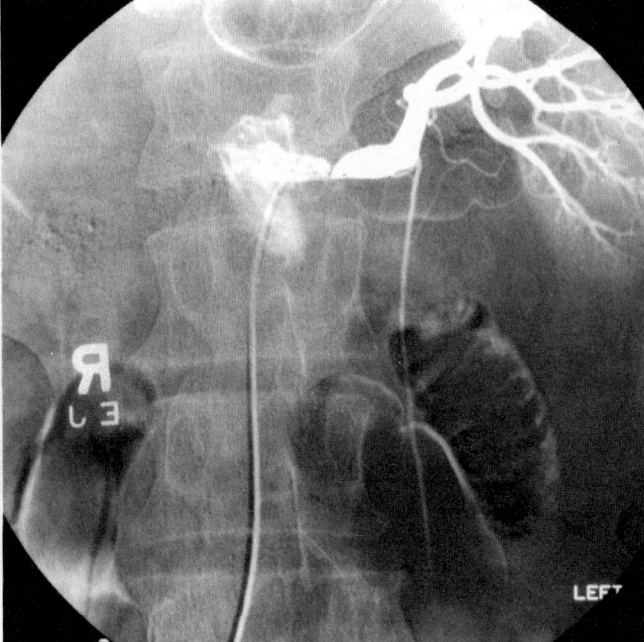

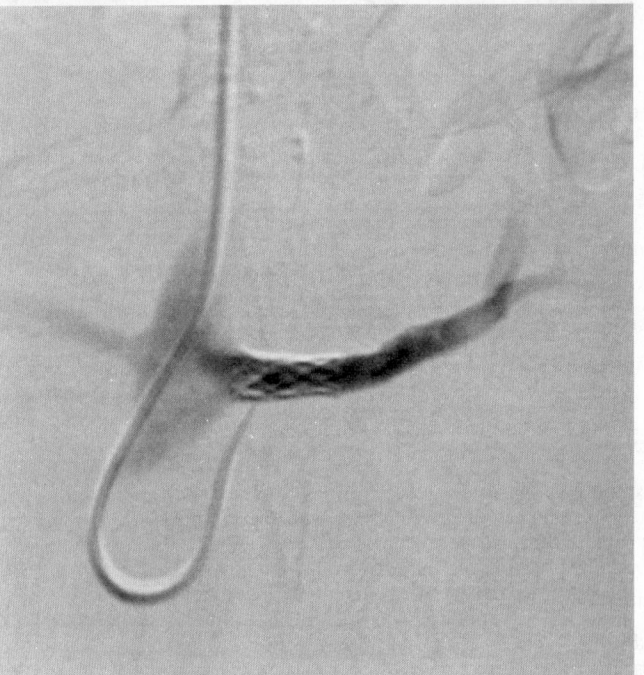

FIGURE 124–1 • *A*, A renal scintigram (scan) without captopril administration. The excretion curves for the left and the right kidneys overlap and appear normal. *B*, Study obtained 30 minutes after administration of captopril reveals marked delay in excretion of the nuclide by the left compared with the right kidney. *C*, The abnormal study shown in *B* combined with a strong clinical suspicion for renovascular hypertension led to selective renal arteriography, which clearly shows stenosis of the proximal left renal artery. *A*, *B*, and *C* are studies from the same patient. *D*, A renal artery stent immediately after placement in a similar patient with discrete unilateral renal artery stenosis.

>1.7 mg/dL). Peripheral vein renin determinations are not generally helpful in the diagnosis or management of renal artery stenosis. Renal vein renin determinations are not usually helpful for screening or diagnosis but may assist with planning the approach to therapy. In unilateral renal artery stenosis, the expected finding for clinically significant disease is a ratio of renin from the affected side to renin from the contralateral renal vein of greater than 1.5. Renin-sodium profiling, assessment of plasma renin activity after captopril administration, and the effect of ACE inhibitor therapy on blood pressure and renal function are not reliable in elderly patients because they do not have renin-dependent hypertension. This testing may be useful in fibromuscular dysplasia, however.

A reasonable diagnostic approach is to screen with a captopril scintigram when the creatinine level is less than 2.0 mg/dL and with MRA when it is greater than 2.0 mg/dL. Arteriography is performed if revascularization is anticipated (see Fig. 124–1*C*). If either test is normal or in the absence of a high degree of clinical suspicion, arteriography is not usually necessary.

Rx **Treatment**

The goal of therapy for renal artery stenosis is to control the blood pressure and stabilize renal function by restoration of renal perfusion. Because considerable controversy surrounds the issue of how best to treat presumed renal artery stenosis, patients should be managed cooperatively by a nephrologist, vascular surgeon, and interventional (vascular) radiologist. Therapeutic options include percutaneous transluminal renal angioplasty (PTRA), percutaneous transluminal renal artery stent placement (PTRAS) (see Fig. 124–1*D*), surgical revascularization, and conservative medical management. The use of aortorenal bypass has declined, whereas celiac or mesenteric to renal bypass has increased in frequency. Mortality is increased when azotemia or bilateral renal disease is present.

Continued

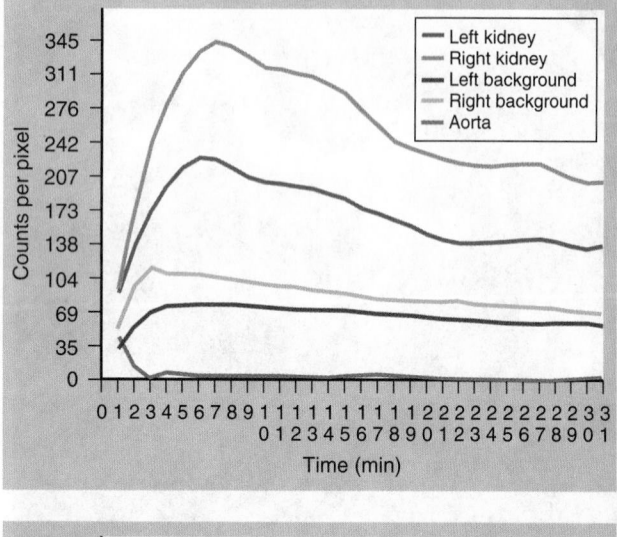

A

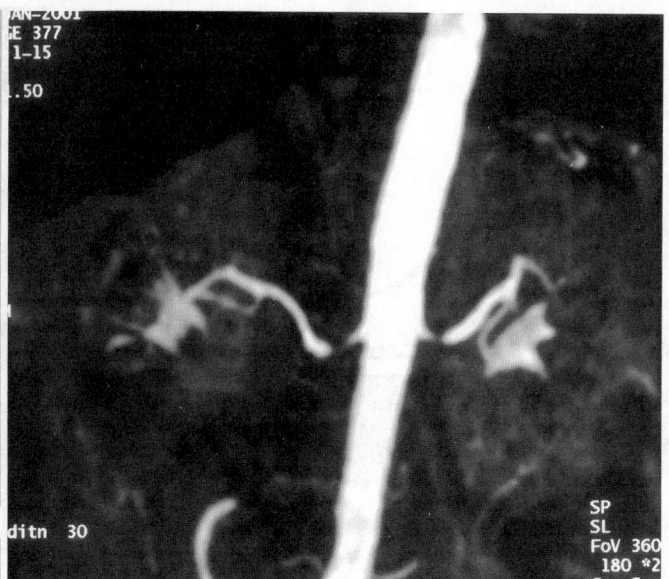

C

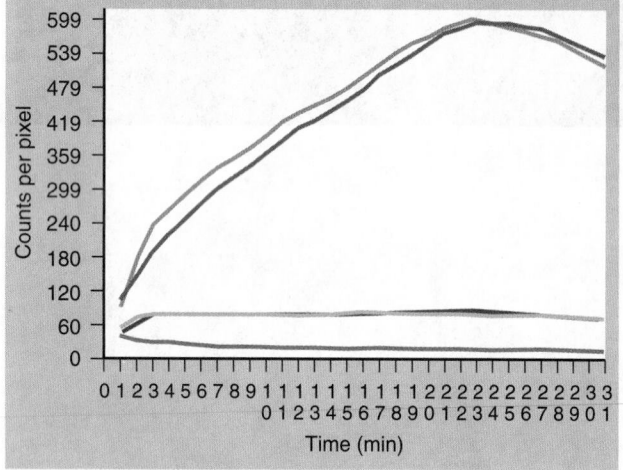

B

FIGURE 124–2 • *A* to *C*, Renal scintigrams before (*A*) and after (*B*) captopril administration in a patient with bilateral renal artery stenosis. This impression was confirmed by magnetic resonance angiography (*C*), obtained because of coexistent renal insufficiency (creatinine 2.1 mg/dL). Subsequent renal sonography in this patient revealed relative preservation of renal size and cortical thickness. Renal artery stenting was performed subsequently (not shown).

Conventional balloon angioplasty is considered the treatment of choice for patients with uncontrolled hypertension and fibromuscular dysplasia. Success rates of 82% to 100% have been reported with recurrence rates of only 10%. Balloon angioplasty is less effective for atherosclerotic renal artery stenosis. Failures can be attributed to complications such as dissection and the rigidity of the lesions, which results in recoil after dilation. Restenosis rates of 10 to 50% have been reported. Stenting or PTRAS is an attractive alternative to PTRA. Final diameter after intervention is an important predictor of the risk for restenosis. Accordingly, follow-up with duplex ultrasonography to assess patency is necessary. Conservative medical management, as primary therapy, was shown in a large multicenter study to compare favorably with angioplasty in patients with hypertension and arterosclerotic renal artery disease but without significant renal failure, according to intention-to-treat criteria at 12 months' follow-up.

Conservative medical management is a crucial component of the continuing care of all patients with atherosclerotic renal artery disease after surgery or PTRA. Medical management includes cessation of smoking, weight loss, exercise, strict blood pressure control with skillful agent selection, and aggressive treatment with lipid-lowering agents. In smaller and less well-controlled studies, endovascular revascularization of renal artery stenosis has been shown to be safe and effective as an alternative to surgical management. PTRA or PTRS is often considered to be the treatment of choice for fibromuscular dysplasia and atherosclerotic renal artery stenosis in many centers, when blood pressure cannot be controlled with at least three antihypertensive agents, or when renal function declines progressively.

Prognosis

PTRA is clearly the initial treatment of choice for hypertension caused by fibromuscular dysplasia inasmuch as the initial success rate for PTRA is high and the restenosis rate is low. PTRA is less effective in atherosclerotic renal artery stenosis if normalization of blood pressure is the outcome to be achieved. Of patients, 50% or more benefit to some extent by improvement in blood pressure. Although PTRA is associated with improved renal function in a significant percentage of patients with sufficient residual renal mass, these observations are based on uncontrolled studies in small series of patients. The progressive nature of atherosclerotic renal artery disease must be taken into consideration when outcomes are assessed. Studies of the ability of revascularization to preserve renal function are severely limited by the small numbers of patients studied, the brief follow-up period, and the uncertainty of outcomes measured. An elevated baseline creatinine is one of the most important independent risk factors for death after renal stenting on longer term follow-up.

Renal function improves with successful percutaneous revascularization in some patients and may delay the necessity for renal replacement therapy by many years. Causes of renal deterioration include volume depletion, contrast nephropathy, and renal embolization. The use of distal balloons to reduce the risk of renal embolization may improve outcomes in the future. In the event that angioplasty fails, PTRAS or surgical revascularization should be considered, but the patient's age and suitability as a surgical candidate must be considered. The risk of surgical reconstruction in younger patients, such as patients with fibromuscular dysplasia, is low. Operative mortality, which is limited to patients with atherosclerosis, has been reported to be 2 to 7%. The risk of surgery is highest in older patients with azotemia, generalized atherosclerosis, and cerebrovascular and cardiac disease.

ARTERIOLES AND MICROVASCULATURE

ATHEROEMBOLIC DISEASE OF THE RENAL ARTERIES

Definition and Etiology

Embolization of cholesterol crystals as a cause of renal artery occlusion occurs almost exclusively in elderly patients with widespread atherosclerosis. Atheroemboli also may occur as a complication of abdominal aorta or renal artery manipulation or surgery or as a consequence of angiography or transluminal angioplasty. This entity may be overlooked because patients at risk for this complication often have other chronic illnesses associated with renal failure, hypertension, and atherosclerosis.

Clinical Manifestations

Renal insufficiency and/or hypertension occur regularly with atheroembolization to the renal vasculature. Evidence of cholesterol embolization in the retina, muscles, or skin (associated with livedo reticularis) can be helpful and obviate the need for a renal biopsy. Evidence of embolization to other organs resulting in cerebrovascular events, acute pancreatitis, ischemic bowel, and gangrene of the extremities may be noted. Urinalysis may not be helpful because cholesterol crystals are not usually present, but mild proteinuria, eosinophiluria, and increased cellularity more often are observed.

Rx Treatment

Therapy for this disorder is often disappointing inasmuch as cholesterol embolization leads to structural changes in the microvasculature without inflammation. Anticoagulants have not proved to be of value and may delay healing of ulcerating atherosclerotic lesions. Dialysis, treating the hypertension with attention to avoiding hypotension, and adequate hydration are the mainstays of treatment.

Prognosis

With adequate blood pressure control for several months or years, renal function may recover sufficiently, even in patients requiring long-term renal replacement therapy, to allow nondialytic conservative management.

HYPERTENSIVE ARTERIOLAR NEPHROSCLEROSIS

Definition and Etiology

Although autoregulation of renal blood flow and GFR occurs throughout a wide range of systemic blood pressure, the renal vasculature is exquisitely sensitive to damage incurred by systemic hypertension when it is transmitted to the glomerular capillary bed (Chapter 111). Unopposed or sustained increases in glomerular capillary hydrostatic pressure eventually result in sclerosis. In *benign nephrosclerosis*, the kidney is the victim of the adverse effects of chronic hypertension over a prolonged period and does not appear to participate in the pathogenesis of the disorder. The vascular injury in the kidney is nonspecific but more pronounced than vascular changes observed systemically. When advanced, these changes can result in end-stage renal disease (ESRD). In *malignant* or *accelerated hypertension,* the vascular changes are unique and severe and lead to renal ischemia, renin production, and exacerbation of the disease, which may terminate in acute renal failure and, if not treated successfully, ESRD. In contrast to benign nephrosclerosis, in which the principal lesion is in the media of the vessels, a unique lesion of the intima characterizes malignant or accelerated hypertension. Renal vascular lesions similar to lesions seen in malignant hypertension also are observed in scleroderma, thrombotic microangiopathy, and renal transplant rejection.

Clinical Manifestations

Patients with benign hypertensive nephrosclerosis have been hypertensive for many years (>10 to 15 years). Kidney size is usually reduced, and the urine sediment is unremarkable except for proteinuria, which is usually less than 1.5 g/day. The sudden development of malignant or accelerated hypertension, in patients with previously established mild-to-moderate hypertension or patients in whom hypertension had not been diagnosed previously, is manifested by an abrupt increase in blood pressure (diastolic usually >130 mm Hg). Papilledema may develop, and renal function may decline rapidly. The kidneys may be enlarged, or the urinary sediment may be active, with gross or microscopic hematuria, and proteinuria is often in the nephrotic range. Microangiopathic hemolytic anemia may be present. Abnormalities in the central nervous system are usually evident and range from headaches to generalized seizures to coma. Malignant hypertension may coexist with cerebrovascular accidents.

The availability of effective antihypertensive medication has reduced sharply the occurrence of this devastating disorder. Benign and malignant hypertensive renal disease and the sequelae of these disorders seem to be more prevalent in blacks.

Rx Treatment

For either benign or malignant hypertension, the primary goal is to control the blood pressure. In benign hypertensive nephrosclerosis, the renal outcome depends on timely initiation of effective therapy, patient compliance, and careful follow-up by a nephrologist. Inadequate treatment may result in irreversible glomerular sclerosis and end-organ damage in the cardiovasculature and central nervous system. Antihypertensives that provide renal protection include ACE inhibitors and ARBs. Even nondihydropyridine calcium channel blockers do not afford protection from progression of renal insufficiency and should be used only in patients who cannot tolerate ACE inhibitor or ARB therapy. Malignant hypertension, by contrast, is a medical emergency and must be approached aggressively. Controlling the blood pressure can reverse the major manifestations in most patients, including the renal functional impairment. Parenteral antihypertensives, such as nitroprusside infused in the critical care setting, may be necessary initially. Blood pressure should be controlled smoothly and gradually but be in the normal range by 36 to 48 hours. Antihypertensive medications should be continued even if renal function continues to deteriorate and renal replacement therapy is required. Some patients experience partial reversal of vascular lesions and return of renal function to levels compatible with nondialytic, conservative management.

Prognosis

With skillful selection of renal-specific antihypertensive agents (ACE inhibitor and ARB therapy) and obsessive control of blood pressure, progression of renal disease can be avoided. Hypertension with nephrosclerosis is the second most common cause of ESRD in the United States. The importance of early recognition and aggressive treatment cannot be overemphasized.

HEMOLYTIC-UREMIC SYNDROME AND THROMBOTIC THROMBOCYTOPENIC PURPURA

Definition and Etiology

Renal failure is a common consequence of hemolytic-uremic syndrome (HUS) and thrombotic thrombocytopenic purpura (TTP). For additional information, see Chapters 116 and 117. These conditions are characterized by platelet and fibrin thrombi within the renal microvasculature, accompanied by thrombocytopenia and microangiopathic hemolytic anemia. Although the vascular lesions are identical, central venous system involvement predominates in TTP, whereas renal involvement is predominant in HUS.

Clinical Manifestations

TTP is suggested by the co-occurrence of hemolysis, thrombocytopenia, fever, purpura, and alternating mental status changes. HUS may be associated with acute renal failure, thrombocytopenia, and microangiopathic hemolytic anemia, most commonly in children after an acute diarrheal illness. Either disorder may be observed in the setting of cancer and infection and during administration of chemotherapeutic agents.

Treatment and Prognosis

Acute implementation of renal replacement therapy has improved survival significantly. The oliguria, degree of renal failure, and severity of hypertension are more pronounced in HUS. Early diagnosis and initiation of dialysis, antihypertensives, supportive transfusions, and control of seizures are essential to a good outcome. Of children with typical HUS, 85% recover with supportive care. For TTP, plasma exchange combined with antiplatelet therapy is recommended and may be required for 1 to 2 weeks.

SCLERODERMA

Clinical Manifestations

The clinical features and progression of scleroderma are highly variable. The various limited skin and systemic manifestations of scleroderma are considered in more detail in Chapter 281. Although it is widely appreciated that the mortality associated with scleroderma increases as a function of the number of organ systems involved, significant renal involvement (which has been reported in 50% of patients with systemic sclerosis of ≥20 years' duration) is the most dreaded complication and is associated with the poorest prognosis. When the kidneys are involved, the typical manifestation is intimal proliferation, medial thinning, and increased collagen deposition in the adventitial layer of small renal arteries. An increase in vasomotor tone at the level of the renal vasculature is probably a renal manifestation of Raynaud's phenomenon and contributes to the reduction in renal blood flow, hypertension, and progressive renal functional impairment. The increase in renin and angiotensin II elaboration contributes to the development of worsening hypertension and hypertensive nephrosclerosis. Most patients with renal scleroderma display mild proteinuria with or without hypertension. When azotemia develops, hypertension may become more difficult to manage, and dialysis is required within 1 to 2 years. Conversely, patients initially may come to medical attention with a "renal crisis" manifested by the abrupt onset of malignant hypertension and renal failure. This manifestation, which occurs in 10 to 25% of patients with type 3 scleroderma, usually of several years' duration, is a medical emergency requiring aggressive antihypertensive therapy.

Treatment and Prognosis

Therapy in patients with scleroderma and renal involvement should be directed primarily toward controlling hypertension in an attempt to slow progression of the renal failure. Referral to a nephrologist is highly recommended. Adequate control may require several drugs in combination, such as ACE inhibitors or angiotensin II receptor antagonists, nondihydropyridine calcium channel blockers, and vasodilators (e.g., minoxidil) and other agents. For patients with manifestations of a renal crisis, intravenous antihypertensive therapy in the critical care setting may be indicated because of the high mortality without therapy. With aggressive management, particularly with ACE inhibitors, progression to ESRD may be slowed significantly. Even in the event that long-term maintenance dialysis is required, there is evidence that with continued aggressive management of hypertension, a small but significant percentage of patients regains sufficient renal function to allow cessation of renal replacement therapy.

SICKLE CELL NEPHROPATHY

Etiology

The hypoxemic and hypertonic environment of the renal medulla (vasa recta) encourages the sickling of red blood cells circulating through this region (Chapter 171). When sickle hemoglobin desaturates, polymerization of hemoglobin can impair or interrupt capillary flow. The major manifestations of sickle cell nephropathy all can be explained by the development of papillary infarction.

Clinical Manifestations

A defect in urinary concentration resulting in a tendency toward volume depletion is one of the best-characterized abnormalities in sickle cell nephropathy. Obliteration of the vasa recta compromises the operation of the medullary countercurrent system and impairs the ability to generate and maintain medullary solute gradients. The concentrating defect also is observed in sickle trait. A defect in urinary acidification is common and manifested as distal renal tubular acidosis with hyperkalemia and hyperchloremic metabolic acidosis (type 4 renal tubular acidosis). The acidification defect usually is not observed in patients with sickle trait. Painless gross hematuria has been estimated to occur in 50% of patients with sickle cell nephropathy. It also occurs in patients with hemoglobin SA or hemoglobin SC. With recurrent papillary infarction, papillary necrosis can occur and progress. Sickle cell "crisis," dehydration, hypoxemia, and the use of nonsteroidal anti-inflammatory drugs predispose to papillary necrosis. Renal papillary necrosis is often "silent," but it may progress to chronic renal insufficiency and predispose the patient to repeated urinary tract infections. Nephrotic syndrome may occur in approximately 4% of patients with sickle glomerulopathy. Findings on renal biopsy usually indicate membranoproliferative glomerulopathy with segmental and global sclerosis. As this disorder progresses, glomerulopathy results in sclerosis and progressive loss of glomerular function, whereas papillary infarction can result in persistent hematuria.

Treatment

Volume depletion should be corrected by isotonic or hypotonic saline intravenously, as dictated by the serum sodium concentration. Hyperkalemia may require potassium exchange resin (sodium polystyrene [Kayexalate]) per rectum or orally. When acidosis accompanies the hyperkalemia, alkali may help correct the hyperkalemia and the acidosis. Long-term administration of Shohl's solution or sodium bicarbonate tablets may be necessary, and loop diuretics may be helpful. Potassium-sparing diuretics, nonsteroidal anti-inflammatory drugs, or potassium supplements should be strictly avoided. Attempts to increase medullary blood flow and reduce medullary tonicity, including the use of distilled water, sodium bicarbonate, and diuretics such as mannitol or loop diuretics, may alleviate the hematuria. Rarely, small doses of ε-aminocaproic acid may be necessary for life-threatening hematuria but can result in thrombosis or ureteral obstruction.

RENAL VEINS

RENAL VEIN THROMBOSIS

Etiology

Unilateral or bilateral thrombosis of the major renal veins or their segments is a common but often subtle disorder that may develop in a variety of conditions. The serious risk for thromboembolic complications and vascular occlusion underscores the need for accurate and timely diagnosis and therapy. The disparate causes of renal vein thrombosis are outlined in Table 124–2. The reported incidence of renal vein thrombosis in patients with nephrotic syndrome is striking, ranging from 5 to 62%. Although some series emphasize a stronger association with membranous nephropathy, a prospective study of 26 patients with nephrotic syndrome showed an association of renal vein thrombosis with a variety of glomerulopathies, including membra-

Table 124–2 • CAUSES OF RENAL VEIN THROMBOSIS

Nephrotic syndrome
Renal cell carcinoma with renal vein invasion
Pregnancy or estrogen therapy
Volume depletion (especially in infants)
Extrinsic compression (lymph nodes, tumor, retroperitoneal fibrosis, aortic aneurysm)

noproliferative, membranous, and proliferative glomerulonephritis and focal glomerular sclerosis. Renal vein thrombosis also has been reported in patients with sickle cell nephropathy, amyloidosis, diabetic nephropathy, renal vasculitis, lupus nephritis, and allograft rejection. Predisposing factors include abnormalities in coagulation or fibrinolysis, and attention has focused on components of clotting parameters in the blood or urine of patients with nephrotic syndrome. Antithrombin III levels are depressed as a result of loss of antithrombin III in the urine of nephrotic patients, and the association between low antithrombin III levels and renal vein thrombosis has been reported in some but not all studies. Circulating levels of proteins S and C also may be altered in nephrotic syndrome and contribute to the tendency toward thromboembolic complications. Renal vein thrombosis in infancy usually occurs in the setting of severe volume depletion and impaired renal blood flow. Extrinsic compression from retroperitoneal sources, such as lymph nodes, retroperitoneal fibrosis, abscess, aortic aneurysm, or tumor, may lead to renal vein thrombosis as a result of sluggish renal venous flow. Acute pancreatitis, trauma, and retroperitoneal surgery also may predispose to renal vein thrombosis. Renal cell carcinoma characteristically invades the renal vein and compromises venous flow, resulting in renal vein thrombosis.

Clinical Manifestations

The manifestations of renal vein thrombosis depend on the extent and rapidity of the development of renal venous occlusion. Patients with acute renal vein thrombosis may have nausea, vomiting, flank pain, leukocytosis, hematuria, renal function compromise, and an increase in renal size. Adult nephrotic patients with chronic renal vein thrombosis may have more subtle findings, such as a dramatic increase in proteinuria or evidence of tubule dysfunction, including glycosuria, aminoaciduria, phosphaturia, and impaired urinary acidification.

Diagnosis

Supportive data may be provided by noninvasive studies such as MRA. Doppler ultrasound is not adequately sensitive for segmental thrombosis. The diagnosis is established by selective renal venography. Evidence of parenchymal edema—stretching of calyces and notching of the ureters—on intravenous pyelography is much less reliable.

Rx Treatment

The most widely accepted form of therapy for acute and chronic renal vein thrombosis is anticoagulation with heparin, which can be converted to oral warfarin (Coumadin) after 7 to 10 days and maintained long-term. Therapy usually is continued for at least 1 year. In patients with recurrence or continued risk factors, anticoagulation might be continued indefinitely. In a pediatric patient with volume depletion and acute renal vein thrombosis, attention to restoration of fluid and electrolyte balance is essential. Fibrinolytic therapy might be considered in patients with acute renal vein thrombosis associated with acute renal failure.

1. Nordmann AJ, Woo K, Parkes R, et al: Balloon angioplasty or medical therapy for hypertensive patients with atherosclerotic renal artery stenosis? A meta-analysis of randomized controlled trials. Am J Med 2003;114:44–50.

SUGGESTED READINGS
Edwards MS, Hansen KJ, Craven TE, et al: Relationships between renovascular disease, blood pressure, and renal function in the elderly: A population-based study. Am J Kidney Dis 2003;41:990–996. *Multivariate analyses showed significant and independent associations of renovascular disease with increasing systolic blood pressure, increasing serum creatinine levels, and renal insufficiency.*
Goto A, Kawauchi N: Images in clinical medicine. Captopril-augmented renal scan. N Engl J Med 2001;344:430. *Part of the Images in Clinical Medicine Series. A picture is worth a thousand words.*
Matthews GJ, Hall S: Images in clinical medicine. Renal-vein thrombosis. N Engl J Med 2000;343:701. *Also part of the Images in Clinical Medicine Series.*
Muller BT, Reiher L, Pfeiffer T, et al: Surgical treatment of renal artery dissection in 25 patients: Indications and results. J Vasc Surg 2003;37:761–768. *Surgical revascularization is effective in the absence of renal infarction or a major decline in renal function.*
Radermacher J, Chavan A, Bleck J, et al: Use of Doppler ultrasonography to predict the outcome of therapy for renal-artery stenosis. N Engl J Med 2001;344:410–417. *Patients with a resistance index value of at least 80 did not show improvement in renal function, renal survival, or blood pressure with angioplasty or surgery.*
Safian RD, Textor SC: Renal-artery stenosis. N Engl J Med 2001;344:431–442. *A comprehensive evaluation of diagnosis and treatment.*
Turi ZG, Jaff MR: Renal artery stenosis: Searching for the algorithms for diagnosis and treatment. J Am Coll Cardiol 2003;41:1312–1315. *A brief evidence-based review.*

125 HEREDITARY CHRONIC NEPHROPATHIES: GLOMERULAR BASEMENT MEMBRANE DISEASES

Manuel Martinez-Maldonado

This chapter discusses three disorders: Alport's syndrome, the nail-patella syndrome (NPS), and benign familial hematuria (BFH), also called *thin basement membrane nephropathy*, all of which are or may be caused by defects in type IV collagen. Some hereditary disorders of renal tubular function are described in Chapter 122. Other genetic disorders that may be associated with renal disease are listed in Table 125–1 and discussed in Part XVI, Metabolic Diseases.

ALPORT'S SYNDROME

Definition

Alport's syndrome, or chronic hereditary nephritis, is characterized by the familial occurrence in successive generations of a progressive nephritis that is more severe in males, manifested invariably by hematuria, and frequently associated with a sensorineural hearing deficit.

Genetics

The mode of transmission in most kindreds is consistent with X-linked dominant inheritance; mutations in *COL4A5*, a gene located in Xq22 that codes for the α5 chain of type IV collagen, are responsible (see Table 125–1 for further details). Deletions also occur and tend to result in more severe renal disease and more severe hearing loss. Alport's disease is termed *juvenile* when early onset occurs in males and termed *adult* when renal failure occurs in middle age. Juvenile kindreds tend to be small and frequently arise from new mutations; adult kindreds are large and exhibit few new mutations.

Table 125–1 • MOLECULAR GENETICS OF ALPORT'S SYNDROME

INHERITANCE	LOCUS	CHROMOSOME	AFFECTED GENE PRODUCT
X-linked dominant	COL4A5	X	α5(IV)
X-linked dominant + leiomyomatosis	COL4A5 + COL4A6	X	α5(IV) + α6(IV)
Autosomal recessive	COL4A3	2	α3(IV)
	COL4A4	2	α4(IV)
Autosomal dominant*	COL4A3[†]	2	α3(IV)[†]
	COL4A4[†]	2	α4(IV)[†]

*Small number of patients.
[†]Not fully worked out.

Table 125–2 • CLINICAL AND GENETIC CHARACTERISTICS OF THE INHERITED GLOMERULAR BASEMENT MEMBRANE DISEASES

CHARACTERISTIC	ALPORT'S SYNDROME	NAIL-PATELLA SYNDROME	BENIGN FAMILIAL HEMATURIA
Inheritance	85% X-linked; approximately 15% autosomal dominant; autosomal recessive (rare)	Autosomal dominant	Autosomal dominant
Clinical findings	Hematuria (100%)*—dysmorphic RBCs are common, especially after exercise or respiratory infection; proteinuria (70%), nephrotic range, 30-40%; sensorineural hearing loss,[†] anterior lenticonus, perimacular flecks (15-40%); thrombocytopathia (rare): thrombocytopenia with giant platelets, bruising, epistaxis, gastrointestinal bleeding, prolonged bleeding time; leiomyomatosis (rare)	Hematuria (33%),* proteinuria (42%), nail hypoplasia (98%); patellar aplasia/hypoplasia (90%); "iliac horns" (80%); elbow deformities (90%); Lester's sign (50%)[‡]	Term BFH should be used for familial, nonprogressive hematuria (100%) that may be lifelong. Hypertension, proteinuria, and ESDR unusual; extrarenal manifestations rare; no gender differences. TBMN patients may exhibit proteinuria, hypertension, and renal insufficiency
Histology	Thickened GBM up to 3× normal with splitting of the lamina densa ("basket weave" appearance) by electron microscopy is pathognomonic. Glomerular crescents may be found in the juvenile form. Electron-dense deposits of the immune complex type are absent	Light microscopy shows glomerular, cellular proliferation; mesangial sclerosis; and basement membrane thickening. Electron microscopy reveals areas of rarefaction in the lamina densa of the GBM filled with bundles of curvilinear fibrils having the typical periodicity of collagen (moth-eaten appearance)	Thin GBM with attenuation of the lamina densa that persists over time; does not undergo the progressive thickening and multilamellation pathognomonic of Alport's syndrome
Clinical course	Males: all progress to ESRD, hypertension, azotemia; predilection for those with massive proteinuria. Females: usually do not progress to ESRD, some may exhibit decline in renal function during pregnancy	Kidney involvement in 40% of patients; 28% reach ESRD by age 33 yr	Rarely progresses to ESRD

*Prevalence of clinical finding.
[†]May require audiometric testing and may progress to clinical deafness; high-frequency range, 4000 to 8000 Hz, 40% to 60% of patients, predominantly in males (81% male; 19% female). Tinnitus is present in some cases.
[‡]Lester's sign: heterochromia of the iris. The pale appearance of the outer zone of the iris in contrast to a darker central portion results in a "cloverleaf" arrangement. BFH = benign familial hematuria; ESRD = end-stage renal disease; GBM = glomerular basement membrane; RBCs = red blood cells; TBMN = thin-basement-membrane nephropathy.

Incidence and Prevalence

Several hundred kindreds of all races and geographic origins exist. With an incidence of approximately 1 in 5000 people, Alport's syndrome accounts for nearly 5% of patients with end-stage renal disease.

Pathology and Pathogenesis

Normal or large kidneys may exist at the onset, but they shrink with progression of the disease. Although glomeruli may be normal (light microscopy), hypertrophy of epithelial cells and an increase in mesangial matrix may be seen (Table 125–2).

The cause of Alport's syndrome seems to be the absence of a 28-kD peptide component of the noncollagenous (NC1) domain of the α3 chain of type IV collagen in the glomerular basement membrane. This peptide is also called the *Goodpasture antigen* (see later).

Clinical Manifestations

Alport's syndrome is discovered in 70% of patients by age 6 years; the rest of the cases are discovered at any age thereafter up to and well into adulthood. Persistent or intermittent microscopic hematuria, sensorineural hearing loss, and ocular disorders are typical of the syndrome (see Table 125–2).

Diagnosis

Progressive renal disease in a patient with hematuria and the aforementioned clinical features suggest Alport's syndrome. If these features are found in a family member—other than the proband—or in a relative younger than age 50 years, the diagnosis is probable. The diagnosis is established if monoclonal antibodies to α3, α4, and α5 chains of type IV collagen show absence of these chains from glomerular basement membrane and distal tubule basement membrane in a kidney biopsy specimen. Expression of α5 (IV) on a skin biopsy in a male with a history suggesting X-linked Alport's syndrome may obviate the need for kidney biopsy, but a normal result does not exclude the diagnosis. Skin biopsy is the first diagnostic step if risks exist against performing kidney biopsy. The differential diagnosis is shown in Table 125–3.

 Treatment

No specific treatment is available for Alport's syndrome, and no therapy exists to alter its course. Control of hypertension is necessary. Peritoneal dialysis or hemodialysis and related or cadaveric donor kidney transplantation have been used with degrees of success that match the results obtained in other renal disorders. Improvement of the hearing deficit and no recurrence of the renal lesion have been observed after transplantation. Goodpasture's syndrome has developed in the renal graft of 3% to 4% of transplanted males with deafness, and end-stage renal disease has developed before age 30, within the first year after transplantation. This is the result of an antibody directed against the basement membrane antigen that is absent in Alport's syndrome (see earlier). Genetic counseling may be useful but is complicated in view of the genetic heterogeneity of Alport's syndrome.

Table 125–3 • DIFFERENTIAL DIAGNOSIS OF ALPORT'S SYNDROME

CONDITION	CHARACTERISTICS
Benign familial hematuria	Nonprogressive disorder, uniformly thin glomerular basement membrane
Berger's disease	IgA nephropathy; mesangial proliferative glomerulonephritis with mesangial deposits of IgA and variable amounts of C3, IgM, or IgG; strong IgA immunofluorescence in mesangial regions

NAIL-PATELLA SYNDROME

Also called *osteo-onychodysplasia*, NPS is characterized by atrophic or absent fingernails, hypoplasia or aplasia of the patella, and other bone anomalies. Table 125–2 summarizes the mode of inheritance and the clinical findings in NPS. The *COL5A1* gene, which encodes the pro α1(V) chain of fibrillar type V collagen, has been located within the segment 9q34.2 to 9q34.3, which places the gene near the NPS locus, which also maps to 9q34; it is not clear whether the *COL5A1* gene is aberrant in NPS. Alteration of the LIM-homeodomain protein *Lmx1b*, disruption of which leads to skeletal defects and renal dysplasia in animals, has been implicated in NPS. The *LMX1B* gene maps to the NPS locus, and de novo heterozygous mutations in this gene have been found in NPS patients. No specific therapy exists for this disorder. Renal transplantation has been done without evidence of recurrence of the disease in the transplanted organ. An enzyme deficient in NPS (e.g., adenylate kinase) may be replenished by transplantation because dystrophic nails have grown back completely post-transplant.

BENIGN FAMILIAL HEMATURIA

BFH also is known erroneously as *thin basement membrane nephropathy*, but thin basement membrane nephropathy is descriptive of several disorders that differ molecularly. BFH is characterized by thinning of the basement membrane and normal renal function. Genetic and clinical characteristics are listed in Table 125–2. A glycine-to-glutamic acid substitution has been identified in the collagenous region of the *COL4A4* gene, but BFH is genetically heterogeneous. Patients with BFH can be carriers of autosomal recessive Alport's syndrome.

SUGGESTED READINGS

Heidet L, Bongers EM, Sich M, et al: In vivo expression of putative LMX1B targets in nail-patella syndrome kidneys. Am J Pathol 2003;163:145–155. *NPS is inherited as an autosomal dominant trait and caused by heterozygous loss of function mutations in LMX1B, a member of the LIM homeodomain protein family.*

Hudson BG, Tryggvason K, Sundaramoorthy M, et al: Alport's syndrome, Goodpasture's syndrome, and type IV collagen. N Engl J Med 2003;348:2543–2556. *A comprehensive overview.*

Ishiguro C, Yaguchi Y, Funabiki K, et al: Serum IgA/C3 ratio may predict diagnosis and prognostic grading in patients with IgA nephropathy. Nephron 2002;91:755–758. *The serum IgA/C3 ratio appears to increase according to the prognostic grading, and its measurement may be useful for diagnosis and prognosis.*

Lemmink HH, Nillesen WN, Mochizuki T, et al: Benign familial hematuria due to mutation of the type IV collagen α4 gene. J Clin Invest 1996;98:1114–1118. *First demonstration of a genetic defect of type IV collagen in thin basement membrane disease.*

Liapis H, Gokden N, Hmiel P, et al: Histopathology, ultrastructure, and clinical phenotypes in thin glomerular basement membrane disease variants. Hum Pathol 2002;33:836–845. *A practical review.*

126 RENAL CALCULI (NEPHROLITHIASIS)

Irmantas Juknevicius
Keith A. Hruska

Epidemiology

A kidney stone is a crystalline mass occurring within the urinary tract that has achieved a size such that it causes symptoms or is visible on imaging studies. It has been estimated that about 12% of U.S. men and 5% of U.S. women have at least one kidney stone by the age of 70. Nephrolithiasis is a major cause of morbidity in the United States, and it is becoming an increasing problem in Western Europe, Japan, and other industrialized countries. In underdeveloped countries, stone disease is more common in children and primarily manifests as bladder stones composed of uric acid. In the developed nations, nephrolithiasis occurs in adults and is seen in the upper urinary tract as calcium stones. This change in presentation has been attributed to changes in diet with a direct relationship between the level of affluence and dietary protein intake. The economic impact of the morbidity associated with kidney stones is related to surgical extraction or fragmentation and loss of productivity. Kidney stones are two to three times more common in men than women and are distinctly uncommon in African Americans and Asians. There is also a geographic distribution of nephrolithiasis with the highest incidence in the southeastern United States. Kidney stones are becoming more frequent in the pediatric population, and in that population the preceding epidemiologic statements may not hold true.

General Clinical Considerations

The pain associated with passing a kidney stone is referred to as *renal colic*. It begins suddenly and quickly becomes an unbearable pain that may cause nausea and vomiting. The distribution of the pain resembles that of the path of the stone to the bladder, beginning in the flank and curving anteriorly toward the groin. Urinary frequency and dysuria occur as the stone reaches the ureterovesical junction. When the stone passes into the bladder or moves in the ureter to decompress the urinary system, the pain vanishes. Unique symptoms develop when the stone passes into the urethra.

Hematuria from nephrolithiasis is common and disturbing to patients. Occasionally, the hematuria is associated with flank pain without detectable obstruction. Nephrolithiasis may be associated with obstructive uropathy (Chapter 121), especially if the stone is not painful and remains undetected for long periods. Obstruction predisposes to infection, especially in women.

Radiologic techniques are used to diagnose stone disease. The radiographic appearance of stones may help identify stone type and guide further evaluation. Calcium phosphate and calcium oxalate stones are radiodense, and struvite (magnesium ammonium phosphate), when it complexes with calcium carbonate or phosphate, is also visible. Cystine stones are usually poorly visualized, and uric acid stones are radiolucent, requiring computed tomography (CT), ultrasonography, or intravenous urography for detection.

The application of helical noncontrast CT for the evaluation of suspected renal colic has been one of the major radiologic advances. It has replaced intravenous urography as the initial step in evaluating patients with suspected renal colic. Because of its superior sensitivity and specificity, it allows nephrolithiasis to be excluded or confirmed expeditiously and without administration of potentially nephrotoxic radiocontrast material. Intravenous urography can also be used as the first step in evaluating patients with renal colic, although there is concern regarding use of this test in patients with renal insufficiency. It is the most useful test to define the degree and extent of urinary tract obstruction.

Renal ultrasonography, which is the safest approach, is useful to rule out significant hydronephrosis or hydroureter; however, it may not detect stones unless they are relatively large. Ultrasonography does not delineate the site of obstruction.

Retrograde pyelography allows visualization of the urinary tract without intravenously administering contrast dye. This test requires cystoscopy and is usually performed during endourologic procedures or when intravenous pyelography is contraindicated (in patients with renal insufficiency or contrast dye allergy).

CT scanning is the modality most useful for defining radiolucent stones not detectable by other means. Pure uric acid stones and, in some cases, cystine stones can be identified by CT scanning with or without contrast material.

TREATING RENAL COLIC

Treatment should focus on relieving pain and urinary tract obstruction. A stepwise scheme for management of renal colic is presented in Figure 126–1. Careful analgesic therapy, hydration, and radiologic assessment are the cornerstones. If significant obstruction is detected, the patient is observed during hydration for movement of the stone. If evidence does not suggest that the stone will pass within 2 to 3 days, urologic intervention is indicated. Stones lodged in the ureteropelvic junction or in the proximal ureter are best pushed into the renal pelvis and disrupted by extracorporeal shock wave lithotripsy (ESWL). Moving the stone backward requires cystoscopy and passing a catheter up the ureter. If the stone cannot be pushed back, it can be bypassed with a stent to provide drainage and disrupted in situ with ESWL. Percutaneous nephrolithotomy is required if lithotripsy fails. Surgical ureterolithotomy is largely an operative procedure of the past.

Stones that are smaller than 2 cm but larger than 5 mm in diameter are best treated with ESWL alone. Stones larger than 2 cm or those larger than 1 cm and in the lower poles may be best treated with percutaneous nephrostolithotomy because with lithotripsy alone residual stones are left in 35 to 50% of cases. Percutaneous

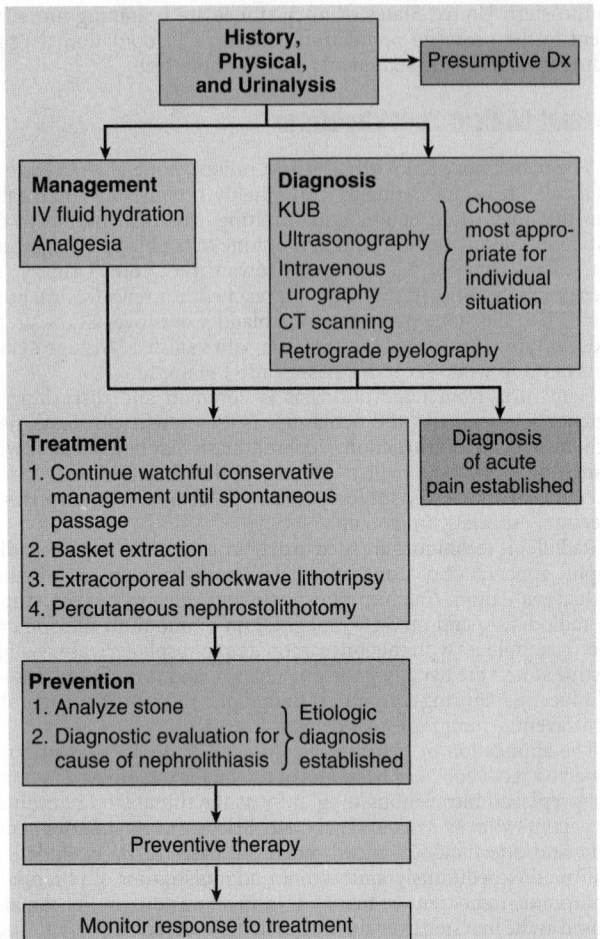

FIGURE 126–1 • Flow diagram for management of renal colic. See text for a description of the approach to patients with acute stone episodes. CT = computed tomography; Dx = diagnosis; KUB = plain radiograph of kidney, ureter, and bladder.

nephrostolithotomy succeeds in most cases. Asymptomatic kidney stones smaller than 5 mm in diameter should be left untreated. The guidelines for ESWL and percutaneous nephrostolithotomy hold for struvite and uric acid stones. Because lithotripsy disrupts cystine stones poorly, percutaneous nephrostolithotomy is often required.

PREVENTING RECURRENT NEPHROLITHIASIS

Careful correlation of stone counts with the clinical history and information from hospital emergency department and past office records determine whether a stone is a new episode or the passage of an existing stone. Nephrolithiasis prevention is a multistep process beginning with accurate diagnosis of the cause of nephrolithiasis (Table 126–1). Diagnosis requires crystallographic analysis of the stones and a battery of urine and blood tests that are begun after the patient has fully recovered from an episode of renal colic and has resumed normal activity and diet for approximately 2 weeks. Because of inherent day-to-day variation in urinary excretion of salts, repeated sampling of 24-hour urine specimens from patients taking their normal diets and

Table 126–1 • **OUTLINE OF STONE PREVENTION PRACTICE**
Stone analysis
Urinalysis
Blood analysis
Diagnoses
Treatments
Follow-up/compliance assessment
Outcomes/continuous quality control

sampling after prescribed interventions are required. The analyses performed on urine specimens include determining volume, pH, calcium, magnesium, potassium, sodium, ammonia, phosphorus, citrate, oxalate, chloride, sulfate, uric acid, urinary urea nitrogen, and creatinine. Measuring the full panel allows calculation of relative supersaturation for calcium oxalate, apatite, brushite, urate, and struvite. The addition of exogenous calcium oxalate or phosphate helps determine formation products for various crystal nucleation events. Cystine screening should be performed in all patients. Blood samples should be assayed for electrolytes (sodium, potassium, chloride, and bicarbonate), calcium, phosphorus, parathyroid hormone, and calcitriol.

The analyses performed on blood specimens should include electrolyte, calcium, phosphorus, parathyroid hormone, and calcitriol levels. The stone, urine, and blood analyses are pooled to make a diagnosis of stone pathogenesis, and treatment recommendations are based on the diagnoses. Follow-up includes repeated urinalyses and assessment of compliance. Compliance parameters in the 24-hour urine specimen include the volume, creatinine, sodium, urea nitrogen, sulfate, and potassium that can be used to monitor adherence to therapy. The assumption of therapy is that normalization of the metabolic abnormalities detected in reaching the diagnosis prevents stone recurrence. This assumption has been shown to be true in the vast majority of cases.

The report of a 1989 National Institutes of Health consensus conference recommended limited evaluation after the first stone episode. However, later studies indicated that recurrence is common in patients with a first stone and detectable metabolic abnormalities. Because repeated stone episodes cause pain, morbidity, and time loss from work, prevention is clearly the recommended approach (see later) and it should be applied with all stone formers.

Pathogenesis of Nephrolithiasis

STONE COMPOSITION. Stone composition should be analyzed in every patient, as it is the cornerstone of preventive therapy. About three fourths of all kidney stones are composed of calcium oxalate: 35% of stones are pure calcium oxalate (calcium oxalate monohydrate or calcium oxalate dihydrate or both), 40% are calcium oxalate with hydroxyapatite or carbonate apatite, and 1% are calcium oxalate with uric acid. Four per cent of all stones are apatite or hydroxyapatite $[Ca_{10}(PO_4)_6(OH)_2]$ and 1% are brushite $(CaHPO_4 \cdot 2H_2O)$. The non–calcium-containing crystal types are struvite, 8% of all stones, although carbonate apatite is always intermixed in the struvite stone. Eight per cent of all stones are composed of uric acid, and 2% are composed of cystine. Rarely, stones composed of acid ammonium urate or xanthine or proteinaceous matrix of potentially insoluble drugs (especially ephedrine) are observed. Determination of the composition of stones requires polarization microscopy, x-ray diffraction, or infrared spectrometry. The latter two procedures surpass microscopy in precision and sensitivity but are more costly.

PHYSICAL CHEMISTRY OF NEPHROLITHIASIS. For a stone to form, the following requirements have to be met: (1) formation of a nidus through nucleation, (2) retention of the nidus within the urinary tract, and (3) growth of the nidus to a size sufficient to cause symptoms or be visible on imaging. The solubility product describes a level of saturation of urine by salts at which solid-phase material exists in equilibrium with a liquid phase. At this level, the concentration product of the constituents in the liquid phase is high enough to prevent the crystals from dissolving but not high enough to allow them to grow. If the concentration is lower than the solubility product, the solution is undersaturated and the crystal can dissolve. Concentrations exceeding the solubility product are defined as supersaturated. The formation product describes the level of supersaturation at which materials no longer remain in solution and precipitate out spontaneously, a process called homogeneous nucleation. Nucleation can take place at a lower level of supersaturation if another material is introduced into the solution, a process called heterogeneous nucleation.

Normal urine has concentrations of calcium oxalate four times as high as its solubility. Hence, urine is supersaturated in regard to calcium oxalate. Calcium oxalate crystalluria occurs in both stone formers and non–stone formers. Studies suggest that calcium oxalate crystal formation occurs by heterogeneous nucleation. Potential nucleating agents are calcium phosphate crystals, uric acid crystals, and cellular debris. In the loop of Henle, calcium phosphate supersaturation can reach such high levels that homogeneous nucleation can take place. Calcium phosphate can then serve as a nucleating material for calcium oxalate. Indeed, calcium phosphate is commonly present in stones composed primarily of calcium oxalate. By a similar mechanism, heterogeneous nucleation, hyperuricosuria contributes to calcium oxalate stone formation.

The factors influencing the degree of urinary supersaturation include the amount of the constituent salts excreted per unit of time, urine volume, presence of inhibitors of crystallization, and urine pH. If a defined amount of salt excretion per 24 hours is obligatory, the urine volume in which that salt is to be dissolved becomes of paramount importance with regard to supersaturation. A low urine volume, which is a function of water intake, is a risk factor for all kinds of kidney stones. pH exerts variable effects on supersaturation. Acidic urine (pH less than 5.5) markedly decreases the solubility of uric acid because of protonation of uric acid (see "Uric Acid Stones") and is a major risk factor for uric acid stones. Uric acid crystals formed in acid urine can then nucleate calcium oxalate. An alkaline urine pH increases the amount of divalent and trivalent phosphates, which can bind and precipitate with calcium or ammonium. Thus, a persistently alkaline urine pH predisposes to formation of calcium phosphate and struvite (ammonium magnesium phosphate) stones. In the case of struvite stones, a high ammonium concentration is achieved in the presence of urease-producing bacteria, which split urinary urea into ammonia and carbon dioxide.

The presence of inhibitors of crystallization also affects supersaturation. Citrate complexes with calcium to form soluble calcium citrate. By doing so, it makes calcium unavailable to precipitate out as calcium oxalate or calcium phosphate. Hypocitraturia, a common finding among calcium stone formers, is a significant risk factor for calcium stone formation.

CRYSTAL ATTACHMENT. Crystal attachment to epithelial surfaces is also crucial for forming at least some stones. Normal subjects often have crystalluria without forming stones. Crystal binding appears to depend on the physicochemical structure of urothelial cell surfaces because the chemically injured urinary bladder binds more calcium oxalate than the uninjured bladder. In addition, there exist specific calcium oxalate crystal receptors on renal tubular epithelial cells.

DEFICIENT URINARY INHIBITORS. Although most recurrent stone formers tend to have an increased risk of nucleation, 1% or more of stone formers exhibit no detectable abnormality. Many healthy subjects, patients with cancer, and normal pregnant women exhibit hypercalciuria but do not form kidney stones. Thus, factors besides supersaturation are crucial in the pathogenesis of kidney stones. Macromolecular inhibitors of crystal growth and aggregation, particularly the growth and aggregation of calcium oxalate, have been identified (Table 126–2). Nephrocalcin, a renal isoform of osteocalcin, is a powerful inhibitor of calcium oxalate crystal growth and appears to act by binding to crystal surfaces. This substance is apparently defective when isolated from the urine of calcium stone formers. Urinary osteopontin (uropontin) is perhaps the most potent calcium oxalate crystal growth inhibitor, and its post-translational

Table 126–2 • ETIOLOGY OF CALCIUM STONES	
High urinary solute concentration	↑ Ca, ↑ Ox, ↓ UV
Deficient inhibitor	Citrate, uropontin, nephrocalcin
Excess promotor	Uric acid
Crystal attachment	Epithelial crystal receptors

Ox = urinary oxalate.
UV = urine volume.

modifications may be affected in nephrolithiasis because its rate of excretion appears normal. Tamm-Horsfall mucoprotein, the most abundant protein in human urine, may inhibit crystal growth but at times promotes calcium oxalate crystal aggregation. Some patients with recurrent nephrolithiasis produce Tamm-Horsfall mucoprotein that self-aggregates and loses its ability to inhibit aggregation of calcium oxalate crystals. Prothrombin fragment 1, a crystal matrix protein found in renal stones, is a peptide generated by cleavage of prothrombin by factor Xa and thrombin. This peptide inhibits calcium oxalate aggregation and growth and is expected to protect against stone formation. Its role in human nephrolithiasis is not known.

Pathogenesis of Calcium, Oxalate, and Apatite Stones

HYPERCALCIURIA

As noted previously, calcium is a constituent of 85 to 95% of kidney stones. After low urinary volumes, hypercalciuria is the most frequently observed abnormality of the urine from stone formers (Fig. 126–2). The definition of hypercalciuria varies with body size and diet. In general, the normal upper limit for urinary calcium is 4 mg of calcium per kilogram of body weight per day for a diet containing 1000 mg of calcium per day (280 mg/day, males; 240 mg/day, females) and 200 mg/day for a diet with a daily composition of 400 mg of calcium and 100 mEq or less of sodium. Dietary sodium is important because calcium reabsorption parallels that of sodium in the proximal nephron so that high rates of sodium excretion are calciuric and must be considered in the diagnosis of hypercalciuria.

Hypercalciuria can be idiopathic or result from a disorder leading to hypercalcemia. Hypercalcemia imposes an increased filtered load of calcium on the nephron and results in hypercalciuria. The disorders resulting in hypercalcemia and associated with calcium nephrolithiasis include the following:

1. Primary hyperparathyroidism, which is caused by adenoma in 85% of cases. Excess parathyroid hormone causes hypercalcemia, which may be mild. All patients with stones with hypercalciuria should be screened for primary hyperparathyroidism. Recurrent calcium nephrolithiasis in a patient with primary hyperparathyroidism is an indication for a parathyroidectomy.

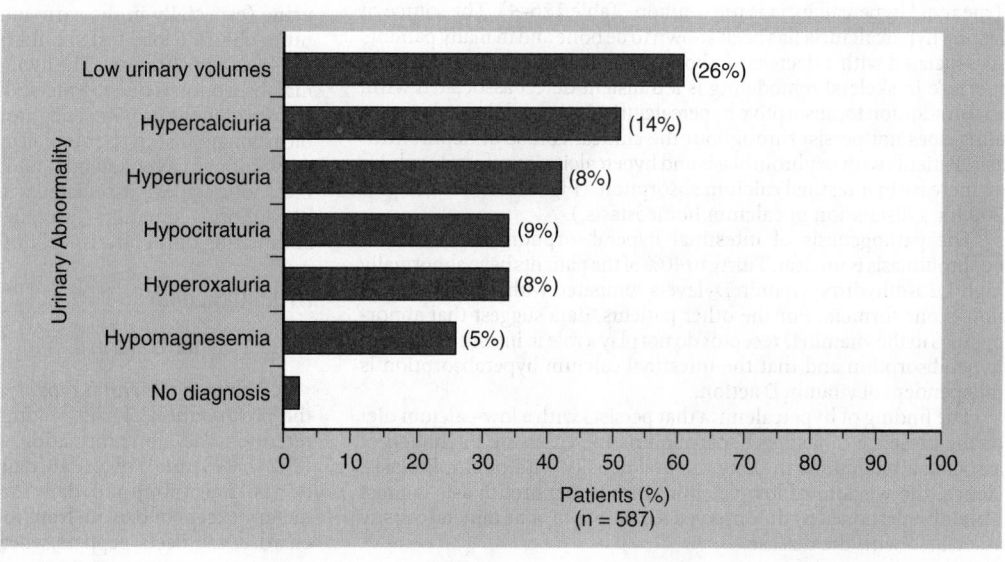

FIGURE 126–2 • Causes of urinary supersaturation in patients with nephrolithiasis: 587 consecutive patients seen in the stone center of St. Louis, Missouri, from 1987 to 1992 were evaluated with a standardized approach described in the text section on preventing recurrent nephrolithiasis. Numbers in parentheses indicate sole occurrence of abnormality. (Data from Seltzer J, Winborn K, Hruska K, unpublished observation.)

Table 126–3 • POTENTIAL MECHANISMS OF HYPERCALCIURIA

Increased intestinal calcium absorption
Direct
Excess 1,25-dihydroxyvitamin D_3
Decreased renal mineral reabsorption
Calcium
Phosphorus
Enhanced bone demineralization

Table 126–4 • PATHOGENESIS OF HYPERCALCIURIA IN NEPHROLITHIASIS

FACTOR	FREQUENCY (%)
Idiopathic absorptive ± skeletal remodeling defect	95
Primary hyperparathyroidism	3
Sarcoidosis	<1
Renal tubular transport defects	
Calcium	1–2
Phosphorus	<1

2. Granulomatous disorders such as sarcoidosis or tuberculosis. Granulomatous tissue is capable of hydroxylating 25-vitamin D_3 into 1,25-dihydroxyvitamin D_3, the physiologically active form of vitamin D, hence increasing intestinal reabsorption of calcium and resulting in hypercalcemia.
3. Other disorders: malignancy, immobilization, thyrotoxicosis.

Idiopathic Hypercalciuria

Idiopathic hypercalciuria is a familial disorder affecting both sexes in which hypercalciuria is not attended by hypercalcemia. Historically, hypercalciuria was thought to stem from one of the following: (1) enhanced absorption of calcium from dietary intake, (2) primary renal transport defects leading to excess calcium excretion and secondary enhanced calcium absorption, (3) excessive resorption of calcium from storage in bone, or (4) a combination of these (Table 126–3). Since the late 1980s, a consensus has emerged that the hypercalciuria of nephrolithiasis is a more uniform defect than was previously thought. The basis for this change is the fact that hypercalciuria is the most frequent abnormality found in patients with a family history of nephrolithiasis, suggesting a genetic basis for hypercalciuria. In addition, it has been found that fasting hypercalciuria, observed in 20 to 30% of patients who have nephrolithiasis and hypercalciuria, is not due to a renal transport defect (renal leak) as previously thought. True renal hypercalciuria is uncommon (Table 126–4). The source of fasting hypercalciuria has been shown to be bone and in many patients is associated with a decrease in bone mineral density. This presumed increase in skeletal remodeling is a transient defect associated with, and in addition to, absorptive hypercalciuria. Increased skeletal remodeling does not persist throughout the clinical course of nephrolithiasis. Patients with nephrolithiasis and hypercalciuria uniformly exhibit an increase in intestinal calcium absorption. (Fig. 126–3; see Chapter 260 for a discussion of calcium homeostasis.)

The pathogenesis of intestinal hyperabsorption of calcium in nephrolithiasis is unclear. Thirty to 40% of the patients have abnormally high 1,25-dihydroxyvitamin D_3 levels compared with a population of non–stone formers. For the other patients, data suggest that abnormalities in the vitamin D receptor do not play a role in intestinal calcium hyperabsorption and that the intestinal calcium hyperabsorption is independent of vitamin D action.

The finding of hypercalciuria that persists with a low-calcium diet or the presence of fasting hypercalciuria increases the likelihood of associated reductions in bone mineral density with nephrolithiasis. Hence, the wisdom of low-calcium diets in nephrolithiasis is most certainly questioned by the observed reductions in bone mineral density associated with the disease.

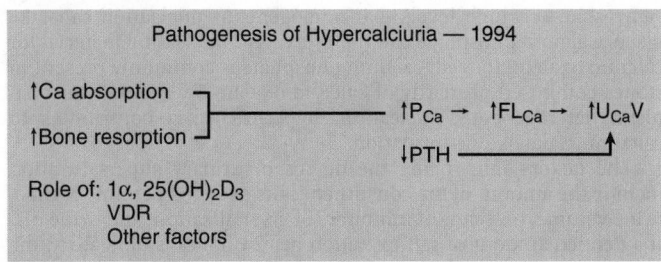

FIGURE 126–3 • Current concepts of the pathogenesis of idiopathic hypercalciuria link intestinal hyperabsorption and transient elevations of skeletal remodeling as the basis of hypercalciuria, accounting for the approximately 20% of patients who exhibit fasting hypercalciuria during evaluation. $1\alpha,25(OH)_2D_3 = 1\alpha,25$-dihydroxyvitamin D_3; PTH = parathyroid hormone; VDR = vitamin D receptor.

Genetic Disorders Associated with Hypercalciuria

Advances in molecular biology have allowed determination of subsets of patients with genetic defects associated with hypercalciuria. Mutations in the CLCN5 chloride channel, present in the proximal renal tubular cells, medullary thick ascending limb, and alpha intercalated cells, result in hypercalciuria and stone formation as well as low-molecular-weight proteinuria. This disorder is X linked and was previously known as Dent's disease.

Autosomal dominant hypocalcemia stems from an activating mutation of the calcium-sensing receptor that is present not only on the parathyroid cells but also on the basal side of the renal tubular cells in the thick ascending limb of the loop of Henle. The activating mutation results in increased detection of ambient free calcium levels and diminished reabsorption of calcium and magnesium in the thick ascending limb and, hence, leads to hypercalciuria, hypocalcemia, hypomagnesemia, and recurrent nephrolithiasis.

Despite these molecular advances, the molecular basis of idiopathic hypercalciuria remains enigmatic. Mutations and polymorphisms in a large number of candidate genes have been excluded. The disorder is probably polygenic, and its genetic basis is proving to be complex.

HYPOCITRATURIA

Reductions in urinary citrate excretion are a common trait in patients who form stones. This hypocitraturia may be (1) idiopathic; (2) due to defective urinary acidification; (3) due to small bowel malabsorption; (4) due to hypokalemia, especially iatrogenic; or (5) due to metabolic acidosis. Hypocitraturia, defined as less than 300 mg/day in women and less than 250 mg/day in men, was observed in 30 to 40% of patients with nephrolithiasis (see Fig. 126–2). More women than men exhibited hypocitraturia. Hypocitraturia often overlaps with hypercalciuria owing to the high prevalence of idiopathic hypercalciuria in nephrolithiasis. In patients who do not spontaneously acidify urine (especially in the early morning) to pH 5.5 or less, an ammonium chloride load test should rule out an acidification defect as the cause of hypocitraturia. The hypocitraturia associated with small bowel malabsorption is due to a metabolic acidosis and stimulation of citrate transport in the proximal nephron. The metabolic acidosis stems from bicarbonate lost in the stool. Treating nephrolithiasis with thiazides may induce hypokalemia and a secondary hypocitraturia. The metabolic acidosis associated with excess consumption of sulfur- and phosphorus-containing protein may also cause hypocitraturia by stimulating citrate transport in the proximal tubule.

HYPEROXALURIA

Dietary Hyperoxaluria

Oxalate is the anion most frequently associated with calcium in the precipitation of salts leading to crystal formation, growth, and retention and stone formation. Normal people excrete 20 to 40 mg (222 to 444 μmol) of oxalate daily. A reasonable upper limit of excretion is 45 mg (500 μmol) daily for men and 40 mg for women. A simple dietary excess of oxalate from foods such as spinach, rhubarb, Swiss chard, cocoa, beets, peppers, wheat germ, pecans, peanuts, okra, chocolate, and lime peel commonly increases urinary oxalate to 50 to 60 mg (556 to 667 μmol) daily. This form of hyperoxaluria is frequently observed in nephrolithiasis (see Fig. 126–2), and treatment consists of altering the diet to avoid an excess of oxalate. However, no clinical trials have proved the efficacy of avoiding oxalate for treating nephrolithiasis.

Enteric Hyperoxaluria

Small bowel malabsorption from any cause, including resection, intrinsic disease, and jejunal ileal bypass, often leads to hyperoxaluria. The pathogenesis is exposure of the colonic mucosa to detergents—in the form of bile salts—and fatty acids, which nonselectively increase the permeability to numerous molecules, including oxalate. These detergents also bind calcium and magnesium, making oxalate more available for transport. The hyperoxaluria from small bowel malabsorption often exceeds 100 mg (1111 μmol) daily, provoking frequent stone formation and even tubulointerstitial renal disease from intrarenal calcifications. A consistent metabolic pattern is observed in the urine of patients with enteric hyperoxaluria, consisting of low urinary volumes and a tendency toward hypocalciuria, hypocitraturia, and hyperoxaluria. Treatment includes reducing dietary oxalate and fat; taking oral calcium supplements, cholestyramine, and oral citrate supplements; and high fluid intake (see later).

Primary Hyperoxaluria

Two genetic disorders lead to hyperoxaluria (Chapter 215). Type I primary hyperoxaluria, an autosomal recessive trait, results from molecular abnormalities that reduce the activity of hepatic peroxisomal alanine glyoxylate aminotransferase, thereby increasing the availability of glyoxylate, which is irreversibly converted to oxalic acid. The second form (type II), resulting from a deficiency of D-glycerate dehydrogenase or glyoxylate reductase, is much rarer than type I. Both forms cause a high level of oxalate production and corresponding urinary oxalate excretion above 135 to 270 mg (1523 μmol) daily. Stone formation often begins in childhood, but tubulointerstitial nephritis progressing to renal failure is the more important and dominant expression of the disease.

HYPERURICOSURIA

Hyperuricosuria (Chapter 288) is a common finding associated with hypercalciuria in patients with calcium oxalate nephrolithiasis. The relationship between hyperuricosuria and calcium oxalate precipitation remains controversial. Some evidence suggests that urate crystals increase the nucleation of calcium oxalate by the process of heterogeneous nucleation and epitaxial growth. However, urate crystals are uncommon in urine compared with the frequency of calcium oxalate crystallization, and the epitaxial theory remains to be proved. Well-controlled studies demonstrate that allopurinol, a drug that decreases urate synthesis, significantly reduces the rate of recurring calcium oxalate stones. Because allopurinol has no direct effect on calcium oxalate crystallization, it is likely that this effect is produced by reduced urinary uric acid excretion. Because an excess of purine in the diet causes hyperuricosuria, normal levels of dietary purine should also be protective.

NEW PROTEIN INHIBITORS OF CALCIUM OXALATE STONE FORMATION

See the discussion of various inhibitors of calcium oxalate stone formation in the section on the physical chemistry of nephrolithiasis.

RENAL STRUCTURAL ABNORMALITIES

Were crystalline particles not retained within the kidney, their forming and passing would be no more than a common urologic curiosity. Crystal adherence promoting crystal growth and aggregation, especially in areas of relatively diminished urinary flow, is crucial in the development of urinary stones. Little is known regarding the process of crystal growth attachment. The role of urinary stasis has not been quantified. Other structural abnormalities, such as medullary sponge kidney, ectopic kidney, polycystic kidney, and horseshoe kidney, may be associated with nephrolithiasis. Medullary sponge kidney probably represents a process that occurs or develops as a result of nephrocalcinosis. It is probably not a specific disease in itself but a process associated with acidification defects and other causes of calcium oxalate nephrolithiasis, especially hypercalciuria. The other structural abnormalities pose a major risk for stones related to urinary stasis and infection.

 Treatment

CALCIUM OXALATE OR APATITE STONES

The first tenet of therapy for preventing nephrolithiasis is an increase in the urinary volume (Table 126–5). Urinary volumes between 2 and 3 L must be maintained. Helpful clues to assist the patient with increasing urinary volume include avoiding urinary concentration at night and taking a metered amount of water to the workplace.

DIET. With careful attention to diet, most calcium oxalate stones could be prevented, but long-term dietary compliance is essential (see Table 126–5). Recurrent calcium nephrolithiasis should be considered a disease of dietary excess superimposed on the genetic predispositions produced by hypercalciuria, renal tubular acidosis, gout, and cystinuria. In patients with hypercalciuria and calcium oxalate stones, diets with reduced sodium and animal protein but normal calcium appear to be more effective than a traditional low calcium diet in preventing recurrent stones.◻

THIAZIDE DIURETICS. Thiazide diuretics are useful pharmacologic approaches to preventing nephrolithiasis. They lower urinary calcium excretion by increasing calcium reabsorption in the proximal nephron because of volume contraction. They also directly stimulate calcium reabsorption through their actions on the luminal Na^+/Cl^- transporter of the diluting segment of the nephron. The relative importance of the two actions is heavily weighted toward the proximal nephron–volume contraction effects. Thus, an adequate response to thiazide diuretics requires controlling sodium intake. Retention of calcium by the kidney results in a secondary suppression of intestinal calcium hyperabsorption. Some reports suggest that this secondary action on the intestine is lost after 2 to 3 years of therapy. This loss may result in thiazide resistance during long-term treatment of absorptive hypercalciuria. Thiazide diuretics tend to improve calcium balance, and the result is observed as an increase in bone mineral density related to increased bone formation (see Table 126–5).

ORAL PHOSPHATE. In patients with absorptive hypercalciuria, 1500 mg of neutral potassium phosphate per day in three to four divided doses lowered urinary calcium excretion in some trials as effectively as thiazide diuretics. However, compliance is more difficult to achieve because of the frequency of dosing and intestinal side effects such as diarrhea and bloating. Studies estimating the efficacy of oral phosphate therapy (see Table 126–5) reported relapses of 9% and 25%. A new slow-release formulation has been developed that avoids many of the side effects and the dosing frequency required with earlier preparations. This new agent reached clinical trials, but it is no longer under development.

SODIUM CELLULOSE PHOSPHATE. A calcium-binding resin, sodium cellulose phosphate, reduces calcium absorption when taken with meals. This approach has not had a high success rate, possibly because of reflex hyperoxaluria. In addition, a negative calcium balance may lead to additional bone mineral loss.

TREATMENT OF HYPOCITRATURIA. Because citrate lowers calcium oxalate supersaturation by binding calcium and, to some extent, by reducing calcium excretion, correcting hypocitraturia should reduce the recurrence of nephrolithiasis. No carefully controlled trials of citrate therapy have been reported. Uncontrolled studies suggest an efficacy of approximately 88% over a 2-year period (see Table 126–5). Citrate therapy may be useful for patients who experience hypocitraturia as a result of thiazide diuretic therapy. Furthermore, in patients with inflammatory bowel disease or renal tubular acidosis, citrate therapy seems a rational replacement for the losses of alkali.

Continued

Table 126–5 • SUMMARY OF TREATMENT OPTIONS FOR DIFFERENT TYPES OF RENAL STONES*

INDICATION	TREATMENT	EXPECTED RESULTS (90% SUCCESSFUL TREATMENT)
All stones	High fluid intake	Unknown
Calcium oxalate and brushite (CaOx/CaHPO₄) stones		
Idiopathic hypercalciuria	1. Controlled protein Na and Ca diets	Unknown
	2. Thiazide diuretics and related drugs	85–90%
	3. Oral phosphate	Unknown
	4. Na cellulose phosphate	Low
Hypocitraturia	Potassium citrate	88%
Renal tubular acidosis	Potassium citrate	Unknown
Ileostomy or small bowel malabsorption	Potassium citrate	Unknown
Hyperoxaluria		
Dietary	Reduced oxalate diet	Unknown
Enteric	Low-fat diet, calcium supplement, cholestyramine	Unknown
Primary	Pyridoxine	Only in a small fraction
Hyperuricosuria	Allopurinol	86%
	Potassium citrate	Unknown
Uric acid stones	Allopurinol	Unknown
	Potassium citrate	88%
Struvite stones	ESWL or percutaneous nephrostolithotomy	30–40% with stones <2 cm
	Acetohydroxamic acid	Control of stone growth if tolerated
Cystine stones/cystinuria	Tiopronin	Unknown
	Penicillamine	Unknown

*Each type of renal stone is listed under indication, and the expected success rate per 100 patients is listed under expected results and described in the text. ESWL = extracorporeal shock wave lithotripsy.

Because of the volume expansion effects, sodium bicarbonate or sodium citrate does not have the required actions of potassium citrate to lower urinary calcium and improve calcium balance.

TREATMENT OF HYPEROXALURIA

Dietary. Normal people excrete 20 to 40 mg (222 to 444 µmol) of oxalate daily. A simple dietary excess of oxalate from foods may increase urinary oxalate, and a low-calcium diet may further increase excretion. Treating this mild form of dietary hyperoxaluria associated with calcium oxalate stones consists of altering the diet to avoid foods that contain high concentrations of oxalate. No carefully controlled trials have proved the efficacy of this approach, however.

Enteric. Hyperoxaluria observed in patients with inflammatory bowel disorders and intestinal bypass is usually associated with hypocitraturia. Patients exhibiting hypocalciuria should be treated with a low-fat diet in addition to calcium supplements. Cholestyramine, a nonresorbable resin that binds fatty acids, bile acids, and oxalate (4 to 16 g/day in four divided doses with meals); oral citrate supplements; and high fluid intake are the mainstays of therapy. These patients may also exhibit magnesium deficiency and hypomagnesuria. Magnesium replacement may be important to increase urinary citrate excretion in response to exogenous potassium alkali.

Primary Hyperoxaluria. Type I primary hyperoxaluria occasionally responds to pyridoxine supplement (2 to 200 mg/day). High urinary volume and supplemental citrate, thiazide diuretics, and possibly oral phosphate supplements can also be used. After renal transplantation, a special protocol is required to avoid accelerated renal oxalosis. Liver transplantation restores the missing enzymes, and many patients with hyperoxaluria have been treated in this manner.

HYPERURICOSURIA. Because an excess of purine in the diet causes hyperuricosuria, normal levels of dietary purine should prevent stones. However, careful studies documenting a response to low-purine diets are not available. Compelling evidence that hyperuricosuria contributes to the formation of calcium oxalate stones comes from a prospective double-blind trial that demonstrated a reduction in stone formation with allopurinol compared with placebo (see Table 126–5).

URIC ACID STONES

Uric acid is the final product of purine metabolism and is excreted in the urine. The pK$_a$ of the uric acid is 5.35. At this pH, half of the uric acid is fully protonated and the other half exists in the form of an anion urate. Protonated uric acid is poorly soluble. Low urine pH makes uric acid supersaturation easy to achieve at normal excretion rates of 600 to 800 mg (3.6 to 4.8 mmol) per day. For example, at a urinary pH of 7.0, the solubility of the uric acid is 200 mg/dL and most of the uric acid exists in a form of a soluble urate anion. It falls to 15 mg/dL at a urine pH of 5.0, at which more than half of the uric acid exists in the protonated form. Acid urine (pH less than 5.5) is a common finding in patients with uric acid stones and is one the major risk factors contributing to uric acid nephrolithiasis. The other risk factors associated with formation of uric acid stones are low urine volume and increased uric acid excretion. Persistently low urine pH and low urine volumes occur in chronic diarrheal states. Increased uric acid excretion (hyperuricosuria) is linked to overproduction of uric acid, which occurs in cases of excessive purine intake or myeloproliferative disorders such as polycythemia vera. Excessive purine intake results in hyperuricosuria, and attendant excessive protein intake imposes an increased acid load resulting in a low urine pH. Not infrequently, patients with uric acid stones also suffer from gout. Hyperuricosuria is also a risk factor for calcium stones, as uric acid crystals often serve as a nidus for calcium oxalate aggregation.

Uric acid stones are radiolucent on plain abdominal radiographs and in excretory urograms are seen as filling defects in the urinary tract, which should be differentiated from a clot or a tumor. Uric acid stones, like all stones, can be detected by abdominal CT. Chemical analysis of the stone provides the definitive diagnosis. Treatment of uric acid nephrolithiasis is based on attempts to increase the solubility of uric acid or decrease its excretion. Alkalinization of urine to a pH greater than 6.5 markedly increases the solubility of uric acid. Potassium citrate is the preferred alkalinizing agent because, unlike sodium alkaline salts, it does not augment urinary calcium excretion. However, avoidance of temporary periods of acidification sufficient to nucleate uric acid or uric acid and calcium oxalate is difficult to achieve. The patients should maintain urine volume higher than 2.5 L per day. Allopurinol, a xanthine oxidase inhibitor, blocks the conversion of xanthine to uric acid. Xanthine and hypoxanthine, which are more soluble than uric acid, become the final products of purine degradation. Allopurinol is well tolerated and effective in reducing urinary uric acid excretion.

STRUVITE STONES

Struvite stones are composed of ammonium and magnesium phosphate. They form in the presence of a urinary infection with urease-producing bacteria such as *Proteus, Pseudomonas,* and *Enterococcus.* Urease splits urinary urea into ammonia and CO_2. Ammonia readily becomes protonated to ammonium, NH_4^+, resulting in a persistently high urine pH (>7). Alkaline pH favors precipitation of phosphate salts, and the bacteria provide ample ammonium. The constellation of these factors results in supersaturation of urine for struvite—magnesium ammonium phosphate. Struvite stones may exist as pure struvite or in combination with calcium stones. The latter occurs in calcium stone formers who become infected with urease-producing bacteria. Pure struvite stones occur more commonly in women and are not associated with other metabolic derangements leading to calcium stone formation. Conversely, mixed struvite and calcium stones occur more often in men with idiopathic hypercalciuria when calcium stones become secondarily infected, resulting in formation of struvite, or alkaline urine becomes supersaturated for calcium phosphate.

Struvite stones are often large and can fill the entire renal pelvis (staghorn calculi). They often cause bleeding, obstruction, and infection and do not pass spontaneously. They may result in renal parenchymal damage and chronic renal insufficiency. The diagnosis of struvite stones is made by chemical analysis of the stone or by the finding in the urine of ammonium magnesium phosphate crystals that have a typical "coffin lid" appearance.

Bacteria adhere to stones and become incorporated into the stone, rendering antibiotics ineffective. Consequently, initial management requires removal of the struvite stones. When patients are free of stones, they benefit from antibiotics directed against the predominant urinary organism, although no control studies support this reasonable approach. ESWL and percutaneous nephrostolithotomy are the approaches used to reduce the damage caused by growth and spread of these stones. Acetohydroxamic acid, a urease inhibitor, has limited use because of patients' intolerance related to side effects.

CYSTINE STONES

Cystine stones are caused by cystinuria, a hereditary disorder of dibasic amino acid transport in the proximal renal tubule. It is inherited as an autosomal recessive trait and results in urinary wasting of the dibasic amino acids cystine, ornithine, arginine, and lysine. Cystinuria should not be confused with cystinosis, a lysosomal disorder resulting in Fanconi's syndrome and chronic renal failure. Cystine, a disulfide of amino acid cysteine, is poorly soluble in urine. Patients suffering from cystinuria often excrete as much as 480 to 3600 mg (2 to 15 mmol) of cystine per day. The solubility limit for cystine in the urine is only 300 mg/L (1.25 mmol/L). Supersaturation of urine with cystine results in stone formation. The stones can become very large and occupy the entire renal pelvis (staghorn calculi).

Approximately 2% of patients attending renal stone clinics exhibit this hereditary defect. Determining the chemical composition of a retrieved stone or demonstrating increased urinary excretion of cystine makes the diagnosis of cystinuria. Microscopic urinalysis often reveals hexagonal cystine crystals. Once formed, cystine stones often require surgical removal. Medical therapy is directed toward prevention of further stone formation. High fluid intake can prevent stones only in some patients with low levels of cystine excretion. Most patients require treatment with penicillamine or tiopronin. Both combine with cysteine to form soluble disulfides that reduce, through competition, the formation of cystine. The ability of these treatments to reduce stone frequency is not quantitatively known, although they are effective. However, there is a high rate of intolerance related to severe side effects, which require careful surveillance. Captopril, an angiotensin-converting enzyme inhibitor, also forms a soluble disulfide with cysteine. However, in quantitative terms, treatment with captopril alone is insufficient to achieve the desired reduction in urinary cystine excretion.

 Grade A

1. Borghi L, Schianchi T, Meschi T, et al: Comparison of two diets for the prevention of recurrent stones in idiopathic hypercalciuria. N Engl J Med 2002;346:77–84.

SUGGESTED READINGS
Bushinsky DA: Nephrolithiasis: Site of the initial solid phase. J Clin Invest 2003;111:602–605. *Explains the underlying pathophysiology of the initiation of stone formation.*
Goldfard DS: Increasing prevalence of kidney stones in the United States. Kidney Int 2003;63:1951–1952. *This editorial accompanies the report below by KK Stamatelou et al published in Kidney International.*
Krishnamurthy MS, Hruska KA, Chandhoke PS: The urinary response to an oral oxalate load in recurrent calcium stone formers. J Urol 2003;169:2030–2033. *This study demonstrates the effect of low calcium diets on oxalate absorption in patients with nephrolithiasis.*
Odvina CV, Preminger GM, Lindberg JS, et al: Long-term combined treatment with thiazide and potassium citrate in nephrolithiasis does not lead to hypokalemia or hypochloremic metabolic alkalosis. Kidney Int 2003;63:240–247. *Co-administration of potassium citrate did not induce hypokalemia or hypochloremic metabolic alkalosis in thiazide-treated patients.*
Pak CY, Heller HJ, Pearle MS, et al: Prevention of stone formation and bone loss in absorptive hypercalciuria by combined dietary and pharmacological interventions. J Urol 2003;169:465–469. *This study demonstrates the effectiveness of a modern safe approach to nephrolithiasis.*
Stamatelou KK, Francis ME, Jones CA, et al: Time trends in reported prevalence of kidney stones in the United States: 1976–1994. Kidney Int 2003;63:1817–1823. *This report demonstrates the marked increase in prevalence of kidney stones associated with American obesity and changes in our diet portion size.*

127 CYSTIC KIDNEY DISEASES

M. Amin Arnaout

Definitions and Epidemiology

The term *cystic kidney diseases* refers to a heterogeneous group of hereditary and acquired disorders characterized by the presence of unilateral or bilateral renal cysts. They include the polycystic kidney diseases, acquired cystic kidney disease, the medullary cystic diseases, and two rare systemic disorders in which renal cyst formation is usually a minor component (tuberous sclerosis and von Hippel-Lindau

syndrome). *Renal cysts* are defined as fluid-filled sacs lined by a single layer of epithelial cells. When acquired singly or in small numbers and in the absence of any other pathology, these renal cysts are termed *simple cysts.* These are present in approximately 50% of individuals older than 40 years of age, are usually not loculated, and tend to bulge out from the renal surface (Fig. 127–1). The *polycystic kidney diseases* (PKDs), by comparison, constitute a clinically important group of

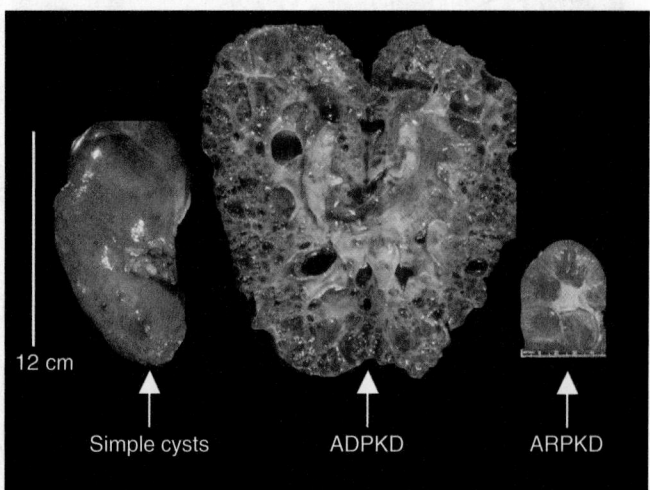

12 cm

Simple cysts   ADPKD   ARPKD

FIGURE 127–1 • Gross pathology of selected cystic kidney diseases. *A,* Photograph of a kidney with multiple simple cysts. The cysts bulge out from the surface of a normal-sized kidney. *B,* Sagittal cross section of a kidney from an adult with autosomal dominant polycystic kidney disease (ADPKD). Multiple macroscopic cysts have resulted in an enlarged but still reniform kidney. (Note the evidence of prior hemorrhage within some of the cysts). *C,* Sagittal cross section of a kidney segment from a neonate with autosomal recessive polycystic kidney disease (ARPKD). The kidney is enlarged with numerous small-sized cysts. (Photographs courtesy of Dr. Robert Colvin, Massachusetts General Hospital.)

genetically mediated disorders that are characterized by prominent, expanding, bilateral renal cysts. They are classified based on inheritance pattern as *autosomal dominant* (ADPKD) or *autosomal recessive* (ARPKD). ADPKD, with prevalence rates of between 1:400 and 1:1000, is the most common monogenetic disease of humans. In common with simple cysts, ADPKD develops in an age-dependent manner and affects mainly adults. ARPKD, by contrast, is a relatively rare childhood disorder that appears every 1:6000 to 1:50,000 live births. Collectively the hereditary PKDs are the fourth leading cause of end-stage renal disease (ESRD) in the United States, affect both genders and all races equally, and cost more than $1 billion annually to manage in the United States alone. *Acquired cystic kidney disease* (ACKD) refers to the appearance of multiple bilateral renal cysts that develop in patients who already have kidney disease. It appears in 90% of patients who have been receiving renal replacement therapy for 8 years or longer and is significant mainly for increased rates of development of renal cell carcinoma (RCC).

Pathogenesis of Cyst Formation

A variety of spontaneously occurring and targeted-mutant rodent models of PKD have shed light on the common cellular processes that lead to cyst formation. Cysts originate as outpouchings of tubules. Any portion of the nephron can undergo this focal dilation, although the preponderance of tubule site of origin depends on the underlying disease. The impetus for tubular dilation has not been identified but must occur hundreds or even thousands of times as up to 1% of nephrons in PKD kidneys undergo cystic conversion. The outpouchings expand and eventually separate from the parent tubules, yielding cysts (Fig. 127–2). Monoclonal proliferation of the cyst-lining cells and abnormal solute transport leading to net luminal secretion of chloride and sodium are implicated in cyst initiation and expansion. In most cystic models, this propagation is also accompanied by increased apoptotic rates of the cyst-lining epithelial cells, by changes in amount and distribution of surrounding extracellular matrix and secretory proteins, and by interstitial fibrosis. Altered expression levels of key regulators of proliferation, apoptosis, extracellular matrix (ECM) composition, fluid secretion, and fibrosis are documented in animal models of PKD (Table 127–1). The contributions of each of these abrogations to the initiation and propagation of cyst formation vary with each model.

Secondary cyst infection and cyst hemorrhage or rupture are frequent complications, which contribute to interstitial fibrosis and to the cellular debris seen within some cysts. Progressive cyst formation and expansion in the hereditary PKDs lead to enlarged (sometimes massively enlarged) kidneys (see Fig. 127–1). When enough normal renal parenchyma has been encroached on by voluminous cysts and by interstitial fibrosis, renal insufficiency and ESRD ensue.

AUTOSOMAL DOMINANT POLYCYSTIC KIDNEY DISEASE

Genetics

ADPKD is a systemic disorder characterized by cyst formation in multiple organs and by the development of abnormalities in the cardiovascular system. Heterogeneous mutations in at least two genes lead to ADPKD. Mutations in the first identified gene, *PKD1*, account for 85 to 90% of cases. This 54-kilobase (kb) gene is located adjacent to the tuberous sclerosis 2 (*TSC2*) gene on chromosome 16. It has 43 exons and encodes polycystin-1, the first described member of an expanding group of proteins termed *polycystins*. Heterogeneous mutations in the 68-kb *PKD2*, located on chromosome 4, contribute a further 10 to 15% of ADPKD cases. *PKD2* transcribes 15 exons, which encode polycystin-2. Aside from a slower rate of progression, the clinical features of *PKD2*-associated ADPKD are indistinguishable from *PKD1*-associated ADPKD. A small minority of ADPKD cases do not have demonstrable *PKD1* or *PKD2* mutations, suggesting that a third defective gene is involved.

Polycystin-1 and -2

Polycystin-1 is comprised of 4302 amino acids, with 11 predicted membrane-spanning segments connecting a large extracellular amino terminus and a short cytoplasmic carboxyl terminus. Multiple functional motifs are predicted and implicate polycystin-1 in cell-cell

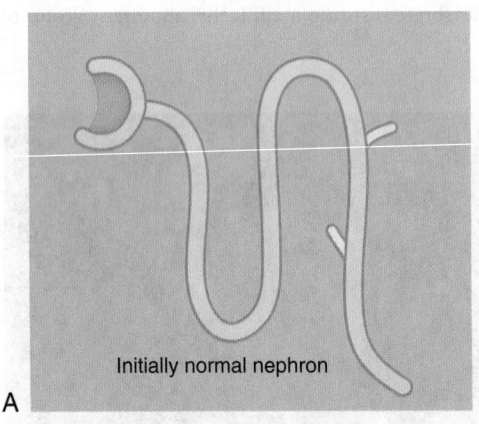

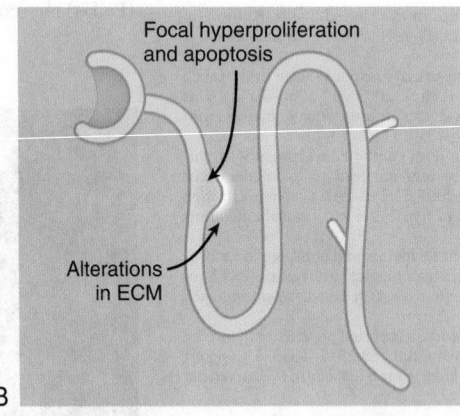

Focal hyperproliferation and apoptosis

Alterations in ECM

Initially normal nephron

A

B

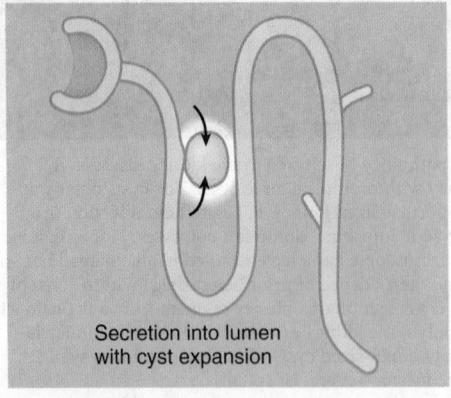

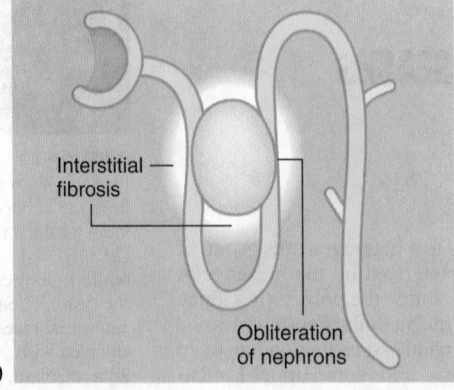

Secretion into lumen with cyst expansion

Interstitial fibrosis

Obliteration of nephrons

C

D

FIGURE 127–2 • *A* to *D*, Steps involved in cyst formation: Schematic of the sequence of events leading to renal cyst formation. Note that this process occurs hundreds or thousands of times during the natural history of polycystic kidney disease. ECM = extracellular matrix. (Adapted from Arnaout MA, in Cooper D [ed]: Nature Encyclopedia of the Human Genome, Nature Publishing Group, 2003.)

Table 127–1 • SELECTED RODENT MODELS OF POLYCYSTIC KIDNEY DISEASE

SPECIES	MODEL	INHERITANCE	CHROMOSOME ASSIGNMENT	PROGRESSION	RENAL*	EXTRARENAL	INCREASED PROLIFERATION	INCREASED APOPTOSIS	CHANGE IN ECM
Mouse	cpk	AR	12	Rapid	PT, <u>CD</u>	Biliary cysts in old heterozygotes	Yes	Yes	Yes
Mouse	bpk	AR	10	Rapid	PT, <u>CD</u>	Biliary dysgenesis	Yes	—	Yes
Mouse	CFWwd	AD	—	Slow	G, PT, LH, DT, CD	Hepatic cysts; thoracic aortic aneurysms	—	—	—
Mouse	pcy	AR	9	Slow	PT, LH, <u>DT</u>, <u>CD</u>	Cerebral aneurysms	—	—	Yes
Mouse	krd	AD	19	Variable	M	Retinal defects	—	—	—
Rat	Han: SPRD	AD	5	Slow	<u>PT</u>, LH, DT, CD	Hepatic and pancreatic cysts in older females	—	—	Yes
Rat	pck	AR	9	Slow	<u>LH</u>, <u>DT</u>, <u>CD</u>, PT	Hepatic cysts	Yes	Yes	Yes
Rat	ARPK	AR	—	Slow	CD	Skeletal deformities	Yes	—	Yes

*Nephron sites predominantly involved in the disease process are underlined. —, not determined.

AD = autosomal dominant; AR = autosomal recessive; CD = collecting duct; DT = distal tubule; ECM = extracellular matrix; G = glomerulus; LH = loop of Henle; M = medulla; PT = proximal tubule.

Modified from Lager DJ, Qian Q, Bengal RJ, et al: The pck rat: A new model that resembles human autosomal recessive polycystic kidney and liver disease. Kidney Int 2001;59:126–136.

and/or cell-matrix adhesion as well as signal transduction functions (Fig. 127–3). Polycystin-2, composed of 963 amino acids, has cytoplasmic amino and carboxy termini and six transmembrane spanning segments. It has been shown to function as a nonselective voltage-dependent gated calcium channel. Polycystin-1 and -2 are widely distributed proteins that, despite only partial co-expression, interact in a common pathway that appears important for the maintenance of mature epithelial and endothelial structures. Mouse embryos homozygous mutant for either of these proteins die in the perinatal period from a variety of causes that relate to the nature of the mutant alleles. In addition to PKD, these causes include congenital cardiac abnormalities, widespread microvascular defects, and generalized edema.

Pathogenesis

ADPKD-associated cysts develop in organs that are (at least initially) heterozygous for *PKD1* or *PKD2* mutations. Approximately 10% of these germline mutations are believed to have arisen spontaneously. There is evidence that subsequent acquired mutations in the normal allele ("second hits") cause PKD. For this to be the sole pathogenic mechanism for cyst formation in ADPKD, however, presupposes high somatic mutation rates of *PKD1* and *PKD2* that have not yet been demonstrated. Mutation analyses of cysts from ADPKD patients reveal loss of heterozygosity in *PKD1* or *PKD2* in only about 20% of examined cysts. Also, the recent demonstration that transgenic mice overexpressing functional polycystin-1 develop PKD is

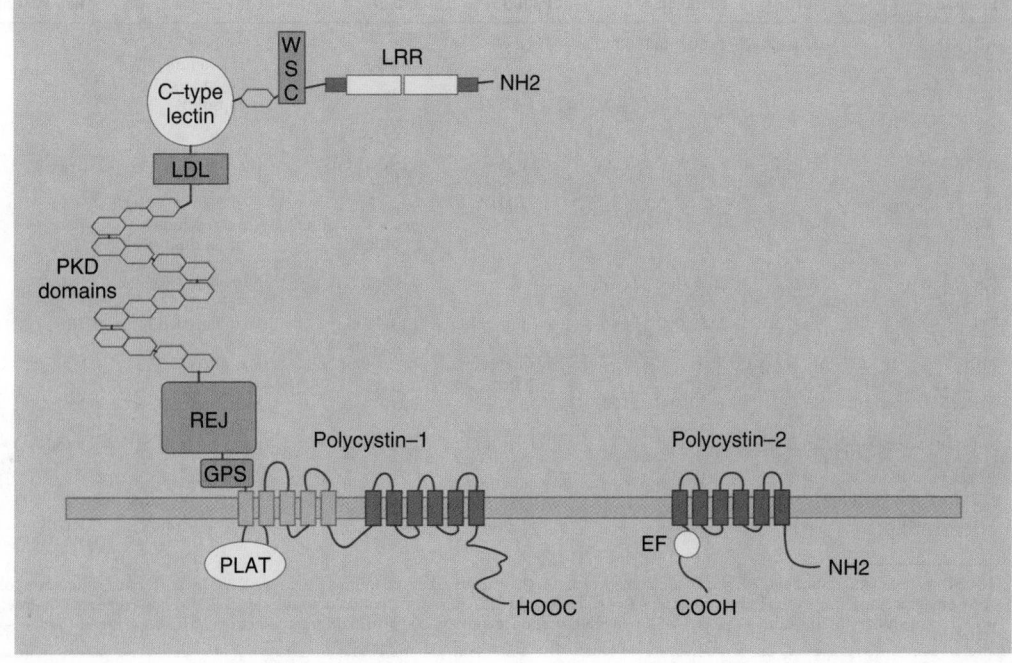

FIGURE 127–3 • Proteins responsible for selected heritable polycystic kidney diseases. *Polycystin-1 domains:* GPS = G protein–coupled receptor proteolytic site; LDL = low-density lipoprotein-like region; LRR = leucine-rich region; PLAT = polycystin-1–lipoxygenase-α toxin; REJ = receptor for egg jelly domain; WSC = cell wall and stress component. *Polycystin-2 domain:* EF = calcium-binding motif consisting of two helixes, E and F. The last six transmembrane regions of polycystin-1 (dark purple) are homologous to those of polycystin-2.

incongruent with the second-hit hypothesis. These data suggest that other genetic mechanisms contribute to cyst formation in ADPKD. It is likely that other gene products modify the rate of disease progression. For example, the gene product of *TSC2* (tuberin) has recently been shown to aid in normal membrane targeting of polycystin-1, and individuals with contiguous *PKD1* and *TSC2* mutations develop early and aggressive ADPKD.

The pathogenesis of aneurysm formation in ADPKD is poorly understood. Hypertension, which is common in ADPKD, has been postulated to play a causal role. However, this link has not been confirmed in cohorts of ADPKD patients screened for cerebral aneurysms. In addition, animal models of ADPKD suggest that the vascular ailment in ADPKD is primary.

Clinical Manifestations

ADPKD has a highly variable presentation, even within families. Thus, despite an estimated 100% penetrance by age 90 years, only half of individuals with heterozygous mutations in *PKD1* or *PKD2* are ever diagnosed with ADPKD. Of these, the majority present in the third or fourth decade of life with symptoms referable to renal cystic disease. However, ADPKD can develop at any age (including infancy) and can have a nonrenal presentation. Renomegaly may predominate the clinical picture with abdominal distention, discomfort, or pain but can also be discovered incidentally on physical examination or after radiographic studies of the abdomen. Urinary concentrating defects (presenting as nocturia), recurrent urinary tract infection, and recurrent kidney stone formation (calcium oxalate or uric acid stones) all are more common in patients with ADPKD. *Hypertension* is present in approximately 50% of cases and can precede the onset of renal disease. Anemia features less prominently than in other renal diseases, an observation that probably stems from relatively well-preserved erythropoietin secretion. Proteinuria also features less prominently than in other renal diseases. Cyst infection, usually by common urinary tract–infecting organisms, is characterized by flank or abdominal pain, fevers, rigors, leukocytosis, and occasionally sepsis. Cyst rupture and hemorrhage occur spontaneously or after trauma and present as sharp pain and hematuria.

An estimated 4 to 15% of individuals with ADPKD develop saccular *cerebral aneurysms*, a prevalence rate that is 4 to 10 times greater than in the general population. These aneurysms tend to

segregate in families, making ADPKD one of a group of diseases characterized by autosomal dominant–inherited familial cerebral aneurysms. As in these other conditions, ADPKD-associated aneurysms tend to rupture at a smaller size and in individuals approximately 10 years younger than those in the general population. Although usually clinically silent, intact cerebral aneurysms can present with focal neurologic symptoms and headaches. By contrast, aneurysms that rupture lead to subarachnoid hemorrhage and have dramatic presentations that include severe headaches, seizures, altered sensorium, and death.

Although almost never severe enough to cause end-stage liver disease, age-dependent *hepatic cysts* occur in 30 to 80% of patients with ADPKD and can also lead to signs and symptoms of mass effect, infection, hemorrhage, and rupture. Multiparous women are disproportionately affected, developing larger and more symptomatic cysts. The cysts that occasionally form in other organs such as pancreas, spleen, brain, ovaries, and testes are usually asymptomatic. *Mitral valve prolapse* with or without mitral regurgitation is reported in 25% of patients. Abdominal aortic aneurysms and inguinal hernias all have been reported to be more prevalent in patients with ADPKD. The previously described increased prevalence of colonic diverticula were not confirmed in a recent report.

Diagnosis

To account for the common age-dependent appearance of simple cysts, PKD is diagnosed if two renal cysts (distributed in one or both kidneys) are present in individuals younger than 30 years of age, if two renal cysts are present in each kidney in individuals aged between 30 and 59 years, or if four renal cysts are present bilaterally in individuals older than 60 years of age. A renal ultrasound, computed tomographic (CT) scan, or magnetic resonance imaging (MRI) scan all are highly sensitive and specific for detection of PKD. The specific diagnosis of ADPKD requires consideration of the characteristics of associated extrarenal manifestations, age at presentation, and family history (Table 127–2). Because only about 60% of individuals give a family history of PKD, ultrasound screening of asymptomatic parents or grandparents may be required to uncover diagnostically relevant silent PKD. Currently, genetic testing is performed mainly for research purposes and is not widely available.

Table 127–2 • COMPARING CLINICAL FEATURES OF CYSTIC KIDNEY DISEASES

DISEASE	FAMILY HISTORY	FREQUENCY	GENE PRODUCT	AGE OF ONSET	CYST ORIGIN	RENOMEGALY	CAUSE OF ESRD	OTHER MANIFESTATIONS
ADPKD	Yes (AD)	1:400–1:1000	Polycystin-1 (85%) Polycystin-2 (~15%)	20s and 30s	Anywhere (including Bowman's capsule)	Yes	Yes	Liver cysts Cerebral aneurysms Hypertension Mitral valve prolapse Kidney stones UTIs
ARPKD	Yes (AR)	1:6000–1:10,000	Fibrocystin/ polyductin (100%)	First year of life	Distal nephron, CD	Yes	Yes	Hepatic fibrosis Pulmonary hypoplasia Hypertension
ACKD	No	90% of ESRD patients at 8 years	—	Years after onset of ESRD	Proximal and distal tubules	Rarely	No	None
Simple cysts	No	50%>age 40 years	—	Adulthood	Anywhere (usually cortical)	No	No	None
FN	Yes (AR)	1:80,000	Nephrocystins	Childhood adolescence	Medullary DCT	No	Yes	Retinal, bone, cerebellar anomalies
MCKD	Yes (AD)	Rare	Uromodulin, others	Early adulthood	Medullary DCT	No	Yes	Hypertension
MSK	No	1:5000–1:20,000	—	30s	Medullary CD	No	No	Kidney stones Hypercalciuria
Tuberous sclerosis	Yes (AD)	1:10,000	Hamartin (TSC1), tuberin (TSC2)	Childhood	Loop of Henle, DCT	Rarely	Rarely	Renal cell carcinoma Tubers, seizures Angiomyolipomas Hypertension
VHL syndrome	Yes (AD)	1:40,000	VHL protein	20s	Cortical nephrons	Rarely	Rarely	Renal cell carcinoma Pheochromocytoma

AD = autosomal dominant; AR = autosomal recessive; ACKD = acquired cystic kidney disease; ADPKD = autosomal dominant polycystic kidney disease; ARPKD = autosomal recessive polycystic kidney disease; CD = collecting duct; DCT = distal convoluted tubule; ESRD = end-stage renal disease; FN = familial nephronophthisis; MCKD = medullary cystic kidney disease; MSK = medullary sponge kidney; UTI = urinary tract infection; VHL, von Hippel-Lindau; — = no known genetic susceptibility.

Prevention and Treatment

There are currently no strategies to prevent the formation and progression of renal or hepatic cysts. Management strategies aim instead at monitoring for and treating complications and providing counseling as appropriate.

Frequent blood pressure monitoring is recommended since hypertension accelerates decline in renal function. The goals of blood pressure control are the same as for any other patient with renal disease and include the attainment of a symptom-free blood pressure of 125/75 mm Hg or less. Although all available antihypertensive agents have been used with roughly equivalent success, theoretical considerations and preliminary data suggest that angiotensin-converting enzyme inhibitors or receptor blockers may be more efficient at delaying the rate of progression to ESRD.

Urinary tract infection and nephrolithiasis treatment are no different than in the general population and include standard antimicrobial therapy and increased fluid intake, respectively. Renal or hepatic cyst infections are optimally treated with lipophilic antibiotics that possess cyst-penetrating capabilities. These include ciprofloxacin, trimethoprim, clindamycin, and vancomycin. The results of blood or urine cultures and sensitivities should be used to guide the choice of antibiotic therapy. Cyst hemorrhage and rupture, with resultant pain and hematuria, are usually managed conservatively with rest and non-NSAID analgesics. Patients with enlarged kidneys should be advised to avoid playing contact sports, and those with massively enlarged kidneys should refrain even from wearing belts and seatbelts. Some patients with unusually painful cysts respond to cyst fluid aspiration, cyst deroofing, or ethanol-induced sclerosis. Nephrectomies are rarely indicated before the onset of ESRD.

Cerebral aneurysms are increasingly being detected with magnetic resonance angiography (MRA) rather than CT scanning with intravenous contrast. The former is more sensitive for posterior circulation anomalies and does not risk worsened renal function. Four-vessel cerebral angiography remains the gold standard and is often used for surgical planning. Performance of a cerebral MRA in all patients at time of diagnosis of ADPKD was shown to be cost effective and to lead to improved morbidity and mortality in a decision analysis model. It was further suggested that those individuals with familial cerebral aneurysms (defined as aneurysms in two or more first- to third-degree relatives) undergo screening MRA every 3 years. Individuals shown to have cerebral aneurysms should be referred to a neurosurgeon for consideration of clipping. An annual screening MRA to assess for aneurysmal growth is recommended in all patients with untreated aneurysms.

Renal replacement therapies including renal transplantation for ADPKD are at least as effective as they are in other causes of ESRD.

COUNSELING. The wide variability in disease presentation and the tendency to late onset of disease-associated morbidity make considerations for therapeutic abortion less pressing. Still, patients should be advised that their children have a 50% probability of inheriting a disease-causing mutation. The decision to screen by renal ultrasound the children of parents with ADPKD is made only after consideration of the potential psychological and economical implications. These include a sense of helplessness and increased medical and life insurance costs.

Prognosis

Approximately 50% of patients with ADPKD develop ESRD by 60 years of age. The rate of progression of renal disease is highest in men with poorly controlled hypertension, an early age at diagnosis, and with mutations in *PKD1* alone or in both *PKD1* and *TSC2*. Approximately 5% of all ADPKD patients with cerebral aneurysms die from aneurysmal rupture. The longevity of patients with ADPKD is reduced, with an average lifespan of approximately 55 and 65 years for patients with *PKD1* and *PKD2* mutations, respectively.

AUTOSOMAL RECESSIVE POLYCYSTIC KIDNEY DISEASE

Genetics and Pathogenesis

ARPKD is a multisystem disorder characterized by severe and early PKD, pulmonary failure, and hepatic fibrosis. In contrast to ADPKD,

ARPKD has been linked to heterogeneous mutations in only one gene, the recently cloned *PKHD1*, an orthologue of the rat gene causing PKD (see Table 127–1). Located on chromosome 6, *PKHD1* transcribes a 16-kb fragment that encodes a unique type I membrane protein comprised of 4074 amino acids. Its large extracellular segment contains at least 10 copies of an immunoglobulin-like domain also found in plexins and certain transcription factors, suggestive of a role in cell adhesion or proliferation. The almost simultaneous publication of the *PKHD1* gene product by two different groups has resulted in two different names being given: *fibrocystin* and *polyductin*. The messenger RNA (mRNA) is variably spliced, and in the most complete form is predicted to possess a large extracellular amino terminus, a single spanning trasmembrane region, and a short cytoplasmic carboxy terminus. The shorter variants lack the membrane-spanning region, indicating that they are secreted. *PKHD1* mRNA is detected mostly in kidney, but also in pancreas, lung, and liver, all organs affected in ARPKD. Sequence homologies predict a receptor function that, on the bases of inheritance pattern and disease phenotype, likely aids in distal tubule, collecting duct, and biliary differentiation.

Clinical Manifestations

In common with ADPKD, ARPKD has a highly variable mode of presentation. Although ARPKD can present as radiographically discovered renal cysts antenatally or during adulthood, it usually manifests as bilateral abdominal masses and renal insufficiency in infancy. Findings related to tubular dysfunction may be present and include polyuria, enuresis, hyponatremia, and hyperchloremic metabolic acidosis. ESRD is expected but can take up to 20 years to develop and may in rare instances never occur. Oligohydramnios, presumably linked to in utero renal disease, is often present and likely accounts for the severe pulmonary hypoplasia that causes most of the deaths in the first year of life. Hepatic fibrosis, a prominent feature of ARPKD, commonly progresses to portal hypertension and its attendant complications of bleeding esophageal varices and hepatosplenomegaly. Pancreatic fibrosis is only rarely a clinical concern. Hypertension is almost universal and probably accelerates renal function decline. Cyst complications of infection and rupture also occur, although hematuria is an infrequent finding.

Diagnosis

The demonstration by abdominal ultrasound or CT scan of both enlarged polycystic kidneys and hepatic fibrosis is sufficient to diagnose ARPKD. Aside from an occasional affected sibling, a family history is often not elicited. Distinguishing ARPKD from ADPKD may rarely require a liver biopsy to document otherwise undetectable hepatic fibrosis. The discovery of the causative gene defect should now aid in genetic counseling.

Prevention and Treatment

As with ADPKD, there is no specific therapy for ARPKD. Management goals include early detection and treatment of the complications of hypertension, urinary tract or cyst infection, and portal hypertension. Treatment of the latter may require liver transplantation or portosystemic shunting. As in all children with ESRD, attention to the issues of nutrition and renal osteodystrophy is paramount.

Prognosis

ARPKD-affected patients suffer their highest mortality rates during the first year of life. Following this, the survival to 15 years of age is approximately 50 to 80%.

ACQUIRED CYSTIC KIDNEY DISEASE

ACKD is largely confined to the ESRD population on dialysis. Cysts arise from proximal and distal tubule dilations in small, end-stage kidneys, regardless of etiology, mode of dialysis, or presence of a functioning kidney transplant. Identifiable risk factors include duration of ESRD, male gender, black race, and chronic hypokalemia.

Clinical Manifestations

Acquired cystic kidney disease is usually asymptomatic. However, it can occasionally lead to enlarged kidneys with associated abdominal discomfort and pain. Cyst hemorrhage is more common than cyst infection and presents with flank pain, anemia, or hematuria. The most significant complication of ACKD is malignant conversion of cysts into RCC. These commonly present as hematuria and are 2 to 200 times more common in patients with ACKD than in the general dialysis population.

Diagnosis

A diagnosis of ACKD is relatively straightforward and entails ultrasound or CT scan demonstration of bilateral renal cysts in a patient with preexistent chronic renal failure or ESRD. In contrast to ADPKD and ARPKD, the kidneys are usually not enlarged and there is no family history of PKD. A renal CT or MRI scan is preferable for detecting cysts in small kidneys and in assessing for malignant conversion.

Rx Prevention and Treatment

As with other PKDs, there are no strategies to prevent the appearance or delay the expansion of renal cysts. Alterations in dialysis dose do not modify the course. New or frank hematuria raises the concern for RCC and requires both enhanced and nonenhanced CT or MRI scans to rule this out. Any evidence for septa formation, solid material, or contrast enhancement within a cyst is suspicious for RCC and warrants consideration of nephrectomy.

Prognosis

Although RCCs in patients with ACKD are less often metastatic at time of diagnosis than in other patients with RCC, the 5-year mortality rates are greater. This likely relates to the almost invariable coexistence of ESRD. Asymptomatic ACKD does not affect survival.

MEDULLARY AND MISCELLANEOUS CYSTIC KIDNEY DISORDERS

The *medullary cystic kidney diseases* comprise two rare but clinically significant hereditary disorders (familial nephronophthisis [FN] and medullary cystic kidney disease [MCKD]), and the common but usually benign developmental condition, medullary sponge kidney (see Table 127–2). Recessively acquired mutations in one of four identified genes result in FN. *NPHP1* and *NPHP4* cause juvenile FN and encode nephrocystin-1 and -4, respectively. These two cytoplasmic proteins interact and are involved in cellular adhesion and signal transduction. The gene products of *NPHP2* and *-3* that cause the infantile and adolescent forms of FN are not yet determined. FN presents in early childhood and adolescence with tubular dysfunction that inexorably progresses to ESRD before age 20 years. Approximately 20% of patients exhibit eye, bone, or cerebellar anomalies. MCKD is similar to FN but is rarer, appears in young adulthood, and has an autosomal dominant inheritance pattern. At least two genes, *MCKD1* and *MCKD2*, cause MCKD. The gene product of *MCKD1* is not yet determined; *MCKD2* encodes uromodulin, an 85-kD urinary protein secreted by the thick ascending limb of the loop of Henle. Medullary sponge kidney is characterized by congenitally acquired inner medullary and papillary collecting duct dilations and hypercalciuria. Although it can present as an incidental finding on intravenous pyelogram (with characteristic pooling of contrast within the cystically dilated collecting ducts), medullary sponge kidney also presents as hematuria and recurrent kidney stones. The pathogenesis of MCKD is unknown. It may be associated with a variety of congenital anomalies suggestive of a genetic predisposition.

Renal cyst formation is seen in two rare autosomal dominant inherited conditions: *tuberous sclerosis* and *von Hippel-Lindau (VHL) syndrome*. These are systemic disorders whose cardinal features usually do not relate to cystic kidney disease and are thus discussed in further detail elsewhere. Cyst formation in tuberous sclerosis is commonly associated with hypertension, can resemble ADPKD (sometimes with severe PKD leading to ESRD), and has an increased incidence of RCC (~5%). Cyst formation in von Hippel-Lindau syndrome can also lead

to features of ADPKD but, more important, is associated with a 25% incidence of clear RCC.

FUTURE DIRECTIONS

Cyst formation is clearly a complex multistep process that resembles, and in some instances leads to, neoplastic transformation. It requires an initiating event (presumably at the single-cell level) followed by a series of propagating steps to become clinically significant. The initiating events that lead to cyst formation can occur many times and, in the case of ADPKD, in disparate organ systems. Future directions will therefore include identification of the key pathogenetic or pathophysiologic events necessary to initiate cyst and aneurysm formation, as well as the signaling processes that propagate cyst and aneurysm expansion, hepatic fibrosis, and tumor genesis. Elucidation of the signaling pathways that include polycystin-1 and -2, fibrocystin/polyductin, and nephrocystin as key participants obviously is central to these goals and should rationalize future targeted drug development.

SUGGESTED READINGS

Arnaout MA: Molecular genetics and pathogenesis of autosomal dominant polycystic kidney disease. Annu Rev Med 2001;52:93–123. *An extensive review of the molecular genetics of ADPKD.*

Chapman AB, Guay-Woodford LM, Grantham JJ, et al: Renal structure in early autosomal-dominant polycystic kidney disease (ADPKD): The Consortium for Radiologic Imaging Studies of Polycystic Kidney Disease (CRISP) cohort. Kidney Int 2003;64:1035–1045. *Magnetic resonance imaging is an accurate method to measure cysts.*

Lager DJ, Qian Q, Bengal RJ, et al: The pck rat: A new model that resembles human autosomal recessive polycystic kidney and liver disease. Kidney Int 2001;59:126–136. *Characterization of a new model of polycystic kidney disease and polycystic liver disease.*

Schrier RW, McFann KK, Johnson AM: Epidemiological study of kidney survival in autosomal dominant polycystic kidney disease. Kidney Int 2003;63:678–685. *Blood pressure control with ACE inhibitors has been associated with slower progression of disease.*

Sutters M, Germino GG: Autosomal dominant polycystic kidney disease: Molecular genetics and pathophysiology. J Lab Clin Med 2003;141:91–101. *A clear, concise overview.*

Ward CJ, Hogan MC, Rossetti S, et al: The gene mutated in autosomal recessive polycystic kidney disease encodes a large, receptor-like protein. Nat Genet 2002;30:259–269. *Discusses the structure and putative function of the protein responsible for ARPKD.*

128 ANOMALIES OF THE URINARY TRACT

Lisa M. Guay-Woodford

DEVELOPMENT OF THE KIDNEY AND URINARY TRACT

The human kidney and the urogenital tract develop from three principal embryonic structures: the metanephric mesenchyme, the mesonephric (wolffian) duct, and the cloaca (Fig. 128–1). At 4 to 5 weeks of gestation, the ureteric bud originates as a diverticulum of the mesonephric duct. Reciprocal interactions between the branching ureteric bud and the metanephric mesenchyme induce kidney development, with the metanephros undergoing an epithelial transformation to form the glomeruli and the proximal and distal tubules. The ureteric bud branches give rise to the collecting ducts, the renal pelvis, the ureter, and the bladder trigone. Nephrogenesis is completed by 34 weeks of gestation.

Concurrent with the initial nephrogenic events, the urorectal fold divides the cloaca into the urogenital sinus and the future rectum. The mesonephric duct opening into the bladder becomes the vesicoureteric orifice of the trigone. Between 5 and 6 weeks of gestation, the second genital duct (mullerian duct) appears and runs in parallel with the wolffian duct. In males, the mullerian duct subsequently regresses, whereas the wolffian duct development proceeds to form the epididymis, the vas deferens, the seminal vesicle, and the ejaculatory duct. In the female, wolffian duct regresses. The mullerian ducts fuse to form the ureterovaginal primordium, which merges with the urogenital sinus, and eventually gives rise to the uterus, the oviducts, and the proximal vagina. The remnants of the allantois form the urachus, a fibrous cord that connects the bladder to the umbilicus.

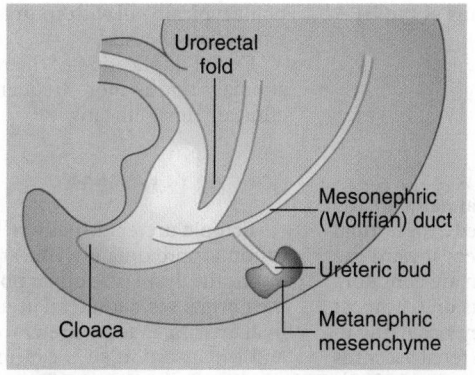
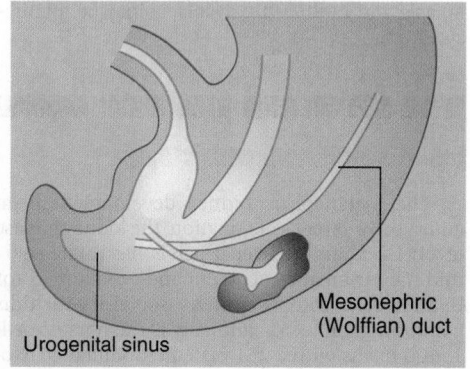
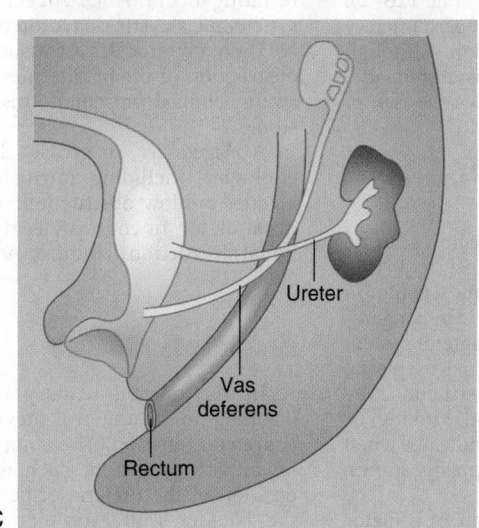
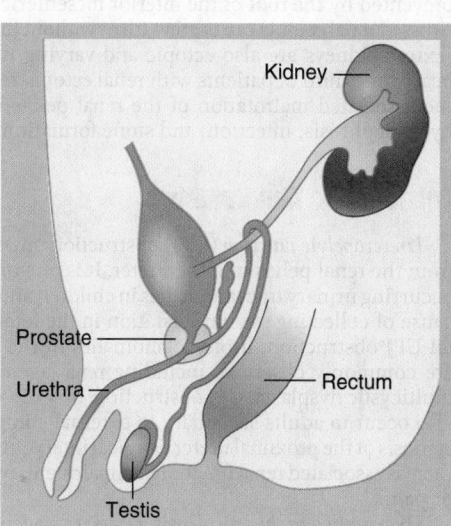

FIGURE 128–1 • Key events in the development of the urinary tract. In the 4-week embryo, the ureteric bud emerges from the wolffian duct (*A*). Reciprocal interactions between the branching ureteric bud and the metanephric mesenchyme induce kidney development. Concurrently, the cloaca is divided by the urorectal fold into the urogenital sinus and the future rectum (*B*). In the 8-week male embryo, the wolffian duct begins to give rise to the epididymis, seminal vesicles, and the caudal part of the vas deferens (*C*). By 9 weeks, axial growth of the fetal spine prompts the developing kidney to ascend from the pelvis to its final lumbar position. The external genitalia develop between 8 and 16 weeks and testicular descent begins in month 7 of gestation (*D*).

Developmental abnormalities of the kidney and urinary tract are relatively common, affecting approximately 10% of newborns and accounting for almost one third of all congenital malformations. Some are asymptomatic and inconsequential, but many renal tract malformations are important causes of infant mortality and of morbidity in older children and adults, including the progression to renal failure.

RENAL PARENCHYMAL MALFORMATIONS

Congenital defects in renal development may result in the absence of a kidney or abnormalities in kidney size, structure, or position. Irregularities in the renal contour may arise from the persistence of fetal lobulation or a depression on the mid-pole of the left kidney by the spleen (a "dromedary hump"). Neither irregularity causes renal functional impairment.

Renal Agenesis

Renal agenesis reflects a complete failure of nephrogenesis. Unilateral agenesis can occur as an isolated abnormality or as a component of syndromic disorders, such as Turner syndrome. As an isolated entity, the complete absence of one kidney occurs in 1 : 500 to 1 : 1000 individuals. The incidence is higher in males and occurs somewhat more frequently on the left side. Absence of the ipsilateral ureter and hemitrigone occur in about half the patients. The remaining kidney is usually enlarged owing to compensatory hypertrophy but may be ectopic or malrotated. Vesicoureteral reflux (VUR) on the contralateral side is observed in about 30% of patients.

Renal agenesis is commonly associated with genital anomalies, suggesting that the anomaly represents a developmental field defect. In females, absence of the ipsilateral oviduct and malformation of the uterus and vagina result from maldevelopment of mullerian duct, whereas in males, wolffian duct–derived structures, such as the vas deferens and the seminal vesicles, are often absent. Other associated anomalies include cardiovascular malformations, vertebral defects, and imperforate anus.

Bilateral renal agenesis is associated with the "Potter's phenotype," which includes pulmonary hypoplasia, a characteristic facies, and deformities of the spine and limbs. At birth, these neonates have a critical degree of pulmonary hypoplasia that is incompatible with survival.

The familial association of unilateral and bilateral renal agenesis, renal dysplasia, and congenital hydronephrosis occurs in hereditary renal adysplasia (HRA) syndrome, an autosomal dominant disorder with variable penetrance.

Renal Hypoplasia

Renal hypoplasia describes small kidneys with apparently normal renal parenchyma. True hypoplasia results from impaired postnatal nephron growth. *Oligomeganephronia* describes a form of bilateral renal hypoplasia with marked reduction in nephron number and associated hypertrophy of individual glomeruli and tubules. This abnormality occurs sporadically as an isolated developmental defect that must be differentiated from acquired renal atrophy and the nephronophthisis–medullary cystic disease complex. Renal function declines slowly, with progression to end-stage renal failure in the second to third decade of life.

Renal Dysplasia

Renal dysplasia, regardless of renal size, indicates abnormal metanephric differentiation resulting in anomalous and incompletely differentiated renal elements. Small dysplastic kidneys are commonly referred to as *aplastic*. Large dysplastic kidneys are often cystic, with the most common type being *multicystic dysplasia*.

Unilateral dysplasia may be asymptomatic well into adult life. Small aplastic and large multicystic dysplastic kidneys are nonfunctioning and can be distinguished with imaging studies from renal agenesis. The ipsilateral ureter is typically atretic. Contralateral malformations, including obstruction and VUR, are common. Unilateral multicystic kidneys involute over time and often disappear. As noted, unilateral aplasia and multicystic dysplasia may be manifestations of the HRA syndrome.

RENAL AND URETERAL STRUCTURAL ANOMALIES

Renal Malrotation and Ectopia

The metanephric kidney development begins caudally in the embryo. By 9 weeks of gestation, the kidney has ascended to its normal level (L1-3) and the renal pelvis has rotated 90 degrees toward the midline. Anomalies of ascent and/or failure of rotation are common. Bilateral renal ectopia is often associated with kidney fusion. The most common renal fusion anomaly is the horseshoe kidney, occurring in 1 : 400 births with a 2 : 1 male predominance. Normal renal ascent is prevented by the root of the inferior mesenteric artery (Fig. 128–2). Crossed renal ectopia can occur with or without fusion. Supernumerary (extra) kidneys are also ectopic and varying in location. Although nearly one third of patients with renal ectopia remain asymptomatic, the associated malrotation of the renal pelvis increases the risk of hydronephrosis, infection, and stone formation.

Pelviureteric Abnormalities

Ureteropelvic junction (UPJ) obstruction impedes the flow of urine from the renal pelvis into the ureter. It is one of the most frequently occurring urinary tract anomalies in children and is the most common cause of collecting system dilatation in the fetal kidney. In congenital UPJ obstruction, urologic anomalies in the contralateral system are commonly observed, including renal agenesis, renal dysplasia, multicystic dysplasia, UPJ obstruction, or VUR. UPJ obstruction may also occur in adults secondary to external compression, kinking, or stenosis of the proximal ureter. Surgical intervention is indicated when there is associated renal functional impairment, pyelonephritis, stones, or pain.

Hydrocalyx or *hydrocalcosis* refers to the dilatation of a major calyx that occurs in the context of intrinsic obstruction, such as infundibular stenosis, or extrinsic compression of the pelvis, such as by a vessel or a parapelvic cyst. In comparison, *megacalycosis* represents a nonobstructive, dysplastic lesion, primarily observed in males, in which the calyces are dilated and usually increased in number. Associated renal medullary hypoplasia causes malformation of the renal papillae.

Calyceal diverticula are cystic structures connected by a narrow channel to an adjacent minor calyx. In imaging studies, these diverticula typically fill with contrast, which distinguishes them from renal parenchymal cysts.

Partial duplication of the renal pelvis and the ureter is a common anomaly that is more frequent in females, typically unilateral, and clinically insignificant.

Ureteric Anomalies

Ectopic ureters usually reflect complete ureteric and renal duplication. Approximately 10% are bilateral. The ectopic ureter typically drains the dysplastic upper pole of a duplex kidney and inserts below the normal vesicoureteral junction into the lower trigone or the proximal urethra. Ectopic ureters occur much more frequently in females, and the insertion sites can include the vagina and the vulva, with resulting incontinence. An ectopic ureter often is associated with an *ureterocele*, a cystic dilatation of the terminal ureter (Fig. 128–3). In children, ureteroceles are associated with urinary tract infection and obstruction of the bladder neck or even the contralateral ureter. In adults, clinical presentation is prompted by infection and ureteric stones.

A *megaureter*, or grossly dilated ureter, has multiple potential etiologies, including intrinsic ureteric obstruction by a stone, bladder outflow obstruction, VUR, or external compression of the distal ureter. In contrast, a *primary megaureter* results from a functional obstruction of the distal ureter caused by an aperistaltic segment (Fig. 128–4).

Vesicoureteral Reflux

In the normal urinary tract, the urinary reflux from the bladder into the ureters is prevented by valve mechanism at the vesicoureteral junction. The competence of this valve is dependent on several critical factors, such as the intramural length of ureter, the position of the ureteric orifice in the bladder, and the integrity of the bladder wall musculature. Primary VUR results from the incompetence of the vesicoureteral junction due to the short length of the ureter submucosal segment and the lateral, ectopic position of its orifice. As the intramural ureter lengthens with age, primary VUR tends to remit or disappear. Genetic factors appear to contribute to the pathogenesis of primary VUR, as there is a 30- to 50-fold increased risk of VUR in immediate relatives of an index case. VUR can also occur secondary to obstructive maldevelopment of the lower urinary tract, such as triad syndrome and posterior urethral valves.

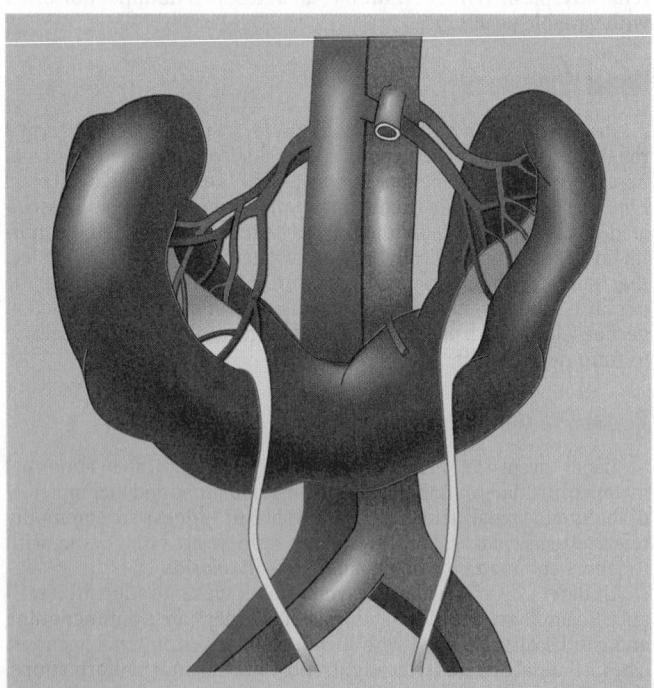

FIGURE 128–2 • Horseshoe kidney.

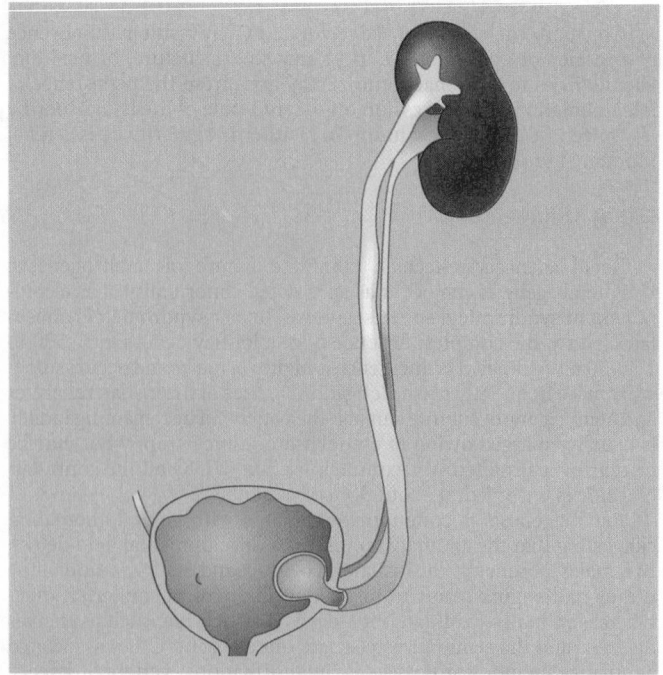

FIGURE 128–3 • Ectopic ureter associated with an ureterocele.

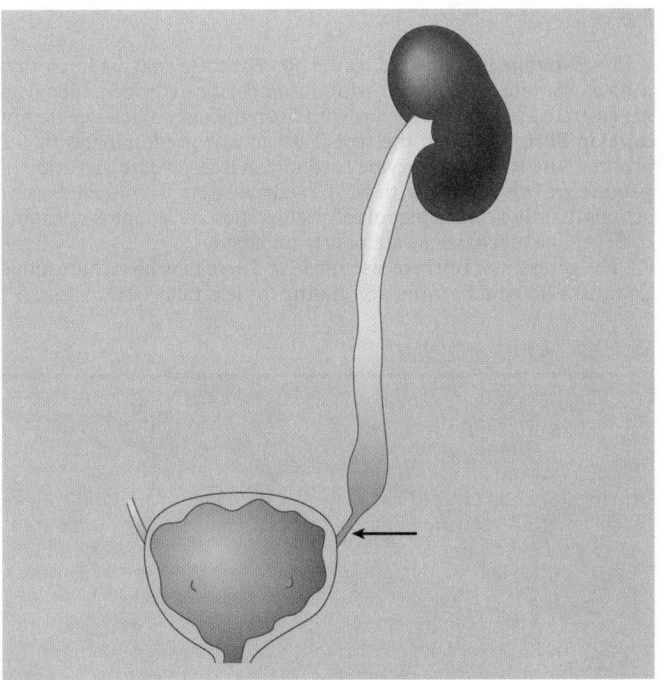

FIGURE 128–4 • Megaureter with the aperistaltic segment (arrow).

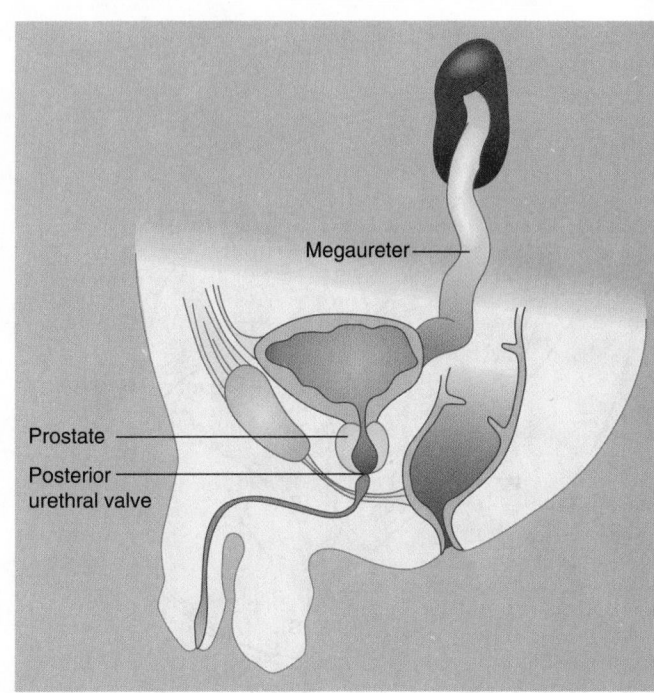

FIGURE 128–5 • Bladder outlet obstruction due to posterior urethral valves.

In both primary and secondary VUR, intrarenal reflux can lead to the development of *reflux nephropathy*, a tubulointerstial lesion associated with gross scarring at the renal poles. In addition, the development of a glomerular lesion consistent with focal and segmental glomerulosclerosis can cause proteinuria, hypertension, and a progressive loss of renal function.

LOWER URINARY TRACT ABNORMALITIES

Triad Syndrome (Prune Belly Syndrome or Eagle-Barrett Syndrome)

Triad syndrome, also referred to as the *prune belly syndrome* or *Eagle-Barrett syndrome,* involves a constellation of anomalies including congenital absence/deficiency of the abdominal wall musculature, gross ureteral dilatation, hypotonic bladder, prostatic hypoplasia, and bilateral undescended testes (cryptorchidism). The full syndrome is expressed only in males, and surviving individuals are typically infertile. Among patients with an incomplete syndrome involving anomalies of the abdominal wall musculature, bladder, and upper urinary tract, 3% are females. Although the specific molecular events have yet to be defined, defects in mesenchymal development appear to cause poor prostatic and bladder differentiation, ureteral smooth muscle aplasia with consequent ureteral aperistalsis, and varying degrees of renal dysplasia. Three fourths of the patients have associated malformations in the cardiopulmonary system, gastrointestinal tract, and the skeleton. In the immediate postnatal period, prognosis depends on the severity of extragenitourinary anomalies. Long-term outcome correlates with the degree of renal dysplasia and the success of urodynamic management.

Bladder Abnormalities

Bladder exstrophy results from a midline closure defect involving the lower anterior abdominal wall, the bladder, and the external genitalia. These abnormalities have been attributed to a primary defect in the differentiation of cloacal membrane, but the precise molecular events are unclear. In severe cases, bladder exstrophy may be associated with imperforate anus and rectal atresia. However, other congenital anomalies are rarely associated. Clinical data indicate a correlation between the success of bladder reconstruction and long-term preservation of renal function.

In adults, *neuropathic bladder* has numerous etiologic contributants, such as central nervous system trauma, stroke, or disorders such as Parkinson's disease; spinal trauma or multiple sclerosis; or peripheral nerve damage due to trauma or surgery. In children, myelomeningocele (spina bifida) is the most common cause of neurogenic bladder dysfunction. Other forms of myelodysplasia, such as spinal dysraphism (spina bifida occulta) and sacral agenesis, are less common causes.

Posterior Urethral Valves

In male infants, posterior urethral valves (PUVs) are the most common cause of bladder outflow obstruction with resulting bilateral hydronephrosis and megaureters. However, among all infants with hydronephrosis, only 10% have PUVs. The urethral obstruction results from a defective reabsorption of mucosal folds in the posterior urethra, just distal to the verumontanum. As a result, there is dilatation of the proximal urethra, bladder wall hypertrophy and trabeculation, associated VUR, and varying degrees of renal dysplasia (Fig. 128–5). Patient survival and long-term renal outcome depend on the severity of the associated renal dysplasia.

SUGGESTED READINGS

Bauer SB: Anomalies of the upper urinary tract. *In* Walsh PC, Retik AB, Vaughan ED, Wein AJ (eds): Campbell's Urology, 8th ed. Philadelphia, WB Saunders, 2002, pp 1885–1924. *A comprehensive urologic discussion of upper urinary tract malformations.*

Neid GH: Congenital abnormalities of the renal tract. *In* Johnson RJ, Feehally J (eds): Comprehensive Clinical Nephrology. London, Harcourt Publishers, 2000, pp 9.55.1–9.55.16. *A concise discussion of congenital urinary tract anomalies and the associated developmental defects.*

Park LM: Normal and anomalous development of the urogenital system. *In* Walsh PC, Retik AB, Vaughan ED, et al (eds): Campbell's Urology, 8th ed. Philadelphia, WB Saunders, 2002, pp 1737–1764. *An excellent, up-to-date discussion of urogenital system development.*

Woolf AS: A molecular and genetic view of human renal and urinary tract malformations. Kidney Int 2000;58:500–512. *An integrated review of the developmental defects and genetic factors that contribute to human urinary tract malformations.*

129 BENIGN PROSTATIC HYPERPLASIA AND PROSTATITIS

Michael J. Barry
Mary McNaughton Collins

The prostate gland, the largest accessory gland in the male reproductive system, surrounds the prostatic urethra below the bladder.

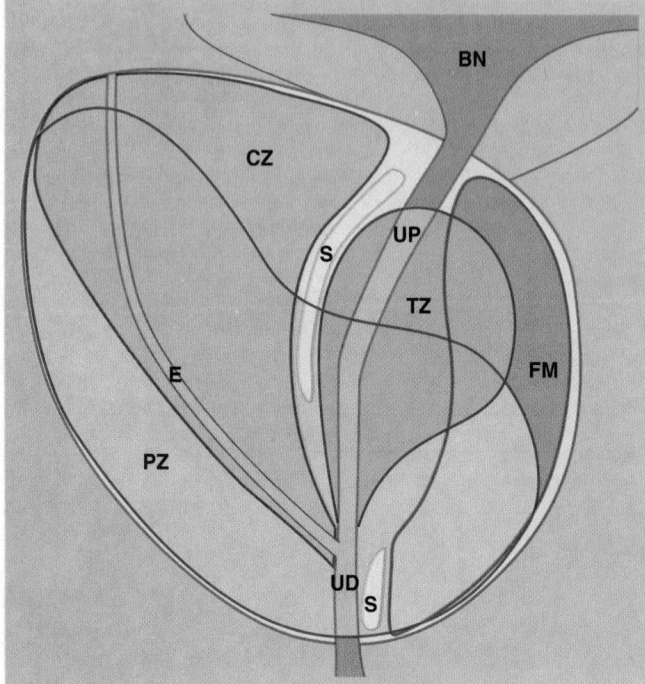

FIGURE 129–1 • Sagittal diagram of distal prostatic urethral segment (UD), proximal urethral segment (UP), and ejaculatory ducts, showing their relationships to a sagittal section of the anteromedial nonglandular tissues (bladder neck [BN], anterior fibromuscular stroma [FM], preprostatic sphincter [S], distal striated sphincter [S]). These structures are shown in relation to a three-dimensional representation of the glandular prostate: central zone (CZ), peripheral zone (PZ), and transitional zone (TZ). (From McNeal J: Normal histology of the prostate. Am J Surg Pathol 1988;12:619–633, with permission.)

Superiorly, its base is contiguous with the bladder neck; inferiorly, its apex adjoins the urogenital diaphragm. The prostatic urethra is angulated at the verumontanum, the union with the two ejaculatory ducts. In younger men, the prostate weighs about 20 grams. As men age, the prostate enlarges and develops a characteristic zonal anatomy (Fig. 129–1). Its acini communicate with the urethra via prostatic ducts, supplying about 20% of semen volume. Prostatic fluid is rich in citrate, zinc, and polyamines, although their roles in reproduction are poorly defined.

BENIGN PROSTATIC HYPERPLASIA

Definition

Benign prostatic hyperplasia (BPH) is defined histologically by hyperplasia of both epithelial and stromal cells, beginning in the periurethral area. With aging, multiple small hyperplastic nodules grow, coalesce, and compress normal tissue outwards against the true prostatic capsule, creating a surgical capsule bounding the expanding adenoma.

Epidemiology

The hyperplastic process often begins in the 30s; by age 80, 85% of men have BPH. The age-specific prevalence of BPH at autopsy is remarkably similar among men of different ethnicities. Aging and functioning testes are the dominant risk factors. The onset of clinical manifestations of BPH before age 65 in a first-degree relative is also a risk factor. The prevalence of clinical manifestations is uncertain because of lack of consensus on a working definition. Nevertheless, about one third of U.S. men age 40 to 79 years have moderate to severe lower urinary tract symptoms, of which a majority are attributable to BPH.

Pathobiology

Testosterone is converted by the 5α-reductase enzyme into dihydrotestosterone (DHT), the major intraprostatic androgen. Men who are castrated before puberty or with 5α-reductase deficiency do not develop BPH. Although the type 2 isoenzyme predominates in the prostate, the type 1 isoenzyme predominates elsewhere. An array of peptide growth factors, with DHT, mediate stromal–epithelial interactions that alter the balance of cell proliferation and apoptosis, leading to BPH. The mechanisms are poorly understood.

The genetics of BPH are also unclear. There may be an autosomal dominant hereditary form, accounting for less than 10% of cases.

Clinical Manifestations

The morbidity of BPH is conferred through bothersome lower urinary tract symptoms. Traditionally, voiding symptoms, such as hesitancy, straining, a sense of incomplete emptying, intermittency, a weak stream, and postvoid dribbling, were considered a consequence of mechanical bladder outlet obstruction. Filling symptoms, such as frequency, nocturia, urgency, and urge incontinence, were considered due to secondary uninhibited detrusor contractions. However, poor correlations among symptom severity, prostate size, degree of obstruction, and detrusor instability suggest their origin is more complex. The key lower urinary tract symptoms of BPH can be quantified using the seven symptom questions in the International Prostate Symptom Score (IPSS) (Fig. 129–2).

Bladder outlet obstruction due to BPH has both static and dynamic components. The static component is due to the enlarged prostate, whereas the dynamic component is due to increased adrenergic tone in the prostate, where α_2-adrenoreceptors predominate.

In the setting of obstruction, increased detrusor pressure can result in detrusor hypertrophy and, eventually, fibrosis. Complications of BPH include acute urinary retention, which may result from prostatic infarction. Postvoid residual urine probably increases the risk of urinary tract infection or stone formation. With longstanding obstruction, hydroureter and hydronephrosis may develop and, eventually, renal failure. Men with BPH may have hematuria, as there is often a complex of veins stretched over the enlarged prostate; however, other causes, especially malignancy, need to be considered.

Diagnosis

Usually, a working diagnosis of symptomatic BPH is made when an older man presents with lower urinary tract symptoms. These symptoms should be quantified with the IPSS (see Fig. 129–2). Scores of 0 to 7 represent mild symptoms; 8 to 19, moderate symptoms; and 20 to 35, severe symptoms. The pattern of individual responses should be noted. When frequency and nocturia are the dominant symptoms, a voiding diary, in which the patient records the times and amounts of each void over several days, may be helpful. For example, if the diary documents nocturnal polyuria alone, causes other than BPH should be strongly considered. Men with BPH tend to have a balance of voiding and filling symptoms that slowly progress with age. Rapid onset, presentation before age 50, or filling symptoms without voiding symptoms are "red flags" suggesting alternative causes. A complete list of medications should be obtained, as many, especially over-the-counter sympathomimetics and anticholinergics, can affect the urinary tract.

Although lower urinary tract symptoms in older men are often due to BPH, the differential includes systemic diseases causing frequency and nocturia, such as diabetes and hypercalcemia; bladder outlet obstruction due to urethral strictures; and neurologic diseases affecting the bladder. A general medical history and the pattern of symptoms should provide clues to systemic diseases. Men with strictures have usually had genitourinary instrumentation or sexually transmitted diseases. Primary bladder problems should be suspected in men with prior stroke, Parkinson's disease, or diabetic neuropathy.

The physical examination should include a digital rectal examination (DRE) and a focused neurologic examination looking for

	Not at all	Less than 1 time in 5	Less than half the time	About half the time	More than half the time	Almost always
1. Over the past month or so, how often have you had a sensation of not emptying your bladder completely after you finished urinating?	0	1	2	3	4	5
2. Over the past month or so, how often have you had to urinate again less than two hours after you finished urinating?	0	1	2	3	4	5
3. Over the past month or so, how often have you found you stopped and started again several times when you urinated?	0	1	2	3	4	5
4. Over the past month or so, how often have you found it difficult to postpone urination?	0	1	2	3	4	5
5. Over the past month or so, how often have you had a weak urinary stream?	0	1	2	3	4	5
6. Over the past month or so, how often have you had to push or strain to begin urination?	0	1	2	3	4	5

7. Over the last month, how many times did you most typically get up to urinate from the time you went to bed at night until the time you got up in the morning?

| 0 | none | 1 | 1 time | 2 | 2 times | 3 | 3 times | 4 | 4 times | 5 | 5 or more times |

Total IPSS Score = sum of questions 1–7 = ____ ____

Quality of life due to urinary symptoms

If you were to spend the rest of your life with your urinary condition just the way it is now, how would you feel about that?

Delighted	Pleased	Mostly satisfied	Mixed—about equally satisfied and dissatisfied	Mostly dissatisfied	Unhappy	Terrible
0	1	2	3	4	5	6

FIGURE 129–2 • International Prostate Symptom Score (IPSS). The seven symptom questions compose a scale initially developed as the American Urological Association symptom index. The eighth question about symptom bother is scored separately. (From Barry MJ, Fowler FJ Jr, O'Leary MP, et al: The American Urological Association symptom index for benign prostatic hyperplasia: The Measurement Committee of the American Urological Association. J Urol 1992;148:1549.)

evidence of peripheral neuropathy or saddle-area anesthesia (the S2-4 segments innervate the bladder) that might suggest an underlying neuropathic bladder. The DRE should assess the size and consistency of the prostate. Classically, BPH causes a symmetrically enlarged, firm prostate, the consistency of the tip of the nose. Asymmetry or frank nodules suggest prostate cancer; however, prostate cancer can be present even when the prostate feels normal. Clinicians tend to underestimate prostate size; if the prostate feels enlarged, it usually is.

A urinalysis should be performed for evidence of pyuria or hematuria. Optional studies include creatinine measurements, uroflow rates, and prostate-specific antigen (PSA) levels. Peak uroflows are often measured in urologists' offices but are unreliable with low voided volumes (<150 mL). Peak flows of less than 10 mL/sec are more suggestive of outlet obstruction, whereas flows greater than 15 mL/sec are less suggestive; unfortunately, men can have good flows with obstruction and forceful bladder contractions, and poor flows without obstruction with weak bladder contractions.

PSA tests are used for early detection of prostate cancer; however, PSA has relatively poor specificity in this situation. Moreover, early detection of prostate cancer with PSA has not as yet been shown to reduce prostate cancer mortality in randomized trials. If a PSA is ordered, generally a level greater than 4 ng/mL should trigger an ultrasonography-guided prostate biopsy. Although about 50% of men with PSA levels greater than 10 ng/mL have prostate cancer at biopsy, only about 25% with levels of 4.1 to 10.0 ng/mL have cancer. Most authorities doubt the value of early detection of nonpalpable prostate cancer in men with a life expectancy of less than 10 years or after about age 75 for men with average comorbidity. Many men who present with BPH are older. However, for medical-legal reasons, it is wise to discuss the possibility of an underlying prostate cancer with any older man presenting with lower urinary tract symptoms. A PSA, probably by serving as a proxy for prostate size, can also help stratify the future risk of progression to surgery or acute urinary retention, with higher values predicting greater risks.

The "gold standard" test for the diagnosis of bladder outlet obstruction is the documentation of increased bladder pressure relative to uroflow. The role of pressure-flow studies in the evaluation of men with lower urinary tract symptoms is debated. These tests should be considered in men who have atypical presentations or with diseases that increase their risk of primary bladder problems or who fail invasive therapy. Because findings at pressure-flow studies can predict responses to invasive therapy, albeit imperfectly, some authorities also consider them for men for whom medical therapy fails.

Prevention and Treatment

As yet, there are no documented effective preventive strategies for BPH.

Men with IPSS scores in the mild range are rarely bothered enough to treat. Similarly, an enlarged prostate alone is not an indication for treatment. The key step in decision-making for men with moderate or severe symptoms is to assess the degree to which they are bothering the patient. The last IPSS question (see Fig. 129–2) can serve as an entree into this discussion.

For men with little bother, "watchful waiting" is appropriate. The patient's situation should be periodically reassessed. Avoidance of offending medications is also wise.

MEDICAL THERAPY. Most men with bothersome symptoms initially choose medical therapy. α_1-Adrenergic blockers and the 5α-reductase inhibitor finasteride are the available prescription options. α-Blockers attack the dynamic component of BPH and have been shown to reduce symptoms in multiple clinical trials of up to 4 years' duration.[1] The response to α-blockers is independent of prostate size. In general, doses should be increased toward the maximum until the therapeutic effect is optimal unless side effects are limiting. Doxazosin and terazosin are effective for the treatment of both BPH and hypertension; however, α-blocker monotherapy can no longer be considered optimal for hypertension. The effect of α-blockers on the risks of acute retention or progression to surgery over 4 years is not significant.[2]

In general, side effects of α-blockers include orthostatic hypotension, dizziness, and asthenia. Tamsulosin and alfuzosin appear more specific for the α_{1a}-receptor subtype that dominates in the prostate. Both agents appear to have little or no effect on blood pressure. However, because the dizziness and asthenia seen with α-blockers are not primarily mediated through hypotension, a lack of head-to-head comparisons makes it unclear whether these agents have advantages other than a lower risk of orthostatic hypotension.

Finasteride and dutasteride are the 5α-reductase inhibitors available to date (Table 129–1). These agents block conversion of testosterone to DHT by the type 2 isoenzyme (finasteride) or both isoenzymes (dutasteride). Prostate size decreases by 15 to 20% over 1 year of treatment with either agent.[2,3] Finasteride and dutasteride reduce lower urinary tract symptoms more than placebo in trials of 2 to 4 years in duration, although symptom relief is more modest than that for α-blockers. In addition, these agents reduce the rate of progression to surgery and acute urinary retention for men with larger prostates.[4] PSA levels can be used to stratify the preventive benefit of finasteride. The "number needed to treat" for 4 years to prevent an episode of acute retention or surgery is about 30 for men with PSA levels of less than 1.4 ng/mL, about 20 for PSA levels of 1.4 to 3.2 ng/mL, and about 10 for PSA levels of greater than 3.2 ng/mL.

The main side effect of finasteride and dutasteride is sexual or ejaculatory dysfunction in about 5% of men. Both agents lower PSA levels by about 50%. Although they do not appear to interfere with the detection of prostate cancer,[3] PSA levels must be interpreted differently. The simplest strategy is to double the measured PSA and interpret it as usual.

Given the different mechanisms of α-blockers and 5α-reductase inhibitors, combination therapy is attractive. In a trial of 1 year's duration, finasteride offered no additional symptomatic benefit over α-blockers.[5] When men present with symptomatic BPH, an α-blocker is a reasonable first choice for medical therapy. Finasteride or dutasteride can be offered as well to men with palpably enlarged prostates or higher PSA levels for added preventive benefit.

SURGERY. Transurethral prostatectomy (TURP) is still considered the "gold standard" for treating BPH, offering symptom reductions substantially greater than that achieved with medical therapy. TURP generally requires a brief hospital stay and an indwelling catheter at first. In a randomized trial comparing TURP with watchful waiting, both symptoms and BPH complications were substantially reduced with surgery.[6] Moreover, the risks of sexual dysfunction and incontinence were no greater with TURP. Standard TURP uses a wire electrode to resect obstructing tissue. Newer variations use a rolling electrode or laser energy to vaporize prostate tissue. These procedures appear to result in less short-term bleeding, but their long-term effectiveness is undefined.

OTHER TREATMENTS. Minimally invasive techniques have been developed to relieve symptoms without hospitalization. Transurethral microwave thermotherapy (TUMT) heats and coagulates prostate tissue using a microwave antenna surrounded by a cooling jacket to protect the urethra. Transurethral needle ablation (TUNA) uses radiofrequency needles placed directly into the prostate to generate heat and cause coagulation. The mechanisms by which these treatments work are poorly understood. However, they appear to produce an initial level of symptom relief intermediate between drug therapy and TURP. Their long-term effectiveness remains unclear.

Prognosis

Lower urinary tract symptoms attributable to BPH generally progress slowly over time, but individuals vary. For example, in one study of men with symptom scores in the moderate range who elected watchful waiting, after 4 years of follow-up, 13% had only mild symptoms, 46% still had moderate symptoms, 17% had severe symptoms, and 24% had opted for surgery. The risk of acute urinary retention for such men is 1 to 2% per year. More serious complications appear to be exceedingly rare.

Future Directions

Future directions in medical therapy include the development of dual type 1 and type 2 5α-reductase inhibitors, which may result in lower DHT levels than achievable with finasteride. Trials are ongoing to determine whether combination therapy with α-blockers and finasteride has added benefit over the long run. Newer, less invasive surgical therapies are being developed in an attempt to marry the durable symptom relief of TURP with the ease and minimal side effects of medical therapy.

PROSTATITIS

Definition

The validity of the traditional etiology-based classification of prostatitis has never been confirmed. A newly established National Institutes of Health (NIH) chronic prostatitis classification system incorporates the terminology "chronic pelvic pain syndrome" to reflect uncertainty over whether chronic nonbacterial prostatitis and prostatodynia are in fact even related to the prostate (Table 129–2).

Epidemiology

Two million outpatient visits are made annually in the United States for prostatitis. The histologic prevalence ranges widely from 6 to 98%.

Table 129–1 • MEDICATIONS USED IN THE TREATMENT OF MEN WITH LOWER URINARY TRACT SYMPTOMS ATTRIBUTED TO BENIGN PROSTATIC HYPERPLASIA

DRUG	TABLET/CAPSULE SIZES (mg)	RECOMMENDED DOSE STEPS
α-Blockers		
Alfuzosin*	2.5	2.5 mg tid
Alfuzosin XL*	10	10 mg qd
Doxazosin	1, 2, 4, 8	1, 2, 4, 8 mg qd
Doxazosin gastrointestinal therapeutic system (GITS)*	4, 8	4, 8 mg qd
Tamsulosin	0.4	0.4, 0.8 mg qd
Terazosin	1, 2, 5, 10	1, 2, 5, 10 mg qd
5α-Reductase inhibitors		
Finasteride	5	5 mg qd
Dutasteride	0.5	0.5 mg qd

*This drug has not been approved by the U.S. Food and Drug Administration at the time of publication.

Renal and Genitourinary Diseases

Table 129–2 • CLASSIFICATION AND DEFINITION OF PROSTATITIS

TRADITIONAL CLASSIFICATION		NATIONAL INSTITUTE OF DIABETES AND DIGESTIVE AND KIDNEY DISEASES CLASSIFICATION	
Category	Definition	Category	Definition
Acute bacterial prostatitis	Recovery of bacteria from prostatic fluid, purulence of fluid, and systemic signs of infectious illness (fever, chills, myalgia)	Type I (acute bacterial prostatitis)	Acute infection of the prostate
Chronic bacterial prostatitis	Recovery of bacteria in significant numbers from prostatic fluid in the absence of concomitant urinary infection or significant systemic signs (as in acute bacterial prostatitis)	Type II (chronic bacterial prostatitis)	Recurrent infection of the prostate
		Type III (chronic abacterial prostatitis/chronic pelvic pain syndrome)	No demonstrable infection
Nonbacterial prostatitis	No recovery of significant numbers of bacteria from prostatic fluid, but the fluid consistently reveals microscopic purulence	Type IIIA (inflammatory chronic pelvic pain syndrome)	Leukocytes in serum, expressed prostatic secretions, or post–prostatic massage urine
Prostatodynia	No recovery of significant bacteria or purulence in the prostatic fluid, but patients have persistent urinary urgency, dysuria, poor urinary flow, and prostatic discomfort	Type IIIB (noninflammatory chronic pelvic pain syndrome)	No leukocytes in serum, expressed prostatic secretions, or post–prostatic massage urine
		Type IV (asymptomatic inflammatory prostatitis	No subjective symptoms; detected by prostate biopsy or by the presence of leukocytes in expressed prostatic secretions or semen during evaluation for other disorders

The prevalence of current prostatitis-like symptoms or a prior physician diagnosis of prostatitis is about 10%.

Pathobiology

Both type I (acute bacterial) and type II (chronic bacterial) prostatitis account for 5 to 10% of cases. Like urinary tract infections, 80% are due to strains of *Escherichia coli*; 10 to 15% are due to *Pseudomonas aeruginosa, Serratia, Klebsiella,* and *Proteus* species; and 5 to 10% are due to enterococci.

The remainder (>90%) of prostatitis cases are type III (chronic abacterial/chronic pelvic pain syndrome) prostatitis, but the pathogenesis of this type remains uncertain. Type III prostatitis is further divided into inflammatory (type IIIA) and noninflammatory (type IIIB) subtypes, based on the presence of leukocytes in expressed prostatic secretions and prostatic urine.

Theories for the etiology of type IIIA (inflammatory chronic abacterial) prostatitis include infectious agents, such as *Mycoplasma hominis, Ureaplasma urealyticum, Trichomonas vaginalis, Chlamydia trachomatis,* viruses, anaerobic bacteria, and coagulase-negative staphylococci; proinflammatory cytokines; autoimmune mechanisms; and chemical irritation. The pathogenesis of the presumed inflammation in type IIIA prostatitis focuses on the intraprostatic reflux of urine. Type IIIB (noninflammatory chronic abacterial) is thought to result from increased tension in the muscles of the bladder neck and prostatic urethra or from a tension myalgia of the pelvic floor. Psychological factors have also been implicated.

Clinical Manifestations

Type I prostatitis is characterized by the acute onset of fever, chills, and malaise, low back or perineal pain, and urinary symptoms, particularly dysuria, frequency, and urgency. The presentation is generally dramatic, and the patient may appear toxic. DRE often reveals a markedly tender gland.

Type II prostatitis generally occurs in older men in association with recurrent urinary tract infections. The presentation is less dramatic but involves similar lower urinary tract symptoms, pelvic pain, and sexual dysfunction. On DRE, the prostate may be normal, swollen, firm, or tender.

Type III prostatitis is characterized by pelvic pain, often associated with lower urinary tract symptoms and pain during or after ejaculation. DRE findings also vary.

Type IV prostatitis is, by definition, asymptomatic.

Because the hallmark of chronic prostatitis is a complex of symptoms that wax and wane, a brief, self-administered index has been developed and validated (NIH Chronic Prostatitis Symptom Index) to quantify them.

Diagnosis

Although acute prostatitis is relatively straightforward to diagnose, chronic prostatitis is more challenging. The symptom complexes of chronic prostatitis and BPH overlap, such that older men with chronic prostatitis may be misdiagnosed as having BPH. Also, because prostatitis can increase PSA levels, unnecessary prostate biopsies and detection of clinically insignificant prostate cancer may result. In addition to BPH and prostate cancer, the differential diagnosis for chronic prostatitis includes sexually transmitted disease, urethritis, epididymitis, orchitis, urethral stricture, urinary tract infection, kidney stone, bladder cancer, pudendal artery insufficiency, sphincter dyssynergy, neurogenic bladder, and depression.

Type I prostatitis is diagnosed primarily based on clinical findings and a positive urine culture. Prostate massage is not recommended because of concern for bacteremia.

Type II and type III prostatitis are traditionally diagnosed using the four-glass test. This segmented, quantitative culture technique involves culturing initial-stream urine, mid-stream urine, expressed prostatic secretions after massage, and postmassage urine. The simplified two-glass test involves culture and microscopic examination of urine obtained before and after prostatic massage; it is easier for all concerned, with similar operating characteristics.

Type IV prostatitis is usually diagnosed incidentally by prostate biopsy or by finding leukocytes in prostatic secretions collected for infertility evaluations.

Prevention and Treatment

There is no proven preventive strategy for any type of prostatitis.

Type I prostatitis is relatively easy to treat. Antibacterial agents that normally diffuse poorly into prostatic fluid work well, probably because intense inflammation enhances penetration. The choice of antimicrobial is driven by culture results. Parenteral antibiotics are necessary for sicker patients, but oral fluoroquinolones or trimethoprim-sulfamethoxazole is adequate for outpatients. Treatment for 4 weeks is generally recommended.

Type II prostatitis is more difficult to treat because prostatic fluid becomes alkaline with chronic inflammation, reducing antibiotic penetration. The fluoroquinolones and trimethoprim-sulfamethoxazole penetrate the prostate, but the penicillins, cephalosporins, aminoglycosides, and nitrofurantoin do not. Recommendations for the duration of therapy range from 1 to 3 months. The addition of an α-blocker may improve symptoms and reduce recurrences.

Type III prostatitis often engenders frustration on the part of the physician and confusion and dissatisfaction on the part of the patient. Although some experts recommend an empirical course of antibiotics for chronic abacterial prostatitis, this practice is not supported by the existing evidence, nor is α-blocker therapy. In small studies, TUMT,[7] the bioflavanoid quercetin,[8] and rofecoxib[9] appear to have clinically significant benefit; further evaluation is merited.

For type IV prostatitis, no treatment is recommended.

Prognosis

The untreated natural history of all types of prostatitis is poorly defined. Most patients with type I prostatitis respond well to antibiotics, but some may progress to chronic prostatitis. Complications of type I prostatitis include prostatic abscess, acute urinary retention, septicemia, and, rarely, vertebral osteomyelitis. Type II prostatitis can cause repeated urinary tract infections. Both type II and type III prostatitis have been associated with decreased fertility, although this relationship is not certain.

Future Directions

The Chronic Prostatitis Collaborative Research Network, funded by the NIH/National Institute of Diabetes and Digestive and Kidney Diseases, is a multi-disciplinary, multi-institutional effort to provide more information about the etiology, diagnosis, and treatment of prostatitis. As a first step, a longitudinal Chronic Prostatitis Cohort study has been established. In addition, the first of a series of randomized clinical trials of therapy is under way.

1. Djavan B, Marberger M: A meta-analysis of the efficacy and tolerability of alpha1-adrenoreceptor antagonists in patients with lower urinary tract symptoms suggestive of benign prostatic obstruction. Eur Urol 1999;36:1–13.
2. McConnell JD, et al: The long-term effects of medical therapy on the progression of BPH: Results from the MTOPS trial. J Urol 2002;167(Suppl):265–267.
3. McConnell JD, Bruskewitz R, Walsh P, et al: The effect of finasteride on the risk of acute urinary retention and the need for surgical treatment among men with benign prostatic hyperplasia. N Engl J Med 1998;338:557–563.
4. Roehrborn CG, Boyle P, Nichol JC, et al: Efficacy and safety of a dual inhibitor of 5-alpha-reductase types 1 and 2 (dutasteride) in men with benign prostatic hyperplasia. Urology 2002;60:434–441.
5. Lepor H, Williford WO, Barry MJ, et al: The efficacy of terazosin, finasteride, or both in benign prostatic hyperplasia. N Engl J Med 1996;335:533–539.
6. Wasson JH, Reda DJ, Bruskewitz RC, et al: A comparison of transurethral surgery with watchful waiting for moderate symptoms of benign prostatic hyperplasia. N Engl J Med 1995;332:75–79.
7. Nickel JC, Sorensen R: Transurethral microwave thermotherapy for nonbacterial prostatitis: a randomized double-blind sham controlled study using new prostatitis specific assessment questionnaires. J Urol 1996;155:1950–1955.
8. Shoskes DA, Zeitlin SJ, Shahed A, et al: Quercetin in men with category III chronic prostatitis: a preliminary prospective, double-blind, placebo-controlled trial. Urology 1999;54:960–963.
9. Nickel JC, Pontari M, Moon T, et al: A randomized placebo controlled multicenter study to evaluate the safety and efficacy of rofecoxib in the treatment of chronic nonbacterial prostatis. J Urol 2003;169:1401–1405.

SUGGESTED READINGS

AUA Practice Guidelines Committee: AUA guideline on management of benign prostatic hyperplasia (2003). Chapter 1: Diagnosis and treatment recommendations. J Urol 2003;170(2 Pt 1):530–547. *Consensus guidelines.*

Barry MJ, Roeherborn CG: Extracts from "Clinical Evidence": Benign prostatic hyperplasia. BMJ 2002;323:1042–1046. *A concise, thorough, evidence-based review of BPH therapeutics.*

Krieger JN: Prostatitis revisited: new definitions, new approaches. Infect Dis Clin North Am 2003;17:395–409. *A practical overview.*

Roehrborn CG, Bartsch G, Kirby R, et al: Guidelines for the diagnosis and treatment of benign prostatic hyperplasia: A comparative, international overview. Urology 2001;58:642–650. *A critical comparison of current guidelines for BPH management promulgated from different developed countries.*

Thorpe A, Neal D: Benign prostatic hyperplasia. Lancet 2003;361:1359–1367. *Overview of the pathophysiology and current approaches to diagnosis and management.*

Wagenlehner FM, Naber KG: Prostatitis: The role of antibiotic treatment. World J Urol 2003;21:105–108. *Overview of the role of antibiotics according to the stage of the disease.*

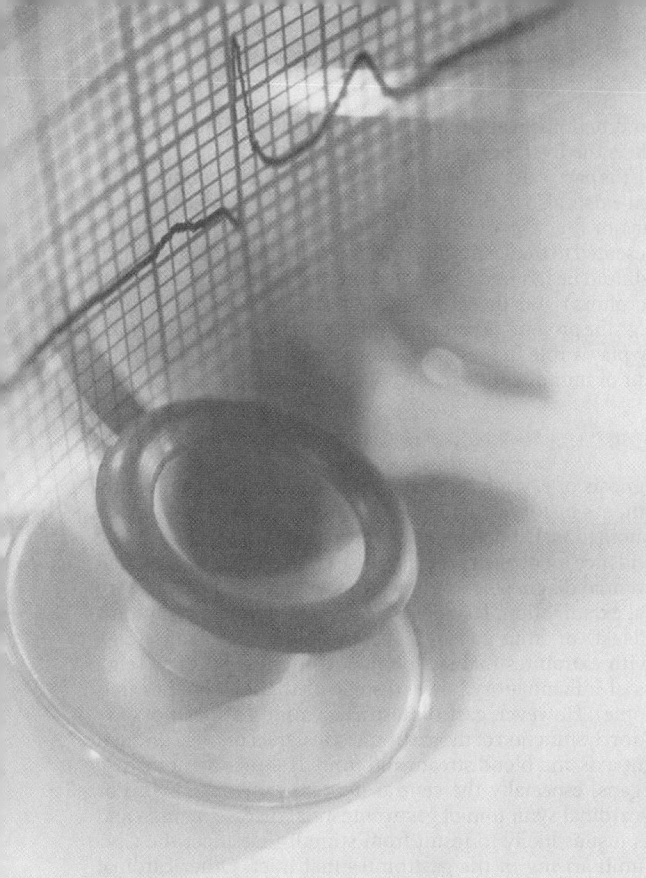

part XII

Gastrointestinal Diseases

130 APPROACH TO THE PATIENT WITH GASTROINTESTINAL DISEASE

Don W. Powell

Epidemiology

Diseases of the gastrointestinal tract and liver together account for about 10% of the total burden of illness, more than 50 million office visits, and nearly 10 million hospital admissions annually in the United States. Colorectal cancer (Chapter 200) is the second most common cause of cancer in men and women, and, when all of the gastrointestinal organs are combined, gastrointestinal malignancies are the most common of any organ system.

The cost of gastrointestinal diseases depends on their prevalence, direct cost (professional fees, hospital charges, pharmaceutical costs), and indirect cost (time lost from work). The most prevalent gastrointestinal diseases are the non–food-borne infections and food-borne illnesses (combined, greater than one episode per year per U.S. citizen) (Chapter 323), gastroesophageal reflux disease (GERD) (Chapter 136), gallbladder disease (Chapter 158), and irritable bowel syndrome (IBS) (Chapter 135), with each occurring in 10% or more of the U.S. population. The most costly diseases (total cost in 2000 dollars) are GERD ($10.1 billion), gallbladder disease ($6.5 billion), colorectal cancer ($5.3 billion), peptic ulcer disease ($3.4 billion; Chapter 138), and diverticular disease ($2.7 billion; Chapter 143). Finally, gastrointestinal diseases as a group account for approximately 10% of all deaths in the United States each year.

Overview of the Gastrointestinal Tract

The major function of the gastrointestinal tract is to process and absorb water and nutrients while food moves physically from mouth to colon, where nonabsorbable wastes are stored for periodic elimination. Dysfunction of the epithelial absorptive function and of the smooth muscle contractile function causes the major pathologic processes related to the gastrointestinal tract. The epithelial lining of the gastrointestinal tract is a huge surface area, greater than that of a tennis court; it interacts with the food, water, and xenobiotics of the external environment and with the intestinal microflora. The epithelium allows the absorption of fluid, electrolytes, and nutrients in health and the secretion of huge volumes of fluid and electrolytes in disease. The rapid turnover of the epithelial cells, which have a life span of 3 to 7 days, allows environmental interaction with genes that may lead to the development of neoplasia. Some of the most common diseases affecting the gastrointestinal tract are disorders of integrated function controlled by secreted hormones, paracrine mediators, and the enteric nervous system. Disruption of this neuroendocrine control is much more likely to cause symptom-complexes (e.g., functional diseases such as IBS and nonulcer dyspepsia) than anatomically defined disease.

However, it would be a mistake to view the gastrointestinal tract only as a muscular tube with an epithelial lining. The enteric nervous system contains between 10 and 100 million neurons, a conglomerate equal to the total number in the spinal cord. If the total number of enteroendocrine cells were put together into a single organ, it would probably be the largest endocrine gland in the body. The gastrointestinal tract's immune cells, which make up the gastrointestinal-associated lymphoid system (GALT), constitute the largest immune organ of the body. These three systems allow the smooth integration of the function of this complex organ, but they also represent points of dysfunction, which can cause both local and even systemic disease.

The enteric nervous system is, for all intents and purposes, an independent nervous system. A growing body of evidence suggests that interaction of the sensory nerves with the spinal cord and brain causes functional gastrointestinal disorders. Current lack of understanding of the enteric nervous system may compromise the management of the 15 to 20% of the population who present with IBS and/or non-ulcer dyspepsia (Chapter 135).

The enteroendocrine system of the gastrointestinal tract is unique because it responds to intraluminal stimuli as well as to systemic stimuli presented to it from either the nervous system or the blood. The secretions of these endocrine cells not only affect epithelial, smooth muscle,

and vascular function but also have poorly understood effects on distal organs such as the liver, pancreas, and brain.

The GALT is part of a common mucosa-associated lymphoid tissue (MALT) that exists also in the lung, the breast, and the genitourinary tract. The major function of the GALT is to recognize the myriad of antigens presented to the gastrointestinal tract, differentiating between those that should be ignored (e.g., the proteins of nutrients and commensal microflora) and those that should excite a major immune response (e.g., the proteins of pathogenic bacteria). The enteric immune system may play a role in systemic autoimmune diseases and in the development of immune tolerance.

Clinical Approach to Gastrointestinal Disease

The diagnosis of gastrointestinal diseases derives predominantly from the patient's history and, to a lesser extent, from the physician's physical examination. Laboratory tests and imaging studies can provide objective evidence for or against a given disease among those included in the differential diagnosis raised by an accurate and expert history and physical examination. Diagnoses arise out of specific symptoms (e.g., dysphagia) or from pairing gastrointestinal complaints (e.g., diarrhea) with extraintestinal symptoms or physical findings (e.g., the arthritis of inflammatory bowel disease or the flushing of carcinoid syndrome). However, gastrointestinal symptoms arise not only from disease or dysfunction of the gastrointestinal tract but also through the brain-gut axis and blood stream and from dysfunction or disease of other organs, especially the central nervous system (CNS). For example, a cardinal symptom of gastrointestinal disease, nausea and vomiting, is just as likely to result from stimuli that affect the CNS as from stimuli arising in the gastrointestinal tract. Other cardinal symptoms are abdominal pain, weight loss, bleeding, diarrhea, and constipation.

CARDINAL SYMPTOMS

Nausea and Vomiting

To understand nausea and vomiting, it is first necessary to differentiate these symptoms from closely related phenomena such as hunger, appetite, satiety, and anorexia. Both *hunger* and *appetite* refer to the desire to eat. The determinants of *hunger* are usually physiologic signals coming from the complex interaction between adrenergic receptors in the medial hypothalamus of the CNS and the serotoninergic, dopaminergic, and β-adrenergic receptors in the lateral hypothalamus. *Appetite* is closely related to hunger, but it is thought to be influenced predominantly by environmental and psychological processes (e.g., the aroma, appearance, and taste of food, as well as the patient's mood). *Satiety* refers to the gratification of hunger and appetite, mediated in part by cholecystokinin and bombesin, which appear to act both peripherally through the vagus nerve and centrally in the hypothalamic satiety center. The discovery of the *Ob* gene and its peptide hormone leptin in adipocytes has improved our understanding of the homeostasis of body mass. Leptin and insulin act on the hypothalamus to inhibit release of anabolic substances such as neuropeptide Y and peptides called orexins that promote feeding and weight gain. Leptin also stimulates release of catabolic substances such as melanocortin and corticotropin-releasing factor, which reduce feeding behavior. *Anorexia* is a clinical symptom characterized by the absence of hunger or appetite. It may be caused by CNS, systemic, or gastrointestinal disease or by emotional processes that initiate functional disorders.

Satiety and anorexia must be differentiated from *nausea*, which is the unpleasant feeling that one is about to vomit, and *vomiting* (or *emesis*), which is the forceful ejection of contents of the upper gut through the mouth. In contrast, *retching* involves coordinated, voluntary muscle activity of the abdomen and thorax—in effect, a forced respiratory inspiration against a closed mouth and glottis without discharge of gastric contents from the mouth. *Regurgitation* is the effortless return of gastric or esophageal contents into the mouth without nausea, and it occurs without spasmodic abdominal, thoracic, or gastrointestinal muscular contractions. *Rumination* (merycism) is the effortless but purposeful regurgitation of food from the stomach into the mouth, where it is rechewed and reswallowed, often several times during or after a meal.

The coordinated events that allow the process of vomiting begin in the reticular areas of the medulla and include the dorsal vagal complex nuclei, which was formerly called the "vomiting center." More recent investigations indicate that multiple brain stem sites mediate emesis, and there is no single "vomiting center." Indeed, several brain stem nuclei are necessary to integrate the various responses of the gastrointestinal, respiratory, pharyngeal, and somatic systems in the act of vomiting. The brain stem control of nausea and vomiting has sensory input from at least four additional areas: (1) the chemoreceptor trigger zone; (2) the vestibular nucleus mediating input from the inner ear and through the cerebellum; (3) the gastrointestinal tract itself, as well as other viscera within the peritoneal cavity; and (4) the upper cortical regions of the CNS. These four areas, through various neurons and receptors of the serotoninergic (5-HT$_3$), dopaminergic (D$_2$), histaminergic (H$_1$), muscarinic (M$_1$), and vasopressinergic (V$_1$) type, respond to environmental and internal stimuli to signal and then activate the vomiting center(s).

The chemoreceptor trigger zone is in the area postrema in the floor of the fourth ventricle. This area lacks a tight blood-brain barrier, so blood-borne agents can penetrate it. The chemoreceptor trigger zone also receives neural input from the upper centers of the brain and the peripheral nerves, and it responds to certain systemic medications and to metabolic diseases. Motion sickness and inner ear disease, such as Ménière's disease (Chapter 470), act through the vestibular nucleus, which contains H$_1$ and M$_1$ receptors. The vagus and sympathetic nerves, via the nodosum ganglion and the nucleus tractus solitarius, mediate nausea that arises from gastric irritants such as salicylates or staphylococcal enterotoxin; gastric, small intestinal, colonic, or bile duct distention; and inflammation or ischemia of bowel, liver, pancreas, and peritoneum. Higher cortical centers also may affect the vomiting center and mediate nausea and vomiting induced by intense emotions or stress, as well as the classic anticipatory nausea and vomiting seen with administration of cancer chemotherapy.

To understand the causes of nausea and vomiting, stimuli arising from the CNS must be differentiated from those originating in the gastrointestinal tract. Historical information concerning the duration, precipitation, and pattern of nausea and vomiting as well as the nature of the vomitus is not sufficient; the physician must also seek signs and symptoms of gastrointestinal diseases (e.g., abdominal pain, diarrhea, constipation, bleeding, or weight loss) and of CNS diseases (e.g., headache, changes in mental status, change in neuromuscular function, symptoms related to the inner ear, drug ingestion, or a history of emotional or environmental stress).

Medications are among the most common causes of nausea and vomiting. Apomorphine, opiates, digitalis, levodopa, bromocriptine, and anticancer drugs act on the chemoreceptor trigger zone. Drugs that frequently cause nausea through other mechanisms include nonsteroidal anti-inflammatory drugs, erythromycin, cardiac antiarrhythmic medications, antihypertensive drugs, diuretics, oral antidiabetic agents, oral contraceptives, and gastrointestinal medications such as sulfasalazine. Chemotherapeutic agents most likely to induce vomiting are cisplatin, nitrogen mustard, and dacarbazine (Chapter 191). *Gastrointestinal and systemic infections,* both viral and bacterial, are probably the second most common cause of nausea and vomiting. Infections may be at fault through the release of bacterial enterotoxins or the inflammation initiated by the pathogen. *Obstruction* of the gastrointestinal tract or organs—stomach, small intestine, colon, pancreas, or biliary tract—and ischemia or inflammation of these organs or the liver or peritoneum are the third most common cause. In addition to *labyrinthine disorders* (motion sickness, space sickness, viral labyrinthitis, acoustic tumors, and Ménière's disease; Chapter 470), a major CNS cause of nausea and vomiting is diseases that increase intracranial pressure (Chapter 428). *Emotional responses* to unpleasant smells or taste and severe psychogenic stress are additional CNS causes. *Metabolic causes* such as uremia, diabetic ketoacidosis, hypercalcemia, hypoxemia, hyperthyroidism, Addison's disease, and radiation therapy cause nausea by stimulating the chemoreceptor trigger zone. The first trimester of *pregnancy* causes vomiting in approximately 70% of pregnant women. *Postoperative nausea and vomiting* complicate up to 40% of surgical operations.

Effective antiemetics for nausea and vomiting include those that block the major receptors of (1) the area postrema (D$_2$, 5-HT$_3$, H$_1$, and M$_1$ receptors) and (2) the H$_1$, M$_1$, 5-HT$_{1A}$, and 5-HT$_3$ receptors of brain stem nuclei (the vomiting center) that receive input from the vestibular nucleus, the vagus, and the sympathetic nerves. Phenothiazines act on D$_1$, H$_1$, and M$_1$ receptors; metoclopramide, domperidone, and ondansetron affect 5-HT$_3$ and 5-HT$_4$ receptors; scopolamine is an M$_1$-receptor antagonist; and diphenhydramine

(Dramamine) and cyclizine (Marezine) are H$_1$ antagonists. The most effective of the antinausea drugs for chemotherapy-induced vomiting are the 5-HT$_3$ receptor antagonists ondansetron, granisetron, and dolasetron. In the chemotherapy setting, a 5-HT$_3$ receptor antagonist may be combined with other medications (a corticosteroid, phenothiazine/butyrophenone, substituted benzamide, or cannabinoid) for maximal antiemetic action.

Abdominal Pain

This symptom complex arises from intra-abdominal, nociceptive impulses that are variously modulated by input from the spinal cord and the CNS. Abdominal pain is either acute or chronic; when chronic, it may be intermittent (e.g., recurrent biliary colic), unrelenting (e.g., chronic pancreatitis or pancreatic cancer), or intractable but of unclear cause (e.g., the functional abdominal pain syndromes).

In the gastrointestinal tract, nociceptive pain receptors are present in the walls (lamina propria and muscle layers) of the hollow organs, in serosal structures (the visceral peritoneum and the capsules of the solid organs), and within the mesentery that supports and surrounds the abdominal organs. These receptors respond to distention, contraction, traction, compression, torsion, and stretch; to inflammatory mediators such as bradykinin, substance P, serotonin, histamine, and prostaglandins; and to chemicals such as hydrochloric acid, potassium chloride, and hypertonic saline. These receptors do not respond to classic nociceptive stimuli such as pinching, burning, stabbing, or cutting or to electrical or thermal stimulation. As a result, the gastroenterologist can biopsy or thermally coagulate the gastrointestinal mucosa with impunity, yet a patient notes severe pain with contraction or distention of the viscera or with traction and pulling on the mesentery and abdominal organs. The cell bodies of the sensory receptors of the gut and viscera are in the dorsal root ganglion of the spinal cord. These neurons synapse in the dorsal horn and then either cross the cord to ascend in the contralateral spinal thalamic tract or ascend in the contralateral posterior column to reach the reticular formation of the brain stem or the thalamus, where they synapse and project to the limbic system and frontal lobe or to the somatosensory cortex, respectively.

In the embryo, the gut and organs are present in the midline and receive innervation from both sides of the spinal canal. Thus, stimuli arising in the gastrointestinal tract (e.g., from inflammation, ischemia) are often perceived as midline pain until the process (e.g., appendicitis or cholecystitis) extends to the adjacent parietal peritoneum, where laterally localizing nerves project the pain to the brain.

The synapses of the pain fibers from the viscera and the dorsal horn of the spinal cord allow the CNS and somatic nerves to modulate the perception of visceral pain. Descending inhibitory neurons arising in the CNS, when activated, stimulate interneurons in the cord that inhibit the firing of the second-order and visceral pain neurons, which travel up the cord to the brain. The balance of these excitatory and inhibitory forces determines the degree to which the nociceptive information is transmitted to the CNS. This process is called the *gate control theory of pain;* it explains how acupuncture might inhibit the perception of visceral pain.

A new and important concept is the role of sensitization in the pathophysiology of the functional gastrointestinal diseases (Chapter 135). Inflammation and/or prolonged and excessive motor events in the gut are thought to induce molecular changes, both in the periphery (enteric nervous system) and centrally (in the spinal cord and brain), that lead the patient to experience a greater than normal amount of discomfort for a given stimulus (hyperalgesia) or a perception of pain with gut stimuli that normally are not perceived as painful (allodynia).

The location of painful sensations is determined by the spinal segments in which the afferent nerves from the abdominal viscera enter the spinal cord. For example, foregut structures, such as the esophagus, stomach, proximal duodenum, liver, biliary tree, and pancreas, are innervated at T5 to T9; pain from these structures is perceived between the xiphoid and the umbilicus. Pain from midgut structures, such as the small intestine, appendix, and ascending and proximal two thirds of the transverse colon, is transmitted from T8 to L1 and is perceived as periumbilical. Pain from hindgut structures, which include the distal one third of the transverse colon, the descending colon, and the rectosigmoid, is transmitted from T11 to L1 and is perceived between the umbilicus and the pubis. Referred pain is pain perceived in the skin or muscle in the same cutaneous dermatomes as those nerve roots where the innervation of the abdominal organ enters the spinal cord. Referred pain is a helpful phenomenon to diagnose the cause of acute abdominal pain: gallbladder pain may be perceived in the right shoulder or scapula, and pain from retroperitoneal processes such as pancreatitis is referred to the back.

In addition to the location of pain and the presence of referred pain, the character of the pain (burning, steady, or colic), its duration, its time to reach peak intensity, and its relieving and aggravating factors (such as eating or passing gas or stool) are helpful components of the medical history. Esophagitis is classically described as substernal burning pain relieved by antacids and aggravated by lying down (Chapter 136). Peptic ulcer pain occurs when the stomach is empty (often 4 AM), and it is relieved by eating or taking antacids (Chapter 138). Gallbladder colic (Chapter 158) is perceived either in the midline or right upper quadrant, reaches a peak intensity within minutes to an hour, and usually persists for 1 to 4 hours. In contrast, the pain of cholecystitis and pancreatitis (Chapter 145) reaches its peak more slowly, becomes sustained, and lasts for days. Intestinal obstruction causes colicky pain that waxes and wanes over the course of minutes and is usually periumbilical (Chapter 143).

Chronic intermittent abdominal pain may be due to obstructed viscera, such as in recurrent cholelithiasis or intestinal obstruction; to metabolic or genetic diseases, such as acute intermittent porphyria (Chapter 223) or familial Mediterranean fever (Chapter 181); to neurologic diseases, such as diabetic reticulopathy (Chapter 462), abdominal migraine (Chapter 428), or vertebral nerve root compression (Chapter 429); or to miscellaneous inflammatory diseases, such as Crohn's disease (Chapter 142), endometriosis (Chapter 250), lead poisoning (Chapter 20), and mesenteric ischemia (Chapter 144).

Functional abdominal pain, now thought to result from visceral hyperalgesia, includes three major types: (1) IBS, in which recurrent abdominal pain is accompanied by changes in gastrointestinal function (constipation, diarrhea, or alternating constipation and diarrhea; Chapter 135); (2) nonulcer dyspepsia, which is defined as ulcer-like symptoms in the absence of endoscopically definable anatomic or histologic evidence of inflammation (Chapter 135); and (3) chronic, intractable abdominal pain, in which pain is not accompanied by other symptoms of organ dysfunction. These functional diseases are quite common and may account for up to 50% of patients who present with gastrointestinal symptoms to either the primary care physician or gastroenterologist.

Weight Loss

Continued, unexplained weight loss greater than 5% of body weight is of concern to the patient and physician. Contrary to usual thought, malignancy is not the most common cause and, when it is, it is usually diagnosed early in the course of evaluation. Gastrointestinal disorders, with their attendant anorexia, fear of eating (sitophobia), malabsorption and/or inflammation, and psychogenic causes, are at least as common as cancer. Diseases of the other organ systems make up the remainder of the diverse etiologies. In the elderly, weight loss often can be attributed to the 10 "D"s: dentition, dysgeusia, dysphagia, diarrhea, disease (chronic), depression, dementia, dysfunction, drugs, and "don't know." In the young, eating disorders (anorexia nervosa and bulimia; Chapter 232) must be considered. Evaluation in both the young and old requires a careful history and physical examination with attention to clues or findings that suggest systemic or organ system disease. A careful neuropsychiatric evaluation should also be performed, with appropriate input from caregivers and friends. Screening laboratory tests are useful: complete blood cell count, urinalysis, metabolic panel, chest radiograph, thyroid-stimulating hormone assay, erythrocyte sedimentation rate, celiac disease antibody test, HIV tests (if risk factors are present), and fecal occult blood test. If cancer is suspected but there are no localizing clues, helpful tests include a cervical Pap smear and mammography in women, a prostate-specific antigen in men, and colonoscopy/barium enema or abdominal/pelvic computed tomography in either gender.

Gastrointestinal Bleeding

Bleeding from a gastrointestinal tract may be occult, that is, requires testing of the stool to be detected, or gross and evident as hematemesis, melena, or hematochezia (Chapter 133). It is always a serious symptom that requires investigation. Hemoccult, the most commonly used test to detect occult bleeding, requires blood loss of 10 mL/day

to give a positive test 50% of the time. Endoscopy is the most effective way to diagnose occult bleeding (Chapters 132 and 133). Upper endoscopy should be performed first if the patient's symptoms suggest upper tract disease; colonoscopy should be performed first in those with lower tract symptoms or in those who are asymptomatic. Melena, which requires 150 mL of blood in the gastrointestinal tract to be manifest, and hematemesis occur when the bleeding site is proximal to the ligament of Treitz. Upper endoscopy is indicated for these signs. Hematochezia may occur after massive upper tract bleeding or minor bleeding from anorectal sources. Hematochezia should be investigated with colonoscopy after an urgent bowel preparation if the bleeding has been significant.

Diarrhea

Death from fluid and electrolyte losses may be the outcome of diarrhea in developing countries but, in developed nations, it is usually more of economic significance due to loss of time from work. For diagnostic purposes, diarrhea (Chapter 141) may be categorized as watery, malabsorption (steatorrhea), or inflammatory. However, the causes in each case may be due to either the presence of ingested, poorly absorbed osmotic substances in the bowel, stimulation of water and electrolyte secretion, or malabsorption of nutrients.

Constipation

Constipation is so common a complaint that it is often not considered to be a symptom of disease. It may occur secondary to endocrine, metabolic, neurologic, or anorectal diseases. More commonly, it is idiopathic. When severe and intractable, two general pathophysiologic mechanisms are sought: colonic inertia (slow transit) and functional outlet obstruction.

PHYSICAL EXAMINATION

In acute abdominal pain, the physical examination is targeted quite differently than in patients with chronic gastrointestinal complaints. The goal of the examination in acute abdominal pain is to determine the presence of surgical disease. Observation of facial expression is key to determining the presence and severity of pain. Distention, particularly if tympanic, suggests bowel obstruction, but simple obesity and ascites are more likely causes of distention without tympany. The character of bowel sounds (absent in peritonitis, high-pitched tinkles in intestinal obstruction) can be important, but any bowel sounds that are hypoactive, hyperactive, or present in one quadrant or another are of little consequence. The most useful part of the examination is palpation, which gives clues to the presence of severe peritoneal inflammation, as manifested by involuntary guarding, abdominal rigidity, or rebound tenderness; when these symptoms are accompanied by absent bowel sounds, perforation and peritonitis must be suspected (Chapter 143). Palpation with the stethoscope rather than with the hand can sometimes differentiate true abdominal rebound tenderness from a response that is either feigned or imagined.

In the patient with chronic gastrointestinal complaints, the goal of the physical examination is to determine the presence or absence of other systemic findings that might suggest the underlying disease, to determine the size of the abdominal viscera, and to detect any abnormal masses. For example, the presence of jaundice and spider telangiectasia suggests liver disease (Chapter 156) and perhaps varices as a cause of gastrointestinal bleeding. Large joint arthritis and aphthous ulcers of the mouth might suggest celiac disease (Chapter 141) or inflammatory bowel disease (Chapter 142). The abdominal examination might reveal epigastric, right upper quadrant, right lower quadrant, or left lower quadrant tenderness to complement a compatible history for peptic ulcer disease (Chapter 138), cholecystitis (Chapter 158), Crohn's disease (Chapter 142), or diverticulitis (Chapter 143), respectively. An epigastric mass might suggest a pancreatic neoplasm (Chapter 201) or pseudocyst (Chapter 145), whereas right lower quadrant and left lower quadrant masses suggest abscess due to inflammatory bowel disease and diverticulitis, respectively, or colonic cancer. Examination of the liver (Chapter 148) should focus primarily on its breadth and consistency. Auscultation is useful to determine the presence of bruits indicative of vascular disease or friction rubs that suggest pancreatic or hepatic cancer (Chapters 201 and 202).

The physical examination is not complete without a digital rectal examination. The examiner should not forget to sweep the finger posterially to search for anorectal carcinoma and masses in the pouch of Douglas and anteriorly to determine the size and consistency of the prostate (Chapter 129). Tenderness and masses laterally can occur in appendicitis (Chapter 143), inflammatory bowel disease, or diverticulitis, as well as abdominal cancers. The character and color of the stool and the presence of fecal occult blood should be assessed.

LABORATORY TESTS AND IMAGING PROCEDURES

A complete blood cell count, liver chemistries, and erythrocyte sedimentation rate can be useful screening tests in assessing gastrointestinal disease. The choice of endoscopy versus barium contrast radiographs depends on the acuteness of the gastrointestinal disease and the diseases being sought (Chapters 131 and 132). Although endoscopy is relatively expensive and should never be used indiscriminately, it often can expedite definitive diagnosis and provide definitive therapy.

SUGGESTED READINGS

Bonen DK, Cho JH: The genetics of inflammatory bowel disease. Gastroenterology 2003;124:521–536. *New concepts of the genetic factors that play a role in the susceptibility to develop inflammatory bowel disease, particularly the NOD2/CARD15 gene, are reviewed.*

Braverman IM: Skin signs of gastrointestinal disease. Gastroenterology 2003;124:1595–1614. *Excellent photographs of the more common external manifestations of gastrointestinal diseases.*

Grady WH: Genetic testing for high-risk colon cancer patients. Gastroenterology 2003;124:1574–1594. *About 20 to 30% of all colon cancers have a potentially definable genetic cause.*

Quigley EMM, Hasler WL, Parkman HP: AGA technical review on nausea and vomiting. Gastroenterology 2001;120:261–263. *This is an authoritative review on the causes, diagnosis, and treatment of nausea and vomiting.*

Schiller LR: Review article: The therapy of constipation. Aliment Pharmacol Ther 2001;15:749–763. *This review focuses on the treatment of constipation, rather than its pathophysiology and causes.*

131 DIAGNOSTIC IMAGING PROCEDURES IN GASTROENTEROLOGY

Gerhard R. Wittich

Long-established techniques, such as plain film radiography and barium studies, continue to play an important role as efficient and cost-effective imaging methods in gastroenterology. In addition, ultrasonography, nuclear medicine, computed tomography (CT), and magnetic resonance imaging (MRI) have greatly improved gastroenterologic diagnosis and have stimulated a number of image-guided interventions.

Plain Film Radiography

Plain film radiography remains a valuable tool for the diagnosis of several abdominal disorders. The acute abdominal series, consisting of supine and upright views of the abdomen, readily provides information regarding abnormal gas patterns. Demonstration of gas/fluid levels within dilated loops of bowel may suggest obstruction or adynamic ileus. This technique is a reliable method to confirm or exclude the presence of intraperitoneal bowel perforation, since as little as 5 mL of air can be detected with proper radiographic technique. Plain film radiography of the abdomen is also useful to detect abnormal calcifications such as calcified gallstones (Chapter 158), pancreatic calcifications (Chapter 145), calcified aneurysms (Chapter 75), and calcified hydatid cysts of the liver.

Barium Studies

Barium studies of the upper gastrointestinal tract allow diagnosis of inflammatory, neoplastic, and motility disorders and of lesions that cause stenosis or obstruction. In the hands of experienced investigators who take advantage of the diagnostic capabilities of optimized single- and double-contrast studies, the sensitivity of barium studies for the detection of gastric ulcers or esophageal or gastric neoplasms approaches that of endoscopic examination. In the esophagus, barium studies cannot quite match the almost 100% sensitivity of

diagnostic endoscopy. However, the lower cost of barium studies and their noninvasive nature make them excellent initial tests for many suspected disorders of the upper gastrointestinal tract. For example, in a subgroup of immunocompromised patients with dysphagia, double-contrast evaluation of the esophagus allows detection of candida esophagitis (Chapter 136), characterized by a granular mucosa and plaquelike lesions, in about 90% of cases. Alternatively, barium study of the esophagus may reveal ulcerative changes suggesting herpes esophagitis or infection with cytomegalovirus or human immunodeficiency virus. Although endoscopy is more sensitive and may allow a specific diagnosis by obtaining samples for microbial cultures, it may be more economical to reserve endoscopy for patients with equivocal or negative radiographic studies. In patients with symptoms of reflux esophagitis (Chapter 136), double-contrast barium examination demonstrates ulcerations and possible stricture formation in advanced cases, but barium studies are inferior to endoscopy in the earlier stages of the disease, and barium studies cannot diagnose or follow Barrett's esophagus.

High-quality double-contrast techniques remain a reasonable alternative as initial imaging studies for the evaluation of the stomach and duodenum, because the vast majority of gastric and duodenal ulcers (Chapter 138) are readily displayed radiographically, and barium studies are safer and less expensive than endoscopy. An indication for primary, endoscopic evaluation is acute upper gastrointestinal hemorrhage: whereas barium studies may reveal the source of bleeding in 70 to 80% of cases, the ability to control hemorrhage by endoscopic intervention clearly makes it the preferred method (Chapter 133).

Because routine endoscopy of the small bowel is not feasible, the most common techniques to image this organ are the small bowel follow-through study with intermittent fluoroscopic evaluation and enteroclysis, which is intubation of the proximal jejunum followed by infusion of contrast material. Enteroclysis, which should be restricted to patients with a high level of suspicion of small bowel disease, has several advantages over the small bowel follow-through study. It is independent of the activity of the pylorus, so a high-quality study can usually be completed in less than 30 minutes. Double-contrast enteroclysis, which includes the use of barium and methylcellulose, allows complete evaluation of all loops of small bowel, including ileal loops that often are superimposed on one another within the pelvis. Common indications for enteroclysis include partial mechanical small bowel obstruction, suspected peritoneal neoplasms (Chapter 146), suspected radiation enteritis (Chapter 143), unexplained, intermittent lower gastrointestinal bleeding (Chapter 133), Crohn's disease being considered for surgery (Chapter 142), and malabsorption possibly due to small bowel disease (Chapter 141).

Endoscopic and radiographic studies play a complementary role in evaluation of the colon. Single-contrast studies are sufficient for documentation of large colon carcinomas, but double-contrast enemas are required for detection of more subtle lesions, such as small polyps or early mucosal changes in patients with inflammatory bowel disease (Chapters 142 and 200). With meticulous double-contrast technique, the detection rate of colonic polyps is approximately 90% and approaches the sensitivity of colonoscopy (Fig. 131–1). Typical indications for barium enemas include symptoms of colon carcinoma (Chapter 200), diverticular disease (Chapter 143), and inflammatory bowel disease (Chapter 142). In addition, double-contrast barium enema is part of one of the alternate strategies to screen asymptomatic patients for colon cancer (Chapter 200).

Ultrasonography

Ultrasonography has many applications in patients with gastroenterologic disorders, but a disadvantage is its inability to penetrate gas-filled structures. For example, ultrasonography can yield exquisite images of the pancreatic parenchyma and the pancreatic duct in thin patients, but it may be difficult to evaluate this retroperitoneal organ in obese patients with a large amount of bowel gas within the transverse colon and stomach.

The sensitivity of ultrasonography for detection of gallbladder stones is greater than 90%. In the jaundiced patient (Chapter 149), ultrasonography allows quick differentiation of obstruction of the intrahepatic and extrahepatic bile ducts (Fig. 131–2) from other causes of jaundice, such as hepatitis. Both the level of obstruction and its cause often can be determined. For example, lesions in the pancreatic head or the porta hepatis or a stone within the common bile duct can be detected.

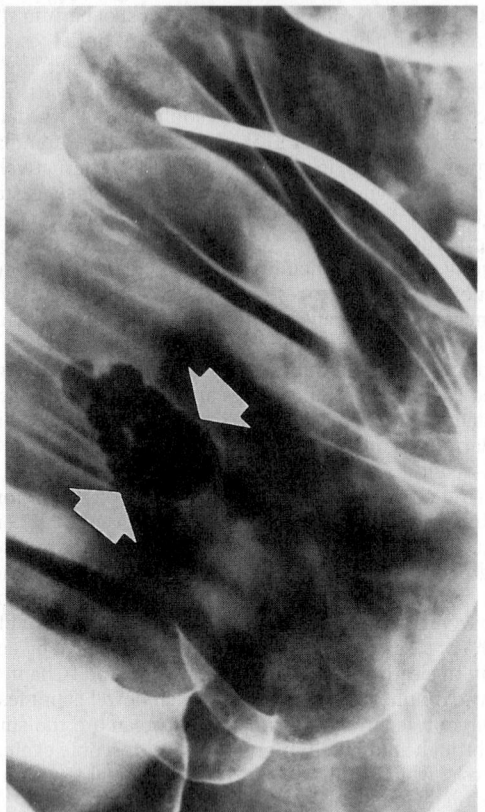

FIGURE 131–1 • Graded compression during double-contrast barium enema demonstrates a small, lobulated, sessile polyp (arrows) on the posterior wall of the ascending colon.

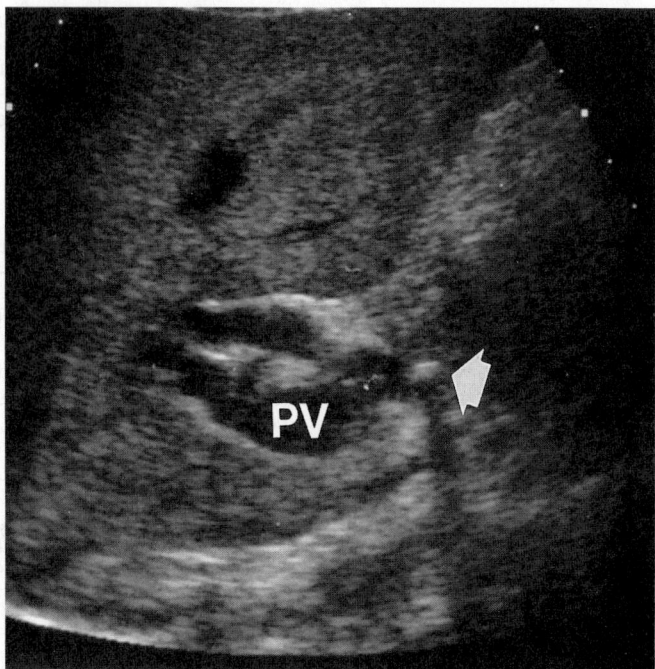

FIGURE 131–2 • Choledocholithiasis. Sagittal scan through the porta hepatis demonstrates a dilated common bile duct anterior to the portal vein (PV). Note the obstructing stone within the distal portion of the common bile duct (arrow).

Because of its anatomic position posterior to the pancreatic head, the distal common bile duct may be obscured by gas within the duodenum, transverse colon, or gastric antrum. Additional studies such as magnetic resonance cholangiography, endoscopic retrograde cholangiopancreatography, or percutaneous transhepatic cholangiography may be necessary.

Ultrasonography is also an excellent imaging tool for the evaluation of the hepatic parenchyma. It allows detection of fatty liver (Chapter 155) as well as textural changes of cirrhosis (Chapter 156), and it has a sensitivity between 80 and 90% for detection of hepatic neoplasms (Chapter 202). Cystic lesions within the liver and hepatic abscesses are easily detected.

The spleen is readily imaged by ultrasonography to determine its size as well as to image intrasplenic or perisplenic fluid collections or mass lesions. Doppler and color Doppler studies can evaluate portal venous flow in patients with portal hypertension before and after placement of a transjugular intrahepatic portosystemic shunt (TIPS).

Computed Tomography

The development of fast CT scanners, which use helical scanning techniques, has enhanced the role of CT for evaluation of abdominal organs. Single images can be obtained in 100 to 500 msec (depending on the scanner), and the abdomen can be imaged in a single breathhold in less than 30 seconds. This speed permits optimal utilization of contrast material. For example, the entire liver can be imaged during the arterial phase after injection of a contrast bolus to detect hypervascular lesions such as hepatomas (Chapter 202) that typically enhance more than normal hepatic parenchyma (Fig. 131–3). Less

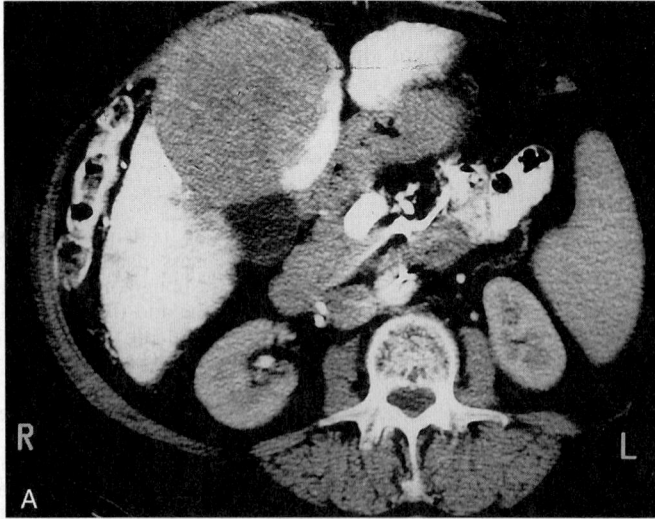

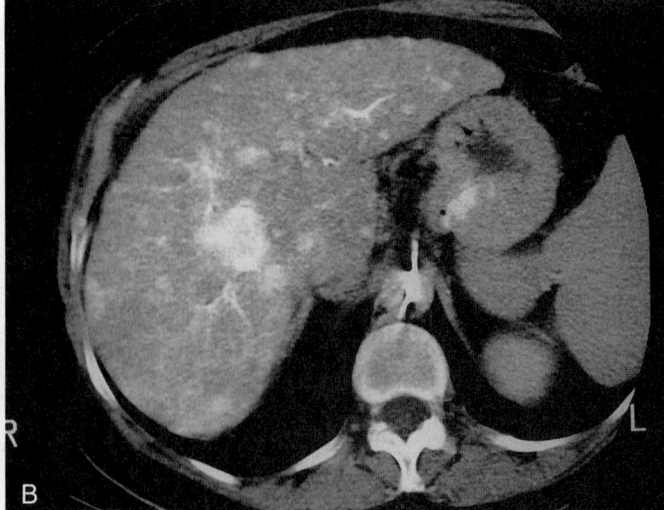

FIGURE 131–3 • *A*, A computed tomography (CT) scan through the lower portion of the liver obtained during the portal venous phase shows a simple large hypodense lesion. Percutaneous biopsy confirmed a hepatoma. *B*, CT scan through the cranial portion of the liver during the arterial phase demonstrates multiple additional hypervascular lesions, suggesting an unresectable, multicentric hepatoma.

vascular lesions such as metastases from a colon carcinoma can typically be detected as low-density lesions during the portal venous phase because they receive significantly less blood than normal parenchyma through the portal system.

An additional benefit of rapid-sequence CT scanning is the possibility to use specialized software for three-dimensional display of organ systems such as the vascular system. This technique, called CT angiography, is of particular value for the noninvasive evaluation of liver transplant recipients (Chapter 157). Application of this technique to the colon has been termed *virtual colonoscopy* (Fig. 131–4). Initial results indicate that this is a useful noninvasive screening test for colonic polyps—at the least in patients in whom conventional colonoscopy has failed.

Computed tomography is also an essential tool for evaluating and staging abdominal mass lesions; for diagnosis of hepatic, pancreatic, and splenic abscesses; and for detecting abscesses associated with disorders of the bowel such as appendicitis, diverticulitis, or Crohn's disease (Chapters 142 and 143). In patients with biliary obstruction, CT is very useful to determine the cause of obstruction, including carcinoma of the pancreatic head or the ampulla (Chapters 158 and 201), particularly when ultrasonographic evaluation remains inconclusive. Another important use of CT is to guide abdominal interventions such as percutaneous needle aspiration of mass lesions

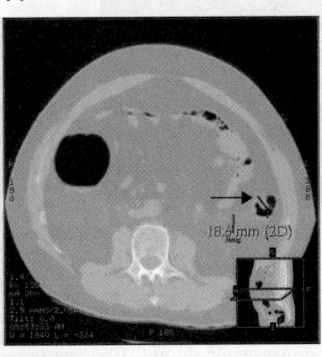

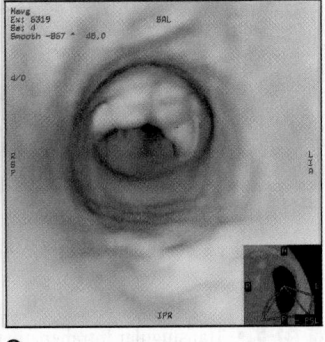

FIGURE 131–4 • Virtual colonoscopy (colonography) is accomplished by taking multiple thin (2–3 mm) two-dimensional images of the air-filled colon in several planes (e.g., axial, coronal) and then reconstructing the cuts into a three-dimensional image. *A*, A conventional barium enema spot film shows an intraluminal tumor (arrow) in the descending colon. *B*, An axial (two-dimensional; 2D) source image of a virtual colonography taken at the level of the tumor (arrow) in the same patient. *C*, The reconstructed three-dimensional virtual colonography shows the tumor viewed from a position distal to it. (Courtesy of Dr. R. Ernst, Galveston, Texas.)

or abnormal fluid collections, placement of needles and probes for percutaneous tumor ablation, and drainage of abdominal abscesses.

Magnetic Resonance Imaging

The more water and hence the more protons a specific tissue contains, the greater is its signal intensity. This property results in a contrast resolution that is superior to that of CT and ultrasonography. Additional advantages of MRI include its noninvasiveness, the absence of ionizing radiation, and the ability to obtain images in multiple planes, such as cross-sectional, sagittal, and coronal displays.

Drawbacks of MRI compared with ultrasonography and CT are the significantly higher cost of equipment, the longer imaging times, the need to exclude patients with ferromagnetic intracranial metallic clips or cardiac pacemakers, and the tunnel-like gantry design of conventional scanners that causes some patients to become claustrophobic (Chapter 7). Low-and mid-field scanners (0.5 to 1.0) have reduced the cost of equipment and provide good-quality images, albeit still at relatively long scanning times.

Magnetic resonance cholangiography has evolved as an alternative to diagnostic endoscopic retrograde cholangiopancreatography or percutaneous transhepatic cholangiography. Magnetic resonance angiography, which can image the vascular supply of the liver, is of particular value in liver transplant patients (Chapter 157). It produces images similar to CT angiography and is of particular value if patients cannot receive iodinated contrast material because of a history of allergies or renal failure.

Magnetic resonance imaging is often used when ultrasonography or CT is inconclusive. For example, MRI can differentiate cavernous hemangiomas (Chapter 202) from other liver lesions, owing to their very long T2 value. The use of contrast agents such as gadolinium-diethylenetriaminepenta-acetic acid gives MRI a high sensitivity for detecting hepatic tumors, but its specificity has not reached a level that would obviate the need for percutaneous biopsies, except in certain lesions such as hemangiomas.

Radionuclide Imaging

Scintigraphic studies are rarely used as the primary method to image abdominal disorders, but they are indicated to solve certain diagnostic problems. Cavernous hemangiomas (Chapter 202), which are found in 1 to 7% of autopsies, must be differentiated from hepatomas, metastases, or other lesions. Technetium-99m (^{99m}Tc)–labeled red blood cell studies represent a noninvasive, economic method to diagnose a cavernous hemangioma. The sensitivity for detection of small lesions (less than 2 cm) has been increased with the introduction of single-photon emission computed tomography. ^{99m}Tc pertechnetate allows detection of ectopic gastric musosa in patients with symptomatic Meckel's diverticulum, which is of particular value in pediatric patients. Of clinical importance is localization of the source of gastrointestinal hemorrhage (Chapter 133) with labeled red cell scintigraphy. This study is often indicated before angiography for patients in whom endoscopy has failed to localize and control bleeding.

Biliary scintigraphy with ^{99m}Tc-HIDA is often useful in patients with clinical symptoms of acute cholecystitis (Chapter 158). In a normal patient, radionuclide uptake can be seen in the liver, bile ducts, gallbladder, and bowel within 60 minutes after intravenous injection. The absence of radionuclide uptake in the region of the gallbladder despite the presence of radionuclide within the remainder of the biliary system suggests obstruction of the cystic duct and supports the diagnosis of acute cholecystitis.

Positron emission tomography, has evolved from an expensive research tool to a widely accepted economical and clinically useful tool for oncologic imaging. Applications of this imaging technique include tumor staging in patients with esophageal or colorectal cancer.

Vascular Interventions

Although noninvasive imaging by ultrasonography, CT, or MRI has largely replaced angiography for the diagnostic evaluation of hepatic and pancreatic masses, angiography remains valuable for tumor therapy (Chapter 202). Catheter delivery systems are useful for chemoembolization to palliate unresectable primary or secondary liver tumors, particularly large tumors, which may not be suitable for percutaneous ablation with radiofrequency.

Selective angiography of the celiac and mesenteric vessels has long been important for the management of acute and chronic ischemia due to vascular stenosis, thrombosis, and embolism (Chapter 144). Local, catheter-directed thrombolysis may revascularize branches of the superior mesenteric artery if an embolic event is suspected and diagnosed within a few hours of the acute event and before irreversible ischemic damage mandates surgical intervention. Balloon angioplasty and stenting may obviate the need for surgical correction of a hemodynamically significant stenosis. Catheter angiography also remains an important tool for management of acute gastrointestinal hemorrhage (Chapter 133); it should be considered when endoscopic attempts to control gastroduodenal bleeding fail. Selective embolization of arteries that feed bleeding sources in the stomach and duodenum is highly effective in controlling active hemorrhage with a low risk of tissue infarction. The role of angiography in acute and massive lower gastrointestinal hemorrhage is primarily for precise preoperative localization of the bleeding source and to temporize surgery by local infusion of a vasoconstrictor. Bleeding is controlled in more than 70% of patients, thereby making them candidates for elective rather than more risky emergency surgery. In a subgroup of patients who remain at high risk for surgery, selective embolization may be considered. This method is also highly effective in controlling lower gastrointestinal hemorrhage but carries about a 10% risk of bowel infarction.

Patients with coagulopathy should be considered for transjugular liver biopsy if a tissue diagnosis is required for management. Refinements in biopsy devices allow retrieval of adequate tissue samples in more than 90% of cases with minimal morbidity.

The use of TIPS has rapidly evolved as standard treatment for patients with complications of cirrhosis (Chapter 156), such as refractory ascites or hemorrhage from esophageal varices after failure of endoscopic sclerotherapy. The technical success rate of this method is more than 90%, and its rates of morbidity and mortality are lower than those of emergency surgical portacaval shunts. Although the long-term success of this method is currently somewhat limited by shunt stenosis or occlusion, close surveillance with periodic visits (3- to 6-month intervals) and color Doppler ultrasonography can often discover shunt stenosis before recurrent episodes of bleeding. Angiographic reintervention may be required to maintain portal decompression (Fig. 131–5). Although the primary patency rate of TIPS at

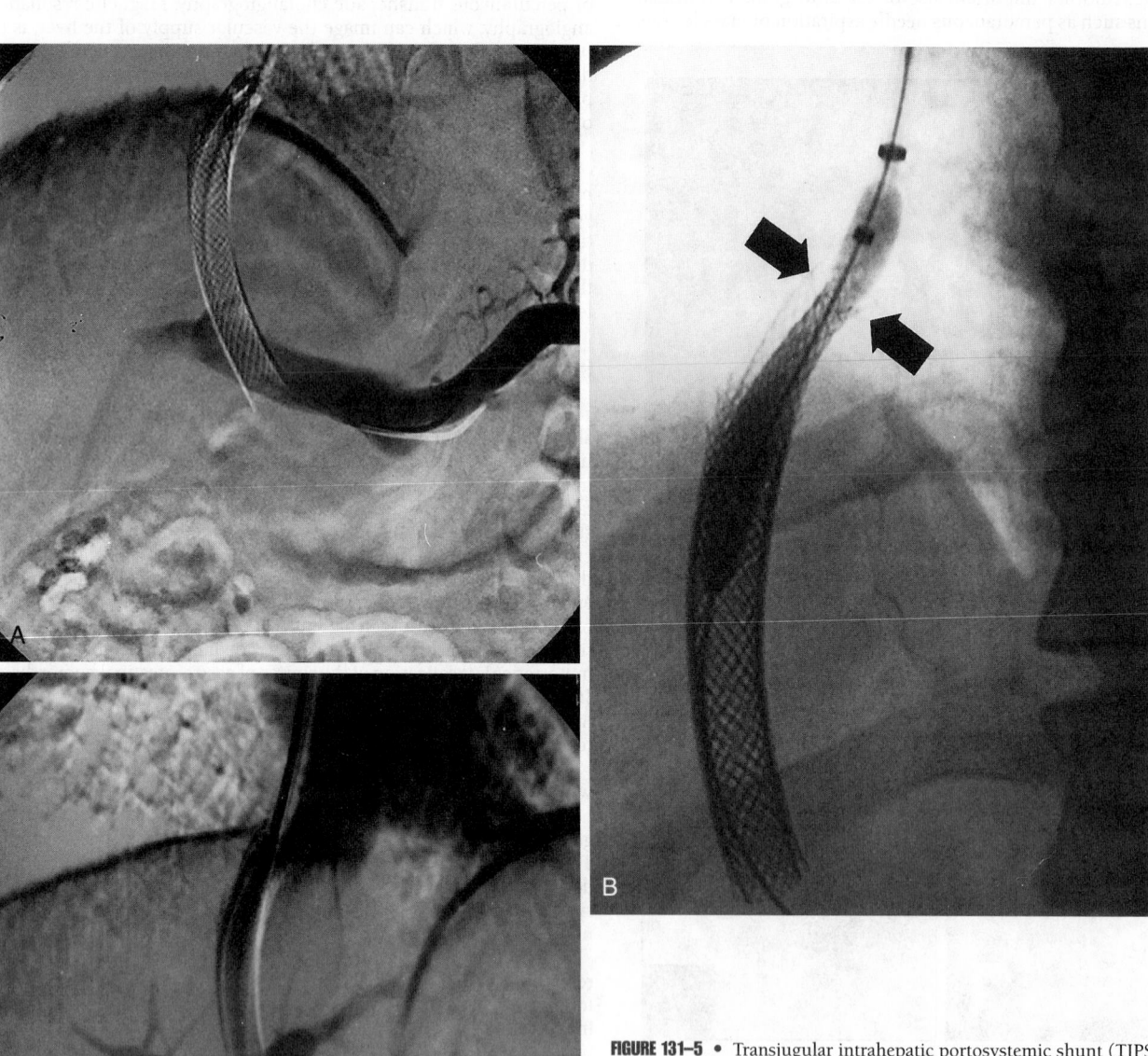

FIGURE 131–5 • Transjugular intrahepatic portosystemic shunt (TIPS) revision in a patient with recurrent variceal bleeding, 3 years after a successful TIPS procedure. *A*, With the use of a transjugular approach, a guidewire has been advanced through the occluded stent. Contrast medium injection demonstrates a patent splenic and portal vein but no flow through the shunt. The portal venous pressure was elevated to 21 mm Hg. *B*, Balloon dilatation of the occluded shunt. The waist of the balloon (arrows) was completely abolished after inflation to 15 atmospheres. *C*, Contrast medium injection into the portal vein now shows excellent flow through the shunt into the right atrium. The pressure gradient between the portal vein and the right atrium was reduced to 10 mm Hg.

1 year is approximately 50%, reinterventions such as balloon dilatation of stenotic shunts can result in a secondary patency rate of more than 90% after 1 year and more than 80% after 3 years. Early results of clinical trials with coated stents suggest that longer patency of shunts can be achieved in the future.

Nonvascular Interventions

Percutaneous ultrasonography or CT guided biopsy of hepatic, pancreatic, or other abdominal mass lesions has become standard practice. The sensitivity of fine needle biopsy of abdominal neoplasms is greater than 90%, with a complication rate that is less than 1%. Similar techniques can be used for nerve blocks, such as celiac ganglion blocks in patients with intractable pain secondary to advanced pancreatic carcinoma (Chapter 201) or chronic pancreatitis (Chapter 145).

Percutaneous catheter drainage combined with antibiotic treatment has been accepted as first-line therapy of hepatic and other abdominal abscesses, with success rates exceeding 90%. For example, patients who have diverticular abscesses without peritonitis (which requires emergency surgical exploration) can undergo diagnostic CT scanning with intravenous contrast, followed by percutaneous CT-guided abscess drainage. After the septic episode is controlled, patients may undergo endoscopic evaluation or a barium enema to determine the extent of disease of the colon and to exclude an underlying perforated neoplasm. Subsequently, most patients will be referred for elective bowel resection. This approach reduces morbidity and mortality when compared with a two- or three-step surgical approach consisting of emergency surgical drainage and colostomy followed by bowel resection and reversal of colostomy. Similarly, patients with appendiceal abscesses may benefit from percutaneous drainage followed by elective appendectomy. Primary surgical intervention can usually be reserved for very complex infectious processes such as infected pancreatic necrosis or multiloculated collections combined with high output bowel fistulae.

Percutaneous tumor ablation may be indicated in patients who are at high risk for surgery. Techniques include percutaneous alcohol injection and ablation with radiofrequency, laser, or cryotherapy probes. Three-year survival rates greater than 50% have been achieved.

Percutaneous biliary interventions (Chapter 158) under fluoroscopic control are complementary to endoscopic and surgical procedures. Transhepatic techniques are of particular value when endoscopic techniques fail or are contraindicated, such as in patients whose prior surgical interventions in the biliary system make endoscopic access impossible. Transhepatic insertion of an indwelling expandable metallic prosthesis is well established as palliation for malignant biliary obstructions and may avoid endoscopic treatment or palliative surgery. Emergency percutaneous biliary drainage may be necessary in patients with acute cholangitis. Transhepatic stone removal is useful in patients with hepatolithiasis. Transhepatic balloon dilation has a greater than 70% long-term success rate in patients with benign biliary strictures. Percutaneous cholecystostomy is useful for initial decompression of the gallbladder in patients with acute calculous or acalculous cholecystitis, particularly if patients are considered to be at high risk for emergency surgery, and permits subsequent elective cholecystectomy. Alternatively, percutaneous methods can be used for fragmentation and removal of stones from the gallbladder in patients who remain at high risk for surgery.

Gastrointestinal interventions such as balloon dilation of benign strictures of the esophagus or placement of an endoprosthesis for palliative treatment of malignant obstructions of the esophagus (Chapter 132) or colon (Chapter 139) can be performed by interventional endoscopists or interventional radiologists. Similarly, percutaneous radiologic gastrostomy has a high success rate because high-grade or complete esophageal obstruction is not a contraindication to this method.

SUGGESTED READINGS

Balthazar EJ: Acute pancreatitis: Assessment of severity with clinical and CT evaluation. Radiology 2002;223:603–613. *The role of contrast-enhanced CT for management of acute pancreatitis.*

Ruers TJ, Langenhoff BS, Neeleman N, et al: Value of positron emission tomography with (F-18) fluorodeoxyglucose in patients with colorectal liver metastases: A prospective study. J Clin Oncol 2002;20:388–395. *Fluorodeoxyglucose positron emission tomography staging improves therapeutic management of these patients.*

Solbiati L, Livraghi T, Goldberg SN, et al: Percutaneous radio-frequency ablation of hepatic metastases from colorectal cancer: Long-term results in 117 patients. Radiology 2001;221:159–166. *Radiofrequency ablation is an effective method to treat hepatic metastases, with a 3-year survival rate of 46%.*

Svensson MH, Svensson E, Lasson A, et al: Patient acceptance of CT colonography and conventional colonoscopy: Prospective comparative study in patients with or suspected of having colorectal disease. Radiology 2002;222:337–345. *CT colonography was less painful than conventional colonoscopy.*

132 GASTROINTESTINAL ENDOSCOPY

Pankaj Jay Pasricha

Technological advances in radiologic and endoscopic imaging have transformed medicine in the past few decades. With its remarkable accessibility, the gastrointestinal tract, perhaps more than any other organ system, has particularly benefited from the endoscopic approach. The major advantages of endoscopy over contrast radiography in evaluation of diseases of the alimentary tract include direct visualization, resulting in a more accurate and sensitive evaluation of mucosal lesions; the ability to obtain biopsy specimens from superficial lesions; and the ability to perform therapeutic interventions. These advantages make endoscopy the procedure of choice in most cases in which mucosal lesions or growths are suspected. Conversely, contrast radiography may be indicated when extrinsic or intrinsic distortions of anatomy are suspected, such as volvulus, intussusception, subtle strictures, or complicated postsurgical changes. For most upper gastrointestinal lesions, however, the sensitivity (about 90%) and specificity (nearly 100%) of endoscopy are far higher than those of barium radiography (about 50 and 90%, respectively).

Diagnostic endoscopy (Table 132–1) is usually a remarkably safe and well-tolerated procedure. However, complications do occur and need to be carefully explained to the patient as part of the informed consent process; patients must also be prepared appropriately to reduce complication rates (Table 132–2).

LUMINAL ENDOSCOPY: SPECIFIC INDICATIONS

Most indications for gastrointestinal endoscopy are based on the presenting symptoms of the patient (e.g., dysphagia, bleeding, diarrhea). In other instances, endoscopy is required to evaluate specific lesions found by other diagnostic imaging, such as a gastric ulcer or colon polyp discovered by barium radiography. Finally, screening endoscopy is often performed in asymptomatic individuals on the

Table 132–1 • ENDOSCOPIC PROCEDURES AND GENERAL APPLICATIONS

	THERAPEUTIC APPLICATIONS
LUMINAL ENDOSCOPY	
Common procedures	Hemostasis
Esophagogastroduodenoscopy (EGD)	Luminal restoration (dilation, ablation, stenting)
Colonoscopy	Lesion removal (e.g., poylpectomy, mucosal ablation)
Flexible sigmoidoscopy	Provision of access (percutaneous endoscopic gastrostomy and jejunostomy)
	Barrier strengthening (antireflux procedures)
Less common procedures	
Enteroscopy	
Capsule endoscopy	
PANCREATOBILIARY IMAGING	
Endoscopic retrograde pancreatocholangiography (ERCP)	Lesion (stone) removal
	Luminal restoration (dilation, stenting)
	Provision of access (sphincterotomy)
	Drainage (bile, pancreatic pseudocyst)
TRANSLUMINAL IMAGING	
Endoscopic ultrasound (EUS)	Analgesic block
	Delivery of therapeutic agents (experimental)

Table 132–2 • COMPLICATIONS OF ENDOSCOPY

ENDOSCOPIC COMPLICATION	INCIDENCE (%)	SPECIFIC PROPHYLAXIS
GENERAL COMPLICATIONS		
Complications related primarily to sedation (cardiovascular and respiratory depression, aspiration)	0.06–0.07	Airway protection with massive upper gastrointestinal bleeding Preprocedure medical evaluation, intra- and postprocedure monitoring Anesthesiology consultation for high-risk patients
Perforation	0.01–0.03 (upper endoscopy) 0.14–0.25 (colonoscopy)	None (except careful technique)
Bleeding	0.03 (upper endoscopy) 0.7–2.5 (poylpectomy)	Discontinue anticoagulant use prior to therapeutic endoscopy
Bacteremia and infectious complications (endocarditis, bacterial ascites)	<0.01	Antibiotics for patients at risk for: Endocarditis (patients with artificial valves, pulmonary-systemic shunts, previous history of endocarditis) Bacterial ascites (cirrhotics)
Death	0.006 (upper endoscopy) 0.02 (colonoscopy)	
COMPLICATIONS ASSOCIATED WITH SPECIALIZED PROCEDURES		
Pancreatitis (ERCP)	3–20	Not well established/experimental
Cholangitis (ERCP)	0.1–2	Preprocedure antibiotics
Wound infections (PEG)	3–4	Preprocedure antibiotics

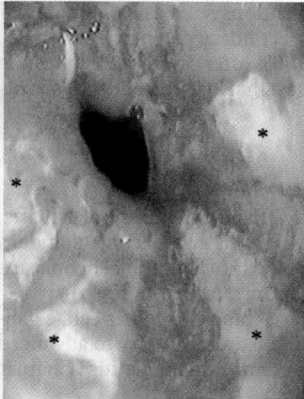 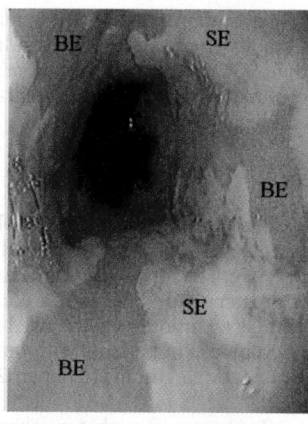

FIGURE 132–1 • Severe reflux esophagitis (*left*) with mucosal erythema and linear ulcers with yellow exudates (*). It is thought that such changes eventually lead to Barrett's esophagus (*right*) in which the normal white squamous epithelium (SE) is replaced by red columnar epithelium (BE). These pictures are from different patients.

esophagitis and hence a risk for complications. Finally, if Barrett's esophagus is discovered (see Fig. 132–1), most experts recommend some form of periodic surveillance endoscopy as these patients are at increased risk for the development of adenocarcinoma.

Barrett's esophagus, once established, does not generally regress despite adequate control of reflux. Because of the small but definite risk of cancer associated with this lesion, various methods to ablate this epithelium have been attempted, with the rationale that under conditions of acid suppression the esophageal lining is reconstituted by squamous epithelium. Ablation can be achieved by a variety of thermal means that include techniques such as electrical cautery, argon plasma coagulation, and high-energy lasers. Other techniques include mucosal resection and photodynamic therapy, which involves the destruction of tumor tissue through the interplay between a tumor-sensitizing drug, usually derived from hematoporphyrins (such as porfimer sodium [Photofrin]), and an activating low-energy laser. For patients who have high-grade dysplasia and who are at high risk for surgery, such procedures may be curative and are considered to be reasonable alternatives to esophagectomy. In patients without dysplasia, the benefit (i.e., reduction in the risk of cancer) remains to be established, and ablation should be considered experimental in this setting.

Endoscopic techniques for the therapy of GERD have been introduced, with the common principle of narrowing of the gastroesophageal junction. One technique uses radio frequency energy to produce a scar at the gastroesophageal junction; another relies on an innovative suturing device to restructure this area. Other procedures under development include variations on these themes as well as injection of polymers to "bulk up" the gastroesophageal junction. It should be cautioned that clinical trials of these procedures have been performed only in small numbers of carefully selected patients, and it is too soon to know whether they are safe and effective for general use.

In contrast to that in the general population, heartburn in immunocompromised patients often indicates an esophageal infection. The most common causes in patients with human immunodeficiency virus (HIV) infection are *Candida,* cytomegalovirus (CMV), herpesvirus, and idiopathic esophageal ulcers. Because most patients with the acquired immunodeficiency syndrome and esophagitis have candidiasis, an empirical 1- to 2-week course of antifungal therapy may be justified. Patients who do not respond to this approach, however, should almost always have an endoscopy and biopsy so that more specific therapy can be instituted.

basis of their risk for commonly occurring and preventable conditions such as colon cancer (see later).

Implicit in the decision to perform endoscopy is the assumption that it will have a bearing on future management strategy. In dealing with the evaluation of gastrointestinal symptoms, several questions need to be addressed by the referring physician and the endoscopist: *Which* patients need endoscopy? *When* should the endoscopy be done? *What* is the endoscopist looking for? What *endoscopic therapy*, if any, should be planned?

GASTROESOPHAGEAL REFLUX AND HEARTBURN (Chapters 135 and 136). Gastroesophageal reflux disease (GERD) is an extremely common condition in the general population. The fact that its cardinal symptom, heartburn, is relatively specific for this condition justifies an empirical approach of treatment using a combination of lifestyle modifications and over-the-counter or even prescription drugs. Endoscopy is not therefore necessary to make the diagnosis of GERD. Indeed, a negative endoscopy does not rule out the diagnosis of GERD because the overall sensitivity of endoscopy in GERD is only about 70%. If necessary, further evaluation with ambulatory pH monitoring may be indicated to establish the diagnosis. However, there are several circumstances in which endoscopy should be considered for patients with reflux, including patients with associated warning symptoms ("red flags") such as dysphagia, odynophagia, regurgitation, weight loss, gastrointestinal bleeding, or frequent vomiting (Fig. 132–1). These symptoms imply either the development of a GERD-related complication (erosive esophagitis, stricture, or adenocarcinoma) or another disorder masquerading as GERD (esophageal cancer or a gastric-duodenal lesion such as cancer or peptic ulcer). Another group of patients who are candidates for endoscopy are those with severe or persistent or frequently recurrent symptoms that suggest significant

DYSPHAGIA (Chapter 136). Dysphagia can often be categorized as *oropharyngeal* on the basis of the clinical features of nasal regurgitation, laryngeal aspiration, or difficulty in moving the bolus out of the mouth. These symptoms are usually associated with a lesion in the central or peripheral nervous system. Although endoscopy is often performed in these patients, videofluoroesophagography (modified barium swallow or cine-esophagogram) is the procedure of choice as it allows a frame-by-frame evaluation of the rapid sequence of events involved in transfer of the bolus from the mouth to the esophagus. Common causes of *esophageal* dysphagia include malignant as well as benign processes (peptic strictures secondary to reflux, Schatzki's rings) and motility disturbances of the esophageal body or the lower esophageal sphincter. Endoscopic examination is considered mandatory in all patients with esophageal dysphagia. However, contrast esophagography may also be helpful; it can provide guidance for an endoscopy that is anticipated to be difficult (e.g., a patient with a complex stricture), suggest a disturbance in motility, and occasionally detect subtle stenoses that are not appreciated on endoscopy (the scope diameter is typically 10 mm or less, whereas some symptomatic strictures can be considerably wider).

Endoscopic treatment options are available for many causes of esophageal dysphagia. Tumors may be dilated mechanically, ablated by thermal means (cautery or laser), or stented with prosthetic devices. Metallic expandable stents have become the palliative procedure of choice for most patients with symptomatic esophageal cancer. Benign lesions of the esophagus, such a strictures or rings, can also be dilated endoscopically, usually with excellent results. Finally, some motility disturbances such as achalasia are best approached endoscopically with the use of large balloon dilators for the lower esophageal sphincter or sometimes with the local injection of botulinum toxin.

DYSPEPSIA (Chapter 135). Dyspepsia, which is chronic or recurring pain or discomfort centered in the upper abdomen, is a common condition that can be caused by a variety of disorders, including peptic ulcer, reflux esophagitis, gallstones, gastric dysmotility, and, rarely, gastric or esophageal cancer. However, up to 60% of patients with chronic (>3 months) dyspepsia belong to the so-called functional category in which there is no definite structural or biochemical explanation for the symptoms. Although *Helicobacter pylori* gastritis is found frequently in these patients, there is no definite evidence to prove a cause-and-effect relationship between these two findings. The optimal diagnostic approach to dyspepsia is somewhat controversial and is still evolving (see Fig. 135–2). If a diagnostic test is to be performed, endoscopy, sometimes with biopsies to detect *H. pylori,* is clearly the procedure of choice, with an accuracy of about 90% (compared with about 65% for double-contrast radiography). There has been a move toward empirical approaches to dyspepsia because only a minority of patients with dyspepsia have peptic ulcers and gastric cancer is extremely rare in Western countries. However, dyspepsia is a recurrent condition, and patients who do not respond to empirical therapy eventually almost always undergo endoscopy. Many gastroenterologists therefore opt for early endoscopy, if only for the reassurance that a negative examination provides.

UPPER GASTROINTESTINAL BLEEDING (Chapter 133). Acid-peptic disease (including ulcers, erosions, and gastritis), variceal bleeding, and Mallory-Weiss tears account for the vast majority of all cases of upper gastrointestinal bleeding. Other less common but important lesions include angiomas or the rarer Dieulafoy's lesion (a superficial artery that erodes through the gut mucosa). Finally, upper gastrointestinal cancers are occasionally associated with significant bleeding. Endoscopy is mandatory in all patients with upper gastrointestinal bleeding, with the rare exception being the terminally ill patient in whom the outcome is unlikely to be affected. Endoscopy is able to detect and localize the site of the bleeding in 95% of cases and is clearly superior to contrast radiography (with an accuracy of only 75 to 80%). The endoscopic appearance of bleeding lesions can also help predict the risk of rebleeding, thus facilitating the triage and treatment process. Bleeding can be effectively controlled during the initial endoscopy itself in the majority of cases. The risk of recurrent

bleeding is diminished, resulting in a shorter duration of hospital stay as well as a reduction in the need for surgery.

In general, endoscopy should be performed only after adequate stabilization of hemodynamic and respiratory parameters. The role of gastric lavage before endoscopy is controversial; some endoscopists prefer that it be done, occasionally even using a large-bore tube, whereas others avoid such preparation because of the fear of producing artifact. The timing of subsequent endoscopy is dependent on two factors: the severity of the hemorrhage and the risk status of the patient. Patients with active, persistent, or severe bleeding (>3 units of blood) require urgent endoscopy. Endoscopy in these patients is best performed in the intensive care unit because they are at particular risk for aspiration and may require emergent intubation for respiratory protection and ventilation. Patients with slower or inactive bleeding may be evaluated by endoscopy in a "semielective" manner (usually within 12 to 20 hours), but a case can be made to perform endoscopy early even in these stable patients (perhaps in the emergency department itself) to allow more confident triage and efficient resource management.

Most bleeding from upper gastrointestinal lesions can be effectively controlled endoscopically. The endoscopist considers factors such as age (older patients have a higher risk of rebleeding) and the severity of the initial hemorrhage (which has a direct correlation with the risk of rebleeding) in addition to the appearance of the lesion when determining the need for endoscopic therapy. Nonvariceal bleeding vessels can be treated by a variety of means including injections of various substances (epinephrine, saline, sclerosants), thermal coagulation (laser or electrocautery), or mechanical means (clipping). In the United States, the most popular approach to a bleeding peptic ulcer lesion is a combination of injection with dilute epinephrine and electrocoagulation. Initial hemostasis can be achieved in 90% or more of cases; rebleeding, which may recur in up to 20% of cases, responds about half of the time to a second endoscopic procedure. Patients who continue to bleed (typically patients with large ulcers in the posterior wall of the duodenal bulb) are usually managed angiographically (with embolization of the bleeding vessel) or surgically.

Variceal bleeding is also effectively managed endoscopically, with a success rate similar to that with bleeding ulcers (Fig. 132–2). Hemostasis is achieved using band ligation (Fig. 132–3), sclerotherapy, or a combination of both. Increasingly, patients who do not respond to endoscopic treatment are considered candidates for a transjugular intrahepatic portosystemic shunt (TIPS); traditional shunt surgery for bleeding varices is rarely performed. Even if initial endoscopic hemostasis is successful, long-term prevention of rebleeding requires a program of ongoing endoscopic sessions until variceal obliteration is complete. Ligation is the preferred approach in this setting because it is associated with fewer side effects. An ongoing area of investigation is whether endoscopic therapy, in the form of ligation, should be performed in patients with large esophageal varices who have never bled (primary prophylaxis). Meta-analysis of the published literature suggests that such therapy may offer some advantages over the current mainstay of treatment, β-blocker drugs.

ACUTE LOWER GASTROINTESTINAL BLEEDING (Chapter 133). The most common cause of acute lower gastrointestinal bleeding is angiodysplasia, followed by diverticulosis, neoplasms, and colitis. In about 10% of patients presenting with hematochezia, a small bowel lesion may be responsible. In contrast to upper gastrointestinal bleeding, there is no single best test for acute lower gastrointestinal bleeding (Fig. 132–4). In young patients (<40 years) with minor bleeding,

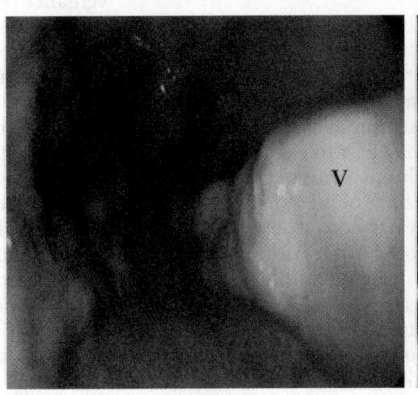
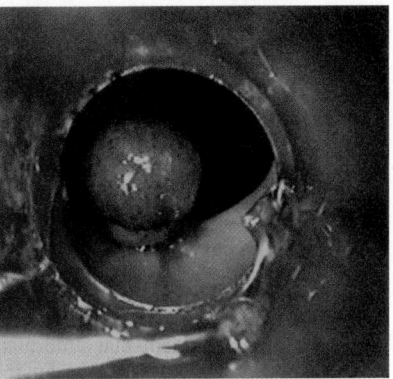

FIGURE 132–2 • Endoscopic view of esophageal varices (*left*) in the wall of the esophagus (V). *Right,* Image of a varix that has been endoscopically ligated with a band.

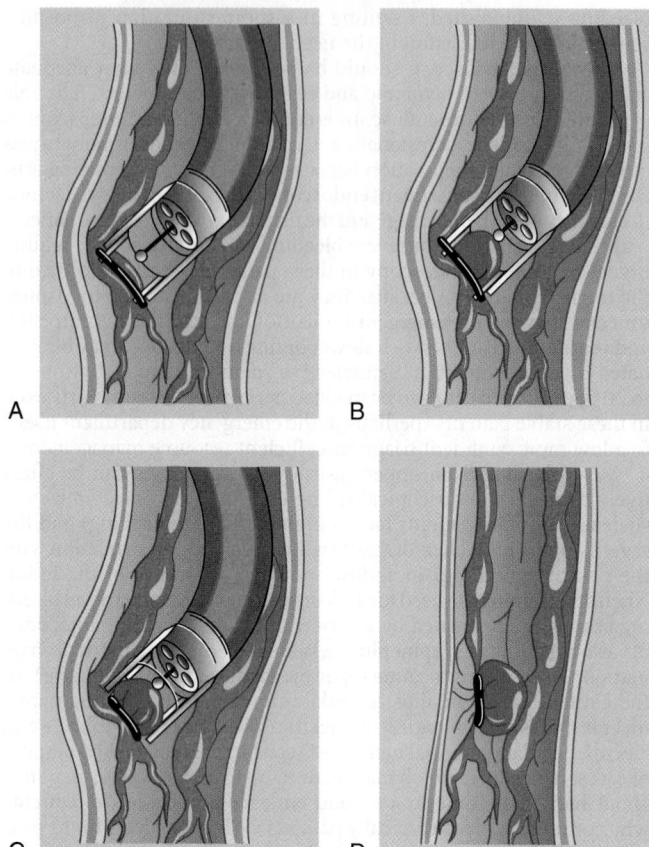

FIGURE 132–3 • Endoscopic variceal ligation technique. *A,* The endoscope, with attached ligating device, is brought into contact with a varix just above the gastroesophageal junction. *B,* Suction is applied, drawing the varix-containing mucosa into the dead space created at the end of the endoscope by the ligating device. *C,* The tripwire is pulled, releasing the band around the aspirated tissue. *D,* Completed ligation.

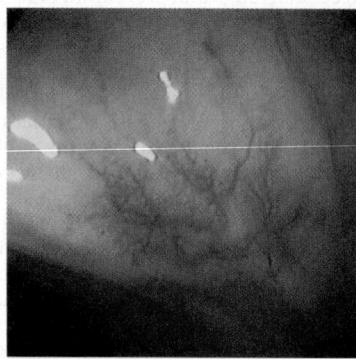

FIGURE 132–4 • Mucosal telangiectasia (arteriovenous malformation, or AVM) in the colon. The patient presented with hematochezia. The lesion was subsequently cauterized endoscopically.

features that are highly suggestive of anorectal origin (e.g., blood on the surface of the stool or on the wipe) may warrant only a flexible sigmoidoscopy. Conversely, patients presenting with hemodynamic compromise may need an upper endoscopy first to exclude a lesion in the upper gastrointestinal tract (typically postpyloric) that is bleeding so briskly that it arises as hematochezia. Colonoscopy has traditionally been recommended after bleeding has slowed or stopped and the patient has been given an adequate bowel purge. However, a disadvantage of delaying endoscopy is that when a pathologic lesion such as an arteriovenous malformation (see Fig. 132–4) or diverticulum is found, it may be impossible to implicate it confidently as the site of bleeding (complementary information by radiography or scintigraphy becomes particularly important in this situation). Some experts

therefore recommend an urgent diagnostic endoscopy with little or no preparation for acute lower gastrointestinal hemorrhages and have reported success rates of 50%.

OCCULT GASTROINTESTINAL BLEEDING OR IRON DEFICIENCY ANEMIA (Chapter 133). Normal fecal blood loss is usually less than 2 to 3 mL/day. Most standard fecal occult blood tests detect only blood loss of 10 mL/day or more. Therefore, even if this test is negative, patients with iron deficiency anemia and no other obvious source of blood loss should always undergo aggressive gastrointestinal evaluation, which uncovers a gastrointestinal lesion in the majority of cases. Although most lesions that cause overt gastrointestinal bleeding can also cause occult blood loss, occult bleeding should almost never be ascribed to diverticulosis or hemorrhoids. Endoscopy is always preferable to radiographic studies for evaluation of occult blood loss or iron deficiency anemia because of its ability to detect flat lesions, particularly vascular malformations, which may be found in 6% or more of patients. If both upper and lower endoscopies are negative, a small bowel radiographic series (preferably an enteroclysis) to look for gross lesions often completes the evaluation. If the patient continues to have symptomatic bleeding, enteroscopy (the use of a very long upper endoscope to intubate the small bowel) and capsule endoscopy (see later) may be helpful to detect small bowel lesions such as tumors or angiomas.

An innovation has been the development of "capsule endoscopy," which consists of a disposable capsule that can be swallowed and that takes color video images as it travels through the digestive tract. These images are received and recorded by a device that the patient wears as a belt while carrying out his or her routine activities. At the end of the procedure, the information is downloaded to a computer, processed, and scanned for detectable abnormalities. The capsule itself passes out harmlessly in the stool. The capsule is not useful, in its present form, as a method for imaging the upper gastrointestinal tract or the colon; further, it has no therapeutic utility. Nevertheless, with the help of this procedure, physicians can now visualize the mucosa of the entire small bowel in detail, facilitating the detection of uncommon but important lesions such as vascular malformations or small tumors that can be missed by alternative imaging methods.

COLORECTAL NEOPLASMS (Chapter 200). Colonoscopy is the most accurate test for detecting mass lesions of the large bowel that are suspected on clinical or radiologic grounds. However, the greatest impact of endoscopy on colorectal neoplasia may be in the area of screening and prevention. The adenoma-to-carcinoma sequence of progression in colorectal cancer provides a relatively unique opportunity for prophylaxis. Thus, if screening programs can identify patients with polyps and if these polyps are removed, cancer can largely be prevented. Various techniques are available for safe and effective polypectomy, depending upon the size, presence of a stalk, and location (Fig. 132–5). Colonoscopy is being increasingly accepted as the procedure of choice for screening patients at average risk, that is, anybody older than 50 years. When patients have been found to harbor adenomatous polyps, they should be entered into a surveillance program; the frequency of colonoscopic examinations is still not settled but varies in practice from 1 to 3 years.

More aggressive screening strategies are required for patients considered at high risk for colorectal cancer, including patients with well-defined hereditary syndromes as well as those with a history of colorectal cancer in a first-degree relative. In addition, patients with ulcerative colitis with long-standing (more than 8 years) disease affecting the entire colon have an increased risk for developing colon cancer, about 0.5 to 3% after 20 years. Periodic colonoscopic surveillance (every 1 to 2 years with biopsies) is therefore recommended for patients with long-standing disease (8 years with pancolitis, 12 to 15 years with left-sided colitis); the discovery of dysplasia or cancer is an indication for colectomy.

"Virtual colonoscopy," which involves the digital construction of an endoluminal view of the colon on the basis of data from abdominal computed tomography (CT), is quite sensitive but currently has a prohibitively high false-positive rate, preventing its adoption for general screening.

CHRONIC DIARRHEA (Chapter 141). Endoscopy may be a valuable aid in the evaluation of patients with persistent diarrhea. The timing of the endoscopy in these patients often depends on the clinical features of the illness. Patients with bloody diarrhea should have lower endoscopy as part of their initial evaluation to look for inflammatory bowel disease (Chapter 142). In most patients with chronic diarrhea, endoscopy is often done when initial routine testing does not yield a

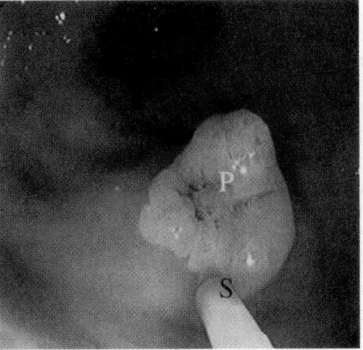
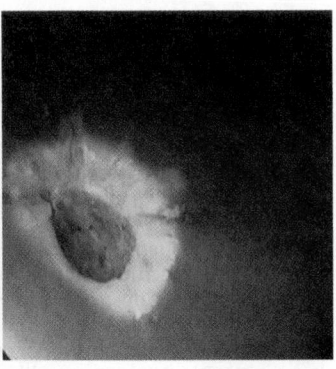

FIGURE 132–5 • Endoscopic polypectomy. *Left*, A snare (S) has been passed through the endoscope and positioned around the polyp (P). *Right*, Subsequently, cautery was applied and the polyp guillotined, leaving behind a clean mucosal defect.

specific diagnosis. Both upper and lower endoscopies may be used, depending on the clinical presentation. Thus, the patient suspected of having a malabsorptive process may require an upper endoscopy with jejunal or duodenal biopsies to look for celiac sprue or rarer lesions such as lymphoma or Whipple's disease (endoscopic biopsy has largely replaced blind intestinal biopsies for these conditions). Conversely, patients suspected to have a secretory cause of diarrhea require a colonoscopy with biopsies to look for overt inflammatory bowel disease or more subtle variants such as microscopic or lymphocytic colitis, in which cases the diagnosis requires careful examination of the biopsy specimens.

The endoscopic approach to diarrhea in immunocompromised patients, such as those with HIV infection, is guided by the degree of immunosuppression and the need to find treatable infections. When routine stool tests are negative, patients with CD4 counts less than 100/mm^3 should undergo endoscopic evaluation to detect pathogens such as CMV, *Mycobacterium avium* complex, and microsporidiosis. Small-volume stools with tenesmus suggest a proctocolitis, for which sigmoidoscopy (rather than a full colonoscopy) with biopsies is usually adequate. In patients with upper gastrointestinal symptoms (large-volume diarrhea, bloating, and dyspepsia), an upper endoscopy with biopsy may be attempted first.

MISCELLANEOUS INDICATIONS. The upper endoscope has provided a relatively quick and noninvasive means for removal of accidentally or deliberately ingested foreign bodies. Timing is critical for removal, however, because objects are usually beyond endoscopic retrieval when they reach the small bowel. Any foreign object that is causing symptoms should be removed, as should potentially dangerous devices such as batteries or sharp objects. In general, objects greater than 2.5 cm in width or 13 cm in length are unlikely to leave the stomach and so should also be removed. Occasionally, patients with food impacted in the esophagus require endoscopic removal (Fig. 132–6). This condition almost always indicates an underlying functional or structural problem (Chapter 136) and should prompt a thorough diagnostic evaluation after the acute problem has been addressed.

Because of the relatively poor correlation between oropharyngeal lesions and more distal visceral injury, upper endoscopy is usually recommended urgently in patients with *corrosive ingestion* (Chapter 106). Endoscopy allows patients to be divided into high- or low-risk groups for complications, with institution of appropriate monitoring and therapy.

Among the myriad causes of *nausea and vomiting,* a few, such as mucosal lesions or unsuspected reflux disease, are amenable to endoscopic diagnosis. Patients with new-onset *constipation* (Chapter 134), particularly those who are older than 40 years, should also undergo a colonoscopic evaluation to exclude an obstructing carcinoma. Colonoscopy is also useful in patients with pseudo-obstructive (nonobstructive) colonic dilation or *Ogilvie's syndrome* (Chapter 134); such patients are at risk for colonic rupture at diameters above 9 to 12 cm, and colonoscopic decompression is often required, sometimes on an emergent basis.

Malignant obstruction of the gastrointestinal lumen including the esophagus (Fig. 132–7), pylorus or duodenum, and colon can now be safely and effectively palliated endoscopically using expandable metal stents, avoiding the need for surgery in these patients. A major advance in enteral feeding has been the introduction of percutaneous endoscopic gastrostomy (PEG), a relatively quick, simple, and safe endoscopic procedure that has virtually eliminated surgical placement of gastric tubes. A variation of PEG is percutaneous endoscopic jejunostomy (PEJ), in which a long tube is passed through the gastric tube, past the pylorus, and into the jejunum. The most common indication for these procedures is the need for sustained nutrition in patients with neurologic impairment of swallowing or with head and neck cancers. Patients with a very short life expectancy are not suitable candidates for PEG and can be managed by nasoenteral tubes. PEJ was originally introduced to prevent aspiration, but it does not prevent this complication; the major indication for PEJ is significant impairment of gastric emptying. Retrograde tube migration with PEJ is quite common, however, and PEJ may require frequent replacement.

PANCREATOBILIARY ENDOSCOPY (IMAGING)

Endoscopic retrograde cholangiopancreatography (ERCP) involves a special side-viewing endoscope (the duodenoscope) that is used to gain access to the second part of the duodenum. A small catheter is then introduced into the bile or pancreatic duct, and radiographic

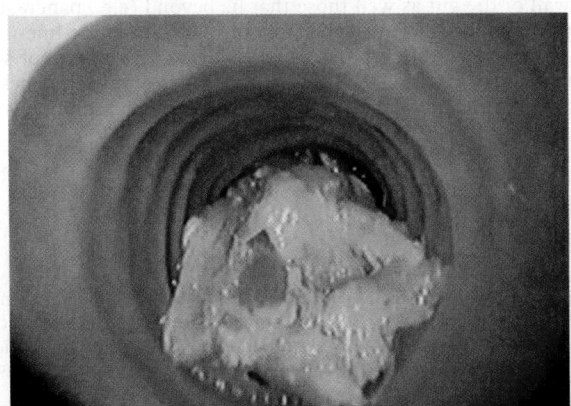

FIGURE 132–6 • Impacted food bolus in a young male who was found to have a ringed esophagus on endoscopy. This presentation is characteristic and may be either congenital or acquired secondary to reflux-induced or eosinophilic esophagitis.

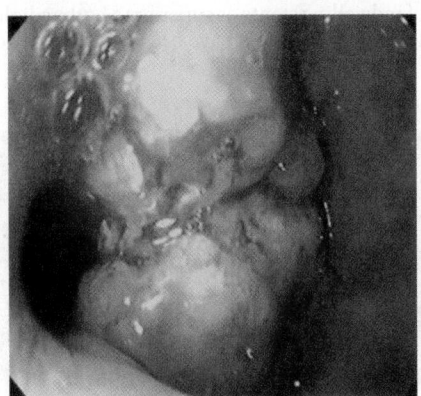

FIGURE 132–7 • Large malignant mass at the gastroesophageal junction as seen endoscopically.

contrast medium is injected under fluoroscopic monitoring. Successful cannulation and imaging can be achieved in up to 95% of cases. In some centers, a very fine caliber "baby" endoscope can also be introduced into the duct of interest (cholangioscopy or pancreaticoscopy), allowing the direct visualization of intraductal pathology. ERCP is perhaps the technically most demanding of gastrointestinal endoscopic procedures, and it is associated with the highest risk of serious complications (notably pancreatitis, in about 5% of cases).

SUSPECTED BILIARY PATHOLOGY (Chapters 148 and 158). The diagnostic approach to patients with cholestasis begins with an attempt to differentiate obstructive from hepatocellular causes. The most common causes of obstructive jaundice are common bile duct stones and tumors of the pancreatic and bile ducts. Less invasive conventional imaging with ultrasonography, CT, or magnetic resonance imaging (MRI) demonstrates dilated bile ducts and mass lesions but is not very sensitive or specific in detecting or delineating pathology in the distal common bile duct and pancreas, two regions where the majority of obstructing lesions are found. Furthermore, some biliary diseases, such as sclerosing cholangitis, do not result in dilated ducts but have a characteristic appearance on cholangiography. Finally, the ability to use devices such as cytology brushes and biopsy forceps during cholangiography provides an additional aid in the diagnosis of biliary lesions. Both percutaneous and endoscopic cholangiographic techniques are associated with a high rate of success in experienced hands, but the endoscopic approach allows visualization of the ampullary region and the performance of sphincterotomy, and it also avoids the small risk of a biliary leak associated with puncture of the liver capsule.

In the last few years, magnetic resonance cholangiopancreatography (MRCP), a digital reconstruction technique based on an abdominal MRI scan, has become popular as an imaging modality for the pancreatobiliary system, with excellent sensitivity and specificity. Because of its relative safety, many experts now advocate this procedure for screening patients with a low likelihood of disease. In those with a higher probability, ERCP is still the procedure of choice because of its therapeutic options.

Of the approximately 600,000 patients undergoing cholecystectomy in this country, 5 to 10% may present with bile duct stones before or after the surgery. Endoscopic stone removal is successful in 90% or more of these cases and usually requires a sphincterotomy (Fig. 132–8). The sphincter of Oddi is a band of muscle that encircles the distal common bile duct and pancreatic duct in the region of the ampulla of Vater; cutting of this muscle, or sphincterotomy, is one of the mainstays of endoscopic biliary treatment and is accomplished using a special tool called a papillotome or sphincterotome. This procedure is often sufficient for the treatment of small stones in the bile ducts, but larger stones may require additional procedures, such as mechanical, electrohydraulic, or laser lithotripsy, all of which can be performed endoscopically. In addition to stone disease, sphincterotomy can be curative for patients with papillary stenosis or muscle spasm (termed *sphincter of Oddi dysfunction*). Finally, by enlarging the access to the bile duct, sphincterotomy facilitates the passage of stents and other devices into the bile duct. Sphincterotomy carries an additional small risk of bleeding, but its associated morbidity is about one third that of surgical exploration and its cost is only about 20% as high.

Endoscopic therapy has also revolutionized the palliative approach to malignant biliary obstruction. The technique, which requires the placement of indwelling stents, is superior to both radiologic and surgical techniques. Plastic stents have been the mainstay of treatment, but metal stents last longer and are perhaps preferred in patients with longer life expectancies.

PANCREATIC DISEASE (Chapters 145 and 201). ERCP is also useful in patients with pancreatic diseases that do not always arise with obstructive jaundice, such as pancreatic cancer of the body and tail and, less commonly, chronic pancreatitis. It is also indicated for patients with acute or recurrent pancreatitis without any obvious risk factors on history or routine laboratory evaluation. Imaging of the pancreatic duct may delineate anatomic abnormalities that may be responsible for the pancreatitis, such as congenital variants (pancreas divisum, annular pancreas), intraductal tumors, or possibly sphincter of Oddi dysfunction. In such cases, bile can be collected from the bile duct for microscopic examination for crystals (so-called microlithiasis) that can result in pancreatitis in some patients even in the absence of macroscopic stones. In patients with chronic pancreatitis, which is most often due to excessive alcohol intake, pancreatography can confirm the diagnosis, provide useful information about the severity of the disease, and identify ductal lesions that may be amenable to therapy by either endoscopic (see later) or surgical means. In more subtle cases, collection and analysis of pancreatic juice after stimulation with secretin may be useful in establishing exocrine impairment and hence in confirming chronic pancreatic injury.

ERCP also has a role in some patients with *acute* pancreatitis (Chapter 145) that is probably caused by obstructing biliary stones. Patients presenting with severe biliary pancreatitis may benefit from an urgent ERCP early in their course, with the intention of detecting and removing stones from the common bile duct. Similarly, patients who have smoldering acute pancreatitis that does not appear to be improving satisfactorily with conservative treatment may require ERCP to identify and treat any obstructing lesions in the pancreatic or distal biliary duct.

Therapeutic endoscopy for pancreatic disease is still evolving. Relief of ductal obstruction (e.g., by endoscopic removal of pancreatic stones or dilation of strictures) can provide short to intermediate pain relief in some patients with chronic pancreatitis. Endoscopic pseudocyst drainage by a variety of techniques is now technically feasible, with results that appear to be comparable to those of surgical or radiologic techniques. Patients with ductal disruptions (e.g., those with pancreatic ascites) can often be treated with endoscopic stent placement. Pancreatic papillotomy may also be useful for selected cases of recurrent pancreatitis, such as those with pancreas divisum or pancreatic sphincter dysfunction. Although the ability to approach these difficult clinical entities by the relatively less invasive endoscopic techniques represents a major accomplishment, the exact role of the various treatment modalities (surgical, radiologic, and endoscopic) in the treatment of pancreatic diseases remains to be determined.

TRANSLUMINAL IMAGING: ENDOSCOPIC ULTRASONOGRAPHY

The development of endoscopic ultrasonography (EUS), or endosonography, has been a major technological achievement in gastroenterology. The incorporation of an ultrasonic transducer in the tip of a flexible endoscope or the use of stand-alone ultrasound probes has now made it possible to obtain images of gastrointestinal lesions that are not apparent on superficial views, including lesions within the wall of the gut as well those that lie beyond (e.g., pancreatic or lymph node lesions). A further role of EUS is to guide fine-needle aspiration, which often provides pathologic confirmation of suspicious lesions (Fig. 132–9). In many cases, this approach appears to be even more accurate than conventional radiologic techniques such

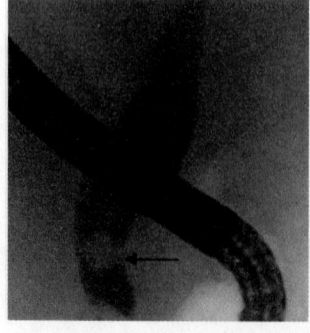
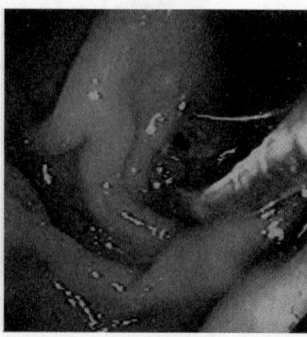
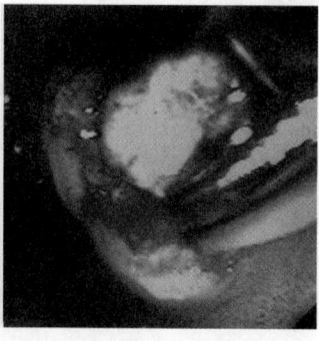

FIGURE 132–8 • Biliary sphincterotomy and stone removal from the bile duct. *Left,* Endoscopic retrograde cholangiographic image showing stones (arrow) in the distal common bile duct. *Center,* Endoscopic image of a sphincterotome in the bile duct with the wire cutting the roof of the ampulla (sphincter). *Right,* A stone is being removed from the bile duct using an endoscopically passed basket

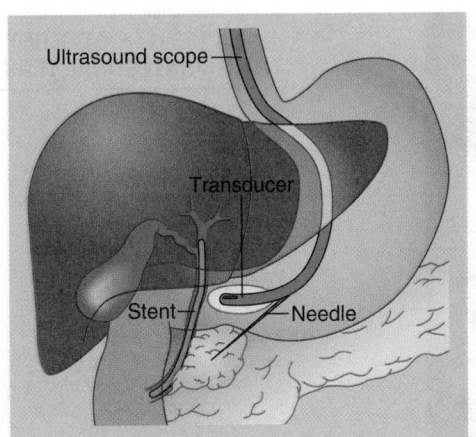
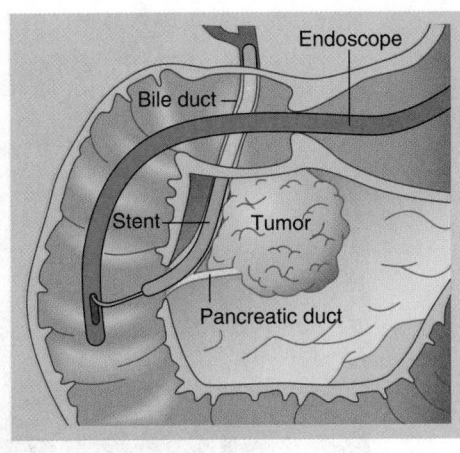

FIGURE 132–9 • Biopsy of a pancreatic mass guided by endoscopic ultrasonography (*A*) and the placement of a stent into a malignant bile duct stricture with endoscopic retrograde cholangiopancreatography (*B*). (From Brugge WR, Van Dam J: Pancreatic and biliary endoscopy. N Engl J Med 1999;341:1808–1816. Copyright © 1999 Massachusetts Medical Society. All rights reserved.)

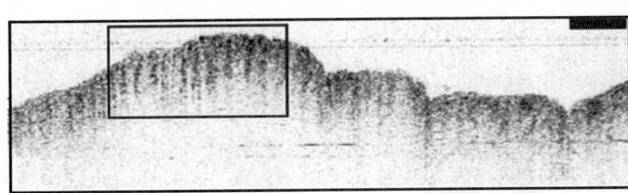
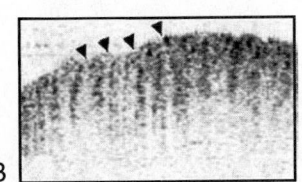
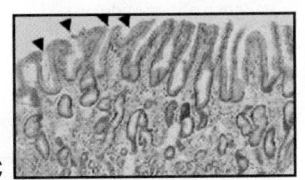

FIGURE 132–10 • *A*, Optical coherence tomography of the stomach, an endoscopic procedure currently under investigation that provides high-resolution images of the superficial epithelium comparable to those of microscopy. Scale bar 500 μm. *B*, Magnified view of *A*. Gastric pits can be clearly identified as areas of relatively low reflectance within the glandular epithelium (arrowheads). *C*, Histology corresponding to *B*. Gastric pits are marked by arrowheads (H&E, original magnification × 40). (From Bouma BE, Tearney GJ, Compton CC, Nishioka NS: High-resolution imaging of the human esophagus and stomach in vivo using optical coherence tomography. Gastrointest Endosc 2000;51:467–474.)

as abdominal ultrasonography or CT. Thus, EUS is probably the single best test for diagnosing pancreatic tumors (Chapter 201), particularly the small endocrine varieties, with sensitivities approaching 95%. It is also the procedure of choice for imaging submucosal and other wall lesions of the gastrointestinal tract (overall accuracy of 65 to 70%) as well as for staging of a variety of gastrointestinal tumors (overall accuracy of 90% or more). Preoperative staging is a critical element in the management strategy for tumors such as esophageal and pancreatic cancer, and EUS can complement more conventional radiologic tests to help determine the resectability and curative potential of surgery in these cases.

In addition to its valuable diagnostic role, EUS is rapidly emerging as a therapeutic tool. One example is EUS-directed celiac plexus neurolysis, a technique that appears to be effective for the treatment of pain in patients with pancreatic cancer. Unfortunately, this approach does not appear to work as well in patients with chronic pancreatitis.

FUTURE DIRECTIONS

Traditional endoscopy, encompassing the procedures described here, is based on the simple reflection of light from tissue. However, light interacts with tissue in many other ways, including fluorescence, absorbance, and scatter. Many instruments are being developed that take advantage of these diverse interactions and provide information on the biology of the tissue that goes beyond a simple endoscopic image. These techniques, termed optical biopsy (Fig. 132–10) or

bioendoscopy, are rapidly undergoing testing as complementary modalities to current endoscopic techniques and promise to take this already valuable technique to new levels of accuracy.

SUGGESTED READINGS

Keymling M: Colorectal stenting. Endoscopy 2003;35:234–238. *Endoscopic stents can relieve malignant colorectal obstruction and avoid high-risk emergency laparotomy and resection.*

Pearce CB, Duncan HD: Enteral feeding. Nasogastric, nasojejunal, percutaneous endoscopic gastrostomy, or jejunostomy: Its indications and limitations. Postgrad Med J 2002;78:198–204. *Review of the current status of enteral feeding.*

Ransohoff DF, Sandler RS: Screening for colorectal cancer. N Engl J Med 2002;346: 40–44. *Evidence supporting various strategies for colorectal cancer screening, followed by a review of formal guidelines.*

Triadafilopoulos G: Endoscopic therapies for gastroesophageal reflux disease. Curr Gastroenterol Rep 2002;4:200–204. *Review of new endoscopic treatments.*

133 GASTROINTESTINAL HEMORRHAGE AND OCCULT GASTROINTESTINAL BLEEDING

David J. Bjorkman

Gastrointestinal hemorrhage is a common clinical disorder. Bleeding from the gastrointestinal tract may present clinically as acute upper tract bleeding (proximal to the ligament of Treitz), acute lower tract bleeding (distal to the ligament of Treitz), or as evidence of occult blood loss either by iron deficiency anemia or a positive stool test for blood.

UPPER GASTROINTESTINAL BLEEDING

Upper gastrointestinal bleeding (proximal to the ligament of Treitz) is responsible for 250,000 to 300,000 hospital admissions and $2.5 billion in costs in the United States each year. The most common causes of upper gastrointestinal bleeding are peptic ulcers (Chapter 138) and esophagogastric varices. Variceal bleeding (Fig. 133–1) most commonly occurs in the setting of portal hypertension (Chapter 156). Less common causes of upper gastrointestinal bleeding are Mallory-Weiss tears (Fig. 133–2), malignancy, erosive disease, and vascular abnormalities (Table 133–1).

Diagnosis

Most cases of acute upper gastrointestinal bleeding present as hematemesis, although brisk bleeding can present as hematochezia. Gastrointestinal endoscopy (Chapter 132) remains both the diagnostic and therapeutic procedure of choice for upper gastrointestinal bleeding. Despite progressive advances in diagnosis, the mortality from acute upper gastrointestinal bleeding requiring hospitalization remains near 4% for young patients and has been reported to be as high as 15% in the elderly.

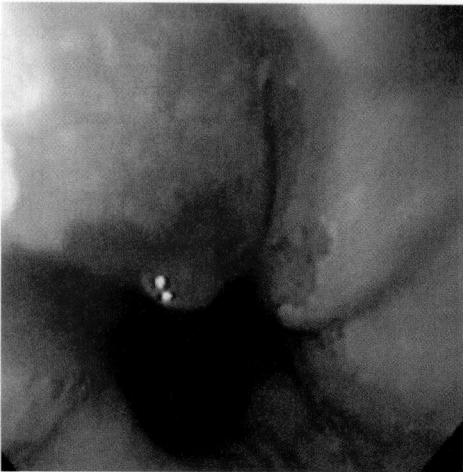

FIGURE 133–1 • Bleeding esophageal varix at the gastroesophageal junction. (Courtesy of Pankaj Jay Pasricha, MD.)

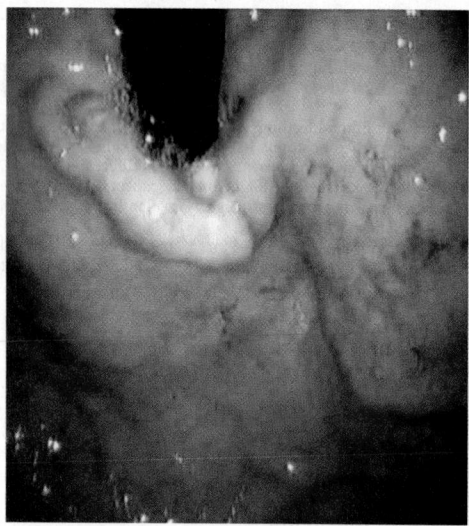

FIGURE 133–2 • Retroflexed endoscopic image of a Mallory-Weiss tear at the gastroesophageal junction.

Table 133–1 • ETIOLOGY AND SEVERITY OF UPPER GASTROINTESTINAL TRACT HEMORRHAGE*

	SEVERITY OF HEMORRHAGE	
SOURCE OF HEMORRHAGE	**Mild–Moderate (246 Patients)**	**Severe (140 Patients)**
Esophagus		
Esophagitis	12%	7%
Ulcer	2%	2%
Mallory-Weiss tear	5%	19%
Esophageal varices	5%	31%
Total esophagus	24%	59%
Stomach		
Gastric ulcer	15%	14%
Prepyloric ulcer	2%	4%
Pyloric channel ulcer	4%	2%
Gastric erosions	2%	0
Gastritis	7%	0
Varices	1%	2%
Portal-hypertensive gastropathy	2%	0
Gastric cancer	2%	0
Polyp	0	2%
Dieulafoy lesion	0	0
Total stomach	35%	24%
Duodenum		
Ulcer	30%	15%
Duodenitis	8%	0
Aortoenteric fistula	0	2%
Pancreatic pseudocyst	2%	0
Post-sphincterotomy	1%	0
Total duodenum	41%	17%
	100%	100%

*All patients underwent diagnostic endoscopy at San Francisco General Hospital over 3 years.

Adapted from Cello JP: Gastrointestinal hemorrhage and occult gastrointestinal bleeding. In Goldman L, Bennett JC (eds): Cecil Textbook of Medicine, 21st ed. Philadelphia, WB Saunders, 2000.

EMERGENCY EVALUATION AND TREATMENT. The initial focus for any patient with significant blood loss should be the evaluation and restoration of intravascular volume, which begins with careful evaluation of blood pressure and pulse, including special attention to any orthostatic changes. Blood hemoglobin concentration and hematocrit are unreliable markers of acute blood loss, but they are helpful as baseline values. Intravenous access and vigorous volume replacement decrease the morbidity of acute upper gastrointestinal bleeding and should be initiated immediately in all patients with significant gastrointestinal bleeding. Initial volume restoration can be accomplished with the infusion of isotonic electrolyte solutions until vital signs become stable. Blood products should be based on the patient's clinical condition.

ASSESSING THE LEVEL OF BLEEDING. Endoscopy (Chapter 132) is the method of choice for establishing the site of gastrointestinal bleeding. An upper gastrointestinal source can be assumed when there is a history of hematemesis with frank blood or coffee grounds–like material. A history of melena alone is suggestive but not pathognomonic of a bleeding source proximal to the ligament of Treitz. In patients with a small bowel or a proximal colonic source of bleeding, delayed colonic transit may result in dark stool that may be difficult to distinguish from melena. Hematochezia is more suggestive of a bleeding site in the lower gastrointestinal tract, but, in as many as 10% of cases, it may also result from vigorous upper gastrointestinal bleeding.

When an acute bleeding source is suspected to be in the upper gastrointestinal tract, nasogastric aspiration is 80% sensitive for the presence of an actively bleeding lesion, and evidence of blood in a nasogastric aspirate suggests bleeding proximal to the ligament of Treitz. False-negative aspirates may occur in 20% of patients because the tube is improperly positioned or the reflux of blood from the duodenum is prevented by pylorospasm or obstruction. Nasogastric suction is also useful to determine whether bleeding is persistent or recurrent and to estimate the rapidity of bleeding.

DIAGNOSTIC ENDOSCOPY. After hemodynamic stabilization, endoscopy is indicated in consenting patients unless the risks of the procedure outweigh its potential benefits, at least temporarily (e.g., patients in shock) or its results would not alter the outcome or care of the patient. Endoscopy has a sensitivity of 92% for identifying the site of upper gastrointestinal bleeding, with a specificity that approaches 100%. The sensitivity of endoscopy may be limited by retained blood and clots in the stomach. In this situation, vigorous gastric lavage using a large-bore orogastric tube is critical prior to the procedure. Endoscopy has the added advantage of guiding biopsies to test for *Helicobacter pylori* infection (Chapters 137 and 138) and to diagnose malignancy (Chapter 199). By comparison, barium radiography has a sensitivity of only 54%. Barium radiography is contraindicated in acute upper gastrointestinal bleeding because it interferes with subsequent endoscopy, angiography, or surgery.

Careful endoscopic examination not only identifies the source of upper gastrointestinal bleeding but also is the most accurate predictor of prognosis (probability of rebleeding, morbidity, and mortality). Additional clinical risk factors for higher morbidity and mortality include older age, shock, volume of bleeding, need for transfusion, onset of bleeding in the hospital, and the presence of comorbid clinical conditions. A scoring system (Table 133–2), which uses clinical factors to predict rebleeding and mortality, has been developed and validated.

Table 133–2 • CLINICAL RISK SCORE*

CHARACTERISTIC	SCORE FOR FINDING				POINTS FOR THIS VARIABLE
	0	1	2	3	
Age	<60 years	≥60 and ≤79 years	≥80 years		(Maximum = 2)
Shock	Heart rate < 100 beats per minute and systolic blood pressure ≥ 100 mm Hg	Heart rate ≥ 100 beats per minute and systolic blood pressure ≥ 100 mm Hg	Systolic blood pressure <100 mm Hg		(Maximum = 2)
Comorbidity	None	None	Heart failure Myocardial or ischemia Malignancy (not disseminated) Other comorbidity	Renal failure Liver disease Disseminated malignancy	(Maximum = 3)
Total Score					(Maximum = 7)

*Mortality of acute upper gastrointestinal bleeding based on characteristics assessed at the initial presentation. A score of ≤3 indicates a low clinical risk (mortality ≤12%), whereas a score of ≥4 indicates a high clinical risk (mortality >20%).

Adapted from Rockall TA, Logan FRA, Devlin HB, Northfield TC, Steering committee of the National Audit of Acute Upper Gastrointestinal Hemorrhage. Risk assessment after acute upper gastrointestinal haemorrhage. Gut 1996;38:316–321.

Table 133–3 • RISK OF REBLEEDING AND DEATH BASED ON ENDOSCOPIC FINDINGS

ENDOSCOPIC FINDING	RISK OF REBLEEDING (%)	MORTALITY (%)
Active bleeding	55	11
Visible vessel	43	11
Adherent clot	22	7
Flat spot	10	3
Clean base	5	2

Adapted from Laine L, Peterson WL: Bleeding peptic ulcer. N Engl J Med 1994;331:717–727.

Endoscopic classification of ulcers has been shown repeatedly to predict accurately the rates of rebleeding, morbidity, and mortality (Table 133–3). Patients without high-risk stigmata (those with a clean ulcer base or flat, pigmented, spots) have an extremely low rate of rebleeding and a negligible mortality.

Endoscopic Triage: Cost-Effective Care for Low-Risk Patients

Although it may seem intuitively obvious that endoscopy would improve outcomes, randomized trials have indicated that *diagnostic* endoscopy alone does not improve mortality, rebleeding rates, the need for surgery, or hospital stay. The overwhelming majority (75 to 80%) of patients with bleeding ulcers stop bleeding spontaneously, limiting the impact of early endoscopy for these patients. Nevertheless, recent prospective studies show that urgent endoscopy in all patients with acute nonvariceal upper gastrointestinal bleeding identifies 20 to 30% of patients who meet both clinical and endoscopic criteria for a low risk of rebleeding and morbidity (see Tables 133–2 and 133–3); these patients can be safely treated as outpatients, thereby dramatically reducing the cost of care. Conversely, patients with a high risk of rebleeding, using the same criteria, can undergo early endoscopic therapy, ideally prior to admission, and be triaged to more intensive hospital care. Urgent endoscopy as a triage tool is rapidly becoming the standard of cost-effective care in upper gastrointestinal bleeding (Fig. 133–3). ∎

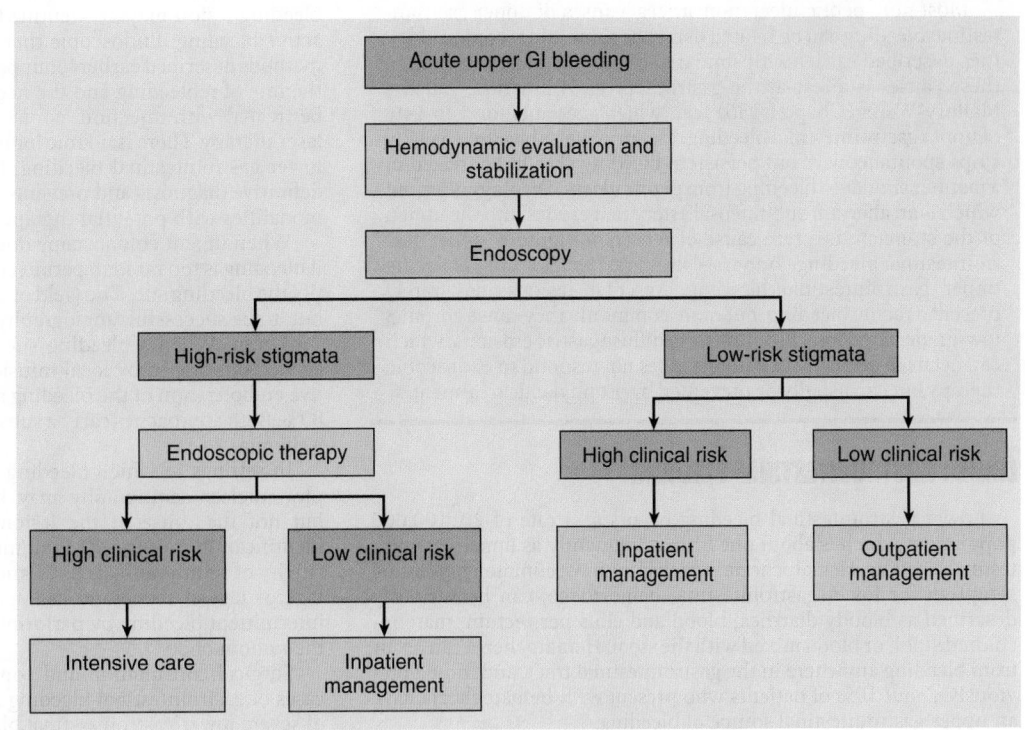

FIGURE 133–3 • Endoscopic triage in acute upper gastrointestinal (GI) bleeding. Flow chart for the cost-effective use of endoscopic triage to determine the level of care required for patients with acute upper gastrointestinal bleeding. Patients who have no clinical risk factors for rebleeding and who have ulcers with low-risk stigmata (clean base, flat pigmented lesions) may be treated as outpatients. Patients with high-risk lesions (active bleeding, a nonbleeding visible vessel) and clinical risk factors should receive endoscopic therapy and hospitalization in a unit based upon their individual risk. Definitions for clinical and endoscopic risk factors are listed in Tables 133–2 and 133–3.

Rx Treatment

ENDOSCOPIC THERAPY. In the 20% of patients with nonvariceal upper gastrointestinal bleeding who have persistent or recurrent bleeding as determined by nasogastric lavage or endoscopy, endoscopic therapy reduces both morbidity and mortality. All available endoscopic techniques appear to have similar results but vary in their approach to sealing the bleeding vessel and maintaining hemostasis. The major methods may be divided into thermal coagulation, injection therapy, and mechanical compression. The most common thermal methods use electrical current (multipolar or bipolar electrode) or direct application of a heated device (heater probe) to seal the vessel with thermal energy. Using these methods, hemostasis can be achieved in 90% of patients with active bleeding, and rebleeding rates are significantly reduced by more than 50%.[2]

The least expensive method of endoscopic therapy for upper gastrointestinal bleeding is to inject the bleeding site with saline or diluted epinephrine. This approach yields initial results that are generally similar to those of thermal therapy but may not be as effective for long-term hemostasis.[3,4] Thermal therapy and injection can be combined to control bleeding and to treat the lesion definitively. Mechanical methods to treat bleeding include hemostatic clips and the use of rubber band ligation. Both of these methods appear to have an efficacy similar to thermal therapy. In the few patients who have recurrent bleeding after initial endoscopic therapy, a second attempt has a significant success rate and can reduce the need for surgery.[5]

MEDICAL THERAPY. The most common causes of peptic ulcer disease are *H. pylori* infection and anti-inflammatory drug (NSAID) use (Chapter 138). NSAIDs should be discontinued and *H. pylori* infection should be treated in all patients with bleeding ulcers.

Data are now compelling that profound acid suppression reduces rebleeding in patients with high-risk endoscopic stigmata for rebleeding. Studies using high doses of both intravenous and oral omeprazole have demonstrated a significant improvement in outcome (rebleeding, hospital stay, transfusion requirement) compared with H_2-receptor antagonists. This effect is likely due to improvement of coagulation and platelet aggregation by increasing intragastric pH. Vigorous acid suppression should be provided to all patients with acute upper gastrointestinal bleeding.[6]

NONULCER ACUTE UPPER GASTROINTESTINAL BLEEDING. Variceal bleeding is the most common cause of nonulcer upper gastrointestinal hemorrhage. The approach to variceal bleeding is a combination of pharmacologic (octreotide, somatostatin), endoscopic (band ligation, sclerotherapy), and mechanical (balloon tamponade) approaches (see Fig. 156–2).

Most non–peptic ulcer, nonvariceal causes of upper gastrointestinal bleeding can be treated using the same endoscopic modalities described earlier with similar success. The most common of these causes is a tear at the gastroesophageal junction, called a Mallory-Weiss (Chapter 136) tear, which accounts for 5 to 14% of upper gastrointestinal bleeding. Mallory-Weiss bleeding usually stops spontaneously, but persistent bleeding should be treated in a manner similar to bleeding from peptic ulcers. Dieulafoy's lesion, which is an aberrant submucosal artery that erodes into the lumen of the stomach, is a rare cause of recurrent vigorous upper gastrointestinal bleeding. Tumors also are rare (<1%) causes of acute upper gastrointestinal bleeding. Vascular lesions may rarely present as acute bleeding, but more commonly they cause chronic, low-grade blood loss. Bleeding from diffuse gastric erosions, which can occur in critically ill patients, does not respond to endoscopic therapy but can usually be prevented by prophylactic treatment.[7]

LOWER GASTROINTESTINAL BLEEDING

Lower gastrointestinal bleeding occurs at a rate of 20 : 100,000 population, which is about one fifth as frequently as upper gastrointestinal bleeding. Hematochezia, which is the most common presenting symptom for lower gastrointestinal hemorrhage, can be variously described as bloody diarrhea, blood and clots per rectum, maroon-colored stool, or blood mixed with the stool. Hematochezia can occur from bleeding anywhere in the gastrointestinal tract, and, noted previously, about 10% of patients who present with hematochezia have an upper gastrointestinal source of bleeding.

Table 133–4 • FINAL DIAGNOSIS IN 219 PATIENTS HOSPITALIZED FOR ACUTE LOWER GASTROINTESTINAL BLEEDING

DIAGNOSIS	n (%)
Colonic diverticulosis	91 (42)
Colorectal malignancy	20 (9)
Ischemic colitis	19 (9)
Acute colitis, unknown cause	11 (5)
Hemorrhoids	10 (5)
Postpolypectomy hemorrhage	9 (4)
Colonic angiodysplasia	6 (3)
Crohn's disease	5 (2)
Other*	22 (10)
Unknown	26 (12)

*Stercoral ulcer, 3; small bowel tumor, 3; infectious colitis, 2; radiation proctitis, 2; small-vessel vasculitis, 2; acute ileitis, unknown cause, 1; benign colonic tumor, 1; colonic diverticulitis, 1; colonic hematoma, 1; Meckel's diverticulum, 1; ulcerative proctitis, 1; indeterminate sources in the rectum, 1; ileum, 1; colonic hepatic flexure, 1; ileocolonic anastomosis, 1.

Adapted from Longstreth GF; Epidemiology and outcome of patients hospitalized with acute lower gastrointestinal hemorrhage: A population-based study. Am J Gastroenterol 1997;92:419–424.

The most common causes of lower gastrointestinal bleeding are colonic diverticula (Chapter 143), vascular ectasias (Chapter 144), and tumors (Chapter 200), all of which increase in prevalence with age (Table 133–4). As a result, lower gastrointestinal bleeding is most commonly a disorder of the elderly, with a dramatically increased incidence with advancing age. The initial approach to the patient should be the same as in upper gastrointestinal bleeding, with careful assessment of vital signs and vigorous volume replacement. A history of prior bleeding, inflammatory bowel disease, radiation therapy, and NSAID use may be helpful but does not identify the bleeding lesion.

Identification and treatment of the bleeding lesion should be attempted after the patient is hemodynamically stable (Fig. 133–4). It may be difficult to diagnose colonic angiodysplasia, which is now thought to be about as common a cause of lower gastrointestinal bleeding as are colonic diverticula. Since many elderly patients have colonic diverticula, bleeding due to undiagnosed angiodysplasia may sometimes be mistakenly attributed to diverticula. Urgent colonoscopy after a vigorous cleansing of the colon can help determine whether the bleeding is from diverticula or angiodysplasia. In many cases, the bleeding lesion may be identified by the presence of a fresh clot or active bleeding. Endoscopic therapy of these lesions, similar to the methods described earlier for upper gastrointestinal bleeding, reduces the rate of rebleeding and the need for surgery. Vascular lesions can be treated with injection, contact thermal methods, or endoscopic laser therapy. There is no role for barium enema in the setting of acute lower gastrointestinal bleeding, because it is unlikely to provide a definitive diagnosis and prevents or delays more accurate diagnostic modalities with potential therapeutic benefits.

When urgent colonoscopy does not identify a bleeding source or if bleeding is too rapid to permit colonoscopy, angiography may identify the bleeding site. The yield of angiography ranges from 40 to 80%, but, to be successful, angiography requires a bleeding rate of at least 1 mL/min. When a bleeding site is identified, the bleeding can be slowed or stopped by local infusion of vasoconstrictors or by selective embolization of the bleeding artery, with success rates exceeding 80%. Both approaches carry a substantial (>10%) risk of causing local ischemia.

In settings in which bleeding is not rapid enough for angiography, nuclear scintigraphy may be helpful in identifying the site but not the cause of the lesion. The bleeding rate required for identification is at least 0.1 mL/min. In optimal conditions, the sensitivity of scintigraphy is 85%, and its specificity is 70%. One advantage of tagged red blood cell scintigraphy is the ability to detect intermittent bleeding by performing serial scans over the lifetime of the radionuclide.

Surgical consultation and comanagement are appropriate in all cases of gastrointestinal bleeding and are most critical in the setting of severe lower gastrointestinal bleeding. Vigorous efforts should be

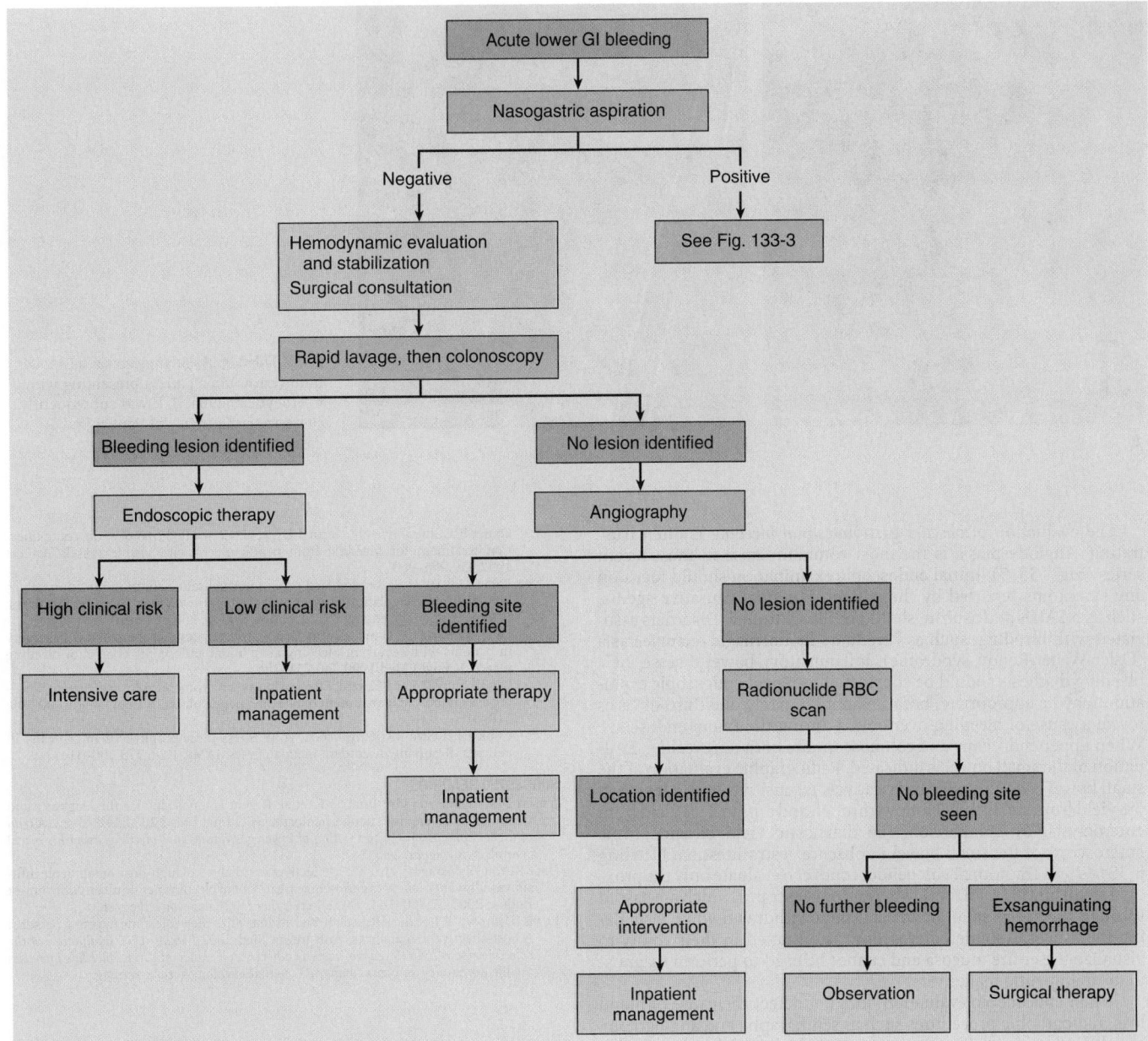

FIGURE 133–4 • Approach to acute lower gastrointestinal bleeding. Nasogastric aspiration is indicated to exclude an upper gastrointestinal source. The optimal diagnostic approach is rapid colonic lavage followed by colonoscopy, which can also be therapeutic. When colonoscopy does not reveal the bleeding lesion and bleeding persists at a brisk volume, angiography may identify and control the bleeding vessel. In the absence of vigorous bleeding, a radionuclide red blood cell scan may identify the site of slower bleeding lesions and guide further evaluation and therapy. Close observation is indicated in patients whose bleeding has stopped spontaneously without a definitive diagnosis. Surgical consultation early in the course is indicated. Surgical therapy, however, should be reserved for patients with an identified lesion, or those with exsanguinating bleeding that cannot be controlled any other way. GI = gastrointestinal; RBC = red blood cell.

made to diagnose the bleeding lesion, and if that is not possible, at least the involved segment of the colon to guide surgical therapy. Surgery directed at a lesion identified endoscopically or radiographically is often curative. Empirical total or right hemicolectomy should be reserved for life-threatening bleeding that could not be localized and has not responded to available therapeutic approaches.

OCCULT AND OBSCURE GASTROINTESTINAL BLEEDING

Occult bleeding is defined as the detection of asymptomatic blood loss from the gastrointestinal tract, generally by routine fecal occult blood testing (FOBT) or the presence of iron deficiency anemia. *Obscure* gastrointestinal bleeding is defined as bleeding of unknown origin that persists or recurs after a negative initial endoscopic evaluation of both the upper and lower gastrointestinal tracts. Both of these entities may be presentations of recurrent or chronic bleeding.

The initial approach to evidence of *occult* gastrointestinal blood loss should be endoscopic evaluation. In the setting of an isolated positive FOBT, colonoscopy is indicated as the first test (Chapter 200). The yield of colonoscopy in these patients is approximately 2% for cancer and 30% for one or more colonic polyps.

The initial approach to a patient with *iron deficiency anemia* depends on the presence of symptoms referable to either the upper or lower gastrointestinal tract. Regardless of the findings on the initial upper or lower endoscopic examination, all patients should have both upper and lower endoscopy because the complementary endoscopic examination has a yield of 6% even if the first one was positive. For premenopausal women, a positive FOBT requires full evaluation, as does iron deficiency anemia. Barium radiographs of the upper and lower gastrointestinal tract have limited utility in the setting of occult bleeding because of their inability to biopsy or treat lesions that are identified.

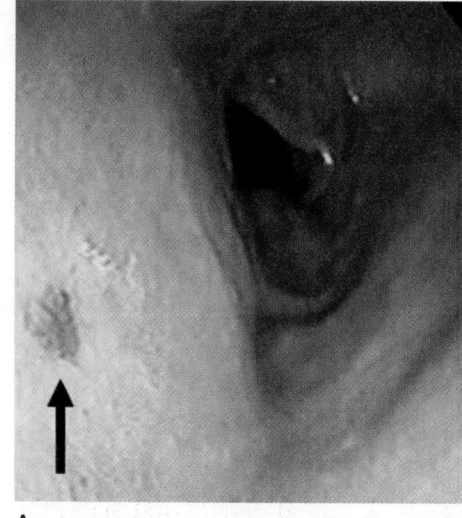
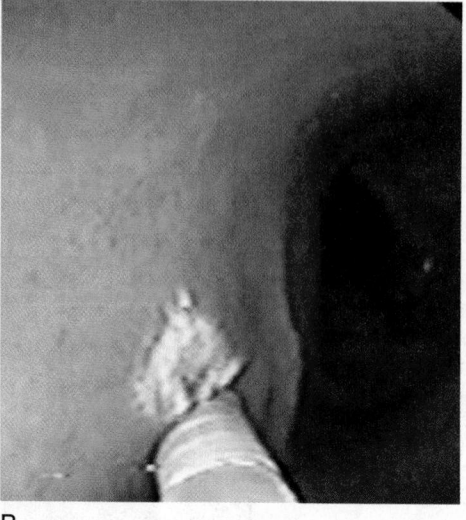

A   B

FIGURE 133–5 • *A*, Telangiectasia in duodenum (arrow) in a patient presenting with microcytic anemia. *B*, It was subsequently cauterized. (Courtesy of Pankaj Jay Pasricha, MD.)

The evaluation of *obscure gastrointestinal bleeding* is often frustrating. Angiodysplasia is the most common cause in most recent series (Fig. 133–5). Initial endoscopic examination should focus on any symptoms reported by the patient. Potential causative agents, such as NSAIDs and aspirin, should be discontinued. Disorders associated with bleeding, such as hereditary hemorrhagic telangiectasia (Osler-Weber-Rendu syndrome), inflammatory bowel disease, or a bleeding diathesis should be considered. A repeat endoscopic evaluation may be appropriate, because approximately one third of cases reveal a cause of bleeding overlooked during the initial endoscopy. When upper endoscopy and colonoscopy are both unrevealing, evaluation of the small bowel is indicated. Radiographic evaluation of the small bowel is noninvasive but relatively insensitive, with a less than 6% yield from small bowel follow-through and a 10 to 21% yield from enteroclysis. By comparison, the diagnostic yield of endoscopic enteroscopy of the small bowel in obscure gastrointestinal bleeding is 38 to 75%. Traditional videoendoscopes can evaluate only the proximal small bowel (≤150 cm), whereas longer scopes, which are passed through the entire small bowel and then withdrawn while visualizing the mucosa (sonde enteroscopy), are limited in their ability to visualize the entire mucosa and cannot be used to perform diagnostic or therapeutic maneuvers.

When endoscopic evaluation does not detect the cause of blood loss, radiographic procedures such as scintigraphy and angiography should be considered. Provocative angiography using heparin or thrombolytic agents has been suggested by some authorities, but this approach has the potential risk of precipitating major bleeding.

In the face of continued blood loss and no identified etiology, intraoperative endoscopy may provide simultaneous diagnosis and therapy. During the procedure, the surgeon plicates the bowel over the endoscope. As the scope is withdrawn, endoscopic findings can be identified for surgical resection or treatment. The yield of this procedure exceeds 70%. In some clinical situations, the site of bleeding cannot be identified, and the patient requires long-term transfusion therapy.

FUTURE DIRECTIONS

A new device for visualizing the entire gastrointestinal mucosa consists of a small camera in an ingestable capsule that transmits images to receivers attached to the patient's abdomen and mapped to identify the location of the image. The diagnostic yield of capsule enteroscopy is not yet clear, but this approach may potentially visualize segments of the small bowel that were previously inaccessible. No therapeutic maneuvers are possible with the device.

1. Lee JG, Turnipseed S, Romano PS, et al: Endoscopy-based triage significantly reduces hospitalization rates and costs of treating upper GI bleeding: A randomized controlled trial. Gastrointest Endosc 1999;50:755–761.
2. Cook DJ, Guyatt GH, Salena BJ, et al: Endoscopic therapy for acute nonvariceal upper gastrointestinal hemorrhage: A meta-analysis. Gastroenterology 1992; 102:139–148.
3. Oxner RB, Simmonds NJ, Gertner DJ, et al: Controlled trial of endoscopic injection treatment for bleeding from peptic ulcers with visible vessels. Lancet 1992;339:966–968.
4. Laine L, Estrada R: Randomized trial of normal saline solution injection versus bipolar electrocoagulation for treatment of patients with high-risk bleeding ulcers: Is local tamponade enough? Gastrointest Endsoc 2002;55:6–10.
5. Lau JYW, Sung JJY, Lam Y-H, et al: Endoscopic retreatment compared with surgery in patients with recurrent bleeding after initial endoscopic control of bleeding ulcers. N Engl J Med 1999;340:751–756.
6. Lau JY, Sung JJ, Lee KK, et al: Effect of intravenous omeprazole on recurrent bleeding after endoscopic treatment of bleeding peptic ulcers. N Engl J Med 2000;343:310–316.
7. Cook DJ, Reeve BK, Guyatt GH, et al: Stress ulcer prophylaxis in critically ill patients: Resolving discordant meta-analyses. JAMA 1996;275:308–314.

SUGGESTED READINGS

Jensen DM, Machicado GA, Jutabha R, et al: Urgent colonoscopy for the diagnosis and treatment of severe diverticular hemorrhage. N Engl J Med 2000;342:78–82. *A trial of urgent colonoscopy in the setting of lower gastrointestinal bleeding using historical controls as a comparison.*

Lee KK, You JH, Wong IC, et al: Cost-effectiveness analysis of high-dose omeprazole infusion as adjuvant therapy to endoscopic treatment of bleeding peptic ulcer. Gastrointest Endosc 2003;57:160–164. *This effective therapy is also worth the cost.*

Lewis JD, Brown A, Localio AR, et al: Initial evaluation of rectal bleeding in young persons: A cost-effectiveness analysis. Ann Intern Med 2002;136:99–110. *Evaluation of the colon of persons 25 to 45 years of age with otherwise asymptomatic rectal bleeding increases the life expectancy at a cost comparable to that of colon cancer screening.*

134 DISORDERS OF GASTROINTESTINAL MOTILITY

Michael Camilleri

Motility disorders result from impaired control of the neuromuscular apparatus of the gastrointestinal tract. Associated symptoms include recurrent or chronic nausea, vomiting, bloating, abdominal discomfort, and constipation or diarrhea in the absence of intestinal obstruction.

PHYSIOLOGY OF GASTROINTESTINAL MOTOR FUNCTION

NEUROENTERIC CONTROL. Motor function of the gastrointestinal tract depends on the contraction of smooth muscle cells and their integration and modulation by enteric and extrinsic nerves. *Neurogenic modulators* of gastrointestinal motility include the central nervous system, autonomic nerves, and enteric nervous system.

Extrinsic neural control of gastrointestinal motor function consists of the cranial and sacral parasympathetic outflow (excitatory to nonsphincteric muscle) and the thoracolumbar sympathetic supply (excitatory to sphincters, inhibitory to nonsphincteric muscle). The cranial outflow is predominantly through the vagus nerve, which innervates the gastrointestinal tract from the stomach to the right colon. Sympathetic fibers to the stomach and small bowel arise from T5 to

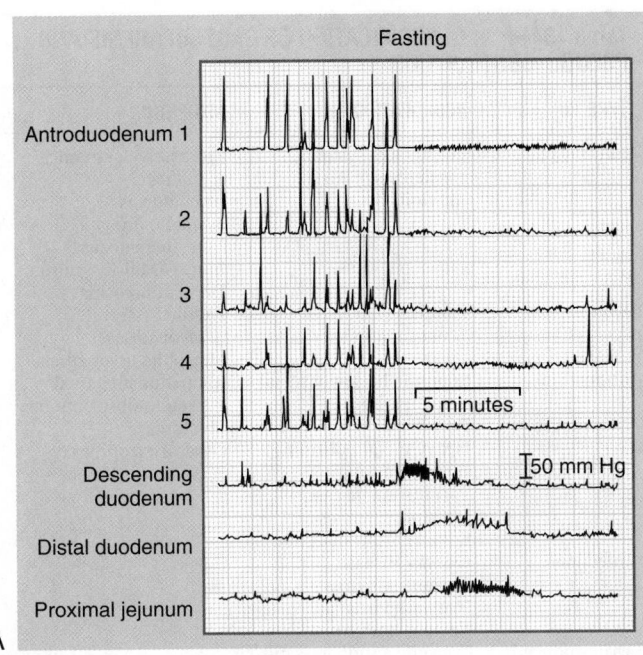
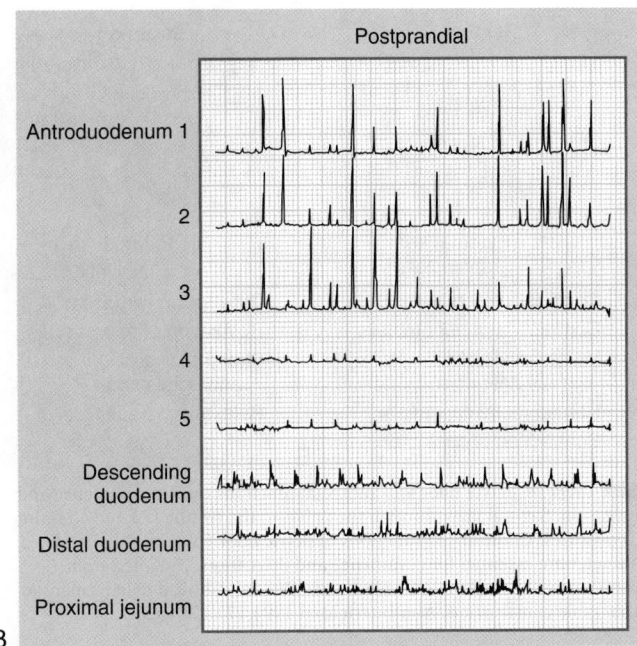

FIGURE 134–1 • Fasting and postprandial gastroduodenal manometric recording in a healthy volunteer. A 535-kcal meal is ingested during the study. Note the cyclic interdigestive migrating motor complex (left panel) and the sustained, high-amplitude but irregular pressure activity after a meal (right panel). (From Coulie B, Camilleri M: Intestinal pseudo-obstruction. Annu Rev Med 1999;50:37–55.)

T10 of the intermediolateral column of the spinal cord. The prevertebral ganglia play an important role in the integration of afferent impulses between the gut and the central nervous system and in the reflex control of abdominal viscera.

The enteric nervous system is an independent nervous system consisting of approximately 100 million neurons organized into ganglionated plexuses. The larger myenteric, or Auerbach's, plexus is situated between the longitudinal and circular muscle layers of the muscularis externa; this plexus contains neurons responsible for gastrointestinal motility. The submucosal, or Meissner's, plexus controls absorption, secretion, and mucosal blood flow. The enteric nervous system also plays an important role in visceral afferent function.

Myogenic factors regulate the electrical activity generated by gastrointestinal smooth muscle cells. *Interstitial cells of Cajal* form a nonneural pacemaker system located at the interface of the circular and longitudinal muscle layers of the intestine and function as intermediaries between the neurogenic enteric nervous system and myogenic control system. Electrical control activity spreads through the contiguous segments of the gut through neurochemical activation by excitatory (e.g., acetylcholine, substance P) and inhibitory (e.g., nitric oxide, somatostatin) transmitters.

GASTRIC AND SMALL BOWEL MOTILITY. The motor functions of the stomach and small intestine are characterized by distinct manometric patterns of activity in the fasting and postprandial periods (Fig. 134–1). The *fasting* or *interdigestive period* is characterized by a cyclic motor phenomenon, the interdigestive migrating motor complex. In healthy individuals, one cycle of this complex is completed every 60 to 90 minutes. The complex has three phases: a period of quiescence (phase I), a period of intermittent pressure activity (phase II), and an activity front (phase III) during which the stomach and small intestine contract at highest frequencies (3 per minute in the stomach, 12 per minute in the duodenum, 8 per minute in the ileum). Another characteristic interdigestive motor pattern seen in the distal small intestine is the giant migrating complex, or power contraction, which empties residue from the ileum into the colon in bolus transfers.

With eating, the proximal stomach accommodates food by reduction in its tone, facilitating the ingestion of food without an increase in pressure. This reflex is vagally mediated and involves an intrinsic nitrergic neuron. *Liquids empty* from the stomach in an exponential manner. The half-emptying time for non-nutrient liquids in healthy individuals is usually less than 20 minutes. Solids are retained selectively in the stomach until particles have been triturated to a size of less than 2 mm in diameter. Gastric emptying of solids is characterized

by an initial lag period followed by a linear postlag emptying phase. The small intestine transports solids and liquids at approximately the same rate. As a result of the lag phase for the transport of solids from the stomach, liquids typically arrive in the colon before solids. Chyme moves from ileum to colon intermittently in boluses.

In the *postprandial period,* the interdigestive migrating motor complex is replaced by an irregular pattern of variable amplitude and frequency. This pattern, which enables mixing and absorption, is observed in the regions in contact with food. The maximum frequency of contractions is lower than during phase III of the interdigestive motor complex, and the duration of this period is proportional to the number of calories consumed during the meal (about 1 hour for each 200 kcal ingested). Segments of the small intestine that are not in contact with food continue with interdigestive motor patterns.

Vomiting is characterized by a stereotypic sequence of motor events, including contractions of the stomach, abdominal muscles, and diaphragm. In humans, this sequence is followed immediately by a process similar to the migrating motor complex in the proximal small bowel.

COLONIC MOTILITY. The normal colon displays short-duration (phasic) contractions and a background contractility or tone. Nonpropagated phasic contractions have a role in segmenting the colon into haustra, which compartmentalize the colon and facilitate mixing, retention of residue, and formation of solid stool. High-amplitude propagated contractions, which are characterized by an amplitude greater than 75 mm Hg, propagation over a distance of at least 15 cm, and a propagation velocity of 0.15 to 2.2 cm/sec, contribute to the mass movements in the colon. In health, these contractions occur on average five to six times per day, most often postprandially and between 6 AM and 2 PM.

Colonic transit is a discontinuous process, slow most of the time and rapid at other times. Residue may be retained for prolonged periods in the right colon, and a mass movement may deliver the contents to the sigmoid colon in seconds. Movement of colonic content is stimulated by feeding (gastrocolonic response). In health, the average mouth-to-cecum transit time is about 6 hours, and transit times through the right colon, left colon, and sigmoid colon are about 12 hours each. As dietary fiber is increased, mean colonic transit time decreases, stool frequency increases, and stool consistency becomes softer. Decreased caloric intake slows colonic transit. Outlet obstruction in patients with pelvic floor dysfunction or voluntary suppression of defecation often is associated with slow colonic transit and decreased motor response to feeding.

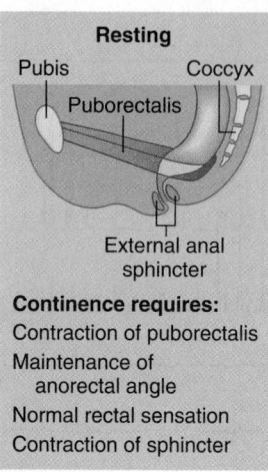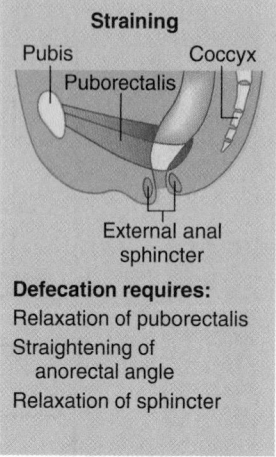

FIGURE 134–2 • Pelvic floor and anorectal functions during continence and defecation. Sagittal view through the pelvis in the resting (*A*) and straining (*B*) postures. Coordinated functions of pelvic floor (puborectalis) and anal sphincter are essential for continence and defecation. (Adapted from Camilleri M, Thompson WG, Fleshman JW, et al: Clinical management of intractable constipation. Ann Intern Med 1994;121:520–528.)

Fluid reabsorption influences gastrointestinal transit. Approximately 9 L of fluid enter the gut from oral intake and endogenous secretions. The small intestine delivers about 1.5 L of fluid to the colon, where most is reabsorbed, leaving a maximum of 200 mL of water excreted in normal stool. Up to 3 L of fluid can be reabsorbed by the colon in a 24-hour period, unless the rate of ileocolonic flow or colonic motility overwhelms the colon's capacity and/or reabsorptive ability.

DEFECATION AND CONTINENCE. Normal defecation requires a series of coordinated actions of the colon, rectum, pelvic floor, and anal sphincter muscles (Fig. 134–2). Filling of the rectum by a volume of 10 mL may be sensed, although the rectum can accommodate 300 mL before a sense of fullness and urge to defecate develop. Distention of the rectum results in the relaxation of the internal anal sphincter (rectoanal inhibitory reflex) and simultaneous contraction of the external anal sphincter to maintain continence. The anal transition zone can sense the difference between solid or liquid stool compared with gas.

DISEASES OF SLOW TRANSIT THROUGH THE STOMACH AND SMALL BOWEL

Gastrointestinal motility disturbances (Table 134–1) result from disorders of the extrinsic nervous system, enteric nervous system, interstitial cells of Cajal (or intestinal pacemakers), or smooth muscle. Combined disorders occur in systemic sclerosis, amyloidosis, and mitochondrial cytopathy, which initially can present with neuropathic patterns and later display myopathic characteristics with disease progression.

Genetic defects include abnormalities of *cRet*, the gene that encodes for the tyrosine kinase receptor; the endothelin B system, which tends to retard development of neural elements, facilitating colonization of the entire gut from the neural crest; Sox_{10}, a transcription factor that enhances maturation of neural precursors; and *ckit*, a marker for the interstitial cells of Cajal. *cRet*, endothelin B, and Sox_{10} defects are associated with the phenotypic picture recognized as Hirschsprung's disease, whereas *ckit* defects have been associated with idiopathic hypertrophic pyloric stenosis and congenital megacolon.

EXTRINSIC NEUROPATHIC DISORDERS

Extrinsic neuropathic processes include vagotomy, trauma, Parkinson's disease (Chapter 443), diabetes (Chapter 242), amyloidosis (Chapter 290), and a paraneoplastic syndrome usually associated with small cell carcinoma of the lung. Another common "neuropathic" problem in clinical practice results from the effect of medications, such as α_2-adrenergic agonists and anticholinergics, on neural control.

Table 134–1 • CLASSIFICATION OF GASTROPARESIS AND PSEUDO-OBSTRUCTION

TYPE	NEUROPATHIC	MYOPATHIC
Infiltrative	Progressive systemic sclerosis Amyloidosis	Progressive systemic sclerosis Amyloidosis Systemic lupus erythematosus Ehlers-Danlos syndrome Dermatomyositis
Familial	Familial visceral neuropathies	Familial visceral myopathies Metabolic myopathies
Idiopathic	Sporadic hollow visceral myopathy	Idiopathic intestinal pseudo-obstruction
Neurologic	Porphyria Heavy metal poisoning Brainstem tumor Parkinson's disease Multiple sclerosis Spinal cord transection	Myotonia Other dystrophies
Infectious	Chagas' disease Cytomegalovirus Norwalk virus Epstein-Barr virus	
Drug-induced	Tricyclic antidepressants Narcotic agents Anticholinergic agents Antihypertensives Dopaminergic agents Vincristine Laxatives	
Paraneoplastic	Small cell lung cancer Carcinoid syndrome	
Postsurgical	Postvagotomy with or without pyloroplasty/gastric resection	
Endocrine	Diabetes mellitus Hypothyroidism/hyperthyroidism Hypoparathyroidism	

Damage to the autonomic nerves by trauma, infection, neuropathy, and neurodegeneration may lead to motor, secretory, and sensory disturbances, most frequently resulting in constipation. Patients with spinal cord injury above the level of the sacral segments have delayed proximal and distal colonic transit attributable to parasympathetic denervation. In these patients, fasting colonic motility and tone are normal, but the response to feeding generally is reduced or absent. Spinal cord lesions involving the sacral segments and/or damage to the efferent nerves from these segments disrupt the neural integration of rectosigmoid expulsion and anal sphincter control. In patients with these injuries, there is loss of contractile activity in the left colon and decreased rectal tone and sensitivity, which may lead to dilation and fecal impaction. *Parkinson's disease and multiple sclerosis* frequently are associated with constipation. *Diabetes mellitus* is associated with gastroparesis (see later), pylorospasm, intestinal pseudo-obstruction, diarrhea, constipation, and fecal incontinence. All of these manifestations may be caused by autonomic dysfunction, although more recent evidence points to the importance of acute changes in glycemia and, more importantly, to changes in the structure and function of the enteric nervous system. The prevalence of constipation is 22% among diabetic patients with neuropathy but only 9.2% in diabetic patients without neuropathy, a rate that is not significantly different from healthy controls.

ENTERIC AND INTRINSIC NEUROPATHIC DISORDERS

Disorders of the enteric nervous system are usually the result of a degenerative, immune, or inflammatory process. Viral-induced gastroparesis (e.g., rotavirus, Norwalk virus, cytomegalovirus, or Epstein-Barr virus) is associated with infiltration of the myenteric plexus with inflammatory cells. In idiopathic chronic intestinal pseudo-obstruction, there is no disturbance of the extrinsic neural control and no identified cause for the enteric nervous system abnormality. Full-thickness biopsy specimens of the intestine may be required to evaluate the myenteric plexus and interstitial cells of Cajal.

SMOOTH MUSCLE DISORDERS

Disturbances of smooth muscle may result in significant disorders of gastric emptying and of transit through the small bowel and colon. These disturbances include, in descending order of prevalence, systemic sclerosis, amyloidosis, dermatomyositis, dystrophia myotonica, and metabolic muscle disorders. Motility disturbances may be the result of metabolic disorders, such as hypothyroidism and hyperparathyroidism, but these patients more commonly present with constipation. Scleroderma may result in focal or general dilation, diverticula, and delayed transit. The amplitude of contractions is reduced, and bacterial overgrowth may result in steatorrhea or pneumatosis intestinalis. Mitochondrial neurogastrointestinal encephalomyopathy, or familial visceral myopathy type II, is an autosomal recessive condition that may present with hepatic failure in neonates, seizures or diarrhea in infants, and hepatic failure or chronic intestinal pseudo-obstruction in adults.

GASTROPARESIS AND PSEUDO-OBSTRUCTION

The clinical features of gastroparesis and chronic intestinal pseudo-obstruction are similar and include nausea, vomiting, early satiety, abdominal discomfort, distention, bloating, and anorexia. In severe cases, there may be considerable weight loss, with depletion of mineral and vitamin stores. Diarrhea and constipation indicate that the motility disorder extends beyond the stomach. Vomiting may be complicated by aspiration pneumonia or Mallory-Weiss esophageal tears, and patients with a generalized motility disorder may have abnormal swallowing or delayed colonic transit.

A careful family and medication history is essential. Review of systems may reveal an underlying collagen vascular disease (e.g., scleroderma) or disturbances of extrinsic neural control, including orthostatic dizziness, difficulties with erection or ejaculation, recurrent urinary tract infections, dry mouth, dry eyes, dry vagina, difficulties with visual accommodation in bright lights, and absence of sweating.

On physical examination, a succussion splash indicates stasis, typically in the stomach. The hands and mouth may show signs of Raynaud's phenomenon or scleroderma. Testing of pupillary responses (to light and accommodation), external ocular movements, blood pressure in the lying and standing positions, and general features of a peripheral neuropathy can identify patients with an associated neurologic disturbance (e.g., diabetic neuropathy) or with the oculogastrointestinal dystrophy that typically is found with mitochondrial cytopathies (see under smooth muscle disorders). The differential diagnosis includes mechanical obstruction, functional gastrointestinal disorders, anorexia nervosa, and the rumination syndrome, which typically presents as early (0 to 30 minutes) postprandial, effortless regurgitation of undigested food after virtually every meal.

Diagnosis

A motility disorder of the stomach or small bowel should be suspected whenever large volumes are aspirated from the stomach, particularly after an overnight fast, or when undigested solid food or large volumes of liquids are observed during an esophagogastroduodenoscopy. The clinician should assess the acuity of the symptoms and the patient's state of hydration and nutrition. The goals of the evaluation are to determine what regions of the digestive tract are malfunctioning and whether the symptoms are due to a neuropathy or a myopathy (Fig. 134–3). Key steps include the following:

1. *Suspect and exclude mechanical obstruction.* In symptomatic patients with pseudo-obstruction, plain radiographs of the abdomen typically show dilated loops of small bowel with associated air-fluid levels. Mechanical obstruction should be excluded by upper gastrointestinal endoscopy and barium studies, including a small bowel follow-through. Barium

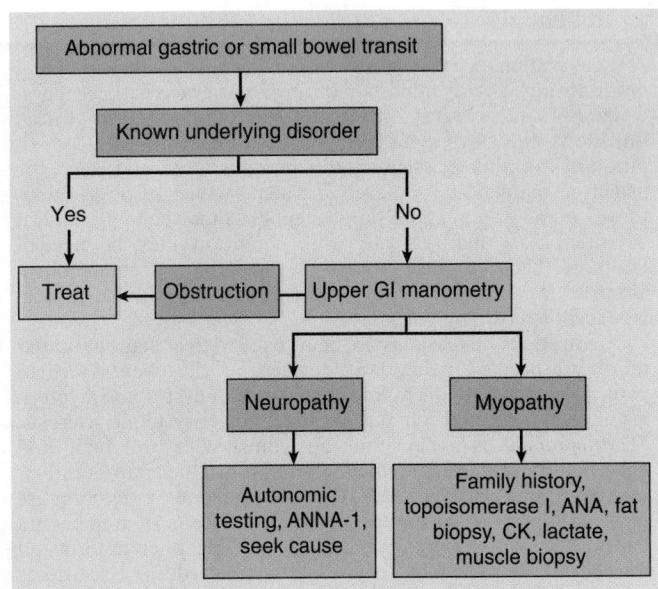

FIGURE 134–3 • Flow diagram outlines steps involved in diagnosing idiopathic gastroparesis and intestinal pseudo-obstruction. ANA = antinuclear antibody; ANNA-1 = antineuronal nuclear antibodies; CK = creatine kinase; GI = gastrointestinal.

studies may suggest the presence of a motor disorder, particularly if there is gross dilation, dilution of barium, or retained solid food within the stomach. These studies rarely identify the cause, however, except for systemic sclerosis, which is characterized by megaduodenum and packed valvulae conniventes in the small intestine.

2. *Assess gastric and small bowel motility.* After mechanical obstruction and alternative diagnoses such as Crohn's disease (Chapter 142) have been excluded, a transit profile of the stomach and/or small bowel should be performed. In a gastric emptying study, ingestion of a radiolabeled meal is followed by scanning at 0, 1, 2, 3, 4, and 6 hours. If the cause of the motility disturbance is obvious, such as gastroparesis in a patient with long-standing diabetes mellitus, it is usually unnecessary to pursue further diagnostic testing. If the cause is unclear, gastroduodenal manometry using a multilumen tube with sensors in the distal stomach and proximal small intestine can differentiate a neuropathic process (normal amplitude contractions, but abnormal patterns of contractility) from a myopathic process (low-amplitude contractions in the affected segments).

3. *Identify the pathogenesis* (Table 134–1). In patients with *neuropathic* causes of uncertain origin, tests should assess autonomic dysfunction (Chapter 460), measure type 1 antineuronal nuclear autoantibodies (ANNA-1) associated with paraneoplastic syndromes, and consider the possibility of a brainstem lesion. In patients with a *myopathic* disorder of unclear cause, the evaluation should consider amyloidosis (immunoglobulin electrophoresis, fat aspirate, or rectal biopsy; Chapter 290), systemic sclerosis (topoisomerase I; Chapter 281), and thyroid disease (Chapter 239). In appropriate settings, porphyria (Chapter 223) and Chagas' disease (Chapter 394) may need to be excluded. In refractory cases, referral to a specialized center may result in genetic testing and/or full-thickness biopsy of the small intestine to identify metabolic muscle disorders and mitochondrial myopathies.

4. *Identify complications of the motility disorder, including bacterial overgrowth, dehydration, and malnutrition.* In patients presenting with diarrhea, it is important to assess nutritional status and to exclude bacterial overgrowth by culture of small bowel aspirates (Chapter 143). Bacterial overgrowth is relatively uncommon in neuropathic disorders but is found more often in myopathic conditions, such as scleroderma, that are associated more often with dilation or low-amplitude contractions. An empirical trial of antibiotics (see later) often is used instead of formal testing.

Gastrointestinal Diseases

 Treatment

Rehydration, electrolyte repletion, and nutritional supplementation are particularly important during acute exacerbations of gastroparesis and chronic intestinal pseudo-obstruction. Initial nutritional measures include low-fiber supplements with the addition of iron, folate, calcium, and vitamins D, K, and B$_{12}$ at the usually recommended daily levels. In patients with more severe symptoms, enteral or parenteral supplementation may be required. If it is anticipated that enteral supplementation may be needed for more than 3 months, a jejunostomy tube is recommended. Gastrostomy tubes should be avoided in patients with gastroparesis except for venting purposes.

Medications increasingly are being used to treat neuromuscular motility disorders, but there is little evidence of effectiveness in myopathic disturbances except for the rare case of dystrophia myotonica affecting the stomach and for small bowel systemic sclerosis. *Metoclopramide* is a dopamine antagonist with prokinetic and antiemetic properties. Antiemetic effects are due in part to its anti–5-hydroxytryptamine type 3 (HT$_3$) antagonist actions. Long-term use of metoclopramide is limited by the side effects of tremor and Parkinson-like symptoms. It is available in tablet or elixir form and typically is taken 30 minutes before meals and at bedtime. Usual doses are 5 to 20 mg four times daily, but patients may experience side effects (changes in affect, anxiety) at relatively low doses (30 to 40 mg/day).

Erythromycin, a macrolide antibiotic that stimulates motilin receptors at higher doses (250 to 500 mg) and cholinergic mechanisms at lower doses (40 to 80 mg), results in the dumping of solids from the stomach, accelerates gastric emptying in gastroparesis, increases the amplitude of antral contractions, and improves antroduodenal coordination. Erythromycin is most effective when it is used intravenously (3 mg/kg every 8 hours) during acute exacerbations of gastroparesis.■ For oral erythromycin, tolerance and gastrointestinal side effects often prevent use for longer than 1 month, but sometimes liquid erythromycin can be tolerated at 40 to 80 mg three times daily before meals.

Octreotide, a cyclized analogue of somatostatin, induces small intestinal activity that mimics phase III of the interdigestive migrating motor complex. It retards gastric emptying, decreases postprandial gastric motility, and inhibits small bowel transit. Octreotide seems to be useful in the treatment of dumping syndromes associated with accelerated transit. Octreotide may be used at night to induce migrating motor complex activity and avoid bacterial overgrowth. If required during the daytime, octreotide often is combined with oral erythromycin to "normalize" the gastric emptying rate.

Antiemetics, including diphenhydramine, trifluoperazine, and metoclopramide, can treat nausea and vomiting in patients with gastroparesis and intestinal pseudo-obstruction. The more expensive serotonin 5-HT$_3$ antagonists (e.g., ondansetron) have not proved to be of greater benefit than these less expensive alternatives.

Antibiotic therapy is indicated in patients with documented, symptomatic bacterial overgrowth. Although formal clinical trials have not been conducted, it is common practice to use different antibiotics for 7 to 10 days each month, in an attempt to avoid resistance. Common antibiotics include doxycycline, 100 mg twice daily; metronidazole, 500 mg three times daily; ciprofloxacin, 500 mg twice daily; and double-strength trimethoprim-sulfamethoxazole, two tablets twice daily. Use of antibiotics in patients with diarrhea and fat malabsorption secondary to bacterial overgrowth results in significant symptomatic relief.

Surgical decompression is rarely necessary in patients with chronic pseudo-obstruction. Venting enterostomy (jejunostomy) is effective, however, in relieving abdominal distention and bloating and in reducing the frequency with which nasogastric intubations and hospitalizations are required for acute exacerbations relative to the period before vent placement. Access to the small intestine by enterostomy also provides nutrients and should be considered in patients with intermittent symptoms. Surgical treatment should be considered whenever the motility disorder is localized to a resectable portion of the gut: duodenojejunostomy or duodenoplasty for patients with megaduodenum, completion gastrectomy for patients with post–gastric surgical stasis syndrome, and colectomy with ileorectostomy for intractable constipation associated with chronic colonic pseudo-obstruction.

Gastric electrical stimulation, an approved treatment, may improve gastric emptying and symptoms in patients with severe gastroparesis, but data on efficacy are inconclusive. Small bowel transplantation currently is limited to patients with intestinal failure who have reversible liver disease induced by total parenteral nutrition or have life-threatening or recurrent catheter-related sepsis.

DISEASES OF RAPID TRANSIT THROUGH STOMACH AND SMALL BOWEL

DUMPING SYNDROME AND ACCELERATED GASTRIC EMPTYING

Dumping syndrome and accelerated gastric emptying typically follow truncal vagotomy and gastric drainage procedures (Chapter 139). With the widespread use of highly selective vagotomy and the advent of effective anti–acid secretory therapy, these problems are becoming rare. A high caloric (usually carbohydrate) content of the liquid phase of the meal evokes a rapid insulin response with secondary hypoglycemia. These patients also may have impaired antral contractility and gastric stasis of solids, which paradoxically may result in a clinical picture of gastroparesis (for solids) and dumping (for liquids).

The management of dumping syndrome and accelerated gastric emptying emphasizes dietary maneuvers, such as avoidance of high-nutrient liquid drinks and possibly addition of guar gum or pectin to retard gastric emptying of liquids. Rarely, pharmacologic treatment with octreotide, 25 to 100 μg subcutaneously before meals, is needed to retard intestinal transit and inhibit the hormonal responses that lead to hypoglycemia.

RAPID TRANSIT DYSMOTILITY OF THE SMALL BOWEL

Rapid transit of material through the small bowel may occur in the setting of the irritable bowel syndrome (Chapter 135), post-vagotomy diarrhea (Chapter 139), short bowel syndrome (Chapter 141), diabetic diarrhea (Chapter 242), and carcinoid diarrhea (Chapter 245). With the exception of irritable bowel syndrome, these conditions may cause severe diarrhea and result in significant losses of fluid and electrolytes. Idiopathic bile acid catharsis may represent an inability of the distal ileum to reabsorb bile acids because of rapid transit and reduced contact time with the ileal mucosa; this condition may induce colonic secretion and secondary diarrhea. Accelerated transit may be confirmed by scintigraphic studies.

Treatment goals are to restore hydration and nutrition and to slow small bowel transit. Dietary interventions include avoiding hyperosmolar drinks and replacing them with iso-osmolar or hypo-osmolar oral rehydration solutions. The fat content in the diet should be reduced to approximately 50 g/day to avoid delivery of unabsorbed fat to the colon. All electrolyte and nutritional deficiencies of calcium, magnesium, potassium, and water-soluble and fat-soluble vitamins should be corrected. In patients with less than 1 m of residual small bowel, it may be impossible to maintain fluid and electrolyte homeostasis without parenteral support. In patients with a longer residual segment, oral nutrition, pharmacotherapy, and supplements are almost always effective.

The opioid agent loperamide (4 mg 30 minutes before meals and at bedtime for a total dose of 16 mg/day) suppresses the motor response to feeding and improves symptoms but may be ineffective or cause side effects (e.g., hypotension). Verapamil (40 mg twice daily) and/or clonidine (0.1 mg twice daily) may be used in addition to loperamide. Octreotide (50 μg subcutaneously three times daily before meals) may be used in patients for whom the oral agents are ineffective or poorly tolerated. 5-HT$_3$ antagonists (e.g., alosetron) may be efficacious in the treatment of carcinoid diarrhea and diarrhea-predominant irritable bowel syndrome.

COLONIC MOTILITY DISORDERS

CONSTIPATION

Epidemiology and Pathophysiology

Constipation is a common clinical problem, reported by about 20% of the population, and 40% of Americans report needing to strain excessively to pass their bowel movements. It is essential to distin-

Table 134–2 • CLINICAL CLUES SUGGESTIVE OF AN EVACUATION DISORDER

HISTORY
Prolonged straining to expel stool
Taking up unusual postures on the toilet to facilitate stool expulsion
Support of perineum or digitation of rectum or vagina to facilitate rectal emptying
Inability to expel enema fluid
Constipation after subtotal colectomy for constipation

RECTAL EXAMINATION (WITH PATIENT IN LEFT LATERAL POSITION)
Inspection
Anus "pulled" forward during attempts to simulate strain during defecation
Anal verge descends <1 cm or >4 cm during attempts to simulate strain during defecation
Perineum balloons down during straining, and rectal mucosa prolapses through anus

Palpation
High anal sphincter tone at rest precludes easy entry of examining finger (in absence of painful perianal condition, e.g., anal fissure)
Anal sphincter pressure during voluntary squeeze is minimally higher than tone at rest
Perineum descends <1 cm or >4 cm during attempts to simulate strain during defecation
Puborectalis muscle palpable through posterior rectal wall is tender
Palpable mucosal prolapse during straining
"Defect" in anterior wall of the rectum, suggestive of rectocele

ANORECTAL MANOMETRY AND BALLOON EXPULSION (WITH PATIENT IN LEFT LATERAL POSITION)
Average anal sphincter resting tone >80, *or* squeeze pressure >240 cm H₂O
Failure of balloon expulsion despite addition of 200 g weight

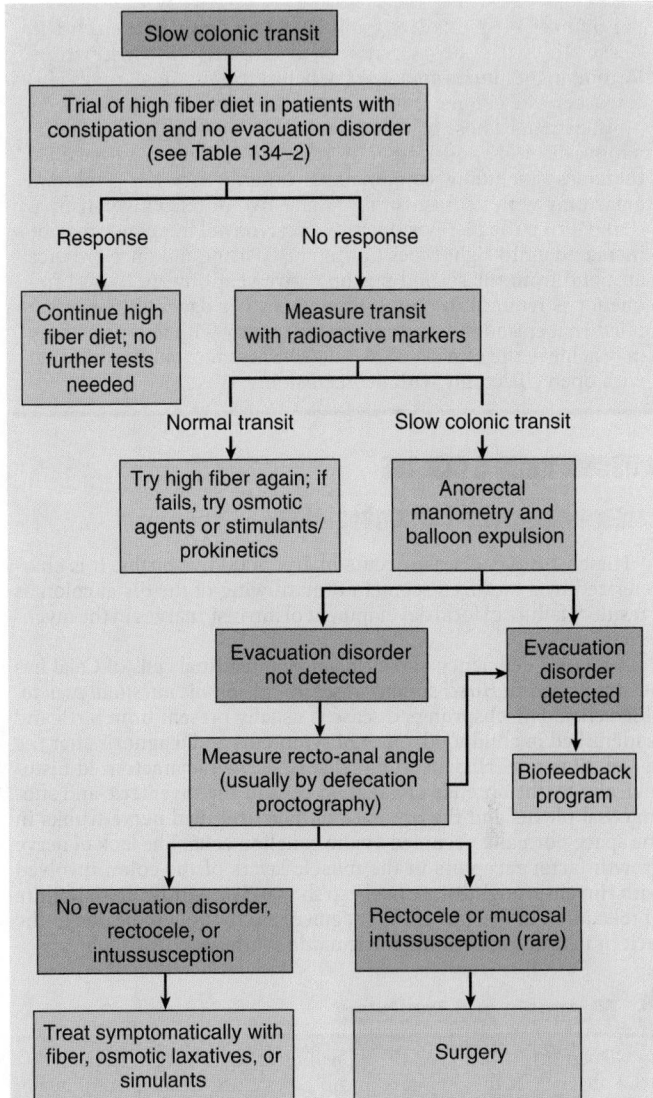

FIGURE 134–4 • Flow diagram outlines steps involved in managing constipation.

guish an evacuation disorder, also called *functional outlet obstruction* (Table 134–2), from constipation resulting from slow transit or other causes. In one study in a tertiary center, 50% of 70 patients with severe, unresponsive constipation had impaired evacuation, and the remainder had constipation associated with either normal transit (also called *functional constipation*) or delayed colonic transit (also called *slow transit constipation*).

In *functional constipation,* transit is normal, and there is no evacuation disorder. These patients may have pain in association with constipation, and there may be overlap with constipation-predominant irritable bowel syndrome (Chapter 135). In patients with *acquired slow transit constipation,* unassociated with colonic dilation, the number of interstitial cells of Cajal in the different layers of the sigmoid colon is reduced compared with controls.

Idiopathic megarectum and megacolon can be either congenital or acquired; an enteric nervous system defect is suspected. In megacolon, the dilated segment shows normal phasic contractility but decreased colonic tone, with smooth muscle hypertrophy and fibrosis of the muscularis mucosa, circular muscle, and longitudinal muscle layers.

Acquired defects in the enteric nervous system may result in constipation in *Chagas' disease* (Chapter 394), which is caused by infection with *Trypanosoma cruzi* and results in the destruction of myenteric neurons. Acquired aganglionosis also has been reported with *circulating antineuronal antibodies,* with or without associated neoplasm.

℞ Diagnosis and Treatment

Characterization of constipated patients (Fig. 134–4) relies on the measurement of transit with radiopaque markers. It is important to identify evacuation disorders because a biofeedback treatment program with muscle relaxation of the anal sphincters and pelvic floor results in a 70% or greater cure rate for the constipation. The response to this treatment program is influenced by comorbidity, such as the coexistence of eating disorders or a psychological or psychiatric diagnosis. Surgical strategies used in the past for evacuation disorders have been shown to be either unnecessary or damaging to patients, resulting in incontinence. An evacuation disorder frequently is associated, however, with delayed overall colonic transit, not simply delayed transit in the distal colon.

The average daily fiber intake is around 12 g/day. In patients with slow transit constipation, drug-induced constipation, or evacuation disorders, supplementation of 30 g of fiber per day does not result in any improvement in constipation. In patients with normal transit constipation, however, 12 to 30 g/day is effective in relief of constipation. By definition, 50% of people have fiber intake less than 12 g/day; the first line of therapy in all patients presenting with constipation is to increase fiber intake to at least 12 g/day. A second step is to add an osmotic laxative, such as a magnesium salt, to enhance the retention of fluid within the lumen by osmotic forces, to increase the fluidity, and to ease aboral transport of colonic content. Polyethylene glycol solutions (such as GoLYTELY, NuLytely, MiraLax, OCL solution) are used frequently as a second-line therapy. If these measures do not suffice, a prokinetic or stimulant agent, such as bisacodyl (5 to 10 mg every 1 to 2 days) may be added. When these approaches do not work, the patient should be reassessed to exclude an evacuation disorder.

Newer medications include the 5-HT₄ agonist, prucalopride, which accelerates colonic transit in healthy participants and in patients with functional constipation.**2** It significantly increased

Continued

the number of spontaneous and complete bowel movements in phase III trials of patients with functional constipation. Recombinant human analogues of neurotrophins (e.g., r-met-Hu) can accelerate colonic transit time and relieve constipation.[3]

In patients whose constipation is not associated with an evacuation disorder and does not respond to aggressive medical therapies (including combinations described earlier), subtotal colectomy with ileorectostomy is effective in relieving constipation. During the first postoperative year, bowel frequency may be increased up to eight times during the daytime and once or twice at night; from the second postoperative year onward, bowel frequency is reduced to one to three times per day with few or no nocturnal episodes. Laparoscopic colectomy with ileorectostomy may achieve the same success rate with less morbidity compared with open colectomy with ileorectostomy.

HIRSCHSPRUNG'S DISEASE

Epidemiology and Pathophysiology

Hirschsprung's disease occurs in 1 in 5000 live births. It is characterized by a localized segment of narrowing of the distal colon as a result of failure of local development of intrinsic nerves in the myenteric plexus.

A relative deficiency of *c-kit*-positive interstitial cells of Cajal has been reported in *Hirschsprung's disease* and *chronic intestinal pseudo-obstruction*. Hirschsprung's disease is usually present from birth and is identified in childhood; onset of symptoms and diagnosis after the age of 10 is rare. Hirschsprung's disease is well characterized histologically by the absence of ganglion cells in the myenteric and submucosal plexus and the presence of hypertrophied nerve trunks in the space normally occupied by the ganglion cells. The lack of nerve growth factor receptors in the muscle layers of the colon involved with Hirschsprung's disease has been shown. The narrowing and failure of relaxation in the aganglionic segment are thought to be due to the lack of neurons containing nitric oxide synthase.

Rx Diagnosis and Treatment

Diagnosis is based on the typical focal narrowing of the colon, the absence of the rectoanal inhibitory reflex (relaxation of anal sphincter pressure at rest during distention of a balloon in the rectum depends on natural preservation and maturation of intrinsic nerves in the distal bowel), and a deep rectal biopsy specimen showing absence of submucosal neurons with hypertrophied nerve trunks. Treatment involves excision of the affected bowel segment or a pull-through procedure by which normal bowel is anastomosed to the cuff of the rectum, just above the anal sphincters.

1. Janssens J, Peeters TL, Vantrappen G, et al: Improvement of gastric emptying in diabetic gastroparesis by erythromycin: Preliminary studies. N Engl J Med 1990;322:1028–1031.
2. Bouras EP, Camilleri M, Burton DD, et al: Prucalopride accelerates gastrointestinal and colonic transit in patients with constipation without a rectal evacuation disorder. Gastroenterology 2001;120:354–360.
3. Coulie B, Szarka LA, Camilleri M, et al: Recombinant human neurotrophic factors accelerate colonic transit and relieve constipation in humans. Gastroenterology 2000;119:41–50.

SUGGESTED READINGS

Bytzer P, Talley NJ, Leemon M, et al: Prevalence of gastrointestinal symptoms associated with diabetes mellitus: A population-based survey of 15,000 adults. Arch Intern Med 2001;161:1989–1996. *Population-based epidemiologic study of gastrointestinal symptoms in patients with diabetes mellitus.*

Camilleri M: Enteric nervous system disorders: Genetic and molecular insights for the neurogastroenterologist. Neurogastroenterol Motil 2001;13:277–295. *Review of genetic and molecular disorders resulting in gastrointestinal syndromes secondary to disturbed function of enteric nerves.*

Camilleri M: Advances in diabetic gastroparesis. Rev Gastroenterol Disord 2002;2:47–56. *Review of the mechanisms and manifestations of upper gastrointestinal syndromes in patients with diabetes mellitus.*

Chaussade S, Minic M: Comparison of efficacy and safety of two doses of two different polyethylene glycol-based laxatives in the treatment of constipation. Aliment Pharmacol Therap 2003;17:165–172. *A well-sructured trial comparing different formulations and doses of osmotic laxatives that are commonly used in clinical practice.*

Maleki D, Locke GR III, Camilleri M, et al: Gastrointestinal tract symptoms among persons with diabetes mellitus in the community. Arch Intern Med 2000;160:2808–2816. *Population-based epidemiologic study of gastrointestinal symptoms in patients with diabetes mellitus.*

Talley NJ, Spiller R: Irritable bowel syndrome: A little-understood organic bowel disease. Lancet 2002;360:555–564. *Overview of a condition affecting up to 10% of the population.*

135 FUNCTIONAL GASTROINTESTINAL DISORDERS: IRRITABLE BOWEL SYNDROME, NONULCER DYSPEPSIA, AND NONCARDIAC CHEST PAIN

Nicholas J. Talley

In clinical practice, most patients who present with chronic or recurrent gastrointestinal symptoms do not have a structural or biochemical explanation identified by routine diagnostic tests. These patients are labeled as having a *functional gastrointestinal disorder*. Functional does not imply a psychiatric disturbance or absence of disease but rather a known or suspected underlying disorder of gut function. Based on clinical and epidemiologic studies, functional gastrointestinal disorders have been classified according to the presumed anatomic site of the disorder (Table 135–1). The most widely recognized functional gastrointestinal disorders are irritable bowel syndrome (IBS), functional (or nonulcer) dyspepsia, and functional (or noncardiac) chest pain.

Table 135–1 • ROME CLASSIFICATION OF FUNCTIONAL GASTROINTESTINAL DISORDERS AND ESTIMATED PREVALENCE IN THE UNITED STATES

DISORDER	APPROXIMATE U.S. PREVALENCE (%)
FUNCTIONAL BOWEL DISORDERS	
Irritable bowel syndrome	15
Abdominal pain or discomfort, relieved with defecation or associated with a change in the frequency or consistency of stools	
Functional abdominal bloating	30
Functional constipation	<5
Functional diarrhea	<5
FUNCTIONAL GASTRODUODENAL DISORDERS	
Functional (nonulcer) dyspepsia	15*
Chronic or recurrent pain or discomfort centered in the upper abdomen (i.e., epigastrium); endoscopy fails to identify a definite structural cause	
Aerophagia	20
FUNCTIONAL ESOPHAGEAL DISORDERS	
Noncardiac chest pain	15
Rumination syndrome	10
Globus	10
FUNCTIONAL ABDOMINAL PAIN	<5
FUNCTIONAL BILIARY PAIN (BILIARY DYSKINESIA)	<1
FUNCTIONAL ANORECTAL DISORDERS	
Functional incontinence	5
Functional anorectal pain	
Levator syndrome	5
Proctalgia fugax	10
Pelvic floor dyssynergia	10

*Assumes one third with dyspepsia have a structural explanation and are excluded.

IRRITABLE BOWEL SYNDROME

Definition

Previously, most patients with unexplained abdominal pain or bowel dysfunction were labeled as having IBS, but IBS now is considered to be characterized by chronic or recurrent abdominal pain and an erratic disturbance of defecation. Bloating is also common.

Epidemiology

Symptoms consistent with IBS are reported by one in six Americans, and similar prevalence rates have been found in Europe, Australia, and Asia. The prevalence is greater in women but is similar in whites and blacks; it is lower in people older than age 60 years. Approximately 30% of persons with IBS become asymptomatic over time.

Only about one third of persons with IBS consult a physician, but the condition still accounts for about 12% of primary care visits. The first presentation is typically between the ages of 30 and 50 years. Persons who seek care for IBS tend to have more severe abdominal pain; a greater frequency and severity of nongastrointestinal symptoms, such as headache, fatigue, or menstrual pain; and greater psychological distress.

Pathogenesis

Accumulating evidence suggests that IBS represents a true disorder of function. The symptoms are neither imagined nor the result of a psychiatric disorder.

ABNORMAL MOTOR FUNCTION. IBS is associated with a generalized disorder of smooth muscle function; the colon, small bowel, upper gastrointestinal tract, gallbladder, and urinary tract may be affected. Basal colonic motility is normal in IBS, but these patients tend to have an abnormally responsive colon to meals, drugs, gut hormones (e.g., cholecystokinin), and stress. The motility of the distal colon after meals (the gastrocolonic response) is augmented in patients with IBS and may explain why postprandial cramps or discomfort is common. Increased fasting colonic contractions and rapid colonic transit in the proximal colon have been linked to diarrhea, whereas a reduction of high-amplitude propagated contractions in the left colon has been linked to constipation (Chapter 134).

Abdominal pain in IBS has been associated with an exaggerated ileal response with high postprandial pressure waves (prolonged propagated contractions). Fasting clusters of jejunal pressure waves (discrete clustered contractions) occur in some patients with IBS, appear to coincide with abdominal pain, and disappear during sleep.

DISTURBED SENSATION. The vagal (and spinal) afferent nerves conduct sensory information from the gut through the dorsal horn neurons to the brain. Abnormal perception of gut sensation (visceral hypersensitivity) is a characteristic finding in IBS. In response to rectal or colonic distention by a balloon, a subset of patients with IBS sense the distention at lower volumes and/or pressures than healthy persons. Many patients complain of unsatisfactory defecation or incomplete rectal emptying, which may be a direct result of excess rectal sensitivity. Repetitive rapid sigmoid distentions induce rectal hypersensitivity in patients with IBS but not in healthy controls. The mechanisms that lead to increased gut visceral sensitivity are unclear, and patients with IBS do not have generalized lower pain thresholds in other parts of their bodies.

CENTRAL NERVOUS SYSTEM. The brain modulates gut sensory and motor function and vice versa. Normal subjects activate the anterior cingulate gyrus (the part of the limbic system that may help reduce sensory input) in response to rectal distention, but patients with IBS may not. These abnormalities may help to explain why patients with IBS have visceral hypersensitivity.

A high proportion of patients with a diagnosis of IBS in tertiary referral centers (40 to 60%) have coexisting psychiatric disease, including depression or panic disorder, or a history of sexual or physical abuse. Patients seen by primary care physicians and persons with IBS who do not seek medical help have a lower prevalence of psychiatric comorbidity. Stressful life events, personality, level of social support, and childhood experiences influence how a patient responds to a chronic illness such as IBS.

INFECTION. Approximately 20% of patients with IBS identify a history of traveler's diarrhea or gastroenteritis (e.g., *Salmonella* or *Campylobacter*) preceding the onset of symptoms. Prospective studies of patients who develop gastroenteritis suggest that one fourth continue to have chronic bowel symptoms, and one in eight develops IBS. *Candida* does not cause IBS.

DIET. True food allergy seems to be rare, but food intolerance may be more important. Lactase deficiency may coexist with IBS, and lactose intolerance may exacerbate symptoms. Excess ingestion of sorbitol or fructose may induce diarrhea and bloating. Short-chain fatty acids may stimulate prolonged propagated contractions in the ileum. Dietary exclusion has resulted in symptomatic improvement in approximately 50% of patients with functional diarrhea (in whom pain is not a prominent feature), but a response is probably less frequent in diarrhea-predominant IBS. No single food group has been implicated, although foods high in amines and salicylates may be most important.

Clinical Manifestations

Chronic or recurrent abdominal pain or discomfort is always a feature of IBS. The pain commonly occurs in the lower abdomen but may occur at any location and tends to be variable in quality, severity, and duration. Classically the pain is cramplike or aching and occurs in episodes. The pain of IBS is relieved by defecation or is associated with a change in stool frequency or consistency. Pain from IBS rarely awakens the patient from sleep. Pain related to exercise, urination, or menstruation is unlikely to be due to IBS. Chronic unremitting pain for more than 6 months unrelated to defecation is never due to IBS but most often represents a chronic pain syndrome (functional abdominal pain).

An irregular disturbance of defecation (predominant constipation or diarrhea or an alternating bowel pattern) is also a key feature of IBS, and its absence excludes the diagnosis. Constipation may refer to a decreased frequency of stools, passage of hard stools or lumps, excessive straining, or an inability to empty the rectum adequately. To a patient, diarrhea may mean loose or watery stools, an increased stool frequency, passage of mucus, urgency, or even fecal incontinence.

Bloating is a common symptom in IBS. There may be visible abdominal distention so that patients can see their abdomen is distended or feel they have to loosen their clothes. Sometimes, women complain that they look pregnant.

Symptoms of gastroesophageal reflux (heartburn or acid regurgitation) are reported by one third of patients with IBS. One third of patients also report dyspepsia (epigastric pain or discomfort). Nausea, usually without vomiting, is a common complaint. Some patients report difficulty swallowing, but the complaint is most often the sensation of a lump in the throat between meals (globus). Urinary frequency, dysuria, nocturia, and urinary urgency may occur, as may dyspareunia and dysmenorrhea. Fatigue, headache, and back pain are common. None of these extraintestinal symptoms is helpful diagnostically, however.

Transient bowel symptoms should not be confused with IBS. Patients who recently have had to rest in bed, had a surgical procedure, or lost weight may become constipated. Similarly, patients who have been under acute stress may develop "nervous diarrhea." Pregnancy, various dietary indiscretions, traveler's diarrhea, food poisoning, and viral or bacterial gastroenteritis all may cause temporary bowel disturbances.

Physical examination is useful to exclude organic disease. Patients with IBS may have abdominal scars because of their higher rates of cholecystectomy, appendectomy, and hysterectomy, in part because of a failure to recognize the condition. Abdominal tenderness is a common, nonspecific finding; localized abdominal tenderness that persists after tensing the abdominal wall muscles (e.g., by asking the patient to do a half sit-up) usually indicates abdominal wall pain (e.g., from nerve entrapment, muscle strain, or myositis), which should not be confused with functional gastrointestinal pain and typically responds to infiltration with a local anesthetic and/or steroid.

Diagnosis

It is important to make a positive clinical diagnosis of IBS by careful history and physical examination. In older patients and in patients with "red flags" (e.g., unexplained weight loss, persistent vomiting, prominent diarrhea, bleeding, anemia, steatorrhea, fever, strong family

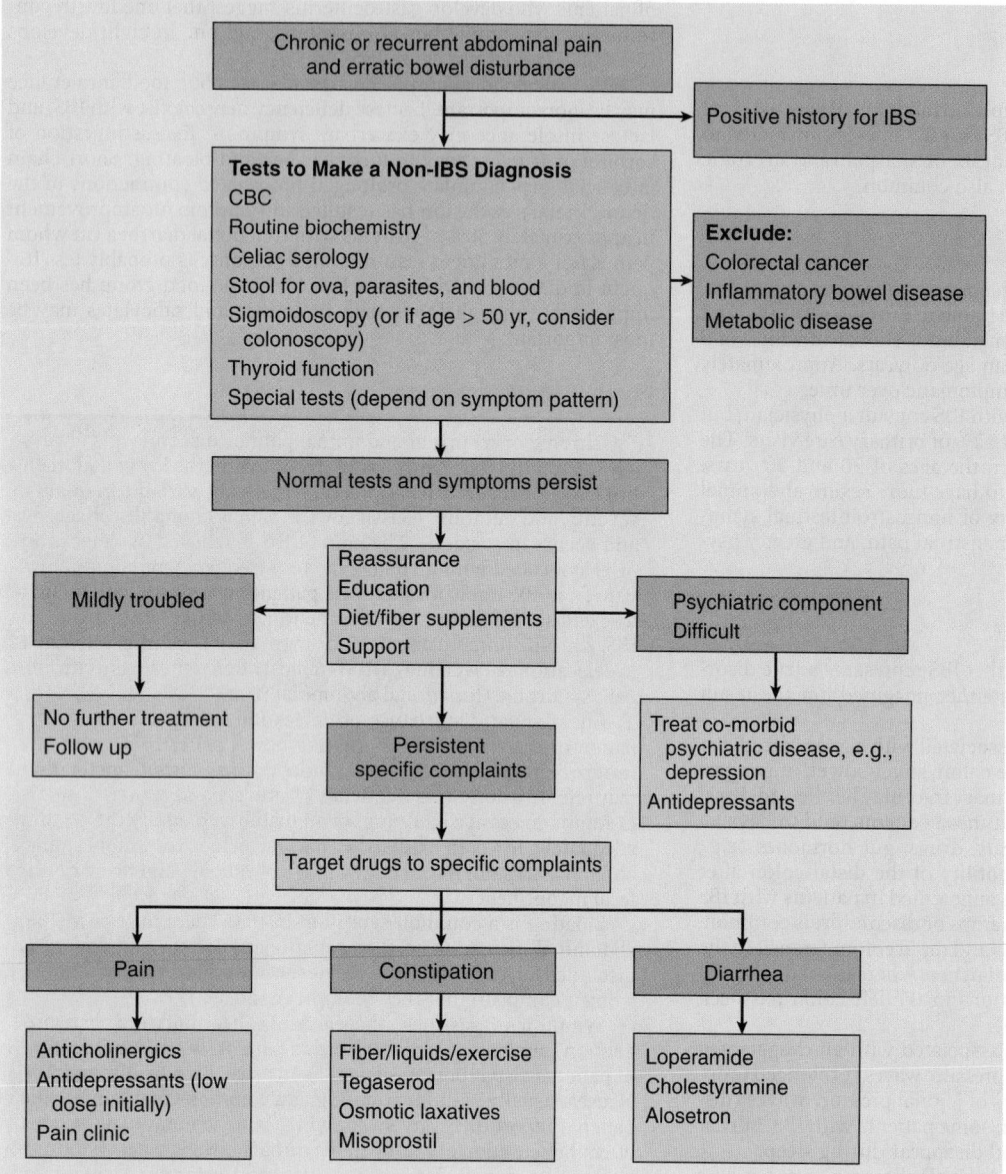

FIGURE 135–1 • Algorithm for the evaluation of suspected irritable bowel syndrome (IBS). CBC = complete blood count.

history of colon cancer), investigations are mandatory to exclude important diseases that may be confused with IBS (Fig. 135–1). Otherwise, investigations have a low yield and may be omitted based on clinical judgment; exhaustive testing before making IBS the diagnosis of exclusion should be discouraged. Flexible sigmoidoscopy is useful to exclude ulcerative colitis but is not required routinely. Rectal biopsy specimens may be obtained in patients with predominant diarrhea to exclude collagenous or microscopic colitis, but the yield is low and unlikely to be cost-effective. In patients older than age 50 with new-onset symptoms, either a colonoscopy or a double-contrast barium enema with flexible sigmoidoscopy is mandatory.

The yield from laboratory tests is low in the presence of typical symptoms and no red flags. Of patients with typical IBS symptoms, up to 5% may have undiagnosed celiac disease (Chapter 141). Screening for celiac disease (e.g., antiendomysial or tissue transglutamase antibodies) should be considered, especially if the patient has predominant diarrhea or bloating. Less commonly, celiac disease can present with constipation-type IBS symptoms. Positive screening tests are an indication for obtaining a small bowel biopsy specimen. Thyroid-stimulating hormone level should be measured if there is clinical suspicion of hyperthyroidism (diarrhea) or hypothyroidism (constipation). Lactose intolerance causes diarrhea and bloating and is common in certain racial groups (e.g., blacks, Asians, Native Americans, and Jews); a substantial amount of lactose usually needs to be ingested to induce symptoms. A resolution of symptoms with a 2-week trial of a lactose-free diet suggests clinically relevant lactase

deficiency; the diagnosis can be confirmed with a lactose hydrogen breath test.

If severe pain is predominant, a plain abdominal radiograph is indicated during an acute episode to exclude bowel obstruction or another pathologic process. Gynecologic examination may detect evidence of endometriosis or fibroids. Endometriosis classically causes mid–menstrual cycle pain that can be associated with disturbed defecation; pelvic ultrasonography is a helpful screening test, but laparoscopy often is required. Pelvic inflammatory disease should be considered if a vaginal discharge is present. When a firm diagnosis of IBS has been made, subsequent testing has an extremely low yield and should not be undertaken unless symptoms have changed.

Differential Diagnosis

CONSTIPATION. *Colonic inertia* (Chapter 134) is characterized by the passage of stools once a week or less, usually affects women, and may be diagnosed by a radiopaque marker study, such as having the patient ingest 24 radiopaque markers on 3 separate days and obtaining a single plain abdominal radiograph on the fourth day. By counting the number of markers retained, total colonic transit can be calculated in hours. A total colonic transit time greater than 72 hours is grossly abnormal and suggests colonic inertia.

Patients with *chronic idiopathic intestinal pseudo-obstruction* typically present with recurrent abdominal pain, visible distention, vomiting, and either constipation (because of colonic and/or small bowel inertia) or diarrhea (because of bacterial overgrowth). This diagnosis must be considered in patients with colonic inertia. A small bowel barium follow-through to look for dilation of the small intestine is the initial investigation of choice. Small bowel and colonic transit can be measured scintigraphically and usually is delayed in intestinal pseudo-obstruction. Small bowel manometry is confirmatory. A definitive diagnosis requires a full-thickness small intestinal biopsy at laparoscopy or laparotomy.

Dyschezia refers to difficult defecation, which the patient may describe as straining, feelings of incomplete evacuation or anal blockage, or having to assist defecation by digitally pressing in or around the anus. The symptoms may be part of IBS. Dyschezia also may be due to mechanical causes, such as rectal prolapse or disease (e.g., aganglionosis of the bowel in Hirschsprung's disease).

Pelvic floor dysfunction refers to the paradoxical contraction or failure of relaxation of the pelvic floor during attempts to defecate. The failure to relax the external anal sphincter and/or puborectalis muscle obstructs defecation and causes constipation. Pelvic floor function can be evaluated by anorectal manometry, ability to expel a balloon, and rectal sensation during balloon distention. Stool softeners and habit retraining are the first steps in management, but biofeedback to teach relaxation of the pelvic floor during straining is also worthwhile.

DIARRHEA. Patients with persistent diarrhea (Chapter 141) should have stools screened for ova, cysts, and parasites, although the yield is low. If stool volume is increased (>400 mL/24 hr), additional tests are indicated. Laxative abuse must be excluded, especially in women with recalcitrant symptoms. Osmotic laxatives can be detected by measuring the stool electrolytes and osmolality and detecting an osmotic gap. A small bowel barium radiograph is useful to rule out Crohn's disease. Bacterial overgrowth, detectable by hydrogen breath testing and confirmed by a small bowel aspirate and quantitative culture, may occur in patients with small bowel diverticula or impaired small bowel motility.

ANAL PAIN. Sudden severe pain in the anal area persisting for seconds or minutes, then completely resolving is usually due to *proctalgia fugax*, which should not be confused with IBS. The attacks are typically infrequent and require no treatment. Local application of heat or pressure to the perianal area may be helpful. Nitrates and quinidine have been used. Proctalgia fugax should be distinguished from the *levator ani syndrome,* which is characterized by chronic or recurrent rectal pain or aching in episodes typically lasting 20 minutes or longer. Treatment is difficult, but sitz baths, digital massage of the levator ani muscle, muscle relaxants, or biofeedback may be helpful. Levator ani syndrome can be distinguished from coccygodynia, in which there is tenderness on pressing over the coccyx.

Rx Treatment

GENERAL MANAGEMENT

A good physician-patient relationship is therapeutic in IBS. Reassurance and explanation remain essential components of management. It is important to provide the patient with a positive diagnosis and explain the likely pathogenesis. Although there is some debate whether IBS is a real disease, most clinicians accept that it is and patients should be so advised. It is important to tell the patient that the symptoms are real. Patients need to be advised that IBS is not life-threatening and does not cause cancer. Although symptoms may be lifelong, they tend to come and go, sometimes with prolonged remissions. Physicians who order an extensive battery of tests without explanation then tell their patients that they do not believe there is a serious underlying disease are likely to engender confusion.

A change in medications may improve symptoms, and unnecessary drugs should be avoided. Constipation may be aggravated by anticholinergics, opiates, psychotropics, aluminum-containing antacids, bile acid–binding resins, calcium channel blockers, or nonsteroidal anti-inflammatory drugs (NSAIDs). Diarrhea may be exacerbated by magnesium-containing antacids, sorbitol-containing cough syrups, antibiotics, and laxatives. Heavy alcohol use and caffeine or decaffeinated products may precipitate symptoms. Persons who drink excess diet drinks or chew gum may ingest enough sorbitol to induce symptoms. Reduction of stress may be helpful.

Fear of serious disease or coexistent psychiatric disease frequently precipitates the decision to seek medical attention and must be identified and addressed. Panic disorder is characterized by abrupt discrete episodes of extreme fear or apprehension associated with other symptoms that may include abdominal pain, nausea, palpitations, chest pain, dyspnea, dizziness, flushing, a choking or smothering sensation, sweating, and fainting. Depression may cause sleep disturbances, mood alterations, and weight loss and may coexist with IBS. If gastrointestinal symptoms are a minor component in patients with a multitude of generalized symptoms, somatization disorder should be considered.

DIETARY RECOMMENDATIONS

Increasing dietary fiber with unprocessed bran makes stools bulkier, softer, and easier to pass and can relieve constipation. Urgency also may improve. The effect is maximal if at least 30 g of fiber is taken daily, approximately double the normal American dietary fiber intake. Fiber content must be increased slowly to reduce the bloating and flatulence that often is induced initially. Some patients with IBS and diarrhea or abdominal pain also improve on increased dietary fiber, whereas others may get worse. Many patients prefer a bulking agent (e.g., psyllium fiber supplement), which should be started at a low once-daily dose of approximately 5 g and increased slowly every 1 to 2 weeks until a total of 15 to 20 g is being ingested in divided doses two to three times per day. A gluten-free diet is of uncertain value in IBS in the absence of celiac disease, although the few patients with latent sprue should respond.

Fad diets and high-fat diets should be avoided. Cabbage, beans, legumes, and lentils may be worth avoiding because they are fermented in the colon and may increase flatus.

Avoidance of milk products may be helpful even in some patients without lactose intolerance. An elimination diet and double-blind reintroduction of foods may be undertaken in patients with suspected food sensitivity and diarrhea, but patient compliance is often poor. Regular exercise and an adequate fluid intake are important in patients with predominant constipation. Follow-up in 3 to 6 weeks allows the physician to determine the response to initial therapy, reassess psychosocial issues, and continue to support the patient.

DRUG THERAPY

The placebo response in IBS is 30 to 60%, in part because of the fluctuating nature of IBS symptoms and the tendency for patients to present when their symptoms are worse, then improve spontaneously. Drugs must be used sparingly in IBS because unequivocal evidence of benefit over placebo is generally lacking.∎

In patients who complain of postprandial abdominal pain, antispasmodics may be useful when administered 30 to 60 minutes before meals to reduce the gastrocolonic response. Alternatives include hyoscyamine (e.g., one to two sustained-release capsules twice daily), belladonna (0.6 mL four times daily), dicyclomine (20 to 40 mg four times daily), and propantheline bromide (7.5 or 15 mg four times daily). Anticholinergic side effects, including dry mouth, blurred vision, and urinary retention, may require dose reduction. Peppermint oil also may be modestly useful for IBS symptoms in some patients.

Patients who do not respond to dietary fiber for treatment of constipation may benefit from lactulose or milk of magnesium, the dose of which can be titrated depending on the clinical response. Misoprostol (200 μg four times a day), the prostaglandin analogue that commonly induces diarrhea, is sometimes empirically useful in severe cases. Stimulant laxatives, such as phenolphthalein, bisacodyl, senna, and docusate, generally should be avoided because of potential harmful effects, such as water and electrolyte loss and, theoretically, long-term damage to the colonic myenteric plexus, although this risk probably has been exaggerated. Polyethylene glycol solutions can be useful in resistant cases. Metoclopramide and domperidone are not efficacious in constipation. Tegaserod (6 mg twice daily) is a new prokinetic agent; it is a well-tolerated 5–hydroxytryptamine type 4 (HT₄) agonist, and in clinical trials it has shown

Continued

a convincing 5 to 15% therapeutic gain in terms of global relief over placebo in women with constipation-predominant IBS.[2] Colchicine (0.6 mg three times daily) sometimes improves constipation and other symptoms of the IBS but may rarely cause a neuromyopathy.

The pharmacologic agent of choice for predominant diarrhea initially is loperamide at a dose of 2 to 4 mg three to four times per day. Loperamide slows intestinal transit and increases intestinal water absorption; it is best taken to prevent diarrhea and not after the event. It causes rebound constipation on cessation in some cases. Loperamide in combination with simethicone may be more efficacious. Abdominal pain is not relieved. Diphenoxylate can cause sedation. A bile acid–sequestering agent such as cholestyramine (4 g two to four times daily) may be helpful, particularly in postcholecystectomy patients with refractory diarrhea caused by idiopathic bile acid malabsorption. Aluminum hydroxide or bismuth subsalicylate used intermittently can be useful, but long-term use should be avoided.

In severe unresponsive cases of diarrhea, alosetron (starting at 1 mg daily), a 5-HT$_3$ antagonist, is available on a limited-access basis. The drug is superior to placebo in women with diarrhea-predominant IBS.[3] Side effects include severe constipation and ischemic colitis, and it is contraindicated in patients with constipation. Patients who have fecal incontinence may respond to loperamide or biofeedback treatment depending on the underlying cause.

Simethicone usually is not helpful for bloating. Activated charcoal can reduce flatus after a lactulose challenge in normal persons, but whether it is of benefit in IBS is not established. Alpha-D-galactosidase may be helpful in some patients after a vegetable meal to reduce flatus. Treatment of constipation may reduce bloating. *Lactobacillus* may reduce pain and flatus but not bloating. Antibiotics should not be prescribed for the symptoms, although a few studies have reported short-term benefits.

Some patients fail to respond to usual pharmacologic therapy. Shotgun testing should be avoided, and the physician should emphasize positive, realistic goals with brief, regular visits to provide key psychosocial support. These patients should be encouraged to join a local IBS support group.

Most patients with functional gastrointestinal complaints do not wish to see a psychiatrist. If referral to a mental health professional is contemplated, patients should be reassured that this is part of a team approach to promote patient motivation. Relaxation therapy, hypnosis, cognitive behavioral therapy, and psychotherapy seem to be of value particularly in patients with moderate symptoms who are motivated and who can identify a link between emotional difficulties or stressful events and their symptoms. Diarrhea and abdominal pain generally respond better than abdominal distention or constipation. Conversely, patients with chronic, constant pain for many years and patients who are resistant to the idea that psychological factors are related to their illness are unlikely to respond.

Tricyclic antidepressants are particularly useful in resistant patients or patients with chronic pain because of their anticholinergic effects and/or central modulation of sensation. Benefits may occur within 3 to 4 weeks even in patients without symptoms of depression. Tricyclic antidepressants should be started at a low dose in the evening (e.g., amitriptyline or desipramine, 10 or 25 mg). If this dose fails, the dose can be titrated slowly upward, although the drugs may worsen constipation. Amitriptyline causes a high incidence of anticholinergic side effects, whereas desipramine causes fewer anticholinergic problems. Other side effects include nausea, weight gain, drowsiness, tremor, postural hypotension, arrhythmias, and rarely cholestasis. Although there is less experience with selective serotonin re-uptake inhibitors (e.g., fluoxetine, paroxetine, sertraline) in IBS, these drugs may be useful when begun once daily in the morning (e.g., fluoxetine or citalopram, 20 mg); side effects are less than with tricyclic antidepressants but include nausea, diarrhea, and weight loss. If antidepressant therapy is successful, it usually should be continued for 3 to 12 months, then the dose should be tapered.

Anxiolytics may induce a rebound effect on withdrawal, are potentially habituating, and interact with other drugs and alcohol; they should be avoided in most patients. Leuprolide acetate, a gonadotropin-releasing hormone analogue, initially seemed to improve some symptoms in women with severe functional gastrointestinal complaints, but in clinical practice the drug is rarely used because of its side effects.

Prognosis

When a positive diagnosis of IBS has been made, it rarely is altered later. Most patients continue to be intermittently symptomatic. The life expectancy of patients with IBS is no different than that of the background population.

FUNCTIONAL (NONULCER) DYSPEPSIA

Definition

Dyspepsia refers to persistent or recurrent epigastric pain or subjective upper abdominal discomfort that may be characterized by early satiety, postprandial fullness, bloating, or nausea. Heartburn is distinct from dyspepsia. Dyspepsia is not restricted to meal-related symptoms because patients with peptic ulcer disease often report pain unrelated to meals. With the widespread availability and use of endoscopy, it has become evident that a structural explanation is found in a few patients with new-onset dyspepsia, and most patients have functional (or nonulcer) dyspepsia (see Table 135–1).

Epidemiology

Population-based studies from around the world indicate that the prevalence of dyspepsia is about 25%. In the United States, only one person in four with dyspepsia seeks medical care, however.

Pathogenesis

MUCOSAL INFLAMMATION AND *HELICOBACTER PYLORI.* *Helicobacter pylori* infection is the most common cause of histologic gastritis in humans and is linked causally to peptic ulcer disease and gastric cancer (Chapters 137, 138, and 199). Symptoms in patients with functional dyspepsia are indistinguishable from the symptoms encountered in

patients with peptic ulcer disease. *H. pylori* gastritis is found in 30 to 60% of patients with functional dyspepsia but also is common in totally asymptomatic subjects in the general population, so a link between *H. pylori* and functional dyspepsia is not established, although it may be important in a small subgroup of patients.

GASTRIC ACID. Basal and peak acid output is normal in patients with functional dyspepsia, but acid secretion in response to gastrin-releasing peptide may be significantly higher in *H. pylori*–positive patients with functional dyspepsia. Overall, 50% of infected patients with functional dyspepsia may have a similar disturbance of stimulated acid secretion as observed in duodenal ulcer. Whether the mucosa is more sensitive to acid in patients with functional dyspepsia is unknown.

DISTURBED MOTOR FUNCTION. Of patients seen at tertiary referral centers with functional dyspepsia, 40% have delayed gastric emptying for solids, and a similar number have antral hypomotility after meals. The prevalence of gastric motility disturbances in patients with functional dyspepsia seen in primary care is unknown but may be lower. Reflux of bile into the stomach is not more frequent in functional dyspepsia than in healthy controls. Up to 40% of such patients may have a stiff fundus that does not relax postprandially and thereby causes fullness and an inability to finish a meal.

In patients with otherwise unexplained nausea, slow and rapid sequences of gastric slow waves with either a regular or an irregular rhythm have been observed. Gastric arrhythmias occur in some patients with functional dyspepsia and also have been documented in patients with severe nausea caused by gastroesophageal reflux disease.

DISTURBED SENSORY FUNCTION. Patients with functional dyspepsia have a decreased pain threshold during balloon distention of the stomach. No major differences in sensory thresholds between *H. pylori*–positive and *H. pylori*–negative patients with functional dyspepsia have been observed. Sensory thresholds are lower after intraduodenal lipid, but not glucose infusion, which may explain why fatty meals induce symptoms in some patients with functional dyspepsia. Lowered duodenal sensory thresholds also occur, as do abnormal rectal and esophageal sensory thresholds in some patients with functional dyspepsia.

CENTRAL NERVOUS SYSTEM DISTURBANCES. In general, patients who present for medical care with functional dyspepsia are more anxious and depressed than healthy controls and have higher neuroticism and somatization scores. The prolactin response to buspirone, an azaspirone that stimulates central serotoninergic-1(A) receptors, may be greater in patients with functional dyspepsia compared with healthy controls.

Acute stress may result in decreased gastric contractility, but it is not known whether chronic dyspeptic symptoms are explained by these mechanisms. Patients with functional dyspepsia with or without antral hypomotility have normal autonomic and humoral responses to acute experimental stressors. The role of major life stress, such as bereavement or divorce, in the pathogenesis of functional dyspepsia is controversial.

DIET AND ENVIRONMENTAL FACTORS. Some patients with functional dyspepsia complain of specific food intolerances, but a convincing relationship between diet and chronic dyspepsia remains to be shown. Coffee may induce symptoms in approximately 50% of patients with functional dyspepsia compared with one in five healthy controls, perhaps because coffee acts as a direct irritant, stimulates acid secretion, or precipitates gastroesophageal reflux.

Aspirin and other NSAIDs cause asymptomatic mucosal lesions in 30 to 60% of chronic users and can cause dyspepsia. Cyclooxygenase-2-selective NSAIDs also cause dyspepsia. Smoking and alcohol are not important risk factors for functional dyspepsia.

Clinical Manifestations

It has been suggested that patients with functional dyspepsia can be subdivided into patients with typical ulcer symptoms, such as epigastric pain related to meals or waking the patient from sleep (ulcer-like dyspepsia), and patients with symptoms suggestive of gastric stasis, such as postprandial bloating or early satiety (dysmotility-like dyspepsia). Although this categorization is used in clinical practice, standardized symptom questionnaires have shown considerable overlap among categories. Dyspepsia often is associated with minor classic reflux symptoms, in particular heartburn; if reflux symptoms dominate, the diagnosis is symptomatic gastroesophageal reflux disease until proved otherwise.

Differential Diagnosis

The major organic causes to consider are chronic peptic ulcer disease, gastroesophageal reflux (with or without esophagitis), and, rarely but importantly, malignancy (Fig. 135–2).

PEPTIC ULCER. The most important condition to exclude is peptic ulcer disease because definitive therapy is now available. The type or pattern of symptoms discriminates poorly between peptic ulcer disease and functional dyspepsia. In clinical practice, peptic ulcer disease must be excluded by upper gastrointestinal endoscopy before functional dyspepsia can be diagnosed firmly (Chapter 132).

GASTROESOPHAGEAL REFLUX. Gastroesophageal reflux (Chapter 136) should be suspected strongly in patients with predominant epigastric or retrosternal burning pain or discomfort that radiates up toward the throat and is relieved by antacids at least transiently. More than 50% of patients with pathologic gastroesophageal reflux confirmed by 24-hour esophageal pH testing have no visible esophagitis at endoscopy; these patients should not be misclassified as having functional dyspepsia.

GASTRIC AND ESOPHAGEAL CANCER. In people younger than age 55 in most Western countries, cancer is a rare cause of dyspepsia; overall, gastric cancer is found in only about 1% of patients with new-onset dyspepsia (Chapters 136 and 199). Nevertheless, a neoplasm must be considered as a possible cause of dyspepsia because delayed diagnosis can affect prognosis adversely.

BILIARY TRACT DISEASE. Cholelithiasis causes biliary pain, which is typically severe, constant pain in the epigastrium or right upper quadrant that persists for hours and occurs episodically (Chapter 158). In the absence of characteristic biliary pain, there is no evidence that gallstones are linked to dyspepsia. At ultrasonography, gallstones may be found in 1 to 3% of patients with chronic dyspepsia but are usually incidental. The prevalence of incidental gallstones increases with age; they are three times more prevalent in women. Biliary dyskinesia also causes biliary-type pain and is due to a motility disorder of the sphincter of Oddi. It usually is recognized after cholecystectomy.

PANCREATIC DISEASE. Chronic pancreatitis or pancreatic carcinoma (Chapters 145 and 201) may cause symptoms that occasionally are confused with functional dyspepsia. These patients tend to have severe pain, however, that is persistent and often radiates through to the back; they may have a history of risk factors for pancreatitis, such as excess alcohol use.

DRUG-INDUCED DYSPEPSIA. Drugs that may produce upper abdominal symptoms include NSAIDs, alendronate, iron or potassium supplements, digitalis, theophylline, and oral antibiotics, especially erythromycin and ampicillin. Reducing the dose or discontinuing drug therapy usually relieves the dyspepsia.

OTHER DISORDERS. Diabetes mellitus can cause postprandial fullness, early satiety, nausea, and vomiting in the presence or absence of gastroparesis (Chapter 242). Diabetic radiculopathy of the thoracic nerve roots can cause upper abdominal pain. Metabolic disturbances (e.g., hypothyroidism, hypercalcemia) can produce upper gastrointestinal distress. Ischemic heart disease sometimes presents as upper abdominal pain induced by exertion. Intestinal angina (chronic mesenteric ischemia) should be considered in older patients, particularly smokers; it typically presents as postprandial pain that is associated with a fear of eating and significant weight loss (Chapter 144). Colon cancer, gastric lymphoma or sarcoma, and ampullary cancer rarely cause upper abdominal distress that initially may be confused with functional dyspepsia. Infiltrative diseases of the stomach, including eosinophilic gastritis, Crohn's disease, sarcoidosis, tuberculosis, and syphilis, also rarely may produce dyspepsia. Abdominal wall pain can be confused with functional dyspepsia.

AEROPHAGIA. Air swallowing with belching is normal and occurs three to four times per hour. Aerophagia is characterized by excessive unconscious swallowing of air that results in abdominal distention or bloating; patients usually report transient improvement of symptoms after belching. The diagnosis of aerophagia is suggested by a specific history and can be confirmed by observing excessive air swallowing between meals and repetitive belching. Because excessive gas is probably not present, either disturbed upper gastrointestinal tract motility or psychopathology probably explains the symptoms.

 **Treatment**

GENERAL MANAGEMENT

In patients with documented functional dyspepsia after endoscopy, a positive clinical diagnosis and firm reassurance are the key steps in management. Not all patients want or require medication for functional dyspepsia after a confident diagnosis has been made. A careful explanation of the meaning of the symptoms and their benign nature can have positive therapeutic effects; some patients lose their symptoms spontaneously after a positive diagnosis. It is useful to ask the patient with long-standing functional dyspepsia symptoms why he or she decided to present for care on this occasion; allaying the patient's unwarranted fears is effective therapy. Patients with functional dyspepsia may improve by eating low-fat meals or by ingesting more frequent but smaller meals throughout the day.

DRUG THERAPY

There is a considerable response to placebo in functional dyspepsia, ranging from 30 to 60%. This placebo response may not reflect a nonspecific effect of treatment but rather in part spontaneous regression of the disease. The course of functional dyspepsia typically is characterized by relapsing and remitting symptoms, but over a 1-year period more than 70% continue to be symptomatic.

ANTACIDS AND ACID INHIBITORS. Antacids commonly are used by patients with functional dyspepsia, but randomized controlled studies

Continued

Gastrointestinal Diseases

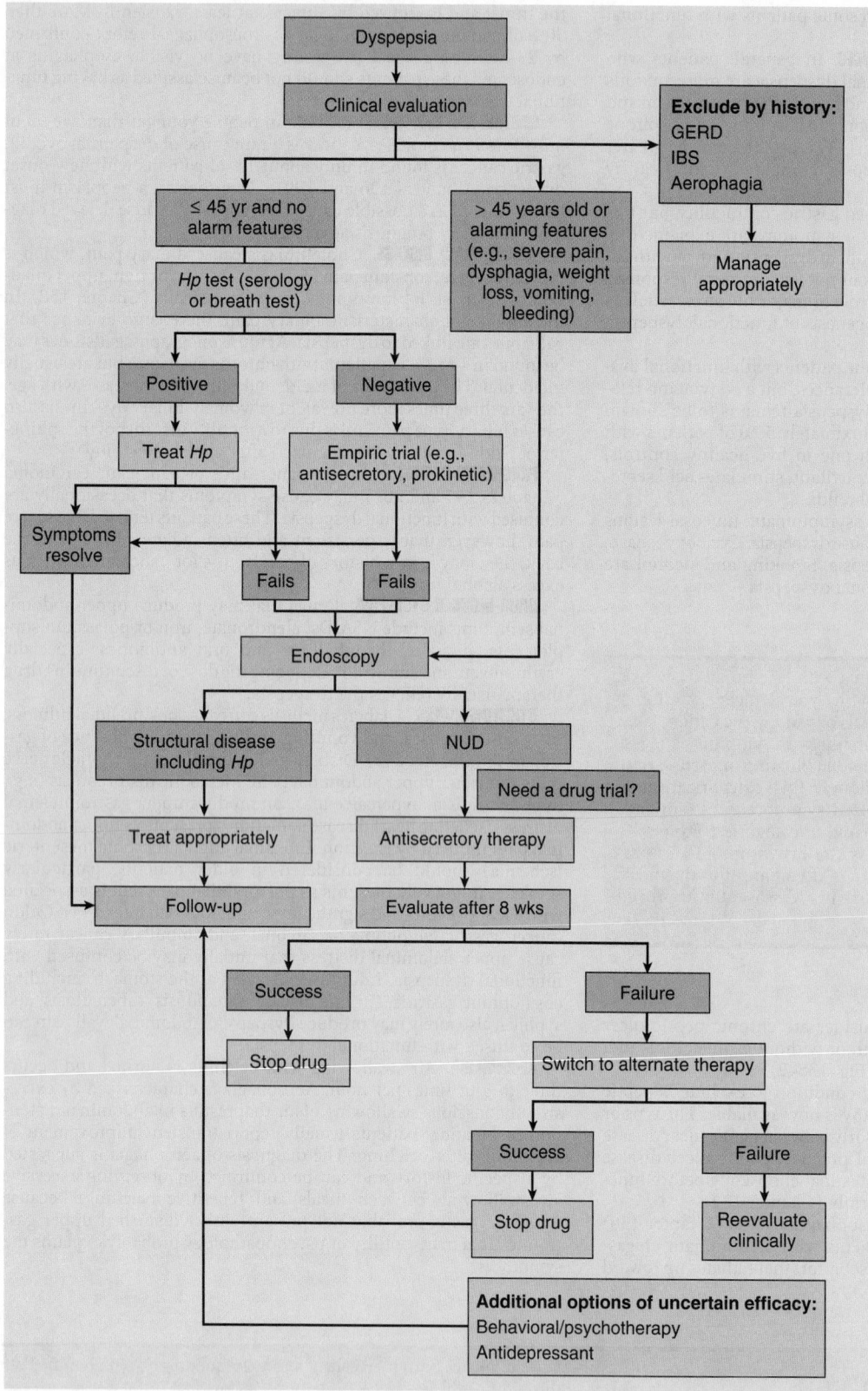

FIGURE 135–2 • Algorithm for the evaluation of dyspepsia. GERD = symptomatic gastroesophageal reflux disease; *Hp* = *Helicobacter pylori*; IBS = irritable bowel syndrome; NUD = nonulcer dyspepsia.

all have failed to show a significant benefit over placebo. The results of controlled trials testing full-dose H_2-receptor antagonists have been conflicting. A meta-analysis suggested an approximately 20% benefit of H_2-receptor antagonists over placebo, but only selected trials could be included. These drugs should be prescribed twice daily (e.g., ranitidine or nizatidine, 150 mg, or famotidine, 20 mg) initially; the value of over-the-counter H_2 blockers is unknown. Reports have described promising improvement of ulcer-like dyspepsia during treatment with a proton-pump inhibitor (e.g.,

omeprazole, 20 mg/day, or lansoprazole, 15 or 30 mg/day) compared with placebo. ◪

PROKINETICS. The dopaminergic receptor blockers metoclopramide (and domperidone) and the serotonin type 4 receptor agonist cisapride have been used in functional dyspepsia, and evidence from randomized controlled trials shows that prokinetics are superior to placebo. Cisapride, although efficacious, is available only on a limited-access program and seldom is prescribed because of rare life-threatening arrhythmias. Metoclopramide (10 to 20 mg before meals and at bedtime) can induce side effects, owing to its central anti-dopaminergic effects, including dystonic reactions, drowsiness, and increased prolactin levels. Rarely, tardive dyskinesia may occur, particularly in the elderly, and in some cases it is not reversible. Erythromycin, a motilin agonist, is of little therapeutic value in functional dyspepsia. Tegaserod, a prokinetic, may have modest efficacy, and trials are in progress. Alosetron also may improve symptoms, but its side-effect profile limits its use.

CYTOPROTECTION. Sucralfate and bismuth subsalicylate may be useful for intermittent dyspepsia but are not clearly superior to placebo. Misoprostol is not efficacious in functional dyspepsia.

TREATMENT TARGETING *H. PYLORI*. Several large trials have assessed the long-term outcome of *H. pylori* eradication therapy with mixed results. One in 15 patients treated may have symptom relief that persists. ☑ *H. pylori* eradication can be considered for infected patients but often fails as initial therapy.

ANTISPASMODICS. Theoretically, anticholinergic agents might be of value in patients with pyloric or antral spasm, but these disturbances have not been documented in functional dyspepsia. Anticholinergic drugs have been evaluated formally in small studies in which dicyclomine was not more efficacious than placebo.

ANTINAUSEA DRUGS. In addition to prokinetics, antinausea drugs include antihistamines, phenothiazines (e.g., prochlorperazine), and others with an uncertain mechanism of action (e.g., trimethobenzamide). Benzodiazepines also may help reduce nausea by their sedative effects. The 5-HT$_3$ receptor antagonist ondansetron and other similar agents are not of established value but may be worth a trial in difficult cases.

ANTIDEPRESSANTS. There are few formal randomized placebo-controlled trials on the effects of antidepressants in functional dyspepsia, but tricyclics (in low dose) are probably of value in patients with resistant symptoms even in the absence of depression.

MANAGEMENT GUIDELINES

NEW-ONSET (UNINVESTIGATED) DYSPEPSIA. The medical history is key (see Fig. 135–2). The physician should inquire about typical reflux symptoms; if heartburn or acid regurgitation is the predominant complaint, a diagnosis of gastroesophageal reflux should be made and appropriate treatment instituted. If there is uncertainty, a short trial of high-dose proton-pump inhibitor therapy (e.g., omeprazole, 20 mg twice daily for 14 days) is useful as a diagnostic test for distinguishing reflux, in which symptoms typically are abolished, from other causes of upper gastrointestinal symptoms (Chapter 136). Similarly, if bowel dysfunction is linked directly to the epigastric pain or discomfort, a diagnosis of IBS should be considered.

Older patients (>45 years old) with new, unexplained dyspepsia and patients with alarm symptoms (e.g., vomiting, bleeding, weight loss, dysphagia) have an increased risk of organic disease and should undergo prompt upper endoscopic evaluation. In younger patients without alarm symptoms, management depends on the degree of uncertainty that the patient and physician are willing to accept. Use of a locally validated noninvasive *H. pylori* test (e.g., serology, breath test, or fecal antigen test) and initiation of anti–*H. pylori* treatment in infected subjects is a reasonable initial approach as an alternative to routine endoscopy. This management approach should relieve symptoms in most patients with peptic ulcer disease and in some with functional dyspepsia (Chapter 138).

In *H. pylori*–negative patients, who are most likely to have functional dyspepsia, the major first-line drugs are a proton-pump inhibitor or an H$_2$ blocker. Some clinicians prefer initially to treat ulcer-like dyspepsia with an antisecretory agent and dysmotility-like dyspepsia with a prokinetic agent. Therapy can be switched if there is no benefit after 1 month. Patients require endoscopy if they fail to respond within 8 weeks or relapse rapidly.

REFRACTORY PATIENT WITH DOCUMENTED FUNCTIONAL DYSPEPSIA. Failure to respond to treatment raises the possibility that the diagnosis of functional dyspepsia was incorrect or that the chosen treatment was suboptimal. Simethicone and antispasmodics may be worth a trial but often fail. If early satiety or fullness is prominent, drugs that relax the gastric fundus (e.g., sumatriptan, buspirone, or clonidine) may be tried. Another option is to initiate low-dose tricyclic antidepressant treatment. In patients who need continuous therapy to avoid incapacitating or unremitting symptoms, drug holidays can confirm that current therapy is still of value.

AEROPHAGIA. Treatment of excessive unconscious air swallowing is difficult. Stress reduction and dietary modifications (avoiding sucking sweets or chewing gum, eating slowly, encouraging small swallows at mealtime, and avoiding diet beverages) occasionally may help. Simethicone and activated charcoal are not of established value. Tranquilizers or prokinetics sometimes may be of benefit.

Prognosis

A firm diagnosis of functional dyspepsia after endoscopy generally excludes ulcer or other structural disease, reduces a patient's fears, and may improve the prognosis. Some patients may be symptom-free for years. Patients seen at tertiary centers for functional dyspepsia represent a subgroup with more intractable symptoms, and spontaneous remissions are less common.

NONCARDIAC (FUNCTIONAL) CHEST PAIN

One third to one half of patients presenting to an emergency department with chest pain do not have coronary artery disease. Angina-like chest pain in these patients most often is caused by gastroesophageal reflux and occasionally by motor disorders of the esophagus. Musculoskeletal chest pain and psychiatric disease (e.g., panic attacks) also are important causes to consider (Chapter 46). Microvascular angina explains some cases too, but these conditions all can overlap, making management a challenge.

Clinical evaluation should be directed initially at excluding cardiac causes of chest pain (Chapter 46). The history should screen for psychiatric disease and especially panic disorder, which may present as recurrent chest pain. Pain aggravated by movement may be musculoskeletal and can be confirmed by reproducing the patient's typical pain with palpation of the sternum or chest wall.

In patients who do not have cardiac, musculoskeletal, or psychiatric disease, the possibility of esophageal disease must be evaluated (Chapter 136). Ambulatory 24-hour esophageal pH monitoring and endoscopy are useful in diagnosing reflux. In the remaining patients, esophageal manometry may be considered, but the yield is low.

Manometry rules out achalasia (<1% of patients with chest pain) and esophageal spasm (<5% of patients with chest pain). "Nutcracker esophagus" refers to high-amplitude distal contractions (mean >180 mm Hg) with normal peristalsis. Other less common, nonspecific motor abnormalities include a hypertensive lower esophageal sphincter or exaggerated esophageal body contractions. Although 30% of patients with chest pain have a nonspecific motor abnormality, they rarely coincide with spontaneous chest pain, and the relevance of the manometric disturbances is highly questionable.

Treatment relies on reassurance and explanation. An aggressive trial of acid suppression with proton-pump inhibitors should be prescribed if there is any suspicion of reflux, with the dose doubled if there is no response after 1 to 2 weeks (Chapter 136). Calcium channel blockers, such as nifedipine (10 to 20 mg four times daily) or diltiazem (30 to 60 mg four times daily), may be tried in unexplained cases, but their efficacy is questionable; use of nitrates (short-acting and long-acting) and anticholinergic agents has been disappointing. Tricyclic antidepressants (starting at a low dose, e.g., imipramine, 25 mg) are of particular value, in part because a subset of patients have esophageal hypersensitivity. Behavioral therapy is valuable in patients with and without panic disorder who have unexplained chest pain.

1. Jailwala J, Imperiale TF, Kroenke K: Pharmacologic treatment of the irritable bowel syndrome: A systematic review of randomized, controlled trials. Ann Intern Med 2000;133:136–147.
2. Muller-Lissner SA, Fumagalli I, Bardhan KD, et al: Tegaserod, a 5HT(4) receptor partial agonist, relieves symptoms in irritable bowel syndrome patients with abdominal pain, bloating and constipation. Aliment Pharmacol Ther 2001;15: 1655–1666.

3. Camilleri M, Chey WY, Mayer EA, et al: A randomized controlled clinical trial of the serotonin type 3 receptor antagonist alosetron in women with diarrhea-predominant irritable bowel syndrome. Arch Intern Med 2001;161:1733–1740.
4. Moayyedi P, Deeks J, Soo S, et al: Pharmacological interventions for non-ulcer dyspepsia. Cochrane Database Syst Rev 2003;1:CD002096.
5. Moayyedi P, Soo S, Deeks J, et al: Systematic review and economic evaluation of *Helicobacter pylori* eradication treatment for non-ulcer dyspepsia. Dyspepsia Review Group. BMJ 2000;321:659–664.

SUGGESTED READINGS

Bytzer P, Talley NJ: Dyspepsia. Ann Intern Med 2001;134:815–822. *Overview of symptoms and their utility in diagnosis.*
Fang J, Bjorkman D: A critical approach to noncardiac chest pain: Pathophysiology, diagnosis and treatment. Am J Gastroenterol 2001;96:958–968. *An up-to-date summary of the literature.*
Talley NJ: Pharmacologic therapy for the irritable bowel syndrome. Am J Gastroenterol 2003;98:750–758. *Emphasizes newer therapies.*
Talley NJ, Spiller R: Irritable bowel syndrome: A poorly understood organic disease? Lancet 2002;360:555–564. *An up-to-date review of the pathophysiology, diagnosis, and management of irritable bowel syndrome.*

136 DISEASES OF THE ESOPHAGUS

Roy C. Orlando

The esophagus is a 22- to 25-cm conduit whose upper third is skeletal muscle and lower two thirds are smooth muscle. Its function is to transport food from the oral cavity to the stomach. When not swallowing, the esophagus is closed at the upper end by the upper esophageal sphincter (UES), or cricopharyngeus muscle, which creates a high-pressure zone that prevents inspired air from entering the esophagus. The lower esophageal sphincter (LES) creates a high-pressure zone that prevents gastric contents from entering the esophagus. On swallowing, the swallowing center located in the medulla oblongata coordinates peristalsis in the pharynx and esophagus with relaxation of the UES and LES, enabling food to be propulsed in a caudad direction to the stomach. The motor signals from the swallow center (nucleus ambiguous) to the end plates on skeletal muscle or to Auerbach's neuronal plexus in smooth muscle are carried by preganglionic or postganglionic cholinergic fibers in the vagus nerve. Contraction of esophageal muscle is elicited by the release of acetylcholine, and its relaxation is induced either by inhibition of acetylcholine release or by release of nitric oxide and vasoactive intestinal peptide. The esophagus must transport food from mouth to stomach, and, at the same time, protect itself from gastric acid reflux. The esophagus is protected by a three-pronged system: antireflux barriers (limits reflux frequency), luminal clearance mechanisms (limits duration within the esophagus), and tissue resistance (limits damage on epithelial contact).

ESOPHAGEAL SYMPTOMS

Heartburn, odynophagia, and dysphagia are symptoms with a high degree of specificity for the esophagus (Chapter 130). Chest pain, though common in esophageal disease (Chapter 135), has a far broader differential, including cardiac disease (Chapter 46).

Dysphagia means *difficulty swallowing.* When dysphagia arises from disease of skeletal muscle, it is called *oropharyngeal dysphagia.* Oropharyngeal dysphagia is characteristically accompanied by failure to transport a bolus from mouth to esophagus, by nasal regurgitation owing to lack of occlusion of the nasal air passages by the soft palate, and by coughing with swallowing owing to aspiration resulting from failure to elevate the larynx and lower the epiglottis. When dysphagia arises from disease affecting smooth muscle, the impairment of bolus transport is perceived substernally and called *esophageal dysphagia.* Esophageal dysphagia is not accompanied by failure of bolus transport from mouth to esophagus, by nasal regurgitation, or by aspiration. Further, esophageal dysphagia is readily separated into (1) diseases that cause dysphagia for solids only, indicating a lumen-narrowing (mechanical) lesion, such as peptic stricture, cancer, or Schatzki's ring (Fig. 136–1A to C) as compared with (2) those that cause dysphagia for liquids as well as solids, indicating motor dysfunction, such as achalasia or diffuse esophageal spasm.

Heartburn is a symptom complex characterized by episodic substernal pain, worse after meals and on reclining, and relieved at least temporarily by antacids. The quality of the discomfort is often burning, and it commonly radiates toward the mouth. Heartburn is often accompanied by complaints of a bitter taste in the mouth (regurgitation) or a welling up in the mouth of a salty tasting (salivary-derived) fluid (waterbrash). When typical symptoms recur at least once per week over an extended period, history alone permits the diagnosis of gastroesophageal reflux disease (GERD). The term *indigestion* is used by some of the lay public as a surrogate for *heartburn,* whereas others use the term *heartburn* to describe symptoms without these characteristics. For this reason, the diagnosis of GERD requires a careful history to ensure that the symptom pattern contains features essential for a diagnosis of heartburn.

Odynophagia means painful swallowing and implies an acute and severe form of esophagitis, usually with mucosal ulceration. Odynophagia is experienced substernally as an aching or stabbing pain that is characteristically aggravated by the act of swallowing, even swallowing saliva. It is common in esophagitis caused by infection, pills, and radiation, but it is rare in esophagitis caused by reflux.

Chest pain, distinctive from heartburn and odynophagia, is common in esophageal disease. It is termed *atypical* because it has some but not all characteristics suggestive of angina. For example, the pain is usually substernal or parasternal; can radiate to the neck, jaw or arms; may worsen with meals; and may be relieved by nitroglycerin (Chapter 46). Such similarities are not surprising given the overlapping pattern of sensory innervation between the heart and esophagus. When such pain is accompanied by dysphagia, odynophagia or heartburn, the origin is likely the esophagus. In the absence of these associated symptoms, patients with chest pain should initially have a cardiac evaluation. If cardiac disease is excluded, the patient is said to have *noncardiac chest pain,* which may be attributed to GERD or diffuse esophageal spasm.

ESOPHAGEAL BLEEDING

Upper gastrointestinal bleeding may present in many forms, such as hematemesis, melena, coffee-ground emesis, Hematest-positive stool, iron deficiency anemia, and, when massive, hematochezia (Chapter 133). When transfusions are required, the most common esophageal causes are ruptured esophageal varices and Mallory-Weiss tears. Less commonly, deep esophageal ulcers from cytomegalovirus (CMV) or human immunodeficiency virus (HIV) infection may cause significant bleeding. Lower rates of bleeding leading to iron deficiency anemia can be a reflection of GERD.

GASTROESOPHAGEAL REFLUX DISEASE

Definition

Gastroesophageal reflux is a physiologic process that refers to the effortless movement of gastric contents from stomach to esophagus. It occurs in everyone, multiple times every day, usually without producing symptoms or signs of damage. Reflux can also be pathologic, producing symptoms and signs of tissue injury to esophagus, oropharynx, larynx, and respiratory tract. Reflux damage to the esophagus (reflux esophagitis) is the commonest form of GERD, most often recognized by recurrent heartburn. In almost all patients with heartburn, there is identifiable esophageal mucosal pathology, though only about 40% have endoscopically detectable erosions. The remaining 60% of patients with heartburn but no erosions have nonerosive GERD.

Epidemiology

GERD is one of the commonest diseases in the Western world based on the prevalence of heartburn. In the United States, about 45% of adults have heartburn at least once a month, about 20% once a week, and about 10% daily. Heartburn affects men twofold to threefold more often than it affects women and is more common in whites than blacks. Although GERD rarely causes death, it reduces quality of life and has a serious morbidity rate of 10 to 15% due to ulceration, bleeding, stricture, Barrett's esophagus, and adenocarcinoma. The overall risk of esophageal adenocarcinoma in patients with heartburn is low, with estimates of 1:2500 cases per year for those with daily heartburn to 1:10,000 cases per year for those with monthly heartburn.

FIGURE 136-1 • Barium esophagrams demonstrate three common causes of dysphagia for solids only: peptic stricture (A), Schatzki's ring (B), and malignant stricture (C). The malignant stricture produces rapidly progressive dysphagia for solids in association with both anorexia and weight loss. The peptic stricture occurs in reflux patients and produces slowly progressive dysphagia for solids in the absence of anorexia and weight loss. The Schatzki's ring produces either intermittent, nonprogressive dysphagia for solids or acute food impaction in the absence of anorexia or weight loss. (From Feldman M [ed]: Gastroenterology and Hepatology: The Comprehensive Visual Reference. New York, Churchill Livingstone, 1997.)

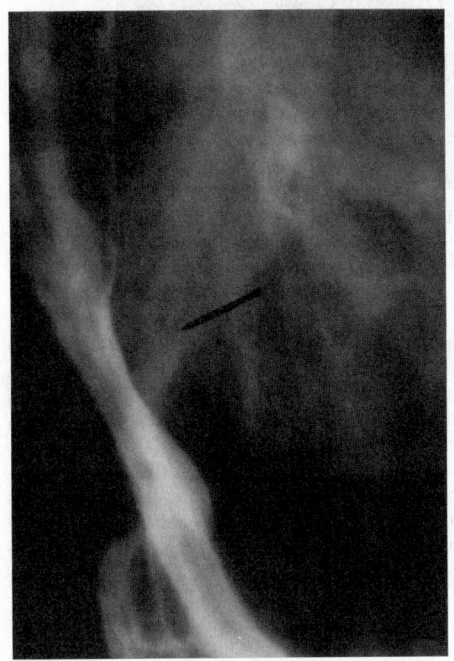

A

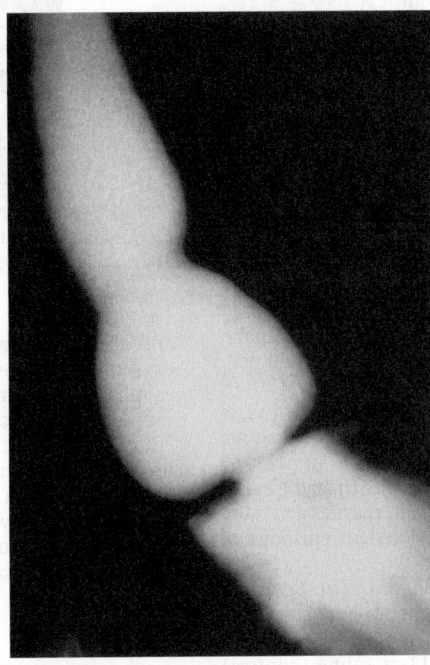

B

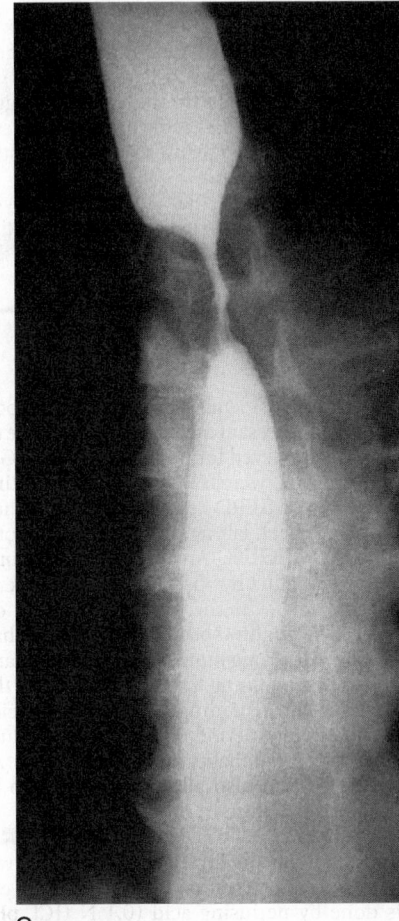

C

Pathobiology

GERD develops when acidic gastric contents reflux into the esophagus and remain there long enough to overcome the resistance of the esophageal epithelium. Based on 24-hour esophageal pH monitoring, GERD develops in at least two fundamentally different ways: (1) under conditions in which there is prolonged contact of the esophageal epithelium with refluxed gastric acid, and (2) under conditions in which the esophageal epithelium is damaged despite a normal duration of contact with refluxed gastric acid. Prolonged acid contact results from defects in the antireflux barriers and/or luminal clearance mechanisms, with an increased frequency of transient LES relaxations accounting for more than 50% of reflux events. These relaxations are non-swallow induced, reflex relaxations of the LES due to gastric fundic distention. They are associated with reflux because these LES relaxations are twice as long as relaxations with swallowing and are unaccompanied by lumen-obliterating esophageal peristalsis. The cause of the increase in transient relaxations is unclear but is unrelated to delayed gastric emptying or *Helicobacter pylori* infection. In erosive esophagitis, transient LES relaxations account for less than 50% of reflux episodes, with most occurring across a mechanically weak LES. Whether LES weakness causes erosive esophagitis or is a consequence of it remains unclear. Similarly, hiatal hernias and impaired peristalsis are common in patients with erosive esophagitis, but whether they are cause or consequence is also unclear since esophagitis can cause both esophageal shortening (by sustained contraction of the longitudinal muscle) and peristaltic dysfunction (by weakening circular muscle contractility). Patients with heartburn despite normal acid contact time presumably have primary defects in tissue resistance.

Clinical Manifestations

SYMPTOMS. Recurrent heartburn, which is the hallmark of reflux esophagitis and GERD, enables a diagnosis of GERD to be made by history alone. However, the frequency, severity, or duration of heartburn does not predict the endoscopic severity of disease. GERD is also associated with dysphagia, which is called an *alarm symptom* since it raises concern about the development of a peptic stricture or adenocarcinoma arising in a Barrett's esophagus. For this reason, dysphagia in a patient with heartburn is an indication for early endoscopy.

SIGNS. The damage in reflux esophagitis is best assessed by upper endoscopy, which may reveal erythema, edema, friability, erosions, ulcers, strictures, or Barrett's esophagus. In the 40% of patients with more advanced disease, biopsy findings include epithelial cell edema and necrosis, with intraepithelial neutrophils and occasional eosinophils. A barium swallow or upper gastrointestinal series (Chapter 131) may also detect ulcers, strictures, and hiatal hernias, but it does not reliably detect inflammation, erosions, or Barrett's esophagus.

EXTRAESOPHAGEAL MANIFESTATIONS. Although GERD is often used synonymously with reflux esophagitis, GERD includes reflux damage to the oropharynx, larynx, and respiratory tract. Consequently, symptoms and signs of GERD can include pharyngitis, earache, gingivitis, globus sensation, eroded tooth enamel, laryngitis, chronic cough, asthma (Chapter 84), and aspiration pneumonia (Chapter 92). With the exception of aspiration pneumonia, which occurs with gross regurgitation of gastric content,

Continued

reflux damage to the oropharynx, larynx, and airways is mediated by acid. Asthma (wheezing) and chronic cough may arise by either direct contact between acid and airway epithelium (microaspiration) or indirectly through an esophagopulmonary vagal reflex initiated by acid contact with esophageal epithelium. The frequency with which GERD causes hoarseness, asthma, chronic cough, and laryngitis is unknown.

ASSOCIATED CONDITIONS. GERD can develop as a consequence of other conditions, such as Zollinger-Ellison syndrome (Chapter 140), scleroderma (Chapter 281), diabetes mellitus (Chapter 242), nasogastric intubation, and pregnancy.

Diagnosis

A history of recurrent heartburn and a positive response to antacids or acid-suppressant medication is adequate to diagnose GERD. Specific testing is reserved for patients who have GERD plus *alarm symptoms* of dysphagia, weight loss, or gastrointestinal bleeding and for those suspected of GERD because of atypical chest pain or the presence of oropharyngeal, laryngeal, or airway symptoms.

TESTS FOR REFLUX. An *upper gastrointestinal series* can detect grossly abnormal reflux by observing the movement of barium from stomach to esophagus with the patient in the head-down position. When positive, it is highly specific; however, it has low sensitivity (20%). *Esophageal pH monitoring*, the gold standard for identifying reflux, is performed by fixing a small pH probe in the esophagus, 5 cm above the LES, and recording all episodes of acid reflux (drop in pH < 4) over a 24-hour period. The number and duration of each acidic event yield a total esophageal acid contact time. An event marker activated by the patient also allows symptoms to be related to episodes of esophageal acidity.

TESTS FOR ESTABLISHING GERD AS CAUSE FOR SYMPTOMS. The *Bernstein test* is one means for assessing a causal relationship between chest pain and esophageal acidification and, by extension, GERD. This test is done by perfusing acid (0.1 N HCl, pH 1.1) or saline (control) through a catheter positioned in mid-esophagus. If symptoms typical of those that occur spontaneously develop during acid, but not saline, perfusion, the test is considered positive for GERD. However, the preferred method for establishing GERD as the cause of any given symptom (e.g. chest pain, wheezing) is an *empiric trial of acid suppression*, based on the ability of proton pump inhibitor (PPI) therapy (e.g., omeprazole 20 mg twice daily) to control gastric acidity in more than 90% of subjects. In some instances, a bedtime dose of a histamine-2 (H_2)-receptor antagonist (e.g., ranitidine 300 mg) is added to reduce the possibility of nocturnal acid breakthrough. The treatment period in which to expect a response is 3 to 4 weeks for chest pain and 2 to 3 months for inflammatory disease of the airway. The resolution of symptoms supports GERD as causal. Confirmation may be obtained by relapse when medication is withdrawn and by a subsequent positive response to retreatment. Failure of symptoms to improve is strong evidence against GERD.

TESTS FOR ESOPHAGEAL INJURY. See earlier Signs section.

TESTS OF ESOPHAGEAL MOTOR FUNCTION. An upper gastrointestinal series or barium swallow is valuable for identifying gross reflux and marked abnormalities of esophageal peristaltic and sphincter function. More subtle abnormalities, however, require esophageal manometry. When mean LES pressure is low (<10 mm Hg), it is highly specific for GERD, but 60% of patients may have normal valves. Currently, the major uses of manometry in GERD are to exclude motor disease (achalasia, scleroderma) and to quantify peristaltic amplitude, the latter for use in determining whether to perform a complete (Nissen) or partial (Belsey, Dor, Toupet) fundoplication.

Clinical Course

Heartburn caused by GERD usually remains stable for long periods but may have short periods of exacerbation and remission. Antacids and acid-suppressing medication effectively control symptoms; however, relapse is common when medication is stopped. When endoscopy has documented the absence of erosions or inflammatory changes, progression to erosive esophagitis is uncommon (~15%), and stricture, Barrett's esophagus, and adenocarcinoma are unlikely to occur. When endoscopy documents erosive esophagitis, the clinical course is more variable; maintenance therapy is often required,

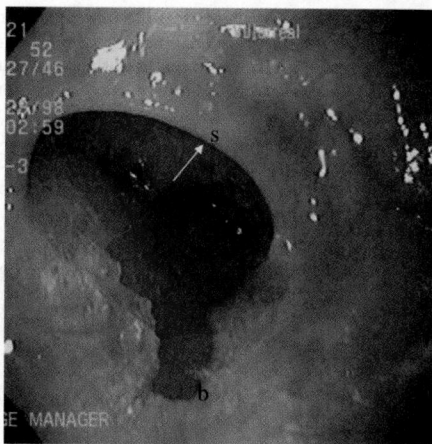

FIGURE 136–2 • Endoscopic view of the distal esophagus from a patient with gastroesophageal reflux disease showing a tongue of Barrett's mucosa (b) and a Schatzki's ring(s) (arrow).

and a repeat endoscopy is often desirable to ensure healing and to exclude Barrett's esophagus. When healing occurs without Barrett's esophagus, Barrett's is unlikely to develop in the future. When Barrett's esophagus is identified on endoscopy, it too generally follows a benign course (life expectancy similar to the general population), remaining unchanged for years to decades irrespective of the type or presence of treatment. Nonetheless, given that the presence of Barrett's esophagus is known to carry a 10% lifetime risk (incidence 0.5% per year) of developing an esophageal adenocarcinoma, periodic endoscopic surveillance is recommended.

Complications

The two major complications of GERD are peptic stricture formation and Barrett's esophagus (frequency, 5 to 15%). *Peptic stricture* is a lumen-narrowing lesion that occurs in erosive esophagitis due to edema, inflammation, and fibrosis of the distal esophagus (Fig. 136–1A). When present, strictures produce dysphagia for solids, a symptom that progresses slowly over months to years. Anorexia and weight loss are absent. Diagnosis is by barium swallow or upper endoscopy, the latter permitting biopsy to exclude malignancy. *Barrett's esophagus* is replacement of reflux-damaged squamous epithelium in the distal esophagus by metaplastic, specialized columnar epithelium. It is found in 10 to 15% of patients with GERD, principally in whites. Barrett's metaplasia, which is more acid-resistant than squamous epithelium, produces no symptoms. The lesion is suspected on endoscopy by the presence of reddish epithelium extending from the stomach into the tubular lumen of the esophagus (Fig. 136–2). When its length is 3 cm or more, it is called *long-segment Barrett's*, and when the length is less than 3 cm, it is referred to as *short-segment Barrett's*. Confirmation is by biopsy. Barrett's metaplasia is a premalignant lesion that increases the risk of esophageal adenocarcinoma 30-fold to 125-fold over that of the general population (see Esophageal Tumors). The incidence of cancer in Barrett's in patients with GERD, which has increased 350% in white men over the last 30 years, is 0.5% per year, with a lifetime prevalence of about 10%. Factors that increase the risk of malignancy in Barrett's include white race, male sex, alcohol and tobacco use, obesity, and Barrett's length. Nonetheless, life expectancy with Barrett's is similar to that of the general population because the cancer rate in the United States is low (6000 cases/year) and because of the late age (mean: mid-60s) at which it develops.

℞ Treatment

MEDICAL. Treatment of GERD is primarily medical, the mainstays being lifestyle modifications (Table 136–1) and drug therapy (Table 136–2). The goal of treatment is to relieve symptoms and prevent complications. All patients are initially advised about lifestyle changes that will improve symptoms. Antacids or antacid-alginate combination are recommended for safe, inexpensive, convenient, and effective relief of occasional heartburn. The same agents, however, are poorly suited for regular use because of poor

Table 136–1 • LIFESTYLE MODIFICATIONS FOR REFLUX ESOPHAGITIS

Elevate the head of the bed 6 inches
Stop smoking
Stop excessive alcohol consumption
Reduce dietary fat
Reduce meal size
Avoid bedtime snacks
Weight reduction (if overweight)
Avoid chocolate, carminatives (spearmint, peppermint), coffee (caffeinated and decaffeinated), tea, cola beverages, tomato juice, citrus fruit juices
Avoid, when possible, anticholinergics, theophylline, diazepam, narcotics, calcium-channel blockers, β-adrenergic agonists (isoproterenol), progesterone (some contraceptives), α-adrenergic antagonists (phentolamine)

Table 136–2 • DRUG THERAPY FOR REFLUX ESOPHAGITIS

AGENT	DOSE
Antacids: Liquid (to buffer HCl and increase LESP)	
For example, Mylanta II/Maalox TC (HCl neutralizing capacity 25 mEq/5 mL)*	15 mL qid 1 hour after meals & at bedtime, or as needed
Gaviscon (to decrease reflux via a viscous mechanical barrier and buffer HCl)	
[Al(OH)$_3$, NaHCO$_3$, Mg trisilicate, alginic acid]	2–4 tabs qid at bedtime, or as needed
H$_2$-Receptor Antagonists (to decrease HCl secretion)	
Cimetidine (Tagamet)	800 mg bid, 400 mg qid, ~13 mL bid
Ranitidine (Zantac)	150 mg qid or 10 mL qid; maintenance dose, 150–300 mg bid, 10 mL bid
Famotidine (Pepcid)	20–40 mg bid or 2.5–5 mL bid
Nizatidine (Axid)	150 mg bid
Prokinetics (to increase LESP and increase gastric emptying)	
Bethanechol (Urecholine)	25 mg qid 30 minutes before meals & at bedtime
Metoclopramide (Reglan)	10 mg qid 30 minutes before meals & at bedtime
Proton Pump Inhibitors (to decrease HCl secretion and gastric volume)	
Omeprazole (Prilosec)	20 mg/day; maintenance dose, 20 mg/day
Lansoprazole (Prevacid)	30 mg/day; maintenance dose, 15 mg/day
Pantoprazole (Protonix)	40 mg/day
Rabeprazole (Aciphex)	20 mg/day
Esomeprazole (Nexium)	20–40 mg/day

*Patients with reflux are not generally hypersecretors of gastric acid, so the therapeutic doses of antacids are based on their capacity to buffer (normal) basal HCl secretion rates of ~1–7 mEq/hr (mean 2 mEq/hr) and peak meal-stimulated HCl secretion rates of ~10–60 mEq/hr (mean 30 mEq/hr).

HCl = hydrochloric acid; LESP = lower esophageal sphincter pressure.

palatability, durability, and side effects, such as diarrhea, constipation, and possible magnesium or aluminum toxicity in renal patients. Recurring heartburn is treated with acid-suppressing medication. H$_2$-receptor antagonists and PPIs are the drugs of choice. H$_2$-receptor antagonists inhibit one of three acid-stimulating receptors on the basolateral membrane of the parietal cell and so reduce gastric acid secretion. When prescribed twice a day, they can control symptoms in about 50% of GERD patients and heal erosions in about 30%. PPIs irreversibly inhibit the H,K,ATPase or proton pump, the final common pathway for acid secretion on the apical membrane of the parietal cell. Consequently, PPIs markedly reduce gastric acidity with once-a-day dosing, providing relief of symptoms and healing lesions in about 85 to 90% of GERD patients. H$_2$-receptor antagonists (>25 years) and PPIs (~10 years) have

excellent safety profiles. PPI safety beyond 10 years remains unclear owing to uncertainty about the long-term risk of chronic hypoacidity and hypergastrinemia.

SURGICAL. The primary indications for antireflux surgery in GERD are (1) as an alternative to medical maintenance for younger patients who are good operative risks and (2) as a means for controlling regurgitation and its attendant risk of aspiration pneumonia. Surgery is generally not indicated for failure of medical therapy because PPI therapy has such a high success rate, and its failure often indicates that the symptoms arise from diseases other than GERD. The operative procedure of choice is the laparoscopic Nissen fundoplication, a procedure that can also be performed open. It has a success rate (~85 to 90%) equivalent to that of flexible dose PPI therapy.[1] Mortality (~0.2%) and morbidity (2 to 8%) rates are acceptable, and postoperative complications, such as dysphagia and the gas-bloat syndrome (inability to belch or vomit), are manageable. Operation, however, is neither a cure for symptoms, since more than 50% of patients require medical therapy again, nor effective to prevent the subsequent development of esophageal adenocarcinoma.[2] A partial (Belsey, Dor, Toupet) fundoplication is preferred for patients with manometrically defined weak peristaltic amplitudes (<30 mm Hg) to reduce the risk of postoperative dysphagia.

ENDOSCOPIC ANTIREFLUX PROCEDURES. In April 2000 two novel endoscopic therapies—Stretta and EndoCinch procedures—were approved by the U.S. Food and Drug Administration for the treatment of GERD. The Stretta uses thermocoagulation of the LES region, whereas EndoCinch provides suture plication of the gastric cardia. The early results are encouraging in that both procedures can reduce reliance on drug therapy in about 30 to 50% of GERD patients, yet long-term safety and effectiveness are unknown.

STRATEGY. Patients with heartburn are empirically treated with lifestyle modifications and drug therapy (Fig. 136–3). Early endoscopy is indicated for those with alarm symptoms. Endoscopy is indicated for patients who fail once-a-day PPI therapy to confirm the diagnosis and assess severity, including Barrett's esophagus. Testing for *H. pylori* is not recommended since the organism is not etiologic in GERD and, when eradicated, may make treatment more difficult. Failures on once-a-day PPI are treated with twice-daily PPI with or without H$_2$-receptor antagonists at bedtime for 6 to 8 weeks, with patients who fail on this regimen having esophageal pH monitoring *on therapy* to assess the control of esophageal acidity. If acidity is controlled, symptoms are not acid mediated. Effective therapy is often accompanied by relapse when medication ceases, especially in patients with erosive esophagitis, in whom maintenance therapy is indicated. Patients requiring maintenance therapy should have at least one endoscopy to determine the presence or absence of Barrett's esophagus. Surgery is a reasonable alternative to lifelong medical therapy in good operative candidates and is superior to medical therapy for control of regurgitant symptoms.

TREATMENT OF COMPLICATIONS. *Strictures* that narrow the esophageal lumen to less than 15 mm are often symptomatic (dysphagia). When associated with active and marked inflammation of the distal esophagus, they may respond to medical therapy alone. However, when fibrotic, dilation is required at varying intervals. PPI therapy is useful after dilation to reduce recurrent stricturing and the need for more frequent dilation. Difficult strictures may be dilated by a surgeon under general anesthesia or require partial esophagectomy with esophagogastrostomy and protective fundoplication.

Barrett's esophagus patients with heartburn or erosive esophagitis are treated like other patients with GERD without Barrett's esophagus. Whether treatment is beneficial for asymptomatic Barrett's esophagus is unclear. Weight control and cessation of smoking and alcohol are recommended because they are identifiable risk factors for malignancy. Esophagectomy to remove all metaplasia is likely to be effective, but the risk is too high (morbidity of 25 to 40% and mortality of 7%) for the relatively low risk of malignancy (0.5% per year). Moreover, endoscopic surveillance allows detection of phenotypic (dysplasia) and genetic (p53, aneuploidy, increase in G2 tetraploidy) abnormalities before progression to adenocarcinoma and permits cancer to be detected at an early enough stage (T0 to T2) for curative esophagectomy. Currently,

Continued

endoscopic surveillance is recommended every 2 to 3 years, with four-quadrant biopsies obtained every 2 cm throughout the length of the Barrett's. High-grade dysplasia on biopsy is an indication for esophagectomy because frank adenocarcinoma is found in about one third of cases. In poor surgical candidates, high-grade dysplasia or cancer in situ can be ablated using endoscopic laser therapy, with or without an oral or intravenous photosensitizing agent; after treatment, high-dose PPIs are required to enable replacement of the destroyed tissue by stratified squamous epithelium. Notably, laser therapy carries a mortality of about 1% and stricture rates of up to 50%.

INFECTIOUS ESOPHAGITIS

Infectious esophagitis occurs principally, but not exclusively, in the immunocompromised patient, the latter usually from cancer chemotherapy, post-transplant antirejection medication, and acquired immunodeficiency syndrome (AIDS) (especially if CD4 counts are < 200 mm^3) (Chapter 416). *Candida albicans*, herpes simplex virus (HSV)-1, and CMV are the most common causes, and coinfections with more than one agent may occur. In AIDS, CMV esophagitis may coexist with CMV retinitis or colitis.

Clinical Manifestations

Odynophagia may be severe. Dysphagia, weight loss, and gastrointestinal bleeding are common. Complications are infrequent but may include tracheobronchial fistula, perforation, and hemorrhage. Esophageal candidiasis in AIDS is associated with oral candidiasis (thrush) in only about two thirds of cases, and HSV esophagitis is associated with oral herpetic lesions in about one third of cases. In the immunocompetent host, infectious esophagitis is primarily due to HSV or *Candida*.

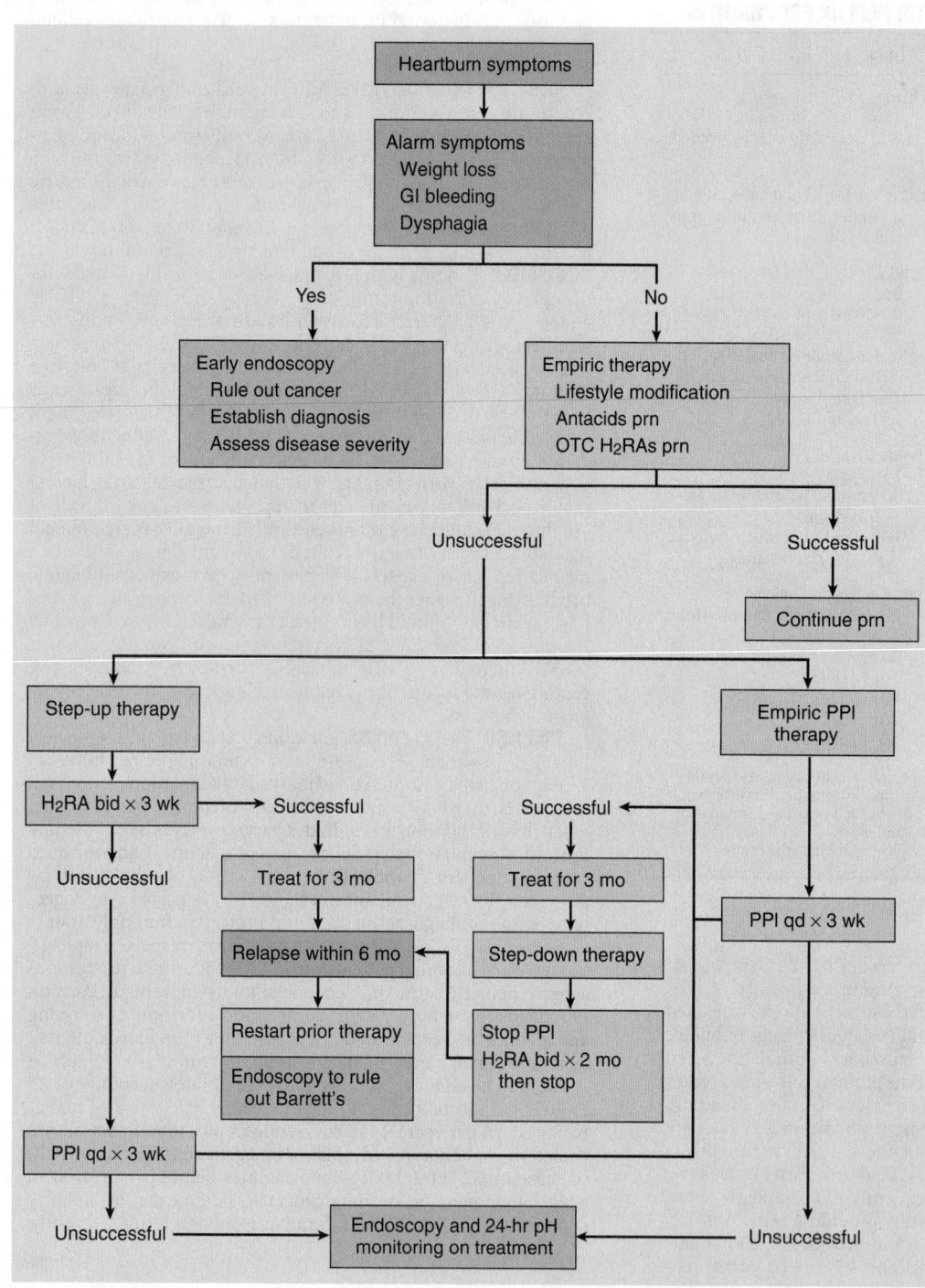

FIGURE 136–3 • Algorithm for management of a patient with heartburn. GI = gastrointestinal; OTC H$_2$RA = over-the-counter H$_2$-receptor antagonist; PPI = proton pump inhibitor; Rx = treatment. (From Orlando L, Orlando RC: Reflux esophagitis: Evaluation of drug management strategies. Formulary 2002;37:140–146. Reprinted with permission from Formulary. Formulary is a copyrighted publication of Advanstar Communications Inc. All rights reserved.)

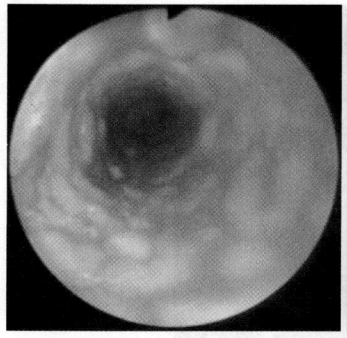 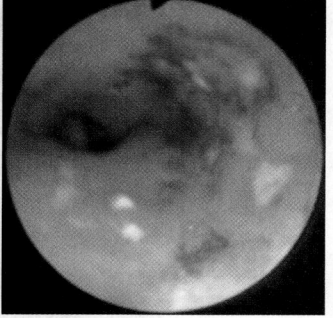

A   **B**

FIGURE 136–4 • Infectious esophagitis in patients with acquired immunodeficiency syndrome. *A,* Esophageal candidiasis. The multiple small white plaques of *Candida* are seen on the background of abnormally reddened esophageal mucosa. Patients with esophageal candidiasis may also present with a smaller number of plaques or with a more or less confluent white coating of the mucosa (which must not be confused with a coating of barium if the patient has recently undergone a barium study). *B,* Herpes simplex ulceration of the lower esophagus. Note the multiple shallow ulcers in the lower part of the esophagus. This appearance is not diagnostic of herpes simplex infection, because a similar appearance may be seen with other causes of ulceration, including some drugs (such as potassium supplements). The presence of vesicles in the mucosa (not shown here) is virtually diagnostic of herpes simplex. (*A* and *B,* From Forbes CD, Jackson WF: Color Atlas and Text of Clinical Medicine, 3rd ed. London, Mosby, 2003.)

Diagnosis

On barium swallow, a "shaggy" mucosa suggests *Candida*; numerous small, volcanic-shaped ulcers suggest HSV, and large, deep linear ulcers suggest CMV (or HIV). Endoscopy with brushings, biopsy, and viral cultures are necessary for definitive diagnosis. *Candida* esophagitis is characterized on endoscopy by numerous, small, white-yellow mucosal plaques containing microorganisms, inflammatory cells, and necrotic mucosa (Fig. 136–4*A*). Positive brushings and biopsy demonstrate *Candida* pseudohyphae with periodic acid-Schiff reagent or special silver stains. HSV esophagitis on endoscopy begins as numerous vesicles that ulcerate to yield small (<2 cm), shallow, volcano-shaped ulcers (Fig. 136–4*B*). Positive biopsy and brushings from the ulcer edge demonstrate the characteristic cytopathic effect of HSV in squamous cells. CMV esophagitis is characterized by large (>2 cm), deep, often linear ulcers. A positive biopsy establishes the diagnosis.

Rx Treatment

In non-AIDS patients, *Candida* esophagitis may be treated with oral nystatin, 1 to 3 million units four times a day, or clotrimazole, 100 mg tablets dissolved in the mouth three to five times a day, but patients with AIDS require an azole antifungal, such as oral or intravenous fluconazole 100 to 200 mg/day for 10 to 14 days (Chapter 416). Ketoconazole and itraconazole are also effective, but, unlike fluconazole, require normal gastric acidity for absorption. In resistant cases, low-dose intravenous amphotericin, 0.3 to 0.5 mg/kg/day, for 10 to 20 days is effective. HSV esophagitis is treated with a nucleoside analogue, such as acyclovir orally 200 to 400 mg five times a day or intravenous 250 mg/m² every 8 hours for 2 weeks. Valacyclovir and famciclovir are alternatives; for resistant cases, intravenous foscarnet 60 mg/kg every 8 hours for 2 to 4 weeks is effective. CMV esophagitis is treated with intravenous ganciclovir, 5 mg/kg every 12 hours for 2 to 4 weeks; for resistant cases, intravenous foscarnet is used at 60 mg/kg every 8 hours intravenous for 2 to 4 weeks. Idiopathic HIV-associated ulcers are treated with prednisone 40 mg/day, tapering by 10 mg/week for 1 month; thalidomide, 200 mg per day, may also be effective. Relapse of all forms of infectious esophagitis is common in the immunocompromised patient and may require maintenance therapy.

OTHER CAUSES OF ESOPHAGITIS

Alkaline reflux esophagitis is an uncommon clinical entity that develops from repeated and prolonged contact of the esophageal epithelium with nonacidic gastric or intestinal contents, usually in subjects with a destroyed pylorus following total gastrectomy or a Billroth II gastroenterostomy. Treatment is bile salt–binding or mucosal-coating agents, such as cholestyramine, sucralfate, or colloidal bismuth. Surgical fundoplication (intact stomach) or creation of a Roux-en-Y limb (post-gastrectomy) is used in refractory cases.

Pill-induced esophagitis develops commonly in patients, particularly the elderly, taking medication improperly (i.e., while supine or with too little liquid). It also occurs in patients with a preexisting abnormality, such as a stricture, diverticulum, or motor disorder. Pills adhere to the esophageal mucosa and cause necrosis and ulceration by the topical release of a caustic medication. Among the common offenders are doxycycline, tetracycline, vitamin C, potassium chloride, nonsteroidal anti-inflammatory drugs, quinidine, alendronate and other bisphosphonates, and iron. Odynophagia is characteristic and commonly accompanied by dysphagia. Ulceration may lead to hemorrhage, perforation, and stricture. Upper endoscopy is indicated in nonobvious cases to exclude infectious esophagitis. Discontinuation of the offending medication and treatment with sucralfate suspension (1 g orally four times a day for 1 to 2 weeks) or a cocktail (equal parts viscous lidocaine, antacid, and diphenhydramine [Benadryl]) may control symptoms. Once-a-day PPI therapy is useful to prevent aggravation by reflux. Education about the proper method for taking medication may prevent recurrence.

Radiation esophagitis occurs from radiation therapy to the chest at dose levels that exceed 30 Gy (3000 rads). At levels higher than 60 Gy, severe esophagitis and ulceration can develop, leading to hemorrhage, perforation, or fistula. Concomitant chemotherapy with cytotoxic agents (e.g., doxorubicin [Adriamycin]) can potentiate radiation injury. Substernal pain, odynophagia, and dysphagia are typical. Barium swallow and endoscopy can demonstrate the extent and severity of mucosal inflammation, ulceration, and luminal narrowing; endoscopy has the added benefit of biopsy for exclusion of infectious esophagitis. Liquid diet or intravenous fluids plus the treatments described for pill-induced esophagitis are helpful. Strictures may require bougienage for dilation or even esophagectomy with a colonic or jejunal interposition.

Eosinophilic esophagitis is an uncommon entity that may be due to topical food allergy or represent part of a systemic atopic condition. Chest pain, heartburn, dysphagia, and food impaction can occur. Esophageal biopsy characteristically shows high (>20/high-power field) concentrations of mucosal eosinophils. Skin testing and RAST for allergy should be performed to identify and remove the offending agent. Elemental diets or therapy with oral cromolyn or glucocorticoids may also control symptoms.

Caustic esophagitis (Chapter 106) occurs from accidental ingestion in children and from suicidal attempts in adults. Among the more common materials ingested are drain cleaners (sodium hydroxide), bleach (sodium hypochlorite), detergents (sodium tripolyphosphates), and disc batteries (sodium hydroxide). Sodium hydroxide (lye) produces a liquefaction necrosis on contact with the oropharynx and esophagus, potentially causing acute ulceration, perforation, and later stricture formation. When perforation is excluded by contrast (diatrizoate [Gastrografin] and, if negative, barium) swallows, endoscopy may be of value to assess esophageal injury, but passage of the scope beyond an area of severe injury is not recommended to avoid perforation. Emergency esophagogastrectomy is indicated for free perforation and mediastinitis. In the absence of these complications, esophagitis is treated supportively with intravenous fluids and prophylactic antibiotics. Steroids in tapering dosage are often given but are without proven efficacy. A feeding tube is passed under direct vision to provide nutrition and to provide a means for later dilation of a tight stricture.

ESOPHAGEAL MOTOR DISORDERS

Esophageal motor disease may present with chest pain, dysphagia, or both. Dysphagia is for liquids as well as solids. Chest pain may mimic cardiac disease (Chapter 46), which must be excluded before esophageal motor disease is evaluated.

Oropharyngeal dysphagia is due to neuromuscular disorders of the oropharynx and the skeletal muscle portion of the esophagus, including stroke, Parkinson's disease, amyotrophic lateral sclerosis, multiple sclerosis, myasthenia gravis, polymyositis, and myotonic dystrophy. It is characterized by difficulty in bolus transfer from mouth to esophagus, with nasal regurgitation or coughing (from aspiration) with swallowing. Oropharyngeal dysphagia commonly occurs amid other signs and symptoms of the underlying neuromuscular disorder. A modified barium swallow with videofluoroscopy is the procedure of choice. The swallows are performed using barium of different consistencies and with the subject swallowing in different head and body positions. Nutritional support via diet, swallow maneuvers, feeding tubes, or percutaneous endoscopic gastrostomy is appropriate, whereas primary therapy is directed at the primary neuromuscular disorder.

Esophageal dysphagia is due to disease of the smooth muscle–lined portion of the esophagus. Dysphagia is not accompanied by failure of bolus transfer from mouth to esophagus, nasal regurgitation, or coughing with swallowing. Dysphagia characteristically occurs with liquids as well as solids, indicating a lack of discrimination for bolus size. Achalasia and diffuse esophageal spasm are primary esophageal motor disorders, whereas scleroderma (Chapter 281) is the most common secondary disorder. Nutcracker esophagus, hypertensive LES, and ineffective peristalsis are best viewed as manometric abnormalities found in association with, but not necessarily causative for, symptoms. Manometry is the diagnostic procedure of choice because it yields both quantitative and qualitative information about peristaltic and sphincter function.

ACHALASIA. Achalasia is the most common primary esophageal motor disorder, with a prevalence of about 10/100,000 population. Its etiology is unknown, and it can occur at any age but usually between ages 30 and 60 years. Achalasia is characterized histopathologically by degeneration of the nerves in Auerbach's plexus, though changes also occur in the vagus nerve and swallowing center. The consequences of neuronal injury are an increase in LES pressure, incomplete relaxation of the LES with swallowing (achalasia means "failure to relax"), and complete (100%) aperistalsis in the esophageal body. Failure of the LES to relax produces an obstruction at the gastroesophageal junction that leads to esophageal retention. Dilation of the esophageal body occurs due to the increase in intraluminal pressure and the presence of weak, aperistaltic contractions. Symptoms are chronic.

Dysphagia for liquids and solids is the primary complaint. Regurgitation is common, and nocturnal cough suggests aspiration on reclining. Atypical chest pain and heartburn occur in about one third of cases due to increased intraesophageal pressure and stasis-induced mucosal inflammation, respectively. Weight loss is highly variable and should raise concerns about adenocarcinoma of the esophagus or gastric cardia. Chagas' disease, due to *Trypanosoma cruzi* and prevalent in South America (Chapter 394), can mimic achalasia by producing a megaesophagus.

The chest radiograph may show a widened mediastinum, air-fluid level, and absent gastric air bubble. Barium swallow characteristically shows a dilated esophagus, air-fluid level, delayed esophageal emptying, and a smooth, tapered "bird's beak" deformity at the LES (Fig. 136–5). Confirmation is by esophageal manometry showing the characteristic incomplete relaxation of the LES with swallows and complete aperistalsis in the esophageal body. LES pressure may or may not be elevated. However, neither radiographic nor manometric criteria can effectively exclude achalasia secondary to cancer. For this reason, endoscopy must be performed prior to treatment. A muscle relaxant, such as nifedipine 10 mg sublingually before meals, may be helpful. More effective treatment requires either endoscopic injection of botulinum toxin into the LES (20 units per quadrant), pneumatic dilation, or surgical Heller myotomy. The benefits of botulinum toxin are relatively short lived (3 to 6 months) compared with pneumatic dilation, so repeated injections are necessary for the life of the patient.[3] Pneumatic dilation under conscious sedation inflates a balloon (3- to 4-cm diameter) placed across the LES to rupture its musculature; repeated treatment may be necessary for maximum benefit. A surgical Heller myotomy, which involves direct incision of the LES, is usually done laparoscopically. Success rates with pneumatic dilation or Heller myotomy are comparable, with excellent relief of symptoms for 5 to 10 years in about 85% of subjects. The major risk of pneumatic dilation is esophageal perforation (average ~3%), and the major side effect of Heller myotomy is reflux esophagitis (~25%). Many surgeons currently combine an antireflux procedure with the Heller myotomy to reduce the risk of postoperative GERD.

DIFFUSE ESOPHAGEAL SPASM. This uncommon motor disorder presents clinically with chest pain, dysphagia, or both. It remains one of the most commonly sought (but uncommonly found) conditions in

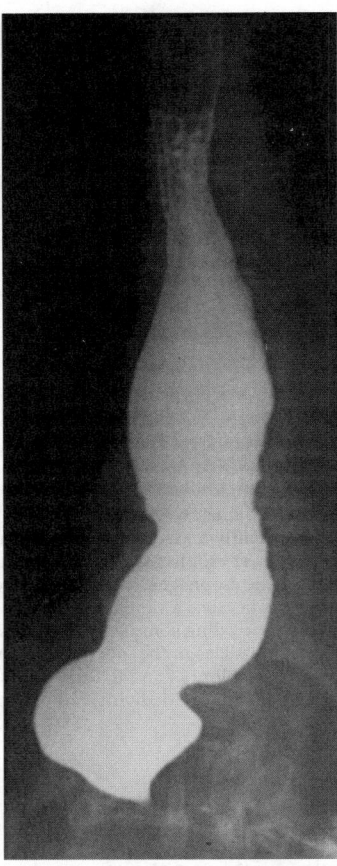

FIGURE 136–5 • Esophagram of a patient with idiopathic achalasia. Note the dilated esophagus with air-fluid level and distal tapering providing a "bird's beak" deformity in the area of the LES. (From Feldman M, Friedman LS, Sleisenger MH [eds]: Sleisenger and Fordtran's Gastrointestinal and Liver Disease: Pathophysiology, Diagnosis, Management, 7th ed. Philadelphia, WB Saunders, 2002.)

patients with noncardiac chest pain. Further, since its symptoms and signs are intermittent, diagnosis may be difficult on routine testing. Like achalasia, diffuse esophageal spasm is associated with degeneration of the nerves in Auerbach's plexus, and, in rare instances, diffuse esophageal spasm has been reported to evolve to achalasia. On barium swallow, idiopathic diffuse esophageal spasm has prominent, spontaneous, nonpropulsive, tertiary contractions that can give rise to the appearance of a "corkscrew" esophagus (Fig. 136–6). This appearance, however, is not pathognomonic since it is also observed in asymptomatic elderly patients, hence the term *presbyesophagus*. The criteria for diagnosing diffuse esophageal spasm on esophageal manometry also lack precision. Although multipeaked and repetitive contractions are reasonably specific, the manometric diagnosis of diffuse esophageal spasm requires exclusion of similar manometric abnormalities from diseases such as diabetes mellitus (Chapter 242), amyloid (Chapter 290), scleroderma (Chapter 281), idiopathic pseudo-obstruction, and reflux esophagitis.

Therapy is principally supportive and empirical. Recommendations include reassurance of the benign nature of the disease, a trial of smooth muscle relaxants (e.g., isosorbide 10 mg, nifedipine 10 mg, or dicyclomine [Bentyl] 20 mg before meals) or a trial of an antidepressant (e.g., amitriptyline 25 to 75 mg at bedtime, imipramine 25 to 50 mg at bedtime, and trazodone 50 mg three times a day). In some instances, relaxation exercises, biofeedback, and psychological counseling are helpful adjuncts to drug therapy.

SCLERODERMA. The esophagus is the gastrointestinal organ most often affected in scleroderma (Chapter 281), resulting in a characteristic manometric pattern of low LES pressure and weak aperistaltic contractions in the smooth muscle part of the esophageal body. UES and skeletal muscle–lined upper esophageal contractions are normal. Esophageal involvement in scleroderma results in dysphagia, regurgitation, and heartburn. When dysphagia for solids is prominent, it likely reflects a peptic stricture or adenocarcinoma in Barrett's

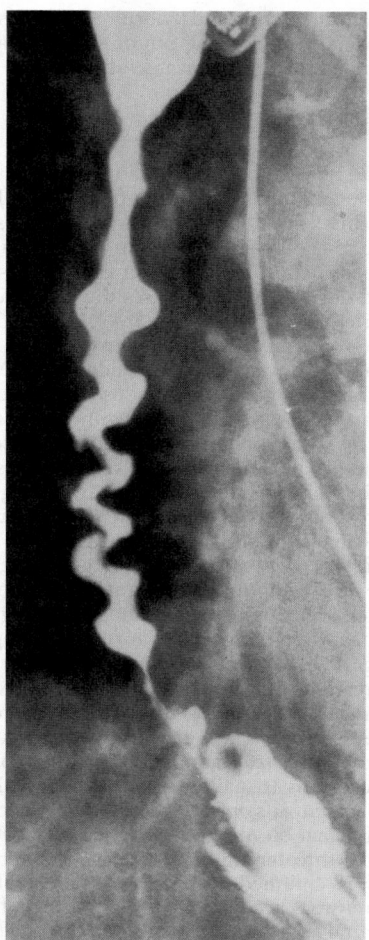

FIGURE 136–6 • Barium esophagram showing a "corkscrew" esophagus in a patient with diffuse esophageal spasm. The patient had dysphagia and chest pain and a normal endoscopy. (From Feldman M [ed]: Gastroenterology and Hepatology: The Comprehensive Visual Reference. New York, Churchill Livingstone, 1997.)

esophagus. Patients with scleroderma should be treated prophylactically as recommended for GERD.

NUTCRACKER ESOPHAGUS. *Nutcracker esophagus* is a term given to a relatively common manometric pattern found in patients with noncardiac chest pain. This pattern consists of normal peristalsis but with contractions of very high amplitude (average > 180 mm Hg). However, reduction in contraction amplitude by calcium-channel blockers has no consistent effect on chest pain, and chest pain can be relieved by medications (e.g., trazodone) having no effect on amplitude. Patients with chest pain and nutcracker esophagus commonly exhibit symptoms and signs of depression or anxiety. Treatment of these disorders with (1) amitriptyline (25 to 75 mg at bedtime), imipramine (25 to 50 mg at bedtime), and trazodone (50 mg three times a day), or (2) alprazolam (0.25 to 0.5 mg three times a day) and clonazepam (0.5 to 1 mg twice a day) may relieve chest pain.

ESOPHAGEAL TUMORS

Tumors of the esophagus may be benign or malignant. Benign tumors are uncommon and include fibrovascular polyps, leiomyomas, papillomas, lipomas, neurofibromas, and granular cell tumors. When large, benign tumors can cause dysphagia or chest pain from obstruction or stretch. Malignant tumors of the esophagus in the United States occur currently at a rate of about 12,000 cases per year, divided about equally between squamous cell carcinomas and adenocarcinomas. Rare primary malignancies include leiomyosarcoma, melanoma, lymphoma, and plasmacytoma. Tumors metastatic to esophagus usually originate from breast, lung, or skin (melanoma).

SQUAMOUS CELL CARCINOMA. The incidence of squamous cell carcinoma in the United States is about 2.6/100,000, with men having a threefold to fourfold higher risk than women and blacks having a fourfold to fivefold higher risk than whites. Regions of high risk also exist in the Transkei of South Africa, China's Linxian and Yangcheng provinces, and Kashmir and Bombay in India. The risk for squamous cancer is higher with heavy alcohol and tobacco use, papillomavirus infection, lye ingestion, achalasia, Plummer-Vinson syndrome, tylosis, celiac disease, and radiation exposure. Clinical presentation typically is with rapidly progressive dysphagia for solids, anorexia, and weight loss. Less commonly, squamous cell carcinoma presents with hypercalcemia (pseudohyperparathyroidism), hoarseness (recurrent laryngeal nerve paralysis), or tracheoesophageal fistula. A barium swallow usually reveals a bulky, eroded, partially obstructing esophageal mass that is proven to be squamous cell carcinoma by endoscopic biopsy. Adjacent lymph node invasion is common because the esophagus lacks a serosal layer. Hematogenous metastases usually spread to liver, lungs, kidney, heart, and bone. Endoscopic ultrasonography and/or computed tomographic (CT) scans are used for staging. Squamous cell carcinoma is radiosensitive, and chemoradiation, with or without subsequent surgery, can improve outcome.■ Nonetheless, late-stage presentation is the rule, so overall 5-year survival is only 20 to 30%. Palliation for inoperable, obstructing cancers may be achieved by bougienage, tumor ablation by laser, heater probe or alcohol injection, or endoscopic stent placement.

ADENOCARCINOMA. Although squamous cell carcinoma was the dominant form of esophageal malignancy 30 years ago, a rapid rise in incidence of esophageal adenocarcinoma over this period, particularly in white men, has made their current cancer rates (~6000 cases per year) about equal. Adenocarcinomas, unlike squamous cancers, arise principally in the distal esophagus (see Fig. 132–7) because the predominant risk of adenocarcinoma comes from the presence of Barrett's esophagus, a complication of GERD. Since only one half of those with Barrett's have heartburn, one half the Barrett's population is undiagnosed and so not subject to endoscopic surveillance. Lymphatic spread is common. Adenocarcinomas are radioinsensitive; although chemoradiation and surgery may improve survival,[4] the 5-year survival rates are less than 10%. Palliation is the same as for inoperable squamous cell carcinoma.

STRUCTURAL ABNORMALITIES

PHARYNGOESOPHAGEAL DIVERTICULA. Esophageal diverticula include Zenker's diverticula, mid-esophageal and epiphrenic diverticula, and intramural pseudodiverticulosis. *Zenker's diverticulum* is an outpouching of pharyngeal mucosa in an area of muscular weakness (Killian's triangle) just proximal to the cricopharyngeus muscle (UES). It results from an incoordination between pharyngeal peristalsis and UES opening. When small, the Zenker's diverticulum produces no symptoms; but when large, it leads to dysphagia, regurgitation of undigested food, halitosis, neck pain and swelling, and aspiration. The diagnosis is made by barium swallow (Fig. 136–7), and treatment is cricopharyngeal myotomy with or without diverticulectomy. *Midesophageal and epiphrenic diverticula* are uncommon and arise either from pulsion, such as esophageal motor disorder, or traction, such as paraesophageal inflammatory or neoplastic disease. Most are small, wide-mouthed outpouchings and are asymptomatic. When large, they may be associated with dysphagia, regurgitation, aspiration, or chest pain. Diagnosis is made on barium swallow or endoscopy, and treatment is by surgical diverticulectomy. *Esophageal intramural pseudodiverticulosis* is an uncommon condition noted on barium swallow in which numerous, small flask-shaped outpouchings are evident within the esophageal wall. These outpouchings represent dilation of the secretory ducts of the esophageal submucosal glands and arise in the setting of mucosal inflammation or esophageal obstruction. The pseudodiverticula produce no symptoms but occur in the setting of chest pain, dysphagia, heartburn, and odynophagia, reflecting the associated underlying disease. Treatment is directed at the underlying disease.

ESOPHAGEAL RINGS AND WEBS. The distal esophagus contains two rings, designated as the *A ring* and *B ring*, which on barium swallow demarcate the proximal and distal borders of the esophageal vestibule, respectively. The A ring is a broad (4- to 5-mm) band of hypertrophied muscle covered by squamous epithelium. It is rare and usually asymptomatic; but when associated with dysphagia, it can be treated by bougienage or by endoscopic injection with botulinum toxin. The *B,* or *Schatzki's, ring,* a thin (2-mm) membrane consisting of mucosa and submucosa, is localized to the squamocolumnar junction. It is found in about 15% of barium studies and is often asymptomatic.

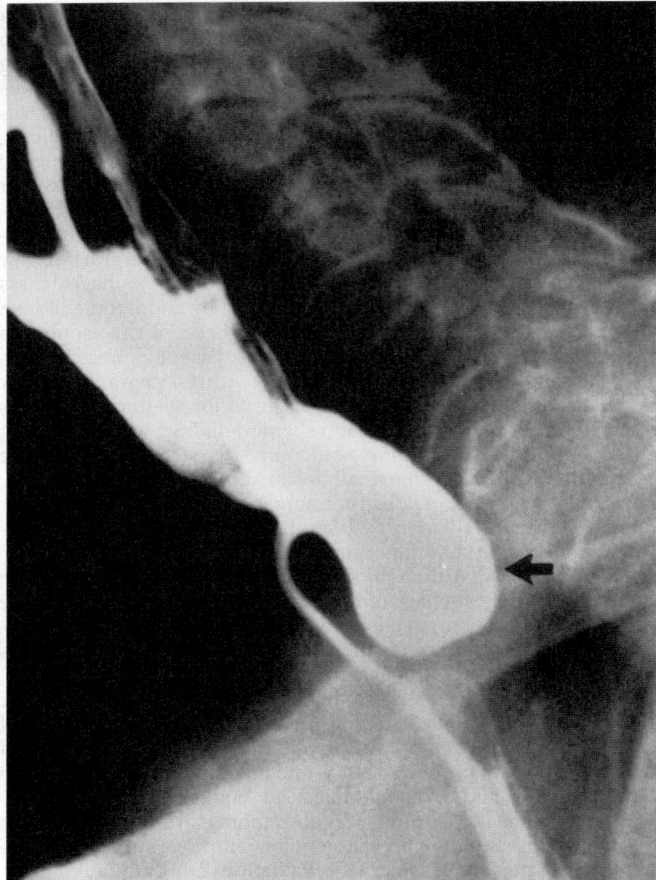

FIGURE 136–7 • Barium esophagram showing a Zenker's diverticulum (arrow). This elderly patient complained of dysphagia, choking with eating, and recurrent pneumonia. (From Feldman M [ed]: Gastroenterology and Hepatology: The Comprehensive Visual Reference. New York, Churchill Livingstone, 1997.)

Schatzki's rings are probably congenital in origin. When the ring constricts the esophageal lumen to less than 15 mm, dysphagia for solids usually occurs. Diagnosis is by barium swallow (see Fig. 136–1B), often aided by swallowing a marshmallow or barium tablet. When symptomatic, treatment is to fracture the ring by esophageal bougienage. *Esophageal webs* are thin, fragile membranes of stratified squamous epithelium that occur in the upper and mid-esophagus. Unlike rings, these congenital anomalies rarely encircle the lumen but instead protrude, as a shelf, from the anterior wall. Webs are usually asymptomatic and diagnosed incidentally on barium swallow. Upper endoscopy can detect the webs but may rupture them without awareness of their presence. Webs, like rings, can cause dysphagia for solids only and, when symptomatic, are treated by esophageal bougienage. Cervical webs associated with dysphagia and iron deficiency anemia are part of the Plummer-Vinson or Paterson-Kelly syndrome (Chapter 167). This syndrome occurs primarily in women and is associated with an increased risk of sprue and squamous cell carcinoma of the pharynx and esophagus.

HERNIAS. The two major types are sliding hiatal hernias and paraesophageal hernias. A *hiatal hernia* is an acquired anomaly in which the esophagogastric junction and stomach project above the diaphragm and into the chest. It is identified in about 15% of upper gastrointestinal series, usually as an incidental finding. Hernias are thought to arise from age-related loss of elasticity of the phrenoesophageal ligament or widening of the right crus of the diaphragm. Hiatal hernias are common in GERD. They also occasionally cause gastric erosions, iron deficiency anemia, and gastrointestinal bleeding due to ischemia or mechanical trauma to the herniated gastric mucosa. Treatment is usually medical (acid inhibitors, mucosal-coating agents), but surgical correction is necessary in refractory cases. *Paraesophageal hernias* are uncommon and result from a defect in the phrenoesophageal membrane. Since the gastroesophageal junction remains fixed, the stomach then herniates into the chest, causing close apposition of

the gastroesophageal junction and pylorus. Symptoms may be absent, but pain, dysphagia, and bleeding can occur. Surgical repair is generally recommended to prevent incarceration.

MISCELLANEOUS CONDITIONS

FOREIGN BODIES. Foreign bodies commonly lodge in the esophagus either at regions of anatomic narrowing (e.g., UES, LES, aorta or left mainstem bronchus) or regions of pathology (e.g., stricture, ring). Symptoms include neck pain, chest pain, dysphagia, or odynophagia. Complete obstruction by the object carries a risk of aspiration pneumonia, and delayed relief increases the risk of ulceration, perforation, and stricture.

In the absence of clinical evidence for perforation, foreign bodies are diagnosed and removed by upper endoscopy. During removal, airway protection is essential. Rigid endoscopy under general anesthesia by an otolaryngologist is an alternative means for the safe retrieval of objects from the hypopharynx or proximal esophagus. Meat impaction in the distal esophagus may respond to smooth muscle relaxation by administration of 1 mg of intravenous glucagon; ingestion of a papain solution is not recommended because of potential for coincident damage to the esophageal wall.

ESOPHAGEAL TRAUMA. The esophagus, though protected by the bony thorax, is subject to being torn or ruptured by blunt chest trauma (e.g., motor vehicle accident) or a penetrating sharp (e.g., knife) wound. However, most tears and perforations are either iatrogenic, resulting from esophagogastric diagnostic or therapeutic instrumentation, or from abrupt increases in intraluminal pressure during vomiting, retching, and coughing. When increased intraluminal pressure causes a mucosal tear just below or through the esophagogastric junction, it is called a *Mallory-Weiss tear;* and when it causes complete rupture of the distal esophagus (usually on the left side), the condition is referred to as *Boerhaave's syndrome.* The consequence of a mucosal tear is gastrointestinal bleeding, which may stop spontaneously or continue with life-threatening hemorrhage (Chapter 133). Cervical rupture usually is confined and leads to periesophageal abscess. Intrathoracic rupture is accompanied by chest pain, fever, soft tissue emphysema, pleural effusion, pneumothorax, and mediastinitis. Intraabdominal segment rupture leads to peritonitis and sepsis. For tears with bleeding, upper endoscopy is the procedure of choice, both for diagnosis and, when needed, for control of bleeding by epinephrine injection and cautery (Chapters 132 and 133). If endoscopic control fails, emergency angiography with embolization or vasopressin infusion, exploratory laparotomy to oversew the tear, or balloon tamponade with a Sengstaken-Blakemore or Minnesota tube can be lifesaving. For esophageal perforations, diagnosis is by physical examination and chest radiograph to demonstrate extraluminal air, confirmed by a leak on a diatrizoate swallow. If diatrizoate swallow is negative, barium may be used. CT scanning also can be helpful. Early recognition (first 24 hours) of an esophageal rupture should prompt primary surgical closure, external drainage, and antibiotics. Later recognition in a clinically stable patient with a walled-off abscess in the neck or mediastinum may be treated medically with nasogastric suction, antibiotics, and parenteral nutrition.

DEVELOPMENTAL ANOMALIES. Congenital anomalies of the esophagus are relatively common at 1 : 3000 to 1 : 4500 live births. Most are diagnosed in childhood or early adolescence. However, an *aberrant right subclavian artery* can present later in life with dysphagia arising from vascular compression of the esophagus. Diagnosis is suggested by barium esophagogram showing a pencil-like indentation near the fourth thoracic vertebra. The diagnosis is confirmed by CT scan, magnetic resonance imaging, or endoscopic ultrasound. Treatment is often by diet modification, but in refractory cases, surgery is required to reanastomose the artery to the ascending aorta.

1. Lundell L, Miettinen P, Myrvold HE, et al: Long-term management of gastroesophageal reflux disease with omeprazole or open antireflux surgery: Results of a prospective, randomized clinical trial. The Nordic GORD Study Group. Eur J Gastroenterol Hepatol 2000;12:879–887.
2. Spechler SJ, Lee E, Ahnen D, et al: Long-term outcome of medical and surgical therapies for gastroesophageal reflux disease: Follow-up of a randomized controlled trial. JAMA 2001;285:2331–2338.
3. Vaezi MF, Richter JE, Wilcox CM, et al: Botulinum toxin versus pneumatic dilatation in the treatment of achalasia: A randomised trial. Gut 1999;44:231–239.
4. Cooper JS, Guo MD, Herskovic A, et al: Chemoradiotherapy of locally advanced esophageal cancer: Long-term follow-up of a prospective randomized trial (RTOG 85-01). Radiation Therapy Oncology Group. JAMA 1999;281:1623–1627.

SUGGESTED READINGS

Baden LR: Gastrointestinal infections in the immunocompromised host. Infect Dis Clin North Am 2001;15:639–670. *Diagnosis and treatment of common causes of infectious esophagitis in the immunocompromised host.*

Corley DA, Kerlikowske K, Verma R, et al: Protective association of aspirin/NSAIDs and esophageal cancer: A systematic review and meta-analysis. Gastroenterology 2003;124:47–56. *Chronic use of aspirin and nonsteroidal anti-inflammatory drugs may reduce the risk of esophageal adenocarcinoma and squamous cell carcinoma.*

Orlando L, Orlando RC: Reflux esophagitis: Evaluation of drug management strategies. Formulary 2002;37:140–146. *A timely overview of modern drug therapy for patients with gastroesophageal reflux disease.*

Richter JE: Oesophageal motility disorders. Lancet 2001;358:823–828. *Overview of conditions that fall under the broad category of esophageal motor disease.*

Shaheen N, Ransohoff DF: Gastroesophageal reflux, Barrett esophagus, and esophageal cancer: Scientific review. JAMA 2002;287:1972–1981. *Insufficient evidence exists to endorse routine endoscopic screening of patients with chronic GERD symptoms.*

137 GASTRITIS AND HELICOBACTER PYLORI

David Y. Graham

Robert M. Genta

Gastritis is defined as inflammation of the gastric mucosa, regardless of its etiology. The term *gastropathy* is reserved for mucosal alterations resulting from chemical injuries or vascular disturbances. Although gastropathies may be mediated by inflammatory mechanisms, mucosal infiltration by polymorphonuclear or mononuclear cells is not a key histopathologic feature. The modern classification of gastritis incorporates etiology and morphologic and topographic attributes (Table 137–1).

HELICOBACTER PYLORI–INDUCED GASTRITIS

Helicobacter pylori is a gram-negative microaerophilic organism with many attributes that allow it to have a unique ecologic niche in the human stomach (Table 137–2). The inflammation induced by *H. pylori* is usually superficial, preferentially located in the foveolar or gastric pit region and upper portion of the lamina propria, and consists of mononuclear cells and polymorphonuclear leukocytes. This mixed infiltrate is commonly termed *chronic active inflammation*. The antrum consistently is involved, whereas inflammation in the acid-secreting gastric body and fundus is more variable. *H. pylori* infection is causally associated with gastritis, duodenal and gastric ulcer (Chapter 138), gastric adenocarcinoma (Chapter 199), and primary gastric B-cell lymphomas of mucosa-associated lymphoid tissue

Table 137–2 • FEATURES OF THE UNIQUE ECOLOGIC NICHE FOR *HELICOBACTER PYLORI*

Colonization
Motility
Urease
Adhesion to surface epithelial cells
Virulence (noninvasive, owing to release of bacterial factors)
Epithelial cytolysis and tight junction disruption by cytotoxins
Induction of inflammatory immune response: chemotaxins, lipopolysaccharide, immune modulators, antigenic stimulation, epithelial cytokines
Persistence
Inaccessibility
Immune evasion

Table 137–1 • CLASSIFICATION OF CHRONIC GASTRITIS BASED ON TOPOGRAPHY, MORPHOLOGY, AND ETIOLOGY

TYPE OF GASTRITIS	ETIOLOGIC FACTORS	GASTRITIS SYNONYMS
Nonatrophic	H. pylori	Superficial
	? Other factors	Diffuse antral gastritis
		Chronic antral gastritis
		Interstitial—follicular
		Hypersecretory
		Type B
Atrophic		
Autoimmune	Autoimmunity	Type A
	? H. pylori	Diffuse corporeal
		Pernicious anemia–associated
Multifocal atrophic	H. pylori	Type B, type AB
	Environmental factors	Environmental
		Metaplastic
		Atrophic pangastritis
		Progressive intestinalizing pangastritis
Special forms		
Chemical	Chemical irritation	Reactive
	Bile	Reflux
	NSAIDs	
	? Other agents	
Radiation	Radiation injury	
Lymphocytic	? Idiopathic	Varioliform
	? Autoimmune mechanisms	Celiac disease–associated
	? Gluten	
	Drugs	
	? H. pylori	
Noninfectious granulomatous	Crohn's disease	
	Sarcoidosis	
	Wegener's granulomatosis	
	Foreign substances	
	? Idiopathic	Isolated granulomatous
Eosinophilic	Food sensitivity	Allergic
	? Other allergies	
Other infectious gastritides	Bacteria (other than H. pylori)	Phlegmonous, syphilitic
	Viruses	Cytomegalovirus
	Fungi	Anisakiasis
	Parasites	

NSAID = nonsteroidal anti-inflammatory drug.

(MALT) (Chapter 195). Infected subjects have about a one in six life-time risk of peptic ulcer; the lifetime risk of gastric cancer varies from 1 to 3% in the United States to more than 12% in Japan.

Epidemiology

H. pylori causes a chronic, serious infection. *H. pylori* shares with syphilis and tuberculosis the features of a long latent period, a small proportion of infected individuals experiencing clinical illness, and a male predominance of clinical disease despite equal infection rates in both sexes. Humans are the only known reservoir. Transmission is opportunistic in that any method that allows the organism access to the stomach is likely to be a mode of transmission. The most common modes of transmission involve lapses in household hygiene or ingestion of contaminated food or water; water-borne infection has been documented but not in the United States. Infection may result from exposure to gastric juice of infected individuals (*oral-gastric*), including contaminated nasogastric tubes or endoscopes. The infection typically is acquired in childhood; adults tend to become infected when children are in the family. The epidemiology of *H. pylori* reflects a pattern typical of person-to-person transmission with high prevalence at a young age in developing countries and in impoverished subpopulations in developed countries. Because the rate of acquisition has been decreasing in developed countries, older individuals have a higher prevalence than younger individuals, reflecting their higher rates of acquisition at a young age. This decrease possibly is related to the increasingly high levels of hygiene, which limit transmission, and the widespread use of antibiotics for other infections, which may cure a portion of the existing *H. pylori* infections. In the United States and other developed countries, the decrease in prevalence of *H. pylori* infection parallels the decrease in the incidence of peptic ulcer and noncardiac gastric adenocarcinoma.

Clinical Course

ACUTE *HELICOBACTER PYLORI* GASTRITIS. With acute *H. pylori* infection, a diffuse gastritis develops, often in association with epigastric pain, nausea, and vomiting. The diagnosis rarely is considered because the symptoms generally last for a few days to a week. Clinically, acute *H. pylori* gastritis can be diagnosed by a positive urea breath test or by the combination of positive histology and negative serology for anti–*H. pylori* IgG.

DISTRIBUTION AND PROGRESSION: RELATION TO PEPTIC ULCER AND GASTRIC CANCER. *H. pylori* causes progressive damage to the gastric structure and function. Follow-up histopathology of subjects with gastritis over extended periods (years to decades) shows that gastritis, initially confined to the antrum (Fig. 137–1), often expands proximally to involve the entire stomach (pangastritis). *H. pylori* pangastritis is the phenotype that carries the highest risk for gastric adenocarcinoma (Chapter 199). The rate of progression varies in different regions of the world, being rapid in regions with high rates of gastric cancer and slow in regions where duodenal ulcer is common. The pattern of gastritis predicts clinical outcome. Duodenal ulcer is associated with antrum-predominant gastritis (Chapter 138), with minimal involvement of the

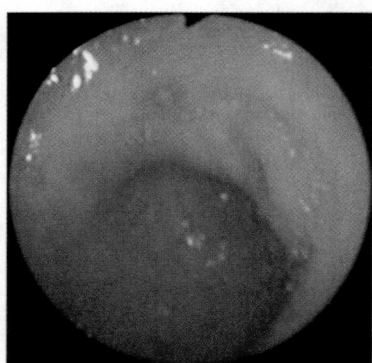

FIGURE 137–1 • Gastric erosions. The patient had been experiencing dyspeptic symptoms for 2 months. Endoscopy revealed numerous small "aphthous erosions," and antral biopsy revealed *Helicobacter pylori* infection. The patient responded to "triple therapy." (From Forbes CD, Jackson WF: Color Atlas and Text of Clinical Medicine, 3rd ed. London, Mosby, 2003, with permission.)

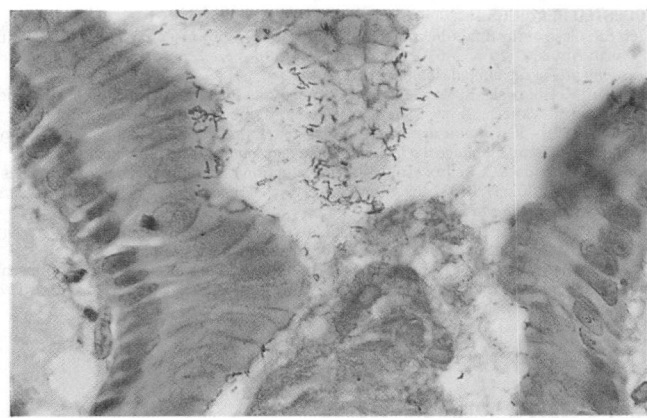

FIGURE 137–2 • *Helicobacter pylori* infection demonstrated on gastric antral biopsy (Warthin-Starry/Alcian green stain). Numerous black-staining organisms are seen in the mucous layer on the epithelial surface and in the crypt at bottom left. The mucus protects the organisms from attack by gastric acid and by antimicrobial therapy. (From Forbes CD, Jackson WF: Color Atlas and Text of Clinical Medicine, 3rd ed. London, Mosby, 2003, with permission.)

fundic gland mucosa; progression occurs at a slow rate. The clinical correlate is that patients with duodenal ulcer secrete acid at high-normal or high rates and have a lower risk of gastric cancer. In contrast to patients with duodenal ulcer, patients with gastric ulcer tend to have more severe antral gastritis, more frequent superficial fundic gland gastritis, and low-normal acid secretion. The variability in the distribution and progression of *H. pylori* gastritis among individuals is probably due to interactions among the infecting strain, the host, and the environment.

Pangastritis eventually causes destruction of the oxyntic glands, which may be replaced by fibrosis, pseudopyloric metaplasia (the parietal and chief cells of fundic glands are replaced by mucus glands indistinguishable from normal antrum), and intestinal metaplasia (mucin-containing goblet cells, absorptive cells, and occasionally rudimentary villi). Metaplasia can progress to dysplastic epithelial changes as part of the evolution to gastric cancer (Chapter 199). Pangastritis and atrophic gastritis usually are associated with a decrease in maximal acid secretion.

Diagnosis

H. pylori can be detected using "noninvasive" modalities: serology with an enzyme-linked immunosorbent assay for IgG or IgA antibodies, ^{13}C-urea or ^{14}C-urea breath tests, or stool antigen testing (Chapter 138). Tests requiring endoscopy and biopsy include histologic examination (Fig. 137–2), urease testing of antral biopsy specimens, or culture (which is not routinely available). The optimal method depends on circumstances, local expertise, and availability. All tests have good sensitivity and specificity, but false-positive and false-negative determinations occur. In tests that depend on the number of organisms (testing breath and gastric biopsy specimens for urease activity, histology, and culture), false-negative results occur especially when the organism has been suppressed by antibiotics, proton-pump inhibitors, or bismuth. Therapy may need to be discontinued for several weeks before these tests become positive.

Rx Treatment

H. pylori infection is typically latent. *H. pylori* gastritis is found, however, in patients with dyspepsia more frequently than in age-matched controls. Nonetheless, cure of the infection resolves symptoms in only about 10% of patients with nonulcer dyspepsia. Because antibiotic therapy for *H. pylori* is less expensive and probably safer than additional diagnostic studies and long-term continuous antacid therapy, cure of *H. pylori* infection is a reasonable option for patients with persisting symptoms. In addition, cure of the infection reduces the risk of subsequent peptic ulcer and gastric cancer and eliminates the individual as a carrier who can transmit the infection. *H. pylori* testing and treatment are appropriate for new-onset or previously undiagnosed dyspepsia without alarm features (Chapters 135, 138, and 139).

ATROPHIC GASTRITIS

ATROPHIC PANGASTRITIS CAUSED BY *HELICOBACTER PYLORI*

The progressive destruction of oxyntic and antral glands that occurs during the course of *H. pylori*–associated pangastritis eventually may lead to atrophy. The resulting functional alterations are expressed first by hypochlorhydria and, in some subjects, achlorhydria. This change in the gastric environment disrupts the unique ecologic niche of *H. pylori* and allows the overgrowth of other bacteria. *H. pylori* eventually may disappear from the atrophic, metaplastic, and hypochlorhydric stomach. IgG and IgA antibodies to *H. pylori* usually begin to decrease within months after loss of the organism, but it may take years for the test to become negative. Autoimmune markers are generally absent from patients with *H. pylori* pangastritis, and only a small (and undefined) proportion of subjects develop secondary vitamin B_{12} deficiency. The contribution of other factors and the overlap with autoimmune gastritis and pernicious anemia remain to be clarified.

PERNICIOUS ANEMIA

Pernicious anemia (Chapter 175) is one of the late complications of autoimmune gastritis, which is characterized by severe chronic inflammation of the oxyntic mucosa, which results in the progressive loss of parietal cells, destruction of the oxyntic glands, and development of atrophy (with decreased or absent glandular elements and mucosal thinning) and extensive intestinal and pseudopyloric metaplasia. When glands atrophy, the inflammatory infiltrate may be minimal. Even with sufficient fundic gland atrophy to produce achlorhydria, some patchy nests of parietal and chief cells may persist. In pure autoimmune gastritis (i.e., without concurrent or previous *H. pylori* infection), the antrum remains normal so that many sick patients develop marked hypergastrinemia because there is no feedback inhibition of acid on gastrin release.

About 90% of patients with pernicious anemia have antibodies against parietal cells. Antibodies reacting with intrinsic factor block the vitamin B_{12} binding site, leading to depleted serum levels and body stores of vitamin B_{12} and a megaloblastic anemia (Chapter 175). Pernicious anemia also is associated with other immunologic disorders (e.g., Hashimoto's thyroiditis, hyperthyroidism, insulin-dependent diabetes mellitus, and vitiligo). Genetic factors are important in pernicious anemia; family members of patients have an increased incidence of atrophic gastritis, achlorhydria, vitamin B_{12} malabsorption, and antibodies to parietal cells and intrinsic factor.

Clinical Manifestations

Patients with pernicious anemia may develop symptoms secondary to vitamin B_{12} deficiency. Macroscopic endoscopic findings are nonspecific, and diagnosis requires gastric mucosal biopsies of the antrum and corpus. The ratio of pepsinogen I (present in fundic chief cells) to pepsinogen II (present in chief cells and surface epithelial cells) falls in proportion to glandular atrophy.

Enterochromaffin-like cells undergo hyperplasia in atrophic gastritis because the elevated gastrin levels exert trophic effects on them. These endocrine cells in the fundic gland mucosa contain histamine and are distinguished by characteristic granules and silver-staining properties. Enterochromaffin-like cells can form carcinoid tumors in atrophic gastritis. Enterochromaffin-like cell hyperplasia also occurs in Zollinger-Ellison (gastrinoma) syndrome (Chapter 140), but carcinoid tumors are largely restricted to patients with multiple endocrine neoplasia type I. Enterochromaffin-like cells do not contain serotonin, and these tumors do not produce the classic carcinoid syndrome found with tumors composed of serotonin-containing enterochromaffin cells (Chapter 245). Enterochromaffin-like carcinoids associated with hypergastrinemia are usually indolent, multifocal tumors that generally are managed by endoscopic excision. Antrectomy may be necessary in cases of multiple recurrences. In contrast, gastric carcinoids found without hypergastrinemia are solitary, aggressive tumors.

Rx Treatment

Other than replacing vitamin B_{12}, no specific therapy exists for pernicious anemia. It is reasonable to evaluate family members for gastritis and vitamin B_{12} deficiency. Gastric adenocarcinomas (Chapter 199) may occur more frequently in patients with pernicious anemia, but the assessment of increased risk is variable, ranging from none to threefold in different series. At the time of an initial diagnosis, endoscopic biopsy usually is recommended to obtain sufficient antral and fundic gland tissue to assess the severity of intestinal metaplasia and epithelial dysplasia; although the predictive value of these features is uncertain, they are the best available indicators of the cancer risk. Using this approach, only patients with dysplasia warrant close follow-up and/or surgical intervention. Otherwise, no recommendations regarding screening have been established.

EROSIVE-HEMORRHAGIC GASTROPATHY

CHEMICAL (OR REACTIVE) GASTROPATHY. An association between the presence of bile in the stomach and gastric mucosal damage (duodenogastric reflux) first was postulated by Beaumont in 1859, and several subsequent clinical observations led to the development of surgical techniques to prevent or minimize the regurgitation of duodenal contents into the stomach. The original term *bile reflux* has been replaced by *chemical gastritis,* to include nonsteroidal anti-inflammatory drug (NSAID)–induced changes in the gastric mucosa. The terms *reactive gastritis* and *chemical gastropathy* also have been used. Three categories of patients may exhibit the endoscopic and histologic changes of chemical gastropathy: (1) patients with alkaline reflux after a partial gastrectomy, (2) patients with duodenogastric bile reflux as part of a poorly understood dysmotility syndrome, and (3) patients who take NSAIDs.

Postgastrectomy alkaline reflux may present with a syndrome characterized by burning midepigastric pain unresponsive to antacids and aggravated by eating. Bilious vomiting, anemia, and weight loss may occur. Endoscopic confirmation of bile reflux and the characteristic histopathologic findings support the diagnosis, and corrective surgery (e.g., creation of a 40- to 50-cm Roux-en-Y gastrojejunostomy) is successful in about half of all cases.

Duodenogastric bile reflux owing to gastroduodenal dysmotility or to cholecystectomy is believed to be rare in patients with an intact stomach. This controversial condition rarely is considered in the differential diagnosis of dyspepsia. The frequency of endoscopic or histologic changes of chemical gastropathy in these patients is unknown. Duodenogastric reflux (with alkaline pancreaticoduodenal secretions and acids, bile salts, and lysolecithin) results in disruption of the mucus barrier and direct damage of chemicals to the gastric surface epithelium. Loss of the mucus barrier may allow back-diffusion of hydrogen ions, leading to accelerated exfoliation of surface epithelial cells and a histamine-mediated vascular response that manifests as edema and hyperemia. Persistent epithelial damage may lead to the release of other proinflammatory agents, such as platelet-derived growth factor, which among its many actions stimulates smooth muscle and, subsequently, fibroblastic proliferation.

Millions of people take daily doses of NSAIDs for indefinite periods, in many cases for life, to control pain caused by osteoarthritis, rheumatoid arthritis, or other chronic conditions. Histologically detectable reactive gastropathy has been documented in 10 to 45% of long-term users of NSAIDs, but no relationship has been established between the appearance of the mucosa and dyspeptic symptoms.

Epithelial injury after exposure to NSAIDs (Fig. 137–3) seems to be mediated by reduced prostaglandin synthesis. Prostaglandins are important cytoprotective agents in the gastric mucosa and exert their effects by maintaining mucosal blood flow, by increasing secretion of mucus and bicarbonate ions, and by augmenting epithelial defense against cytotoxic injury. NSAID-inflicted injury can be partially prevented by simultaneous administration of prostaglandin analogues, such as misoprostol, and by suppression of gastric acid production. New selective cyclooxygenase type 2 inhibitors are better tolerated by the gastric mucosa (Chapter 32).

The histopathologic changes of reactive gastropathy include evidence of epithelial regeneration, foveolar hyperplasia, edema of the lamina propria, and expansion of the smooth muscle fibers into the upper third of the mucosa, an area in which they normally are not

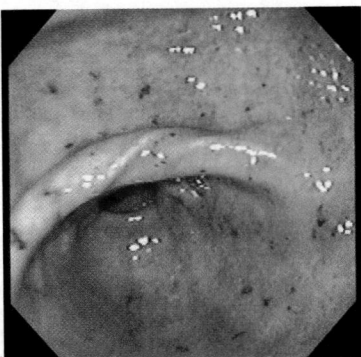

FIGURE 137–3 • Gastropathy caused by nonsteroidal anti-inflammatory drugs. Note the petechial hemorrhages.

found. *H. pylori* infection induces some of the same features traditionally considered characteristic of chemical gastropathy, however. The pathologist can suspect chemical gastropathy and communicate this suspicion to the clinician, but a firm diagnosis can be made only when supportive clinical data are available and *H. pylori* infection is absent.

STRESS-RELATED MUCOSAL DAMAGE AND ULCERS. See Chapter 138.

ALCOHOL GASTROPATHY. Characteristic subepithelial (intramucosal) hemorrhages, with the endoscopic appearance of "blood under a plastic wrap," sometimes are found in individuals who abuse alcohol. Termed *hemorrhagic gastritis*, these lesions are composed of hemorrhage and edema in the interstitial space under the surface epithelium, without accompanying inflammation. Clinical bleeding usually does not occur. When bleeding is found, associated lesions, such as portal hypertension, peptic ulcer, or a Mallory-Weiss tear, should be sought (Chapter 133).

SPECIAL FORMS OF GASTRITIS

PHLEGMONOUS GASTRITIS. Phlegmonous gastritis is a rare, purulent process involving the gastric submucosa and wall. α-Hemolytic streptococci, staphylococci, *Escherichia coli*, and *Proteus* have been implicated. The course is usually fulminant, and medical management is generally ineffective; surgery is usually unavoidable.

OTHER INFECTIONS. Herpes simplex virus type 1 has been implicated as a cause of ulcer disease in normal hosts (Chapter 138). The *Ascaris*-like larva, *Anisakis* (Chapter 404), present in raw fish, may penetrate the gastric mucosa, producing pain and dyspepsia. Rare cases of disseminated *Strongyloides stercoralis* infection (Chapter 404) have involved the stomach.

In immunocompromised hosts, a variety of types of infectious gastritis occur. Gastric tuberculosis (Chapter 341), diagnosed by caseating granulomas and positive cultures, occurs in acquired immunodeficiency syndrome. Secondary syphilis (Chapter 349) may involve the stomach with thickened folds and erosions. Cytomegalovirus also can involve the stomach. Whether *Candida* causes gastric ulcers is controversial; mycelia may occur at the margins of gastric ulcers, but healing does not seem to be impaired, and antifungal therapy does not accelerate healing, suggesting colonization rather than an infectious cause.

CHRONIC EROSIVE (DIFFUSE VARIOLIFORM) GASTRITIS. In chronic erosive vasculitis, multiple gastric erosions occur on the top of small nodules, usually involving the body and fundus more than the antrum. The multiplicity and chronicity distinguish this entity from occasional isolated antral erosions found without symptoms. In most instances, this appearance is related to *H. pylori* or the use of NSAIDs. Symptoms are nonspecific and include abdominal pain, nausea, vomiting, anorexia, weight loss, and, sometimes, bleeding.

LYMPHOCYTIC GASTRITIS. Lymphocytic gastritis is characterized by large numbers of mature lymphocytes infiltrating the surface and foveola. Lymphocytic gastritis also may be found in endoscopically normal stomachs and in patients with celiac disease; chronic erosive (varioliform) gastritis, with numerous thickened folds capped by small nodules that contain a central erosion or ulceration, is associated with *H. pylori* infection. Lymphocytic gastritis is relatively rare, found in 1 to 4% of subjects who undergo endoscopy with biopsy. It is diagnosed most commonly in the 50s and seems to affect men and women equally. Patients with the varioliform type of lymphocytic gastritis are often symptomatic with rapid weight loss and anorexia; epigastric pain is not as common. Hypoproteinemia, hypoalbuminemia, and peripheral edema suggesting a protein-losing gastroenteropathy have been documented in approximately 20% of affected patients. Lymphocytic gastritis is a chronic disease, but spontaneous resolution can occur. When it is associated with gluten enteropathy, signs, symptoms, and clinical course are those of *celiac disease* (Chapter 141).

Lymphocytic gastritis generally is diagnosed if more than 25 intraepithelial lymphocytes are seen per 100 epithelial cells on a biopsy specimen. If *H. pylori* infection is present, immunohistochemistry to detect CD8+ T cells may be helpful; in pure lymphocytic gastritis, most intraepithelial lymphocytes are CD8+, whereas a heterogeneous infiltrate characterizes *H. pylori* gastritis.

When concurrent *H. pylori* infection is present, eradication should be attempted because it may resolve the inflammation. Patients with gluten enteropathy benefit from standard dietary limitations for this condition (Chapter 141). For patients with "pure" lymphocytic gastritis and severe mucosal lesions, no therapy is currently available.

EOSINOPHILIC GASTRITIS. Eosinophils may infiltrate the gastrointestinal mucosa and muscular layers, especially in the antrum. Thickening of gastric folds and rigidity of the gastric wall are common. Antral motility may be altered, leading to gastric retention. Patients may present with eosinophilia, nausea, vomiting, or pain. Rarely, serosal involvement results in ascites. Milk-sensitive enteropathy of infancy, connective tissue disorders, and parasitic infections should be excluded. Glucocorticoid therapy may be useful, and surgery may be needed if mechanical outlet obstruction occurs.

GRANULOMATOUS GASTRITIS. Granulomas may occur in the gastric mucosa with generalized diseases such as sarcoidosis, Crohn's disease, or infections. Crohn's disease (Chapter 142) may involve the duodenum, pylorus, antrum, and gastric body (in that order), usually in association with disease in the small intestine or colon. Mucosal granulomas may occur in eosinophilic granulomas or in isolated, idiopathic granulomatous gastritis, or they may be incidental findings. Involved portions of the stomach may be rigid or narrow or have thickened folds on radiograph; these findings must be distinguished from malignancy. The antrum is involved most often, and granulomas may occur in all layers of the stomach. Ulcerated lesions may perforate. Patients often undergo surgery because it is difficult to differentiate this entity from malignancy. When the diagnosis is made, it is important to exclude potentially curable diseases (e.g., tuberculosis, histoplasmosis, syphilis) or treatable processes (e.g., sarcoidosis, Crohn's disease). If malignancy and associated diseases have been excluded, the patient can be observed without specific treatment because spontaneous resolution has been reported.

MÉNÉTRIER'S DISEASE

Ménétrier's disease is defined by four features: (1) giant folds in the gastric fundus and body, (2) diminished acid secretory capacity, (3) hypoalbuminemia secondary to protein-losing gastropathy, and (4) histologic features of foveolar hyperplasia (gastric pit region) and a marked increase in mucosal thickness combined with glandular atrophy and cystic dilation. Tortuous gastric folds may resemble the cerebral cortex. Hypochlorhydria is generally present, but a hypersecretory variant, which may be an unrelated entity, has been described. Symptoms are variable and may include abdominal pain, nausea, vomiting, weight loss, and edema. The disease is more common in men than in women, and it generally presents after age 50, although a childhood form exists. Typically, biopsy confirms the diagnosis, but variant patterns warrant the less specific diagnosis of idiopathic hypertrophic gastropathy. Variant cases that do not include all of the typical features are more common than classic cases. The differential diagnosis includes gastrinoma syndrome, infiltrating carcinoma, lymphoma, and amyloidosis. Large gastric folds and a picture of hypertrophic gastritis may be associated with *H. pylori* infection, especially in children; if present, the infection should be treated. If *H. pylori* is not present, any accompanying ulcers and erosions usually respond to standard antiulcer therapy. No increased risk of cancer has been established.

GASTRIC ISCHEMIA

Ischemic gastric injury is rarely recognized, although erosive changes have been reported with vasculitis and atheromatous embolization. Whether chronic gastric ulcers have an ischemic component remains speculative.

HEMORRHAGIC GASTRITIS AND VASCULAR GASTROPATHIES

Hemorrhagic gastritis and vascular gastropathies are a heterogeneous group of conditions. Acute hemorrhagic gastritis is characterized by diffuse mucosal hyperemia with bleeding erosions and ulcers, precipitated by a sudden stress-induced imbalance between aggressive and protective factors involved in the maintenance of mucosal integrity. Vascular gastropathies are defined as endoscopically distinct alterations of the gastric mucosal vessels accompanied by little or no inflammation. The most important vascular gastropathies are the watermelon stomach syndrome and portal hypertensive gastropathy.

ACUTE HEMORRHAGIC GASTRITIS. Acute hemorrhagic gastritis has been a recognized nosologic entity for at least a century, when Curling documented the association between severe burns and duodenal ulceration—Curling's ulcer (Chapter 138). Ingestion of large doses of aspirin or other NSAIDs may induce acute mucosal injury ranging from edema and hyperemia to multiple erosions and ulcerations. Acute hemorrhagic gastritis is characterized by a hyperemic edematous mucosa with erosions and various degrees of active bleeding. The clinical history (e.g., shock, burns, ingestion of large doses of aspirin) rather than the widely overlapping nature of the lesions helps the endoscopist determine the precipitating factors. The pathogenesis of stress-induced hemorrhagic gastritis is not known, but luminal acid seems to be essential.

VASCULAR GASTROPATHIES. *Watermelon stomach,* or *gastric antral vascular ectasia,* is a rare condition of unknown etiology frequently associated with gastric atrophy and autoimmune and connective tissue disorders. More than 70% of cases occur in women older than age 65. Occult bleeding is seen at presentation in almost 90% of the cases; melena or hematemesis is seen in 60%. In most patients, the chronic blood loss causes iron-deficiency anemia. Watermelon stomach has a characteristic histopathologic appearance, particularly in the antrum. The lamina propria, usually devoid of inflammation, appears expanded owing to smooth muscle proliferation and some fibrosis; it also contains markedly dilated mucosal capillaries, which are not increased in number but show a significant increase in cross-sectional area. In most cases, fibrin thrombi are found within the dilated capillaries. The presence of these thrombi is particularly important for excluding other causes of mucosal congestion and, although not pathognomonic, is highly suggestive of gastric antral vascular ectasia. Treatment is empirical; iron supplements are sufficient in patients with limited bleeding, but therapeutic endoscopy with obliteration of the dilated vessels or antrectomy may be necessary in severe cases.

Portal hypertensive gastropathy, which is a dilation of the mucosal vessels especially in the proximal stomach, occurs in a high proportion of patients with portal hypertension. The endoscopic appearance of portal hypertensive gastropathy is nonspecific and does not correlate well with the degree of portal hypertension. The endoscopic patterns have been described variously as snakeskin, scarlatina rash, cherry-red spots, and mosaic. The mosaic pattern was found by a consensus conference to be the most reliable indicator of mild portal hypertensive gastropathy with a low risk of hemorrhage. Red marks suggest a more severe degree of hypertension and a greater risk of hemorrhage. Patients with the most severe portal hypertension usually have diffuse lesions and gastric bleeding. β-Blockers may reduce the risk of hemorrhage.

SUGGESTED READINGS

El Zimaity HM, Ota H, Graham DY, et al: Patterns of gastric atrophy in intestinal type gastric carcinoma. Cancer 2002;94:1428–1436. *Using intestinal metaplasia as a marker of atrophy may significantly underestimate the extent and severity of atrophy in the precancerous stomach.*

Genta RM: A year in the life of the gastric mucosa. Gastroenterology 2000;119:252–254. *A discussion of the feasibility of controlled clinical trials to determine whether eradication of* H. pylori *infection from a population can decrease the incidence of gastric cancer.*

Uemura N, Okamoto S, Yamamoto S, et al: Helicobacter pylori infection and the development of gastric cancer. N Engl J Med 2001;345:784–789. *A large study in Japan showing that gastric cancer occurred in persons infected with* H. pylori *but not in uninfected persons.*

138 PEPTIC ULCER DISEASE

David Y. Graham

Epidemiology

The most common causes of peptic ulcer disease are infection with *Helicobacter pylori* and use of nonsteroidal anti-inflammatory drugs (NSAIDs) (Table 138–1). Clinically the natural history of peptic ulcer disease is one of exacerbation and remission; unless the causative factor is eliminated, the recurrence rate is 60 to 90% per year. By comparison, elimination of the causative factor effectively cures the disease and prevents recurrence.

Incidence, Prevalence, and Relative Risk

Before 1900, gastric ulcer was more common than duodenal ulcer. The incidence of duodenal ulcer began to increase in the early 1900s, reached a peak about the 1950s, and progressively decreased thereafter. This change in the location of ulcer was associated with a change in the pattern of gastritis that underlies *H. pylori*–associated peptic ulcers. Gastric ulcer is associated with a pangastritis and, generally, with lower than normal acid secretion. The site of a gastric ulcer is typically on the lesser curvature at or near the border of the advancing atrophic gastritis (pseudopyloric metaplasia). Duodenal ulcer is associated with antral-predominant gastritis, which spares the acid-secreting gastric corpus so that acid secretion is typically in the high-normal or definitely increased range. The change in the pattern of gastritis was likely a reflection of changes in diet, especially new methods of food preservation, a reduction in the use of salt, and the availability of fresh fruits and vegetables year-round rather than just in season. The continuing decrease in prevalence of duodenal ulcer after 1950 seems to be related to a decline in the prevalence of *H. pylori* infection associated with improvements in sanitation and standards of living. Nevertheless, ulcer disease has remained common because the decline in *H. pylori*–related ulcer has been offset by the marked increase in NSAID use and NSAID-associated ulcers. NSAID-associated ulcers may decline as traditional NSAIDs give way to the selective cyclooxygenase-2 (COX-2) inhibitors (see later).

The risk of developing a peptic ulcer is about one in six among persons who are infected with *H. pylori*, and the risk is higher in men

Table 138–1 • CAUSES AND ASSOCIATIONS OF PEPTIC ULCER

COMMON FORMS OF PEPTIC ULCER
Helicobacter pylori–associated
NSAID-associated
Stress ulcer

UNCOMMON SPECIFIC FORMS OF PEPTIC ULCER
Acid hypersecretion
    Gastrinoma: inherited—multiple endocrine neoplasia I, sporadic
Increased mast cells/basophils
    Mastocytosis: inherited and sporadic
    Basophilic leukemias
Antral G-cell hyperfunction/hyperplasia

OTHER INFECTIONS
Viral infection: herpes simplex virus type I, cytomegalovirus
Other infections (?)

OTHER CAUSES
Duodenal obstruction/disruption (congenital bands, annular pancreas)
Vascular insufficiency: crack cocaine–associated perforations
Radiation-induced
Chemotherapy-induced (hepatic artery infusions)
Rare genetic subtypes (?)
Amyloidosis type III (Van Allen–Iowa) (?)
Tremor-nystagmus-ulcer syndrome of Neuhauser (?)

NSAID = nonsteroidal anti-inflammatory drugs.
Modified from Soll AH: Gastric, duodenal, and stress ulcer. *In* Sleisinger M, Fordtran J (eds): Gastrointestinal Disease, 5th ed. Philadelphia, WB Saunders, 1993, p 580.

than women. Until more recently, the "point prevalence" (percentage of the population with ulcer) in the United States was about 1 to 2%, but the prevalence has declined. The onset of duodenal ulcer is most commonly between age 25 and 55, whereas gastric ulcer is most frequent between age 40 and 70.

Daily use of NSAIDs significantly increases the risk of ulcer disease (relative risk 10-fold to 20-fold) and is related to the systemic effects of the drugs to suppress prostaglandin synthesis. The risk of ulcer disease is remarkably less with the selective COX-2 inhibitors (Chapter 32). Theoretically a new class of NSAIDs that are in trial, NSAIDs bound to nitric oxide, also would provide effective relief of arthritic pain with few untoward gastrointestinal effects. Although the introduction of effective, but safer NSAIDs undoubtedly would reduce the magnitude of the problem, aspirin, even low-dose aspirin, is associated with a 1 to 2% risk of bleeding peptic ulcer per year. Until an effective, safe alternative antiplatelet drug with similar benefits becomes available, aspirin-induced ulcers and ulcer complications will remain significant problems.

The direct costs (i.e., physician visits, hospitalizations, medications) of peptic ulcer (gastric and duodenal ulcer) disease have been estimated to be greater than $10 billion, with equivalent indirect costs (principally resulting from time lost from work). The annual mortality rate secondary to ulcer disease is low (<15,000), and deaths are due to ulcer complications, principally hemorrhage.

Genetics

Genetic factors seem to play a role in ulcerogenesis possibly related to differences in acid secretion and in susceptibility to *H. pylori* infection. If one monozygotic twin develops an ulcer, the concordant twin has about a 50% chance of developing an ulcer. First-degree relatives of ulcer patients have about a three-fold greater chance of developing ulcer because of genetic susceptibility, common environment and source of *H. pylori,* or a combination of these factors. Rare genetic syndromes associated with duodenal ulcer include multiple endocrine neoplasia type 1 (Chapter 242), gastrin-secreting pancreatic tumor associated with another endocrine tumor (e.g., hyperparathyroidism; Chapters 140 and 260), and systemic mastocytosis (increased circulating levels of histamine; Chapter 272).

Pathophysiology

Peptic ulcers are mucosal defects extending through the muscularis mucosa and into the muscularis propria of the esophagus, stomach, or duodenum. Chronic peptic ulcers are primarily a failure of normal wound healing.

ULCERS RESULTING FROM *HELICOBACTER PYLORI*

The fine details of the pathophysiology of development of peptic ulcer are unclear. More than a century of work has confirmed a prominent role for acid secretion. Maximal gastric acid output is elevated in about one third of duodenal ulcer patients and is in the high-normal range in the remaining patients. Duodenal ulcer is virtually nonexistent if maximal gastric output is less than about 12 mEq/hr.

DUODENAL ULCER. A unifying hypothesis for *H. pylori* duodenal ulcer is based on the fact that *H. pylori* growth is inhibited by bile acids; *H. pylori* should not be able to thrive in the duodenal bulb, but in patients with duodenal ulcer, it does. A high duodenal acid load is one of the physiologic characteristics of duodenal ulcer disease. Glycine conjugated bile acids are precipitated by acid, and it is likely that the high duodenal acid load reduces the concentration of bile acids in the duodenal bulb and allows *H. pylori* to grow. *H. pylori*–associated inflammation causes a dysregulation of gastric acid secretion, including defective feedback inhibition, which results in prolonged acid secretion after meals. Smoking and stress also increase acid secretion and the duodenal acid load. Smoking also indirectly increases the duodenal acid load by its inhibition of the ability of the duodenal mucosa and the pancreas to produce bicarbonate and further compromises the duodenal bulb's ability to neutralize the acid emptied from the stomach. The normal duodenal bulb also contains areas of heterotopic gastric mucosa, which provide sites for attachment of *H. pylori* and may secrete acid locally. Healing of duodenal injury promotes patches of gastric metaplasia, which may become colonized by *H. pylori*. The inflammatory reaction resulting from colonization with *H. pylori* can result in a vicious cycle of damage, gastric metaplasia,

and more sites for colonization, all of which produce more damage and eventuate in a large patch of inflamed intestinal metaplasia that may ulcerate and produce the peptic ulcer. The continuing presence of the infection and the resulting inflammation may retard wound healing and produce the chronic ulcer. The presence of duodenal bulb inflammation further reduces the ability of the duodenal mucosa to produce bicarbonate in response to acid and indirectly accentuates the duodenal acid load. Cure of the *H. pylori* infection results in disappearance of mucosal inflammation and reversal of the dysregulation of acid secretion and recovery of the ability of the duodenal bulb to secrete bicarbonate. Although cure of the infection in duodenal ulcer patients reduces the duration of acid secretion to a meal, it has a minimal effect on the maximal ability of the stomach to secrete acid, consistent with the fact that corpus gastritis is minimal in duodenal ulcer patients. The importance of the duodenal acid load is consistent with the notion that the ability to secrete more than a normal amount of acid is a risk factor of duodenal ulcer disease.

GASTRIC ULCER. The pathogenesis of gastric ulcer remains an enigma, and any patient with a gastric ulcer must be evaluated carefully to exclude gastric cancer (Chapter 199). Gastric ulcers tend to occur at the junction between the antral-type and corpus epithelium (i.e., a junctional epithelium) and on the lesser curvature of the stomach. There are few theories or observations to identify which patients are at risk or why. Similar to duodenal ulcer, the actual ulcer results in a failure in the normal healing process. If a strip of mucosa is removed near the ulcer, the defect heals rapidly, whereas the ulcer heals slowly and recurs. Ulcer healing is accelerated by antisecretory therapy. In gastric and duodenal ulcer, cure of *H. pylori* infection results in a marked reduction in ulcer recurrence and effectively cures the chronic disease.

ULCERS RESULTING FROM NONSTEROIDAL ANTI-INFLAMMATORY DRUGS

The other common form of ulcer disease is related to use of NSAIDs. The point prevalence of ulcers is more than 15% of chronic NSAID users, and 1 to 4% of patients taking NSAIDs develop gastrointestinal complications during the course of 1 year of NSAID use. Because all the subjects taking NSAIDs are exposed to the same damaging effects, a fascinating, unanswered question is why only a few treated subjects develop clinically significant ulcer disease.

INHIBITION OF PROSTAGLANDIN PRODUCTION. Traditional NSAIDs and aspirin inhibit the enzyme COX-1, which catalyzes the formation of the prostaglandin precursor endoperoxide from arachidonic acid that is derived from cell membrane phospholipids (Chapter 32). In animal models, ulcers also are produced by antibodies to prostaglandins but not to inactive prostaglandin analogues, further supporting the conclusion that endogenous prostaglandins are important elements in mucosal defense.

HELICOBACTER PYLORI VERSUS NONSTEROIDAL ANTI-INFLAMMATORY DRUG ULCERS. NSAIDs cause clinically relevant ulcers in patients who do not have *H. pylori,* and neither *H. pylori* nor gastritis is a prerequisite for NSAID ulcer development. There does seem to be an interaction between NSAID use and *H. pylori,* however, because studies have shown that curing *H. pylori* infection reduces the risk of ulcers and ulcer complications during subsequent NSAID therapy. This finding has led to the current recommendation that it may be worthwhile to test prospective long-term NSAID or aspirin users for *H. pylori* and to eradicate the infection when it is present.

RISK OF GASTROINTESTINAL COMPLICATIONS WITH NONSTEROIDAL ANTI-INFLAMMATORY DRUGS. NSAID use is reported in 40 to 60% of patients presenting with the ulcer complications of bleeding or perforation (Chapter 139). Although the magnitude of the risk of complications from NSAIDs is uncertain, in a controlled study, aspirin (1 g/day) caused a 9-fold to 10-fold increased risk of hospitalization for duodenal ulcer and gastric ulcer. The risk begins within days after treatment, is slightly higher within the first 3 months of therapy, and persists indefinitely. Ulcer risk is increased with even low-dose aspirin (81 mg daily). An important component of bleeding, especially with aspirin, is platelet dysfunction resulting from inhibition of thromboxane production. A thorough evaluation is appropriate in any patient who bleeds while on NSAID therapy because the probability of finding lesions other than ulcers (Chapter 139) is at least as high as in subjects who are not taking NSAIDs.

RISK FACTORS FOR NONSTEROIDAL ANTI-INFLAMMATORY DRUG ULCERS. Age is an independent risk factor for hospitalization secondary to ulcer complications. Corticosteroids alone cause little risk of ulcer disease, but when they are combined with NSAIDs their added risk is significant (Chapter 31). Anticoagulant cotherapy also increases the risk of gastrointestinal complications. The most important risk factor for NSAID ulcers is a history of prior peptic ulcer disease, owing to either *H. pylori* or NSAIDs. This finding is not surprising considering that the risk of an ulcer complication in *H. pylori* alone is 1 to 2% per year and increases to 10 to 36% per year after a complication such as hemorrhage from an ulcer. This risk emphasizes the importance of finding and eliminating the cause of ulcer in any patient who has had an ulcer complication.

STRESS ULCERS

Superficial mucosal damage (petechiae and erosions) is found in most patients within a few hours after major operations or within 24 hours of the onset of major multisystem illness. This damage remains silent in most patients and rarely results in clinically significant acute bleeding unless complicated by severe coagulopathy. Major bleeding associated with severe and prolonged physiologic stress occurs with discrete ulcers rather than from superficial mucosal lesions. Stress-related mucosal damage is independent of *H. pylori*. Risk factors that constitute an indication for preventive intervention with antiulcer agents include mechanical ventilation for more than 5 days and coagulopathy, which are the clearest predictors of major hemorrhage. Prolonged hospitalizations with hepatic or renal failure, sepsis, and shock also are important predictors of stress ulcer risk, especially when complicated by prolonged, multisystem failure. Acute stress ulcers also occur in characteristic clinical settings, such as with extensive third-degree burns (Curling's ulcers; Chapter 108) and after head trauma (Cushing's ulcers; Chapter 431). The rates of stress ulcer complications have decreased dramatically, for example, from about 30% in serious burn patients in the 1970s to less than 1 to 2% today, reflecting improved overall management (e.g., control of sepsis and respiratory care) and rapid institution of enteral or, when necessary, parenteral nutrition. Patients with stress ulcer–induced gastrointestinal bleeding have greatly increased mortality, in part because of the severity of the underlying disease and superimposed multiorgan failure, which simultaneously increase mortality and the risk of stress ulcer bleeding.

Currently the risks are so low in unselected patients in the intensive care unit that pharmacologic intervention does not improve outcomes sufficiently to justify routine use. Preventive therapy is appropriate, however, in high-risk patients or in patients with a history of peptic ulcer or gastrointestinal bleeding when they are exposed to severe, prolonged physiologic stress. Although there has been concern over increased rates of nosocomial pneumonia in patients placed on antisecretory agents, the data are conflicting, and the effects are probably modest, at most.

UNUSUAL CAUSES OF ULCERS

Gastrinoma, an uncommon form of ulcer disease, is caused by excessive secretion of gastrin by a tumor and gastric acid hypersecretion (Chapter 140). *Retained antrum* is an unusual complication of peptic ulcer surgery, in which the antrum is excluded from acid, preventing the downregulation of gastrin secretion and producing a form of pseudogastrinoma (Chapter 139). *Antral G-cell hyperfunction* is a rare form of duodenal ulcer disease in which acid hypersecretion is caused by enhanced secretion of antral gastrin. Fasting gastrin levels usually are elevated only modestly, but the response to a meal is greatly exaggerated. In contradistinction to patients with gastrinoma, intravenous secretin does not elevate gastrin blood levels. Although controversial, this entity appears in a *H. pylori*–independent form and as the end of the spectrum of *H. pylori*–induced hypergastrinemia and acid hypersecretion. In the *H. pylori*–dependent form, cure of the infection reverses the phenomenon.

Mastocytosis and basophilic leukemia are unusual conditions that can be associated with peptic ulcer as the result of release of the acid secretagogue histamine from the malignant cells. *Congenital disorders of the duodenum*, such as annular pancreas and congenital bands, have been associated with duodenal ulcer and acid hypersecretion. The mechanisms accounting for these associations remain to be established. *Herpes simplex virus type 1* ulcers have been documented in the mucosa near ulcers in a small proportion of ordinary peptic ulcer patients with normal immunocompetence. Although the studies are intriguing, causality in ulcer pathogenesis has not been established. The eradication of *H. pylori* from the population would allow identification and study of this currently rare cause of ulcer disease.

Clinical Manifestations

Classically an ulcer was considered likely when pain was located in the epigastric area, was burning in quality, occurred on an empty stomach 2 to 4 hours after meals and/or at night, was relieved by antacids and/or meals, and tended to wax and wane over months. This pattern has been called *acid dyspepsia* because it occurs when acid is unbuffered by food and is relieved with neutralizing acid or inhibiting acid secretion. It had been assumed that most patients with ulcer disease had epigastric abdominal distress. With the availability of upper gastrointestinal endoscopy, however, it now is recognized that most patients (approximately 70%) with epigastric distress (dyspepsia) do not have evidence of active ulcer disease (Chapter 135); conversely 40% of patients with an active ulcer crater deny abdominal pain (Table 138–2). Patients can present with an ulcer-related complication, particularly hemorrhage in chronic NSAID users, without antecedent symptoms. Nevertheless, despite being insensitive and nonspecific, the symptom of epigastric abdominal pain, particularly burning after meals or at night and relieved with food or antacid, suggests the possibility of ulcer disease and warrants an evaluation (see later).

Diagnosis

PHYSICAL EXAMINATION. Physical examination is of limited value in patients with uncomplicated ulcer (e.g., epigastric tenderness on deep palpation) because the sensitivity, specificity, and positive and negative predictive value all are approximately 50% or less. Many patients with nonulcer diseases also have epigastric tenderness on physical examination (see later). In patients with free perforation or ulcer penetration into the pancreas, findings of peritonitis are usually present (Chapter 146), whereas in patients with gastric retention who have been fasting for a few hours, a succussion splash (produced by auscultating the abdomen while rocking the patient back and forth) suggests retained gastric contents.

DIFFERENTIAL DIAGNOSIS. Epigastric abdominal pain can be caused by many processes (Chapter 130), including, most frequently, nonulcer dyspepsia (Chapter 135), gastroesophageal reflux (Chapter 136), biliary tract disease (Chapter 158), pancreatitis (Chapter 145), coronary and/or mesenteric vascular insufficiency (Chapter 144), intra-abdominal neoplasms (particularly gastric, pancreatic, and hepatic; Chapters 199, 201, and 202), functional bowel syndrome (Chapter 135), inflammatory bowel disease (Chapter 142), and others. Symptoms of indigestion can be associated with gastric dyskinesia (gastroparesis, slow gastric emptying) or with gastric dysesthesia (hypersensitivity to gastric distention or specific foods). Delayed gastric emptying can be secondary to diabetic neuropathy, drugs, or connective tissue diseases, although it is most commonly part of the spectrum of functional bowel disorders.

Table 138–2 • DIAGNOSIS OF ULCER DISEASE BY SYMPTOMS ALONE*

	PREVALENCE (%)		
SYMPTOM	Duodenal Ulcer	Gastric Ulcer	Nonulcer Dyspepsia
Epigastric pain	~70	~70	~70
Nocturnal pain	50–80	30–45	25–35
Food causes pain relief	20–65	5–50	5–30
Episodic pain	50–60	10–20	30–40
Belching/bloating	30–65	30–70	40–80

*Ulcers occur without symptoms (10–40%), and ulcer symptoms occur without ulcer (30–60%).

Modified from Isenberg JI, Walsh JH, Johnson LR: Peptic ulcer diseases. AGA Undergraduate Teaching Project–Unit 23. Timonium, MD, Milner-Fenwick, 1991.

ENDOSCOPY VERSUS RADIOGRAPHY. The diagnosis of ulcer disease can be suspected only based on the history and physical examination. Diagnostic confirmation requires either upper gastrointestinal endoscopy (Fig. 138–1) or barium contrast gastrointestinal radiography. Endoscopy establishes the diagnosis more accurately than conventional radiography, but it also has a greater cost and a small risk of untoward events (<1 in 1000 procedures) (Chapters 131 and 132). Although highly skilled radiologists using air-contrast radiography may be as accurate as endoscopy, radiology has lost favor in that there are now more skilled endoscopists than gastrointestinal radiologists, and endoscopy provides an opportunity for immediate biopsy.

Duodenal ulcers are almost never malignant and do not require biopsies or repeat endoscopy to ensure healing. Ulcerating lesions within the stomach may be due to gastric cancer, however; 4% of lesions that appear to be benign by endoscopy (Fig. 138–2) are malignant (Table 138–3). In most circumstances, it is prudent to obtain multiple biopsy specimens of gastric ulcers. There is controversy

Table 138–3 • FACTORS INFLUENCING THE DECISION FOR EARLY ENDOSCOPY IN GASTRIC ULCER DISEASE

EARLY ENDOSCOPY	DELAYED ENDOSCOPY
Advanced age	Young patient
Long history	Short history
Weight loss	No weight change
Anorexia	Normal appetite
UGI bleeding/anemia	Normal blood cell count
Significant vomiting	No vomiting
No ulcerogenic drugs	NSAID use and positive *Helicobacter pylori* serology
Equivocal UGI series	Unequivocal UGI series

NSAID = nonsteroidal anti-inflammatory drug; UGI = upper gastrointestinal.

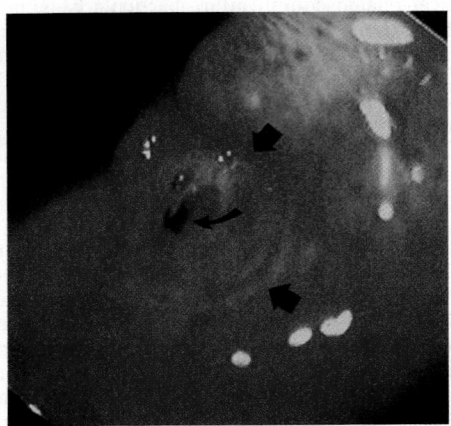

FIGURE 138–1 • Duodenal bulbar ulcer. A white excavated base is noted just inside the pylorus (large arrows) containing a dark red central artery oozing blood (small arrow).

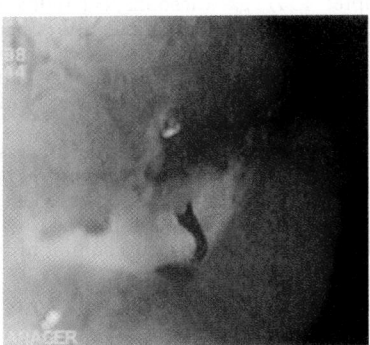

FIGURE 138–2 • Gastric ulcer (white base) with bleeding vessel.

regarding the necessity of repeat endoscopy to ensure complete healing after 8 to 12 weeks of medical treatment. Repeat endoscopy has a low yield if the initial endoscopy revealed a benign-appearing ulcer and adequate biopsy specimens (4 with jumbo forceps or 6 or 7 with regular forceps) were reviewed carefully and found to be negative for malignancy. Repeated endoscopy also is unnecessary in young patients (<50 years old) with an adequate biopsy specimen of gastric ulcer in the setting of regular NSAID intake.

IS A PRECISE DIAGNOSIS OF ULCER REQUIRED? One of the major tenets of medicine has been to establish a precise diagnosis and apply the appropriate and specific therapy. This principle has come into question for ulcer disease. Most patients who have dyspepsia and who undergo endoscopy do not have active ulcer disease but instead have either nonulcer dyspepsia or evidence of esophagitis (Chapters 131 and 136). Current recommendations are for patients with uncomplicated dyspepsia to have *H. pylori* testing and for patients with positive results to be treated to eradicate *H. pylori*. In patients who require NSAIDs on a regular basis or who have persistent or systemic symptoms (e.g., anorexia, weight loss, back pain), the diagnosis should be established, preferably by endoscopy. Endoscopy not only permits a firm diagnosis, but also provides opportunity to obtain biopsy specimens of the lesion and/or gastric antrum to test for *H. pylori* and to exclude gastric cancer (Chapter 199).

MEASURING SERUM GASTRIN AND GASTRIC SECRETORY TESTING. Determination of fasting and secretin-stimulated serum gastrin is indicated in patients who have intractable ulcer disease, patients who are to undergo elective duodenal ulcer surgery, and patients in whom a diagnosis of Zollinger-Ellison (gastrinoma) syndrome is a consideration (Chapter 140). Gastric secretory testing is performed rarely, and the current general unavailability of pentagastrin has made the test impractical. Because of the lack of clinical utility of gastric secretory testing, it has become obsolete as a diagnostic tool except in patients who have hypergastrinemia or in whom gastrinoma or another cause of acid hypersecretion is considered (Chapter 140).

DIAGNOSTIC TESTS FOR *HELICOBACTER PYLORI*. *H. pylori* can be identified using tests that directly assess the presence of the bacteria and by indirect tests (Tables 138–4 and 138–5). Direct tests include breath tests (e.g., ^{13}C-urea breath test), tests of the release of ammonia (NH_3) from gastric mucosal biopsy specimens, histologic identification of the microorganism, and culture. Indirect tests include an

Table 138–4 • DIAGNOSTIC TESTS FOR *HELICOBACTER PYLORI*

TEST	SENSITIVITY (%)	SPECIFICITY (%)	COMMENTS
Rapid urease test	89–98	93–98	Requires endoscopy
Histology	93–99	95–99	Requires endoscopy
Culture	77–92	100	Requires endoscopy
Serologic tests			
ELISA	88–99	86–95	Unsuitable for follow-up
Quick office test	94–96	88–95	Inexpensive, rapid
Urea breath test	90–100	89–100	Good for diagnosis and follow-up
Stool antigen test	90–100	89–100	Good for diagnosis and follow-up

ELISA = enzyme-linked immunosorbent assay.

Table 138–5 • CLUES SUGGESTIVE OF SPECIFIC CAUSES OF PEPTIC ULCER

	H. PYLORI	NSAIDS	ZOLLINGER-ELLISON SYNDROME
One or more			
Serology	Positive	Negative	Negative
Urea breath test	Positive	Negative	Negative
Histology	Positive	Negative	Negative
NSAID use			
History	Absent	Positive	Absent
Elevated serum salicylate	Absent	Positive	Absent
Unusual location, multiple	Absent	Absent	Present
Severe esophagitis	Absent	Absent	Present
Diarrhea	Absent	Absent	Present

NSAIDs = nonsteroidal anti-inflammatory drugs.

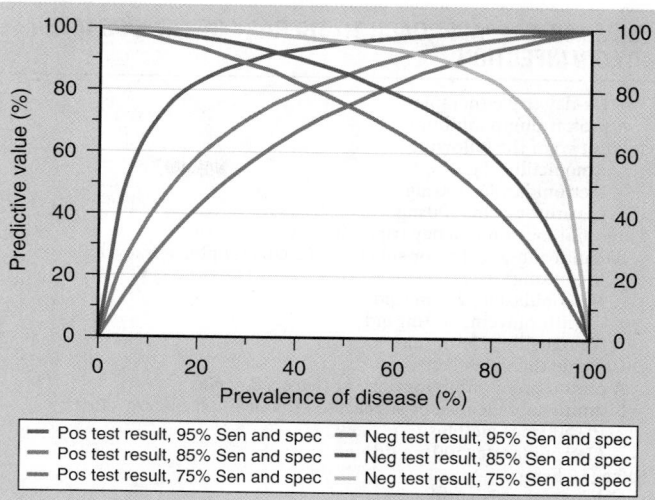

FIGURE 138–3 • Effect of frequency of *H. pylori* in a population on the predictive value of a positive or negative test. The effect is shown for tests with specificity and sensitivity of 95%, 85%, and 75%. Low prevalence of *H. pylori* results in an increasing proportion of false-positive tests with high accuracy of negative tests. In contrast, when the prevalence of *H. pylori* is expected to be high (e.g., in duodenal ulcer), false-negative tests become more prevalent. Even at low or high prevalence of *H. pylori* infection, the tests retain their stated specificity and sensitivity. (From Miehlke S, Bayerdorffer E, Graham DY: Treatment of *Helicobacter pylori* infection. Semin Gastrointest Dis 2001;12:167.)

immunologic response by enzyme-linked immunosorbent assay, a rapid serologic test, and stool antigen testing. Direct tests and stool antigen testing require the patient to discontinue all drugs that suppress *H. pylori* (antibiotics, bismuth, and proton pump inhibitors [PPIs]) for at least 2 weeks. Antibody tests remain positive for many months to years after successful therapy and cannot be used clinically to assess the effectiveness of therapy.

The choice of test depends on the clinical situation. Two questions are important in this regard: (1) Does the patient need endoscopy, and (2) what is the pretest probability of a *H. pylori* infection? When endoscopy is indicated (e.g., a patient with signs or symptoms suggesting a gastric malignancy), one or more of the endoscopic tests (e.g., histology with special stains) should be used. When endoscopy is not needed, serology often seems to be the most convenient test because it can be ordered along with other indicated blood tests. Serology can be used reliably, provided that the likelihood of the presence of the infection is taken into account and any unexpected results are confirmed (Fig. 138–3). Interpretation of the results of any test depends critically on the pretest probability of the infection (Chapter 6). When the pretest probability is high (e.g., a patient with a known active duodenal ulcer), false-positive results are rare (right side of the plot), and one can prescribe therapy reliably based on serologic test results. In contrast, the prevalence of *H. pylori* in young white Americans with gastroesophageal reflux is less than 20%. In these patients, a positive serologic test result must be confirmed with a direct test, such as a ^{13}C-urea breath test, before initiating therapy. In contrast, a negative serologic test in a patient with duodenal ulcer would have a reasonable chance of being false negative (see Fig. 138–3). A rule of thumb is that low pretest probabilities rarely are associated with false-negative test results but commonly are associated with false-positive results. High pretest probabilities are the opposite (Chapter 6). The ^{13}C-urea breath test and the stool antigen test have become widely available, reducing the indications for serology. These direct tests provide reliable evidence for the presence of an active infection and are the best method for confirmation of the presence of an active infection and determination of whether the infection has been cured (see later).

Rx Treatment

Although traditional therapies that neutralize or suppress gastric acid are effective in accelerating ulcer healing, they do not change the natural history of the disease, and ulcers recur soon after therapy is discontinued. The current recommendation is to tailor therapy to the cause of the disease and to eliminate the causative factor.

GOALS. The goals of ulcer therapy are to relieve symptoms, to heal the ulcer, and to cure the disease (*H. pylori* ulcers) and/or prevent recurrence (NSAID ulcers). Treatment should be aimed at curing *H. pylori* infection, if it is present. In addition, neutralizing acid with antisecretory agents, such as H_2-receptor antagonists, PPIs, or prostaglandins, relieves pain rapidly and accelerates ulcer healing. Antacids and surface-active agents, such as sucral-

fate, are considered outmoded now as primary therapies for ulcer disease.

ANTISECRETORY DRUGS. Antisecretory therapy accelerates the healing of ulcers regardless of their cause. The H_2-receptor antagonists available in the United States include cimetidine (Tagamet), ranitidine (Zantac), famotidine (Pepcid), and nizatidine (Axid). The main difference is potency, not effectiveness. When administered with the evening meal, the clinically equivalent doses are 800 mg of cimetidine, 300 mg of ranitidine or nizatidine, and 20 mg of famotidine. Choice should be based on cost. Cimetidine is associated with prolongation of the metabolism of warfarin, theophylline, and phenytoin, and the dosage of these drugs may have to be adjusted if they are administered with cimetidine.

Available PPIs include omeprazole (Prilosec, 20 to 40 mg/day), lansoprazole (Prevacid, 30 mg/day), pantoprazole (Protonix, 40 mg), rabeprazole (Aciphex, 20 mg), and esomaprazole (Nexium, 40 mg). The PPIs have direct antibacterial activity against *H. pylori* but do not cure the infection when used alone. PPI therapy reduces the *H. pylori* load in the stomach and can result in negative diagnostic tests. PPIs are the most effective antisecretory agents and work by inhibiting the hydrogen-potassium adenosine triphosphatase responsible for acid secretion. Their main disadvantage is their higher cost.

Misoprostol is the only synthetic prostaglandin available in the United States. It is a relatively weak antisecretory drug; 200 µg of misoprostol is slightly less potent as an antisecretory drug than 300 mg of cimetidine. Misoprostol is not a first-line therapy for treating peptic ulcers. Its primary role is to prevent ulcers and ulcer complications in NSAID users.

ANTIMICROBIAL THERAPY. *H. pylori* is sensitive in vitro to a variety of antimicrobial agents but, similar to tuberculosis, requires multidrug combination therapy. Many effective treatment regimens are available, and several have been approved by the U.S. Food and Drug Administration. The best results have been obtained with combination therapies using three or four drugs (Table 138–6). Antimicrobial agents used in combination therapies include bismuth subsalicylate or subcitrate, ranitidine bismuth citrate, tetracycline, metronidazole, amoxicillin, furazolidone, and clarithromycin. Doxycycline cannot be substituted for tetracycline, and other macrolides (e.g., erythromycin or azithromycin) cannot

Continued

Table 138–6 • APPROACH TO THERAPY OF *HELICOBACTER PYLORI* INFECTION

Twice-a-day triple therapies
  A proton-pump inhibitor
  Plus two of the following
    Amoxicillin, 1 g
    Metronidazole, 500 mg
    Clarithromycin, 500 mg
Three and four times a day triple therapy
  Bismuth subsalicylate or subcitrate (2 tablets) plus tetracycline
    (500 mg) *plus*
  Metronidazole, 250 mg qid
  Clarithromycin, 500 mg qid
  Amoxicillin, 750 mg qid
Quadruple therapies
  A proton pump inhibitor once or twice a day *plus*
  Bismuth subsalicylate or subcitrate (2 tablets) *plus* tetracycline
    (500 mg) qid *plus*
  Metronidazole, 500 mg tid
Salvage Therapy
  Omeprazole 40 mg tid
  Amoxicillin 1 g tid

be substituted for clarithromycin. Where available, tinidazole can substitute for metronidazole. PPIs have some in vivo anti–*H. pylori* activity and have a potential benefit over H_2-receptor antagonists in that they more effectively control pH. Nevertheless, head-to-head comparisons have shown that H_2-receptor antagonist cotherapy is approximately equal to PPIs as adjuvant therapy for *H. pylori* infection. The primary reasons to include antisecretory therapy with antimicrobial agents are to increase the intragastric pH because many antibiotics become increasingly less effective as the pH falls to less than 7.4, to relieve pain, and to accelerate ulcer healing. Typically the PPIs are more effective in all these goals than the H_2-receptor antagonists, and they generally are preferred.

TREATING THE *HELICOBACTER PYLORI* ULCER PATIENT. The steps in the treatment of *H. pylori* infection are to diagnose (test), treat, and confirm cure. The widespread availability of noninvasive testing (e.g., urea breath or stool antigen tests) have made pretreatment and posttreatment testing easy and have eliminated any controversy about appropriateness. The minimal duration of antibiotic therapy is unknown. *H. pylori* is a bacterial infection; the goal is to cure all the patients, and theoretically cure rates should exceed 95%. Triple therapy including a PPI yields an eradication rate of 72 to 84%, rising as high as 91% among patients who comply with the full protocol.[2] Studies in the United States and in Europe generally have shown that 14 days of therapy provide better cure rates than therapies of either 7 or 10 days' duration. Practically, the minimum duration of therapy should be at least 10 days. The simplest approach for *H. pylori*–related ulcers is to combine antisecretory therapy with antimicrobial therapy for 10 days to 2 weeks. Antisecretory therapy provides rapid relief of pain, accelerates ulcer healing, and, with many drug combinations, improves the cure rate. Antisecretory therapy can be discontinued at the same time as the antibiotics unless the patient has a history of prior ulcer complications, in which case H_2-receptor antagonists or PPIs should be continued until cure of the infection is confirmed.

Many combination therapies are available that reliably cure *H. pylori* infections (see Table 138–6). The major factors reducing effectiveness of therapy are the presence of antibiotic-resistant *H. pylori* and poor compliance with the regimens. Therapies can be divided into first-line, second-line, and salvage therapies (see Treatment Failures).

Confirmation of Results of Therapy. Although confirmation of successful treatment of *H. pylori* infection generally is indicated, testing must be delayed until any remaining bacteria have had an opportunity to repopulate the stomach. Failure to cure the infection in a patient with peptic ulcer leads to return of symptoms, recurrent ulcer disease, continuing risk of ulcer complications, and the need for more tests and additional treatment. The patient also remains a reservoir for transmission of the infection, especially to family members. If the patient declines post-therapy testing, the discussion should be recorded in the chart to protect the physician if ulcer complications should occur. Although a positive test at any time after the end of therapy indicates failure, the most reliable results are obtained 4 or more weeks after ending antimicrobial therapy. Noninvasive testing with the ^{13}C-urea breath test or a stool antigen test is preferred, unless there is a compelling reason for endoscopy, such as the need to re-evaluate a "suspicious" gastric ulcer or the status of pyloric stenosis. Because PPIs inhibit growth of *H. pylori*, they must be discontinued at least 1 week (preferably 2 weeks) before testing to confirm that the therapy was successful. H_2-receptor antagonists do not affect culture, histology, or the ^{13}C-urea breath test and can be continued, if necessary, up to the day before testing. The stool antigen test requires a longer delay after the end of antibiotic therapy than does breath testing and is best deferred for 6 to 8 weeks after antibiotic therapy.

Treatment Failure. Failure of therapy to cure the infection is an increasing problem. In general, failure to cure means that the organism was or has become resistant to one of the major antibiotics used (e.g., clarithromycin or metronidazole). A drug combination that does not use the suspect drug should be given for the second attempt. If the combination of a PPI, clarithromycin, and amoxicillin failed, the next attempt would avoid clarithromycin (amoxicillin resistance is rare even after treatment failure). Ideally, pretreatment culture and susceptibility testing guide therapy, but culture is not routinely available. Salvage therapy, or therapy for patients who have failed more than two attempts, is handled best by referral to a specialized center. Alternatively, quadruple therapy with a PPI, tetracycline (500 mg four times daily), metronidazole (500 mg three times daily), and bismuth (e.g., bismuth subsalicylate, 2 tablets four times daily) for 14 days is often successful. Because this regimen generally has a higher initial cure rate than traditional triple therapies, it also can be an initial therapy. An alternative salvage therapy uses high-dose omeprazole (40 mg three times daily) plus amoxacillin (1 gm three times daily). Either approach has a high rate of success, even in the face of metronidazole resistance.

NONSTEROIDAL ANTI-INFLAMMATORY DRUG ULCERS. Because continued NSAID use delays ulcer healing, it is generally best to stop the NSAID and use antisecretory therapy to heal the ulcer. Patients who are NSAID users and who also are infected with *H. pylori* should receive therapy for *H. pylori* infection. Many elderly patients with osteoarthritis receive potent NSAIDs when they actually require only analgesia (Chapter 287). Stopping the NSAID provides a reverse therapeutic challenge that allows the physician to assess whether the NSAID was needed. For patients with rheumatoid arthritis (Chapter 278) who require active anti-inflammatory therapy, prednisone (5 to 10 mg/day) can be given without apparently adversely affecting ulcer healing (Chapter 31). After ulcer healing, patients requiring NSAID therapy can be prescribed a selective COX-2 inhibitor (a coxib; Chapter 32) or be given a traditional NSAID with concomitant misoprostol with or without a PPI or H_2-receptor antagonist. Clinically, in NSAID users without *H. pylori* infection, H_2-receptor antagonists, PPIs, and misoprostol all are approximately equally effective in preventing endoscopic NSAID ulcers. Their relative merits in non–*H. pylori*–infected individuals for the prevention of NSAID-induced ulcer complications are unknown because only misoprostol and the selective COX-2 inhibitors have been evaluated and shown to be effective in reducing ulcer complications.

Prevention of Nonsteroidal Anti-Inflammatory Drug Ulcers. The large multicenter studies of omeprazole for prevention of NSAID ulcers seem to have provided misleading impressions of effectiveness, in part because of failure to separate *H. pylori*–infected and non–*H. pylori*–infected NSAID users.[3] The results with misoprostol among patients without complicating *H. pylori* infection are superior to results with omeprazole. Omeprazole and ranitidine are approximately equal for ulcer prevention in that patient population. Subsequent studies in non–*H. pylori*–infected NSAID users confirmed that PPI therapy (lansoprazole) was superior to placebo and slightly less effective than full-dose misoprostol. When one considers the higher proportion of dropouts among misoprostol users, the two strategies (PPI or misoprostol) were clinically equal. Currently the combination of low-dose misoprostol (400 µg) and a H_2-receptor antagonist or PPI seems to provide the highest level of protection with traditional NSAIDs. [4] It is probably best to avoid traditional NSAIDs for long-term use and to consider selective COX-2 inhibitors. Low-dose ibuprofen (e.g., 200 to 400 mg), which is a potent analgesic with low anti-inflammatory effect (at these doses), generally can be used safely for acute pain at a low cost (Chapter 32). The remaining problem is with aspirin, with which the risk of an ulcer complication is 1 to 2% per year among chronic users even with low-dose aspirin (Chapter 33). Nevertheless, the risk-to-benefit ratio for aspirin for prophylaxis of cardiovascular events is decidedly on the side of aspirin. The best strategy for prevention is unclear, but *H. pylori* eradication is likely to play a role in the ultimate approach.

Preventing *Helicobacter pylori* Ulcer Recurrence. Curing *H. pylori* infection cures *H. pylori* ulcers; maintenance antisecretory therapy is not needed. For patients with resistant infections, antisecretory therapy can be continued at approximately one half of the healing dose to reduce ulcer recurrence and prevent ulcer complications.

SPECIAL SITUATIONS. Because patients with a history of ulcer complications such as bleeding have a high probability of having another complication, it is important not to discontinue antisecretory therapy until it has been confirmed that the *H. pylori* infection has been cured. In patients with large ulcers, especially ulcers that have recently bled; patients who have had balloon dilation of gastric outlet obstruction for ulcer disease; or in frail patients with major comorbid disease, PPIs are preferred until the ulcer heals. In patients who require long-term aspirin therapy, chronic treatment with a PPI can reduce recurrent ulcer complications. [5]

Complications of Peptic Ulcer

Patients with ulcer disease are at risk of developing ulcer complications, such as bleeding, perforation, or obstruction. The risk for *H. pylori*–infected ulcer patients who have never suffered a complication is 1% per year; the likelihood of a complication sometime during the life history of peptic ulcer disease is 20 to 30%. When a complication has occurred, the risk of a subsequent complication increases to approximately 1 to 3% per month.

INTRACTABILITY. Intractability is defined as failure of an ulcer to heal despite successful treatment of *H. pylori* infection and adequate antisecretory therapy. Intractability is rare and suggests a complicating factor, such as Zollinger-Ellison syndrome (Chapter 140); concomitant, and often covert, NSAID use; or another disease, such as Crohn's disease, masquerading as a peptic ulcer. Evaluation should include a determination of the serum gastrin and calcium levels and requestioning about drug use, especially regarding over-the-counter medications that contain aspirin. Assessment of gastric secretory function with a gastric analysis occasionally may be necessary to exclude hypersecretory states. This problem is infrequent enough that referral to a gastroenterologist with particular interest in peptic ulcer disease is probably indicated. Ultimately, surgery may be necessary (Chapter 139).

HEMORRHAGE. For major upper gastrointestinal bleeding (Chapter 133), the incidence rate is 150 per 100,000 population; the mortality rate is 5 to 10%, in part because of bleeding in older and sicker patients. Peptic ulcer disease remains the most common cause of major upper gastrointestinal bleeding; 15 to 20% of ulcer patients experience hemorrhage during the course of disease. NSAIDs are now responsible for an increasingly large percentage of upper gastrointestinal bleeding because of the increasing use of these drugs and the decreased prevalence of *H. pylori* infection.

Approximately 80% of patients relate a history of symptomatic ulcer disease before the onset of bleeding, about 33% have had a previous hemorrhage, and about 10% have bled more than once. At presentation, hematemesis and/or melena are evident in more than 95%; 15% present in shock. Clinical features that suggest a poor outcome are age older than 60 years, hematemesis, presence of shock, severe bleeding requiring multiple transfusions, and presence of clinically active comorbid disease (particularly cardiovascular, respiratory, hepatic, or malignant). Physical examination should assess circulatory status, determine the presence of comorbid disease, and search for features suggesting other causes of hemorrhage, such as the presence of chronic liver disease or cutaneous telangiectasia.

Management. The management steps are resuscitation, diagnosis, therapy, and a plan for long-term management (Chapter 133). For serious bleeding, outcome is best if initial management is in an intensive care unit and if decisions are made by a team experienced in managing gastrointestinal hemorrhage. Resuscitation takes precedence over diagnosis, and one of the first steps for the patient with significant bleeding is to restore the vascular and the oxygen-carrying capacity of the blood. A systolic blood pressure less than 100 mm Hg or pulse greater than 100 beats per minute is suggestive of volume depletion of 20% or more. A positive tilt test (defined as a systolic blood pressure decrease >10 mm Hg or an increase in pulse rate >20 beats per minute on standing or sitting) suggests an acute blood loss greater than 1 L. An intravenous catheter should be inserted in all patients, and 0.9% saline should be infused as rapidly as the patient's cardiopulmonary status allows. Blood should be obtained for a complete blood cell count; assessment of coagulation status; and determination of serum electrolyte, blood urea nitrogen (BUN), and creatinine levels. In most instances, it also is prudent to send blood for typing and crossmatching. Transfusions generally should be given to maintain the hemoglobin at about 10 g/dL; overtransfusion should be avoided. The response of the blood pressure to postural changes usually provides a reasonably reliable indication of whether the intravascular volume is unstable. The hematocrit is not reliable after acute hemorrhage. An elevated BUN concentration and a normal serum creatinine value in the presence of melena strongly suggests a significant upper gastrointestinal site of bleeding. The rate of normalization in the BUN is a useful gauge of the effectiveness of volume replacement because correction of the deficit in the vascular volume results in a rapid return of the BUN to normal. Most clinicians would insert a nasogastric tube to ascertain whether there is fresh blood or clots within the stomach. Lavage of the stomach with ice water no longer is thought to be of value and is not recommended.

Bleeding from a peptic ulcer is usually self-limited; about 5% do not stop bleeding. Rebleeding occurs in 20 to 25%, with 80 to 90% of rebleeding episodes occurring within 48 hours of presentation. After the patient's condition has stabilized, attention can focus on the site of bleeding. Endoscopy provides rapid diagnosis, and endoscopic therapy has become the method of choice for initial management of upper gastrointestinal bleeding. All patients with clinical evidence of major bleeding, such as hemodynamic instability, need for transfusions, or decreasing hematocrit, should undergo early endoscopy; patients with endoscopic evidence of active bleeding, adherent clot, or visible vessel should receive endoscopic therapy. Most also would begin ulcer therapy with an H_2-receptor antagonist or PPI administered intravenously by continuous infusion. Endoscopy increasingly is being used to triage patients into subgroups who can be sent home compared with patients who require a regular medical-surgical bed or intensive care (Chapter 133).

Management After Bleeding. Patients who have bled should be investigated for *H. pylori* status and for NSAID use. Maintenance antisecretory therapy reduces the incidence of subsequent complications and should not be withdrawn until it has been confirmed that the *H. pylori* infection has been treated successfully. If the patient was receiving NSAIDs and does not have *H. pylori* infection, traditional NSAIDs should be prescribed with great caution in the future. If NSAIDs are required, a selective COX-2 inhibitor may be tried, or the lowest possible dose of a conventional NSAID should be used along with cotherapy with a PPI, misoprostol, or a combination. For cardiovascular indications, newer antiplatelet medications (Chapter 33) should be considered as a substitute for aspirin if possible; if aspirin is used, the dose should be as low as possible, and antisecretory therapy or misoprostol cotherapy should be considered.

The recognition that *H. pylori* peptic ulcer disease can be cured has eliminated gastric surgery as an acceptable first-line therapy (Chapter 139). If an operation is required to control hemorrhage, simple oversewing of the ulcer and, if possible, a highly selective vagotomy is the treatment of choice (Chapter 139). Gastrectomy should be avoided whenever possible.

PERFORATION. The incidence of ulcer perforation is 7 to 10 per 100,000 population per year. Perforation is more common in men than in women (4 to 8:1), although that ratio appears to be changing as the frequency of gastric perforation is increasing in association with NSAID use in elderly women. The most common presentation is an abrupt onset of severe abdominal pain followed rapidly by signs of peritoneal inflammation (Chapter 146). The typical patient appears to be acutely and seriously ill, lying immobile in bed with grunting and shallow respiration. Abdominal tenderness is usually most pronounced in the epigastrium; spasm of the abdominal musculature usually approaches boardlike rigidity. Loss of hepatic dullness, if present, is a valuable clue to the correct diagnosis. The possibility of a perforated viscus should be the differential diagnosis in any patient with unexplained shock.

Leukocytosis appears rapidly. Blood chemistries are usually normal, with the exception of the serum amylase value, which may be slightly increased. The suspected diagnosis can be confirmed by the identification of free intraperitoneal air, which is demonstrable in about 80% of cases and is seen best on erect chest radiograph or a left decubitus film of the abdomen rather than a plain abdominal film. When the diagnosis is suspected and radiographs are negative, it is worthwhile to repeat the radiographic evaluation after several hours. The diagnosis may be confirmed by an upper gastrointestinal series using a radiopaque contrast medium (Gastrografin), especially if it is combined with computed tomography to enhance the ability to identify the perforation and exclude other pathology.

Management. Initial management is to prepare the patient for presumed surgery (Chapter 139). The steps include resuscitation by correction of fluid and electrolyte abnormalities; treatment of complications; continuous nasogastric suction; parenteral administration of broad-spectrum antibiotics (e.g., an ampicillin/sulbactam combination and gentamicin); and, if a tension pneumoperitoneum is present, needle aspiration of the peritoneal cavity. Nasogastric suction is a mainstay of therapy, and it is important to confirm that the aspirating ports of the nasogastric tube are positioned in the most dependent portion of the stomach. A randomized trial comparing nonoperative treatment with emergency surgery showed that an initial period of nonoperative observation yielded similar outcome, and the decision not to operate immediately could be based on the age and clinical condition of the patient. **6** If there is evidence of increasing peritoneal irritation after 6 hours of treatment, it is best to declare nonoperative therapy a failure and to proceed to surgery. Alternatively, surgery may be chosen immediately in any patient in whom there is not good evidence that the perforation has sealed. Simple closure of the perforation and proximal selective gastric vagotomy is the preferred operation.

The long-term plan for a patient who has survived a perforation and is ready to be discharged from the hospital depends on whether the patient received a definitive ulcer operation, had simple closure of the perforation, or was managed with conservative medical therapy and whether the perforation was a complication of concomitant NSAID use. H. pylori status should be determined, and if present, the infection should be treated even if the patient received a definitive ulcer operation. Because treatment of H. pylori infection cures peptic ulcer disease, it is likely that it also will prevent the complication from recurring. Recommendations regarding future NSAID and aspirin use are the same as for patients who have survived an ulcer hemorrhage (see earlier).

OBSTRUCTION. Approximately 2% of ulcer patients develop gastric outlet obstruction; 90% are caused by previous or coexistent duodenal or channel ulcers. Inflammatory swelling surrounding the ulcer, muscular spasm associated with nearby ulcer, and cicatricial narrowing with fibrosis are the factors responsible for the obstruction. The mainstay of initial resuscitation and therapy is conservative medical management with decompression of the obstructed stomach; correction of fluid, electrolyte, and acid-base abnormalities; and intravenous H_2-receptor antagonist therapy. Endoscopic balloon dilation and treatment of H. pylori infection have reduced the need for surgery to relieve obstruction. Resuscitation and antisecretory therapy usually provide rapid relief for most patients in whom the obstruction is related functionally to edema. For patients with stricture, endoscopic balloon dilation of the pylorus combined with antisecretory therapy (e.g., full-dose PPI therapy) and followed by treatment of the H. pylori infection is usually effective. For patients in whom the stricture rapidly recurs, missed gastric cancer becomes a likely diagnosis, and endoscopic biopsy is required and often is followed by surgery.

1. Malfertheiner P, Megraud F, O'Morain C, et al: Current concepts in the management of *Helicobacter pylori* infection—the Maastricht 2-2000 consensus report. Aliment Pharmacol Ther 2002;16:167–180.
2. Ulmer HJ, Beckerling A, Gatz G: Recent use of proton pump inhibitor-based triple therapies for the eradication of *H. pylori*: A broad data review. Helicobacter 2003;8:95–104.
3. Graham DY: Critical effect of *Helicobacter pylori* infection on the effectiveness of omeprazole for prevention of gastric or duodenal ulcers among chronic NSAID users. Helicobacter 2002;7:1–8.
4. Graham DY, Agrawal NM, Campbell DR, et al: Ulcer prevention in long-term users of nonsteroidal anti-inflammatory drugs: Results of a double-blind, randomized, multicenter, active- and placebo-controlled study of misoprostol vs lansoprazole. Arch Intern Med 2002;162:169–175.
5. Lai KC, Lam SK, Chu KM, et al: Lansoprazole for the prevention of recurrences of ulcer complications from long-term low-dose aspirin use. N Engl J Med 2002;346:2033–2038.
6. Crofts TJ, Park KGM, Steele RJC, et al: A randomized trial of nonoperative treatment for perforated peptic ulcer. N Engl J Med 1989;320:970–973.

SUGGESTED READINGS

Graham DY, Qureshi WA: Markers of infection. *In* Mobley HLT, Mendz GL, Hazell SL (eds): *Helicobacter pylori*: Physiology and Genetics. Washington, DC, ASM Press, 2001, pp 499–510. *Review of the pros and cons of the various methods of diagnosis of* H. pylori *infection.*

Huang JQ, Sridhar S, Hunt RH: Role of *Helicobacter pylori* infection and non-steroidal anti-inflammatory drugs in peptic-ulcer disease: A meta-analysis. Lancet 2002; 359:14–22. *Meta-analysis shows that there is likely an interaction between* H. pylori *and NSAIDs and that eradication of* H. pylori *should be considered in long-term NSAID users.*

Rostom A, Wells G, Tugwell P, et al: The prevention of chronic NSAID induced upper gastrointestinal toxicity: A Cochrane collaboration metaanalysis of randomized controlled trials. J Rheumatol 2000;27:2203–2214. *Meta-analysis of the available trials of studies in long-term NSAID users.*

139 PEPTIC ULCER DISEASE: SURGICAL THERAPY

Susan Orloff
Haile Debas

The overall role of surgery in ulcer therapy has declined over the past two decades because of a decrease in the natural incidence of peptic ulcer disease, the advent of effective pharmacologic therapies, the understanding of the central role of *Helicobacter pylori* in the etiology of peptic ulcer disease, and the dramatic reduction of ulcer recurrence after *H. pylori* eradication. Although the rate of emergent complications of peptic ulcer (bleeding and perforation) has not changed, the incidence of surgical intervention has, because of the advent of improved endoscopic therapies (Chapters 132 and 133). The use of nonsteroidal anti-inflammatory drugs (NSAIDs) continues to be an important and growing cause of peptic ulcer and its complications (Chapter 138).

Indications

Indications for elective surgical treatment for ulcers are few and include intractable disease due to NSAIDs or persistent disease despite

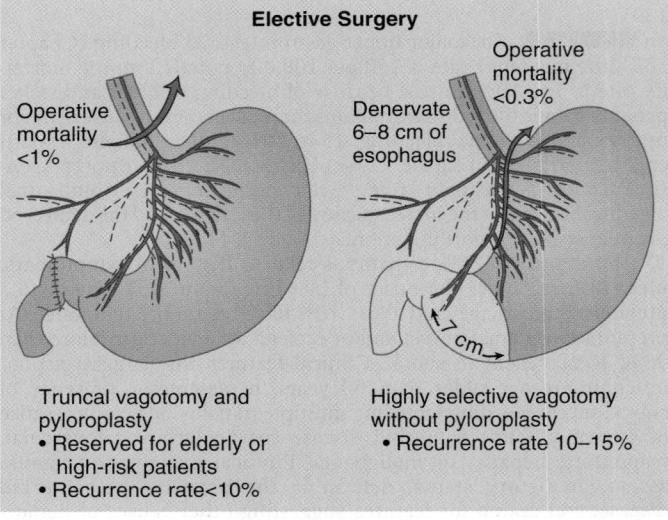

FIGURE 139–1 • Model illustrating the most common surgical procedures used for peptic ulcer disease.

total eradication of *H. pylori* and several courses of antiulcer therapies. A second indication is the high cost of prolonged ulcer therapy in economically disadvantaged countries. Less than 10% of patients admitted with bleeding duodenal ulcer require endoscopic or surgical intervention.

Indications for emergent or urgent operative intervention are more common and include perforation, bleeding, and gastric outlet obstruction. The incidence of gastric outlet obstruction has decreased as a result of *H. pylori* eradication.

A patient clearly needs surgery if there is acute peritonitis due to a perforated peptic ulcer. In patients with equivocal signs of peritonitis or in those who present more than 48 hours after a perforation, nonoperative management is indicated as long as the perforation is sealed and the patient is not septic. Otherwise, an operative approach is recommended.

Operative Procedures

The most appropriate and commonly used procedures are highly selective vagotomy and truncal vagotomy and pyloroplasty (Fig. 139–1). Either of these surgical procedures can be done by the open technique or laparoscopically.

Choice of Operative Procedure

Elective surgical therapy is rarely required for peptic ulcer because failure to heal is unusual and because most cases of gastric cancer are diagnosed at the original endoscopy (Fig. 139–2).

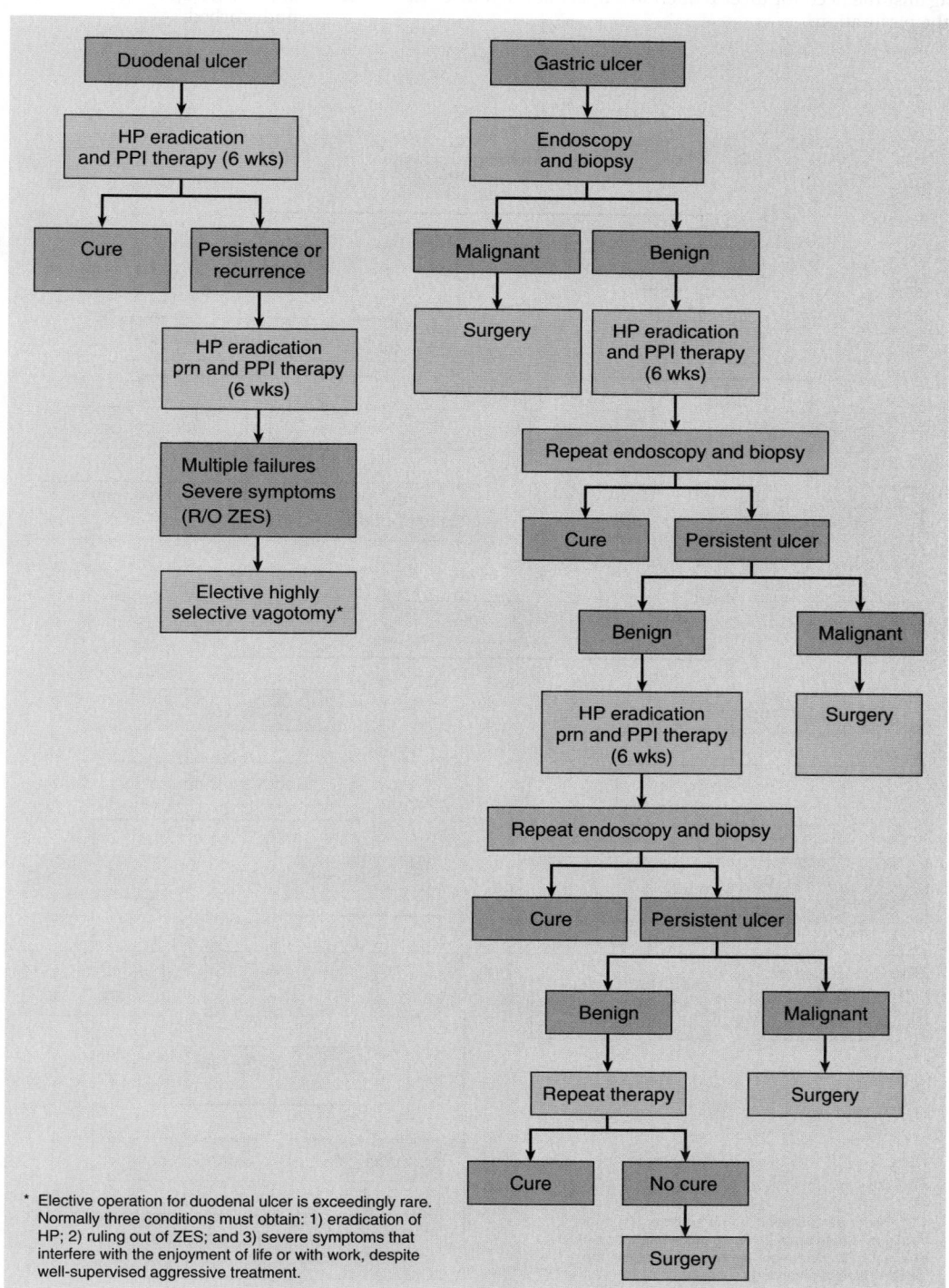

FIGURE 139–2 • Role of surgery in the management of uncomplicated ulcer. HP = *Helicobacter pylori*; PPI = proton pump inhibitors; R/O = rule out; ZES = Zollinger-Ellison syndrome.

* Elective operation for duodenal ulcer is exceedingly rare. Normally three conditions must obtain: 1) eradication of HP; 2) ruling out of ZES; and 3) severe symptoms that interfere with the enjoyment of life or with work, despite well-supervised aggressive treatment.

DUODENAL ULCER

Elective Surgery

The elective procedures of choice for intractable duodenal ulcer are shown in Figure 139–1.

Emergent/Urgent Surgery

PERFORATION. The primary goal of surgery is to close the perforation and prevent continuing peritoneal contamination and infection (Fig. 139–3). Prospective, randomized clinical trials have shown that adding routine, highly selective vagotomy is associated with a significant decrease in ulcer recurrence and subsequent need for operation but no increase in morbidity or mortality.[1] A recent randomized trial has also shown that eradication of *H. pylori* prevents ulcer recurrence after simple closure of perforation.[2] This finding argues against the need for ulcer reduction surgery at the time of closure of the perforation.

BLEEDING. The standard approach to bleeding ulcer is endoscopic control (see Fig 139–3). Controlled trials have shown that once endoscopic hemostasis is achieved, *H. pylori* eradication significantly prevents further bleeding.[3] Surgery is indicated only if repeated attempts at endoscopic control are unsuccessful.[4] The preferred emergent operation for bleeding is suture control of bleeding by means of duodenotomy and highly selective vagotomy, except in the unstable patient in whom truncal vagotomy and pyloroplasty may be used. Simple control of bleeding either laparoscopically or with an open procedure without vagotomy is becoming a potentially acceptable option, because eradication of *H. pylori* is known to prevent further bleeding after endoscopic control of bleeding. However, this specific surgical approach has not been assessed in randomized trials.

OBSTRUCTION. Truncal vagotomy and antrectomy with gastroduodenal anastomosis (Billroth I) is the surgical treatment of choice in gastric outlet obstruction. If the duodenum is involved in an inflammatory mass or is otherwise severely distorted, truncal vagotomy and gastrojejunostomy should be done, leaving the duodenum undisturbed.

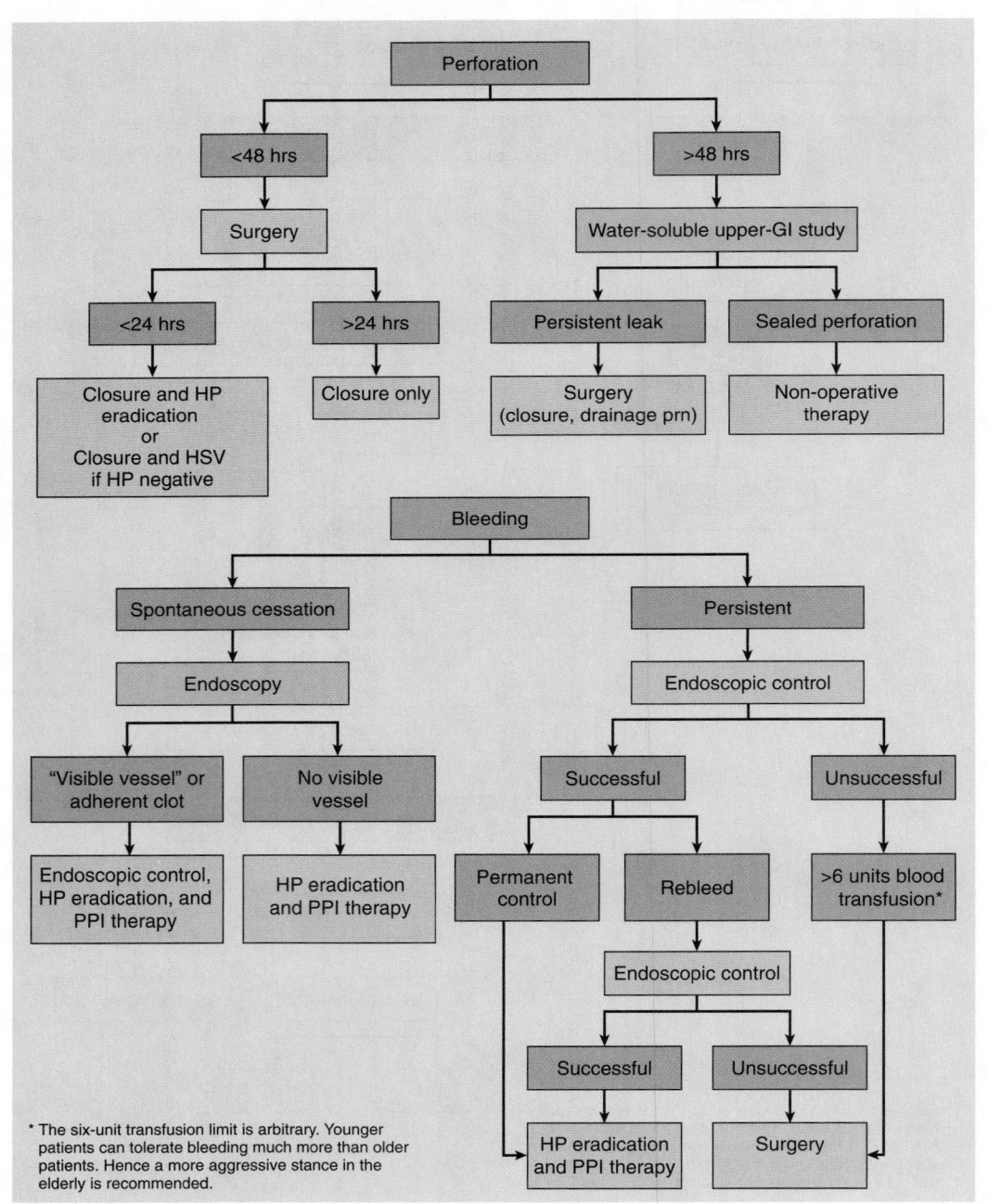

* The six-unit transfusion limit is arbitrary. Younger patients can tolerate bleeding much more than older patients. Hence a more aggressive stance in the elderly is recommended.

FIGURE 139–3 • Role of surgery in the management of ulcer complication. GI = gastrointestinal; HP = *Helicobacter pylori*; HSV = highly selective vagotomy; PPI = proton pump inhibitor.

GASTRIC ULCER

Elective Operation

The choice of elective operation depends on the type of gastric ulcer (Table 139–1). The problem of an ulcerated cancer masquerading as a benign ulcer is more common than a benign gastric ulcer degenerating into a malignant one. With the advent of endoscopy, fewer patients diagnosed as having a benign ulcer have an ulcerated cancer. In the United States, carcinoma has been found in only 3% of resected gastric ulcers.

Emergent Operation

BLEEDING. Bleeding is a more serious complication in gastric ulcers than in duodenal ulcers. Surgery (open or laparoscopic) is indicated if endoscopic control fails. In a stable patient, the preferred procedure is distal gastrectomy that removes the ulcer and creates a gastroduodenal (Billroth I) anastomosis. In the less stable patient, ulcer excision with or without vagotomy and pyloroplasty is recommended. If the ulcer cannot be excised, bleeding should be controlled by suture ligation; biopsy specimen may be obtained if deemed safe or it may be postponed to subsequent endoscopy.

PERFORATION. In the stable patient, the preferred and definitive procedure is distal gastrectomy with Billroth I anastomosis. Definitive operation should be avoided if the perforation is older than 24 hours, if the patient is frail or unstable, or if there is severe peritoneal contamination. In these circumstances, a lesser procedure may be considered, such as ulcer excision with vagotomy and pyloroplasty. In extremely ill patients, the ulcer should be sampled in four quadrants and patched with omentum, without the addition of an acid-reducing procedure. Studies of perforated duodenal ulcers suggest that this latter approach combined with a postoperative *H. pylori* eradication regimen may be an effective long-term treatment.

Gastrointestinal Diseases

Table 139–1 • SURGICAL OPTIONS FOR GASTRIC ULCERS

TYPE	LOCATION	INCIDENCE	TREATMENT OF CHOICE	COMMENTS
I	Body (lesser curve)	55–60%	Antrectomy (Billroth I)	Ulcer resected with specimen. Mortality/recurrence rate of 2%. Highly selective vagotomy and ulcer excision is a less optimal approach.
II	In association with duodenal ulcer	20–25%	Vagotomy and antrectomy	Acid reduction and ulcer excision accomplished
III	Prepyloric	20%	Vagotomy and antrectomy	Behaves like duodenal ulcer
IV	High-lying near gastroesophageal junction	<5%	Resection and esophagogastrojejunostomy (Csendes)	More common in South America

---

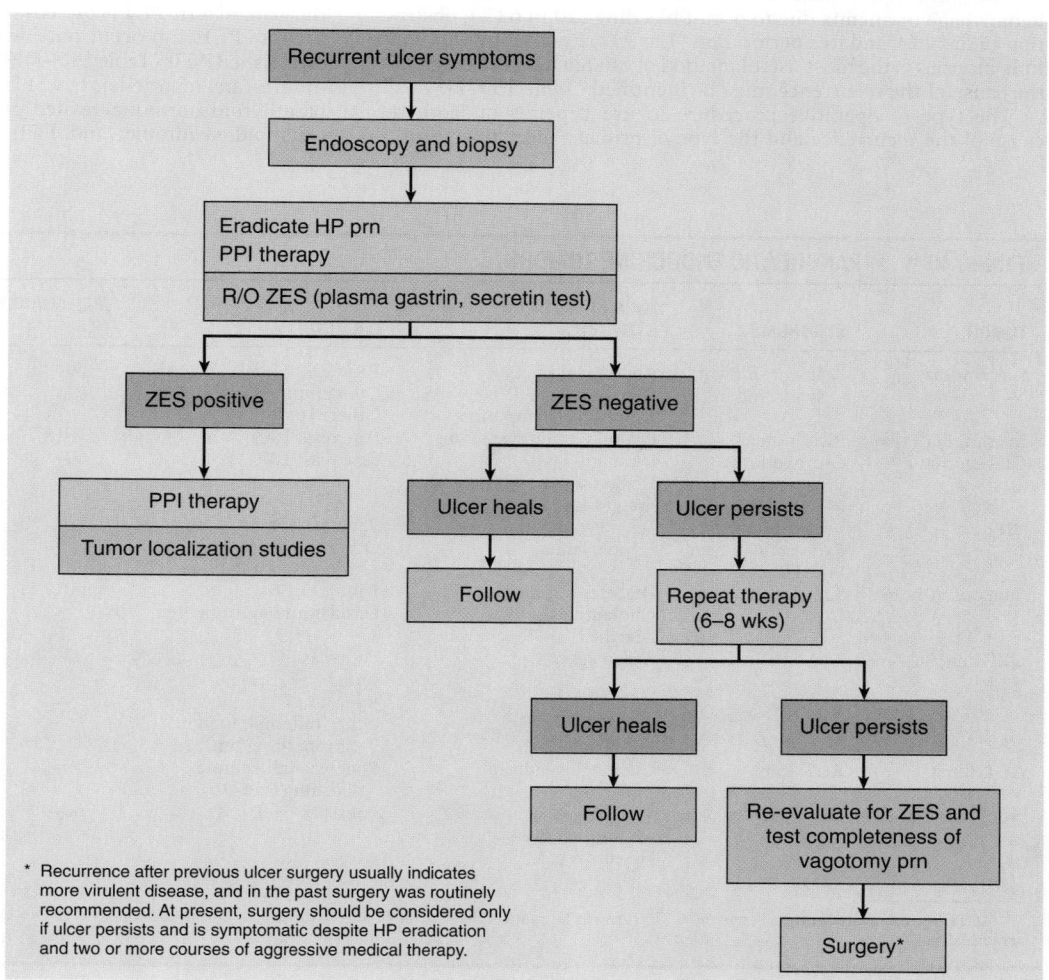

FIGURE 139–4 • Management of ulcer recurrence after previous ulcer surgery. HP = *Helicobacter pylori*; PPI = proton pump inhibitors; R/O = rule out; ZES = Zollinger-Ellison syndrome.

* Recurrence after previous ulcer surgery usually indicates more virulent disease, and in the past surgery was routinely recommended. At present, surgery should be considered only if ulcer persists and is symptomatic despite HP eradication and two or more courses of aggressive medical therapy.

Table 139–2 • CAUSES OF POSTOPERATIVE ULCER RECURRENCE

Persistent *Helicobacter pylori* infection
Inappropriate primary operation
   Highly selective vagotomy for gastric and prepyloric ulcer
Inadequate operation
   Incomplete vagotomy
   Inadequate drainage
   Inadequate resection
   Retained antrum
Hypersecretory states
   Gastrinoma
   Multiple endocrine neoplasia I syndrome
   G-cell hyperplasia
   Hypercalcemia
Ulcerogenic drugs
   Nonsteroidal anti-inflammatory drugs
   Steroids
   Reserpine

RECURRENT ULCER AFTER SURGERY

H_2-receptor antagonists and proton pump inhibitors (PPIs) have been shown to be effective in treating recurrent ulcer, particularly after previous vagotomy (Fig. 139–4). Eradication therapy of *H. pylori* has further improved medical treatment of recurrent ulcer. In recurrent ulcers, the incidence of *H. pylori* positivity has been reported to range from 5 to 50% (compared with 75 to 90% incidence in primary ulcer disease). In the absence of a surgically treatable cause of the recurrence (retained antrum, gastrinoma), medical therapy (especially *H. pylori* eradication) should be attempted; surgery should be considered only if medical therapy fails.

The clinical presentation of recurrent ulcer includes pain (95%), hemorrhage or anemia due to occult bleeding (20 to 63%), obstruction (5 to 19%), and free perforation (1 to 9%). Endoscopy with multiple biopsies is the most useful method of establishing the diagnosis; the cause of the recurrence must be identified (Table 139–2).

The type of operative procedure to use depends on both the cause of the recurrence and the type of primary ulcer operation. If gastrinoma (Zollinger-Ellison) is diagnosed and identified by localization studies, the tumor should be resected. If the tumor cannot be identified by localization studies, including thorough surgical exploration of the pancreas, duodenum, and retroperitoneum, the treatment of choice is long-term PPI therapy. Total gastrectomy is reserved for PPI failure or intolerance. In most patients, however, none of these causes is identified and the treatment should be a more extensive antiulcer operation to include revagotomy and resection or re-resection of the antrum.

1. Boey J, Braniki FJ, Alagaratam TT, et al: Proximal gastric vagotomy: The preferred operation for perforations in acute duodenal ulcer. Ann Surg 1988;208:169–174.
2. Ng EK, Lam YH, Sung JJ, et al: Eradication of *Helicobacter pylori* prevents recurrence of ulcer after simple closure of duodenal ulcer perforation. Randomized controlled trial. Ann Surg 2000;231:153–158.
3. Graham DY, Hepps KS, Ramirez FC, et al: Treatment of *Helicobacter pylori* reduces the rate of rebleeding in peptic ulcer disease. Scand J Gastroenterol 1993;28:939–942.
4. Lau JY, Sung JJ, Lam YH, et al: Endoscopic retreatment compared with surgery in patients with recurrent bleeding after initial endoscopic control of bleeding ulcers. N Engl J Med 1999;340:751–756.

SUGGESTED READINGS

Stabile BE: Redefining the role of surgery for perforated duodenal ulcer in the *Helicobacter pylori* era. Ann Surg 2000;231:159–160. *A cogent editorial opinion addressing the role of* H. pylori *and controversies in surgical management of perforated duodenal ulcer.*
Towfigh S, Chandler C, Hines OJ, et al: Outcomes from peptic ulcer surgery have not benefited from advances in medical therapy. Am Surg 2002;68:385–389. *Since 1981, operations for peptic ulcers decreased by more than 50%, but the 30-day mortality rate is unchanged.*

140 PANCREATIC ENDOCRINE TUMORS

Robert T. Jensen

Pancreatic endocrine tumors (PETs) also are called *islet tumors* or *islet cell tumors*; however, because the cell of origin of most is unknown, the general term *PET* is preferred. This term is also a slight misnomer because PETs can occur outside the pancreas. There are eight well-established PETs (Table 140–1). Three additional functional PET syndromes are reported rarely: PETs causing hypercalcemia (usually parathyroid hormone–related peptide secreting), PETs causing the carcinoid syndrome, and PETs secreting renin (one case). PETs

Table 140–1 • PANCREATIC ENDOCRINE TUMORS

TUMOR	SYNDROME	MAIN SIGNS OR SYMPTOMS	LOCATION (%)	MALIGNANCY (%)	HORMONE CAUSING SYNDROME
Gastrinoma	Zollinger-Ellison syndrome	Abdominal pain Diarrhea Esophageal symptoms	Pancreas: 30 Duodenum: 60 Other: 10	60–90	Gastrin
Insulinoma	Insulinoma	Hypoglycemic symptoms	Pancreas: 100	5–15	Insulin
Glucagonoma	Glucagonoma	Dermatitis Diabetes/glucose intolerance Weight loss	Pancreas: 100	60	Glucagon
VIPoma	Verner-Morrison Pancreatic cholera WDHA	Severe watery diarrhea Hypokalemia	Pancreas: 90 Other (neural, adrenal, periganglionic tissue): 10	80	VIP
Somatostatinoma	Somatostatinoma	Diabetes mellitus Cholelithiasis Diarrhea	Pancreas: 56 Duodenum/jejunum: 44	60	Somatostatin
GRFoma	GRFoma	Acromegaly	Pancreas: 30 Lung: 54 Jejunum: 7 Other (adrenal, foregut, retroperitoneum): 13	30	GRF
ACTHoma	ACTHoma	Cushing's syndrome	Pancreas (all ectopic Cushing's): 4–16	>95	ACTH
Nonfunctioning	Nonfunctional PPoma	Weight loss Abdominal mass Hepatomegaly	Pancreas: 100	60–90	None—pancreatic polypeptide or chromogranin released but no known symptoms caused by hypersecretion

ACTH = adrenocorticotropic hormone; GRF = growth hormone–releasing factor; VIP = vasoactive intestinal peptide; WDHA = watery diarrhea, hypokalemia, and achlorhydria.

synthesizing neurotensin, calcitonin, and ghrelin also are reported, but no distinct syndrome has been described. PETs each share many features. PETs are classified as *APUDomas* (*a*mine *p*recursor *u*ptake and *d*ecarboxylation), and they share cytochemical features with carcinoid tumors, melanomas, and many other endocrine tumors (pheochromocytomas and medullary thyroid cancer). Except for insulinomas, PETs are frequently malignant. All PETs appear similar histologically; have few mitotic figures; and have dense granules containing peptides, amines, and products of neuroendocrine differentiation (neuron-specific enolase, chromogranins, and synaptophysins). The presence of chromogranin immunoreactivity in the tumor is used widely to identify these tumors as endocrine tumors.

PETs frequently are classified as functional or nonfunctional depending on whether a clinical syndrome secondary to the autonomously released hormone is present (gastrinoma, insulinoma, glucagonoma, VIPoma [caused by vasoactive intestinal peptide (VIP)], somatostatinoma, GRFoma [caused by growth hormone–releasing factor (GFR)], and ACTHoma [caused by adrenocorticotropic hormone (ACTH)]). Nonfunctional PETs frequently release other hormones and peptides (pancreatic polypeptide, neurotensin, chromogranin A, and breakdown products) that cause no distinct clinical syndromes.

PETs are uncommon, having a prevalence of less than 10 per 1 million population. Insulinomas, gastrinomas, and nonfunctional PETs are the most common, with an incidence of one to three new cases per 1 million population. Insulinomas are discussed in Chapter 243.

ZOLLINGER-ELLISON SYNDROME (GASTRINOMAS)

The Zollinger-Ellison syndrome (ZES) is a clinical syndrome caused by a gastrin-releasing endocrine tumor, usually located in the pancreas or duodenum and characterized by clinical symptoms and signs resulting from gastric acid hypersecretion (peptic ulcer disease, diarrhea, esophageal reflux disease).

ZES occurs most frequently between ages 35 and 65 and is slightly more common in men (60%). Abdominal pain resulting from a peptic ulcer is the most common symptom (>80%). Most ulcers occur in the duodenum (>85%), but they occasionally occur in the postbulbar area, jejunum, or stomach and occasionally are in multiple locations. The pain is usually similar to that of patients with typical peptic ulcers (Chapter 138), especially early in the disease course. With time, the symptoms become persistent and, in general, respond poorly to conventional doses of H₂-receptor antagonists, to proton-pump inhibitors, to conventional surgical treatments, and to treatments aimed at eliminating the bacterium *Helicobacter pylori,* which are commonly used for routine duodenal ulcer disease. Heartburn secondary to reflux of gastric acid into the esophagus is also common (20%). Diarrhea (60 to 70%) occurs frequently and may precede peptic ulceration in some patients (10 to 20%). Of patients, 20 to 25% have ZES as part of the multiple endocrine neoplasia type I (MEN I) syndrome, an autosomal dominant inherited disease (Chapter 244). These patients have hyperplasia or tumors of multiple endocrine glands and most commonly have parathyroid hyperplasia (>90%), pituitary tumors (60%), and PETs (80%). ZES is the most common functional PET syndrome these patients develop (54%). Patients typically first develop renal stones secondary to hypercalcemia from hyperparathyroidism or have elevated prolactin levels secondary to pituitary tumors and only later develop ZES.

Pathology and Pathophysiology

In older studies, gastrinomas were found primarily in the pancreas. In more recent large surgical series, gastrinomas are found two to five times more frequently in the duodenum. Duodenal gastrinomas are generally small (<1 cm), whereas pancreatic gastrinomas are generally larger. Occasionally, ZES is due to a gastrinoma in the splenic hilum, mesentery, stomach, or lymph node or to a gastrin-releasing tumor of the ovary. Extrapancreatic gastrinomas producing ZES have been reported secondary to small cell lung cancer. Approximately one third of patients have metastatic liver disease at presentation, but less than 20% of other patients developed metastatic disease to the liver during a 10-year follow-up period. The exact percentage of malignant gastrinomas is unclear. Similar to other PETs, malignancy can be determined reliably only by showing the presence of metastatic disease, and no light microscopic or ultrastructural finding can establish malignant behavior clearly. These patients usually have metastatic gastrinoma in the liver, have ZES without MEN I, and have a poor prognosis. Approximately 25% of gastrinomas show aggressive growth. More recent studies show the most important prognostic predictor is the development of liver metastases. The presence of a large primary, a pancreatic tumor, bone metastases, or high fasting gastrin levels is associated with more aggressive growth.

Gastrin stimulates parietal cells to secrete acid and has a growth effect (trophic) on cells of the gastric mucosa. Chronic hypergastrinemia leads to increased gastric mucosal thickness, prominent gastric folds, and increased numbers of parietal cells and gastric enterochromaffin-like (ECL) cells. Patients with gastrinomas have increased basal acid output and an increased maximal acid output, which is a measure of the total number of parietal cells. Almost all of the symptoms are due to the effects of gastric acid hypersecretion, but, late in the disease, patients can develop cachexia, weight loss, and pain owing to extensive liver metastases. In contrast to patients with routine peptic ulcers, *H. pylori* seems not to be important in the pathogenesis of ulcer disease in ZES. Diarrhea (Chapter 141) is due to the large-volume gastric acid output leading to small intestinal structural damage (inflammation, blunted villi, edema), interference with fat transport, inactivation of pancreatic lipase, and precipitation of bile acids. These same mechanisms, if prolonged, can lead to steatorrhea. If acid hypersecretion is controlled medically, surgically, or with nasogastric suction, the diarrhea stops at once. Of patients with ZES, 5% develop Cushing's syndrome (Chapter 240) resulting from ACTH secretion by the gastrinoma.

Diagnosis and Differential Diagnosis

ZES should be suspected in any patient whose peptic ulcer disease is recurrent; is nonhealing with treatment; is multiple or in unusual locations; is not associated with *H. pylori* infection; or is associated with a complication (e.g., bleeding, obstruction, esophageal stricture), with chronic secretory diarrhea, with a pancreatic tumor, with large gastric folds on radiography or endoscopy, with a family or personal history of renal stones or endocrinopathies, or with a laboratory finding of hypercalcemia, hypergastrinemia, or gastric acid hypersecretion. When the diagnosis is suspected, a fasting serum gastrin level, which is elevated in 99 to 100% of patients with ZES, should be obtained. There are other causes of hypergastrinemia, however, including a physiologic response to achlorhydria or hypochlorhydria because of pernicious anemia, atrophic gastritis, renal failure, *H. pylori* infection, or the use of proton-pump inhibitors, which suppress acid for 1 week after discontinuation. If the serum gastrin level is elevated, the fasting gastric pH should be determined. If the serum gastrin level is greater than 1000 pg/mL (normal <100 pg/mL) and the pH is less than 2.5, the patient almost certainly has ZES. If the gastrin level is elevated less than 10-fold and the pH is less than 2.5, basal acid output and a secretin test should be done. Basal acid output is increased in patients with ZES (>10.6 mEq/hr in men and >5.6 mEq/hr in women), and more than 95% of ZES patients have a value greater than 15 mEq/hr if no previous gastric acid–reducing surgery has been performed.

A secretin test can exclude *H. pylori* infection, retained gastric antrum syndrome, antral G cell hyperfunction/hyperplasia, chronic renal failure, and gastric outlet obstruction that may mimic ZES. Normal individuals show an increase of less than 200 pg/mL in the serum gastrin level after intravenous secretin, whereas 87% of ZES patients with an elevated fasting gastrin increased less than 10-fold have a positive secretin test (i.e., >200 pg/mL increase in serum gastrin after a bolus injection of secretin). No false-positive results have been reported except in patients with achlorhydria. In all patients with ZES, evaluation must exclude MEN I (Chapter 244) syndrome by determining if there is a family history of endocrinopathies and by excluding hyperparathyroidism and pituitary adenomas.

Rx Treatment

Therapy is directed at controlling the gastric acid hypersecretion and at the gastrinoma itself. Proton-pump inhibitors (e.g., omeprazole, lansoprazole, rabeprazole, pantoprazole) are the drugs of choice. Because of their long duration of action, acid hypersecretion can be controlled in all patients with once-daily or twice-daily dosing. The recommended starting dose for omeprazole or

Continued

lansoprazole is 60 mg once a day. In 30% of patients, higher doses are needed, particularly in patients with MEN I, previous gastric surgery, or a history of severe esophageal reflux. Patients need to be treated indefinitely unless they are cured surgically. Long-term therapy is safe, with patients being treated for 15 years with omeprazole without loss of efficacy, although decreased vitamin B_{12} levels have been reported with prolonged treatment. H_2-receptor antagonists also are effective, but frequent dosing (every 4 to 6 hours) and high doses are needed. Total gastrectomy, the classic treatment for this disease, now is performed only for patients who cannot or will not take oral antisecretory medications. Selective vagotomy (Chapter 139) effectively reduces the acid secretion, but many patients continue to require a low dose of drug. Parathyroidectomy should be performed in patients with hyperparathyroidism, ZES, and MEN I because it markedly reduces acid secretion and increases the sensitivity to antisecretory drugs.

All patients should have imaging studies to localize the tumor. Somatostatin receptor scintigraphy (SRS) using single-photon emission computed tomography after injection of ^{111}In-[DTPA-DPhe^1]octreotide is the localization method of choice. SRS identifies 60% of primary gastrinomas and greater than 90% of metastatic disease in the liver; its sensitivity is equal to all conventional imaging studies combined (magnetic resonance imaging, computed tomography, ultrasound, and angiography). For pancreatic gastrinomas, endoscopic ultrasound is particularly sensitive. Small duodenal gastrinomas (<1 cm) frequently are not detected by any imaging modality but can be found at surgery if routine duodenotomy is performed.

Tumors are found in 95% of patients at surgery. Surgical exploration for cure now is recommended in all patients without liver metastases, MEN I, or complicating medical conditions limiting life expectancy. Surgical resection decreases the metastatic rate and results in a 5-year cure rate of 30%. Patients with metastatic gastrinoma in the liver have a poor prognosis, with a 5-year survival rate of 30%. If the metastatic disease is increasing in size or is symptomatic, treatment with octreotide alone or in combination with α-interferon is effective in inhibiting further tumor growth in 50 to 60% of patients. If this treatment fails, chemotherapeutic agents (streptozotocin, 5-fluorouracil, and doxorubicin [Adriamycin]) are recommended. Liver transplantation (Chapter 157) is used occasionally in the rare patient with metastases limited to the liver.

GLUCAGONOMAS

Glucagonomas are endocrine tumors of the pancreas that ectopically secrete glucagon, which causes a specific clinical syndrome whose cardinal features are a distinct dermatitis called *necrolytic migratory erythema* (70 to 90% of patients), diabetes mellitus or glucose intolerance (40 to 90%), weight loss (70 to 96%), anemia (30 to 85%), hypoaminoacidemia (80 to 90%), thromboembolism (10 to 25%), diarrhea (15 to 30%), and psychiatric disturbances (≤20%). The characteristic skin rash (Fig. 140–1) usually is found at intertriginous and periorificial sites, especially in the groin and buttocks. It is initially erythematous, then becomes raised with central bullae; the tops of the bullae detach, and the eroded areas become crusty. Healing occurs with hyperpigmentation.

Pathology and Pathophysiology

Glucagonomas are generally large when discovered (mean size 5 to 10 cm). The most frequent location is in the pancreatic tail (>50%), and liver metastases are present at diagnosis in 45 to 80% of patients. Excess glucagon secretion explains the glucose intolerance. The exact cause of the rash is unclear, but a role for possible zinc deficiency has been proposed because of the similarity of the rash to that seen with zinc deficiency (acrodermatitis enteropathica) and because the rash sometimes improves with zinc therapy. The hypoaminoacidemia is thought to be caused by the effect of altered gluconeogenesis on amino acid metabolism. The wasting and weight loss, which are intrinsic parts of the glucagonoma syndrome, seem to be caused by an anorectic substance distinct from glucagon.

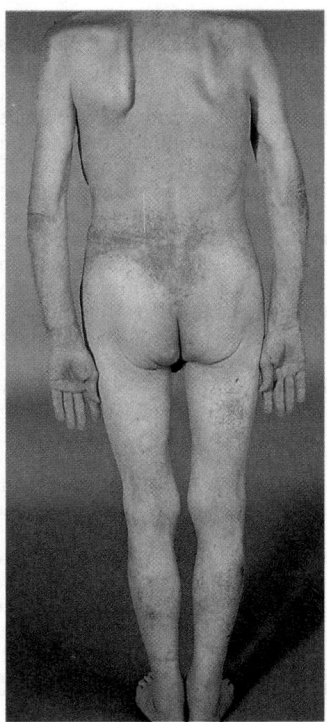

FIGURE 140–1 • Glucagonoma syndrome usually is associated with a characteristic rash, the cause of which is obscure. The rash evolves through stages of erythema, blistering, and crusting and may ultimately be much more severe than in this patient. Note the accompanying weight loss. (From Forbes CD, Jackson WF: Color Atlas and Text of Clinical Medicine, 3rd ed. London, Mosby, 2003, with permission.)

Diagnosis and Differential Diagnosis

The diagnosis is established by showing elevated plasma glucagon levels. Normal levels are 150 to 200 pg/mL; in patients with glucagonomas, levels usually (>90%) are greater than 1000 pg/mL. In some more recent studies, 40% of patients had plasma glucagon values of 500 to 1000 pg/mL. Increased plasma glucagon levels are reported in renal insufficiency, acute pancreatitis, hypercorticism, hepatic diseases, severe stress (trauma, exercise, diabetic ketoacidosis), prolonged fasting, and familial hyperglucagonemia. In these conditions, the level does not usually exceed 500 pg/mL, however, except in patients with hepatic diseases such as cirrhosis or familial hyperglucagonemia.

Rx Treatment

Subcutaneous administration of the synthetic long-acting somatostatin analogue octreotide controls the rash in 80% of patients; improves weight loss, diarrhea, and hypoaminoacidemia; but usually does not improve diabetes mellitus. Zinc supplementation or infusion of amino acids also can diminish the severity of the rash. After tumor localization, surgical resection is preferred; even debulking of metastatic tumor may be of benefit. For advanced disease, chemotherapy with dacarbazine or streptozotocin and doxorubicin, hepatic embolization, or chemoembolization may control symptoms in refractory cases.

VIPomas

The VIPoma syndrome (also called the *Verner-Morrison syndrome, pancreatic cholera,* and *WDHA syndrome* [watery diarrhea, hypokalemia, and achlorhydria]) is due to an endocrine tumor, usually in the pancreas (in adults), that ectopically secretes VIP. The cardinal clinical feature is severe, large-volume, watery diarrhea (>1 L/day) (100%), which is secretory in nature and occurs during fasting (Chapter 141). Hypokalemia (80 to 100%) and dehydration (83%) commonly occur because of the volume of the diarrhea. Achlorhydria sometimes occurs, but hypochlorhydria is usually found (54 to 76%). Flushing occurs in 20% of patients, hyperglycemia in 25 to 50%, and hypercalcemia in 25 to 50%. Steatorrhea is uncommon (16%) despite the volume of diarrhea.

Pathology and Pathophysiology

VIPomas in adults are in the pancreas in 80 to 90% of cases, with rare cases secondary to intestinal carcinoids, ganglioneuromas, ganglioneuroblastomas, or pheochromocytomas. Characteristically in children younger than 10 years old but in less than 5% of adults, the VIPoma syndrome is due to ganglioneuromas or ganglioneuroblastomas at extrapancreatic sites. VIPomas are usually large and solitary, 50 to 75% occur in the pancreatic tail, and 40 to 70% have metastasized at diagnosis. VIPomas frequently secrete VIP and peptide histidine methionine, but VIP is responsible for the symptoms. VIP is a potent stimulant of secretion in the small and large intestine. VIP also relaxes gastrointestinal smooth muscle, an action that may contribute to the dilated loops of bowel and atonic gallbladder often found in this syndrome. Hypochlorhydria is thought to be due to the inhibitory effect of VIP on acid secretion, flushing is due to the vasodilatory effects of VIP, and hyperglycemia is caused by the glycogenolytic effect of VIP. The mechanism of hypercalcemia is unclear.

Diagnosis and Differential Diagnosis

The diarrhea of VIPomas characteristically persists during fasting and is large in volume (>3 L/day in 70 to 80% of patients); the diagnosis is excluded when fasting stool volume is less than 700 mL/day. To differentiate VIPomas from other causes of large-volume, fasting diarrhea, fasting plasma VIP levels should be determined. The normal value in most laboratories is less than 190 pg/mL, and elevated levels are present in 90 to 100% of patients with VIPomas. The differential diagnosis of large-volume, fasting diarrhea (>700 mL/day) includes ZES, diffuse islet cell hyperplasia, surreptitious use of laxatives, pseudopancreatic cholera syndrome, and, rarely, human immunodeficiency virus (HIV) infections. Elevated serum gastrin level identifies patients with ZES, and plasma VIP levels are normal in most patients who abuse laxatives, in 82% of patients with pancreatic islet cell hyperplasias, and in patients with HIV-induced severe secretory diarrhea.

 Treatment

> The symptoms caused by the VIP can be controlled in greater than 85% of patients by octreotide, but increased doses may be needed over time. After tumor localization studies, surgical resection should be attempted, if possible, to remove all visible tumor; however, more than 50% of patients have generalized liver metastases, so resection may not be possible. For advanced cases with refractory symptoms, chemotherapy with streptozotocin and doxorubicin, hepatic chemoembolization, and hepatic embolization have been beneficial.

SOMATOSTATINOMAS

Somatostatinomas are endocrine tumors that occur in the pancreas or upper small intestine and ectopically secrete somatostatin, which causes a distinct clinical syndrome of diabetes mellitus, gallbladder disease, diarrhea, steatorrhea, and weight loss. These symptoms occur three to four times more commonly (80 to 95% of all cases) in patients with pancreatic than in patients with intestinal somatostatinomas. Duodenal somatostatinomas frequently are reported in patients with von Recklinghausen's disease (Chapter 459) and frequently are asymptomatic. Although von Recklinghausen's tumors commonly are called *somatostatinomas* because of the immunocytochemical finding of somatostatin in the tumor, the plasma somatostatin usually is not elevated, and they rarely cause the clinical somatostatinoma syndrome.

Pathology and Pathophysiology

Of somatostatinomas, 60% occur in the pancreas and 40% in the duodenum/jejunum. Pancreatic somatostatinomas occur in the pancreatic head in 60 to 80% of cases; 70 to 92% have metastasized at diagnosis, and they are usually large (mean 5 cm), solitary tumors. In contrast, duodenal somatostatinomas are smaller (mean 2.4 cm), frequently are associated with psammoma bodies on histologic examination, and less frequently have metastases at diagnosis (30 to 40%). Of duodenal somatostatinomas without von Recklinghausen's disease, 70% have elevated plasma somatostatin levels. In the gastrointestinal tract, somatostatin inhibits basal and stimulated acid secretion; pancreatic secretion; intestinal absorption of amino acids; gallbladder contractility; and release of numerous hormones, including cholecystokinin and gastrin.

Diagnosis and Differential Diagnosis

Somatostatinomas usually are found by accident, particularly at exploratory laparotomy for cholecystectomy, during endoscopy, or on imaging studies. The presence of psammoma bodies on histologic examination of a duodenal endocrine tumor or any duodenal lesions in patients with von Recklinghausen's disease should raise the suspicion of a duodenal somatostatinoma. The diagnosis requires the demonstration of increased plasma and tumor concentrations of somatostatin-like immunoreactivity, which also has been reported with endocrine tumors outside of the pancreas or intestine, including small cell lung cancer, medullary thyroid carcinoma, pheochromocytomas, and paragangliomas.

 Treatment

> Treatment with octreotide can improve symptoms. Somatostatinomas can be imaged using SRS or, if needed, other conventional imaging studies to assess tumor location and extent. Surgery, if possible, or chemotherapy, hepatic chemoembolization, or hepatic embolization may be of value.

GRFomas

GRFomas, which are endocrine tumors that frequently originate in the pancreas but also occur in other extrapancreatic locations, ectopically release GRF that causes acromegaly that is clinically indistinguishable from that resulting from a pituitary adenoma (Chapter 237). GRFomas are an uncommon cause of acromegaly, occurring in 0 of 177 unselected patients with acromegaly in one study. The intraabdominal features of GRFomas are due to its metastases and are typical of any malignant PET.

Pathology and Pathophysiology

GRFomas most commonly occur in the lung (54%), with most of the remainder occurring in the gastrointestinal tract, including 30% in the pancreas. Pancreatic GRFomas are usually large (mean 6 cm); 39% are metastatic at diagnosis, 40% occur in combination with ZES, and 33% are associated with MEN I.

Diagnosis and Differential Diagnosis

Any patient who has acromegaly with abdominal complaints, without a pituitary tumor, or with hyperprolactinemia (which occurs in 70% of GRFomas) should be suspected of having a GRFoma. The diagnosis is confirmed by performing a plasma assay for GRF and growth hormone.

Treatment

> The effects of the GRF can be controlled with octreotide in more than 90% of patients. Treatment also needs to be directed at the GRFoma per se, as described for the other, more frequent PETs.

NONFUNCTIONAL PANCREATIC ENDOCRINE TUMORS

Nonfunctional PETs are endocrine tumors that originate in the pancreas and either secrete no peptides or secrete products that cause no clinical symptoms. Symptoms and signs are due to the tumor per se, including abdominal pain, hepatosplenomegaly, cachexia, and jaundice. In 20% of asymptomatic patients, tumors are found incidentally at surgery.

Pathology and Pathophysiology

More than 60% of tumors have metastasized to the liver at presentation. Of tumors, 70% are large (>5 cm), and 70% occur in the pancreatic head. Frequently secreted, nonfunctional peptides include chromogranin A (100%), chromogranin B (100%), pancreatic polypeptide (60%), and the α-subunit (40%) and β-subunit (20%) of human chorionic gonadotropin. Immunocytochemically an even higher percentage contain these peptides and insulin (50%), glucagon (30%), and somatostatin (13%). Malignancy correlates with vascular or perineural invasion, proliferative index greater than 2%, mitotic rate equal to or greater than 2, size equal to or greater than 4 cm, capsular penetration, nuclear atypia, lack of progesterone receptors, and the presence of calcitonin immunoreactivity in the tumor.

Diagnosis and Differential Diagnosis

Nonfunctional PETs frequently are diagnosed only after patients present with symptoms or signs of metastatic disease and a liver biopsy specimen reveals a metastatic neuroendocrine tumor. Any patient with a long survival (>5 years) after a diagnosis of metastatic pancreatic adenocarcinoma (Chapter 201) should be suspected of having a nonfunctional PET. An elevated plasma chromogranin A or pancreatic polypeptide level or positive SRS is strong evidence that a pancreatic mass is a PET.

Rx Treatment

Tumor localization; surgical resection; and, for advanced cases, chemotherapy with streptozotocin and doxorubicin, hepatic embolization, and chemoembolization are useful, as described earlier.

ACTHomas AND OTHER UNCOMMON PANCREATIC ENDOCRINE TUMORS

PETs ectopically secreting ACTH comprise 4 to 16% of the causes of ectopic Cushing's syndrome (Chapter 240). Cushing's syndrome occurs in 5% of all cases of ZES; in patients with sporadic ZES, it is invariably a late feature, occurring in patients with metastatic disease to the liver. Its development is associated with a poor prognosis and poor response to chemotherapy; however, occasional patients benefit from the use of octreotide.

Paraneoplastic hypercalcemia can result from a PET releasing parathyroid hormone–related peptide or an unknown hypercalcemic substance. Tumors are generally large and metastatic to the liver at diagnosis. Octreotide may help control the hypercalcemia, but surgery, chemotherapy, hepatic embolization, and chemoembolization are the mainstays of treatment.

PETs causing the carcinoid syndrome (Chapter 245) are usually large, and 68 to 88% are malignant. Octreotide may control the symptoms; surgery, chemotherapy, or hepatic embolization or chemoembolization may be helpful.

A single case of a renin-secreting PET in the pancreas was described. The patient presented with severe hypertension. After the tumor was localized with SRS, symptoms were improved significantly by tumor resection.

SUGGESTED READINGS

Alexander RA, Jensen RT: Pancreatic endocrine tumors. In DeVita VT, Hellman S, Rosenberg SA (eds): Cancer: Principles and Practice of Oncology, 6th ed. Philadelphia, Lippincott Williams & Wilkins, 2001, pp 1788–1813. *A general chapter covering treatment of pancreatic endocrine tumors.*

Hung PD, Schubert ML, Mihas AA: Zollinger-Ellison syndrome. Curr Treat Options Gastroenterol 2003;6:163–170. *A comprehensive review.*

Jensen RT: Endocrine tumors of the pancreas. In Alpers DH, Owyang C, Powell DW, Silverstein FE (eds): Textbook of Gastroenterology, 4th ed. Philadelphia, Lippincott Williams & Wilkins, 2002. *A general chapter covering all aspects of pancreatic endocrine tumors.*

141 APPROACH TO THE PATIENT WITH DIARRHEA AND MALABSORPTION

Carol E. Semrad
Don W. Powell

Definitions of Diarrhea

Normal stool frequency ranges from three times a week to three times a day. Although individuals rarely cite increases in frequency alone as the definition of diarrhea, a decrease in stool consistency (increased fluidity) and stools that cause urgency or abdominal discomfort are likely to be termed *diarrhea. Consistency* is defined as the ratio of fecal water to the water-holding capacity of fecal insoluble solids, which are composed of bacterial mass and dietary fiber. One half of the dry weight of stool is bacteria. Because it is difficult to measure stool consistency and because stool is predominantly (60 to 85%) water, stool weight becomes a reasonable surrogate of consistency.

Physicians often define diarrhea as a physical sign, 24-hour stool excretion by weight or volume, rather than as a symptom. Daily stool weights of children and adults are less than 200 g, and greater stool weights are an objective definition of diarrhea; however, this definition misses 20% of diarrheal symptoms in patients with loose stools less than this daily weight.

Acute diarrheas are those of less than 2 to 3 weeks', and rarely 6 to 8 weeks', duration. The most common cause of acute diarrheas is infectious agents. *Chronic diarrheas* are those of at least 4 weeks', and more usually greater than 6 to 8 weeks', duration. There are three categories of chronic diarrhea: osmotic (malabsorptive) diarrhea, secretory diarrhea, and inflammatory diarrhea.

Epidemiology

The number of deaths from acute diarrhea in infants and children in developing nations has decreased from 4.6 million in 1980 to 1.5 million in 1999 largely as a result of the widespread use of oral rehydration therapy. Children who live in extreme poverty with inadequate sewage disposal and water supplies, insufficient food, lack of refrigeration, poor education, and lack of access to health care remain at risk. The incidence of infant and child diarrheal deaths in the United States decreased by 75% between 1968 and 1985. Since 1999, about 300 deaths have been reported each year, most occurring in very-low-birth-weight infants.

The elderly have the highest mortality; about 1600 deaths per year occur in individuals older than age 74 years. In the United States, diarrheal diseases are frequent and severe enough to result in 250,000 hospital admissions, 8 million visits to physicians, and 90 million episodes that last at least 1 full day and result in loss of time from school or work. Total yearly costs are greater than $23 billion.

Although improvements in sanitation and education in the United States have decreased rates for infectious parasitic diarrheas, diarrheas resulting from person-to-person contact (e.g., rotavirus) and from food-borne transmission (e.g., *Salmonella, Campylobacter,* caliciviruses) doubled in the 1990s. More recently, however, rates of infection from all the common food-borne bacteria (*Salmonella, Shigella, Listeria, Escherichia coli,* and *Yersinia*), but not the vibrios, have declined by 20 to 35%. Most likely, this more recent decline is the result of increased attention by the government, industry, and consumers to food safety.

Appropriate population studies have not been done to determine the incidence or prevalence of chronic diarrhea. The best estimate is that chronic diarrhea occurs in approximately 5% of the U.S. population.

Pathophysiology

ABNORMALITIES OF FLUID AND ELECTROLYTE TRANSPORT

Diarrhea previously was thought to be caused principally by abnormal gastrointestinal motility. It is now clear, however, that most diarrheal conditions are due primarily to alterations of intestinal fluid and electrolyte transport and less to smooth muscle function.

Each 24 hours, 8 to 10 L of fluid enters the duodenum with 800 mEq sodium (Na^+), 700 mEq chloride (Cl^-), and 100 mEq potassium (K^+). The diet supplies 2 L of this fluid; the remainder comes from salivary, stomach, liver, pancreatic, and duodenal secretions. The small intestine normally absorbs 8 to 9 L of this fluid and presents 1.5 L to the colon for absorption. Of the remaining fluid, the colon absorbs all but approximately 100 mL, which contains 3 mEq, 8 mEq, and 2 mEq of Na^+, K^+, and Cl^-. Diarrhea can result from decreased absorption or increased secretion by either the small intestine or the colon. If either deranged electrolyte transport or the presence of non-absorbable solutes in the intestinal lumen reduces the absorptive capacity of the small intestine by 50%, the volume of fluid (50% of 10 L, or 5 L) presented daily to the normal colon would exceed its maximum daily absorptive capacity of 4 L. Stool excretion of 1000 mL would

result, which by definition is diarrhea. Alternatively, if the colon is deranged so that it cannot absorb even the 1.5 L normally presented to it by the small intestine, a stool volume of greater than 200 mL/24 hours would result, again defined as diarrhea.

At the cellular level, excess intraluminal fluid volumes occur when there is a derangement of electrolyte transport capabilities of the small or large intestine or when osmotic solutes in the bowel lumen create an adverse osmotic gradient that the normal electrolyte absorptive mechanisms cannot overcome. Na^+ transport by the epithelium from lumen to blood (by Na^+-coupled sugar and amino acid transport in the small intestine, by $Na^+:H^+$ exchange proteins in the small intestine and proximal colon, and by aldosterone-regulated Na^+ channels in the distal colon) creates a favorable osmotic gradient for absorption (Fig. 141–1A and B). Oral rehydration solutions, which are used

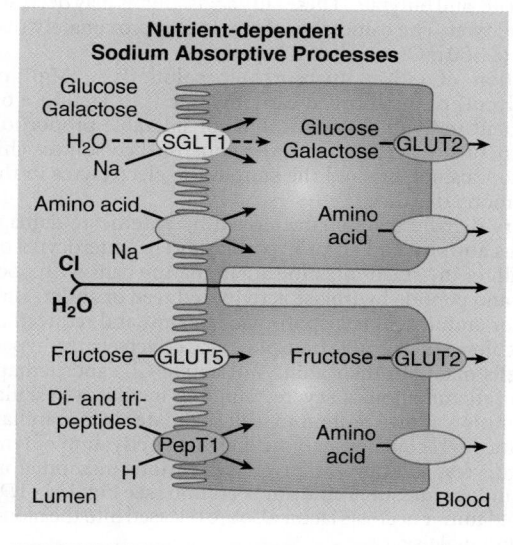

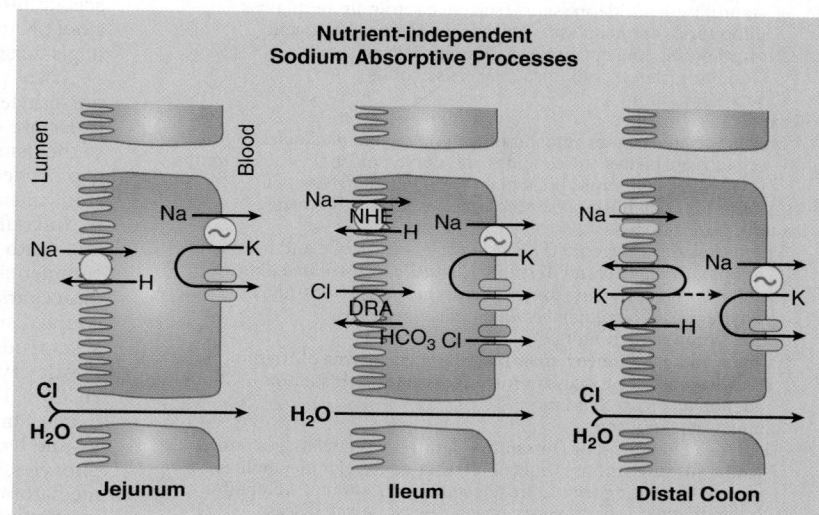

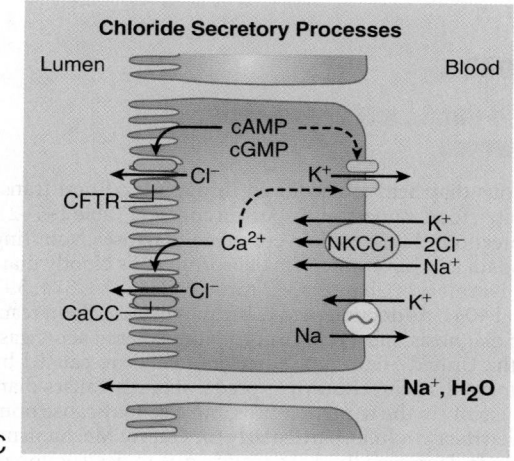

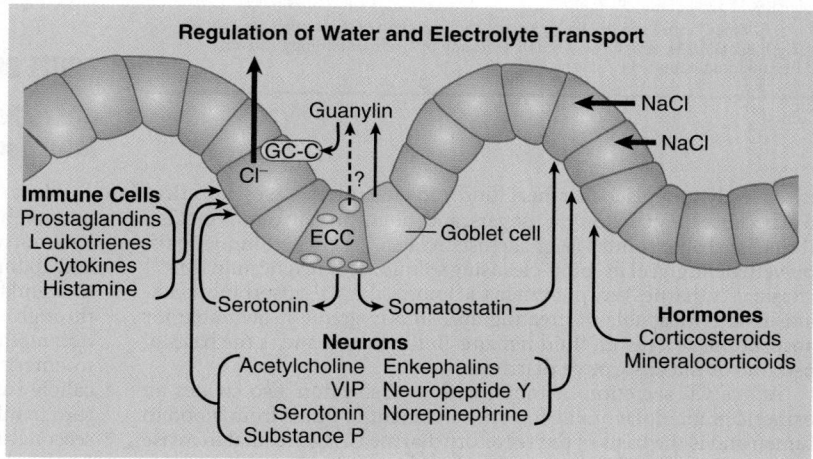

FIGURE 141–1 • *A,* Intestinal sodium absorption. Sodium is actively absorbed in villus cells of the small intestine and surface cells of the colon. The Na^+,K^+-ATPase present on the cell basolateral membrane maintains a low intracellular Na^+ concentration and an electronegative cell interior favoring Na^+ movement across the apical membrane from lumen into cell. In the small intestine, glucose and galactose are taken up with sodium and water at the apical membrane by the sodium-glucose ligand transporter (SGLT1). Several different sodium-dependent amino acid carriers, some with overlapping substrate specificities, transport cationic, anionic, and neutral amino acids into villus cells. Dipeptides and tripeptides are transported by a hydrogen-coupled oligopeptide carrier, PepT1, that is driven by luminal hydrogen ions generated by the epithelial Na/H exchanger. Fructose is taken up by the facilitative glucose transporter (GLUT5). *B,* Sodium also is absorbed by nutrient-independent transport processes in the small intestine and colon. The Na/H (NHE) and Cl/HCO₃ (DRA) exchangers are inhibited by agents that elevate intracellular cAMP, cGMP, or calcium. *C,* Chloride secretion by intestinal crypt cells. Chloride can be secreted actively throughout the small intestine and colon. Intracellular mediators of secretion (cAMP, cGMP, Ca^{2+}) open apical Cl^- channels (cystic fibrosis transmembrane conductance regulator [CFTR], calcium-activated chloride channel [CaCC]) and basolateral K^+ channels. Chloride moves from crypt cells into the intestinal lumen, favoring movement of Cl^- from the blood into cells by the Na/K/2Cl cotransporter (NKCC1). Bicarbonate also may be secreted via the CFTR channel. *D,* Regulation of intestinal water and electrolyte transport. Normally the intestine is in a net absorptive state under the control of extrinsic adrenergic nerves from the sympathetic nervous system. Guanylin, the natural ligand for the *Escherichia coli* stable-toxin receptor (membrane-bound guanylyl cyclase [GC-C]) may be important in regulating local chloride secretion. The normal tone of the intestine is modified by the enteric nervous system, endocrine and inflammatory cells in the intestinal mucosa, and circulating hormones. The enteric nervous system releases a variety of neurotransmitters, some stimulate chloride secretion (e.g., vasoactive intestinal peptide [VIP], acetylcholine), and others promote sodium absorption (e.g., enkephalins, neuropeptide Y). Hormones produced locally from enterochromaffin cells (ECC) in the intestinal epithelium and inflammatory mediators released from immune cells directly affect enterocytes and nearby nerves. Circulating hormones (e.g., aldosterone, glucocorticoids) enhance sodium absorption in the intestine. Glucocorticoids also inhibit arachidonic acid release and prostaglandin production by inflammatory cells.

Table 141–1 • AGENTS THAT CAUSE INTESTINAL SECRETION

Laxatives
Phenolphthalein, anthraquinones, bisacodyl, oxyphenisatin, senna, aloe, ricinoleic acid (castor oil), dioctyl sodium sulfosuccinate; endogenous laxatives such as dihydroxy bile acids and long-chain fatty acids

Medications/drugs
Diuretics (furosemide, thiazides), coffee, tea, or cola (caffeine and other methylxanthines); asthma medication (theophylline); thyroid preparations; type II diabetes drug (metformin)
Cholinergic drugs, glaucoma eye drops and bladder stimulants (acetylcholine analogues or mimetics); myesthenia gravis medication (cholinesterase inhibitors); cardiac drugs (quinidine and quinine); gout medication (colchicine); antihypertensives (angiotensin-converting enzyme inhibitors); H_2 blocker (ranitidine); antidepressants (selective serotonin reuptake inhibitors), antineoplastic drugs, chenodeoxycholic acid
Prostaglandins (misoprostol); di-5-aminosalicylic acid (azodisalicylate); gold (also may cause colitis)
Protease inhibitors

Toxins
Metals (arsenic); plant (mushroom, e.g., *Amanita phalloides*); organophosphates (insecticides and nerve poisons); seafood toxins (ciguatera; scombroid poisoning; paralytic, diarrhetic, or neurotoxic shellfish poisoning); monosodium glutamate

Bacterial enterotoxins
Vibrio cholerae, toxigenic *Escherichia coli* (heat-labile and heat-stable toxins), *Campylobacter, Yersinia, Klebsiella, Clostridium difficile, Staphylococcus aureus* (toxic shock syndrome), *Clostridium perfringens, Clostridium botulinum, Bacillus cereus*

Hormone-producing tumors
Vipoma and ganglioneuromas; medullary carcinoma of thyroid (calcitonin and prostaglandins); mastocytosis (histamine), villous adenoma (prostaglandins)

Inflammatory conditions
Allergy and anaphylaxis (histamine, serotonin, platelet-activating factor, prostaglandins); infection (reactive oxygen metabolites, platelet-activating factor, prostaglandins, histamine); idiopathic inflammation, inflammatory bowel disease, celiac disease

Ischemic colitis

Adapted from Powell DW: Approach to the patient with diarrhea. *In* Yamada T, Alpers DH, Owyang C, et al (eds): Textbook of Gastroenterology, 3rd ed. Philadelphia, Lippincott-Raven, 1999.

extensively to replace diarrheal fluid and electrolyte losses, are effective because they contain Na^+, sugars, and, often, protein (amino acids). If unabsorbable solutes (e.g., lactose in lactase-deficient individuals, polyethylene glycol in colon-cleansing solutions, or magnesium [Mg^{2+}] citrate in cathartics) are present in the lumen, the Na^+-absorbing mechanisms are incapable of creating an osmotic gradient favorable for absorption; as a result, fluid remains in the lumen and is the basis of osmotic or malabsorptive diarrhea.

Active Cl^- secretion or inhibited Na^+ absorption also creates an osmotic gradient favorable for the movement of fluids from blood to lumen and is the basis of the secretory diarrheas. Agents that increase enterocyte cyclic adenosine monophosphate (cAMP), cyclic guanosine monophosphate (cGMP), or intracellular ionized calcium (Ca^{2+}) (e.g., cholera toxin, *E. coli* enterotoxins, prostaglandin, vasoactive intestinal peptide [VIP]) all inhibit Na^+ absorption and stimulate Cl^- secretion (Fig. 141–1C and Table 141–1). Secretion is controlled by neurotransmitters, hormones, and inflammatory mediators (Fig. 141–1D).

CLASSIFICATION OF DIARRHEA

To understand the three general categories of diarrhea—malabsorption (osmotic diarrheas), secretory diarrheas, and inflammatory diarrheas—it is necessary to understand how the normal intestine handles fluid and solutes in health and disease. Regardless of whether a subject ingests a hypotonic meal, such as a steak, or a hypertonic meal, such as milk and doughnut, the volume of the meal is augmented by gastric, pancreatic, biliary, and duodenal secretions. The permeable duodenum then renders the meal approximately isotonic with an

electrolyte content similar to that of plasma by the time it reaches the proximal jejunum. As the chyme moves toward the colon, the Na^+ concentrations in the luminal fluid remain constant, but Cl^- is reduced to 60 to 70 mmol/L, and bicarbonate (HCO_3^-) is increased to a similar concentration as the result of the Cl^- and HCO_3^- transport mechanisms in the enterocyte and HCO_3^- secretion in the ileum (see Fig. 141–1B and C). In the colon, K^+ is secreted, and the Na^+ transport mechanism of the colonocyte and the low epithelial permeability extract Na^+ and fluid from the stool. As a result, the Na^+ content of stool decreases to 30 to 40 mmol/L; K^+ increases from 5 to 10 mmol/L in the small bowel to 75 to 90 mmol/L; and poorly absorbed divalent cations, such as Mg^{2+} and Ca^{2+}, are concentrated in stool to values of 5 to 100 mmol/L. The anion concentrations in the colon change drastically because bacterial degradation of carbohydrate (i.e., unabsorbed starches, sugars, and fiber) creates short-chain fatty acids that attain concentrations of 80 to 180 mmol/L. At colonic pH, these are present as organic anions, such as acetate, propionate, and butyrate. These fatty acids/anions may decrease stool pH to 4 or lower. The osmolality of stools is approximately that of plasma (280 to 300 mOsm) when it is passed.

With ingestion of either unabsorbable solute (i.e., Mg^{2+} or polyethylene glycol) or unabsorbed carbohydrate (i.e., lactulose or, in lactase-deficient individuals, lactose), a considerable proportion of the osmolality of stool results from the nonabsorbed solute. This gap between stool osmolality and the sum of the electrolytes in the stool causes osmotic diarrhea.

Inflammatory diarrheas are characterized by enterocyte damage and death, villus atrophy, and crypt hyperplasia. The enterocytes on rudimentary villi of the small intestine are immature cells with poor disaccharidase and peptide hydrolase activity, reduced or absent Na^+-coupled sugar or amino acid transport mechanisms, and reduced or absent sodium chloride absorptive transporters. Conversely, the hyperplastic crypt cells maintain their ability to secrete Cl^- (and perhaps HCO_3^-). If the inflammation is severe, immune-mediated vascular damage or ulceration allows protein to leak (exudate) from capillaries and lymphatics and contribute to the diarrhea. Activation of lymphocytes, phagocytes, and fibroblasts releases various inflammatory mediators that induce intestinal chloride secretion (see Fig. 141–1D). Interleukin-1 and tumor necrosis factor also are released into the blood, causing fever and malaise.

ACUTE DIARRHEAS

Sporadic, Food-Borne, and Water-Borne Infectious Diarrhea

Most infectious diarrheas are acquired through fecal-oral transmission from water, food, or person-to-person contact (Table 141–2). Patients with infectious diarrhea often complain of nausea, vomiting and abdominal pain and have watery, malabsorptive, or bloody diarrhea and fever (dysentery) (Chapters 323 through 331, 373, 374, 397 through 400, and 404). As documented using polymerase chain reaction methods of diagnosis, most outbreaks of nonbacterial acute gastroenteritis in the United States and other countries are caused by caliciviruses (Norwalk agent). Rotavirus predominantly causes diarrhea in infants, usually in the winter months, but also may cause nonseasonal acute diarrhea in adults, particularly the elderly. Mechanisms for diarrhea include decreased fluid absorption due to destruction of villus enterocytes and stimulation of fluid secretion by NSP4 rotatoxin and viral activation of the enteric nervous system.

Some of the short-lived watery diarrheas ascribed to "viral gastroenteritis" are likely to be mild, sporadic, food-borne bacterial infections. In addition to enteric infections, certain systemic infections (e.g., hepatitis, listeriosis, and legionellosis) may cause substantial diarrhea.

The incidence of food-borne illness in the United States is estimated to be 76 million cases per year, with 325,000 hospitalizations and 5000 deaths annually. The incidence may be underestimated because most patients present with sporadic diarrhea rather than as part of a clear epidemic, and most epidemic diarrheas are not reported. Emerging food-borne diseases in the United States include the *enteritidis* serotype of *Salmonella, Campylobacter jejuni, E. coli* O157:H7, and *Cyclospora* infections. Fish can become contaminated in their own environment (especially the filter-feeding bivalve mollusks, such as mussels, clams, oysters, and scallops) or by food handlers. Organisms

Table 141–2 • EPIDEMIOLOGY OF ACUTE INFECTIOUS DIARRHEA AND INFECTIOUS FOOD-BORNE ILLNESS

VEHICLE	CLASSIC PATHOGEN
Water (including foods washed in such water)	*Vibrio cholerae,* caliciviruses (Norwalk agent), *Giardia,* and *Cryptosporidium*
Food	
Poultry	*Salmonella, Campylobacter,* and *Shigella* species
Beef, unpasteurized fruit juice	Enterohemorrhagic *Escherichia coli*
Pork	Tapeworm
Seafood and shellfish (including raw sushi and gefilte fish)	*V. cholerae, V. parahaemolyticus,* and *V. vulnificus; Salmonella* and *Shigella* species; hepatitis A and B viruses; tapeworm; and anisakiasis
Cheese, milk	*Listeria* species
Eggs	*Salmonella* species
Mayonnaise-containing foods and cream pies	Staphylococcal and clostridial food poisonings
Fried rice	*Bacillus cereus*
Fresh berries	*Cyclospora* species
Canned vegetables or fruits	*Clostridium* species
Sprouts	Enterohemorrhagic *Escherichia coli* and *Salmonella* species
Animal-to-person (pets and livestock)	*Salmonella, Campylobacter, Cryptosporidium,* and *Giardia* species
Person-to-person (including sexual contact)	All enteric bacteria, viruses, and parasites
Day care center	*Shigella, Campylobacter, Cryptosporidium,* and *Giardia* species; viruses, *Clostridium difficile*
Hospital, antibiotics or chemotherapy	*C. difficile*
Swimming pool	*Giardia* and *Cryptosporidium* species
Foreign travel	*E. coli* of various types; *Salmonella, Shigella, Campylobacter, Giardia,* and *Cryptosporidium* species; *Entamoeba histolytica*

Adapted from Powell DW: Approach to the patient with diarrhea. *In* Yamada T, Alpers DH, Owyang C, et al (eds): Textbook of Gastroenterology, 3rd ed. Philadelphia, Lippincott-Raven, 1999.

that are specific for seafood include *Vibrio parahaemolyticus,* which causes either watery or bloody diarrhea, and *V. vulnificus,* which causes watery diarrhea and, especially in patients with liver disease, a fatal septicemia. Ingestion of meat contaminated by anthrax (Chapter 333) causes fever, diffuse abdominal pain, and bloody stool or vomitus. Anthrax invades the intestinal mucosa; the organism, or anthrax toxin, causes inflammation, ulceration, and necrosis. Ascites develops, and death results from blood loss, dehydration and electrolyte imbalance, intestinal perforation, or toxemia.

Food-Borne and Water-Borne Poisonings

Food poisoning occurs with environmental chemicals, such as monosodium glutamate (used in Asian food), heavy metals (arsenic from rat poison), or insecticides, and with natural toxins found in mushrooms and seafood (fin fish or shellfish). Most of these toxins cause varying combinations of gastrointestinal and neurologic symptoms. Arsenic (Chapter 20) also induces cardiovascular collapse at higher, acute doses; one form of mushroom (*Amanita*) poisoning (see Chapter 106) can cause acute liver and kidney failure.

Diarrhea and neurologic symptoms (tingling and burning around the mouth, facial flushing, sweating, headache, palpitations, and dizziness) of seafood poisoning may be caused by histamine release from the decaying flesh of blood fish (mahi-mahi, tuna, marlin, or mackerel) after it is caught. This form of seafood poisoning is called *scombroid.* Plankton, algae, or dinoflagellates ingested by tropical fish (amberjack, snapper, grouper, or barracuda) produce a toxin (ciguatoxin) that causes seafood poisoning called *ciguatera.* Fish from the Albemarle-Pamlico estuary (eastern United States) ingest toxic dinoflagellates that cause *Pfisteria piscicida* poisoning. The dinoflagellate toxins cause nausea; vomiting; abdominal pain;

diarrhea; and neurologic symptoms such as weakness, pruritus, circumoral paresthesias, temperature reversal (hot drinks taste cold and vice versa), and psychiatric abnormalities and memory loss. Shellfish poisonings are also due to algae or dinoflagellates ingested by bivalve mollusks; these different toxins may cause predominantly and occasionally severe neurologic symptoms (paralytic, neurotoxic, or amnestic shellfish poisonings) or predominantly gastrointestinal symptoms (diarrhetic shellfish poisoning). Puffer fish poisoning (tetrodotoxin) causes neurologic symptoms, respiratory paralysis, or death.

High-Risk Groups

ANTIBIOTIC-ASSOCIATED DIARRHEAS. Diarrhea may occur in 20% of patients receiving broad-spectrum antibiotics; about 20% of these diarrheas are due to *Clostridium difficile* (Chapter 319). The A and B toxins produced by *C. difficile* can cause diarrhea. In animal models, substance P mediates toxin A–stimulated intestinal fluid secretion. *C. difficile* can cause severe diarrhea, pseudomembranous colitis or toxic megacolon. Patients may have a relapsing course after seemingly successful therapy with metronidazole or vancomycin. Non–*C. difficile* diarrhea is mild and self-limited, and it clears spontaneously or in response to cholestyramine therapy.

TRAVELER'S DIARRHEA. North American travelers to developing countries and travelers on airplanes and cruise ships where errors in food preparation occur are at high risk for acute infectious diarrhea. Bacterial agents account for 85% of traveler's diarrhea. Enterotoxic *E. coli* is the most common cause. *E. coli* heat-stable toxin binds to guanylate cyclase in the enterocyte brush-border membrane, resulting in elevation of intracellular cGMP. *E. coli* heat-labile toxin, similar to cholera toxin, binds to the monosialoganglioside GM_1 in the brush-border membrane, resulting in the activation of adenylate cyclase and elevation of intracellular cAMP. cAMP and cGMP stimulate intestinal chloride secretion (see Fig. 141–1*C*) and inhibit nutrient-independent sodium and chloride absorption (see Fig. 141–1*B*). Sodium-glucose absorption is not affected, hence the basis for oral rehydration therapy. Cholera toxin permanently binds to adenylate cyclase (until the natural turnover [5 to 7 days] of the intestinal epithelium), resulting in persistent secretion and severe diarrhea. Of the 10 to 15 cases of cholera reported in the United States each year, about 60% are travel associated.

SEXUALLY TRANSMITTED AND AIDS DIARRHEAS. Men who have sex with men and prostitutes develop infectious diarrhea through the oral-fecal route. The incidence of infectious diarrhea among men who have sex with men (gay bowel syndrome) has decreased markedly, but the decline has been more than offset by the high incidence and seriousness of enteric infections in acquired immunodeficiency syndrome (AIDS) (Chapter 416). In patients with human immunodeficiency virus (HIV) disease receiving highly active antiretroviral therapy, diarrhea is more likely to be due to protease inhibitors than enteric infection.

DAYCARE DIARRHEA. More than 6 million children in the United States attend daycare, and diarrhea from organisms that colonize at a low inoculum dose (e.g., *Shigella, Giardia, Cryptosporidium*) or organisms that are spread easily (e.g., rotavirus, astrovirus, adenovirus) is extremely prevalent in this setting. The secondary attack rate for parents and siblings is 10 to 20%.

Diagnosis of Acute Infectious Diarrhea

The differential diagnosis of acute watery diarrhea includes food toxins, infections, medications, and diseases (Fig. 141–2 and see Table 141–2) (Chapters 323 through 331, 373, 374, 397 through 400, and 404). The use of the laboratory to make the diagnosis of infectious diarrhea can be reduced if the evaluation focuses on *Campylobacter, Salmonella, Shigella,* and *C. difficile* and if only liquid stools are cultured. Organisms that can cause diarrhea and that are not sought routinely by most clinical microbiology laboratories unless specifically requested include *Yersinia, Plesiomonas,* enterohemorrhagic *E. coli* serotype O157:H7, *Aeromonas, Cryptosporidium, Cyclospora, Microsporidia,* and noncholera *Vibrio.* Parasites such as *Giardia* and *Strongyloides* and enteroadherent bacteria may be difficult to detect in stool but may be diagnosed by intestinal biopsy. Even with the use of all available laboratory techniques, the cause of 20 to 40% of all acute infectious diarrheas remains undiagnosed.

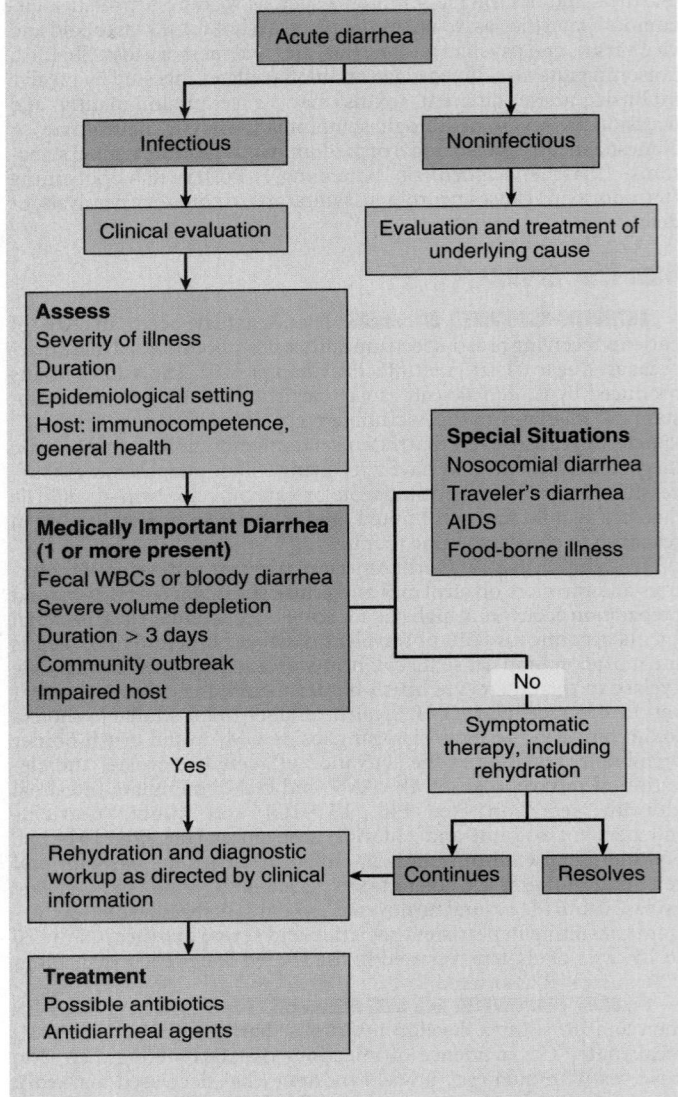

FIGURE 141–2 • Algorithm for the diagnostic approach to acute diarrhea. AIDS = acquired immunodeficiency syndrome; WBCs = white blood cells. (Adapted from Park SI, Giannella R: Approach to the patient with acute diarrhea. Gastroenterol Clin North Am 1993;22:483–497.)

Rx Treatment

The treatment of diarrhea can be symptomatic (fluid replacement and antidiarrheal agents) and/or specific (antimicrobial therapy). Because death in acute diarrhea is caused by dehydration, an important principle is to assess the degree of dehydration and replace fluid and electrolyte deficits. Severely dehydrated individuals should be rehydrated with intravenous Ringer's lactate or saline solutions to which additional K^+ and $NaHCO_3^-$ may be added as necessary. Alert patients should be given oral rehydration solutions. In mild-to-moderate dehydration, oral rehydration solutions can be given to infants and children in volumes of 50 to 100 mL/kg over 4 to 6 hours; adults may need to drink 1000 mL/hr. Glucose-based oral rehydration solutions, although effective in rehydrating the patient, may worsen the diarrhea. In contrast to glucose-based solutions, rice-based oral rehydration solutions decrease diarrhea in cholera victims; rice is digested to many glucose monomers that aid in the absorption of intestinal secretions.[1] These solutions may be less effective in decreasing stool output in noncholera diarrheas. After the patient is rehydrated, oral replacement solutions are given at rates equaling stool loss plus insensible losses until the diarrhea ceases.

Bismuth subsalicylate (Pepto-Bismol) is safe and efficacious in bacterial infectious diarrheas. Because of the possibility of

worsening the colonization or invasion of infectious organisms by paralyzing intestinal motility, and because of evidence that the use of motility-altering drugs may prolong microorganism excretion time, neither opiates nor anticholinergic drugs are recommended for infectious diarrheas. Loperamide can be useful and safe, however, in acute or traveler's diarrhea, provided that it is not given to patients with dysentery (high fever, with blood or pus in the stool), and especially when administered concomitantly with effective antibiotics. A combination of loperamide plus simethicone may reduce the abdominal cramps and duration of traveler's diarrhea. Racecadotril, an intestinal enkephalinase inhibitor that is antisecretory but does not paralyze intestinal motility, is effective in the treatment of acute diarrhea in children[2] and adults.[3] Anxiolytics and antiemetics that decrease sensory perception may make symptoms more tolerable and are safe.

Some foods or food-derived substances (green bananas,[4] pectins [amylase-resistant starch], zinc[5]) lessen the amount and/or duration of diarrhea in children. Unabsorbed amylase-resistant starches are metabolized in the colon to short-chain fatty acids that enhance fluid absorption. Zinc supplementation is effective in preventing recurrences of diarrhea in malnourished children.[6] Copper deficiency is a potential complication of prolonged zinc therapy.

Probiotics are live, nonpathogenic, human microorganisms that provide a health benefit. Most species are lactic acid bacteria. *Lactobacillus GG* added to an oral replacement solution decreases the duration of diarrhea in children with acute diarrhea, particularly with rotavirus infection.[7] *Lactobacillus GG* and other organisms (*Lactobacillus reuteri, Enterococcus faecium, Lactobacillus acidophilus, Streptococcus thermophilus*, bifidobacteria) also may be effective in the prevention of antibiotic-associated diarrhea in children. Their role in the treatment of acute infectious and antibiotic-associated diarrheas in adults is less clear. Some commercially available probiotic preparations contain dead microorganisms and may not be effective.

Certain infectious diarrheas should be treated with antibiotics: shigellosis, cholera, traveler's diarrhea, pseudomembranous enterocolitis, parasitic infestations, and sexually transmitted diseases. Antibiotics are not usually indicated in viral diarrhea and cryptosporidiosis because they are not effective. Treatment of *E. coli* serotype O157:H7 infection is not recommended at present because current antibiotics do not seem to be helpful, and the incidence of complications (hemolytic uremic syndrome) may be greater after antibiotic therapy. Regardless of the cause of infectious diarrhea, patients should be treated if they are immunosuppressed; have valvular, vascular, or orthopedic prostheses; have congenital hemolytic anemias (especially if salmonellosis is involved); or are extremely young or old.

While the clinician is awaiting stool culture results to guide specific therapy (Chapter 323), the fluoroquinolones (e.g., ciprofloxacin) are the treatment of choice. If the symptom complex suggests *Campylobacter*, erythromycin should be added. Trimethoprim-sulfamethoxazole is second-line therapy. Fluoroquinolone-resistant and trimethoprim-sulfamethoxazole–resistant strains of *E. coli*, *Salmonella*, and *Campylobacter* have emerged.

Nosocomial Hospital Diarrheas

Diarrhea is either the first or the second most common nosocomial illness among hospitalized patients and residents in long-term care facilities. Fecal impaction and medication are common causes. Magnesium-containing laxatives and antacids, sulfate and phosphate laxatives, and lactulose cause osmotic diarrheas. Colchicine, neomycin, para-aminosalicylic acid, and cholestyramine damage the enterocyte and/or bind bile salts, resulting in malabsorption. Radiation therapy and drugs such as gold cause intestinal inflammation and diarrhea. Liquid formulations of any medication may cause diarrhea (elixir diarrhea) because of the high content of sorbitol used to sweeten the elixir. Patients prescribed liquid medications through feeding tubes may receive more than 20 g of sorbitol daily. An important but poorly understood cause of diarrhea is enteral (tube) feeding (Chapter 229), particularly in critically ill patients, who often develop diarrhea. Dysmotility, increased intestinal permeability, and low sodium content in enteral formulas may be contributing factors. The diarrhea often can be managed with pectin or, if there are no contraindications, lo-peramide and is not a reason to stop tube feeding unless stool volumes exceed 1 L.

Patients in mental institutions and nursing homes have high incidences of nosocomial infectious diarrheas (e.g., hemorrhagic *E. coli* and *C. difficile* infections). Infectious diarrhea (mostly caused by *C. difficile*) is also common in acute-care hospitals, accounting for more than 20% of nosocomial infections and being second only to respiratory infections on pediatric wards and in intensive care units. The likelihood of a nosocomial infection caused by *Salmonella, Shigella,* or parasites in the hospital is now so low that routine evaluation for these agents is not cost-effective if diarrhea begins at least 3 days after hospital admission and the patient does not have neutropenia, HIV infection, or signs of enteric infection or is older than age 65 with comorbid disease (modified 3-day rule). Immunosuppressed patients are susceptible to nosocomial diarrhea, especially viral infections (rotavirus, astrovirus, adenovirus, and coxsackievirus).

The incidence of acute, mild diarrhea with cancer chemotherapy or radiation therapy is high, approaching 100% with some agents, such as amsacrine, azacitidine, cytarabine, dactinomycin, daunorubicin, doxorubicin, floxuridine, 5-fluorouracil, 6-mercaptopurine, methotrexate, plicamycin, and irinotecan (CPT-11). Interleukin-2 therapy and the combination of 5-fluorouracil plus leucovorin are frequent causes of severe watery diarrhea. Current treatment for chemotherapy-induced and radiation-induced diarrhea is symptomatic and includes loperamide and nonsteroidal anti-inflammatory drugs (NSAIDs). In patients with severe diarrhea, octreotide may be an effective treatment.

Runner's Diarrhea

Gastrointestinal disturbances including anorexia, heartburn, nausea, vomiting, cramps, urgency, and diarrhea occur in 10 to 25% of persons who exercise vigorously, particularly women marathon runners and triathletes. The pathophysiology in runner's diarrhea is unclear but may involve release of intestinal secretogogues or hormones by ischemia. Loperamide and NSAIDs are taken prophylactically by many runners, but it is not clear whether they are effective.

CHRONIC DIARRHEA

The goal in evaluating a patient with chronic diarrhea is to make a definitive diagnosis as quickly and inexpensively as possible (Fig. 141–3). In 25 to 50%, expert history and physical examination may be sufficient. The addition of stool culture and examination for ova and parasites, determination of stool fat, and flexible sigmoidoscopy with biopsy raises the diagnostic rate to about 75%. The remaining 25% of patients with severe or elusive chronic diarrhea may need hospitalization and extensive testing.

Prolonged, Persistent, and Protracted Infectious Diarrheas

Stool culture and examination may detect organisms that often cause protracted infectious diarrhea in adults: enteropathogenic (enteroadherent) *E. coli, Giardia, Entamoeba, Cryptosporidium, Aeromonas,* and *Yersinia enterocolitica.* If none of these organisms is found, a therapeutic trial of metronidazole or trimethoprim-sulfamethoxazole may be indicated. Persistent infectious diarrhea lasting more than 3 to 4 weeks occurs in 3% of returned travelers; if trimethoprim-sulfamethoxazole or the fluoroquinolones have been unsuccessful, tetracycline or metronidazole should be tried.

Of patients, 25% experience pain, bloating, urgency, a sense of incomplete evacuation, and loose stools for 6 months or longer after documented infectious diarrhea. This syndrome of infectious diarrhea–induced irritable bowel syndrome, also called *Brainerd's diarrhea,* is a prolonged, often severe diarrhea initiated by unidentified organisms. Some patients respond to cholestyramine.

Visitors residing in the tropics for 1 to 3 months may develop tropical sprue (see later). A severe postinfectious diarrhea syndrome (severe protracted diarrhea) may develop in infants and children in developing nations and can occur in milder forms (postenteritis syndrome) in infants and children in developed countries. Malnutrition and death (mortality 50%) can occur in severe disease. Treatment includes dietary lactose exclusion in mild disease or total parenteral nutrition in severely

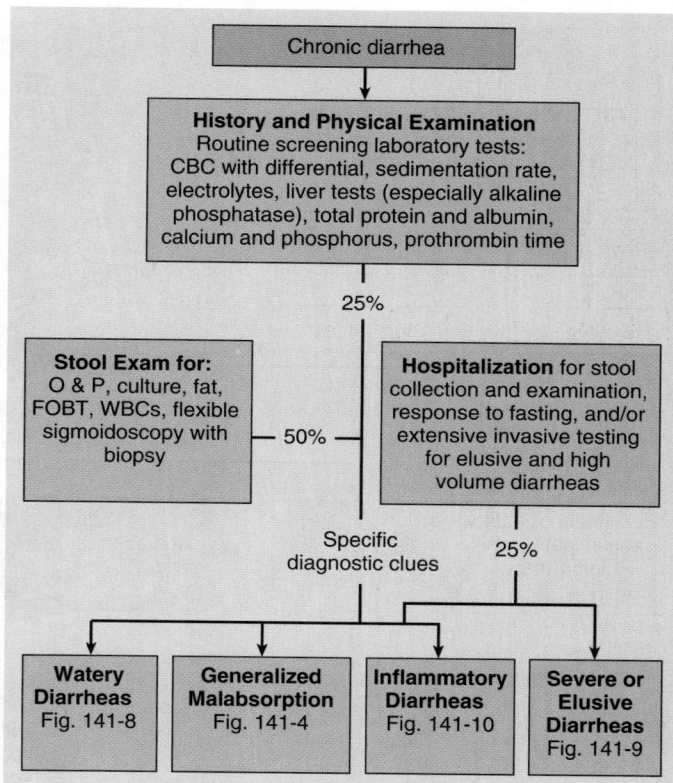

FIGURE 141–3 • Approach to the evaluation of chronic diarrhea. CBC = complete blood count; O & P = ova and parasites; FOBT = fecal occult blood test; WBCs = white blood cells. (Adapted from Powell DW: Approach to the patient with diarrhea. *In* Yamada T, Alpers DH, Owyang C, et al [eds]: Textbook of Gastroenterology, 3rd ed. Philadelphia, Lippincott-Raven, 1999.)

affected patients. Metronidazole, tetracycline, trimethoprim-sulfamethoxazole, folic acid, and zinc therapy also may help.

Malabsorptive Syndromes

Malabsorption is caused by many different diseases, drugs, or nutritional products that impair intraluminal digestion, mucosal absorption, or nutrient delivery to the systemic circulation (Fig. 141–4 and Tables 141–3 and 141–4). Dietary fat is the nutrient most difficult to absorb. Fat is predominantly insoluble in the aqueous milieu of the intestine and critically depends on all phases of digestion, absorption, and delivery for its assimilation. Steatorrhea (excess fat in the stool) is the hallmark of malabsorption; a stool test for fat is the best screening test for malabsorption. Malabsorption does not always cause diarrhea. Clinical signs of vitamin or mineral deficiencies may occur in the absence of diarrhea (Table 141–5). A careful history is crucial in guiding further testing to confirm the suspicion of malabsorption and to make a specific diagnosis (see Fig. 141–4). The goals of treatment are to correct or treat the underlying disease and to replenish water, electrolyte, and nutritional losses.

CONDITIONS THAT IMPAIR INTRALUMINAL DIGESTION

Most nutrient digestion and absorption occurs in the small intestine (Fig. 141–5). Pancreatic proteases (trypsinogen, chymotrypsinogen, proelastase, and procarboxypeptidases) are secreted from acinar cells in inactive forms. The cleavage of trypsinogen to trypsin by the duodenal brush-border peptidase enteropeptidase (enterokinase) allows trypsin to cleave the remaining trypsinogen and other proteases to their active form. Neutralization of acid in the small intestinal lumen by bicarbonate secreted from pancreatic duct cells is physiologically important because pancreatic enzyme activity and bile salt micelle formation is optimal at a luminal pH of 6 to 8.

Carbohydrates and most dietary proteins are water-soluble and readily digested by pancreatic enzymes. Most dietary lipids (long-chain

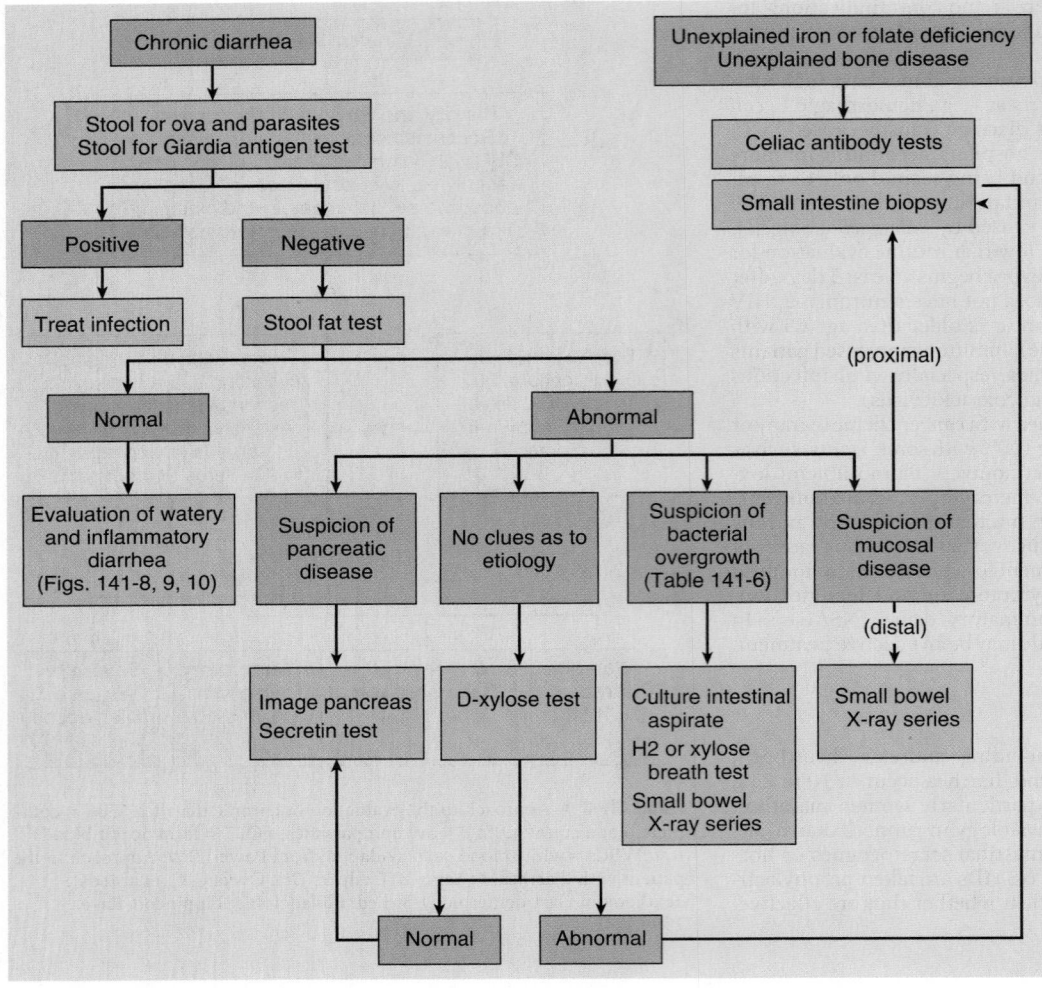

FIGURE 141–4 • Approach to the diagnosis of malabsorption.

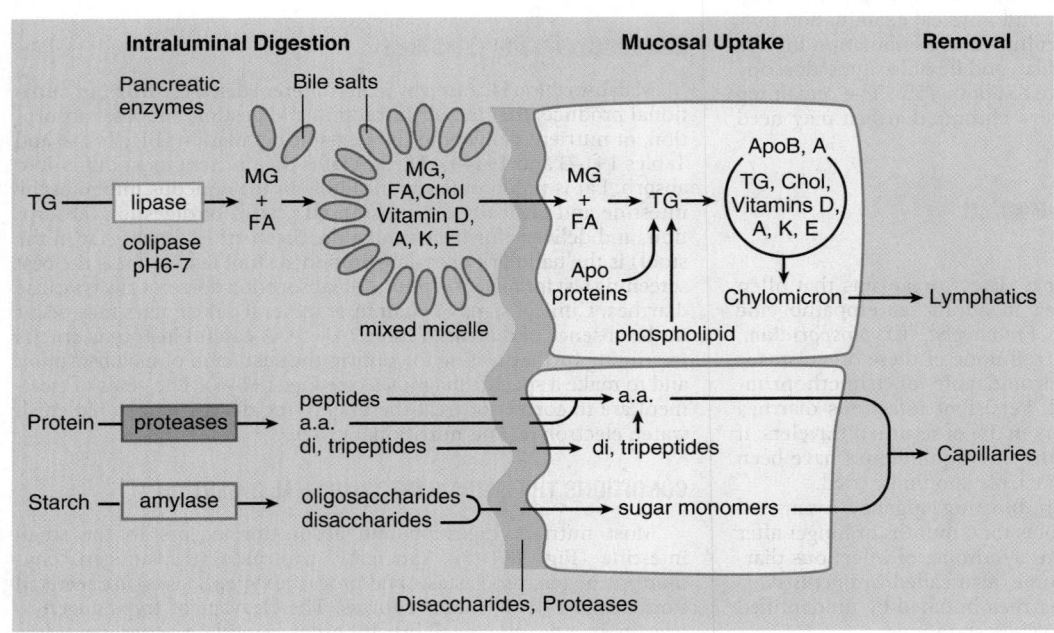

FIGURE 141–5 • Phases of intestinal digestion and absorption of dietary fat, protein, and carbohydrate. TG = triglycerides; a.a. = amino acids; MG = monoglycerides; FA = fatty acids; chol = cholesterol.

triglycerides, cholesterol, phosphatidylcholine [lecithin], and fat-soluble vitamins) are water-insoluble and must undergo lipolysis and incorporation into mixed micelles before they can be absorbed across the intestinal mucosa. Pancreatic lipase, in the presence of its cofactor, colipase, cleaves long-chain triglycerides into fatty acids and mono-

glycerides. The products of lipolysis interact with bile salts and phospholipids to form mixed micelles, which also incorporate cholesterol and fat-soluble vitamins (D, A, K, E) in their hydrophobic centers.

IMPAIRED MIXING. Surgical alterations, such as partial gastrectomy with gastrojejunostomy (a Billroth II anastomosis) or Roux-en-Y gastric

Table 141–3 • CAUSES OF MALABSORPTION

CONDITIONS THAT IMPAIR MIXING
Partial gastrectomy with gastrojejunostomy
Gastric bypass surgery

CONDITIONS THAT IMPAIR LIPOLYSIS
Chronic pancreatitis
Pancreatic cancer
Congenital pancreatic insufficiency
Congenital colipase deficiency
Gastrinoma

CONDITIONS THAT IMPAIR MICELLE FORMATION
Severe chronic liver disease
Cholestatic liver disease
Bacterial overgrowth
Crohn's disease
Ileal resection
Gastrinoma

CONDITIONS THAT IMPAIR MUCOSAL ABSORPTION
Congenital, primary, and secondary lactase deficiency
Congenital enterokinase deficiency
Abetalipoproteinemia
Giardiasis
Celiac disease
Tropical sprue
Agammaglobulinemia
Amyloidosis
AIDS-related (infections, enteropathy)
Radiation enteritis
Graft-versus-host disease
Whipple's disease
Eosinophilic gastroenteritis
Megaloblastic gut
Collagenous sprue
Ulcerative jejunitis
Lymphoma
Bacterial overgrowth
Short bowel syndrome
Mastocytosis

CONDITIONS THAT IMPAIR NUTRIENT DELIVERY
Congenital intestinal lymphangiectasia
Lymphoma
Tuberculosis
Constrictive pericarditis
Severe congestive heart failure

CONDITIONS IN WHICH THE MECHANISM OF MALABSORPTION IS UNKNOWN
Hypoparathyroidism
Adrenal insufficiency
Hyperthyroidism
Carcinoid syndrome

AIDS = acquired immunodeficiency syndrome.

Table 141–4 • DRUGS AND DIETARY PRODUCTS THAT IMPAIR NUTRIENT ABSORPTION

DRUG	MECHANISM	NUTRIENT MALABSORBED
Cholestyramine	Bile salt binder	Iron and cobalamin
High fiber, phytates	Chelator	Iron, calcium, magnesium
Tetracycline	Chelator	Calcium
Antacids	Chelator	Calcium, phosphate
Olestra	Nonabsorbable fat (lipophilic)	Fat-soluble vitamins
Orlistat	Lipase inhibitor	Fat, fat-soluble vitamins
Metformin	?Mechanism	Glucose, cobalamin, folate
Acarbose	Competitive inhibitor of intestinal α-glucosidases	Carbohydrate
Colchicine	?Altered membrane trafficking	Carbohydrate, fat, cobalamin
Neomycin	Inhibitor of protein synthesis Binds bile salts	Carbohydrate, fat, protein
Methotrexate	Villus blunting	Carbohydrate, fat, protein
Phenytoin	Decreases folate absorption	Folate
Sulfasalazine	Inhibits folate hydrolase ?Inhibits folate transporter	Folate

Table 141–5 • CLINICAL CONSEQUENCES OF NUTRIENT AND WATER AND ELECTROLYTE MALABSORPTION

NUTRIENT MALABSORBED	CLINICAL MANIFESTATION
Protein	Wasting Edema
Carbohydrate and fat	Diarrhea Abdominal cramps and bloating Weight loss/growth retardation
Fluid and electrolytes	Diarrhea Dehydration
Iron	Anemia Cheilosis Angular stomatitis
Calcium/vitamin D	Bone pain Fractures Tetany
Magnesium	Paresthesias Tetany
Vitamin B$_{12}$/folate	Anemia Glossitis Cheilosis Paresthesias Ataxia (vitamin B$_{12}$ only)
Vitamin E	Paresthesias Ataxia Retinopathy
Vitamin A	Night blindness Xerophthalmia Hyperkeratosis
Vitamin K	Ecchymoses
Riboflavin	Angular stomatitis Cheilosis
Zinc	Dermatitis Hypogeusia Diarrhea
Selenium	Cardiomyopathy
Essential fatty acids	Dermatitis

bypass for morbid obesity, result in the release of biliary and pancreatic secretions into the intestine at a site remote from the site of entry of gastric chyme into the jejunum. This imbalance can result in impaired lipolysis and impaired micelle formation, with subsequent fat malabsorption. Absorption of iron, calcium, and cobalamin is impaired as well. Rapid transit through the jejunum contributes to the malabsorption of nutrients. Individuals with these conditions also have surgical anastomoses that predispose to bacterial overgrowth.

IMPAIRED LIPOLYSIS. A deficiency in pancreatic lipase can be due to the congenital absence of pancreatic lipase or due to destruction of the pancreatic gland from alcohol-related pancreatitis, cystic fibrosis, or pancreatic cancer. Pancreatic lipase also can be denatured by excess secretion of gastric acid (e.g., Zollinger-Ellison syndrome).

Chronic pancreatitis (Chapter 145) is the most common cause of pancreatic insufficiency and impaired lipolysis. In the United States, chronic pancreatitis is most commonly due to alcohol abuse; in contrast, tropical (nutritional) pancreatitis is most common worldwide. Malabsorption of fat does not occur until more than 90% of the pancreas is destroyed. Individuals typically present with bulky, fat-laden stools (usually >30 g of fat per day), abdominal pain, and diabetes, although some present with diabetes in the absence of gastrointestinal symptoms. Stools are not usually watery because undigested

triglycerides form large emulsion droplets with little osmotic force and, in contrast to fatty acids, do not stimulate water and electrolyte secretion in the colon. Deficiency of fat-soluble vitamins is seen only rarely, presumably because gastric and residual pancreatic lipase generates enough fatty acids for some micelle formation. Clinical manifestations of carbohydrate and protein malabsorption also are rare in pancreatic insufficiency. In severe disease, subclinical protein malabsorption, manifested by the presence of undigested meat fibers in the stool, and subclinical carbohydrate malabsorption, manifested by gas-filled, floating stools, can occur. Weight loss, when it occurs, is usually due to decreased oral intake to avoid abdominal pain or diarrhea and less commonly to malabsorption. About 30 to 40% of individuals with chronic pancreatitis secondary to alcohol abuse have calcifications on abdominal radiographs. A qualitative or quantitative test for fecal fat is positive in individuals whose pancreas is more than 90% destroyed.

Pancreatic enzyme replacement and analgesics are the mainstays of treatment. It is difficult to correct fat malabsorption completely with exogenous pancreatic enzymes because of their inactivation by acid and pepsin in the stomach. Normally, 28,000 U of lipase is present in the duodenal lumen with each meal. A high lipase—containing pancreatic enzyme preparation (25,000 to 40,000 U of lipase in the form of uncoated enzymes or enteric-coated, pH-sensitive microspheres) should be prescribed with each meal. Pancreatic proteases present in enzyme preparations may reduce abdominal pain by inactivating CCK-releasing factor in the duodenum. Uncoated preparations may be more effective in pain relief because coated preparations release enzymes predominantly distal to the duodenum. An H_2-receptor antagonist should be added to uncoated pancreatic enzyme replacement therapy in patients with a poor response.

IMPAIRED MICELLE FORMATION. Bile salt concentrations in the intestinal lumen can fall to less than the critical concentration (5 to 15 mM) needed for micelle formation because of decreased bile salt synthesis (severe liver disease), decreased bile salt delivery (cholestasis), or removal of luminal bile salts (bacterial overgrowth, terminal ileal disease or resection, cholestyramine therapy, acid hypersecretion). Fat malabsorption resulting from impaired micelle formation is generally not as severe as malabsorption resulting from pancreatic lipase deficiency, presumably because fatty acids and monoglycerides can form lamellar structures, which to a certain extent can be absorbed. Malabsorption of fat-soluble vitamins (D, A, K, E) may be marked, however, because micelle formation is required for their absorption.

Decreased Bile Salt Synthesis and Delivery. Malabsorption can occur in individuals with cholestatic liver disease or bile duct obstruction. The clinical consequences of malabsorption are seen most often in women with primary biliary cirrhosis because of the prolonged nature of the illness. Although these individuals can present with steatorrhea, bone disease is the most common presentation. Osteoporosis is more common than osteomalacia. The cause of bone disease in these individuals is poorly understood and often not related to vitamin D deficiency. Treatment of bone disease is with calcium supplements (and vitamin D if a deficiency is documented), weight-bearing exercise, and hormone therapy.

Intestinal Bacterial Overgrowth. In health, only small numbers of lactobacilli, enterococci, gram-positive aerobes, or facultative anaerobes can be cultured from the upper small bowel lumen. Motility and acid are the most important factors in keeping the number of bacteria in the upper small bowel low. Any condition that produces local stasis or recirculation of colonic luminal contents allows development of a predominantly "colonic" flora (coliforms and anaerobes, such as *Bacteroides* and *Clostridium*) in the small intestine (Table 141–6). Anaerobic bacteria cause impaired micelle formation by releasing cholylamidases, which deconjugate bile salts. The unconjugated bile salts, with their higher pKa, are more likely to be in the protonated form at the normal upper small intestinal pH of 6 to 7 and can be absorbed passively. As a result, the concentration of bile salts decreases in the intestinal lumen and can fall to less than the critical micellar concentration to cause fat and fat-soluble vitamin malabsorption. Vitamin B_{12} deficiency and carbohydrate malabsorption also can occur with generalized bacterial overgrowth. Anaerobic bacteria ingest vitamin B_{12} and release proteases that degrade brush-border disaccharidases. Lactase is the disaccharidase normally present in lowest abundance and is the first affected. Although anaerobic bacteria use vitamin B_{12}, they synthesize folate. Individuals with bacterial overgrowth usually have low serum vitamin B_{12} levels but normal or high folate levels, which help distinguish bacterial overgrowth from tropical sprue, in which vitamin B_{12} and folate levels are usually low owing to decreased mucosal uptake.

Individuals with bacterial overgrowth can present with diarrhea, abdominal cramps, gas and bloating, weight loss, and signs and symptoms of vitamin B_{12} and fat-soluble vitamin deficiency. Watery

Table 141–6 • ABNORMALITIES CONDUCIVE TO BACTERIAL OVERGROWTH

STRUCTURAL
Surgical
  Afferent loop dysfunction after gastrojejunostomy
  Ileocecal valve resection
  Surgical loops (end-to-side intestinal anastomoses)
Anatomic
  Duodenal and jejunal diverticula
  Obstruction
    Strictures (Crohn's disease, radiation enteritis)
    Adhesions (postsurgical)
  Gastrojejunocolic fistulas

MOTOR
Scleroderma
Diabetes mellitus
Idiopathic pseudo-obstruction

HYPOCHLORHYDRIA
Atrophic gastritis
Proton-pump inhibitors
Acquired immunodeficiency syndrome
Acid-reducing surgery for peptic ulcer disease

MISCELLANEOUS
Immunodeficiency states
Pancreatitis
Cirrhosis

diarrhea occurs because of the osmotic load of unabsorbed carbohydrates and stimulation of colonic secretion by unabsorbed fatty acids. The diagnosis of bacterial overgrowth should be considered in the elderly and in individuals with predisposing underlying disorders (see Table 141–6). The identification of greater than 10^5 colony-forming units/mL in a culture of small intestinal aspirate remains the gold standard in diagnosis. The noninvasive tests with a sensitivity and specificity equal to intestinal culture are the glucose hydrogen breath test and the $[^{14}C]D$-xylose breath test; in individuals with low vitamin B_{12} levels, a Schilling test before and after antibiotic therapy can be diagnostic (Table 141–7).

The goal of treatment is to correct the structural or motility defect if possible, eradicate offending bacteria, and provide nutritional support. Acid-reducing agents should be stopped if possible. Treatment with antibiotics should be based on culture results when possible; otherwise, empirical treatment is given. Tetracycline (250 to 500 mg orally four times a day) or a broad-spectrum antibiotic against aerobes and enteric anaerobes (ciprofloxacin, 500 mg orally twice a day; amoxicillin/clavulanic acid, 250 to 500 mg orally three times a day; cephalexin, 250 mg orally four times a day; with metronidazole, 250 mg three times a day) should be given for 14 days. Prokinetic agents such as metoclopramide (10 mg orally four times a day) or erythromycin (250 to 500 mg orally four times a day) can be tried to treat small bowel motility disorders but often are not efficacious. Octreotide (50 µg subcutaneously every day) may improve motility and reduce bacterial overgrowth in individuals with scleroderma. When the structural abnormality or motility disturbance cannot be corrected, patients are at risk for malnutrition and vitamin B_{12} and fat-soluble vitamin deficiencies. Cyclic treatment (1 week out of every 4 to 6 weeks) with rotating antibiotics may be required in these patients to prevent recurrent bouts of bacterial overgrowth. If supplemental calories are needed, medium-chain triglycerides should be given because they are not dependent on micelle formation for their absorption. Monthly treatment with vitamin B_{12} should be considered, along with supplemental vitamins D, A, K, and E and calcium.

Ileal Disease or Resection. Disease of the terminal ileum is most commonly due to Crohn's disease (which also may lead to ileal resection) but also can be caused by radiation enteritis, tropical sprue, tuberculosis, *Yersinia* infection, and idiopathic bile salt malabsorption. These diseases cause bile salt wasting in the colon.

The clinical consequences of bile salt malabsorption are related directly to the length of the diseased or resected terminal ileum. In an adult, if less than 100 cm of ileum is diseased or resected, watery diarrhea results owing to stimulation of colonic fluid secretion by unabsorbed bile salts. Fat absorption remains normal because

Table 141–7 • TESTS FOR THE EVALUATION OF MALABSORPTION*

GENERAL TESTS OF ABSORPTION	COMMENTS
Quantitative stool fat test	Gold standard test of fat malabsorption with which all other tests are compared. Requires ingestion of a high-fat diet (100 g) for 2 days before and during the collection. Stool is collected for 3 days. Normally <7 g/24 hr is excreted on a high-fat diet. Borderline abnormalities of 8–14 g/24 hr may be seen in secretory or osmotic diarrheas that are not due to malabsorption. There are false-negative findings if fat intake is inadequate. False-positive results can occur if mineral oil laxatives or rectal suppositories (cocoa butter) are given to the patient before stool collection
Qualitative stool fat test	Sudan stain of a stool sample for fat. Many fat droplets per medium power (40×) field constitute a positive test result. The test depends on an adequate fat intake (100 g/day). High sensitivity (90%) and specificity (90%) with fat malabsorption of >10 g/24 hr. Sensitivity drops with stool fat in the range of 6–10 g/24 hr
D-xylose test	A test of small intestinal mucosal absorption, which is used to distinguish mucosal malabsorption from malabsorption due to pancreatic insufficiency. An oral dose of D-xylose (25 g/500 mL water) is administered, and D-xylose excretion is measured in a 5-hr urine collection. Normally >4 g of D-xylose is excreted in the urine over 5 hr. The test also may be positive in bacterial overgrowth owing to metabolism of D-xylose by bacteria in the intestinal lumen. False-positive test results occur with renal failure, ascites, and an incomplete urine collection. Blood levels at 1 and 3 hr improve sensitivity. May be normal with mild or limited mucosal disease
Hydrogen breath test	Most useful in the diagnosis of lactase deficiency. An oral dose of lactose (1 g/kg body weight) is administered after measurement of basal breath hydrogen levels. The sole source of H_2 in the mammal is bacterial fermentation; unabsorbed lactose makes its way to colonic bacteria resulting in excess breath H_2. A *late peak* (within 3–6 hr) of >20 ppm of exhaled hydrogen after lactose ingestion suggests lactose malabsorption. Absorption of other carbohydrates (e.g., sucrose, glucose, fructose) can be tested as well
SPECIFIC TESTS FOR MALABSORPTION **Tests for Pancreatic Function**	
Secretin stimulation test	The gold standard test of pancreatic function. Requires duodenal intubation with a double-lumen tube and collection of pancreatic juice in response to IV secretin. Allows measurement of HCO_3^- and pancreatic enzymes. A sensitive test of pancreatic function, but labor intensive and invasive
Fecal elastase-1 test	Stool test for pancreatic function. Equal sensitivity to the secretin stimulation test for the diagnosis of moderate-to-severe pancreatic insufficiency. More specific than the fecal chymotrypsin test. Unreliable with mild insufficiency. False-positive test results occur with increased stool volume and intestinal mucosal diseases
Tests for Bacterial Overgrowth	
Quantitative culture of small intestinal aspirate	Gold standard test for bacterial overgrowth. Greater than 10^5 colony-forming units/mL in the jejunum suggests bacterial overgrowth. Requires special anaerobic sample collection, rapid anaerobic and aerobic plating, and care to avoid oropharyngeal contamination. False-negative results occur with focal jejunal diverticula or when overgrowth is distal to the site aspirated
Hydrogen breath test	The 50-g glucose breath test has a sensitivity of 90% for growth of 10^5 colonic-type bacteria in the small intestine. When bacterial overgrowth is present, increased hydrogen is excreted in the breath. An *early peak* (within 2 hr) of >20 ppm of exhaled hydrogen suggests bacterial overgrowth
Tests for Mucosal Disease	
Small bowel biopsy	Obtained for a specific diagnosis when there is a high index of suspicion for small intestinal disease. Several biopsy specimens (4–5) must be obtained to maximize the diagnostic yield. Distal duodenal biopsy specimens are usually adequate for diagnosis, but occasionally enteroscopy with jejunal biopsy specimens is necessary. Small intestinal biopsy provides a specific diagnosis in some diseases (e.g., intestinal infection, Whipple's disease, abetalipoproteinemia, agammaglobulinemia, lymphangiectasia, lymphoma, and amyloidosis). In other conditions, such as celiac disease and tropical sprue, the biopsy specimen shows characteristic findings, but the diagnosis is made on improvement after treatment
Permeability studies	A test of mucosal integrity. These tests are gaining favor as screening tests for small intestinal disease and to follow response to treatment. The study is performed by administering an oral dose of nonabsorbable markers (e.g., mannitol/lactulose or lactulose/^{51}Cr-EDTA), and measuring urinary excretion. Currently a research tool
Tests of Ileal Function	
Schilling test	A test of vitamin B_{12} absorption. Performed as part I, followed by parts II, III, and IV if needed Part I: A saturating dose (1 mg IM) of vitamin B_{12} is given followed by an oral dose of radioactive cyanocobalamin (0.5–2 μg). Urine is collected for 24 hr because of a poorly understood delay in the passage of cobalamins across ileal cells. Part I is abnormal in all individuals with vitamin B_{12} deficiency except those with dietary deficiency and food-cobalamin malabsorption Part II: The test is repeated with a dose of intrinsic factor. Distinguishes lack of intrinsic factor from other causes of vitamin B_{12} malabsorption Part III: The test is repeated with pancreatic enzymes. Can be used as a test for pancreatic insufficiency. In such individuals, administration of exogenous enzymes frees cyanocobalamin from R-proteins, reverting the Schilling test to normal Part IV: The test is repeated with antibiotics. When values for parts I and II are low, bacterial overgrowth can be distinguished from ileal disease by repeating the test after a 5-day course of antibiotics

*Not all of these tests are readily available. A strong suspicion for any disease may warrant forgoing an extensive work-up and obtaining the test with highest diagnostic yield. In some cases, empirical treatment, such as removing lactose from the diet of an otherwise healthy individual with lactose intolerance, is warranted without any testing.

increased bile salt synthesis in the liver compensates for bile salt losses, and micelle formation is preserved. Bile acid diarrhea responds to cholestyramine (2 to 4 g taken at breakfast, lunch, and dinner). When more than 100 cm of ileum is diseased or resected, bile salt losses (>3 g/day) in the colon exceed the capacity for increased bile salt synthesis in the liver, the bile salt pool shrinks, and micelle formation is impaired. As a result, steatorrhea ensues, and fatty acid—induced intestinal secretion synergizes with the bile acid—induced secretion to cause diarrhea. Treatment is with a low-fat diet, vitamin B_{12} injections, dietary supplements of calcium, and a multiple vitamin-mineral supplement. An antimotility agent should be given for diarrhea. Bile

salt binders may worsen diarrhea. Screening for fat-soluble vitamin deficiencies (vitamins A and E, 25-(OH) vitamin D, and prothrombin time) and bone disease (bone densitometry, serum calcium, and intact parathyroid hormone) should be done.

Three long-term complications of chronic bile salt wasting and fat malabsorption are renal stones, bone disease (osteoporosis and osteomalacia), and gallstones. Oxalate renal stones occur as a consequence of excess free oxalate absorption in the colon. Free oxalate is generated when unabsorbed fatty acids bind luminal calcium, which is then unavailable for binding oxalate. Renal oxalate stones sometimes can be avoided with a low-fat, low-oxalate diet and calcium supplements.

Bone disease is due to impaired micelle formation with a resulting decrease in absorption of vitamin D; year-round sun exposure reduces this complication. Vitamin D and calcium supplements should be given to susceptible individuals, but vitamin D levels and serum and urinary calcium should be monitored for response to treatment because excess vitamin D can be toxic. The mechanism of gallstone formation in these individuals is unclear; pigmented gallstones are most common.

CONDITIONS THAT IMPAIR MUCOSAL ABSORPTION

Nutrients are absorbed along the entire length of the small intestine with the exception of iron and folate, which are absorbed predominantly in the duodenum and proximal jejunum, and bile salts and cobalamin, which can be absorbed only in the distal ileum. The efficiency of nutrient uptake at the mucosa is influenced by the number of villus absorptive cells, the presence of functional hydrolases and specific nutrient transport proteins on the brush-border membrane, and transit time. Transit time determines the contact time of luminal contents with the brush-border membrane and influences the efficiency of nutrient uptake across the mucosa.

Long-chain fatty acids are transported across the microvillus membrane of villus epithelial cells by the fatty acid transport protein FATP4; are resynthesized into triglycerides; and combine with cholesterol ester, fat-soluble vitamins, phospholipid, and apoproteins to form chylomicrons. The bile salts from mixed micelles remain in the intestinal lumen and are absorbed in the distal ileum by sodium-dependent cotransport.

Oligosaccharides and larger oligopeptides (products of pancreatic enzyme digestion), sucrose and lactose, are hydrolyzed further by enzymes present in the brush-border membrane of villus epithelial cells before they are absorbed. Although only sugar monomers (glucose, galactose, fructose) can be taken up at the apical epithelial cell membrane, dipeptides and tripeptides are readily taken into the cell. Defects in amino acid uptake in Hartnup disease and cystinuria are characterized by renal and intestinal malabsorption of neutral and basic amino acids. In the intestine, these defects are offset by the absorption of these amino acids as dipeptides and tripeptides.

Water-soluble vitamins are readily absorbed throughout the small intestine. Fat-soluble vitamins, cobalamin, and minerals are more difficult to absorb because of the requirement for micelle formation (vitamin D, A, K, E), a divalent charge (magnesium, calcium, iron), or select sites of uptake in the intestine (iron, folate, cobalamin). Calcium is absorbed best in the proximal small intestine by a vitamin D—dependent uptake process. Magnesium from the diet and endogenously secreted magnesium from biliary, gastric, and pancreatic juices are absorbed by the small intestine (throughout its length) by a poorly understood mechanism. Ferrous iron is transported into intestinal epithelial cells by a proton-coupled metal-ion transporter (Nramp2) that has specificity for Fe^{2+} and other divalent cations (Zn^{2+}, Mn^{2+}, Co^{2+}, Cd^{2+}, Cu^{2+}, Ni^{2+}, and Pb^{2+}). The absorption of calcium and nonheme iron is enhanced by solubilization with hydrochloric acid. Intraluminal compounds, such as oxalate, phytates, and long-chain fatty acids, bind to calcium and magnesium, decreasing their absorption. Individuals with severe mucosal disease or short-bowel syndrome with high fecal fluid outputs lose magnesium from endogenous secretions.

Folates (Chapters 175 and 231) are taken in the diet and produced by bacteria in the colon. Deficiency can be due to poor intake or malabsorption secondary to intestinal disease or drugs. Dietary folates are absorbed in the proximal small intestine. A reduced folate carrier (RFC1), expressed in the small intestine and colon, suggests folate might be absorbed in the colon and the small intestine.

The cobalamins (Chapters 175 and 231) are high-molecular-weight, water-soluble molecules that contain a porphyrin-like corrin ring with a cobalt atom in its center. The supplemental form contains a cyanide group attached to the cobalt atom; hence the name cyanocobalamin (vitamin B_{12}). The cobalamins are readily abundant in foods containing animal proteins (e.g., meat, seafood, eggs, and milk), so cobalamin deficiency in industrialized countries is rarely due to poor dietary intake but rather reflects the inability to absorb cobalamin in the ileum. This inability may be due to a lack of intrinsic factor, consumption of cobalamin by overgrowth of anaerobic bacteria in the small bowel lumen, or ileal disease or resection. Large amounts of cobalamin are present in the liver (2 to 5 mg), and cobalamin is reabsorbed from bile via the enterohepatic circulation, limiting daily losses to only 0.5 to 1 µg. It usually takes 10 to 12 years for cobalamin deficiency to develop when it is eliminated from the diet, but deficiency can occur more rapidly (2 to 5 years) with malabsorptive syndromes. When lack of gastric acid causes food-cobalamin malabsorption, treatment with oral cyanocobalamin is curative.

Mucosal malabsorption can be caused by specific (usually congenital) brush-border enzyme or nutrient transporter deficiencies or by generalized diseases that damage the small intestinal mucosa or result in surgical resection or bypass of small intestine. The nutrient(s) malabsorbed in these general malabsorptive diseases depend on the site of intestinal injury (proximal, distal, or diffuse) and the severity of damage. The main mechanism of malabsorption in these conditions is a decrease in surface area available for absorption. Some conditions (infection, celiac disease, tropical sprue, food allergies, and graft-versus-host disease [GVHD]) are characterized by intestinal inflammation and villus flattening; other conditions are characterized by ulceration (ulcerative jejunitis, NSAIDs), infiltration (amyloidosis), or ischemia (radiation enteritis, mesenteric ischemia).

LACTASE DEFICIENCY. Acquired lactase deficiency is the most common cause of selective carbohydrate malabsorption. Most individuals, except those of northern European descent, begin to lose lactase activity by the age of 2 years. The prevalence of lactase deficiency is highest (85 to 100%) in Asians, blacks, and Native Americans. In most individuals, lactase deficiency is due to decreased synthesis of the enzyme. In some, intracellular transport and glycosylation of lactase is defective, however. Adults with lactase deficiency typically complain of gas, bloating, and diarrhea after the ingestion of milk or dairy products but do not lose weight. Unabsorbed lactose is osmotically active, drawing water followed by ions into the intestinal lumen. On reaching the colon, bacteria metabolize lactose to short-chain fatty acids, carbon dioxide, and hydrogen gas. Short-chain fatty acids are transported with sodium into colonic epithelial cells, facilitating the reabsorption of fluid in the colon. If the colonic capacity for the reabsorption of short-chain fatty acids is exceeded, an osmotic diarrhea results (see Carbohydrate Malabsorption under Watery Diarrheas).

The diagnosis of lactase deficiency can be made by empirical treatment with a lactose-free diet, which results in resolution of symptoms, or by the hydrogen breath test after oral administration of lactose. Many intestinal diseases cause secondary reversible lactase deficiency, such as viral gastroenteritis, celiac disease, giardiasis, and bacterial overgrowth.

CONGENITAL ENTEROPEPTIDASE (ENTEROKINASE) DEFICIENCY. Enteropeptidase is a brush-border protease that cleaves trypsinogen to trypsin, triggering the cascade of pancreatic protease activation in the intestinal lumen. The rare congenital deficiency of enteropeptidase results in the inability to activate all pancreatic proteases and leads to severe protein malabsorption. It manifests in infancy as diarrhea, growth retardation, and hypoproteinemic edema.

ABETALIPOPROTEINEMIA. Formation and exocytosis of chylomicrons at the basolateral membrane of intestinal epithelial cells are necessary for the delivery of lipids to the systemic circulation. One of the proteins required for assembly and secretion of chylomicrons is the microsomal triglyceride transfer protein, which is mutated in individuals with abetalipoproteinemia. Children with this disorder have fat malabsorption and the consequences of vitamin E deficiency (retinopathy and spinocerebellar degeneration). Biochemical tests show low plasma levels of apoprotein B, triglyceride, and cholesterol. Membrane lipid abnormalities result in red blood cell acanthosis (burr cells). Intestinal biopsy is diagnostic and characterized by engorgement of epithelial cells with lipid droplets. Calories are provided by treatment with a low-fat diet containing medium-chain triglycerides. Medium-chain fatty acids are easily absorbed and released directly into the portal circulation, bypassing the defect of abetalipoproteinemia. Poor absorption of long-chain fatty acids sometimes can result in essential fatty acid deficiency. High doses of fat-soluble vitamins, especially vitamin E, often are needed. Mutations in the apolipoprotein B gene (hypobetalipoproteinemia) and intracellular retention of chylomicrons (Anderson's disease) cause a similar although less severe clinical syndrome.

CELIAC DISEASE. Celiac disease, also called *celiac sprue, nontropical sprue,* and *gluten-sensitive enteropathy,* is an inflammatory condition of the small intestine precipitated by the ingestion of wheat, rye, and barley in individuals with certain genetic predispositions. The prevalence of celiac disease in the United States, based on the number of individuals presenting with typical gastrointestinal symptoms, is estimated at 1 : 4500. Screening studies for the antigliadin (AGA), antiendomysial (EMA), and anti–tissue transglutaminase (anti-tTG) antibodies that are associated with celiac disease suggest a much higher prevalence in Northern Ireland (1:122), Europe (about 1:250), and the United States (about 1:133). High-risk groups for celiac disease include first-degree relatives and individuals with type I diabetes mellitus and autoimmune thyroid disease. About 10% of patients diagnosed with irritable bowel syndrome have celiac disease.

Environmental and genetic factors are important in the development of celiac disease. The alcohol-soluble protein fraction of wheat gluten, the gliadins, and similar prolamins in rye and barley trigger intestinal inflammation in susceptible individuals. Oat grains, which have prolamins rich in glutamine but not proline, are not toxic. A 33-mer peptide that is a natural digestion product of α_2-gliadin may be important in the pathogenesis of celiac disease. This peptide resists terminal digestion by intestinal brush-border proteases and contains three previously identified antigenic epitopes. It also reacts with tissue transglutaminase and stimulates HLA DQ2–restricted intestinal T cell clones from individuals with celiac disease.

Approximately 15% of first-degree relatives of affected individuals are found to have celiac disease. Predisposition to gluten sensitivity has been mapped to the HLA-D region on chromosome 6. More than 90% of individuals with celiac disease have the DQ2 heterodimer encoded for by alleles DQA1*0501 and DQB1*0201 compared with 20 to 30% of controls. A smaller group carries HLA-DQ8. Genome-wide searches support a strong susceptibility locus for celiac disease in the HLA-D region. Non-HLA loci have been implicated but not yet identified. The DQ2 protein is expressed on antigen-presenting cells, but the site on DQ2 that interacts with gliadin and host T-cell receptors, sensitizing the intestine to gluten, has not been identified. tTG (the autoantigen recognized by EMA) may enhance intestinal inflammation by deamidation of select glutamine residues in gliadin; in the deamidated form, gliadin is a more potent stimulant of gluten-sensitized T cells.

The diagnosis of celiac disease is made by characteristic changes found on small intestinal biopsy specimen and improving when a gluten-free diet is instituted (Figs. 141–6 and 141–7). Mucosal flat-

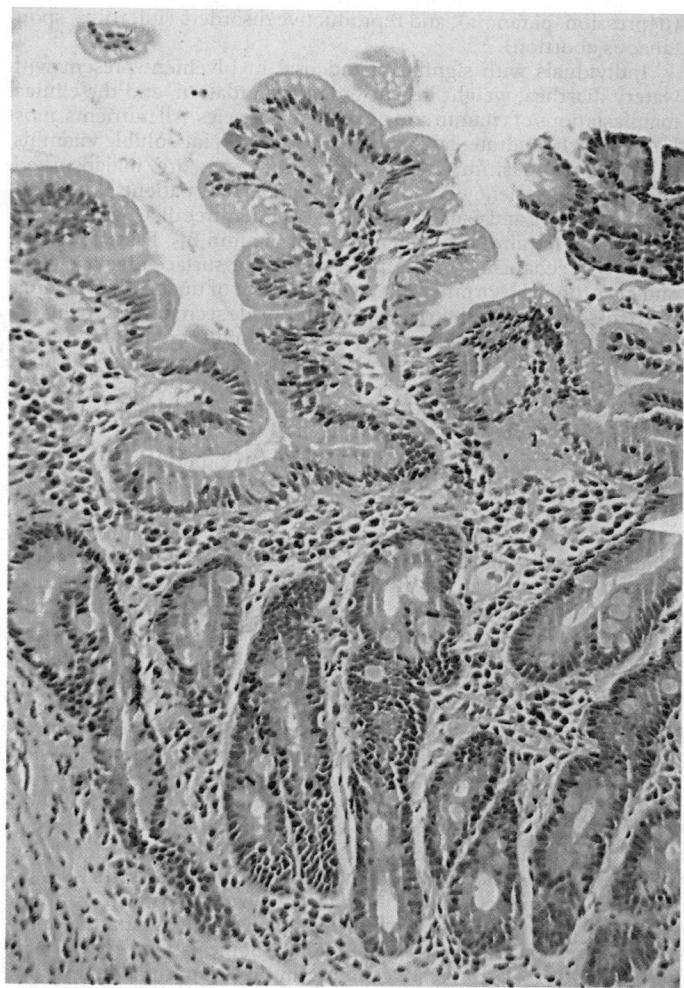

FIGURE 141–7 • Regeneration of villi 4 weeks after initiation of a gluten-free diet. (Courtesy of Heidrun Rotterdam, MD.)

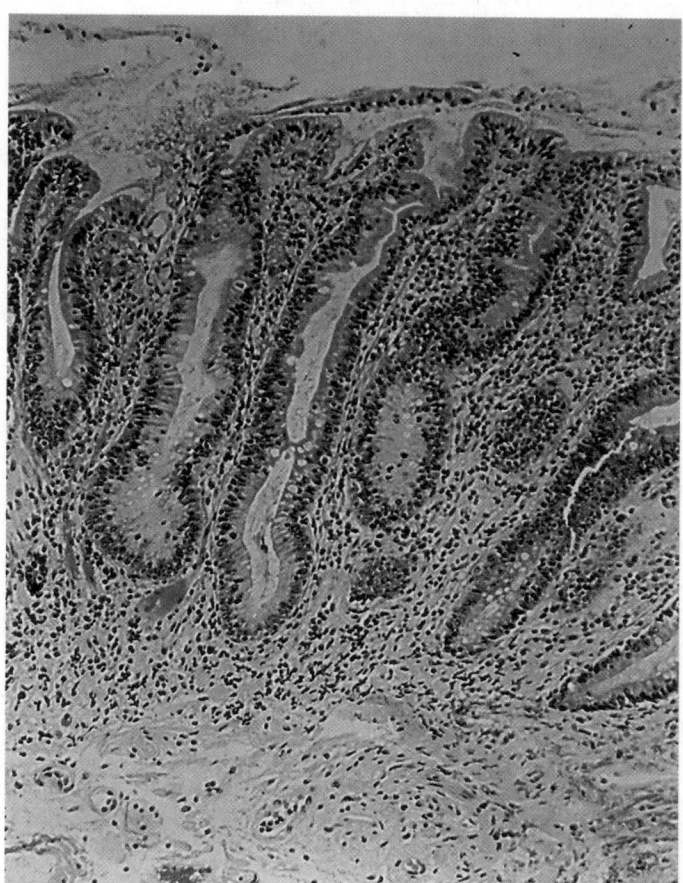

FIGURE 141–6 • Intestinal biopsy appearance of flattened villi and hyperplastic crypts. (Courtesy of Heidrun Rotterdam, MD.)

tening can be observed endoscopically as reduced duodenal folds or duodenal scalloping. Characteristic features found on intestinal biopsy include the absence of villi, crypt hyperplasia, increased intraepithelial lymphocytes, and infiltration of the lamina propria with plasma cells and lymphocytes.

Serologic markers for celiac disease are useful in supporting the diagnosis, in screening first-degree relatives, and in following the response to a gluten-free diet. AGA IgA and IgG antibodies are sensitive but not specific. EMA IgA antibodies, detected by indirect immunofluorescence, are highly sensitive (90%) and specific (90 to 100%) for active celiac disease in skilled laboratory testing. An enzyme-linked immunosorbent assay (ELISA) test to detect antibodies against tTG has equal sensitivity to the EMA test and is less operator dependent. Anti-tTG, EMA, and AGA IgA antibodies tests are negative in individuals with selective IgA deficiency. In these patients, anti-tTG IgG antibodies may be helpful in diagnosis. A new dot blot assay against recombinant human tTG reacts to IgA and IgG antibodies, increasing the specificity to nearly 100%. Patients with mild disease may have negative antibody studies, so intestinal biopsy remains the gold standard for diagnosis, provided that the pathologist can recognize milder degrees of villus atrophy.

Celiac disease usually manifests early in life at about 2 years of age, after wheat has been introduced into the diet, or later in the second to fourth decades of life but can occur at any age. About half of adults with celiac disease in the United States present with anemia or osteoporosis without diarrhea or other gastrointestinal symptoms. These individuals likely have proximal disease that impairs iron, folate, and calcium absorption but an adequate surface area in the remaining intestine for absorption of other nutrients. Other extraintestinal manifestations of celiac disease include rash (dermatitis herpetiformis), neurologic disorders (myopathy, epilepsy), psychiatric disorders (depression, paranoia), and reproductive disorders (infertility, spontaneous abortion).

Individuals with significant mucosal involvement present with watery diarrhea, weight loss or growth retardation, and the clinical manifestations of vitamin and mineral deficiencies. All nutrients, most notably carbohydrate, fat, protein, electrolytes, fat-soluble vitamins, calcium, magnesium, iron, folate, and zinc, are malabsorbed. Cobalamin deficiency is more common (10% of patients) than previously thought and usually corrects on a gluten-free diet. Symptomatic individuals require supplementation of vitamin B_{12}. Diarrhea is due to many mechanisms, including a decreased surface area for water and electrolyte absorption, the osmotic effect of unabsorbed luminal nutrients, an increased surface area for chloride secretion (crypt hyperplasia), and the stimulation of intestinal fluid secretion by inflammatory mediators and unabsorbed fatty acids. Some individuals have impaired pancreatic enzyme secretion caused by decreased mucosal cholecystokinin release or bacterial overgrowth that may contribute to diarrhea.

Treatment consists of a lifelong gluten-free diet. Wheat, rye, and barley grains should be excluded from the diet. Rice, corn, and oat grains are tolerated (if not contaminated by wheat grain). Early referral to a celiac support group is often helpful in maintaining dietary compliance. Owing to secondary lactase deficiency, a lactose-free diet should be recommended until symptoms improve. All individuals with celiac disease should be screened for vitamin and mineral deficiencies and have bone densitometry. Of individuals with celiac disease, 70% have osteopenia. Documented deficiencies of vitamins and minerals should be replenished (Table 141–8), and women of childbearing age should take folic acid supplements.

Of patients with celiac disease treated with a gluten-free diet, 90% experience symptomatic improvement within 2 weeks. The most common cause of a poor dietary response is continued ingestion of gluten. Other possibilities include an overlooked intestinal infection, other food allergies (cow's milk, soy protein), ulcerative jejunitis, or intestinal lymphoma. A small percentage of patients on a strict gluten-free diet have persistent enteropathy and no other diagnosis is found, so-called refractory sprue. Rarely, collagen deposition is found beneath the surface epithelium (collagenous sprue), or a hypoplastic mucosa shows villus and crypt atrophy. Some patients have antienterocyte antibodies indicative of autoimmune enteritis. Others have a monoclonal population of intraepithelial T cells with an aberrant phenotype or clonal T-cell receptor–γ gene rearrangements predictive of enteropathy-associated T-cell lymphoma. Although patients with collagenous sprue and autoimmune enteritis may respond to steroid treatment, a hypoplastic mucosa indicates irreversible (end-stage) intestinal disease. Individuals with celiac disease are at increased risk for intestinal T-cell lymphoma and carcinomas and increased mortality; a strict gluten-free diet for life may lessen this risk. Lymphoma should be suspected in individuals who have abdominal pain, recurrence of symptoms after initial response to a gluten-free diet, and refractory sprue.

TROPICAL SPRUE. Tropical sprue is an inflammatory disease of the small intestine associated with the overgrowth of predominantly coliform bacteria. It occurs in residents or travelers to the tropics, especially India and Southeast Asia. Individuals classically present with diarrhea and megaloblastic anemia secondary to vitamin B_{12} and folate deficiency, but some have anemia only. Intestinal biopsy characteristically shows subtotal and patchy villus atrophy in the proximal and distal small intestine, which may be due to the effect of bacterial toxins on gut structure or to the secondary effects of vitamin B_{12} deficiency on the gut (megaloblastic gut). Diagnosis is based on history, documentation of vitamin B_{12} and/or folate deficiency, and the presence of an abnormal small intestinal biopsy report. Treatment is a prolonged course of broad-spectrum antibiotics, oral folate, and vitamin B_{12} injections until symptoms resolve. Relapses occur mainly in natives of the tropics.

INFECTION. *Giardia lamblia* infection, the most common protozoal infection in the United States, can cause malabsorption in individuals infected with many trophozoites, especially the immunocompromised or IgA-deficient host. Malabsorption occurs when many organisms cover the epithelium and cause mucosal inflammation, which results in villus flattening and a decrease in absorptive surface area. Stool for ova and parasites at this stage of infection is often negative because of the attachment of organisms in the proximal small intestine. Diagnosis can be made by a stool antigen capture ELISA test but may require duodenal aspiration and biopsies.

Table 141–8 • VITAMIN AND MINERAL DOSES USED IN THE TREATMENT OF MALABSORPTION

	ORAL DOSE	PARENTERAL DOSE
Vitamin A*	Water-soluble A 25,000 U/day[§]	
Vitamin E	Water-soluble E 400–800 U/days[§]	
Vitamin D[†]	25,000–50,000 U/day	
Vitamin K	5 mg/day	
Folic acid	1 mg/day	
Calcium[‡]	1500–2000 mg elemental calcium/day	
	Calcium citrate, 500 mg calcium/tablet[§]	
	Calcium carbonate, 500 mg calcium/tablet[§]	
Magnesium	Liquid magnesium gluconate[§] 1–3 tbsp (12–36 mEq magnesium) in 1–2 L of ORS or sports drink sipped throughout the day	2 mL of a 50% solution (8 mEq) both buttocks IM
Zinc	Zinc gluconate[§] 20–50 mg elemental zinc/day[‖]	
Iron	150–300 mg elemental iron/day Polysaccharide-iron complex[§] Iron sulfate or gluconate	Iron dextran as calculated for anemia (IV or IM)[¶]
B-complex vitamins	1 megadose tablet/day	
Vitamin B_{12}	2 mg/day	1 mg IM or SC/mo[#]

*Monitor serum vitamin A level to avoid toxicity, especially in patients with hypertriglyceridemia.
[†]Monitor serum calcium and 25-OH vitamin D levels to avoid toxicity.
[‡]Monitor 24-hr urine calcium to assess adequacy of dose.
[§]Form best absorbed or with least side effects.
[‖]If intestinal output is high, additional zinc should be given.
[¶]Parenteral therapy should be given in a supervised outpatient setting because of the risk of fatal reactions.
[#]For vitamin B_{12} deficiency 1 mg IM or SC twice a week for 4 weeks, then once a month.
ORS = oral rehydration solution.

Diarrhea, malabsorption, and wasting are common in individuals with AIDS but are seen less frequently with improved antiretroviral therapy (Chapter 416). Malabsorption is usually due to infection with cryptosporidia, *Mycobacterium avium-intracellulare* complex, *Isospora belli,* and microsporidia. An organism can be identified by stool examination or intestinal biopsy about 50% of the time. *AIDS enteropathy* (a term used when no organism is identified) also can cause malabsorption. Mechanisms of malabsorption and diarrhea include villus atrophy, increased intestinal permeability, rapid small bowel transit (in patients with protozoal infection) and ultrastructural damage of enterocytes (in AIDS enteropathy). In individuals with AIDS and diarrhea, fecal fat and D-xylose absorption study results are frequently abnormal. Serum albumin, vitamin B_{12}, and zinc levels are often low. Low serum levels of vitamin B_{12} also have been reported in HIV-infected individuals without AIDS. Vitamin B_{12} deficiency is due mainly to ileal disease, but low intrinsic factor (IF) and decreased transcobalamin (TC) II may be contributing factors. Management of malabsorption should focus on restoring the immune system by treating the underlying HIV infection with antiviral therapy. When possible, the offending organism should be treated with antibiotics. If the organism cannot be eradicated, chronic diarrhea and malabsorption result; treatment in these cases consists of antimotility agents and a lactose-free, low-fat diet. Pancreatic enzyme replacement therapy can be tried in HIV-infected individuals who are taking highly active antiretroviral therapy or nucleoside analogues and who have fat malabsorption of obscure origin. If supplemental calories are needed, liquid oral supplements that are predigested and high in medium-chain triglycerides (semielemental) are tolerated best. Vitamin and mineral deficiencies should be screened for and treated.

Whipple's disease, a rare cause of malabsorption, manifests with gastrointestinal complaints in association with systemic symptoms, such as fever, joint pain, or neurologic manifestations. About a third of patients have cardiac involvement, most commonly culture-negative endocarditis. Occasionally, individuals present with ocular or neurologic disease without gastrointestinal symptoms. Men are affected more commonly than women, particularly white men. The organism responsible for causing Whipple's disease is a gram-positive actinomycete, *Tropheryma whippelii*. The epidemiology and pathogenesis of Whipple's disease are poorly understood. The prevalence of the disease is higher in farmers compared with other workers, which suggests the organism lives in the soil. Using polymerase chain reaction, *T. whippelii* has been detected in sewage and in duodenal biopsy specimens, gastric juice, saliva, and stool of individuals without clinical disease. Whether the last-mentioned represents a carrier state or the presence of nonpathogenic organisms is not known. Immunologic defects and an association with the HLA-B27 gene may be disease factors. Small intestinal biopsy shows villus blunting and infiltration of the lamina propria with large macrophages that stain positive with the periodic acid–Schiff method and are filled with the organism. It is important to distinguish these macrophages from macrophages infected with *Mycobacterium avium-intracellulare* complex, which stain positive on acid-fast staining and are found in individuals with AIDS. Treatment is with a prolonged course of broad-spectrum antibiotics. Relapses are common.

GRAFT-VERSUS-HOST DISEASE. Diarrhea occurs frequently after allogeneic bone marrow or stem cell transplantation. Immediately after transplant, diarrhea is due to the toxic effects of cytoreductive therapy on the intestinal epithelium. At 20 to 100 days after transplant, diarrhea is usually due to GVHD or infection. Patients with GVHD present clinically with a skin rash, buccal mucositis, anorexia, nausea, vomiting, abdominal cramps, and diarrhea. The diagnosis of GVHD in the gastrointestinal tract can be made on biopsy of the stomach, small intestine, or colon. In mild cases, the mucosa appears normal on inspection at endoscopy, but apoptosis of gastric gland or crypt cells can be found on biopsy. In severe cases, denuding of the intestinal epithelium results in diarrhea and malabsorption and often requires parenteral nutritional support. Octreotide (50 to 250 µg subcutaneously three times a day) may be helpful in controlling voluminous diarrhea. Treatment of GVHD is with steroids and antithymocyte globulin combined with parenteral nutritional support until intestinal function returns.

SHORT-BOWEL SYNDROME. Malabsorption caused by small bowel resection or surgical bypass is called the *short-bowel syndrome*. The most common causes in the United States are Crohn's disease, radiation enteritis, and mesenteric ischemia. The severity of malabsorption depends on the site and extent of resection, the capacity for bowel adaptation, and the function of the residual bowel. Adaptive changes to enhance absorption in the remaining bowel include hyperplasia, dilation, and elongation. Mechanisms of malabsorption after small bowel resection include a decreased absorptive surface area, decreased luminal bile salt concentration, rapid transit, and bacterial overgrowth. Limited jejunal resection usually is tolerated best because bile salt and vitamin B_{12} absorption remain normal. Ileal resection is less well tolerated because of the consequences of bile salt wasting and the limited capacity of the jejunum to undergo adaptive hyperplasia.

When fewer than 100 cm of jejunum remain, the colon takes on an important role in caloric salvage and fluid reabsorption. Malabsorbed carbohydrates are digested by colonic bacteria to short-chain fatty acids, which are absorbed in the colon. Parenteral nutrition may be avoided by a diet rich in complex carbohydrates, oral rehydration solution, and an antimotility agent. In comparison, individuals with fewer than 100 cm of jejunum and no colon have high jejunostomy outputs and often require intravenous fluids or parenteral nutrition to survive. These individuals waste sodium, chloride, bicarbonate, magnesium, zinc, and water in their ostomy effluent. Dietary modifications should include a high-salt, nutrient-rich diet given in small meals and taken separately from fluids. An oral rehydration solution with a sodium concentration greater than 90 mmol is absorbed best. Oral vitamin and mineral doses higher than the usual U.S. recommended daily allowances are required (see Table 141–8). Vitamin B_{12} should be given parenterally. Magnesium deficiencies are often difficult to replenish with oral magnesium because of its osmotic effect in the intestinal lumen. A liquid magnesium preparation added to an oral rehydration solution and sipped throughout the day may minimize magnesium-induced fluid losses. Potent antimotility agents, such as tincture of opium, often are needed to slow transit and maximize contact time for nutrient absorption. High-volume jejunostomy outputs can be lessened by inhibiting endogenous secretions with a proton-pump inhibitor and, in severe cases, octreotide. The benefit of octreotide may be offset by its potential to inhibit intestinal adaptation and impair pancreatic enzyme secretion with doses greater than 300 µg/day. In the most severe cases, supplemental calories must be provided by nocturnal tube feeding or parenteral nutrition. Long-term complications include bone disease, renal stones (oxalate stones if the colon is present, urate stones with a jejunostomy), gallstones, bacterial overgrowth, fat-soluble vitamin deficiencies, essential fatty acid deficiency, and D-lactic acidosis. Small bowel transplantation should be considered in individuals who require parenteral nutrition to survive and then develop liver disease or venous access problems.

CONDITIONS THAT IMPAIR NUTRIENT DELIVERY TO THE SYSTEMIC CIRCULATION

Insoluble lipids (present in chylomicrons) are exocytosed across the basolateral membrane of epithelial cells into the intestinal lymphatics. From there, they enter the mesenteric lymphatics and the general circulation via the thoracic duct. Sugar monomers, amino acids, and medium-chain fatty acids are transported across the basolateral membrane of intestinal epithelial cells into capillaries and into the portal circulation. Sugar monomers are transported across the basolateral membrane by the facilitative glucose transporter isoform (GLUT2) and amino acids by facilitative amino acid carriers (see Fig. 141–1A).

IMPAIRED LYMPHATIC DRAINAGE. Diseases that cause intestinal lymphatic obstruction, such as primary congenital lymphangiectasia (malunion of intestinal lymphatics), or diseases that result in secondary lymphangiectasia (lymphoma, tuberculosis, Kaposi's sarcoma, retroperitoneal fibrosis, constrictive pericarditis, severe heart failure) result in fat malabsorption. The increased pressure in the intestinal lymphatics leads to leakage and sometimes rupture of lymph into the intestinal lumen with the loss of lipids, gamma globulins, albumin, and lymphocytes. The diagnosis of lymphangiectasia can be made by intestinal biopsy, but the specific cause may be more difficult to identify. Individuals with lymphangiectasia malabsorb fat and fat-soluble vitamins and have protein loss into the intestinal lumen. The most common presentation is hypoproteinemic edema. Nutritional management includes a low-fat diet and supplementation with medium-chain triglycerides, which are absorbed directly into the portal circulation. Fat-soluble vitamins should be given if deficiencies develop.

Watery Diarrheas

See Figures 141–8 and 141–9 for algorithms concerning evaluation of watery diarrheas.

INGESTION OF NONABSORBABLE SOLUTES: MAGNESIUM AND SODIUM PHOSPHATE/SULFATE DIARRHEAS

Individuals ingesting significant amounts of Mg^{2+}-based antacids or high-potency multimineral/multivitamin supplements or individuals surreptitiously taking Mg^{2+}-containing laxatives or nonabsorbable anion laxatives, such as Na_2PO_4 (neutral phosphate) or Na_2SO_4 (Glauber's or Carlsbad salt), may develop significant osmotically induced, watery diarrhea.

CARBOHYDRATE MALABSORPTION

SORBITOL AND FRUCTOSE DIARRHEA. Chewing gum and elixir diarrhea can result from the chronic ingestion of dietetic foods, candy, chewing gum, or medication elixirs that are sweetened with unabsorbable carbohydrates such as sorbitol. Excessive consumption of pears, prunes, peaches, and apple juice, which also contain sorbitol and fructose, also results in diarrhea. Fructose may be malabsorbed if ingested in high concentrations, and an occasional patient may have diarrhea related to ingestion of large volumes of fruit juice or soft drinks that are sweetened with fructose-containing corn syrup.

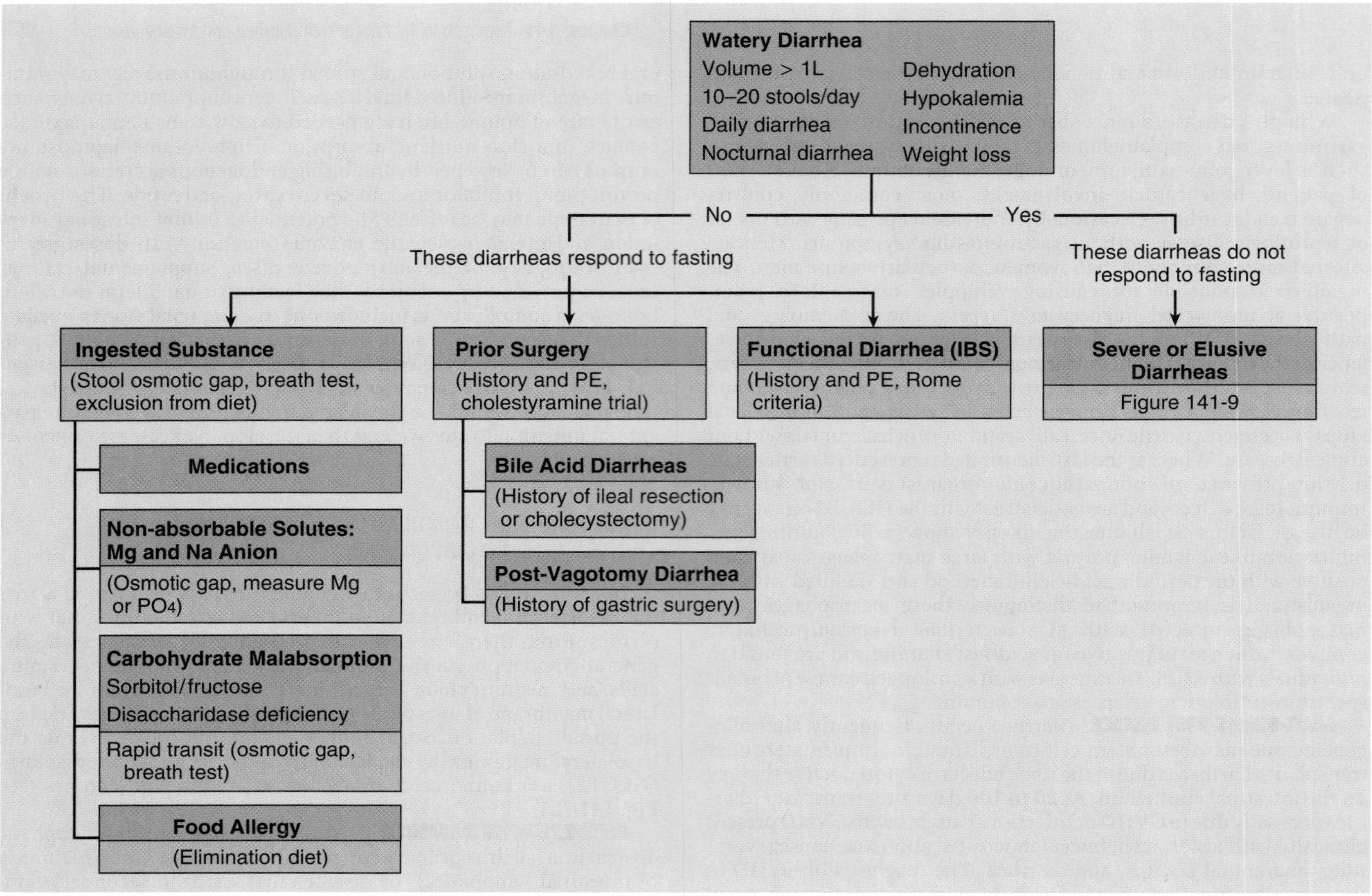

Figure 141-8

Watery Diarrhea

Volume > 1L	Dehydration
10–20 stools/day	Hypokalemia
Daily diarrhea	Incontinence
Nocturnal diarrhea	Weight loss

No — These diarrheas respond to fasting

Yes — These diarrheas do not respond to fasting

Ingested Substance
(Stool osmotic gap, breath test, exclusion from diet)

- **Medications**
- **Non-absorbable Solutes: Mg and Na Anion**
  (Osmotic gap, measure Mg or PO_4)
- **Carbohydrate Malabsorption**
  Sorbitol/fructose
  Disaccharidase deficiency
  Rapid transit (osmotic gap, breath test)
- **Food Allergy**
  (Elimination diet)

Prior Surgery
(History and PE, cholestyramine trial)

- **Bile Acid Diarrheas**
  (History of ileal resection or cholecystectomy)
- **Post-Vagotomy Diarrhea**
  (History of gastric surgery)

Functional Diarrhea (IBS)
(History and PE, Rome criteria)

Severe or Elusive Diarrheas
Figure 141-9

FIGURE 141–8 • Approach to the evaluation of watery diarrheas. IBS = irritable bowel syndrome; PE = physical examination. (Adapted from Powell DW: Approach to the patient with diarrhea. *In* Yamada T, Alpers DH, Owyang C, et al [eds]: Textbook of Gastroenterology, 3rd ed. Philadelphia, Lippincott-Raven, 1999.)

Figure 141-9

Severe or Elusive Diarrheas
High volume watery diarrhea, or undiagnosed malabsorption, inflammatory or low volume watery diarrheas

Stool collection (48–72 hr) on regular diet and then on 48 hr fast. Measure stool fat, Na^+, K^+, osmolality and calculate osmotic gap; laxative screen

Stool <500 mL(g)/24 hr
Responds to fast

- **Functional Diarrhea**
  No osmotic gap

Stool 500–3000 mL(g)/24 hr
May or may not respond to fast

- **Inflammatory Diarrheas**
  Microscopic/collagenous colitis, eosinophilic gastroenteritis, IBD
  No osmotic gap, diagnose with endoscopy and biopsy
- **Diabetic or Alcoholic Diarrhea**
  Suspect in patients with these diseases.
  Diagnoses of exclusion
- **Factitious Osmotic Diarrhea**
  Osmotic gap present, increased Mg^{++}, PO_4
  Room search positive

Stool >1000 mL(g)/24 hr and often >3000 mL(g)/24 hr
Does not respond to fast. All have normal osmotic gap

- **Endocrine malignancies**
  - **VIPoma or WDHA Syndrome**
    >3L/day, serum VIP elevated
  - **Carcinoid Syndrome**
    Increased urinary 5-HIAA
  - **Medullary CA of Thyroid**
    Serum calcitonin elevated
- **Nonendocrine malignancies**
  - **Gastrinoma**
    Serum gastrin elevated
  - **Glucagonoma**
    Serum glucagon elevated
  - **Villous Adenoma**
    Hypokalemia, colonoscopy and biopsy is diagnostic
  - **Mastocytosis**
    Urinary histamine elevated
- **Factitious Secretory Diarrheas**
  Female > Male
  Laxative screen positive
  Room search positive
- **Chronic Idiopathic Diarrhea or Pseudo-Pancreatic Cholera**
  Diagnosis of exclusion, completely negative workup for secretory diarrhea

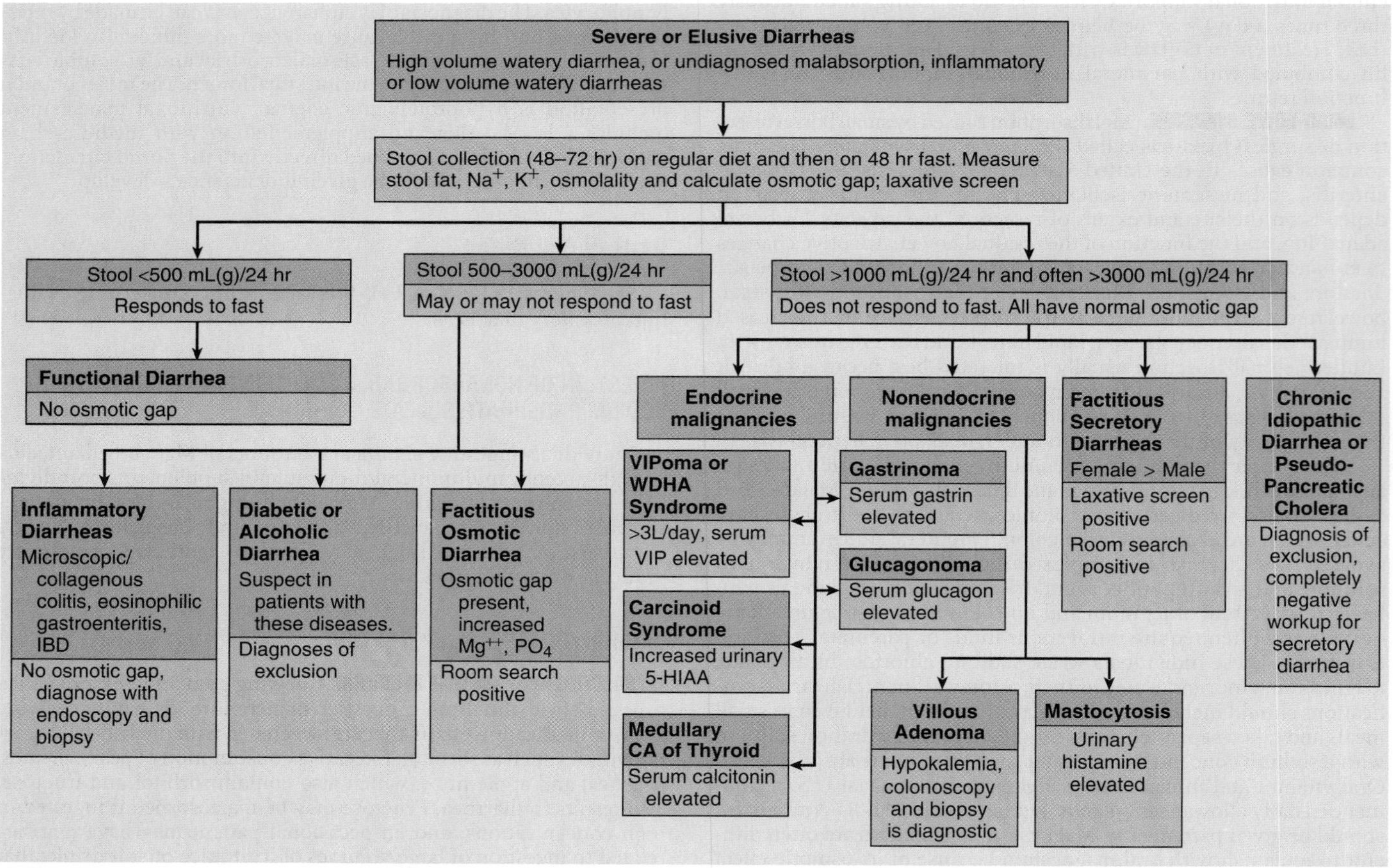

FIGURE 141–9 • Approach to the evaluation of severe or elusive diarrheas. WDHA = watery diarrhea hypokalemia achlorhydria; VIP = vasoactive intestinal polypeptide; IBD = inflammatory bowel disease; 5-HIAA = 5-hydroxyindoleacetic acid; CA = cancer. (Adapted from Powell DW: Approach to the patient with diarrhea. *In* Yamada T, Alpers DH, Owyang C, et al [eds]: Textbook of Gastroenterology, 3rd ed. Philadelphia, Lippincott-Raven, 1999.)

RAPID INTESTINAL TRANSIT. Approximately 25% of the normal 200-g carbohydrate diet may be unabsorbed by the normal small intestine. When passed into the colon, it is metabolized to osmotically active short-chain fatty acids by colonic flora. Diets high in carbohydrate and low in fat may allow rapid gastric emptying and rapid small intestinal motility, leading to carbohydrate malabsorption and osmotic diarrhea. Rapid orocecal transit time also occurs in thyrotoxicosis. Because carbohydrate is metabolized also to H_2 and CO_2 by colonic bacteria, the symptoms of excess flatus, abdominal bloating, and cramping abdominal pain may be important clues to the diagnosis of carbohydrate malabsorption.

GLUCOSE-GALACTOSE MALABSORPTION AND DISACCHARIDASE DEFICIENCIES. Lactase deficiency and congenital absence of enterocyte brush-border carbohydrate hydrolases and transport proteins may cause diarrheas. Lactase deficiency should be considered in cases of unexplained watery diarrhea, especially if accompanied by abdominal cramps, bloating, and flatus (see earlier). Patients with symptoms on ingesting mushrooms may have trehalose deficiency.

PRIOR SURGERY: BILE ACID DIARRHEA

There are three types of bile acid–induced diarrhea. Type 1 results from severe disease (e.g., Crohn's disease), resection, or bypass of the distal ileum, which allows dihydroxy bile salts to escape absorption (see earlier). Type 2 bile acid diarrhea, or primary bile acid malabsorption, may be congenital or acquired. This form of diarrhea often responds to cholestyramine. Type 3 bile acid diarrhea is caused by measured increases in fecal bile acids in patients with postcholecystectomy diarrhea. It is unclear why interruption of gallbladder storage would lead to increased bile acid wastage. Although many patients respond to cholestyramine, some do not. Another cause of type 3 bile acid diarrhea is truncal vagotomy combined with a drainage procedure (postvagotomy diarrhea), after which 20 to 30% of patients develop diarrhea. Many patients do not respond to cholestyramine, but motility-altering drugs (opiates and anticholinergics) may be of benefit. Celiac disease also may appear first after gastric surgery or vagotomy.

FUNCTIONAL WATERY DIARRHEAS (IRRITABLE BOWEL SYNDROME)

About 25% of patients with irritable bowel syndrome have a symptom complex of predominantly painless diarrhea (Chapter 135), but many patients are discovered to have other conditions, such as occult lactose intolerance, celiac disease, collagenous or microscopic/lymphocytic colitis, rapid transit with carbohydrate-wasting diarrhea, malabsorption of fructose or sorbitol, or even primary bile acid malabsorption (type 2).

True Secretory Diarrheas

See Figure 141–9.

ENDOCRINE TUMOR DIARRHEAS

CARCINOID SYNDROME. Patients with metastatic carcinoid tumors of the gastrointestinal tract or, rarely, primary nonmetastatic carcinoid tumors of the bronchial epithelium may develop a watery diarrhea and cramping abdominal pain in addition to these other symptoms (Chapter 245). Because one third of these patients do not have other symptoms at the time the diarrhea begins, carcinoid should be considered in patients with secretory diarrhea.

GASTRINOMA. Diarrhea occurs in one third of patients with Zollinger-Ellison syndrome (Chapter 140), may precede the ulcer symptoms, and in about 10% of patients may be the major pathophysiologic manifestation. The diarrhea is caused by high volumes of hydrochloride secretion (it can be reduced by nasogastric aspiration or effective antisecretory therapy) and by maldigestion of fat due to pH inactivation of pancreatic lipase and precipitation of bile acids.

VIPOMA OR WATERY DIARRHEA HYPOKALEMIA ACHLORHYDRIA SYNDROME. Non–β cell pancreatic adenomas may secrete various peptide secretagogues, including VIP that produces all of the symptoms of this disease (Chapter 140). Patients with this syndrome have secretory diarrhea, with 70% of patients having more than 3 L of stool per day and virtually all having more than 700 mL/day. Stool electrolyte losses account for the dehydration, hypokalemia, and acidosis that give this syndrome its name.

MEDULLARY CARCINOMA OF THE THYROID. This cancer may present in sporadic form, or it may present as part of the multiple endocrine neoplasia type II syndrome with pheochromocytomas and hyperparathyroidism in 25 to 50% of cases. Watery (secretory) diarrhea is caused by the secretion of calcitonin by the tumor; however, these tumors also elaborate other secretogogues, such as prostaglandins, VIP, and serotonin. By the time watery diarrhea occurs, the tumor has metastasized, and this symptom portends a poor prognosis.

NONENDOCRINE MALIGNANCIES

VILLOUS ADENOMAS. Large (4 to 10 cm) villous adenomas of the rectum or rectosigmoid may cause a secretory form of diarrhea of 500 to 3000 mL/24 hours characterized by hypokalemia, chloride-rich stool, and metabolic alkalosis. Secretogogues such as prostaglandins have been found in the tumor and rectal effluent of patients, and indomethacin administration reduces the diarrhea in some.

SYSTEMIC MASTOCYTOSIS. The diarrhea of systemic mastocytosis (Chapter 272) may be malabsorptive, secondary to mast cell infiltration of the mucosa with resulting villus atrophy, or intermittent and secretory. Histamine or another mast cell mediator may be the secretogogue responsible for these symptoms and for the secretory diarrhea, by either stimulating gastric acid secretion (such as in Zollinger-Ellison syndrome) or by having a secretory effect on the intestine. Antihistamines (H_1 blockers), H_2 blockers, proton-pump inhibitors, and cyclooxygenase inhibitors may be helpful. Blockade of mast cell degranulation with disodium cromoglycate may reduce all the symptoms and the diarrhea, but not the steatorrhea, which may be treated better with corticosteroids.

FACTITIOUS DIARRHEA

Approximately 15% of patients referred to secondary or tertiary centers for diarrhea and 25% of patients with proven secretory diarrheas are found to be ingesting either laxatives or diuretics surreptitiously. These patients present with severe chronic watery, often nocturnal, diarrhea and may have abdominal pain, weight loss, nausea, vomiting, hypokalemic myopathy, acidosis, or protein-losing enteropathy. Patients may have 10 to 20 bowel movements per day, with 24-hour stool volumes in the range of 300 to 3000 mL. Phenolphthalein, now removed from the market; bisacodyl; and anthraquinone (senna, cascara, aloe, rhubarb, frangula, and danthron) ingestion and osmotic laxatives (neutral phosphate, epsom salts, and magnesium citrate) can cause this syndrome. Because there is no readily available assay for the stool softener dioctyl sodium sulfosuccinate (the docusate salts), one of the more common laxatives, it is unclear how often it contributes. Some patients ingest large quantities of diuretics, such as furosemide or ethacrynic acid.

More than 90% of patients are women, and two different clinical syndromes are most common: (1) women younger than 30 years of age, in whom eating disorders such as anorexia nervosa or bulimia may be part of the psychic abnormality, and (2) middle-aged to elderly women, who have extensive medical histories and are more likely to be health care workers. Factitious diarrhea is sufficiently common to warrant laxative screening to exclude this syndrome before initiating extensive medical evaluation for the other causes of diarrhea.

CHRONIC IDIOPATHIC DIARRHEA AND PSEUDOPANCREATIC CHOLERA SYNDROME

Patients in whom extensive evaluation for a cause of secretory diarrhea is negative are said to have either chronic idiopathic diarrhea or pseudopancreatic cholera syndrome, depending on whether the fasting stool volumes are less than or greater than 700 mL/24 hours. If no diagnosis is found after thorough testing and a search for surreptitious laxative abuse, a therapeutic trial with bile salt—binding drugs, NSAIDs, or opiates is warranted. Follow-up studies suggest that the diarrhea is usually self-limited and disappears spontaneously in 6 to 24 months.

DIABETIC DIARRHEA

Of young to middle-aged diabetics with type I diabetes, particularly men between 20 and 40 years old whose diabetes has been poorly controlled for more than 5 years, 20% may have a profuse watery, urgent diarrhea, often occurring at night with incontinence. These patients usually have concomitant neuropathy, nephropathy, and retinopathy. Exocrine pancreatic insufficiency is sometimes the cause, and bacterial overgrowth occasionally is present because of the motility disturbance of the autonomic neuropathy. Type I diabetic patients must have an appropriate evaluation to exclude other causes of diarrhea, especially celiac disease. If no other cause is found, clonidine may be helpful. Patients with neuropathy frequently have impaired anal sphincter function, and high-dose loperamide may improve the incontinence. A common cause of diarrhea in type II diabetics is therapy with metformin.

ALCOHOLIC DIARRHEA

Binge drinking of alcohol causes a brief episode of diarrhea that usually lasts less than 1 day. Chronic alcoholics often have a severe watery diarrhea that persists for days or weeks after hospitalization. Various physiologic abnormalities have been described in alcoholics as a cause of diarrhea but none have been proven. With abstinence, renourishment, and replenishment of vitamin deficiencies, the diarrhea slowly improves.

Inflammatory Diarrheas

See Figure 141–10 for an algorithm for evaluation of inflammatory diarrheas.

INFLAMMATORY BOWEL DISEASE. Patients with Crohn's disease or ulcerative colitis have diarrhea with stool volumes usually less than 1 L/24 hours (Chapter 142). Occasional patients with severe ulcerative colitis may have more severe diarrhea with water and electrolyte secretion in the unaffected small intestine, suggesting the presence of circulating secretogogues originating from the inflamed colon. Pouchitis (inflammation of the ileal reservoir) is a common cause of diarrhea in patients who have ulcerative colitis with an ileoanal anastomosis after colectomy. The cause is unknown. Antibiotic therapy is effective, but relapses are common. A probiotic compound containing lactobacilli, bifidobacteria, and *S. thermophilus* may be effective at preventing relapses. [8]

EOSINOPHILIC GASTROENTERITIS. Infiltration of various layers of the gastrointestinal tract with eosinophils is a recognized clinical entity that is accompanied by diarrhea in 30 to 60% of patients. Peripheral eosinophilia is present in 75% of these patients. The disease may involve the entire gastrointestinal tract from esophagus to anus, or it may be isolated to a segment. Abdominal pain, nausea, vomiting, weight loss, steatorrhea, and protein-losing enteropathy are other prominent signs and symptoms of this disease. The cause of this disease is unknown, but approximately 50% of patients have atopic (allergic) histories, and food allergy is suspected. Corticosteroids are the mainstay of therapy; sodium cromoglycate may be useful. Infestation with nematodes must be excluded before making this diagnosis.

MILK AND SOY PROTEIN INTOLERANCE AND FOOD ALLERGY. Intolerance to cow's milk and soy protein is a well-established cause of enterocolitis in infants. Approximately 50% of patients who are allergic to one of these proteins are also allergic to the other. The role of food allergy in causing diarrhea in adults is less clear, however. Commonly suspected allergens include milk, eggs, seafood, nuts, artificial flavors, and food coloring.

COLLAGENOUS AND MICROSCOPIC COLITIS. These two conditions may or may not be the same or variants of the same disease. Microscopic (lymphocytic) colitis is equally prevalent in men and women, whereas collagenous colitis occurs 10 times more often in middle-aged or elderly women. There is an increased prevalence (15%) of microscopic colitis in individuals with celiac sprue. These diseases may be categorized as either inflammatory or secretory diarrheas. An epidemiologic relationship to long-term NSAID use has been reported, and increased luminal prostaglandin levels may cause the diarrhea. Either food hypersensitivity or intraluminal bile has been proposed as a trigger for prostaglandin release from lymphocytes. The disease disappears with fecal stream diversion. Budesonide and bismuth subsalicylate therapy has been successful in small studies. [9] Corticosteroids and 5-aminosalicylates may be useful in refractory disease.

PROTEIN-LOSING ENTEROPATHY. Severe protein loss through the gastrointestinal tract caused by ulceration, obstructed lymphatics, and immune-related vascular injury occurs in a variety of disease states: bacterial or parasitic infection, gastritis, gastric cancer, collagenous colitis, inflammatory bowel disease, congenital intestinal lymphangiectasia, sarcoidosis, lymphoma, mesenteric tuberculosis, Ménétrier's disease, sprue, eosinophilic gastroenteritis, systemic lupus erythematosus, chronic peritoneal dialysis, or food allergies. The condition usually responds to corticosteroids or immunosuppressive therapy.

RADIATION ENTERITIS. Patients receiving pelvic radiation for malignancies of the female urogenital tract or the male prostate may develop

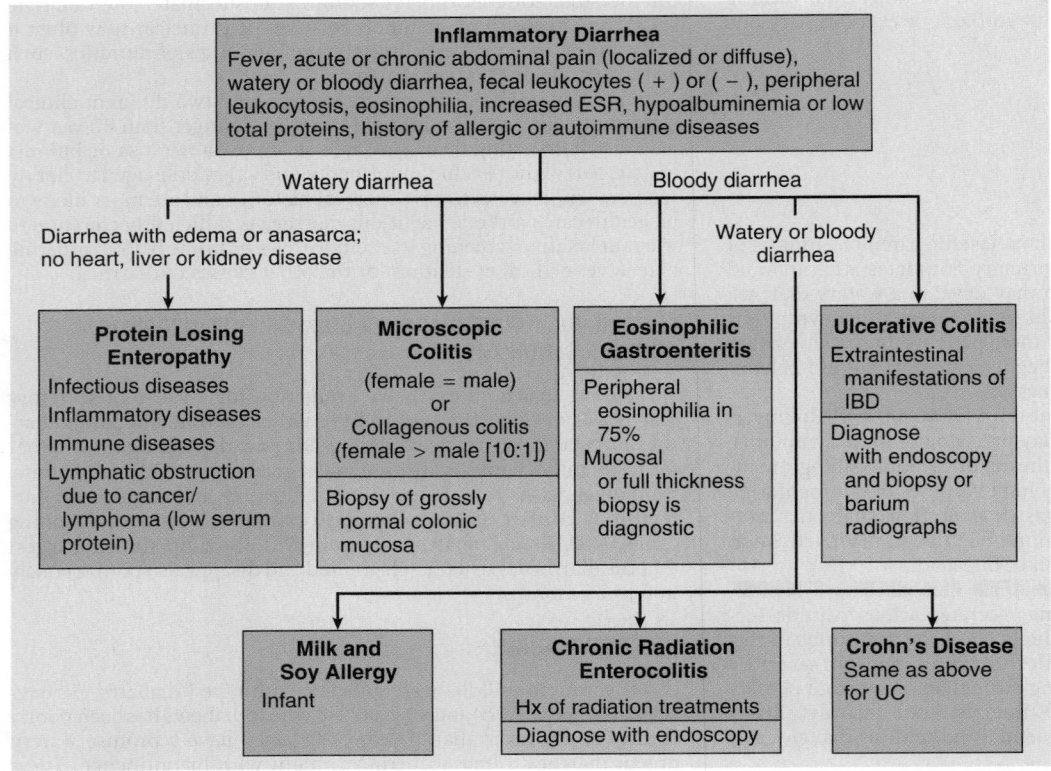

FIGURE 141–10 • Approach to the evaluation of inflammatory diarrheas. ESR = erythrocyte sedimentation rate; IBD = inflammatory bowel disease; UC = ulcerative colitis. (Adapted from Powell DW: Approach to the patient with diarrhea. *In* Yamada T, Alpers DH, Owyang C, et al [eds]: Textbook of Gastroenterology, 3rd ed. Philadelphia, Lippincott-Raven, 1999.)

chronic radiation enterocolitis 6 to 12 months after total doses of radiation greater than 40 to 60 Gy (Chapters 19 and 143). Symptoms can develop 20 years after treatment, however. In irradiated animal models, early abnormalities include an increase in inflammatory mediators, an increase in cholinergic stimulation of intestinal tissue, and endothelial cell apoptosis that precedes epithelial cell apoptosis. The last finding suggests that vascular injury is the primary event. Vascular endothelial growth factor, basic fibroblast growth factor, and interleukin-11 protect animal intestine from radiation damage. Diarrhea may be caused by bile acid malabsorption if the ileum is damaged, by bacterial overgrowth if radiation causes small intestine strictures or bypass, or by radiation-induced chronic inflammation of the small intestine and colon. Rapid transit also may contribute to malabsorption and diarrhea. Treatment is often unsatisfactory. Anti-inflammatory drugs (sulfasalazine, corticosteroids) and antibiotics have been tried with little success. Cholestyramine and NSAIDs may help, as may opiates.

MISCELLANEOUS DISEASES. Although acute mesenteric arterial or venous thrombosis presents as an acute bloody diarrhea, chronic mesenteric vascular ischemia may present as watery diarrhea. Gastrointestinal tuberculosis and histoplasmosis present as diarrhea that may be either bloody or watery, as do certain immunologic diseases, such as Behçet's syndrome or Churg-Strauss syndrome. All of these diseases may be misdiagnosed as inflammatory bowel disease. Diarrhea, the hallmark of acute GVHD after allogeneic bone marrow transplantation, presents with the triad of dermatitis, hepatic cholestasis, and enteritis (see earlier). Neutropenic enterocolitis, an ileocolitis occurring in neutropenic leukemic patients, sometimes is caused by *C. difficile* infection.

Diagnosis of Chronic Diarrhea

HISTORY AND PHYSICAL EXAMINATION

A detailed history, physical examination, and certain screening tests can lead to a diagnosis in 75% of patients with watery diarrheas (see Table 141–1 and Figs. 141–3 and 141–8). A history of 10 to 20 bowel movements per day suggests secretory diarrhea (see Fig. 141–9). A history of peptic ulcer should suggest gastrinoma or systemic mastocytosis. Physical examination is helpful only if the thyromegaly of medullary carcinoma, the cutaneous flushing of the neuroendocrine tumors and systemic mastocytosis, the dermatographism of systemic mastocytosis, or the migratory necrolytic erythema of glucagonoma is evident. Scars from previous surgery may suggest postvagotomy diarrhea or terminal ileal resection with bile acid diarrhea. Autonomic dysfunction (e.g., postural hypotension, impotence, gustatory sweating) is almost invariably present in diabetic diarrhea.

Evaluation for malabsorption begins with a careful history of bowel habits, weight loss, travel, food or milk tolerance, underlying gastrointestinal or liver diseases, abdominal surgery, radiation or chemotherapy treatments, family history, and drug and alcohol use. Patients with malabsorption can present with a variety of gastrointestinal or extraintestinal manifestations (see Table 141–5). Significant malabsorption of fat and carbohydrate usually causes chronic diarrhea, abdominal cramps, gas, bloating, and weight loss. Steatorrhea (fat in the stool) manifests as oily, foul-smelling stools that are difficult to flush down the toilet. Stools may be large and bulky (e.g., pancreatic insufficiency) or watery (e.g., bacterial overgrowth, mucosal diseases). Individuals with malabsorption also can present with manifestations of vitamin and mineral deficiencies. Dyspnea can be due to anemia from iron, folate, or vitamin B_{12} deficiency. Cheilosis, angular stomatitis, or a scaly rash can be due to many vitamin and mineral deficiencies or essential fatty acid deficiency (see Table 141–5). Dermatitis herpetiformis is a blistering, burning, itchy rash on the extensor surfaces and buttocks associated with celiac disease. Manifestations of calcium, magnesium, or vitamin D malabsorption include paresthesias and tetany owing to hypocalcemia or hypomagnesemia and bone pain owing to osteomalacia or osteoporosis-related fractures. Paresthesias and ataxia are manifestations of cobalamin and vitamin E deficiency.

The important clinical manifestations of inflammatory diarrheas are the signs and symptoms of inflammation and/or the effects of severe chronic protein loss (see Fig. 141–10). Diarrhea in these inflammatory diseases may be meager (e.g., the pseudodiarrhea of proctitis), or it may be fairly severe (e.g., as in GVHD). Systemic

manifestations of inflammatory bowel disease include oral aphthous ulcers, polymigratory arthritis, uveitis, erythema nodosum, pyoderma gangrenosum, and the palpable purpura of vasculitis.

SCREENING LABORATORY EXAMINATIONS

Blood levels (see Fig. 141–3) of iron, folate, vitamin B_{12}, vitamin D, or prothrombin time (vitamin K) help evaluate malabsorption. Although serum carotene levels may be low simply from poor intake, values less than $50\,\mu g/dL$ suggest malabsorption. Peripheral blood findings of leukocytosis, eosinophilia, elevated erythrocyte sedimentation rate, hypoalbuminemia, or low total serum proteins suggest inflammatory diarrheas, whose hallmark is the presence of blood, either gross or occult, and leukocytes in the stool. There are no bedside screening tests to establish the diagnosis in watery diarrheas.

RADIOGRAPHY

Radiography should be viewed as an adjunct to the diagnosis of diarrheal diseases and not a primary test. Malabsorption may be suggested by a flat plate of the abdomen that shows pancreatic calcification. Some diseases (e.g., previous gastric surgery, gastrocolic fistulas, blind loops from previous intestinal anastomoses, small intestine strictures, multiple jejunal diverticula, and abnormal intestinal motility that could lead to bacterial overgrowth) may be shown by an upper gastrointestinal series with small intestine follow through. Certain diseases may present radiographically as uniform thickening of the intestinal folds (e.g., amyloidosis, lymphoma, Whipple's disease); others, such as lymphoma or lymphangiectasia, show uniform or patchy abnormalities. Patients with celiac disease show dilation of the small intestine, with little mucosal abnormality, and segmentation of the barium column as a result of precipitation or flocculation of the barium. Routine contrast radiographs of the gastrointestinal tract are not usually helpful in the diagnosis of watery diarrheas, unless they show a previous vagotomy, extensive small bowel resection or cholecystectomy, the presence of a tumor (carcinoid or villous adenoma), or a bowel filled with fluid (endocrine tumor). Contrast radiography may show diagnostic evidence of inflammatory bowel disease or changes suggestive of eosinophilic gastroenteritis or radiation enterocolitis. Early or mild gut inflammation may be missed entirely by radiography. Somatostatin receptor scintigraphy with indium-111–labeled octreotide can be useful in localizing gastrinomas, pancreatic endocrine tumors, and carcinoid tumors.

ENDOSCOPY AND BIOPSY

Upper endoscopy with distal duodenal biopsy should be undertaken if serologic tests for celiac disease are positive or diagnostic clues suggest small bowel mucosal malabsorption. Patients with severe watery or elusive diarrhea should have a flexible sigmoidoscopy or, preferably, a colonoscopy to exclude villous adenomas of the rectosigmoid and biopsy to exclude microscopic or collagenous colitis, mastocytosis, or early inflammatory bowel disease. Colonoscopy and biopsy also may reveal melanosis coli secondary to chronic anthracene laxative use. Terminal ileal biopsy may indicate inflammatory bowel diseases.

LABORATORY TESTING

MALABSORPTION. If chronic diarrhea is the presenting symptom, a stool for ova and parasites and a stool antigen capture ELISA test for *Giardia* should be obtained. A stool test for fat is the best available screening test for malabsorption (see Table 141–7). If the fecal fat test result is negative, selective carbohydrate malabsorption or other causes of diarrhea should be considered. If the fecal fat test result is positive (Fig. 141–11), further testing should be based on clinical suspicion for particular diseases. If pancreatic insufficiency is suspected, imaging studies of the pancreas should be performed. If proximal mucosal damage is suspected, multiple small intestinal biopsy specimens should be obtained. If there are no clues as to the cause of malabsorption, a D-xylose test may help to distinguish mucosal disease from pancreatic insufficiency. The D-xylose test result also can be abnormal in individuals with bacterial overgrowth; if this condition is suspected, culture of an intestinal aspirate or a breath test should be obtained (see Table 141–7). A small bowel barium study is useful in detecting ileal disease and structural abnormalities that predispose

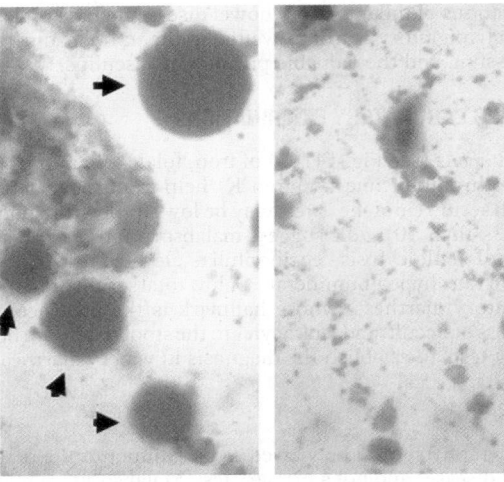

Positive   Negative

FIGURE 141–11 • Sudan stain of stool for fat. The positive stain (left) shows larges globules of unabsorbed fat (arrows).

to bacterial overgrowth. Some individuals with celiac disease present with selective nutrient deficiencies without diarrhea. In these cases, AEA or tTG antibody tests and intestinal biopsy should be performed. When malabsorption is suspected in patients hospitalized for severe diarrhea or malnutrition, a more streamlined evaluation usually includes a stool for culture, ova and parasites, and fat; an abdominal imaging study; and a biopsy of the small intestine.

WATERY DIARRHEA. *Breath tests* to measure the respiratory excretion of labeled CO_2 after oral administration and metabolism of radioactive carbon-labeled substrates or of H_2 after administration of carbohydrates can assess fat, carbohydrate, and bile salt malabsorption or bacterial overgrowth (see Table 141–7).

The diagnosis of endocrine tumors, such as carcinoids, gastrinoma, VIPoma, medullary carcinoma of the thyroid, glucagonoma, somatostatinoma, and systemic mastocytosis, is made by showing elevated blood levels of serotonin or urinary 5-hydroxyindoleacetic acid and serum levels for gastrin, VIP, calcitonin, glucagon, somatostatin, histamine, or prostaglandins (Chapter 140). Somatostatin receptor scintigraphy has proved to be sensitive and useful in the diagnosis and evaluation of Zollinger-Ellison syndrome (Chapter 140).

INFLAMMATORY DIARRHEA. Indium-labeled leukocyte scans occasionally may detect bowel inflammation not evident by endoscopy or conventional barium contrast radiography. Fecal white blood cells can be detected in stool smears with a methylene blue stain. Stool excretion of lactoferrin (a constituent of leukocytes) also can be used as a quantitative index of fecal leukocyte loss. The most sensitive test for certain inflammatory diarrheas is measurement of intestinal protein loss by 24-hour stool excretion or clearance of chromium-51–labeled albumin or α_1-antitrypsin.

ELUSIVE DIARRHEA. An important adjunct to diagnosing the cause of diarrhea is to look at the stool. The greasy bulky stool of steatorrhea and the bloody stool of gut inflammation are distinctive. Patients with steatorrhea sometimes also have severe watery diarrhea, however. Qualitative tests on outpatient spot stool collections and quantitative tests (stool fat, electrolytes, and osmolality) on 48- to 72-hour stool collections can help define the causes of diarrhea, especially severe or elusive diarrheas (see Table 141–7 and Fig. 141–9). Stool collections can be analyzed for appearance, weight, quantitative fecal fat, electrolytes (Na^+, K^+, and, if thought necessary, Cl^-, PO_4^{2-} and Mg^{2+}), osmolality, fecal pH, and laxative screen. Stool or urine can be analyzed for emetine (a component of ipecac), bisacodyl, castor oil, or anthraquinone. Stool SO_4, PO_4^{2-}, and Mg^{2+} analysis detects factitious diarrheas caused by osmotic cathartics.

Carbohydrate malabsorption lowers stool pH because of colonic fermentation of carbohydrate to short-chain fatty acids. Stool pH less than 5.3 usually means pure carbohydrate malabsorption, whereas in generalized malabsorptive diseases, stool pH is greater than 5.6 and usually greater than 6.0.

The normal stool osmotic gap, which is the difference between stool osmolality (or 290 mOsm) and twice the stool Na^+ and K^+ concentrations, is 50 to 125. In secretory diarrheas, the solutes causing the movement of water from blood to bowel lumen are the secreted Na^+ and K^+ ions; stool Na^+ concentrations are usually greater than 90 mmol/L, and the osmotic gap is less than 50. In osmotic diarrhea, the ingestion of nonabsorbable (or nonabsorbed) solutes displaces Na^+ from the stool and causes the osmotic gap and the diarrhea (see Pathophysiology); stool Na^+ is less than 60 mmol/L, and the osmotic gap is greater than 125. Stools with Na^+ concentration between 60 and 90 mmol/L and calculated osmotic gaps between 50 and 100 can result from either secretory or malabsorptive abnormalities. Patients with Mg^{2+}-induced diarrhea can be diagnosed by fecal Mg^{2+} values greater than 50 mmol/L. Sodium anion–induced diarrheas mimic secretory diarrhea because the stool Na^+ content is high (>90 mmol/L), and there is no osmotic gap; this diarrhea can be diagnosed by determining stool Cl^- concentration because these anions displace stool Cl^-, and the resulting stool Cl^- value is usually less than 20 mmol/L.

Rx Antidiarrheal Therapy

Antidiarrheal agents are of two types: agents useful for mild-to-moderate diarrheas and agents helpful in secretory and other severe diarrheas. The bulk-forming agents (kaolin-pectin, psyllium, and methylcellulose) increase the consistency of stool and have no antisecretory activity. Pectin has been shown to have proabsorptive activity.[1] Other antidiarrheal agents have only mild proabsorptive or antisecretory action, and most have antidiarrheal activity by altering the intestinal motility. Bismuth salicylates, opiates, loperamide, clonidine, phenothiazine, and somatostatin have mild antisecretory activity but also cause dilation of the small intestine and colon and decrease peristalsis. The opiates also increase anal sphincter tone. The therapeutic mechanism of these drugs is to trap fluid within the intestine and put it in contact with the mucosa for a greater period of time, allowing more complete absorption.

The opiates may be symptomatically useful in mild diarrheas. Paregoric, deodorized tincture of opium, codeine, and diphenoxylate with atropine largely have been supplanted by loperamide. Loperamide does not pass the blood-brain barrier and has a high first-pass metabolism in the liver; it has a high therapeutic-to-toxic ratio and is essentially devoid of addiction potential. It is safe in adults, even in total doses of 24 mg/day. The usual dose is 2 to 4 mg two to four times daily. When giving opiates, stool output is not a reliable gauge for replacing fluid losses because the antimotility effects of opiates cause fluid to sequester in the bowel lumen (third space). The antimotility effects are a problem in infectious diarrheas because stasis may enhance bacterial invasion and delay clearance of the microorganisms from the bowel, increasing carriage time. Opiates and anticholinergics also are dangerous in severe inflammatory bowel disease, where they may precipitate megacolon. Racecadotril does not seem to affect motility, so it may prove to be a useful, opiate-like antidiarrheal.[2]

The use of drugs with potentially serious side effects can be justified for treatment of severe secretory diarrheas. The somatostatin analogue octreotide has its major antisecretory effect in carcinoid syndrome and in neuroendocrine tumors because it inhibits hormone secretion by the tumor. New long-acting preparations are now available, easing its use. Octreotide may be of only limited usefulness in short-bowel syndrome and AIDS diarrhea. Agents such as phenothiazine, calcium channel blockers, or clonidine can have serious side effects but may be tried if octreotide fails. Clonidine can be useful in the diarrhea of opiate withdrawal and occasionally in patients with diabetic diarrhea. Indomethacin, a cyclooxygenase blocker that inhibits prostaglandin production, occasionally may be useful in neuroendocrine tumors, irritable bowel syndrome, and food allergy and is most useful in patients with diarrhea caused by acute radiation, AIDS, and villous adenomas of the rectum or colon. Cyclooxygenase blockers may be harmful in inflammatory bowel disease. Glucocorticoids reduce prostaglandin and leukotriene production in inflammatory bowel disease and have a proabsorptive effect on the intestine that is demonstrable by 5 hours after administration. The new anti–tumor necrosis factor antibodies are useful in Crohn's disease that is unresponsive to conventional therapy (Chapter 142).

1. Fontaine O, Gore SM, Pierce NF: Rice-based oral rehydration solution for treating diarrhoea. Cochrane Database Syst Rev 2000;(2):CD001264.
2. Salazar-Lindo E, Santisteban-Ponce J, Chea-Woo E, Gutierrez M: Racecadotril in the treatment of acute watery diarrhea in children. N Engl J Med 2000;343:463–467.
3. Vetel JM, Berard H, Fretault N, Lecomte JM: Comparison of racecadotril and loperamide in adults with acute diarrhea. Aliment Pharmacol Ther 1999;13(Suppl 6):21–26.
4. Rabbani GH, Teka T, Zaman B, et al: Clinical studies in persistent diarrhea: Dietary management with green banana or pectin in Bangladeshi children. Gastroenterology 2001;121:554–560.
5. Sazawal S, Black RE, Bhan MK, et al: Zinc supplementation in young children with acute diarrhea in India. N Engl J Med 1995;333:839–844.
6. Bhutta ZA, Black RE, Brown KH, et al: Prevention of diarrhea and pneumonia by zinc supplementation in children in developing countries: Pooled analysis of randomized controlled trials. Zinc Investigators' Collaborative Group. J Pediatr 1999;135:689–697.
7. Szajewska H, Mrukowicz JZ: Probiotics in the treatment and prevention of acute infectious diarrhea in infants and children: A systematic review of published randomized, double-blind, placebo-controlled trials. J Pediatr Gastroenterol Nutr 2001;33(Suppl 2):S17–S25.
8. Gionchetti P, Rizzello F, Venturi A, et al: Oral bacteriotherapy as maintenance treatment in patients with chronic pouchitis: A double-blind, placebo-controlled trial. Gastroenterology 2000;119:305–309.
9. Bonderup OK, Hansen JB, Birket-Smith L, et al: Budesonide treatment of collagenous colitis: A randomized, double blind, placebo controlled trial with morphometric analysis. Gut 2003;52:248–251.

SUGGESTED READINGS

Bartlett JG: Antibiotic-associated diarrhea. N Engl J Med 2002;346:334–339. *A concise, up-to-date review of C.* difficile*–related and unrelated antibiotic-associated diarrheas.*

Bauer TM, Lalvani A, Fehrenbach J, et al: Derivation and validation of guidelines for stool cultures for enteropathogenic bacteria other than* Clostridium difficile *in hospitalized adults. JAMA 2001;285:313–319. Nosocomial infection with* Salmonella, Shigella, *and parasites is so rare that routine evaluation for them is not recommended if diarrhea begins after 3 days of hospitalization, unless the patient has other high-risk characteristics.*

Farrell RJ, Kelly CP: Celiac sprue. N Engl J Med 2002;346:180–188. *A complete, modern review of celiac disease that includes epidemiology, pathogenesis, treatment, and complications of the disease.*

Field M: Intestinal ion transport and the pathophysiology of diarrhea. J Clin Invest 2003;111:931–943. *This is a superb review of intestinal ion transport physiology and pathophysiology.*

Powell DW: Approach to the patient with diarrhea. In Yamada T, Alpers DH, Owyang C, et al (eds): Textbook of Gastroenterology, 4th ed. Philadelphia, Lippincott Williams & Wilkins, 2003. *This is an expanded and detailed version of the chapter presented here.*

Vesa TH, Marteau P, Korpela R: Lactose intolerance. J Am Coll Nutr 2000;19:165S–175S. *This review points out that the syndrome of lactose intolerance is much more clinically complicated than one would think.*

142 INFLAMMATORY BOWEL DISEASE

William F. Stenson

Definition

Inflammatory bowel diseases (IBDs), including ulcerative colitis and Crohn's disease, are chronic inflammatory diseases of the gastrointestinal tract. They are diagnosed by a set of clinical, endoscopic, and histologic characteristics, but no single finding is absolutely diagnostic for one disease or the other. Moreover, some patients have a clinical picture that falls between the two diseases and are said to have indeterminate colitis.

The inflammatory response in ulcerative colitis is largely confined to the mucosa and submucosa, but in Crohn's disease the inflammation extends through the intestinal wall from mucosa to serosa. Ulcerative colitis is confined to the colon, and colectomy is a curative procedure. Crohn's disease, in contrast, can involve any part of the gastrointestinal tract, although the distal small bowel and the colon are most commonly involved. Resection of the inflamed segment is not curative in Crohn's disease, and inflammation is likely to recur.

Epidemiology

The incidence and prevalence of Crohn's disease and ulcerative colitis vary with geographic location; the highest rates are for white populations in northern Europe and North America, where the incidence for each disease is about 5 per 100,000 and the prevalence is about 50 per 100,000. Rates in central and southern Europe are lower, and in South America, Asia, and Africa, they are lower still. Crohn's disease and ulcerative colitis are both more common in Jews than non-Jews. In the United States, the incidence of IBD in the black population has been one fifth to one half that in the white population, but in recent years that gap has narrowed. In northern Europe and North America, the incidence of ulcerative colitis has leveled off but that of Crohn's disease is still increasing. For both diseases, the incidence is equal in men and women. The peak age at onset is between 15 and 25 years of age, with a second, lesser peak between 55 and 65 years of age. Both diseases occur in childhood, although the incidence before 15 years of age is low.

The risk of developing ulcerative colitis is increased among both nonsmokers and former smokers compared with current smokers. Whether initiation of smoking improves symptoms is unclear, although success has been reported with nicotine patches. In contrast, the incidence of smoking is higher among Crohn's disease patients than the general population, and patients who continue to smoke may be less likely to respond to medical therapy.

Etiology and Pathogenesis

The most important risk factor for IBD is a positive family history. Approximately 15% of IBD patients have affected first-degree relatives, and the incidence among first-degree relatives is 30 to 100 times that of the general population. The best estimates of the lifetime risk of developing IBD among first-degree relatives of affected individuals are 3 to 9%. The increased incidence among first-degree relatives contrasts to the absence of an increased incidence in spouses of patients. Dizygotic twins have the same rate of concordance as would be expected for siblings, whereas monozygotic twins have higher rates of concordance for both diseases. Mutations in *NOD2*, a gene that codes for a protein that acts as an intracellular receptor for lipopolysaccharide, are seen in about 15% of Crohn's disease patients.

In IBD, the lamina propria is infiltrated with lymphocytes, macrophages, and other cells of the immune system. An intensive search for the antigens that trigger the immune response has yet to identify a specific microbial pathogen. Anticolon antibodies of unclear significance have been identified in the sera of ulcerative colitis patients. IBD may also be related to a failure to suppress (or "downregulate") the normal, finely tuned, low-grade chronic inflammation of the intestinal lamina propria in response to its chronic exposure to luminal antigens.

Whatever the antigenic trigger, activated lamina propria T cells are involved in the pathogenesis of IBD. In Crohn's disease, the activated lymphocytes appear to be primarily Th1 lymphocytes that produce interferon (IFN)-γ. Proinflammatory cytokines including interleukin (IL)-1 and tumor necrosis factor (TNF)-α amplify the immune response. Intravenous infusion of an antibody to TNF-α is clinically effective in Crohn's disease. Large numbers of neutrophils enter the inflamed mucosa attracted by chemotactic agents including IL-8 and leukotriene B₄. Epithelial injury in IBD appears to be due to reactive oxygen species from neutrophils and macrophages, as well as to cytokines including TNF-α and IFN-γ.

Mice develop colitis when the genes for IL-2, IL-10, or TGFβ1 are knocked out or when there are certain T-cell receptor mutants, and transgenic rats develop colitis if the human HLA-B27 gene has been introduced. If the same animals are raised in a germ-free environment, colitis does not develop.

Pathology

Ulcerative colitis and Crohn's disease each have a characteristic pathologic appearance, but in any given case the pathologic picture may not be specific enough to distinguish between them or to differentiate them from other diseases such as infectious colitis or ischemic colitis (Table 142–1). In IBD, the pathologic assessment of disease activity may not correlate with the clinical and endoscopic assessments.

In ulcerative colitis, inflammation begins in the rectum, extends proximally a certain distance, and then abruptly stops, with a clear demarcation between involved and uninvolved mucosa. In mild disease, there are superficial erosions, whereas in more severe disease, ulcers may be large but superficial, penetrating the muscularis mucosa

Table 142–1 • COMPARISON OF ULCERATIVE COLITIS AND CROHN'S DISEASE

FEATURE	ULCERATIVE COLITIS	CROHN'S DISEASE
PATHOLOGY		
Rectal involvement	Always	Common
Skip lesions	Never	Common
Transmural involvement	Rare	Common
Granulomas	Occasional	Common
Perianal disease	Never	Common
Cobblestone mucosa	Rare	Common
RADIOLOGY		
"Collar button" ulcers	Common	Occasional
Small intestinal involvement	Never	Common
Discontinuous involvement	Never	Common
Fistulas	Never	Common
Strictures	Occasional	Common
ENDOSCOPY		
Aphthous ulcers	Never	Common
Discontinuous involvement	Never	Common
Rectal sparing	Never	Common
Linear or serpiginous ulcers	Never	Common
Ulcers in terminal ileum	Never	Common

Table 142–2 • CRITERIA FOR SEVERITY IN INFLAMMATORY BOWEL DISEASE

Mild	Fewer than four bowel movements per day with little or no blood, no fever, and sedimentation rate less than 20 mm/hr
Moderate	Between mild and severe
Severe	Six or more bowel movements per day with blood, fever, anemia, and sedimentation rate greater than 30 mm/hr

addition to signs of acute activity, there are also signs of chronicity, with lymphoid aggregates, plasma cells, mast cells, and eosinophils in the lamina propria.

In Crohn's disease, the bowel wall is thickened and stiff. The mesentery, which is thickened, edematous, and contracted, fixes the intestine in one position. Transmural inflammation may cause loops of intestine to be matted together. All layers of the intestine are thickened, and the lumen is narrowed. "Skip lesions" with two involved areas separated by a length of normal intestine suggest Crohn's disease. Colonic inflammation with rectal sparing is more consistent with Crohn's disease than with ulcerative colitis. The earliest lesion of Crohn's disease is the aphthous ulcer, which typically occurs over Peyer's patches in the small intestine and over lymphoid aggregates in the colon. As the disease progresses, aphthous ulcers enlarge and become stellate or serpiginous. Eventually, the stellate ulcers coalesce to form longitudinal and transverse linear ulcers. The remaining islands of nonulcerated mucosa give a cobblestone appearance. Fissures develop from the base of ulcers and extend down through the muscularis to the serosa. Lymphoid aggregates are found in the submucosa and external to the muscularis propria. Granulomas are common in Crohn's disease but not in ulcerative colitis.

only in very severe disease. Inflammatory polyps or pseudopolyps may be present. Most of the pathologic findings in ulcerative colitis are limited to the mucosa and submucosa; the muscularis propria is affected only in fulminant disease. Active ulcerative colitis is marked by neutrophils in the mucosa and submucosa and clumps of neutrophils in crypt lumens (crypt abscesses). There is mucus depletion, mucosal edema, and vascular congestion with focal hemorrhage. In

Clinical Manifestations

ULCERATIVE COLITIS. The dominant symptom in ulcerative colitis is diarrhea, which is usually associated with blood in the stool (Table 142–2). Bowel movements are frequent but small in volume as a result of irritability of the inflamed rectum. Urgency and fecal incontinence may limit the patient's ability to function in society. Other symptoms include fever and pain, which may be in either lower quadrant or in the rectum. Systemic features—fever, malaise, and weight loss—are more common if all or most of the colon is involved and may have a greater effect than diarrhea on the patient's ability to function. Some patients, especially elderly persons, complain of constipation rather than diarrhea because rectal spasm prevents the passage of stool. The initial attack of ulcerative colitis may be fulminant with bloody diarrhea, but more commonly the disease begins indolently, with nonbloody diarrhea progressing to bloody diarrhea. Ulcerative colitis can present initially with any extent of anatomic involvement, from disease confined to the rectum to pancolitis. Most commonly, ulcerative colitis follows a chronic intermittent course with long periods of quiescence interspersed with acute attacks lasting weeks to months; however, a significant percentage of patients suffer a chronic continuous course.

In ulcerative colitis of mild to moderate severity, there may be tenderness over the affected area of the colon, and rectal examination may reveal tenderness or blood on the glove. In severe disease, the patient is more likely to be febrile and tachycardic.

Anemia and an elevated leukocyte count and erythrocyte sedimentation rate are useful in confirming severe disease and in following the clinical course of a severe exacerbation. Electrolyte disorders, particularly hypokalemia, are seen with severe diarrhea.

CROHN'S DISEASE. Crohn's disease presents with one of three major patterns: (1) disease in the ileum and cecum (40% of patients), (2) disease confined to the small intestine (30%), and (3) disease confined to the colon (25%). Much less commonly, Crohn's disease involves more proximal parts of the gastrointestinal tract—the mouth, the tongue, the esophagus, the stomach, and the duodenum.

The predominant symptoms are diarrhea, abdominal pain, and weight loss; any of these three symptoms may be most prominent in a given individual. The initial presentation may not be dramatic; patients may complain for months or years with vague abdominal pain and intermittent diarrhea before the diagnosis is considered. Diarrhea occurs in almost all those with Crohn's disease, but the pattern varies with the anatomic location of the disease. In patients with colonic disease, especially with rectal involvement, diarrhea is of small volume and associated with urgency and tenesmus. Inflammation in the rectum causes a loss of distensibility; the entry of even a small amount of stool into a nondistensible rectum causes an immediate and urgent need to defecate. Prolonged inflammation and scarring in the rectum can leave it so rigid and nondistensible that the patient is incontinent. In disease confined to the small intestine, stools are of larger volume and not associated with urgency or tenesmus. Patients with severe involvement of the terminal ileum and those who have had surgical resections of the terminal ileum may have bile salt diarrhea or steatorrhea.

The location and pattern of pain correlate with disease location. In patients with ileal disease, cramping right lower quadrant pain occurs after eating and is related to partial intermittent obstruction of a narrowed intestinal lumen. Abdominal distention, nausea, and vomiting may accompany the pain. Weight loss of some degree, which occurs in most patients with Crohn's disease regardless of anatomic location, is a product of malabsorption or diminished intake because of pain, diarrhea, or anorexia. Fever and chills often accompany disease activity; a low-grade fever may be the patient's first warning sign of a flare. Induction of remission by drugs or surgery is invariably associated with increased energy and a sense of well-being. Crohn's disease, like ulcerative colitis, is a relapsing and remitting disease. About 30% of placebo-treated patients with Crohn's disease of mild to moderate activity go into remission within 4 months. Conversely, of patients in remission and on no therapy, about 30% relapse within 1 year and 50% at 2 years.

Physical findings in Crohn's disease vary with the distribution and severity of the disease. Aphthous ulcers of the lips, gingiva, or buccal mucosa are common. The abdomen may be tender, typically over the area of disease activity. Thickened bowel loops, thickened mesentery, or an abscess may cause a mass, often in the right lower quadrant. The presence of perianal disease is suggested by fistulous openings, induration, redness, or tenderness near the anus.

Laboratory findings are largely nonspecific. Anemia may result from chronic disease, blood loss, or nutritional deficiencies of iron, folate, or vitamin B_{12}. A modestly elevated leukocyte count is indicative of active disease, but a marked elevation suggests the presence of an abscess or other suppurative complication. The erythrocyte sedimentation rate has been used to follow disease activity, and it tends to be higher in colonic disease than in ileal disease. Hypoalbuminemia is an indication of malnutrition. Ileal disease or resection of more than 100 cm of ileum results in a diminished serum vitamin B_{12} level because of malabsorption.

EXTRAINTESTINAL MANIFESTATIONS. Although IBD primarily involves the bowel, it is associated with manifestations in other organ systems. The extraintestinal manifestations (e.g., sclerosing cholangitis or ankylosing spondylitis) may be more problematic than the bowel disease. The extraintestinal manifestations can be divided into two major groups: (1) those in which the clinical activity follows the activity of the bowel disease and (2) those in which the clinical activity is unrelated to the clinical activity of the bowel disease.

The most common extraintestinal manifestation of IBD is arthritis, including colitic arthritis and ankylosing spondylitis. Colitic arthritis, a migratory arthritis that affects knees, hips, ankles, wrists, and elbows, parallels the course of the bowel disease; successful treatment of the intestinal inflammation results in improvement in the arthritis. Ankylosing spondylitis (Chapter 279) presents with morning stiffness, low back pain, and stooped posture; it can be relentlessly progressive and crippling. Patients with ulcerative colitis have a 30-fold increase in the incidence of ankylosing spondylitis compared with the general population. Nonsteroidal anti-inflammatory drugs reduce inflammation and pain but do not halt the progression of the disease. Medical treatment of the IBD and colectomy are not helpful in managing ankylosing spondylitis. Sacroiliitis, which is inflammation of the joint between the sacrum and the ilium, occurs in conjunction with ankylosing spondylitis but is more often seen alone. In ulcerative colitis, 15% of patients have radiographs consistent with sacroiliitis but most patients are asymptomatic.

The hepatic complications of IBD include fatty liver, pericholangitis, chronic active hepatitis, and cirrhosis. The biliary tract complications are sclerosing cholangitis (ulcerative colitis) and gallstones (Crohn's disease). Cholesterol gallstones occur in patients with ileal disease or ileal resections because of malabsorption of bile salts and the resultant decrease in the size of the bile salt pool. Pericholangitis is the most common hepatic complication of IBD; patients with pericholangitis are usually asymptomatic. Elevations of alkaline phosphatase are seen frequently; elevations of bilirubin are less common.

Sclerosing cholangitis (Chapter 157) is a chronic cholestatic liver disease marked by fibrosing inflammation of the intrahepatic and extrahepatic bile ducts. Even though it occurs in only 1 to 4% of patients with ulcerative colitis and with lower frequency in Crohn's disease, the majority of patients with sclerosing cholangitis have IBD. Colectomy and medical therapy of the bowel disease do not ameliorate the course; sclerosing cholangitis is one of the most common indications for liver transplantation (Chapter 157) in adults.

The two common dermal complications of IBD are pyoderma gangrenosum and erythema nodosum (Chapter 476). The lesions of pyoderma gangrenosum almost always develop during a bout of acute colitis and usually resolve with control of the colitis by oral corticosteroids or with intradermal corticosteroids; in rare cases, colectomy is required. The activity of erythema nodosum, which is seen particularly in association with Crohn's disease in children, follows the activity of the bowel disease.

The ocular complications of IBD are uveitis and episcleritis (Chapter 465). Local therapy with corticosteroids and agents that dilate the pupil helps to prevent scarring and blindness.

Diagnostic Tests

RADIOGRAPHY. In both ulcerative colitis and Crohn's disease, radiographic findings may not correlate well with disease activity. The patient's clinical response or endoscopic findings are more useful for this purpose.

In early ulcerative colitis, the barium enema may be normal or there may be limited distensibility of the involved segment, resulting in a narrowed, shortened, and tubular form of the lumen. The haustral markings disappear, and the normally tortuous appearance of the colon is straightened (Fig. 142–1). Air contrast examination reveals a fine granular appearance to the mucosa, with a slightly irregular surface. In more severe disease, the granularity becomes coarser and eventually nodular; ulcers penetrate through the mucosa and can be seen in profile as small collar-button collections of barium extending beyond the colonic lumen.

The earliest form of Crohn's disease detectable by air contrast barium enema is marked by the presence of aphthous ulcers, which appear as small discrete collections of barium surrounded by radiolucent halos of inflammatory infiltrate. These small ulcers are usually multiple, and the intervening mucosa is normal. As Crohn's disease becomes more severe, the aphthous ulcers enlarge, deepen, and connect with one another to form linear ulcers; the intervening mucosa develops a nodular appearance on a radiograph, a process termed *cobblestoning*. Progressive deepening of ulcers can lead to abscess formation or fistulization. Contrast studies are more likely than endoscopic studies to identify fistulas. Transmural inflammation and fibrosis lead to limited distensibility, with decreased luminal diameter and stricture formation. Like fistulas, strictures are more easily appreciated on radiographic studies than by endoscopy. Transmural inflammation and fibrosis result in thickening of the bowel wall, with wide gaps between the barium-filled lumens of loops of inflamed small bowel (Fig. 142–2). Small bowel Crohn's disease can be evaluated by small bowel follow-through or by enteroclysis. Computed tomography and ultrasonography are useful in identifying abscesses and other fluid collections and in assessing the thickness of the bowel wall.

ENDOSCOPY. The earliest endoscopic manifestations of ulcerative colitis are the development of diffuse erythema and loss of the fine vascular pattern seen in the normal rectal mucosa (Fig. 142–3). Erythema is usually accompanied by mucosal edema, which is manifested endoscopically by blunting of the rectal valves, loss of normal vasculature, and development of granular-appearing mucosa. Inflammation is associated with the presence of yellowish exudate on the mucosa. The inflamed mucosa bleeds easily if touched with the endoscope; this easy bleeding is termed *friability*. In more severe disease, the mucosa bleeds spontaneously and small ulcerations appear. An important aspect of the endoscopic findings in ulcerative colitis is their distribution: inflammation begins in the rectum, extends proximally a certain

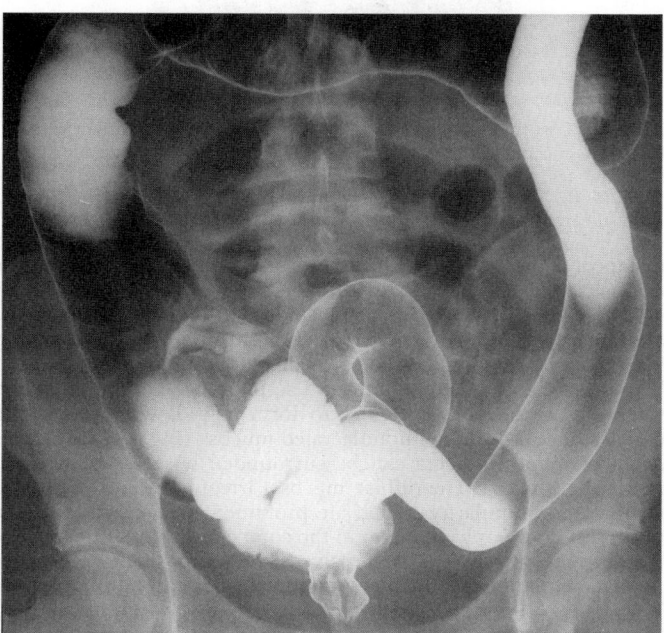

FIGURE 142–1 • Air contrast barium enema demonstrating luminal narrowing and loss of haustral markings in the sigmoid and descending colon in a patient with ulcerative colitis.

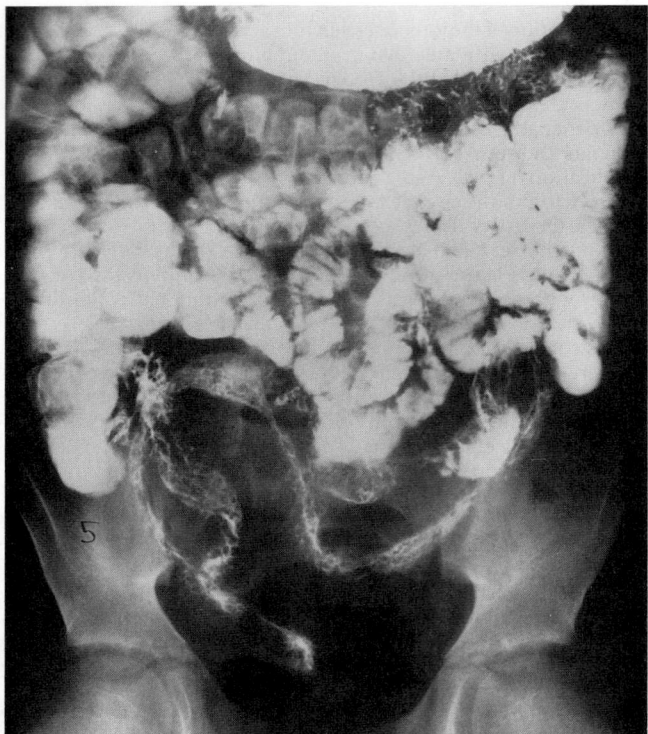

FIGURE 142–2 • Small bowel follow-through in a patient with Crohn's disease of the ileum demonstrating luminal narrowing, mucosal ulceration, and separation of the barium-filled loops due to thickening of the bowel wall.

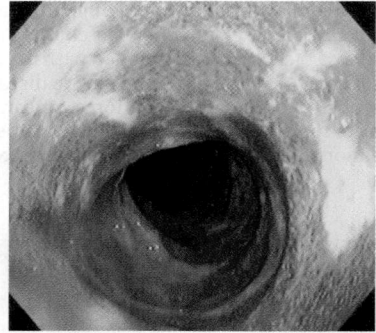

FIGURE 142–3 • Endoscopic view of the colonic mucosa in a patient with idiopathic ulcerative colitis, showing a friable mucosa, extensive ulceration, and exudates.

distance, and then stops; all the mucosa proximal to that point is normal, and all the mucosa distal to it is abnormal.

The earliest endoscopic manifestation of Crohn's disease is the aphthous ulcer, a small discrete ulcer a few millimeters in diameter surrounded by a thin red halo of edematous tissue (Fig. 142–4). Ulcers may be rounded or long and serpiginous. Longitudinal and transverse ulcers may intersect to form a grid with intervening cobblestone-like areas of nonulcerated mucosa (Fig. 142–5). Large, deep, penetrating ulcers can be surrounded by areas of normal-appearing mucosa. The diffuse mucosal irregularities of erythema, edema, and granularity, which are prominent in ulcerative colitis, occur less commonly and later in the course of Crohn's disease. The rectum may or may not be involved in Crohn's disease. Areas of involvement are typically interspersed with normal "skip" areas.

Differential Diagnosis

For many therapeutic decisions, it is not particularly important to know whether the patient has ulcerative colitis or Crohn's disease.

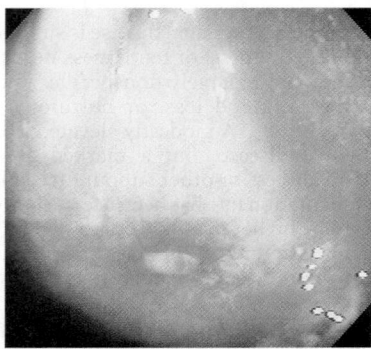

FIGURE 142–4 • A single aphthous ulcer, the earliest endoscopic finding in Crohn's disease.

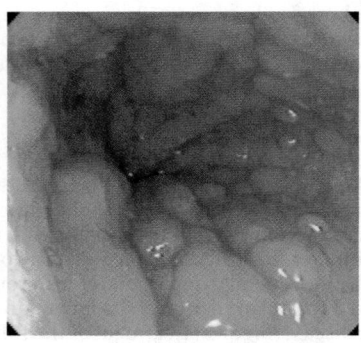

FIGURE 142–5 • Crohn's disease in the colon. Multiple edematous inflammatory polyps give a "cobblestone" appearance to the mucosa. Similar changes may be seen in ulcerative colitis. (From Forbes CD, Jackson WD: Color Atlas and Text of Clinical Medicine, 3rd ed. London, Mosby, 2003, with permission.)

However, when surgery is contemplated, the distinction is important. For example, a colectomy and ileoanal anastomosis could be recommended as a curative procedure if the physician were confident the patient had ulcerative colitis rather than Crohn's colitis.

The anatomic distribution of the inflammatory response may be helpful in distinguishing ulcerative colitis from Crohn's disease. In ulcerative colitis, inflammation is seen in the rectum and extends proximally for some distance; in extensive disease, inflammation extends to the cecum. Although ulcerative colitis does not involve the small intestine, there may be a few centimeters of inflamed mucosa without ulceration in the terminal ileum. If the rectum is spared or if there are areas of uninflamed mucosa (skip areas) between areas of inflamed mucosa, then Crohn's colitis is more likely. Ulcerative colitis is not only continuous along the longitudinal axis of the colon, but the degree of inflammation is also consistent and symmetric circumferentially at any level. In contrast, in Crohn's colitis, deep linear ulcers may be separated by areas of normal mucosa. A major distinguishing mark in favor of Crohn's disease is the presence of transmural inflammatory changes; in ulcerative colitis, inflammation is confined to the mucosa and submucosa. Extensive perianal involvement with fistulas and abscesses point to Crohn's disease. The presence of noncaseating granulomas suggests Crohn's disease, but even in Crohn's disease, most patients have no granulomas on biopsy. Despite all these differences, there is a small but significant number of patients with IBD who cannot be assigned with confidence to one disease category or the other; these patients are considered to have indeterminate colitis.

Infections with *Shigella, Amoeba, Giardia, Escherichia coli* O157:H7, and *Campylobacter* organisms can present with bloody diarrhea, cramps, and an endoscopic picture identical to ulcerative colitis (Chapter 323). An important distinction between these infectious diseases (except amebiasis) and IBD is that the diarrhea in the infectious diseases tends to be limited to a period of days to a few weeks, whereas the diarrhea of IBD is typically of longer duration. Stool cultures for bacterial pathogens and serologic tests for amebiasis help distinguish infectious diarrhea from IBD. In patients who present with

Table 142–3 • PREPARATIONS OF 5-AMINOSALICYLIC ACID

PREPARATION	DELIVERY	DISTRIBUTION	DOSE*
TOPICAL			
Mesalamine suppository	Direct	Rectum	500 mg once or twice a day
Mesalamine enema	Direct	Left colon	4 g in 60 mL at bedtime
ORAL			
Sulfasalazine	Bacterial azo reductase	Colon	4–6 g in divided doses
Dipentum	Bacterial azo reductase	Colon	1.5–3.0 g in divided doses
Asacol	Release at pH > 7	Distal ileum, colon	2.4–4.8 g in divided doses
Pentasa	Time-release ethyl cellulose microgranules	Ileum, colon	3–4 g in divided doses

*Doses given are for active disease; similar doses can be given for maintenance therapy, although some practitioners use lower doses for maintenance.

prolonged diarrhea, other protozoal diseases, such as giardiasis, must be considered. Pseudomembranous colitis presents as profuse watery diarrhea and may last from a few days to months; the presence of small membranous plaques adherent to the mucosa on sigmoidoscopy is pathognomonic. As part of the initial evaluation of patients with acute exacerbation of IBD, it is appropriate to check the stool for *Clostridium difficile* toxin, especially if there has been recent antibiotic exposure.

Mild ulcerative colitis, in which rectal bleeding is the primary manifestation, can be confused with hemorrhoids or anal fissures (Chapter 143). The presence of urgency or diarrhea is more consistent with ulcerative colitis. Sigmoidoscopy should easily differentiate ulcerative colitis from these perianal problems.

Collagenous colitis is a chronic inflammatory disease marked pathologically by the presence of a thick collagen deposition in the subepithelial layer of the colonic mucosa (Chapter 141). The typical clinical presentation is chronic watery diarrhea in a middle-aged woman. Endoscopically, the mucosa appears mildly inflamed or, more commonly, absolutely normal; biopsy with histology provides the diagnosis. Ischemic colitis is part of the differential diagnosis of the initial bout of IBD and should be considered in elderly persons or others at particular risk for ischemic disease (Chapter 144). Diverticulitis, which may be difficult to separate from acute Crohn's colitis, tends to be a more acute problem without a chronic inflammatory state (Chapter 143). Intestinal lymphoma can mimic the symptoms of Crohn's disease; in lymphoma, small bowel radiographs may show diffuse involvement with masses in the bowel wall. If Crohn's disease has a long, indolent course with relatively mild symptoms, it may be difficult to differentiate from IBS, and some patients may have both (Chapter 135).

 Treatment

DRUGS USED IN INFLAMMATORY BOWEL DISEASE

GENERAL SUPPORTIVE THERAPY. Antidiarrheal agents, usually loperamide or diphenoxylate, are useful in patients with mild IBD to reduce the number of bowel movements and to relieve rectal urgency. Anticholinergics (tincture of belladonna, clidinium, propantheline bromide, and dicyclomine hydrochloride) may reduce cramps, pain, and rectal urgency. An especially effective combination of an antidiarrheal and an antispasmodic is powdered opium (25 mg) and belladonna (15 mg). Antidiarrheal agents and antispasmodics are contraindicated in severe colitis because of the risk of precipitating toxic megacolon. The chronic use of narcotics for pain should not be part of the management of IBD. Sometimes antidepressants can be helpful. Nonsteroidal anti-inflammatory drugs can exacerbate the clinical activity of IBD and should be used cautiously.

Nutritional management plays only a small role in ulcerative colitis. Patients should avoid specific foods (typically high-fiber foods) that worsen their symptoms. Nutritional management plays a much larger role in Crohn's disease, in which many patients have diminished caloric intake and vitamin B_{12}, vitamin D, calcium, magnesium, zinc, and iron may be malabsorbed. Both total parenteral nutrition and elemental enteral diets can decrease intestinal inflammation by reducing the antigen load in the lumen.

AMINOSALICYLATES. Sulfasalazine is composed of 5-aminosalicylic acid (5-ASA) joined by an azo bond to sulfapyridine (Table 142–3). Colonic bacteria split the azo bond to release 5-ASA, the active ingredient, into the colonic lumen. 5-ASA is not absorbed from the colon; it appears to have a local therapeutic effect by acting intraluminally. Sulfasalazine has been used successfully as a single agent in mild to moderate acute attacks of ulcerative colitis and Crohn's colitis; it is the drug of choice in mild cases. Success rates with sulfasalazine are dose related, with better success rates at doses of 4 g/day or more. Patients who respond to sulfasalazine usually do so in 2 to 3 weeks, although some take 4 weeks or longer to respond. Dose-related toxic effects (headache, nausea, vomiting, and abdominal discomfort) are related to serum sulfapyridine levels, but hypersensitivity reactions (rash, fever, aplastic anemia, pancreatitis, lupus-like rash, nephrotoxicity, hepatitis, agranulocytosis, and autoimmune hemolysis) are not. Sulfasalazine commonly causes changes in sperm morphology and number, leading to reversible infertility. Sulfasalazine inhibits folic acid absorption and is a competitive inhibitor of folate conjugase in the jejunal brush border; folic acid supplementation of 1 to 2 mg/day is commonly recommended.

If 5-ASA alone is administered orally, it is rapidly absorbed, and significant luminal concentrations are not achieved. 5-ASA is available in the United States as an enema and as a suppository. Several oral formulations provide 5-ASA to the colon by binding two 5-ASAs through an azo linkage, by coating 5-ASA in granules that dissolve at pH 7 or above in the colon and terminal ileum, or by encapsulating 5-ASA in a semipermeable membrane that releases 65% of its 5-ASA in the colon and 35% in the small intestine.

CORTICOSTEROIDS. Oral corticosteroids are effective in mild to moderate ulcerative colitis and Crohn's disease. Parenteral therapy is reserved for moderate to severe disease. The typical initial dose of prednisone is 40 mg/day in moderate to severe disease. The patient is left on high doses of corticosteroids until symptoms begin to diminish, after which the dose is gradually reduced. If an inadequate initial dose of prednisone is used because of the fear of side effects, the likelihood of a positive response diminishes. In some patients, disease activity flares when the dose of prednisone is reduced to less than a certain level (steroid dependence). For most patients, administration of oral prednisone in a single morning dose is as effective as divided doses. Corticosteroids should not be used in patients with undrained abscesses or when symptoms are due to a stricture or fibrotic process. Maintenance therapy with corticosteroids is ineffective to prevent recurrences in ulcerative colitis or Crohn's disease in remission. The many side effects of corticosteroids (Chapter 31) constitute the major factor limiting their use in IBD.

IMMUNOMODULATORS. Immunomodulator drugs act by blocking lymphocyte proliferation, activation, or effector mechanisms. There is extensive experience with azathioprine and its metabolite 6-mercaptopurine (6-MP) to treat IBD and lesser experience with cyclosporine and methotrexate. Azathioprine and 6-MP are effective in treating active Crohn's disease and in maintaining remission; their roles in ulcerative colitis are less clear. Typical initial doses are 1 to 1.5 mg/kg for 6-MP and 2.0 to 2.5 mg/kg for azathioprine. The delay between the initiation of therapy and the clinical response is typically 3 to 4 months. These drugs are used in patients who have

Continued

active disease that is unresponsive to corticosteroids (refractory patients) and in corticosteroid-dependent patients. In these patients, 6-MP or azathioprine is added to corticosteroid therapy; after 3 or 4 months, when the 6-MP and azathioprine are likely to have taken effect, the dose of corticosteroids is gradually tapered. Most clinicians maintain patients on 6-MP or azathioprine for several years if remission is induced by these drugs. Some patients are maintained on these drugs indefinitely. The major limiting factor in the use of 6-MP and azathioprine is their toxicity; both commonly cause leukopenia, may cause pancreatitis, and may increase the risk of lymphoma. Methotrexate, given either orally or parenterally, is effective in active Crohn's disease. Cyclosporine, given intravenously, is effective in reducing inflammation in patients with severe ulcerative colitis who are facing colectomy.

ANTIBIOTICS. Except in cases of overt sepsis, there is little role for antibiotics in the management of ulcerative colitis. Antibiotics do not affect the remission rate; moreover, the risk of inducing antibiotic-associated pseudomembranous colitis must be considered. Antibiotics play a larger role in Crohn's disease; they are used in the management of the suppurative complications, especially abscess formation and perianal disease, although surgical drainage is the primary therapy for abscesses. Metronidazole (10 to 15 mg/kg/day) is effective in perianal Crohn's disease and is as effective as sulfasalazine in Crohn's colitis. The major side effect of metronidazole is peripheral neuropathy, which is dose dependent and usually resolves when the drug is discontinued. Ciprofloxacin at 500 mg twice a day for a few weeks is also effective in some patients.

MEDICAL MANAGEMENT OF ULCERATIVE COLITIS (Fig. 142–6)

PROCTITIS. For active ulcerative proctitis, a relatively effective and rapidly acting approach is the nightly administration of 5-ASA retention enemas or suppositories, often supplemented with an oral aminosalicylate. Corticosteroid enemas can also be used. Either 5-ASA suppositories or corticosteroid foam is appropriate for disease of up to 20 cm of distal colon; 5-ASA or corticosteroid retention enemas can be used for active disease, involving up to 60 cm of distal colon. Another approach to proctitis or distal colitis is an oral aminosalicylate, although a response may not be evident for 3 to 4 weeks.

EXTENSIVE COLITIS. For patients with colitis of mild to moderate activity and extension proximal to the sigmoid colon, the initial drug of choice is an oral aminosalicylate; efficacy increases with increasing doses. For patients with more active disease (>5 to 6 bowel movements per day), patients in whom a more rapid response is desired, or patients who have not responded to 3 to 4 weeks of aminosalicylates, the treatment of choice is oral prednisone. Patients with severe diarrhea, systemic symptoms, or significant amounts of blood in the stool should be started on 40 mg/day; most patients respond to oral corticosteroids within a few days. After the symptoms are controlled, prednisone can be gradually tapered by 5 to 10 mg every 1 to 2 weeks. Patients who respond to oral prednisone and can be fully withdrawn from it should be maintained on an aminosalicylate.

For patients who do not respond to corticosteroids (steroid refractory) or who do respond but whose disease flares whenever the corticosteroids are withdrawn (steroid dependent), options include indefinite corticosteroid therapy, an immunomodulator (azathioprine or 6-MP), or colectomy. Continuation of high-dose corticosteroid therapy for too long a time is the most common serious error in the management of ulcerative colitis. If the patient is on a substantial dose (>15 mg/day of prednisone) for more than 6 months, a trial of an immunomodulator or colectomy should be given serious consideration.

The most common reason for hospitalization is intractable diarrhea, although blood loss is also a common problem. Patients with severe active ulcerative colitis should be evaluated for toxic megacolon. Anticholinergics and antidiarrheal agents are contraindicated in severe ulcerative colitis because of the risk of precipitating toxic megacolon. The mainstays of therapy for severe ulcerative colitis are bedrest, rehydration with intravenous fluids, and intravenous corticosteroids (hydrocortisone 300 mg/day; prednisolone, 60 to 80 mg/day, or methylprednisolone, 48 to 60 mg/day). Total parenteral nutrition may be necessary if there is malnutrition. Patients with peritoneal signs or signs of systemic infection should be treated with parenteral antibiotics. Patients who do not improve in 7 to 10 days should be considered for either colectomy or a trial of intravenous cyclosporine.

MAINTENANCE THERAPY. Aminosalicylates reduce the incidence of recurrences in patients with ulcerative colitis; almost all patients should receive maintenance therapy. The efficacy of sulfasalazine at 3 to 4 g/day is greater than the efficacy of 2 g/day even though 2 g/day is the usual recommended maintenance dose. Corticosteroids are not effective as maintenance therapy and should not be used. Most of the experience with 6-MP as maintenance therapy in ulcerative colitis is in patients whose acute disease has been brought under control with 6-MP; withdrawal of 6-MP from these patients results in a high incidence of exacerbation.

MEDICAL MANAGEMENT OF CROHN'S DISEASE (Fig. 142–7)

GENERAL APPROACH. It is difficult to develop generally applicable guidelines for the management of Crohn's disease because of the great variety of anatomic locations, clinical presentations, and gastrointestinal complications such as fistulas, abscesses, strictures, and perforations. Response to therapy is monitored by empirical clinical assessment directed at the problem that is most troublesome for the patient.

A common problem in the management of Crohn's disease is a marked discrepancy between the severity of the patient's symptoms and the objective signs of disease activity. Patients with severe pain and diarrhea may have minimal findings on endoscopy or radiographic studies. Patients who have undergone ileal resections may have significant diarrhea on the basis of their surgery alone.

ACTIVE DISEASE. For colonic or ileocolic Crohn's disease with mild to moderate activity, an aminosalicylate is a reasonable first therapy. Pentasa, an oral 5-ASA preparation with greater availability of 5-ASA in the ileum than sulfasalazine or Asacol, may be a better choice for patients with ileitis or ileocolitis. Metronidazole (10-15 mg/kg/day) and/or ciprofloxacin (500 mg twice daily) are alternatives to prednisone. Prednisone is the drug of choice for patients who have failed to respond to aminosalicylates or antibiotics, for patients with ileal disease, and for patients with highly active colonic

Condition	Treatment				
Proctitis	5-ASA enemas or 5-ASA suppositories or oral 5-ASA drugs or corticosteroid enemas	*Continued activity* →	Prednisone or immunomodulators	*Continued activity* →	Colectomy
Mild to moderate pancolitis	Oral 5-ASA drugs	*Continued activity* →	Prednisone	*Continued activity or Steroid dependence* →	Immunomodulators or colectomy
Severe or fulminant pancolitis	Parenteral steroids	*Continued activity* →	Cyclosporine or colectomy		
Disease in remission	Maintenance with oral 5-ASA drugs				

FIGURE 142–6 • Treatment algorithm for ulcerative colitis. ASA = aminosalicylic acid.

Condition	Treatment
Colitis or ileocolitis	Oral 5-ASA drug or metronidazole and/or ciprofloxacin —*Continued activity*→ Prednisone —*Continued activity or Steroid dependence*→ Immunomodulator —*Continued activity*→ Surgery or infliximab
Ileitis	Prednisone —*Continued activity*→ Immunomodulator —*Continued activity*→ Surgery or infliximab
Fistula	TPN or immunomodulator or infliximab —*Failure to close*→ Surgery
Abscess	Antibiotics, drainage, and resection
Obstruction due to inflammation	IV fluids, nasogastric suction, parenteral steroids —*Failure to respond*→ Surgery
Obstruction due to scarring	IV fluids, nasogastric suction —*Failure to respond*→ Surgery
Perianal disease	Antibiotics and surgical drainage
Disease in remission	Maintenance with oral 5-ASA drugs or immunomodulators

FIGURE 142–7 • Treatment algorithm for Crohn's disease. ASA = aminosalicylic acid; IV = introvenous; TPN = total parenteral nutrition.

or ileocolic disease. The response to prednisone is usually more rapid than that to aminosalicylates. Before corticosteroids are given to a Crohn's disease patient with abdominal pain, fever, and a high leukocyte count, an abdominal computed tomographic scan should be obtained to exclude an abscess.

For patients who have been brought into clinical remission on corticosteroids, the rate at which the dose is tapered is arbitrary and not defined by controlled trials. Usually the prednisone dose can be tapered from 40 mg/day to 20 mg/day relatively rapidly (5 to 10 mg/L to 2 weeks) without inducing a flare of disease activity. If the patient has not been on a 5-ASA preparation, one should be added to increase the likelihood of a successful corticosteroid withdrawal. Once the dose of prednisone has reached 20 mg/day, the taper is slowed to 5 mg every 10 to 14 days; if symptoms flare, the dose of prednisone is increased. At this point, the best approach for most patients is a trial of an immunomodulator, either 6-MP or azathioprine; corticosteroid therapy is continued for 3 to 4 months and then tapered gradually. Approximately 60% of corticosteroid-dependent patients are able to withdraw from corticosteroids using this approach; the alternative is surgery if there is a stricture or a focal area of involvement.

Infliximab, a mouse-human chimeric monoclonal IgG1 antibody directed against TNF, is effective in closing fistulas and in treating active Crohn's disease.[1] Infliximab is largely reserved for patients who have failed therapy with azathioprine or 6-MP. Future use of infliximab is likely to include combination therapy with immunomodulators, but there are currently no published studies on combination therapy. A newer option is natalizumab, an integrin-specific human monoclonal antibody, which has been effective in a randomized trial of patients with active Crohn's disease.[2]

The approach to severe Crohn's disease is similar to the approach to severe ulcerative colitis. The patient is hospitalized, given nothing by mouth, rehydrated with intravenous fluids, and given parenteral corticosteroids. Patients who respond to parenteral corticosteroids are switched to high-dose oral corticosteroids (prednisone 40 mg/day), and the dose of prednisone is gradually reduced. Patients with severe Crohn's disease who do not respond to parenteral corticosteroids within a week should be considered for surgery. A course of total parenteral nutrition may be useful as adjunctive therapy.

MAINTENANCE THERAPY. Maintenance therapy with aminosalicylates is recommended for those brought into remission on corticosteroids or with surgery; however, the efficacy of aminosalicylates as maintenance therapy is less well established in Crohn's disease than in ulcerative colitis. Maintenance with 6-MP or azathioprine is recommended for patients brought into remission on those drugs or who were corticosteroid dependent and then converted to those drugs. There is no role for corticosteroids as maintenance therapy.

SURGERY

Twenty per cent to 25% of patients with extensive ulcerative colitis eventually undergo colectomy, usually because their disease has not responded adequately to medical therapy. In ulcerative colitis, colectomy is a curative procedure. Emergency colectomy may be required in toxic megacolon or in a severe fulminant attack without toxic megacolon. The standard operation for ulcerative colitis is a proctocolectomy and Brooke's ileostomy. The most popular alternative operation is the proctocolectomy and ileoanal anastomosis; in this procedure, a pouch is constructed from the terminal 30 cm of ileum, and the distal end of the pouch is pulled through the anal canal. Ileoanal anastomosis is sometimes complicated by inflammation in the ileal pouch, which can be treated with probiotics.[3] The decision for or against colectomy is influenced by the patient's age, social circumstances, and duration of disease. The risk of developing malignancy enters into the equation when considering colectomy in those with long-standing ulcerative colitis; if the other indications are equivocal, the risk of malignancy may push the balance in favor of colectomy.

Within 10 years of diagnosis, approximately 60% of patients with Crohn's disease undergo surgery for their disease. Because surgical resection is not curative in Crohn's disease and recurrences are likely, the approach is more conservative in terms of the amount of tissue removed. Failure of medical management is a common cause for resection in Crohn's disease, as it is in ulcerative colitis, but complications (e.g., obstruction, fistula, abscess) are often indications for resection in Crohn's disease. Surgery is also performed to allow patients to stop taking medications (usually corticosteroids). For small bowel Crohn's disease, the most common surgical procedure is segmental resection for obstruction or fistula. The incidence of recurrence severe enough to need repeat surgery after ileal or ileocolic resection is about 50% after 10 years and 75% after 15 years. Endoscopic and histologic surgical approaches to Crohn's colitis include segmental resection, subtotal colectomy with ileoproctostomy, and total colectomy with ileostomy. For patients with extensive colonic disease including the rectum, the procedure of choice is total proctocolectomy with a Brooke's ileostomy. Total colectomy with ileoanal anastomosis is not appropriate in Crohn's colitis because recurrence of Crohn's disease in the ileal segment forming the new pouch would require a repeat operation and loss of a long segment of ileum.

Complications

The most severe complication of ulcerative colitis is toxic megacolon, that is, dilatation of the colon to a diameter of greater than 6 cm associated with a worsening of the patient's clinical condition and the development of fever, tachycardia, and leukocytosis. Physical examination may reveal postural hypotension, tenderness over the distribution of the colon, and absent or hypoactive bowel sounds. Antispasmodics and antidiarrheal agents are likely to initiate or exacerbate toxic megacolon. Medical therapy is designed to reduce the likelihood of perforation and to return the colon to normal motor activity as rapidly as possible. The patient is given nothing by mouth, and nasogastric suction is begun. Intravenous fluids should be administered to replete water and electrolytes, broad-spectrum antibiotics are given in anticipation of peritonitis resulting from perforation, and parenteral corticosteroids are given at a dose equivalent to more than 40 mg of prednisone per day. Signs of improvement include a decrease in abdominal girth and the return of bowel sounds. Deterioration is marked by the development of rebound tenderness, increasing abdominal girth, and cardiovascular collapse. If the patient does not begin to show signs of clinical improvement during the first 24 to 48 hours of medical therapy, the risk of perforation increases markedly, and surgical intervention is indicated.

Abscesses and fistulas, which are common complications in Crohn's disease, are products of the extension of a mucosal fissure or ulcer through the intestinal wall and into extraintestinal tissue. Leakage of intestinal contents through a fissure into the peritoneal cavity results in an abscess. Extension of the inflammatory process through the wall of adjacent viscera or through the abdominal wall to the exterior results in a fistula. Abscesses occur in 15 to 20% of patients with Crohn's disease and are especially common in the terminal ileum. The typical clinical presentation of intra-abdominal abscess is fever, abdominal pain, tenderness, and leukocytosis. Abdominal abscess is most often diagnosed by computed tomography. Broad-spectrum antibiotic therapy, including anaerobic coverage, is indicated. Percutaneous drainage of abscesses in patients with Crohn's disease may improve the clinical picture but does not provide adequate therapy because of persistent communication between the abscess cavity and the intestinal lumen. Resection of the portion of involved intestine containing the communication is usually required for definitive therapy. The prevalence of fistulas is 20 to 40% in Crohn's disease. Most fistulas are enteroenteric or enterocutaneous, with smaller numbers that are enterovesical or enterovaginal. Total parenteral nutrition or immunomodulator therapy may induce fistula closure; however, the fistulas often recur after the total parenteral nutrition or immunomodulator is stopped. Surgical therapy includes resection of the segment involved with active disease.

Obstruction is a common complication of Crohn's disease, particularly in the small intestine, and is a leading indication for surgery. Small bowel obstruction in Crohn's disease may be caused by mucosal thickening from acute inflammation, by muscular hyperplasia and scarring as a result of previous inflammation, or by adhesions. Obstruction may also occur because of impaction of a bolus of fibrous food in a stable, long-standing stricture. Obstruction presents with cramping abdominal pain and diarrhea that worsen after meals and resolve with fasting. Strictures may be evaluated by oral contrast studies, barium enema, or colonoscopy, depending on anatomic location. Corticosteroids are useful if acute inflammation is an important component of the obstructive process, but not if the obstruction is due to fibrosis. A common error in the management of Crohn's disease is treatment with long courses of corticosteroids in patients who have obstructive symptoms from fixed anatomic lesions. If the obstruction does not resolve with nasogastric suction and corticosteroids, surgery is necessary.

Perianal disease is an especially difficult complication of Crohn's disease. A complex of problems is caused by ulcers in the anal canal and the resulting fistulas. The fistulous openings are most commonly in the perianal skin but can be in the groin, the vulva, or the scrotum. Fistulas present as drainage of serous or mucous material. If the fistula does not drain freely, there is local accumulation of pus (perianal abscess) with redness, pain, and induration. The pain of perianal abscess is exacerbated by defecation, sitting, or walking. The typical physical presentation of abscess is redness with tenderness on digital examination. Adequate evaluation of perianal disease usually requires proctoscopic examination under anesthesia. Computed tomography is useful in defining the presence and extent of perianal abscesses. The goals of therapy in perianal disease are relief of local symptoms and preservation of the sphincter. Limited disease can be approached with sitz baths and metronidazole, but in most cases adequate external drainage is also required. Persistent severe perianal Crohn's disease can result in destruction of the anal sphincter and fecal incontinence.

Colon Cancer, Dysplasia, and Colonoscopic Surveillance

Patients with extensive ulcerative colitis have a markedly increased risk for colon cancer compared with the general population beginning 8 to 10 years after diagnosis and increasing with time. The risk of malignancy is also a function of the anatomic extent of the disease; the risk is much greater with pancolitis than with left-sided disease. Patients with long-standing ulcerative colitis are at risk for developing cancer even if their symptoms have been relatively mild; that is, colon cancer is seen in patients whose disease has been quiescent for 10 to 15 years. In ulcerative colitis, colon cancers are frequently submucosal and may be missed at colonoscopy. Colon cancer in ulcerative colitis is associated with dysplastic changes in the mucosa at other sites in the colon. Dysplasia cannot be identified by visual inspection; microscopic examination of biopsy specimens is required. Some practitioners perform surveillance colonoscopies with random biopsies in patients with long-standing ulcerative colitis beginning 8 to 10 years after the onset of disease and repeated every 1 to 2 years. If the specimens show dysplasia, the patient is sent for colectomy. Although it is clear that dysplasia is associated with colon cancer in ulcerative colitis, the utility of surveillance colonoscopy has not been firmly established. The risk of colon cancer in Crohn's colitis is less than in ulcerative colitis but greater than in the general population. The utility of surveillance in Crohn's colitis is unproven.

Pregnancy and Inflammatory Bowel Disease

Fertility in women with IBD is normal or only minimally impaired, and the incidences of prematurity, stillbirth, and developmental defects in IBD are similar to those of the general population. The incidence of fetal complications may be somewhat higher in cases in which the mother's disease is clinically active, regardless of drug therapy. Previous proctocolectomy or the presence of an ileostomy is not an impediment to the successful completion of a pregnancy. Many women have taken sulfasalazine throughout the course of pregnancy, and there is no evidence for its causing harm to the fetus. Pregnant women have an increased requirement for folic acid, and sulfasalazine interferes with folate absorption. Therefore, women taking sulfasalazine who are pregnant or considering pregnancy should receive folate supplementation (1 mg twice daily) to ensure that the fetus receives amounts adequate for normal development. The use of corticosteroids by pregnant women with IBD is not associated with an increased rate of fetal complications. In general, it appears that the risks to the pregnancy of treatment with sulfasalazine or corticosteroids are less than the risks of allowing disease activity to go untreated. Most of the data on azathioprine and 6-MP in pregnancy come from the transplant literature and involve higher doses than are commonly used in IBD. Reported fetal effects in the transplant population include congenital malformations, immunosuppression, prematurity, and growth retardation; risks in the IBD population are not known. The effects of pregnancy on IBD depend on disease activity. If the patient's disease is inactive at the time of conception, it is likely that it will remain inactive during the course of the pregnancy. If the disease is active at the time of conception, the course is harder to predict. Ulcerative colitis that is active at the time of conception tends to worsen. In two thirds of Crohn's disease cases that are active at conception, the degree of activity remains the same; among the other third, some improve clinically and others deteriorate.

1. Hanauer SB, Feagan BG, Lichtenstein GR, et al: Maintenance infliximab for Crohn's disease: The ACCENT 1 randomized trial. Lancet 2002;359:1541–1549.
2. Ghosh S, Goldin E, Gordon FH, et al: Natalizumab Pan-European Study Group: Natalizumab for active Crohn's disease. N Engl J Med 2003;348:24–32.
3. Gionchetti P, Rizzello F, Venturi A, et al: Oral bacteriotherapy as maintenance treatment in patients with chronic pouchitis: A double-blind placebo controlled trial. Gastroenterology 2000;119:305–309.

SUGGESTED READINGS
Farrell RJ, Peppercorn MA: Ulcerative colitis. Lancet 2002;359:331–340. *Overview with emphasis on emerging therapies.*
Podolsky DK: Inflammatory bowel disease. N Engl J Med 2002;347:417–429. *A comprehensive review.*
Shanahan F: Crohn's disease. Lancet 2002;359:62–69. *Overview of pathogenesis, diagnosis, and therapy.*

143 APPENDICITIS, DIVERTICULITIS, AND MISCELLANEOUS INTESTINAL INFLAMMATORY CONDITIONS

C. Mel Wilcox

ACUTE APPENDICITIS

Etiology and Pathogenesis

Appendicitis is an acute inflammatory disorder of the vermiform appendix. It is uncommon at the extremes of age, with the highest incidence in the second and third decades. Although not demonstrable in all cases, obstruction of the appendiceal lumen by a fecalith is the usual inciting event. Less common causes include neoplasms (carcinoid tumors, adenocarcinoma, Kaposi's sarcoma) and infections (*Enterobius vermicularis,* cytomegalovirus). With appendiceal obstruction, normally secreted mucus becomes impacted and causes appendiceal distention, thrombosis, and, subsequently, bacterial invasion of the wall; the end result is gangrene and perforation.

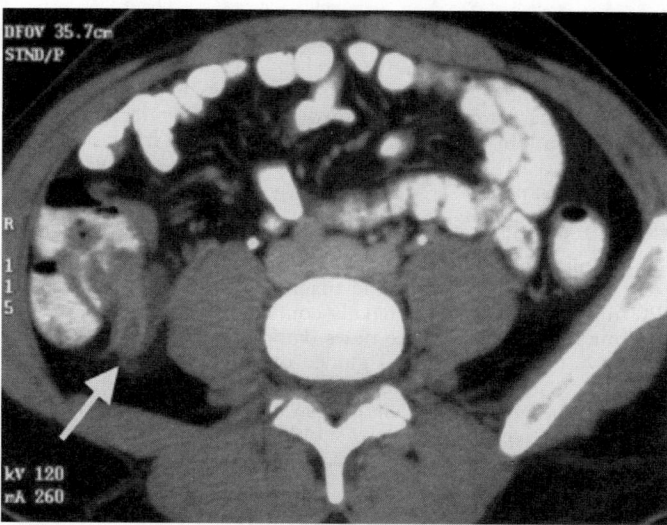

FIGURE 143–1 • Computed tomographic scan showing acute appendicitis. The appendix is edematous and there is surrounding stranding of the mesenteric fat (arrow).

Clinical Manifestations

The clinical manifestations follow a stereotypic course paralleling these pathologic events. Almost invariably, abdominal pain is the first manifestation. It is often poorly localized to the periumbilical area or epigastrium and may be discounted as indigestion. Appendiceal distention results in this poorly localized, visceral type of periumbilical discomfort. The pain is at first colicky, then steady, and increases in severity as the inflammatory process progresses. When the parietal peritoneum becomes inflamed, usually hours after the initial onset of symptoms, the pain becomes localized. Right iliac pain is the typical location of appendicitis; however, pelvic pain (pelvic appendix) or right upper quadrant pain may result, depending on the location of the appendix. Anorexia is frequent, and the urge to eat argues against the diagnosis of appendicitis. Vomiting is not a prominent symptom.

Diagnosis

PHYSICAL EXAMINATION. Physical findings depend on the stage of the inflammatory process, location of the appendix, and, in some cases, the age of the patient. Acute abdominal conditions have notoriously atypical manifestations in elderly persons and in patients receiving corticosteroid therapy. The most consistent physical finding is tenderness in the right iliac region at McBurney's point (one fingerbreadth from the anterosuperior iliac spine toward the umbilicus). The area of tenderness, however, corresponds to the location of the inflamed appendix. With a retrocecal appendix, tenderness may be mild. Rectal examination may disclose tenderness anteriorly with a pelvic appendix or a bulge in the pelvic wall from an abscess. An inflamed parietal peritoneum results in localized rebound tenderness and rigidity. Only with generalized peritonitis are diffuse rebound tenderness and peritoneal signs elicited. Rarely, a mass is palpable in the right lower quadrant. Rotating a flexed right hip when supine (obturator sign) or raising a straightened leg against resistance (psoas sign) may elicit pain. Bowel sounds can be heard unless peritonitis and ileus are present. Fever occurs only in the later stages of inflammation; fever at the onset of abdominal pain should suggest another diagnosis.

LABORATORY AND IMAGING STUDIES. Leukocytosis with increased polymorphonuclear leukocytes is a consistent finding only in the later stages of appendicitis. Urinalysis is usually normal. Standard abdominal radiography is frequently normal, although it may demonstrate localized loops of bowel, obliteration of the psoas shadow, or a soft tissue mass; however, the latter findings represent abscess formation. Fewer than 10% of patients have a calcified fecalith seen in the region of the appendix by abdominal imaging. Appendiceal computed

tomography (CT) examination can be highly accurate in diagnosing appendicitis∎ and should usually be performed prior to laparotomy (Fig. 143–1). The overall accuracy of CT is 98%, and it has a 90% positive predictive value for diagnosing necrotizing appendicitis.

DIFFERENTIAL DIAGNOSIS OF APPENDICITIS AND THE ACUTE ABDOMEN. Although the differential diagnosis of acute appendicitis and acute abdomen is broad, a systematic history and physical examination, combined with selected laboratory tests and abdominal imaging studies, in most cases lead to a diagnosis. For an acutely ill patient, early surgical consultation is mandatory. Despite improvements in abdominal imaging with ultrasonography and CT, surgical exploration reveals a normal appendix in approximately 15% of laparotomies for presumed acute appendicitis; this rate is entirely acceptable given the increase in morbidity and mortality with appendiceal rupture.

A variety of disorders cause a subacute to acute right lower quadrant pain syndrome mimicking acute appendicitis (Table 143–1). In young children, bacterial infections, including *Campylobacter* (Chapter 327) or *Yersinia* (Chapter 331), may mimic appendicitis or may result in a mesenteric adenitis. Terminal ileitis can involve the right colon. Crohn's ileitis or ileocolitis frequently masquerades as acute appendicitis (Chapter 142). Meckel's or cecal diverticulitis may be impossible to distinguish from acute appendicitis. Special consideration should be given to female patients. Pelvic inflammatory disease (Chapters 345 and 346) is infrequently unilateral but may mimic appendicitis. Ectopic pregnancy, ruptured endometrioma (Chapter 250), or torsion of an ovarian cyst (Chapters 205 and 249) may cause unilateral pain. A ruptured graafian follicle occurs in midcycle without fever and leukocytosis (Chapter 250). Appendicitis may be difficult to diagnose during pregnancy because the appendix moves toward the right upper quadrant.

Table 143–1 • CAUSES OF RIGHT LOWER QUADRANT PAIN SYNDROMES

INFLAMMATORY DISORDERS	NEOPLASMS	OTHER
Appendicitis	Carcinoid	Gynecologic
Crohn's ileitis/colitis	Lymphoma	disorders
Cecal diverticulitis	Cecal adenocarcinoma	
Meckel's diverticulitis	(perforated)	
Yersinia ileocolitis		
Amebic colitis		
Tuberculous colitis		

Gastrointestinal Diseases

Rx Treatment

Surgical therapy is curative, and laparoscopic surgery is as safe and effective as open laparotomy.[2,3] Mortality is minimal when the diagnosis is rapidly established and the appendectomy performed. Mortality rates increase significantly with frank perforation, particularly in elderly patients. Although the history may be typical, most patients, especially elderly ones, should have a confirmatory abdominal imaging study prior to surgical intervention. When the diagnosis is in doubt, careful observation for 6 to 12 hours may be diagnostic. Broad-spectrum antibiotics directed toward gram-negative rods and anaerobes (such as ciprofloxacin 200 mg intravenously twice daily combined with metronidazole 250 mg intravenously three times daily) should be given before surgery or at the time of CT-guided drainage. In some patients, acute appendicitis resolves with localized perforation alone; however, because subsequent relapse is frequent (chronic appendicitis), elective appendectomy should be performed.

OTHER CAUSES OF THE ACUTE ABDOMEN

Differential Diagnosis

Acute severe abdominal pain most often results from perforation of an abdominal viscus (peptic ulcer; Chapter 138), small bowel obstruction, choledocholithiasis (Chapter 158), nephrolithiasis (Chapter 126), or rupture and dissection of an abdominal aortic aneurysm (Chapter 75). Subacute onset of pain is more typical of intestinal ischemia (Chapter 137), cholecystitis (Chapter 158), pancreatitis (Chapter 145), diverticulitis, Crohn's disease (Chapter 142), and appendicitis. Pain of a constant nature is seen with cholecystitis, pancreatitis, intestinal ischemia, and other inflammatory disorders. Colicky pain occurs with nephrolithiasis or intestinal obstruction. Although more typical of nephrolithiasis, pain radiating to the groin may rarely be seen in appendicitis. Radiation of pain to the back suggests pancreatitis, peptic ulcer disease, or biliary tract disease. Shoulder pain results from diaphragmatic irritation (pancreatitis, cholecystitis). Significant vomiting is seen with pancreatitis or obstruction of the stomach or small bowel.

PHYSICAL EXAMINATION. Careful observation of the patient may provide clues to the cause. With peritonitis (Chapter 146), the patient attempts to lie quietly. In contrast, patients with intermittent visceral-type pain (nephrolithiasis or choledocholithiasis) are restless during the attack. Tachycardia is nonspecific. Hypotension suggests bleeding (ruptured aneurysm), sepsis, or severe pancreatitis. Low-grade fever occurs with any inflammatory process, including acute pancreatitis. Abdominal inspection should include attention to scars that may suggest hernias or to masses (aneurysm, abscess). Absence of bowel sounds suggests ileus, whereas "rushes and tinkles" occur with small bowel obstruction. Abdominal palpation should begin opposite the point of subjective pain to minimize voluntary guarding, which may limit the examination. Coughing may cause local pain with peritonitis. Diffuse abdominal rigidity, unequivocal rebound tenderness, or severe localized tenderness with rebound represents generalized peritonitis and indicates a need for urgent surgical exploration. Involuntary guarding or referred rebound suggests a focal peritoneal process. Abdominal ischemia causes subjective pain disproportionate to the findings on examination until infarction and perforation occur. Abdominal distention and tympany are found with dilation of either the large or small bowel. Femoral artery or abdominal bruits suggest vascular disease (ischemic disease or aneurysms). Rectal and pelvic examinations may help evaluate for a pelvic appendix, peritonitis, and gynecologic disorders.

LABORATORY STUDIES. A complete blood cell count with differential, serum electrolytes, blood urea nitrogen and creatinine, serum amylase, liver chemistry tests, urinalysis, and a pregnancy test in women of childbearing potential are useful tests in patients with an acute abdomen. An elevated polymorphonuclear leukocyte count points to infection (appendicitis, cholecystitis), tissue necrosis (bowel infarction), or other inflammatory processes (pancreatitis). Anemia may result from gastrointestinal bleeding secondary to carcinoma or peptic ulcer. Pyuria and bacteriuria indicate a urinary tract infection, and microscopic or gross hematuria suggests nephrolithiasis. Fecal white blood cells or blood in the stool is seen with colitis (ischemia, inflammatory bowel disease, infection); fecal white cells are not present in acute appendicitis. A mildly elevated serum amylase level (less than two times the upper limit of normal) is nonspecific and occurs with a variety of intra-abdominal disorders (Chapter 145).

ABDOMINAL IMAGING. Radiographic films of the chest and a supine-upright abdominal series are useful to evaluate for free peritoneal air, bowel gas pattern, and the presence of calculi (nephrolithiasis, 80%; gallstones, 15%; appendicolith, 5%; or pancreatic calcification). Pneumonia or another basilar pulmonic process may mimic an abdominal syndrome. Abdominal sonography may demonstrate gallstones and a thickened gallbladder wall (acute cholecystitis), a dilated common bile duct (choledocholithiasis), pancreatic calcifications (chronic pancreatitis), or a noncompressible, abnormally thickened appendix greater than 6 mm in diameter (appendicitis).

Abdominal CT scanning has been invaluable in the evaluation of patients with an acute abdomen. Localized inflammatory processes of the right lower quadrant may suggest appendicitis or possibly Crohn's disease if the terminal ileum and/or right colon is thickened; however, overlap between these two entities may occur. CT also helps exclude diverticulitis, acute pancreatitis, biliary obstruction, luminal disorders such as small bowel or colonic infarction, and aortic dissection as well as unsuspected processes of the liver and spleen. Because of its ability to evaluate essentially all intra-abdominal organs, CT has become the imaging modality of choice for patients with an acute abdomen. Helical CT with both oral and intravenous contrast agents, if no contraindications are present, has the highest diagnostic yield.

A variety of other nonsurgical conditions may cause an acute abdominal pain syndrome. Disorders "above the diaphragm" include myocardial infarction (Chapter 69), bacterial pneumonia (Chapter 92), and acute pericarditis (Chapter 74). Severe right heart failure and a distended liver (Chapter 55) may cause mild to moderate right upper quadrant pain. Acute hepatitis (Chapter 151) rarely results in severe abdominal pain and should be suspected from marked elevations of serum aminotransferase concentrations. Marked transient elevations in serum aminotransferases, however, are commonly seen with acute biliary obstruction (choledocholithiasis; Chapter 158). Systemic disorders with abdominal manifestations include sickle cell crisis (Chapter 171), acute intermittent porphyria (Chapter 223), diabetic neuropathy (Chapter 242), heavy metal poisoning (Chapter 20), and cutaneous herpes zoster (Chapter 475).

Rx Treatment

Treatment of the patient with an acute abdomen is determined in consultation with a general surgeon and is usually guided by the diagnosis: laparotomy for appendicitis and appropriate therapy for cholecystitis (Chapter 158), cholangitis (Chapter 158), pancreatitis (Chapter 145), ischemic bowel (Chapter 144), diverticulitis (see later), nephrolithiasis (Chapter 126), Crohn's disease (Chapter 142), bowel obstruction, and a perforated viscus. Exploratory laparotomy may be required when the diagnosis is unclear and the physical examination confirms an acute abdomen. Broad-spectrum antibiotic coverage for gram-negative rods and anaerobes is warranted in all patients until a diagnosis is established.

DIVERTICULITIS OF THE COLON

Colonic diverticula are mucosal outpouchings that occur where arteries penetrate the muscularis to reach the submucosa and mucosa. Because these areas are inherently weak and under stress, prolapse of mucosa and submucosa may occur. Diverticula form throughout the entire colon, although more commonly in the left colon, particularly the sigmoid. Diverticulitis results when a fecalith becomes impacted in a diverticulum, with erosion through the serosa resulting in perforation.

Clinical Manifestations

Diverticulitis of the colon typically affects patients 50 years and older because the prevalence of diverticulosis increases with age. The pain is usually subacute and constant, and it is typically located in the left lower quadrant (sigmoid diverticulitis). However, the location of pain depends on the colonic segment involved, and right-sided diverticulitis is often misdiagnosed. Fever is almost invariably present. High-grade fever and sepsis occur when the perforation is not contained or when the peritonitis is generalized (Chapter 146). Constipation or loose stools may be reported. Rectal bleeding is distinctly unusual.

Diagnosis

DIFFERENTIAL DIAGNOSIS. Constant left lower quadrant pain and fever in elderly persons are highly suggestive of acute diverticulitis. Lower abdominal pain, fever, and bloody diarrhea suggest a bacterial colitis (*Shigella, Salmonella, Campylobacter*), ischemic colitis, or other inflammatory bowel disease (Chapters 325 to 327). With generalized peritonitis, the differential diagnosis becomes that of the acute abdomen (see earlier). Gynecologic disorders (Chapters 248 and 345) may be localized to the left lower quadrant and should always be considered in females.

LABORATORY AND IMAGING STUDIES. Leukocytosis is common, although nonspecific. Urinalysis may demonstrate nonspecific findings such as protein or rare white blood cells. If significant diarrhea is reported, fecal leukocytes should be sought.

Abdominal radiographs may indicate a displaced colon, extraluminal gas, or colonic mucosal abnormalities. These studies are probably more helpful in excluding other potential causes of left lower quadrant pain. Abdominal CT, which is the test of choice, may demonstrate bowel wall thickening, abscess formation, and diverticula (Fig. 143–2). Diagnostic barium enema is safe when carefully performed. Typical findings include spiculation of the mucosa, spasm, or frank perforation and abscess (Fig. 143–3A). These findings are relatively specific for acute diverticulitis but may be difficult to differentiate from carcinoma. CT and barium enema are complementary because neither is 100% sensitive or specific.

Endoscopic examination, which is contraindicated with diverticulitis because of the theoretical potential to exacerbate perforation, can detect diverticulosis before or between attacks (Fig. 143–3B). However, when carcinoma (Chapter 200) or inflammatory bowel disease (Chapter 142) is highly suspected, sigmoidoscopy is appropriate.

Rx Treatment

Initial therapy includes broad-spectrum antibiotics such as a third-generation cephalosporin (ceftriaxone 1.5 mg intravenously daily) combined with anaerobic coverage (metronidazole 250 mg intravenously three times daily) during hospitalization. At the time of discharge, oral antibiotics (ciprofloxacin and metronidazole) can be given to complete a 14-day course. For mild disease, oral antibiotics, such as ciprofloxacin (500 mg twice daily) combined with metronidazole (250 mg three times daily) for 14 days, and bowel rest can be used in the outpatient setting. Early surgical consultation is important, especially in the presence of more significant pain or an acute abdomen. If CT imaging identifies a large abscess, percutaneous catheter drainage can be a temporary measure before subsequent definitive surgical therapy. Complications of diverticulitis include colonic stricture, bleeding, or fistula formation to the small bowel, colon, bladder, or vagina. These complications may require surgical therapy. Recurrence of diverticulitis is well recognized and occurs in approximately one third of patients. With recurrent disease, surgical resection should be strongly considered.

SMALL BOWEL INFECTIONS

Small bowel bacterial overgrowth is a clinically uncommon disorder that typically manifests as diarrhea with or without weight loss. Contamination of the normally sterile small bowel may result from multiple diverticula, fistulas to the colon, and motility disorders. Malabsorption (Chapter 141) results from bacterial deconjugation of bile salts, and vitamin B_{12} deficiency is frequent because bacteria utilize this vitamin (Chapter 175). If surgical correction of any anatomic defects is not possible, intermittent use of broad-spectrum antibiotics is required.

Whipple's disease (Chapter 141), caused by the bacterium *Tropheryma whipplii*, is a multisystem disease affecting the small intestine, joints, heart, lymph nodes, and central nervous system. The clinical presentation is variable depending upon the organs involved. Malabsorption is the principal manifestation of small intestinal involvement. The diagnosis of intestinal disease is established by small bowel biopsy to identify periodic acid–Schiff–positive macrophages containing the organisms. Therapy should include a 2-week course of intravenous antibiotics such as parenteral penicillin G (1.2 million units per day) and streptomycin (1 g/day for 10 to 14 days) to treat any central nervous system involvement, followed by 1 year of oral antibiotics, such as trimethoprim-sulfamethoxazole (TMP-SMX, one double-strength tablet twice daily). In older studies in which TMP-SMX was not used, up to one third of patients suffered relapse, usually neurologic. Relapse seems to be less common today with TMP-SMX, which crosses the blood-brain barrier; nevertheless, close clinical follow-up is mandatory.

Intestinal tuberculosis (Chapter 341) is a rare disease observed primarily in the developing world. *Mycobacterium tuberculosis* may involve any portion of the gastrointestinal tract, but small bowel involvement is usually ileocecal in location and manifested by ulceration, stricture, and fistula formation. The clinical manifestations are nonspecific, including fever, abdominal pain, weight loss, and diarrhea. Radiographic studies using barium or CT may suggest the diagnosis. Colonoscopy with biopsy can often obtain tissue for culture, but laparotomy may be required; appropriate staining of biopsy specimens is critical. The prognosis is good, and cure is often achieved using standard antituberculous therapy even in patients with the acquired immunodeficiency syndrome.

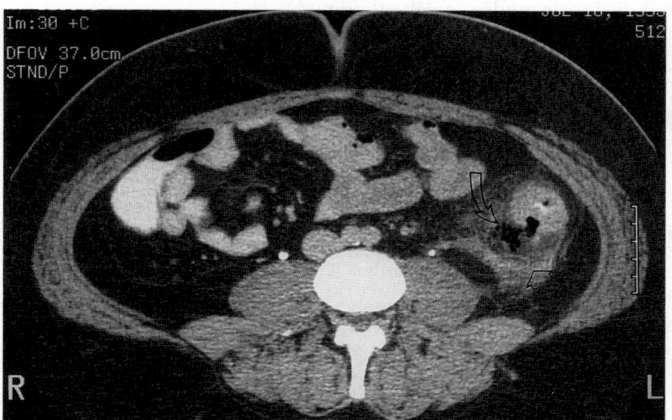

FIGURE 143–2 • Computed tomographic scan showing marked thickening of the distal end of the descending colon with surrounding inflammatory changes (straight arrow) and extraluminal gas (curved arrow) diagnostic of diverticulitis.

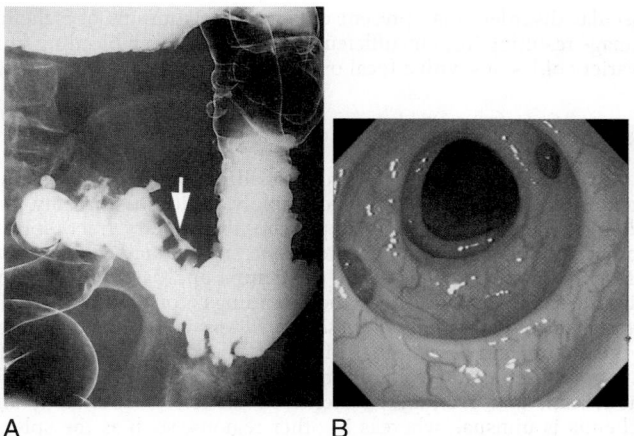

A   **B**

FIGURE 143–3 • *A*, Diverticular disease of the colon with sinus formation. The barium enema shows multiple diverticula, and a communicating sinus is clearly seen (arrow). This appearance is diagnostic of local abscess formation. *B*, Severe diverticular disease viewed through the colonoscope. Wide-mouthed openings to diverticula are present and were seen throughout the sigmoid colon in this patient. Colonoscopy may be difficult and hazardous when diverticula are large enough to admit the tip of the scope. (From Forbes CD, Jackson WF: Color Atlas and Text of Clinical Medicine, 3rd ed. London, Mosby, 2003.)

RADIATION ENTEROCOLITIS

Pathogenesis

Given the high turnover rate of gastrointestinal epithelium, it is not unexpected that the gut, particularly replicating cells in the crypts, would be affected by radiation (Chapter 19). If the dose of radiation does not exceed 50 Gy, minor mucosal injury (edema, erosions) may be temporary. With more intense therapy, damage to submucosal blood vessels results in an arteritis and, secondarily, mucosal ischemia. Late complications include fibrosis, strictures, and diffuse vascular ectasia in the affected segments.

Clinical Manifestations

During the early phases of radiation therapy, the symptoms of acute radiation are nausea, vomiting, and diarrhea, which may be bloody. Symptoms caused by the late complications of high-dose radiation are not seen for months or even years following therapy and include intestinal ulcerations with bleeding, obstruction from fibrosis and stricture, fistulas to other pelvic organs or to abscesses, or chronic gastrointestinal bleeding and anemia from vascular ectasia. If a significant amount of small bowel is in the radiation field, malabsorption may be noted.

Diagnosis

In the acute setting, the diagnosis is relatively straightforward based on the symptoms and signs. Endoscopic features in acute disease include mucosal edema and ulceration (Fig. 143–4). Late complications are suggestive by symptoms and by diffuse vascular ectasia and stricture on endoscopy. Although nonspecific, barium enema may demonstrate mucosal edema, fistula formation, and strictures. In an older patient with a stricture, carcinoma must be excluded.

Rx Treatment

Treatment options are limited. Patients with iron deficiency anemia from bleeding (vascular ectasia) should be treated with chronic iron therapy, and endoscopic therapies should be considered. For symptomatic distal colonic strictures, dilation may be attempted, although surgery is usually required. Diarrhea can be treated with antimotility agents. Abscess and fistulas require surgical resection, but surgery should be performed only when necessary because of the potential for later complications owing to delayed involvement of adjacent bowel segments.

INTESTINAL AND COLONIC ULCERATION

Except in patients with inflammatory bowel disease (Chapter 142), small intestinal or colonic ulceration is uncommon. The location

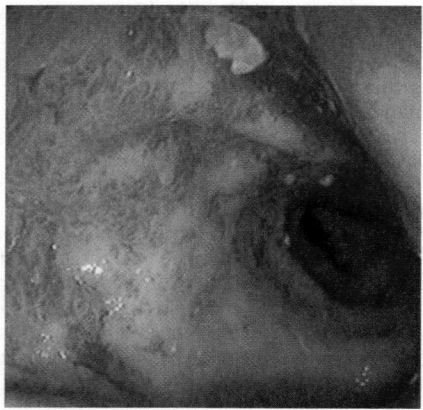

FIGURE 143–4 • Radiation proctitis in a patient with hematochezia. Note the extensive neovascularization of the mucosa. (Courtesy of Pankaj Jay Pasricha, MD.)

and the character of the ulcers suggest the underlying cause. Isolated proximal small bowel ulcerations are most commonly caused by medications, such as slow-release potassium pills or nonsteroidal anti-inflammatory drugs (NSAIDs), and ulcerated neoplasms. Multiple ulcers may be caused by Zollinger-Ellison syndrome (Chapter 140) and have been associated with celiac disease (Chapter 141). In some cases they are idiopathic.

Because of their small size, small bowel ulcers are difficult to identify by routine barium radiographs; enteroclysis (Chapter 131) is more sensitive. Small bowel enteroscopy has been the best method to visualize the distal duodenum and proximal jejunum, although capsule endoscopy is becoming an alternative (Chapter 132).

Diffuse colonic ulcerations are seen in infections and collagen vascular diseases, including Behçet's disease (Chapter 291), systemic lupus erythematosus (Chapter 280), and polyarteritis nodosa (Chapter 284). Ulcerations in the right colon resulting from NSAIDs may cause strictures. Infections such as tuberculosis (Chapter 341), amebiasis (Chapter 399), or rarely bacterial infections may produce right colonic ulceration. Ischemia (Chapter 144) usually produces diffuse segmental ulceration. Distal colonic ulcers result from ischemia, infections, or inflammatory bowel disease, particularly Crohn's colitis (Chapter 142). Rectal ulcers, when solitary, may be seen with chronic constipation (stercoral ulcer) or trauma or may be idiopathic (Chapter 147).

Barium enema may suggest Crohn's disease or ischemia. Colonoscopy with ulcer biopsy is the diagnostic procedure of choice, and diagnosis guides specific therapy.

1. Kaiser S, Frenckner B, Jorulf HK: Suspected appendicitis in children: US and CT a prospective randomized study. Radiology 2002;223:633–638.
2. Hellberg A, Rudberg C, Kullman E, et al: Prospective randomized multicentre study of laparoscopic versus open appendectomy. Br J Surg 1999;86:48–53.
3. Sauerland S, Lefering R, Neugebaur EA: Laparoscopic versus open surgery for suspected appendicitis. Cochrane Database Syst Rev 2002;CD001546.

SUGGESTED READINGS

Flum DR, Morris A, Koepsell T, Dellinger EP: Has misdiagnosis of appendicitis decreased over time? A population-based analysis. JAMA 2001:286:1748–1753. *No evidence of improvement in the sensitivity or specificity of the preoperative diagnosis of appendicitis despite newer diagnostic techniques.*
Paulson EK, Kalady MF, Pappas TN: Suspected appendicitis. N Engl J Med 2003;348: 236–242. *A practical approach to this common clinical challenge.*

144 VASCULAR DISORDERS OF THE INTESTINE

Lawrence J. Brandt

Vascular disorders may present either with symptoms of ischemic damage resulting from insufficient blood flow or with bleeding from a variety of lesions with a focal or diffuse increase in vascularity.

ISCHEMIC DISORDERS

Three major vessels supply almost all of the blood to the gastrointestinal tract, albeit with incredible variation in anatomy. The *celiac axis* and its branches supply the liver, biliary tract, spleen, stomach, duodenum, and pancreas; the *superior mesenteric artery* (SMA) gives off branches to the duodenum and pancreas and supplies the entire small intestine, the ascending colon, and a part of the transverse colon; the *inferior mesenteric artery* (IMA) delivers blood to the rectum and descending colon and anastomoses with the SMA to supply the transverse colon. In some areas, such as the stomach, duodenum, and rectum, collateral circulation is abundant, and ischemia is unusual, whereas in other regions, such as the splenic flexure and sigmoid ("watershed" areas), anastomoses are limited, and segmental ischemic damage is common. Ischemic injury of the bowel is influenced by the adequacy of cardiac output, the integrity of the aorta, the potential for collateral flow, the response of the vasculature to autonomic stimuli and circulating vasoactive substances, local modulation of blood flow, and a host of exogenous agents causing vasoconstriction (digitalis glycosides, vasopressin, and α-adrenergic agonists) or vasodilation (β-adrenergic agonists, papaverine, calcium channel blockers, and aminophylline).

The types of intestinal ischemia and their approximate incidences are colonic (60%), acute mesenteric (30%), focal segmental (5%), and chronic mesenteric (5%). Ischemic injury may be *venous* or *arterial,* and arterial forms of ischemia may be occlusive (caused by an anatomic obstruction to blood flow) or nonocclusive (mediated by vasoconstriction), but these two processes often coexist. When a major artery is suddenly occluded, collaterals open immediately in response to the decrease in arterial pressure. Increased blood flow through these collaterals continues as long as the pressure in the vascular bed distal to the obstruction remains below systemic pressure. After several hours of ischemia, vasoconstriction develops in the involved vascular bed, elevating its pressure and reducing collateral flow. If the ischemia and vasoconstriction are prolonged, the vasoconstriction can persist even after the cause of the ischemia is corrected. The bowel may tolerate a remarkable reduction in blood flow without damage. Normal oxygen consumption can be maintained with only 20 to 25% of normal blood flow, but below this crucial level, oxygen consumption decreases because increased oxygen extraction no longer can compensate for diminished blood flow. Ischemic damage results from hypoxia and from reperfusion injury. Most injury from brief periods of ischemia occurs during reperfusion. As the duration of ischemia lengthens, hypoxia becomes more detrimental than reperfusion.

ACUTE MESENTERIC ISCHEMIA

Intestinal ischemia can be acute or chronic and of venous or arterial origin. Acute mesenteric ischemia is much more common than chronic mesenteric ischemia, and ischemia of arterial origin is much more frequent than venous disease.

Arterial Forms

Acute mesenteric ischemia is caused by SMA embolus (50%), nonocclusive mesenteric ischemia (25%), SMA thrombosis (10%), focal segmental ischemia (5%), and acute mesenteric venous thrombosis (10%). SMA emboli usually originate from a left atrial or ventricular thrombus and lodge distal to the origin of a major vascular branch. Common sources of emboli include the left atrium in patients with atrial fibrillation or flutter (Chapter 59); the left ventricle in patients with mural thrombus owing to myocardial infarction (Chapter 69), heart failure (Chapters 55 and 56), or cardiomyopathy (Chapter 73); valvular vegetations or thrombus in patients with bacterial endocarditis (Chapter 310) or marantic endocarditis (Chapter 79); and, occasionally, paradoxical emboli in patients with right-to-left shunts (Chapter 65). Many patients with SMA emboli have had previous peripheral emboli, and approximately 20% have synchronous emboli to other arteries. Nonocclusive mesenteric ischemia usually results from splanchnic vasoconstriction hours to days after some cardiovascular event (e.g., acute myocardial infarction [Chapter 69], heart failure [Chapter 55], severe arrhythmias [Chapter 59], or shock [Chapter 103]). Patients with chronic renal diseases, especially patients requiring hemodialysis and patients undergoing major cardiac or intra-abdominal operations, are also at risk. SMA thrombosis occurs at severe atherosclerotic narrowings, most often at the SMA origin. In patients with SMA thrombosis, the acute episode commonly is superimposed on chronic ischemia, and 20 to 50% of these patients have a history suggesting intestinal angina during the weeks to months preceding the acute event.

Clinical Manifestations

Sudden severe abdominal pain developing in a patient with heart disease and arrhythmias, long-standing and poorly controlled heart failure, recent myocardial infarction, or hypotension should suggest the possibility of acute mesenteric ischemia. Early on, the pain is accompanied by a paucity of physical findings. Increasing abdominal tenderness and muscle guarding indicate infarcted bowel. Right-sided abdominal pain associated with maroon or bright red blood in the stool, although characteristic of colonic ischemia, also can be due to acute mesenteric ischemia because the blood supply to the right colon and the small bowel originates from the SMA.

Leukocytosis; metabolic acidemia; and elevations of serum phosphate, amylase, lactate dehydrogenase, creatine kinase, and intestinal alkaline phosphatase are seen with advanced ischemic bowel injury. Early in the course of disease, plain films of the abdomen usually are normal. Later, formless loops of small intestine, ileus, or "thumbprinting" of the small bowel or right colon secondary to submucosal hemorrhage may develop.

Diagnosis and Management

The approach to diagnosing and managing acute mesenteric ischemia is based on several observations: (1) If the diagnosis is not made before intestinal infarction, the mortality rate is 70 to 90%; (2) occlusive and nonocclusive forms can be diagnosed by angiography; (3) vasoconstriction may persist even after the initial cause of the ischemia is corrected; and (4) vasoconstriction can be relieved by vasodilators infused into the SMA. Early and liberal use of angiography and the incorporation of intra-arterial papaverine are the cornerstones in the treatment of occlusive and nonocclusive mesenteric ischemia.

Duplex ultrasonography of the celiac axis and SMA may show partial or complete occlusion of these vessels but is not reliable to evaluate peripheral splanchnic blood flow. Abdominal computed tomography (CT) is helpful in some cases, especially cases caused by mesenteric venous thrombosis, but early signs are nonspecific, and later signs develop only with necrosis and gangrene. Magnetic resonance angiography has great potential, but as available currently in most medical centers, can evaluate only the proximal portions of the splanchnic vessels. Selective mesenteric angiography is the mainstay of diagnosis and initial treatment of occlusive and nonocclusive acute mesenteric ischemia.

Initial management of patients suspected of having acute mesenteric ischemia includes resuscitation, abdominal plain films or CT study, and selective angiography. Resuscitation includes relieving acute heart failure and correcting hypotension, hypovolemia, and cardiac arrhythmias. Mesenteric blood flow cannot be improved if low cardiac output, hypovolemia, or hypotension persists. Broad-spectrum antibiotics are begun immediately. Plain films of the abdomen are obtained, not to establish the diagnosis of acute mesenteric ischemia, but to exclude other causes of abdominal pain. A normal plain film does *not* exclude acute mesenteric ischemia. If no alternative diagnosis is made on the abdominal films, selective SMA angiography is performed. Based on the angiographic findings and the presence or absence of peritoneal signs, treatment can be planned (Fig. 144-1).

Even when the decision to operate has been made based on clinical findings, a preoperative angiogram should be obtained. Relief of mesenteric vasoconstriction is essential in treating emboli, thromboses, and low-flow states and is accomplished by infusing papaverine at 30 to 60 mg/hr through an indwelling SMA angiography catheter (Fig. 144-2). Patients with splanchnic vasoconstriction only and selected patients with major or minor emboli may be managed angiographically without surgery (see Fig. 144-1).

Laparotomy is performed in acute mesenteric ischemia to restore arterial flow after an embolus or thrombosis and/or to resect irreparably damaged bowel. Except in the case of mesenteric venous thrombosis, heparin should not be used immediately postoperatively. Late thrombosis after embolectomy or arterial reconstruction occurs frequently enough, however, that anticoagulation 48 hours postoperatively is advisable. Survival is in the range of 55%; 90% of patients in whom acute mesenteric ischemia is diagnosed angiographically before the development of peritonitis survive.

Mesenteric Venous Thrombosis

Mesenteric venous thrombosis accounts for 5 to 10% of intestinal ischemia. Underlying causes have been identified in more than 80% of patients and include prothrombotic disorders such as antithrombin III; protein S and C deficiencies; and hypercoagulable states associated with polycythemia vera, anticardiolipin antibodies, myeloproliferative disorders, pregnancy, and neoplasms (Chapter 180). Oral contraceptives account for less than 10% of cases. About 60% of patients have a history of peripheral vein thromboses (Chapter 78). Mesenteric venous thrombosis can have an acute, subacute (weeks to months), or chronic onset; the last-mentioned is unaccompanied

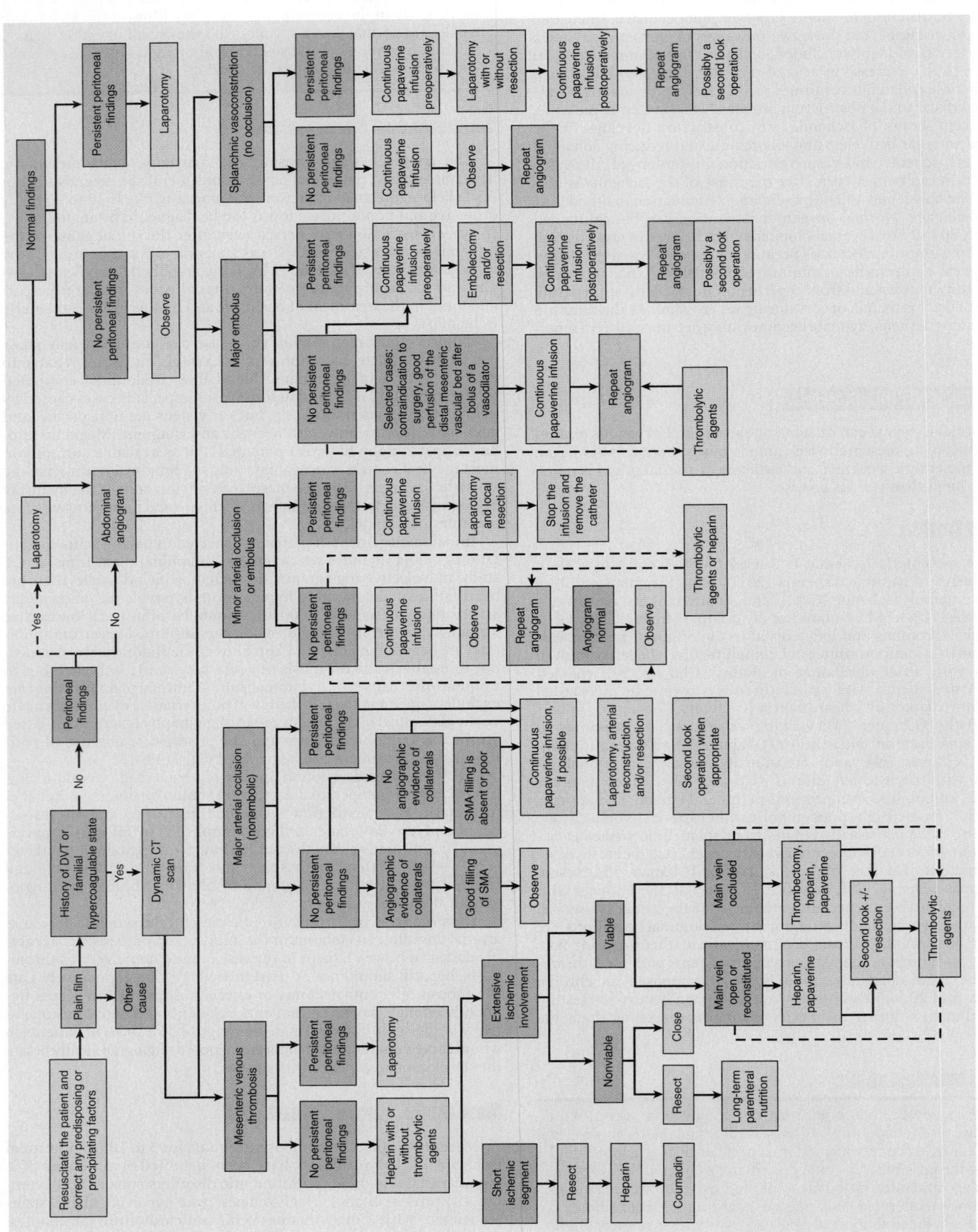

FIGURE 144–1 • Algorithm for managing patients with suspected acute mesenteric ischemia: diagnosis and management. Solid lines indicate accepted management plan; dashed lines indicate alternate management plan. CT = computed tomography; DVT = deep venous thrombosis; SMA = superior mesenteric artery. (From American Gastroenterological Association Medical Position Statement: Guidelines on Intestinal Ischemia. Gastroenterology 2000;118:951–953 [corrected algorithm in Gastroenterology 2000;119:281].)

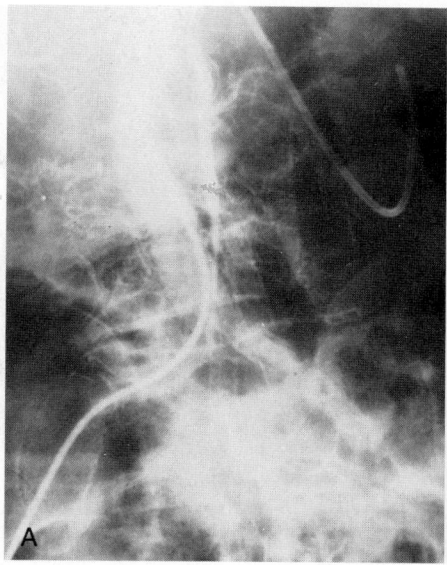
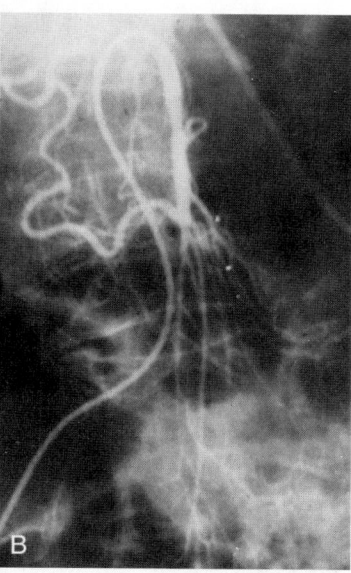

FIGURE 144–2 • Selected films from a superior mesenteric angiogram. *A,* Diffuse vasoconstriction characteristic of nonocclusive mesenteric ischemia. *B,* Intra-arterial infusion of papaverine (30 to 60 mg/hr) resulted in vasodilation.

by symptoms unless and until late complications occur. *Acute mesenteric venous thrombosis* resembles arterial forms of acute mesenteric ischemia; it presents as abdominal pain that, early on, is typically out of proportion to the physical findings. The tempo of illness is slower than that with arterial ischemia, however, and the mean duration of pain before hospital admission is 5 to 14 days. Nausea and vomiting are common, and lower gastrointestinal bleeding or hematemesis indicating bowel infarction is found in 15%. Abdominal plain film signs of mesenteric venous thrombosis are similar to those of other forms of acute mesenteric ischemia and almost always reflect the presence of infarcted bowel. Chronic ischemic colitis has recently been described in patients with phlebosclerosis, e.g., calcification of the mesenteric veins. Characteristic findings on small bowel series include luminal narrowing from congestion and edema of the bowel wall, separation of loops owing to mesenteric thickening, and "thumbprinting" secondary to submucosal hemorrhage and edema. Selective mesenteric arteriography can differentiate venous thrombosis from arterial forms of ischemia, but ultrasonography, CT, and magnetic resonance imaging (MRI) are used more commonly to show thrombi in the superior mesenteric vein (SMV) and portal vein. If patients with suspected acute mesenteric ischemia have features suggesting mesenteric venous thrombosis, a contrast-enhanced CT scan is obtained before SMA angiography; a history of deep vein thrombosis or a family history of a thrombotic disorder also suggests CT as the initial imaging study. In the few patients with no physical findings of intestinal infarction in whom a diagnosis of mesenteric venous thrombosis is made by ultrasonography, CT, or MRI, a trial of anticoagulant or thrombolytic therapy is worthwhile. All other patients should have prompt laparotomy, resection of nonviable bowel, and anticoagulation with heparin (see Fig. 144–1). The mortality of acute mesenteric venous thrombosis is lower than that of the other forms of acute mesenteric ischemia, varying from 20 to 50%. Recurrence rates of 20 to 25% fall to 13 to 15% if heparin is begun promptly.

Subacute mesenteric venous thrombosis is a condition in which patients have abdominal pain for weeks to months but have no intestinal infarction. It is caused either by extension of thrombosis at a rate rapid enough to cause pain but slow enough to allow collaterals to develop before infarction occurs or by acute thrombosis of a sufficiently small portion of the venous drainage system to permit recovery from ischemic injury. Diagnosis usually is made on imaging studies done for other suspected diagnoses. Nonspecific abdominal pain usually is the only symptom, and physical examination and laboratory tests are normal. In *chronic mesenteric venous thrombosis,* there usually are no symptoms at the time of thrombosis, and the patient may remain asymptomatic or may develop gastrointestinal bleeding. If the portal vein is involved, physical findings are those of portal hypertension, but if only the SMV is involved, there may be no abnormal findings. Laboratory studies may show hypersplenism with pancytopenia or thrombocytopenia. Treatment of chronic mesenteric venous thrombosis is aimed at controlling bleeding, which is usually

from esophageal varices (Chapters 133 and 136). No treatment is indicated for patients with asymptomatic chronic mesenteric venous thrombosis. The natural history of chronic mesenteric venous thrombosis is not known, but from postmortem studies it seems that almost 50% of patients do not have bowel infarction, and most are without symptoms.

FOCAL SEGMENTAL ISCHEMIA OF THE SMALL BOWEL

Vascular insults to short segments of small bowel produce a broad spectrum of clinical features without the life-threatening complications associated with more extensive ischemia. Focal segmental ischemia usually is caused by atheromatous emboli, strangulated hernias, vasculitis, blunt abdominal trauma, radiation, or oral contraceptives. With focal segmental ischemia, there usually is adequate collateral circulation to prevent transmural infarction, and patients present with one of three clinical patterns: (1) acute enteritis often simulating appendicitis (Chapter 143), (2) chronic enteritis resembling Crohn's disease (Chapter 142), and (3) intestinal obstruction often with bacterial overgrowth and a blind loop syndrome. Treatment is resection of the involved bowel.

COLON ISCHEMIA (ISCHEMIC COLITIS)

Ischemic colitis is the most common ischemic injury to the gastrointestinal tract. A spectrum of colon ischemic injury is recognized, including reversible colopathy (submucosal or intramural hemorrhage; at least 30 to 40%), transient colitis (at least 15 to 20%), chronic ulcerating colitis (20 to 25%), stricture (10 to 15%), gangrene (15 to 20%), and fulminant universal colitis (<5%). In most cases, no specific cause is identified, and what finally triggers the presenting episode is usually unknown. Colonic blood flow is lower than that of any other intestinal segment, decreases with functional motor activity, and is affected greatly by autonomic stimulation—a combination that may make the colon especially susceptible to ischemia. More than 90% of patients are older than age 60, although ischemic colitis has been documented in young patients with vasculitis (especially systemic lupus erythematosus; Chapter 280), sickle cell disease (Chapter 171), prothrombotic conditions (Chapter 180), medication-induced reactions (estrogens, danazol, vasopressin, psychotropic drugs), cocaine abuse (Chapter 30), and long distance running. A small percentage of patients with ischemic colitis have a distal and potentially obstructing colonic or rectal lesion, including carcinoma (Chapter 200), diverticulitis (Chapter 143), stricture, or fecal impaction. Ischemic colitis is a complication of elective aortic surgery in 1 to 7% of cases (Chapter 75); but after surgery for ruptured abdominal aortic aneurysm, it may occur in 60%.

Pathologic abnormalities are varied. Mildest changes include mucosal and submucosal hemorrhage and edema with or without

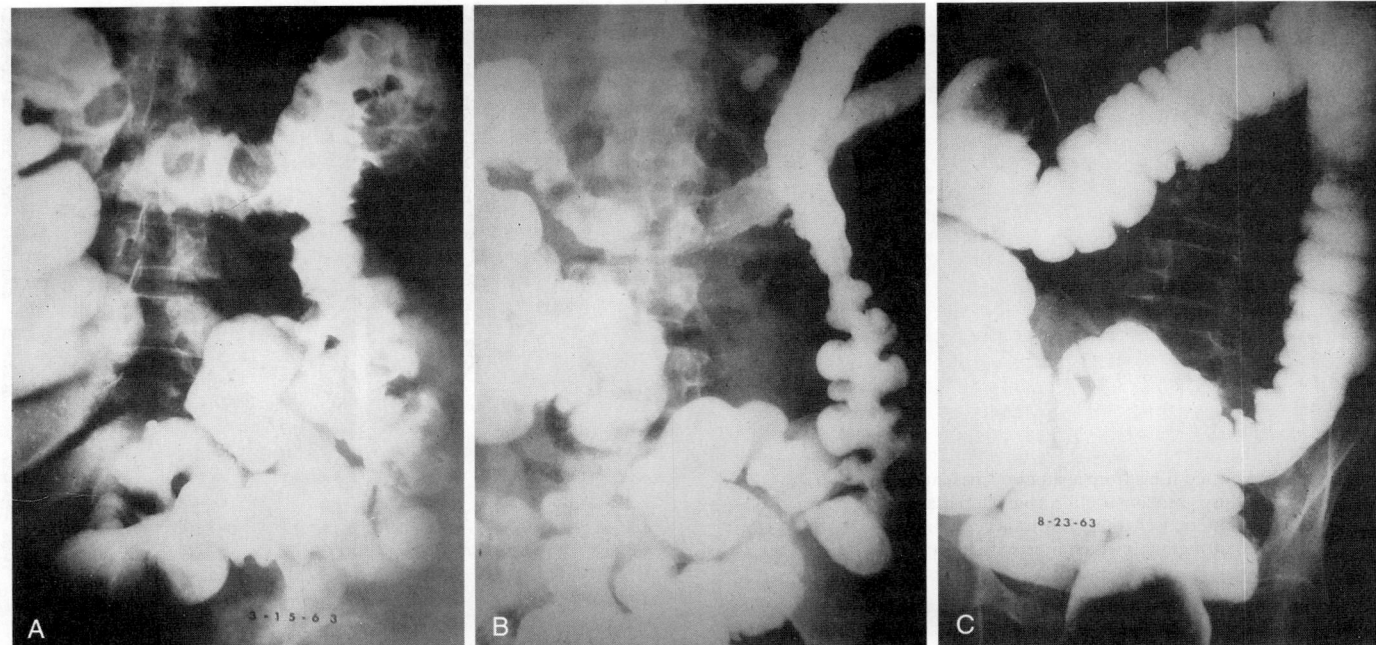

FIGURE 144–3 • Ischemic changes in the transverse colon and splenic flexure. *A*, Initial study shows dramatic thumbprints throughout the involved area. *B*, Eleven days later, thumbprints have resolved, and a segmental colitis has developed. *C*, Five months after onset, there is a complete return to normal. The patient was asymptomatic 3 weeks after her illness. (From Boley SJ, Schwartz SS, Williams FL [eds]: Vascular Disorders of the Intestine. New York, Appleton-Century-Crofts, 1971.)

partial mucosal necrosis. Hemorrhages subsequently are resorbed, or the overlying mucosa breaks down or sloughs, forming an ulcer. Multiple ulcers manifest clinically as a transient segmental colitis. With more severe injury, the mucosa and submucosa are replaced by granulation tissue. Later the mucosa may regenerate over the edematous submucosa, which contains granulation and fibrous tissue and iron-laden macrophages. Moderately severe ischemic colitis can produce chronic ulcerations separated by normal bowel, a picture that mimics inflammatory bowel disease (Chapter 142). With more severe and prolonged ischemia, the muscularis propria is damaged and replaced by fibrous tissue, forming a stricture. The most severe cases show transmural infarction with gangrene and perforation.

Clinical Manifestations

In contrast to acute mesenteric ischemia, most ischemic colitis is not associated with either a major vascular occlusion or a period of low cardiac output. Ischemic colitis usually presents with sudden, mild, crampy, left lower abdominal pain; an urge to defecate; and passage of bright red or maroon blood mixed with the stool within 24 hours. Bleeding is not severe, and blood loss requiring transfusion suggests another diagnosis. Physical examination usually reveals only mild-to-moderate abdominal tenderness over the involved segment of bowel. Any part of the colon may be affected, but the splenic flexure and sigmoid are involved most commonly. Systemic low-flow states usually involve the right colon; local nonocclusive ischemic injuries involve the "watershed" areas of the colon (i.e., the splenic flexure and rectosigmoid), whereas ligation of the IMA produces changes in the sigmoid.

Diagnosis

If ischemic colitis is suspected and the patient has no signs of peritonitis, colonoscopy or the combination of sigmoidoscopy and a gentle barium enema should be performed on the unprepared bowel within 48 hours of the onset of symptoms; colonoscopy is more sensitive in diagnosing mucosal abnormalities, and biopsy specimens may be obtained. Hemorrhagic nodules seen at colonoscopy represent submucosal bleeding and appear as filling defects called *thumbprints* on barium enema examination (Fig. 144–3). The initial diagnostic study should be performed within 48 hours because thumbprinting

disappears as the submucosal hemorrhages are resorbed or the overlying mucosa breaks down or sloughs. Studies performed 1 week after the initial study should show evolution of the injury: normalization of the colon or replacement of the thumbprints with segmental ulceration. Mesenteric angiography usually is *not* indicated in ischemic colitis because colonic blood flow has returned to normal by the time of presentation. Angiography may be indicated, however, when the clinical presentation does not allow a clear distinction between ischemic colitis and acute mesenteric ischemia or if only the right side of the colon is involved, a situation indicating disease in the distribution of the SMA and implying the possibility of coincident or subsequent acute mesenteric ischemia. In such situations, because untreated acute mesenteric ischemia rapidly becomes irreversible and because optimal management requires angiography, acute mesenteric ischemia must be excluded before barium studies, which would preclude an adequate angiographic examination.

℞ Treatment

In general, symptoms of ischemic colitis subside within 24 to 48 hours, and healing is seen within 2 weeks. Two thirds of patients with reversible disease exhibit intramural and submucosal hemorrhage (reversible colopathy), whereas one third manifest a transient colitis. More severe reversible damage may take 6 months to resolve, although symptoms still should subside within weeks. Irreversible damage occurs in less than 50% of patients, of whom approximately two thirds develop gangrene with or without perforation. The prognosis of patients with ischemic colitis complicating shock, heart failure, myocardial infarction, or severe dehydration is particularly poor, perhaps because of associated acute mesenteric ischemia.

When physical examination does not suggest gangrene or perforation, the patient is treated expectantly. The bowel is placed at rest, broad-spectrum antibiotics are given, cardiac function is optimized, and medications that cause mesenteric vasoconstriction are withdrawn if possible. Serial radiographic or endoscopic evaluations of the colon and continued monitoring of the hemoglobin, white blood cell count, and electrolytes are performed. Increasing abdominal tenderness, guarding, rising temperature, and paralytic ileus indicate colonic infarction and mandate expedient laparotomy and colon resection. If, as usual, ischemic colitis completely resolves within 1 to 2 weeks, no further therapy is indicated. When segmental colitis develops, corticosteroid therapy does not seem to be beneficial and may predispose to perforation. Asymptomatic patients with evidence of persistent disease should have frequent examinations to determine if the colon is healing, has persisting inflammation, or is developing a stricture. Recurrent fevers, leukocytosis, and septicemia in otherwise asymptomatic patients with unhealed segmental colitis usually are caused by the diseased bowel, and elective resection is indicated. Because patients with diarrhea or rectal bleeding for more than 2 weeks usually develop irreversible disease, often with colonic perforation, resection should be considered. Ischemic colitis may not produce symptoms during the acute insult but cause a chronic colitis frequently misdiagnosed as inflammatory bowel disease. Involvement is segmental, resection is not followed by recurrence, and the response to corticosteroid therapy usually is poor. Ischemic strictures that produce no symptoms should be observed; some disappear over 12 to 24 months without specific therapy, but resection is required for strictures that cause obstruction. For the rare form of fulminant ischemic colitis involving all or most of the colon and rectum, management is similar to that of other fulminant colitides.

CHRONIC MESENTERIC ISCHEMIA

Atherosclerosis (Chapters 47 and 66) is almost always the cause of chronic mesenteric ischemia or "abdominal angina." Abdominal pain probably results from a meal-induced increase in gastric blood flow that, in the presence of a fixed splanchnic arterial inflow, "steals" blood from the small bowel and makes it ischemic. Although autopsy and angiographic studies frequently show partial or complete occlusions of the major splanchnic vessels, chronic mesenteric ischemia is rare; many patients with occlusion of two or even all three of these vessels remain asymptomatic. The clinical significance of an angiogram showing an occlusion of one or more of these vessels in an individual patient varies. The lack of available and reliable means to determine the inadequacy of intestinal blood flow before morphologic changes of ischemia occur has been the major obstacle to identifying patients with chronic mesenteric ischemia.

Clinical Manifestations

The one consistent clinical feature of chronic mesenteric ischemia is abdominal discomfort or pain, which most commonly occurs 10 to 30 minutes after eating, gradually increases in severity, reaches a plateau, then slowly abates over 1 to 3 hours. The pain is usually dull, gnawing, or cramping and is located periumbilically or in the epigastrium. Initially the pain follows only a large meal, but it characteristically increases in frequency and severity so that the patient reduces the meal size ("small meal syndrome"), becomes reluctant to eat, and often loses substantial weight. Bloating, flatulence, constipation, and diarrhea are frequent. Physical findings are limited and nonspecific. Patients with advanced disease appear chronically ill with marked weight loss. The abdomen is usually soft and nontender even during episodes of pain. A systolic bruit is usually present in the upper abdomen but is nonspecific. Many patients have coincident cardiac (Chapters 67, 68, and 69), cerebral (Chapter 440), or peripheral vascular insufficiency (Chapter 76).

Diagnosis

There is no specific reliable diagnostic test for abdominal angina; the diagnosis is based on clinical symptoms, arteriographic demonstration of splanchnic arterial occlusions, and the exclusion of other gastrointestinal disease. Conventional examinations of the gastrointestinal tract usually are unremarkable or show nonspecific abnormalities. Studies for malabsorption often show increased fecal fat and decreased D-xylose excretion (Chapter 141). Duplex ultrasound can detect a 70% stenosis of the celiac axis or SMA with a sensitivity of 97 and 87%. Angiographic evaluation includes flush aortography and selective injections of the SMA, celiac axis, and, if possible, the IMA.

The presence of stenosis of a major vessel with prominent collateral vessels indicates that the stenosis is hemodynamically significant and chronic. In a comprehensive review of patients with chronic mesenteric ischemia, 91% had occlusion of at least two vessels, and 55% had involvement of all three; 7 and 2% had isolated occlusion of the SMA and celiac axis. *Stenosis or occlusion of one or two or all of the major vessels does not by itself establish the diagnosis of chronic mesenteric ischemia, however, and patients with even three occluded vessels may be asymptomatic.* Techniques to measure the effect of eating on mesenteric blood flow include Duplex ultrasound of the celiac axis and SMA, MRI of blood flow in the SMA and SMV, and balloon tonometry to determine intestinal intramural pH. Intestinal blood flow normally increases after eating, whereas in patients with intestinal ischemia, it does not; intramural pH decreases in patients with intestinal ischemia when postcibal blood flow is insufficient to sustain the increased metabolic processes that accompany digestion.

A patient with typical pain and unexplained weight loss, whose diagnostic evaluation has excluded other gastrointestinal disease and whose angiogram shows occlusion of at least two of the three major arteries, should undergo revascularization. Patients with chronic mesenteric ischemia who are otherwise relatively healthy probably should be treated by surgical revascularization, whereas patients at higher risk probably should have an initial attempt at percutaneous mesenteric angioplasty with or without stenting to relieve symptoms. After surgical revascularization, cumulative 5-year survival rates are 81 to 86%.

VASCULAR LESIONS

Through the widespread use of endoscopy and angiography, vascular lesions of the gastrointestinal tract are being recognized with increasing frequency as causes of hemorrhage. They may be solitary or multiple, exist as isolated abnormalities, or be part of a syndrome or systemic disorder.

Colonic vascular ectasia (angiodysplasia) is the most common vascular abnormality of the gastrointestinal tract. These degenerative lesions are associated with aging and are not associated with other cutaneous or visceral lesions. They almost always are confined to the cecum or ascending colon, are usually multiple, and rarely can be identified at operation or on routine histologic sections; they usually can be diagnosed by angiography or colonoscopy.

Colonic vascular ectasias are one of the most common causes of recurrent lower gastrointestinal bleeding in the elderly (Chapter 133). Patients may have bright red blood, maroon-colored stools, and melena on separate occasions. Bleeding is usually low grade, but about 15% of patients present with massive hemorrhage; in 20 to 25% of episodes, only tarry stools are passed. In 10 to 15% of patients, bleeding is evidenced only by iron-deficiency anemia with stools that are intermittently positive for occult blood. In more than 90% of cases, bleeding stops spontaneously.

When patients with colonic vascular ectasias have been studied carefully with enteroscopy or angiography, concomitant vascular lesions in the small intestine have been seen in approximately 20% of cases. Colonic vascular ectasias also have been reported to occur with higher frequency in patients with von Willebrand's disease (Chapter 178) and renal failure (Chapter 117). In most cases, careful histologic study of these lesions is lacking. Upper gastrointestinal bleeding from these vascular lesions occurs in one third of affected patients with renal failure. The lesions are usually small, multiple, and located mainly in the stomach and duodenum. Rebleeding also is common. Their occurrence has been attributed to clotting disorders and other comorbid illnesses. The association of colonic vascular ectasias with von Willebrand's disease has been linked to a deficiency of factor VII:vWF in the endothelial cells and an inability to allow platelets to adhere and form platelet plugs. Prospective study is required to determine the true incidence of vascular lesions in these disorders and to obtain sufficient tissue specimens to understand their cause and natural history.

Approximately 50% of patients with bleeding colonic vascular ectasias have evidence of cardiac disease, and 25% have been reported to have aortic stenosis (Chapter 72). The interrelationships of aortic stenosis, gastrointestinal bleeding, and colonic vascular ectasias are obscure, however. Histologic identification of colonic vascular ectasia is difficult without special techniques. Colonic vascular ectasias consist of dilated, distorted, thin-walled veins, venules, and capillaries. The earliest abnormality noted is the presence of a dilated, tortuous, submucosal vein, which often exists in areas where the mucosal vessels are normal. More extensive lesions show increasing numbers of dilated and deformed vessels involving the mucosa until, in the most severe lesions, the mucosa is replaced by a maze of distorted, dilated vascular channels.

Studies using special injection and clearing techniques indicate that colonic vascular ectasias are degenerative lesions associated with aging, probably caused by intermittent, low-grade obstruction of submucosal veins, where they pierce the colonic muscle layers of the cecum. Dilation and tortuosity of the submucosal vein and later the venules and capillaries of the mucosal units draining into it lead to a small arteriovenous fistula, which is responsible for the "early filling vein" that was the original angiographic hallmark of this lesion. The prevalence of colonic vascular ectasias in the right colon has been attributed to the greater tension in the cecal wall than in other parts of the colon.

Angiography was formerly the primary method to identify ectasias, but currently colonoscopy is preferable (Chapter 133). The endoscopist's ability to diagnose the specific nature of a vascular lesion is limited, however, by the similar appearance of many disparate lesions (e.g., spider angiomas, hereditary hemorrhagic telangiectasia, angiomas, and the focal hypervascularity of various colitides). Biopsy specimens of vascular lesions obtained during endoscopy usually are nonspecific, and the risk of biopsy is not justified. The appearance of vascular lesions is influenced by the patient's blood pressure, blood volume, state of hydration, and medications (e.g., meperidine) administered during colonoscopy. Colonic vascular ectasias may not be evident in patients with severely reduced blood volumes or patients who are in shock, so accurate evaluation may not be possible until red blood cell and volume deficits are corrected. Angiography can determine the site and nature of lesions during active bleeding and can identify colonic vascular ectasias even when bleeding has ceased if a slowly emptying and tortuous submucosal vein, a vascular tuft, or an early filling vein is present.

The natural history of colonic vascular ectasias is not known precisely. It has been estimated that less than 10% of patients with these lesions eventually bleed, supporting the recommendation not to treat incidental colonic vascular ectasias. Almost half of the patients with vascular ectasias may not bleed again after the initial bleeding episode. Laser therapy, sclerosis, electrocoagulation, the argon plasma coagulator, and the heater probe all have been used to ablate colonic vascular ectasias. None has been established as superior, but the heater probe and bipolar coagulation are used most commonly. No data prove that endoscopic ablation of colonic vascular ectasias changes their natural history. Under emergent conditions, angiographic methods have been used to arrest bleeding from colonic vascular ectasias, and intra-arterial (SMA) vasopressin infusions stop hemorrhage in more than 80% of patients in whom extravasation is shown. Right hemicolectomy is performed if the bleeding continues and an experienced endoscopist is not available or endoscopic ablation has been unsuccessful. The extent of colonic resection is not altered by the presence or absence of diverticulosis in the left colon; only the right half of the colon is removed. Because 80% of bleeding diverticula are located in the right side of the colon (Chapter 143), the risks of leaving a left colon containing diverticula are outweighed by the increased morbidity and mortality of the larger procedure, a subtotal colectomy. Recurrent bleeding can be expected in 20% of patients so treated. Subtotal colectomy should be performed only as a last resort: that is, in the patient in whom active colonic bleeding persists, the angiogram is completely normal, and colonoscopy either yields negative findings or is not helpful (Chapter 133).

HEREDITARY HEMORRHAGIC TELANGIECTASIA (OSLER-WEBER-RENDU DISEASE).

This autosomal dominant familial disorder is characterized by telangiectases of the skin and mucous membranes and by recurrent gastrointestinal bleeding. The gene for hereditary hemorrhagic telangiectases, localized to chromosome 9q3, is the gene for endoglin, a membrane glycoprotein that binds transforming growth factor (TGF)-β. Perturbation of one or more of the processes modulated by TGF-β may cause vascular dysplasia. Lesions frequently are noticed in the first few years of life, and recurrent epistaxis in childhood is characteristic. By age 10, about half of patients have some gastrointestinal bleeding, but severe hemorrhage is unusual before age 30 and has a peak incidence in the 50s. In most patients, bleeding presents as melena; hematochezia and hematemesis are less frequent. Lesions are usually present on the lips, oral and nasopharyngeal membranes, tongue, and periungual regions. Telangiectases occur in the colon but are more

common in the stomach and small bowel, where they also are more likely to cause significant bleeding. Telangiectases are seen easily on endoscopy as millet seed–sized, cherry-red hillocks, although, in the presence of severe anemia and blood loss, they may become transiently invisible or less obvious. Angiography may be normal or may show arteriovenous communications, conglomerate masses of abnormal vessels, phlebectasias, and aneurysms. Pathologically the major changes involve the capillaries and venules, but arterioles also may be affected. Lesions consist of irregular ectatic tortuous blood spaces lined by a single layer of endothelial cells and supported by a fine layer of fibrous connective tissue. No elastic lamina or muscular tissue is present in these vessels, so they cannot contract, perhaps explaining why they tend to bleed. Arterioles show intimal proliferation, often with thrombi. Many forms of treatment have been recommended for bleeding telangiectases, including estrogens, endoscopic ablation, and resection of involved bowel.

In the absence of contraindication to their use, estrogens are a reasonable form of systemic therapy that can diminish bleeding episodes. Endoscopic therapy, whether it be argon plasma coagulation, bipolar coagulation, heater probe, laser, or any other form of endoscopic ablation, can be used only if these lesions are within reach of the endoscope, essentially limiting their use to lesions in the stomach and duodenum. Resection is a last resort; because of the diffuse distribution of the lesions, surgery is best used when bleeding has been shown to come from a specific site. No attempt should be made to remove all the lesions, but rather only the lesions believed to be clinically significant.

PROGRESSIVE SYSTEMIC SCLEROSIS. Vascular lesions are a prominent feature of progressive systemic sclerosis, especially in the CREST variant with *c*alcinosis, *R*aynaud's phenomenon, *e*sophageal dysmotility, *s*cleroderma, and *t*elangiectasia (Chapter 281). These lesions may be the source of occult or clinically significant bleeding and are treated best by endoscopic ablation if within reach of the endoscope.

WATERMELON STOMACH. The term *watermelon stomach* describes an unusual vascular lesion of the gastric antrum consisting of tortuous dilated vessels radiating outward from the pylorus like spokes from a wheel and resembling the dark stripes on the surface of a watermelon. This lesion produces acute and chronic occult bleeding, and its cause is unknown; gastric peristalsis may cause prolapse of the loose antral mucosa with consequent elongation and ectasia of the mucosal vessels. The lesion is seen particularly in middle-aged or older women and is associated with achlorhydria, atrophic gastritis, cirrhosis, and a variety of autoimmune disorders. The cirrhosis and portal hypertension found in almost half of the reported cases of watermelon stomach suggest that it may be an expression of portal gastropathy (Chapter 137). Microscopic features include dilated capillaries with focal thrombosis, dilated tortuous submucosal venous channels, and fibromuscular hyperplasia. Corticosteroid treatment is unsuccessful, and antrectomy or, preferably, transendoscopic therapy is more likely to be successful.

DIEULAFOY'S ULCER. An increasingly diagnosed cause of massive gastrointestinal hemorrhage (Chapter 133), Dieulafoy's ulcer usually is found in the stomach and sometimes in the small or large bowel. Dieulafoy's lesion is twice as common in men as in women and presents at a mean age of 52 years. An artery of extramural caliber is present in the submucosa and, in some instances, the mucosa, typically with a small overlying mucosal defect. It is believed that focal pressure from this large-caliber vessel erodes the overlying mucosa, destroying the exposed vascular wall and resulting in hemorrhage. There is sudden onset of massive hematemesis or melena, usually followed by intermittent bleeding over several days. The bleeding site is usually 6 cm distal to the cardioesophageal junction, where the arteries are largest. The mortality rate for elderly patients with this lesion can be high, but angiographic and endoscopic techniques to localize and treat bleeding lesions decrease the need for emergent surgery, and the prognosis is likely to improve.

HEMANGIOMAS. Hemangiomas occur throughout the gastrointestinal tract and are the second most common vascular lesions of the colon. Hemangiomas may be of cavernous, capillary, or mixed types. Most are small and appear as polypoid, reddish-purple mounds, ranging from a few millimeters to 2 cm; larger lesions occur, especially in the rectum, where they may be associated with phleboliths. Bleeding from hemangiomas is usually slow, producing occult blood loss with anemia or melena. Hematochezia is less common except in large cavernous hemangiomas of the rectum. Diagnosis is established best by endoscopy, including enteroscopy, because radiographic studies, including angiography, are frequently normal. The new videocapsule, which enables tubeless and wireless imaging of the small intestine, offers great promise to detect not only hemangiomas, but also other bleeding lesions in the small bowel. Small hemangiomas that are solitary or few and can be approached endoscopically are locally ablated. Large or multiple lesions usually require resection of either the hemangioma alone or the involved segment of colon.

BLUE RUBBER BLEB NEVUS SYNDROME. The term *blue rubber bleb nevus syndrome* describes a particular type of cutaneous vascular nevus associated with similar cavernous hemangiomas of the gastrointestinal tract. A familial history is infrequent, although a few cases of autosomal dominant transmission have been reported. The lesions are distinctive: blue and raised, 0.1 to 5.0 cm, and leaving a characteristic wrinkled sac when the contained blood is emptied by direct pressure. Lesions may be single or innumerable and usually are found on the trunk, extremities, and face but not on mucous membranes; they are most common in the small intestine. Diagnosis and treatment are as for the hemangiomas (see earlier).

CONGENITAL ARTERIOVENOUS MALFORMATIONS. Congenital arteriovenous malformations are developmental anomalies that are found mainly in the extremities but potentially are located anywhere in the vascular tree. They may be small and resemble ectasias or large and involve a long segment of bowel. Characteristically, there is "arterialization" of the veins (i.e., tortuosity, dilation, and thick walls with smooth muscle hypertrophy), primarily in the submucosa, with intimal thickening or sclerosis. Angiography is the primary means of diagnosis. Patients with significant bleeding should have resection of the involved segment.

KLIPPEL-TRENAUNAY-WEBER SYNDROME. This syndrome consists of a vascular nevus involving the lower limb, varicose veins limited to the affected side and appearing at birth or in childhood, and hypertrophy of all tissues of the involved limb (especially the bones). Edema of the involved leg is common, and if the thigh is involved, a variety of lymphatic abnormalities may be present (e.g., chylous mesenteric cysts, chyloperitoneum, and protein-losing enteropathy). Symptomatic gastrointestinal or genitourinary involvement is rare and manifests as mild or severe hemorrhage, which may be recurrent and is usually due to a rectal or vaginal hemangioma, localized rectovaginal varices caused by an obstructed internal iliac system, or portal hypertension with varices. Physical examination is diagnostic, and a variety of imaging techniques can define the anatomy and guide surgical repair. Prognosis depends on the severity of the disorder and the extent and location of the gastrointestinal or genitourinary lesions.

SUGGESTED READINGS

Brandt LJ, Boley SJ: AGA technical review on intestinal ischemia. Gastroenterology 2000;118:954–968. *A comprehensive review of the world's literature structured in the form of responses to the questions most frequently asked about intestinal ischemia.*

Iwashita A, Yao T, Schlemper RJ, et al: Mesenteric phlebosclerosis: A new entity causing ischemic colitis. Dis Colon Rectum 2003;46:209–220. *A newly described cause of chronic ischemic colitis.*

145 PANCREATITIS

Chung Owyang

ACUTE PANCREATITIS

Definition and Classification

Acute pancreatitis, which is an inflammatory disease of the pancreas, is characterized by a discrete episode of abdominal pain and elevated serum amylase and lipase levels. In contrast to chronic pancreatitis, which is characterized by changes in pancreatic structure and by persistence of dysfunction after the precipitating cause has been corrected, acute pancreatitis is distinguished by complete restitution of the pancreas morphologically and functionally after the derangements that precipitated the attack have been corrected.

The incidence of acute pancreatitis ranges from one to five cases per 10,000 population per year. Pathologically, two morphologic classifications are recognized: acute interstitial pancreatitis and acute hemorrhagic pancreatitis. The latter type is associated with much higher morbidity and mortality.

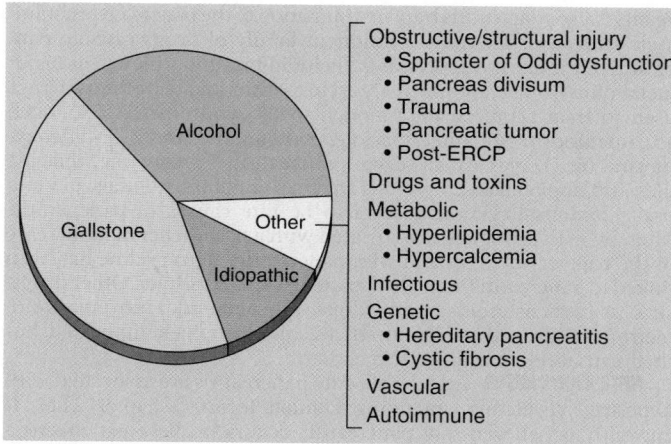

FIGURE 145–1 • Factors associated with acute pancreatitis. ERCP = endoscopic retrograde cholangiopancreatography.

Etiology

The list of causative factors of acute pancreatitis is long (Fig. 145–1). Alcoholism and biliary tract disease are most frequent, accounting for more than 70% of cases. Rare causes are responsible for about 10% of cases; in the remainder, the cause remains unknown.

ALCOHOL. Alcohol-induced acute pancreatitis usually occurs in patients who consume large quantities of alcohol for 5 to 10 years before the first attack (Chapter 17). Among individuals who consume large amounts of alcohol, only 5 to 10% develop acute pancreatitis, suggesting that additional factors, such as smoking and consumption of a high-fat diet, may affect a person's susceptibility to the disease.

Several mechanisms may contribute to the development of alcoholic pancreatitis, including abnormal sphincter of Oddi spasm in the presence of stimulated pancreatic secretion, obstruction of small ductules by proteinaceous plugs, and direct toxic effects of alcohol metabolic byproducts. Alcohol also may change the amounts of potentially damaging proteases in pancreatic secretions. Increased amounts of lysosomal enzymes and an increased trypsinogen-to-pancreatic trypsin ratio have been reported in the pancreatic juice of alcoholic patients.

GALLSTONES. The frequency of acute pancreatitis is inversely proportional to the size of gallstones (Chapter 158). Persistence of stones in the bile duct or ampulla is associated with more severe disease. An impacted gallstone may permit the reflux of bile into the pancreatic duct or occlude the duct's orifice.

Microlithiasis (crystals in the bile) may cause recurrent pancreatitis, although the precise mechanism is unknown. Microlithiasis is common after prolonged fasting, total parenteral nutrition (Chapter 230), rapid weight loss, and use of drugs such as octreotide or ceftriaxone. Microlithiasis may be identified by the presence of sludge on ultrasound or the presence of birefringent cholesterol crystals in the bile; the diagnosis should be considered in patients who have recurrent bouts of apparently idiopathic pancreatitis.

PANCREATIC OBSTRUCTION. Obstruction of pancreatic secretion is a less common cause of acute pancreatitis. Sphincter of Oddi dysfunction is associated with increases in sphincter pressure caused by increased smooth muscle tone or fibrotic stricturing. Pancreas divisum results from failure of the ventral and dorsal ducts to join during fetal development; the small accessory duct of Santorini and minor papilla may produce a high outflow resistance. Sphincter of Oddi dysfunction or pancreas divisum has been reported in more than 25% of patients with idiopathic pancreatitis in some series, but whether this association is causal or coincidental is difficult to determine. Pancreatitis has been reported in 10% of patients with pancreatic cancer (Chapter 201), but it is usually mild. Older patients with unexplained pancreatitis should have a careful evaluation to exclude a minute pancreatic cancer amenable to resection.

DRUGS AND TOXINS. Toxins and drugs that have been implicated in acute pancreatitis include insecticides, methanol, organophosphates, and the venom of a scorpion found in the West Indies. Some of these agents cause pancreatitis by overstimulation of the pancreas via cholinergic pathways. The most prominent family of drugs causing pancreatitis are immunosuppressants, including azathioprine and its major metabolite (6-mercaptopurine), cyclosporine, and tacrolimus. Drugs used to treat acquired immunodeficiency syndrome (AIDS), such as trimethoprim-sulfamethoxazole, pentamidine, and 2',3'-dideoxyinosine (ddI), may cause severe pancreatitis. Furosemide, thiazide diuretics, angiotensin-converting enzyme inhibitors, sulfasalazine, and oral 5-aminosalicylic acid seem to be rare causes of pancreatitis. Therapy with estrogens is associated with a dose-dependent increase in the triglyceride level and with pancreatitis. Tetracycline has been linked to pancreatitis, usually in patients with fatty liver. Other drugs, such as corticosteroids, methyldopa, procainamide, nitrofurantoin, metronidazole, and interleukin (IL)-2, also have been implicated, but their causal relationship is less certain.

METABOLIC CAUSES. Attacks of acute pancreatitis are associated with hypertriglyceridemia, including familial forms (Chapter 211). It currently is believed that pancreatitis occurs in these patients as a result of the harmful effects of fatty acids released into the pancreatic circulation or parenchyma by the action of pancreatic lipase. Hypercalcemia owing to hyperparathyroidism, immobilization, multiple myeloma, or total parenteral nutrition has been linked to hyperamylasemia but probably causes pancreatitis infrequently.

GENETIC DISORDERS. In patients with a family history of pancreatitis, the possibility of familial pancreatitis should be considered. This autosomal dominant disorder has a penetrance of about 80%. Most patients have their first symptoms before reaching age 20 years, with attacks frequently precipitated by alcohol use, high fat intake, or emotional stressors. Patients with this disorder also have a higher risk of developing pancreatic cancer. The most common genetic defect is an arginine-histidine substitution at 7q35, the site of the trypsinogen gene, which results in resistance to trypsin hydrolysis. Mutations in the pancreatic trypsin inhibitor gene also may predispose to pancreatitis.

Mutations in the cystic fibrosis transmembrane regulator (*CFTR*) (Chapter 86) cause two types of pancreatitis. Classically, cystic fibrosis results in pulmonary disease and pancreatic insufficiency, but it rarely results in pancreatitis. All cystic fibrosis patients have elevated sweat chloride levels and diminished *CFTR* function in the nasal mucosa. A second pancreatic phenotype not associated with pulmonary disease has been identified. These patients are not homozygous but are predisposed to develop acute and chronic pancreatitis.

TRAUMA AND IATROGENIC DISEASE. Most cases of trauma-induced pancreatitis occur as a result of blunt rather than penetrating injury. Postoperative pancreatitis most frequently is associated with procedures that involve manipulation of the pancreas and/or the periampulla region. Reduced vascular perfusion (e.g., shock) of the pancreas, as may occur when surgical procedures are associated with hypotension or hypoperfusion, also can precipitate acute pancreatitis. Hyperamylasemia and abdominal pain are common after endoscopic retrograde cholangiopancreatography (ERCP) (Chapter 132), but evidence of significant pancreatitis occurs in less than 5% of patients undergoing ERCP.

MISCELLANEOUS CAUSES. Other unusual causes of pancreatitis include autoimmune diseases, renal and cardiac transplantation, and infections with mumps (Chapter 368) and coxsackieviruses (Chapter 373). Cytomegalovirus infection (Chapter 370) can cause acute inflammation of the pancreas in patients with AIDS (Chapter 416).

In 10 to 15% of patients with pancreatitis, no obvious cause can be identified; these patients are considered to have idiopathic pancreatitis. In these patients with recurrent episodes of pancreatitis, ERCP to search for gallstones and biliary drainage to examine bile for cholesterol crystals should be performed even if the abdominal ultrasound examination is negative.

Pathophysiology

Little is known about the precise mechanisms responsible for acute pancreatitis, but the fundamental mechanism for transforming the initial injury into pancreatitis seems to be activation of digestive enzymes and autodigestion. Alcohol, drugs, and infectious agents damage acinar cells. Although the pancreas has little ability to metabolize alcohol, acetaldehyde (its toxic metabolite) may reach the pancreas and may cause premature activation of pancreatic enzymes within acinar cells. In experimental models, hyperstimulation of the pancreas may result in fusion of lysosome and zymogens within large vacuoles, followed by activation of enzymes and acute intracellular injury. Cathepsin B is a lysosomal enzyme capable of activating the conversion of trypsinogen to trypsin. Trypsin then catalyzes the conversion of many proenzymes to their active forms, which are responsible for the major systemic complications of acute pancreatitis.

During pancreatitis, inflammatory mediators, including cytokines (such as tumor necrosis factor-α and platelet-activating factor) and chemokines (such as IL-6), are generated and released. These agents stimulate the recruitment of inflammatory cells, enhance the activation and adherence of inflammatory cells to the vascular wall, or cause direct cell injury. Generation of proinflammatory mediators can lead to the systemic inflammatory response syndrome (SIRS) (Chapters 102 and 104). Marked leukocyte activation can lead to distant organ injury and the development of multisystem organ failure. SIRS and pancreatic infection are the two major causes of death from acute pancreatitis.

Clinical Manifestations

The typical symptoms of acute pancreatitis are abdominal pain, nausea, and vomiting. Pain usually develops first and remains constant, without the waxing and waning pattern typical of intestinal or renal colic (Chapter 130). The pain frequently is located in the epigastrium with radiation to the midback; it typically lasts hours to days and is not relieved by vomiting. Abdominal findings vary with the severity of the attack, from minimal local tenderness to marked generalized rebound tenderness, guarding, and abdominal distention. Bowel sounds frequently are diminished or absent owing to intestinal ileus. Jaundice can occur in cases without stone-induced pancreatitis owing to compression of the common bile duct by the edematous pancreas. With severe attacks, hypotension, tachypnea, tachycardia, and hyperthermia may be noted. Fever is usually less than 38.5 °C. Examination of the skin may reveal tender areas of induration and erythema resulting from subcutaneous fat necrosis. In severe necrotizing pancreatitis, large ecchymoses occasionally may appear in the flanks (Grey Turner's sign; Fig. 145–2) or the umbilical area (Cullen's sign); these ecchymoses are caused by blood dissecting from the retroperitoneally located pancreas along the fascial planes.

Diagnosis

SERUM AMYLASE. The diagnosis of acute pancreatitis is based on clinical findings and supported by an elevation of serum amylase and lipase. Most, but not all, patients with acute pancreatitis have hyperamylasemia. Typically the serum amylase level rises rapidly over the initial 2 to 12 hours of an attack, then slowly declines to its normal values over the next 3 to 5 days. The magnitude of hyperamylasemia has no prognostic value. Hyperamylasemia is not specific to pancreatitis, although the greater the elevations of the serum amylase, the more it tends to signify acute pancreatic damage. Apart from acute pancreatitis, hyperamylasemia may result in small bowel obstruction, perforation, or infarction; a perforated duodenal ulcer; or liberation

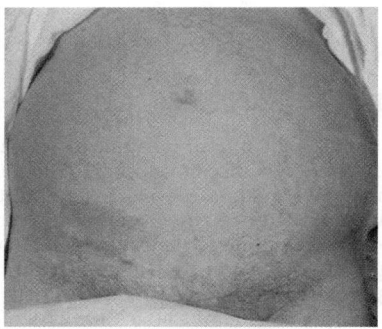

FIGURE 145–2 • Grey Turner's sign in acute pancreatitis. This characteristic discoloration in both flanks results from the tracking of blood from the pancreatic area of the retroperitoneum. (From Forbes CD, Jackson WF: Color Atlas and Text of Clinical Medicine, 3rd ed. London, Mosby, 2003, with permission.)

Table 145–1 • CAUSES OF INCREASED AMYLASE AND LIPASE LEVELS

	AMYLASE	LIPASE
Pancreatitis	↑	↑
Intestinal injury/obstruction	↑	↑
Biliary stone	↑	↑
Tubo-ovarian disease	↑	Normal
Renal failure	↑	↑
Macroamylasemia	↑	Normal
Parotitis	↑	Normal

of amylase into the circulation from nongastrointestinal sources, such as the lung, fallopian tubes, and salivary glands (Table 145–1). Alternatively, hyperamylasemia may be caused by release of amylase from certain tumors or reduced renal clearance of amylase owing to renal failure. Pancreatic hyperamylasemia can occur after ERCP or after passage of common duct stones even in the absence of pancreatitis. Macroamylasemia, an unusual but not rare condition, occasionally can cause isolated elevation of the serum amylase level. In this condition, amylase is bound to an abnormal serum protein: The complex is not cleared by the kidney and results in hyperamylasemia. Macroamylasemia should be suspected when hyperamylasemia is associated with low urinary amylase levels. Hypertriglyceridemia may depress serum amylase measurements spuriously; diluting the serum unmasks the increased serum amylase level.

Amylase activity in blood is composed of isoenzymes from the pancreas and salivary glands. Pancreatic isoamylase normally accounts for approximately 40% of total serum amylase activity. In acute pancreatitis, serum pancreatic isoamylase increases substantially. These increases also can occur in conditions other than acute pancreatitis, including intestinal injury and renal insufficiency, rendering its measurement nonspecific.

SERUM LIPASE. During acute pancreatitis, serum lipase levels increase in parallel with serum amylase levels. The lipase level remains elevated longer and may help to diagnose pancreatitis after an attack has passed. Additionally, lipase levels are normal in macroamylasemia and parotitis. Although not entirely specific for pancreatitis, serum lipase has supplanted amylase as the single test of choice for the diagnosis of pancreatitis.

OTHER BLOOD TESTS. Routine laboratory tests in patients with moderate-to-severe acute pancreatitis usually reveal leukocytosis. Transient mild hyperglycemia is common and occurs when excess glucagon is released from the α cells of the islets of Langerhans. Hypocalcemia usually is caused by extravasation of nonionized, albumin-bound calcium from inflamed retroperitoneal and, at times, peritoneal surfaces; this form of hypocalcemia is common, usually causes no symptoms, and requires no treatment. In necrotizing pancreatitis, hypocalcemia can be more severe owing to loss of ionized calcium within areas of fat necrosis in the pancreas and peripancreatic tissue. Hyperbilirubinemia and elevations in serum aminotransferase and alkaline phosphatase levels are seen in 50% of patients resulting from either compression of the common bile duct by the inflamed pancreas or nonobstructive cholestasis that accompanies severe illness. Hypoalbuminemia may occur as a result of extravasation of albumin from inflamed retroperitoneal and peritoneal surfaces. The serum triglyceride level should be measured in all patients because of its etiologic implications and to interpret unexpectedly normal serum amylase levels. Serum triglyceride levels greater than 1000 mg/dL may precipitate attacks of acute pancreatitis, and lowering serum triglyceride levels to less than 200 mg/dL can prevent pancreatitis. Serum triglyceride levels of less than 500 mg/dL are unlikely to be a cause of pancreatitis. Most individuals who abuse alcohol have moderate but transient elevations of triglyceride levels that likely represent an epiphenomenon rather than the cause of pancreatitis.

URINE TESTS. The urinary amylase-to-creatinine clearance ratio increases from 3% to approximately 10% in acute pancreatitis. Moderate renal insufficiency interferes with the accuracy and specificity of this test. Urinary amylase excretion is not increased in macroamylasemia. Other than to diagnose macroamylasemia, urinary amylase and the amylase-to-creatinine clearance ratio are not used clinically.

CHEST AND ABDOMINAL RADIOGRAPHS. Standard and upright chest and abdominal radiographs should be obtained in patients suspected to have acute pancreatitis. Chest radiographs may show pleural effusions and basilar atelectasis. Bilateral pulmonary opacification with a normal size heart is the hallmark of adult respiratory distress syndrome (ARDS) (Chapter 99). Abdominal radiographs should be obtained to exclude nonpancreatic diseases, such as intestinal perforation. Intestinal gas patterns may indicate ileus, which sometimes may appear as an isolated dilated loop of small bowel overlying the pancreas (a sentinel loop) or dilation of the transverse colon with abrupt termination of the gas column at the splenic flexure (colon cutoff sign) when the inflammatory process affects the phrenicocolic ligament.

ULTRASONOGRAPHY AND COMPUTED TOMOGRAPHY. Ultrasound and computed tomography (CT) play important roles in the diagnosis and management of acute pancreatitis. Ultrasound is the best noninvasive test for detecting cholelithiasis, although it is less reliable for direct visualization of a bile duct stone. An inflamed pancreas may appear hypoechoic on ultrasound because of edema in the parenchyma. Pancreatic visualization is limited, however, by intestinal gas or adipose tissue in 30 to 40% of patients.

The CT scan is the primary modality for evaluating the extent and local complications of pancreatitis. Pancreatic inflammation may be seen as pancreatic enlargement, inhomogeneity of the pancreatic parenchyma, or fluid infiltrating the peripancreatic fat in 90% of patients (Fig. 145–3). Dynamic CT during bolus administration of intravenous contrast material is useful to evaluate the severity of pancreatitis because it can show poor pancreatic perfusion, which suggests pancreatic necrosis (Fig. 145–4). The CT finding of

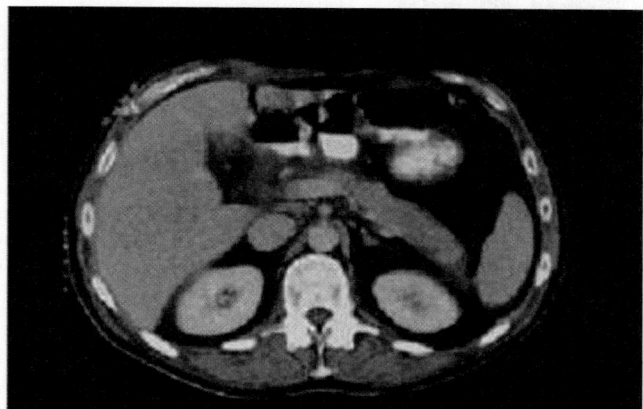

FIGURE 145–3 • Typical computed tomography scan in acute non-necrotizing pancreatitis. After intravenous contrast injection, the normally enhancing pancreatic parenchyma is separated from the nonenhancing peripancreatic fluid surrounding the pancreatic tail. (Courtesy of Poonputt Chotiprasidhi.)

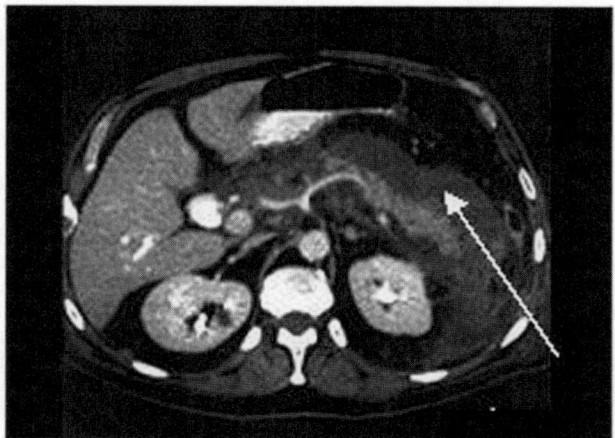

FIGURE 145–4 • Typical computed tomography scan in necrotizing pancreatitis. Peripancreatic and retroperitoneal edema are obvious. Large nonenhancing areas of necrosis are visible in the body and tail of the pancreas (arrow). Pancreatitis is grade D by computed tomography criteria (see Table 145–2). (Courtesy of Poonputt Chotiprasidhi.)

necrosis identifies patients who are at higher risk for pancreatic infection and death (see Table 145–2).

MAGNETIC RESONANCE IMAGING AND ENDOSCOPIC CHOLANGIOPANCREATOGRAPHY. Magnetic resonance imaging (MRI) is probably equivalent to CT for imaging the acutely inflamed pancreas. Although more expensive and less accessible, MRI is preferred in patients who are pregnant or have allergies to contrast material. In patients with suspected biliary pancreatitis, MRI cholangiopancreatography may identify greater than 90% of bile duct stones.

ERCP is not useful for establishing the diagnosis of acute pancreatitis, but it is useful for diagnosing and treating persistent bile duct stones in acute pancreatitis. It also should be used in the investigation of patients with unexplained recurrent pancreatitis. It is especially useful for the diagnosis of mild chronic pancreatitis, pancreas divisum, or sphincter of Oddi disease. Pancreatitis occurs in about 5% of patients undergoing ERCP, however. The risk of pancreatitis increases significantly in female patients with normal serum bilirubin levels, patients suspected to have sphincter of Oddi dysfunction, and patients with a previous history of post-ERCP–induced pancreatitis. Patients with the least probability of harboring truly obstructive pathology are at highest risk of post-ERCP–induced pancreatitis, even if the procedure is for diagnosis alone. Because new techiques such as MRI cholangiopancreatography and endoscopic ultrasound (EUS) have accuracy rates rivaling ERCP, they may be preferable to ERCP for patients with equivocal evidence of biliary obstruction, especially patients at high risk for post-ERCP–induced pancreatitis.

Differential Diagnosis

Acute pancreatitis must be distinguished from many conditions that cause upper abdominal pain, nausea, and vomiting, especially perforated viscus, bowel obstruction, mesenteric ischemia, and cholecystitis (Chapters 143, 144, and 158). Each of these processes can present with elevated serum amylase and lipase levels and be difficult to distinguish from acute pancreatitis. Features that favor the diagnosis of acute pancreatitis include greater than twofold elevation of the serum amylase level, CT evidence of pancreatic inflammation, lack of free air on the abdominal plain radiograph or CT scan, and improvement with nonoperative treatment. If doubt persists and clinical deterioration continues, surgical intervention may be necessary to establish the diagnosis.

Evaluation of Severity

It is important to establish the severity of acute pancreatitis to predict the patient's course and anticipate complications. Prognostic information from specific laboratory tests, clinical and physiologic assessment, and CT should guide the use of prophylactic antibiotics, urgent bile duct imaging, and early ERCP.

LABORATORY TESTS. Routine blood tests, such as serum amylase and lipase and white blood cell counts, provide little prognostic information, whereas markers such as serum or urinary trypsinogen activation peptide and C-reactive protein may help separate mild pancreatitis from severe pancreatitis. The trypsinogen activation peptide assay, which is an indirect measure of the amount of active trypsin, seems to discriminate between mild and severe disease. Neuron-specific elastase and IL-6 are released from inflammatory cells and are elevated in the blood during the first 12 hours of acute pancreatitis; their elevation correlates with the severity of pancreatitis. C-reactive protein is induced by IL-6 and is a later marker to distinguish patients with severe disease on the second hospital day.

CLINICAL AND PHYSIOLOGIC EVALUATION. Many scoring systems can predict the morbidity and mortality of acute pancreatitis. Ranson's criteria, which are the most well known (Table 145–2), include 11 characteristics. The five characteristics that are assessed at admission reflect the intensity of the inflammatory response, whereas the six evaluated during the initial 48 hours reflect serious complications, including fluid shifts, cardiovascular instability, and end-organ failure. In general, patients with fewer than two criteria have less than 1% mortality. Conversely, patients with more than six positive criteria have an increased likelihood of pancreatic necrosis and infection and a higher mortality rate. The Glasgow system, which can be calculated anytime within the first 48 hours of hospitalization, measures only eight parameters (see Table 145–2) but seems to have prognostic accuracy similar to that of Ranson's criteria. The Acute Physiology and Chronic Health

Table 145–2 • PROGNOSTIC CRITERIA FOR ACUTE PANCREATITIS

RANSON CRITERIA*	SIMPLIFIED GLASGOW CRITERIA†	COMPUTED TOMOGRAPHY CRITERIA‡
On admission	**Within 48 hr of admission**	Normal
Age >55 yr	Age >55 yr	Enlargement
WBC >16,000/μL	WBC >15,000/μL	Pancreatic inflammation
AST >250 U/L	LDH >600 U/L	Single fluid collection
LDH >350 U/L	Glucose >180 mg/dL	Multiple fluid collection
Glucose >200 mg/dL	Albumin <3.2 g/dL	
48 hr after admission	Ca²⁺ <8 mg/dL	
hematocrit decrease by >10%	Arterial PO₂ <60 mm Hg	
BUN increase by >5 mg/dL	BUN >45 mg/dL	
Ca²⁺ <8 mg/dL		
Arterial PO₂ <60 mm Hg		
Base deficit >4 mEq/L		
Fluid sequestration >6 L		

*Three or more Ranson's criteria predict a complicated clinical course. Data from Ranson JH, Rifkind KM, Turner JW: Prognostic signs and nonoperative peritoneal lavage in acute pancreatitis. Surg Gynecol Obstet 1976;143:209–219.

†Data from Blamey SL, Imrie CW, O'Neill J, et al: Prognostic factors in acute pancreatitis. Gut 1984;25:1340–1346.

*‡Grades A and B represent mild disease with no risk of infection or death. Grade C represents moderately severe disease with a minimal likelihood of infection and essentially no risk of mortality. Grades D and E represent severe pancreatitis with an infection rate of 30 to 50% and mortality rate of 15%. Data from Balthazar EJ, Robinson DL, Megibow AJ, Ranson JH: Acute pancreatitis: Value of CT in establishing prognosis. Radiology 1990;174:331–336.

AST = aspartate aminotransferase; BUN = blood urea nitrogen; LDH = lactate dehydrogenase; WBC = white blood cells.

Evaluation (APACHE) II system uses 14 routinely measured parameters to produce a numerical score based on a patient's deviation from the normal range; however, it is more complex and difficult to use outside of an intensive care unit.

COMPUTED TOMOGRAPHY. Standard CT and contrast-enhanced CT provide useful prognostic information. The CT Severity Index (see Table 145–2) correlates with the Ranson criteria for assessing severity. Contrast-enhanced CT evaluates the presence and extent of pancreatic necrosis, which correlates well with morbidity and mortality. In non-necrotizing acute pancreatitis (see Fig. 145–3), infection is rare and mortality is less than 1%. Conversely, necrotizing pancreatitis (see Fig. 145–4) is associated with a 30 to 50% rate of infection, and mortality is 10 to 30%.

 Treatment

Because there is no proven therapy that directly affects pancreatic inflammation, the main treatment goal for acute pancreatitis is to provide supportive care, including fluid resuscitation, maintenance of optimal fluid balance, and close monitoring for signs of local and systemic complications (Fig. 145–5). More than 80% of patients with acute pancreatitis have mild disease with no complications. Patients should not receive any oral fluids or food until abdominal pain and tenderness have subsided and bowel sounds have returned. Nasogastric suction is not necessary in mild pancreatitis, but it is recommended in the presence of vomiting and ileus. The patient should receive sufficient analgesic medications for pain control. Abdominal pain may be treated with 50 to 100 mg of meperidine every 4 hours as needed. More severe pain requires hydromorphone, which has a longer half-life than meperidine and may be given parenterally by a patient-controlled anesthesia pump. Neither total parenteral nutrition nor prophylactic antibiotic therapy is indicated in uncomplicated acute pancreatitis. Severe intravascular volume contraction and hypovolemia, which can be caused by the exudation of fluid into the inflamed peripancreatic retroperitoneum and by the gastrointestinal fluid losses owing to vomiting and nasogastric suction, should be corrected promptly. Most patients with gallstone pancreatitis have a mild episode, do well, and can undergo cholecystectomy during the same admission. Patients with severe gallstone pancreatitis and evidence that gallstones remain impacted at the duodenal ampulla often benefit from early ERCP, sphincterotomy, and stone extraction; however, surgical intervention may be needed. Hypertriglyceridemia may cause 1 to 4% of cases of acute pancreatitis. Every attempt should be made to lower serum triglyceride levels to less than 200 mg/dL.

Patients who are still hypotensive after adequate volume replacement require placement of central catheters to allow more precise assessment and management of fluid and electrolyte requirements. Patients with severe necrotizing pancreatitis frequently have a high cardiac index and low peripheral vascular resistance typical of SIRS. The major indication for early surgical intervention is diagnostic uncertainty in the presence of an acute abdomen. Intestinal perforation or necrosis, which sometimes mimics hemorrhagic acute pancreatitis, can be confirmed and corrected only when a laparotomy is performed. Infected necrosis (see later) also requires urgent intervention. Surgical débridement and drainage are usually necessary.

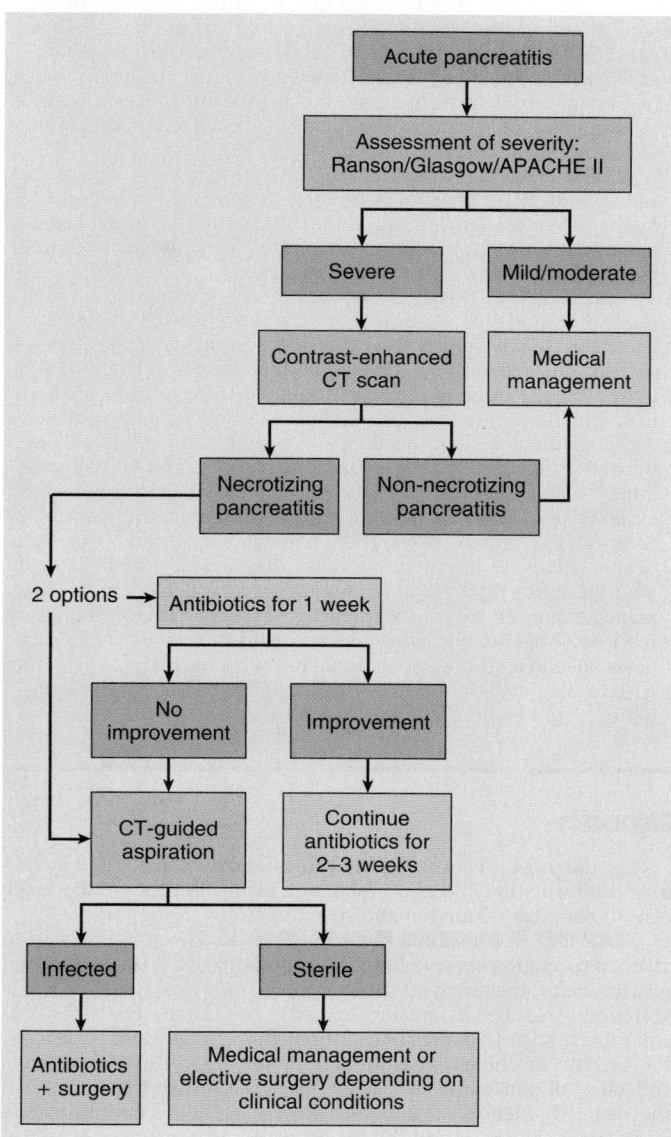

FIGURE 145–5 • Approach to the patient with suspected or proven acute pancreatitis. CT = computed tomography.

Complications

In patients who show evidence of smoldering persistent pancreatitis, every effort should be made to exclude infected pancreatic necrosis, an impacted gallstone in the duodenal ampulla, and a pseudocyst. If the ultrasound does not show a pseudocyst or an enlarged pancreas, a CT scan is indicated. The CT scan often reveals structural abnormalities, such as pseudocyst, pancreatic necrosis, or dilated ducts, that may have escaped detection.

LOCAL COMPLICATIONS. Infected pancreatic necrosis should be suspected in patients who have moderate-to-severe acute pancreatitis; who have worsening of symptoms after initial improvement; and who develop new fever (especially >38.5 °C), marked leukocytosis, positive blood cultures, or other evidence of sepsis (see Fig. 145–5). If necrotic pancreatitis is suspected, an emergency abdominal CT scan with intravenous contrast enhancement should be performed; any fluid collection of phlegmonous masses should be subjected to aspiration for Gram stain and culture. Alternatively, antibiotic treatment may be given for 1 week; if there is no improvement, a CT-guided aspiration should be performed. The demonstration of polymorphonuclear cells and bacteria suggests infected pancreatic necrosis and should lead to urgent surgical intervention because the mortality of conservatively treated patients with infected pancreatic necrosis is greater than 60%. Antibiotic therapy should be initiated or continued to cover gram-negative enteric and anaerobic organisms[1]; antibiotics with high penetration into pancreatic tissue include imipenem/cilastatin, fluoroquinolones, and metronidazole. Standard regimens include imipenem, 500 mg intravenously three times a day; pefloxacin (a fluoroquinolone), 400 mg intravenously two times a day; or metronidazole, 500 mg three times a day for 10 to 14 days.[2] The management of clinically sterile pancreatic necrosis is controversial; the necrotic tissue may resolve or evolve gradually into a pseudocyst or a region of organized pancreatic necrosis. Among patients with persistent necrosis, 40% or more become infected during the course of their disease; others may experience persistent organ failure despite prolonged supportive care. Careful clinical monitoring and repeated dynamic CT scans are recommended in these patients to monitor the progression of necrotizing pancreatitis. If the condition deteriorates, surgery should be contemplated.

Pancreatic pseudocysts occur in 10 to 20% of cases of acute pancreatitis. Diagnosis is made most easily by abdominal ultrasound or CT scan. Smaller cysts tend to disappear without specific treatment. Cysts that have been present for more than 6 weeks and are greater than 5 cm in diameter usually require treatment. The presence of severe pain, rapid expansion, or complications such as bleeding, leakage, or rupture may accelerate the need to intervene. Internal surgical drainage into the stomach or small intestine is the most widely used treatment, but endoscopic or percutaneous drainage can be attractive nonsurgical options.

Acute pancreatitis can cause true pancreatic ascites as defined by the presence of large amounts of fluid that is rich in pancreatic amylase and protein and that results from a communication between the pancreatic duct or a pseudocyst and the peritoneal cavity (Chapters 143 and 156). The site of ductal disruption usually is identified by ERCP. Acute pancreatitis infrequently may cause bleeding or thrombosis of peripancreatic vessels. Arterial hemorrhage occurs when a pseudocyst erodes into a pancreatic artery and transforms the pseudocyst cavity into a pseudoaneurysm. The diagnosis is made by CT scan and angiography; the bleeding artery often can be treated by embolization, but surgical intervention sometimes is required. The most common venous complication of pancreatitis is occlusion of the splenic vein, which may result in splenomegaly and gastric varices.

SYSTEMIC COMPLICATIONS. The two most important systemic complications of acute pancreatitis are renal and respiratory failure. Renal failure usually occurs as a result of hypovolemia and decreased renal perfusion (Chapter 116). The prevention and treatment of pancreatitis-associated renal failure depends, to a large extent, on correction of fluid and electrolyte abnormalities. Mild and transient respiratory failure is believed to be the result of infradiaphragmatic inflammation, splinting of respiration, and atelectasis. Arterial hypoxemia with an arterial P_{O_2} value less than 70 mm Hg is often associated with mild respiratory alkalosis and frequently is noted in patients with severe acute pancreatitis; it usually is detected within the first 2 or 3 days of an attack. Hypoalbuminemia and fluid overload probably are important contributory factors. In most cases, respiratory failure usually improves as the acute phase of pancreatitis ends. Some patients progress, however, to a more severe form of respiratory failure that resembles ARDS (Chapter 99). This poor prognostic sign frequently is associated with a complicated clinical course and/or death. Pancreatitis-associated ARDS results from injury to the alveolar membrane and/or degradation of surfactant by circulating enzymes, such as phospholipase, that may be released from the inflamed pancreas. Treatment is mainly supportive because specific therapy for pancreatitis-associated ARDS has not been defined.

Prognosis

The natural history of pancreatitis is unpredictable and depends on the causes. In gallstone pancreatitis, cholecystectomy prevents further attacks. Hyperparathyroidism, hypertriglyceridemia, and implicated drugs may cause or contribute to pancreatitis; elimination of these precipitants should prevent reoccurrence. With the exception of alcoholic pancreatitis, progression from acute to chronic pancreatitis is rare. In most cases of alcoholic pancreatitis, structural and functional abnormalities usually already have occurred, so the impact of abstinence from alcohol is still unpredictable. Nevertheless, the natural history of alcoholic pancreatitis usually is influenced favorably by discontinuation of alcohol consumption. After alcohol abstinence, pancreatic structure and function may continue to deteriorate but at a slower pace. Abstinence also should reduce the recurrence of acute attacks.

CHRONIC PANCREATITIS

Definition and Classification

Chronic pancreatitis is an inflammatory disease of the pancreas characterized by the presence of permanent and progressive morphologic or functional damage to the pancreas. Many patients have intermittent flares of acute pancreatitis. Sometimes the clinical distinction between acute recurrent pancreatitis, with restoration of normal pancreatic function and structure between attacks, and chronic pancreatitis may be difficult without structural or functional studies of the pancreas. The prevalence of chronic pancreatitis in autopsy series is 0.04 to 5%, although it may be much higher in alcoholics. Chronic pancreatitis can be subdivided into calcifying chronic pancreatitis and obstructive chronic pancreatitis. Chronic calcifying pancreatitis is characterized by irregular distribution of fibrosis and calcification within the pancreas, with varying degrees of obstruction of the primary and secondary pancreatic ducts. It is the most common form of chronic pancreatitis and may be associated with chronic alcoholic pancreatitis, tropical pancreatitis (see later), hereditary pancreatitis, pancreatitis secondary to hypercalcemia or hyperlipidemia, and idiopathic pancreatitis. Obstructive chronic pancreatitis is characterized by dilation of the ductal system, diffuse atrophy of the acinar parenchyma, and uniform fibrosis. Obstructive chronic pancreatitis may be caused by pancreatic tumors, duct strictures, and possibly pancreas divisum. In contrast to other forms of chronic pancreatitis, intraductal plugs or stones are rare or absent, and structural and functional changes may improve when the obstruction is relieved.

Etiology

In the United States, alcohol consumption is the principal cause of chronic pancreatitis, accounting for approximately 70% of all cases. In contrast to acute pancreatitis, gallstones do not cause chronic pancreatitis. Malnutrition-induced (tropical) pancreatitis is the most prevalent form of chronic pancreatitis in developing Asian and African countries. Consumption of cassava, a plant indigenous to these regions, may contribute to pancreatic injury by increasing serum thiocyanate levels, which subsequently increase cellular free radical production. Ingestion of a diet deficient in micronutrients and antioxidants exposes the pancreas to injury by unopposed free radicals. In a few cases, chronic pancreatitis results from trauma or from prolonged metabolic disturbances, such as hypercalcemia and hypertriglyceridemia. In rare instances, pancreatitis can be inherited as an autosomal dominant disease, presenting as acute or chronic pancreatitis with prominent pancreatolithiasis. Approximately 20% of cases are believed to be idiopathic. A bimodal age distribution in adolescents and the elderly suggests that there may be two distinct pathophysiologic causes.

Clinical studies indicate an increased incidence of heterozygotic mutations in the *CFTR* gene in idiopathic chronic pancreatitis. In contrast to patients with cystic fibrosis, who usually present with painless pancreatic insufficiency, these patients experience recurrent pancreatitis despite normal sweat tests and pulmonary function.

Pathophysiology

The pathophysiologic mechanism responsible for chronic pancreatitis is unclear. In experimental animal models, chronic alcoholism causes an increase in the basal secretion of pancreatic proteins and a decrease of trypsin inhibitor. The proteins in the pancreatic juice precipitate as protein plugs and block small ductules in a random fashion, activating pancreatic enzymes that result in episodes of acute pancreatitis. In time, calcium is complexed to protein plugs, resulting in further structural deterioration of pancreatic ducts and acinar tissue, infiltration of inflammatory cells, and eventual acinar atrophy and fibrosis of the exocrine tissue. Lack of normal secretion of specific proteins that inhibit calcium carbonate stone formation has been proposed as a cause of stone formation and chronic pancreatitis.

Clinical Manifestations

ABDOMINAL PAIN. Abdominal pain, which is the major symptom of chronic pancreatitis, occurs in about 80% of patients. Pain may be intermittent or chronic, and it may continue, diminish, or disappear completely over time. Pain may improve as the severity of pancreatitis worsens. In about 15% of patients, chronic pancreatitis is relatively painless. Possible causes of the pain include inflammation of the pancreas, increased intrapancreatic pressure, neural inflammation, and extrapancreatic causes, such as stenosis of the common bile duct and duodenum.

WEIGHT LOSS. Weight loss occurs in more than 50% of patients. Initially the major cause of weight loss is decreased caloric intake owing to fear of aggravating abdominal pain. In advanced chronic pancreatitis, weight loss is usually due to pancreatic insufficiency with malabsorption or uncontrolled diabetes.

MALABSORPTION. Diarrhea and steatorrhea secondary to inadequate digestion of fats occur when pancreatic lipase is reduced to less than 10% of normal levels, a reduction that indicates extensive structural damage (Chapter 141). Amylase deficiency results in diminished carbohydrate digestion and leads to osmotic diarrhea. Maldigestion of proteins is caused by deficiency of protease. Although maldigestion affects all nutrients, the most clinically significant problem concerns maldigestion of fat and fat-soluble vitamins (A, D, E, and K).

DIABETES MELLITUS. Although glucose intolerance is common early in the course of chronic pancreatitis, clinical diabetes occurs relatively late in the disease. Ketoacidosis and diabetic neuropathy are relatively uncommon in this form of diabetes. The management of pancreatic diabetes is often difficult because the loss of insulin and glucagon makes for a brittle form of diabetes. Insulin requirements are usually lower than for most patients with genetic diabetes because insulin receptors are not downregulated, and insulin antibodies initially are not present (Chapter 242).

Diagnosis

The diagnosis of chronic pancreatitis usually is suggested by historical information and confirmed by imaging studies or laboratory tests of pancreatic function and structure.

ASSESSMENT OF PANCREATIC EXOCRINE FUNCTION. The simplest way to assess pancreatic exocrine function is quantitative 72-hour fecal fat measurement. Increased fat in the stool (>7 g/day) occurs if exocrine secretion is reduced by greater than 90%, but the test is neither sensitive nor specific (Chapter 141). Among the pancreatic function tests, the secretin or cholecystokinin stimulation test with simultaneous collection of pancreatic secretions through a catheter positioned in the distal duodenum is most sensitive (sensitivity approximately 90 to 95%). The collected fluid is assayed for bicarbonate (secretin stimulation) or lipase and trypsin. This test is time-consuming (2 hours), however, and is not widely available.

STRUCTURAL STUDIES. The demonstration of diffuse, speckled calcification of the pancreas on a plain abdominal film is diagnostic of chronic pancreatitis, but the sensitivity of this finding is only 30 to 40%. Ultrasound has a sensitivity of approximately 70% and specificity of 90%, and the finding of chronic pancreatitis on ultrasound usually requires no confirmatory testing. Findings associated with mild chronic pancreatitis include irregular contour of the gland, reduction in echogenicity or echogenic foci in the parenchyma, and mild dilation of the duct. Calcification and dilation of the main pancreatic duct suggest more severe chronic pancreatitis. CT scan is more sensitive than ultrasound with comparable specificity. The most common diagnostic findings of chronic pancreatitis on CT include ductal dilation, calcifications, and cystic lesions. Other findings include enlargement or atrophy of the pancreas and heterogeneous density of the parenchyma.

ERCP commonly is considered to be the most sensitive (approximately 90%) and specific (approximately 100%) diagnostic test for chronic pancreatitis. In minimal chronic pancreatitis, the branches and fine ducts show dilation and irregularity. Moderate pancreatitis is characterized by the additional finding of dilation, tortuosity, and stenosis of the main pancreatic duct. Advanced pancreatitis is defined by marked dilation of the main duct with total loss of the normal, tapered appearance; the secondary ducts are similarly dilated and blunted. ERCP should be reserved for patients in whom the diagnosis cannot be established by other imaging techniques or who have recurrent acute pancreatitis without an obvious cause.

EUS has sensitivity and specificity equivalent to ERCP without the risk of inducing pancreatitis. EUS-guided fine-needle aspiration can differentiate chronic pancreatitis from malignancy. As with ERCP, EUS should be used only when less invasive procedures fail to substantiate the diagnosis of chronic pancreatitis.

DIAGNOSTIC APPROACH. If chronic pancreatitis is suspected, imaging techniques such as ultrasound and CT may reveal diagnostic information in approximately 70 to 90% of the cases. If these tests are equivocal or negative, ERCP should be performed to view abnormalities of the pancreatic duct that may not be visible by other imaging techniques. Less invasive EUS can be used in place of ERCP. If ultrasound, CT, and ERCP or EUS are normal, a secretin/cholecystokinin stimulation test, which may disclose evidence of mild chronic pancreatitis, can be used in selected cases.

Rx Treatment and Prevention of Recurrences

Medical treatment is aimed mainly at the control of pain and correction of malabsorption with adequate enzyme replacement.

PAIN CONTROL. Control of pain includes avoidance of alcohol, use of analgesics, and celiac plexus block (Fig. 145–6). Elevated triglycerides (>500 mg/dL) and drugs such as azathioprine can cause pancreatitis. It makes sense to eliminate these precipitants as possible causes of ongoing inflammation and pain. The same is true for alcohol, the most common cause of chronic pancreatitis. On abstinence from alcohol, the structure and function of the pancreas may stabilize in some patients. An initial trial of acetaminophen or nonsteroidal anti-inflammatory drugs is preferable, but patients may require opiate analgesics (Chapter 29). Concerns about addiction should not interfere with the goal of pain relief; a strong patient-physician relationship may prevent abuse of prescribed narcotics. Percutaneous radiographically or sonographically guided celiac plexus block can control pain from pancreatic cancer (Chapter 201), but the procedure's occasional benefits almost never persist for more than a few months in chronic pancreatitis.

Oral pancreatic enzymes can reduce pain in about 75% of patients, perhaps because the administration of trypsin or chymotrypsin can inhibit the intrinsic secretion of cholecystokinin and pancreatic enzymes. Patients who have mild-to-moderate nonalcoholic chronic pancreatitis are most likely to respond. Non–enteric-coated enzyme supplements, which provide more protease activity in the proximal duodenum, may be more effective than supplements that are coated.

The somatostatin analogue octreotide inhibits pancreatic secretion and has visceral analgesic effects. Clinical trials are in progress to ascertain the utility of this drug in patients with painful chronic pancreatitis. Octreotide also may have a role in the management of refractory pancreatic fistulas or pseudocysts.

Endoscopic therapy can control pain in some patients who have a prominent stricture in the proximal pancreatic duct. In most

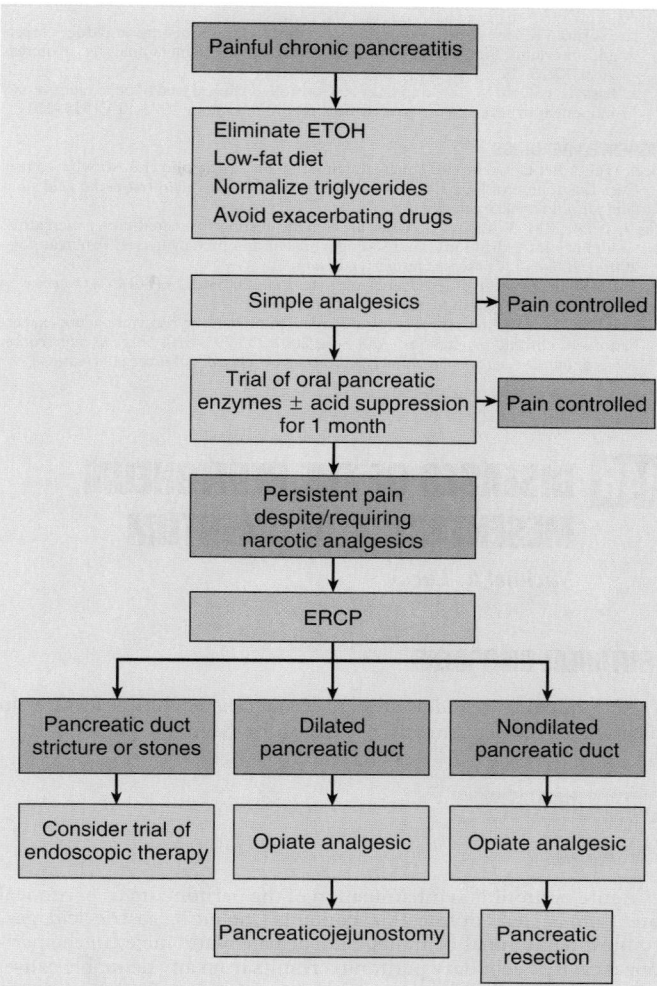

FIGURE 145–6 • Approach to the patient with painful chronic pancreatitis. ERCP = endoscopic retrograde cholangiopancreatography; ETOH = alcohol.

cases, dilation is followed by stent placement across the stricture. Pain improves in 55 to 100% of patients during a follow-up period of 2 to 69 months.

If all measures fail to relieve pain, surgery should be considered. Patients who have ductal dilation have a 60% chance of obtaining pain relief if they undergo either a partial resection with pancreaticojejunostomy or a lateral pancreaticojejunostomy (modified Puestow procedure). In patients who have ductal obstruction and dilation, the modified Puestow pancreaticojejunostomy relieves pain in about 60% of patients with morbidity less than 5% and mortality less than 2%. For patients with moderate-to-severe parenchymal disease and no ductal dilation, partial pancreatic resection can reduce pain in about 50% of cases.

MANAGEMENT OF PANCREATIC INSUFFICIENCY. Pancreatic steatorrhea should be treated with pancreatic enzyme replacement. At least 25,000 to 30,000 U of lipase per meal are necessary to provide adequate lipolysis, so patients must take 2 to 10 pills with each meal, depending on the preparation. Most patients on this regimen achieve satisfactory nutritional status and become relatively asymptomatic. A reduction in dietary fat also can help alleviate symptoms. In some patients, the use of enteric-coated preparations may be necessary because their gastric acid can destroy pancreatic enzymes; an H_2 receptor antagonist or proton pump inhibitor should be reserved for patients who cannot achieve adequate relief by these maneuvers. If all the aforementioned measures are ineffective, the diagnosis must be reaffirmed (by pancreatic function testing), and other contributing causes (celiac sprue, terminal ileal disease, or bacterial overgrowth) must be excluded.

1. Sharma VK, Howden CW: Prophylactic antibiotic administration reduces sepsis and mortality in acute necrotizing pancreatitis: A meta-analysis. Pancreas 2001;22:28–31.
2. Bassi C, Falconi M, Talamini G, et al: Controlled clinical trial of pefloxacin versus imipenem in severe acute pancreatitis. Gastroenterology 1998;115:1513–1517.

SUGGESTED READINGS

Boeck WG, Adler G, Gress TM: Pancreatic function tests: When to choose, what to use. Curr Gastroenterol Rep 2001;3:95–100. *The secretin-caerulein test is the gold standard for mild to moderate disease.*

Ellis J, Lerch MM, Whitcomb DC, et al: Genetic testing for hereditary pancreatitis: Guidelines for indications, counselling, consent and privacy issues. Pancreatology 2001;1:405–415. *Consensus recommendations.*

Mitchell RM, Byrne MF, Baillie J: Pancreatitis. Lancet 2003;361:1447–1455. *Overview of the genetics, pathogenesis, diagnosis, and treatment.*

Nealon WM, Matin S: Analysis of surgical success in preventing recurrent acute exacerbations in chronic pancreatitis. Ann Surg 2001;233:793–800. *Surgical intervention seems to improve outcome in patients with recurrent episodes of acute pancreatitis.*

146 DISEASES OF THE PERITONEUM, MESENTERY, AND OMENTUM

Michael R. Lucey

PERITONEAL DISORDERS

Abdominal pain and ascites are characteristic clinical features in disorders of the peritoneum. Ascites is discussed in Chapter 156.

ACUTE PERITONITIS

Definition

Acute peritonitis is inflammation of the peritoneum or peritoneal fluid from bacteria or intestinal contents (including gastric acid, gastrointestinal luminal contents, bile, or pancreatic juice) in the peritoneal cavity. Secondary peritonitis results from any definable cause, such as perforation of a viscus owing to acute appendicitis or diverticulitis, perforation of an ulcer (peptic ulcer, Crohn's disease, malignancy), and trauma, including iatrogenic intervention (e.g., surgery, needle biopsies). Primary peritonitis, including spontaneous bacterial peritonitis (SBP), refers to peritonitis arising without a recognizable preceding cause. Tertiary peritonitis, which is persistent intra-abdominal sepsis without a discrete focus of infection, generally follows surgical treatment of prior severe peritonitis and occurs in severely ill patients in intensive care units, especially patients who are immunosuppressed.

Prognostic Factors

Peritonitis after acute appendicitis or a perforated peptic ulcer occurring in an otherwise healthy patient is associated with a low mortality, whereas peritonitis after elective surgery, trauma, or pancreatitis has a high mortality regardless of the patient's overall clinical setting. The prognosis for severe peritonitis has not changed in 50 years despite the advent of broad-spectrum antibiotics, critical care units, and radical approaches to eliminate bacterial contamination of the peritoneal cavity. The outcome in severe peritonitis is dictated by the patient's overall health, including nutritional status, immunocompetence, and systemic factors, such as cardiac and renal function.

Clinical Manifestations

The classic features of acute peritonitis are abdominal pain, abdominal tenderness, and the absence of bowel sounds. Severe, sudden-onset abdominal pain suggests a ruptured viscus. The clinical signs of peritoneal irritation include abdominal tenderness, rebound tenderness, and eventually abdominal rigidity. In florid cases, these signs and symptoms are accompanied by fever, hypotension, tachycardia, and acidosis. Although this clinical pattern is characteristic, acute peritonitis frequently may lack these features.

SBP arising in ascites is often subtle in manifestation (see later). Acute peritonitis arising in elderly or immunosuppressed patients may lack the features of peritoneal irritation or systemic decompensation. Similarly, in patients with tertiary peritonitis, classic signs and symptoms may be absent or suppressed, and the diagnosis may be suggested only by persistent leukocytosis or fever. In these atypical circumstances, a high index of suspicion is necessary.

Diagnosis

Plain abdominal radiographs can determine the presence of free air in the abdominal cavity, a characteristic finding of a perforated viscus. Computed tomography (CT) and/or ultrasonography can identify the presence of free fluid or an abscess. When peritonitis is associated with ascites, paracentesis is mandatory.

Rx Treatment

The three key elements of therapy for acute peritonitis are resuscitation, laparotomy, and antibiotics. Resuscitation with intravenous fluids and correction of metabolic and electrolyte disturbances are the initial steps. Laparotomy is a cornerstone of therapy for secondary or tertiary acute peritonitis to identify and repair the cause of the acute catastrophe, to evacuate pus, and to irrigate the peritoneal cavity. In some patients, when biliary peritonitis is accompanied by little systemic disturbance, careful conservative management with intravenous fluids and broad-spectrum antibiotics is adequate, and laparotomy can be avoided. The threshold for proceeding to laparotomy should be low, however, even in these circumstances. Broad-spectrum systemic antibiotics are crucial to cover bowel flora, including anaerobic species. Studies have shown cure rates of 80% or greater for a wide range of antibiotic regimens, including (1) ciprofloxacin plus metronidazole intravenously, (2) ciprofloxacin plus metronidazole intravenously with conversion to oral ciprofloxacin and metronidazole when oral feeding is resumed, (3) cefepime and metronidazole intravenously, and (4) single-agent administration of imipenen-cilastatin sodium or clinafloxacin intravenously. When peritonitis persists despite all standard measures, antifungal agents (e.g., amphotericin B or fluconazole) are appropriate for possible candidal infections.

PERITONEAL CARCINOMATOSIS

Peritoneal carcinomatosis is usually a result of metastatic spread from a gastrointestinal tumor or another intra-abdominal malignancy (Table 146–1). Less common causes include lymphoma, or other metastatic tumors; primary peritoneal mesotheliomas are rare.

Table 146–1 • CAUSES OF PERITONEAL CARCINOMATOSIS

PRIMARY DISORDERS OF THE PERITONEUM
Mesothelioma

METASTATIC SPREAD FROM
Gastrointestinal tumors
  Stomach
  Colon
  Pancreas
  Carcinoid
Other intra-abdominal organs
  Ovary
  Pseudomyxoma peritonei
Extra-abdominal primary tumors
  Breast
  Lung
Hematologic malignancy
  Lymphoma

SPONTANEOUS BACTERIAL PERITONITIS

Definition

SBP (Chapter 156), which has no obvious precipitating cause, occurs almost exclusively in cirrhotic patients but occasionally may complicate acute hepatic failure. SBP is a marker of severe hepatic failure and usually occurs in patients with low ascitic fluid protein content and elevated serum bilirubin. SBP develops in approximately 25% of patients with an ascitic fluid total protein content of less than 1 g/dL during 3 years of subsequent observation. The development of SBP is related to deficient opsonic activity in ascitic fluid. The offending organisms almost always are enteric gram-negative aerobes, such as *Escherichia coli* or *Klebsiella pneumoniae*, or gram-positive aerobes, particularly *Streptococcus pneumoniae*. Anaerobic organisms rarely cause SBP.

Clinical Manifestations

The clinical manifestations of SBP are often subtle. SBP must be suspected not only whenever a cirrhotic patient has fever and abdominal pain more typical of acute peritonitis, but also whenever a cirrhotic patient with ascites has a sudden deterioration in hepatic or renal function, worsening malaise, encephalopathy, or unexplained persistent leukocytosis, even in the absence of abdominal signs or symptoms typical of acute peritonitis. A high index of suspicion is also necessary whenever a patient with known established liver disease has features of sepsis or hepatic deterioration despite the absence of clinical ascites; small pockets of infected ascites may be present and detectable only by ultrasound or CT, and a presumptive diagnosis of SBP followed by empirical antibiotic therapy may be the wisest course.

Diagnosis

The key to establishing SBP is diagnostic paracentesis in which the ascitic fluid is found to have 250 or more polymorphonuclear cells per cubic millimeter. A greatly elevated polymorphonuclear cell count in ascites (e.g., >5000/mm³) suggests an intra-abdominal abscess or a secondary cause of peritonitis. Showing an organism in the ascitic fluid is helpful but not required for diagnosis. The chances of identifying an organism in ascites are enhanced by directly transferring ascitic fluid to blood culture media bottles before incubation, but even then no organism is identified in 30 to 50% of cases. SBP usually is caused by a single species so that multiple organisms on ascitic culture suggest a perforated viscus. In addition to inspecting and culturing ascitic fluid, all patients suspected of having SBP should have blood cultures, chest radiography, and urine microscopy and culture to identify blood-borne sepsis and to look for additional sites of infection.

℞ Treatment

Antibiotics are the cornerstone of managing SBP, and laparotomy has no place in therapy for SBP. Intravenous treatment with a broad-spectrum antibiotic regimen, such as cefotaxime, for 3 to 5 days is usually adequate, at which time efficacy can be determined by estimating the ascitic fluid polymorphonuclear cell count; the use of intravenous antibiotics can be discontinued if the polymorphonuclear cell count is less than 250/mm³. The most important negative prognostic factors are the presence of renal failure, onset of SBP while in the hospital, and elevated serum aminotransferase levels.

SBP recurs in 70% of patients in the first year after the initial episode, unless prophylactic antibiotics are used. The frequency of recurrence is greatest in patients with a low ascitic fluid total protein content and impaired hepatic synthetic function. The incidence of SBP can be reduced markedly in patients who are at risk for a first episode and in patients who already have had SBP with prophylactic antibiotics that cleanse the gut microflora, such as quinolones (norfloxacin once per day or ciprofloxacin once per week) or trimethoprim-sulfamethoxazole. Although prophylaxis reduces the incidence of SBP, mortality is related to the underlying hepatic dysfunction and is not affected.

PERITONEAL TUBERCULOSIS

Tuberculosis (Chapter 341) is an important cause of peritonitis worldwide and, with the advent of the acquired immunodeficiency syndrome epidemic, has re-emerged in the developed world (Table 146-2). Patients with peritoneal tuberculosis frequently have concomitant cirrhosis (Chapter 156), which may be implicated incorrectly as the source of ascites and obscure the presence of tuberculous peritonitis. The serum-ascites albumin gradient is low in patients with peritoneal tuberculosis without portal hypertension or cirrhosis, but it is variably high or low in cirrhotic patients with tuberculosis. Tuberculosis in human immunodeficiency virus (HIV)–infected patients is characterized by newly acquired infection rather than a recrudescence of quiescent infection, a high likelihood of tuberculosis among at-risk persons who are exposed to tuberculosis, a high rate of clinical rather than quiescent tuberculosis, rapidly progressive tuberculosis that frequently has extrapulmonary involvement, and the emergence of tuberculosis strains that are resistant to one or more of the standard antituberculous chemotherapeutic agents.

Clinical Manifestations

Ascites is almost invariable, whereas abdominal swelling and pain are common (Table 146-3). Many patients have accompanying systemic signs and symptoms, such as fever, weight loss, and anemia. A high index of suspicion is necessary because intra-abdominal tuberculosis may mimic malignancy. Examples include peritoneal tuberculosis associated with an elevated serum CA 125 in women being misdiagnosed as having ovarian cancer or intra-abdominal tuberculosis arising in recipients of solid organ transplants being construed as post-transplant lymphoproliferative disorder.

Diagnosis

Paracentesis reveals a lymphocytosis but rarely shows acid-fast bacilli on smear (Table 146-4). Culture of ascitic fluid has a higher diagnostic yield but with a 4- to 6-week delay; the potential

Table 146-2 • RISK FACTORS FOR INTRA-ABDOMINAL TUBERCULOSIS

HIV infection
Imunosuppressive therapy
Advanced age
Intravenous drug use/alcoholism/cirrhosis
Immigration from an endemic area
Poverty
Incarceration/long-stay care
Peritoneal dialysis

HIV = human immunodeficiency virus.

Table 146-3 • CLINICAL CHARACTERISTICS OF PERITONEAL TUBERCULOSIS*

FEATURE	%
Ascites	80–100
Abdominal swelling	65–100
Abdominal pain	36–93
Weight loss	37–87
Fever	56–100
Diarrhea	9–27
Abdominal tenderness	65–87
Anemia	46–68
Positive PPD test	55–100

*The percentages represent the frequency with which these features have been observed in peritoneal tuberculosis. These data antedate studies of tuberculosis in human immunodeficiency virus–infected persons.
PPD = purified protein derivative.

Table 146–4 • DIAGNOSTIC TESTS OF PERITONEAL TUBERCULOSIS

DIAGNOSTIC TEST	COMMENT
Paracentesis	
With smear	<3% positive
With culture	<20–80% positive
With ascitic ADA measurement	>30.0 U/L
	Low ascitic protein (i.e., cirrhosis) may cause false-negative results
	Not validated in U.S. patients
With LDH >90 U/L	
Laparoscopy with biopsy	Best test
	Up to 100% positive
Needle biopsy of the peritoneum	Largely replaced by laparoscopy
Diagnostic laparotomy	Should be considered if laparoscopy not available

ADA = adenosine deaminase; LDH = lactate dehydrogenase.

immediate value of molecular diagnostic methods has not yet been defined. An elevated ascitic concentration of adenosine deaminase, a marker of T-lymphocyte and macrophage activation, has been reported to be a sensitive and specific diagnostic test for tuberculous peritonitis in developing countries where laparoscopy and other diagnostic tests are scarce; a cutoff level of 30 U/L corresponded to sensitivity and specificity of 94 and 92%, respectively, in one series from South Africa. The value of adenosine deaminase in diagnosing tuberculous peritonitis in the United States is less clear, however. An ascitic fluid lactate dehydrogenase level greater than 90 U/L may be a useful indicator of peritoneal tuberculosis regardless of the presence of cirrhosis and portal hypertension. A definitive diagnosis of peritoneal tuberculosis is made best by laparoscopy and directed peritoneal biopsy. The occasional patient with fibroadhesive tuberculous peritonitis without ascites should not undergo laparoscopy.

Rx Treatment

Treatment of tuberculous peritonitis involves standard protocols using two or three drugs, usually for 9 months (Chapter 341). All tuberculosis isolates must be tested for drug susceptibility. HIV-infected persons who are coinfected with a strain of tuberculosis that is susceptible to first-line chemotherapeutic agents usually respond well to standard therapeutic protocols, but HIV-infected persons with resistant strains have a high mortality.

PERITONITIS IN CONTINUOUS AMBULATORY PERITONEAL DIALYSIS

Infection in the washout dialysate is common in patients undergoing continuous ambulatory peritoneal dialysis, often unaccompanied by systemic disturbance and characterized by mild abdominal pain and low-grade fever (Chapter 118). Cytologic analysis of the cloudy effluent shows a high white cell count. Most causative organisms are gram positive, especially *Staphylococcus epidermidis*, followed by *Staphylococcus aureus* and streptococci. Treatment should be started promptly after recognizing a cloudy effluent before culture results are available. Treatment consists of infusing broad-spectrum antibiotics into the peritoneum through the abdominal wall catheter; the catheter is not removed, and dialysis is not interrupted. For the few patients who fail to respond to prompt outpatient therapy, intravenous antibiotics and catheter removal are necessary.

MISCELLANEOUS FORMS OF PERITONITIS

In familial Mediterranean fever (Chapter 181), the most common recurring feature is peritonitis, which affects more than 90% of symptomatic patients. It is manifested as episodic abdominal pain and fever. Colchicine may reduce the frequency and severity of attacks. Systemic vasculitic syndromes, such as systemic lupus erythematosus, occasionally may involve the peritoneum and present as unexplained ascites.

Table 146–5 • DISORDERS OF THE MESENTERY AND OMENTUM

MESENTERY
Primary inflammatory diseases
  Mesenteric lipodystrophy
  Mesenteric panniculitis
  Retractile mesenteritis
Mesenteric cysts
  Embryonic
  Traumatic/acquired
  Neoplastic
  Infective
Mesenteric tumors
  Benign: lipoma, hemangioma, leiomyoma, ganglioneuroma, fibroma (Gardner's syndrome)
  Malignant: various sarcomas; metastatic tumors
Mesenteric vascular insufficiency
  Acute
  Chronic

OMENTUM
Tumor
  Benign: fibroma, lipoma, hemangioma, neuroma, lymphangioma, leiomyoma, mesothelioma
  Malignant: primary metastases—especially ovary, stomach, colon
Cysts
Vascular insufficiency
  Torsion
  Infarction
Inflammation: usually secondary to peritonitis

DISEASES OF THE MESENTERY AND OMENTUM

Mesenteric lipodystrophy, mesenteric panniculitis, and retractile mesenteritis (Table 146–5) probably represent different manifestations of the same rare idiopathic disorder. Mesenteric panniculitis consists of diffuse fatty infiltration of the mesentery, which is replaced by fat necrosis, fibrosis, and calcification. Retractile mesenteritis is at the fibrotic end of this spectrum. Patients with these conditions have intermittent abdominal pain, abdominal swelling, and an abdominal mass. Many patients are asymptomatic, however, and changes suggesting mesenteric fat deposition or fibrosis may be detected serendipitously on CT scanning. Otherwise the diagnosis usually is made at laparotomy. When recognized, surgical resection should not be undertaken unless the fibrosis is causing intestinal obstruction.

Cysts and tumors, including desmoid mesenteric fibromas that are part of Gardner's syndrome, rarely are seen. Rare diseases of the omentum include mass lesions, acute vascular insufficiency from torsion or infarction, and inflammatory processes.

SUGGESTED READINGS

Burgess LJ, Swanepoel CG, Taljaard JJ: The use of adenosine deaminase as a diagnostic tool for peritoneal tuberculosis. Tuberculosis 2001;81:243–248. *Ascitic fluid adenosine deaminase levels greater than 30 U/L have a high sensitivity and specificity for tuberculous peritonitis.*

Daskalogiannaki M, Voloudaki A, Prassopoulos P, et al: CT evaluation of mesenteric panniculitis: Prevalence and associated diseases. AJR Am J Roentgenol 2000;174:427–431. *In more than 7600 abdominal computed tomography scans, 49 patients had mesenteric panniculitis: 34 with coexisting malignancies, 11 with coexisting benign disorders, and 4 idiopathic.*

Salvaggio MR, Pappas PG: Current concepts in the management of fungal peritonitis. Curr Infect Dis Rep 2003;5:120–124. *Approach to this unusual form of peritonitis.*

147 DISEASES OF THE RECTUM AND ANUS

Heidi Nelson

Anatomy

The anal canal is a 2- to 4-cm long muscular cuff (Fig. 147–1). It is distinctly different from the rectum, but some of its components,

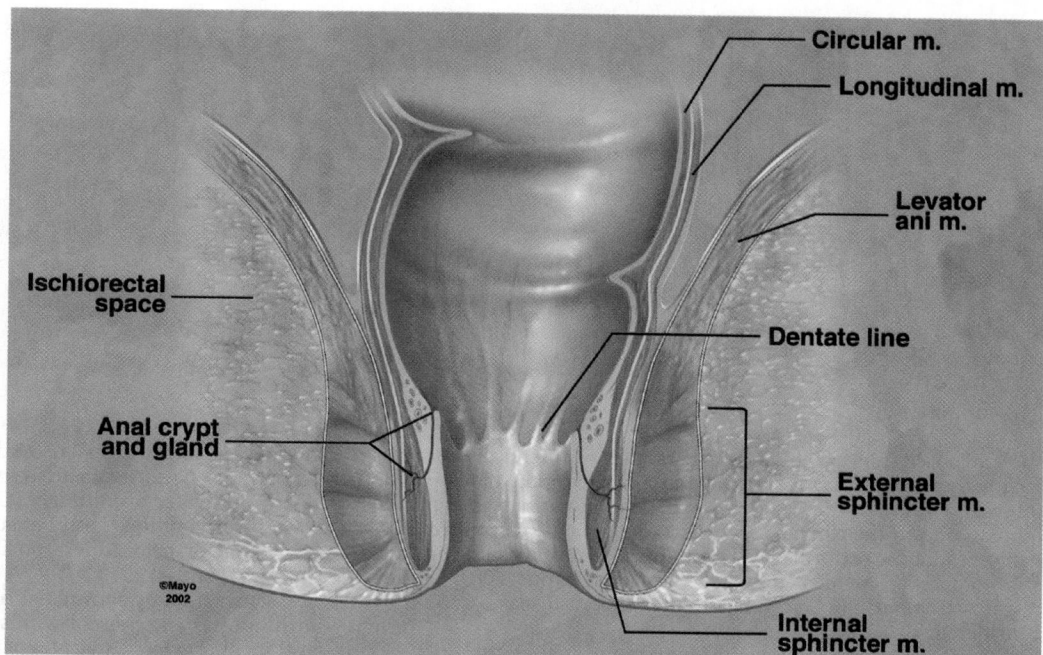

FIGURE 147–1 • Anorectal anatomy. m = muscle. (By permission of Mayo Foundation.)

such as the mucosal lining, are essentially a continuance of rectal structures, and they work together to regulate defecation. The internal sphincter, which is an involuntary muscle innervated by the autonomic nervous system, must relax for rectal emptying. The external sphincter, which is a voluntary skeletal muscle innervated by the internal pudendal nerve, can contract for a short period of time to delay rectal emptying.

The anal canal transitions from rectal columnar epithelium and sensory responses to distention, to perianal skin with squamous epithelium and responses to thermal and traumatic cutaneous stimuli. The dentate line represents the transition point between these two types of linings. Accordingly, ulcerative colitis, adenocarcinomas, and internal hemorrhoids occur cephalad to the dentate line, whereas squamous carcinomas, hidradenitis suppurativa, and external hemorrhoids occur caudad to this line.

Diagnostic Evaluation

For acute problems, the history should focus on the duration, intensity, and character of symptoms. For chronic and recurring problems, the possibility of underlying inflammatory bowel disease (Chapter 142) or cancer (Chapter 200) should be considered, and diagnostic tests should be ordered accordingly. The anus can be examined with the patient lying in the left lateral decubitus position or lying prone in the jackknife position. Gentle retraction of the buttocks allows for inspection followed by palpation of the anal canal to assess for skin conditions, sphincter strength, and the presence of masses or inflammation. A rigid proctoscope or anoscope best visualizes the anal canal and distal rectum. Flexible sigmoidoscopy or colonoscopy best evaluates the proximal bowel (complete evaluation is particularly indicated for bleeding or changes in bowel habits).

Hemorrhoids

The normal anal canal contains cushions located typically in the left lateral, right anterior, and right posterior positions within the canal. Anal cushions are discrete areas of thickened submucosa containing blood vessels, smooth muscle, and elastic and connective tissues. Repetitive downward pressure gradually exaggerates the cushion and produces a hemorrhoid. Internal hemorrhoids originate above the dentate line and therefore rarely cause pain; they typically present with symptoms of bleeding or prolapse. Anoscopy and inspection with straining give the best assessment of the location and extent of prolapse. The severity of the symptoms dictates the management (Table 147–1). For fourth degree prolapse, urgent hemorrhoidectomy may be required to prevent tissue necrosis.

Table 147–1 • INTERNAL HEMORRHOIDS: GRADING AND MANAGEMENT

GRADE	SYMPTOMS AND SIGNS	MANAGEMENT
First degree	Bleeding; no prolapse	Dietary modifications* Rubber band ligation Coagulation
Second degree	Prolapse with spontaneous reduction Bleeding, seepage	Rubber band ligation Coagulation Dietary modifications
Third degree	Prolapse requiring digital reduction Bleeding, seepage	Surgical hemorrhoidectomy Rubber band ligations Dietary modifications
Fourth degree	Prolapsed, cannot be reduced Strangulated	Surgical hemorrhoidectomy Urgent hemorrhoidectomy

*Dietary modifications include increasing consumption of fiber, bran, or psyllium and water. Dietary modifications are always appropriate for the management of hemorrhoids and to prevent recurrence after banding and/or surgery.

From Nelson H, Dozois RR: Anus. *In* Townsend CM (ed): Sabiston Textbook of Surgery, 16th ed. Philadelphia, WB Saunders, 2001, p 979, with permission.

In contrast, external hemorrhoids originate distal to the dentate line and typically present as swellings and problems with hygiene. Thrombosis of the underlying vessels can cause severe anal pain (Fig. 147–2). Stool softeners, sitz baths, and excision can ameliorate symptoms.

Anal Fissures

Anal fissure is one of the most common causes of anal pain (see Fig. 147–2). Anal fissures typically occur as linear ulcers just inside the anal verge, most commonly with a posterior commissure. The classic symptoms of pain and bleeding on defecation may be severe and have acute onset, or they may be insidious and chronic.

An initiating event, such as strain from constipation, probably produces a small tear in the anal lining. Local anal pain from the tear generates spasm of the underlying internal sphincter muscle, and this hypertonia reduces blood flow, thereby causing mucosal ischemia.

The diagnosis can be confirmed by gentle retraction near the anal verge to expose and visualize the ulcer. Acute ulcers tend to be red with rough edges, whereas chronic fissures tend to be white and

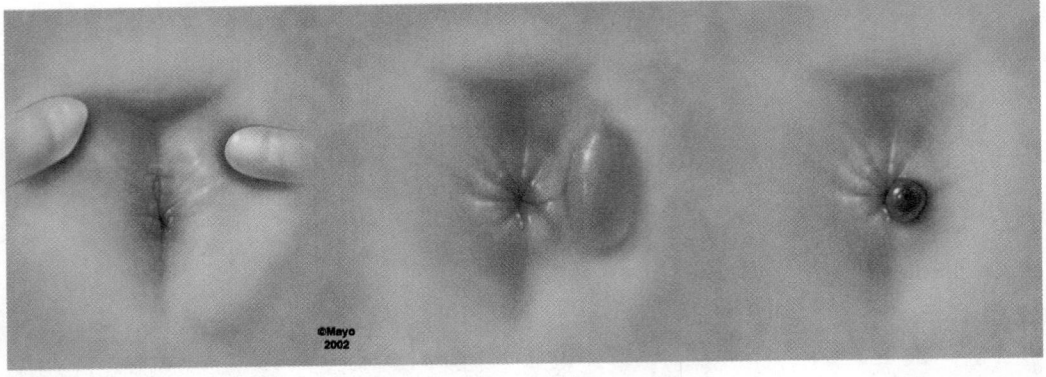

FIGURE 147–2 • Causes of anal pain. (By permission of Mayo Foundation.)

show exposed internal sphincter fibers; they also tend to be associated with a sentinel tag externally and a hypertrophied anal papilla internally. The resting tone of the anal sphincter is typically quite tense and the pain so severe that digital and anoscopic examinations cannot be performed. When fissures are multiple, have unusual appearances, or are located laterally, cancer (Chapter 200), Crohn's disease (Chapter 142), or sexually transmitted diseases should be considered.

Medical management of acute and chronic anal fissures includes sitz baths and the topical applications of anesthetics. Long-term preventive measures are modifications of diet and bowel habits, as well as the use of bulking agents or temporary stool softeners. The internal sphincter can be relaxed by nitric oxide donors (e.g., either nitroglycerin 0.2% twice daily or isosorbide-dinitrate 2.5 mg three times daily as topical therapy for 4 to 8 weeks).[1] Approximately 70% heal and require no further management. Those who fail can be treated with botulinum injections or with a surgical sphincterotomy.[2]

Anorectal Abscess

Anorectal abscess should always be considered in patients with acute anal pain because a delay in diagnosis can lead to necrotizing infections, particularly in the immunocompromised host. Most anorectal infections arise from an obstructed crypt and an infected gland (see Fig. 147–1). The infection can present as a superficial perianal or ischiorectal abscess, both of which are usually easy to diagnose because of obvious erythema and a tender, fluctuant mass (see Fig. 147–2). In the otherwise healthy, nontoxic patient, these abscesses can be incised and drained in the office. A deep abscess may require needle localization before incision and drainage. More difficult to diagnose are abscesses in the intersphincteric, intermuscular, postanal, and supralevator spaces; these abscesses commonly require drainage under anesthesia. In rare circumstances, an abscess in the anorectal tissues may originate from an intra-abdominal process such as malignancy, Crohn's disease, or diverticulitis.

Anorectal Fistula

Approximately 30% of patients who are treated acutely for an anorectal abscess subsequently develop a chronic fibrous tract that typically follows the course of the previous suppuration, from the internal crypt to the external opening where drainage occurred spontaneously or surgically. Treatment is indicated to manage symptoms of purulent or feculent drainage and to prevent the recurrent infections that occur whenever the tract becomes occluded and fecal material accumulates.

Although it is typically easy to identify the external opening of an anorectal fistula (also called fistula in ano), it may be difficult to visualize the internal opening. Sometimes a fibrous tract can be palpated or located via a probe in the office, but other fistulas can be delineated only in the operating room. For anterior fistulas in which the external opening is close to the anus, the internal opening is typically in a straight radial line toward the anus. For posterior fistulas, or those with a horseshoe-type or long tract, the opening is usually in the posterior midline.

For simple fistulas arising from cryptoglandular sources, treatment is fistulotomy, seton placement, or fibrin glue injection. For complex or refractory anal fistulas, or those associated with an internal opening proximal to the dentate line, the diagnosis of Crohn's disease must be entertained; the gastrointestinal tract should be evaluated and treated accordingly (Chapter 142). Surgical drainage and seton placement for control of suppuration, antibiotics, anti–tumor necrosis factor medications, and fibrin glue injections can treat Crohn's anorectal fistulas.

Rectovaginal or anovaginal fistulas often occur following childbirth injuries and present with sphincter damage and symptoms of fecal incontinence. Surgical repair is required.

For fistulas distal to the dentate line, hidradenitis suppurativa should be considered. This condition is a chronic inflammatory skin process that can affect the perianal tissues, with apocrine gland obstruction leading to local abscesses and sinuses. In addition to acute treatment of the infections, preventive measures, such as frequent hygiene, should be instituted.

On rare occasions, neglected rectal cancers present as perianal fistulas. Alternatively, cancers can develop in chronic fistula tracts.

Pruritus Ani

Pruritus ani or perianal itching can be associated with diverse conditions ranging from simple hygiene problems to systemic diseases, such as diabetes mellitus. The history should focus on changes in health status, such as new systemic illnesses, new medications, and/or changes in bowel habits or diet. Excoriation suggests intense itching. Biopsies are indicated if there is a suspicion of dermatologic conditions, particularly Bowen's or Paget's disease. For new-onset pruritus, endoscopy may be useful to exclude a rectal neoplasm, such as a large mucous-secreting villous polyp.

Unless a specific cause is discovered, management is symptomatic. Insufficient hygiene can cause itching owing to residual fecal material, but excessive hygiene removes the protective natural oils from the perianal skin. Optimal cleansing is with warm water without soaps, followed by gentle drying, preferably using warm air rather than abrasive towels. Cornstarch or talc powder may be applied to maintain moisture-free perianal conditions.

Stool bulking agents and modifications in diets may be required to improve daily bowel function. If food diaries suggest that certain foods (e.g., citrus fruits and juices, colas, coffees, teas, alcoholic beverages, nuts, popcorn, and milk) are associated with the pruritus, their reduction or elimination may alleviate symptoms.

Sexually Transmitted Diseases

Sexually transmitted diseases involve the rectum and anus primarily in persons who practice anal intercourse. Nonviral sexually transmitted diseases (Chapter 345) may produce pruritus, bloody or mucopurulent rectal discharge, pain, diarrhea, and fever. Etiologic agents include *Neisseria gonorrhoeae* (Chapter 346), *Treponema pallidum* (Chapter 349), *Chlamydia* (Chapter 345), *Shigella* (Chapter 326), *Campylobacter* (Chapter 327), and *Haemophilus ducreyi* (Chapter 364). Endoscopic evaluations and cultures of stool or anorectal swabs facilitate diagnosis and treatment based on the causative agent.

Viral sexually transmitted diseases most typically present as pain, discharge, and/or bleeding with physical features characteristic of the specific causative agents. Herpes simplex, which presents as vesicles and/or ulcers, can be diagnosed with cultures and treated with acyclovir. Human papillomavirus-6 and -11 are commonly associated with benign warts or condyloma acuminata. Human papillomavirus-16 and -18 are more often associated with dysplasia and malignancy. Condyloma may be small and external only, or they may be extensive, coalescing, and internal (Fig. 147–3). Medical managements include podophyllin (0.5% self-applied sequentially for 3 days) and imiquimod (5% cream applied nightly, three times per week for 6 weeks). Surgical therapies include excision, laser, and cauterization; excised specimens should be examined histologically to exclude malignancy. The lesions of molluscum contagiosum are painless, round, and umbilicated. Human immunodeficiency virus infections involving the anus can present as painful anal ulcers or with lower gastrointestinal symptoms, such as bleeding, proctalgia, and diarrhea.

Parasitic sexually transmitted diseases are associated with systemic symptoms such as abdominal cramping, fever, and bloody diarrhea. Common agents include *Entamoeba histolytica* (Chapter 399), *Giardia lamblia* (Chapter 398), and *Isospora belli* (Chapter 416).

Fecal Incontinence

Fecal incontinence is the inability of the sphincter complex to contract sufficiently to control the release of gas, stool, or diarrhea. In patients with symptoms of leakage or incontinence, the evaluation should focus on testing the pressure, nerve, and anatomic profiles of the anal sphincter muscles (Fig. 147–4). Diet and bulking agents may improve the consistency and regularity of bowel function. In difficult or extreme cases of diarrhea, constipating medications, such as Imodium may be required. If constipation is complicating the ability to control bowel evacuation, laxatives or enemas may be helpful.

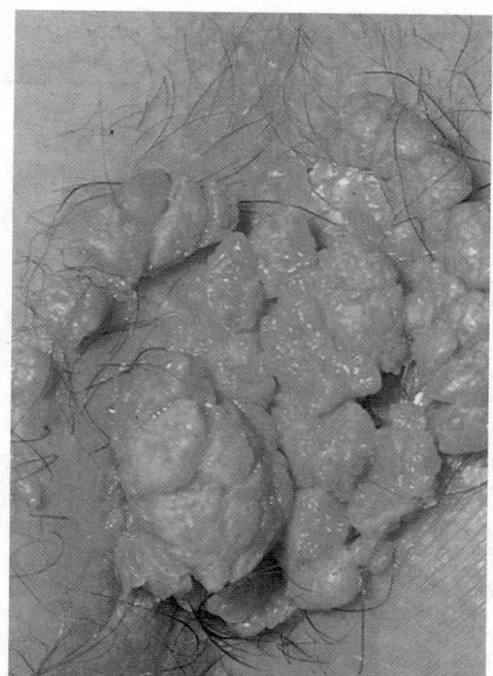

FIGURE 147–3 • Perianal condylomata resulting from human papillomavirus infection. They are usually sexually transmitted and are most common in homosexual men. (From Forbes CD, Jackson WF: Color Atlas and Text of Clinical Medicine, 3rd ed. London, Mosby, 2003, with permission.)

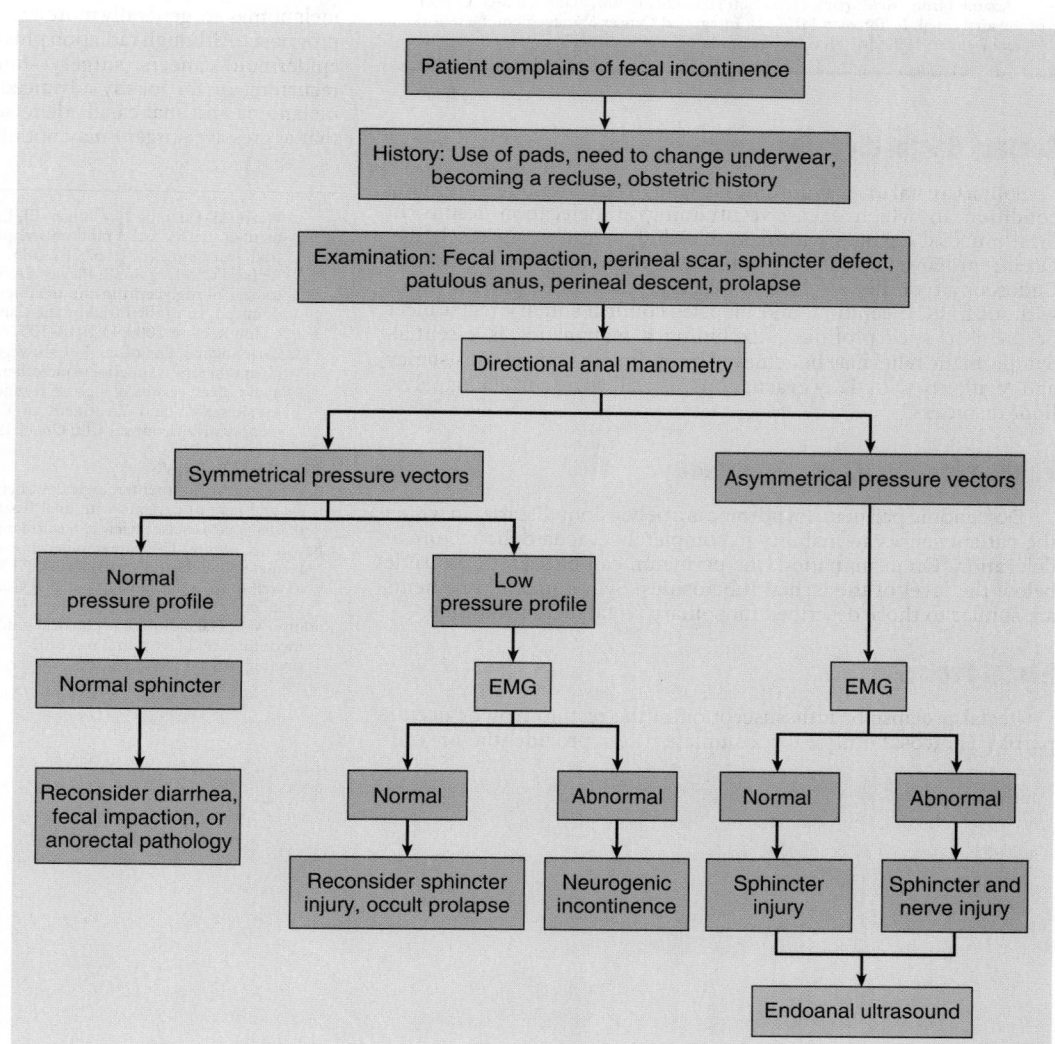

FIGURE 147–4 • Algorithm for the investigation of fecal incontinence. EMG = electromyogram. (From Sagar PM, Pemberton JH: Anorectal and pelvic floor function: relevance to continence, incontinence, and constipation. Gastroenterol Clin North Am 1996;25:163–182.)

Table 147–2 • SUMMARY OF THERAPIES FOR ANAL NEOPLASMS*

Bowen's disease (intraepithelial squamous cell carcinoma)
  Accurate lesion mapping
  Wide local excision with flap repair as indicated
  Exclude presence of locally invasive component and underlying
    gynecologic malignancy
Paget's disease (intraepithelial adenocarcinoma)
  Accurate lesion mapping
  Wide local excision with flap repair as indicated
  Exclude underlying malignancy
  APR and chemoradiation if invasive adenocarcinoma present
Basal cell and anal margin squamous cell carcinoma
  Local excision with clear margins
  Radiation or chemotherapy in poor prognosis lesions or recurrence as
    indicated
Verrucous carcinoma
  Wide local excision; APR if very extensive
  Combined modality therapy if transformation to SCC has occurred
Epidermoid cancer
  Combined modality, external-beam radiation therapy plus 5-FU +
    mitomycin
  Local excision if favorable T1
  APR if incontinent, or local treatment failure or recurrence after
    combined chemoradiation
  Triple-modality therapy in bulky T3 and T4 lesions (role of APR
    controversial)
Adenocarcinoma
  APR with 5-FU and radiation therapy as indicated, based on stage
Melanoma
  APR or local excision (controversial) if potentially curable

*APR = abdominal perineal resection; SCC = squamous cell carcinoma; 5-FU = 5-fluorouracil; T1 = tumor 2.0 cm or less than greatest dimension; T3 = tumor >5.0 cm; T4 = tumor of any size that invades adjacent organs.
Adapted from McMurrick PJ, Nelson H, Goldberg RM, Haddock MG: Cancer of the anal canal. *In* Torosian MH (ed): Integrated Cancer Management. New York, Marcel Dekker, 1999, p 200. Courtesy of Marcel Dekker, Inc.

Solitary Rectal Ulcer Syndrome

Solitary rectal ulcer syndrome is a benign but oftentimes disabling condition in which excessive straining at defecation results in focal mucosal changes with pain, bleeding, and mucous discharge. Occult prolapse or internal intussusception may be implicated. Endoscopy typically discloses a raised erythematous patch with or without frank ulceration, and biopsies confirm solitary rectal ulcer or colitis cystica profunda. Excluding a malignancy is essential. Symptomatic relief may be achieved by optimizing bowel consistency and regularity with daily evacuations, as well as by correcting pelvic floor disorders.

Descending Perineum Syndrome

Descending perineum syndrome is a pelvic floor disorder in which the patient senses an inability to completely evacuate the rectum at defecation. On examination, the perineum can be seen to protrude below the level of the ischial tuberosities. Symptomatic treatments are similar to those described for solitary rectal ulcer syndrome.

Rectal Prolapse

Rectal prolapse or intussusception of the rectum may be occult, partial (mucosal only), or complete (i.e., procidentia or full-thickness protrusion beyond the anus). It tends to occur more often in women, in patients with straining conditions, or in patients with chronic mental conditions. The patient typically describes a rectal bulge while straining, and this sign may be reproduced during the examination to determine the degree and extent of prolapse, which may be few to several centimeters in length.

Full-thickness rectal prolapse should be surgically corrected with a perineal or abdominal procedure. Patients recover more rapidly after a perineal approach, but its higher recurrence rate makes it best suited for the frail, elderly, or high-risk patient. The abdominal approach, which typically involves resection and/or rectopexy and can be done laparoscopically, offers the best chance for prolonged relief.

Neoplasms of the Anus

Anal tumors are rare, representing only a small fraction of lower gastrointestinal tract malignancies, and they are highly diverse (Table 147–2). Tumors of the anal margin occur in the hair-bearing perianal skin, outside or beyond the anal verge; they include Bowen's, Paget's, basal cell, and verrucous carcinomas. Some squamous cell carcinomas also occur in this region and should be treated as skin tumors, whereas more proximal squamous cell carcinomas behave more aggressively and require more radical treatments.

There is often a continuum between benign and malignant neoplasms. For example, verrucous carcinomas are best considered as intermediate lesions between benign condyloma acuminata and malignant squamous cell carcinomas. Similarly, although Bowen's disease is an intraepithelial neoplasm, it is rarely associated with malignancy and rarely metastasizes. In contrast, Paget's disease is often associated with underlying malignancy, and it has a poor prognosis.

Tumors of the anal canal, including epidermoid (squamous, basaloid, cloacogenic, or mucoepidermoid) cancers, adenocarcinomas, and melanomas are generally more aggressive and associated with a poorer prognosis. Although radiation plus chemotherapy is standard for most epidermoid cancers, surgery should be considered for refractory, recurrent, or for locally advanced lesions (see Table 147–2). **3** For melanoma and anal canal adenocarcinoma, the prognosis is so poor that aggressive surgery may not offer benefit over local excision.

1. Werre AJ, Palamba HW, Bilgen EJ, Eggink WF: Isosorbide dinitrate in the treatment of anal fissure: A randomised, prospective, double blind, placebo-controlled trial. Eur J Surg 2001;167:382–385.
2. Richard CS, Gregoire R, Plewes EA, et al: Internal sphincterotomy is superior to topical nitroglycerin in the treatment of chronic anal fissure. Results of a randomized, controlled trial by the Canadian Colorectal Surgical Trials Group. Dis Colon Rectum 2000;43:1048–1057.
3. Bartelink H, Roelofsen F, Eschwege F, et al: Concomitant radiotherapy and chemotherapy is superior to radiotherapy alone in the treatment of locally advanced anal cancer: results of a phase II randomized trial of the European Organization for Research and Treatment of Cancer Radiotherapy and Gastrointestinal Cooperative Groups. J Clin Oncol 1997;15:2040–2049.

SUGGESTED READINGS

AGA (American Gastroenterological Association): AGA technical review of the diagnosis and care of patients with anal fissure. Gastroenterology 2003;124:235–245. *A thorough yet concise review of medical and surgical management.*
Chawla AK, Willett CG: Squamous cell carcinoma of the anal canal and anal margin. Hematol Oncol Clin North Am 2001;15:321–344. *Anatomy and histology of the anus, as well as the epidemiology, pathology, and clinical management of tumors of the anal canal and anal margin.*
Rudolph WR, Galandiuk S: A practical guide to the diagnosis and management of fecal incontinence. Mayo Clin Proc 2002;77:271–275. *Current practices of diagnosing and treating patients with fecal incontinence, with an emphasis on surgical options.*

148 APPROACH TO THE PATIENT WITH LIVER DISEASE

Don W. Powell

The scope of practice of liver diseases has expanded dramatically in the past decade, primarily because of the success of liver transplantation (1-year survival rate of 90% and 5-year survival rate of 75%; Chapter 157), the development of effective drug treatment for viral hepatitis (Chapters 151 and 152), and safer techniques for diagnosing liver disease and treating obstructive jaundice (Chapter 158).

The current epidemic of hepatitis C, which involves more than 4 million people infected through contaminated blood transfusions (before its serologic identification) and injection drug use, will lead to the development of cirrhosis or hepatocellular carcinoma (Chapter 202) in a significant percentage. As effective and simpler therapeutic approaches develop, the primary care physician is likely to play an increasingly important role.

The major function of the liver is to synthesize and metabolize proteins, carbohydrates, and fats, as well as to detoxify normal metabolic wastes (e.g., urea) and ingested drugs and chemicals. Except for gamma globulin, which is synthesized by B lymphocytes, and some natural anticoagulants or coagulants, such as von Willebrand's factor, which is produced by the endothelium, most of the plasma proteins are synthesized by the liver. Albumin is made at a rate of 15 g/d, but its long half-life, about 20 days, maintains plasma albumin levels for a substantial period of time, even if synthesis ceases because of nutritional deficiencies or cytokines produced in hepatic disease. The liver synthesizes 11 of the 13 blood-coagulating factors, including fibrinogen (I), prothrombin (II), and factors V, VII, IX, X, XII, and XIII (Chapter 178). Factors II, VII, IX, and X, as well as the antithrombotic proteins S and C synthesis, are vitamin K dependent. Vitamin K is a fat-soluble vitamin that requires adequate intraluminal bile and micelle formation for absorption from the intestine. Thus, dietary deficiency that often occurs in chronic alcoholics, obstructive jaundice that leads to poor micelle formation, and severe parenchymal liver disease that prohibits utilization of vitamin K may all cause a prolonged prothrombin time. Severe liver disease can be differentiated from inadequate vitamin K intake or absorption by the response of the prothrombin time to a single parental injection of vitamin K (Chapters 149 and 178). The prothrombin time is not a sensitive index of the presence of liver disease, but it has prognostic importance regarding the severity of acute liver disease and functional importance regarding the propensity of patients with chronic liver disease to bleed after surgical or diagnostic procedures. α_1-Antitrypsin synthesis may be important in preventing damage in the liver or in distant sites such as the lungs (Chapter 85). Ceruloplasmin deficiency results in abnormalities of copper metabolism, as in Wilson's disease (Chapter 224).

The liver plays a critical role in glucose homeostasis (Chapters 242 and 243). The liver is the major site of gluconeogenesis from red blood cell–derived pyruvate and lactate and from amino acid precursors. Glucose and, to a lesser extent, fructose and galactose are converted by the liver to amino acids, fatty acids, or glycogen, the major storage form of glucose. Hepatic glycogen is the major storage site for the metabolic fuel for glucose-dependent organs such as erythrocytes, retina, renal medulla, and brain. Through glycogenolysis and gluconeogenesis, hepatic glucose production keeps pace with glucose consumption by the brain and other peripheral organs. The sympathetic nerves, as well as glucagon and insulin, play critical roles in maintaining blood glucose levels. This control becomes abnormal in cirrhosis (Chapter 156), a disease in which 60% of patients have glucose intolerance and 20% have overt diabetes mellitus. At the other end of the spectrum, fulminate hepatic failure (Chapter 157) or inherited glycogen storage diseases (Chapter 213) can lead to profound hypoglycemia through impaired gluconeogenesis or glycolysis.

Fatty acid metabolism is a central function of the liver. Excess glucose can be converted to fatty acids, which can be stored in the liver and serve as energy sources through mitochondrial β-oxidation or peroxisomal oxidation. Alternatively, the fatty acids can be combined with apoproteins synthesized by the liver and transported in the blood as lipoproteins to distant organs for metabolism or storage as adipose tissue. Abnormalities in β-oxidation lead to microvesicular fat accumulation in many hepatic diseases of childhood, such as

inherited or acquired Reye's syndrome. Abnormalities of mitochondrial β-oxidation fatty acids are mirrored in adulthood by the acute fatty liver of pregnancy or the hypertension/hemolysis, elevated liver enzyme, and low platelet (HELLP) syndrome of pregnancy. Macrovesicular fat accumulation, or steatosis, is an important feature of viral hepatitis C and is the most dramatic feature of alcoholic liver disease. A condition of increasing incidence in this era of affluent, overfed, and underexercised Americans is nonalcoholic hepatic steatonecrosis (Chapter 155), which is a complex syndrome characterized by increased delivery of fatty acid to the liver and by insulin resistance. The disease is more commonly now being termed *nonalcoholic fatty liver disease* to describe the entire spectrum from simple fatty liver, through steatohepatitis, to fibrosis and cirrhosis. It is becoming clear that nonalcoholic fatty liver disease is part of the constellation known as *syndrome X* (insulin resistance, obesity, hyperlipidemia, and hypertension; Chapter 242). Given the liver's role in lipoprotein formation, it is not surprising that dyslipoproteinemias develop with chronic liver diseases. The most common form is hypertriglyceridemia with alcoholic and viral liver diseases. Cholestatic disorders cause elevated cholesterol and lipid levels, thereby leading to xanthoma formation. Severe chronic liver diseases decrease serum cholesterol esters, leading to alterations in cell membrane lipids and abnormal red blood cell morphology.

Ammonia (NH_3) is toxic to the central nervous system if it is not detoxified into urea by hepatic synthesis (Chapter 157). Elevated NH_3 levels due to inherited defects in the urea cycle enzymes (Chapter 219) or acquired Reye's syndrome may cause episodes of hyperammonemic encephalopathy that can lead to permanent neurologic dysfunction. This relationship of NH_3 to encephalopathy has made NH_3 the leading suspect as a cause of hepatic encephalopathy (Chapter 157) in adult liver diseases, despite the fact that blood NH_3 levels are not always elevated in cases of hepatic encephalopathy, and administration of NH_3 to cirrhotic patients may not cause acute hepatic encephalopathy. These findings have led to the theory that other substances, such as abnormal neurotransmitters (glutamate, γ-aminobutyric acid, endogenous benzodiazepines, endogenous opioids, monoamines [5-HT] or imbalances in blood amino acids), not the intestinal absorption of proteinaceous substances or ammonia, are the actual cause of hepatic encephalopathy. Regardless of the precise etiology, maneuvers that tend to decrease gut NH_3 absorption or production (enemas or cathartics, low-protein diet, antibiotics, or the creation of an acidic environment by administration of lactulose) seem to be effective in the treatment of hepatic encephalopathy (Chapter 157).

Drug detoxification and excretion by the liver is a multistep process (Chapter 27). Phase I reactions are oxidations carried out by one of the three P-450 enzymes, CYP 1, 2, or 3, of which there may be multiple families (A, B, C, etc.) and species (1, 2, 3, etc.). Phase I reactions are likely to make the drug more toxic, so it then must be detoxified by phase II reactions through conjugation with glutathione, glucuronate, sulfate, glycine, or water. Phase II reactions make the compound more water soluble, and thus more easily transported into the blood or bile. If P-450 metabolites are not rapidly detoxified by phase II, hepatic injury may ensue. Genetic mutations in P-450 result in some individuals inheriting the properties of being "poor metabolizers" and others being "hypermetabolizers" of drugs. Furthermore, some medications inhibit and others induce P-450 enzymes, potentially resulting in serious drug interactions that either increase or decrease blood levels of one of the two interacting medications. Hepatic disease may also alter metabolism of the sex hormones through changes in these phase I and II reactions, leading to either feminization (gynecomastia) in males or abnormal menses and infertility in females, as well as osteoporosis in persons of both genders.

The liver's anatomic position as a filter of splanchnic blood flow makes it a critical determinant of the pharmacodynamics of drugs and crucial for the detoxification of absorbed metabolic poisons from the colon. When hepatic blood flow is obstructed, the shunting of mesenteric blood around the liver creates encephalopathy and hemorrhage from esophageal or gastric varices.

History

The recognition of liver disease is not difficult when the patient presents with classic manifestations, such as overt jaundice, or with the classic stigmata of chronic liver disease, such as ascites, spider angiomata, liver palms, and asterixis. However, the mettle of the physician is tested by the fact that liver disease can have so many occult manifestations. Easy fatigability and malaise may be the only manifestations of chronic liver disease, and even these symptoms may be so mild that the patient is not aware of the illness until ascites, altered mental status, and even coma develop. Although jaundice may be the earliest manifestation of liver disease in some patients, it is often noticed by the patient or family members as scleral icterus (yellow discoloration of the conjunctiva) or even similar discoloration of the gums and tongue. Pruritus may develop first in the course of obstructive jaundice (cholestasis) because retention of bile salts can occur before significant retention of bilirubin. As jaundice progresses, patients develop light-colored stools and dark urine when the excretion of bile pigments is diverted from the gastrointestinal tract to the kidney.

Abdominal complaints may be absent or mild. An enlarging liver from inflammation or passive congestion may present only as mild right upper quadrant tenderness. Abdominal distention, due to the development of ascites, may be detected only by a change in belt size, and it may be intermittent, related to cyclic alcohol intake. As ascites progress, peripheral edema may develop.

Liver diseases may manifest as symptoms related to other systems. For example, early hepatic encephalopathy may manifest as changes in sleep pattern or mild alterations in personality long before confusion, combativeness, obtundation, and ataxia develop (Chapters 156 and 157). Hepatitis C can manifest as glomerulonephritis or hemorrhagic skin lesions, owing to the presence of cryoglobulinemia (Chapter 152). Patients with hemochromatosis sometimes present with arthralgias, diabetes, or cardiac disease without the overt manifestations of hepatic involvement (Chapter 225). Hemolytic anemias and psychic aberrations can be the presenting symptoms of Wilson's disease (Chapters 154 and 224). Bleeding esophageal varices may be the first manifestation of cirrhosis. Surgical jaundice due to obstruction from common duct stones may manifest as atypical abdominal pain or even as silent jaundice, whereas the obstructive jaundice of pancreatic cancer may manifest as mental depression (Chapters 158 and 201). In special settings such as pregnancy or diabetes mellitus, liver abnormalities may portend inconsequential or even dangerous hepatocyte lipid accumulation (Chapter 155). Mild increases in aminotransferases in the asymptomatic patient may be the only manifestation of hepatitis C, the ongoing inflammation of which silently destroys the liver. Silent cirrhosis may be discovered after the finding of asymptomatic thrombocytopenia caused by the congestive splenomegaly of portal hypertension. Thus, the effective physician must not only understand the classic presentations of the various liver diseases but also have a firm grasp on the atypical presentations.

In the United States, the two major epidemiologic settings for liver disease are alcohol ingestion (Chapters 155 and 156) and exposure to hepatitis virus (Chapters 151 and 152). Thus, the medical history should seek the presence of occult alcoholism, even to the extent of questioning family members. Exposure to or contact with jaundiced persons or those with hepatitis is important to elicit. Hepatitis exposure from foreign travel, ingested shellfish, prior blood transfusions, and employment in the health care professions is not nearly as important as the history of injection drug use with even a single, one-time, experimental use of shared needles. Sexual promiscuity is unequivocally a risk factor for the viral hepatitides, particularly among male homosexuals. Family history of liver diseases is a clue to genetic diseases such as Wilson's disease, hemochromatosis, or α_1-antitrypsin deficiency.

Physical Examination

The skin can be an important clue implicating liver disease. Spider angiomata (Fig. 148–1) occur on the upper trunk and face. Palmar erythema (Fig. 148–2), except in the setting of pregnancy, may signal the presence of chronic liver disease. Scleral icterus and icterus of the gums or the tympanic membranes may be detected before bilirubin levels of 3 to 4 mg/dL are manifested by jaundice of the skin. Xanthomata and xanthelasmas are more common in lipid disorders than in obstructive jaundice but may be a sign of prolonged cholestasis. Chronic liver disease leads to changes in estrogen and testosterone metabolism, resulting in the development of gynecomastia, the loss of hair, particularly on the shins, and reduction in the size or consistency of the testes. Chronic portal hypertension may lead to development of collateral circulation, which is manifested as caput medusa in the region of the umbilicus and epigastrium.

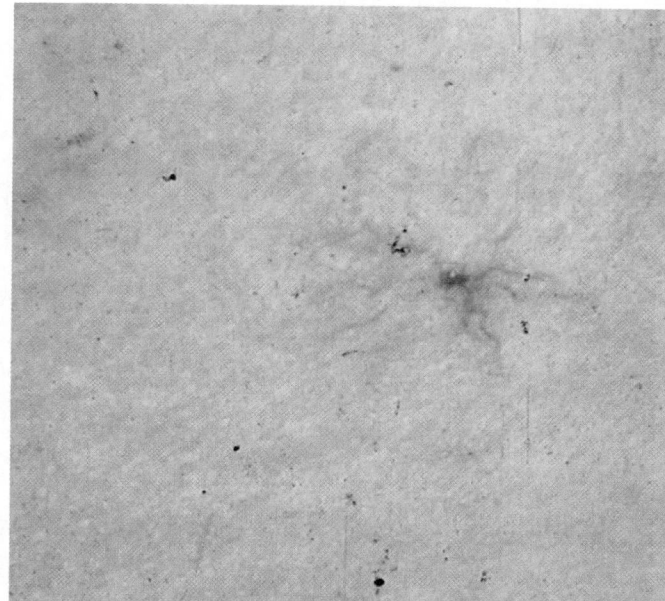

FIGURE 148–1 • Close-up view of a spider angioma of the skin in a patient with liver disease. Note the central, punctate filling vessel and the "spider-like" vessels emanating from it. (Courtesy of Telfer Reynolds, MD.)

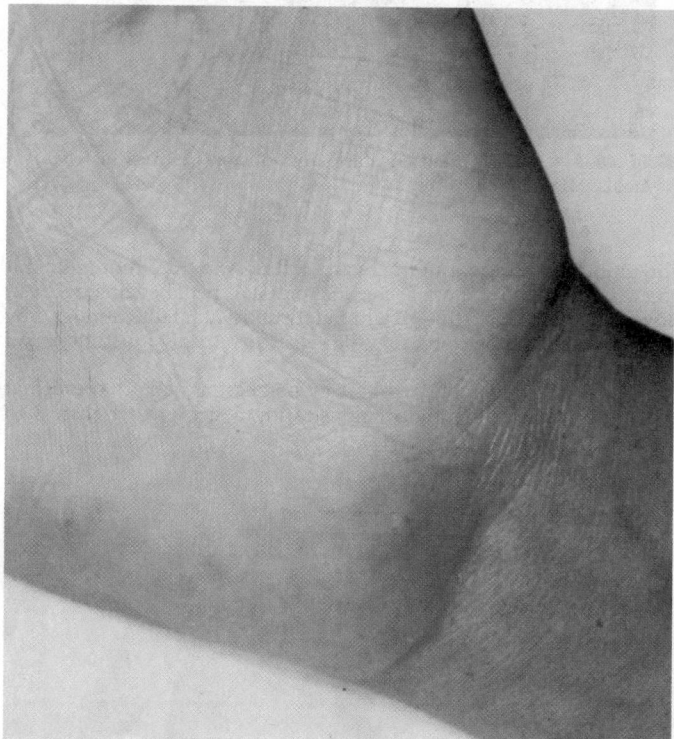

FIGURE 148–2 • Liver palms: thenar and hypothenar erythema in a patient with chronic liver disease. (Courtesy of Telfer Reynolds, MD.)

Abdominal examination should focus first on the presence or absence of ascites and then on the size and characteristics of the liver. Distention from ascites (Fig. 148–3) is sometimes difficult to differentiate from truncal obesity. Ascites can be determined most easily by the demonstration of flank dullness. By percussing first at the umbilicus, which is usually tympanic due to accumulated gas-filled loops of bowel, and then progressing radially toward the flanks, one can detect the fluid interface with the air-filled bowel loops as a ring of dullness in the flanks and lower abdomen at a uniform distance from

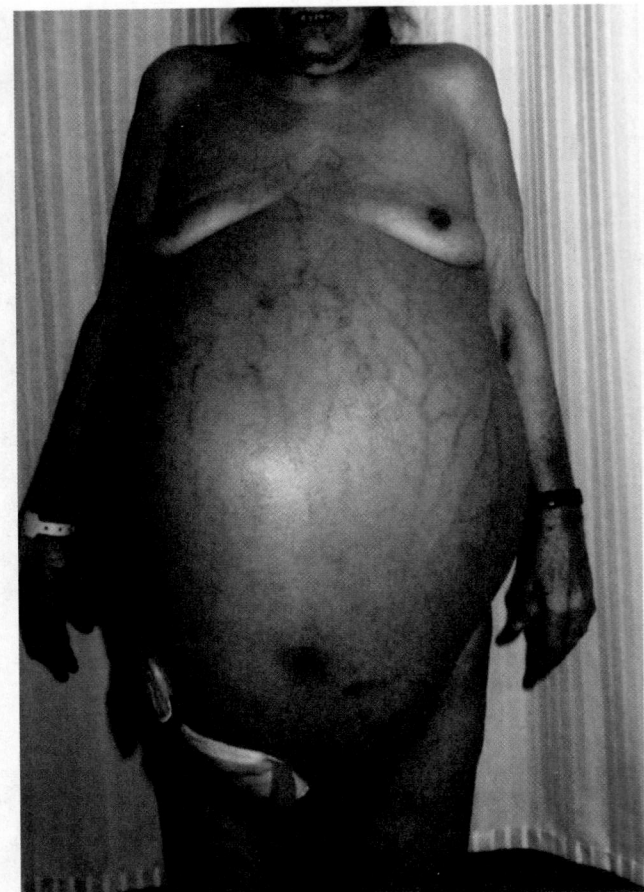

FIGURE 148–3 • Massive ascites in an elderly woman. (Courtesy of Telfer Reynolds, MD.)

the umbilicus. Shifting dullness and a fluid wave are more difficult to elicit and require more ascites. Scrotal and pedal edema occur in advanced cases (Fig. 148–4). Ultimately, abdominal ultrasonography or computed tomography may be necessary to demonstrate small amounts of ascites.

Hepatomegaly is detected best by percussing hepatic breadth at the midclavicular line and demonstrating a size greater than 8 to

10 cm. How far the liver extends below the costal margin is of less importance, particularly in patients with emphysema and flattened diaphragms. Liver consistency can often be determined; the smooth liver with the sharp edge can be differentiated from the nodular liver of cirrhosis, the rock-hard liver of metastatic cancer, the tender liver of hepatitis or chronic passive congestion, and the pulsating liver of severe tricuspid insufficiency. Liver tenderness can be determined by having the patient inspire, which pushes the liver into the examining hand that is positioned below the liver, or by lightly punching a hand that is placed on the rib cage laterally over the right lobe of the liver. At times, a visible or palpable gallbladder, which may be somewhat tender, can be detected below the liver margin in patients with cystic or common bile duct obstruction. In pancreatic carcinoma with common bile duct obstruction, the presence of the palpable gallbladder in the jaundiced patient is known as Courvoisier's sign. When liver disease is expected, splenomegaly should be sought. Its presence is usually confirmation of portal hypertension.

Evaluation for possible hepatic encephalopathy is crucial in the physical examination in the patient with suspected liver disease. Early in the course of encephalopathy, manifestations are subtle and include personality change, mild confusion, and lethargy. At this point, a formal mental status examination and fine motor testing (e.g., drawing stars, connecting dots) may be necessary to show early mental aberration. Later, a flapping tremor (asterixis) develops. To elicit this neurologic sign, it is necessary to have the patient extend his or her hands against gravity and look for the release phenomenon that causes the flap. If the patient cannot follow this command, the patient can grasp two fingers of the examiner's hand and be asked to sustain the grasp; the release phenomenon might be thus elicited. Advanced encephalopathy manifests as severe coma, often with decerebrate rigidity; but any neurologic presentation, including lateralization of signs, may be seen (Chapter 157).

Clinical Approach to Diagnosis

In the setting of frank jaundice without stigmata of chronic liver disease, immediate diagnostic imaging (ultrasonography and computed tomography) is indicated to differentiate so-called surgical jaundice, which requires either operative or endoscopic intervention or even urgent transplantation, from medical jaundice, in which the diagnosis may be made from laboratory tests or biopsy and for which the management involves medications or watchful waiting. The approach to patients with abnormal liver test results or with signs and symptoms of cirrhosis is directed toward excluding medically treatable diseases, remembering that some diseases causing "surgical" jaundice can manifest this way as well (Chapter 149).

The diagnosis of liver diseases will likely change in the future. The advent of improved imaging techniques such as nuclear magnetic resonance imaging of the biliary ducts may make conventional visualization of the hepatobiliary ducts by endoscopic retrograde cholangiopancreatography an archaic test. Such techniques, however, will not obviate the need for endoscopy as a mode to deliver therapy.

SUGGESTED READINGS
Alpini G, McGill JM, LaRusso NF: The pathobiology of biliary epithelia. Hepatology 2002;35:1256–1268. *Biliary tract diseases (cholangiopathies) are important causes of acute and chronic liver disease, as are diseases of the hepatocytes (hepatopathies). An overview of the biology of the biliary epithelium and how it is deranged by disease is given.*

Kane GC, Lipsky JJ: Drug–grapefruit juice interactions. Mayo Clin Proc 2000;75:933–942. *P-450 drug metabolizing enzymes are present in the gastrointestinal tract as well as in the liver. The major P-450 enzyme present in the small bowel enterocyte is CYP 3A4, which can be inhibited for up to 3 days by ingestion of a single glass of grapefruit juice. As a result, certain drugs normally metabolized by the intestinal P-450s may be absorbed in increased amounts and significantly increase blood levels. This can be important in patients taking the statins, saquinavir, nifedipine, buspirone, and cyclosporin A.*

Marchesini G, Brizi M, Bianchi G, et al: Nonalcoholic fatty liver disease: A feature of the metabolic syndrome. Diabetes 2001;50:1844–1850. *The relationships between nonalcoholic fatty liver disease and the insulin resistance of syndrome X.*

Stolz A: Liver physiology and metabolic function. In Feldman M, Friedman LS, Sleisenger MH (eds): Gastrointestinal and Liver Disease: Pathophysiology/Diagnosis/Management, 7th ed, Vol. 2. Philadelphia, WB Saunders, 2002, pp 1202–1226. *A brief review of the physiologic and metabolic functions of the liver and how they are altered by disease.*

Watkins PB: Drug metabolism in the liver and intestines. In Yamada T, Alpers DH, Laine L, et al (eds): Textbook of Gastroenterology, 4th ed. Philadelphia, Lippincott, Williams & Wilkins, 2003, pp 592–604. *A clear and readable review of the important aspects of human drug metabolism.*

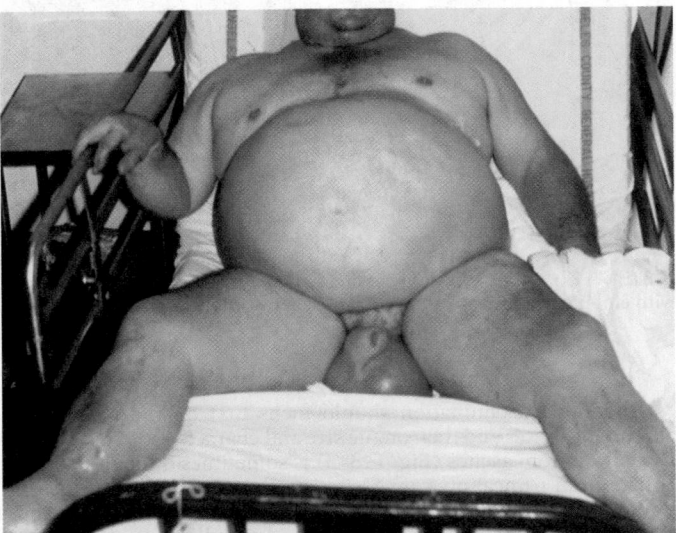

FIGURE 148–4 • Ill patient with alcoholic cirrhosis and portal hypertension. Note the parotid hypertrophy, distended abdomen from ascites, and scrotal and pedal edema. (Courtesy of Telfer Reynolds, MD.)

149 APPROACH TO THE PATIENT WITH JAUNDICE OR ABNORMAL LIVER TESTS

Paul D. Berk

Jaundice, from the French *jaune* (yellow), is the yellow-orange discoloration of the skin, conjunctivae, and mucous membranes that results from elevated concentrations of bilirubin in plasma. Mild hyperbilirubinemia may be clinically undetectable, but jaundice becomes evident at plasma bilirubin concentrations of 3 to 4 mg/dL, depending on the patient's normal pigmentation, the conditions of observation, and the bilirubin fraction that is elevated. Optimal interpretation of an elevated plasma bilirubin concentration is based on an appreciation of its sources and disposition.

BILIRUBIN METABOLISM

BILIRUBIN PRODUCTION. Bilirubin is the degradation product of the heme moiety of hemoproteins, a class of proteins involved in the transport or metabolism of oxygen (Fig. 149–1). Normal adults produce about 4 mg of bilirubin per kilogram of body weight per day. Between 70 and 90% of bilirubin is derived from the hemoglobin of erythrocytes, which are sequestered and destroyed by the mononuclear phagocytic cells of the reticuloendothelial system, principally in the spleen, liver, and bone marrow. The remainder results primarily from the turnover of nonhemoglobin hemoproteins such as myoglobin, the P-450 cytochromes, catalase, and peroxidase, principally in the liver; a minor fraction reflects ineffective erythropoiesis, which is the premature destruction of newly formed erythrocytes within the bone marrow.

The two-step conversion of heme to bilirubin begins with the opening of the heme molecule at its α bridge carbon by the microsomal enzyme *heme oxygenase*, a process that results in the formation of equimolar quantities of carbon monoxide and the green tetrapyrrole biliverdin. This nontoxic, water-soluble pigment is the main excretory product of heme in birds, reptiles, and amphibians. However, biliverdin cannot cross the placenta. Accordingly, its reduction to bilirubin in mammals by a second enzyme, *biliverdin reductase*, allows its transplacental removal from the fetus into the maternal circulation. The unconjugated bilirubin produced in the periphery is transported to the liver in plasma. Because of its insolubility in aqueous media, it is kept in solution by tight but reversible binding to albumin. A number of compounds, including sulfonamides, furosemide, and radiographic contrast agents, competitively displace bilirubin from its binding sites on albumin, a phenomenon that is of little clinical significance except in neonates, in whom the resulting increased concentration of unbound bilirubin raises the risk of kernicterus.

DISPOSITION OF BILIRUBIN BY THE LIVER. Excretion of bilirubin from the body is a major function of the liver (see Fig. 149–1), where specialized microanatomy enhances the extraction of tightly protein-bound compounds from the circulation. Hepatic translocation of bilirubin from blood to bile involves four distinct steps: (1) uptake of unconjugated bilirubin, principally by an incompletely characterized facilitated transport process and to a lesser extent by diffusion; (2) intracellular binding, mainly to various cytosolic proteins of the glutathione-*S*-transferase family; (3) conversion of unconjugated bilirubin to bilirubin mono- and diglucuronides by a specific UDP-glucuronosyltransferase isoform designated UGT1A1, encoded by the *UGT1* gene complex; and (4) transfer of bilirubin mono- and diglucuronides into bile by a canalicular membrane adenosine triphosphate (ATP)–dependent transporter designated multidrug resistance–associated protein 2 (MRP2) or canalicular multispecific organic anion transporter (cMOAT). MRP2/cMOAT is a member of the MRP gene family, other members of which pump certain types of drug conjugates, as well as unmodified anticancer drugs, out of cells.

Conjugation of unconjugated bilirubin to bilirubin mono- and diglucuronides is a critical process that greatly increases the aqueous solubility of bilirubin and thereby enhances its elimination from the body while simultaneously reducing its ability to diffuse across biologic membranes, including the blood-brain barrier. In newborn infants, a decreased capacity to conjugate bilirubin leads to

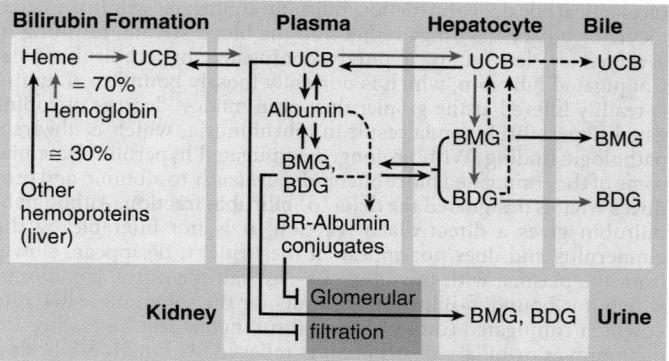

FIGURE 149–1 • Overview of bilirubin metabolism. Unconjugated bilirubin (UCB) formed from the breakdown of heme from hemoglobin and other hemoproteins is transported in plasma reversibly bound to albumin and is converted in the liver to bilirubin monoglucuronide (BMG) and diglucuronide (BDG), the latter being the predominant form secreted in bile. BMG and BDG together normally account for less than 5% of serum bilirubin. In patients with hepatobiliary disease, BMG and BDG accumulate in plasma and appear in urine. Bilirubin glucuronides in plasma also react nonenzymatically with albumin and possibly other serum proteins to form protein conjugates, which do not appear in urine and have a plasma half-life similar to that of albumin.

unconjugated hyperbilirubinemia (physiologic jaundice of the newborn). If severe, this hyperbilirubinemia may lead to irreversible central nervous system toxicity. Phototherapy by exposure to blue light converts bilirubin to water-soluble photoisomers that are readily excreted in bile, thereby protecting the central nervous system from bilirubin toxicity. Gilbert's syndrome and Crigler-Najjar syndrome types 1 and 2, which result from genetic defects in bilirubin conjugation, are characterized by unconjugated hyperbilirubinemia; in contrast, Dubin-Johnson syndrome, which results from inheritable defects in MRP2/cMOAT (see later), is characterized by conjugated or mixed hyperbilirubinemia.

BILIRUBIN IN PLASMA. The total plasma bilirubin concentration in normal adults is less than 1 to 1.5 mg/dL, depending on the measurement method that is used. Modern analytic techniques show that normal plasma contains principally unconjugated bilirubin, with only traces of conjugates. Clinical laboratories typically quantify plasma bilirubin by a reaction in which bilirubin is cleaved by a diazo reagent, such as diazotized sulfanilic acid, to azodipyrroles that are readily quantitated spectrophotometrically. Bilirubin conjugates react rapidly ("prompt" or "direct"-reacting bilirubin). Unconjugated bilirubin reacts slowly because the site of attack by the diazo reagent is protected by internal hydrogen bonding. Accordingly, accurate measurement of the total plasma bilirubin concentration requires addition of an accelerator, such as ethanol or urea, to disrupt this internal hydrogen bonding and to ensure complete reaction of any unconjugated bilirubin. The "indirect"-reacting bilirubin is calculated by subtracting the direct-reacting bilirubin from the total. Although physicians traditionally equate the direct-reacting fraction of bilirubin in plasma with conjugated bilirubin and the indirect fraction with unconjugated bilirubin, this approach is, at best, a rough approximation. The 10 to 20% of bilirubin in normal plasma that gives a prompt (direct) diazo reaction is an artifact of the kinetics of the diazo reaction; unqualified interpretation of the direct and indirect fractions as reflecting conjugated and unconjugated bilirubin, respectively, may lead to diagnostic errors, particularly in the diagnosis of the isolated, hereditary hyperbilirubinemias.

Interpretation of Clinical Measurements of Plasma Bilirubin Concentration. At virtually any total bilirubin concentration, a direct-reacting fraction of less than 15% of total bilirubin can be considered as essentially all unconjugated. When the direct-reacting fraction is greater than 15%, a simple dipstick test for bilirubinuria may clarify the situation. Unconjugated bilirubin is not excreted in urine regardless of the height of its plasma concentration because its binding to albumin is too tight for effective glomerular filtration and it is not secreted by the tubules. The canalicular transport mechanism for excretion of bilirubin conjugates is especially sensitive to injury. Accordingly, in hepatocellular disease, as well as with either cholestasis or mechanical bile duct obstruction, bilirubin conjugates within the hepatocyte or biliary tract may reflux into the blood stream, resulting in a mixed or, less often, a purely conjugated hyperbilirubinemia. Conjugated bilirubin, which is normally loosely bound to albumin, is readily filtered at the glomerulus; even modest degrees of conjugated hyperbilirubinemia result in bilirubinuria, which is *always* a pathologic finding. With prolonged conjugated hyperbilirubinemia, some of the conjugated bilirubin binds *covalently* to albumin and produces what is designated the delta (δ) bilirubin fraction. Although δ-bilirubin gives a direct diazo reaction, it is not filterable by the glomerulus and does not appear in the urine; it disappears slowly from the plasma, with the 14- to 21-day half-life of the albumin to which it is bound. δ-Bilirubin accounts for the sometimes slow rate at which conjugated (direct) hyperbilirubinemia resolves as hepatitis improves or biliary obstruction is relieved. Although δ-bilirubin is not easily measured, its presence can be inferred when an elevated direct-reacting bilirubin persists after bilirubinuria resolves.

BILIRUBIN IN BILE. Normal bile contains an average of less than 5% unconjugated bilirubin, 7% bilirubin monoconjugates, and 90% bilirubin diconjugates. The proportion of monoconjugates increases with either an increased bilirubin load (hemolysis) or reduced bilirubin conjugating capacity (e.g., Crigler-Najjar type 1).

POSTHEPATIC ASPECTS OF BILIRUBIN DISPOSITION. Unconjugated bilirubin ordinarily does not reach the gut except in neonates or, by ill-defined alternative pathways, in the presence of severe unconjugated hyperbilirubinemia (e.g., Crigler-Najjar type 1). In these circumstances, unconjugated bilirubin is reabsorbed from the gut, thereby amplifying the hyperbilirubinemia. Following canalicular secretion, conjugated bilirubin traverses the biliary tree, reaches the duodenum, and passes down the gastrointestinal tract without reabsorption by either the gallbladder or intestinal mucosa. Although some bilirubin reaches the feces, most is converted to urobilinogen and to related compounds by bacteria within the ileum and colon, where the urobilinogen is reabsorbed, returns to the liver through the portal circulation, and is reexcreted into bile in a process of enterohepatic recirculation. Any urobilinogen that is not taken up by the liver reaches the systemic circulation, from which it is cleared by the kidneys. Normal urine urobilinogen excretion is 4 mg/day or less. With hemolysis, which increases the load of bilirubin entering the gut and therefore the amount of urobilinogen formed and reabsorbed, or with liver disease, which decreases the hepatic extraction of bilirubin, plasma urobilinogen levels rise, and more urobilinogen is excreted in the urine. Severe cholestasis, bile duct obstruction, or broad-spectrum antibiotics that reduce or eliminate the bacterial conversion of bilirubin to urobilinogen markedly decrease the formation and urinary excretion of urobilinogen.

DIFFERENTIAL DIAGNOSIS OF HYPERBILIRUBINEMIA AND JAUNDICE. Hyperbilirubinemia and jaundice (Fig. 149–2) may result from isolated disorders of bilirubin metabolism, liver disease, or obstruction of the biliary tract. Jaundice represents the most visible sign of hepatobiliary disease of many causes (Table 149–1).

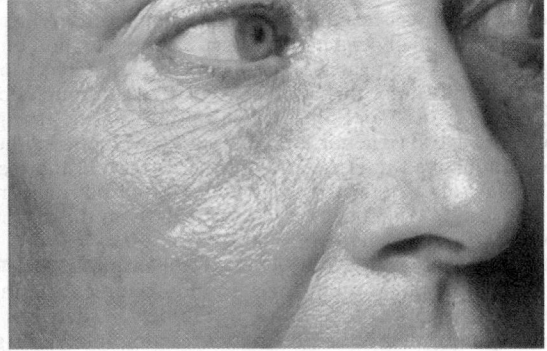

FIGURE 149–2 • Severe cholestatic jaundice in a patient with primary biliary cirrhosis. The high level of conjugated bilirubin, maintained over a long period, gives a characteristic dark brown-orange pigmentation to the skin and sclerae. Patients with primary biliary cirrhosis usually develop large xanthelasmas and corneal arcus as a consequence of disordered lipid metabolism. (From Forbes CD, Jackson WF: Color Atlas and Text of Clinical Medicine, 3rd ed. London, Mosby, 2003.)

Table 149–1 • **DIFFERENTIAL DIAGNOSIS OF HYPERBILIRUBINEMIA AND JAUNDICE**

ISOLATED DISORDERS OF BILIRUBIN METABOLISM
Unconjugated hyperbilirubinemia
  Increased bilirubin production
    Examples: hemolysis, ineffective erythropoiesis, blood transfusion, resorption of hematomas
  Decreased hepatocellular uptake
    Examples: drugs (e.g., rifampin)
  Decreased conjugation
    Examples: Gilbert's and Crigler-Najjar syndromes, physiologic jaundice of the newborn, breast milk jaundice, HIV protease inhibitors
Conjugated or mixed hyperbilirubinemia
  Decreased canalicular transport: Dubin-Johnson syndrome
  Mechanism uncertain: Rotor's syndrome

LIVER DISEASE
Acute or chronic hepatocellular dysfunction
  Acute or subacute hepatocellular injury
    Examples: viral hepatitis A,B,C, hepatotoxins (e.g., ethanol, acetaminophen, mushroom [*Amanita phalloides*] poisoning), drugs (e.g., isoniazid, α-methyldopa), metabolic diseases (e.g., Wilson's disease, Reye's syndrome), pregnancy-related (e.g., acute fatty liver of pregnancy, preeclampsia), hepatic ischemia (e.g., hypotension, postoperative, hepatic artery thrombosis)
  Chronic hepatocellular disease
    Examples: hepatitis B and C, hepatotoxins (e.g., ethanol, vinyl chloride, vitamin A), autoimmune hepatitis, metabolic disease (Wilson's disease, hemochromatosis, α1-antitrypsin deficiency)
Hepatic disorders with prominent cholestasis
  Familial cholestatic disorders
  Single gene disorders
    Examples: benign recurrent intrahepatic cholestasis; progressive familial intrahepatic cholestasis types 1–3
  Familial cholestatic disorders of unknown pathogenesis
    Examples: Aagenaes syndrome, Navajo neurohepatopathy, North American Indian cholestasis
  Diffuse infiltrative disorders
    Examples: granulomatous diseases (e.g., mycobacterial and fungal infections, sarcoidosis, lymphoma, drugs, Wegener's granulomatosis), amyloidosis, infiltrative malignancies
  Inflammation of intrahepatic bile ductules and/or portal tracts
    Examples: primary biliary cirrhosis, liver allograft rejection, graft-versus-host disease, drugs (e.g., chlorpromazine, erythromycin)
  Miscellaneous conditions
    Examples: uncommon presentations of viral or alcoholic hepatitis, intrahepatic cholestasis of pregnancy, contraceptive jaundice, estrogens, anabolic steroids, postoperative cholestasis, total parenteral nutrition, bacterial infections, drugs

OBSTRUCTION OF THE BILE DUCTS
Choledocholithiasis
  Examples: cholesterol gallstones, pigment gallstones
Diseases of the bile ducts
  Inflammation/infection
    Examples: primary sclerosing cholangitis, AIDS cholangiopathy, hepatic arterial chemotherapy, postsurgical strictures
  Neoplasms (e.g., cholangiocarcinoma)
Extrinsic compression of the biliary tree
  Neoplasms
    Examples: pancreatic carcinoma, metastatic lymphadenopathy, hepatoma
  Pancreatitis with or without pseudocyst formation
  Vascular enlargment (e.g., aneurysm, cavernous transformation of portal vein)

AIDS = acquired immunodeficiency syndrome; HIV = human immunodeficiency syndrome.

DISORDERS OF BILIRUBIN METABOLISM

Pure hyperbilirubinemia may result either from extrahepatic factors or from inherited or acquired defects in specific aspects of hepatic bilirubin disposition.

Unconjugated Hyperbilirubinemia

The plasma unconjugated bilirubin concentration ([UCB]) is determined by a balance between the bilirubin production rate

(BRP) and hepatic bilirubin clearance (C_{BR}) according to the relationship:

$$[UCB] \approx BRP/C_{BR} \qquad (1)$$

C_{BR} is analogous to the creatinine clearance in the test of kidney function; it is a measure of the rate at which bilirubin is extracted from plasma, and it is a true quantitative test of liver function. Whereas BRP and C_{BR} are not easily quantified, investigative measurements have yielded useful pathophysiologic insights. Equation 1 indicates that [UCB] increases linearly with an increase in BRP or hyperbolically with a decrease in C_{BR}, thereby providing a basis for classifying unconjugated hyperbilirubinemias according to their pathogenesis.

INCREASED BILIRUBIN PRODUCTION

An increased production of bilirubin and a resulting unconjugated hyperbilirubinemia can be caused by hemolysis, an accelerated destruction of transfused erythrocytes, resorption of hematomas, or ineffective erythropoiesis (e.g., lead poisoning, megaloblastic anemias related to deficiency of either folic acid or vitamin B_{12}, sideroblastic anemia, congenital erythropoietic porphyria, or myeloproliferative or myelodysplastic diseases). In these settings, other liver tests are typically normal and the hyperbilirubinemia is modest, rarely exceeding 4 mg/dL; higher values imply concomitant hepatic dysfunction. However, following brisk blood transfusion or resorption of massive hematomas caused by trauma, the increased bilirubin load may be transiently sufficient to lead to frank jaundice. The causes of hemolysis are numerous (Chapters 169 and 171). Besides specific blood disorders, mild hemolysis accompanies many acquired diseases. In the setting of systemic disease, which may include a degree of hepatic dysfunction, hemolysis may produce a component of conjugated hyperbilirubinemia in addition to an elevated unconjugated bilirubin concentration. Prolonged hemolysis may lead to the formation of bilirubin gallstones, which may cause cholecystitis, obstruction, or any other biliary tract consequence of calculous disease (Chapter 158).

DECREASED HEPATIC BILIRUBIN CLEARANCE

DECREASED BILIRUBIN UPTAKE. Several drugs (e.g., rifampin, flavaspidic acid, novobiocin, and various cholecystographic contrast agents) competitively inhibit the hepatocellular uptake of bilirubin. The resulting unconjugated hyperbilirubinemia resolves with cessation of the medication. Decreased hepatic bilirubin uptake is also believed to contribute to the unconjugated hyperbilirubinemia of Gilbert's syndrome, although the principal molecular basis for this syndrome is a reduction of the conjugation of bilirubin.

IMPAIRED BILIRUBIN CONJUGATION. The most frequent cause of decreased bilirubin clearance is a decrease in bilirubin conjugating activity. Bilirubin conjugation with glucuronic acid is catalyzed by a specific UDP-glucuronosyltransferase, which is designated UGT1A1 and encoded by the *UGT1* gene complex. The *UGT1A1* gene is assembled by alternative splicing of a bilirubin-specific variant of exon 1, designated exon A_1, with four common exons (exons 2 to 5) that encode the shared carboxyl terminal end of all *UGT1*-encoded proteins. Its promoter region normally contains an A(TA)$_6$TAA TATA box–like construct.

Genetic Disorders of Bilirubin Conjugation. The hereditary hyperbilirubinemias (Table 149–2) are a group of five syndromes in which hyperbilirubinemia occurs as an isolated biochemical abnormality, without evidence of either hepatocellular necrosis or cholestasis. The molecular defects have been identified in all but Rotor's syndrome.

Crigler-Najjar syndrome types 1 and 2 and *Gilbert's syndrome* are hereditary forms of unconjugated hyperbilirubinemia that result from mutations in *UGT1A1*. In Crigler-Najjar type 1, essentially no functional enzyme activity is present, whereas patients with Crigler-Najjar type 2 have up to 10% of normal and patients with Gilbert's syndrome have 10 to 33% of normal, leading to bilirubin concentrations of 18 to 45, 6 to 25, and 1.5 to 4 mg/dL, respectively (see Table 149–2). Because total UGT1A1 enzymatic activity must be reduced to less than 50% of normal to produce unconjugated hyperbilirubinemia, phenotypic expression of mutations in this enzyme requires either homozygosity or double heterozygosity. Thus, despite earlier reports

to the contrary, each of these disorders is inherited as an autosomal recessive trait. Patients with Crigler-Najjar types 1 and 2 are either homozygotes or double heterozygotes for structural mutations within the coding region. In Western countries, patients with Gilbert's syndrome are typically homozygous for an A(TA)$_7$TAA promoter mutation. Structural mutations causing modest reductions in UGT1A1 enzymatic activity have been reported in some Japanese patients with Gilbert's syndrome.

Crigler-Najjar type 1 is characterized by striking unconjugated hyperbilirubinemia that appears in the neonatal period, persists for life, and is unresponsive to phenobarbital. The majority of patients (type 1A) exhibit defects in the glucuronide conjugation of a spectrum of substrates in addition to bilirubin as the result of mutations in one of the common exons (2 to 5) of the *UGT1* complex. In a smaller subset (type 1B), a mutation in the bilirubin-specific exon A1 limits the defect to bilirubin conjugation. More than 30 structurally diverse *UGT1A1* mutations can cause Crigler-Najjar type 1; their common feature is that they all encode proteins with absent or, at most, traces of enzymatic activity. Prior to the availability of phototherapy, most patients with Crigler-Najjar type 1 died of bilirubin encephalopathy (kernicterus) in infancy or early childhood. Optimal treatment for a neurologically intact patient includes (1) about 12 hours/day of phototherapy from birth throughout childhood, perhaps supplemented by exchange transfusion in the neonatal period; (2) use of tin-protoporphyrin to blunt transient episodes of increased hyperbilirubinemia; and (3) early liver transplantation, prior to the onset of brain damage. Transplantation with isolated allogenic hepatocytes is being evaluated as an experimental therapeutic approach.

Bilirubin concentrations are typically lower in Crigler-Najjar type 2, and plasma bilirubin levels can be reduced to 3 to 5 mg/dL by phenobarbital. At least 10 different mutations of *UGT1A1* have been associated with Crigler-Najjar type 2; all encode a bilirubin-UDP-glucuronosyltransferase with markedly reduced but detectable enzymatic activity. Although uncommon in Crigler-Najjar type 2, kernicterus has occurred at all ages, typically associated with factors that temporarily raise the plasma bilirubin concentration above baseline (e.g., fasting, intercurrent illness). For this reason, phenobarbital therapy is often recommended; a single bedtime dose usually maintains clinically safe plasma bilirubin concentrations.

Gilbert's syndrome is the most common of the hereditary hyperbilirubinemias, with a genotypic prevalence of 12% or less and a phenotypic prevalence of 7% or less. Its high prevalence may explain the frequency of mild unconjugated hyperbilirubinemia in liver transplant recipients. Plasma bilirubin concentrations are most often less than 3 mg/dL, although both higher and lower values are frequent, with increases of two- to three-fold commonly occurring with fasting and intercurrent illness. The phenotypic distinction between mild Gilbert's syndrome and a normal state is often blurred. Phenobarbital normalizes both the bilirubin concentration and C_{BR}. Oxidative drug metabolism and the disposition of most xenobiotics that are metabolized by glucuronidation appear to be normal in Gilbert's syndrome. A critical exception is the antitumor agent irinotecan (CPT-11), whose active metabolite (SN-38) is glucuronidated specifically by UGT1A1. In patients with Gilbert's syndrome, CPT-11 can cause intractable diarrhea, myelosuppression, and other serious toxicities. Unconjugated hyperbilirubinemia related to selective inhibition of UGT1A1 also occurs with several human immunodeficiency virus (HIV) protease inhibitors (e.g., indinavir). Abnormal disposition of menthol, estradiol benzoate, acetaminophen, tolbutamide, rifamycin SV, and other agents has not been associated with significant complications, but prudence should be exercised in prescribing agents that are metabolized by glucuronidation to patients with Gilbert's syndrome.

Unconjugated Hyperbilirubin in the Newborn Period. Most neonates develop mild unconjugated hyperbilirubinemia between days 2 and 5 after birth because of hepatic immaturity and low levels of UGT1A1. Peak bilirubin levels are typically less than 5 to 10 mg/dL, and levels return to normal within 2 weeks as mechanisms of bilirubin disposition mature. Prematurity, with hemolysis or hepatic immaturity, is associated with higher bilirubin levels that may require phototherapy. The progestational steroid 3α,20β-pregnanediol and certain fatty acids that are found in breast milk (but not serum) of some mothers inhibit bilirubin conjugation and can cause excessive neonatal hyperbilirubinemia (*breast milk jaundice*). By comparison, *transient familial neonatal hyperbilirubinemia* (Lucey-Driscoll

Table 149–2 • PRINCIPAL FEATURES OF THE HEREDITARY DISORDERS OF BILIRUBIN METABOLISM

FEATURE	CRIGLER-NAJJAR SYNDROME		GILBERT'S SYNDROME	DUBIN-JOHNSON SYNDROME	ROTOR'S SYNDROME
	Type I	Type II			
Incidence	Very rare	Uncommon	Up to 12% of population	Uncommon	Rare
Total serum bilirubin (mg/dL)	18–45 (usually >20), unconjugated	6–25 (usually ≤20), unconjugated	Typically ≤4 in absence fasting or hemolysis; mostly unconjugated	Typically 2–5, less often ≤25; about 60% direct reacting	Usually 3–7, occasionally ≤20; about 60% direct reacting
Defect(s) in bilirubin metabolism	Bilirubin UDPGT activity markedly reduced: trace to absent	Bilirubin UDPGT activity reduced: ≤10% of normal.	Bilirubin UDPGT activity typically reduced to 10–33% of normal; reduced bilirubin uptake in some cases; mild hemolysis in up to 50% of patients	Impaired canalicular secretion of conjugated bilirubin due to MRP2/cMOAT mutation	Impaired hepatic secretion or storage of conjugated bilirubin; molecular defect not known
Routine liver tests	Normal	Normal	Normal	Normal	Normal
Serum bile acids	Normal	Normal	Normal	Usually normal	Normal
Plasma Sulfobromophthalein removal (% retention of 5 mg/kg dose at 45 min)*	Normal	Normal	Usually normal (<5%); mild 45-min (<15%) retention in some patients.	Slow initial decline in plasma concentration (retention ≤20% at 45 min) with secondary rise at 90–120 min	Very slow initial decline in plasma concentration (45-min retention = 30–45%) without secondary rise
Oral cholecystography	Normal	Normal	Normal	Faint or nonvisualization of gallbladder	Usually normal
Pharmacologic responses/special features	No response to phenobarbital	Phenobarbital reduces bilirubin by ≤75%	Phenobarbital reduces bilirubin, often to normal	Increased bilirubin concentration with estrogens; diagnostic urine coproporphyrin isomer pattern (total is normal, with isomer I increased to ≥80% of total)	Characteristic urine coproporphyrin excretion pattern (total is increased ≥2.5-fold in ~65% of cases but isomer I always <80% of total)
Major clinical features	Kernicterus in infancy if untreated; may occur later despite therapy	Rare late-onset kernicterus with fasting	None	Occasional hepatosplenomegaly	None
Hepatic morphology/histology	Normal	Normal	Normal; occasionally increased lipofucin pigment	Liver grossly black; coarse, dark centrilobular pigment	Normal
Bile bilirubin fractions†	>90% unconjugated	Largest fraction (mean 57%) monoconjugates	Mainly diconjugates but monoconjugates are increased (mean 23%)	Mixed conjugates, reported increase in diconjugates	Increased conjugates
Inheritance (all autosomal)	Recessive	Recessive	Promoter mutation is recessive; missense mutation often dominant	Recessive; rare kindred appears dominant	Recessive
Diagnosis	Clinical and laboratory findings, lack of response to phenobarbital	Clinical and laboratory findings, response to phenobarbital	Clinical and laboratory findings; promoter genotyping; liver biopsy rarely necessary	Clinical and laboratory findings; liver biopsy unnecessary if coproporphyrin studies available; BSP disappearance	Clinical and laboratory findings; urine coproporphyrin analysis; BSP disappearance
Treatment	Phototherapy or tin protoporphyrin as short-term therapy; liver transplantation definitive	Consider phenobarbital if baseline bilirubin ≥8 mg/dL	None necessary	Avoid estrogens; no other therapy necessary	No treatment necessary

*Sulfobromophthalein studies: may be useful in distinguishing Dubin-Johnson and Rotor syndromes if coproporphyrin isomer studies are not available.
†Bilirubin in normal bile: <5% unconjugated bilirubin, with an average of 7% bilirubin monoconjugates and 90% bilirubin diconjugates.
BSP = sulfobromophthalein; UDPGT = uridine diphosphate glucuronosyltransferase.

syndrome) is caused by a UGT1A1 inhibitor that is found in maternal serum.

Acquired Conjugation Defects. A modest reduction in bilirubin conjugating capacity occurs in advanced hepatitis or cirrhosis (Chapters 156 and 157). However, in this setting, conjugation is better preserved than other aspects of bilirubin disposition, such as canalicular excretion. Pharmacologic and metabolic perturbations may also lead to acquired reductions in bilirubin conjugation. Various drugs (e.g., pregnanediol, novobiocin, chloramphenicol, gentamycin, and several HIV protease inhibitors) may cause unconjugated hyperbilirubinemia by inhibiting UGT1A1. In all settings in which UGT1A1 inhibitors cause unconjugated hyperbilirubinemia, the hyperbilirubinemia is greater in patients with underlying Gilbert's syndrome.

Conjugated or Mixed Hyperbilirubinemia

Two phenotypically similar but mechanistically distinct inherited disorders, Dubin-Johnson syndrome and Rotor's syndrome, are characterized by conjugated or mixed hyperbilirubinemia with normal values for other standard liver tests (see Table 149–2). Dubin-Johnson syndrome results from any of several mutations in the gene encoding the ATP-dependent canalicular organic anion transporter MPR2/cMOAT (see Fig. 149–1). The molecular defect in Rotor's syndrome remains unknown, although some data suggest that it is precanalicular. Despite the conjugated hyperbilirubinemia, patients with these syndromes are not cholestatic and can be distinguished noninvasively by analysis of urine coproporphyrins (see Table 149–2), so liver biopsy is not required. Both syndromes carry a benign prognosis without specific therapy.

LIVER AND BILIARY TRACT DISEASE

Jaundice is a common sign of generalized hepatobiliary dysfunction, both acute and chronic. Icteric hepatobiliary disease is readily distinguished from the isolated disorders of bilirubin metabolism because the increase in plasma bilirubin concentration occurs in association with abnormalities in other standard liver tests. Liver diseases can be categorized as those in which the primary injury results from inflammation and hepatocellular necrosis as compared with those in which the central feature is inhibition of bile flow (cholestasis) and retention of bile constituents, some of which (e.g., bile acids) may be toxic. Although an accurate classification into one these two broad categories is possible in most patients on the basis of clinical findings and standard biochemical studies (see later), the further classification of patients with a predominantly cholestatic picture into those with decreased hepatocellular bile secretion and those with mechanical obstruction to the biliary tree may be more difficult. These diagnostically challenging conditions include several familial cholestatic syndromes; infiltrative disorders, particularly those involving the intrahepatic biliary tree; certain other inflammatory or neoplastic conditions; and drug reactions (see Table 149–1 and Chapters 150 to 156).

FAMILIAL CHOLESTASIS SYNDROMES. Benign recurrent intrahepatic cholestasis is a rare, autosomal recessive disorder characterized by recurrent attacks of malaise, pruritus, and jaundice beginning either in childhood or adulthood and varying in duration from weeks to months. Intervals between attacks may vary from months to years. This benign disorder does not progress to chronic liver disease or cirrhosis, and there is complete resolution between episodes; treatment during the cholestatic episodes is symptomatic. The familial intrahepatic cholestasis 1 (*FIC1*) gene, which is mutated in this condition, encodes a protein that transports aminophospholipids from the outer to the inner leaflet of various cell membranes; the gene is expressed strongly in the small intestine but only weakly in the liver. *Progressive familial intrahepatic cholestasis* describes three phenotypically related syndromes of cholestasis during infancy and end-stage liver disease during childhood. In contrast to the selective bilirubin transport defect in Dubin-Johnson syndrome, the conjugated hyperbilirubinemia in these syndromes is caused by generalized bile secretory failure.

POSTOPERATIVE JAUNDICE. This multifactorial syndrome can be caused by increased bilirubin production (e.g., breakdown of transfused erythrocytes, resorption of hematomas) and/or decreased hepatic clearance (e.g., bacteremia, endotoxemia, parenteral nutrition, perioperative hypoxia). Hyperbilirubinemia, which is the main biochemical feature, is often accompanied by a several-fold increase in the alkaline phosphatase and/or γ-glutamyl transpeptidase (GGT) levels. Aminotransferases are, at most, minimally elevated, and synthetic function is typically normal. The differential diagnosis includes biliary obstruction (Chapter 158) or hepatocellular injury related to shock, anesthetic injury (Chapter 150), or post-transfusion hepatitis (Chapter 151). Postoperative jaundice per se is not a threat to the patient, and it usually resolves in parallel with the patient's overall condition.

JAUNDICE IN PREGNANCY. Jaundice in pregnancy (Chapter 253) may result from any liver disease that also affects nonpregnant women or from conditions unique to pregnancy. The unique conditions include a generally modest and self-limited elevation of the aminotransferase and bilirubin levels during the first trimester, often in patients with hyperemesis gravidarum; intrahepatic cholestasis of pregnancy, which occurs during the second and third trimesters and resolves spontaneously after delivery; or acute fatty liver or the HELLP (hemolysis, elevated liver enzymes, and low platelets) syndrome, in association with preeclampsia in the third trimester (Chapters 154, 179, and 253). Acute fatty liver may resemble fulminant hepatic failure, with early delivery a prerequisite to maternal recovery; a defect in the oxidation of fatty acids is found in some infants born after these pregnancies.

Diagnostic Tools for the Evaluation of Liver Disease

Accurate diagnosis and the distinction between acute and chronic disease are often dependent on appropriate selection and interpretation of a spectrum of laboratory and imaging studies.

Tests used in initial evaluation of liver disease fall into two categories: (1) tests that indicate injury, such as release of intracellular enzymes, and (2) tests that measure, or at least reflect, actual function. Tests that reflect injury do not measure liver function and should not be called liver function tests.

The important functions of the liver include clearance, biotransformation and detoxification of potentially toxic metabolites and exogenous compounds, synthesis and export of various plasma proteins, and a critical integrative role in the intermediary metabolism of carbohydrates, amino acids, and lipids (Chapter 148). In specific diseases, some of these functions may be markedly compromised, whereas others are little affected. Liver tests must be chosen with care and interpreted within the total clinical context. In specific situations, serial determinations are often helpful to assess the course of disease or the effects of therapy.

SERUM ENZYME TESTS

The levels of hepatic enzymes found in plasma are a measure of hepatocyte turnover or injury. Enzymes released during normal hepatocyte turnover are believed to be the basis for normal circulating levels. Cell injury and cell death activate phospholipases that create holes in the plasma membrane, thereby increasing the release of intracellular contents.

AMINOTRANSFERASES. The aminotransferases (formerly called transaminases) catalyze transfer of the α-amino group of aspartate (aspartate aminotransferase, AST) or alanine (alanine aminotransferase, ALT) to the α-keto group of ketoglutarate. Serum levels are normally 40 IU/L or less (Chapter 478) but can exceed 1000 IU/L in acute hepatocyte injury, for example, from viral infection (Chapter 151) or toxins (Chapter 150). ALT is a purely cytosolic enzyme. Distinct isoforms of AST are present in cytosol and mitochondria. Expression of the mitochondrial isoform and its physiologic export from the hepatocyte are upregulated by ethanol. Circulating levels of AST and ALT are elevated in most hepatic diseases, and the degree of aminotransferase activity roughly reflects the current activity of the disease process. There are, however, critical exceptions. In even the most severe cases of alcoholic hepatitis, aminotransferase levels greater than or equal to 200 to 300 IU/L are uncommon (Chapter 155). By contrast, aminotransferase activities of 1000 IU/L or greater are often present in even mild acute viral hepatitis (Chapter 151) or shortly after acute biliary obstruction, for example, during passage of a gallstone (Chapter 158). Conversely, aminotransferase levels may decline during the course of massive hepatic necrosis because liver injury is so extensive that little enzyme activity remains (Chapter 157).

Aminotransferase levels are useful in several distinct ways. First, they provide a relatively specific screening test for hepatobiliary disease. Although AST levels may be increased with disease of other organs (notably myocardial and skeletal muscle), values 10 times or greater than the upper limit of normal almost invariably indicate hepatobiliary pathology. Moreover, in the total clinical context, the source of increased aminotransferase activity is usually obvious. Aminotransferase levels are also used to monitor the activity of an acute or chronic parenchymal liver disease and its response to therapy. However, levels in a given patient may correlate poorly with the severity of the disease as assessed by liver biopsy, particularly in chronic hepatitis C (Chapter 152). Aminotransferases are also often normal in advanced cirrhosis (Chapter 156), in which they are of limited prognostic value. Finally, aminotransferase levels may provide diagnostic clues. AST levels 15 or more times normal are unusual in *chronic* bile duct obstruction without cholangitis, and AST levels 6 or more times normal are uncommon in alcoholic liver disease in the absence of other causes. In most liver diseases, the ratio of AST to ALT is usually less than or equal to 1. However, ratios are typically 2 or higher in alcoholic fatty liver and alcoholic hepatitis (Chapters 155 and 156), reflecting increased synthesis as well as secretion of mitochondrial AST into plasma and selective loss of ALT activity because of the pyridoxine deficiency commonly seen in alcoholism. An elevated AST/ALT ratio also occurs in fulminant hepatitis related to Wilson's disease (Chapter 224).

ALKALINE PHOSPHATASE. Alkaline phosphatases are widely distributed enzymes (e.g., liver, bile ducts, intestine, bone, kidney, placenta, and leukocytes) that catalyze the release of orthophosphate from ester substrates at an alkaline pH. The normal activity level in adult serum is highly dependent on the measurement method, age, and sex. Two methods in current use have upper limits of normal in adults of 85 and 110 IU/L (Chapter 478). Higher levels are normal in children and in pregnancy. Results must always be compared with the appropriate normal range. In bone, alkaline phosphatase participates in the deposition of hydroxyapatite in osteoid. In other sites, including liver, its phosphatase activity may facilitate movement of molecules across cell membranes. Serum alkaline phosphatase activity usually reflects principally the hepatic and bone isozymes; the intestinal form may account for 20 to 60% of the total after a fatty meal. There is a substantial placental contribution to the alkaline phosphatase level late in pregnancy; the *Regan isozyme,* a variant that appears identical to the placental form, is associated with hepatomas, lung cancer, and other tumors (Chapter 202).

Elevations in the serum alkaline phosphatase activity in cholestatic hepatobiliary disease result from two distinct mechanisms: increased synthesis and secretion of the enzyme and solubilization from the apical (canalicular) surface of hepatocytes and the luminal surface of biliary epithelial cells by the increased local concentrations of bile acids that occur with cholestasis. Serum alkaline phosphatase activity may also be increased in bone disorders (e.g., Paget's disease [Chapter 263], osteomalacia [Chapter 259], bone metastases [Chapter 208]), during rapid bone growth in children, in the later stages of pregnancy, with chronic renal failure (Chapter 117), and, occasionally, in the presence of malignancy not involving bones or liver. The source is often obvious, but when it is not, methods such as heat stability and electrophoretic separation can distinguish hepatobiliary alkaline phosphatase from other forms. A simpler alternative is to measure serum levels of GGT or 5′-nucleotidase (5-NT), which tend to parallel levels of alkaline phosphatase in hepatobiliary disease but are usually not increased in bone disease. With a serum half-life of approximately 1 week, serum alkaline phosphatase levels may remain elevated for days to weeks after resolution of biliary obstruction. This delay may be especially misleading when it is accompanied by prolonged direct-reacting hyperbilirubinemia owing to delayed clearance of δ-bilirubin.

Modest increases in serum alkaline phosphatase activity (≤3 times normal) occur in many hepatic parenchymal disorders, including hepatitis and cirrhosis. In the absence of bone disease, larger increases (3 to 10 times normal) usually indicate obstruction of bile flow. Although the highest levels usually reflect obstruction of the common bile duct, major elevations also occur with intrahepatic cholestasis and with infiltrative or mass lesions (primary or metastatic cancer, lymphoma, leukemia, sarcoidosis, or infection with *Mycobacterium avium-intracellulare*). A normal serum bilirubin in the setting of chronic elevation of the alkaline phosphatase level can occur early in primary biliary cirrhosis (Chapter 156), but this combination also suggests localized infiltrative disease or obstruction of a portion of the biliary tree related to other localized lesions, such as stricture or tumor (Chapter 158). Alkaline phosphatase is a relatively sensitive screening test for primary or metastatic tumors of the liver, but up to one third of patients with isolated elevations of hepatobiliary alkaline phosphatase have no detectable liver or biliary disease.

OTHER HEPATIC ENZYMES. *5′-NT* is a plasma membrane enzyme that cleaves orthophosphate from the 5′ position on the pentose sugar of adenosine or inosine phosphate. *Leucine aminopeptidase (LAP)* is a ubiquitous cellular peptidase. The serum levels of both usually increase in cholestasis. Accordingly, their major use is to confirm whether an elevated serum alkaline phosphatase is hepatic in origin. Both enzymes may be increased late in normal pregnancy.

γ-Glutamyl transpeptidase is present in many tissues. Its serum activity increases in hepatobiliary disease but also after myocardial infarction; in neuromuscular diseases, pancreatic disease (even in the absence of biliary obstruction), pulmonary disease, and diabetes; and during the ingestion of ethanol and other inducers of microsomal enzymes. Nevertheless, because serum GGT levels are usually normal in bone disease, the enzyme may be helpful in confirming the hepatic origin of alkaline phosphatase. Measurement of GGT has been proposed as a sensitive screening test for hepatobiliary disease and for monitoring abstinence from ethanol. Because of its low specificity, many persons who test positive have no identifiable liver disease on further study. GGT offers no clear advantage over LAP or 5′-NT for identifying the source of increased serum alkaline phosphatase activity except in pregnancy. Serum GGT levels may be normal despite elevated hepatobiliary alkaline phosphatase levels in certain rare disorders, including benign recurrent intrahepatic cholestasis and progressive familial intrahepatic cholestasis types 1 and 2 (see earlier and Chapter 154).

Lactate dehydrogenase levels are often elevated in liver disease but are usually not helpful diagnostically because this enzyme is also found in most other body tissues.

TESTS BASED ON CLEARANCE OF METABOLITES AND DRUGS

A major function of the liver is to remove various metabolites and toxins from the blood (Chapter 150). In liver disease, clearance of such molecules may be impaired because of loss of parenchymal cells, diminished bile secretion, biliary obstruction, decreased cellular uptake or metabolism, or reduced or heterogeneous hepatic blood flow. When a metabolite is produced at a relatively constant rate (e.g., bilirubin), its serum level can be a sensitive indicator of liver function. The removal rate from plasma of certain exogenous drugs and dyes can be similarly interpreted.

BILIRUBIN. The differential diagnosis of hyperbilirubinemia (see earlier) includes generalized liver disease, inherited disorders of bilirubin metabolism (e.g., Gilbert's and Crigler-Najjar syndromes), and nonhepatic conditions (e.g., hemolysis). Higher bilirubin levels correlate with a poorer prognosis in alcoholic hepatitis (Chapter 155), primary biliary cirrhosis (Chapter 156), and fulminant hepatic failure (Chapter 157).

AMMONIA. Ammonia, a byproduct of amino acid metabolism, is removed from blood by the liver, converted to urea in the Krebs-Henseleit cycle, and excreted by the kidneys (Chapter 219). In the setting of portosystemic shunting or severe hepatic dysfunction (e.g., fulminant hepatic failure), ammonia levels rise. Measurements of blood ammonia are principally used to confirm a diagnosis of hepatic encephalopathy and to monitor the success of therapy, but the correlation of ammonia levels with the degree of encephalopathy is only approximate (Chapter 157). Correlations may be somewhat better if the measurement is made rapidly on an iced arterial blood sample. Elevated ammonia levels also occur when ammonia production is increased by intestinal flora (e.g., after a high-protein meal or gastrointestinal bleeding), by the kidney (in response to metabolic alkalosis or hypokalemia), or in rare genetic diseases that affect the pathway of urea synthesis (Chapter 219).

DRUG CLEARANCE. The rate of hepatic clearance of compounds such as sulfobromophthalein, lidocaine, and aminopyrine from the circulation can be measured chemically or with radiolabeled tracers. Although such tests can quantify hepatic function, they are rarely used in clinical practice.

TESTS REFLECTING HEPATIC SYNTHETIC FUNCTION

Coagulation Tests (Chapter 178)

PROTHROMBIN TIME. The prothrombin time (PT) reflects the plasma concentrations of both extrinsic and common pathway factors, that is, factors VII, X, and V, prothrombin, and fibrinogen. A prolonged PT most often results from vitamin K deficiency, liver disease, or both. Vitamin K, a fat-soluble vitamin, is found in many foods and is also synthesized by gut bacteria (Chapter 179). Vitamin K deficiency can be caused by poor dietary intake and malabsorptive states, including the fat malabsorption that results from cholestasis, and it also occurs with antibiotic suppression of gut flora, particularly in patients who receive inadequate vitamin K replacement.

The half-lives of clotting factors are typically less than 1 day. Factor VII, which has the shortest half-life, is usually the earliest and most severely depressed during periods of defective hepatic synthesis. Because the PT is dependent on the level of factor VII, it responds rapidly with changes in hepatic synthetic function; it is useful for following the course of acute liver diseases, in which a significant or growing prolongation of the PT may indicate a poor prognosis (Chapter 151). An abnormal PT that is due solely to vitamin K deficiency usually becomes normal within 24 to 48 hours after parenteral repletion. However, if decreased synthesis of clotting factors reflects hepatocyte dysfunction, there may be little or no response to vitamin K. Finally, prolongation of the PT may also reflect disseminated intravascular coagulation (Chapter 179), which should always be considered in the context of both acute liver failure and end-stage chronic liver disease.

PARTIAL THROMBOPLASTIN TIME. This test reflects both the intrinsic and common pathway factors, that is, all of the classical clotting factors except factor VII, and is, therefore, complementary to the PT. It is especially useful in detecting circulating anticoagulants (Chapter 179) but adds little to the PT in evaluating hepatic synthetic function.

Albumin

Albumin is produced solely by the liver. Its plasma concentration reflects a balance between its synthetic rate of about 100 to 200 mg/kg/day and its plasma half-life of about 21 days. The synthetic rate is affected by the patient's nutritional state, thyroid and gluco-corticoid hormone levels, plasma colloid osmotic pressure, exposure to hepatotoxins (e.g., alcohol), and presence of systemic disorders and/or liver disease. Many conditions increase albumin losses and shorten its plasma half-life, including nephrotic syndrome (Chapter 119), protein-losing enteropathy (Chapter 141), severe burns (Chapter 108), exfoliative dermatitis, and major gastrointestinal bleeding (Chapter 133). In cirrhosis with ascites (Chapter 156), hypoalbuminemia indicates diminished synthesis or redistribution into ascitic fluid. Thus, a reduced serum albumin concentration can be considered an indicator of decreased hepatic synthetic function only when these factors are not involved.

EXAMINATIONS OF URINE AND STOOL

Bilirubinuria always indicates a pathologic increase in plasma conjugated bilirubin levels. It is frequently seen with plasma conjugated bilirubin concentrations of 2 to 3 mg/dL, often appearing before the onset of clinical jaundice and persisting after jaundice has resolved. The quantification of urobilinogen in urine or feces is of limited clinical value. By contrast, stool culture or examination for ova and parasites may provide important information in selected patients. Testing of stool for occult blood may lead to discovery of a gastrointestinal lesion related to hepatobiliary disease (e.g., tumors metastatic to liver, ulcerative colitis associated with sclerosing cholangitis) or may explain the onset or worsening of hepatic encephalopathy.

HEMATOLOGIC TESTS IN LIVER DISEASE

In moderate to severe acute liver diseases, mild anemia may reflect low-grade hemolysis or marrow depression; modest leukopenia, often with atypical lymphocytes, and mild thrombocytopenia are also common. Bone marrow suppression may be caused by ethanol or drugs, and aplastic anemia may sometimes complicate acute viral hepatitis (Chapters 151 and 174). Zieve's syndrome (hemolytic anemia and hypertriglyceridemia) is a rare but well-characterized complication of alcoholic liver disease (Chapter 156). Coagulopathy frequently complicates both acute and chronic liver failure owing to depressed hepatic synthesis of clotting factors and/or disseminated intravascular coagulation (Chapters 178 and 179).

Chronic liver disease, especially if cholestatic, may be accompanied by target cells in the peripheral blood smear. Target cells are erythrocytes with an expanded cell membrane that reflects abnormalities in serum lipids. Spur cells (acanthocytes), most often found in advanced alcoholic cirrhosis, reflect a still greater increase in membrane cholesterol. Red blood cells, white blood cells, and platelets may all be decreased in the presence of portal hypertension related to hypersplenism (Chapters 156 and 164).

TESTS FOR SPECIFIC LIVER DISEASES

Patients who present with a picture of acute or chronic parenchymal liver disease are most likely to fall into one of three categories:

viral or toxic hepatitis, including alcoholic liver disease; autoimmune liver disease; or an inherited metabolic disorder (Chapters 150 to 152, 154, 155, and 369 to 371). Specific tests for viral antigens, nucleic acids, and antibodies are available for the conventional hepatitis viruses (Chapter 151) as well as Epstein-Barr virus (Chapter 371), cytomegalovirus (Chapter 370), and herpesviruses (Chapter 453), which are well-established but less common causes of liver disease. The major autoimmune diseases of the liver include primary biliary cirrhosis (Chapter 156), autoimmune hepatitis (Chapter 152), and various overlap syndromes. The starting point for establishing a specific diagnosis within this category is the search for specific autoantibodies in serum, including antimitochondrial antibodies against epitopes of the pyruvate dehydrogenase complex, which are virtually diagnostic of primary biliary cirrhosis (Chapter 156), and antinuclear, anti–smooth muscle, and anti–liver microsomal antibodies, which suggest a diagnosis of one of the subtypes of autoimmune hepatitis (Chapters 152, 156, and 158). The most prevalent of the hereditary metabolic disorders affecting the liver include hemochromatosis (Chapters 225), α_1-antitrypsin deficiency (Chapter 154), and Wilson's disease (Chapter 224).

LIVER BIOPSY

Liver biopsy can be of great help in the diagnosis of diffuse or localized parenchymal diseases, including chronic hepatitis, cirrhosis, and primary or metastatic malignancy in the liver. The value of liver biopsy in acute hepatitis or acute cholestatic jaundice may be primarily prognostic because the histologic changes in these settings may be nonspecific. However, toxic hepatitis related to certain medications may display diagnostic features. Liver biopsy for assessment of diffuse disease can be performed by the blind percutaneous technique or ultrasonographic visualization. When specific lesions, such as tumors, must be sampled, the biopsy can be guided by ultrasonographic or radiographic imaging or performed under direct visualization during laparoscopy or laparotomy. Relative or absolute contraindications include coagulopathy, high-grade biliary obstruction, biliary sepsis, ascites, and right pleural disease.

APPROACH TO THE PATIENT WITH JAUNDICE OR ABNORMAL LIVER TESTS

History, Physical Examination, and Initial Laboratory Studies

Patients with liver disease may present with jaundice or with other signs or symptoms, or the disease may be detected in the asymptomatic patient by the finding of abnormal liver tests during a routine evaluation. Regardless of how the patient comes to medical attention, the diagnostic approach (Fig. 149–3) begins with a careful history, physical examination, screening laboratory studies (complete blood cell count, measurement of plasma bilirubin concentration, assay of ALT, AST, and alkaline phosphatase levels, and PT), and formulation of an initial differential diagnosis. The ability to distinguish expeditiously between liver disease and extrahepatic biliary tract obstruction is the major goal of the initial evaluation, in part because the latter may call for prompt surgical intervention. Appropriate selection of second-level laboratory tests and imaging studies leads to a definitive diagnosis in most patients. Care in selecting tests, particularly imaging studies, can both maximize the likelihood of making a correct diagnosis and protect the patient from unnecessary discomfort, risk, and expense.

If the patient is asymptomatic and hepatic tests other than bilirubin are normal, hemolysis or an isolated disorder of bilirubin metabolism should be considered. If signs, symptoms, or laboratory abnormalities indicate hepatobiliary disease, certain patterns of findings help to distinguish intrinsic liver disease from biliary obstruction (Table 149–3). Pain in the right upper quadrant accompanied by a predominant increase in serum alkaline phosphatase activity suggests biliary obstruction (Chapter 158), as does a history of prior biliary surgery, right upper quadrant scars, or an abdominal mass. Fever and rigors, indicative of cholangitis, strengthen this conclusion. The incidences of gallstone disease and malignant neoplasm increase with age, although risk factors such as obesity or recent extensive diet-induced weight loss increase the risk of gallstones. Other risk factors (e.g., hepatitis exposure, transfusions, intravenous drug

Diseases of the Liver, Gallbladder, and Bile Ducts

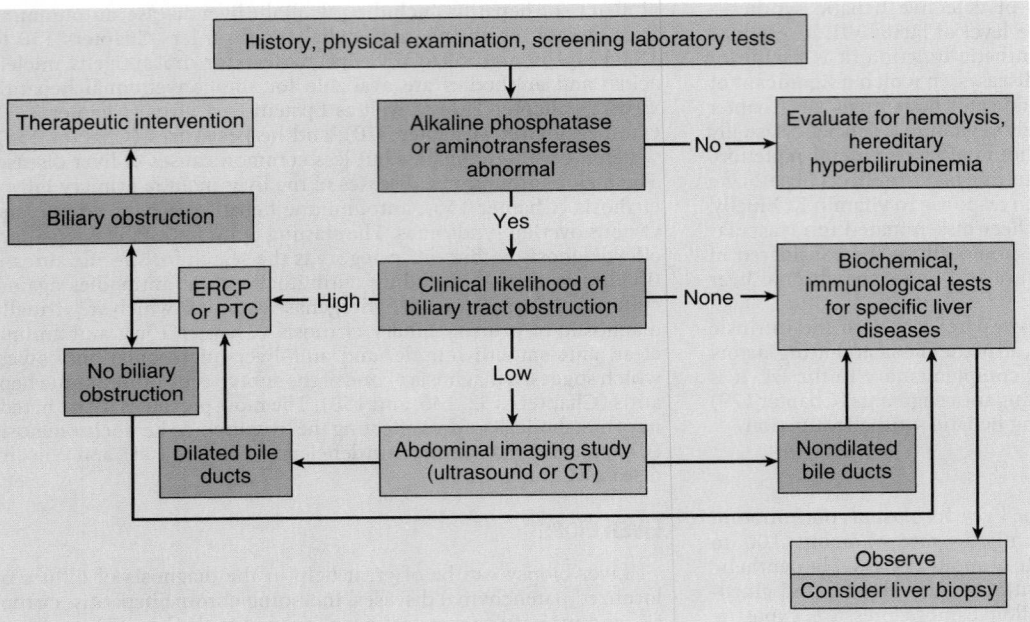

FIGURE 149–3 • Diagnostic algorithm for the evaluation of hyperbilirubinemia and other liver test abnormalities and/or signs and symptoms suggestive of liver disease. CT = computed tomography; ERCP = endoscopic retrograde cholangiopancreatography; PTC = percutaneous cholangiogram. (Modified from Lidofsky SD, Scharschmidt BF: Jaundice. *In* Feldman M, Scharschmidt BF, Sleisenger MH [eds]: Gastrointestinal and Liver Disease, 6th ed. Philadelphia, WB Saunders, 1998, p 227.)

Table 149–3 • OBSTRUCTIVE JAUNDICE VERSUS CHOLESTATIC LIVER DISEASE

FEATURE	SUGGESTS OBSTRUCTIVE JAUNDICE	SUGGESTS PARENCHYMAL LIVER DISEASE
History	Abdominal pain Fever, rigors Prior biliary surgery Older age Acholic stools	Anorexia, malaise, myalgias, suggestive of viral prodrome Known infectious exposure Receipt of blood products, use of intravenous drugs Exposure to known hepatotoxin Family history of jaundice
Physical examination	High fever Abdominal tenderness Palpable abdominal mass Abdominal scar	Ascites Other stigmata of liver disease (e.g., prominent abdominal veins, gynecomastia, spider angiomata, asterixis, encephalopathy, Kayser-Fleischer rings)
Laboratory studies	Predominant elevation of serum bilirubin and alkaline phosphatase Prothrombin time that is normal or normalizes with vitamin K administration Elevated serum amylase	Predominant elevation of serum aminotransferases Prolonged prothrombin time that does not correct with vitamin K administration Blood tests indicative of specific liver disease

use, alcohol use, certain medications, and family history of genetic diseases) and a predominant elevation in serum aminotransferase levels favor a diagnosis of parenchymal liver disease. Physical evidence of cirrhosis (e.g., spider angiomas, gynecomastia, ascites, splenomegaly) supports the diagnosis of chronic parenchymal disease.

Despite the general validity of these patterns, many exceptions exist. In particular, parenchymal disorders with prominent cholestasis may mimic biliary obstruction. Both alkaline phosphatase and GGT are usually elevated in patients with cholestasis; the combination of an elevated alkaline phosphatase and normal GGT suggests that the alkaline phosphatase is from bone. Conversely, an isolated elevation

of GGT may result from certain drugs (e.g., diphenylhydantoin) or alcohol even in the absence of liver disease. Because of the risk of life-threatening infection in the setting of unrelieved biliary tract obstruction, this possibility must always be considered and excluded if an alternative diagnosis is not definitely established.

Imaging Studies

If extrahepatic obstruction is suspected, it should be possible to determine its site and nature in virtually all patients (see Fig. 149–3). A reasonable initial step is the use of a noninvasive study such as ultrasonography (US) or computed tomography (CT) to determine whether the intrahepatic and/or extrahepatic biliary system is dilated, implying mechanical obstruction. Because of its lesser expense, lack of radiation exposure, portability, and convenience, US is often the procedure of choice and is substantially better than CT for detecting gallstones. CT may be preferred when better anatomic definition and information about the general level of obstruction are desired. Still more precise resolution may be obtained with magnetic resonance imaging cholangiopancreatography (MRCP), but this test is not generally used as the initial study because of its cost. Each of these techniques can fail to identify dilated ducts, particularly in patients with cirrhosis or primary sclerosing cholangitis. Conversely, a modest degree of ductal dilatation is common in a patient with a previous cholecystectomy and does not necessarily signify current obstruction. US has the disadvantage of being highly operator dependent, whereas optimal CT imaging requires the use of intravenous contrast agents that may be nephrotoxic.

If dilated ducts are found, the biliary tree should be examined by endoscopic retrograde cholangiopancreatography (ERCP) or percutaneous transhepatic cholangiography (PTC) (Chapter 132). ERCP involves positioning an endoscope in the duodenum, inserting a catheter through the ampulla of Vater, and injecting contrast medium into the distal common bile duct and/or pancreatic duct. PTC involves percutaneous passage of a needle through the hepatic parenchyma into a peripheral bile duct, followed by injection of contrast medium into the biliary tree through the peripheral duct. The choice of procedure is based on the suspected site of obstruction (proximal vs. distal); the presence of coagulopathy or a history of prior gastroduodenal surgery that might preclude PTC or ERCP, respectively; the likely need for a therapeutic procedure (e.g., stent placement or endoscopic sphincterotomy); and the skills of available staff.

SELECTION OF IMAGING TESTS

If the likelihood of obstruction is negligible on the basis of the clinical findings and laboratory test results, no imaging studies are required. Conversely, if obstruction is considered very likely, direct cholangiography by ERCP or PTC may be an appropriate initial choice. If obstruction is considered possible but not highly likely, noninvasive imaging with US or CT is a reasonable first study. Individual radiology suites have different levels of expertise for these procedures, and the local radiology staff may be quite helpful in recommending the best procedure for a given patient.

APPROACH TO THE ASYMPTOMATIC PATIENT WITH ABNORMAL LIVER TESTS

The apparently healthy patient with an isolated abnormality of the aminotransferase or alkaline phosphatase levels requires careful evaluation to identify any underlying disease while avoiding unneeded testing. Often, no significant disease is found despite extensive evaluation. Common causes of abnormal enzyme tests include obesity, alcohol consumption, chronic hepatitis C, steatohepatitis, bone disease, and muscle injury.

ASYMPTOMATIC AMINOTRANSFERASE ELEVATION. Epidemiologic data suggest that up to 25% of asymptomatic adult Americans have a mild to moderate elevation of aminotransferase levels. The incidental discovery of such abnormalities is currently the most frequent means by which liver disease is first recognized. Whereas up to one third of such patients have no elevation on subsequent testing, many others prove to have steatohepatitis (Chapter 155) or chronic hepatitis C (Chapter 152) (Fig. 149–4). Further evaluation is generally indicated only in patients with persistent abnormalities. Initial screening should include a careful history of exposure to hepatotoxins (alcohol, prescription drugs, over-the-counter medications, herbs, chemicals, and occupational exposures). If the abnormal test was an AST determination, a hepatic origin for the enzyme elevation should be confirmed with an ALT determination. If the ALT is normal, a muscle source is likely. If the ALT level is abnormal, the patient should be screened serologically for hepatitis B and C; young women should also be screened for markers of autoimmune liver disease. Older persons should be screened for hemochromatosis with an iron and transferrin level (Chapter 225), whereas younger persons should be screened with ceruloplasmin and urine copper for Wilson's disease (Chapter 224). If these tests are negative, screening for alpha$_1$-antitrypsin

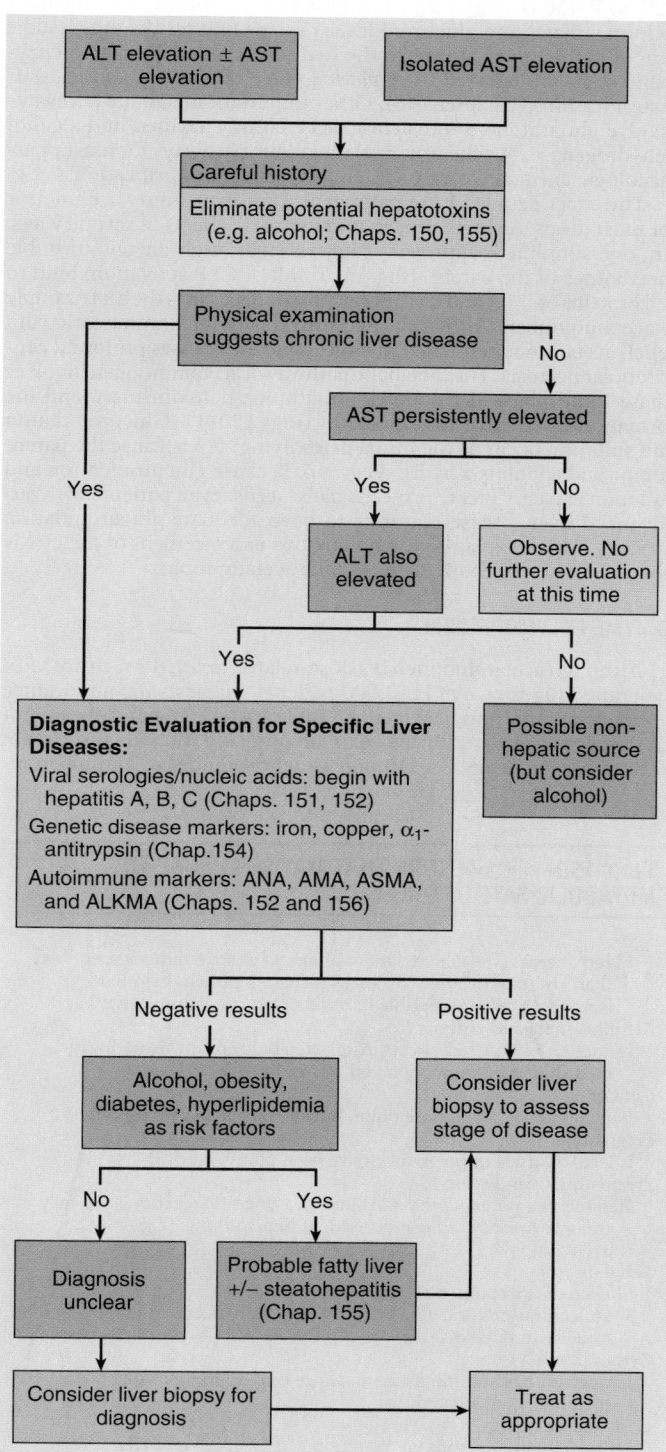

FIGURE 149–4 • Approach to the evaluation of isolated elevated levels of serum alanine aminotransferase (ALT) and/or aspartate aminotransferase (AST) in the asymptomatic patient. ANA = antinuclear antibody; AMA = antimitochondrial antibody; ASMA = anti–smooth muscle antibody; ALKMA = anti–liver/kidney microsomal antibody.

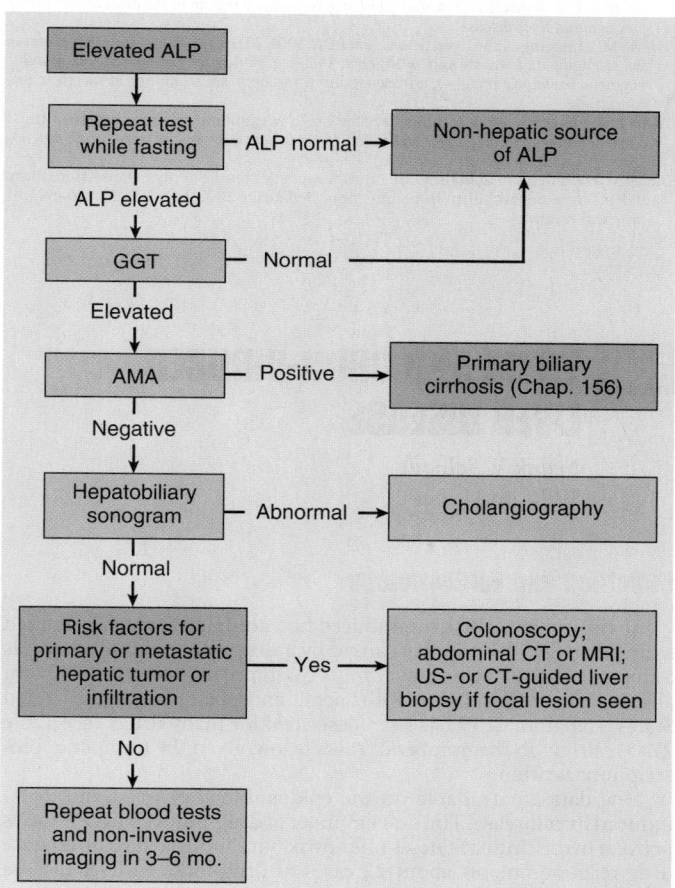

FIGURE 149–5 • Approach to the asymptomatic patient with isolated elevated levels of serum alkaline phosphatase (ALP). AMA = antimitochondrial antibody; CT = computed tomography; GGT = γ-glutamyl transpeptidase; MRI = magnetic resonance imaging; US = ultrasonography.

deficiency is indicated (Chapter 85). Malaria (Chapter 392), schistosomiasis (Chapter 402), and other parasitic diseases should be considered in appropriate settings. A substantial fraction of patients prove to have fatty liver, with or without nonalcoholic steatonecrosis (NASH; Chapter 155). AST abnormalities caused by alcohol-induced steatosis should become normal with several weeks of abstinence. If the abnormalities persist for 6 to 12 months without an apparent cause, liver biopsy should be considered.

ASYMPTOMATIC ALKALINE PHOSPHATASE ELEVATION (Fig. 149–5). Many patients with isolated elevation of the alkaline phosphatase level have nonhepatic causes, such as pregnancy or bone disease. The origin of an elevated alkaline phosphatase should be confirmed with a fasting sample because intestinal alkaline phosphatase may be elevated after a meal. A hepatic source is highly likely if the serum GGT is also abnormal. Women should be screened with an antimitochondrial antibody test; a positive result suggests primary biliary cirrhosis (Chapter 156). A careful history identifies patients at risk for intrahepatic cholestasis related to drugs or toxins. Essentially all other patients with persistently abnormal alkaline phosphatase should receive a hepatobiliary sonogram or other noninvasive imaging test. Demonstration of dilated intrahepatic or extrahepatic bile ducts should prompt direct visualization of the biliary tract by ERCP or PTC (Chapters 132 and 158). Evidence of an intrahepatic mass should prompt thorough evaluation for possible malignancy (Chapters 202 and 158). Because colon cancer often metastasizes to liver, colonoscopy or barium enema may be useful in appropriate cases (Chapter 200). Infiltrative diseases, including schistosomiasis and granulomatous hepatitis (Chapter 153), should be considered. Liver biopsy may be useful in patients whose abnormalities persist without an apparent cause.

SUGGESTED READINGS

Dufour DR: Evaluation of liver function and injury. *In* Henry JB (ed): Clinical Diagnosis and Management by Laboratory Methods, 20th ed. Philadelphia, WB Saunders, 2001, pp 264–280. *A detailed review of the role of laboratory testing in the evaluation of liver function and liver disease.*

Federle MP: Imaging of the liver. Semin Liver Dis 2001;21:133–291. *Reviews that examine the strengths and weaknesses of different imaging modalities (computed tomography, magnetic resonance imaging, ultrasonography, radionuclide scanning) in specific clinical settings.*

Green RM, Flamm S: AGA technical review on the evaluation of liver chemistry tests. Gastroenterology 2002;123:1367–1384. *An excellent overview of tests for the diagnosis and evaluation of liver disease.*

Kaplan M, Hammerman C, Maisels MJ: Bilirubin genetics for the nongeneticist: Hereditary defects of neonatal bilirubin conjugation. Pediatrics 2003;111(4 Pt 1):886–893. *A practical review.*

150 TOXIC AND DRUG-INDUCED LIVER DISEASE

Frank V. Schiødt
William M. Lee

Definition and Epidemiology

Toxin-induced and drug-induced hepatotoxicity, which is defined as any degree of liver injury caused by a drug or a toxic substance, is a frequent cause of acute liver injury, comprising more than 50% of all cases of acute liver failure with hepatic encephalopathy in the United States. Hepatotoxicity has been described for many drugs (see Table 27–5), although the number of cases is low, given the number of prescriptions written.

Few data are available on the epidemiology of toxic and drug-induced liver disease. The exact number of drug-induced liver injuries per year in the United States is unknown, but European data on adverse drug reactions report about 22 cases of drug-induced liver disease per 1 million people/year. In developing parts of the world, drug-induced liver disease is much less common and related to fewer drugs. In all parts of the world, probably only a small fraction of actual cases are reported, and a true estimate of the incidence of toxic and drug-induced liver disease may be impossible to obtain.

Pathogenesis

The liver, which is situated between the absorptive surface of the gastrointestinal tract and the targets of drugs throughout the body, is central to the metabolism of foreign substances. Most drugs and xenobiotics cross the intestinal brush border because they are lipophilic. *Biotransformation* is the process whereby lipophilic therapeutic agents are rendered more hydrophilic by the liver, resulting in drug excretion in urine or bile. In most instances, biotransformation changes a nonpolar to a polar compound through several steps. Foremost are oxidative pathways (e.g., hydroxylation) mediated by the cytochromes (CYPs) P-450 (Chapter 27). The next step is typically esterification to form sulfates and glucuronides, a process that results in the addition of highly polar groups to the hydroxyl group. These two enzymatic steps are referred to as *phase I* (CYP oxidation) and *phase II* (esterification) (Chapter 148). Other important metabolic pathways involve glutathione-S-transferase, acetylating enzymes, and alcohol dehydrogenase, but the principal metabolic pathways for most pharmacologic agents involve CYPs and subsequent esterification.

The exact details of the pathogenesis of liver injury are unclear for most drugs. A single drug may cause toxic effects in several ways. An oversimplified approach suggests that high-energy unstable metabolites of the parent drug, the result of CYP activation, bind to cell proteins or DNA and disrupt cell function. Perhaps the best example is acetaminophen. Although used universally for non-narcotic pain relief, acetaminophen taken in large quantities causes profound centrilobular necrosis. The metabolic pathway of acetaminophen involves phase I and phase II reactions, glutathione detoxification, and the formation of reactive intermediates (Fig. 150–1). Glucuronidation and sulfation occur as the initial detoxifying step because the parent compound contains a hydroxyl group. Because glucuronidation and sulfation capacity greatly exceeds daily needs, even patients with far-advanced liver disease continue to have adequate glucuronidation capacity, which explains why no obvious enhancement of toxicity is observed when cirrhotic patients take acetaminophen.

ENZYME POLYMORPHISM

Although acetaminophen is a dose-related toxin, the rarity of idiosyncratic drug toxicity (1 : 10,000 patients) suggests the importance of environmental and host factors (Table 150–1). Genetically variant CYP isoenzymes partially may explain observed individual variation in responses to drugs. An example is debrisoquine, an antihyperten-

---

Table 150–1 • FACTORS THAT MAY INFLUENCE THE METABOLIC FATE OF DRUGS

Age
    Elderly seem to be affected more often. Adults are more susceptible than children in some instances (acetaminophen, halothane, isoniazid), less susceptible in others (aspirin, valproic acid)

Alcohol, acute and chronic
    Induction of CYP2E1 affects drugs metabolized by this pathway, including acetaminophen and isoniazid

Gender
    Females are affected more often, but the mechanism is unknown

Pregnancy
    Effects of drugs in pregnancy have been poorly studied

Preexisting liver disease
    Hepatic disease may *protect* against idiosyncratic reactions and may *enhance* toxicity in dose-dependent hepatotoxins (e.g., acetaminophen)

Renal disease
    Slowed disappearance of parent compound yields higher concentrations and affects P-450 (e.g., enhancement of tetracycline toxicity in renal disease)

Certain foods
    Grapefruit has an unknown substance that interferes with the metabolism of some drugs

Concomitant drugs
    Drug-drug interactions are common causes of adverse effects (e.g., valproate and chlorpromazine together lead to enhanced cholestasis)

Genetic factors
    Enzyme polymorphisms (e.g., enhanced phenytoin liver disease in patients with defective epoxide hydrolase activity), HLA phenotypes (e.g., nitrofurantoin susceptibility)

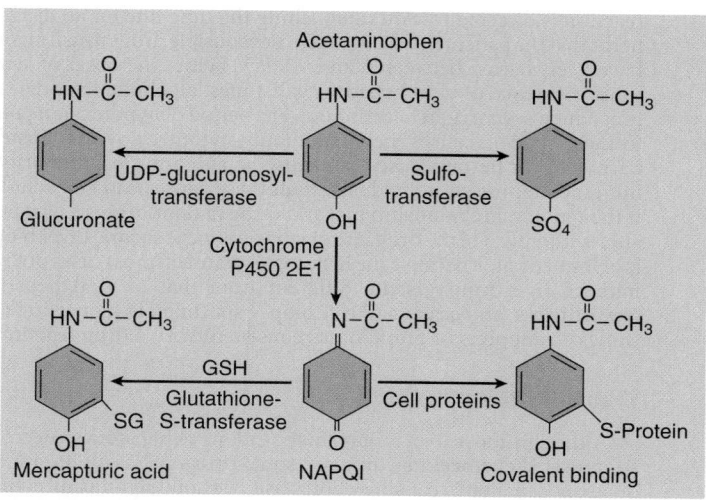

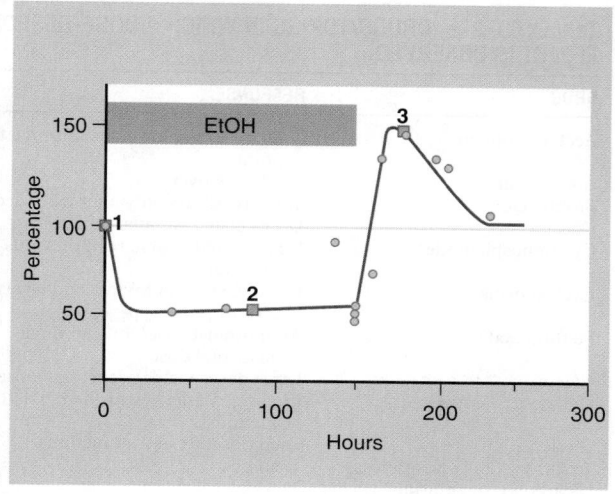

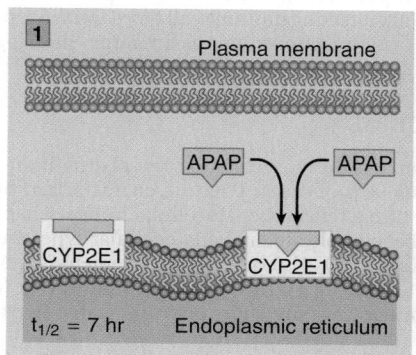

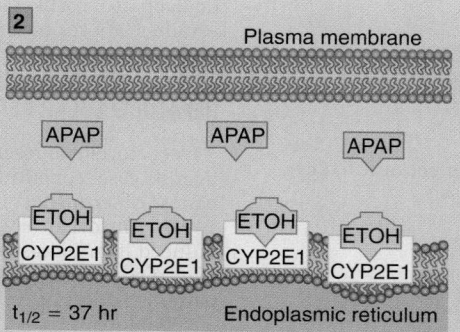

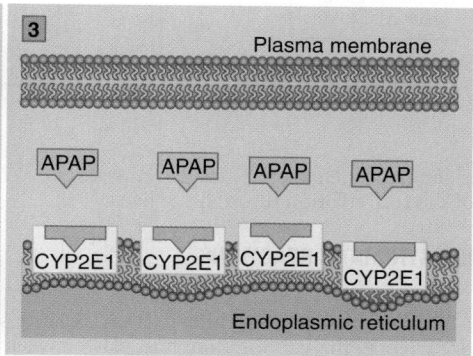

FIGURE 150–1 • Acetaminophen metabolism. Although acetaminophen is metabolized largely by sulfation or glucuronidation under normal conditions, exceeding recommended doses increases the proportion metabolized by cytochrome P-450 2E1, which leads to the highly reactive intermediate N-aminoparaquinoneamine (NAPQI) (A). This compound leads to liver injury unless scavenging by glutathione yields the inert, water-soluble mercapturic acid. The presence of alcohol (EtOH), which competes for cytochrome P-450 2E1, not only inhibits NAPQI formation, but also induces the enzyme so that the half-life is slowed and more enzyme is present (B and C). After cessation of alcohol, NAPQI formation is enhanced by the presence of the induced enzyme and the lack of competition from alcohol. Toxicity is a dynamic process and may be most pronounced in the 24 hours after cessation of alcohol. (Adapted from Thummel KE, Slattery JT, Ro H, et al: Ethanol exposure and acetaminophen hepatotoxicity: Inhibition and induction of hepatotoxic metabolite formation. Clin Pharmacol Ther 2000;67:5991–5999.)

sive drug marketed in Europe, which is hydroxylated by CYP2D6, an isoform that is totally absent in 5% of normal individuals. Lack of CYP2D6 greatly prolongs the half-life of the parent compound in affected individuals. Another example is the phenomenon of fast compared with slow acetylation, which affects whole races and has been implicated in variation in the metabolism of isoniazid. Most known genetic variants that occur relatively frequently cannot explain, however, the formation of a toxic intermediate in only a rare individual.

Most drugs are small organic compounds, unlikely to evoke an immune response. Although some toxic drug reactions are associated with an obvious allergic response, most are not. Nevertheless, immune mechanisms not associated with systemic allergic IgE reactions or skin hypersensitivity might be involved. Studies suggest that the products of cytochrome P-450 metabolism, the highly reactive intermediates that are formed within the microsomes, covalently bind to the enzyme itself to form a drug-hapten adduct that disables the enzyme and injures the cell. Haptenization then evokes an immune response directed against the newly formed antigen or neoantigen. P-450s have been shown to traffic to the plasma membrane, allowing the drug-P-450 adduct to become the target of a subsequent cytolytic attack. Whether these adducts or smaller peptides processed and presented by the major histocompatibility complex class I and class II schemes are the targets is unclear. The association among neoantigens, autoantibodies, and hepatotoxic drugs implicates an immunologic mechanism.

Whether or not an individual drug causes significant cell necrosis, the P-450-drug adducts can evoke the immune response. Any subsequent P-450-drug adduct present on the hepatocyte surface would evoke a further response. Responses may be antibody-mediated or occur from direct cytolytic attack by primed T cells.

Specific genetically determined components of the immune response may be important. A specific HLA haplotype has been associated with amoxicillin-clavulanate–induced hepatitis, and polymorphisms have been identified for the interleukin-10 promoter and for tumor necrosis factor-α. A multistep, immune-based mechanism would explain best the rarity of idiosyncratic reactions and their severity and the findings of mild, nonprogressive liver injury in some patients—those with "protective" phenotypes.

OTHER MECHANISMS

In drug-induced cholestasis, disruption of specific transport proteins or processes in hepatocytes or cholangiocytes may be the key events. Estrogen may cause multiple canalicular membrane transport changes, affecting, among others, the canalicular bile salt pump. Uncoupling or inhibition of mitochondrial respiration may lead to microvesicular steatosis.

Classification of Hepatotoxic Agents

Although there are a few dose-related toxins, most drugs involved in liver disease cause idiosyncratic, unpredictable toxicity.

INTRINSIC (DOSE-DEPENDENT) AGENTS

Acetaminophen (see later) and a few other agents seem to have a clear dose-response effect, although idiosyncrasy also usually plays a role (Table 150–2). Some toxins, such as α amanitine produced by Amanita mushrooms, cause dose-related injury. Amanita poisoning may occur after ingestion of the mushrooms Amanita phalloides (death cap) or Amanita virosa (deadly agaric). The dose-dependent toxic effect to the liver is attributed to amatoxin, an ingredient of the mushrooms that further enhances the toxic effect by its enterohepatic

Table 150–2 • DRUGS/TOXINS IN WHICH A DOSE-RESPONSE EFFECT IS OBSERVED

DRUG	RESPONSE
Acetaminophen	Total dose, single versus multiple time points
Amiodarone	Total dose over time
Bromfenac	Toxicity occurs only after extended use
Cocaine	Dose-related vascular collapse
Cyclophosphamide	Dose related, worse with previous ALT elevations
Cyclosporine	Cholestasis with toxic blood levels, CYP3A phenotype
Methotrexate	Aminotransferase/fibrosis; single dose/total dose
Niacin	Large doses yield vascular collapse
Oral contraceptives	Prolonged usage yields hepatic adenomas
Tetracycline	Total dose, renal dysfunction
Toxins (yellow phosphorus, carbon tetrachloride, amanita toxin, bacterial toxins)	Total dose

ALT = alanine aminotransferase.

recirculation characteristics, exerting the toxic effect on each cycle of the recirculation through the liver.

IDIOSYNCRATIC REACTIONS

Most drug reactions occur in 1 in 1000 to 1 in 200,000 patients. Characteristics of these idiosyncratic reactions include infrequent occurrence, the varying time intervals between the initial exposure and the action, and the varying severity of reactions among affected individuals. There also are similarities such as "class effects" (similar drugs exhibit similar features) (see Table 27–5), a pattern consistent for each drug, and the fact that rechallenge with a responsible agent usually leads to a more severe reaction with a shorter latency compared with the initial exposure.

Nonsteroidal anti-inflammatory drugs (NSAIDs), antibiotics, and anticonvulsants are associated more frequently with drug-induced liver disease, whereas hormones, antihypertensive drugs, digoxin, and antiarrhythmic drugs are implicated rarely. Idiosyncratic reactions occur infrequently enough that some drugs continue to be used when their effectiveness or uniqueness make the risk acceptable. An example is isoniazid, which is among the few drugs implicated in drug-induced liver injury in developing countries. Of individuals receiving isoniazid as a single agent for tuberculosis prophylaxis, 15 to 20% may develop increased aminotransferase levels, but only 0.1 to 1% develop severe hepatic necrosis (Chapter 341)—a rate that is high compared with other idiosyncratic drug reactions, yet low enough that isoniazid, because of its effectiveness, remains a key drug. NSAIDs, including the newer cyclooxygenase type 2 inhibitors, and antibiotics are the most common class of drugs associated with idiosyncratic hepatotoxic reactions (see Table 150–1).

Diagnosing Drug Reactions

Patients often have few or nonspecific complaints, but typically they have elevated aminotransferase levels, often out of proportion to the reported symptoms. Clinical features include nausea, fatigue, occasional right upper quadrant pain, and nonspecific symptoms similar to other forms of hepatitis (Chapter 151). Fever or pharyngitis (typically seen in phenytoin reactions) may be present. No specific physical findings are present except possibly for a skin rash to raise suspicion for drug toxicity. Any patient who develops jaundice is at risk for having a severe or fatal outcome.

Abnormal aminotransferases with the use of a new drug should raise suspicion of a drug-induced reaction and prompt immediate discontinuation of the drug rather than waiting for further diagnostic tests to confirm or exclude the diagnosis. This rapid discontinuation of medication at the first sign of liver disease can prevent most fatal liver injuries. The evaluation of the patient with suspected drug

reaction is directed toward establishing the time line for all drugs or herbs that the patient may have taken. Responsible drugs usually would have been started between 5 and 90 days before the onset of symptoms. Evidence of viral hepatitis, gallstones, alcoholic liver disease, pregnancy, severe right heart failure, or a period of hypotension points to these specific causes. Less commonly, cytomegalovirus, Epstein-Barr virus, or herpesviruses can cause hepatic injuries, primarily in immunosuppressed individuals. If all these causes can be excluded, if the temporal relationship fits, and if the patient begins to improve after withdrawal of the drug, the diagnosis is more secure. Liver biopsy is of limited value because the histologic picture of most cases of drug-induced liver injury is not different from that of viral hepatitis. Nevertheless, an occasional liver biopsy specimen in a puzzling case shows eosinophils or granulomas consistent with a drug reaction.

Types of Drug Reactions

Although most liver injury involves direct hepatocyte necrosis/apoptosis (hepatocellular injury), some drugs primarily injure bile ducts or canaliculi, causing cholestasis without significant damage to hepatocytes. Other drugs affect sinusoidal cells or present a particular pattern of liver injury affecting multiple cell types (mixed type). Another approach to drug reactions emphasizes the histologic changes involved and the cell type (Table 150–3 and Fig. 150–2).

HEPATOCELLULAR REACTIONS

Hepatocellular reactions are the most common type of drug-induced liver disease, constituting 90% of cases. They are characterized by a pattern of serum liver tests that reflects hepatocellular injury (Chapter 149). Many drugs have been implicated in hepatocellular-type, drug-induced liver disease (Table 150–4). Usually, improvement is quick after discontinuation of the drug (1 to 2 months), and only a few patients develop fulminant, acute liver failure with hepatic encephalopathy.

Histologic findings include necrosis and cellular infiltration. Necrosis may be zonal (e.g., acetaminophen-induced or carbon tetrachloride–induced) or diffuse (e.g., halothane-induced), and the inflammatory response consists of lymphocytes or eosinophils. Massive necrosis may cause acute liver failure and death.

Acetaminophen toxicity is the most common form of acute liver failure observed in the United States and has been the best understood example of direct hepatocyte toxicity. The incidence of acetaminophen poisoning varies widely throughout the world, but it is becoming more frequent and widespread. Liver injury occurs pre-

Table 150–3 • TYPES OF TOXIC AND DRUG REACTIONS

Autoimmune (*attack on cell surface markers*)
  Lovastatin, methyldopa, nitrofurantoin
Cholestatic (*attack on bile ducts*)
  Anabolic steroids, carbamazepine, chlorpromazine, estrogen, erythromycin
Fibrosis (*activation of stellate cells leads to fibrosis*)
  Methotrexate, vitamin A excess
Granulomatous (*macrophage stimulation*)
  Allopurinol, diltiazem, nitrofurantoin, quinidine, sulfa drugs
Hepatocellular (*damage to smooth endoplasmic reticulum and immune cell surface*)
  Acetaminophen, *Amanita* poisoning, diclofenac, isoniazid, lovastatin, nefazodone, trazodone, venlafaxine
Immunoallergic (*cytotoxic cell attack on surface determinants*)
  Halothane, phenytoin, sulfamethoxazole
Mixed (*see above*)
  Amoxicillin/clavulanate, carbamazepine, cyclosporine, herbs, methimazole
Oncogenic (*hepatic adenoma formation*)
  Oral contraceptives, androgenic agents
Steatohepatitis (*mitochondrial dysfunction: β-oxidation and respiratory chain*)
  Amiodarone, perhexiline maleate, tamoxifen
Vascular collapse (*ischemic damage*)
  Cocaine, ecstasy, nicotinic acid
Veno-occlusive disease (*endotheliitis of sinusoidal endothelial cells*)
  Busulfan, cytoxan

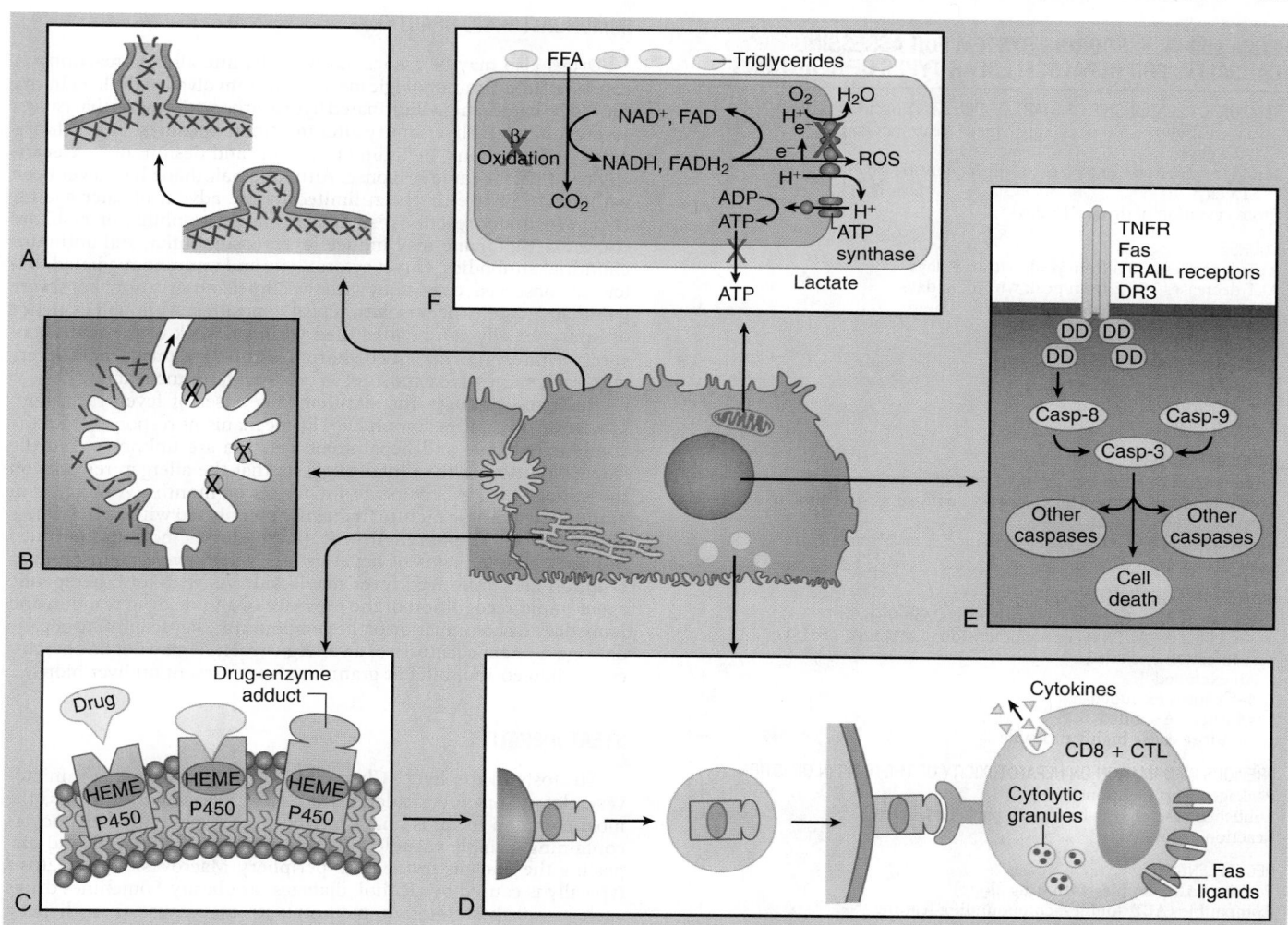

FIGURE 150–2 • Mechanisms of liver injury. Each form of liver injury targets specific organelles, although multiple organelles may be affected. The hepatocyte in the center may be affected in at least six ways: *A*, Disruption of intracellular calcium leads to actin fibril disassembly at the hepatocyte surface, resulting in blebbing of the cell membrane and subsequent rupture and cell lysis. *B*, In cholestatic diseases, disruption of actin filaments may occur with loss of villus processes. Interference with ion pumps limits excretion of bilirubin and other organic compounds. *C*, Most hepatocellular reactions involve the cytochrome P-450 system. The high-energy reaction involved may lead to binding of drug to enzyme, creating a new adduct. *D*, Enzyme-drug adducts may traffic to the cell surface and serve as target immunogens for cytolytic attack by T cells. *E*, Activation of apoptotic pathways results in cell death. *F*, Inhibition of beta oxidation or respiration in mitochondria results in microvesicular fat accumulation and lactic acidosis, a pattern characteristic of a variety of agents, including nucleoside analogues, tetracycline, and aspirin. (*A* adapted from Farrell GC: Drug-Induced Liver Disease. Edinburgh, Churchill Livingstone, 1994, p 44. *B* adapted from Trauner M, Meier PJ, Boyer J: Mechanisms of disease: Molecular pathogenesis of cholestasis. N Engl J Med 1998;339:1217–1227. *C* adapted from Watkins Zimmerman HJ: Hepatotoxicity, 2nd ed. Philadelphia, Lippincott Williams & Wilkins, 2000. *D* reprinted from Journal of Hepatology, Vol 26, Supplement 1, Robin M-A, Le Roy M, Descatoire V, Pessayre D, Plasma membrane cytochromes P450 as neoantigens and autoimmune targets in drug-induced hepatitis, Pages 23–30, Copyright 1997, with permission from Elsevier Science. *E* reprinted from Trends in Molecular Medicine, Vol 7, Reed JC, Apoptosis-regulating proteins as targets for drug discovery, Pages 314–319, Copyright 2001, with permission from Elsevier Science. *F* adapted from Pessayre D: Personal communication.)

dictably after intentional suicidal overdose; it also occurs when acetaminophen is used in excessive doses or sometimes even in therapeutic doses for pain relief. Enhanced toxicity occurs when patients are fasting or are chronic alcohol users, owing to enzyme induction and depletion of glutathione by alcohol and fasting; by comparison, acute alcohol intake may protect against acetaminophen toxicity during the period of alcohol ingestion. Thereafter, a rebound increase in available CYP2E1 results in increased toxicity in the 12 hours after ingestion because of enzyme induction (see Fig. 150–1). Patients with accidental acetaminophen overdose may fare worse than suicidal patients because the former present for treatment later in their course, even though suicidal patients take larger doses. The better outcome in acute overdose may be explained by earlier presentation and the use of N-acetylcysteine, an effective antidote. Nevertheless, one fifth of acetaminophen suicidal attempts are associated with severe liver injury and the potential for a fatal outcome.

The extremely elevated aminotransferase values (often >6000 IU/L and sometimes as high as 30,000 U/L) observed in suicidal and accidental acetaminophen ingestion help distinguish these cases from

viral hepatitis or other drug injury. The antidote N-acetylcysteine should be given by nasogastric tube on admission and for the ensuing 72 hours to provide glutathione substrate. In Europe, intravenous N-acetylcysteine is the standard treatment, beginning with a dose of 140 mg/kg in 300 mL of 5% dextrose over 1 hour, followed by a dose of 70 mg/kg in 5% dextrose over 1 hour given every 4 hours for 48 hours. An oral regimen is used in the United States because the intravenous formulation never received FDA approval: 140 mg/kg is given orally as a loading dose followed by 70 mg/kg every 4 hours for 17 doses (72 hours). Expected survival is greater than 80%, although liver transplantation occasionally is required.

CHOLESTATIC REACTIONS

Cholestatic reactions have been described for many drugs. Cholestasis is defined best as failure of the bile to reach the duodenum, and common symptoms are jaundice and pruritus. *Pure cholestasis* with no signs of hepatocellular necrosis is seen almost exclusively in patients taking oral contraceptives, anabolic steroids, or sex

Table 150–4 • SCORING SYSTEM FOR ASSESSING CAUSALITY FOR HEPATOCELLULAR TYPES OF REACTIONS

TEMPORAL RELATIONSHIP OF START OF DRUG TO START OF ILLNESS	
Initial treatment 5–90 days; subsequent treatment course: 1–15 days	+2
Initial treatment <5 or >90 days; subsequent treatment course: >15 days	+1
From cessation of drug: ≤15 days*	+1
COURSE	
ALT decreases ≥50% from peak within 8 days	+3
ALT decreases ≥50% from peak within 30 days	+2
If the drug is continued, inconclusive	0
RISK FACTORS	
Alcohol[†]	+1
No alcohol[†]	0
Age ≥55 years	+1
Age <55 years	0
CONCOMITANT DRUG	
Concomitant drug with suggestive time of onset	−1
Concomitant drug known hepatotoxin with suggestive time of onset	−2
Concomitant drug with further evidence of involvement (rechallenge)	−3
NUMBER OF NONDRUG CAUSES	
Hepatitis A, B, or C; biliary obstruction; alcoholism (AST ≥ 2× ALT); recent hypotension; CMV, EBV, or HSV infection excluded	
All excluded	+2
4–5 causes excluded	+1
<4 causes excluded	−2
Nondrug cause highly probable	−3
PREVIOUS INFORMATION ON HEPATOTOXICITY OF THE DRUG IN QUESTION	
Package insert mentions	+2
Published case reports but not in package label	+1
Reaction unknown	0
RECHALLENGE	
Positive (ALT doubles with drug alone)[‡]	+2
Compatible (ALT doubles, compounding features)[‡]	+1
Negative (increase in ALT but ≤2× ULN)[‡]	−2
Not done	0

For cholestatic reactions: *≤30 days; [†]alcohol or pregnancy; [‡]Read AP (or TB) instead of ALT.

Highly probable (score >8), *probable* (score 6–8), *possible* (score 3–5), *unlikely* (score 1–2), or *excluded* (score ≤ 0).

ALT = alanine aminotransferase; AP = alkaline phosphatase; AST = aspartate aminotransferase; CMV = cytomegalovirus; EBV = Epstein-Barr virus; HSV = herpes simplex virus; TB = total bilirubin; ULN = upper limits of normal.

Adapted from Danan G, Benichou C: Causality assessment of adverse reactions to drugs: I. A novel method based on the conclusions of international consensus meetings: Application to drug-induced liver injuries. J Clin Epidemiol 1993;46:1323–1330; and Benichou C, Danan G, Flahault A: Causality assessment of adverse reactions to drugs: II. An original model for validation of drug causality assessment methods: Case reports with positive rechallenge. J Clin Epidemiol 1993;46:1331–1336.

hormone antagonists, such as tamoxifen. Acute *cholestatic hepatitis* is characterized histologically by cholestasis (dilated canaliculi, brown granules in cytoplasm of hepatocytes), some degree of liver cell necrosis and bile duct injury, and inflammatory infiltration with polymorphonuclear leukocytes. Drugs that cause this type of reaction include carbamazepine, trimethoprim-sulfamethoxazole, and captopril.

Generally, drug-induced cholestasis requires a longer time to resolve than hepatocellular drug reactions. In some cases, segments of the intrahepatic biliary tree may be destroyed progressively, the so-called *vanishing bile duct syndrome* that occurs after a protracted course (>6 months) of drug-induced cholestasis. The result is a state of chronic cholestasis, resembling primary biliary cirrhosis (Chapter 158). Approximately 30 drugs have been implicated in the vanishing bile duct syndrome, including chlorpromazine and ajmaline. A sclerosing cholangitis–like syndrome with jaundice caused by intrahepatic and extrahepatic strictures of the bile ducts sometimes is observed in patients receiving intra-arterial floxuridine chemotherapy for hepatic metastases of colorectal cancer.

IMMUNOALLERGIC REACTIONS

Drugs also may be associated with definite allergic reactions. A combined toxic/immunologic mechanism is involved in the liver injury caused by halothane, a fluorinated hydrocarbon anesthetic that causes severe, often fatal liver injury after multiple exposures. Other fluorinated hydrocarbons, including isoflurane and desflurane, occasionally result in the same response. Although halothane has never been withdrawn, its use has been limited by the advent of safer agents. Hypersensitivity reactions, such as fever, eosinophilia, or rash, are common. Halothane may induce fever, eosinophilia, and antimitochondrial antibodies. Direct cytotoxicity and immune-mediated toxicity are observed, consistent with the clinical observation that severe halothane toxicity occurs with repeat exposures. Although evidence of injury usually can be identified within 1 week of the first exposure, the interval to toxicity is shortened and the damage more severe with each successive exposure, as befits an immune reaction.

Phenytoin induces the simultaneous onset of fever, rash, lymphadenopathy, and eosinophilia. The mechanisms responsible for the combined allergic and hepatotoxic reaction are unknown, but the slow resolution of the illness suggests that the allergen remains on the surface of the hepatocyte for weeks or months. A concurrent mononucleosis-like picture frequently is confused with a viral illness or streptococcal pharyngitis. If phenytoin is not discontinued promptly despite signs of hepatitis, a severe Stevens-Johnson drug eruption and prolonged fever may result. As with any therapeutic agent, rapid recognition of the presence of a toxic drug reaction and immediate discontinuation of the compound are key to limiting hepatic damage. Systemic features of an allergic reaction may not be obvious, even when eosinophilia or granulomas are present on liver biopsy.

STEATOHEPATITIS

Steatosis in the liver (Chapter 155) can be present in a microvesicular or macrovesicular pattern. Macrovesicular steatosis, the most common form, is characterized histologically by hepatocytes containing a single vacuole of fat filling up the hepatocyte and displacing the nucleus to the cell's periphery. Macrovesicular steatosis typically is caused by alcohol, diabetes, or obesity. Sometimes drugs such as corticosteroids or methotrexate may cause these hepatic changes. Amiodarone (Chapter 62) has been associated with a picture resembling alcoholic hepatitis, sometimes with progression to cirrhosis. The pathophysiology involves accumulation of phospholipids in the liver, eyes, thyroid, and skin. Treatment is primarily withdrawal of the drug and observation, although the half-life of amiodarone is prolonged. Tamoxifen, which has been used in long-term regimens for prevention of recurrent breast cancer (Chapter 204), also has been associated with a steatohepatitis picture evolving to cirrhosis.

In microvesicular steatosis, hepatocytes contain numerous small fat vesicles that do not displace the nucleus. Valproic acid, an anticonvulsant (Chapter 434), causes hepatotoxicity, either as microvesicular fat deposition resembling Reye's syndrome or in a more chronic indolent fashion associated with macrovesicular fat accumulation. Toxicity is more severe and frequent in children. These lesions are associated with disruption of mitochondrial DNA, with resulting anaerobic metabolism that leads to lactic acidosis in the most severe cases. Macrovesicular and microvesicular lesions may be observed concomitantly in some patients, and the microvesicular lesions are associated more often with a poor prognosis. Hepatocellular necrosis also may be present. Acute fatty liver of pregnancy (Chapter 154) and Reye's syndrome are two examples of severe liver diseases caused by microvesicular steatosis.

Drugs involved in microvesicular steatosis include valproate, tetracycline, and fialuridine. Aspirin use in children has been associated with Reye's syndrome, and the incidence of Reye's syndrome has decreased dramatically since warnings were issued concerning aspirin use in children.

EFFECTS OF SEX STEROIDS

Anabolic steroids, such as methyltestosterone, may cause cholestasis. Androgens may cause peliosis hepatis and benign or malignant tumors. Oral contraceptives may cause cholestasis, hepatic adenomas, or Budd-Chiari syndrome (hepatic vein thrombosis).

Antiandrogens used to treat prostate cancer, such as flutamide and nilutamide, and antipituitary drugs, such as cyproterone acetate, also have been associated with severe hepatocellular injury.

OTHER DRUG REACTIONS

Other less severe drug reactions involving the liver include granulomatous reactions, fibrosis, ischemic injury, and chronic autoimmune liver injury (Table 150–3). The type of reaction observed can be helpful in determining the likely agent because most drugs have a specific injury profile.

A pattern of veno-occlusive disease with obliteration of small intrahepatic veins, sinusoidal congestion, and necrosis is observed frequently in bone marrow transplant patients who receive chemotherapy with cyclophosphamide (Cytoxan) or busulfan. Symptoms including rapidly accumulating ascites, painful hepatomegaly, and jaundice develop soon after the chemotherapeutic regimen has begun. Rarely, herbal medicines such as pyrrolizidine alkaloids (*Crotolaria* and *Senecio* found in Jamaican bush tea) may cause veno-occlusive disease.

Toxins are associated with direct injury to hepatocytes in a dose-dependent fashion. Organic solvents, such as carbon tetrachloride and trichloroethylene, cause centrilobular injury. Yellow phosphorus, found in firecrackers and rat poisons, is a rare cause of liver injury either from accidental or from intentional exposure. Symptoms from poisoning are similar to those of any other types of hepatitis.

Mushroom poisoning, which follows ingestion of *Amanita phylloides* and related species, typically occurs in amateur mushroom fanciers in a dose-related fashion. The associated muscarinic effects predominate in the first hours after ingestion with severe diarrhea, vomiting, and profuse sweating. Hepatic failure follows if antidotes (see later) are not given. The overall prognosis for spontaneous recovery is poor; liver transplantation may be life-saving.

Differential Diagnosis

The differential diagnoses of toxic and drug-induced liver injury include almost the entire spectrum of liver diseases. Because the clinical picture of drug-induced liver injury ranges from pure hepatocellular to pure cholestatic variants, a high index of suspicion must be maintained, even when toxic or drug-induced liver injury is not obvious initially.

For dose-dependent hepatotoxins, the diagnosis may be easier to establish than for idiosyncratic drug reactions. Serum levels of acetaminophen, a thorough history, and characteristic biochemical abnormalities (high aminotransferase levels) usually reveal acetaminophen overdose, whereas a diagnosis of *Amanita* poisoning depends on history, symptoms of gastroenteritis (muscarinic reaction), and a positive mushroom identification.

For idiosyncratic drug reactions, the diagnosis sometimes is more difficult to establish. A standardized reporting form developed by an international panel provides a worthwhile causality assessment scoring system, called the *RUCAM* (Roussel Uclaf *c*ausality *a*ssessment *m*ethod; Table 150–4). These guidelines outline the steps an experienced clinician might use to assess likelihood of drug reactions. Causality assessment methods typically include temporal relationship, course after cessation of drug, risk factors, concomitant drugs, a search for nondrug causes (viral hepatitis), previous information concerning the drug, and response to rechallenge, which usually is not attempted.

Prevention

It is wise to defer embracing new drugs during their first year of introduction, particularly if they show no unique advantages over accepted formulations. Physicians must strive to instill in their patients a healthy level of alertness with regard to drug-induced liver injury, particularly for agents with known hepatotoxicity. Monitoring aminotransferase levels is suggested for known hepatotoxins, such as isoniazid or diclofenac, on a monthly basis but is unlikely to be cost-effective when an adverse reaction occurs less frequently, such as in only 1 in 50,000 patients. Because many drug reactions develop within days, monitoring provides no guarantee. Most fatal drug reactions could be prevented if the offending agent were withdrawn immediately, at the first sign of illness.

 **Treatment**

Prompt discontinuation of a suspected drug is mandatory. Available antidotes should be used for acetaminophen (*N*-acetylcysteine) and *Amanita* poisoning (penicillin, 250 mg/kg/day and thioctic acid, 5 to 100 mg every 6 hours intravenously, have been recommended, but there are no controlled trials). General supportive therapy ranges from intravenous fluid replacement to the intensive monitoring and treatment of patients with acute liver failure hepatic encephalopathy (Chapter 157). Liver transplantation is performed in more than 50% of patients with idiosyncratic drug-induced acute liver failure because the survival in this setting without transplantation is less than 20%.

Future Directions

Research in *pharmacogenomics* may allow the patient's own genetic information to guide individualized drug therapy and idiosyncratic drug reactions. The genetic information likely would concentrate initially on enzymes with variant alleles associated with a poor metabolism, such as CYP1A2 or CYP2C19 for isoniazid, CYP2C9 for piroxicam, or CYP2D6 for nortriptyline. Better postmarketing surveillance of all drugs should be a high priority to identify drugs whose hepatotoxicity was not previously appreciated.

SUGGESTED READINGS
Chitturi S, George J: Hepatotoxicity of commonly used drugs: Nonsteroidal anti-inflammatory drugs, antihypertensives, antidiabetic agents, anticonvulsants, lipid-lowering agents, psychotropic drugs. Semin Liver Dis 2002;22:169–184. *A good summary of current agents causing liver damage.*
Kaplowitz N: Causality assessment versus guilt-by-association in drug hepatotoxicity. Hepatology 2001;33:189–192. *Review of the problem of assessing causality in drug-related liver injury.*
Ostapowicz G, Fontana RJ, Schiødt FV, et al: Results of a prospective study of acute liver failure at 17 tertiary care centers in the United States. Ann Intern Med 2002;137:947–954. *The initial report of the Acute Liver Failure Study Group, describing the condition and the importance of drugs in causing severe hepatic failure in the United States.*
Stedman C: Herbal hepatotoxicity. Semin Liv Dis 2002;22:195–206. *This review provides an update on the various herbs implicated in liver injury.*

151 ACUTE VIRAL HEPATITIS

Jay H. Hoofnagle
Karen L. Lindsay

Acute viral hepatitis is at least five different diseases caused by five or more distinct and unrelated viruses. The disease is characterized clinically by symptoms of malaise, nausea, poor appetite, vague abdominal pain, and jaundice; biochemically by marked increases in serum bilirubin and aminotransferase levels; serologically by the presence of a hepatitis viral genome in liver and serum followed by development of antibodies to viral antigens; and histologically by varying degrees of hepatocellular necrosis and inflammation. Acute viral hepatitis typically is self-limited and resolves completely without residual liver injury or viral replication. A proportion of some forms of hepatitis can result, however, in a persistent infection with chronic liver injury. The five forms of viral hepatitis are similar clinically but can be distinguished by serologic assays.

The five known causes of acute hepatitis are the hepatitis A (HAV), B (HBV), C (HCV), D or delta (HDV), and E (HEV) viruses (Table 151–1). All except HBV are RNA viruses. Hepatitis A and E are forms of *infectious* hepatitis; they are spread largely by the fecal-oral route, are associated with poor sanitary conditions, are highly contagious, occur in outbreaks and sporadically, and cause self-limited hepatitis only. Hepatitis B, C, and D are forms of *serum* hepatitis; they are spread largely by parenteral routes and less commonly by intimate or sexual exposure; they are not highly contagious but instead occur sporadically, rarely causing outbreaks; and they are capable of leading to chronic hepatitis and, ultimately, to cirrhosis and hepatocellular carcinoma. Cases of an acute viral hepatitis–like syndrome that cannot be identified as being due to a known hepatitis virus occur and are termed acute *non-A, non-B, non-C, non-D, non-E (non-A–E) hepatitis* or *acute hepatitis of unknown cause.*

Table 151–1 • FIVE CAUSES OF ACUTE VIRAL HEPATITIS

HEPATITIS VIRUS	SIZE (nm)	GENOME	SPREAD	INCUBATION PERIOD (DAYS)	FATALITY RATE	CHRONIC RATE	ANTIBODY
A	27	RNA	Fecal-oral	15–45 mean 25	1%	None	Anti-HAV
B	45	DNA	Parenteral Sexual	30–180 mean 75	1%	2–7%	Anti-HBs Anti-HBc Anti-HBe
C	60	RNA	Parenteral	15–150 mean 50	<0.1%	70–85%	Anti-HCV
D (delta)	40	RNA	Parenteral Sexual	30–150	2–10%	2–7% 50%	Anti-HDV
E	32	RNA	Fecal-oral	30–60	1%	None	Anti-HEV

Epidemiology

Acute viral hepatitis is a common disease, affecting 0.5 to 1% of persons in the United States each year. The annual incidence of acute hepatitis fluctuates largely as a result of hepatitis A. Cases of hepatitis B and C have been decreasing since 1990. In population-based surveys, the viral causes of acute hepatitis were hepatitis A in 48%, hepatitis B in 34%, and hepatitis C in 15% of cases. Hepatitis D is rare in the United States (<1% of acute cases), and only imported cases of hepatitis E have been reported. In 3% of cases, the cause of hepatitis cannot be ascertained even after extensive testing. In clinical practice, other nonviral forms of acute hepatitis must be considered, especially mononucleosis (Chapter 371); secondary syphilis (Chapter 349); drug-induced liver disease (Chapter 150); acute cholecystitis (or acute biliary obstruction; Chapter 158); Wilson's disease (Chapter 224); and various forms of ischemic, malignant, or toxic hepatic injury (Chapters 153–156).

Pathogenesis

The pathogenesis of the liver injury in viral hepatitis is not well understood. None of the five agents seems to be directly cytopathic, at least at levels of replication found during typical acute and chronic hepatitis. The timing and histologic appearance of hepatocyte injury in viral hepatitis suggest that immune responses, particularly cytotoxic T-cell responses to viral antigens expressed on hepatocyte cell membranes, may be the major effectors of injury. Other proinflammatory cytokines, natural killer cell activity, and antibody-dependent cellular cytotoxicity also may play modulating roles in cell injury and inflammation during acute hepatitis virus infection. Recovery from hepatitis virus infections usually is accompanied by appearance of rising titers of antibody against envelope antigens, such as anti-HAV, anti-HBs, anti-HCV-E1 and anti-HCV-E2, and anti-HEV; these antibodies may provide at least partial immunity to reinfection.

Clinical Manifestations

The course of acute hepatitis is highly variable, ranging in severity from a transient, asymptomatic infection to a severe or fulminant disease. The disease can be self-limited and resolve, run a relapsing course, or lead to a chronic infection. In a typical, clinically apparent course of acute resolving viral hepatitis (Fig. 151–1), the incubation period varies from 2 to 20 weeks, largely on the basis of viral etiology and dose of exposure. During this phase, virus becomes detectable in blood, but serum aminotransferase and bilirubin levels are normal, and antibody is not detected.

The preicteric phase of illness is marked by the onset of fatigue, nausea, poor appetite, and vague right upper quadrant pain. Viral-specific antibody usually first appears during this phase, which typically lasts 3 to 10 days. In patients with subclinical or anicteric forms of acute hepatitis, this phase constitutes the entire course of illness. Viral titers are generally highest at this point, and serum aminotransferase levels start to increase. The onset of dark urine marks the icteric phase of illness, during which jaundice appears, and symptoms of fatigue and nausea worsen. Typically, acute viral hepatitis rarely is diagnosed correctly before onset of jaundice. If jaundice is severe, stool color lightens, and pruritus may appear. Anorexia, dysgeusia, and weight loss of 20 lb also may occur.

Physical examination usually shows jaundice and hepatic tenderness. In more severe cases, hepatomegaly and splenomegaly may be present.

Serum bilirubin levels (total and direct) rise, and aminotransferase levels usually are greater than 10 times the upper limit of normal, at least at the onset. During the icteric, symptomatic phase, levels of hepatitis virus begin to decrease in serum and liver.

The duration of clinical illness is variable; it typically lasts 1 to 3 weeks. Recovery first is manifested by return of appetite and is accompanied by resolution of the serum bilirubin and aminotransferase elevations and clearance of virus. Convalescence can be prolonged, however, before full degrees of energy and stamina return. Neutralizing antibodies usually appear during the icteric phase and rise to high levels during convalescence.

Complications of acute viral hepatitis include chronic infection, fulminant hepatic failure, relapsing or cholestatic hepatitis, and extrahepatic syndromes. Chronic hepatitis (Chapter 152), usually defined as at least 6 months of illness, eventuates in approximately 5% of adults with hepatitis B and in 75% of adults with hepatitis C. Hepatitis B, C, and D are said to be chronic if viremia persists for more than 3 months after onset of symptoms.

Acute liver failure or fulminant hepatitis occurs in 1 to 2% of patients with symptomatic acute hepatitis, perhaps most commonly with hepatitis B and D and least commonly with hepatitis C. The disease is called fulminant if hepatic encephalopathy appears; however, the initial symptoms (changes in personality, aggressive behavior, or abnormal sleep patterns) may be subtle or misunderstood. The most reliable prognostic factor in acute hepatic failure is the degree of prolongation of prothrombin time; other signs of poor prognosis are persistently worsening jaundice, ascites, and decreases in liver size. Serum aminotransferase levels and viral titers have little prognostic value and often decrease with worsening hepatic failure.

A proportion of patients with acute hepatitis develop a cholestatic pattern of illness, with prolonged and fluctuating jaundice and pruritus. Patients may have one or more clinical relapses. Patients may feel relatively well despite marked jaundice. Cholestatic hepatitis is generally benign and ultimately resolves.

Of patients, 10 to 20% develop a serum sickness–like syndrome during the preicteric phase of acute hepatitis, with variable combinations of rash, hives, arthralgias, and fever. This immune complex–like syndrome often is attributed mistakenly to other illnesses until the onset of jaundice, at which time the fever, hives, and arthralgias quickly resolve. Other extrahepatic manifestations of acute hepatitis are uncommon but include severe headaches, encephalitis, aseptic meningitis, seizures, acute ascending flaccid paralysis, nephrotic syndrome, and seronegative arthritis.

Liver histology in acute viral hepatitis is characterized by widespread parenchymal inflammation and spotty necrosis. Inflammatory cells are predominantly lymphocytes, macrophages, and histiocytes. Fibrosis is absent. Immunohistochemical stains for hepatitis antigens are usually negative during acute disease, and there are no reliably distinctive features that separate the five viral forms of acute hepatitis from each other. Because serologic tests are usually adequate for diagnosis, liver biopsy is not recommended in acute hepatitis, unless the diagnosis remains unclear and a therapeutic decision is needed.

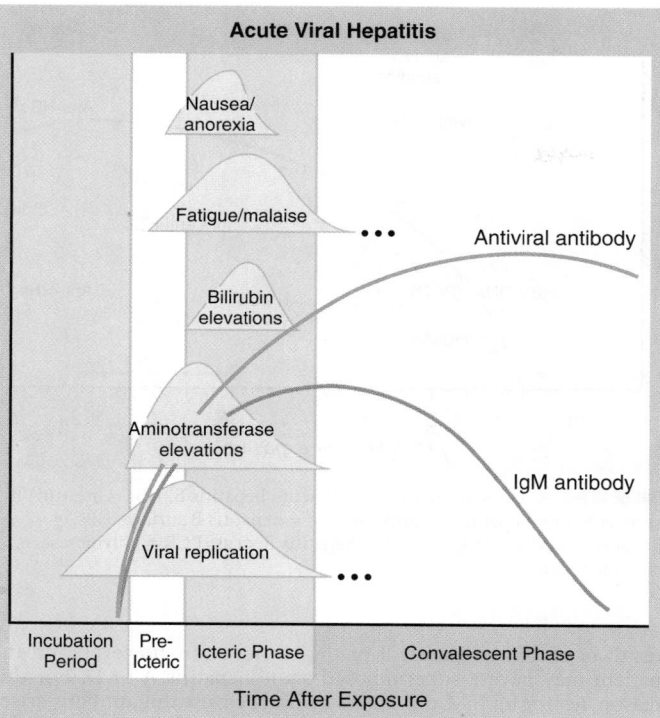

FIGURE 151–1 • The typical course of acute viral hepatitis.

Diseases of the Liver, Gallbladder, and Bile Ducts

℞ **General Treatment**

Although there are no specific therapies for the various forms of acute viral hepatitis, there are nonspecific recommendations for all patients. Bedrest and sensible nutrition are recommended in patients who are symptomatic and jaundiced. Alcohol should be avoided until convalescence. Sexual contacts should be limited until partners receive prophylaxis. In hepatitis A, all household contacts should be given immune globulin, and initiation of HAV vaccination is appropriate. In hepatitis B, family members should be vaccinated; for recent sexual contacts, hepatitis B immune globulin also should be given. Patients who develop any signs of fulminant hepatic failure (prolongation of prothrombin time and/or personality changes or confusion) should be evaluated quickly for possible liver transplantation (Chapter 157). The success of transplantation for severe, acute viral hepatitis often depends on early referral and careful attention to all details of clinical management in the context of an experienced team of physicians. Follow-up of acute hepatitis should be adequate to show that resolution has occurred, particularly for patients with hepatitis C. Finally and importantly, all cases of acute hepatitis should be reported to the local or state health department as soon as possible after diagnosis.

HEPATITIS A

HAV is a small RNA virus that belongs to the family of Picornaviridae (genus *Hepatovirus*). The viral genome is 7.5 kb in length and has a single large open-reading frame that encodes a polyprotein with structural and nonstructural components. The virus replicates largely in the liver and is assembled in the hepatocyte cytoplasm as a 27-nm particle with a single RNA genome and an outer capsid protein (HAVAg). The virus is secreted into the bile and, to a lesser extent, the serum. Highest titers of HAV are found in stool (10^6 to 10^{10} genomes per gram) during the incubation period and early symptomatic phase of illness.

Hepatitis A is highly contagious and is spread largely by the fecal-oral route, especially when there are poor sanitary conditions. Hepatitis A has become the most common cause of acute hepatitis in the United States, occurring largely as sporadic, rather than epidemic cases. Investigation of the source of hepatitis A cases reveals that most are due to direct person-to-person exposure and, to lesser extent, to direct

fecal contamination of food or water. Consumption of shellfish from contaminated waterways is a well-known but uncommon source of hepatitis A. Rare instances of spread of hepatitis A from blood transfusions and from pooled plasma products have been described. High-risk groups for acquiring hepatitis A include travelers to developing areas of the world, children in day care centers (and secondarily their parents), men who have sex with men, injection drug users, hemophiliacs given plasma products, and persons in institutions.

The clinical course of typical acute hepatitis A (Fig. 151–2) begins with an incubation period that is typically 15 to 45 days (mean 25 days). Jaundice occurs in 70% of adults infected with HAV but in smaller proportions of children. Antibody to HAV (anti-HAV), which appears in all patients infected with the virus, is first apparent shortly before the onset of symptoms, rises to high titer, and persists for life. The finding of anti-HAV can indicate previous infection and immunity and ongoing acute hepatitis A. The diagnosis of acute hepatitis A can be made by testing for IgM-specific anti-HAV, which arises early in the disease and persists for 4 to 12 months. Acute hepatitis A is invariably a self-limited infection; the virus can persist for months, but it does not lead to a chronic infection, chronic hepatitis, or cirrhosis. Severe and fulminant cases of hepatitis A can occur, particularly in the elderly and in patients with preexisting chronic liver disease. Hepatitis A is the most common cause of relapsing cholestatic hepatitis.

The diagnosis of acute hepatitis A can be made based on the finding of IgM anti-HAV in the serum of a patient with the clinical and biochemical features of acute hepatitis. Testing for total anti-HAV is not helpful in diagnosis but is a means of assessing immunity to hepatitis A.

A safe and effective HAV vaccine is available and is recommended for patients at high risk of acquiring hepatitis A, including travelers to endemic areas of the world, children in communities with high rates of infection (e.g., Alaskan Natives or Native Americans on reservations), men who have sex with men, injection drug users, and hepatitis and primate-research workers. HAV vaccine also is recommended for all patients with chronic liver disease and recipients of pooled plasma products, such as hemophiliacs. The universal use of HAV vaccine in childhood and in food handlers is still being evaluated.

Two formulations of HAV vaccine are available in the United States; both consist of inactivated hepatitis A antigen purified from cell culture. Havrix (GlaxoSmithKline, Philadelphia, PA) is recommended as two injections 6 to 12 months apart in an adult dose of 1440 ELISA units (1.0 mL) and a pediatric (ages 2 to 18 years) dose of 720 ELISA units (0.5 mL). Vaqta (Merck, West Point, PA) is recommended as two injections at least 6 months apart in an adult dose of 50 U (1.0 mL) and a pediatric dose (2 to 17 years) of 25 U (0.5 mL). A combination HAV and HBV vaccine (Twinrix; GlaxoSmithKline) is also available; it is recommended for adults who require vaccination against both forms of hepatitis and is given in a three-injection schedule, at 0, 1, and 6 months. HAV vaccines have an excellent safety record, with serious complications occurring in less than 0.1% of recipients. Seroconversion

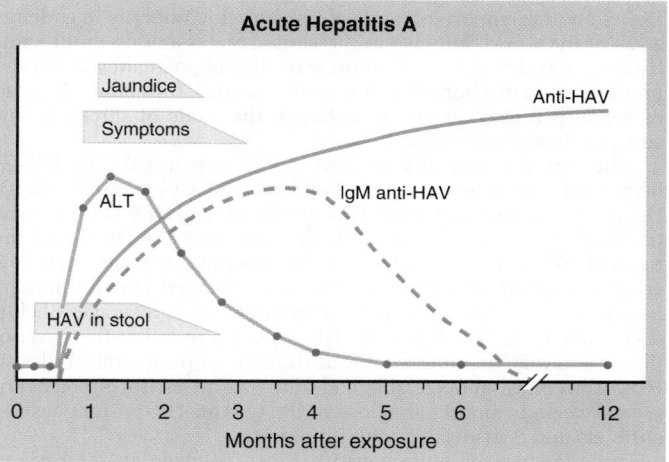

FIGURE 151–2 • The serologic course of acute hepatitis A. ALT = alanine aminotransferase; HAV = hepatitis A virus.

rates after HAV vaccine are greater than 90% but are lower in the elderly and in patients with chronic liver disease. Nevertheless, neither follow-up testing for anti-HAV nor late-booster inoculations currently are recommended.

Postexposure prophylaxis with immune globulin still is recommended for household and intimate contacts of persons with acute hepatitis A. The dose is 2 mL in adults and 0.02 mL/kg in children, given intramuscularly within 2 weeks of exposure. Concurrent HAV vaccination is appropriate.

There are no specific therapies for hepatitis A that have been shown to shorten or ameliorate the course of illness. An important element of management should be prophylaxis for contacts. Persons with fulminant hepatitis should be referred early for possible liver transplantation (Chapter 157).

HEPATITIS B

HBV is a double-shelled, enveloped DNA virus belonging to the family Hepadnaviridae (genus *Orthohepadnavirus*). The viral genome consists of partially double-stranded DNA, is 3.2 kb in length, and possesses four partially overlapping open-reading frames that encode the genes for hepatitis B surface antigen (*S* gene, HBsAg), hepatitis B core antigen (*C* gene, HBcAg), the HBV polymerase (*P* gene), and a small protein that seems to have transactivating functions (*X* gene, HBxAg). The *S* gene has three start codons and is capable of producing three different sizes of HBsAg (small, medium, and large *S*). The *C* gene has two start codons and can produce two antigenically distinct products: the HBcAg that is retained in hepatocytes until assembled as core particles and incorporated into HBV virions and the HBeAg that is secreted into the serum as a small soluble protein. The virus infects only humans and higher apes and replicates predominantly in hepatocytes and perhaps to a lesser extent in stem cells in pancreas, bone marrow, and spleen. During acute and chronic infection, patients with hepatitis B have large amounts of HBsAg in serum, most in the form of incomplete 20-nm virus-like spherical and tubular particles. The intact virion is a double-shelled particle with an envelope of HBsAg, an inner nucleocapsid of HBcAg, and an active polymerase enzyme that is linked to a single molecule of double-stranded HBV DNA. Persons who produce large amounts of HBV in serum also typically produce HBeAg, making this a surrogate marker for high levels of viral replication.

Hepatitis B is spread predominantly by the parenteral route or by intimate personal contact. It is endemic in many areas of the world, such as Southeast Asia, China, Micronesia, and sub-Saharan Africa. Lesser rates occur in the Indian subcontinent and the Middle East. In the United States, hepatitis B is the second most common cause of acute hepatitis, and chronic infection affects approximately 0.5% of the population. Investigations of the source of hepatitis B reveal that most adult cases are due to sexual or parenteral contact. Hepatitis B is common among injection drug users, heterosexuals with multiple sexual partners, and men who have sex with men. Blood transfusion and plasma products are now rarely infectious for hepatitis B because of the institution of routine screening of blood donations for HBsAg and antibody to HBcAg, anti-HBc. Maternal-infant spread of hepatitis B is another important mode of transmission not only in endemic areas of the world, but also in the United States among immigrants from these endemic areas. Routine screening of pregnant women and prophylaxis of newborns are now recommended. Intrafamilial spread of hepatitis B also can occur, although the mode of spread in this situation is not well defined.

The typical course of acute, self-limited hepatitis B (Fig. 151–3) begins with an incubation period of 30 to 150 days (mean 75 days). During the incubation period, HBsAg, HBeAg, and HBV DNA become detectable in serum and rise to high titers, with the virus reaching titers of 10^8 to 10^{11} virions/mL. By the onset of symptoms, anti-HBc arises, and serum aminotransferase levels are elevated. Jaundice appears in one third of adults with hepatitis B and lesser percentages of children. Generally, HBV DNA and HBeAg begin to fall at the onset of illness and may be undetectable at the time of peak clinical illness. HBsAg becomes undetectable and anti-HBs arises during recovery, several weeks to months after loss of HBsAg. Anti-HBs is a long-lasting antibody and is associated with immunity.

The diagnosis of acute hepatitis B can be made on the basis of finding HBsAg in the serum of a patient with the clinical and biochemical features of acute hepatitis. HBsAg also may be present as a

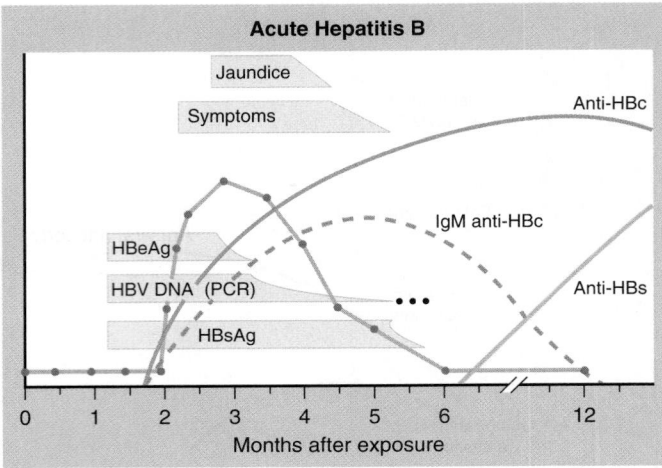

FIGURE 151–3 • The serologic course of acute hepatitis B. HBc = hepatitis B core; HBeAg = hepatitis B e antigen; HBs = hepatitis B surface; HBsAg = hepatitis B surface antigen; HBV = hepatitis B virus; PCR = polymerase chain reaction.

result of chronic hepatitis B or the carrier state, however, and the patient may have a superimposed acute hepatitis A or D. For this reason, testing for IgM anti-HBc is helpful because this antibody arises early and is lost within 6 to 12 months of onset of illness. Testing for HBeAg, anti-HBe, HBV DNA, and anti-HBs is generally not helpful in the diagnosis of hepatitis B but may be valuable in assessing prognosis. Persons who remain HBV DNA– and/or HBeAg-positive 6 weeks after onset of symptoms are likely to develop chronic hepatitis B. Loss of HBeAg or HBV DNA is a favorable serologic finding. Similarly, loss of HBsAg and development of anti-HBs denote recovery.

Chronic hepatitis B (Chapter 152) develops in 2 to 7% of adults infected with HBV, more commonly in men and in immunosuppressed individuals. The risk of chronic infection also correlates with age, occurring in 90% of newborns infected with HBV, in approximately 30% of infants, but in less than 10% of adults. Chronic hepatitis B is still the third or fourth most common cause of cirrhosis (Chapter 156) in the United States and is an important cause of liver cancer (Chapter 202).

Hepatitis B is also an important cause of fulminant hepatitis. Factors associated with severe outcomes of acute hepatitis B include advanced age, female sex, and perhaps some strains of virus. There are variants of HBV that lack the ability to produce HBeAg because of a mutation in the precore region of the viral genome. These precore or HBeAg-negative mutants are associated with atypical forms of acute and chronic hepatitis B. Several clusters of severe or fulminant hepatitis B have been associated with infection with the HBeAg-negative forms of virus.

Vaccination against HBV now is recommended for all newborns and children. Adults, especially in groups at high risk for acquiring HBV, also should be vaccinated. Two formulations of HBV vaccine are available in the United States; both are made from recombinant techniques using cloned HBV *S* gene expressed in *Saccharomyces cerevisiae*. For adults, the recommended regimen is three injections of 1.0 mL (20 µg of Energix-B [GlaxoSmithKline] or 10 µg of Recombivax HB [Merck]) given intramuscularly in the deltoid muscle at 0, 1, and 6 months. A combined HAV and HBV vaccine (GlaxoSmithKline) is given by the same schedule. The dose in newborns, children, and adolescents is less (Table 151–2). The seroconversion rate is greater than 80% in adults but may be less in smokers, in the obese, in the elderly, and in patients who are immunocompromised, who may require higher doses and more injections. Prevaccination screening for anti-HBs is not recommended except for adults in high-risk groups (injection drug users or men who have sex with men). In addition, postvaccination testing for anti-HBs to document seroconversion is not recommended routinely except for persons who are at highest risk for continued exposures. At present, booster doses are not recommended, but they may be appropriate for high-risk individuals if titers of anti-HBs fall below what is considered protective (10 IU/mL).

Postexposure prophylaxis with hepatitis B immune globulin (HBIG) is recommended for newborns and patients with parenteral exposure

Table 151–2 • HEPATITIS B VIRUS VACCINATION RECOMMENDATIONS

GROUP	NO. DOSES	SCHEDULE (MO)	RECOMBIVAX-HB	ENERGIX-B
Infants	3	0, 1, and 6	5.0 μg (0.5 mL)	10 μg (0.5 mL)
Infants born to HBsAg+ mother	3	0*, 1, and 6	5.0 μg (0.5 mL)	10 μg (0.5 mL)
Children (1–10 yr)	3	0, 1, and 6	5.0 μg (0.5 mL)	10 μg (0.5 mL)
Adolescents (11–19 yr)†	3	0, 1, and 6	5.0 μg (0.5 mL)	10 μg (1.0 mL)
Adults	3	0, 1, and 6	10 μg (1.0 mL)	20 μg (1.0 mL)
Adults on dialysis‡	4	0, 1, 2, and 6	40 μg (1.0 mL)	40 μg (2.0 mL)

*Hepatitis B immune globulin (HBIG) and initial vaccination should be given within 12 hours of birth.
†Adolescents ages 11–15 years can receive an alternative regimen of two doses of 10 μg (1.0 mL) at 0 and 4–6 months.
‡Recombivax HB is available in a dialysis formulation of 40 μg/mL; Energix-B must be given as two 1.0 mL injections to achieve a dose of 40 μg.

to a patient with acute or chronic hepatitis B. A single dose of HBIG (0.5 mL in newborns, 2 mL in adults) should be given as soon as possible after exposure, and HBV vaccination should be started immediately. For patients with sexual or household contact with a patient with acute or chronic hepatitis B, vaccination alone may be appropriate, although HBIG often is recommended if the exposure is to a patient with acute hepatitis B.

There is no evidence that early therapy for acute hepatitis B with interferon-α or antiviral agents decreases the rate of chronicity or speeds recovery. Most patients with acute, icteric hepatitis B recover without residual injury or chronic hepatitis. Management of acute hepatitis B should focus on avoidance of further hepatic injury and prophylaxis of contacts. The patient should be followed with repeat testing for HBsAg and alanine aminotransferase levels 3 to 6 months later to determine whether chronic hepatitis B develops (Chapter 152).

HEPATITIS C

HCV is an RNA virus that belongs to the family Flaviviridae (genus *Hepacivirus*). HCV originally was identified by molecular techniques, and the virus has not been well visualized. HCV probably circulates as a double-shelled enveloped virus, 50 to 60 nm in diameter. The genome is a positively stranded RNA molecule, which is approximately 9.6 kb in length and contains a single, large open-reading frame that encodes a large polyprotein that is post-translationally modified into three structural and several nonstructural polypeptides. The structural proteins include two highly variable envelope antigens (E1 and E2) and a relatively conserved nucleocapsid protein (C). HCV replicates largely in the liver and is detectable in serum in titers of 10^5 to 10^7 virions/mL during acute and chronic infection.

Hepatitis C is spread predominantly by the parenteral route. At highest risk are injection drug users and persons with multiple parenteral exposures. Sexual transmission of hepatitis C occurs but is not common. Prospective follow-up of spouses and sexual partners of patients with chronic hepatitis C shows the risk of sexual transmission to be low (<1% per year of exposure). Maternal-infant spread occurs in approximately 5% of cases, usually to infants whose mothers have high levels of HCV RNA in serum. Other potential sources of HCV are needlestick accidents and either contamination or inadequate sterilization of reusable needles and syringes. Since the introduction of routine screening of blood for anti-HCV, post-transfusion hepatitis C has become rare. Inactivation procedures performed on plasma products have made transmission of HCV from clotting factor concentrates uncommon. There remain, however, many persons with chronic hepatitis C who were infected with this virus by these means in the past. Current studies of acute hepatitis C indicate that more than 60% of cases are attributable to injection drug use; 15 to 20% of cases to sexual exposure (usually involving multiple sexual partners); and only a small proportion of cases to maternal-infant spread, needlestick accidents, and iatrogenic causes. Approximately 10% of cases have no history of potential exposure and remain unexplained.

The clinical course of acute hepatitis C (Fig. 151–4) begins with an incubation period that ranges from 15 to 120 (mean 50) days. During the incubation period, often within 1 to 2 weeks of exposure, HCV RNA can be detected by sensitive assays such as reverse-transcriptase polymerase chain reaction (PCR). HCV RNA persists until well into the clinical course of disease. Antibody to HCV (anti-HCV) arises late in the course of acute hepatitis C and may not be

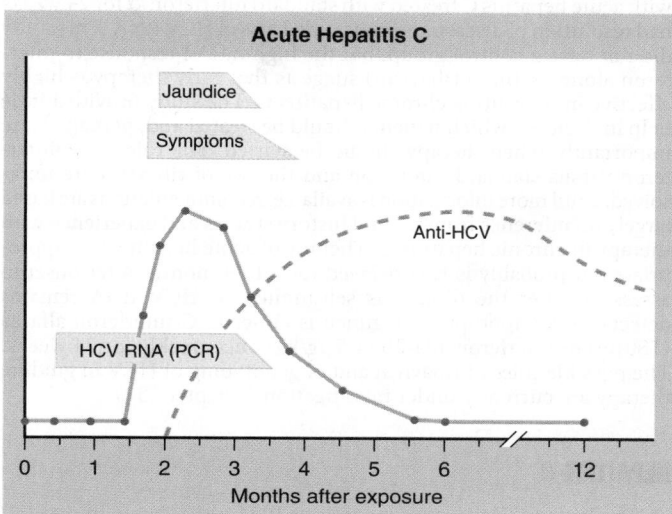

FIGURE 151–4 • The serologic course of acute hepatitis C. HCV = hepatitis C virus; PCR = polymerase chain reaction.

present at the time of onset of symptoms and serum aminotransferase elevations. If the hepatitis is self-limited, HCV RNA soon becomes undetectable in serum; in this situation, titers of anti-HCV are generally modest and eventually may fall to undetectable levels as well.

The major complication of acute hepatitis C is the development of chronic hepatitis. The clinical course depicted in Figure 151–4 is not typical because hepatitis C does not resolve in 70% of cases but rather progresses to chronic infection (Chapter 152). In this situation, HCV RNA remains detectable, and aminotransferases usually remain elevated, although often in a fluctuating pattern. In some instances, aminotransferase levels become normal despite persistence of viremia. Other complications include development of immune complex phenomena and cryoglobulinemia, although these are more typical of chronic disease. Fulminant hepatitis resulting from HCV is rare; in several large surveys of acute liver failure, none of the cases could be attributed to HCV.

The diagnosis of acute hepatitis C generally is made based on the finding of anti-HCV in serum in a patient with the clinical and biochemical features of acute hepatitis. Some patients do not develop detectable levels of anti-HCV, however, until weeks or months after onset of illness, so retesting for anti-HCV during convalescence or direct tests for HCV RNA are necessary to exclude the diagnosis of acute hepatitis C in a patient who tests negative for all serologic markers. At least one commercial test for HCV RNA is now licensed and is reliable in detecting HCV RNA at levels greater than 100 copies/mL. Tests that quantify the HCV RNA level are also available, but measuring viral levels is not clinically useful in diagnosis or monitoring of acute hepatitis C.

At present, there are no means of prevention of hepatitis C other than avoidance of high-risk behaviors and appropriate use of universal precautions. Injection drug use is currently the most common cause of newly acquired cases of hepatitis C. In this regard, needle exchange programs and education regarding the risks of drug use including intranasal cocaine and the role of reusable equipment are important.

Accidental needlestick exposure is perhaps the most frequent issue in prevention of transmission. At present, neither immune globulin nor preemptive therapy with antiviral agents or interferon is recommended in this situation. Monitoring using aminotransferase levels, HCV RNA, and anti-HCV testing (at 1 and 6 months after exposure) is appropriate. This approach allows for early intervention and treatment.

Therapy with pegylated interferon-α and ribavirin has been shown to be beneficial in chronic hepatitis C (Chapter 152), leading to sustained clearance of virus and resolution of disease in slightly more than 50% of cases. The role of therapy during the acute infection is still unresolved. Because 60 to 75% of patients with acute disease progress to chronic infection, the issue of early therapy often arises. In a single, multicenter study from Germany, more than 95% of patients with acute hepatitis C treated with standard interferon-α for 24 weeks had resolution of disease and a sustained loss of HCV RNA. This study did not have a control group, but the high rate of response to interferon alone (without ribavirin) suggests that early therapy is highly effective in preventing chronic hepatitis C. The study provided little help in deciding which patients should be treated and, perhaps more importantly, when therapy should be started. The role of peginterferon versus standard interferon and the use of ribavirin are unresolved. Until more information is available, recommendations are based largely on inference from natural history studies and experience with therapy in chronic hepatitis C. Therapy of acute hepatitis C is appropriate but probably is best delayed for 2 to 4 months after onset to assess whether the disease is self-limited. If HCV RNA remains detectable, an appropriate regimen is either PEG-interferon alfa-2a (180 μg) or interferon alfa-2b (1.5 μg/kg) once weekly for 24 weeks. The possible roles of ribavirin and of genotyping of HCV in guiding therapy are currently under investigation (Chapter 152).

HEPATITIS D

The hepatitis delta virus is a unique RNA virus that requires HBV for replication. The viral genome is a short, 1.7-kb circular single-stranded molecule of RNA that has a single open-reading frame and a highly conserved nontranslated region that resembles the self-replicating element of viroids. The single open-reading frame encodes delta antigen, and RNA editing can vary the size of the molecule to produce either a small (195 amino acids) or large (214 amino acids) delta antigen. The small delta antigen promotes replication of HDV RNA; the large delta antigen promotes viral assembly and secretion into the serum as the mature 36-nm delta viral particle.

Hepatitis D is linked to hepatitis B, and consequently its epidemiology is similar. HDV can be spread by the parenteral route and sexually. Persons at greatest risk are chronic carriers of hepatitis B and persons who have repeated parenteral exposures. In the United States and Western Europe, delta hepatitis is most common among injection drug users and, before the routine screening of blood donations, recipients of blood products, including persons with hemophilia and thalassemia. Delta hepatitis is endemic in the Amazon basin and central Africa and is common in some European and Mediterranean countries, including Southern Italy and Greece, and in Eastern Europe.

Delta hepatitis occurs in two clinical patterns, termed *coinfection* and *superinfection*. Delta coinfection is the simultaneous occurrence of acute HDV and acute HBV infections. It resembles acute hepatitis B but may manifest a second elevation in aminotransferase levels associated with the period of delta virus replication. The diagnosis of acute delta coinfection can be made in a patient presenting with clinical features of acute hepatitis who has HBsAg, anti-HDV, and IgM anti-HBc in serum. Immunoassays for anti-HDV are commercially available and reliable, although antibody may appear late during the illness. In patients suspected of having delta hepatitis, repeat testing for anti-HDV during convalescence is appropriate.

Acute delta superinfection is the occurrence of acute HDV infection in a chronic HBsAg carrier. The diagnosis of acute delta superinfection can be made in a patient presenting with clinical features of acute hepatitis who has HBsAg and anti-HDV but no IgM anti-HBc in serum. Superinfection with HDV is more frequent than coinfection and is far more likely to lead to chronic delta hepatitis. Other tests that are helpful in making the diagnosis of ongoing HDV

infection are serum HDV RNA (detectable by PCR) and HDV antigen (detectable by immunoblot); both of these tests are currently research assays and not standardized. Delta antigen also can be detected readily in liver biopsy specimens using immunohistochemical stains.

Delta hepatitis tends to be more severe than hepatitis B alone and is more likely to lead to fulminant hepatitis and more likely to cause severe chronic hepatitis and ultimately cirrhosis. There are no specific means of therapy for acute delta hepatitis. Most cases of acute coinfection resolve; patients with superinfection should be treated when it is clear that chronic delta hepatitis has supervened.

Delta hepatitis can be prevented by preventing hepatitis B. The severity of delta hepatitis provides the rationale for routine hepatitis B vaccination in areas of the world where delta hepatitis is endemic. There are no means of prevention of delta hepatitis in a person who is already an HBsAg carrier; in this situation, avoidance of further exposures is important.

HEPATITIS E

HEV is a small nonenveloped, single-stranded RNA virus that is similar to the caliciviruses but is currently unclassified. The viral genome is 7.5 kb in length and encodes three open-reading frames, the first (ORF1) for the nonstructural proteins responsible for viral replication, the second (ORF2) for the capsid protein (HEV antigen), and the third (ORF3) for a short protein of unknown function. The virus and HEV antigen can be detected in hepatocytes during acute infection. Highest levels of virus are detectable in the stool during the incubation period of disease. Viruses similar to HEV are found in other species, and strains found in domesticated swine may be infectious in humans.

Hepatitis E is responsible for epidemic and endemic forms of non-A, non-B hepatitis that occur in lesser developed areas of the world. Large outbreaks have been described from India, Pakistan, China, Northern and Central Africa, and Central America. In studies from India and Egypt, hepatitis E has accounted for a high proportion of cases of sporadic acute hepatitis. In the United States and Western Europe, hepatitis E is rare, most cases being imported or due to zoonotic spread from swine or rats that harbor a similar virus. HEV is spread by the fecal-oral route, and most cases can be traced to exposure to contaminated water under poor hygienic conditions. Hepatitis E seems to be less contagious than hepatitis A, the other form of infectious hepatitis, and secondary cases are rare.

The clinical course of hepatitis E resembles that of other forms of hepatitis. The incubation period is 15 to 60 days (mean 35 days). The disease is frequently cholestatic, with prominence of bilirubin and alkaline phosphatase elevations. Hepatitis E also tends to be more severe than other forms of epidemic jaundice, with a fatality rate of 1 to 2% and a particularly high rate of acute liver failure in pregnant women. HEV virions and antigen can be detected in stool and liver during the incubation period and early symptomatic phase, but these tests are not practical means for diagnosis. Enzyme-linked immunoassays (ELISAs) for IgM and IgG antibody to HEV (anti-HEV) have been developed and are reactive in at least 90% of patients at the onset of clinical illness. These tests are neither generally available nor standardized, however. In addition, anti-HEV is found in 1 to 2% of the normal population, which may represent resolved subclinical cases of hepatitis E acquired during travel or as a result of exposure to livestock or other infected animals.

The diagnosis of hepatitis E should be considered in a patient who presents with acute hepatitis and has traveled recently to an endemic area, particularly if tests for other forms of hepatitis are nonreactive. The finding of anti-HEV, particularly of the IgM subclass, is sufficient to make the diagnosis in this situation. Hepatitis E is rare in the United States and Western world, however, so testing for anti-HEV is rarely necessary.

There are no known means of prevention or treatment of hepatitis E. Immune globulin, even when prepared from the plasma of populations with a high rate of hepatitis E, does not seem to be effective. No specific means of treatment have been evaluated. Travelers to areas of the world (particularly pregnant women) where hepatitis E is endemic should be cautioned regarding drinking water and uncooked food. Recombinant vaccines against HEV have been developed and shown to be effective in animal models of hepatitis E. Efficacy trials of an HEV vaccine are now under way in endemic areas.

DIFFERENTIAL DIAGNOSIS

The diagnostic approach to the patient with the clinical features of acute hepatitis (Table 151–3) begins with a careful history for risk factors and possible exposure; for medication use, including herbal and over-the-counter drugs; and for alcohol use. The onset and progression of symptoms may give clues to other causes of liver disease, such as alcohol or gallstones. Biochemical laboratory tests, including serum bilirubin, alanine and aspartate aminotransferases, alkaline phosphatase, lactic dehydrogenase, albumin, complete blood cell counts, and prothrombin time, are valuable in defining whether the clinical picture is typical of acute hepatitis (high aminotransferases, normal or modest elevations in alkaline phosphatase and lactic dehydrogenase) or resembles that of obstructive jaundice or alcoholic liver disease. In atypical cases, testing for antinuclear antibodies to evaluate autoimmune hepatitis and a Venereal Disease Research Laboratory test to exclude secondary syphilis (Chapter 349) are needed. The presence of fever and atypical lymphocytosis should suggest mononucleosis (Chapter 371). The presence of hemolysis should suggest Wilson's disease (Chapter 224). Serologic tests that are helpful in all cases of acute hepatitis include IgM anti-HAV, HBsAg and/or IgM anti-HBc, and anti-HCV. Follow-up testing for anti-HDV or anti-HCV can be useful in making the diagnosis of delta hepatitis (in a patient with HBsAg) or hepatitis C (in a patient initially testing negative for all viral antibodies).

HEPATITIS NON-A–E

Cases of acute hepatitis that appear viral in etiology but that cannot be attributed to any known virus are called *hepatitis non-A–E*. Various candidate viruses have been reported in association with this disease, including paramyxoviruses, togaviruses, flaviviruses (GBV-C, hepatitis G, and the TT virus), but none has been linked clearly to this disease. In serologic surveys of cases of acute hepatitis in Western countries, 2 to 20% of cases cannot be attributed to any of the five known hepatitis viruses. Animal inoculation and tissue culture studies in search of the agent of hepatitis non-A–E have been unrevealing.

The clinical features of non-A–E hepatitis are similar to features of known forms of acute hepatitis. Most cases of non-A–E hepatitis have no clear source of exposure. Cases are rare after blood transfusion and are no more common than in control, nontransfused subjects. The absence of typical risk factors for viral hepatitis suggest that some cases of non-A–E hepatitis may be due to nonviral causes, such as an environmental exposure, drug, or autoimmune process.

The syndrome of non-A–E hepatitis has been particularly associated with the complications of acute liver failure and aplastic anemia. Hepatitis non-A–E is a more common cause of fulminant hepatic failure than hepatitis A or B combined, often accounting for 30 to 40% of cases. Approximately one third of patients with non-A–E hepatitis develop chronic hepatitis, and a small percentage ultimately develop cirrhosis.

Non-A–E hepatitis is a diagnosis of exclusion, usually made on the basis of an acute hepatitis occurring in a patient without anti-HAV, HBsAg, anti-HBc, HCV RNA, or anti-HCV and without any other known cause of acute hepatic injury. Testing of serum during convalescence is helpful in excluding hepatitis C with delayed seroconversion. Tests for anti-HEV are generally not necessary unless there is a history of travel to an endemic area or exposure to swine. The most important diagnoses to exclude are infectious mononucleosis and the nonviral causes of an acute hepatitis–like syndrome, most particularly drugs, over-the-counter medications, herbal preparations, toxins, alcoholic liver injury, acute cholecystitis, autoimmune hepatitis, and Wilson's disease. A careful history of exposure to drugs and toxins, abdominal ultrasonography to exclude gallstone disease, and tests for antinuclear antibodies and ceruloplasmin (and urine copper if necessary) are helpful in fully defining a case of non-A–E hepatitis.

There are no means of either treatment or prevention of non-A–E hepatitis. A viral etiology of this syndrome is being investigated, particularly in the situation of acute liver failure and aplastic anemia.

SUGGESTED READINGS

Centers for Disease Control and Prevention: Recommendations for prevention and control of hepatitis C virus (HCV) infection and HCV-related chronic disease. Morb Mortal Wkly Rep Recomm Rep 1998;47:1–33. *Recommendations for screening, diagnosis, management, and prevention of acute and chronic hepatitis C.*

Centers for Disease Control and Prevention: Prevention of hepatitis A through active or passive immunization: Recommendations of the Advisory Committee on Immunization Practices. Morb Mortal Wkly Rep Recomm Rep 1999;48:1–37. *Recommendations for hepatitis A vaccination and use of immune globulin and rationale for each.*

Hoofnagle JH: Course and outcome of hepatitis C. Hepatology 2002;36(5 Suppl 1):S21–S29. *Emphasizes good short-term outcome but higher rate of chronic manifestations.*

Jaeckel E, Cornberg M, Wedemeyer H, et al: Treatment of acute hepatitis C with interferon alfa-2b. N Engl J Med 2001;345:1452–1457. *Treatment prevents chronic infection.*

Vinholt Schiodt F, Davern TJ, Obaid Shakil A, et al: Viral hepatitis–related acute liver failure. Am J Gastroenterol 2003;98:448–453. *Viral hepatitis now comprises only one-eighth of all cases of acute liver failure in the United States; hepatitis B carries a worse prognosis than hepatitis A.*

152 CHRONIC HEPATITIS

Karen L. Lindsay
Jay H. Hoofnagle

Definition

Chronic hepatitis comprises several diseases that are grouped together because they have common clinical manifestations and are marked by chronic necroinflammatory injury to the liver that can lead insidiously to cirrhosis and end-stage liver disease (Table 152–1). The disease is defined as *chronic* if there is evidence of ongoing injury for 6 months or more. The strict definition of chronic hepatitis is based on histologic features, but the diagnosis usually can be made from clinical features and blood test results alone. Chronic hepatitis has multiple causes, including viruses, medications, metabolic abnormalities, and autoimmune disorders. The most common forms are chronic hepatitis B and C and autoimmune hepatitis. Drug-induced (Chapter 150) or metabolic (Chapter 154) liver diseases, alcoholic steatohepatitis (Chapter 155), and nonalcoholic steatohepatitis (Chapter 155) also can cause chronic necroinflammatory lesions of the liver. Despite extensive testing, some cases cannot be attributed to any known cause.

Epidemiology

The incidence and prevalence of chronic hepatitis in the general U.S. population have not been well defined. In population-based surveys, 2.3% of Americans have elevations in serum alanine aminotransferase (ALT) level, 0.2% are seropositive for hepatitis B surface

Table 151–3 • SEROLOGIC DIAGNOSIS OF ACUTE HEPATITIS

DIAGNOSIS	SCREENING ASSAYS	SUPPLEMENTAL ASSAYS
Hepatitis A	IgM anti-HAV	None needed
Hepatitis B	HBsAg, IgM anti-HBc	HBeAg, anti-HBe HBV DNA
Hepatitis C	Anti-HCV by EIA	HCV RNA by PCR; anti-HCV by Immunoblot
Hepatitis D	HBsAg	Anti-HDV
Hepatitis E	History	Anti-HEV
Mononucleosis	History, white blood cell differential counts	Monospot test Heterophil antibody
Drug-induced hepatitis	History	

Table 152–1 • MAJOR CAUSES OF CHRONIC HEPATITIS

Chronic hepatitis B
Chronic hepatitis D
Chronic hepatitis C
Autoimmune hepatitis
Drug-induced chronic hepatitis
Wilson's disease
Cryptogenic hepatitis (non-A–E hepatitis)

antigen (HBsAg), and 1.8% are reactive for antibody to hepatitis C virus (anti-HCV). Not all ALT elevations are due to chronic hepatitis, however, and not all HBsAg-positive or anti-HCV–positive individuals have active liver disease. A fair estimate is that chronic hepatitis affects 2% of the population, but these diseases tend to occur mostly in high-risk groups rather than the general population. For hepatitis B, high-risk groups include recent immigrants from endemic areas of the world (Africa, Eastern Europe, Southeast Asia), men who have sex with men, persons with multiple sexual partners, hemophiliacs, oncology and renal dialysis patients, and health care workers. For hepatitis C, high-risk groups include recipients of blood or blood products before 1992, injection drug users, renal dialysis patients, health care workers, and persons with multiple sexual partners. Chronic hepatitis B and C probably cause 10,000 to 12,000 deaths yearly, and about another 2000 patients with these diseases undergo liver transplantation annually for end-stage liver failure.

Clinical Manifestations

The *clinical symptoms* of chronic hepatitis are typically nonspecific, intermittent, and mild; a large proportion of patients have no symptoms of liver disease. The most common symptom is fatigue, which may be intermittent. Some patients have sleep disorders or difficulty in concentrating. Right upper quadrant pain, if present, is usually mild, intermittent, and aching in character. In many cases, the diagnosis of chronic hepatitis is made in a person without any symptoms after liver test abnormalities are identified when blood is drawn for a routine health evaluation, during assessment for an unrelated health problem, or at the time of voluntary blood donation (Chapter 149). Symptoms of advanced disease or an acute exacerbation include nausea, poor appetite, weight loss, muscle weakness, itching, dark urine, and jaundice. When cirrhosis is present, weakness, weight loss, abdominal swelling, edema, ready bruisability, gastrointestinal bleeding, and hepatic encephalopathy with mental confusion may arise.

The *clinical signs* of liver disease in patients with chronic hepatitis also are usually minimal. The most common physical finding is liver tenderness. In patients with severe or advanced disease, other findings may include a firm liver or enlargement of the spleen, spider angiomata (see Fig. 148–1), and palmar erythema (see Fig. 148–2). When cirrhosis is present, signs may include muscle wasting, ascites (see Fig. 148–3), edema, skin excoriations or bruises, and hepatic fetor.

Although symptoms and signs are not particularly useful in identifying chronic hepatitis, biochemical and hematologic blood test results are reliable. Most typical are elevations in ALT and aspartate aminotransferase (AST) levels with little or no elevation in alkaline phosphatase level. The elevations are usually in the range of one to five times the upper limit of normal, and the ALT level is generally higher than the AST level, unless cirrhosis is present. Serum aminotransferase levels can be normal when the disease is mild or inactive but also can be markedly elevated in the range typical of acute hepatitis (10 to 25 times the upper limit of normal) during acute exacerbations. Although there may be major discrepancies between the height of the liver enzyme elevations and the histologic estimates of activity as shown by liver biopsy, monitoring of these values over time generally provides a reasonable estimate of the severity of disease and likelihood of progression.

In general, alkaline phosphatase and γ-glutamyltranspeptidase elevations are minimal in chronic hepatitis, unless cirrhosis is present. Creatine kinase and lactate dehydrogenase levels are normal. Serum bilirubin and albumin levels and prothrombin time are normal in patients with chronic hepatitis, unless the disease is severe or advanced. Any elevation in serum direct bilirubin level or decrease in albumin level should be considered evidence of serious disease activity or injury. Serum immunoglobulin levels are mildly elevated or normal in chronic viral hepatitis but may be strikingly elevated in chronic autoimmune hepatitis. Blood counts are normal in chronic hepatitis, unless cirrhosis or portal hypertension is present with associated decreases in white blood cell and platelet counts. Serial determinations of platelet counts may provide the earliest clinical evidence of progression of chronic hepatitis to advanced fibrosis and cirrhosis.

Imaging with ultrasound can define hepatic texture and size, determine the presence of hepatic masses, assess the gallbladder and intrahepatic bile ducts, define the size of the spleen, and determine the presence of collateral vessels and portal venous flow. Computed tomography and magnetic resonance imaging of the liver are less helpful unless a mass or other abnormality is found by ultrasound.

Hepatic histologic characteristics include spotty hepatocellular necrosis, chronic inflammatory cell infiltration in portal areas, and variable degrees of fibrosis. The hepatocellular necrosis is typically eosinophilic degeneration or ballooning degeneration. The necrosis is spotty throughout the parenchyma, but activity is usually greater in the periportal area; the pattern is termed *piecemeal necrosis* or *interface hepatitis*. The hepatocellular necrosis seems to be mediated largely by apoptosis in association with cytotoxic lymphocytes. Chronic inflammatory cells (CD4+ and CD8+ lymphocytes and plasma cells, histiocytes, and macrophages) are found in the areas of necrosis and in sinusoids but most prominently in portal areas. Fibrosis occurs insidiously during the course of chronic hepatitis and typically begins in the periportal regions. Ultimately, bands of fibrosis can link up adjacent portal areas or portal and central areas (bridging fibrosis), distort the hepatic architecture, and lead to cirrhosis and portal hypertension.

Hepatic histologic analysis is useful for grading the severity of necroinflammation and for staging the degree of fibrosis in chronic hepatitis and usually is obtained to confirm the diagnosis made through the patient's history, physical examination, and blood test results. The hepatic histologic evaluation may help to confirm the diagnosis of autoimmune hepatitis and clarify the role of α_1-antitrypsin deficiency or Wilson's disease. Most importantly, liver histologic analysis can exclude other diagnoses that can mimic chronic hepatitis clinically or cause similar patterns of liver enzyme level elevations, including fatty liver, alcoholic liver disease (Chapter 156), steatohepatitis (Chapter 155), drug-induced liver disease (Chapter 150), sclerosing cholangitis (Chapter 158), iron overload (Chapter 225), and veno-occlusive disease.

The *grade* of chronic hepatitis refers to the activity of the disease in terms of necrosis and inflammation; the grade of disease fluctuates and is reversible. The *stage* of disease refers to how advanced the fibrosis process is and whether cirrhosis is present; stages of disease previously have been considered irreversible, but it is now clear that successful treatment of chronic hepatitis caused by hepatitis B, hepatitis C, or autoimmune processes can result in reversal of hepatic fibrosis. The most commonly used system of grading and staging is the histology activity index, in which the combined scores for periportal necrosis and inflammation (0 to 10), lobular necrosis and inflammation (0 to 4), and portal inflammation (0 to 4) define the grade or activity of disease. Disease stage is defined by scores between 0 and 4 for fibrosis, with 4 indicating cirrhosis. A modification of the histology activity index system scores fibrosis from 0 to 6 (Ishak score), with stages 3 and 4 indicating bridging hepatic fibrosis and stages 5 and 6 representing incomplete and established cirrhosis.

Differential Diagnosis

Chronic hepatitis can be caused by several diseases that are similar clinically but that respond differently to therapy and must be managed individually. Patients with suspected chronic hepatitis should be evaluated carefully for fatty liver, alcohol-induced (Chapter 155) or drug-induced liver disease (Chapter 150), and metabolic liver diseases (Chapter 154) not only because these disorders mimic disorders that cause chronic hepatitis, but also because they can coexist with the disorders that cause chronic hepatitis. After taking a history designed to elucidate risk factors for viral hepatitis, specific and appropriate serologic tests (Table 152–2) can be used to make the diagnosis. Liver biopsy with special stains is used to confirm the diagnosis, assess the activity and severity of injury, and stage the disease. A

Table 152–2 • DIFFERENTIAL DIAGNOSIS IN CHRONIC HEPATITIS

DIAGNOSIS	SCREENING TESTS	CONFIRMATORY TESTS	COMMENTS
Chronic hepatitis B	HBsAg	HBV DNA, HBeAg, or HBcAg in liver	
Chronic hepatitis C	Anti-HCV	HCV RNA (using PCR)	Immunoblot for anti-HCV can be used to confirm antibody reactivity
Chronic hepatitis D	Anti-HDV	HDV RNA or HDV antigen in liver	
Autoimmune hepatitis	ANA (Anti-LKM 1)	Exclusion of other causes and pattern of clinical disease	Suggested by raised IgG levels and by response to corticosteroid therapy
Drug-induced liver disease	History	Rechallenge if necessary and considered safe	Medications most suspect include isoniazid, NSAIDs, methyldopa, nitrofurantoin
Wilson's disease	Ceruloplasmin	Urine and hepatic copper concentration	Suggested by hemolysis or severe chronic hepatitis in child or adolescent
Cryptogenic	Exclusion of other causes		Major differential is with autoimmune hepatitis and drug-induced liver disease

ANA = antinuclear antibody; HBcAg = hepatitis B core antigen; HBeAg = hepatitis B e antigen; HBsAg = hepatitis B surface antigen; HBV = hepatitis B virus; HCV = hepatitis C virus; HDV = hepatitis D virus; IgG = immunoglobulin G; LKM 1 = liver-kidney microsomal 1 antibody; NSAIDs = nonsteroidal anti-inflammatory drugs.

treatment strategy should arise from a careful consideration of the diagnosis and grade and stage of disease. With advances currently being made in antiviral and immunomodulatory therapeutics, it is anticipated that the considerable progress made in treating these diseases in the 1990s will continue in the future.

CHRONIC HEPATITIS B

Chronic hepatitis B is caused by infection with the hepatitis B virus (HBV), a medium-sized DNA virus belonging to the family Hepadnaviridae (Chapter 152). The diagnosis of chronic hepatitis B usually is suspected on the basis of HBsAg in the serum of a patient with chronic hepatitis and confirmed by the finding of HBV DNA in serum or hepatitis B core antigen (HBcAg) in liver. Most patients with chronic hepatitis B also have hepatitis B e antigen (HBeAg) in serum, reflecting high levels of viral replication. Some patients have active liver disease with HBsAg and high levels of HBV DNA but no HBeAg in serum. These patients usually harbor a mutant HBV that replicates efficiently and is pathogenic but does not produce HBeAg.

In the typical course of chronic hepatitis B, HBsAg, HBeAg, and HBV DNA become detectable in serum during the incubation period and gradually rise in titer (Fig. 152–1). Symptoms appear 30 to 152 days after exposure (mean incubation period 75 days), usually at the time of peak viral levels. Symptoms are mild and nonspecific, and jaundice is rare. Appearance of jaundice during the course of acute infection is highly predictive of eventual recovery. In chronic hepatitis, serum ALT levels decrease after the acute phase of infection but persist at levels between 1 and 10 times the upper limit of normal. HBsAg, HBeAg, and HBV DNA persist, generally in high levels; the finding of HBeAg more than 2 months after onset of symptoms indicates evolution to chronicity. Levels of HBV DNA are usually in the range of 10^7 to 10^{11} genome copies/mL, levels readily detectable by hybridization techniques.

The subsequent course of chronic hepatitis B is highly variable. Some patients continue to have active viral replication with high levels of HBV DNA and HBeAg in serum and progressive liver injury; cirrhosis and end-stage liver disease soon may develop. In other patients, the disease is more indolent, leading insidiously to cirrhosis in decades. In a large proportion of patients, the outcome is more benign, however; the disease eventually goes into remission spontaneously, symptoms (if present) resolve, serum aminotransferase levels decrease into the normal range, and liver histologic characteristics improve. Remission often is preceded by a transient flare of disease and can be precipitous, coinciding with a major decrease in level of HBV DNA and seroconversion from HBeAg to anti-HBe. HBsAg persists in serum at levels lower than before this seroconversion, and HBV DNA can be detected at low levels (generally $<10^5$ genome copies/mL) if sensitive techniques, such as the polymerase chain reaction (PCR), are used.

With the decrease in viral levels and loss of HBeAg, the disease seems to go into remission, suggesting that there has been a transition from chronic hepatitis B to an "inactive" carrier state with no symptoms, normal serum aminotransferase levels, and inactive liver disease indicated by biopsy findings. The loss of HBeAg is not always followed by permanent resolution of disease, however. In some patients, reactivation occurs with reappearance of HBeAg; in others, an HBV mutant develops and replicates efficiently but cannot produce HBeAg. These patients with HBeAg-negative chronic hepatitis B can have severe disease and often have multiple clinical relapses.

There are two general forms of chronic hepatitis B: typical, HBeAg-positive chronic hepatitis B, in which there is HBsAg, HBeAg, and high levels of HBV DNA in serum, and the less common HBeAg-negative form, in which there is HBsAg and anti-HBe without HBeAg in serum. Patients with HBeAg-negative chronic hepatitis B often have moderate or fluctuating levels of HBV DNA in serum. These forms of chronic hepatitis B should be distinguished from the inactive (which has been inappropriately referred to as *healthy*) HBsAg carrier state, in which HBsAg persists in serum without active liver disease and minimal or no detectable viral replication (Table 152–3); in the inactive carrier state, HBV DNA is not detectable in serum using conventional hybridization assays sensitive to levels of 10^6 viral copies/mL. Testing for HBV DNA by the more sensitive PCR assays usually shows low levels of viral genome (rarely $>10^4$ viral copies/mL) in serum of patients with the inactive carrier state, however, suggesting that the difference in their disease is quantitative rather than qualitative. Liver injury and pathogenesis of chronic hepatitis B are believed to be immunologically mediated so that the severity and course of disease do not correlate well with the level of virus in serum or antigen

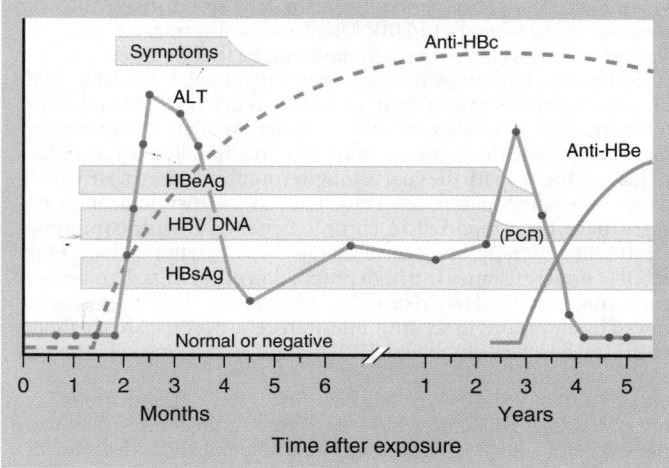

FIGURE 152–1 • The typical serologic course of chronic hepatitis B. ALT = alanine aminotransferase; HBc = hepatitis B core antigen; HBeAg, HBe = hepatitis B e antigen; HBsAg = hepatitis B surface antigen; HBV = hepatitis B virus; PCR = polymerase chain reaction.

Table 152–3 • THREE FORMS OF CHRONIC HEPATITIS B VIRUS INFECTION

PATTERN	HBsAg	HBeAg	HBV DNA* (titer: range)	HBcAg IN LIVER	CHRONIC HEPATITIS
Typical chronic hepatitis B	Positive	Positive	Positive 10^7–10^{11}	Positive (nuclear)	Active
HBeAg-negative chronic hepatitis B	Positive	Negative	Positive 10^5–10^9	Positive (cytoplasmic)	Active (relapsing)
Inactive HBsAg carrier state	Positive	Negative	Positive 10^1–10^5	Negative	Inactive

*Positive or negative result by hybridization techniques (sensitive to a titer of 10^6 genome-equivalents/mL). Titers less than 10^6 genome-equivalents/mL generally require polymerase chain reaction assays for detection.
HBcAg = hepatitis B core antigen; HBeAg = hepatitis B e antigen; HBsAg = hepatitis B surface antigen; HBV = hepatitis B virus.

expression in liver. Antigen-specific cytotoxic T cells are believed to mediate the cell injury in hepatitis B and account for ultimate viral clearance. Specific cytokines produced by cytotoxic and other T cells also have antiviral effects on hepatocytes, contributing to viral clearance without cell death. The progression of acute to chronic hepatitis B is attributed to lack of a vigorous cytotoxic T-cell response to hepatitis B antigens. Similarly, spontaneous seroconversion from HBeAg to anti-HBe during chronic hepatitis B may be immunologically mediated, as is suggested from the transient flare of disease that often immediately precedes clearance of HBeAg. Viral factors also may affect outcome: Some HBV strains may be more pathogenic and more likely to lead to chronic infection because they are less immunogenic or more resistant to T-cell attack. Seroconversion may be due to spontaneous mutations in the predominant HBV species to forms that produce HBsAg without HBeAg (e-negative mutant) and that are less efficient in replication and less pathogenic.

The extrahepatic manifestations of chronic hepatitis B include mucocutaneous vasculitis, glomerulonephritis, and polyarteritis nodosa. The glomerulonephritis of hepatitis B occurs more commonly in children than adults and usually is characterized by nephrotic syndrome with little decrease in renal function. Polyarteritis nodosa (Chapter 284) occurs primarily in adults and is marked by sudden, severe onset of hypertension, renal disease, and systemic vasculitis with arteritis in vessels of the kidney, gallbladder, intestine, or brain.

 Treatment

Nonspecific recommendations for management of chronic hepatitis B include vaccination of all household and sexual contacts. Patients should be counseled on the modes of transmission of hepatitis B and means of prevention of spread. Vaccination against hepatitis A also is recommended. Patients with hepatitis B should avoid all but the most necessary use of immunosuppressive medications. Severe flares of hepatitis B and even deaths have followed short courses of corticosteroids or cancer chemotherapy.

The standard treatment of chronic hepatitis B is a 4- to 6-month course of interferon-α given by subcutaneous injection in doses of 5 million U daily or 10 million U three times weekly, a regimen that results in clearance of HBeAg in 30 to 40% of patients and of HBsAg in 10% of patients. These are high doses of interferon, and therapy often is tolerated poorly. More recently, pegylated forms of interferon-α (peginterferon) have been developed; because of decreased renal clearance, they can be given once weekly rather than daily. Studies suggest that peginterferon is more effective than standard interferon in hepatitis B, and these forms of interferon are likely to replace standard interferon. The proper dose regimen of peginterferon for chronic hepatitis B remains to be established, but excellent results have been obtained in preliminary studies using 100 μg (approximately 1.5 μg/kg) weekly for 24 weeks.

Therapy with interferon is indicated in patients who have chronic hepatitis B with HBsAg and HBV DNA in serum and elevations in serum aminotransferase levels. Interferon therapy is contraindicated in patients with advanced cirrhosis, in solid-organ transplantation recipients, in immunosuppressed patients, and in patients with other serious major illnesses. Interferon therapy is not recommended in patients with normal or near-normal serum aminotransferase levels (even if HBeAg is present) largely because interferon therapy is usually ineffective in this situation. The other major factors associated with response to interferon-α in chronic hepatitis B are initial high levels of serum aminotransferases, relatively low levels of HBV DNA, and absence of immunosuppression. The potential benefits and risks of interferon therapy should be discussed thoroughly before treatment. The major side effects of interferon include fatigue, muscle aches, fever, depression, and irritability; uncommon severe side effects include suicide, psychosis, renal and cardiac failure, bacterial infections, and induction of autoimmune disorders (see the discussion of treatment of chronic hepatitis C).

With initiation of treatment, levels of HBV DNA usually decrease. In patients with a beneficial response (as defined by loss of HBeAg with treatment), the disease typically flares with elevations of serum ALT to levels two to three times the baseline after 2 to 3 months of therapy, coinciding with a precipitous fall in HBV DNA levels and loss of HBeAg. Serum aminotransferase levels decrease to normal, and a proportion of patients lose HBsAg, often many months to several years after loss of HBeAg. Reactivation of disease with rises in aminotransferase levels and reappearance of HBeAg and high levels of HBV DNA occurs rarely.

Oral nucleoside analogues, including lamivudine, adefovir dipivoxil, entecavir, and clevudine (L-FMAU), have been shown to have potent effects against HBV. Two of these agents are currently approved for use in the United States (see later): lamivudine and adefovir dipivoxil. Lamivudine is a negative enantiomer of a 3′ sulfated cytidine analogue and has major activity against HBV and human immunodeficiency virus (HIV). Lamivudine is recommended in a dose of 100 mg/day for 1 year. Initiation of therapy is followed rapidly by marked falls in HBV DNA by 4 to 6 $\log_{10}$ units to levels less than 10^5 viral copies/mL within the first 3 to 6 months of starting therapy. Prolonged therapy (≥1 year) is associated with loss of HBeAg in 15 to 30% of patients. With loss of HBeAg and development of anti-HBe, lamivudine can be stopped; relapses are uncommon when seroconversion occurs. Most patients remain HBeAg-positive, however, despite improvements in HBV DNA and aminotransferase levels. Lamivudine is well tolerated; in randomized trials, side effects were no more common with lamivudine than with placebo. The lack of side effects of lamivudine and the improvements in HBV DNA and serum aminotransferase levels that occur with therapy often convince physicians and patients to continue lamivudine indefinitely despite the lack of loss of HBeAg, with the goal of long-term suppression of HBV replication. Instances of long-term biochemical and histologic improvement have been reported in chronic hepatitis B with continuous lamivudine therapy. Long-term therapy is associated with development of viral resistance in a high proportion of patients. Lamivudine resistance is marked by a rise of HBV DNA toward baseline levels followed by elevations in serum aminotransferase levels. Most patients with viral resistance harbor an HBV mutant with amino acid changes in the conserved region of the polymerase gene (YMDD mutates to either YIDD or YVDD). Typically, patients with YMDD mutations have lower levels of HBV DNA and serum aminotransferases than were present before therapy, suggesting that the mutant HBV is less efficient in replication and less pathogenic than the wild-type virus. Lamivudine resistance develops in 20 to 25% of patients in each year of therapy so that after 4 to 5 years of treatment, more than two thirds of patients have HBV mutants.

Adefovir dipivoxil is a nucleotide analogue (*bis*-POM-PMEA) that acts as a prodrug of adefovir with enhanced oral availability. Adefovir has activity in vitro against the wild-type and lamivudine-resistant HBV strains. For this reason, adefovir has been used to treat patients with lamivudine resistance. Monotherapy with adefovir dipivoxil itself (given in a dose of 10 mg daily) leads to marked decreases in HBV DNA levels (by 3 to 4 $\log_{10}$ units), however, and subsequent improvements in serum aminotransferase levels and hepatic histology in more than half of patients. [2] Similar trials have been carried out in patients with HBeAg-negative chronic hepatitis B, in whom improvements in serum aminotransferases and liver histology occurred in more than 60% of patients. [3] Stopping therapy usually is followed by relapse, however, and return of disease activity. Long-term trials of adefovir dipivoxil therapy are now under way, but studies of treatment for 1 to 2 years show no clinical or genetic evidence of viral resistance, a unique and unexpected finding for any antiviral agent. The safety of 10 mg daily of adefovir has been shown in randomized trials in which side effects were no more common with adefovir than placebo. Higher doses of adefovir have been associated, however, with renal toxicity (renal tubular acidosis) that arises after 6 to 12 months of treatment. The dose of adefovir must be kept to 10 mg daily or less, and patients should be monitored for increases in serum creatinine; any elevation of greater than 0.5 mg/dL above baseline levels should lead to an immediate modification of dose or temporary withholding of therapy. The safety of adefovir dipivoxil in patients with preexisting renal disease has not been shown.

There are no clear guidelines for use of antiviral therapy in hepatitis B. Studies of combination therapy (peginterferon with lamivudine or lamivudine with adefovir) are under way, as are studies of long-term treatment. Lamivudine and adefovir are easy to administer and are well tolerated. The long-term benefits of treatment have yet to be proved, however, and the decision of whether to stop or continue therapy after 1 to 2 years is often difficult. Withdrawal of therapy with nucleoside or nucleotide analogues usually results in a rapid return of HBV DNA levels toward baseline; this return of viral replication can be associated with a transient exacerbation of disease, which in some instances can be severe and symptomatic and ultimately may reverse any benefit of years of treatment. Management of lamivudine resistance is particularly challenging; often it is appropriate to stop therapy when resistance develops.

At present, monotherapy with lamivudine or adefovir should be limited to patients who have moderate-to-severe chronic hepatitis B as shown by liver biopsy histology or by clinical features. Patients with HBeAg-positive chronic hepatitis B probably should be treated first with interferon, either standard interferon-α or peginterferon. Lamivudine or adefovir monotherapy should be reserved for HBeAg-positive patients who fail to respond to or cannot tolerate a course of interferon. Because of the high rate of viral resistance, therapy should not be continued for more than 1 year in patients with typical, compensated HBeAg-positive chronic hepatitis B. Continuous, long-term therapy with lamivudine or adefovir should be reserved for patients who are immunosuppressed and patients who have severe disease, such as decompensated chronic hepatitis B. Monotherapy with lamivudine or adefovir dipivoxil may be appropriate for patients with HBeAg-negative chronic hepatitis B, although the long-term efficacy of this treatment has yet to be shown. Patients with lamivudine resistance should be reevaluated for the necessity of therapy and perhaps are best switched to adefovir dipivoxil therapy (stopping lamivudine). Lamivudine and adefovir should not be used in patients with mild or minimal disease; the exception is a patient with chronic hepatitis B or the inactive carrier state who requires therapy with a pulse or short course of immunosuppression or corticosteroids, as with cyclic cancer chemotherapy. Use of lamivudine in this situation is directed at preventing hepatitis reactivation, which can be severe and even life-threatening. These patients should be treated with lamivudine (100 mg/day) for the duration of the immunosuppressive therapy. Recommendations regarding indications and regimens and duration of therapy will change as more effective combination antiviral therapies are developed.

CHRONIC HEPATITIS D

Hepatitis D is caused by combined infection with hepatitis B and the hepatitis D virus (HDV), a defective RNA virus that replicates and spreads efficiently only in the presence of HBsAg (Chapter 150). Hepatitis D is the least common form of chronic viral hepatitis but also is the most severe. On average, cirrhosis develops in 70% of patients with chronic hepatitis D, generally at a younger age than in patients with hepatitis B alone.

The diagnosis of chronic hepatitis D usually is made on the basis of finding antibody to HDV (anti-HDV) in a patient with chronic hepatitis and HBsAg in serum. The diagnosis can be confirmed by the identification of HDV antigen in liver or by detection of HDV RNA in serum, a research test not generally available. Most patients with chronic hepatitis D have HBsAg without serologic markers of active viral replication (i.e., they have a negative result for HBeAg and either low levels [<10^5 viral copies/mL] or no detectable HBV DNA). Replication of HDV seems to suppress replication of HBV.

 Treatment

Therapy of hepatitis D is difficult. A prolonged course of high doses of interferon-α (5 to 10 million U/day or three times weekly) results in improvements in serum aminotransferase levels and liver histology in approximately one third of patients. With the exception of patients who become HBsAg-negative during treatment, however, most patients have a relapse when therapy is stopped. Trials of long-term therapy with peginterferon are currently under way. Neither corticosteroids nor lamivudine or adefovir is helpful. General management recommendations for hepatitis D are the same as for hepatitis B.

CHRONIC HEPATITIS C

Chronic hepatitis C is caused by infection with the hepatitis C virus (HCV), a small RNA virus classified in genus *Hepacivirus*, family Flaviviridae (Chapter 149). The diagnosis of chronic hepatitis C usually is based on the finding of anti-HCV in a patient with serum aminotransferase elevations or a risk factor for hepatitis C (Table 152–4). The typical test for anti-HCV is an enzyme immunoassay, which occasionally can yield a false-positive result. A recombinant immunoblot assay can be used to confirm anti-HCV reactivity. The diagnosis of hepatitis C is confirmed more aptly, however, by a qualitative test for HCV RNA in serum using a sensitive assay, such as a reverse-transcriptase PCR. If anti-HCV is present without HCV RNA, recovery from hepatitis C rather than persistent infection probably has occurred. Several commercial assays are available to quantify HCV RNA levels in serum, but these tests have been difficult to standardize. Most patients with chronic hepatitis C have 10^5 to 10^7 IU of HCV RNA in serum, and levels are usually stable over time. HCV RNA levels should be measured before and during therapy, but otherwise there is little clinical value to following levels of HCV RNA.

HCV has marked genetic heterogeneity, with nucleotide variability between different isolates ranging from 1 to 50%. Phylogenetic analyses indicate that there are at least 6 different genotypes of HCV (differing by 30 to 50% in sequence) and more than 90 subtypes (differing by 15 to 30%). Different isolates of a single genotype can vary by 5 to 15%, and virions isolated from a single individual often differ by 1 to 5%, a phenomenon that is termed *quasispecies diversity* and that may account for the propensity of this virus to lead to chronic infection. The most common genotypes in the United States are *1a* and *1b* (approximately 75%), *2a* and *2b* (approximately 15%), and *3a* (approximately 7%). Genotype 4 occurs typically in Africa and the Middle East and is uncommon in the United States. Genotype 5 is rare outside of South Africa, and genotype 6 is rare outside of Southeast Asia. Infections with different genotypes do not differ in clinical expression or disease severity, but responses to interferon-based therapies depend on genotype of the infection.

Hepatitis C is spread largely by the parenteral route, most commonly as a result of injection drug use or receipt of blood transfusions before the introduction of routine screening of blood for anti-HCV (in 1992) or receipt of plasma products before the introduction of inactivation procedures (in 1986). Hepatitis C also occurs after

Table 152–4 • INTERPRETATION OF SEROLOGIC MARKERS FOR HEPATITIS C				
ANTI-HCV (EIA)	**ANTI-HCV (RIBA)**	**HCV RNA (PCR)**	**ALT**	**INTERPRETATION**
Positive	Positive	Positive	Elevated	Acute or chronic hepatitis C
Positive	Positive	Positive	Normal	Chronic hepatitis C
Positive	Positive	Negative	Normal	Resolved hepatitis C
Positive	Negative	Negative	Normal	False-positive EIA assay result

ALT = alanine aminotransferase; Anti-HCV = antibody to hepatitis C virus; EIA = enzyme immunoassay; HCV RNA = hepatitis C viral RNA; PCR = polymerase chain reaction; RIBA = recombinant immunoblot assay.

accidental needle sticks and is an occupational hazard for health care workers. In 10 to 30% of patients, a parenteral source of infection cannot be identified, even after careful questioning. These sporadic cases of hepatitis C probably are related to sexual contact or "inapparent" parenteral spread. Sexual spread of hepatitis C can occur, but the risk is low, and sexual transmission has been described primarily in individuals with multiple partners. Maternal-infant spread of HCV occurs in approximately 5% of cases of mothers with chronic hepatitis C. Neither breast-feeding nor type of delivery correlates with transmission.

In the typical course of chronic hepatitis C (Fig. 152–2), HCV RNA becomes detectable soon after exposure and remains present throughout the course of the acute illness and thereafter. Approximately one third of patients experience symptoms during the acute episode, and a similar percentage are jaundiced. Aminotransferase levels vary widely but after the acute episode are usually less than 10 times the upper limit of normal. In 30 to 50% of infected individuals, serum aminotransferase levels decrease and remain in the normal range despite persistence of HCV RNA. These individuals nevertheless have chronic hepatitis on liver biopsy. Anti-HCV rises after the onset of ALT elevations and symptoms, and it usually persists at high titers. Anti-HCV may not become detectable in patients who have renal failure, are immunosuppressed, or have hypogammaglobulinemia or agammaglobulinemia.

The natural history of hepatitis C is highly variable. A small proportion of patients have severe and progressive disease, and cirrhosis and end-stage liver disease develop within a few years; other patients have a benign outcome. In patients followed from the time of acute infection (e.g., after blood transfusion or receipt of contaminated blood products), approximately 55 to 85% have chronic infection, but cirrhosis develops in only 5 to 20% within the first 20 years. In these patients, there is little or no increase in hepatitis C–related mortality rate during the first 2 decades of infection. When patients with established chronic hepatitis C are followed prospectively from the time of initial presentation, 30 to 50% have cirrhosis, however, and morbidity and mortality rates are substantial, with development of end-stage liver disease or hepatocellular carcinoma, particularly in patients with cirrhosis or severe fibrosis indicated on initial liver biopsy. At the time of diagnosis, the average patient probably has had the infection for 10 to 20 years (dating onset from time of presumed exposure).

Factors associated with the risk of development of cirrhosis in chronic hepatitis C include age, male sex, alcohol use, and coinfection with other hepatitis viruses or HIV. Factors associated with increased rate of development of hepatocellular carcinoma are cirrhosis or advanced fibrosis on liver biopsy, age, male sex, and alcohol abuse. In some retrospective studies, treatment with interferon-α, even without a sustained virologic response, has been associated with a lower rate of development of liver cancer.

The pathogenesis of viral persistence and the cause of hepatic injury in chronic hepatitis C infection are unknown, but cytotoxic T

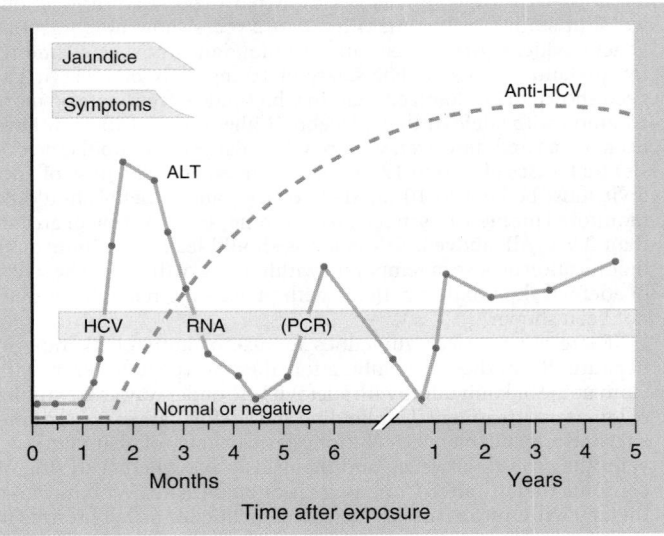

FIGURE 152–2 • The typical serologic course of chronic hepatitis C. HCV = hepatitis C virus; ALT = alanine aminotransferase; PCR = polymerase chain reaction.

lymphocyte–mediated responses are probably important. In general, the degree of liver injury does not correlate with the level or genotype of virus but tends to increase with duration of infection. Nevertheless, some individuals remain infected with HCV for decades yet have minimal changes on liver biopsy. Alcohol ingestion and other causes of liver injury (e.g., iron overload, nonalcoholic steatohepatitis, or concurrent hepatitis virus infection) may augment liver injury in chronic HCV infection.

The extrahepatic manifestations of chronic hepatitis C include cryoglobulinemia (Chapter 196), glomerulonephritis (Chapter 119), mucocutaneous vasculitis (Chapter 284), sicca syndrome (Chapter 282), non-Hodgkin's B-cell lymphoma (Chapter 195), porphyria cutanea tarda (Chapter 223), lichen planus (Chapter 474), and perhaps fibromyalgia (Chapter 289). Cryoglobulinemia, which is the most common and well-defined complication of hepatitis C, occurs in approximately 1% of adults with this infection. Typical manifestations are fatigue, myalgias, arthralgias, skin rash (purpura, hives, and leukocytoclastic vasculitis), neuropathy, and renal disease (glomerulonephritis). Laboratory testing reveals high levels of rheumatoid factor and of cryoglobulins containing anti-HCV and HCV RNA, with low levels of complement. Cryoglobulinemia can be severe and lead to end-stage renal disease or severe neuropathies.

Rx Treatment

The management of patients with chronic hepatitis C should include counseling to abstain from alcohol and evaluation for hepatitis A and B vaccination. The therapy of hepatitis C is rapidly evolving. Interferon-α (recombinant and natural) has been used successfully to treat chronic hepatitis C for more than a decade, but the overall sustained virologic response rate to a course of interferon-α monotherapy is only 10 to 20%. Combination therapy using interferon-α and ribavirin increases the sustained virologic response rate considerably to 35 to 45%. A 48-week course of the combination of peginterferon and ribavirin yields an overall virologic response rate of 54 to 56%.

Pretreatment factors associated with a beneficial response to combination therapy include short duration of disease, lack of severe hepatic fibrosis or cirrhosis, low level of HCV RNA, and viral genotypes 2 and 3. Sustained virologic responses also correlate with early clearance of HCV RNA (within 3 months of starting therapy) and with more prolonged courses of treatment. Among patients with genotypes 2 and 3, the sustained response rates are 70 to 80%, and these rates can be achieved by a 24-week course of therapy using a lower dose of ribavirin (800 mg daily). In contrast, among patients with genotype 1, sustained responses are more common with a 48-week course of therapy (40 to 45%) than with a 24-week course, and optimal response rates require a full dose of ribavirin (1000 to 1200 mg daily).

The usual criteria used to define a beneficial response to therapy in chronic hepatitis C are (1) eradication of HCV RNA from serum, (2) normalization of serum aminotransferase levels, and (3) improvements in liver histology. The most accurate end point in defining a beneficial response to treatment is absence of detectable HCV RNA (by a reliable and sensitive PCR technique) for at least 6 months after stopping therapy, a sustained virologic response that is highly predictive of long-term remission and resolution of the liver disease and may indicate eradication of the infection.

With combination therapy, HCV RNA levels typically decrease rapidly with starting treatment and, in responders, become undetectable within 1 to 3 months (Fig. 152–3). Serum aminotransferase levels become normal in most patients with virologic response by the end of treatment. In patients who have a relapse, HCV RNA and elevations in serum ALT level reappear soon after therapy is stopped. In nonresponders, ALT levels may decrease and become normal, but HCV RNA remains detectable. In contrast, in some patients HCV becomes RNA–negative during therapy, but aminotransferase levels remain elevated; these patients often have a sustained response, and serum ALT levels may become normal when interferon is stopped.

At present, therapy is recommended for patients with chronic hepatitis C with HCV RNA in serum, raised serum aminotransferase levels, chronic hepatitis of at least moderate severity on liver biopsy specimen (presence of fibrosis or moderate degrees of inflammation and necrosis), and no contraindications to treatment. The contraindications to peginterferon and ribavirin combination therapy are decompensated liver disease, renal failure, severe immunosuppression, solid-organ transplantation, cytopenia, severe psychiatric disease, and active substance abuse. Ribavirin therapy is contraindicated in patients with hemolysis, anemia, significant coronary or cerebrovascular disease, or renal insufficiency. Because ribavirin is teratogenic, it is essential that adequate contraception be practiced during therapy of men and women and for at least 6 months thereafter. Patients with genotype 1 should receive a 48-week course of peginterferon (1.5 µg/kg of alfa-2b, or 180 µg of alfa-2a) weekly in combination with ribavirin in a dose of 1000 mg if body weight is less than 75 kg and 1200 mg if body weight is greater than 75 kg. Patients with genotype 2 or 3 may be able to receive a 24-week course of peginterferon (in the same dose as for genotype 1 patients) and ribavirin in a dose of 800 mg/day. The side effects of interferon and ribavirin must be reviewed carefully before starting therapy. Interferon induces an influenza-like syndrome with the first several doses. Thereafter, the major side effects are fatigue, malaise, depression, difficulty in concentrating, bone marrow suppression, and, in rare instances, bacterial infections or induction of autoimmune disease. Side effects of ribavirin include a dose-related hemolysis that usually results in a 5 to 15% decrease in hemoglobin level, mild itching, and nasal congestion. Dose modification frequently is required during therapy.

Even with combination therapy, the overall sustained virologic response rate to interferon treatment in hepatitis C is only 50%, and many patients find the therapy difficult to tolerate. For patients with decompensated liver disease secondary to hepatitis C, liver transplantation (Chapter 157) is indicated. Potential future approaches include specific inhibitors of HCV protease, helicase, and polymerase enzymes and agents that block uptake, membrane attachment, or translation initiation of HCV.

AUTOIMMUNE HEPATITIS

Autoimmune hepatitis is a chronic inflammatory disorder of the liver of unknown cause. It is characterized by presence of autoantibodies, high levels of serum immunoglobulins, and frequent association with other autoimmune diseases. The disease has been given a variety of names since it first was described in the 1950s, but in 1992 the International Autoimmune Hepatitis Group recommended the term *autoimmune hepatitis* and established diagnostic criteria. Two types of autoimmune hepatitis have been described: type 1 (or classic) autoimmune hepatitis and type 2 autoimmune hepatitis. Both forms are more common among women than men and have similar clinical and serum biochemical features. Type 2 autoimmune hepatitis is found largely in Europe and typically affects young women or girls.

Autoimmune hepatitis is one of the three major autoimmune liver diseases, along with primary biliary cirrhosis and primary sclerosing cholangitis (Chapters 156 and 158). Also within this group of autoimmune liver diseases are variant forms of autoimmune hepatitis, which have been termed *overlap syndromes* because they share features of autoimmune hepatitis and another type of chronic liver disease, and *outlier syndromes,* which have features of autoimmune hepatitis but do not meet criteria established by the International Autoimmune Hepatitis Group.

The pathogenesis of autoimmune hepatitis is not known, but it is believed to be caused by autoimmune reactions against normal hepatocytes. The disease seems to occur among genetically predisposed individuals on exposure to as yet unidentified noxious environmental agents, triggering an autoimmune process directed at liver antigens. In patients with autoimmune hepatitis, primary associations are seen with the human leukocyte antigen (HLA) class I B8 and class II DR3 and DR52a loci. Among Asians, autoimmune hepatitis is associated with HLA-DR4, an association that is less common among Western patients.

Autoimmune hepatitis is a heterogeneous disease with a wide spectrum of clinical manifestations. It tends to be more severe and florid in onset than chronic hepatitis B or C. Autoimmune hepatitis is usually progressive and leads to end-stage liver disease if not treated with immunosuppression. The disease is more common in women than men and typically has its onset either in childhood and young adulthood (between ages 15 and 25) or around the time of menopause (between ages 45 and 60). The disease, particularly type 2 autoimmune hepatitis, can occur in young children. In some patients, it is detected before the onset of symptoms and jaundice if elevated serum aminotransferase levels are found on a routine health evaluation. More typically, patients present with jaundice and fatigue. Abnormalities in routine liver test results are also similar to abnormalities found in other forms of chronic hepatitis with elevations in serum aminotransferase levels. Elevations in bilirubin or alkaline phosphatase levels indicate more severe or advanced disease. Perhaps most characteristic of autoimmune hepatitis are striking elevations in serum gamma globulin and specifically in immunoglobulin G (IgG) levels, accompanied by the autoantibodies directed at non–organ-specific cellular

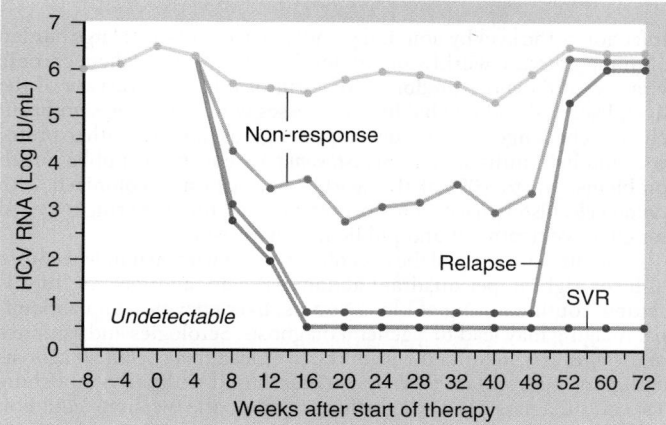

FIGURE 152–3 • Virologic responses to treatment of chronic hepatitis C for 48 weeks. HCV = hepatitis C virus; SVR = sustained virologic response.

constituents, the detection of which forms the basis for the diagnosis of the disease.

The presence of serum autoantibodies is the basis for the diagnosis of the two types of autoimmune hepatitis: Type 1 (classic) autoimmune hepatitis is characterized by the detection of antinuclear (ANA), anti–smooth muscle (SMA), antiactin, and antiasialoglycoprotein receptor antibodies. Type 2 autoimmune hepatitis is characterized by the detection of anti–liver-kidney microsomal 1 antibodies (anti-LKM1) and anti-liver cytosol 1 antibodies and the absence of ANA or SMA. To meet criteria for the diagnosis of autoimmune hepatitis, these antibodies should be present in titers of at least 1:80 in adults and 1:20 in children.

Liver biopsy specimens in patients with autoimmune hepatitis show features characteristic of chronic hepatitis (as described earlier). Plasma cell infiltrates, which are rare in other forms of chronic hepatitis, are characteristic of autoimmune hepatitis.

Rx Treatment

Most typical of autoimmune hepatitis is a rapid clinical response to corticosteroid therapy, in terms of resolution of clinical symptoms and improvements in serum aminotransferase and serum bilirubin elevations. Prednisone should be initiated in a dose of 20 to 30 mg/day. A biochemical response with fall of serum aminotransferase levels into the normal or near-normal range should occur within 1 to 3 months. A lack of biochemical or clinical response should lead to a reevaluation of the diagnosis. To prevent the side effects of long-term prednisone therapy, azathioprine, 50 to 100 mg, can be combined with prednisone, starting at the same time or added later. In the typical patient, prednisone can be tapered slowly to a maintenance regimen of 5 to 10 mg/day combined with azathioprine, 50 to 150 mg/day. In some patients, azathioprine alone, in a dose of 2 mg/kg body weight/day, can be used instead of prednisone as maintenance therapy. The long-term side effects of azathioprine (immune suppression, bone marrow suppression, and risk of cancer) need to be considered. Corticosteroid or immunosuppressive therapy usually is continued indefinitely; attempts can be made to withdraw therapy in some patients, but these trials should be monitored carefully thereafter because severe and even fatal flares of disease can occur weeks to months after stopping prednisone. Prognosis in this disease generally is related to the histologic stage of disease at the time of diagnosis and initiation of therapy, but patients whose disease responds to immunosuppressive therapy can do well for many years. Patients with autoimmune hepatitis that progresses to end-stage liver disease have excellent survival rates after liver transplantation (Chapter 157).

VARIANT FORMS OF AUTOIMMUNE HEPATITIS

Patients who have features of autoimmune hepatitis but do not meet the criteria established by the International Autoimmune Hepatitis Group for definite or probable autoimmune hepatitis are considered to have a variant form of autoimmune hepatitis. These patients may have features associated with autoimmune hepatitis and another type of chronic liver disease (overlap syndromes).

Three overlap syndromes are recognized: autoimmune hepatitis with concurrent features of primary biliary cirrhosis, autoimmune hepatitis with concurrent features of primary sclerosing cholangitis, and autoimmune hepatitis with concurrent features of chronic viral hepatitis. In each of these syndromes, the clinical manifestations, laboratory findings, and liver histologic characteristics share features of each of the two diseases. In general, treatment regimens are designed in relation to the more dominant of the two disorders. In another variant, *autoimmune cholangitis* (also called *antimitochondrial antibody–negative primary biliary cirrhosis*), patients have features of hepatitis and cholangitis; prednisone and ursodeoxycholic acid have been used to treat the disease with variable success.

CRYPTOGENIC CHRONIC LIVER DISEASE

The term *cryptogenic chronic liver disease* generally is reserved for patients with chronic hepatitis or cirrhosis of unknown cause.

Cryptogenic hepatitis is a diagnosis of exclusion and should be made only after hepatitis B, C, and D; autoimmune hepatitis; and other causes of a chronic hepatitis-like syndrome are excluded (see Table 152–1). It is most important to exclude drug-induced liver disease (Chapter 150) and inherited metabolic liver diseases (Chapter 154), such as Wilson's disease (by serum ceruloplasmin and, if necessary, urine and liver copper concentrations) and α_1-antitrypsin deficiency (by serum levels of α_1-antitrypsin and phenotyping). Diseases that can resemble chronic hepatitis on blood test results but are excluded readily by liver biopsy histologic findings include alcoholic liver disease (Chapter 156), fatty liver, nonalcoholic steatohepatitis (Chapter 155), hemochromatosis (Chapter 225), primary biliary cirrhosis (Chapter 156), and sclerosing cholangitis (Chapter 157). Cryptogenic cirrhosis may represent the end stage of any of these diseases, but particularly nonalcoholic steatohepatitis, which in its later stages may be associated with little or no fat and loss of the other usual characteristics of the disease.

1. Dienstag JL, Perrillo RP, Schiff ER, et al: A preliminary trial of lamivudine for chronic hepatitis B infection. N Engl J Med 1995;333:1657–1661.
2. Marcellin P, Chang T-T, Lim SG, et al, for the Adefovir Dipivoxil 437 Study Group: Adefovir dipivoxil for the treatment of hepatitis B e antigen–positive chronic hepatitis B. N Engl J Med 2003;348:808–816.
3. Hadziyannis SJ, Tassopoulos NC, Heathcote EJ, et al, for the Adefovir Dipivoxil 438 Study Group: Adefovir dipivoxil for the treatment of hepatitis B e antigen–negative chronic hepatitis B. N Engl J Med 2003;348:800–807.
4. Manns MP, McHutchison JG, Gordon SC, et al, and the International Hepatitis Interventional Therapy Group: Peginterferon alfa-2b plus ribavirin compared with interferon alfa-2b plus ribavirin for initial treatment of chronic hepatitis C: A randomised trial. Lancet 2001;358:958–965.
5. Fried MW, Shiffman MC, Reddy KR, et al: Peginterferon alfa-2a plus ribavirin for chronic hepatitive virus infection. N Engl J Med 2002;347:975–982.

SUGGESTED READINGS

Czaja A, Manns MP, McFarlane IG, Hoofnagle JH: Autoimmune hepatitis: The investigational and clinical challenges. Hepatology 2000;31:1194–1200. *A concise summary of a conference on the current understanding of the pathogenesis, natural history, and therapy of autoimmune hepatitis.*

Lauer GM, Walker BD: Hepatitis C virus infection. N Engl J Med 2001;345:41–52. *Excellent and concise summary of the virology, immunopathogenesis, epidemiology, and natural history of hepatitis C.*

Lok AS, Heathcote EJ, Hoofnagle JH: Management of hepatitis B: 2000: Summary of a workshop. Gastroenterology 2001;120:1828–1853. *Summary of natural history and therapy of hepatitis C using interferon and newer nucleoside analogues.*

Seeff LB, Hoofnagle JH: Management of hepatitis C, 2002: Proceedings of the 2002 National Institutes of Health Consensus Development Conference. Hepatology 2002;36(Suppl 1):1, 2. *Review articles on the important virology, clinical features, epidemiology, natural history, complications, and treatment of hepatitis C.*

153 BACTERIAL, PARASITIC, FUNGAL, AND GRANULOMATOUS LIVER DISEASES

Brent A. Neuschwander-Tetri

Infection of the liver by nonviral pathogens accounts for a large burden of human disease worldwide. In developed countries where chronic viral hepatitis is the predominant form of infectious disease of the liver, bacterial and amebic liver abscesses continue to be significant clinical challenges. In less-developed regions, amebae, other protozoa, and helminths such as *Schistosoma* are enormous public health problems. Up to 10% of the world's population is colonized with *Entamoeba histolytica* or schistosomal species, underscoring the need for effective treatment and public health measures.

Nonviral infections of the liver often present with an indolent course of fever, right upper quadrant abdominal pain, and malaise. In this setting, routine testing of blood counts, liver enzymes, and abdominal imaging may lead to a general diagnosis. Serologies and aspirates of focal lesions identified within the liver lead to a specific diagnosis and guide appropriate therapy. A common difficulty in establishing a specific diagnosis is distinguishing between the two more common problems in developed countries, amebic liver abscess as compared with bacterial (pyogenic) liver abscess. Other nonviral infectious diseases and granulomatous liver diseases also often present as diagnostic challenges

BACTERIAL INFECTIONS OF THE LIVER

BACTERIAL (PYOGENIC) ABSCESS

Definition

A *bacterial*, or *pyogenic*, liver abscess is a focal accumulation of purulent necroinflammatory debris within the liver parenchyma caused by single or multiple bacterial pathogens.

Epidemiology

Because bacterial liver abscesses are caused by seeding from biliary tract infections (Chapter 158), other intra-abdominal infections, such as diverticulitis and appendicitis (Chapter 143), or extra-abdominal infections, such as bacterial endocarditis (Chapter 310) or infections of the oral cavity, their incidence shows no major gender, ethnic, or geographic influence. The typical age of patients is 50 to 70 years, an age when diverticulitis and biliary tract occlusion by stones or malignancy are more prevalent.

Pathobiology

Bacterial liver abscesses most commonly develop as a result of seeding of the liver through an infected biliary tract (cholangitis) or bacteremia (Table 153–1). Bacteremia of the portal blood flow is caused by focal infections in regions drained by the mesenteric circulation. Appendicitis and diverticulitis are two infections associated with liver abscesses. Inflammatory bowel disease, especially Crohn's disease (Chapter 142), is a major risk factor because of the compromised mucosal barrier separating enteric bacteria from the circulation. Cirrhosis (Chapter 156) is also a risk factor for liver abscess formation, probably because of the impaired clearance of transient portal bacteremia by the cirrhotic liver. Systemic bacteremia caused by untreated infections of the oral cavity or bacterial endocarditis predispose to the development of bacterial liver abscesses. Less common causes include blunt or penetrating trauma to the liver and extension of an adjacent abscess into the liver parenchyma. Penetrating trauma may be obvious, as in the case of a knife wound, or less obvious, such as penetration of an ingested toothpick or fish bone from the duodenum into the liver. Bacterial liver abscesses are multifocal in about 50% of patients.

The organisms responsible for bacterial liver abscesses reflect the underlying source of bacteremia. Colonic flora such as *Escherichia coli*, *Klebsiella pneumoniae*, and viridans streptococci are common pathogens when primary colonic infections such as diverticulitis, appendicitis, and inflammatory bowel disease are the predisposing processes. Such abscesses are typically polymicrobial and may involve coexisting enteric anaerobes such as *Bacteroides* species. Abscesses in the setting of endocarditis are typically monomicrobial and reflect responsible organisms such as *Staphylococcus aureus*.

Clinical Manifestations

The symptoms of a bacterial liver abscess are nonspecific. Fever, malaise, loss of appetite, and weight loss are the most common. Surprisingly, fever is absent in 5 to 20% of patients. Right upper quadrant abdominal pain is helpful in leading to an appropriate evaluation, but it is present in less than half of patients. Jaundice is even less common unless the underlying infection is cholangitis due to biliary obstruction. About one third of patients have nausea and vomiting.

Diagnosis

Identifying the presence of a liver abscess as a cause of nonspecific constitutional symptoms requires a high index of suspicion. Physical examination reveals right upper quadrant abdominal tenderness and hepatomegaly in 50% of patients. Laboratory testing typically reveals a leukocytosis. Blood cultures may be negative. Liver enzymes are usually normal to mildly elevated unless biliary obstruction is present, in which case the alkaline phosphatase can be substantially elevated. The chest radiograph may identify an elevated right hemidiaphragm. Imaging of the abdomen by ultrasonography (US) or computed tomography (CT) with intravenous contrast (Fig. 153–1) identifies single or multiple abscesses within the liver. CT has a somewhat better sensitivity, and both US and CT are superior to technetium sulfur colloid scanning.

The greatest challenge facing the clinician in the management of a liver abscess is distinguishing a bacterial abscess from an amebic abscess (Table 153–2) and an echinococcal cyst. In the absence of fever and leukocytosis, a noninvasive approach for obtaining imaging studies and serologic tests for *E. histolytica* and *Echinococcus granulosus* is reasonable. If these tests are negative, if fever and leukocytosis are present, or if a focal lesion is suspected of being a bacterial abscess, US- or CT-guided needle aspiration, with Gram's stain and culture of the aspirate, is indicated.

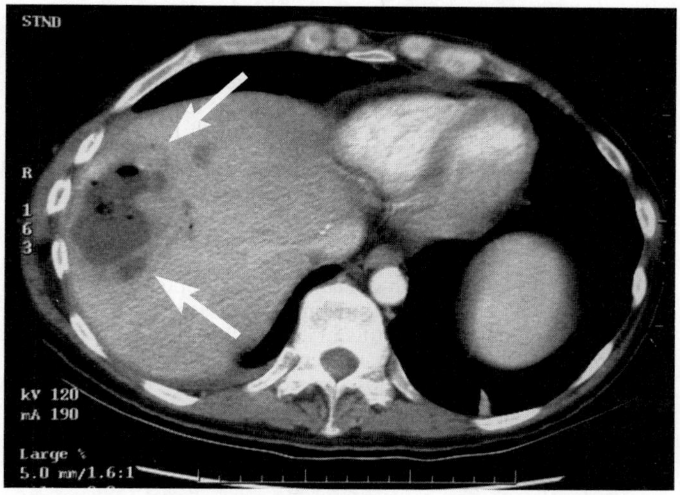

Table 153–1 • CONDITIONS THAT PREDISPOSE TO BACTERIAL LIVER ABSCESSES

MAJOR
Bacterial cholangitis (biliary tract manipulation, duct obstruction by stones, malignancy, *Ascaris lumbricoides*)
Diverticulitis
Appendicitis
Alcoholism
Diabetes

LESS COMMON
Inflammatory bowel disease
Peptic ulcer
Cirrhosis
Necrotizing pancreatitis
Omphalitis
Bacterial endocarditis
Pneumonia
Pelvic inflammatory disease
Hemorrhoidal abscess
Poor oral hygiene
Iatrogenic bacteremia (line sepsis)
Penetrating liver trauma
Liver necrosis (blunt trauma, sickle crisis)
Tumor necrosis within the liver
Neutrophil defects (chronic granulomatous disease, leukemia)
Hemochromatosis (*Yersinia enterocolitica*)

FIGURE 153–1 • Abdominal computed tomography scan obtained after intravenous contrast administration demonstrates an irregular hypodense area containing gas bubbles in the right lobe of the liver (arrows). Aspiration revealed purulent material from which *Klebsiella pneumoniae* organisms were cultured.

Table 153–2 • DISTINGUISHING FEATURES OF BACTERIAL AND AMEBIC ABSCESSES OF THE LIVER

	BACTERIAL LIVER ABSCESS	AMEBIC LIVER ABSCESS
Demographics	Age: 50–70 yr Equal gender ratio	Age: 20–40 yr Strong male predominance (>10:1)
Major risk factors	Recent bacterial infection, especially intra-abdominal Biliary obstruction/manipulation Diabetes mellitus	Travel to or living in an endemic area (even in the remote past)

Symptoms	Right upper quadrant abdominal pain, fever, chills,
	    rigors, weakness, malaise, anorexia, weight loss,
	    diarrhea, cough, pleuritic chest pain
		Acute presentation: fever, chills, abdominal pain
		Subacute presentation: weight loss; fever and abdominal pain
		    less common
		Typically no symptoms of enteric colonization or colitis

Signs	Tender hepatomegaly, abdominal mass, jaundice	Variable right upper quadrant abdominal tenderness

Laboratory testing	Leukocytosis, anemia, elevated liver enzymes (alkaline
	    phosphatase more than aminotransferases),
	    elevated bilirubin, hypoalbuminemia
	Blood cultures positive in 50–60%
		Positive amebic serologies (70–95%)
		Variable leukocytosis and anemia
		No eosinophilia
		Alkaline phosphatase elevated but aminotransferases usually
		    normal

Imaging	Abscesses are multifocal in 50% Usually right lobe Irregular margins	Typically single abscess in 80% Usually right lobe Round or oval, can be septated Wall enhancement on computed tomography scan with intravenous contrast
Aspirate	Purulent Organisms on Gram's stain Culture positive in 80% with proper handling	Variable consistency and color Sterile Trophozoites rarely visualized

Rx Treatment

Once a bacterial abscess of the liver is suspected, treatment with antibiotics should also be initiated. In the setting of a known predisposing infection such as *S. aureus* endocarditis, antibiotic therapy can be tailored immediately to the likely organism. In most circumstances, however, empirical therapy directed at enteric flora including anaerobes should be initiated soon after detection of a likely abscess. Using metronidazole to treat possible anaerobic coinfection offers the additional advantage of also effectively treating *E. histolytica* if an amebic abscess has not been excluded. Undue delay in initiating therapy while arranging for aspiration and culture should be avoided. Most bacterial abscesses of the liver should be treated with percutaneous drainage as well as antibiotics, but small abscesses in patients who are not severely ill can be successfully managed with antibiotics alone. Multiple large abscesses and abscesses not responding to percutaneous drainage may require surgical drainage. Effective drainage of an obstructed biliary tract, either endoscopically or percutaneously, is also necessary when cholangitis has led to liver abscess formation.

Prognosis

Bacterial abscesses respond well to drainage and appropriate antibiotic therapy. However, if appropriate diagnostic testing does not lead to effective treatment in a timely fashion, death from sepsis is the most likely outcome.

OTHER BACTERIAL LIVER INFECTIONS

ENTERIC INFECTIONS. *Listeria monocytogenes* (Chapter 335) infection commonly involves the liver in neonates and occasionally causes a clinical picture of acute hepatitis in adults. Preexisting liver disease is a major risk factor for liver involvement, which presents with liver enzyme elevations and is diagnosed by positive blood cultures. *Yersinia enterocolitica* (Chapter 331) infection may cause multiple liver abscesses when patients with underlying cirrhosis, diabetes, or hemochromatosis develop active enteric infection, usually manifested as terminal ileitis. If abscesses are large, drainage as well as antibiotics are indicated. *Salmonella typhi* and *paratyphi* infections (Chapter 325) can be associated with aminotransferase elevations that range from mild to severe, sometimes mimicking viral hepatitis. Jaundice is occasionally seen.

LEGIONELLA PNEUMOPHILA. Legionnaire's disease (Chapter 307) causes mild elevations of the aminotransferase and alkaline phosphatase levels in more than half of cases. Direct liver infection can be seen on liver biopsy, but a biopsy is rarely indicated because the hepatic abnormalities gradually improve with appropriate antibiotic treatment.

EHRLICHIA SPECIES. Ehrlichiosis (Chapter 355) usually causes aminotransferase elevations that range from mild to severe, even suggesting acute viral hepatitis. Alkaline phosphatase and bilirubin elevations are less common, although severe cholestasis has been reported. The presence of fever, neutropenia, and thrombocytopenia suggest the diagnosis. Improvement is seen after treatment with doxycycline.

Q FEVER. Although Q fever (Chapter 355) is often thought of as a cause of granulomatous hepatitis, acute infection is commonly associated with mild elevations of aminotransferase and alkaline phosphatase levels. Q fever should be suspected in individuals with an exposure to cattle, sheep, goats, unprocessed milk, or raw goat cheese.

FRANCISELLA TULARENSIS. Tularemia (Chapter 332) is commonly associated with mild to moderate elevations of aminotransferase levels. In severe disease, markedly elevated aminotransferase levels, jaundice, hepatomegaly, and ascites may develop.

NEISSERIA GONORRHOEAE. Liver enzyme elevations, most commonly of the alkaline phosphatase, are common in gonococcal infections (Chapter 346). Jaundice is occasionally seen. Although these abnormalities may represent nothing more than the response of the liver to systemic infection, they may also be a manifestation of infection of the liver capsule (perihepatitis, or the Fitz-Hugh–Curtis syndrome), which commonly reflects intra-abdominal spread of pelvic gonococcal infection in women. Gonococcal perihepatitis presents with sudden right upper quadrant pain and liver tenderness. Although cholecystitis is often a consideration, coexisting arthritis, pericarditis, and/or myocarditis may suggest gonococcal disease that is confirmed by vaginal swabs. A history of prior gonococcal infection, sometimes years earlier, is often elicited.

SPIROCHETE AND RICKETTSIAL INFECTIONS. Syphilitic involvement of the liver is most common with secondary syphilis (Chapter 349). It presents as tender hepatomegaly with enzyme elevations in a predominantly cholestatic pattern. The abnormalities gradually improve over weeks after effective therapy.

Leptospirosis (Chapter 353) causes a range of abnormalities from minor enzyme elevations to severe jaundice, with the latter occurring in the severe form of leptospirosis known as Weil's disease. Liver failure is not a manifestation of the infection, and the hepatic abnormalities gradually resolve after the infection subsides.

Lyme disease, caused by tick-transmitted *Borrelia burgdorferi* (Chapter 352), is sometimes associated with mild aminotransferase elevations, usually only during the early phase of the infection.

Infections by the *Borrelia* species responsible for relapsing fever (Chapter 351) commonly involve the liver. In severe forms, the liver infection is manifested by tender hepatosplenomegaly, jaundice, and even hepatic failure. The diagnosis is established by manual examination of the peripheral blood smear.

Rocky Mountain spotted fever, caused by *Rickettsia rickettsii* (Chapter 355), is usually associated with mild to moderate aminotransferase elevations. Rarely, infection leads to marked vasculitic involvement of the liver with jaundice, and increased mortality.

MYCOBACTERIAL INFECTIONS. See information on granulomatous liver disease later.

HEPATIC MANIFESTATIONS OF SYSTEMIC BACTERIAL INFECTIONS

Abnormalities of liver function can develop in the setting of systemic bacterial infection in the absence of direct involvement of the liver. The most common clinical problem is cholestasis of sepsis. Bacterial endotoxins exert an inhibitory effect on hepatocellular bilirubin secretion, leading to predominately conjugated hyperbilirubinemia. Total bilirubin levels of 10 mg/dL to as high as 30 mg/dL can occur. The alkaline phosphatase can also become elevated, but the aminotransferase levels typically remain normal or only mildly elevated. Most commonly implicated organisms are *Streptococcus pneumoniae* and enteric Gram-positive and Gram-negative bacteria. Jaundice is a common manifestation of *S. aureus* infections, such as toxic shock syndrome, and is an occasional manifestation of gangrene caused by *Clostridium perfringens*. The keys to diagnosing the cholestasis of sepsis are recognizing the underlying infection, excluding biliary tract obstruction by imaging, and observing gradual resolution following appropriate antibiotic therapy. The possibility of a cholestatic drug reaction must also be considered (Chapter 150) in this setting, and potentially offending drugs should be discontinued if the diagnosis is uncertain.

PARASITIC PROTOZOAL AND HELMINTHIC INFECTIONS OF THE LIVER

AMEBIC LIVER ABSCESS (Chapter 399)

Definition

An amebic liver abscess is a focal accumulation of fluid and proteinaceous debris within the liver parenchyma surrounded by a rim of granulomatous inflammation caused by invading *E. histolytica* trophozoites.

Epidemiology

About 10% of the world's population is colonized by *E. histolytica*, and amebic infection is second only to malaria as a protozoan cause of death. Persons at highest risk live in or travel to an endemic area, but men who have sex with men, immunosuppressed individuals, and institutionalized, mentally retarded persons are also at risk. Ingestion of cysts and colonization of the gastrointestinal tract may occur years before the development of a liver abscess. Alcohol abuse is a significant risk factor and may explain the greater frequency of amebic liver abscess in men compared with women.

Pathobiology

Humans are the principal host of *E. histolytica*, a motile nonflagellated protozoan parasite. Shedding of cysts in stool with subsequent ingestion of fecally contaminated food or water perpetuates the organism's life cycle. Cysts mature into trophozoites in the intestinal lumen, and the trophozoites are responsible for human disease. Only a minority of infected individuals develop amebic colitis, and the development of colitis is not necessary for the development of a liver abscess. Invasion of trophozoites through the colonic mucosa into the portal circulation, with or without clinically evident colitis, leads to liver abscess formation.

Clinical Manifestations

Amebic liver abscesses can present with an acute clinical picture or a more indolent course. Patients with symptoms of less than 10 to 14 days typically have high temperatures, chills, abdominal tenderness, leukocytosis, relatively low alkaline phosphatase levels but higher aspartate aminotransferase levels, and a higher chance of multifocal disease in the liver. Patients with indolent symptoms of 2 weeks to up to 6 months are more likely to have a solitary abscess, higher alkaline phosphatase levels, and anemia; fever and abdominal pain are less common, and leukocytosis generally is not present. Untreated amebic abscesses can spontaneously rupture into the peritoneal cavity or erode into the pleural or pericardial spaces.

Diagnosis

Most patients have a history of prior travel to endemic areas at some previous time. The physician should have a low threshold for obtaining abdominal US, CT, or magnetic resonance imaging in patients who have unexplained fever. Serologic testing, which can be a valuable adjunct in diagnosing amebic abscess, has a 90% sensitivity. However, serologic testing is less useful for residents or migrants from endemic regions because of a high prevalence of preexisting seropositivity.

Stool should be evaluated for *E. histolytica* using commercially available tests that specifically detect antigens of this *Entamoeba* species. Even with such highly sensitive stool tests, however, colonization with *E. histolytica* is often missed. Routine microscopic stool evaluation for ova and parasites lacks adequate sensitivity and specificity and is no longer recommended as a means of detecting colonization.

Aspiration may be needed to exclude a primary bacterial abscess or secondary bacterial infection of an amebic abscess. The aspirate is variable in appearance and viscosity, ranging from thin yellow fluid to thick brown fluid.

℞ Treatment and Prevention

The cornerstone of treatment is oral or parenteral metronidazole (500 to 750 mg orally three times daily or 15 mg/kg loading dose followed by 7.5 mg/kg every 6 hours IV). The recommended duration of treatment is 5 to 10 days, and most patients improve clinically within 3 days. At some point during treatment, intestinal cysts must be eradicated by the administration of a luminal agent such as iodoquinol, 650 mg three times daily, for 20 days to prevent continued colonization and possible recurrence of the abscess. Failure to obtain a clinical response within 3 to 5 days should prompt percutaneous cyst drainage to exclude secondary bacterial infection and prevent rupture of large abscesses. Because the response to treatment is excellent, follow-up imaging studies to verify resolution generally are not needed. Moreover, abscesses typically require 6 months and up to 2 years to resolve fully. Interim imaging in the clinically improved patient may lead to unwarranted concern and unnecessary procedures. Abscesses that erode into adjacent tissue spaces respond equally well to treatment, and no further intervention is generally needed unless organ function is compromised.

Prevention of infection requires boiling of water used for drinking and preparing food. Iodine treatment can be ineffective. Prophylactic antibiotic use during travel to endemic areas is not recommended. Household contacts of infected individuals should have stool antigen tests to detect colonization.

Prognosis

With appropriate antibiotic therapy, amebic liver abscesses resolve fully without sequelae. If diagnosis and appropriate treatment are delayed, amebic liver abscesses may rupture or become secondarily infected. Mortality rates can reach 13% without treatment; overall mortality is highest in patients who present acutely with high fevers and abdominal pain.

OTHER PROTOZOAL LIVER DISEASES

The key features of the other major protozoal diseases affecting the liver are shown in Table 153–3.

HELMINTHIC LIVER DISEASES

ECHINOCOCCOSIS (Chapter 401). Hepatic infection with *E. granulosus* is sometimes called hydatid disease because of the watery cysts that characterize the infection. The liver cysts may be septated or multiple, and they grow at an average rate of 1 to 5 cm per year. Because of this slow growth, diagnosis may be delayed for months to years after initial infection. Infection occurs worldwide. Canids such as dogs and wolves are the primary hosts and serve as reservoirs for intestinal tapeworms that shed *Echinococcus* eggs in the feces. Humans become accidental secondary hosts by ingesting food or water that is fecally contaminated with eggs. Because sheep and other livestock are the usual secondary hosts, human contact with canids such as sheepdogs, which are in frequent contact with livestock, represents a major risk for infection. Hydatid cysts may cause abdominal pain, nausea, hepatomegaly, or a palpable mass. Liver enzymes are generally normal or near normal, and eosinophilia is not reliably present. Cysts may rupture or become secondarily infected with bacteria. Intraabdominal rupture can cause pruritus and anaphylaxis. The diagnosis is suggested by the presence of septated liver cysts or cysts that have adjacent daughter cysts. Serologic tests can be helpful but lack sufficient sensitivity to exclude the diagnosis. Fine-needle aspiration under US guidance can establish the diagnosis after antihelminthic therapy has been started. Treatment is challenging and usually relies on a combination of a skilled surgical approach with antihelminthic therapy.

SCHISTOSOMIASIS (Chapter 402). Although infection with schistosomiasis does not occur in the United States, the enormous burden of infection with this parasite (5% of the world's population) makes it a major international public health issue and cause of disease in immigrants. Worms lodge in the tributaries of the portal vasculature, where they induce a granulomatous and fibrotic reaction. The end result is presinusoidal portal hypertension, marked splenomegaly, ascites, and gastroesophageal varices. In the late phase of the disease, the diagnosis is established by examination of a rectal biopsy for eggs. Liver biopsy can also be helpful. Infection is treated with antischistosomal agents; decompression of portal hypertension may be needed to prevent recurrent variceal hemorrhage.

OTHER HELMINTHIC LIVER DISEASES. The key features of other helminthic infections are outlined (see Table 153–3). A careful history of travel and dietary habits may identify important risk factors for these infections.

FUNGAL DISEASES OF THE LIVER

CANDIDIASIS (Chapter 385). Hepatic infection with *Candida albicans* is seen primarily in patients with severe, prolonged neutropenia. Unexplained fever, often already treated with broad-spectrum antibiotics and even amphotericin, is invariably present. Liver enzymes may be elevated in a cholestatic pattern, and contrast-enhanced CT scanning may identify focal low-density areas in the liver parenchyma. Diagnosis is confirmed by identification of fungal elements on liver biopsy or by culture of liver biopsy specimens. However, the sensitivity of these diagnostic tests is poor, especially if the patient has already received amphotericin. Eradication of hepatic candidal infection is difficult and may require prolonged amphotericin administration even after reconstitution of the immune system.

OTHER FUNGAL DISEASES. Clinically significant hepatic involvement with other fungal pathogens is unusual and is typically manifested as hepatic granulomas in the immunocompromised host (Table 153–4).

GRANULOMATOUS DISEASES OF THE LIVER

In patients with abnormal aminotransferase or alkaline phosphatase levels, granulomas are frequently found on liver biopsy. The recommended evaluation to establish an underlying cause depends on the patient's clinical status, coexisting diseases, and exposure history. The evaluation of the asymptomatic patient is usually limited, whereas the patient with constitutional symptoms or signs should be evaluated by obtaining cultures, serologic testing, and imaging as indicated by the travel history, immunologic competence, and other risk factors (see Table 153–4).

Definition

Granulomas are focal aggregates of epithelioid cells, macrophages, and other inflammatory cells (Fig. 153–2). The macrophages of granulomas may coalesce to form multinucleated giant cells. Central necrosis, or caseation, may also develop, especially in tuberculous granulomas (Fig. 153–3). *Granulomatous hepatitis* is a poorly defined term that is generally used to describe an illness characterized by cholestatic liver enzyme abnormalities and granulomatous inflammatory changes as the predominant histologic manifestation.

Epidemiology

Up to 10% of liver biopsies show granulomas, either as an incidental finding or as part of the primary process. Sarcoidosis (Chapter 91) accounts for up to one third of cases, and about two thirds of patients with sarcoidosis have hepatic granulomas.

Pathobiology

Granuloma formation is the response of the immune system to the presence of foreign substances that are nondigestable by enzymes

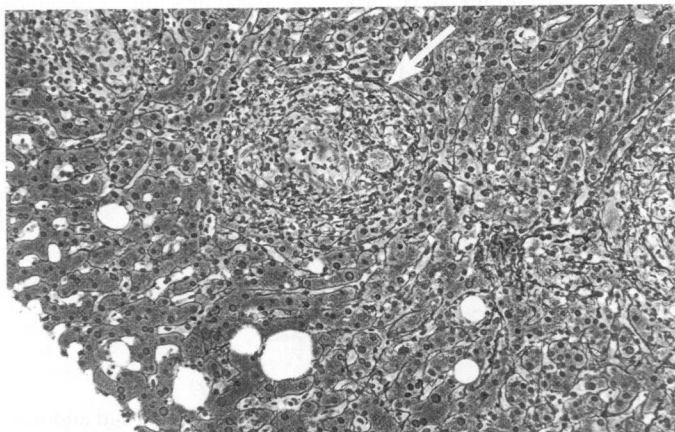

FIGURE 153–2 • Well-defined non-necrotizing granulomas (e.g., arrow) in the liver of a 48-year-old man with unexplained fevers (original magnification, ×20). (Courtesy of E. M. Brunt)

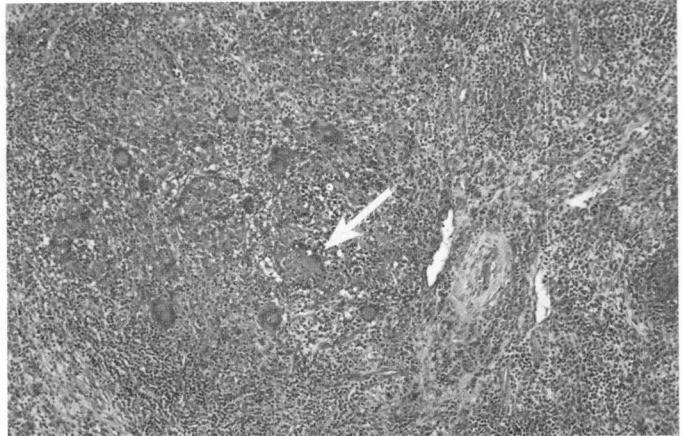

FIGURE 153–3 • Large necrotizing hepatic granuloma from a patient with active *Mycobacterium tuberculosis* infection fills this entire field. Several focal aggregates of histiocytes are present (e.g., arrow). Although tissue sections did not reveal organisms by acid-fast staining, culture of the tissue confirmed the diagnosis (original magnification, ×20). (Courtesy of E. M. Brunt.)

Table 153–3 • PARASITIC INFECTIONS INVOLVING THE LIVER

	CHARACTERISTICS	MAJOR HEPATIC MANIFESTATIONS	RISK FACTORS AND ENDEMIC AREAS
MAJOR PROTOZOA			
Entamoeba histolytica	Ingested cysts develop into invasive trophozoites that colonize the colon and occasionally spread to the liver by the portal blood	Amebic liver abscesses develop as a tissue response to trophozoite invasion with acute and chronic presentations (see text)	Mexico, regions of Central and South America, India, and regions of Africa
OTHER PROTOZOA			
Cryptosporidium spp. and microsporidia family	Ingested cysts develop into trophozoites in intestinal mucosa	Biliary tract infection with obstruction and cholangitis	AIDS; worldwide distribution
Toxoplasma gondii	Ingestion of oocysts in contaminated soil or water, or in infected meat; systemic spread of tachyzoites in circulation	Immunocompetent: asymptomatic or hepatomegaly and mild enzyme elevations Immunocompromised: occasional overt hepatitis	Worldwide distribution
Leishmania spp.	Sand fly bite transmits promastigotes; proliferation in reticuloendothelial system	Hepatosplenomegaly months to years after infection	Worldwide distribution
Plasmodium spp.	Mosquito (*Anopheles*) bite transmits sporozoites	Proliferation in hepatocytes causes hepatomegaly, enzyme elevations, and jaundice	Exposure to anopheline mosquito bites in multiple regions throughout the world
Babesia microti	Tick bite transmits the agent which parasitizes erythrocytes	Mild liver enzyme elevations	Asplenia is a risk for fatal hepatic failure, especially bovine babesiosis (Europe)
MAJOR HELMINTHS			
Schistosoma spp.	Cercaria in fresh water penetrate the skin, travel by circulation to portal vein radicals	Progressive presinusoidal blood flow obstruction, periportal fibrosis, portal hypertension, varices, ascites, splenomegaly	Contact with fresh water in regions of Africa, Asia, South America, and Caribbean
Echinococcus granulosus	Eggs of small (5–10 mm) tapeworms in stool of canid hosts; ingested eggs produce larval oncospheres that migrate to the liver and form cysts in sheep, humans, and other intermediate hosts	Liver cysts that increase in diameter by 1–5 cm yearly and cause variable abdominal pain, hepatomegaly, and variable eosinophilia; occasional cyst rupture, secondary bacterial infection	Ingestion of food or water contaminated by dog or other canid feces; worldwide distribution, found especially in areas where dogs are in contact with livestock
Fasciola spp.	Leaf-shaped flukes up to 13 × 30 mm derived from ingested cysts; the fluke excysts in the duodenum, migrates directly across the bowel wall into the peritoneal cavity, and burrows directly into the liver (or occasionally out to the skin)	Acute: fever, abdominal pain, eosinophilia Chronic: symptomatic biliary obstruction, variable eosinophilia	Consumption of fresh water or aquatic plants contaminated by colonized livestock; worldwide distribution
Clonorchis sinensis *Opisthorchis* spp.	Flukes of 8–25 mm derived from ingested cysts; the fluke excysts in the duodenum and migrates into the bile ducts	Acute: typically asymptomatic Chronic: abdominal pain, fever, anorexia, tender hepatomegaly, sometimes eosinophilia Late sequelae: intermittent biliary obstruction, cholelithiasis, cholecystitis, cholangitis, secondary bacterial abscesses, cholangiocarcinoma	Consumption of raw, pickled, dried, smoked, or salted freshwater fish or crayfish originating from east Asia or, in the case of *O. felineus*, Russia and eastern Europe
Toxocara spp.	Nematode infection disseminates to cause visceral larva migrans after ingestion of soil contaminated with dog or cat feces	Often an asymptomatic cause of eosinophilia (exclude *Trichinella*, *Strongyloides*, filaria, hookworm, schistosomiasis); hepatomegaly is common but nonhepatic manifestions dominate the clinical picture	Consumption of food contaminated with soil containing eggs; distributed throughout United States, highest prevalence in southeast United States
OTHER HELMINTHS			
Ascaris lumbricoides	Ingested eggs develop into larva that migrate to the lungs, are coughed and swallowed; develop into roundworms 15-30 mm long in the small intestine	Colonization is typically asymptomatic with eosinophilia; biliary migration of worms can cause symptomatic biliary obstruction, cholangitis, cholecystitis, and secondary bacterial liver abscess	Consumption of fecally contaminated food or water; 20% of world's population is colonized
Capillaria hepatica	Ingested eggs develop into larva in the intestinal mucosa; larva migrate to the liver by portal blood flow and develop into short-lived roundworms	Fever, eosinophilia, and hepatomegaly; subsequent foci of liver fibrosis, granulomas, and calcification in involved areas	Consumption of food contaminated with rodent feces; human infection is rare
Strongyloides stercoralis	Ingested eggs develop into 1.5- to 2.5-mm nematodes that invade the hepatic vasculature, lymphatics, and biliary tract	Hepatic disease in the setting of immunosuppression: jaundice, abdominal pain; eosinophilia is uncommon	Consumption of food contaminated with soil containing eggs in warm, moist climates

Table 153–4 • CAUSES OF GRANULOMATOUS LIVER DISEASE

UNDERLYING DISEASE PROCESS	FACTORS AND COEXISTING CONDITIONS THAT SUGGEST THE DIAGNOSIS
Sarcoidosis	Evidence of pulmonary sarcoidosis, African-American ancestry, elevated angiotensin-converting enzyme level
Primary biliary cirrhosis	Female, positive anti–mitochondrial antibody
Other immunologic disorders (Wegener's granulomatosis, chronic granulomatous disease, temporal arteritis, polymyalgia rheumatica, Crohn's disease, ulcerative colitis, idiopathic hypogammaglobulinemia, allergic granulomatosis, erythema nodosum, systemic lupus erythematosus, AIDS)	Specific serologic findings, prior established diagnosis
Malignancy (Hodgkin's lymphoma, non-Hodgkin's lymphoma, carcinoma)	Adenopathy, known primary disease
Mycobacterium tuberculosis	Fever, active pulmonary or miliary tuberculosis, caseating granulomas on biopsy
Other mycobacteria (*M. leprae*, atypical, bacille Calmette-Guérin)	Exposure history, HIV infection
Other bacterial infections (syphilis, Q-fever, brucellosis, Whipple's disease, tularemia, yersiniosis, melioidosis, listeriosis, nocardiosis, actinomycosis, typhoid fever, cat-scratch disease, psittacosis, ehrlichiosis, Lyme disease)	Fever, specific risk factors for unusual infections
Parasitic infections (schistosomiasis, fascioliasis, toxocariasis, capillariasis, strongyloidiasis, amebiasis, toxoplasmosis, malaria, leishmaniasis)	Travel to endemic regions, positive serologic testing
Fungal infections (histoplasmosis, candidiasis, cryptococcosis, coccidioidomycosis, blastomycosis, aspergillosis, mucormycosis)	Fever, immunocompromised
Viral infections (cytomegalovirus, Epstein-Barr virus, influenza B, coxsackievirus)	Characteristic clinical illness, positive serologies for acute or recent exposure
Drug reactions (allopurinol, carbamazepine, hydralazine, penicillins, phenylbutazone, procainamide, quinidine, sulfonamides)	Prior or ongoing exposure to the suspected drug
Toxins (beryllium, copper sulfate, thorotrast)	Prior exposure history
Foreign body reactions (talc, mineral oil)	Talc: history of intravenous drug use, birefringent crystals in granulomas

of inflammatory cells and macrophages. Such substances are typically derived from infectious organisms (e.g., mycobacteria and schistosomes) or from injected or ingested materials (e.g., talc and mineral oil). The response may also be elicited by hypersensitivity reactions to drugs and toxins. The stimulus in sarcoidosis remains uncertain. Sometimes the collagen deposition in and around a granuloma forms a fibrin ring, which is a characteristic finding in brucellosis (Chapter 339). Lipogranulomas are associated with hepatic steatosis (Chapter 155) and may be due to ingestion by macrophages of large, unmetabolizable lipid droplets that originate in hepatocytes.

Clinical Manifestations

Hepatic granulomas are typically asymptomatic. Constitutional symptoms such as fever, weight loss, anorexia, and night sweats are more often manifestations of any underlying disease process rather than of the liver involvement itself. Laboratory evaluation most commonly reveals lower enzyme elevations in a cholestatic pattern with the alkaline phosphatase being higher than the aminotransferases. Jaundice occasionally develops in severe granulomatous hepatitis. Imaging of the liver may reveal hepatomegaly. Focal lesions on imaging studies are unusual but can be seen with coalescence of sarcoid granulomas or extensive mycobacterial granulomas in an immunocompromised host.

Diagnosis

Incidentally encountered granulomas require minimal further evaluation. Tuberculosis should be excluded, and sarcoidosis should be considered. The antimitochondrial antibody titer should be measured to identify primary biliary cirrhosis (Chapter 158). Granulomas discovered during the evaluation of systemic illness or unexplained liver enzyme elevations require more extensive diagnostic testing, often guided by the exposure history (see Table 153–4). Potentially causative drugs should be stopped if possible (see Table 153–4). Certain pathologic features, often revealed by additional staining such as Gomori's methenamine silver stain for fungal elements or acid-fast staining for mycobacteria, can point to specific underlying processes.

Rx Treatment

Treatment of granulomatous liver disease depends on the underlying cause and clinical status of the patient. Granulomas associated with sarcoidosis do not require treatment unless they are associated with significant constitutional symptoms or severe cholestasis, in which case corticosteroid therapy may be indicated (Chapter 91).

Prognosis

Incidental hepatic granulomas in the absence of sarcoidosis, primary biliary cirrhosis, or other specific underlying causes do not cause progressive liver disease. Sarcoidosis is usually an asymptomatic manifestation of the primary disease, but it can occasionally progress to biliary cirrhosis with portal hypertension, ascites, and variceal hemorrhage.

SUGGESTED READINGS

Alvarez Perez JA, Gonzalez JJ, Baldonedo RF, et al: Clinical course, treatment, and multivariate analysis of risk factors for pyogenic liver abscess. Am J Surg 2001;181:177–186. *A well-characterized European experience with liver abscesses in 133 patients over 12 years.*

Baughman RP, Lower EE, du Bois RM: Sarcoidosis. Lancet 2003;361:1111–1118. *A good review of newer treatment options.*

Bica I, Hamer DH, Stadecker MJ: Hepatic schistosomiasis. Infect Dis Clin North Am 2000;14:583–604. *Review of the key clinical aspects of liver disease caused by schistosomiasis.*

Haque R, Huston CD, Hughes M, et al: Amebiasis. N Engl J Med 2003;348:1565–1573. *A concise review of pathogenesis and treatment.*

Hughes MA, Petri WA Jr: Amebic liver abscess. Infect Dis Clin North Am 2000;14:565–582. *Concise review of amebic liver abscesses.*

Valla DC, Benhamou JP: Hepatic granulomas and hepatic sarcoidosis. Clin Liver Dis 2000;4:269–285. *Concise review of granulomatous liver disease.*

154 INHERITED, INFILTRATIVE, AND METABOLIC DISORDERS INVOLVING THE LIVER

Jacquelyn J. Maher

A variety of inherited, infiltrative, and metabolic diseases affect the liver and involve multiple organs. In some cases, the hepatic component dominates the clinical picture, and in other cases, it plays a contributory or relatively minor role.

α₁-ANTITRYPSIN DEFICIENCY

α₁-Antitrypsin (A₁AT) is a circulating glycoprotein whose primary function is to inhibit neutrophil proteinases (Chapter 85). This 52-kD protein, which comprises the α₁-globulin fraction of serum, is synthesized primarily by hepatocytes. Deficiencies in circulating A₁AT are caused by mutations in the A₁AT gene and lead to either single amino acid substitutions or more extensive frameshifts or deletions. A₁AT production is controlled by codominant alleles; the protease inhibitor (Pi) phenotype of an individual is designated by the allelic pair. The normal allele is *M*, with the most common abnormal alleles being *S* and *Z*. Individuals who are PiMM have circulating levels of antitrypsin in the range of 200 mg/dL. Individuals who are PiZZ have only 15% of this amount. Heterozygous combinations of 75 or more alleles permit a wide range of A₁AT levels in serum.

Pulmonary disease in patients with A₁AT deficiency is linked directly to the amount of functional A₁AT in the serum. Liver disease is not due to A₁AT deficiency, but instead is related to accumulation of abnormal A₁AT within hepatocytes. Liver involvement occurs almost entirely in PiZZ homozygotes: These individuals produce a protein that folds improperly and cannot pass from the endoplasmic reticulum to the Golgi apparatus. Although all PiZZ homozygotes exhibit impaired hepatocellular trafficking of A₁AT, only 10% develop liver disease. Individuals who escape liver disease manage to degrade the abnormal A₁AT within the endoplasmic reticulum. Individuals who develop liver disease are unable to degrade the retained protein and accumulate massive amounts of abnormal A₁AT in hepatocytes. The mechanism by which retained A₁AT causes hepatocyte injury is unknown.

Liver disease in PiZZ infants typically presents as cholestasis or neonatal hepatitis. Approximately 2% of PiZZ infants progress to childhood cirrhosis. PiZZ homozygotes who escape liver disease in childhood have a 10% chance of developing cirrhosis as adults. Males are at higher risk for adult-onset cirrhosis than females. Patients who develop liver disease have an unusually high incidence of liver cancer.

A₁AT deficiency should be suspected in adults with cirrhosis of unknown origin. Emphysema need not be present to entertain the diagnosis. A₁AT deficiency can be detected by measuring the enzyme in serum or by directly analyzing Pi phenotype. Liver biopsy specimens in individuals inheriting a Z allele show globular deposits of abnormal A₁AT within the rough endoplasmic reticulum of hepatocytes. Because the inclusions are present in heterozygotes and homozygotes, their presence alone is not pathognomonic of A₁AT-induced liver disease.

The only treatment for hepatic cirrhosis secondary to A₁AT deficiency is liver transplantation (Chapter 157). After transplantation, the A₁AT in serum assumes the phenotype of the donor. Genetic strategies to prevent liver disease, such as the use of ribozymes to degrade RNA molecules that encode misfolded A₁AT, are under consideration.

WILSON'S DISEASE

Wilson's disease is an autosomal recessive disorder characterized by accumulation of copper in the liver and other organs (Chapter 224). The disease is caused by several different mutations in the WND gene on chromosome 13. WND encodes a copper-transporting adenosine triphosphatase that is expressed predominantly in liver and kidney. Affected patients exhibit impaired biliary excretion of copper and ineffective incorporation of copper into ceruloplasmin. The initial consequence of disease is accumulation of copper in the liver. In later stages, copper is released into the circulation, permitting deposition in the brain, cornea, and kidneys. Patients with Wilson's disease begin to accumulate hepatic copper in infancy but rarely develop symptoms before age 5.

Symptoms of liver disease are the presenting complaint in approximately half of affected individuals. The most common syndrome is postnecrotic cirrhosis with hepatic dysfunction and portal hypertension. A few (10 to 30%) patients have chronic active hepatitis. Rarely the disease manifests as fulminant hepatic failure; in patients with massive liver necrosis, there can be coincident hemolysis, which may provide an important clue to the diagnosis.

No single biochemical test can establish the diagnosis. A serum ceruloplasmin value of less than 20 mg/dL is highly suggestive; however, 28% of patients with symptomatic Wilson's liver disease may have normal ceruloplasmin levels. Even Kayser-Fleischer rings are not pathognomonic because they can occur in chronic cholestatic liver disease. For screening purposes, it is useful to test the copper levels in urine. All symptomatic patients with Wilson's disease should have abnormally high urinary copper excretion in a 24-hour collection. Patients suspected to have disease based on noninvasive testing should undergo liver biopsy to confirm and quantify hepatic copper accumulation. More than 250 μg of copper per gram of dry liver tissue is required to make the diagnosis. Genetic testing also is available, although the large number of mutations in the WND gene makes screening by genetic methods impractical.

Copper chelation (Chapter 224) improves survival but does not reverse cirrhosis. When initiated, therapy must be continued for life; discontinuation can result in rapid deterioration of liver function. In patients with fulminant hepatic failure or decompensated cirrhosis, liver transplantation provides effective therapy by correcting the primary metabolic defect.

HEMOCHROMATOSIS

Hereditary hemochromatosis (Chapter 225) is an autosomal recessive disorder characterized by iron overload in the liver, heart, pancreas, pituitary gland, and joints. A gene for the disease, HFE, has been identified on chromosome 6 near the human leukocyte antigen-A (HLA-A) allele. Of whites, 60% or more with a clinical syndrome suggestive of hereditary hemochromatosis are homozygous for a single mutation in HFE designated C282Y. A much smaller proportion are compound heterozygotes for C282Y and a second HFE mutation termed H63D. Rare individuals have no mutation in HFE; consequently a search for other genetic causes of iron overload remains active. Patients with HFE mutations absorb excessive amounts of iron from the gut and deposit the metal in many organs, where it can injure cells. Only C282Y homozygotes develop clinically significant hepatic iron overload; heterozygotes accumulate some hepatic iron but do not develop liver injury in the absence of an independent insult.

In hereditary hemochromatosis, iron accumulation is progressive from birth but rarely leads to symptoms before age 40. The onset of disease is delayed further in women because of loss of iron in menstrual blood and a lower intake of dietary iron. Presenting symptoms are often vague, with abdominal pain reported in 16 to 58% of patients. Despite the variability of symptoms, signs of liver disease (particularly hepatomegaly) can be found in more than 75% of patients.

Biochemical abnormalities that suggest hereditary hemochromatosis in symptomatic individuals include elevations in transferrin saturation (≥45%) and ferritin (more than twice normal). Both of these parameters are prone to false-positive elevations, however, and must be interpreted with caution. Transferrin saturation can be falsely elevated in nonfasting patients, in patients with active liver necrosis, and in heterozygotes for hemochromatosis. Ferritin also increases nonspecifically with hepatocellular necrosis and systemic inflammatory disease and may cause particular confusion in patients with alcoholic liver disease. Diagnostic algorithms for hemochromatosis call for HFE mutation analysis in all individuals with iron saturation equal to or greater than 45%. C282Y homozygotes who are older than age 40 or have abnormal liver enzymes should have a liver biopsy to stage disease. C282Y homozygotes who are younger than 40 with normal liver enzymes can be treated without liver biopsy. Patients with iron saturation equal to or greater than 45% who are not C282Y homozygotes should undergo liver biopsy for quantitation of hepatic iron. Significant iron overload is diagnosed if the hepatic iron index (micromoles of hepatic iron per gram of dry tissue divided by age in years) is greater than 1.9. Histology also is useful for determining the distribution of hepatic iron (parenchymal versus nonparenchymal).

Treatment of hemochromatosis consists of phlebotomy (Chapter 225), the goal being to reduce transferrin saturation to less than 50% and serum ferritin to less than 50 ng/mL. Phlebotomy has the potential to prevent or reverse hepatic fibrosis. Patients with cirrhosis are at high risk of developing hepatocellular carcinoma, whether or not they undergo iron depletion therapy. Hepatocellular carcinoma is currently the leading cause of death among patients with hereditary hemochromatosis.

Family members of probands are screened by genetic testing and by serial measurements of transferrin saturation and ferritin. Because of the high frequency of the genetic defect in the general population, the benefit of widespread *HFE* screening is currently under study.

PROTOPORPHYRIA

Protoporphyria is an inherited disorder marked by a profound reduction in ferrochelatase, the final enzyme in the pathway of heme synthesis. The mode of inheritance is debated. The primary clinical features of protoporphyria are cutaneous photosensitivity and scarring of sun-exposed skin; patients also can develop pigment gallstones, frequently at a young age. Parenchymal liver disease has been reported in fewer than 30 patients.

Protoporphyria can be diagnosed by measuring elevated protoporphyrin levels in erythrocytes or feces. Patients with the highest levels of protoporphyrin (>1000 μg/dL in erythrocytes) may be predisposed to liver disease and should undergo liver biopsy. Histology reveals birefringent deposits of protoporphyrin in hepatocytes and Kupffer cells. Development of jaundice predicts rapid deterioration and demise.

Treatment of the liver disease of protoporphyria is aimed at reducing production and increasing excretion of protoporphyrin. Hematin seems to decrease protoporphyrin production and has been useful in selected patients. Cholestyramine and activated charcoal bind protoporphyrin in the gut, preventing enterohepatic recirculation and promoting excretion. For patients with severe liver disease and jaundice, liver transplantation should be considered.

CYSTIC FIBROSIS

Cystic fibrosis (Chapter 86) manifests rarely in infants as a syndrome of obstructive jaundice. Older children and adolescents are more likely to develop liver disease, although the reported prevalence varies from 2.2 to 16%. Patients usually have established hepatic fibrosis at the time of diagnosis. Biochemical tests often fail to predict liver injury; a catastrophe such as variceal hemorrhage is sometimes the first evidence for hepatic disease. Because chronic liver disease may be the initial manifestation of cystic fibrosis, the diagnosis should be considered in any child or adolescent with hepatic fibrosis of unknown cause. Therapy for portal hypertension follows that for other liver diseases.

GLYCOGEN STORAGE DISEASES

Most of the glycogen storage diseases (Chapter 213) are accompanied by hepatic glycogen accumulation and hepatomegaly. Only four of these (types O, I, III, and IV) result in clinical liver disease. Type O (glycogen synthetase deficiency) is extremely rare. Type IV (α-1,4-glucan-6-glycosyltransferase deficiency) leads to mortality from cirrhosis in early childhood. Types I and III are the two most likely to be encountered in adults.

Type I glycogenosis (glucose-6-phosphatase deficiency) is characterized by hepatic glycogen accumulation and marked hepatic steatosis. Biochemical studies reveal profound hypoglycemia and hypertriglyceridemia. Hepatic aminotransferases are only mildly increased. Patients treated with a high glucose diet can survive to adulthood but are at extremely high risk for developing hepatic adenomas. Adenomas are present in 75% of patients by age 30; malignant transformation is rare. Rigorous therapy designed to maintain the blood glucose level greater than 75 mg/dL at all times may prevent or reverse adenoma formation.

Type III glycogenosis (debrancher enzyme deficiency) differs from type I in that hypoglycemia and hyperlipidemia are much milder. Liver biopsy does not reveal steatosis but frequently shows fibrosis, which rarely progresses to cirrhosis or portal hypertension. Supplemental feedings are recommended for patients with progressive liver injury.

AMYLOIDOSIS

Hepatic involvement is common in patients with systemic amyloidosis (Chapter 290). Localized disease in the liver is rare but has been reported. Features of hepatic amyloidosis include hepatomegaly

and increased serum alkaline phosphatase, which are found in 60% of patients with biopsy-proven liver involvement; clinical liver disease is rarely encountered, however. A few patients with hepatic amyloidosis develop severe intrahepatic cholestasis with jaundice. This syndrome portends a poor prognosis, although death results from extrahepatic (primarily renal) disease.

Liver biopsy is not required to confirm hepatic involvement in patients with known systemic amyloidosis. If the diagnosis is uncertain, liver biopsy may be useful and can be performed safely if clotting parameters are normal and any history of a bleeding disorder is excluded.

SARCOIDOSIS

See Chapter 91.

COMPLICATIONS OF TOTAL PARENTERAL NUTRITION

The most common hepatobiliary complication of total parenteral nutrition (TPN) (Chapter 230) is hepatic steatosis. Fatty liver occurs in 25 to 100% of patients receiving TPN; the lesion is heralded by an increase in serum aminotransferase levels with a smaller increase in alkaline phosphatase. Steatosis is completely reversible on cessation of the infusion.

Long-term TPN poses a risk of chronic liver injury in adults. The most common abnormality is steatohepatitis; cholestasis and hepatic fibrosis also have been observed. Because steatohepatitis and cholestasis can progress to hepatic fibrosis, their development is considered by many an indication to discontinue therapy. Chronic liver injury may be prevented by providing a balance of calories from carbohydrate and fat,[1] by infusing TPN cyclically, and by providing small amounts of enteral nutrition when possible. Supplementing TPN solutions with choline also reduces liver enzyme abnormalities in patients requiring long-term TPN.[2]

Adults receiving TPN for more than 30 days also are at risk of forming biliary sludge and gallstones. Of patients, 50% develop sludge after 6 weeks, and virtually 100% of patients are affected after 3 months. Acalculous and calculous cholecystitis can occur. Although the pathophysiology of sludge and stone formation in the setting of TPN is due in part to decreased bile flow, gallbladder stasis plays an important role. Stasis may be ameliorated by cholecystokinin, by pulsed infusions of amino acids, or by small enteral feedings.

LIVER DISEASE IN PREGNANCY

Pregnant women are susceptible to the full range of hepatic diseases. For the most part, pregnancy does not pose an increased risk of acute liver disease, and it does not alter the natural history of hepatic illnesses contracted during gestation. Notable exceptions are viral hepatitides caused by the herpes simplex, herpes zoster, and hepatitis E viruses. Herpes simplex hepatitis has a higher incidence in pregnant women than in the population at large. All three agents can provoke severe illness in pregnant women, with mortality rates of 20% in the case of hepatitis E.

LIVER DISEASES UNIQUE TO PREGNANCY. Transient elevations in hepatic aminotransferase levels may accompany hyperemesis gravidarum (Table 154–1). Biochemical cholestasis, defined as an increase in circulating bile acids, can be detected in 10% of normal gestations. Symptomatic cholestasis occurs in only 1 to 5% of pregnant women and generally is confined to the second and third trimesters. Most patients complain only of pruritus (pruritus gravidarum); a few exhibit a more severe syndrome with disabling pruritus, jaundice, and steatorrhea. Patients with severe symptoms may have an inherited predisposition toward cholestasis, with women of South American Indian and Swedish descent being at high risk. Cholestasis of pregnancy is a self-limited syndrome that resolves spontaneously after delivery. Although mild disease poses no risk to either mother or fetus, severe disease places women at increased risk of premature delivery and fetal death. Symptoms of mild gestational cholestasis can be treated with antihistamines or cholestyramine. Severe disease warrants close monitoring and possible early delivery. Patients should be counseled that the syndrome often recurs with future pregnancies.

Acute fatty liver of pregnancy is characterized by microvesicular fat accumulation in hepatocytes and hepatic necrosis. It mimics diseases caused by impairment of mitochondrial fatty acid oxidation and

Table 154–1 • LIVER DISEASES UNIQUE TO PREGNANCY

	TRIMESTER OF ONSET	SYMPTOMS	LABORATORY ABNORMALITIES	RECURRENCE WITH FUTURE PREGNANCIES
Hyperemesis gravidarum	1	Nausea, vomiting	Elevated AST/ALT (60–1000 U/L), occasionally hyperbilirubinemia	
Cholestasis	2, 3	Pruritus	Bile acids >8 µM, elevated AST/ALT and bilirubin in more severe cases	Common
Acute fatty liver	3	Nausea, vomiting, abdominal pain	Elevated AST/ALT (100–1000 U/L), bilirubin >5 mg/dL, prolonged prothrombin time*	Rare
HELLP syndrome	2, 3, or postpartum	Abdominal pain, nausea, vomiting	Elevated AST/ALT (60–1500 U/L), platelets <100,000/mm³, LDH >600 U/L, microangiopathic anemia	3–25%

*Useful diagnostic distinction from HELLP syndrome, in which prothrombin time, partial thromboplastin time, and fibrinogen are usually normal.
ALT = alanine aminotransferase; AST = aspartate aminotransferase; HELLP = hemolysis, elevated liver enzymes, and low platelet count; LDH = lactate dehydrogenase.

in some instances has been linked to fetal long-chain 3-hydroxyacyl-CoA dehydrogenase (LCHAD) deficiency. The incidence is estimated from 1 in 6500 to 1 in 13,000 gestations. Approximately half of affected women are primiparas. A specific diagnosis can be made only by showing microvesicular fat droplets in hepatocytes; liver biopsy is not essential, however, for management and may be precluded by coagulopathy. Because acute fatty liver almost always resolves spontaneously postpartum, prompt delivery of the fetus is the treatment of choice. Patients deteriorating despite delivery should be considered for liver transplantation. Fatty liver of pregnancy tends not to recur with subsequent gestations, although with fetal LCHAD deficiency, the predicted recurrence rate is 25%.

HELLP syndrome is the name given to a disorder of pregnancy characterized by *h*emolysis, *el*evated *l*iver enzymes, and *l*ow *p*latelets. This microangiopathic disorder of the liver occurs in severe preeclampsia or eclampsia with a frequency of 2 to 12%. Older, multiparous patients are at increased risk of HELLP syndrome; the classic triad of hypertension, proteinuria, and edema need not be present to make the diagnosis. Patients can develop HELLP syndrome in the second or third trimester or postpartum. Symptoms are similar to those of acute fatty liver of pregnancy, including abdominal pain, nausea, and vomiting. In rare instances, subcapsular hematomas can occur and lead to hepatic rupture and circulatory collapse. Laboratory abnormalities are not specific but often include anemia (hematocrit <30%), increased aminotransferase levels, and depressed platelet count (<100,000/mm³). Lactate dehydrogenase is commonly greater than 600 U/L. Prothrombin time, partial thromboplastin time, and fibrinogen are usually normal and may provide some distinction from acute fatty liver of pregnancy. Blood smear suggests intravascular hemolysis. Liver biopsy, when performed, reveals focal hepatocellular necrosis and fibrin deposits within the sinusoids.

Prompt delivery is the treatment of choice. In gestations of less than 37 weeks, corticosteroids can be given to promote fetal lung maturity, to permit delivery as early as practical, and to improve the mother's health.◼ The syndrome usually resolves rapidly postpartum; in patients with persistent thrombocytopenia, plasmapheresis may be successful. The recurrence rate of HELLP syndrome in two large series was 3 to 25%.

PREGNANCY WITH CHRONIC LIVER DISEASE. Fertility is reduced in women with chronic liver disease, particularly in women with cirrhosis. Nevertheless, pregnancies can occur in women with advanced liver disease and are encountered with some frequency in women with mild-to-moderate liver disease. In general, pregnancy does not alter the course of underlying liver disease. Nevertheless, severe underlying liver disease places the mother at risk of gestational complications such as variceal hemorrhage and fetal death. Prophylaxis of gastrointestinal bleeding is not warranted in patients with cirrhosis. Patients receiving specific medications, such as corticosteroids for autoimmune chronic active hepatitis or copper chelators for Wilson's disease, should continue them throughout gestation.

1. Buchmiller CE, Kleiman-Wexler RL, Ephgrave KS, et al: Liver dysfunction and energy source: Results of a randomized clinical trial. J Parenter Enteral Nutr 1993;17:301–306.
2. Buchman AL, Ament ME, Sohel M, et al: Choline deficiency causes reversible hepatic abnormalities in patients receiving parenteral nutrition: Proof of a human choline requirement: A placebo-controlled trial. J Parenter Enteral Nutr 2001;25:260–268.
3. Magann EF, Bass D, Chauhan SP, et al: Antepartum corticosteroids: Disease stabilization in patients with the syndrome of hemolysis, elevated liver enzymes, and low platelets (HELLP). Am J Obstet Gynecol 1994;171:1148–1153.

SUGGESTED READINGS
Bacon BR: Hemochromatosis: Diagnosis and management. Gastroenterology 2001;120:718–725. *A scientific and clinical review with practical algorithms for diagnosis and treatment.*
Morrison ED, Brandhagen DJ, Phatak, et al: Serum ferritin level predicts advanced hepatic fibrosis among U.S. patients with phenotypic hemochromatosis. Ann Intern Med 2003;138:627–633. *If the ferritin is <1000 µg/L, cirrhosis is unlikely.*
Riordan SM, Williams R: The Wilson's disease gene and phenotypic diversity. J Hepatol 2001;34:165–171. *A review addressing the relationship between gene mutations in WND and the diverse clinical features of the disease.*

155 ALCOHOLIC AND NONALCOHOLIC STEATOHEPATITIS

Anna Mae Diehl

Definition

Steatohepatitis is an intermediate stage in the spectrum of fatty liver disease, an entity that ranges from relatively clinically benign steatosis to cirrhosis. Alcoholic steatohepatitis develops in some individuals who consume alcohol habitually. Nonalcoholic steatohepatitis shows the same histopathology and is strongly associated with insulin-resistant states, including obesity (Chapter 233), type 2 diabetes mellitus (Chapter 242), generalized lipodystrophy, and use of certain drugs (see later).

Steatohepatitis is the accumulation of lipid droplets within hepatocytes that are surrounded by spotty accumulations of acute and chronic inflammatory cells (Fig. 155–1). Some of these hepatocytes may contain Mallory bodies, which are ropelike condensations of ubiquitinated cytokeratins. Steatohepatitis, which should be distinguished from simple steatosis, is often associated with the accumulation of fibrous tissue (type 1 collagen) along hepatic sinusoids and around terminal hepatic venules. Therefore, steatohepatitis may progress to cirrhosis.

Epidemiology

The overall incidence and prevalence of alcoholic steatohepatitis and nonalcoholic steatohepatitis are unknown, but the prevalence of fatty liver disease diagnosed by abdominal ultrasonography is about 20% in the adult populations of Japan, Western Europe, and the United States. Studies of asymptomatic individuals referred for liver biopsy to evaluate mild elevations of serum aminotransferase levels demonstrate that steatosis is roughly twice as common as steatohepatitis. Assuming that this relationship is maintained within less selected cohorts, then about 14% of the general adult population has steatosis and 6% has steatohepatitis. Evidence suggests that 10 to 50% of

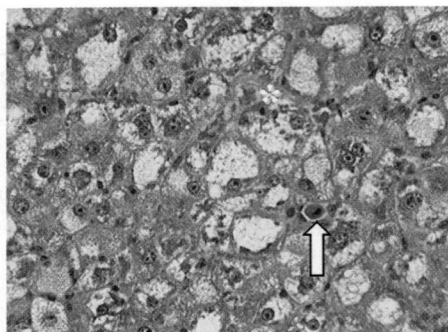

FIGURE 155–1 • Histology typical of steatohepatitis. The hepatocytes have accumulated lipid droplets. Small foci of inflammatory cells are apparent, and a few ballooned hepatocytes contain Mallory bodies.

those with steatohepatitis will develop cirrhosis, so that as many as 3% of the adult population may have cirrhosis related to fatty liver disease.

Pathobiology

According to the "multiple hit" hypothesis for the pathogenesis of fatty liver disease, steatosis is an initial insult (i.e., "hit") that enhances hepatic vulnerability to secondary insults, which lead to steatohepatitis. Steatohepatitis, in turn, enhances vulnerability to further insults, which eventually result in cirrhosis.

In experimental animals, the progression from steatosis to steatohepatitis is promoted by a number of factors that induce the formation of reactive oxygen species, thereby increasing the expression of tumor necrosis factor (TNF) α, a proinflammatory cytokine, within the liver. In humans, steatosis can progress rapidly to steatohepatitis in some obese patients with fatty livers who undergo jejunal ileal bypass in which the intestinal blind loop leads to bacterial overgrowth and malabsorption, which expose liver cells to portal blood endotoxins that induce TNF-α and other proinflammatory cytokines while simultaneously reducing antioxidant defenses. Polymorphisms of TNF-α or one of its receptors are more prevalent in individuals with steatohepatitis than in those with simple steatosis.

Clinical Manifestations

Individuals with alcoholic or nonalcoholic steatohepatitis may be entirely asymptomatic, but vague constitutional complaints, such as malaise and weakness, are common. Careful physical examination detects hepatomegaly in almost 75% of patients. When sufficient fibrosis has developed to cause portal hypertension, patients may have splenomegaly, spider telangiectases, palmar erythema, gynecomastia, ascites, lower extremity edema, portal hypertensive bleeding, or hepatic encephalopathy. Severe steatohepatitis can also lead to jaundice, coagulopathy, or fever.

Classically, severe alcoholic steatohepatitis is characterized by sudden development of tender hepatomegaly, jaundice, and fever in an individual who has been drinking heavily. Often, the illness is associated with a flulike prodrome that includes malaise, anorexia, and weakness. These symptoms sometimes prompt reduced alcohol ingestion, which in turn may precipitate alcohol withdrawal (Chapter 17). Some individuals require hospitalization because of decompensated liver disease or associated conditions, such as alcohol withdrawal, gastrointestinal bleeding, infection, or pancreatitis. Although most people gradually recover during early abstinence, others deteriorate despite abstinence and aggressive management of their associated problems.

Serum concentrations of TNF-α, interleukin-1α, interleukin-6, and interleukin-8 are increased in most patients with severe alcoholic steatohepatitis, and the greatest mortality rates occur in those with the highest cytokine levels. Similarly, serum cytokines gradually fall during recovery.

Diagnosis

The diagnosis of alcoholic and nonalcoholic steatohepatitis requires a combination of noninvasive and invasive tests because there is no single test that is perfectly sensitive or specific. Patients generally have elevated alanine and aspartate aminotransferase levels that are detected incidentally on blood tests, as well as γ-glutamyl transpeptidase levels, but some have hepatomegaly or the incidental finding of a fatty liver on abdominal ultrasonogram. Occasionally, a patient with liver disease first presents with hypersplenism, gastrointestinal bleeding, or encephalopathy.

HISTORY AND PHYSICAL EXAMINATION. Risk factors for viral hepatitis (Chapter 151) should be sought. Although the rare hepatitis C genotype 3 may cause steatosis, a diagnosis of chronic hepatitis B or C (Chapter 152) generally excludes alcoholic or nonalcoholic steatohepatitis; however, these diseases may coexist.

Information about lifetime alcohol consumption should be obtained. More than 60 g/day in men or 20 g/day in women increases the risk for alcoholic steatohepatitis, and lower levels may potentiate liver damage in cases of nonalcoholic steatohepatitis. A history of exposure to any drugs that have been associated with nonalcoholic steatohepatitis (Table 155–1) should be elicited. Obesity, type 2

Table 155–1 • POTENTIAL CAUSES OF NONALCOHOLIC STEATOHEPATITIS
Drugs
Cytotoxic/cytostatic drugs
L-Asparaginase
Azacitidine
Azaserine
Azauridine
Bleomycin
Methotrexate
Antibiotics
Puromycin
Tetracycline
Other drugs
Amiodarone
Coumadin
Dichloroethylene
Ethionine
Ethyl bromide
Estrogens
Flectol H
Glucocorticoids
Hydrazine
Hypoglycin
Orotate
Perhexilene maleate
Safrole
Total parenteral nutrition
Inherited and acquired metabolic conditions
Inborn errors of metabolism
Abetalipoproteinemia
Congenital generalized lipodystrophy
Familial hepatosteatosis
Galactosemia
Glycogen storage disease
Hereditary fructose intolerance
Homocystinuria
Prader-Willi syndrome
Systemic carnitine deficiency
Tyrosinemia
Refsum's syndrome
Shwachman's syndrome
Weber-Christian syndrome
Wilson's disease
Acquired metabolic disorders
Diabetes mellitus, type 2
Lipodystrophy—drug induced
Inflammatory bowel disease
Jejunoileal bypass
Kwashiorkor and marasmus
Obesity

diabetes, and other insulin-resistance syndromes (e.g., lipodystrophy, dyslipidemia, polycystic ovary syndrome) and other, more rare, inherited conditions have also been associated with nonalcoholic steatohepatitis.

The history and physical examination should also include a thorough search for clues of other types of chronic liver diseases, including autoimmune hepatitis (Chapter 152), hemochromatosis (Chapters 154 and 225), α_1-antitrypsin deficiency (Chapter 154), Wilson's disease (Chapters 154 and 224), primary biliary cirrhosis (Chapter 156), or primary sclerosing cholangitis (Chapter 158).

The severity of any underlying liver damage is assessed by evidence of cirrhosis (Chapter 156), such as jaundice, dark urine, acholic stools, pruritus, gastrointestinal bleeding, ascites or lower extremity edema, or personality changes, insomnia, decreased memory or ability to concentrate, asterixis, lethargy, confusion, or coma.

BLOOD TESTS. Serum alanine aminotransferase, aspartate aminotransferase, and γ-glutamyl transpeptidase values are generally increased less than four-fold; elevations greater than 10-fold are very unusual and suggest either an alternative diagnosis or superimposed drug- or virus-induced liver injury. The liver enzyme values correlate poorly with the severity of the underlying liver disease and cannot predict which patients have steatosis rather than steatohepatitis, with or without cirrhosis. The aspartate aminotransferase value tends to be at least twice the alanine aminotransferase value in many patients with alcoholic steatohepatitis, whereas this pattern of liver enzyme values generally does not occur until patients with nonalcoholic steatohepatitis develop cirrhosis. γ-Glutamyl transpeptidase elevations are common in cases of both alcoholic and nonalcoholic steatohepatitis, and increased γ-glutamyl transpeptidase values may be a sensitive marker of insulin resistance. Steatosis is often present with normal enzyme levels. Some patients with alcoholic steatohepatitis or nonalcoholic steatohepatitis also have accompanying, minor (generally, 1.5- to 2-fold) elevations in serum alkaline phosphatase values. Greater increases in alkaline phosphatase values should prompt suspicion of associated biliary tract disease or a hepatic infiltrative process (Chapters 154 and 158). Levels of bilirubin, albumin, and ammonia, prothrombin time, and the platelet count help estimate the severity of liver disease.

Hyperglycemia and dyslipidemia (increased total and low-density lipoprotein levels, decreased high-density lipoprotein levels, and hypertriglyceridemia) are associated with alcoholic and nonalcoholic steatohepatitis. Classically, patients with alcoholic and nonalcoholic steatohepatitis test negative for autoantibodies and have normal values for viral markers, the α_1-antitrypsin phenotype, transferrin saturation, and ceruloplasmin. However, some patients with alcoholic steatohepatitis may also have chronic viral hepatitis. Hyperferritinemia and increased transferrin saturation have also been noted in many individuals with nonalcoholic steatohepatitis, even in the absence of detectable mutations in the *HFe* gene.

IMAGING STUDIES. Abdominal ultrasonography is the most common imaging test used to screen for hepatic steatosis, but fatty liver on an ultrasonogram has a positive predictive value of only 77% and a negative predictive value of only 67% compared with liver biopsy. Computed tomography is less sensitive than ultrasonography. Abdominal magnetic resonance imaging provides the most reliable noninvasive approach for detecting and quantifying hepatic steatosis. Most importantly, none of these imaging modalities can distinguish simple steatosis from steatohepatitis nor identify cirrhosis until hepatic fibrosis has caused overt portal hypertension.

LIVER BIOPSY. Liver biopsy is the gold standard for confirming the clinical suspicion of alcoholic and nonalcoholic steatohepatitis, particularly in patients who have physical findings or blood test results that suggest the presence of more than one type of liver disease. Biopsy is also the most sensitive means for staging fatty liver disease because histology distinguishes steatohepatitis from steatosis and permits the identification of hepatic fibrosis long before overt sequelae of portal hypertension develop. It is indicated whenever a definitive diagnosis will influence patient management. Because this is most likely to occur in individuals who are at greatest risk for liver-related morbidity and mortality, many practitioners reserve biopsy for patients who are older than 45 years of age and who are obese or diabetic, because these patients are at highest risk for advanced hepatic fibrosis.

Prevention

PRIMARY PREVENTION. Abstinence from alcohol is the primary prevention for alcoholic steatohepatitis. In humans with fatty livers, diet modification and exercise to improve insulin resistance may reduce the fatty liver state that is the substrate for nonalcoholic steatohepatitis.

SECONDARY PREVENTION. In individuals who have already developed alcoholic or nonalcoholic fatty liver disease, situations that increase hepatic oxidative stress promote the progression from steatosis to steatohepatitis. Such patients should discontinue alcohol consumption and consider supplemental antioxidants or treatments that inhibit endogenous factors that promote TNF-α production; however, the data for such interventions are currently limited to experimental animal models.

 Treatment (Table 155–2)

ALCOHOLIC STEATOHEPATITIS. In humans hospitalized with severe alcoholic steatohepatitis, prospective, randomized, placebo-controlled trials have demonstrated the efficacy of corticosteroids[1,2] and pentoxifyllin.[3] Both agents are known to inhibit either the production or the activities of proinflammatory cytokines, and each reduces acute liver-related mortality by about 50%. Patients with severe alcoholic steatohepatitis should be treated with corticosteroids (40 mg prednisolone PO every day for 4 weeks) or pentoxifylline (400 mg PO three times a day for 4 weeks) if they have no contraindications; maintenance therapy is not recommended. All patients with alcoholic steatohepatitis are strongly urged to discontinue alcohol consumption; referral to alcohol rehabilitation services may improve long-term success (Chapter 17). Actively drinking individuals with alcoholic steatohepatitis are advised to take supplemental B vitamins and to eat a nutritious diet.

NONALCOHOLIC STEATOHEPATITIS. Virtually nothing is known about the impact of treatment on the natural history of nonalcoholic steatohepatitis. Nevertheless, it is reasonable to suggest dietary modification and exercise. Even very minor reductions in body weight (i.e., about 10 to 20%) improve insulin sensitivity and may also improve nonalcoholic steatohepatitis. By comparison, rapid, extreme weight loss may accelerate the progression of nonalcoholic steatohepatitis to cirrhosis and also increases the risk of gallstone disease. Vitamin E is probably safe at doses of 400 to 600 IU/day, but its efficacy is unproven. Insulin-sensitizing agents, such as metformin or a second-generation thiazolidinedione, are indicated in patients with overt type 2 diabetes or polycystic ovary syndrome. Treatment of dyslipidemia is appropriate (Chapter 211), and reductions in triglyceride levels might theoretically be beneficial in patients with nonalcoholic steatohepatitis; ursodeoxycholic acid has also been suggested for refractory patients.

Progression to Cirrhosis

Among patients hospitalized because of severe alcoholic steatohepatitis, up to 50% develop cirrhosis within 5 years, an outcome that is more common in patients who have severe liver damage by histology, patients who continue drinking alcohol, and women. Cirrhosis also can develop in relatively asymptomatic individuals with alcoholic or nonalcoholic steatohepatitis in whom the hepatic fibrosis evolves gradually over 1 to 2 decades and can be unrecognized until an overt manifestation of portal hypertension, such as hypersplenism or ascites, develops. About 10 to 50% of patients with alcoholic steatohepatitis develop advanced fibrosis or cirrhosis within 5 to 10 years. Nonalcoholic steatohepatitis probably has similar rates of progression; age, obesity, and type 2 diabetes portend a worse prognosis.

The natural history of patients with cirrhosis is similar, regardless of whether the cirrhosis resulted from alcoholic or nonalcoholic steatohepatitis (Chapter 156). In well-compensated cirrhotic patients without overt clinical manifestations of advanced liver disease (i.e., ascites, jaundice, encephalopathy, or gastrointestinal bleeding), one or more of these complications develops at a rate of about 25 to 30% per decade. Nevertheless, until liver-related complications occur, death from liver disease is rare, with a 10-year risk of liver-related

Table 155–2 • APPROACH TO TREATMENT

MILD-MODERATE*	SEVERE†
ALCOHOLIC STEATOHEPATITIS	
Discontinue alcohol	Discontinue alcohol
Nutritious diet	Enteral or parenteral nutrition
	Treat alcoholic steatohepatitis
	Prednisolone (40 mg PO qd)† or
	Pentoxifylline (400 mg PO tid)
	Treat comorbid conditions

BODY MASS INDEX <27		BODY MASS INDEX >27	
No Diabetes	**Diabetes**	**No Diabetes**	**Diabetes**
NONALCOHOLIC STEATOHEPATITIS			
Vitamin E	Metformin or thiazolidiendione Vitamin E	Diet/exercise Vitamin E	Diet/exercise Metformin or thiazolidiendione Vitamin E

*4.6 × (patient's prothrombin time – control prothrombin time) + bilirubin (mg/dL) ≤ 32.

†4.6 × (patient's prothrombin time – control prothrombin time) + bilirubin (mg/dL) > 32.

†Contraindicated in patients with active, systemic infection.

mortality of less than 10% in patients with well-compensated cirrhosis. However, once a cirrhotic patient has suffered a liver-related complication, the 5-year risk of liver-related mortality jumps to about 50%. Alcohol abuse accelerates the rate of hepatic decompensation and doubles the risk of liver-related mortality in patients with cirrhosis.

Once a diagnosis of cirrhosis has been established, patients should be monitored carefully for the appearance of varices, ascites, encephalopathy, or liver tumors and then treated accordingly. General treatments to prevent or palliate the complications of cirrhosis (Chapter 156) are effective in patients with alcoholic and nonalcoholic steatohepatitis. For example, β-blockers and nitrates reduce the incidence of portal hypertensive bleeding in patients with large esophageal or gastric varices; dietary sodium restriction and diuretics reduce ascites and edema formation; lactulose improves hepatic encephalopathy; and norfloxacin reduces the risk of recurrent spontaneous bacterial peritonitis. Hepatitis A and B vaccination protects nonimmune cirrhotic patients from infection with these viruses. Regular screening with abdominal ultrasonography and serum tests for α-fetoprotein improve the early detection of hepatocellular carcinoma. Ultimately, liver transplantation (Chapter 157) improves the survival of patients who have decompensated cirrhosis or small hepatocellular carcinomas that are confined to the liver.

Most transplant centers do not recommend transplantation for patients with alcoholic liver disease unless patients have demonstrated at least 6 months of abstinence from alcohol. However, in sober patients who undergo liver transplantation for alcoholic liver disease, post-transplant survival is outstanding, with 5-year survival rates approaching 85%.

1. Carithers RL, Herlong HF, Diehl AM, et al: Methylprednisolone therapy in patients with severe alcoholic hepatitis: A randomized multicenter trial. Ann Intern Med 1989;110:685–690.
2. Ramond MJ, Poynard T, Rueff B, et al: A randomized trial of prednisolone in patients with severe alcoholic hepatitis. N Engl J Med 1992;326:507–512.
3. Akrividis E, Botla R, Briggs W, et al: Pentoxifylline improves short-term survival in severe acute alcoholic hepatitis: A double-blind, placebo-controlled trial. Gastroenterology 2000;119:1637–1648.

SUGGESTED READINGS
Angulo P: Nonalcoholic fatty liver disease. N Engl J Med 2002;346:1221–1231. *A comprehensive review.*
Bui Han SH: Alcoholic hepatitis. Curr Treat Options Gastroenterol 2001;4:511–516. *Summarizes the clinical features and treatment options for alcoholic steatohepatitis.*
Chitturi S, Farrell GC: Etiopathogenesis of nonalcoholic steatohepatitis. Semin Liver Dis 2001;21:27–41. *Summarizes and interprets animal and human data to suggest mechanisms that are likely to mediate the pathogenesis of nonalcoholic steatohepatitis.*
Falck-Ytter Y, Younossi ZM, Marchesini G, McCullough AJ: Clinical features and natural history of nonalcoholic steatosis syndromes. Semin Liv Dis 2001;21:17–26. *A concise but comprehensive review of the clinical literature about nonalcoholic steatohepatitis.*
Marchesini G, Bugianesi E, Forlani G, et al: Nonalcoholic fatty liver, steatohepatitis, and the metabolic syndrome. Hepatology 2003;37:917–923. *Clues obtained by noninvasive testing can be used to predict the risk for histologically advanced forms of NAFLD.*

156 CIRRHOSIS AND ITS SEQUELAE

Scott L. Friedman
Thomas D. Schiano

OVERVIEW

Definition and General Features

Cirrhosis consists of fibrosis of the hepatic parenchyma, resulting in nodule formation. It represents the consequences of a sustained wound-healing response to chronic liver injury from a variety of causes (Table 156–1). The clinical manifestations of cirrhosis vary widely, from no symptoms whatsoever to liver failure, and are determined by both the nature and severity of the underlying liver disease as well as the extent of hepatic fibrosis. Clinical manifestations can be broadly classified into those resulting from impaired hepatocellular function, such as jaundice and coagulopathy, and those that result from physical disruption of the parenchyma, such as gastroesophageal varices and ascites (Table 156–2).

Epidemiology

Up to 40% of patients with cirrhosis are asymptomatic. In these individuals, cirrhosis may be discovered during routine examination or at autopsy. The overall prevalence of cirrhosis in the United States is estimated at 360 per 100,000 population, or 900,000 total patients, the large majority of whom have either alcoholic liver disease (Chapters 17 and 157) or chronic viral infection (Chapter 152).

Cirrhosis is a major cause of mortality worldwide and is the most common non-neoplastic cause of death among hepatobiliary and digestive diseases in the United States, accounting for approximately 30,000 deaths per year. An additional 10,000 deaths occur due to liver cancer (Chapter 202), the majority of which involve underlying cirrhosis,

Table 156–1 • CAUSES OF CIRRHOSIS

Autoimmune hepatitis
Alcohol-induced liver injury
Drug- or toxin-induced liver injury (e.g., amiodarone, carbon tetrachloride, methotrexate, vitamin A)
Viral hepatitis B, C, or D

Metabolic diseases
   α_1-Antitrypsin deficiency
   Carbohydrate disorders (e.g., glycogen storage disease, galactosemia)
   Hemochromatosis and other iron disorders
   Tyrosinemia
   Wilson's disease

Nonalcoholic steatohepatitis (NASH) or fatty liver
Vascular derangements
   Chronic right-sided heart failure
   Budd-Chiari syndrome
   Long-standing portal vein thrombosis
   Hereditary hemorrhagic telangiectasia (Osler-Weber-Rendu)

Biliary disorders
   Primary biliary cirrhosis
   Cystic fibrosis
   Sarcoidosis
   Bile acid disorders (e.g., Byler's disease)
   Biliary cirrhosis secondary to chronic large bile duct obstruction
   Primary sclerosing cholangitis
   Biliary atresia
   Congenital paucity of intrahepatic ducts
   Progressive familial intrahepatic cholestasis

Malnutrition and postjejunoileal bypass surgery
Cryptogenic disease

Table 156–2 • SEQUELAE OF CIRRHOSIS

CONSEQUENCES OF HEPATIC SYNTHETIC FAILURE
Hypoalbuminemia and coagulopathy
Jaundice
Susceptibility to infection
Protein-calorie malnutrition
Renal dysfunction
Cholelithiasis
Pruritus
Altered drug metabolism
Hepatic osteodystrophy
Gonadal failure

CONSEQUENCES OF PORTAL HYPERTENSION
Splenomegaly with hypersplenism
Gastrointestinal bleeding
   Esophageal/gastric varices
   Ectopic varices
   Portal gastropathy
Ascites
   Spontaneous bacterial peritonitis
   Hepatic hydothorax
   Hernias
Hepatorenal syndrome
Hepatic encephalopathy
Hepatopulmonary syndrome/portopulmonary hypertension

HEPATOCELLULAR CARCINOMA (Chapter 202)

and deaths due to liver cancer have increased in the past decade. Cirrhosis is the most common indication for liver transplantation (Chapter 157).

Pathophysiology

The chemical composition of the scar tissue in cirrhosis is similar regardless of etiology and consists of the extracellular matrix molecules, collagen types I and III (i.e., "fibrillar" collagens), sulfated proteoglycans, and glycoproteins. These scar constituents accumulate from a net increase in their deposition in liver and not simply collapse of existing stroma. Although the cirrhotic bands surrounding nodules are the most easily seen form of scarring, it is actually the early deposition of matrix molecules in the subendothelial space of Disse—so-called capillarization of the sinusoid—that more directly correlates with diminished liver function (Fig. 156–1).

Efforts to identify the cellular source of scar constituents in cirrhosis have established that the hepatic stellate cell is the main producer of matrix. In both human disease and animal models, these mesenchymal cells undergo characteristic activation from a resting perisinusoidal cell rich in vitamin A to a proliferating and fibrogenic cell with reduced vitamin A content. Stellate cell activation is common to all forms of experimental liver injury, including chronic biliary obstruction. Increased matrix produced by stellate cells in liver injury results from increased cell numbers as well as enhanced matrix production per cell. Cell proliferation is regulated primarily by the cytokine platelet-derived growth factor, whereas fibrogenesis is stimulated by transforming growth factor-β, whose messenger RNA levels are markedly increased in human cirrhosis. Activated stellate cells can also contract and secrete proteases, which can remodel the hepatic extracellular matrix. At present, there is no established treatment to arrest or reverse scar formation in chronic liver injury, so removal of the primary insult, when possible, remains the most effective way to prevent irreversible scarring and may yield dramatic improvement.

Diagnosis and Prognosis of Cirrhosis

Liver biopsy is the "gold standard" for documenting cirrhosis, identifying a cause, and assessing the extent of scar formation. Biopsy specimens should be large enough to identify portal tracts and central areas. Ultrasound and computed tomography (CT) can delineate the characteristic features of a cirrhotic liver (nodularity, decrease in size, prominence of the left lobe) and the presence of portal hypertension (splenomegaly, varices, reversal of portal vein blood flow) but are not diagnostic. Noninvasive (i.e., serum) markers of fibrosis are under development but are not yet suitable for widespread use.

With hepatocellular destruction, residual hepatic parenchyma may produce proteins such as albumin and clotting factors as a result of the large reserve capacity of the healthy liver. Extensive liver damage usually must occur before this hepatic reserve is lost.

Both the Child-Pugh-Turcotte classification (Child's score) and the Model for End-Stage Liver Disease scoring system (Table 156–3) use parameters of hepatic synthetic dysfunction to help assess prognosis in patients with advanced liver disease. To date, no dynamic tests of hepatic functional reserve have been validated or widely adopted. Patients with cirrhosis have an increased risk for morbidity and mortality when undergoing any type of surgery, a risk that correlates well with their preoperative Child's score.

POSTVIRAL CIRRHOSIS

Chronic hepatitis B virus (HBV) and hepatitis C virus (HCV) infections are among the leading causes of cirrhosis in the Western world and the leading cause in Asia and Africa (Chapter 152). In chronic HBV infection, the rate of progression to cirrhosis is influenced by

FIGURE 156–1 • Sinusoidal events during fibrosing liver injury. Changes in the subendothelial space of Disse and sinusoid as fibrosis develops in response to liver injury include alterations in both cellular responses and extracellular matrix composition. Stellate cell activation leads to accumulation of scar (fibril-forming) matrix. This, in turn, contributes to the loss of hepatocyte microvilli and sinusoidal endothelial fenestrae, which results in deterioration of hepatic function. Kupffer cell (macrophage) activation accompanies liver injury and contributes to paracrine activation of stellate cells (From Friedman SL: Molecular regulation of hepatic fibrosis; an integrated cellular response to tissue injury [mini-review]. J Biol Chem 2000;275:2247–2250, with permission.)

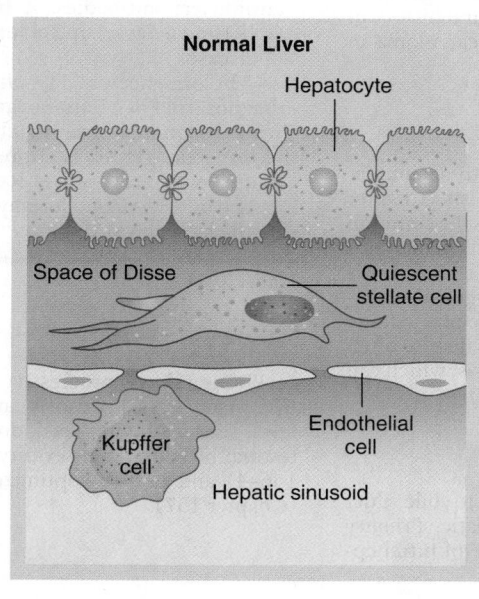

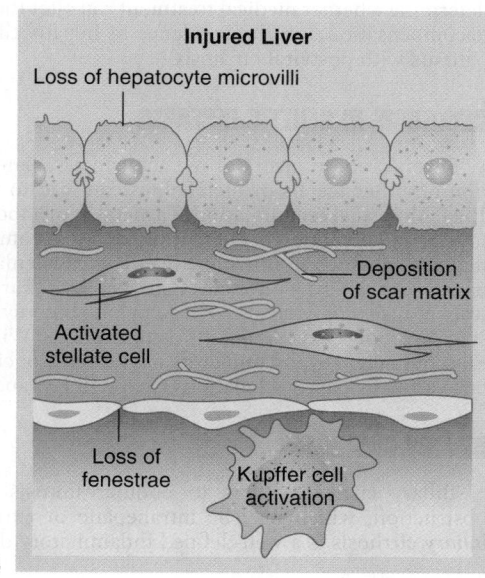

Table 156–3 • MODIFIED CHILD-PUGH CLASSIFICATION AND THE MELD SURVIVAL MODEL

	NUMERICAL SCORE		
PARAMETER	**1**	**2**	**3**
Ascites	None	Slight	Moderate/Severe
Encephalopathy	None	Grade 1–2	Grade 3–4
bilirubin (mg/dL)	<2.0	2.0–3.0	>3.0
Albumin (mg/L)	>3.5	2.8–3.5	<2.8
Prothrombin time (seconds increased)	1–3	4–6	>6.0

Total Numerical Score	Child-Pugh Class
5–6	A
7–9	B
10–15	C

MELD = (0.957 × log (creatinine) + 0.378 × log (bilirubin)
         + 1.12 × log (INR) + 0.643) × 10*

*See http://www.mayo.edu/int-med/gi/model/mayomodl-5-unos.htm to calculate MELD score directly.
MELD = Model for End-Stage Liver Disease.

the degree of inflammation and lobular distortion. These parameters, in turn, are determined by the replicative activity of the virus and whether there has been superinfection by hepatitis delta virus (HDV). Concurrent liver injury from other causes (e.g., alcohol) may also amplify the degree of inflammation and hasten the onset of cirrhosis. Similarly, in chronic HCV, progression to cirrhosis is influenced by the degree of liver damage at initial biopsy, as well as the age at initial exposure and duration of infection. The development of cirrhosis in most patients with chronic HBV or HCV infection is insidious over many years. The average rate of progression from HCV infection to cirrhosis has been estimated at 30 years, with older age, male gender, human immunodeficiency virus or HBV coinfection, and concurrent alcohol use identified as the major risk factors. Particularly rapid progression to cirrhosis has also been seen in patients with recurrent HBV or HCV infection after liver transplantation. Approximately 25% of cases of chronic HCV infection progress to cirrhosis.

One of the goals of treating chronic viral hepatitis B and C is to decrease the degree of hepatic inflammation and thus potentially prevent the development of cirrhosis. In fact, dramatic reversal of hepatic fibrosis and cirrhosis have occurred in select groups of hepatitis B patients treated with lamivudine and hepatitis C patients treated with α-interferon/ribavirin (Chapter 152). Studies are ongoing to determine whether medical treatment can alter the natural history of decompensation and the incidence of hepatocellular carcinoma in patients with postviral cirrhosis.

CIRRHOSIS IN GENETIC DISEASES

Several inborn errors of metabolism associated with accumulation of either metals or metabolites can lead to cirrhosis (Chapter 154). Abnormal accumulation of a metal or metabolite is the common link, as inflammation is often minimal. Most common is hemochromatosis, in which the cirrhotic liver is greatly enlarged and cirrhosis usually develops over decades (Chapter 225). Early diagnosis is critical because removing excess iron by phlebotomy in the precirrhotic stage prevents cirrhosis and its complications. Wilson's disease often is accompanied by inflammatory liver disease or cirrhosis, which can be averted by copper chelation (Chapters 154 and 224).

BILIARY CIRRHOSIS

Biliary cirrhosis refers to nodular fibrosis due to bile duct obstruction, which may be intrahepatic or extrahepatic. *Primary biliary* cirrhosis is a well-defined inflammatory disease of intrahep-

atic bile ducts. *Secondary biliary cirrhosis* encompasses other causes of biliary obstruction, including long-standing mechanical obstruction, sclerosing cholangitis, and genetic or developmental diseases in which cholestasis is prominent (e.g., cystic fibrosis, biliary atresia).

PRIMARY BILIARY CIRRHOSIS

Primary biliary cirrhosis (PBC) is an immune-mediated disorder of unknown cause characterized by progressive destruction of intrahepatic bile ducts and the presence of antimitochondrial antibodies. The disease has a strong female preponderance (10:1). Although it is most common in whites from North America and Europe, cases have occurred in all races. An autoimmune attack against the bile duct is probably an important pathogenic element, but the precipitating event and relative contribution of genetic and environmental factors are not known. Apoptosis of bile duct epithelium and cell surface expression of cell-derived proteins may contribute to autoimmune attack. The disease is commonly associated with other autoimmune disorders, including sicca complex, CREST syndrome (Chapter 281), rheumatoid arthritis (Chapter 278), thyroiditis Chapter 239), pernicious anemia (Chapter 175), and renal tubular acidosis (Chapter 113).

Clinical Manifestations

PBC typically presents in middle-aged females, either as an incidental three-fold to four-fold elevation of alkaline phosphatase or during evaluation of complaints such as fatigue and pruritus. Mild (two-fold to three-fold) elevation of transaminase levels is common. Identifying antimitochondrial antibody (AMA) in serum usually leads to liver biopsy, which establishes the diagnosis. Atypical presentations include women with negative AMA but compatible biochemistry and biopsy (about 5%), women with positive AMA and compatible biopsy but normal liver biochemistries (about 15%), and disease in men (about 10%).

Insidious onset of pruritus is the most characteristic symptom. Its etiology is uncertain, and it may appear at any stage of the disease. Fatigue is also common. Symptoms resulting from malabsorption of fat-soluble vitamins may be evident. Other symptoms may be attributable to other autoimmune diseases, especially dry eyes or mouth and arthritis. As the disease progresses, jaundice develops, the skin becomes dry, xanthomas appear, and the liver and spleen enlarge but are nontender. Once cirrhosis develops, symptoms of portal hypertension and liver failure may predominate. Osteoporosis and osteomalacia may lead to fractures.

In addition to AMA, characteristic laboratory abnormalities include increased serum IgM (95%), hypercholesterolemia, and other autoantibodies, including rheumatoid factor (70%), anti–smooth muscle antibodies (65%), and thyroid-specific or antinuclear antibodies. A high international normalized ratio (INR) and a decreasing albumin level characterize the late stages of disease.

The presence of AMA and a compatible biopsy establish the diagnosis of PBC. Extrahepatic ductal disease should be excluded with abdominal imaging, but endoscopic retrograde cholangiopancreatography is not required unless there are atypical laboratory or clinical features. Rare cases of progressive bile duct injury caused by drugs may clinically resemble PBC but are distinguishable by the lack of AMA.

Prognosis

PBC is a slowly progressive disease, usually leading to liver failure over many years. Prognosis can be predicted (based on age, bilirubin level, serum albumin level, prothrombin time, presence of gastrointestinal bleeding, and severity of edema and biopsy findings; Table 156–4) and used to optimize the timing of liver transplantation (Chapter 157).

Table 156–4 • ESTIMATING PROGNOSIS IN PATIENTS WITH PRIMARY BILIARY CIRRHOSIS (PBC)

MAYO PBC RISK SCORE

R = 0.871 log (serum bilirubin in mg/dL) −
2.53 × log (albumin in g/dL) + 0.039 + (age in years) + 2.38 ×
log (prothrombin time in seconds) + 0.859 (if edema present)

Risk score is translated into a survival function to estimate survival for the individual patient with PBC. Other models have emphasized variceal bleeding as an important additional clinical prognosticator.

PROGNOSTIC INDEX FOR SURVIVAL AFTER LIVER TRANSPLANTATION IN PATIENTS WITH PBC

PI = 0.60 × log (serum bilirubin in mg/dL) +
0.82 × log (serum urea in mmol/L) + 1.14 +
(transplantation before 1985) − 0.92 (diuretic-responsive ascites)
+ 1.70

Risk Score	4-Month Survival
<8.6	91%
8.6–9.9	78%
>9.9	57%

Rx Treatment

Ursodeoxycholic acid (UDCA), a hydrophilic bile acid, can slow the progression of PBC and improve survival free of liver transplantation in patients with moderate or severe disease, possibly by reducing the concentration of toxic bile acids in the hepatic pool, but long-term follow-up (>4 years) is lacking. Management should include supplementation of fat-soluble vitamins (vitamins A, D, E, and K) and calcium. Bisphosphonates should be considered in patients with osteoporosis (Chapter 258). Pruritus is usually treated with cholestyramine; more severe cases may require rifampicin, phenobarbital, naltrexone, or even plasmapheresis. Liver transplantation is usually curative, but PBC may recur after transplantation.

SECONDARY BILIARY CIRRHOSIS

Secondary biliary cirrhosis occurs in response to chronic biliary obstruction from a variety of causes (Chapter 158). At least 6 months of obstruction are generally required to induce cirrhosis, but shorter intervals have been reported. Cholestasis may be intrahepatic or extrahepatic, the latter also referred to as "mechanical" cholestasis.

Etiology

Primary sclerosing cholangitis is the most common cause of intrahepatic cholestasis after PBC (Chapter 158). The majority of patients with primary sclerosing cholangitis are men who have ulcerative colitis or, less frequently, Crohn's colitis (Chapter 142). Cholestasis is incomplete but progressive and leads to cirrhosis, usually within 20 years. There is no correlation between the activity of underlying inflammatory disease and the course of primary sclerosing cholangitis. Cholangiocarcinoma (Chapter 158) may complicate primary sclerosing cholangitis and lead to clinical decompensation or cholangitis.

In cystic fibrosis (Chapter 86), intrahepatic cholestasis with focal biliary cirrhosis may complicate up to 25% of cases by the time of death, although liver disease is often asymptomatic. The precirrhotic lesion is marked by biliary proliferation and ductal occlusion.

Extrahepatic cholestasis in adults most commonly results from structural or mechanical obstruction. Common lesions include choledocholithiasis, biliary or pancreatic cancer, iatrogenic stricture, choledochal cyst, or chronic pancreatitis (Chapters 145, 158, and 201).

Clinical and Laboratory Manifestations

Clinical consequences of secondary biliary cirrhosis are initially determined by the underlying disease. With progression, jaundice may become the prominent symptom. Pruritus is variable in severity. Fat malabsorption with steatorrhea and deficiencies of vitamins A, D, E, and K occur in long-standing obstruction. Osteomalacia or osteoporosis may occur because of vitamin D malabsorption and calcium deficiency.

Disproportionately increased hepatic alkaline phosphatase (four-fold to five-fold increase) relative to other liver tests is typical. The γ-glutamyl transpeptidase and 5′-nucleotidase may be similarly elevated. Aminotransferase levels usually are increased less than two-fold. Hypercholesterolemia is common. Associated markers of immunologic disease or bacterial cholangitis may be evident in patients with sclerosing cholangitis or mechanical obstruction, respectively.

Rx Treatment

Recognizing and treating the underlying cause of cholestasis is the mainstay of therapy. For extrahepatic obstruction, biliary decompression, either by surgical drainage or by placement of a biliary stent for neoplasms, is usually required and occasionally leads to reversal of severe fibrosis and cirrhosis. Intrahepatic cholestasis is less amenable to surgical drainage, with management limited to treating complications; UDCA improves biochemical parameters but does not retard disease progression. Liver transplantation is highly successful in most patients with deteriorating liver function (Chapter 157).

MISCELLANEOUS DISORDERS ASSOCIATED WITH CIRRHOSIS

Long-standing right-sided heart failure due to cardiomyopathy (Chapter 73), tricuspid valve insufficiency (Chapter 72), pulmonary disease (Chapter 64), or pericardial constriction (Chapter 74) can rarely lead to hepatic fibrosis. The clinical picture is usually dominated by cardiac or pulmonary dysfunction. Liver abnormalities may be typical of hepatic congestion, with disproportionate elevation of bilirubin (up to ten-fold) and INR, but modest aminotransferase elevations (less than three-fold).

Nonalcoholic steatohepatitis (NASH) is remarkably similar to alcoholic liver disease, but it occurs in the absence of alcohol use (Chapter 155). Cirrhosis may result if the underlying condition is not corrected. Its incidence is steadily rising in parallel with the increasing prevalence of obesity in the United States and Western Europe. It is now believed that many cases of cryptogenic cirrhosis actually represent long-standing NASH.

In addition to medications associated with nonalcoholic steatonecrosis, drug-induced hepatic fibrosis may also be seen in patients taking isoniazid or antimetabolites, especially methotrexate (Chapter 150). The latter is associated with dose-dependent fibrosis in patients treated for psoriasis (Chapter 474) or rheumatoid arthritis (Chapter 278) for at least 2 years. Continuous therapy is more fibrogenic than intermittent dosing, and coexisting liver disease or heavy alcohol intake amplifies the risk of fibrosis. Surveillance liver biopsies are required in patients whose cumulative dose exceeds 1.5 to 2 g, because considerable fibrosis may develop in the absence of symptoms.

CONSEQUENCES OF HEPATIC SYNTHETIC FAILURE

HYPOALBUMINEMIA AND COAGULOPATHY. Low serum albumin levels are almost always found in cirrhosis. Albumin, however, is an imperfect indicator of liver function. The plasma concentration of albumin is also affected by fluid and nutritional status. Albumin loss through proteinuria may be a consequence of several renal diseases (e.g., membranoproliferative glomerulonephritis owing to hepatitis C) associated with cirrhosis. Hypoalbuminemia results in reduced plasma oncotic pressure, which permits the leakage of fluid from the vascular space and promotes tissue edema.

Another consequence of impaired hepatic protein synthesis is coagulopathy, because all protein clotting factors except factor VIII are synthesized by the liver (Chapter 178). Bleeding risk is further increased because of concurrent thrombocytopenia, the result of hypersplenism. The magnitude of prolongation of the INR is generally a better marker of the severity of liver dysfunction than is the serum albumin. Consumptive coagulopathy (disseminated intravascular coagulopathy [DIC]) associated with sepsis can be distinguished from the coagulopathy of cirrhosis by assaying factor VIII levels, which are decreased only in DIC (Chapter 179).

JAUNDICE (Chapter 149). The extent of hyperbilirubinemia often parallels the severity of liver disease. Jaundice occurs in parenchymal failure because the ability of the hepatocyte to conjugate and excrete bilirubin into bile is reduced, leading to elevated indirect and direct serum bilirubin. Hepatic enzyme systems responsible for detoxification and metabolism are impaired, thereby making the patient with cirrhosis more susceptible to drug toxicity or overdose.

PROTEIN-CALORIE MALNUTRITION. Malnutrition increases morbidity and mortality in cirrhosis and in those individuals undergoing liver transplantation. Contributing factors in cirrhotic patients include malabsorption of nutrients because of intestinal edema, diarrhea, and decreased bile flow, and reduced hepatic stores of many water-soluble vitamins and trace elements. Anorexia and decreased oral intake result from fatigue, dysgeusia, nausea, and early satiety due to ascites and decreased gastric emptying. Glucose intolerance and diabetes are common.

Cirrhotic patients are prone to rapid protein wasting during periods of decreased oral intake. Frequent feeding and the avoidance of prolonged fasting may improve nutritional balance. Low-grade encephalopathy should not be considered a contraindication to nutritional intervention.

SUSCEPTIBILITY TO INFECTION. Facultative gram-negative bacilli appear to be increased in the jejunal flora of many patients with cirrhosis, some of whom have decreased motility. This change in intestinal flora may increase the risk of gram-negative bacteremia by way of translocation through the gut wall and a disruption of the normal intestinal permeability barrier. Hypoalbuminemia and ascites contribute to gut wall edema, predisposing to bacterial translocation. The activity of the reticuloendothelial system is reduced in cirrhosis. Serum opsonic activity is also reduced, probably as a consequence of decreased serum complement and fibronectin. Decreased opsonic activity in ascites may predispose to bacterial peritonitis (Chapter 146). The phagocytic and bacterial killing capacity of neutrophils is also impaired.

Cirrhotics are at increased risk for developing infection as a result of the sequelae of portal hypertension. In particular, in patients with variceal hemorrhage, 20% are already infected upon presentation and 50% develop an infection during hospitalization. Short-term antibiotic prophylaxis in these patients can significantly decrease the incidence of infection and improve survival. Patients are also at risk for aspiration during bouts of hepatic encephalopathy. Anasarca and malnutrition predispose to poor wound healing and soft tissue infection. Because patients with cirrhosis may be hypothermic and their peripheral white blood cell counts are frequently depressed because of hypersplenism, infection may present without fever and leukocytosis.

RENAL DYSFUNCTION. Early in cirrhosis there is diminished renal ability to excrete a sodium load. As cirrhosis and portal hypertension progress, renal sodium excretional capacity decreases, resulting in fluid retention, ascites, and dilutional hyponatremia (Chapter 112). Sodium retention leads to compensatory activity of the renin-angiotensin-aldosterone axis and sympathetic nervous system. Renal perfusion and the glomerular filtration rate become impaired, related in part to further compensatory increases in plasma levels of antidiuretic hormone, renin, and norepinephrine. These pathophysiologic changes predispose patients with cirrhosis to develop renal failure (Chapter 116). Methods for measuring creatinine clearance generally overestimate renal functional capacity in cirrhosis, in part because of the protein malnutrition and muscle wasting that diminish their urea and creatine production. Effective arterial blood volume can be decreased even in the presence of substantial peripheral edema.

MAJOR SEQUELAE OF CIRRHOSIS

PORTAL HYPERTENSION

Features of the Portal Circulation and Classification of Portal Hypertension

The portal circulation is a low-pressure system (<10 mm Hg) formed by the venous drainage from intraperitoneal viscera, including the luminal gastrointestinal tract, spleen, gallbladder, and pancreas. Veins from these sites merge to form the splenic vein and superior and inferior mesenteric veins, which, in turn, merge to create the portal vein. Portal hypertension occurs when portal venous pressure exceeds the pressure in the nonportal abdominal veins (e.g., inferior vena cava) by at least 5 mm Hg; portosystemic collateral vessels develop in an effort to equalize pressures between these two venous systems. These collateral vessels, or varices, most commonly develop in the esophagus and proximal stomach, where they can cause clinically significant bleeding.

Increased portal pressure in cirrhosis results primarily from increased resistance to blood flow through the shrunken, fibrotic liver. Increased intrahepatic resistance results both from fixed obstruction to flow by extracellular matrix and from dynamic organ and sinusoidal contraction by activated stellate cells (also referred to as myofibroblasts). Because pressure is a function of both resistance and flow, independent increases in portal inflow due to the hyperdynamic circulation of cirrhosis and to splanchnic arteriolar vasodilation also elevate portal pressure.

In cirrhosis, which is the most common cause of portal hypertension, the lesion is intrahepatic and primarily sinusoidal. Portal hypertension may also arise from presinusoidal obstruction, either outside (e.g., portal vein thrombosis) or within (e.g., schistosomiasis) the liver. Similarly, lesions leading to portal hypertension may be postsinusoidal, either within the liver (e.g., veno-occlusive disease) or distal to it (e.g., Budd-Chiari syndrome, right-sided heart failure). In rare circumstances, portal hypertension can develop despite a normal liver in a patient with markedly increased inflow beyond the capacity of the compliant portal vessels to absorb; examples include arterial-portal fistulas and massive splenomegaly due to infection or neoplasm.

Clinical Manifestations

> Splenomegaly and/or distention of abdominal wall veins (caput medusae) may be initial or associated findings. Patients with noncirrhotic portal hypertension generally have well-preserved liver function, so clinical manifestations primarily reflect altered hemodynamics. In patients with presinusoidal lesions such as schistosomiasis or portal vein thrombosis, variceal hemorrhage and splenomegaly are prominent. In postsinusoidal obstruction, such as veno-occlusive disease or Budd-Chiari syndrome, typical presenting symptoms are hepatomegaly and rapid onset of ascites and weight gain.

Diagnosis

Portal hypertension should be suspected in any patient with ascites, splenomegaly, encephalopathy, or gastroesophageal varices. Portal vein pressure is indirectly estimated by "wedging" a catheter into a small branch of the hepatic vein to measure hepatic sinusoidal pressure and thus, indirectly, that of the portal vein. Portal pressure is estimated by the difference between the wedged hepatic venous pressure and the free hepatic venous pressure. Cirrhosis leads to both an increase in hepatic sinusoidal pressure and an increase in portal pressure gradient (difference between the portal vein and the inferior vena cava). Varices form when this gradient exceeds 10 to 12 mm Hg. However, the risk of hemorrhage does not correlate with the extent of elevation beyond this threshold. Portal hypertension leads to pooling of blood in vascular beds that normally empty into the portal vein. Sequestration of blood in the spleen causes splenomegaly and congestion, with secondary thrombocytopenia, neutropenia, and anemia.

VARICEAL HEMORRHAGE

Hemorrhage from gastroesophageal varices (Chapter 133) is often the initial complication of portal hypertension. Less commonly, ectopic variceal hemorrhage occurs from portosystemic collateral vessels in the duodenum, rectum, or the peristomal area in patients with ostomies following bowel surgery.

Bleeding from varices accounts for one third of all deaths in patients with cirrhosis. Esophageal varices develop at a rate of 50% per year and ultimately occur in up to 90% of all patients with cirrhosis. Patients with cirrhosis should thus be screened endoscopically for the presence of varices upon initial presentation. Patients should be screened semiannually, especially in the presence of significant portal hypertension, as reflected in the degree of thrombocytopenia. The prevalence of varices in cirrhosis is proportional to the severity of portal hypertension and the underlying liver disease. For patients who survive the initial episode of variceal bleeding, the risk of recurrent bleeding approaches 70%, with most episodes occurring within 6 months of the index bleed. The mortality for each episode of variceal hemorrhage is 30 to 50%, with the risk of dying directly related to the severity of the underlying liver condition.

Esophageal variceal hemorrhage typically occurs as painless, large-volume hematemesis or melena with minimal abdominal pain (Chapter 133). Signs of significant volume depletion, including orthostasis and pallor, are common. In a patient with known varices, risk factors that correlate with increased likelihood of bleeding include (1) variceal size (large varices have increased wall tension and thus greater thinning of the vessel wall); (2) endoscopic signs (known as red wales or cherry-red spots) overlying the varix and believed to represent hemorrhage within the vessel wall; and (3) poor liver function with ascites and/or jaundice. Patients who are actively drinking alcohol or who have a large hepatocellular carcinoma also are at increased risk for hemorrhage.

Patients with esophageal varices may bleed from associated gastric varices. A gastric variceal hemorrhage is more difficult to diagnose because gastric varices are not easily distinguished from prominent rugae. A rare cause of gastric variceal hemorrhage that should not be overlooked is splenic vein thrombosis due to pancreatic or retroperitoneal disease. In this setting, localized obstruction of short gastric veins leads to hemorrhage from gastric varices in the absence of esophageal varices. Splenectomy and splenic vein resection are curative. Hemorrhage from portal hypertensive gastropathy, also known as congestive gastropathy, refers to bleeding in the stomach from submucosal veins engorged as a result of portal hypertension. Bleeding from this lesion may be clinically indistinguishable from variceal hemorrhage.

Rx Diagnosis and Treatment

Stabilizing blood pressure is the first requirement in suspected variceal hemorrhage (Fig. 156–2). Replacing fluid and blood is essential in the orthostatic or hypotensive patient, but overexpanding volume with fresh-frozen plasma should be avoided in the stabilized individual because it may increase portal pressure and accelerate hemorrhage. Endotracheal intubation to protect the airway is essential in the obtunded or inebriated patient to avoid aspiration and to facilitate emergent endoscopy.

Once the patient's condition is stabilized, vigorous gastric lavage followed by emergent endoscopy (Chapter 132) is necessary to establish the source of hemorrhage, even if acute bleeding has subsided. Nearly half (30 to 50%) of bleeding episodes in patients with varices originate from nonvariceal sources. Concurrent bleeding from more than one lesion is not unusual.

INITIAL CONTROL OF VARICEAL HEMORRHAGE

Two thirds of variceal hemorrhage episodes cease spontaneously, but rapid onset of rebleeding is significant. Thus, endoscopic hemostasis is required, either when varices are actively bleeding or when they display endoscopic evidence of recent bleeding. Two endoscopic methods are equally effective in arresting active hemorrhage in more than 95% of patients: (1) direct or paravariceal injection with 1 to 2 mL of a sclerosant or (2) band ligation, in which a rubber ligature is placed around the varix. Band ligation is associated with a lower incidence of complications such as esophageal ulceration, bacterial mediastinitis, and esophageal strictures, and with more rapid variceal obliteration than is sclerotherapy. Endoscopic therapy has no effect on the pathophysiologic mechanisms that underlie portal hypertension, so varices eventually recur.

Pharmacologic therapy can be initiated as soon as variceal hemorrhage is suspected, even before diagnostic endoscopy is performed because its safety profile is excellent. In the United States, vasopressin 0.1 to 0.4 units/min and octreotide 50 to 100 μg/hr are the most commonly used agents and control variceal hemorrhage in 75 to 80% of cases. Vasopressin is limited by its frequent side effects; its efficacy and safety are significantly improved by the addition of intravenous nitroglycerin (40 to 400 μg/min). Octreotide carries less systemic hemodynamic side effects than vasopressin does and, when used in conjunction with endoscopy, may reduce the risk of rebleeding better than does endoscopic therapy alone.

Despite urgent endoscopic and pharmacologic therapy, variceal bleeding cannot be controlled or recurs early in about 10 to 20% of patients. For such patients, transjugular intrahepatic portosystemic shunting (TIPS) has supplanted emergent surgical portal decompression and balloon tamponade. TIPS is an angiographically placed shunt between a hepatic vein and portal vein to decompress the portal circulation. TIPS can effectively control acute variceal hemorrhage by lowering the portal vein–inferior vena caval pressure gradient to less than 10 mm Hg. Portal vein thrombosis, which may occur in the setting of cirrhosis or secondary to hepatocellular carcinoma, generally precludes TIPS placement. Chronic problems associated with TIPS are hepatic encephalopathy and stent occlusion.

Surgical decompression for acute variceal hemorrhage is generally avoided because of high perioperative morbidity and mortality rates, especially in patients with Child's B or C cirrhosis. It is usually undertaken in patients who have Child's A cirrhosis and who are not expected to have short-term progression of their hepatic synthetic dysfunction.

PREVENTING INITIAL OR RECURRENT VARICEAL HEMORRHAGE

PRIMARY PREVENTION. In the patient with moderate or large varices and well-preserved liver function, prophylactic use of β-blockers (propranolol [40 to 200 mg/day] or nadolol [40 to 160 mg/day]) to reduce resting heart rate by 25% lessens the risk of a first variceal hemorrhage. β-Blockers also reduce the risk of bleeding from congestive gastropathy and gastric varices associated with portal hypertension. Despite this efficacy in treating portal hypertension, β-blockade has no effect on mortality. Prophylactic sclerotherapy and band ligation do not reduce the likelihood of initial bleeding.

SECONDARY PREVENTION. In patients who have already survived an episode of hemorrhage from varices or congestive gastropathy, β-blockers significantly reduce the risk of rebleeding but must be discontinued in up to 25% of patients because of adverse effects (e.g., bronchoconstriction, impotence, lethargy, heart failure). In patients in whom β-blockers fail or cannot be tolerated, endoscopic sclerotherapy or band ligation is equally effective; multiple sessions are required to eliminate varices initially, and regular endoscopic surveillance every 3 to 6 months is needed. Combining endoscopic therapy with β-blockade is rational because β-blockers protect against rebleeding in the period before variceal obliteration can prevent variceal recurrence. Patients who rebleed during pharmacologic/endoscopic therapy should be considered for shunting, either surgical or TIPS, as well as for urgent liver transplantation.

ASCITES

Ascites, which is the accumulation of excess fluid in the abdomen, is often among the first signs of decompensation in patients with chronic liver disease (Chapter 146). Cirrhosis is the underlying cause of ascites in at least 80% of patients, but other factors (e.g., heart failure, constrictive pericarditis, nephrotic syndrome, tuberculous peritonitis, peritoneal malignancy, and pancreatic duct leak) must also be considered. Approximately 50% of patients with cirrhosis develop ascites within 10 years. The development of ascites in the setting of cirrhosis is an important landmark in the natural history of chronic liver disease, because approximately 50% of patients die within 2 years.

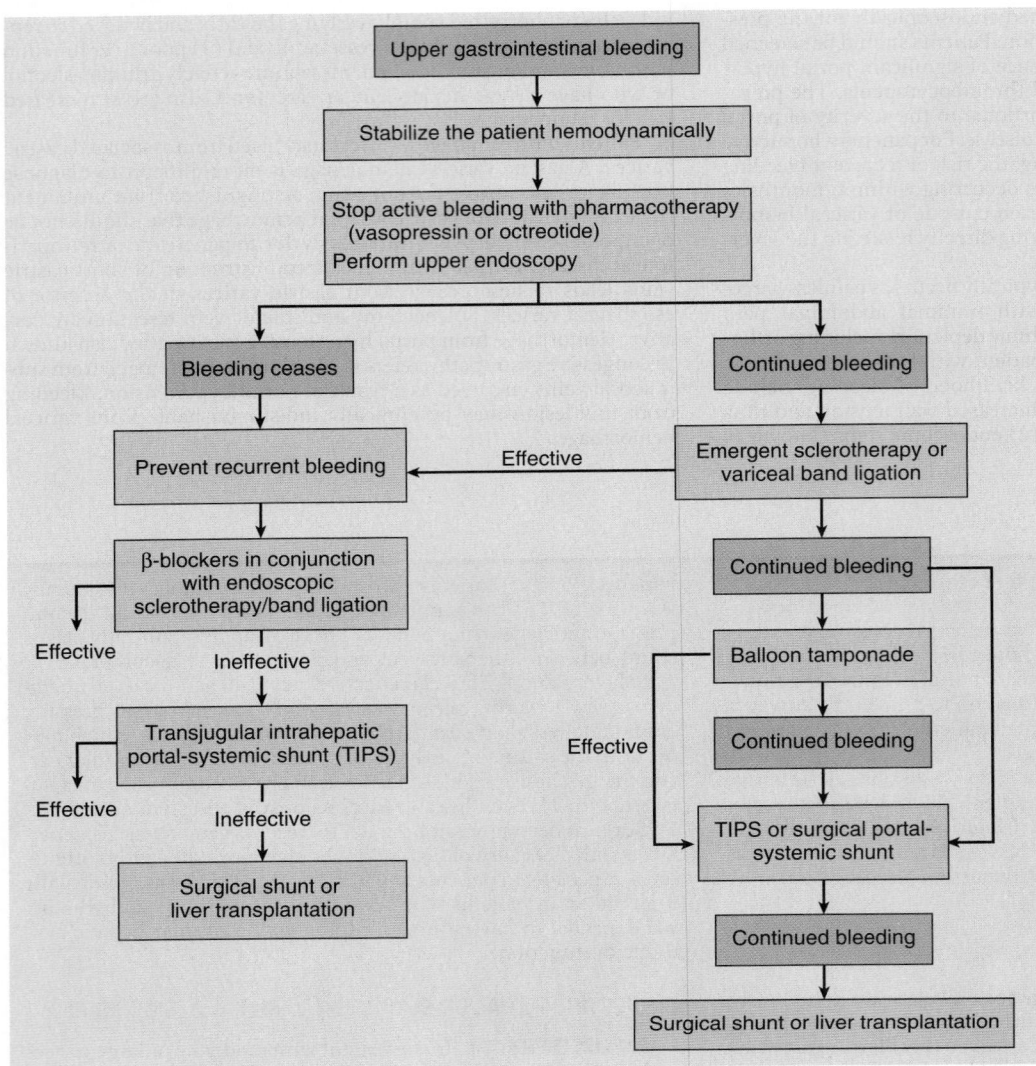

FIGURE 156–2 • Management algorithm for variceal bleeding.

Pathogenesis

Many factors contribute to ascites formation in chronic liver injury. Sinusoidal hypertension expands plasma volume and increases portal inflow. Initially, albumin traverses the porous sinusoidal endothelium along with fluid, but as fibrosis progresses, only protein-free fluid can escape the sinusoid, from where it enters hepatic lymphatics. Continued accumulation of lymph overcomes the capacity for lymphatic drainage, and the excess fluid "weeps" from the liver into the peritoneal cavity. Hypoalbuminemia worsens with advancing liver dysfunction and decreases oncotic pressure. Increased sodium reabsorption by the kidneys and splanchnic arteriolar vasodilation increase portal flow. Finally, despite the increasing accumulation of ascites, the capacity of the peritoneum to absorb fluid is fixed.

Diagnostic Evaluation

All patients with new-onset ascites or requiring hospitalization with ascites should undergo diagnostic paracentesis with cell count, albumin determination, Gram stain, and culture.

The serum ascites albumin gradient (SAAG), calculated by subtracting the ascites albumin concentration from the serum value, is the most accurate method of classifying ascites. An SAAG value of greater than 1.1 g/dL predicts a portal hypertensive cause with more than 95% accuracy. Values less than 1.1 g/dL are associated with neoplasms, tuberculosis, pancreatitis, or bile leak; the ascitic fluid should be tested, as indicated, for amylase, cytology, and mycobacterial culture.

Rx Treatment

Treatment of ascites does not significantly improve survival. Most patients with cirrhotic ascites respond to dietary sodium restriction (<2000 mg/day) and a diuretic. Sodium retention in cirrhosis is mainly the result of increased renal distal tubular reabsorption, so aldosterone antagonists are the initial diuretics of choice. Spironolactone should be started at 50 to 100 mg/day and can be advanced up to 400 mg to achieve a daily weight loss of 0.5 to 0.75 kg in patients without peripheral edema; more rapid weight loss is safe if peripheral edema is present. Furosemide can be used instead of or in combination with spironolactone, beginning at a dose of 40 mg/day, although there is a greater incidence of azotemia than with spironolactone. Single morning dosing of both drugs maximizes compliance. Treatment with diuretics may result in dehydration, severe muscle cramping, hyponatremia, and hepatic encephalopathy.

Some patients with ascites (10%) fail to respond to standard therapy, either because fluid cannot be mobilized or because of associated prerenal azotemia. In these patients, therapeutic paracentesis is safe and can remove 4 to 6 L or more per procedure in patients with peripheral edema. In nonedematous patients, safe paracentesis requires infusing 6 to 8 g of albumin per liter of ascites removed. Repeated paracentesis may increase the risk of bacterial peritonitis. In patients with ascites, TIPS is more effective in controlling the ascites than is medical therapy or large volume paracentesis,[1] and it may improve survival in patients with refractory ascites.[2] Peritoneovenous shunting, performed by surgically placing a subcutaneous catheter between the superior vena cava and peritoneum, is as effective as therapeutic paracentesis in treating refractory ascites. However, low-grade DIC, catheter infection, and shunt occlusion are frequent complications that reduce long-term efficacy substantially. The use of these shunts appears limited to those patients who are not liver transplant candidates. Liver transplantation remains the most definitive therapy for liver disease with ascites; it should be considered when ascites develops and becomes urgent when complications of ascites appear, particularly spontaneous bacterial peritonitis (SBP).

Complications

SBP (Chapter 146) is an ominous complication of late-stage liver disease because it portends a 2-year survival of less than 50%. The pathogenesis is uncertain but is believed to reflect altered gut wall permeability to bacteria, impaired capacity of hepatic and splenic macrophages to clear portal bacteremia, and/or the presence of a large volume of peritoneal fluid conducive to bacterial growth. The clinical presentation is subtle, and frank peritoneal pain or tenderness is uncommon. Thus, clinicians must have a high index of suspicion to recognize SBP before it is fatal. Typical findings include fever, altered gastrointestinal motility, signs of sepsis, or decompensation of previously stable liver function manifested by new encephalopathy, worsening jaundice, or azotemia. Common causative organisms include *Escherichia coli, Pneumococcus, Klebsiella,* and anaerobes. Gram stain of peritoneal fluid is not used for diagnosis, because ascites Gram stain is rarely positive. If the absolute polymorphonuclear (PMN) count is greater than 250/mm³ (percent PMN times total white blood count [WBC]), a presumptive diagnosis should be made, and empirical antibiotic therapy (e.g., cefotaxime, 1 to 2 g intravenously every 6 to 8 hours, or ceftriaxone, 500 to 1000 mg intravenously every 12 hours) should be given for 5 to 7 days. Adequate response to therapy should be documented by demonstrating a 50% reduction in ascites WBC. Culture-negative neutrophilic ascites (i.e., ascites WBC > 250/mm³) is common, especially if ascitic fluid has not been promptly inoculated into blood culture broth; these patients should be treated for presumed SBP, and the response to antibiotics should be documented with repeat paracentesis. Use of intravenous albumin as an adjunct to antibiotic therapy may lower the incidence of renal failure and improve survival, particularly in patients with poor baseline liver and renal function. The recurrence rate of SBP is more than 70% in 1 year but can be reduced if patients are treated prophylactically, such as with norfloxacin, 400 mg/day. Prophylaxis may be appropriate for high-risk patients even before the first episode of SBP (i.e., those with gastrointestinal bleeding or low-protein ascites), especially if the patient is a candidate for liver transplantation.

Hydrothorax results from direct passage of ascitic fluid into the pleural space via defects in the diaphragm, perhaps drawn by negative intrathoracic pressure. Hepatic hydrothorax, which may occur even without demonstrable ascites, is generally right-sided and transudative. A CT scan of the chest should be obtained to exclude other mediastinal, pulmonary, or pleural disease. Treatment with diuretics, thoracocentesis, or TIPS is usually tried but is often ineffective. Chest tube placement is contraindicated because of significant associated morbidity. Patients typically have advanced liver disease and should be considered candidates for liver transplantation.

Abdominal wall hernias expose cirrhotic patients to potentially life-threatening complications, such as strangulation and rupture. Prevention of hernias is based on adequate control of ascites.

HEPATORENAL SYNDROME

Hepatorenal syndrome, also known as functional renal failure, is defined as renal failure associated with severe liver disease without an intrinsic abnormality of the kidneys. Ascites is invariably present. Hepatorenal syndrome can develop in the absence of any precipitating factors or can follow events that reduce effective arterial blood volume (e.g., dehydration, gastrointestinal bleeding). The development of hepatorenal syndrome is associated with a poor prognosis, with more than 95% of patients dying within a few weeks of the onset of azotemia. Spontaneous recovery of renal function is rare. Hepatorenal syndrome represents the extreme expression of circulatory

dysfunction associated with portal hypertension, occurring in the setting of increased plasma volume and cardiac output, accompanied by increased resistance in all major arterial vascular beds except the splanchnic circulation, where resistance is low. Renal hypoperfusion and hepatorenal syndrome represent the extreme consequence of the underfilling of the arterial circulation caused by this splanchnic vasodilation. The diagnosis is established in patients with cirrhosis by documenting very low urine sodium (<10 mEq/L) and oliguria in the absence of intravascular volume depletion. The syndrome must therefore be distinguished from prerenal azotemia by an empirical fluid challenge (1000 mL saline) or by measurement of pulmonary wedge pressure. Other likely causes of renal failure must be excluded, such as acute tubular necrosis or renal impairment from aminoglycosides and contrast agents, although these conditions typically lead to high sodium excretion (Chapter 116). Patients with liver disease are especially sensitive to inhibition of renal vasodilation by nonsteroidal anti-inflammatory drugs (NSAIDs) and aminoglycosides. The most effective treatment for hepatorenal syndrome is to correct the underlying liver disease by liver transplantation if appropriate. Treating any underlying infections and optimizing volume status are important adjunctive measures. Potentially nephrotoxic drugs, especially NSAIDs, should be withdrawn. There are isolated reports of response to peritoneovenous shunt, TIPS, and combination treatments using midodrine, octreotide with albumin, or continuous intravenous infusion of renal dose dopamine with terlipressin, but no randomized trials are available.

HEPATIC ENCEPHALOPATHY

Hepatic encephalopathy is a neuropsychiatric disorder caused by hepatic insufficiency characterized by changes in personality, cognition, motor function, or level of consciousness. It is usually reversible and portends a poor prognosis, with a 1-year survival of 40%. The precise pathogenesis of hepatic encephalopathy is unknown. Nitrogenous gut-derived substances accumulate and produce adverse effects on brain function. In chronic liver disease, increased arterial levels of ammonia are commonly seen, but there is little correlation between blood levels and the severity of neuropsychiatric impairment despite the fact that ammonia appears to play a role in the pathogenesis of hepatic encephalopathy. Hepatic encephalopathy may cause mild cognitive abnormalities recognizable only by psychometric testing, or it can present as recurrent or chronic cognitive or motor disorders. Asterixis and psychomotor retardation may be clues to the diagnosis, but they are not specific, and their absence does not exclude the diagnosis. Altered mentation or level of consciousness can range from subtle personality changes to lethargy to coma (Chapters 436 and 458). Subclinical encephalopathy occurs in 50 to 80% of patients with cirrhosis, with the most common symptoms being insomnia, reversal of the day-night sleep cycle, and subtle deficits in concentration and hand-eye coordination that contribute to falls and traffic accidents.

Because the manifestations of hepatic encephalopathy are so variable, it should be suspected in any cirrhotic patient with a neuropsychiatric abnormality. Many other conditions must be considered in the differential diagnosis of hepatic encephalopathy (Table 156–5).

Rx Treatment

A comprehensive search to identify and eliminate any precipitating factors is a key initial step to treating hepatic encephalopathy (Table 156–6). Supportive care and prevention of falls must be provided to all patients when at home or while hospitalized. Medical treatment is based on efforts to control the generation of putative neuroactive toxins. Nonabsorbable disaccharides, such as lactulose (30 g two to four times daily), are used as laxatives, to decrease ammoniagenesis, and to reduce ammonia absorption from the gastrointestinal tract. Antibiotics, such as neomycin (1 to 3 g per day) or metronidazole (250 mg four times per day), which may be alternatives or adjuncts to lactulose, work by altering colonic flora. The medications may not be well tolerated, so noncompliance is a major problem.

Table 156–5 • DIFFERENTIAL DIAGNOSIS OF HEPATIC ENCEPHALOPATHY

Alcohol-related disorders (Chapter 17)
  Intoxication
  Korsakoff's syndrome
  Wernicke's encephalopathy
  Withdrawal
Drug toxicity (sedatives or other psychoactive drugs)
Infections
  Encephalitis
  Meningitis
  Sepsis
Intracranial lesions
  Abscess
  Hemorrhage
  Infarct
  Tumor
Metabolic encephalopathies
  Acidosis (e.g., hypercarbia, ketoacidosis)
  Dehydration
  Electrolyte imbalances
  Hyperglycemia or hypoglycemia
  Uremia
Postictal encephalopathy
Primary neuropsychiatric disorders

Table 156–6 • PRECIPITATING FACTORS FOR HEPATIC ENCEPHALOPATHY

Azotemia and dehydration
Constipation
Electrolyte abnormalities, usually from diuretic use
Excessive dietary protein intake
Gastrointestinal bleeding
Hepatic injury (viral infection, toxic damage, surgery, hepatocellular carcinoma)
Infection (especially spontaneous bacterial peritonitis)
Noncompliance with lactulose and neomycin
Portosystemic shunts (e.g., transjugular intrahepatic portosystemic shunting)
Sedative and opiate analgesic use

HEPATOPULMONARY SYNDROME AND PORTOPULMONARY HYPERTENSION

Hepatopulmonary syndrome is defined as hypoxemia occurring in the setting of advanced liver disease related to intrapulmonary vascular dilatation in the absence of intrinsic cardiopulmonary disease. Portal hypertension appears to be centrally involved in the pathophysiology of the hepatopulmonary syndrome, but the cause remains unknown. An imbalance between potential pulmonary vasodilators and vasoconstrictors is likely. Most patients have no respiratory symptoms but do have an increased alveolar-arterial gradient when breathing room air. Patients with more severe disease have dyspnea on exertion and may have substantial hypoxemia. Characteristics of hepatopulmonary syndrome are dyspnea, which occurs when the patient assumes the standing position (platypnea), and hypoxemia, which typically is worse when changing from the supine to the standing position (orthodeoxia), reflecting pulmonary vascular dilation that occurs predominantly in the lung bases. Contrast-enhanced transthoracic echocardiography establishes the presence of intrapulmonary shunting, and pulmonary angiography allows for the identification of discrete intrapulmonary vascular dilatation and may allow for therapeutic intervention. It is vital to exclude pulmonary hypertension as a cause of the oxygenation defects and symptoms. Oxygen supplementation can improve symptoms but does not reverse the vascular defects. The gas exchange abnormalities often resolve after liver transplantation.

Rarely, patients with cirrhosis and portal hypertension may develop pulmonary hypertension (Chapter 64). Portopulmonary hypertension and hepatopulmonary syndrome are distinct entities. Individuals may have respiratory symptoms, but more frequently the diagnosis is made by echocardiography, which demonstrates high right-sided cardiac pressures (Chapter 51). The pulmonary pathophysiology of portopulmonary hypertension is similar to that of primary pulmonary hypertension, but the inciting factors for its development are unknown. Patients typically exhibit hemodynamic features of both primary pulmonary hypertension (elevated mean pulmonary artery pressure and vascular resistance) and cirrhosis (elevated cardiac output and depressed systemic vascular resistance). It is imperative to diagnose portopulmonary hypertension before proceeding with liver transplantation; its presence is a strict contraindication to transplantation because of high intraoperative and postoperative mortality secondary to cardiopulmonary failure. Recently, epoprostenol, a prostaglandin analogue (Chapter 64), has been successfully used in some patients to lower pulmonary arterial pressures sufficient enough to allow for liver transplantation.

1. Sanyal AJ, Genning C, Reddy KR, et al: North American Study for the Treatment of Refractory Ascites Group. The North American Study for the Treatment of Refractory Ascites. Gastroenterology 2003;124:634–641.
2. Rössle M, Ochs A, Gülberg V, et al: A comparison of paracentesis and transjugular portosystemic shunting in patients with ascites. N Engl J Med 2000;342:1701–1707.
3. Aldeguer X, Planas R, Ruiz del Arbol L, et al: Effect of intravenous albumin on renal impairment and mortality in patients with cirrhosis and spontaneous bacterial peritonitis. N Engl J Med 1999;341:403-409.

SUGGESTED READINGS
Albanis E, Friedman SL: Hepatic fibrosis. Pathogenesis and principles of therapy. Clin Liver Dis 2001;5:315-334. *Review of the intricacies of hepatic fibrosis, how it produces disease, and how potential treatments might be developed in the future.*
Blei AT, Cordoba J: The Practice Parameters Committee of the American College of Gastroenterology. Practice guidelines. Hepatic encephalopathy. Am J Gastroenterol 2001;96:1968-1976. *An excellent review on current management principles.*
Garcia-Tsao G: Current management of the complications of cirrhosis and portal hypertension: Variceal hemorrhage, ascites and spontaneous bacterial peritonitis. Gastroenterology 2001;120:726-748. *Outstanding review of the complications of portal hypertension, especially of ascites and spontaneous bacterial peritonitis.*
Heathcote EJ: Management of primary biliary cirrhosis. The American Association for the Study of Liver Diseases practice guidelines. Hepatology 2000;31:1005-1013. *Recommendations made by experts in the field for management of primary biliary cirrhosis.*
Lee Y-M, Kaplan MM, and the Practice Guidelines Committee of the ACG: Management of primary sclerosing cholangitis. Am J Gastroenterol 2002;97:528-534. *Practical review of the clinical manifestations, natural history, and treatment of patients with primary sclerosing cholangitis.*
Sharara AI, Rockey DC: Gastroesophageal variceal hemorrhage. N Engl J Med 2001;345:669-681. *Excellent review of all aspects of variceal bleeding, from pathophysiology to prevention and treatment.*

157 HEPATIC FAILURE AND LIVER TRANSPLANTATION

Emmet B. Keeffe

The first liver transplantations in humans were attempted in 1963, but relatively few transplantations were performed before 1980. Nearly 5000 liver transplantations were performed in the United States in 2001, while the waiting list grew to more than 18,000 patients. With modern immunosuppressive drug regimens, technical advances, and improved perioperative care, the current 1-year patient survival rates after liver transplantation are 85 to 90% except in cases of hepatic malignancies, for which the 1-year survival is 72% (Table 157–1). Many studies show that liver transplantation significantly improves the physical, cognitive, and psychological functioning of the recipients. In recent years, the rapidly escalating disparity between a limited supply of cadaver donor organs and an increased need for liver transplantation has resulted in an increased number of deaths of patients listed for transplantation and created a mandate to optimize resources.

Indications and Selection Criteria for Liver Transplantation

The indications and contraindications for liver transplantation, the most appropriate candidates to receive a transplant, and the organ

Table 157–1 • SURVIVAL AFTER ADULT LIVER TRANSPLANTATION BY DIAGNOSIS

DIAGNOSIS	SURVIVAL (%)		
	1 yr	**4 yr**	**7 yr**
Primary sclerosing cholangitis	91	84	78
Primary biliary cirrhosis	89	84	79
Autoimmune hepatitis	86	81	78
Chronic hepatitis C	86	75	67
Alcoholic liver disease	85	76	63
Cryptogenic cirrhosis	84	76	67
Chronic hepatitis B	83	71	63
Malignancy	72	43	34

UNOS Database 1987–1998; *n* = 24,900 patients.

Data from Seaberg EC, Belle SH, Beringer KC, et al: Liver transplantation in the United States from 1987–1998: updated results from the Pitt-UNOS liver transplant registry. *In* Cecka JM, Terasaki PI (eds): Clinical Transplants 1998. Los Angeles, UCLA Tissue Typing Laboratory, 1999, pp. 17–37.

Table 157–3 • KING'S COLLEGE CRITERIA FOR LIVER TRANSPLANTATION IN FULMINANT HEPATIC FAILURE

ACETAMINOPHEN PATIENTS
pH < 7.3, or
Prothrombin time >6.5 (INR) and serum creatinine >3.4 mg/dL

NONACETAMINOPHEN PATIENTS
Prothrombin time >6.5 (INR), or
Any three of the following:
1. Age: <10 or >40 years
2. Etiology: non-A, non-B hepatitis, halothane hepatitis; idiosyncratic drug reaction
3. Duration of jaundice before encephalopathy: >7 days
4. Prothrombin time: >3.5 (INR)
5. Serum bilirubin: >17.6 mg/dL

*INR = international normalized ratio.

Adapted from O'Grady JG, Alexander GJ, Hayllar KM, Williams R: Early indicators of prognosis in fulminant hepatic failure. Gastroenterology 1989; 97:439–445.

allocation scheme continue to evolve. The diseases for which liver transplantation is performed in adults includes cirrhosis with end-stage liver disease, acute liver failure, hepatic malignancies (particularly hepatocellular carcinoma), and metabolic diseases in which the inborn error of metabolism resides in the hepatocytes (e.g., hemochromatosis, α_1-antitrypsin deficiency, and Wilson's disease). The most common indications for liver transplantation are chronic hepatitis C infection and alcoholic liver disease in adults (together accounting for approximately 40% of transplantations), and biliary atresia and α_1-antitrypsin deficiency in children.

General selection criteria that should be considered in the referral of patients for liver transplantation include (1) the absence of alternative forms of therapy that may reverse liver failure and defer the need for liver transplantation, (2) the absence of any absolute contraindication to transplantation (discussed later), (3) expected compliance with longitudinal follow-up care, and (4) the ability to provide for the financial costs of liver transplantation and follow-up care, including medications that may be expensive. Insurance coverage for transplantation is typically determined before referral by a financial counselor at the transplant center.

Referral for Liver Transplantation

Patients with chronic (Table 157–2) or acute (Table 157–3) liver disease should be referred when hepatic decompensation first develops. The greatest likelihood of survival and return to an excellent

Table 157–2 • BIOCHEMICAL AND CLINICAL INDICATIONS FOR LIVER TRANSPLANTATION IN CHRONIC LIVER DISEASE

CHOLESTATIC LIVER DISEASE
Bilirubin >10 mg/dL
Intractable pruritus
Progressive cholestatic bone disease
Recurrent bacterial cholangitis

HEPATOCELLULAR LIVER DISEASE
Serum albumin <3.0 g/dL
Prothrombin time >3 seconds above control

BOTH CHOLESTATIC AND HEPATOCELLULAR LIVER DISEASES
Recurrent or severe hepatic encephalopathy
Refractory ascites
Spontaneous bacterial peritonitis
Recurrent portal hypertensive bleeding
Severe chronic fatigue and weakness
Progressive malnutrition
Development of hepatorenal syndrome
Detection of small hepatocellular carcinoma

From Keeffe EB: Selection of patients for liver transplantation. *In* Maddrey WC, Sorrell MF, Schiff ER (eds): Transplantation of the Liver, 3rd ed. Philadelphia, Lippincott Williams & Wilkins, 2001, pp. 5–34, with permission.

quality of life occurs in patients who undergo liver transplantation before the onset of multiorgan failure. Meticulous attention to medical management of the complications of cirrhosis, such as avoidance of excessive diuretic therapy or aminoglycosides to protect renal function in patients with ascites or spontaneous bacterial peritonitis, is critically important. Blood loss in patients with gastrointestinal bleeding should be judiciously replaced with blood products to avoid fluid overload and pulmonary edema.

For the long-term management of patients with chronic liver disease who may ultimately become transplantation candidates, nonsurgical interventions (e.g., transjugular intrahepatic portosystemic shunt [TIPS] for refractory portal hypertensive bleeding and endoscopic or radiologic approaches to dominant biliary strictures in patients with primary sclerosing cholangitis) are preferable to abdominal procedures that may cause adhesions.

CHRONIC LIVER DISEASE

Although the survival of patients with compensated cirrhosis is good (approximately 90% 5-year survival rate), the development of decompensation with ascites, portal hypertensive bleeding, or encephalopathy implies a lower 5-year survival of about 50%. A patient with a Child-Turcotte-Pugh (CTP) score of 5 or 6 (Child's A cirrhosis; see Table 156–4) without a history of portal hypertensive bleeding or spontaneous bacterial peritonitis is likely to remain stable for a considerable period of time and does not require listing for transplantation. Criteria for listing should be clinical decompensation and/or biochemical deterioration of synthetic function that yield a CTP score of 7 or greater (Child's class B or C).

Liver transplantation for hepatocellular carcinoma (Chapter 202) is reserved for selected patients who have advanced cirrhosis, who do not have the hepatic reserve to undergo resection, and who have no evidence of extrahepatic tumor after thorough evaluation. Risks for recurrent hepatocellular carcinoma after transplantation include advanced stage disease as defined by lymph node involvement, gross vascular invasion by imaging studies, tumor size greater than 5 cm, multiple lesions, and/or involvement of more than one lobe. In low-risk patients, the actuarial survival rate is about 75% at 4 years, whereas the survival in higher risk patients is about 50% at 4 years.

ACUTE LIVER FAILURE

Liver transplantation is a major advance in the management of severe acute liver failure. *Fulminant hepatic failure* refers to the presence of acute liver failure with superimposed hepatic encephalopathy developing within 2 to 8 weeks of the onset of illness in a patient without preexisting liver disease. *Subfulminant hepatic failure* (or *late-onset hepatic failure*) is applied to a syndrome developing more slowly after 2 to 8 weeks up to 3 to 6 months. The selection of patients with acute liver failure who are likely to die and therefore would benefit from liver transplantation is challenging but can be predicted by certain biochemical and clinical features, the most popular of which was established at King's College Hospital in London (see Table 157–3).

Aggressive supportive care is necessary in patients with fulminant hepatic failure to prevent and treat bleeding, infection, cerebral edema, renal failure, and respiratory failure. These complications are the main reasons that transplantation may not be possible and may also contribute to postoperative morbidity and mortality. Alternative treatment strategies for fulminant hepatic failure include auxiliary hepatic support with filtration devices or hepatocyte transplantation and heterotopic auxiliary liver transplantation. Hepatic support devices remain experimental but theoretically could serve either as a bridge to liver transplantation or as definite therapy. Heterotopic liver transplantation presents a number of technical problems that limits its widespread application.

Patients with fulminant hepatic failure should be treated in an intensive care unit, with the patient's head elevated at 20 to 30 degrees. Although lactulose is the cornerstone of treatment of chronic hepatic encephalopathy, it is less effective in patients with acute encephalopathy, and the role of antibiotics such as neomycin is unknown. However, a trial of lactulose is worthwhile, and the drug may need to be administrated by nasogastric tube or by rectal enema. Factors precipitating hepatic encephalopathy, such as gastrointestinal bleeding, hypokalemia, or sepsis, should be identified and treated.

Cerebral edema is frequently manifested by hypertension, bradycardia, and neurologic findings such as decerebrate posturing or abnormal pupillary reflexes. These findings may occur late; thus, monitoring of intracranial pressure (ICP) with institution of therapy to maintain ICP less than 20 mm Hg is preferred. ICP may be monitored with either a subdural or epidural transducer, and the risk of hemorrhage as a complication of placement is outweighed by the benefit of monitoring and early intervention.

Initial treatment of increased ICP is with mannitol (100 to 200 mL of a 20% solution by intravenous infusion over 5 minutes). Repeated doses of mannitol may be required to treat recurrent increases in ICP. Mannitol can only be given if the serum osmolality is less than 320 mOsm/L. Caution is advised in patients with renal failure, and mannitol may need to be administered in combination with hemodialysis or continuous arteriovenous hemofiltration. Other useful therapies include elevation of the head 20 to 30 degrees above the horizontal, disturbing the patient as little as possible, controlling agitation, and administering moderate hyperventilation to a partial carbon dioxide pressure of 25 to 30 mm Hg. A persistent ICP greater than 40 mm Hg that is refractory to treatment precludes liver transplantation.

Listing for Liver Transplantation

Before final selection and listing for liver transplantation, prospective candidates with acute or chronic liver disease undergo a pretransplant evaluation to define the current status of systemic diseases and to determine whether absolute or relative contraindications are present. Routine evaluation includes blood bank and hematologic studies, complete liver and kidney chemistry profiles, viral serology assays (hepatitis A, B and C viruses, human immunodeficiency virus [HIV], cytomegalovirus [CMV]), chest radiograph, and abdominal computed tomography or ultrasound with Doppler of the hepatic vasculature. Additional routine tests include skin testing for tuberculosis, creatinine clearance, electrocardiogram, and, in presence of lung disease, pulmonary function testing. Patients at risk for coronary artery disease undergo cardiology consultation and, when indicated, stress testing, and/or cardiac catheterization. Cancer screening, depending on age and gender, includes Papanicolaou smear, mammogram, occult fecal blood testing, and lower gastrointestinal endoscopy. Consultations with a social worker, financial counselor, and psychiatrist are routinely performed at the transplant center.

Patients are generally assigned to one of four categories by the liver transplant center selection committee: (1) suitable and ready, with listing for transplantation; (2) suitable but too well, with placement on inactive status and continued follow-up with the referring physician; (3) potentially reversible relative contraindication, with treatment and recategorization at a later date; and (4) absolute contraindication, with denial of transplantation. Patients who are approved for liver transplantation are then listed for a donor organ with the United Network for Organ Sharing (UNOS), and final approval by the insurance carrier or third party payer is sought.

Allocation of Donor Organs

New organ allocation policies that emphasize disease severity and de-emphasize waiting time were established by UNOS in early 2002. The Model for End-Stage Liver Disease (MELD; Table 157–4) was selected to replace the former allocation system that employed a combination of CTP score and waiting time.

Absolute Contraindications to Liver Transplantation

The list of absolute contraindications to transplantation is short: advanced cardiopulmonary disease, active untreated sepsis, extrahepatic malignancy, active alcoholism or substance abuse, and anatomic abnormality precluding transplantation. Patients are not candidates for liver transplantation if they have poor ventricular function or severe valvular heart disease. Coronary artery disease, if anatomically reversible by angioplasty or bypass surgery, is not a contraindication to listing if left ventricular function is adequate.

Half of all liver transplant candidates have abnormal arterial oxygenation, but only patients with advanced chronic obstructive pulmonary diseases or pulmonary fibrosis are precluded from liver transplantation. Previous tuberculosis is not a contraindication to liver transplantation. Active tuberculosis should be treated for at least 2 to 3 weeks and preferably several months before and up to 1 year following liver transplantation. Hepatopulmonary syndrome (Chapter 156), which is diagnosed on the basis of the triad of chronic liver disease with portal hypertension, intrapulmonary vascular dilatation with right-to-left shunting, and arterial hypoxemia, may be reversed by liver transplantation. In contrast, portopulmonary hypertension is associated with high operative mortality; for example, patients with a mean pulmonary artery pressure of 50 mm Hg or greater have a postoperative mortality that approaches 100%. Conversely, patients with mean pulmonary artery pressures less than 35 mm Hg do not have increased perioperative mortality.

Active untreated infection should be controlled before proceeding with liver transplantation. In the setting of spontaneous bacterial peritonitis, most transplant programs defer transplantation until antibiotic treatment has been administered for 48 hours and resolution of infection is documented on repeat paracentesis. Sepsis and pneumonia remain absolute contraindications to liver transplantation. Serious chronic infections such as osteomyelitis, chronic fungal diseases, and abscesses preclude transplantation unless they can be treated effectively. Patients who are HIV-positive are undergoing transplantation, but only in a few centers.

Liver transplantation is not performed in the presence of extrahepatic malignancy, except perhaps for patients with isolated liver metastases from slow-growing neuroendocrine tumors (Chapter 140), such as gastrinoma, insulinomas, glucagonomas, somatostatinomas, and carcinoid tumors. The results of liver transplantation are so poor with cholangiocarcinoma (Chapter 158) that most centers consider this diagnosis an absolute contraindication.

Most programs accept patients with alcoholic liver disease as liver transplant candidates only after proven alcohol abstinence for at least 6 months, and completion of an inpatient or outpatient rehabilitation program. Isolated portal vein thrombosis, previously considered an absolute contraindication, is only a relative problem in light of novel reconstructive innovations, including thrombectomy or jump grafts.

Table 157–4 • RELATIONSHIP BETWEEN MELD AND 3-MONTH MORTALITY IN HOSPITALIZED CIRRHOTIC PATIENTS

MELD	MORTALITY (%; NUMBER/TOTAL)
≤9	4 (6/148)
10–19	27 (28/103)
20–29	76 (16/21)
30–39	83 (5/6)
≥40	100 (4/4)

Adapted from Wiesner RH, McDiarmid SV, Kamath PS, et al: MELD and PELD: application of survival models to liver allocation. Liver Transpl 2001; 7:567–580.

RELATIVE CONTRAINDICATIONS. Patient selection should be based on an assessment of biologic age rather than arbitrary chronologic age cutoff. Patients undergoing evaluation for liver transplantation may have the hepatorenal syndrome, chronic renal failure, or reversible acute renal failure that may be related to intercurrent events such as spontaneous bacterial peritonitis, gastrointestinal bleed, or excessive diuresis; however, these conditions are not contraindications to transplantation. Chronic renal failure secondary to intrinsic kidney disease is not a contraindication to liver transplantation but necessitates consideration for dual transplantation of liver and kidney. Transient deterioration in renal function due to an acute injury is usually not a problem unless complicated by the development of hepatorenal syndrome, which is reversible only if urgent liver transplantation can be performed.

The Transplant Procedure

Donors and recipients are matched according to blood type and body size. In general, organs are transplanted into recipients in keeping with standard ABO compatibility rules. Most surgeons believe that a satisfactory size match exists if the donor's and recipient's body weights are within 20% of one another. The donor organ is harvested according to standard protocols to ensure that the physiologic condition of the donor is close to normal when the organ is removed and to limit warm ischemia time. The cold ischemia time while the organ is in a preservation solution is also kept as short as possible; the usual goal is less than 12 hours to minimize the risk of delayed graft function or nonfunction.

The recipient undergoes bilateral subcostal incision with upper midline extension. The standard hepatectomy includes removal of both the vena cava and the liver, often with use of a pump-driven venovenous bypass to return the inferior vena cava and portal venous flow to the heart through the axillary vein. A popular alternative method is to preserve the retrohepatic vena cava during hepatectomy. After hepatectomy, the donor liver is put in place, with repair of the inferior vena cava if it was interrupted, portal reperfusion, hepatic arterial reconstruction, and, finally, duct-to-duct reconstruction of the common bile duct. A Roux-en-Y choledochojejunostomy is used when a duct-to-duct anastomosis is not suitable, such as in patients who have primary sclerosing cholangitis, in whom the diseased common bile duct is removed in its entirety.

Evolving Approaches to Liver Transplantation

The growing discrepancy between the available organs and the need for transplantation has led to increasing application of novel approaches to liver replacement, including cadaver split liver transplantation and adult living donor liver transplantation. Xenotransplantation and hepatocyte transplantation are future hopes.

Split liver transplantation allows two liver transplants from a single cadaver liver, usually a right lobe implanted into an adult recipient and left lobe or left lateral segment implanted into a pediatric recipient. This technique has the potential to provide grafts to the majority of listed pediatric patients and to decrease substantially the adult waiting time.

Living donor liver transplantation uses the left lateral segment for adult-to-child donation, with a very low risk to the adult donor, who usually is a parent. Good results also have been achieved in recent years with elective adult-to-adult living donor liver transplantation using four right lobe segments or three left lobe segments for small recipients, and four right lobe segments and the medial segment of the left lobe for larger recipients to ensure adequate liver volume. This operation has also been applied to urgent cases with good outcomes. Patients with small hepatocellular carcinomas and those with primary sclerosing cholangitis at risk of cholangiocarcinoma are excellent candidates for a timely living donor liver transplantation. Unfortunately, adult-to-adult living donor liver transplantation is just a partial solution to the donor shortage for adult liver transplantation, because only about 15% of potential donors are satisfactory candidates after complete evaluation. The morbidity and mortality to the donor averages 10 and 0.5%, respectively, thereby making the operation formidable and necessitating careful informed consent from the donor.

Rx Post-transplantation Management

Allograft dysfunction is the most important complication following liver transplantation. Liver biopsy is critical in differentiating the various causes of dysfunctions, in that many of them share similar but nonspecific clinical and biochemical presentations. Diagnostic evaluations may also include a cholangiogram and duplex ultrasound of the vessels supplying the liver.

STANDARD MEDICAL THERAPIES

In general, all patients receive corticosteroids in large intravenous doses during the operation. Steroid doses are rapidly reduced over 5 days and can be discontinued by 3 to 12 months after transplantation in many patients depending on the underlying disease and the presence or absence of rejection. Either cyclosporine or tacrolimus is initiated at the time of liver transplantation and is used long-term to prevent acute and chronic allograft rejection. Other routine medications after liver transplantation include those used for preemptive prevention of viral and fungal infection (see later text).

EARLY COMPLICATIONS AFTER LIVER TRANSPLANTATION. Problems that may occur in the first few days after liver transplantation include hepatic artery thrombosis, portal vein thrombosis, primary graft nonfunction, and hyperacute rejection. Hepatic artery thrombosis occurs in about 2 to 8% of adults and in 3 to 20% of children who undergo liver transplantation. Hepatic artery thrombosis typically presents early after transplantation as fulminant liver failure; occasionally, it occurs 1 to 2 months after transplantation and manifests with stenosis or intimal hyperplasia with eventual rearterialization from collaterals. Early hepatic artery thrombosis is first treated by immediate revascularization via thrombectomy or use of a surgical conduit, but it often requires urgent retransplantation. Hepatic artery stenosis without thrombosis is usually associated with multiple ischemic biliary strictures and presents somewhat later. Retransplantation is indicated when biliary sepsis or graft failure develops.

Portal vein thrombosis complicates only 1 to 3% of liver transplant cases. Early acute portal vein thrombosis leads to fulminant liver failure and requires immediate revascularization or urgent retransplantation. Conversely, late portal vein thrombosis manifests as portal hypertension.

Primary graft nonfunction, or delayed ischemia-reperfusion injury, is the most common cause of graft loss within the early postoperative period after a technically successful liver transplantation. Clinical presentation resembles fulminant liver failure with persistent or new hepatic encephalopathy and elevated serum aminotransferases greater than 2500 IU/L.

Initial poor graft function is characteristic of a marginally functioning graft that typically recovers adequate function after days to weeks after transplantation. This syndrome has a milder clinical presentation than primary nonfunction, and serum aminotransferases are usually less than 2500 IU/L. Treatment is largely supportive, and most grafts eventually recover.

ACUTE AND CHRONIC ALLOGRAFT REJECTION. The most common cause of allograft dysfunction after the first postoperative week is acute cellular rejection, which occurs in two thirds of cases and is seen between the 5th day and the first 3 weeks after transplantation. An acute rejection episode occurring beyond 6 weeks after transplantation should raise suspicion for a subtherapeutic immunosuppressive regimen or for noncompliance with the medical regimen. The patient is usually asymptomatic and presents with increases in serum bilirubin, alkaline phosphatase, and γ-glutamyltransferase in the early post-transplant course and predominant elevations in the serum aminotransferases when acute rejection occurs several weeks following transplantation. However, recipients can also present with fever, malaise, abdominal pain, or portal hypertensive changes such as ascites. Histologic examination reveals a mixed portal or periportal inflammatory infiltrate (with neutrophils, eosinophils, plasma cells, and lymphocytes) leading to destructive suppurative cholangitis and endotheliitis. Treatment, which reverses 65 to 85% of episodes, consists of high-dose intravenous corticosteroids, usually 1 g of methylprednisolone, followed by oral prednisone with a rapid taper over 7 days.

Chronic ductopenic rejection occurs in about 3% of recipients and has been decreasing in incidence among adult recipients, largely because of earlier diagnosis and improved immunosuppressive drug regimens. It most commonly occurs between 6 weeks and 6 months following transplantation. Cholestatic enzymes, such as alkaline phosphatase and γ-glutamyltransferase, gradually increase for weeks to months before the onset of jaundice that signals the late stage of chronic ductopenic rejection. Histologic evaluation reveals sparse lymphocytic portal inflammation but progressive loss of interlobular and septal bile ducts in at least half of the portal tracts—a condition known as vanishing bile duct syndrome. Approximately 15 to 20% of retransplantations are due to chronic ductopenic rejection.

BILIARY COMPLICATIONS FOLLOWING LIVER TRANSPLANTATION. The biliary tree has very poor regenerative and reparative capacity when damaged and is the most common site for technical complications following transplantation. Biliary complications occur in 10 to 25% of all recipients, with more than two thirds of cases diagnosed within 1 month and 80% within 6 months of transplantation. Causes of biliary complications include technical factors, preservation injury, hepatic artery thrombosis, immunologic factors, and infection, particularly with CMV. Bile leaks and strictures are the most common presentations of biliary complications in the first 3 months postoperatively.

Choledochocholedochostomy and choledochojejunostomy are the two methods of primary biliary reconstruction in liver transplantation. The more commonly performed choledochocholedochostomy, or duct-to-duct anastomosis, preserves the sphincter of Oddi and endoscopic access to the biliary tree following transplantation. Choledochojejunostomy, or Roux-en-Y anastomosis, is used for retransplantation, transplanting small liver grafts, and in patients with intrinsic disease of the extrahepatic bile ducts, such as primary sclerosing cholangitis.

Bile leak occurs in up to 25% of all recipients and can be diagnosed by cholangiogram or biliary scintigraphy if the leak is sufficiently large. Patients may present with fever, abdominal pain, peritonitis, hypotension, or sepsis with biloma. For patients who suffer from bile leak after T-tube removal, endoscopic placement of nasobiliary drain or internal plastic stent allows the leakage to heal as the bile flows preferentially through the ampulla. Surgical creation or revision of choledochojejunostomy should be performed only after failure of endoscopic or radiologic interventions.

Anastomotic biliary stricture, which affects 4 to 10% of all recipients, occurs within the first 6 months of transplantation. Clinical presentation is typical of cholangitis but may be asymptomatic with only elevation of cholestatic enzymes (predominantly alkaline phosphatase and γ-glutamyltransferase). Balloon dilatation or stenting endoscopically or radiologically should be attempted before resorting to surgery. Nonanastomotic biliary strictures, affecting up to 20% of all recipients, occur within the first 4 months of transplantation. The biliary strictures are usually multiple and may be associated with extrahepatic bile leaks and intrahepatic bile leaks. Management of these strictures depends on their number, location, and severity, as well as liver function. Diffuse strictures in the setting of bile leaks and bilomas indicate the need for retransplantation. Focal intrahepatic strictures may benefit from repeated sessions of balloon dilatation and stenting performed endoscopically or radiologically.

INFECTIONS

Most infections occur within the first 2 months after transplantation when recipients are receiving a high-dose induction immunosuppressive regimen. Bacteria and fungi cause more than 90% of infections during this period. Pneumonia, urinary infection, intraabdominal and hepatic abscesses, peritonitis, wound infection, line sepsis are the most common infections. *Candida albicans* is the most common infecting fungal agent in the immediate posttransplantation period. Other frequently seen fungi include *Aspergillus fumigatus* and non-*Albicans candida* species. Despite its nephrotoxicity, amphotericin B is the treatment of choice for invasive fungal infections. Oral fluconazole prevents most fungal infections and is the standard antifungal prophylaxis used for the first 6 weeks after transplantation.

The routine use of trimethoprim-sulfamethoxazole prophylaxis has made infection with *Pneumocystis carinii* rare in liver transplant recipients. Inhalational pentamidine and oral dapsone are alternative prophylactic regimens in patients allergic to sulfa. Prophylaxis lasts for 1 year after transplantation but should be extended for an extra year if the patient received additional high-dose immunosuppressants (e.g., steroid boluses, muromonab-CD3, increased tacrolimus) during the first year after transplantation.

Reactivation of herpes simplex virus as oral and genital lesions may occur within the first month of transplantation. Prophylaxis with oral acyclovir is advocated for the first 3 months. Reactivation of varicella zoster virus may present as localized dermatomal vesicles and, in patients who were seronegative before transplantation, as cutaneous and visceral dissemination; treatment is with high-dose acyclovir.

By 6 months after liver transplantation, recipients who have normal allograft function and are receiving standard doses of immunosuppressive drugs share the same risks as immunocompetent hosts for community-acquired infections and are not at increased risks for opportunistic infections. Conversely, recipients who have been on high-dose immunosuppressive drug regimens for antirejection therapy continue to be at high risk for life-threatening opportunistic infections.

Long-Term Follow-Up

Long-term management of liver transplant recipients requires continuing communication and cooperation between the transplant center and the primary care physician. These patients require careful routine medical management, screening for malignancy, and immunization updates and boosters.

Hypertension (Chapter 63) occurs among 30 to 90% of all recipients and is related to cyclosporine and tacrolimus, which cause vasoconstriction in the systemic and renal vasculature, and corticosteroids, which result in sodium retention, increased plasma volume, and weight gain. Management of hypertension in liver transplant recipients follows a stepwise approach. Dietary sodium restriction, resumption of physical activity, and weight reduction are the first steps. Due to the pathophysiology of vasoconstriction, calcium channel blockers are the drugs of first choice. The preferred calcium channel blockers belong to the dihydropyridine class, such as nifedipine. Verapamil, diltiazem, and nicardipine are also effective, but they increase the drug levels of cyclosporine and tacrolimus. Second-line antihypertensive agents include diuretics, β-blockers, and α-adrenergic blockers. Angiotensin-converting enzyme inhibitors should be used with caution because they may aggravate hyperkalemia and can rarely exacerbate leukopenia. Hypertension may improve with time as corticosteroids are discontinued and the dose of cyclosporine or tacrolimus is lowered.

Diabetes mellitus (Chapter 242) develops in more than one third of liver recipients after transplantation, with the majority of cases being insulin-dependent. The pathogenesis is multifactorial, including genetic predisposition and use of tacrolimus, cyclosporine, and corticosteroids. Steroid tapering is the key to managing of early posttransplant hyperglycemia. Management is otherwise similar to that for the nontransplanted population.

Hyperlipidemia (Chapter 211) develops in approximately one fourth of all liver recipients following transplantation. The management of hyperlipidemia includes appropriate dietary restrictions of fat and carbohydrate, weight reduction, regular exercise, and smoking cessation. The preferred medication for patients with resistant hyperlipidemia is 3-hydroxy-3-methylglutaryl coenzyme A (HMG-CoA) reductase inhibitors. Pravastatin is known to be safe and effective in these patients.

Bone mineral density decreases during the first few months following transplantation but eventually regains its preoperative level. Fractures most frequently involve trabecular bones such as the vertebrae and the ribs. *Osteonecrosis or avascular necrosis* of the hips and, less often, the knees and the humerus bones, may occur. Contributing risk factors to bone disease include preexisting osteopenia, prolonged bed rest, malnutrition, corticosteroids, cyclosporine, tacrolimus, furosemide, and the original diagnosis of primary biliary cirrhosis or primary sclerosing cholangitis with associated metabolic osteodystrophy. Management includes regular exercise and pharmacologic therapies such as calcium supplementation, vitamin D derivatives, bisphosphonates, and, for postmenopausal women, consideration of estrogen replacement (Chapter 258).

Skin cancer (Chapter 209) is the most common malignancy occurring in the setting of solid-organ transplantation and immunosuppression. Squamous cell carcinoma is more common than basal cell carcinoma or malignant melanoma in this population, and some recipients may develop hundreds of squamous cell carcinomas. Patients should seek medical attention if they have a skin growth that bleeds or crusts, increases in size or thickness, or changes in color or texture.

Sunscreen with a sun protection factor of at least 15 is recommended. Patients should undergo at least annual skin examinations depending on previous history of skin cancers.

Colon cancer (Chapter 200) is a common *de novo* neoplasia following transplantation. Colonoscopic surveillance with multiple biopsies every 6 months for the first 2 years after transplantation followed by annual examination has been recommended for high-risk patients with ulcerative colitis.

If not given before liver transplantation, hepatitis A, hepatitis B, and pneumococcal vaccines (Chapter 16) should be given. Other immunizations include influenza vaccine annually and tetanus toxoid booster every 5 years. Vaccines based on live or attenuated microorganisms should be avoided, including those for measles, mumps, rubella, chickenpox, polio, and BCG.

SUGGESTED READINGS

Carithers RL: Liver transplantation. American Association for the Study of Liver Diseases. Liver Transpl 2000;6:122–135. *This evidenced-based consensus guideline developed by the Standards of Practice Committee of the American Association for the Study of Liver Diseases addresses all aspects of the practice of liver transplantation.*

Farmer DG, Anselmo DM, Ghobrial RM, et al: Liver transplantation for fulminant hepatic failure: Experience with more than 200 patients over a 17-year period. Ann Surg 2003;237:666–676. *Long-term survival was nearly 70%, and the serum creatinine level was the single most important predictor of survival.*

Keeffe EB: Liver transplantation: current status and novel approaches to liver replacement. Gastroenterology 2001;120:749–762. *This review summarizes the current status of liver transplantation, including organ allocation, and concisely reviews the use of split livers and the evolving practice of living donor liver transplantation.*

Wiesner RH, McDiarmid SV, Kamath PS, et al: MELD and PELD: application of survival models to liver allocation. Liver Transpl 2001;7:567–580. *This review outlines the rationale and logistics of the Model for End-Stage Liver Disease and how it will impact the organ allocation system in the United States.*

158 DISEASES OF THE GALLBLADDER AND BILE DUCTS

Nezam H. Afdhal

The biliary tract consists of the intrahepatic biliary canaliculus, the small, medium, and large intrahepatic bile ducts, the common bile duct, the gallbladder, the cystic duct, and the ampulla of Vater. The primary functions of the biliary system are secretion and storage of bile salts that solubilize intestinal lipids, excretion of cholesterol to maintain cholesterol homeostasis, excretion of excess bilirubin, and excretion of organic ions, including drug metabolites.

ANATOMY AND PATHOPHYSIOLOGY OF THE BILIARY SYSTEM

BILE FORMATION AND THE ENTEROHEPATIC CIRCULATION.
In the liver, hepatocytes are organized into cribriform, anastomosing plates along the sinusoids. At the apical pole, between adjacent hepatocytes, is the 1- to 2-μM biliary canaliculus or space. Each hepatocyte can have multiple canaliculi (up to three), which are characterized by microvilli that protrude into the canalicular lumen.

Bile consists of water, electrolytes, and organic solutes (Table 158–1). It is continuously modified both by the cholangiocytes that line the bile ducts and by the gallbladder mucosa, so gallbladder bile is markedly different than hepatic bile. The gallbladder mucosa absorbs water and concentrates bile, so that the total lipid content of gallbladder bile is much higher than that of hepatic bile (10 g/dL compared with 3 g/dL, respectively).

The major primary bile acids are cholic and chenodeoxycholic acid. The secondary bile acids, lithocholic and deoxycholic acids, which are derived from the intestinal breakdown of primary bile acids, are more hydrophobic, increase in cholestasis, and can be toxic to hepatocytes. Amidation with glycine or taurine results in the formation of bile salts, which are preferentially secreted into bile. Bile salts are amphiphilic detergent-like molecules that are synthesized from cholesterol via a pathway dependent on 7α-hydroxylase or a pathway dependent on sterol 27-hydroxylase. Bile salt synthesis accounts for approximately 50% of the liver metabolism of cholesterol. Bile salts are secreted into the canalicular space by an energy-dependent bile salt export pump (Fig. 158-1). In the canalicular membrane, bile salts exist as simple (bile salt only) or mixed (with phosphatidylcholine

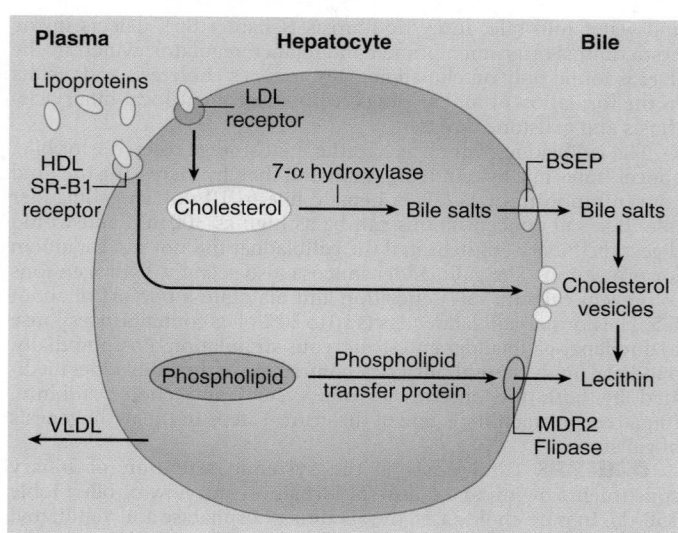

FIGURE 158–1 • Schematic diagram of metabolism of phospholipid and cholesterol by the hepatocyte. BSEP = bile salt export pump; MDR2 = multidrug resistant receptor 2, a phospholipid lipase highly selective for phosphatidylcholine or lecithin.

Table 158–1 • CONSTITUENTS OF HUMAN CANALICULAR BILE

Bile salts 12 g/L	Cholates 35%
Glycine conjugates 75%	Chenodeoxycholates 35%
Taurine conjugates 24.8%	Deoxycholates 25%
Free bile acids 0.2%	Lithocholates 1%
	Miscellaneous 40%
Phospholipids 5 g/L	Phosphatidylcholine 96%
	Phosphatidyl ethanolamine 3%
Cholesterol 1 g/L	Free, unesterified 99%
Bilirubin 0.2 g/L	Diglucuronide 80%
	Monoglucuronide 18%
	Unconjugated 2%
Proteins 2 g/L	Albumin 50%
	Immunoglobulins 23%
	Calcium binding protein/ anionic peptide fraction 17%
	Serum proteins 9%
	Canalicular proteins 1%
Electrolytes	Sodium 150 mEq/L
	Magnesium 2 mEq/L
	Calcium 3 mEq/L
	Potassium 5 mEq/L
	Chloride 110 mEq/L
	Bicarbonate 30 mEq/L

and cholesterol) micelles and are transported into the gallbladder. A fatty meal results in contraction of the gallbladder, with expulsion of bile salts into the duodenum, where they form micelles with intraluminal fat. About 95% of bile acids are absorbed by a sodium-dependent bile acid transporter in the terminal ileum. The total bile acid pool is circulated four to six times per day, and the volume of biliary secretion is approximately 1 liter per day. The major phospholipid in bile is phosphatidyl choline, also called lecithin. Phosphatidyl choline in bile is derived from newly synthesized hepatic phosphatidyl choline, which is then transported through the hepatocyte by a phosphatidyl choline transfer protein and delivered to MDR3, a phosphatidyl choline–specific transporter for final secretion into bile (see Fig. 158-1).

The current concept for cholesterol secretion is that the high bile salt concentrations in the canaliculus leach cholesterol from the plasma membrane as preformed cholesterol vesicles that are then rapidly solubilized. Gallstone disease is predominantly an inability to maintain free cholesterol in solution in bile.

As canalicular bile passes down the bile duct system, cholangiocytes maintain bile flow and volume by secreting chloride, bicarbonate, and water into bile. In cystic fibrosis (Chapter 86), defects in the cystic fibrosis transmembrane conductance regulator, which in the liver is found only on cholangiocytes, reduces choleresis and results in the formation of mucus plugs, with subsequent focal biliary cirrhosis and gallstone disease.

The gallbladder, which acts as the final storage reservoir for bile, concentrates bile by removing water and thereby increasing the lipid concentration from 3 g/dL in hepatic bile to 10 g/dL in gallbladder bile. Bile salt concentrations can be as high as 300 mM and would digest the biliary epithelium if the gallbladder did not secrete mucin for protection. The gallbladder mucosa also secretes hydrogen ions to prevent calcium salt deposition and maintain a bile pH of about 6.5. The normal gallbladder ejects 10 to 20% of its contents in response to duodenal-gallbladder enteric nervous stimulation. Postprandially, duodenal lipids cause about a 70% contraction of the gallbladder mediated by both the enteric nervous system and cholecystokinin. Impaired contractility is one of the critical steps in the pathogenesis of gallstones.

CHOLESTASIS. Cholestasis is the systemic retention of biliary constituents owing to a failure of formation and flow of bile (Table 158–2). In pure cholestasis, the alkaline phosphatase and γ-glutamyl transferase (GGT) levels are elevated significantly, whereas the aminotransferase levels are normal or only mildly increased (Chapter 149). Bilirubin may be elevated but can be normal even in severe intrahepatic cholestasis until the very late stages of disease.

Dilation of the intrahepatic ducts on ultrasonography (US) suggests *extrahepatic obstructive cholestasis*. The clinical manifestations depend on the location and etiology of the obstructive process and the degree to which an associated increase in proinflammatory cytokines decreases bile salt synthesis and secretion. *Intrahepatic cholestasis* is usually the result of either hepatocellular dysfunction (Chapter 149) or injury to the small and medium bile ducts owing to viruses (Chapters 151 and 152), alcohol (Chapters 155 and 156), and drugs (Chapter 120).

Bile salt retention can lead to an excess of hydrophobic bile salts, such as deoxycholate, which are hepatotoxic. These retained bile salts can overflow out of the liver and lead to increased levels of bile salts in the serum and skin. Bile acid binders or sequestrants, such as cholestyramine, can lower bile acid concentration (Table 158–3).

Replacement of hydrophobic bile salts with hydrophilic bile salts, such as ursodeoxycholic acid, treats all forms of intrahepatic cholestasis and the associated pruritus. The sensorineural pathway can also be blocked using opioid antagonists. In some cases of intractable pruritus, marijuana or its synthetic form, Marinol, has been useful in controlling symptoms.

In cholestasis, excess cholesterol is deposited in all tissues, particularly as tendinous xanthomas and periorbital xanthelasmas. Clinically significant atherosclerosis is uncommon. No medical treatment is effective in reducing cholesterol significantly in this condition.

In cholestasis, concentrations of intestinal bile salts are inadequate to solubilize dietary lipids; the result is the excretion of excess non-absorbed fat. Long-chain dietary fats also irritate the colonic mucosa. Steatorrhea, which is characterized by greasy, foul-smelling diarrhea, develops (Chapter 141). Steatorrhea is suggested by the presence of stainable fat in the stool (see Fig. 141–11) and confirmed by quantitative analysis of a 32-hour stool collection (Table 141–7).

Malabsorption of fat-soluble vitamins A, D, E, and K can result in deficiency syndromes; fat-soluble vitamins and essential fatty acids should be given as dietary supplements. A combination of osteomalacia and osteoporosis is a serious consequence of cholestasis and chronic liver disease. Supplementation of calcium, 1500 mg daily, plus vitamin D is essential. If bone density scans show osteopenia, therapy with bisphosphonates should be instituted (Chapter 258).

Therapy should also attempt to remove the cause of cholestasis, such as bypassing an obstructing pancreatic cancer (Chapter 201) with surgery or a stent. In the progressive cholestasis of intrahepatic biliary disease (e.g., primary biliary cirrhosis; Chapter 156), liver transplant (Chapter 157) may be the only recourse.

GALLSTONE DISEASE

Definition

There are three different types of gallstones: cholesterol gallstones, mixed gallstones, and pigment stones, which can be further divided into black and brown stones. Cholesterol and mixed stones account for 80% of gallstone disease in the United States. Cholesterol stones contain more than 70% cholesterol, whereas mixed stones also contain significant amounts of pigments, such as bilirubin. Black pigment stones, which are usually associated with hemolytic diseases, contain calcium salts, bilirubin, and proteins. Brown pigment stones are more common in Asia, where they are associated with intrahepatic cholangitis and infection; in the United States, brown stones are seen postcholecystectomy, especially when they present as choledocholithiasis.

Epidemiology

Approximately 30 million people in the United States have gallstones, and the estimated annual cost of gallstone disease is $15 billion. In Europe, large ultrasound studies in subjects between ages 30 and 65 years have shown gallstones in 18.8% of women and 9.5% of men. In a study in which 1930 subjects were followed up for 10 years, the cumulative incidence of new stones was 4.6%.

Age is a major risk factor for gallstone disease (Table 158–4); less than 2% of cholecystectomies for gallstones are performed in

Table 158–2 • CAUSES OF CHOLESTASIS

EXTRAHEPATIC	INTRAHEPATIC
Choledocholithiasis	Viral hepatitis
Bile duct stricture	Alcoholic hepatitis
Cholangiocarcinoma	Drug induced
Pancreatic carcinoma	Ductopenia syndromes
Chronic pancreatitis	Primary biliary cirrhosis
Papillary stenosis	Benign recurrent intrahepatic cholestasis
Ampullary cancer	Byler's disease
Primary sclerosing cholangitis	Primary sclerosing cholangitis
Choledochal cysts	Alagille's syndrome
Parasites (e.g., ascaris, clonorchis)	Sarcoid
Acquired immunodeficiency syndrome cholangiography	Lymphoma
Biliary atresia	Postoperative
Portal lymphadenopathy	Total parenteral nutrition
Mirrizzi's syndrome	α1-Antitrypsin deficiency

Table 158–3 • CLINICAL FEATURES OF AND THERAPY FOR CHOLESTASIS

CLINICAL SYNDROME	TREATMENT
Pruritus	Bile salt binders (e.g., cholestyramine), ursodeoxycholic acid, rifampin, naltrexone, carbinolds
Hypercholesterolemia	Bile salt binders (e.g., cholestyramine) Statins—poor effect
Malabsorption	Medium chain triglycerides, fat-soluble vitamins (A, D, E, K), essential fatty acids
Osteopenia	Calcium, vitamin D, bisphosphonates

Table 158–4 • RISK FACTORS FOR GALLSTONE DISEASE

Age
Female gender
Parity
Obesity
Rapid weight loss
Hypertryglyceridemia
Genetic (e.g., Pima Indians, Chileans)
Medications: estrogen, clofibrate, ceftriaxone, sandostatin
Terminal ileal resection
Gallbladder hypomotility: pregnancy, diabetes, postvagotomy
Somatostatinoma
Total parenteral nutrition
Spinal cord injury

children, usually because of hemolytic diseases. However, the increased prevalence of obesity in children may result in an earlier incidence of gallstone disease.

The age-adjusted female-to-male ratio for gallstone disease is 2.9 between ages 30 and 39 years but decreases to 1.2 between the ages of 50 and 59 years. Women with gallstone disease also appear to be more likely to have a cholecystectomy compared with men. Pregnancy appears to be the major risk factor for the increased prevalence of gallstones in younger women, with a prevalence of 1.3% in nulliparous women compared with 13% in multiparous women. Estrogen use is also associated with a higher risk of symptomatic gallstones and cholecystectomy, with a relative risk of 2.1 to 3.7 compared with no estrogen use. The mechanisms of increased risk include an estrogen-induced increase in cholesterol secretion, a progesterone-induced reduction in gallbladder contraction, and a pregnancy-induced alteration in hydrophobic/hydrophilic bile salt balance.

Obesity increases the risk for gallstones owing to enhanced cholesterol absorption, synthesis, and secretion. The risk is higher in women and in the morbidly obese, but rapid weight reduction by very low-calorie diets is also associated with gallstones.

Genetics

Family history studies have shown that gallstones are twice as common in first-degree relatives of gallstone patients compared with age- and sex-matched control subjects. In the United States, descendants of the original Amerindians have markedly increased prevalence of gallstones, with the highest rates in female Pima Indians older than age 25 years, who have a 75% prevalence of cholesterol gallstones. Amerindians in South America and Mexico also have very high prevalence of gallstones, and these populations have the highest rate of complications of gallstone disease, such as gallbladder cancer, in the world. South Americans of Hispanic origin have much lower rates of gallstone disease.

No specific gallstone genes have been found in humans, but lithogenic genes, including the bile salt export pump gene, have been described in gallstone-susceptible mice. Human gallstone disease is probably a combination of complex multigene susceptibility and environmental factors.

Pathogenesis

CHOLESTEROL GALLSTONES. Cholesterol gallstones contain 50 to 90% cholesterol and are the most common form of stones in countries with a Western diet that is high in protein and fat. Cholesterol is an intensely hydrophobic molecule that can remain soluble in aqueous solution only as saturated micelles and vesicles in conjunction with bile salts and lecithin. Cholesterol in gallbladder bile is in multiple phases; in the presence of cholesterol supersaturation, unstable cholesterol vesicles nucleate to form cholesterol crystals (Fig. 158–2). Nucleation is promoted by a variety of factors, including proteins and lipids.

Increased biliary secretion of cholesterol results in cholesterol supersaturation of bile. The result is excess secretion of mucus into the gallbladder, the formation of a gel layer, and stasis that causes cholesterol to nucleate and cholesterol crystals to be deposited.

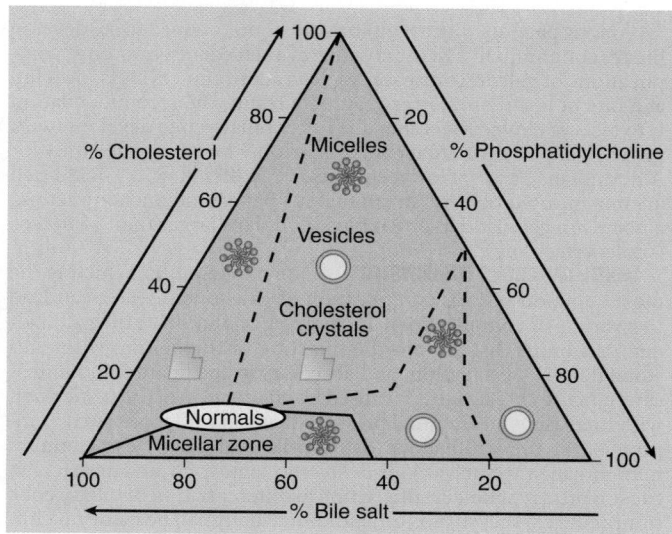

FIGURE 158–2 • Equilibrium phase diagram for a lithogenic model bile system with a total lipid content of 10 g/dL.

Cholesterol monohydrate crystals are only several hundred microns in size and should be easily expelled through the cystic duct. However, the mucus sludge containing calcium salts, bilirubin, mucin, and crystals is not easily expelled by contraction of the gallbladder. Biliary sludge, also known as microlithiasis, can be seen as an echogenic, freely mobile mass in the gallbladder on US. Biliary sludge can cause the symptoms of gallstone disease, including cholecystitis, cholangitis, and pancreatitis.

Biliary sludge can resolve, persist, or progress to stones when its crystals grow to form plates owing, in part, to an impairment of gallbladder contractility. Cholesterol supersaturation of bile is associated with increased absorption of cholesterol by the gallbladder smooth muscle, a process that impairs smooth muscle contractility and reduces the response of the gallbladder to cholecystokinin.

PIGMENT GALLSTONES. Black pigment stones contain 10 to 90% calcium bilirubinate in combination with a variety of other calcium salts, such as hydroxyapatite and carbonate. These stones are common in India (40%) but rare in Minnesota (5%). Older age is associated with a higher incidence of pigment stones, as are total parenteral nutrition and hemolytic diseases.

Brown pigment stones comprise 30% of gallstones in Japan and up to 90% of gallstones in rural China. They are related to low-calorie, high-vegetable diets, occur in both the biliary tract and the liver, and have strong association with recurrent pyogenic cholangitis and cholangiohepatitis. In the United States, these stones are seen as postcholecystectomy cholelithiasis, presumably owing to stasis and infection. Bacterial enzymes deconjugate bilirubin from its glucuronide and hydrolyze phospholipids, thereby leading to the precipitation of calcium, bilirubin, and free fatty acids. These stones, which are often soft and easy to crush endoscopically, are commonly treated by endoscopic extraction.

Clinical Manifestations

SYMPTOMATIC VERSUS SILENT GALLSTONES. The symptoms caused by gallstones are often nonspecific and include nausea, bloating, and right upper quadrant pain. Biliary pain, which is described as an intermittent right upper quadrant or epigastric pain occurring 15 to 30 minutes after a meal, often with radiation to the back, is unpredictable, severe, and usually constant rather than a true colic. The pain persists for 3 to 4 hours and may be associated with nausea and vomiting. In uncomplicated cholecystitis, fever and leukocytosis are absent, the pain usually can be adequately treated with a single dose of narcotic analgesics or nonsteroidal anti-inflammatory agents (NSAIDs), and the pain usually subsides within 6 hours. Attacks of colic may be separated by days or months.

Asymptomatic gallstones, which are frequently diagnosed by US performed for other indications, comprise about 85% of gallstones. Patients with asymptomatic stones have a similar incidence of nonspecific symptoms of nausea and bloating as the general population and rarely develop complications of gallstone disease. Biliary colic, however, is more predictive of gallstones, and it is an indicator of an increased risk of cholecystitis or other complications. Obesity, lack of exercise, female gender, and estrogen use may all lead to more symptomatic gallstones. Because the current standard of care is to treat only symptomatic stones, it is critically important to determine whether any symptoms are related to gallbladder stones.

Continued

Among patients with asymptomatic stones, about 2 to 3% develop biliary colic annually. In the absence of antecedent symptoms, complications of gallstone disease, such as acute cholecystitis, develop at a rate of less than 1% per year. As a result, the recommendation is to reserve cholecystectomy until after biliary colic develops, with prophylactic or incidental cholecystectomy recommended only for Amerindians, transplant recipients, or patients with sickle cell anemia, morbid obesity, an anomalous pancreatic ductal junction, a porcelain gallbladder, or gallbladder polyps larger than 1 cm (see Cholecystectomy).

ACUTE CALCULOUS CHOLECYSTITIS. Acute cholecystitis, which is the most common serious complication of gallstone disease, can lead to a variety of complications, including perforation of the gallbladder, peritonitis, fistula into the intestine or duodenum with gallstone ileus or obstruction, and abscesses in the liver or abdominal cavity. Acute cholecystitis is caused by obstruction of the cystic duct, with increased intraluminal pressure that can lead to vascular compromise of the gallbladder. Salmonella and other less common microorganisms, such as *Vibrio cholerae*, leptospira, and listeria, can cause a primary cholecystitis. Clinical differentiation of biliary colic from acute cholecystitis is difficult but usually can be made on clinical and radiologic findings (Table 158–5).

In uncomplicated acute cholecystitis, laboratory testing usually shows leukocytosis but otherwise is not very helpful. Elevated liver enzyme levels, hyperbilirubinemia, and elevated amylase or lipase levels are not common in cholecystitis and suggest other complications of gallstone disease, such as cholangitis or pancreatitis. When acute cholecystitis is accompanied by an inflammatory mass, the gallbladder can compress the common duct and lead to bile duct obstruction (Mirrizzi's syndrome).

Right upper quadrant US noninvasively diagnoses gallstones in 95% of patients with cholecystitis (Fig. 158–3). US can also exclude common bile duct obstruction and may occasionally show bile duct stones. In cholecystitis, the gallbladder wall may be thickened, and free pericholecystic fluid may be present. Murphy's sign is also useful and can be elicited by the ultrasonographer or on physical examination. Gentle pressure is placed by the probe or hand at the border of the rectus sheath in the right upper quadrant, and the patient is asked to inspire. The gallbladder moves down with inspiration onto the examiner's hand or ultrasound probe, and the patient complains of pain when the inflamed gallbladder comes into contact with the examining hand. US can also exclude gangrenous cholecystitis with free air in the gallbladder wall, perforation, and abscess. The most specific test for acute cholecystitis is a technetium-labeled hydroxyl iminodiacetic acid (HIDA) scan. Intravenously, HIDA is normally taken up by the liver, excreted into the biliary tract, and concentrated in the gallbladder. When a stone obstructs the cystic duct, the gallbladder fails to fill with HIDA; the sensitivity of HIDA scan is 95%, but the specificity varies markedly and can be as poor as 50% in critically ill or jaundiced patients.

Table 158–5 • CLINICAL FEATURES OF BILIARY COLIC COMPARED WITH ACUTE CHOLECYSTITIS

CLINICAL FINDINGS	BILIARY COLIC	ACUTE CHOLECYSTITIS
Right upper quadrant pain	Present	Present
Abdominal tenderness	Absent or mild	Moderate to severe, especially over liver and/or gallbladder (Murphy's sign)
Fever	Absent	Usually present
Leukocytosis	Absent	Usually >11,000 μL
Duration of symptoms	<4 hr	>6 hr
Ultrasound	Gallstones	Gallstones, thickening of the gallbladder wall
HIDA scan	Gallbladder visualized within 4 hr	No filling of the gallbladder

HIDA = hydroxyl iminodiacetic acid.

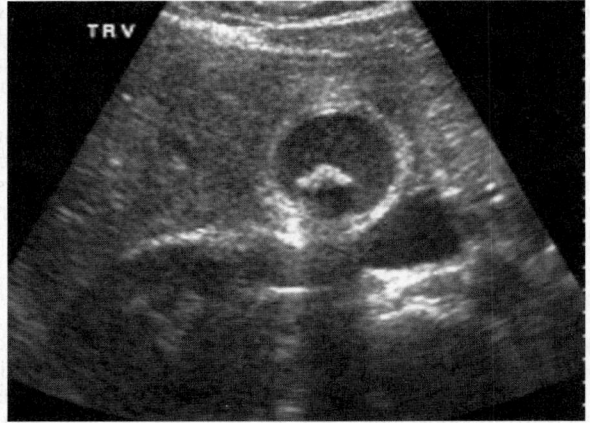

FIGURE 158–3 • Ultrasound showing a gallstone.

℞ Treatment

MEDICAL STABILIZATION OF ACUTE CHOLECYSTITIS. The treatment for uncomplicated acute cholecystitis is intravenous fluids, antibiotics for 7 to 10 days, and bowel rest. Antibiotic choices include ampicillin (2 g intravenously every 6 hours) and an aminoglycoside (gentamicin 5.1 mg/kg every 24 hours), but cephalosporins (ceftriaxone 1 to 2 g once daily) and ampicillin-sulbactam (1.5 to 3 g every 6 hours) can also be used. Broader coverage should be used in immunosuppressed patients, including the addition of metronidazole (500 mg every 8 hours), piperacillin-tazobactam (3.375 g every 6 hours), and levofloxacin (500 mg to 1 g once daily). Early cholecystectomy (at the time of first admission) is usually recommended.◻

CHOLECYSTECTOMY. Laparoscopic cholecystectomy has now all but replaced conventional open cholecystectomy as the procedure of choice for gallstones. The advantages of laparoscopic cholecystectomy include less pain, early discharge (usually 1 day after the procedure), fewer wound infections, earlier return to work, and lower costs. Nationally, the lower cost per procedure largely has been offset by the increasing number of procedures performed. The indications for cholecystectomy include biliary colic, acute and chronic cholecystitis, and acalculous cholecystitis. Diabetic patients may have fewer symptoms owing to their neuropathy, so their cholecystitis more frequently may be complicated by gangrene and perforation; however, prophylactic cholecystectomy is not recommended in patients with diabetes.

Operative cholangiography can be performed during laparoscopic cholecystectomy, and bile duct stones can be removed concurrently or subsequently by the endoscopic retrograde cholangiopancreatographic (ERCP) approach. The incidence of unsuspected, retained common bile duct stones after laparoscopic cholecystectomy is about 2.3%.

Complications of laparoscopic cholecystectomy can be from the procedure itself or from the induced pneumoperitoneum. The pneumoperitoneum can cause liver function impairment, bowel ischemia, and hernias. The most serious complication of the procedure itself is bile duct injury, which varies from 0.62 to 1.6%, is more common when the indication for surgery is acute cholecystitis, and is less common after a surgeon has performed more than 25 laparoscopic surgeries. Bile duct injuries include cystic duct leak, laceration to the duct, complete transection of the duct, and thermal injuries to the duct. Early recognition permits primary open bile duct repair. Leakage from the cystic duct is usually recognized as jaundice, fever, and abdominal pain several days after the procedure; it can be treated successfully by ERCP with insertion of an endoscopic stent or by sphincterotomy.

In less than 10% of cases, a planned laparoscopic approach is changed to open cholecystectomy, usually because of difficulty in identifying critical anatomic structures such as the cystic or common bile ducts.

GALLSTONE DISSOLUTION THERAPIES. In patients who have relative or absolute contraindications to laparoscopic cholecystectomy, such as concomitant advanced cardiopulmonary or liver disease, a combination of chenodeoxycholic acid with ursodeoxycholic acid (UDCA) or UDCA alone can dissolve multiple small (<5 mm) stones in up to 60% of patients with a functioning gallbladder. If computed tomography (CT) scan shows the stones as calcified, the efficacy is lower, and complete dissolution is seen in only about 10% of patients. Gallstones generally dissolve at a rate of 1 mm per month. After dissolution, gallstones recur at a rate of 10% per year for 5 years, but recurrence is unusual after that time. Continuous therapy may be necessary, thereby making this therapy unattractive except in selected patients in whom cholecystectomy cannot be performed safely.

Extracorporeal shock wave lithotripsy, which uses a focused ultrasound beam, can fragment larger stones. The fragmented stones can be passed through the cystic duct and expelled into the common bile duct. The fragments that remain behind in the gallbladder should be treated with UDCA for dissolution. Gallstones disappear in more than 50% of patients, but recurrences occur in 50% of successfully treated patients, particularly in those with multiple stones and poorly functioning gallbladders.

Topical dissolution therapy involves insertion of a catheter into the gallbladder under ultrasound guidance; stones are dissolved using methyl terbutyl ether or ethyl propionate. The technique is still experimental but may soon be ready for widespread testing.

Choledocholithiasis

Common bile duct stones can decend from the gallbladder or arise de novo in a tortuous, dilated common bile duct owing to infection and biliary stasis (usually cholesterol stones) or they can occur in the postcholecystectomy patient (usually brown stones), in whom they are frequently missed at surgery (2% of cholecystectomies). The clinical presentation is cholangitis, pancreatitis, or biliary obstruction; large, obstructing stones can cause jaundice.

Acute bacterial cholangitis, which is most frequently caused by common duct stones that obstruct the common bile duct and raise intrabiliary pressure, is a medical emergency. The bile in these patients is usually infected with *Escherichia coli*, *Bacteroides*, *Klebsiella*, or *Clostridium* species, and the increase in pressure results in transient bacteremia. Patients present with Charcot's triad of jaundice, abdominal pain, and fever with rigors. Severe renal dysfunction and disseminated intravascular coagulation can complicate severe cholangitis. Fluids and antibiotics with broad gram-negative coverage (e.g., ceftriaxone, 1 to 2 g once daily; ampicillin-sulbactam, 1.5 to 3 g every 6 hours; piperacillin-tazobactam, 3.375 g every 6 hours; levofloxacin, 500 mg to 1 g once daily) are recommended. Aminotransferase, bilirubin, and alkaline phosphatase levels are usually increased. The diagnosis of common bile duct stones can be made using US, which usually shows dilated bile ducts and occasionally identifies a stone. Magnetic resonance cholangiopancreatography (MRCP) can identify 95% of stones larger than 1 cm (Fig. 158–4). ERCP remains the "gold standard" for the diagnosis and treatment of common bile duct stones. If cholangitis is suspected, ERCP should be performed; endoscopic therapy includes sphincterotomy and stone extraction with a balloon or basket. Small (<2 cm) stones can be removed easily, whereas larger stones may be crushed with mechanical or US lithotriptors before removal. In the acutely ill patient, an initial decompression of a pus-filled common bile duct with a stent may be the first line of treatment, followed subsequently by definitive endoscopic or surgical therapy. After successful endoscopic therapy, laparoscopic cholecystectomy should be performed routinely because of the high risk of recurrent biliary events.[2]

In certain situations, such as after a Roux-en-Y choledochojejunostomy, ERCP may not be possible. Alternative approaches include a radiologic percutaneous transhepatic (PTC) approach or open exploration of the common bile duct. At PTC, the radiologist can decompress the bile ducts with catheters or stents, and stones can subsequently be removed through the fistula tract by direct cholangiography.

Gallstone pancreatitis (Chapter 145) is more common in patients with multiple small stones; it has also been associated with microlithiasis and biliary sludge. Patients present with acute epigastric pain radiating into the back, hyperamylasemia, and an imaging study that demonstrates an edematous or necrotic pancreas. Concomitant cholangitis or jaundice can rarely be seen if the stone is obstructive. Clinical features that suggest gallstone pancreatitis include elevated aspartate aminotransferase and alkaline phosphatase levels. Early ERCP with sphincterotomy and stone extraction within 24 hours of suspected acute gallstone pancreatitis reduces morbidity and

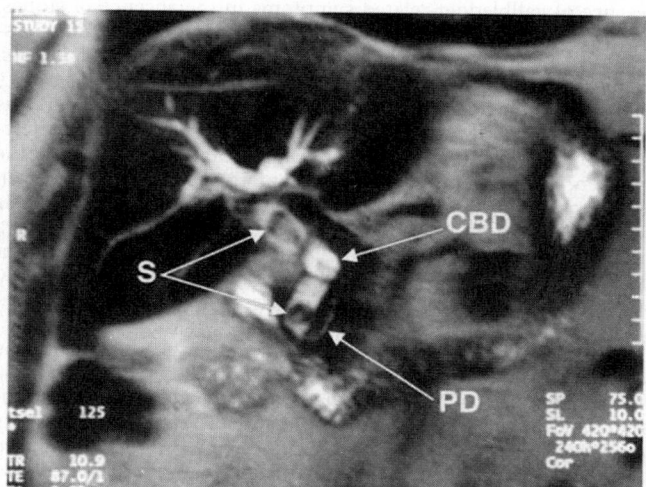

FIGURE 158–4 • Magnetic resonance cholangiopancreatogram of a dilated biliary tract showing the common bile duct (CBD), pancreatic duct (PD), and two large common duct stones (S).

mortality, but in 50% of cases the stones are not visible or have passed by the time of ERCP. After successful treatment of common duct stones, patients who still have a gallbladder should have it removed electively.

Unusual Complications of Gallstones

Vascular compromise to the gallbladder and the presence of gasforming bacteria, which are more common in patients who have diabetes or who are immunocompromised, can cause *gangrenous or emphysematous cholecystitis*. Clinically, patients are usually very ill with high temperature, features of systemic sepsis, and obtundation. US may show air in the gallbladder or gallbladder wall; perforation of the gallbladder with peritonitis may then occur. Emergency cholecystectomy is required.

If a fistula develops from the gallbladder to the duodenum, stomach, or colon, a large gallstone can pass through the fistula and into the bowel. If obstruction occurs at the duodenum or the ileocecal valve, *gallstone ileus* presents with symptoms and signs of intestinal obstruction. A plain abdominal radiograph shows bowel obstruction with free air in the gallbladder or biliary tract. Treatment is usually cholecystectomy and removal of the obstructing gallstone.

Prevention

Ursodeoxycholic acid, 600 mg at night, markedly reduces gallstone formation in patients on low-fat, low-calorie diets. Primary prevention of cholesterol gallstones is based on dietary alteration to avoid cholesterol supersaturation (i.e., a diet rich in whole grains and roughage and low in cholesterol and saturated fats). Secondary prevention includes using bile acid therapy with UDCA to reduce cholesterol supersaturation, improving gallbladder motility with cholecystokinin analogues, and reducing mucin secretion with aspirin and NSAIDs. All these strategies have been used effectively in high-risk groups, such as patients on low-calorie diets or patients on total parenteral nutrition.[3]

Prognosis

Overall the prognosis of gallstone disease is excellent for younger and otherwise healthy patients. However, with the aging population, there is a higher prevalence of complicated gallstone disease with common duct stones, cholangitis, and pancreatitis, each of which is associated with substantial morbidity and mortality.

ACALCULOUS CHOLECYSTITIS

Acalculous cholecystitis is inflammation of the gallbladder or the presence of gallbladder-related symptoms in the absence of stones. Acute acalculous cholecystitis accounts for 2 to 17% of all cholecystectomies. Ischemia, infections, chemical injury by biliary contents, and obstruction of the cystic duct have all been implicated as causes (Table 158–6). Primary infections may present as acute cholecystitis with unexplained fever, right upper quadrant pain, or clinical deterioration postoperatively or after transplantation, trauma to the abdomen, chemotherapy, or total parenteral nutrition. Pain, fever, leukocytosis, and abnormal liver enzyme tests are common. Diagnosis is confirmed by US that shows a distended gallbladder, often with a thin wall, pericholecystic fluid, or a positive Murphy sign (see earlier text) in the absence of gallstones. Sludge may be present. Intraluminal gas or bubbles, the so-called champagne sign, indicates emphysematous cholecystitis.

Treatment includes intravenous fluids, antibiotics as for gallstone disease, and general supportive measures. Because gangrene and perforation are more common in acalculous than calculous cholecystitis, urgent cholecystectomy is recommended. Postcholecystectomy complications such as leaks, abscess, and wound infection are also more common and reflect the underlying multisystemic problems. In severely ill patients in whom cholecystectomy is contraindicated,

radiologic decompression of the gallbladder via a percutaneous cholecystostomy can be performed. The overall mortality of acute acalculous cholecystitis is 5 to 20%.

Chronic acalculous cholecystitis is a poorly understood clinical syndrome in which patients present with symptoms of biliary colic in the absence of gallstones. The gallbladder may be normal or show changes of chronic inflammation. Cholesterolosis may also be present, with deposits of cholesterol in the mucosa and muscle layers of the gallbladder. Affected patients, who are often young and female, have abdominal pain and nonspecific symptoms such as nausea and fatty food intolerance. Biliary dyskinesia may be diagnosed by a food-cholecystokinin–stimulated US or HIDA scan; in 80 to 90% of patients with abnormal stimulated motility, symptoms are relieved by cholecystectomy.

GALLBLADDER CANCER

Gallbladder cancer constitutes 0.76 to 1.2% of all cancers and is the most common biliary cancer, with about 7200 new cases reported in the United States each year. The highest incidence occurs in Amerindians, particularly in Chile, Mexico, and Colombia. Gallbladder cancer is a disease of the elderly and is more common in women than men. There is a strong association with cholelithiasis, chronic cholecystitis, and inflammation; 90% of patients with gallbladder cancer have concomitant stones. Patients who have porcelain gallbladder, in which there is calcification of the gallbladder wall, have a 25% risk of developing gallbladder cancer, and patients with an anomalous pancreatic ductal junction, where the pancreatic duct drains into the lower common bile duct instead of the ampulla, have an increased risk of gallbladder cancer. Both of these lesions are indications for prophylactic cholecystectomy.

About 90% of gallbladder cancers are adenocarcinomas; the remainder are squamous cell or other cancers. Gallbladder cancer spreads locally, with invasion of the liver, and to the local lymph nodes and peritoneal cavity. About 90% of patients present with symptoms and signs suggestive of cholecystitis. Surgery, which is the only therapeutic option, can be curative when the tumor is confined to the gallbladder. Adjuvant radiotherapy and chemotherapy have not been shown to be effective. The median survival for all patients with gallbladder cancer is 3 months, with a 1-year survival of 14% and a 5-year survival of 5%.

BILIARY TRACT DISEASES

Lesions of the intrahepatic and extrahepatic biliary tree, including the ampulla of Vater, are rare.

BILIARY ATRESIA. Biliary atresia is a fibro-obliterative process that affects the perinatal bile ducts from the hilar bifurcation to the duodenum in 1 in every 13,000 live births in the United States. Associated genetic abnormalities in 25% of cases include polysplenia, anomalies of the portal vein and hepatic artery, abdominal situs inversus, intestinal malrotation, and cardiovascular and urinary tract anomalies. The clinical presentation is jaundice with acholic stools persisting for 2 weeks after birth. Diagnosis can be suspected by ERCP or MRCP but is usually confirmed by laparotomy. Surgical correction by a portoenterostomy should be performed within the first 60 days of life. About 80% of children grow normally through the first years of life, but subsequent stenosis of the anastomosis with progressive biliary cirrhosis and liver failure is common and is an indication for liver transplantation.

Choledochal Cysts

Choledochal cysts are congenital ductal ectasias involving either a segment or the entirety of the biliary tree. The incidence is 1 per 13,000 live births in the Unites States but is 13 times higher in Japan and Asia. Female gender carries a four-fold greater prevalence, and there is an association of cysts with an abnormal pancreatic ductal junction and congenital hepatic fibrosis. The usual clinical presentation is a right upper quadrant mass, jaundice, and pain. Acute pancreatitis, cholangitis, variceal hemorrhage, and cyst rupture are alternative presentations. Diagnosis is usually by imaging studies including US, CT scan, MRCP, and ERCP. Therapy is usually surgical excision of the cyst with a Roux-en-Y hepaticojejunostomy because of the high (3 to 26%) incidence of malignant transformation of

---

Table 158–6 • RISK FACTORS AND PRIMARY ORGANISMS ASSOCIATED WITH ACALCULOUS CHOLECYSTITIS

RISK FACTORS
Fasting
Total parenteral nutrition
Septicemia, biliary infections
Major trauma
Burns
Major nonbiliary surgery
Childbirth
Multiple blood transfusions
Mechanical ventilation
Opiates
Immunosuppression—chemotherapy, human immunodeficiency virus infection, transplantation
Diabetes
Ischemic heart disease
Malignancy

ORGANISMS IMPLICATED AS A PRIMARY CAUSE
Salmonella typhi
Vibrio cholera
Staphylococcus
Leptospira
Listeria
Pneumocystis carinii
Mycobacteria sp.
Cytomegalovirus
Candida
Ascaris
Echinococcus

the cysts into cholangiocarcinoma. When there is extensive intrahepatic ductal dilation (Caroli's disease), recurrent cholangitis and intrahepatic stones are common, and liver transplantation is the optimal therapy.

Oriental Cholangiohepatitis

Recurrent cholangitis with hepatolithiasis is endemic in East Asia, especially in Taiwan where the incidence is as high as 13% in areas where infection with *Ascaris lumbricoides* (Chapter 404) and *Clonorchis sinensis* (Chapter 403) are common. These worms cause local strictures and dilation of the intrahepatic biliary tree. Biliary stasis ensues, and the bile becomes infected with bacteria that are able to deconjugate bilirubin and cause brown stones to be formed. Recurrent cholangitis is the usual presentation, but malignant transformation to cholangiocarcinoma can also occur. Diagnosis is made by US or CT. Treatment includes intravenous fluids and antibiotics. Endoscopic stone removal and clearance of infected biliary segments is a primary option, but surgical resection of localized segments of the liver may be necessary.

Primary Sclerosing Cholangitis

Primary sclerosing cholangitis is a chronic cholestatic condition characterized by segmental fibrosing inflammation of the intrahepatic and extrahepatic bile ducts. The etiology remains unknown, but primary sclerosing cholangitis is thought to be a primary autoimmune disease. The disease is progressive, with obliteration of small, medium, and large bile ducts leading to three distinct clinical syndromes: (1) cholestasis with eventual biliary cirrhosis, (2) recurrent cholangitis and large duct strictures, and (3) cholangiocarcinoma. The multiple causes of secondary sclerosing cholangitis can cause symptoms and signs that are indistinguishable from the primary form (Table 158–7).

Primary sclerosing cholangitis is associated with both ulcerative colitis and Crohn's disease of the colon (Chapter 142). Between 70 and 90% of primary sclerosing cholangitis patients have clinical or microscopic colitis, and between 1.3 and 13% of colitis patients have primary sclerosing cholangitis. Inflammatory bowel disease usually precedes primary sclerosing cholangitis, but in some cases the colitis is asymptomatic and only discovered by subsequent colonoscopy and biopsy. There is also a crossover syndrome between primary sclerosing cholangitis and primary autoimmune hepatitis (Chapter 152).

The prevalence of primary sclerosing cholangitis is 1 to 6 cases per 100,000 in the U.S. population, with a male-to-female ratio of 2.3:1. The mean age at diagnosis is 32 to 40 years of age, but children can be affected.

The most common laboratory finding is an elevated alkaline phosphatase level, which is present in 90% of patients, and mildly elevated aminotransferase levels. The bilirubin level is initially normal in 60% of patients but increases over time and is an important prognostic factor. Autoantibodies, including antinuclear antibodies and anti–smooth muscle antibodies, are seen in 22% of patients, but a positive antimitochondrial antibody is rare and suggests primary biliary cirrhosis (Chapter 156). The antineutrophilic cytoplasmic antibody (pANCA) is positive in 90% of patients with primary sclerosing cholangitis and colitis, but pANCA is nonspecific and is also found in ulcerative colitis and in autoimmune hepatitis without primary sclerosing cholangitis.

The diagnosis is based on pathologic and radiologic findings, and all patients should have both a liver biopsy and cholangiogram. Liver biopsy shows an obliterative cholangitis with inflammation and characteristic periductular onion ring fibrosis. As the disease progresses, ductopenia and secondary biliary cirrhosis predominate. In stage I, inflammation is confined to portal tracts; in stage II, there is hepatitis and portal fibrosis; in stage III, bridging fibrosis appears; and stage IV is characterized by biliary cirrhosis and regenerative nodules. Large duct disease, which is diagnosed most frequently by ERCP or MRCP, includes strictures, beading, and dilation. Associated conditions include pancreatitis (15% of patients), perihepatic lymphadenopathy, and cholangiocarcinoma (27 to 41% of patients at autopsy or transplantation).

The natural history is variable. Some patients have severe recurrent cholangitis, whereas others progress to biliary cirrhosis. The median survival to death or transplantation is approximately 12 years, with a range up to 21 years. Actuarial survival is greater for asymptomatic patients (10-year survival of 80%) than for symptomatic patients (10-year survival of 50%).

No treatment slows disease progression, prevents cholangiocarcinoma, or increases survival. Medical therapy includes treatment of cholangitis and endoscopic therapy of large strictures by balloon dilation and stent insertion. Surgery is avoided, if possible, because it increases the risk of recurrent cholangitis. Immunosuppressive therapy is not effective. In randomized trials, UDCA (15 mg/kg/day) has improved bilirubin, alkaline phosphatase, and albumin levels but provided no definite benefit on survival or time to liver decompensation. Higher doses (20 mg/kg) are often used because some preliminary reports have suggested a better biochemical response to these doses.

Liver transplantation, which is the only potentially curative therapy, provides an actuarial survival of 83% at 1 year and 73% at 5 years. All patients with primary sclerosing cholangitis who undergo transplantation should be screened periodically for colon carcinoma because they have chronic colitis (Chapter 200). Recurrent primary sclerosing cholangitis after transplantation is rare and difficult to distinguish from other causes of bile duct injury. If small (<1 cm), incidental cholangiocarcinomas are found at transplantation, survival is not affected, but larger cholangiocarcinomas (>2 cm) detected in the pretransplant evaluation by CT or MRI are a contraindication to liver transplantation. Patients with primary sclerosing cholangitis should be screened for possible cholangiocarcinoma by cholangiography of strictures every 6 to 12 months with brushings and biopsies. If cholangiocarcinoma is detected, patients should be offered surgical resection or radiotherapy (see later text).

Vanishing Bile Duct Syndromes

Vanishing bile duct syndromes are characterized by a paucity of intrahepatic bile ducts and by eventual cholestasis and biliary cirrhosis. Causes include primary biliary cirrhosis (Chapter 156), primary sclerosing cholangitis, autoimmune hepatitis (Chapter 152), graft-versus-host disease, chronic liver allograft rejection (Chapter 157), ischemia, intrahepatic chemotherapy, drug toxicity (e.g., ampicillin, amoxicillin, flucloxacillin, erythromycin, tetracycline, doxycycline, cotrimoxazole), HIV infection (Chapter 416), sarcoidosis (Chapter 91), idiopathic or paraneoplastic bile duct paucity, and histiocytosis. Almost all of these conditions present with chronic cholestasis and elevations in the alkaline phosphatase level. Treatment is for the complications of cholestasis, and UDCA (15 mg/kg) is given to increase bile flow. Most of these conditions are slowly progressive and result in biliary cirrhosis, which ultimately requires liver transplantation.

Cholangiocarcinoma

Cholangiocarcinoma accounts for less than 0.2% of all human malignancies. Its incidence, however, has increased significantly in

Table 158–7 • DISEASES ASSOCIATED WITH SCLEROSING CHOLANGITIS

PRIMARY SCLEROSING CHOLANGITIS	SECONDARY SCLEROSING CHOLANGITIS
Ulcerative colitis	Choledocholithiasis
Crohn's colitis or ileocolitis	Infections in immunocompromised
Type 1 autoimmune hepatitis	patients (*Cryptosporidium*, *Trichosporon*, cytomegalovirus, *Cryptococcus*, visceral protothecosis)
	HTLV-1–associated myelopathy
	Ischemic injury to the hepatic artery or arterioles
	Trauma
	Neoplasia
	Toxic injury
	Floxuridine (hepatic artery injection)
	Formalin injection of echinococcal cysts
	Congenital abnormalities
	Celiac sprue

the United States over the past 2 decades, with a parallel increase in the associated mortality to about 2500 to 3000 deaths per year. Tumors can occur at any point along the bile ducts, with 40 to 60% occurring at the hepatic hilum as so-called Klatskin's tumors. Risk factors for cholangiocarcinoma include primary sclerosing cholangitis, congenital choledochal cysts, Caroli's disease, hepatolithiasis, parasitic infection, and toxic exposure. Genetic factors have been suggested by mutations in certain oncogenes, such as p53 and K-Ras. More than 90% of malignant tumors are adenocarcinomas of high-grade scirrhous, nodular, or papillary forms. Patients commonly present with cholestasis, abdominal pain, insidious weight loss, marked increases in the serum alkaline phosphatase level, and variable increases in serum bilirubin and aminotransferase levels. A novel tumor marker, CA19-9, is elevated in up to 80% of cholangiocarcinomas. Type I tumors are confined to the inferior aspect of the bile duct confluence; type II tumors involve the superior aspect and prevent communication between the right and left ductal systems; type IIIa and IIIb tumors extend into the segmental branches of the right and left main hepatic ducts, respectively; and type IV tumors involve the segmental branches of both right and left hepatic ducts.

Abdominal CT, angiography, and MRCP or cholangiography are used to stage the disease and determine resectability. Bilateral involvement of secondary radicles, encasement or occlusion of the hepatic artery or portal vein, and lung, liver, or peritoneal metastases are contraindications to surgery. Surgery, which is the optimal therapy in patients without contraindications, should include bile duct excision and hepatic resection. Following complete surgical excision, adjuvant radiation alone or combined with chemotherapy is aimed at preventing local recurrence, but there is little demonstrable survival benefit.

In the 50 to 90% of patients who present with unresectable disease, palliative treatment is focused on the alleviation of pain, pruritus, and jaundice and on improving the quality of life. Surgical bypass gives the best results but carries a high procedure-related complication and mortality rate, so endoscopic biliary drainage and endoprosthesis insertion via ERCP or PTC may be preferred in many patients. Photodynamic therapy may benefit some patients who fail stent insertion. Liver transplantation is disappointing because recurrence is almost universal.

Disorders of the Ampulla of Vater

The ampulla of Vater represents the final sphincter that controls the entry of bile into the duodenum. Hormonal control of the sphincter is mediated by cholecystokinin, which causes the gallbladder to contract and the ampulla to relax. The most common disorder of the ampulla is stenosis or dysfunction after cholecystectomy, the so-called sphincter of Oddi dysfunction.

SPHINCTER OF ODDI DYSFUNCTION OR BILIARY DYSKINESIA.
In true sphincter stenosis, the sphincter is narrowed by inflammation and fibrosis owing to pancreatitis, passage of a gallstone through the papilla, intraoperative trauma, infection, or adenomas. Sphincter stenosis can present with abdominal pain and pancreatitis. The common bile duct is often dilated above the stenosis, and treatment is a large sphincterotomy performed at ERCP.

In sphincter of Oddi dyskinesia, a functional disorder of the sphincter leads to intermittent biliary obstruction. Most patients have had cholecystectomies and present with recurrent biliary pain or, less frequently, pancreatitis. Diagnosis is usually by ERCP, which can demonstrate delayed excretion of contrast. In patients who have pain associated with abnormal aminotransferases on two or more occasions, a dilated common bile duct, and delayed drainage of contrast, sphincterotomy is recommended. Patients without all three of these criteria are usually given a trial of relaxants, such as nitrates or calcium channel blockers.

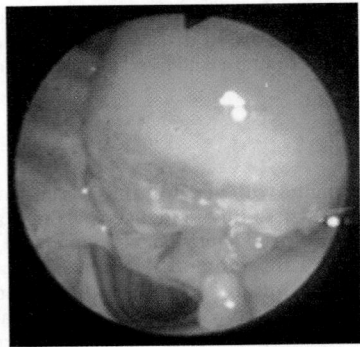

FIGURE 158–5 • Carcinoma of the ampulla of Vater. The carcinoma is seen toward the bottom of the picture. The bulging swelling above is the grossly dilated common bile duct, which is obstructed by the carcinoma. (From Forbes CD, Jackson WF: Color Atlas and Text of Clinical Medicine, 3rd ed. London, Mosby, 2003, with permission.)

AMPULLARY TUMORS. Adenocarcinoma of the ampulla has an incidence of 3 per million. Adenomas appear as protruding ampullary lesions, may grow either inside the ampulla or into the duodenum, and can transform into adenocarcinomas (Fig. 158–5). The cancer tends to be locally invasive. Ampullary adenomas are associated with familial polyposis coli (Chapter 200) and the FAP gene: almost 80% of patients with the FAP gene have adenomas of the ampulla, and their risk of ampullary cancer is 100-fold that of the normal population.

The average age at diagnosis is 50 years, with a peak at 70 years; there is no gender predilection. About 80% of patients present with jaundice, which is usually progressive and associated with abdominal pain and weight loss. Liver enzymes are usually abnormal, and the diagnosis is suggested by US or CT findings of dilated biliary and pancreatic ducts all the way to the ampulla. Confirmation is by endoscopy with biopsy and brushings. Staging of the tumor, particularly for lesions growing into the ampulla, can be best performed by endoscopic US. Adenomas and small cancers can be removed by endoscopic ampullectomy. The standard recommended curative operation is a pancreaticoduodenectomy (the Whipple procedure), which provides a 25 to 55% 5-year survival depending on the extent of the tumor. Adjuvant chemotherapy and radiotherapy have no proven benefit in the therapy of ampullary lesions.

1. Lo C, Liu C, Lai E, et al: Early versus delayed laparoscopic cholecystectomy for treatment of acute cholecystitis. Ann Surg 1996;223;37–42.
2. Boerma D, Rauws EA, Keulemans YC, et al: Wait-and-see policy or laparoscopic cholecystectomy after endoscopic sphincterotomy for bile-duct stones: A randomised trial. Lancet 2002;360:761–765.
3. Shiffman ML, Kaplan GD, Brinkman-Kaplan V, Vickers FF: Prevention of gallstone formation with ursodeoxycholic acid in patients participating in a very low calorie diet program. Ann Intern Med 1995;122:899–905.
4. Lindor KD: Ursodiol for primary sclerosing cholangitis. Mayo Primary Sclerosing Cholangitis-Ursodeoxycholic Acid Study group. N Engl J Med 1997;336:691–695.

SUGGESTED READINGS
Afdhal NH (ed): Gallbladder and Biliary Tract Disease. Marcel Dekker, New York, 2000. *A comprehensive review of basic physiology, pathology, and clinical diseases of the gallbladder and biliary tract.*
Byrnes V, Afdhal NH: Cholangiocarcinoma of the hepatic hilum (Klatskin tumor). Current Treatment Options in Gastroenterology 2002;6:87–94. *A complete review of treatment options for cholangiocarcinoma.*
Hawn MT: Gallbladder and biliary tract disease in the intensive care unit. Semin Gastrointest Dis 2003;14:28–33. *A lucid overview.*

part XIV

Hematologic Diseases

159 HEMATOPOIESIS AND HEMATOPOIETIC GROWTH FACTORS

Peter J. Quesenberry

The production of hematopoietic and lymphoid cells is complex but tightly regulated. The system is exquisitely responsive to functional needs. Red blood cell (erythroid) production changes with tissue oxygen levels; neutrophil and monocyte production responds to noxious foreign stimuli, especially bacterial infection; and platelet levels respond to blood loss, tissue damage, and platelet deficiency.

Lymphohematopoietic cells, which are produced by a very small number of marrow cells, termed *stem cells*, proliferate, differentiate, and self-renew. Stem cells respond to inductive stimuli and differentiate to progenitor cells (Table 159–1) that are progressively restricted in their potential for proliferation, differentiation, and self-renewal

but that have increasing functional characteristics as defined by their specific lineages (Fig. 159–1). An alternative cell-cycle model postulates that stem cells may represent phenotypic shifts in a reversible continuum and that differentiation comes from different phenotypes in the continuum (Fig. 159–2).

In either model, differentiation results in the cell lineages recognizable by standard Wright-Giemsa stains as erythroid, granulocytic, monocytic, lymphoid, or megakaryocytic. These events occur continuously with a large turnover of differentiated cells, as illustrated by the blood lifespan of human erythrocytes (120 days), platelets (10 days), and granulocytes (9 hours). The lifespans of lymphocytes (T and B cells) vary tremendously from hours to years. The production of different types of blood cells occurs predominantly in the bone marrow, but the spleen, lymph nodes, and accessory lymphoid tissues are also ongoing sites of lymphoid cell production; under stress, myeloid cell production also occurs at these sites. The end cells produced in the marrow are released into the blood stream under various stimuli and circulate in the blood. With the exception of erythrocytes and platelets, these cells emigrate to tissues where they have variable

Table 159–1 • STEM AND PROGENITOR CELLS (HIERARCHICAL MODEL)

CHARACTERISTIC	STEM CELL	PROGENITOR CELL
Proliferative potential	Tremendous	More limited
Renewal	On a population basis	Probably none
Potential for differentiation	All lymphohematopoietic lineages	Restricted
Differentiated characteristics	Minimal—lineage negative	Progressively increases
Functional characteristics	Rapid directed motility and expression of proteopodia; homing	Less defined
Cycle status	Dormant	Cycling
Cytokine responsiveness	Large number of cytokines needed for expression of phenotype	Restricted
Cell of origin	Unknown	Stem cell
Staining with rhodamine and Hoechst dyes (partial measure of p170 pump activity)	Active p170 pump—stains dimly	Less active p170 pump—rhodamine "bright"
Producing long-term hematopoiesis after in vivo transplant	Defines cells	Limited to none
Adheres to marrow stroma	Yes	No or limited

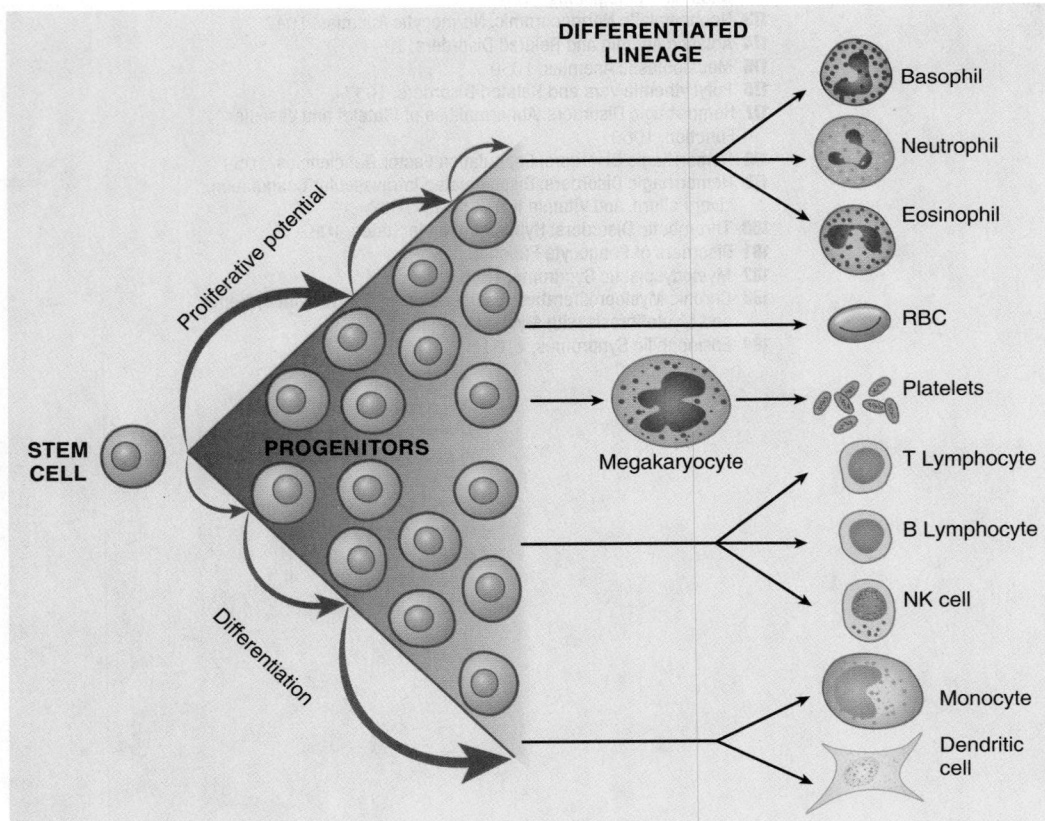

FIGURE 159–1 • Hierarchical model of lymphohematopoiesis. NK = natural killer cell; RBC = red blood cell.

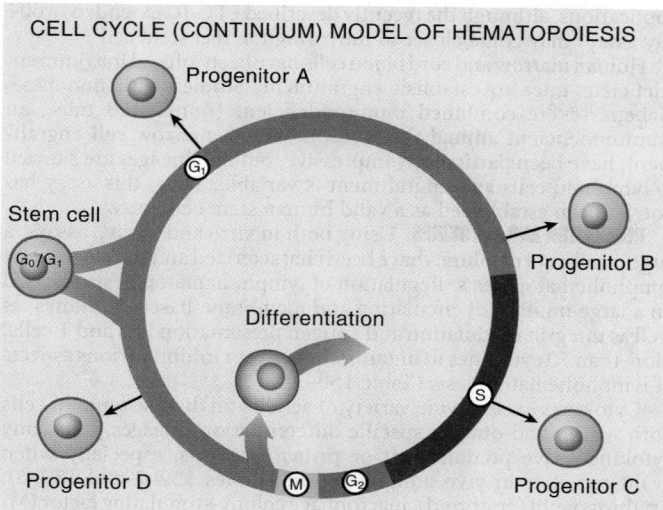

CELL CYCLE (CONTINUUM) MODEL OF HEMATOPOIESIS

FIGURE 159–2 • Cell-cycle–based model of stem cell regulation.

lifespans: days for granulocytes and weeks to years for monocytes, macrophages, and lymphocytes.

Lymphohematopoiesis

The classically recognizable differentiated marrow lineages represent the end stages of a carefully orchestrated production system. Progenitors and possibly stem cells (the continuum model) feed into the various blast compartments (myeloblast, proerythroblast, lymphoblast, and megakaryoblast), which, in turn, feed into lineages that show increasingly differentiated characteristics while losing proliferative potency. Myeloblasts become promyelocytes, which then differentiate into myelocytes, the stage at which neutrophilic (Fig. 159–3), eosinophilic, and basophilic lineages are distinguished. Erythrocyte and platelet lineages result in anucleate functional cells, whereas B, T, and NK lymphocyte lineages give rise to a variety of effector cell populations. This system is an irreversible in-out production system, with final demise of end cells occurring in the blood stream (platelets and red cells) or tissues (all others).

Stem Cell Ontogeny

Early multipotent stem cells are present in the yolk sac and in mesenchymal tissues. These stem cells subsequently traffic predominantly to the liver (and to a lesser extent the kidney), followed by the establishment of marrow as the major site of active hematopoiesis. The earlier in ontogeny that stem cells are harvested, the greater their proliferative potential, as illustrated by the proliferative

and growth potential of fetal liver and cord blood cells in clinical transplantation.

The hematopoietic cell in both murine and human species has been characterized regarding its surface proteins and physical, metabolic, and cell cycle characteristics; these characteristics have been used physically to purify stem cells (Fig. 159–4). Early stem cells differentially express more than 2000 nonredundant genes involved with energy metabolism, signaling pathways, cell cycle regulation, chromatin, the translational apparatus, DNA metabolism, transcription factors, surface proteins, cytoskeleton, the mitochondria apparatus, and membrane trafficking. Early stem cells do not express many differentiated cell functions, but they do express functions involving movement and membrane deformation, probably as part of their homing function. Recent work indicates a high degree of functional plasticity with cell cycle transit and reversible fluctuations of cell surface–based markers such as CD34. The most primitive marrow stem cells are either slowly cycling or intermittently entering the cell cycle, and their phenotype changes reversibly with cell cycle. Traditionally, primitive stem cells have been thought to give rise to committed progenitors (the hierarchical model) (Figs. 159–1 and 159–5), but recent data suggest that there may be a continuum whereby stem cells convert to progenitor cells and then back to stem cells (see Fig. 159–2); if so, progenitor cells might not be a discrete class of cells. Some cells may divide to give rise to two stem cells, and some divide into two differentiating cells, but the most common outcome is probably an asymmetrical stem cell division in which the stem cell divides and gives rise to another stem cell and a differentiating cell. Apoptosis presumably also modifies the system.

LYMPHOHEMATOPOIETIC STEM CELL (CLASSIC SYSTEM). The existence of a stem cell common to all lymphoid and myeloid lineages was established by studies in mice in which the infusion of a single cytogenetically or retrovirally marked stem cell gave rise to all cell lineages, which then persisted over time. Sustained in vivo engraftment is the "gold standard" for the true stem cell, although different subpopulations may show different engraftment kinetics, ranging from weeks to more than a year in the mouse. The engrafting cell, which is quiescent or dormant but slowly cycling over time, appears to have high p170 pump activity (stains low for rhodamine, a p170-pumped dye). The existence of a similar multipotent stem cell in humans was inferred from studies of marrow and blood cells from patients with chronic myelogenous leukemia, in whom all lineages were marked with the Philadelphia chromosome, and from glucose-6-phosphate dehydrogenase studies of patients with myeloproliferative disorders.

There is not an in vivo engraftment assay in humans, but three in vitro assays appear to measure relatively primitive multilineage cells and have been proposed as true surrogates for the long-term renewable lymphohematopoietic stem cell. The colony-forming unit–blast (an assay in which marrow cells give rise to small colonies of primitive blast cells), with extensive proliferative and differentiative potential, may in fact be a good surrogate, but few laboratories have mastered this technique, so it is not generally applicable. The high proliferative potential colony-forming cell, an assay in which marrow cells proliferate in the presence of combinations of growth factors to give rise to large (>0.5 mm) colonies in vitro, also appears to be

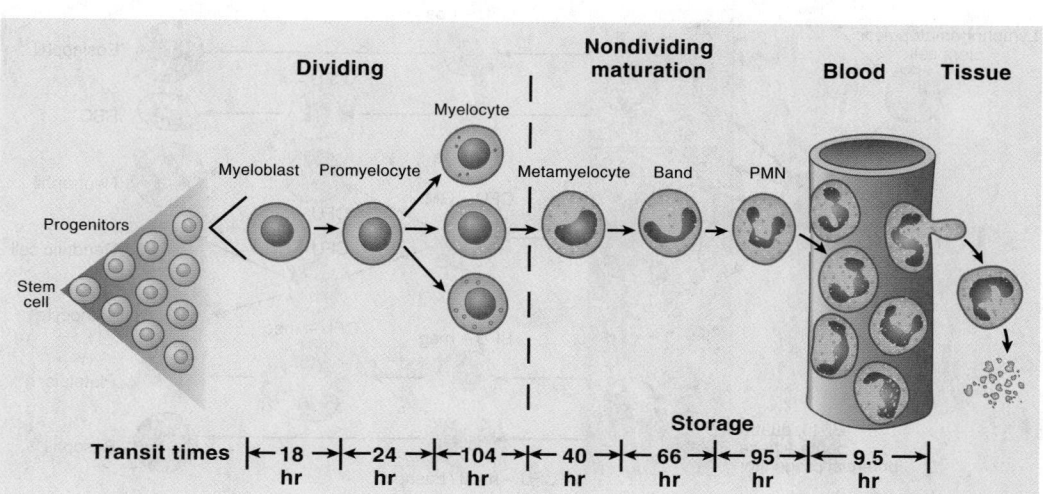

FIGURE 159–3 • Neutrophil production system. PMN = polymorphonuclear leukocyte.

Transit times	⊢ 18 →	← 24 →	← 104 →	← 40 →	← 66 →	← 95 →	← 9.5 →
	hr	hr	hr	hr	hr	hr	hr

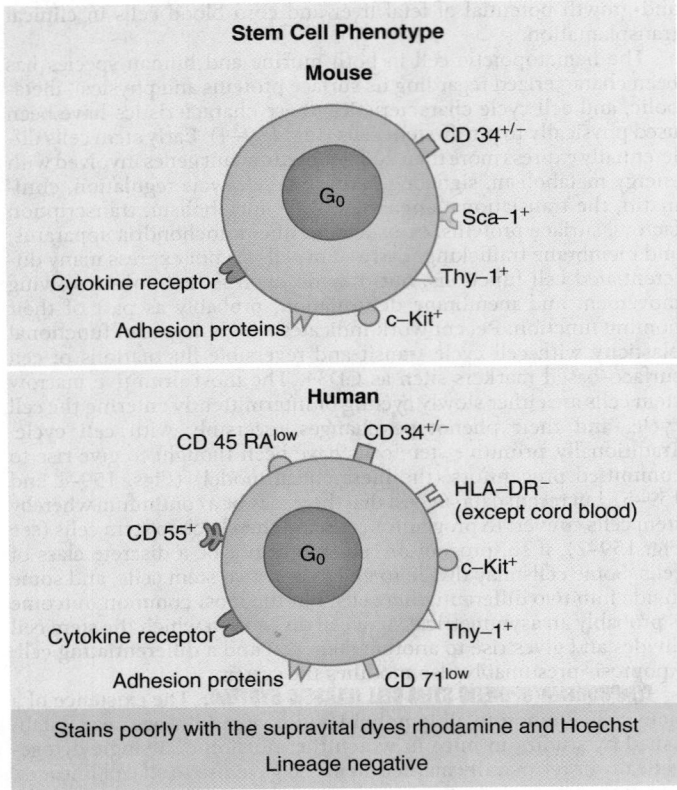

Stem Cell Phenotype

Mouse

G_0

CD 34$^{+/-}$

Sca–1$^+$

Thy–1$^+$

c–Kit$^+$

Cytokine receptor

Adhesion proteins

Human

CD 45 RA^{low} CD 34$^{+/-}$

HLA–DR$^-$
(except cord blood)

CD 55$^+$

G_0

c–Kit$^+$

Thy–1$^+$

CD 71^{low}

Cytokine receptor

Adhesion proteins

Stains poorly with the supravital dyes rhodamine and Hoechst

Lineage negative

FIGURE 159–4 • Characteristics of the lymphohematopoietic stem cell.

a reasonable surrogate and is probably the best generally available. The stromal-based assays, long-term culture-initiating cell (LTC-IC) and cobblestone-forming assays, are of interest, but appear to monitor both primitive and more differentiated cells and are difficult to reproduce. These assays, in which marrow cells grow on an adherent stromal layer, remain interesting research areas without practical

applications, although the recently described LTC-IC extended (a 60+ day assay) may come closer to mirroring the real stem cell.

Human marrow and cord blood cells have been infused into immunodeficient mice to establish engraftment. Studies with nonobese, diabetic severe combined immunodeficient (non-SCID) mice, an immunodeficient animal that accepts human marrow cell engraftment, have been particularly impressive, but the lineages are skewed to lymphoid cells and engraftment is variable. Thus, this assay has not yet been established as a valid human stem cell assay.

REGULATION AND CYTOKINES. Using both in vitro and in vivo assays, a large number of cytokines have been characterized and shown to affect lymphohematopoiesis. Regulation of lymphohematopoiesis is based on a large number of circulating and membrane-based cytokines, as well as integrin modulation and antigen presentation to B and T cells. More than 70 cytokines maintain, stimulate, or inhibit various aspects of lymphohematopoiesis (Table 159–2).

Cytokines exert a wide variety of actions on diverse types of cells both within and outside specific differentiation lineages, but many cytokines have predominant or primary actions, especially when evaluated after in vivo administration (Tables 159–2 and 159–3). Erythropoietin (erythroid), macrophage colony-stimulating factor (M-CSF), and granulocyte-CSF (G-CSF) are cytokines with a relatively high degree of specificity. Most cytokines, however, have multiple actions. Examples include interleukin (IL)-6, which acts on primitive stem cells as well as lymphoid, granulocyte, megakaryocyte, and macrophage lineages, and IL-3, which impacts virtually all lineages. IL-1 induces many other cytokines and illustrates the difficulty in ascertaining primary or secondary effects, especially with the potential for paracrine or autocrine loops.

Most cells produce multiple cytokines, which can be differentially induced by various stimuli, including other cytokines, such as IL-1. The suggestion that "everything makes everything" is perhaps too drastic, but also not too far off target. The key is differential production in response to different stimuli, and probably in local production. Monocytes, T lymphocytes, endothelial cells, fibroblasts, and "marrow stromal" cells are important sources of lymphohematopoietic cytokines. Erythropoietin is an exception to the general rule, because it is largely produced in the kidney in response to hypoxia, although it can also be produced by the liver. Stimuli that induce white blood cell formation are, in general, related to exposure to foreign or noxious agents, whereas platelet production occurs in response to hemorrhage, anemia, and thrombocytopenia.

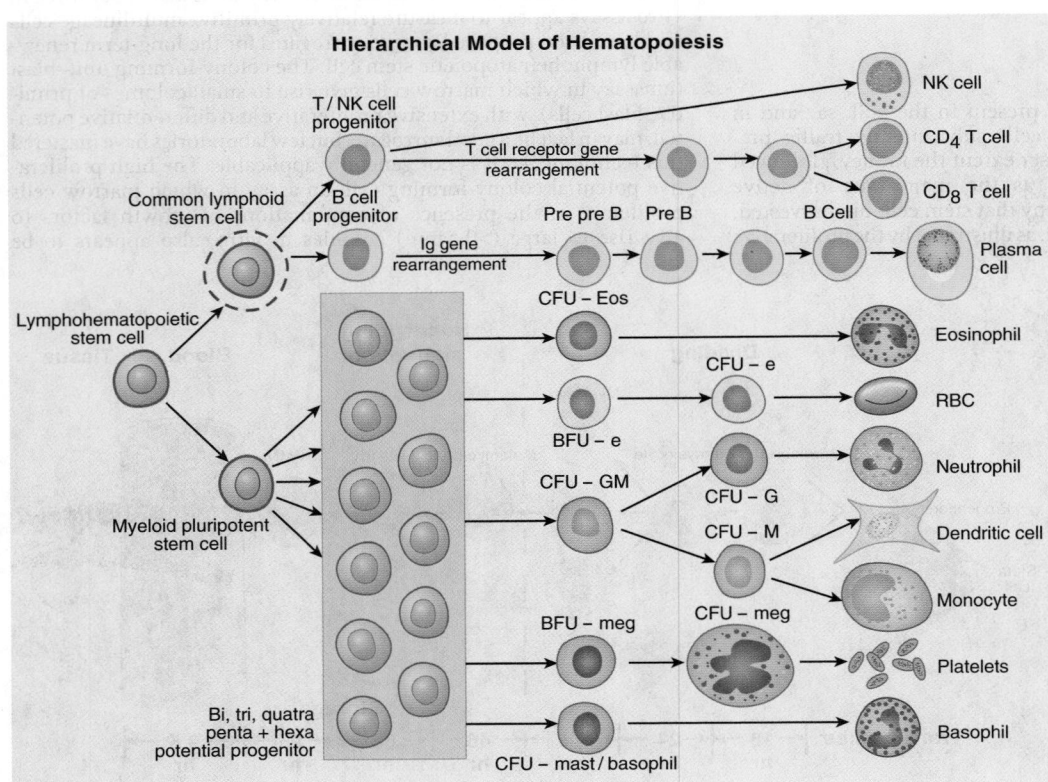

Hierarchical Model of Hematopoiesis

T / NK cell progenitor

NK cell

T cell receptor gene rearrangement

CD$_4$ T cell

CD$_8$ T cell

Common lymphoid stem cell

B cell progenitor

Pre pre B   Pre B   B Cell

Ig gene rearrangement

Plasma cell

Lymphohematopoietic stem cell

CFU – Eos

Eosinophil

CFU – e

RBC

BFU – e

CFU – GM

CFU – G

Neutrophil

Myeloid pluripotent stem cell

CFU – M

Dendritic cell

Monocyte

BFU – meg

CFU – meg

Platelets

Bi, tri, quatra penta + hexa potential progenitor

Basophil

CFU – mast / basophil

FIGURE 159–5 • Hierarchical model of stem cell regulation.

Table 159–2 • CYTOKINES ACTIVE ON LYMPHOHEMATOPOIETIC STEM CELLS

CYTOKINE	PRINCIPAL OR HIGHLIGHTED ACTIVITY
INTERLEUKINS	
IL-1	Induces production of other cytokines from many cells: co-stimulates early stem cells with other cytokines; modulates immune response.
IL-2	T-cell growth factor; inhibits myelopoiesis and erythropoiesis.
IL-3	Multilineage stimulator—myeloid, erythroid, lymphoid, and megakaryocytic; in vivo increases blood monocytes and granulocytes including eosinophils and platelets.
IL-4	Stimulates B cells and dendritic cells and modulates immune response; co-stimulates CFU-GM and CFU-E.
IL-5	Simulates B cells and eosinophils.
IL-6	Stimulates megakaryopoiesis and synergizes with IL-1, IL-2, IL-3, IL-4, GM-CSF, and CSF-1; enhances plasma cell proliferation; role in Castleman's disease and atrial myxoma.
IL-7	Stimulates pre-B cells (with steel factor) and early stem cells.
IL-8	Stimulates production and function of neutrophils; acts as proinflammatory factor.
IL-9	Co-stimulates CFU-GM and CFU-MIX; stimulates BFU-E with erythropoietin; enhances T-cell production and, with IL-3, mast cell production.
IL-10	Inhibits cytokine production, modulates immune cells, and stimulates mast cells.
IL-11	Shares most of activities of IL-6; increases neutrophils and platelets in blood in primate model.
IL-12	Increases generation of immunocompetent cells.
IL-13	Enhances steel factor–induced proliferation of Lin– Sca+ murine marrow stem cells; inhibits cytokine production by monocytes; stimulates B cells and activates T cells.
IL-14	B-cell growth factor.
IL-15	Modulates T-cell activity.
IL-16	Acts as immunomodulator.
IL-17	Induces production of other cytokines such as IL-6, IL-8, and G-CSF, and enhances expression of adhesion molecules.
IL-18	Induces GM-CSF and interferon-γ production; inhibits IL-10 production.
COLONY-STIMULATING FACTORS, ERYTHROPOIETIN, AND EARLY-ACTING FACTORS	
CSF-I	Enhances production and function of monocytes.
G-CSF	Stimulates granulocyte production and function; co-stimulates early progenitors in synergy with a number of cytokines; stimulates pre-B cells; in vivo stimulates granulocyte production.
GM-CSF	Stimulates GM-CFC and production of monocytes, granulocytes, eosinophils, and basophils; synergizes with IL-4 to produce dendritic cells; co-stimulates many types of progenitors, including early multipotent stem cells.
Erythropoietin	Stimulates erythrocyte production in vitro and in vivo; co-stimulates BFU-E and CFU-MEG and stimulates CFU-E.
FLT-3 ligand	Co-stimulates multipotential stem cells, especially with thrombopoietin and steel factor; stimulates generation of dendritic cells.
Steel factor	Similar to FLT-3; enhances generation of mast cells.
Thrombopoietin, c-mpl ligand	Major regulator of proliferation and differentiation of megakaryocytes; co-stimulates multipotential stem cells in combination with steel factor and IL-11; promotes erythropoiesis in synergy with erythropoietin.
CYTOKINE INHIBITORY FACTORS AND OTHERS	
MIP-1 α	Inhibits early multipotent colony formation but stimulates that of committed precursors.
TGF-β	Suppresses early multipotent progenitors but stimulates later progenitors.
MCAF, platelet factor 4, H-ferritin	Similar to TGF-β
TNF-α	Similar to TGF-β, but a more pronounced effect on BFU-E and CFU-E.
Activin	Enhances IL-3 and erythropoietin-stimulated BFU-E and CFU-E; inhibits IL-3–stimulated CFU-GM.
Inhibin	Inhibits CFU-MIX, CFU-GM, and BFU-E.
Interferon-α, β, and γ	Co-inhibits CFU-MIX, CFU-GM, and BFU-E; inhibits production of cytokines; immune modulator.
Prostaglandin E₂	Suppresses CFU-M with less or no activity on CFU-GM and CFU-G; enhances BFU-E indirectly through CD8+ lymphocytes.
Glu-Glu-Asp-Asp-Lys (pentapeptide)	Inhibits CFU-S proliferation and CFU-GM.
N-acetyl-Ser-As-Lys-Pro (tetrapeptide)	Inhibits CFU-S and other progenitors' entry into cell cycle.
Leukemia inhibitory factor	Inhibits GM-CSF– and G-CSF–stimulated CFU-GM and CFU-G, respectively.
Insulin-like growth factor II	Stimulates erythroid and granulocyte progenitors.
Hepatocyte growth factor (scatter factor)	Synergistic activity on progenitors.
Basic fibroblast growth factor	Acts in concert with other cytokines on early multipotential and megakaryocyte progenitors.
Platelet-derived growth factor	Stimulates erythroid and granulocyte progenitors.

BFU-E = blast-forming unit–erythroid; CFU-E = colony-forming unit–erythroid; CFU-G = colony-forming unit–granulocyte; CFU-GM = colony-forming unit–granulocyte-macrophage; CFU-M = colony-forming unit–macrophage; CFU-MEG = colony-forming unit–megakaryocytes; CFU-S = colony-forming unit–spleen; G-CSF = granulocyte colony-stimulating factor; GM-CFC = granulocyte-macrophage colony-forming cell; GM-CSF = granulocyte-macrophage colony-stimulating factor; MIP-1 = macrophage inhibitory protein-1; TGF-β = transforming growth factor-beta; TNF-α = tumor necrosis factor-alpha.

Perhaps the best way to define the cytokine responsiveness of a particular cell class is to characterize its cytokine receptor expression. Each cytokine has its private receptor, but different cytokines may share class-specific signal transducers. Many receptors dimerize on cytokine binding and then activate tyrosine kinase, thereby promoting phosphorylation of intracellular proteins; other receptors do not have intrinsic enzymatic activity but induce protein phosphorylation through associated non–receptor-type tyrosine kinase activities, such as JAK2, Fes, and Lyn. Receptors are expressed in low numbers and do not exceed a few hundred per cell. The multipotent repopulating stem cell possesses receptors for most cytokines, but more mature cells have a more restricted distribution of receptors.

Two major receptor families have been described. First, the hematopoietic receptor family includes IL-2, IL-3, IL-4, IL-5, IL-6, IL-7, IL-9, G-CSF, granulocyte-macrophage CSF (GM-CSF), and erythropoietin. The extracellular binding domains of these receptors contain four conserved cysteine residues and a WS-X-WS motif (X is a variable nonconserved amino acid). Some also have an immunoglobulin-like structure. Receptors for GM-CSF, IL-3, and IL-5 each contain specific low-affinity α-chains, but a high-affinity β-chain is shared by all three receptors. The common β-chain plays a role in the competitive binding of these ligands. Second, the tyrosine kinase receptor family includes receptors for FLT3-ligand, steel factor (c-*kit* ligand), CSF-1, and thrombopoietin. These receptors have an

Table 159–3 • CHARACTERISTICS OF LYMPHOHEMATOPOIETIC CYTOKINES

Are glycoproteins

Act on cell surface receptors

Initiate complex second messenger and transcriptional and post-transcriptional regulation

May act on stem cells, progenitor cells, and differentiated cells of the same lineage

May act on multiple different lineages (e.g., erythroid, granulocyte, and lymphoid)

Stimulate or inhibit proliferation, apoptosis, differentiation, or function

Usually act on neoplastic counterpart of normal target cell

---

immunoglobulin-like structure and 10 conserved cysteines in the extracellular domain, with tyrosine kinase activity in the cytoplasmic domain. Receptors not fitting into these families include those for IL-1 and IL-8.

Signaling through these receptors activates transcription factors that then may direct differentiation toward specific lineages. For example, GATA-1 and FOG promote erythroid and megakaryocyte differentiation, whereas SCL, AML-1, and GATA-2 regulate primitive stem cell differentiation. A sequential pathway determining myeloid and lymphoid development appears to work through jagged-based signaling to notch then activating PU.1; PU.1 (and GATA-1) then signals development of myeloid differentiation. Conversely, low PU.1 levels in concert with Ikarios expression signal lymphoid differentiation. Physical combinations of various transcription factors appear critical for mediating these effects.

Adhesion molecules function both to bind cells or extracellular matrix and as signaling molecules. Steel factor, IL-3, and GM-CSF activate very late antigens 4 and 5 (VLA-4 and VLA-5), which are adhesion molecules expressed on CD34-positive cells. This activation results in promotion of the ability of VLA-4 and VLA-5 to bind fibronectin. Other adhesion proteins important in hematopoiesis include stromal-derived growth factor-1 (SDF1) and CD44. Stromal or microenvironmental cells are major regulators of hematopoiesis, both by positioning stem/progenitor cells and by signaling with secreted and membrane-based cytokines. Homing studies indicate that long-term repopulating lymphohematopoietic stem cells move closely adjacent to osteogenic surfaces; others have suggested that bone cells are major stem cell regulators.

These regulatory influences affect hematopoietic lineages in a variety of ways. An important effect of erythropoietin on erythrocyte progenitors and precursors is to prevent apoptosis and thus maintain the viability of these cells. Cell cycle transit and the induction of proliferation are major effects of many of the early acting cytokines, such as steel factor, and all lineages exhibit cytokine-modulated differentiation. Erythropoietin induces erythroid hemoglobinization, G-CSF causes the acquisition of myeloid enzymes in granulocytes, and thrombopoietin induces the expression of platelet-specific proteins. Thus, differentiation is a general feature, although whether this is specifically cytokine-mediated induction from a multipotent cell or simply a manifestation of survival of cells with a genetic probability of differentiation into a specific lineage remains an area of controversy. Regulatory influences also affect the function of many end cells, such as granulocytes, monocytes, T cells, B cells, NK cells, and dendritic cells. These data are consistent with either a hierarchical or continuum model of hemopoiesis.

STEM CELL PLASTICITY: FUNCTIONAL AND HIERARCHICAL.

Recent studies indicate that bone marrow–derived hematopoietic stem cells have much greater potential than previously realized. Marrow cells are capable of giving rise to cardiac myocytes, keratinocytes, pneumocytes, hepatocytes, neural cells, skeletal muscle, and a variety of mesenchymal cells including cartilage, fat, and bone. Several murine studies have shown quantitatively significant replacement of cardiac and hepatic cells in models of cardiac ischemia and liver failure. More importantly, improved cardiac and hepatic function was also seen. In one intriguing study, a single purified marrow hematopoietic stem cell was shown by limiting dilution techniques to give rise to hematopoietic cells and to a wide variety of nonhematopoietic cells; such cells might possibly be used to restore tissue in various disease states. Other studies have suggested that muscle, neural, or hepatic cells could give rise to hematopoietic cells.

Another form of hematopoietic plasticity is functional plasticity tied to the cell cycle. Continuing studies have indicated that all stem cells continuously or intermittently enter the cell cycle; during cell cycle transit, the stem cell phenotype continually and reversibly changes. These data suggest that a primitive stem cell and a progenitor may present a phenotypic continuum rather than being part of a hierarchy and, in fact, that there may not be a discrete population of hematopoietic progenitors.

MOBILIZATION OF STEM/PROGENITOR CELLS.

Engraftable, long-term repopulating stem cells and their progenitors are easily mobilized into the peripheral blood by a number of cytokines, including G-CSF, steel factor, FLT-3, IL-11, IL-12, IL-3, IL-8, IL-7, MIP-1α, and erythropoietin. In addition, previous exposure to cyclophosphamide or other cytotoxic agents also mobilizes stem cells, presumably through the actions of cytokines. Pretreatment with cyclophosphamide followed by treatment with steel factor and G-CSF may be the most potent regimen for mobilizing stem/progenitor cells. In general, mobilized stem/progenitor cells appear to restore hematoopoiesis more rapidly than unstimulated marrow, although marrow that has been primed with in vivo cytokines may be equivalent to mobilized peripheral blood cells for rapid engraftment. Whether these mobilized stem cells have the same long-term repopulation capacity as marrow cells remains to be established.

STEM/PROGENITOR CELL EXPANSION.

The ability to expand lymphohematopoietic stem cells in vitro has immediate implications for strategies of repetitive transplant, immunotherapy, and gene therapy. A large number of studies have established that exposure of marrow cells to a variety of cytokines in liquid culture leads to differentiation and progenitor cell expansion. These cells can also be effective in transplantation, but as yet no study has established expansion of long-term engraftable stem cells, and studies have shown that cytokine stimulation of marrow stem cells can lead to fluctuations in engraftment phenotype that are reversible and correlate with phase of cell cycle; engraftment tends to be lost in the late S/early G_2 phase.

HOMING AND ENGRAFTMENT OF STEM CELLS.

Historic dogma had contended incorrectly that marrow transplant recipients needed to be treated with cytotoxic agents, usually irradiation and/or cytotoxic drugs, to open space in the marrow for stem cells to engraft. In fact, marrow stem cells engraft quantitatively in nontreated hosts, and the final ratio of donor to host cells after transplantation appears to be determined simply by the ratio of donor to host stem cells (Chapter 166). Homing to marrow appears complete within several hours, and engrafted stem cells rapidly enter the cell cycle after intravenous infusion (within 12 hours). They move to the bone surface, giving rise to both hematopoietic and bone cells. The blood stream clears quickly of stem cells, and there appears to be virtually no primary thymic engraftment, although secondary engraftment of the thymus occurs later. These observations form the basis for the current minitransplant approaches, although additional steps are necessary in the allogeneic setting to ensure engraftment and avoid graft-versus-host disease.

Therapeutic Uses of Stem Cells and Cytokines

DIAGNOSIS.

A number of diseases appear to be caused by abnormalities of stem cells or cytokines. Diseases of deranged or deficient stem cells are usually manifest as cancers or as cell deficiency states (Table 159–4).

THERAPY.

Marrow transplantation (Chapter 166) represents one of the major therapeutic advances of the past 30 years. It has been successfully used to cure marrow deficiency states (e.g., aplastic anemia), genetic marrow diseases (hemoglobinopathies, enzymopathies), osteopetrosis, and a variety of predominantly marrow or lymphoid malignancies. It was initially used to restore deficient cell production (or deficient products from cells) or to restore cell populations after otherwise lethal damage by high-dose radiotherapy/chemotherapy was used to eliminate malignant cell populations; marrow transplantation circumvented the first barrier (killing of marrow stem cells) to dose escalation. More recent studies have indicated that a graft-versus-tumor effect is a major component of the therapeutic efficiency of allogeneic transplantation, thus indicating that transplantation may work in part by mediating a cellular immune attack against cancer cells. Graft-versus-tumor effects may also be operative in autologous stem cell transplantation. Marrow cells were the initial source of stem cells for transplantation, but pheresis of peripheral blood stem cells

Table 159–4 • STEM CELL DISEASES

DISEASE	MECHANISM
Aplastic anemia	Deficient multipotent stem cell: multiple causes (cell killing or immune)
Neutropenia—Kostmann's, cyclic, and others	Genetic deficiency or regulatory abnormality
Myelodysplastic syndrome	Marrow damage progressing to neoplasm
Acute myelogenous leukemia	Cytogenetic abnormality at stem cell level
Paroxysmal nocturnal hemoglobinuria	Defective glycosylphosphatidylinositol-anchored membrane proteins and mutation in the *PIG-A* gene
Chronic myelogenous leukemia	9:22 translocation moves *abl* oncogene adjacent to *bcr*
Myeloproliferative disorders: polycythemia vera, myelofibrosis, myeloid metaplasia, primary thrombocytosis	Neoplasms of multipotent stem cells
Congenital amegakaryocytic thrombocytopenia	Mutation of *cmpl* gene

Table 159–5 • INDICATIONS FOR THERAPY WITH ERYTHROPOIETIN

DISEASE/CONDITION	THERAPEUTIC EFFICACY
Anemia of renal failure	Improves quality of life and decreases transfusion requirement; there is clinical benefit
Anemia with human immunodeficiency virus induced by zidovudine with erythropoietin levels <500/mL	Approved for use in United States but clinical benefit not clear
Chemotherapy-induced anemia	Approved in United States for nonmyeloid malignancies. May be of use in selected cases with possible increased quality of life; overall benefit in this setting still unclear
Anemia of inflammation (rheumatoid arthritis and inflammatory bowel disease)	Increases hematocrit without clinical benefit; should not be used
Other conditions under evaluation: perioperative setting; autologous blood collection; anemia of prematurity; anemia of myelodysplasia, lymphoma, or leukemia; anemia with allogeneic transplantation: anemia of pure red cell aplasia; induction of hemoglobin F in sickle cell anemia or thalassemia; and adjuvant for phlebotomy	May be considered in selected individuals but benefit not established (perioperative setting with restrictions has Food and Drug Administration approval)

has supplemented marrow in autologous transplantation and is rapidly replacing it in allogeneic transplantation. Fetal liver has been used as a source of stem cells, and umbilical cord blood is becoming a major source of cells, especially for unrelated pediatric transplantation. Stem cells from these sources are also the most attractive vehicles for a variety of gene therapy approaches.

Cytokines in Therapy

The first successful use of a cytokine for a cytokine deficiency state was the use of erythropoietin to treat the anemia of renal failure. Administration of erythropoietin to patients with renal failure corrects or partially corrects the anemia and restores a better state of well-being. Erythropoietin is also used in other settings, where its benefits are less clear (Table 159–5).

Unfortunately, other cytokine deficiency states have been hard to document, and the results of cytokine therapy for other diseases (despite Food and Drug Administration [FDA] approval) are equivocal at best. A major emphasis has been placed on the use of G-CSF and GM-CSF (Table 159–6) to expedite marrow recovery after cytotoxic therapy for cancer. Initial trials indicated that administration of G-CSF enhanced granulocyte recovery and decreased febrile infectious complications. Unfortunately, the use of G-CSF or GM-CSF has not led to better control of cancer or its outcomes and may not be cost-effective. Despite FDA approval, G-CSF and GM-CSF are best considered as experimental therapies at this time. Neither G-CSF nor GM-CSF has proven effective in other conditions, such as in active infection, presumably because endogenous levels of G-CSF are already quite high in neutropenic and infected patients.

G-CSF, probably with steel factor, helps mobilize stem cells and appears effective in certain severe chronic neutropenic states, including Kostmann's neutropenia and cyclic neutropenia (Chapter 163). Evolution to leukemia in patients with Kostmann's neutropenia, however, is a concern. The malignant counterparts of the marrow cells usually retain the cytokine responsiveness of the normal cells, and many neoplastic cells proliferate in response to cytokines. Tumor progression is a risk, but cytokine manipulation of tumor growth, possibly in concert with therapy to kill cycling cells, is an opportunity. GM-CSF has been combined with cytosine arabinoside as an effective therapy for myelodysplasia (Chapter 182). G-CSF and GM-CSF stimulate a wide variety of cell types of both hematopoietic and nonhematopoietic origin and, not surprisingly, have a wide variety of side effects, including bone pain, fever, chills, pleural and pulmonary effusions/infiltrates, vasculitis, splenic enlargement, proteinuria, and rashes, including neutrophilic dermatitis (Sweet's syndrome). Thrombopoietin and IL-11 can stimulate platelet production but their clinical usefulness is not documented.

Table 159–6 • G-CSF AND GM-CSF USE IN CLINICAL THERAPY

CONDITION	ESTABLISHED BENEFIT	
	G-CSF	GM-CSF
Chronic neutropenia (cyclic, idiopathic, and Kostmann's)	Yes	No
Cancer chemotherapy–induced neutropenia	Uncertain	Uncertain
Stem cell mobilization	Yes	Yes
Active infection	No	No
Other inflammatory conditions	No	No
Drug-induced (not chemotherapy) neutropenia	No	No

SUGGESTED READINGS

Ho AD, Punzel M: Hematopoietic stem cells: Can old cells learn new tricks? J Leukoc Biol 2003;73:547–555. *Overview of the clinical reality of stem cell therapy.*
Quesenberry PJ, Colvin G, Lambert JF: The Chiaroscuro stem cell: a unified stem cell theory. Blood 2002;100:4266–4271. *Marrow cells can change their surface receptor expressions and respond to external stimuli at various stages of the cell cycle.*

160 APPROACH TO THE ANEMIAS

Kenneth S. Zuckerman

Definitions

Anemia is defined as a reduction in the number of circulating erythrocytes. It is a common manifestation of primary bone marrow disorders (resulting in impaired production of erythrocytes), primary abnormalities of erythrocytes (resulting in increased rate of destruction), immunologic disorders, nutritional deficiencies, and a broad spectrum of systemic diseases that secondarily result in anemia. Any condition that can impair the production or increase the rate of destruction or loss of erythrocytes can result in anemia, if the bone marrow is unable to compensate for the rate of loss of red blood cells (RBCs). At least some degree of anemia is detectable in 20 to 40% of hospitalized patients.

Electronic, automated blood cell counters provide a considerable amount of information that is useful in determining severity, pathophysiology, and etiology of anemia (Table 160–1). The hemoglobin (Hgb), measured in grams per deciliter, represents the total amount of hemoglobin in all of the erythrocytes in 100 mL of blood. The hematocrit (Hct) is the percentage of the total blood volume that is composed of erythrocytes. The mean corpuscular or cell volume (MCV) is measured directly on automated cell counters but can be calculated as MCV (μ^3 or fL) = Hct (%) × 10/RBC count (× 10^6/μL of whole blood). The mean cell hemoglobin (MCH) is calculated by automated cell counters as MCH (pg) = Hgb (g/dL) × 10/RBC (× 10^6/μL). The mean cell hemoglobin concentration (MCHC) is calculated by automated cell counters as MCHC = Hgb (g/dL) × 100/Hct (%). The MCH and MCHC are of limited value because of relatively poor sensitivity for any individual disorders, whereas the MCV is extremely useful in classification and determination of the cause of anemia. The RBC distribution width (RDW/CV) is a ratio of the width of the RBC size distribution curve at 1 standard deviation from the mean size divided by the MCV. Because this value is a ratio with the MCV as denominator, it tends to magnify any variation in cell size in patients with microcytosis but is relatively insensitive to mild or early macrocytosis. A less frequently used value, the RDW/SD, is the width of the RBC size distribution curve, encompassing 80% of the erythrocytes in the measured population. This latter measurement is particularly sensitive even to small populations of microcytic or macrocytic RBCs. In addition to these standard measurements, automated absolute reticulocyte counts per microliter of blood or evaluations of new methylene blue–stained peripheral blood smears for the percent of positive-staining erythrocytes (reticulocytes) give a measure of the number of newly released (generally 1- to 2-day-old) erythrocytes. These newly formed erythrocytes still contain residual ribosomal RNA, which can be recognized easily on supravital staining with new methylene blue. Because the ribosomal RNA is lost from the cell within the first 1 to 2 days in the circulation and erythrocytes in the blood survive an average of about 120 days, reticulocytes comprise about 1 to 2% of all erythrocytes in the circulation; a normal, nonanemic adult has 40,000 to 100,000 reticulocytes per microliter of blood. Automated blood cell counters also provide total white blood cell (WBC) count, WBC differential count, and platelet count. All of this information is useful in assessing the mechanism of anemia.

Table 160–1 • NORMAL VALUES FOR RED BLOOD CELL MEASUREMENTS

MEASUREMENT	UNITS	NORMAL RANGE (APPROXIMATE)*
Hemoglobin	g/dL	Males: 13.5–17.5 Females: 12.0–16.0
Hematocrit	%	Males: 40–52 Females: 36–48
Red blood cell (RBC) count	×10^6/μL of blood	Males: 4.5–6.0 Females: 4.0–5.4
Mean cell volume (MCV)	fL	81–99
Mean cell hemoglobin (MCH)	pg	30–34
Mean cell hemoglobin concentration (MCHC)	g/dL	30–36
Red blood cell size distribution width		
RDW-CV	%	12–14
RDW-SD	fL	37–47
Reticulocyte count (absolute number)	No./μL of blood	40,000–100,000
Reticulocyte percentage	% of RBCs	0.5–1.5

*Actual normal ranges for many of these values may vary slightly, depending on factors such as the location and type of equipment used, altitude above sea level, and patient age.

Etiology and Pathogenesis

NORMAL ERYTHROPOIESIS

The circulating erythrocyte under normal conditions has an average lifespan of approximately 120 days. It is a non-nucleated, nondividing cell, in which more than 90% of the protein content is the oxygen-carrying molecule hemoglobin. The erythrocyte's sole responsibility is to deliver oxygen to the tissues of the body. The primary consequence of anemia is tissue hypoxia. Erythropoiesis is driven by a feedback loop. Oxygen-sensing cells in the area of the juxtaglomerular apparatus of the kidney respond to local tissue hypoxia by increasing production of erythropoietin (EPO), which is the primary regulatory hormone for erythropoiesis. EPO plays little, if any, role in maintaining or producing early hematopoietic precursors or even the earliest detectable erythroid progenitor cells, known as *burst forming units–erythroid* (BFU-E); however, EPO is essential for the maturation of BFU-E to late erythroid progenitor cells, known as *colony-forming units–erythroid* (CFU-E), and to proerythroblasts in the bone marrow. The main mechanism of action of EPO is to prevent apoptosis, also called *programmed cell death,* of erythroid precursor cells and to permit their proliferation and maturation. When erythroid precursor cells mature to the level of proerythroblasts, further maturation to normoblasts, reticulocytes, and mature erythrocytes no longer requires the presence of EPO. Under normal circumstances, the RBC mass is maintained at a nearly constant level by means of the EPO feedback loop's ability to match new erythrocyte production to the rate of natural senescence and loss of RBCs. Although total absence of EPO in the circulation never or almost never occurs, severe depression of circulating EPO levels results in near-cessation of erythrocyte production.

Hypoxia, as sensed in the kidney, results in increased production of EPO, which leads to increased erythrocyte production by the bone marrow. When the local tissue hypoxia is due to a reduction in the number of circulating erythrocytes and amount of hemoglobin and the consequent decreased total-body oxygen-carrying capacity, the increased EPO produced by the kidney stimulates the bone marrow to produce increased numbers of erythrocytes to compensate for the existing deficiency of RBCs. When an increase in EPO levels in the circulation occurs in response to acute onset of anemia, new proerythroblasts and normoblasts appear in the bone marrow within 2 to 4 days, and new reticulocytes begin to appear in the peripheral blood within 3 to 7 days. Reestablishment of normal numbers of circulating erythrocytes and normal tissue oxygenation results in reduced production of EPO and a reduced rate of production of erythrocytes back to the normal basal level that is required to maintain a stable, normal number of erythrocytes in the blood. When hypoxia is caused by decreased ambient oxygen concentration, impaired delivery of oxygen through the lungs and to hemoglobin molecules in erythrocytes, venous-to-arterial shunting of blood, hemoglobin mutants with increased oxygen affinity and decreased ability to release oxygen in the tissues, or localized renal disease that the renal sensor cannot distinguish from generalized hypoxemia, the increase in EPO results in increased erythropoiesis, erythrocytosis, and secondary polycythemia.

PATHOGENESIS OF ANEMIAS

The basic mechanisms of anemia can be divided into conditions that result in accelerated destruction or loss of RBCs and conditions in which the primary abnormality is impaired ability of the bone marrow to produce sufficient numbers of erythrocytes to replace the erythrocytes that are lost. Although this classification makes it easier to understand the pathophysiology of anemia and to determine the proper diagnostic studies to perform, more than one mechanism may occur simultaneously in many patients.

Anemias Caused by Impaired Production of Erythrocytes by the Bone Marrow

If there is a reduced erythrocyte mass secondary to impaired production of erythroid precursors and mature RBCs by the bone marrow, the number of reticulocytes in the circulating blood and the number of normoblasts in the bone marrow would be lower than would be appropriate in the presence of the existing degree of anemia. A wide variety of conditions can be responsible for impaired erythropoiesis (Table 160–2).

ERYTHROPOIETIN DEFICIENCY. Insufficient production of EPO results in failure of an otherwise normal bone marrow to produce the required number of erythrocytes, despite the production of normal numbers of other hematopoietic cells, such as neutrophils and platelets. The prototype for impaired EPO production is renal failure (with particularly severe EPO deficiency after bilateral nephrectomies), in which only low levels of EPO, generally less than 10% of normal, are produced (Chapter 117). The small amount of EPO produced in patients after nephrectomies is derived from the liver and is sufficient to generate only a small portion of the required numbers of erythrocytes. Patients with chronic renal failure and particularly patients who have had bilateral nephrectomies have severe anemia, with hemoglobin values less than 5 g/dL in the absence of exogenous EPO therapy or RBC transfusions. Rare patients with autoantibodies against EPO have extremely low to undetectable circulating EPO levels and severe anemia, with pure RBC aplasia in the bone marrow. Patients with chronic infectious or inflammatory diseases or cancer also can have anemia that is associated with inappropriately low levels of EPO for the degrees of anemia; in these circumstances, cytokines such as interleukin (IL)-1, IL-6, or tumor necrosis factor-α may be responsible, at least in part, for the impaired EPO production.

QUANTITATIVE DEFICIENCY OF HEMATOPOIETIC STEM CELLS AND/OR COMMITTED ERYTHROID PROGENITOR CELLS. A second mechanism of anemia caused by reduced production of cells by the bone marrow is deficiency of hematopoietic stem cells and/or committed erythroid progenitor cells. Any condition that is characterized by a deficiency of hematopoietic stem cells and/or committed erythroid precursor cells also results in anemia. Even if EPO production is appropriately increased for the degree of anemia, anemia results if the target marrow precursor cells are deficient in number. In almost all such cases, the defect is a more generalized bone marrow abnormality that results in reduced production of all lineages of bone marrow–derived cells, particularly erythrocytes, granulocytes, and platelets. Idiopathic bone marrow failure, commonly called *aplastic anemia,* is the prototype of these disorders (Chapter 174). Bone marrow aplasia or hypoplasia also may occur as a result of toxic substances such as benzene; cancer chemotherapeutic agents; other pharmacologic agents, such as chloramphenicol or gold salts; ionizing radiation; or certain viral infections, such

as Epstein-Barr virus, human immunodeficiency virus (HIV), hepatitis (non-A, non-B, non-C) virus, or dengue virus. Other conditions, such as bone marrow fibrosis (myelofibrosis; Chapter 183) or extensive replacement of the bone marrow by neoplastic cells, also can result in deficiencies of hematopoietic stem and progenitor cells and/or impaired ability of these cells to proliferate and to differentiate into mature hematopoietic cells. Patients with severe malnutrition (Chapter 228), including anorexia nervosa, also may have bone marrow hypoplasia. A few patients with myelodysplasia (Chapter 182) or paroxysmal nocturnal hemoglobinuria also have significant bone marrow hypoplasia. Selective anemia also is seen in pure RBC aplasia; this disorder usually has an immunologic basis, with selective immune-mediated destruction of erythroid progenitor cells and absence or near-absence of detectable nucleated erythroid precursors in the bone marrow despite elevated levels of circulating EPO. Viral infection, particularly with parvovirus B19, which selectively infects committed erythroid progenitor cells, also can cause transient or prolonged pure RBC aplasia because of the cytotoxic effect of this virus on the infected erythroid precursor cells.

IMPAIRED ABILITY OF ERYTHROID PROGENITORS TO RESPOND TO ERYTHROPOIETIN. A third general mechanism responsible for reduced erythrocyte production by the bone marrow is impaired responsiveness of erythroid precursors to appropriate circulating EPO concentrations. This category covers a broad range of disorders, including intrinsic erythrocyte abnormalities, exogenous inhibitory effects, and nutritional deficiencies. No mutations or abnormalities of EPO receptors or in EPO-related signal transduction pathways in erythroid precursors have been identified as causes of anemia thus far. There are many potential ways to categorize this large, diverse group of anemias. One method is to divide these conditions pathophysiologically into conditions in which there is impaired DNA synthesis and cell division and conditions in which there is impaired synthesis of hemoglobin.

Disorders Characterized by Impaired DNA Synthesis: Megaloblastic Anemias. Impaired DNA synthesis and the resulting impaired cell division by erythroid precursors result in RBC macrocytosis (increased MCV) and variable degrees of anemia (see Chapter 175). These abnormalities may occur whenever there is a significant deficiency of key substrates in the DNA synthetic pathways, as is caused by deficiencies of cobalamin (vitamin B_{12}) and folate. Folate deficiency frequently may be due to insufficient dietary intake but also may be due to diffuse intestinal disorders and to drugs that interfere with folate metabolism, such as ethanol, sulfonamides or sulfa-related drugs, trimethoprim, methotrexate, anticonvulsants, and possibly oral contraceptives. Folate deficiency may occur in individuals with an increased requirement for folate, such as patients with chronic hemolytic anemias, pregnant women, and children. In addition, severe alcoholics, patients with general malnutrition from any cause, and patients with certain unconventional dietary habits are susceptible to developing folate deficiency. A severely folate-deficient diet results in clinically significant folate deficiency within about 6 weeks. Cobalamin deficiency almost never occurs because of lack of dietary cobalamin intake; instead, it most often is due to impaired absorption of cobalamin due to lack of intrinsic factor, gastric atrophy, and abnormalities of cobalamin absorption in the terminal ileum. Because of substantial stores and low daily requirements for cobalamin in normal individuals, deficiency of cobalamin usually takes at least 3 to 5 years to become manifest. In patients with myelodysplasia, one of the mechanisms of anemia and other hematopoietic cell deficiencies can be a moderately severe to severe impairment of DNA synthesis, with development of megaloblastosis and macrocytosis. A broad range of cancer chemotherapeutic agents impair DNA synthesis in the short term, and some cause stem cell damage that can result in a long-term adverse effect on DNA synthesis, which may result in mild-to-moderate anemia or may be manifested only by an increased MCV. In association with the reduced DNA synthesis and delays in or decreased number of cell divisions in megaloblastic anemias, there generally is intramedullary death of hematopoietic precursors, predominantly by apoptosis, and reduced numbers of mature erythrocytes and sometimes granulocytes and platelets released into the blood. This condition of hypercellular bone marrow combined with death of precursors before full maturation of hematopoietic cells is called *ineffective hematopoiesis* or, in the case of RBCs alone, ineffective erythropoiesis.

Impaired Hemoglobin Synthesis: Disorders Characterized by Diminished Heme Synthesis. Impaired hemoglobin synthesis occurs with disorders in which there is reduced production of either heme or globin

---

Table 160–2 • PATHOPHYSIOLOGIC CLASSIFICATION OF ANEMIAS CAUSED BY IMPAIRED PRODUCTION OF ERYTHROCYTES BY THE BONE MARROW

Erythropoietin (EPO) deficiency (normocytic anemias)
  Renal insufficiency (worse after bilateral nephrectomies)
  Pure red cell aplasia due to anti-EPO antibodies (extremely rare)
  Anemia of chronic disease (inappropriately low EPO level is a partial contributing factor)
Quantitative deficiency of hematopoietic/erythroid progenitor cells (normocytic anemias)
  Idiopathic bone marrow aplasia/hypoplasia
  Secondary bone marrow aplasia/hypoplasia (drugs, toxins, infections, radiation, malnutrition)
  Myelofibrosis (primary or secondary)
  Bone marrow replacement by neoplastic cells (myelophthisis)
  Myelodysplasia (minority of myelodysplasia patients)
  Paroxysmal nocturnal hemoglobinuria (10–15% of PNH patients)
  Pure red cell aplasia (anti–erythroid precursor cell antibodies, parvovirus B19 infection)
Impaired erythroid precursor cell division and DNA synthesis (macrocytic/megaloblastic anemias)
  Cobalamin (vitamin B_{12}) deficiency
  Folate deficiency
  Myelodysplasia
  Cancer chemotherapeutic drugs and some immunosuppressive and antimicrobial drugs
Impaired heme synthesis in differentiating erythroid cells (microcytic anemias)
  Iron deficiency
  Anemia of chronic disease/inflammation
  Sideroblastic anemias (particularly hereditary forms)
Impaired globin synthesis in differentiating erythroid cells (microcytic anemias)
  Thalassemias

and, when sufficiently severe, results in microcytic anemias (decreased MCV; Chapter 167). Most or all of the rare disorders collectively called *hereditary sideroblastic anemias* seem to be due to mutations in the coding regions of genes for the erythroid-specific forms of heme synthetic pathway enzymes or erythroid-specific promoters (especially ALA synthase, HMB synthase, and possibly ferrochelatase); the result is reduced heme synthesis in erythroid cells. Iron is required for the final stage of synthesis of heme, and iron deficiency impairs heme synthesis and results in anemia. Although iron deficiency anemia is associated classically with microcytosis, most patients with mild iron deficiency anemia actually have normocytic erythrocytes. Over time, iron-deficient patients commonly have a progressive decrease in the MCV within the normal range, and microcytosis occurs generally in the most severe 20 to 30% of cases. In patients with chronic infectious or inflammatory diseases or with cancer, the responsiveness of erythroid precursors to endogenous and exogenous EPO may be impaired. The mechanism for this impaired responsiveness to EPO is unknown, but it is thought to be due to inhibitory cytokines and chemokines. One of the hallmarks of anemia of chronic disease or inflammation is impaired transfer of iron into developing erythroid cells, resulting in a functional iron deficiency in normoblasts even when iron stores in the bone marrow and the rest of the body are adequate. The result is impaired heme synthesis and a mild-to-moderate normocytic or microcytic anemia. In many of the circumstances in which anemia of chronic disease/inflammation occurs, there may be concomitant iron deficiency.

Impaired Hemoglobin Synthesis: Disorders Characterized by Impaired Globin Synthesis—Thalassemias.
Impaired synthesis of α-globin chains in α-thalassemias or β-globin chains in β-thalassemias results in unbalanced synthesis of globin chains and a reduction in the number of hemoglobin $\alpha2/\beta2$ tetramers (Chapter 168). Because of the reduced numbers of hemoglobin tetramer molecules in each cell, thalassemia patients have a microcytic anemia. The unpaired excess β-chains in the erythrocytes of patients with α-thalassemia and unpaired excess α-chains in patients with β-thalassemia tend to aggregate, precipitate, and form insoluble cytoplasmic inclusion bodies that result in oxidative damage to the membranes of developing normoblasts and death of a large proportion of these developing erythroid cells within the marrow, leading to anemia secondary to ineffective erythropoiesis. The normoblasts that do survive produce erythrocytes that contain similar inclusions (Heinz bodies), which lead to premature destruction of these cells in the spleen and liver, resulting in a hemolytic component of the anemia. The overall degree of anemia is related to the severity of the defect in globin synthesis so that patients who have deletion of only one of their four α-globin genes generally have microcytosis but no anemia, patients with deletion of two α-globin genes have microcytosis and mild anemia, and patients who are heterozygous for β-thalassemia have microcytosis and mild anemia.

INEFFECTIVE ERYTHROPOIESIS.
Ineffective erythropoiesis is defined as anemia with increased numbers of erythroid precursor cells in the bone marrow but decreased numbers of mature circulating erythrocytes being released from the bone marrow. In ineffective erythropoiesis, there are inappropriately low numbers of reticulocytes in the blood. This condition usually is caused by defects that are present in the maturing proerythroblasts and normoblasts in the bone marrow and result in their premature death within the bone marrow. The most common causes of anemia secondary to ineffective erythropoiesis are myelodysplasia, megaloblastic anemias, and thalassemias.

Anemias Caused by Accelerated Destruction, Consumption, or Loss of Circulating Erythrocytes

Any intrinsic defects of erythrocytes or extrinsic conditions that cause erythrocytes to be damaged intravascularly, removed from the circulation prematurely by the spleen or liver, or lost through bleeding result in increased EPO production, increased numbers of maturing erythroid precursors in the bone marrow, and release of increased numbers of newly formed reticulocytes into the blood. In a patient with normal bone marrow, accelerated loss of circulating erythrocytes always is associated with increased erythropoiesis, which can be judged by the presence of an increased reticulocyte count. An increased reticulocyte count implies that there is at least a mildly increased rate of loss or destruction of erythrocytes. If the bone marrow is able to keep up with the increased demand for replacement erythrocytes, the patient will not have a decreased RBC mass. Anemia occurs only if the rate of production of erythrocytes by the bone marrow

is unable to compensate completely for the loss or destruction of RBCs. Although chronic hemolysis or blood loss is associated with compensatory increased erythropoiesis (assuming no additional abnormalities of bone marrow, kidney, or required nutrients), signs of compensatory increased erythropoiesis do not appear until several days after acute hemolysis or blood loss.

HEMOLYTIC ANEMIAS CAUSED BY INTRINSIC RED BLOOD CELL MEMBRANE DEFECTS.
Abnormalities of RBC membrane proteins and lipids lead to deformed erythrocytes, which are prone to be removed prematurely from the circulation, primarily by the filtering functions of the spleen (see Chapter 170). The most common membrane protein abnormalities involve spectrin, ankyrin, band 3 protein, and protein 4.1 and lead to the RBC membranopathies known as *hereditary spherocytosis*, *hereditary elliptocytosis*, and *hereditary pyropoikilocytosis*. In each of these disorders, the decreased deformability of RBCs results in their premature clearance from the blood, primarily in the spleen. Abnormalities of the lipid bilayer of the erythrocyte membrane lead to bizarrely shaped RBCs, which have poor deformability and cytoplasmic projections and result in an increased rate of destruction of erythrocytes, primarily in the spleen. One abnormality of the lipid bilayer is acanthocytosis or spur cell anemia, which may be caused by hereditary lipoprotein defects, such as abetalipoproteinemia, cholesterol metabolism abnormalities that occur in patients with severe liver disease, or the McLeod phenotype of severely deficient Kell blood group antigen on erythrocytes. Stomatocytes or xerocytes result from imbalance in the size of the outer and inner portions of the membrane lipid bilayer and dehydration of erythrocytes; abnormalities of membrane phospholipids or absence of Rh antigens on the surface of RBCs (Rh null phenotype) result in these morphologic abnormalities, which may lead to mild hemolysis. In paroxysmal nocturnal hemoglobinuria, a defect in a crucial membrane-anchoring molecule (glycosylphosphatidylinositol), which is responsible for anchoring many cell surface proteins, results in the absence of at least three surface proteins that are crucial to prevention of complement-mediated cell damage and lysis. The absence or significant reduction in decay accelerating factor (DAF, CD55), membrane inhibitor of reactive lysis (MIRL, CD59), and C8-binding protein results in variably increased susceptibility of these defective cells to lysis by complement.

HEMOLYTIC ANEMIAS CAUSED BY INTRINSIC RED BLOOD CELL ENZYMOPATHIES.
RBC enzymopathies (see Chapter 170) that may lead to hemolytic anemia generally fall into two groups. Defects in enzymes in the hexose monophosphate shunt (e.g., glucose-6-phosphate dehydrogenase) or enzymes responsible for maintaining reduced glutathione (e.g., γ-glutamylcysteine synthetase) to prevent oxidative injury to RBCs tend most frequently to be associated with episodic hemolysis during times of physiologic stresses, such as surgery, infections, or oxidants in foods or pharmacologic agents. The oxidant damage causes Heinz body formation. In contrast, deficiencies of enzymes in the Embden-Meyerhof pathway (e.g., pyruvate kinase and glucose phosphate isomerase) or enzymes responsible for supporting nucleotide metabolism (e.g., adenosine deaminase and pyrimidine 5′-nucleotidase) tend to cause chronic hemolytic anemias, presumably as a result of adenosine phosphate deficiency, which leads to impaired homeostasis of water, sodium, potassium, and calcium. Because erythrocytes are unable to synthesize new proteins, older erythrocytes are most likely to have the lowest levels of enzymes that are susceptible to intracellular degradation and are the most likely to be removed from the circulation.

HEMOLYTIC ANEMIAS CAUSED BY HEMOGLOBIN VARIANTS WITH REDUCED SOLUBILITY OR PROTEIN INSTABILITY.
More than 100 different structural variants of hemoglobin exhibit either reduced solubility (e.g., hemoglobins S, C, O-Arab, and D-Los Angeles) or a higher susceptibility than normal to oxidation of amino acids within the globin chains (e.g., hemoglobins Zurich, Köln, Hammersmith, and Gun Hill) (Chapter 172). The less soluble and unstable hemoglobins tend to form abnormal hemoglobin polymers or crystals, to precipitate, and to form cytoplasmic Heinz bodies, which then become attached to the cell membrane and decrease erythrocyte deformability; the result is membrane damage, followed by sequestration and destruction of erythrocytes in the spleen.

HEMOLYTIC ANEMIAS CAUSED BY ABNORMALITIES EXTRINSIC TO THE RED BLOOD CELL.
Erythrocytes can be sequestered or destroyed prematurely as a result of other conditions that secondarily cause damage to otherwise normal RBCs. In autoimmune hemolytic anemia, antibodies form against RBC membrane antigens (most commonly Rh-D antigen for so-called warm IgG antibodies and I or i antigen for so-called cold,

complement-fixing IgM antibodies) (Chapter 169). These antibody-coated erythrocytes are recognized by Fc or complement receptors on macrophages in the spleen (especially IgG) or liver (especially C3 complement). IgG-coated RBCs usually undergo repeated partial phagocytosis with progressive loss of RBC membrane until the cells that survive and reenter the circulation are spherocytes, which have decreased deformability and eventually are sequestered and removed permanently from the circulation. A long list of drugs can result in hemolysis by similar mechanisms by causing antierythrocyte antibodies or by causing antidrug antibodies that lead to subsequent immune complex deposition on erythrocytes, which also results in hemolysis by similar mechanisms. Alloimmune hemolysis may result from transfusion of blood with "minor" blood group mismatches into recipients previously sensitized to those antigens by prior transfusions and/or pregnancies. Severe acute intravascular hemolysis (see Chapter 169) can occur from transfusion of ABO incompatible blood and less commonly from transfusion of blood that has Rh or so-called minor blood group antigen mismatches. Microangiopathic hemolysis with fragmented erythrocytes, intravascular release of hemoglobin and other erythrocyte contents, and intravascular and splenic destruction of RBCs occurs in the presence of fibrin deposition in small arterioles, in conditions such as thrombotic thrombocytopenic purpura and disseminated intravascular coagulation, and in the presence of diffuse small vessel vasculitis, eclampsia, or malignant hypertension. Prosthetic heart valves or arterial grafts with roughened endothelial surfaces also can cause mechanical fragmentation of erythrocytes. Other causes of mechanical damage to otherwise normal erythrocytes are trauma (e.g., march hemoglobinuria), thermal injury from severe burns, and osmotic lysis secondary to freshwater drowning or mistaken intravenous infusion of high volumes of hypotonic fluids. Certain infections, such as malaria, bartonellosis, and babesiosis, can cause direct intravascular destruction of infected erythrocytes, and clostridial sepsis can result in release of toxins that directly damage RBC membrane phospholipids and lyse the cells. Certain snake and spider venoms can cause hemolysis (i.e., cobra venom via phospholipases that destroy the erythrocyte membrane and pit viper and brown recluse spider venoms via induction of disseminated intravascular coagulation). Finally, many drugs and ingested toxins, including nitrofurantoin, phenazopyridine, sulfones, amyl nitrite, naphthalene mothballs, paraquat, and hydrogen peroxide, can cause direct oxidative damage to erythrocytes. Several cancer chemotherapeutic agents also probably cause oxidant and/or membrane damage, which can result in anemia within a few days after drug administration.

BLOOD LOSS. Although acute blood loss can result in anemia, it may be much more difficult to document slow, chronic blood loss, in which case the bone marrow almost always is able to compensate until the patient becomes iron deficient. The gastrointestinal tract is a major site of chronic blood loss: Malignancies, gastritis, peptic ulcer disease, inflammatory bowel disease, diverticulitis, proctitis, hemorrhoidal bleeding, angiodysplasia, arteriovenous malformations, and hereditary hemorrhagic telangiectasia (Osler-Weber-Rendu syndrome) are among the major causes of chronic or intermittent gastrointestinal blood loss (Chapter 133). Chronic excessive menstrual blood loss, chronic urinary tract bleeding, and recurrent epistaxis also can lead to iron deficiency and anemia. Because of the substantial consumption of maternal iron by the developing fetus, multiple pregnancies also may contribute to the development of iron deficiency and anemia. Patients with chronic intravascular hemolysis (e.g., paroxysmal nocturnal hemoglobinuria, malaria, or traumatic hemolysis from a prosthetic cardiac valve) lose hemoglobin in the urine and may become iron deficient and anemic. The blood drawn from and lost by a hospitalized patient also can contribute to an otherwise unexplained recent anemia, especially in patients who are unable to mount an erythropoietic response.

Dilutional Pseudoanemia

Certain conditions lead to an expansion of plasma volume, which results in a decreased hemoglobin, hematocrit, and RBC count without any decrease in the patient's total RBC mass. The chronic intravascular volume expansion that occurs in pregnancy can reduce the hemoglobin to 10 g/dL. Acute volume overload also can cause a dilutional decrease in the concentration of RBCs, which resolves after equilibration and diuresis occur. Certain medications, particularly some cytokines, such as IL-2, IL-11, and granulocyte-macrophage colony-stimulating factor, also may cause acute dilutional pseudoanemias.

Clinical Manifestations

There are three main types of clinical manifestations of anemia. In anemia that has developed rapidly, symptoms related to hypotension may develop as a result of loss of blood volume. In chronic and acute anemias, tissue and organ hypoxia is a major source of symptoms, although eventually orthostatic and nonorthostatic hypotension and tachycardia may occur secondary to chronically decreased blood volume. In hemolytic anemias, the toxicity of products of lysed erythrocytes also may cause specific clinical findings. The signs and symptoms of anemia may vary widely from patient to patient with the same degree and tempo of anemia. The major factors that determine the specific response of each individual to anemia include severity of anemia, rapidity of onset of anemia, age of the patient, overall physical condition, and comorbid events or disorders. Mild anemia often is associated with no clinical symptoms and may be discovered only when a complete blood cell count is done for another reason. The earliest clinical symptoms of mild-to-moderate anemia tend to be a sense of fatigue, generalized weakness, and loss of stamina, followed by tachycardia and exertional dyspnea. In young, healthy patients, these symptoms frequently are not noticed until the hemoglobin level decreases to less than 7 or 8 g/dL. In elderly patients and patients with cardiovascular or pulmonary disease, symptoms may occur even with modest degrees of anemia and hemoglobin levels of 9 to 11 g/dL.

PHYSIOLOGIC COMPENSATORY MECHANISMS. The five main physiologic compensatory responses to anemia vary in prominence depending on rapidity of onset and duration of anemia and the condition of the patient. First, in acute-onset anemia with severe loss of intravascular volume, peripheral vasoconstriction and central vasodilation preserve blood flow to vital organs. Second, over time and with increasingly severe anemia, systemic small vessel vasodilation results in increased blood flow to ensure better tissue oxygenation. These vascular compensations result in decreased systemic vascular resistance, increased cardiac output, and tachycardia, which result in a higher rate of delivery of oxygen-bearing erythrocytes to the tissues. Third, RBCs develop an increased level of 2,3-diphosphoglycerate, which interacts with hemoglobin molecules to cause a rightward shift of the hemoglobin oxygen dissociation curve, which in turn enhances the release of oxygen to the tissues at any given partial pressure of oxygen. Fourth, in chronic anemias, there is a compensatory increase in plasma volume, which maintains the total blood volume and enhances tissue perfusion. The fifth compensatory response in otherwise normal individuals is stimulation of EPO production, which in turn stimulates new erythrocyte production. The latter occurs if the stem cells and erythroid precursors are normal, the erythroid precursors are able to respond normally to EPO, and the developing normoblasts are normal.

CLINICAL MANIFESTATIONS OF CHRONIC ANEMIA. Weakness, fatigue, lethargy, decreased stamina, palpitations, dyspnea on exertion, and orthostatic light-headedness are common symptoms in patients with chronic anemia, although the compensatory mechanisms described earlier may prevent these symptoms from being manifested in mild or moderate anemias. Occasional patients with slowly developing or long-standing anemia may report being asymptomatic with hemoglobin levels of 5 or 6 g/dL, although virtually all such patients notice a distinct improvement in their performance status after correction of anemia. As is true of acute anemias, comorbid conditions, particularly with impaired blood supply or oxygenation of specific organs, may result in symptoms and signs secondary to organ-specific dysfunction. Anemic patients with prior myocardial dysfunction may have more pronounced edema, dyspnea, orthopnea, tachycardia, fatigue, and loss of stamina. In patients with coronary artery disease, anemia may result in onset or worsening of angina or may precipitate a myocardial infarction. Anemic patients with significant peripheral arterial disease may develop new or worsening claudication. Anemic patients with cerebrovascular disease may experience more frequent or severe transient ischemic attacks or strokes.

Continued

In patients who are anemic without an immediately obvious cause, careful probing of the patient's past medical history and family history is essential. In particular, it is important to obtain results of previous blood cell counts to determine whether the anemia is of recent to even lifelong duration. A careful, in-depth discussion of personal and family history can be helpful, particularly if positive for anemia, splenectomy, cholecystectomy, gallstones, or jaundice at birth or later in life. The new mutation rate for congenital/hereditary hemolytic anemias is sufficiently high, however, that a lack of family history should not deter one from the search for these conditions, if the remainder of the clinical picture is compatible with a congenital hemolytic anemia. Mild hereditary and congenital hemolytic anemias sometimes escape detection until patients are elderly or until a second event compromises the ability of the patient's bone marrow to compensate for the chronic, excessive rate of destruction of erythrocytes. In some patients, past treatment may have been inappropriate or ineffective because of inadequate evaluation and incorrect diagnosis.

The most prominent general physical examination findings that may occur in patients with significant anemia include pallor of skin and mucosal surfaces (Fig. 160–1), orthostatic hypotension, resting or orthostatic tachycardia, systolic ejection murmur, increased prominence of the cardiac apical impulse, bounding pulses, and wide pulse pressure. The presence of splenomegaly or history of prior splenectomy raises the possibility of a chronic hemolytic anemia. A right upper quadrant surgical scar or history of gallstones and/or cholecystectomy also should raise the possibility of a chronic hemolytic state with formation of bilirubin-containing gallstones.

GENERAL CLINICAL MANIFESTATIONS OF ACUTE DEVELOPMENT OF ANEMIA FROM BLOOD LOSS OR HEMOLYSIS.

In a patient with severe acute hemolysis or blood loss, prominent early symptoms include resting or orthostatic hypotension resulting from a decrease in total blood volume, with subsequent light-headedness or syncope, exertional and/or resting tachycardia and palpitations, diaphoresis, anxiety, agitation, generalized severe weakness and lethargy, and possibly decreased mental function. All of the physical examination findings described earlier for chronic anemias tend to be more pronounced with anemias of rapid onset that also are complicated by acute loss of intravascular blood volume. Depending on the severity of the anemia and blood volume depletion, comorbid conditions, age, and overall health, there also may be signs of oxygen deprivation in one or multiple organ systems. Loss of 25 to 35% of the total blood volume in 12 to 24 hours cannot be ameliorated by the normal compensatory mechanisms, and loss of more than 40% of blood volume in 12 hours leads to profound symptoms resulting more from intravascular volume depletion than from anemia.

DISEASES OF OTHER BODY SYSTEMS THAT CAN CAUSE OR BE ASSOCIATED WITH ANEMIA.

A broad spectrum of disorders of other organ systems can give rise to anemia. Any chronic infection, chronic inflammatory disease, or malignant disease can result in anemia of chronic disease or inflammation. Patients with lymphoproliferative and rheumatologic diseases may develop autoimmune hemolytic anemia. Moderate-to-severe renal insufficiency can cause anemia secondary to impaired EPO production. Any cause of marked splenomegaly, including myeloproliferative and lymphoproliferative disorders, certain chronic infectious diseases (e.g., malaria, tuberculosis), portal vein thrombosis, or portal hypertension may cause excessive RBC sequestration and destruction. Gastritis, peptic ulcer disease, gastrointestinal angiodysplasia, and hereditary hemorrhagic telangiectasia frequently are associated with chronic blood loss that leads to iron deficiency and anemia. Iron deficiency also can be caused by removal or significant dysfunction (e.g., Whipple's disease, Crohn's disease) of the duodenum, which is the major site of iron absorption. Anti–gastric parietal cell antibodies, gastric achlorhydria, prior gastrectomy, intestinal bacterial overgrowth, or dysfunction (e.g., inflammatory bowel disease) or surgical removal of the terminal ileum can result in cobalamin deficiency and anemia. Gastroduodenal bypass surgery for treatment of obesity frequently causes chronic iron deficiency, owing to loss of duodenal absorption, and chronic vitamin B_{12} deficiency, owing to loss of intrinsic factor. Patients with hypopituitarism or hypothyroidism may have a mild macrocytic anemia. Severe alcoholics may develop folate deficiency from poor dietary intake, iron deficiency from chronic gastric blood loss, or toxic suppression of the bone marrow, resulting in decreased erythropoiesis. Patients with severe liver disease often have shortened RBC survival secondary to splenomegaly caused by portal hypertension or secondary to excess deposition of unesterified cholesterol on erythrocyte membranes and the resulting formation of acanthocytes and schistocytes that are cleared from the blood prematurely. Anemia is a common manifestation of HIV infection and may be multifactorial, including contributions from cytokine-mediated anemia of chronic disease, relative EPO deficiency, malnutrition, myelodysplastic changes in the bone marrow, bone marrow fibrosis and necrosis, immune-mediated hemolysis, and drug-induced (e.g., zidovudine) myelosuppression.

Diagnosis

The initial diagnostic evaluation (Fig. 160–2) of anemia is based on using readily available information, including a careful in-depth evaluation of the patient's past medical history and family history (Table 160–3), physical examination (splenomegaly is the most important physical finding in the anemic patient), complete blood cell count, reticulocyte count, and microscopic evaluation of the peripheral blood smear (Table 160–4). More specialized laboratory tests are indicated only after these screening studies have been obtained. In a patient with anemia, the first distinction to be made is whether the primary cause of the anemia is failure of the bone marrow to produce sufficient numbers of erythrocytes or accelerated loss or destruction of erythrocytes. A single test, the reticulocyte count, often provides the answer to this question. An elevated absolute reticulocyte count in an anemic patient indicates that the bone marrow is responding to the requirement for new erythrocyte production to replace prematurely destroyed or lost erythrocytes from hemolysis or blood loss. A reticulocyte count that is below normal or below the level expected for the degree of anemia indicates inability of the bone marrow to maintain the rate of production of RBCs required to compensate for those lost or destroyed and is the primary cause or a major contributing factor of the anemia.

Microscopic examination of the morphology of RBCs in a peripheral blood smear is an essential part of the evaluation of defective production and excessive destruction of RBCs (see Fig. 161–1). In a patient with an elevated reticulocyte count, specific morphologic changes in the RBCs observed on microscopic examination often make the diagnosis readily apparent or reduce the list of possible diagnoses considerably. The finding of sickle cells should lead to a hemoglobin electrophoresis, which confirms the type of sickling disorder (see Fig. 161–8). A predominant finding of spherocytes means that the patient almost certainly has autoimmune or alloimmune hemolysis or hereditary spherocytosis (Fig. 160–3). The evaluation includes a careful past medical and family history (for duration of anemia; medications; history of blood transfusions; anemia in other family members; and

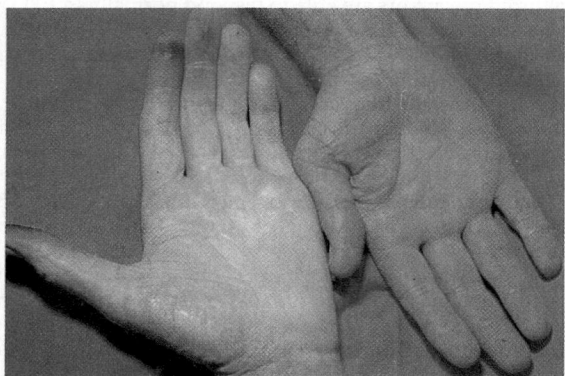

FIGURE 160–1 • Pallor of the hand in anemia is obvious in this patient, especially when compared with the physician's hand on the right. The patient's hemoglobin was 7 g/dL. The hand also shows that the patient was a heavy smoker. His anemia resulted from chronic blood loss from a carcinoma in the esophagus, a site where the risk of carcinoma is increased in smokers. (From Forbes CD, Jackson WF: Color Atlas and Text of Clinical Medicine, 3rd ed. London, Mosby, 2003, with permission.)

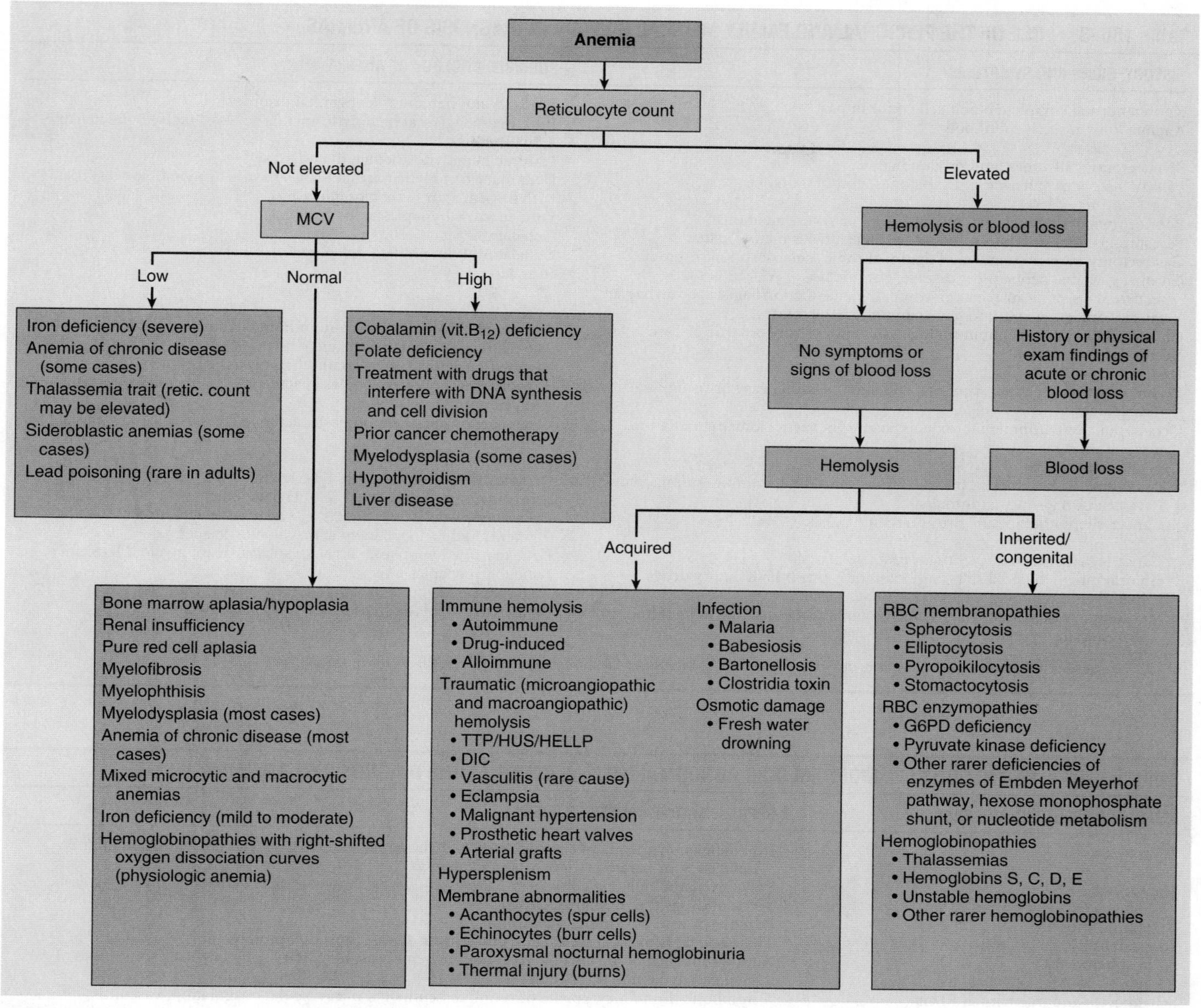

```
                              ┌─────────────┐
                              │   Anemia    │
                              └──────┬──────┘
                                     ↓
                              ┌──────────────────┐
                              │ Reticulocyte count│
                              └──────┬───────────┘
```

FIGURE 160–2 • Algorithm for diagnosis of anemias. DIC = disseminated intravascular coagulation; HELLP = *h*emolysis, *e*levated *l*iver (function tests), *l*ow *p*latelets; HUS = hemolytic uremic syndrome; TTP = thrombotic thrombocytopenic purpura.

Anemia → Reticulocyte count

Not elevated → MCV
- **Low:** Iron deficiency (severe); Anemia of chronic disease (some cases); Thalassemia trait (retic. count may be elevated); Sideroblastic anemias (some cases); Lead poisoning (rare in adults)
- **Normal:** Bone marrow aplasia/hypoplasia; Renal insufficiency; Pure red cell aplasia; Myelofibrosis; Myelophthisis; Myelodysplasia (most cases); Anemia of chronic disease (most cases); Mixed microcytic and macrocytic anemias; Iron deficiency (mild to moderate); Hemoglobinopathies with right-shifted oxygen dissociation curves (physiologic anemia)
- **High:** Cobalamin (vit.B₁₂) deficiency; Folate deficiency; Treatment with drugs that interfere with DNA synthesis and cell division; Prior cancer chemotherapy; Myelodysplasia (some cases); Hypothyroidism; Liver disease

Elevated → Hemolysis or blood loss
- **No symptoms or signs of blood loss** → Hemolysis
  - **Acquired:** Immune hemolysis (Autoimmune, Drug-induced, Alloimmune); Traumatic (microangiopathic and macroangiopathic) hemolysis (TTP/HUS/HELLP, DIC, Vasculitis (rare cause), Eclampsia, Malignant hypertension, Prosthetic heart valves, Arterial grafts); Hypersplenism; Membrane abnormalities (Acanthocytes (spur cells), Echinocytes (burr cells), Paroxysmal nocturnal hemoglobinuria, Thermal injury (burns)); Infection (Malaria, Babesiosis, Bartonellosis, Clostridia toxin); Osmotic damage (Fresh water drowning)
  - **Inherited/congenital:** RBC membranopathies (Spherocytosis, Elliptocytosis, Pyropoikilocytosis, Stomactocytosis); RBC enzymopathies (G6PD deficiency, Pyruvate kinase deficiency, Other rarer deficiencies of enzymes of Embden Meyerhof pathway, hexose monophosphate shunt, or nucleotide metabolism); Hemoglobinopathies (Thalassemias, Hemoglobins S, C, D, E, Unstable hemoglobins, Other rarer hemoglobinopathies)
- **History or physical exam findings of acute or chronic blood loss** → Blood loss

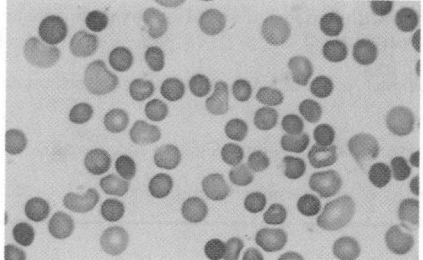

FIGURE 160–3 • Hereditary spherocytosis. Peripheral smear shows a predominance of microspherocytes (small, densely staining red blood cells with loss of the central areas of pallor) alongside larger, grayish, "polychromatic" cells that probably represent reticulocytes.

history of splenectomy, cholecystectomy, gallstones, and jaundice in the patient and family members). Examination of the patient (for splenomegaly, jaundice, or signs of autoimmune disorders) may be helpful.

Laboratory studies play a crucial role in diagnosis of the specific cause of anemia. The direct antiglobulin (Coombs) test or more sensitive tests of antierythrocyte antibodies help to diagnose autoimmune hemolytic anemia, and the indirect antiglobulin test helps to diagnose alloimmune hemolysis. Elevated levels of total and particularly indirect hyperbilirubinemia support a general diagnosis of hemolysis. Microcytic RBCs in a patient without an elevated reticulocyte count suggest iron deficiency (see Fig. 161–7), anemia of chronic disease, or thalassemia trait (or, in more severe cases, homozygous β-thalassemia or hemoglobin H disease) as the most likely cause. Sideroblastic anemia with or without myelodysplasia and lead poisoning are rare causes of microcytic anemia in adults. In microcytic anemia, helpful clues include the duration and severity of the anemia; prior menstrual and pregnancy history in women; dietary history; occupational history; history of gastric, duodenal, or ileal surgery; history of gastrointestinal, upper respiratory, or urinary tract bleeding; history of chronic infections or autoimmune or chronic inflammatory disorders; response to prior therapy for anemia; and family history of anemia. A low or low normal RBC count and normal RDW favor anemia of chronic disease, an elevated RDW favors iron deficiency, and a high normal or elevated RBC count and normal RDW favor thalassemia. Serum iron, iron-binding capacity, and particularly ferritin levels often can distinguish between anemia of chronic disease and iron deficiency anemia (Table 160–5); in patients with anemia of chronic disease, an elevated serum soluble transferrin receptor level favors the associated presence of iron deficiency. Determination of marrow iron stores on bone marrow aspiration or biopsy, the gold

Hematologic Diseases

Table 160–3 • USE OF THE PERSONAL AND FAMILY MEDICAL HISTORY IN DIAGNOSIS OF ANEMIAS

HISTORY: SIGNS AND SYMPTOMS	POSSIBLE ETIOLOGY OF ANEMIA
Known normal complete blood cell count in past	Probably not hereditary/congenital disorder
Anemia known since childhood	Inherited/congenital hemolytic anemia or (less likely) bone marrow hypoplasia
Splenectomy, gallstones, and/or jaundice	Chronic hemolytic anemia, liver disease
Family history of splenectomy, gallstones, and/or jaundice	Hereditary hemolytic anemia (RBC enzyme or membrane disorder, thalassemia, or hemoglobinopathy)
Poor or unconventional diet, malnutrition, or severe alcoholism	Bone marrow hypoplasia, folate deficiency
Paresthesias, foot numbness, loss of balance, altered mental status	Cobalamin (vitamin B_{12}) deficiency
Gastrectomy, surgical removal of ileum, chronic malabsorption disorder	Cobalamin (vitamin B_{12}) deficiency
Chronic gastritis, peptic ulcer disease, chronic use of ASA or NSAID, recurrent epistaxis or rectal bleeding, melena, menorrhagia, metrorrhagia, multiple pregnancies, duodenal surgery, gastrectomy	Iron deficiency
Chronic rheumatologic, immunologic, infectious, or neoplastic disease	Anemia of chronic disease, autoimmune hemolytic anemia
Decreased urine output	Anemia due to renal insufficiency
Dark urine	Hemolytic anemia (intravascular hemolysis)
Recent onset of infections, mucosal and skin bleeding, easy bruising, oral ulcerations	Bone marrow aplasia/hypoplasia, acute leukemia, myelodysplasia, myelophthisis
Occupational/environmental toxin exposure (benzene, ionizing radiation, lead)	Bone marrow aplasia/hypoplasia, acute leukemia, myelodysplasia, lead poisoning
Drug/medication exposure:	
Penicillin, cephalosporin, procainamide, quinidine, quinine, sulfonamide	Drug-induced immune hemolytic anemia
Fava beans, dapsone, naphthalene	Oxidant-induced hemolysis (G6PD deficient)
Cancer chemotherapeutic drugs (recent use)	Bone marrow aplasia/hypoplasia, oxidant damage, fluid retention/dilutional anemia, megaloblastic anemia
Cancer chemotherapeutic drugs (past use)	Bone marrow hypoplasia, myelodysplasia, acute myeloid leukemia
Chloramphenicol, gold salts, sulfonamides, anti-inflammatory drugs	Bone marrow aplasia/hypoplasia
Ethanol, chloramphenicol	Acute reversible bone marrow toxicity
Methotrexate, azathioprine, pyrimethamine, trimethoprim, zidovudine, sulfa drugs, hydroxyurea	Bone marrow aplasia/hypoplasia, megaloblastic anemia

ASA = aspirin; G6PD = glucose-6-phosphate dehydrogenase; NSAID = nonsteroidal anti-inflammatory drug; RBC = red blood cell.

Table 160–4 • RED BLOOD CELL MORPHOLOGIC ABNORMALITIES AS CLUES TO THE DIAGNOSIS OF ANEMIAS

RED BLOOD CELL (RBC) MORPHOLOGY	REPRESENTATIVE CAUSES OF ANEMIA
Microcytosis	Iron deficiency, anemia of chronic disease, thalassemia, and (rarely) lead poisoning, vitamin B_6 deficiency, or hereditary sideroblastic anemias
Macrocytosis	Polychromatophilia (reticulocytes), vitamin B_{12} (cobalamin) or folate deficiency, myelodysplasia, use of drugs that inhibit DNA synthesis
Basophilic stippling	Hemolysis, lead poisoning, thalassemia
Target cells	Thalassemia, hemoglobins C, D, E, and S, liver disease, abetalipoproteinemia
Microspherocytes	Autoimmune hemolytic anemia, alloimmune hemolysis, hereditary spherocytosis, some cases of Heinz body hemolytic anemias
Schistocytes and fragmented RBCs	Thrombotic thrombocytopenic purpura, disseminated intravascular coagulation, vasculitis, malignant hypertension, eclampsia, traumatic hemolysis due to prosthetic heart valve or damaged vascular graft, thermal injury (burns), post-splenectomy
Teardrop cells	Myelofibrosis, myelophthisis (bone marrow infiltration by neoplastic cells)
Sickle cells	Hemoglobin SS, SC, or S-β-thalassemia
Acanthocytes (spur cells)	Severe liver disease, malnutrition, McLeod blood group phenotype
Echinocytes (burr cells)	Renal failure, hemolysis due to malnutrition with hypomagnesemia and hypophosphatemia, pyruvate kinase deficiency, common in vitro artifact
Stomatocytes	Alcoholism, hereditary stomatocytosis
"Bite" cells or "blister" cells	Glucose-6-phosphate dehydrogenase deficiency, other oxidant-induced hemolysis, unstable hemoglobins
Howell-Jolly bodies	Postsplenectomy, hyposplenism
Intraerythrocytic parasitic or bacterial inclusions	Malaria (parasites), babesiosis (parasites), bartonellosis (gram-negative coccobacilli)
Agglutinated RBCs	Cold agglutinin disease, in vitro artifact
Rouleaux formation	Multiple myeloma, monoclonal gammopathy of undetermined significance

standard for determining iron stores, rarely is required for this purpose now.

The diagnosis of myelodysplasia requires microscopic examination of bone marrow cell morphology, and diagnosis of sideroblastic anemia (see Fig. 167–2) also requires Prussian blue staining (for detection of iron) of normoblasts in the bone marrow (Table 160–6). If there is microcytosis and mild anemia with substantial numbers of target cells, thalassemia trait is the most likely diagnosis. β-Thalassemia heterozygotes almost always can be distinguished from α-thalassemia heterozygotes on the basis of an elevated hemoglobin A_2 level, as measured by chromatography (estimates of hemoglobin A_2 levels on starch gel electrophoresis are much less accurate). More sophisticated tests, including direct sequencing of the β-globin gene, may be needed to determine the specific type of β-thalassemia. α-Thalassemia can be diagnosed definitively only with globin chain synthesis studies, Southern blotting, polymerase chain reaction, or α-globin gene sequencing; however, a normal hemoglobin A_2 level in a patient with microcytosis, target cells, and no or mild anemia strongly suggests one or two gene deletion α-thalassemia trait.

Patients often have multiple potential causes of anemia. A patient with a rheumatologic or lymphoproliferative disease may have anemia of chronic disease but also may have a marked change in the

Table 160–5 • LABORATORY TESTS TO DISTINGUISH IRON DEFICIENCY ANEMIA FROM ANEMIA OF CHRONIC DISEASE (ACD)

MEASUREMENT	UNITS	NORMAL VALUES	IRON DEFICIENCY	ACD	ACD + IRON DEFICIENCY
Serum iron	μg/dL	50–150	↓	Low normal–↓	↓
Serum total iron-binding capacity	μg/dL	250–400	↑	Low normal–↓	Low normal–↓
Transferrin saturation	%	20–50	↓	Normal–↓	Low normal–↓
Serum ferritin	μg/L	20–350	↓	Normal–↑	Normal–↓
Serum soluble transferrin receptor	nM	9–28	↑	Normal	↑
Bone marrow iron stores	0–4+	2–3+	↓	Normal	↓
Iron-containing normoblasts in the bone marrow	%	20–80%	↓	↓	↓

Table 160–6 • SELECTED LABORATORY STUDIES THAT ARE USEFUL IN THE DIAGNOSIS OF ANEMIAS

IF THIS IS CONSIDERED TO BE A POSSIBLE CAUSE OF A PATIENT'S ANEMIA	THESE ARE POTENTIALLY USEFUL DIAGNOSTIC LABORATORY TESTS
HYPOPROLIFERATIVE ANEMIAS	
Bone marrow aplasia/hypoplasia or myelophthisis	Platelet count, white blood cell count with differential, bone marrow aspirate and biopsy
Myelodysplasia	Bone marrow aspirate and biopsy (including Prussian blue stain of iron), karyotype analysis
Acute leukemia	Bone marrow aspirate and biopsy, flow cytometry, immunohistochemical staining, karyotype analysis
Myelofibrosis	Bone marrow biopsy with stains for collagen (trichrome stain) and reticulin (silver stain)
Iron deficiency	Serum iron, TIBC, ferritin, soluble transferrin receptor (± bone marrow iron stain)
Anemia of chronic disease/inflammation	Serum iron, TIBC, ferritin, soluble transferrin receptor (± bone marrow iron stain)
Folate deficiency	Red blood cell folate level, serum folate level, bone marrow aspirate
Vitamin B$_{12}$ (cobalamin) deficiency	Serum vitamin B$_{12}$ level, urine (± serum) methylmalonic acid level, bone marrow aspirate, Schilling tests
HEMOLYTIC ANEMIAS	
General measures of hemolysis (intravascular [I] and extravascular [E])	Reduction in serum haptoglobin (I > E), presence of urine hemoglobin (I) and/or urine hemosiderin (I), increased serum LDH (I > E), and serum unconjugated bilirubin (I > E)
Thalassemias	Hemoglobin electrophoresis, hemoglobin A$_2$ and hemoglobin F levels, globin DNA analysis (Southern blotting, polymerase chain reaction, sequencing), globin chain synthesis ratios
Sickle cell disorders	Hemoglobin electrophoresis
Autoimmune hemolysis	Direct antiglobulin (Coombs) test, quantitation of red blood cell surface antibodies, cold agglutinin titer
Alloimmune hemolysis	Direct and indirect antiglobulin (Coombs) test with specificity analysis of eluted antibodies
Truamatic (microangiopathic or macroangiopathic) hemolysis	History and physical examination findings of hypertension, pregnancy, prosthetic heart valves or vascular grafts, systemic vasculitis, neurologic changes, fever; schistocytes, anemia, and destructive thrombocytopenia; BUN and creatinine; urinalysis; DIC panel
Hereditary spherocytosis, elliptocytosis, pyropoikilocytosis, and stomatocytosis	Primarily morphologic diagnoses; specific mutations detected by sequencing spectrin, ankyrin, band 3 or protein 4.1 DNA
Red blood cell enzymopathies	G6PD assay (1–2 months after acute hemolysis), Heinz body prep, specific enzyme assays
Unstable hemoglobins	Heat/isopropanol denaturation tests, hemoglobin electrophoresis
Paroxysmal nocturnal hemoglobinuria	Acid hemolysis (Ham) or sucrose hemolysis test, flow cytometry analysis of GPI-anchored cell surface proteins (e.g., CD55, 59)

BUN = blood urea nitrogen; DIC = disseminated intravascular coagulation; G6PD = glucose-6-phosphate dehydrogenase; GPI = glycosylphosphatidylinositol; TIBC = total iron-binding capacity.

severity of the anemia because of the development of autoimmune hemolysis. A patient with chronic hemolytic anemia, such as sickle cell disease, thalassemia, or hereditary spherocytosis, may develop folate deficiency or become infected with parvovirus B19, which prevents the bone marrow from continuing to overproduce erythrocytes and leads to a decreased number of reticulocytes and a resulting marked increase in the severity of the anemia. If the entire clinical picture cannot be explained by a single cause, the physician must search for secondary factors that may be important contributing components to the patient's anemia.

SUGGESTED READINGS

Erslev AJ: Clinical manifestations and classification of erythrocyte disorders. In Beutler E, Coller BS, Lichtman MA, et al (eds): Williams Hematology, 6th ed. New York, McGraw-Hill, 2001, pp 369–374. *Excellent review of the systemic manifestations of anemia.*

Hillman RS, Ault KA: Clinical approach to anemia. In: Hematology in Clinical Practice, 3rd ed. New York, McGraw-Hill, 2002, pp 17–37. *Excellent summary of practical approaches to the evaluation and management of anemias.*

Schnall SF, Berliner N, Duffy TP, Benz EJ Jr: Approach to the adult and child with anemia. In Hoffman R, Benz EJ Jr, Shattil SJ, et al (eds): Hematology: Basic Principles and Practice, 3rd ed. New York, Churchill Livingstone, 2000, pp 367–382. *Comprehensive review of the pathophysiology and evaluation of anemias.*

161 THE PERIPHERAL BLOOD SMEAR

John M. Bennett

Examination of a properly prepared and well-stained peripheral blood smear is an important component of the evaluation of patients with an abnormal blood count, especially when anemia is found with an abnormal white blood cell count or platelet count. The increased use of automated counters that can analyze red blood cell (RBC) size and perform white blood cell differential counts has led many hospitals to abandon routine Wright-Giemsa staining of the peripheral blood smear (Fig. 161–1).

Examination of the Blood Smear

The peripheral blood smear should be examined using a systematic approach. Scanning with a 10× or 20× objective can ensure that the stain is of good quality, with the erythrocytes being salmon pink, platelets with purple-blue cytoplasm and red-purple granules, and eosinophils with distinct orange granules (Fig. 161–2). The pattern of the RBCs should be examined to determine whether there is

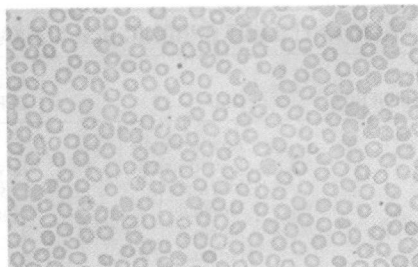

FIGURE 161–1 • Normal peripheral blood smear. The red blood cells are normocytic (normal size) and normochromic (normal hemoglobin pigment), with central areas of pallor that should occupy less than one half of the diameter of the cells. (Courtesy of Andrew Schafer, MD.)

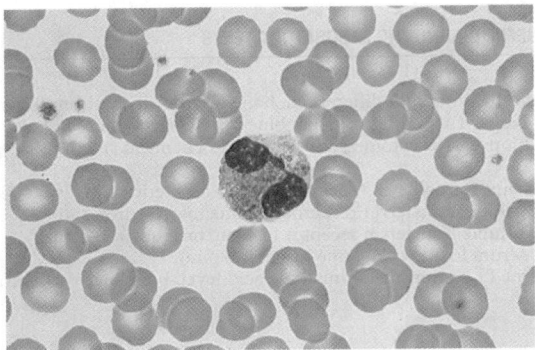

FIGURE 161–2 • Salmon pink red blood cells and orange granules of the eosinophil (×400). (Courtesy of Jean Shafer.)

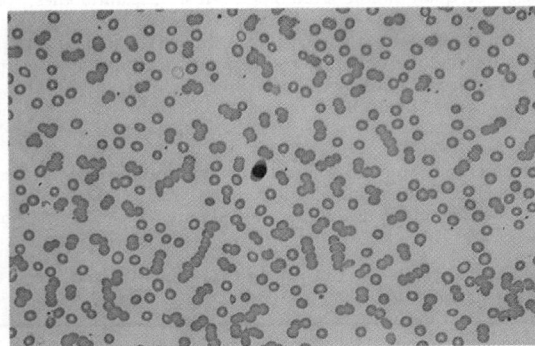

FIGURE 161–3 • Short stacks or rows of red blood cells, typical for rouleaux formation as seen with elevated globulin levels (×100). (Courtesy of Jean Shafer.)

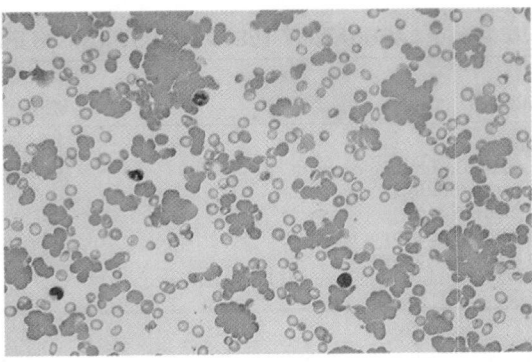

FIGURE 161–4 • Large amorphous aggregates (agglutination) of red blood cells as seen in *Mycoplasma pneumoniae* (×100). (Courtesy of Jean Shafer.)

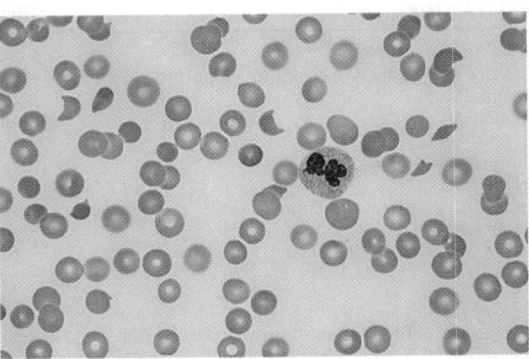

FIGURE 161–5 • Polychromatophilic macrocytes, helmet cells, rare schistocytes, and spherocytes (×250).

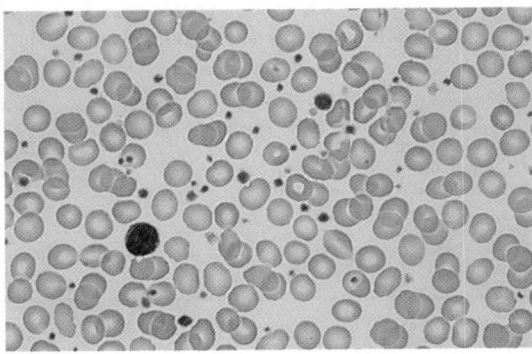

FIGURE 161–6 • Numerous small and one large platelet (×250). (Courtesy of Jean Shafer.)

evidence of rouleaux formation (Fig. 161–3) to suggest elevated globulin levels, as found in multiple myeloma (Chapter 196), or autoagglutination (Fig. 161–4), as is seen with cold agglutinins typical of *Mycoplasma pneumoniae* (Chapter 169). The smear should be scanned to determine whether nucleated RBCs are present.

The normal RBC is 7 to 8 μ in diameter, and two thirds of the diameter is hemoglobinized (normocytic, normochromic). The RBCs should be reviewed for size, shape, polychromasia, and hemoglobin content. The observation of "fragmented" cells may indicate an angiopathic hemolytic anemia (Chapter 169) or alcoholic cirrhosis (Fig. 161–5).

The examiner should review a minimum of 100 leukocytes with high power (usually under oil immersion with 100× lens). Special attention should be paid to the maturity of granulocytes; any increase in the number of basophils, eosinophils, monocytes, or lymphocytes; and the presence of any reactive lymphocytes or blast cells.

An estimate of the platelet count can be performed by multiplying the average number of platelets in 10 oil immersion fields by 20,000. The presence of macroplatelets (>5%) can reflect overproduction, splenic hypofunction, or the absence of a spleen (Fig. 161–6). The presence of too many microplatelets may indicate marrow failure (Chapter 174) or iron deficiency anemia (Chapter 167).

Specific Disease Entities

ERYTHROCYTES

Abnormalities of the erythrocytes can provide important clues regarding the presence of a variety of disorders, including hemoglobinopathies (Chapters 171 and 172), congenital and hemolytic anemias (Chapters 168 through 170), potentially reversible megaloblastic states (Chapter 175), iron deficiency (Chapter 167), and myelodysplastic syndromes (Chapters 182 and 183). Hypochromic microcytic cells are seen typically in chronic iron deficiency anemia (Chapter 167) or thalassemia minor (Fig. 161–7; Chapter 168). Target cells are associated with liver disease or hemoglobinopathies (Fig. 161–8; Chapters 170 through 173). Polychromasia implies retained RNA and should prompt consideration of hemolysis, often resulting from an increased reticulocyte count (Chapter 169). Increased numbers of macrocytes

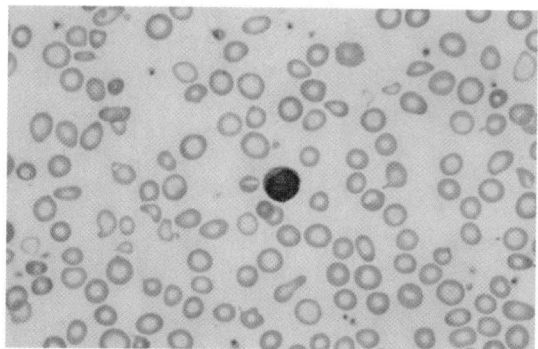

FIGURE 161–7 • Solitary small lymphocyte surrounded by hypochromic microcytic red blood cells (×250). (Courtesy of Jean Shafer.)

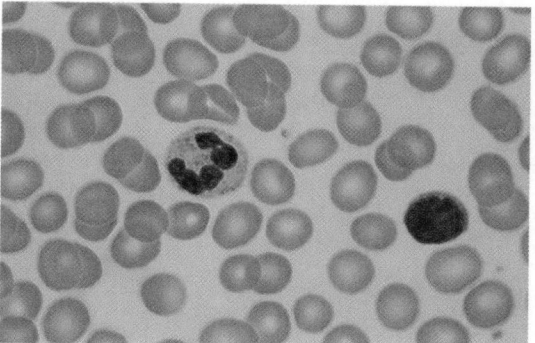

FIGURE 161–10 • Mature neutrophil with three lobes and small lymphocyte (×400). (Courtesy of Jean Shafer.)

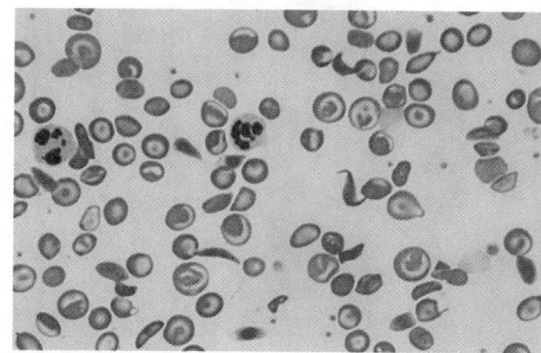

FIGURE 161–8 • Many target cells and sickle cells, typical of sickle cell anemia (×200). (Courtesy of Jean Shafer.)

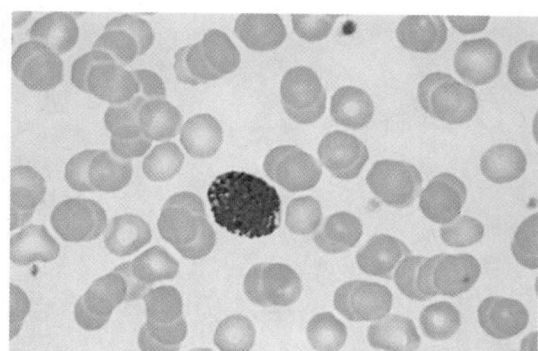

FIGURE 161–11 • A single basophil with prominent basophilic granules (×400). (Courtesy of Jean Shafer.)

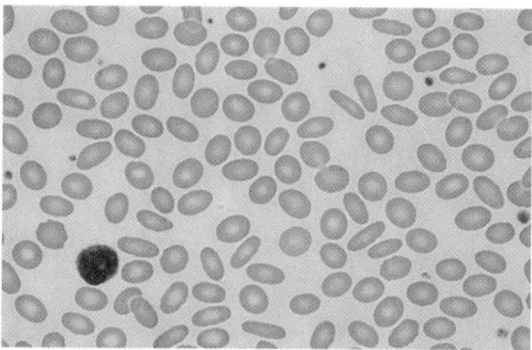

FIGURE 161–9 • Oval-shaped red blood cells, typical of hereditary elliptocytosis (×250). (Courtesy of Jean Shafer.)

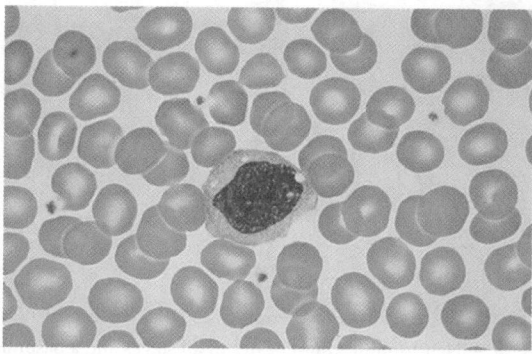

FIGURE 161–12 • Monocyte with abundant cytoplasm, occasional vacuoles, a few azurophilic granules, and cerebriform nucleus (×400). (Courtesy of Jean Shafer.)

are seen in benign disorders (pernicious anemia, folate deficiency; Chapter 175) or in myelodysplastic syndromes (Chapters 182 and 183). Elliptocytes (ovalocytes) are seen in familial disorders (Fig. 161–9; Chapter 170), whereas sickle cells are specific for sickle cell trait or disease. The presence of fragmented erythrocytes (schistocytes, helmet or "bitten" cells) implies a shearing effect in small vessels, which reflects an angiopathic disorder, but also is found in myelodysplasia and myelofibrosis (Chapters 182 and 183). Nucleated RBCs indicate bone marrow stromal disruption and can be seen in severe hypoxia, hemolysis, marrow fibrosis, metastatic disease, and extramedullary hematopoiesis.

LEUKOCYTES

A normal differential count includes mature neutrophils (56% ± 10%) (Fig. 161–10): band neutrophils (5% ± 3%), eosinophils (3% ± 2%) (see Fig. 161–2), basophils (<1%) (Fig. 161–11), monocytes (6%

± 4%) (Fig. 161–12), lymphocytes (30% ± 10%), and rarely plasma cells (<0.5%). An increase in band neutrophils or toxic cytoplasmic granules (Fig. 161–13) suggests infection, whereas hypersegmentation (five or more lobes) implies folate or vitamin B$_{12}$ deficiency (Fig. 161–14; Chapter 175). Increased eosinophils often represent an allergic reaction (Chapter 184), whereas an increase in basophils usually is present only in myeloproliferative disorders.

An elevated granulocyte count (e.g., neutrophils, bands, metamyelocytes, basophils) without an obvious infection can represent a leukemoid reaction (Chapter 163) or chronic myelogenous leukemia (Chapter 192). In chronic myelogenous leukemia, the morphology of the granulocytes is usually normal, but there are usually immature granulocytes, an occasional blast, and often basophils (Fig. 161–15). The presence of dysplastic granulocytes (pseudo Pelger-Huët cells with hyperdense chromatin, with or without a hypogranular or agranular cytoplasm) should prompt consideration of a myelodysplastic syndrome (Chapters 192 and 193), acute myelogenous leukemia

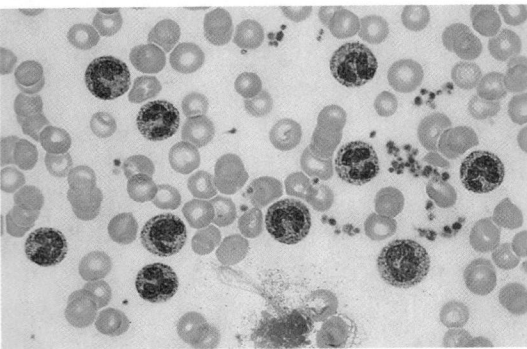

FIGURE 161–13 • Prominent toxic granules in the neutrophils (×250). (Courtesy of Jean Shafer.)

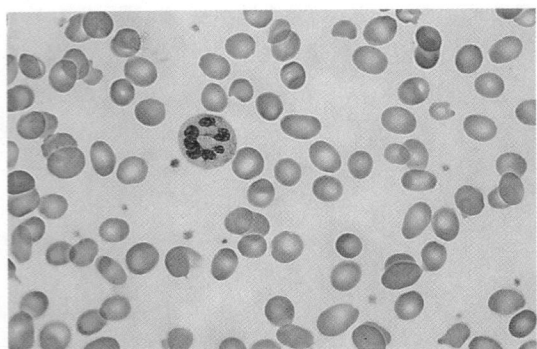

FIGURE 161–14 • One seven-lobed neutrophil and oval macrocytes, typical of folate or vitamin B$_{12}$ deficiency (×250). (Courtesy of Jean Shafer.)

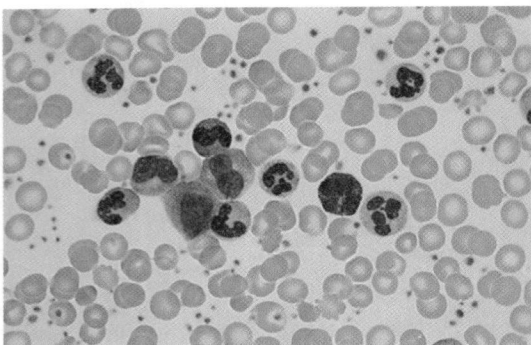

FIGURE 161–15 • Neutrophilic granulocytes of all stages and a basophil, typical of chronic myelogenous leukemia (×250). (Courtesy of Jean Shafer.)

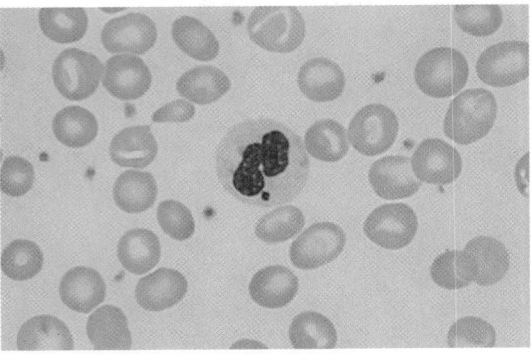

FIGURE 161–16 • Pseudo Pelger-Huët neutrophil with agranular cytoplasm (×400). (Courtesy of Jean Shafer.)

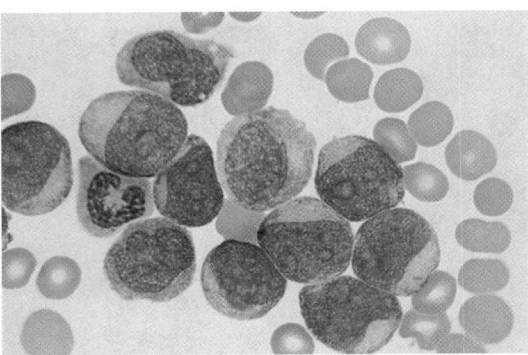

FIGURE 161–17 • Many blasts with prominent nucleoli and one with a thin Auer rod, typical of acute myelogenous leukemia (×400). (Courtesy of Jean Shafer.)

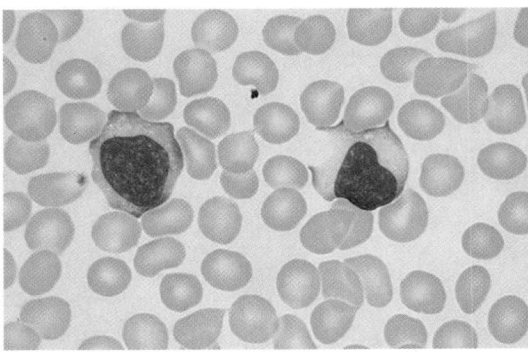

FIGURE 161–18 • Two reactive lymphocytes with low nuclear-to-cytoplasmic ratio, typical of infectious mononucleosis (×400). (Courtesy of Jean Shafer.)

(Chapter 193), or an accelerated phase of chronic myelogenous leukemia (Fig. 161–16; Chapter 192). The presence of myeloblasts (immature cells with occasional primary granules or Auer rods) indicates acute myelogenous leukemia or a high-risk myelodysplastic syndrome (Fig. 161–17; Chapter 192).

An increased number of lymphocytes or reactive lymphocytes (irregular outline of cytoplasm, low nuclear-to-cytoplasm ratio, peripheral basophilia, or convoluted nuclear shape) suggests a viral illness (i.e., infectious mononucleosis; Chapter 371) (Fig. 161–18). In the absence of other indications of a viral illness, immature lymphocytes raise the question of acute lymphocytic leukemia (Fig. 161–19; Chapter 193). An elevated lymphocyte count (>5000/μL) consisting of small, well-differentiated lymphoid cells implies chronic lymphocytic leukemia (Fig. 161–20; Chapter 192) or a related disorder. Confirmation by flow cytometry can determine the immunologic phenotype.

Increased numbers of monocytes can be seen in chronic disease states, such as tuberculosis (Chapter 341) or cancer (Chapter 194). Unexplained monocytosis raises suspicion of a myelodysplastic or

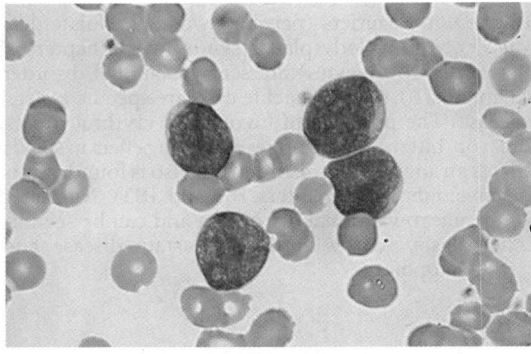

FIGURE 161–19 • Four blasts with high nuclear-to-cytoplasmic ratio and rare indistinct nucleoli, indicative of acute lymphocytic leukemia (×400). (Courtesy of Jean Shafer.)

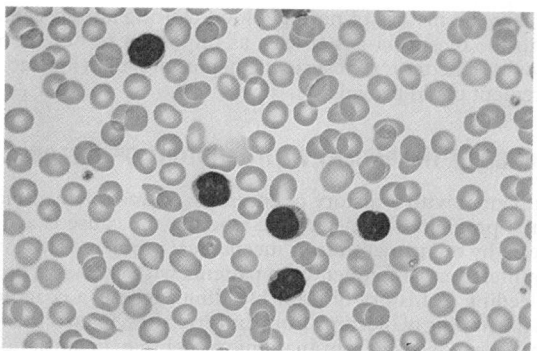

FIGURE 161–20 • Small well-differentiated lymphoid cells, in this case in a patient with B-cell chronic lymphocytic leukemia (×250). (Courtesy of Jean Shafer.)

myeloproliferative disorder, including myelomonocytic leukemia (Chapter 193). The presence of immature monocytes or monoblasts invariably indicates either acute myelomonocytic leukemia or acute monocytic leukemia (Chapter 193).

162 APPROACH TO THE PATIENT WITH BLEEDING AND THROMBOSIS

Andrew I. Schafer

Mechanisms of Hemostasis and Thrombosis

The intimal surface of the vasculature throughout the circulatory tree is lined by a monolayer of endothelial cells. These cells constitutively express anticoagulant properties that promote blood fluidity under normal circumstances. At a site of vascular injury, however, endothelial cells either are activated and are converted from an antithrombotic to a prothrombotic state or become detached to expose circulating blood to thrombogenic constituents of the subendothelial vessel wall. These processes result in the rapid formation of a hemostatic plug that consists of platelets and fibrin. Activation of platelets and formation of fibrin occur essentially simultaneously and interdependently to effect hemostasis. Subsequently, vessel wall repair is accomplished by thrombolysis and recanalization of the occluded site.

In the presence of intact endothelium, platelets are repelled from the vessel wall and circulate passively. Prostacyclin and nitric oxide are among the potent, locally active platelet inhibitors (and vasodilators) that are elaborated by normal endothelial cells to promote blood fluidity. At a site of vascular damage, these antiplatelet substances are lost, and platelets adhere to the de-endothelialized intimal surface. Platelet adhesion (platelet–vessel wall interaction) is mediated by von Willebrand's factor, which anchors the platelets to the vessel wall by binding to its platelet receptors located in membrane glycoprotein Ib. Adherent platelets undergo the "release reaction," during which they discharge constituents of their storage granules, including adenosine diphosphate (ADP), and synthesize thromboxane A_2 from arachidonic acid by means of the aspirin-inhibitable cyclooxygenase reaction. ADP, thromboxane A_2, and other components of the release reaction act in concert to recruit and activate additional platelets from the circulation to the site of vascular injury. These activated platelets expose binding sites for fibrinogen by forming the surface membrane glycoprotein IIb/IIIa complex. In the process of platelet aggregation (platelet-platelet interactions), fibrinogen (or von Willebrand's factor under conditions of high shear stress) mediates the formation of an occlusive platelet plug.

The fibrin, which anchors the hemostatic platelet plug, is formed from soluble plasma fibrinogen by the action of the potent protease enzyme thrombin (Fig. 162–1). The fibrin mesh is stabilized by covalent cross-linking mediated by factor XIII. Thrombin is formed from its inactive (zymogen) plasma precursor, prothrombin, by the action of activated factor X (Xa) and its cofactor, factor Va. This

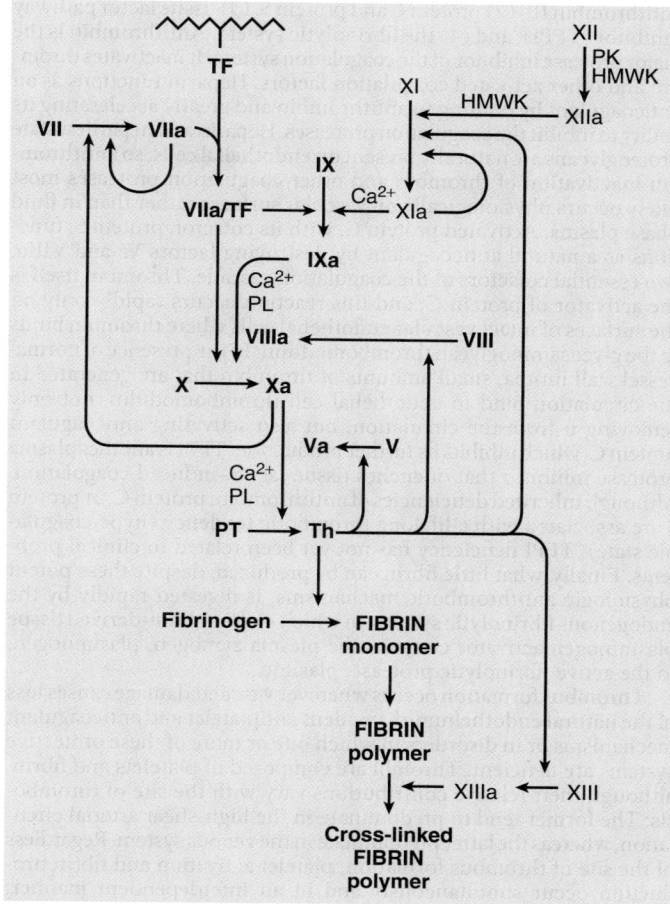

FIGURE 162–1 • The coagulation cascade. This scheme emphasizes understanding of (1) the importance of the tissue factor pathway in initiating clotting in vivo, (2) the interactions between pathways, and (3) the pivotal role of thrombin in sustaining the cascade by feedback activation of coagulation factors. HMWK = high-molecular-weight kininogen; PK = prekallikrein; PL = phospholipid; PT = prothrombin; TF = tissue factor; Th = thrombin. (From Schafer AI: Coagulation cascade: An overview. *In* Loscalzo J, Schafer AI [eds]: Thrombosis and Hemorrhage. Cambridge, MA, Blackwell Scientific Publications, 1994, pp 3–12.)

sequence of reactions classically has been referred to as the *common pathway* of coagulation. Factor X can be activated by either the tissue factor (extrinsic) pathway or the contact activation (intrinsic) pathway of coagulation. The former is initiated by the complex of tissue factor and factor VIIa. The latter involves a series (or cascade) of zymogen-protease reactions that are initiated by contact activation of factor XII to XIIa. High-molecular-weight kininogen and prekallikrein are two other plasma protein components of the contact activation system that leads to the generation of factor XIIa. Factor XIIa converts factor XI to XIa, followed by factor XIa–mediated activation of factor IX to IXa. Factor IXa serves as the enzyme to convert factor X to Xa, a reaction that requires factor VIIIa as a cofactor.

In the interpretation of screening in vitro laboratory tests of coagulation, it is still convenient to separate the extrinsic and intrinsic pathways of coagulation that converge as alternative mechanisms to activate factor X, leading to the common pathway that culminates in fibrin formation. It now is understood, however, that this is an inaccurate oversimplification of the situation in vivo. Factor IX (an intrinsic factor) can be activated by factor VII (an extrinsic factor). The absence of any clinical bleeding problems in patients with inherited deficiencies of the contact activation factors (high-molecular-weight kininogen, prekallikrein, factor XII) has cast doubt, however, on the physiologic importance of the intrinsic pathway in hemostasis.

Intact, normal endothelium promotes blood fluidity by inhibiting platelet activation, and it likewise plays a crucial role in naturally anticoagulating blood by preventing fibrin accumulation. Among the physiologic antithrombotic systems that produce this effect are (1)

Hematologic Diseases

antithrombin III, (2) protein C and protein S, (3) tissue factor pathway inhibitor (TFPI), and (4) the fibrinolytic system. Antithrombin is the major protease inhibitor of the coagulation system: It inactivates thrombin and other activated coagulation factors. Heparin functions as an anticoagulant by binding to antithrombin and greatly accelerating its ability to inhibit the coagulation proteases. Heparin and heparin sulfate proteoglycans are naturally present on endothelial cells, so antithrombin inactivation of thrombin and other coagulation proteases most likely occurs physiologically on vascular surfaces rather than in fluid phase plasma. Activated protein C, with its cofactor, protein S, functions as a natural anticoagulant by destroying factors Va and VIIIa, two essential cofactors of the coagulation cascade. Thrombin itself is the activator of protein C, and this reaction occurs rapidly only on the surfaces of intact vascular endothelial cells where thrombin binds to the glycosaminoglycan thrombomodulin. In the presence of normal vessel wall intima, small amounts of thrombin that are generated in the circulation bind to endothelial cell thrombomodulin, not only removing it from the circulation, but also activating anticoagulant protein C, which inhibits its further production. TFPI is another plasma protease inhibitor that quenches tissue factor–induced coagulation. Although inherited deficiencies of antithrombin, protein C, or protein S are associated with a lifelong thrombotic tendency (hypercoagulable state), TFPI deficiency has not yet been related to clinical problems. Finally, what little fibrin can be produced, despite these potent physiologic antithrombotic mechanisms, is digested rapidly by the endogenous fibrinolytic system, in which endothelium-derived tissue plasminogen activator converts the plasma zymogen, plasminogen, to the active fibrinolytic protease, plasmin.

Thrombus formation occurs wherever vascular damage causes loss of the natural endothelium-dependent antiplatelet and anticoagulant mechanisms or in disorders in which one or more of these protective systems are deficient. Thrombi are composed of platelets and fibrin, although their relative contributions vary with the site of thrombosis: The former tend to predominate in the high-shear arterial circulation, whereas the latter predominate in the venous system. Regardless of the site of thrombus formation, platelet activation and fibrin production occur simultaneously and in an interdependent manner: Thrombin generation occurs most efficiently on the surfaces of activated platelets, whereas thrombin itself is a potent stimulus for further platelet activation.

Evaluation of the Patient with a Possible Bleeding Disorder

A thorough history is paramount in evaluating a patient for a possible systemic bleeding disorder. Not only should the patient be asked about spontaneous bleeding episodes in the past, but also the response to specific hemostatic challenges should be recorded. A bleeding tendency may be suspected if a patient has experienced excessive hemorrhage after previous surgery or trauma, including commonly encountered events, such as circumcision, tonsillectomy, labor and delivery, menses, dental procedures, vaccinations, and injections.

Conversely, the history of normal blood clotting after specific challenges in the recent past is at least as important to note because it may provide a better test of systemic hemostasis than any laboratory measurement could provide.

EVALUATION OF THE PATIENT WITH A HISTORY OF BLEEDING

In a patient with a history of excessive or unexplained bleeding, the initial problem is to determine whether the cause is a systemic coagulopathy or an anatomic or mechanical problem. This situation is encountered most frequently in patients with excessive postoperative bleeding. A history of prior bleeding suggests a coagulopathy, as does the finding of bleeding from multiple sites. Even diffuse bleeding may arise, however, from anatomic rather than hemostatic abnormalities (e.g., recurrent mucosal hemorrhage in patients with hereditary hemorrhagic telangiectasia). Conversely, a single episode of bleeding from an isolated site may be the initial manifestation of a systemic coagulopathy.

The history must include a survey of coexisting systemic diseases and drug ingestion that may affect hemostasis. Renal failure and the myeloproliferative disorders are associated with impaired platelet–vessel wall interactions and qualitative platelet abnormalities, connective tissue diseases and lymphomas are associated with thrombocytopenia, and liver disease causes a complex coagulopathy. Ingestion of aspirin and other nonsteroidal anti-inflammatory drugs (NSAIDs) that cause nonselective inhibition of cyclooxygenase leads to platelet dysfunction; these drugs often are contained in over-the-counter preparations that patients may neglect to report without specific questioning. Other drugs, such as antibiotics, also may be associated with a bleeding tendency by causing abnormal platelet function or thrombocytopenia. Finally, it is important to elicit a family history of bleeding problems. Although a positive history provides a clue to a possible inherited coagulopathy, a negative history does not exclude a familial cause; 20% of patients with classic hemophilia have a completely negative family history of bleeding.

Patterns of clinical bleeding, as revealed by the history and physical examination, may be characteristic of certain types of coagulopathy (Table 162–1). In general, patients with thrombocytopenia or qualitative platelet and vascular disorders present with bleeding from superficial sites in the skin and mucous membranes; these may involve petechiae, which are pinpoint cutaneous hemorrhages that appear particularly over dependent extremities (characteristic of severe thrombocytopenia), ecchymoses (common bruises), purpura, gastrointestinal and genitourinary tract bleeding, epistaxis, and hemoptysis. In these disorders, bleeding from these sites tends to occur spontaneously or immediately after trauma. In contrast, patients with inherited or acquired coagulation factor deficiencies, such as hemophilia or therapeutic anticoagulation, tend to bleed from deeper tissue sites (e.g., hemarthroses, deep hematomas, retroperitoneal hemorrhage) and in a delayed manner after trauma.

Four simple screening tests generally are used in the initial evaluation of patients with a suspected coagulopathy: (1) platelet count,

Table 162–1 • CHARACTERISTIC PATTERNS OF BLEEDING IN SYSTEMIC DISORDERS OF HEMOSTASIS

| TYPE OF DISORDER | SITES OF BLEEDING | | | | ONSET OF BLEEDING | CLINICAL EXAMPLES |
	General	Skin	Mucous Membranes	Others		
Platelet-vascular disorders	Superficial surfaces	Petechiae, ecchymoses	Common: oral, nasal, gastrointestinal, genitourinary	Rare	Spontaneous or immediately after trauma	Thrombocytopenia, functional platelet disorder, vascular fragility Disseminated intravascular coagulation, liver disease
Coagulation factor deficiency	Deep tissues	Hematomas	Rare	Common: joint, muscle, retroperitoneal	Delayed after trauma	Inherited coagulation factor deficiency, acquired inhibitor, anticoagulation Disseminated intravascular coagulation, liver disease

(2) bleeding time, (3) prothrombin time (PT), and (4) activated partial thromboplastin time (aPTT). Thrombocytopenia, reported by electronic particle counting, should be verified by examination of the peripheral smear. Pseudothrombocytopenia, a laboratory artifact of ex vivo platelet clumping, may be caused by the ethylenediamine tetraacetic acid anticoagulant used in tubes for blood cell counts, other anticoagulants, or cold agglutinins acting at room temperature; it should be suspected whenever a low platelet count is reported in a patient who does not exhibit any clinical bleeding. Pseudothrombocytopenia is indicated by the finding of platelet clumps on the peripheral smear, and the diagnosis is supported by the finding of simultaneously normal platelet counts in blood samples obtained by finger-stick, in tubes containing other anticoagulants, or when the tube of blood is maintained at 37°C before platelet counting. Examination of the blood smear in patients with thrombocytopenia also can reveal clues to the cause, such as fragmented red blood cells in thrombotic thrombocytopenic purpura.

The bleeding time is the most widely used clinical screening test for disorders of platelet–vessel wall interactions. It measures the time to cessation of bleeding after a standardized incision over the volar aspect of the forearm, now most commonly performed by disposable automated devices. The bleeding time is prolonged in (1) thrombocytopenia, (2) qualitative platelet abnormalities, (3) defects in platelet–vessel wall interactions (e.g., von Willebrand's disease), or (4) primary vascular disorders. The bleeding time usually is not prolonged in patients with coagulation factor deficiencies. The test is prone to problems, however, of reproducibility, sensitivity, and specificity.

The PT measures the integrity of the extrinsic and common pathways of coagulation (factors VII, X, and V; prothrombin; and fibrinogen) (Fig. 162–2). The aPTT measures the integrity of the intrinsic and common pathways of coagulation (high-molecular-weight kininogen; prekallikrein; factors XII, XI, IX, VIII, X, and V; prothrombin; and fibrinogen). The sensitivity of the PT and aPTT in detecting coagulation factor deficiencies may vary with the reagents used to perform these tests, and each laboratory must determine its own reference standards.

With a few notable exceptions, as follows, normal results for all four of the screening tests of hemostasis essentially exclude any clinically significant systemic coagulopathy. Patients with factor XIII deficiency may have a serious bleeding diathesis but have normal screening tests; specific tests for factor XIII deficiency should be performed when this disease is suspected. The PT and aPTT detect only more severe deficiencies of coagulation factors, generally involving levels of less than 30% of normal; specific factor levels should be determined if a mild coagulation factor deficiency is suspected. Patients with von Willebrand's disease sometimes have normal bleeding times and usually do not have sufficiently reduced levels of factor VIII to affect the aPTT. Rare disorders of fibrinolysis also may be associated with normal screening tests, necessitating more specialized tests when indicated. Abnormalities in the screening tests of hemostasis may be pursued by more specialized tests to establish a specific diagnosis (Chapters 177 through 180).

A prolonged bleeding time in the absence of thrombocytopenia initially should be approached by determining if the patient is taking any drugs that might interfere with platelet function (e.g., aspirin, other NSAIDs) or has coexisting diseases that might explain the finding (e.g., renal failure) (Fig. 162–3). If these conditions are not found or if the bleeding time fails to correct after discontinuing any potential offending drugs, further specialized testing may include platelet aggregation studies to identify specific qualitative abnormalities of platelet function and specific assays to exclude one of the types of von Willebrand's disease.

The finding of a prolonged PT and/or aPTT indicates that there is a deficiency of one or more coagulation factors or an inhibitor, usually an antibody, directed at one or more components of the coagulation system (Fig. 162–4). These two possibilities can be distinguished by performing an inhibitor screen, which involves a 1:1 mix of the patient's plasma and normal plasma. The premise of the test is that even if a patient's plasma is completely deficient (0% level) in a certain factor, mixing it 1:1 with normal plasma (100% level) should bring the concentration of the factor to 50% in the mixture, which, as noted earlier, is sufficient to correct the prolonged PT and/or aPTT; individual coagulation factor levels should be assayed for a specific deficiency state. If the 1:1 mix fails to correct the prolonged PT and/or aPTT, an inhibitor is likely to be present in the patient's plasma and to be interfering with coagulation in the patient's plasma and normal plasma; specific assays should be performed to determine if there is a true inhibitor against a coagulation factor (e.g., factor VIII antibody) or if the inhibitor is a lupus anticoagulant.

EVALUATION OF THE ASYMPTOMATIC PATIENT WITH ABNORMAL COAGULATION TESTS

In asymptomatic individuals who are discovered incidentally to have abnormalities in screening laboratory tests of hemostasis, the

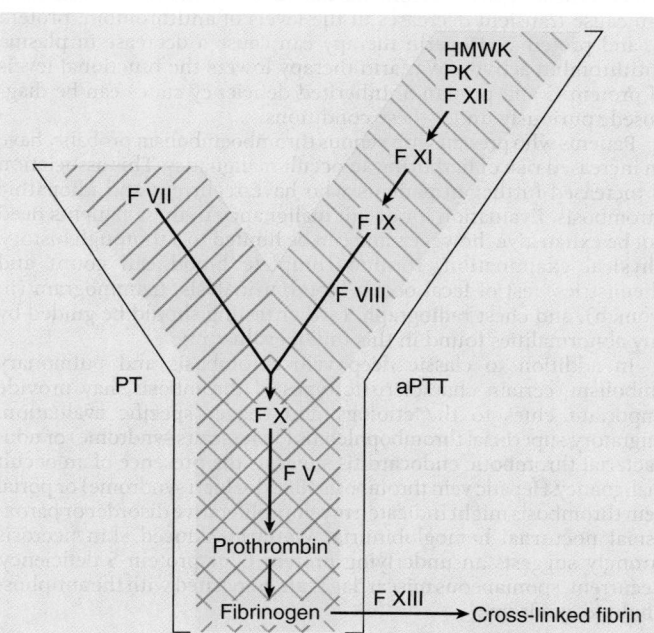

FIGURE 162–2 • Classic coagulation cascade, in which the prothrombin time (PT) measures the integrity of the extrinsic and common pathways, whereas the activated partial thromboplastin time (aPTT) measures the integrity of the intrinsic and common pathways. Factor (F) XIII deficiency is not detected by the PT or aPTT. HMWK = high-molecular-weight kininogen; PK = prekallikrein.

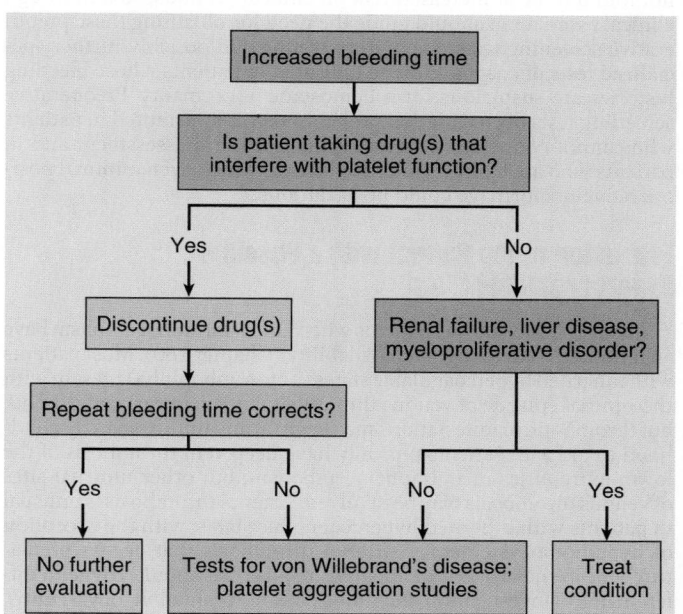

FIGURE 162–3 • Algorithm for diagnostic decisions in evaluating patients with a prolonged bleeding time. The scheme assumes that the platelet count is normal because thrombocytopenia itself can prolong the bleeding time.

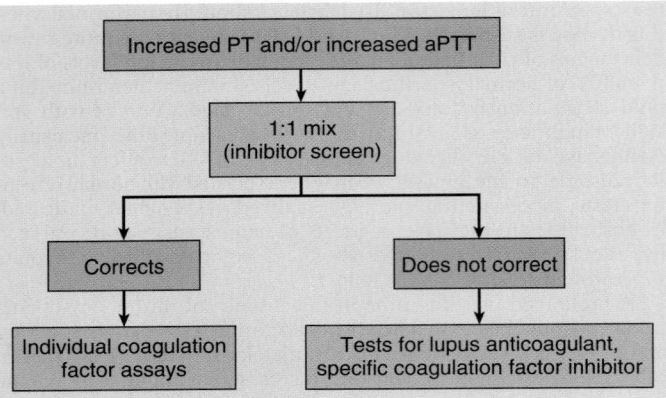

FIGURE 162-4 • Approach to evaluating patients with prolonged prothrombin time (PT) and/or activated partial thromboplastin time (aPTT).

Table 162-2 • CLINICAL CHARACTERISTICS OF PATIENTS WITH INHERITED HYPERCOAGULABLE STATES

Venous thromboembolism (>90% of cases)
   Deep vein thrombosis of lower limbs (common)
   Pulmonary embolism (common)
   Superficial thrombophlebitis
   Mesenteric vein thrombosis (rare but characteristic)
   Cerebral vein thrombosis (rare but characteristic)
Frequent family history of thrombosis*
First thrombosis usually at young age (<40 yr)*
Frequent recurrences*
Neonatal purpura fulminans (homozygous protein C and protein S deficiency)

*All these features are less evident in patients with activated protein C resistance, who appear to be less severely affected clinically.
From De Stefano V, Finazzi G. Manucci PM: Inherited thrombophilia: Pathogenesis, clinical syndromes, and management. Blood 1996;87:3531–3544.

first crucial question is whether the findings are clinically relevant. Patients with inherited deficiencies of one of the contact activation coagulation factors (factor XII, high-molecular-weight kininogen, prekallikrein) characteristically have a markedly prolonged aPTT, yet they do not have a clinical bleeding tendency. Likewise, patients with lupus anticoagulants typically have prolongations of the aPTT and sometimes the PT; they more often have thrombotic rather than bleeding complications. In patients with heparin-induced thrombocytopenia, a marked decrease in the platelet count sometimes is associated with arterial and venous thrombosis. It is crucial to view the clinical setting, history, physical examination, and screening laboratory tests as complementary facets of the approach to patients with suspected coagulopathies.

EVALUATION OF THE PREOPERATIVE PATIENT

The platelet count, bleeding time, PT, and aPTT have become widely ingrained in surgical practice as components of a coagulation panel to screen patients for bleeding risk before elective surgery. Increasing evidence from many studies now indicates, however, that this routine screening of all preoperative patients is not only uninformative, but also may be counterproductive when follow-up testing causes unnecessary expense and delays in surgery. Preoperative bleeding time, PT, and aPTT do not predict surgical bleeding risk in patients who are not found to be at increased risk on clinical grounds, so a thorough clinical assessment should guide the need for obtaining these preoperative screening tests. Laboratory testing and possibly further specialized tests of coagulation are indicated in patients whose bleeding histories are suspicious for a hemostatic abnormality. Preoperative screening tests of coagulation probably also are warranted in patients who cannot cooperate with an adequate clinical assessment and in patients who are to undergo procedures in which even minimal postoperative hemorrhage could be hazardous.

Evaluation of the Patient with a Possible Hypercoagulable State

Many (possibly most) patients with venous thromboembolism have an inherited basis for hypercoagulability (Chapter 180). Most patients with inherited hypercoagulable states (or thrombophilia) present with their initial episode of venous thromboembolism in early adulthood, but thrombotic manifestations may begin at any time from early childhood to old age. Patients typically have deep vein thrombosis of the lower extremities or pulmonary embolism, but other unusual sites of venous thrombosis may be involved. Arterial thrombosis is unusual in patients with inherited hypercoagulable states, with the exception of hyperhomocysteinemia. Arterial thrombosis that occurs prematurely or in the absence of apparent risk factors should trigger a different line of investigation, including possible evaluation for vasculitis, myeloproliferative disorders, antiphospholipid syndrome, and other acquired disorders as well as potential sources of systemic embolization.

The primary or hereditary hypercoagulable states (see Table 180–1) result from specific mutations or polymorphisms, leading to decreased levels of physiologic antithrombotic proteins or increased levels of procoagulant proteins. The hereditary form of heterozygous hyperhomocysteinemia, which often presents in adulthood with venous or arterial thrombosis, is caused by discrete mutations in the enzymes that mediate homocysteine metabolism. In contrast, the secondary or acquired hypercoagulable states (see Fig. 180–1) are a heterogeneous group of disorders that predispose to thrombosis by complex mechanisms. Venous thrombosis often is precipitated by the combination of a hypercoagulable genotype and an acquired prothrombotic, hypercoagulable state, such as pregnancy, immobilization, or the postoperative state. Certain clinical characteristics suggest the presence of an inherited hypercoagulable state (Table 162–2). Patients with recurrent thrombosis should be tested for these disorders and, in most cases, committed to lifelong prophylactic anticoagulation. It is not clear at this time whether or not it is essential to order these tests after a single episode of venous thromboembolism. Even when patients are not maintained on long-term anticoagulation, patients with diagnosed primary hypercoagulable states should receive prophylactic anticoagulation during situations that pose a high risk for thrombosis, such as the peripartum period. There is no simple screening test for primary hypercoagulable states, and the timing of obtaining these tests is crucial to avoid erroneous diagnoses. Acute thrombosis itself can cause transient decreases in the levels of antithrombin, protein C, and protein S. Heparin therapy can cause a decrease in plasma antithrombin activity. Warfarin therapy lowers the functional levels of protein C and protein S. Inherited deficiency states can be diagnosed spuriously under these conditions.

Patients who present with venous thromboembolism probably have an increased risk of harboring an occult malignancy. This association is increased further in patients who have recurrent and idiopathic thrombosis. Evaluation for occult malignancy in these patients need not be exhaustive, however, and can be limited to a thorough history, physical examination, routine complete blood cell count and chemistries, test of fecal occult blood, urinalysis, mammogram (in women), and chest radiograph; further testing should be guided by any abnormalities found in this initial evaluation.

In addition to classic deep vein thrombosis and pulmonary embolism, certain characteristic types of thrombosis may provide important clues to the etiology and trigger specific evaluation. Migratory, superficial thrombophlebitis (Trousseau's syndrome) or nonbacterial thrombotic endocarditis suggests the presence of an occult malignancy. Hepatic vein thrombosis (Budd-Chiari syndrome) or portal vein thrombosis might indicate a myeloproliferative disorder or paroxysmal nocturnal hemoglobinuria. Warfarin-induced skin necrosis strongly suggests an underlying protein C or protein S deficiency. Recurrent, spontaneous miscarriages are associated with the antiphospholipid syndrome.

SUGGESTED READINGS

Barger AP, Hurley R: Evaluation of the hypercoagulable state: Whom to screen, how to test and treat. Postgrad Med 2000;108:59–66. *Practical, clinical guidelines in approaching the diagnosis of thrombosis-prone patients.*
Crowther MA, Kelton JG: Congenital thrombophilic states associated with venous thrombosis: A qualitative overview and proposed classification system. Ann Intern Med 2003;138:128–134. *Practical guide to the inherited hypercoagulable states and the increas-*

ing recognition that genetic causes of venous thromboembolism may involve not only reduced levels of the inhibitors of the coagulation cascade but also increased function of the coagulation factors.

Federman DG, Kirsner RS: An update on hypercoagulable disorders. Arch Intern Med 2001;161:1051–1056. *Up-to-date diagnostic approach to patients with suspected thrombophilia.*

163   LEUKOPENIA AND LEUKOCYTOSIS

Grover C. Bagby, Jr.

The normal peripheral white blood cell count ranges from 5.0 to 10.0×10^9/L, and a low total white blood cell count (less than 4.5×10^9/L) is known as *leukopenia*. When leukopenia is discovered, the single most important first step is to determine which type of white blood cell is at lower levels than normal. Circulating leukocytes consist of heterogeneous cell types (neutrophils, monocytes, basophils, eosinophils, B lymphocytes, T lymphocytes, and natural killer cells), each of which serves a unique purpose and each of which represents a different fractional component of the total body leukocyte population. Taking this leukocyte heterogeneity into account, patients may be either severely neutropenic or lymphocytopenic despite having total white blood cell counts that fall within the normal range. Consequently, in a number of clinical settings (e.g., patients with an acute infection or those with recurrent infections) differential white blood cell counts are important even in the absence of leukopenia.

NEUTROPENIA

Definition

The clinical consequences of prolonged phagocyte dysfunction can be life threatening. Fortunately, acquired and inherited phagocyte dysfunction syndromes are rare. However, a reduction in the number of circulating phagocytes is more common in clinical practice, the most life-threatening instances of which result from bone marrow failure. Neutropenia is said to exist when a patient's peripheral *neutrophil* count is less than 2.0×10^9/L. Because the normal range

in Yemenite Jews and black individuals is somewhat lower, neutropenia in these populations is defined as counts less than 1.5×10^9/L. The role of the neutrophil in phagocytic defense of the host is generally met if the neutrophil count is above 1.0×10^9/L. If the neutrophil count drops further, particularly below 0.5×10^9/L, the threat of recurrent, severe, life-threatening, and difficult-to-treat infections increases enormously.

Pathophysiology

The causes of neutropenia are best described in the context of normal neutrophil kinetics. Neutrophils arise from a pool of marrow precursor cells through serial divisions and synchronous maturation steps (Fig. 163–1). The rate of neutrophil production is high: more than 10^{11} cells/day. In the bone marrow, neutrophil precursors that retain replicative potential (myeloblasts, promyelocytes, and myelocytes) constitute the mitotic pool. Later differentiation stage cells (metamyelocytes, bands, and segmented neutrophils) do not replicate and therefore form a nonmitotic precursor pool. A retained pool of fully developed neutrophils form a neutrophil storage pool within the bone marrow. These cells are held in reserve, ready for rapid release into the circulating blood when environmental conditions call for their release.

Released after a few days' sojourn in the bone marrow, neutrophils move through the blood in one of two pools. Half of the cells circulate freely for a few hours; this circulating pool contains all of the neutrophils sampled in the white blood cell count. The other half (the marginated pool) literally roll along the endothelium, held loosely in place by shear forces of blood flow and by interaction of families of adhesion molecules on the neutrophil surface with ligand molecules on the endothelial cell surface; these cells are not counted as part of the white blood cell count but can be recruited to circulate instantaneously by various stimuli (e.g., epinephrine). Ultimately, virtually all neutrophils leave the circulation in a matter of 6 to 12 hours and move into the extravascular space, looking for organisms and debris to destroy. However, because the circulating pool is measured and the marginated pool is not, the true intravascular neutrophil number, consisting of the circulating and the marginated pools, is

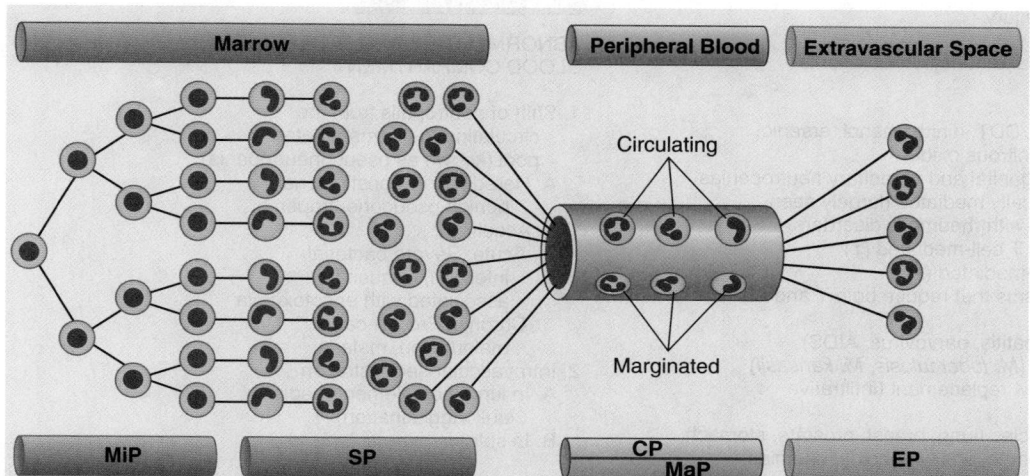

FIGURE 163–1 • Production and distribution of neutrophils involve three compartments: marrow, peripheral blood, and extravascular space. Unlike red blood cells, phagocytes are destined to function primarily in the extravascular space. The critical issue for clinicians to consider is whether the delivery of phagocytes to this space is adequate. Stem cells, committed progenitor cells, and morphologically recognizable bone marrow precursor cells proliferate and mature; they differentiate under the influence of a variety of humoral regulatory factors that govern the production of neutrophils (granulocyte colony-stimulating factor), monocytes (macrophage colony-stimulating factor), and eosinophils (interleukin-5). These replicative responses occur in the mitotic pool (MiP). Once more differentiated cells reach the intermediate maturation stage known as the metamyelocyte, they stop replicating but continue differentiating into bands and segmented neutrophils. These cells, although capable of leaving the marrow when needed (e.g., in the setting of an acute bacterial infection), spend up to 5 days in the marrow in the storage pool (SP). The neutrophils then enter the blood stream. Half of these circulating cells adhere to endothelial cells and compose the marginated pool (MaP). The nonmarginated cells make up the circulating pool (CP). After their very brief sojourn in the peripheral blood, the neutrophils invade the extravascular compartments of most organs, where they are used as defenders or garbage disposal devices (a process that involves both destruction of the offending organism and self-destruction), or they die within 1 to 2 days. EP = extravascular pool.

ordinarily twice that measured by the neutrophil count. Taking these kinetic considerations into account, a simple pathophysiologic classification of neutropenia can be derived from the three-compartment model: (1) the marrow compartment, (2) the peripheral blood compartment, (3) the extravascular compartment, or (4) combinations of these three (Fig. 163–2).

ABNORMALITIES IN THE MARROW COMPARTMENT. Bone marrow defects (failure to produce and release neutrophils at a normal rate) account for the majority of neutropenias in clinical practice. Failure of the marrow compartment can occur as a result of direct injury to either hematopoietic progenitors and stem cells or cells in the hematopoietic microenvironment. With both types of injury, the marrow usually contains fewer than normal numbers of hematopoietic cells; or, maturation defects of hematopoietic cells result in normal or increased numbers of morphologically abnormal hematopoietic cells. In either case, neutropenia of this type frequently occurs along with abnormalities in the number of platelets and red blood cells.

Marrow injury can occur as a consequence of a variety of diseases, but drug-induced injury is most common (Table 163–1). Antineoplastic, certain antiviral, and some immunosuppressive agents are generally designed to inflict injury on a nonmyeloid cell population (e.g., neoplastic cells); myelosuppressive toxicity is the rule but is generally predictable because its intensity varies directly with the dose. Drugs that usually are not myelosuppressive and well tolerated in the majority of patients can sometimes induce either marrow injury or peripheral neutrophil destruction. These idiosyncratic drug-induced reactions can result from direct drug-mediated cytotoxicity or from an immune mechanism in which (1) neutrophils are destroyed in extramedullary sites as a result of antineutrophil antibodies (e.g., the penicillins) or (2) the marrow compartment is injured (e.g., procainamide, chloramphenicol, dapsone, tocainide).

Radiation (Chapter 19) may result in acute self-limited bone marrow injury and chronic marrow failure. Chronic radiation-induced injury can also result in the later development of myelodysplasia and non-lymphocytic leukemia, both of which may manifest with neutropenia. Benzene toxicity can also result in acute or chronic neutropenia and, like radiation-induced marrow failure, is associated with a high risk of acute nonlymphocytic leukemia.

Immune-mediated bone marrow failure can be mediated by autoantibodies or by T lymphocytes that inhibit the growth of bone marrow precursor cells. Apart from those with acquired aplastic anemia (often immunologically mediated; see Chapter 174), most patients with immune-mediated leukopenia have concurrent rheumatic or autoimmune diseases, which are especially likely if the neutropenia is the only severe hematologic defect in patients with normal red blood cell and platelet counts. Infection of the marrow per se is unusual and most often does not result in neutropenia; some exceptions include mycobacterial infections (especially those caused by *Mycobacterium tuberculosis* and *Mycobacterium kansasii*; see Chapters 341 and 342) and certain viral infections.

Bone marrow invasion by abnormal cells can result in neutropenia. Carcinoma of the lung (Chapter 198), breast (Chapter 204), prostate (Chapter 207), and stomach (Chapter 199) as well as malignant hematopoietic disorders can occupy enough of the medullary space to cause global marrow failure. Similarly, in certain of the myeloproliferative diseases and leukemias, bone marrow fibroblasts can proliferate significantly in the marrow (myelofibrosis) and contribute to bone marrow failure (see Fig. 163–2). This type of global marrow dysfunction nearly always results in both neutropenia and anemia, while platelet counts can be variable, particularly in the syndromes associated with myelofibrosis.

Maturation arrest can result in functional bone marrow failure even though the bone marrow is full of granulocyte precursors. In the bone marrows of patients with folate or vitamin B_{12} deficiency, for example, numerous morphologically abnormal granulocyte precursors fail to mature normally and therefore suffer a high rate of intramedullary death because of the effects of the vitamin deficiency

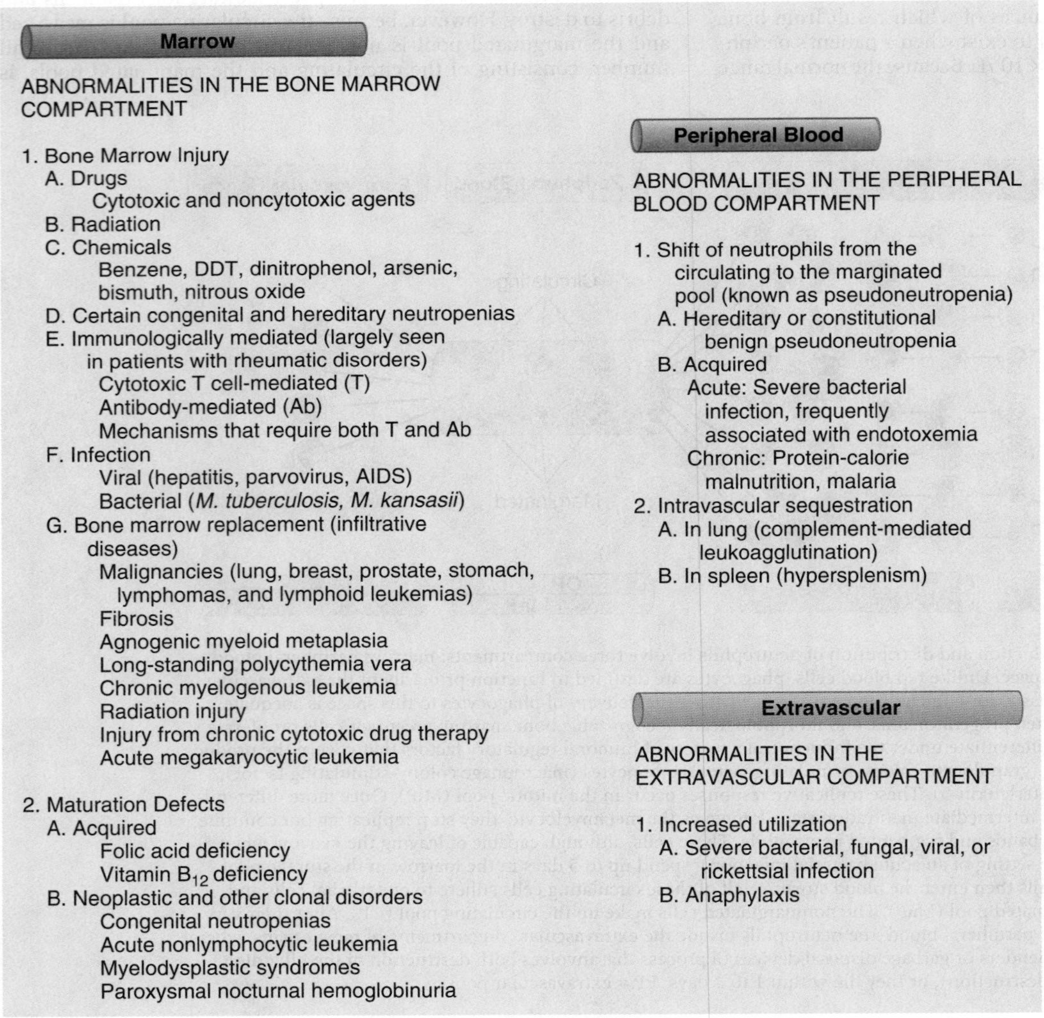

Marrow

ABNORMALITIES IN THE BONE MARROW COMPARTMENT

1. Bone Marrow Injury
   A. Drugs
      Cytotoxic and noncytotoxic agents
   B. Radiation
   C. Chemicals
      Benzene, DDT, dinitrophenol, arsenic, bismuth, nitrous oxide
   D. Certain congenital and hereditary neutropenias
   E. Immunologically mediated (largely seen in patients with rheumatic disorders)
      Cytotoxic T cell-mediated (T)
      Antibody-mediated (Ab)
      Mechanisms that require both T and Ab
   F. Infection
      Viral (hepatitis, parvovirus, AIDS)
      Bacterial (*M. tuberculosis, M. kansasii*)
   G. Bone marrow replacement (infiltrative diseases)
      Malignancies (lung, breast, prostate, stomach, lymphomas, and lymphoid leukemias)
      Fibrosis
      Agnogenic myeloid metaplasia
      Long-standing polycythemia vera
      Chronic myelogenous leukemia
      Radiation injury
      Injury from chronic cytotoxic drug therapy
      Acute megakaryocytic leukemia

2. Maturation Defects
   A. Acquired
      Folic acid deficiency
      Vitamin B_{12} deficiency
   B. Neoplastic and other clonal disorders
      Congenital neutropenias
      Acute nonlymphocytic leukemia
      Myelodysplastic syndromes
      Paroxysmal nocturnal hemoglobinuria

Peripheral Blood

ABNORMALITIES IN THE PERIPHERAL BLOOD COMPARTMENT

1. Shift of neutrophils from the circulating to the marginated pool (known as pseudoneutropenia)
   A. Hereditary or constitutional benign pseudoneutropenia
   B. Acquired
      Acute: Severe bacterial infection, frequently associated with endotoxemia
      Chronic: Protein-calorie malnutrition, malaria
2. Intravascular sequestration
   A. In lung (complement-mediated leukoagglutination)
   B. In spleen (hypersplenism)

Extravascular

ABNORMALITIES IN THE EXTRAVASCULAR COMPARTMENT

1. Increased utilization
   A. Severe bacterial, fungal, viral, or rickettsial infection
   B. Anaphylaxis

FIGURE 163–2 • The causes of neutropenia have been arranged according to the compartment with which the pathophysiologically relevant mechanism is linked. One should begin the approach to the neutropenic patient by determining which of the three major compartments is likely the critical pathophysiologic point. The approach to the neutropenic patient whose neutrophil production is reduced is entirely different than that taken for neutropenic patients whose production is normal and whose rate of delivery to the extravascular compartment is normal or appropriately increased in the context of an acute infection.

Table 163–1 • DRUGS THAT CAUSE NEUTROPENIA

Antiarrhythmics
   Tocainide, procainamide, propranolol, quinidine
Antibiotics
   Chloramphenicol, penicillins, sulfonamides, para-aminosalicylic acid
      (PASA), rifampin, vancomycin, isoniazid, nitrofurantoin,
      ganciclovir
Antimalarials
   Dapsone, quinine, pyrimethamine
Anticonvulsants
   Phenytoin, mephenytoin, trimethadione, ethosuximide,
      carbamazepine
Hypoglycemic agents
   Tolbutamide, chlorpropamide
Antihistamines
   Cimetidine, brompheniramine, tripelennamine
Antihypertensives
   Methyldopa, captopril
Anti-inflammatory agents
   Aminopyrine, phenylbutazone, gold salts, ibuprofen, indomethacin
Antithyroid agents
   Propythiouracil, methimazole, thiouracil
Diuretics
   Acetazolamide, hydrochlorothiazide, chlorthalidone
Phenothiazines
   Chlorpromazine, promazine, prochlorperazine
Immunosuppressive agents
   Antimetabolites
Cytotoxic agents
   Alkylating agents, antimetabolites, anthracyclines, vinca alkaloids,
      cisplatin, hydroxyurea, dactinomycin
Other agents
   Recombinant interferons, allopurinol, ethanol, levamisole,
      penicillamine, zidovudine, streptokinase, carbamazepine, clozapine

state on nuclear replication (Chapter 175). The marrow is hypercellular but is packed with peculiar cells exhibiting dys-synchronous nuclear and cytoplasmic maturation (e.g., primitive nuclei and very differentiated cytoplasm [the hallmark of megaloblastic change]). Hematopoietic activity in the primitive cell population is intensely active, but the proliferative activity is ineffective at delivering terminally differentiated cells into the blood stream—the process is known as *ineffective hematopoiesis*. Certain congenital neutropenias also represent maturation abnormalities, as do the acute nonlymphocytic leukemias, myelodysplastic syndromes, and paroxysmal nocturnal hemoglobinuria.

ABNORMALITIES IN THE PERIPHERAL BLOOD COMPARTMENT. Perturbations of the peripheral blood compartment result from shifts from the marginated to the circulating pool and vice versa (see Figs. 163–1 and 163–2). In one form of pseudoneutropenia, neutrophil production and utilization are normal, but the size of the marginated pool is increased and the circulating pool is decreased. Because these marginated cells, while hidden from the counting machine, maintain their capacity to migrate to sites of infection, patients with pseudoneutropenia are not at increased risk of infection unless a neutrophil function abnormality coexists. Acquired pseudoneutropenia often occurs as an acute or subacute response to systemic infections; it is generally associated with acute changes in other compartments (Fig. 163–3) and resolves when the infection is appropriately treated or spontaneously abates. Finally, a truly artifactual type of pseudoneutropenia can be seen as a result of EDTA (the anticoagulant in the CBC tube)-induced clumping of neutrophils, which can be eliminated by adding kanamycin to the sample.

DEMANDS OF THE EXTRAVASCULAR COMPARTMENT. Neutrophils and their precursors respond to a number of environmental cues in a highly regulated fashion. The most frequent of these cues evolve in response to infections. These responses are governed by a variety of hematopoietic growth factors, adhesion molecules, and interleukins, including two granulopoietic factors, granulocyte-macrophage colony stimulating factor (GM-CSF) and granulocyte colony stimulating factor (G-CSF), and an important chemokine, interleukin (IL)-8. These factors, along with IL-1 and tumor necrosis factor-α, cytokines that induce synthesis and release of granulopoietic factors and adhesion molecules on both neutrophils and endothelial cells, account for (1) a prompt increase in the rate of production of neutrophils in the mitotic compartment, a response mediated by a complex network of cellular and humoral regulatory interactions; (2) early release of neutrophils from the marrow storage pool to the peripheral blood pool; (3) an increase in the rate of neutrophil egress from the peripheral blood pool to the invaded tissue or tissues; and (4) increased phagocytic and bactericidal activity of the neutrophils. Rarely, increased demand for neutrophils in the extravascular compartment can lead to transient neutropenia, especially in patients with severe acute infections (see Fig. 163–3). In such cases, the immediate demand for neutrophils in the zone of infection calls forth such a substantial release response that the marrow storage pool is used up before it can be restored by increased proliferative activity of granulocyte progenitor cells. This kind of neutropenia is not uncommon in cases of typhoid fever salmonella (Chapter 324), in which leukopenia is common in the acute phase. In such cases, for a brief period (sometimes up to 5 to 6 days), the infected tissue serves as a sink for neutrophils. Ultimately, under even these conditions, the neutrophil count generally rises well above normal within a few days because the bone marrow is highly effective in responding to infectious events, so that the demand for neutrophils almost never exceeds the capacity of the mitotic pool to supply them if the bone marrow is completely normal. In contrast, neutrophil consumption in patients with autoimmune neutropenia and hypersplenism can outstrip marrow production regularly.

Clinical Manifestations

Neutropenia can occur as a manifestation of a wide variety of systemic diseases (see Fig. 163–2), the manifestations of which may dominate the clinical picture. Many neutropenic patients remain asymptomatic, most often those whose neutrophil count exceeds 1.0×10^9/L or those whose neutropenia is acute and/or of brief duration. When symptoms do occur, they generally result from recurrent, often severe, bacterial infections because of the pivotal importance of the neutrophil in the defense of the host against microorganisms (Chapter 181).

This risk of bacterial infection increases slightly as the peripheral neutrophil count falls below 1.0×10^9/L but is substantially increased at levels below 0.5×10^9/L. The degree to which monocytosis compensates for neutropenia may modify the risk. Some patients with severe congenital neutropenia have such substantial compensatory monocytosis that their clinical course is very mild. Because of the capacity of the extra monocytes to "cover" for neutrophil deficiencies, such rare patients have few bacterial infections. Lungs, genitourinary system, gut, oropharynx, and skin are the most frequent sources of infection in neutropenic patients. The infecting organisms are the "usual suspects" for the given anatomic site, with the caveat that, for patients who have recurrent infections and require prolonged and recurrent antibacterial therapy, unusual (often hospital-acquired) organisms can colonize and subsequently cause infection. Consequently, the antibiotic history of infected neutropenic patients is important to obtain.

One must look carefully for infections in neutropenic patients because the usual signs and symptoms of infection are often diminished or absent, owing to the reduction in the cells that mediate much of the inflammatory responses to infection. Thus, neutropenic patients with severe bilateral bacterial pneumonia can present, initially, with minimal infiltrates demonstrable on chest radiograph (sometimes no infiltrates at all until about 3 or 4 days of full-blown symptoms) and can have benign-looking, nonpurulent sputum; patients with pyelonephritis may not exhibit much pyuria; patients with bacterial pharyngitis may not have purulence in the oropharynx; and patients with severe bacterial infection of the skin may present only with some mild erythroderma rather than furunculosis. In the neutropenic patient, infections that in an otherwise normal individual might have been well localized become quickly disseminated. Therefore, not only does the infected neutropenic patient represent a diagnostic problem but in addition, because any given infection is more likely to be widespread at the time of diagnosis, these patients are often gravely ill at the time they initially present to their caregivers.

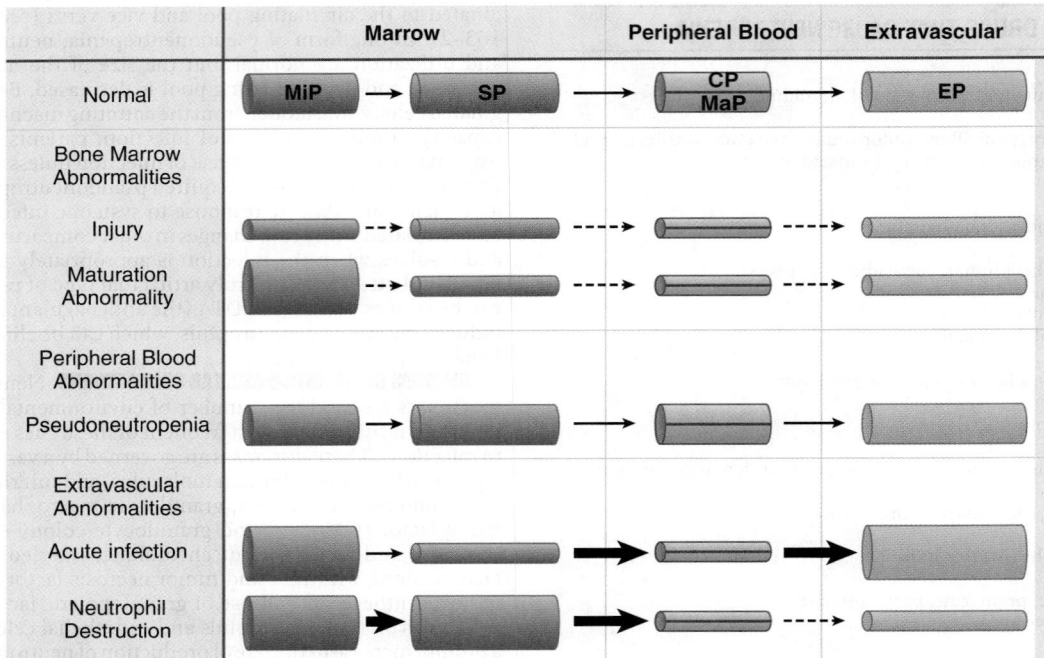

	Marrow		**Peripheral Blood**	**Extravascular**
Normal	MiP →	SP →	CP / MaP →	EP
Bone Marrow Abnormalities				
Injury				
Maturation Abnormality				
Peripheral Blood Abnormalities				
Pseudoneutropenia				
Extravascular Abnormalities				
Acute infection				
Neutrophil Destruction				

FIGURE 163–3 • Pathophysiologic mechanisms of neutropenia. The size of a given compartment is represented by the size of the corresponding cylindrical pool. The relative number of cells leaving one compartment and headed for the next (highly variable from case to case) is represented by the size of the arrow between those compartments. Flow between compartments is unidirectional. MiP = mitotic pool; SP = storage pool; CP = circulating pool; MaP = marginated pool; EP = extravascular pool. Notice that in every case the circulating neutrophil pool is small, but the size of the other pools is variable. In marrow injury, there is a global decline in the size of all pools. A maturation abnormality (e.g., folic acid or vitamin B_{12} deficiency), however, is characterized by an increase in the number of precursor cells that do not mature, resulting in an absolute decrease in mature neutrophils in the marrow, blood, and tissues. Pseudoneutropenia is characterized by a movement of circulating neutrophils to the marginated pool, but, because delivery of the cells to the extravascular space is usually normal, such patients are not at increased risk of infections. In patients who have acute infections, the demand for neutrophils in the infected extravascular site can result in a transient loss of storage pool neutrophils before the hypercellular (but as yet immature) mitotic compartments can renew the storage pool. This kind of neutropenia is very transient and occurs most often in cases of overwhelming infection, although certain organisms (e.g., *Salmonella typhosa*) seem to induce this kind of response more than others. Excessive destruction of neutrophils can also result in neutropenia, but this is not particularly common, except in cases of human immunodeficiency virus infection.

Diagnosis

The diagnostic evaluation of neutropenia is influenced by its severity and the clinical setting in which it occurs. The assessment of patients with neutrophil counts of less than 0.5 to 1.0×10^9/L must proceed briskly. The patient with fever, sepsis, or both in whom neutropenia is discovered for the first time presents a particularly difficult problem. In such patients, it is impossible to determine immediately whether the neutropenia antedated sepsis, a situation with both prognostic and therapeutic implications, or whether the neutropenia is merely a short-lived response to the infection itself (see Fig. 163–3). Examination of the peripheral blood smear and differential white blood cell count can be helpful in such cases. An increase in the fraction of circulating band neutrophil forms to levels above 20% suggests that marrow granulopoietic activity is responding appropriately (Fig. 163–4). Although the clinical context is more important to consider than this single data point, colloquially known as "bandemia," it is, nonetheless, a data point more compatible with the notion that the bone marrow of the patient is in the midst of recovering from injury or that the neutropenia is derived from a transient shift to the marginated pool or to the extravascular compartment.

The diagnostic evaluation of neutropenia must first address the question of severity and then whether the patient has fever, sepsis, or both. The patient with sepsis and severe neutropenia should be treated promptly with intravenous antibiotics after obtaining appropriate cultures but without waiting for the results of those cultures. Once these important initial questions are answered, the remainder of the diagnostic evaluation can proceed (Fig. 163–5): (1) identifying any potential drugs and toxins to which the patient might have been exposed (see Table 163–1); (2) determining, if possible, the

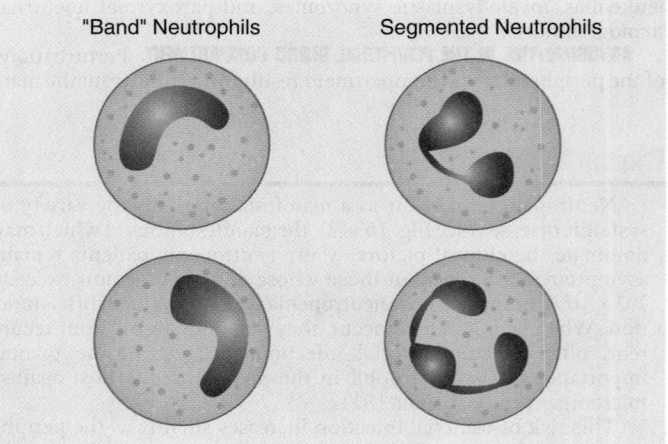

"Band" Neutrophils   Segmented Neutrophils

FIGURE 163–4 • The nuclear lobes in a segmented form are separated by fine filaments absent in the band. Band neutrophils are "younger" forms than segmented neutrophils. In time, bands residing in the bone marrow undergo segmentation. Normally, band neutrophils account for less than 4% of total circulating neutrophils. Band percentages greater than 6 to 7% suggest that the storage pool is releasing granulocytes early under the influence of increased levels of granulopoietic factors and that neutrophils are being consumed in the periphery. Alternatively, if neutropenia is the result of bone marrow failure, the bone marrow may be in the midst of an early recovery.

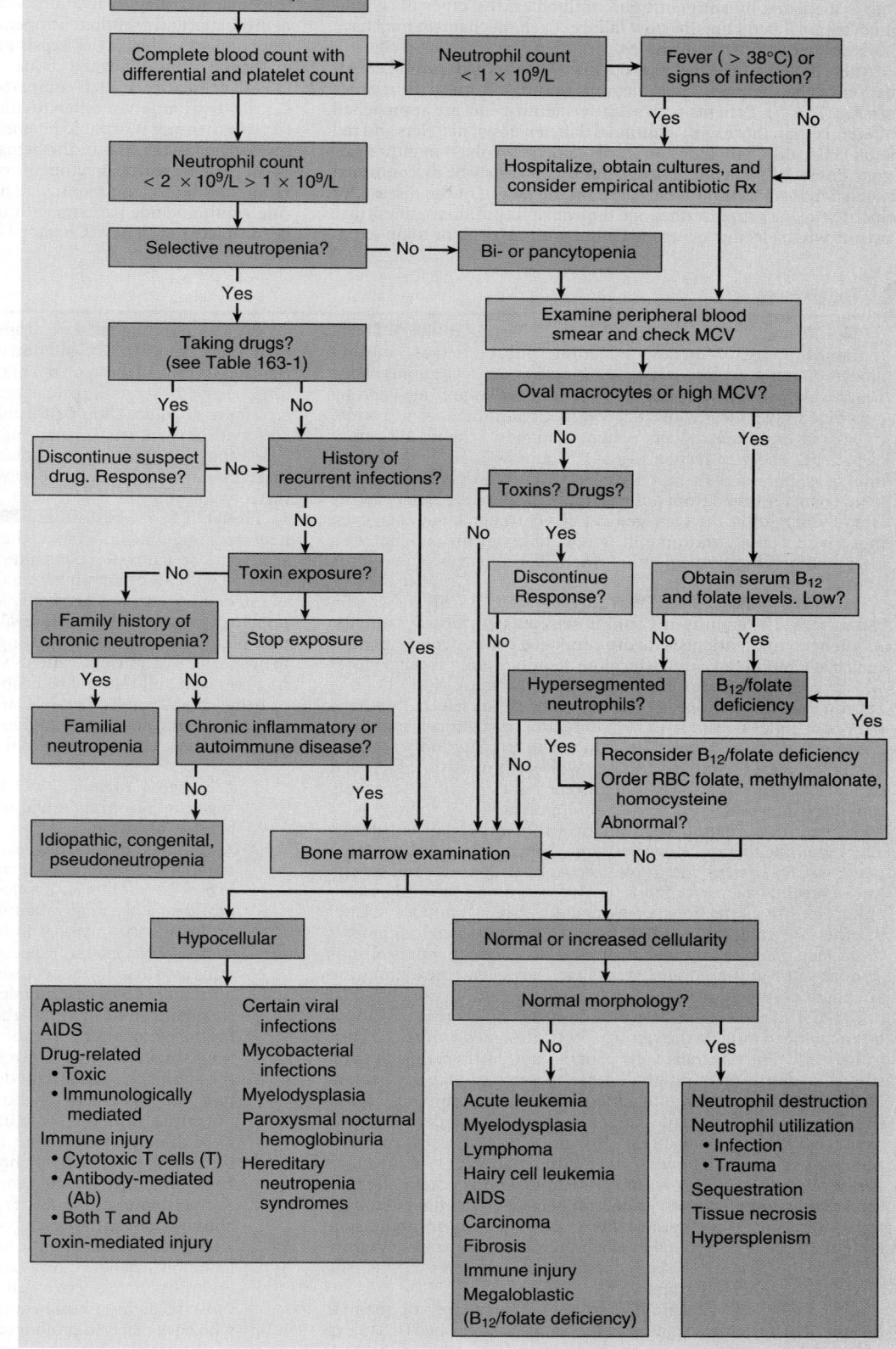

FIGURE 163–5 • A practical algorithm for the evaluation of patients with neutropenia. The fundamental diagnostic principle is that for patients with severe neutropenia or for those with bicytopenia or pancytopenia, bone marrow examination will likely be necessary unless the following diagnoses are made: (1) a nutritional (folate or vitamin B_{12}) deficiency or (2) drug or toxin-induced neutropenia in a patient whose neutropenia resolves after discontinuation of the offending agent. AIDS = acquired immunodeficiency virus; MCV = mean corpuscular volume; RBC = red blood cell.

chronicity of the neutropenia (e.g., seeking evidence as to whether the patient ever had a normal white blood cell count and when); (3) ascertaining whether there have been recurrent infections; (4) identifying any underlying systemic disease that might be causative; and (5) examining the blood counts and blood and bone marrow morphology (marrow examination is virtually always warranted unless a diagnosis is clear based on simple blood tests, e.g., serum folate, homocysteine, methylmalonate, or vitamin B_{12} levels) to determine the most likely pathophysiologic explanation. In some cases, specialized bone marrow studies (e.g., progenitor cell colony assays before and after removing T lymphocytes from the sample) are warranted even with a clear diagnosis. Felty's syndrome, for example, a well-recognized syndrome of neutropenia in patients with rheumatoid arthritis (Chapter 278), is caused by one of two pathophysiologic mechanisms. One is mediated by antineutrophil antibodies, the other by T lymphocyte–mediated bone marrow failure. Each mechanism may have different therapeutic implications.

After the severity of the neutropenia is determined, careful examination of the peripheral blood counts and blood smear is in order (see Fig. 163–5). Patients with selective neutropenia are approached differently than those with additional deficiencies of platelets and red blood cells, although drugs or toxins may be involved in either category. Potentially offending drugs should obviously be discontinued if such a maneuver is possible based on the nature of the disease for which the agent was prescribed and the availability of alternative drugs. Patients with selective neutropenia but with no drug or toxin expo-

sure, no history of recurrent sepsis, and no underlying chronic inflammatory or autoimmune disease may have stable and benign neutropenia; this category includes some cases of familial and congenital neutropenia and pseudoneutropenia. Any patient with selective neutropenia with a history of sepsis and all patients with known toxin exposure should have a bone marrow examination to assess (1) the cellularity of each compartment (storage and mitotic pools), (2) the distribution of differentiation stages found in each pool, and (3) whether any morphologic abnormality (e.g., acute leukemia or myelodysplasia) exists in the hematopoietic cells.

In patients with pancytopenia or bicytopenia, bone marrow aspiration and biopsy are required. The only arguable exception to this rule would include patients with unambiguous evidence of vitamin B_{12} or folate deficiency (Chapter 175).

 Treatment

TREATMENTS SPECIFICALLY DESIGNED TO INCREASE THE NEUTROPHIL COUNT. Immunosuppressive therapy, including glucocorticoids, antithymocyte globulin, cyclosporin, or azathioprine, very commonly elicits a favorable response in patients with marrow failure mediated by cytotoxic T lymphocytes. In vitro clonogenic cultures of bone marrow cells in severely neutropenic patients can aid in the identification of patients likely to respond to such therapy. Some responses to immunosuppressive therapy have also occurred in patients whose neutropenia resulted from antineutrophil antibodies. Splenectomy is rarely helpful in the management of neutropenic patients, even those with Felty's syndrome; it is now reserved for patients with unambiguous hypersplenism in whom bone marrow function is normal.

RECOMBINANT HUMAN GRANULOPOIETIC FACTORS. GM-CSF and G-CSF can increase the neutrophil count in selected neutropenic patients. As a general rule, patients with drug-induced neutropenia (e.g., after cancer chemotherapy) recover more rapidly if they receive either GM-CSF or G-CSF. However, other than the settings of (1) bone marrow transplantation, (2) the management of selected patients with congenital neutropenia, (3) induction of stem cell mobilization from marrow to peripheral blood in preparation for transplantation, and (4) combined therapy with erythropoietin for selected patients with myelodysplastic syndromes, the role of these agents in clinical practice is unclear. Granulopoietic factor therapy is in widespread use to support bone marrow recovery in cancer patients after cytotoxic therapy. However, large clinical studies indicate that while G-CSF hastens neutrophil recovery, it does not reduce the rate of hospitalization for febrile episodes, prolong survival, reduce culture-positive infections, or reduce the costs of supportive care, whether given preemptively or to treat neutropenic fever. In summary, in selected cases, the use of G-CSF or GM-CSF treatment is of substantial value and no doubt saves lives; however, considering the attendant costs of growth factor therapy, the routine use of G-CSF or GM-CSF to prevent infection in neutropenic cancer patients cannot be encouraged outside the setting of well-designed controlled clinical trials.■ For nontransplant patients not participating in such studies, it seems most rational to use these granulopoietic factors in those patients undergoing cytotoxic chemotherapy only if the dose intensity of the chemotherapeutic agents has a demonstrated impact on overall survival (e.g., Hodgkin's disease, germ cell neoplasms) *and* one of following three criteria apply: (1) the patient has developed, in prior rounds of therapy, serious potentially life-threatening complications of neutropenia (e.g., documented bacterial infection); (2) prior probability for prolonged myelosuppression is high (e.g., patients seropositive for human immunodeficiency virus-1); or (3) the patient's persistent neutropenia interferes with scheduled doses of chemotherapy.

BONE MARROW TRANSPLANTATION. In cases of severe aplastic anemia, the role of bone marrow transplantation is well established (Chapters 166 and 174). Other marrow failure states (e.g., myelodysplastic

syndromes and congenital neutropenias) may also respond to transplantation. Before transplantation is seriously considered, the duration and severity of the neutropenia must be assessed; marrow failure must be established as the primary cause, and immunologically mediated marrow failure should probably be excluded. If the patient has an identical twin, transplantation might be attempted with fewer constraints, but allogeneic transplantation should always be reserved for individuals with severe and symptomatic neutropenia caused by marrow failure.

TREATMENT OF THE INFECTED NEUTROPENIC PATIENT. Each patient with neutropenia should understand the function of neutrophils, the consequences of neutrophil deficiency, and the importance of communicating with his or her physician the moment signs and symptoms of infection occur. If a neutropenic patient is afebrile and there is no sign of sepsis, the diagnostic evaluation of the neutropenia should take place in the outpatient setting to avoid unnecessary exposure to nosocomial organisms. Patients with severe neutropenia and fever, however, generally should be hospitalized (Chapter 298). Cultures of urine, blood, and other relevant sites should be obtained, but broad-spectrum antibiotics should be given without waiting for the results of these cultures. One of three responses will be seen:

1. A causative organism will be identified, in which case the spectrum of antimicrobial agents can be promptly and appropriately narrowed.
2. A candidate organism will not be found, but the patient still improves with empiric therapy. In this situation, a full course of broad-spectrum antibiotics should be given. Moreover, after a full course of parenteral antibiotics, some of which may be given on an outpatient basis, another 7 to 14 days of oral antibiotics should be considered, especially in patients with invasive infections associated with necrosis, slow responses to initial antibiotic therapy, or recurrent infections in the same anatomic site.
3. No organism is found, and the clinical picture has not changed for the better after 3 days of empirical treatment. This unsettling situation occurs with some regularity in practice, and the approach at this point depends on the seriousness of the infection. For a patient who has localized disease and who is not critically ill, it is sometimes helpful for empirical therapy to be discontinued and for repeat cultures to be obtained. If the patient is critically ill, however, antibiotics should be discontinued only if other antibiotics are substituted. Among the antibiotics to consider under these circumstances are antiviral and antifungal agents. Antifungal agents should be added to the therapeutic regimen for patients with acute leukemia, diabetes, dysphagia and/or esophagitis, endophthalmitis, or defective cell-mediated immunity (including those receiving immunosuppressive therapy) and for those who have received prolonged treatment with broad-spectrum antibacterial agents in the recent past.

DEFICIENCIES OF OTHER CIRCULATING PHAGOCYTES

Monocytopenia, eosinopenia, and basophilopenia are seen in most of the bone marrow failure states associated with neutropenia. Isolated monocytopenia, however, is very unusual. In view of the heterogeneous and critical roles played by the monocyte-macrophage in normal physiology, complete failure of monocyte production for a period

of more than 9 to 10 months (the estimated lifespan of tissue macrophages) is probably incompatible with life.

Eosinopenia and basophilopenia are more common than monocytopenia in clinical practice and most often represent redistributional mechanisms resulting from stress, including acute infections, widespread neoplasms, and severe injury (e.g., burns). A variety of humoral factors, including glucocorticoids, prostaglandins, and epinephrine, are released in such settings and are known to induce eosinopenia. In fact, because of the reliable reduction of peripheral eosinophils during infectious events, if a patient with bacterial infection does not have eosinopenia, one should consider that adrenocortical insufficiency or a primary myeloproliferative syndrome may coexist.

LYMPHOCYTOPENIA

Lymphocyte production and traffic are difficult to assess because (1) both T and B lymphocytes replicate in heterogeneous anatomic sites, including the lymph nodes, spleen, tonsils, and bone marrow; and (2) lymphocytes are capable of leaving and then later re-entering a given compartment. Given these variables, it is surprising that the lymphocyte counts in the peripheral blood are so tightly regulated; normal counts range from 2 to 4×10^9/L; approximately 20% are B lymphocytes and 70% are T lymphocytes. Lymphocytopenia is defined as a peripheral blood lymphocyte count below 1.5×10^9/L, but severe lymphocytopenia is considered to be less than 0.7×10^9/L.

Etiology and Pathogenesis

Lymphocytopenia can result from three types of abnormalities: (1) lymphocyte production, (2) lymphocyte traffic, and (3) lymphocyte loss and destruction (Table 163–2).

REDUCED PRODUCTION OF LYMPHOCYTES. The most common cause of reduced lymphocyte production in the world is protein-calorie malnutrition. Immune paresis resulting from malnutrition (Chapter 228) contributes to the high incidence of infection in malnourished populations. Radiation (Chapter 19) and immunosuppressive agents (Chapter 191), including alkylating agents and antithymocyte globulin, can induce lymphocytopenia by injuring the progenitor pool and inhibiting replication of more well-differentiated cells. T-cell deficiencies have been found in some long-term survivors of intensive chemotherapy for childhood cancers. A variety of congenital lymphocytopenic immunodeficiency states exist, some of which result in selective deficiencies of B lymphocytes, some of T cells, and some of combined deficiencies of both T cells and B cells. The mechanisms by which production and maturation of B and T lymphocytes are impaired in these patients are heterogeneous; many remain ill defined, although in some cases inactivating mutations of receptors for lymphopoietic factors are the cause. Even in the absence of lymphocytopenia, immunodeficiency states can clearly exist because of abnormal lymphocyte function or selective deficiency of a component of the circulating lymphocyte population.

Certain viruses are capable of inducing lymphocytopenia; some of these agents infect lymphoid cells and cause their destruction. Such viruses include measles, polio, varicella zoster, and human immunodeficiency virus. Human immunodeficiency virus does not frequently cause lymphocytopenia, but it infects the helper (CD4+) subset of T lymphocytes and destroys them, a process that results in a marked decline in the absolute numbers of helper (CD4+) T cells in the peripheral circulation (Chapter 419). Patients with untreated Hodgkin's disease occasionally have lymphocytopenia, especially during the late stages of the disease or in instances associated with the least favorable histologic subtypes (Chapter 194).

ALTERATIONS IN LYMPHOCYTIC TRAFFIC. Traffic redistribution is common and most frequently represents transient responses to a variety of stressful events, including bacterial infections, surgery, trauma, and hemorrhage. These responses are likely mediated by high levels of endogenous glucocorticoids that induce rapid declines in circulating levels of B and T lymphocytes. In hospitalized patients with lymphocytopenia, glucocorticosteroid therapy (Chapter 31) is the third most common cause, after acute bacterial or fungal infections and surgery. The lymphocytopenic response to this type of steroid results from a self-limited shift of lymphocytes away from the peripheral blood compartment. Lymphocyte values generally return to normal within 24 to 48 hours. For this reason, the transient declines induced by endogenous steroid production are not associated with functional immunologic deficiency. Certain viruses can also bind to lymphocyte populations and cause their departure from the blood compartment into other sites.

More persistent lymphocytopenia has been described in patients with widespread granulomatous disease, a phenomenon that is likely multifactorial, deriving from both inhibition of production and alterations of traffic. Patients with these disorders are often difficult to treat. In daily practice, establishing a cause-and-effect relationship between the infection and lymphocytopenia can be difficult when one considers that the reverse might just as easily be true; consider, for example, the frequency of mycobacterial infection in patients with the acquired immunodeficiency syndrome.

INCREASED DESTRUCTION OF LYMPHOCYTES. Viral infections or antilymphocyte antibodies, especially in patients with underlying autoimmune or rheumatic diseases, increase lymphocyte destruction. Losses of viable lymphocytes can also occur because of structural defects in sites of high-density lymphocyte traffic (e.g., via thoracic duct fistulas). In such patients, both T cells and B cells decline in the peripheral blood. Loss of lymphocytes from intestinal lymphatics can occur in cases of protein-losing enteropathies, severe heart failure, or primary diseases of the gut or intestinal lymphatics (see Table 163–2).

Clinical Manifestations and Diagnosis

There are no specific clinical manifestations of lymphocytopenia per se. Whether the patient exhibits signs of immunologic deficiency depends on the pathophysiology of the disorder, the duration of the disease, the type of lymphocytes affected, the intactness of nodal tissues, and the degree to which cellular or humoral immunity is functionally perturbed. Accordingly, unless the clinical setting is clearly one in which transient lymphocytopenia is likely, the approach to diagnosis should involve comprehensive assessment of the integrity of the immune apparatus. Specifically, the subsets of lymphocytes remaining in the circulating blood should be quantified, including B cells, helper-inducer T cells (CD4+), and cytotoxic-suppressor T cells (CD8+). In addition, quantitative immunoglobulin levels should be measured in the serum and a series of skin tests should be performed to detect deficiencies of cell-mediated immunity.

Table 163–2 • CAUSES OF LYMPHOCYTOPENIA

Abnormalities of Lymphocyte Production	Alterations in Lymphocyte Traffic
Protein-calorie malnutrition	Acute bacterial/fungal infection
Radiation	Surgery
Immunosuppressive therapeutic agents	Trauma
Glucocorticosteroids	Hemorrhage
Cyclosporine	Glucocorticosteroid therapy
Congenital immunodeficiency states	Viral infection
Wiskott-Aldrich syndrome	Widespread granulomatous infection
Nezelof's syndrome	Hodgkin's disease
Adenosine deaminase deficiency	**Lymphocyte Destruction or Loss**
Viral infections	Viral infection (e.g., human immunodeficiency virus)
Hodgkin's disease	Antibody-mediated lymphocyte destruction
Multiple myeloma	Protein-losing enteropathy
Widespread granulomatous infection (mycobacterial, fungal)	Chronic right ventricular failure
Cytotoxic chemotherapy	Thoracic duct drainage or rupture
Direct dose-related effects (e.g., fludarabine)	Extracorporeal circulation
Long-term effects (e.g., cyclophosphamide)	Graft-versus-host disease
Idiosyncratic drug reactions (e.g., quinine)	

Rx Treatment

Because lymphocytopenia ordinarily represents a response to an underlying disease, primary attention must be paid to establishing the nature of that disease and instituting therapy for it. Patients whose lymphocytopenia is accompanied by hypogammaglobulinemia may benefit significantly from administration of intravenous immunoglobulin, which often reduces the incidence of infectious events. The treatment of severe deficiencies of cell-mediated immunity remains experimental. Responses have been described with transplantation of allogeneic bone marrow, fetal liver, or thymic epithelial cells. Some syndromes may respond in the future to gene therapy.

LEUKOCYTOSIS AND LEUKEMOID REACTIONS

Circulating leukocytes consist of neutrophils, monocytes, eosinophils, basophils, and lymphocytes (T cells, B cells, and natural killer cells). Any one or all of these cell types can increase to abnormal levels in peripheral blood in response to various stimuli. Each type of leukocyte is produced in the bone marrow (and in the case of lymphocytes, in lymph nodes, spleen, and thymus as well) in response to specific growth factors, and in the case of some lymphocytes, in response to antigenic stimuli. The term *leukocytosis* is used to describe a total leukocyte count above $11.0 \times 10^9/L$; it is a common and diagnostically important finding in clinical practice. Once leukocytosis is discovered, it is first essential to examine the differential white blood cell count so that one can determine which white blood cell types are increased. The terms *neutrophilia* (neutrophilic leukocytosis), *monocytosis*, *lymphocytosis*, *eosinophilia*, and *basophilia* suggest specific sets of diagnostic considerations.

Leukocytosis is a common finding in acutely ill patients. When the leukocyte count exceeds 25 to $30 \times 10^9/L$, the condition is sometimes termed a *leukemoid reaction*. Leukemoid reactions generally reflect the response of healthy bone marrow to cytokines released by auxiliary cells (lymphocytes, macrophages, and stromal cells) exposed to infection or trauma. Leukemoid reactions are not synonymous with *leukoerythroblastosis*, which indicates the presence of immature white blood cells and nucleated red blood cells in the peripheral blood, irrespective of the total leukocyte count. Leukoerythroblastosis is less common than leukemoid reactions but often, especially in the adult patient, reflects serious marrow dysfunction (Table 163–3). Consequently, the finding of leukoerythroblastosis represents a clear indication to perform bone marrow aspiration and biopsy, unless the clinical setting is specifically an acute severe hemolytic anemia, sepsis in a patient with hyposplenism, or acute massive trauma with multiple fractures.

Table 163–3 • CAUSES OF LEUKOERYTHROBLASTOSIS

Normal Bone Marrow
  Severe acute hemolytic anemia
  Acute infection in hyposplenic patients
Abnormal Bone Marrow
  Marrow infiltration
  Metastatic malignancy (e.g., carcinoma of lung, breast, prostate, or
    stomach)
  Hematologic malignancies
    Acute leukemia
    Multiple myeloma
    Chronic myeloproliferative diseases (e.g., myeloid metaplasia or
      chronic myelogenous leukemia)
    Lymphoma
  Granulomatous diseases
    Mycobacterial infection
    Fungal diseases
Other Disorders
  Osteopetrosis
  Gaucher's disease
  Amyloidosis
  Paget's disease of bone
  Severe tissue hypoxia
  Multiple fractures

NEUTROPHILIA

Pathophysiology

The number of neutrophil precursors in the marrow mitotic pool (Fig. 163–6) is largely influenced by the hematopoietic growth factors, the most neutrophil lineage specific of which is the granulopoietic factor G-CSF. G-CSF not only functions to stimulate the growth and differentiation of granulocyte progenitor cells but also functionally activates neutrophils, enhancing their capacity to kill ingested organisms. The same holds true for macrophage colony-stimulating factor (the growth factor for mononuclear phagocytes) and IL-5 (the growth factor for eosinophils).

The marrow storage pool can provide the periphery with neutrophils for about 5 days in the steady state, even if it received no input from the mitotic pool. Neutrophils are released from the storage pool into the circulating pool in response to a variety of physiologic stresses, including endogenous glucocorticoids (see Fig. 163–6B). Neutrophilia can result from a shift of neutrophils from the marginated to the circulating pool, termed *demargination* (see Fig. 163–6C). This response is rapid and can be induced by injections of epinephrine and glucocorticosteroids. In patients with acute inflammatory illnesses, storage pool release and demargination usually occur together (see Fig. 163–6D).

Neutrophilic leukocytosis is the most common type of leukocytosis in clinical practice. It evolves in response to the release of factors that govern the production and traffic of this cell type, including G-CSF and the factors that augment the mitotic activity of G-CSF, including IL-3 and Steel factor. These factors are produced by a network of auxiliary cells in the bone marrow, including mononuclear phagocytes, microvascular endothelial cells, fibroblasts, and lymphocytes. These growth factor–producing cells respond to acute inflammatory events by augmenting production of the critically important colony stimulating factors. The colony stimulating factors stimulate replication of granulopoietic progenitor cells, which leads to expansion of the neutrophil storage pool and subsequent neutrophilia (see Fig. 163–6E). In response to the infection and the induced cytokines and adhesion molecules, the transit time of neutrophils in the mitotic and postmitotic pools in the bone marrow is shorter than in the uninfected state, and immature neutrophils (bands and metamyelocytes) are released from the storage pool. This new high level of production persists until the inflammatory process resolves.

Causes

Neutrophilia (neutrophil counts greater than $7.5 \times 10^9/L$), a common finding in clinical practice, usually reflects the inflammatory response to acute or subacute infections (Fig. 163–7; Table 163–4), so it should trigger a diagnostic search for its cause. Such searches usually involve a careful history and physical examination and just a few inexpensive laboratory tests (the nature of which depends on the findings on physical examination), because in most cases the cause will become apparent and usually proves to be an active infectious process.

When neutrophilia occurs in the absence of evidence of acute inflammation or illness, three explanations should be considered: (1) chemical effects, including agents such as glucocorticoids, lithium chloride, or epinephrine; (2) malignant tumors, in which cancer cells may inappropriately express certain of the genes encoding granulopoietic factors (e.g., G-CSF or IL-5); and (3) chronic myeloproliferative disorders, including chronic myelogenous leukemia, agnogenic myeloid metaplasia, essential thrombocytosis, and polycythemia vera.

Diagnosis

The diagnostic approach to patients with neutrophilia (see Fig. 163–7) leads quickly to the performance of bone marrow aspiration and biopsy for patients with leukoerythroblastosis. In patients without leukoerythroblastosis, neutrophilic leukocytosis generally results from acute toxic, inflammatory, or traumatic stresses, and it is usually best to observe the course of neutrophilia to determine its degree of linkage with the underlying disease. If the underlying disease resolves and the neutrophilia does not, other, less common explanations must be pursued.

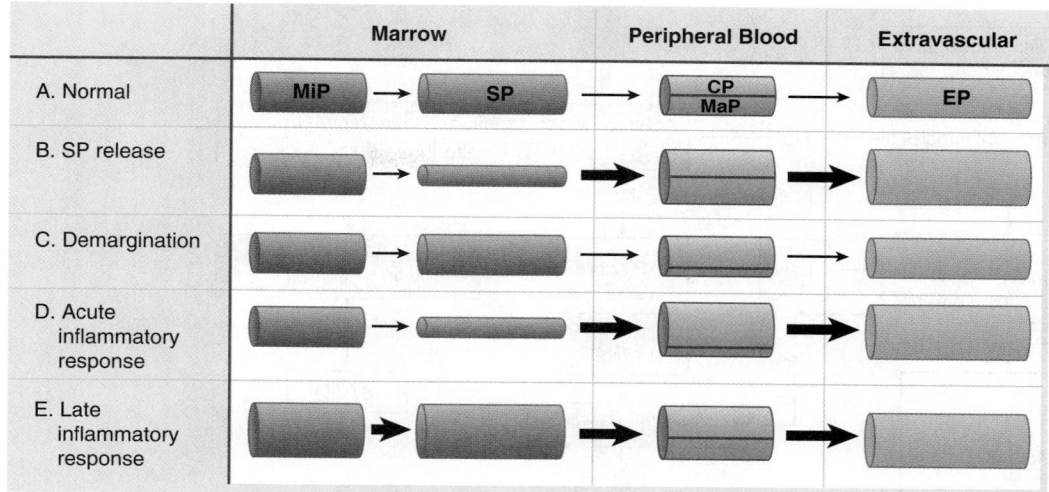

	Marrow		Peripheral Blood	Extravascular
A. Normal	MiP	SP	CP / MaP	EP
B. SP release				
C. Demargination				
D. Acute inflammatory response				
E. Late inflammatory response				

FIGURE 163–6 • Pathophysiologic mechanisms of neutrophilia. *A,* In this figure, the size of a given compartment is represented by the relative size of the cylinder shaped "pool." The absolute number of cells leaving one pool for the next is represented by the size of the arrows between the pools. MiP = the mitotic pool of neutrophil precursor cells; SP = the neutrophil storage pool; CP = the circulating granulocyte pool; MaP = the marginated pool; EP = the extravascular pool. Notice that the circulating neutrophil pool is large (necessarily true for patients with neutrophilic leukocytosis), but the size of the other pools is variable. *B,* A variety of stresses, such as infection, can result in the release of storage pool granulocytes, probably mediated through the actions of glucocorticosteroids or the granulopoietic factors granulocyte colony stimulating factor and granulocyte-macrophage colony stimulating factor. *C,* The circulating granulocyte pool can also increase in size because of a shift of neutrophils from the marginated to the circulating pool. The demargination response can be regularly elicited by the administration of epinephrine. This is a response that also occurs in infections, but generally not without other dynamic alterations of other pools. *D,* In most bacterial infections and other inflammatory processes, the demand for neutrophils in the infected extravascular site results in the simultaneous release of storage pool neutrophils and demargination. *E,* Later in the inflammatory response, after the hematopoietic growth factors released in response to the inflammatory stimulus have induced a few days of proliferation in the mitotic pool, the content of neutrophils in all pools increases and delivery to the tissues is maximized.

Table 163–4 • COMMON CAUSES OF NEUTROPHILIC LEUKOCYTOSIS

Infections
  Bacteria
  Viruses
  Fungi
  Parasites
  Rickettsia
Rheumatic and Autoimmune Disorders
  Rheumatoid arthritis
  Vasculitis
  Autoimmune hemolytic anemia
  Inflammatory bowel disease
  Gout
Neoplastic Disorders
  Pancreatic, gastric, bronchogenic, breast, and renal cell carcinoma
  Melanoma
  Any cancer metastatic to bone marrow
  Lymphoma, especially Hodgkin's disease
  Chronic myeloproliferative disorders (chronic myelogenous leukemia, agnogenic myeloid metaplasia, essential thrombocytosis, polycythemia vera)
  Myelodysplastic disorders and acute leukemia
Chemicals
  Mercury poisoning
  Venoms (reptiles, insects, jellyfish)
  Ethylene glycol
  Histamine

Trauma
  Thermal injury
  Hypothermia
  Crush injury
  Electrical injury
Endocrine and Metabolic Disorders
  Ketoacidosis
  Lactic acidosis
  Thyrotoxicosis
Hematologic Disorders (Non-neoplastic)
  Acute hemolytic anemias and transfusion reactions
  Postsplenectomy
  Recovery from marrow failure
Other Disorders
  Tissue necrosis
  Pregnancy
  Eclampsia
  Exfoliative dermatitis
  Hypoxia
Drugs
  Corticosteroids
  Lithium
  Epinephrine
  Granulocyte colony stimulating factor
  Granulocyte-macrophage colony stimulating factor

NEUTROPHIL MORPHOLOGY. Neutrophil morphology can lead to early diagnosis. Toxic granulation of neutrophils, the presence of Döhle bodies, and the presence of vacuoles in the neutrophil cytoplasm suggest that overt or subclinical inflammation, toxin exposure, trauma, or neoplasia exists. Because glucocorticoids induce prompt eosinopenia and basophilopenia, these cells are almost universally absent in the blood of the acutely injured or infected patient. Thus, their presence should indicate that (1) the acutely ill patient may have concomitant adrenocortical insufficiency, (2) the neutrophilia derives from the inappropriate production of GM-CSF or interleukin-5 (e.g., by

malignant cells), or (3) the neutrophilia is one manifestation of a hematopoietic neoplasm (a chronic myeloproliferative disorder, myelodysplastic syndrome, lymphoma, or acute nonlymphocytic leukemias associated with eosinophilia).

LEUKOCYTE ALKALINE PHOSPHATASE. Leukocyte alkaline phosphatase (LAP) is an enzyme found in neutrophils. When neutrophilia represents a reaction to an acute illness, the LAP levels usually increase substantially. In cases of chronic myelogenous leukemia (CML; Chapter 192), however, the LAP score is markedly decreased. A low LAP level in a patient with neutrophilia should therefore

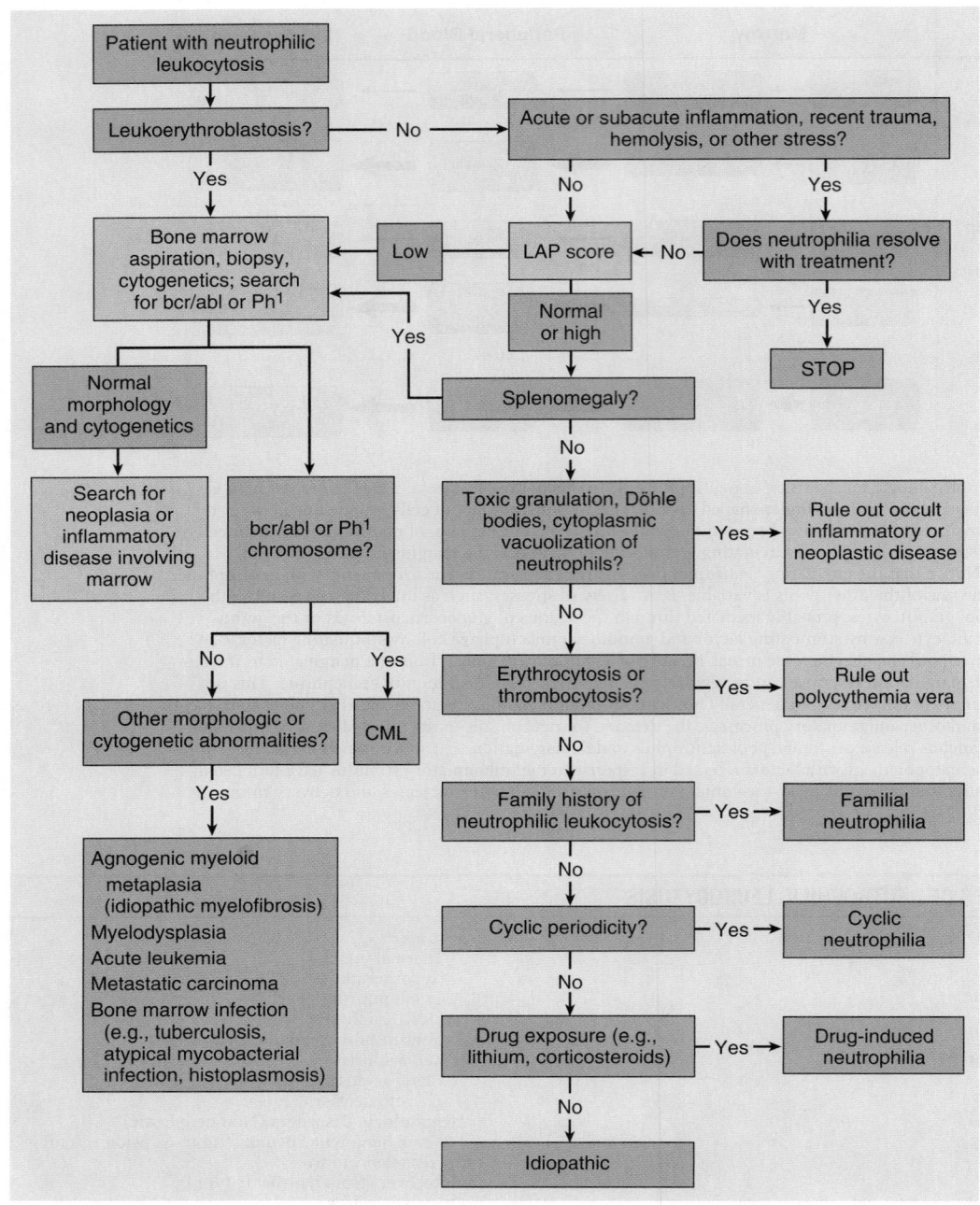

FIGURE 163–7 • Evaluation of patients with neutrophilic leukocytosis. bcr/abl = the translocation of the c-*abl* gene from chromosome 9 to the *bcr* gene on chromosome 22q; CML = chronic myelogenous leukemia; LAP = leukocyte alkaline phosphatase; Ph[1] = Philadelphia chromosome.

lead to a diagnostic evaluation designed to exclude CML (Table 163–5).

DIFFERENTIAL DIAGNOSIS OF NEUTROPHILIC LEUKEMOID REACTIONS. Neutrophilic leukemoid reactions generally occur in patients who are obviously systemically ill. When the neutrophil count exceeds 80×10^9/L or when the mildness of the systemic illness seems discordant with the extremely high level of neutrophils in the peripheral blood, the diagnosis most often considered is CML or chronic myelomonocytic leukemia. A number of additional features distinguish leukemoid reactions from CML and chronic myelomonocytic leukemia (see Table 163–5). The diagnostic tests for CML are those designed to identify the classic balanced chromosomal rearrangement (a chromosome 9;22 translocation) either morphologically (cytogenetic analysis) or by molecular methods (identification of the bcr/abl DNA, mRNA, or protein).

MONOCYTOSIS

Monocytosis is defined as absolute peripheral blood monocyte counts greater than 0.80×10^9/L in children and greater than 0.50×10^9/L in adults. Monocytes present processed antigens to lymphocytes, mediate cellular cytotoxicity, release procoagulants, participate in bone remodeling and wound repair, dispose of damaged cells, and regulate immune and hematopoietic responses by producing IL-1, tumor necrosis factor-α, G-CSF, IL-6, and certain interferons. The most specific growth/survival factor for mononuclear phagocytes is macrophage colony-stimulating factor (known as CSF-1 in the mouse) (see Fig. 163–7) produced by stromal cells, including endothelial cells and fibroblasts. Macrophage colony-stimulating factor knockout mice have monocytopenia and macrophage deficiency, but GM-CSF knockout mice do not. The cytokine IL-13 also induces monocytosis.

The mononuclear phagocyte is more sluggish than the neutrophil in moving toward and killing bacteria but is as effective, if not more so, in killing obligate intracellular parasites such as fungi, yeast, and viruses. In addition, the mononuclear phagocyte participates in all types of granulomatous inflammation. Accordingly, monocytosis is often seen in patients with tuberculosis, syphilis, fungal infections, ulcerative and granulomatous colitis, and sarcoidosis (Table 163–6). Mild monocytosis is common in patients with Hodgkin's disease and a variety of cancers. High levels of monocytes in the blood are most often seen in patients with hematopoietic malignancies, including acute and chronic myelomonocytic leukemia, acute monocytic leukemia, and chronic myelogenous leukemia of the juvenile type.

EOSINOPHILIA

Eosinophilic leukocytosis (eosinophilia) exists when the eosinophil count in the peripheral blood exceeds $0.4 \times 10^9/L$ (Chapter 184). Eosinophils are produced by progenitor cells in the marrow, largely under the influence of IL-5, a protein that also stimulates the growth and differentiation of B lymphocytes. Eosinophils not only function as phagocytes but also play an extraordinarily important role in modulating the potentially toxic effects of mast cell degranulation in hypersensitivity reactions.

LYMPHOCYTOSIS

Lymphocytosis (Table 163–7) is defined as a lymphocyte count in excess of $5.0 \times 10^9/L$. Atypical lymphocytosis is present when atypical lymphocytes account for more than 20% of the total peripheral blood lymphocyte population. A number of humoral factors induce growth of T lymphocytes (IL-2, IL-3, IL-7, IL-15), natural killer cells (IL-2, IL-12, IL-1), and B lymphocytes (IL-10, IL-6, IL-5, IL-4, IL-7, IL-13, IL-14, IL-15).

Diagnosis

Mild to moderate lymphocytosis (lymphocyte counts $<12 \times 10^9/L$) is most commonly caused by viral infections, including infectious mononucleosis and viral hepatitis. Careful examination of the peripheral blood lymphocyte morphology can help distinguish between these two disorders. In cases of infectious mononucleosis, many of the lymphocytes are large, with abundant cytoplasm and a "ballerina skirt"–like cytoplasmic border; these are the characteristic "atypical" lymphocytes that exceed 20% of the total lymphocyte population during the course of this disease (Fig. 163–8). Interestingly, whereas the B lymphocyte is the target of the causative Epstein-Barr virus, the majority of the cells in the peripheral blood of patients with this disease are T lymphocytes. This proliferation of T lymphocytes in response to Epstein-Barr virus infection of B cells plays a role in eradicating the infected B-cell population. This response is a critical one in view of the oncogenic potential of this virus.

Acute bacterial infections rarely cause lymphocytosis. One exception is pertussis (seen almost exclusively in children), in which profound lymphocytosis (up to $60 \times 10^9/L$) is sometimes seen. It has

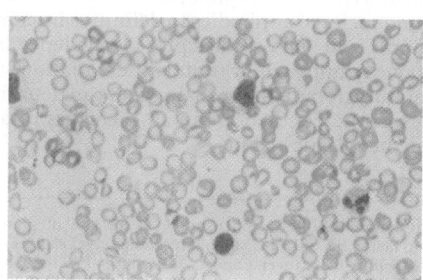

FIGURE 163–8 • Infectious mononucleosis. Peripheral smear shows pleomorphic, atypical (or reactive) lymphocytes.

Table 163–5 • DISTINCTIONS BETWEEN NEUTROPHILIC LEUKEMOID REACTIONS AND CHRONIC MYELOGENOUS LEUKEMIA (CML)

FINDING/RESULT	LEUKEMOID REACTION	CML
Presence of fever or other manifestations of acute or subacute inflammation	Usual*	Infrequent†
Splenomegaly	Rare	Frequent
Natural course of neutrophilia	Resolution linked with abatement of underlying disease	Progressive slow increase over time
Peripheral blood basophilia	Rare‡	Common
LAP score	High	Low§
Philadelphia chromosome	Absent	Frequent (>85%)
bcr/abl translocation	Absent	Frequent (>90%)

*Exceptions include patients with leukemoid reactions associated with certain cancers.

†Patients with CML can also develop infections. The time to evaluate this possibility is when the inflammatory process resolves and the neutrophilia does not.

‡Patients with acute allergic reactions and patients with parasitic diseases are exceptions to this rule.

§LAP scores can be normal in some CML patients, particularly after splenectomy.

CML = chronic myelogenous leukemia; LAP = leukocyte alkaline phosphatase.

Table 163–7 • CAUSES OF LYMPHOCYTOSIS

High ($>15 \times 10^9/L$)
 Infectious mononucleosis
 Pertussis
 Acute infectious lymphocytosis
 Chronic lymphocytic leukemia and variants thereof
 Acute lymphocytic leukemia
Moderate ($<15 \times 10^9/L$)
 Many viral infections
 Infectious mononucleosis
 Measles
 Varicella
 Hepatitis
 Coxsackievirus
 Adenovirus
 Mumps
 Cytomegalovirus
 Human immunodeficiency virus-1 (acute lymphadenopathy)
 Other infectious diseases
 Toxoplasmosis
 Brucellosis
 Tuberculosis
 Typhoid fever
 Syphilis (secondary)
 Neoplastic disorders
 Carcinoma
 Hodgkin's disease
 Acute lymphocytic leukemia (early)
 Chronic lymphocytic leukemia
 Thymoma
 Sjögren's syndrome
 Graves' diseases
 Drug reactions (e.g., tetracycline)

Table 163–6 • CAUSES OF MONOCYTOSIS

Infections	Neoplastic Diseases	Gastrointestinal Disorders
Tuberculosis	Hodgkin's disease	Ulcerative colitis
Brucellosis	Carcinoma (many varieties)	Granulomatous colitis
Endocarditis	Acute and chronic myelomonocytic leukemia	Cirrhosis
Typhoid and paratyphoid	Juvenile chronic myelomonocytic leukemia	Sarcoidosis
Syphilis	Acute monocytic leukemia	Drug reactions
Fungal	Myelodysplasia	Recovery from marrow suppression
Recovery from acute infections	Myeloma and Waldenström's macroglobulinemia	Congenital neutropenia
Protozoal	Chronic lymphocytic leukemia (rare)	
Viral (e.g., varicella)		

been known for 30 years that specific soluble factors derived from the causative organism *Bordetella pertussis* induce lymphocytosis in experimental animals. Perhaps with the exception of patients with early chronic lymphocytic leukemia, most patients with lymphocytosis and especially substantial lymphocytosis (>12 to 15×10^9/L) have overt signs of an underlying illness involving anatomic sites other than the lymphohematopoietic system. The diagnostic approach depends simply on establishing a tissue diagnosis to exclude malignant disease in patients who do not have clear-cut evidence of one of the more benign disorders. Bone marrow aspiration and biopsy are required when lymphocytosis coexists with leukoerythroblastosis, peripheral lymphocytes are immature (lymphoblasts), and the lymphocytosis is persistent in a patient who has no evidence of acute or subacute infection.

Immunophenotyping ("lymphocyte markers") should be performed using monoclonal antibodies to definitive integral membrane proteins. Not only will such studies provide evidence for or against dominance of one lymphocyte type and differentiation stage, but also analyses of immunoglobulin light chain types can determine whether B lymphocytes in the circulation are all members of a single (and therefore likely neoplastic) clone.

1. Rusthoven J, Bramwell V, Stephenson B, et al: Use of granulocyte colony-stimulating factor (G-CSF) in patients receiving myelosuppressive chemotherapy for the treatment of cancer. Cancer Care Ontario Practice Guideline Initiative CPG 12–2, 2002 (http://www.ccopebc.ca/guidelines/sys/cpg12_f.html).

SUGGESTED READINGS

Basu S, Hodgson G, Katz M, Dunn AR: Evaluation of role of G-CSF in the production, survival, and release of neutrophils from bone marrow into circulation. Blood 2002;100:854–861. *Review of the control points for the differentiation of granulocytes.*
Berghmans T, Paesmans M, Lafitte J, et al: Therapeutic use of granulocyte and granulocyte-macrophage colony-stimulating factors in febrile neutropenic cancer patients: A systematic review of the literature with meta-analysis. Support Care Cancer 2002;10:181–188. *The routine use of G-CSF or GM-CSF in neutropenic cancer patients who present with fever is not supported by the literature.*
Ward AC, Loeb DM, Soede-Bobok AA, et al: Regulation of granulopoiesis by transcription factors and cytokine signals. Leukemia 2000;14:973–990. *This concise review looks at the molecular processes by which lineage commitment, cell survival, self-replication, and differentiation occur in granulocyte progenitor cells and their progeny.*
Weisman MH: What are the risks of biologic therapy in rheumatoid arthritis? An update on safety. J Rheumatol Suppl 2002;65:33–38. *The inhibition of interleukin-1 and tumor necrosis factor-α can be associated with adverse effects, thereby documenting their importance for the normal immune response and the production and function of leukocytes.*

164 APPROACH TO THE PATIENT WITH LYMPHADENOPATHY AND SPLENOMEGALY

James O. Armitage

LYMPHADENOPATHY

Physiology and Anatomy

Lymph nodes are found throughout the body along the course of lymphatics, strategically located to allow filtering of lymphatic fluid and interdiction of microorganisms and abnormal proteins. Lymphatic fluid enters the node in afferent lymphatic vessels that empty into the subcapsular sinus. The fluid then transverses the node to exit in a single efferent lymphatic vessel. In doing so, the lymph and its contents are exposed to immunologically active cells throughout the node. Lymph nodes are populated predominantly by macrophages, dendritic cells, B lymphocytes, and T lymphocytes. B lymphocytes are located primarily in the follicles and perifollicular areas, whereas T lymphocytes are found primarily in the interfollicular or paracortical areas of the lymph node. These cells function together to provide antigen processing, antigen presentation, antigen recognition, and proliferation of effector B and T lymphocytes as part of the normal immune response to microorganisms or foreign proteins.

Because the normal immune response leads to proliferation and expansion of one or more of the cellular components of lymph nodes, it also often leads to significant lymph node enlargement. In young children, who are continuously undergoing exposure to new antigens, palpable lymphadenopathy is the rule. In fact, the absence of palpable lymphadenopathy would be considered abnormal. In adults, lymph nodes larger than 1 to 2 cm in diameter are generally considered abnormal. However, lymph nodes 1 to 2 cm in diameter in the groin are sufficiently frequent to often be considered "normal."

Lymphoid proliferation is a normal response to exposure to foreign antigens. The location of the enlarged lymph nodes will often reflect the site of invasion. For example, cervical lymphadenopathy would be typical in a patient with pharyngitis. Generalized immune proliferation and lymphadenopathy can occur with a systemic disorder of the immune system, disseminated infection, or disseminated neoplasia. Malignancies of the immune system might be manifested as localized or disseminated lymphadenopathy.

Differential Diagnosis

The differential diagnosis of lymphadenopathy (Table 164–1) is vast, with the underlying causes responsible for either proliferation of immunologically active cells or infiltration of the lymph node by foreign cells or substances. In practice, the cause of enlarged lymph nodes is often not certain even in retrospect; in these cases, unrecognized infectious processes are generally blamed.

Infections by bacteria, mycobacteria, fungi, chlamydiae, parasites, and viruses are the major causes of lymph node enlargement. Lymph nodes in the drainage area of essentially all pyogenic infections can enlarge. In certain infections such as bubonic plague caused by *Yersinia pestis*, dramatic regional lymph node enlargement with fluctuant lymph nodes (i.e., buboes) can be a hallmark of the disease (Chapter 331). Other bacterial infections have lymph node enlargement as a prominent feature (e.g., cat-scratch disease) and can mimic lymphoproliferative disorders (Chapter 357). Mediastinal lymphadenopathy is seen in inhalational anthrax (Chapter 333). In some parts of the world, cervical lymphadenopathy is a sufficiently frequent manifestation of tuberculosis to lead to the institution of antituberculosis therapy rather than biopsy. Disseminated lymphadenopathy can be seen in cases of infection by a variety of organisms such as *Toxoplasma*, Epstein-Barr virus (i.e., infectious mononucleosis), cytomegalovirus, and human immunodeficiency virus.

A variety of nonmalignant disorders of the immune system can lead to localized or disseminated lymphadenopathy (Chapter 273). Autoimmune diseases such as rheumatoid arthritis and systemic lupus erythematosus often have accompanying lymphadenopathy, which can pose a diagnostic challenge because of the increased incidence of lymphoma in patients with these disorders. In the lymphadenopathy that occurs as a reaction to drugs such as phenytoin, lymph node

Table 164–1 • CAUSES OF LYMPHADENOPATHY
Infection
Bacterial (e.g., all pyogenic bacteria, cat-scratch disease, syphilis, tularemia)
Mycobacterial (e.g., tuberculosis, leprosy)
Fungal (e.g., histoplasmosis, coccidioidomycosis)
Chlamydial (e.g., lymphogranuloma venereum)
Parasitic (e.g., toxoplasmosis, trypanosomiasis, filariasis)
Viral (e.g., Epstein-Barr virus, cytomegalovirus, rubella, hepatitis, human immunodeficiency virus)
Benign disorder of the immune system (e.g., rheumatoid arthritis, systemic lupus erythematosus, serum sickness, drug reactions such as to phenytoin, Castleman's disease, sinus histiocytosis with massive lymphadenopathy, Langerhans' cell histiocytosis, Kawasaki syndrome, Kimura's disease)
Malignant disorders of the immune system (e.g., chronic and acute myeloid and lymphoid leukemia, non-Hodgkin's lymphoma, Hodgkin's disease, angioimmunoblastic-like T-cell lymphoma, Waldenström's macroglobulinemia, multiple myeloma with amyloidosis, malignant histiocytosis)
Other malignancies (e.g., breast carcinoma, lung carcinoma, melanoma, head and neck cancer, gastrointestinal malignancies, germ cell tumors, Kaposi's sarcoma)
Storage diseases (e.g., Gaucher's disease, Niemann-Pick disease)
Endocrinopathies (e.g., hyperthyroidism, adrenal insufficiency, thyroiditis)
Miscellaneous (e.g., sarcoidosis, amyloidosis, dermatopathic lymphadenitis)

biopsy findings can sometimes be confused with those of lymphoma. Benign proliferative diseases of the immune system that can also be confused with lymphoma include Castleman's disease (angiofollicular lymph node hyperplasia), sinus histiocytosis with massive lymphadenopathy, and disorders seen more frequently in Asia, such as Kawasaki syndrome and Kimura's disease.

All of the cells in the immune system can become malignant. Several of these malignancies are usually manifested as lymphadenopathy, and it can be seen in all. Lymphadenopathy as the initial manifestation is the rule for Hodgkin's disease and non-Hodgkin's lymphoma and is common in Waldenström's macroglobulinemia and B-cell chronic lymphocytic leukemia, but it is only occasionally seen in the myeloid leukemias (Chapters 192 through 196). Malignancies of all organ systems can metastasize to the lymph nodes and cause lymphadenopathy, which is usually seen in the drainage area of the primary tumor, for example, axillary lymph nodes in patients with breast cancer, hilar and mediastinal lymph nodes in patients with lung cancer, and cervical lymph nodes in patients with head and neck cancer. However, widespread lymphadenopathy can also be seen with many solid tumors.

Other disorders that can have lymphadenopathy as an initial finding include storage diseases such as Gaucher's disease (Chapter 222), endocrinopathies such as hyperthyroidism (Chapter 239), sarcoidosis (Chapter 91), and dermatopathic lymphadenitis. Amyloidosis (Chapter 290) can cause lymphadenopathy in patients with multiple myeloma, hereditary amyloidosis, or amyloidosis associated with chronic inflammatory states.

Among patients with lymphadenopathy actually seen in practices in the United States, diagnoses will not be determined in a high proportion of them (Table 164–2). In these cases, the lymphadenopathy will usually be blamed on infection. When the lymphadenopathy is in the drainage site of a known infection (e.g., cervical lymphadenopathy in a patient with pharyngitis) or the patient has a known infection associated with lymphadenopathy (e.g., infectious mononucleosis; see Chapter 371), this infectious assumption is usually correct. Alternatively, if a patient has an immunologic disorder that is known to cause lymphadenopathy, such as rheumatoid arthritis, this disorder is usually an acceptable explanation; however, progressive lymphadenopathy in such patients should trigger a biopsy because these patients are at an increased risk for lymphoma. Localized, progressive lymphadenopathy, particularly when associated with fever, sweats, or weight loss, requires biopsy to exclude lymphoma.

Lymph Node Evaluation

Evaluation of a patient with lymphadenopathy includes a careful history, a thorough physical examination, laboratory tests, and sometimes imaging studies to determine the extent and character of the lymphadenopathy (Table 164–3). The age of the patient and any associated systemic symptoms might be important hints in the evaluation. Cervical lymphadenopathy in a child would be much less worrisome than equally prominent lymphadenopathy in a 60-year-old adult. The occurrence of fever, sweats, or weight loss raises the possibility of a malignancy of the immune system. The explanation for the lymphadenopathy might become apparent by identification of a site of infection, a particular medication, a travel history, or a previous malignancy.

Physical examination allows the identification of localized versus widespread lymphadenopathy. The particular sites of involvement can be important hints to the diagnosis inasmuch as infections and carcinomas are likely to cause lymphadenopathy in the lymphatic drainage

of the site of the disorder. In general, lymph nodes that are tender are more likely to be due to an infectious process, whereas painless adenopathy raises the concern of malignancy. Lymph node consistency can also aid in the diagnosis: typically, lymph nodes containing metastatic carcinoma are rock hard, lymph nodes containing lymphoma are firm and rubbery, and lymph nodes enlarged in response to an infectious process are soft.

The larger the lymph node is, the more likely it is that a serious underlying cause exists; lymph nodes greater than 3 to 4 cm in diameter in an adult are very worrisome. Physical examination to assess lymph node size is only marginally accurate and reproducible, although it is by far the most widely used method. More precise methods are available with various imaging techniques.

Imaging studies using routine radiographs or computed tomography (CT), ultrasonography, lymphangiography, magnetic resonance imaging, gallium scans, and positron emission tomography provide the only methods to assess the extent of lymphadenopathy in the chest and abdomen (Table 164–4). Chest radiographs provide the most economical and easiest method to assess mediastinal and hilar lymphadenopathy but are not as accurate as CT of the chest. Although the technique is no longer widely available, lymphangiography provides an extremely accurate assessment of the lower abdominal lymph nodes and, because of retained contrast material, allows repeat examinations and assessment of the response to therapy. CT and ultrasonography provide the most useful ways to assess abdominal and retroperitoneal lymphadenopathy. In most patients, CT is probably the most accurate approach, but ultrasonography has the advantage of being less expensive and not requiring radiation exposure. Magnetic resonance imaging and gallium scanning are not first-line studies for the assessment of lymphadenopathy. Gallium scans are frequently positive in patients with Hodgkin's disease and aggressive non-Hodgkin's lymphomas and can assess the presence of active lymphoma in patients with lymphadenopathy and a proven diagnosis; they are especially useful for re-evaluating patients after therapy because the lymph nodes do not always regress to normal size after therapy, particularly in the mediastinum and retroperitoneum.

Lymph node aspiration or biopsy is often necessary for an accurate diagnosis of the cause of the lymphadenopathy. Fine-needle aspiration is currently popular and is often an accurate way to diagnose infection or carcinoma involving a lymph node. Although lymphomas can sometimes be diagnosed with this approach, it is inappropriate as an initial diagnostic maneuver for lymphoma. Cutting needle

---

Table 164–3 • FACTORS TO CONSIDER IN THE DIAGNOSIS OF LYMPHADENOPATHY

Associated systemic symptoms
Patient age
History of infection, trauma, medications, travel experience, previous malignancy, etc.
Location: cervical, supraclavicular, epitrochlear, axillary, intrathoracic (hilar versus mediastinal), intra-abdominal (retroperitoneal versus mesenteric versus other), iliac, inguinal, femoral
Localized versus disseminated
Tenderness/inflammation
Size
Consistency

Table 164–2 • MOST FREQUENT CAUSES OF LYMPHADENOPATHY IN ADULTS IN THE UNITED STATES

Unexplained
Infection
   In drainage area of infection (e.g., cervical adenopathy with pharyngitis)
   Disseminated (e.g., mononucleosis, human immunodeficiency virus infection)
Immune disorders (e.g., rheumatoid arthritis)
Neoplasms
Immune system malignancies (e.g., leukemia and lymphomas)
Metastatic carcinoma or sarcoma

Table 164–4 • METHODS OF LYMPH NODE EVALUATION

Physical examination
Imaging
   Chest radiography
   Lymphangiography
   Ultrasonography
   Computed tomography
   Magnetic resonance imaging
   Gallium scanning
   Positron emission tomography
Sampling
   Needle aspiration
   Cutting needle biopsy
   Excisional biopsy

biopsies will occasionally provide sufficient material for an unequivocal diagnosis and subtyping of the lymphoma. In general, however, excisional biopsy, which is most likely to provide the pathologist with adequate material to perform histologic, immunologic, and genetic studies, is the most appropriate approach.

An Approach to the Patient with Lymphadenopathy

Patients with lymphadenopathy (Table 164–5) come to medical attention in several ways. Perhaps the most common is a patient who has felt a lymph node in the neck, axilla, or groin and then seeks a physician's opinion. Lymphadenopathy might also come to medical attention as an unexpected finding on routine physical examination or as part of the evaluation of another complaint. Finally, patients might be found to have unexpected lymphadenopathy on imaging studies of the chest or abdomen. When the nodes are multiple or larger than 2 to 3 cm, biopsy using mediastinoscopy, paramediastinal incision, laparoscopy, or laparotomy is often required for diagnosis.

The approach to a patient complaining of newly discovered lymphadenopathy in the neck, axilla, or groin depends on the size, consistency, and number of enlarged lymph nodes and the patient's general health. In general, very large or very firm lymph nodes in the presence of systemic symptoms such as unexplained fever, sweats, or weight loss should lead to a lymph node biopsy. Patients who have lymph nodes in the drainage area of a previously treated malignancy (e.g., neck nodes in a patient with a history of head and neck cancer) might be best approached by lymph node aspiration. Carcinoma can often be diagnosed in this manner, although it is a poor approach for the diagnosis of lymphoid malignancies. For cervical lymph nodes, excisional biopsy should be delayed in a patient who has head and neck cancer as a diagnostic consideration (Chapter 197). These patients should initially undergo careful ear, nose, and throat examinations to avoid performing a biopsy that complicates the patient's subsequent therapy.

For the most common situation, in which a lymph node is soft and not larger than 2 to 3 cm and the patient has no obvious systemic illness, observation for a brief period is usually the best approach. Performance of a complete blood cell count and examination of a peripheral smear can be helpful in recognizing a systemic illness (e.g., infectious mononucleosis) (see Fig. 163–9). These patients are often also given antibiotics. If the lymph node does not regress over the course of a few weeks or if it grows in size, a biopsy should be performed.

Part of the care of such patients involves the art of medicine and responsiveness to the patient's particular needs. For example, a biopsy might be done more quickly in a patient who is very anxious about malignancy or who needs a definitive diagnosis expeditiously.

SPLENOMEGALY

Physiology and Anatomy

The spleen is the largest lymphatic organ in the body and is sometimes approached clinically as though it were a very large lymph node. However, although it also participates in the primary immune response to invading microorganisms and foreign proteins, the spleen has many other functions. It functions as a filter for the blood and is

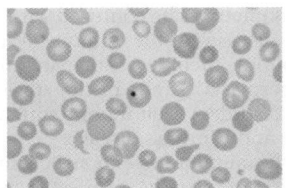

FIGURE 164–1 • A Howell-Jolly body in an erythrocyte, evidence of splenectomy or a nonfunctional spleen.

Table 164–6 • CAUSES OF SPLENOMEGALY

Infection
  Bacterial (e.g., endocarditis, brucellosis, syphilis, typhoid, pyogenic abscess)
  Mycobacterial (e.g., tuberculosis)
  Fungal (e.g., histoplasmosis, toxoplasmosis)
  Parasitic (e.g., malaria, leishmaniasis)
  Rickettsial (e.g., Rocky Mountain spotted fever)
  Viral (e.g., Epstein-Barr virus, cytomegalovirus, human immunodeficiency virus, hepatitis)
Benign disorders of the immune system (e.g., rheumatoid arthritis with Felty's syndrome, systemic lupus erythematosus, drug reactions such as to phenytoin, Langerhans' cell histiocytosis, serum sickness)
Malignant disorders of the immune system (e.g., acute or chronic myeloid or lymphoid leukemia, non-Hodgkin's lymphoma, Hodgkin's disease, Waldenström's macroglobulinemia, malignant histiocytosis)
Other malignancies (e.g., melanoma, sarcoma)
Congestive splenomegaly (e.g., portal hypertension secondary to liver disease, splenic or portal vein thrombosis)
Hematologic disorders (e.g., autoimmune hemolytic anemia, hereditary spherocytosis, thalassemia major, hemoglobinopathies, elliptocytosis, megaloblastic anemia, extramedullary hematopoiesis)
Storage diseases (e.g., Gaucher's disease)
Endocrinopathies (e.g., hyperthyroidism)
Miscellaneous (e.g., sarcoidosis, amyloidosis, tropical splenomegaly, cysts)

responsible for removing from the circulation senescent red blood cells, as well as blood cells and other cells coated with immunoglobulins. Blood enters the spleen, filters through the splenic cords, and is exposed to the immunologically active cells in the spleen.

The splenic red pulp occupies more than half the volume of the spleen and is the site where senescent red cells are identified and destroyed and red blood cell inclusions are removed by a process known as *pitting*. In the absence of splenic function, basophilic inclusions known as *Howell-Jolly bodies* are seen in circulating red blood cells. The presence of Howell-Jolly bodies (Fig. 164–1) in the peripheral blood indicates that the patient has had a splenectomy or has a process that has rendered the spleen nonfunctional.

The white pulp of the spleen contains macrophages, B lymphocytes, and T lymphocytes, participates in the recognition of microorganisms and foreign proteins, and is involved in the primary immune response. Absence of this splenic function makes individuals particularly sensitive to certain infections, including sepsis with encapsulated organisms such as *Streptococcus pneumoniae*.

Causes

As with lymphadenopathy, the conditions associated with splenomegaly are extremely numerous (Table 164–6). A wide variety of infections can lead to splenomegaly (Chapter 294). Certain bacterial infections such as endocarditis (Chapter 310), brucellosis (Chapter 339), and typhoid fever (Chapter 324) have splenomegaly as a frequent manifestation. Disseminated tuberculosis (Chapter 341) is often associated with splenomegaly, and splenomegaly can also be seen in cases of disseminated histoplasmosis (Chapter 379) and toxoplasmosis (Chapter 396). Splenomegaly is an almost constant accompaniment of malaria (Chapter 392). Rickettsial disorders such as Rocky Mountain spotted fever are frequently associated with splenomegaly. A wide variety of viral infections usually cause splenomegaly (Chapter 357), including infectious mononucleosis associated with Epstein-Barr virus (Chapter 371) and viral hepatitis (Chapter 151). Splenomegaly can accompany human immunodeficiency virus infection.

Table 164–5 • AN APPROACH TO THE PATIENT WITH LYMPHADENOPATHY

1. Does the patient have a known illness that causes lymphadenopathy? Treat and monitor for resolution.
2. Is there an obvious infection to explain the lymphadenopathy (e.g., infectious mononucleosis)? Treat and monitor for resolution.
3. Are the nodes very large and/or very firm and thus suggestive of malignancy? Perform a biopsy.
4. Is the patient very concerned about malignancy and unable to be reassured that malignancy is unlikely? Perform a biopsy.
5. If none of the preceding are true, perform a complete blood cell count and if it is unrevealing, monitor for a predetermined period (usually 2 to 6 weeks). If the nodes do not regress or if they increase in size, perform a biopsy.

Splenic abscesses, which are usually the result of hematogenous spread of pyogenic organisms, represent an unusual and difficult to diagnose cause of splenomegaly.

Splenomegaly is also seen in a variety of benign disorders of the immune system (Chapter 273), including rheumatoid arthritis (Chapter 278), in which some patients will have Felty's syndrome and accompanying granulocytopenia. Splenomegaly is frequently seen in patients with systemic lupus erythematosus (Chapter 280), certain drug reactions, and serum sickness.

Malignancies of the immune system and nonimmune organs can also lead to splenomegaly. Splenomegaly is usually seen in patients with chronic myeloid leukemia and is frequent in chronic lymphoid leukemia (Chapter 192). It can be seen in patients with acute myeloid or lymphoid leukemia, non-Hodgkin's lymphoma, Hodgkin's disease, and Waldenström's macroglobulinemia (Chapters 194 through 196). The condition previously known as angioimmunoblastic lymphadenopathy, which is now known usually to represent a T-cell lymphoma, often has splenomegaly as one manifestation. Metastasis of carcinomas and sarcomas to the spleen is unusual except for malignant melanoma; even in melanoma, however, palpable splenomegaly is an unusual finding.

Splenomegaly can develop from increased pressure in the splenic circulation, especially in portal hypertension, caused by a variety of hepatic disorders, including alcoholic cirrhosis (Chapter 156). However, it also can be due to splenic or portal vein thrombosis.

Hematologic disorders that can lead to palpable splenomegaly include autoimmune hemolytic anemia, hereditary spherocytosis, and a number of other anemias (Chapters 169 through 171). In cases of idiopathic myelofibrosis, the spleen is frequently a site of extramedullary hematopoiesis (Chapter 183).

A variety of less common conditions can lead to splenomegaly. The storage disorder Gaucher's disease (Chapter 222) is usually manifested as splenomegaly. Splenomegaly can be seen in endocrinopathies such as hyperthyroidism (Chapter 239). Sarcoidosis (Chapter 91) and amyloidosis (Chapter 290) can be manifested as splenomegaly. *Tropical splenomegaly* is a term used to describe the palpable spleens found in patients who live in tropical areas and might have numerous causes.

Evaluation of Splenic Size and Function

The ability to perform an accurate physical examination and determine the presence of an enlarged spleen (Table 164–7) is an important skill, but it is not easily learned. Physical examination of the spleen can be performed with the patient supine or in the right lateral decubitus position. Inspection, percussion, auscultation, and palpation can all be important in accurate assessment. It is rare to have a spleen so large that it is visible and can be seen to move with respiration. However, in patients with such a condition, it is possible to miss the splenomegaly by failing to start palpation sufficiently low to find the edge. Occasionally, percussion of the left upper quadrant will help identify an area of dullness that moves with respiration and can lead to the identification of splenomegaly. Splenic size is usually recorded as the number of centimeters that the spleen descends below the left costal margin in the midclavicular line on inspiration. Although auscultation is not usually a regular part of splenic examination, the existence of a splenic rub on inspiration can lead to the diagnosis of splenic infarct. The left kidney is sometimes confused with the spleen on physical examination, but its failure to

move with respiration in the way typical for the spleen will usually allow distinction.

Laboratory studies are frequently valuable in assessing splenic function. In patients with an absent spleen or a nonfunctional spleen, Howell-Jolly bodies will be seen in circulating red blood cells (see Fig. 164–1). Splenic hyperfunction (a condition often referred to as *hypersplenism*) is associated with cytopenias: the spleen is the normal reservoir for a significant proportion of platelets, and this reservoir function can lead to thrombocytopenia in patients with splenomegaly. Patients with autoimmune hemolytic anemia usually have palpable splenomegaly, but patients with idiopathic (immune) thrombocytopenic purpura usually do not.

The spleen can be imaged with ultrasonography, CT, traditional radionuclide scans, and positron emission tomography. Ultrasonography can provide accurate determination of splenic size and is easy to repeat. CT will frequently give a better view of the consistency of the spleen and can identify splenic tumors or abscesses that would otherwise be missed. Radionuclide scans such as gallium scans can identify active lymphoma or infections. The technetium liver-spleen scan can be important in identifying liver disease as the cause of splenomegaly; in patients with cryptogenic cirrhosis, a technetium liver-spleen scan that shows higher activity in the spleen than the liver might be the initial hint of liver disease.

Because of the spleen's location and its propensity to bleed, needle aspiration or cutting needle biopsy of the spleen is rarely performed. In general, a splenic "biopsy" involves splenectomy, which can be performed at the time of laparotomy or with laparoscopy. However, a splenectomy done via laparoscopy leads to maceration of the organ and can reduce the diagnostic information. In very young children, in whom splenectomy causes a high risk for serious infections such as pneumococcal septicemia, partial splenectomy can sometimes be performed. Patients who undergo splenectomy at the time of splenic trauma and rupture can have seeding of splenic cells to other sites in the abdomen. Some patients have additional small or accessory spleens. Persistent, functional splenic tissue can be the explanation for recurrent immune thrombocytopenia after splenectomy and might be recognized by the absence of Howell-Jolly bodies in circulating red blood cells.

An Approach to the Patient with Splenomegaly

(Table 164–8)

Patients with splenomegaly may come to medical attention for a variety of reasons. Patients may complain of left upper quadrant pain or fullness or of early satiety. A splenic infarct, which typically manifests with left upper quadrant pain that sometimes radiates to the left shoulder, can be the first clue to the existence of an enlarged spleen. Rarely, splenomegaly can initially manifest with the catastrophic symptoms of splenic rupture. Some patients are found to have splenomegaly as a result of evaluation for unexplained cytopenias. Splenomegaly can be discovered incidentally on physical examination. In recent years, splenomegaly has been frequently discovered on imaging studies of the abdomen performed for other purposes.

The presence of a palpable spleen on physical examination is almost always abnormal. The one exception to this rule is a palpable spleen tip in a slender, young woman. In general, the presence of a palpable spleen should be considered a serious finding, and an explanation should be sought. It is less clear that the same rules would apply to

---

Table 164–7 • METHODS FOR EVALUATING THE SPLEEN

Physical examination
Imaging
  Ultrasonography
  Computed tomography
  Liver-spleen scanning
  Gallium scanning
  Positron emission tomography
Biopsy
  Needle aspiration
  Splenectomy
    Laparotomy (total or partial splenectomy)
    Laparoscopy

Table 164–8 • AN APPROACH TO THE PATIENT WITH SPLENOMEGALY

1. Does the patient have a known illness that causes splenomegaly (e.g., infectious mononucleosis)? Treat and monitor for resolution.
2. Search for an occult infection (e.g., infectious endocarditis), hematologic disorder (e.g., hereditary spherocytosis), occult liver disease (e.g., cryptogenic cirrhosis), autoimmune disease (e.g., systemic lupus erythematosus), or storage disease (e.g., Gaucher's disease). If found, manage appropriately.
3. If systemic symptoms are present and suggest malignancy and/or focal replacement of the spleen is seen on imaging studies and no other site is available for biopsy, splenectomy is indicated.
4. If none of the above are true, monitor closely and repeat studies until the splenomegaly resolves or a diagnosis becomes apparent.

borderline splenomegaly discovered incidentally on routine imaging studies.

The approach to a patient with an enlarged spleen should focus initially on excluding a systemic illness that could explain the splenomegaly. Infectious mononucleosis, leukemia or lymphoma, rheumatoid arthritis, sarcoidosis, cirrhosis of the liver, malaria, or a host of other illnesses would be accepted as a reasonable explanation for the splenomegaly. The systemic condition should be treated and then the spleen should be re-evaluated. If the systemic illness can be treated successfully, the spleen should regress to normal size over time.

Patients with no obvious explanation for an enlarged spleen present a difficult diagnostic problem. Careful follow-up of these patients sometimes reveals occult liver disease or an autoimmune process that initially defied diagnosis. Concerns about malignancy, particularly in patients with systemic symptoms such as fever, sweats, or weight loss or in patients in whom imaging studies show a focal abnormality, are sometimes indications for splenectomy. However, in the absence of such findings, it is generally preferable to monitor patients closely with repeated attempts to establish the diagnosis by approaches other than splenectomy. It is particularly important to avoid splenectomy in a patient with occult liver disease and portal hypertension.

Splenectomy was once performed routinely as part of the staging evaluation for Hodgkin's disease or other lymphomas (Chapters 194 and 195). Today, this procedure is rarely needed to choose the correct therapy, and it generally should be avoided. Splenectomy can be an effective therapy for immune thrombocytopenic purpura (Chapter 177) and can occasionally be an appropriate therapy to relieve cytopenias in other conditions such as advanced myelofibrosis (Chapter 183).

SUGGESTED READINGS

Fritscher-Ravens A, Mylonaki M, Pantes A, et al: Endoscopic ultrasound-guided biopsy for the diagnosis of focal lesions of the spleen. Am J Gastroenterol 2003;98:1022–1027. *An approach to the diagnosis of unknown splenic lesions when CT- or US-guided biopsy fails.*

Grover SA, Barkun AN, Sackett DL: Does this patient have splenomegaly? JAMA 1993;270:2218–2221. *A practical approach to the evaluation of possible splenomegaly.*

165 TRANSFUSION MEDICINE

Jay E. Menitove

Introduction

BLOOD DONATION AND COMPONENT THERAPY

Volunteer blood donors are screened to detect donors who might be harmed by donating blood and who might pose a risk to the potential recipient. Whole blood (500 mL) is collected into plastic blood containers, or various blood components (e.g., red blood cells [RBCs], platelets, and plasma) are collected using automated cell separator devices (apheresis technology).

After donation, aliquots of the donor's blood undergo testing for ABO and Rh type; antibodies to hepatitis B core (anti-HBc), hepatitis C virus (anti-HCV), human immunodeficiency virus (anti-HIV) 1 and 2, and human T-lymphotropic virus (anti-HTLV) I and II; syphilis; and the hepatitis B surface antigen (HBsAg). Nucleic acid testing for HIV and HCV detects RNA viral sequences approximately 12 days and 25 days, respectively, after exposure. Selected donations are tested for antibodies to cytomegalovirus (anti-CMV). Donations with reactive test results are destroyed because the presence of antibodies indicates potential infectivity rather than convalescence. RBCs can be stored for 42 days at 1° C to 6° C, platelets for 5 days at 20° C to 24° C, and frozen plasma for 1 year at −18° C.

LEUKOCYTE REDUCTION

RBC and pooled platelet concentrates derived from whole blood collections contain 10^8 to 10^9 white blood cells (WBCs). These contaminating leukocytes cause febrile, nonhemolytic transfusion reactions and alloimmunization to human leukocyte antigen (HLA) and other non-RBC alloantigens. They also serve as a reservoir of intracellular infectious agents, such as CMV and HTLV.

Leukocyte-reduction filters and apheresis technologies permit the routine preparation of RBCs and platelets with less than 5×10^6 WBC per unit, the presumed threshold for the beneficial effects of leukocyte reduction. For the most part, plasma components contain less than 10^6 WBCs. Leukocyte reduction shortly after collection also prevents accumulation of various cytokines (e.g., interleukin [IL]-1, IL-6, IL-8, and tumor necrosis factor-α) produced by WBCs during storage in platelet concentrates. Some patients who are taking angiotensin-converting enzyme inhibitors and who receive blood undergoing leukocyte reduction by bedside filtration develop vasodilation and precipitous hypotension linked to bradykinin that is produced as plasma interacts with the filter polymers. In current practice, 50% or more of RBC transfusions are leukocyte-reduced by filtration conducted at blood centers before storage. Apheresis platelets, in general, are leukocyte-reduced during preparation.

IRRADIATION

Gamma (25 Gy at the midplane of the blood containers) radiation and less frequently x-ray irradiation are used to prevent graft-versus-host disease (GVHD) by eliminating the proliferative potential of T lymphocytes contained in RBCs, platelets, and granulocytes. Patients at risk for GVHD include bone marrow, peripheral blood progenitor cell, or umbilical cord blood transplant recipients (Chapter 166); patients with congenital immunodeficiency syndromes; infants weighing less than 1000 g at birth; fetuses receiving intrauterine transfusions; neonates who receive intrauterine transfusions; patients with Hodgkin's disease, non-Hodgkin's lymphoma, and hematologic and solid tumor malignancies who are profoundly immunosuppressed by chemotherapy; recipients of transfusions from blood relatives; and recipients of HLA-selected components.

INFORMED CONSENT TO RECEIVE A TRANSFUSION

The informed consent process involves a discussion of transfusion-associated risks (including risks related to not receiving a transfusion), benefits, and alternatives. Physicians should present this information in conjunction with an opportunity to answer questions.

ALTERNATIVES TO ROUTINE ALLOGENEIC TRANSFUSION

AUTOLOGOUS TRANSFUSION. Autologous blood transfusions are indicated for patients who are scheduled for surgical procedures for which transfusion is likely. Blood donation occurs preoperatively as frequently as every 3 days, up to 72 hours before a scheduled surgery, provided that the hemoglobin concentration is greater than 11 g/dL. The blood may be stored for 42 days. Oral iron supplementation (ferrous sulfate, 325 mg orally three times daily at least through surgery) is given to replete iron losses of 200 to 250 mg per unit. Autologous transfusion also can be accomplished by salvaging blood during surgery by sterile collection. Currently in the United States, autologous blood accounts for about 5% of units collected and 3% of units transfused.

DIRECTED DONATIONS. Directed donations refer to blood from donors (usually family members or friends) selected by a patient. Collection of directed units has declined from 3.2% of the U.S. blood supply in 1992 to about 1% at present. In general, there is no evidence that blood from designated donors is safer than blood collected routinely.

ERYTHROPOIETIN. Release of inflammatory cytokines or replacement of the bone marrow with tumor cells blunts the erythroid response to endogenous erythropoietin (EPO) in anemic patients with solid tumors, chronic lymphocytic leukemia (Chapter 192), lymphoma (Chapters 194 and 195), and myeloma (Chapter 196). Exogenous EPO therapy effectively increases the hemoglobin concentration in patients with these disorders and avoids transfusion in about 15 to 35% of patients who are undergoing treatment for cancer. EPO also decreases allogeneic transfusions in patients with chronic renal failure (Chapter 117); patients undergoing therapy for HIV (Chapter 419); patients scheduled for elective, noncardiovascular surgery with low hemoglobin levels; and patients donating multiple units of autologous blood before elective surgery.

THROMBOPOIETIN. Recombinant thrombopoietin (TPO) therapy is effective only in patients with intact marrow reserves. TPO increases platelet counts in patients with chronic idiopathic thrombocytopenic purpura (Chapter 177) or HIV-associated idiopathic thrombocytopenic purpura (Chapter 419), and it permits platelet donors to provide greater quantities of platelets for transfusion. In patients who have relatively intact marrow reserves while undergoing nonmyeloablative therapy for solid tumors, TPO therapy achieves only modest decreases in platelet nadirs, duration of thrombocytopenia, and number of platelet transfusions. TPO is not useful for reducing platelet transfusions in patients who have acute leukemia or who are undergoing progenitor cell transplantation. In some patients who receive multiple injections of TPO, autoantibodies develop and diminish the clinical utility of this growth factor.

ADVERSE EVENT REPORTING/HEMOVIGILANCE. The risk of noninfectious serious hazards of transfusion, such as ABO/Rh-incompatible transfusions and transfusion-related acute lung injury, pose a greater threat to transfusion safety than does viral transmission. Efforts to reduce these complications involve nonpunitive systems that encourage physicians to identify, report, and analyze the cause of these events. Technologic improvements may help ensure accurate matching of the blood container with the intended transfusion recipient.

Indications for Red Blood Cell Components

WHOLE BLOOD

With the exception of labile clotting factors V and VIII, the plasma in whole blood contains normal levels of all other coagulation factors. It is appropriate to consider whole blood transfusions when there is a concomitant deficiency of oxygen-carrying capacity, coagulation factors, and blood volume. In practice, these combined deficits occur infrequently.

RED BLOOD CELLS

RBC transfusions increase hemoglobin concentration and augment oxygen-carrying capacity. They are indicated when signs and symptoms of anemia are present, and physiologic mechanisms for enhancing tissue oxygen delivery no longer provide adequate compensation. The cause of anemia should be investigated and treated, if appropriate, with iron, folate, vitamin B_{12}, exogenous EPO, or other medications before giving RBC transfusions unless the patient's condition requires acute intervention (Chapter 160).

Signs and symptoms attributable to anemia include fatigue, dyspnea on exertion, decreased exercise capacity, angina, postural hypotension, impaired mentation, syncope, transient ischemic attack, tachycardia, increased respiratory rate, and pallor. Compensatory mechanisms that permit patients to tolerate modest degrees of anemia include increasing cardiac output by raising stroke volume or heart rate; redistributing blood to areas requiring more oxygen; enhancing oxygen extraction by peripheral tissue; increasing coronary artery blood flow, ventilatory volume, and respiratory rates; and augmenting oxygen unloading as a result of elevated 2,3-diphosphoglycerate levels. The presence of cardiovascular, cerebrovascular, and pulmonary impairment or dysfunction limits the effectiveness of these responses and requires transfusion at higher hematocrit and hemoglobin levels than generally recommended. The myocardium extracts 60 to 75% of oxygen delivered through the coronary circulation. Normally, coronary artery blood flow increases in response to higher myocardial oxygen requirements. For patients with coronary stenoses, however, myocardial ischemia may occur at higher hemoglobin levels than observed in patients without stenotic lesions.

The threshold for RBC transfusion is uncertain in many clinical situations. In critically ill patients randomized to receive RBC transfusions when the hemoglobin concentration fell to less than 7.0 g/dL (maintenance 7.0 to 9.0 g/dL) compared with patients who received transfusions when the hemoglobin concentration decreased to 10.0 g/dL (maintenance 10.0 to 12.0 g/dL), there was no difference in 30-day mortality. In a subgroup of patients younger than 55 years old or less acutely ill, the less aggressive transfusion strategy was associated with a lower 30-day mortality.[1]

In nonrandomized observation studies, patients who have postoperative hemoglobin levels less than or equal to 5.0 g/dL and who refuse transfusion on the basis of religious beliefs have significantly higher mortality rates than patients with higher levels. Retrospective data suggest that elderly patients with acute myocardial infarctions have lower mortality rates when hematocrits lower than 30 to 33% are treated with transfusions. For heart failure, a randomized trial showed benefit in terms of survival, exercise tolerance, and left ventricular function when EPO and iron therapy were used to increase

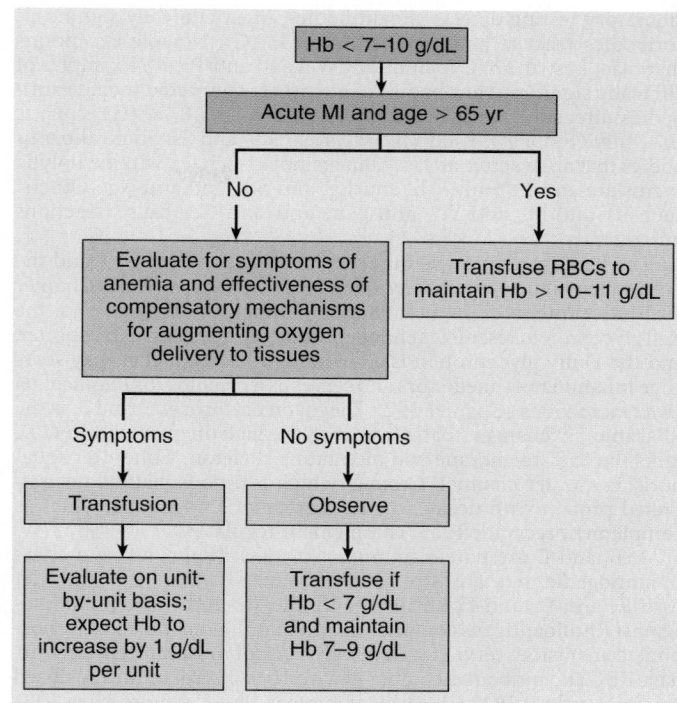

FIGURE 165–1 • Guideline for deciding when to administer red blood cell (RBC) transfusions. Hb = hemoglobin.

chronic hemoglobin levels to greater than 12.5 g/dL.[2] Taken together, these data suggest RBC transfusions are indicated when the hemoglobin concentration falls to 7.0 g/dL (maintenance level 7.0 to 9.0 g/dL), with the exception of patients with acute myocardial infarctions or heart failure, in whom transfusions or other hemoglobin-raising therapies are indicated at a higher level (Fig. 165–1).

One unit of transfused RBCs raises the hemoglobin concentration by 1 g/dL and the hematocrit by 3%. In patients without effective bone marrow erythropoietic activity, the hemoglobin concentration and hematocrit decline an average of 1 transfused unit per week. If transfusion requirements exceed this level, blood loss or hemolysis should be considered.

WASHED RED BLOOD CELLS

Washed RBCs are prepared by adding saline to the container, followed by centrifugation, decanting the supernatant plasma/saline solution, and subsequent suspension of the remaining RBCs in normal saline. This process removes plasma proteins, including IgA. Washed RBCs are indicated for patients who have allergic reactions, including IgA-deficient patients who have anti-IgA antibodies.

RED BLOOD CELLS STORED IN THE FROZEN STATE

Adding the cryoprotectant glycerol to RBCs followed by appropriate freezing permits storage of RBCs for 10 years. When the cells are needed, the unit is thawed and washed to remove the glycerol. This cumbersome and expensive procedure is reserved primarily for maintaining repositories of uncommon RBC phenotypes needed by patients with alloantibodies against frequently occurring RBC antigens; it also is used by the military to maintain emergent blood supplies.

Immunohematology: Red Blood Cell Transfusions

RED BLOOD CELL BLOOD GROUP ANTIGENS

The 25 blood group systems found on RBCs (e.g., ABO, Rh, K, MNS, Fy), contain more than 250 antigens. Some are common (e.g., Vel, u), whereas others are rarely found on RBCs (e.g., ScZDi[a], Co[b], Wr[a]). Patients who lack an alloantigen may form alloantibodies directed against the antigen that is missing from their cells. Pretransfusion laboratory testing detects alloantibodies. Most clinically significant antibodies react at body temperature (37° C). Notable exceptions that react best at 22° C include anti-Vel and anti-PP1^{pk}. Examples of clinically significant antibodies frequently encountered include antibodies directed against blood groups such as A, B, Rh (D, c, C, e, E), Duffy (Fy^a, Fy^b), Kidd (Jk^{a}Jk^b), Kell (K), and Ss. Some alloantibodies that are reactive at 37° C but are not associated with hemolytic events are anti-Le^b, anti-Ch, anti-Rg, anti-Sd^a, and anti-Xg^a. Others, such as anti-M, anti-Yt^a, anti-Lan, and anti-Ge, cause reactions infrequently.

The P antigen serves as the receptor for parvovirus B19, and the Le^a antigen is the epithelial receptor for *Helicobacter pylori* (Chapter 137). Rh proteins show homology to ammonium transporters, the Kell glycoprotein resembles endopeptidases, Kidd is a urea transporter, and the Duffy glycoprotein is a chemokine receptor that may scavenge inflammatory mediators and serves as a receptor for *Plasmodium vivax* merozoites (Chapter 392). Diego, on erythrocyte band 3, is the RBC anion exchanger, that, along with Gerbich on glycophorin C/D, links the RBC membrane and membrane skeleton. Colton on aquaporin is a water channel. Cromer, which is a phosphatidylinositol-linked protein with decay accelerating factor, and Knops, which is complement receptor 1, are complement regulators.

A, B, and D are potent immunogens. Kell (K), c, and E are less immunogenic but are stronger antigenically than Fy^a and Jk^a. Anti-K, anti-D, anti-E, and anti-Fy^a and anti-Jk^a and other antibodies against Rh alloantigens comprise most alloantibodies detected by hospital transfusion services. Generally, 1% of hospitalized patients have RBC alloantibodies compared with 10 to 30% of multitransfused patients; only 0.1% of healthy, volunteer blood donors have RBC alloantibodies.

COMPATIBILITY TESTING

RBC donor and recipient ABO types must be compatible; Rh-compatible RBCs should be given, especially to women of childbearing age. Plasma from group A donors contains anti-B, plasma from B donors contains anti-A, and plasma from O donors contains anti-A and anti-B. Group O (universal donor) RBCs may be given to A, B, or O patients. Group AB patients (universal recipients) may receive RBCs from group A, B, AB, or O donors. Rh-negative patients should receive blood from Rh-negative donors. Rh-positive patients may receive blood from Rh-positive or Rh-negative donors.

An electronic crossmatch uses a computer algorithm to match the donor with previously typed donor blood. If alloantibodies are present, a full crossmatch is conducted in which donor RBCs, lacking blood group antigens corresponding to alloantibodies contained in the patient's serum, are incubated with the patient's serum.

If a physician is concerned that a transfusion delay would unduly jeopardize a patient, blood is issued before completion of pretransfusion testing, provided that the records contain a signed statement from the physician indicating that the clinical status was sufficiently urgent to require emergency release. If the ABO group is not known, group O RBCs should be provided. If the ABO type has been determined, ABO group compatible RBCs should be given.

Indications for Platelet Transfusions

A 50,000/μL platelet count, in the absence of other coagulation abnormalities, provides adequate coverage for patients undergoing most minor surgical procedures. Higher platelet counts, approximately 100,000/μL, are preferred for patients having central nervous system or ocular surgeries. Recommended platelet count levels for performing specific invasive procedures, such as lumbar punctures, organ biopsies, dental extractions, and central venous catheter insertions, range from 20,000/μL to 50,000/μL. Bone marrow aspirations and biopsies can be performed safely at platelet counts of less than 20,000/μL.

The prophylactic platelet transfusion threshold for patients with acute leukemia is 10,000/μL (Chapters 177 and 193). Transfusion at a higher level should be considered in patients with signs of hemorrhage, high fever, rapidly falling platelet counts, high WBC counts, or other coagulation abnormalities (Fig. 165–2). For patients with chronic, stable, severe thrombocytopenia, such as aplastic anemia (Chapter 174), thresholds lower than 10,000/μL may be appropriate (Chapter 177). The 10,000/μL guideline seems appropriate for patients

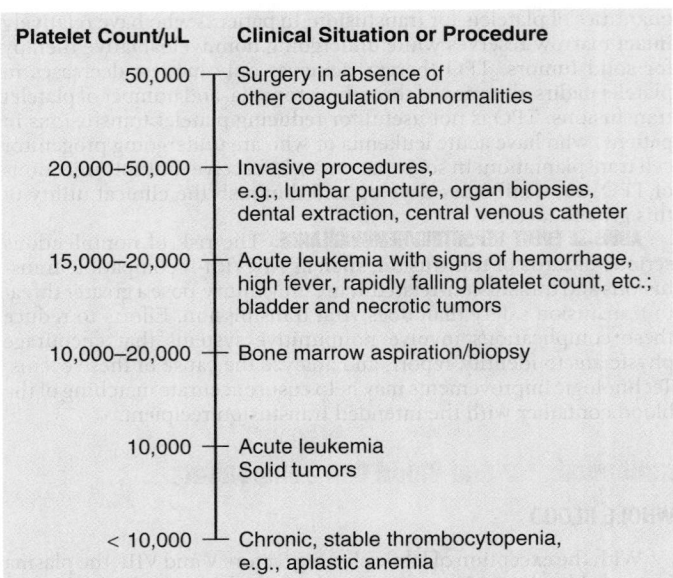

Platelet Count/μL	Clinical Situation or Procedure
50,000	Surgery in absence of other coagulation abnormalities
20,000–50,000	Invasive procedures, e.g., lumbar puncture, organ biopsies, dental extraction, central venous catheter
15,000–20,000	Acute leukemia with signs of hemorrhage, high fever, rapidly falling platelet count, etc.; bladder and necrotic tumors
10,000–20,000	Bone marrow aspiration/biopsy
10,000	Acute leukemia Solid tumors
< 10,000	Chronic, stable thrombocytopenia, e.g., aplastic anemia

FIGURE 165–2 • Threshold for providing platelet transfusions in thrombocytopenic patients.

with solid tumors, although patients treated for bladder cancer (Chapter 203) or necrotic tumors may benefit from platelet transfusions at higher levels.

The routine platelet transfusion dose is achieved by pooling 4 to 6 units of whole blood–derived platelets, that is, 1 unit per 10 to 12 kg body weight or, more commonly, infusing 1 unit of apheresis platelets. Platelet count monitoring determines if the target platelet count has been reached and if subsequent platelet transfusions are needed. Additional platelet transfusions should be available for prompt infusion in the event that procedure-related bleeding occurs. Studies are under way to determine whether higher platelet doses result in fewer bleeding episodes, longer intervals between platelet transfusions, and lower numbers of total platelet transfusions.

The usual expected increment in the platelet count is 30,000/μL at 10 to 60 minutes post-transfusion, with a minimally expected increment of 12,000/μL. Lower increments occur in the presence of alloimmunization (e.g., anti-HLA antibodies), splenomegaly, and severe disseminated intravascular coagulation (Chapter 179). Platelet counts obtained 18 to 24 hours after transfusion reflect platelet survival and are lower in patients with fever, infection, and other inflammatory conditions.

In contrast to RBC transfusions, routine platelet transfusions do not involve compatibility testing, but platelet transfusions should be given from donors with similar ABO types. If Rh-negative donors receive platelet transfusions from Rh-positive donors, anti-D immunoprophylaxis should be considered for Rh-negative women with childbearing potential.

Approximately 25 to 35% of frequently transfused patients with acute leukemia (Chapter 193) develop alloantibody-mediated (usually anti-HLA) refractoriness (i.e., platelet count increments <10,000 to 12,000/μL at 10 minutes after at least two ABO-compatible platelet transfusions). Alloimmunization against HLA antigens occurs less frequently among patients who receive leukocyte-reduced RBC and platelet transfusions. Platelet transfusions from donors with HLA-A and HLA-B antigens similar to the patient or from donors selected by platelet crossmatching techniques are recommended for alloimmunized patients.

Indications for Fresh-Frozen Plasma

One unit of frozen plasma contains 180 to 300 mL, whereas apheresis-derived plasma may exceed 400 mL. A standard fresh-frozen plasma (FFP) unit contains approximately 200 units of each coagulation factor or 7% of the coagulation factor activity of a 70-kg patient.

Coagulation factor concentrations of 20 to 30% and a fibrinogen concentration greater than 75 mg/μL generally maintain hemostasis (Chapter 178). Plasma transfusions of 10 to 15 mL/kg body weight should raise coagulation factor levels to 30%. Repeat dosing should be based on follow-up coagulation test results and the clinical setting. Based on observational data, indications for FFP include treatment of hemorrhage in patients with congenital or acquired coagulation factor deficiencies (e.g., factor II, V, X, XI, or XIII). The risk of hemorrhage increases when the prothrombin and partial thromboplastin times exceed 1.5 to 1.8 times control values or there is a proportionate increase in the international normalized ratio (INR). For patients with severe liver disease and active bleeding or patients undergoing invasive procedures, FFP sometimes is recommended if the INR is greater than 1.6 and certainly is recommended if it is greater than 2.0. Recombinant factor VIIa, used to treat hemophilic patients with inhibitors, is under study for treating hemorrhagic complications in patients with liver disease and prolonged INRs in the setting of bleeding associated with severe trauma. FFP is not the primary modality for treating coagulation factor deficiencies, such as factors VIII and IX, for which virally inactivated or recombinant concentrates are available.

Parenteral vitamin K administration reverses the warfarin anticoagulation effect. For patients who have active bleeding, are facing emergency surgery, or need an invasive procedure within the 6 hours before vitamin K correction, FFP provides active coagulation factors. FFP is the preferred replacement fluid for patients undergoing plasma exchange therapy for thrombotic thrombocytopenic purpura (Chapter 177).

Indications for Cryoprecipitate

Cryoprecipitate is the cold-insoluble precipitate formed by thawing frozen plasma at 4° C and decanting the liquid supernatant. The precipitate suspended in a small amount of plasma is refrozen and stored at −18° C or colder for 1 year. It contains more than 150 mg of fibrinogen, more than 80 units of factor VIII, significant amounts of von Willebrand factor, and some fibronectin and factor XIII.

Cryoprecipitate is used predominately to replace fibrinogen or to prepare fibrin sealants. A dose of 1 unit (bag) of cryoprecipitate per 5 kg body weight raises fibrinogen levels by at least 75 mg/dL. The half-life of fibrinogen is 3 to 5 days; additional doses should be given on the basis of laboratory test results. Fibrin sealant prepared by adding thrombin to cryoprecipitate is used to promote hemostasis and adhesion during cardiovascular, neurosurgical, and other procedures. Commercially prepared fibrin sealants are available currently and may replace cryoprecipitate except when fibrinogen replacement specifically is required.

Indications for Granulocytes

Granulocyte transfusions are obtained from donors given corticosteroids, granulocyte colony-stimulating factor, or both to increase the number of granulocytes. In patients undergoing stem cell transplantation, granulocyte transfusions may reduce the mortality rate from bacterial and stable fungal infections and candidemia, but not invasive fungal infections, if their absolute granulocyte count is 100 to 500/μL. Additional studies are in progress to quantitate the potential benefit.

Granulocyte transfusions contain RBCs and must be ABO compatible with the donor. Irradiation is recommended, as is selection of CMV-seronegative donors for seronegative patients. Alloimmunization against WBC antigens results in febrile reactions. An interval of 12 hours between granulocyte transfusions and amphotericin or the use of liposomal amphotericin is suggested to reduce the risk of acute respiratory distress.

Transfusion-Associated Adverse Reactions

NONINFECTIOUS SERIOUS HAZARDS OF TRANSFUSIONS

INCOMPATIBLE BLOOD TRANSFUSIONS. Acute hemolytic reactions involving antibody-mediated intravascular hemolysis cause more than 50% of transfusion-associated fatalities. ABO incompatible transfusions, which occur at a rate of 1 per 38,000 units transfused, account for most of those morbid events (Table 165-1). Symptoms occur in 40% of these episodes; fewer than 5% result in death. Hemolysis follows infusion of ABO incompatible plasma in platelet concentrates at a rate of 1 per 9000 such episodes. Signs and symptoms associated with

Table 165-1 • TRANSFUSION-ASSOCIATED ADVERSE REACTIONS

	RISK PER UNIT INFUSED
ABO incompatible blood transfusions	1:38,000
Symptoms	40%
Fatalities	1:1,800,000
Delayed serologic reactions	1:1600
Delayed hemolytic reactions	1:6700
Transfusion-related acute lung injury	1:5000
Graft-versus-host disease	Infrequent
Fluid overload	?
Febrile, nonhemolytic transfusion reactions	
Red blood cells (nonleukocyte reduced/leukocyte reduced)	1:200/1:300
Platelets (nonleukocyte reduced/ leukocyte reduced)	1:5–20/1:25–50
Allergic reactions	1:30–100
Anaphylactic reactions	1:150,000
Iron overload	After 80–100 U
Post-transfusion purpura	Rare
Immunosuppressive effects	?

intravascular hemolysis include fever and/or chills; pain in the flanks, back, chest, head, or infusion site; nausea and/or vomiting; dyspnea; and tachycardia. Clinical complications of hypotension, renal failure, and intravascular coagulation occur in response to complement activation, cytokine release, and endothelial interaction.

Extravascular hemolysis, which is removal of antibody-opsonized RBCs by the spleen, liver, and marrow, occurs with noncomplement–binding antibodies directed against Rh, Kell, Duffy, S, and other antigens. Jaundice is the common presentation; nausea, vomiting, pain, dyspnea, and tachycardia are less frequent.

Laboratory investigation involves an identification check to determine whether the correct patient received the implicated unit, examination of a post-transfusion plasma specimen for a reddish or pinkish hue (hemolysis), and performance of a direct antiglobulin test seeking evidence of RBC opsonization. The differential diagnosis includes febrile nonhemolytic transfusion reactions (see later); nonimmune causes of hemolysis, such as coinfusion of RBCs with hypotonic or other noncompatible fluids or malfunctioning blood warmers or infusion pumps; congenital hemolytic anemias and hemoglobinopathies; microangiopathic hemolytic anemias such as thrombotic thrombocytopenic purpura; and infections that cause hemolysis (e.g., *Clostridium welchii*, malaria, babesiosis).

Recognition of a potential hemolytic reaction is imperative and should lead to immediate cessation of the RBC infusion. Fluid infusion and vasopressor support are appropriate if hypotension occurs. Patients should be monitored for disseminated intravascular coagulation, renal impairment, and volume overload. The risk of renal failure may be diminished by the use of sodium bicarbonate (250 to 500 mg intravenously over 1 to 4 hours) to maintain urinary pH greater than 7.0 and by the use of osmotic or other diuretics (e.g., 20% mannitol, 100 mL/m² given over 30 to 60 minutes followed by 30 mL/m²/hour for 12 hours, or furosemide, 40 to 120 mg intravenously). Exchange transfusion can reduce the number of incompatible RBCs.

DELAYED SEROLOGIC REACTIONS. Alloantibodies arising against newly infused alloantigens or through an anamnestic response related to previous transfusions or pregnancies are recognized by laboratory testing 3 to 21 days after transfusion. These events, considered delayed serologic transfusion reactions, follow approximately 1 per 1600 units transfused. Patients develop alloantibodies resulting in positive direct antiglobulin tests that reflect RBC sensitization, but clinical hemolysis does not occur. For example, 40% of Rh, Kell (K), Kidd (Jk), and Duffy (Fy) alloantibodies do not reduce RBC survival.

DELAYED HEMOLYTIC REACTIONS. Newly formed or anamnestically stimulated alloantibodies leading to hemolysis occur after approximately 1 per 6700 units transfused. Presenting signs and symptoms include fever, a decrease in hemoglobin concentration of at least 1 g/dL, an increase in indirect bilirubin or serum creatinine, and an unexplained decrease in urine output. Serious complications occur infrequently, although 10% of fatal hemolytic transfusion events involve delayed reactions. The direct antiglobulin test is positive and is sustained in some patients, possibly as a result of autoantibody formation months after transfusion. Alloantibodies frequently associated with delayed hemolytic or delayed serologic transfusion reactions include anti-Rh antibodies and anti-Kidd (Jk), anti-Duffy (Fy), and anti-Kell (K) antibodies.

Patients with sickle cell anemia (Chapter 171) who have acute or delayed hemolytic transfusion reactions are at risk for severe pain suggestive of sickle cell crisis, diminished RBC production, more severe anemia than present before transfusion, and possibly recurrence of these problems after subsequent transfusions. This syndrome occurs predominantly in patients with multiple RBC alloantibodies despite transfusion of crossmatch-compatible RBCs. Although the direct antiglobulin test is often negative, hemolysis of autologous RBCs (bystander immune hemolysis) plays a role in negating the expected post-transfusion increase in the hemoglobin level. Despite profound anemia, further transfusions should be withheld, if possible, and the patient should be given corticosteroids (e.g., prednisone, 1 to 2 mg/kg/day). In routine practice, extended RBC phenotypic matching of donors with recipients reduces the alloimmunization rate six-fold and hemolytic transfusion reactions by 90% and may reduce the incidence of delayed hemolytic transfusion reactions in patients with sickle cell anemia.

TRANSFUSION-RELATED ACUTE LUNG INJURY. Transfusion-related acute lung injury is the third leading cause of transfusion-associated fatalities, accounting for about 13% of deaths. Most deaths have been associated with FFP transfusions, but all blood components are implicated. The clinical syndrome consists of dyspnea, hypotension, and fever occurring shortly after transfusions and 4 to 6 hours later. The chest radiograph shows bilateral pulmonary infiltrates consistent with pulmonary edema but without evidence of fluid overload. The differential diagnosis includes pneumonia and adult respiratory distress syndrome.

Treatment consists of appropriate respiratory and ventilatory support. Three quarters of patients require ventilatory support, and 100% require oxygen supplementation. The hypoxemia and radiographic abnormalities resolve within 72 hours. Diuretics are not indicated because the pathophysiology involves microvascular injury, not fluid overload. Mortality approaches 5 to 10%.

GRAFT-VERSUS-HOST DISEASE. Transfusion-associated GVHD occurs when there are differences in HLA antigens between donor and recipient; immunocompetent cells are transfused; and the host, whether an immunocompetent patient undergoing surgery or an immunocompromised patient, does not reject the immunocompetent cells. CD4+ cells appear to be involved causally, whereas CD8+ and natural killer cells offer protection. Patients at high risk include those with impaired CD8+ and natural killer function. Fever occurs 4 to 23 (median 10) days after transfusion, followed by a rash, generalized erythroderma, bullae formation, and epidermolysis. The mortality rate approximates 90% at 3 to 4 weeks post-transfusion. GVHD is prevented by irradiating cellular blood components for at-risk patients (see earlier discussion of irradiated blood).

FLUID OVERLOAD. Patients with impaired myocardial reserve are at risk of hypervolemia. Routine transfusion rates are 2 to 4 mL/kg/hour, but rates should be reduced to 1 mL/kg/hour in susceptible patients.

FEBRILE, NONHEMOLYTIC TRANSFUSION REACTIONS. The initial presentation of a febrile nonhemolytic transfusion reaction or chill/fever reaction overlaps with the less frequent hemolytic events. The patient's temperature rises 1° C or more, usually associated with chills, rigors, a rise in diastolic blood pressure, and headache 45 to 60 minutes after starting the RBC transfusion. At the time of presentation, this process is not distinguished easily from more serious reactions; however, the symptoms, usually treated with antipyretics, do not progress and resolve within a few hours. Less than 15% of patients have a recurrence when subsequently transfused. Leukocyte reduction usually prevents a recurrence.

Chill/fever reactions have been reported to occur after 10 to 38% of platelet transfusions, with severe reactions after 1 to 8%. In contrast to RBCs, platelets are stored at room temperature, promoting the accumulation of various biologic response modifiers. Infusion of these cytokines results in febrile reactions. Leukocyte reduction to less than 5×10^6 WBCs before storage effectively reduces the incidence of chill/fever reactions associated with platelet transfusions.

ALLERGIC AND ANAPHYLACTIC REACTIONS

Allergic reactions, which commonly present as pruritic urticarial eruptions, result from an interaction of recipient IgE antibodies with donor plasma proteins. The reactions, usually mild, follow 1 to 3% of transfusions and generally respond to antihistamines and a brief cessation of the transfusion.

Anaphylactic reactions occur infrequently and are marked by sudden decreases in blood pressure, bronchospasm, laryngeal or facial edema, shock, facial flushing, vomiting, or diarrhea. These reactions appear immediately to 45 minutes after beginning the transfusion. The differential diagnosis includes transfusion-related acute lung injury, circulatory overload, acute hemolytic reaction, and septic shock. With anaphylactic reactions, urticaria or angioedema may occur, but fever is unusual.

Isolated IgA deficiency (approximately 1 per 500 to 1000 persons) in the presence of IgE or IgG anti-IgA antibodies is associated with anaphylactic reactions. Treatment includes epinephrine and corticosteroids for profound reactions. Future transfusions must be saline washed to remove IgA or must be obtained from IgA-deficient donors.

IRON OVERLOAD

Clinical features of transfusion-associated iron overload include increased skin pigmentation, liver disease, diabetes mellitus, cardiac dysfunction, arthropathy, and gonadal insufficiency. Each unit of RBCs contains 200 to 250 mg of iron. After receiving 100 units of RBCs, patients are at risk for cardiac and possibly liver, pancreatic, and endocrine dysfunction if they have not received iron chelation therapy (Chapter 225).

POST-TRANSFUSION PURPURA

Patients with post-transfusion purpura develop profound thrombocytopenia 5 to 14 days after transfusion. Most cases occur in women with a history of prior pregnancy, and almost all have platelet-specific alloantibodies. The treatment of choice is intravenous gammaglobulin infusion, but therapeutic plasma exchange is an alternative.

IMMUNOSUPPRESSIVE EFFECTS OF BLOOD TRANSFUSION

Patients receiving transfusions perioperatively may have a 20 to 30% increased risk of postoperative infections and a lower rate of tumor-free interval after cancer surgery. Any cause-and-effect relationship is controversial, however. Blood transfusions, including leukocyte-reduced transfusions, do not activate HIV, CMV, or cytokines in patients with advanced HIV infection. ◼

Transfusion-Transmitted Diseases

BACTERIAL CONTAMINATION

The second leading cause of reported transfusion-associated fatalities involves bacterial contamination of platelets and RBCs (Table 165–2). Most RBC and platelet contamination occurs as a result of transient bacteremia in the blood donor or ineffective antisepsis of the phlebotomy site during blood collection. The risk is greater in platelets stored at room temperature than RBCs stored at 1° C to 6° C. Bacterial contamination commonly includes group B streptococcus (Chapter 308), *Staphylococcus aureus* (Chapter 311), *Pseudomonas rettgeri* (Chapter 319), *Escherichia coli* (Chapter 329), *Enterobacter cloacae* (Chapter 323), and *Serratia marcescens* (Chapter 310) for platelets and *Staphylococcus epidermidis* (Chapter 311), *Yersinia enterocolitica* (Chapter 331), and *Serratia liquefaciens* for RBCs.

Patients develop rigors, fever, tachycardia, nausea/vomiting, shortness of breath, decreased or increased blood pressure, and lumbar pain 5 to 230 minutes (median 45 minutes) after receiving 10 to 550 mL (median 150 mL) of transfusion. The reported 40% mortality rate reflects reactions to gram-negative endotoxins.

Treatment involves early recognition, discontinuation of the transfusion, administration of broad-spectrum antibiotics, and other clinically indicated support. Organisms are identified by Gram stain in most, but not all, episodes. Cultures should be obtained. The differential diagnosis includes hemolytic reactions, febrile nonhemolytic reactions, and exacerbation of the underlying illness.

VIRUSES AND OTHER AGENTS

Nucleic acid testing detects HCV RNA and reduces the interval from an average 82 days to detect anti-HCV antibody to 25 days.

Table 165–2 • TRANSFUSION-ASSOCIATED INFECTIOUS RISKS

	RISK PER UNIT INFUSED
Bacterial contamination	
Bacterial culture positive	
Red blood cells	1 : 30,000
Platelets	
Whole blood derived	1 : 2000–3000
Apheresis	1 : 2400–5000
Observed	
Red blood cells	1 : 500,000
Platelets	1 : 2500–13,000
Fatal	
Red blood cells	1 : ≥700,000
Platelets	1 : 17,000–65,000
Hepatitis	
A	Infrequent
B	1 : 205,000–488,000
C	1 : 1,935,000
Retrovirus	
HIV	1 : 2,135,000
HTLV	1 : 2,993,000
Herpesviruses	
CMV	Varies with clinical situation
HHV 6,7,8	None documented
Parvovirus	?
Malaria	1 : 4,000,000
Babesiosis	Infrequent
Chagas' disease	Infrequent
Creutzfeldt-Jakob disease	None reported
Variant CJD	None reported
Syphilis	No recent cases

CMV = cytomegalovirus; HHV = human herpesvirus; HIV = human immuno-deficiency virus; HTLV = human T-cell lymphotropic virus.

Despite improvement in testing for HBsAg, mutant strains are not detected by current tests. Hepatitis A is not associated with a long-term carrier state, so only persons with acute hepatitis A infections transmit it by transfusion.

Nucleic acid testing for HIV-1 reduces the "window period" from 22 days to 12 days. HTLV I and II are intracellular viruses that are transmitted by RBC and platelet components but not by plasma and cryoprecipitate (i.e., noncellular components).

CMV-seronegative (Chapter 370) cellular blood components have a 1 to 4% risk of transmitting CMV, a risk similar to that associated with leukocyte-reduced components. CMV risk-reduced blood components, either leukocyte-reduced or from a CMV-seronegative donor, should be given to CMV-seronegative allogeneic and autologous progenitor cell transplant recipients; CMV-seronegative, HIV-positive patients; CMV-seronegative recipients of solid organ transplants from CMV-seronegative donors; CMV-seronegative patients who are potential progenitor cell transplant recipients; and CMV-seronegative pregnant women.

Parvovirus B19 causes fifth disease. The acute infection is self-limited, but approximately 1 per 3300 to 40,000 donors is viremic. Some patients with RBC hemolytic disorders, HIV infection, and solid organ transplants develop aplastic or hypoplastic anemia after infection (Chapter 174). Fetal loss may follow acute parvovirus infection during the second trimester of pregnancy. Nucleic acid testing can reduce the risk of transmission.

Approximately three transfusion-associated cases of malaria (Chapter 392) occur per year in the United States as a result of donations by asymptomatic carriers. The incubation period after transfusion ranges from 7 to 50 days (average 20 days). The differential diagnosis includes babesiosis (Chapter 400), which is transmitted by asymptomatic carriers via transfusion. Symptoms begin 7 days to 9 weeks post-transfusion. Treatment includes appropriate antimicrobial agents; exchange transfusion has been used successfully. At least six cases of transfusion-transmitted Chagas' disease (Chapter 394) have been reported in North America, most involving platelet transfusions and donors from Central and South America.

Transmission of prions (Chapter 456) by blood transfusion, although theoretically possible, has not been observed. Proactive inter-

ventions include deferral of donors at potential risk of Creutzfeldt-Jacob disease (CJD), such as individuals with a genetic predisposition or iatrogenic exposure. To reduce the theoretical risk of variant CJD transmission by transfusion, residents of the United Kingdom for more than 3 months between 1980 and 1996 and residents of Europe for more than 5 years between 1980 and the present are deferred from blood donation.

Future Directions

Techniques under development inactivate cell-free and cell-associated enveloped and nonenveloped viruses, bacteria, and parasites. These techniques also block T-lymphocyte proliferation, suggesting effectiveness in preventing transfusion-associated GVHD. Synthetic oxygen-carrying compounds have the potential for universal compatibility and immediate availability. Their safety and efficacy have not been proved, however.

1. Herbert PC, Wells G, Blajchman MA, et al: A multicenter, randomized, controlled clinical trial of transfusion requirements in critical care. N Engl J Med 1999;340:409–417.
2. Silverberg DS, Wexler D, Sheps D, et al: The effect of correction of mild anemia in severe, resistant congestive heart failure using subcutaneous erythropoietin and intravenous iron: A randomized controlled study. J Am Coll Cardiol 2001;37:1775–1780.
3. TRAP Study Group: Leukocyte reduction and ultraviolet B irradiation of platelets to prevent alloimmunization and refractoriness to platelet transfusion. N Engl J Med 1997;337:1861–1869.
4. Collier AC, Kalish LA, Busch MP, et al: Leukocyte-reduced red blood cell transfusions in patients with anemia and human immunodeficiency virus infection. JAMA 2001;285:1592–1601.

SUGGESTED READINGS

Dodd RY, Notari EP, Stramer SL: Current prevalence and incidence of infectious disease markers and estimated window period risk in the American Red Cross blood donor population. Transfusion 2002;42:975–979. *The risk of transfusion-transmitted infections decreased in response to recently introduced blood test improvement.*
Hebert PC, Fergusson D, Blajchman MA, et al: Clinical outcomes following institution of the Canadian universal leukoreduction program for red blood cell transfusions. JAMA 2003;289:1941–1949. *A national program can decrease post-transfusion fever and, potentially, mortality.*
Kopko PM, Marshall CS, MacKenzie MR, et al: Transfusion-related acute lung injury: Report of a clinical look-back investigation. JAMA 2002;287:1968–1971. *This report emphasizes the importance of recognizing and reporting these complications.*
Schiffer CA, Anderson KC, Bennett CL, et al: Platelet transfusion for patients with cancer: Clinical practice guidelines of the American Society of Clinical Oncology. J Clin Oncol 2001;19:1519–1538. *These practice guidelines provide an excellent review of the clinical settings for platelet transfusions.*
Wu WC, Rathore SS, Wang Y, et al: Blood transfusion in elderly patients with acute myocardial infarction. N Engl J Med 2001;345:1230–1236. *In contrast to routine guidelines for maintaining the hemoglobin concentration between 7 and 9 g/dL, blood transfusion was associated with lower short-term mortality rates in elderly patients having an acute myocardial infarction with admission hematocrit levels of 30 to 33%.*

166 HEMATOPOIETIC STEM CELL TRANSPLANTATION

Steven Z. Pavletic
Julie M. Vose

Hematopoietic stem cell transplantation is the process of collection and infusion of hematopoietic stem cells obtained from the bone marrow (bone marrow transplantation [BMT]) or the peripheral blood (blood stem cell transplantation). High-dose chemotherapy followed by subsequent BMT or peripheral blood progenitor (stem cells) transplantation is used increasingly for the treatment of many hematologic, immunologic, and neoplastic diseases. Hematopoietic stem cells can be obtained directly from the bone marrow by multiple aspirations from the pelvic bones while the patient is under general anesthesia (BMT). Alternatively, hematopoietic stem cells can be obtained from the peripheral blood after stimulation with hematopoietic growth factors, such as granulocyte colony-stimulating factor (G-CSF), followed by leukapheresis (peripheral blood stem cell transplantation). The subsequent availability of hematopoietic stem cell transplantation permits the administration of supralethal chemotherapy or radiotherapy to patients with malignancies in an attempt to increase the destruction of malignant cells. Additionally, the healthy transplanted cells may reconstitute the patient's immune system to provide an antitumor effect or, in the case of BMT for congenital diseases, provide cells that are no longer deficient in certain vital components.

Allogeneic and Syngeneic Transplantation

Allogeneic BMT or peripheral blood transplantation involves the transfer of stem cells from a donor to another person. A syngeneic transplant, which occurs in about 1% of transplants, is the special rare case of a donor and a recipient who are genetically identical twins. Allogeneic transplants usually are considered for patients no older than age 55 to 60 years, but older patients occasionally are treated. The results tend to be poorer in older patients because of the increasing incidence of graft-versus-host disease (GVHD) with age. The decision in any patient must take into account all factors, including not only the patient's chronologic age, but also his or her physiologic age. Donor and recipient must be matched for human leukocyte antigens (HLA); the most important gene pairs include HLA-A, HLA-B, HLA-C, and DR loci, all of which are linked closely on chromosome 6 and are inherited in haplotypes. The chance of having an HLA match from a sibling is one in four; however, as a result of the relatively small size of families in the United States, only about 30% of patients have an HLA-matched sibling. For patients who lack an HLA-identical sibling donor, there are two possible solutions: to identify an unrelated but closely HLA-matched person through the National Marrow Donor Program (NMDP) or to use a partially matched, related donor. The genes encoding HLA antigens are numerous, and the odds that any two unrelated individuals are HLA-identical for main loci are less than 1 in 10,000. About 4 million volunteer donors have been HLA-typed through the NMDP registry, however, and a donor can be found for about 50% of patients for whom a search is initiated. To locate an unrelated donor usually requires about 4 months, a waiting time that may be too long for some patients with rapidly progressive malignancies. Allogeneic partially matched sibling or placental/umbilical cord blood is an alternative source of stem cells. Umbilical cord blood stem cells already are stored in cord blood banks, and no additional harvest procedures are needed. Because of the unique immature biology of the umbilical cord blood stem cells, these transplants are associated with less GVHD; the HLA-matching requirements are less strict. The small volume of the cord blood stem cells often makes these transplants unsuitable for adult recipients.

When an adequate donor has been identified, the patient is prepared for the allogeneic or syngeneic transplant with high doses of chemotherapy, alone or combined with radiotherapy. This treatment is designed to destroy any remaining malignant cells, to provide sufficient immunosuppression to allow engraftment of the new cells, and to clear the marrow space for engraftment of the new cells. The preparative agents must have few toxicities at doses that are much greater than their hematologic effects. High doses of anthracyclines are often impractical because of their cardiac toxicities (Chapter 191). Most regimens consist of total body irradiation combined with alkylating agents, etoposide, or cytarabine.

An integral part of the regimens for allogeneic transplantation is immunosuppression to prevent GVHD and graft rejection. Because the recipient's immune system is ablated with high-dose chemotherapy and radiotherapy, graft rejection is a rare event. The drugs that are used most commonly to prevent GVHD include tacrolimus, mycophenolate mofetil, rapamycin, and the combination of cyclosporine and methotrexate. For allogeneic hematopoietic stem cell transplantation, prophylactic immunosuppression is not lifelong; when immunologic tolerance is established, immunosuppressives can be discontinued. Another approach to prevent GVHD is to deplete the donor's T cells from the graft; the disadvantage of this approach is that it is associated with increased rates of disease relapse and infections; overall survival also does not seem to be improved. To accelerate engraftment, hematopoietic growth factors, such as G-CSF, are administered after the transplant until the neutrophil count recovers. Allogeneic transplantation regimens also include prophylactic antiviral drugs (acyclovir, ganciclovir), antifungal drugs (fluconazole), broad-spectrum antibiotics (cephalosporins, fluoroquinolones), and anti-*Pneumocystis* drugs (trimethoprim-sulfamethoxazole, dapsone, pentamidine).

Leukemias (Chapters 192 and 193) that relapse after allogeneic stem cell transplantation sometimes can be controlled by further infusions of lymphocytes from the same allogeneic donor. The donor T lymphocytes destroy leukemia cells by an immune mechanism called the *graft-versus-leukemia effect.* For solid tumors, a graft-versus-tumor effect sometimes can be shown. These observations have led to the development of a new approach to allogeneic stem cell transplantation: nonmyeloablative transplantation regimens, based on the philosophy that allogeneic stem cell transplantation is a form of immunotherapy by which the donor lymphocytes eradicate the malignant disease, with high-dose chemotherapy and irradiation not necessary for success.

Autologous Bone Marrow Transplantation

Autologous BMT infuses the patient's own hematopoietic cells to reestablish bone marrow function after the administration of high-dose chemotherapy and radiotherapy. These reinfused hematopoietic cells can come from the patient's bone marrow and/or peripheral blood. Because a major limitation to the use of allogeneic BMT is that only a few patients have an HLA-matched sibling donor, the use of autologous hematopoietic cells greatly increases the number of patients eligible for transplantation. Autologous transplantation also can be used safely in older patients because of the absence of GVHD, which is a major concern with older patients. A disadvantage of autologous hematopoietic cell transplantation is the risk of contaminating the graft with viable tumor cells. Although patients undergoing autologous transplant have higher relapse rates than patients undergoing allogeneic transplants, the lower rate of other complications with autologous transplantation seems to translate into similar long-term outcomes (Table 166–1). A variety of methods have been developed to decrease the contamination of autologous grafts with tumor cells (graft "purging"), but no prospective data yet confirm that these interventions are beneficial because most relapses originate from incompletely eradicated disease in the host.

Indications for Transplantation

For many diseases, hematopoietic stem cell transplantation is now part of standard therapy (Table 166–2). More than 17,000 allogeneic and autologous transplants are performed per year for various diseases in the United States (Fig. 166–1).

LYMPHOPROLIFERATIVE MALIGNANCIES

NON-HODGKIN'S LYMPHOMA. Autologous transplantation has been used for the treatment of intermediate-grade and high-grade non-Hodgkin's lymphoma (Chapter 195). Patients with relapsed disease seem to benefit most from this therapy if they have transplantation when they still have chemotherapy-sensitive disease.■ Patients who have high-risk characteristics and have transplantation as part of their planned therapy early in the course of disease in first partial or complete response seem to have a better outcome than similar patients treated with conventional therapy. The use of high-dose chemotherapy and radiotherapy and autologous transplantation in indolent disease is associated with a failure-free survival of 40 to 60% at a median follow-up of 3 years; because late relapses are common, much longer follow-up is necessary to assess the long-term results of this treatment.

HODGKIN'S DISEASE. High-dose therapy followed by autologous hematopoietic stem cell transplantation has been accepted widely for patients with relapsed Hodgkin's disease (Chapter 194). Allogeneic transplantation has not been used as extensively because of its increased morbidity and mortality. The outcome is poorer in patients who have received multiple chemotherapy regimens than in patients who have undergone less pretreatment. In a small randomized trial, patients

Table 166–1 • COMPARISON OF ALLOGENEIC AND AUTOLOGOUS TRANSPLANTATION

FEATURE	ALLOGENEIC	AUTOLOGOUS
Upper age limits	55–60	60–70
Availability	40–60% of patients	Only limitation may be the ability to collect enough stem cells
Main cause of failure	Graft-versus-host disease Infections	Disease relapse

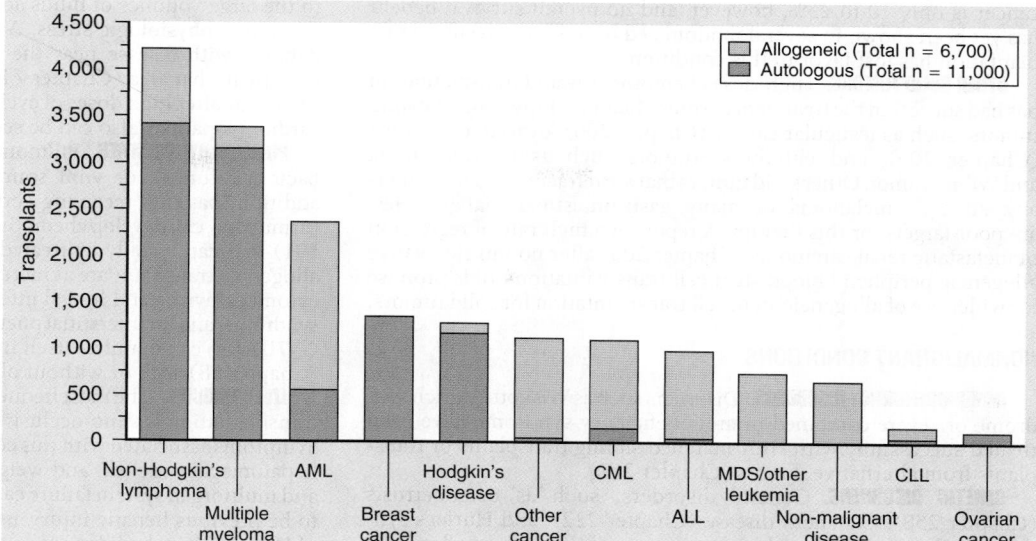

FIGURE 166–1 • Indications for blood and marrow transplantation in North America in 2000. ALL = acute lymphocytic leukemia; AML = acute myelogenous leukemia; CLL = chronic lymphocytic leukemia; CML = chronic myelogenous leukemia; MDS = myelodysplastic syndrome. (Information reprinted with permission of the International Bone Marrow Transplant Registry/Autologous Blood and Marrow Transplant Registry.)

Table 166–2 • RESULTS OF STANDARD OF CARE ALLOGENEIC OR AUTOLOGOUS STEM CELL TRANSPLANTATION IN SPECIFIC DISEASES*

	THREE-YEAR SURVIVAL (%)	
	Allogeneic	**Autologous**
HEMATOLOGIC MALIGNANCIES		
Acute myelogenous leukemia	37–60	24–59
Chronic myelogenous leukemia	46–69	NU
Myelodysplastic syndrome	25–73	NU
Acute lymphocytic leukemia	28–61	12–44
Chronic lymphocytic leukemia	47	84
Hodgkin's disease	NU	55–81
Follicular lymphoma	60	63–81
Diffuse large cell lymphoma	24–46	42–68
Multiple myeloma	38–47	48–59
Neuroblastoma	NU	41–53
NONMALIGNANT CONDITIONS		
Aplastic anemia	32–76	NA
Fanconi's anemia	16–81	NA

*Information based on the International Bone Marrow Transplantation Registry report for patients transplanted between 1994 and 1999. Results typically are better in patients younger than 20 years old, patients in earlier stages of the disease, and recipients of HLA-identical sibling transplants.
NA = not applicable; NU = not routinely used.

who received high-dose carmustine and etoposide followed by autologous transplantation had a better outcome than patients who received lower doses of the same drugs without transplantation. Autologous transplantation performed in first remission is being evaluated in patients with B symptoms, disseminated disease with bone marrow or pulmonary involvement, and other high-risk features.

MULTIPLE MYELOMA. Autologous and allogeneic transplantation have been performed successfully in patients with multiple myeloma (Chapter 196). The major concern with conventional myeloablative allogeneic transplantation has been its high mortality rate. With improvements in supportive care, however, the transplant-related mortality of autografts for multiple myeloma has been reduced to 1%, and a randomized trial confirmed the better survival after autologous stem cell transplantation when compared with conventional chemotherapy.[2] Autologous transplantation for multiple myeloma is more successful in patients who undergo less pretreatment and have a smaller tumor burden.

ACUTE LYMPHOBLASTIC LEUKEMIA. The results of conventional induction and consolidation chemotherapy for acute lymphoblastic leukemia (ALL) in children are excellent except in a few clinical circumstances, such as ALL associated with the Philadelphia chromosome (Chapter 193). The use of transplantation for ALL in children

usually is reserved for these high-risk patients and patients who relapse after initial therapy. In adults, the indications for transplantation are similar, although a much higher percentage of adults fail after initial therapy.

CHRONIC LYMPHOCYTIC LEUKEMIA. Selected younger patients with B-cell chronic lymphocytic leukemia (B-CLL) that is refractory or has relapsed more than once might benefit from transplantation from a related or unrelated donor; durable disease-free survival is 40 to 60% (Chapter 192). Because the allogeneic graft-versus-leukemia effect seems to be especially important against B-CLL, this disease has become one of the most popular indications for nonmyeloablative allogeneic transplantation. Autologous transplantation also yields high rates of remission in pretreated B-CLL patients, but relapse rates are high, and the eventual survival may not be improved.

MYELOPROLIFERATIVE MALIGNANCIES

ACUTE MYELOGENOUS LEUKEMIA. Because patients with good-risk or average-risk acute myelogenous leukemia (AML) can be cured with conventional chemotherapy, most centers use transplantation only for (1) relapsed AML in adults or (2) as part of the initial therapy for patients with known poor prognostic characteristics, such as certain high-risk chromosomal abnormalities, including complex abnormalities or deletions of chromosomes (Chapter 193). Most studies show a decreased relapse rate with allogeneic transplantation, but long-term overall survival is not as improved because of the morbidity and mortality of the transplantation itself.

MYELODYSPLASTIC SYNDROMES. Myelodysplastic syndromes in young, otherwise healthy patients are treated best with an allogeneic transplant from an HLA-identical sibling donor (Chapter 182). Most patients with myelodysplastic syndromes are elderly, which often precludes use of this successful therapy.

CHRONIC MYELOGENOUS LEUKEMIA. Allogeneic transplantation from an HLA-matched sibling donor produces long-term disease-free survival in 55 to 75% of patients with Philadelphia chromosome–positive chronic myelogenous leukemia (CML) (Chapter 192). The results seem to be better when the patients are younger, undergo transplantation within the first year of diagnosis, have received hydroxyurea rather than busulfan, and have not received extensive interferon. When an HLA-matched related donor is not available, the use of alternative donors can yield a cure in about 50% patients with chronic-phase CML. The development of effective and nontoxic tyrosine kinase inhibitors for the treatment of BCR-ABL–positive CML is tempering enthusiasm for allogeneic transplantation in CML, however.

SOLID TUMORS

BREAST CANCER. The use of high-dose chemotherapy for the treatment of metastatic breast cancer can result in a higher complete response rate than with conventional treatment (Chapter 204). The reported disease-free survival in chemotherapy-sensitive stage IV breast cancer is only 10 to 25%, however, and no overall survival benefit has yet been shown in several randomized trials.[3] As a result, transplantation has lost favor in this condition.

OTHER SOLID TUMORS. High-dose chemotherapy and transplantation has had success in the treatment of some chemotherapy-sensitive solid tumors, such as testicular cancer (Chapter 206), ovarian carcinoma (Chapter 205), and childhood tumors such as neuroblastoma and Wilms' tumor. Other solid tumors that are refractory to chemotherapy, such as melanoma or many gastrointestinal malignancies, are poor targets for this therapy. A report of a high rate of regression of metastatic renal carcinoma (Chapter 203) after nonmyeloablative allogeneic peripheral blood stem cell transplantation holds promise for wider use of allogeneic stem cell transplantation for solid tumors.

NONMALIGNANT CONDITIONS

IMMUNODEFICIENCY DISORDERS. Disorders such as Wiskott-Aldrich syndrome or severe combined immunodeficiency syndrome have been treated successfully with HLA-matched sibling transplants or transplants from alternative donors (Chapter 267).

GENETIC DISORDERS. Genetic disorders, such as osteopetrosis (Chapter 258), Gaucher's disease (Chapter 222), and Hurler's syndrome (Chapter 276), can be treated successfully with an allogeneic transplant. Other indications for allogeneic transplant include hemoglobinopathies, such as sickle cell anemia (Chapter 171) and thalassemia (Chapter 168), and acquired blood disorders such as paroxysmal nocturnal hemoglobinuria (Chapter 169). The transplant must be performed before the onset of secondary organ failure.

APLASTIC ANEMIA. Allogeneic transplant can lead to long-term disease-free survival in more than 50% of patients with severe aplastic anemia (Chapter 174). Compared with standard immunosuppressive therapy, allogeneic transplant is more likely to produce a complete and durable reversal of hematologic abnormalities. For patients with less severe aplastic anemia, patients older than age 40 years, and patients without a matched sibling donor, a trial of immunosuppression therapy is usually appropriate before consideration of an allogeneic transplant.

AUTOIMMUNE DISEASE. Autologous stem cell transplantation to engraft a tolerant immune system has had promising results in selected patients with systemic lupus erythematosus, rheumatoid arthritis, scleroderma, and multiple sclerosis. Randomized prospective trials comparing conventional treatments currently are being planned.

Complications

INFECTIONS. Infections are a major cause of morbidity and mortality after hematopoietic stem cell transplantation, especially allogeneic transplantation, owing to prolonged immunosuppression for the prevention or treatment of GVHD (Chapter 298). Bacterial infections frequently are related to the central venous catheters. Among fungal infections, infections with *Aspergillus* typically occur in patients on prolonged therapy with high-dose steroids for the treatment of GVHD. Viral infections include reactivation cytomegalovirus (Chapter 370), human herpesvirus 6, and Epstein-Barr virus (Chapter 371). These patients are also susceptible to seasonal respiratory viruses.

At 1 year after allogeneic or autologous transplant, patients should receive the following vaccinations: diphtheria, tetanus, *Haemophilus influenzae* type b, hepatitis B, 23-valent pneumococcal polysaccharide, hepatitis A virus, seasonal influenza virus, inactivated poliovirus, and, only in areas of outbreaks, meningococcal vaccine (Chapter 16). Live vaccines against measles, mumps, and rubella should not be administered until 2 years after transplantation and only in the absence of chronic GVHD and immunosuppressive therapy. Family members may receive routine vaccines, including influenza virus vaccine, but patients should avoid contact with a child who has received oral poliovirus vaccine for about 1 month after vaccination. Despite these recommendations, vaccines may not always induce protective immunity in an immunodeficient patient with chronic GVHD or on immunosuppression.

CARDIAC TOXICITY. Most transplant centers screen potential patients for underlying cardiac abnormalities that would place them at potential increased risk during the procedure. Nevertheless, a few patients experience cardiotoxicity, either acutely during the transplant or at a later time, manifested as arrhythmias, heart failure, or ischemia owing

to the large volumes of fluids administered during the procedure or the added physiologic stress. A pericardial effusion can develop in patients with disease near the pericardium or receiving radiation therapy in that area (Chapter 74). An idiosyncratic cardiomyopathy can occur after high doses of cyclophosphamide (Chapter 191). Viral cardiomyopathies also can be seen.

PULMONARY TOXICITIES. Pulmonary toxicities include infections from bacterial, fungal, or viral sources during the transplantation. In addition, patients receiving certain chemotherapy agents, such as carmustine, can develop chemotherapy-induced lung damage (Chapter 191) that can usually be treated with steroids. Patients undergoing allogeneic transplant are at increased risk for pneumonitis caused by cytomegalovirus and fungal infections, for adult respiratory distress syndrome, and for interstitial pneumonia of unknown etiology. Chronic GVHD also can manifest itself in the lung as bronchiolitis obliterans (Chapter 88) with or without obstructive pneumonia.

LIVER TOXICITY. The most frequent liver complication associated with transplantation is veno-occlusive disease of the liver (Chapter 150). Symptoms associated with this complication include jaundice, tender hepatomegaly, ascites, and weight gain. Progressive hepatic failure and multiorgan system failure can develop. Predisposing factors seem to be previous hepatic injury, use of estrogens, and perhaps the use of HLA-mismatched donors.

RENAL TOXICITY. Acute renal failure requiring dialysis occurs infrequently during the transplant. The judicious use of nephrotoxic agents can decrease the incidence of this complication. An idiopathic or cyclosporine-induced hemolytic-uremic syndrome (Chapter 177) can be a serious complication after allogeneic stem cell transplantation, with a high risk of end-stage renal disease or death.

GRAFT-VERSUS-HOST DISEASE. In the allogeneic transplant setting, acute GVHD is manifested by symptoms in the skin, gastrointestinal tract, and liver within the first 100 days after transplantation. The skin manifestations range from a maculopapular rash to generalized erythroderma or desquamation. The severity of liver disease is scored on the basis of the bilirubin, and the severity of the gastrointestinal disease is graded by the quantity of diarrhea per day. Patients who receive transplants from unrelated donors are at increased risk, and the incidence and severity of GVHD rise with the age of the patient. Other risk factors include a female donor (particularly a multiparous donor), advanced age, and cytomegalovirus seropositivity of the donor or patient. Prophylaxis with cyclosporine or tacrolimus, with or without methotrexate, corticosteroids, or mycophenolate mofetil, reduces incidence and severity. Treatment for acute GVHD includes high-dose corticosteroids, antithymocyte globulin, or various monoclonal antibodies.

Chronic GVHD occurs more than 100 days after the transplant and is most likely to develop in older patients who also had acute GVHD. Symptoms include the sicca syndrome, chronic sinusitis, rashes, scleroderma-like skin thickening, diarrhea, wasting syndrome, and liver abnormalities. Patients are also at greatly increased risk for infectious complications, resulting from either the GVHD itself or the treatment for it. Adverse prognostic factors for survival include thrombocytopenia, a progressive clinical presentation, involvement of more than 50% of the skin, poor performance status, and elevated bilirubin. Treatment for chronic GVHD includes corticosteroids, cyclosporine, tacrolimus, mycophenolate mofetil, thalidomide, ultraviolet light treatments, and other immunosuppressive agents.

GRAFT REJECTION. Graft rejection occurs when immunologically competent cells of host origin destroy the transplanted cells of donor origin. This complication is rare after a fully matched, related donor transplant and occurs more commonly in patients who receive transplants from alternative donors or in T cell–depleted transplants. Graft rejection is less likely in nontransfused patients with aplastic anemia.

Late Complications

As the number of long-term survivors after transplantation increases, complications that develop years later are beginning to be recognized.

SECONDARY MALIGNANCIES. One complication of the chemotherapy and/or radiotherapy used to treat malignancy is the development of a secondary malignancy. There have been several reports of the development of secondary AML or myelodysplastic syndrome after autologous transplantation. Some studies have suggested that total body irradiation may increase the risk of these complications. After allogeneic transplantation, the overall incidence of secondary malignancies is 2.2% at 10 years and 6.7% at 15 years after transplantation. Within the first 1 to 2 years, the most common malignancies are Epstein-Barr virus–related lymphoproliferative disorders; solid tumors are more likely to occur more than 3 years after transplantation. Risk factors include the use of antithymocyte globulin to treat GVHD, the use of a T cell–depleted graft, HLA incompatibility, and perhaps total body irradiation.

INFERTILITY AND HYPOGONADISM. The risk of gonadal failure is likely to be lower with the increased use of nonmyeloablative preparative regimens. The use of total body irradiation almost always is associated with sterility, but successful pregnancies have occurred in some patients after other regimens. Gynecomastia (sometimes tender) occasionally occurs in males. To address all the complexities of functional castration from high-dose therapy, a reproductive endocrinologist should be consulted before transplant in patients for whom future fertility is an issue.

ENDOCRINE DYSFUNCTION. Iatrogenic Cushing's syndrome is commonly due to long-term steroid therapy in patients with chronic GVHD (Chapters 31 and 240). Particularly disabling are consequences such as steroid-induced myopathy, avascular necrosis of the hip, and osteoporosis. Because many patients are on steroids for many months, tapering can be associated with malaise, nausea, hypotension, and musculoskeletal pains. In these situations, slower tapering over several months or reintroduction of physiologic replacement doses (e.g., 7.5 to 10 mg/day of prednisone) is appropriate. Hypothyroidism (Chapter 239) typically is related to the use of total body irradiation or to local irradiation to the head and neck for lymphoma or other cancer. Osteoporosis (Chapter 258) occurs in 50 to 60% of patients after hematopoietic stem cell transplantation. The major contributing causes include hypogonadism, secondary hyperparathyroidism caused by low serum calcium, and post-transplant steroid therapy. Bone mineral density should be evaluated before and after transplantation; osteopenia should be treated as appropriate with bisphosphonates, calcium, vitamin D, estrogen, and testosterone.

OTHER COMPLICATIONS. The long-term incidence of cataracts is about 20 to 50%; the risk is related to the use of total body irradiation and corticosteroids (Chapter 465). About 50% of patients with cataracts require surgical therapy. Alopecia is typically reversible, but in rare cases it can be irreversible, especially after busulfan-containing preparative regimens.

Future Directions

The safety and efficacy of transplantation may be improved by the use of hematopoietic cytokines to stimulate immunologic reconstitution, ex vivo expansion of progenitors, genetic modulation of cells, improved supportive care for transplant patients, better prophylaxis against GVHD, better HLA, typing, and newer anti-cancer agents. Whether stem cells can be infused to improve the function of adult organs is an area of active investigation.

1. Philip T, Guglielmi C, Hagenbeek A, et al: Autologous bone marrow transplantation as compared with salvage chemotherapy in relapses of chemotherapy-sensitive non-Hodgkin's lymphoma. N Engl J Med 1995;333:1540–1545.
2. Attal M, Harousseau JL, Stoppa AM, et al: A prospective, randomized trial of autologous bone marrow transplantation and chemotherapy in multiple myeloma. N Engl J Med 1996;335:91–97.
3. Stadtmauer EA, O'Neill A, Goldstein LJ, et al: Conventional-dose chemotherapy compared with high-dose chemotherapy plus autologous hematopoietic stem-cell transplantation for metastatic breast cancer. Philadelphia Bone Marrow Transplant Group. N Engl J Med 2000;342:1069–1076.

SUGGESTED READINGS
Antin JH: Long-term care after hematopoietic-cell transplantation in adults. N Engl J Med 2002;347:36–42. *A comprehensive, concise, and up-to-date review on the topic.*
Childs R, Chernoff A, Contentin N, et al: Regression of metastatic renal-cell carcinoma after nonmyeloablative allogeneic peripheral-blood stem cell transplantation. N Engl J Med 2000;343:750–758. *A first unequivocal clinical demonstration of the allogeneic graft-versus–solid tumor effect.*
Goldman JM, Druker BJ: Chronic myeloid leukemia: Current treatment options. Blood 2001;98:2039–2042. *An up-to-date summary of the treatment strategies for CML in the era of the tyrosine kinase inhibitors.*
Latham RJ, Oettgen P: Bone marrow transplantation for the heart: Fact or fiction. Lancet 2003;361:11–12. *Overview of this rapidly-evolving field.*
Vogelsang G: How I treat chronic graft-versus-host disease. Blood 2001;97:1196–1201. *A practical summary for the clinician.*

167 MICROCYTIC AND HYPOCHROMIC ANEMIAS

Thomas P. Duffy

Hematologic Diseases

Hemoglobin synthesis for the needs of normal red blood cell (RBC) production requires an adequate supply of iron and intact metabolic pathways for the generation of heme and globin molecules. Any deficiency in this triad of iron, heme, and globin may result in RBCs with a deficient mean corpuscular hemoglobin concentration. These hemoglobin-deficient RBCs are usually microcytic with a reduced mean corpuscular volume that is attributable to additional divisions in the RBC maturation sequence in bone marrow in the setting of a low hemoglobin concentration. This combination of small and hypochromic RBCs can be detected on examination of the peripheral smear (Fig. 167–1) when the process is advanced and can be confirmed by indices generated from measurements of RBC size by electronic Coulter counters. An emerging population of microcytic RBCs at an early stage of iron deficiency anemia can be recognized by studying the RBC distribution width, in which any small cells constitute a peak separate from RBCs of normal size (Chapter 160).

Characterization of anemia as hypochromic and microcytic narrows the possible causes of the RBC deficiency to some abnormality in iron, heme, or globin metabolism. Low values for mean corpuscular volume and hemoglobin concentration generated by the electronic counter delimit a small number of possible lesions as the cause of this type of anemia.

IRON DEFICIENCY ANEMIA

Definition

Iron, as the core of the hemoglobin molecule responsible for the oxygen-carrying capabilities of blood, is the most precious element within the body; an efficient system of conservation and recycling of this valuable resource guarantees the amount of iron necessary for daily hemoglobin synthesis. Storage depots of iron (as ferritin and hemosiderin) exist within the reticuloendothelial cells of the liver, spleen, and bone marrow and the parenchymal cells of the liver, and these stores are depleted before any restriction in hemoglobin synthesis occurs. Iron deficiency anemia is the final temporal development in the chronology of progressive iron deficiency within the body. Because this anemia does not supervene until iron stores are mobilized to maintain an optimal hemoglobin mass, absence of iron stores on examination of the marrow is specific confirmation that iron deficiency is contributing to any anemia that is present.

Prevalence

Iron deficiency is the most common cause of anemia throughout the world and one of the most common medical problems that confronts the general physician. Its geographic distribution is determined by dietary deficiencies and intestinal parasitism, especially in developing countries; hookworm infection (Chapter 404) has created the same lesion in the southern United States.

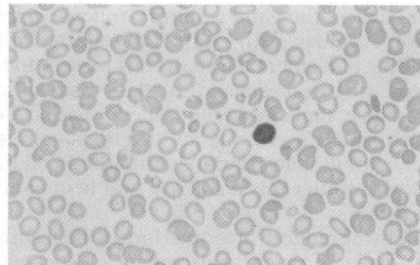

FIGURE 167–1 • Iron deficiency anemia. Many red blood cells are microcytic (smaller than the nucleus of the normal lymphocyte near the center of the field) and hypochromic (with central areas of pallor that exceed half of the diameter of the cells).

The prevalence of iron deficiency is much higher in women than in men because of the toll of menstruation and pregnancy on the iron stores of women. The expansion of the blood pool that occurs during adolescence also leads to low iron stores that may be depleted further as a result of inadequate dietary intake. The latter factor contributes to the iron-deficient state in many women, even in affluent societies, as they embark on pregnancy.

Iron Metabolism

Mechanisms exist to ensure that the total body iron content is maintained within a defined range. In specific contrast to other body constituents, control of iron content is imposed by limiting its entrance into the body rather than by increasing the excretion of any excess. When iron has entered the plasma after absorption from the gastrointestinal tract or from the breakdown of transfused RBCs, it can be removed only by the withdrawal of blood or by the more laborious process of iron chelation therapy. The normal metabolism of iron is weighted strictly in favor of ensuring adequate iron reserves even at the cost of iron overload, which may result in hemochromatosis (Chapter 225) with organ damage created by the tissue accumulation of excess elemental iron.

The major locus of iron within the body is at the center of the hemoglobin molecule within RBCs and as part of the myoglobin molecule in muscle; a smaller fraction is a constituent of important tissue-based enzymes. Storage pools of iron in the form of ferritin and hemosiderin are present within the liver, spleen, and bone marrow. These reserves of approximately 1000 mg in men and 500 mg in women are derived from the breakdown of senescent RBCs within the reticuloendothelial system and from any surplus of absorbed iron beyond that needed for hemoglobin synthesis. The disparity in the size of these stores in men and women is attributable to the previously mentioned demands of menstruation and pregnancy in women.

The tiniest compartment of iron within the body is transport iron (7 mg), in which iron travels while linked to the transport protein transferrin. Although transport iron is the smallest compartment, it is kinetically the most active and turns over several times a day as iron is transported to its various destinations within the body. Transferrin picks up iron from the gastrointestinal cells and delivers it primarily to cells engaging in hemoglobin synthesis. Transferrin also picks up iron from the storage depots in the daily recycling of iron stores.

This system of conservation and recycling of iron provides a constant supply of iron for the needs (30 to 35 mg) of daily hemoglobin synthesis. Only a tiny fraction of iron (1 mg) is lost each day by the pathway of sweating and epidermal shedding from the gut and urinary tract; this minuscule amount can be replaced easily from the food in a normal diet. The major source of iron for hemoglobin synthesis is derived from the breakdown of RBCs, which after survival for 90 to 120 days in peripheral blood undergo phagocytosis by splenic macrophages; the iron released from these senescent RBCs is immediately available for the needs of hemoglobin synthesis, with the excess stored as ferritin and hemosiderin. The vector of normal iron transport is always in the direction of providing iron to fulfill the body's needs in maintaining an optimal RBC mass.

Absorption

The normal diet in the United States contains approximately 15 to 30 mg of iron each day, with every 1000 calories in the diet containing about 6 mg of elemental iron. Iron is present in food as a portion of the heme ring in meats and in a less easily absorbable form as ferric hydroxide complexes in other foods. The acid environment of the stomach and its enzymatic secretions emulsify ingested food and liberate iron for absorption within the small intestine; pancreatic secretions counter this acidic pH and help control excessive absorption of iron.

Iron must be in the reduced or ferrous form to be absorbed. Ingestion of reducing substances, such as ascorbate or succinate, enhances iron absorption because of their effect on iron valence. Other substances, such as phytates in cereals, tannates in tea, antacids, and certain antibiotics (tetracycline), may complex with iron and hinder its absorption. Maximal absorption of iron occurs in the duodenum and upper portions of the jejunum. Ferric iron is reduced to a ferrous form by a duodenal ferric reductase. Malabsorptive states or bypass of these areas by gastrojejunostomy may contribute to iron deficiency.

Iron absorption can be adjusted over a broad range according to the body's needs. In normal health, the body must guard itself against iron overload by absorbing only one tenth of the iron available in the diet. The mechanism whereby such a limitation or "mucosal curtain" is imposed on iron absorption is still not defined; it seems to be regulated by some aspect of dynamic iron turnover because hemolytic anemias, ineffective erythropoiesis, and hypoxemic states all have increased iron turnover, and all are associated with increased iron absorption. The mucosal curtain is lowered by imposing a limit on the amount of iron that crosses the gastrointestinal membranes. Whatever iron is not needed by the body is diverted into storage molecules within gastrointestinal mucosal cells; this iron is lost from the body as these cells are exfoliated during the normal cycle of cell turnover. In the presence of iron deficiency, the body can increase its absorption efficiency at least fivefold to compensate easily and rapidly for any deficiency. In iron-deficient states, in which iron needs are exaggerated, little iron is diverted to the storage form, and most of the absorbed iron passes directly through the cells for plasma transport linked to transferrin. The gene product of the hemochromatosis *HFE* gene influences the efficiency of intestinal iron absorption with serum transferrin receptors acting as a ligand for *HFE*.

Failure of this interaction is thought to be the explanation for iron accumulation in primary hemochromatosis (Chapter 225); these patients continue to absorb iron even in the face of total body iron overload. Increased iron absorption also occurs with pancreatic insufficiency (Chapter 145) because of absence of the pH alteration contributed by normal pancreatic secretions; absence of this restraint on iron absorption explains in part the iron overload that often occurs in chronic alcoholic states (Chapter 17).

Transport

Transferrin, a glycoprotein with a molecular weight of approximately 80,000, is produced by liver parenchymal cells in inverse proportion to the iron stores within these cells. This matching of transferrin production to iron needs explains in part the elevated transferrin levels or iron-binding capacity that characterizes iron deficiency. Transferrin can bind one or two molecules of ferric iron, a process accompanied by the simultaneous attachment of an equal number of bicarbonate ions; the latter molecules facilitate the uncoupling of iron from the binding protein.

Transferrin binding of iron protects the body against the toxicity of elemental iron and increases the solubility of this molecule within plasma. Transferrin receptors are present on the surface of developing RBCs in direct proportion to their potential for hemoglobin synthesis; a small amount of transferrin receptor also is present in serum. Transferrin-bound iron links to the cellular receptors, and the complex enters the RBC by endocytosis; dissociation of the complex occurs after a pH alteration in the vesicle. Iron is released to enter the cycle of heme synthesis, and transferrin leaves the cell to scavenge for other iron molecules. Transferrin is measured in the plasma by quantifying the amount of iron-binding sites available, a measurement called the *total iron-binding capacity of plasma*. Under normal circumstances, total iron-binding capacity is only one third saturated, with the total amount of transferrin within the plasma being approximately 300 mg/dL.

Iron levels vary diurnally, with the highest levels present in the morning; normal iron levels are usually within 60 to 180 mg/dL. A small amount of iron also is present in plasma in the form of the storage molecule ferritin, with the concentration of this molecule generally mirroring the stores of iron within the marrow. Iron also complexes with lactoferrin, which is an iron-binding protein liberated from neutrophilic granules and which is thought to play a role in defense against infection. Lactoferrin rapidly sequesters iron in reticuloendothelial cells, depriving microorganisms of iron, which is an essential growth factor for most microorganisms.

Iron Kinetics

Ferrokinetic measurements using radiolabeled iron-59 can quantify iron absorption, the marrow transit time of iron, and plasma and erythrocyte iron turnover. These studies permit in vivo localization of any defect in the uptake, transport, or delivery of iron; these measurements are now primarily investigative tools and are not used in routine clinical situations.

Pathogenesis

Conservation and recycling of iron within the body provide an excellent buffer to fulfill the daily needs of iron for hemoglobin synthesis. Iron deficiency anemia occurs only after an extended period of negative iron balance, a period during which the storage pool is exhausted of its reserves. Although this depletion may result from decreased ingestion or absorption of iron, the most common causes of iron deficiency are blood loss from lesions in the gastrointestinal tract or from the demands of menstruation and pregnancy.

DECREASED IRON UPTAKE. To maintain iron balance within the body, a man needs to absorb only 1.0 to 1.5 mg of iron each day; a woman needs to absorb a larger amount (2 to 3 mg) because of iron losses from menstruation. Each 1 mL of blood contains approximately 0.4 mg of iron so that the monthly menstrual loss of approximately 60 mL creates the need for an additional 20 to 30 mg of iron absorption each month. Pregnancy, with its expansion of the maternal blood pool and additional needs for fetal hemoglobin synthesis, frequently overwhelms an already marginal iron storage pool and requires supplemental iron as a prophylactic measure against the development of frank anemia.

Because the iron-to-calorie ratio of the normal U.S. diet is 6 mg iron for every 1000 calories, men usually have no shortage of dietary iron; the restricted diets of some women may not provide a comparable surfeit and may give rise to an iron-deficiency state without frank anemia. Diet-related iron deficiency may be aggravated by gastric achlorhydria, with its negative effect on iron absorption, but achlorhydria alone rarely causes iron deficiency anemia (Chapter 137).

Gastrojejunostomies and sprue (Chapter 141) may result in iron deficiency as a result of loss of the necessary mucosal surface and/or increased intestinal transit time. After gastrojejunal bypass procedures, blood loss from mucosal lesions ulcerated at the anastomotic site is the principal cause of iron deficiency.

The modern shift to non–iron-containing cooking utensils has eliminated this rich source of iron from the diet. Vegetarian diets also may lessen the amount of dietary iron.

A vicious cycle may occur in which patients with iron deficiency acquire an appetite for bizarre foods. This phenomenon, pica, is the only known example of a compulsive appetite or behavior created by the lack of a normal body element. Its victims may ingest clay (geophagia), which may potentiate the problem by chelating iron within the gut; ice (pagophagia); or starch (amylophagia). Iron replacement corrects the problem, which may or may not be accompanied by anemia.

INCREASED IRON LOSS. The most common cause of iron deficiency anemia in men and women is blood loss; this loss most frequently has its source in gastrointestinal bleeding in the former and menstrual bleeding in the latter. The implication of the discovery of iron deficiency anemia in men and postmenopausal women is the same; the gastrointestinal tract harbors the causal lesion until proved otherwise (Chapter 133). Even in the absence of occult blood in the stool or a history of melena, it is still imperative to examine the gastrointestinal tract because of its frequent involvement when iron deficiency is present. Iron deficiency may be the initial manifestation of an otherwise occult carcinoma of the gut (Chapter 200), with right-sided colon tumors frequently having this clinical picture. Multiple other gastrointestinal lesions, such as large hiatal hernias (Chapter 136), ulcer disease (Chapter 138), inflammatory bowel disease (Chapter 142), or angiodysplasias (Chapter 144), all may be characterized by iron deficiency.

Ingestion of aspirin and nonsteroidal anti-inflammatory drugs, often in the treatment of arthritic conditions, may be complicated by gastrointestinal blood loss. Less common causes of excessive iron loss include urinary tract bleeding and renal filtration of hemoglobin released from the breakdown of RBCs; individuals with mechanical heart valves have traumatic rupture of RBCs as they flow across the artificial surfaces of these valves. Pulmonary sequestration of iron also occurs after some pulmonary hemorrhagic states, with no mechanism available to the body to recapture this closeted iron. The stores of iron also may be depleted by frequent blood donations.

Clinical Manifestations

Iron deficiency anemia is characterized by a degree of fatigue that may be disproportionate to the severity of the anemia, apparently because of depletion of essential tissue-based, iron-containing enzymes with an attendant reduction in energy generation by muscle. Transfusion of RBCs to correct this anemia reverses the symptoms only in part; iron repletion is the definitive treatment for this fatigue.

Iron deficiency has several characteristic clinical manifestations, but all of them are rare relative to the high incidence of this condition. A sore tongue (glossitis; Fig. 167–2), atrophy of the lingual papillae, and erosions at the corners of the mouth (angular stomatitis; Fig. 167–3) are oral manifestations of iron deficiency; atrophy of the gastric mucosa with achlorhydria is a further extension of the same process. An atrophic rhinitis with a foul nasal discharge (ozena) may progress to anosmia in iron-deficient individuals. A greenish hue to the complexion (chlorosis) is an accompaniment of the same deficiency, especially in adolescent girls in Victorian literature. Brittle, fragile fingernails and spooning of the nails (koilonychia) are peripheral clues to the disorder.

Dysphagia, attributable to an esophageal web, occurs most frequently in elderly women with iron deficiency; this lesion, the Plummer-Vinson or Paterson-Kelly syndrome, may be complicated later by the development of esophageal carcinoma (Chapter 136). The web may not disappear with iron replacement, and these patients may require dilation for relief of symptoms.

Splenomegaly has been described as an accompaniment of iron deficiency, although an independent or concomitant thalassemia trait may be the true cause of the enlargement (Chapter 164). Pseudotumor cerebri also has been described as a rare accompaniment of iron deficiency.

Laboratory Findings

The laboratory findings in full-blown iron deficiency anemia include a reduction in all three parameters (mean corpuscular volume, hemoglobin, hemoglobin concentration) that are generated from the Coulter counter. In contrast, early iron deficiency anemia has normochromic, normocytic indices because the iron-deficient population of RBCs constitutes only a small percentage of the RBC mass. Only when the hematocrit falls to less than 31 to 32% do the RBC indices become microcytic; a normochromic, normocytic anemia is the earliest form of anemia with iron deficiency.

Coulter counter indices generally have replaced examination of peripheral blood smears (see Fig. 167–1) in the recognition of hypochromia and microcytosis in iron deficiency. Serum iron and transferrin (total iron-binding capacity) levels help confirm the diagnosis of iron deficiency, with a low serum iron and an elevated transferrin level resulting in a transferrin saturation of less than 10 to 15%. Transferrin levels are increased in iron-deficiency states because of increased hepatic synthesis of the protein and greater liberation

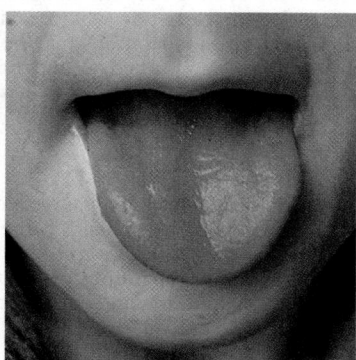

FIGURE 167–2 • Iron deficiency anemia commonly leads to pallor of the face, lips, and tongue, and when chronic to atrophic glossitis and angular stomatitis. All these are seen in this young woman whose iron deficiency anemia resulted from excessive menstrual bleeding. She responded to oral iron supplementation. (From Forbes CD, Jackson WF: Color Atlas and Text of Clinical Medicine, 3rd ed. London, Mosby, 2003, with permission.)

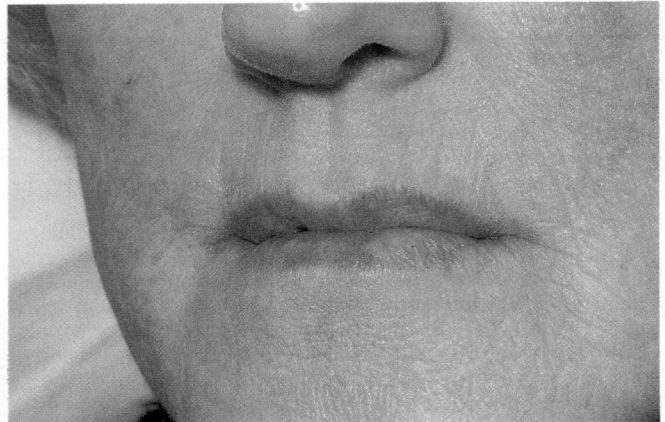

FIGURE 167–3 • Angular stomatitis in a patient with iron deficiency anemia. Like other signs of anemia, this is nonspecific, but it is an indication for the performance of a complete blood study. (From Forbes CD, Jackson WF: Color Atlas and Text of Clinical Medicine, 3rd ed. London, Mosby, 2003, with permission.)

of apotransferrin (the transport protein without iron) from hemoglobin-synthesizing sites. Serum transferrin receptor levels also are increased in iron-deficient states, and their measurement is a possible, but usually unnecessary, means of making a diagnosis of iron deficiency. A low iron level is not in itself diagnostic of iron deficiency because many other systemic insults can alter the serum level of iron. Ferritin levels also permit recognition of iron deficiency, with a reduction in this serum protein to less than 10 ng/mL in uncomplicated iron deficiency. The final step in heme synthesis is the incorporation of iron into a protoporphyrin ring; deficient delivery of iron to RBCs results in elevated levels of free erythrocyte protoporphyrin as an additional marker of iron-deficient erythropoiesis.

Diagnosis of iron deficiency is usually possible by using the combination of RBC indices and serum measurement of transferrin saturation or ferritin levels. Because both of these levels are altered by perturbations as varied as infection, inflammation, malignancy, and starvation, however, bone marrow iron stores remain the final arbiter when any uncertainty exists regarding the presence of iron deficiency; the marrow is devoid of macrophage iron, and fewer than 10% of the RBC precursors contain siderotic granules. Absence of iron stores categorically confirms the presence of iron deficiency and is the gold standard for making the diagnosis. Serum transferrin receptor levels also help discriminate iron deficiency from the anemias of chronic disease.

 Treatment

Recognition and treatment of iron deficiency anemia require the identification and reversal, if possible, of its cause; the anemia is a critical sign of an underlying lesion that may be as benign as aspirin ingestion or as threatening as an occult malignancy. Treating the anemia without identifying its cause may mean loss of the only opportunity to discover a malignancy at a potentially curable stage.

Treatment of iron deficiency anemia is made difficult by the frequent induction of nausea, dyspepsia, constipation, and diarrhea by medicinal iron. These symptoms are usually proportional to the iron content of the prescribed oral iron preparation; the most commonly administered preparation is ferrous sulfate tablets, 300 mg, which contain 60 mg of elemental iron in each tablet. The drug is absorbed best on an empty stomach, but it frequently is prescribed with meals so that it is tolerated better. Most patients tolerate starting with once-daily dosing and escalating to a final dose of three times daily. Persistent intolerance can be addressed by switching to ferrous gluconate, but its lower elemental iron content requires a longer period of iron administration to correct the deficiency state; charting serum ferritin levels permits the ascertainment of adequate replacement with either preparation.

Innumerable iron preparations are marketed, but there is little to recommend these preparations over the cost-effective ferrous sulfate pills. Although ascorbate and succinate enhance the absorption of iron, the addition of these agents to iron preparations is costly and unnecessary in light of the body's efficiency in iron absorption under normal circumstances. Enteric-coated iron tablets may be contraindicated because the coating may shield against absorption in the upper portions of the small intestine, where maximal iron absorption takes place. Liquid iron preparations may be tolerated better by some patients and better absorbed in patients with gastrojejunostomies or rapid intestinal transit times; because iron salts can stain the teeth, iron solutions should be ingested through a straw.

At the time that iron therapy is initiated, a baseline reticulocyte count and ferritin level should be obtained. With iron replacement, the symptoms of fatigue and lassitude improve in the first week, but maximal reticulocytosis does not occur for 7 to 10 days. The hemoglobin level does not rise for 2 to 2.5 weeks, and it requires about 2 months of daily iron therapy for the hemoglobin level to return to normal. Measurement of ferritin levels determines when iron stores have been reconstituted and when iron therapy should be discontinued; return of ferritin levels to normal documents that iron stores have been restocked.

Successful treatment of presumed iron deficiency anemia with iron permits confirmation of the diagnosis. This diagnostic-therapeutic trial is used commonly in young women with menometrorrhagia. Documentation of a reticulocyte response at 7 to 10 days after the initiation of iron therapy and a subsequent return of the hematocrit to normal proves the diagnosis of iron deficiency in an inexpensive and simple fashion.

In the rare patient who cannot tolerate or cannot absorb iron from the gastrointestinal tract and in individuals who require large iron boluses to compensate for chronic blood loss, the preferred parenteral approach is intravenous administration of ferric gluconate. A test dose of 2 mL (25 mg elemental iron) in 50 mL of normal saline over 60 minutes is indicated to identify any hypersensitivity to the drug. For patients on dialysis, a serum ferritin level of greater than 100 µg/L is the desired target level to ensure an optimal response to erythropoietin administration. An older alternative, which is less safe and is not recommended if ferric gluconate is available, is iron dextran.

Prognosis

The prognosis in iron deficiency anemia is related strictly to the underlying cause of the anemia. Iron deficiency per se does not usually alter the prognosis because it is treated easily when recognized. The importance of the diagnosis is recognition of the need to identify the underlying cause of the condition and correct this lesion so that the anemia does not recur (Chapter 133).

HYPOCHROMIC ANEMIAS NOT CAUSED BY IRON DEFICIENCY

Because characterization of an anemia as hypochromic restricts its cause to some abnormality in iron, heme, or globin metabolism, the elimination of iron deficiency as the cause narrows the choices to these other components of hemoglobin metabolism. Abnormalities in globin chain synthesis, the thalassemias, are a more prominent consideration when hypochromic anemia occurs in the appropriate ethnic groups (Chapter 168). The sideroblastic anemias are iron-loading anemias caused by abnormalities in heme synthesis; a clue to their presence is nearly total saturation of serum transferrin levels, a striking departure from the findings in iron deficiency. Confirmation of the diagnosis requires bone marrow documentation of ringed sideroblasts, the pathognomonic lesion in this condition.

ANEMIA OF CHRONIC DISEASE

Although iron deficiency is the most common anemia in general, anemia of chronic disease is the most common anemia in hospitalized patients. This condition represents a shared hematologic response to systemic insults as varied as infection, inflammation, malignancy, and trauma. The anemia is moderate in degree, with the hematocrit usually in the range of 28 to 32%. The morphology is normochromic, normocytic in 60 to 70% of patients, with the remainder having a mild hypochromic microcytic anemia. Hypoferremia is characteristic of anemia of chronic disease in the face of marrow iron overload. Confusion of anemia of chronic disease with iron deficiency anemia results from the overlapping of microcytosis and hypoferremia in both disorders. In anemia of chronic disease, the lesion includes deficient delivery of iron to developing RBCs, in addition to other derangements in RBC production.

Etiology and Pathogenesis

At least three different pathophysiologic mechanisms contribute to anemia of chronic disease, an anemia that develops within a few weeks of the onset of systemic disease and is independent of any marrow involvement or specific hematologic complication of the systemic disease. Accelerated RBC breakdown, abnormalities in iron mobilization and delivery, and cytokine inhibition of erythropoiesis all have been implicated to various degrees. A modest shortening of RBC survival is noted, probably resulting from extravascular sequestration by a stimulated reticuloendothelial system. The degree of hemolysis in anemia of chronic disease is modest, and failure of the host to mount an appropriate reticulocyte response to compensate for the anemia indicates that a hypoproliferative defect rather than hemolysis is the major lesion.

Iron studies reveal low serum iron and transferrin levels in anemia of chronic disease, in contrast to the elevated transferrin levels in iron deficiency. Nevertheless, the transferrin saturation levels in anemia of chronic disease may overlap with those of iron deficiency, further adding to the confusion of these two entities. Anemia of chronic disease is a sideropenic anemia in the face of reticuloendothelial iron overload; serum ferritin levels and bone marrow iron stores are increased in anemia of chronic disease.

The cause of the hypoferremia in anemia of chronic disease is not strictly defined. The disproportionate incorporation of iron into ferritin in storage depots may explain ferritin elevation as an acute phase reactant in all the conditions associated with anemia of chronic disease. Another explanation for the hypoferremia in this type of anemia is a form of nutritional deficiency because microorganisms and malignancies require iron for growth and proliferation. In the face of infection and malignancies, normal iron metabolism is subverted to bolster the body's defenses against these assaults; lactoferrin, the product of polymorphonuclear leukocytes, redirects the vector of iron delivery away from RBCs, which lack lactoferrin receptors, to cells of the reticuloendothelial system. Malignancies may alter the vector of iron delivery because many tumors contain siderophores, which are molecules that effectively can extract iron from the surrounding plasma. This closeting of iron explains the fall in serum iron in anemia of chronic disease, although hypoferremia is unlikely to be the primary cause of the anemia. Administration of iron to these patients does not correct the anemia and is not indicated in its management. The hypoferremia is considered an advantage to the body in restraining bacterial or tumor cell growth; the anemia is the cost of the body's defense against invasion.

Elevated ferritin production and lactoferrin linkage are not the only factors causing hypoferremia in patients with anemia of chronic disease; the low serum iron level now is thought to be only part of a more generalized response to infection, malignancy, or inflammation. These systemic threats to the body start a cascade of cytokines initiated by interleukin-1 release from macrophages. Anabolic and catabolic responses result, with an elevation in acute phase reactants (C-reactive protein, haptoglobin, ceruloplasmin, fibrinogen, ferritin) and a reduction in serum iron and hematocrit levels. Playing an important role in the production of anemia is the liberation of tumor necrosis factor, or cachectin, a product of macrophages and part of the cytokine network. Injection of these substances creates the anorexia, debilitation, and weight loss of chronic disease and inhibits the growth of erythroid precursor cells; a hypoerythropoietin state results from an absolute deficiency of the hormone or a dampening of its effect on the marrow. Anemia of chronic disease represents "cachexia" of the marrow, a sharing by marrow in the defense of the body against the threat of infection, malignancy, or inflammatory disorders.

Clinical Manifestations

Anemia of chronic disease is not itself usually a cause of symptoms. The anemia is mild and well tolerated unless it is superimposed on other threatening conditions. The importance of recognizing anemia of chronic disease is in identifying its underlying cause. This type of anemia is frequently the initial evidence that otherwise occult disease is present.

Diagnosis

Anemia of chronic disease is a moderate (hematocrit usually 28 to 32%), normochromic, normocytic anemia that supervenes during the early course of disorders as diverse as malignancy, infection, inflammation, or trauma. Iron indices usually reveal hypoferremia and a reduced iron-binding capacity. Confusion occurs with iron deficiency anemia because microcytic anemia occurs in 30 to 40% of these cases, and transferrin saturation may be reduced to levels seen in iron deficiency. Serum ferritin and serum transferrin receptor levels help distinguish iron deficiency anemia from anemia of chronic disease. Iron-deficient states have elevated serum transferrin receptors relative to a marked lowering of ferritin levels; anemia of chronic disease is characterized by an elevation in ferritin levels, usually greater than 100 ng/mL. When iron deficiency and anemia of chronic disease are present, as occurs in some patients with rheumatoid arthritis (Chapter 278), elevated serum transferrin receptor levels permit recognition of iron deficiency that otherwise would be masked by the alterations in iron/transferrin levels in the anemia of chronic disease. Bone marrow iron stores also distinguish the two because of the presence of marrow iron in anemia of chronic disease; iron deficiency anemia is the only cause of hypochromic, microcytic RBCs in which iron stores are absent from the marrow.

 Treatment

Anemia of chronic disease is a secondary manifestation of an underlying disorder, and its successful reversal requires recognition and correction of that disorder. Although hypoferremia is present, iron therapy does not correct the anemia and contributes to the usual iron overload in this condition. Blood transfusions frequently are not necessary because the anemia is modest and usually well tolerated. Because anemia of chronic disease results from a cytokine-induced hypoerythropoietin state, the defect can be overridden with erythropoietin administration; however, erythropoietin is commonly not appropriate because anemia of chronic disease is not usually severe.

SIDEROBLASTIC ANEMIAS

Sideroblastic anemias, which are uncommon causes of hypochromic anemia, have their origins in altered production of the heme component of the hemoglobin molecule. The final step in heme synthesis involves the incorporation of iron into the protoporphyrin ring, which is synthesized in and around the mitochondria of developing RBCs. Any defect in the multistep generation of protoporphyrin creates a mismatch between iron delivery and iron incorporation into heme. This mismatch results in iron overloading of the mitochondria because heme, the feedback inhibitor of further RBC iron uptake, is deficient. Cells are designated "ringed" sideroblasts when the iron-laden mitochondria occupy a perinuclear distribution within the developing RBCs; Prussian blue staining of the RBCs within the marrow shows these siderotic granules surrounding the nucleus (Fig. 167–4). The siderotic granules of normal siderocytes are fewer in number and are distributed throughout the cytoplasm of the cell. Mitochondrial accumulation of iron is what distinguishes the sideroblastic anemias.

A clue to the presence of these anemias is the paradoxical finding of hyperferremia and nearly total transferrin saturation in a patient with a hypochromic anemia. The hypochromia has its origin in deficient protoporphyrin ring synthesis, which leads to less hemoglobin in affected cells.

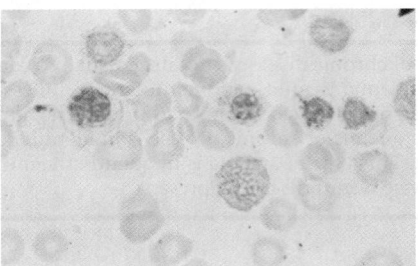

FIGURE 167–4 • Sideroblastic anemia. Prussian blue iron stain of the bone marrow shows ringed sideroblasts, which are nucleated red blood cell precursors with perinuclear rings of iron-laden mitochondria.

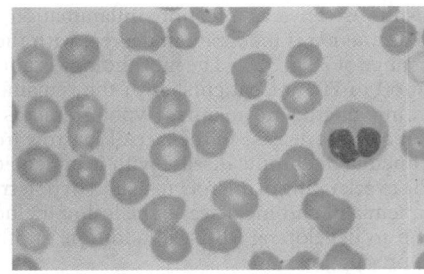

FIGURE 167–5 • Pelger-Huët anomaly. Mature neutrophil with a two-lobed nucleus that has a dumbbell or "pince-nez" appearance. Pseudo–Pelger-Huët anomaly occurs in acquired conditions (e.g., myelodysplasia, myeloproliferative disorders, infections).

Pathogenesis and Classification

Protoporphyrin ring synthesis is a multistep process that depends on several sequential enzymatic reactions occurring in and around the surface of cell mitochondria. A lesion at any stage in this sequence, whether caused by an enzymatic deficiency or an abnormality in mitochondrial structure or function, may result in faulty protoporphyrin synthesis. These lesions may occur as inherited or acquired defects in the pathway. The inherited forms have mitochondrial and nuclear genetic mutations as their cause. As with disturbances in other metabolic pathways within the body, drugs and toxins are the major causes of acquired sideroblastic anemia; a less common form of acquired sideroblastic anemia is a clonal disorder that is a subgroup of the myelodysplasias.

The primary lesion in sideroblastic anemia results in a mismatch between iron delivery and its incorporation into heme. The unincorporated iron accumulates in the mitochondria and damages these crucial organelles. This iron loading of the mitochondria further contributes to ineffective erythropoiesis. In some patients, cautious phlebotomy may improve the anemia by unloading iron from the mitochondria and correcting this secondary lesion.

The morphologic evidence for the sideroblastic process in peripheral blood is a population of hypochromic RBCs. Transferrin levels are saturated, and ferritin levels are increased, although not usually to the same degree as in hemochromatosis. Rare RBCs containing sideriotic granules, or Pappenheimer bodies, also may circulate in the peripheral blood. The diagnosis of sideroblastic anemia is confirmed by the presence of ringed sideroblasts within marrow stained for iron; these forms are nucleated RBCs with a perinuclear collection of iron granules.

ACQUIRED SIDEROBLASTIC ANEMIA

IDIOPATHIC REFRACTORY SIDEROBLASTIC ANEMIA. A hypochromic anemia, frequently with slightly macrocytic (rather than microcytic) indices, develops in elderly individuals as a predominantly erythroid manifestation of a myelodysplastic syndrome (Chapter 182) The RBC population is often dimorphic, with a varying proportion of hypochromic and normochromic cells; the hypochromic cells have their origin in a clonal population of ringed sideroblasts within the marrow. The cause of the disorder is not known, although its occurrence after chemotherapy suggests that damage to the chromosomal material responsible for normal erythroid development creates this picture.

The lesion is chronic and may remain restricted to the erythroid line with ineffective erythropoiesis in addition to the defect in heme synthesis. The lesion also may evolve into leukemia, but with no firm predictors of whether or when this transition will occur (Chapter 193). Common antecedents to leukemia transformation are an associated leukopenia, especially when accompanied by leukocyte developmental abnormalities (pseudo–Pelger-Huët anomaly) and alterations in platelet number (Fig. 167–5).

Treatment of the disorder remains experimental. Pharmacologic doses of pyridoxine, a vitamin necessary for the initial step in heme synthesis, usually have no benefit; androgens and erythropoietin also are rarely helpful. The process may be chronic, with no need for RBC transfusion until late in the course, but prolonged support with RBC transfusions may lead to secondary hemochromatosis and require chelation therapy with deferoxamine.

Sideroblastic anemia may be discovered in the setting of a large variety of medical conditions, including rheumatoid disease, malignancies, and endocrine disorders. The relation to these disorders is probably not causal because treatment or correction of the underlying disorder does not correct the anemia. It is more likely that the medical condition unmasks an otherwise undetected anemia.

SIDEROBLASTIC ANEMIA ASSOCIATED WITH DRUGS OR TOXINS. Consumption of large amounts of alcohol (Chapter 17) over a several-week period can induce sideroblastic anemia in the absence of any concomitant vitamin deficiency. The lesion is thought to have its origin in the interference of alcohol with pyridoxine metabolism and its essential role as a coenzyme in the δ-aminolevulinic acid synthase step in porphyrin synthesis. Alcohol is also a mitochondrial toxin, and the anemia may be related to damage to mitochondrial function.

In alcoholics with sideroblastic anemia, the marrow lesion persists for 7 to 10 days after the withdrawal of alcohol. Other insults to this metabolic pathway include lead (Chapter 20), chloramphenicol, and several antituberculous drugs. All these agents interfere with the initial step in protoporphyrin ring synthesis, with lead also hindering a second site where heme synthetase catalyzes the incorporation of iron into the heme ring in the final step in this pathway.

HEREDITARY SIDEROBLASTIC ANEMIAS

Hereditary sideroblastic anemia is most commonly a moderate-to-severe hypochromic, normocytic anemia inherited in a sex-linked recessive fashion. A point mutation resulting in an amino acid change near the pyridoxal phosphate binding site of the erythrocytic δ-aminolevulinic acid synthase isoenzyme is the underlying defect in some kindreds with this disorder. The anemia does not usually become evident until early adulthood and responds to varying doses of pyridoxine, which are usually much larger than the daily requirements for this vitamin.

Mitochondrial cytopathies also may be responsible for congenital disorders when a sideroblastic anemia is linked to pancreatic, liver, and kidney dysfunction, as in Pearson's syndrome. These rare syndromes affect infants and are thought to be due to inherited mutations in mitochondrial DNA that result in defective oxidative phosphorylation in the involved organs.

SUGGESTED READINGS

Alcindor T, Bridges KR: Sideroblastic anaemias. Br J Haematol 2002;116:733–743. *A comprehensive overview of pathophysiology and clinical implications.*
Fishbone S, Wagner J: Sodium ferric gluconate complex in the treatment of iron deficiency for patients on dialysis. Am J Kidney Dis 2001;37:879–883. *An intravenous iron replacement option that is associated with fewer adverse effects than iron dextran.*
Ioannou GN, Rockey DC, Bryson CL, et al: Iron deficiency and gastrointestinal malignancy: A population-based cohort study. Am J Med 2002;113:276–280. *Gastrointestinal malignancy is uncommon in iron-deficient premenopausal women with or without anemia.*
Means RT Jr.: Recent developments in the anemia of chronic disease. Curr Hematol Rep 2003;2:116–121. *This syndrome has expanded beyond traditional chronic infectious, inflammatory, or neoplastic diseases to include other, often acute, syndromes in which the same pathogenetic mechanisms are operating.*

168 HEMOGLOBINOPATHIES: THE THALASSEMIAS

Griffin P. Rodgers

The *thalassemia syndromes* are a heterogeneous group of inherited anemias characterized by defects in the synthesis of one or more globin chain subunits of the adult hemoglobin tetramer (Hb A). Patients with β-thalassemia have a decrease in β-chain production relative to α-chain production; the converse is the case in α-thalassemia. The clinical syndromes associated with thalassemia arise from the combined effects of inadequate hemoglobin production and unbalanced accumulation of globin subunits. The former causes hypochromia and microcytosis; the latter leads to ineffective erythropoiesis and hemolytic anemia. Clinical manifestations are diverse and range from asymptomatic hypochromia and microcytosis to profound anemia leading to death in utero or in early childhood if untreated. This clinical heterogeneity reflects the variable severity of the primary biosynthetic defect and coinherited modulating factors, such as accelerated synthesis of fetal hemoglobin subunits, the overall effectiveness of a wide range of cellular and circulatory adaptive factors, and perhaps not yet appreciated environmental factors. These disorders differ from the hemoglobinopathies that result from mutations in the coding sequences of the α-globin or β-globin genes; these mutations alter protein structure and lead to other disease manifestations (e.g., Hb S in sickle cell disease) (Chapters 171 and 172). These disorders are not mutually exclusive in that some mutations (e.g., Hb E and Hb Constant Spring) alter the structure of a globin chain and the rate at which it is produced. Table 168–1 presents a clinical classification and distinguishing characteristics of specific thalassemia syndromes.

Molecular Genetics

Many structural genes encode for the globin polypeptides in maturing human erythroid cells. Normal functional hemoglobin consists of a tetramer of two α-like and two β-like globin polypeptide chains. Two clusters of closely linked genes encode the globin chains. The non-α (β-like) genes reside on chromosome 11 and include the two adult genes δ and β, the two similar fetal genes (differing by one amino acid, alanine or glycine) Aγ and Gγ, and the single embryonic ε-gene. On chromosome 16 is found the α-like genes, including the duplicated and almost identically functional α-genes ($\alpha_2\alpha_1$), which are present in the fetal and adult stages of erythropoiesis, and the embryonic ζ-gene. A θ-gene downstream from the α_1-gene has been shown to be a pseudogene incapable of producing normal messenger RNA. High-level tissue and developmentally specific globin gene expression is governed in large part by novel upstream regulatory elements designated HS-40 and LCR for the α-globin and β-globin clusters, respectively. As the descriptors of these genes imply, several distinct hemoglobin species are present during the transition from intrauterine to adult life (Fig. 168–1).

On a smaller scale, individual α-like and β-like globin genes share many general features. Each gene consists of three coding sequences (exons) interrupted by two intervening sequences (introns). As with other eukaryotic genes, globin genes have short segments of 5′ and 3′ untranslated regions, appropriate recognition sequences at the intron/exon junctions to facilitate normal splicing, and polyadenylation sequences in the 3′ untranslated regions. In the 5′ promoter region are three elements crucial for normal globin gene expression, including the ATA, CCAAT, and CACCC boxes. Enhancers and silencing elements also have been recognized in these 5′ and 3′ flanking sequences. Mutations (or deletions) in any of these important elements in the promoters, enhancers, or intron-exon junctions lead to a decrease in overall gene transcription.

Table 168–1 • CLINICAL CLASSIFICATION OF THALASSEMIAS

CLASSIFICATION	GENOTYPE	CLINICAL SEVERITY*	TREATMENT
α-THALASSEMIA SYNDROMES			
α+-Carrier (silent)	$-\alpha/\alpha\alpha$†	Silent	None
α-Thalassemia trait	$-\alpha/-\alpha; --/\alpha\alpha$	Mild	None
Hemoglobin H disease	$-\alpha/--$	Mild–moderate; hemolytic anemia	Folic acid; avoidance of oxidant drugs; transfusion support and splenectomy, as indicated
Hydrops fetalis	$--/--$	Lethal	Early referral to high-risk obstetric service
Hemoglobin Constant Spring genotypes	$\alpha\alpha^{cs}/\alpha\alpha$	Silent–mild	None
β-THALASSEMIA SYNDROMES			
β-Thalassemia minor (trait)	β/β^{++}	Silent	None
β-Thalassemia intermedia	$\beta/\beta^0; \beta^+/\beta^+; \beta^+/\beta^0 = \beta^+$ Hemoglobin E/β^0	Moderate–severe	Folic acid; periodic blood transfusion support and/or splenectomy, as indicated
β-Thalassemia major	$\beta^0/\beta^0 = \beta^0$	Severe	Early referral for hematopoietic stem cell transplantation, if feasible; regular blood transfusions and iron chelation therapy; splenectomy, as indicated
COMPLEX β-THALASSEMIA SYNDROMES			
Coinherited β-thalassemia†	Various combinations of α- and β-thalassemia syndromes		
Hereditary persistence of fetal hemoglobin	Various point mutations or deletions in or around γ-globin gene	Mild–moderate	Folic acid; periodic blood transfusion support and/or splenectomy, as indicated
γ-Thalassemia	Deletion of ≥1 γ-genes		
δ-Thalassemia	Deletion of ≥1 δ-genes		
γδβ-Thalassemia	Complex deletions of ≥1 γ-, δ-, β-genes in tandem		

Silent, normal or minimally abnormal hematology values; *mild*, hemoglobin level normal or slightly reduced with disproportionate microcytic hypochromic indices; *moderate*, hemolytic anemia, icterus, splenomegaly, although no regular transfusion requirement; *severe*, profound anemia with transfusion dependency, extramedullary hematopoiesis, growth retardation, bone abnormalities, hemosiderosis; *lethal*, death in utero from anemic congestive heart failure.

†The α-thalassemia syndromes usually result from deletions in one or more α-genes, indicated by the minus sign, or from mutations in the coding sequence (e.g., α-Constant Spring, α^{cs}).

†The β-thalassemia syndromes are typically the consequence of mutations that lead to a *decreased* level of normal β-chain production (β^+) or *absence* of β-chain production (β^0). Various combinations of these mutations give rise to syndromes of increasing severity.

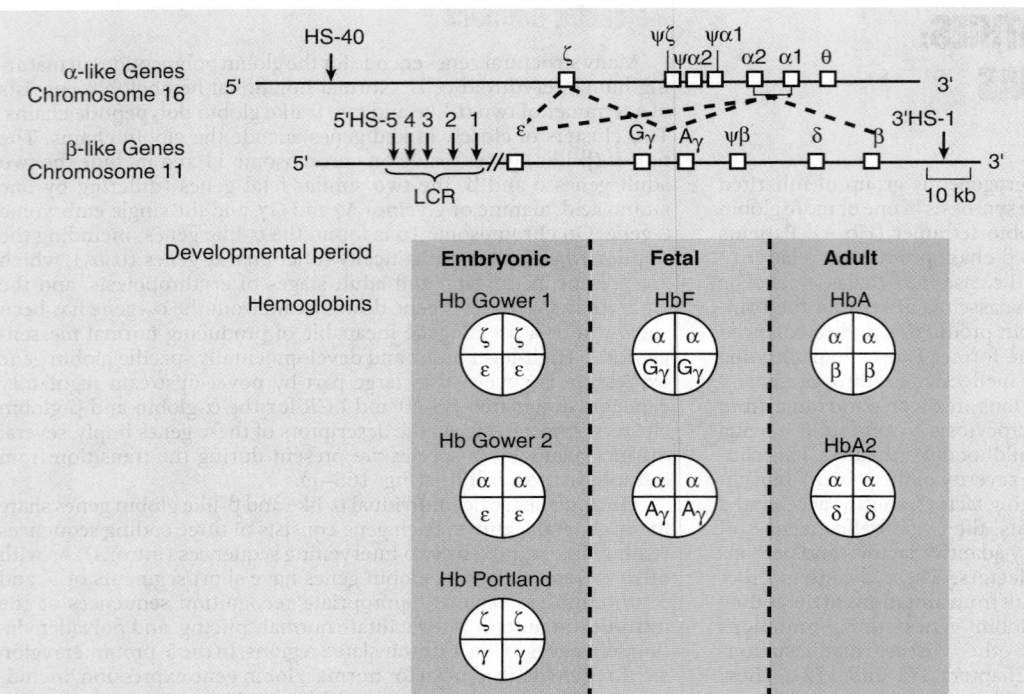

FIGURE 168–1 • Organization and expression of the human globin genes. The human globin genes consist of two clusters of closely linked genes on two separate chromosomes encoding the globin chains. The genes are arranged with the same transcriptional orientation arrayed from 5′ to 3′ in the order that they are sequentially expressed during development. The α- and β-globin gene clusters also contain several pseudogenes, indicated by the ψ θ prefix. Upstream (5′) of these clusters are major transcriptional control elements, HS-40 → (α), LCR → (β), that are crucial for high-level expression in a developmentally specific manner. Hb = hemoglobin.

These mutations or deletions in and around the α-globin and β-globin genes or in the α-HS-40 or β-LCR may lead to disease manifestations ranging from inconsequential laboratory findings (microcytosis and hypochromia in α-thalassemia and β-thalassemia trait) to events incompatible with normal intrauterine growth and development (hydrops fetalis) (Fig. 168–2; see Table 168–1).

Molecular Defects

α-Thalassemia syndromes have been classified by defects resulting in severe (α-thalassemia type 1) and mild (α-thalassemia type 2) forms (Fig. 168–3). This nomenclature gradually is being replaced to reflect the current classification scheme of the β-thalassemias into two groups: α°-thalassemia and α⁺-thalassemia. The α°-thalassemias result in completely abolished production of α-globin chains by the affected chromosome, whereas the α⁺-thalassemias are defined by a variable amount of globin chain production resulting from the remaining α-globin genes on the chromosome. The a°-thalassemias usually result from deletion of the α_2-globin and α_1-globin genes *in cis* (on the same chromosome), the entire cluster together with the main regulatory sequence (HS40), or the HS40 regulatory element alone. Other less frequent causes of α°-thalassemia include the occurrence of nonsense mutations within a single α-gene *in cis* and deletion of the other α-globin locus.

α⁺-Thalassemia usually results from deletion of a single α-gene within the cluster or, less frequently, a thalassemic-generating point mutation in either the α_1-genes or the α_2-genes. The point mutation in the 3′ untranslated region (α Constant Spring) is an example of a thalassemic hemoglobinopathy in which a structural variant renders the hemoglobin unstable and effectively diminishes the α-globin–to–β-globin chain ratio.

In contrast to the α-thalassemia syndromes, the β-thalassemias rarely are caused by major structural gene deletions (Fig. 168–4). Deletions that have been described include deletions in individuals who are heterozygous (with removal of all or a substantial portion of the regulatory elements in the β-LCR); large structural deletions, including the α-δ-β or β-genes (or some subset thereof); and deletions within the crucial elements in the β-promoter described previously. The more common cause of β-thalassemia is the so-called nondeletional variant, which affects gene function in many ways, including abnormalities in transcription, RNA processing, or RNA translation of the β-globin gene.

Despite the large number of these mutations—more than 200 β-thalassemia alleles have been characterized—probably only 20

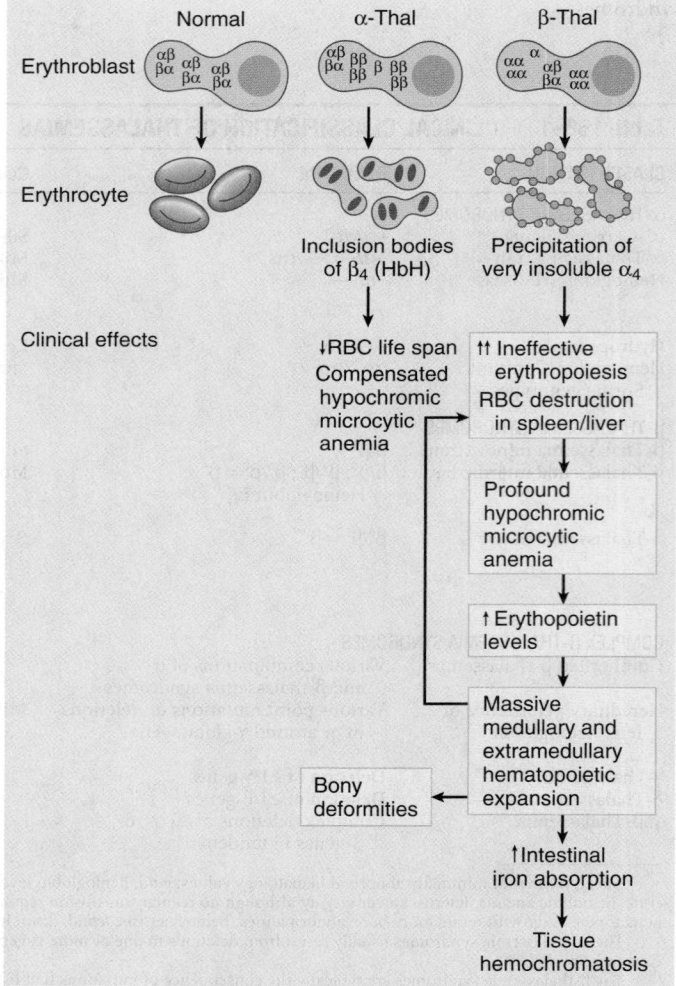

FIGURE 168–2 • Schematic representation of the pathophysiology of the clinically significant α- and β-thalassemia (Thal) syndromes. RBC = red blood cell.

α-Globin Gene		Genotype	Phenotype	No. of Functional α-Genes
α2 α1	αα/αα	Normal	Normal	4
α2 α1	−α/αα	α⁺-thal heterozygote (mild)	Silent carrier α-thal trait	3
α2 α1	−−/αα	α⁰-thal heterozygote (moderate)	Microcytosis α-thal trait	2
α2 α1	−α/−α	α⁺-thal heterozygote (moderate)	Microcytosis α-thal trait	2
α2 α1	−−/−α	α⁰-thal × α⁺-thal (severe)	Hb H disease	1
α2 α1	−−/−−	α⁰-thal homozygote (lethal)	Hydrops fetalis with Hb Bart's	0

FIGURE 168–3 • The genetic bases of the more common forms of α-thalassemia. The hematologic and clinical severity is directly proportional to the number of deleted α-globin genes, as indicated. (Adapted from Gelehrter TD, Collins FS: Principles of Medical Genetics. Baltimore, Williams & Wilkins, 1990.)

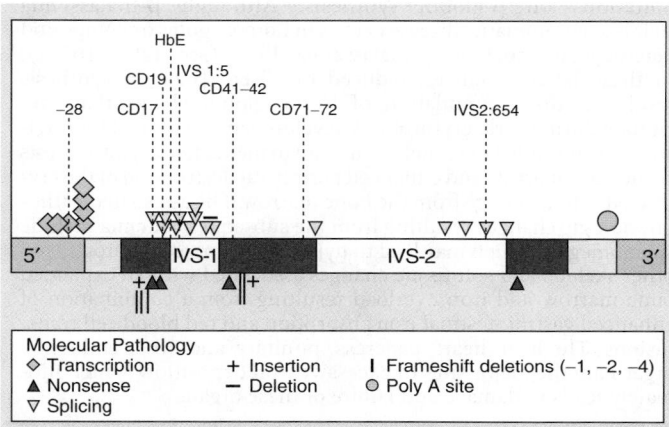

FIGURE 168–4 • General structure of the human β-globin gene and the sites (and bases) of some of the more common recessively inherited β-thalassemia mutations. (Adapted from Stamatoyannopoulos G, Neinhuis AW, Leder P, Majerus PW: The Molecular Basis of Blood Disease. Philadelphia, WB Saunders, 1987.)

β-thalassemic alleles account for greater than 80% of the β-thalassemia mutations. Transcriptional mutants result from mutations either in the promoter of regulatory elements, generally between position −101 and position −28, or in the 5′ untranslated regions, especially in the region of the canonical CAP site. An example of such a transcriptional mutant is the −28 point mutation, which is common in blacks and Southeast Asians and gives rise to a β⁺-phenotype. RNA processing abnormalities, perhaps the most common of all mutations thus characterized, occur near splice junctions next to the consensus splice site (e.g., the IVS 1:5 mutation common in Mediterranean populations, Northern Europeans, and Algerians), in cryptic splice sites in introns (e.g., IVS II:654 producing β⁰-thalassemia or β⁺-thalassemia in Chinese, Southeast Asians, and Japanese), or in cryptic splice sites in exons (e.g., codon 19 in Southeast Asians). A mutation in codon 26 (GTA GTG) results in Hb E, prevalent among Southeast Asians, and gives rise to a quantitative reduction in normal β-globin gene mRNA because of activation of a cryptic splice donor site and a qualitative abnormality of the β-globin chain because of substitution of a lysine for the normal glutamic acid (Chapter 171). The third major category of mutations results in RNA translation abnormalities. These mutations produce a β⁰-thalassemia phenotype and include abnormalities in the initiation (ATG) codon; the production of nonsense codons (codon 39 in Mediterranean populations); or frameshift mutations such as the codon 41/42 mutations common in Chinese,

Southeast Asian, and Asian Indian populations or the codon 71/72 mutations in Chinese populations.

Pathophysiology

Patients with α-thalassemia have a decrease in α-globin chain production relative to β-globin chain, with the formation of β₄ (Hb H) inclusion bodies. Red blood cells bearing these inclusion bodies are removed rapidly from the circulation by the reticuloendothelial system, shortening their survival. The resulting mild anemia is compensated partially by an increase in red blood cell production.

In contrast, patients with β-thalassemia have a decrease in β-globin chain production relative to α-globin chain production, which leads to an excess of α-globin chains. Although this decrease in β-synthesis is compensated slightly by the γ-globin and δ-globin chains, the combined β-globin, δ-globin, and γ-globin chains are insufficient to match the number of α-globin chains present. Unbound α-globin chains are extremely insoluble and precipitate in red blood cell precursors and their progeny, a process leading to defective erythroid maturation (ineffective erythropoiesis). The few cells that do emerge into the peripheral circulation are removed rapidly in the spleen and liver. Progressive splenomegaly occurs in an attempt to entrap these abnormal red blood cells and further exacerbates the anemia by virtue of hemodilution. The resulting profound anemia increases circulating erythropoietin levels and causes a massive expansion of medullary and extramedullary hematopoietic tissue. This expansion leads to skeletal abnormalities and various growth and metabolic derangements. The expanded erythroid marrow induces signals (yet uncharacterized) that increase intestinal iron absorption. This process, along with the iatrogenic iron overload (secondary to long-term transfusions), leads to tissue hemochromatosis and its attendant complications.

Clinical Manifestations

α-THALASSEMIAS. Deletion of one or both α-globin genes on chromosome 16 is the most common mutation of the human genome. The α-globin gene cluster is a dynamic locus in which tandemly duplicated long blocks of nucleotide sequences promote nonhomologous recombination between chromosomes during meiosis. The α-thalassemia syndromes are predominately due to deletions of one or more of the four genes coding for the α-chain, although nondeletional forms also have been described. These disorders have their highest prevalence in Africans and their descendants (30%), in whom a single α-gene or two α-genes *in trans* (opposite chromosomes) may be deleted. In contrast, in Southeast Asian populations, where the prevalence may reach 40%, more typically two α-genes *in cis* (on the same chromosome) may

Continued

be deleted, although single α-gene deletions also are seen (see Fig. 168–3).

The clinical spectrum of the α-thalassemia syndromes is related directly to the number of functioning α-globin genes. Accordingly, deletions of one (αα/–α) or two (–α/–α, – –/αα) α-globin genes, which occur frequently in many parts of the world, are virtually asymptomatic. Correct diagnosis of these genotypes allows for the identification of couples at risk for pregnancies with homozygous fetuses (see later). In addition, proper recognition of these syndromes provides a molecular basis for microcytosis and hypochromia (and possibly mild anemia) and averts the injudicious and often exten ded use of iron supplementation for the erroneous diagnosis of iron deficiency (Chapter 167). Hb H disease, which is caused by deletions of three genes (– –/– α), is manifested as a moderately severe anemia with splenomegaly and a hypochromic, microcytic blood film appearance (see Table 168–1). Hb H (β₄) is demonstrable by special staining of the red blood cell and by hemoglobin electrophoresis. Generally, however, the hemolytic anemia in Hb H disease is compensated partially, with an average hemoglobin value of 8 to 10 g/dL, and long-term transfusion therapy may not be required. Hb H is prone to precipitation in red blood cells during oxidative stress and under conditions of increased temperature, however, and consequently the hemolytic anemia may be exacerbated in these patients by agents known to induce oxidant injury or by infections. Accordingly the same drugs that induce hemolysis in glucose-6-phosphate dehydrogenase–deficient patients (Chapter 169), especially the sulfonamides, should be avoided in susceptible patients with Hb H disease.

In its most severe form, in which all four genes are deleted, α-thalassemia is incompatible with life, and the fetus is stillborn or critically ill with hydrops fetalis. Reports indicate that mothers carrying affected fetuses have a high incidence of pregnancy-induced hypertension (75%), seizures, postpartum hemorrhage (10%), and other peripartum complications. Accordingly, every effort should be made to identify these women (typically Asians or Asian-Americans) during the early course of their pregnancy for appropriate referral.

β-THALASSEMIAS. The β-thalassemia syndromes represent the classic molecular paradigm in which disparate defects in a eukaryotic structural gene can culminate in decreased to absent (β) polypeptide chain production. This diverse group of disorders for the most part is due to single nucleotide changes in or around either or both of the two β-globin genes. Some of the molecular mechanisms accounting for the thalassemic phenotype include nonsense, frameshift, splicing, and polyadenylation mutations and insertions and deletions (see Fig. 168–4). These alterations give rise to significant changes in the level of gene transcription that lead to absent (β°) or markedly diminished (β⁺) amounts of β-globin gene mRNA (see Table 168–1). In addition, long deletions lead to more complex forms of β-thalassemia syndromes, such as β-thalassemia or hereditary persistence of fetal hemoglobin. These large deletions in the β-globin cluster occur less commonly, however, than in the α-globin cluster.

The condition is ubiquitous, but is especially common in Mediterranean, Asian, and African populations (and their American descendants), in whom the high gene frequency has been thought to reflect geographic areas with a high malaria prevalence. Within a given ethnic group, relatively few genotypes account for most cases, each of which now has been defined by DNA analysis. At a lower level of resolution, the pattern of DNA resolved on gel electrophoresis after restriction enzyme digestion has been used to define certain haplotypes or restriction fragment length polymorphisms. Specific β-globin cluster haplotypes are linked genetically to certain of these thalassemic mutations, and haplotype analysis has been used to define mutation prevalence in various populations and to assess population migration.

The clinical spectrum of disease severity in the β-thalassemia syndromes is related directly to the quantitative effect of individual mutations on β-globin synthesis. Although β-thalassemia trait is asymptomatic, disease occurs in homozygotes or compound heterozygotes such as β-thalassemia/Hb E (see Table 168–1). In these latter instances, reduced or absent β-globin synthesis results in the accumulation of free α-globin chains that precipitate during early erythroblast development because of their relative insolubility. These inclusions lead to ineffective erythropoiesis in the bone marrow and enhanced peripheral destruction of the erythrocytes that emerge from the bone marrow. The associated pathophysiologic changes resulting from the subsequent anemia include splenomegaly, which may lead to hypersplenism, osteoporosis, and other skeletal and soft tissue changes associated with an expanded bone marrow and iron overload resulting from a combination of enhanced gastrointestinal iron absorption and red blood cell transfusions. The liver, heart, pancreas, pituitary, and other endocrine organs are the major sites of excessive iron deposition, which ultimately leads to damage and failure of these organs.

Laboratory Diagnosis

Historically the diagnosis of β-thalassemia and α-thalassemia has relied heavily on clinical and hematologic features (Fig. 168–5). Often the patients were referred for the evaluation of anemia and/or microcytosis or in the context of neonatal or population screening. The discovery of low mean corpuscular volume and hemoglobin on automated complete blood counts has increased the number of these referrals. In the presence of normal iron status, increased levels of Hb A₂ (to 4 to 6%) and/or increased Hb F (to 5 to 20%) by quantitative hemoglobin analysis support the diagnosis. Differentiation between iron-deficiency anemia and β-thalassemia or α-thalassemia trait can be difficult in practice if no reciprocal increases in Hb A₂ levels and/or Hb F are present. In the presence of concomitant iron deficiency, Hb A₂ levels in individuals with β-thalassemia may fall into the normal range. In these instances, the demonstration of a modified β-globin-to-α-globin synthetic chain ratio, generally using ³H-leucine to analyze globin chain production in reticulocytes, would be required for a conclusive diagnosis.

In the contemporary era of DNA technology, reference laboratories can swiftly clone and directly sequence the α-globin or β-globin genes or perform other techniques of DNA analysis on patients suspected to have thalassemia syndromes. This approach, which has revolutionized prenatal diagnosis of the severe thalassemia syndromes, can be performed at 14 weeks' gestation on amniotic fluid cells and at 10 weeks if chorionic villus sampling is performed. These procedures generally carry a risk of miscarriage of 1% and 5%, respectively.

A hydrops fetalis (– –/– –) genotype can be shown by the complete absence of α-globin genes in the DNA with the use of α-globin–specific probes. For β-thalassemia mutations, antenatal diagnosis can be made by polymerase chain reaction gene amplification of white blood cell–derived DNA and hybridization with a panel of DNA probes specific for common mutations within the patient's ethnic group. Other DNA-based methods to diagnose and differentiate the thalassemia syndromes include the ligase chain reaction, denaturing gradient electrophoresis, color complementation assay, and direct DNA sequencing. These methods all use an initial step of polymerase chain reaction gene amplification.

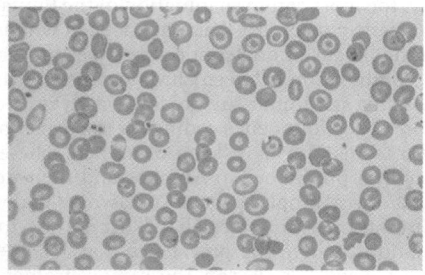

FIGURE 168–5 • Thalassemia minor. Smear shows hypochromic red blood cells with many target cells.

℞ Treatment

α-THALASSEMIA. Some deletions of one ($\alpha\alpha/-\alpha$) or two ($-\alpha/-\alpha,- -/\alpha\alpha$) α-globin genes are asymptomatic, and no therapy is indicated. For Hb H disease (three-gene deletion, $--/-\alpha$), folic acid, 1 mg orally, should be administered daily to compensate for folate loss from accelerated red blood cell turnover. Splenectomy may be indicated for progressive anemia and often is associated with a mean rise in hemoglobin of 2 to 3 g/dL.

β-THALASSEMIA. Despite a nearly comprehensive understanding of the molecular and cellular pathogenesis of the β-thalassemia syndromes, a widely available curative form of treatment for homozygotes remains elusive. Nonetheless, dramatic improvement in life expectancy and morbidity has been observed since the 1980s, primarily because of aggressive transfusion support and the institution of effective iron chelation therapy in these regularly transfused patients. Except for curative allogeneic bone marrow transplantation (Chapter 166), therapy is considered symptomatic and supportive. Treatment of compound heterozygotes for Hb S is discussed in Chapter 171.

Transfusion. As treatment of severe β-thalassemia has improved, so have morbidity and median survival. Although nontransfused patients in the 1920s had a median survival of 2 years, transfusion therapy aimed at maintenance of a hemoglobin concentration of 11 to 13 g/dL (pretransfusion level, >10 g/dL) has been shown to extend the average survival into the second decade and to minimize the bony abnormalities and improve sexual development. Transfusion support generally is initiated when the hemoglobin level decreases to less than 7 g/dL and remains there in the absence of infection or blood loss. To minimize febrile reactions and so as not to prejudice the potential future application of bone marrow transplantation (see later), leukocyte-poor red blood cells should be administered (Chapter 165). An accurate record of the date and amount of blood administered, along with pretransfusion and post-transfusion hemoglobin levels and the occurrence of any transfusion reactions, facilitates optimal therapy. Patients should be tested for the presence of hepatitis B antibodies; patients testing negative should be immunized (Chapter 16). Splenectomy usually is recommended in children (approximately 6 to 7 years old) or adolescents when their transfusion requirements exceed 1.5 times normal (e.g., >200 mL/kg/yr). Before elective splenectomy, all patients should receive polyvalent pneumococcal vaccine, and children also should be given *Haemophilus influenzae* and *Neisseria meningitidis* vaccines.

Iron Chelation. Although intensive transfusion programs have led to markedly improved survival, patients die of iron overload unless chelation therapy is instituted and maintained (Chapter 225). Currently, this therapy involves subcutaneous deferoxamine, a parenterally administered iron chelator, although a search for an effective oral chelator is currently under way. Many patients can be placed in iron balance by receiving a 12- to 24-hour infusion of deferoxamine 5 or 6 days a week. Chelation therapy should be individualized according to age, risks, compliance history, and other factors. For younger patients who are not yet at risk for the complications of iron overload, 1.5 to 2.0 g/day 5 to 6 days per week should be administered. Individuals aged 13 years or older should receive 2.0 to 2.5 g/day, depending on their ability to tolerate subcutaneous infusions. Patients with high liver iron concentrations (>6000 µg/g dry tissue) and patients with evidence of cardiac involvement (i.e., heart failure,

arrhythmias) require more intensive intravenous therapy and should be managed at specialized medical centers caring for large numbers of patients requiring long-term transfusion support. Periodic assessment of the effectiveness of chelation therapy should include an estimate of iron burden (e.g., serum iron, total iron-binding capacity, ferritin) and an estimate of liver iron concentration by the judicious use of percutaneous liver biopsy or ideally by validated noninvasive testing. At present, the options include superconducting quantum interference device (SQUID) susceptometry or, potentially, magnetic resonance susceptometry. A yearly cardiac evaluation should be done in an effort to detect clinical evidence of cardiac disease and should include a complete history and physical examination, electrocardiogram, echocardiogram, and chest radiograph. A Holter monitor should be used in any patient who complains of palpitations or who is noted on physical examination to have an irregular heartbeat. Potential iron-induced damage to the endocrine glands should be evaluated by glucose tolerance testing, thyroid function tests, and cortisol determinations. Hormone replacement therapy is dictated by the results of basal and/or provocative endocrine function studies.

Complications associated with the use of deferoxamine include visual disturbances, tinnitus, and renal dysfunction (azotemia and proteinuria). All of these complications are reversible on discontinuation of treatment with the drug and generally do not recur when the drug subsequently is given at lower doses. For these reasons, annual ophthalmologic and audiologic evaluations are strongly recommended for patients receiving long-term deferoxamine therapy.

Stem Cell Transplantation and Experimental Therapies. Allogeneic bone marrow transplantation (Chapter 166) is increasingly effective for patients with homozygous β-thalassemia. Among good-risk children (defined by good compliance with chelation and the absence of hepatomegaly and portal fibrosis), the 3-year event-free survival rate is 95%. Older patients or patients exhibiting one or more risk factors have rejection-free survival rates of less than 75%. Currently, bone marrow transplantation can be recommended as a reasonable option only for selected good-risk pediatric candidates who have an HLA-matched donor.

One alternative form of therapy involves the manipulation of globin gene expression with drugs such as 5-azacytidine, hydroxyurea, erythropoietin, or butyrate analogues. The rationale for these trials is that these agents are known to stimulate fetal hemoglobin synthesis and that γ-globin chain augmentation may compensate for the reduced β-chain synthesis, normalizing the ratio of α-chain to non–α-chain; the result could be decreased transfusion requirements, decreased extramedullary hematopoiesis, and reduced iron overload. Although some patients have responded impressively to these therapies, the overall low response rate and the requirement for frequent parenteral administration have tempered enthusiasm for this approach. Nonetheless, these initial successes have led investigators to examine the efficacy of related classes of orally administered agents to stimulate Hb F production.

Finally, gene therapy has been directed at replacing or compensating for the defective β-globin alleles, especially in view of the comparative ease of obtaining hematopoietic stem cells. Although this approach remains theoretically attractive, methodologic and logistic hurdles remain.

SUGGESTED READINGS

Lucarelli G, Andreani M, Angelucci E: The cure of thalassemia by bone marrow transplantation. Blood Rev 2002;16:81–85. *A new and successful option for thalassemia.*

Nisbet-Brown E, Olivier NF, Giardina PJ, et al: Effectiveness and safety of JCL670 in iron-loaded patients with thalassaemia: A randomised, double-blind, placebo-controlled, dose-escalation trial. Lancet 2003;361:1597–1602. *A promising pilot study of a new, oral chelation agent.*

Rodgers GP, Rachmileuritz EA: New therapies of sickle cell anemia and β-thalassemia. Semin Hematol 2001;38:299–392 (entire issue). *Review of the molecular, cellular, and clinical aspects of thalassemia.*

Weatherall DJ, Provan AB: Red cell: I: Inherited anemias. Lancet 2000;355:1169–1175. *Review of the genetic mechanisms underlying the thalassemias.*

169 AUTOIMMUNE AND INTRAVASCULAR HEMOLYTIC ANEMIAS

Alan D. Schreiber

In autoimmune hemolytic anemia, hemolysis is largely extravascular, although a substantial intravascular component can occur in paroxysmal nocturnal hemoglobinuria (PNH) and in cold agglutinin disease. In contrast, intravascular hemolysis predominates in microangiopathic hemolytic anemia and hemolysis caused by exertional trauma, chemical or thermal agents, osmotic perturbations, infections, venoms, or prosthetic intravascular material.

IMMUNE HEMOLYTIC ANEMIAS

Autoimmune hemolytic anemia comprises a group of disorders in which individuals produce antibodies directed toward one or more of their own erythrocyte membrane antigens. This process leads to the destruction of antibody-coated erythrocytes by tissue macrophages.

The most effective way to approach autoimmune hemolytic anemia is to determine which class of antibody is responsible for the hemolysis. In general, two major classes of antierythrocyte antibodies produce hemolysis in humans, IgG and IgM. The pattern of red blood cell (RBC) clearance, the site of organ sequestration, the response to therapy, and the prognosis all relate to the class of antierythrocyte antibody involved.

Pathophysiology of Immune Hemolysis

IgG-INDUCED IMMUNE HEMOLYTIC ANEMIA. Human erythrocytes are relatively resistant to the lytic action of complement (Chapter 45), and their hemolysis, which is mediated by antibody (and enhanced by complement), is primarily extravascular. IgG-coated erythrocytes are cleared from the circulation in the absence of complement activation. Two molecules of IgG antibody need to be in close proximity to one another on the erythrocyte surface for the first component of complement (C1) to bind and initiate activation of the classic complement pathway. With antigens that are widely distributed on the erythrocyte surface, such as the antigens recognized by most antierythrocyte antibodies, many IgG antibody molecules must be deposited on the erythrocyte membrane before two bind sufficiently close to one another to permit complement activation.

IgG-sensitized erythrocytes are removed progressively from the circulation and are sequestered predominantly in the spleen. Erythrocyte survival is determined in part by the number of antibody molecules per cell; increasing the number of IgG molecules per cell progressively increases the splenic sequestration of these cells. Complement activation enhances the clearance of the IgG-coated cells.

In the absence of the third component of complement (C3), the complement activation sequence does not proceed through C3, and erythrocytes do not become coated with C3 in vivo. Nevertheless, in this circumstance, IgG-coated erythrocytes still are cleared from the circulation in an accelerated manner, predominantly by macrophages in the spleen.

Although IgG-coated erythrocytes are cleared predominantly by the spleen regardless of whether complement activation occurs, the liver becomes the predominant organ of clearance when large amounts of IgG are bound to the erythrocytes. In vitro studies showed that macrophages of the reticuloendothelial system have several classes of surface receptors for the Fc domain of IgG antibodies (Fcγ receptors). These receptors are responsible for the binding and phagocytosis of IgG-coated erythrocytes. One of the Fcγ receptor isoforms is a high-affinity receptor present on macrophages and monocytes, FcγRI. Two low-affinity receptors also are located on macrophages, FcγRIIA and FcγRIIIA. Fcγ receptors are largely responsible for the clearance of IgG-coated cells. Erythrocytes coated with multiple IgG molecules interact with macrophages that have multiple Fcγ receptors even if they are low affinity; this interaction leads to the binding of the erythrocytes to the surface of the macrophage, which induces phagocytosis.

Macrophages can alter IgG-coated and/or C3b-coated erythrocytes in a manner that causes the RBCs to form microspherocytes. These spherocytes are less able to pass through the splenic cords and sinuses and have decreased survival; their presence in the circulation indicates ongoing immune hemolysis. Macrophages also have receptors, designated *CR1* and *CR3*, for the activated third component of complement, which recognize the C3b and iC3b forms of C3b and which are capable of binding C3b-coated erythrocytes. The receptors for the various C3 fragments do not recognize native C3; they recognize only fragments of C3 after C3 has undergone activation. These receptors are capable of efficient function in the presence of normal plasma concentrations of C3. Fcγ receptors and C3b receptors can interact synergistically in their binding of IgG-coated and C3b-coated cells, and the clearance of erythrocytes coated with IgG and C3b is greater than that of erythrocytes coated with IgG alone.

IgM-INDUCED IMMUNE HEMOLYTIC ANEMIA. A single molecule of IgM antibody bound to an erythrocyte membrane can bind C1, which is the first component of complement, and activate the classic complement pathway. Complement is required for the clearance of IgM-coated cells. Erythrocyte survival is proportional to the number of IgM molecules per RBC. IgM-coated cells are cleared rapidly within the liver rather than the spleen.

Macrophages do not have receptors for the Fc domain of IgM antibody, in contrast to their abundant receptors for the Fc domain of IgG antibody. Activation of the complement sequence by IgM results in the deposition of C3b on the erythrocyte surface. Erythrocyte-bound C3b and iC3b can interact with hepatic macrophage C3b and iC3b receptors. This interaction with complement is responsible for the clearance of IgM-coated erythrocytes.

IgM-coated and C3b-coated erythrocytes are sequestered rapidly within the liver. Subsequently the coated RBCs undergo phagocytosis and are destroyed, or they are released from their hepatic macrophage C3b receptor attachment sites back into the circulation, where they survive normally, even though they still are coated with C3. This release of IgM-coated and C3-coated erythrocytes from the macrophage C3 receptor attachment sites is not due to elution of the antibody from the surface. Rather the C3b/iC3b inactivator system, which involves several circulating plasma proteins, including factor I and factor H, causes the release of C3-coated erythrocytes from the macrophage C3b and iC3b receptor attachment sites. These released C3-coated cells have on their surfaces an antigenically altered form of C3 (C3d) that no longer is recognized by macrophage C3b receptors. These C3d-coated erythrocytes survive normally. Increasing the concentration of IgM per erythrocyte accelerates sequestration by liver macrophages and decreases the number of erythrocytes released from the hepatic macrophage receptor binding sites. Pretreatment of IgM-coated and C3-coated erythrocytes with a source of serum C3 inactivator system proteins alters the erythrocyte cell-bound C3 and improves erythrocyte survival.

The two major classes of antibody that cause autoimmune hemolytic anemia, IgG and IgM, differ markedly in their biologic effects. IgG-coated erythrocytes are cleared predominantly in the spleen, whereas IgM-coated erythrocytes are sequestered predominantly within the liver. Splenic macrophage Fcγ receptors and C3 receptors are responsible for the clearance of IgG-coated cells. IgG-coated erythrocytes do not require complement for their clearance. Complement accelerates the clearance of IgG-coated erythrocytes in the spleen, however. Blood flow in the spleen is relatively slow, with close contact between sinusoidal macrophages and circulating RBCs. This close contact facilitates IgG-mediated splenic macrophage clearance.

The pattern of clearance of IgM-coated erythrocytes is different from that of IgG-coated cells. IgM-coated cells are cleared rapidly by hepatic macrophage C3 receptors. The clearance is complement dependent, and in the absence of complement activation, these cells survive normally. The C3 inactivator system serves as an important control mechanism for the clearance of IgM-coated cells by mediating the release of IgM-coated cells from their hepatic macrophage C3 receptor attachment sites. Exposure of IgM-coated and C3-coated erythrocytes to C3 inactivator system proteins can attenuate the clearance of these C3-coated cells by hepatic macrophages.

Etiology

IgG-INDUCED AUTOIMMUNE HEMOLYTIC ANEMIA. Autoimmune hemolytic anemia is caused most commonly by IgG antibodies. The antigen to which the IgG antibody is directed is usually one of the Rh erythrocyte antigens, although often its precise specificity is not defined easily. This antibody usually has its maximal activity at 37° C, and this entity has been termed *warm antibody—induced hemolytic anemia*.

IgG-induced immune hemolytic anemia can occur without an apparent underlying disease (idiopathic autoimmune hemolytic anemia); however, it also can occur with an underlying immunoproliferative disorder, either malignant or nonmalignant, such as chronic lymphocytic leukemia (Chapter 192), non-Hodgkin's lymphoma (Chapter 195), or systemic lupus erythematosus (Chapter 280). In certain patients with immunodeficiency, such as agammaglobulinemia (Chapter 267), autoimmune hemolytic anemia can develop as well. Rarely, IgG-induced immune hemolytic anemia also has been observed in patients with an underlying malignant disease that is not an immunoproliferative disorder (Table 169–1). Additionally,

Table 169–1 • DISEASES ASSOCIATED WITH AUTOIMMUNE HEMOLYTIC ANEMIA

INFECTIONS
Viral infections, especially respiratory infections
Infectious mononucleosis and cytomegalovirus infection
Mycoplasma, especially pneumonia
Tuberculosis

NONMALIGNANT DISORDERS
Systemic lupus erythematosus
Rheumatoid arthritis
Thyroid disorders
Ulcerative colitis
Chronic active hepatitis

IMMUNODEFICIENCY SYNDROMES
X-linked agammaglobulinemia
Dysgammaglobulinemia
Common variable hypogammaglobulinemia
IgA deficiency
Wiskott-Aldrich syndrome

MALIGNANCIES
Non-Hodgkin's lymphoma
Hodgkin's disease
Acute lymphocytic leukemia
Carcinoma
Thymoma
Ovarian cysts and tumors

bacterial infections, such as tuberculosis (Chapter 341); viral infections, such as cytomegalovirus (Chapter 370); and chronic inflammatory conditions, such as ulcerative colitis (Chapter 142), have been described as associated conditions. The incidence of idiopathic IgG-induced autoimmune hemolytic anemia varies in different series. Overall, approximately half of the patients with IgG-induced immune hemolysis do not have a detectable underlying cause at the time of diagnosis. Regardless of cause, some patients have immune thrombocytopenia (Chapter 177) in conjunction with IgG-induced autoimmune hemolytic anemia (Evans' syndrome), and some have immune granulocytopenia (Chapter 163) as well. It is not clear whether these IgG antibodies directed against blood cells recognize a common blood cell antigen or represent antibodies with different specificities.

In IgG-induced autoimmune hemolytic anemia, many IgG molecules are needed on the erythrocyte surface to bind and activate a single molecule of C1, the first component of complement, because two IgG molecules in close proximity to each other (a doublet) are required. When C1 is bound and activated, C4 and C2 activation occurs in a manner similar to that described for IgM antibody (see later), and C3 convertase is formed. C3 cleavage results, and C3b is deposited on the erythrocyte surface.

Macrophages within the reticuloendothelial system have receptors not only for C3b, but also for the Fc fragment of IgG (Fcγ receptors). These macrophage Fcγ receptors bind IgG-coated erythrocytes and mediate spherocyte formation and phagocytosis of the IgG-coated RBCs. Patients who have IgG on the erythrocyte surface in insufficient numbers or distributed in such a way not to allow C1 binding and activation still have a substantial decrease in erythrocyte survival. When sufficient IgG is present on the erythrocyte surface so that C1 activation occurs, however, erythrocyte clearance is accelerated further. In such a circumstance, clearance is due to the macrophage Fcγ receptors and the macrophage C3b receptors. These receptors interact synergistically to induce the binding of erythrocytes coated with IgG and C3b. IgG-coated erythrocytes are cleared progressively from the circulation, primarily in the spleen, and hemolysis is almost always extravascular.

IgM-INDUCED AUTOIMMUNE HEMOLYTIC ANEMIA. In humans, IgM-induced autoimmune hemolytic anemia is caused by an IgM antibody that reacts most efficiently with erythrocytes in the cold; this disorder also has been called *cold hemagglutinin disease*. The IgM antibody in cold hemagglutinin disease usually is directed against the I antigen or related antigens on the human erythrocyte membrane. As with all IgM antibodies, agglutinating activity is particularly efficient because of the multiple antigen-combining sites on the IgM molecule. The IgM antibody has a particular affinity for its RBC antigen at 0° to 10° C, and the affinity is lower at higher temperatures. Similar to warm antibody

(i.e., IgG-mediated) autoimmune hemolytic anemia, cold hemagglutinin disease can be divided into cases considered primary or idiopathic and cases associated with the presence of an underlying disease (secondary).

Chronic cold hemagglutinin disease is due to clonal expansion of lymphocytes in which a monoclonal antibody is produced and recognizes a polysaccharide antigen, termed I or i, on RBCs. The most common form of chronic cold hemagglutinin disease, which is the primary or idiopathic form, is usually a disease of older persons, with a peak incidence in the 50s and 60s. Most often this condition initially causes fatigue, anemia, and occasionally jaundice in an elderly individual, but it may be associated with the development of acrocyanosis from sludging of blood in peripheral vessels on exposure to cold or with acute hemolysis. This disease is associated with the presence of a monoclonal IgM antibody, usually exhibiting a high cold agglutinin titer (>1:1000). This IgM antibody binds to erythrocytes avidly in the cold but shows little or no binding activity at 37° C. In most, but not all, patients, the antibody is of the κ light-chain type and has specificity for the I antigen present on the erythrocytes of most adults. The I antigenic determinants are related closely to the ABO core antigenic determinants. Although present on the erythrocytes of almost all persons, the antigenic groupings recognized by the antibody develop during childhood and are not present on blood taken from the umbilical vein of the newborn. Operationally, specificity is established by the ability of the antibody to agglutinate the blood of almost all adults but an inability to agglutinate the erythrocytes of newborns. Although the monoclonal antibody responsible for development of the cold hemagglutinin syndrome presumably reflects the expansion of a single clone of B cells, the symptom complex associated with multiple myeloma or Waldenström's macroglobulinemia (Chapter 196) does not develop in these patients. The monoclonal antibody seems to be a highly restricted clonal response to the I antigen. Although each patient usually has only a single antibody with a single amino acid sequence, the antibodies among patients virtually always differ. Nevertheless, these antibodies tend to share idiotypic determinants consistent with their uniform recognition of the I antigen.

Secondary cold hemagglutinin disease, or IgM-induced immune hemolytic anemia, is associated most commonly with an underlying *Mycoplasma* infection (Chapter 304), particularly *Mycoplasma pneumoniae,* in which antibody with typical anti-I specificity is produced. It also may occur with other infections, however, such as infectious mononucleosis (Chapter 371), cytomegalovirus (Chapter 370), and mumps (Chapter 368). With infectious mononucleosis, anti-i (antibody to an antigen related to I but present on cord blood cells) cold hemagglutinins are produced, but overt hemolysis is unusual. Under most circumstances with an underlying infection, the cold hemagglutinin (IgM antibody) is polyclonal, that is, immunochemically heterogeneous.

Cold hemagglutinin disease also can be seen in patients with an underlying immunoproliferative disorder, such as chronic lymphocytic leukemia (Chapter 192) and non-Hodgkin's lymphoma (Chapter 195), or in patients with an underlying connective tissue disease, such as systemic lupus erythematosus (Chapter 280). As in idiopathic cold hemagglutinin disease, patients with an underlying malignant immunoproliferative disorder, such as one of the non-Hodgkin's lymphomas, have a cold hemagglutinin that is commonly monoclonal or of restricted heterogeneity (oligoclonal). Waldenström's macroglobulinemia (Chapter 196) also at times is associated with the formation of IgM antibody against RBCs. Anti-i also may be seen in malignant lymphocytic neoplasias.

The plasma of healthy adults and children contains low levels of antierythrocyte antibodies, that is, low levels of IgM cold hemagglutinins. Rarely, cold-reacting autoantibodies have been observed with specificity directed against RBC antigens other than I or i (i.e., the P and the PR antigens). Also rarely, IgA cold hemagglutinins have been observed.

The reason for the preferential reaction of cold hemagglutinin with the human RBC membrane in the cold is not completely understood. Most cold hemagglutinins have no measurable activity at temperatures greater than 30° C. Although it has been postulated that either the antibody or the antigen may undergo a structural change on exposure to cold, most data suggest that the antigen on the erythrocyte surface is altered in the cold.

As in all patients with autoimmune hemolytic anemia, erythrocyte survival is generally proportional to the amount of antibody on the erythrocyte surface. In cold hemagglutinin disease, the extent of hemolysis is a function of the titer of the antibody (cold agglutinin titer), the thermal amplitude of the IgM antibody (the highest temperature at which the antibody is active), and the level of the circulating control proteins of the C3 inactivator system.

In cold hemagglutinin disease, the IgM antibody in the circulation of patients with the disease interacts with the erythrocyte surface after the cells have circulated to areas below body temperatures, then activates the early steps of the classic complement pathway. When C1, the first component of complement, is bound to the IgM molecule and activated, it sequentially binds and activates the fourth and second components of complement. The first of these two steps takes place at temperatures as low as 0° C. When the cells return to body temperature, activation proceeds, even though the cold hemagglutinin antibody can dissociate from the erythrocyte. The C3 convertase (C142) generated cleaves C3 into two antigenic fragments, one of which, C3b (and iC3b), binds to the erythrocyte surface. At this step, the IgM effect is considerably amplified, with a single C142 classic pathway C3 convertase capable of cleaving many C3 molecules and depositing many C3b molecules on the erythrocyte surface. In some cases, the complement sequence of reactions may be completed with resulting hemolysis, but this event is unusual because of the presence of membrane-bound proteins that restrict complement action. The C3b-coated erythrocytes are recognized by hepatic macrophage complement receptors. The macrophage C3b and iC3b receptors bind, sphere, and may mediate phagocytosis of the C3b-coated erythrocytes. Because no receptors on macrophages are capable of interacting with IgM-coated cells in the absence of complement, IgM-coated RBCs have normal survival in the absence of an intact classic complement pathway.

In humans, clearance of IgM-plus-complement–coated cells has been shown to be rapid and takes place primarily in the liver. When large numbers of IgM molecules are present on the erythrocyte surface, however, sufficient terminal complement components (C5 through C9) are generated occasionally to lyse the erythrocytes in the intravascular space.

Control proteins involved in the C3 inactivator system are particularly important in cold hemagglutinin disease because cell destruction is mediated entirely by C3 and the later complement components. The level of the C3 inactivator proteins in plasma plays an important role in determining hemolysis by regulating the number of active C3 fragments on the cell surface. The C3-coated erythrocytes interacting with C3 inactivator system proteins are degraded to C3dg or C3d. C3dg-coated or C3d-coated erythrocytes are not bound by macrophage C3 receptors and have normal survival. The presence of C3 (C3dg or C3d)-coated erythrocytes in cold hemagglutinin disease explains the earlier observation of normal erythrocyte survival in patients who still have C3 on their erythrocyte membranes, as detected by the Coombs antiglobulin test.

The thermal amplitude of the IgM cold agglutinin is important in determining the extent of hemolysis in cold hemagglutinin disease. At a relatively low level of cold agglutinin sensitization, patients whose antibodies have a higher thermal amplitude (antibodies that possess activity at temperatures approaching 37° C) still may have considerable hemolysis. These patients have been described as having a low-titer cold hemagglutinin syndrome with a high-thermal amplitude antibody. The correct diagnosis in these patients is important because they seem to respond to glucocorticoid therapy in a manner different from the usual patient with high-titer cold hemagglutinin disease. Some unusual patients have an IgG cold agglutinin. The presence of such an IgG antibody is potentially important inasmuch as it seems to indicate responsiveness to steroids and splenectomy.

Epidemiology and General Features

In large centers, 15 to 30 cases of autoimmune hemolytic anemia are seen yearly, with an annual incidence of approximately 1 case per 75,000 to 80,000 persons in the general population. As with any disease that may require careful serologic study for diagnosis, the level of sophistication and diagnostic capability of the institution influence the reported incidence. There seems to be little genetic predisposition to the development of autoimmune hemolytic anemia except in patients who have a family history of other autoimmune diseases, such as autoimmune thrombocytopenia (Chapter 177), rheumatoid arthritis (Chapter 278), and glomerulonephritis (Chapter 119). Although warm antibody (IgG-induced) immune hemolytic anemia can occur at any age, the peak incidence occurs in the

50-year-old age group. In contrast, idiopathic cold hemagglutinin disease occurs predominantly in the elderly. Autoimmune hemolytic anemia does not seem to be more prevalent in any particular racial group.

Patients with autoimmune hemolytic anemia vary considerably in their clinical courses, which may be either indolent or fulminant. In general, the course of autoimmune hemolytic anemia is more acute in children, in whom complete resolution often occurs, than in adults. The fall in hemoglobin may occur over hours to days, with resolution of the disease often within 3 months.

The Donath-Landsteiner cold hemolysin is an unusual IgG antibody with anti-P specificity that originally was noted in cases of congenital or acquired syphilis (Chapter 349). The disease it causes is called *paroxysmal cold hemoglobinuria*. Hemolysis in this syndrome most commonly occurs intravascularly, after the antibody has passed through a cell attachment phase in the lower temperatures of the peripheral circulation. The intravascular hemolysis is due to the unusual complement-activating efficiency of this IgG antibody. As its name implies, this antibody is associated with cold hemoglobinuria. This antibody, although uncommon, is found most frequently in children with viral infections. Hemolysis, although sometimes severe, is usually mild and tends to resolve as the infection clears.

Mortality in the pediatric age group has ranged from 9 to 29%. Death during the acute stage is usually due to severe anemia or hemorrhage from associated thrombocytopenia. Mortality in chronic cases or in adults is higher and usually occurs because of an underlying serious disorder, such as Hodgkin's disease (Chapter 194) or non-Hodgkin's lymphoma (Chapter 195), or as a complication of therapy. Fatal sepsis has been observed after splenectomy.

Estradiol, in contrast to cortisol, enhances the clearance of IgG-coated erythrocytes by splenic macrophages in a dose-dependent manner. Conversely, estradiol does not alter the splenic macrophage clearance of heat-altered erythrocytes or the hepatic macrophage clearance of IgM-coated and C3b-coated erythrocytes. During pregnancy, estrogen concentrations rise to a level similar to that necessary to accelerate the clearance of IgG-coated erythrocytes; as a result, the course of IgG-induced autoimmune hemolytic anemia accelerates.

Clinical Manifestations

Many of the symptoms of autoimmune hemolytic anemia, such as weakness, malaise, and light-headedness, are caused by the presence of anemia. Patients who have underlying cardiovascular disease may have significant dyspnea on exertion and peripheral edema and angina pectoris. If the hemolysis is significant, mild jaundice may be noted, particularly in the presence of hepatic dysfunction. In addition, patients with an underlying disease often have the symptoms associated with that disease (e.g., fever and weight loss with an underlying malignant disease or joint symptoms secondary to an underlying systemic vasculitis). Physical findings also are generally referable to the underlying disease. In patients with an underlying non-Hodgkin's lymphoma, hepatosplenomegaly and lymphadenopathy are common. Mild splenomegaly may be present in patients with severe autoimmune hemolytic anemia. Massive splenomegaly suggests an underlying disorder, such as lymphoma. Other signs that may result from the anemic state include those caused by heart failure (edema, ascites, or pulmonary congestion). Severe jaundice is uncommon.

The common initial symptoms are pallor, jaundice, dark urine, abdominal pain, and fever. Pallor may precede the appearance of jaundice. The clinical status depends on the rapidity of the hemolysis and the severity of the anemia. In mild cases, fatigue may be the only symptom. In severe cases, the patient may appear acutely ill or moribund, with tachycardia, tachypnea, signs of hypoxia, and cardiovascular collapse. In severe IgM-induced cold hemagglutinin disease, the skin may have a livedo reticularis pattern, and the patient may show acrocyanosis on exposure to cold.

Diagnosis

Laboratory data reveal the presence of anemia, reticulocytosis (if bone marrow function is adequate), and a positive result on the direct Coombs test. Autoantibodies directed against early erythroid precursors are believed to be responsible for the reticulocytopenia in some patients. Examination of the peripheral blood smear may show

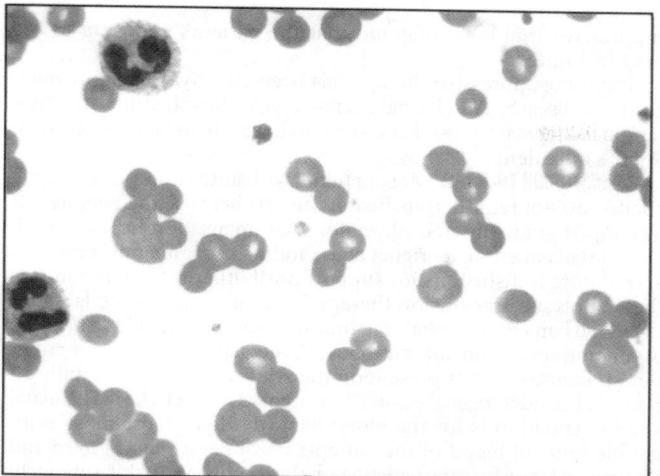

FIGURE 169–1 • Representative peripheral blood smear in a patient with autoimmune hemolytic anemia visible. (Courtesy of Thomas K. Chacko.)

spherocytes, polychromasia, nucleated RBCs, and erythrophagocytosis (Fig. 169–1). Rosetting of RBCs around white blood cells may be visible in a buffy coat preparation. Agglutination of RBCs may be evident in cold hemagglutinin disease. In severe cases, macroagglutination is visible on the microscope slide or in a capillary tube. The white blood cell count is usually normal or elevated. Autoimmune hemolysis also is associated with thrombocytopenia and/or leukopenia in a few patients. Indirect hyperbilirubinemia is common.

The diagnosis of autoimmune hemolytic anemia is established most effectively by directly examining the patient's circulating RBCs for the presence of antibody and/or complement components on their surface, most easily with a direct Coombs antiglobulin test. Classically, in this test, the patient's RBCs are made to interact with a rabbit or goat antihuman serum globulin reagent, then agglutination of the patient's RBCs is assessed. It is also possible to use antibody to human immunoglobulin or complement components as a more specific test reagent. In this case, agglutination induced by anti-IgG (a γ-Coombs test) indicates the presence of IgG on the surface of the RBCs, whereas agglutination with anti-C3 or anti-C4 (a non-γ-Coombs test) is used to test for the presence of C3 and C4. In IgG-induced hemolytic anemia, IgG or IgG plus complement components is found on the surface of erythrocytes. These patients usually have a positive result on the γ-Coombs' test but may have a positive result on the non-γ-Coombs test as well. In IgM-induced hemolytic anemia (cold hemagglutinin disease), IgG is not found on the RBCs, and the IgM cold agglutinin, because of its low affinity for RBC antigens at 37° C, is not found either. In contrast, C3, stably bound at 37° C, is detected on the RBC membrane. In cold hemagglutinin disease, usually a positive result is observed in only the non-γ (C3) Coombs test. Rarely, patients with IgG-induced immune hemolysis have levels of IgG per erythrocyte undetectable by the standard Coombs test, which requires the presence of hundreds of molecules of IgG on the erythrocyte surface for the result to be positive. When this phenomenon originally was described, the small amounts of RBC-bound IgG antibody were detected with a complex antiglobulin consumption test. Now, however, Coombs test using radiolabeled anti-IgG, which is 10 times more sensitive than the standard Coombs test, also may be used to detect the antibody.

Testing with the Coombs antisera shows several patterns of reactivity. The RBCs may be coated with IgG in the presence or absence of detectable complement (warm antibody IgG-mediated autoimmune hemolytic anemia) or with complement protein alone (IgM-induced hemolysis, i.e., cold hemagglutinin disease). It is not possible to predict the chronicity or severity of autoimmune hemolytic anemia from the Coombs testing pattern.

A cold agglutinin titer also is diagnostically helpful. This test is performed by examining the patient's plasma for agglutinating activity directed against normal ABO compatible erythrocytes containing the I antigen at 0° C. The cold agglutinin titer is the highest dilution of antibody that still agglutinates normal RBCs in the cold. Most patients with immune hemolysis secondary to cold hemagglutinin disease have cold agglutinin titers greater than 1:1000.

Rx Treatment

In many patients with IgG-induced or IgM-induced immune hemolytic anemia, no therapeutic intervention is necessary because the hemolysis is mild. If an underlying disease is present, control of this disease often brings the hemolytic anemia under control as well. If the patient has significant anemia secondary to hemolysis, therapeutic intervention is in order.

GLUCOCORTICOIDS. Patients with IgG antibody–mediated autoimmune hemolytic anemia or immune thrombocytopenic purpura treated with glucocorticoids often respond within days of initiating therapy in dosages equivalent to 1 to 2 mg of prednisone per kg body weight per day. Glucocorticoids are believed to decrease hemolysis in IgG-induced hemolytic anemia by three major mechanisms. First, glucocorticoids decrease production of the abnormal IgG antibody. This effect is common and gradual and can be expected to begin to produce a gradual decrease in the strength of the Coombs test result and a rise in the hemoglobin level by 4 to 6 weeks. Second, glucocorticoids are reported to be associated with a fall in the amount of antibody detected by the direct Coombs test and a rise in the amount detected by the indirect Coombs test, as though they induce a decrease in antibody affinity; this result is probably an uncommon effect of glucocorticoid therapy. Third, glucocorticoids have been shown in vitro and in vivo to decrease the expression of the macrophage Fcγ receptors responsible for erythrocyte clearance from the circulation. The effect improves erythrocyte survival despite the continued presence of IgG on the erythrocyte surface. The Coombs test in some patients may remain positive in the face of improved erythrocyte survival and a rising hemoglobin concentration. This effect of glucocorticoids may be rapid and may be responsible for the rise in hemoglobin noted to occur in some patients within 1 to 4 days of glucocorticoid therapy. Most patients respond to glucocorticoid therapy within 2 to 3 weeks. Some patients do not respond until after 4 to 6 weeks of therapy.

Approximately 60 to 70% of patients have an initial response to high-dose glucocorticoids. In some patients with acute autoimmune hemolytic anemia and in a small proportion of patients with chronic autoimmune hemolytic anemia, the anemia remains in remission if the steroid dose is tapered and stopped. In other patients, the hemolytic process can be controlled with continued low-dose to medium-dose steroid therapy. Alternate-day therapy may be less effective in autoimmune hemolytic anemia than in some of the inflammatory autoimmune diseases, and patients should be monitored carefully for exacerbation. Great care should be taken in stopping glucocorticoid therapy if the patient continues to show a positive result on direct Coombs test. For patients who are steroid dependent, the initial and long-term side effects of glucocorticoids must be considered.

In some patients, the presence of a mild hemolytic anemia may be preferable to splenectomy or other treatment options. The initial goal of therapy is to return the patient to normal hematologic values and nontoxic levels of glucocorticoid therapy. In some patients, a modified goal of improvement in hemolysis to a clinically asymptomatic state with minimum glucocorticoid side effects is more realistic.

Glucocorticoids are not usually effective in cold hemagglutinin disease, probably because these patients generally have large amounts of IgM antierythrocyte antibody and large numbers of C3 molecules deposited on their RBCs. Macrophage C3b receptors, in contrast to Fcγ receptors, are less responsive to glucocorticoid therapy. In addition, some of the hemolysis may be intravascular, and glucocorticoids do not inhibit complement-mediated cell lysis. A few patients with a low-titer cold hemagglutinin disease syndrome, in which the antierythrocyte antibody has activity at temperatures approaching 37° C, do respond to steroid therapy. In addition, the few patients described with an IgG cold agglutinin seem to respond to steroids and splenectomy. Patients with cold hemagglutinin disease

Continued

respond best to the avoidance of cold and control of the underlying disease. In many patients, hemolytic anemia is mild.

SPLENECTOMY. The spleen with its resident macrophages is the major site for sequestration of IgG-coated blood cells in humans, as in animals. Splenectomy markedly decreases the sequestration of IgG-sensitized cells. Splenectomy also may lead to a decrease in the production of IgG antierythrocyte antibody because the spleen contains a large B-lymphocyte pool. As the antibody concentration is increased, however, splenectomy becomes less effective in preventing the clearance of IgG-coated cells because the liver becomes the dominant organ for erythrocyte clearance.

Splenectomy should be considered in patients who are not responsive to steroids or who require more than 10 to 20 mg of prednisone per day or substantial dosages of steroid every other day for maintenance. Each patient requires individual evaluation of underlying diseases, surgical risk, extent of anemia, and steroid intolerance.

The response rate to splenectomy in IgG-mediated disease is approximately 50 to 70%; however, most responses are partial remissions. Probably the patients who are least responsive to splenectomy are patients whose erythrocytes are coated with large amounts of IgG. In this circumstance, the liver plays a larger role in clearance. The partial remissions that occur with splenectomy are often helpful in that they result in lessening of the hemolytic rate, with a rise in the hemoglobin concentration, and/or allow a reduction in the amount of glucocorticoid needed to control the hemolytic anemia. Because of the increased risk of sepsis, patients should be selected carefully. Patients who are unresponsive to steroids, require moderate-to-high maintenance doses, or have glucocorticoid intolerance can be considered for splenectomy. ^{51}Cr-labeled RBC kinetic studies are probably not helpful because the procedure is time-consuming, expensive, and not a reliable indicator of response to splenectomy in most cases. Immunization with pneumococcal vaccine should be performed before splenectomy to decrease the likelihood of postsplenectomy pneumococcal infection.

Splenectomy, similar to glucocorticoid therapy, is usually not effective in patients with cold hemagglutinin disease because IgM-coated erythrocytes are cleared predominantly in the liver. An occasional patient with an apparent IgM-induced hemolytic anemia may respond to splenectomy, perhaps because of decreased production of IgM antibody by the spleen or the presence of an IgG cold agglutinin.

IMMUNOSUPPRESSIVE AGENTS. The immunosuppressive agents most commonly used include the thiopurines (6-mercaptopurine, azathioprine, and thioguanine) and alkylating agents (cyclophosphamide and chlorambucil). Immunosuppressive agents act by decreasing the production of antibody, and it generally takes at least 4 weeks before any therapeutic result is observed. A reasonable clinical trial consists of 3 to 4 months of therapy. These drugs rarely are needed in the treatment of childhood autoimmune hemolytic anemia.

Patients are selected for immunosuppressive therapy when a clinically unacceptable degree of hemolytic anemia persists after glucocorticoid therapy and splenectomy. Alternatively, patients may be glucocorticoid resistant or intolerant and be at high surgical risk for splenectomy. Clinical benefit has been noted in about 50% of patients. The drug dose should be adjusted to maintain the leukocyte count greater than 4000/µL, the granulocyte count greater than 2000/µL, and the platelet count greater than 50,000/µL to 100,000/µL. Side effects require that the clinical indications for an immuno-suppressive trial be strong and that the patient's exposure to the drug be limited.

Immunosuppressive therapy has been effective in cold hemagglutinin disease. Alkylating agents (cyclophosphamide or chlorambucil) have been used and seem to have a beneficial effect in 50 to 60% of patients.

TRANSFUSION THERAPY. Most patients with autoimmune hemolytic anemia do not require transfusion therapy because the anemia has developed gradually, and physiologic compensation has occurred. Occasional patients experience acute and/or severe anemia, however, and require transfusions for support until other treatment reduces the hemolysis. Transfusion therapy is complicated by the fact that the blood bank may be unable to find any "compatible" blood because of the presence of an autoantibody directed at a core component of the Rh locus, which is present on the erythrocytes of essentially all potential donors, regardless of Rh subtype (Chapter 165). The usual recommendation is for the blood bank to identify the most compatible units of blood of the patient's own major blood group and Rh type and transfuse the patient with these units. With this approach, it is unlikely that the donor blood would have a dramatically shortened RBC survival.

In cold hemagglutinin disease, it is important to prewarm all intravenous infusions, including whole blood, to 37° C because a decrease in temperature locally in a vein can enhance binding of the IgM antibody to RBCs and accelerate the hemolytic process. Hemagglutination of transfused chilled or room temperature cells in small peripheral blood vessels can result in severe ischemia and vascular compromise.

MISCELLANEOUS THERAPY. Intravenous gamma globulin, which has been used extensively in the treatment of immune thrombocytopenic purpura, may be effective in patients with IgG-induced immune hemolytic anemia, probably by interfering with the clearance of the IgG-coated cells. Treatment regimens vary from 400 mg/kg/day for 5 days to 2 g/kg given over 2 days, with additional treatment as needed to maintain the effect. Currently, data are incomplete, but gamma globulin seems less effective in autoimmune hemolytic anemia than in immune thrombocytopenic purpura.

Plasmapheresis or exchange transfusion has been used in patients with severe IgG-induced immune hemolytic anemia but has met with limited success, possibly because more than half of the IgG is extravascular, and the plasma contains only small amounts of the antibody (most of the antibody being on the RBC surface). Plasmapheresis has been effective in IgM-induced hemolytic anemia (cold hemagglutinin disease), however, because IgM is a high-molecular-weight molecule that remains predominantly within the intravascular space, and at 37° C, most of the IgM is in the plasma fraction. Plasmapheresis is useful only as short-term therapy, but it may be life-saving in the rare patient with severe, uncontrollable hemolysis.

Other measures that have been used effectively in some patients with IgG-induced immune hemolysis are vincristine, vinblastine, and hormonal therapy. Because of the limited side effects (limited masculinizing effects and mild weight gain), danazol is an additional agent for use in some patients with IgG-induced immune hemolytic anemia. The results of these agents in IgM-induced hemolysis suggest that this treatment is ineffective. Folic acid should be given to avoid depletion of folate stores by chronic hemolysis caused by either IgG or IgM antibodies.

IMMUNE PANCYTOPENIA

Evans' syndrome is an autoimmune hemolytic anemia accompanied by thrombocytopenia. It occurs in a small percentage of adults and children with acute autoimmune hemolytic anemia. In an even smaller percentage of patients, it also is associated with marked neutropenia. Antibodies directed against RBCs, leukocytes, and platelets have been shown in some patients with immune pancytopenia. Suppression of hematopoietic cell maturation by T cells also has been observed. Autoimmune hemolytic anemia in the presence of thrombocytopenia and/or neutropenia is associated more commonly with a chronic or relapsing course. Many patients have associated disorders, such as chronic lymphadenopathy or dysgammaglobulinemia. Some patients are hematologically normal between relapses, which may involve depressions in any of the three cell lines. Usually glucocorticoid therapy is effective in controlling the acute episodes and is not needed between relapses. Some patients have persistent immune cytopenia, however, and require prolonged steroid treatment or more aggressive therapy. Splenectomy may result in improvement, but the risk of infection may be higher in children and adults with pancytopenia than in patients with autoimmune hemolytic anemia alone, and relapses are more common.

PAROXYSMAL NOCTURNAL HEMOGLOBINURIA

PNH is an acquired disorder initially thought to consist of paroxysms of intravascular hemolysis causing nocturnal hemoglobinuria. It now is recognized that chronic intravascular hemolysis is the more frequent clinical presentation. PNH is a primary bone marrow disorder that not only affects the RBC lineage, but also affects the platelet, leukocyte, and pluripotent hematopoietic stem cell lines. It is believed to be a disorder of stem cells of a clonal nature and can arise from or evolve into other dysplastic bone marrow diseases, including aplastic anemia, sideroblastic anemia, and myelofibrosis. Rarely, PNH also evolves into acute leukemia. A major clue to the cause of this disease was provided by the finding that patients have a somatic mutation in the DNA of the X chromosome coding for a protein (phosphatidylinositol 1 glycan class A [PIGA or GPI]) that is important in the pathway that controls the formation of the phosphatidylinositol anchor of various membrane proteins, including the complement control proteins. Many different mutations of the PIGA gene have been reported.

Although PNH is often a disease of young adults, it can occur in any age group and in persons of either sex. Chronic intravascular hemolysis of varying severity is the most common presentation. The severity of the hemolysis and the degree of hemoglobinuria depend on the number of circulating abnormal RBCs and the degree of expression of the membrane abnormality among these cells. Two to three populations of abnormal RBCs, termed *PNH type I, II, and III cells,* may be present simultaneously and differ in their expression of GPI-linked proteins and their lytic susceptibility. Patients commonly also have iron deficiency anemia because of the large amount of iron lost in the urine during intravascular hemolysis with persistent hemoglobinuria and hemosiderinuria. Other frequent clinical complaints include abdominal, back, and musculoskeletal pain. This pain may be associated with intravascular hemolysis and hemoglobinuria, or it may be ischemic, secondary to the complication of venous thrombosis of major or minor vessels. Thromboses of the hepatic veins (Budd-Chiari syndrome) and of portal, splenic, mesenteric, cerebral, and other veins may occur and are a common cause of death. Acute intestinal infarction requiring surgical resection has been reported (Chapter 144), and thrombotic episodes may require anticoagulant therapy. Platelets and leukocytes also seem to have unusual susceptibility to lysis, and thrombocytopenia or granulocytopenia or both are commonly present and may be the initial manifestations of the disease. The bone marrow is usually hyperplastic, but it may be hypocellular, consistent with aplastic anemia. The clinical course is variable and depends on the occurrence of the life-threatening complications of progressive bone marrow disease or venous thrombosis.

PNH should be considered in anyone who has aplastic anemia (Chapter 174). In general, patients are not predisposed to the development of infection. At least half of these patients live for many years.

Diagnosis

The diagnosis rests on the clinical picture and clinical laboratory measurement of a population of circulating cells with unusual sensitivity to complement-mediated lysis. This sensitivity is shown most readily by fluorescence-activated cell sorter analysis of DAF, CD59, or other GPI-anchored molecules that are deficient in PNH. The deficiency of GPI-linked proteins is determined by flow cytometry using monoclonal antibodies. The size of the affected clonal population and the extent of GPI protein deficiency are important determinants of clinical symptoms. PNH also can be diagnosed by a positive sugar-water test or Ham acidified serum test. In the sugar-water test, the patient's serum is mixed with 5% dextrose in water and incubated with the patient's cells; in PNH, hemolysis ensues. Everyone has antibody molecules that recognize their own cells under conditions of low ionic strength. These antibodies activate the classic complement pathway. Normal erythrocytes resist lysis, but PNH erythrocytes are susceptible to lytic attack. In the Ham test, the patient's cells are incubated in acidified serum. Under these conditions, the alternative complement pathway is triggered, and lysis of PNH, but not normal cells, follows. The Ham test result is also positive with some, but not all, normal sera from patients with the syndrome of congenital dyserythropoietic anemia (hereditary erythrocytic multinuclearity with positive acidified serum [HEMPAS]).

Pathogenesis

Patients with PNH have an unusual sensitivity of their erythrocytes and often granulocytes and platelets to the lytic action of complement. Activation of complement by either the classic or alternative pathway results in the deposition of larger numbers of complement molecules on the PNH blood cell surface than on normal cells. The excessive binding of complement to blood cells in PNH is due to more efficient alternative pathway C3 convertase activity on the cell surface. The surface of a PNH erythrocyte is a better acceptor for C3 than is the surface of a normal cell, so there is more activation of the termi-

nal complement components C5 to C9, causing more cell lysis than with normal cells. PNH cells are damaged more effectively by the C5 through C9 complex generated on the erythrocyte surface because the C5b through C9 lytic complex penetrates the PNH cell membrane more efficiently than the normal cell membrane.

Patients with PNH lack the complement regulatory proteins present on the membranes of all normal blood cells, causing the increased susceptibility to complement lysis of PNH erythrocytes. The fundamental feature of blood cells in PNH patients is that they are deficient in proteins linked to the membrane by a GPI anchor. DAF and CD59 are the complement regulatory proteins that are GPI linked and that are deficient in hematopoietic cells in patients with PNH. Many patients with PNH have several populations of abnormal erythrocytes. The complement lysis sensitivity test, which examines the susceptibility of antibody-sensitized erythrocytes to complement-mediated lysis, can be used to define the various PNH cell populations. PNH type 1 cells have a moderate increase in susceptibility to complement attack; they commonly express close to normal levels of GPI-linked proteins. PNH type 2 cells exhibit decreased expression of GPI-linked proteins. These erythrocytes seem to have decreased levels of DAF, but they do not have the membrane deficit (CD59) that leads to sensitivity to attack by the C5b complex. PNH type 3 cells are highly susceptible to complement attack; they seem to lack phosphatidylinositol-linked control proteins completely, lacking DAF and CD59. As noted, the platelets and leukocytes in PNH are also abnormally sensitive to complement-mediated lysis, and this abnormality is likely to have the same cause.

 Treatment

In some patients, hemolysis can be controlled with prednisone at a dose of 15 to 40 mg every other day. During acute episodes, a higher dose given daily for a short period may help to control the hemolysis. In patients with anemia, androgens, including the anabolic steroid danazol at variable doses, may be effective. Bone marrow transplantation, which is the only curative therapy, has been successful in some patients, but in general the treatment of PNH has not been satisfactory. PNH patients may be iron deficient, but iron replacement, especially acutely, may result in increased hemolysis because of the formation and release of a new cohort of sensitive RBCs. Oral iron replacement should be used if possible, but parenteral iron therapy may be necessary when iron losses are large.

DRUG-INDUCED IMMUNE HEMOLYSIS

Drug-induced immune hemolytic anemia may be divided into three primary pathophysiologic entities. The clinical signs and symptoms are identical to those of autoimmune hemolytic anemia. Patients may have chronic hemolytic anemia or, occasionally, catastrophic intravascular hemolysis (quinidine type). Many autoimmune or drug-related hemolytic anemias are accompanied by thrombocytopenia and/or neutropenia as a result of similar pathophysiologic processes. The diagnosis is established primarily by history and in vitro assay.

α-METHYLDOPA TYPE. α-Methyldopa, levodopa, and their derivatives produce a clinical syndrome virtually identical to IgG-induced immune hemolytic anemia. These drugs stimulate production of IgG warm-reactive antibodies with anti-Rh specificity. A primary mode of action of these drugs in this disorder may be an alteration in immunoregulation that allows B lymphocytes that produce Rh antibodies to escape suppression.

Much of the information regarding this type of hemolytic anemia is derived from patients taking α-methyldopa, which rarely is used today. Antinuclear antibodies develop in 15% of patients receiving α-methyldopa therapy. Of patients exposed to α-methyldopa, 25% have a positive result on the Coombs test for IgG. Of diagnostic importance is that almost all patients have IgG antierythrocyte antibodies present in their plasma as well. Sufficient IgG coating for hemolysis does not develop in most patients, but patients with the highest amount of erythrocyte-associated IgG seem to have the most significant hemolysis. Overall, significant hemolysis and hemolytic anemia develop in approximately 0.8% of patients 3 to 37 months after the onset of therapy. The diagnosis can be made by examining patient's RBCs and plasma. In vitro, it is not necessary to have the drug present for the patient's plasma to deposit IgG antibody on donor erythrocytes. The Coombs test result can remain positive in some patients 2 years after withdrawal of the drug. A similar syndrome has been reported with mefenamic acid.

HAPTEN TYPE. The hapten type of drug-induced immune hemolysis classically develops in patients exposed to high doses of penicillin. A portion of the penicillin molecule or its active metabolites combines with the erythrocyte surface, acts as a hapten, and induces an antibody response directed against the penicillin-coated erythrocyte membrane. This response usually involves IgG; complement activation is common. The erythrocytes become coated with IgG and often with C3. This syndrome rarely develops unless patients have received 10 to 20 million units of penicillin per day. The diagnosis can be established by incubating the patient's serum with donor erythrocytes preincubated with penicillin. Deposition of IgG antibody occurs only in the presence of penicillin and can be detected with the Coombs test.

Nonspecific coating of the erythrocyte surface has been observed with the cephalosporin antibiotics. Cephalothins become bound to the erythrocyte membrane and cause the RBC to be coated by many plasma proteins. The Coombs test result is positive. Hemolytic anemia does not occur. Cephalothin can cause hemolytic anemia by acting as a hapten, however, by a mechanism similar to that of penicillin.

QUINIDINE TYPE. The quinidine type of autoimmune hemolytic anemia usually occurs with quinidine, but it has been reported with quinine, stibophen, chlorpromazine, and sulfonamides. Commonly called an *innocent-bystander reaction*, it is thought to be due to an antibody that is directed against quinidine or its derivatives and that has a low affinity for the RBC surface. Presumably the drug binds weakly to cell glycoprotein. The antibody recognizes the complex, and this interaction results in activation of the classic complement pathway and deposition of C3 on the erythrocyte surface. It is believed that the immune complex transiently adheres to the RBC surface, activates complement, then dissociates. With quinidine or its analogues, an IgM antibody seems to be involved. The diagnosis can be established in vitro by examining deposition of complement on donor erythrocytes by patient serum, which occurs only in the presence of the drug. The Coombs test is used to detect complement deposition on the erythrocyte surface.

In all these drug-induced processes, patients respond to withdrawal of the offending drug. If necessary, a brief course of glucocorticoid therapy can be administered.

INTRAVASCULAR HEMOLYSIS

Although intravascular hemolysis can occur with RBC abnormalities such as sickle cell disease (Chapter 171) or severe autoimmune hemolytic anemias, most intravascular hemolysis is caused by external damage to previously normal RBCs. The peripheral blood smear typically shows damaged, fragmented RBCs, which are variably described as schistocytes, burr cells, or helmet cells after they are injured and deformed.

Pathogenesis and Clinical Syndromes

HEMOLYSIS RELATED TO ABNORMALITIES OF THE HEART AND LARGE VESSELS

Mechanical hemolysis secondary to a prosthetic heart valve (Chapter 72) is a classic example in which intrinsically normal RBCs are injured during their circulation through the heart or large vessels (Table 169–2). As in microangiopathic hemolytic anemias, the generation of fragmented RBCs or schistocytes (Fig. 169–2) is a hallmark

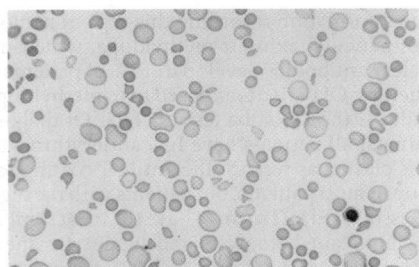

FIGURE 169–2 • Microangiopathic hemolytic anemia. Peripheral smear shows fragmental red blood cells or schistocytes in a variety of shapes and sizes.

Table 169–2 • CAUSES OF INTRAVASCULAR HEMOLYSIS
Prosthetic materials
Heart valves
Ventricular or atrial septal patches
Left ventricular assist devices
Vascular grafts
Transjugular intrahepatic portosystemic shunts
Thrombotic thrombocytopenic purpura
Hemolytic uremic syndrome
Disseminated intravascular coagulation
Disseminated carcinomatosis
Chemotherapy (e.g., mitomycin C)
Solid organ transplantation
Bone marrow transplantation
Malignant hypertension
Scleroderma
Systemic lupus erythematosus
Eclampsia, preeclampsia, HELLP syndrome
Trauma to small vessels (e.g., exercise-related)
Burn-related
Venoms
Bacterial infection (e.g., clostridia)
Copper

of the disorder. The hemolysis is typically intravascular, resulting in hemoglobinuria and hemosiderinuria. If persistent, the urinary loss of iron can cause iron deficiency. Significant hemolytic anemia is less common with modern prosthetic valves, but a low level of hemolysis still can be detected in many patients. Valves in the aortic position are involved more often than mitral valves, presumably because RBCs are subjected to a higher velocity and to a higher shear stress through the aortic rather than through the mitral opening. Bioprostheses are less likely to cause hemolysis. Valve dysfunction or defects such as paravalvular leaks can worsen the RBC fragmentation significantly and always should be excluded. Valve replacement or repair should be strongly considered if mechanical dysfunction is found in patients with severe anemia. The treatment is otherwise supportive, including folic acid supplementation, iron therapy if prolonged hemosiderinuria has occurred, and transfusions if needed. Because an increased cardiac output is known to worsen the hemolysis, rest is recommended in severe cases.

Other intravascular devices also can cause hemolysis. Examples include synthetic patches used to close ventricular or atrial septal defects, left ventricular assist devices, vascular grafts, and transjugular intrahepatic portosystemic shunts. Less frequently, RBC fragmentation also can be observed in the absence of prosthetic material (e.g., in valvular or congenital heart disease).

MICROANGIOPATHIC HEMOLYTIC ANEMIAS

Thrombotic thrombocytopenic purpura and hemolytic uremic syndrome (Chapter 177) are part of a spectrum of disorders characterized by microangiopathic hemolytic anemia. Microangiopathic hemolytic anemia also occurs in malignancies, often with advanced disseminated disease. The pathogenesis is thought to involve microvascular abnormalities related to the tumor, perhaps as a result of direct invasion by tumor cells. Certain chemotherapeutic agents, such as mitomycin C (Chapter 191), also can trigger microangiopathic hemolytic anemia, most likely by direct toxicity to the endothelium. Plasma infusion or exchange is tried sometimes but usually is not helpful. Treatment of the malignancy, if possible, is usually the only available therapy.

Microangiopathic hemolytic anemia also can occur after solid organ and bone marrow transplantation. Calcineurin inhibitors such as cyclosporine and FK-506 (tacrolimus) are potential triggers. In bone marrow transplantation, endothelial injury from the conditioning regimen is thought to play an important role. Treatment usually involves withdrawal of the offending agent, supportive care, and a trial of plasma exchange therapy. Human immunodeficiency virus infection also can cause microangiopathic hemolytic anemia, with clinical features resembling classic thrombotic thrombocytopenic purpura (Chapter 419); plasma exchange is the treatment of choice. Thrombotic microangiopathies also occur with increased frequency during pregnancy and the postpartum period (Chapter 253), when preeclampsia/eclampsia and the HELLP syndrome (*hemolysis, ele-*

vated *liver* enzymes, *low* platelets) occur and may mimic thrombotic thrombocytopenic purpura. Microangiopathic hemolytic anemia also occurs in patients with malignant hypertension (Chapter 63), patients with scleroderma (Chapter 281), and sometimes patients with systemic lupus erythematosus (Chapter 280). It is less common with other glomerular diseases.

HEMOLYSIS CAUSED BY OTHER DIRECT PHYSICAL OR CHEMICAL INJURY TO THE RED BLOOD CELLS

Mechanical destruction of the RBCs occurs with long-distance running or prolonged strenuous exercise (e.g., exertional hemolysis or march hemoglobinuria). The RBC destruction is thought to occur as a result of direct trauma to the small vessels of the feet.

Hemolytic anemia also has been reported in victims of extensive burns (Chapter 108), presumably from direct thermal injury to the erythrocytes. The acute hemolysis typically occurs within 24 to 48 hours after the burn. The most heat-damaged RBCs undergo intravascular hemolysis, whereas other erythrocytes acquire major membrane alterations and are removed by tissue macrophages, predominantly in the spleen. Less frequent causes of heat injury include accidental overheating of blood transfusions or of dialysis material.

Some insect, spider, or snake bites (Chapters 406 through 408) cause acute intravascular hemolysis as a result of direct injury to the RBCs by toxins or in the setting of disseminated intravascular coagulation. Infection with clostridial sepsis (Chapter 318) releases bacterial enzymes with a phospholipase activity that damages the erythrocyte membrane; the resulting hemolysis can be acute and profound.

A variety of chemicals cause hemolytic anemia by toxic nonoxidant mechanisms. Acute copper intoxication and Wilson's disease (Chapter 224) cause direct toxicity to the RBC, either by interference with RBC metabolism or by damage to the RBC on membranes. In patients who survive freshwater near-drowning (Chapter 90) or are exposed to hypotonic fluids (e.g., during prostate surgery), RBCs may lyse owing to osmotic forces.

Clinical Manifestations

Intravascular hemolysis may present as anemia, elevation of the unconjugated bilirubin level, or jaundice. The lactate dehydrogenase level typically is elevated and correlates with the severity of the hemolysis. A low serum haptoglobin level confirms intravascular hemolysis. The peripheral blood smear typically shows fragmented RBCs and spherocytes (see Fig. 169–2). Hemoglobinuria is found during periods of active hemolysis, and chronic intravascular hemolysis can cause hemosiderinuria. If the bone marrow is not involved with tumor, and if the patient is not deficient in iron or folate, the reticulocyte count is elevated as the patient attempts to compensate for the hemolytic anemia.

Because microangiopathic hemolytic anemias can be associated with disseminated intravascular coagulation, thrombotic thrombocytopenic purpura, or the hemolytic uremic syndrome, evaluation of the patient with intravascular hemolysis should include a platelet count, prothrombin time, partial thromboplastin time, fibrinogen level, and other tests to exclude these diagnoses (Chapters 177 and 179). Pernicious anemia (Chapter 175) is associated with ineffective erythropoiesis and can present with many findings similar to intravascular hemolysis; however, patients with pernicious anemia commonly have hypersegmented granulocytes and a low reticulocyte count.

Rx Treatment

The treatment of intravascular hemolysis must focus on addressing any precipitating conditions, which also determine the ultimate prognosis. As with any form of serious hemolysis, folate supplementation is recommended. For patients with chronic intravascular hemolysis, such as found with prosthetic heart valves, urinary iron losses may be sufficient to require oral iron supplementation. In patients with tumor-associated intravascular hemolysis, thrombotic complications are common and may require long-term anticoagulation (Chapter 188).

SUGGESTED READINGS

Rosse WF, Nishimura J: Clinical manifestations of paroxysmal nocturnal hemoglobinuria: Present state and future problems. Int J Hematol 2003;77:113–120. *A comprehensive review.*

Schreiber AD: Autoimmune hemolytic anemia. *In* Samter M, Austen KF, Frank MM, et al (eds): Immunological Diseases, 6th ed. Philadelphia, Lippincott Williams & Wilkins, 2001, pp 738–749. *An in-depth review of autoimmune hemolytic anemia.*

170 HEMOLYTIC ANEMIAS: RED CELL MEMBRANE AND METABOLIC DEFECTS

David E. Golan

NORMAL RED CELL MEMBRANE

Structure

MEMBRANE LIPIDS. The red cell membrane, which was the first biologic membrane to be characterized biochemically, consists of an asymmetrically organized lipid bilayer in which some membrane proteins are embedded and to which other membrane proteins are attached. The lipids consist principally of a mixture of phospholipids and unesterified cholesterol in an approximately 1:1 molar ratio. The cholesterol is randomly distributed between the inner and outer leaflets of the bilayer, but the phospholipids are asymmetrically arranged such that the amino phospholipids (phosphatidylserine and phosphatidylethanolamine) and phosphatidylinositols are localized mainly in the inner leaflet whereas the choline phospholipids (phosphatidylcholine and sphingomyelin) are mainly in the outer leaflet. This phospholipid asymmetry is maintained by the action of a selective amino phospholipid translocase, or "flippase," that uses the energy of adenosine triphosphate (ATP) hydrolysis to translocate phosphatidylserine and phosphatidylethanolamine vectorially from the outer to the inner bilayer leaflet. The action of the translocase is functionally important because exposure of phosphatidylserine and phosphatidylethanolamine at the outer surface of the circulating red cell not only activates the coagulation pathways but also promotes mononuclear phagocyte adhesion, which leads to hemolysis. Red cell membrane lipids appear to exchange freely with those in plasma lipoproteins.

MEMBRANE PROTEINS. Like membrane phospholipids, red cell membrane proteins are asymmetrically arranged to optimize membrane structure and function (Fig. 170–1). The major integral membrane proteins, which penetrate and/or span the lipid bilayer and are commonly decorated with carbohydrate on their extracellular surfaces, include functionally important transport proteins such as band 3 (the anion-exchange protein) and proteins that carry cell-surface antigens such as the glycophorins. The major peripheral membrane proteins, which do not penetrate the lipid bilayer but are instead attached to the intracellular surface of the bilayer by virtue of binding interactions with one or more integral proteins, include structural proteins such as spectrin and actin and some glycolytic enzymes such as glyceraldehyde-3-phosphate dehydrogenase.

The structural proteins are organized into a dense, two-dimensional fibrous meshwork that laminates the inner membrane surface but does not extend into the cytoplasm of the cell. The principal components of this meshwork are spectrin, actin, and protein 4.1. Spectrin is a long, flexible, rod-shaped heterodimer consisting of an α- and a β-chain that wrap around one another. These heterodimers associate with one another to form spectrin heterotetramers (and a few higher-order oligomers) at the "head" (self-association) end of the heterodimers and with short filaments of actin at the "tail" end of the heterodimers. The spectrin-actin binding interaction is strengthened by protein 4.1, which binds to both actin and the spectrin β-chain. Because each actin filament can accommodate the binding of about six spectrin heterodimers (this assembly is sometimes called the "junctional complex"), the spectrin-actin-protein 4.1 complex can extend as a two-dimensional "membrane skeleton" around the entire inner membrane surface.

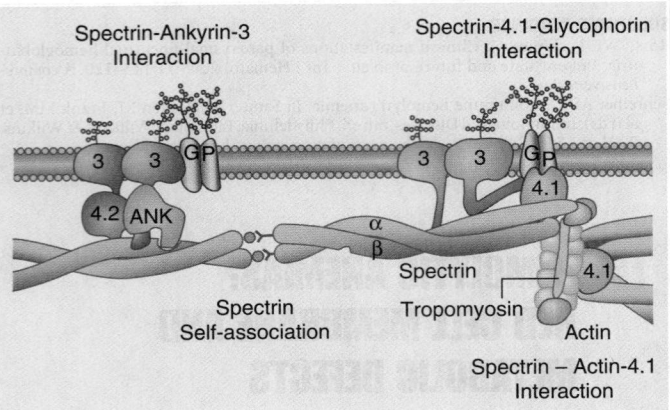

FIGURE 170–1 • Molecular binding interactions among the major proteins of the red cell membrane. 3 = Band 3; 4.1 = protein 4.1; 4.2 = protein 4.2; ANK = ankyrin; GP = glycophorins.

The membrane skeleton is coupled to the overlying lipid bilayer by the action of several "linking" proteins. The most important linking action is provided by ankyrin, which binds to the spectrin β-chain near the self-association site and to the cytoplasmic domain of the integral protein band 3. Protein 4.2 may play a role in strengthening the spectrin-ankyrin interaction. Other linking mechanisms, the importance of which was demonstrated by the existence of intact (albeit abnormal) red cells in mammalian species that are completely lacking in band 3 protein, include binding interactions between protein 4.1 and glycophorins (especially glycophorin C) and interactions between skeletal proteins (especially spectrin) and inner leaflet membrane lipids.

Function

MEMBRANE STRENGTH AND DEFORMABILITY. The exquisite mechanical coupling between the membrane skeleton and the overlying lipid bilayer confers on the normal red cell its remarkable properties of strength and deformability. On release from the bone marrow, mature red cells must withstand the high pressure and shear forces in the heart and large arteries and also traverse the small-diameter microcirculatory vessels for 120 days. The ability of the skeleton-bilayer couple to withstand high shear and to deform readily allows normal red cells to perform these tasks. Abnormal red cells with defective membrane skeletons and/or defective coupling between the skeleton and the overlying bilayer fragment spontaneously in the circulation, which leads to the clinical picture of nonimmune hemolytic anemia.

CATION AND VOLUME HOMEOSTASIS. The red cell uses protein pumps and channels in its lipid bilayer membrane to control intracellular concentrations of sodium, potassium, and calcium ions and thereby regulate cell volume. Normal intracellular concentrations of Na^+, K^+, and Ca^{2+} are about 10 mmol/L, 100 mmol/L, and 100 nmol/L, respectively. The physiologically most important pumps include the ATP-dependent Na^+/K^+ exchanger, which uses the energy provided by ATP hydrolysis to pump Na^+ outward against its concentration gradient and K^+ inward against its concentration gradient, and the ATP-dependent Ca^{2+} pump, which pumps Ca^{2+} outward against its concentration gradient. The activities of these pumps counteract the small passive leaks of Na^+, K^+, and Ca^{2+} down their concentration gradients through the relatively impermeable lipid bilayer. Pathologic increases in the passive leak rates of these three cations—or decreases in the activities of these two pumps—can have deleterious effects. A net gain of intracellular cations obligates net water entry and causes cells to swell, whereas a net loss of intracellular cations dehydrates cells. The free flow of water molecules in both directions across the lipid bilayer is mediated by the aquaporin-1 water channel protein. An increase in intracellular Ca^{2+} concentration can be especially harmful by (1) activating a Ca^{2+}-dependent K^+ channel (the Gardos channel) that mediates K^+ efflux and cell dehydration and (2) at very high concentrations, activating a Ca^{2+}-dependent transglutaminase that cross-links membrane proteins and thereby (among other effects) decreases cell deformability.

CELL SHAPE. The biconcave disc shape of normal red cells is maintained by a balance of forces within the membrane skeleton and between the skeleton and the lipid bilayer. These forces are sufficiently robust to allow normal red cells to deform without fragmenting in the normal circulation. Alterations in membrane skeleton integrity, skeleton-bilayer coupling, intracellular cation and water content, transmembrane protein organization, and hemoglobin denaturation and polymerization can all affect red cell morphology. One major determinant of red cell shape is the ratio between the surface area and volume of the cell; decreases and increases in this ratio lead to the formation of sphere-shaped (spherocyte) and cup- (stomatocyte) or target-shaped red cells, respectively. Irreversible shape change can also be mediated by permanent deformation of the membrane skeleton; orderly plastic deformation causes the formation of elliptical or oval red cells (elliptocytes or ovalocytes), whereas random membrane injury with denatured hemoglobin precipitation on the skeleton and oxidative cross-linking of proteins leads to the formation of spiculated (echinocyte), irreversibly sickled, and other abnormal red cell forms.

ANION EXCHANGE. The red cell membrane plays an important physiologic role in carbon dioxide (CO_2) transport. CO_2 handling is facilitated by red cell enzyme-mediated conversion of this molecule to bicarbonate in the tissues and back to CO_2 for excretion in the lungs. To increase the HCO_3^- carrying capacity of the blood, some of the HCO_3^- is carried in the plasma. Movement of HCO_3^- in and out of red cells is facilitated by the presence of about 1 million anion-exchange proteins (the band 3 protein) in each red cell membrane. Band 3 mediates the passive bidirectional exchange of HCO_3^- for Cl^-; no energy is required for this process. Band 3 therefore serves at least two important roles in red cell membrane structure and function: coupling the membrane skeleton to the overlying lipid bilayer and mediating anion exchange across the membrane.

INTERACTIONS WITH THE SPLEEN: RED CELL SENESCENCE. Most normal red cells are removed from the circulation by the spleen after a 120-day lifespan. The fenestrations between splenic cords and sinuses provide mechanical stress as red cells squeeze through these openings, whereas the low-oxygen, low-glucose, low-pH environment of the splenic cords places metabolic stress on the cells. The spleen uses two major mechanisms to sequester and remove aged red cells. First, as red cells become less deformable with age, they are less able to traverse the splenic fenestrations. Second, as red cells age, their membranes are progressively decorated with autoantibodies and/or complement proteins that bind to receptors on mononuclear phagocytes in the spleen; these autoantibodies may be directed against clustered and/or proteolytically altered band 3 at the red cell surface.

RED CELL MEMBRANE DISORDERS

HEREDITARY SPHEROCYTOSIS

ETIOLOGY AND INCIDENCE. Hereditary spherocytosis is an inherited hemolytic anemia caused by a defect in one of the proteins that couples the red cell membrane skeleton to the overlying lipid bilayer. These proteins include spectrin (either the α- or the β-chain), ankyrin, band 3, and protein 4.2. Some mutations in these proteins have been identified, and others are the subject of current investigation. Many of the mutations defined to date are unique, thus indicating that no one mutation is common. Autosomal dominant, autosomal recessive, new mutations, and nonclassic patterns of inheritance have been observed; approximately 75% of families exhibit the autosomal dominant pattern. The incidence of hereditary spherocytosis is between 1:2000 and 1:5000 among northern European people, although the disease can occur in any population.

PATHOGENESIS. Molecular defects in spectrin, ankyrin, band 3, and protein 4.2 lead to spectrin deficiency as the "final common pathway" that characterizes all red cells with hereditary spherocytosis. This molecular phenotype results either from a primary deficiency of spectrin or, more commonly, from a deficiency of one of the proteins that allows spectrin to bind with high affinity to the overlying lipid bilayer. Spectrin deficiency appears to cause the spherocytic cellular phenotype by weakening "vertical" interactions between the membrane skeleton and the bilayer and thereby leading to "unsupported" areas of lipid that are spontaneously lost as red cells traverse the circulation. Spherocytic red cells are less able than normal cells to squeeze through the fenestrations between splenic cords and sinuses, and the

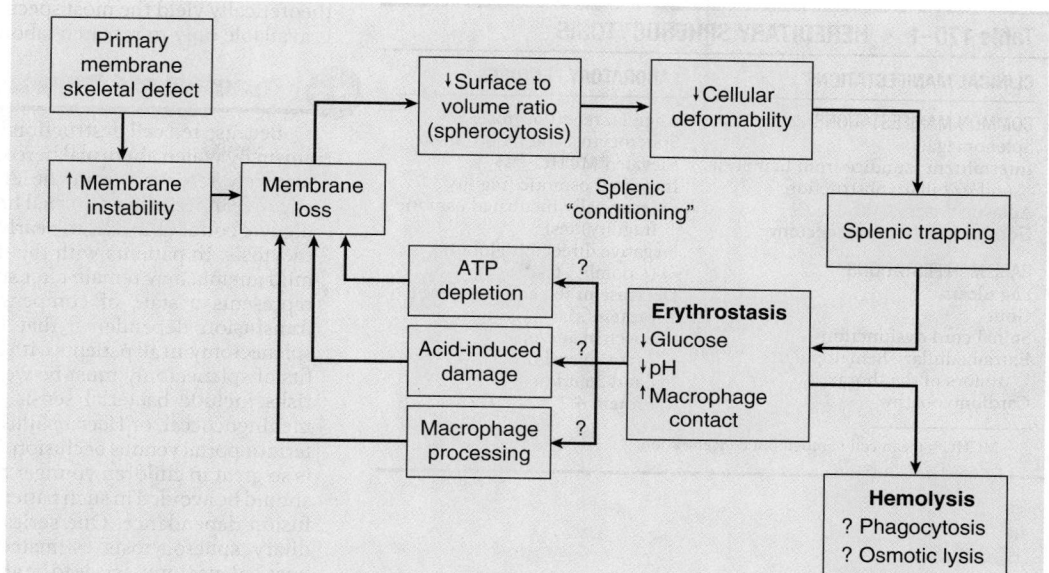

FIGURE 170–2 • Model of the pathophysiology of spherocytosis and hemolysis in hereditary spherocytosis.

increased metabolic stress placed on the cells in the environment of the cords leads to further membrane loss. Although some hyperchromic microspherocytes eventually escape back into the peripheral circulation, many of these cells are hemolyzed in the spleen (Fig. 170–2).

The discovery that spectrin deficiency is the sine qua non of hereditary spherocytic red cells led some to hypothesize that primary defects in spectrin would be found in most cases of hereditary spherocytosis. Surprisingly, mutations in α-spectrin (autosomal recessive hereditary spherocytosis) and β-spectrin (autosomal dominant hereditary spherocytosis) are each present in only about 10% of patients with hereditary spherocytosis. Instead, mutations in ankyrin (autosomal dominant and recessive hereditary spherocytosis; about 40 to 50% of cases) and band 3 (autosomal dominant hereditary spherocytosis; about 20% of cases) are much more common. Mutations in protein 4.2 (autosomal recessive hereditary spherocytosis) are relatively rare except in Japan, where a number of families have been described. The severity of hemolysis correlates with the cellular spectrin content in spherocytic red cells, providing strong evidence in support of the pathogenetic mechanisms described above.

Clinical Manifestations

GENERAL. The clinical manifestations of hereditary spherocytosis can vary from a clinically insignificant hemolytic state that is fully compensated by increased marrow erythropoiesis to a life-threatening hemolytic state that is dependent on red cell transfusion. This variation in clinical phenotype is a reflection of the variation in the molecular consequences of the mutations in spectrin, ankyrin, band 3, or protein 4.2, all of which result in weakened interaction between the membrane skeleton and the overlying lipid bilayer. In general, an autosomal recessive inheritance pattern is associated with clinically more severe disease, whereas an autosomal dominant pattern is associated with a milder phenotype. Although all cases of hereditary spherocytosis are present from birth, the diagnosis can be made at any age. Clinical manifestations common in hereditary spherocytosis include jaundice and splenomegaly (Table 170–1). Approximately 50% of neonates experience marked jaundice that may require exchange transfusion, and some infants may require periodic red cell transfusions to maintain an adequate hematocrit. The potential for erythropoietin therapy to obviate the need for red cell transfusions in neonates and infants with hereditary spherocytosis is under investigation. By several months of age, most patients with hereditary spherocytosis achieve a partially compensated hemolytic state characterized by mild to moderate anemia (hemoglobin, 9 to 11.5 g/dL), intermittent jaundice (exacerbated by viral infection), and splenomegaly. Even in patients with fully compensated hemolysis, states associated with splenic enlargement and/or increased splenic blood flow (e.g., infectious mononucleosis and, occasionally, intense physical activity) may provoke severe hemolysis and anemia. Previously compensated elderly patients with hereditary spherocytosis may experience more severe anemia with aging because of a decline in compensatory bone marrow activity.

COMPLICATIONS. Common clinical complications of hereditary spherocytosis include occasional crises and the formation of bilirubinate gallstones. Hemolytic crisis appears to be caused by the increased activity of the mononuclear phagocyte (reticuloendothelial) system associated with many infections; such crises are typified by a small decrease in the hematocrit that is not clinically significant. Aplastic crisis is most often associated with parvovirus B19 infection (Chapter 160); such crises may be clinically severe and require prompt red cell transfusion. Fortunately, infection with parvovirus B19 generally produces lifelong immunity, so most patients are subjected to no more than one such crisis in a lifetime. Megaloblastic crisis is caused by a relative lack of folic acid in the diet; because of the increased need for this vitamin during pregnancy, such crises are especially common in pregnant women. The increased generation of bilirubin associated with ongoing hemolysis leads to the formation of bilirubinate gallstones in most untreated teenagers and adults with hereditary spherocytosis. The incidence of this complication increases from about 5% in children 0 to 10 years old, to about 45% in patients aged 11 to 50 years, and to about 65% in older patients. Because a large fraction of bilirubinate gallstones are not radiopaque, abdominal ultrasonography is the most reliable imaging method to detect these stones.

Relatively rare clinical complications of hereditary spherocytosis in adults include gout, rashes and ulcers of the lower extremities, and extramedullary hematopoietic tumors of the thorax. The gout and lower extremity complications usually disappear after splenectomy (see later), but the tumors commonly undergo fatty change after splenectomy and therefore persist on routine chest film. Several families with hereditary spherocytosis and either spinocerebellar degeneration or cardiomyopathy have been described, perhaps suggesting a common genetic basis for these disorders in these families.

Table 170–1 • HEREDITARY SPHEROCYTOSIS

CLINICAL MANIFESTATIONS	LABORATORY FEATURES
COMMON MANIFESTATIONS Splenomegaly Intermittent jaundice from hemolysis and/or biliary obstruction Aplastic crises Good response to splenectomy	Anemia, reticulocytosis Spherocytosis on blood smear Elevated MCHC Increased osmotic fragility (especially incubated osmotic fragility) test Negative direct antiglobulin (Coombs) test
RARE MANIFESTATIONS Leg ulcers Gout Spinal cord dysfunction Extramedullary hematopoietic tumors of the thorax Cardiomyopathy	Decrease in red cell membrane protein(s): Spectrin and/or Ankyrin and/or Band 3 and/or Protein 4.2

MCHC = mean cell hemoglobin concentration.

Diagnosis

Laboratory features common to all cases of hereditary spherocytosis include an elevated reticulocyte count and the presence of spherocytes on the blood smear (Fig. 160–2). Patients with very mild disease may not be anemic or manifest hyperbilirubinemia, although many patients with hereditary spherocytosis do exhibit mild to moderate anemia and an elevated indirect bilirubin level. The differential diagnosis of spherocytosis includes a number of clinical entities (Table 170–2), but the most common other clinical state characterized by spherocytosis—autoimmune hemolytic anemia—can be readily distinguished from hereditary spherocytosis by the direct antiglobulin (Coombs) test. The laboratory test most commonly used to confirm the presence of spherocytosis is the osmotic fragility test, which measures the ability of red cells to withstand swelling in solutions of decreasing osmotic strength. Because spherocytes have a decreased ratio of surface area to volume, these cells are less able to swell in a hypotonic environment than normal discocytes are. Thus populations of red cells containing a significant proportion of spherocytes exhibit increased osmotic fragility when compared with normal red cell populations. In some cases of mild hereditary spherocytosis, however, neither striking spherocytosis on the blood smear nor an abnormal osmotic fragility test is apparent. The most reliable test in this situation is the incubated osmotic fragility test, in which red cells are metabolically stressed by incubation in the absence of glucose for 24 hours. Whereas normal red cells can withstand this treatment without significant membrane damage, hereditary spherocytic red cells shed bilayer lipids under these conditions and become less able to remain intact in a hypotonic environment. Finally, because hereditary spherocytic red cells tend to be dehydrated, an elevated mean cell hemoglobin concentration (MCHC) can be a helpful clue in the diagnosis of hereditary spherocytosis; even in patients with hereditary spherocytosis but no increase in MCHC, the presence of a subpopulation of dehydrated cells can usually be observed by using laboratory instruments that provide a histogram of MCHC values. Biochemical quantification of spectrin, ankyrin, band 3, and protein 4.2, which could

Table 170–2 • DISEASES CHARACTERIZED BY PROMINENT SPHEROCYTOSIS ON THE BLOOD SMEAR

COMMON
Hereditary spherocytosis
Autoimmune hemolytic anemia (warm antibody type)
ABO incompatibility (neonates)

UNCOMMON TO RARE
Hemolytic transfusion reaction
Clostridial sepsis
Severe burn
Spider, bee, and snake venom
Acute red cell oxidant injury
Severe hypophosphatemia
Bartonellosis

theoretically yield the most specific test for hereditary spherocytosis, is available only in research laboratories.

Treatment and Prognosis

Because red cell destruction in the spleen is the primary mechanism by which abnormal hereditary spherocytic red cells are prematurely removed from the circulation, splenectomy is highly effective in restoring a normal hematocrit and a near-normal reticulocyte count (1 to 3%) to nearly all patients with hereditary spherocytosis. In patients with the most severe form of the disease, a mild anemia may remain after splenectomy; however, this anemia represents a state of compensated hemolysis rather than the transfusion dependence that characterizes such patients presplenectomy. In all patients with hereditary spherocytosis, the benefits of splenectomy must be weighed against its risks. The major risks include bacterial sepsis, often caused by pneumococcal, meningococcal, or *Haemophilus influenzae* B bacteria, and mesenteric or portal venous occlusion. The risk of postsplenectomy sepsis is so great in children younger than 3 to 5 years that splenectomy should be avoided in such patients even with the necessity of transfusion dependence. One series of 226 adult patients with hereditary spherocytosis estimated the lifetime risk of fulminant post-splenectomy sepsis to be about 2%. After splenectomy, a small but significant increase in the risk of ischemic heart disease has also been reported.

Most hematologists recommend splenectomy for children with severe hereditary spherocytosis, defined as a hemoglobin concentration less than 8 g/dL and a reticulocyte count greater than 10%, and for children with moderate disease (hemoglobin, 8 to 11 g/dL; reticulocyte count, 8 to 10%) if the degree of anemia compromises physical activity. In adults with moderate hereditary spherocytosis, additional indications for splenectomy include a degree of anemia that compromises oxygen delivery to vital organs, the development of extramedullary hematopoietic tumors, and the occurrence of bilirubinate gallstones, which could predispose to cholecystitis and biliary obstruction. Splenectomy is generally deferred in patients with mild hereditary spherocytosis (hemoglobin greater than 11 g/dL; reticulocyte count less than 8%).

Several European groups have advocated the use of subtotal splenectomy as a compromise operation that ameliorates most of the extravascular hemolysis associated with splenic function while retaining some immune and phagocytic activity of the normal spleen. In 40 children treated with this operation, the success rate in relieving hemolysis over a 1- to 14-year follow-up period was adequate (although less than that achieved with total splenectomy), and the rate of complications has been low; however, data are currently too limited to recommend this procedure in the general hereditary spherocytosis population.

All patients undergoing splenectomy should receive polyvalent pneumococcal vaccine, preferably several weeks before the operation; children should also receive meningococcal and *H. influenzae* B vaccines. In the first several years after splenectomy, many patients are treated with prophylactic oral penicillin to protect against pneumococcal sepsis, although the emergence of penicillin-resistant pneumococci may force a change in this practice over the coming years. All patients with hereditary spherocytosis should be given 1 mg folate as a daily supplement to prevent megaloblastic crisis.

After splenectomy, the blood smear in patients with hereditary spherocytosis acquires several characteristic alterations. Howell-Jolly bodies, acanthocytes, target cells, and siderocytes normally mark red cells for removal by the spleen, but such cells now remain in the circulation. Although spherocytes are still present, the microspherocytes formed by splenic conditioning disappear. Failure of splenectomy to ameliorate the degree of hemolysis in hereditary spherocytosis, either immediately after the operation or many years later, is often due to the presence of an accessory spleen. The presence of this structure, which is found in about 15 to 20% of patients with hereditary spherocytosis, can be revealed by the disappearance of Howell-Jolly bodies from the blood smear and/or by laboratory abnormalities associated with hemolysis such as an increased reticulocyte count. The radionuclide liver-spleen scan can be a useful imaging modality when searching for an accessory spleen.

HEREDITARY ELLIPTOCYTOSIS

Etiology and Incidence

Hereditary elliptocytosis comprises a family of inherited hemolytic anemias caused primarily by defects in one or more of the proteins that make up the two-dimensional membrane skeletal network. The four clinical phenotypes of hereditary elliptocytosis appear to be caused by different sets of molecular defects. Mild hereditary elliptocytosis and hereditary pyropoikilocytosis arise most often from α- and/or β-spectrin chain defects that affect the ability of spectrin heterodimers to self-associate and from protein 4.1 defects that affect the strength of binding in the ternary spectrin-actin-protein 4.1 complex. Spherocytic hereditary elliptocytosis can be caused by defects in the β-chain of spectrin that may affect spectrin-ankyrin binding as well as spectrin self-association; other mutations are the subject of current investigation. In general, mild hereditary elliptocytosis and spherocytic hereditary elliptocytosis are inherited as autosomal dominant traits, and hereditary pyropoikilocytosis is inherited in an autosomal recessive pattern. The incidence of mild hereditary elliptocytosis is about 1 : 2500 among northern Europeans and as common as 1 : 150 in some areas of Africa, although the disease can occur in any population. Hereditary pyropoikilocytosis and spherocytic hereditary elliptocytosis are considerably more rare. Southeast Asian ovalocytosis (SAO) is caused by a specific deletion in band 3 that allows the mutant protein to form linear aggregates in the plane of the lipid bilayer. The incidence of this autosomal dominant disorder is as common as 1 : 3 among some lowland aboriginal populations of Indonesia, Malaysia, Melanesia, and the Philippines, although SAO is rare in other areas of the world.

Pathogenesis

In mild hereditary elliptocytosis, a molecular defect near the "head" region of the spectrin heterodimer (i.e., a mutation near the N terminus of α-spectrin or the C terminus of β-spectrin) leads to weakening of the "horizontal" interactions that give the red cell membrane skeleton its properties of strength and deformability. Heterozygous deficiency of protein 4.1—or a mutation that prevents formation of the spectrin-actin-protein 4.1 ternary complex at the "tail" region of the spectrin heterodimer—has a similar mechanical effect. In both cases, red cells are released from the bone marrow with a normal discocytic shape, but the membrane skeletons (and consequently, the red cells themselves) undergo plastic deformation to a permanent elliptocytic shape as the cells traverse the microcirculation. Because the "vertical" interactions that couple the membrane skeleton to the overlying lipid bilayer remain intact in these cells, membrane loss does not occur, and the cells may have a relatively normal lifetime in the circulation. Hereditary pyropoikilocytosis, in contrast, results from either a homozygous or a compound heterozygous defect in spectrin (typically, α-spectrin) or protein 4.1. In addition to the defects described above, coinheritance of an α-spectrin mutation with the spectrin α^{LELY} polymorphism can cause the hereditary pyropoikilocytosis phenotype. In spectrin α^{LELY}, α-spectrin mRNA splicing is altered such that the resulting protein chains lose the ability to pair with β-spectrin. Because α-spectrin is synthesized in excess of β-spectrin in normal erythropoiesis, the spectrin α^{LELY} polymorphism is silent by itself. When paired in *trans* with an α-spectrin coding region mutation, however, the polymorphism causes the majority of spectrin heterodimers at the membrane to carry the hereditary elliptocytosis defect, which leads to the much more severe hereditary pyropoikilocytosis phenotype.

In spherocytic hereditary elliptocytosis, the molecular defect in the spectrin β-chain appears to affect both "horizontal" interactions at the spectrin self-association site and "vertical" interactions at the spectrin-ankyrin binding site. This combined defect results in features of both hereditary elliptocytosis (because of the "horizontal" interaction defect) and hereditary spherocytosis (because of the "vertical" interaction defect). The linear aggregates of mutant band 3 protein in SAO red cells are thought to cause extreme rigidification of the membrane by preventing the local expansions and contractions of the membrane skeletal network that are responsible for membrane deformability. Membrane rigidity is likely to be the mechanism by which SAO red cells resist invasion by malaria parasites, which accounts for the high prevalence of this variant in certain areas of Southeast Asia. Interestingly, unlike the nondeformable spherocytes found in hereditary spherocytosis and autoimmune hemolytic anemias, the rigid SAO red cells are not removed prematurely from the circulation. The mechanisms by which SAO cells survive normally in the circulation remain to be elucidated. The SAO mutation must have some deleterious effect on red cell membrane structure and function, however, because the homozygous state appears to be lethal.

Clinical Manifestations and Diagnosis

The great majority of individuals with mild hereditary elliptocytosis are heterozygous carriers of a dominantly inherited molecular and cellular defect that is clinically insignificant. These individuals have no anemia, little or no hemolysis (reticulocyte count, 1 to 3%), and no splenomegaly. Diagnosis is based on the presence of prominent elliptocytosis (often greater than 40%) on the blood smear (Fig. 161–9), a normal osmotic fragility test, and a positive family pedigree. Individuals who inherit a mild α-spectrin defect in *trans* with spectrin α^{LELY} may exhibit mild chronic hemolysis and some fragmented red cells on the blood smear. Mild hereditary elliptocytosis can be associated with significant hemolysis in patients in whom splenic enlargement develops from, for example, viral infection or portal hypertension. Neonates with mild hereditary elliptocytosis often exhibit a syndrome, called transient infantile poikilocytosis, characterized by a moderately severe hemolytic anemia for the initial 6 to 12 months of life. The increased hemolysis in the neonatal and early infant period appears to result from the increase in intracellular 2,3-diphosphoglycerate (2,3-DPG) concentration that is present in fetal red cells. Elevated levels of this normal metabolite weaken the ternary spectrin-actin-protein 4.1 binding interaction and thereby exacerbate the spectrin self-association defect caused by the mild hereditary elliptocytosis mutation. As fetal red cells are lost from the circulation, the intracellular 2,3-DPG concentration falls and the clinical condition spontaneously reverts to that of mild hereditary elliptocytosis.

Hereditary pyropoikilocytosis is a recessively inherited disorder that is clinically manifested by a severe (sometimes life-threatening) hemolytic anemia in which the blood smear contains bizarre poikilocytes and red cell fragments. The mean cell volume is markedly decreased (45 to 75 fL), and because spectrin deficiency and spherocytosis are often secondary consequences of the combined molecular defects, osmotic fragility is increased. The name is derived from the property of hereditary pyropoikilocytosis red cells to fragment at 45 to 46° C rather than the normal 49° C; this abnormal heat sensitivity is most often due to a lowering of the temperature at which the mutant spectrin chains denature. As implied by the name, spherocytic hereditary elliptocytosis has clinical and diagnostic features of both hereditary spherocytosis and mild hereditary elliptocytosis. Patients manifest mild to moderate hemolytic anemia with splenomegaly and intermittent jaundice, the blood smear contains rounded elliptocytes and sometimes spherocytes, and osmotic fragility is increased. In contrast, individuals with the SAO mutation are clinically normal, with little to no anemia or hemolysis; the blood smear shows characteristic rounded elliptocytes that often exhibit a transverse bar dividing the central clear area.

 ## Treatment and Prognosis

Mild hereditary elliptocytosis and SAO are clinically insignificant variants that require no treatment and have no effect on life-span (other than the beneficial protection against malaria afforded to SAO individuals). Spherocytic hereditary elliptocytosis should be treated like hereditary spherocytosis, with the considerations for and against splenectomy as noted above. Virtually all patients with hereditary pyropoikilocytosis require splenectomy, which ameliorates but does not completely cure the hemolytic anemia. As in treating patients with moderate to severe hereditary spherocytosis, it is important to defer splenectomy until 3 to 5 years of age if possible, especially because of the possibility that a severe poikilocytic anemia in the neonatal and infant period could represent transient infantile poikilocytosis rather than true hereditary pyropoikilocytosis.

HEREDITARY DEFECTS IN MEMBRANE PERMEABILITY

HEREDITARY XEROCYTOSIS. The hallmark of this rare autosomal dominant disorder is an alteration in red cell membrane cation permeability that leads to a net loss of intracellular cations and water and to cell dehydration. The molecular defect responsible for this phenotype remains to be elucidated. The dehydrated red cells appear on the blood smear as target cells and/or spiculated acanthocytes, and the increased MCHC leads to relatively nondeformable cells that can be sequestered and removed by the spleen. The differential diagnosis of dehydrated red cells also includes the much more common sickle cell syndromes, hereditary spherocytosis, and hemoglobin C disease. Splenectomy is contraindicated in patients with hereditary xerocytosis because of the high risk of postprocedure thrombosis.

HEREDITARY STOMATOCYTOSIS. This rare autosomal dominant disorder appears to be due to an inherited defect in Na^+ permeability that leads to a net influx of Na^+ and water and to cell swelling. Several molecular defects are probably responsible for this phenotype because some families with this disorder experience severe hemolytic anemia, whereas others have clinically mild disease. The swollen red cells appear on the blood smear to have a "mouth"-like invagination in the membrane and are therefore called stomatocytes. The differential diagnosis of stomatocytosis also includes the much more common acquired effects of acute alcoholism and/or liver disease. Patients with the severe form of hereditary stomatocytosis often respond well to splenectomy, but some patients have developed severe hypercoagulability and catastrophic thrombosis after splenectomy.

NORMAL RED CELL METABOLISM

Glycolysis

Normal mature red cells have lost the cellular machinery responsible for oxidative phosphorylation, and the metabolism in these cells is almost entirely anaerobic. The major red cell energy source is glucose, which is metabolized primarily by the glycolytic pathway (also called the Embden-Meyerhof pathway) and secondarily by the pentose phosphate pathway (also called the hexose monophosphate shunt) (Fig. 170–3). The glycolytic pathway converts 90 to 95% of the metabolized glucose in red cells to lactate, in the process generating 2 mol of ATP per mol of glucose consumed. Although this rate of ATP generation is inefficient when compared with that provided in other cells by the tricarboxylic acid cycle, it is sufficient in normal red cells to renew 150 to 200% of the total red cell ATP per hour. ATP is an essential energy source that is used to maintain homeostasis by cation pumps and channels, by protein kinases, and by enzymes that regulate glycolysis, glutathione synthesis, and nucleotide salvage in red cells. Two important metabolic cofactors generated in the glycolytic pathway are reduced nicotinamide adenine dinucleotide (NADH) and 2,3-DPG. NADH is an essential cofactor for the enzyme methemoglobin reductase, which maintains heme iron in the ferrous (Fe^{2+}) state, necessary for the ligation of molecular oxygen by hemoglobin. 2,3-DPG, generated by the Rapoport-Luebering shunt, regulates the affinity of hemoglobin for oxygen and thereby increases oxygen delivery to tissues.

Pentose Phosphate Pathway and Glutathione Metabolism

The pentose phosphate pathway handles 5 to 10% of metabolized glucose in normal red cells, in the process generating 2 mol of reduced nicotinamide adenine dinucleotide phosphate (NADPH) for each mol of glucose metabolized. NADPH is an essential cofactor for the enzyme glutathione reductase, which maintains glutathione in the reduced state necessary for detoxification of toxic oxygen products such as superoxide anion (O_2^-), hydrogen peroxide (H_2O_2), and hydroxyl radical (OH·). Normal red cells are continually subjected to these products as a result of intracellular heme oxidation. In addition, certain drugs can markedly enhance oxidant generation by red cells, and many infections can induce oxidant generation by phagocytic cells in the circulation. In the absence of reduced glutathione, toxic oxygen products can damage red cell lipids and proteins and result in hemolysis. Under conditions of oxidative stress, the pentose phosphate pathway can increase in activity to use 50% or more of the available

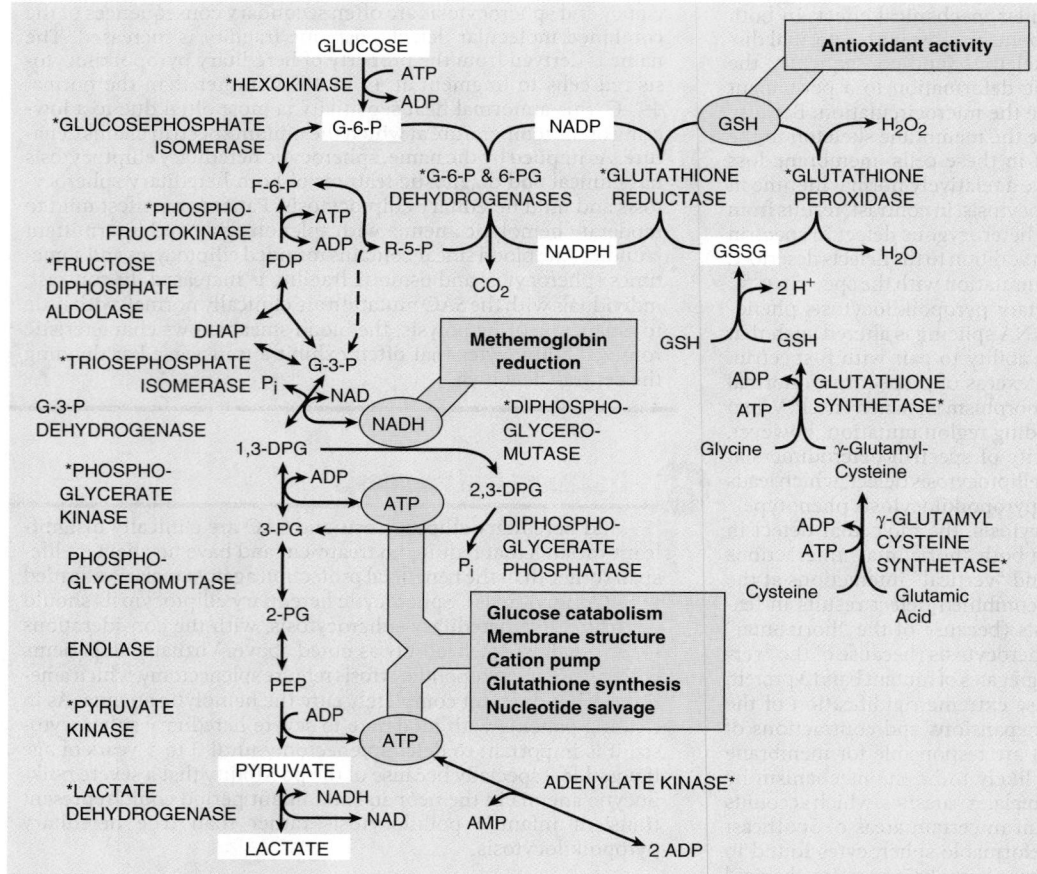

FIGURE 170–3 • Biochemical glycolysis, pentose phosphate, and glutathione pathways in human red cell metabolism. Asterisks denote enzymes that have been shown to be deficient in hereditary metabolic defects. ATP = adenosine triphosphate; ADP = adenosine diphosphate; G-6-P = glucose-6-phosphate; NADP = nicotinamide-adenine dinucleotide phosphate; GSH = reduced glutathione; 6-PG = 6-phosphogluconate; F-6-P = fructose-6-phosphate; FDP = fructose-1,6-diphosphate; R-5-P = ribose-5-phosphate; NADPH = reduced NADP; GSSG = oxidized glutathione; DHAP = dihydroxyacetone phosphate; G-3-P = glyceraldehyde-3-phosphate; 1,3-DPG = 1,3-diphosphoglycerate; 3-PG = 3-phosphoglycerate; PEP = phosphoenolpyruvate; AMP = adenosine monophosphate; NAD = nicotinamide-adenine dinucleotide; NADH: reduced NAD. (From Valentine WN: Hemolytic anemia and inborn errors of metabolism. Blood 1979;54:549.)

glucose. This increase in activity is stimulated by NADP and inhibited by NADPH, thereby tightly coupling intracellular antioxidant supply and demand.

Glutathione is a tripeptide that is synthesized in relatively high amounts (2 mmol/L steady-state concentration) from the amino acids cysteine, glutamic acid, and glycine by mature red cells. Two enzymes catalyze this synthetic pathway, and two other enzymes couple glutathione metabolism to NADPH oxidation (Fig. 170–3).

RED CELL METABOLISM DISORDERS

DEFECTS IN THE PENTOSE PHOSPHATE PATHWAY AND GLUTATHIONE METABOLISM

GLUCOSE-6-PHOSPHATE DEHYDROGENASE DEFICIENCY

Etiology and Incidence

Glucose-6-phosphate dehydrogenase (G6PD) deficiency, which is by far the most common enzyme defect associated with hereditary hemolytic anemia, affects hundreds of millions of individuals from all races around the world. More than 140 molecular G6PD variants have been described. The most common normal variants of the enzyme are called $G6PD^B$ or Gd^B, found in 99% of whites and about 70% of blacks, and Gd^{A+}, found in about 20% of blacks. The most common abnormal variants of the enzyme are called Gd^{A-}, found in about 10% of American blacks and a number of black African populations, and Gd^{Med}, found in Mediterranean (Arabs, Greeks, Italians, Sephardic Jews, and others), Indian, and Southeast Asian populations. Both Gd^{A-} and Gd^{Med} represent mutant enzymes that differ from the respective normal variants by a single amino acid. The prevalence of G6PD deficiency in African black, Mediterranean, Indian, and Southeast Asian populations is thought to derive from the relative protection afforded G6PD heterozygotes against *Plasmodium falciparum* malaria. Although the electrophoretic mobilities of the Gd^B and Gd^{Med} enzymes are identical, and those of the Gd^{A+} and Gd^{A-} isoforms are also identical, the overall catalytic activity of each abnormal variant is markedly less than that of the corresponding normal variant (see below).

Because the G6PD gene is located on the X chromosome, the inheritance pattern of G6PD deficiency is sex linked. Thus, whereas males have either a normal or an abnormal G6PD variant, females can exhibit either homozygous or heterozygous G6PD deficiency. Although relatively rare, homozygous G6PD deficiency in females is phenotypically identical to hemizygous deficiency in males. Even in female heterozygotes, each individual red cell is either normal or abnormal (i.e., there is no intermediate state) because only one X chromosome is active in each somatic cell (according to the Lyon hypothesis). The overall effect of G6PD deficiency in female heterozygotes may be mild, moderate, or severe, depending on the proportion of red cells in which the abnormal G6PD enzyme is expressed.

Pathogenesis

The primary metabolic consequence of G6PD deficiency is the diminished ability of the variant enzyme to generate sufficient NADPH to keep up with the requirement for reduced glutathione in a red cell population stressed by oxidizing agents. Depletion of cellular glutathione allows toxic oxygen products to damage red cell macromolecules, including hemoglobin, band 3, spectrin, membrane lipids, and other molecules. Oxidation of the heme iron of hemoglobin generates methemoglobin, which is incapable of ligating molecular oxygen. Oxidative denaturation of the globin chain produces intracellular hemoglobin precipitates called Heinz bodies that localize to the inner surface of the red cell membrane, probably through specific binding interactions between denatured hemoglobin and the cytoplasmic domain of band 3. Heinz bodies cause further oxidative damage to the membrane, manifested by clustering of band 3 proteins into large aggregates, which can be recognized by low-affinity autoantibodies and thereby targeted for removal by the mononuclear phagocyte system, and by increasing membrane cation permeability, which is accompanied by changes in cell hydration and deformability. Oxidative cross-linking of spectrin is likely to contribute to the decreased deformability of oxidatively stressed G6PD-deficient red cells, and peroxidation of membrane lipids may be a major contributing factor in the intravascular hemolysis that accompanies acute hemolytic episodes.

Normal and abnormal G6PD variants differ in both the stability and the catalytic activity of the various enzymes. Normal Gd^B and Gd^{A+} enzymes are slowly degraded over the lifetime of a normal red cell in vivo, such that intracellular G6PD activity falls to half its original value in about 60 days. This slow decline in enzyme activity over time is clinically inconsequential, because even the oldest normal red cells in the circulation retain sufficient G6PD activity to maintain intracellular reduced glutathione levels and to withstand nearly all oxidant stresses (Fig. 170–4). The catalytic activity of the Gd^{A-} variant is only mildly reduced when compared with the normal enzyme; the major defect in Gd^{A-} red cells is the more rapid degradation of Gd^{A-} in comparison with the normal enzyme, such that G6PD activity falls to half its original value in only 13 days. Thus young Gd^{A-} red cells are capable of withstanding oxidant stresses, whereas old Gd^{A-} red cells are not. This cellular heterogeneity allows a substantial fraction of Gd^{A-} red cells to survive even severe oxidant stress, and the acute hemolytic episode is therefore self-limited and usually not life-threatening. In contrast, both the catalytic activity and the stability of Gd^{Med} are much less than those of either the normal enzymes or Gd^{A-}; this feature renders nearly all Gd^{Med} red cells susceptible to oxidant-induced hemolysis and results in potentially life-threatening acute hemolytic episodes. Chronic ongoing hemolysis is not observed even in Gd^{Med} red cells in vivo, thus suggesting that endogenous oxidant activity must be low in the absence of oxidant stresses such as drugs and infections.

In a Gd^{A-} individual treated with an oxidant drug, the acute hemolytic episode occurs immediately after initiation of drug therapy, and is indicated by progressive anemia, hemoglobinuria, and reticulocytosis (Fig. 170–5); during this phase, the older red cells with low G6PD activity are hemolyzing. Despite continuation of the offending drug, however, the hemolysis spontaneously abates, red cell survival improves, and the hematocrit increases; during this phase, the bone marrow is compensating for the acute hemolytic episode by increasing its production of young Gd^{A-} red cells, which have sufficient G6PD activity to withstand the ongoing oxidant stress. Although the individual now appears to be resistant to drug-induced hemolysis, this "resistance" actually results from increased bone marrow erythropoiesis, which compensates for the ongoing hemolysis. The individual's continuing vulnerability to the effects of the drug is unmasked by withdrawing use of the drug for several months to allow the rate of red cell production by the bone marrow to fall to its original value;

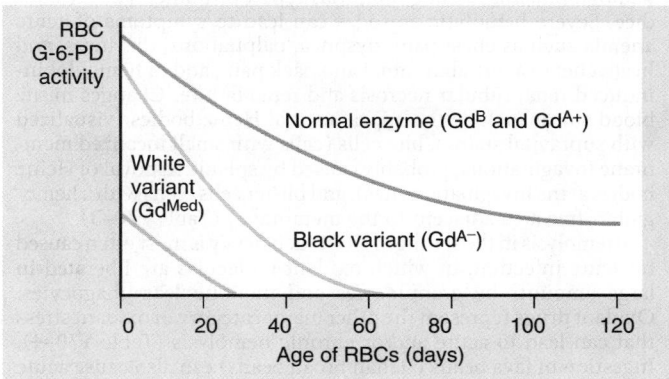

FIGURE 170–4 • Decline in red cell glucose-6-phosphate dehydrogenase (G6PD) activity as a function of cell age. Shown are curves for the normal Gd^B and Gd^{A+} enzymes and for the unstable Gd^{A-} and Gd^{Med} variants. Note that although the activity of the normal enzyme declines as red cells age, even the oldest cells have a sufficient level of activity to provide protection against oxidative damage and hemolysis. In contrast, very few Gd^{Med} red cells have sufficient enzyme activity to prevent such damage, whereas a substantial fraction of young Gd^{A-} red cells are so protected. Under oxidative stress, then, nearly all Gd^{Med} cells but only the oldest Gd^{A-} cells are susceptible to hemolysis. Assuming a normally functioning bone marrow, individuals with Gd^{A-} red cells can compensate by increasing the reticulocyte count and thereby populating the red cell pool with younger cells. In this way, G6PD screening assays may be falsely negative in Gd^{A-} males immediately after a hemolytic episode. (Adapted from Lux SE: Hemolytic anemias. Metabolic defects. *In* Beck WS [ed]: Hematology, 4th ed. Cambridge, MA, MIT Press, 1985, p 223.)

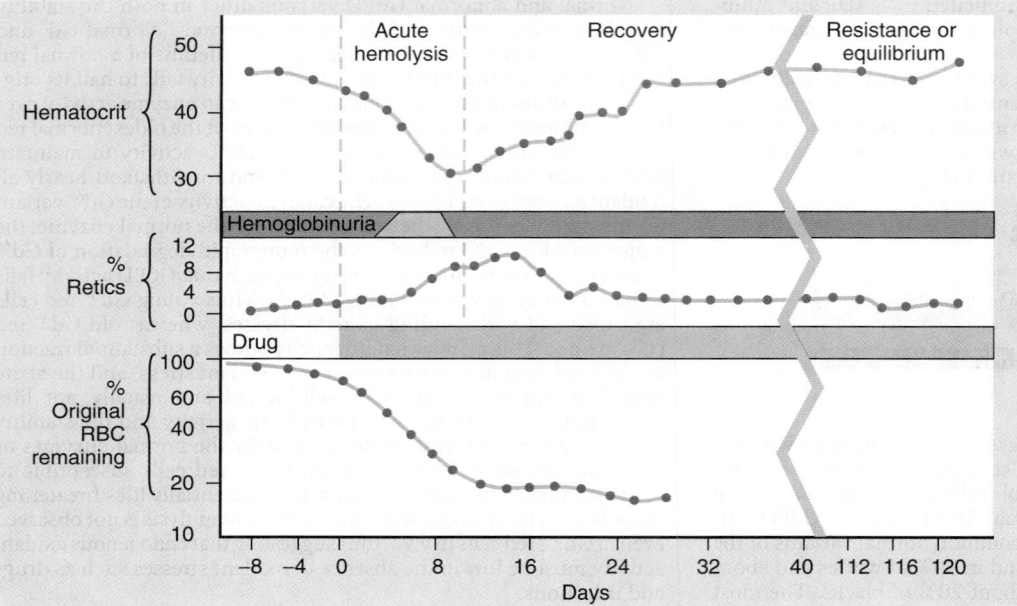

FIGURE 170–5 • Time course of primaquine-induced hemolysis in an individual with Gd^{A-} glucose-6-phosphate dehydrogenase (G6PD) deficiency. Drug was administered from day 0 through day 120. Note that hemolytic anemia, hemoglobinuria, and reticulocytosis develop shortly after starting the drug, but that red cell survival stabilizes and hemolysis abates shortly thereafter because of repopulation of the red cell pool with young cells that have sufficient G6PD activity to protect against oxidative damage and hemolysis. (Modified from Alving AS: Bull World Health Organ 1960;22:621.)

during this phase, the older red cells are again allowed to survive, and the red cell population is again rendered sensitive to drug-induced hemolysis.

Clinical Manifestations

Except in a few rare cases (see later), the clinical manifestations of G6PD deficiency occur only under conditions of oxidant stress. In the absence of such stress, individuals with the Gd^{A-} and Gd^{Med} variants have a normal blood smear and no hemolysis. In the presence of such stress, individuals with G6PD deficiency manifest hemolysis that can range from a chronic low-level hemolytic state, with a modest (3 to 4 g/dL) decrease in hemoglobin concentration and a modest increase in the reticulocyte count, to an acute episode of intravascular hemolysis characterized by anemia, hemoglobinemia, hemoglobinuria, hyperbilirubinemia, and jaundice. Severe hemolytic episodes can lead to symptoms of acute anemia such as chest pain, dyspnea, palpitations, dizziness, and headache; to acute abdominal and back pain; and to hemoglobin-induced renal tubular necrosis and renal failure. Changes in the blood smear include the appearance of Heinz bodies (visualized with supravital stains), bite cells (cells with small localized membrane invaginations, probably caused by splenic removal of Heinz bodies at the invagination sites), and blister cells (cells with a hemoglobin-free area adjacent to the membrane) (Table 170–3).

Hemolysis in the setting of G6PD deficiency is most often caused by acute infection, in which oxidant molecules are liberated in large amounts by granulocytes and mononuclear phagocytes. Oxidant drugs represent the other major category of oxidant stress that can lead to acute and/or chronic hemolysis (Table 170–4). Ingestion of fava beans (Italian broad beans) can also cause acute hemolysis in some patients with Gd^{Med}, probably because of the presence of high levels of oxidant pyrimidine analogues in the beans. Many neonates with G6PD deficiency manifest jaundice at 1 to 4 days of age; although this complication can occasionally require exchange transfusion, it is usually managed successfully with phototherapy. A few rare patients with extremely unstable and/or low-activity G6PD variants have chronic ongoing hemolysis in the absence of oxidant stress.

Diagnosis

The most widely used screening tests for G6PD deficiency rely on a change in NADPH-induced dye decolorization or in methylene blue-mediated methemoglobin reduction to detect a decrease in enzyme activity. These tests suffer from low sensitivity, however, because 30

Table 170–3 • COMMON FORMS OF ABNORMAL GLUCOSE-6-PHOSPHATE DEHYDROGENASE (G6PD)

FEATURE	GD^{A-}	GD^{Med}
Frequency	Common in African populations	Common in Mediterranean populations
Chronic hemolysis	None	None
Degree of acute hemolysis	Moderate	Severe
Abnormal G6PD activity	Old red cells	All red cells
Hemolysis with		
Drugs	Unusual	Common
Infection	Common	Common
Need for transfusions	Rare	Sometimes

to 40% of the cells in the sample must be deficient for the abnormal state to be detected and most if not all of the deficient cells may be hemolyzed (especially in Gd^{A-} individuals) following an acute oxidant stress. More sensitive than these screening tests is the specific enzyme assay, which relies on a direct measurement of NADPH generation; however, even this assay requires that 20 to 30% of the cells be deficient to yield an abnormal result, although careful comparison between the activity of G6PD and that of other age-dependent enzymes in the sample may allow the diagnosis to be made immediately after an acute hemolytic episode. The most sensitive test for G6PD deficiency is the G6PD-tetrazolium cytochemical test, which requires that only 1 to 5% of the cells be deficient to discriminate an abnormal result; this test is capable of not only making the diagnosis after a hemolytic episode but also detecting the enzyme deficiency in female heterozygotes.

Rx Treatment and Prognosis

Because all but a few rare individuals with G6PD deficiency are hematologically normal in the absence of an exogenous oxidant stress, no treatment is required for the deficiency itself. Mild to moderate episodes of acute hemolysis can often be managed by removal of the offending drug or by treatment of the concurrent infection. Severe hemolytic episodes in individuals with Gd^{Med} and other unstable G6PD variants may require red cell transfusions to alleviate the signs and symptoms of acute anemia, as well as measures designed to protect against the potential renal complications of hemoglobinuria.

Table 170–4 • DRUGS THAT COMMONLY CAUSE HEMOLYSIS IN GLUCOSE-6-PHOSPHATE DEHYDROGENASE (G6PD) DEFICIENCY*

SULFONAMIDES AND SULFONES
Sulfisoxazole (Gantrisin)
Trimethoprim-sulfamethoxazole (Septra)
Salicylazosulfapyridine (Azulfidine, sulfasalazine)
Sulfanilamide
Sulfapyridine
Sulfadimidine
Sulfacetamide (albucid)
Diaminodiphenylsulfone (dapsone)†
Sulfoxone†
Glucosulfone sodium (Promin)

OTHER ANTIBACTERIALS
Nitrofurans
 Nitrofurantoin (Furadantin)
 Nitrofurazone (Furacin)
 Furazolidone
Chloramphenicol
p-Aminosalicylic acid
Nalidixic acid‡

ANTIMALARIALS
Primaquine§
Pamaquine

ANTHELMINTICS
β-Naphthol
Stibophen
Niridazole

ANALGESICS‡‡
Acetylsalicylic acid (aspirin) (can give moderate doses)
Acetophenetidin (phenacetin)

MISCELLANEOUS
Probenecid
Vitamin K analogues (1 mg phytonadione can be given to infants)
Dimercaprol (BAL)
Mepacrine (quinacrine HCl)
Methylene blue
Toluidine blue
Naphthalene (mothballs)†

*Persons with all forms of G6PD deficiency should avoid the drugs listed in bold print; G6PD-deficient persons of Mediterranean, Middle Eastern, and Asian origin should avoid the drugs listed in bold and plain print.
†These drugs or chemicals may cause hemolysis in normal persons if given in large doses.
‡This drug applies only to individuals with GdA−.
§Persons with GdA− may take this drug at reduced dosage (15 mg/day or 45 mg twice weekly) under surveillance.
**Chloroquine may be used under surveillance when required for prophylaxis or treatment of malaria.
‡‡Acetaminophen (paracetamol) is a safe alternative.
Adapted from WHO Working Group: Glucose-6-phosphate dehydrogenase deficiency. Bull World Health Organ 1989;67:601–611.

DEFECTS IN GLUTATHIONE METABOLISM

Deficiencies in all of the enzymes responsible for glutathione synthesis and metabolism have been described (see Fig. 170–3). Red cells deficient in either γ-glutamylcysteine synthetase or glutathione synthetase, the two enzymes that catalyze glutathione synthesis, have abnormally low levels of glutathione and are sensitive to drug- and infection-induced oxidant hemolysis. Deficiencies of these two enzymes are rare, and the clinical syndromes are similar to G6PD deficiency. Inherited defects in glutathione reductase are also rare; the clinical consequence of this deficiency is uncertain, however, because no case of glutathione reductase–associated hemolysis has been carefully documented. Deficiencies in glutathione peroxidase are relatively common, but this disorder appears not to be associated with hemolytic anemia by virtue of the ability of glutathione to reduce hydrogen peroxide by a nonenzymatic as well as an enzymatic route.

DEFECTS IN GLYCOLYSIS

PYRUVATE KINASE DEFICIENCY
Etiology and Incidence

Pyruvate kinase deficiency, which is the most common hereditary defect in the glycolytic pathway, affects hundreds to thousands of individuals worldwide. The disease is inherited in an autosomal recessive pattern; homozygotes manifest clinically significant hemolytic anemia, whereas heterozygote carriers are phenotypically normal.

Pathogenesis

Hemolysis in pyruvate kinase deficiency is thought to result from an intracellular deficiency of ATP, which leads to alterations in many of the biochemical pathways responsible for cellular homeostasis (see Fig. 170–3). These inherent biochemical abnormalities are magnified in the stressful environment of the splenic cords. Depending on the level of residual enzyme activity, the degree of hemolysis can range from mild (compensated hemolysis without anemia) to severe (red cell transfusion dependent). One factor that may mitigate the deleterious effects of pyruvate kinase deficiency on ATP generation is the two- to three-fold increase in 2,3-DPG that results from the distal block in the glycolytic pathway (see later).

Clinical Manifestations

Pyruvate kinase deficiency, unlike G6PD deficiency, results in a chronic hemolytic anemia that is not affected by drugs or other oxidant-producing states. Splenomegaly is a common feature of the disorder, probably because the ATP-deficient red cells are not capable of rapidly traversing the splenic fenestrations. The clinical sequelae of hemolytic anemia in pyruvate kinase deficiency are often milder than those seen in other conditions with the same degree of anemia, perhaps because the elevated levels of 2,3-DPG in pyruvate kinase–deficient red cells permit more efficient delivery of oxygen to the tissues for the same concentration of hemoglobin in the blood.

Diagnosis

Pyruvate kinase deficiency is most conveniently diagnosed by spectrophotometric assays of enzyme activity and by measurements of enzyme substrate and product concentrations in the affected red cells. Measurement of red cell ATP content is not a reliable method for determination of pyruvate kinase activity, perhaps because the most severely affected cells with the lowest ATP content are quickly removed from the circulation and because the young reticulocytes that remain in the circulation have a high ATP content. Similarly, the morphology of pyruvate kinase–deficient red cells is often relatively normal in the presence of a functioning spleen.

Rx Treatment and Prognosis

In moderate to severe pyruvate kinase deficiency, splenectomy ameliorates the hemolysis, although the improvement may not be as marked as that seen in diseases such as hereditary spherocytosis. After splenectomy, a "paradoxical reticulocytosis" (sometimes with a reticulocyte count of 50 to 70%) often occurs despite an improvement in the anemia. This striking finding is thought to be due to improved survival of the pyruvate kinase–deficient reticulocytes, which must depend on mitochondrial oxidative phosphorylation for ATP generation and are therefore susceptible to accelerated splenic "conditioning" (see Fig. 170–2) and extravascular hemolysis in the hypoxic environment of the splenic cords.

OTHER DEFECTS IN GLYCOLYSIS

Although abnormalities in most of the other enzymes in the glycolytic pathway have been described (see Fig. 170–3), the incidence of these deficiencies is so rare that together they affect only 5 to 10% of the number of individuals with pyruvate kinase deficiency. Like pyruvate kinase deficiency, the inheritance pattern of most of these defects is autosomal recessive; the only exception is phosphoglycerate kinase deficiency because the gene coding for this enzyme is located on the X chromosome. The pathogenesis, clinical manifestations, diagnosis, and treatment of these deficiencies are generally similar to those described above for pyruvate kinase deficiency.

DEFECTS IN RED CELL NUCLEOTIDE METABOLISM

Two rare defects in red cell nucleotide metabolism can cause chronic hereditary hemolytic anemia. Pyrimidine-5′-nucleotidase deficiency is inherited in an autosomal recessive pattern. Lack of this enzyme prevents red cell precursor cells from degrading pyrimidine nucleotides to cytidine and uridine, which allows the intracellular accumulation of partially degraded RNA that appears in the mature red cells as basophilic stippling. (This mechanism may also explain the basophilic stippling seen in lead poisoning because the same enzyme is also inhibited by lead.) Although splenomegaly is common in this disorder, splenectomy is of little benefit, thus indicating that the mechanism of hemolysis may be fundamentally different from that involved in the other hereditary anemias discussed in this chapter. Overproduction of adenosine deaminase also causes chronic hemolytic anemia, apparently by depleting the intracellular pool of adenine to the point that ATP synthesis is affected; the molecular mechanism responsible for overexpression of this apparently normal protein remains to be elucidated.

SUGGESTED READINGS

Bader-Meunier B, Gauthier F, Archambaud F, et al: Long-term evaluation of the beneficial effect of subtotal splenectomy for management of hereditary spherocytosis. Blood 2001;97:399–403. *Suggests that subtotal splenectomy can ameliorate hemolysis in patients with hereditary spherocytosis while preserving phagocytic and immune functions of the spleen.*

Walensky LD, Narla M, Lux SE: Disorders of the red blood cell membrane. *In* Handin RI, Lux SE, Stossel TP (eds): Blood: Principles and Practice of Hematology, 2nd ed. Philadelphia, Lippincott Williams & Wilkins, 2003, pp 1709–1858. *Comprehensive review of red cell membrane structure, function, and disorders, especially hereditary spherocytosis and hereditary elliptocytosis. See also periodic updates of recently described membrane protein variants in the electronic journal* Blood Cells Molecules and Diseases.

171 SICKLE CELL ANEMIA AND ASSOCIATED HEMOGLOBINOPATHIES

Stephen H. Embury

Definition

Sickle cell disease is an inherited multisystem disorder caused by the abnormal properties of red blood cells (RBCs) containing mutant sickle cell hemoglobin (Hb S). Chronic hemolytic anemia, recurrent painful episodes, and acute and chronic organ dysfunction are the cardinal features of this disease. Sickle cell disease's attributes include an A→T nucleotide substitution in the sixth codon of the β-globin gene, a β-globin Val→Glu substitution on the surface of the Hb S

tetramer, the abnormal solubility and polymerization of Hb S when deoxygenated, the impaired deformability and sickling of polymer-containing erythrocytes, the occlusion of the microvasculature by poorly deformable RBCs, and numerous mechanisms that are independent of polymerization (Fig. 171–1).

The different sickle cell syndromes that result from distinct inheritance patterns of the sickle cell gene (β^S gene) are divided into sickle cell disease and sickle cell trait. The former is associated with chronic anemia and recurrent pain; the latter is largely asymptomatic. Common varieties of sickle cell disease are inherited as homozygosity for the β^S gene, called *sickle cell anemia* (Hb SS), or as compound heterozygosity of the β^S gene with another mutant β-globin gene: sickle cell–β°-thalassemia (Hb S-β° thal), sickle cell–Hb C disease (Hb SC disease), and sickle cell–β$^+$-thalassemia (Hb S-β$^+$ thal). Sickle cell trait is inherited as simple heterozygosity for the β^S gene (Hb AS).

Epidemiology

The stable frequency of the sickle cell gene in areas of hyperendemic falciparum malaria is a function of the balance between gene exclusion due to early death of homozygotes and gene selection resulting from protection of heterozygotes against death from malaria (Chapter 392). Mechanisms for this "heterozygous advantage" are effected at a stage of the symbiotic parasite-erythrocyte relationship occurring after initial parasitization. The worldwide distribution of sickle cell anemia mirrors the "malaria belt." In the United States, more than 90% of patients are African American.

Near the β-globin gene on chromosome 11 are a series of restriction fragment length polymorphisms, combinations of which define ethnogeographic-specific β-globin haplotypes. The association of the β^S gene with five different haplotypes demonstrates the multiple occurrence of the sickle cell mutation among peoples of Senegal, Benin, Bantu, Cameroon, and Arab-Indian origins. The effect of glucose-6-phosphate dehydrogenase (G6PD) deficiency, another common African polymorphism, on the sickle cell gene remains controversial, but there is no apparent higher frequency of the mutant G6PD gene, greater hemolysis, or more frequent pain among male subjects with coexistent sickle cell disease and G6PD deficiency.

The prevalence of sickle cell trait is 8 to 10% among African American newborns in the United States. An estimated 50,000 to 60,000 patients with sickle cell disease are living in the United States, and 4000 to 5000 pregnancies are at risk for sickle cell disease each

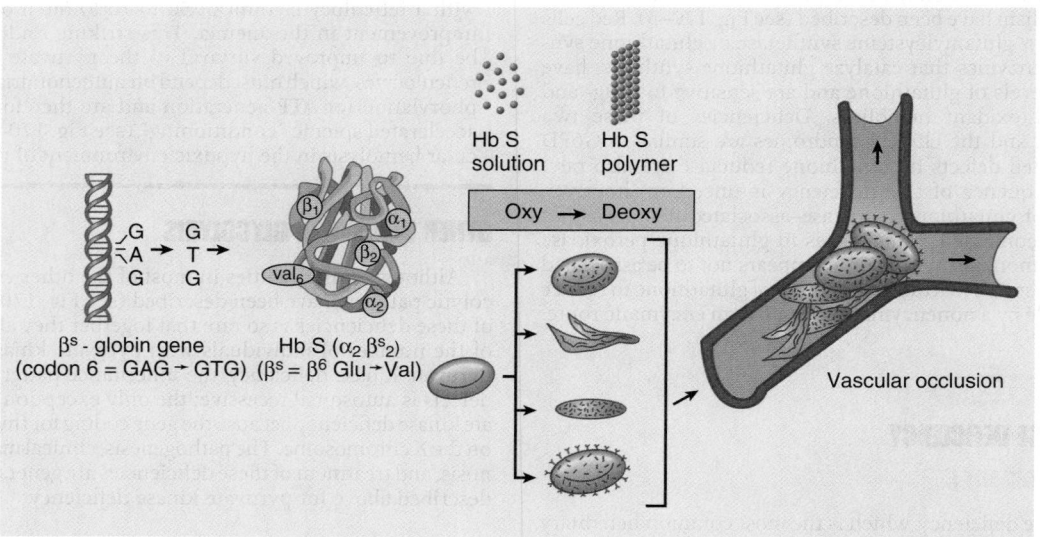

FIGURE 171–1 • A schematic view of the pathophysiologic characteristics of sickle cell disease. The double-stranded DNA molecule on the left represents a β-globin gene in which a GAG→GTG substitution in the sixth codon has created the sickle cell gene. The product of this gene is the β^S-globin variant, in which valine is substituted for glutamic acid as the sixth amino acid. The mutant hemoglobin tetramer α$_2$β$^S_2$ is Hb S, which loses solubility and polymerizes when deprived of oxygen. Upon deoxygenation, most sickle cells accumulate polymer and lose deformability; some cells sickle; a fraction of cells become dehydrated, irreversibly sickled, and poorly deformable; and a few cells accrue cytoadherence molecules on their surface. Dehydrated and highly adherent cells also may be generated by polymerization independent processes. Vasoocclusion, shown on the right, is initiated by adherent cells sticking to the vascular endothelium, thereby creating a nidus that traps rigid cells and facilitates polymerization.

year. In western Africa, the prevalence of sickle cell trait is 25 to 30%, and 120,000 babies are born with sickle cell disease in Africa each year.

Pathobiology

Deoxygenation-induced polymerization of Hb S, sickling of RBCs, and increased viscosity of blood are the sine qua non of sickle cell disease. However, additional pathophysiologic processes are required for the full expression of the disorder.

Hb S POLYMER. Although oxygenated Hb S and normal Hb A are equally soluble, the solubility of deoxygenated Hb S is severely reduced owing to the presence of valine rather than glutamic acid as the sixth amino acid of β^S globin and to the resultant increased surface hydrophobicity of Hb S molecules. The intermolecular bonding of deoxy-Hb S generates polymer filaments, which associate into bundles that can be discerned by electron microscopy. One of the two β^S valines forms a lateral contact with the β^{85} phenylalanine and β^{88} leucine within a hydrophobic pocket of an adjacent Hb S tetramer. The other valine is uninvolved in intermolecular bonding. Additional intermolecular bonds make axial and lateral contacts between other amino acid residues.

POLYMERIZATION. The solubility of deoxy-Hb S is 17 g/dL, far less than the usual 34 g/dL concentration of hemoglobin within sickled RBCs. Deoxygenation promotes rapid supersaturation, aggregation, and polymerization, with the progression from nuclear aggregation to polymer formation having a delay time inversely related to the 30th power of the deoxy-Hb S concentration. Resultant polymer fibers provide additional nuclei for further polymer formation. Because delay times in polymerization usually exceed capillary transit times, sickle cells usually do not accumulate significant amounts of polymer until they are in large veins where they cannot elicit vasoocclusion; local vascular perturbations that cause unusual delays in the transit time allow cellular sickling and vascular occlusion in small vessels.

INHERITED INFLUENCES ON POLYMERIZATION. The switch from γ- to β-globin production begins in the fetus and results in replacement of fetal hemoglobin (Hb F) by adult Hb S. The retardant effect of Hb F on Hb S polymerization and cellular sickling masks the expression of sickle cell disease until approximately 6 months of age, when Hb S levels increase to about 75%. Syndromes in which high Hb F levels persist into adulthood, such as hereditary persistence of fetal hemoglobin (HPFH) and Hb S-β thalassemia, similarly mitigate the course of sickle cell disease. Polymerization is also influenced by elevated levels of Hb A$_2$ in Hb S-β^0 thalassemia and Hb S-β$^+$ thalassemia and by Hb A levels of 5 to 30% in Hb S-β$^+$ thalassemia. In this regard, Hb F inhibits polymerization 100 to 10,000 times more actively than Hb A does. Another influence retarding polymerization in sickle cell-β-thalassemia is the lower intraerythrocytic Hb S concentration as reflected by the reduced mean corpuscular hemoglobin concentration (MCHC).

α-Thalassemia (Chapter 168) also reduces the MCHC and influences certain aspects of sickle cell disease. The silent carrier of α-thalassemia syndrome (genotype −α/αα) exists in about 30% of African Americans and α-thalassemia trait (genotype −α/−α) in 2%. The lower intraerythrocytic concentrations of Hb S associated with these two genotypes modulate, after 7 years of age, the hematologic, pathophysiologic, and clinical manifestations of disease, particularly the severity of anemia. Average hemoglobin levels associated with different α-globin genotypes in adults are 7.9 g/dL for αα/αα, 8.7 g/dL for −α/αα, and 9.0 g/dL for −α/−α.

CELLULAR SICKLING. Deoxygenation of sickle cells results in generation of deoxy-Hb S polymer, alteration of cellular morphologic char-

acteristics, and increased viscosity. Accrual of polymer is prompt and precedes changes in cell morphologic properties during deoxygenation. Polymer is lost before cells regain normal shape during reoxygenation. During slow deoxygenation, classic crescent-shaped cells with a single domain of highly aligned polymer arise by homogeneous nucleation from a single nucleus; with faster deoxygenation, holly leaf–shaped cells with a greater number of less aligned domains are generated by heterogeneous nucleation from a few nuclei; and with very rapid deoxygenation, granular cells with multiple poorly aligned domains are derived by heterogeneous nucleation from many nuclei. Shear stress applied from the beginning of polymerization creates more nucleation sites, shortens the delay time, and increases cell viscosity; shear applied after polymerization has begun breaks the polymer and diminishes viscosity.

IRREVERSIBLY SICKLED CELLS. Those cells that do not unsickle when reoxygenated, the *irreversibly sickled cells*, are the least deformable sickle cells and have the shortest circulatory survival. Their rheologic impairment is related more to the effects of severe cellular dehydration on intraerythrocytic Hb S concentration, cytoplasmic viscosity, and polymerization tendency than to rigidly deformed skeletal proteins.

Sickled forms seen on the peripheral blood smear (see Figs. 161–8 and 171–3) are irreversibly sickled. Their number does not change with complications of disease (such as the acute painful episode), is generally constant in individual patients, and correlates mainly with the degree of anemia. Their quantification is generally not useful diagnostically in the assessment of whether a patient is experiencing a pain crisis. These cells exist in all sickle cell disease genotypes but not in sickle cell trait.

CATION HOMEOSTASIS AND CELL DEHYDRATION. During their brief survival in the circulation, sickle cells become dehydrated, some achieving MCHC greater than 50 g/dL, which greatly enhances polymerization. The predominant mechanism of cell dehydration involves the interdependent actions of calcium-dependent potassium loss and potassium chloride cotransport on a population of calcium-sensitive reticulocytes. Potassium efflux lowers the intracellular pH, thereby activating the volume-regulatory K-Cl cotransport activity, which further depletes cells of potassium and water.

The hematuria and diminished concentrating ability of subjects with sickle cell trait demonstrate that even Hb AS cells can sickle and occlude vessels when dehydrated osmotically in the extremely hypertonic renal medulla. The clinical manifestations of Hb SC disease demonstrate that even heterozygous amounts of Hb S can cause morbidity when the Hb S is sufficiently concentrated within the cell; the cellular dehydration effected by Hb C–induced potassium chloride cotransport increases the intraerythrocytic Hb S concentration and causes sufficient polymerization to result in anemia and pain. The complex interaction between α-thalassemia and sickle cell anemia demonstrates the importance of polymerization-independent pathophysiologic interpretations. The less severe anemia associated with coexistent α-thalassemia is related to better cell hydration, lower MCHC, fewer dense and irreversibly sickled cells, and greater deformability of α-thalassemic sickle cells—all consistent with a retardant effect on polymerization. Yet, coexistent α-thalassemia is associated with more severe vasoocclusion—more frequent pain and osteonecrosis, and a higher mortality rate after the age of 20 years. These conflicting influences of α-thalassemia demonstrate the presence of pathophysiologic processes beyond polymerization alone.

OXIDATIVE DAMAGE. In addition to having abnormal electrophoretic and solubility properties, Hb S is unstable. Its oxidation results in

---

Table 171–1 • TYPICAL HEMATOLOGIC VARIABLES ASSOCIATED WITH SICKLE CELL ANEMIA, THE SICKLE CELL–β-THALASSEMIA SYNDROMES, AND SICKLE CELL–HEREDITARY PERSISTENCE OF FETAL HEMOGLOBIN

GENOTYPE	%HB	%HB A	%HB F	%HB A$_2$	MCV	%RETICULOCYTES
Hb SS	7.8	0	4.6	2.9	85.9	10.18
Hb S-β^0 thal	8.9	0	5.9	5.0	69.3	7.2
Hb S-β$^+$ thal	8.4–11.6	3–25	5.1–6.8	4.7–4.9	64–73	1.3–9.7
Hb S-HPFH	14.6	0	25.8	1.95	81.7	2.4

MCV = mean corpuscular volume; Hb SS = homozygosity for the β^S gene: sickle cell anemia; Hb S-β^0 thal = compound heterozygosity of the β^S gene with the β^0-thalassemia gene; Hb S-β$^+$ thal = compound heterozygosity-β^S gene with the β$^+$-thalassemia gene; Hb S-HPFH = compound heterozygosity-β^S gene with the hereditary persistence of fetal hemoglobin gene.

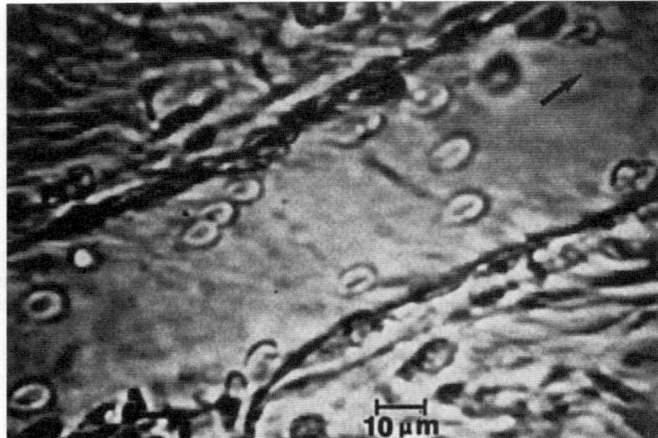

A

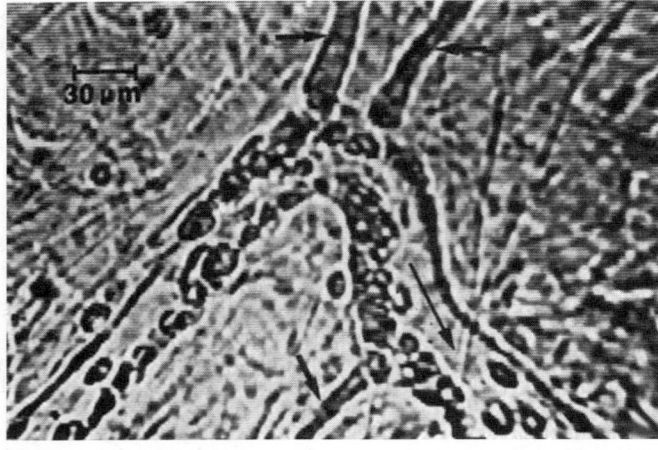

B

FIGURE 171–2 • Adhesion of sickle erythrocytes in venules. *A*, Adherent discocytic sickle cells tethered to the endothelial wall of a venule and aligned in the direction of the flow (arrow). *B*, Increased adherence of sickle cells at a venule or bending and at junctions of smaller diameter postcapillary venules. The postcapillary vessels (small arrows) are totally blocked. Large arrow indicates flow direction. (From Kaul DK, et al: Microvascular sites and characteristics of sickle cell adhesion to vascular endothelium in shear flow conditions: Pathophysiologic implications. Proc Natl Acad Sci U S A 1989;86:3356, with permission.)

increased generation of methemoglobin, heme, and oxidative radicals. Resultant oxidative stresses affect RBC metabolism, membrane lipids, membrane proteins, and Hb S itself. Hemoglobin oxidation results in hemichrome aggregation on the cytoplasmic portion of the transmembrane protein, band 3, which initiates coclustering of these molecules within the cell membrane, assembly of immunoglobulin G and complement on band 3 extracellular domains, and sickle cell adherence to macrophages and endothelial cells. Oxidation of membrane proteins and lipids damages cell membranes and contributes to the loss of phosphatidylinositol-anchored complement regulatory proteins of the membrane.

SICKLE CELL ADHESION. The two-step process of sickle cell vasoocclusion is initiated by the adherence of a more adhesive population of sickle RBCs to the vascular endothelium. Occlusion is completed by the log-jamming of polymerization-prone sickle cells and poorly deformable irreversibly sickled cells behind the nidus of occlusion (Fig. 171–2). In addition to the cascade of adhesion molecules that mediates the adherence of sickle cells to the endothelium, it appears that adhesion of leukocytes may precede and mediate the adhesion of sickled RBCs. In patients with Hb SS, there is a direct relationship between the leukocyte count and the rates of mortality, hemorrhagic stroke, and acute chest syndrome; the clinical response to hydroxyurea also correlates with reductions in the polymorphonuclear neutrophil leukocyte (PMN) count. The mechanisms by which PMNs influence vasoocclusion may involve their poor deformability, their increased adherence to endothelium and frequent upregulation of CD64 during pain crisis, and their activation by sickled erythrocytes. Platelets may also be activated in sickle cell disease and form aggregates with sickled RBCs.

COAGULATION ABNORMALITIES. The continuous perturbation and activation of the hemostatic system in sickle cell disease is evidenced by ongoing platelet activation, which is increased during acute vasoocclusive episodes. The activation of coagulation in sickle cell disease is demonstrated by increased thrombin generation, the evidence for which includes elevated levels of thrombin-antithrombin III complexes, prothrombin activation fragment 1.2, and fibrinopeptide A. The most likely cause of hemostatic activation is the production of tissue factor by the interaction of activated endothelial cells and monocytes. Tissue factor is also expressed by circulating endothelial cells that have been dislodged from their vascular moorings during the course of vascular perturbations in this disease.

PATHOPHYSIOLOGIC MECHANISMS OF VASOOCCLUSION. Polymerization is necessary but not sufficient for vasoocclusion. Sickle cells become deoxygenated more frequently than once a minute, demonstrating that "sickling" is a constant, unrelenting process rather than an occasional cataclysmic one; there probably is no normal "steady-state" blood flow in sickle cell disease. Despite the considerable effect of a high MCHC on polymerization, there is no greater frequency of pain in patients with high numbers of irreversibly sickled cells, which have the highest MCHC. The cells that adhere to initiate vasoocclusion are those with lower MCHC, which further indicates the importance of polymerization-independent events.

MECHANISMS OF HEMOLYSIS. Hemolysis of sickle cells is both extravascular and intravascular. The former is due to the effects of unstable Hb S and recurrent sickling on causing oxidative damage to cell membranes. Binding of oxidatively denatured Hb S to the cytosolic portion of band 3 induces adherence of IgG and complement to extracellular band 3, thereby promoting cell recognition by macrophages. Also, the very rigid irreversibly sickled cells that are generated by recurrent sickling and by sickling-independent cell dehydration are trapped extravascularly, accounting for their short circulatory survival and correlation with the severity of anemia. Elevated free plasma hemoglobin levels suggest that one third of sickle cell hemolysis is intravascular. One mechanism relates to complement-mediated lysis, which is the result of depletion from the cell membrane of complement-regulatory proteins during sickling-induced exovesiculation of vesicles enriched in phosphatidylinositol-anchored membrane proteins. A second mechanism involves the mechanical fragility of cells, which accounts for accelerated hemolysis during exercise.

IMMUNE DEFICIT. The propensity of children with sickle cell disease to *Streptococcus pneumoniae* infection relates to their impaired splenic function and diminished serum opsonizing activity. The function of the spleen is deficient even before its eventual autoinfarction, but prior to the second decade function is restorable by transfusion. The greater the rate of hemolysis, the earlier the age at which splenic function is lost: sickle cell anemia before Hb SC disease before sickle cell–β⁺-thalassemia. The decreased titer of antibody against *S. pneumoniae* antigens following splenectomy in individuals without sickle cell disease suggests that splenic hypofunction may mediate opsonic deficiency in sickle cell disease.

Clinical Manifestations

Clinical manifestations of sickle cell disease vary greatly between and among the disease genotypes. Even within the most severe genotype, sickle cell anemia, asymptomatic patients may be detected incidentally, whereas others are disabled by complications of the disease. The typical patient is anemic but asymptomatic except during painful episodes. In addition, most organ systems are subject to chronic and acute vasoocclusion, which results in characteristic acute and chronic effects. Important clinical features less directly related to vasoocclusion are growth retardation, psychosocial problems, and susceptibility to infection. Therapeutic interventions are directed to specific complications.

LIFE EXPECTANCY. The current mean survival is 42 years for men and 48 years for women with sickle cell anemia. This improved life expectancy compared with that of earlier eras is mainly the result of better general medical care, such as prophylactic penicillin therapy for preventing *S. pneumoniae* bacteremia in children.

CHRONIC ANEMIA. Sickle cells are destroyed randomly and have a mean lifespan of 17 days. The degree of anemia is most severe in sickle cell anemia and Hb S-β° thalassemia, milder in Hb S-β⁺ thalassemia and Hb SC disease, and, among patients with sickle cell anemia, less severe in those who have coexistent α-thalassemia. In addition to hemolysis, inappropriately low erythropoietin levels contribute to the anemia.

EXACERBATIONS OF ANEMIA. The reasonably constant level of hemolytic anemia may be exacerbated by several different causes, most commonly aplastic crises. Aplastic crises are transient arrests of erythropoiesis characterized by abrupt falls in hemoglobin levels, reticulocytes, and RBC precursors in the marrow. Anemia becomes severe as hemolysis continues in the absence of RBC production. These episodes, which typically last only a few days, are associated with the inflammation that occurs in all types of infections. Parvovirus B19 specifically invades proliferating erythroid progenitors and accounts for approximately two thirds of aplastic crises in children with sickle cell disease; the subsequent development of protective antibodies makes parvovirus a less frequent cause in adults. Bone marrow necrosis, with attendant fever, bone pain, reticulocytopenia, and leukoerythroblastic response, is another cause of aplastic crisis; it is sometimes associated with parvovirus infection and sometimes with marrow embolus to the lungs. High oxygen tensions during oxygen inhalation suppress erythropoietin production promptly and, within 2 days, impair RBC production. RBC transfusion is the main treatment for aplastic crises. When transfusion is necessitated by cardiorespiratory symptoms, a single transfusion usually suffices, as reticulocytosis soon resumes spontaneously. Transfusion sometimes can be avoided by enforcing bed rest and avoiding unnecessary oxygen therapy.

Acute splenic sequestration is characterized by acute exacerbation of anemia, persistent reticulocytosis, a tender enlarging spleen, and sometimes hypovolemia. Patients whose spleens have not undergone fibrosis are at risk, such as young patients with sickle cell anemia and adults with Hb SC disease or sickle cell-β⁺ thalassemia. Splenic sequestration occurs in 30% of children, and 15% of the attacks are fatal. Transfusion is given to restore blood volume and RBC mass. Splenic sequestration recurs in half the cases, so splenectomy is recommended after the acute event. Acute sequestration also may occur in the liver.

Apparent hyperhemolytic crises usually represent occult splenic sequestration or aplastic crises detected during the resolving reticulocytosis. Actual hyperhemolysis may occur with coexistent G6PD deficiency.

Chronic worsening of anemia may be related to incipient renal insufficiency or lack of folic acid or iron. Inadequate erythropoietin production in renal failure limits compensation for hemolysis. Transfusion therapy is usually required, but it may be forestalled by using hydroxyurea and/or recombinant human erythropoietin. Chronic hemolysis consumes folic acid stores, potentially resulting in megaloblastic crises. The combination of nutritional deficiency and urinary iron losses may result in iron deficiency, which may be obscured by the elevated serum iron levels associated with hemolysis; low serum ferritin or elevated serum transferrin levels help make the diagnosis.

THE ACUTE PAINFUL EPISODE. Acute pain is often the first symptom of disease, is the most frequent complication after the newborn period, and is the most common reason that patients seek medical attention. Although there is a general association between vasoocclusive severity and genotype, tremendous variability exists within genotypes and in the same patient over time. One third of patients with sickle cell anemia rarely have pain, one third are hospitalized for pain two to six times per year, and one third have more than six pain-related hospitalizations per year; 5% of patients account for one third of emergency department visits. The frequency of pain is highest in the third and fourth decades. After the second decade, frequent pain is associated with increased mortality rates. Factors associated with more frequent pain include high hemoglobin levels, α-thalassemia, and low Hb F levels. The frequency of pain is decreased during chronic transfusion therapy.

Painful episodes are caused by vasoocclusion and may be precipitated by cold, dehydration, infection, stress, menses, or alcohol consumption, but the cause of most episodes cannot be determined. Pain can affect any area of the body, most commonly the back, chest, extremities, and abdomen. Severity varies from trifling to agonizing, and the duration is usually a few days. Frequent pain may cause despair, depression, and apathy, which predispose the patient to an existence that revolves around pain—a chronic debilitating pain syndrome.

Half of painful episodes are associated with objective clinical signs—fever, swelling, tenderness, tachypnea, hypertension, nausea, and vomiting. Potential laboratory indicators are a decline in the dense fraction of sickle cells and an increase in overall RBC deformability, levels of acute phase reactants, serum lactate dehydrogenase, interleukin 1, tumor necrosis factor, and serum viscosity.

Diagnosis

General diagnostic methods include hemoglobin electrophoresis, solubility testing, review of the peripheral blood smear (Fig. 171–3), and DNA testing for mutations.

The purpose of diagnosis is to identify older children or adults who have the disease or trait and who need treatment or counseling. Hb S, G, and D have the same electrophoretic mobility on cellulose acetate electrophoresis at pH 8.4, but Hb S has a different mobility on citrate agar electrophoresis at pH 6.2. The solubility test (Sickledex) also distinguishes Hb S, which is not soluble, from Hb D

and G, which are. Thin-layer isoelectric focusing separates Hb S, D, and G but also requires confirmatory solubility testing. The "sickle cell prep" using metabisulfite or dithionite is currently of historical interest only.

In cases of sickle cell anemia and sickle cell–β°-thalassemia, Hb S constitutes nearly all the hemoglobin present. Useful indicators of sickle cell–β°-thalassemia are microcytosis or one parent lacking Hb S. Sickle cell–β⁺-thalassemia and sickle cell trait both have Hb A and Hb S. In sickle cell trait, there is neither anemia nor microcytosis; the Hb A fraction exceeds 50%. In sickle cell–β⁺-thalassemia, there is anemia, microcytosis, and a Hb A fraction of only 5 to 25%. Solubility tests yield positive findings in both sickle cell–β⁺-thalassemia and sickle cell trait, but sickled forms occur on the peripheral smear only in sickle cell–β⁺-thalassemia, not in sickle cell trait. In Hb SC disease, nearly equal amounts of Hb S and C are present.

OTHER LABORATORY TESTING. The hemolytic anemia of sickle cell disease is associated with mildly to moderately reduced hematocrit, hemoglobin, and RBC levels; reticulocytosis of approximately 3 to 15%; unconjugated hyperbilirubinemia; elevated lactate dehydrogenase levels; and low haptoglobin levels. The peripheral blood smear reveals polychromasia related to reticulocytosis and Howell-Jolly bodies indicative of hyposplenia. Sickle cells are normochromic, except with coexistent thalassemia or iron deficiency. Hb F levels are slightly to moderately elevated, with average values of 5 to 6%. White blood cell (WBC) and platelet counts tend to be elevated in patients with sickle cell anemia but not in those with Hb SC disease or sickle cell–β⁺-thalassemia.

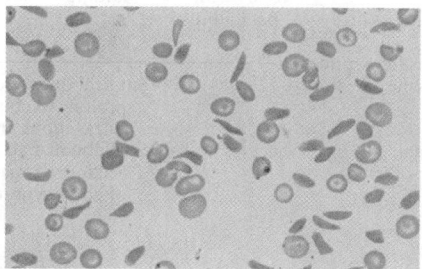

FIGURE 171–3 • Sickle cell anemia. Homozygous SS disease with a predominance of sickled red blood cells in the peripheral smear.

Complications

GROWTH AND DEVELOPMENT. Growth retardation affects weight more than height and has no clear gender difference. By adulthood, normal height is achieved, but weight remains abnormally low. More severe growth delay is noted in children with sickle cell anemia and sickle cell–β^0-thalassemia than in those with Hb SC disease. Skeletal maturation is also delayed. Delayed sexual maturation is associated with elevated gonadotropin levels for the stage of sexual development and, in girls, with delayed menarche. Retarded sexual maturation in males can be the result of primary hypogonadism, hypopituitarism, or hypothalamic insufficiency. Impaired development can be reversed after splenectomy in children. In severely delayed growth and development, hormonal therapy should be tailored to the specific deficiency.

INFECTIONS. Infectious complications of sickle cell disease are a major cause of morbidity and mortality (Table 171–2). *S. pneumoniae*, the most common cause of bacteremia in children with sickle cell disease, may be accompanied by aplastic crisis, disseminated intravascular coagulation, and a 20 to 50% mortality rate. The second most common cause of bacteremia, *Haemophilus influenzae* type b, affects older children, is less fulminant, but also may be fatal. Vaccination and regular reimmunization are recommended. Prophylactic penicillin beginning in infancy has reduced the incidence of *S. pneumoniae* bacteremia in newborns by 84%, and its use is recommended through the age of 5 years. Penicillin-resistant microorganisms have emerged, and local patterns of resistance vary. Patients with a history of previous *S. pneumoniae* bacteremia should not be treated as outpatients, and vancomycin should be used in areas in which antibiotic resistance is frequent. Urinary tract infections and bacteremia in older patients are more likely due to *Escherichia coli* and other gram-negative organisms.

Meningitis in sickle cell anemia is primarily a problem of infants and young children, and *S. pneumoniae* is the most frequent cause. Because meningitis occurs commonly in association with bacteremia, rapid administration of antibiotics for bacteremia has resulted in a much lower incidence of meningitis. *H. influenzae* type b is a less common cause of meningitis.

Bacterial pneumonia is one cause of the acute chest syndrome. Patients with any combination of dyspnea, cough, chest pain, fever, tachypnea, or leukocytosis should be evaluated by chest radiograph, arterial blood gas measurement, blood and sputum culture, cold agglutinins, and serologic study for *Mycoplasma pneumoniae*, *Chlamydia pneumoniae*, and *Legionella* species. *Mycoplasma pneumoniae* and *Chlamydia pneumoniae* account for approximately 20% of cases of acute chest syndrome. *S. pneumoniae* and *H. influenzae* type b are less common causes. Treatment of suspected bacterial pneumonia is with a broad-spectrum cephalosporin, such as ceftriaxone, and a tetracycline or macrolide.

Osteomyelitis occurs more commonly in sickle cell disease, probably as a result of infection of infarcted bone. Among sickle cell patients, osteomyelitis is commonly caused by *Salmonella* species. *S. aureus* accounts for less than 25% of cases. Infection is often at multiple sites in long bones. Diagnosis is made by culture of blood or infected bone. Articular infection is less common and is often due to *S. pneumoniae*.

NEUROLOGIC COMPLICATIONS. Neurologic complications occur in 25% of patients with sickle cell disease. Common events are transient ischemic attacks, cerebral infarction, cerebral hemorrhage, seizures, and unexplained coma. Cerebrovascular accident (CVA) may occur spontaneously or intercurrently with complications, such as pneumonia, aplastic crises, painful episodes, or dehydration. Patients at higher risk for CVA are those with more severe anemia, higher reticulocyte counts, lower Hb F levels, higher WBC counts, and sickle cell anemia rather than Hb SC disease or sickle cell–β-thalassemia. Cerebral thrombosis accounts for 70 to 80% of CVAs and is due to large vessel obstruction rather than the typical microvascular occlusion of sickle cell disease. Thrombotic CVAs, which may be heralded by focal seizures or transient ischemic attacks, are fatal in approximately 20% of cases, recur within 3 years in nearly 70%, and frequently cause motor and cognitive impairment.

Many patients with sickle cell disease develop collateral vessels that appear as puffs of smoke (*moyamoya* in Japanese) on angiograms. These friable pseudomoyamoyas are vulnerable to both thrombosis and hemorrhage. Improved treatment of this complication has been achieved with surgical extracranial-intracranial shunting. Coma is more frequently associated with hemorrhage than with thrombosis, and the combination of coma and seizures without hemiparesis is strongly suggestive of hemorrhage. Although the mortality rate with hemorrhage is 50%, the morbidity of survivors is low. The favorable neurosurgical outcome in subarachnoid hemorrhage from ruptured aneurysm justifies aggressive diagnosis, transfusion, vasodilatory therapy, and surgery.

Patients presenting with symptoms and signs of CVA should be evaluated immediately by computed tomographic scanning or magnetic resonance imaging (MRI) to distinguish among transient ischemic attack, cerebral thrombosis, and hemorrhage. In hemorrhage, angiography is indicated after a partial exchange transfusion to prevent complications associated with injected contrast material. In thrombosis, prompt partial exchange transfusion is indicated, and chronic transfusion to maintain the Hb S level below 30% is initiated to prevent recurrent thrombosis and promote resolution. Transfusion therapy provides the best means of preventing recurrence. Transfusion may be required indefinitely for patients with persistent flow abnormalities after 5 years of transfusion and for those in whom thrombosis recurs soon after chronic transfusion therapy is discontinued.

Silent cerebral infarcts have been determined to cause neurodevelopmental abnormalities. These subclinical cerebral infarcts are detectable by MRI and transcranial Doppler flow studies. The ability to predict the occurrence of strokes by detecting arterial stenosis with transcranial Doppler ultrasonography and to prevent the occurrence of such strokes with chronic transfusion has led to the recommendation that transcranial Doppler ultrasonography be used for routine screening and that transfusion be instituted upon detection of arterial stenosis. ▮

PULMONARY COMPLICATIONS. The *acute chest syndrome* consists of dyspnea, chest pain, fever, tachypnea, leukocytosis, and a pulmonary infiltrate on the chest radiograph. It affects approximately 30% of

---

Table 171–2 • ORGAN-RELATED INFECTION IN SICKLE CELL DISEASE

PRIMARY SITES OF INFECTION	MOST COMMON PATHOGENS	OTHER PATHOGENS	PATHOPHYSIOLOGY	PREVENTION	MANAGEMENT
Septicemia	*Staphylococcus pneumoniae*	*Haemophilus influenzae* type b *Escherichia coli* *Salmonella* spp.	Defective splenic function; deficiency of opsonic antibody	Vaccines* Prophylactic penicillin	Empirical intravenous antibiotics for fever
Meningitis	*S. pneumoniae*	← Same as for Septicemia →			
Osteomyelitis and septic arthritis	*Salmonella* spp. *S. pneumoniae*	*E. coli* *Proteus* spp. *S. aureus*	Ischemic or infarcted tissue	—	Surgical drainage; prolonged course of intravenous antibiotics
Pneumonia	*Mycoplasma pneumoniae* Respiratory viruses	*Chlamydia pneumoniae* *S. pneumoniae*	Concomitant infection and intrapulmonary vasoocclusion leading to infarction and/or sequestration	Vaccines*	See Pulmonary Complications section for management of chest syndrome

*Against *S. pneumoniae* and *H. influenzae* type b.
From Buchanan GR: Infections. *In* Embury SH, Hebbel RP, Mohandas N, Steinberg MH (eds): Sickle Cell Disease: Basic Principles and Clinical Practice. New York, Raven Press, 1994, pp 567–587.

patients with sickle cell disease and may be life-threatening. The usual causes are vasoocclusion, infection, and pulmonary fat embolus from infarcted marrow. Microbial pathogens are more commonly isolated in children, in whom the mortality rate is one fourth that in adults. Premorbid events in the 2 weeks preceding the acute chest syndrome are likely to be febrile events in children and acute painful events in adults. Often, when common pathogens are not detected on culture, one of the "atypical" agents, *Mycoplasma, Chlamydia,* or *Legionella,* is responsible. Pulmonary fat embolism has a severe clinical course and can be diagnosed by a positive stain for fat in sputum macrophages (Chapter 94). When arterial oxygen tension cannot be maintained above 70 mm Hg with the use of inhaled oxygen, partial exchange transfusion is indicated. Emerging reports of clinical improvement associated with the use of inhaled nitric oxide suggest a possible role for this treatment. Mechanical ventilation is indicated for a progressive course associated with severely decreased arterial oxygen tension. Extracorporeal membrane oxygenation may be required for extreme cases that do not respond to the above-mentioned interventions.

Evaluation of chronic pulmonary status of patients with sickle cell anemia may reveal restrictive lung disease, hypoxemia, and pulmonary hypertension, singly or in combination. These complications are often preceded by a history of acute chest syndrome. Blood gas and pulmonary function measurements should be obtained as baseline data. Airway hyper-reactivity and sleep apnea are more common in sickle cell disease and are treatable causes of morbidity. A recent study suggests that the oral administration of L-arginine, the precursor molecule for nitric oxide synthesis, lowers the pulmonary artery pressure in sickle cell patients with pulmonary hypertension.

HEPATOBILIARY COMPLICATIONS. Pigmented gallstones develop as a result of the chronic hemolysis in at least 70% of patients. Laparoscopic cholecystectomy has become a feasible approach for asymptomatic gallstones to prevent subsequent confusion of gallbladder pain with acute painful episodes.

Chronic hepatomegaly and liver dysfunction caused by trapping of sickle cells, transfusion-acquired viral infection, and iron overload are associated with centrilobular parenchymal atrophy, accumulation of bile pigment, periportal fibrosis, hemosiderosis, and cirrhosis. In acute hepatic events, the combination of hemolysis, hepatic dysfunction, and renal tubular defects often results in dramatically high serum bilirubin levels, sometimes exceeding 100 mg/dL. Acute hepatic complications may result from viral hepatitis, benign cholestasis (which causes severe hyperbilirubinemia but not fever, pain, or mortality), and ischemic hepatic crisis (which causes severe hyperbilirubinemia, fever, pain, abnormal liver function test results, and hepatic failure). Hepatitis C occurs with high frequency. Autoimmune liver disease has been treated successfully in patients with sickle cell disease with immune suppression. Liver transplantation has been used successfully for patients with hepatic failure.

OBSTETRIC AND GYNECOLOGIC ISSUES. Fetal complications of pregnancy relate to impaired placental blood flow and include spontaneous abortion, intrauterine growth retardation, low birth weight, preeclampsia, and death. Maternal complications include increased rates of painful episodes and infections, severe anemia, preeclampsia, and death. Prophylactic transfusions do not improve fetal outcome, and their routine application is not recommended. Oral contraceptives containing low-dose estrogen are a safe and recommended method of birth control. Barrier methods and injections of medroxyprogesterone every 3 months also may be useful.

RENAL COMPLICATIONS. Occlusion of the vasa recta compromises blood flow to the medulla, causing impaired urinary concentrating ability, papillary infarction, hematuria, incomplete renal tubular acidosis, and abnormal potassium clearance. Isosthenuria is reversible with RBC transfusions up to the age of 8 years.

Sickle cell trait is a common cause of hematuria among African Americans. When patients who have sickle cell disease or trait also have hematuria, they should be evaluated by ultrasonography or MRI to exclude life-threatening causes, such as medullary carcinoma, which has been reported increasingly in patients with sickle cell disease. Therapeutic options for hematuria include standard hydration, alkalization of the urine, and diuresis. In unresponsive cases, ε-aminocaproic acid, vasopressin, intravenous distilled water, and nephrectomy have been used. Proximal tubular dysfunction may result in hyperuricemia and is aggravated by chronic use of analgesics.

Glomerular abnormalities result from vasoocclusion, hyperperfusion, immune complex nephropathy, and parvovirus B19 infection.

Hypertension, proteinuria, hyperkalemia, and worsening anemia may herald chronic renal insufficiency, the average age of onset of which is 23 years in patients with sickle cell anemia and 50 years in patients with Hb SC disease. Angiotensin-converting enzyme inhibitors diminish hyperperfusion and proteinuria but do not increase glomerular filtration rate. Renal transplantation is effective therapy for end-stage renal disease.

PRIAPISM. Priapism, an unwanted painful erection, has been reported to affect 6.4 to 42% of males with sickle cell disease and strikes most commonly between the ages of 5 to 13 years and 21 to 29 years. Its onset can be acute, recurrent, chronic, or "stuttering." In the priapism of sickle cell disease, the corpora cavernosa are usually engorged, and the glans penis and corpus spongiosum are spared. In a minority of patients, there is tricorporal priapism, which can be diagnosed by nuclear scanning of the penis.

Recurrent priapism can be prevented by oral self-administration of the α-adrenergic agent etilefrine and by its intracavernous injection for episodes lasting more than an hour. Recurrences can be prevented by diethylstilbestrol.

Patients not responding to these treatments should be hospitalized. If there is no response of intracavernous pressure to 12 hours of intravenous hydration and analgesia, partial exchange transfusion is used. If there is still no resolution within 12 hours, corporal aspiration with saline solution and α-adrenergic agents is used. If there is no response within the next 12 hours, a fistula is created surgically between the glans penis and the corpora cavernosa by insertion of a large-bore needle through the glans. In 45% of patients who experience priapism, some degree of impotence develops.

OCULAR COMPLICATIONS. Ophthalmologic features include tortuosity of conjunctival vessels, anterior chamber ischemia, retinal artery occlusion, angioid streaks, proliferative retinopathy, and retinal detachment and hemorrhage. The earlier onset and greater frequency of proliferative retinopathy in patients with Hb SC disease and sickle cell-β⁺ thalassemia than in patients with sickle cell anemia and sickle cell-β⁰ thalassemia suggest that retinal vessels are particularly vulnerable to occlusion by more viscous blood, rather than to the rigidity of individual sickle cells. Annual retinal examination is part of routine health care maintenance. Peripheral sickle retinopathy may require therapy with laser photocoagulation.

BONE COMPLICATIONS. Osteonecrosis may cause compression of vertebrae, shortening of cuboidal bones of the hands and feet, and acute aseptic or avascular necrosis. The painful bone infarction of the hand-foot syndrome in children is often the first symptom of sickle cell disease. Nuclear medicine scintigraphy and MRI are sensitive means of detecting bone infarcts. Bone marrow infarction can be distinguished from osteomyelitis by triple scans that specifically identify osteoclasts, bone marrow macrophages, and inflammatory cells, but cultures taken directly from the affected tissue should be obtained before antibiotic therapy for osteomyelitis is started.

Osteonecrosis is most sensitively detected by MRI. Necrosis of femoral heads commonly progresses to joint destruction, which can be prevented or delayed by core decompression surgery to relieve increased intraosseous pressure. In cases of advanced disease, major reconstructive therapy can be attempted to prevent permanently limited joint mobility. Among the sickle cell syndromes, osteonecrosis occurs most frequently in patients with sickle cell anemia and coexistent α-thalassemia.

Arthritic pain, swelling, and effusion may be the result of periarticular infarction or gouty arthritis. Nonsteroidal anti-inflammatory agents are useful therapies.

Bone marrow infarction may cause reticulocytopenia, exacerbation of anemia, a leukoerythroblastic appearance, and sometimes pancytopenia. It may also cause pulmonary fat embolism, which has a severe clinical course. This constellation of events may be caused by parvovirus B19 infection.

DERMATOLOGIC COMPLICATIONS. Leg ulcers begin spontaneously or result from trauma, arise near the medial or lateral malleolus, and frequently occur bilaterally. They may become infected and cause systemic infection, osteomyelitis, or tetanus. They rarely occur before the age of 10 years and are less frequent in patients who have coexistent α-thalassemia. Male patients have a three-fold greater incidence. Ulcers are resistant to healing and recur in well over half the cases. Treatment requires weeks for healing. Initial therapy is intended to remove nonviable, superficial tissue by use of wet to dry dressings or adhesive hydrocolloid dressings (DuoDerm). After débridement, zinc oxide-impregnated Dome-paste bandages (Unna's boots) are applied.

Bed rest, elastic stockings, and leg elevation control edema and facilitate healing.

The myofascial syndrome consists of soft tissue swelling and subcutaneous edema, which may cause a peau d'orange appearance. These lesions may be large or only a few centimeters in diameter, are probably the result of dermal or subdermal vasoocclusion, and are treated symptomatically.

CARDIAC COMPLICATIONS. Beginning in childhood, the chronic anemia of sickle cell disease is compensated for by increased cardiac output, stroke and chamber volumes, and heart size. Despite diminished exercise capacity and progressive loss of cardiac reserve, overt heart failure is uncommon in sickle cell patients unless they are stressed with volume overload, exacerbations of anemia, or hypertension. Myocardial infarction occurs in the absence of coronary disease; in one autopsy series, evidence of such events was found in 10% of patients, perhaps as a result of increased oxygen demand exceeding limited oxygen-carrying capacity or of microcirculatory impairment. Septal hypoperfusion affecting the atrioventricular node and bundle of His can cause second-degree atrioventricular block during a painful episode, and it has been suggested that cardiac autonomic dysfunction accounts for the increased rate of sudden death observed in sickle cell disease patients.

Variant Sickle Cell Syndromes

In addition to homozygous sickle cell anemia, sickle cell syndromes result from simple heterozygous inheritance of the sickle cell gene (i.e., sickle cell trait) and from its compound heterozygous inheritance with other mutant β-globin genes (e.g., Hb SC disease, sickle cell–β-thalassemia). Brief descriptions of these syndromes follow.

SICKLE CELL TRAIT. The approximate prevalence of sickle cell trait is 9% among African Americans and 25 to 30% in regions of western Africa. Those heterozygous for the sickle cell gene number approximately 2.5 million in the United States and 30 million worldwide. Sickle cell trait is a benign carrier condition with no hematologic manifestations. Sickle forms are not seen on the peripheral blood smear. The fractional partition of Hb A and Hb S is usually 60:40 as a result of a greater post-translational affinity of α-globin chains for β^A than for β^S chains. Coinherited α-thalassemia reduces the availability of α chains, thereby enhancing this preferential affinity and decreasing the percentages of Hb S according to the number of α-globin genes deleted (i.e., 40, 35, 29, and 21% Hb S, respectively, for the genotypes αα/αα, –α/αα, –α/–α, and ––/–α).

Few clinical complications are associated with sickle cell trait. Splenic infarction at high altitude affects whites with sickle cell trait more frequently than it does those of African ancestry. Sickle cell trait is a common cause of hematuria among African Americans. The impaired urinary concentrating ability is directly related to the intraerythrocytic concentration of Hb S, inversely related to the presence of α-thalassemia, and reversed by transfusion up to the age of 8 years. There is no increased incidence of anesthetic complications. The 30-fold greater frequency of unexplained sudden death in military recruits during basic training appears to be the result of exercise-induced vasoocclusion and rhabdomyolysis.

Despite its known complications, the rare clinical events do not justify regarding sickle cell trait as anything but a benign carrier condition. When newborn screening programs identify infants with sickle cell trait, their parents require genetic counseling. Parents must understand that their child has a benign hereditary condition, not a disease, but that there may a risk for a subsequent child to be born with sickle cell disease.

If individuals who appear to have sickle cell trait are symptomatic, the diagnosis must be verified. Rare hemoglobins other than Hb S may polymerize and explain the symptoms, that is, heterozygous Hb S^Antilles and Hb Quebec-CHORI. Many symptomatic individuals with Hb SC disease or sickle cell–β-thalassemia have been misdiagnosed as having sickle cell trait.

Hb SC DISEASE. The frequency of the Hb C gene ($\alpha_2\beta_2^{6Glu\rightarrow Lys}$) among African Americans is approximately one third the frequency of the β^S gene, resulting in a prevalence for Hb SC disease that is one third the prevalence of sickle cell anemia. Although oxy-Hb C forms intraerythrocytic crystals, Hb C does not participate in deoxy-Hb S polymerization. The fundamental contribution of Hb C to sickle erythrocyte pathobiologic mechanisms is the sustained potassium-

chloride cotransport that induces cellular desiccation, thereby raising intraerythrocytic Hb S concentrations to levels that support polymerization, sickling, and clinical symptoms.

The β^c mutation affects the same codon as Hb S, the sixth codon of the β-globin gene, but the GAG→AAG substitution results in lysine instead of glutamic acid as the sixth amino acid. Hemoglobin C is poorly soluble when oxygenated and forms intraerythrocytic oxy-Hb C crystals.

As a result of a longer circulatory survival of Hb SC RBCs (i.e., 27 days compared with 17 days for Hb SS RBCs), the degree of anemia and reticulocytosis is frequently milder. Target cells predominate on the peripheral smear (Fig. 171–4). The clinical course is generally milder than that of sickle cell anemia: the frequency of painful episodes is approximately half, the life expectancy is 20 years longer, the persistence of splenic function is extended, and the incidence of fatal bacterial infection is lower. There is a higher incidence of proliferative sickle retinopathy.

Simple heterozygosity for Hb C (Hb AC) is not associated with anemia, hemolysis, or splenomegaly. Target cells are present on the peripheral smear. On electrophoresis, there is about 50 to 60% Hb A and 40 to 50% Hb C.

Homozygosity for Hb C (Hb CC) results in mild to moderate hemolytic anemia, with hematocrit values ranging from 25 to 37%, and moderate reticulocytosis. Splenomegaly is usual, gallstones are common, and aplastic crisis may occur. Cell dehydration elevates the MCHC to approximately 38 g/dL. Prominent spherocytes, target cells, a few Hb C crystals, and folded RBCs are observed on the peripheral smear.

Compound heterozygosity for Hb C and β-thalassemia results in moderately severe hemolytic anemia with microcytosis, hypochromia, and target cells. Both Hb C-β^0 thalassemia and Hb C-β^+ thalassemia are associated with a risk for gallstones and aplastic crisis. Although both Hb C-β^0 thalassemia and Hb CC are characterized by predominantly Hb C on electrophoresis, the former is distinguishable by its lower mean corpuscular volume (MCV) (55 to 70 versus 72 fL), lower mean corpuscular hemoglobin (18 to 21 versus 27 pg), and higher Hb F level (3 to 10% versus <3%). A characteristic electrophoresis pattern for Hb C-β^+ thalassemia is 65 to 80% Hb C, 20 to 30% Hb A, and 2 to 5% Hb F.

SICKLE CELL–β-THALASSEMIA. The frequency of β-thalassemia genes among African Americans is one tenth the frequency of the β^S gene, resulting in a prevalence for compound heterozygous sickle cell–β-thalassemia that is one tenth the prevalence of sickle cell anemia. Sickle cell–β-thalassemia encompasses sickle cell–β^+-thalassemia and sickle cell–β^0-thalassemia, which have, respectively, reduced amounts of or no Hb A present. The percentage of Hb A present in sickle cell–β^+-thalassemia varies from 3 to 25%, according to the degree to which specific thalassemia mutations impair β-globin gene expression. Eighty per cent of cases of β-thalassemia in African Americans is due to the mild -88 (C→T) and -29 (A→G) promoter region mutations, which generate relatively large amounts of Hb A.

Sickle cell–β-thalassemia RBCs are hypochromic and microcytic. The clinical nature of sickle cell–β^+-thalassemia is more benign than that of sickle cell–β^0-thalassemia, as reflected by its higher rate of incidental diagnosis, later age of presentation, less frequent leg ulcers, half as frequent acute chest syndrome, lower frequency of priapism and aplastic crisis, and less severe retardation of growth and development. Splenomegaly occurs in approximately one third of both groups.

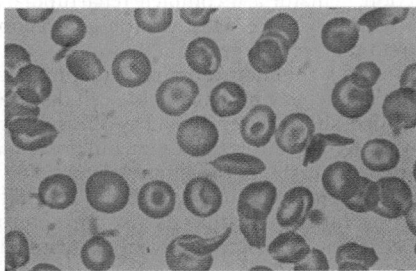

FIGURE 171–4 • Hemoglobin SC disease. Peripheral smear shows frequent target cells interspersed with sickled red blood cells that are sometimes more plump in appearance than the sickled cells in SS disease.

SICKLE CELL ANEMIA WITH COEXISTENT α-THALASSEMIA. The α-globin gene deletion responsible for α-thalassemia among African Americans has a frequency of 0.16 in this population—nearly one in three are silent carriers of α-thalassemia (genotype −α/αα), and 2% have α-thalassemia trait due to homozygous α-thalassemia 2 (genotype −α/−α). The powerful effect of Hb S concentration on polymerization results in milder anemia in sickle cell anemia associated with the deletion of either one (genotype −α/αα) or two (genotype −α/−α) α-globin genes.

Coinherited α-thalassemia also results in a decreased incidence of leg ulcers but an *increased* incidence of osteonecrosis, frequency of acute painful episodes, incidence of CVA, and mortality rate after the age of 20 years. The conflicting clinical correlates of α-thalassemia demonstrate the vagaries of trying to predict clinical severity by using formulas of polymerization tendencies.

SICKLE CELL−δβ-THALASSEMIA AND SICKLE CELL−HEREDITARY PERSISTENCE OF FETAL HEMOGLOBIN. δβ-Thalassemia and HPFH are the result of large deletions of the δ- and β-globin genes. The δβ-thalassemia deletion allows the switch from fetal to adult hemoglobin production, which in this case is an attempted switch in expression to genes that are not present. Sickle cell−δβ⁰-thalassemia is an uncommon compound heterozygous condition in which Hb S, F, and A_2 exist. The 15 to 25% Hb F is distributed unevenly in the RBC population (heterocellularly). Anemia is mild, and clinical complications are infrequent. Classic HPFH results from large deletions that retard the switch from the production of Hb F to adult hemoglobin. The gene frequency of deletional HPFH among black Americans is 0.0005, resulting in an incidence of sickle cell-HPFH that is 1/100 that of sickle cell anemia. These individuals have pancellular distribution of 25% Hb F and are neither anemic nor afflicted with vasoocclusive manifestations as a result of Hb F inhibiting Hb S polymerization. The hemoglobin electrophoresis finding of Hb S, F, and A_2 is distinguished from sickle cell anemia and sickle cell−β-thalassemia by the pancellular distribution of 15 to 35% Hb F and Hb A_2 levels less than 2.5%.

SICKLE CELL-Hb LEPORE DISEASE. Hb Lepore is a crossover fusion product of the δ- and β-globin genes that has the same electrophoretic mobility as Hb S. Thalassemic expression of the Hb Lepore gene results in only 12% Hb Lepore in simple heterozygotes. Compound heterozygous Hb S-Hb Lepore is similar to sickle cell anemia or sickle cell−β⁰ thalassemia on electrophoresis, but the anemia is less severe. The combination of predominantly Hb S with microcytosis resembles sickle cell−β-thalassemia, but low to low-normal Hb A_2 levels (due to crossover incapacitation of one δ-globin gene) suggest Hb S-Hb Lepore. Vasoocclusive complications and splenomegaly occur.

SICKLE CELL-Hb D DISEASE. Hb SD disease was mistaken for sickle cell anemia, because Hb D^Punjab or Hb D^Los Angeles ($\alpha_2\beta_2^{121Glu\rightarrow Gln}$) has an alkaline electrophoretic mobility similar to that of Hb S. Hb D is distinguishable from Hb S by acid electrophoresis or isoelectric focusing. There is moderately severe hemolytic anemia, irreversibly sickled cells on the peripheral smear, and clinical manifestations similar to those of sickle cell anemia.

SICKLE CELL-Hb E DISEASE AND OTHER Hb E SYNDROMES. Hb E ($\alpha_2\beta_2^{26Glu\rightarrow Lys}$) is a β-thalassemic hemoglobinopathy found predominantly among Southeast Asians. Hb E has an electrophoretic mobility similar to that of Hb A_2, C, and O Arab under alkaline conditions, but it can be distinguished by acid electrophoresis or isoelectric focusing. Hb E is classified as a thalassemic hemoglobinopathy because of its having features both of quantitatively reduced production and of structural aberrance. Because of the thalassemic expression, Hb E constitutes only 30% of the hemoglobin in Hb SE disease, and there is mild microcytosis.

Simple heterozygosity for Hb E (Hb AE) is not associated with anemia, hemolysis, or splenomegaly but usually is characterized by mild microcytosis (average MCV ~74 fL) and target cells on the peripheral smear. The imbalanced proportions of Hb E (27 to 30%) and Hb A (70 to 73%) on electrophoretic analysis are largely the result of the thalassemic synthesis of β^E globin and Hb E, and this lower proportion of Hb E provides a clue for distinguishing carriers of Hb E and C, which co-migrate on standard alkaline electrophoresis.

In cases of homozygous Hb E (Hb EE) there is no or mild anemia. Microcytosis is more pronounced than in Hb AE (average MCV ~67 fL), and there are more target cells on the peripheral smear.

The most significant clinical syndrome associated with Hb E is the compound heterozygous condition Hb E-β thalassemia. Because of the thalassemic quality of both the β^E and β^Thal alleles, the clinical severity of this condition usually resembles that of homozygous β-thalassemia major. The high frequencies of these two genes in Southeast Asia make this combination the most common cause of thalassemia major. The most frequent β-thalassemia alleles in this population completely abolish β-globin production, so there is no Hb A. This condition is associated with severe transfusion-requiring hemolytic anemia (average Hb = 6.4 g/dL), reticulocytosis, and microcytosis. The remarkably abnormal peripheral smear is notable for microcytosis, hypochromia, target cells, poikilocytosis, anisocytosis, nucleated RBCs, and a variable degree of basophilic stippling. Clinical features are those of β-thalassemia major (Chapter 168). Both Hb E-β⁺-thalassemia and Hb AE have Hbs A and E, but the former is readily distinguishable by its greater clinical severity.

 Screening, Prevention, and Treatment

NEWBORN SCREENING. Incentive for early identification of infants with sickle cell disease derives from the tremendous reduction in the rate of mortality effected by the use of prophylactic penicillin and comprehensive medical care in the first 5 years of life. Universal screening of newborns of all ethnic backgrounds is recommended.

PREVENTION. The limited efficacy of current treatments for sickle cell disease emphasizes the importance of preventing sickle cell disease, which can be achieved through genetic counseling and prenatal diagnosis. In current clinical practice, fetal DNA samples are obtained by chorionic villus sampling at 8 to 10 weeks' gestation. However, sampling DNA from fetal cells in the maternal circulation and preimplantation diagnosis have been used successfully.

HEALTH CARE MAINTENANCE. Routine outpatient visits are important for patients with sickle cell disease to establish baseline data for comparison at times of clinical exacerbations, relationships with health care professionals, and RBC phenotypes for individualized blood bank files. Counseling about the disease, genetic characteristics, and psychosocial issues is best done during routine visits. Folic acid, 1 mg/day orally, is administered. Noninvasive surveillance of cerebral blood flow using transcranial Doppler assessment is a useful predictor of CVA and should be performed regularly to identify those patients in whom chronic transfusion should be initiated to prevent this outcome. Retinal evaluation is begun at school age and continued routinely. Sexually active women receive routine pelvic examinations. Oral contraception with low-dose estrogen can be administered safely. Immunization using conjugated vaccines for

S. pneumoniae and *H. influenzae* type b should be employed. Reimmunization for *S. pneumoniae* is recommended every 6 to 8 years.

PSYCHOSOCIAL ISSUES. Particular challenges to psychosocial adjustment are recurrent pain and the response to it, limitation of activity due to painful episodes, misinterpretation of the meaning of pain, and depression leading to learned helplessness. Some patients become addicted to narcotics, but addiction is uncommon and most often the result of social influences rather than appropriate analgesia therapy. Signs of good adjustment are active coping strategies and support from the family and the extended family unit. Interventional approaches emphasize recognizing and reinforcing individual strengths, confronting pathologic behavior, and establishing coping skills. Attention to psychosocial welfare is critical to health and integration into society.

INFECTIONS. Outpatient ceftriaxone is recommended for children with fevers higher than 38.5° C unless they appear toxic, have temperature higher than 40° C, are not receiving prophylactic penicillin, have previously documented *S. pneumoniae* bacteremia, or live in areas where antibiotic-resistant *S. pneumoniae* has evolved. In these situations, the patient should be hospitalized, have culture samples of blood and cerebrospinal fluid taken, and receive treatment with antibiotics likely to be effective against local strains of *S. pneumoniae*. Treatment of meningitis should cover *S. pneumoniae* and *H. influenzae* type b and be continued for at least 2 weeks.

Antibiotic therapy for the acute chest syndrome should provide coverage for *S. pneumoniae, H. influenzae* type b, *Mycoplasma pneu-*

Continued

moniae, and *Chlamydia pneumoniae.* Cefuroxime combined with tetracycline or a macrolide is recommended.

The diagnosis of osteomyelitis is confirmed by culture of blood or infected bone, after which parenteral antibiotics that cover *Salmonella* species and *S. aureus* are administered. Antibiotic therapy is tailored by using culture and sensitivity results and continued for 2 to 6 weeks. Surgical drainage or sequestrectomy may be required.

TRANSFUSION THERAPY. Patients with sickle cell disease have requirements for transfusion similar to those of other patients (Chapter 165), but they also have indications unique to their disease: protection from imminent danger (e.g., acute chest syndrome, septicemia, metabolic acidosis) and improved rheologic properties of blood (e.g., prevention of recurrent CVA, priapism, preoperatively). The routine acute painful crisis is not an indication for transfusion. Transfusion complications include alloimmunization, iron overload, transmission of viral illness, and the hyperviscosity associated with increasing the RBC mass to a level at which the hematocrit exceeds 30% or the hemoglobin concentration exceeds 10 g/dL. Antibodies against the Rh (E, C), Kell (K), Duffy (Fya, Fyb), and Kidd (Jk) antigens present the greatest problem in transfusion of these patients. Transfusing extended-matched, phenotypically compatible blood has been documented to diminish alloimmunization rates. Deferoxamine chelation should be considered for patients with elevated total body iron levels reflected by serum ferritin levels that exceed 2000 ng/mL.

Preoperative transfusion to reduce Hb S to less than 60% and raise the hemoglobin level to near 10 g/dL reduces the incidence of acute chest syndrome perioperatively. Partial exchange transfusion to reduce Hb S to less than 30% may be advantageous in cases of Hb SC disease. Partial exchange transfusion in adults is accomplished by phlebotomizing 500 mL, infusing 300 mL normal saline solution, phlebotomizing another 500 mL, and infusing 4 to 5 units of packed RBCs. After transfusion, the hematocrit should not exceed 30%, and the hemoglobin concentration should not exceed 10 g/dL.

PAIN MANAGEMENT. Acute painful episodes are the most common reason that sickle cell patients seek medical care. The physician must exclude causes other than vasoocclusion, maintain optimal hydration by oral or intravenous fluid administration, and use analgesics aggressively but cautiously. RBC transfusion is not routinely indicated, and oxygen is recommended only for patients who are hypoxemic.

Optimal treatment of patients in pain (Table 171–3) should be in a familiar setting if possible. The treatment of severe pain may require hospitalization, intravenous fluid administration, and narcotics (Chapter 29). Intravenous morphine or oxycodone is recommended for prompt pain relief, and patient-controlled analgesia is an excellent means of subsequent pain control. Patients with sickle cell disease metabolize narcotics more rapidly than normal and may respond poorly to conventional doses of analgesia. Comprehensive approaches to the biopsychosocial experience of pain includes psychosocial support systems, local anesthetics, epidural anesthetics, combinations of nonsteroidal anti-inflammatory agents and narcotics, and antidepressive drugs. Ketorolac (Toradol) can be given by injection or orally, provides analgesia superior to that of parenteral meperi-

---

Table 171–3 • RECOMMENDED DOSE AND INTERVAL OF ANALGESICS NECESSARY TO OBTAIN ADEQUATE PAIN CONTROL IN SICKLE CELL DISEASE

	DOSE/RATE	COMMENTS
SEVERE/MODERATE PAIN		
Morphine	Parenteral: 0.1–0.15 mg/kg/dose every 3–4 hours. Recommended maximum single dose 10 mg PO: 0.3–0.6 mg/kg/dose every 4 hours	Drug of choice for pain, lower doses in the elderly and infants and in patients with liver failure or impaired ventilation
Meperidine (Demerol)	Parenteral: 0.75–1.5 mg/kg/dose every 2–4 hours. Recommended maximum dose 100 mg PO: 1.5 mg/kg/dose every 4 hours	Increased incidence of seizures. Avoid in patients with renal or neurologic disease or those who receive monoamine oxidase inhibitors
Hydromorphone	Parenteral: 0.01–0.02 mg/kg/dose every 3–4 hours	
Oxycodone	PO: 0.04–0.06 mg/kg/dose every 4 hours. Recommended maximum dose: 0.15 mg/kg/dose every 4 hours	
Ketorolac	**Intramuscular:** Adults: 30 or 60 mg initial dose, followed by 15 to 30 mg every 6–8 hours Children: 1 mg/kg load, followed by 0.5 mg/kg every 6 hours	Equal efficacy to 6 mg MS; helps narcotic-sparing effect; not to exceed 5 days. Maximum 150 mg first day, 120 mg maximum subsequent days. May cause gastrointestinal irritation
Butorphanol	**Parenteral:** Adults: 2 mg every 3–4 hours	Agonist-antagonist. Can precipitate withdrawal if given to patients who are being treated with agonists
MILD PAIN		
Codeine	PO: 0.5–1 mg/kg/dose every 4 hours Maximum dose 60 mg	For mild-to-moderate pain not relieved by aspirin or acetaminophen; can cause nausea and vomiting
Aspirin	PO: Adults: 0.3–0.6 g/dose every 4–6 hours Children: 10 mg/kg/dose every 4 hours	Often given with a narcotic to enhance analgesia. Can cause gastric irritation. Avoid in febrile children
Acetaminophen	PO: Adults 0.3–0.6 g every 4 hours Children: 10 mg/kg/dose	Often given with a narcotic to enhance analgesia
Ibuprofen	PO: Adults: 300–400 mg/dose every 4 hours Children: 5–10 mg/kg/dose every 6–8 hours	Can cause gastric irritation
Naproxen	PO: Adults: 500 mg/dose initially, then 250 mg/dose every 8–12 hours Children: 10 mg/kg/day (5 mg/kg every 12 hours)	Long duration of action. Can cause gastric irritation
Indomethacin	PO: Adults: 25 mg/dose every 8 hours Children: 1–3 mg/kg/day given in three to four divided doses	Contraindicated in psychiatric, neurologic, renal diseases. High incidence of gastric irritation. Useful in gout

Adapted from Charache S, Lubin B, Reid C, et al: Management and Therapy of Sickle Cell Disease, 3rd ed. NIH publication #95-2117. Bethesda, MD, National Institutes of Health, 1995, pp 1–114.

dine, especially for bone pain, and avoids respiratory depression. Tramadol causes minimal respiratory depression and has a low potential for abuse or addiction.

HYDROXYUREA. In a large multicenter study, hydroxyurea reduced leukocyte, PMN, reticulocyte, and sickle cell counts and increased levels of hemoglobin, hematocrit, MCV, Hb F, F cells, and F reticulocytes. The result was a lower rate of acute painful episodes, longer interval to first and second acute painful episodes, decrease in episodes of acute chest syndrome, and a diminished transfusion requirement.[2] The therapeutic benefit of hydroxyurea may be related to its lowering of the PMN count. After 9 years of treatment, hydroxyurea appears to reduce mortality.[3] General guidelines recommend administration of hydroxyurea to patients who consider themselves impaired by painful episodes, who are willing to comply with frequent monitoring for myelosuppression, and who will adopt a program that may improve their quality of life. Optimal administration of the agent is once daily by mouth in a dose beginning at 15 mg/kg and escalating to maximum tolerated dose.

BONE MARROW TRANSPLANTATION. Bone marrow transplantation (Chapter 166) is useful for severe sickle cell anemia, particularly in children, in whom bone marrow transplantation from matched sibling donors yielded a 94% survival rate and an 84% event-free survival rate. In nearly all patients who had stable donor engraftment, complications of sickle cell disease remitted, including pain crises, CVA, and acute chest syndrome. Bone marrow transplantation has not yet been applied widely to adults. Given the high annual cost of care for patients with sickle cell disease, bone marrow transplantation may become a cost-effective option.

NITRIC OXIDE. There is increasing evidence for a potential role of nitric oxide in the treatment of sickle cell disease. In addition to its powerful vasodilatory activity, nitric oxide inhibits platelet function and reduces the adhesivity of vascular endothelial cells. In a controlled trial, inhaled nitric oxide was found to reduce the narcotic requirement of patients having acute painful episodes,[4] and there are reports of its beneficial effects for the treatment for the acute chest syndrome. The oral administration of the nitric oxide precursor L-arginine has beneficial effects in sickle cell patients with pulmonary hypertension.

Future Directions

Oral administration of agents that inhibit the cellular dehydration, such as the imidazole compound clotrimazole, or magnesium supplements that inhibit potassium-chloride cotransport have shown promise in pilot studies. Antiadhesion therapies using monoclonal antibodies may block the adhesivity of endothelial integrin molecules. Unfractionated heparin, which blocks sickle cell adhesion to P-selectin, is a compelling candidate for clinical trials. Artificial surfactant can inhibit the adherence of sickle cells to the vascular endothelium and may have a therapeutic role for acute painful episodes. Gene therapy is a promising but unproven possibility.

1. Adams RJ, McKie VC, Hsu L, et al: Prevention of a first stroke by transfusions in children with sickle cell anemia and abnormal results on transcranial Doppler ultrasonography. N Engl J Med 1998;339:5–11.
2. Charache S, Terrin ML, Moore RD, et al: Effect of hydroxyurea on the frequency of painful crises in sickle cell anemia. N Engl J Med 1995;332:1317–1322.
3. Steinberg MH, Barton F, Castro O, et al: Effect of hydroxyurea on mortality and morbidity in adult sickle cell anemia: Risks and benefits up to 9 years of treatment. JAMA 2003;289:1645–1651.
4. Weiner DL, Hibberd PL, Betit P, et al: Preliminary assessment of inhaled nitric oxide for acute vaso-occlusive crisis in pediatric patients with sickle cell disease. JAMA 2003;289:1136–1142.

SUGGESTED READINGS
Hebbel RP: Clinical implications of basic research: Blockade of adhesion of sickle cells to endothelium by monoclonal antibodies. N Engl J Med 2000;342:1910–1912. *An insightful perspective on the application of antiadhesion therapy for the prevention of sickle cell vasoocclusion.*
Pawliuk R, Westerman KA, Fabry ME, et al: Correction of sickle cell disease in transgenic mouse models by gene therapy. Science 2001;294:2368–2371. *A successful collaboration in which a group of experts brought their respective expertise to bear on an elusive disease target.*
Vichinsky E: New therapies in sickle cell disease. Lancet 2002;360:629–631. *A succinct overview.*
Walters MC, Storb R, Patience M, et al: Impact of bone marrow transplantation for symptomatic sickle cell disease: An interim report. Blood 2001;95:1918–1924. *Transplantation restored normal erythropoiesis in 22 of 26 transplanted patients in whom engraftment was successful.*

172 HEMOGLOBINOPATHIES: METHEMOGLOBINEMIAS, POLYCYTHEMIAS, AND UNSTABLE HEMOGLOBINS

Josef T. Prchal
Xylina Gregg

METHEMOGLOBINEMIAS

Methemoglobin Formation

Methemoglobin is the derivative of hemoglobin in which the iron of the heme group is oxidized from the ferrous (Fe^{2+}) to the ferric (Fe^{3+}) state. The oxidation state of the iron moiety in hemoglobin determines its oxygen-carrying capacity. The iron in deoxyhemoglobin is in the ferrous form, which allows oxygen to bind to it easily. In contrast, the ferric hemes of methemoglobin are unable to bind oxygen. In addition, the oxygen affinity of the accompanying ferrous hemes in the hemoglobin tetramer is increased. As a result, the oxygen dissociation curve is left-shifted, and oxygen delivery is impaired.

Methemoglobin is generated physiologically as a consequence of deoxygenation. During deoxygenation, some oxygen leaves hemoglobin as a superoxide (O_2^-) radical, leaving the iron in a ferric state and creating methemoglobin. This reaction is called *hemoglobin autooxidation* and occurs spontaneously at a rate of about 3% per day. Endogenous enzymatic hemoglobin reduction mechanisms reduce the methemoglobin, however, to maintain a low steady-state blood methemoglobin level (<1% of total hemoglobin). Increased levels of methemoglobin above this steady state, termed *methemoglobinemia*, result from either enhanced methemoglobin production or decreased methemoglobin reduction.

Although several potential mechanisms exist to reduce methemoglobin back to hemoglobin, only the reaction catalyzed by the reduced form of nicotinamide-adenine dinucleotide (NADH)/cytochrome b_5 reductase (b_5R) is physiologically important. Electrons are transferred from NADH (generated by glyceraldehyde 3-phosphate in the glycolytic pathway) to an enzyme, NADH cytochrome b_5R, then to cytochrome b_5. In hemoglobin-containing red blood cells (RBCs), cytochrome b_5 transfers electrons directly to methemoglobin to reduce it to hemoglobin. In nucleated cells and reticulocytes, cytochrome b_5 transfers electrons to stearyl-CoA desaturase (Fig. 172–1).

A minor alternative pathway of methemoglobin reduction uses the reduced form of nicotinamide-adenine dinucleotide phosphate (NADPH), which is generated by glucose-6-phosphate dehydrogenase (G6PD) in the pentose phosphate pathway. Under normal physiologic conditions, electron transfer by NADPH-dependent reductase

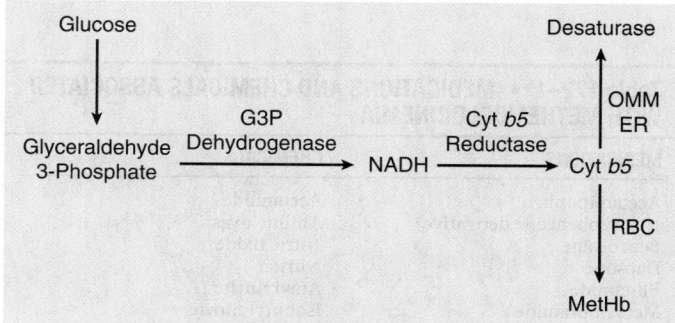

FIGURE 172–1 • Pathway of electron transfer. Glucose catabolism through the anaerobic Embden-Meyerhof pathway generates the reduced form of nicotinamide-adenine dinucleotide (NADH), which serves as a physiologic cofactor for cytochrome b_5 reductase. Two electrons are transferred by means of NADH/cytochrome b_5 reductase to cytochrome b_5. In the red blood cell (RBC), these electrons are transferred to methemoglobin (MetHb); in the outer mitochondrial membrane (OMM) and endoplasmic reticulum (ER), these electrons are transferred to stearyl-CoA desaturase.

to methemoglobin is not functionally significant because of the lack of an electron acceptor for this reductase. Methylene blue, ascorbic acid, and free flavin all can act as exogenous electron acceptors from NADPH reductase in vivo, however. The NADPH-dependent pathway of methemoglobin reduction is crucial in the treatment of toxic methemoglobinemia. Because the reduction of methemoglobin by methylene blue depends on NADPH generated by G6PD, methylene blue may be ineffective in the treatment of methemoglobinemia in individuals with G6PD deficiency. Administration of methylene blue to these patients is potentially dangerous because it may produce hemolysis, presumably as a result of redox cycling by methylene blue to generate reactive oxygen species.

Types of Methemoglobinemia

ACQUIRED

The most frequent type of methemoglobinemia is acquired or acute toxic methemoglobinemia, usually induced by drugs and other chemicals that increase methemoglobin formation (Table 172–1). Methemoglobinemia may occur as a result of medication overdoses, but also may occur at standard doses, particularly in individuals with impaired methemoglobin reduction caused by partial deficiencies of cytochrome b_5R. Infants are particularly susceptible because their erythrocyte cytochrome b_5R activity is normally 50 to 60% of adult activity. One scenario leading to symptomatic methemoglobinemia is an infant who receives formula that is diluted with well water that is contaminated with nitrates. In infants, diarrheal illnesses without toxin exposure also are associated with methemoglobinemia. In adults, methemoglobinemia usually presents as acute shortness of breath and cyanosis, often mistaken for pulmonary embolism, in a susceptible patient exposed to offending agents. Local anesthetics, such as benzocaine, are a frequent cause of acute toxic methemoglobinemia. When the evaluation fails to confirm hypoxia, methemoglobinemia should be suspected. These individuals are often heterozygous for cytochrome b_5R deficiency and respond rapidly to methylene blue.

CONGENITAL

TYPE I CYTOCHROME b_5R DEFICIENCY. The most common form of congenital methemoglobinemia is due to a deficiency of cytochrome b_5R and is inherited in an autosomal recessive pattern (Table 172–2). These individuals have a decreased ability to reduce the methemoglobin that is formed continuously at physiologic rates because of a deficiency in cytochrome b_5R, which, along with NADH, catalyzes the reduction of methemoglobin in normal human erythrocytes. Cytochrome b_5R is a constitutively expressed enzyme, a product of a single gene that produces multiple transcripts.

Most cases of enzymopenic congenital methemoglobinemia are type I, in which the deficiency of cytochrome b_5R is isolated to erythrocytes. Type I cytochrome b_5R deficiency is found worldwide, but it is endemic in some populations, such as the Athabascan Indians, Navajo Indians, and Yakutsk natives of Siberia. In other ethnic and racial groups, the defect occurs sporadically.

Table 172–1 • MEDICATIONS AND CHEMICALS ASSOCIATED WITH METHEMOGLOBINEMIA

MEDICATIONS	CHEMICALS
Acetaminophen (nitrobenzene derivative)	Acetanilide
	Aniline dyes
Benzocaine	Nitric oxide
Dapsone	Nitrites
Flutamide	Amyl nitrite
Metoclopramide	Isobutyl nitrite
Nitroglycerin	Sodium nitrite
Phenacetin	Nitrates (bacterial conversion to
Phenazopyridine (Pyridium)	nitrites)
Primaquine	Nitrobenzenes/nitrobenzoates
Sulfamethoxazole	Nitroethane (nail polish remover)
	Nitrofurans
	4-Amino-biphenyl
	Paraquat/monolinuron

Table 172–2 • TYPES OF METHEMOGLOBINEMIA

Acquired methemoglobinemia
   Medication/chemicals
   Premature infants and infantile diarrhea
Congenital methemoglobinemia
   Autosomal recessive
      Cytochrome b_5 reductase deficiency
      Cytochrome b_5 deficiency
   Autosomal dominant
      Hemoglobin M disease

Homozygotes or compound heterozygotes have methemoglobin concentrations of 10 to 35% and appear cyanotic but are usually asymptomatic even with levels of 40%. Symptoms of headache and easy fatigability have been reported by some patients. Life expectancy is not shortened, and pregnancies occur normally. Significant compensatory elevation of hemoglobin concentration (polycythemia, erythrocytosis) is observed sometimes. Although of cosmetic significance only, the cyanosis can be treated effectively with methylene blue or ascorbic acid, both of which facilitate the reduction of methemoglobin through alternative pathways (NADPH-dependent reductase).

The cytochrome b_5R activity of the erythrocytes of *heterozygotes* is approximately 50% of normal. Although this activity level is sufficient to maintain normal methemoglobin levels during normal conditions, oxidant stress can overwhelm the erythrocyte's capacity to reduce methemoglobin and produce acute symptomatic methemoglobinemia.

TYPE II CYTOCHROME b_5R DEFICIENCY. Of cases of enzymopenic congenital methemoglobinemia, 10 to 15% are type II, which is caused by a general deficiency of cytochrome b_5R in all cell types. Type II cytochrome b_5R deficiency is found sporadically worldwide. The main symptoms are cyanosis, mental retardation, and severe developmental delay. Life expectancy is significantly shortened. The cyanosis can be treated effectively with methylene blue or ascorbic acid, as in type I cytochrome b_5R deficiency; however, treatment is not indicated except for cosmetic reasons because it has no effect on the neurologic aberrations. Amniotic cells contain easily measurable cytochrome b_5R activity; prenatal diagnosis of homozygous cytochrome b_5R deficiency is feasible.

Because the cytochrome b_5R enzyme is coded by a single gene, the suggested explanation for the two types of cytochrome b_5R deficiency is that in type I the abnormal gene product is produced at a normal rate but is unstable; as a result, only mature RBCs, which cannot synthesize proteins, are affected. By contrast, when mutations cause enzyme inactivation or underproduction of the enzyme, the cytochrome b_5R deficiency is generalized (type II).

CYTOCHROME b_5 DEFICIENCY. Deficiency of cytochrome b_5 is a rare disorder that also causes congenital methemoglobinemia. Only one well-documented case of cytochrome b_5 deficiency has been described compared with more than 500 reported cases of cytochrome b_5R deficiency.

HEMOGLOBIN M DISEASE. Hemoglobin M also causes congenital methemoglobinemia and is distinguishable from cytochrome b_5R deficiency and cytochrome b_5 deficiency by its autosomal dominant inheritance. Mutations of α-globin, β-globin, and γ-globin genes have been described; most result in substitution of tyrosine for either the proximal or the distal histidine residue that binds to the iron atom of heme. These amino acid substitutions stabilize iron in the oxidized form, making it resistant to reduction by endogenous enzyme mechanisms or reducing agents (e.g., methylene blue). Affected patients present with asymptomatic cyanosis. Individuals with α-globin variants are cyanotic at birth, whereas individuals inheriting β-globin variants do not develop cyanosis until fetal hemoglobin is replaced by adult hemoglobin in later infancy. Infants with γ-globin variants have transient cyanosis in the first few weeks of life. Hemoglobin M usually is associated with normal RBC morphology and may not be detected on routine hemoglobin electrophoresis; sophisticated evaluation in a specialized laboratory may be required. No therapy is effective or necessary.

DIFFERENTIAL DIAGNOSIS

To distinguish among the hereditary forms of methemoglobinemia, biochemical analyses and interpretation of family pedigrees are required. Because of its dominant inheritance pattern, cyanosis in successive generations suggests the presence of hemoglobin M disease, whereas normal parents and possibly affected siblings implies the presence of the autosomal recessive cytochrome b_5 or cytochrome b_5R deficiencies. Incubation of blood with small amounts of methylene blue differentially distinguishes cytochrome b_5R deficiency from hemoglobin M disease because this treatment results in the rapid reduction of methemoglobin through alternative pathways in cytochrome b_5R deficiency; this reduction does not occur in hemoglobin M disease. To distinguish cytochrome b_5 deficiency from cytochrome b_5R deficiency, measurement of the amount of cytochrome b_5 and the level of cytochrome b_5R activity is required.

Diagnosis of Methemoglobinemia

Methemoglobinemia may be suspected clinically by cyanosis, the slate-blue color of the skin, in the presence of a normal partial pressure of arterial oxygen. Other clinical symptoms of methemoglobinemia generally are seen only in acute toxic (acquired) methemoglobinemia and include headache, fatigue, dyspnea, and lethargy. Respiratory depression, altered consciousness, shock, seizures, and death may occur as levels of methemoglobin increase, and oxygen delivery to tissues is impaired. Clinically discernible cyanosis is caused by methemoglobinemia when the absolute level of methemoglobin exceeds 1.5 g/dL (corresponding to 10 to 15% methemoglobin). Methemoglobin measurements are expressed as a percentage of the total hemoglobin concentration so that the proportion of methemoglobin necessary to cause cyanosis in anemic or polycythemic individuals may be higher or lower than 10 to 15%.

Clinically discernible cyanosis also is associated with sulfhemoglobin when its absolute concentration exceeds 0.5 g/dL. Sulfhemoglobin is an abnormal complex pigment with a different absorption spectrum and usually is produced by methemoglobin degradation in toxic methemoglobinemia. A more commonly encountered clinical situation is cyanosis resulting from desaturated oxyhemoglobin caused by deoxyhemoglobin levels greater than 4 g/dL.

The blood in methemoglobinemia is dark red or a characteristic "chocolate" color, and the color does not change with the addition of oxygen. Pulse oximetry is inaccurate in monitoring oxygen saturation in the presence of methemoglobinemia. The laboratory diagnosis of methemoglobinemia is based on analysis of its absorption spectra. A fresh specimen always should be tested because methemoglobin levels tend to increase with storage. Methemoglobin has its peak absorbance at 631 nm. The microprocessor-controlled, fixed-wavelength co-oximeter commonly used to assay methemoglobin interprets all readings in the 630-nm range as methemoglobin; false-positive results may occur in the presence of other pigments, including sulfhemoglobin and methylene blue. For specific diagnosis and accurate quantification, a spectrophotometric assay should be used to confirm methemoglobinemia.

℞ Treatment

Offending agents should be discontinued in the patient with acquired or toxic methemoglobinemia. If the patient is symptomatic, which is often the case in deliberate or accidental overdoses or in toxin ingestion, specific therapy is required. Methylene blue, 1 to 2 mg/kg over 5 minutes, provides an artificial electron acceptor for the reduction of methemoglobin by means of the NADPH reductase–dependent pathway. Response is usually rapid; the dose may be repeated in 1 hour but frequently is unnecessary. Caution should be exercised to avoid overdosage because large (>7 mg/kg) cumulative doses have been reported to cause dyspnea, chest pain, and hemolysis. Co-oximetry should not be used to follow methemoglobin levels because this method does not distinguish methylene blue from methemoglobin. Patients with G6PD deficiency should not receive methylene blue but can receive ascorbic acid. For severe cases, hyperbaric oxygen and exchange transfusion have been reported anecdotally to be effective.

Treatment of cyanosis in individuals with type I and II cytochrome b_5R deficiency is indicated for cosmetic reasons only. Treatment options include methylene blue, 100 to 300 mg/day orally, or ascorbic acid, 300 to 1000 mg/day orally in divided doses, although this therapy has been associated with formation of renal calculi. The use of riboflavin (20 to 30 mg/day) also has been

reported to be effective. There is currently no therapy for the neurologic disorder associated with type II cytochrome b_5R deficiency. There is also no treatment for methemoglobinemia resulting from hemoglobin M disease, but because the patients are asymptomatic, no therapy is warranted.

POLYCYTHEMIA CAUSED BY MUTANT HEMOGLOBINS AND CONGENITAL RED BLOOD CELL ENZYME DEFICIENCY

The polycythemias (also known as *erythrocytosis*) comprise a group of etiologically diverse disorders characterized by increased RBC mass (Chapter 176). Absolute polycythemias may be either primary, resulting from an intrinsic defect of hematopoietic progenitors, or, more commonly, secondary, resulting from stimulation of normal hematopoietic progenitors by extrinsic factors, particularly erythropoietin (Epo). Although most polycythemias are acquired, some are congenital.

Primary Familial and Congenital Polycythemias

Primary familial and congenital polycythemia (PFCP) (also called *familial erythrocytosis*) is characterized by elevated RBC mass, normal leukocyte and platelet counts, hypersensitivity of erythroid progenitors to Epo in serum containing clonogenic cultures, low serum Epo level, normal oxygen affinity of hemoglobin, absence of progression to leukemia, and typically autosomal dominant inheritance. The molecular basis of PFCP in some families is various gain-of-function mutations of the Epo receptor (*EPOR*) gene. The lack of downregulation of the *EPOR* gene after ligand binding results in increased proliferation of cells expressing these abnormal receptors. In most PFCP families, however, the PFCP phenotype is not linked to the *EPOR* gene, and the cause of the syndrome remains unclear.

Familial Congenital Secondary Polycythemias

MUTANT HEMOGLOBINS WITH INCREASED OXYGEN AFFINITY. Mutant hemoglobins with increased oxygen affinity are a rare cause of congenital polycythemia. Mutations of α-globin and β-globin genes can lead to autosomal dominant polycythemia. More than 50 variants have been described; they all are characterized by an increased oxygen affinity of hemoglobin. The hemoglobin tetramer oscillates between the R (relaxed; fully oxygenated hemoglobin) and T (tense; fully deoxygenated hemoglobin) state of the quaternary protein conformation requiring the cooperative interaction of globin subunits. Mutations affecting the equilibrium between R and T states result in a change of oxygen affinity. Many high oxygen–affinity mutants are located in the α_1/β_2 interface of the hemoglobin tetramer. Some mutations interfere with binding of 2,3-bisphosphoglycerate (2,3-BPG) to hemoglobin, whereas others have an amino acid substitution that is located at the C-terminus of one of the globin subunits and that interferes with binding of heme. The functional consequences of the change of oxygen affinity and a decreased P_{50} are a shift in the oxygen saturation curve (Fig. 172–2). The result is decreased delivery of oxygen into the peripheral tissues and compensatory polycythemia. Patients inheriting these mutations are generally asymptomatic because compensatory polycythemia ensures normal oxygen delivery to tissues. It would be expected that individuals inheriting α-globin variants have elevated hemoglobin at birth, whereas individuals inheriting β-globin variants would have detectable abnormalities after fetal hemoglobin ($\alpha_2\gamma_2$) is largely replaced by adult hemoglobin A ($\alpha_2\beta_2$) in later infancy.

2,3-BISPHOSPHOGLYCERATE DEFICIENCY. One rare cause of congenital secondary polycythemia is familial 2,3-BPG (formerly called *2,3-diphosphoglycerate*) deficiency, which results from a deficiency of the RBC enzyme bisphosphoglyceromutase. Present in a high concentration in RBCs, 2,3-BPG binds hemoglobin, allosterically changing the hemoglobin conformation and modulating its ability to bind oxygen. A decreased 2,3-BPG level shifts the hemoglobin oxygen dissociation curve to the left (and increases hemoglobin affinity for oxygen). The resultant increased hemoglobin oxygen affinity decreases the amount of oxygen released peripherally, leading to a compensatory polycythemia. The deficiency has been reported as either an autosomal dominant or an autosomal recessive disease. Some of the heterozygous individuals are not polycythemic.

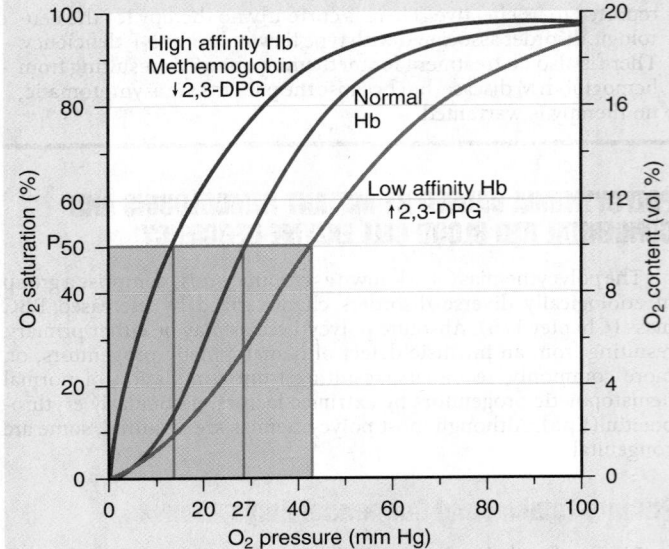

FIGURE 172–2 • Hemoglobin (Hb) oxygen dissociation curve. Left-shifted curve is characteristic of mutant hemoglobins with increased oxygen affinity or decreased 2,3-bisphosphoglycerate (formerly called 2,3-diphosphoglycerate [2,3-DPG]) levels and low P_{50}, whereas the right-shifted curve is characteristic of mutant hemoglobins with decreased oxygen affinity or increased 2,3-DPG levels and increased P_{50}. Normal P_{50} value is 27 mm Hg.

Determination of hemoglobin oxygen association kinetics is the best initial screening laboratory test for suspected congenital secondary polycythemia. A decreased P_{50} suggests a mutant hemoglobin. In contrast to patients inheriting unstable hemoglobins, subjects inheriting stable high oxygen–affinity hemoglobin mutants have normal RBC morphology. Definite identification of the mutant globin requires specialized analytic techniques. When a hemoglobin mutant has been excluded, a biochemical assay of freshly obtained erythrocytes may be used to detect decreased erythrocyte 2,3-BPG. If 2,3-BPG deficiency is found, it should be followed by an assay of bisphosphoglyceromutase activity. Because inheritance of this defect is sometimes autosomal recessive, a family history of this rare deficiency may not be present.

Congenital High Erythropoietin States with Normal P_{50} and Normal Oxygen Saturation

Congenital high Epo states with normal P_{50} and normal oxygen saturation are heterogeneous disorders. The best understood is an autosomal recessive polycythemia present among an ethnic minority in Russia: Chuvash polycythemia. This disorder may affect hundreds to thousands of individuals and seems to be inherited as an autosomal recessive disorder. It is due to a defect in the oxygen-sensing Epo-production pathway caused by a mutation of the von Hippel–Lindau (*VHL*) gene. This mutation impairs the interaction of *VHL* with the α subunit of transcription factor HIF-1 that regulates many hypoxia-controlled genes. This *VHL* mutation reduces the rate of HIF-1α degradation, resulting in increased expression of downstream target genes, including Epo. Other *VHL* mutations have been found in children who have congenital polycythemia without other characteristics of the von Hippel–Lindau syndrome.

HEMOGLOBIN MUTANTS ASSOCIATED WITH HEMOLYTIC ANEMIA: UNSTABLE HEMOGLOBINS

Approximately 100 different globin mutations have been reported to cause unstable hemoglobins. These mutations interfere with the binding of heme, the secondary structure of hemoglobin, the stabilization of hemoglobin hydrophobic interactions, the tertiary structure that disturbs the hydrophobic interior of hemoglobin, or the quaternary structure of hemoglobin because of

deletions of one to five amino acids in one of the globin subunits of hemoglobin.

The hemolysis in this syndrome is inherited as an autosomal dominant phenotype. Most of these patients have enlarged spleens. In some patients, hemolysis is so severe that it may be associated with intravascular hemolysis and hemoglobinuria. Most α-globin mutations that lead to unstable hemoglobins are present at birth. The unstable hemoglobins resulting from β-globin mutations are noticed after the fetal hemoglobin ($\alpha_2\gamma_2$) is replaced by adult hemoglobin A ($\alpha_2\beta_2$). The β-globin mutants generally are noticed within 6 months of birth. A rare γ-globin mutant has been reported in which the hemolytic anemia was present at birth but disappeared after the fetal hemoglobin was replaced fully by hemoglobin A (hemoglobin F pool). Because hemoglobin is present at almost saturated concentrations in the RBCs, the significant change of its conformation may lead to its decreased solubility and precipitation. Hemoglobin precipitates within RBCs are visualized microscopically as Heinz bodies. These rigid particles interfere with the plasticity of RBCs and create hindrance in the microcirculation, especially in the spleen, which leads to RBC destruction.

The mechanism of hemoglobin destruction also involves autooxidation of hemoglobin, which leads to release of superoxide radicals and further disturbance of the hemoglobin molecule by its oxidative damage. Fever and many oxidant drugs, such as sulfonamides, lead to exacerbation of hemolysis and acute hemolytic crisis. During infections, oxygen radicals are produced in greater amounts by neutrophils, diffuse into RBCs, further accentuate the hemolytic process, and may lead to acute hemolytic crisis.

The diagnosis of hemolysis resulting from unstable hemoglobin is suspected by demonstration of Heinz bodies in the RBCs. These inclusions are visualized specifically by supravital stains, such as methyl violet or brilliant cresyl blue. Hemoglobin electrophoresis is not a reliable way of making a diagnosis because some of these hemoglobin mutants are electrophoretically normal. The definitive diagnosis uses either the isopropanol test or the heat test (incubation of hemolysate at 50° C).

SUGGESTED READINGS

Novaro GM, Aronow HD, Militello MA, et al: Benzocaine-induced methemoglobinemia: Experience from a high-volume transesophageal echocardiography laboratory. J Am Soc Echocardiogr 2003;16:170–175. *Benzocaine-induced methemoglobinemia occurred after transesophageal echocardiography in 0.115% (95% confidence interval 0.037–0.269) of patients.*

Pastore YD, Prchal JT: Classification and consequences of polycythemias (erythrocytoses). *In* Jelkmann W (ed): Molecular Biology and Clinical Uses of Erythropoietin. Johnson City, TN, FP Graham, 2002, pp 245–266. *Review of the congenital polycythemias.*

Prchal JT, Gregg XT: Red cell enzymopathies. *In* Hoffman R, Benz E (eds): Hematology: Basic Principles and Practice. Philadelphia, WB Saunders, 2000, pp 861–876. *A detailed description of enzyme disorders leading to methemoglobinemias, hemolytic anemias, and polycythemic disorders.*

173 NONHEMOLYTIC NORMOCHROMIC, NORMOCYTIC ANEMIAS

Thomas P. Duffy

An optimal red blood cell (RBC) mass is maintained within the body by a feedback loop whereby the hormonal stimulus for RBC production, erythropoietin (EPO), is released in response to the hemoglobin needs of the body. EPO is a glycoprotein secreted by renal interstitial cells that respond to the oxidative state of hematin in RBCs perfusing the kidney. As anemia develops, this sensing device within the kidney causes increased EPO secretion, with overdrive of the erythroid component of the marrow. EPO causes amplification of erythroid precursors within the marrow, hastens their differentiation and release from the marrow, and inhibits apoptosis in the erythroid cell line. Under heightened EPO stimulation, normal marrow responds with erythroid hyperplasia and accelerated release of reticulocytes. These reticulocytes can be recognized by supravital staining of their residual polyribosomal reticulated network, which is the marker for these young RBCs in the peripheral blood.

Under normal conditions, the marrow compensates for the 1 to 1.5% of the RBC mass that is lost each day through senescence by

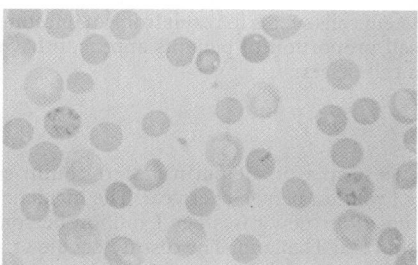

FIGURE 173–1 • Reticulocytes. Special supravital (methylene blue) staining of the blood smear reveals dark purple reticulin, representing residual RNA in immature red blood cells.

replacing it with reticulocytes. When anemia occurs, a physiologic "surge" in reticulocytes should follow if the marrow is capable of responding appropriately to EPO overdrive. This normal response is evidenced by an elevated reticulocyte count, significantly above the normal 1 to 1.5%. If an anemia has its origin within the marrow or is secondary to inadequate EPO stimulation, an appropriate reticulocytosis is not mounted to compensate for the anemia. This reticulocytopenic response indicates that the anemia is due to problems in RBC production within the marrow rather than accelerated RBC loss or destruction in the periphery.

Knowledge of this feedback EPO loop and the reticulocyte count permits a broad dissection of the cause of the anemia (Chapter 159). Absence of an appropriate reticulocyte response in patients with anemia is the hallmark of hyporegenerative anemias. These conditions have myriad causes, including a lack of marrow precursors (stem cell or pure RBC aplasia), lack of necessary building blocks (iron, vitamin B_{12}, folate), lack of adequate EPO stimulation, and abnormalities in proliferation and differentiation of RBCs (leukemia, myelodysplasias, infiltrative disorders of the marrow). The lesion in hyporegenerative anemias is within the marrow, and bone marrow aspiration and biopsy are the definitive procedures for investigation of these anemias if serum and RBC measurements (serum iron, iron-binding capacity, vitamin B_{12}, RBC folate, ferritin, EPO) do not provide an answer.

The presence of an elevated reticulocyte count has the opposite implications regarding the cause of the anemia (Fig. 173–1). Reticulocytosis indicates the presence of a hyperregenerative anemia in which the marrow is able to respond appropriately to the stimulus of anemia. This lesion has its locus in the periphery, with accelerated loss of RBCs from either premature RBC destruction secondary to hemolysis or excessive loss of blood secondary to bleeding.

Measurement of the mean corpuscular volume (MCV) of RBCs, a value derived from the electronic Coulter counter, can further define anemias with a low reticulocyte count. Anemia with small, or microcytic, RBCs (MCV, <80 fL) is most commonly due to iron deficiency (Chapter 167). Anemia with large, or macrocytic, cells (MCV, >95 fL) is usually due to abnormalities in nucleic acid metabolism, with vitamin B_{12} or folate deficiency most commonly responsible (Chapter 175). Anemias with RBCs of normocytic size (MCV, 80 to 95 fL) have numerous causes ranging from faulty production to infiltrative disorders; low EPO states also result in normocytic anemias. The early stages of most anemias are also normochromic/normocytic because of continued presence of the original, normal RBC population manufactured before the new pathologic lesion appeared.

BLOOD LOSS ANEMIA

The hematologic manifestations of bleeding depend on the interval that separates the acute event from measurement of the hematocrit or hemoglobin concentration. Immediately after an acute bleed, the hematocrit is normal because hemodilution has not yet had time to occur and compensate for any reduction in blood volume. Early evidence of acute blood loss may be apparent only in postural changes in blood pressure and pulse rate. After about 24 hours, volume re-expansion corrects this defect by mobilization of extravascular fluid into the intravascular compartment; the result is a decrease in hematocrit that parallels the degree of blood loss. After 3 to 5 days, the reticulocyte count rises to compensate for the anemia; this reticulo-

cytosis may lead to confusion with hemolytic anemia because acute blood loss and hemolytic anemia are normochromic, normocytic anemias with high reticulocyte counts. The MCV may be increased in both conditions because reticulocytes are polychromatophilic macrocytes that may elevate the MCV. The two anemias can be distinguished by the byproducts of accelerated RBC breakdown in hemolytic anemias, in which hyperbilirubinemia is frequently, but not always, the marker of hemolysis. Evidence of bleeding is usually clear, but with bleeding into soft tissues or into a body cavity, such as the retroperitoneum, resorption of blood may be associated with hyperbilirubinemia; the clinical picture may be confusing until the hematoma extends to the surface as an ecchymosis or a radiographic study identifies retroperitoneal bleeding. Individuals receiving anticoagulants especially are candidates for this complication.

The normochromic, normocytic anemias of hemolysis and acute posthemorrhagic states often are accompanied by leukocytosis and thrombocytosis; these responses represent cytokine stimulation of all cell lines within the marrow in response to the anemia.

OTHER NORMOCYTIC, NORMOCHROMIC ANEMIAS

ANEMIA OF CHRONIC RENAL INSUFFICIENCY. Chronic renal failure leads to anemia because of the progressive absence of adequate EPO production in the feedback loop for maintenance of erythropoiesis (Chapter 117). No strict correlation exists between the degree of azotemia and the severity of this anemia, although anemia usually supervenes when the creatinine clearance decreases to less than 20 to 40 mL/minute. A modest shortening of RBC survival also occurs as a result of a metabolic lesion incurred from uremia. This abbreviated RBC survival is only a minor contribution to the anemia of renal disease, however, because the uncomplicated anemia of renal disease can be reversed with the administration of EPO. EPO usually is administered as epoetin alfa three times weekly, either subcutaneously or intravenously, after dialysis treatments. Treatment is initiated with EPO doses of 150 units/kg three times weekly and reduced to 50 to 100 units/kg per dose when the desired response has been obtained. Weekly EPO administration is also effective but requires larger amounts (40,000 units) of the recombinant factor. A long-acting EPO, darbepoetin, is now available that allows hemoglobin maintenance with weekly to tri-weekly administration of the drug.

An essential adjunctive therapy for renal failure patients is intravenous iron in patients with serum ferritin less than 100 mg/mL or transferrin saturation less than 20%. A new form of intravenous iron, sodium ferric gluconate, has been shown to be a safe and effective alternative to iron dextran for this purpose. With EPO therapy, the anemia of renal failure has been largely eliminated.

Many other factors also may contribute to the development of anemia in renal failure. Bleeding may occur from angiomatous malformations that develop in the gastrointestinal tract in uremia, and the hemostatic platelet defect of renal failure may exaggerate this threat. Significant iron loss also occurs as a byproduct of hemodialysis, and folate stores may be compromised by loss of this dialyzable vitamin. Aluminum toxicity interferes with iron metabolism, and a microcytic anemia may develop in patients whose dialysate baths contain high concentrations of this metal. A microangiopathic process often develops with malignant hypertension, and this same RBC lesion is a hallmark of hemolytic-uremic syndrome and thrombotic thrombocytopenic purpura.

ANEMIA OF LIVER DISEASE. After their release from marrow, RBCs' membranes are remodeled by splenic macrophages, and the lipid constituents of the membrane remain in dynamic equilibrium with plasma lipoproteins. Advanced stages of liver disease (Chapters 156 and 157) are complicated by progressive lipoprotein abnormalities that result in the sequential transformation of normochromic, normocytic RBCs into macrocytes, target cells, echinocytes, and, at the final and most severe stage, acanthocytes. Acanthocytes, or spur cells, are converted into spherocytes by the spleen; their lifespan is significantly shortened because the lipid deposition in their membranes interferes with the normal plasticity or deformability of RBCs. In liver disease associated with portal hypertension, hypersplenism may shorten RBC survival even in the absence of any membrane lipid abnormality.

Anemia in liver disease also may have its origin in the several other insults that often accompany hepatic damage; the many insults explain the 50% incidence of anemia in liver disease. Alcohol, with its effect on folate metabolism, may create a macrocytic, megaloblastic anemia (Chapter 175). The same toxin may interfere with mitochondrial heme metabolism and produce a sideroblastic anemia (Chapter 167); vacuolization of erythroid precursors represents this morphologic effect of alcohol on the marrow. A metabolic product of alcohol, acetaldehyde is a direct inhibitor of erythropoiesis in vitro. Iron deficiency also is common in liver disease because of blood loss from varices, alcohol-induced gastritis, and the coagulopathy resulting from defective synthesis of coagulation factors. Wilson's disease (Chapter 224) is associated with hemolytic anemia caused by copper-induced damage to the RBC membrane.

ANEMIA OF ENDOCRINE DISORDERS. Dysfunction in hormonal regulation has systemic effects that include the production and survival of RBCs. An anemia, usually normocytic but sometimes macrocytic, accompanies hypothyroidism because of physiologic responses to decreased metabolic needs (Chapter 239). Menometrorrhagia occurs frequently in hypothyroidism and can lead to iron deficiency anemia. Erythrocytosis may be a feature of Cushing's disease (Chapter 240) because of androgen overdrive of the marrow; a reduction in RBC mass occurs in Addison's disease, but anemia is not usually evident because of a concomitant reduction in plasma volume caused by mineralocorticoid deficiency. Hypopituitary states (Chapter 237) are complicated by mild anemias; growth hormone has a growth-stimulating effect on RBC mass.

Anemia is not a feature of uncomplicated diabetes mellitus but usually occurs in the course of the disease as renal complications develop. Anemia occurs early in diabetic renal disease because of EPO deficiency. Severe hemolysis may occur in diabetic ketoacidosis if significant hypophosphatemia appears after insulin treatment.

ANEMIA OF STEM CELL FAILURE. Deficiencies of stem cells, as occurs with aplastic/hypoplastic anemias, cause a normochromic, normocytic (sometimes slightly macrocytic) anemia that is usually part of a pancytopenia with attendant leukopenia and thrombocytopenia (Chapter 174). Pure RBC aplasia, caused by drugs, parvovirus infection of RBC precursors, or humoral or cellular immune mechanisms, may produce a normochromic, normocytic anemia without increase in reticulocytes. Leukemias and lymphomas may replace and inhibit the marrow and cause normochromic, normocytic anemia.

ANEMIA OF CHRONIC DISEASE. Most patients with anemia of chronic disease have normochromic, normocytic RBC indices. The remainder have a mild hypochromic, microcytic anemia (Chapter 167).

SUGGESTED READINGS

Astor BC, Muntner P, Levin A, et al: Association of kidney function with anemia. Arch Intern Med 2002;162:1401–1408. *When the glomerular filtration rate falls to less than 60 mL/minute, the prevalence of anemia increases progressively with worsening renal function.*

Dikow R, Schwenger V, Schomig M, et al: How should we manage anaemia in patients with diabetes? Nephrol Dial Transplant 2002;17:67–72. *In diabetes, anemia is caused mostly by a diminished production of EPO.*

Wilkinson TJ, Warren MR: What is the prognosis of mild normocytic anaemia in older people? Intern Med J 2003;33:14–17. *A mild normocytic anemia in older people, in the absence of an obvious cause, appears to be a marker of frailty but not necessarily of poorer survival.*

174 APLASTIC ANEMIA AND RELATED DISORDERS

Hugo Castro-Malaspina
Richard J. O'Reilly

APLASTIC ANEMIA

Definition

Aplastic anemia is a disorder of hematopoiesis characterized by pancytopenia and marked reduction or depletion of erythroid, granulocytic, and megakaryocytic cells in the bone marrow. Hematopoiesis (Chapter 159) is markedly decreased as shown by the near absence of myeloid elements and by the absence or low numbers of CD34 cells and colony-forming cells in the bone marrow. In aplastic anemia, hematopoietic stem cells are unable to proliferate, differentiate, or give rise to mature blood cells and their precursors. In most cases,

this failure of stem cells seems to result from an immune mechanism, whereas a small proportion of patients appear to have an acquired intrinsic stem cell defect.

Epidemiology

The incidence of aplastic anemia in western countries is about two new cases per 1 million persons per year. The incidence is higher in Asia, with almost four new cases per 1 million persons per year in Bangkok and in rural Thailand. The disease occurs at all ages but is more common in young adults ages 15 to 30 years and in persons over age 60. The incidence is similar in males and females.

Etiology

Aplastic anemia may occur as the result of inherited abnormalities, such as Fanconi's anemia, but most cases are acquired. Causative factors include drugs, viruses, organic compounds, and radiation (Table 174–1). For over 50% of patients, however, no cause can be determined. Even when a well-defined association exists between an exposure and the subsequent development of aplastic anemia (e.g., chloramphenicol), it remains unclear why only a small proportion of exposed individuals develop the disease. Furthermore, the mechanisms by which certain agents or classes of agents (e.g., viruses, drugs) contribute to the pathogenesis of aplastic anemia are still poorly understood.

DRUGS. Population-based studies have demonstrated an association between certain drugs and aplastic anemia. Drug-induced aplastic anemia is most commonly caused by anticonvulsants, antibacterial agents, antidiabetic drugs, diuretics, sulfonamides, antimetabolites, antimitotic agents, and synthetic antithyroid drugs (Table 174–2). Many other drugs have been linked to aplastic anemia, but the current data are less convincing. For antineoplastic drugs, antimetabolites, and sulfonamides, the myelotoxicity is dose dependent. For the other agents, however, and particularly for chloramphenicol, phenylbutazone, oxyphenbutazone, indomethacin, and gold salts, aplasias are idiosyncratic and not dose related. The mechanisms contributing to aplasia are unclear. For example, chloramphenicol produces both a dose-related reversible suppression of erythropoiesis during treatment and an idiosyncratic dose-independent global marrow suppression many weeks or months after cessation of therapy.

RADIATION. Acute exposure to total body irradiation causes a dose-related transient marrow suppression, which is reversible at low doses but permanent and life-threatening at high doses (Chapter 19). Total body irradiation exceeding 700 to 1000 cGy can induce persistent aplasia by eradicating hematopoietic cells depending on the radiation energy and the dose rate. At a dose exceeding 4000 cGy, the marrow microenvironment in sites of radiation does not support hematopoiesis. Chronic exposure to low dose and extensive localized radiation may cause late permanent marrow failure; for example, patients irradiated for ankylosing spondylitis (Chapter 279) have a higher incidence of aplastic anemia. However, the incidence of aplastic anemia has not been increased in long-term survivors of the atomic bombings in Hiroshima and Nagasaki.

BENZENE AND INSECTICIDES. Benzene, which was the first organic solvent linked to aplastic anemia, has a dose-dependent effect, and chronic exposure has been associated with the development of aplastic anemia and leukemias. Benzene and related aryl hydrocarbons may generate

Table 174–1 • CAUSES OF APLASTIC ANEMIA
ACQUIRED
Drugs: antimetabolites, antimitotic agents, chloramphenicol, phenylbutazone, sulfonamides
Radiation
Chemicals: benzene, solvents, insecticides
Viruses: non-A, non-B, non-C hepatitis, Epstein-Barr virus
Paroxysmal nocturnal hemoglobinuria
Miscellaneous: pregnancy, connective tissue disorders
HEREDITARY
Fanconi's anemia
Dyskeratosis congenita
Schwachman syndrome
IDIOPATHIC: 50 TO 65% OF CASES

Table 174–2 • DRUGS ASSOCIATED WITH APLASTIC ANEMIA

Antineoplastic drugs
  Antimetabolites: fluorouracil, mercaptopurine, methotrexate
  Alkylating agents: busulfan, cyclophosphamide, nitrogen mustard melphalan
Cytotoxic antibiotics: daunorubicin, doxorubicin, mitoxantrone
Sulfonamides and derivatives
  Antibacterials: sulfonamides
  Diuretic: acetazolamide, chlorothiazide, furosemide
  Hypoglycemic: chlorpropamide, tolbutamide
Other antimicrobial drugs
  Antibacterials: chloramphenicol, dapsone, β-lactam antibiotics
  Antifungals: amphotericin, flucytosine
  Antiprotozoals: quinacrine, chloroquine, pyrimethamine, mepacrine
Anti-inflamatory drugs: phenylbutazone, oxyphenbutazone, indomethacin, ibuprofen, naproxen, sulindac
Antiarthritic drugs: gold salts, colchicine
Anticonvulsant drugs: carbamazepine, hydantoins, ethosuximide, pirimidone
Analgesic drugs: phenacetin, salicylamide, aspirin
Antiarrhythmic drugs: quinidine, tocainimide
Antithyroid drugs: carbimazole, methimazole, methylthiouracil, potassium perchlorate, propylthiouracil, sodium thyocyanate
Antihypertensive drugs: captopril, enalapril, methyldopa
Antihistamine drugs: chlorpheniramine, pyrilamine, tripelennamine
Sedatives: chlordiazepoxide, chlorpromazine, lithium, meprobamate
Antiplatelet drugs: ticlopidine

because the proportion of PNH cells in the blood may be too small to be detected by the Ham test; flow cytometric studies using antibodies against cell surface proteins, such as CD55 and CD59, which are lacking in PNH, are helpful in establishing the diagnosis.

OTHER ACQUIRED CAUSES. Eosinophilic fasciitis (Chapter 463), which is a rare connective tissue disease characterized by painful swelling and induration of the skin and subcutaneous tissue, has been associated with aplastic anemia. Suppression of marrow function in this condition is thought to be antibody mediated. A similar mechanism has been implicated in the rare case reports of patients with systemic lupus erythematosus (SLE) (Chapter 280) who develop spontaneous aplastic anemia. However, patients with SLE and other autoimmune diseases are often treated with anti-inflammatory drugs and gold salts, both of which have been linked to aplastic anemia; as a consequence, the independent role of SLE in the pathogenesis of a secondary aplasia is uncertain. In recipients of allogeneic stem cell transplants (Chapter 166), graft-versus-host disease (GvHD) may cause severe marrow suppression. Aplasia has also been documented in rare patients with congenital or acquired immunodeficiency (Chapter 267) and in recipients of organ allografts who have been engrafted with HLA-mismatched T cells derived from nonirradiated blood products or allografts. Certain disorders of the immune system, including thymoma, X-linked lymphoproliferative disorder, and T gamma lymphocyte proliferation, have also been associated with marrow failure. Aplastic anemia may also, in rare instances, precede acute leukemia. The hypocellular variant of the myelodysplastic syndrome (Chapter 182) may present with clinical and pathologic features that are difficult to distinguish from aplastic anemia.

catabolites that are directly toxic to stem cells, and they may also induce formation of haptens that may stimulate immune responses.

VIRUSES. The most common viral infection associated with aplastic anemia is viral hepatitis (Chapters 151 and 152). Approximately 1 to 5% of cases of aplastic anemia follow an overt hepatitis. Although hepatitis A, B, C, and G viruses have been implicated in aplastic anemia in a small number of cases, most cases are not related to these viruses. Although hepatitis viruses may induce lytic infection of primitive hematopoietic stem cells, the remissions of aplasia induced by immunosuppressive therapies in a proportion of cases of posthepatitic aplasia have suggested that immune responses induced by infection may play a central role.

Parvovirus B19, the etiologic agent of exanthema subitum, can cause transient erythroid aplasia in patients with underlying spherocytic anemias and hemoglobinopathies. This virus infects and lyses erythroid progenitor cells. Persistent infection results from the inability to mount an adequate antibody response. Epstein-Barr virus–induced infectious mononucleosis (Chapter 371) is rarely associated with aplastic anemia, and blood counts usually recover spontaneously in most patients. Cytomegalovirus (CMV) infections in newborns and immunocompromised individuals commonly cause neutropenia and/or thrombocytopenia (Chapter 370). CMV has also been associated with marrow failure, particularly in recipients of marrow transplants. Evidence suggests that certain strains of CMV may infect the bone marrow's stromal cells, which support hematopoietic cell growth, thereby inducing secondary aplasia. The human immunodeficiency virus (HIV) (Chapter 409) can also suppress erythropoiesis.

PREGNANCY. Case reports have documented that some women develop aplastic anemia during pregnancy. In some cases, aplasia has resolved with natural or premature termination of pregnancy but has recurred with a subsequent pregnancy. The pathogenesis and causal relationship between pregnancy and aplastic anemia remains unknown.

PAROXYSMAL NOCTURNAL HEMOGLOBINURIA. Paroxysmal nocturnal hemoglobinuria (PNH) (Chapter 169) is a clonal disease caused by acquired mutations in the *PIG-A* gene, which results in partial or complete inability to construct a glycosyl phosphatidyl inositol (GPI) anchor for the attachment of membrane proteins such as CD55, CD59, and others. Aplastic anemia can be the initial hematologic presentation of PNH. Conversely, PNH can develop in patients with aplastic anemia months to years after immunosuppressive therapy. This clinical observation and laboratory studies have shown that a PNH clone can expand in a marrow that is depleted of normal stem cells. A history of thrombosis and evidence of hemolysis in a patient with an aplastic anemia picture suggest PNH. However, the diagnosis may be difficult to make

Pathobiology

Early clinical observations suggested that acquired aplastic anemia results from two main pathogenic mechanisms: an acquired intrinsic stem cell defect and/or an immune suppressive mechanism. The observations that 40 to 50% of syngeneic transplants for aplastic anemia can achieve hematologic reconstitution without pretransplantation immunosuppression are consistent with an isolated stem cell defect. Conversely, the fact that the other 50 to 60% of the recipients of syngeneic grafts fail to engraft but can achieve hematologic reconstitution if adequate immunosuppression is given before a second transplantation strongly suggests that an immune mechanism contributes to the disease. This suggestion is further supported by documentation of autologous recovery in patients who receive allogeneic marrow transplants after immunosuppressive conditioning or antithymocyte globulin (ATG) and/or cyclosporine. Moreover, the observation that approximately 25% of patients with aplastic anemia are cured by immunosuppressive therapy suggests that, in some patients, the disease is due to an isolated reversible immune defect that induces a quantitative deficiency of healthy hematopoietic stem cells. Conversely, the observation that 20 to 30% of patients with aplastic anemia who achieve a partial or, less commonly, a complete reconstitution of hematopoiesis after treatment with ATG and/or cyclosporine develop a clonal disease, either PNH (10 to 13%) or a myelodysplastic syndrome (10 to 15%), months to years after completion of immunosuppressive therapy suggests that these patients develop aplastic anemia as a manifestation of an immune response directed against preexisting abnormal hematopoietic stem cells or that these abnormal hematopoietic stem cells preferentially recover after immunosuppressive therapy.

In vitro studies have confirmed that the pancytopenia in acquired aplastic anemia results from a quantitative deficiency of early hematopoietic stem cells, as documented by colony-forming cell assays, long-term marrow cultures, and quantification of marrow cells expressing the CD34 antigen. This stem cell deficiency is due to the cytotoxic and/or suppressive effect of the patient's own T cells, but the nature of the antigen(s) causing this pathologic immune response and the intimate mechanisms triggering this abnormal response are not known. In vitro studies have also demonstrated that activated cytotoxic T cells derived from the blood and the marrow of a significant proportion of patients with aplastic anemia cause a Fas-mediated death of stem cells and that they overproduce TH1 cytokines, specifically interferon-γ and tumor necrosis factor β, that suppress hematopoietic progenitors. In patients who respond to immunosuppressive therapy, these colony-inhibiting and interferon γ–producing T cells are no longer detected in the marrow.

Clinical Manifestations

The most common presenting symptoms of aplastic anemia are caused by anemia and thrombocytopenia: progressive weakness, fatigue, headaches, dyspnea on exertion, petechia, ecchymoses, epistaxis, metrorrhagias, and gum bleeding. Even when the neutropenia is very severe, infection is rarely a presenting symptom. The most frequent physical findings are cutaneous and conjunctival pallor and hemorrhages (petechia, ecchymoses, and gum bleeding). If anemia is severe, the patient may be tachycardic and have cardiac murmurs associated with high flow states. Hepatosplenomegaly and lymphadenopathy are notably absent.

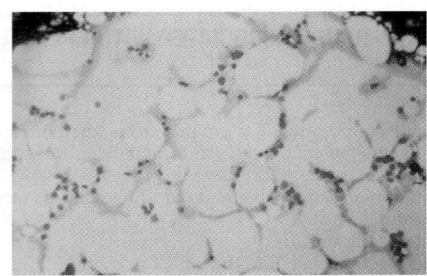

FIGURE 174–1 • Aplastic anemia. Bone marrow biopsy shows a virtually empty marrow. (Courtesy of Andrew Schafer, MD.)

Diagnosis

DIAGNOSTIC EVALUATION. The diagnosis of aplastic anemia should be considered if a pancytopenic patient has a normochromic, normocytic (or slightly macrocytic), and aregenerative anemia; thrombocytopenia with normal size platelets; neutropenia, and no abnormal cells in the leukocyte differential. The absolute reticulocyte count is low because the anemia is secondary to reduced or absent red cell production. Confirmation of the diagnosis requires morphologic and cytogenetic evaluation of the bone marrow.

The bone marrow typically shows numerous spicules with empty fatty spaces and a few hematopoietic cells (Fig. 174–1). The hypocellularity is due to a marked decrease in megakaryocytes and in granulocytic and erythroid cells. Lymphocytes, plasma cells, and mast cells are relatively increased and, in severe cases, constitute over 65% of the cells. Although erythroid cells may exhibit megaloblastic changes, the morphology of marrow elements is usually normal. The presence of overt dysplasia favors the diagnosis of hypocellular myelodysplasia (Chapter 182). Sometimes the cellularity may appear normal because of isolated foci (hot spots) of hematopoiesis. The marrow biopsy allows a better assessment of the cellularity, and it permits evaluation for the presence of tumor cells, hairy cells, and fibrosis. Cytogenetic studies are important to distinguish aplastic anemia from myelodysplasia: the presence of clonal chromosomal abnormalities favors myelodysplasia, but a normal karyotype does not exclude it.

Lactic dehydrogenase and serum haptoglobin levels, Ham's test, and flow cytometric analysis of peripheral blood cells using antibodies against the GPI-linked proteins are useful to establish or exclude the diagnosis of PNH (Chapter 169). In younger patients, cytogenetic studies of marrow cells in the presence or absence of diepoxybutane (DEB) should be performed, because patients with Fanconi's anemia may not have a family history or other clinical findings of the disease.

DIFFERENTIAL DIAGNOSIS. Patients with *hypocellular myelodysplastic syndrome* (Chapter 182) also have pancytopenia and a hypocellular bone marrow. However, review of blood smears may show the presence of immature granulocytes or nucleated red cells. The few myeloid elements in the marrow have dysplastic changes, and the marrow karyotype may show a clonal abnormality. The differential diagnosis may be difficult when the dysplastic changes are subtle and there are no chromosomal abnormalities. *Hypocellular acute leukemia* (Chapter 193) can be misdiagnosed as aplastic anemia when the few mononuclear cells present in the bone marrow are not identified as blasts. Although *hairy cell leukemia* (Chapter 192) usually presents with splenomegaly and a hypercellular marrow, occasionally it presents without these features; this diagnosis is established by recognizing the few hairy cells by their typical morphology, as well as their cytochemical and phenotypic characteristics.

DETERMINATION OF SEVERITY. Aplastic anemia can be categorized as moderate, severe, or very severe based upon the degree of pancytopenia. Severe aplastic anemia is defined by two or more of the following criteria: neutrophils of less than 500/mL, platelets of less than 20,000/mL, and reticulocytes of less than 20,000/mL; these patients have an 80% risk of death by 2 years postdiagnosis if treated with supportive care alone. The very severe form meets the above criteria and in addition has a neutrophil count of less than 200/mL; this very severe form has the worst prognosis, with a lower response rate and a poorer survival rate following immunosuppressive therapy. Patients with less profound cytopenias (neutrophils >500/mL, platelets >20,000/mL, and reticulocytes >20,000/mL) are classified as having a moderate form of aplastic anemia.

℞ Treatment

Prompt and aggressive treatment is indicated for most patients. If a specific cause is suspected, withdrawal of the etiologic agent is the most direct approach to treatment. Discontinuation of the suspected drug, thymectomy in patients with thymoma (Chapter 266), and delivery or therapeutic abortion in pregnancy-associated aplastic anemia may result in recovery of blood counts. Aplastic anemia that develops after hepatitis B may resolve if the virus is cleared with lamivudine therapy (Chapter 152). Unfortunately, however, remissions are observed in only a small proportion of patients.

Once the diagnosis of aplastic anemia is established, family HLA typing should be performed as soon as possible, particularly in younger patients (<50 years), because these patients are most likely to benefit from stem cell transplantation from a histocompatible sibling (Chapter 166). Transplantation is a curative treatment, but it is associated with an early mortality risk ranging from 10% in children and young adults to over 20% in older patients. Transplantation is the preferred therapy in children who have a histocompatible sibling. Transfusions of blood products from family members should be avoided in transplant candidates to prevent sensitization to minor antigens because sensitization increases the risk of graft rejection after transplantation. Whenever possible, only CMV-negative blood products should be given to CMV-seronegative potential transplant candidates to reduce the incidence of CMV infection in the post-transplant period. At diagnosis and during the interval between diagnosis and response to immunosuppressive therapy and allogeneic transplantation, supportive care, including judicious use of red cell and platelet transfusions and aggressive treatment of infections with parenteral antimicrobial agents, is essential in the treatment of patients with aplastic anemia.

Immunosuppression is the most common therapy used in aplastic anemia because only 25 to 30% of patients have a histocompatible sibling. In older adult patients, the choice between immunosuppression and allogeneic stem cell transplantation is sometimes difficult because of differences in short- and long-term complications. Immunosuppression has a low early mortality rate (<10%), but it is not curative and carries a 30 to 50% risk of relapse and a 20 to 30% probability of developing a myelodysplastic syndrome or PNH.

IMMUNOSUPPRESSIVE THERAPY. ATG alone or in combination with cyclosporine is the treatment of choice for aplastic patients who lack a histocompatible sibling or who are over age 40 years. Prospective trials have demonstrated that ATG in combination with cyclosporine induces a higher response rate (60 to 80% versus 40 to 60%) and a more rapid response (median of 60 days versus 80 days) compared with ATG alone, but the rates of relapse, development of secondary clonal diseases, and survival are similar. ∎ Combined ATG and cyclosporine is recommended for patients with the severe and very severe forms of aplastic anemia, whereas ATG alone is often used for patients with moderate aplastic anemia.

The exact mechanism for the response to immunosuppressive therapy in aplastic anemia is unclear. The licensed ATG preparations contain purified and concentrated IgG from hyperimmune sera derived from horses or rabbits immunized with human thymocytes or thoracic duct lymphocytes. These antibodies may delete an abnormal clone of T cells. Cyclosporine induces immunosuppression by inhibiting the first phase of T-cell activation. Response to immunosuppressive therapy is slow and progressive and may not be detected until 12 weeks after its administration. Response rates and post-treatment survival correlate with severity of the disease; patients with the very severe forms have a lower response rate.

Of the 60 to 80% of patients responding to immunosuppression, about 20 to 30% achieve a complete and durable recovery of blood counts. The other 50 to 70% achieve a partial response and become transfusion-independent with platelet counts exceeding 20,000/mL and neutrophil counts exceeding 500/mL. About 10 to 40% of responders to immunosuppressive therapy require chronic immunosuppression with cyclosporine therapy to maintain adequate blood counts.

Of the 20 to 40% of patients who fail to respond to an initial course of combined immunosuppressive therapy with ATG and cyclosporine, about 75% can respond to second course of immunosuppression with rabbit ATG and cyclosporine. Similarly, 30 to 50% of patients who initially respond to immunosuppressive therapies later relapse, particularly if they have achieved only a partial response. Retreatment with a second course of immunosuppressive therapy can induce a second response in over 50 to 75% of patients.

Overall, the quality of the initial response is a strong predictor of ultimate outcome. Of patients who achieve a complete remission, 90% survive event free. In contrast, only 50 to 60% of the patients who have partial responses or who relapse survive 5 years.

Major long-term complications of immunosuppressive therapy include the development of overt myelodysplastic syndrome or PNH in 20 to 30% of patients many months to years after therapy; both are markedly more frequent in patients who achieve only a partial response. ATG is associated with a higher incidence of secondary solid tumors, similar to what is observed among patients who have aplastic anemia and who are prepared for allogeneic stem cell transplantaion with radiation-containing regimens. Whether there is an increase in the incidence of solid tumors in patients treated with a more intensive immunosuppression remains to be determined.

In a prospective randomized trial, a standard course of ATG and cyclosporine was better than cyclophosphamide, which caused more toxicity, fungal infections, and deaths. Although very high dose corticosteroids (10 to 20 mg/kg) can induce responses in a small proportion of patients with aplastic anemia, corticosteroids are no longer used as single agents because of their side effects and the better response rates achieved with ATG and cyclosporine. Treatment with androgens is not beneficial in aplastic anemia.

ALLOGENEIC STEM CELL TRANSPLANTATION. Allogenic stem cell transplantation from an HLA compatible sibling is a curative treatment for aplastic anemia (Chapter 166). Unfortunately, this approach is applicable only to a minority of patients because the proportion of patients who have an HLA matched sibling is in the order of 25 to 30%. Current survival rates achievable with transplant, which are about 70 to 90%, reflect improvements in the management of transplant related complications, particularly graft failure and GvHD. Early studies reported a 20 to 30% incidence of graft failure in multiply transfused patients who were prepared for transplantation with cyclophosphamide alone. In contrast, the risk of graft failure in patients who had not been transfused was <5%. Subsequently, several approaches incorporating total body or total lymphoid irradiation in addition to cyclophosphamide were explored in an attempt to reduce the incidence of graft failure in sensitized patients. Although these treatments reduced the incidence of graft failure, the long-term survival was not improved because of the added transplant related morbidity and mortality associated with these regimens.

The preparative regimen that is currently considered the standard of care for allogeneic transplantation in aplastic anemia consists of pretransplant immunosuppression with high dose cyclophosphamide and ATG, followed by post-transplant immunosuppression with cyclosporine and methotrexate as prophylaxis against GvHD. Marrow transplants from HLA-matched siblings administered with this regimen are associated with a low (<5%) incidence of graft failure and a 30 to 50% incidence of grade III/IV acute GvHD; the long-term survival is up to 90% at 2 years posttransplantation. The relative effectiveness of granulocyte-colony stimulating factor (G-CSF)–mobilized peripheral blood stem cell transplants has not yet been evaluated in aplastic anemia.

Marrow or peripheral blood stem cell transplants from a related single HLA allele-mismatched donor or an HLA-matched unrelated donor are an accepted form of therapy for aplastic anemia when patients have no histocompatible siblings, have failed immunosuppressive therapy, and are refractory to platelet transfusions. Transplants from such donors are associated with a higher incidence of acute and chronic GvHD as well as a high incidence of transplant-related complications. As a result, the usually reported survival rates (30 to 50%) have not been as good as those achieved following HLA-matched sibling transplants. Nevertheless, these survival rates are superior to those seen in otherwise refractory patients on supportive therapy. The outcome of unrelated donor transplants has improved as a result of the use of less toxic preparative regimens and the better selection of donors by high-resolution DNA-based HLA-typing. Now, disease-free survival rates in aplastic children who receive matched unrelated marrow grafts may approach the rates achieved with matched sibling transplants.

SUPPORTIVE THERAPY. Red cell and platelet transfusions should be used with caution because of short-term and long-term complications. The risk of bleeding should be carefully assessed, and platelet transfusions should be given only when the platelet count is less than 10,000/mL or if there is active bleeding with a higher platelet count (Chapter 165). Pooled-donor platelets are usually used until sensitization occurs. Ideally, single donor platelets should be used from the beginning to minimize the risk of sensitization, but in practice this alternative is difficult to implement. Refractoriness to platelet transfusions is a major problem with long-term transfusion support; such patients may require HLA-compatible platelet transfusions. Menstruating female patients should be placed on suppressive doses of birth control pills to avoid severe blood losses.

Packed red cells also should be transfused when the hemoglobin value is less than 7 gm/dl. Younger patients may tolerate lower values, whereas a higher threshold may be clinically indicated in older patients. To reduce sensitization, packed red cells should be filtered to remove leukocytes and platelets. Chronic administration of red cell transfusions results in secondary hemochromatosis because each unit has approximately 200 to 250 mg of iron. Serum ferritin values should be monitored, and chelation therapy with deferoxamine therapy should be given to treat iron overload (Chapter 225).

Patients with aplastic anemia who develop sepsis or other severe bacterial or fungal infections require intensive treatment with parenteral antibacterial and antifungal agents (Chapter 298). Leukocyte transfusions are indicated only in severely neutropenic (<200/mL) patients who have documented fungal or bacterial infections that are caused by organisms that are resistant to first-line antifungal or antibacterial therapy. Prophylactic use of antibiotics in afebrile neutropenic patients has no benefits and increases the emergence of resistant strains.

A common drawback to immunosuppressive treatments is that recovery of blood counts does not occur until 12 to 16 weeks after ATG treatment. The resulting significant early mortality is usually due to infections. Hematopoietic growth factors, particularly G-CSF, may stimulate a more rapid correction of severe neutro-penia. However, when patients with aplastic anemia have been maintained on long-term G-CSF, the long-term incidence of myelodysplastic syndromes with clonal chromosomal abnormalities is increased.

When used as first-line therapy, recombinant hematopoietic growth factors improve blood counts, particularly the neutrophil count, in only a small proportion of patients. Unfortunately, these increments are entirely dependent on the presence of residual hemopoietic progenitors, so patients with very severe neutropenia (<200/mL) rarely respond to growth factors. In patients who do respond, blood counts drop to pretreatment values following discontinuation of growth factor administration.

Hematologic Diseases

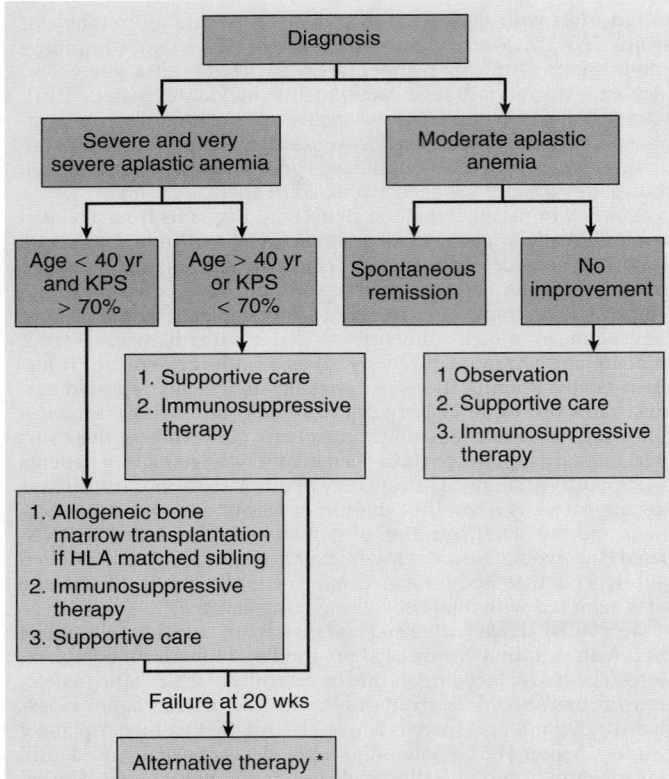

FIGURE 174–2 • Management of aplastic anemia. KPS = Karnofsky performance status score. *Alternative therapy includes a second course of immunosuppressive therapy and allogenic stem cell transplantation from an HLA-matched sibling for older patients and from an unrelated donor, or a partially matched related donor for younger and older patients who are refractory to immunosuppressive therapies and also are severely thrombocytopenic and refractory to platelet transfusions.

Prognosis and Therapeutic Recommendations

The pancytopenia of aplastic anemia is progressive and life-threatening. Prognosis at diagnosis is closely correlated with the severity of neutropenia. The risk of infection (mainly bacterial and fungal) and associated mortality is high in patients with very severe aplastic anemia. Before the advent of immunosuppressive therapy and allogeneic bone marrow transplantation, more than 25% of patients with severe aplastic anemia died within 4 months of diagnosis, 50% within 1 year, and up to 80% within 18 to 24 months despite supportive care with or without androgens.

The introduction of allogeneic bone marrow transplantation and immunosuppressive therapy has radically improved prognosis, and the results achieved with each of these treatments have progressively improved. HLA-matched related bone marrow transplantation is curative in 80 to 90% of patients, but it carries a substantial risk of early morbidity and mortality (Chapter 166). Furthermore, a proportion of long-term survivors may have chronic GvHD. In contrast, immunosuppressive therapy has fewer early risks and can induce at least partial remission in 60 to 80% of patients. However, it is not curative, so a large proportion of patients may relapse and can develop secondary clonal diseases. The success of allogeneic bone marrow transplantation correlates with age and degree of matching. The upper age limit for marrow transplantation continues to increase as better approaches are developed to prevent or treat transplant-related complications. However, allogeneic bone marrow transplantation should be used as a first line of therapy only in younger patients. There is no consensus regarding the definition of a younger patient, but it is well accepted that patients who are below age 20 years and who have an HLA-matched sibling should be treated with allogeneic stem cell transplantation. It is also well accepted that patients above age 50 years should be treated with immunosuppressive therapy. Patients who do not respond to

immunosuppression can be maintained with supportive therapy, but their prognosis is poor. Transplants from partially matched family members or matched unrelated donors are an increasingly effective option for these patients. However, at this time, the higher rates of transplant-associated morbidity and mortality associated with such grafts continue to argue against their use in the front-line management of severe aplastic anemia.

FANCONI'S ANEMIA AND OTHER CONGENITAL CYTOPENIAS

Fanconi's anemia is an autosomal recessive disorder characterized by a progressive pancytopenia, diverse congenital abnormalities, an increased predisposition the malignancy, and increased chromosomal fragility or cellular hypersensitivity to mutagenic chemicals. The most widely recognized features include short stature, café-au-lait spots, kidney and urinary tract abnormalities, microphthalmia, mental retardation, and skeletal abnormalities, most often affecting the thumb and radius. However, many patients with Fanconi's anemia have no morphologic abnormalities and present with anemia or progressive aplasia as the only manifestation of disease. Cells from patients with Fanconi's anemia are uniquely hypersensitive to the clastogenic effect of DNA cross-linking agents, such as diepoxybutane (DEB) and cyclophosphamide; the increased chromosomal breakage resulting from DEB exposure establishes the diagnosis. At least eight different genetic defects may induce Fanconi's anemia; six of these genes have been cloned, and the respective encoded proteins have been characterized. Specific mutations within the common variant of Fanconi's anemia, type C, are associated with earlier onset of severe aplasia. In addition, Fanconi type G and specific mutations of type C are associated with a high risk of secondary myelodysplasia and acute myelogenous leukemia.

Aplastic anemia also may occur as the result of other inherited disorders such as Shwachman-Diamond syndrome and dyskeratosis congenita. Patients with Shwachman syndrome have pancreatic insufficiency, malabsorption, neutropenia, and a tendency to develop aplastic anemia. Dyskeratosis congenita is a rare X-chromosome dermatologic syndrome characterized by reticular hyperpigmentation, mucous membrane leukoplakia, and dystrophic nails; about 50% of patients develop aplastic anemia.

Rx Treatment

Patients with Fanconi's anemia and dyskeratosis congenita are now most commonly detected early in life in families of known predisposition, at which time they may have normal hematologic indices, mild anemia, or neutropenia. Up to 75% of patients with moderate to severe Fanconi's anemia may attain improved hemoglobin levels when treated with androgens, with or without corticosteroids. Androgen therapy may also lead to temporary partial recovery of hematopoiesis in up to 50% of patients with dyskeratosis congenita. However, long-term androgen use in these patients is associated with significant complications, including hepatocellular carcinoma. Prompt improvements of neutrophil counts have also been observed with G-CSF or GM-CSF. Daily to thrice weekly doses of these cytokines can sustain neutrophil counts for many months.

A bone marrow transplant from a normal HLA-matched sibling can cure aplastic anemia in 70 to 80% of patients with Fanconi's anemia or dyskeratosis congenita. In small series, comparable results have been achieved with cord blood transplants from HLA-matched related siblings.

PURE RED CELL APLASIA

Pure red cell aplasias (PRCAs) are rare disorders that selectively affect the growth and differentiation of erythroid precursors in the marrow. Affected patients present with varying degrees of anemia. Myeloid, megakaryocytic, and lymphoid lineages appear normal. Several distinctive forms of red cell aplasia are recognized, including a congenital form, Blackfan-Diamond anemia, which is usually diagnosed at or shortly after birth, and acquired forms, which may have their onset at any time but are usually first detected in older children and adults.

BLACKFAN-DIAMOND ANEMIA

Blackfan-Diamond anemia is a rare form of hypoplastic anemia characterized by intrinsic abnormalities of erythroid progenitor differentiation resulting in varying degrees of a normochromic or macrocytic anemia and either absence or severely reduced erythroid elements in the marrow. Red cell hypoplasia is associated with craniofacial dysmorphologies, malformations of the thumb or upper limbs, atrial or ventricular septal defects of the heart, and abnormalities of the urogenital system. A family history consistent with an autosomal dominant or, less commonly, a recessive disorder is detected in 10 to 20% of cases. Of the patients with the autosomal dominant or the sporadic forms, approximately 25% have mutations involving a gene on chromosome 19q13.2 that encodes the ribosomal protein S19. An etiologic role for such mutations is suggested because transduction of CD34+ marrow progenitor cells from these patients with a retroviral vector encoding a normal gene for the S19 protein increases formation of erythroid colonies in vitro by over threefold.

The severity of anemia in Blackfan-Diamond anemia is variable. Approximately 60% of affected patients achieve a partial or full remission when treated with low-dose steroids over periods of years. Patients with severe refractory anemia require transfusions. In phase II trials, 15 to 30% of such patients have achieved partial or complete remissions when treated with interleukin (IL)-3 or with the prolactin-inducing drug metoclopramide. In contrast, erythropoietin is ineffective. Approximately 2% of patients have ultimately developed leukemia. Transplants of marrow from HLA-matched siblings administered after myeloablative and immunosuppressive conditioning can reconstitute normal donor-derived hematopoiesis and provide an 87% disease-free survival at 5 years post-transplantation. Unfortunately, the success rate for transplants from unrelated or HLA disparate related donors is still poor.

ACQUIRED FORMS

Acquired PRCA may develop for unknown reasons, but more commonly it develops in association with specific types of malignancy, infection, or drugs. Most commonly, acquired PRCA develops as a complication of a neoplastic process such as a thymoma (Chapter 266), B- or T-cell chronic lymphocytic leukemia (Chapter 192), non-Hodgkin's lymphoma (Chapter 195), or an autoimmune disorder such as rheumatoid arthritis (Chapter 278) or SLE (Chapter 280). When PRCS is a complication of lymphoreticular malignancies or chronic Epstein-Barr virus infection, interferon γ–secreting T cells that inhibit erythroid colony growth in vitro can often be isolated from the blood or marrow. In patients with B-cell chronic lymphocytic leukemia or autoimmune diseases who develop PRCA, antibodies that suppress erythropoiesis have often been identified. In rare instances, these antibodies have been shown to neutralize erythropoietin.

The development of T or B cells that are active against erythroid progenitors has also been hypothesized to play an etiologic role in the PRCA that develops in patients treated with specific drugs such as phenytoin, chlorpropamide, isoniazid, and azathioprine. However, certain agents, such as chloramphenicol and the antibiotic linezolid, may induce a dose-dependent selective inhibition of red cell production.

Acquired PRCA may also result from a lytic infection of erythroid progenitors by human parvovirus B19, the etiologic agent of fifth disease. Erythroid cells are selectively targeted by virtue of their expression of globoside, the blood group P antigen that is expressed on a proportion of erythroid colony-forming units and all more differentiated erythroid elements. In normal individuals, such infections likely occur, but anemia is not observed because of the rapidity of the immune response and the regrowth of normal erythroid elements. However, in patients with spherocytosis or sickle cell anemia whose erythroid cell production is already stressed by chronic hemolysis, red cell aplastic crises may develop. Similarly, acquired PRCA may develop after parvovirus B19 infection in patients with AIDS due to impairment in viral clearance ascribable to their immunodeficiency.

Acquired PRCA may also be the first manifestation of a myelodysplastic syndrome (Chapter 182), reflecting a clonal disorder of erythropoiesis rather than a sequela of a secondary immune response. Consistent with this hypothesis is the low rate of response to immunosuppressive therapy in these patients.

 Treatment

The therapy of acquired PRCA is usually suggested by the disorder co-associated with its development. Removal of a thymoma, treatment of an underlying malignancy or cessation of an instigating drug may induce remission. For patients with autoimmune forms, treatment with prednisone usually improves erythropoiesis. Refractory patients may also respond to cyclosporine or low-dose cyclophosphamide. Studies indicate that the CD20-specific monoclonal antibody rituximab can induce durable remissions in patients whose PRCA is refractory to these agents. In contrast, for patients with parvovirus B19 infection–induced aplasia, brief treatment with high doses of intravenous immunoglobulin alone usually fosters rapid recovery of normal erythropoiesis by providing significant doses of parvovirus-specific antibody and thereby hastening viral clearance. For patients with AIDS, chronic parvoviremia may necessitate repeated doses of immunoglobulin.

MYELOPHTHISIC ANEMIAS

Deposition of fibrous tissue in the bone marrow (myelofibrosis) usually causes leukoerythroblastosis in the peripheral blood (immature granulocytes, nucleated red cells, and teardrop-shaped red cells). This process can occur as a primary hematologic disease, called *myelofibrosis with myeloid metaplasia* (Chapter 183), or as a secondary process, called *myelophthisis*, which is often associated with anemia. Myelophthisis represents a reaction of the marrow tissue to invading tumor cells, infectious agents (particularly mycobacteria or fungi), lipid storage diseases (notably Gaucher's disease [Chapter 222]), or other granulomatous diseases such as sarcoidosis (Chapter 91). Tumors associated with myelophthisis are both of hematopoietic (acute leukemias, chronic myeloproliferative disorders, hairy cell leukemia, Hodgkin's disease, and non-Hodgkin's lymphomas, multiple myeloma) and epithelial (breast, lung, prostate, and stomach adenocarcinomas) origin. Myelophthisis can also occur as a result of osteopetrosis (Chapter 264), a congenital disease that is characterized by the failure of osteoclasts to remodel bone, thereby resulting in obliteration of the marrow space with bone and fibrous tissue. Marrow fibrosis results from an overproduction of collagen by marrow stromal cells as a consequence of abnormal concentrations of cytokines that are produced by tumor cells or inflammatory cells and that control collagen metabolism.

The blood smear in myelophthisis is characterized by a normocytic and normochromic anemia with low reticulocyte counts, teardrop-shaped red cells, and circulating erythroblasts. Platelet counts are usually decreased, whereas the granulocyte count, which includes immature forms, is normal or increased. The marrow fibrosis is often associated with extramedullary hematopoiesis and sometimes hepatosplenomegaly. Marrow is often inaspirable (dry tap), but the biopsy reveals fibrosis; the primary process is usually apparent, but it is extremely important to exclude an infectious cause. Therapy is aimed at the primary cause; infections can be successfully treated, whereas metastatic marrow disease is more difficult to treat.

FUTURE DIRECTIONS

In patients with aplastic anemia and in some patients with acquired PRCAs, research is focused on a characterization of the T cells that contribute to marrow suppression. Identification of genes responsible for dyskeratosis congenita, Fanconi's anemia, and an increasing fraction of Diamond-Blackfan anemia cases permits antenatal screening in affected families, in vitro selection of unaffected conceptuses, and potential gene replacement therapy for affected individuals. The introduction of T-cell–depleted transplants and novel nonmyeloablative preparative regimens has improved the results of allogeneic marrow transplants, reduced the risk of transplant-associated mortality, and fostered increasingly effective transplant strategies for patients who lack an HLA-matched sibling donor.

 1. Frickhofen N, Heimpel H, Kaltwasser JP, et al: Antithymocyte globulin with or without cyclosporin A: 11-Year follow-up of a randomized trial comparing treatments of aplastic anemia. Blood 2003;101:1236–1242.

SUGGESTED READINGS

Horowitz MM: Current status of allogeneic bone marrow transplantation in acquired aplastic anemia. Semin Hematol 2000;37:30–42. *An overview of the outcomes and risks of marrow transplant in aplastic anemia.*

Kojima S, Ohara A, Tsuchida M, et al: Risk factors for evolution of acquired aplastic anemia into myelodysplastic syndrome and acute myeloid leukemia after immunosuppressive therapy in children. Blood 2002;100:786–790. *Failure to respond to immunosuppressive therapy and longer duration of G-CSF therapy increases the likelihood of evolution into myelodysplasia or leukemia.*

Young NS: Acquired aplastic anemia. Ann Intern Med 2002;136:534–546. *A comprehensive review..*

175 MEGALOBLASTIC ANEMIAS

Sally P. Stabler
Robert H. Allen

Definition

Megaloblastic anemias are caused by various defects in DNA synthesis that lead to a common set of hematologic abnormalities of bone marrow and peripheral blood. The term *megaloblastic* refers to a morphologic abnormality of cell nuclei that is readily recognizable but difficult to describe. The erythrocytic, granulocytic, and megakaryocytic cell lines all are involved, and pancytopenia may develop. Recognition of megaloblastic anemia is important because two of its most common causes, cobalamin (vitamin B_{12}) deficiency and folate deficiency, are completely corrected with appropriate therapy. Recognition of cobalamin deficiency is particularly important because it also causes a wide variety of neurologic and psychiatric abnormalities that are preventable or reversible if the diagnosis is made at an early stage.

Etiology

Etiologic categories of megaloblastic anemia are cobalamin deficiency, folate deficiency, drugs, and miscellaneous causes, including rare enzyme deficiencies and unexplained disorders (Table 175–1). The cause of cobalamin deficiency can be subdivided into causes of decreased ingestion, impaired absorption, or impaired usage of the vitamin. Folate deficiency also can be caused by decreased intake, impaired absorption, or impaired usage or by many conditions with an increased requirement for folic acid or an increased loss of folic acid. Drugs causing megaloblastosis can be categorized as those that are purine or pyrimidine antagonists and those that inhibit some

Table 175–1 • ETIOLOGIC CLASSIFICATION OF THE MEGALOBLASTIC ANEMIAS

CATEGORY	ETIOLOGIC MECHANISMS
I. Cobalamin deficiency	
A. Decreased ingestion	Poor diet, lack of animal products, strict vegetarianism
B. Impaired absorption	1. Failure to release cobalamin from food protein
	Old age
	Gastrectomy (partial)
	2. Intrinsic factor deficiency
	Pernicious anemia
	Gastrectomy (total)
	Destruction of gastric mucosa by caustics
	Congenital abnormal or absence of intrinsic factor molecule
	3. Chronic pancreatic disease
	4. Competitive parasites
	Bacteria in diverticula of bowel, blind loops
	Fish tapeworm infestations (*Diphyllobothrium latum*)
	5. Intrinsic intestinal disease
	Ileal resection, Crohn's disease, radiation ileitis
	Tropical sprue, celiac disease
	Infiltrative intestinal disease (e.g., lymphoma, scleroderma)
	Drug-induced malabsorption
	Congenital selective malabsorption (Imerslund-Gräsbeck syndrome)
C. Impaired utilization	Congenital enzyme deficiencies
	Lack of transcobalamin II
	Nitrous oxide administration
II. Folate deficiency	
A. Decreased ingestion	Poor diet, lack of vegetables
	Alcoholism
	Infancy
B. Impaired absorption	Intestinal short circuits
	Tropical sprue, celiac disease
	Anticonvulsants, sulfasalazine, other drugs
	Congenital malabsorption
C. Impaired utilization	Folic acid antagonists: methotrexate, triamterene, trimethoprim, pyrimethamine, ethanol
	Congenital enzyme deficiencies
D. Increased requirement	Pregnancy, infancy
	Hyperthyroidism
	Chronic hemolytic disease
	Neoplastic disease, exfoliative skin disease
E. Increased loss	Hemodialysis
III. Drugs—metabolic inhibitors	Purine synthesis: methotrexate, 6-mercaptopurine, 6-thioguanine, azathioprine
	Pyrimidine synthesis: methotrexate, 6-azauridine
	Thymidylate synthesis: methotrexate, 5-fluorouracil
	Deoxyribonucleotide synthesis: hydroxyurea, cytosine arabinoside
IV. Miscellaneous	
A. Inborn errors	Lesch-Nyhan syndrome
	Hereditary orotic aciduria
	Others
B. Unexplained disorders	Pyridoxine-responsive megaloblastic anemia
	Thiamine-responsive megaloblastic anemia
	Some cases of myelodysplastic syndrome
	Some cases of acute myelogenous leukemia

other aspect of DNA synthesis. The miscellaneous category includes enzyme defects and some cases of myelodysplastic syndrome and acute leukemia.

It is important to determine the correct etiologic factor in megaloblastic anemia. If a myelodysplastic syndrome is misdiagnosed in a cobalamin-deficient patient, chemotherapy might result in the early death of a patient who could have been cured completely with cobalamin therapy. Similarly, some causes of cobalamin and folate deficiency require therapy for the underlying disease, in addition to replacement therapy with the appropriate vitamin.

Incidence and Prevalence

COBALAMIN DEFICIENCY. The term *pernicious anemia,* often used as a synonym for cobalamin deficiency, should be reserved for conditions in which a gastric mucosal defect results in insufficient intrinsic factor to facilitate the absorption of physiologic amounts of cobalamin. This lack of intrinsic factor, which is the most common cause of severe cobalamin deficiency in the Western hemisphere, occurs in individuals as early as in their 20s and can develop in all ethnic groups. Clinically recognized pernicious anemia develops in about 1% of individuals in the United States at some time during their lives. Approximately 10% of the U.S. population, especially the elderly, have low or low-normal serum cobalamin levels *and* metabolic evidence of cobalamin deficiency (elevated levels of serum methylmalonic acid and homocysteine that fall to normal with cobalamin therapy). The cause and hematologic and neuropsychiatric significance of these findings are unknown at present, although there is increasing evidence of a strong correlation between serum homocysteine levels and all forms of vascular disease, cognitive dysfunction, and various cancers.

FOLATE DEFICIENCY, DRUGS, AND OTHER CAUSES. The incidence of folate deficiency and drug-related megaloblastic anemia is less well established. Through its association with alcoholism (Chapter 17), folate deficiency is not a rare condition. The marked increase in the use of chemotherapeutic agents (Chapter 191) to treat malignant disease and immune disorders suggests that these drugs now may be the most common cause of megaloblastic anemia in the Western hemisphere.

Pathogenesis and Pathology

MECHANISM OF MEGALOBLASTOSIS

FOLATE DEFICIENCY. Folate functions to transfer one-carbon units, such as methyl, methylene, and formyl groups, to various substrates in a variety of enzymatic reactions that are intimately related to the synthesis of DNA, RNA, and proteins. In folate deficiency, all forms of folate are diminished within cells; the result is impaired growth and maturation of rapidly growing cells, such as cells in the bone marrow. Thymidylate synthase catalyzes the synthesis of thymidine from deoxyuridine and 5,10-methylenetetrahydrofolate, a step that is required for DNA synthesis.

COBALAMIN DEFICIENCY. Cobalamin functions as an essential cofactor for only two enzymes in human cells, methionine synthase and L-methylmalonyl coenzyme A (CoA) mutase. Methionine synthase catalyzes the recycling of homocysteine to methionine; this reaction requires 5-methylcobalamin as a coenzyme (Fig. 175–1). Methionine, an essential amino acid for protein synthesis, also serves in the form of *S*-adenosylmethionine as the major methyl donor in numerous important enzymatic reactions. In cobalamin deficiency, increasing amounts of intracellular folate are converted to 5-methyltetrahydrofolate in an attempt to prevent intracellular methionine deficiency. The "trapping" of intracellular folate as 5-methyltetrahydrofolate is augmented by the fact that this substance is the major component of plasma folate and is the form that enters cells and must be converted to tetrahydrofolate by methionine synthase before it can enter the folate pool. Cobalamin deficiency results in secondary intracellular deficiency of all forms of folate except 5-methyltetrahydrofolate. As a result, the activities of all of the enzymes using folate to transfer one-carbon moieties, including thymidylate synthase, are impaired. This concept of *methylfolate trapping* explains why cobalamin deficiency and folate deficiency produce indistinguishable hematologic abnormalities and why the hematologic abnormalities seen in cobalamin deficiency sometimes can be reversed completely by pharmacologic amounts of folic acid. The latter oxidized, nonphysiologic form of folate can be reduced directly to tetrahydrofolate

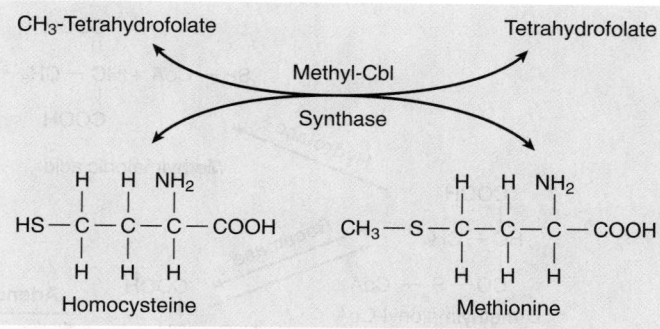

FIGURE 175–1 • Reaction catalyzed by methionine synthase that requires methylcobalamin (Methyl-Cbl) and transfers the methyl group of 5-methyltetrahydrofolate (CH$_3$-tetrahydrofolate) to homocysteine to form methionine and tetrahydrofolate. Homocysteine accumulates in cobalamin deficiency because of a lack of methylcobalamin and in folate deficiency because of a lack of 5-methyltetrahydrofolate.

without initially being converted to 5-methyltetrahydrofolate. This concept also explains why the hematologic abnormalities caused by folate deficiency respond only slightly, if at all, to large amounts of cobalamin.

DRUGS AND OTHER CAUSES. Drugs cause megaloblastic anemia by inhibiting a variety of enzymes involved in DNA synthesis. 5-Fluorouracil (5-FU) inhibits thymidylate synthase directly. The addition of 5-formyltetrahydrofolate (leucovorin) to 5-FU regimens increases the inhibition of thymidylate synthase because 5-formyltetrahydrofolate is converted to 5,10-methylenetetrahydrofolate, which is involved in the formation of inhibitory ternary complexes between 5,10-methylenetetrahydrofolate, 5-FU, and thymidylate synthase. Why megaloblastic changes occur in some cases of the myelodysplastic syndrome (Chapter 182) and acute leukemias (Chapter 193) is unknown but is probably due to a variety of mutations that alter DNA synthesis.

MECHANISM OF NEUROPSYCHIATRIC ABNORMALITIES IN COBALAMIN DEFICIENCY

A wide variety of neuropsychiatric abnormalities are seen in cobalamin deficiency and seem to be due to an undefined defect involving myelin synthesis. Because these abnormalities are not seen in folate deficiency, it has been tempting to ascribe them to deficient activity of the second cobalamin-dependent enzyme, L-methylmalonyl-CoA mutase, which is unrelated to any folate-dependent enzyme or pathway. This enzyme catalyzes the conversion of L-methylmalonyl-CoA to succinyl-CoA by using adenosylcobalamin as a required coenzyme (Fig. 175–2). Abnormal odd-carbon and branched-chain fatty acids are formed when the mutase is impaired. The neuropsychiatric abnormalities of cobalamin deficiency are not seen, however, in individuals with genetic defects of the mutase reaction caused either by primary defects in the enzyme itself or by defects in the formation of adenosylcobalamin. Impairment of methionine synthase also has been postulated as the cause of neuropsychiatric abnormalities in view of the importance of methionine and *S*-adenosylmethionine for the many methylation reactions occurring in the nervous system. As noted, however, the neuropsychiatric abnormalities caused by cobalamin deficiency are not seen in folate deficiency, although methionine synthase seems to be equally impaired in both vitamin deficiencies (based on similar marked elevations in serum homocysteine concentrations). Genetic defects in which the synthesis of adenosylcobalamin and methylcobalamin is impaired do lead to neuropsychiatric abnormalities of the kind seen in cobalamin deficiency. These observations suggest that both cobalamin-dependent enzymes must be impaired for neuropsychiatric abnormalities to develop and that the two cobalamin-dependent enzymes or pathways are connected or interrelated in a way that is not yet understood.

MECHANISMS OF COBALAMIN DEFICIENCY

Cobalamin is not present in plants; until more recently, humans obtained their cobalamin exclusively from animal products. Cobalamin is synthesized only by certain microorganisms. During the last half

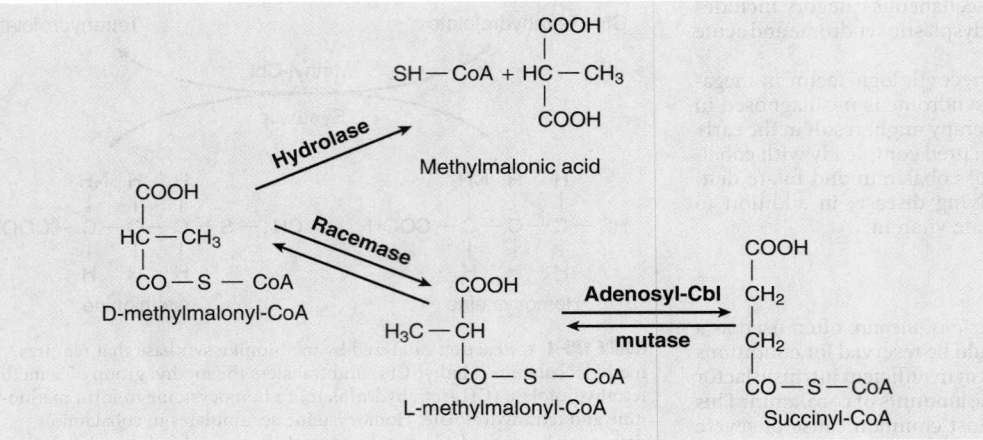

FIGURE 175-2 • Reactions involved in the metabolism of D-methyl-malonyl–coenzyme A (CoA) and L-methylmalonyl-CoA. Methylmalonic acid accumulates in cobalamin deficiency because of a lack of adenosylcobalamin (Adenosyl-Cbl), which leads to an increase in L-methylmalonyl-CoA, which is converted to D-methyl-malonyl-CoA and hydrolyzed to methylmalonic acid.

of the 20th century, humans have received increasing amounts of dietary cobalamin from multivitamin supplements taken in the form of pills and as additives to many food preparations. Most cobalamin in animal products is tightly bound to proteins (i.e., the two cobalamin-dependent enzymes) and is released from them in the stomach by the concerted action of hydrochloric acid and pepsin. The stomach is also the site of synthesis of intrinsic factor, which binds free cobalamin with high affinity and plays an essential role in cobalamin absorption. Gastric juice contains another cobalamin binding protein that originates in saliva and has a more rapid or R-type electrophoretic mobility than does intrinsic factor. R protein binds cobalamin with a higher affinity than does intrinsic factor, particularly at an acid pH.

Under normal conditions of gastric acidity, dietary cobalamin enters the duodenum bound to R protein. Additional cobalamin bound to R protein enters the duodenum after secretion into bile by the liver (the only significant route by which cobalamin is lost from the body). Pancreatic proteases partially degrade salivary and biliary R protein–cobalamin complexes in the jejunum; cobalamin is bound to intrinsic factor only after this process occurs. The intrinsic factor–cobalamin complex remains intact until it reaches the distal end of the ileum, where it binds with high affinity to specific receptors located on ileal mucosal cells. Cobalamin then enters these cells and reaches the portal plasma, which contains three cobalamin binding proteins known as *transcobalamin I, II, and III* (Table 175–2). Although it contains only about 10% of the plasma cobalamin, transcobalamin II is the important transport protein because of its rapid clearance and its ability to deliver cobalamin to all cells within the body. Transcobalamin II–cobalamin is taken up by cells by endocytosis during a process in which the transcobalamin II moiety is degraded and the cobalamin is reduced and eventually converted to its two coenzyme forms, methylcobalamin and adenosylcobalamin. Cobalamin is not stored intracellularly; the entire intracellular vitamin is bound to the aforementioned two enzymes, which are present in greater amounts than is cobalamin.

Many acquired and genetic diseases affect the pathway of cobalamin absorption and transport and result in cobalamin deficiency. Strict vegetarians, who ingest neither meat nor other animal products such as milk, cheese, or eggs and who do not ingest multivitamin supplements, become cobalamin deficient on a dietary basis. Because absorption of biliary cobalamin remains intact, 10 to 15 years is required for the development of clinical signs of dietary cobalamin deficiency. The secretion of biliary cobalamin ranges from 5 to 10 μg/day, and approximately 90% is reabsorbed by strict vegetarians and other normal individuals. Only 0.5 to 1.0 μg of the 5 to 10 μg of cobalamin present in a normal diet must be absorbed each day to maintain the total body content of cobalamin in the normal range of 2000 to 5000 μg. Breast-fed infants of even mildly deficient mothers can develop life-threatening cobalamin deficiency within the first year of life.

Achlorhydria and the loss of pepsin secretion are common in elderly subjects (>50% of individuals >70 years old) and in subjects with partial gastrectomy. Cobalamin deficiency develops in these individuals because of an inability to liberate cobalamin from its protein-bound form in foods of animal origin. Secretion of intrinsic factor is reduced, but because it normally is formed in vast excess, sufficient intrinsic factor usually remains for the reabsorption of biliary R protein–cobalamin, which is not dependent on hydrochloric acid and pepsin. The same time span of 10 to 15 years is required for these subjects to acquire clinical signs of cobalamin deficiency as for subjects who have deficient diets. Cobalamin deficiency never develops in many of these subjects, apparently because of the availability of free, non–protein-bound cobalamin in multivitamin pills and supplements and because some natural animal products contain small amounts of free cobalamin.

A complete lack of intrinsic factor occurs in individuals who have undergone total gastrectomy or who have pernicious anemia; these individuals have idiopathic and essentially complete atrophy of the gastric mucosa in association with autoantibodies to parietal cells and intrinsic factor. Only about 3 to 5 years is required for clinical signs of cobalamin deficiency to develop under these circumstances because these individuals show malabsorption of biliary and all forms of dietary cobalamin.

Cobalamin malabsorption occurs commonly in severe pancreatic exocrine insufficiency because of an inability to degrade R protein–cobalamin complexes in the jejunum. Clinically evident cobalamin

Table 175–2 • DISTRIBUTION OF ENDOGENOUS COBALAMIN AMONG THE VARIOUS TRANSCOBALAMINS AND THEIR RELATIVE IMPORTANCE TO COBALAMIN TRANSPORT*

COBALAMIN TRANSPORT PROTEIN	ENDOGENOUS COBALAMIN (pg/mL)	HALF-LIFE FOR COBALAMIN CLEARANCE (hr)	COBALAMIN CLEARANCE (pg/mL 24 hr)	SITE OF SPECIFIC UPTAKE
R proteins[†]				
Transcobalamin I	425–450	240.0	30	None
Transcobalamin III	0–25	0.1	0–4000	Hepatocytes
Transcobalamin II[‡]	50	0.1	8000	All cells

*In a typical normal subject with a serum cobalamin level of 500 pg/mL.

[†]In congenital R-protein deficiency, the total serum cobalamin level is low, but no hematologic abnormalities are present because R proteins do not transport cobalamin to rapidly dividing cells, such as those in the bone marrow.

[‡]In congenital transcobalamin II deficiency, the total serum cobalamin level is well within the normal range, but severe megaloblastic anemia develops because only transcobalamin II transports cobalamin to rapidly dividing cells, such as those in the bone marrow.

deficiency rarely occurs, however, probably because oral therapy with pancreatic extract usually is instituted in these patients during the 3 to 5 years necessary for the signs of cobalamin deficiency to develop.

The abnormal presence of high concentrations of bacteria and certain parasites in the small intestine can result in cobalamin malabsorption inasmuch as these organisms can avidly take up and retain cobalamin. Diseases interfering with the integrity of the distal ileal mucosa also can result in cobalamin malabsorption, which occurs invariably after surgical removal of the distal 100 cm of ileum.

Many genetic disorders involve the plasma transport of cobalamin, its intracellular conversion to its coenzyme forms, or its use by the two cobalamin-dependent enzymes. These disorders usually appear within the first few weeks of life.

The general anesthetic nitrous oxide causes multiple defects in cobalamin usage, including the following: (1) rapid (within minutes) inhibition of methionine synthase activity with slow (over several days) recovery when nitrous oxide administration is stopped, (2) displacement of cobalamin from methionine synthase, (3) decrease in the level of methylcobalamin, (4) irreversible conversion of cobalamin to inactive and inhibitory cobalamin analogues, (5) gradual (over many weeks) development of cobalamin deficiency, (6) an eventual decrease in L-methylmalonyl-CoA mutase activity, and (7) a further decrease in methionine synthase activity. General anesthesia with nitrous oxide can precipitate clinical signs of cobalamin deficiency in individuals whose cobalamin status is low or marginal.

MECHANISMS OF FOLATE DEFICIENCY

Folate is distributed widely in plants and in products of animal origin; green vegetables are particularly rich sources of folate. Excessive cooking destroys or removes a high percentage of folate in foods. Folate is missing or is present only in amounts of 800 µg or less in most nonprescription multivitamin pills and supplements because of long-standing concern that its presence in larger amounts might mask the diagnosis of cobalamin deficiency by correcting the associated hematologic abnormalities without having any beneficial effect on the neuropsychiatric abnormalities. Folates in natural foods are conjugated to chains of polyglutamic acid. Enzymes in the lumen of the small intestine convert the polyglutamate forms of folate to the monoglutamate and diglutamate forms, which are absorbed readily in the proximal portion of the jejunum. Absorption involves active and passive transport. Most of the folate in plasma is present as 5-methyltetrahydrofolate in the monoglutamate form. Most is bound loosely to albumin, from which it is readily taken up by the high-affinity folate receptors present on cells throughout the body. When it enters the cell, 5-methyltetrahydrofolate must be converted to tetrahydrofolate by the cobalamin-dependent enzyme methionine synthase before it can be converted to the polyglutamate form and take part in the other folate-dependent enzymatic reactions. In addition to being secreted into bile and reabsorbed in the small intestine, folates are degraded and excreted in the urine.

Table 175–3 • HEMATOLOGIC AND OTHER ABNORMALITIES THAT MAY BE DUE TO ANY OF THE VARIOUS CAUSES OF MEGALOBLASTIC ANEMIA

HEMATOLOGIC	OTHER
Anemia	Glossitis
Reticulocytopenia	Stomatitis
Macrocytosis (increased MCV)	Gastrointestinal symptoms
Neutropenia	Hyperpigmentation
Thrombocytopenia	Infertility
Peripheral blood smear	Orthostatic hypotension
Neutrophil hypersegmentation	Weight loss
Erythrocyte	
Variation in size	
Variation in shape	
Macro-ovalocytes	
Serum	
Elevated lactate dehydrogenase	
Elevated bilirubin	
Elevated iron	
Decreased haptoglobin	
Bone marrow	
Hypercellular	
Megaloblastic morphology	
Giant bands and metamyelocytes	

MCV = mean corpuscular volume.

Decreased intake is the most common cause of folate deficiency. Normal individuals have approximately 5000 to 20,000 µg of folate in body stores. Because folate is degraded within the body and is excreted in bile and urine, 50 to 200 µg must be absorbed each day from the average Western diet, which contains about 200 to 500 µg of folate. The amount of dietary folate has increased at least 100 µg/day in the United States because of the mandatory fortification of all grain products to reduce the incidence of neural tube defects. Clinical signs of folate deficiency develop after approximately 4 months of decreased intake, as can occur in chronic alcoholism.

Absorption of folate is impaired in a variety of diseases affecting the jejunal mucosa, including tropical sprue and celiac disease (Chapter 141). Certain drugs, such as anticonvulsants and sulfasalazine, may impair folate absorption in some individuals. Ethanol and drugs such as triamterene impair the use of folate. Certain conditions associated with hypermetabolism or rapid cell growth lead to an increased requirement for folate that often cannot be met by a normal diet; these conditions include hyperthyroidism (Chapter 239), pregnancy, chronic hemolysis (Chapter 117), and various exfoliative skin diseases. Hemodialysis causes an increased loss of folate from the body.

Clinical Manifestations

HEMATOLOGIC MANIFESTATIONS. All causes of megaloblastic anemia produce a common set of hematologic, laboratory, and other abnormalities (Table 175–3). None of the abnormalities are specific for the various diseases that cause megaloblastic anemia, and each may be present in any combination that may vary greatly from patient to patient. In addition, none of the abnormalities are always seen in conditions that cause megaloblastic anemia, and the absence of any one or more of them cannot be used to exclude any of the diseases that cause megaloblastic anemia in a given patient, including cobalamin or folate deficiency.

Megaloblastic anemia typically develops over many months and may not cause symptoms until the hematocrit decreases to less than 20%. The reticulocyte count is not elevated, in either absolute or relative (percentage) terms, even when the anemia is severe. The mean cell volume is often increased (normal, 80 to 100 fL), with values as high as 140 fL. A review of previous blood counts often reveals a steady increase in mean cell volume over several months or years.

Neutropenia and thrombocytopenia occur less commonly than anemia and are not usually severe. Occasionally, however, neutrophil counts of less than 1000/µL and platelet counts of less than 50,000/µL may be seen. A peripheral blood smear frequently shows neutrophil hypersegmentation (Fig. 175–3), which may be documented by observing one or more of the following: (1) the presence of at least one neutrophil containing 6 or more lobes, (2) the presence of 5% or more of 5-lobe neutrophils, or (3) an increase above the normal neutrophil lobe average of fewer than 3.4 lobes per neutrophil. Erythrocytes often vary markedly in size and shape, and macro-ovalocytes (large, oval erythrocytes) frequently are present. When the hematocrit is low, nucleated red blood cells may be seen on the peripheral smear and permit detection of the megaloblastic morphology of the nuclei without the need to perform bone marrow aspiration or biopsy.

Although the reticulocyte count may be normal or low, many serum abnormalities often suggest hemolytic anemia: elevated serum levels of lactate dehydrogenase, indirect bilirubin, and iron and decreased levels of haptoglobin. These findings are consistent with the markedly increased red blood cell production and destruction seen in megaloblastic anemia but confined to the bone marrow and termed *intramedullary hemolysis* or *ineffective erythropoiesis*.

The bone marrow is usually hypercellular with an increase in all cellular elements. Megaloblastic morphologic changes often are seen

Continued

in all cells within the bone marrow but usually are more prominent in the erythroid series. All cells in the erythroid series are larger than their normal counterparts, their cytoplasm appears more mature than their nuclei (nuclear-cytoplasmic asynchrony), and the nuclear chromatin has a distinctive open and fine-grained texture (Fig. 175–4). Similar abnormalities are seen in neutrophil precursors and usually are most striking at the metamyelocyte and band stages, in which "giant metamyelocytes" and "giant bands" are seen. All these features are much more prominent in a Wright-stained smear of bone marrow aspirate than in fixed sections from the bone marrow biopsy specimen. Use of the latter alone can lead to disastrous clinical consequences because even the most experienced hematopathologist can, on the basis of fixed bone marrow sections only, experience difficulty in distinguishing the hypercellularity and abnormal morphology of megaloblastosis from the changes seen in the myelodysplastic syndromes and some cases of acute leukemia. Coexisting iron deficiency also may cause diagnostic problems inasmuch as all of the erythroid megaloblastic changes may be absent, even in Wright-stained smears of aspirated bone marrow. The diagnosis of megaloblastic anemia should never be excluded after bone marrow examination unless bone marrow aspirates have been examined and the presence of bone marrow iron has been established.

Megaloblastic abnormalities may occur in other proliferating body cells, all of which share the underlying defect in DNA synthesis. These changes have been documented in the epithelial cells of the buccal mucosa, stomach, intestine, and vagina and account for phenomena such as glossitis, stomatitis, and secondary malabsorption. Similar changes may account for the infertility that sometimes is seen.

Few, if any, patients with cobalamin or folate deficiency or other causes of megaloblastic anemia show all or even most of the classic hematologic or other abnormalities. Even anemia and increased mean cell volume are frequently absent in patients with otherwise severe deficiencies of cobalamin or folate. In a prospective study of 86 consecutive patients with low serum cobalamin levels (<200 pg/mL) *and* one or more objective hematologic and/or neuropsychiatric responses to cobalamin therapy, 44% did not have anemia, 36% had a mean cell volume of 100 fL or less, 86% had a normal white blood cell count, 79% had a normal platelet count, 33% had a normal peripheral smear on routine laboratory study, 43% had normal serum lactate dehydrogenase levels, and 83% had normal serum bilirubin levels.

NEUROPSYCHIATRIC ABNORMALITIES CAUSED BY COBALAMIN DEFICIENCY.
Cobalamin deficiency, in contrast to folate deficiency and other causes of megaloblastic anemia, produces a wide variety of neuropsychiatric abnormalities (Table 175–4) (Chapter 458). None of these abnormalities are specific for cobalamin deficiency, and any of them may be present alone or in any combination and may vary greatly from patient to patient. None of the abnormalities are always seen in cobalamin deficiency, and the absence of any one or a combination of them does not exclude cobalamin deficiency. The neuropsychiatric abnormalities may occur early or late in the course of

cobalamin deficiency and with or without any of the hematologic or other abnormalities listed in Table 175–3. How the deficiency of a single substance, such as cobalamin, can produce a clinical picture with such wide variations in severity and dissociation of various hematologic and neuropsychiatric abnormalities is unknown.

Pathologic studies show loss of myelin with axonal degeneration, most frequently in the dorsal and lateral columns of the spinal cord, but also in peripheral and cranial nerves and the cerebral cortex. *Combined systems disease* designates a spinal cord disorder marked by the insidious beginning and gradual progression of demyelination, initially of the dorsal (proprioceptive afferent) and later the lateral (corticospinal efferent) columns. Axonal degeneration affects the same pathways as a late, irreversible change. Demyelinative neuropathy of large peripheral fibers may precede or develop concurrently with the cord changes. Signs and symptoms are usually symmetrical and often include paresthesias in the extremities and impaired vibration and position sense that may progress to an abnormal gait, spastic ataxia, and quadriparesis. Urinary and fecal incontinence and impotence may be seen. Cerebral and cranial nerve abnormalities include irritability, memory loss, disorientation, obtundation, and changes in taste and smell; changes in vision can progress to severe optic atrophy and near-blindness. Psychiatric abnormalities, which may be prominent and isolated, include depression, hallucinations, agitation, marked personality change, abnormal behavior, and suicide.

The neuropsychiatric abnormalities caused by cobalamin deficiency frequently bear no relationship to the presence or degree of hematologic abnormalities. The severity of neuropsychiatric abnormalities bears a striking *inverse correlation* to the degree of anemia. The frequency with which hematologic and neuropsychiatric abnormalities are dissociated is often unappreciated. Several clinical studies document that a normal hematocrit and/or mean cell volume occur in at least 25 to 50% of patients whose neuropsychiatric abnormalities are caused by cobalamin deficiency *and* respond partially or completely to cobalamin therapy. Other hematologic and laboratory abnormalities of the kind outlined in Table 175–3 are lacking in a similar or even higher percentage of these patients.

DELETERIOUS EFFECTS ASSOCIATED WITH HYPERHOMOCYST(E)INEMIA CAUSED BY COBALAMIN AND FOLATE DEFICIENCY.
Hyperhomocyst(e)inemia resulting from inborn errors of metabolism has long been associated with thrombosis and accelerated vascular disease. Elevated total homocyst(e)ine also is associated with mortality from cardiovascular disease and death from all causes (Chapters 47 and 231). Patients with vascular disease and with hyperhomocyst(e)inemia have inadequate folate and/or cobalamin status and respond to vitamin replacement therapy. Six months of oral therapy with cobalamin, folate, and vitamin B_6 significantly decreased the incidence of major adverse events (at 6 months and 1 year) after percutaneous coronary intervention.■ Other prospective treatment studies with folate and cobalamin are ongoing in patients with cerebrovascular and cardiovascular disease.

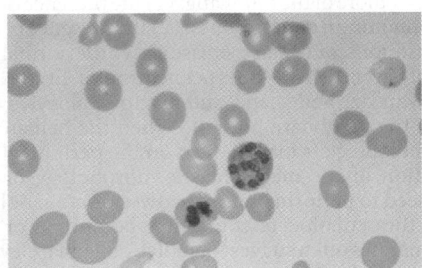

FIGURE 175–3 • Megaloblastic anemia. Peripheral blood with oval macrocytes (large red blood cells) and marked neutrophil hypersegmentation.

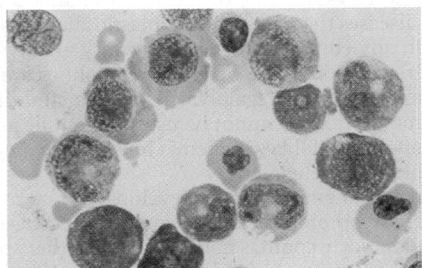

FIGURE 175–4 • Megaloblastic anemia. Bone marrow aspirate shows red blood cell precursors that are giant megaloblasts, with nuclear-cytoplasmic dissociation (nuclear maturation lagging behind cytoplasmic maturation). Megaloblastic changes in the leukocyte series are shown by the "giant metamyelocyte."

Table 175–4 • NEUROPSYCHIATRIC ABNORMALITIES* THAT MAY BE CAUSED BY COBALAMIN DEFICIENCY

NEUROLOGIC ABNORMALITIES	PSYCHIATRIC ABNORMALITIES
Paresthesia	Depression
Impaired vibration sense	Paranoia
Impaired position sense	Listlessness
Impaired touch or pain perception	Acute confusional state
Ataxia	Hallucinations
Abnormal gait	Delusions
Fatigue	Insomnia
Memory loss	Apprehensiveness
Disorientation	Psychosis
Obtundation	Slow mentation
Decreased reflexes	Paraphrenia
Weakness	Mania
Decreased muscle strength	Panic attacks
Romberg's sign	Personality change
Increased reflexes	Suicide
Spasticity	
Babinski's sign	
Lhermitte's sign	
Urinary or fecal incontinence	
Urinary urgency or nocturia	
Impotence	
Abnormal smell or taste	
Decreased vision or optic atrophy	

*These abnormalities may be present in any number or combination in a given patient. They are seen frequently with *or without* any of the hematologic or other abnormalities listed in Table 175–3.

Diagnosis

INDICATIONS. If drugs are excluded as a cause, the differential diagnosis of megaloblastic anemia in adults usually is limited to the important task of distinguishing between cobalamin deficiency and folate deficiency and firmly establishing the presence of one or the other (Table 175–5). Patients always should be evaluated for these two conditions in the presence of any unexplained hematologic or other abnormality of the kind listed in Table 175–3. In addition, patients always should be investigated for cobalamin deficiency in the presence of any unexplained neuropsychiatric abnormality of the kind listed in Table 175–4, regardless of the presence or absence of hematologic abnormalities. The yield may be relatively low because of the nonspecific nature of these worrisome abnormalities, but these studies are justified by the fact that all of the hematologic abnormalities caused by cobalamin or folate deficiency are completely corrected by safe and inexpensive therapy with the proper vitamin. In addition, the neuropsychiatric abnormalities caused by cobalamin deficiency usually are

Table 175–5 • DIAGNOSTIC APPROACH TO PATIENTS WITH COBALAMIN OR FOLATE DEFICIENCY

I. **Initial approach**
  A. Indications
    1. Any unexplained hematologic or other abnormality of the kind listed in Table 175–3 (cobalamin and folate deficiency)
    2. Any unexplained neuropsychiatric abnormality of the kind listed in Table 175–4 (cobalamin deficiency)
  B. Initial tests
    1. Serum cobalamin (normal 200–900 pg/mL)
    2. Serum folate (normal 2.5–20 ng/mL)
II. **Follow-up**
  A. Indications
    1. Serum cobalamin <350 pg/mL *or*
    2. Serum folate <5 ng/mL *or*
    3. Clinical condition
      a. Serious unexplained hematologic or neuropsychiatric abnormalities *or*
      b. Suggestive of cobalamin or folate deficiency
  B. Follow-up tests
    1. Serum methylmalonic acid (normal 70–270 nmol)—elevated in cobalamin deficiency
    2. Serum homocysteine (normal 5–14 μmol)—elevated in cobalamin and folate deficiency

corrected partially or completely by cobalamin therapy, and in the few patients who do not improve, cobalamin therapy always prevents subsequent worsening. It is particularly important that the diagnosis of cobalamin deficiency be established with a high degree of certainty because cobalamin therapy almost always must be given for the lifetime of the patient. The distinction between cobalamin deficiency and folate deficiency is also important because treatment of cobalamin deficiency with folate does not improve the neuropsychiatric abnormalities, although hematologic improvements often occur.

SERUM COBALAMIN AND FOLATE. Competitive binding assays for serum cobalamin and serum folate still are used often as the initial screening tests because they are widely available and relatively inexpensive. Essentially all serum cobalamin assays today use purified intrinsic factor, which neither binds nor measures the serum cobalamin analogues that caused problems with earlier assays.

Normal ranges are defined as the mean ± 2 standard deviations for normal subjects and include only 95% of normal individuals. These normal ranges are approximately 200 to 900 pg/mL for serum cobalamin and approximately 2.5 to 20 ng/mL for serum folate. By definition, 2.5% of normal subjects who have no evidence of cobalamin deficiency and who would not benefit in any way from cobalamin therapy have low serum cobalamin values of less than 200 pg/mL. Serum cobalamin and folate levels cannot be used alone to establish the diagnosis of cobalamin or folate deficiency unequivocally. The problem is compounded by the fact that not all patients with clinically confirmed cobalamin or folate deficiency (defined as patients who have objective clinical responses to appropriate therapy) have low values for serum cobalamin or folate. The following distribution of serum cobalamin levels has been noted in clinically confirmed cobalamin-deficient patients: less than 100 pg/mL, approximately 50%; 100 to 200 pg/mL, approximately 40%; 200 to 350 pg/mL, approximately 10%; and higher than 350 pg/mL, approximately 0.1 to 1%. The distribution of serum folate levels in patients with clinically confirmed folate deficiency has been less well studied, but currently available data indicate that only about 75% of these patients have serum folate levels lower than 2.5 ng/mL, with almost all of the remaining 25% falling in the 2.5 to 5.0 ng/mL range.

Many patients with clinically confirmed cobalamin or folate deficiency have serum vitamin levels within the normal range. Both vitamins function within cells and not in plasma. In the case of cobalamin, serum levels of the vitamin are influenced greatly by levels of plasma binding proteins, which bear no relationship to cellular cobalamin levels. Transcobalamin I has no apparent function. Assays for serum cobalamin and serum folate are useful as initial screening tests that allow the physician to exclude from consideration almost all patients with serum cobalamin levels of 350 pg/mL or greater and serum folate levels of 5.0 ng/mL or greater. Additional follow-up tests are required for serum cobalamin levels less than 350 pg/mL, serum folate levels less than 5.0 ng/mL, or clinical conditions that are serious or suggestive of cobalamin or folate deficiency. Examples of these conditions include (1) marked myelodysplasia in a patient who is about to start a regimen of chemotherapy, (2) incapacitating urinary and fecal incontinence of unknown cause in a young patient, (3) pancytopenia with an increased mean cell volume and serum lactate dehydrogenase level, and (4) symmetrical paresthesias in the hands and feet in a patient who also has spastic ataxia and a recent change in personality.

SERUM METHYLMALONIC ACID AND HOMOCYSTEINE. The most useful follow-up tests for diagnosing and distinguishing between cobalamin and folate deficiency are serum levels of methylmalonic acid (normal, 70 to 270 nmol/L) and homocysteine (normal, 5 to 14 nmol/L). For homocysteine, what is actually measured is *total homocysteine,* which consists of the sum of homocysteine and homocysteine that is linked via disulfide bond formation in a variety of compounds that include homocystine (homocysteine-homocysteine disulfide), homocysteine-cysteine mixed disulfide, proteins via their cysteine moieties, and peptides such as glutathione via their cysteine moieties. Tests of methylmalonic acid and homocysteine can be performed on serum that remains after cobalamin and folate levels have been determined; these tests are now widely available. The serum methylmalonic acid level is elevated in more than 95% of patients with clinically confirmed cobalamin deficiency. Values of 2 million nmol/L have been observed, with a median value in the range of 3500 nmol/L. Serum methylmalonic acid levels are not elevated in folate deficiency. In contrast, serum homocysteine concentrations are elevated in cobalamin and folate deficiency. Values of 500 μmol/L have been observed in cobalamin deficiency, with a median value of 70 μmol/L; values of

250 µmol/L have been observed in folate deficiency, with a median value of 50 µmol/L. Broad-spectrum antibiotics can lower an elevated serum methylmalonic acid level to normal in patients with cobalamin deficiency by inhibiting the gut microflora, an important source of precursors of methylmalonic acid. Antibiotics do not affect elevated homocysteine levels in these patients, and they do not change any clinical parameters.

Elevated levels of methylmalonic acid and homocysteine resulting from cobalamin deficiency return to normal within 5 to 10 days of starting cobalamin therapy. Elevated levels of homocysteine caused by folate deficiency decrease to normal during the same period after folate therapy. Elevations in serum methylmalonic acid and homocysteine secondary to cobalamin deficiency do not respond to pharmacologic doses of folate even in cobalamin-deficient patients, in whom folate causes a marked hematologic improvement (together with no response or a worsening of neuropsychiatric abnormalities). Elevations in homocysteine caused by folate deficiency do not respond to pharmacologic doses of cobalamin. Elevations in methylmalonic acid and homocysteine resulting from renal insufficiency or intravascular volume depletion are not corrected by therapy with either vitamin unless vitamin deficiency coexists. Repeat determinations of serum methylmalonic acid and homocysteine levels after a short course of therapy with a single vitamin may provide additional information of diagnostic usefulness.

With few exceptions, patients with serum cobalamin levels less than 350 pg/mL or serum folate levels less than 5.0 ng/mL do not show objective hematologic or neuropsychiatric responses to cobalamin or folate therapy if their serum levels of methylmalonic acid and homocysteine are normal. The use of serum levels of cobalamin and folate as initial screening tests, together with the use of serum methylmalonic acid and homocysteine determinations as follow-up tests, makes it possible to diagnose cobalamin or folate deficiency and to distinguish between them in most patients (see Table 175–5). If in doubt, one always can start empirical therapy, but these therapeutic trials can be difficult to perform (see later) and should be monitored carefully in an attempt to establish a definitive diagnosis. As an alternative, patients can be observed carefully with repeat determinations of methylmalonic acid and homocysteine after 6 months or 1 year. The usual patterns of serum cobalamin, folate, methylmalonic acid, and homocysteine concentrations in cobalamin and folate deficiency are summarized in Table 175–6.

OTHER TESTS. Many other tests have been used as diagnostic or follow-up tests in cobalamin deficiency. Serum antibodies to intrinsic factor are present in about 50% of patients with pernicious anemia (Chapter 137) and are highly specific for that condition. They fail to diagnose about 50% of cases, however, as well as all cases with other causes of cobalamin deficiency. The standard Schilling test (see Table 141–7 for a complete description of this test) requires a reliable 24-hour urine collection, and because it uses free (i.e., non–protein-bound) cobalamin, it fails to diagnose cobalamin deficiency not only in patients who are strict vegetarians, but also, much more commonly, in patients who malabsorb cobalamin from food sources. The intrinsic factor antibody test and the Schilling test provide information about the cause of cobalamin deficiency rather than information about the presence or absence of cobalamin deficiency per se. The cause of cobalamin deficiency (and folate deficiency) should be pursued in patients with unusual cases and patients with gastrointestinal symptoms that do not respond to cobalamin therapy because these studies may disclose the presence of a disease that requires additional therapy. It is

acceptable practice to institute lifetime cobalamin therapy in individuals with anti–intrinsic factor antibodies or abnormal Schilling tests who lack evidence of current cobalamin deficiency because they probably will become deficient in the future. A normal result with either test should never be used, however, to exclude the diagnosis of cobalamin deficiency or to withhold lifetime therapy.

 Treatment

COBALAMIN DEFICIENCY. Oral cobalamin, 1 to 2 mg/day, is the treatment of choice for most patients.[2] This dose is as effective and possibly superior to a parenteral regimen in all causes of cobalamin deficiency because 1 to 2% of an oral dose is always absorbed by diffusion. For patients who may not be compliant, intramuscular or subcutaneous cyanocobalamin can be given. One approach consists of injections of 1 mg of cyanocobalamin once per week for 8 weeks, then once per month for life. More frequent injections often are used in hospitalized patients or patients with marked neuropsychiatric abnormalities, but no evidence of incremental benefit has been shown. When the weekly injections are completed, the patient or a family member or friend can be taught to give the monthly injections. Parenteral and high-dose oral regimens give prompt and equivalent hematologic and neurologic responses, but post-treatment serum cobalamin levels are significantly higher and post-treatment methylmalonic acid levels are significantly lower with the oral regimen. With either the parenteral or the oral regimens, the absolute requirement of lifetime therapy must be well understood by the patient and the patient's family. Because cobalamin is inexpensive and free of side effects, it is better to give too much than too little.

FOLATE DEFICIENCY. Therapy usually is administered orally in the form of 1-mg tablets of folic acid. Oral therapy is almost always satisfactory, even in the presence of intestinal malabsorption. The usual dose is 1 to 2 mg daily. Therapy limited to several weeks is usually adequate in an alcoholic who begins to eat a normal diet. In patients with chronic conditions, such as malabsorption, hemolysis, exfoliative skin diseases, or renal failure requiring hemodialysis, oral folate is continued indefinitely and usually given prophylactically.

ADVANTAGES OF COMBINED COBALAMIN AND FOLATE THERAPY. Because at least 25% of patients with cobalamin deficiency also have or develop folate deficiency, oral therapy with at least 1 mg of each vitamin is an attractive and increasingly popular option. This option is also useful in patients with folate deficiency because it ensures that the neuropsychiatric abnormalities caused by cobalamin deficiency will not be masked and untreated.

COBALAMIN OR FOLATE DEFICIENCY. Red blood cell transfusions rarely are required because of the well-compensated state of moderately and even severely anemic patients. Transfusions should be avoided if possible because of the associated cost and risk. If a transfusion is required, it should be given slowly because fluid overload is common and may precipitate lethal congestive heart failure. The only additional therapy is that required for certain underlying causes of cobalamin or folate deficiency, such as antibiotics in bacterial overgrowth or dietary changes in celiac disease.

DRUGS OR OTHER CAUSES. When drugs are responsible for cobalamin or folate deficiency, either administration of them can be stopped or the dosages can be reduced if necessary. When methotrexate is used for rheumatic conditions (Chapter 278), 1 mg of folic acid is often given daily. In other causes, pyridoxine or thiamine can be tried in pharmacologic doses because occasional patients respond.

Prognosis

The hematologic abnormalities caused by cobalamin or folate deficiency respond rapidly to therapy with the appropriate vitamin. Reticulocytosis begins by day 5, followed shortly by an increase in the hematocrit, which returns to normal within several months. Neutrophil and platelet counts and other laboratory abnormalities usually return to normal within 7 to 10 days. If complete correction of all hematologic abnormalities does not occur, a search should be made for other conditions, such as iron deficiency or hypothyroidism.

The response of neuropsychiatric abnormalities caused by cobalamin deficiency is less predictable. Cobalamin therapy always pre-

Table 175–6 • TYPICAL SERUM FINDINGS IN MEGALOBLASTIC ANEMIA

COMPONENT	NORMAL LEVELS	DEFICIENCY Cobalamin	Folate
Cobalamin	200–900 pg/mL	↓*	N
Folate	2.5–20 ng/mL	N	↓*
Methylmalonic acid	70–270 nmol	↑↑	N
Homocysteine	5–14 µmol	↑↑	↑↑

*Many patients with cobalamin deficiency have serum cobalamin levels in the lower portion of the normal range (see text). The same is true with respect to folate deficiency and serum folate levels.

vents these patients from getting worse and most often results in partial or complete correction. Responses may be seen within several days but may take 12 or 18 months. Patients with pernicious anemia have an approximately twofold increased risk of gastric carcinoma and an increased association with hyperthyroidism, hypothyroidism, and other manifestations of the polyglandular failure syndrome.

1. Schnyder G, Roffi M, Flammer Y, et al: Effect of homocysteine-lowering therapy with folic acid, vitamin B_{12}, and vitamin B_6 on clinical outcome after percutaneous coronary intervention. The Swiss Heart Study: A randomized controlled trial. JAMA 2002;288:973–979.
2. Kuzminski AM, Del Giacco EJ, Allen RH, et al: Effective treatment of cobalamin deficiency with oral cobalamin. Blood 1998;92:1191–1198.

SUGGESTED READINGS

Clark R, Refsum H, Birks J, et al: Screening for vitamin B_{12} and folate deficiency in older persons. Am J Clin Nutr 2003;77:1241–1247. *Documents how common these deficiencies are in elderly persons, their diagnosis, and their clinical consequences.*

Vollset SE, Refsum H, Tverdal A, et al: Plasma total homocysteine and cardiovascular and noncardiovascular mortality: The Hordaland Homocysteine Study. Am J Clin Nutr 2001;74:130–136. *This population-based study shows a strong relationship between total homocysteine and mortality, both all-cause and due to cardiovascular disease.*

176 POLYCYTHEMIA VERA AND RELATED DISORDERS

Ayalew Tefferi

The word *polycythemia* is Greek-derived and literally translates as *too many blood cells*. However, in conventional terminology, polycythemia refers to either a real (*true polycythemia*) or spurious (*apparent polycythemia*) increase in red blood cell mass. *True polycythemia* may represent either a clonal myeloproliferative disorder polycythemia vera or a nonclonal increase in red blood cell mass that is often mediated by erythropoietin (EPO; secondary polycythemia). *Apparent polycythemia* may result from either a reduction in plasma volume (relative polycythemia) or an inaccurate interpretation of hemoglobin and hematocrit values that are greater than the 95th percentile range of reference intervals (Fig. 176–1).

APPARENT POLYCYTHEMIA

Most conditions that cause acute plasma volume depletion (i.e., relative polycythemia) are clinically obvious (e.g., severe dehydration, diarrhea, vomiting, use of diuretics, capillary leak syndrome, severe burns) and do not require diagnostic confirmation with the use of specialized tests. Conversely, the existence of chronic plasma volume contraction, such as postulated for both *Gaisbock's syndrome* (relative polycythemia associated with hypertension and nephropa-

thy) and *stress polycythemia* (relative polycythemia associated with emotional stress) is controversial. Accurate reference to the race- and sex-adjusted normal laboratory values should minimize the inappropriate use of the term *apparent polycythemia* in normal persons with hematocrit values that lie in the upper percentiles of the normal distribution. In such instances, the performance of costly diagnostic tests, including the measurement of red blood cell mass, is unwarranted.

SECONDARY POLYCYTHEMIA

Normal red blood cell production requires erythroid progenitor cell stimulation by EPO. This hematopoietic growth factor is a 35-kD glycosylated protein that is synthesized in response to hypoxia, mainly by the peritubular capillary endothelial cells of the renal cortex by means of an intricate oxygen-sensing mechanism. EPO acts at both the late burst-forming unit erythroid (BFU-E) and colony-forming unit erythroid (CFU-E) levels of erythropoiesis (Chapter 159). Stimulants of physiologic EPO production include both anemia and hypoxia.

Secondary polycythemia may or may not be associated with increased EPO production (Table 176–1). EPO-mediated secondary polycythemia may be classified as a hypoxia-driven or hypoxia-independent process. Usually, serum EPO level is increased in hypoxia-independent secondary polycythemia and is not affected by fluctuations in the hemoglobin level. In contrast, in hypoxia-driven secondary polycythemia, the serum EPO level is affected by the hemoglobin response and is often within the normal reference range after the hemoglobin level has stabilized at a higher level. Most cases of EPO-mediated secondary polycythemia are acquired. Exceptions include the autosomal-dominant, high-oxygen affinity hemoglobinopathies (e.g., hemoglobin Chesapeake, hemoglobin Heathrow; see Chapter 172) as well as an autosomal-recessive red cell enzymopathy (2,3-diphosphoglycerate [DPG] mutase deficiency; see Chapter 170).

Some patients with autosomal-dominant congenital polycythemia carry an activating mutation of the EPO receptor gene that results in

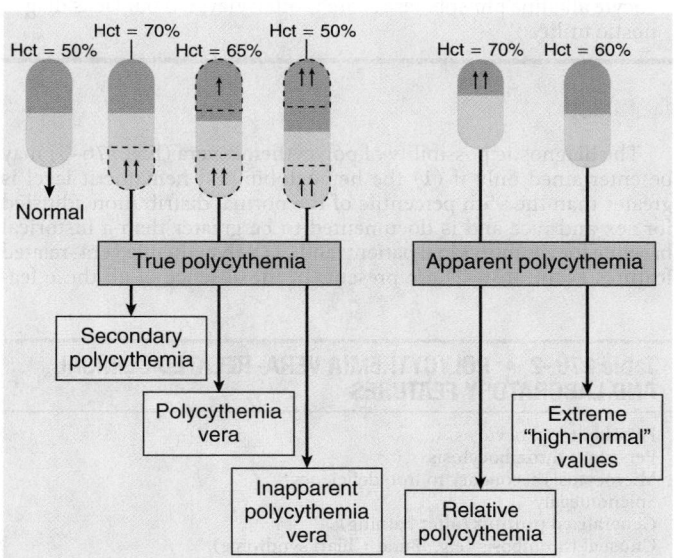

FIGURE 176–1 • Clonal and nonclonal causes of polycythemia.

Table 176–1 • CAUSES OF SECONDARY POLYCYTHEMIA

ERYTHROPOIETIN (EPO)-MEDIATED
Hypoxia-Driven
Central hypoxic process
    Chronic lung disease
    Right-to-left cardiopulmonary vascular shunts
    High-altitude habitat
    Chronic carbon monoxide exposure (e.g., smoking)
    Hypoventilation syndromes including sleep apnea
Peripheral hypoxic process
    Localized
        Renal artery stenosis or an equivalent renal pathology
    Diffuse
        High-oxygen-affinity hemoglobinopathy (congenital; autosomal dominant)
        2,3-Diphosphoglycerate mutase deficiency (congenital; autosomal recessive)

Hypoxia-Independent (Pathologic EPO Production)
Malignant tumors
    Hepatocellular carcinoma
    Renal cell cancer
    Cerebellar hemangioblastoma
Nonmalignant conditions
    Uterine leiomyomas
    Renal cysts
    Postrenal transplantation
    Adrenal tumors

EPO RECEPTOR–MEDIATED
Activating mutation of the erythropoietin receptor
Some cases of autosomal dominant congenital polycythemia

DRUG-ASSOCIATED
EPO Doping
Treatment with Androgen Preparations

UNKNOWN MECHANISMS
Most Cases of Autosomal Dominant Congenital Polycythemia
Autosomal-Recessive Congenital Polycythemia Including Chuvash Type

a C-terminal truncated receptor that is more efficient in signal transduction, possibly because of defective recruitment of regulatory phosphatases. The serum EPO level is usually low in such cases. However, mutations of the EPO receptor are not found in most patients with autosomal-dominant congenital polycythemia or with the autosomal-recessive form, including Chuvash polycythemia that is endemic in Russia. The underlying molecular lesions in the latter forms of congenital polycythemia are not known. In general, serum EPO levels are either normal or increased in such cases. Finally, it is essential to include a drug-induced process (e.g., EPO doping, androgens) in the differential diagnosis of secondary polycythemia.

Evaluation

The serum EPO level does not reliably differentiate among the different causes of secondary polycythemia. If family history suggests a congenital cause, it is essential to measure P_{50} (oxygen pressure at 50% hemoglobin-oxygen saturation). A low P_{50} is consistent with either a high oxygen affinity hemoglobinopathy or 2,3-DPG mutase deficiency (Chapter 170). A normal P_{50} in the presence of congenital polycythemia suggests either autosomal-dominant or autosomal-recessive congenital polycythemia (Chapter 172).

In acquired secondary polycythemia, initial laboratory tests should include the measurement of arterial hemoglobin-oxygen saturation. In the absence of a central hypoxic state, renal vascular studies should be performed to exclude the possibility of renal artery stenosis (Chapter 124). Imaging studies of the kidney, liver, and central nervous system may be considered when either the aforementioned studies are unrevealing or serum EPO level is persistently elevated. For suspected EPO doping, immunoblotting techniques can differentiate endogenous EPO from exogenously administered recombinant EPO.

Rx Treatment

Both the frequency and severity of thrombotic and nonthrombotic complications of polycythemia are significantly less in secondary polycythemia than in polycythemia vera. Therefore, prophylactic phlebotomy is recommended at a higher hematocrit target level (55 to 60%) in secondary polycythemia than in polycythemia vera (40 to 45%). Angiotensin-converting enzyme inhibitors and angiotensin II receptor blockers can significantly reduce hematocrit levels in secondary polycythemia that is associated with either renal transplantation or chronic obstructive lung disease [1,2] by inducing apoptosis in erythroid precursor cells.

POLYCYTHEMIA VERA

Polycythemia vera is currently classified with essential thrombocythemia and agnogenic myeloid metaplasia as a chronic myeloproliferative disorder (Chapter 183). Accordingly, polycythemia vera is a clonal stem cell disease with growth factor–independent erythroid proliferation that results in increased red blood cell mass.

Epidemiology

Population-based epidemiologic studies suggest a stable prevalence of polycythemia vera at approximately 2.3 per 100,000 population. A higher incidence has been suggested in persons of Jewish ancestry and among parent-offspring pairs, but no known environmental exposures have been implicated. Median age at diagnosis is approximately 60 years, with a slight male preponderance. Approximately 7% of patients are diagnosed before age 40, and rare cases have occurred in children.

Pathogenesis

Polycythemia vera is a clonal stem cell disease, but the underlying molecular lesion remains elusive. The growth of erythroid progenitors in polycythemia vera is not only EPO-independent but also hypersensitive to insulin-like growth factor (IGF)-1, interleukin-3, granulocyte-monocyte colony-stimulating factor, stem cell factor, and thrombopoietin (TPO). These observations suggest

an aberrant signal transduction pathway that may also be responsible for the increased baseline phosphorylation of the IGF-1 receptor as well as the abundance in erythroid precursors of antiapoptotic proteins (Bcl-x_L).

Clinical Manifestations

More and more patients with polycythemia vera are being diagnosed at an asymptomatic stage based on routine blood counts. When symptoms are present (Table 176–2), they fall into three major categories: vasomotor, thrombohemorrhagic, and other nonvascular symptoms. Vasomotor symptoms include headache, lightheadedness, transient neurologic or ocular disturbances, tinnitus, atypical chest discomfort, paresthesias, and erythromelalgia (Fig. 176–2). Erythromelalgia occurs in less than 5% of the patients and may represent small vessel platelet-endothelium interaction with associated inflammation and transient thrombotic occlusion. It is sometimes difficult to distinguish vasomotor disturbances from symptoms of hyperviscosity that include head fullness, dizziness, flushing, visual disturbances, tinnitus, epistaxis, dyspnea, and increased blood pressure.

Approximately 20% of patients with polycythemia vera present with thrombosis, and another 20 to 30% experience recurrent thrombosis in the first decade after diagnosis. Arterial events are more frequent than venous events and include transient ischemic attack or stroke, myocardial infarction, and digital ischemia. There is an approximately 10% incidence of abdominal large vessel thrombosis including Budd-Chiari syndrome and portal vein thrombosis (Chapter 144). Other venous events include cavernous sinus thrombosis and pulmonary embolism. Major hemorrhage is much less frequent but may be precipitated by the use of aspirin or aspirin-like drugs. Minor mucocutaneous bleeding episodes are much more frequent and include epistaxis, gingival bleeding, and ecchymoses.

Nonvascular symptoms include pruritus and hypercatabolic symptoms. Pruritus that is often exacerbated by water contact (aquagenic) occurs in more than 50% of patients with polycythemia vera and may be sufficiently severe to prevent patients from taking daily showers. Hypercatabolic symptoms include weight loss, fatigue, diaphoresis, and night sweats. Patients may present with peptic ulcer symptoms or toe or joint pain secondary to gouty arthritis.

An untreated patient with polycythemia vera may display plethora or ruddiness (a red and congested facial complexion), palmar erythema, and sausage-shaped distention of retinal veins. Palpable splenomegaly occurs in approximately 70% of the patients and may be associated with early satiety. Laboratory findings may include leukocytosis (20 to 43%), thrombocytosis (48 to 63%), microcytosis (50 to 80%), and increased serum levels of uric acid, lactate dehydrogenase (a general indicator of high cell turnover), vitamin B_{12}, and vitamin B_{12} binding capacity. The leucocyte alkaline phosphatase score is often elevated but lacks diagnostic utility.

Diagnosis

The diagnostic possibility of polycythemia vera (Fig. 176–3) may be entertained only if (1) the hemoglobin and hematocrit level is greater than the 95th percentile of the normal distribution adjusted for sex and race and is documented to be greater than a historical baseline for the individual patient; and (2) polycythemia vera–related features (Table 176–2) are present. In the absence of all these fea-

Table 176–2 • POLYCYTHEMIA VERA–RELATED CLINICAL AND LABORATORY FEATURES

Persistent leukocytosis
Persistent thrombocytosis
Microcytosis secondary to iron deficiency
Splenomegaly
Generalized pruritus (after bathing)
Unusual thrombosis (e.g., Budd-Chiari syndrome)
Erythromelalgia (acral dysesthesia and erythema); see Figure 176–2.

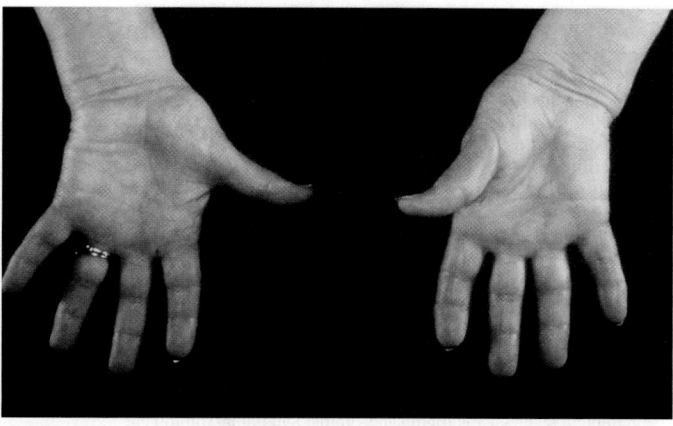

FIGURE 176–2 • Erythromelalgia refers to a painful red discoloration of the hands or toes (Chapter 77).

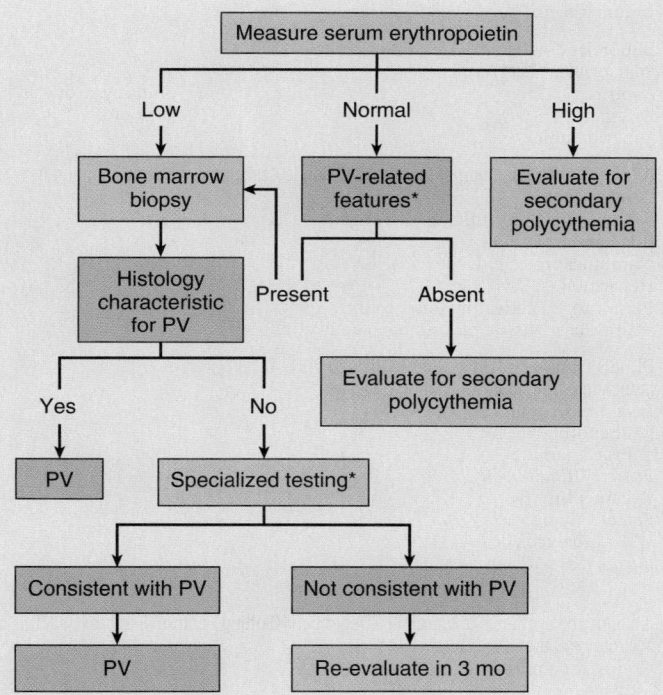

FIGURE 176–3 • A diagnostic algorithm for polycythemia vera (PV). (See Table 176–2 for polycythemia vera–related features.) *Specialized testing includes bone marrow immunohistochemistry for the thrombopoietin receptor (c-Mpl) and reverse transcriptase-polymerase chain reaction (RT-PCR) for neutrophil expression of polycythemia rubra vera (PRV)-1 gene.

tures, a repeat blood test should be performed in 3 months. In the presence of one of these features, a serum EPO level should be obtained. The serum EPO level is low in most patients with polycythemia vera, and polycythemia vera is unlikely to be associated with an increased serum EPO level. In suspicious cases with a low or normal serum EPO level, a bone marrow examination may reveal characteristic changes (including hypercellularity), increased numbers of megakaryocytes (sometimes including clusters of giant megakaryocytes), mild reticulin fibrosis, and decreased bone marrow iron stores. In equivocal cases, the demonstration of markedly decreased megakaryocyte expression of c-Mpl supports the histologic diagnosis. In contrast, cytogenetic studies have limited diagnostic value. A peripheral blood neutrophil assay for PRV-1 expression can distinguish polycythemia vera (high expression) from secondary polycythemia (not detectable), but the assay is not widely available.

Rx Prognosis and Treatment

Life expectancy in polycythemia vera exceeds 10 years but is worse than the sex- and age-matched control population owing to premature death from fatal thrombohemorrhagic complications and to transformation into myelofibrosis with myeloid metaplasia (Chapter 183) and acute myeloid leukemia (AML, Chapter 193). Age older than 60 years, history of thrombosis, and treatment with phlebotomy alone are considered adverse risk factors (Table 176–3). The estimated rates of recurrent thrombosis in low- and high-risk patients are 5 and 30%, respectively. The incidences of myeloid metaplasia and AML in the first decade of the disease are approximately 10 and 5%, respectively. A higher proportion of patients experience disease transformation in the second decade of the disease.

At present, treatment of polycythemia vera is primarily directed at preventing thrombotic complications. Aggressive phlebotomy and modern supportive care are credited with a marked improvement in the median survival. The addition of oral chlorambucil or intravenous radioactive phosphorus (^{32}P) to phlebotomy significantly reduces the rate of early thrombotic complications but also significantly lessens survival because of an increased incidence of acute leukemia.[3] Hydroxyurea appears to lower the risks of thrombosis compared with phlebotomy alone, with a lower risk of acute leukemia compared with either chlorambucil or radioactive phosphorus, but these data are not from randomized trials.

Based on these observations, the mainstay of therapy in polycythemia vera remains phlebotomy, with a goal of keeping the hematocrit below 45% in white men and 42% in women and African-American men. These levels reduce blood hyperviscosity, improve cerebral blood flow, and lower the rate of thrombotic complications. The current consensus is to supplement phlebotomy with hydroxyurea only in those patients who are at high risk for thrombosis (Table 176–4; see Table 176–3). Whether specific therapy modifies the risk of transformation into myeloid metaplasia is not clearly ascertained.

Pipobroman (not available in the United States) is as effective as hydroxyurea in the treatment of polycythemia vera without being more or less leukemogenic.[4] In nonrandomized settings, both busulfan and interferon alfa have shown activity against polycythemia vera, but they have not been compared rigorously with hydroxyurea. Anagrelide has also been used in a noncontrolled setting, and its role currently is not clear.

High doses of aspirin (300 mg three times a day) in combination with dipyridamole (75 mg three times a day) do not alter the risk of thrombosis but do increase the risk of gastrointestinal bleeding in randomized trials. However, more recent studies have suggested a decreased risk of bleeding with lower doses of aspirin, and this low-dose approach is currently being investigated in a large randomized study. Low-dose aspirin (81 to 325 mg/day) is most effective in the treatment of vasomotor symptoms. Paroxetine, a selective serotonin reuptake inhibitor, is effective in the treatment of polycythemia vera–associated pruritus.

Although there is wide agreement on the supplemental use of cytoreductive drug therapy for the purpose of minimizing thrombotic complications in high-risk patients (see Table 176–3), controversy remains in the management of younger patients who do not have a history of thrombosis but who have either cardiovascular symptoms or extreme thrombocytosis. The value of cytoreductive therapy in such patients is unclear unless the platelet count exceeds 1.5 million/μL, in which case the concern is for a bleeding diathesis rather than thrombosis.

Table 176–3 • RISK STRATIFICATION IN POLYCYTHEMIA VERA

LOW RISK
Age <60 years, *and*
No history of thrombocytosis, *and*
Platelet count <1.5 million/μL

INTERMEDIATE RISK
Age <60 years, *and*
No history of thrombocytosis, *and*
either
Platelet count >1.5 million/μL, *or*
The presence of cardiovascular risk factors, especially smoking

HIGH RISK
Age ≥60 years, *or*
A history of thrombosis

Table 176–4 • TREATMENT ALGORITHM IN POLYCYTHEMIA VERA

RISK CATEGORY	AGE < 60 YEARS	AGE ≥ 60 YEARS	WOMEN OF CHILDBEARING AGE
Low risk	Phlebotomy alone*	Not applicable	Phlebotomy alone*
Indeterminate risk	Phlebotomy alone*†	Not applicable	Phlebotomy alone*
High risk	Phlebotomy + Hydroxyurea or α-interferon‡	Phlebotomy + Hydroxyurea†	Phlebotomy + Interferon α†§

*Use of low-dose aspirin is optional and not evidence-based.
† Use of aspirin is discouraged if the platelet count is >1.5 million/μL, in which case a cytoreductive agent may be used to control symptomatic thrombocytosis.
‡ There is some preliminary evidence to support the use of low-dose aspirin in addition to cytoreductive therapy.
§ Based on anecdotal evidence of safety.

1. Yildiz A, Cine N, Akkaya V, et al: Comparison of the effects of enalapril and losartan on posttransplantation erythrocytosis in renal transplant recipients: Prospective randomized study. Transplantation 2001;72:542–544.
2. Vlahakos DV, Marathias KP, Kosmas EN: Losartan reduces hematocrit in patients with chronic obstructive pulmonary disease and secondary erythrocytosis. Ann Intern Med 2001;134:426–427.
3. Berk PD, Wasserman LR, Fruchtman SM, et al: Treatment of polycythemia vera: A summary of clinical trials conducted by the Polycythemia Vera Study Group. *In* Wasserman LR, et al (eds): Polycythemia Vera and the Myeloproliferative Disorders. Philadelphia, WB Saunders, 1995, pp 166–194.
4. Najean Y, Rain JD: Treatment of polycythemia vera: The use of hydroxyurea and pipobroman in 292 patients under the age of 65 years. Blood 1997;90:3370–3377.

SUGGESTED READINGS
Diehn F, Tefferi A: Pruritus in polycythaemia vera: prevalence, laboratory correlates and management. Br J Haematol 2001;115:619–621. *A comprehensive study of prevalence, severity, and outcomes of treatment.*
Fairbanks VF: Myeloproliferative disease: Polycythemia vera: The packed cell volume and the curious logic of the red cell mass. Hematology 2000;4:381–395. *A critical appraisal of the relationship between hematocrit and the red cell mass.*
Prchal JT: Pathogenetic mechanisms of polycythemia vera and congenital polycythemic disorders. Semin Hematol 2001;38(1 Suppl 2):10–20. *A detailed review of the different causes of secondary polycythemia, with emphasis on congenital causes.*
Tefferi A: Polycythemia vera: A comprehensive review and clinical recommendations. Mayo Clin Proc 2003;78:174–194. *Evidence-based recommendations.*

177 HEMORRHAGIC DISORDERS: ABNORMALITIES OF PLATELET AND VASCULAR FUNCTION

Marc Shuman

The normal sequence of events leading to clotting is initiated by trauma to the vessel, which constricts to reduce blood flow. Platelets adhere to the subendothelial matrix in the injured vessel, and platelet aggregation and thrombus formation begin simultaneously (Chapter 162). A variety of drugs can interfere with different aspects of hemostasis

Table 177–1 • DRUGS THAT MAY ALTER HEMOSTASIS

DRUGS REPORTED TO CAUSE THROMBOCYTOPENIA
Immune Mechanism Proposed*

Quinine/quinidine	Ranitidine
Sulfa compounds	Cimetidine
Ampicillin	Danazol
Penicillin	Procainamide
Thiazide diuretics	Carbamazepine
Furosemide	Acetaminophen
Chlorthalidone	Phenylbutazone
Phenytoin	p-Aminosalicylate
α-Methyldopa	Rifampin
Heparin	Acetazolamide
Digitalis derivatives	Anazoline
Aspirin	Arsenicals
Valproic acid	

Nonimmune Mechanisms (Hemolytic-Uremic Syndrome/Thrombotic Thrombocytopenic Purpura)

Mitomycin C	Cisplatin
Ticlopidine	Cyclosporine

Mechanism Undefined
Gold compounds
Indomethacin

DRUGS THAT ALTER PLATELET FUNCTION
Primary Antiplatelet Agents

Aspirin	Sulfinpyrazone
Dextran	Ticlopidine
Dipyridamole	

Drugs in Which Inhibition of Platelet Function Is Associated with Prolongation of Bleeding Time
Nonsteroidal anti-inflammatory agents
β-lactam antibiotics
ε-aminocaproic acid (>24 g/d)
Heparin
Plasminogen activators (streptokinase, urokinase, tissue plasminogen activator)

DRUGS THAT AFFECT COAGULATION FACTORS
Induction of Antibodies Inhibiting Function
Lupus anticoagulant†‡
  Phenothiazines
  Procainamide
Factor VIII antibodies
  Penicillin
Factor V antibodies
  Aminoglycosides
Factor XIII antibodies
  Isoniazid

Inhibitors of Synthesis of Vitamin K–Dependent Clotting Factors (Factors II, VII, IX, X, Proteins C and S)
Coumarin compounds
Moxalactam

Inhibitor of Fibrinogen Synthesis
L-asparaginase‡

*List is limited to drugs for which there are multiple reports and there is in vitro or in vivo evidence for antiplatelet antibodies.
†Does not cause bleeding.
‡May cause thrombosis.

(Table 177–1), and therefore a medication history is particularly important.

PATHOLOGIC HEMOSTASIS. Thrombus formation is similar to normal hemostasis except that abnormalities in activation, inhibition, or fibrinolysis result in pathologic clots. Derangements may occur in (1) the vessel wall (e.g., atherosclerosis), (2) platelets (e.g., myeloproliferative disorders), and (3) regulation of the coagulation system (e.g., antithrombin III deficiency, factor V Leiden). Anatomic and/or biochemical alterations of the vascular intima are by far the most frequent causes of pathologic thrombosis. The endothelium normally provides antithrombotic mechanisms that are dominant during homeostasis. Thus, in an unperturbed state, the vascular endothelium inhibits activation of platelets and coagulation. Endothelial cells secrete tissue plasminogen activator, the primary activator of fibrinolysis in blood. Moreover, these cells manufacture potent inhibitors of platelet activation, including prostacyclin and ecto-ADPase/CD39, which rapidly metabolize adenosine diphosphate (ADP) released from activated platelets, thereby preventing further platelet activation and recruitment. Finally, the luminal surface of endothelial cells expresses thrombomodulin, protein S, and the receptor for protein C. Thrombin bound to thrombomodulin acts paradoxically as an inhibitor of activation of coagulation by activating protein C. Activated protein C (APC) and its cofactor, protein S, degrade activated factors V and VIII, thus stopping coagulation.

In contrast, a variety of pathologic alterations of the vessel wall modify endothelial function in a prothrombotic fashion. At one extreme, the endothelial lining may be physically disrupted, with exposure of circulating blood to extracellular matrix and tissue factor. Also, several substances may induce the intact endothelium to promote thrombosis. Thus, interleukin-1, tumor necrosis factor, and endotoxin increase both endothelial plasminogen activator inhibitor-1, an inhibitor of fibrinolysis, and endothelial tissue factor. Moreover, endothelial cells express receptors for several of the coagulation factors, including factors Va, IXa, and Xa, so that once coagulation is initiated, it can be amplified on endothelial cells. It is not difficult to imagine how rupture of an atherosclerotic plaque results in pathologic initiation of clotting, terminating in vascular occlusion (Chapter 66).

BLOOD PLATELETS

Formation and Kinetics

Platelets are disc-shaped cells, 2 to 4mm in diameter, normally found in the peripheral blood (150,000 to 300,000 per microliter). In Wright's-stained blood smears, they are identified by their blue-gray cytoplasm and red (lysosomal) granules and by lack of a nucleus.

Platelets are formed in the bone marrow from giant polyploid cells called *megakaryocytes*. Megakaryocytes mature by a series of nuclear replications within a common cytoplasm (endomitosis), leading to four- to six-lobed nuclei, and by elaboration of specific granules in the cytoplasm. Following maturation, the cytoplasm of the megakaryocyte becomes demarcated into platelet subunits, and the platelets are released into the circulation through the marrow sinusoids. Thrombopoietin is a hematopoietic growth factor specific for megakaryocytes. Recombinant thrombopoietin is currently being tested for potential clinical uses.

Interleukin-11(IL-11) also stimulates platelet production. IL-11 has been approved for use in patients with hypoproliferative thrombocytopenia resulting from high-dose chemotherapy.

Ordinarily, each megakaryocyte produces 1000 to 3000 platelets. Normally, 3 to 10 megakaryocytes are seen in bone marrow smears under low-power magnification, but none appear in peripheral blood. Platelets circulate for 9 to 10 days. Approximately one-third reside in a splenic pool, which exchanges freely with the circulating pool. In diseases associated with platelet antibodies, the spleen is frequently the site of destruction. In disorders causing secondary splenic enlargement, thrombocytopenia may result from splenic sequestration (Chapter 164). Conversely, following splenectomy, the platelet count may increase transiently to $10^6/\mu L$ or greater.

An estimate of platelet number in the peripheral blood film (normal, increased, decreased) is useful in detecting abnormally low platelet counts. Normally, 3 to 10 platelets per high-power (oil immersion) field are seen on a peripheral smear (Chapter 161). Platelets are counted directly by an automated particle counter.

Platelet Function

Platelets contain three types of secretory granules: *lysosomes*, α-*granules*, and *dense bodies* (electron-dense organelles). α-Granules contain platelet-specific proteins: platelet factor 4; β-thromboglobulin; and several growth factors, including platelet-derived growth factor (PDGF), endothelial cell growth factor (PD-ECGF), and transforming growth factor-β (TGF-β). α-Granules also contain several hemostatic proteins, including fibrinogen, factor V, and von Willebrand factor, which is synthesized by megakaryocytes. Dense bodies (δ-granules) contain adenosine triphosphate (ATP), ADP, Ca^{2+}, and serotonin.

In addition to release of potent vasoconstrictors from intracellular granules in response to a variety of substances and aggregation to form a plug at the site of vessel injury, platelets provide a surface for

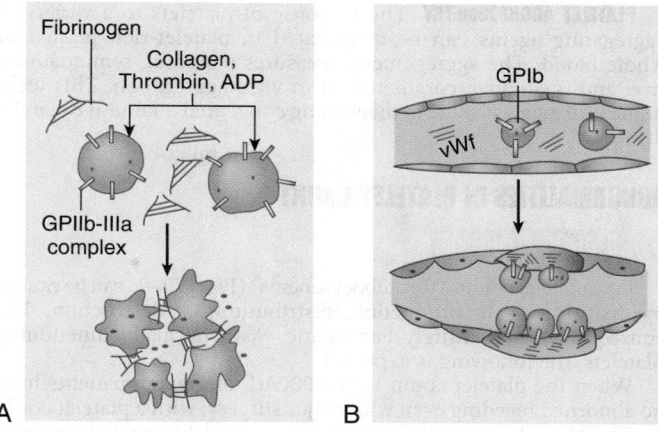

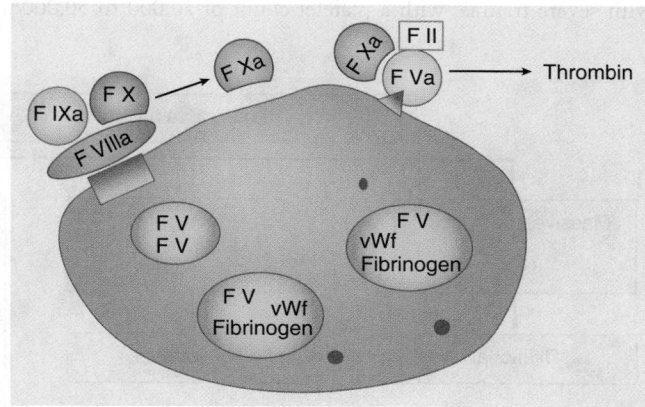

FIGURE 177–1 • Platelet adhesion, aggregation and enhancement of coagulation. *A*, Platelet aggregation. Activation of platelets by several physiologic stimuli results in fibrinogen binding to specific receptors, GPIIb-IIIa. Binding of fibrinogen is followed by platelet aggregation. *B*, Platelet adhesion. Injury to the vascular endothelium results in exposure of extracellular matrix. Under high shear, von Willebrand factor (vWf) binds to the platelet receptor GPIb. The platelet-vWf complex then adheres to the subendothelium. *C*, Amplification of thrombin formation by platelets. Coagulation factors IXa, VIIIa, and X form a Ca^{2+}-dependent trimolecular complex on the platelet surface. Activation of factor X is amplified several hundred thousand–fold. Coagulation factors Xa and Va and prothrombin form a Ca^{2+}-dependent trimolecular complex on platelets. Thrombin formation is amplified several hundred thousand–fold.

the activation of soluble coagulation factors (Fig. 177–1). Activated platelets expose specific receptors that bind factors Xa and Va and in this way increase their local concentration, thus accelerating prothrombin activation. Factor X is also activated by factors IXa and VIII (antihemophilic factor) on the surface of the platelet.

Platelets contain a membrane phospholipase C, which, upon stimulation by activating agents, hydrolyzes endogenous phosphatidylinositol to form a diglyceride. The diglyceride is converted to arachidonic acid by a diglyceride lipase. Arachidonic acid is a substrate for prostaglandin synthetase (cyclooxygenase; Chapter 32), a reaction inhibited by aspirin and nonsteroidal anti-inflammatory drugs, and is subsequently converted to prostaglandins. The prostaglandin endoperoxide PGG_2 is required for ADP-induced aggregation and release; both PGG_2 and thromboxane A_2 are potent platelet-aggregating agents.

Platelet Function Tests

BLEEDING TIME (Chapter 162). Bleeding time is prolonged when the platelet count goes below 90,000/mL or when a functional platelet abnormality exists. Von Willebrand disease prolongs the bleeding time not as a result of a platelet defect but rather because of the lack of a plasma factor important for normal platelet function (Chapter 178). Although imperfect, the bleeding time is the only test of platelet function that correlates with susceptibility to bleeding. Even though patients with a prolonged bleeding time are at risk for increased bleeding with surgery, not all have abnormal bleeding.

PLATELET AGGREGOMETRY. The response of platelets to a variety of aggregating agents can be quantitated in platelet-rich plasma or whole blood. The aggregometer measures temporal, semiquantitative, and qualitative parameters of in vitro aggregation. This technique is of greatest value in diagnosing congenital qualitative platelet disorders.

ABNORMALITIES IN PLATELET COUNT

THROMBOCYTOPENIA

Low platelet counts (thrombocytopenia) (Fig. 177–2) can be caused by disturbances in production, distribution, or destruction. The consequences are entirely hemostatic. With normally functioning platelets, the following is expected:

When the platelet count is 100,000/μL or greater, patients have no abnormal bleeding even with major surgery; with a platelet count of 50,000 to 100,000/μL, patients may bleed longer than normal with severe trauma; with a platelet count of 20,000 to 50,000/μL, bleeding occurs with minor trauma, but spontaneous bleeding is unusual; with a platelet count less than 20,000/μL, patients may have spontaneous bleeding; when the platelet count is less than 10,000/μL, patients are at high risk for severe bleeding.

Decreased Production of Platelets

Hypoplasia of hematopoietic stem cells may cause thrombocytopenia (Table 177–2). Examination of the bone marrow reveals decreased numbers of megakaryocytes and either an overall decrease in cellularity or infiltration by abnormal cells.

Decreased production of platelets may also be due to abnormal maturation of megakaryocytes. Deficiency of either vitamin B_{12} or folate can cause thrombocytopenia owing to ineffective thrombocytopoiesis (Chapter 175). Similarly, abnormal platelet production is common in hematopoietic dysplasias (Chapters 174 and 182). In both disorders, megakaryocytes are usually increased. In hematopoietic dysplasia, megakaryocytes may be abnormal in appearance, such as micromegakaryocytes occasionally with a single-lobed nucleus.

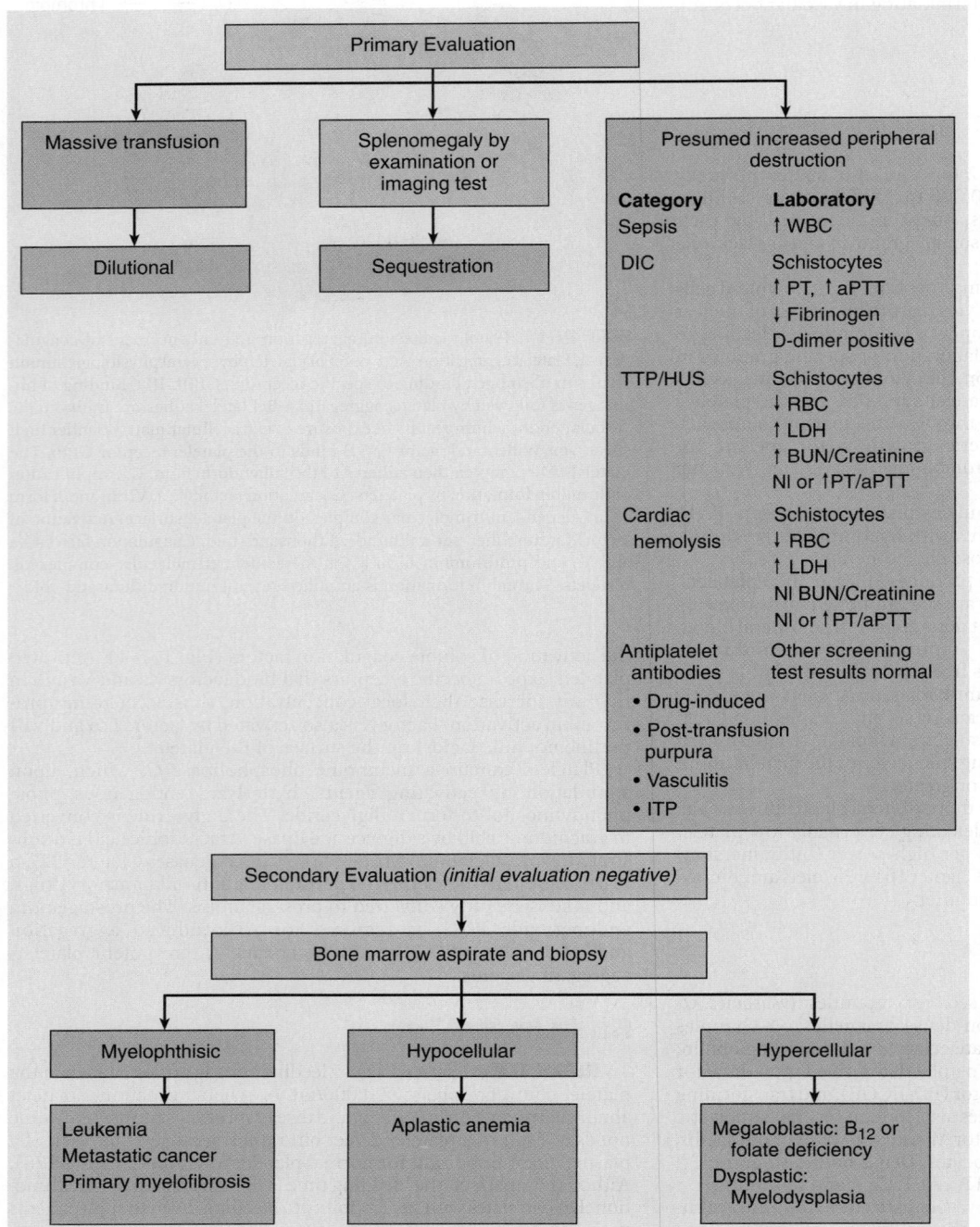

FIGURE 177–2 • Evaluation of thrombocytopenia. Abn = abnormal; aPTT = activated partial thromboplastin time; BUN = blood urea nitrogen; LDH = lactate dehydrogenase; Nl = normal; PT = prothrombin time.

Table 177–2 • DISORDERS ASSOSIATED WITH THROMBOCYTOPENIA

HYPOPLASIA OF HEMATOPOIETIC STEM CELLS
Aplastic anemia
Marrow damage from drugs, chemicals, ionizing radiation, alcohol, infection
Congenital and hereditary thrombocytopenias
Thrombocytopenia with absent radii syndrome
Wiskott-Aldrich syndrome
May-Hegglin anomaly

REPLACEMENT OF NORMAL MARROW
Leukemias
Metastatic tumor (prostate, breast, lymphoma)
Myelofibrosis

INEFFECTIVE THROMBOCYTOPOIESIS (NORMAL OR INCREASED NUMBERS OF MEGAKARYOCYTES)
Cobalamin or folate deficiency
Hematopoietic dysplastic syndromes

INCREASED DESTRUCTION OF PLATELETS
Immune disorders
  Idiopathic thrombocytopenic purpura
  Secondary causes:
    Cancer: chronic lymphocytic leukemia, lymphoma, systemic autoimmune disorders (SLE, polyarteritis nodosa)
    Infectious diseases: infectious mononucleosis, CMV, HIV
    Drugs: quinine/quinidine, heparin, sulfa compounds (see Table 177–1)
Nonimmune disorders
  Disseminated intravascular coagulation
  Cavernous hemangioma
  Thrombotic thrombocytopenic purpura
  Hemolytic-uremic syndrome
  Sepsis
  Malaria
  Paroxysmal nocturnal hemoglobinuria
  Congenital cyanotic heart disease
  Acute renal transplant rejection

DISORDERS OF DISTRIBUTION
Hypersplenism

DILUTIONAL
Secondary to transfusion

CMV = cytomegalovirus; HIV = human immunodeficiency virus;
SLE = systemic lupus erythematosus.

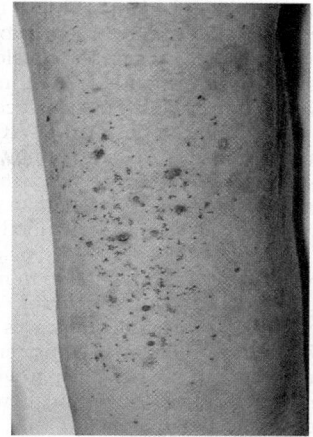

FIGURE 177–3 • Acute idiopathic thrombocytopenic purpura commonly manifests with purpuric lesions of this kind, though they may often be more widespread by the time medical attention is sought. It is important to remember that purpura of identical appearance may result from many other causes. (From Forbes CD, Jackson WF: Color Atlas and Text of Clinical Medicine, 3rd ed. London, Mosby, 2003, with permission.)

Increased Peripheral Destruction of Platelets (See Table 177–2)

IMMUNE DISORDERS

Three types of immunologic reactions cause premature destruction of platelets: (1) development of autoantibodies against platelet-membrane antigens, (2) the binding of immune complexes to platelet Fc receptors, and (3) lysis of platelets because of fixation of complement on their surface.

IDIOPATHIC THROMBOCYTOPENIC PURPURA. Idiopathic thrombocytopenic purpura (ITP; Fig. 177–3) is an autoimmune bleeding disorder characterized by the development of antibodies to one's own platelets, which are then destroyed by phagocytosis in the spleen and, to a lesser extent, the liver. The spleen is the principal reticuloendothelial site of platelet destruction, as well as the major site of synthesis of antibody production in ITP. Childhood ITP is usually acute and follows recovery from a viral infection. The incidence is equal in boys and girls. In adults, the onset is usually more gradual, without a preceding illness and with a chronic course. In a small percentage of adult cases, the disease has an acute onset. Ninety per cent of adults with ITP are younger than age 40 years, and the ratio of women to men is 3 to 4:1. Some patients' sera contain antibodies against platelet glycoproteins IIb and IIIa. Petechiae, ecchymoses, and epistaxis develop in these patients. Menorrhagia may develop in women. The incidence of death, reported in older series to be about 5%, is thought to be significantly lower now. Adverse risk factors are severe thrombocytopenia (platelet count less than 15,000), advanced

age, and concomitant bleeding diathesis. Cerebral bleeding occurs in approximately 1% of cases.

The diagnosis of ITP depends on the exclusion of underlying systemic disorders that result in increased peripheral destruction or decreased production of platelets. On physical examination, the spleen is not enlarged, although it may be in childhood ITP as a consequence of viral infection. In ITP the hemoglobin is normal unless the patient has significant bleeding. Peripheral blood smears reveal normochromic, normocytic red blood cells. Similarly, the leukocyte count and differential are normal, although these values may reflect a preceding viral illness in children. The value of assays for detecting antiplatelet antibodies on the platelet surface is unclear; most of the tests do not distinguish between autoantibodies and immune complexes that bind to the platelet Fc receptor. Furthermore, the assays do not differentiate between specific antiplatelet antibodies and nonspecifically absorbed IgG. In most cases of ITP, the diagnosis is clear-cut, making it unnecessary to confirm the presence of antiplatelet antibodies. In complex cases, the antibody test may be helpful. The level of platelet-associated IgG does not correlate with the severity of thrombocytopenia. In more than 90% of cases of chronic ITP, the antibody is IgG.

If the general clinical evaluation and blood tests do not identify a systemic cause of thrombocytopenia, the bone marrow should be examined. In ITP, the marrow is normal, although megakaryocytes may be increased in number.

In children, ITP is self-limited. Approximately 70% recover within 4 to 6 weeks. In adults, indications for treatment depend on the severity of bleeding and the degree of thrombocytopenia. Asymptomatic patients with platelet counts greater than 40,000/μL can be observed with periodic evaluation to determine the natural fluctuations of their disease. Patients with platelet counts less than 20,000/μL are usually symptomatic and require treatment. Patients with platelet counts greater than 30,000/μL who have bleeding may have an acquired platelet function abnormality caused by the antibody. Initially, bleeding associated with ITP is treated with prednisone at a dose of 1 to 2 mg/kg/day. Prednisone inhibits macrophage ingestion of antibody-coated platelets, in addition to suppressing antibody synthesis. Prednisone has also been shown to have a stabilizing effect on small blood vessels in thrombocytopenic animals. In 80 to 90% of patients, the platelet count increases to hemostatic levels within 2 to 3 weeks. Failure to respond to steroids can be defined by a platelet count less than 50,000/μL after 4 weeks of treatment or a subnormal platelet count. Once the platelet count has reached its apex and is stable, steroids should be tapered slowly. When the dose of prednisone is tapered, however, most patients (>90%) exhibit a relapse of thrombocytopenia. Thus, the primary benefit of prednisone is in the acute management of bleeding.

Another effective approach to managing patients who are actively bleeding or for whom major surgery is necessary is the use of intravenous gamma globulin. Intravenous immunoglobulin (IVIG)

Hematologic Diseases

concentrates elevate the platelet count within 3 to 5 days in most patients and is the most rapidly active agent. However, the therapeutic effect is usually transient, because the platelet count decreases to baseline levels over the next month. In rare instances, repeated infusions of gamma globulin have led to sustained remissions after discontinuation of therapy. It is proposed that IVIG works by blocking Fc receptors on macrophages, thereby inhibiting phagocytosis. The dosage is 1 g/kg/day on 2 successive days. In 80% of patients, subsequent platelet counts increase to more than 50,000/μL. A less expensive alternative is RhoGAM, anti-Rh antibody. The principal is the same as that in IVIG, reticuloendothelial blockade.

Owing to the lack of a sustained remission in most patients with severe thrombocytopenia treated with steroids or IVIG, a more definitive approach is necessary. Splenectomy improves the platelet count in 70% of patients with ITP and induces sustained remission in approximately 60%, but no tests can predict reliably which patients will respond. The platelet count increases within a few days, or at most in 1 to 2 weeks after splenectomy.

A variety of other therapies have been shown to be efficacious in inducing partial or complete remissions in chronic ITP when splenectomy has failed. Danazol, 200 mg three times per day, induces a remission in approximately 40% of chronic ITP. Response is delayed and takes 4 to 6 weeks. The mechanism remains unknown. Intravenous vincristine and vinblastine also elevate the platelet count in ITP, usually within 1 to 2 weeks. Responses are transient and remissions are not sustained.

Immunosuppressive agents—cyclophosphamide and azathioprine—improve the platelet count in 20 to 30% of cases of chronic ITP. The potential benefit of these drugs must be weighed against the risks of toxicity. In one small series, 60% of patients with refractory ITP had complete remissions with combination chemotherapy. Pulsed high-dose dexamethasone has also been reported to be effective therapy in patients with refractory ITP.

Management of ITP in pregnancy is complicated by the additional risk to the fetus of thrombocytopenia secondary to maternal antibodies. Intraventricular hemorrhage, gastrointestinal bleeding, and death have been reported in newborns. Whether the mother had ITP before pregnancy is critical. When ITP initially develops during pregnancy, the risk of serious bleeding in the newborn is negligible. Conversely, neonates born to women with a history of ITP preceding pregnancy have a 20% risk of severe thrombocytopenia. In addition to treating the underlying ITP, cesarean delivery is recommended to decrease the risk of intracranial bleeding in these newborns.

PLATELET ANTIBODIES ASSOCIATED WITH SYSTEMIC DISORDERS. Antibodies directed against platelets and causing thrombocytopenia occur in several types of disorders in which bone marrow megakaryocytes are normal or increased in number. Antibody-mediated destruction of platelets occurs in *lymphoproliferative disorders*, such as chronic lymphocytic leukemia (Chapter 192) and lymphoma (Chapters 194 and 195). Generally, thrombocytopenia improves with treatment of the underlying malignancy. Immune thrombocytopenia has also been associated with nonhematologic tumors, but it is unclear whether these have been chance associations. The platelet count improves with immunosuppressive therapy such as prednisone.

Immune thrombocytopenia is common in *systemic lupus erythematosus* (SLE) (Chapter 280). Whether this association is due to specific antiplatelet antibodies, to antibodies against common antigens also found on platelets, or to immune complexes is unclear. The platelet count is usually mildly to moderately decreased. Treatment is usually directed at SLE, because other manifestations of the disease are present in most cases. Occasionally, immune thrombocytopenia occurs in patients who have serologic evidence of lupus but fail to meet all of the criteria for the diagnosis of SLE. The decision to treat such patients with splenectomy is difficult because other manifestations of SLE may appear subsequently. If the platelet count is severely decreased (<30,000/μL) and no other complications of SLE exist, splenectomy is a reasonable choice. If the platelet count is moderately decreased (23,000 to 40,000/μL) and major bleeding problems are absent, careful observation may be the best course. Monthly intravenous cyclophosphamide, 0.75 to 1.0 g/m² body surface area, has been shown to normalize platelet counts within 2 to 18 weeks in patients with SLE who were also taking prednisone. Such therapy allows substantial reduction in steroid dosage. Newer immunosuppressive drugs (e.g., cyclosporine) and antitumor drugs (e.g., rituximab) have

been reported to be successful in small case series of patients with refractory ITP.

Thrombocytopenia associated with antiplatelet antibodies has been reported in patients with *viral* illnesses, including infectious mononucleosis (Chapter 371), with human immunodeficiency virus (HIV) infection (Chapter 419), and with cytomegalovirus (CMV) infection (Chapter 370). In the case of infectious mononucleosis and CMV infection, thrombocytopenia is usually self-limited, with recovery in 3 to 4 weeks. In patients with severe thrombocytopenia, a short course of glucocorticoids may be indicated. The nature of the immune reaction has not been characterized. In HIV-infected patients, thrombocytopenia is frequent with or without the full acquired immunodeficiency syndrome (AIDS). Frequently, the causes are multifactorial: (1) infection causing increased platelet destruction and/or inhibition of platelet production due to granulomatous replacement of the bone marrow, (2) suppression of hematopoiesis by drugs used to treat AIDS or associated infections, and (3) immune destruction of the patient's own platelets. Antibodies associated with platelets have been demonstrated in these patients, although the cause is unclear. Treatment with prednisone is hazardous owing to the immunocompromised status. Splenectomy has the disadvantage of further compromising the immune system. Zidovudine (AZT) treatment sometimes elevates the platelet count with mild to moderate thrombocytopenia. For acute bleeding, IVIG increases the platelet count within a few days.

More than 50 *drugs* (see Table 177–1) have been reported to cause immune thrombocytopenia, but infrequently with conclusive confirmation. Quinine and quinidine often cause immune thrombocytopenia, and drug-dependent antibodies have been demonstrated. Sulfa compounds, including sulfisoxazole, sulfonamide, sulfamethoxypyridazine, and sulfamethazine, have also been demonstrated to cause immune thrombocytopenia. Reports describe immune thrombocytopenia caused by hydrochlorothiazide, phenytoin, methyldopa, heparin, and digitalis derivatives. In most instances, the drug must be present to cause antibody binding and thrombocytopenia, and the platelet count returns to normal within a few days after discontinuation. Glucocorticoids do not accelerate recovery. Platelet antibody tests with and without the putative offending agent are useful in determining the cause of thrombocytopenia, but they cannot be performed until the drug clears from the plasma. In addition, a drug metabolite, rather than the parent compound, may be responsible for antibody formation and binding to platelets. Unless the metabolite is specifically tested, a negative result is obtained.

The incidence of thrombocytopenia associated with *heparin therapy* appears to be 3 to 5%, with a higher percentage of cases associated with bovine than with porcine preparations. The platelet count usually decreases gradually after the first few days of treatment and seldom induces bleeding. The count corrects rapidly after heparin is discontinued. Nevertheless, if the platelet count decreases to less than 50,000/μL, or if thrombocytopenia is associated with new-onset thrombosis, heparin should be discontinued. Thrombocytopenia has been reported with the usual therapeutic doses as well as with the very low doses used for procedures such as hemodialysis and *flushing* of vascular catheters, or during revascularization procedures. The antibody appears to be against a complex of heparin and platelet factor 4, a glycosaminoglycan α-granule component with high affinity for heparin. Immune thrombocytopenia also occurs with low-molecular-weight heparins (LMWHs): In approximately 50% of patients with immune thrombocytopenia secondary to heparin, the antibody cross reacts with LMWH (Chapter 33). A tentative diagnosis of heparin-induced thrombocytopenia can be confirmed once the heparin has been stopped and cleared from the circulation. The principle of the laboratory test is demonstration of activation of normal platelets by heparin and the patient's serum. Patients with heparin-induced thrombocytopenia are at risk for either arterial and/or venous thrombosis and pose a difficult challenge because treatment with unfractionated heparin or LMWH is contraindicated. Alternative acute anticoagulation can be obtained with low-molecular-weight direct thrombin inhibitors (argatroban), hirudin analogues (lepirudin), and heparinoids (danaparoid) until therapeutic anticoagulation with warfarin can be achieved. Heparin-induced thrombocytopenia patients who have had cardiovascular surgery are more likely to have limb loss; those with renal failure are more likely to die. Overall, the severity of the thrombocytopenia is the best predictor of death, thrombotic progression, and limb amputation.

Table 177–3 • DIFFERENTIAL DIAGNOSIS OF ANEMIA AND THROMBOCYTOPENIA

DIAGNOSTIC STUDY	AUTOIMMUNE DISORDERS (EVANS' SYNDROME, COLLAGEN-VASCULAR DISEASE)	DISSEMINATED INTRAVASCULAR COAGULATION	THROMBOTIC THROMBOCYTOPENIC PURPURA/HEMOLYTIC-UREMIC SYNDROME
Peripheral blood smear	Microspherocytes	Schistocytes (+)	Schistocytes (+++)
Reticulocyte count	Increased (+++)	N/increased (+)	Increased (+++)
Coombs test	Positive	Negative	Negative
Coagulation tests	N	Abn (+++)	N/Abn (+)

Abn = abnormal; N = normal.

NONIMMUNE DISORDERS ASSOCIATED WITH INCREASED CONSUMPTION OF PLATELETS

DISSEMINATED INTRAVASCULAR COAGULATION (Chapter 179). In disseminated intravascular coagulation (DIC), pathologically activated coagulation results in thrombin formation and the subsequent removal of platelets from the circulation.

THROMBOTIC THROMBOCYTOPENIC PURPURA. A rare disease of unknown etiology, thrombotic thrombocytopenic purpura (TTP) is characterized by severe thrombocytopenia, microangiopathic hemolytic anemia (>96% of patients), and neurologic abnormalities (>92% of patients). Fever and renal involvement—proteinuria, hematuria, azotemia, and casts—are present in 98 and 88% of patients, respectively. Renal abnormalities are usually mild; the creatinine rarely exceeds 3.0 mg/dL. Azotemia usually reverses as remission occurs, in contrast to the hemolytic-uremic syndrome (see later discussion). In the involved organs, arterioles and capillaries become occluded by a hyaline material consisting principally of platelet thrombi plus fibrin deposits in the vessel wall. Virtually any organ may be involved.

Recent evidence suggests that many cases of nonfamilial TTP are due to an inhibitor of von Willebrand factor–cleaving protease. The familial form seems to be caused by a constitutional deficiency of the protease. In contrast, patients with the hemolytic-uremic syndrome do not have a deficiency of von Willebrand factor–cleaving protease or a defect in von Willebrand factor that leads to its resistance to protease.

Symptoms frequently wax and wane, presumably owing to platelet aggregation and disaggregation. Thus, patients may have evanescent headache, aphasia, or stupor one moment and be alert the next.

TTP must be considered when thrombocytopenia and anemia occur acutely with microangiopathic changes of red blood cells on the peripheral blood smear (Fig. 177–4) and the lack of evidence of other disorders (Tables 177–3 and 177–4). Although findings in DIC are similar, patients with TTP have minimal changes in coagulation tests. Evans' syndrome, which is the combination of autoimmune hemolytic anemia and autoimmune thrombocytopenia, is characterized by microspherocytes on peripheral smear, rather than by schistocytes, and by a positive Coombs test. Rarely, TTP has been reported to complicate SLE. More commonly, patients with SLE have immune thrombocytopenia and anemia of chronic disease or immune hemolytic anemia (Chapters 169 and 280). TTP has also been reported in association with oral contraceptives and pregnancy.

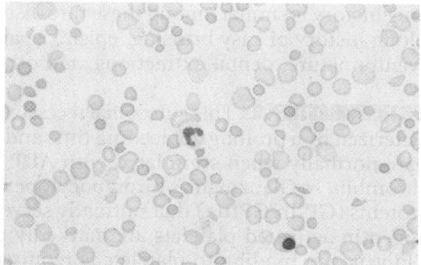

FIGURE 177–4 • Thrombotic thrombocytopenic purpura. Peripheral smear shows fragmented red cells alongside larger, polychromatophilic cells and a nucleated red cell that reflects hemolysis, as well as a paucity of platelets.

Table 177–4 • DISORDERS ASSOCIATED WITH THROMBOCYTOPENIA AND MICROANGIOPATHIC ANEMIA

Thrombotic thrombocytopenic purpura
Hemolytic-uremic syndrome
Disseminated intravascular coagulation
Malignant hypertension
Eclampsia
Vasculitis
  Systemic lupus erythematous
  Polyarteritis nodosa
Cavernous hemangioma (Kasabach-Merritt syndrome)
Disseminated carcinoma
Renal allograft rejection
Prosthetic heart valves
Malignant angioendotheliomatosis

In most cases, the diagnosis of TTP is straightforward. When the diagnosis is uncertain, gum, skin, or bone marrow biopsy may be helpful, with positive results reported in 40 to 60% of cases. It is critical to establish the diagnosis and begin treatment rapidly, because delay can result in severe morbidity or mortality. Most untreated patients die within 3 months. Large-volume plasmapheresis, approximately two plasma volumes, with replacement infusion of normal plasma, is the treatment of choice for TTP; it cures approximately 70% of patients. Infusion of large volumes of plasma without pheresis sometimes induces remission, in which case concomitant plasmapheresis becomes imperative. Furthermore, because repeated courses of plasma infusion are usually necessary, the practical management of TTP is facilitated by plasmapheresis, which prevents excessive expansion of the blood volume and the risk of cardiovascular compromise. The best indication of a successful response is an increase in the platelet count. Plasmapheresis/infusion should be continued until the platelet count becomes normal and stable. Normalization of anemia and neurologic abnormalities usually follows. Approximately 10% of patients have a chronic, relapsing form of TTP. The plasma of patients with chronic TTP in remission contains abnormally large multimers of von Willebrand factor.

There have been several reports of an unusual risk of TTP in patients receiving unrelated donor allogeneic bone marrow transplantation (Chapter 166). Endothelial damage from the intensive conditioning regimens may be contributive, and the development of TTP in this setting portends a poor outcome despite aggressive therapy.

HEMOLYTIC-UREMIC SYNDROME. Primarily a disorder of infants and young children, hemolytic-uremic syndrome rarely occurs in adults. Like TTP, hemolytic-uremic syndrome produces a microangiopathic hemolytic anemia, but thrombocytopenia is mild to moderate, and neurologic abnormalities are absent. Unlike TTP, acute renal failure is a prominent feature in hemolytic-uremic syndrome, frequently requiring hemodialysis. Severe hypertension is also a prominent feature. Children typically present with gastrointestinal signs and symptoms, abdominal pain, and diarrhea. Hemolytic-uremic syndrome may occur in women who are in the postpartum period or who are taking oral contraceptives.

A definite or probable causal relationship for TTP and hemolytic-uremic syndrome–like syndromes is documented for quinine, famotidine, and ticlopidine. For all other reported drugs, other than those causing dose-related toxicity, published case reports do not distinguish between causality and coincidence. TTP and hemolytic-uremic syndrome–like syndromes have also been reported in cancer patients receiving mitomycin C or cisplatin chemotherapy.

SEPSIS. Gram-negative (more commonly than gram-positive) sepsis causes accelerated platelet destruction, presumably due to binding of bacterial immune complexes to the platelet. Severe thrombocytopenia may follow.

Disorders of Distribution of Platelets

With splenic enlargement, platelet pooling increases (e.g., Gaucher's disease, congestive splenomegaly, lymphoma) and may cause thrombocytopenia (Chapter 162). Platelet counts less than 30,000 to 50,000/μL are unusual.

Dilutional Thrombocytopenia

When packed erythrocytes or nonfresh whole blood is transfused to replace blood loss, thrombocytopenia may ensue. Approximately 35 to 40% of platelets remain after replacement of one blood volume; microvascular bleeding due to thrombocytopenia occurs rarely after replacement of one to two volumes. Platelets should be transfused only if thrombocytopenia and bleeding are present.

THROMBOCYTOSIS

Elevation of the platelet count above the normal range reflects increased production, either reactive or the result of a myeloproliferative disorder. Most thrombocytosis occurs secondary to an underlying disorder unassociated with complications. When caused by a primary disorder of hematopoiesis, however, thrombocytosis can cause serious bleeding and/or thrombotic complications, which makes it important to determine its cause.

ESSENTIAL THROMBOCYTHEMIA. Essential thrombocythemia, a myeloproliferative disorder, is discussed in Chapter 183. Other myeloproliferative diseases, such as agnogenic myeloid metaplasia (Chapter 183) and polycythemia vera (Chapter 176), also are associated with an elevated platelet count. The count may be elevated in chronic myelogenous leukemia but rarely results in complications.

REACTIVE THROMBOCYTOSIS. Elevated platelet counts occur secondarily in a number of unrelated disorders, but counts higher than 10^6/μL are unusual: iron deficiency anemia (Chapter 167); hemorrhage; splenectomy (Chapter 164); inflammatory disorders, particularly inflammatory bowel disease (Chapter 142); neoplasms (e.g., lung, gastrointestinal); and leukemoid reaction (Chapter 163).

No convincing evidence exists that reactive thrombocytosis increases the risk of thrombosis. Therefore, it should not be treated. With successful treatment of the primary disease, the count returns to normal.

ABNORMALITIES IN PLATELET FUNCTION

Acquired Disorders of Platelet Function

DRUGS THAT INHIBIT PLATELET FUNCTION (See Table 177–1). *Nonsteroidal anti-inflammatory agents* inhibit platelet function by blocking platelet synthesis of prostaglandins (Chapter 32). Aspirin (acetylsalicylic acid [ASA]) irreversibly acetylates prostaglandin synthetase and, as a result, impairs platelet function for its lifespan (Chapter 33). One ASA tablet (300 mg) is sufficient to cause this effect. Fortunately, in normal people, this effect does not result in excessive bleeding, but in patients with von Willebrand disease or with severe coagulation factor deficiency (factor VIII or IX), serious bleeding can result (Chapter 178). For this reason, aspirin is contraindicated in these disorders.

High doses of the β-lactam antibiotics, such as penicillin and related compounds, induce an abnormality in platelet function that persists for 2 to 3 days after the drug is discontinued. The mechanism is unclear. The bleeding time is prolonged, and patients may have increased bleeding.

RENAL FAILURE. Platelets function abnormally in patients with renal failure (Chapter 117). The uremic metabolites responsible for this

dysfunction are uncertain. Guanidinosuccinic acid and phenolic compounds that accumulate in uremia may inhibit platelet aggregation. Abnormal platelet adhesion and activation may occur in uremia as well as thrombocytopenia. The latter is usually mild and may be due to the underlying cause of renal disease.

Uremic bleeding is usually mucocutaneous and reflects abnormal platelet and/or vascular hemostatic functions. The bleeding time is commonly prolonged, but other causes of prolongation must be excluded (e.g., medication, congenital platelet disorders, and von Willebrand disease). Low hematocrits (<24%) prolong the bleeding time in uremia. Transfusion of packed red blood cells to elevate the hematocrit above 26% improves the bleeding time. Tests of coagulation are normal.

When a uremic patient bleeds, a structural lesion or other hemostatic abnormalities must be suspected; platelet abnormalities are seldom the cause. When the hemostatic defect of renal failure is believed to be a significant contributing factor in bleeding, either peritoneal dialysis or hemodialysis usually can reverse the hemostatic defect. If the bleeding time remains prolonged and the patient is bleeding, low-dose estrogens (e.g., emopremarin 0.6 mg/kg qd × 5 days), 1-deamino-8-D-arginine vasopressin (DDAVP; 0.3 μg/kg once daily × 2 days), or cryoprecipitate (1 bag/7 kg) can be tried. All three raise the plasma levels of factor VIII (antihemophilic factor/von Willebrand factor), but their efficacies have not been firmly established. Platelet transfusion usually has no benefit.

HEPATIC FAILURE (Chapters 156, 157, and 179). Platelet function is sometimes abnormal in liver disease, but why this is so and the extent to which it contributes to bleeding are unclear. The bleeding time may be prolonged in moderately severe liver disease when the platelet count is greater than 90,000/μL. DDAVP has been reported to improve the bleeding time in these circumstances. More commonly in hepatic failure, a bleeding diathesis is due to deficiencies of coagulation factors.

PARAPROTEINEMIAS (Chapter 196). Abnormal platelet function occurs in a subset of patients with multiple myeloma or Waldenström's macroglobulinemia. The bleeding time is usually prolonged, and bleeding can be moderately severe. If the level of the paraprotein is lowered by plasmapheresis and/or chemotherapy, the bleeding time and bleeding improve, suggesting a direct effect of the paraprotein on platelet function. Paraproteins may impair platelet function by inhibiting platelet-fibrinogen interaction.

ACQUIRED STORAGE POOL DISEASE. Patients may develop mild platelet function abnormalities from loss of storage granules. Some of the disorders in which this has been reported include surgeries requiring cardiopulmonary bypass, hairy cell leukemia, and conditions with antiplatelet autoantibodies. Platelet dysfunction following cardiopulmonary bypass is transient and not of clinical importance beyond the first 24 hours after surgery.

MYELOPROLIFERATIVE DISORDERS. Patients with essential thrombocythemia and, less commonly, agnogenic myeloid metaplasia may have abnormalities of platelet function (Chapter 183). In essential thrombocythemia, abnormalities usually occur at platelet counts greater than 10^6/μL and may lead to abnormal bleeding, thrombosis, or both. Although the functional abnormalities are not specific, a prolonged bleeding time indicates that the patient is at risk for bleeding. Treatment of bleeding patients with thrombocytosis should be directed at lowering the platelet count as rapidly as possible.

Hereditary Disorders of Platelet Function

The bleeding history is similar among these rare diseases. Patients provide a lifelong history of easy bruising, epistaxis, and prolonged oozing after venipuncture, dental extractions, and other challenges to hemostasis.

GLANZMANN'S THROMBASTHENIA. This autosomal recessive bleeding disorder is characterized by a prolonged bleeding time and platelets that fail to aggregate normally when stimulated with ADP, epinephrine, collagen, or thrombin. In Glanzmann's thrombocytopenia, two membrane glycoproteins (GPIIb/GPIIIa) that normally serve as the receptor for fibrinogen in activated platelets are markedly deficient (see Fig. 177–1). Fibrinogen binding to platelets is required for platelet aggregation. The diagnosis is confirmed by demonstrating deficiency of platelet GPIIb/GPIIIa. The platelet count is always normal.

BERNARD-SOULIER SYNDROME. This autosomal recessive disorder is caused by a deficiency of a platelet membrane glycoprotein complex, GPIb-IX. As a result, "giant" platelets appear in the peripheral blood smear. Frequently, the platelet count is mildly decreased. In laboratory studies, platelets aggregate normally in response to ADP, collagen, or epinephrine but fail to aggregate in response to ristocetin. Physiologically, platelets fail to adhere normally to subendothelial connective tissue owing to defective binding of von Willebrand factor.

STORAGE POOL DISEASE. In this autosomal dominant disorder, platelet storage granules are decreased in number and/or content, presumably because of abnormal granule formation in megakaryocytes. The bleeding diathesis is mild and affects mostly women. With the deficiency in dense granules, platelets aggregate abnormally owing to inadequate secretion of ADP. Dense-granule storage pool disease is also associated with several other congenital disorders, including oculocutaneous albinism in both the Hermansky-Pudlak syndrome (HPS) and Chédiak-Higashi syndrome, the Wiskott-Aldrich syndrome, and a syndrome, which includes thrombocytopenia and absent radii. Patients with HPS have oculocutaneous albinism and a bleeding diathesis due to the absence of platelet dense granules. Mutations in the *HPS1* gene cause HPS-1 disease, and *ADTB3A* mutations cause HPS-2 disease, which is known to involve abnormal intracellular vesicle formation. A third HPS-causing gene, *HPS3*, was recently identified in Puerto Rico. Patients may also be deficient in α-granules, either in combination with dense granule deficiency or independently. The gray platelet syndrome refers to the latter situation, in which the absence of granule staining confers a gray color to the platelets. Mild thrombocytopenia may also be present.

VON WILLEBRAND DISEASE. This disease, the most common congenital bleeding disorder, is discussed in Chapter 178.

PLATELET TRANSFUSIONS

INDICATIONS. When serious bleeding complicates thrombocytopenia, platelet transfusions (Chapter 165) are effective only when the cause is decreased production. Thrombocytopenia due to increased peripheral destruction or sequestration is usually refractory to platelet transfusion. Bleeding due to qualitative platelet disorders ordinarily responds to platelet transfusions except when it is secondary to uremia or hepatic failure or when an offending drug remains present in the circulation.

For patients with congenital platelet disorders, platelet transfusion must be given judiciously because repeated transfusions stimulate alloantibodies. Eventually, it may become impossible to increase the platelet count through transfusion. Accordingly, platelet transfusions should be reserved for serious bleeding or in preparation for surgery in patients with moderately severe platelet defects.

Platelet transfusions are indicated for patients who are bleeding actively and have either a platelet count less than 50,000/μL or a qualitative platelet abnormality as manifested by a prolonged bleeding time. Platelet transfusions may also be indicated prophylactically before surgery or other invasive procedures. Before surgery, platelet counts should be greater than 50,000/μL in most cases, and greater than 90,000/μL for procedures such as neurosurgery or ophthalmologic surgery in which any abnormal bleeding may cause excessive morbidity. For invasive procedures, such as kidney or liver biopsies, a platelet count greater than 50,000/μL is probably sufficient, assuming normal platelet function.

CHRONIC THROMBOCYTOPENIA. In the absence of active bleeding, recommendations are based on the cause of thrombocytopenia. When thrombocytopenia is due to decreased production, the platelet count should be maintained at more than 10,000 to 20,000/μL. When accelerated destruction of platelets exists, transfusion is seldom effective. Patients with ITP frequently tolerate low platelet counts with little bleeding, presumably, because of younger circulating platelets.

DOSAGE. For patients who require platelet transfusions over the long term, platelets should be obtained from a single donor for each transfusion (generally 6 to 7 units) to reduce the risk of forming multiple alloantibodies. In a 70-kg patient, one unit of platelets usually increases the platelet count by approximately 10,000/μL. The count should be repeated 10 to 60 minutes after transfusion to assess the compatibility of the transfused platelets and to determine whether the desired count has been achieved. In actively bleeding patients, the platelet count should be maintained at greater than 50,000/μL.

ALLOANTIBODIES AGAINST PLATELETS. In approximately 50 to 60% of patients who become refractory to random donor platelets, anti-HLA (human leukocyte antigen) antibodies appear to be responsible. The other presumed antigens have not yet been identified. In one rare form of alloimmunization, antibodies develop against the PL antigen, an epitope on platelet glycoprotein IIIa. The difference between PL^{A1} positive and negative (PL^{A2}) is a single amino acid. Of the normal population, 98% have PL^{A1}-positive platelets.

When PL^{A1}-negative patients are transfused with PL^{A1}-positive blood, they may produce anti-PL^{A1} antibodies and post-transfusion purpura (PTP) may develop (Chapter 165). Previous immunization is necessary, either by transfusion or by pregnancy. Why this syndrome is rare and selectively high in women despite the frequency of PL^{A1} negativity in the population is unknown. These patients not only rapidly clear transfused platelets from their circulation but also destroy their own platelets, becoming thrombocytopenic usually 5 to 10 days after transfusion. If patients with antibodies against the PL^{A1} antigen become severely thrombocytopenic, treatment with plasmapheresis or exchange transfusion is necessary, because bleeding from thrombocytopenia can be life-threatening.

Neonatal Alloimmune Thrombocytopenia. Thrombocytopenia due to maternal alloantibodies against fetal platelet antigens occurs in approximately 1 in 2000 to 4000 fetuses. Affected infants may have intracranial hemorrhages (estimated between 10 and 30%); in families with an affected infant, the risk of recurrence is at least 75%. PL^{A1} antibodies have been identified in most cases as being responsible for thrombocytopenia. Affected infants are treated by transfusion with washed maternal platelets. Women with a prior history of an affected infant should undergo cesarean section. Also, IVIG given to pregnant mothers with a prior affected infant increases fetal platelet counts and reduces the rate of intracranial hemorrhage.

VASCULAR DISORDERS (Table 177–5)

Normal vascular function is necessary for effective hemostasis. Alteration in the integrity or structure of blood vessels can lead to a bleeding diathesis, the symptoms and signs of which are indistinguishable from those of a platelet disorder.

Congenital Vascular Disorders Associated with Bleeding

HEREDITARY HEMORRHAGIC TELANGIECTASIA (RENDU-OSLER-WEBER DISEASE). This disorder, the most common genetic cause of vascular bleeding, is inherited as an autosomal dominant trait. Its most frequent symptom is spontaneous epistaxis. More than half of the patients have epistaxis by age 20 and 90% by age 45. Telangiectasia occurs most frequently on the face in two thirds of patients, on the mouth in half, and on the cheeks, tongue, nose, and lower lip in approximately one third. In about 40%, the hands (Fig. 177–5) and wrists are also involved. Beyond this cutaneous or mucosal involvement, the organ system affected most often is the gastrointestinal tract (>2%). Death from intestinal bleeding (Chapter 144) occurs in 12 to 15% of

---

Table 177–5 • VASCULAR DISORDERS ASSOCIATED WITH BLEEDING

CONGENITAL
Hereditary hemorrhagic telangiectasia
Cavernous hemangioma
Connective tissue disorders
    Ehlers-Danlos syndrome
    Osteogenesis imperfecta
    Pseudoxanthoma elasticum

ACQUIRED DISORDERS AFFECTING VASCULAR HEMOSTATIC FUNCTION
Scurvy
Immunoglobulin disorders
    Cryoglobulinemia
    Benign hyperglobulinemia
    Waldenström's macroglobulinemia
    Multiple myeloma
    Henoch-Schönlein purpura
Glucocorticoid excess
    Cushing's syndrome
    Glucocorticoid therapy

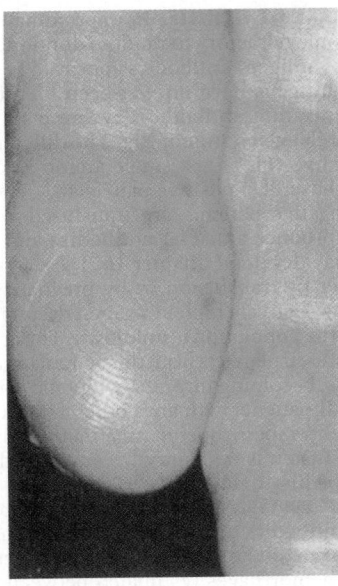

FIGURE 177–5 • Hereditary hemorrhagic telangiectasia. Patients commonly present with lesions on or close to mucous membranes, but the telangiectasia may occur anywhere on the body, as in this patient whose fingers were affected. The lesions are dilated capillaries, and they blanch if pressure is applied with a glass slide. (From Forbes CD, Jackson WF: Color Atlas and Text of Clinical Medicine, 3rd ed. London, Mosby, 2003, with permission.)

symptomatic patients. The liver, lungs, central nervous system, and urinary tract are involved in decreasing order of frequency. Pulmonary arteriovenous fistulas, present in approximately 5% of patients, are manifested by cyanoses, dyspnea, clubbing, and thoracic murmurs. Hemoptysis is unusual. Surgical resection is successful in managing this complication in most instances. Coil embolization of these fistulas has also been used successfully. Stroke may occur with central nervous system involvement, a complication that tends to affect younger patients (mean age, 33 years). Careful inspection of the nose and mouth usually reveals the diagnosis. In other cases, endoscopy or angiography may be necessary. Pathologic examination of involved tissue demonstrates dilated capillaries with loss of subendothelial structures.

The *ENG* gene encoding endoglin is mutated in hereditary hemorrhagic telangiectasia type 1 (HHT 1). Endoglin is a component of the TGF-β receptor complex expressed on endothelial cells and is involved in cardiovascular morphogenesis and vascular remodeling. Mutations in the *ALK-1* gene on chromosome 12 also have been reported. *ENG* abnormalities have been correlated with a higher prevalence of pulmonary arteriovenous malformations.

Platelet function and bleeding time are normal. Although no therapy is consistently effective, conjugated estrogen-progestin therapy may decrease the number of bleeding episodes. Generally, the prognosis is relatively good.

CAVERNOUS HEMANGIOMA (KASABACH-MERRITT SYNDROME). Congenital subcutaneous and visceral hemangiomas may be associated with thrombocytopenia and bleeding in infants and children. Bleeding occurs at the site of the lesions or systemically owing to thrombocytopenia. Platelets are activated within the hemangioma and subsequently removed from the circulation. In addition, mild DIC may occur with consumption of fibrinogen. Thrombocytopenia is more severe than coagulation abnormalities. Spontaneous regression of hemangiomas may occur over a period of years. When thrombocytopenia is severe and tumors are few, surgery and/or radiation therapy may be effective. Intentional thrombosis of hemangiomas by administration of inhibitors of fibrinolysis, with or without cryoprecipitate, has been successful in managing thrombocytopenia in a few cases. Also, interferon-α has been observed to cause significant regression of hemangiomas.

DISORDERS OF CONNECTIVE TISSUE. Genetic abnormalities in structural glycoproteins such as collagen can result in vascular fragility caused by weakening of the vessel wall. Bleeding may be limited to increased bruising or may manifest as internal hemorrhaging. Ehlers-Danlos syndrome, osteogenesis imperfecta, and pseudoxan-

thoma elasticum (Chapter 276) are examples of inherited disorders of connective tissue that may be associated with a bleeding diathesis on this basis.

Acquired Disorders of Blood Vessels Causing Bleeding

SCURVY. Severe vitamin C deficiency (Chapter 231) results in defective collagen formation in small blood vessels. Bleeding may occur in any tissue but is prominent in the lower extremities and is perifollicular in distribution. Other sites where bleeding is common include the gums, the subperiosteum in children, and the muscles.

PURPURA ASSOCIATED WITH IMMUNOGLOBULIN DISORDERS

Cryoglobulinemia (Chapter 196). Patients with all three types of cryoglobulinemia have purpura as a complication of their disease. In type I, bleeding may be due to obstruction of blood flow in the microcirculation at cold temperatures by cryoprecipitates, resulting in increased vascular fragility. In type II and type III cryoglobulinemia, bleeding may be due to leukocytoclastic vasculitis associated with the immune complexes. Purpura occurs most commonly in the distal extremities.

Benign Hyperglobulinemia (Waldenström's Purpura). In this syndrome, patients have polyclonal hyperglobulinemia associated with purpura of the lower extremities. Leukocytoclastic involvement of the vessel wall may account for increased vascular fragility and bleeding. Commonly, the onset of purpura is preceded by a stinging sensation in areas of involvement. Although generally no evidence of systemic vasculitis is seen, the disorder may evolve into Sjögren's syndrome or SLE.

Amyloidosis (Chapter 290). Amyloid deposition in the skin and subcutaneous tissues alters the normal structural support for small blood vessels, resulting in increased vascular fragility. Purpura can occur at any site; for unclear reasons, periorbital hemorrhage is a characteristic finding.

Waldenström's Macroglobulinemia and Multiple Myeloma (Chapter 196). Abnormalities in platelet function may occur with M proteins, as noted earlier. An additional contributing factor is hyperviscosity when it complicates these diseases. Slowing of blood flow and increased hydrostatic pressure may increase vascular fragility, leading to purpura.

Henoch-Schönlein Purpura. Symmetrical purpura and arthralgias of the lower extremities, abdominal pain, and melena characterize this childhood disorder. Rarely, adults are affected. Patients may give a history of a recent infectious illness. The disease has an acute onset with a maculopapular rash evolving into palpable purpura. Other complications include glomerulonephritis and hypertension (both of which are self-limiting) and intussusception. Involved tissues, including the skin, demonstrate vasculitis with immunoglobulin A (IgA) and complement deposition.

Henoch-Schönlein purpura usually remits spontaneously over a period of 1 to 2 months, although the course is often punctuated by flaring of symptoms and signs. Symptomatic improvement is obtained with glucocorticoids.

Miscellaneous Disorders

CUSHING'S SYNDROME. Cushing's disease (Chapter 240) or long-term administration of glucocorticoids (Chapter 31) results in increased bruising, particularly in the extremities. Abnormal bleeding probably results from alterations in the structure of the perivascular matrix, with loss of normal elasticity.

AUTOERYTHROCYTE SENSITIZATION (GARDNER-DIAMOND SYNDROME). This syndrome is characterized by the development of purpura at any site on the body, preceded by pain and burning. It occurs almost exclusively in women. Usually, affected women have a history of severe stress and emotional problems. Tests for abnormalities in hemostasis are all normal.

The diagnostic test is the development of large ecchymoses within 24 to 48 hours at the site of subcutaneous injection of a small amount (~0.1 μL) of the patient's own blood or erythrocytes. Injection should be at sites inaccessible to the patient, and a concurrent control injection should be administered. The primary differential diagnosis is factitious purpura.

PURPURA SIMPLEX. Purpura simplex denotes easy bruising, commonly observed in young children and middle-aged women, affecting primarily the lower extremities. Laboratory evaluation, including the bleeding time, is normal, and no evidence exists of vascular abnormalities. Affected women do not experience excessive bleeding with surgery, nor do they suffer from internal bleeding.

SUGGESTED READINGS

Allford SL, Hunt BJ, Rose P, et al: Guidelines on the diagnosis and management of the thrombotic microangiopathic haemolytic anaemias. Br J Haematol 2003;120:556–573. *A consensus review.*

Grabowski EF: The hemolytic-uremic syndrome—toxin, thrombin, and thrombosis. N Engl J Med 2002;346:58–61. *New understandings of pathophysiology and treatment.*

Kelton JG: Heparin-induced thrombocytopenia: An overview. Blood Rev 2002;16:77–80. *A comprehensive overview of diagnosis and treatment, based on the pathophysiology.*

Moake JL: Thrombotic microangiopathies. N Engl J Med 2002;347:589–600. *Comprehensive overview of pathophysiology, presentation, diagnosis, and treatment.*

Provan D, Newland A: Fifty years of idiopathic thrombocytopenic purpura (ITP): Management of refractory ITP in adults. Br J Haematol 2002;118:933–944. *A systematic approach to this difficult clinical problem.*

Schiffer CA, Anderson KC, Bennett CL, et al: Platelet transfusion for patients with cancer: Clinical practice guidelines of the American Society of Clinical Oncology. J Clin Oncol 2001;19:1519–1538. *Indications for platelet transfusion based on most recent data.*

178 HEMORRHAGIC DISORDERS: COAGULATION FACTOR DEFICIENCIES

Craig M. Kessler

Severe coagulation deficiencies, or coagulopathies, typically are characterized by the development of excessive bleeding precipitated by trivial incidental or surgical trauma. Frequently, these conditions produce life-threatening and limb-threatening complications. Moderate and mild coagulopathies may remain clinically silent until they are detected serendipitously on routine laboratory screening assays for global coagulation (e.g., prothrombin time [PT] or activated partial thromboplastin time [aPTT]) or when these assays are ordered to evaluate the cause of abnormal bleeding or easy bruisability. Much of the morbidity of coagulopathies can be minimized or avoided altogether by advanced awareness and prophylactic replacement of the deficient clotting factor proteins. In contrast to the lifelong clinical manifestations of hereditary/congenital coagulopathies, acquired deficiencies usually occur in previously asymptomatic individuals, may not be suspected immediately on examination, and may remit spontaneously or after eradication of an inciting disease state or withdrawal of treatment with an offending medication. Acquired coagulation disorders often are associated with more severe bleeding than the congenital forms. Coagulopathies predominantly result from quantitative defects in biosynthesis of the coagulation factor proteins, but qualitative defects also can result in bleeding.

HEREDITARY COAGULATION DEFICIENCIES

HEMOPHILIAS

The first written documentation for the existence of a sex-linked hereditary coagulation disorder dates back to a 5th century description in the Talmud and eventually was termed *hemophilia* ("love of bleeding") in the 19th century German medical literature. The pathogenesis of this hemorrhagic process was not elucidated completely until 1952, when a mixture of plasma from two hemophilic individuals with similar clinical and hereditary pictures corrected their respective prolonged clotting assays. This incident eventually resulted in the recognition of hemophilia A, caused by a deficiency of clotting protein VIII (antihemophilic factor), and hemophilia B, caused by a deficiency of factor IX (antihemophilic factor B, plasma thromboplastin component, or Christmas factor, named after an individual with the disease). A deficiency of either of these two intrinsic coagulation pathway components results in inefficient and inadequate generation of thrombin, which cannot be circumvented or supplemented by a normal extrinsic pathway because of the strong modulatory effects of tissue factor pathway inhibitor.

Epidemiology

The sex-linked recessive disorders of hemophilia A and B are estimated to occur in approximately 1 per 5000 and 1 per 30,000 male births. The significantly increased incidence of hemophilia A may be due to the greater amount of DNA "at risk" for mutation in the factor VIII gene (186,000 base pairs) compared with the factor IX gene (34,000 base pairs). Hemophilia A and B are observed throughout all races and ethnic groups. There are more than 20,000 individuals with hemophilia in the United States. Although carrier testing, genetic counseling, and prenatal diagnosis are widely available through the network of Hemophilia Treatment Centers, fecundity rates remain high, and few confirmed carriers elect to terminate their pregnancies even if an affected fetus is detected in utero. These decisions probably are influenced by the efficacy and safety of the currently available coagulation factor replacement products and the prospect for gene therapy to cure the hemophilias. The advent of highly active antiretroviral therapy (Chapter 421) and liver transplantation (Chapter 157) has prolonged the survival of hemophiliacs with acquired immunodeficiency syndrome (AIDS) and chronic hepatitis. A substantial proportion (30%) of cases of hemophilia result from unanticipated new spontaneous mutations. Overall the hemophilias are much more common than the autosomal recessive coagulation disorders, which typically involve progeny from consanguineous relationships and require the inheritance of two defective alleles for the disease to become manifest.

Genetics

As with other sex-linked recessive diseases, the genes for factor VIII and IX are located on the long arm of the X chromosome. Males with a defective allele on their single X chromosome do not transmit this gene to their sons, but all of their daughters become obligate carriers. Female carriers transmit the coagulation disorder to half of their sons, whereas half of their daughters become carriers. Female carriers can manifest hemophilia-like symptoms when the alleles on the X chromosome are unequally inactivated (lyonization); the defective hemophilic allele is expressed in preference to the normal allele, and a phenotypic hemophiliac is produced. Female hemophilia can arise as the result of mating between a hemophilic male and a female carrier (homozygous for the defective factor VIII or IX gene) or in carrier females who have the 45 XO karyotype (Turner's syndrome) (hemizygous for the defective hemophilia gene). Evaluation of hemophilia in a female should address the aforementioned processes and von Willebrand's disease (vWD) and its variants (e.g., type 2 Normandy) and exclude the rare but reported situation of a normal male karyotype associated with testicular feminization.

No single mutation is responsible for the hemophilias, and many missense and nonsense point mutations, deletions, and inversions have been described. Severe molecular defects predominate, with 40% to 50% of all severe hemophilia A evolving from a unique inversion of intron 22 (the largest of the factor VIII introns). This inversion results from the recombination and translocation of DNA within intron 22 of the factor VIII gene, with areas of extragenic but homologous "nonfunctional" DNA located at a distance from intron 22. Other less commonly encountered severe molecular defects include large gene deletions (5 to 10%) and nonsense mutations (10 to 15%). The encoded proteins resulting from these mutations are defective and do not express any factor VIII activity. Mild and moderate hemophilia A commonly is associated with point mutations and deletions. In contrast, factor IX mutations are more diverse, and severe hemophilia B more likely is caused by large deletions. Hemophilia B also may result from mutations altering the γ-glutamyl residues of the factor IX protein, which normally become carboxylated through a vitamin K–dependent process, then assemble on a phospholipid surface for eventual activation. Mutated clotting factor genes responsible for the hemophilias may code for the production of defective nonfunctional proteins that circulate in the plasma and can be detected by immunoassays. Designated *cross-reacting material*, these proteins have no clinical relevance except that individuals without cross-reacting material may be more susceptible to alloantibody inhibitor formation.

Carrier Detection and Prenatal Diagnosis

Carrier detection is particularly useful for women who are related to males with hemophilia and who anticipate becoming pregnant. Coagulation laboratory diagnosis of the carrier state or prenatal involvement is based on measurement of factor IX activity or factor VIII activity compared with von Willebrand factor antigen (vWF:Ag). This

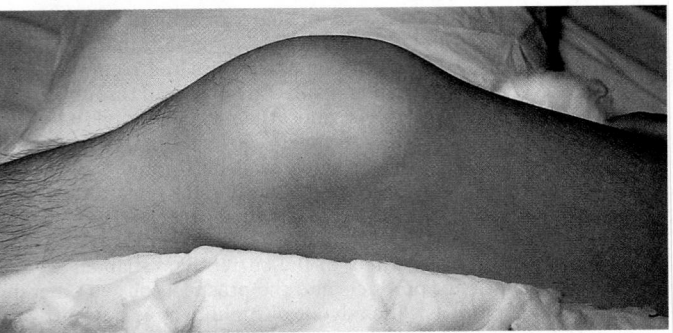

Figure 178–1 • Acute hemarthrosis of the knee is a common complication of hemophilia. It may be confused with acute infection unless the patient's coagulation disorder is known, because the knee is hot, red, swollen, and painful. (From Forbes CD, Jackson WF: Color Atlas and Text of Clinical Medicine, 3rd ed. London, Mosby, 2003, with permission.)

phenotypic approach is 90% accurate but cannot be applied easily to fetal blood specimens or amniotic fluid. Genotypic analysis through restriction fragment length polymorphisms is more accurate if the specific gene defect is known and genetic material is available from the propositus and the carrier. Polymerase chain reaction amplification of DNA and denaturing gradient gel electrophoresis analysis are useful for detection of the intron 22 inversion associated with half of the cases of severe hemophilia A.

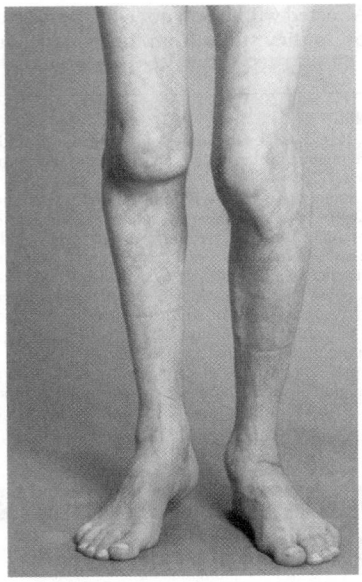

Figure 178–2 • Severe chronic arthritis in hemophilia. The knee is the most commonly affected joint. Both knees are severely deranged in this patient. Note that he is unable to stand with both feet flat on the floor. (From Forbes CD, Jackson WF: Color Atlas and Text of Clinical Medicine, 3rd ed. London, Mosby, 2003, with permission.)

Clinical Manifestations

The clinical pictures of hemophilia A and B are indistinguishable from each other, with their clinical severity corresponding inversely to the circulating levels of plasma coagulant factor VIII or IX activity. Individuals with less than 1% of normal factor VIII or IX activity have severe disease characterized by frequent spontaneous bleeding events in joints (hemarthrosis) and soft tissues and by profuse hemorrhage with trauma or surgery. Spontaneous bleeds are uncommon with mild deficiencies of greater than 5% of normal activity; however, excessive bleeding still can occur with trauma or surgery. A moderate clinical course is associated with factor VIII or IX levels between 1 and 5%. Approximately 60% of all cases of hemophilia A are clinically severe, whereas only 20 to 45% of cases of hemophilia B are severe.

Severe hemophilia typically is suspected and diagnosed during infancy in the absence of a family history. Although the trauma of uncomplicated childbirth (vaginal or cesarean section) rarely produces intracranial hemorrhage, prolonged labor, forceps delivery, and the use of vacuum extraction are major risk factors. Circumcision within days of birth is accompanied by excessive bleeding in fewer than half of severely affected boys. The first spontaneous hemarthrosis usually occurs in severely affected hemophiliacs between 12 and 18 months of age, when ambulation begins, and in moderately affected individuals at about 2 to 5 years of age. The knees are the most prominent sites of spontaneous bleeds, followed by the elbows, ankles, shoulders, and hips; wrists less commonly are involved.

Acute hemarthroses (Fig. 178–1) originate from the subsynovial venous plexus underlying the joint capsule and produce a tingling or burning sensation, followed by the onset of intense pain and swelling. On physical examination, the joint is swollen, hot, and tender to palpation, with erythema of the overlying skin. Joint mobility is compromised by pain and stiffness, and the joint usually is maintained in a flexed position. Replacement of the deficient clotting factor to normal hemostatic levels rapidly reverses the pain. Swelling and joint immobility improve as the intra-articular hematoma resolves. Intra-articular needle aspiration of fresh bleeding is not recommended because of the risk of introducing infection. Short courses of oral corticosteroids may be helpful in reducing the acute joint symptoms in children but rarely are used in adults.

Recurrent or untreated bleeds result in chronic synovial hypertrophy and eventually damage the underlying cartilage, with subsequent subchondral bone cyst formation, bony erosion, and flexion contractures. Abnormal mechanical forces from weight bearing can produce subluxation, misalignment, loss of mobility, and permanent deformities of the lower extremities (Fig. 178–2). These changes are accompanied by chronic pain, swelling, and arthritis. Radiographic and clinical examination of chronic hemarthroses often underestimates the extent of bone and joint damage; serial ultrasonography and magnetic resonance imaging are the most sensitive and specific monitoring and diagnostic techniques.

The pain that accompanies acute hemarthroses responds to immediate analgesic relief, temporary immobilization, restraint from weight bearing, and clotting factor replacement. Narcotic analgesics, such as codeine or synthetic derivatives of codeine, should be prescribed alone or combined with doses of acetaminophen that are low enough (<10 g) to avoid hepatic toxicity in patients with chronic hepatitis. Although these medications do not possess significant anti-inflammatory activity, they are preferable to nonsteroidal anti-inflammatory drugs (NSAIDs) or aspirin, which may exacerbate bleeding complications through their antiplatelet aggregatory effects. The cyclooxygenase type 2 inhibitors seem to be safe and effective for the chronic arthritic symptoms produced by recurrent hemarthroses. Alternative approaches to pain control include acupuncture, transdermal nerve stimulation, and hypnosis, which may reduce narcotic consumption but also may mask joint pain so that proper immobilization and timely replacement therapy are delayed or ignored, with eventual worsening of the joint damage. Strategies intended to prevent end-stage joint destruction should be initiated at an early age. Synovectomy through open surgery or arthroscopy removes the inflamed tissue and should result in substantially decreased pain and recurrent bleeding. Nonsurgical synovectomy (synoviorthesis), which involves the intra-articular administration of a radioisotope, is particularly useful in high-risk patients or patients with alloantibody inhibitors against factor VIII or IX. Neither synovectomy nor synoviorthesis reverses joint damage, but both procedures may delay its progression. Non–weight-bearing exercises, such as swimming and isometrics, are important to periarticular muscle development and maintenance of joint stability for ambulation. Intractable pain and severe joint destruction secondary to repeated hemorrhage require prosthetic replacement. Chronic ankle pain responds best to open surgical or arthroscopic fixation and fusion (arthrodesis).

The ultimate strategy to minimize or eliminate progressive joint destruction by recurrent hemarthroses is predicated on the concept of primary prophylaxis—the planned administration of clotting factor concentrates two (for factor IX products) or three (for factor VIII replacement) times weekly at doses to maintain trough clotting factor activity levels above 1 to 2% of normal. These regimens prevent the development of joint deformities and the need for orthopedic surgery, significantly reduce the frequency of spontaneous bleeds, and translate into increased productivity and improved performance status. Although the short-term costs of clotting factor replacement are greater with primary prophylaxis versus traditional "on-demand" therapy for each acute bleeding event, the substantial long-term benefits derived from primary prophylaxis reduce the overall cost of hemophilia care. Primary prophylaxis is facilitated by the implantation of a permanent indwelling central catheter for venous access.

Intramuscular hematomas account for about 30% of the bleeding events in individuals with hemophilia and are rarely life-threatening. They usually are precipitated by physical or iatrogenic trauma (i.e., after intramuscular injection of vaccines or medications) and can compromise sensory and/or motor function and arterial circulation when they entrap and compress vital structures in closed fascial compartments. Retroperitoneal hematomas may be confused clinically with appendicitis or hip bleeds. Unless these bleeding episodes are treated immediately and aggressively, permanent anatomic deformities, such as flexion contractures and pseudotumors (expanding hematomas that erode and destroy adjacent skeletal structures), may occur. Bleeding from mucous membranes, a frequent and troublesome complication in hemophilia, is due to the degradation of fibrin clots by proteolytic enzymes contained in the secretions. Bleeding involving the tongue or the retropharyngeal space rapidly can produce life-threatening compromise of the airways. Gastrointestinal hemorrhage in hemophiliacs typically originates from anatomic lesions proximal to the ligament of Treitz and can be exacerbated by esophageal varices secondary to cirrhosis and portal hypertension and by the use of NSAIDs for the treatment of hemarthroses. Of hemophiliacs, 90% experience at least one episode of gross hematuria or hemospermia. Spontaneous bleeding in the genitourinary tract secondary to hemophilia is a diagnosis of exclusion after renal stones and infection are ruled out. Ureteral blood clots produce renal colic, which may be worsened by the use of antifibrinolytic agents.

Intracranial bleeds are the second most common cause of death in hemophiliacs after AIDS. They occur in 10% of patients, usually are induced by trauma, and are fatal in 30%. The risk of development of an intracranial hemorrhage is approximately 2% per year. Neuromuscular defects, seizure disorders, and intellectual deficits may ensue.

 Treatment

Reversal and prevention of acute bleeding events in hemophilia A and B are based on replacement of the missing or deficient clotting factor protein to restore adequate hemostasis (Table 178–1). Severely affected adolescents or adults consume an average of 50,000 to 80,000 IU of factor VIII or IX concentrate yearly at a cost ranging from $20,000 to $100,000, depending primarily on the choice of replacement product (e.g., recombinant or plasma derived). Data indicate that the morbidity, mortality, and overall cost of care for individuals with hemophilia are reduced significantly if patients are managed and treated by comprehensive hemophilia centers, where the multispecialty expertise, specialized coagulation laboratory, and diagnostic capabilities exist to coordinate and monitor specific patient needs.

Replacement guidelines (Table 178–2) are intended to achieve plasma levels of factor VIII and IX activity of 25 to 30% for minor spontaneous or traumatic bleeds (e.g., hemarthroses, persistent hematuria), at least 50% clotting factor activity for the treatment or prevention of severe bleeds (e.g., major dental surgery, maintenance replacement therapy after major surgery or trauma), and 80% to 100% activity for any life-threatening or limb-threatening hemorrhagic event (e.g., major surgery, trauma). After major trauma or if visceral or intracranial bleeding is suspected, replacement therapy adequate to achieve 100% clotting factor activity should be administered before initiating diagnostic procedures. Although replacement dosing is often empirical, for each unit of factor VIII administered per kilogram of body weight, plasma factor VIII activity increases about 2% (0.02 U/mL), and for each unit of factor IX administered per kilogram of body weight, factor IX activity increases about 1% (0.01 U/mL). The initial dose of factor IX diffuses into the extravascular space and binds to endothelial cell surfaces to a much greater degree than factor VIII does. A 70 kg individual with severe hemophilia A or B (factor VIII or IX activity <1% of normal) who requires replacement to 100% activity for major surgery initially should receive 3500 U of factor VIII or 7000 U of factor IX concentrate. The circulating kinetics of factors VIII and IX require subsequent dosing every 8 to 12 hours and every 18 to 24 hours, individualized according to the peak recovery increment within 15 to 30 minutes after bolus infusion and according to trough activity levels. The frequency of repeat dosing also is determined by the rapidity of pain relief, recovery of joint function, and resolution of active bleeding. Replacement usually is maintained for 10 to 14 days after major surgery to allow for proper wound healing. Bolus dosing typically results in wide fluctuations in clotting factor activity levels and requires frequent laboratory monitoring to avoid suboptimal troughs. Continuous infusion regimens consisting of 1 to 2 U of factor VIII or IX concentrate per kilogram per hour after a bolus dose maintain a plateau level without the necessity for frequent laboratory testing and reduce total concentrate consumption 30 to 75% in surgical settings. Because of the potential thrombogenicity associated with repeated administration of prothrombin complex concentrates for replacement of factor IX deficiency, high-purity, plasma-derived or genetically engineered IX concentrates, which lack activated vitamin K–dependent clotting factors, are preferred therapies in hemophilia B.

Cryoprecipitate (the precipitate remaining after fresh-frozen plasma [FFP] is thawed at −4°C), which is a rich source of factor VIII, and FFP contain factors VIII and IX, but they are not the optimal replacement products for either hemophilia A or hemophilia B because of their potential to transmit blood-borne pathogens. Plasma-derived clotting factor concentrates are manufactured from the plasma donations of more than 10,000 individual donors and are subjected to various types of viral inactivation techniques. Only lipid-enveloped viruses are susceptible to these procedures, which increases the risk that these products can transmit viruses such as parvovirus B19, hepatitis A, and prions, implicated in new variant Creutzfeldt-Jakob disease (Chapter 456). Most manufacturers in the United States screen donated plasma pools for hepatitis A, B, and C virus (HAV, HBV, HCV); human immunodeficiency virus (HIV); and parvovirus B19 by polymerase chain reaction to enhance the viral safety of the final product. Recombinant factor VIII and IX concentrates (see Table 178–1), which do not transmit blood-borne pathogens, are available in formulations that are free of albumin stabilizers to eliminate theoretical risks of potential transmission of prions or murine viruses. All concentrates available in the United States, whether plasma derived or genetically engineered, are equally efficacious and are considered extremely safe; no concentrate has been implicated in the transmission of prions thus far.

As obligate recipients of clotting factor replacement, virtually all hemophiliacs treated before 1985, when techniques for elimination of lipid-enveloped viruses were introduced, have been exposed to HCV, often with multiple genotypes (Chapter 151). Seropositivity to hepatitis G, caused by another lipid-enveloped virus, has been observed in 15 to 25% of hemophiliacs; similar to HCV, it is believed to be susceptible to current viral attenuation procedures. HBV, also lipid enveloped, is a rare problem for hemophiliacs now because vaccination at an early age is the standard of care; however, approximately 5% of individuals exposed before 1985 are chronic carriers of hepatitis B surface antigen. HAV is not lipid coated and has been transmitted to a small but significant number of patients through solvent detergent–treated factor VIII and IX concentrates; HAV vaccination now should eliminate this risk. Parvovirus B19 seroprevalence approaches 80% in hemophiliacs; although the long-term clinical consequences are unclear, transmission symbolizes the vul-

Continued

nerability of hemophiliacs to blood-borne pathogens that escape viral attenuation processes. Cadaver and living-donor liver transplantation (Chapter 157) have improved the survival of hemophiliacs with chronic hepatitis–induced liver failure and cured the coagulopathy, suggesting that the liver is the predominant source of normal factor VIII and IX synthesis. Liver transplantation may be performed successfully in HIV/HCV-coinfected individuals who have an undetectable HIV viral titer while on highly active antiretroviral therapy.

Ancillary treatment strategies for hemophilias include the use of antifibrinolytic agents (e.g., ε-aminocaproic acid or tranexamic acid) to minimize mucous membrane bleeding and the application of fibrin glues to bleeding sites. Desmopressin (DDAVP) is useful in patients with mild hemophilia A inasmuch as an adequate incremental rise in factor VIII activity can circumvent the use of clotting factor concentrates. Repeated administration of DDAVP (intravenously or by intranasal spray) can be complicated by tachyphylaxis, hyponatremic seizures, and angina.

Prognosis

The life expectancy of severe hemophiliacs approached 62 years by the mid-1980s with the introduction of clotting factor concentrates; however, HIV has tripled the death rate and is currently responsible for more than 55% of all hemophilia deaths. In contrast, the lifetime risk of intracranial hemorrhage is 2 to 8%. More than 75% of adults with hemophilia A and 46% of adults with hemophilia B are HIV positive. The availability of anti-HIV protease inhibitors has

prolonged HIV disease-free survival in infected hemophiliacs. Hemophiliacs coinfected with HCV have a poorer prognosis, however, despite the initiation of interferon-α and ribavirin therapy; the progression of HCV can be exacerbated by alcohol and by hepatotoxic medications prescribed for prophylaxis of opportunistic infections and chronic pain (e.g. large doses of acetaminophen). Otherwise, life expectancy is related to the severity of hemophilia, with the mortality rate of severely affected patients being four to six times greater than that of patients with mild deficiencies. The mortality of patients

Table 178–1 • CLOTTING FACTOR CONCENTRATES FOR HEMOPHILIA A AND B AVAILABLE IN THE UNITED STATES

VIRUCIDAL TECHNIQUE	TYPE/NAME OF PRODUCT (MANUFACTURER)	SPECIFIC ACTIVITY (U/mg PROTEIN DISCOUNTING ALBUMIN)
ULTRAPURE RECOMBINANT FACTOR VIII		
Immunoaffinity chromatography	Recombinate (Baxter) synthesized in Chinese hamster ovary cell lines	>3000
	Refacto (Wyeth-Ayerst/Genetics Institute); B-domain deleted molecule; synthesized in Chinese hamster ovary cell lines; albumin-free formulation; solvent detergent (TNBP/Triton X100) viral attenuation step added	11,200–15,000
	Kogenate FS (Bayer), Helixate FS (Aventis-Behring); both synthesized in baby hamster kidney cell lines; solvent detergent (TNBP/polysorbate 80) viral attenuation step added; albumin-free formulations	>3000
ULTRAPURE PLASMA-DERIVED FACTOR VIII		
Immunoaffinity chromatography and pasteurization (60°C, 10 hr)	Monoclate P (Aventis-Behring)	>3000
Immunoaffinity chromatography, solvent detergent (TNBP/Triton X-100), and terminal heating (25°C, >10 hr)	Hemofil M (Baxter), Monarc M (Baxter, distributed by the American Red Cross, which also provides the donor plasma)	>3000
INTERMEDIATE-PURITY AND HIGH-PURITY PLASMA-DERIVED FACTOR VIII		
Affinity chromatography, solvent detergent (TNBP and polysorbate 80), and terminal heating (80°C, 72 hr)	Alphanate SD (Alpha Therapeutics)	~8–30 (>400 when corrected for von Willebrand factor protein content)
Solvent detergent (TNBP/polysorbate 80)	Koate-HP (Bayer)	~9–22
Pasteurization (60°C, 10 hr)	Humate-P (Aventis-Behring)	~1–2
	Hyate-C (Ibsen/Biopharma) (porcine plasma-derived factor VIII used in treatment of inhibitor patients)	None >50
ULTRAPURE RECOMBINANT FACTOR IX		
Affinity chromatography and ultrafiltration	BeneFix (Wyeth-Ayerst/Genetics Institute) (Chinese hamster ovary cell lines maintained in fetal calf serum-free medium)	>200 (albumin free)
VERY HIGHLY PURIFIED PLASMA-DERIVED FACTOR IX		
Dual-affinity chromatography, solvent detergent (TNBP/polysorbate 80), and nanofiltration	AlphaNine SD (Alpha Therapeutics)	>200
Immunoaffinity chromatography, solvent detergent (sodium thiocyanate), and ultrafiltration	Mononine (Aventis-Behring)	>160 (albumin free)
LOW PURITY PLASMA-DERIVED FACTOR IX COMPLEX CONCENTRATES		
Solvent detergent (TNBP/polysorbate 80)	Profilnine SD (Alpha Therapeutics)	~4.5
Vapor heat (10 hr, 60°C, 1190 mbar pressure plus 1 hr 80°C, 1375 mbar)	Bebulin VH (Immuno, distributed by Baxter)	~2
ACTIVATED PLASMA-DERIVED FACTOR IX COMPLEX CONCENTRATES (RESERVED PRIMARILY FOR INHIBITOR PATIENTS)		
Dry heat (68°C, 144 hr)	Autoplex T (Baxter, distributed by NABI)	~5
Vapor heat (10 hr, 60°C, 1190 mbar plus 1 hr 80°C, 1375 mbar)	FEIBA VH (Immuno, distributed by Baxter)	~0.8
RECOMBINANT FACTOR VIIa (INDICATED FOR INHIBITOR PATIENTS)		
Affinity chromatography	Novoseven (NovoNordisk)	50,000 IU/mg
Detergent viral attenuation step added; albumin-free formulation	Synthesized in baby hamster kidney cells; solvent	

Table 178–2 • COAGULATION PROTEINS AND REPLACEMENT THERAPY

COAGULATION PROTEIN DEFICIENCY	INHERITANCE PATTERN	PREVALENCE	MINIMUM HEMOSTATIC LEVEL	REPLACEMENT SOURCES
Factor I (fibrinogen) Afibrinogenemia Dysfibrinogenemia	Autosomal recessive Autosomal dominant or recessive	Rare (<300 families) Rare (>300 variants)	50–100 mg/dL	Cryoprecipitate/FFP
Factor II (prothrombin)	Autosomal dominant or recessive	Rare (~25 kindreds)	30% of normal	FFP, Factor IX complex concentrates
Factor V (labile factor)	Autosomal recessive	1 per 1 million births	25% of normal	FFP
Factor VII	Autosomal recessive	1 per 500,000 births	25% of normal	FFP, Factor IX complex concentrates, or recombinant Factor VIIa
Factor VIII (antihemophilic factor)	X-linked recessive	1 per 5000 male births	80–100% for surgery/life-threatening bleeds, 50% for serious bleeds, 25–30% for minor bleeds	Factor VIII concentrates (see Table 178–1)
von Willebrand disease Type 1 and 2 variants	Usually autosomal dominant	1% prevalence	>50% vWF antigen and ristocetin cofactor activity	DDAVP for mild to moderate vWD (except 2B. Variable response to 2A); cryoprecipitate and FFP (not preferred except in emergencies); Factor VIII concentrates, viral attenuated, intermediate purity (preferred for vWD unresponsive to DDAVP and for Type 3) (see Table 178–1)
Type 3	Autosomal recessive	1 per 1 million births		
Factor IX (Christmas factor)	X-linked recessive	1 per 30,000 male births	25–50% of normal, depending on extent of bleeding and surgery	Factor IX concentrates; FFP is not preferred except in dire emergencies (see Table 178–1)
Factor X (Stuart-Prower factor)	Autosomal recessive	1 per 500,000 births	10–25% of normal,	FFP or Factor IX complex concentrates
Factor XI (hemophilia C)	Autosomal dominant: severe type is recessive	~4% Ashkenazi Jews; 1 per 1 million general population	20–40% of normal	FFP or Factor XI concentrate
Factor XII (Hageman factor), prekallikrein, high-molecular-weight kininogen	Autosomal recessive	Not available	No treatment necessary	
Factor XIII (fibrin stabilizing factor)	Autosomal recessive	1 per 3 million births	5% of normal	FFP, cryoprecipitate, or viral-attenuated Factor XIII concentrate

DDAVP = desmopressin; FFP = fresh frozen plasma; vWF = von Willebrand factor.

with inhibitors is significantly greater than that of patients without inhibitors. Defects in normal growth and development also are exaggerated in HIV-infected boys, with increased cortical atrophy on magnetic resonance imaging (15% in HIV-positive versus 6.5% in HIV-negative boys) and delayed growth velocity in adolescence. IQ does not seem to be affected by either HIV or hemophilia.

Alloantibody and Autoantibody Inhibitors to Factors VIII and IX

Alloantibody inhibitors arise predominantly in individuals with severe congenital deficiencies of factors VIII or IX and are suspected when replacement therapy does not provide the usual immediate relief in bleeding symptoms. These IgG antibodies (usually IgG4 subclass) completely neutralize clotting factor activity; no or reduced increments in factor VIII or IX levels are observed after the administration of bolus doses of concentrate. These inhibitors are time and temperature dependent. The strength of the inhibitor is quantitated in Bethesda units (BU); 1 BU is defined arbitrarily as the amount of inhibitor that neutralizes 50% of the specific clotting factor activity in normal plasma. Patients with high-titer inhibitor, or "high responders," have greater than 5 BU, and an anamnestic antibody enhancement usually develops 5 to 7 days after subsequent exposure to the antigenic clotting factor protein. Low-titer inhibitor patients (i.e., <5 BU) are "low responders" and do not manifest anamnesis. Low-titer inhibitor patients can be overwhelmed easily by large amounts of human factor VIII or IX concentrate, usually three to four times the usual dose. Treatment of patients with high-titer inhibitor against factor VIII or IX is complicated by the observation that no single approach is uniformly successful. For intermittent bleeds and on-demand regimens, factor IX complex concentrates of the standard inactivated or activated varieties (see Table 178–1) can be used at an empirical dose of 75 U/kg every 12 to 18 hours. Approximately 48 to 64% of bleeding events respond favorably. These products contain activated vitamin K–dependent clotting factors that "bypass" the intrinsic pathway inhibitor. As a result, their use is limited by potential thrombogenicity, and the aPTT and clotting factor assays are useless monitors of adequate hemostasis. Alternatively, for patients with inhibitor titers less than 50 BU against human factor VIII, porcine factor VIII concentrate can be administered at a dose between 50 and 100 U/kg with an 80% excellent or good response rate. Cross-reactivity factor VIII assays should be performed before use to exclude the possibility that the anti–human factor VIII antibodies will neutralize the effectiveness of the porcine factor VIII. Factor VIII activity can be measured after its administration and provides objective laboratory evidence of hemostasis. This product is nonthrombogenic, but anamnestic immune responses can result in increased antibody titers against porcine and human factor VIII. Recombinant factor VIIa seems to be an additional new, effective therapy in patients with high-titer factor VIII and IX inhibitors.

Immune tolerance induction regimens have emerged as a useful adjunctive therapy to eradicate alloantibody inhibitors. Consisting of daily administration of factor VIII or IX concentrates to patients with inhibitors, this regimen is essentially a desensitization process with a 68% success rate. Young age, low-titer inhibitor, and immediate initiation after detection of the inhibitor increase the likelihood of success. When tolerance has been achieved, maintenance prophylaxis with factor concentrate administered two to three times weekly (20 U/kg) is necessary.

Alloantibodies usually are detected in childhood after a median of 9 to 12 days of exposure to clotting factor. These inhibitors occur with an increased incidence in sibships; are more common in individuals with large, multidomain factor VIII and factor IX gene deletions; and manifest a racial predilection. The incidence of factor VIII alloantibodies is 24 to 52%, with an increased frequency in blacks and perhaps Hispanics. Factor IX alloantibodies are observed with a 1.5 to 3% incidence and predominate in Scandinavians. Factor IX inhibitor patients seem to be susceptible to anaphylaxis and the development of nephrotic syndrome with subsequent exposure to sources of factor IX.

Autoantibody inhibitors occur spontaneously in individuals with previously normal hemostasis (nonhemophiliacs). Although approximately 50% have no obvious underlying cause, the remainder are associated with autoimmune diseases, lymphoproliferative disorders, idiosyncratic drug associations, and pregnancy. Patients typically have massive hemorrhagic events, usually much more severe than events produced by alloantibodies; the laboratory expression of autoantibodies is similar to that of alloantibodies except that clotting factor activity is not completely neutralized. Residual clotting factor activities between 3 and 20% of normal frequently are observed in autoantibody patients. The same principles of replacement therapy for alloantibodies also apply to these inhibitors. Porcine factor VIII concentrate is particularly useful in acquired hemophilia A because little cross-reactivity usually occurs even with extremely high titers of anti–human factor VIII antibodies. Immunosuppressive therapy with steroids and cytotoxic agents is a necessary component of the overall treatment to suppress the inhibitor. High-dose intravenous gamma globulin may be a useful adjunctive therapy. Immune tolerance induction is rarely successful in eradicating autoantibody inhibitors and usually is not attempted. For hemorrhagic catastrophes related to either alloantibodies or autoantibodies, extracorporeal plasmapheresis over a staphylococcal protein A column may remove enough of the IgG to allow for replacement therapy with enough factor concentrates to achieve hemostasis.

VON WILLEBRAND DISEASE

In 1926, von Willebrand described an autosomal dominantly inherited hemorrhagic disease affecting both sexes that subsequently was recognized as a deficiency in vWF. vWD has emerged as the most common bleeding disorder, with a prevalence of 1 to 3% of the population without any ethnic predominance. Homozygous patients are rare and are the result of a recessive mutant gene.

Normal vWF is a large multimeric glycoprotein product of the vWF gene, located on chromosome 12. The protein consists of 220,000 D monomeric subunits, and the fully processed protein may reach a total molecular weight of 20 million D, with its platelet agglutination properties mediated predominantly by the highest molecular weight multimers. The phenotypic classification of vWD recognizes three major types of the disease based on their multimeric structure and function of the vWF protein (Table 178–3). Type 1 vWD accounts

for 75 to 80% of patients and is inherited predominantly via an autosomal dominant mode; a qualitative defect is present in which the vWF structure is normal but vWF antigen and activity are concurrently reduced. Type 2 vWD includes approximately 20% of vWD patients, is inherited in either a dominant or a recessive pattern, and is characterized by qualitative and quantitative abnormalities in the vWF protein. Further subclassification is based on multimeric structure and responses in the ristocetin-induced platelet aggregation assay. Up to 30 variants have been described, each with unique aberrations in vWF multimer structure. Type 2A is the most common variant, with loss of the largest and intermediate-sized multimers, and type 2B lacks only the largest vWF multimers. The multimeric patterns in type 2A may result from defective synthesis of the vWF protein or increased susceptibility of vWF to proteolysis in vivo. In type 2B, the highest molecular weight multimers of vWF are adsorbed preferentially and with abnormally high affinity to the glycoprotein Ib receptor binding site on the platelet membrane surface. Alternatively, a structural defect in the glycoprotein Ib platelet receptor binding site for vWF can produce a multimeric pattern similar to that of type 2B by virtue of its preferential adsorption of the highest molecular weight multimers from normal vWF in the circulation. This latter variant is designated *platelet-type pseudo-vWD*. Type 2N (Normandy) is an unusual variant that resembles hemophilia A, although it is inherited in an autosomal dominant pattern. The defective vWF protein is normal from functional and multimeric perspectives but lacks an intact binding site for factor VIII. Unbound factor VIII is cleared from the circulation with a rapid half-life. Finally, type 3 vWD, an exceedingly rare variant that occurs in 1 per 1 million individuals, is characterized by nearly complete absence of circulating vWF.

Clinical Manifestations

Most patients with vWD have mild disease that may go undiagnosed until trauma or surgery. Symptomatic individuals manifest easy bruisability and mucosal surface bleeding, including epistaxis and gastrointestinal hemorrhage. Menorrhagia affects 50% to 75% of women and may be the initial symptom. These symptoms are consistent with platelet-based defects and reflect the crucial role of vWF protein in mediating platelet-platelet and platelet-subendothelial matrix interactions in the process of vascular plug formation and primary hemostasis. The use of aspirin or NSAIDs with antiplatelet aggregation effects may exacerbate the symptoms. Deep subcutaneous and intramuscular bleeds, hemarthroses, and intracranial hemorrhage are unusual in vWD except in the rare type 3 variant. The factor VIII deficiency is due to the absence of vWF protein, which normally complexes with factor VIII, delivers it to sites of ongoing coagulation, and prevents its clearance from the circulation.

Diagnosis

Physical examination usually reveals nonspecific evidence of easy bruising and bleeding. The bleeding time is variably prolonged in patients with vWD and may be influenced by the thrombocytopenia associated with vWD type 2B. As such, it is used predominantly to diagnose vWD but is less useful as a predictor of adequate hemostasis after replacement therapy. The platelet function analyzer (PFA-100; Dade-Behring, Liederbach, Germany) provides a global perspective of vWF and platelet function and may be a helpful substitute for the bleeding time in the diagnosis of vWD; however, similar to the bleeding time, its results do not always correlate with bleeding propensity after replacement therapy. This assay is more sensitive to the vWF stored in the α granule of the platelet rather than therapeutically administered vWF. The aPTT is also variably increased because of concurrent factor VIII deficiency; however, a normal aPTT does not exclude the diagnosis of vWD. The vWF activity assay or ristocetin cofactor activity (vWF:RCoF) is the most specific test for vWF function but may be only slightly decreased in mild vWD. The vWF:Ag assay measures the immunologic expression of vWF and usually is performed via electroimmunoassay or enzyme-linked immunosorbent assay. It is reduced slightly in mild vWD and its variants and virtually absent in type 3. Because these assays are sensitive to the molecular mass of vWF, vWF:RCoF activity is discordantly low as a result of a low-normal or slightly reduced vWF:Ag level in the type 2 variants of vWD. vWF:RCoF and vWF:Ag are acute-phase

Table 178–3 • PATTERNS OF VON WILLEBRAND DISEASE

TYPE	VWF:AG/ VWF:RCOF	RIPA	RIPA–LOW DOSE	MULTIMERIC PATTERN
1 (classic)	↓/↓	±↓	Absent	Uniform ↓ in all multimers
2 (Variant)				
2A	↓/↓↓↓	↓↓	Absent	↓ in large and intermediate multimers
2B	±↓/±↓	Normal	Increased	↓ in large multimers
2N (Normandy)	Normal/ normal	Normal	↓	Normal
Platelet type	±↓/±↓	±↓	Increased	↓ in large multimers
3 (Homozygote or compound heterozygote)	Absent/ absent	Absent	Absent	Absent

vWF:Ag = von Willebrand factor antigen; vWF:RCoF = Willebrand factor ristocetin cofactor activity; RIPA = ristocetin-induced platelet aggregation.

reactants and are increased by exercise, stress, pregnancy, oral contraceptives, and liver disease and decreased with hypothyroidism and in the presence of blood group O. vWD subtypes can be analyzed by in vitro platelet aggregation assays in which the patient's platelet-rich plasma is activated by the addition of standard and low concentrations of ristocetin or cryoprecipitate. Types 1 and 3 vWF show mild or marked hyporesponsiveness to the standard concentration of ristocetin, whereas type 2B and the rare platelet-type pseudo-vWD hyperaggregate with half-standard concentrations of ristocetin. Platelet-type pseudo-vWD can be differentiated from type 2B by observing spontaneous platelet agglutination after the addition of cryoprecipitate. With type 2B vWD, the defect responsible for the high-affinity vWF-platelet interaction is present in the vWF protein, whereas in the platelet type, the defect resides in the platelet glycoprotein Ib/IX complex.

Gene-based assays are the most specific for diagnosing vWF variants via restriction enzyme mapping of the vWF gene. Type 3 vWF has large deletions, whereas the others are caused by variable point mutation defects. Type 2N has defects in the functional domain coding for vWF binding to factor VIII.

 Treatment

The goals of therapy for vWD consist of correcting the deficiencies in vWF protein activity to greater than 50% of normal and factor VIII activity to levels appropriate for the clinical situation. Although cryoprecipitate is licensed by the Food and Drug Administration (FDA) for prophylaxis or treatment of vWD-related bleeding complications, the lack of viral safety relegates its use exclusively to emergency circumstances when no other options are readily available. Replacement therapy with viral-attenuated, intermediate-purity or high-purity factor VIII concentrates containing high-molecular-weight multimers of vWF (e.g., Humate-P or Alphanate) is preferred[1] and should be reserved for patients with type 1 and 2A variants who are unresponsive to DDAVP and for patients with type 2B and type 3 disease. These products also are indicated for the 2N variant and provide a source of normal vWF to complex with the normal intrinsic factor VIII. Dosing of these concentrates for vWD is calculated according to ristocetin cofactor units. On-demand and continuous infusion regimens have been used successfully. An ultrahigh-purity, plasma-derived vWF concentrate is available for clinical research protocols; however, this product would have little value for type 3 individuals, who require simultaneous sources of factor VIII. All these plasma-derived concentrates may precipitate thrombotic complications or exacerbate the thrombocytopenia in platelet-type pseudo-vWD. These individuals should receive transfusions with normal platelets that possess glycoprotein Ib/IX complexes with normal vWF affinity. Otherwise, DDAVP (0.3 μg/kg in 50 mL of normal saline infused over 20 minutes or intranasally at 150 μg per nostril for adults) is the recommended treatment and eliminates potential exposure to blood-borne pathogens.

The adjunctive use of antifibrinolytic agents, such as ε-aminocaproic acid or tranexamic acid, is helpful after DDAVP therapy for bleeds. These agents should not be used for renal bleeds or menorrhagia.

The following important caveats for vWD treatment should be considered: (1) A prolonged bleeding time does not need to be normalized to achieve adequate hemostasis after replacement therapy. Correction of vWF and factor VIII activity suffices and correlates closely with the clinical risk of bleeding. (2) DDAVP administration should be avoided in most individuals with type 2B variant vWD. Their thrombocytopenia may worsen inasmuch as DDAVP induces the release of abnormal vWF into the circulation with additional in vivo platelet agglutination/aggregation. (3) Individuals with variant type 2N may not manifest a sustained response to DDAVP because the vWF released cannot complex with the simultaneously released factor VIII and prevent its clearance from the circulation. (4) Individuals who respond adequately to intravenously administered DDAVP may not respond adequately to the intranasal DDAVP preparation. Ideally, patients should be tested for their responses *before* needing it for surgery. (5) Pregnant women with type 2B variant vWD may experience an exacerbation of thrombocytopenia as pregnancy progresses. Levels of the abnormal vWF increase as estrogen levels increase. (6) Free water intake, whether intravenous or by mouth, should be severely restricted for 4 to 6 hours after DDAVP administration to minimize the risk of hyponatremia and seizures. (7) vWD is associated clinically with Osler-Weber-Rendu syndrome (hereditary hemorrhagic telangiectasia), so gastrointestinal bleeding may occur. (8) Replacement therapy in type 3 vWD occasionally may precipitate the formation of alloantibody inhibitors that neutralize vWF activity.

Acquired vWD is a rare condition and usually occurs as a complication of autoimmune, myeloproliferative, or lymphoproliferative disorders. The acquired vWD associated with neuroblastoma is secondary to proteolysis of vWF by tumor-secreted hyaluronidase. Abnormal vWF multimeric composition is a hallmark of these syndromes. Treatment is similar to that for congenital vWD, but responses are unpredictable.

FACTOR XI DEFICIENCY (HEMOPHILIA C)

Factor XI deficiency occurs at a prevalence of 1 per 1 million in the general population and 1 per 500 births in Ashkenazi Jewish families. Factor XI is the only component of the contact phase system of coagulation (factor XII, prekallikrein, and high-molecular-weight kininogen) that is associated with excessive bleeding complications when a deficient state exists. Factor XI deficiency is diagnosed in the laboratory by a prolonged aPTT, normal PT, and decreased factor XI activity ascertained in a specific quantitative clotting assay (normal range, 60 to 130%). The clinical bleeding tendencies in factor XI deficiency are less severe than the tendencies seen with severe hemophilia A or B and are not correlated with the extent of the deficiency. Most individuals with factor XI levels less than 20% of normal activity experience excessive bleeding after trauma or surgery; however, a few do not bleed. In contrast, bleeding has been observed in approximately 35 to 50% of mildly affected patients with factor XI levels between 20 and 50%. Spontaneous hemorrhagic episodes, hemarthroses, and intramuscular and intracerebral bleeds are unusual; traumatic and surgical bleeds typically involve the mucous membranes. Patients undergoing tonsillectomies, prostatectomies, and dental extractions are at highest risk for bleeding unless replacement therapy is administered. Women may experience significant menorrhagia.

Genetics

Factor XI deficiency is an autosomal disorder that can be inherited in recessive and dominant patterns. The factor XI gene is located on chromosome 4. In Ashkenazi Jewish individuals, two predominant gene mutations occur with equal frequency and are designated *type II* (a stop codon in exon 5) and *type III* (a single base defect in exon 9). The most severe clinical disease is observed in homozygous type II patients, who usually have less than 1% factor XI activity. Homozygous type III individuals also manifest severe symptoms, typically less severe than symptoms in individuals with type II, and have slightly higher factor XI levels of about 10 to 20%. Compound heterozygotes, type II/III, make up the bulk of factor XI–deficient patients and are clinically mild, with factor XI levels between 30 and 50%. Genotypic identification of affected patients is determined practically by factor XI levels rather than by defining their specific gene defect.

 Treatment

FFP remains the mainstay for factor XI replacement (15 to 20 mL/kg); however, it is not virally inactivated. A minimum factor XI level of 40% is essential for major bleeds and major surgery. A dry heated factor XI concentrate is not widely available and may precipitate hypercoagulable events manifested by fatal disseminated coagulation, myocardial infarction, and acute cerebrovascular events; these complications usually have occurred postoperatively in older individuals with preexisting hypercoagulable conditions such as malignancy. Factor XI concentrate should be avoided or administered judiciously in carefully selected patients. Replacement dosing levels should never exceed 70% factor XI activity. Repeat dosing with FFP or factor XI concentrate should be in the context of the long 60- to 80-hour biologic half-life of factor XI in vivo.

Continued

The decision to treat heterozygotes with factor XI at levels greater than 20% is empirical and should be based on the individual's prior history of bleeding after trauma or surgery. Alternatively the family medical history of previous bleeding complications can be considered. For symptomatic patients, the preoperative or post-trauma use of FFP and pooled plasma products can be minimized or avoided by administering DDAVP, 0.3 μg/kg intravenously. Because hemorrhagic complications originate most commonly from mucosal membrane surfaces, antifibrinolytic agents, such as ε-aminocaproic acid or tranexamic acid, are frequently helpful as adjunctive therapy.

The poor correlation between factor XI levels and bleeding risk has prompted a search for concurrent defects in coagulation and platelet function. Preliminary data suggest that individuals with absent platelet factor XI content are at risk. A significant association is seen between an increased bleeding tendency in patients with mild factor XI deficiency and coincident mild vWD.

CONTACT ACTIVATION FACTORS

Although factor XI is important for activating factor IX in the intrinsic pathway generation of thrombin, it is only one of the four components of the contact phase of coagulation. Deficiencies in any of the other three factors (factor XII, prekallikrein, and high-molecular-weight kininogen) produce in vitro laboratory abnormalities but no clinical bleeding and require no replacement therapy. Deficiencies of each of these contact factors prolong the aPTT, which may normalize after prolonged incubation of the patient's plasma at 37°C with a negatively charged activator of the aPTT assay (e.g., kaolin or celite). Specific assays are also available to quantitate each of the contact factors.

Counterintuitively, 8 to 10% of individuals with severe factor XII deficiency (<1% activity) have experienced premature venous thromboembolic events, occasionally fatal in nature. This finding has led to speculation that factor XII deficiency may lead to hypercoagulability through defective participation of the contact phase proteins in the activation of fibrinolysis.

FACTOR XIII (FIBRIN-STABILIZING FACTOR) DEFICIENCY

Factor XIII is a transglutaminase that is activated by thrombin and subsequently cross-links fibrin to protect it from lysis by plasmin. It also is involved in wound healing and tissue repair and seems to be crucial for maintaining a viable pregnancy. Homozygous severe deficiency states are rare and inherited in an autosomal recessive manner with a prevalence of 1 per 3 million births. Consanguinity is common. Typically, patients are seen first shortly after birth with persistent bleeding around the umbilical stump. Intracranial bleeding events, usually precipitated by minimal trauma, occur commonly enough in infants to justify initiating a primary prophylaxis regimen of replacement therapy. Delayed bleeding after surgery and trauma is the hallmark of the disease; however, easy bruisability, poor wound healing with defective scar formation and dehiscence, and hemarthroses are characteristic. Spontaneous abortions are increased in severely affected women. The diagnosis usually is suspected on clinical grounds inasmuch as factor XIII deficiency is not detected by the conventional screening coagulation assays (e.g., the aPTT or the PT). Most laboratories use a rapid screening assay that assesses the ability of a fibrin clot to remain intact with incubation in 5 mol/L of urea or 1% monochloroacetic acid. With factor XIII levels less than 1% of normal, the clot dissolves within 2 to 3 hours.

Replacement therapy for prophylaxis or treatment of acute bleeds can be accomplished by administering cryoprecipitate, FFP, or, preferably, plasma-derived factor XIII concentrate (pasteurized for viral safety and available in the United States via compassionate investigational new drug [IND] use through Centeon Pharma, King of Prussia, PA). Clinical studies are in progress to evaluate a placentally derived product. Normal hemostasis is achieved with a factor XIII level of only 5% of normal. The circulating half-life of factor XIII is 10 days, so prophylaxis replacement can be scheduled every 3 to 4 weeks. Acquired alloantibody inhibitors can develop in severely affected individuals. Autoantibodies also occur, usually in association with systemic lupus erythematosus.

DYSFIBRINOGENEMIA AND AFIBRINOGENEMIA

Approximately 300 abnormal fibrinogens have been described; however, few cause symptoms. Abnormalities usually are detected incidentally when routine coagulation screening assays reveal decreased fibrinogen concentrations and prolonged thrombin clotting times. On further evaluation, discordance between functional and immunologic fibrinogen levels (>50 mg/dL more antigenic than functional) is observed; plasma-based clotting times with substitution of snake venom for thrombin (e.g., reptilase and ancrod) are variably prolonged. Abnormal fibrinogens are rare autosomally inherited proteins. Their characterization has provided valuable structure-function information and better understanding of wound healing and fibrinolysis.

Greater than 50% of the dysfibrinogenemias are asymptomatic, 25% are associated with a mild hemorrhagic tendency (commonly caused by defective release of fibrinopeptide A), and 20% predispose individuals to thrombophilia (usually caused by impaired fibrinolysis). Concurrent bleeding and thrombosis also may occur. The prevalence of dysfibrinogenemia in patients with a history of thromboembolic episodes approaches 0.8%, typically occurring in late adolescence and early adulthood. Women experience a high incidence of pregnancy-related complications, such as spontaneous abortions and postpartum thromboembolic events. Thrombin and reptilase times are not helpful in predicting whether an abnormal fibrinogen will be prothrombotic, prohemorrhagic, or asymptomatic, but clinical history, fibrinopeptide release studies, and fibrin polymerization studies may be useful. Clinically insignificant dysfibrinogenemias may be acquired in association with hepatocellular carcinoma.

In contrast to the hepatic synthesis of a qualitatively abnormal protein in dysfibrinogenemia, congenital afibrinogenemia, an autosomal recessive disorder, represents the markedly deficient production of a normal protein. Severe life-threatening hemorrhagic complications can occur at any site, beginning at birth with umbilical bleeding. Intracranial hemorrhage is a frequent cause of death. Poor wound healing is characteristic. All coagulation-based assays dependent on detection of a fibrin clot end point are markedly prolonged. Afibrinogenemia is usually detectable by either specific functional or immunologic assays. Platelet dysfunction may accompany afibrinogenemia and exacerbate bleeding.

Deficiencies of fibrinogen may be corrected by the administration of FFP or cryoprecipitate; however, viral safety remains an issue. Intermediate-purity factor VIII concentrates from FFP that have been viral attenuated and treated with solvent detergent (when licensed by the FDA) are preferable alternatives. The replacement goal is 100 mg/dL of fibrinogen. With a circulating biologic half-life of at least 96 hours, treatment every 3 to 4 days is adequate. Primary prophylaxis regimens may be useful in afibrinogenemia; on-demand or prophylactic replacement for trauma or surgery is recommended for prohemorrhagic dysfibrinogenemias. Individuals with thrombophilic manifestations should receive anticoagulation indefinitely.

FACTOR V (PROACCELERIN, LABILE FACTOR) DEFICIENCY

Factor V is a component of the prothrombinase complex that assembles factors Va and Xa on the phospholipid membrane of the platelet for prothrombin (factor II) activation to thrombin. Deficiency of factor V is a rare autosomal recessive disorder (1 per 1 million births). The severity of the plasma factor V reduction correlates less well with the risk of clinical bleeding than does the platelet factor V content in the α-granule. This observation illustrates the crucial role of the platelet in promoting adequate hemostasis at bleeding sites and explains why transfusions of normal platelets may be preferred over FFP for the treatment of hemorrhagic episodes secondary to congenital or acquired factor V deficiency. Hemostasis can be maintained without correcting plasma factor V activity (>25% of normal). The factor V Leiden protein, which is responsible for resistance to activated protein C and thrombophilia, does not affect factor V coagulant activity (Chapter 33).

Combined deficiencies of factors V and VIII occur as an autosomal recessive disorder with a prevalence of 1 per 100,000 births in Jews of Sephardic origin. The severity of bleeding is determined by the levels of these factors, usually ranging from 5 to 30% of normal. Replacement therapy should be aimed at normalizing both clotting protein activities. Factors V and VIII are structurally homologous proteins.

Acquired factor V deficiency has been described in individuals exposed to bovine factor V, which contaminates the thrombin preparations used topically to control bleeding during cardiovascular surgery. This abnormality probably represents the development of anti–bovine factor V antibodies that cross-react with the human factor V protein. Profuse bleeding accompanies this complication.

DEFICIENCIES OF VITAMIN K–DEPENDENT COAGULATION FACTORS II, VII, AND X

Congenital deficiencies of factors II, VII, and X are rare autosomally inherited disorders. Heterozygotes (with factor levels approximately 20% of normal) are typically asymptomatic except in the immediate newborn period, when physiologic vitamin K deficiency exacerbates the underlying clotting factor deficiency. Homozygotes with clotting factor levels less than 10% of normal manifest variable symptoms. As with other coagulopathies, these deficiencies usually are suspected after the onset of neonatal umbilical stump bleeding. Thereafter, unless replacement or prophylactic therapy is provided, these patients are subject to mucosal bleeding from epistaxis, menorrhagia, and dental extractions; to hemarthroses and intramuscular hematomas; and to postsurgical and post-trauma bleeding.

In the coagulation laboratory, factor VII deficiency is associated with a prolonged PT and normal aPTT. This pattern localizes the deficiency to the extrinsic pathway. In contrast, deficiencies of factors II and X prolong the PT and the aPTT, with the defects localized to the common pathway of coagulation. A Russell's viper venom–based clotting assay can differentiate between these two deficiencies because as a direct activator of factor X, the Russell's viper venom assay is prolonged with factor X but not factor II deficiency. Mixing patient plasma with normal plasma shows correction of these assays; specific clotting assays using plasma deficient in the coagulation protein to be studied confirm the diagnosis.

Replacement therapy is indicated for acute symptomatic bleeds and for prophylaxis for surgery. In addition to FFP, which has the potential to transmit blood-borne viruses, factor IX complex concentrates can be administered to achieve hemostatic levels of any of these vitamin K–dependent factors (>25 to 30% of normal).

Additional issues that should be considered when a deficiency of these or other coagulation factors is confirmed include the following:

1. Acquired severe deficiency of factor X, often accompanied by deficiencies of other vitamin K–dependent factors, occasionally occurs in individuals with systemic amyloidosis. Because amyloid fibrils in the reticuloendothelial system bind endogenous and exogenous sources of factor X, replacement therapy with FFP or factor IX complex concentrates, even in large quantities, may not always be sufficient. Splenectomy may ameliorate or reverse the bleeding complications.

2. Acquired factor IX deficiency has been associated with Gaucher's disease because factor IX binds to glucocerebroside (Chapter 222).

3. Factor IX deficiency may accompany Noonan's syndrome, an autosomal dominant disease complex characterized by congenital heart disease, abnormal facies, and excessive bleeding or bruising.

4. The genetic factor II variant resulting from a G-to-A mutation at nucleoside 20210 is associated with elevated prothrombin levels and an increased risk of venous and arterial thrombosis (Chapter 33). The PT and aPTT are not affected.

5. Bleeding complications caused by acquired IgG autoantibodies directed against any coagulation factor protein may be reversed rapidly but temporarily by extracorporeal immunoadsorption over a Sepharose-bound polyclonal antihuman IgG or staphylococcal A column with concomitant replacement therapy and initiation of immunosuppression.

6. Acquired factor VII deficiency has been associated with Dubin-Johnson and Gilbert syndromes (Chapter 149).

LUPUS ANTICOAGULANTS

The lupus anticoagulant may be discovered incidentally when routine coagulation assays reveal prolongations in the PT and/or the aPTT, when young women experience recurrent spontaneous miscarriages and/or pregnancy-related thromboembolic events, when young women and elderly men are detected with cerebral arterial thromboses, when patients are affected by systemic lupus erythematosus (20 to 40%) or other autoimmune diseases or lymphoproliferative malignancies, and when patients have been receiving long-term therapy with psychotropic medications (e.g., chlorpromazine). Lupus anticoagulant also can occur with the active opportunistic infections and malignancies associated with AIDS.

The lupus anticoagulant is an IgG or IgM antiphospholipid antibody directed against the phospholipids that function as templates for activation of the prothrombinase complex in vivo and in coagulation assays in vitro. Anticardiolipin antibodies, which are a subset of the antiphospholipid antibody family, can be purified with cardiolipin liposomes and show anticoagulant activity similar to that of lupus anticoagulants. Data suggest, however, that anticardiolipin antibody and lupus anticoagulant may represent separate types of antibodies with different specificities and binding kinetics to phospholipid. Occasionally, individuals may have discordant test results for lupus anticoagulant and the anticardiolipin and antiphospholipid antibodies, particularly during an acute thrombotic event. For practical purposes, one or a combination of these antibodies can be associated with thrombotic complications. These antibodies are diagnosed when mixing studies of patient and normal plasma reveal immediate inhibition of the aPTT or the PT at baseline with no additional prolongation after a 2-hour incubation (in contrast to factor VIII autoantibody). Confirmatory assays include the kaolin clotting time (the most sensitive test), the dilute Russell's viper venom time, the dilute tissue thromboplastin inhibition assay, the textarin:ecarin venom clotting time ratio, and the platelet neutralization assay. All of these laboratory tests depend on the presence of phospholipid; antiphospholipid antibodies block the binding of coagulation factors and the modulators of coagulation (protein S and activated protein C) to their assembly surface template. The lupus anticoagulant precipitates bleeding complications in the presence of acquired prothrombin (factor II) deficiency, probably because of accelerated clearance of lupus anticoagulant–prothrombin complexes from the circulation, and when the lupus anticoagulant targets platelet membranes and produces quantitative and/or qualitative platelet abnormalities.

The pathologic mechanism for thrombotic complications is not clear; however, the lupus anticoagulant may activate platelets and/or damage the endothelial cell so that prostacyclin synthesis is inhibited, tissue factor is released, or thrombomodulin-activated protein C binding is blocked. β_2-Glycoprotein 1, a serum protein that mediates binding of anticardiolipin antibodies to phospholipid, may be crucial to the development of thrombotic complications. β_2-Glycoprotein 1 inhibits coagulation and platelet aggregation, but antiphospholipid/anti–β_2-glycoprotein 1 antibodies interfere with these activities and promote development of thrombotic complications.

The approach to the management of lupus anticoagulant or antiphospholipid antibody varies according to the severity of symptoms and the clinical circumstances. In the setting of pregnancy, treatment with low-dose unfractionated heparin (5000 U subcutaneously every 12 hours) and daily aspirin (81 mg) has resulted in 80% fetal survival.[2] The use of corticosteroids is controversial and is not recommended because of attendant diabetes and hypertension. Supplemental calcium should be administered to minimize the risks of osteoporosis from prolonged heparin use. Clinical trials with low-molecular-weight heparin (LMWH) preparations and immunosuppressive agents such as intravenous gamma globulin are in progress. An FDA-mandated advisory suggested that the use of LMWHs may be associated with a low incidence of teratogenicity and possibly with thrombogenicity; although these complications have not been observed in meta-analyses of LMWH in pregnancy, controlled studies are needed to confirm any potential risk.

Nonpregnant individuals with thrombotic manifestations of lupus anticoagulant or antiphospholipid antibody have a 50% risk of experiencing recurrent events over a 5-year period. Typically, recurrent hypercoagulable episodes occur in a pattern consistent with the initial findings (i.e., venous recurrence follows an initial deep venous thrombosis). Conventional oral anticoagulation to maintain the international normalized ratio (INR) between 2.0 and 3.0 does not effectively prevent recurrent events; a more aggressive regimen intended to achieve an INR of 3.0 to 3.5 is recommended.

The nonvirilizing androgen preparations danazol and stanazol may be helpful in raising depressed factor II levels into the hemostatic range. Asymptomatic individuals may benefit from prophylactic aspirin therapy, which has a favorable risk-to-benefit profile.

COAGULOPATHIES SECONDARY TO ANTICOAGULATION

The most common acquired clinical coagulopathies are secondary to anticoagulation with warfarin and other coumarin analogues and to heparin. Vitamin K–dependent clotting factors II, VII, IX, and X are functionally defective after warfarin because posttranslational carboxylation of their γ-glutamyl residues cannot be accomplished (Chapter 149). The risks for life-threatening bleeding increase proportionally with the intensity of anticoagulation and INRs rising to greater than 6.0. Warfarin effects can be exaggerated by potentiating medications, excessive ethanol use, and simultaneous dietary vitamin K deficiency. Bleeding may be severe or occult and may unmask the presence of pathologic lesions, such as gastrointestinal or genitourinary carcinomas. For acute and profuse bleeding events caused by warfarin with any INR, vitamin K_1, 1 to 5 mg, should be administered subcutaneously or intravenously in conjunction with FFP (10 to 20 mL/kg) or small amounts of factor IX complex concentrates (20 to 50 U/kg). Recombinant factor VIIa concentrate (20 to 30 μg/kg) is a useful salvage therapy to reverse refractory hemorrhage caused by overanticoagulation with warfarin. For minor bleeding or markedly increased INRs without bleeding, warfarin should be withheld for 1 to 2 days and vitamin K_1 administered at 1 or 2 mg subcutaneously or intravenously. A single dose of oral vitamin K_1 (1 mg) also has been used successfully in this scenario, but the INR may not correct significantly for about 48 hours.[3] Administration of FFP may be considered for INRs greater than 9.0 to facilitate reduction of the INR and to minimize potential bleeding in high-risk patients. These maneuvers allow for easy reinitiation of warfarin with appropriate dose adjustment. The frequency of major hemorrhage, the mortality rates, and the incidence of recurrent thromboembolic complications all are reduced greatly when anticoagulated patients on long-term warfarin are managed in anticoagulation clinics. Warfarin effects on the PT can be reversed in vitro by mixing patient plasma with normal plasma. Although the PT is the first coagulation screening parameter that is prolonged after warfarin therapy, this prolongation simply reflects decreased factor VII activity. Protein C activity has a circulating half-life that parallels that of factor VII. In early anticoagulation, a potential paradoxical thrombogenic state is produced despite an increased PT. Simultaneous heparin therapy with a 5-day overlap with warfarin minimizes these risks.

Heparin anticoagulation also can induce life-threatening hemorrhagic complications. The aPTT and thrombin times are prolonged even with minimal amounts of heparin in the circulation or contaminating indwelling catheters from which blood specimens are obtained. The reptilase time can be used to distinguish heparin from other causes of thrombin time prolongation (e.g., fibrin degradation products or abnormal fibrinogens). The PT may be prolonged in the presence of large concentrations of heparin. Heparin functions as a circulating inhibitor so that mixing studies of patient plasma with normal plasma do not result in correction of the aPTT. LMWH preparations do not affect the aPTT but may affect the thrombin time, depending on the thrombin concentration used in the assay (Chapter 33). The anticoagulant properties of LMWHs can be monitored by the anti–factor Xa assay. Acute and profuse bleeding episodes secondary to heparin can be reversed by administering protamine sulfate (1 mg/100 U of residual heparin). Overdosing with protamine sulfate can produce its own coagulopathy. Otherwise, the circulating survival time of standard heparin in plasma is short enough (2 to 4 hours) to allow the anticoagulant state to dissipate on its own. The half-life of LMWH is longer, but bleeding is uncommon unless the patient has renal dysfunction. The anticoagulation effects of LMWH may be reversed with protamine sulfate, although the response may be marginal and unpredictable. Recombinant factor VIIa (30 to 90 μg/kg) has been used anecdotally to reverse refractory bleeding associated with LMWH.

FUTURE DIRECTIONS

The severe hemophilias are well suited for gene therapy because the genes for factors VIII and IX have been cloned; a small incremental rise in the activities of these coagulation factors can ameliorate clinical manifestations greatly; the levels of clotting factor activity are not precisely regulated in vivo; and the close longitudinal follow-up of these patients in Hemophilia Treatment Centers has documented their usual pattern of bleeding and their clotting factor replacement needs. Since 1998, five gene therapy studies have been initiated in the United States to establish the proof of principle that hemophilia A and hemophilia B can benefit from this approach. So far, these efforts have shown undetectable to small incremental increases in clotting factor activity levels in plasma, but no rise has been durable. Many patients in these clinical trials, even patients without rises in coagulation activity, report fewer bleeds and reduced use of clotting factor concentrates; a placebo effect cannot be excluded. Multiple vectors have been used without establishing clear benefit for any one approach.

1. Mannucci PM, Chediak J, Hanna W, et al: Treatment of von Willebrand disease with a high-purity factor VIII/von Willebrand factor concentrate: A prospective, multicenter study. Blood 2002;99:450–456.
2. Rai R, Cohen H, Dave M, Regan L: Randomized controlled trial of aspirin and aspirin plus heparin in pregnant women with recurrent miscarriage associated with phospholipid antibodies (or antiphospholipid antibodies). BMJ 1997;314:253–257.
3. Crowther MA, Douketis JD, Schnurr T, et al: Oral vitamin K lowers the international normalized ratio more rapidly than subcutaneous vitamin K in the treatment of warfarin-associated coagulopathy: A randomized, controlled trial. Ann Intern Med 2002;137:251–254.

SUGGESTED READINGS
DiMichele D: Inhibitors: Resolving diagnostic and therapeutic dilemmas. Haemophilia 2002;8:280–287. *Review of the epidemiology, immunology, predisposing factors, and therapeutic options for alloantibody inhibitors in hemophilia A and B.*

Evatt BL, Farrugia A, Shapiro AD, Wilde JT: Haemophilia 2002: Emerging risks of treatment. Haemophilia 2002;8:221–229. *A complete review of potential complications of hemophilia treatment, including infectious agents, alloantibody inhibitor formation, thrombotic and infectious complications, and the effects of protease inhibitors on the bleeding complications of hemophilia.*

Hirsh J, Fuster V, Ansell J, et al: American Heart Association/American College of Cardiology Foundation guide to warfarin therapy. J Am Coll Cardiol 2003;41:1633–1652. *Consensus guidelines.*

Miller DG, Stamatoyannopoulos G: Gene therapy for hemophilia. N Engl J Med 2001;344:1782–1784. *A detailed examination of the different approaches to gene therapy in hemophilia A and B and a discussion of the accomplishments to date and expectations.*

179 HEMORRHAGIC DISORDERS: DISSEMINATED INTRAVASCULAR COAGULATION, LIVER FAILURE, AND VITAMIN K DEFICIENCY

Andrew I. Schafer

DISSEMINATED INTRAVASCULAR COAGULATION

Disseminated intravascular coagulation (DIC), also referred to as *consumptive coagulopathy* or *defibrination*, is caused by a wide variety of serious disorders (Table 179–1). In most patients, the underlying process dominates the clinical picture, but in some cases (e.g., occult malignancy, envenomation), DIC may be the initial manifestation of the disorder.

Pathophysiology

DIC is primarily a thrombotic process, although its clinical manifestation may be widespread hemorrhage in acute, fulminant cases. The basic pathophysiology (Fig. 179–1), regardless of cause, is entry into the circulation of procoagulant substances that trigger systemic activation of the coagulation system and platelets and lead to the disseminated deposition of fibrin-platelet thrombi. In most cases, the procoagulant stimulus is tissue factor, a lipoprotein that is not normally exposed to blood. In DIC, tissue factor gains access to blood by tissue injury, its elaboration by malignant cells, or its expression on the surfaces of monocytes and endothelial cells by inflammatory mediators. Tissue factor triggers generation of the coagula-

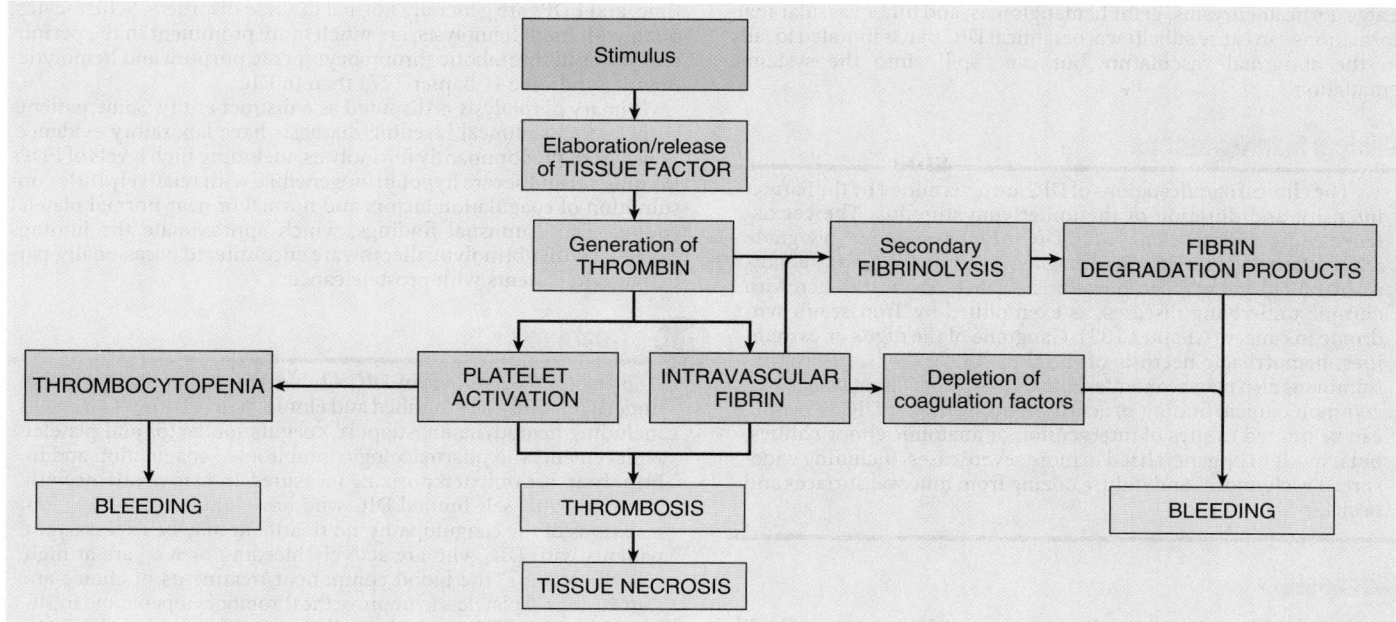

FIGURE 179–1 • Pathophysiology of bleeding, thrombosis, and ischemic manifestations in disseminated intravascular coagulation.

Table 179–1 • **MAJOR CAUSES OF DISSEMINATED INTRAVASCULAR COAGULATION**

Infections
  Gram-negative bacterial sepsis
  Other bacteria, fungi, viruses, Rocky Mountain spotted fever, malaria
Obstetric complications
  Amniotic fluid embolism
  Retained dead fetus
  Abruptio placentae
  Toxemia, preeclampsia
  Septic abortion
Malignancies
  Pancreatic carcinoma
  Adenocarcinomas
  Acute promyelocytic leukemia
  Other neoplasms
Liver failure
Acute pancreatitis
Envenomation
Transfusion reactions
Respiratory distress syndrome
Trauma, shock
  Brain injury
  Crush injury
  Burns
  Hypothermia/hyperthermia
  Fat embolism
  Hypoxia, ischemia
  Surgery
Vascular disorders
  Giant hemangioma (Kasabach-Merritt syndrome)
  Aortic aneurysm
  Vascular tumors

---

tion protease thrombin, which induces fibrin formation and platelet activation. In some specific cases of DIC, procoagulants other than tissue factor (e.g., a cysteine protease or mucin in certain malignancies) and proteases other than thrombin (e.g., trypsin in pancreatitis, exogenous proteins in envenomation) provide the procoagulant stimulus.

In acute, uncompensated DIC, coagulation factors are consumed at a rate in excess of the capacity of the liver to synthesize them, and platelets are consumed in excess of the capacity of bone marrow megakaryocytes to release them. The resulting laboratory manifestations are a prolonged prothrombin time (PT) and activated partial thromboplastin time (aPTT) and thrombocytopenia. Increased fibrin formation in DIC stimulates the compensatory process of secondary fibrinolysis, in which plasminogen activators generate plasmin to digest fibrin (and fibrinogen) into fibrin(ogen) degradation products (FDPs). FDPs are potent circulating anticoagulants that contribute further to the bleeding manifestations of DIC. Intravascular fibrin deposition can cause fragmentation of red blood cells and lead to the appearance of schistocytes in blood smears; however, frank hemolytic anemia is unusual in DIC. Microvascular thrombosis in DIC can compromise the blood supply to some organs and lead to multiorgan failure, particularly when accompanied by systemic hemodynamic and metabolic derangements.

Etiology

DIC always has an underlying etiology, which generally must be identified and eliminated to treat the coagulopathy successfully. The development of DIC in many of these disorders is associated with an unfavorable outcome. Infection is the most common cause of DIC. The syndrome particularly is associated with gram-negative or gram-positive sepsis, although it can be triggered by a variety of other bacterial, fungal, viral, rickettsial, and protozoal microorganisms. The placenta and uterine contents are rich sources of tissue factor and other procoagulants that normally are excluded from the maternal circulation; a spectrum of clinical manifestations of DIC may accompany obstetric complications, especially in the third trimester. These syndromes range from acute, fulminant, and often fatal DIC in amniotic fluid embolism to chronic or subacute DIC with a retained dead fetus. Other obstetric problems associated with DIC include abruptio placentae, toxemia, and septic abortion. Chronic forms of DIC accompany a variety of malignancies, particularly pancreatic cancer (Chapter 201) and mucin-secreting adenocarcinomas of the gastrointestinal tract (Chapter 200), in which thrombotic manifestations predominate. Treatment with all-*trans*-retinoic acid has reduced greatly the incidence of severe DIC in patients with acute promyelocytic leukemia (Chapter 193). It is not known whether liver failure can cause DIC or whether its coexistence merely exacerbates intravascular coagulation because of impaired clearance of activated clotting factors, plasmin, and FDPs. Snake venom contains a variety of substances that can affect coagulation and endothelial permeability. Bites from rattlesnakes and other vipers can induce profound DIC by introducing these exogenous toxins and by endogenous tissue factor released by tissue necrosis. The likelihood and degree of DIC caused by trauma, surgery, and shock are related to the extent of tissue damage and the organs involved; the brain is a particularly rich source of tissue factor so that traumatic brain injury can precipitate acute DIC.

Large aortic aneurysms, giant hemangiomas, and other vascular malformations can cause subclinical or clinical DIC that is initiated locally in the abnormal vasculature but can "spill" into the systemic circulation.

Clinical Manifestations

The clinical manifestations of DIC are determined by the nature, intensity, and duration of the underlying stimulus. The coexistence of liver disease enhances DIC of any etiology. Low-grade DIC is often asymptomatic and diagnosed only by laboratory abnormalities. Thrombotic complications of DIC occur most often with chronic underlying diseases, as exemplified by Trousseau's syndrome in cancer (Chapter 188). Gangrene of the digits or extremities, hemorrhagic necrosis of the skin (Fig. 179–2), or purpura fulminans also may be manifestations of DIC. Bleeding is the most common clinical finding in acute, uncompensated DIC. Bleeding can be limited to sites of intervention or anatomic abnormalities, but it tends to be generalized in more severe cases, including widespread ecchymoses and diffuse oozing from mucosal surfaces and orifices.

Diagnosis

The laboratory diagnosis of severe, acute DIC is not usually difficult. Consumption and inhibition of the function of clotting factors cause prolongation of the PT, aPTT, and thrombin time. Consumption of platelets causes thrombocytopenia. Secondary fibrinolysis generates increased titers of FDPs, which can be measured by latex agglutination or D-dimer assays. Some schistocytes may be seen in the peripheral blood smear, but this finding is neither sensitive nor specific for DIC. Chronic or compensated forms of DIC are more difficult to diagnose, with highly variable patterns of abnormalities in "DIC screen" coagulation tests. Increased FDPs and prolonged PT are generally more sensitive measures than are abnormalities of the aPTT and platelet count. Overcompensated synthesis of consumed clotting factors and platelets in some chronic forms of DIC may cause shortening of the PT and aPTT and/or thrombocytosis, even while elevated levels of FDPs indicate secondary fibrinolysis in such cases.

The most difficult differential diagnosis of DIC occurs in patients who have coexisting liver disease. The coagulopathy of liver failure is often indistinguishable from that of DIC, partly because advanced hepatic dysfunction is accompanied by a state of DIC. In liver failure, the combination of decreased synthesis of clotting factors, impaired clearance of activated clotting factors, secondary fibrinolysis, and thrombocytopenia from portal hypertension and hypersplenism may make the coagulopathy practically impossible to differentiate from DIC. In thrombotic microangiopathies, including thrombotic thrombocytopenic purpura and hemolytic-uremic syndrome, platelet consumption and thrombocytopenia are not accompanied by activation of clotting factors or secondary fibrinolysis; the PT, aPTT, thrombin

time, and FDPs are generally normal in these disorders. Schistocytes, often with frank hemolysis, are much more prominent in the peripheral smear in thrombotic thrombocytopenic purpura and hemolytic-uremic syndrome (Chapter 177) than in DIC.

Primary fibrinolysis is disputed as a distinct entity. Some patients with a serious clinical bleeding diathesis have laboratory evidence, however, of predominantly fibrinolysis, including high levels of FDPs (D-dimers) and severe hypofibrinogenemia, with relatively little consumption of coagulation factors and normal or near-normal platelet counts. These unusual findings, which approximate the findings expected with fibrinolytic therapy, are encountered occasionally, particularly in patients with prostate cancer.

Rx Treatment

Successful treatment of DIC (Table 179–2) requires that the underlying cause be identified and eliminated. All other therapies, including hemodynamic support, coagulation factor and platelet replacement, and pharmacologic inhibitors of coagulation and fibrinolysis, are only temporizing measures. In many patients with asymptomatic, self-limited DIC who have only laboratory manifestations of the coagulopathy, no treatment may be necessary. In patients with DIC who are actively bleeding or who are at high risk of bleeding, the blood component treatments of choice are transfusions of platelets to improve the thrombocytopenia and fresh-frozen plasma (FFP) to replace all consumed coagulation factors and correct the prolonged PT and aPTT. Large volumes of plasma (e.g., 6 U/24 hours) may be required to ameliorate bleeding in severe cases. The theoretical concern that these blood products may "fuel the fire" and exacerbate the DIC has not been supported by clinical experience. In some patients who have particularly profound hypofibrinogenemia, the additional transfusion of cryoprecipitate, a plasma concentrate that is enriched in fibrinogen, may be useful. The infusion of antithrombin III concentrate may be considered as an adjunctive measure in selected cases, particularly in DIC associated with sepsis.

The use of pharmacologic inhibitors of coagulation and fibrinolysis in DIC is controversial. Heparin is of theoretical benefit because it blocks thrombin activity and quenches intravascular coagulation and the resultant secondary fibrinolysis. In practice, heparin might exacerbate the bleeding tendency in acute DIC. Heparin usually is reserved for special forms of DIC, including forms manifested by thrombosis or acrocyanosis and forms that accompany cancer, vascular malformations, retained dead fetus, and possibly acute promyelocytic leukemia. Antifibrinolytic agents, including ε-aminocaproic acid and tranexamic acid, generally are contraindicated in DIC. By blocking the secondary fibrinolytic response to DIC, these drugs cause unopposed fibrin deposition and may precipitate thrombosis. Antifibrinolytic agents may be effective in decreasing life-threatening bleeding in DIC, however, particularly in extreme cases in which aggressive blood component replacement fails to control the hemorrhage; the simultaneous infusion of low doses of heparin may reduce the risk of thrombosis in these situations.

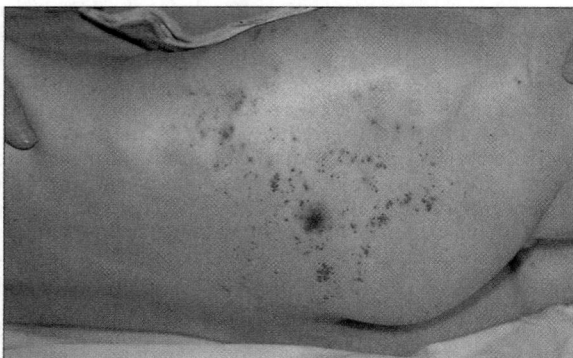

FIGURE 179–2 • Disseminated intravascular coagulation resulting from staphylococcal septicemia. Note the characteristic skin hemorrhage ranging from small purpuric lesions to larger ecchymoses. (From Forbes CD, Jackson WF: Color Atlas and Text of Clinical Medicine, 3rd ed. London, Mosby, 2003, with permission.)

Table 179–2 • TREATMENT OF DISSEMINATED INTRAVASCULAR COAGULATION

Identify and eliminate the underlying cause
No treatment if mild, asymptomatic, and self-limited
Hemodynamic support, as indicated, in severe cases
Blood component therapy
  Indications: Active bleeding or high risk of bleeding
    Fresh-frozen plasma
    Platelets
    In some cases, consider cryoprecipitate, antithrombin III
Drug therapy
  Indications: Heparin for DIC manifested by thrombosis or
    acrocyanosis; antifibrinolytic agents generally contraindicated
    except with life-threatening bleeding and failure of blood
    component therapy

DIC = disseminated intravascular coagulation.

LIVER FAILURE

Bleeding complications in patients with advanced liver disease (Chapters 156 and 157) can be severe and even fatal, directly accounting for about 20% of the deaths associated with hepatic failure. The extent of the bleeding tendency depends on the severity and type of liver disease involved. About one third of deaths in patients undergoing liver transplantation are attributable to perioperative hemorrhage.

Pathophysiology

The pathophysiology of bleeding in liver failure is complex and multifactorial. Anatomic abnormalities are frequently the major cause of gastrointestinal bleeding in patients with liver disease. These changes usually result from portal hypertension. Upper gastrointestinal bleeding can be caused by esophageal varices or hemorrhagic gastritis (congestive gastropathy), whereas lower gastrointestinal bleeding, although seldom life-threatening, can be due to hemorrhoids. Conversely, portal hypertension may result from primary coagulation abnormalities (i.e., thrombosis), as may occur in the myeloproliferative disorders and paroxysmal nocturnal hemoglobinuria (Chapter 180).

The complexity of the systemic coagulopathy of liver failure is not surprising inasmuch as the liver is the principal organ site for the synthesis of coagulation and fibrinolytic factors and their protein inhibitors (Table 179–3). Hepatocytes produce all of the clotting factors except von Willebrand factor, and advanced parenchymal liver disease results in impaired synthesis of these proteins (Chapter 178). Liver disease also can produce impairment in vitamin K–dependent γ-carboxylation of the procoagulant factors II, VII, IX, and X. Functional abnormalities of fibrinogen, termed *dysfibrinogenemias*, frequently are found in various forms of liver disease, particularly in hepatomas. Most forms of advanced liver disease are accompanied by some degree of DIC caused by impaired synthesis of inhibitors of blood coagulation and defective hepatocellular clearance of activated coagulation factors. DIC is an especially important potential complication of LeVeen shunts used to treat intractable ascites because this procedure introduces procoagulant-rich ascitic fluid into the systemic circulation. In many of these cases, shunt ligation is required to terminate the DIC. DIC and bleeding risk are exacerbated by the enhanced fibrinolytic activity of liver disease that is caused by increased levels of tissue plasminogen activator accompanied by decreased synthesis of inhibitors of plasminogen activator and plasmin.

Quantitative and qualitative abnormalities of platelets also contribute to the bleeding diathesis of liver failure. Congestive splenomegaly secondary to portal hypertension causes increased pooling of platelets in the spleen (hypersplenism). The resultant thrombocytopenia, the degree of which generally correlates with spleen size, rarely causes a reduction in the platelet count to less than 50,000/mm³. In alcoholic patients, suppression of bone marrow thrombopoiesis by the acute toxic effects of alcohol or folate deficiency may contribute to the thrombocytopenia. Qualitative platelet abnormalities also have been described in patients with liver disease.

Liver transplantation (Chapter 157) poses special problems to the coagulation system. During the anhepatic stage of surgery, which lasts about 2 hours, the complete cessation of synthesis of coagulation factors causes further prolongations in the PT and aPTT. Release of tissue plasminogen activator from the newly grafted liver leads to increased fibrinolysis and transient exacerbation of bleeding risk in the postoperative period.

Table 179–3 • COAGULATION ABNORMALITIES IN LIVER DISEASE

ABNORMALITIES OF COAGULATION
Decreased synthesis of coagulation factors
Impaired vitamin K–dependent γ-carboxylation
Dysfibrinogenemia
Disseminated intravascular coagulation
Increased fibrinolytic activity

ABNORMALITIES OF PLATELETS
Thrombocytopenia (hypersplenism)
Abnormal platelet function

Clinical Manifestations

The most common hemorrhagic complication of liver disease is gastrointestinal bleeding, which usually is caused by anatomic abnormalities and exacerbated by the systemic coagulopathy of liver failure. Bleeding from other mucosal sites, extensive ecchymoses, or more serious hemorrhage into the retroperitoneum or central nervous system generally indicates more significant derangements of the coagulation system.

Severe coagulopathy in liver disease makes liver biopsy a potentially hazardous procedure. The PT and platelet count are the best guides to bleeding risk. In general, liver biopsy can be performed safely if the PT and aPTT do not exceed 1.5 times control and the platelet count is greater than 50,000/mm³. FFP can be infused to correct the prolonged PT and aPTT. Bleeding time is not a reliable predictor of bleeding risk after biopsy.

Diagnosis

Although the PT and the aPTT are often prolonged in advanced liver disease, the former tends to be a more sensitive assay early in the course; a disproportionate prolongation of the aPTT should raise suspicion of a coexisting coagulation abnormality, such as a lupus anticoagulant or clotting factor inhibitor. The prolonged PT is also a useful prognostic indicator of poor outcome in patients with cirrhosis, acute acetaminophen hepatotoxicity, and acute viral hepatitis; in the latter, it is a better index of prognosis than the serum albumin or transaminases. A disproportionate prolongation of the thrombin time should suggest the presence of dysfibrinogenemia. Hypersplenism, possibly associated with nutritional folate deficiency or the acute toxic effects of alcohol on bone marrow, often causes mild-to-moderate thrombocytopenia in patients with liver disease; however, consideration should be given to other coexisting causes of thrombocytopenia if the platelet count is significantly less than 50,000/mm³.

The coagulopathy of liver failure is sometimes indistinguishable from that of DIC, in part because some degree of DIC is a necessary accompaniment of advanced liver disease. In general, patients with DIC have more marked decreases in levels of factor VIII and increases in titers of FDPs, however, particularly D-dimers, than do patients with liver failure.

 ## Treatment

Therapy for the coagulopathy of liver disease may be directed at preventing the hemorrhagic complications of invasive procedures or treating active bleeding. The most effective treatment is blood component therapy with FFP (which contains all of the coagulation factors) and platelet transfusions (Chapter 165). Some patients require large volumes of FFP (15 to 20 mL/kg) to lower the prolonged PT; rarely, plasmapheresis with plasma exchange is required to avoid fluid overload in these situations. Because of the short half-lives of some clotting factors, FFP may have to be administered every 8 to 12 hours to maintain acceptable coagulation test parameters. In some patients, especially those with cholestasis, parenteral administration of vitamin K can reverse at least partially the coagulation abnormalities; however, in patients with advanced hepatocellular failure, vitamin K is largely ineffective. Prothrombin complex concentrates are relatively contraindicated in liver failure, as in DIC, because of the risk of thrombotic complications. Because of immediate pooling of transfused platelets in the enlarged spleens of patients with hypersplenism, a higher than calculated dose of platelet concentrates usually is required to increase the circulating platelet counts significantly. Desmopressin (DDAVP), which can shorten the bleeding time of patients with cirrhosis, may be used as ancillary therapy.

VITAMIN K DEFICIENCY

Vitamin K is required for γ-carboxylation of glutamic acid residues of the procoagulant factors II (prothrombin), VII, IX, and X and the anticoagulant factors protein C and protein S. This post-translational modification normally renders these proteins functionally active in coagulation. The PT is more sensitive than the aPTT in detecting vitamin K deficiency states because factor VII, the only one of the vitamin K–dependent factors that is in the extrinsic pathway of coagulation, is the most labile of these proteins.

The two major sources of vitamin K are dietary intake and synthesis by the bacterial flora of the intestine. In the absence of malabsorption, nutritional deficiency alone rarely causes clinically significant vitamin K deficiency. This condition can arise, however, when eradication of gut flora is combined with inadequate dietary intake. This situation typically occurs in critically ill patients in intensive care units who have no oral intake and are receiving broad-spectrum antibiotics for prolonged periods. Vitamin K deficiency also can develop in patients receiving total parenteral nutrition unless the infusions are supplemented with vitamin K.

Vitamin K is absorbed predominantly in the ileum and requires the presence of bile salts. Clinically significant vitamin K deficiency occurs with malabsorption of fat-soluble vitamins secondary to obstructive jaundice (Chapter 158) or with malabsorption caused by intrinsic small bowel diseases, including celiac sprue, short-bowel syndrome, and inflammatory bowel disease (Chapters 141 and 142). Finally, warfarin acts as an anticoagulant by competitive antagonism of vitamin K.

Correction of vitamin K deficiency, when clinically significant, can be achieved with oral supplementation, unless malabsorption is present. In the latter case, parenteral vitamin K (10 mg subcutaneously daily) should be administered. Emergency treatment of bleeding caused by vitamin K deficiency is transfusion of FFP.

SUGGESTED READINGS

Amitrano L, Guardascione MA, Brancaccio V, Balzano A: Coagulation disorders in liver disease. Semin Liver Dis 2002;22:83–96. *Reviews mechanisms, clinical manifestations, and therapeutic approach to the coagulopathy of liver disease.*

Bick RL: Disseminated intravascular coagulation: Current concepts of etiology, pathophysiology, diagnosis, and treatment. Hematol Oncol Clin North Am 2003;17:149–176. *A comprehensive review.*

Crowther MA, Douketis JD, Schnurr T, et al: Oral vitamin K lowers the international normalized ratio more rapidly than subcutaneous vitamin K in the treatment of warfarin-associated coagulopathy. A randomized, controlled trial. Ann Intern Med 2002;137:251–254. *Clinical guidelines for strategies to reverse excessive warfarin anticoagulation.*

Toh CH: Laboraory testing in disseminated intravascular coagulation. Semin Thromb Hemost 2002;27:653–656. *Discusses the advantages and disadvantages of available assays in DIC.*

180 THROMBOTIC DISORDERS: HYPERCOAGULABLE STATES

Andrew I. Schafer

The *hypercoagulable states* encompass a group of inherited or acquired disorders that cause a pathologic thrombotic tendency or risk of thrombosis. These conditions also are known as *prethrombotic* states. A hereditary tendency to thrombosis, regardless of its cause, sometimes is referred to as *thrombophilia*.

The primary hypercoagulable states (Chapter 162) are caused by quantitative or qualitative abnormalities of specific coagulation proteins that induce a prothrombotic state. Most of these disorders involve inherited mutations that lead to either (1) deficiency of a physiologic antithrombotic factor or (2) increased level of a prothrombotic factor (Table 180-1). Particularly when combined with other prothrombotic mutations (multigene interactions), these primary hypercoagulable states are associated with a lifelong predisposition to thrombosis. The trigger for a discrete, clinical thrombotic event is often the development of one of the acquired, secondary hypercoagulable states superimposed on an inherited state of hypercoagulability. The secondary hypercoagulable states, a diverse group of mostly acquired conditions (Fig. 180-1), cause a thrombotic tendency by complex, often multifactorial mechanisms.

PRIMARY HYPERCOAGULABLE STATES

Molecular Mechanisms and Frequency

ANTITHROMBIN III DEFICIENCY. Inherited quantitative or qualitative deficiency of antithrombin III leads to increased fibrin accumulation and

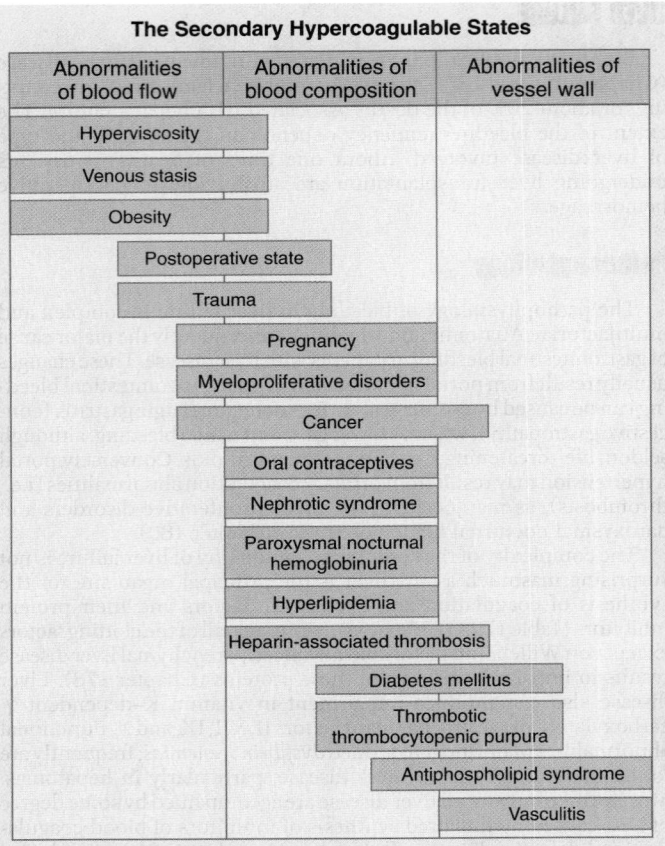

The Secondary Hypercoagulable States

Abnormalities of blood flow	Abnormalities of blood composition	Abnormalities of vessel wall
Hyperviscosity		
Venous stasis		
Obesity		
Postoperative state		
Trauma		
	Pregnancy	
	Myeloproliferative disorders	
	Cancer	
	Oral contraceptives	
	Nephrotic syndrome	
	Paroxysmal nocturnal hemoglobinuria	
	Hyperlipidemia	
	Heparin-associated thrombosis	
		Diabetes mellitus
		Thrombotic thrombocytopenic purpura
		Antiphospholipid syndrome
		Vasculitis

FIGURE 180–1 • Secondary hypercoagulable states. The pathophysiologic basis of thrombotic risk in these diverse disorders is complex and multifactorial. Predominant mechanisms of thrombosis for the different secondary hypercoagulable states shown are based on Virchow's triad of thrombogenesis: abnormalities in blood flow, abnormalities in blood composition, and abnormalities of the vessel wall. (Modified from Schafer AI: The primary and secondary hypercoagulable states. *In* Schafer AI [ed]: Molecular Mechanisms of Hypercoagulable States. New York, Chapman & Hall, 1997, p 16.)

Table 180–1 • MOST COMMON PRIMARY HYPERCOAGULABLE STATES

DEFICIENCY OF ANTITHROMBOTIC FACTORS
Antithrombin (III) deficiency
Protein C deficiency
Protein S deficiency

INCREASED PROTHROMBOTIC FACTORS
Factor Va (activated protein C resistance; factor V Leiden)
Prothrombin (prothrombin G20210A mutation)
Hyperhomocysteinemia
Factors VIII, XI, IX, fibrinogen, thrombin-activatable fibrinolysis inhibitor

a lifelong propensity to thrombosis (Chapter 162). Antithrombin is the major physiologic inhibitor of thrombin and other activated coagulation factors, and its deficiency leads to unregulated protease activity and fibrin formation. Patients with type I antithrombin deficiency have proportionately reduced plasma levels of antigenic and functional antithrombin that result from a quantitative deficiency of the normal protein. Impaired synthesis, defective secretion, or instability of antithrombin in type I antithrombin–deficient individuals is caused by major gene deletions, single nucleotide changes, or short insertions or deletions in the antithrombin gene. Patients with type II antithrombin deficiency have normal or nearly normal plasma antigen accompanied by low activity levels, indicating a functionally defective molecule. Type II antithrombin deficiency is subdivided further into subtypes in which abnormalities affect the reactive protease inhibitory activity, the heparin binding site, or both. Type II deficiency usually is caused by specific point mutations leading to single amino acid substitutions that produce a dysfunctional protein. More than 80 different mutations causing type I or type II antithrombin deficiency have been recognized to date.

The pattern of inheritance of antithrombin deficiency is autosomal dominant. Most affected individuals are heterozygotes whose antithrombin levels are typically about 40 to 60% of normal but may have the full clinical manifestations of hypercoagulability. Rare homozygous antithrombin-deficient patients usually have type II deficiency with reduced heparin affinity, a variant that is associated with a low risk of thrombosis in its heterozygous form.

The frequency of asymptomatic heterozygous antithrombin deficiency in the general population may be 1 in 350. Most of these individuals have clinically silent mutations and never have thrombotic manifestations. The frequency of symptomatic antithrombin deficiency in the general population has been estimated to be between 1 in 2000 and 1 in 5000. Among all patients seen with venous thromboembolism, antithrombin deficiency is detected in only about 1%, but it is found in about 2.5% of selected patients with recurrent thrombosis and/or thrombosis at a younger age (<45 years old).

PROTEIN C DEFICIENCY. Protein C deficiency leads to unregulated fibrin generation because of impaired inactivation of factors VIIIa and Va, two essential cofactors in the coagulation cascade. As with antithrombin deficiency, two general forms of protein C deficiency are recognized: type I, with proportionate decreases in protein C antigen and activity, and type II, in which qualitative defects in protein C are associated with disproportionately reduced protein C relative to antigen. More than 160 mutations are known to cause protein C deficiency. In the more common type I deficiency, frame-shift, nonsense, or missense mutations cause premature termination of synthesis or loss of protein C stability. In type II deficiency, different mutations can cause abnormalities in protein C activation or function.

The mode of inheritance of protein C deficiency is autosomal dominant. As in antithrombin deficiency, most affected individuals are heterozygotes. The prevalence of protein C deficiency in the general population is 1 in 200 to 1 in 300 when an antigenic assay is used and 1 in 500 when a functional assay with confirmatory DNA analysis is used. Protein C deficiency is found in 3 to 4% of all patients with venous thromboembolism.

PROTEIN S DEFICIENCY. Protein S is the principal cofactor of activated protein C (APC), and its deficiency mimics that of protein C in causing loss of regulation of fibrin generation by impaired inactivation of factors VIIIa and Va. In contrast to protein C, protein S circulates in plasma partly in complex with C4b binding protein; only free protein S, which normally constitutes about 35 to 40% of total protein S, can function as a cofactor of APC. As in antithrombin and protein C deficiencies, quantitative (type I) and qualitative (type II) forms of inherited protein S deficiency are known. In addition, type III protein S deficiency is characterized by normal plasma levels of total protein S but low levels of free protein S.

Relatively few specific mutations of the protein S gene have been described to date, most involving frame-shift, nonsense, or missense point mutations. The prevalence of protein S deficiency in the general population is unknown. Its frequency among all patients evaluated for venous thromboembolism (2 to 3%) is comparable, however, to that of protein C deficiency.

ACTIVATED PROTEIN C RESISTANCE. Inherited APC resistance causing thrombophilia originally was detected by the finding that the activated partial thromboplastin times (aPTTs) of the plasma of affected individuals could not be prolonged appropriately by the addition of exogenous APC in vitro. It subsequently was recognized that most subjects with functional APC resistance have a single, specific point mutation in the factor V gene. This mutation, termed *factor V Leiden,* replaces guanine with adenine at nucleotide 1691 (G1691A), which leads to the amino acid substitution of Arg504 by Gln and renders factor Va incapable of being inactivated by APC. Heterozygosity for the autosomally transmitted factor V Leiden increases the risk of thrombosis by a factor of 5 to 10, whereas homozygosity increases the risk by a factor of 50 to 100.

The factor V Leiden mutation is remarkably frequent (3 to 7%) in healthy white populations but seems to be far less prevalent or even nonexistent in certain black and Asian populations. In various studies, APC resistance was found in a wide range of frequencies (10 to 64%) in patients with venous thromboembolism.

PROTHROMBIN GENE MUTATION. The substitution of G for A at nucleotide 20210 of the prothrombin gene has been associated with elevated plasma levels of prothrombin and an increased risk of venous thrombosis. The allele frequency for the prothrombin gene mutation is 1.2% in a Dutch population, which makes it second only to factor V Leiden as a genetic risk factor for venous thrombosis, at least in certain white populations. The prothrombin G20210A mutation is found in 6 to 8% of all patients with venous thromboembolism.

OTHER PRIMARY HYPERCOAGULABLE STATES. Elevated levels of factor VIII coagulant activity are a significant risk factor for venous thrombosis, and family studies suggest that high factor VIII levels often are genetically determined. Increased levels of factors XI and IX, fibrinogen, and thrombin-activatable fibrinolysis inhibitor also may confer increased risk. Many other inherited abnormalities of specific physiologic antithrombotic systems may be associated with a thrombotic tendency. Most of these conditions are limited to case reports or family studies, their molecular genetic bases are less well defined, and their prevalence rates are unknown but are probably much lower than those of the disorders described earlier, however. The other primary hypercoagulable states include heparin cofactor II deficiency, dysfunctional thrombomodulin, and many fibrinolytic disorders that lead to impaired fibrin degradation, including hypoplasminogenemia, dysplasminogenemia, plasminogen activator deficiency, and certain dysfibrinogenemias that cause a thrombotic rather than a bleeding diathesis.

HYPERHOMOCYSTEINEMIA. Hyperhomocysteinemia is due to elevated blood levels of homocysteine, a sulfhydryl amino acid derived from methionine by a transmethylation pathway (Fig. 180–2).

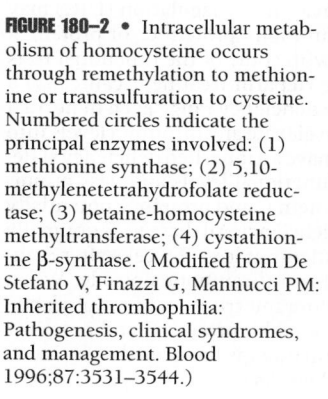

FIGURE 180–2 • Intracellular metabolism of homocysteine occurs through remethylation to methionine or transsulfuration to cysteine. Numbered circles indicate the principal enzymes involved: (1) methionine synthase; (2) 5,10-methylenetetrahydrofolate reductase; (3) betaine-homocysteine methyltransferase; (4) cystathionine β-synthase. (Modified from De Stefano V, Finazzi G, Mannucci PM: Inherited thrombophilia: Pathogenesis, clinical syndromes, and management. Blood 1996;87:3531–3544.)

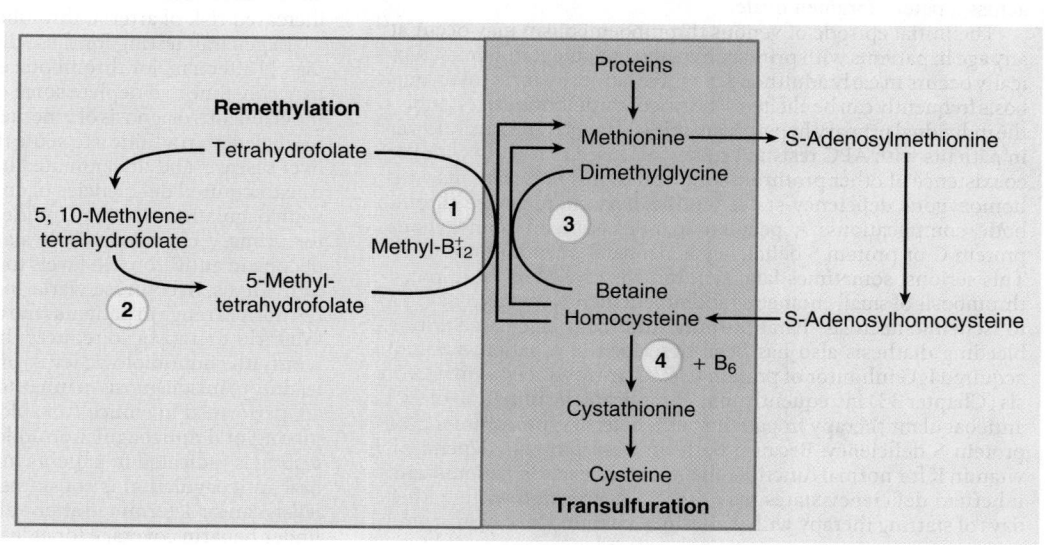

Homocysteine is remethylated into methionine or catabolized into cystathionine. The major remethylation pathway requires folate and cobalamin (vitamin B$_{12}$) and involves the action of methylenetetrahydrofolate reductase (MTHFR); a minor remethylation pathway is mediated by betaine-homocysteine methyltransferase. Alternatively, homocysteine is converted to cystathionine in a transsulfuration pathway catalyzed by cystathionine β-synthase (CBS), with pyridoxine used as a cofactor. Inherited hyperhomocysteinemia most commonly is caused by deficiency of cystathionine β-synthase, whereas a few cases are caused by hereditary defects in the remethylation pathways.

Homozygous CBS deficiency states that lead to severe hyperhomocysteinemia (homocystinuria) cause premature arterial atherosclerotic disease and venous thromboembolism and mental retardation, neurologic defects, lens ectopy, and skeletal abnormalities. Adults with heterozygous CBS deficiency, with resultant mild-to-moderate hyperhomocysteinemia, may have only venous or arterial thrombotic manifestations, however. The frequency of heterozygous CBS deficiency, which can be due to any of several point mutations in the CBS gene, is about 0.3 to 1.4% in the general population. Hyperhomocysteinemia resulting from inherited remethylation pathway defects usually involves reduced MTHFR activity. In homozygous individuals with the autosomal recessive C677T mutation of the *MTHFR* gene, which occurs in 15% of certain populations, moderate hyperhomocysteinemia, which is correctable with folic acid, may occur. Its relation to venous thrombosis is controversial, however. Acquired causes of hyperhomocysteinemia in adults most commonly involve nutritional deficiencies of the cofactors required for homocysteine metabolism, including pyridoxine, cobalamin, and folate.

Acquired and inherited hyperhomocysteinemia is a likely risk factor for arterial and venous thrombosis (Chapters 47 and 78). The mechanism of homocysteine-induced thrombosis and atherogenesis involves complex, probably multifactorial effects on the vessel wall. Homocysteine can cause vascular endothelial injury, conversion of the endothelial surface of blood vessels from an antithrombotic to a prothrombotic one, and smooth muscle cell proliferation. These toxic effects of homocysteine on the vessel wall may be mediated by oxidant stress.

Clinical Manifestations

The primary hypercoagulable states are associated with predominantly venous thromboembolic complications (Chapter 78). Deep vein thrombosis of the lower extremities and pulmonary embolism are the most frequent clinical manifestations. More unusual sites of venous thrombosis include superficial thrombophlebitis and mesenteric and cerebral vein thrombosis (see Table 162–2). Arterial thrombosis involving the coronary, cerebrovascular, and peripheral circulations is not linked to any of the primary hypercoagulable states except hyperhomocysteinemia, although some reports have described their occurrence with protein S deficiency and homozygous antithrombin deficiency. Venous thrombosis also may result in arterial occlusion by paradoxical embolism across a patent foramen ovale.

The initial episode of venous thromboembolism may occur at any age in patients with primary hypercoagulable states, but it typically occurs in early adulthood. Positive family histories of thrombosis frequently can be elicited. The risk of thrombosis varies among the individual primary hypercoagulable states and is relatively lower in patients with APC resistance; it is increased markedly with the coexistence of other prothrombotic mutations. Rare patients with homozygous deficiency states tend to have more severe thrombotic complications. A peculiar manifestation of homozygous protein C or protein S deficiency is neonatal purpura fulminans. This serious, sometimes fatal syndrome is caused by widespread thrombosis of small cutaneous and subcutaneous vessels that leads to ischemic necrosis. Fatal purpura fulminans associated with a bleeding diathesis also has been described in a patient with an acquired IgG inhibitor of protein C. Warfarin-induced skin necrosis (Chapter 33) infrequently may complicate the initiation of oral anticoagulant therapy in patients with heterozygous protein C or protein S deficiency. Because both of these proteins depend on vitamin K for normal function, their plasma levels in patients with inherited deficiency states may drop to nearly zero within a few days of starting therapy with warfarin, a vitamin K antagonist, and

lead to a transient prothrombotic imbalance and skin necrosis caused by dermal vascular thrombosis. Nevertheless, oral anticoagulation provides effective long-term antithrombotic prophylaxis in these patients.

In most patients with primary hypercoagulable states, discrete clinical thrombotic complications seem to be precipitated by acquired prothrombotic events (e.g., pregnancy, use of oral contraceptives, surgery, trauma, immobilization), many of which are the secondary hypercoagulable states discussed subsequently. In particular, thrombosis complicates pregnancy, especially in the puerperium, in about 30 to 60% of women with antithrombin deficiency, 10 to 20% with protein C or protein S deficiency, and almost 30% with APC resistance, unless prophylactic anticoagulation is administered during this period. The clinical manifestations and circumstances of venous thromboembolism in hyperhomocysteinemia are essentially indistinguishable from those of the other primary hypercoagulable states. In contrast to the other disorders, hyperhomocysteinemia is also an independent risk factor for arterial thrombosis, including myocardial infarction, stroke, and peripheral arterial disease (Chapter 47).

Diagnosis

Laboratory diagnosis (Chapter 162) of the primary hypercoagulable states requires testing for each of the disorders individually because no general screening test is available to determine whether a patient may have such a condition. At this time, functional, immunologic, or DNA-based assays are available to test for antithrombin deficiency, protein C deficiency, protein S deficiency, APC resistance (factor V Leiden), the prothrombin G20210A mutation, and hyperhomocysteinemia.

The detection of a primary hypercoagulable state (thrombophilia) in an individual who has suffered a single episode of venous thromboembolism has uncertain therapeutic implications. It does not alter the initial anticoagulant therapy. Because it is not established that the presence of a prothrombotic mutation increases the risk of recurrent thrombosis, it also may not modify the duration of prophylactic anticoagulation prescribed after a single venous thromboembolic event. Screening for hereditary thrombophilia may be useful, however, in these patients to help identify other affected relatives and to guide the approach to preventing thrombosis whenever high-risk situations are encountered (e.g., to administer antithrombotic prophylaxis during surgery, pregnancy, or immobilization or possibly to recommend avoiding oral contraceptives or hormone replacement therapy). A reasonable diagnostic approach at this time is to screen at least all "strongly thrombophilic" patients after an episode of venous thromboembolism: individuals with documented events occurring before age 50 or individuals with a positive family history or a history of recurrent thrombosis. Individuals with arterial thrombosis generally should not be tested for any of these disorders except hyperhomocysteinemia and the antiphospholipid syndrome because other primary hypercoagulable states (see Table 180–1) are not associated clearly with an increased risk of arterial thrombosis.

In general, testing for these disorders is not recommended immediately after a major thrombotic event. Active thrombosis transiently may consume and deplete some of the proteins in plasma and lead to the erroneous diagnosis of inherited antithrombin, protein C, or protein S deficiency. In addition to acute thrombosis, pregnancy, estrogen use, liver disease, and disseminated intravascular coagulation (DIC) may cause acquired deficiencies of antithrombin, protein C, or protein S. Anticoagulation also may interfere with some of the functional tests for primary hypercoagulable states. Heparin treatment can cause a decline in antithrombin levels to the deficiency range even in normal individuals. In contrast, warfarin can elevate antithrombin levels into the normal range in patients who do have an inherited deficiency state. Warfarin therapy also reduces the functional levels and, less prominently, the immunologic levels of protein C and protein S, potentially leading to misdiagnosis of inherited deficiency. All these tests optimally are performed in clinically stable patients at least 2 weeks after completing oral anticoagulation following a thrombotic episode. When testing is indicated in patients in whom interruption of prophylactic oral anticoagulation is considered too risky, protein C and protein S levels can be determined after warfarin therapy has been discontinued under heparin coverage for at least 2 weeks.

Table 180–2 • LONG-TERM MANAGEMENT OF PATIENTS WITH PRIMARY HYPERCOAGULABLE STATES

RISK CLASSIFICATION	MANAGEMENT
High risk ≥2 spontaneous thromboses 1 spontaneous life-threatening thrombosis 1 spontaneous thrombosis at an unusual site (e.g., mesenteric, cerebral venous) 1 spontaneous thrombosis in the presence of more than a single hypercoagulable state	Indefinite anticoagulation or lifelong chronic anticoagulation
Moderate risk 1 thrombosis with an acquired prothrombotic stimulus	Vigorous prophylaxis during high-risk situations
Asymptomatic	

Modified from Bauer K: Approach to thrombosis. *In* Loscalzo J, Schafer AI (eds): Thrombosis and Hemorrhage, 2nd ed. Baltimore, Williams & Wilkins, 1998, pp 477–490.

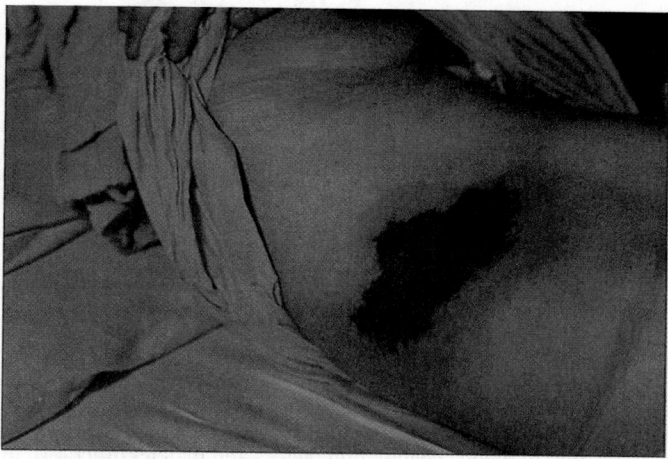

FIGURE 180–3 • Acute skin necrosis in a patient with protein C deficiency who was treated with heparin and warfarin for a deep vein thrombosis that occurred after elective hip surgery. Warfarin treatment was withdrawn, and anticoagulation continued with heparin. Skin grafting to the affected area was required. (From Forbes CD, Jackson WF: Color Atlas and Text of Clinical Medicine, 3rd ed. London, Mosby, 2003, with permission.)

Functional assays are the best screening tests for antithrombin, protein C, and protein S deficiencies because these assays detect quantitative and qualitative defects; antigenic (immunologic) assays detect only quantitative deficiencies of these proteins. Functional coagulation assays for protein C and protein S may yield spuriously low values, however, if APC resistance is present. APC resistance can be diagnosed by the newer, high-sensitivity and high-specificity coagulation assays or by DNA analysis of peripheral blood mononuclear cells for the factor V Leiden mutation. Hyperhomocysteinemia cur-

rently is diagnosed by measurement of total plasma homocysteine after an overnight fast (Chapter 213). Discrimination of affected individuals from normal subjects can be improved if the fasting plasma homocysteine level increment is measured after ingestion of a standardized oral methionine load. DNA diagnosis of the C677T *MTHFR* mutation is also available, but this genetic variant is not established as a significant prothrombotic risk factor.

Rx Treatment

The initial treatment of acute venous thrombosis or pulmonary embolism in patients with primary hypercoagulable states is not different from that in patients without genetic defects (Chapters 33 and 78). As in patients without known thrombophilia, thrombolytic therapy should be considered after massive venous thrombosis or pulmonary embolism. Acute management is initiated with at least 5 days of unfractionated or low-molecular-weight heparin. **1** Oral anticoagulation with warfarin can be started on the first day of heparin use and continued for at least 6 months in patients with venous thromboembolism in the absence of triggering factors (e.g., postoperative state), with regulation of the dose to maintain an international normalized ratio (INR) of the prothrombin time between 2.0 and 3.0.

Continuing oral anticoagulant prophylaxis beyond the initial 6 months after an acute episode of venous thromboembolism must be weighed against continued exposure of the individual patient to the significant risk of bleeding complications. **2** Patients with primary hypercoagulable states who have had two or more thrombotic events should receive lifelong prophylactic anticoagulation with warfarin (Chapter 78). Indefinite or lifelong anticoagulation probably is indicated for individuals with recurrent thrombosis even in the absence of identifiable primary hypercoagulable states.

The decision to continue prophylactic oral anticoagulation beyond the initial period after the first episode of thrombosis is more difficult (Table 180–2). After a single episode of thrombosis, patients with inherited hypercoagulable states probably should receive indefinite or lifelong anticoagulation if their initial episodes were life-threatening or occurred in unusual sites (e.g., mesenteric, cerebral venous thrombosis) or if they have more than one prothrombotic genetic abnormality (Chapter 78). In the absence of these characteristics, particularly if the initial episode was precipitated by a transient acquired prothrombotic situation (e.g., pregnancy, postoperative state, immobilization), it is reasonable at this time to discontinue warfarin therapy after 6 months and to administer subsequent prophylactic anticoagulation only during high-risk periods.

Asymptomatic individuals with known thrombophilia who have not had previous thrombotic complications do not require

prophylactic anticoagulation except during periods of high risk for thrombosis. Because about half of the first-degree relatives of a patient with a primary hypercoagulable state should be affected, these individuals should be counseled about the implications of making a diagnosis.

The management of pregnancy in women with primary hypercoagulable states requires special consideration because of the high risk of thrombosis, particularly in the puerperium. Women with thrombophilia who have had previous thrombosis—and probably also asymptomatic women with thrombophilia—should receive prophylactic anticoagulation throughout pregnancy and for 4 to 6 weeks postpartum, a particularly high-risk period. Heparin is presently the anticoagulant of choice because of the risk of embryopathy in the first trimester and bleeding late in pregnancy with the use of warfarin. The options are adjusted-dose unfractionated heparin given by subcutaneous injection every 8 or 12 hours, with doses adjusted to maintain a midinterval aPTT of 1.5 times the control INR, or fixed-dose, low-molecular-weight heparin.

Because warfarin-induced skin necrosis (Fig. 180–3) is a rare problem, screening of all patients for inherited protein C or protein S deficiency, conditions that are known to predispose to this complication, is not indicated before starting warfarin therapy. Most cases can be avoided by not initiating warfarin therapy with high loading doses and by concomitant coverage with heparin. When the complication does occur, as manifested by painful red and subsequently dark, necrotic skin lesions within a few days of starting warfarin, warfarin therapy must be discontinued immediately, vitamin K administered, and heparin started (Chapter 33). The use of fresh-frozen plasma or purified protein C concentrate to normalize protein C levels rapidly can improve results. Despite this rare complication, warfarin is an effective, long-term prophylactic anticoagulant in patients with inherited protein C or protein S deficiency.

Antithrombin III concentrate purified from normal human plasma may be a useful adjunct to anticoagulation in "heparin-resistant" patients, who represent unusual cases of type II antithrombin deficiency, and in antithrombin-deficient patients with recurrent thrombosis despite adequate anticoagulation. Antithrombin concentrate

Continued

infusion also can be considered in some perioperative or obstetric settings in which anticoagulation poses an unacceptable bleeding risk.

It is not clear at this time whether comparable guidelines for anticoagulation are applicable to patients with hyperhomocysteinemia and venous thrombosis. Vitamin supplementation with folate, pyridoxine, and cobalamin can normalize elevated blood levels of homocysteine, but it is not known whether this treatment reduces the risk of thrombosis. Until this information becomes available, the safety and low cost of supplementation make this treatment advisable for patients with hyperhomocysteinemia associated with thrombosis. The recommended daily doses are folate, 1 mg; pyridoxine, 100 mg; and cobalamin, 0.4 mg.

SECONDARY HYPERCOAGULABLE STATES

The secondary hypercoagulable states (see Fig. 180–1) are diverse, mostly acquired disorders that predispose patients to thrombosis by complex, multifactorial pathophysiologic mechanisms. Many of these conditions also represent the acquired precipitating stimuli for clinical thrombotic events in individuals with a genetic predisposition (primary hypercoagulable states). Although each disorder causes thrombosis primarily through abnormalities in blood flow (rheology), composition of blood (coagulation factors and platelet function), or the vessel wall, multiple overlapping mechanisms are operative in many of them.

MALIGNANCY. Multiple abnormalities of hemostasis are involved in the hypercoagulable state in cancer patients, many of which initiate a systemic process of chronic DIC (Chapters 179 and 188). The thrombotic tendency of patients with cancer also may be related to mechanical factors, such as immobility or a bulky tumor mass compressing vessels, and to comorbid conditions, such as liver dysfunction secondary to metastases, sepsis, surgery, and the prothrombotic effects of certain antineoplastic agents.

The incidence of thrombotic complications in cancer patients depends in part on the type of malignancy. Hypercoagulability seems to be most prominent in patients with pancreatic cancer (Chapter 201), adenocarcinomas of the gastrointestinal tract (Chapters 199 and 200) or lung (Chapter 198), and ovarian cancers (Chapter 205). The presence of underlying malignancy compounds the independent risk of thrombosis in the postoperative state. Although thrombosis most commonly occurs in patients with established malignancy, it also can antedate the diagnosis by months or years (Chapters 78 and 188). There is an increased incidence of occult malignancy in patients who present with idiopathic venous thromboembolism in the absence of known risk factors.

The most common thrombotic manifestations in patients with neoplasms are deep vein thrombosis and pulmonary embolism, but more unusual and distinctive thrombotic complications also are found. Trousseau's syndrome, characterized by migratory superficial thrombophlebitis of the upper or lower extremities, is linked strongly to cancer. Nonbacterial thrombotic endocarditis involves fibrin-platelet vegetations on heart valves, which produce clinical manifestations by systemic embolization (Chapter 188). Of cases of nonbacterial thrombotic endocarditis, 75% have underlying malignancies at autopsy. Trousseau's syndrome and nonbacterial thrombotic endocarditis are highly associated with adenocarcinomas. The occurrence of either syndrome in patients without known cancer demands a more vigorous search for occult malignancy than in patients with deep vein thrombosis or pulmonary embolism. Thrombotic microangiopathy, characterized by hemolysis with red blood cell fragmentation, thrombocytopenia, and microvascular thrombosis with involvement of target organs, occurs in about 5% of patients with metastatic carcinomas, most commonly with gastric, lung, and breast (Chapter 204) primary sites.

Treatment of acute venous thromboembolism in cancer patients should be initiated as in other patients, but subsequent prophylactic anticoagulation should be continued while active malignancy is present. Anticoagulation can be difficult in many cancer patients; these patients may be resistant to warfarin prophylaxis. Anticoagulation also can be complicated by bleeding into tumors. In some cases, only continuous heparin infusion, delivered by pump, is effective in suppressing the thrombotic process.

MYELOPROLIFERATIVE DISORDERS AND PAROXYSMAL NOCTURNAL HEMOGLOBINURIA. Thrombosis and, apparently paradoxically, bleeding are major causes of morbidity and mortality in the myeloproliferative disorders (Chapters 176 and 183) and in the related stem cell disorder, paroxysmal nocturnal hemoglobinuria (Chapter 169). In uncontrolled polycythemia vera (Chapter 176), increased whole blood viscosity contributes to the thrombotic tendency. Thrombocytosis, abnormal platelet function, and other less well understood factors also probably are involved in the hemostatic defect of the myeloproliferative disorders and paroxysmal nocturnal hemoglobinuria.

In addition to deep vein thrombosis and pulmonary embolism, some distinctive thrombotic manifestations are seen. Hepatic vein thrombosis (Budd-Chiari syndrome) (Chapter 156) and portal and other intra-abdominal venous thromboses (Chapter 194) are associated with myeloproliferative disorders and paroxysmal nocturnal hemoglobinuria and may be the initial manifestations of the disease. Myeloproliferative disorders, particularly polycythemia vera and essential thrombocythemia, may cause erythromelalgia, a syndrome of microvascular thrombosis that is manifested by intense pain accompanied by warmth, duskiness, and mottled erythema, sometimes resembling livedo reticularis, in a patchy distribution in the extremities, most prominently in the feet; digital microvascular ischemia progressing to vascular insufficiency and gangrene may ensue (Chapters 77 and 176; see also Fig. 176–3). A wide spectrum of neurologic manifestations may be caused by cerebrovascular ischemia, especially in essential thrombocythemia.

Treatment of venous thromboembolism in the myeloproliferative disorders and paroxysmal nocturnal hemoglobinuria should be initiated as in patients without these hematologic disorders. In patients with thrombosis associated with polycythemia vera, the hematocrit should be maintained in the normal range with phlebotomies and/or chemotherapy; in patients with essential thrombocythemia, cytoreduction of the elevated platelet count should be achieved with chemotherapy. Long-term prophylaxis of recurrent thrombosis in these patients also may be achieved with antiplatelet (aspirin) therapy, but caution should be exercised because of the increased risk of bleeding complications.

ANTIPHOSPHOLIPID SYNDROME. The antiphospholipid syndrome is characterized by venous and arterial thrombosis, recurrent spontaneous abortions (which also may be due to thrombosis), thrombocytopenia, and a variety of neuropsychiatric manifestations. The syndrome is associated with a heterogeneous group of autoantibodies that bind to anionic phospholipid-protein complexes, the crucial protein cofactor of which is probably β_2-glycoprotein I. Patients with this syndrome have any combination of positive tests to detect different plasma antiphospholipid-protein antibodies (e.g., anticardiolipin antibodies) and/or phospholipid-based clotting tests (lupus anticoagulants). The predominant prothrombotic effects of these antibodies probably are directed to the vessel wall.

Deep vein thrombosis and pulmonary embolism are the most common venous thrombotic events in these patients. Cerebrovascular events are the most common arterial thrombotic complications and are manifested as stroke, transient ischemic attacks, multiinfarct dementia, or retinal artery occlusion. Peripheral and intraabdominal vascular occlusion is encountered more rarely. About one third of these patients have nonbacterial heart valve vegetations (Libman-Sacks endocarditis). The most prominent obstetric complications are recurrent spontaneous abortions and fetal growth retardation, which probably are due to thrombosis of placental vessels. Occasional patients present with "catastrophic" antiphospholipid syndrome, involving a series of acute and sometimes fatal vascular occlusive events, or "thrombotic storm." Thrombotic complications are limited largely to patients with primary antiphospholipid syndrome or patients in whom the antibodies are associated with collagenvascular disease, not with drugs or infections.

Acute management of thrombosis in these patients is essentially the same as that in other individuals. Monitoring of heparin anticoagulation is difficult in patients who have a lupus anticoagulant because they already have a prolonged aPTT at baseline; the use of low-molecular-weight heparin, which does not require monitoring, can circumvent this problem. Warfarin is effective in preventing recurrent thrombosis but usually requires prolonged therapy with intermediate-intensity to high-intensity doses to achieve an INR greater than 2.6, with a target INR of 3.0. No established treatment of women with antiphospholipid syndrome has been shown to prevent recurrent fetal loss. Treatment during pregnancy with prednisone and aspirin is not effective in promoting live birth and may increase the risk of prematurity.

PREGNANCY, ORAL CONTRACEPTIVES, AND HORMONE REPLACEMENT THERAPY. The pathophysiology of hypercoagulability associated with pregnancy (Chapter 253) involves a progressive state of DIC throughout the course of pregnancy. Activation of the coagulation system is initiated locally in the uteroplacental circulation, where the placenta is the source of increased thrombin generation. Platelet activation and increased platelet turnover also occur during normal pregnancy, and about 8% of healthy women at term have mild thrombocytopenia. Simultaneously the fibrinolytic system is progressively blunted throughout pregnancy because of the action of placental plasminogen activator inhibitor type 2. The net effect of these coagulation changes is to produce a state of hypercoagulability that makes pregnant women vulnerable to thrombosis, particularly in the puerperium. These systemic alterations are compounded by prothrombotic mechanical and rheologic factors in pregnancy, including venous stasis in the legs caused by the gravid uterus, pelvic vein injury during labor, and the trauma of cesarean section. Oral contraceptives induce a prothrombotic state by increased procoagulant effects and decreased physiologic anticoagulant effects. Postmenopausal hormone replacement use increases the risk of deep venous thromboembolism by a factor of 2 to 3.5, at least during the first year.

Deep vein thrombosis and pulmonary embolism are the most common thrombotic complications of pregnancy and of the use of oral contraceptives or hormone replacement therapy. Coexisting primary hypercoagulable states are an additive risk factor in all of these settings. In the absence of a clear family history of venous thromboembolism, there is little justification, however, to screen for prothrombotic mutations with pregnancy or before starting hormone replacement therapy or oral contraceptives. Increasing age, increasing parity, cesarean delivery, prolonged bed rest or immobilization, obesity, and previous thromboembolism are additional prothrombotic risk factors in pregnant women. Most thrombotic events associated with pregnancy occur in the peripartum period, especially after delivery.

POSTOPERATIVE STATE, IMMOBILIZATION, AND TRAUMA. Postoperative thrombosis is caused by a combination of local mechanical factors, including decreased venous blood flow in the lower extremities, and systemic changes in coagulation (Chapter 78). The level of risk of postoperative thrombosis depends largely on the type of surgery performed. It probably is compounded by coexisting risk factors, such as an underlying inherited primary hypercoagulable state or malignancy, advanced age, and prolonged procedures. Postoperative deep vein thrombosis and pulmonary embolism, the most common thrombotic complications, are often asymptomatic but detectable by noninvasive studies. The incidence of deep vein thrombosis after general surgical procedures is about 20 to 25%, with almost 2% of these patients having clinically significant pulmonary embolism. The risk of deep vein thrombosis after hip surgery and knee reconstruction ranges from 45 to 70% without prophylaxis, and clinically significant pulmonary embolism occurs in 20% of patients undergoing hip surgery. Postoperative thrombosis risk after urologic and gynecologic surgery more closely approximates that found after general surgery. Although the process of thrombosis usually begins intraoperatively or within a few days of surgery, the risk of this complication can be protracted beyond the time of discharge from the hospital, particularly in hip replacement patients.

Patients who are bedridden or experiencing prolonged air travel are at increased risk of venous thromboembolism. Venous thromboembolism is also one of the most common causes of morbidity and mortality in survivors of major trauma, and asymptomatic deep vein thrombosis of the lower extremities has been detected by venography in more than 50% of hospitalized trauma patients (Chapter 108). The risk of venous thrombosis after trauma is increased by advanced age, need for surgery or transfusions, and the presence of lower extremity fractures or spinal cord injury.

1. Hull RD, Raskob GE, Rosenbloom D, et al: Heparin for 5 days as compared with 10 days in the initial treatment of proximal venous thrombosis. N Engl J Med 1990;322:1260–1264.
2. Agnelli G, Prandoni P, Santamaria MG, et al: Warfarin Optimal Duration Italian Trial Investigators. Three months versus one year of oral anticoagulant therapy for idiopathic deep venous thrombosis. Warfarin Optimal Duration Italian Trial Investigators. N Engl J Med 2001;345:165–169.

SUGGESTED READINGS
Bauer KA: The thrombophilias: Well-defined risk factors with uncertain therapeutic implications. Ann Intern Med 2001;135:367–373. *Practical discussion of the clinical approach to thrombosis-prone individuals, including diagnostic and therapeutic implications.*
Durand P, Prost M, Loreau N, et al: Impaired homocysteine metabolism and atherothrombotic disease. Lab Invest 2001;81:645–672. *Comprehensive review of the pathophysiology of thrombosis in hyperhomocysteinemia.*

Matei D, Brenner B, Marder VJ: Acquired thrombophilic syndromes. Blood Rev 2001;15:31–48. *Current concepts of acquired hypercoagulable states, including antiphospholipid syndrome, myeloproliferative disorders, and malignancies.*
Prandoni P, Bilora F, Marchiori A, et al: An association between atherosclerosis and venous thrombosis. N Engl J Med 2003;348:1435–1441. *This strong relationship suggests that atherosclerosis may activate coagulation or the two conditions may share common risk factors.*
Seligsohn U, Lubetsky A: Genetic susceptibility to venous thrombosis. N Engl J Med 2001;344:1222–1231. *Mechanisms, epidemiology, clinical features, diagnosis, and management of patients with inherited thrombophilia.*

181 DISORDERS OF PHAGOCYTE FUNCTION

Laurence A. Boxer

Neutrophils and mononuclear phagocytes are essential components of the host defense system. Both cell types are made in the bone marrow, and both accomplish most of their purpose by protecting and maintaining the organism's internal biologic environment. Mononuclear phagocytes are versatile cells whose functions include the consumption and destruction of invading pathogens, elimination of debris from the blood stream and sites of tissue damage, remodeling of normal tissue, release of immune regulators, and presentation of antigens to lymphocytes. Neutrophils remain dedicated primarily to the destruction of invading microbes. To appreciate the deranged function of phagocytes, the normal physiology of the phagocytes must be considered.

THE NEUTROPHIL

ORIGIN. Like other cells in the circulation, neutrophils originate from pluripotential stem cells in the bone marrow. Depending on environmental influences, pluripotential stem cells may give rise to the committed progenitors of blood cells. Partial purification of human pluripotential stem cells has been accomplished by using an antibody to the cell surface antigen CD34, which marks cells that are used in human stem cell transplantation. These pluripotential stem cells give rise to more mature stem cells that are committed to either lymphoid or myeloid development. Myelopoiesis begins with about 10^6 stem cells in the bone marrow; these cells undergo both self-renewal and differentiation to produce all the individual types of blood cells. The individual types of blood cells arise from the ability of their precursors to express lineage-specific growth factor receptors. These single-lineage progenitors proliferate and differentiate into their respective precursors in response to the growth factors that bind to their unique receptors. The proliferation, differentiation, and survival of immature hematopoietic progenitor cells are governed by a family of glycoproteins termed the *hematopoietic growth factors* (Chapter 159). The mechanism that determines whether a stem cell simply self-renews or differentiates is probably governed by the different signaling pathways used between cell surface receptors and the cell nucleus, but the precise pathway for each cytokine remains poorly defined. Cell proliferation and differentiation are also influenced by interleukins and the local hematopoietic microenvironment, which is defined by extracellular matrix proteins and their stromal elements. Colony-stimulating factors are rarely lineage specific and usually influence multiple steps in hemolymphopoiesis, often in synergy with as many as four or five other factors. As cells mature, they lose receptors for most cytokines, especially those that influence early cell development such as stem cell factor. However, once the cells have matured, they express receptors for chemokines, which help direct the cells to sites of inflammation.

NEUTROPHIL MATURATION AND KINETICS. Based on kinetic studies, four cellular compartments containing myeloid cells are generally recognized: (1) the marrow mitotic compartment; (2) the marrow postmitotic and storage compartment; (3) the vascular compartment, which in the case of neutrophils is divided into a circulating pool and a marginating pool; and (4) the tissue compartments. During infection, tissue macrophages can engage the invading microbes, release cytokines such as interleukin-1 (IL-1) and tumor necrosis factor (TNF) that activate stromal cells, and activate T lymphocytes to produce additional growth factors. Early progenitor cells in the marrow are then stimulated to proliferate and differentiate. This step markedly shortens the time of maturation of myeloid precursors through the postmitotic pool. Increased numbers of neutrophils are then released from the marrow storage compartment into the circulation. These same neutrophils are then primed by either granulocyte (G-CSF) or granulocyte-macrophage colony-stimulating factor (GM-CSF) for enhanced bactericidal activities.

The bone marrow microenvironment supporting the progenitors and precursors must provide for the normal steady-state rates of renewal of the cellular elements of blood through its ability to provide growth and differentiation factors generated by stromal cells themselves. The growth factors such as G-CSF and GM-CSF not only stimulate cell division but also affect the synthesis of many cytoplasmic components of the neutrophil as well as expression of transcription factors that are necessary for myeloid cell differentiation. Transcription factors such as PU.1, SP-1, C/EBPα, and Oct-1 affect myeloid differentiation. For example, the promoter for the myeloblastin gene has a binding site for PU.1, which is engaged following activation of myeloid progenitor cells with G-CSF. Normally, the production rates precisely equal destruction rates. Granulocytes survive intravascularly for 6 to 12 hours. To maintain a level of circulating granulocytes of $5 \times 10^3/\mu L$ requires a daily production of $2 \times 10^4/\mu L$ of blood.

STRUCTURE. The neutrophil is a terminally differentiated, nondividing cell that is well equipped for removing microorganisms. The cell is packed with granules whose contents kill and degrade target microorganisms. The granules are primarily of three types. Azurophil granules contain proteases and other hydrolytic enzymes, defensins, other microbicidal peptides, and myeloperoxidase, a Cl^--oxidizing enzyme. Specific granules contain, among other things, apolactoferrin, collagenase, and an as-yet unidentified enzyme that releases C5a from complement component C5. The membranes of the granules contain receptors for chemoattractants, extracellular matrix proteins, and cytochrome b_{558}. Gelatinase granules contain gelatinase, and the membranes bear the CD11/CD18 receptor essential to cell adhesiveness. In addition to granules are vesicles that bear membranes containing the CD11/CD18 receptor, cytochrome b_{558}, and CR1, a receptor for the complement component C3b. The nucleus is a vestigial structure that can no longer replicate its DNA. The plasma membrane contains some of the neutrophil's killing equipment, sensors that locate the microorganisms to which the neutrophil responds, such as chemokines, chemotactic factors, and adhesion molecules. The cytoskeleton of the neutrophil is a complex system of microfilaments and microtubules and is responsible for the orderly movement of this highly motile cell.

FUNCTION. Chemotactic factors generated by interactions with antigens and with chemokines released by activated T cells attract neutrophils from the blood to sites of infection. Plasma, in addition to elaborating chemoattractants, provides antibodies and complement that coat microorganisms in a process called *opsonization*. Neutrophils ingest the opsonized microorganisms by surrounding them with moving pseudopodia that fuse to enclose the microbe within a vesicle called the *phagosome*. The cytoplasmic granules of the neutrophil fuse with the phagosome and discharge their contents through the membrane, a process called *degranulation*. The neutrophil reduces molecular oxygen enzymatically to generate "activated" metabolites, such as superoxide (O_2^-) and hydrogen peroxide (H_2O_2), which join with material discharged into the phagosome from the granules to destroy the ingested microbes. Granule contents and oxygen metabolites under certain circumstances may leak from the activated neutrophil into extracellular fluid, where they can injure surrounding tissue and engender tissue inflammation.

Adhesion. Because neutrophils move by crawling, they must adhere to surfaces to migrate through the tissues to an inflammatory site. Activated neutrophils enter postcapillary venules adjacent to inflammatory foci and develop low-avidity, adhesive interactions with inflamed endothelium via specific classes of adhesion molecules that include L-selectin, E-selectin (ELAM-1), and P-selectin (GMP-140) (Fig. 181–1). Endothelial cells inducibly express selectins following exposure to inflammatory cytokines (TNF and IL-1). Specific oligosaccharide molecules expressed on the neutrophil membrane glycolipids and glycoproteins serve as counter-receptors for E-selectin and P-selectin (sialyl-Lewis X and Lewis X, respectively). In conjunction with neutrophil membrane L-selectin, which recognizes oligosaccharide molecules expressed by endothelial cells, the selectins promote low-affinity neutrophil-endothelial binding under flow conditions termed neutrophil "rolling." Subsequent to neutrophil rolling, high-affinity interactions are induced by a separate class of adhesion molecules (e.g., intracellular adhesion molecule types 1 and 2 [ICAM-1 and -2]) whose functional affinity is increased by high and prolonged local concentrations of TNF and IL-1. ICAM-1 and -2 serve as recognition receptors for the neutrophil β_2-integrin counter-receptors CD11/CD18. This latter agent's relative affinity for ICAM-1 and -2 is increased by exposure to neutrophil-activating stimuli, including platelet activating factor expressed by the inflamed endothelium, as well as by soluble chemotactic stimuli (formyl bacterial peptides, C5a, IL-8, and leukotriene B_4). During neutrophil activation, a

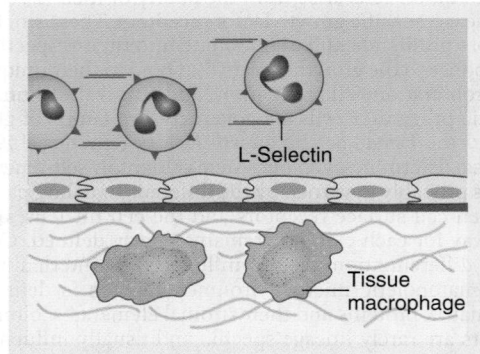

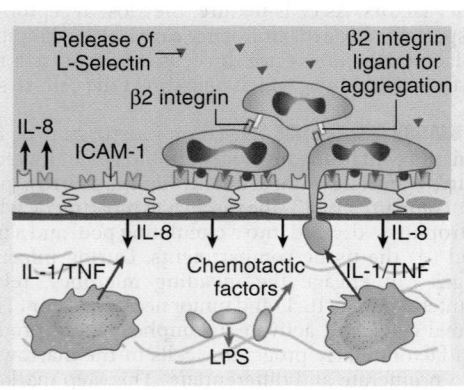

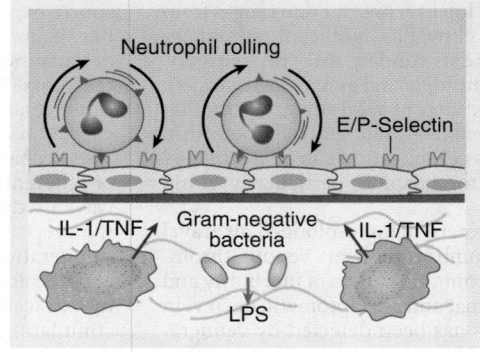

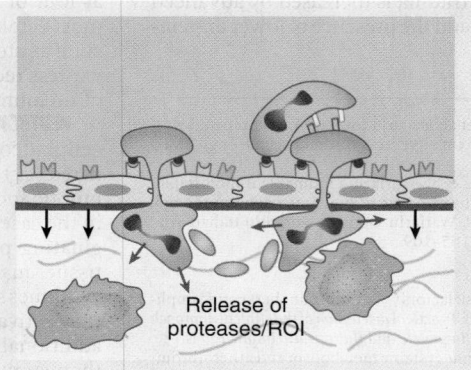

FIGURE 181–1 • The neutrophil-mediated inflammatory response (see the text for details). *A,* Unstimulated neutrophils (expressing L-selectin) entering a postcapillary venule. *B,* Invasion of gram-negative bacteria stimulates low-avidity neutrophil rolling. *C,* Leukocyte spreading and the start of transendothelial migration. *D,* Neutrophils invade through the vascular basement membrane with the release of proteases and reactive oxidative intermediates (ROI). ICAM = intracellular adhesion molecule; IL-1 = interleukin-1; LPS = lipopolysaccharide; TNF = tumor necrosis factor. (Redrawn from Smolen JE, Boxer LA: Functions of neutrophils. *In* Beutler E, Lichtman MA, Coller BS, et al [eds]: Hematology, 6th ed. New York, McGraw-Hill, 2001, p 763.)

reciprocal relationship between the expression of L-selectin and β_2-integrin on the plasma membrane leads to a release of L-selectin, followed by a dramatic increase in the number and affinity of surface CD11/CD18 receptors. Once the neutrophils adhere through their β_2-integrin receptors to the endothelium, subsequent transendothelial migration by neutrophils occurs in response to local gradients of chemotactic factors.

Chemotaxis. The neutrophil finds its target through a chemical sensor that detects substances known as chemotactic factors. These factors are continuously released at sites where microorganisms have invaded tissue, thereby establishing a concentration gradient. Circulating neutrophils recognize this gradient and travel toward its source by migrating between endothelial cells and penetrating the subendothelial basement membrane. Once outside the capillaries, they continue their directed migration, eventually reaching the microorganism-invaded site in which the chemotactic factors originated.

Ingestion. Contact between the neutrophil and the microorganism sets the stage for ingestion. This step proceeds as the neutrophil recognizes opsonins on the surface of the invading microorganisms and attaches to them. The opsonins themselves consist of antibodies belonging to the IgG subclass and the complement components C3b and C3bi (an important stable opsonin formed by the cleavage of C3b by C3b inactivator). The actual binding takes place between opsonic antibodies and the Fc receptors FcR11 and FcR111, plus the C3b and C3bi receptors on the surface membrane of the neutrophils. As the opsonic target attaches to the neutrophil surface, ingestion begins. The neutrophilic membrane and the region of the attached complement particle invaginate into the cell. Once fully internalized, the invagination closes at its neck to form an internal phagocytic vesicle that is lined with the neutrophil plasma membrane and kills the ingested organisms.

Bactericidal Killing. Killing involves two separate actions on the part of neutrophils: degranulation and activation of the respiratory burst. Degranulation refers to a calcium-dependent process by which the granule membranes fuse with the plasma membrane and release the granule contents into either a phagocytic vesicle or the external environment. Azurophil granules degranulate almost exclusively into the phagocytic vesicles, so their microbicidal proteins destroy the ingested microorganisms; myeloperoxidase reacts with H_2O_2 and a halide to produce hypochlorous acid (HOCl). Specific granules degranulate into both the phagocytic vesicles and the external environment to destroy their ingested microorganisms.

The respiratory burst refers to a metabolic event that produces potent microbicidal oxidants through partial reduction of oxygen. The burst is activated by the same stimuli that provoke degranulation of the specific granules—namely, primary contact with ingestible particles and exposure to chemotactic factors. These stimuli initiate the translocation of 47- and 67-kD cytosolic proteins along with a low-molecular-weight G protein (Rac-2) to the membrane containing cytochrome b_{558}. This step initiates the reduction of oxygen to $O_2^{\bullet-}$ at the expense of the reduced form of nicotinamide adenine dinucleotide phosphate (NADPH). Most of the $O_2^{\bullet-}$ reacts with itself to yield H_2O_2, and NADPH is regenerated concurrently by way of the hexose monophosphate shunt. A portion of the H_2O_2 oxidizes Cl^- to the highly microbicidal HOCl, a reaction catalyzed by myeloperoxidase. Another portion of the H_2O_2 is converted to the reactive hydroxyl radical ($\cdot$OH) in an iron-catalyzed reaction with $O_2^{\bullet-}$. These and related oxidants attack and kill ingested microorganisms by oxidizing their cellular constituents.

MONONUCLEAR PHAGOCYTES

ORIGIN AND STRUCTURE. The first recognizable monocyte precursor is the monoblast. The next stage is the promonocyte, a somewhat larger cell with cytoplasmic granules and an indented nucleus containing freely divided chromatin. Finally, the fully developed monocyte appears. Larger than the neutrophil and with a large horseshoe-shaped nucleus containing dispersed chromatin, the mature monocyte has a cytoplasm filled with granules whose content includes hydrolytic enzymes and other proteins necessary for the cell's activities (see Fig. 161–12). The transition from monoblast to mature circulating monocyte requires about 5 days.

Unlike neutrophils, monocytes have a limited capacity to divide, and they undergo considerable further differentiation. After circulating in the blood stream, they enter the tissues, where they differentiate into mature macrophages that live for weeks to months. Topologic factors seem to influence their final differentiation and endow each type with particular metabolic and structural features. Those in the liver, for example, become the Kupffer cells, spidery phagocytes that bridge the sinusoids separating adjacent plates of hepatocytes. Those in the lungs become large ellipsoid alveolar macrophages.

Macrophages are important components of the inflammatory reactions elicited by microorganisms and foreign bodies. Some of the macrophages that appear at a site of inflammation are recruited from the surrounding tissue, whereas others are derived from monocytes that have migrated from the blood stream. Once at the inflamed site, macrophages can be stimulated by opsonized particles. Monocytes and macrophages share the receptors described for neutrophils and, in addition, express other receptors. The contact between a suitable particle and its receptor on the surface of the macrophage elicits the transient production of compounds that include reactive oxygen species, nitric oxide, and arachidonate metabolites. Besides phagocytosable particles, many soluble substances can activate macrophages to release a number of mediators or affect their own signal transduction. Some activators, such as, interferon-γ (IFN-γ), also confer the ability to kill tumor cells and inactivate specific pathogens.

FUNCTIONS. Despite their functional specialization, macrophages have at least three major functions in common: presentation of antigens, phagocytosis, and immunomodulation.

Antigen Presentation. Activation of mononuclear phagocytes by IFN-γ is one of a series of mutually potentiating interactions between these cells and lymphocytes that take place at sites of inflammation (Fig. 181–2). Both T and B lymphocytes participate in these interactions.

Phagocytosis. Mononuclear phagocytes ingest material for two purposes: to eliminate waste and debris (scavenging) and to kill invading pathogens. In their role as general scavengers, mononuclear phagocytes dispose of effete cells, a process exemplified by splenic phagocytes disposing of aged red blood cells or by macrophagic destruction of cells that have not undergone programmed cell death (apoptosis). Similarly, phagocytes remove foreign material from the blood stream and clean up debris at sites of infection or tissue damage.

A dense network of resident macrophages lying chiefly in the liver and spleen remove material from the blood stream. Bacterial

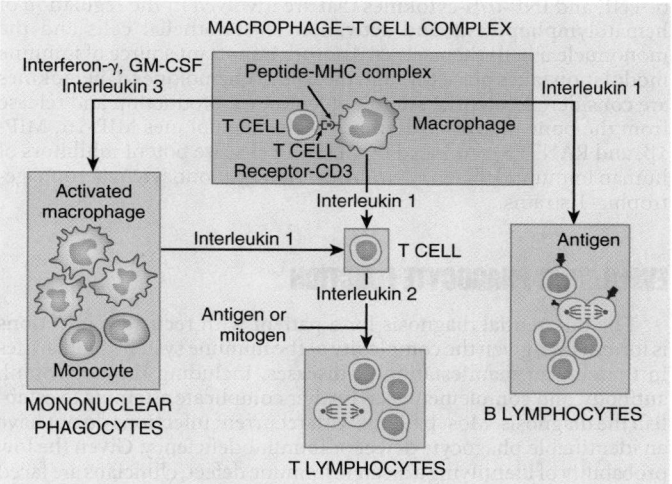

FIGURE 181–2 • Macrophage-lymphocyte interactions. The macrophage, acting in its capacity as an "accessory cell," presents a peptide to a T cell equipped with specific receptors that recognize the complex between the peptide and a class II major histocompatibility complex (MHC) molecule on the macrophage surface. The T cell to which the antigen has been presented undergoes activation and begins to secrete lymphokines. The lymphokines include interferon-γ, granulocyte-macrophage colony-stimulating factor (GM-CSF), and interleukin-3; they cause macrophages to accumulate and undergo activation at the site of the initial macrophage–T cell interaction. Macrophages so activated secrete interleukin-1, a potent mediator capable, among other things, of inducing the proliferation of both B and T cells. B cells are directly stimulated by interleukin-1 to proliferate and differentiate into antibody-secreting plasma cells. T cells, however, proliferate under the influence of a mediator known as interleukin-2 (T-cell growth factors), itself a T-cell product. Interleukin-1 promotes the proliferation of T cells indirectly by inducing them to secrete interleukin-2.

products such as lipopolysaccharide that enter the blood stream from the large intestine are removed principally by the Kupffer cells of the liver during the process of gastrointestinal venous drainage. Similarly, macrophages recruited to the damaged area dispose of dead cells and tissue fragments at sites of infection or injury. Activated macrophages also secrete neutral proteases that break down damaged connective tissue and fibrin mesh to clear the way for the reconstitution of injured tissues.

Mononuclear phagocytes also eliminate from the circulation denatured proteins, protein fragments, and activated clotting factors. Some proteins are eliminated through pinocytosis, a process in which the detritus is taken into the cell by an invagination of the cell membrane that buds off and enters the cytoplasm as a pinocytotic vesicle. Other proteins are eliminated by receptor-mediated endocytosis. For instance, the lipids of atherosclerotic lesions are derived from lipoproteins that have been taken into the macrophage by receptor-mediated endocytosis. On occasion, monocytes will ingest oxidized lipoproteins, which transform them into foam cells and contribute to the generation of atherosclerotic plaque.

Killing. Mononuclear phagocytes can kill invading microorganisms. Like neutrophils, monocytes can adhere to endothelial cells by multiple adhesion molecules, including the selectins and β_2-integrins. Monocytes differ importantly from neutrophils in that they express significant levels of β_1 (VLA) integrin receptors, including VLA-4, which binds to VCAM-1 on activated endothelial cells. Neutrophils are initially the predominant leukocytes at sites of acute inflammation, with the peak of immigration generally occurring in the first several hours. Subsequently, mononuclear phagocytes derived from blood monocytes become the most abundant cell type. These differences in the kinetics of immigration and accumulation can be explained by the elaboration of particular cytokines and chemoattractants in the inflamed tissue that alter the affinity of leukocyte integrin receptors or induce upregulation or downregulation of both leukocyte and endothelial cell adhesion molecules. Neutrophils generally find their targets by responding to chemotactic gradients, whereas fixed tissue macrophages have their targets brought to them by the blood stream. Unlike neutrophils, monocytes and macrophages also express the CD4 antigen, which is involved in human immunodeficiency virus uptake and infection.

Immunomodulation. Activated monocytes also release IL-1 and IL-6, TNF, and INF-α/β-cytokines that are involved in the regulation of hematolymphopoiesis and activation of endothelial cells and the mononuclear cells themselves. Another important source of immune modulation takes place through the role of chemokines. Chemokines are considered potential stimuli of leukocyte production and release from the bone marrow. Additionally, the chemokines MIP-1α, MIP-1β, and RANTES, produced by CD8+ T cells, are potent inhibitors of human immunodeficiency virus infection by monocyte/macrophage-trophic-1 strains.

EVALUATING PHAGOCYTE FUNCTION

The differential diagnosis for a patient with recurrent infections is formidable, given the complexity of the immune system. Similarities in the clinical manifestation of diseases, including the neutrophil, antibody, and complement, can further complicate attempts to establish the diagnosis. Most patients with recurrent infections do not have an identifiable phagocyte defect or immunodeficiency. Given the low probability of identifying a discrete immune defect, clinicians are faced with the difficult question of deciding which patients merit a complete evaluation. In general, evaluation should be initiated for those who, within a 1-year period, have had at least one of the following clinical features: (1) more than two systemic bacterial infections (e.g., sepsis, meningitis, osteomyelitis); (2) three serious respiratory infections (e.g., pneumonia, sinusitis) or three bacterial infections (e.g., cellulitis, draining otitis media, lymphadenitis); (3) the presence of an infection at an unusual site (e.g., hepatic or brain abscess); (4) infections with unusual pathogens (e.g., *Aspergillus* pneumonia, disseminated candidiasis, or infection with *Serratia marcescens*, *Nocardia* spp., or *Burkholderia cepacia*); (5) infections of unusual severity; and (6) dissemination of recurrent mycobacterial infection.

Neutrophils have a particularly important role in protecting the skin, the mucous membranes, and the lining of the respiratory and gastrointestinal tracts. As such, they form the initial line of defense against microbial invasion. During the critical 2- to 4-hour period

following invasion by microbial organisms, neutrophils must arrive at the site of invasion if infection is to be contained. Patients whose neutrophils have defects in adhesion or cell motility generally suffer cutaneous abscesses with common pathogens such as *Staphylococcus aureus* or have mucous membrane lesions caused by microbes such as *Candida albicans*. A profound defect in adhesion and chemotaxis is often reflected by a paucity of neutrophils at the site of inflammation. Disorders of phagocyte microbicidal activity, especially as observed in cases of chronic granulomatous disease (CGD), are also associated with cutaneous abscesses and pulmonary infections.

Once the decision is reached that a phagocyte evaluation is warranted, a thorough clinical history, physical examination, and laboratory testing (Fig. 181–3) should provide the diagnosis and help formulate an appropriate therapeutic plan. Despite the rarity of the inherited disorders, the understanding gleaned from evaluating their molecular mechanisms has contributed immensely to our knowledge of normal neutrophil function.

ACQUIRED DISORDERS OF PHAGOCYTE FUNCTION

Neutrophils may exhibit decreased adhesiveness and chemotaxis after exposure to a variety of drugs, the most common being corticosteroids (Chapter 31) and epinephrine. Clinically, the diminished adhesiveness induced by these drugs is manifested by a dramatic rise in the total neutrophil count in the blood as cells from the marginating pool are quickly released into the circulating pool. Although the mechanism by which corticosteroids alter adherence remains unknown, epinephrine exerts its effects indirectly by causing endothelial cells to release cyclic adenosine monophosphate, which impairs the ability of neutrophils to adhere to endothelium. In contrast, the adhesiveness of neutrophils can be dramatically enhanced in a variety of clinical conditions that generate biologically active complement fragments (e.g., C5a), cytokines (e.g., TNF and IL-1), and chemokines (e.g., IL-8). Disorders associated with gram-negative bacterial sepsis, severe thermal injury, pancreatitis, trauma, and exposure of neutrophils to artificial membrane surfaces during hemodialysis and cardiopulmonary bypass can all be associated with activation of neutrophils and, in extreme cases, lead to adult respiratory distress syndrome. In these various conditions, generation of C5a and cytokines promotes enhanced neutrophil adhesiveness, possibly because of enhanced expression of β_2-integrins. Under these conditions, neutrophils undergo increased aggregation with each other and become trapped within the capillary beds of the lungs. It is believed that the aggregated neutrophils then generate toxic oxygen radicals and release proteases that damage structural proteins such as collagen and elastin.

Immune complexes are found in association with disorders such as rheumatoid arthritis (Chapter 278) and systemic lupus erythematosus (Chapter 280) as well as after bone marrow transplantation (Chapter 166). Immune complexes can bind to Fc receptors on neutrophils and impair their motility. In turn, diminished motility of neutrophils may be associated with recurrent pyogenic infections.

INHERITED DISORDERS OF PHAGOCYTE FUNCTION

HYPERIMMUNOGLOBULIN E SYNDROME

The hyperimmunoglobulin E syndrome (Table 181–1) is characterized by reduced neutrophil motility accompanied by markedly elevated levels of serum IgE that lead to chronic dermatitis and recurrent sinopulmonary infections (Chapter 268). Skin infections in these patients are remarkable for their absence of surrounding erythema and subsequent formation of "cold abscesses." Neutrophils and monocytes from patients with this syndrome exhibit a variable, but at times profound, chemotactic defect that appears to be extrinsic to the neutrophil. The clinical manifestations of hyperimmunoglobulin E syndrome can begin as early as 1 to 8 weeks of age. This syndrome is characterized by chronic eczematoid rashes, which are typically papular and pruritic and often involve the face and extensor surface of the arms and legs. Most frequently the offending pathogen is *Staphylococcus aureus*. Patients have serum IgE levels exceeding 2500 IU/mL, but unlike atopic patients who may have similarly elevated IgE levels, those with hyperimmunoglobulin E syndrome have serum IgE antibodies directed to *S. aureus*. Patients may also develop septic arthritis, cellulitis, osteomyelitis, or recurrent pneumonias with pneumatoceles. Other associated features include coarse facial features

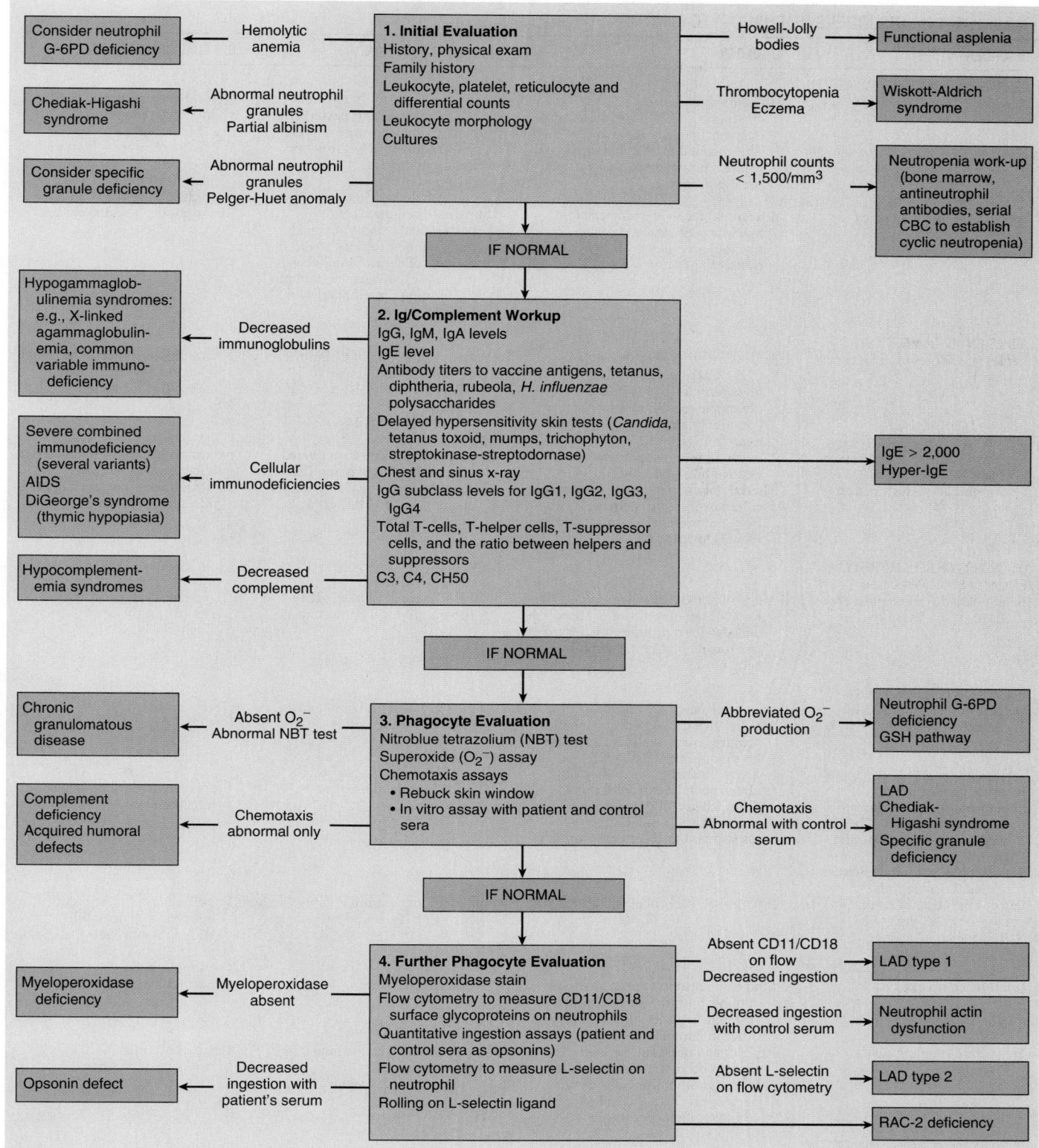

FIGURE 181–3 • Algorithm for the evaluation of patients with recurrent infections. Ig = immunoglobulin; G6PD = glucose-6-phosphate dehydrogenase; GSH = glutathione; LAD = leukocyte adhesion deficiency; RAC = member of Rho family of GTPases. (Modified from Curnutte JT, Boxer LA: Clinical significant phagocyte cell defects. *In* Remington JS, Swartz MN [eds]: Current Clinical Topics in Infectious Diseases, 6th ed. New York, McGraw-Hill, 1985, p 144.)

manifested by a broad nasal bridge, prominent nose, dental abnormalities, and irregular but proportional cheeks and jaw. The molecular basis for the syndrome remains unknown. However, there is growing evidence that a defective IL-12–IFN-γ pathway leads to the preferential activation of the Th$_2$ T cells and increased IgE synthesis. Treatment is supportive.

FAMILIAL MEDITERRANEAN FEVER

Familial Mediterranean fever is an autosomal recessive, recurrent, inflammatory disease prevalent among people of the Near East—Arabs, Turks, Armenians, and Sephardic Jews. It is transmitted as an autosomal recessive trait. The disease is characterized by acute self-limited

Table 181–1 • DISORDERS OF PHAGOCYTE FUNCTION

DISORDER	ETIOLOGY	IMPAIRED FUNCTION	CLINICAL CONSEQUENCE
DEGRANULATION ABNORMALITIES			
Chédiak-Higashi syndrome	Autosomal recessive; disordered coalescence of lysosomal granules. Responsible gene found at 1q42–45. The encoded protein has structural features homologous to a vacuolar sorting protein	Decreased neutrophil chemotaxis, degranulation, and bactericidal activity; platelet storage pool defect; impaired NK function, failure to disperse melanosomes	Neutropenia; recurrent pyogenic infections; propensity to develop marked hepatosplenomegaly in the accelerated phase; pigment dilution in the skin and fundus
Specific granule deficiency	Autosomal recessive; abnormal regulation of various myeloid granule genes by a transacting factor	Impaired chemotaxis and bactericidal activity; bilobed nuclei in neutrophils; reduced content of neutrophil defensins, gelatinase, collagenase, vitamin B_{12}-binding protein, and lactoferrin	Recurrent deep-seated abscesses
ADHESION ABNORMALITIES			
Leukocyte adhesion deficiency type 1	Autosomal recessive; absence of CD11/CD18 surface adhesive glycoprotein (β_2-integrins) on leukocyte membranes most commonly arising from failure to express CD18 mRNA	Decreased binding of C3bi to neutrophils and impaired adhesion to ICAM-1 and ICAM-2	Neutrophilia; recurrent bacterial infection associated with a lack of pus formation
Leukocyte adhesion deficiency type 2	Autosomal recessive; absence of neutrophil sialyl-Lewis X	Decreased adhesion to activated endothelium expressing ELAM	Neutrophilia; recurrent bacterial infection without pus
Neutrophil actin dysfunction	Altered polymerization of neutrophil cytoplasmic actin; perhaps arising from the presence of an inhibitor to F-actin formation	Impaired neutrophil adhesion, chemotaxis, and bacterial killing	Neutrophilia; recurrent bacterial infections without pus
DISORDERS OF CELL MOTILITY			
Enhanced Motile Responses			
Familial Mediterranean fever (FMF)	Autosomal recessive gene responsible for FMF on chromosome 16, which encodes for a protein called "pyrin"; pyrin may modify neutrophil activation	Excessive accumulation of neutrophils at inflamed sites	Recurrent fever, peritonitis, pleuritis, arthritis amyloidosis
Depressed Motile Responses			
Defects in the generation of chemotactic signals	IgG deficiencies; C3 and properdin deficiency can arise from genetic or acquired abnormalities; mannose binding protein deficiency predominantly in neonates	Deficiency of serum chemotaxis and opsonic activities	Recurrent pyogenic infections
Intrinsic defects of the neutrophil, e.g., leukocyte adhesion deficiency, Chédiak-Higashi syndrome, specific granule deficiency, neutrophil actin dysfunction, neonatal neutrophils	In the neonatal neutrophil there is diminished ability to express β_2-integrins and a qualitative impairment in β_2-integrin function	Diminished chemotaxis	Propensity to develop pyogenic infections
Direct inhibition of neutrophil mobility, e.g., drugs	Ethanol, glucocorticoids, cyclic AMP	Impaired locomotion and ingestion. Impaired adherence	Possible cause for frequent infections; neutrophilia seen with epinephrine is the result of cyclic AMP release from endothelium
Immune complexes	Bind to Fc receptors on neutrophils in patients with rheumatoid arthritis, systemic lupus erythematosus, and other inflammatory states	Impaired chemotaxis	Recurrent pyogenic infections
Hyperimmunoglobulin E syndrome	Autosomal dominant; variable expression of a soluble inhibitor from mononuclear cells affecting neutrophil chemotaxis; high levels of antistaphylococcal IgE	Impaired chemotaxis; impaired IgG opsonization of *Staphylococcus aureus*	Recurrent skin and sinopulmonary infections
DEFECTS OF MICROBICIDAL ACTIVITY			
Chronic granulomatous disease	X-linked and autosomal recessive; failure to express functional gp91^{phox} in the phagocyte membrane in p22^{phox} (autosomal recessive). Other autosomal recessive forms of CGD arise from failure to express protein p47^{phox} or p67^{phox}	Failure to activate neutrophil respiratory burst leading to failure to kill catalase-positive microbes	Recurrent pyogenic infections with catalase-positive microorganisms
G6PD deficiency	Less than 5% of normal activity of G6PD	Failure to activate NADPH-dependent oxidase	Infections with catalase-positive microorganisms
Myeloperoxidase deficiency	Autosomal recessive; failure to process modified precursor protein arising from missense mutation	H_2O_2-dependent antimicrobial activity not potentiated by myeloperoxidase	None

Table 181–1 • DISORDERS OF PHAGOCYTE FUNCTION—cont'd

DISORDER	ETIOLOGY	IMPAIRED FUNCTION	CLINICAL CONSEQUENCE
Rac-2 deficiency	Autosomal recessive; dominant negative inhibitor by mutant protein of Rac-2-mediated functions	Absent receptor-mediated O_2^- generation and chemotaxis Impaired neutrophil rolling on endothelium	Neutrophilia; recurrent bacterial infections
Deficiencies of glutathione reductase and glutathione synthetase	Failure to detoxify H_2O_2	Excessive formation of H_2O_2	Minimal problems with recurrent pyogenic infections
IMPAIRED MACROPHAGE FUNCTION			
Defects in the interferon-γ–IL-12 axis	Interferon-γ–receptor ligand-binding chain, interferon-γ–receptor signalling chain, IL-12–receptor β1 chain, IL-12p40 deficiency; the interferon-γ–receptor abnormalities may be autosomal dominant or recessive; the IL-γ-12 receptor and IL-12 are autosomal recessives	Impaired killing of microorganisms. Fatal BCG infection secondary either to inability to produce IL-12 by dendritic cells and macrophages or to depressed bactericidal activity of macrophages lacking normal function of interferon-γ receptor	Infection with atypical mycobacteria, *Salmonella*, and *Listeria*
IMPAIRED SPLEEN FUNCTION			
Splenic absence or splenic dysfunction	Congenital absence of spleen, removal of spleen, vascular occlusion of spleen	Removal or impaired function of splenic macrophages	Propensity to infection with encapsulated bacteria

Modified from Boxer LA: Quantitative abnormalities of granulocytes. *In* Beutler E, Lichtman MA, Coller BS, et al (eds): Williams Hematology, 6th ed. New York, McGraw-Hill, 2001, p 836.

AMP = adenosine phosphate; BCG = bacille Calmette-Guérin; CGD = chronic granulomatous disease; G6PD = glucose-6-phosphate dehydrogenase; ICAM = intracellular adhesion molecule; IL = interleukin; NADPH = nicotinamide-adenine dinucleotide phosphate; NK = natural killer; phox = phagocyte oxidase.

attacks of fever often accompanied by pleuritis, peritonitis, arthritis, pericarditis, inflammation of the tunica vaginalis of the testes, and erythematous skin lesions. The first attacks may begin in infancy, although more commonly they begin in childhood or adolescence. Most patients have the first attack by 20 years of age.

Epidemiology

The gene responsible for familial Mediterranean fever, *MEFV*, is located on chromosome 16. It encodes for a 781-amino acid protein called pyrin. Homology searches indicate that pyrin is a new member of the RetRo gene family and suggests that pyrin itself may be a transcription factor that presumably regulates the expression of target genes, at least some of which are probably involved in the suppression of inflammation. The gene is expressed in neutrophils and monocytes. Missense mutations have been found in exons 2 and 10 in most of the affected patients, but other mutations are likely to be discovered.

Pathology

The pathologic findings in familial Mediterranean fever are those of nonspecific acute inflammation. Neutrophilic infiltration predominates, and exudates develop in the peritoneal, pleural, and/or joint spaces at the time of acute attacks. In about 25% of affected patients, a form of renal amyloidosis (Chapter 290) develops in which the amyloid is derived from a normal serum protein called serum amyloid A (amyloidosis of the AA type). Amyloidosis usually progresses over a period of years to renal failure, and almost all causes of death in patients with familial Mediterranean fever can be attributed to this complication.

Clinical Manifestations

The duration and frequency of attacks vary considerably, even in the same patient. Acute attacks frequently last 24 to 48 hours and recur once or twice per month. In some patients, attacks may recur as frequently as several times a week or as infrequently as once a year, and symptoms may persist for as long as a week during individual episodes. Some patients experience spontaneous remis-

sion that persists for years, followed by recurrence of frequent attacks. Peritonitis secondary to familial Mediterranean fever may resemble an acute abdomen (Chapter 146), thereby leading to potential uncertainties about the clinical management of acute abdominal episodes.

Pleuritic pain occurs during attacks in 75% of patients. Symptoms of pleuritis may sometimes precede abdominal pain, and a few patients experience pleuritic attacks without abdominal symptoms. Mild arthralgia is a common feature of febrile attacks; monarticular or oligoarticular arthritis may occur. Arthritis usually affects the large joints, the knee in particular, and effusions are common.

As many as one third of patients experience transient erysipelas-like skin lesions that typically appear on the lower part of the leg, ankle, or dorsum of the foot. These painful erythematous areas of swelling usually subside within 24 to 48 hours.

Laboratory findings in familial Mediterranean fever are non-specific. During acute attacks, prominent leukocytosis (up to 30,000/mm^3) is present, and the erythrocyte sedimentation rate is increased. Between attacks, the leukocyte count is normal.

Diagnosis

The diagnosis of familial Mediterranean fever is based primarily on clinical findings and the patient's history. In individuals of appropriate ethnic background with typical recurrent, self-limited attacks, diagnosis is not difficult; in such individuals, delay in recognizing the disease usually occurs because the diagnosis is not considered.

Rx Treatment

Prophylactic colchicine, 0.6 mg orally two or three times per day, prevents or substantially reduces acute attacks of familial Mediterranean fever in 75 to 90% of patients and may prevent the development of amyloidosis. Some patients can abort attacks with intermittent doses of colchicine beginning at the onset of attacks (0.6 mg orally every hour for 4 hours, then every 2 hours for 4 hours, and then every 12 hours for 2 days).

Prognosis

With colchicine, most patients can be maintained almost entirely symptom-free and have a normal longevity. Amyloidosis can manifest as the nephrotic syndrome or uremia, with a high likelihood of death from renal failure unless the patient receives a renal transplant.

ADHESION ABNORMALITIES

Leukocyte adhesion deficiency (LAD) is a rare autosomal recessive disorder of leukocyte function. LAD-1 affects about 1 in 10^6 individuals; it is characterized by recurrent bacterial and fungal infections as well as a depressed inflammatory response despite striking blood neutrophilia.

Epidemiology

Individuals with LAD-1 have mutations of the gene on chromosome 21q22.3 encoding CD18, the 95-kD β_2-integrin subunit. The lack of a β-chain prevents active $\alpha\beta$-dimers from forming. Diminished or absent surface expression of these proteins accounts for the failure of patients' neutrophils to migrate to specific sites of inflammation.

Clinical Manifestations

LAD-1 is characterized by recurrent soft tissue infections, delayed wound healing, and severe impaired pus formation despite a striking blood neutrophilia. The onset of clinical manifestations begins in the newborn period and is usually characterized by delayed separation of the umbilical cord, with patients often not surviving beyond the toddler age. Patients with moderate disease can survive into adulthood. The diagnosis is most readily made by flow cytometric measurement of surface CD11/CD18 in stimulated and unstimulated neutrophils by using monoclonal antibodies directed against CD11/CD18.

In contrast to LAD-1 patients, three patients have been described with neutrophilia, recurrent bacterial infections, and an inability to form pus. Both patients had the Bombay blood phenotype, short-limbed dwarfism, and mental retardation. Functionally, their neutrophils were unable to adhere to cytokine-activated endothelial cells expressing E-selectin. This disorder is recognized as LAD-2.

 Treatment

Treatment of LAD-1 is largely supportive. Patients with a history of recurrent infections can take prophylactic trimethoprim-sulfamethoxazole. Marrow transplantation from HLA-compatible siblings or parental donors has resulted in engraftment and restoration of neutrophil function and remains the treatment of choice in patients with the severe phenotype of LAD-1.

DEGRANULATION ABNORMALITIES

Chédiak-Higashi syndrome is a rare autosomal recessive disease in which neutrophils, monocytes, and lymphocytes contain giant cytoplasmic granules. About 200 cases have been reported. The disorder is characterized by generalized cellular dysfunction involving increased fusion of cytoplasmic granules. Affected patients with this disorder are usually recognized in infancy, and only a few patients survive into early adulthood.

Pathogenesis

The mutated gene for Chédiak-Higashi syndrome, known as *LYST*, is located on chromosome 1q42-q44 and has structural features homologous to a vacuolar sorting protein termed VPS15 in yeast. Almost all cells of patients with Chédiak-Higashi syndrome show some aspect of oversized and dysmorphic lysosomes, storage granules, or related vesicular structures. This abnormality in melanocytes leads to the macroscopic impression of hair that is lighter than expected from parental coloration and to the partial ocular albinism associated with light sensitivity. Patients with this syndrome exhibit an increased susceptibility to infection that can be explained in part by the presence of giant neutrophil granules that alter cell motility by compromising neutrophils' ability to traverse the narrow passages between endothelial cells.

Clinical Manifestations

Features of the disease include neutropenia arising from ineffective myelopoiesis, a platelet defect associated with a mild bleeding disorder, natural killer cell abnormalities, and peripheral neuropathies. The most serious clinical problem, however, is caused by abnormalities in neutrophil chemotaxis, degranulation, and bactericidal activity. In the accelerated phase of the disorder, polyclonal T-cell proliferation in the liver, spleen, and bone marrow leads to hepatosplenomegaly and high fever in the absence of bacterial sepsis. Pronounced pancytopenia often leads to hemorrhage and further increased susceptibility to infection.

Diagnosis

The diagnosis is made by demonstrating giant granules in neutrophils and eosinophils. Diagnosis of the accelerated phase depends on finding the characteristic infiltrate of T cells in a biopsy sample of involved tissue.

 Treatment

Management of the early stage of Chédiak-Higashi syndrome amounts to the management of infectious complications. Prophylactic antibiotics (trimethoprim-sulfamethoxazole) should be given, and infections should be treated vigorously with appropriate antibiotic therapy. Ascorbic acid (20 mg/kg/day) has corrected the microbicidal defect in some patients with Chédiak-Higashi syndrome. Bone marrow transplantation is the treatment of choice during progression to the accelerated phase.

DEFECTS OF MICROBICIDAL ACTIVITY: CHRONIC GRANULOMATOUS DISEASE

Chronic granulomatous disease affects 4 to 5 per 1 million humans. Neutrophils and monocytes from affected individuals ingest but do not kill catalase-positive microorganisms because of their inability to generate antimicrobial oxygen metabolites. CGD is caused by genetic defects affecting one X-linked and three autosomal recessive chromosomes encoding the components of NADPH oxidase.

Pathogenesis

Approximately two thirds of affected patients lack the membrane-bound component of the oxidase cytochrome b_{558}. The gene for the heavy chain of this protein (gp91-kd protein), which is a heterodimeric protein, is located on the X chromosome. Other patients with CGD lack one of two identified cytosolic factors, either a 47-kD protein or 67-kD protein or the genes responsible for expression of the light chain of cytochrome b_{558}; these three deficiencies are inherited in an autosomal recessive pattern.

Clinical Manifestations

Several clinical features suggest the diagnosis of CGD. Any patient with recurrent lymphadenitis should be considered to have CGD. Additionally, bacterial hepatic abscesses, osteomyelitis at multiple sites or in the small bones of the hands and feet, and a family history of recurrent infections or unusual catalase-positive microbial infections all suggest the disorder. The onset of clinical signs and symptoms may occur from early infancy to young adulthood. The severity and frequency of infections vary widely. The most common offending organism is *S. aureus*, although any catalase-positive microorganism may be involved. Infection with *S. marcescens*, *Burkholderia cepacia*, *Aspergillus* species, *C. albicans* or *Salmonella* spp. occur frequently. Pneumonias, lymphadenitis, and skin infections remain the most commonly encountered infections. Often the infections are characterized by microabscesses and granuloma formation. Patients may suffer from the sequelae of chronic infection, including anemia of chronic disease, lymphadenopathy, hepatosplenomegaly, chronic purulent dermatitis, restrictive lung disease, gingivitis, hydronephrosis, and gastrointestinal narrowing.

Diagnosis

The diagnosis is usually suggested with use of the nitroblue tetrazolium (NBT) test, in which the yellow, water-soluble tetrazolium dye is reduced to a blue and insoluble formazan pigment by O_2^- generated from activated normal phagocytes. Phagocytes from patients with CGD fail to reduce NBT because they cannot produce O_2^-. Because carriers of X-linked CGD are mosaics, only a fraction of their neutrophils stain on the NBT test. The NBT test is rapidly being replaced by the more accurate flow cytometry test, which detects oxidant production because it increases fluorescence when oxidized by H_2O_2.

Leukocytes from patients with CGD have normal glucose-6-phosphate dehydrogenase (G6PD) activity. A few individuals with apparent CGD, however, have neutrophils that lack almost all G6PD activity. Erythrocytes from these patients also lack G6PD and are subject to chronic hemolysis.

In cases of suspected X-linked CGD, further analysis is not necessary if the fetus is an XX female. Fetal blood sampling or DNA analysis of amniotic fluids or chorionic villus biopsy samples are options for prenatal diagnosis of CGD.

Prevention and Treatment

Marrow transplantation is the only cure for CGD. As part of the supportive care, patients with CGD should be given daily oral trimethoprim-sulfamethoxazole, 5 mg trimethoprim/kg/day for infection prophylaxis. INF-γ (50 μg/m², three times/week) can reduce the number of serious infections. Cultures should be obtained as soon as infection is suspected. Empirical treatment with broad-spectrum parenteral antibiotics is often required while awaiting culture results. Granulomas may be sensitive to low doses of prednisone (0.5 mg/24 hr); treatment should be tapered over several weeks.

Prognosis

The overall mortality rate for CGD is about 2% per year. The mortality rate is highest in young children, and the long-term prognosis has improved greatly over the past 20 years, owing to close surveillance as well as aggressive surgical and medical interventions.

Future Directions

New approaches to stem cell transplantation using low-intensity marrow conditioning and T-cell depletion of the allograft are being evaluated. Early clinical experience suggests that gene transfer therapy can be effective for 6 months, but long-term success requires future therapeutic improvements.

MYELOPEROXIDASE DEFICIENCY

Deficiency of myeloperoxidase, an autosomal recessive disorder, is the most common inherited disorder of neutrophil function, with an incidence of 1 in 4000 individuals. A missense mutation in the myeloperoxidase gene leads to a myeloperoxidase precursor that does not incorporate heme. Partial or complete myeloperoxidase deficiency leads to diminished production of HOCl and HOCl-derived chloramines. Lack of HOCl in the phagosome causes a delay in the microbicidal activity of neutrophils early after the ingestion of microorganisms. Eventually, however, effective killing occurs. Myeloperoxidase-deficient neutrophils accumulate more hydrogen peroxide than do normal neutrophils, which improves the bactericidal activity of affected neutrophils.

Clinically, myeloperoxidase deficiency is almost completely silent. The most frequent problem is an increase in *Candida* infections in occasional patients with coincident diabetes mellitus. The diagnosis is made from a peroxidase stain of the blood film. In cases of myeloperoxidase deficiency, peroxidase activity is missing from neutrophils and monocytes but is present in the eosinophils. No specific treatment is needed.

SUGGESTED READINGS

Drenth JPH, van der Meer JWM: Hereditary periodic fever. N Engl J Med 2001;345:1748–1757. *Overview of the periodic fever syndrome with a strong emphasis on the molecular abnormalities underlying these disorders.*

Holland SM: Update on phagocytic defects. Pediatr Infect Dis J 2003;22:87–88. *Recent insights, including the role of mononuclear phagocytes in mycobacterial infections.*

Lekstrom-Himes JA, Gallin JI: Immunodeficiency diseases caused by defects in phagocytes. N Engl J Med 2000;343:1703–1714. *A review of the inherited defects of neutrophils and monocytes with a strong emphasis on the molecular abnormalities underlying these disorders.*

Winkelstein JA, Marino MC, Johnston RB Jr, et al: Chronic granulomatous disease: Report on a national registry on 368 patients. Medicine 2000;79:155–169. *Summary of the clinical and laboratory findings of a large number of CGD patients enrolled in a registry sponsored by the National Institutes of Health.*

182 MYELODYSPLASTIC SYNDROME

D. Gary Gilliland

Definition

Myelodysplastic syndrome (MDS) refers to a heterogeneous group of acquired bone marrow disorders characterized by dysplastic growth of hematopoietic progenitors, a hypercellular bone marrow with peripheral cytopenia, and propensity to progress to acute myelogenous leukemia (AML; Chapter 193).

Epidemiology

Although rare kindreds have an inherited predisposition to develop MDS, most cases are sporadic. In most instances, the etiology of de novo MDS is unknown, although exposure to chemical solvents, including benzene, and to pesticides have been identified as risk factors. De novo MDS occurs only rarely in young patients, but therapy-related MDS and acute myelogenous leukemia (t-MDS/AML) is increasingly recognized as a potentially fatal complication of chemotherapy and/or radiation therapy for other malignancies. De novo MDS is rare, occurring at a frequency of approximately 1 per 100,000 per year in the general population. However, the incidence increases dramatically with age, with an incidence of 25 to 50 per 100,000 per year in populations older than age 60 years. In this age group, the incidence approximates other common hematologic malignancies, such as chronic lymphocytic leukemia and multiple myeloma. As longevity increases in developed countries, the prevalence of MDS will increase. Similarly, with advances in technology that include the use of stem cell support and hematopoietic growth factors, the intensity and duration of treatment for cancer have increased dramatically; to the extent that these therapeutic maneuvers are successful in eradicating the underlying disease, the incidence of t-MDS/AML is likely to increase.

The treatment of Hodgkin's disease (Chapter 194) and non-Hodgkin's lymphoma (NHL; Chapter 195) is an example of the problem. Autologous bone marrow transplantation (BMT; Chapter 166) has proven to be a significant advance in the treatment of Hodgkin's disease and NHL, with cure rates approaching 40 to 50% in subgroups of patients in whom the expected survival had been lower than 20%. The counterpoint to the success of intensive therapy has been an increased risk of t-MDS/AML in this population. Because autologous BMT is a relatively new procedure and follow-up is not sufficiently long, the exact incidence of secondary t-MDS/AML in this population is not known. However, reported actuarial incidences of t-MDS/AML in patients undergoing autologous BMT for Hodgkin's disease and NHL range from 4 to 25%.

Pathobiology

CLONALITY. MDS is a clonal disorder with an acquired somatic mutation that affects an early hematopoietic progenitor and gives rise to clonally derived neutrophils, red cells, and platelets. There is no convincing evidence for clonal involvement of B and T cells.

CYTOGENETIC ABNORMALITIES. Identification of mutant genes in MDS has been difficult, in part because MDS is characterized by loss of genetic material, in contrast to the balanced reciprocal chromosomal translocations typical of de novo AML. Consistent loss of genetic material has led to the hypothesis that MDS is caused by homozygous loss of genes with tumor suppressor activity. The most common cytogenetic abnormalities in MDS are deletions of the long arm of chromosomes 5, 7, and 20. 5q– is present in approximately 15% of de novo MDS and 50% of t-MDS, and abnormalities of 5q and/or 7 are present in 70% of t-MDS. It has been hypothesized that tumor suppressor genes reside in these loci in which one allele is deleted and that there is concomitant loss of function of the residual allele through point mutation or epigenetic influences. Despite significant progress in identifying the critically deleted regions on chromosomes 5 and 7, genes meeting criteria for classic tumor suppressors associated with 5q–, 7q–, or 20q– have not yet been identified. Recent evidence indicates that MDS may be associated with loss of a single allele, or haploinsufficiency, of the *AML1* gene (see later discussion), thereby suggesting that loss of a single copy of a critical gene or genes located on 5q, 7q, or 20q may be sufficient for MDS.

Rare but recurring chromosomal translocations are also associated with MDS. For example, the *MLL (HRX)* gene localized to chromosome 11q23 has been implicated in the pathogenesis of de novo AML and in t-MDS/AML. The t(11;16)(q23;p13) is exclusively associated with t-MDS/AML and results in fusion of *MLL* to the transcriptional coactivator *CBP* (CREB binding protein).

The t(3;21)(q22;q22) translocation, which is associated with some cases of t-MDS/AML as well as with chronic myelogenous leukemia (CML) in blast crisis, results in fusion of *AML1* with one of several fusion partners on chromosome 3, including *EAP, EVI1,* and *MDS1*. *AML1*, which is also involved in the t(8;21) translocation in de novo AML, contains a highly conserved DNA binding domain that regulates expression of myeloid specific genes, including myeloperoxidase and neutrophil elastase. It has been suggested that the t(3;21) and t(8;21) fusions disrupt *AML1* function and thereby inhibit early myeloid differentiation.

t(5;12)(q33;p13) is a rare recurring translocation associated with chronic myelomonocytic leukemia (CMML) (see Classification). The consequence of the translocation is fusion of the tyrosine kinase domain of the platelet-derived growth factor-β receptor (PDGFRβ) to a member of the ETS family of transcription factors, TEL. Fusion of TEL to PDGFRβ constitutively activates the tyrosine kinase domain of PDGFRβ, leading to abnormal myeloid proliferation. It has subsequently been demonstrated that a spectrum of chromosomal translocations associated with a CMML phenotype all result in constitutive activation of a tyrosine kinase, including the TEl/ABL, HIP1/PDGFβR, RAP5E/PDGFβR, TEL/JAK2, and H4/PDGFβR fusions.

Many of the chromosomal translocations associated with AML have also been observed in MDS, including the t(15;17), t(8;21), and inv(16) giving rise to the PML/RARα, AML1/ETO, and CBFβ/SMMHC fusions, respectively, suggesting that MDS and AML are a continuum of the same disease.

POINT MUTATIONS. Activating mutations, which confer transforming potential to the *RAS* gene family, occur in 5 to 15% of patients with MDS. Mutations are rare in *p53*, in the macrophage colony-stimulating receptor gene (*M-CSFR*), and in the neurofibromatosis gene *NF1*, which acts in the *RAS* signal transduction pathway. However, some patients with MDS harbor mutations in the hematopoietic receptor tyrosine kinase FLT3, resulting in constitutive activation of FLT3. FLT3 and RAS may therefore be therapeutic targets of FLT3 and farnesyl transferase inhibitors, respectively.

Loss of function point mutations may occur in hematopoietic transcription factors in MDS, including the *AML1 (RUNX1)* gene. *AML1* is required for normal hematopoietic development; thus, loss of function mutations associated with inherited forms of MDS, such as the FPD/AML syndrome (familial platelet disorder with propensity to develop acute myelogenous leukemia) and in sporadic cases of MDS, would be expected to impair hematopoiesis.

CELL CULTURE ANALYSIS. Hematopoietic progenitors from patients with MDS grow poorly in culture, although poor growth can be partially overcome by addition of exogenous growth factors such as granulocyte-macrophage colony-stimulating factor (GM-CSF). There are functional defects in neutrophils (decreased phagocytosis, chemotaxis, microbicidal activity), red cells (ringed sideroblasts with defective iron processing, qualitative defects in red cell glycolytic enzymes), and platelets (defects in aggregation and morphology). Most patients have normal T- and B-cell numbers and normal levels of immunoglobulins and hence are not particularly prone to opportunistic infections unless they have been treated with immunosuppressive agents.

Clinical Manifestations

The clinical presentation of MDS is frequently related to cytopenia in one or more hematopoietic cell lineages, with neutropenia occurring in 24 to 39% of patients, anemia in 45 to 93%, and thrombocytopenia in 28 to 45% in various series. In the geriatric population, patients may present with symptoms related to comorbid illnesses. For example, a patient with coronary artery disease may present with mild anemia associated with an increase in the frequency and duration of angina. Other common presenting symptoms include easy bruising, epistaxis or petechiae, and signs and symptoms of infection. Because infection may itself suppress myelopoiesis, any patient with a mild cytopenia (Chapter 163) in the setting of infection should have follow-up blood cell counts to determine whether the cytopenia persists after the infection has resolved. This evaluation is particularly important because MDS confers not only a quantitative defect in the production of myeloid lineage cells but also a qualitative defect in function of those cells. Therefore, a patient with a mild leukopenia may have MDS and be highly susceptible to bacterial infections owing to abnormal neutrophil function. Patients with MDS usually have normal number and function of T and B cells and rarely present with evidence of opportunistic infections. Infections due to opportunistic pathogens are usually seen only in MDS patients who have been heavily treated with antibacterial antibiotics for extended periods of time or who have received marrow suppressive therapy for MDS.

The clinical course of MDS is characterized by inexorably progressive pancytopenia. Although the rate of decline of peripheral blood cell counts is highly variable and may affect one hematopoietic lineage more than another, a clinically significant improvement in blood cell counts rarely, if ever, occurs during the course of MDS. The clinical problems encountered during the course of MDS depend in part on comorbid illness and the extent to which each of the hematopoietic lineages is involved. For example, although it is relatively easy to provide red cell transfusion therapy for patients with isolated macrocytic anemia as the primary manifestation of MDS, anemia may be a significant and life-threatening problem in an elderly MDS patient with coexistent severe coronary artery disease. Similarly, an elderly MDS patient with diabetes may encounter little difficulty with anemia or thrombocytopenia but may have recurrent life-threatening infections requiring frequent hospitalization from persistent neutropenia in the setting of diabetes. Because de novo MDS occurs most commonly in the elderly, about 30% of patients die of underlying medical conditions unrelated to MDS. About 40% of patients die of complications of marrow failure, such as infection or bleeding, and about 30% die of transformation to acute leukemia.

Diagnosis and Classification of MDS

Examination of the peripheral blood smear is often helpful in establishing the diagnosis of MDS. Granulocytes are poorly granulated and may be hyposegmented and display the Pelger-Huët anomaly (see Fig. 161–16). Red cells are usually hypochromic with polychromasia. Other abnormalities in red cell morphology can include teardrop-shaped cells, especially in the subset of MDS patients with bone marrow fibrosis, as well as red cell fragments and nucleated cells. Mild macrocytosis is a hallmark of MDS, with mean corpuscular volume (MCV) in the 100 to 110 range. MCVs outside this range make a diagnosis of MDS less likely. Platelets may be large, and megakaryocyte fragments may be present.

A bone marrow aspirate and biopsy are required to provide a definitive diagnosis. Evidence of dysmyelopoiesis can include abnormal granules, such as large primary granules or decreased numbers of granules, the presence of bizarre nuclear forms in myeloid lineage cells, the Pelger-Huët anomaly, and Auer rods (see Fig. 161–17). Signs of dyserythropoiesis may include multinuclear forms, nuclear fragments, megaloblastic changes, nuclear:cytoplasmic dyssynchrony, and ringed sideroblasts. Finally, dysplasia affecting megakaryocyte lineage cells can include bizarre nuclear figures, decreased ploidy, separated nuclei (so-called pawn ball nuclei), and micro-megakaryocytes. The percentage of myeloblasts may be increased and is used as part of the classification of MDS. The bone marrow cellularity is usually normal or increased, despite the fact that most patients present with peripheral blood cytopenia.

Characteristic cytogenetic abnormalities are another helpful clue in the diagnosis of MDS, although normal cytogenetics do not exclude the diagnosis. Most cytogenetic abnormalities in MDS are characterized by loss of genetic material through deletions. Nonrandom chromosomal abnormalities associated with MDS include 5q–, which occurs in approximately 15% of de novo MDS and 50% of secondary MDS, monosomy 7, trisomy 8, 21q–, 17q–, and 20q–. As many as 80% of patients have detectable chromosomal abnormalities.

A diagnosis of MDS requires the exclusion of other disorders that may cause peripheral cytopenias (Table 182–1). The evaluation of a patient with unexplained cytopenia (Chapters 163 and 174) should always include exclusion of congenital disorders associated with cytopenia, vitamin deficiencies, and, toxic drugs. Whenever possible, patients should be taken off any medications that can cause cytopenia for at least 6 to 8 weeks. A careful physical examination should search for evidence of hypersplenism, with attention to various potential underlying causes, such as myelofibrosis, hepatic cirrhosis, and other hematologic disorders (e.g., hairy cell leukemia or primary splenic lymphoma). Alcoholic patients may present with a combination of vitamin deficiency, alcoholic myelosuppression, and hypersplenism that may resemble MDS (Chapter 156). Some physicians incorporate testing for autoimmune diseases, such as antinuclear antibody tests, in the evaluation of cytopenia, although it is rare that cytopenia is the only presenting finding for autoimmune disorders (Chapters 163 and 174). When the initial physical examination, laboratory evaluation, and removal of potentially causative drugs fail to disclose a cause for a cytopenia, bone marrow aspiration and biopsy with cytogenetic analysis should be performed to address the possibility that the patient may have MDS or another cause of the

cytopenia, such as aplastic anemia, leukemia, or marrow infiltration by malignant cells.

MDS is currently classified by a scheme developed by the World Health Organization (Table 182–2). Although these categories carry prognostic information, the International Prognostic Scoring System (IPSS; Table 182–3) provides the most reliable estimates of survival and likelihood of progression to AML.

Table 182–1 • DIFFERENTIAL DIAGNOSIS OF MYELODYSPLASTIC SYNDROME

CONGENITAL DISORDERS
Hereditary sideroblastic anemia
Fanconi's anemia
Diamond-Blackfan syndrome
Kostmann's syndrome
Shwachman syndrome
Down syndrome

VITAMIN DEFICIENCY
B_{12}, folate, or iron deficiency

DRUG TOXICITY
Marrow suppression from oral or parenteral medications
Toxins
Chemotherapy and/or radiation therapy
Alcohol

ANEMIA OF CHRONIC DISEASE
Renal failure
Chronic infection, including tuberculosis
Rheumatologic disorders

VIRAL MARROW SUPPRESSION
Including Epstein-Barr virus, parvovirus B19, human immunodeficiency virus, and others

MARROW INFILTRATION
Acute and chronic leukemias
Metastatic solid tumor infiltration

PAROXYSMAL NOCTURNAL HEMOGLOBINURIA

HYPERSPLENISM

 Treatment

Supportive care remains the mainstay of therapy, including transfusion of red cells (Chapter 165) with chelation therapy to prevent iron overload, prevention and treatment of infection, and transfusion of platelets for clinically significant bleeding. Pyridoxine, a cofactor in heme biosynthesis, is nontoxic and is often given for 3 months in patients with anemia from MDS; responses are rare. There is no clear role for corticosteroids, androgens, or other vitamins in the therapy of MDS, despite anecdotal reports of response.

HEMATOPOIETIC STEM CELL TRANSPLANTATION (Chapter 166). Related or unrelated donor hematopoietic stem cell transplantation (HSCT) remains the only known cure for MDS and should be considered the treatment of choice for patients who meet age and donor criteria. Disease-free survivals can exceed 15 years. Allogeneic HSCT, especially including experimental nonmyeloablative HSCT, is being used in older (age 55 to 66 years) patients; as a result, as many as 50% of patients with MDS may be candidates for HSCT, usually without prior chemotherapy. Age younger than 40 years and a short duration of disease before transplantation are favorable prognostic indicators.

Overall long-term survival after HSCT is about 46%, and patients who have refractory anemia and receive transplants with fully-matched related donors have as high as 75% long-term, disease-free survival. Even in patients ages 55 to 66 years, overall 3-year, disease-free survival is greater than 53%. The risk of relapse is higher in patients with worse IPSS scores (see later text).

DIFFERENTIATION AGENTS. 5-Azacytidine, which interferes with DNA methylation, prolongs median time to progression to AML and median survival.∎ Other drugs that promote differentiation of hematopoietic progenitors, such as low-dose cytarabine, low-dose

etoposide, retinoic acid derivatives including all-*trans* retinoic acid, vitamin D_3 derivatives, interferon, and hexamethylene bisacetamide have been tested extensively without evidence of benefit in clinical trials. Amifostine, a phosphorylated organic thiol, has been associated with responses in small, uncontrolled trials, but further investigation is necessary before advocating its routine use.

HEMATOPOIETIC GROWTH FACTORS. There is no known survival benefit from administration of any hematopoietic growth factor either alone or in combination. About 20% of patients respond to erythropoietin (EPO), usually when their pretreatment serum EPO levels were less than 500 mU/mL. A trial of 150 to 300 U/kg of EPO three times per week by subcutaneous injection is reasonable, especially in patients with low serum EPO levels relative to their degree of anemia. Granulocyte colony-stimulating factor (G-CSF) given alone almost invariably results in hematologic responses, but a large randomized trial showed no survival benefit.

CONVENTIONAL CHEMOTHERAPY. Remission rates for MDS or secondary AML (evolving from MDS) range from 18 to 44% with standard antileukemia regimens; treatment-related deaths occur in as many as half of patients. More recently, treatment with fludarabine 30 mg/m², ara-C (cytarabine) 2 g/m², daily for 5 days, and G-CSF has provided complete response rates comparable to those for induction chemotherapy for de novo AML. However, duration of remission is brief, and it is not yet clear whether intensive chemotherapy prolongs survival. Intensive chemotherapy, with or without growth factor support, can be recommended only under the auspices of a clinical trial.

IMMUNOSUPPRESSIVE THERAPY. Several clinical observations have suggested a link between MDS and aplastic anemia (Chapter 174), which

Continued

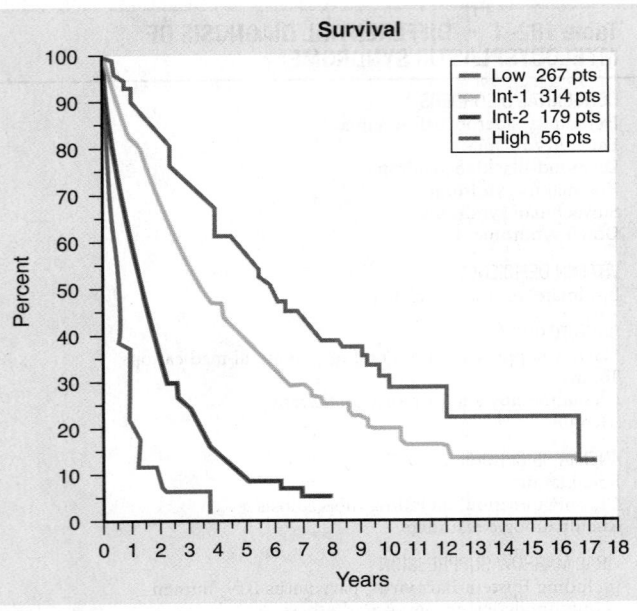
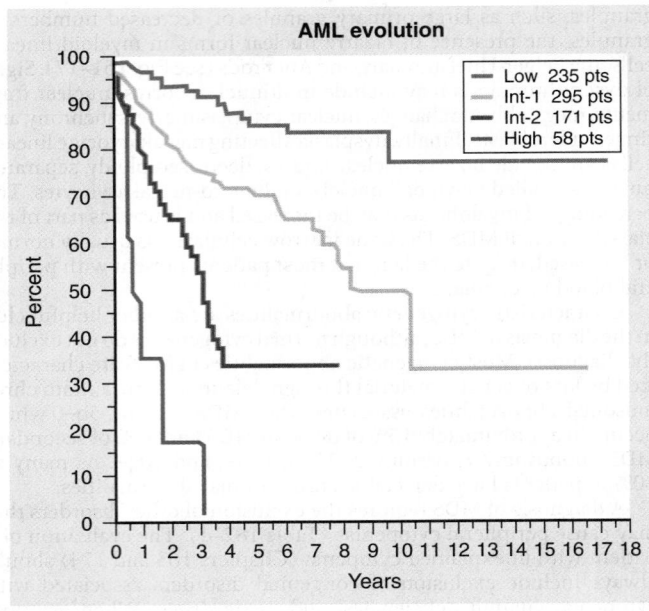

FIGURE 182–1 • International myelodysplastic syndrome risk classification by International Prognostic Scoring System for survival and evolution to acute myelogenous leukemia. (From Greenberg P, Cox C, LeBeau MM, et al: International scoring system for evaluating prognosis in myelodysplastic syndromes. Blood 1997;89:2079–2088.)

Table 182–2 • WORLD HEALTH ORGANIZATION CLASSIFICATION OF MYELODYSPLASTIC SYNDROME

CATEGORY	PERIPHERAL BLOOD	BONE MARROW
1a. RA without dysplasia	Blasts <1%; monocytes <1000/mm^3	Blasts <5%; ringed sideroblasts <15%
1b. RA with dysplasia	Same + dysgranulocytes and/or giant platelets	Same + dysgranulocytes and/or dysmegakaryocytes
2a. RARS without dysplasia	Blasts <1%; monocytes <1000/mm^3	Blasts <5%; ≥15% ringed sideroblasts
2b. RARS with dysplasia	Same + dysgranulocytes and/or giant platelets	Same + dysgranulocytes and/or dysmegakaryocytes
3a. RAEB-I	Blasts 1–4%; monocytes <1000/mm^3	Blasts 5–10%
3b. RAEB-II	Blasts 5–19%; monocytes <1000/mm^3	Blasts 11–19%

RA = refractory anemia; RAEB = refractory anemia with excess blasts; RARS = refractory anemia with ringed sideroblasts.

Table 182–3 • INTERNATIONAL PROGNOSTIC SCORING SYSTEM

	SCORE VALUE				
PROGNOSTIC VARIABLE	0	0.5	1.0	1.5	2.0
Bone marrow blasts (%)	<5	5–10	—	11–21	21–30
Karyotype*	Good	Intermediate	Poor		
Cytopenias†	0 or 1	2 or 3			

*Karyotype scores: Good: normal-Y, del(5q), del(20q); poor: complex (≥3), any abnormality of chromosome 7; intermediate: any other cytogenetic abnormality.

†Cytopenias: Hemoglobin <10 g/dL, absolute neutrophil count <1500/μL; platelet count <100,000/μL.

Scores for each of the three variables are summed for an overall score. Overall scores for risk groups are low: 0, intermediate-1: 0.5–1.0; intermediate-2: 1.5–2.0; and high: >2.5.

From Greenberg P, Cox C, LeBeau MM, et al: International scoring system for evaluating prognosis in myelodysplastic syndromes. Blood 1997;89:2079–2088.

often responds to immunosuppressive therapy with antithymocyte globulin (ATG) and/or cyclosporin A. Several Phase II trials have suggested that ATG and/or cyclosporine A is well tolerated and effective in some patients with MDS, but treatment should be undertaken only in the context of a clinical trial.

MOLECULAR THERAPIES. RAS inhibition using farnesyl transferase inhibitors and FLT3 inhibition using small molecule ATP analogues are being tested in clinical trials.

Prognosis

An IPSS (see Table 182–3) assigns points for blast percentage, karyotype, and the presence of cytopenias; the resulting overall score correlates well with overall survival and likelihood of progression to AML (Fig. 182–1). The IPSS may also be useful to identify high-risk patients who are most likely to benefit from intensive therapy with curative intent, such as HSCT.

Future Directions

Significant strides in the understanding of the molecular pathophysiology of MDS may lead to novel therapies. In the interim, advances in HSCT, especially nonmyeloablative transplant strategies, hold the greatest promise for improving long-term, disease-free survival.

1. Silverman LR, Demakos EP, Peterson BL, et al: Randomized controlled trial of azacitidine in patients with the myelodysplastic syndrome: A study of the cancer and leukemia group B. J Clin Oncol 2002;20:2429–2440.

SUGGESTED READINGS

Bennett JM: World Health Organization classification of the acute leukemias and myelodysplastic syndrome. Int J Hematol 2000;72:131–133. *An overview of the new WHO classification scheme for MDS.*

Deeg HJ, Appelbaum FR: Hemopoietic stem cell transplantation for myelodysplastic syndrome. Curr Opin Oncol 2000;12:116–120. *Summary of the use of hematopoietic stem cell transplantation for MDS.*

Steensma DP, Tefferi A: The myelodysplastic syndromes: A perspective and review highlight current controversies. Leuk Res 2003;27:95–120. *Concise overview of the pathophysiology and diagnostic approach to MDS, with a discussion of the new WHO criteria.*

183 CHRONIC MYELOPROLIFERATIVE DISORDERS: ESSENTIAL THROMBOCYTHEMIA AND MYELOFIBROSIS WITH MYELOID METAPLASIA

Ayalew Tefferi

Definition

Essential thrombocythemia and myelofibrosis with myeloid metaplasia are currently classified with polycythemia vera (Chapter 176) as chronic myeloproliferative disorders. The chronic myeloproliferative disorders have biologic and phenotypic similarity to other chronic myeloid diseases, including chronic myeloid leukemia (CML; Chapter 192) and the myelodysplastic syndrome (MDS; Chapter 182). X-linked glucose-6-phosphate dehydrogenase cell assays initially established the clonal (neoplastic) nature of trilineage myeloproliferation in both chronic myeloproliferative disorders and CML, and many other myeloid disorders are now known to arise from clonal stem cells (Fig. 183–1). Unlike CML, however, the specific disease-causing mutations in the chronic myeloproliferative disorders have yet to be identified. Current diagnosis is, therefore, based on a constellation of clinical findings, bone marrow histology, and cytogenetics.

Epidemiology

The chronic myeloproliferative disorders are rare, with approximate annual incidences of 0.2 to 2.5, 0.8 to 2.8, and 0.4 to 1.3 per 100,000 for essential thrombocythemia, polycythemia vera, and myeloid metaplasia, respectively. The median age at presentation across the three disorders is similar (55 to 65 years), with a slight male preponderance (1.2 : 1) in polycythemia vera and myeloid metaplasia and female preponderance (2 : 1) in essential thrombocythemia. All three disorders have infrequently been described in children. No convincing evidence links specific environmental exposures to these diseases.

Pathogenesis

Clonal myeloproliferation involving granulocytes, monocytes, erythroid cells, and platelets has been demonstrated in most patients with chronic myeloproliferative disorders, including essential thrombocythemia and myeloid metaplasia, using X chromosome–linked DNA or gene product analysis. Such assays, however, reveal "polyclonal" hematopoiesis in a substantial minority of patients with essential thrombocythemia and reveal "monoclonal" hematopoiesis in some normal elderly control subjects. Regardless, the cytokine-independent (clonal) nature of platelet production in essential thrombocythemia is further supported by the failure of antibodies against interleukin (IL)-3, IL-6, granulocyte-macrophage colony-stimulating factor, and thrombopoietin (TPO) to inhibit endogenous megakaryocyte growth. Furthermore, patients with essential thrombocythemia have not been shown to carry mutations for either TPO (the major megakaryocyte growth and development factor) or its receptor (c-Mpl). In contrast, some forms of familial thrombocytosis are associated with activating mutations of the TPO gene. Recent studies suggest that megakaryocytes or their precursors may be hypersensitive to TPO and may underexpress c-Mpl.

Clonal myeloproliferation in myeloid metaplasia is associated with intense bone marrow stromal reaction that consists of excess deposition of extracellular matrix proteins including collagen, angiogenesis (new blood vessel formation), and osteosclerosis (osteoblast proliferation and new bone formation). These observations, and the finding that bone marrow fibroblasts in myeloid metaplasia are polyclonal, form the basis for the current assumption that the bone marrow stromal changes in myeloid metaplasia represent a reactive process that is mediated by cytokines that are furnished by cellular components of the clonal process (Fig. 183–2).

ESSENTIAL THROMBOCYTHEMIA

Diagnosis

In routine clinical practice, more than 80% of cases of thrombocytosis are considered reactive and are not associated with a clonal hematologic disorder (Table 183–1). It is important to distinguish reactive thrombocytosis from essential thrombocythemia (Fig. 183–3), because there is an increased risk of thrombosis associated with essential thrombocythemia but not with reactive thrombocytosis. The degree of thrombocytosis, platelet morphology, and platelet function tests are neither specific nor sensitive enough to distinguish essential from reactive thrombocytosis.

However, serum levels of both ferritin and C-reactive protein may help address the possibility of iron deficiency anemia (Chapter 167) and occult inflammatory process, respectively, as causes of possible reactive thrombocytosis. Essential thrombocythemia is characterized by normal C-reactive protein. A normal serum ferritin level excludes iron deficiency–associated reactive thrombocytosis, but a low level does not exclude the possibility of essential thrombocythemia. Howell-Jolly bodies on the peripheral blood smear suggest surgical or

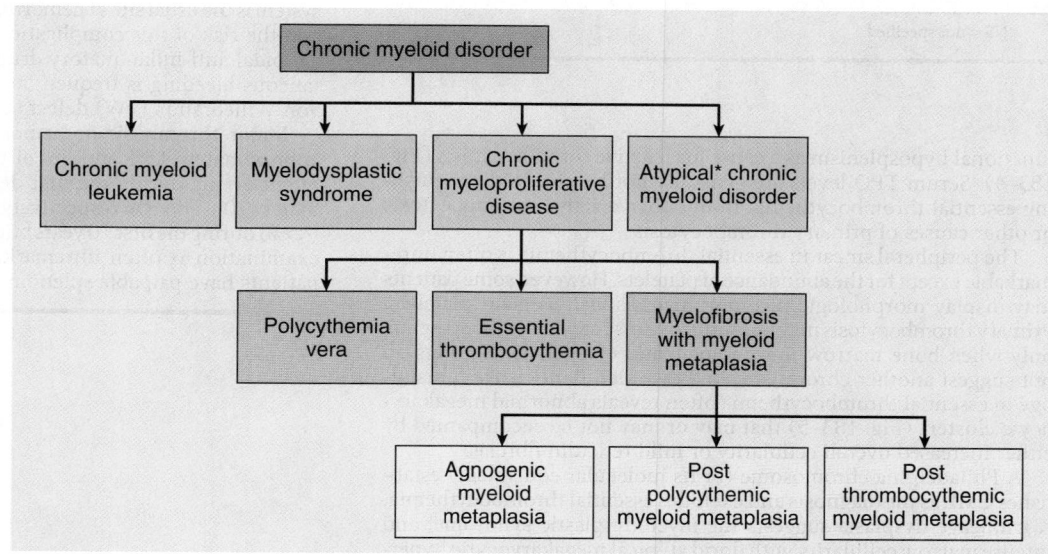

FIGURE 183–1 • A working classification of chronic myeloid disorders. Chronic myeloid leukemia and the myelodysplastic syndrome are specifically characterized by the presence of the Philadelphia chromosome (or its molecular equivalent) and trilineage dysplasia, respectively. *Atypical chronic myeloid disorders include chronic neutrophilic leukemia, chronic eosinophilic leukemia, mast cell disease, and a chronic myeloid process that displays overlapping features of both myelodysplastic syndrome and chronic myeloproliferative disorder. (From Tefferi A: Myelofibrosis with myeloid metaplasia. N Engl J Med 2000; 342:1255–1265, with permission.)

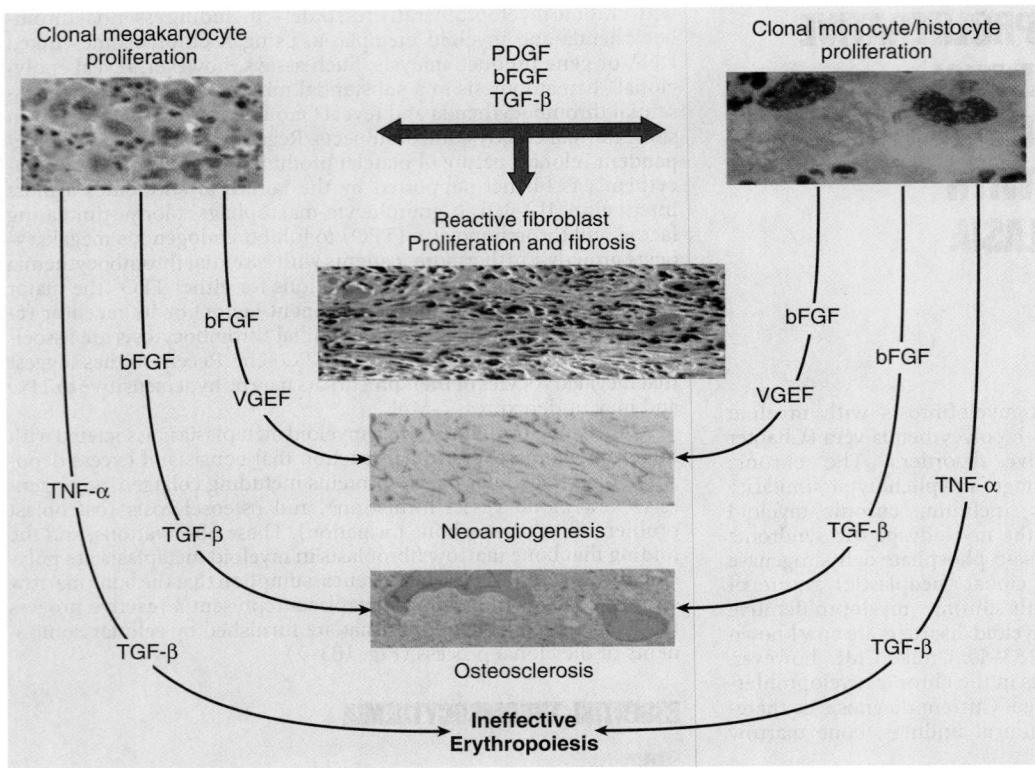

Clonal megakaryocyte proliferation

PDGF
bFGF
TGF-β

Clonal monocyte/histocyte proliferation

Reactive fibroblast Proliferation and fibrosis

bFGF

bFGF

bFGF

bFGF

VGEF

VGEF

TNF-α

TNF-α

TGF-β

TGF-β

Neoangiogenesis

TGF-β

TGF-β

Osteosclerosis

Ineffective Erythropoiesis

FIGURE 183–2 • Potential pathogenetic mechanisms in myelofibrosis with myeloid metaplasia. (Tefferi A: Myelofibrosis with myeloid metaplasia. N Engl J Med 2000;342:1255–1265, with permission.)

Table 183–1 • CAUSES OF THROMBOCYTOSIS (PLATELET COUNT >500,000/μL OR ABOVE IN UNSELECTED COHORTS OF CONSECUTIVE PATIENTS (APPROXIMATE PERCENTAGES)

CONDITION	ADULTS	PLATELET COUNT OF 1 MILLION/μL OR ABOVE	CHILDREN
Infection	22%	31%	31%
Rebound thrombocytosis	19%	3%	15%
Tissue damage (surgery)	18%	14%	15%
Chronic inflammation	13%	9%	4%
Malignancy	6%	14%	2%
Renal disorders	5%	NS	4%
Hemolytic anemia	4%	NS	19%
Postsplenectomy	2%	19%	1%
Blood loss	NS	6%	NS
Primary thrombocythemia	3%	14%	0%

NS = not specified.

functional hyposplenism as a cause for reactive thrombocytosis (Fig. 183–4). Serum TPO levels are generally not helpful in distinguishing essential thrombocythemia from either reactive thrombocytosis or other causes of primary thrombocytosis.

The peripheral smear in essential thrombocythemia is often unremarkable except for the abundance of platelets. However, some patients may display morphologic pleomorphism as well as giant platelets. Primary thrombocytosis may be ascribed to essential thrombocythemia only when bone marrow morphologic and cytogenetic findings do not suggest another chronic myeloid disorder. Bone marrow histology in essential thrombocythemia often reveals abnormal megakaryocyte clusters (Fig. 183–5) that may or may not be accompanied by either increased overall cellularity or mild reticulin fibrosis.

A Philadelphia chromosome (or its molecular equivalent) establishes CML as the diagnosis and excludes essential thrombocythemia. A trilineage dysplasia suggests the myelodysplastic syndrome, and intense marrow cellularity with florid atypical megakaryocytic hyperplasia suggests "cellular phase" myeloid metaplasia.

Clinical Manifestations

Approximately 50% of patients with essential thrombocytosis may be asymptomatic at presentation. Vasomotor disturbances (headaches, lightheadedness, visual symptoms, palpitations, atypical chest pain, erythromelalgia, distal paresthesia) are the most frequent symptoms, occurring in 25 to 50% of patients. It is believed that these symptoms, especially erythromelalgia (see Fig. 176–2), are the result of small vessel platelet-endothelium interaction with associated inflammation and transient thrombotic occlusion. The life-threatening complications of essential thrombocythemia are thrombosis, hemorrhage, and transformation into myeloid metaplasia or acute myeloid leukemia (AML; Chapter 193).

Arterial thrombosis (e.g., cerebrovascular or cardiovascular ischemia or infarcts, digital gangrene) is more frequent than venous thrombosis (pulmonary embolism, Budd-Chiari syndrome, portal vein thrombosis, deep vein thrombosis) in both essential thrombocythemia and polycythemia vera. The upper gastrointestinal system is the usual site of hemorrhage in essential thrombocythemia, and the risk of this complication is enhanced by the use of nonsteroidal anti-inflammatory drugs (NSAIDs). Increased mucocutaneous bleeding is frequent and may be related to an acquired von Willebrand's (vW) defect (Chapter 178).

Major thrombosis or hemorrhage occurs at presentation in approximately 15% and 5% of the patients, respectively; subsequent events during the first decade of the disease are approximately 20% and 5%, respectively. Leukemic transformation is rare (<5%) during the first 10 years but may be higher thereafter. Physical examination is often unremarkable, but approximately 25% of patients have palpable splenomegaly at diagnosis.

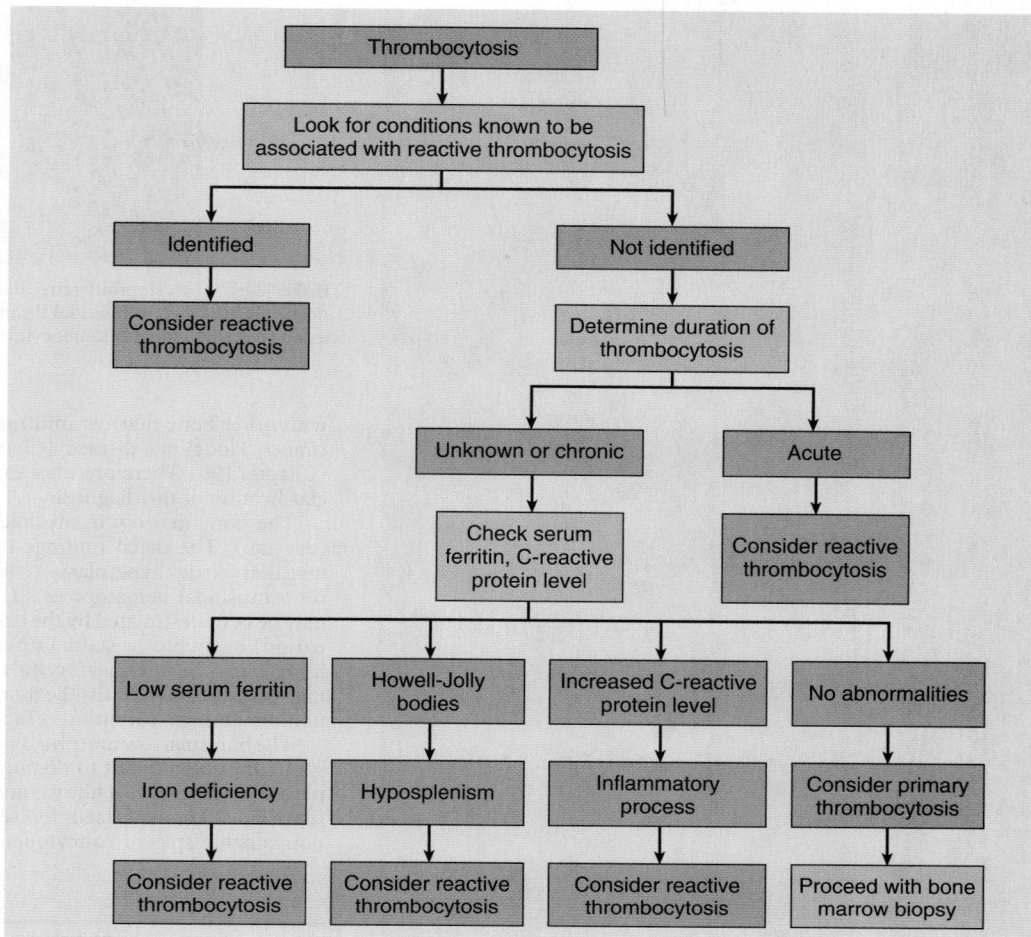

FIGURE 183–3 • Diagnostic evaluation of thrombocytosis in routine clinical practice.

Rx Treatment and Prognosis

The key guide to long-term management of essential thrombocythemia is the patient's risk of thrombosis based on a history of prior thrombosis and age older than 60 years (Table 183–2). The overall incidence of superficial or deep thrombosis in essential thrombocythemia is 20 to 40%, but major thrombosis (stroke, myocardial infarct, deep vein thrombosis, pulmonary embolism, digital arterial occlusion) occurs in only 10 to 20% of patients.

Cytoreductive (platelet-lowering) therapy reduces the risk of thrombosis in high-risk patients, in whom the platelet count may need to be reduced to 400,000/μL or lower. In other patients, the use of platelet-lowering agents is not supported. Only hydroxyurea (Table 183–3) has been shown prospectively to reduce the risk of thrombosis in essential thrombocythemia. ◻ Additional randomized trials are ongoing. In the meantime, it is reasonable to substitute anagrelide for hydroxyurea in patients who are intolerant to hydroxyurea. In high-risk women who are or wish to be pregnant, cytoreductive therapy with interferon alfa has been safe and effective in anecdotal reports.

Acute thrombosis in essential thrombocythemia requires an immediate reduction of the platelet count to less than 400,000/μL. If the platelet count is more than 800,000/μL, platelet apheresis is indicated, usually combined initially with hydroxyurea, which can be switched to an alternative platelet-lowering agent later. Systemic anticoagulation, with full-dose heparin followed by warfarin (with an international normalized ratio goal of 2 to 2.5) should also be started, and warfarin may be switched to low-dose aspirin after 6 months of treatment if thrombocytosis has been adequately controlled.

More than one third of patients with essential thrombocythemia may have first trimester spontaneous miscarriage, which may be unrelated to the platelet count or use of aspirin. Complications late in pregnancy are unusual and appear not to be reduced by prophylactic platelet apheresis during delivery. High-risk women (see Table 183–2) with essential thrombocythemia require cytoreductive therapy to protect the mother from a thrombotic complication, and anecdotal evidence suggests use of interferon alfa as the preferred therapy in such patients.

Low-dose aspirin (81 to 325 mg per day) may not increase the bleeding diathesis of patients with essential thrombocythemia and is currently recommended as a supplement to cytoreductive therapy in high-risk patients as well as an optional consideration in most patients with essential thrombocythemia in the absence of risk factors for bleeding, such as acquired vW disease and a history of upper gastrointestinal bleeding.

Vasomotor disturbances are effectively treated with low-dose aspirin (one baby aspirin, 81 mg, per day). If aspirin is not adequate, a platelet-lowering (cytoreductive) therapy may be indicated, with the goal being a platelet count level that provides symptom relief. In general, the use of aspirin or other NSAIDs is discouraged in the presence of platelet counts greater than 1 million/μL because of the danger of bleeding from acquired vW disease. Cytoreductive therapy may be indicated in the presence of a greater than 50% reduction in large vW factor multimers.

Life expectancy in the first decade of the disease may not be significantly different than the age- and sex-matched control population, in part because the risk of early leukemic transformation is well below 10%. The subsequent risk of leukemia is thought to be higher, however, and natural history studies suggest a poorer survival compared with age-matched control subjects after the first decade.

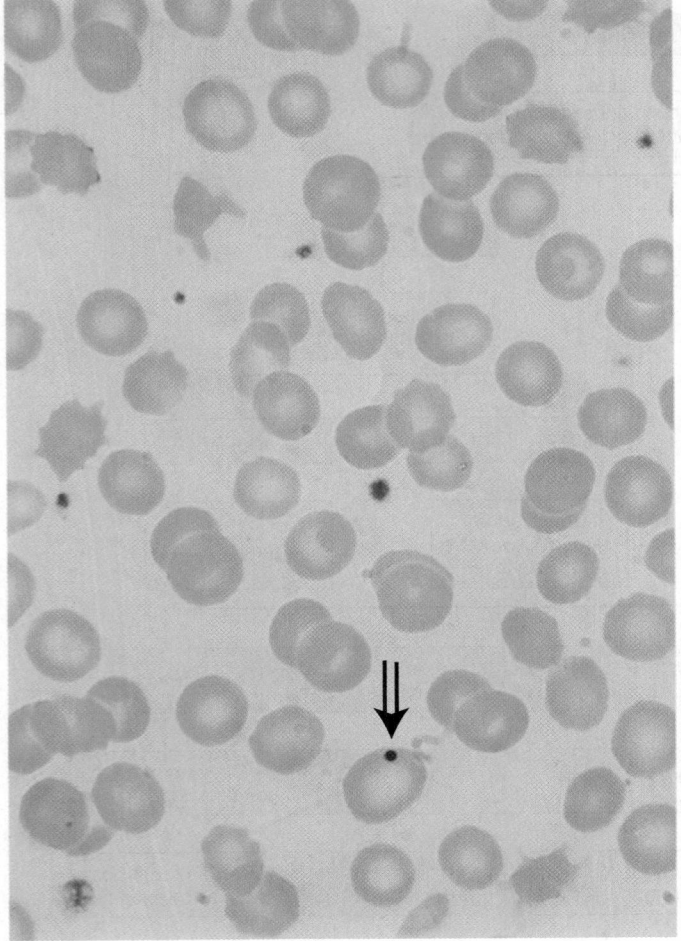

FIGURE 183–4 • Peripheral smear shows Howell-Jolly bodies (arrow) in the red blood cells, a finding typical for surgical or functional hyposplenism.

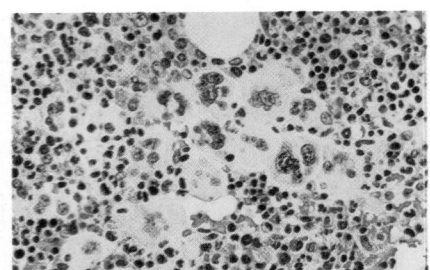

FIGURE 183–5 • Myeloproliferative disorder. Bone marrow shows megakaryocytic clusters seen in essential thrombocythemia and other conditions associated with clonal thrombocytosis.

with other bone marrow infiltrating processes including metastatic cancer, Hodgkin's disease (Chapter 194), and multiple myeloma (Chapter 196). Therefore, a bone marrow biopsy is essential for further clarification of the diagnosis.

The bone marrow in myeloid metaplasia is not easily aspirated (dry tap). The usual findings in the core biopsy include atypical megakaryocyte hyperplasia, collagen fibrosis, osteosclerosis, and intrasinusoidal hematopoiesis (Fig. 183–7). The degree of fibrosis may be better estimated by the use of either a reticulin (silver impregnation) or trichrome stain. Occasionally, the degree of bone marrow fibrosis may be minimal ("cellular phase" myeloid metaplasia). Bone marrow fibrosis may also be associated with other hematologic and nonhematologic conditions (Table 183–4).

The bone marrow morphologic features of myeloid metaplasia may sometimes be difficult to distinguish from those of both myelodysplastic syndrome with fibrosis and acute myelofibrosis. Acute myelofibrosis is characterized by severe constitutional symptoms, a nonpalpable spleen, pancytopenia, and the presence of circulating

MYELOFIBROSIS WITH MYELOID METAPLASIA

Diagnosis

The diagnosis of myeloid metaplasia is actively considered when anemia or splenomegaly is accompanied by a "myelophthisic" blood picture, with immature granulocytes, nucleated red cells, and teardrop-shaped red blood cells (dacryocytes) on the peripheral blood smear (Fig. 183–6). However, myelophthisis may also be associated

Table 183–2 • THERAPY OF ESSENTIAL THROMBOCYTHEMIA BASED ON THE RISK OF THROMBOSIS

Risk category	Low risk*	High risk†	Intermediate risk‡ +Cardiovascular risk factors +Extreme thrombocytosis
Cytoreductive therapy	No	Yes	No Sometimes
Aspirin therapy	Optional	Yes	Yes No

*Age <60 years *and* no history of thrombosis, extreme thrombocytosis (platelet count ≥1,500,000/μL), or cardiovascular risk factors (smoking, hyperlipidemia).
†Age ≥60 years *or* a history of thrombosis.
‡Neither low risk nor high risk.

Table 183–3 • CLINICAL PROPERTIES OF PLATELET-LOWERING AGENTS

DRUG (CLASS)	HYDROXYUREA (MYELOSUPPRESSIVE)	ANAGRELIDE (PLATELET-SPECIFIC)	INTERFERON ALFA (MYELOSUPPRESSIVE)
Mechanism of action	Antimetabolite	Unknown	Biologic agent
Pharmacology	Half-life ≅ 5 hours, renal excretion	Half-life ≅ 1.5 hours, renal excretion	Kidney is main site of metabolism
Starting dose	500 mg PO bid	0.5 mg PO tid	5 million units SC 3×/week
Onset of action	≅3–5 days	≅6–10 days	1–3 weeks
Frequent side effects	Leukopenia, oral ulcers, anemia, hyperpigmentation, nail discoloration, xeroderma	Headache, palpitations, diarrhea, fluid retention, anemia	Flulike syndrome, fatigue, anorexia, weight loss, lack of ambition, alopecia
Infrequent side effects	Leg ulcers, nausea, diarrhea, alopecia, skin atrophy	Arrhythmias, lightheadedness, nausea	Confusion, depression, autoimmune thyroiditis, myalgia, arthritis
Rare side effects	Fever, cystitis, platelet oscillations	Cardiomyopathy	Pruritus, hyperlipidemia, transaminasemia
Absolute contraindications	Pregnancy	Pregnancy	
Relative contraindications		Congestive heart failure	
Cost*	Annual = $1714 for 500 mg tid dose	Annual = $8500 for 0.5 mg qid dose	Annual = $10,500, for 3 million units 5 days/week

*Estimated cost to patient in 2003.

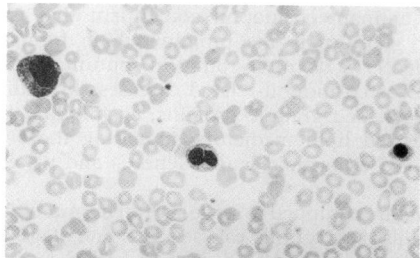

FIGURE 183–6 • Myeloproliferative disorder. A peripheral blood smear in agnogenic myeloid metaplasia showing a leukoerythroblastic picture. The characteristic findings are teardrop-shaped red blood cells (dacryocytes), nucleated red blood cells (erythroblasts), and immature granulocyte precursors.

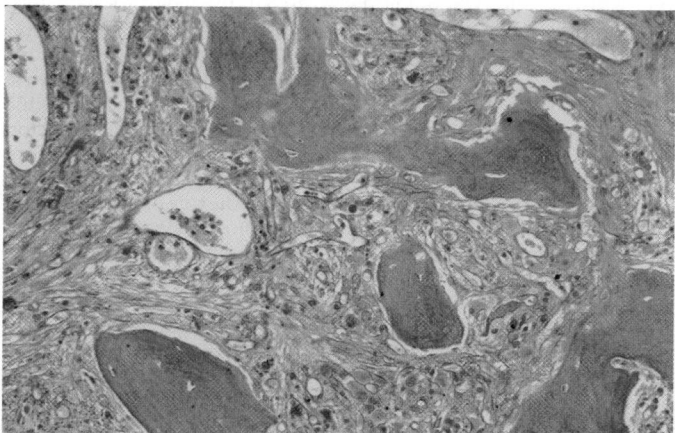

FIGURE 183–7 • A bone marrow biopsy in myelofibrosis with myeloid metaplasia showing reticulin fibrosis, osteosclerosis, and intrasinusoidal hematopoiesis.

Table 183–4 • CAUSES OF BONE MARROW FIBROSIS

MYELOID DISORDERS
Myelofibrosis with myeloid metaplasia
Metastatic cancer
Chronic myeloid leukemia
Myelodysplastic syndrome
Atypical myeloid disorder
Acute megakaryocytic leukemia
Other acute myeloid leukemias
Gray platelet syndrome

LYMPHOID DISORDERS
Hairy cell leukemia
Multiple myeloma
Lymphoma

NONHEMATOLOGIC DISORDERS
Connective tissue disorder
Infections (tuberculosis, kala-azar)
Vitamin D–deficiency rickets
Renal osteodystrophy

blasts. Some cases of acute myelofibrosis are classifiable as acute megakaryoblastic leukemia. Compared with myeloid metaplasia, both myelodysplastic syndrome with fibrosis and acute myelofibrosis are associated with shorter survival rates and may require more aggressive treatment.

Cytogenetic studies are most important in excluding atypical forms of CML that may present with substantial bone marrow fibrosis. At diagnosis, approximately one third of patients with myeloid metaplasia display karyotypic abnormalities including del(13q), del(20q), trisomy 8, and abnormalities of chromosomes 1 and 7. However, none of these cytogenetic markers carries diagnostic specificity.

Clinical Manifestations

The typical clinical presentation in myeloid metaplasia is anemia and marked splenomegaly. The causes of anemia include ineffective hematopoiesis, the replacement of normal hematopoietic tissue with collagen fibrosis, and hypersplenism. Hepatosplenomegaly in myeloid metaplasia is secondary to extramedullary hematopoiesis and may be associated with hypercatabolic symptoms (profound fatigue, weight loss, night sweats, low-grade fever), peripheral edema, diarrhea, early satiety, and, occasionally, portal hypertension. Some patients may experience splenic infarcts with severe pain that may be referred to the left shoulder.

Most patients also have leukocytosis at presentation, but less than half have thrombocytosis. Serum levels of lactate dehydrogenase are often elevated. Nonhepatosplenic extramedullary hematopoiesis may occur in the lymph nodes, pleura (effusion), peritoneum (ascites), lung (interstitial process), and the paraspinal and epidural spaces (spinal cord and nerve root compression). Diagnostic tests include tissue biopsy, cytologic analysis (a transudate with megakaryocytes and granulocyte precursors), a technetium sulfur colloid scan, and spinal magnetic resonance imaging.

Prognosis

The most frequent disease-related causes of death in myeloid metaplasia are infection and leukemic transformation. The latter occurs in approximately 20% of patients over the first 10 years. The presence of anemia (hemoglobin <10 g/dL), hypercatabolic symptoms, left-shifted granulocytosis (white blood cell count >30,000/μL or the presence of circulating blasts), and advanced age may predict a median survival that is less than 2 years. In the absence of all these adverse features, the anticipated median survival may exceed 10 years. Furthermore, a recent study has suggested that the presence of some (+8,12p-) but not other (13q-,20q-) karyotypic abnormalities may adversely affect survival. In general, the degree of either hepatosplenomegaly or bone marrow fibrosis may not affect survival.

Treatment

CONVENTIONAL TREATMENT. Conventional therapy in myeloid metaplasia is largely palliative and has not been shown to improve survival. Anemia is often treated with an androgen preparation (oral fluoxymesterone 20 mg/day) with or without the addition of corticosteroids (oral prednisone 30 mg/day). Response occurs in less than one third of the patients and lasts for less than a year. Before instituting androgen therapy, the possibility of occult prostate cancer should be excluded. Furthermore, female patients should be warned about possible virilizing side effects, and all patients should be periodically monitored for serum liver chemistries.

Hydroxyurea (500 mg three times a day) remains the drug of choice for the control of leukocytosis, thrombocytosis, or organomegaly. Hydroxyurea-refractory splenomegaly, if symptomatic, may require surgical removal. Other indications for splenectomy include disabling constitutional symptoms associated with marked splenomegaly, symptomatic portal hypertension, and the need for frequent red cell transfusions. Approximately one fourth of the patients with transfusion-requiring anemia may derive durable benefit from splenectomy. However, the perioperative mortality rate may be as high as 9%, and overall survival may not be affected (median postsplenectomy survival is approximately 2 years).

After splenectomy, approximately 16, 16, and 22% of the surgical survivors may develop acute leukemia, marked hepatomegaly, and extreme thrombocytosis, respectively, with the latter being significantly associated with perioperative thrombosis. Therefore, prophylactic hydroxyurea is strongly advised to prevent the postsplenectomy elevation in platelet count. In poor surgical candidates with symptomatic splenomegaly, palliative splenic irradiation is reasonable (approximately 300 cGy given in 10 fractions). Splenic irradiation may also be used in the management of splenic infarcts that are refractory to opiate analgesics. Treatment of nonsplenic extramedullary hematopoiesis requires low doses of involved field irradiation (100 to 150 cGy) given in multiple fractions.

Continued

INVESTIGATIONAL TREATMENT. Among many drugs that have recently been evaluated for the treatment of myeloid metaplasia, thalidomide has given the most promising results. A dose of 200 mg/day or more is poorly tolerated, but a dose of 50 mg/day has about a 20% response rate for anemia and splenomegaly with tolerable toxicity.

Allogeneic hematopoietic stem cell transplantation has provided durable disease remission in approximately one third of patients with myeloid metaplasia who have undergone such treatment. However, the substantial mortality and morbidity (approximately 50%) of the procedure currently limit it to poor-risk young patients. Autologous hematopoietic stem cell transplantation may have a role as palliative treatment, with a greater than 50% rate of benefit.

FUTURE DIRECTIONS

In essential thrombocythemia, the most important goal may be the identification of patients who are at risk for either thrombohemorrhagic complications or clonal evolution to guide selection for specific treatment. In myeloid metaplasia, the immediate goal is to identify the causal genetic mutation. The spectacular benefits of imatinib mesylate in CML (Chapter 192) suggest that targeted therapy with small molecules may provide great benefit in chronic myeloproliferative disorders.

Grade A

1. Cortelazzo S, Finazzi G, Ruggeri M, et al: Hydroxyurea for patients with essential thrombocythemia and a high risk of thrombosis. N Engl J Med 1995;332:1132–1136.

SUGGESTED READINGS

Anderson JE, Tefferi A, Craig F, et al: Myeloablation and autologous peripheral blood stem cell rescue results in hematologic and clinical responses in patients with myeloid metaplasia with myelofibrosis. Blood 2001;98:586–593. *A novel treatment approach for disease palliation.*

Storen EC, Tefferi A: A long-term use of anagrelide in young patients with essential thrombocythemia. Blood 2001;97:863–866. *Emphasis on both short-term and long-term side effects of anagrelide in the treatment of essential thrombocythemia.*

Tefferi A: Treatment approaches in myelofibrosis with myeloid metaplasia: The old and the new. Semin Hematol 2003;40(1 Suppl 2):18–21. *A comprehensive overview.*

Tefferi A, Murphy S: Current opinion in essential thrombocythemia: Pathogenesis, diagnosis, and management. Blood Rev 2001;15:121–131. *A comprehensive review of the biology and clinical aspects of essential thrombocythemia.*

184 EOSINOPHILIC SYNDROMES

Peter F. Weller

Eosinophilia, often with heightened production of eosinophils as well as increased blood and tissue eosinophil accumulation, is associated with distinctive disease processes that include helminth parasitic infections, allergic diseases, and a diversity of diseases of often ill-defined etiology (Chapters 265 and 391). In comparison with other leukocytes, eosinophils are distinguished by their morphology, constituents, products, and associations with specific diseases.

Eosinophils are produced in the bone marrow. The cytokine interleukin-5 specifically promotes the development and terminal differentiation of eosinophils and is principally responsible for increases in eosinophilopoiesis. Normally, eosinophils are primarily tissue-dwelling cells; the greatest numbers of eosinophils are found in tissues with a mucosal epithelial interface with the environment, including the respiratory, gastrointestinal, and lower genitourinary tracts. The lifespan of eosinophils is longer than that of neutrophils, and eosinophils may survive for weeks within tissues. Eosinophils, similarly sized to neutrophils but with usually bilobed nuclei, are morphologically characterized by their cytoplasmic granules (see Fig. 161–2). Specific granules, the most numerous of several types of cytoplasmic granules, have unique, ultrastructurally distinct crystalloid cores and contain eosinophil-specific cationic proteins. These cationic granule proteins, which bind acidic dyes such as eosin, are responsible both for the tinctorial properties of eosinophils and for many of the functional properties of eosinophils. The four eosinophil cationic proteins are major basic protein, eosinophil peroxidase, eosinophil cationic protein, and eosinophil-derived neurotoxin. Preformed stores of many cytokines are also present in the granules of eosinophils.

Another predominant eosinophil constituent that is not derived from specific granules is the protein, which forms bipyramidal Charcot-Leyden crystals, often found in sputum, feces, and tissues as a hallmark of eosinophil-related diseases. In addition to their content of preformed granule proteins, eosinophils also elaborate newly synthesized lipid mediators, including the 5-lipoxygenase pathway–derived eicosanoid leukotriene C_2 and platelet activating factor.

Eosinophils are equipped to serve several immunologic functions. Like neutrophils, eosinophils can serve as end-stage effector cells, but eosinophils have specialized roles in host defense and act primarily against multicellular parasites that cannot be eradicated by phagocytosis. Although eosinophils are capable of phagocytosing and killing bacteria and other small microbes, eosinophils do not have a major role in vivo in host defense against such microbial pathogens and cannot constitute an effective defense against bacterial infections in situations in which neutrophil function is deficient. Rather, eosinophils function in host defense against large, nonphagocytosable organisms, most notably the multicellular, helminth parasites. Eosinophils can invoke several mechanisms, including their cytotoxic cationic granule proteins, for antiparasitic host defense.

Pertinent to the involvement of the eosinophil in allergic diseases, including asthma, is the capacity of eosinophils to elaborate specific lipid mediators, including leukotriene C_4 and platelet activating factor, which can contract airway smooth muscle, promote mucus secretion, alter vascular permeability, and elicit eosinophil and neutrophil infiltration. Some of the mechanisms beneficial in the role of the eosinophil in host defense can prove detrimental to the host. Released eosinophil cationic proteins are toxic to host cells, and the dysfunction and damage elicited by eosinophil granule proteins may contribute to the pathogenesis of diseases in which heightened numbers of eosinophils are found within involved tissues. The effector functions of mature eosinophils, whether they are mediated by release of preformed granule proteins or by the synthesis of new lipid mediators, can be stimulated by cytokines, including interleukin-5 and granulocyte-macrophage colony-stimulating factor. Additional immunologic functions, based on the capabilities of the eosinophil to interact with lymphocytes and other cells, are beginning to be defined and may further contribute to the understanding of eosinophil participation in normal mucosal immune responses and in eosinophil-related diseases.

Blood eosinophil numbers do not always reflect the extent of eosinophil involvement in affected tissues in various diseases. Eosinophils usually number less than 450/μL in the blood; the count has a mild diurnal variation, being higher in the early morning and decreasing as endogenous glucocorticosteroid levels increase. Eosinopenia occurs with corticosteroid administration and is also frequent with active bacterial and viral infections. In patients with eosinophilia of various etiologies, circulating blood eosinophils can exhibit morphologic and functional changes consequent to their activation. In some patients with sustained blood eosinophilia, organ damage can develop, especially cardiac damage, as found in the idiopathic hypereosinophilic syndrome. Undoubtedly, the development of such complications of sustained eosinophilia reflects not just heightened numbers of eosinophils but also some activating events, as yet ill defined, that promote eosinophil-mediated tissue damage. Patients with sustained eosinophilia should be monitored for evidence of cardiac disease.

DISEASES ASSOCIATED WITH EOSINOPHILIA (Table 184–1)

PARASITIC DISEASES. Eosinophilia is not elicited by infections with single-celled protozoan parasites (with the exception of the intestinal coccidian parasites *Isospora belli* [Chapter 400] and *Dientamoeba fragilis*), but rather by the multicellular helminth parasites. The level of eosinophilia tends to parallel the magnitude and extent of tissue invasion, especially by larvae. Eosinophilia may be absent in established infections that are well contained within tissues or solely intraluminal in the gastrointestinal tract (e.g., *Ascaris*, tapeworms). Even with severe helminth diseases such as disseminated strongyloidiasis (Chapter 404), superimposed bacterial infections can suppress eosinophilia. In evaluating a patient with unexplained eosinophilia, geographic and dietary histories are germane in indicating potential exposure to helminth parasites. Stool examinations for diagnostic ova and larvae should be performed, and for evaluation of *Strongyloides* infection, an enzyme-linked immunosorbent assay for antibodies

Table 184–1 • DISEASES ASSOCIATED WITH EOSINOPHILIA

"Allergic" Diseases
Atopic and related diseases
Medication-related eosinophilias

Infectious Diseases
Parasitic infections, mostly with helminths
Specific fungal infections: allergic bronchopulmonary aspergillosis, coccidioidomycosis (acute and sometimes disseminated)
Other infections—infrequent, including human immunodeficiency virus-1 and human T-cell leukemia virus-1

Hematologic and Neoplastic Disorders
Hypereosinophilic syndrome
Leukemia
Lymphomas, including nodular sclerosing Hodgkin's disease
Tumor associated
Mastocytosis

Diseases with Specific Organ Involvement
Skin and subcutaneous diseases, including urticaria, bullous pemphigoid, eosinophilic celluitis (Well's syndrome), episodic angioedema with eosinophilia
Pulmonary diseases, including acute or chronic eosinophilic pneumonia, allergic bronchopulmonary aspergillosis
Gastrointestinal diseases, including eosinophilic gastroenteritis
Neurologic diseases (e.g., eosinophilic meningitis)
Rheumatologic diseases, especially Churg-Strauss vasculitis; eosinophilic fasciitis
Cardiac diseases (e.g., endomyocardial fibrosis)
Renal diseases, including drug-induced interstitial nephritis, eosinophilic cystitis, dialysis

Immunologic Reactions
Specific immune deficiency diseases: Hyper-IgE syndrome, Omenn syndrome
Transplant rejection: lung, kidney, liver

Endocrine
Hypoadrenalism: Addison's disease, adrenal hemorrhage

Other
Atheroembolic disease
Irritation of serosal surfaces, including peritoneal dialysis
Inherited

---

should be performed. In addition, for a number of helminth parasites that cause eosinophilia, diagnostic parasite stages are never present in feces. Hence negative stool examinations do not necessarily exclude a helminth etiology for eosinophilia, and examination of blood or appropriate tissue biopsy material, as guided by the clinical findings and exposure history, may be needed to diagnose specific tissue or blood-dwelling infections, including trichinosis, filarial infections, and in children, visceral larva migrans.

OTHER INFECTIOUS DISEASES. The characteristic response in acute bacterial and viral infections is eosinopenia, although in the convalescent phase of these diseases eosinophil numbers return to normal and at times to above normal, as seen with scarlet fever. Two fungal diseases may be associated with eosinophilia: (1) aspergillosis (Chapter 386), but only in the form of allergic bronchopulmonary aspergillosis and not as invasive disease, and (2) coccidioidomycosis (Chapter 380), following primary infection, especially in conjunction with erythema nodosum and at times with progressive disseminated disease.

ALLERGIC DISEASES. Allergic rhinitis and asthma (Chapters 84 and 268) are commonly associated with blood eosinophilia of less than 1500/µL. Hypersensitivity drug reactions can elicit eosinophilia without accompanying manifestations such as drug fever or organ dysfunction. When organ dysfunction develops, cessation of drug administration is necessary. Drug-induced interstitial nephritis (Chapter 120) may be accompanied by blood eosinophilia and eosinophils in the urine.

MYELOPROLIFERATIVE AND NEOPLASTIC DISEASES. Idiopathic hypereosinophilic syndrome is a myeloproliferative disease characterized by sustained overproduction of eosinophils. The four diagnostic criteria for this disorder are (1) eosinophilia in excess of 1500/µL persisting for longer than 6 months; (2) lack of an identifiable parasitic, allergic, or other etiology for eosinophilia; (3) signs and symptoms

of organ involvement; (4) lack of association with other, often idiopathic, yet clinically distinct eosinophilic syndromes (e.g., chronic eosinophilic pneumonia). Not all patients with prolonged eosinophilia develop organ involvement, and many have benign courses. Moreover, the aforementioned diagnostic criteria are sufficiently broad potentially to include eosinophilic disorders of other etiologies, currently unrecognized, that may have more favorable courses. The presence of angioedema is a good prognostic sign in hypereosinophilic patients, and this finding may be related to the more recent identification of a distinct clinical syndrome of recurrent episodic angioedema with eosinophilia, not complicated by the development of hypereosinophilic cardiac disease.

The clinical signs and symptoms of hypereosinophilic syndrome can be heterogeneous because of the diversity of potential organ involvement. One of the most serious and more frequent complications in this disorder is cardiac disease secondary to endomyocardial thrombosis and fibrosis. Mitral and tricuspid regurgitation may result from progressive fibrotic damage to the chordae tendineae (Chapter 72), and heart failure can develop from valvular incompetence and endomyocardial fibrosis (Chapter 73). Cardiac involvement in hypereosinophilic syndrome, which may require surgical valve replacement, has developed in association with eosinophilias of other recognized etiologies, occasionally including parasitic infections. A pathologically similar disease, Löffler's endocarditis and endomyocardial fibrosis, has been noted in tropical regions, where it is possible that antecedent parasite-elicited eosinophilias were responsible for the development of this cardiac disease. Echocardiography can facilitate detection and monitoring of these changes. Neurologic involvement can take three forms: embolic disease originating from the heart, diffuse encephalopathy, and peripheral neuropathy, especially mononeuritis multiplex. Other organ systems that can be involved include the skin, liver, spleen, gastrointestinal tract, and lungs. For patients with prominent organ involvement, mortality without therapy is about 75% after 3 years. Therapy is aimed at suppressing eosinophilia and is initiated with corticosteroids, to which about one third of patients will respond. In those unresponsive to corticosteroids, hydroxyurea, and interferon-α have also proved beneficial.

Eosinophilic leukemia is distinctly uncommon. Eosinophilia may accompany chronic myelogenous leukemia (Chapter 192), often with basophilia, and some subtypes of acute myelogenous leukemia (Chapter 193), but it is uncommon with acute lymphoblastic leukemia (Chapter 193). In a minority of patients with Hodgkin's disease (Chapter 194), blood eosinophils are elevated, occasionally to high levels. Increases in marrow and lymph node eosinophilia are more common. A small proportion of patients with carcinomas, especially of mucin-producing epithelial cell origin, have associated blood eosinophilia. Eosinophilia develops in some patients with mastocytosis (Chapter 272).

CUTANEOUS DISEASES. In addition to the neoplastic involvement of skin, a number of cutaneous diseases can be associated with increased blood eosinophils, including scabies (Chapter 406), bullous pemphigoid (Chapter 475), and two diseases associated with pregnancy: herpes gestationis and the syndrome of pruritic urticarial papules and plaques of pregnancy. In episodic angioedema with eosinophilia (Chapter 269), recurrences are marked by blood eosinophilia and prominent angioedema, at times with significant weight gain from fluid retention, and less frequently by fever. This entity is responsive to corticosteroids.

PULMONARY EOSINOPHILIAS. Blood eosinophilia can infrequently accompany pleural fluid eosinophilia, which is a nonspecific response seen with various disorders, including trauma and even repeated thoracenteses.

GASTROINTESTINAL DISEASES. Eosinophilic gastroenteritis (Chapter 143) is often associated with blood eosinophilia. Eosinophils are often present in the lesions of ulcerative colitis, and increased blood eosinophilia is occasionally found in both ulcerative colitis and Crohn's disease (Chapter 142).

IMMUNE DISEASES. Of the various forms of vasculitis (Chapter 284), only two are commonly associated with eosinophilia: hypersensitivity vasculitis and allergic granulomatous angiitis, or the Churg-Strauss syndrome, in which asthma, eosinophilia, and pulmonary and neurologic involvement are frequent. Although eosinophilia may uncommonly accompany rheumatoid arthritis (Chapter 278), any associated eosinophilia is more commonly due to medications used to treat the disease. Cholesterol embolization (Chapter 124) is at times associated with eosinophilia and hypocomplementemia, thus suggesting a secondary immunologic component. Some primary immunodeficiency syndromes are associated with eosinophilia, including the hyper-IgE syndrome and Omenn syndrome. Eosinophilic fasciitis is commonly associated with blood eosinophilia.

OTHER DISEASES. Irritation of serosal surfaces can be associated with eosinophilia, and related diseases can include Dressler's syndrome; eosinophilic pleural effusions; peritoneal and, at times, blood eosinophilia developing during chronic peritoneal dialysis; and, perhaps, the eosinophilia that follows abdominal irradiation. Two notable, apparently toxic diseases, the eosinophilia-myalgia syndrome caused by contaminated L-tryptophan (Chapter 463) and the earlier toxic oil syndrome in Spain, were prominently associated with

eosinophilia. Loss of normal adrenoglucocorticosteroid production in Addison's disease (Chapter 240), adrenal hemorrhage, or hypopituitarism can cause blood eosinophilia.

SUGGESTED READINGS

Cools J, De Angelo DJ, Gotlib J, et al: A tyrosine kinase created by fusion of the PDGFRA and FIP1L1 genes as a therapeutic target of imatinib in idiopathic hypereosinophilic syndrome. N Engl J Med 2003;348:1201–1204. *In nine of 11 patients, the eosinophil count returned to normal for more than 3 months.*

Weller PF: Eosinophilia and eosinophil-related disorders. *In* Adkinson NF Jr, Yunginger JW, Busse WW, et al (eds): Allergy: Principles and Practice, 6th ed. St. Louis, Mosby, 2003. *Provides a comprehensive review of clinical conditions associated with eosinophilia.*

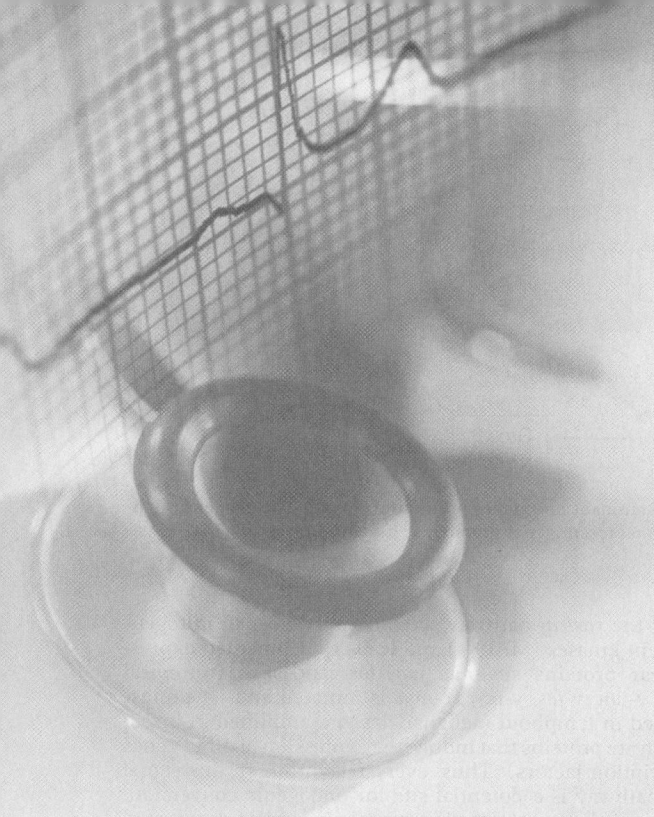

part XV

Oncology

185 ONCOGENES AND SUPPRESSOR GENES: GENETIC CONTROL OF CANCER

Edison T. Liu

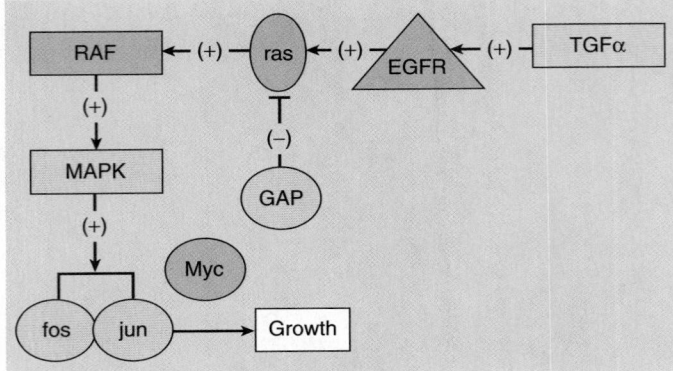

FIGURE 185–1 • Dominant oncogenes promoting growth. The elements highlighted in brown represent genes mutated in human cancers

THE ONCOGENE THEORY AND HUMAN CANCERS

Oncogenes encode proteins that, when activated, induce cancer; by contrast, tumor suppressor genes cause cancer when their function is blocked. The observation that mutant chicken and mouse oncogenes not only are associated with but also are causal in human cancers provided the first concrete evidence that human and animal cancers follow the same genetic rules. This observation also led to a new cancer model that stressed the importance of mutations in resident genes (also called proto-oncogenes) rather than the introduction of foreign genes. The concept that genes involved in cancer are the same as those controlling normal cellular processes further generalized the malignant process as a part of normal biology. Since these seminal observations, our understanding of the genetic basis of cancer has dramatically expanded. Cellularly, cancer cells can be characterized by uncontrolled growth either by augmentation of growth signals or by crippling of normal restraining checkpoints, bypass of senescence or programmed cell death, and inability to repair DNA damage and replication errors leading to genetic instability. In all cases, abnormalities in signaling mechanisms or the maintenance of genetic integrity are the root causes of cancer. The picture today reveals interacting webs of pathways controlling cellular functions critical to maintaining the cancer characteristics. Each node of this web is a candidate agent for cancer induction.

The primacy of genes and pathways in defining cellular behavior would predict that the mutational profile of a cancer cell may presage clinical outcome or at least explain cancer cell behavior. Indeed, this prediction has become reality. Moreover, in some cases, this molecular knowledge of the oncogenic events leads to the discovery of new and very specific therapies. Thus, in this process of discovery, a more unified theory explaining normal and malignant biology has emerged that also has significant clinical implications.

THE MANY ROADS TO CANCER

Aberrations of Signaling Pathways

Viral oncogenes were the first evidence that endogenous genes can directly cause cancer. Normal cellular genes (proto-oncogenes, designated by the "c" prefix) are transduced or captured by the retrovirus and mutated through the error-prone replicative process of the retroviral life cycle. The result is a viral oncogene (v-*onc*) that is often structurally distinct from its normal cellular counterpart and is functionally arrested in a biochemically activated form. Extensions of these early investigations revealed that the oncogene precursors, the proto-oncogenes, act as biochemical switches in cellular command and control processes, specifically relaying signals from the outside of the cell to the nucleus. The progressive and controlled transfer of extracellular signals is bypassed when one of the relay members is rendered constitutively activated, resulting in a characteristic of a cancer cell: unmanaged growth.

Nature has provided ample evidence for oncogenic mutations in members of signaling pathways (Fig. 185–1). The receptor tyrosine kinase epidermal growth factor receptor (EGFR, mutated or overexpressed in brain and epithelial cancers; homologous retroviral oncogene = v-*erbB*), when stimulated with one of its ligands, transforming growth factor-α (TGF-α; found to be overexpressed in some human cancers), interacts with *ras* (retroviral homologue = v-H-*ras*, or v-K-*ras*, mutated in 10 to 20% of all human cancers, including 40 to 50% of colon cancers and 20% of acute myelogenous leukemias) through bridging proteins. *Ras*, in turn, is controlled by guanosine triphosphate–activating proteins (GAPs, oncogenic homologue = *NF1*, the gene mutated in neurofibromatosis) and transmits signals through activation of *raf* (retroviral homologue, v-*raf*; the *BRAF* gene has been found to be mutated and activated in 66% of malignant melanomas).

Stimulation of the *ras/raf* pathway activates a number of mitogen-activated protein kinases (MAPKs) and leads to augmented expression of nuclear proteins such as *jun, fos,* and *myc* (retroviral homologues = v-*jun*, v-*fos*, v-*myc*; c-*myc* is mutated and its expression deregulated in lymphoid malignancies and amplified in breast cancers), which are proteins that induce the expression of other genes (called transcription factors). Thus, every relay node in this signal transduction pathway is a potential site for oncogenic conversion. The complexity of the transformation process is further augmented by the existence of multiple parallel signaling pathways that are promiscuous in their selection of biochemical partners. For example, the receptor tyrosine kinase HER-2 forms dimers either with itself or with related receptor tyrosine kinases, such as EGFR, HER-3, and HER-4. It is the activation through binding with heterodimerization that recruits the RAS pathway in this signaling stream. Thus, mutations in genetic members of oncogenic pathways are important in the genesis of human cancers.

THE WRONG PLACE AT THE WRONG TIME. In human cancers, mutations in proto-oncogenes lead to altered function. However, another avenue to cancer is the inappropriate expression of structurally normal proteins. Several transcription factors fall into this category: *myc, tal-1*/SCL, *lyl-1, Ttg-1,* and *Ttg-2*. These oncoproteins are structurally identical to their normal forms but are expressed either inappropriately in the cell cycle or in inappropriate tissues. *myc* is ubiquitously expressed in cells and plays a role in cell division and differentiation. Activation of *myc* related to the t(8;14)(q24;q32) seen in Burkitt's lymphomas and B-cell acute lymphoblastic leukemias (ALLs) deregulates *myc* expression such that the exquisite control of *myc* transcription is lost. In lymphoid tissues, the result is expansion of the pre–B-cell compartment in *myc*-containing transgenic mice and ultimately to the emergence of a monoclonal lymphoid malignancy. By contrast, the other members on this list (*tal-1*/SCL, *lyl-1, Ttg-1,* and *Ttg-2*) are linked to T-cell ALL. In this group, oncogenic potential is activated by expression in an inappropriate cell type: *tal-1* is normally expressed in erythroid and myeloid precursors and not T cells; *lyl-1* is expressed only in myeloid and B-lymphoid cells; and *Ttg-2* transcripts are found in liver, spleen, and kidney but not in activated T cells. The exception is *Ttg-1,* which is mainly a neurally associated transcription factor that is expressed at low levels in normal T cells; however, in T-cell leukemias with the t(11;14) translocation, *Ttg-1* RNA levels are extraordinarily high. In each case, the inappropriate expression of a transcription factor serves as a molecular switch to induce a malignancy.

Release of Suppression

Whereas proto-oncogenes are identified by a gain of function after mutational damage, another class of cancer genes, tumor suppressor genes, contribute to malignancy by a loss of function. To this end, well-known tumor suppressor genes such as the retinoblastoma gene (*Rb*) and *p53* can act as "brakes" to cellular proliferation, and each appears to function through distinct pathways. *Rb* negatively regulates an important transcription factor, E2F, and the deletion of the *Rb* gene (as seen in congenital retinoblastoma) or sequestration of its protein product (as seen in the presence of the adenovirus E1A protein or the human papilloma viral protein, E7) releases the suppression of E2F, thereby activating transcription. *p53*, functioning as a transcription factor, enhances the expression of *p21/CIP1*, which is a potent suppressor of cell cycle regulatory kinases, the cyclin-dependent kinases (CDKs). Activation of these CDKs is necessary for progression through the cell cycle, and CDK inhibitors block this process. The loss of *p53* and the associated loss of *p21/CIP1* expression control result in unmanaged progression through the cell cycle (Fig. 185–2). Mutations that disrupt function of the *p53* gene are among the most commonly seen in human cancers, occurring in over 50%, and the presence of a mutant *p53* in the germline of transgenic mice or in individuals affected with the Li-Fraumeni syndrome renders the mutation carrier susceptible to a host of cancers. These observations point to the importance of p53 in maintaining the noncancerous state. It is therefore not surprising that a number of biochemical controls are placed on p53 function. For example, MDM2 is a protein that binds to p53 and enhances p53 degradation. p53 induces the expression of MDM2, and thus p53 extinguishes itself through the induction of MDM2. MDM2 is overexpressed or amplified in 15% of human tumors and would be equivalent to a loss of *p53*.

That both *Rb* and *p53* are involved in the genesis of cancer is supported by the identification of germline mutations in patients with cancer predisposition syndromes such as congenital retinoblastoma (*Rb*) and the Li-Fraumeni multicancer syndrome (*p53*). As is the case with transforming oncogenes, the presence of a single abnormal tumor suppressor allele is insufficient for cancer to form; lesions at other genetic loci are necessary. For example, both *Rb* and *p53* may need to be inactivated for some primary cells to be rendered immortal, one of the first steps in transformation. The DNA tumor virus human papillomavirus (HPV), which is etiologic in cervical, anal, and penile carcinomas, has engineered itself to degrade both of these critical proteins by binding with the HPV viral proteins E6 (with *p53*) and E7 (with *Rb*). Through this mechanism, HPV biochemically achieves the same outcome that carcinogens accomplish by inactivating genetic mutations. In colon cancers, mutations in *p53* frequently accompany several other genetic lesions, including those involved in signal transduction (*APC* gene responsible for familial adenomatous polyposis, and *ras*) and cellular adhesion (*DCC* gene in colon cancers), for an invasive cancer to emerge.

By using the definition of a tumor suppressor gene as any gene whose loss of function contributes to cancer progression, functional categories of molecules involved in maintaining cellular "containment" can be devised. One category of suppressor genes includes the inhibitors of the cyclin-dependent kinases (CDKs). CDKs are kinases that control progression through the cell cycle. They, in turn, are controlled by protein activators (called cyclins) and inhibitors (called CDK inhibitors). The loss of expression of CDK inhibitors such as *p16^INK4A*, *p21*, *p27*, and *p57* has been associated with a wide range of

cancers, including cancers of lung, head and neck, breast, and pancreas, as well as melanoma. In malignant melanoma, the loss of both *p16^INK4A* alleles identified in most primary tumors led to the finding that inactivating germline mutations in *p16^INK4A* are constitutively found in patients with familial melanoma and with some familial pancreatic cancer syndromes. Therefore, CDK inhibitors such as *p16^INK4A* maintain the normal cellular phenotype by regulating cell proliferation, and abrogation of inhibitor function leads to cancer. The story of *p16^INK4A* reiterates the importance of viewing cancer genetics in the context of signaling relays. Rb acts to inhibit cell proliferation. Biochemically, cyclin D activates CDK4, the kinase that phosphorylates Rb. Phosphorylation of Rb inhibits its inherent growth-suppressive function, resulting in cellular proliferation. *p16^INK4A* blocks CDK4-dependent Rb phosphorylation, and therefore inactivating mutations of *p16^INK4A* allow the cyclin D/CDK4 complex to phosphorylate Rb, thus releasing a block to cell cycle progression (see Fig. 185–2).

Within the *p16^INK4A* gene is another gene whose protein product, *p14^ARF*, uses a different reading frame. Although *p14^ARF* and *p16^INK4A* are transcribed from overlapping segments of DNA, their protein products are distinct from each other. Interestingly, *p14^ARF*, like *p16^INK4A*, is also involved in the control of cellular growth: *p14^ARF* biochemically blocks the negative regulatory action of MDM2 on p53. Thus, crippling of *p14^ARF* found in lymphomas and leukemias augments MDM2 and would lead to a functional loss of *p53*. In many tumors, homozygous deletions of the entire p16 locus are observed. Genetically, this loss results in the concurrent loss of *p16^INK4A* and *p14^ARF* and ultimately the abrogation of *p53* and *Rb* function through the respective pathways. Thus, this single deletion inactivates the two "sentries" for cellular senescence, *p53* and *Rb*, accomplishing genetically exactly what HPV does on a biochemical basis with the E6 and E7 oncoproteins. Taken together, on a cellular level, *Rb*, CDK4, cyclin D, *p16^INK4A*, and *p14^ARF* are components of a signaling "relay station" that regulates traverse through the G1 portion of the cell cycle. Inactivating mutations in *Rb* and in *p16^INK4A*, deletions of *p14^ARF*, activation of CDK4 through mutation, amplification of MDM2, and amplification or overexpression of cyclin D have all been observed in human cancers (see Fig. 185–2).

Block in Cell Death and Bypass of Senescence

The accumulation of cancer cells can be accomplished by a decrease in cell death as well as by an increase in cellular proliferation. Current evidence suggests that the abrogation of programmed cell death (apoptosis) may be an important concomitant to neoplastic transformation. Certain cellular events, such as cytokine signaling (e.g., tumor necrosis factor, interleukin-3 withdrawal) or DNA damage, can trigger a cascade of events culminating in activation of intracellular proteases (caspases) leading to the regulated cleavage of cellular constituents, DNA fragmentation, and ultimately to cell death. Central to these events is the induction of mitochondrial outer membrane permeabilization whereby certain mitochondrial contents, notably cytochrome *c*, are inappropriately released into the cytoplasm. This event triggers activation of Apaf-1 (apoptotic protease activating factor-1), which, in turn, activates specific members of the caspase family. The cell exerts exquisite control of this process using redundant systems to induce or to block apoptosis, and some of these control switches are involved in cancer induction and in the response to cancer treatment.

The clearest example of an oncogene modulating the apoptotic process is *bcl-2*, found to be the important oncogene in patients with the t(14q;18q) translocation frequently detected in follicular lymphomas. *Bcl-2* blocks apoptosis when overexpressed or inappropriately expressed, and, in lymphomas, perturbations in *bcl-2* may be among the earliest oncogene abnormalities acting to prolong the lifespan of cells that are prone to accumulate genetic mutations. In experimental lymphomas, *bcl-2* does not cause cancer directly but allows the cell to survive to undergo subsequent mutations involving rearrangements at other oncogenes, such as c-*myc*, that result in accelerated progression of the lymphoma. This *bcl-2/myc* interaction underscores another principle of oncogene action: more than one cancer gene must be perturbed for a malignancy to arise. Other *bcl-2*–related proteins have been identified, all capable of physically interacting with each other as homodimers or heterodimers: *bcl-X_L* and *bcl-w*, like *bcl-2*, are antiapoptotic; however, overexpression of *bax, bak, bid, bim,* and *bad* actually induces apoptosis (proapoptotic). The emerging thinking is that the bcl family of proteins are fundamental

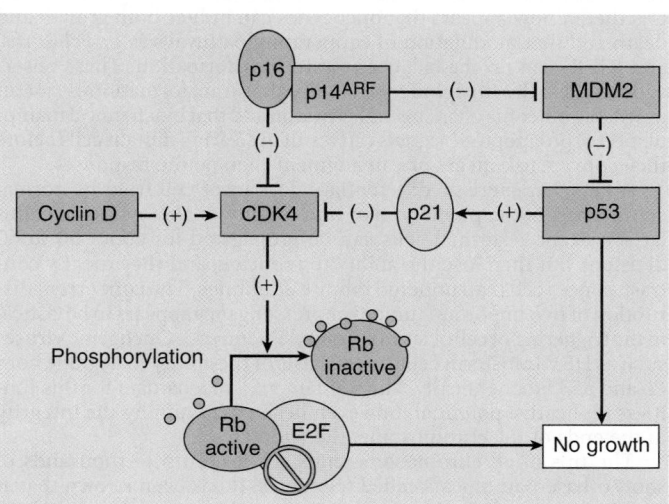

FIGURE 185–2 • Cancer genes involved in the control of the cell cycle. The elements highlighted in brown represent genes mutated in human cancers. Rb, p53, p16, and p14^ARF have deletions or mutations that disrupt function, whereas MDM2 and cyclin D are amplified.

Oncology

regulators of the mitochondrial outer membrane permeabilization: antiapoptotic members such as *bcl-2* and *bcl-X*$_L$ block mitochondrial membrane permeability, whereas proapoptotic members, such as *bak* and *bax*, promote this mitochondrial permeability and subsequent cytochrome *c* release. Thus, the ratio of antiapoptotic to proapoptotic factors of related structure determines the cell's "set point" that triggers apoptosis (Fig. 185–3). Significantly, this set point is associated with responsiveness to irradiation and chemotherapy.

Growth factor receptors and other surface signaling molecules have also been directly linked with the control of apoptosis. Many receptor kinase systems such as platelet-derived growth factor receptor (PDGFR), insulin-like growth factor receptor (IGFR), and *met* recruit and activate the phosphatidylinositol 3-kinase (PI 3-kinase). PI 3-kinase is now known to activate the *Akt* protein kinase, which supports cell survival through its phosphorylation and inactivation of BAD, a *bcl-2*–related protein that promotes cell death. Therefore, augmented *Akt* function or expression induced by either certain ligand-receptor interactions (increased IGF levels are associated with risk for breast and prostate cancers) or gene amplification (*akt* amplification seen in ovarian cancers) is predicted to have a significant antiapoptotic effect and may be involved in the induction of cancer.

The direct involvement of the PI 3-kinase/AKT pathway in cancer induction is exemplified in mutations found in the gene responsible for Cowden's syndrome. Cowden's syndrome is characterized by gastrointestinal hamartomas, cutaneous trichilemmomas, and increased rates of thyroid (3 to 10%) and breast cancers (25 to 50%), as well as uterine leiomyomas. The gene responsible for this syndrome has been mapped to 10q23 and was found to be *PTEN/MMAC*. Intriguingly, the function of PTEN is as a multifunctional phosphatase that removes phosphate groups from tyrosine and serine residues (thus countering the effects of oncogenic kinases) as well as from phosphatidylinositols, especially phosphatidylinositol 3,4,5-triphosphate. Its major function is to disarm the PI 3-kinase/AKT pathway leading to a heightened proapoptotic state. Thus, inactivating mutations in *PTEN* as is seen in Cowden's syndrome render a cell more resistant to

apoptotic signals. Biologically, artificial introduction of a normal copy of the PTEN complementary DNA reduces growth and induces cell spreading in established cancer cell lines. Moreover, mice with one disrupted PTEN allele have a high rate of lymphomas, teratocarcinomas, and liver and prostatic cancer. Thus, PTEN satisfies the classical definition of a tumor suppressor.

The most important biochemical consequence of PTEN action is to disarm the PI 3′-kinase/AKT pathway. Specifically, mutations in *PTEN* are associated with an increase in AKT activity. The intersect of antiapoptotic pathways is seen in the observation that AKT phosphorylates and inactivates the BCL2 proapoptotic homologue, BAD, resulting in a block to apoptosis. Thus, *PTEN* mutations render cells more resistant to cell death signals potentially by blocking the activity of the BAD protein (see Fig. 185–3). Although germline *PTEN* mutations are operative in a relatively rare disorder, somatic mutations leading to the loss of PTEN function are found in a large number of sporadic cancers including high-grade gliomas, thyroid cancers, and endometrial cancers and are circumstantially associated with gastrointestinal, breast, and prostate cancers as well. Why certain tumors such as lymphomas directly alter *bcl-2* to modulate apoptotic potential whereas others primarily use alternative pathways (as in Cowden's syndrome) to accomplish the same ends is unclear. In addition, the finding that patients with Cowden's syndrome do not suffer higher rates of lymphoma despite the logic of the biochemical pathways suggests that there are intricacies in the signaling network that gross biochemistry cannot discern. Nevertheless, the underlying are principle is that normal cells have self-policing mechanisms that activate suicide programs: when the mutational load of a cell exceeds a critical level, self-destruct processes are activated. Cancer, however, may result when genetically aberrant cells are not cleared but rather are permitted to proliferate, thus accumulating mutations in important cancer genes.

A second principle that has emerged is that many of the common oncogenes known to transform cells and to induce growth paradoxically also have proapoptotic functions. For example, *myc* is capable of transforming rat fibroblasts; however, in situations of cellular stress, such as starvation or when coupled with exposure to certain chemotherapeutic agents, *myc* triggers cell death in the same cells. Activated *ras* oncogenes, which are potent transforming genes in immortalized cell lines, also induce apoptosis under similar stress conditions. The characteristic of one protein having such diametrically opposed biologic functions as growth and death has been termed *antagonistic pleiotropy*. This characteristic has been considered nature's mechanism for preventing runaway proliferative conditions, such as cancer, by a single gene. Mechanistically, both RAS and MYC oncoproteins induce p14^{ARF}, which, by blocking MDM2 action, results in augmentation of normal p53 activity. This antagonistic pleiotropy, however, can be bypassed: when *myc* and *ras* are cointroduced into primary murine fibroblasts, unequivocal transformation occurs. When the biochemical components necessary for apoptosis were investigated for *myc*, it was found that *bcl-2* overexpression or specific activation of IGFR by IGF-1 can block *myc*-induced apoptosis. Taken together, it now appears that oncogenes can induce both growth and death and that modulation of cooperating pathways (e.g., *bcl-2*, *ras*, and IGFR) can tip the balance toward transformation. These observations raise the intriguing possibility that transformation is not an inevitable outcome of oncogene activation and that biochemical manipulation of proapoptotic signals can result in clearing mutant cells before they convert to cancers or can augment therapeutic responses.

A key characteristic differentiating a cancer cell from its normal counterpart is the phenotype of immortality or the bypass of cellular senescence. Normal cells can be propagated for about 50 to 60 divisions but then lose the ability to replicate, and they die. By contrast, cancer cells can undergo infinite doublings. The concurrent disruption of two important tumor suppressor genes appears to be critical in the triggering of cellular immortality: *Rb* and *p53*. Oncogenic viruses such as HPV transform cells on the basis of the ability to degrade both *Rb* and *p53* biochemically. The fundamental mechanism for this limitless replicative potential, however, lies in maintaining the integrity of the ends of the chromosome, the telomeres.

The tips of all chromosome ends are made up of thousands of short 6-base-pair repeats called telomeres. It has been known that at each replicative cycle, tips of chromosomes shorten by about 100 base pairs at the telomeres because of the inability of DNA polymerases to copy completely the entire 3′ ends of the chromosomes. Thus, after each division of a normal cell, the chromosomes shorten until, as with a fuse, a critical length is achieved, and the chromosomes lose

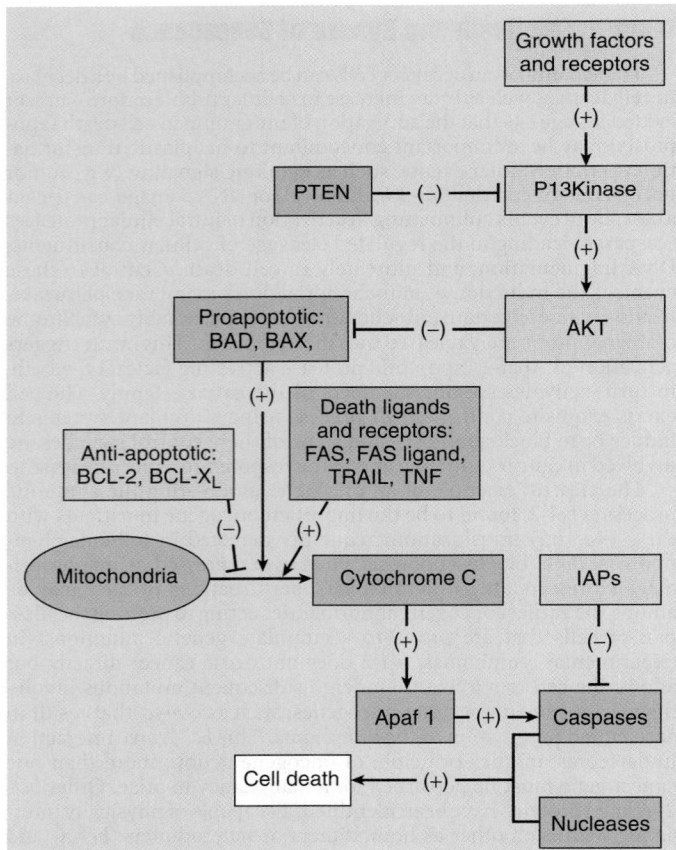

FIGURE 185–3 • Genes involved in cellular apoptosis. The elements highlighted in brown are proapoptotic whereas the others are antiapoptotic.

the ability to maintain their integrity. The result is chromosomal fusions and other evidence of cytogenetic damage that leads to cell death by triggering distress signals such as p53. All cancer cells, however, have evaded this central mechanism of senescence and biochemically maintain telomeric length. The vast majority accomplish this by turning on an enzyme complex called telomerase, which reverses the telomere shortening by adding back telomeric sequences at the ends of chromosomes. Normal cells do not exhibit telomerase activity, but cells with unlimited replicative potential, stem cells and cancer cells, do. When telomerase is artificially introduced in normal cells, senescence is abrogated and the cells exhibit unlimited replicative capability. The in vitro transformation of normal human fibroblasts can also be accomplished by the simultaneous introduction of a minimum of just three genetic events: the upregulation of telomerase, the activation of ras, and the inactivation of p53 and Rb. The role of telomerase in cancer was confirmed when it was observed that mice that were genetically engineered to disrupt telomerase activity exhibited progressive chromosomal aberrations and susceptibility to cancer development. Thus, genes central to aging and senescence are intimately linked to cancer induction.

Abnormalities in Genetic Stability and DNA Repair

A characteristic of a cancer cell is its inherent ability to undergo and to sustain genetic mutations. Normal cells have the ability not only to identify and repair DNA damage but also to prevent the propagation of mutation-laden daughter cells by suicide mechanisms such as apoptosis. It has long been suspected that defects in DNA repair, found in rare disorders such as xeroderma pigmentosum and ataxia-telangiectasia, are associated with the risk of cancer. Now, it is recognized that abnormalities in maintaining genetic integrity are causative in common epithelial tumors and are, in fact, one of the essential characteristics of cancer. An example is hereditary non-polyposis colon cancer (HNPCC), an inherited syndrome characterized by increased risk for colon cancer without associated polyposis and for endometrial cancer. It was found that affected individuals show signs of a defect in the repair of DNA mismatches; additions or reductions in the number of dinucleotide repeats (called microsatellite instability) were clonally detected in their tumors. Although DNA mutations are commonly seen in cancer cells, this type of abnormality is a signature for a specific kind of repair defect previously studied mainly in bacteria and in yeast. When incorrectly paired nucleotides occur within a DNA duplex, through either misincorporations, nucleotide damage, or faulty genetic recombination, cells use a mismatch repair (MMR) system to identify and to excise the mismatch. This recognition is mediated by the mammalian protein products of the *MSH2, MSH3, MSH6, MLH1, PMS1,* and *PMS2* genes. Patients with HNPCC primarily have mutations in *MSH2* and *MLH1,* although mutations in the others are also found in a smaller proportion of the patients. That mutations in the MMR genes lead to cancer has been confirmed in mice genetically engineered to have deleted the *MSH2, MLH1, PMS1,* and *PMS2* homologues. These animals have a high potential for developing hematopoietic malignancies and intestinal adenocarcinomas and adenomas (Chapter 200). The clinical consequence of this molecular defect in humans is the emergence of colon cancers that differ from the sporadic variety and are characterized by fewer *ras* and p53 mutations and a better prognosis than sporadic colon cancers. This observation suggests that the genetic point of origin of a cancer results from different pathways of carcinogenesis and even in different outcomes.

In breast cancer, evidence is accumulating that defects in DNA repair are the primary factors in the genesis of the disease. *BRCA1* and *BRCA2* are the two genes that, when crippled by inactivating mutations in the germline, dramatically increase the risk of breast and ovarian cancer (Chapters 204 and 205). Carriers of mutant *BRCA1* and *BRCA2* genes account for about 50% of clear-cut hereditable breast cancers. Although *BRCA1* and *BRCA2* reside in different chromosomes and are poorly related by amino acid sequence, both have primary functions in DNA repair and specifically in the rejoining of broken DNA. BRCA1 and BRCA2 are found to be associated with other proteins involved in DNA repair such as p53 and RAD51 and even to augment the transcriptional activity of p53 in response to DNA-damaging agents (Fig. 185–4). Moreover, tissues with disrupted *BRCA1* or *BRCA2* genes exhibit increased sensitivity to irradiation and a propensity for chromosomal aberrations related to illegitimate

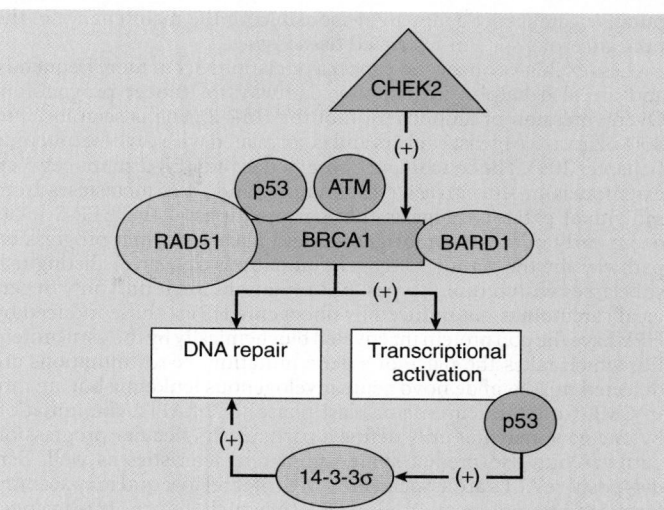

FIGURE 185–4 • Interconnections of *BRCA1* with DNA repair and transcriptional machinery. The elements highlighted in brown are genes that have been found mutated in human cancer.

recombination of DNA in the repair process. Other genes involved in the DNA repair process are also involved in breast cancer susceptibility. Carriers of germline *p53* mutations (Li-Fraumeni syndrome) have increased risk for the development of breast cancers. In response to DNA damage, CHEK2, a cell cycle checkpoint kinase, phosphorylates BRCA1 and p53 and is thought to augment their function. Inactivating mutations in *CHEK2* have been found to account for up to 6% of familial breast cancers without *BRCA1* or *BRCA2* mutations, often with a Li-Fraumeni syndrome phenotype. Taken together, the primary mechanisms for human breast carcinogenesis appear to be aberrant DNA repair and inability to clear damaged cells through apoptosis (PTEN, see earlier) but not excessive proliferative drive.

ONCOGENES AS POINTS OF ORIGIN: MOLECULAR PATHWAYS DEFINE A CANCER

Certain oncogenes are closely associated with specific malignancies, suggesting that they may be causative for those diseases. Chronic myelogenous leukemia (CML) is characterized by a genetic rearrangement juxtaposing the beginning of the *bcr* gene on chromosome 22 with the *abl* proto-oncogene on chromosome 9. The resultant bcr-abl hybrid protein activates the tyrosine kinase activity of *abl* and, in animal models, has been shown to be the direct cause of the CML phenotype (Chapter 192). Intriguingly, 10 to 25% of patients with de novo ALL also harbor the same t(9;22) translocation, but the rearrangement occurs at a slightly different genetic location to generate a distinctly smaller hybrid *bcr-abl* oncoprotein with increased biochemical activity. Thus, not only does the *bcr-abl* induce a specific hematologic disease, CML, but also minor alterations of the same aberrant protein result in a different clinical picture, ALL. Another example of specific oncogene-cancer associations is the t(15;17) translocation found exclusively in acute promyelocytic leukemia (APL); it causes the aberrant fusion of the retinoic acid receptor α (RARA) with another transcription factor, PML. This abnormal protein is seen in no other cancers. Lastly, rearrangements of the *bcl-2* locus and translocations involving the *myc* proto-oncogene are found solely in lymphomas.

In solid tumors, genetic perturbations that activate the *ret* oncogene have been identified only in sporadic thyroid cancers. Moreover, germline mutations of this receptor tyrosine kinase give rise to the heritable multiple endocrine neoplasia (MEN2) syndrome characterized by pheochromocytomas, medullary carcinomas of the thyroid, and parathyroid tumors as well as a more restricted syndrome of familial medullary thyroid carcinomas. Germline *APC* mutations give rise predominantly to colorectal cancers, and constitutive *BRCA1* and *BRCA2* mutations result mainly in breast and ovarian cancers. The near exclusivity of the involvement of some of these genes with the induction of specific cancers suggests a potential "gatekeeper" function for these genes. Although the exact mechanism is unclear, such putative gatekeeper genes are responsible for the maintenance of the noncancerous state in restricted tissue types.

Less exclusive oncogene-cancer associations occur more frequently and are also helpful in mapping pathways of cancer progression. Overexpression or amplification of the *HER-2* gene is seen in 20 to 30% of invasive breast cancers and is correlated with a worse outcome (Chapter 204). The concordance observed in the HER-2 status between carcinomas in situ, invasive carcinomas, and their metastases from individual patients suggests that perturbations at the *HER-2* locus occur early in breast tumorigenesis and mark a distinct progression pathway for the tumor. Oncogene mutations appear to distinguish subclasses within tumor types: *p53* mutations are found only in cervical carcinomas not induced by oncogenic HPVs; those induced by HPV have the p53 protein inactivated biochemically by the viral protein E6, which takes the place of a gene mutation. N-*ras* mutations are detected in 20% of de novo acute myelogenous leukemia but are rare in CML (in either chronic or blast phase) or in APL. The initiation by one gene may not only define a particular molecular progression pathway but also predict some tumor characteristics as well. *Bcr-abl*–positive ALLs are associated with earlier relapse and may account for the poorer prognosis in adult ALL (in which the *bcr-abl* rearrangement is seen in 25 to 40% of patients) compared with childhood ALL (in which only 5% are *bcr-abl* positive). HER-2 overexpression or amplification is found frequently in ductal breast carcinomas but rarely in lobular carcinomas. N-*myc* amplification remains one of the most potent predictors of poorer survival in childhood neuroblastomas. Thus, oncogene mutations can be used not only in cancer diagnostics but also as useful markers of prognosis.

CONVERGENCE OF PATHWAYS: TOWARD A UNIFYING EXPLANATION OF CANCER

The many oncogenes involved in malignancies highlight the complexity of the cancer process. However, the dissection of the biochemical pathways used by these oncogenes is uncovering interactions that may begin to unify empirical observations of human tumor biology. One example is found in *ras*. Ras activity is down-regulated by GAP, and oncogenic *ras* is resistant to the effects of GAP, suggesting that mutations abrogating GAP's negative effects on *ras* might promote cancer. Although abnormalities in *ras*-GAP have not been found, the gene associated with congenital neurofibromatosis, *NF1*, is structurally a guanosine triphosphate–activating protein that functionally interacts with *ras*. Mutations in *NF1*, seen in neurofibromatosis, block its ability to downregulate *ras* activity. This biochemical interaction between *ras* and *NF1* is manifested clinically in an unusual form of leukemia. Mutations in *ras* are a common genetic abnormality in adult acute myelogenous leukemia (AML). Interestingly, children with neurofibromatosis have a higher rate of developing a rare myeloproliferative syndrome that often progresses to AML. The biochemical pathway, therefore, predicts the clinical convergence.

How the molecular pathways explain some clinical manifestations of a disease can also be found in the example of von Hippel–Lindau (VHL) disease (Chapter 459). VHL disease is a heritable disorder characterized by renal cell carcinomas, retinal and cerebellar hemangioblastomas, pancreatic cysts, pheochromocytomas, and endolymphatic sac tumors. Linkage analysis led to the identification of the *VHL* gene as causative in the syndrome and as the important gene within the 3p deletions seen in the majority of sporadic renal cell cancers. Many of the VHL tumors, notably the renal cell carcinomas and the retinal and cerebellar hemangioblastomas, are highly vascular tumors. This finding is particularly pertinent because the VHL protein product is now thought to be involved in the post-translational processing of regulatory proteins, particularly those produced in response to hypoxic stress. The presence of an intact VHL protein induces the degradation of the hypoxia-inducible factors, HIF-1α and HIF-2α, which are transcription factors that augment the expression of hypoxia-inducible genes such as those encoding the angiogenic factor, vascular endothelial growth factor (VEGF), and erythropoietin (EPO). Mutations in the *VHL* gene seen in both hereditary and sporadic renal cell carcinoma frequently result in higher levels of VEGF and EPO. These higher levels explain, to a great extent, the highly vascular nature of renal cell carcinomas and the generation of vascular tumors such as hemangioblastomas in individuals with the VHL syndrome (related to the VEGF) and the association of elevated red blood cell mass in patients with renal cell carcinoma (related to the EPO).

A more dramatic example of the confluence of oncogenic processes has been uncovered in the analysis of the TGF-β pathway in gastrointestinal carcinogenesis. It has long been known that the peptide factor TGF-β can inhibit tumor formation and that tumor progression is associated with loss of response to TGF-β. This loss of response now appears to be due to the disruption of the type II TGF-β receptor. TGF-β acts by heterodimerizing the cognate type I and II receptors (TGFβRI and TGFβRII), leading to phosphorylation of the type I receptor and engagement of the downstream pathway (see later). Many tumors, especially colorectal cancers, have frameshift mutations in a short polyadenine tract within the gene that generates a truncated TGF-β receptor protein lacking kinase activity. Interestingly, this frameshift mutation occurs most commonly in cancers that are abnormal in MMR such as those from patients with HNPCC. This is because in the normal course of DNA replication, errors occur in copying these short repeating segments of DNA. It is as if the polymerase "lost its place" when reading DNA. These errors are corrected by the MMR system, which is defective in patients with HNPCC. That the TGFβRII gene mutation occurs at the switch from colonic adenoma to malignant carcinoma locates the biologic point of control of TGF-β in the carcinogenic process (Fig. 185–5). This association is so specific that this mutation in the TGFβRII gene is almost synonymous with an aberration of MMR.

The TGF-β signaling pathway requires engagement and phosphorylation by the activated receptors with cytoplasmic SMAD proteins. Activated SMADs form heterodimers between SMAD1 or SMAD2 with SMAD4, enter the nucleus, and interact with DNA binding proteins to induce transcription of TGF-β responsive genes. The importance of this sequence is that *SMAD4*, which is an essential component in the signaling pathway, is a major tumor suppressor gene found to be disrupted in 50% of human pancreatic cancers and to a lesser extent in gastric, breast, ovarian, and prostatic cancers. Thus, the TGF-β pathway alone involves three functional nodes that have significant roles in human cancers: MMR, TGFβRII, and SMAD4.

FRUIT FLIES AND HUMAN CANCER. One aspect of biology and medicine that has become apparent is that seemingly unrelated fields and biologic systems are uncovering common truths through the study of related genes. The underlying principle is that any biochemical switch can be usurped to control oncogene processes. This principle is evident in the observation that many oncogenes function as genetic switches in the development of diverse systems such as *Drosophila melanogaster* (fruit fly).

As is the case for all oncogenes, their nononcogenic counterparts, the proto-oncogenes, act as switches for normal cellular functions

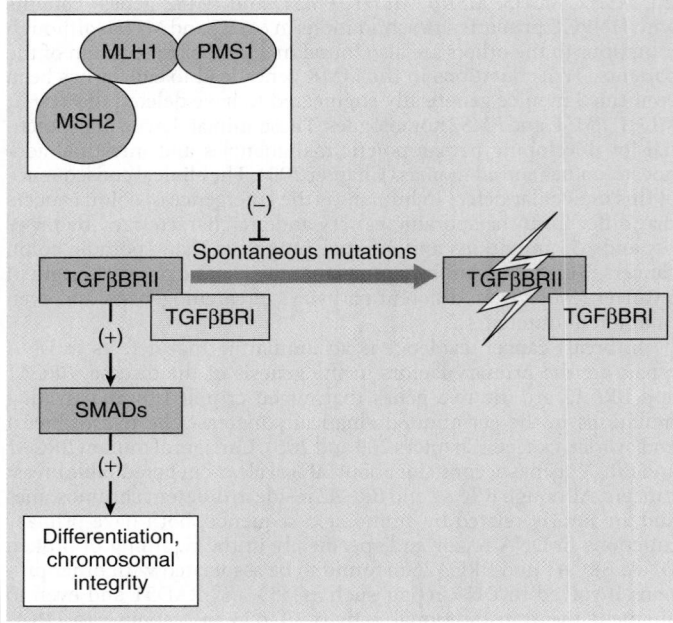

FIGURE 185–5 • Interaction between mismatch repair mechanism and tumor suppressor functions of the TGF-β receptor. The elements highlighted in brown represent genes mutated in human cancers.

especially in embryonic development. In the fruit fly, body segmentation during embryogenesis is controlled by the regulated expression of a series of related genes called homeobox (HOM) genes. Abnormalities in one such molecular switch are found in the homeotic mutation called antennapedia, which induces a condition in which legs develop where antennae are normally found. The human homologues are called *HOX* genes, and 22 of the 39 human *HOX* genes are expressed in different subpopulations of hematopoietic progenitor cells, functioning as signals for hematopoietic differentiation. As might be predicted, abnormalities in some of the *HOX* genes are associated with human leukemias; for example, the HOXA9-NUP98 fusion transcript is generated in the t(7;11) translocation, and the *HOX11* gene is activated in the t(10q;14q) translocation. Intriguingly, the genes that interact or control HOM expression in *Drosophila* are also specifically and frequently implicated in human leukemia. The translocated genes involved in t(8;21)(q22;q22) of AML-M2 include *AML1* (now called *RUNX1*), which is related to the *Drosophila* pair rule gene, *runt*, that acts temporally and spatially to regulate the expression of specific patterns of the HOM genes.

That *RUNX1* is involved in the genesis of leukemia is supported by the fact that hereditable germline mutations in the *RUNX1* gene predispose to thrombocytopenia and acute myeloid leukemia. The normal RUNX1 binds to a protein partner called CBFβ to perform its physiologic function as a transcription factor; specifically, CBFβ dramatically augments the ability of the RUNX1/AML1 to induce gene expression. Remarkably, CBFβ is also involved in leukemias with eosinophilia harboring the inv(16) translocation that generates the fusion protein CBFβ–MYHII. In both the *AML1/RUNX1* and the *CBFβ* translocations, the resultant fusion proteins act as dominant suppressors of the normal RUNX1- CBFβ transcriptional complex. The biologic consequence of inhibiting the normal transcriptional cassette of RUNX1-CBFβ is a blockade of hematopoietic differentiation. Intriguingly, the clinical responsiveness of leukemias with either *AML1/RUNX1* or *CBFβ* translocation is high. Thus, the association through a biochemical pathway appears to predict related clinical characteristics, an example of clinical convergence based on biochemical pathways. Extending these findings further, investigations have shown the importance of other *RUNX* genes in human cancers. There are three *RUNX* genes in humans: *RUNX1, RUNX2,* and *RUNX3*. Disruption of *RUNX3* in engineered mice led to intestinal hyperplasia and a reduced rate of apoptosis. This finding led to the observation that many human gastric cancers exhibit a reduction in gene dosage and gene expression of *RUNX3* and that this is associated with the virulence of the tumors. Because all the RUNX isoforms dimerize with CBFβ to perform its function, again, the biochemical pathway predicts the clinical outcome of cancer.

Similarly, rearrangements involving the t(4q21;11q23) translocation observed in both AML and ALL create fusion oncogenes mutating the *ALL1/MLL* gene (residing on 11q23). *ALL1/MLL* is homologous

to another *Drosophila* gene, *trithorax,* that maintains the cell type–specific expression patterns of the HOM genes. Although this translocation was originally thought to be unusual in leukemias, detailed molecular studies reveal that aberrations in *ALL1,* including internal duplication of a portion of the gene, are actually common, especially in secondary leukemias that arise from prior carcinogen exposure. Once expressed, HOM proteins interact with the extradenticle (exd) protein to exert its physiologic effects. In the related human situation, the mammalian counterpart to *exd, PBX1,* is rearranged to form the E2A-PBX1 fusion oncoprotein seen in pre–B-cell leukemias. Thus, at every node of signaling control, perturbations induce aberrations of differentiation and growth.

Genes involved in more common human cancers also have parallel networks in *Drosophila*. Germline mutations in the *APC* gene on 5q are responsible for the syndrome of familial adenomatous polyposis, which predisposes to colon cancer. Moreover, almost all sporadic colorectal cancers and sporadic adenomas involve somatic mutations in *APC,* suggesting a critical role for this gene in the genesis of the common colorectal malignancy. The structure of APC provided few clues to the mode of action of this protein. It was the discovery that the *Drosophila* homologue of APC binds to *Drosophila* β-catenin that quickly advanced our understanding of an important cancer-associated signaling pathway that links the cytoskeleton with nuclear signals and the central role of β-catenin in this process (Fig. 185–6).

In humans, E-cadherin is a surface receptor that is involved in cell-cell adhesion, particularly in epithelial cells. The intracellular domain of E-cadherin binds to catenins, and this interaction is essential for E-cadherin's function of forming and maintaining epithelial structures. Mutations in E-cadherin and in β-catenin are found in epithelial cancers, and germline mutations in E-cadherin are associated with familial gastric cancers. β-Catenin, in a different cellular compartment, has a role as a transcription factor. β-catenin also binds to APC in a complex that includes a kinase called GSK-3β, which leads to the phosphorylation of β-catenin and its subsequent degradation. When APC is inactivated, as in the case of most colon cancers, or when GSK-3β is further activated, β-catenin is stabilized and is free to bind with transcription factor TCF/LEF1. The β-catenin/TCF complex translocates to the nucleus and activates gene expression. This induction of specific gene expression, related to the release of inhibition by inactivating *APC* mutations, is thought to be the driver for colonic transformation.

In *Drosophila,* the mapping of genes responsible for morphologic mutants led to the discovery of a number of signaling pathways in which each signaling node is a gene that, when mutated, can result in a phenotype. The β-catenin homologue is called Armadillo. Armadillo is phosphorylated by Zeste-White 3 (homologue of the mammalian GSK-3β), which is, in turn, inhibited by the Wingless/Frizzled ligand-receptor interaction. Of importance is that the

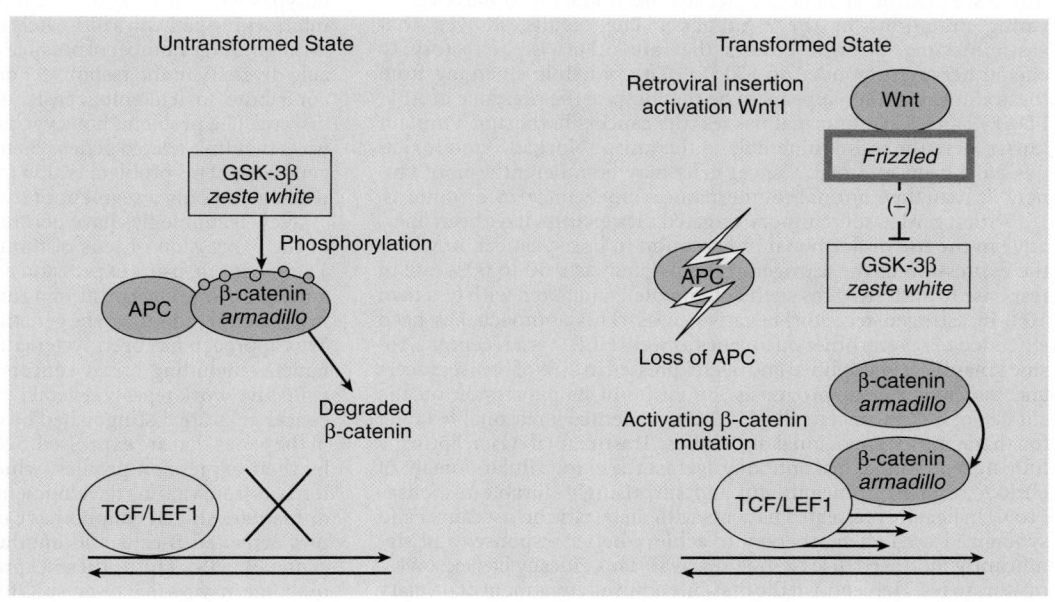

FIGURE 185–6 • The wnt/APC signaling pathway. The elements highlighted in brown represent genes mutated in cancers.

mammalian equivalent of Wingless is the protein product of the *wnt-1* gene, which is a well-known oncogene activated by retroviral insertion and responsible for certain mammary cancers in mice (see Fig. 185–6). Thus, the interconnections involving the β-catenin/Armadillo signaling pathway are implicated in human colon cancers, in murine mammary cancers, and in determining the morphologic condition in fruit flies.

These examples point out that a molecular switch that is functional in one setting may be disastrous in another. Specifically, inappropriate expression, either in developmental time or in tissue distribution, of genes involved in cell signaling may lead to cancerous consequences.

ONCOGENES AND CANCER TREATMENT

A goal of oncogene research has been the potential targeting of oncogenes as specific therapies for cancer. Some of the most mature forms of antioncogene therapeutics are seen in the treatment of human leukemias, such as the use of all-*trans* retinoic acid in the treatment of APL (Chapter 193) and the anti–BCR-ABL kinase inhibitor STI571 in the treatment of CML (Chapter 192). APL is characterized by the t(15;17) translocation that generates a fusion protein between PML and RARA. Normal myeloid differentiation appears to require an intact RARA that is active as a transcription factor. The PML-RARA fusion results in aberrant protein that is defective in signaling, leading to an arrest in myeloid differentiation. This defect is corrected by interaction with the retinoic acid–related ligand all-*trans* retinoic acid, which is an effective single-agent treatment for APL resulting in a 90% response rate. In conjunction with standard induction chemotherapy, all-*trans* retinoic acid results in an increase in the complete remission rate from 75 to 90% and in intermediate disease-free survival from 35 to 45% to 70 to 80%, making adult APL one of the most curable malignancies.

The specificity of the bcr-abl translocation to CML and the vulnerability of kinases to pharmacologic intervention led to the development of STI571 (imatinib mesylate, Gleevec). STI571 is a small molecule directed against the kinase domains of the BCR-ABL, PDGFR, and KIT oncoproteins. In clinical trials against CML in chronic phase, STI571 achieved complete hematopoietic responses in 95% of 532 cases. Significantly, only 9% experienced relapses within 18 months of therapy, and 41% achieved complete cytogenetic remission. In myeloid blast crisis, of the 232 patients, 52% responded, but only 22% maintained the complete remission at the 1-year milestone (Chapter 192). Direct inhibition of the BCR-ABL kinase is the mechanism of action for STI571 because leukemic cells from patients who become resistant to the drug either harbor further mutations in the *bcr-abl* gene that inhibit the binding between STI571 and the BCR-ABL oncoprotein or show overexpression of the BCR-ABL kinase through gene amplification. Because STI571 is also active against the KIT receptor tyrosine kinase, it was tested on patients bearing gastrointestinal stromal tumors that have been known to harbor activating mutations in the c-*kit* gene. The results showed that gastrointestinal stromal tumors that are otherwise refractory to chemotherapy responded to STI571. The principle emerging from these clinical studies appears to be that despite the presence of ABL, PDGFR, and KIT in normal tissues, the cancers harboring a mutant kinase were the most vulnerable to the kinase blockade, and toxicities have been minimal. Cancer cells may be inherently more vulnerable than their normal counterparts to biochemical interruptions.

With regard to solid tumors, targeted therapeutics have been operative in the use of hormonal intervention in breast cancer, in which the expression of the estrogen receptor predicts a 50 to 60% rate of response to antiestrogens such as tamoxifen compared with less than 10% in estrogen receptor–negative cases. This approach has been extended to several other oncogenes as well. HER-2 is a receptor tyrosine kinase that is amplified and overexpressed in 20% of breast cancers and indicates a poor prognosis. By virtue of its expression on the surface of breast cancer cells, HER-2 represented a reasonable target for therapeutic monoclonal antibodies. Trastuzumab (Herceptin), a humanized monoclonal antibody against the extracellular domain of HER-2, resulted in meaningful and surprisingly durable responses (16%) in heavily pretreated patients with metastatic breast cancer and synergized with chemotherapy to achieve better responses and significantly increased disease-free survival. This efficacy has led investigators to test Herceptin in the first-line adjuvant treatment of primary breast cancer. Although Herceptin is able to block HER-2 signaling, resulting in cessation of in vitro cancer cell growth, studies show that a major mechanism underlying the tumor response in vivo appears to be the ability of the antibody to induce a targeted immune response through antibody-dependent cytotoxicity.

Intracellular tumor suppressor genes such as *p53* have also been targeted for therapies. However, these targets are not readily accessible to antibodies or small molecules. Adenoviruses are double-stranded DNA viruses that, upon replication, can cause death in cancer cells and, when engineered, function as vehicles for gene therapy. After initial infection with a wild-type virus, *p53* is normally upregulated and can block viral replication through cell cycle arrest. This response would limit the cellular lysis by the virus except that the adenoviral gene *E1B* binds to and inactivates *p53*, thereby allowing completion of the replication cycle, resulting in cell lysis. A molecularly engineered adenovirus, Onyx-015, has specifically deleted the *E1B* gene. Thus, in normal cells with wild-type or normal *p53*, viral replication is aborted and no lysis occurs; however, in cells mutant in *p53*, replication proceeds, leading to cell death. Because a large number of cancers harbor *p53* mutations whereas normal cells do not, this engineered virus may provide antitumor specificity based on a single molecular mutation. Thus, knowledge of the *p53* biochemical pathways uncovered a novel therapeutic approach.

Aside from being targets, oncogenes can function as markers of cancer behavior that help in defining optimal cytotoxic therapy. For example, the presence of either the t(8;21) or the inv(16) translocation in AMLs (resulting in abnormalities in the AML1 and CBFβ transcription factors, respectively) predicts a good response to standard leukemic chemotherapy. The presence of 11q23 abnormalities with mutations in the *ALL1* gene and of a *bcr-abl* rearrangement are markers of inherent resistance to standard treatment and may indicate a requirement for transplantation. HER-2 amplification and overexpression are seen in about 20% of primary breast cancers and have historically been associated with a worse outcome even after standard adjuvant chemotherapy. Work arising from the national cooperative clinical trials group, Cancer and Leukemia Group B (CALGB), revealed that the presence of HER-2 overexpression and amplification predicts worse survival when patients are treated with suboptimal doses of adjuvant doxorubicin-based chemotherapy but that the bad outcome can be overcome by increasing the dose intensity of the drug. Thus, the presence of poor prognostic factors may not necessarily mean irreversibly unfavorable outcomes; instead, the profile of oncogene abnormalities in a particular tumor may be used to choose optimal therapy.

WHOLE GENOME INTEGRATION AND THE CELL BIOLOGY OF CANCER

Our standard reductionist approach to biology is to investigate one gene and its biologic consequences. This approach has led to an appreciation of the primacy of biochemical pathways in defining phenotypes with all its subtle manifestations. We know, however, that interlocking pathways ultimately determine the cellular response and, through a large number of possible combinations, can provide a remarkable diversity in the response. For example, many genetic mutations contribute to leukemogenesis, all converging on a single clinical disease. The problem, however, is how to parse out the critical pathways that link related genes when the analysis is on a single gene-by-gene basis. This problem is akin to identifying the origin of a painting when given only a segment of the whole picture.

New technologies have permitted the simultaneous interrogation of the expression of tens of thousands of genes in a single sample. The approach, using expression microarrays, fundamentally captures an expression fingerprint of a tumor. In this manner, a detailed but integrated "readout" of the genetic profile of a cancer can be obtained. This approach has been systematically applied to a number of malignancies including breast cancers, leukemias, and lymphomas. The collective work reveals several intriguing findings. First, normal and cancer cells are distinguished by only a fraction (less than 5 to 10%) of the genes that are expressed. Second, the cancers can be catalogued by their expression profiles, which resemble normal cellular counterparts from varying developmental or activation states. For example, diffuse large B-cell lymphomas can be divided into a form that resembles activated B cells and another that resembles resting germinal center B cells. Third, these expression profiles can predict clinical outcome in ways that test results for individual genes cannot: in diffuse large B-cell lymphomas, the activated B-cell variety has a worse prognosis than the germinal center B cell–like forms. Aside from providing a unique and powerful tool for the discovery of diagnostic markers, the expression arrays yield insight into how the various oncogenic pathways interact and converge to generate defined clinical manifestations.

MOLECULAR ONCOLOGY AND PUBLIC HEALTH

In the past, oncogene sciences have centered on understanding molecular mechanisms and applications to clinical care. Advances have placed oncogenes more prominently in public health and, in the process, have moved the field into the realm of cancer prevention. This fusion of disciplines has been necessitated by the identification of a growing number of cancer susceptibility genes and by the finding that oncogene mutations in some cases may represent "signatures" of carcinogen exposure. Data from molecular epidemiologic investigations have identified predictable mutations in the p53 gene associated with aflatoxin in hepatocellular carcinoma and with ultraviolet light exposure in skin cancers. Cancer susceptibility genes for colon cancer (APC, MSH2, MLH1), for breast cancer (BRCA1 and BRCA2), for retinoblastoma (Rb), for the Li-Fraumeni syndrome (p53), for the VHL syndrome (VHL), for the MEN syndrome (RET and MEN1), and for neurofibromatosis (NF1) have already been cloned and can be used for direct screening for cancer susceptibility (Table 185–1). The availability of these genetic tests raises some interesting and, simultaneously, troubling questions: Who should be tested, and at how young an age? What are the environmental factors modifying the genetic risk? Do all mutations in the susceptibility gene result in the same cancer phenotype? What kind of screening or surveillance is optimal? What is the best timing for surgical prophylaxis? Is surgical prophylaxis efficacious? What safeguards of privacy can we provide for our patients?

Answers to these questions are being formulated on the basis of studies of genetically at-risk individuals, and much has been accomplished. Because of the high rate of malignant thyroid cancers, prophylactic thyroidectomy is recommended even in children of MEN2 families with ret mutations. In almost all cases of confirmed carriers of ret mutations, precancerous or cancerous thyroid abnormalities are found in the resected material. Compared with historical management, prophylactic thyroidectomy prevents the occurrence of life-threatening metastatic and recurrent disease. Germline carriers of BRCA1 and BRCA2 mutations are associated with a 50 to 80% lifetime probability of developing breast cancer. Prophylactic mastectomy appears to be associated with a reduction of breast cancer in BRCA1 and BRCA2 carriers by 90%, and prophylactic oophorectomy reduces the incidence of ovarian cancer to almost the same extent. However, troubling concerns remain in the treatment of individuals at genetic risk for cancer. First, in the absence of a functional assay, it was not clear what constituted a mutation that changed protein activity compared with what constituted a simple polymorphism that has no functional impact. Unforeseen, often adverse, psychological effects were noted in patients who were tested regardless of the outcome of the genetic test; moreover, relationships within families can change when test results are disclosed. Even when firm linkages can be established between a truncation mutation and cancer susceptibility, the therapeutic options remain limited in syndromes with multiple or widespread cancers such as the Li-Fraumeni syndrome (sarcomas, brain tumors, and leukemias) or those in which the affected organs are vital such as the VHL syndrome, where the kidneys and the brain are involved, or hereditary retinoblastoma, where the eyes are involved. Moreover, as the genetic tests for carrier status become more available, social concerns about confidentiality and insurability severely restrict their clinical application.

LESSONS LEARNED AND FUTURE CHALLENGES

Our understanding of cancer genes has dramatically altered the conceptual landscape of basic biology. The most striking change is that the study of single genes has given way to the study of genes linked in pathways and in complex cellular processes, and this knowledge is directly affecting the clinical care of cancer patients. The integration of the individual pieces of genetic knowledge reveals only a small number of processes critical to the genesis of cancer. First is dysregulated growth, second is abrogation of programmed cell death, third is the establishment of cellular immortality, fourth is genetic instability, and the remainder, although not discussed in this chapter, are also important in the totality of the cancer phenotype: sustained angiogenesis, invasion and metastasis, and evasion of immunologic surveillance. Each of these cancer processes presents diagnostic opportunities and new therapeutic options. Intriguingly, in the past 10 years, the challenge in cancer biology and cancer medicine has become not the discovery of the molecular components of carcinogenesis but the logistic limitations of bringing these discoveries to clinical practice. The promise for more precise and effective therapy and for more rational preventive measures is being realized. The challenge in the future, however, will be to determine the safest and most expeditious approach to bringing these discoveries to clinical practice. Equally challenging is extending this process to the public health arena with all its attendant social and legal implications.

Table 185–1 • KEY GENES INVOLVED IN CANCER SUSCEPTIBILITY

DISORDER	GENE	FUNCTION
Ataxia-telangiectasia	ATM	DNA repair
Bloom's syndrome	BLM	DNA repair
Cowden's disease	PTEN	Protein phosphatase
Familial leukemias	RUNX1	Transcription factor
Familial adenomatous polyposis	APC	Associated with protein degradation
Familial breast and ovarian cancer	BRCA1, BRCA2	DNA repair
Familial melanoma	p16INK4A	Cyclin-dependent kinase inhibitor
Familial papillary renal cell carcinoma	MET	Receptor tyrosine kinase
Familial retinoblastoma	Rb	Transcription regulator
Hereditary diffuse gastric cancers	E-cadherin	Cytoskeletal protein
Hereditary nonpolyposis colorectal cancer (HNPCC)	MSH2, MLH1, PMS1, PMS2	DNA repair
Li-Fraumeni syndrome	p53 CHEK2	Transcription factor Cell cycle kinase
Multiple endocrine neoplasia I (MEN1)	MEN1/menin	Nuclear factor
Multiple endocrine neoplasia II (MEN2)	RET	Receptor tyrosine kinase
Neurofibromatosis	NF1	GTPase activating protein
	NF2	Cytoskeletal protein
Nevoid basal cell carcinoma syndrome	PTCH	Transmembrane receptor
von Hippel–Lindau syndrome	VHL	Protein degradation
Werner's syndrome	WRN	DNA repair
Wilms' tumor	WT-1	Transcription factor
Xeroderma pigmentosum	XPB, XPD, XPG	DNA repair

GTPase = guanosine triphosphatase.

SUGGESTED READINGS
Oncogenes and Their Role in Human Cancer
Markowitz SD, Dawson DM, Willis J, Willson JKV: Focus on colon cancer. Cancer Cell 2002;1:233–236. *A succinct review of colon cancer as a paradigm for molecular pathogenesis.*
Malumbres M, Barbacid M: Timeline: RAS oncogenes: The first 30 years. Nat Rev Cancer 2003;3:459–465. *An updated review of this important class of oncogenes.*
Venkitaraman AR: Cancer susceptibility and the functions of BRCA1 and BRCA2. Cell 2002;108:171–182. *Shows how disruption of the biologic functions of the BRCA proteins induces susceptibility to specific cancers.*

Cancer Genes and Cancer Treatment
Druker BJ: Perspectives on the development of a molecularly targeted agent. Cancer Cell 2002;1:31–36. *An example of how molecularly targeted therapy may revolutionize cancer treatment.*
Rosenwald A, Wright G, Chan WC, et al: The use of molecular profiling to predict survival after chemotherapy for diffuse large B-cell lymphoma. N Engl J Med 2002;346:1937–1947. *Demonstrates the power of molecular profiling for classification and prognosis.*

Cancer Susceptibility Genes and Cancer Prevention

Hartmann LC, Sellers TA, Schaid DJ, et al: Efficacy of bilateral prophylactic mastectomy in BRCA1 and BRCA2 gene mutation carriers. J Natl Cancer Inst 2001;93:1633–1637. *Prophylactic mastectomy is associated with less breast cancer in women with known BRCA1 or BRCA2 mutations.*

Pharoah PD, Antoniou A, Bobrow M, et al: Polygenic susceptibility to breast cancer and implications for prevention. Nat Genet 2002;31:33–36. *Genetic-risk profiles may provide significant improvements in programs to reduce the incidence of cancer and other diseases.*

186 EPIDEMIOLOGY OF CANCER

William J. Blot

Descriptive Patterns

GEOGRAPHY OF CANCER. Cancer affects all the world's populations, with nearly a four-fold difference between areas with the highest and lowest age-adjusted rates for all cancers combined. The geographic variation differs widely by cancer type. For certain cancers, the difference between high and low incidence exceeds 100-fold (Table 186–1). One of the most distinctive geographic patterns is seen for esophageal cancer (Chapter 136), with pockets of exceptionally high mortality in areas of north central China, the Caspian littoral of Iran, and South Africa. In Linxian, China, for as yet unknown reasons, esophageal/gastric cardia cancer is the most common cause of death, causing more than one third of all fatalities among adults. Clustering of elevated esophageal cancer rates also has been observed in parts of Europe and the United States, primarily due to heavy alcohol intake.

Geographic variation for other tumors is also noteworthy. Rates of oral cancer (Chapter 197) are highest in India and parts of south central Asia. Within the United States, elevated oral cancer mortality among women is found in the southern states, especially in rural areas. In both instances, the cause is the same, namely, high use of smokeless tobacco. In southeastern China, nasopharyngeal cancer is the most common malignancy; it is also a leading cancer among Alaskan Aleuts and Eskimos and occurs more frequently among Chinese than white or black Americans. A major cause of nasopharyngeal cancer in southern China appears to be consumption of salted fish,

especially during weaning and early childhood. The importance of early life events is also suggested by the up to three-fold higher rates of nasopharyngeal cancer among Chinese-Americans born and raised in China than among those born and raised in the United States. Similar migrant effects are seen for stomach cancer (Chapter 199): Japanese-Americans born in Japan, where rates of stomach cancer are among the highest in the world, have a two- to three-fold higher incidence of this cancer than Japanese-Americans born in the United States but who still have more than double the incidence of stomach cancer of white Americans. Such differences in rates imply the influence of environmental factors.

The most common cancers in Western countries, those of the lung, large bowel, and breast, also vary geographically. Within the United States, the highest rates of lung cancer (Chapter 198) are now found in southern rural counties, where lung cancer mortality in the 1980s surpassed that in northern cities, reversing a long-standing pattern. These shifts follow changes in cigarette smoking (Chapter 14), which is now more prevalent in the South than elsewhere in the United States. In addition, certain southern port and coastal areas have had excess lung cancer rates among men as a legacy of occupational exposures to asbestos in shipyards during World War II, when shipbuilding was the largest manufacturing industry in the United States, although the effect of such exposures has waned. In contrast, for colon and breast cancer, higher rates occur in the Northeast and lower rates in the South for reasons that remain unclear.

CANCER RATES AND TRENDS. It was estimated that in 2002 nearly 1.3 million Americans would develop and approximately 550,000 would die of cancer (Fig. 186–1). Cancer, excluding basal and squamous cell skin cancers, is newly diagnosed annually in about 450 of every 100,000 males and 350 of every 100,000 females. Cancer is now the leading cause of death, surpassing heart disease among Americans ages 40 to 79. The lifetime probability of developing cancer (again excluding the aforementioned skin cancers) has reached 43% among males and 38% among females. The most common cancers among men are those of the prostate, lung, and colon/rectum, whereas among women the top three are breast, colon/rectum, and lung. If mortality rather than incidence data are considered, the order shifts. Among males, lung cancer is by far the leading cause of cancer death (approximately 89,000 deaths expected in 2002), followed by prostate (30,000 deaths) and colon/rectum (28,000 deaths) cancer. Among females, deaths from lung cancer (66,000 deaths) now exceed those for breast (40,000 deaths) and colon/rectum (29,000 deaths) cancer.

For nearly all cancers, the incidence rates are higher among men than women, the exceptions being gallbladder and thyroid cancers. For some cancers, explanations for the male excess are evident (e.g., higher tobacco and alcohol intake account for most of the higher rates of oral, esophageal, laryngeal, and lung cancer among males), but for others (e.g., stomach cancer, leukemia), the reasons are enigmatic.

Rates of most cancers, particularly those deriving from epithelial tissue, increase steadily with advancing age, often exponentially. Some cancers show a bimodal age distribution. Leukemia and nervous system tumors display an early childhood (younger than 5 years) peak, then rates decline before increasing again in late middle age. Testis cancer occurs primarily between the ages of 20 and 40 years, whereas Hodgkin's disease incidence is highest at ages 20 to 30 years, declines somewhat, then increases after age 50 years.

Racial differences in cancer occurrence are sometimes marked. Total cancer incidence from 1989 to 1999 was higher among black than white males by 23%, whereas rates were higher among white than black females by 5%. The black/white differences among males were particularly pronounced for esophageal, stomach, pancreas, and lung cancer and for multiple myeloma, with age-adjusted incidence from 50 to 160% higher among blacks than whites. Reasons for the excess cancer occurrence among blacks are poorly understood. Racial differences tend to be even more pronounced for cancer mortality than incidence

Rates of several cancers have changed over the past decades (see Fig. 186–1). Most notable have been the trends in lung cancer (Chapter 198). Lung tumors were rarely diagnosed before the early 1900s, but incidence and mortality began a steady increase in the 1920s, which has continued until recently. The epidemic increase in lung cancer, almost entirely attributable to cigarette smoking, ended among males in the late 1980s. Rates among males are now declining, whereas the leveling off has just taken place among females. Rates of stomach and cervical cancers, the leading tumors early in this century, have declined, the former for reasons not yet fully understood, the latter, at least in

Table 186–1 • INTERNATIONAL VARIATION IN AGE-ADJUSTED INCIDENCE RATES FOR SELECTED CANCERS

CANCER SITE	HIGH-RATE AREAS* AND POPULATIONS	RATE†	BASELINE RATE‡
Oral cavity	France, India	35–45	1–2
Nasopharynx	China, Hong Kong	30	<1
Esophagus	China, Iran	100+	1–2
Stomach	Japan	80–90	5
Colon/rectum	U.S., Japan, New Zealand	50–60	6
Liver	China, Japan, Thailand	40–90	1
Pancreas	U.S. blacks	15	1
Larynx	Brazil, Italy, Spain	15–20	2
Lung	U.S. blacks, New Zealand Maori	110–120	6
Skin melanoma	Australia	30	<1
Breast	U.S.	100	20
Uterine cervix	Brazil, Paraguay, Peru, Colombia, India	40–50	4
Ovary	Norway, Iceland, Switzerland	15	4
Prostate	U.S. blacks	120+	2
Bladder	U.S. whites, Italy, Spain	25–35	2
Thyroid	Pacific Islands	25	<1
Non-Hodgkin's lymphoma	Switzerland, U.S., Canada	10–15	1
Hodgkin's disease	Ireland, Italy	4	<1
Multiple myeloma	U.S. blacks	10	<1
Leukemia	Canada	12	2–3

*Country in which high-rate areas occur is listed. The high rates do not necessarily persist throughout the country.

†Approximate age-adjusted (world standard) incidence rate per year 100,000 population among males (except for breast, cervix, and ovarian cancers). Data collection periods vary by area but typically center around the mid-1980s.

‡Approximate age-adjusted incidence rate in typical low-rate areas.

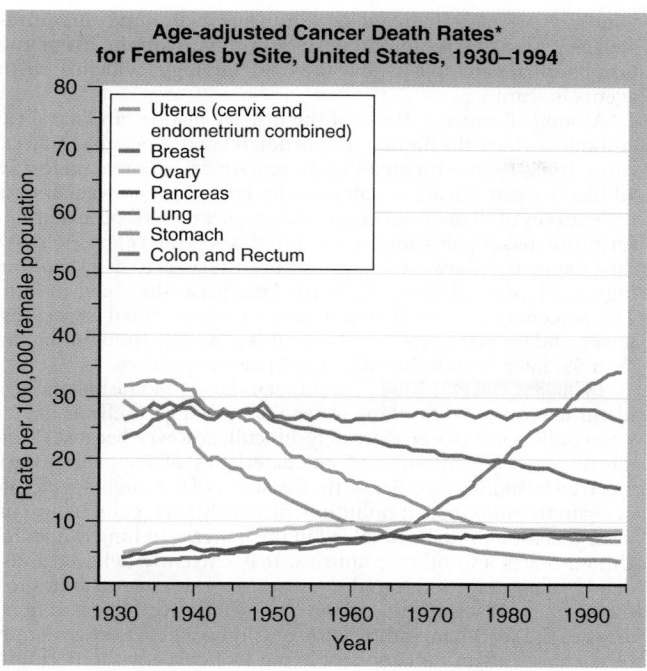

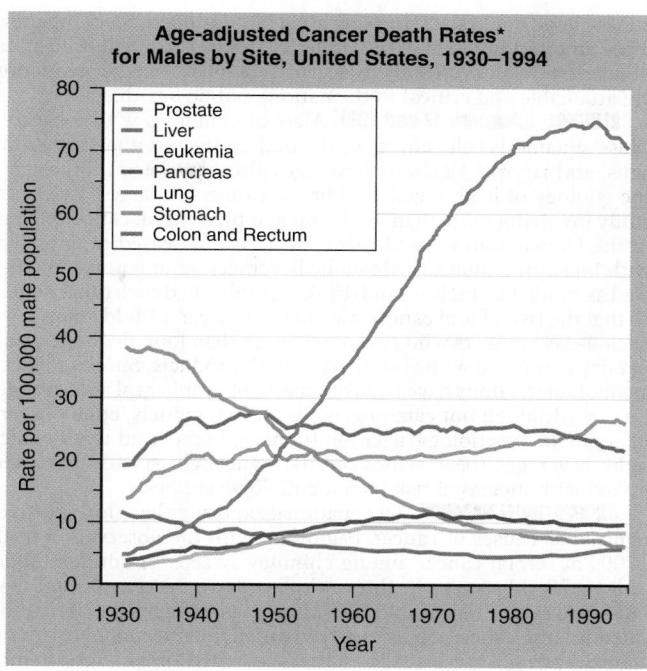

FIGURE 186–1 • Trends during 1930 to 1998 in age-adjusted mortality rates for selected cancers in the United States for females (*A*) and males (*B*). Rates are per 100,000 population and are age-adjusted to the 1970 U.S. standard population. Because of changes in the International Classification of Disease (ICD) coding, numerator information has changed over time. Rates for cancer of the uterus, ovary, lung, liver, and colon and rectum are affected by these coding changes. (From Jamal A, Thomas A, Murray T, Thun M: Cancer statistics, 2002. CA Cancer J Clin 2002;52:23–47, with permission; based on data from the Vital Statistics of the United States, 1997.)

part, due to cytologic screening for cervical pathology. The decreases in these tumors are beginning to end, however, and rates of gastric cardia cancer are increasing (Chapters 199 and 205).

Although not shown in Figure 186–1, there has been nearly a doubling in incidence of melanoma (Chapter 209) and a 50% increase in non-Hodgkin's lymphomas (Chapter 195) among whites since the early 1970s. In addition, among blacks the excess in lung, oral, laryngeal, and esophageal cancer has been increasing. For esophageal cancer (Chapter 136), however, striking differences exist by cell type: rates of adenocarcinomas of the esophagus have been increasing, especially among whites, and account for the large majority of esophageal cancers among white men, whereas squamous cell carcinomas of the esophagus still predominate among black men. The increase in esophageal adenocarcinoma appears in part related to the increasing prevalence of obesity, but full explanations remain to be discovered.

In the United States, a sharp increase in the incidence of prostate cancer (Chapter 207) occurred from the late 1980s to early 1990s, owing mainly to the increased detection of early tumors because of expanded screening with prostate-specific antigen testing. The result was a far greater incidence for prostate cancer than for any other malignancy (see Fig. 186–1). The spike ended around 1992, and both prostate cancer incidence and mortality rates have since been declining.

Causes of Cancer

Cancer is believed to be largely preventable. The causes of most cancers of the oral cavity and pharynx, esophagus, liver, larynx, lung, and uterine cervix are now known. Risk factors also have been identified for other cancers, but the search continues to clarify the factors that account for the bulk of malignancies in the United States and around the world. Most current information on risk factors for cancer has come from case-control studies assessing various characteristics and exposures of patients with individual cancers and from cohort studies determining rates of cancer among groups exposed to particular agents suspected of carcinogenic potential. The leads for these epidemiologic investigations often have arisen from descriptive studies of cancer rates and statistics and from alert clinical observations.

The striking variation in cancer rates within and between countries, the differing rates among migrants from one place to another,

and the often marked trends over time suggest that environmental factors (using the term *environmental factors* in its broadest sense to encompass all exogenous, nongenetic exposures) induce most cancers, perhaps through interaction with host susceptibility traits.

TOBACCO (Chapters 14 and 190). Cigarette smoking is the dominant cause of the leading cancer (i.e., lung cancer) in the United States and many other Western nations. The association was first suspected by clinical observations that new lung cancer patients were often smokers and then confirmed in the 1950s by case-control and cohort studies in the United States and Great Britain. In the years since the first U.S. Surgeon General's report on smoking in 1964, additional evidence has documented that risks of lung cancer increase in proportion to both duration of smoking and amount smoked per day, with risks of lung cancer more than 20 times greater among long-term heavy smokers than among nonsmokers. Lifelong filter smokers have experienced a somewhat lesser risk than lifelong nonfilter smokers, but the greatest protection comes from smoking cessation. Risks 10 years after quitting are typically only one third or less those of continuing cigarette smokers. Smoking affects all major types of lung cancer, but squamous and small cell carcinomas are affected more so than adenocarcinomas. Cigarette smoking also is a principal cause of cancer of the oral cavity and pharynx, esophagus, larynx, and renal pelvis; is a major contributor to cancers of the pancreas, bladder, and kidney; and is implicated to a moderate degree in cancers of the stomach and uterine cervix. Smoking also increases the chances of developing intestinal adenomatous polyps and thus may be involved in the early states of colorectal cancer. Smokeless tobacco is the predominant cause of buccal mucosa cancers in some populations. In total, tobacco use is thought to account for nearly one third of all cancers in the United States and thus is the largest single preventable cause of cancer.

Although the effects of smoking are far greater for smokers themselves, the consensus of evidence from multiple epidemiologic studies conducted in various countries since the early 1980s indicates that long-term exposure to environmental tobacco smoke also increases the risk of lung cancer among nonsmokers. The excess risk of lung cancer among nonsmoking women married to smokers averages about 20 to 30% (in contrast to more than a 1000% excess among smokers themselves). Because of tobacco's harmful effects, efforts to induce smokers to quit and to encourage nonsmokers, particularly

Oncology

adolescents, not to start smoking must be continued. Smoking prevalence among adult men in the United States has declined from a peak of nearly 60% in the 1950s to nearly 25% today. Further reductions are attainable and critical to the nation's public health.

ALCOHOL (Chapters 17 and 190). Alcohol combines with tobacco to cause squamous cell cancers of the oral cavity and pharynx, esophagus, and larynx. Alcoholic beverages also have been implicated in the etiology of liver, rectal, and breast cancers. A large case-control study involving more than 1100 oral and pharyngeal cancer patients in the United States found that cancer risk increased progressively with increasing intake of alcoholic beverages among nonsmokers as well as smokers. Smoking and drinking multiplied each other's effects so that the risk of oral cancer was increased over 35-fold among two-pack-a-day smokers who consumed more than four alcoholic drinks per day compared with abstainers of both products. Similar tobacco-alcohol interactions have been observed for esophageal and laryngeal cancer. Although not carcinogenic in animal models, ethanol seems likely to be the etiologic agent in humans, because all types of alcoholic beverages (beer, wine, and dark and light spirits) have been linked with increased risk in epidemiologic studies.

OCCUPATIONAL HAZARDS. Occupational exposures have long been recognized as causes of cancer, beginning with the observation in the 1700s of scrotal cancer among chimney sweeps in London. Today, at least 20 substances in the workplace have been associated with increased cancer risk (Table 186–2). About one half have been implicated in lung cancer, occasionally in an interactive manner with cigarette smoking. Asbestos exposure has accounted for the largest number of occupational cancers, although its impact is diminishing because of curtailments in asbestos exposure instituted more than 2 decades ago. Increased rates of lung cancer and mesothelioma have been found among asbestos miners and millers; factory workers handling asbestos, textile, and other products; shipyard, railroad, and construction workers; and employees working in other industries that manufacture or use this material. Rates of lung cancer and mesothelioma vary, however, according to intensity and type of asbestos exposure, with the large majority of asbestos-related tumors being caused by high levels of exposure to amphibole fibers.

Radon and its daughter products (Chapter 190), another group of potent carcinogens, exist in high levels in underground mines throughout much of the world. More than 20-fold increases of lung cancer have been reported in some groups of radon-exposed miners, most of whom are also smokers, with the excesses most pronounced for small cell anaplastic carcinomas. Several chemicals, including inorganic arsenic, benzene, β-naphthylamine and other aromatic amines, bischloromethylether, mustard gas, certain nickel compounds, and polycyclic hydrocarbons, also have induced cancer in exposed workers. All except arsenic are carcinogenic also in animals, with the carcinogen often inducing similar tumors in animals as in humans.

Some reviews have included beryllium and cadmium compounds, as well as 2,3,7,8-tetrachlorodibenzo-para-dioxin, on the list of known occupational carcinogens, but the epidemiologic evidence for these agents is scanty.

Among all cancers, those of the urinary bladder and nasal cavity and sinuses have the highest proportion related to occupational exposures. It has been estimated that among American men, up to 25% of all bladder cancers are occupationally related. In a Swedish nationwide survey of all nasal adenocarcinomas, nearly 25% occurred among furniture makers, possibly as a result of wood dust exposures. Wood dust exposures, however, have not been related to as exceptionally high a risk of nasal cancer in North America as they have in Europe. The percentages of other tumors due to occupational exposures are lower, and for all cancers combined it is generally thought that fewer than 5% have been induced by workplace exposures.

ENVIRONMENTAL POLLUTION. Carcinogens have in some instances been identified in air and drinking water. Quantifying the effects of air and water pollution has been extremely difficult, however, because of uncertainty over the amount and characteristics of exposures actually received by individuals. Before the discovery of the carcinogenic effects of cigarette smoking, air pollution, primarily from combustion products, was thought to be involved in the increase in lung cancer in the United States and other countries. It is currently believed that the degree of air pollution found in most urban areas contributes to less than 10% of cases of this cancer. The percentage increases in some areas of the world, including parts of China, where excessive rates of lung cancer affect nonsmokers living in houses without chimneys and in homes heavily polluted by coal-burning heating systems. Mesotheliomas have been diagnosed among women married to asbestos workers, presumably from handling clothing or otherwise being exposed to fibers brought home by their husbands. Concern has arisen over possible health risks from much lower levels of asbestos exposure that may occur in homes, schools, and other public places, but few such environmentally induced cancer cases seem likely. Pollutants in drinking water also have aroused concern. Rates of bladder cancer have correlated with levels of halogenated compounds in municipal water supplies; some of these agents have shown carcinogenicity in animal studies. Laboratory tests also indicate an increased risk of osteogenic sarcomas after high levels of exposure to fluoride in exposed animals, but epidemiologic investigations have found no significant or unexpected changes in cancer rates after fluoridation of water supplies.

MEDICINAL AGENTS. Among chemicals considered to be causally associated with cancer in humans, nearly one half are medications (Table 186–3), including drugs used in cancer treatment (Chapter 191). The occurrence of second primary cancers in 5 to 10% or more of patients who have received chemotherapy suggests that risks as well as benefits of such agents must be carefully assessed, particularly for patients

---

Table 186–2 • OCCUPATIONAL EXPOSURES RECOGNIZED AS HUMAN CARCINOGENS

EXPOSURE	SITE OF CANCER
4-Aminobiphenyl	Bladder
Arsenic	Lung, skin
Asbestos	Lung, pleura, peritoneum
Benzene	Leukemia
Benzidine	Bladder
β-Naphthylamine	Bladder
Bischloromethylether	Lung
Chromium (hexavalent) compounds	Lung
Coal tars and pitches	Lung, skin
Mineral oils	Skin
Mustard gas	Pharynx, lung
Nickel compounds	Lung, nasal sinuses
Radon	Lung
Soot, tars, and oils (polycyclic hydrocarbons)	Lung, skin
Strong inorganic acid mists containing sulfuric acid	Lung
Talc containing asbestiform fibers	Lung
Vinyl chloride	Liver
Wood dusts (furniture)	Nasal sinuses

Table 186–3 • MEDICINAL AGENTS RECOGNIZED AS HUMAN CARCINOGENS

DRUG	SITE OF CANCER
Azathioprine	Lymphoma, skin, soft tissue sarcoma
Chlornaphazine	Bladder
Cyclosporine	Lymphoma
1,4-Butanediol dimethanesulfonate (Myleran)	Leukemia
Combined chemotherapy for lymphoma, including MOPP	Leukemia
Chlorambucil	Leukemia
Cyclophosphamide	Leukemia, bladder
Estrogens-conjugated	Endometrium
Estrogens-synthetic (diethylstilbestrol)	Vagina, cervix
Estrogens-steroid contraceptives	Benign liver tumors
Melphalan	Leukemia
Methoxsalen with ultraviolet A therapy (PUVA)	Skin
Phenacetin-containing analgesics	Renal pelvis
Tamoxifen	Uterus
Thiotepa	Leukemia
Treosulfan	Leukemia

MOPP = nitrogen mustard, vincristine, procarbazine (Oncovin), and prednisone.

Oncology

whose long-term prognosis is otherwise highly favorable. Exogenous estrogens have been implicated in cancer risk. Diethylstilbestrol taken during pregnancy has resulted in vaginal adenocarcinomas in offspring exposed in utero. Unopposed estrogens given to menopausal women in the 1970s induced an increasing rate of endometrial cancer, and rates decreased abruptly when combined estrogen-progestogen therapy was substituted. Aggregate data, however, suggest an increased risk of breast cancer among long-term users of combined estrogen plus progestogen therapy. Indeed, a large national clinical trial was stopped in 2002 before its scheduled end because of an increased risk of breast cancer found among postmenopausal women receiving combined estrogen-progestogen therapy.[1] Use of tamoxifen or raloxifene has been shown in clinical trials to reduce the risk of estrogen receptor–positive breast cancer, especially in high-risk women, although the benefit is partially offset by increased rates of thromboses and endometrial cancer.[2] Extended use of oral contraceptives before a first pregnancy also has been reported to increase subsequent risk of breast cancer, but the widespread introduction of oral contraceptives in the 1960s has not significantly influenced national rates of breast cancer in the United States. Combined (estrogen plus progestogen) oral contraceptives have been associated with a reduced risk of endometrial and ovarian cancer. Immunosuppressive agents sharply increase the risk of cancer; for example, renal transplant recipients have a more than 30-fold increased risk of subsequent lymphomas. The excess risk begins within months of starting immunosuppressive therapy, the fastest onset of any environmentally induced cancer.

Some common medications may have beneficial effects on cancer risk. Recent epidemiologic studies have shown that aspirin and other nonsteroidal anti-inflammatory drugs are associated with a lowered rate of gastrointestinal cancer, particularly colon cancer, perhaps through their effects on cyclooxygenase enzymes. Randomized trials are underway to evaluate the chemopreventive potential of these drugs.

RADIATION (Chapter 19). Follow-up of survivors of the atomic bombs of Hiroshima and Nagasaki and of groups of patients receiving radiation therapy for ankylosing spondylitis, cancer, and certain other conditions demonstrates that ionizing radiation can induce cancer in humans as it does in lower animals. Leukemia is the initial carcinogenic consequence, occurring most frequently 5 to 10 years after exposure, with increased risks of a variety of solid tumors, particularly breast, thyroid, and lung cancers, following thereafter. Significantly increased risks of breast cancer have been detected among atomic bomb survivors at doses somewhat less than 0.5 Gy, and head and neck tumors have followed less than 0.1 Gy of scalp irradiation for tinea capitis in Israeli children. The findings suggest the need for prudence in the use of medical irradiation. Improvements in radiologic equipment, however, have resulted in lower radiation doses. Thus, for example, risks associated with mammography are now believed to be low enough to justify routine periodic screening for breast cancer among U.S. women age 50 and older.

Ultraviolet radiation from sun exposure is the dominant cause of basal and squamous cell carcinoma and melanoma of the skin (Chapter 209). The key to prevention is reduced solar exposure, even though there is uncertainty regarding variations in effect according to extent and timing of exposure. For melanoma, intermittent heavy sun exposures, particularly during childhood and adolescence, may carry the greatest risk.

DIET AND NUTRITION (Chapters 12 and 190). Strong evidence indicates that diet and nutrition can influence cancer risk. Clearest are the inverse associations between risk of certain epithelial cancers, particularly oral, esophageal, stomach, and lung cancers, and intake of fresh fruits and vegetables. Epidemiologic studies have shown that the risk of these cancers among persons in the highest quartile of consumption is lower than among those in the lowest quartile of intake, although the magnitude of the decrease has varied between studies. The ingredients responsible for any protective effects in humans remain to be clarified. The epidemiologic data indicate that carotenoids, but not animal sources of vitamin A (retinols), link fairly consistently to reduced cancer risk, but vitamins C and E, which can inhibit the formation of carcinogenic N-nitroso compounds in vivo, folate, selenium and other possibly protective nutrients also have been identified. In a randomized clinical trial in an area of China characterized by chronic nutrient deficiencies, daily supplementation with a combination of β-carotene, vitamin E, and selenium reduced cancer mortality. Selenium supplementation also was associated with reduced risk of several cancers in a smaller randomized trial in the United States. No similar benefit, however, was observed in trials of cigarette smokers in Finland taking supplements of β-carotene or vitamin E, of American physicians taking β-carotene, or of American smokers and asbestos workers taking β-carotene plus retinol. Indeed, the Finnish and American smokers' trials showed small but significant increases in lung cancer among those supplemented with β-carotene. This unexpected result cautions against supplementation with high levels of β-carotene among smokers and indicates that the link between diet and cancer is more complex than was originally believed.

Recent studies in China and Italy suggest that garlic, onions, and other allium vegetables may reduce the risk of stomach cancer. Compounds in allium vegetables exhibit strong anticancer effects in experimental animals. Animal studies also show protection against cancer by polyphenols and other compounds in tea and certain other foods. Several epidemiologic studies have shown lower risk of some cancers in tea drinkers, but the evidence is mixed. Some food products may also contain substances that may increase cancer risk; for example, some food contaminants, including aflatoxins sometimes found in moldy peanuts or grains, are strong animal carcinogens. Rates of liver cancer tend to be high in parts of Asia and Africa where aflatoxin contamination is common, but information on the effect of these substances in humans is scanty.

Dietary fat, particularly saturated fat, and calories have been implicated in the risk of colon and other cancers, although the etiologic nature of the associations is still not well established. The relationship between dietary fiber and the risk of colon cancer is unclear, but it has been estimated that a high percentage of colorectal cancers have a dietary etiology. Diet and breast cancer have been linked, in part because of the much higher rates of these cancers in Western nations with high-fat, low-fiber diets, but the evidence is inconsistent. Despite the uncertainty about the precise role of diet and nutrition in cancer cause and prevention, past and recent estimates suggest that one third or more of all cancers may be related to dietary and nutritional practices.

INFECTIOUS AGENTS. Several viral agents have been associated with human cancer, particularly cancers of the liver in endemic areas and of the uterine cervix worldwide. Hepatitis B virus (HBV) is the primary cause of hepatocellular carcinoma in China and other areas where infections are prevalent (Chapter 202). Prospective follow-up studies show large increases in risk, with nearly all liver cancers arising among persons with prediagnosis HBV surface antigen positivity. Childhood hepatitis vaccination campaigns in some of these areas in the 1980s appear to be resulting in lowered liver cancer incidence at young ages, an effect that should persist as the cohort of vaccinees ages. The epidemiologic patterns of cervical cancer (with risks elevated among those with multiple sexual partners and/or early age at coitus) have long suggested a venereal component to etiology (Chapter 205). Only recently have laboratory techniques enabled detection of human papillomavirus (HPV) as the likely etiologic agent in a high percentage of cases. Herpes simplex virus type 2 has been associated with cervical cancer, but its independent or interactive role with HPV remains to be clarified. The Epstein-Barr virus has been implicated in both nasopharyngeal cancer (Chapter 197) and Burkitt's lymphoma (Chapter 195), whereas certain human retroviruses have been associated with adult T-cell leukemias in Japan and the Caribbean. The human immunodeficiency virus, the cause of acquired immunodeficiency syndrome, is associated not only with Kaposi's sarcomas but also with clearly increased risk of lymphoma among survivors of AIDS. Infection with *Schistosoma haematobium* has been implicated in increased risk of bladder cancer in parts of Africa, and infection with the liver fluke (*Opisthorchis viverrini*) has been linked to liver cancers, predominantly cholangiosarcomas, in Thailand. Recently, sufficient data have accumulated to declare that infection with *Helicobacter pylori* increases risk of gastric cancer, including gastric lymphomas (Chapter 199). *H. pylori* thus becomes the first bacterial agent to be recognized as a cause of human cancer.

GENETIC SUSCEPTIBILITY. A history of cancer in the family often is associated with increased cancer risk. The increases for common cancers such as those of the lung, colon, and breast are typically on the order of two- to three-fold. Shared environmental factors may contribute to the familial clustering, but strong associations among subgroups with early age at onset of cancer or bilateral presentation of breast cancer indicate a genetic predisposition. The most marked genetic effects are seen for skin cancer, with tumors rarely appearing in persons inheriting darkly pigmented skin. A few cancers show mendelian inheritance patterns, including retinoblastomas and melanomas arising from familial dysplastic nevi. In addition, certain

Oncology

hereditary precancerous syndromes have been linked to increased cancer risk: neurofibromatosis and other phacomatoses (associated with nervous system cancer), xeroderma pigmentosum and albinism (skin cancer), ataxia-telangiectasia and certain other immunodeficiency syndromes (lymphoma, leukemia, and other cancers), Bloom's syndrome (lymphoma, leukemia, and other cancers), and Fanconi's anemia (leukemia).

Investigations of families with unusually large numbers of members with the same or different cancers have provided insight into genetic patterns. In larger epidemiologic studies, increasing attention is being paid to systematic evaluations of genetic factors, such as polymorphisms in genes involved in the activation of compounds to carcinogenic form and the detoxification of carcinogenic agents, as reliable markers of host susceptibility become available. The search for indicators of individual susceptibility to specific carcinogenic exposures has intensified in hopes of identifying persons at high risk of cancer who could then be counseled to avoid exposure and be examined for early detection of cancer. The process of establishing relevant markers is complex, and promising leads sometimes fail to materialize. Nevertheless, the rapid expansion of research in genomics, proteomics, and susceptibility factors should prove highly fruitful in understanding the mechanisms of carcinogenesis as well as delineating groups and individuals at high risk for targeted interventions.

1. Writing Group for the Women's Health Initiative Investigators: Risks and benefits of estrogen plus progestin in healthy postmenopausal women. JAMA 2002;288:321–333.
2. Kinsinger LS, Harris R, Woolf SH, Sox HC, et al: Chemoprevention of breast cancer: A summary of the evidence for the U.S. Preventive Services Task Force. Ann Intern Med 2002;137:59–69.

SUGGESTED READINGS

Adami HO, Hunter D, Trichopoulos D: Textbook of Cancer Epidemiology. New York, Oxford University Press, 2002. *A review of the patterns of cancer and a summary of known and suspected causes of the major cancers affecting human populations.*

Bingham SA, Day NE, Luben R, et al: Dietary fibre in food and protection against colorectal cancer in the European Prospective Investigation into Cancer and Nutrition (EPIC): An observational study. Lancet 2003;361:1496–1501. *A doubling of dietary fiber intake from foods was associated with a significant 40% reduction in clorectal cancer.*

International Agency for Research on Cancer: Overall evaluations of carcinogenicity: An updating of IARC Monographs Volumes 1 to 42. Monographs on the Evaluation of Carcinogenic Risks to Humans. Supplement 7. Lyon, World Health Organization, 1987, and Volumes 43 to 80, 1987 to 2002. *A systematic review of epidemiologic and experimental evidence regarding carcinogenicity of over 150 substances.*

Jamal A, Thomas A, Murray T, Thun M: Cancer statistics, 2002. CA Cancer J Clin 2002;52:23–47. *Cancer frequency, incidence, mortality, and survival data for the United States.*

187 ENDOCRINE MANIFESTATIONS OF TUMORS: "ECTOPIC" HORMONE PRODUCTION

Robert F. Gagel

It is now commonly accepted that genetic abnormalities cause disordered cell growth that leads to the transformation of the phenotype. A corollary of this fundamental tenet is that changes in a handful of important cellular genes can result in altered expression of other genes, leading to the production of cellular proteins not normally expressed in the differentiated cell type. Among the more interesting and clinically relevant types of abnormal protein are those associated with "ectopic" hormone syndromes, a small but clinically important group of disorders.

There are several patterns of ectopic hormone production. The most common is the production of small polypeptide hormones by tumors derived from a specific class of neuroendocrine cells. These neuroendocrine cells are widely dispersed throughout the lung, gastrointestinal tract, pancreas, thyroid gland, adrenal medulla, breast, prostate, and skin; they share several common cytologic and biochemical characteristics (amine precursor uptake and decarboxylation), are often derived from the neural crest, and normally produce both biogenic amines and small polypeptide hormones. The list of hormones produced by tumors derived from members of this group of neuroendocrine cells includes corticotropin (ACTH), calcitonin, vasoactive intestinal peptide, growth hormone–releasing hormone, corticotropin-releasing hormone (CRH), somatostatin, and other small peptides. A second group of tumors, generally derived from squamous epithelium, produce parathyroid hormone–related protein (PTHrp) and vasopressin.

Current evidence suggests that aberrant hormone production is due to reversion to an earlier state of differentiation and an earlier developmental pattern of transcription factor expression. Expression of human achaete-scute homologue, a helix-loop-helix transcription factor, is necessary for differentiation of pulmonary neuroendocrine cells, the cell type involved in small cell carcinoma of the lung (SCCL). This factor is not expressed normally in the differentiated cell type, but it is expressed at high levels in SCCL. Recent studies have shown that a negative regulator of human achaete-scute homologue, hairy enhancer of split-1, is expressed at low levels in SCCL and that overexpression of this gene in SCCL and other neuroendocrine carcinoma cell lines returns the cell to a more differentiated phenotype. These results suggest that a perturbation in a normal differentiation factor is involved not only in the development of the transformed phenotype but also in the aberrant expression of several small polypeptide hormones.

In a second common hormonal syndrome, hypercalcemia caused by ectopic production of PTHrp, activation of the *ras*-MAP kinase signaling pathway, through mutation, appears to be responsible for PTHrp production by squamous epithelium. For example, normal fibroblasts can be stimulated to overexpress PTHrp by combined expression of an activated *ras* gene and a mutated tumor suppressor gene, p53. In this example, a combinatorial effect of common genetic changes in human cancer apparently results in abnormal expression of this hypercalcemic peptide.

CLINICAL SYNDROMES

The clinical syndromes associated with ectopic hormone production are important because they are often difficult diagnostic dilemmas, they are a major cause of morbidity and death in cancer patients, and their therapy can be challenging (Table 187–1). Management of these clinical syndromes is often difficult because of the necessity to treat both the cancer and the syndrome caused by excessive hormone production.

HUMORAL HYPERCALCEMIA OF MALIGNANCY

Hypercalcemia is one of the most common hormonal syndromes associated with cancer and one of the most difficult to manage. Hypercalcemia is the final common manifestation for several different pathophysiologic processes, so each patient must be approached in an organized manner to facilitate correct diagnosis and treatment. Measurement of an intact serum parathyroid hormone (PTH) level provides a useful starting point (Fig. 187–1). An elevated parathyroid hormone level in the context of hypercalcemia should prompt further evaluation for parathyroid disease (Chapter 260). However, in the majority of cancer patients with hypercalcemia, the intact PTH value is suppressed, indicating that the malignancy is generating the hypercalcemia. Several different clinical syndromes have been elucidated.

Parathyroid Hormone–Related Protein

Parathyroid hormone–related protein is normally involved in chondrocytic and dermatologic differentiation. Eight of the first 16 amino acids of PTHrp are homologous with PTH, and both peptides exert their various effects through interaction with the osteoblast PTH receptor. Activation of this receptor increases the expression of an osteoblast-specific cell surface protein, RANK ligand. Cell-to-cell communication of RANK ligand with the RANK receptor on the undifferentiated osteoclast causes increased osteoclast differentiation, bone resorption, and hypercalcemia. Ectopic production of PTHrp by a wide variety of tumors is one of the most common causes of hypercalcemia associated with malignancy. The clinical syndrome is nearly identical to that observed with hyperparathyroidism and includes

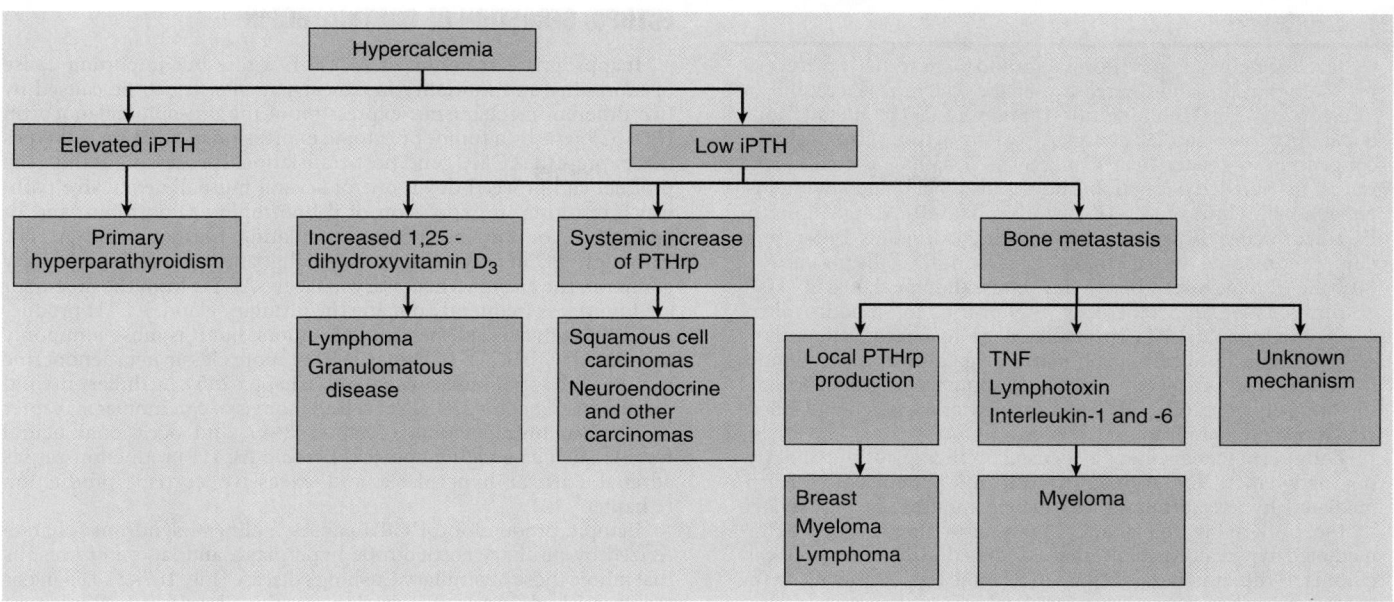

FIGURE 187-1 • A strategy for the evaluation of hypercalcemia in the context of malignancy based on measurement of intact parathyroid hormone (iPTH). PTHrp = parathyroid hormone–related protein; TNF = tumor necrosis factor.

Table 187-1 • SOME CLINICAL SYNDROMES OF ECTOPIC HORMONE PRODUCTION

Humoral hypercalcemia
  Parathyroid hormone-related protein
    Squamous cell carcinoma
    Breast cancer
    Neuroendocrine tumors
    Renal cell cancer
    Melanoma
    Prostate cancer
  Increased calcitriol
    Lymphoma
    Benign conditions: sarcoid, berylliosis, tuberculosis, fungal
      infections
Corticotropin (ACTH)
  Pro-opiomelanocortin
    Small cell lung cancer
    Pulmonary carcinoid
    Medullary thyroid cancer
    Islet cell tumor
    Pheochromocytoma
    Ganglioneuroma
  Corticotropin-releasing hormone
    Medullary thyroid cancer
    Paraganglioma
    Prostate cancer
    Islet cell tumors
Human chorionic gonadotropin
  Choriocarcinoma
  Testicular embryonal cell carcinoma
  Seminoma
Hypoglycemia
  Insulinoma
  Sarcomas or large retroperitoneal tumors
Inappropriate antidiuretic hormone secretion
  Small cell lung cancer
  Squamous cell head and neck cancer
Erythropoietin
  Renal cell cancer
  Hepatoma
  Pheochromocytoma
  Benign conditions: cerebellar hemangioblastoma, uterine fibroids

increased osteoclast-mediated bone resorption as well as an increase in renal tubular calcium resorption and a decrease in renal phosphorus resorption. The only significant clinical difference between PTHrp and PTH-mediated hypercalcemia is the finding of increased serum calcitriol (1,25-dihydroxycholecalciferol) levels in hyperparathy-roidism and low or normal values in PTHrp-mediated hypercalcemia, presumably because of inhibitory effects of cancer on the enzyme that produces calcitriol, 1α-hydroxylase. PTHrp production is most commonly associated with squamous cell carcinomas (Chapter 198), although production has been observed in other types of tumors, including breast (Chapter 204), neuroendocrine (Chapter 140), renal (Chapter 203), melanoma (Chapter 209), and prostate tumors (Chapter 207).

Increased Production of Calcitriol

Increased production of calcitriol occurs in a high percentage of patients with lymphoma (Chapters 194 and 195). There is compelling evidence for increased expression of 1α-hydroxylase by lymphomatous tissue. Other granulomatous conditions such as sarcoid (Chapter 91), berylliosis (Chapter 89), tuberculous (Chapter 341), or fungal infections (Chapter 378) may also cause this clinical syndrome. Other clinical features in this group of patients include a suppressed intact PTH level (see Fig. 187–1), an increased or normal serum phosphorus level, hypercalciuria, and no evidence of bone metastasis. An elevated serum calcitriol concentration is found in approximately one half of these patients.

Bone Metastasis

Bone metastasis should always be considered in the differential diagnosis of hypercalcemia in the cancer patient. Bone metastases are frequently associated with local production of cytokines, PTHrp, or other substances that cause increased bone resorption. Indeed, the distinctions between humoral hypercalcemia of malignancy and localized osteolysis have become blurred because of evidence that tumors such as breast carcinoma (Chapter 204) or myeloma (Chapter 196) cause localized osteolysis by local production and secretion of PTHrp. In breast carcinoma, there is considerable evidence supporting a local regulatory loop between transforming growth factor β and PTHrp production. Transforming growth factor β is a normal component of bone matrix. Local PTHrp production by breast carcinoma cells can stimulate osteoclastic bone resorption and transforming growth factor β release, which in turn stimulate greater PTHrp production, thereby accelerating the osteolytic process. Other activators of bone resorption, including tumor necrosis factor, lymphotoxin, interleukin (IL)-1, and IL-6, can be produced by other tumors that metastasize to (renal cell carcinoma) or reside in (myeloma) bone.

Treatment

Management of hypercalcemia should focus initially on reversing dehydration and increasing urine calcium excretion by infusion of normal saline solution at rates of 100 to 300 mL/hour, depending upon cardiac status. A patient with a serum calcium concentration greater than 13 mg% (3.25 mM/L), altered mental status, or renal dysfunction should also be treated with bisphosphonate (intravenous [IV] pamidronate 60–90 mg/4 hours or IV zoledronate, 4 mg over 30 min), glucocorticoids (40–60 mg/day prednisone or methylprednisolone), gallium nitrate (200 mg/M^2/day, infused for 7 days), or salmon calcitonin (100–200 units, IV or subcutaneously [SQ] every 6 to 12 hours) alone or in combination. PTHrp-mediated or localized osteolysis is most responsive to bisphosphonates or gallium nitrate; vitamin D–mediated hypercalcemia is most responsive to glucocorticoid therapy (Chapter 260). Intravenous zoledronate is generally more effective than pamidronate.

Long-term management is focused on therapy of the underlying malignancy. The average survival in a patient with PTHrp-mediated hypercalcemia is less than 3 months, in part related to the underlying malignancy. Long-term therapy of PTHrp-mediated hypercalcemia, like that associated with parathyroid carcinoma, is difficult: patients tend to become less responsive to the effects of bisphosphonate or salmon calcitonin therapy over time and may experience renal toxicity from gallium nitrate therapy when it is used for extended periods.

The identification of the aforementioned RANK ligand/RANK receptor system has led to the identification of osteoprotegrin, a soluble receptor that is produced by osteoblasts and that binds to RANK ligand, thereby preventing activation of the RANK receptor. Preliminary human studies with the recombinant protein indicate that osteoprotegrin is effective for the short-term treatment of hypercalcemia caused by activation of the RANK receptor, including hyperparathyroidism and PTHrp overproduction.

ECTOPIC SECRETION OF CORTICOTROPIN

Inappropriate secretion of ACTH is a rare but important cause of morbidity and mortality in cancer patients. It can be caused by two different mechanisms: expression of the pro-opiomelanocortin (POMC) gene by a tumor or ectopic expression of CRH. In cell types that express the POMC gene, post-translational processing of this gene product can proceed down one of several mutually exclusive pathways, resulting in expression of β-lipotropin, γ-lipotropin, and β-endorphin, or big melanocyte-stimulating hormone and ACTH. Although POMC expression by malignant tumors is relatively common, the enzymes necessary to cleave ACTH from the precursor are found less frequently outside the pituitary gland. ACTH production occurs in a broad spectrum of tumors, but it is most commonly associated with SCCL (Chapter 198) or more classic neuroendocrine tumors such as pulmonary carcinoid (Chapter 245), medullary thyroid carcinoma (Chapter 239), islet cell adenomas or carcinomas (Chapter 243), pheochromocytoma (Chapter 241), and occasional neural tumors such as ganglioneuroma. Ectopic ACTH production causes adrenal cortical hyperplasia and excessive cortisol production (Chapter 240).

Ectopic production of CRH causes a clinical syndrome characterized by pituitary corticotrope hyperplasia and laboratory results that mimic those of pituitary Cushing's disease (Fig. 187–2). Diagnosis requires a high index of suspicion, combined with either measurement of CRH in the blood or identification of a neoplasm outside the pituitary. Some neoplasms produce both ACTH and CRH. Tumors reported to produce CRH include medullary thyroid carcinoma, paragangliomas, prostate cancer, and islet cell neoplasms.

Hypercorticism associated with ectopic ACTH syndrome may manifest with classic features of Cushing's syndrome, such as easy bruisability, centripetal obesity, muscle wasting, hypertension, diabetes, and metabolic alkalosis (Chapter 240). In other patients, particularly those with rapidly growing SCCL, the clinical picture may be dominated by profound hypokalemic metabolic alkalosis and hypertension without the other clinical findings of Cushing's syndrome.

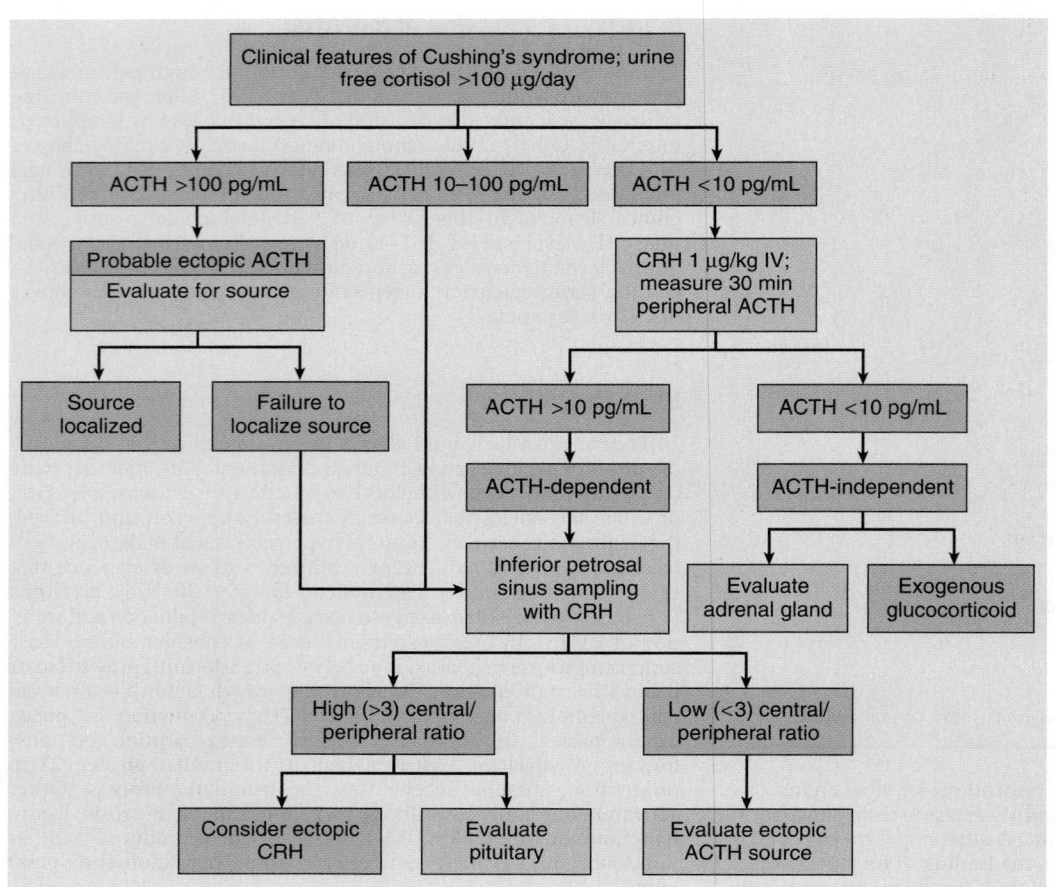

FIGURE 187–2 • An evaluation strategy for a patient with Cushing's syndrome and suspected ectopic corticotropin (ACTH) production. In patients with a plasma ACTH concentration greater than 100 pg/mL, ectopic ACTH concentration should be considered, although some patients with pituitary Cushing's disease may have values in this range. In patients with a plasma ACTH concentration between 10 and 100 pg/mL, inferior petrosal sinus sampling for ACTH should be performed after peripheral corticotropin-releasing hormone (CRH) injection (Chapter 240) to separate a pituitary (high central/peripheral ACTH ratio) from an ectopic ACTH (low central/peripheral ACTH ratio) source. In patients with a low basal peripheral ACTH value (<10 pg/mL), a low-dose CRH test (1 μg/kg) should be performed, followed by inferior petrosal sinus sampling in individuals whose plasma ACTH concentration rises to greater than 10 pg/mL.

Diagnosis

Several different approaches have evolved for the evaluation of Cushing's syndrome (Chapter 240). One approach (see Fig. 187–2) is based on the plasma ACTH measurement in a patient with clinical and laboratory features of Cushing's syndrome. The finding of a marked elevation of the plasma ACTH concentration (>100 pg/mL) should prompt a search for an ectopic source of ACTH. In a patient with a plasma ACTH value greater than 10 pg/mL but less than 100 pg/mL, a more detailed evaluation is appropriate. The differentiation between a pituitary and an ectopic source may require stimulation of ACTH secretion by CRH combined with measurement of ACTH in blood from the pituitary venous drainage (inferior petrosal sinus sampling). Lack of an increase in the inferior petrosal sinus ACTH concentration (more than three times the peripheral ACTH concentration) following peripheral CRH stimulation should prompt a search for an ectopic source. In patients who have an increased (more than three times the peripheral level) inferior petrosal sinus ACTH concentration following CRH, a pituitary source is likely. Ectopic CRH can yield confusing results and may not be diagnosed unless the clinician considers the possibility and measures a plasma CRH or looks for an ectopic source.

Other approaches have also been applied to the diagnosis of ectopic ACTH syndrome. For example, ACTH production from an ectopic source is not generally suppressed by high-dose dexamethasone. In a patient with an ACTH concentration greater than 10 pg/mL, administration of a single 8-mg oral dose of dexamethasone at 11:00 PM followed by measurement of serum cortisol level at 8:00 AM can differentiate between a pituitary and an ectopic source. The serum cortisol level in patients with pituitary Cushing's syndrome is generally suppressed 50% after dexamethasone administration, whereas levels in patients with ectopic ACTH generally are not suppressed. However, false-positive or false-negative results occur with each of these testing procedures, making the differential diagnosis of Cushing's syndrome among the most challenging in medicine.

 Treatment

Hypercortisolism associated with ectopic ACTH can be managed by removal of the ACTH- or CRH-producing tumor or by inhibition of cortisol synthesis with metyrapone (1 to 4 g/day orally [PO]), aminoglutethimide (250 mg PO four times a day with upward titration), or ketoconazole (200 to 400 mg PO twice a day). Parenteral etomidate, used for sedation and induction of anesthesia, rapidly inhibits cortisol synthesis at subhypnotic concentrations. It is titrated from 0.3 to 4 mg/kg/hour to normalize serum cortisol measurements and has been used to rapidly reverse hypercorticism in a small number of patients. Replacement glucocorticoid therapy is needed to prevent adrenal insufficiency. If surgical removal of an ACTH- or CRH-producing tumor is not possible and inhibition of cortisol synthesis is inadequate, bilateral adrenalectomy (with replacement glucocorticoid and mineralocorticoid therapy) may be required. In patients with a rapidly progressive SCCL and ectopic ACTH syndrome, the oncologic imperative to initiate immediate cytotoxic therapy must be counterbalanced by the desire to improve cell-mediated immunity by normalizing cortisol secretion, hypokalemia, and metabolic alkalosis. Cytotoxic chemotherapy generally should be delayed, if possible, until the serum cortisol level is normalized, because of the high rate of infection in neutropenic patients with hypercortisolism. If oncologic therapy is initiated, prophylactic therapy for pulmonary *Pneumocystis carinii* and fungal infections should be considered.

HUMAN CHORIONIC GONADOTROPIN PRODUCTION

Two different genes encode the α- and β-subunits of human chorionic gonadotropin (hCG). The β-subunit is common to all of the pituitary glycoprotein hormones (luteinizing hormone, follicle-stimulating hormone, thyroid-stimulating hormone, and hCG), whereas each of these hormones has a unique β-subunit gene. Inappropriate production of the α-subunit occurs in a variety of pituitary and nonpituitary tumors and does not cause any discernible clinical syndrome. The β-subunit confers biologic specificity. Production of intact hCG occurs commonly in trophoblastic tumors

(choriocarcinomas, testicular embryonal carcinomas, and seminomas; Chapter 206) and less commonly in other tumors such as lung and pancreas. Clinical syndromes associated with production of hCG include precocious puberty, gynecomastia, and hyperthyroidism. Hyperthyroidism results from the low-affinity interaction of hCG with the thyroid-stimulating hormone receptor when β-hCG is present at high concentrations. β-hCG concentrations that are several orders of magnitude higher than normal interact with the thyroid-stimulating hormone receptor, increasing thyroid hormone production, thereby suppressing endogenous thyroid-stimulating hormone production below normal.

 Treatment

Therapy for precocious puberty and gynecomastia is directed toward removal or treatment of the underlying tumor. Hyperthyroidism is treated by inhibition of thyroid hormone synthesis, usually with thionamide therapy, followed by therapy for the underlying tumor. Treatment of hyperthyroidism by surgical removal of the thyroid gland or ablation with radioactive iodine is rarely required, since the hyperthyroidism resolves rapidly after successful treatment of the underlying tumor.

HYPOGLYCEMIA ASSOCIATED WITH CANCER

Tumor-associated hypoglycemia is a rare but important cause of morbidity for cancer patients. Three different clinical syndromes cause most cancer-related hypoglycemia. The first is production of insulin by an islet tumor. Although primary insulinomas are rare, dedifferentiation and bulky hepatic metastasis of an islet cell carcinoma may be associated with excessive insulin production (Chapter 243). A second cause of hypoglycemia, insufficient gluconeogenesis to maintain the plasma glucose concentration in the fasting state, is caused by near-complete replacement of the liver by metastatic tumor. A third cause of hypoglycemia is increased concentrations of insulin-like growth factor (IGF) II, a ligand that interacts with the insulin receptor. This peptide is produced by large abdominal tumors, most commonly fibrosarcomas, hemangiopericytomas, or hepatomas. This increase appears to be due to the failure to form normal IGF binding protein 3 and the acid labile subunit complex that normally binds IGF-II; the result is an increase in free IGF-II concentrations.

 Treatment

In all three types of hypoglycemia, the patient is at greatest risk for symptoms during periods of fasting, most commonly during sleeping hours. Therapy should focus on surgical excision, where possible, or antineoplastic therapy directed at the tumor. Initial therapy of hypoglycemia is focused on frequent meals, and patients may occasionally be maintained symptom-free if awakened for one or more snacks during sleeping hours. If there is progression of the tumor or the patient's caloric intake is inadequate, additional measures may be required. In patients in whom hepatic replacement by tumor is evident, a continuous infusion of 20% dextrose through a central line may be required, especially during sleeping hours. In patients with insulin-producing or large retroperitoneal tumors, glucagon infusion (0.5-2 mg/hour) stimulates hepatic gluconeogenesis and prevents hypoglycemia, although in rare patients the rash associated with glucagonoma may develop. A glucose response to a single injection of glucagon (1 mg) should be documented before therapy is initiated. In patients with large retroperitoneal tumors, treatment with growth hormone (3 to 6 μg/kg SQ) or glucocorticoids (20 to 40 mg/day) may reverse hypoglycemia, possibly by facilitating IGF binding protein 3/acid labile subunit complex formation, thereby reducing free serum IGF-II levels. Growth hormone doses as high as 2600 μg/day have been administered in patients with this condition, although long-term treatment with this dose may cause acromegalic side effects. Somatostatin analogues (octreotide or lanreotide) are generally not effective for normalizing the plasma glucose level in patients with islet cell tumors; diazoxide (3 to 8 mg/kg/day in two or three divided doses) may be effective, but problems with fluid retention frequently preclude its long-term use.

SYNDROME OF INAPPROPRIATE ANTIDIURETIC HORMONE SECRETION

Ectopic production of vasopressin by head and neck tumors (3%), SCCL (15%), and other lung carcinomas (1%) causes a clinical syndrome characterized by hyponatremia, hypo-osmolality, excessive urine sodium excretion, an inappropriately high urine osmolality for the low serum osmolality, and normal function of the kidneys, adrenal glands, and thyroid (Chapter 239). Other malignant neoplasms (primary brain tumors; hematologic neoplasms; skin tumors; gastrointestinal, gynecologic, breast, and prostate cancers; and sarcomas) are rare causes of this clinical syndrome. In most cases, the hyponatremia is asymptomatic, although altered mental status and seizures may develop when the serum sodium concentration falls below 120 mEq/L; hyponatremic women of the reproductive age may experience profound cerebral degeneration (Chapter 112). Fluid restriction may be effective for short-term management but is difficult to maintain over long periods. Treatment with demeclocycline, 150 to 300 mg/day can block the effects of vasopressin on the kidney and is the most effective long-term therapy in patients with cancer. Vasopressin receptor antagonists are in clinical trials but are not currently available.

RARE ECTOPIC HORMONE SYNDROMES

Oncogenic osteomalacia, a clinical syndrome characterized by profound hypophosphatemia, muscle weakness, and osteomalacia (Chapter 259) can be produced by mesenchymal tumors (osteoblastomas, giant cell osteosarcomas, hemangiocytomas, and, rarely, prostate and lung carcinoma). Recent studies have shown that fibroblast growth factor 23, mutated in cases of autosomal dominant hypophosphatemic rickets, is overexpressed in neoplasms causing this disorder. Therapy is directed toward correction of hypophosphatemia with either oral or intravenous supplementation and vitamin D treatment. Surgical removal of the tumor is curative. The identification of an overexpression of fibroblast growth factor 23 as a cause may lead to the development of specific antagonists.

HEMATOLOGIC SYNDROMES

The kidney is the primary site of erythropoietin production, and, therefore, the relatively common erythropoietin production by benign or malignant renal tumors is not an "ectopic" hormone syndrome. Production of erythropoietin by cerebellar hemangioblastoma, uterine fibroids, pheochromocytomas, and ovarian and hepatic tumors is generally considered "ectopic." Patients with excessive erythropoietin production may or may not have polycythemia (Chapter 172). Other ectopic syndromes, less well defined, include production of thrombopoietin, leukopoietin, or colony-stimulating factor by some tumors (Chapter 159). These conditions are treated by removal of the tumor or by appropriate chemotherapy.

HYPERTENSION

Renal (Wilms' tumor, renal cell carcinoma, or hemangiopericytoma), lung (SCCL, adenocarcinoma), hepatic, pancreatic, and ovarian carcinomas may produce renin. The clinical presentation in patients with these conditions can include hypertension, hypokalemia, and evidence of increased aldosterone production. Therapy with spironolactone (Aldactone) or angiotensin-converting enzyme inhibitors may be effective.

GROWTH HORMONE AND PROLACTIN PRODUCTION

Rare examples of growth hormone production have been identified in cases of lung and gastric adenocarcinoma. Ectopic production of growth hormone–releasing hormone has been documented for islet cell tumors, bronchogenic carcinoids, and SCCL. Increased prolactin production is a rare phenomenon associated with lymphoma or with lung, colon, oral, and renal carcinoma; it produces galactorrhea and amenorrhea in women and produces hypogonadism and gynecomastia in men. Treatment with dopamine agonists (bromocriptine, quinagolide or cabergoline), effective in pituitary prolactinoma, should be tried, but is most commonly ineffective.

SUGGESTED READINGS

Gagel RF: Hypoglycemia and insulinomas. *In* Besser CM, Thorner MO (eds): Comprehensive Clinical Endocrinology, 3rd ed. Edinburgh, Elsevier Science, 2002, pp 255–265. *A comprehensive review of tumor-related hypoglycemia.*

Reimondo G, Paccotti P, Minetto M, et al: The corticotrophin-releasing hormone test is the most reliable noninvasive method to differentiate pituitary from ectopic ACTH secretion in Cushing's syndrome. Clin Endocrinol (Oxf). 2003;58:718–724. *CRH levels correctly classified 86% of cases.*

White KE, Jonsson KB, Carn G, et al: The autosomal dominant hypophosphatemic rickets (ADHR) gene is a secreted polypeptide overexpressed by tumors that cause phosphate wasting. J Clin Endocrinol Metab 2001;86:497–500. *Initial description of fibroblast growth factor 23 overproduction by tumors causing hypophosphatemic rickets.*

188 PARANEOPLASTIC SYNDROMES AND OTHER NON-NEOPLASTIC EFFECTS OF CANCER

Hope S. Rugo

The clinical manifestations of cancer are usually due to local effects of tumor growth, either in the primary site or at a distant site, or are nonspecific such as anorexia, malaise, weight loss, night sweats, and fever. The term *paraneoplasia*, which means *along side cancer*, has been commonly used to denote the remote effects that cannot be attributed either to direct invasion or distant metastases. These syndromes may be the first sign of a malignancy and may affect up to 15% of patients with cancer; however, if patients with cachexia are excluded, the incidence likely drops to only a few percent.

Paraneoplastic syndromes are important clinically for a number of reasons. First, they may be the initial presenting sign or symptom of an underlying malignancy. Up to two thirds of paraneoplastic syndromes present before an associated malignancy is diagnosed. In some cases, the paraneoplastic syndrome may be associated with relatively small tumors; recognition of these associations may lead to earlier diagnosis and better therapy. Second, one of the hallmarks in defining a paraneoplastic syndrome is that the course of the syndrome generally parallels the course of the tumor. Therefore, effective treatment of the underlying malignancy is often accompanied by improvement or resolution of the syndrome. Conversely, recurrence of the cancer may be heralded by return of systemic symptoms. One exception is the neurologic paraneoplastic syndromes, in which damage to structures within the nervous system may not be reversible. Third, the clinical manifestations of the paraneoplastic syndrome (or the toxic effects of electrolyte disturbances) may constitute a more urgent hazard to life or have a greater impact on quality of life than the underlying cancer.

In a patient who presents with symptoms or signs of a paraneoplastic syndrome, the screening evaluation (Table 188–1) should focus on the most common associated malignancies. If the initial

---

Table 188–1 • EVALUATION AND DIAGNOSIS OF PARANEOPLASTIC SYNDROMES

Characterize abnormality; obtain laboratory studies and biopsy as necessary.
Carefully elicit any additional symptoms and signs.
Eliminate common causes.
If there is no obvious etiology, consider a paraneoplastic syndrome.
If findings are consistent with a known syndrome, screen for underlying malignancy.
If signs and symptoms are consistent with a known paraneoplastic syndrome, undertake a search for an unknown primary cancer or recurrence or progression of a known primary tumor.
Screening should include a careful physical examination including breast, gynecologic, and prostate evaluations; basic hematology, chemistry, and urine studies; chest radiograph, and mammogram. Computed tomography of the abdomen and pelvis is indicated if there are any suspicious symptoms, signs, or laboratory abnormalities. Antibody testing for paraneoplastic neurologic syndromes and/or skin biopsy should be performed as indicated.
Consider treatment of cancer and/or appropriate palliative treatment including immunosuppressive therapy for paraneoplastic symptoms when possible.

evaluation is unrevealing, a repeat evaluation should be considered after several months. If the relationship between the syndrome and malignancy is less clear or less frequently observed, the evaluation should be focused on the patient's individual risks and symptoms.

Paraneoplastic syndromes may be caused by a variety of mechanisms; the endocrine (Chapter 187) and neurologic syndromes are the best understood. Possible etiologies include (1) secretion of proteins that are not associated with the normal tissue equivalent of the cancer (e.g., ectopic endocrine syndromes, local destruction of tissues by tumor-secreted cytokines), (2) antibodies that are directed against aberrantly expressed antigens on the tumor cell that cross react with antigens that are normally expressed on other tissues (e.g., neurologic syndromes), and (3) effects due to unknown mechanisms, such as unidentified tumor products or circulating immune complexes stimulated by the tumor (e.g., osteoarthropathy owing to bronchogenic carcinoma; Chapter 198). Clinical findings may resemble those of primary metabolic, hematologic, dermatologic, or neuromuscular disorders, or be specific to a cancer-related syndrome. Even such nonspecific symptoms as fever and weight loss are truly paraneoplastic and are due to the production of specific factors (e.g., tumor necrosis factor) by tumor cells or by normal cells in response to the tumor (see later text).

The most common cancer associated with paraneoplastic syndromes is small-cell cancer of the lung (Chapter 198), likely because of its neuroectodermal origin. Other neoplasms commonly associated with paraneoplastic syndrome include carcinomas of the breast (Chapter 204) and ovary (Chapter 205), lymphoproliferative diseases (especially Hodgkin's disease; Chapter 194), and thymoma (Chapter 266).

NEUROLOGIC PARANEOPLASTIC SYNDROMES

Research over the past 4 decades has helped to elucidate the underlying mechanisms of neurologic syndromes associated with cancer; increasing evidence suggests that most effects are autoimmune in origin (Table 188–2). Tumors express antigens that are normally isolated to the nervous system and are found on neurons, referred to as "onconeuronal antigens." Antineuronal antibodies that are produced against the new tumor cell antigen circulate in serum and spinal fluid, and, at least in some patients, cause damage at the primary site of normal antigen expression. Pathologically, perivascular and interstitial lymphocytic infiltrates are found in the affected area of the brain (Fig. 188–1). Indirect immunofluorescence of serum detects antibodies reactive with neurons.

Neurologic paraneoplastic syndromes may involve the brain, cranial nerves, spinal cord, dorsal root ganglia, peripheral nerves, neuro-

muscular junction, muscle, or multiple levels of the nervous system. Perhaps because of cross-reactivity of antibodies, it is not uncommon for patients to develop more than one paraneoplastic syndrome, making the diagnosis of a particular syndrome more difficult. Therapy includes treatment of the underlying tumor as well as immunosuppressive therapy with or without plasmapheresis, although this approach usually results in only modest, if any, improvement of the neurologic deficit.

The differential diagnosis of neurologic paraneoplastic syndromes includes idiopathic presentations of the same syndrome, side effects of chemotherapy (Chapter 191) and radiation therapy (Chapter 19; Table 188–3), infections (usually associated with lymphoproliferative diseases), vascular disease (including infarction and hemorrhage), and metabolic and nutritional abnormalities (including hormonal paraneoplastic syndromes).

A high degree of specificity of an antibody for a particular syndrome does not prove that the antibody is pathogenic. Finding a circulating antibody is useful but not diagnostic of any particular syndrome; patients can have circulating antibodies without the associated clinical syndrome, and the majority of lung cancers as well as many breast and gynecologic malignancies express neuronal antigens. It is unclear what susceptibility factors lead to development of a neurologic paraneoplastic syndrome. In addition to direct antibody-mediated damage, there is evidence that cellular-mediated autoimmune mechanisms may also contribute. The finding of CD8+ T lymphocytes infiltrating neurologic tissue in postmortem studies of patients with neurologic paraneoplastic syndromes combined with data that patients with antibodies (with or without neurologic paraneoplastic syndromes) may have longer survival rates than otherwise similar patients without circulating antibodies, suggests that CD8+ T lymphocytes play a beneficial role in tumor-directed immune responses. This immune response may be mediated by aberrant expression of native antigens. Diagnosis of a neurologic paraneoplastic syndrome should instigate a reasonable search for the commonly associated malignancy (see Table 188–1).

Lambert-Eaton Myasthenic Syndrome—Anti-VGCC Antibodies

The Lambert-Eaton myasthenic syndrome is one of the first recognized and most common neurologic paraneoplastic syndromes, and it is one of the only syndromes with direct evidence to support the role of autoantibodies in producing clinical disease. This disorder affects 1 to 2% of patients with small-cell cancer of the lung, and two thirds of the cases are associated with an underlying malignancy. Clinically, patients present with proximal lower limb weakness, with improvement in strength after several seconds of sustained voluntary contraction. Autonomic symptoms, including dry mouth, ptosis, and impotence, are also common. Lambert-Eaton myasthenic syndrome is associated with a defect in the release of neurotransmitters (acetylcholine) from the presynaptic neurons at the neuromuscular junction and other sites. Acetylcholine release is mediated by P-type voltage-gated calcium channels (VGCCs); antibodies to VGCC are found in the serum of more than 85% of patients with Lambert-Eaton myasthenic syndrome. The diagnosis is made by an electromyogram, which shows *increased* muscle action potential with repeated nerve stimulation greater than 10 HZ (the opposite of myasthenia gravis; Chapter 464). Treatment consists of a combination of plasmapheresis, intravenous immunoglobulin (IVIG) to bind circulating antibodies, and immunosuppression (to remove antibodies and suppress their production), as well as treatment of the underlying malignancy. Pharmacologic facilitation of neuromuscular transmission with pyridostigmine, 3,4-diaminopyridine, and guanidine may be useful. Patients may also have associated central nervous system (CNS) dysfunction, such as encephalomyelitis, cerebellar dysfunction, and peripheral neuropathy resulting from cross-reactivity or the presence of combinations of antibodies.

Paraneoplastic Encephalomyelitis/Subacute Sensory Neuropathy—Anti-HU Antibodies

This heterogeneous group of disorders can affect the cerebral hemispheres, limbic system, cerebellum, brain stem, spinal cord, dorsal root, and autonomic ganglia. The most common manifestations are related to subacute sensory neuropathy, with patchy or asymmetrical numbness, burning or aching paresthesias, and sensory ataxia with

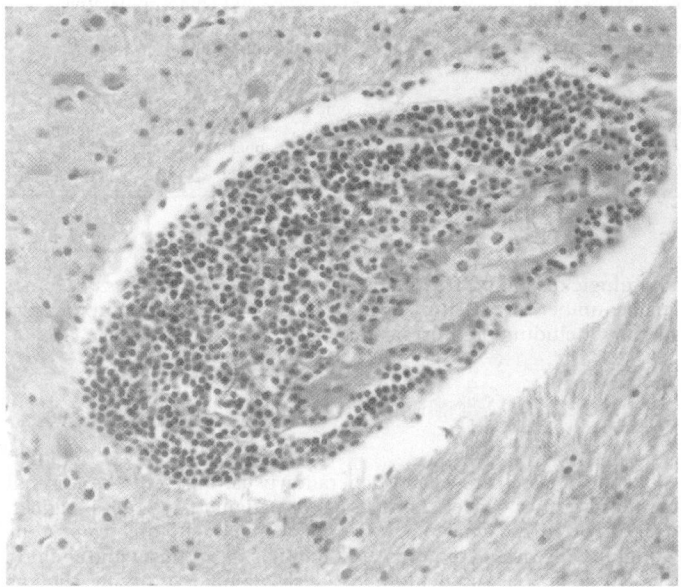

FIGURE 188–1 • Perivascular lymphocytic cuffing in the basal ganglia of a patient with anti-Hu antibodies and paraneoplastic encephalitis. (Courtesy of Dr. Ian Sutton, Department of Neurology, University of Sydney.)

Oncology

Table 188–2 • SOME PARANEOPLASTIC NEUROLOGIC SYNDROMES, ASSOCIATED ANTIBODIES, AND MALIGNANCIES

NEUROLOGIC SYNDROME	CLINICAL PRESENTATION	ANTIBODY	ASSOCIATED MALIGNANCY
Lambert-Eaton myasthenic syndrome	See text	Anti-VGCC	SCLC (>80%)
Paraneoplastic encephalomyelitis/subacute sensory neuropathy	See text	Anti-Hu	SCLC (75–80%), neuroblastoma
		Anti-amphiphysin	SCLC, breast
		Anti-Ma	Various carcinomas
Paraneoplastic cerebellar degeneration	See text	Anti-Yo	Breast, ovarian, and other gynecologic malignancies
		Anti-Ri	Breast (50%)
		Anti-Hu	SCLC
		Anti-Tr, Anti-GluR	Hodgkin's lymphoma
		Anti-Ma	Various carcinomas
Limbic encephalopathy	Subacute amnestic syndrome, affective disorder, seizures. DDX: Herpes encephalitis. Improvement common with treatment of underlying tumor; immunosuppression is of unclear benefit	Anti-Hu, anti-amphiphysin, others	SCLC
		Anti-Ta	Testicular, breast
Opsoclonus/myoclonus	Saccadic eye movements with ataxia and myclonus. Majority occur in children with neuroblastomas. Pathology reveals diffuse dropout of Purkinje cells. Treatment of underlying tumor may improve symptoms; ACTH, steroids, and IVIG may also benefit	Anti-Ri	Breast (70%), ovarian
		Anti-Hu	SCLC, neuroblastoma (50%)
		Anti-amphiphysin	SCLC
		Anti-Ta	Testicular
Stiff-person syndrome	Progressive muscle stiffness and rigidity, with intermittent and painful muscle spasms. EMG: continuous firing of motor unit potentials. Treat with muscle relaxants; may improve with cancer therapy	Anti-amphiphysin	Breast, SCLC
		Anti-GAD	Breast
Neuromyotonia	Diffuse muscle stiffness and cramps; may be associated with myasthenia gravis. Responds to treatment of tumor and immunosuppression	Anti-VGCC	Thymoma
VISUAL SYNDROMES			
CAR	Gradual to acute and progressive visual loss	Anti-retinal, anti-recoverin	SCLC
MAR	Reports of response to immunosuppressive therapy, and plasmapheresis	Anti-bipolar cell	Melanoma
Bilateral diffuse melanocytic proliferation		?	Gynecologic malignancy
SYNDROMES WITH NO ASSOCIATED ANTIBODY IDENTIFIED			
Demyelinating neuropathies (including CDP, mononeuritis multiplex)	Sensory more common than motor or both. May improve with treatment of paraprotein, plasmapheresis	IGM paraprotein may cross react with MAG, cryoglobulins	Plasma cell and lymphoproliferative neoplasms, osteosclerotic myeloma, POEMS, amyloid, SCLC, other carcinomas
Necrotizing myelopathy	Symptoms associated with specific levels of spinal cord dysfunction. Rapid deterioration and death		Variety of carcinomas and lymphomas
Motor neuron disease	Similar to ALS with progressive weakness; may improve with plasmapheresis and treatment of paraproteinemia		Plasma cell and lyphoproliferative neoplasms
Polymositis/dermatomyositis	Unclear relationship to cancer, higher risk with dermatomyositis. May improve with treatment of cancer, otherwise treat as idiopathic		Variety of carcinomas

ACTH = adrenocorticotropic hormone; ALS = amytotrophic lateral sclerosis; CAR = carcinoma-associated retinopathy; CDP = chronic demyelinating polyneuropathy; DDX = differential diagnosis; EMG = electronyogram; GAD = glutamic acid decarboxylase; amphiphysin = synaptic vesicle-associated protein; IVIG = intravenous immunoglobulin; MAG = myelin-associated glycoprotein; MAR = melanoma-associated retinopathy; POEMS = polyneuropathy, organomegaly, endocrinopathy, monoclonal protein, and skin changes associated with osteosclerotic myeloma; SCLC = small-cell lung cancer; VGCC = voltage-gated calcium channels.

loss of proprioception and vibration sense. Patients may also present primarily with subacute cerebellar degeneration or brain stem encephalitis, and nearly all patients have evidence of multifocal involvement of the CNS and dorsal root ganglia. About 75 to 80% of paraneoplastic encephalomyelitis/subacute sensory neuropathy is associated with small-cell lung cancer, with a variety of other neoplasms representing the remainder. The majority of patients have circulating antineuronal "anti-HU" autoantibodies; a small number have either no antibodies or antibodies to other proteins. Although neuronal loss is accompanied by perivascular and leptomeningeal infiltration of lymphocytes, the pathogenesis of this syndrome is unknown.

The diagnosis is made on clinical grounds and is aided by finding circulating antibody in serum. Magnetic resonance (MR) scans are usually normal, and the cerebrospinal fluid (CSF) can show elevated protein levels with a lymphocytosis. The usual course is deterioration over weeks to months, with stabilization at a level of severe neurologic disability. Treatment has been largely unsuccessful, but a small number of patients have improved with immunosuppressive therapy including prednisone and IVIG.

Paraneoplastic Cerebellar Degeneration—Anti-YO Antibodies

Paraneoplastic cerebellar degeneration usually presents as the initial manifestation of cancer. About 90% of patients have breast cancer, ovarian or other gynecologic tumors, small-cell lung cancer, or Hodgkin's disease. Symptoms are often abrupt in onset and include dysarthria, ataxia, and oculomotor dysfunction. Syndromes such as paraneoplastic encephalomyelitis or Lambert-Eaton myasthenic syndrome may be superimposed. Patients with paraneoplastic cerebellar degeneration and carcinomas of the breast, ovary, or other

Table 188–3 • NEUROLOGIC COMPLICATIONS OF THERAPEUTIC RADIATION

LATENCY PERIOD (TIME FOLLOWING RADIATION)	SITE OF INJURY	CLINICAL FINDINGS
Immediate	Brain	Acute encephalopathy (self-limited)
Early (1-4 months)	Brain	Somnolence syndrome (steroid responsive)
		Focal neurologic signs
	Spinal cord	Lhermitte's sign (shocklike sensation down the spine when bending the neck so the chin meets the chest)
Delayed (months to years)	Brain	Cognitive dysfunction
		Focal neurologic signs
	Spinal cord	Transverse myelopathy
	Peripheral nerves	Peripheral neuropathy, decreased function
Secondary effects at other organ sites (years)	CNS including nerve sheaths	Secondary malignancy
	Arteries	Premature atherosclerosis
		Telangiectasias (increased risk for hemorrhage)
	Thyroid or parathyroid	Hypothyroid or hypoparathyroid (hyperthroidism or hyperparathyroidism may be an early symptom)

CNS = central nervous system.

gynecologic cancers have been found to have high titers of an anti-Purkinje cell antibody, anti-YO, in the serum and CSF, but other antibodies that react against Purkinje cell antigens can also be found (see Table 188–2). Autopsy reveals near complete loss of cerebellar Purkinje cells, with occasional inflammatory infiltrates. The diagnosis is based on clinical signs and may be aided by the presence of circulating antibody; however, anti-YO antibodies are also found in patients who have a variety of cerebellar disorders but no evidence of cancer even on follow-up. CSF may reveal a pleocytosis and an elevated protein level or may be normal. MR scans may show diffuse cerebellar atrophy, but they are often normal. Treatment of the underlying malignancy occasionally results in significant improvement of cerebellar function. Rarely, responses have been seen to immunosuppressive therapy.

Neurologic Complications of Therapeutic Radiation

Although improvements in technique have significantly reduced the neurologic complications of radiation therapy (Chapter 19),

profound side effects can still occur and may be seen more frequently as patients with advanced cancers enjoy longer survival owing to improved systemic treatment (see Table 188–3). Complications may be acute or delayed, and delayed reactions can be seen within 1 to 4 months or up to months to years following completion of treatment. The risk of any reaction is related to the total dose, the extent of the radiation field, the dose of radiation per fraction, and the length of time over which the radiation was given. Lowering the dose per fraction and extending the duration of treatment decreases both short- and long-term risks, but variations in susceptibility among individuals are not well understood. Treatment is generally supportive, except for the somnolence syndrome, which may respond to corticosteroids. Rarely, radiation-induced tumors, including meningiomas or gliomas, may occur many years after successful cranial irradiation.

DERMATOLOGIC PARANEOPLASTIC SYNDROMES

Recognition of cutaneous manifestations of malignancy can be critical for the early diagnosis and successful treatment of malignancy, but some abnormalities are seen only with advanced, incurable disease. Cutaneous manifestations include direct involvement of the skin with tumor as well as the remote effects of cancer.

Benign skin changes may be the only sign of genetic syndromes that predispose to an increased risk for malignancy over a lifetime (Table 188–4). Recognition of these syndromes is critical for screening, early diagnosis, and genetic counseling of affected family members.

Associations between cutaneous syndromes and underlying malignancies may be difficult to confirm. Generally, and unlike neurologic paraneoplastic syndromes, the skin condition and cancer should follow a parallel course, and the two diagnoses should be made at about the same time (Table 188–5). Some skin lesions are almost always associated with malignancy. Others, however, are nonspecific and are most commonly seen with nonmalignant conditions, thereby making it difficult or impossible to connect the skin disease with the underlying malignancy.

One of the most well-known paraneoplastic syndromes is acanthosis nigricans (Fig. 188–2), a velvety, verrucous hyperpigmentation of the neck, axilla, groin, and mucosal membranes, including the lips, periocular area, and anus. Although this lesion clearly occurs as a benign entity, its appearance in older adults, especially when it includes mucosal lesions, has been highly associated with malignancies of the gastrointestinal tract. The lesions often regress with successful treatment of the underlying tumor. The pathogenesis of acanthosis nigricans is unclear, although cytokines (transforming growth factor [TGF]-α) and insulin resistance have been implicated.

The diagnosis of a new skin lesion that is almost always associated with an underlying malignancy (e.g., Bazex' syndrome, erythema gyratum repens) should prompt a directed evaluation for that tumor. In contrast, diagnosis of a common problem that only occasionally is associated with cancer (e.g., pruritus, dermatomyositis) should prompt a careful physical examination and routine cancer screening.

Table 188–4 • GENETIC SYNDROMES WITH CUTANEOUS MANIFESTATIONS ASSOCIATED WITH AN INCREASED RISK OF SYSTEMIC CANCERS

GENETIC SYNDROME	SKIN LESION	ASSOCIATED CANCERS	RISK
Torre's	Multiple sebaceous gland tumors, basal cell cancers	GI and GU cancers	High
Gardner's	Multiple epidermal/sebaceous cysts of face and scalp, desmoid tumors of skin, osteomas of face and head, GI polyps	GI cancers	High
Cowden's	Multiple hamartomas of skin, mucous membranes (trichilemmomas), lipomas	Breast, thyroid cancers	High
MEN IIB	Multiple papular mucosal neuromas on lips, oropharynx, conjunctiva	Medullary carcinoma of thyroid, pheochromocytoma	High
Ataxia-telangiectasia	Telangiectasias over face, conjunctiva	Lymphomas	Medium
Neurofibromatosis	Café au lait spots, axillary freckles, neurofibromas	Neurofibrosarcoma, pheochromocytoma, acoustic neuromas	Low
Peutz-Jeghers	Pigmented macules on the lips, oral mucosa, hands, feet; hamartomatous GI polyps	GI, pancreas, ovary, testes	Low
Basal cell carcinoma nevus	Multiple basal cell cancers	Medulloblastoma, fibrosarcoma	Low
Bloom's	Telangiectatic redness of skin in photoexposed areas, stunted growth	Lymphomas, leukemias	Medium

GI = gastrointestinal; GU = genitourinary; MEN = multiple endocrine neoplasia.

Oncology

Table 188–5 • EXAMPLES OF CUTANEOUS AND RHEUMATOLOGIC LESIONS ASSOCIATED WITH MALIGNANT DISEASE

SYNDROME	CLINICAL PRESENTATION	ASSOCIATED MALIGNANCY	DEGREE OF ASSOCIATION/RISK
CUTANEOUS			
Acanthosis nigricans	Velvety, verrucous, brown hyperpigmentation involving body folds and mucosal membranes	Gastric cancer (also endocrinopathies)	High
Acquired tylosis	Hyperkeratosis of palms	Lung cancer	Likely low
Bazex's syndrome	Acral hyperkeratotic papulosquamous lesions, onychodystrophy	Squamous cell carcinomas of the oropharynx, larynx, bronchi, esophagus	High
Extramammary Paget's	Nonhealing superficial dermatitis	Genitourinary and rectal cancers	Moderate to high
Sign of Lesar-Trélat	Diffuse eruption of seborrheic keratoses	Gastrointestinal cancers (also seen with aging)	Likely moderate
Tripe palms	Thickened, velvety palms	Lung and gastric cancers (almost always seen with acanthosis nigricans)	High
Necrolytic migratory erythema	Circinate erosive erythematous rash, stomatitis	Glucagonoma	Likely moderate
Erythema gyratum repens	Concentric rings on trunk and proximal extremities; may have pruritus	Lung cancer	High
Erythroderma	Diffuse erythema	Lymphoma	Low to moderate
Paraneoplastic pemphigus	Painful erythematous lesions with blistering; mucous membrane ulcerations	Lymphoma	High
Sweet's syndrome	Red nodules or plaques, fever, dermal neutrophilic infiltrates	Acute myelogenous leukemia (also seen with infection)	Moderate
Pruritus	Excoriations	Lymphoma and myeloproliferative disease	Low
CUTANEOUS WITH ARTHRITIS OR MYOPATHY			
Amyloidosis	Waxy papules and nodules, occasionally with associated symmetrical arthritis; renal insufficiency	Multiple myeloma	Moderate
Palmar fasciitis-polyarthritis	Thickening of the palmar fascia; inflammatory distal symmetrical arthritis	Ovarian cancer	Low
Panniculitis-arthritis	Erythematous subcutaneous tender nodules; inflammatory monoarticular or polyarticular arthritis	Cancer of the pancreas (also pancreatitis)	Low
Eosinophilic fasciitis	Edema, thickening of the dermis and fascia associated with joint contractures	Breast cancer, myeloproliferative disease, lymphoproliferative disease	Low
Dermatomyositis/polymyositis	Heliotrope rash (erythema in periorbital area); Gottron's papules (erythematous papules over phalangeal joints); proximal myopathy	Various tumors, primarily adenocarcinomas	Low to moderate, more with dermatomyositis
ARTICULAR			
Digital clubbing	Loss of nail bed angle	Lung cancer (also seen with benign cardiopulmonary disorders)	Low
Hypertrophic pulmonary osteoarthropathy	Periostosis of long bones; pain and swelling in distal joints	Lung cancer	High
Carcinoma polyarthropathy	Sudden onset of seronegative arthritis at a late age	Cancers of the breast and lung	Low to moderate
Gout	Classic acute painful gouty arthritis	Acute leukemias, lymphomas associated with rapid tumor cell turnover and tumor lysis	Low
VASCULAR			
Leukocytoclastic vasculitis	Palpable purpura, urticaria, maculopapular rash with or without arthritis	Myeloproliferative and lymphoproliferative diseases, myelodysplasia; rarely with adenocarcinoma and melanoma	Low to moderate
Polyarteritis nodosa	Cutaneous and/or mesenteric vasculitis; fever, mylagia; arthritis; mononeuritis multiplex	Hairy cell leukemia	Low
Raynaud's syndrome	Classic Raynaud's with progression to digital necrosis or gangrene common	Lymphoma, leukemia, myeloma, and cancers of the lung, ovary, small bowel, breast, pancreas, kidney	Low to moderate in patients older than age 50 years
Erythromelalgia	Painful, erythematous digits, relieved by aspirin	Myeloproliferative disease	Moderate to high

The etiology of most dermatologic paraneoplastic syndromes is not well understood, except in paraneoplastic pemphigus (Chapter 475). This recently described syndrome is manifested by ulcerative and blistering mucocutaneous lesions with acantholysis; it is primarily associated with lymphoma, other lymphoproliferative diseases, and thymic cancers. Patients have high titers of autoantibodies that react against tumor antigens and cross react with antigens at the epidermal cell junction; indirect immunofluorescent staining shows immunoglobulin (Ig)G autoantibody deposition on the surface of epidermal cells. Antibody titers may correlate with the severity of the skin disease and its response to therapy.

RHEUMATOLOGIC PARANEOPLASTIC SYNDROMES

A wide variety of rheumatologic paraneoplastic syndromes have been associated with underlying malignancies, but almost all of these syndromes are identical to their benign counterparts (see Table 188–5). The rheumatologic paraneoplastic syndromes can be classified as cutaneous with arthritis, articular, and vasculitic. Paraneoplastic rheumatologic syndromes may either coincide with the diagnosis of malignancy or precede it by several years. In general, when a rheumatologic paraneoplastic syndrome is suspected, screening should include a physical examination, laboratory tests, and standard radiographic

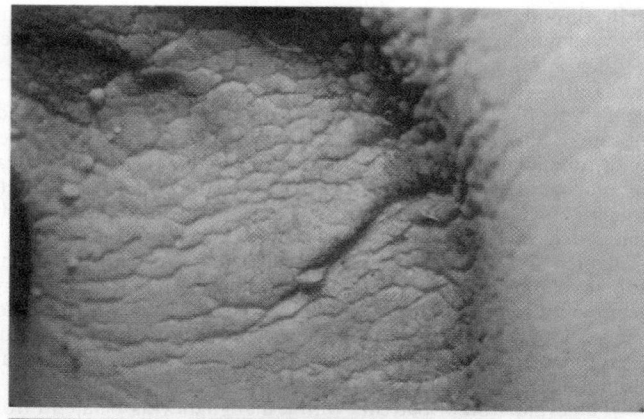

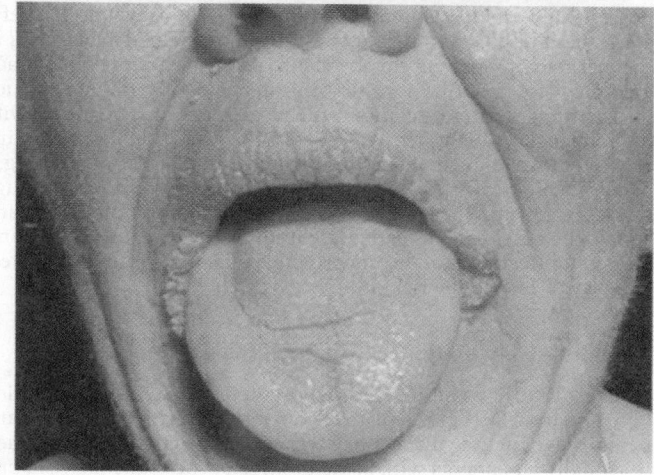

FIGURE 188–2 • *A,* Paraneoplastic acanthosis nigricans with a velvety hyperpigmented rash in the axilla in a patient with gastric cancer. *B,* Acanthosis nigricans of the oral mucosa. This pattern of involvement is almost always associated with cancer. (Courtesy of Dr. Timothy Berger, Professor of Clinical Dermatology, University of California, San Francisco.)

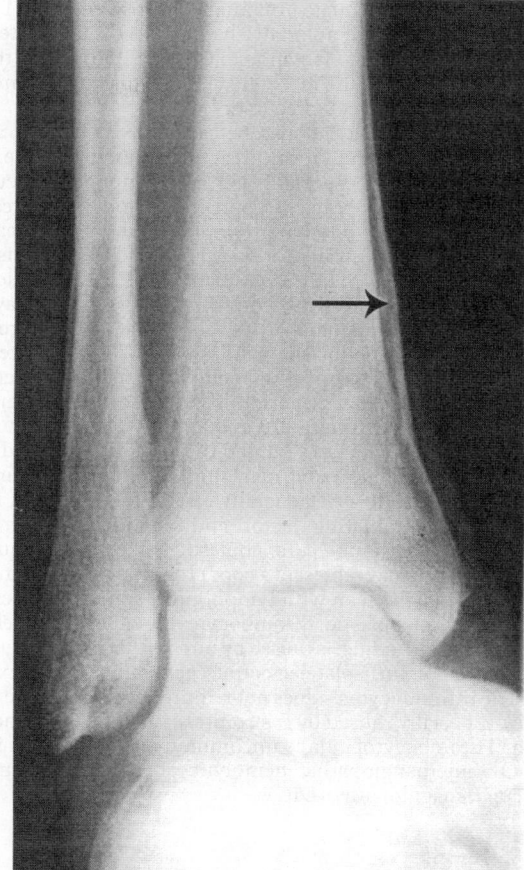

FIGURE 188–3 • Hypertrophic pulmonary osteoarthropathy characterized by periosteal elevation of the tibia (arrow). (Courtesy of Dr. Lynne S. Steinbach, Professor of Clinical Radiology, University of California, San Francisco.)

tests, such as a mammogram. An increased risk of subsequent malignancy may exist in patients with a variety of rheumatologic diseases. For example, Sjögren's syndrome (Chapter 282) is associated with a slightly increased risk of lymphoproliferative disease, although the cause for this relationship remains unclear.

In contrast to the nonparaneoplastic rheumatologic syndromes, rheumatologic paraneoplastic syndromes are associated with rapid onset, late age at onset (older than age 50 years), negative serologies, and effusions characterized by the absence of inflammatory markers. Considerable overlap exists among the rheumatologic, dermatologic, and neurologic paraneoplastic syndromes. Osteosclerotic myeloma (Chapter 196) associated with the POEMS syndrome (*p*olyneuropathy, *o*rganomegaly, *e*ndocrinopathy, *m*onoclonal protein and *s*kin changes suggestive of scleroderma) is a rare condition that has features of all three of the paraneoplastic syndromes owing to the effects of a circulating paraprotein.

One of the more common and specific paraneoplastic syndromes is hypertrophic osteoarthropathy, which presents as an oligoarthritis or polyarthritis of the distal joints with clubbing, tender periostitis of the distal long bones, and noninflammatory synovial effusions. Laboratory studies may reveal an elevation in the erythrocyte sedimentation rate; bone radiographs show linear ossification of the distal long bones separated by a radiolucent zone from the underlying cortex (Fig. 188–3). Hypertrophic osteoarthropathy may affect up to 10% of patients with adenocarcinoma of the lung. It has also been seen with a variety of other pulmonary malignancies, including metastases to the lung. The etiology is unknown, and treatment is symptomatic with anti-inflammatory agents; treatment of the underlying tumor may also improve symptoms.

Dermatomyositis/polymyositis has been reported to be associated with an underlying malignancy in less than 10% to as high as 60% of

cases (Chapter 283). Dermatomyositis has been more closely associated with malignancy than has polymyositis. Studies of patients with dermatomyositis suggest a two- to four-fold increased risk of malignancies, including cancer of the lung, ovaries, breast, gastrointestinal tract, and testes. The true incidence of malignancy in patients diagnosed with dermatomyositis is likely in the range of 10 to 15%. The diagnosis of malignancy is usually made within 1 year preceding or following the diagnosis of dermatomyositis; a longer duration of dermatomyositis substantially decreases the risk of association. Although the etiology is unknown, autoantibodies to muscle have been described in patients with dermatomyositis. These antibodies have not been well characterized and do not appear to be directly related to tumor antigens.

HEMATOLOGIC PARANEOPLASTIC SYNDROMES

Routine blood testing may identify hematologic paraneoplastic syndrome as well as the underlying malignancy. Hematologic paraneoplastic syndromes may involve all three cell lines.

RED CELLS. The most prevalent and commonly recognized paraneoplastic syndrome, seen with many cancers, is a normochromic, normocytic anemia associated with a low reticulocyte count (Chapter 173). This hypoproductive anemia, generally termed anemia of chronic disease, must be differentiated from anemia as a result of side effects of treatment or direct tumor infiltration of the bone marrow. It is associated with inappropriately low erythropoietin levels as well as the inability to reuse iron. Cytokines including interleukin-1 (IL-1), tumor necrosis factor (TNF), and TGF-β released by the tumor or local inflammatory cells mediate this disorder, which may be effectively treated with weekly subcutaneous injections of erythropoietin at a dose of 40,000 units. Adequate iron intake must be ensured. The rare syndrome of pure red cell aplasia (Chapter 174) is associated with cancer of the thymus gland (thymoma; Chapter 266) and is thought to be due to an autoimmune mechanism. Bone marrow examination shows an absence of red cell precursors.

Paraneoplastic anemia can also be caused by hemolytic anemia (Chapter 169) due to warm- or cold-reacting antibodies in the setting of B-cell malignancies, especially chronic lymphocytic leukemia (Chapter 192) and lymphoma (Chapters 194 and 195). Treatment is directed toward the underlying lymphoproliferative disease but may also include splenectomy for warm antibody hemolysis; cold-reacting hemolysis may require plasmapheresis. Microangiopathic hemolytic anemia (Chapter 169) with thrombocytopenia may occur with mucinous adenocarcinomas or after chemotherapy. Erythrocytosis is an uncommon paraneoplastic syndrome that is associated with tumors that produce erythropoietin, including renal cell cancer, hepatocellular carcinoma, and posterior fossa tumors (e.g., cerebellar hemangioblastoma) (Chapters 176 and 187).

LEUKOCYTES. Leukocytosis (Chapter 163) is common in advanced cancer. Although infection and myeloproliferative disease must be excluded, the leukocytosis is generally caused by cytokines, including granulocyte stimulating factor and granulocyte-macrophage stimulating factor. Although paraneoplastic leukocytosis requires no specific treatment, it may represent a poor prognostic sign. Eosinophilia (Chapter 184) may be seen with lymphoproliferative diseases.

PLATELETS. Paraneoplastic thrombocytosis, which is a relatively common laboratory finding, is caused by tumors that produce cytokines (IL-6, thrombopoietin); platelet counts generally do not exceed 1 million. The thrombocytosis does not require specific treatment. Iron deficiency, especially caused by gastrointestinal blood loss, should be excluded. Thrombocytopenia is uncommon except when it is associated with microangiopathic hemolytic anemia or disseminated intravascular coagulopathy (DIC).

Coagulopathies

THROMBOSIS

The best known and one of the first described hematologic paraneoplastic syndromes is Trousseau's syndrome, or the association of venous or arterial thrombosis with malignancy (Fig. 188–4). Although thrombosis frequently complicates progressive cancer, it may also be the first sign of cancer. Deep venous thrombosis may herald an underlying malignancy in approximately 10% of patients, particularly in patients who present with an initial episode without other obvious risk factors, in the setting of recurrent thrombosis despite adequate doses of warfarin (warfarin resistance), or when the thrombosis occurs in usual sites (e.g., subclavian vein, Budd-Chiari syndrome, portal vein thrombosis). It is important to exclude inherited clotting disorders, especially in younger patients who present with a deep venous thrombosis without known underlying cause (Chapters 78 and 180).

Paraneoplastic thrombosis is most commonly associated with adenocarcinomas, particularly of the stomach, breast, and ovary. The etiology of malignant thrombosis is complex and may be due to release of procoagulant mediators (e.g., sialic residues of tumor-secreted mucin) directly by tumor cells or due to tumor-mediated endothelial damage. The thrombosis can be associated with low-grade DIC (Chapter 179) and abnormal platelet activation. As with other hematologic paraneoplastic syndromes, cytokines play a role in the systemic activation of coagulation. Other factors that contribute to a high risk of thrombosis in patients with known malignancy include the procoagulant effects of chemotherapy, indwelling catheters, and immobility.

The evaluation of patients with a malignancy-associated thrombosis should include laboratory testing for DIC, as well as a careful assessment of bleeding risk at sites of tumor, such as metastases to the nervous system or involvement of the gastrointestinal tract. Treatment for thrombosis without evidence of DIC should include initial standard anticoagulation with heparin. Chronic treatment with low-molecular weight heparin is better than warfarin for preventing recurrent thromboembolism without increasing the risk of bleeding, or consideration of venous interruption (Chapters 78 and 94), although this latter therapy is associated with significant complications and should be reserved for patients without other treatment options. Successful treatment of the underlying malignancy is the most effective way to reduce the risk of thrombosis.

HEMORRHAGIC PARANEOPLASTIC SYNDROMES

DIC due to activation of the hemostatic system with consumption of coagulation factors and platelets can result in both thrombosis and hemorrhage. Acute DIC can be seen with a variety of malignancies. Essentially all patients with acute promyelocytic leukemia (Chapter 193) either present with acute DIC and associated hemorrhage or develop it during treatment. Procoagulant material released from the leukemia cells activates the fibrinolytic pathway; treatment with all-trans retinoic acid and low-dose heparin has significantly reduced the complications of hemorrhage with this leukemia.

Other causes of malignancy-associated bleeding disorders include paraproteins that interfere with fibrin polymerization (Chapter 178), amyloid deposits associated with monoclonal gammopathies such as multiple myeloma(Chapters 196 and 290), and, rarely, acquired von Willebrand disease associated with lymphoproliferative and myeloproliferative disorders (Chapter 178). Increased fibrinolysis may be seen in patients with advanced prostate cancer (Chapter 207).

RENAL PARANEOPLASTIC SYNDROMES

Renal involvement in the setting of malignancy may be due to direct tumor infiltration of the renal parenchyma or, less commonly, to a paraneoplastic syndrome. Paraneoplastic syndromes involving the kidney may be caused by tumor-related hormone production (Chapter 187), may directly involve the glomerulus or the microvasculature, may be related to proteins produced by the tumor (e.g., amyloid, paraproteins), or be caused by electrolyte disorders (hyponatremia, hyperuricemia).

The renal paraneoplastic syndrome most clearly linked to malignancy is membranous glomerulonephritis, which is characterized by nephrotic range proteinuria, edema, hypoalbuminema, microscopic hematuria, hypertension, and increased risk of thrombosis (Chapter 119). The course of the disease, as measured by the degree of proteinuria, should parallel the course of the malignancy. Associated cancers include lung (Chapter 198), breast (Chapter 204), stomach (Chapter 199), and others. The pathology is thickening of the glomerular basement membrane owing to subepithelial deposition of tumor antigen that has reacted with circulating immunoglobulins (IgG) and complement. Other glomerular lesions include minimal change nephropathy complicating lymphoproliferative disorders, in particular Hodgkin's disease (Chapter 194); rapidly progressive glomerulonephritis associated with lymphoplasmacytic diseases; and other glomerulopathies (including nephrotic syndrome and minimal change disease) associated with a variety of malignant diseases.

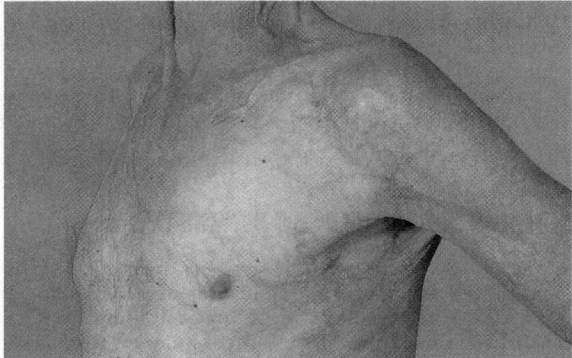

FIGURE 188–4 • Thrombophlebitis in superficial or deep veins is relatively common in many forms of malignant disease, but it is particularly associated with carcinoma of the pancreas, and sometimes it is the presenting feature. In this patient, thrombosis in the veins of the upper arm is associated with an extensive collateral circulation in the superficial veins around the shoulder. Recurrent episodes of thrombophlebitis may precede the diagnosis of carcinoma by many months, and their occurrence in an otherwise apparently fit patient should lead to a search for underlying malignancy, especially in the pancreas. (From Forbes CD, Jackson WF: Color Atlas and Text of Clinical Medicine, 3rd ed. London, Mosby, 2003, with permission.)

Renal microvascular involvement is uncommon and may be due to vasculitis or microangiopathy. Vasculitis may be caused by cryoglobulinemia in patients with hepatitis C–related hepatocellular carcinoma (Chapter 202) or rarely in patients with IgA monoclonal gammopathy in association with cancer of the lung. Thrombotic microangiopathy (hemolytic uremic syndrome) or thrombotic thrombocytopenic microangiopathy (Chapter 177) is most commonly a complication of chemotherapy (Chapter 191), including mitomycin-C, cisplatin, and others, but it may also be seen in association with a variety of adenocarcinomas as well as with promyelocytic leukemia. The etiology is unknown; the underlying malignancy should be treated, if possible, and plasma exchange may be indicated.

HEPATOPATHY

Paraneoplastic hepatopathy is an uncommon disorder characterized by hepatic dysfunction with elevated liver enzymes and abnormal synthetic function with fever and weight loss. This syndrome has been associated with nonmetastatic renal cell cancer (Chapter 203), and is likely due to either autoimmune effects or direct toxicity from tumor related products. This unusual syndrome resolves with resection of the tumor.

FEVER AND CACHEXIA

Fever (Chapter 296), night sweats, and cachexia are nonspecific symptoms that, when paraneoplastic, often suggest the diagnosis of an underlying malignancy. Fever is generally cyclical and may be associated with drenching night sweats. Symptoms resolve with treatment of the underlying tumor, and return of fever usually heralds relapse. When treatment of the tumor is not possible or is ineffective, nonsteroidal anti-inflammatory agents or steroids given around the clock significantly improve quality of life. Although fever is most commonly seen in association with lymphoproliferative disease (Chapters 194 and 195), renal cell carcinoma (Chapter 203), and leukemias (Chapters 192 and 193), it may also occur with other cancers.

Cachexia, or the cancer wasting syndrome, is likely the single most common paraneoplastic syndrome, eventually affecting up to 80% of patients with cancer. This syndrome is characterized by anorexia, muscle wasting, loss of subcutaneous fat, and fatigue. It appears to be caused by a combination of protein wasting, malabsorption, immune dysregulation, and increased glucose turnover in the setting of tumor-induced increased energy expenditure. Successful treatment of the underlying tumor reverses the process, but, in many cases, no treatment is successful. Megestrol acetate given in high concentrations in liquid form (400 to 800 mg/day) can significantly improve appetite and result in weight gain. Corticosteroids may also help.

Cytokines clearly play a pathogenetic role in inducing both fever and cachexia. TNF-α (previously known as cachectin), interleukins (including IL-1 and IL-6), and interferon-γ are produced directly by the tumor or by normal host cells, such as macrophages, in response to inflammation and result in a catabolic state. Cytokines may produce fever directly by acting at the hypothalamic thermoregulatory center (Chapter 296). In addition to the burden of tumor and the production of cytokines, cachexia may be caused or worsened by the side effects of cancer treatment, by intestinal blockage or malabsorption caused by tumor infiltration, and by depression. Although agents that block TNF production are theoretically attractive to treat cancer-related cachexia, there is also concern that such agents may block cytokines that may inhibit tumor growth. In addition, preclinical data suggest that antibodies to parathyroid hormone–related protein may block the production of inflammatory cytokines in cancer; whether this effect is of clinical value remains a research question.

 1. Lee AY, Levine MN, Baker RI, et al: Low-molecular-weight heparin versus a coumarin for the prevention of recurrent venous thromboembolism in patients with cancer. N Engl J Med 2003;349:146–153.

SUGGESTED READINGS
Braverman IM: Skin manifestations of internal malignancy. Clin Geriatric Med 2002;18:1–19. *A concise review of dermatologic paraneoplastic syndromes.*
Fam AG: Paraneoplastic rheumatic syndromes. Bailliere's Clin Rheum 2000;14:515–533. *A comprehensive review of the paraneoplastic rheumatologic syndromes with a discussion of pathogenesis as well as photographs.*
Rosenfeld MR, Dalmau J: Current therapies for paraneoplastic neurologic syndromes. Curr Treat Options Neurol 2003;5:69–77. *The best approach is to treat the tumor, though immunosuppression may help in early stages.*
Sutton I, Winer JB: The immunopathogenesis of paraneoplastic neurological syndromes. Clin Sci 2002;102:475–486. *A comprehensive discussion of antibodies and their relationship to neurologic paraneoplastic syndromes.*

189 TUMOR MARKERS

Dennis L. Cooper

Since the first report of the use of serum carcinoembryonic antigen (CEA) levels in colon cancer, an increasing number of serum tumor markers have been tested for the purpose of assessing prognosis and response to therapy. Tumor markers may also substantially precede other evidence of progression or recurrence of the disease. However, the value of earlier detection afforded by tumor markers is clearly tumor dependent and in some cases may increase costs (by encouraging further testing) without enhancing quality or duration of life. The clinician should be familiar with tumor markers that have proven clinical value for diagnosis or treatment (Table 189–1), but need not be concerned with tissue tumor markers that are important only for the diagnostic pathologist.

COLORECTAL CANCER

Screening

Although an increase in the serum level of CEA was initially thought to be indicative of colorectal cancer (Chapter 200), abnormal CEA levels are observed in a variety of adenocarcinomas (lung, breast, pancreas, and stomach) as well as medullary cancer of the thyroid and some squamous cell cancers of the head and neck. In addition, serum

---

Table 189–1 • USE OF SERUM TUMOR MARKERS FOR SCREENING, PROGNOSIS, MONITORING RESPONSE TO THERAPY, AND DETECTING RECURRENCE

TUMOR	MARKER	UTILITY OF MARKERS			
		Screening	Prognosis	Monitoring	Recurrence
Colorectal	CEA	No	Yes	Yes	Yes
Ovary	CA-125	No	No	Yes	Yes
Breast	CA-15-3, CA-27.29	No	No	Yes	Yes
Prostate	PSA	Yes/No?	Yes	Yes	Yes
Testicle	hCG, AFP	No	In some studies	Yes	Yes
Hepatoma	AFP	No*	No	Yes	Yes
Myeloma	β_2-microglobulin	No	Yes	Yes	Yes
Non-Hodgkin's lymphoma	LDH	No	Yes	No	Yes

*Screening with a combination of ultrasound and AFP have been useful in Asian patients who have known hepatitis infection. In the United States and Europe, patients with cirrhosis are often followed up with AFP and ultrasound, but there are no supportive data for the use of AFP.

AFP = α-fetoprotein; CEA = carcinoembryonic antigen; hCG = human chorionic gonadotropin; LDH = lactate dehydrogenase; PSA = prostate-specific antigen.

CEA is often not increased in early stage colon cancer and may be modestly increased in smokers and in association with a variety of benign conditions, including bronchitis, diverticulitis, peptic ulcer disease, fibrocystic breast disease, and a number of liver disorders. In view of the lack of sensitivity (percentage of patients with disease who have an abnormal test) or specificity (percentage of patients without disease who have a normal test result) for colorectal cancer, CEA is not considered an effective screening test.

Prognosis

Preoperative increases in CEA appear to provide prognostic information independent of Dukes' stage. Thus, in one large study, a preoperative CEA greater than 2.5 ng/mL was associated with an increased risk of recurrence of 1.62 in patients with disease that had not apparently penetrated through the bowel wall. The risk of recurrence increased to 3.25 if the CEA was greater than 10 ng/mL. In patients with recurrent disease, the time to recurrence was also shorter in patients with higher preoperative levels. Nevertheless, from a practical point of view, finding a high preoperative CEA is, at present, of limited value because there are no data to suggest that a different or more intensive therapy, such as adjuvant chemotherapy, will lead to a better outcome.

Monitoring Response to Therapy

In patients undergoing therapy for metastatic colorectal cancer, CEA studies are indicated if no other simple test (physical examination or radiographic study) is available to measure response. In such situations (e.g., peritoneal carcinomatosis), the CEA should be tested every 2 to 3 months during treatment. Two sequential CEA values above baseline are considered adequate to document progression of disease even in the absence of a confirmatory radiographic study.

Increasing Carcinoembryonic Antigen and Surgical Re-exploration

A small percentage of patients with local-regional recurrence or single liver metastases can be cured with second resections, and CEA is perhaps the most cost-effective test to find surgically resectable recurrent disease in patients with a normal postoperative CEA level. CEA should be monitored every 2 to 3 months in patients who would be considered surgical candidates. If an abnormal result is confirmed by a repeat CEA test, more extensive investigation is considered appropriate. Positron emission tomography appears to be a valuable tool for identifying and localizing recurrent disease in patients with an increasing CEA and otherwise normal radiographic studies. In patients who are not considered surgical candidates, no data suggest that an increased CEA should be used to begin chemotherapy.

OVARIAN CANCER

Screening

Analogous to the use of CEA in colon cancer, the serum CA-125 level is neither sensitive nor specific for the diagnosis of ovarian cancer (Chapter 205). Thus, the CA-125 value may be normal in up to 50% of stage I (limited to one ovary) patients and may be increased in patients with other types of adenocarcinomas. In addition, abnormal CA-125 levels are not limited to patients with malignant disease; increased levels have been seen in patients with endometriosis, pelvic inflammatory disease, benign ovarian cysts, the first trimester of pregnancy, menstruation, and liver disease. Because of the limited specificity of CA-125 and the low prevalence of ovarian cancer, it is predicted that less than 5% of women with an abnormal CA-125 value would be found to have ovarian cancer at exploratory laparotomy. Even if CA-125 screening is limited to women with pelvic tumors, the positive predictive value (the percentage of patients with an abnormal CA-125 value who have ovarian cancer) depends on the age of the woman. Thus, because benign conditions associated with an increased CA-125 level are more common in premenopausal women, only 15 to 36% of premenopausal women who have a pelvic mass will be found to have ovarian cancer. Conversely, at ages older than 50 years, 80 to 90% of women who have a pelvic mass and an increased

CA-125 value will be found to have ovarian cancer; if the CA-125 value is greater than 65 U/mL, 93% of such patients will be found to have ovarian cancer. Patients in the latter category are most appropriately referred to a gynecologic oncologist who can perform a definitive procedure at the initial laparotomy.

Importantly, although a high CA-125 measurement in a postmenopausal woman with a pelvic mass is highly suggestive of ovarian cancer, a normal CA-125 measurement does not exclude ovarian cancer. In one study of women with pelvic masses and ovarian cancer, 18 to 28% did not have an abnormal CA-125 result.

Monitoring Response to Therapy

Particularly in patients whose tumors had been optimally debulked surgically, the CA-125 level may be the most sensitive indicator of the response to treatment. In addition, serial tests of CA-125 are less expensive than sequential computed tomography (CT) scans. A 50 to 75% reduction in the CA-125 level is consistent with more than a 50% shrinkage of tumor. Moreover, the rate of decrease of CA-125 also provides prognostic information. In one study, for example, if the CA-125 measurement was less than 10 U/mL after three cycles of therapy, the median survival was 60 months; however, if the CA-125 measurement was greater than 100 U/mL, the median survival was only 7 months.

Nevertheless, CA-125 testing has limited sensitivity for the detection of microscopic disease. Approximately 60% of patients with advanced ovarian cancer and an abnormal CA-125 value respond to therapy as documented by the CA-125 declining to normal levels. However, only about 50% of patients who respond by CA-125 criteria have a complete pathologic response at the time of surgical re-exploration, and approximately 50% of the patients with such a pathologic response eventually relapse. These results suggest that a significant volume of disease is required to produce an abnormal CA-125 level, a finding that also can be inferred by the poor sensitivity of CA-125 testing in patients with early ovarian cancer.

After chemotherapy, a doubling of the CA-125 level indicates progressive disease both in patients who had previously normalized their markers and in those whose markers remained abnormal. An increase in the CA-125 value should be confirmed by a second test at least 1 week later. Although there is an increasing number of second-line treatments for ovarian cancer, early confirmation of progressive disease has not yet been shown to be advantageous in terms of overall survival.

BREAST CANCER

Screening

At present there is no evidence that the most commonly used tumor markers, CA-15-3 or CA-27.29, have any role in screening patients for breast cancer (Chapter 204). These markers are not usually abnormal in early stage disease, nor are they specific for breast cancer.

Monitoring Response to Therapy

Analogous to ovarian cancer, tumor markers could play a potentially important role in monitoring response to therapy in patients whose disease cannot be followed by physical examination or with radiographic studies. For example, in disease limited to bone, the bone scan may lag behind improvements in tumor markers by many months. Similarly, in patients with abdominal carcinomatosis, tumor markers may substitute for more costly CT scans. Limited information suggests that CA-27.29 may be better than CA-15-3 in this setting.

An important caveat to the use of tumor markers in patients on hormonal therapy is that some patients have a "flare" (worsening clinical disease and increase in tumor markers) weeks to months after beginning hormonal therapy. Because these patients predictably go on to have excellent responses, their therapy should not be changed prematurely.

Disease Progression

Levels of CA-15-3 and CA-27.29 may precede other evidence of recurrent disease by several months. Although widely used for this purpose, there are no data that modifying or beginning new treatment based on increasing tumor markers improves survival or quality of life.

PROSTATE CANCER

Screening

Prostate cancer (Chapter 207) is the most frequently diagnosed malignancy in men, with about 190,000 cases per year in the United States. Because disease that spreads outside the prostate is usually incurable, there has been significant enthusiasm for a test that can identify cancer that is confined to the prostate. In large cohorts of asymptomatic men, screening with prostate-specific antigen (PSA) consistently detects approximately one third more cancers than digital rectal examination. Nevertheless, because a variable number of cancers have been found by digital rectal examination alone, both tests are recommended by proponents of screening. However, the routine use of PSA for the detection of organ-confined prostate carcinoma remains controversial (Chapter 11). If a cutoff of 4.0 ng/mL is used to separate normal from abnormal, then 38 to 48% of men with organ-confined cancer will be missed because they fall within the normal range, and only two thirds of men with tumors will have organ-confined disease. Conversely, because of the poor specificity of PSA screening, a great number of men who do not have prostate cancer will be subjected to biopsies, thus causing morbidity and increasing the cost of health care without any benefit. In fact, nearly 75% of men with a PSA between 4 and 10 ng/mL do not have prostate cancer.

Recently, it has been observed that there are different forms of circulating PSA and that PSA produced by prostate carcinoma tends to be bound by plasma proteins, whereas PSA produced by normal cells is more likely to be free. Thus, a high-normal (2.5 to 4.0 ng/mL) or marginally increased (4.0 to 10.0 ng/mL) PSA is of more concern if the percentage of free PSA is relatively low. If biopsies were limited to patients with a low percentage of free PSA, about 20% of biopsies could be avoided in patients with a PSA of 4 to 10 ng/mL but with a slight decrease in the detection of prostate cancer (Chapter 207). Further studies are required to validate the usefulness of the percentage of free PSA.

Despite the favorable stage migration that has occurred as a result of PSA testing, there is little evidence that screening for prostate cancer is responsible for the decline in prostate cancer–related mortality that has been observed over the past 10 years. In addition, because the lifetime risk of prostate cancer (16%) is much higher than prostate cancer–related mortality (3.4%), there is concern that many patients are being overtreated for biologically indolent disease. The latter problem is accentuated by the high incidence of impotence and incontinence secondary to definitive treatment and a lack of consensus of optimal therapy for early stage disease. Accordingly, some authorities do not recommend screening for prostate cancer, whereas others believe the decision should be individualized and would recommend PSA screening only after an extensive discussion about the potential benefits and problems of screening, follow-up diagnostic procedures, and possible definitive treatment (Chapter 11). Because detection of organ-confined cancer is likely to reduce mortality only after more than a decade of follow-up, screening should be limited to patients with a greater than 10-year life expectancy.

Decisions about Initial Therapy

Nearly half of prostate cancers that are resected with curative intent are not organ-confined at the time of surgery. Recently, based on preoperative data from a large cohort of patients, the PSA, Gleason grade, and clinical stage have been combined to construct nomograms to indicate the chance of finding tumor outside the prostate gland (Chapter 207). These data can theoretically be used to counsel patients before attempted definitive therapy, but the most appropriate therapy for various subsets of patients has not been clearly defined.

Assessment of the Adequacy of Definitive Therapy

Because PSA is organ-specific, patients with completely resected prostate cancer should have undetectable levels of PSA. Thus, patients with measurable levels of PSA 6 to 8 weeks after surgery generally have persistent disease. Similarly, the re-emergence of detectable PSA after surgery is indicative of recurrent prostate cancer. After potentially curative radiation, local or systemic spread of cancer is likely if the PSA does not decrease to less than 1.0 ng/mL. However, a consensus has not been reached on appropriate treatment for patients with persistent or recurrent disease.

Monitoring Response to Hormonal Ablation Therapy

Androgen ablation therapy is the most effective treatment for patients with metastatic prostate cancer. Although it has become clear that androgen ablation can reduce the PSA independent of its antitumor effect, the depth of decrease of PSA after androgen ablation correlates with the duration of response. It is rare for patients to have progression of disease in the absence of an increasing PSA.

TESTICULAR CANCER

Screening

Human chorionic gonadotropin (hCG) and α-fetoprotein (AFP) have no value in screening because they are detected in fewer than 20% of patients with stage I testicular tumors (Chapter 206).

Diagnosis

Although 15% of seminomatous germ cell tumors are associated with an increased hCG, high levels of hCG are often associated with a nonseminomatous tumor component, and an increased level of AFP is diagnostic of the presence of nonseminomatous tumor. The importance of this distinction is that nonseminomatous germ cell tumors are treated with chemotherapy, whereas nonbulky seminomas confined to the abdomen may be treated with radiation. In patients with undifferentiated midline tumors (pineal, mediastinal, and retroperitoneum regions), markedly elevated germ cell markers are diagnostic of a testicular or extragonadal germ cell tumor and do not require biopsy for diagnosis. However, low-level elevation of hCG may be seen in lung, breast, gastrointestinal, and ovarian tumors, so hCG is not diagnostic of a germ cell tumor.

Monitoring Response to Therapy

Because either hCG or AFP is increased in 89% of patients with nonseminomatous germ cell tumors, they are useful in monitoring response after chemotherapy or for detecting recurrence after the completion of treatment. During chemotherapy, the hCG generally should decrease by half every 3 days after treatment while the half-life of AFP is 7 days. However, in view of the exquisite sensitivity of germ cell tumors to therapy, it is not unusual for patients to have a temporary elevation in tumor markers early after chemotherapy before a subsequent decline. In patients whose tumor markers do not decline at an appropriate rate, more intensive treatment may be indicated. If the tumor markers do not return to normal after chemotherapy, residual disease is almost invariably present. In patients with very high tumor markers at diagnosis, the tumor markers may not return to normal until a month or two after therapy is completed. Conversely, nearly one third of patients with normal markers and residual masses have residual disease, whereas the remainder have scar tissue or a mature teratoma.

HEPATOCELLULAR CARCINOMA

Screening

At present, the available evidence does not suggest that AFP is an effective screening test for hepatocellular carcinoma (Chapter 202). Smaller cancers rarely cause a significant increase in the AFP measurement, and tumors of all sizes are detected better with ultrasound or spiral CT scans. In patients with masses detected on an imaging study, an elevated AFP level provides supportive evidence of hepatocellular carcinoma. An elevated AFP level is not specific; for example, among patients with chronic hepatitis, only a minority of patients with increases in AFP value have hepatocellular carcinomas.

MULTIPLE MYELOMA

Prognosis

Multiple myeloma is a malignant lymphoproliferative disorder that is inevitably fatal in a period ranging from a few months to several years (Chapter 196). Because of the extreme variability in the aggressiveness of this disease, it is helpful to identify patients who might benefit from more aggressive treatment, including bone marrow transplantation. The β_2-microglobulin (β_2-M) level is the most important (and generally available) prognostic factor in multiple myeloma. In a large cooperative group study, patients with a β_2-M level less than $6 \mu g/mL$ had a median survival of 36 months compared with a median survival of 23 months in patients with a β_2-M level greater than $6 \mu g/mL$. The median survival of patients younger than 60 years with a serum albumin measurement greater than 3.0 and a β_2-M level less than $6 \mu g/L$ was projected at greater than 48 months, whereas older patients with both a low serum albumin measurement and a high β_2-M level had an average survival of just more than 1 year.

Monitoring

After treatment, the β_2-M level generally parallels the decline in serum monoclonal protein, but persistently elevated levels of β_2-M may occasionally identify patients with brief responses. In patients with light chain disease or nonsecretory myeloma without a measurable serum monoclonal protein, the β_2-M level can be used to follow the response to treatment.

NON-HODGKIN'S LYMPHOMA

Prognosis

Clinical stage, performance status, and the serum lactate dehydrogenase (LDH) level are considered the most important prognostic factors in newly diagnosed patients with non-Hodgkin's lymphoma (Chapter 195). High pretreatment serum LDH levels, which have been consistently shown to be an adverse risk factor, presumably reflect the growth rate and tumor burden. Patients with a high LDH level and either advanced stage disease or a poor performance status have less than a 50% probability of durable remission with standard therapy. These patients are considered candidates for clinical trials of more aggressive chemotherapy.

Monitoring Response to Therapy

In contrast to the level of the pretreatment LDH, levels obtained during therapy may be difficult to interpret. In one study, the LDH increased as much as two- to four-fold during therapy and remained elevated for up to 1 month after the conclusion of treatment. In addition, the LDH level is consistently increased in patients treated with hematopoietic colony-stimulating factors, presumably due to increased turnover of progenitor cells in the bone marrow.

TUMORS OF UNKNOWN ORIGIN

Approximately 5 to 10% of patients who present with cancer have tumors of unknown primary (Chapter 210). Although squamous cell histology limits the site of origin to the head and neck, lung, skin, or cervix, it is more common for patients to have adenocarcinoma or a poorly differentiated tumor. Tumor markers are not generally helpful in predicting the site of origin or recommending therapy. Important exceptions are serum PSA levels to detect prostate cancer and AFP and hCG to detect germ cell tumors.

SUGGESTED READINGS

Bast RC Jr, Ravdin P, Hayes DF, et al: 2000 update of recommendations for the use of tumor markers in breast and colorectal cancer: Clinical practice guidelines of the American Society of Clinical Oncology. J Clin Oncol 2001:19:1865–1878. *Consensus guidelines.*

Schrohl AS, Holten-Anderson M, Sweep F, et al: Tumor markers: From laboratory to clinical utility. Mol Cell Proteomics 2003:2:378–387. *A current overview.*

Tanguay S, Begin LR, Elhilali MM, et al: Comparative evaluation of total PSA, free/total PSA, and complexed PSA in prostate cancer detection. Urology 2002:59:261–265. *Use of free PSA and the ratio of free-to-total PSA improves diagnostic accuracy.*

190 CANCER PREVENTION

Gilbert S. Omenn

Cancers are estimated to have claimed about 550,000 lives in the United States during 2001, accounting for 23% of all deaths. An estimated 1.3 million people had newly diagnosed cancer (not including 1 million people with squamous or basal cell skin cancers and more than 100,000 with carcinomas in situ). Fear of cancers, suffering from cancers and their treatments, and the limited benefit of therapy for many common cancers combine to make prevention an increasingly high priority in clinical medicine and public health.

The leading cancer killer by far in both men and women is lung cancer (Chapter 198), followed by cancer of the prostate (Chapter 207), colon and rectum (Chapter 200), and pancreas (Chapter 201) in men and cancer of the breast (Chapter 204), colon and rectum, pancreas, and ovary (Chapter 205) in women (Fig. 190–1). Nine screening-accessible cancers (breast, colon, rectum, cervix, prostate, testis [Chapter 206], tongue [Chapter 197], mouth, and skin [Chapter 209]) are targets for early diagnosis. Currently, no effective screening tests have been validated for pancreatic and pulmonary cancers, although trypsinogen active peptide and spiral computed tomography (CT) scans, respectively, are being investigated. Despite reductions in age-adjusted incidence and death rates in the past decade, total mortality from cancers continues to increase in the aging and expanding American population. Racial disparities must be noted as well: African-American men and women have higher incidence rates and poorer survival than whites for nearly all tumor sites.

The primary modalities for cancer prevention (Table 190–1) require changes in behavior, especially those that involve smoking (Chapter 14), alcohol (Chapter 17), diet (Chapter 12), physical activity (Chapter 13), and infections related to sexual activity (Chapter 345). Reduction of exposures to carcinogenic agents from all environmental sources, including workplace and recreational settings, is a complementary approach. Meanwhile, hormonal, nutritional, vaccine, and pharmacologic interventions are being tested in clinical trials, especially in patients with preneoplastic conditions. New animal models and human genetic markers of high risk for colon and breast cancer offer promising means of screening and testing agents and modifying risk factors on a scientifically sound basis.

Smoking Cessation and Smoking Prevention (Chapter 14)

Diseases related to cigarette smoking represent a 20th century epidemic, which is rapidly spreading globally. Smoking is the primary cause of cancer of the lungs, larynx, oral cavity, and esophagus (approximately 10 to 20 times greater risk than in nonsmokers) and

Table 190–1 • PROPORTIONS OF CANCER DEATHS ATTRIBUTED TO VARIOUS PREVENTABLE FACTORS

FACTOR OR CLASS OF FACTOR	BEST ESTIMATE	RANGE OF ESTIMATES
Tobacco	30	25–40
Alcohol	3	2–4
Diet	35	10–70
Food additives*	<1	–5–2
Reproductive/sexual behavior	7	1–13
Occupation	4	2–8
General pollution	2	1–5
Industrial products	<1	<1–2
Medical procedures	1	0.5–3
Geophysical factors†	3	2–4
Infections	10?	1–?

*Minus indicates potential benefits from antioxidants and other additives.
†Ultraviolet and cosmic radiation included

From Doll R, Peto R: The causes of cancer: Quantitative estimates of avoidable risks of cancer in the United States today. J Natl Cancer Inst 1981;66:1193–1308. These conclusions and estimates were updated and reaffirmed in a special supplement to Cancer Causes & Control 1996; 7(Suppl. 1), edited by Colditz et al.

Leading Sites of New Cancer Cases and Deaths—2003 Estimates*

Estimated New Cases*		Estimated Deaths	
Male	**Female**	**Male**	**Female**
Prostate 220,900 (33%)	Breast 211,300 (32%)	Lung and bronchus 88,400 (31%)	Lung and bronchus 68,800 (25%)
Lung and bronchus 91,800 (14%)	Lung and bronchus 80,100 (12%)	Prostate 28,900 (10%)	Breast 39,800 (15%)
Colon and rectum 72,800 (11%)	Colon and rectum 74,700 (11%)	Colon and rectum 28,300 (10%)	Colon and rectum 28,800 (11%)
Urinary bladder 42,200 (6%)	Uterine corpus 40,100 (6%)	Pancreas 14,700 (5%)	Pancreas 15,300 (6%)
Melanoma of the skin 29,900 (4%)	Ovary 25,400 (4%)	Non-Hodgkin's lymphoma 12,200 (4%)	Ovary 14,300 (5%)
Non-Hodgkin's lymphoma 28,300 (4%)	Non-Hodgkin's lymphoma 25,100 (4%)	Leukemia 12,100 (4%)	Non-Hodgkin's lymphoma 11,200 (4%)
Kidney 19,500 (3%)	Melanoma of the skin 24,300 (3%)	Esophagus 9,900 (4 %)	Leukemia 9,800 (4%)
Oral cavity 18,200 (3%)	Thyroid 16,300 (2%)	Liver 9,200 (3%)	Uterine corpus 6,800 (3%)
Leukemia 17,900 (3%)	Pancreas 15,800 (2%)	Urinary bladder 8,600 (3%)	Brain 5,800 (2%)
Pancreas 14,900 (2%)	Urinary bladder 15,200 (2%)	Kidney 7,400 (3%)	Multiple myeloma 5,500 (2%)
All sites 675,300 (100%)	All sites 658,800 (100%)	All sites 285,900 (100%)	All sites 270,600 (100%)

*Excludes basal and squamous cell skin cancers and in situ carcinoma except urinary bladder.
Percentages may not total 100% due to rounding.

© 2003, American Cancer Society, Inc., Surveillance Research.

FIGURE 190–1 • Leading sites of cancer incidence and death—2003 estimates. (From Cancer Facts and Figures 2003. Atlanta, American Cancer Society, 2003.)

contributes to leukemias and pancreatic, bladder, kidney, stomach, and cervical cancers (about 2 times increased risk). Smoking acts synergistically with chemical and radiation carcinogens in the lung and with alcohol in the esophagus and oral cavity. Former smokers, after a lag of up to 4 years, show a progressively lower relative risk compared with continuing smokers. However, unlike the risk of coronary heart disease, the absolute risk of lung cancer in former smokers probably never declines, certainly not to the level of nonsmokers; the rate of increase seems comparable to the slowly rising rate among never-smokers as they age. Low-tar, low-nicotine, and filtered cigarettes have had little or no protective effect because the smokers of these products tend to inhale more deeply and more frequently. Smokeless tobacco and snuff dipping have been successfully promoted to children and adolescents in recent years. Leukoplakia, a white patch involving the oral mucosa epithelium (Chapter 197), is a telltale premalignant lesion found in up to half of tobacco chewers, with a 5% risk of epidermoid carcinoma. Finally, environmental tobacco smoke, or second-hand smoke, has been declared a definite human carcinogen by the U.S. Environmental Protection Agency; 6000 cases of lung cancer per year are attributed to environmental tobacco smoke by the National Research Council.

A huge literature attests to the difficulty of helping smokers quit and remain abstinent. Each year, about 5% of smokers quit smoking by themselves for at least a 6-month period. Physicians play a key role in urging smokers to quit and in guiding them to self-help materials, classes, or pharmacologic aids, which increase quit rates and reduce relapse rates. Work site, family, community, and physician reinforcement is essential; increased taxes (prices) on tobacco products also reduce smoking, especially in young people, minorities, and women.

Moderation of Alcohol Intake (Chapter 17)

The National Cancer Institute Dietary Guidelines recommend that consumption of alcoholic beverages, if any, be moderate. Alcohol intake is highly associated with cancers of the esophagus, oral cavity, pharynx, larynx, and breast, as well as liver, rectum, and pancreas. Alcohol acts synergistically with cigarette smoking and poor diet, especially in the oral cavity and esophagus.

Diet (Chapter 12)

Guidelines for healthy diets strongly recommend decreases in fat and increases in fiber intake, most easily described as five portions each day of fruits and vegetables. Such advice aims at preventing colon and possibly prostate cancers, as well as heart disease and bowel disorders.

The typical U.S. diet provides 39% of calories from fat, about 150 g/day. In a feasibility study for the Women's Health Trial, women 45 to 69 years old lowered their mean dietary fat intake to less than 25% of energy requirements for 2 years. Reduction in dietary fat intake is a major component of the Women's Health Initiative, a massive trial aimed at reducing breast cancer, heart disease, and osteoporosis in postmenopausal women by means of hormone replacement therapy, calcium, vitamin D, diet, and exercise. High calcium intake also may be protective against colon cancer.■ Analysis of fat intake involves many variables, including percentage of calories, grams per day, saturated versus unsaturated fats and fatty acids, and duration of diet. In the colon, fat may influence bile acids, sterol substrates, and fecal microflora. Each type of cancer possesses other confounding or interacting risk factors. A body mass index $\geq 30 \text{ kg/m}^2$ increases the risk of postmenopausal breast, endometrial, colorectal, renal cell, and gallbladder cancers.

The highest rates of colon cancer occur in Western countries, associated with a high intake of refined carbohydrates as compared with the naturally occurring fiber-rich foods common in African and Asian countries, where colon cancer rates are low. Among Western countries, low colon cancer rates and a mean intake of 31 g of fiber per day in Finland contrast with high colon cancer rates in Denmark and New York and 17 g of fiber per day despite similar fat intake. "Fiber," defined by plant origin and resistance to digestion by human enzymes, is highly heterogeneous, thus making measurement difficult. Soluble fiber (gum, mucilage, pectin, and hemicellulose) delays gastric emptying, slows glucose absorption, and lowers serum cholesterol levels, with lesser effects on bulk and transit time. Insoluble fiber increases fecal bulk and decreases intestinal transit time; cellulose and hemicellulose are prominent in cereals and grains, lignin in berry fruits, and pectin in citrus fruits and apples. Although a number of epidemiologic studies suggested a link between higher dietary fiber intake and lower rates of colorectal cancer, randomized trials of high-fiber diets have failed to reduce rates of polyp recurrence. **2,3**

Increased Physical Activity

Overcoming sedentary or inactive lifestyles benefits the cardiovascular, respiratory, muscular, cognitive, and metabolic systems. Increased physical activity seems to offer significant protection against colon cancer. Physical activity differences may be influential in cross-national and cross-cultural studies and should be carefully monitored in chemoprevention and diet studies.

Reduction of Environmental and Occupational Exposures to Carcinogenic Chemicals, Physical Agents, and Infectious Agents

CARCINOGENIC CHEMICALS. Asbestos fibers, inorganic arsenic compounds, bis-chloromethyl ether, chromium compounds, mustard gas, nickel dust, and polycyclic aromatic hydrocarbons from coal and gasoline combustion are lung carcinogens (Chapter 198); vinyl chloride causes a distinctive angiosarcoma of the liver (Chapter 202); some pesticides are associated with the development of non-Hodgkin's lymphoma (Chapter 195); aromatic amine dyestuffs can cause bladder cancer (Chapter 203); leather production and isopropyl alcohol manufacturing are associated with nasal cancer (Chapter 197); and benzene can cause acute myelogenous leukemia (Chapter 193). Tobacco smoke is the most prevalent chemical carcinogen, probably followed by char-broiled meat and fish.

PHYSICAL AGENTS. Ultraviolet radiation is the primary cause of skin cancer, including melanoma and lip cancer. The risk of squamous cell cancers arising from actinic keratoses is greatly exacerbated in organ transplant and human immunodeficiency virus (HIV)-infected patients who are immunosuppressed after infection; preemptive removal of these precancerous lesions and fastidious sun protection are required in such patients. Ionizing radiation (including radiotherapy) increases rates at essentially all exposed sites (Chapter 19). The Environmental Protection Agency estimates that as many as 21,000 cases of lung cancer (Chapter 198) per year may be attributed to α-particle–emitting radon gas in homes, for which simple testing and venting procedures are available to reduce exposure and risk. Nonionizing radiation and electromagnetic fields, although previously suspected of increasing leukemia (of any type) and brain cancer, seem not to raise risks based on current data.

INFECTIOUS AGENTS (Chapter 186). Certain cancers are causally related to specific infections: primary hepatocellular cancer is associated with chronic hepatitis B and C infections, and with synergistic effects from aflatoxins (Chapter 202); cervical cancer with certain human papillomaviruses (Chapter 205); Burkitt's lymphoma and nasopharyngeal cancer with Epstein-Barr virus (Chapter 197); Kaposi's sarcoma with HHV8 and HIV-1; non-Hodgkin's lymphoma with HIV-1; T-cell leukemia with human T-cell leukemia virus type I (Chapter 193); urinary bladder cancer (*Schistosoma haematobium*) and cholangiocarcinoma of the liver (*Clonorchis sinensis*) with parasites; and gastric cancer with *Helicobacter pylori* (Chapter 199). Environmental control of parasites, antibiotic treatment of *Helicobacter,* interferon treatment of hepatitis, and vaccines to protect against exposures to the viruses and *Helicobacter* should be effective cancer prevention strategies. For example, population-wide neonatal immunization against hepatitis B virus was expected to eliminate the scourge of primary liver cancer in Taiwan until the risks of hepatitis C were recognized; hepatitis C vaccines are under development.

PHARMACEUTICAL AGENTS. Alkylating agents can cause leukemias (Chapter 193); androgens and anabolic steroids, liver cancer (Chapter 202); estrogens, cancer of the vagina and cervix (diethylstilbestrol), breast and endometrium (postmenopausal estrogens), or liver and cervix (steroid contraceptives) (Chapters 202 and 205); azathioprine and cyclosporine immunosuppressants, non-Hodgkin's lymphoma and skin cancer (Chapter 209); and phenacetin-containing analgesics,

renal pelvic tumors. Careful indications for use and surveillance are essential.

CHEMOPREVENTION

Population trials of chemopreventive agents are under way worldwide. From the clinical point of view, agents that can be used in patients identified with preneoplastic conditions are most directly useful. The risks and the potential benefits are much greater than for the general population. Randomized trials of candidate agents are much more cost-effective in such populations. By comparison, primary prevention trials in the general population, or even in populations with increased risk due to identifiable environmental, behavioral, or genetic factors, require larger numbers and much longer durations of intervention and follow-up to accrue end points and detect differences in incidence rates. Many candidate agents are natural products, food constituents, or pharmaceuticals that are already approved for other indications, thereby markedly reducing the development costs. Various agents block activation of procarcinogens, enhance detoxification of carcinogens, block carcinogenic actions, or make cells less responsive to carcinogenic effects.

Antioxidants (vitamins E and C and selenium), isoflavones, phytosterols in soybeans, polyphenols in green tea, organosulfur compounds in onions and garlic, curcumin in curry, and many other plant-derived inhibitors of cellular proliferation or tumor promotion are being investigated in animal models and in phase I and phase II human studies. The most active area of chemoprevention currently is focused on selective inhibition of arachidonic acid metabolism, both the inducible cyclooxygenase (Cox-2) pathway to prostaglandins and thromboxanes and the 12-, 5-, and 8-lipoxygenase (Lox) pathways to leukotrienes and hydroeicosatetraenoic (HETE) acids. This work builds on positive findings with aspirin, piroxicam, sulindac, and other nonsteroidal anti-inflammatory drugs. Celecoxib, rofecoxib, and many other approved and emerging agents directed at these pathways in arthritis and asthma patients have shown promising efficacy against carcinogenesis in cell culture, animal models, and early clinical trials. Numerous agents inhibit carcinogenesis in one experimental setting, but increase carcinogenesis in another, including decaffeinated tea, phenobarbital, vitamin E, retinoic acid, vitamin D_3, estrogens, and tamoxifen. These chemicals commonly have multiple molecular and cellular targets, thereby greatly complicating extrapolation to humans and eventually benefit/risk tradeoffs in patients.

The largest studies of the past 20 years involved β-carotene alone (22,000 low-risk male physicians), β-carotene plus vitamin E (29,000 male smokers in Finland), β-carotene plus vitamin A (14,000 male and female U.S. smokers and 4000 asbestos-exposed workers), and β-carotene plus vitamin E and aspirin (40,000 female health professionals). The Alpha-Tocopherol/Beta-Carotene study in Finland found no benefit from vitamin E or from β-carotene; instead, the men receiving 20 mg/day of β-carotene had an 18% higher rate of lung cancer and 8% higher overall mortality. The Beta-Carotene and Retinol Efficacy Trial (CARET) confirmed these adverse effects (28% higher lung cancer incidence and 17% higher mortality). There were no benefits from β-carotene after 10 to 15 years in the Physicians Health Study and in several other trials against skin, colon, and lung cancers. Subsequent laboratory studies have identified epoxides and ketones of β-carotene that increase the formation of B[a]P-DNA adducts. The adverse effects of β-carotene have stimulated a search for other chemopreventive constituents from fruits and vegetables including folic acid, calcium D-glucarate, and lycopene.

The U.S. Food and Drug Administration (FDA) has approved new indications for celecoxib in persons with familial adenomatous polyposis of the colon, for tamoxifen for ductal carcinoma in situ, for topical 5-fluorouracil and diclofenac for actinic keratoses, and for intravesical BCG and valrubicin for superficial bladder cancer. Agents being considered for approval include Cox-2 inhibitors and aspirin for gastrointestinal polyps, raloxifene for breast cancer, retinoids for head and neck cancer, and several agents for intraepithelial precancerous lesions of the bladder.

CHEMOPREVENTION WITH HORMONES. In the United States, cancers of hormone-responsive tissues account for 20% of the newly diagnosed cancers in men and more than 40% in women. Thus chemoprevention with "antihormones" represents a promising approach. Diethylstilbestrol and luteinizing hormone–releasing hormone agonists are therapeutically effective against metastatic prostate cancer

Oncology

by reducing testosterone-mediated maintenance of prostate tissue (Chapter 207). Finasteride, a testosterone 5α-reductase inhibitor, is being tested in 18,000 men for the primary prevention of prostate cancer. Another long-term prostate cancer prevention trial will test vitamin E with and without selenium in 32,000 men. Although the early sequential oral contraceptives increased endometrial cancer risk, modern estrogen-progesterone combinations are potent chemopreventive agents. Women with 6 or more years of oral contraceptive use have less than one sixth the risk of endometrial cancer when compared with never-users, and the effect lasts at least 15 years after discontinuation of the oral contraceptives. Combination oral contraceptives also suppress gonadotropin levels and ovulation, thereby decreasing the risk for epithelial ovarian cancer by about 40%, independent of parity.

The breast responds differently, however. Postmenopausal estrogens and especially estrogen plus progestin combinations markedly increase the risk of breast cancer. The Women's Health Initiative (see earlier text) randomized 16,608 women aged 50 to 79 to an estrogen/medroxyprogesterone acetate combination or to placebo. After just 5.2 years, the trial was stopped because of an excess incidence of invasive breast cancer and of coronary heart disease, stroke, and venous thromboembolism; dementia rates were also increased. Of note, however, was that the incidences of hip fractures and colorectal cancers, but not endometrial cancers, were decreased. ▨

Antiestrogenic agents such as tamoxifen reduce the incidence of new primary breast cancers in breast cancer survivors. In the largest trial with 13,000 women, tamoxifen halved the rates of invasive and noninvasive breast cancer and of fractures, so the trial was halted after 5 years, 2 years ahead of schedule. However, endometrial cancer rates and venous/pulmonary thromboses were significantly increased among those receiving tamoxifen. ▨ Among newer agents, the 2-arylbenzothiophene raloxifene is a target-site selective estrogen receptor modulator that has estrogen agonist effects on bone and serum lipids but estrogen antagonist effects on the breast and uterus. In the Multiple Outcomes of Raloxifene Evaluation (MORE) trial in 7705 postmenopausal women with osteoporosis, raloxifene, like tamoxifen, dramatically reduced the incidence of estrogen-receptor–positive (but not estrogen-receptor–negative) breast cancer. Women with higher lifetime estrogen exposure (as reflected in higher bone density and higher estradiol levels) and with positive family history also had greater reductions from raloxifene. An excess risk of venous thrombosis and pulmonary embolism continues to be a problem, requiring risk/risk counseling by physicians. ▨ Aromatase inhibitors, which may have a more favorable benefit/risk profile, are under investigation, as are direct comparisons of tamoxifen with raloxifene.

GENETIC SCREENING

Molecular studies of cancer have revealed numerous oncogenes, tumor suppressor genes, and other genes affecting cell division, cell cycle, genomic stability, cell proliferation, and apoptosis (Chapter 185) as potential molecular targets for cancer prevention. Therapeutic agents are being targeted at specific receptors (Her2/neu, EGFR), products of chromosomal translocations (Bcl/Abl), and enzymes (protein farnesylation as a measure of *ras* oncogene inhibition). Advances in the molecular epidemiology of cancers help identify targets for chemoprevention and high-risk populations for interventions. Transgenic and knockout mice are increasingly important models for human cancers, including mice with Apc and Min mutations that lead to intestinal cancers, and mice transgenic for HPV16 that develop intraepithelial neoplasia and squamous carcinoma of the cervix. The FDA and the National Cancer Institute have negotiated a plan to encourage phase II and small phase III clinical trials with such end points. An example is testing of cyclooxygenase-2 inhibitors for the prevention or regression of adenomatous colorectal polyps in patients with familial polyposis coli.

4. Women's Health Initiative Investigators Writing Group: Risks and benefits of estrogen plus progestin in healthy postmenopausal women. Principal results from the Women's Health Initiative randomized controlled trial. JAMA 2002;288:321–333.
5. Early Breast Cancer Trialists' Collaborative Group: Tamoxifen for early breast cancer: An overview of the randomized trials. Lancet 1998;351:1451–1467.
6. Cuzick J, Powles T, Veronesi U, et al: Overview of the main outcomes in breast-cancer prevention trials. Lancet 2003;361:296–300.

SUGGESTED READINGS
American Cancer Society: Cancer Facts and Figures 2003. Atlanta, American Cancer Society, 2003. *Excellent annual update on cancer statistics and advances.*
Lippman M, Krueger KA, Eckert S, et al: Indicators of lifetime estrogen exposure: Effect on breast cancer incidence and interaction with raloxifene therapy in the Multiple Outcomes of Raloxifene Evaluation study participants. J Clin Oncol 2001;19: 3111–3116. *Higher estrogen exposure increases risk, raloxifene reduces risk.*
Steele VE, Hawk ET, Viner JL, et al: Mechanisms and applications of non-steroidal anti-inflammatory drugs in the chemoprevention of cancer. Mutation Res 2003;523: 137–144. *How they work and may be used in the future.*

191 PRINCIPLES OF CANCER THERAPY

Joseph R. Bertino
William Hait

The development of effective anticancer drugs has progressively integrated medical management with surgery and radiation therapy in the multimodal treatment of cancer. New cytotoxic and endocrine agents and the introduction of biologic therapy that includes naked or "armed" antibodies, interferons (IFNs), and cytokines have expanded medical management. The physician also must be familiar with palliative aspects of cancer care, including management of pain (Chapter 29) and treatment of life-threatening complications.

Although current systemic therapy can cure few forms of metastatic cancer, it has become increasingly effective as a component of multimodal management of apparently localized cancers known to have a high frequency of occult micrometastatic spread. Not all patients are candidates for attempts at cancer therapy because of limitations in available drugs or comorbidity from other medical problems. Patients and families must be fully informed about the nature of planned treatment, whether curative or palliative in intent. Inasmuch as prognosis for individual patients is currently based on statistical estimates, the physician must evaluate each patient individually in relation to relevant prognostic factors in attempting to develop a treatment plan.

DEVELOPMENT OF A TREATMENT PLAN

The major clinical features of cancer to be considered in developing a treatment plan include (1) specific histologic diagnosis of the neoplasm, (2) tumor burden and extent of specific organ involvement (stage), and (3) biologic characteristics and other prognostic factors relevant to the specific type of cancer.

Diagnosis

Accurate histologic diagnosis and staging critically influence treatment selection. Increasingly, immunohistochemical and genetic analysis helps in subtyping lymphomas and distinguishing among various morphologically "undifferentiated" neoplasms (Chapter 210). Tumors of diverse histogenesis can have markedly different prognosis and treatment. Electron microscopy sometimes can help by identifying specific morphologic features such as melanosomes (in melanoma) or desmosomes (in carcinomas) that permit more specific classification. Other distinctive biologic markers include immunohistochemistry (e.g., overexpression of cyclin D in mantle cell lymphoma), hormone receptor expression, serum or urinary tumor markers (e.g., β-human chorionic gonadotropin, α-fetoprotein, carcinoembryonic antigen, CA-125, myeloma proteins, urinary 5-hydroxyindole acetic acid), karyotype, or molecular analysis. Molecular biologic methods for DNA analysis also play a role in diagnosis by identifying characteristic gene rearrangements (e.g., Southern blots), tumor suppressor gene deletions and/or mutations, and oncogene expression. Methods to profile the expression of genes in cancer cells, both at the mRNA level and the protein level (proteomics), may permit more selective use of currently available anticancer agents and stimulate new drug development.

1. Baron JA, Beach M, Mandel JS, et al: Calcium supplements for the prevention of colorectal adenomas. N Engl J Med 1999;340:101–107.
2. Schatzkin A, Lanza E, Corle D, et al: Lack of effect of a low-fat, high-fiber diet on the recurrence of colorectal adenomas. N Engl J Med 2000;342:1149–1155.
3. Alberts DS, Martinez ME, Roe DJ, et al: Lack of effect of a high-fiber cereal supplement on the recurrence of colorectal adenomas. N Engl J Med 2000;342:1156–1162.

In the leukemias and lymphomas, such information can be important for selecting appropriate treatment approaches. For example, the approach to treatment of T-cell or B-cell lymphomas differs as a function of cell lineage, which often cannot be identified with standard histologic approaches. Specialized studies sometimes can provide evidence for a treatable or curable form of cancer that might otherwise go unrecognized.

Staging

Assessment of the body burden and spread of cancer by clinical means (staging) is important in developing the treatment plan. Most staging systems assess the size of the primary tumor and define regional lymph node involvement as well as the presence or absence of distant metastatic disease. It is important to distinguish between clinical and pathologic staging and to recognize that pathologic staging by surgical biopsy is generally more accurate. Increasingly, staging can be accomplished by using noninvasive imaging procedures such as chest radiography and magnetic resonance imaging (MRI), computed tomography (CT), and positron-emission tomography (PET) scanning. In the diagnostic evaluation of specific forms of cancer, such as breast or prostate cancer, bone scans can be useful to evaluate advanced disease but have minimal use in early localized disease unless the patient has skeletal symptoms. For multiple myeloma, bone scans are of less use than skeletal radiographs. The temptation to use a variety of redundant and expensive tests such as CT, MRI, PET scanning, and ultrasonography to examine the same site should be avoided. It is important to focus on the benefit-to-risk ratio of invasive procedures such as staging laparotomy. The patient's age, performance status, concomitant medical problems, and histologic diagnosis all must be considered; then the procedure should be performed only if it may influence the treatment plan. For patients who present with life-threatening local complications of cancer (e.g., spinal cord compression, upper airway obstruction, superior vena cava syndrome, or obstructive jaundice), it is usually necessary first to treat the local complication. Even in these cases, a pathologic diagnosis should be established if possible before treatment is started.

Overall Assessment

Once diagnosis and staging have been performed, the information must be integrated into an optimal treatment plan. For patients with apparently localized cancers, multidisciplinary input is important, because a combined-modality approach may be indicated. The biologic characteristics of the specific cancer must be considered. For many tumor types, histopathologic features such as grade of tumor cell differentiation are important, with a less differentiated or undifferentiated phenotype usually indicating a more aggressive neoplasm. For some sites, other biologic factors are of greater value than histologic grade. For example, in breast cancer, the presence or absence of estrogen or progesterone receptors, the overexpression of the *HER-2/neu* gene, and the DNA index and ploidy status as determined by flow cytometry provide useful information in developing a treatment plan (Chapter 204). Some patients with a minimal tumor burden (e.g., stage I) of currently incurable B-cell neoplasms (e.g., chronic lymphocytic leukemia [CLL] and low-grade lymphomas) are best watched expectantly rather than treated. By contrast, almost all patients with diffuse large-cell (intermediate- or high-grade) lymphoma should be treated aggressively with curative intent, regardless of stage, unless they are very elderly and have other major medical problems (Chapter 195).

In any patient, it is important to decide whether curative therapy is available or not, and, if so, whether the patient's age and overall medical condition permit a curative approach. If cure is not an option, one must consider whether palliation with prolongation of survival (and relief of symptoms) can be achieved. For old and infirm patients, a palliative approach may be preferable, particularly if there is significant morbidity associated with the treatment approach under consideration. On the other hand, some forms of cancer therapy are very effective and well tolerated even with advanced age (e.g., use of tamoxifen in adjuvant therapy of postmenopausal breast cancer or of chlorambucil for CLL). For many tumor types, it is important to examine results of recent prospective clinical trials relevant to the patient's diagnosis and clinical setting and, when possible, to enter patients in clinical trials.

THERAPEUTIC MODALITIES

Three primary therapeutic approaches dominate the treatment of cancer: surgery, radiation therapy, and medical therapy. A fourth modality, biologic therapy (cytokines, antibodies, vaccines), has added another dimension to treatment programs.

Surgery

Cancer surgery is used to establish a tissue diagnosis, to excise the primary tumor with clear surgical margins free of tumor, and to determine the extent of cancer with staging procedures. Surgery is a simple and safe means to remove solid tumors when the tumor is confined to a specific anatomic site of origin. However, in the case of some solid tumors, most patients already have metastatic disease at the time of presentation. In evaluating major surgery for an individual patient, it is important to assess the operative risk-to-benefit ratio for the procedure in the context of the patient's general health, the extent of the tumor, and the likelihood that it can be completely removed. Additionally, the technical complexity of the surgical procedure, the type of anesthesia needed, and the experience of the personnel must also be considered.

With advances in both radiation and chemotherapy, the need for radical surgery has diminished. However, surgery remains a major primary approach to curative cancer therapy. For testicular cancer, even in the presence of limited metastatic disease, regional lymphadenectomy after radical orchiectomy can be curative and eliminate the need for chemotherapy in some patients who have metastases only to retroperitoneal lymph nodes (Chapter 206). For many other sites, surgical resection of regional lymph nodes is performed for diagnostic rather than therapeutic purposes. For example, in breast cancer, the presence or absence of axillary lymph node involvement is the single most important factor in evaluating the likelihood of distant recurrence, and this information is currently not reliably obtained by nonsurgical means (Chapter 204). Similarly, surgical staging of nodal involvement in colorectal cancer plays an important role in deciding whether adjuvant systemic chemotherapy is indicated (Chapter 200). A recent advance is the use of "sentinel" lymph node biopsy, most notably in patients with breast cancer or malignant melanoma (Chapters 204 and 209), to decrease the extent of lymph node dissection.

Initial cancer therapy often requires a multimodal approach to maximize the chance of cure while simultaneously reducing the extent of surgery required. Early communication is improved by obtaining histopathologic diagnosis by needle biopsy or local excision of the primary cancer before more extensive therapy. Two examples are of note in this regard: (1) the management of osteogenic sarcoma with limb salvage surgery, irradiation, and adjuvant chemotherapy (Chapter 208) and (2) the management of early breast cancer with lumpectomy, axillary staging followed by primary irradiation, and adjuvant systemic administration of cytotoxic or endocrine agents (Chapter 204). In both instances, the combined approach yields a better cosmetic and functional outcome. Improved plastic surgical techniques have also made breast reconstruction possible for women who either require or prefer mastectomy rather than lumpectomy followed by radiation therapy.

In addition to its use in diagnosis, staging, and primary therapy, cancer surgery also plays an important role in the management of some patients with more extensive cancer. In ovarian cancer, when the gynecologic oncologist "debulks" peritoneal and omental spread and leaves the patient with minimal residual disease, patients become better candidates for systemic chemotherapy and have a better survival (Chapter 205). Additionally, early resection of pulmonary metastases of soft tissue sarcomas or of solitary brain metastases in melanoma, colon, or breast cancer may provide marked palliation and improved survival, albeit with only occasional cures.

Radiation Therapy

Radiation therapy has made major strides in instrumentation, physics, radiobiology, treatment planning, and applications to curative and palliative cancer therapy. Compared with surgery, radiation therapy has distinct advantages in the locoregional treatment of cancer. Radiation causes less acute morbidity and can be curative for some specific sites while preserving organ or tissue structure and function.

An example is the use of radiation for the curative treatment of early stage laryngeal cancer wherein vocal function can be preserved (Chapter 197).

The basic unit of ionizing irradiation is the gray (Gy), which has superseded the rad (1 Gy = 100 rads = 100 cGy) (Chapter 19). By interaction with molecular oxygen, radiation induces the formation of superoxide, hydrogen peroxide, or hydroxyl radicals that damage or break cellular DNA, the critical target for radiation-induced cell death. Both single- and double-strand breaks of the DNA helix can be induced, with the latter constituting lethal damage. Single-strand breaks, if not repaired by the cell, can also result in cell death.

Large, bulky tumors frequently have poorly perfused, hypoxic zones in which radiation often fails to induce needed reactive intermediaries. Various forms of irradiation are used for different therapeutic objectives. For example, electron-beam irradiation deposits most of its energy in the skin and soft tissues and can be useful for superficial therapy of skin neoplasms such as mycosis fungoides. Low-energy (kilovoltage) x-rays expend most of their effects on the overlying tissues above a deep-seated tumor and therefore cause considerable normal tissue damage. By contrast, higher-energy x-rays (megavoltage) or x-irradiation from a cobalt-60 source spare the skin, deposit their energy at greater depth, and provide a better approach to treating deep-seated neoplasms. Use of radioactive implants also can be useful in some settings (e.g., cervical cancer, prostate cancer). The use of multiple irradiation fields reduces the dose to normal tissue while increasing the dose to the tumor. The use of fractionated doses causes less cumulative damage to normal tissues than to the tumor, because the normal tissues are often able to repair sublethal damage more quickly. Additionally, as a tumor shrinks with therapy, its oxygenation can improve and render it more radiosensitive. The selection of treatment is based on the relative radiosensitivity of the tumor and of the normal organs and tissues within the radiation field (Table 191–1).

The combined use of multiple fields, fractionated irradiation, and megavoltage radiation equipment is optimized by treatment individualized to the patient's tumor. Although the major uses of radiation therapy involve local irradiation of sites of tumor involvement, total-body irradiation or total lymphoid irradiation is a valuable part of a preparative regimen for allogeneic or autologous bone marrow transplantation for leukemia or lymphoma (Chapter 166).

Radiation therapy has important palliative applications. Irradiation can also cause sufficient cytoreduction of tumor in bone to permit healing of osteolytic lesions and thereby prevent pathologic fractures of weight-bearing bones. Other examples include tumor shrinkage to relieve postobstructive infection in lung cancer and to suppress bronchial or gastric bleeding secondary to local tumor invasion.

Although modern radiation therapy with megavoltage equipment is extremely useful, even higher energy radiation approaches are currently in development. These include the use of neutrons, charged particles, and heavy ions, which may provide selective advantages for specific tumor sites and reduce the need for oxygenation of tumor tissue. Additionally, several classes of compounds (e.g., halopyrimidines, gemcitabine, paclitaxel, and amifostine) are under study as radiosensitizers to enhance the cytotoxic effects of radiation on tumor cells.

Although the term *radiation* normally refers to ionizing irradiation, several other forms of radiation, such as hyperthermia and photodynamic therapy (PDT), are also used in cancer treatment. Some tumors show thermal sensitivity to temperatures in the range of 41° to 43°C and may be more sensitive than surrounding normal tissues. Hyperthermia appears to work best on bulky tumors with poor blood supply in which the tumor cells are in an acidic environment.

PDT involves the preliminary systemic administration of a photosensitizing compound such as a hematoporphyrin derivative (e.g., dihematoporphyrin ether, photofrin II) that is concentrated in the vicinity of local tumors and can be activated with local exposure to visible red light (usually 630 nm), with a resulting preferential toxicity to cancer cells. The intense light used for PDT can be delivered by means of a fiberoptic probe, which can be used for various internal sites as well as on the skin. Side effects of PDT include hypersensitivity to light (skin and eyes). Locally, PDT induces transient sunburn and hyperpigmentation as well as local tumor necrosis. Tumor sites amenable to PDT include skin recurrences of breast cancer (e.g., chest wall) and malignant lesions in the endobronchus, peritoneal cavity, and bladder.

Medical Therapy

Curative therapy has been developed for a series of relatively uncommon disseminated neoplasms, and useful palliative therapy has been developed for some common forms of cancer (Table 191–2). With rare exceptions, effective therapy has used combinations of anticancer drugs, commonly in concert with surgery and/or irradiation.

Ideally, anticancer drugs should eradicate cancer without harming normal tissues; however, most useful drugs have significant side effects. Most drugs are general antiproliferative agents that are more effective against rapidly proliferating tumors than against some of the more slowly growing solid tumors and that are more toxic to rapidly growing tumors than to normal host tissues. Nevertheless, such generally antiproliferative agents commonly have important toxic side effects on normal tissues that divide rapidly, such as bone marrow, gastrointestinal mucosa, and skin. Newer agents that selectively target abnormalities specific to the tumor cell, such as imatinib mesylate (Gleevec), are generally less toxic (Chapter 192).

CELL KINETICS AND RESPONSE TO CHEMOTHERAPY. A number of related factors, including total tumor burden, cell kinetics, and intrinsic sensitivity, influence the response to anticancer drugs. In both animal models and human tumors, growth occurs in accord with gompertzian kinetics. Initially, growth occurs rapidly, and most tumor cells traverse the complete cell cycle. As the tumor burden grows larger, the

---

Table 191–1 • TOLERANCE OF NORMAL TISSUES TO IRRADIATION

TISSUE	TOXIC EFFECT	LIMITING DOSE (GY)*
Bone marrow	Aplasia	2.5
Lung	Pneumonitis, fibrosis	15.0
Kidney	Nephrosclerosis	20.0
Liver	Hepatitis	25.0
Spinal cord	Infarction, necrosis	45.0
Intestine	Ulceration, fibrosis	45.0
Heart	Pericarditis, myocarditis	45.0
Brain	Infarction, necrosis	50.0
Skin	Dermatitis, sclerosis	55.0

*Radiation in 2.0-Gy fractions to the whole organ for 5 days weekly produces a 5% incidence of the listed toxicities at the limiting doses listed.

Table 191–2 • RESPONSIVENESS OF CANCER TO CHEMOTHERAPY

CURE (>30%) OF ADVANCED DISEASE
Choriocarcinoma
Acute lymphocytic leukemia (childhood)
Malignant lymphoma (Hodgkin's disease, diffuse high-grade or intermediate-grade non-Hodgkin's lymphoma)
Hairy cell leukemia
Testicular cancer
Childhood solid tumors (embryonal rhabdomyosarcoma, Ewing's sarcoma, Wilms' tumor)
Acute myelocytic leukemia
Acute lymphocytic leukemia (adult)
Acute promyelocytic leukemia

SIGNIFICANT PALLIATION, SOME CURES OF ADVANCED DISEASE (5–30%)
Ovarian cancer
Bladder cancer
Small cell lung cancer
Gastric cancer

PALLIATION, PROBABLY INCREASES SURVIVAL
Breast cancer
Multiple myeloma
Head and neck cancer

ADJUVANT TREATMENT LEADING TO INCREASED CURE
Breast cancer
Colon cancer
Osteogenic sarcoma
Early stage large cell lymphoma

Oncology

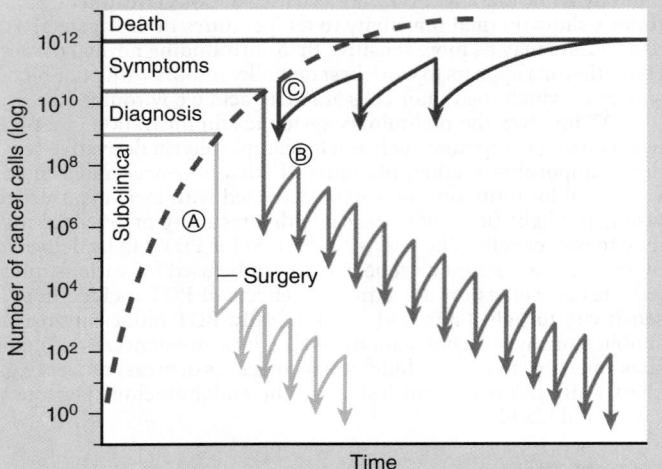

FIGURE 191–1 • The relationship of tumor growth and tumor burden to treatment strategies and outcome with systemic chemotherapy. Human tumors grow in accord with the Gompertz curve (dashed line), with a decreasing doubling time as tumor burden increases. Treatment interventions relate to tumor type and extent of disease. *A,* Surgery followed by pulse courses of adjuvant chemotherapy. Combined modality has curative potential with the addition of chemotherapy after surgery. *B,* Systemic chemotherapy for stage III Hodgkin's disease. Cure is possible with prolonged administration of combination chemotherapy. *C,* Palliative chemotherapy for advanced non–small cell cancer. The patient's tumor burden is too great and the potency of the drugs for this specific form of cancer is inadequate because of development of drug resistance. (Modified from Salmon SE, Sartorelli AC: Cancer chemotherapy. *In* Katzung BG [ed]: Basic and Clinical Pharmacology, 4th ed. Norwalk, CT, Appleton & Lange, 1989, p 685.)

Table 191–3 • RELATIONSHIP OF TUMOR CELL CYCLE TO ACTIVITY OF MAJOR CLASSES OF CYTOTOXIC ANTICANCER DRUGS

CELL CYCLE SPECIFIC AGENTS	CELL CYCLE NONSPECIFIC AGENTS
Antimetabolites (cytarabine, fluorouracil, methotrexate, mercaptopurine, hydroxyurea)	Alkylating agents (busulfan, cyclophosphamide, mechlorethamine, melphalan, thiotepa, chlorambucil)
Anthracyclines (doxorubicin, daunorubicin)	Antibiotics (dactinomycin, mitomycin)
Bleomycin	Platinum compounds (cisplatin, carboplatin)
Camptothecins (irinotecan, topotecan)	Nitrosoureas (BCNU, CCNU)
Plant alkaloids (vincristine, vinblastine, etoposide, taxol)	Dacarbazine
	L-Asparaginase

rate of tumor cell doubling progressively slows (Fig. 191–1), and the fraction of cells traversing the cell cycle decreases as more and more cells remain "hung up" in a G_0 phase. Whereas the population doubling time may be in the range of 1 to 2 days at the subclinical phase (with less than 1 g of tumor), by the time the tumor burden has reached 1 kg or more, the tumor cell population doubling time may be 3 to 6 months. A major problem in the large, solid tumors is that the expanding tumor exhibits a significant degree of heterogeneity; subpopulations of cells exhibit differing biologic, kinetic, antigenic, and drug-sensitivity profiles.

Several important features related to cell kinetics and tumor burden are important with respect to drug dose, scheduling, and response to chemotherapy. Anticancer drugs may be classified as either cell cycle specific (CCS) or cell cycle nonspecific (CCNS) (Table 191–3). CCNS agents have greater effects on cycling than on noncycling cells but nonetheless can exert anticancer effects on noncycling cells, whereas CCS agents do not. Endocrine agents are also in a sense cycle active, because they block the transition of tumor cells from G_1 to the S phase of the cell cycle. However, certain endocrine agents (e.g., tamoxifen,

progestins) suppress growth rather than kill tumor cells. Endocrine agents are therefore often given for many years, whereas cytotoxic agents are usually given over a time course measured in months.

An important concept in cancer chemotherapy is that cellular killing with cytotoxic agents follows first-order kinetics, with a given dose of drug killing only a fraction of the tumor cells. This "fractional kill hypothesis" is particularly relevant to CCNS agents and predicts that the greater the dose of drug administered, the greater the "log kill" of tumor cells that will occur.

The concept of combination chemotherapy was developed to take advantage of the fact that many anticancer agents have differing mechanisms of action and side effects. This concept was based on the hypothesis that giving drugs with differing mechanisms of action may achieve synergistic antitumor effects while simultaneously retarding the rate of development of drug resistance. Optimal results for most tumor types sensitive to chemotherapy have been achieved with drug combinations, often employing CCNS and CCS agents possessing different mechanisms of action and toxicities. For example, cisplatin has clear-cut synergy with etoposide in testicular cancer and small cell lung cancer and with fluorouracil in both head and neck and esophageal cancer. The major potential toxicity for cisplatin is nephrotoxicity, whereas myelosuppression is the major side effect for both etoposide and fluorouracil.

DRUG RESISTANCE. For many of the drug-responsive tumor types (see Table 191–2), major cytoreduction occurs with initial chemotherapy. Some months to years thereafter, however, tumor regrowth occurs and continues even though the same drugs are reinstituted. This observation usually reflects the acquisition of drug resistance by the tumor to the specific drugs. Most drug resistance is considered to result from the high spontaneous mutation rate of cancer cells. One of the most important forms of resistance is multidrug resistance, mediated by a cell membrane glycoprotein (the P-glycoprotein), which functions as an energy-dependent efflux pump that actively extrudes a variety of cytotoxic agents from the cell (Fig. 191–2).

Drugs effluxed from the cancer cell by P-glycoprotein include natural products such as plant alkaloids (vincas, podophyllotoxins, paclitaxel) and antibiotics (dactinomycin, doxorubicin, daunorubicin). P-glycoprotein is normally expressed in tissues such as the gut and the kidney, perhaps to deal with toxic products in the environment. Cancer cells that overexpress the MDR-1 gene, responsible for encoding the P-glycoprotein, show resistance to a wide variety of useful anticancer drugs. Clinical studies suggest that patients whose tumors express P-glycoprotein have a poor prognosis. Culture studies performed on biopsy specimens in vitro have documented that P-glycoprotein—positive tumors usually exhibit resistance to doxorubicin. Tumor types such as sarcoma, neuroblastoma, malignant lymphoma,

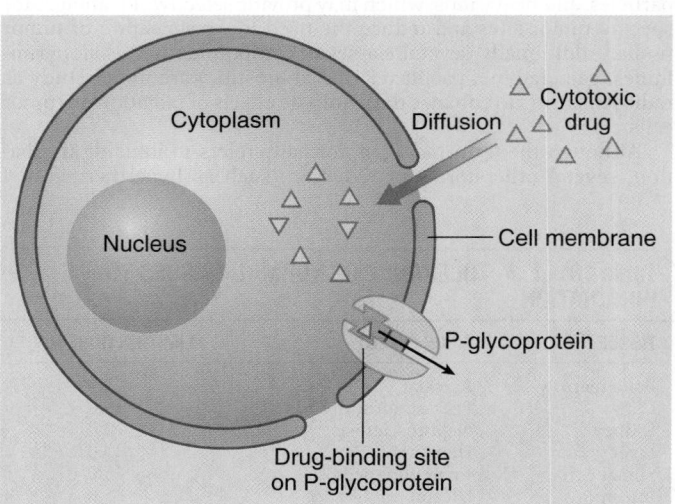

FIGURE 191–2 • Model of cancer cell expressing P-glycoprotein. This transmembrane protein is believed to function as an energy-dependent efflux pump or drug transporter. It has acceptor sites to which various natural product anticancer drugs bind, after which they are pumped out of the cell. Chemosensitizers such as verapamil also bind to the drug acceptor sites on P-glycoprotein and can competitively inhibit its function.

and myeloma are usually P-glycoprotein negative at the time of diagnosis but are frequently positive for P-glycoprotein when the patient relapses from chemotherapy. A series of noncytotoxic drugs has been identified to reverse drug resistance mediated by P-glycoprotein (e.g., verapamil, cyclosporine). In drug-resistant patients with malignant lymphoma and multiple myeloma, high doses of verapamil given simultaneously with vincristine and doxorubicin can reverse resistance to these agents, with some patients regaining remission. Although verapamil is not an ideal chemosensitizer (because of its cardiovascular side effects), other potential chemosensitizers are being tested in an effort to identify more effective and less toxic chemosensitizers. Other mechanisms of multidrug resistance include an increase in proteins, called *MRP* (a family of seven or more proteins).

Drug-specific resistance mechanisms also occur (Table 191–4). For example, intrinsic or natural resistance of patients with acute myelogenous leukemia to methotrexate is attributed to lack of retention of this drug by leukemic blasts. These cells form low levels of methotrexate polyglutamates, the drug species that are retained by cells. In contrast, acute lymphocytic leukemia (ALL) blasts (pre-B, not T cells) convert methotrexate to its polyglutamates efficiently and are sensitive to treatment with this drug. Acquired resistance, which is noted in the minority of patients with this disease treated with combination chemotherapy, is associated with impaired uptake due to abnormalities in the reduced folate carrier transport protein, or to low-level amplification of the dihydrofolate reductase gene, whose product is the target for methotrexate.

PREDICTIVE TESTING IN VITRO.

Many approaches have been developed to assess the probability of relapse after primary therapy or response to a given type or class of endocrine or cytotoxic agents. The "S-phase" fraction of the tumor cell population undergoing DNA synthesis as well as DNA ploidy can be determined by flow cytometry. For several tumor types, patients with a high percentage of tumor cells in DNA synthesis and/or aneuploidy have a high likelihood of relapsing early after local primary cancer therapy. Taken with other prognostic characteristics, such flow cytometry assays may aid in identifying patients who should receive adjuvant chemotherapy. This approach is being applied to patients with stage I breast cancer to determine which patients are at higher risk for recurrence.

Diagnostic laboratories can provide the results of S-phase and DNA ploidy analysis as well as the findings from estrogen and progesterone receptor testing. Estrogen and progesterone receptor assays in breast cancer are used primarily to identify patients likely to respond to endocrine agents in either the adjuvant or recurrent disease setting. The sex steroid hormone receptors are located in the cell nucleus and must bind the hormone and translocate it to cellular DNA to exert endocrine action through gene activation or suppression. Additionally, in the absence of adjuvant therapy, tumors that are estrogen or progesterone receptor positive take longer to recur and have a better overall prognosis than tumors that are receptor negative. Another tumor cell constituent, the *HER-2/neu* oncogene, can be of prognostic value (Chapter 204). Amplification of the number of copies of the *HER-2/neu* gene or increased expression of the gene product by RNA or protein analysis appears to predict a poor prognosis in both breast and ovarian cancer. The protein product of HER-2/neu is expressed on the surface of tumor cells and is a member of the epidermal growth factor tyrosine kinase receptor family. An antibody to this receptor can cause tumor regression in patients whose breast cancers

overexpress this protein. Abnormalities in expression of *p53*, the tumor suppressor gene, have been associated with a worse prognosis when present in a wide variety of solid tumors. Studies indicate that the lack of wild type *p53* protects cells from chemotherapy-induced apoptosis. Lack of the retinoblastoma protein may also decrease the sensitivity of tumor cells to antimetabolites. Other in vitro assays, such as inhibition of thymidine uptake or inhibition of cell growth (clonogenic assays), appear to predict drug resistance but are somewhat less accurate for predicting which drugs will be useful for an individual patient.

PHARMACOKINETIC CONSIDERATIONS.

Although intrinsic drug sensitivity appears to be the most critical determinant of response to chemotherapy, pharmacokinetic factors related to the route of administration, bioavailability, metabolism, and elimination are probably of greater importance in cancer therapy. Many cytotoxic agents have a steep dose-response curve and a resulting narrow therapeutic index. Thus, at too low a concentration within the tumor, no response is seen. On the other hand, at higher doses, host toxicity supervenes and is usually dose limiting. Because of the steep dose-response relationship, doses of most cytotoxic agents are calculated in relation to body surface area, a more accurate approach than dose calculations based on body weight. Patients usually prefer the oral route of drug administration, but marked variations in bioavailability among oral formulations plus inconsistent patient compliance tend to limit such an approach. For example, with the alkylating agent melphalan, more than a ten-fold variation in plasma levels has been documented after standard dosing. Plasma assays are not routinely available for most anticancer drugs, and the only semiquantitative indicator of bioavailability of cytotoxic agents is the occurrence of myelosuppression after drug administration. For patients presenting with hypercalcemia or other complications of myeloma, oral melphalan therefore seems undesirable, because such patients need to achieve effective plasma levels immediately. Similar difficulties are faced with oral administration of fluorouracil, methotrexate, and 6-mercaptopurine. Bioavailability is adequate after oral administration of agents such as tamoxifen, cyclophosphamide, and the 5-fluorouracil prodrug, capecitabine.

The intravenous route of drug administration is preferable for most cytotoxic anticancer drugs, because it ensures adequate plasma levels while minimizing compliance problems. For some agents, continuous intravenous drug administration for 4 days or longer provides better results and less toxicity than do bolus or short-duration infusions because tumor response for many agents can be related to the "area under the plasma disappearance curve (AUC)" for the drug, whereas toxicity generally relates more directly to peak plasma concentrations than to the AUC. With the advent of vascular access devices such as subcutaneous ports, external catheters, and infusion pumps, outpatient continuous infusion chemotherapy can be used for stable drugs such as fluorinated pyrimidines, anthracyclines, and vinca alkaloids. Subcutaneous administration can be used effectively with drugs such as cytarabine, IFN-α, and erythropoietin. Subcutaneous dosing provides more sustained plasma levels than can be obtained with intravenous administration. Depot intramuscular formulations are available for a variety of endocrine agents used in treatment of breast or prostate cancer.

Regional administration of chemotherapy can be effective for several tumor sites. For metastatic colon cancer limited to the liver, hepatic artery catheterization for arterial infusion of 5-fluorodeoxyuridine or 5-fluorouracil can be used effectively by connection of the catheter to an external pump or to an implantable perfusion pump. In either instance, arterial infusions are often administered for 14 days, followed by a similar rest period. A relatively high objective response rate of metastatic colon cancer in the liver can be obtained by this means, but this route is ineffective for metastases outside the liver. Hepatic artery chemotherapy is expensive and associated with complications, including arterial thrombosis, biliary sclerosis, and chemical hepatitis. Nonetheless, it can induce sustained remissions for a year or more in selected patients. Regional infusion or isolated perfusion has been used with melanomas and sarcomas of the lower extremity. With melanoma metastases of the lower extremity, melphalan or cisplatin has been administered in this fashion with or without regional hyperthermia.

Intraperitoneal drug administration has been studied extensively in patients with peritoneal carcinomatosis, where it can induce remissions of established metastatic disease. In ovarian cancer, intraperitoneal chemotherapy is being studied as a follow-up to cytoreductive surgery. Diffusion of intraperitoneally administered drugs is limited

---

Table 191–4 • SOME MECHANISMS OF RESISTANCE TO CHEMOTHERAPY DRUGS

DRUG	MECHANISMS OF RESISTANCE
Methotrexate	Impaired transport or amplification of dihydrofolate reductase
Cytarabine	Decreased deoxycytidine kinase or increase in cytidine deaminase
5-Fluorouracil	Increase in thymidylate synthase
Cisplatin	Decreased uptake; increase in repair enzymes
Taxol, vinca alkaloids	MDR expression; mutations in tubulin (decreased binding)
Doxorubicin	MDR expression; decrease or alterations in topoisomerase II
Irinotecan, topotecan	Decrease in topoisomerase I

to a few millimeters of tumor tissue. Accordingly, intraperitoneal chemotherapy is seldom warranted in patients with bulky tumor masses. Preferred drugs for intraperitoneal administration are those that tend to be limited largely to the peritoneal cavity, have good properties for tumor penetration, and produce little or no local toxicity. Mitoxantrone, fluorodeoxyuridine, and cisplatin have these favorable characteristics and can be quite useful. With each of these drugs, the intraperitoneal concentration can be 1000-fold higher than measured in the systemic circulation. Other agents sometimes used in intraperitoneal administration include thiotepa, fluorouracil, and methotrexate. Intraperitoneal drug administration can be performed at repeated intervals with relative ease if a surgically implanted Tenckoff catheter is connected to a subcutaneous port. Mild to moderate chemical peritonitis and the development of peritoneal adhesions are common complications of intraperitoneal chemotherapy and limit repeated use. Intracavitary drug administration with instillation of a biologic agent such as bacille Calmette-Guérin (BCG) or IFN, or a variety of cytotoxic agents (e.g., thiotepa, doxorubicin, mitomycin, cisplatin) is used to treat superficial bladder cancer.

The intrathecal route can be used to deliver therapy to the meninges. Methotrexate, cytarabine, and thiotepa can be given by this route to prevent meningeal leukemia and treat central nervous system leukemia or lymphoma or meningeal carcinomatosis. Intrathecal methotrexate has been used effectively for acute lymphoblastic leukemia as an adjuvant to initial systemic chemotherapy and has reduced the frequency of central nervous system relapse in patients in complete peripheral remission.

EVALUATION OF RESPONSE. Objective measurement of tumor shrinkage with medical or radiation therapy has prognostic importance. Cure or significant prolongation of survival occurs in patients who achieve complete response (disappearance of all evidence of cancer). When possible, confirmation of response should be obtained pathologically through the use of restaging procedures. Many patients achieve only a partial response, defined as a reduction of tumor burden by 50% or greater. Modest improvements in survival accompany some partial responses.

Tumor markers in the blood or urine can be useful in monitoring response to therapy (Chapter 189). Patients with testicular germ cell tumors and gestational choriocarcinoma cannot be considered potentially cured unless the titer of marker substance goes below the limit of detection. Tumor marker studies are also useful in judging responses in ovarian cancer, prostatic carcinoma, colon cancer, multiple myeloma, neuroblastoma, and the carcinoid syndrome.

CYTOTOXIC ANTICANCER DRUGS

Drug doses are cited for single-agent chemotherapy; when drugs are used in combinations (Table 191–5), lower doses may be required

for some agents. Physicians should use effective and well-established combination protocols with known side-effect profiles rather than improvise combinations.

Alkylating Agents

The major clinically useful alkylating agents (Table 191–6) kill cells by binding to and cross linking DNA through a bis(chloroethyl)amine, ethyleneimine, or nitrosourea moiety. Although these agents likely kill cells by alkylating DNA (primarily at the N7 position of guanine), they also react chemically with nucleophilic molecules (e.g., sulfhydryl, amino, hydroxyl, and phosphate groups). The major acute side effects are gastrointestinal (nausea and vomiting) and hematologic (myelosuppression). Most alkylating agents cause local skin and subcutaneous tissue necrosis when infiltrated into the skin.

All alkylating agents can potentially induce ovarian or testicular failure as well as acute leukemia. Agents such as melphalan and chlorambucil appear to be more leukemogenic than cyclophosphamide, whereas busulfan and the nitrosoureas cause more persistent damage to hematopoietic stem cells and more prolonged myelosuppression. By 15 to 20 years after combination chemotherapy including alkylating agents for lymphoma, there is an increased risk of new solid tumors.

CYCLOPHOSPHAMIDE AND IFOSFAMIDE. Cyclophosphamide (Cytoxan) is the most widely used alkylating agent and is effective in the treatment of both hematologic malignancies and solid tumors. It does not have significant vesicant effects, because it is a prodrug that requires bioactivation in the liver. Metabolism of cyclophosphamide by cytochrome P-450 produces the active metabolite phosphoramide mustard plus acrolein. Cyclophosphamide is available in both intravenous and oral formulations and is well absorbed by the oral route. Cyclophosphamide produces a less severe pattern of myelosuppressive toxicity than other alkylating agents; it can cause severe neutropenia but usually of relatively short duration, and thrombocytopenia is less severe than with other alkylators. Other toxicities of cyclophosphamide include alopecia and immunosuppression. When high doses are used (e.g., for bone marrow transplantation), cyclophosphamide can also cause myocardial necrosis or the syndrome of inappropriate secretion of antidiuretic hormone. Although cyclophosphamide can cause acute nonlymphocytic leukemia and pulmonary fibrosis, these toxicities are more common with other alkylating agents. Both cyclophosphamide and a related analogue, ifosfamide (Ifex), can cause hemorrhagic cystitis. Bladder toxicity can be blocked by administration of the uroprotective agent mesna (Mesnex), which is concentrated in the urine and inactivates the toxic metabolite acrolein. Mesna is administered with ifosfamide, which otherwise may cause bladder toxicity. Ifosfamide causes somewhat less hematologic toxicity than other alkylating agents and at present is used mostly for second-line therapy (e.g., for therapy for testicular cancer, lymphoma, or metastatic sarcomas).

CHLORAMBUCIL. Chlorambucil (Leukeran) has antitumor activity similar to that of cyclophosphamide and is also well absorbed after oral administration. It is used primarily in the treatment of CLL, low-grade lymphomas, macroglobulinemia, and polycythemia vera. Chlorambucil does not cause hemorrhagic cystitis or alopecia, and

Table 191–5 • COMMON COMBINATION CHEMOTHERAPY REGIMENS

ABBREVIATION	DRUGS EMPLOYED	INDICATION
MOPP	Nitrogen mustard (Mustargen), vincristine (Oncovin), prednisone, procarbazine	Hodgkin's disease
ABVD	Doxorubicin (Adriamycin), bleomycin, vinblastine, dacarbazine	Hodgkin's disease
CHOP	Cyclophosphamide, hydroxydaunomycin (doxorubicin), vincristine (Oncovin), prednisone	Non-Hodgkin's lymphomas
CMF	Cyclophosphamide, methotrexate, 5-fluorouracil	Breast cancer
CAF	Cyclophosphamide, doxorubicin (Adriamycin), 5-fluorouracil	Breast cancer
M-VAC	Methotrexate, vinblastine, doxorubicin (Adriamycin), cisplatin	Bladder cancer
PVB	Cisplatin (platinum), vinblastine, bleomycin	Testicular cancer
VAD	Vincristine, doxorubicin (Adriamycin), dexamethasone	Multiple myeloma

Table 191–6 • ALKYLATING ANTICANCER DRUGS

DRUG	MAJOR INDICATIONS
Nitrogen mustard	Hodgkin's disease
Melphalan	Multiple myeloma
Chlorambucil	Chronic lymphocytic leukemia
Busulfan	Chronic myelocytic leukemia
Cyclophosphamide	Lymphoma, breast cancer, bladder cancer
Ifosfamide	Soft tissue sarcoma, lymphoma
Nitrosoureas (carmustine, lomustine)	Brain tumors, lymphoma
Procarbazine	Hodgkin's disease
Dacarbazine	Melanoma, Hodgkin's disease
Temozolomide	Glioblastoma
Cisplatin, carboplatin	Testicular, ovarian, head and neck, lung cancer

its gastrointestinal side effects are mild. However, it is myelosuppressive and potentially carcinogenic. Acute nonlymphocytic leukemia has been reported in patients treated with chlorambucil for polycythemia vera or other disorders and is related to the cumulative dose administered.

MELPHALAN. Melphalan (Alkeran) is L-phenylalanine mustard and gains access to cells through an amino acid transport system. Melphalan is commonly given orally in a dosage of 10 mg/m²/day for 4 days every 3 to 4 weeks. Some patients do not absorb the drug; generally, the only clue, other than drug levels, is the absence of myelosuppression. If myelosuppression does not occur, melphalan dosage should be increased in subsequent courses until moderate myelosuppression is induced. Melphalan is commonly used in the treatment of multiple myeloma and ovarian cancer and occasionally for other tumor types. The drug induces acute nonlymphocytic leukemia in some patients treated for myeloma or ovarian cancer.

BUSULFAN. Busulfan (Myleran) is a methane sulfonate–based alkylating agent that has specificity for myeloid neoplasms and appears to have less antitumor activity in other forms of cancer. It is used primarily for treatment of chronic myeloid leukemia or as part of marrow ablative regimens followed by stem cell transplantation. Busulfan can produce protracted myelosuppression, and hematologic recovery should be complete before the next course is administered. Busulfan can also cause pulmonary fibrosis, hyperpigmentation, weakness, and wasting. Adrenal function remains normal.

NITROSOUREAS. Carmustine (BCNU) and lomustine (CCNU) are rapidly biotransformed through nonenzymatic hydrolysis to release intermediates with alkylating and carbamoylating activities. Carmustine is available for intravenous use, and lomustine is given orally. The major toxicity of nitrosoureas at standard dosage levels is on hematopoietic stem cells; delayed, prolonged myelosuppression can result. At high doses (e.g., in preparative regimens for bone marrow transplantation), nitrosoureas can induce a chemical hepatitis or pneumonitis. Prolonged use with total doses greater than 1500 mg/m² can also result in pulmonary fibrosis or renal failure. Because of their high lipid solubility and ability to cross the blood-brain barrier, the nitrosoureas have some activity against primary brain tumors. The nitrosoureas also are useful in the management of Hodgkin's disease and multiple myeloma.

PLATINUM COMPOUNDS. Cisplatin and carboplatin are platinum-coordination compounds with broad-spectrum antitumor activity and produce synergistic interactions with a variety of other cytotoxic agents, including alkylating agents, antimetabolites, natural products, and the antibody trastuzumab. They act similarly to alkylating agents in terms of their ability to bind to the N7 position of guanine and cross link DNA. However, cross linking with adenine and cytosine also occurs, as does binding to RNA and protein.

Both drugs are administered intravenously. Cisplatin is commonly given in a dose of 100 mg/m² every 3 weeks, whereas the dose of carboplatin is in the range of 450 mg/m² at similar intervals, although larger doses may be tolerated. After intravenous infusion, the major acute toxicity for both cisplatin and carboplatin is nausea and vomiting, which is worse with cisplatin. Satisfactory suppression of the gastrointestinal side effects of platinum compounds requires potent antiemetic agents, often in combination. Large cumulative doses of cisplatin also cause renal toxicity, which can be largely prevented if the patient is well hydrated with simultaneous saline infusions and diuretics. Large cumulative doses can also cause a progressive neuropathy. Myelosuppression is minimal with cisplatin but is dose limiting with carboplatin. Although carboplatin is less toxic than cisplatin, its efficacy is equivalent for some tumors. The lack of myelosuppression favors cisplatin for use in some drug combinations with myelosuppressive agents. A new platinum analogue, oxalaplatin, has activity against colon cancer comparable with that of fluorouracil.

Antimetabolites

The antimetabolites (Table 191–7) are structural analogues of naturally occurring compounds, most of which are involved in DNA or RNA synthesis and generally function as CCS agents.

PYRIMIDINE ANTAGONISTS

Cytarabine (Cytosine Arabinoside, Cytosar-U, Ara-C). Cytarabine is an S-phase–specific agent that is particularly useful in the treatment of acute nonlymphocytic leukemia and, to a lesser extent, in other hematologic malignancies. Its active form, ara-CTP, competitively inhibits DNA polymerase, blocking DNA synthesis. Ara-C also blocks chain

Table 191–7 • ANTIMETABOLITE ANTICANCER DURGS

DRUG	MAJOR INDICATIONS
Folic acid antagonists (methotrexate)	Acute lymphocytic leukemia, choriocarcinoma, breast cancer, bladder cancer, head and neck cancer, lymphoma
5-Fluorouracil	Gastrointestinal cancer, breast cancer, head and neck cancer
5-Fluorodeoxyuridine	Regional therapy (intra-arterial or intraperitoneal) for colon cancer metastasis
Cytarabine	Acute leukemia
Gemcitabine	Cancer of the pancreas
6-Mercaptopurine, 6-thioguanine	Acute leukemia
Fludarabine	Chronic lymphocytic leukemia, low-grade lymphoma
2-Chlorodeoxyadenosine	Hairy cell leukemia, low-grade lymphoma
Deoxycoformycin	Hairy cell leukemia, T-cell lymphoma
Hydroxyurea	Chronic myelocytic leukemia

elongation and ligation of fragments into newly synthesized DNA. Ara-C, which crosses the blood-brain barrier, is given either by continuous infusion or in bolus doses by the intravenous or subcutaneous route for 5 to 7 days. In an alternative schedule that exceeds the manufacturer's recommended maximum, high-dose ara-C is administered in doses of 1 to 3 g every 12 hours for 3 to 5 days and yields higher response rates. Both standard and high-dose ara-C can produce severe myelosuppression. With the high-dose regimen, chemical conjunctivitis is common and can be ameliorated with corticosteroid ophthalmic drops. With rare exception, complete remissions can be achieved in acute leukemia only if ara-C is administered with sufficient intensity to drive the bone marrow to severe hypocellularity and destroy the leukemic blast population. Thereafter, the marrow is repopulated by residual normal progenitors that were suppressed by the leukemia. Ara-C is generally used in combination with daunorubicin in the treatment of acute nonlymphocytic leukemia but also acts synergistically with other drugs, including cisplatin. Cytarabine can also be given intrathecally in doses of 75 to 100 mg as treatment for leukemic or carcinomatous meningitis.

Gemcitabine. Gemcitabine (Gemzar) is a novel nucleoside analogue that is approved for use in patients with advanced pancreatic carcinoma. Gemcitabine significantly improves disease-related symptoms in approximately 25% of patients, and a modest increase in survival was demonstrated in patients with pancreatic carcinoma when compared with treatment with 5-fluorouracil. The drug is well tolerated; reversible myelosuppression, with thrombocytopenia and anemia quantitatively more important than granulocytopenia, is the dose-limiting toxicity. The drug is administered intravenously over 30 minutes, weekly for 3 weeks, followed by 1 week of rest. Recent studies show substantial antitumor activity in combination with other drugs for the treatment of non–small cell lung cancer, bladder cancer, and Hodgkin's disease.

Fluorouracil, Floxuridine, and Capecitabine. Fluorouracil (5-FU) is used to treat a variety of solid tumors, including cancers of the head and neck, esophagus, breast, and colon. It acts synergistically with a variety of agents, including platinum compounds and radiation therapy. "Pulse" or bolus injections of 5-FU are cytotoxic mainly as a result of incorporation into RNA, whereas continuous infusions of this drug (2 or more days) kill cells by inhibiting DNA synthesis and producing "thymine-less death." 5-FU is usually given intravenously by bolus or infusion schedules but can also be used in intra-arterial, intracavitary, and topical therapy. An optimal schedule for 5-FU administration is a 5-day continuous infusion at a dose rate of 1.0 g/m²/day. This schedule causes some gastrointestinal toxicity but only a mild degree of myelosuppression. Full doses of cisplatin can be administered additionally, providing an active treatment program in the neoadjuvant chemotherapy of head and neck and esophageal cancer. Less common toxicities observed with 5-FU include a neurologic syndrome associated with ataxia, chemical conjunctivitis, and a syndrome including chest pain and cardiac enzyme elevation consistent with myocardial ischemia. The bioavailability of 5-FU after oral administration is erratic, and the drug is metabolized mostly during its first pass through the liver.

Both the gastrointestinal toxicity and the antitumor activity of 5-FU can be enhanced by administration of leucovorin, which increases the binding of fluorodeoxyuridine phosphate to thymidylate synthase. This combination appears to increase the antitumor activity of 5-FU in breast and colon cancer. IFN-α and levamisole also appear to enhance 5-FU activity in adjuvant colorectal cancer, and 6 months of treatment with 5-FU and leucovorin in the adjuvant setting is now the regimen of choice for patients with colorectal cancer. Both 5-FU and floxuridine (5-FUDR) can be given by hepatic artery infusion to treat patients with colorectal carcinoma with metastases confined to the liver. With the use of a surgically placed vascular access catheter, outpatient hepatic artery infusions can be administered using either an internal or a portable external pump. A limitation is that either 5-FU or 5-FUDR can induce a chemical hepatitis and biliary sclerosis with jaundice. Hepatic dysfunction can be most readily detected by obtaining liver chemistry readings on day 14 when 5-FUDR is to be discontinued. Studies indicate that the response rate and duration of remission are increased by the addition of leucovorin (folinic acid) or dexamethasone to 5-FUDR.

Capecitabine (Xeloda), a fluorouracil prodrug, has been approved by the Food and Drug Administration (FDA) for the treatment of breast cancer and colorectal cancer. This drug is administered orally, twice daily; when given over 14 days or longer, it generates a constant blood level of 5-FU, thus simulating continuous infusions of 5-FU. Activation to 5-FU is via the enzyme thymidine phosphorylase.

PURINE ANTAGONISTS

6-Mercaptopurine and 6-Thioguanine. In contrast to 6-mercaptopurine (6-MP), some 6-thioguanine (6-TG) metabolites are incorporated into both DNA and RNA. 6-TG has some uses in acute nonlymphocytic leukemia in combination with cytarabine, whereas 6-MP is used primarily in acute lymphoblastic leukemia, particularly in childhood. Absorption of 6-MP is variable, but plasma monitoring can identify poor absorbers who have a high likelihood of developing recurrent leukemia, presumably because of inadequate bioavailability of 6-MP. The 6-MP analogue azathioprine is a useful immunosuppressive agent. Because both 6-MP and azathioprine are catabolized by xanthine oxidase, patients must have their thiopurine doses reduced to 25% of their standard doses if they are also receiving the xanthine oxidase inhibitor allopurinol. 6-TG is not catabolized by xanthine oxidase, and dose correction is not required for allopurinol.

Fludarabine. Fludarabine (Fludara, 5-fluoroadenosine monophosphate) is an analogue of adenine that inhibits DNA polymerase and ribonucleotide reductase. Fludarabine is the single most active agent available in the treatment of CLL and also exhibits some antitumor activity in other indolent lymphomas and macroglobulinemia. Fludarabine is often given intravenously in a dose of 25 mg/m²/day over 30 minutes for 5 days every 4 weeks. The major toxicity is myelosuppression. Higher doses administered in early trials in patients with acute nonlymphocytic leukemia occasionally produced cortical blindness. In the lower-dosage schedule used in CLL and other lymphoid neoplasms, side effects are usually mild and reversible. Fludarabine is also used in combination with cyclophosphamide or mitoxantrone to treat low-grade lymphomas.

Other Purine Antagonists. Additional purine antagonists include deoxycoformycin (DCF) and 2-chlorodeoxyadenosine (2-CDA). Both DCF and 2-CDA are extremely active agents in the treatment of hairy cell leukemia and can produce prolonged remissions after a single course of treatment. Both agents also exhibit some antitumor activity in other low-grade lymphoid neoplasms.

FOLIC ACID ANTAGONISTS.
Methotrexate (MTX) is a structural analogue of folic acid and is currently the only FDA-approved member of this group. MTX can be administered orally, intramuscularly, intravenously, or intrathecally and is useful primarily as a component of chemotherapy combinations for various types of cancer, including acute lymphoblastic leukemia, small cell lung cancer, bladder cancer, head and neck cancer, and breast cancer. When used in high dosage with leucovorin rescue, it exerts antitumor activity in osteogenic sarcoma. Intracellular formation of polyglutamated forms of MTX is important to the action of MTX, because the polyglutamated forms have equivalent ability to inhibit dihydrofolate reductase action but have a longer intracellular retention time than MTX. The polyglutamates also inhibit other folate-dependent enzymes, including thymidylate synthase. Given satisfactory renal function and adequate hydration, MTX is excreted unchanged mainly in the urine within 12 hours of administration.

Major toxicities of MTX are to rapidly dividing tissues, including the bone marrow, gastrointestinal mucosa, and, to a lesser extent, skin. At high dosages or in patients with impaired renal function, MTX also can induce renal toxicity. Chronic extended use of MTX (e.g., for maintenance treatment of patients with ALL or long-term treatment of patients with psoriasis) occasionally leads to liver fibrosis and cirrhosis. The toxic effects on the rapidly dividing tissues can be circumvented by administering the reduced folate leucovorin (folinic acid) within 36 hours after MTX administration. When high-dose (e.g., ≥1500 mg/m²) MTX is administered, leucovorin must be administered 24 to 36 hours after MTX in dosages of 15 to 50 mg/m² every 6 hours for 48 hours, with the duration of rescue contingent on the serum MTX level. Increased leucovorin dosage and longer periods of rescue are needed in patients with impaired renal function. The high-dose MTX/leucovorin rescue regimen therefore requires good renal function and careful monitoring of the plasma concentration and renal function.

NATURAL PRODUCT ANTICANCER DRUGS

The two main classes of natural antitumor products are plant alkaloids and antibiotics (Table 191–8). Resistance to the natural products, with the exception of bleomycin, can be mediated by the P-glycoprotein multidrug resistance mechanism.

Plant Alkaloids

VINCRISTINE AND VINBLASTINE. The vinca alkaloids, which were isolated from the common periwinkle (*Vinca rosacea*), precipitate tubulin and disrupt cellular microtubules. Whereas the primary toxicity of vinblastine (Velban) is hematopoietic, the major toxicity of vincristine (Oncovin) affects peripheral nerves, resulting in sensorimotor and autonomic neuropathies. Common symptoms are paresthesias ("pins and needles sensation") in the digits and progressive muscular weakness with areflexia, particularly in the lower extremities. Footdrop can develop, as can occasional cranial, bladder, or bowel neuropathies. The neurotoxicity subsides slowly after the drug is discontinued, with improvement requiring months, especially if motor function is impaired. The lack of bone marrow toxicity of vincristine has made

Table 191–8 • NATURAL PRODUCT ANTICANCER DRUGS

DRUGS	MAJOR INDICATIONS
PLANT ALKALOIDS	
Vincristine	Lymphoid malignancies
Vinblastine	Hodgkin's disease, testicular cancer
Vinorelbine	Small cell lung cancer
PODOPHYLLOTOXINS	
Etoposide (VP-16)	Small cell lung cancer, lymphoma
Teniposide (VM-26)	Acute lymphocytic leukemia
TUBLIN INHIBITORS	
Paclitaxel (Taxol)	Ovarian cancer, breast cancer
Docetaxel (Taxotere)	Lung cancer
TOPOISOMERASE I INHIBITORS	
CPT-11	Colon cancer
Irinotecan	Ovarian cancer
ANTIBIOTICS	
Anthracyclines	
Doxorubicin	Lymphoma, breast cancer, sarcomas
Daunorubicin	Acute leukemia
Idarubicin	Acute leukemia
Mitoxantrone (synthetic)	Acute leukemia, lymphoma
Mitomycin	Gastrointestinal malignancies
Dactinomycin	Choriocarcinoma, Wilms' tumor, Ewing's sarcoma, rhabdomyosarcoma
Bleomycin	Lymphoma, head and neck cancer
MISCELLANEOUS AGENTS	
Hexamethylmelamine	Ovarian cancer
Asparaginase	Acute lymphocytic leukemia
all-TRANS retinoic acid	Acute promyelocytic leukemia
Arsenic trioxide	Acute promyelocytic leukemia
Gleevec	Chronic myelocytic leukemia

it useful for combination chemotherapy regimens. The vinca alkaloids have vesicant effects and can be administered only intravenously. Both provide antitumor activity in leukemias and lymphomas as well as in selected solid tumors, including small cell lung cancer and breast cancer. Vincristine is used in various drug combinations, including MOPP, CHOP, MACOP-B, and M-BACOD for the treatment of lymphomas (Chapter 195), and VMCP and VAD in the treatment of multiple myeloma (Chapter 196). The greatest use of vinblastine has been in its incorporation into the PVB regimen for the treatment of non-seminomatous testicular cancers (Chapter 247), and in the ABVD regimen to treat Hodgkin's disease (Chapter 194). Vinblastine is also used in combination with cisplatin in non–small cell lung cancer and with mitomycin in metastatic breast cancer.

VINORELBINE. Vinorelbine (Navelbine) is a semisynthetic vinca alkaloid approved for use in the treatment of non–small cell lung cancer and breast cancer. Its spectrum of antitumor activity and its mechanism of action are similar to those of vinblastine and vincristine. In humans, its limiting toxicity, like that of vinblastine, is hematologic.

Podophyllotoxins

ETOPOSIDE. Etoposide (VP-16, VePesid), a semisynthetic glucoside, is produced from extracts of the root of the mayapple or mandrake (*Podophyllum peltatum*). A closely related analogue, teniposide (VM-26), has not been approved in the United States by the FDA. Mechanistically, podophyllotoxins are thought to act as inhibitors of nuclear topoisomerase II, leading to DNA strand breaks. Additional effects include inhibition of nucleoside transport and mitochondrial electron transport. Etoposide is highly lipid soluble and water insoluble and requires a special formulation for intravenous administration. An oral formulation is also available. Good tissue distribution is achieved in all sites other than the brain. A commonly used schedule administers etoposide intravenously for 3 days at a dosage of 150 to 200 mg/m²/day. Etoposide is excreted primarily in the urine and to a lesser extent in the bile. Its dosage should be reduced by half in patients with impaired renal function. The main side effect is myelosuppression, although gastrointestinal toxicity and alopecia also can occur. Etoposide is used primarily to treat metastatic testicular cancer in combination with cisplatin and bleomycin. Etoposide also exerts potent effects against small cell lung cancer, lymphomas, and monocytic leukemia.

PACLITAXEL. The taxanes appear to stabilize tubulin as their major mechanism of action. Paclitaxel (Taxol) has been approved for use in the United States for the treatment of breast cancer and ovarian cancer and is also widely used for other epithelial tumors (head and neck, esophagus, non–small cell lung cancer, and bladder cancer) in combination therapy regimens. For example, the combination of cisplatin and paclitaxel is now first-line treatment with a 10 to 20% cure rate for patients with ovarian cancer, where it improves survival compared with cisplatin and cyclophosphamide. The drug may cause hypersensitivity reactions (e.g., hypotension, dyspnea, bronchospasm, and urticaria). Typically, premedications are administered before paclitaxel administration to prevent these reactions: dexamethasone, 20 mg orally or intravenously, 12 and 6 hours before treatment; diphenhydramine, 50 mg, 30 minutes before treatment; and an H₂ antagonist (e.g., cimetidine), 300 mg, intravenously, 30 minutes before treatment. Other toxicities include neutropenia, which is dose limiting, myalgias, and peripheral neuropathy, the latter of which generally occurs only after multiple courses at conventional doses (135 to 250 mg/m² over 24 hours). The antitumor effects of paclitaxel against metastatic breast cancer are increased when combined with the antibody trastuzumab (Herceptin).

DOCETAXEL. Docetaxel (Taxotere), which is a semisynthetic analogue of paclitaxel, has been approved for use in the treatment of locally advanced or metastatic breast cancer that has progressed during anthracycline-based therapy. This drug also has anticancer activity in patients with non–small cell lung cancer. The recommended dose is 60 to 100 mg/m² intravenously every 3 weeks. Toxicities are similar to paclitaxel but may also include a capillary leak syndrome when given in high doses.

Antitumor Antibiotics

DOXORUBICIN, DAUNORUBICIN, EPIRUBICIN AND IDARUBICIN. These anthracycline antibiotics were isolated from a variant of *Streptomyces peucetius*.

Daunorubicin (daunomycin) is active in the treatment of acute leukemia. Its congener, doxorubicin (Adriamycin), has a broader spectrum of antitumor activity, including both hematologic malignancies and a variety of solid tumors such as carcinoma of the breast and thyroid, lymphoma, and myeloma, as well as osteogenic and soft tissue sarcomas. Daunorubicin is frequently used in combination with cytarabine in the treatment of acute myelocytic leukemia (AML), whereas doxorubicin is incorporated into regimens for solid tumors along with cyclophosphamide, fluorouracil, etoposide, vincristine, or cisplatin. Mechanistically, the anthracyclines intercalate with high affinity into DNA and inhibit the action of topoisomerase II, resulting in DNA strand breaks. Anthracycline cardiac toxicity may also be related in part to the generation of free radicals. Both doxorubicin and daunorubicin must be administered intravenously by either bolus injection or prolonged infusion. Extravasation can lead to severe tissue injury. Immediate topical application of 1.5 mL of 99% dimethylsulfoxide (DMSO) has been reported to prevent subsequent ulceration. For prolonged anthracycline infusions, use of a vascular access catheter is advisable. Ulceration and necrosis after anthracycline extravasation usually require surgical débridement of the damaged tissues plus skin grafting.

The most common acute toxicities of the anthracyclines include alopecia, nausea, vomiting, mucositis, and myelosuppression. A dose-dependent, delayed, and potentially irreversible cardiomyopathy with reduced cardiac contractility can develop in patients who receive large cumulative doses of doxorubicin or daunorubicin (Chapter 73). Acute cardiac arrhythmias are uncommon.

Periodic monitoring for cardiac effects of anthracyclines is normally initiated when a patient has received a total doxorubicin dose of 350 to 400 mg/m²; doxorubicin should be discontinued if the left ventricular ejection fraction decreases by 15 percentage points and to below 50%. Endomyocardial biopsy can also be used. Cardiac toxicity is uncommon with cumulative bolus doses of doxorubicin of less than 550 mg/m², above which the incidence increases progressively. Elderly patients and others with risk factors for cardiac disease (e.g., hypertension) are at somewhat higher risk for anthracycline cardiomyopathy. Anthracyclines are not recommended for patients who have major preexisting heart disease. When doxorubicin is administered by continuous infusion (e.g., for 4 to 5 days), there is less cardiotoxicity, and a significantly larger cumulative dose in the range of 1000 mg/m² usually can be administered. In controlled studies, idarubicin in combination with cytarabine induced higher remission rates in AML than daunorubicin and cytarabine. Epirubicin, recently approved in the United States for the adjuvant treatment of breast cancer in combination with other agents, is less cardiotoxic than doxorubicin.

An agent that protects the heart from anthracycline toxicity, dexrazoxane, has been approved for use by the FDA for patients who are treated with cumulative doses of doxorubicin greater than 300 mg/m². Toxicities associated with dexrazoxane are pain at the injection site and modest neutropenia and thrombocytopenia. The possibility that dexrazoxane may have an adverse effect on tumor response led to the FDA recommendation that treatment with this drug should be initiated only when the cumulative dose of 300 mg/m² of doxorubicin was reached.

Several preparations that encapsulate doxorubicin or daunomycin into liposomes have been introduced, with the goal of lessening toxicity, especially cardiac toxicity, by providing slow release forms of the drug. These preparations may also distribute to tissues differently than the parent drug, and they have different therapeutic profiles. Doxil, a doxorubicin HCL liposome, is approved for the treatment of ovarian cancer refractory to both paclitaxel and platinum-based chemotherapy regimens. Liposomal daunomycin (Daunosome) is also approved for the treatment of Kaposi's sarcoma.

BLEOMYCIN. Bleomycin (Blenoxane) comprises 11 closely related glycopeptide moieties produced by *Streptomyces verticillus*. Bleomycin binds to DNA and generates superoxide and other reactive oxygen species, including hydroxyl radicals. DNA fragmentation appears to result from the oxidation of a DNA-bleomycin-Fe²⁺ complex. The antitumor activity of bleomycin is schedule dependent, acting primarily at the G₂ phase of the cell cycle. It can be administered by subcutaneous, intramuscular, and intravenous routes. Its major uses are in combination therapy to treat carcinoma of the testis and squamous cell carcinomas of the head and neck, cervix, skin, penis, and rectum. It is also used in combination regimens for treatment of lymphomas (ABVD).

Bleomycin has minimal myelosuppressive effects and is useful in combination with drugs that cause leukopenia. Acute toxicities include anaphylactoid reactions and fever associated with hypotension and dehydration. Patients who have not received bleomycin previously should receive a test dose (e.g., 1 to 2 mg) to discover such adverse reactions. Individual therapeutic doses of bleomycin are usually in the range of 5 to 10 units/m^2.

The most serious chronic reaction to bleomycin is pulmonary fibrosis related to the cumulative dose of drug and manifested by cough, dyspnea, and bilateral basilar infiltrates on chest radiography. It is possible to screen for earlier pulmonary abnormalities such as a decline in the diffusion capacity, which is usually detectable at total doses of bleomycin greater than 250 units. If the pulmonary diffusion capacity decreases abnormally, bleomycin should be discontinued. The incidence of pulmonary fibrosis increases at total doses greater than 450 units and is greater in patients with preexisting pulmonary disease, after lung irradiation, and in the elderly. This toxicity may be irreversible, although corticosteroids may be of some use. Other reactions to bleomycin include skin toxicity with blistering, desquamation, hyperkeratosis of the palms, and hyperpigmentation of creases.

MITOMYCIN. Mitomycin (Mutamycin, Mitocin-C, Mitomycin C) is isolated from *Streptomyces caespitosus*. Mitomycin functions as a CCNS alkylating agent after it has been activated in various tissues by the cytochrome P-450 system. Thereafter, it can alkylate DNA to form intrastrand and interstrand cross links resulting in cell death. Mitomycin has "bioreductive" properties, with increased cytotoxic effects on poorly oxygenated tumor cells in solid tumors. It has been used in combination with irradiation to treat patients with cancer of the head and neck. The clinical spectrum of antitumor activity of mitomycin includes breast, lung, gastrointestinal, genitourinary, and gynecologic cancers. Mitomycin has been incorporated into a variety of cytotoxic drug combinations for systemic administration, often as second-line therapy for patients who relapse from initial chemotherapy. It is usually administered intravenously but can be used for intravesical therapy of superficial bladder cancer. Its normal intravenous dosage range is 10 to 15 mg/m^2.

The major toxicity of mitomycin is delayed myelosuppression, usually appearing 4 to 6 weeks after injection. Mitomycin has a cumulative effect on bone marrow stem cells, which can lead to protracted marrow hypoplasia for 3 to 6 months after discontinuing the drug. Nausea, vomiting, and anorexia often occur at the time of administration but can usually be managed effectively with antiemetic agents. Occasionally, mitomycin can induce interstitial pneumonitis, nephrotoxicity, or hemolytic-uremic syndrome.

DACTINOMYCIN. Dactinomycin (Actinomycin D, Cosmegen) binds to the DNA helix by intercalation between adjacent guanine-cytosine base pairs; it inhibits DNA-dependent RNA synthesis and leads to cessation of most protein synthesis in sensitive cells. The drug is administered intravenously, and its major toxicity is myelosuppression, usually appearing 7 to 10 days after injection. Dactinomycin also causes significant gastrointestinal toxicity with abdominal cramps and diarrhea as well as mucositis. The drug also can cause a radiation "recall" reaction in which cutaneous erythema redevelops at a site of prior irradiation. The principal use of dactinomycin is in pediatric oncology in combination chemotherapy for the treatment of Wilms' tumor, Ewing's sarcoma, and embryonal rhabdomyosarcoma. It has some utility in adults in third-line therapy of germ cell tumors of the testis or ovary, gestational choriocarcinoma, and soft tissue sarcomas.

Topoisomerase I Inhibitors

This class of drugs binds to topoisomerase I. Two inhibitors of this enzyme have now been approved for clinical use: irinotecan and topotecan.

IRINOTECAN. Irinotecan (CPT-11, Camptosar) is a prodrug that is rapidly hydrolyzed in vivo to SN-38, a potent inhibitor of topoisomerase I. It has been approved for use in the treatment of patients with colorectal cancer. The dose schedule used most commonly is a single infusion (200 mg/m^2) every 3 weeks, although other dose schedules are being explored. The principal dose-limiting toxicities are nonhematologic, in particular diarrhea. Diarrhea may be seen within the first 24 hours of treatment, or later, occurring 4 to 8 days after treatment. Aggressive treatment with loperamide or octreotide at the first sign of diarrhea has allowed patients to tolerate this drug. Severe neutropenia may also occur. Recent studies in which irinotecan was combined with 5-FU/leucovorin demonstrate activity in colorectal cancer

greater than irinotecan or 5-FU alone. However, this combination produces both severe diarrhea and neutropenia that may be difficult to manage.

TOPOTECAN. Topotecan (Hycamtin) is approved for use in previously treated patients with ovarian cancer. Its mechanism of action is similar to that of irinotecan, namely, inhibition of topoisomerase I. Topotecan also has activity in other tumors, including hematologic malignancies, small cell lung cancer, neuroblastoma, and rhabdomyosarcoma. The recommended dose is 1.5 mg/m^2/day infused intravenously over 30 minutes for 5 consecutive days, every 3 weeks. The dose-limiting and most common toxicity is myelosuppression, especially neutropenia.

MISCELLANEOUS ANTICANCER AGENTS

PROCARBAZINE. Procarbazine (Matulane) is an orally administered methylhydrazine derivative that has antitumor activity in Hodgkin's disease (as part of MOPP combination chemotherapy) and in non-Hodgkin's lymphomas, lung cancer, and brain tumors. Procarbazine is usually given in a dose of 100 mg/m^2/day for 10 to 14 days in each chemotherapy cycle. Procarbazine is activated metabolically to produce a methyldiazonium ion that binds to nucleic acids, proteins, and phospholipids to inhibit macromolecular synthesis. Its mechanism of cytotoxicity is thought to involve DNA strand scission, possibly through generation of H$_2$O$_2$. Principal toxicities of procarbazine are nausea, vomiting, and myelosuppression. One of the metabolites of procarbazine is a monoamine oxidase (MAO) inhibitor that can cause toxicity when the patient is taking other MAO inhibitors. Patients taking procarbazine may develop hypertension if they ingest tyramine-rich foods such as ripe cheese, wine, and bananas. Disulfiram-like reactions are also seen, with sweating and headache after alcohol ingestion. Other infrequent reactions include hemolytic anemia and pulmonary reactions. Procarbazine is also known to be leukemogenic, carcinogenic, and mutagenic and is considered to play a significant role in the development of late leukemias and other second malignancies in patients with Hodgkin's disease. Procarbazine also produces azoospermia and anovulation. Because alternative combinations lacking procarbazine can be used in the treatment of Hodgkin's disease (e.g., ABVD), the benefits versus risks of using this agent must be carefully considered.

DACARBAZINE. Dacarbazine (DTIC, dimethylimidazole carboxamide) is activated by oxidative N-demethylation. A methyl carbonium ion metabolite is thought to be the cytotoxic intermediate with alkylating activity. Dacarbazine is administered intravenously either in a single-day infusion schedule of 750 mg/m^2 or in fractionated bolus doses over 5 days or more. DTIC causes severe nausea and vomiting, and potent antiemetic agents are required. Myelosuppression is relatively mild. Dacarbazine is used in combination chemotherapy for Hodgkin's disease (ABVD), for soft tissue sarcomas in combination with doxorubicin and other agents, and in single-agent chemotherapy for metastatic melanoma.

TEMOZOLOMIDE (TEMODAR). This orally active imidazotetrazine derivative is indicated for the treatment of adult patients with anaplastic astrocytoma (glioblastoma). Temozolomide undergoes rapid nonenzymatic conversion at a physiologic pH to the reactive compound 5-3-methyltriazin-1-yl)imidazole-4-carboximide (MTIC), similar to the metabolism of DTIC. Toxicities are similar to those for DTIC. Both of these agents are potent carcinogens.

HEXAMETHYLMELAMINE (HMM). This agent is available only in an oral formulation because of its sparing solubility. Nausea and vomiting increase with daily use, limiting treatment courses (at doses of up to 12 mg/kg/day) to 2 to 3 weeks. Mild myelosuppression occurs. Additionally, HMM can induce both central and peripheral neurotoxicities, including altered mood, hallucinations, and peripheral neuropathy. HMM is thought to act as an alkylating agent, possibly through the enzymatic hydroxylation of its dimethyl metabolites to cytotoxic methylol compounds. HMM exhibits antitumor activity in alkylating agent–resistant ovarian cancer and, to a lesser extent, in several other neoplasms (lung cancer, breast cancer, lymphomas).

HYDROXYUREA. Hydroxyurea (Hydrea, HU) acts as an inhibitor of ribonucleotide reductase, resulting in intracellular depletion of deoxynucleoside triphosphates and inhibition of DNA synthesis. It is available for clinical use in oral formulation. The major toxicity of HU is to the bone marrow, and it causes transient dose-related myelosuppression. A megaloblastic anemia, which is nonresponsive to vitamin B$_{12}$ or folic acid, can develop at a high dose. Gastrointestinal side effects of nausea and vomiting are also common with high-dose therapy. HU is used primarily to treat CML and polycythemia vera, but it also has some use in head and neck cancer and metastatic melanoma and as a radiosensitizer.

MITOXANTRONE. Mitoxantrone (Novantrone) is a synthetic anthracenedione with a structure similar to that of the anthracyclines. It has been approved by the FDA as a second-line agent for treatment of acute leukemia in relapse but is also useful in the treatment of breast cancer and lymphoma. Mitoxantrone binds to DNA and causes strand breaks and inhibits DNA and RNA synthesis. In terms of cellular response by tumor cells, there is not complete cross reactivity between mitoxantrone and the anthracyclines. Mitoxantrone dosage for acute leukemia is higher than for solid tumors. Comparative studies in patients with advanced breast cancer suggest that it is less active and less toxic than doxorubicin. Its major acute toxicity is myelosuppression. Gastrointestinal side effects, including nausea, vomiting, and mucositis as well as alopecia, are less severe than with the anthracyclines. Mitoxantrone can cause some cardiac toxicities, usually manifest by development of arrhythmia at the time of injection, and can exacerbate preexisting anthracycline-induced cardiomyopathy. It can be used intraperitoneally in patients with ovarian cancer, because most of the drug remains in the peritoneal cavity. This approach reduces systemic toxicity, but it can induce chemical peritonitis and adhesions.

ASPARAGINASE. L-Asparaginase (Crasnitin, Elspar) is a bacterial enzyme isolated from *Escherichia coli* or *Erwinia carotovora*. Its major use is to treat lymphoblastic leukemias and some lymphomas with a deficiency in asparagine synthetase and cellular dependence on exogenous asparagine. L-Asparagine is a nonessential amino acid, and most normal cells can synthesize their required asparagine. Therapeutically, L-asparaginase depletes the plasma of asparagine by converting it to aspartic acid and ammonia. Most patients develop fever and chills as well as nausea and vomiting after administration, but these symptoms can usually be reduced or prevented by premedication with antiemetics and anti-inflammatory agents. Asparaginase toxicity can produce abnormal liver function tests (aspartate aminotransferase, alkaline phosphatase, and bilirubin) as well as hypoalbuminemia and reductions in plasma levels of clotting factors and insulin. Other occasional toxicities include pancreatitis and central nervous system abnormalities, which can lead to confusion or coma. Repeated use of asparaginase leads to the development of antibodies that can inhibit its activity and accelerate its clearance as well as induce hypersensitivity reactions. Patients developing hypersensitivity after asparaginase administration may exhibit hypotension, laryngeal edema, bronchospasm, and urticaria. Switching to an asparaginase derived from a different bacterial species can bypass neutralizing antibodies in hypersensitive patients. The lack of myelosuppressive or gastrointestinal toxicity has facilitated incorporation of L-asparaginase into drug combinations for the treatment of ALL. A useful combination in ALL is methotrexate, followed 24 hours later by L-asparaginase.

Management of Toxicity

Most cytotoxic drugs are also toxic for host cells, and treatment schedules must take this into account.

DOSE ADJUSTMENTS FOR BONE MARROW TOXICITY. Doses of myelosuppressive agents often must be adjusted downward to avoid serious or life-threatening side effects such as granulocytopenic fever and thrombocytopenic bleeding. For most drugs, empirical schedules have been developed for drug administration with single agents or combinations of myelosuppressive drugs normally given every 3 to 4 weeks. The interval between treatments provides time for hematopoietic recovery of normal myeloid progenitors in the bone marrow and avoids cumulative myelosuppression. It is essential to check the patient's white blood cell count, differential, and platelet count immediately before each course of myelosuppressive chemotherapy. During the first few cycles of chemotherapy, and at intervals thereafter, it is useful to check counts between treatment courses, particularly to determine the nadir of absolute granulocyte count (AGC). Decreases in AGC below 1000/μL increase the risk of infection; AGCs less than 500/μL represent a potentially fatal risk. Because hematopoietic recovery can occur rapidly after the nadir, the AGC immediately before the next course can be normal, even though the nadir count may have been very low. For some drug combinations with low but brief AGC nadirs, prophylactic antibiotic agents (e.g., ciprofloxacin, sulfamethoxazole-trimethoprim) that will bracket the AGC nadir can protect against infection secondary to neutropenia. In general, if the AGC immediately before the next course of chemotherapy is less than 2000/μL, the dose of myelosuppressive drugs should be reduced by 50%. With an AGC of less than 1500/μL, doses should be reduced by 75%. If AGC is less than 1000/μL, the drug should be withheld until hematologic recovery occurs. An additional approach to problems of myelosuppression involves the use of bone marrow growth factors (see Biologic Therapy).

DOSE ADJUSTMENTS FOR IMPAIRED HEPATIC OR RENAL FUNCTION. It is important to make downward dosage adjustments for specific drugs when altered hepatic or renal function plays a major role in drug metabolism. The metabolism of doxorubicin depends on good hepatobiliary function. Patients with a serum bilirubin value of greater than 3.0 mg/dL should have their doxorubicin dose reduced by at least 50% until drug tolerance is established.

Cisplatin, methotrexate, etoposide, hydroxyurea, and bleomycin all are cleared predominantly through renal excretion. Doses of these agents should be decreased approximately in proportion to the decline in renal function as determined by creatinine clearance and reflected by the serum creatinine value.

Endocrine Agents

Cancer cells often exhibit susceptibility to hormonal control mechanisms that regulate growth of the normal organ or tissue from which the neoplasm arose. Endocrine therapy (Table 191–9) appears to work through cytostatic and cytotoxic mechanisms and usually requires long-term suppression. Endocrine therapy includes the use of both hormones and "antihormones," which are either antagonists or partial agonists for a given endocrine mechanism. Inasmuch as the effects of hormones are receptor mediated, evaluation of receptors capable of binding hormones has played an important role in assessing both tumor types and individual patients for possible endocrine therapy.

STEROID HORMONES AND ANTIHORMONES. Cancers arising from endocrine organs and the immune system are susceptible to the effects of steroid hormones, steroid hormone antagonists, and hormone deprivation. The sex steroids and their antagonists represent major agents for the treatment of common cancers arising from the breast, prostate gland, and uterus. The role of endocrine ablation procedures (hypophysectomy, adrenalectomy, oophorectomy, orchiectomy) has diminished as systemic agents have been identified to replace surgical procedures. Nonetheless, oophorectomy and orchiectomy are still useful in the treatment of endocrine-sensitive cancers of the breast and prostate, respectively.

Estrogens and Estrogen Receptor Modulators (ERMs): Tamoxifen (Nolvadex), Raloxifene (Evista), and Toremifene (Fareston). Tamoxifen is a nonsteroidal ERM that binds to estrogen receptors in normal and malignant tissues. It is useful for treatment of breast cancers that express hormone receptors (either estrogen or progesterone receptors). Tamoxifen is given orally at a daily single dose of 20 mg to patients with metastatic breast cancer (Chapter 204) or in the treatment of premenopausal or postmenopausal women in the adjuvant setting. In tumors that are strongly hormone-receptor positive, the response rate is greater than 60%; tamoxifen is of little benefit to women whose tumors do not express hormone receptors. A recent breast cancer prevention trial involving more than 1300 women at high risk for breast cancer showed that women taking tamoxifen had a 50% lower incidence of disease than those taking placebo. Raloxifene, a selective estrogen receptor modulator (SERM), decreases the incidence of breast cancer in older women treated for osteoporosis. Toremifene (Fareston), a more potent ERM than tamoxifen, is as effective as tamoxifen in terms of response rate, median duration of response, median time-to-progression, and median survival; short-term side effects were similar, but the risk of endometrial cancer with the long-term use of toremifene has not been determined.

Aromatase Inhibitors: Aminoglutethimide (Cytadren), Anastrazole (Arimidex), Letrozole (Femara), and Exemestane (Aromasin). Inhibition of the enzyme aromatase is an effective treatment for postmenopausal women with breast cancer in whom the greatest source of estrogen is the conversion of androstenedione produced in the adrenal to estrone in liver, muscle, and fat. Aromatase is an enzyme complex made up of two proteins, aromatase cytochrome P-450 (CYP19) and NADPH-cytochrome P-450 reductase; inhibition of aromatase blocks the conversion of androgens to estrone in peripheral tissues including fat, liver, muscle, and breast. The newer aromatase

Oncology

Table 191–9 • HORMONALLY ACTIVE AGENTS IN CANCER TREATMENT

REPRESENTATIVE AGENTS	DOSE (ORAL UNLESS SPECIFIED)	TOXICITY (A = ACUTE; D = DELAYED)	USES
Glucocorticoids			
Prednisone	20–100 mg/day or 50 mg qod (single dose)	A: Fluid retention, hyperglycemia, euphoria, depression, hypokalemia	Leukemia Lymphoma
Dexamethasone	4–16 mg/day or 40 mg/day for 4-day pulses every 2–4 weeks	D: Osteoporosis, immunosuppression, gastrointestinal ulcers, cushingoid appearance, cataracts	Myeloma Breast cancer Brain metastases
Estrogen			
Diethylstilbestrol	5 mg tid (breast); 1–3 mg qd (prostate)	A: Nausea, vomiting, fluid retention, hypercalcemia (flare reaction with bone metastases), uterine bleeding D: Feminization, accelerated coronary artery disease	Breast cancer Prostate cancer
Antiestrogen			
Tamoxifen	20 mg qd	A: Occasional nausea, fluid retention, hot flashes D: Retinal degeneration	Breast cancer
Toremifene			Breast cancer
Aromatase Inhibitors			
Aminoglutethimide (plus hydrocortisone 20 mg bid)	250 mg bid (breast); 250 mg qid (prostate)	A: Dizziness D: Rash (transient)	Breast cancer Prostate cancer
Anastrozole	1 mg/day	A: Nausea, vomiting	
Progestins			
Megestrol acetate	40 mg qid	A: Increased appetite (megestrol), fluid retention	Breast cancer
Medroxyprogesterone acetate	1 g IM weekly	D: Weight gain, thromboembolism	
Androgens			
Fluoxymesterone	10–20 mg qd	A: Cholestatic jaundice (with oral drug)	Breast cancer
Testosterone	600 mg IM q 4–6 wk	D: Virilization	
Antiandrogen			
Flutamide	250 mg tid	D: Gynecomastia	Prostate cancer
Gonadotropin-releasing hormone agonists (depot formulations)			
Leuprolide acetate	7.5 mg SQ monthly	A: Transient flare of symptoms	Prostate cancer
Goserelin acetate	3.6 mg SQ monthly		Breast cancer (?)

inhibitors have much higher affinities for CYP19, are far more selective and less toxic than aminoglutethimide, and do not require glucocorticoid replacement. Anastrazole and letrozole are nonsteroidal, reversible aromatase inhibitors, whereas exemestane is a steroidal, irreversible antagonist. Aromatase inhibitors are approved for use in the treatment of hormone-responsive metastatic breast cancer. Their activity as second-line hormonal agents in patients who have relapsed after tamoxifen is equal to megestrol acetate, but with fewer side effects. Recent studies in both front-line metastatic breast cancer and preliminary data in the adjuvant setting suggest that these newer agents have activity equal to or perhaps greater than tamoxifen. Whereas aminoglutethimide produces glucocorticoid deficiency, mineralocorticoid deficiency, skin rash, lethargy, and orthostatic hypotension, the newer drugs have an excellent toxicity profile and only a small percentage of patients experience nausea, diarrhea, asthenia, headache, hot flushes, or pain at tumor sites. Recommended daily oral doses are anastrazole, 1 mg; letrozole, 2.5 mg; and exemestane, 25 mg.

Antiandrogens: Bicalutamide (Casodex), Flutamide (Eulexin), Nilutamide (Nilandron). Antiandrogens are competitive antagonists of the interaction between androstenedione and the androgen receptor. Antiandrogens are effective treatment for prostate cancer when used in combination with a luteinizing hormone-releasing hormone (LHRH) receptor agonist or orchiectomy. Although the activity of the three agents appears similar, the side effects are different. Androgenic blockade results in feminizing side effects in men including mastodynia, gynecomastia, galactorrhea, hot flashes, and loss of facial hair. Whereas each may produce nausea, diarrhea, and constipation, nilutamide is associated with idiosyncratic reactions including visual disturbances, interstitial pneumonitis, and alcohol intolerance.

PROGESTINS. Progestins are useful in palliative management of metastatic breast or endometrial cancer and can cause tumor regression in endocrine-sensitive disease. No evidence suggests their utility in the adjuvant setting in either of these neoplasms. Occasional patients with prostate cancer also appear to benefit from progestational therapy. The most commonly used progestins include megestrol acetate (Megace), medroxyprogesterone (Provera), and hydroxyprogesterone caproate (Delalutin). Megestrol acetate is useful for second-line endocrine therapy for patients with metastatic breast cancer who initially respond to tamoxifen or an aromatase inhibitor. In patients who experience disturbing side effects from tamoxifen (e.g., severe hot flashes), megestrol acetate may represent a reasonable alternative. In addition to its antitumor effects, megestrol acetate improves appetite in some patients with cancer-induced cachexia.

GLUCOCORTICOIDS. Adrenal steroid hormones of the glucocorticoid class (e.g., prednisone, methylprednisolone, dexamethasone) are useful in treating lymphoid malignancies and may also potentiate the effects of cytotoxic agents in these tumor types as well as in breast cancer and perhaps other neoplasms. The glucocorticoids play an important role in treating complications of cancer (hypercalcemia, cerebral edema). Glucocorticoids are lympholytic and nonmyelosuppressive and have been incorporated into combination chemotherapy for acute and chronic lympholytic leukemia, malignant lymphoma, and multiple myeloma. Glucocorticoids appear to induce cell death in some lymphoid malignancies by apoptosis.

GONADOTROPIN-RELEASING HORMONE (GnRH, LHRH) AGONISTS. Several synthetic analogues of natural GnRH (LHRH) are clinically available. Both leuprolide acetate (Lupron) and goserelin acetate (Zoladex) are available in long-acting parenteral depot formulations. These analogues function more potently than natural GnRH agonists and have an unusual effect on the pituitary, consisting of initial stimulation followed by long-term inhibition of the release of follicle-stimulating hormone and luteinizing hormone. This initial increase in gonadotropins can cause a transient increase in symptoms in patients with bone metastases. The inhibition of release of the gonadotropin reduces testicular androgen synthesis in men and ovarian estrogen production in women. Accordingly, GnRH offers an alternative to surgical orchiectomy in patients with prostate cancer and avoids the gynecomastia, nausea, vomiting, edema, and thromboembolic disease that estrogens may induce. The effectiveness of GnRH agonists is enhanced by administration in combination with an antiandrogen (flutamide), and the combination has been reported to be more effective than a GnRH agonist alone in patients with stage D metastatic prostate cancer. Impotence results from this form of "medical orchiectomy," as it does from surgical orchiectomy, but the effects of medical therapy are potentially reversible if treatment is discontinued. Medical orchiectomy is more expensive but acceptable to patients who decline surgical orchiectomy. GnRH agonists now show promise in combination with antiestrogens as endocrine therapy for premenopausal women with hormone receptor–positive breast cancer. The GnRH agonists are abortifacients in animals and should not be given to women who are or may become pregnant.

Biologic Therapy

A new form of cancer therapy, still in its evolution, is the use of recombinant cytokines, vaccine growth factors, and monoclonal antibodies for the treatment of cancer. The term *biologic therapy* describes this heterogeneous group of agents that either are normal mammalian mediators or achieve antitumor effects through endogenous host defense mechanisms. The biologic agents have also been termed *biologic response modifiers*. Both the cellular and humoral limbs of immunity can be exploited in cancer therapy. The cellular defenses include several classes of cytotoxic lymphocytes (natural killer cells), lymphokine-activated killer (LAK) cells, tumor-infiltrating lymphoma, and cytotoxic T lymphocytes, as well as antibody-dependent cytotoxic cells. The nonspecific cells of the reticuloendothelial system, including activated macrophages, also may be important. Humoral agents with antitumor activities include cytokines such as IFNs and interleukins as well as specific antibodies. Most of these humoral agents interact with specific immune effector cells in a coordinated and synergistic fashion. Antibodies are highly specific and generally interact directly with their tumor targets when they are targeted against cell surface constituents. Some humoral agents, including the tumor necrosis factors α and β, have potent local antitumor properties in preclinical models but have yet to be shown to be clinically useful.

Vaccines based on specific bacterial agents or extracts from bacteria can nonspecifically activate the host immune system. By using BCG, this approach has been applied successfully to intravesical therapy of in situ cancer of the urinary bladder. Specific cancer-associated antigen vaccines are under active investigation.

INTERFERONS. The three major molecular species are IFN-α, -β, and -γ. IFN-α and -β mediate their action by binding to the same cell surface receptor, whereas a second cell-surface receptor mediates the action of IFN-γ. IFN-α is the major species for use in the treatment of hematologic malignancies and solid tumors. Whether IFN-β or -γ will have sufficient advantage over IFN-α in any specific cancer indication to gain regulatory approval is uncertain.

Interferon-α. Recombinant IFN-α (IFN-α_2, Intron-A, Roferon-A), a polypeptide cytokine with antiviral properties, is useful for single-agent treatment of selected hematologic malignancies and solid tumors. IFN activates the transcription of a number of cellular genes and inhibits the synthesis of a number of proteins in sensitive tumor target cells, including ornithine decarboxylase, a rate-limiting enzyme in polyamine metabolism. Although IFN-α also has antiviral and immunoregulatory properties, it is unclear whether these functions influence its antitumor properties. The antitumor properties of IFN-α also appear to be schedule dependent with a cytostatic mode of action. Most remissions induced by IFN are only partial.

IFN-α can be administered parenterally by intravenous, intramuscular, subcutaneous, and intracavitary routes. Its preferred route is by subcutaneous administration, which provides the longest duration of action. The dosage schedules are variable, with higher dosages required for some tumor types. Hairy cell leukemia is the tumor most sensitive to IFN-α. Usual dosages are in the range of 3 million IU administered subcutaneously three times weekly. At these low levels, IFN usually causes only mild side effects such as fever and chills with the first few doses. For Kaposi's sarcoma, far more aggressive and toxic IFN schedules are required and can cause anorexia, weight loss, failure in concentration, and profound weakness. High-dose IFN can

also induce occasional cardiac arrhythmias, nausea, vomiting, leukopenia, myalgias, proteinuria, and hepatic dysfunction. Elderly patients appear to develop more marked side effects at all dosage schedules.

IFN-α is also useful in the treatment of CML, multiple myeloma, some of the low-grade non-Hodgkin's lymphomas, and some cases of metastatic melanoma or renal cell carcinoma. In melanoma, the use of high doses of IFN-α in an adjuvant mode has been shown to decrease the relapse rate. In patients receiving recombinant IFN-α for hairy cell leukemia, CML, or renal cancer, neutralizing antibodies to the recombinant product can develop. IFN-α is also used in combination with *cis*-retinoic acid to treat renal and cervical cancers. In general, IFN therapy has not had the broad-spectrum benefits that were initially envisioned.

INTERLEUKIN-2. Interleukin-2 (IL-2, Proleukin) is an immunomodulatory cytokine that acts on T-cell progenitors to produce LAK cells. Recombinant IL-2 has been approved for therapeutic use in renal cancer. Direct intravenous infusion induces LAK cells in the patient. Additionally, leukapheresis can obtain circulating lymphocytes that can then be exposed to IL-2 in tissue culture to activate lymphoid progenitors into LAK cells, which are then reinfused into the patient. There is now general agreement that either IL-2 or IL-2/LAK can induce tumor regression in 10 to 20% of patients with renal carcinoma or melanoma.

Whereas the infusion of LAK cells causes relatively few side effects, IL-2 induces considerable toxicity. Patients receiving high-dose IL-2 must be in an intensive care unit with close management of blood pressure, fluids, and electrolytes. The high-dose regimens are suitable only for younger patients without other significant disease or impairment of cardiac, pulmonary, hepatic, or renal function. Common side effects of high-dose IL-2/LAK are probably due to lymphoid infiltrates in major organs and an induced capillary leak syndrome. Shortly after initiation of high-dose IL-2 therapy, tachycardia develops, and a significant decrease in arterial blood pressure occurs. As IL-2 administration continues, compensatory fluid retention occurs in association with weight gain, oliguria, and azotemia. Vasopressors are often needed. Even at lower doses that can be used in a conventional hospital or outpatient setting (e.g., 3 million IU/m^2/day by intravenous infusion for 2 weeks), hypotension and fluid retention are not uncommon.

Pulmonary metastases appear to be somewhat more sensitive to IL-2 or IL-2/LAK therapy than are other tumors. With the adoptive immunotherapy approach using IL-2/LAK, a small percentage of patients who had undergone prior removal of the primary tumor achieved complete remission, with all evidence of metastatic disease disappearing for prolonged periods of time.

LEVAMISOLE. Levamisole (Ergamisol) is an anthelmintic agent possessing immunopotentiating properties. When combined with 5-FU, levamisole enhances adjuvant chemotherapy of patients with Dukes' C colon cancer, although this regimen has been largely supplanted by treatment with 5-FU and leucovorin. In patients with overt metastatic colon cancer, levamisole does not appear to be beneficial.

Antitumor Antibody Therapy

RITUXIMAB. Rituximab (Rituxan) is a genetically engineered chimeric murine/human monoclonal antibody directed against the CD20 antigen found on the surface of normal and malignant B lymphocytes. It is the first antibody approved for therapeutic use in humans. Approximately 50% of patients with relapsed or refractory low-grade lymphoma treated with 375 mg/m^2 of this agent given as an IV infusion weekly for four doses had a partial or complete remission lasting 10 to 12 months. Current studies are exploring the use of this antibody together with chemotherapy and/or irradiation. Infusion-related side effects consisting of fever, chills, and rigors occur in the majority of patients during the first infusion. Subsequent infusions are associated with fewer side effects.

TRASTUZUMAB (HERCEPTIN). This genetically engineered monoclonal antibody is directed against cells overexpressing the HER-2 protein, a transmembrane glycoprotein. Approximately 30% of breast cancers overexpress this protein. The response rate to the antibody alone in this group of patients is low (about 15%); however, in combination with Taxol or doxorubicin, augmented response rates have been reported, leading to the approval of this antibody for clinical use by the FDA. An unexpected side effect of this treatment has been an increased incidence of cardiac toxicity when this antibody is used in combination with doxorubicin or Taxol.

GEMTUZABAB OZOGAMICIN (MYLOTARG). This antibody, when directed against the CD33 antigen present in the membrane of AML cells, has been linked to a potent calicheamicin. It is approved for patients who have AML in first relapse, who are 60 years of age or older, and who are not candidates for other cytotoxic chemotherapy. Severe myelosuppression is the major toxicity. In addition, chills, fever, nausea, and vomiting may accompany drug administration. Complete remissions have been achieved in approximately 30% of patients with this agent, with a median duration of 6 months.

ALEMTUZUMAB (CAMPATH). This antibody targets CD52, an antigen present on both T and B lymphocytes. This agent, which recently was approved for the treatment of patients with CLL, can cause severe pancytopenia and opportunistic infections.

BONE MARROW GROWTH FACTORS (Chapter 159). Bone marrow growth factors are glycoproteins that function in an overlapping and hierarchic manner on bone marrow progenitors and not only result in cell proliferation but also activate differentiation and cell trafficking. Several of these recombinant proteins, including granulocyte colony-stimulating factor (G-CSF), granulocyte-macrophage CSF (GM-CSF), and erythropoietin (Epogen, EPO), are widely used in cancer treatment. IL-3, macrophage CSF (M-CSF), and thrombopoietin are at an earlier stage of development, and their role in supportive care is currently uncertain. Clinical trials using subcutaneously administered G-CSF or GM-CSF have shown that either can shorten the duration of granulocytopenia, the frequency of infectious complications, and the duration of hospitalization after chemotherapy combinations that normally require inpatient administration. With bone marrow transplantation in which high-dose chemotherapy and/or total body irradiation is used, both myelosuppressive and nonmyelosuppressive side effects can be diminished with the use of G-CSF or GM-CSF. Preliminary evidence suggests that IL-3 (multi-CSF) can stimulate platelet and red blood cell as well as granulocyte production. The major toxicities of the growth factors that stimulate white blood cell production include bone pain, fever, myalgias, and occasional rashes. Pericarditis has been reported with high-dose GM-CSF or G-CSF.

Recombinant EPO is already in general clinical use for the anemia of renal failure. Preliminary studies also suggest that, when used in pharmacologic doses, EPO can restore normal red blood cell counts in some patients with multiple myeloma and in patients with solid tumors undergoing chemotherapy.

DIFFERENTIATION THERAPY. ALL-Trans retinoic acid (ATRA) is the first effective differentiation agent introduced into routine clinical care. It causes a high percentage of complete remissions in patients with acute promyelocytic leukemia (APL; Chapter 193). Retinoids are also under investigation as chemotherapeutic and chemopreventive agents.

Arsenic trioxide (Trisenox) was first shown to be effective differentiation therapy for patients with APL in China, and its activity was confirmed in trials in the United States and Europe. In patients relapsing after treatment with ATRA, this agent is highly effective and produces complete remissions in more than 70% of patients. APL is now curable in a high percentage of patients with the use of differentiating agents together with anthracycline-based chemotherapy.

ANTIANGIOGENESIS TREATMENTS. An attractive target for anticancer drug development is the neovasculature elicited by growth of tumors. Natural substances derived from precursor proteins (e.g., endostatin, a 20-kD terminal fragment of collagen, and angiostatin, a 38-kD internal fragment of plasminogen), show encouraging antitumor effects in animal models. Several of these are in phase II and phase III clinical trials. Some standard chemotherapeutic agents, including the vinca alkaloids and taxanes, are potent inhibitors of proliferation in human vascular endothelium and are being evaluated as antiangiogenesis agents at very low doses compared with their usual chemotherapeutic doses.

THALIDOMIDE. Thalidomide is active against otherwise refractory multiple myeloma, alone or in combination with dexamethasone. It has direct cytotoxic effects on myeloma cells and can inhibit the upregulation of vascular endothelial growth factor and IL-6 upon binding to bone marrow stromal cells. Thalidomide is approved for the treatment of erythema nodosum leprosum (Hansen's disease), an unusual manifestation of leprosy.

TARGETED TREATMENTS. The striking therapeutic successes of Gleevec, a potent inhibitor of tyrosine kinases overexpressed in chronic myelogenous leukemia and most gastrointestinal stromal tumors, has stimulated the search for other tumor-specific abnormalities that will allow

drug targeting. The ability to interrogate the entire genome of each cancer has given rise to considerable optimism that other specific tumor targets will be found, leading to more selective and less toxic treatments.

SUGGESTED READINGS

DeVita VT, Hellman S, Rosenberg SA: Cancer: Principles and Practice of Oncology, 6th ed. Philadelphia, JB Lippincott, 2000. *A standard reference.*

Emanuel EJ, Young-Xu Y, Levinsky NG, et al: Chemotherapy use among Medicare beneficiaries at the end of life. Ann Intern Med 2003;138:639–643. *A cancer's responsiveness to chemotherapy does not seem to influence whether dying patients receive chemotherapy at the end of life.*

Gabizon A: Emerging role of liposomal drug carrier systems in cancer chemotherapy. J Liposome Res 2003;13:17–20. *A promising new approach for drug delivery.*

Holland JF, Frei E III, Bast RC Jr, et al: Cancer Medicine, 5th ed. Philadelphia, Lea & Febiger, 2000. *A comprehensive textbook covering clinical, diagnostic, and therapeutic approaches for all major forms of cancer. Major modalities of treatment as well as drug combination schedules are delineated in detail in relation to relevant tumor types.*

192 THE CHRONIC LEUKEMIAS

Michael J. Keating
Hagop Kantarjian

CHRONIC MYELOGENOUS LEUKEMIA (CHRONIC MYELOID LEUKEMIA, CHRONIC MYELOCYTIC LEUKEMIA, CHRONIC GRANULOCYTIC LEUKEMIA)

Definition

Chronic myelogenous leukemia (CML) is a disease characterized by overproduction of cells of the granulocytic, especially the neutrophilic, series and occasionally the monocytic series, leading to marked splenomegaly and very high white blood cell (WBC) counts. Basophilia and thrombocytosis are common. A characteristic cytogenetic abnormality, the Philadelphia (Ph[1]) chromosome, is present in the bone marrow cells in more than 95% of cases. The granulocytes usually appear relatively normal, although those of many patients exhibit dysplastic changes, including Pelger-Huët anomalies. Neutrophil functions, such as phagocytosis and bactericidal activity, are largely preserved. Before effective treatment was available, patients survived, on the average, approximately 2 years after diagnosis.

Epidemiology

CML constitutes one fifth of all cases of leukemia in the United States. It is diagnosed in 1 or 2 persons per 100,000 per year and has a slight male preponderance. This incidence has not changed significantly in the past few decades. The incidence of CML increases with age; the median age at diagnosis is 45 to 50 years. Ph[1]-positive CML is uncommon in children and adolescents. Patients older than 60 years have a poorer prognosis. No familial association of CML has been noted.

Usually no etiologic agent can be incriminated in CML. Exposure to ionizing radiation increases the risk of subsequent CML. Survivors of the atomic bomb explosions in Japan in 1945 have had an increased incidence of CML, with a peak occurring 5 to 12 years after exposure and seeming to be dose related. The relative risk has been decreasing since that time but is still above the expected rate for Japan. Radiation treatment of ankylosing spondylitis and cervical cancer has increased the incidence of CML. No increase in the risk of CML has been demonstrated in individuals working in the nuclear industry. Radiologists working without adequate protection before 1940 were more likely to develop myeloid leukemia, but no such association has been found in recent studies. Benzene exposure increases the risk of acute myelogenous leukemia (AML) but not of CML. Patients with CML have an increased frequency of the Cw3 and Cw4 human leukocyte antigens (HLAs). CML is not a frequent secondary leukemia following the treatment of other cancers with radiation and/or alkylating agents.

Molecular Pathogenesis

The striking feature in CML is the presence of the Ph[1] chromosome in the bone marrow cells of more than 90% of patients with

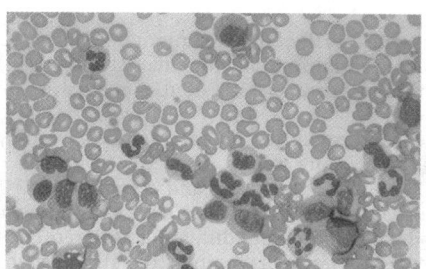

FIGURE 192–1 • Chronic myelogenous leukemia, stable phase. Peripheral smear shows leukemia, stable phase. Peripheral smear shows leukocytosis, with representation by the entire spectrum of leukocyte differentiation, ranging from myeloblasts to mature neutrophils. (Courtesy of Andrew Schafer, MD.)

typical CML (Fig. 192–1). The Ph[1] chromosome results from a balanced translocation of material between the long arms of chromosomes 9 and 22. As more chromosomal material is lost from chromosome 22 than is gained from chromosome 9, the Ph[1] chromosome is a shortened chromosome 22 containing approximately 60% of its normal complement of DNA. The break, which occurs at band q34 of the long arm of chromosome 9, allows translocation of the cellular oncogene C-ABL to a position on chromosome 22 called the breakpoint cluster region (bcr). The breakpoint in the bcr varies from patient to patient but is identical in all cells of any one patient. C-ABL is a homologue of V-ABL, the Abelson virus that causes leukemia in mice. The apposition of these two genetic sequences produces a new hybrid gene (BCR/ABL), which codes for a novel protein of molecular weight 210,000 kd (P210). The P210 protein, a tyrosine kinase, appears to trigger the uncontrolled proliferation of CML cells.

What induces this molecular rearrangement is unknown. Using molecular techniques that amplify detection of BCR/ABL, it can be found in the marrow cells of 25 to 30% of healthy volunteers and 5% of infants, but not in cord blood. Because clinical CML develops in

only 1 to 2 of 100,000 individuals (i.e., 1 to 2 per 25,000 to 30,000 individuals who express BCR/ABL in their bone marrow), immune regulatory processes or additional molecular events may contribute to the development of CML. BCR/ABL is found only in hematopoietic cells, and the incidence of CML is not increased in monozygotic twins or in relatives of patients with CML.

The Ph[1] chromosome occurs in erythroid, myeloid, monocytic, and megakaryocytic cells, less commonly in B lymphocytes, rarely in T lymphocytes, but not in marrow fibroblasts. This extensive cellular distribution places the abnormality in CML close to the pluripotent stem cell. Studies of glucose-6-phosphate dehydrogenase (G6PD) isoenzymes support the finding of multilineage monoclonal proliferation, because a single isoenzyme is present in the aforementioned cells in some patients with CML. Insertion of a retrovirus encoding P210 (BCR/ABL) into cells of mice has led to the development of a disease closely resembling CML in some of these animals, giving credence to the hypothesis that the BCR/ABL hybrid gene is sufficient to cause CML. C-sis, the homologue of the simian sarcoma virus, is also translocated from chromosome 22 to chromosome 9 in CML but is distant from the breakpoint and not expressed in benign-phase CML. C-sis codes for a protein identical to platelet-derived growth factor (PDGF).

The fusion BCR/ABL gene and the P210 protein can be found in many cases of typical CML in which no cytogenetic abnormality occurs or in which changes other than typical t(9;22)(q34;q11) are identified. These patients have a survival rate and a response to therapy that are similar to those in Ph[1]-positive patients. Patients with atypical CML who are Ph[1] and BCR/ABL negative have a different natural history than do patients who are either Ph[1] positive or Ph[1] negative with BCR/ABL positivity. They resemble more closely patients with myelodysplastic syndrome (MDS; Chapter 182). Thus, three groups of patients with CML can be identified: (1) positive for Ph[1] and BCR/ABL, (2) Ph[1] negative but BCR/ABL positive, and (3) negative for Ph[1] and BCR/ABL.

Although 100% of the metaphases on cytogenetic analysis usually show the presence of the Ph[1] chromosome, some normal stem cells must remain. Normal diploid cells emerge on long-term bone marrow culture and after treatment with interferon (IFN), imatinib, high-dose chemotherapy, and autologous bone marrow transplantation (BMT).

Clinical Manifestations

CML is increasingly being diagnosed in asymptomatic patients owing to the use of hematologic studies in routine physical examinations or in evaluations of other illnesses. In these patients, the WBC count may be relatively low at the time of diagnosis. The WBC count correlates well with tumor mass as defined by spleen size. Patients with higher WBC counts and larger spleens have more symptoms. The symptoms of CML, which usually are nonspecific, are caused by anemia, spleen size, or an increased basal metabolic rate, but most patients are asymptomatic or only mildly symptomatic. Fatigue, weight loss, malaise, easy satiety, and a sense of left upper quadrant fullness are the major symptoms of CML. Rarely, bleeding (associated with a low platelet count and/or platelet dysfunction) or thrombosis (associated with thrombocytosis and/or marked leukocytosis) occurs. The serum uric acid level is commonly elevated at diagnosis, and acute gouty arthritis may follow treatment. An elevated blood histamine level (related to the basophil cell mass) can cause upper gastrointestinal ulceration and bleeding. Neutrophil function is usually normal or only modestly impaired, and neutrophil numbers are markedly increased; infections are therefore uncommon at the time of diagnosis. Headaches, bone pain, arthralgias, pain from splenic infarction, and fever are uncommon in the early stages of CML but become more common as the disease progresses. Priapism is occasionally noted, usually in patients with marked leukocytosis or thrombocytosis. Leukostatic symptoms, such as dyspnea, drowsiness, loss of coordination, or confusion, which are due to sludging in the pulmonary or cerebral vessels, are uncommon in the benign (chronic) phase of CML despite WBC counts that may exceed 400,000/μL. These symptoms appear more frequently in later stages of the disease (i.e., in the accelerated or blast crisis phases, in which more immature cells predominate). All symptoms subside if the WBC count decreases and the splenomegaly decreases as a result of effective treatment.

Splenomegaly, by far the most consistent physical sign in CML, occurs in more than 60% of cases. The spleen may extend to the pelvic brim and across the midline of the abdomen. Hepatomegaly is less common and is usually minor (1 to 3 cm below the right costal margin). Lymphadenopathy is uncommon, as is infiltration of skin and other tissues. If present, these findings suggest Ph[1]-negative CML or accelerated phase or blastic crisis of CML.

NATURAL HISTORY. More than 90% of patients present with CML in the benign (chronic) phase, in which the disease behaves in a predictable fashion, with the symptoms, abnormal physical signs, and abnormal blood findings returning to normal after treatment. This satisfactory response is transient; all patients eventually develop a variety of changes in the behavior of the disease. Most frequently there is a "blast crisis," a clinical picture resembling that of acute leukemia (Table 192–1). Rarely, patients initially present in blast crisis. This change can be abrupt, but more frequently it is preceded by a period of progressively greater difficulty in maintaining the WBC count at a level of less than 20,000/μL and of other manifestations, such as increasing splenomegaly, hepatomegaly, and infiltration of nodes, skin, bones, or other tissues; the appearance of blast cells or basophils in the peripheral blood; development of anemia and/or thrombocytopenia; or fever, malaise, and weight loss. These features, termed the *accelerated phase* of CML, demand reevaluation of the bone marrow, which, in the accelerated phase, often shows dysplastic changes in the myeloid and other cell lineages and may show an increase in the percentage of blast cells (5 to 29%) and an increase in basophils. Aspiration of bone marrow may be difficult, especially in patients who have developed myelofibrosis subsequent to the CML. Chromosomal abnormalities in addition to the Ph[1] chromosome occur in both the accelerated and the blastic phases of CML. Blast crisis is diagnosed when 30% or more blast cells are present in the bone marrow and/or peripheral blood.

Continued

When the accelerated phase or blast crisis is suspected (more than 10% blasts in bone marrow), the patient should be further observed in 2 to 4 weeks, because the percentage of blasts in the blood and bone marrow can increase transiently after the treatment of CML is discontinued, especially if the patient had been treated with hydroxyurea or IFN. It is important to be cautious in classifying patients as having blast crisis or accelerated phase because of the adverse prognostic implications. The risk of developing accelerated phase or blast crisis in CML is relatively low in the first 2 years after diagnosis (approximately 10% per year) but then increases and remains constant (15 to 20% per year) thereafter unless therapies such as imatinib mesylate, IFN, or BMT are used.

LABORATORY FINDINGS. All patients with untreated CML have an elevated WBC count, ranging from 10,000/μL to more than 0.5 million/μL. The predominant cells are of the neutrophil series, with a left shift extending to blast cells. In addition, eosinophils and basophils are commonly increased in number. Monocytes may be slightly increased in some cases that overlap with chronic myelomonocytic leukemia (CMML). The bone marrow is hypercellular with marked myeloid hyperplasia and sometimes shows evidence of increased reticulin or collagen fibrosis. The myeloid:erythroid ratio is 15:1 to 20:1. About 15% of patients have 5% or more blast cells in the peripheral blood or bone marrow at diagnosis. T cells (both T helper and T suppressor), but not B cells, are increased in number in CML. A hemoglobin level of less than 11 g/dL is present in one third of patients. The red cells are usually normochromic and normocytic, but nucleated red cells are present in the blood of one fourth of the patients at diagnosis. Autoimmune hemolytic anemia and thrombocytopenia (<100,000/μL) are rare in CML, but thrombocytosis (>450,000/μL) occurs in almost half of the patients.

Biochemical abnormalities in CML include a leukocyte alkaline phosphatase (LAP) score that is markedly decreased in the neutrophils of 90% or more of patients and is zero in 5 to 10% of cases. A low LAP score also occurs in some patients with agnogenic myeloid metaplasia, which is sometimes difficult to differentiate from CML. The serum levels of transcobalamins I and III, cobalamin-binding glycoproteins produced by neutrophils, are elevated in accord with the increased neutrophils. This elevation leads to extremely high serum cobalamin values (e.g., vitamin B₁₂ levels greater than ten times normal). Serum levels of lactate dehydrogenase, uric acid, and lysozyme are often increased. The lysozyme levels are modestly increased in CML compared with CMML, in which the levels in blood and urine are often markedly increased. Kinetic studies show an increased neutrophil production rate related to a markedly expanded myeloid mass. The number of colony-forming cells in the blood in CML is increased, but the number in the bone marrow is in the normal range. Defective feedback control of WBC production is common in CML; some patients demonstrate a cyclic oscillation of the WBC count. The labeling index of myeloblasts in CML is lower than in normal bone marrow, and the generation time is prolonged, confirming the concept that CML is an accumulative rather than a proliferative disease: neutrophils in CML survive slightly longer in the intravascular circulation than do normal granulocytes.

Diagnosis

The diagnosis of typical CML is not difficult. The presence of unexplained myeloid leukocytosis (Fig. 192–2) with splenomegaly should lead to a LAP test on the peripheral blood neutrophils (usually zero or a low value) and bone marrow examination with a cytogenetic analysis. Marrow myeloid hyperplasia and hypercellularity further suggest the diagnosis. The standard diagnostic test remains the cytogenetic analysis; the presence of the Ph¹ chromosome in this clinical setting establishes the diagnosis. When the Ph¹ chromosome is not found in a patient with suspected CML, molecular evidence for the presence of the hybrid *BCR/ABL* gene should be sought, because 25 to 30% of Ph¹-negative patients with CML have *BCR/ABL* rearrangement. The Ph¹ chromosome is usually present in 100% of metaphases, ordinarily as the sole abnormality. Ten to 15% of patients at initial presentation have an additional chromosomal change, such as loss of the Y chromosome, trisomy 8, an additional loss of material from 22q, or an atypical translocation. Many patients who have atypical complex chromosomal changes, which may or may not involve chromosome 9 or chromosome 22 morphologically, demonstrate evidence of the hybrid *BCR/ABL* gene when molecular techniques are used.

CML must be differentiated from leukemoid reactions (Chapter 163), which usually produce WBC counts lower than 50,000/μL, toxic granulation vacuolation, Döhle bodies in the granulocytes, absence of basophilia, a normal or increased LAP level, and a clinical history and physical examination suggesting the origin of the leukemoid reaction. Corticosteroids can rarely cause extreme neutrophilia together with the left shift, but this response is self-limited and short in duration and thus seldom a cause of diagnostic difficulty.

CML may be more difficult to differentiate from other myelodysplastic or myeloproliferative syndromes (Chapters 176, 183, and 187). Patients having agnogenic myeloid metaplasia with or without myelofibrosis have splenomegaly and often have neutrophilia and thrombocytosis. Polycythemia rubra vera with associated iron deficiency, which

---

Table 192–1 • **FEATURES AND DEFINITIONS OF ACCELERATED AND BLASTIC PHASE CHRONIC MYELOGENOUS LEUKEMIA**

Accelerated phase chronic myelogenous leukemia
- Marrow or peripheral blasts 10% or more
- Marrow or peripheral basophils and eosinophils 20% or more
- Frequent Pelger-Huët–like neutrophils, nucleated red cells, or megakaryocytic nuclear fragments
- Increased marrow reticulin or collagen fibrosis
- Leukocytosis (>50,000/mL), anemia (hematocrit <25%), or thrombocytopenia (<10,000/mL) not responsive to antileukemic therapy
- Progressive splenomegaly unresponsive to therapy
- Unexplained fever or bone pain
- Requirement of increased doses of medication
- Documented extramedullary leukemia
- Clonal evolution with new chromosomal changes in addition to the Ph¹ chromosome

Blastic phase chronic myelogenous leukemia
- 30% or more marrow or peripheral blasts
- Extramedullary hematopoiesis with immature blasts

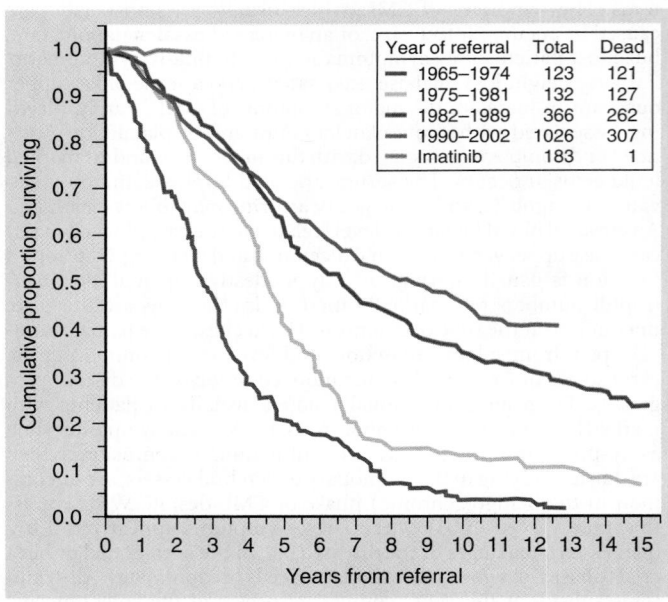

FIGURE 192–2 • Survival of patients with chronic myelogenous leukemia in the chronic phase by year of therapy. (MD Anderson data; patients from 1965 to 2002.)

Year of referral	Total	Dead
1965–1974	123	121
1975–1981	132	127
1982–1989	366	262
1990–2002	1026	307
Imatinib	183	1

causes a normal hemoglobin level and hematocrit value, can manifest with an elevated neutrophil and platelet count. Such patients usually have a normal or increased LAP score, a WBC count less than 25,000/μL, and no Ph[1] chromosome.

The greatest diagnostic difficulty lies with patients who have splenomegaly and leukocytosis but who do not have the Ph[1] chromosome. Many of these patients have the usual blood and marrow findings of Ph[1]-positive CML, and the *BCR/ABL* hybrid gene can be demonstrated despite a normal or atypical cytogenetic pattern. Patients who are Ph[1] negative and *BCR/ABL* negative are considered to have Ph[1]-negative CML or CMML. The cytogenetic findings in patients with CMML are normal or involve an additional chromosome 8 or findings other than the Ph[1] chromosome. Patients with CMML have *ras* mutations in 50 to 60% of cases. Rarely, patients have myeloid hyperplasia, which involves almost exclusively the neutrophil, eosinophil, or basophilic cell lineage. These patients are described as having chronic neutrophilic, eosinophilic, or basophilic leukemia and do not have evidence of the Ph[1] chromosome or *BCR/ABL* gene. Isolated megakaryocytic hyperplasia can give rise to idiopathic thrombocythemia (Chapter 183) with marked thrombocytosis and splenomegaly. These conditions are considered to fall under the general category of myeloproliferative disorders and have a better prognosis than does CML. Some patients who present with clinical characteristics of essential thrombocythemia (with marked thrombocytosis but without marked leukocytosis) actually have CML, with a Ph[1] chromosome and/or the *BCR/ABL* rearrangement (Chapter 183).

Evolution of Chronic Myelogenous Leukemia

Death occurs rarely during the chronic phase of CML, but over time the clinical behavior of the disease changes. One third of patients abruptly develop an acute transformation (blast crisis of CML); the other two thirds respond progressively less well in the control of the WBC count and spleen size with conventional agents such as busulfan and hydroxyurea. This loss of control (accelerated phase) is often associated with an increased proportion of blasts, promyelocytes, and basophils in the peripheral blood and bone marrow and is often accompanied by anemia and thrombocytopenia. Some patients develop bone marrow failure in which anemia and thrombocytopenia are accompanied by increasing evidence of dysplastic changes in the marrow and myelofibrosis. The median survival after developing a blast crisis of CML is only 5 months. The survival after development of the accelerated phase of CML is about 1–2 years if the blood and bone marrow contain more than 30% blasts plus promyelocytes or more than 20% basophils or if the platelet count decreases to less than 100,000/μL. Most patients with blast crisis or accelerated phase have additional chromosomal abnormalities (clonal evolution), such as duplication of the Ph[1] chromosome, trisomy of chromosome 8, or development of an isochromosome 17. Clonal evolution usually presages the accelerated phase or blast crisis of CML. The blast cells in blast crisis are usually myeloblasts, but less commonly erythroid, monocytoid, or megakaryoblastic transformations occur. In one fourth of cases, the blast cells are lymphoid, as demonstrated by cytochemical stains (terminal deoxynucleotidyl transferase), immunophenotyping, and immunoglobulin heavy-chain rearrangement studies. In 10% of cases, the blast cells are completely undifferentiated. Some patients with acute leukemia and the Ph[1] chromosome abnormality presumably have had blast crises that occurred before the diagnosis of CML was made. These cases have the P210 protein and 8.5-kb fusion messenger RNA. Patients with acute lymphoblastic leukemia (ALL) with a Ph[1] chromosome usually have a P190 protein or a 7.0-kb fusion messenger RNA probably restricted to the lymphoid cells. Extramedullary blast crisis of CML can occur in the spleen, lymph nodes, skin, meninges, bone, and other sites. This initial extramedullary transformation is usually shortly followed by evidence of marrow involvement.

CMML and Ph[1]-negative and *BCR/ABL*-negative CML appear to overlap clinically in some instances, and their clinical behavior, progress, and response to therapy resemble those of the myelodysplastic syndromes more than Ph[1]-positive CML (Chapter 182). A male preponderance is noted, splenomegaly is common (60 to 70%), and the WBC count, while elevated, is usually in the 25,000 to 100,000/μL range. Anemia and thrombocytopenia are more common than in Ph[1]-positive CML, and eosinophilia and basophilia are less common. The median survival is 18 to 24 months, with patients dying of infection, bleeding, or transformation to acute leukemia.

 Treatment

Treatment decisions in CML are based on the patient's age and the phase of the disease. Initially, most patients receive cytoreductive therapy with hydroxyurea to provide rapid control of their leukocyte counts. Although busulfan was the first agent shown to provide effective hematologic control in CML, its use should be discouraged except as part of a preparative regimen for allogeneic stem cell transplantation because it is associated with significantly worse survival. Hydroxyurea is an excellent debulking agent, which provides rapid hematologic responses in 50 to 80% of patients, and is an effective adjuvant to more definitive therapies. Cytogenetic responses are rare, however, and hydroxyurea does not significantly modify the natural history of CML. Other palliative strategies include 6-mercaptopurine, 6-thioguanine, cytosine arabinoside, melphalan, and anagrelide. Definitive therapy for patients with CML is divided into transplant and nontransplant alternatives.

NONTRANSPLANT THERAPIES. Single-agent IFN-α has a dose-response effect, but side effects increase with higher doses. Complete hematologic responses occur in 40 to 80% of patients, cytogenetic responses occur in 15 to 58% of patients, and complete cytogenetic responses (undetectable Ph[1]) in 5 to 25% of patients. Median survival ranges from 60 to 90 months, but patients who achieve a complete cytogenetic response have 10-year survival rates of 70 to 80%. In randomized trials, IFN-α has generally provided significantly higher response rates and longer survival than hydroxyurea or busulfan, with most of the benefits noted in lower-risk groups. Randomized trials suggest that the combination of IFN-α plus cytosine arabinoside yields a modest improvement over IFN-α alone.

Imatinib mesylate is revolutionizing the treatment paradigm and prognosis of CML. Early studies in patients with chronic phase CML have shown unprecedented rates of complete cytogenetic responses, but the full impact of such therapy on long-term prognosis remains unknown. However, if the early results persist at long-term follow-up, imatinib will become established as the most effective treatment for CML.

Imatinib is a 2-phenylaminopyrimidine derivative that occupies the kinase pocket of Bcr-Abl, thereby specifically inhibiting the binding site for ATP to the Abl kinase and blocking the phosphorylation of tyrosine residues on substrate protein. Blocking ATP binding inactivates the Abl kinase because it cannot transfer phosphate to its substrate. By inhibiting phosphorylation, imatinib prevents activation of signal transduction pathways that induce leukemic transformation processes that cause CML. Imatinib mesylate inhibits several tyrosine kinases including p210[BCR-ABL], p190[BCR-ABL], v-ABL, c-ABL, c-Kit, and PDGF-R.

Multi-institutional studies of imatinib in patients with chronic phase CML after failure of IFN-α therapy, in patients with accelerated phase CML, and in patients with blastic phase CML have demonstrated its clinical benefits. In patients in chronic phase CML after failure of IFN-α therapy, a 400-mg oral daily dose of imatinib provided major cytogenetic responses in 60% of patients and complete responses in 41%; the estimated 18-month survival rate was 95%. A lower rate of major cytogenetic response was observed in patients with splenomegaly, thrombocytopenia, anemia, longer duration of chronic phase, active disease, clonal evolution, and 100% Ph[1] positivity at the start of therapy. In accelerated phase CML, doses of 400 mg or 600 mg daily yielded hematologic responses in 82% of patients, and complete hematologic responses persisted for at least 4 weeks in 34% of patients; the estimated 12-month progression-free survival and overall survival rates were 59 and 74%, respectively. Compared with 400 mg, the 600 mg daily dose was associated with better cytogenetic responses and longer median survival. In blastic phase CML, patients who received daily doses of 400 to 600 mg of imatinib daily had overall response rates of 40 to 50%,

Continued

but the complete cytogenetic response rate was only 7% and the median survival was just 7 months.

A multinational study randomized 1106 patients with newly diagnosed CML to either imatinib or a combination of IFN-α with cytosine arabinoside.. After 12 months of therapy, imatinib was associated with significantly higher rates of major cytogenetic response (87% versus 35%) and complete cytogenetic response (76% versus 14%), as well as lower rates of progression (8% versus 26%) and transformation (3% versus 9%). Based on these results, imatinib is now considered the standard of care in patients who have CML and are judged not to be suitable for allogeneic stem cell transplantation.

ALLOGENEIC STEM CELL TRANSPLANTATION. Allogeneic stem cell transplantation, which is a potentially curative therapy in selected patients with CML, is most effective during the chronic phase, when it is associated with 3- to 5-year survival rates of 40 to 80% and 10-year survival rates of 30 to 60%. Transplant-related mortality ranges from 5 to 50%, depending on the patient's age, whether the donor is related or unrelated, the degree of matching, the patient's and host's positivity for cytomegalovirus, the preparative and post-transplant regimens, and institutional expertise. Most recent studies report 3- to 5-year survival rates of 50 to 60%, with relapse rates of less than 20%. The risk of relapse plateaus at 5 to 7 years after transplantation. The two most significant factors influencing long-term outcomes are the patient's age and the phase of disease. Disease-free survival rates with related allogeneic stem cell transplantation are 40 to 80% in chronic phase CML, 15 to 40% in accelerated phase CML, and 5 to 20% in blastic phase CML. In chronic phase CML, patients younger than 30 to 40 years of age have disease-free survival rates of 60 to 80% and relapse rates of 20%. By comparison, 5-year survival rates are 30 to 40% in patients older than age 50 years. Toxicity from preparative regimens is observed in 100% of patients (Chapter 166). Acute graft-versus-host disease (GVHD) occurs in 10 to 60% of patients and is the cause of death in 10 to 15%. Chronic GVHD occurs in 75% of patients, and its associated mortality is 10%. A major limitation of allogeneic stem cell transplantation is the availability of related donors. HLA-compatible unrelated donors can be found in about 50% of patients, and the median time from donor search to transplant is 3 to 6 months.

Nonablative preparative regimens (minitransplants) have been developed to expand the indications of allogeneic stem cell transplantation to older patients and to reduce transplant mortality and complications (Chapter 166). Early results in patients not eligible for standard transplant regimens show acceptable degrees of engraftment, less mortality, more persistent residual disease, and perhaps similar degrees of GVHD. The improved results from reduced morbidity and mortality may be offset by the higher incidence of persistent or recurrent disease, which may be responsive to donor lymphocyte infusions, IFN-α, or imatinib mesylate therapy.

TREATMENT OF ACCELERATED AND BLASTIC PHASE CHRONIC MYELOGENOUS LEUKEMIA. Response rates to combination chemotherapy are 20% in nonlymphoid blastic phase CML and 60% in lymphoid blastic phase CML. Median survivals are 3 to 6 and 9 to 12 months, respectively.

Allogeneic stem cell transplantation is the only curative therapy for accelerated and blastic phase CML. Cure rates are in the ranges of 5 to 20%, and 15 to 40%, respectively. Patients with cytogenetic clonal evolution as the only accelerated phase criterion have about a 60% long-term event-free survival with allogeneic stem cell transplantation. Other than allogeneic stem cell transplantation, imatinib is the only approved treatment for accelerated or blastic phase CML. Single-agent imatinib therapy provides good results in accelerated phase CML but not in blastic phase CML (Table 192–2). Patients in accelerated or blastic phases should be encouraged to participate in investigational strategies to improve their prognosis.

SPECIAL THERAPEUTIC CONSIDERATIONS. Patients with severe leukocytosis and leukostatic manifestations may benefit from initial leukapheresis. Severe thrombocytosis uncontrolled with anti-CML measures may respond to anagrelide, thio-TEPA, IFN-α, and leukopheresis. CML during pregnancy may be controlled with pheresis in the first trimester and then with hydroxyurea until delivery. Use of IFN-α during pregnancy has been reported to be safe anecdotally. Little experience exists regarding the use of imatinib during pregnancy. Splenectomy is useful as a palliative measure in patients with massive painful splenomegaly and/or hypersplenism or thrombocytopenia. Splenectomy also may provide palliation in patients with CML in transformation.

Prognosis

The median survival in CML was about 3 years in the 1970s (see Fig. 192–2). With improved therapy and supportive care, the median survival increased to 4 to 5 years with hydroxyurea and to 6 to 7 years with IFN-α. Prognostic models can classify patients into good (30 to 50%), intermediate (30 to 40%), and poor (10 to 20%) risk groups with median survivals of 9 years, 7 years, and 4 to 6 years respectively with modern therapies. Before imatinib therapy was available, the yearly risk of death was 5 to 10% in the first 2 years and 15% subsequently. With allogeneic stem cell transplantation, cures are expected in 40 to 80% of patients in chronic phase CML, in 15 to 40% in accelerated phase CML, and in 5 to 20% in blastic phase CML.

Imatinib therapy has revolutionized the treatment of CML and may have profound favorable prognostic implications that must be

confirmed with longer follow-up (see Table 192–2). However, the estimated 2.5-year mortality with imatinib therapy in chronic phase CML after failure of IFN-α therapy is less than 10% compared with historical annual mortality rates of 15 to 25%. With IFN-α treatment, a complete cytogenetic response was a surrogate marker for excellent long-term survival (80% at 10 years); if the prognostic implications for complete cytogenetic response are similar with imatinib as with IFN-α, the median survival with imatinib therapy in CML might exceed 10 years, with many patients remaining disease-free beyond 10 years.

HAIRY CELL LEUKEMIA

Clinical Manifestations

Hairy cell leukemia (HCL) is uncommon (1 to 2% of all leukemias). The median age at diagnosis is 50 years, and there is a 4:1 male preponderance. Patients have fatigue due to anemia, fever, weight loss, and/or abdominal discomfort produced by splenomegaly. Sometimes the disease is diagnosed when patients have infection secondary to granulocytopenia or monocytopenia. The only consistent physical findings are slight to marked splenomegaly (75 to 80% of cases) caused by massive infiltration of the spleen by hairy cells and slight to moderate hepatomegaly (33% of cases). Clinical lymphadenopathy is very uncommon, although retroperitoneal lymphadenopathy is noted on computed tomography (CT) in 20 to 25% of cases. More than two thirds of patients have anemia (hemoglobin < 10 g/dL), neutropenia (absolute neutrophil count < 1500/μL), thrombocytopenia (platelet count < 100,000/μL), and monocytopenia (absolute monocyte count < 100/μL). The total WBC count is usually lower than 4000/μL at diagnosis, but marked thrombocytopenia is rare. The

Table 192–2 • EARLY RESULTS OF IMATINIB MESYLATE THERAPY IN CHRONIC MYELOGENOUS LEUKEMIA AND COMPARISON TO IFN-α EXPERIENCE

PHASE	CYTOGENETIC RESPONSE		ESTIMATED SURVIVAL
	Complete	Major	
Blastic	7%	11–16%	22–32% at 1 year
Accelerated	17–24%	24–35%	73% at 1.5 years
Chronic, after failure of IFN-α	41–45%	60–62%	95% at 1.5 years
Chronic, newly diagnosed	76%	87%	97% at 1.5 years

cytopenias are due to a combination of bone marrow production failure caused by leukemic infiltration and of hypersplenism. Marrow failure may be due in part to inhibitory factors (e.g., tumor necrosis factor) produced by the leukemic infiltrate, because the pancytopenia is often much more marked than would be anticipated from the degree of leukemic infiltration. During the course of the illness, patients often experience repeated infections and, more rarely, a systemic vasculitis resembling polyarteritis nodosa. Patients also rarely have osteolytic bone lesions, usually affecting the upper femurs. Although gram-positive or gram-negative infections occur as expected with neutropenia, patients with HCL have a predilection to develop tuberculosis, atypical mycobacterial infections, or fungal infections, perhaps related to the severe monocytopenia that is characteristic of this disorder. Pneumonia and septicemia are common causes of death in HCL.

Diagnosis

In conjunction with the described clinical features, examination of the blood often suggests the diagnosis of HCL. In addition to the cytopenias described earlier, the peripheral blood film usually demonstrates relative or absolute lymphocytosis, composed of cells with cytoplasmic projections, giving rise to the name *hairy cell leukemia* (Fig. 192–3). The cytoplasmic projections are best seen using phase contrast or electron microscopy. The hairy cells are 10 to 15 mm in diameter with pale blue cytoplasm and a nucleus with a loose chromatin structure and one or two indistinct nucleoli. Bone marrow aspiration is usually inadequate owing to increased reticulin, collagen, and fibrin deposition; bone marrow biopsy is usually necessary. The biopsy demonstrates increased cellularity with a diffuse or occasionally patchy infiltrate with hairy cells. The infiltrate is loose and spongy, with pale-staining cytoplasm surrounding bland, monotonous round or ovoid nuclei.

Hairy cells exhibit a strong acid phosphatase (isoenzyme 5) cytochemical reaction in 95% of cases, a reaction that is resistant to the inhibitory effect of tartaric acid (TRAP). Other lymphoproliferative diseases are rarely TRAP positive. Electron microscopy exquisitely demonstrates the microvillar projections. Often, ribosomal-lamellar complexes can be identified; these are characteristic, but not diagnostic, of HCL. The peroxidase stain is negative, and lysozyme activity is absent in hairy cells, differentiating the cells from monocytes.

The cell of origin of HCL is the B lymphocyte, as documented by the demonstration of heavy- and light-chain immunoglobulin gene rearrangements. Hairy cells express CD19, CD20, CD11C, CD103, FMC7, and CD22, but not CD21 or CD5. Cell-surface immunoglobulins can be immunoglobulin G (IgG) or immunoglobulin A (IgA), which are rare in chronic lymphocytic leukemia (CLL). The cells demonstrate a κ or λ light-chain phenotype excess. The cells are CD25 (TAC or low-affinity interleukin-2 [IL-2] receptor) positive and anti-HC2 positive, and they are positive for an early plasma cell antigen PCA-1 but not a late plasma cell antigen PC1. These findings suggest that hairy cells are late B lymphocytes or early plasma cells. High levels of soluble IL-2 receptors (more than five times normal) are present in the sera of almost all patients with HCL, with extremely high levels being noted in many cases. Some cases of HCL have a 14q+ cytogenetic abnormality with a breakpoint at 14q32 (the locus

of the Ig heavy chain gene). Hairy cells have a low proliferative index, with fewer than 1% being in the S phase of the cell cycle. Immune dysfunction is wide ranging in HCL. Monocytopenia is universal; B and T lymphocytes are decreased in number; the CD4/CD8 ratio is often inverted; and skin test reactivity to recall antigens is impaired, as is antibody-dependent cellular cytotoxicity. Humoral immunity is relatively preserved with normal immunoglobulin levels. Patients with HCL may have markedly impaired production of IFN-α.

Differential Diagnosis

The differential diagnosis is most difficult between HCL and patients with lymphoma or CLL who have predominant splenomegaly and minimal lymphadenopathy. Some patients with a myelodysplastic or myeloproliferative syndrome have marked splenomegaly and pancytopenia with only a few atypical cells. Patients with other diseases, such as systemic lupus erythematosus and other autoimmune diseases, infiltrative splenomegaly, or tuberculosis, may have splenomegaly and cytopenia, but these diagnoses can usually be made by history, physical examination, and appropriate blood and bone marrow tests. Splenomegaly, cytopenia, and nonaspirable marrow in a male should create a very high index of suspicion for HCL.

Other pathologic conditions to be differentiated from HCL by special tests are HCL variant, splenic lymphoma with villous lymphocytes, B-cell and T-cell prolymphocytic leukemia, and CLL with splenomegaly and no lymphadenopathy. Splenectomy and lymph node biopsy are sometimes necessary to establish the diagnosis in difficult cases. Cases of HCL variant manifest with higher WBC counts, are TRAP negative, have prominent nucleoli, and are only occasionally positive for antibodies against CD25. HCL variant responds poorly to IFN or deoxycoformycin, which are very effective agents in the management of typical HCL.

 ## Treatment

A small proportion (<5%) of patients with HCL do not require therapy. These patients have mild cytopenias, are not transfusion dependent, have no history of infections, and have a low level of marrow infiltration by hairy cells.

Splenectomy, often used in the past as the first treatment of most patients with complications from HCL, temporarily improves blood cell counts in two thirds of patients, usually within 1 to 4 weeks, but does not decrease the infiltration of hairy cells in the marrow or reduce the incidence of infections. Splenectomy is now recommended mainly for patients with splenic infarcts or massive splenomegaly.

2-Chlorodeoxyadenosine (2-CDA), an adenosine analogue that is resistant to deamination by adenosine deaminase, produces complete remissions in more than 90% of HCL patients with a single course of 0.1 mg/kg/day for 7 days by continuous intravenous infusion. Patients for whom previous splenectomy or IFN therapy had failed usually respond to 2-CDA; patients resistant to pentostatin can also respond to 2-CDA. Remissions are durable, and the few patients who experience relapse can attain second remissions after retreatment with 2-CDA. The drug is well tolerated, with a low infection rate. Despite long-lasting suppression of CD4+ lymphocyte counts from 2-CDA, there does not appear to be an increase in late opportunistic infections or second malignancies. The low doses and brief exposure to 2-CDA that are required to treat HCL, and the durability of 2-CDA–induced responses, strongly suggest that this drug is established as the therapy of choice in HCL. An immunotoxin, LMV2 composed of the FC portion of the anti-TAC antibody linked to a pseudomonas exotoxin is effective in patients with refractory HCL. Rituximab has significant activity in patients with relapsed HCL.

Human leukocyte interferon (HuIFN) or r-IFN-α rapidly improves (1 to 3 months) granulocyte, platelet, and hemoglobin levels; reduces spleen size; and consistently decreases marrow infiltration. Peripheral blood cell counts return to normal in 80% of cases, and these patients achieve complete remission (no hairy cells in the marrow) or partial remission (>50% reduction in marrow HCL infiltration). Most patients achieve partial remission by 6 months and complete remission by 12 to 18 months. Lack of response or loss of an initial response may result from the

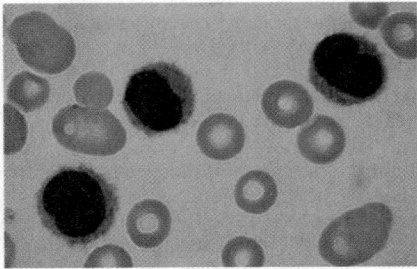

FIGURE 192–3 • Hairy cell leukemia. Peripheral smear shows hairy cells with blue-gray cytoplasm and fine, hairlike projections (resembling ruffles), and oval or slightly indented nuclei with loose chromatin and indistinct nucleoli. (Courtesy of Andrew Schafer, MD.)

Continued

development of neutralizing antibodies to r-IFN-α, especially if the antibody titer is high. When treatment is discontinued, most cases relapse within 1 to 2 years but can respond to retreatment.

Pentostatin, an adenosine deaminase inhibitor, produces complete remissions in 50 to 60% of patients and partial remissions in 40%. The response to treatment is more rapid than for IFN, occurring within 2 to 4 months after the initiation of therapy. Pentostatin is active in patients previously treated with IFN. Responses appear to be more durable than those seen in IFN-treated patients. Toxicity includes nausea and vomiting, infection, renal and hepatic dysfunction, conjunctivitis, and photosensitivity.

Chemotherapy for HCL with alkylating agents, corticosteroids, androgens, and anthracyclines is not effective. Granulocyte colony-stimulating factor (G-CSF) has been reported to correct the granulocytopenia in HCL.

Prognosis

The median survival of patients with HCL before IFN therapy was available was 2 to 3 years. A return to normal leukocyte counts in HCL diminishes the risk of infection and is certain to improve the survival of patients with HCL. More than 90% of patients treated with interferon, 2-CDA, or pentostatin are projected to be alive at 5 years.

CHRONIC LYMPHOCYTIC LEUKEMIA

CLL is a neoplasm characterized by accumulation of monoclonal lymphocytes, usually of B-cell immunophenotype (>95% of cases) and rarely of T-cell immunophenotype. The cells accumulate in the bone marrow, lymph nodes, liver, spleen, and occasionally other organs. CLL is the most common leukemia (one third of all cases) in the Western world and is twice as common as CML. The disease occurs rarely in those younger than 30 years of age; most patients with CLL are older than age 60 years. CLL increases in incidence exponentially with age; by age 80 the incidence rate is 20 cases per 100,000 persons per year. The male:female ratio is approximately 2:1. Asians in Japan and China have an incidence of CLL only 10% of that in the United States and other Western countries. Intermediate incidence rates are seen in persons of Hispanic origin.

Etiology

The cause of CLL is unknown. Ionizing radiation and viruses have not been associated with CLL, although recently hepatitis C infection has been associated with splenic lymphoma with villous lymphocytes (a variant of B-cell CLL). Familial clustering in CLL is more common than in other leukemias; first-degree relatives of patients have a two- to four-fold higher risk and develop CLL at a younger age than does the general population (anticipation). Farmers have a higher incidence of CLL than do those in other occupations, raising the question of the possible etiologic role of herbicides or pesticides. No definite leukemogenic role of chemicals, including benzene, has been established for CLL. Approximately half of the patients with CLL have hypermutation of the Ig heavy chain sequences. Patients with mutated Vh genes usually have a low expression of CD38, whereas unmutated genes have higher expression of CD38. Both mutated Vh genes and CD38 expression in CLL cells are associated with indolent disease with a favorable prognosis.

Pathogenesis

Leukemia cells in CLL are usually remarkably homogeneous. The cells express low-intensity monoclonal surface immunoglobulin (SmIg, usually immunoglobulin M [IgM] ± immunoglobulin D [IgD]) of a single κ or λ light chain phenotype. A number of patients with CLL have SmIg molecules that cross-react with IgM rheumatoid factor paraprotein. CLL cells are early B cells and have lost terminal deoxynucleotidyl transferase activity. The CLL cells express the pan-B cell antigens CD19, CD20, CD23, and CD24 in almost all cases and CD21 (which includes the receptor for the Epstein-Barr virus and the C3D component of complement) in more than 75% of cases. The C3B complement component receptor is expressed in fewer than 20% of cases.

Almost all cells exhibit Ia antigen, receptors for the Fc fragment of IgG, and spontaneously form rosettes with mouse erythrocytes. In 95% of cases, the CLL cells coexpress pan-B cell antigens and CD5 (Leu 1, T1, and T101), a pan-T cell antigen. Other T-cell antigens and common acute lymphocytic leukemia antigen (CD10) are absent. CD25 (TAC, IL-2 receptor) antigen is positive in more than 20% of cells in 20% of cases. Monoclonality of the B cells is demonstrated by marked preponderance of κ or λ light chains, evidence of immunoglobulin gene rearrangement, the presence of monoclonal serum Ig peaks in some cases, and by G6PD isoenzyme studies.

CLL is an accumulative rather than a proliferative disease, because the CLL cells have a low proliferative index. Patients with higher WBC counts and more advanced stages have higher proliferative indices and shorter survivals. Most of the CLL cells in the blood and bone marrow are in the G_0 phase of the cell cycle, with only a small proportion of larger cells in the marrow and lymph nodes being in the other phases. The CLL cells have a longer lifespan in the blood than do normal B cells and have impaired egress from the blood. The CLL B cells have impaired responses to B-cell mitogens and to B-cell growth factors. The cells appear to be blocked in differentiation, with a high content of cytoplasmic IgM but a low surface IgM. Although most of the cells do not secrete immunoglobulins, in about 5% of cases a paraprotein similar to that on the surface of the CLL cells is present in the plasma or urine. The stimulatory effect of the CLL cells is low or absent in allogeneic or autologous mixed lymphocyte cultures. The CLL cells can be stimulated to differentiate into cells resembling hairy cells or plasma cells under the influence of phorbol esters, B-cell mitogens, or growth factors.

T-cell function is invariably abnormal in CLL. T cells are increased in number in the blood, bone marrow, and lymph nodes of patients with CLL at diagnosis; but they are usually polyclonal, and T-cell receptor gene rearrangement is rare. The CD4/CD8 (T-helper/T-suppressor) ratio is often close to unity or is inverted owing to a relatively greater increase in the CD8-positive cells. The T cells have a blunted response to T-cell mitogens in unseparated blood and decreased delayed hypersensitivity reactions to recall antigens. The T-cell defects worsen as the disease progresses to a more advanced stage. Purified T cells have a normal response to T-cell mitogens.

Genetics

Nonrandom cytogenetic abnormalities in CLL include trisomy 12 (40%), 14q+ abnormalities (25%), and abnormalities in the long arm of chromosomes 6, 11, and 13. Single abnormalities are more common in early and recently diagnosed cases, and additional changes develop with time (clonal evolution). The site of the breakpoint on chromosome 14 (q32) is close to the site of the Ig heavy chain gene. Recent molecular and fluorescent in situ hybridization (FISH) studies suggest that deletion of genetic material from chromosome 13q14 occurs in two thirds of the cases. Deletions of chromosome material from 11q and 17p are associated with a poor prognosis. It is probable that deletion of a tumor suppressor gene occurs in association with loss of genetic material from chromosome 13q14.

Clinical Manifestations

Most patients with CLL are asymptomatic, and the disease is diagnosed when absolute lymphocytosis is noted in the peripheral blood (Fig. 192–4) during evaluation for other illnesses or when the patient undergoes a routine physical examination. Symptoms such as fatigue, lethargy, loss of appetite, weight loss, or reduced exercise tolerance are nonspecific. These features, especially fatigue, are occasionally greater than can be explained by the degree of anemia or extent of tumor burden. Many patients have enlarged lymph nodes (usually cervical) noted by themselves or others. Fever, night sweats, and documented infections are uncommon initial symptoms (<5%) but become more prominent as the disease progresses. Sinopulmonary infections occur during the early phases of the disease; but as the disease progresses, the frequency of neutropenia, T-cell deficiency, and hypogammaglobulinemia increases, resulting in gram-negative bacterial, fungal, and viral infections such as herpes zoster or herpes simplex. Cytomegalovirus infections usually occur later in the disease, especially after treatment with purine analogues or alemtuzumab, which deplete T cells.

The major physical findings relate to infiltration of the reticuloendothelial system. Lymphadenopathy with discrete, rubbery, mobile lymph nodes is present in two thirds of patients at diagnosis (Chapter 164). Later, as the lymph nodes enlarge, they can become matted. Enlargement of the liver or spleen is less common at diagnosis (approximately 10 and 40% of cases, respectively). Less commonly, and usually late in the disease, clinically significant infiltration of skin, eyelids, heart, lungs, pleura, or gastrointestinal tract may occur, suggesting MALT or mantle cell leukemia. Organ failure resulting from infiltration with CLL is uncommon, with pulmonary symptoms being most likely to cause clinical problems. Infiltration of the central nervous system in CLL is rare, and central nervous system symptoms are more likely to be due to opportunistic infections, such as cryptococcosis or listeriosis. The extent of involvement varies from only a single node or node group to enlargement of virtually all nodes. Later in the disease, massive adenopathy may develop and cause luminal obstruction, such as obstructive jaundice, obstructive uropathy, dysphagia, or partial bowel obstruction. Unilateral or bilateral leg edema can occur, owing to obstruction of the lymphatic and/or venous systems. Pleural effusions and ascites can also develop and are associated with a poor prognosis.

Diagnosis

CLL is characterized by absolute lymphocytosis in the peripheral blood—a minimal level of more than 5000/μL, but more usually in the range of 25,000 to 150,000/μL. Extreme leukocytosis approaching 1×10^6/μL occurs late in the disease, but hyperviscosity symptoms seldom occur unless the WBC count is higher than 500,000/μL. If the lymphocyte count is 5000 to 15,000/μL, supportive evidence for clonality (κ or λ light chain excess or immunoglobulin gene rearrangement) should be present before the diagnosis is made. Most physicians also document lymphocytosis in the bone marrow (>30% lymphocytes) and perform a bone marrow biopsy. Anemia (hemoglobin < 11 g/dL) is present in 15 to 20% of patients at diagnosis and

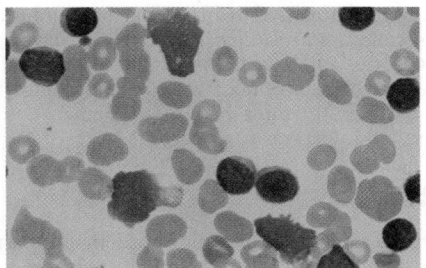

FIGURE 192–4 • Chronic lymphocytic leukemia. Peripheral smear shows that the predominant leukocytes are "normal" mature-appearing lymphocytes, with occasional "smudge" cells. (Courtesy of Andrew Schafer, MD.)

thrombocytopenia (platelet count < 100,000/μL) in 10%. Both bone marrow replacement and hypersplenism contribute to the anemia and thrombocytopenia in most cases. The anemia is usually normochromic and normocytic, and the reticulocyte count is normal unless the patient has autoimmune hemolytic anemia, which usually results from the development of a warm-reacting IgG antibody (Chapter 169). The diagnosis of autoimmune hemolytic anemia, which occurs in the course of 8 to 10% of cases, is confirmed by a positive direct Coombs' test (80 to 90% of cases), reticulocytosis, a low serum haptoglobulinemia, and an elevated unconjugated serum bilirubin level. In such patients, reactive erythroid hyperplasia as a response to the hemolysis may be masked in the bone marrow by the marked lymphocytic infiltration. Cold agglutinin hemolysis occurs rarely in CLL. Autoimmune thrombocytopenia (immune thrombocytopenic purpura [ITP]) can be diagnosed in some cases with a positive test for platelet antibodies (Chapter 177). The antibodies causing the red cell and platelet destruction are not produced by the CLL cells, and the mechanism for the autoimmune diseases is not known. Pure red cell aplasia associated with T-suppressor cell activity is an additional underappreciated cause of anemia in CLL.

The lymphocytes in CLL are indistinguishable on light or electron microscopy from normal small B lymphocytes. On bone marrow aspiration, the proportion of lymphocytes is greater than 30% and may extend up to 100% in patients with newly diagnosed CLL. The remainder of the cells are normal myeloid and erythroid cells. Four patterns of lymphocyte infiltration on bone marrow biopsy occur and have prognostic value in CLL: (1) nodular (15%), (2) interstitial (30%), (3) mixed nodular and interstitial (30%), and (4) diffuse (35%). Most early stage cases have patterns 1, 2, or 3; diffuse histology is most common in advanced stage disease and becomes more prominent as the disease evolves. Only a diffuse histologic pattern confers a poor prognosis regardless of the stage of disease. Hypogammaglobulinemia is common in CLL and predisposes to infections, especially with encapsulated microorganisms. Low levels of IgG, IgA, or IgM occur in 25% of newly diagnosed patients, are more common in advanced stages, and increase in frequency to 50 to 70% as the disease progresses.

Staging

Two major clinical staging systems are used. The Rai staging system (1975) defines five stages and is most frequently used in the United States, whereas the Binet system (1981) defines three stages and is most frequently used in Europe (Table 192–3). Both systems have the advantage of simplicity, low cost, and reproducibility, and both have been prospectively validated. Within the stages, outcome is variable; other prognostic factors, such as the bone marrow histologic pattern, provide additional prognostic information. Patients with anemia and thrombocytopenia (Rai stages III and IV, Binet C) have, on the average, a poor prognosis; patients with lymphocytosis alone (Rai 0, some Binet A patients) have an excellent prognosis. The prognosis of the other patients is heterogeneous and, as might be expected, is worse in patients with a greater tumor burden. Rai stage II patients who have splenomegaly without lymphadenopathy (pure splenic form) have a better prognosis than do other stage II patients. Although useful

Table 192–3 • RAI AND BINET STAGING SYSTEMS IN CHRONIC LYMPHOCYTIC LEUKEMIA

	LYMPHOCYTOSIS	LYMPHADENOPATHY	HEPATOMEGALY OR SPLENOMEGALY	HEMOGLOBIN (g/dL)	PLATELETS × 10³/μL
Rai stage					
0	+	−	−	≥11	≥100
I	+	+	−	≥11	≥100
II	+	±	+	≥11	≥100
III	+	±	±	<11	≥100
IV	+	±	±	Any	<100
Binet stage					
A	+	±	± (<3 Lymphatic groups* positive)	≥10	≥100
B	+	±	± (≥3 Lymphatic groups* positive)	≥10	≥100
C	+	±	±	<10 and/or	<100

*(1) Cervical, axillary, and inguinal nodes; (2) liver; and (3) spleen; each group is considered one group whether unilateral or bilateral.

in the design and analysis of clinical trials, the staging systems are not particularly useful for individual patients because of the heterogeneity of outcome. A group of patients with a lymphocyte count of less than 30,000/µL, hemoglobin higher than 11 g/dL, platelet count higher than 100,000/µL, fewer than three involved node areas, and lymphocyte doubling time of greater than 12 months has been described as having "smoldering" CLL, with a survival equal to that of an age- and sex-matched population. Some studies suggest that serum levels of β_2-microglobulin, thymidine kinase, and soluble CD23 are more strongly predictive for prognosis than stage.

Patients tend to progress through stages, with many patients developing more sites of involvement with time and eventually experiencing marrow failure, but anemia and thrombocytopenia can develop abruptly even without antibody-mediated destruction or increasing tumor burden.

Differential Diagnosis

Many diseases can cause lymphocytosis: pertussis, infectious lymphocytosis, cytomegalovirus, Epstein-Barr virus mononucleosis, tuberculosis, toxoplasmosis, chronic inflammatory disorders, and autoimmune syndromes. Although these conditions may superficially resemble CLL, their clinical pictures are seldom confused with that of B-cell CLL. Many of these patients are younger, have fever or other acute symptoms, or exhibit other clinical features, such as rash and joint symptoms, that are uncommon in CLL. The lymphocytosis (usually <15,000/µL) is not sustained. If doubt persists, immunophenotype or molecular studies distinguish the monoclonal lymphocytosis in CLL from the polyclonal B cell proliferation in the other disorders.

The more difficult differential diagnosis is from other lymphoproliferative disorders, such as *prolymphocytic leukemia* (PLL), splenic lymphoma with villous lymphocytes, HCL, the leukemic phase of mantle cell lymphoma, Waldenström's macroglobulinemia, and T-cell CLL. Whereas certain clinical features are more common in some of these disorders (e.g., marked splenomegaly with minimal or no lymphadenopathy in prolymphocytic leukemia, splenic lymphoma and HCL versus extensive lymphadenopathy with or without splenomegaly in CLL), none of these clinical features is specific. The differential diagnosis therefore depends largely on histopathologic and, more specifically, immunophenotypic features (Table 192–4).

PLL is an uncommon disease (<5% of the incidence of CLL) and its characteristics of massive splenomegaly, minimal lymphadenopathy, and WBC count commonly more than 100,000/µL, with 10 to 90% of the cells being prolymphocytes, distinguish this disease from typical B-cell CLL. Prolymphocytes are larger cells than typical CLL lymphocytes; they have a distinct nucleolus and are often FMC-7 positive. The male:female ratio is 4:1, and the median age at diagnosis is 70 years. Survival is shorter than in CLL (median, 3 years), and response to therapies usually applied in CLL is poor. A monoclonal spike, usually IgG or IgA, is present in one third of cases. The immunoglobulin on the surface of the cells is occasionally IgG or IgA, not IgM ± IgD, as in CLL. Several karyotypic abnormalities have been reported in PLL,

including t(11;14) (q13;q32). Deletions of 11q3, 23, and 17p are more common in B-cell PLL than CLL. P53 abnormalities are found in 75% of B-cell PLL. One fifth of the cases of PLL are of T-cell phenotype.

Small lymphocytic lymphoma (SLL) shares histopathologic and immunophenotypic features with CLL, differing only in lacking absolute monoclonal lymphocytosis in the peripheral blood (Chapter 195). The bone marrow in SLL may or may not have more than 30% lymphocytes. LFA-1 adhesion protein is much more commonly expressed on SLL cells than CLL cells. Occasionally, other lymphomas, such as follicular small cleaved cell lymphoma (FSCCL) and mantle cell lymphoma, manifest a leukemic phase on initial presentation. These cells are often cleaved on light microscopy, have bright staining for SmIg, and are commonly FMC-7 and CD10 positive. Lymph node biopsy should be performed to identify these cases with greater precision. The presence of lymphoma cells in the blood in SLL and FSCCL is more common later in the disease. FSCLL can usually be identified by the presence of the translocation t(14;18) on cytogenetic analysis and consequent *bcl*-2 rearrangement, both of which are rare in CLL. The WBC count in Waldenström's macroglobulinemia (Chapter 196) at diagnosis is usually much lower than in CLL (<10,000/µL), and many patients are leukopenic. The cells have a plasmacytoid appearance, CD38 and PCA-1 positivity, and more SmIg and cytoplasmic Ig. A monoclonal IgM plasma peak is present in almost all cases of Waldenström's macroglobulinemia, common in splenic lymphoma, but rare in CLL.

The predominant clinical manifestation in *Sézary's syndrome* (a CD4+ T-cell malignant disorder related to mycosis fungoides; see Chapter 474) is chronic exfoliative erythroderma with a low number of circulating monoclonal T cells. The clinical and laboratory differential diagnosis from CLL is not difficult. Other T-cell malignant disorders with peripheral blood involvement are *adult T-cell leukemia-lymphoma* and *large granular lymphocytosis* (LGL), also referred to as *large granular lymphoproliferative disorder, T-cell lymphocytosis with neutropenia*, or *T-gamma lymphocytosis syndrome*. Adult T-cell leukemia-lymphoma is associated with a retrovirus (human T-cell leukemia-lymphoma virus [HTLV-I]) and is common in Japan and the Caribbean. It is frequently manifested by lytic bone lesions and hypercalcemia. In T-LGL the absolute lymphocyte count is usually low (<5000/µL), with a CD2+, CD3+, CD8+, and CD16+ (T-suppressor) phenotype (T-gamma cells). These patients often have splenomegaly, neutropenia, and rheumatoid arthritis–like symptoms and serology. Some tumors, called *natural killer* (NK) *cell LGL*, have a natural killer phenotype (CD16–) and have no molecular evidence of T-cell receptor rearrangement. The lymphocytes have abundant cytoplasm with azurophilic granules. In most patients, a benign course is noted, although repeated infections can occur.

Prognostic Factors

In addition to the impact of tumor burden and marrow function on prognosis, as reflected in the Rai and Binet staging systems, other adverse factors include a diffuse pattern of lymphocytic infiltration observed on bone marrow biopsy; an abnormal karyotype (e.g.,

Table 192–4 • DIFFERENTIAL DIAGNOSIS OF INDOLENT LYMPHOPROLIFERATIVE DISORDERS

DISEASE	LYMPHADENOPATHY (%)	SPLENOMEGALY (%)	CELL OF ORIGIN (B/T)	POSITIVE MARKERS*			
				SmIg	CD5	CD19,20 (%)	Other Positives
Chronic lymphocytic leukemia (CLL)	75	50	B (20:1)	Weak	>90%	≥90	Mouse red blood cell (RBC) receptors
Prolymphocytic leukemia (PLL)	33	95	B (4:1)	Bright	T cell PLL	75	FMC-7
Hairy cell leukemia	<10	80	B (T rare)	Bright	—	>90	CD25, CD11C, CD103
Lymphoma (leukemic phase)	90	90	B (T rare)	Bright	Some	>90	CD10
Splenic lymphoma with villous lymphocytes	10	80	B	Bright	20%	>90	FMC-7, CD22
Waldenström's macroglobulinemia	33	33	All B	Weak	Some	Many	CD38, PCA-1
Large granular lymphocytosis	10	10	All T	Absent	—	—	CD2, CD3, CD8

*CD5—pan T cell, B CLL; CD19—early pan B cell; CD20—pan B cell; FMC-7—PLL and hairy cell; CD2—pan T cell; CD3—pan mature T cell; CD8—T cell (suppressor cytotoxic); CD10—early B cell; CD11C—hairy cell, activated T cell, NK cell; CD38—activated B cell, thymocyte, plasma cell; PCA-1—plasma cell; CD25—low-affinity interleukin-2 (IL-2) receptor.

deletion of 11q or 17p or multiple chromosomal abnormalities); advanced age; male sex; elevated serum levels of thymidine kinase, β_2-microglobulin, soluble CD23, uric acid, alkaline phosphatase, or lactate dehydrogenase; rapid lymphocyte doubling time; and an increased proportion of large or atypical lymphocytes in the peripheral blood. A poor response to therapy is an adverse factor in all phases of the disease. As the disease progresses, a worsening of stage and the development of a prolymphocytic transformation (10% of cases), large cell lymphoma, or myelomatous or acute lymphocytic leukemia (rare) are grave prognostic features. Multiple chromosomal abnormalities identify patients at risk of developing a large cell lymphomatous transformation (Richter's syndrome), which occurs in 5 to 10% of CLL patients as a terminal event. Richter's syndrome should be suspected whenever a single lymph node area or the spleen begins to enlarge in CLL or when unexplained clinical deterioration occurs. The transformation does not always share immunophenotypic or cytogenetic features with the original CLL clone and may be a coincidental second tumor. Most sites of large cell lymphomatous transformation are gallium avid on gallium whole body scanning and most are positive on positron-emission tomography scan. Response to therapy in Richter's transformation is not as satisfactory as for de novo large cell lymphoma.

A high incidence of second malignant tumors (10 to 20% of patients) either precedes or follows the diagnosis of CLL, with the roles of therapy versus impaired immune surveillance as causative factors being unclear. Skin cancer, including melanoma, colorectal and lung cancers, and sarcomas are common in patients with CLL. Hypogammaglobulinemia may have an adverse impact on survival. Patients who develop repeated infections fare less well than other patients.

CLL tends to develop in elderly patients; in indolent cases, death often occurs from other intercurrent illnesses of this age group. Patients younger than 60 years of age and patients with progressive disease almost all die as a result of CLL or one of its complications, especially infections. Gram-positive organisms usually cause nonfatal infections early in CLL, but most deaths due to infection are associated with gram-negative bacterial or fungal infections. Infection with other opportunistic organisms, such as *Mycobacterium tuberculosis,* herpesvirus, and *Pneumocystis carinii,* may also be fatal.

Rx Treatment

The major therapeutic questions for CLL are when to treat and which therapeutic regimens to use.

WHEN TO TREAT. Patients with CLL are usually elderly, and the prognosis of the disease is variable (with some early stage cases being stable for 5 to 20 years). Treatment of early stage CLL (Rai 0, Binet A) is delayed until the disease progresses. Early treatment with alkylating agents does not prolong survival and may be associated with a heightened risk of developing second malignant tumors. Treatment of Rai stages III and IV (Binet stage C) is recommended at the time of diagnosis because of the poor survival of these patients (median, 3 years). Treatment of intermediate-stage disease (Rai stages I and II, Binet stage B) is recommended if symptomatic disease (fever, sweats, weight loss, severe fatigue), massive lymphadenopathy, or hepatosplenomegaly is present. Progressive organ and/or node enlargement and lymphocytosis (>100,000/µL) are other common indications for treatment. Development of anemia, thrombocytopenia, or neutropenia associated with infections is usually an indication for systemic antileukemic therapy unless an autoimmune cause of the cytopenia (positive direct Coombs' test, antiplatelet or antineutrophil antibodies) is found. In the latter group of cases, the use of corticosteroids, such as prednisone, should be tried before the initiation of cytotoxic therapy. A doubling of blood lymphocytes in less than 12 months is an adverse prognostic factor and suggests that treatment is indicated.

CHEMOTHERAPY. Chlorambucil (less commonly, cyclophosphamide) is often the first chemotherapeutic agent used. Corticosteroids are often used concurrently, but with no clearly demonstrated advantage in therapeutic response or survival. Chlorambucil regimens vary widely. In the long-term low-dose daily regimen, 0.1 to 0.2 mg/kg/day of chlorambucil is continued for 3 to 6 weeks until the desired effect is obtained or until thrombocytopenia or neutropenia develops. The dose is then adjusted for maintenance and is continued for 6 to 12 months. For intermittent high-dose (pulse) schedules, chlorambucil (0.5 to 2 mg/kg, total dose) is given over 1 to 4 days every 4 weeks or at half dose every 2 weeks. No dosage schedule for chlorambucil has been established as being superior. If prednisone is given concurrently with chlorambucil, the dose is 60 to 100 mg/day in a pulse schedule. Continuous prednisone is not recommended in this elderly population but can be given at a dose of 40 to 60 mg/day for 4 weeks initially, tapering to 10 to 20 mg/day when combined with chlorambucil in the continuous therapy schedule. Myelosuppression is the most common toxicity with chlorambucil, although occasionally rash, nausea, or pulmonary toxicity occurs. After therapy, the condition of many patients remains stable for months to years before disease progression indicates the need for further treatment. The end points for response to therapy have not been well defined, because treatment is usually strictly palliative. Most physicians try to achieve the disappearance of lymphadenopathy and splenomegaly. The WBC count often returns to normal but the bone marrow usually does not (Table 192–5).

Fludarabine monophosphate and 2-CDA, both adenosine analogues, and pentostatin (deoxycoformycin), an adenosine deaminase inhibitor, have exhibited striking therapeutic efficacy in CLL. Fludarabine monophosphate (25 mg/m²/day for 5 days every 4 weeks) leads to complete remission in 25% of untreated patients and 10% of those previously treated with alkylating agents. The dose-limiting toxicity is myelosuppression. The course of therapy may be complicated by infections with organisms usually associated with immunodeficiency syndromes involving T lymphocytes (e.g., those caused by *P. carinii* or herpes viruses). When compared with chlorambucil, fludarabine currently provides a higher complete remission rate, longer remission duration, improved salvage rate on crossover, but no demonstrated survival advantage. ▨ 2-CDA delivers similar results with a lower complete remission rate and more myelosuppression. Deoxycoformycin has not been as widely studied in CLL as in HCL.

The COP regimen (cyclophosphamide, 100 to 300 mg/m²/day given orally on days 1 through 5; vincristine [Oncovin], 2 mg given intravenously on day 1; and prednisone, 100 mg administered orally on days 1 through 5) does not have any advantage over chlorambucil. Regimens using cyclophosphamide, doxorubicin (Adriamycin), and prednisone with vincristine (CHOP) or without vincristine (CAP) have produced response rates of 50 to 70% in previously untreated patients with Binet stage C disease and are well tolerated in CLL despite the advanced age of most patients but do not prolong survival when compared to chlorambucil or fludarabine.

Corticosteroids, usually prednisone (60 to 100 mg/day), are indicated as treatment for Coombs-positive autoimmune hemolytic anemia and for some cases of immune-mediated thrombocytopenia (ITP) in CLL. If there is no response in 3 to 4 weeks, the treatment has failed, and the dose should then be tapered over 1 to 2 weeks. If a response is obtained, the dose is usually reduced by 25% each week over 4 weeks. Patients in whom corticosteroids fail usually respond well to splenectomy and sometimes to intravenous therapy with high doses of immunoglobulin, cyclosporine, or rituximab. Autoimmune hemolytic anemia and immune-mediated thrombocytopenia do not correlate closely with the activity of CLL. Intravenous immunoglobulin (400 mg/kg every 3 to 4 weeks) significantly decreases the incidence of infections of minor to moderate severity in CLL patients with hypogammaglobulinemia, but the cost of this therapy is substantial. Although ineffective in patients with advanced-stage CLL, IFN-α may significantly decrease the lymphocyte count in 50 to 70% of early stage cases.

RADIATION THERAPY. In CLL, radiation therapy is usually restricted to external irradiation of localized nodal masses or an enlarged spleen that has been refractory to chemotherapy. Repeated leukapheresis and extracorporeal irradiation of blood can decrease the tumor burden in CLL and occasionally increase hemoglobin and platelet levels but are not practical for long periods.

Continued

Table 192–5 • DEFINITION OF REMISSION IN CLL: COMPARISON OF THE INTERNATIONAL WORKSHOP IN CLL (IWCLL) AND THE NATIONAL CANCER INSTITUTE WORKING GROUP (NCI-WG) CRITERIA

| | COMPLETE REMISSION | | PARTIAL REMISSION | |
CRITERIA	IWCLL	NCI-WG	IWCLL	NCI-WG
Physical examination				
Nodes	None	None	Shift to a lower Binet stage, e.g., C → A, or B, B → A	≥50% decrease
Liver/spleen	Not palpable	Not palpable		≥50% decrease
Symptoms	None	None		N/A
Peripheral blood				
Neutrophils	≥1500/μL	≥1500/μL		≥1500/μL or ≥50% ↑ from baseline
Platelets	>100,000/μL	>100,000/μL		100,000/μL or ≥50% ↑ from baseline
Hemoglobin	Not specified	>11 g/dL		>11 g/dL or >50% ↑ from baseline
Lymphocytes	<4000/μL	≤4000/μL		>50% decrease
Bone marrow	Normal aspirate and biopsy*			N/A
Lymphocytes		<30%		N/A

*Nodules or focal aggregates of lymphocytes are compatible with complete remission in IWCLL, not NCI-WG.

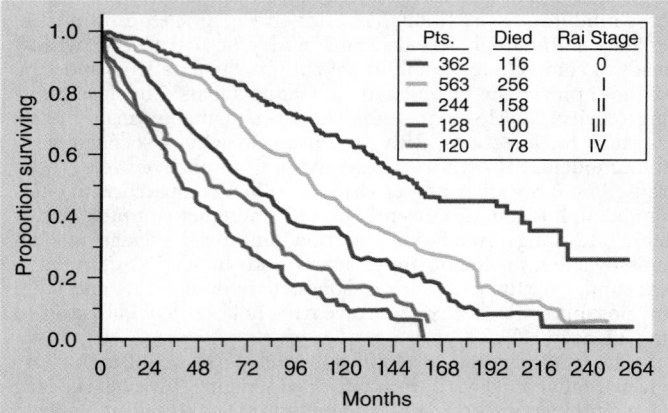

FIGURE 192–5 • Survival of untreated patients with chronic lymphocytic leukemia by Rai stage.

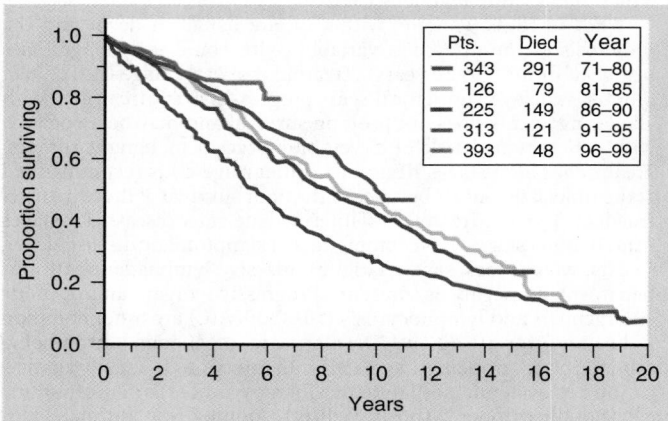

FIGURE 192–6 • Survival of untreated patients with chronic lymphocytic leukemia by time period.

MONOCLONAL ANTIBODIES. Rituximab, a monoclonal antibody directed against CD20, kills CLL by complement lysis, antibody-dependent cellular cytotoxicity, and signal transduction. With conventional doses of 375 mg/m² per week for 4 weeks, the response rate in CLL is 15 to 20%. Higher doses or three times a week schedules are associated with response rates of 40 to 60%. Alemtuzumab (Campath-1H) is a monoclonal antibody directed against CD52. This antigen is present on the surface of the cells of all patients with CLL as well as on normal B and T lymphocytes. Alemtuzumab is extremely active in CLL and has been approved for the management of patients with fludarabine-refractory CLL; one third of such patients can achieve a remission on alemtuzumab. Combinations of these antibodies have been explored and appear to have additive activity.

Rituximab increases the cytotoxicity of a number of chemotherapeutic agents in cell culture. Combinations of fludarabine with or without cyclophosphamide provide very high complete remission rates as initial and salvage therapy in CLL. Rituximab has been combined with fludarabine as simultaneous or sequential therapy in CLL. Simultaneous therapy has resulted in a higher complete response rate than sequential therapy. These combinations are likely to become the new standard of treatment for CLL.

BONE MARROW TRANSPLANTATION. Autologous BMT has been explored as consolidation therapy in CLL patients who have achieved a very good response in the bone marrow. The time-to-treatment failure is prolonged with autologous transplant without any evidence that there is an improvement in survival or long-term disease control. Allogeneic BMTs with full cytoreductive approaches have been explored in patients younger than age 65 years, with a 40 to 50% long-term control rate. Nonablative stem cell transplants have been applied to patients with CLL with success. These transplants can be undertaken in patients up to 70 years of age. The graft-versus-leukemia effect is the major antileukemic action and appears to be able to achieve long-term disease control.

Gene therapy approaches and DNA vaccine trials are under way, as are tests of other new drugs. None of these modalities is established as effective therapies for CLL at this time.

Prognosis

The median survival of patients with CLL is 4 to 5 years after initiation of treatment. As expected, patients with early stage cases (Rai 0 to II) survive significantly longer, a median of 7 to 8 years (Fig. 192–5). There appears to be an improvement in survival over recent years (Fig. 192–6). Whether this is due to better diagnosis, improved supportive care, or improved treatment is not certain.

1. O'Brien SG, Guilhot F, Larson RA, et al: Imatinib compared with interferon and low-dose cytarabine for newly diagnosed chronic-phase chronic myeloid leukemia. N Engl J Med 2003;348:994–1004.

2. Rai KR, Peterson BL, Appelbaum FR, et al: Fludarabine compared with chlorambucil as primary therapy for chronic lymphocytic leukemia. N Engl J Med 2000:343:1750–1757.

3. Byrd JC, Peterson BL, Morrison VA, et al: Randomized phase 2 study of fludarabine with concurrent versus sequential treatment with rituximab in symptomatic, untreated patients with B-cell chronic lymphocytic leukemia: Results from Cancer and Leukemia Group B 9712 (CALGB 9712). Blood 2003;101:6–14.

SUGGESTED READINGS

Druker BJ, Talpaz M, Resta DJ, et al: Efficacy and safety of a specific inhibitor of the BCR-ABL tyrosine kinase in chronic myeloid leukemia. N Engl J Med 2001;344:1031–1037. *First study demonstrating efficacy of imatinib in chronic phase CML.*

Kantarjian H, Sawyers C, Hochhaus A, et al: Hematologic and cytogenetic responses to imatinib mesylate in chronic myelogenous leukemia. N Engl J Med 2002;346:645–652. *Imatinib in chronic phase CML induced high rates of complete cytogenetic response and survival.*

Krober A, Seiler T, Benner A, et al: V_H mutation status, CD38 expression level, genomic aberrations, and survival in chronic lymphocytic leukemia. Blood 2002;100:1410–1416. *Influence of cytogenetics on prognosis.*

Kurzrock R, Kantarjian HM, Druker BJ, et al: Philadelphia chromosome-positive leukemias: From basic mechanisms to molecular therapeutics. Ann Intern Med 2003;138:819–830. *The function of Bcr-Abl and its normal counterparts (Bcr and Abl), and their impact on the development of targeted therapy.*

193 THE ACUTE LEUKEMIAS

Frederick R. Appelbaum

Definition

Normal hematopoiesis requires tightly regulated proliferation and differentiation of pluripotent hematopoietic stem cells that become mature peripheral blood cells. Acute leukemia is the result of a malignant event or events occurring in an early hematopoietic precursor. Instead of proliferating and differentiating normally, the affected cell gives rise to progeny that fail to differentiate and instead continue to proliferate in an uncontrolled fashion. As a result, immature myeloid cells (in acute myeloid leukemia [AML]) or lymphoid cells (in acute lymphoblastic leukemia [ALL]), often called *blasts*, rapidly accumulate and progressively replace the bone marrow; diminished production of normal red cells, white cells, and platelets ensues. This loss of normal marrow function in turn gives rise to the common clinical complications of leukemia: anemia, infection, and bleeding. With time, the leukemic blasts pour out into the blood stream and eventually occupy the lymph nodes, spleen, and other vital organs. If untreated, acute leukemia is rapidly fatal; most patients die within several months of diagnosis. With appropriate therapy, the natural history of acute leukemia can be markedly altered, and many patients can be cured.

Etiology

In most cases, acute leukemia develops for no known reason, but sometimes a possible cause can be identified.

RADIATION. Ionizing radiation (Chapter 19) is leukemogenic. ALL, AML, and chronic myelogenous leukemia (CML) are all increased in incidence in patients given radiation therapy for ankylosing spondylitis and in survivors of the atomic bomb blasts at Hiroshima and Nagasaki. The magnitude of the risk depends on the dose of radiation, its distribution in time, and the age of the individual. Greater risk results from higher-dose radiation delivered over shorter periods to younger patients. In areas of high natural background radiation (often from radon), chromosomal aberrations have been reported to be more frequent, but an increase in acute leukemia has not been consistently found. Recently, concern has been raised about the possible leukemogenic effects of extremely low-frequency nonionizing electromagnetic fields emitted by electrical installations. If such an effect exists at all, the magnitude of the effect is small.

ONCOGENIC VIRUSES. The search for a viral cause of leukemia has been intensely pursued, but none has been found, except for two rare leukemias associated with retroviruses. Human T-cell lymphotropic virus type I (HTLV-I), an enveloped, single-stranded RNA virus, is considered the causative agent of adult T-cell leukemia (Chapter 372). This distinct form of leukemia is found within geographic clusters in southwestern Japan, the Caribbean basin, and Africa. The virus can be spread vertically from mother to fetus or horizontally by sexual contact or through blood products. Although previously rare in the United States, HTLV-I seropositivity has been found with increasing frequency among patients undergoing frequent transfusions and among intravenous drug users. Screening of blood products for antibodies to HTLV-I is routine practice in blood banks in the United States. A second human retrovirus, termed HTLV-II, which is genetically distinct from HTLV-I, has been isolated from several patients with a syndrome resembling hairy cell leukemia. The etiologic link between HTLV-II and malignancy is uncertain.

GENETICS AND CONGENITAL FACTORS. If leukemia develops before 10 years of age in a patient with an identical twin, the unaffected twin has a one in five chance of subsequently developing leukemia. Several syndromes with somatic cell chromosome aneuploidy (Chapter 38), including trisomy 21 (Down), trisomy 13 (Patau), and XXY (Klinefelter; Chapters 38 and 246) are associated with an increased incidence of AML. Other inherited mutations, for example, a mutation at 21q22, have been associated with a high incidence of AML in rare families. Several autosomal recessive disorders associated with chromosomal instability are prone to terminate in acute leukemia, including Bloom syndrome, Fanconi's anemia (Chapter 174), and ataxia-telangiectasia (Chapter 267).

CHEMICALS AND DRUGS. Heavy occupational exposure to benzene and benzene-containing compounds such as kerosene and carbon tetrachloride may lead to marrow damage, which can take the form of aplastic anemia, myelodysplasia, or AML. A link between leukemia and tobacco use has recently been reported.

Prior exposure to alkylating agents such as melphalan and the nitrosoureas is associated with an increased risk of AML (Chapter 191). These so-called secondary leukemias are often manifested as a myelodysplastic syndrome, frequently have abnormalities of chromosomes 5, 7, and 8, but have no distinct morphologic features; they typically develop 4 to 6 years after alkylating agent exposure, and their incidence may be increased with greater intensity and duration of drug exposure. Prolonged exposure to epipodophyllotoxins (teniposide or etoposide) has also been identified as a risk factor for the development of AML. The secondary leukemias associated with epipodophyllotoxin exposure tend to have a shorter latency period (1 to 2 years), lack a myelodysplastic phase, have a monocytic morphology, and involve abnormalities of the long arm of chromosome 11 (band q23). Recently, an association between the development of acute promyelocytic leukemia (APL) and prior treatment for psoriasis with bimolane, a dioxopiperazine derivative, has been reported.

Incidence

The annual new case incidence of all leukemias is 8 to 10 per 100,000. This rate has remained static over the past 3 decades. The relative incidences for the four categories of leukemia are as follows: ALL, 11%; chronic lymphocytic leukemia, 29%; AML, 46%; and CML, 14%. The leukemias account for about 3% of all cancers in the United States. The impact of leukemia is heightened because of the young age of some patients. For example, ALL is the most common cancer and the second leading cause of death in children younger than 15 years. ALL has a maximal incidence between 2 and 10 years of age, with a second, more gradual increase in frequency later in life. The incidence of AML gradually increases with age, without an early peak. Approximately half of AML cases occur in patients younger than 50 years.

Classification

The acute leukemias can be classified in a variety of ways, including morphology, cytochemistry, cell surface markers, cytoplasmic markers, cytogenetics, and oncogene expression (Tables 193–1 and 193–2). The most important distinction is between AML and ALL because these two diseases differ considerably in their clinical behavior, prognosis, and response to therapy. The various subgroups of AML and ALL also have some important differences.

MORPHOLOGY. Leukemic cells in AML are typically 12 to 20 nm in diameter, with discrete nuclear chromatin, multiple nucleoli, and cytoplasm that usually contains azurophilic granules. Auer rods, which are slender, fusiform cytoplasmic inclusions that stain red with Wright-Giemsa stain, are virtually pathognomonic of AML. The French-American-British (FAB) collaborative group has subdivided AML into

Oncology

Table 193-1 • CLASSIFICATION OF ACUTE LEUKEMIAS

| SUBTYPE | MORPHOLOGY | HISTOCHEMISTRY | | | MONOCLONAL REACTIVITY | CYTOGENETIC ABNORMALITIES |
		Myeloperoxidase	Nonspecific Esterase	PAS		
M0, Acute undifferentiated leukemia	Uniform, very undifferentiated	−	−	−		Various
M1, Acute myeloid leukemia with minimal differentiation	Very undifferentiated, few azurophilic granules	+/−	+/−	−		Various
M2, acute myeloid leukemia with differentiation	Granulated blast predominate; Auer rods may be seen	+++	+/−	+	For subtypes M0–M5b, approximately 90% of cases will react with at least one of the following antimyeloid antibodies:	Various, including t(8;21)
M3, acute promyelocytic leukemia	Hypergranular promyelocytes	+++	+	+		t(15;17)
M4, acute myelomonocytic leukemia	Both monoblasts and myeloblasts are present	++	+++	++	anti-CD13 anti-CD14 anti-CD33 anti-CD34	Various, including inv/del(16)
M4E	Like M4 but with eosinophils					
M5, acute monocytic leukemia	Monoblasts predominate					
M5a M5b	Type a, >80% monoblasts; type b, >20% promonocytes	+/−	+++	++		Various, including abnormalities of 11q23
M6, acute erythroleukemia	Erythroblasts and megaloblastic red cell precursors seen	−	−	++	Antiglycopherin, antispectrin	Various
M7, Acute megakaryocytic leukemia	Undifferentiated blasts	−	+/−	+	CD41, 61	Various
L1, Acute lymphoid leukemia, childhood variant	Small, uniform blasts, nucleoli indistinct	−	−	+++	65% react with anti-CD10 (anti-CALLA); 20% react with anti-CD5, 3, or 2 (anti–T cell)	Various including t(9;22), t(4;11), and t(1;9)
L2, Acute lymphoid leukemia, adult variant	Larger, more irregular nucleoli present	−	−	++		
L3, Burkitt-like acute lymphoid leukemia	Large with strongly basophilic cytoplasm and vacuoles	−	−	−	Anti-surface immunoglobulin, anti-CD19 anti-CD20	t(8;14)

PAS = periodic acid–Schiff.

eight subtypes based on morphology and histochemistry: M0, M1, M2, and M3 reflect increasing degrees of differentiation of myeloid leukemic cells; M4 and M5 leukemias have features of the monocytic lineage; M6 has features of the erythroid cell lineage; M7 is acute megakaryocytic leukemia.

The leukemic cells in ALL tend to be smaller than AML blasts and relatively devoid of granules. ALL can be divided, by FAB criteria, into L1, L2, and L3 subgroups. L1 blasts are uniform in size, with homogeneous nuclear chromatin, indistinct nucleoli, and scanty cytoplasm with few, if any, granules. L2 blasts are larger and more variable in size and may have nucleoli. L3 blasts are distinct, with prominent nucleoli and deeply basophilic cytoplasm with vacuoles. The World Health Organization has developed alternative classifications for AML and ALL that add molecular and clinical features to the usual morphologic classification.

CELL SURFACE MARKERS. Monoclonal antibodies reactive with cell surface antigens have been used to classify acute leukemias. Antibodies that react with antigens found on normal immature myeloid cells, including CD13, CD14, CD33, and CD34, also react with blast cells from most patients with AML. Exceptions are the M6 and M7 variants, which have antigens restricted to the red cell and platelet lineage, respectively. Myeloid leukemia blasts also express HLA-DR antigens but usually lack T-cell, B-cell, and other lymphoid antigens. In 10 to 20% of patients, however, AML blasts express antigens usually restricted to B- or T-cell lineage. Expression of lymphoid antigens by AML cells does not change either the natural history or the therapeutic response of these leukemias.

ALL can be divided into several forms based on cell surface antigen expression. The five most common forms are early pre–B-cell, pre–B-cell, B-cell, T-cell, and null-cell ALL. Approximately 60% of cases

of ALL express the common ALL antigen (CALLA) on the cell surface. CALLA (CD10) is a glycoprotein also found on occasional normal early lymphocytes and other nonhematopoietic tissues. Cases of CALLA-positive ALL are thought to represent an early pre–B-cell differentiation state. About 20% of cases of CALLA-positive ALL have intracytoplasmic immunoglobulin and are termed pre–B-cell ALL. B-cell ALL is signified by the presence of immunoglobulin on the cell surface and accounts for fewer than 5% of cases of ALL. About 20% of cases of ALL are of the T-cell phenotype and express antigens found on normal early T cells such as CD5, CD3, or CD2. Approximately 15% of cases of ALL fail to express CALLA or T-cell markers but express CD19, a B-cell marker, and are termed pro-B-ALL. In about 25% of patients with ALL, the leukemic cells also express myeloid antigens. The presence of such antigens defines a group of patients who historically have had a somewhat worse prognosis; with current, more aggressive regimens, however, outcomes seem to be similar.

CYTOGENETICS AND MOLECULAR BIOLOGY. In most cases of acute leukemia, an abnormality in chromosome number or structure is found. These abnormalities are clonal, essentially involving all of the malignant cells in a given patient, are acquired and not found in the normal cells of the patient, and are referred to as "nonrandom" because specific abnormalities are found in multiple cases of AML and are associated with distinct morphologic or clinical subtypes of the disease. These abnormalities may be simply the gain or loss of whole chromosomes, but more often they include chromosomal translocations, deletions, or inversions. When patients with acute leukemia and a chromosomal abnormality are treated and enter into complete remission, the chromosomal abnormality disappears; when relapse occurs, the abnormality reappears.

Table 193–2 • WORLD HEALTH ORGANIZATION CLASSIFICATIONS OF ACUTE LEUKEMIAS

Acute myeloid leukemia (AML)
  AMLs with recurrent cytogenetic translocations
    AML with t(8;21)(q22;q22), AML1 (CBF-alpha)/ETO
    Acute promyelocytic leukemia (AML with t(15;17)(q22;q11–12) and variants, PML/RAR-alpha)
    AML with abnormal bone marrow eosinophils (inv[16][p13q22] or t[16;16][p13;q11], CBFβ/MYH11X)
    AML with 11q23 (MLL) abnormalities
  AML with multilineage dysplasia
    With prior myelodysplastic syndrome
    Without prior myelodysplastic syndrome
  AML and myelodysplastic syndromes, therapy-related
    Alkylating agent–related
    Epipodophyllotoxin-related (some may be lymphoid)
    Other types
  AML not otherwise categorized
    AML minimally differentiated
    AML without maturation
    AML with maturation
    Acute myelomonocytic leukemia
    Acute monocytic leukemia
    Acute erythroid leukemia
    Acute megakaryocytic leukemia
    Acute basophilic leukemia
    Acute panmyelosis with myelofibrosis
Acute biphenotypic leukemias
Acute lymphoid leukemias
  Precursor B-cell acute lymphoblastic leukemia (cytogenetic subgroups)
    t(9;22)(a34;q11); BCR/ABL
    t(v;11q23); MLL rearranged
    t(1;19)(q23;p13) E2A/PBX1
    t(12;21)(p12;q22) ETV/CBF-alpha
  Precursor T-cell acute lymphoblastic leukemia
  Burkitt-cell leukemia

tions (5 to 10%), and tend to be associated with a poorer overall response to therapy. Mutations in FMS, which like FLT3 is a receptor tyrosine kinase, is seen in 10 to 20% of cases of AML, whereas mutations in H-, K-, or N-ras, which are cellular proteins involved with signal transduction, are seen in 15 to 20% of AML cases. These mutations have become of interest not only for their prognostic importance but also because they may serve as targets for newly developed forms of therapy.

The most common cytogenetic abnormality seen in adults with ALL is the Philadelphia (Ph) chromosome [t(9;22)], a translocation that results in fusion of the *bcr* gene on chromosome 22 to the *abl* tyrosine kinase gene on chromosome 9. This translocation appears to result in the constitutive activation of *abl*, but the precise mechanism by which this activity results in the development of leukemia is unclear. The *bcr/abl* fusion is associated with both ALL and CML (Chapter 192), with a minor difference in the breakpoint of *bcr* distinguishing the two. A slightly smaller 190-kD protein is generally found in ALL, whereas a larger 210-kD protein is characteristic of CML. The t(9;22) abnormality is seen in approximately 20% of adult ALL cases and 5% of childhood cases, and is associated with a poor prognosis. The most common translocation seen in childhood ALL is t(12;21), which involves the genes *TEL* and *AML1*. Like the AML-associated translocation t(8;21) and inv(16), t(12;21) is thought to result in abnormal DNA transcription by interfering with the normal function of CBF. The t(12;21) is difficult to diagnose by routine cytogenetics, but by molecular studies it has been shown to account for 25% of childhood ALL and 4% of adult ALL. Other abnormalities sometimes seen in B-cell ALL include t(8;14) and t(8;22), which result in translocation of the *myc* gene on chromosome 8 and immunoglobulin enhancer response genes on chromosomes 14 or 22, and abnormalities involving 11q23. T-cell ALLs are frequently associated with abnormalities of chromosomes 7 or 14 at the sites of T-cell receptor enhancer genes on these chromosomes. The leukemia cells in about 20% of patients with ALL have a propensity to gain chromosomes, sometimes reaching an average of 50 to 60 chromosomes per cell. Patients with such hyperdiploid leukemias tend to respond well to chemotherapy.

Clinical Manifestations

The signs and symptoms of acute leukemia result from decreased normal marrow function and invasion of normal organs by leukemic blasts. Anemia is present at diagnosis in most patients and causes fatigue, pallor, and headache and, in predisposed patients, angina or heart failure. Thrombocytopenia is usually present, and approximately one third of patients have clinically evident bleeding at diagnosis, usually in the form of petechiae, ecchymoses, bleeding gums, epistaxis, or hemorrhage. Most patients with acute leukemia are significantly granulocytopenic at diagnosis. As a result, approximately one third of patients with AML and slightly fewer patients with ALL have significant or life-threatening infections when initially seen, most of which are bacterial in origin.

In addition to suppressing normal marrow function, leukemic cells can infiltrate normal organs. In general, ALL tends to infiltrate normal organs more often than AML does. Enlargement of lymph nodes, liver, and spleen is common at diagnosis. Bone pain, thought to result from leukemic infiltration of the periosteum or expansion of the medullary cavity, is a common complaint, particularly in children with ALL, in many of whom the original diagnosis was juvenile rheumatoid arthritis. Leukemic cells sometimes infiltrate the skin and result in a raised, nonpruritic rash, a condition termed *leukemia cutis*. Leukemic cells may infiltrate the leptomeninges and cause leukemic meningitis. Signs of leukemic meningitis are headache and nausea. As the disease progresses, central nervous system (CNS) palsies and seizures may develop. Although fewer than 5% of patients have CNS involvement at diagnosis, the CNS is a frequent site of relapse, particularly with ALL; because of the so-called blood-brain barrier, the CNS requires special therapy. Testicular involvement is also seen in ALL and the testicles are a frequent site of relapse. In AML, collections of leukemic blast cells, often referred to as *chloromas* or *myeloblastomas*, can occur in virtually any soft tissue and appear as rubbery, fast-growing masses.

In AML, the most frequent changes detectable by routine cytogenetic examination are a gain of chromosome 8 or loss of part or all of chromosome 7 or 5. These abnormalities are each seen in anywhere from 7 to 12% of cases and are not associated with a particular morphologic subtype of AML. They are, however, more frequently seen in patients with secondary leukemia. Abnormalities in chromosomes 7 or 5 are associated with an unfavorable prognosis, whereas isolated changes in chromosome 8 do not change overall prognosis. Whether these abnormalities cause leukemia or occur secondarily is uncertain. Two other chromosomal abnormalities seen in AML, inv(16) and t(8;21), interfere with DNA transcription, which is normally regulated by a protein complex that includes core building factors (CBF) α and β. The t(8;21) results in the fusion of the CBFα subunit on chromosome 21 with the ETO gene on chromosome 8, whereas inv(16) results in the fusion of the CBFβ subunit on the q arm of chromosome 16 with MYH11 gene on the p arm (*CBFβ/MYH11*). Both of these "core binding factor" AMLs are characterized by a high complete response rate and relatively favorable long-term survival. The two differ in that t(8;21) is normally associated with FAB M2, whereas inv(16) is associated with a unique morphologic subtype, M4 with abnormal eosinophils. A third translocation seen in AML, t(15;17), involves two genes, *PML* and *RARα* (a gene encoding the α-retinoic acid receptor) and is invariably associated with APL, the M3 subtype of AML. Leukemia develops in transgenic mice containing the *PML/RARα* fusion gene after a variably long latency period. A final group of translocations involve the *MLL* gene located at chromosome band 11q23. *MLL* is among the most promiscuous oncogene partners in oncology, with more than 30 fusion partners identified. *MLL* gene rearrangements account for as many as 85% of all secondary leukemias arising from exposure to epipodophyllotoxins or topoisomerase II inhibitors.

In addition to the abnormalities detectable by routine cytogenetic analysis, other mutations have recently been detected in the malignant cells of substantial proportions of AML cases. Many of these involve signal transduction pathways. Activating mutations in the FLT3 receptor have been found in 20 to 40% of cases of AML. These mutations may be internal tandem repeats (15 to 30%) or point muta-

Continued

Certain clinical manifestations are unique to specific subtypes of leukemia. Patients with APL (M3) commonly have subclinical or clinically evident disseminated intravascular coagulation (DIC) (Chapter 162) caused by tissue thromboplastins that are present in the leukemic cells and released as these cells die. Acute monocytic or myelomonocytic leukemias are the forms of AML most likely to have extramedullary involvement. M6 leukemia often has a long prodromal phase. Patients with T-cell ALL frequently have mediastinal masses.

Laboratory Findings

Abnormalities in peripheral blood counts are usually the initial laboratory evidence of acute leukemia. Anemia is present in most patients. Most are also at least mildly thrombocytopenic, and up to one-fourth have severe thrombocytopenia (platelets <20,000/μL). Although most patients are granulocytopenic at diagnosis, the total peripheral white cell count is more variable; approximately 25% of patients have very high white cell counts (>50,000/μL), approximately 50% have white cell counts between 5000 and 50,000, and about 25% have a low white cell count (<5000/μL). In most cases, blasts are present in the peripheral blood, although in some patients the percentage of blasts may be quite low or blasts may be absent.

The diagnosis of acute leukemia is generally established by marrow aspiration and biopsy, usually from the posterior iliac crest. Marrow aspirates and biopsy specimens are generally hypercellular and contain 30 to 100% blast cells, which largely replace the normal marrow (Figs. 193–1 and 193–2). Occasionally, in addition to the blast cell infiltrate, other findings are present, including marrow fibrosis (especially with M7 AML) or bone marrow necrosis.

The prothrombin and partial thromboplastin times are sometimes elevated. In APL, reduced fibrinogen and evidence of DIC are also often seen. Other laboratory abnormalities frequently present are hyperuricemia, especially in ALL, and increased serum lactate dehydrogenase. In cases of high cell turnover and cell death, such as ALL-L3, evidence of tumor lysis syndrome may be noted at diagnosis, including hypocalcemia, hyperkalemia, hyperphosphatemia, hyperuricemia, and renal insufficiency. This syndrome, which is more commonly seen shortly after therapy is begun, can be rapidly fatal if untreated.

Differential Diagnosis

The diagnosis of acute leukemia is usually straightforward but can occasionally be more difficult. Both leukemia and aplastic anemia (Chapter 174) can be manifested by peripheral pancytopenia, but the finding of hypoplastic marrow without blasts usually distinguishes aplastic anemia. Occasionally a patient may have hypocellular

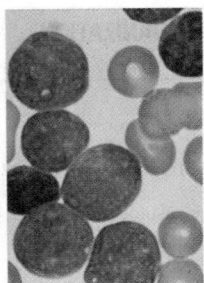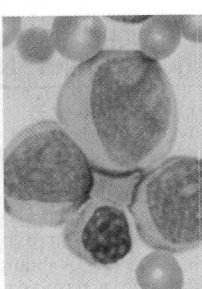

FIGURE 193–1 • Acute leukemia. *Left,* Acute lymphoblastic leukemia (ALL). *Right,* Acute myeloid leukemia (AML). Lymphoblasts in ALL are smaller, with a higher nuclear:cytoplasmic ratio and less distinct nucleoli than myeloblasts in AML. The nucleoli in the myeloblasts are clear and "punched out."

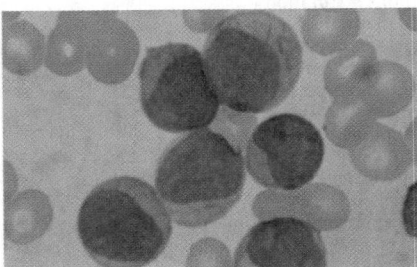

FIGURE 193–2 • Acute nonlymphoblastic leukemia. The myeloblasts in the smear show Auer rods as cytoplasmic inclusions.

marrow and a clonal cytogenetic abnormality, which establishes the diagnosis of myelodysplasia or hypocellular leukemia. A number of processes other than leukemia can lead to the appearance of immature cells in the peripheral blood. Although other small round cell neoplasms can infiltrate the marrow and sometimes mimic leukemia, immunologic markers are effective in differentiating the two. Leukemoid reactions to infections such as tuberculosis can result in the outpouring of large numbers of young myeloid cells, but virtually never does the proportion of blasts in marrow or peripheral blood reach 30% in a leukemoid reaction (Chapter 163). Infectious mononucleosis (Chapter 371) and other viral illnesses can sometimes resemble ALL, particularly when large numbers of atypical lymphocytes are present in the peripheral blood and when the disease is accompanied by immune thrombocytopenia or hemolytic anemia.

 Treatment

With the development of effective programs of combination chemotherapy and advances in marrow transplantation, many patients with acute leukemia can be cured. These therapeutic measures are complex and are therefore best carried out at centers with appropriate support services and experience in treating leukemia. Because leukemia is a rapidly progressive disease, specific antileukemic therapy should be started as soon after diagnosis as possible, usually within 48 hours. Before therapy is started, hemorrhage and infection should be brought under control, if possible. To prevent uric acid nephropathy, patients should be hydrated and given allopurinol, 100 to 200 mg orally three times per day. The diagnosis of leukemia usually comes as a profound psychological shock to the patient and family. Therefore, in addition to stabilizing the patient hematologically and metabolically, it is worthwhile having at least one formalized conference in which the patient and the family are advised about the meaning of the diagnosis of leukemia and the consequences of therapy before treatment is initiated.

MANAGEMENT OF EMERGENCIES

Patients sometimes have treatable emergencies that require immediate attention before specific antileukemic therapy is begun. Severe

bleeding usually results from thrombocytopenia, which can be reversed with platelet transfusions (Chapter 165). Once thrombocytopenic bleeding is stopped, continued prophylactic transfusions of platelets may be warranted to maintain the platelet count above 20,000/μL. Occasionally, patients also have evidence of DIC, usually associated with the diagnosis of M3 AML. If active bleeding is due to DIC (Chapter 179), low doses of heparin (50 U/kg) given intravenously every 6 hours can often be of benefit. Platelets and fresh-frozen plasma (or cryoprecipitate) should be transfused to maintain platelets at more than 50,000/μL and fibrinogen levels at greater than 100 mg/dL until the DIC abates. Whether heparin should be given prophylactically to patients with laboratory evidence of DIC but no active bleeding is an often debated, but unsettled question. Patients with fever and granulocytopenia should have blood cultures obtained; while awaiting culture results, infection should be assumed and broad-spectrum antibiotics begun empirically (Chapters 163 and 298). It is preferable to bring an infection under control before starting initial chemotherapy if the patient has an adequate granulocyte count. However, patients often have infection but essentially no granulocytes; in this situation, delaying chemotherapy is unlikely to be of benefit. Patients with very high blast counts (>150,000/μL) may have symptoms attributable to the effect of masses of these immature cells on blood flow. The leukostasis may evolve into vascular injury and local hemorrhage. If this situation occurs in the CNS, the outcome may be fatal. Leukapheresis, immediate whole-brain irradiation (600 cGy in one dose), and administration of hydroxyurea ($3\,g/m^2$ given orally for 2 or 3 days) can usually prevent this complication. Patients with very high white cell counts may also have uremia and anuria secondary to greatly increased serum uric acid levels, with subsequent intratubular crystallization. Rehydration, urine alkalinization with acetazolamide (500 mg/day), and prevention of uric acid production with allopurinol may lead to improved renal function. If patients do not respond and remain uremic, dialysis should be begun before institution of chemotherapy.

TREATMENT OF ACUTE LYMPHOBLASTIC LEUKEMIA

After the patient's condition has been stabilized, antileukemic therapy should be started as soon as possible. Initial therapy for ALL can be divided into three phases: remission induction, postremission therapy, and CNS prophylaxis.

REMISSION INDUCTION. The initial goal of treatment is to induce complete remission, which is usually defined as the reduction of leukemic blasts to undetectable levels and restoration of normal marrow function. A number of different chemotherapeutic combinations can be used to induce remission; all include vincristine and prednisone, and most add L-asparaginase and/or daunorubicin, administered over a period of 3 to 4 weeks. With such regimens, complete remission is achieved in 90% of children and 75% of adults. Because vincristine, prednisone, and L-asparaginase are relatively nontoxic to normal marrow precursors, the disease often enters complete remission after a relatively brief period of myelosuppression. Failure to achieve complete remission is usually due to either resistance of the leukemic cells to the drugs used or progressive infection. These two complications occur with approximately equal frequency.

POSTREMISSION CHEMOTHERAPY. If no further therapy is given after induction of complete remission, virtually all cases relapse, most within several months. This fact demonstrates the need for further postremission therapy. Chemotherapy after complete remission can be given in a variety of combinations, dosages, and schedules. The term *consolidation chemotherapy* generally refers to short courses of further chemotherapy given at doses similar to those used for initial induction and thus requiring rehospitalization. Attempts are usually made to select different drugs for consolidation than were used to induce the initial remission. In the case of ALL, such drugs include high-dose methotrexate, cyclophosphamide, and cytarabine, among others. Maintenance involves the administration of low-dose chemotherapy on a daily or weekly outpatient basis for long periods. The most commonly used maintenance regimen in ALL combines daily 6-mercaptopurine and weekly or biweekly methotrexate. The optimal duration of maintenance chemotherapy is unknown, but maintenance is usually given for 2 to 3 years. Optimal chemotherapy for ALL requires both consolidation and maintenance chemotherapy.

CENTRAL NERVOUS SYSTEM PROPHYLAXIS. Most chemotherapeutic agents, when given intravenously or orally, do not penetrate the CNS well, thus making it a common site of relapse unless specific measures are taken. Effective regimens for CNS prophylaxis include the use of intrathecal methotrexate alone, intrathecal methotrexate combined with 2400 cGy to the cranium, or 2400 cGy to the craniospinal axis.

PROGNOSIS AFTER INITIAL CHEMOTHERAPY. A number of factors are predictive of outcome in ALL, the most consistent of which are age, white cell count at diagnosis, and cytogenetics. With currently available treatment regimens, 50 to 70% of children and 25 to 45% of adults who initially achieve complete remission maintain complete remission for more than 5 years, and thus these patients are probably cured of their disease. In both children and adults, a low white cell count at diagnosis predicts a favorable outcome, whereas a high white cell count at diagnosis does the reverse. Patients with Ph-positive leukemia, t(4;11), or t(1;19) have a poor prognosis, as do patients with the L3 mature B-cell variant of ALL characterized by t(8;14). Accordingly, these patients are more often treated with marrow transplantation while in first remission.

TREATMENT OF RELAPSED ALL. Most relapses occur within 2 years of diagnosis, and most occur in the marrow. Occasionally, relapse may

initially be found in an extramedullary site such as the CNS or testes. Extramedullary relapse is usually followed shortly by systemic (marrow) relapse and should thus be considered part of a systemic recurrence. With the use of chemotherapeutic regimens similar to those used for initial induction, 50 to 70% of patients achieve at least short-lived second remissions. A small percentage of patients in whom the initial remission was longer than 2 years may be cured with salvage chemotherapy. If the CNS or testes is the initial site of the relapse, specific therapy to that site is also required, along with systemic retreatment. Patients with recurrent Ph-positive ALL respond dramatically, although only briefly, to STI571. Because the prognosis of relapsed leukemia treated with chemotherapy is so poor, marrow transplantation is generally recommended in this setting.

MARROW TRANSPLANTATION. The use of high-dose chemoradiotherapy followed by marrow transplantation (Chapter 166) from an HLA-identical sibling can cure 20 to 40% of patients with ALL who fail to achieve an initial remission or who have a relapse after an initial complete remission. The major limitations of transplantation are graft-versus-host disease, interstitial pneumonia, and disease recurrence. If an HLA-identical sibling is not available, alternative sources are marrow from a partially matched family member, marrow or stored cord blood from an HLA-matched unrelated donor, or autologous marrow that has been removed during remission, treated in vitro to remove contaminating tumor cells, and then subsequently stored. The outcome of transplantation of either autologous marrow or alternative sources of marrow has not been as favorable as that using matched allogeneic family member donors.

TREATMENT OF ACUTE MYELOBLASTIC LEUKEMIA

REMISSION INDUCTION. Treatment with a combination of an anthracycline (daunomycin or idarubicin) and cytarabine leads to complete remission in 60 to 80% of patients with AML. Profound myelosuppression always follows when these agents are used at doses capable of achieving complete remission. Failure to achieve complete remission is usually due to either drug resistance or fatal complications of myelosuppression.

POSTREMISSION THERAPY. Intensive consolidation chemotherapy with repeated courses of daunomycin and cytarabine at conventional doses, high-dose cytarabine, or other agents prolongs the average remission duration and improves the chances for long-term disease-free survival. The best results reported to date with chemotherapy have generally used repeated cycles of high-dose cytarabine. Unlike the situation in ALL, low-dose maintenance therapy is of limited benefit after intensive consolidation treatment. In AML, leukemic recurrence occurs less often in the CNS, being seen in only approximately 10% of cases, most commonly in patients with the M4 or M5 variants. There is no evidence that CNS prophylaxis improves overall disease-free survival in AML.

PROGNOSIS AFTER INITIAL CHEMOTHERAPY. Among patients in whom complete remission is achieved, 20 to 40% remain alive in continuous complete remission for more than 5 years, thus suggesting probable cure. As with ALL, younger patients and those with a low white cell count at diagnosis have a more favorable outcome. Patients whose disease is characterized by certain chromosomal abnormalities, particularly t(8;21), t(15;17), and inv(16), do somewhat better, whereas those with 5q–, –7, 11q23, inv(3), or t(6;9) do worse. Patients who have a preleukemic phase before their condition evolves into acute leukemia and those whose leukemia is secondary to prior exposure to alkylating agents or radiation respond poorly to chemotherapy. Expression of the multidrug resistance gene 1 (*MDR1*) is also associated with a worse outcome.

TREATMENT OF RECURRENT AML. Patients whose AML recurs after initial chemotherapy can achieve second remission in about 50% of cases following retreatment with daunomycin-cytarabine or high-dose cytarabine. Older patients may benefit from gemtuzumab ozogamicin, a form of antibody-targeted chemotherapy. These remissions tend to be short lived, however, and few patients in whom relapse occurs after first-line chemotherapy are cured by salvage chemotherapy.

TREATMENT OF ACUTE PROMYELOCYTIC LEUKEMIA. Recent studies demonstrate that complete remissions can be induced in at least 80% of patients with APL by using all-*trans*-retinoic acid (ATRA). ■ Patients treated with ATRA usually have their coagulation disorders corrected within several days, but up to 2 or 3 months of therapy may be

Continued

required to achieve complete remission. ATRA works by inducing differentiation of leukemic cells. A unique toxicity of ATRA in the treatment of APL is the development of hyperleukocytosis accompanied by respiratory distress and pulmonary infiltrates. The syndrome responds to temporary discontinuation of ATRA and the addition of corticosteroids. If patients are treated for APL with ATRA alone, disease inevitably recurs, which suggests that ATRA should be combined with or followed by other therapy. The best results are achieved if ATRA is combined with an anthracycline-containing induction regimen and if ATRA is added during maintenance.■

BONE MARROW TRANSPLANTATION. For patients with AML in whom an initial remission cannot be achieved or for patients who have a relapse after chemotherapy, bone marrow transplantation (BMT; Chapter 166) from an HLA-identical sibling offers the best chance for cure. If carried out when patients have end-stage disease, approximately 15% of patients can be saved. If the procedure is applied earlier, the outcome with BMT improves: approximately 30% of patients who undergo BMT at first relapse or second remission are cured, and 50 to 60% of patients are cured if BMT is performed in the first remission. Several studies have prospectively compared the outcome of allogeneic BMT with that of chemotherapy in patients with AML in first remission. The trend in all of these studies has been in favor of BMT, although not all studies have shown a statistically significant difference. Currently, BMT is the treatment of choice for patients with AML who have suffered an initial relapse, and it should be strongly considered for patients with high- or intermediate-risk disease while in first remission. The major limitations to allogeneic BMT are graft-versus-host disease, interstitial pneumonia, and disease recurrence. Because the incidence of graft-versus-host disease increases with age, most centers limit BMT to patients age 55 years old or younger. Autologous BMT offers an alternative for patients without matched siblings to serve as donors. In recently completed randomized trials, the use of autologous BMT after consolidation chemotherapy significantly prolonged the duration of disease-free survival and overall survival for patients with AML in first remission,■ but was not of benefit if used as a substitute for intensive consolidation.■

SUPPORTIVE CARE

Treatment of acute leukemia, especially AML, is accompanied by a number of complications, the two most serious and frequent being infection and bleeding. During the granulocytopenic period following induction and consolidation chemotherapy, most patients become febrile, and in approximately 50% of cases a bacterial infection can be documented. The most commonly isolated organisms vary somewhat from medical center to medical center, but generally, gram-positive organisms such as *Staphylococcus epidermidis* and gram-negative enteric organisms such as *Pseudomonas aeruginosa*, *Escherichia coli*, and *Klebsiella/Aerobacter* are the most commonly isolated bacteria. Even if no cause for fever is found, bacterial infection should be assumed, and, in general, all patients with fever and neutropenia should begin receiving broad-spectrum antibiotics (Chapters 163 and 298). Commonly used antibiotic combinations include a cephalosporin and a semisynthetic penicillin or a semisynthetic penicillin and an aminoglycoside. Once begun, antibiotic use should be continued until patients recover their granulocyte count, even if they become afebrile first. If documented bacterial infection persists despite appropriate antibiotics, the physician should consider removing indwelling catheters and giving granulocyte transfusions. It may be possible to reduce the incidence of bacterial infection through the use of selective gastrointestinal decontamination with, for example, ciprofloxacin or a combination of trimethoprim-sulfamethoxazole plus colistin. The use of protective environments can also reduce the incidence of infection, but this approach is costly and has not been shown to influence overall survival.

Frequently, patients taking broad-spectrum antibiotics become afebrile for a time, only to have a second fever develop. Such patients should be carefully reassessed with a high index of suspicion for fungal infection. Granulocytopenic patients who remain febrile for more than a week while taking broad-spectrum antibiotics should be treated empirically with amphotericin for presumed fungal infection. The prophylactic use of fluconazole can reduce the incidence of invasive candidal infections.

In addition to being granulocytopenic, patients undergoing induction chemotherapy for leukemia have deficient cellular and humoral immunity, at least temporarily, and thus are subject to infections common in other immunodeficiency states, including *Pneumocystis carinii* infection and a variety of viral infections. *P. carinii* infection can be prevented by prophylactic use of trimethoprim-sulfamethoxazole. Cytomegalovirus (CMV) infection can be prevented in a CMV-seronegative patient by the sole use of CMV-seronegative blood products (Chapter 370). Herpes simplex (Chapter 369) can often complicate existing mucositis and can be treated successfully with acyclovir. Acyclovir is also useful for the treatment of disseminated varicella-zoster virus infection (Chapter 367).

Myeloid growth factors (granulocyte or granulocyte-macrophage colony-stimulating factor; Chapter 159), if given shortly after the completion of chemotherapy, shorten the period of severe myelosuppression by, on average, approximately 4 days. In most studies, this accelerated recovery has resulted in fewer days with fever and less use of antibiotics, but it has not improved the complete response rate or altered survival.

The platelet count that signals a need for platelet transfusion has been the subject of recent debate. Traditionally, platelet transfusions from random donors were used to maintain platelet counts greater than $20,000/\mu L$, but more recently it has been demonstrated that lowering this threshold to $10,000/\mu L$ is safe in patients with no active bleeding. In 30 to 50% of cases, patients eventually become alloimmunized and require the use of HLA-matched platelets (Chapter 165). Occasionally, cells (presumably T cells) within the blood product can engraft in an immunosuppressed leukemic patient and cause a graft-versus-host reaction. Transfusion-induced graft-versus-host disease is manifested as a rash, low-grade fever, elevated values in liver function tests, and decreasing blood counts. This syndrome can be prevented by irradiating all blood products with at least 1500 cGy before transfusion.

1. Tallman MS, Anderson JW, Schiffer CA, et al: All-trans-retinoic acid in acute promyelocytic leukemia. N Engl J Med 1997;337:1021–1028.
2. Burnett AK, Goldstone AH, Stevens RM, et al, for the UK Medical Research Council Adult and Children's Leukaemia Working Parties: Randomised comparison of addition of autologous bone-marrow transplantation to intensive chemotherapy for acute myeloid leukaemia in first remission: Results of MRC AML 10 trial. Lancet 1998;351:700–708.
3. Cassileth PA, Harrington DP, Appelbaum FR, et al: Chemotherapy compared with autologous or allogeneic bone marrow transplantation in the management of acute myeloid leukemia in first remission. N Engl J Med 1998;339:1649–1656.

SUGGESTED READINGS
Grimwade D, Walker H, Harrison G, et al: The predictive value of hierarchical cytogenetic classification in older adults with acute myeloid leukemia (AML): Analysis of 1065 patients entered into the United Kingdom Medical Research Council AML11 trial. Blood 2001;98:1312–1320. *An extensive analysis of the impact of cytogenetics on outcome of treatment of AML.*
Staudt LM: Molecular diagnosis of the hematologic cancers. N Engl J Med 2003;348:1777–1785. *Gene expression profiling is providing a new framework for the understanding of leukemias and lymphomas.*

Tallman M, Nabhan C, Feusner J, et al: Acute promyelocytic leukemia: Evolving therapeutic strategies. Blood 2002;99:759–767. *An up-to-date review of APL, focusing on issues of clinical relevance.*
Verma A, Stock W: Management of adult acute lymphoblastic leukemia: Moving toward a risk-adapted approach. Curr Opin Oncol 2001;13:14–20. *A review of ALL in adults, with an emphasis on prognostic factors and current therapy based on a risk-adapted approach.*

194 HODGKIN'S DISEASE

Carol S. Portlock
Joachim Yahalom

Hodgkin's disease, a distinct malignant disorder of the lymphatic system that primarily affects the lymph nodes, serves as a paradigm of the successful evolution of modern oncologic concepts. The management of Hodgkin's disease provides a multidisciplinary challenge, from an accurate diagnosis to a comprehensive staging evaluation and appropriate treatment recommendation. Particularly important is the collaboration between the medical and radiation oncologist because treatments often involve combined chemotherapy/radiation strategies, and single-modality alternatives may affect future treatment options if relapse occurs. These complexities make the disease best treated by experienced multidisciplinary teams working in major medical centers.

Epidemiology and Etiology

In the United States, approximately 7500 new cases of Hodgkin's disease are diagnosed annually. In contrast to the increasing incidence of non-Hodgkin's lymphoma, the annual incidence of Hodgkin's disease has remained stable over the past several decades. In developed Western countries, the age-specific incidence of the disease is bimodal, with its greatest peak in the third decade of life and a second, smaller peak after age 50 years. The second peak is decreasing as pathology is better classified and many of the lymphomas in older patients are found to be non-Hodgkin's lymphomas. Hodgkin's disease is more common in males (ratio of 1.3 : 1.0) and less common in African Americans. Genetic factors appear to affect disease expression. Same-sex siblings have a 10 times greater risk of the disorder. In monozygotic twins, risk is 99 times higher than that in dizygotic twins if one affected twin has Hodgkin's disease. Parent-child combinations have been more common than spouse-pairing incidences, which possibly could reflect the influence of an infectious or environmental agent during childhood or early adolescence. Persons who grow up with few siblings or in single-family houses and persons who had early birth order and fewer playmates show a higher risk of Hodgkin's disease. The incidence of clinical infectious mononucleosis is also associated with these factors; indeed, infectious mononucleosis becomes clinically detectable only after early childhood. Some believe that a viral infection at a certain age and host circumstances may induce a malignant transformation. For a short period, it was thought that Hodgkin's disease might be contagious because of reports of clustering, but that concern has been effectively dispelled.

There have been no conclusive studies regarding the possible increased frequency of Hodgkin's disease in patients with human immunodeficiency virus (HIV) infection. However, Hodgkin's disease in HIV-positive patients is associated with advanced stage and poor therapeutic outcome.

A small increase in incidence of Hodgkin's disease has been detected among patients with a history of infectious mononucleosis (Chapter 371). More importantly, perhaps, the proportion of patients with Hodgkin's disease who possess high titers of antibody against the viral-capsid antigen of the Epstein-Barr virus (EBV) was found to be larger than expected. Furthermore, enhanced activation of EBV was shown to precede the development of Hodgkin's disease. A variety of techniques have demonstrated that 50% or more of Hodgkin's biopsy specimens contain the EBV genome, that the EBV nucleic acid is localized to the Reed-Sternberg (R-S) cell and its variants, and that the infected cells are monoclonal. These data suggest that EBV alone or with other carcinogens may contribute directly to the pathogenesis of Hodgkin's disease. Alternatively, it is possible that EBV is only a marker of a more fundamental disruption of the immune system of the host. Hodgkin's disease may represent a final common response to diverse pathologic processes such as viral infection, environmental or occupational exposures (e.g., woodworking), and a genetically determined host response.

Pathology

The diagnosis of Hodgkin's disease requires expert hematopathologic interpretation of a properly processed lymph node specimen. The R-S cell is the diagnostic tumor cell that must be identified within the appropriate cellular milieu of lymphocytes, eosinophils, neutrophils, plasma cells, and histiocytes. Hodgkin's disease is unique pathologically because the tumor cells compose a minority (0.1 to 10%) of the cell population, whereas normal inflammatory cells are the major cell component. As a result, it sometimes may be difficult to identify the diagnostic R-S cells. Also, other lymphoproliferations may have cells that resemble R-S cells. The R-S cell is characterized

by its large size and classic binucleated structure with large eosinophilic nucleoli. The malignant Hodgkin cells may also be mononuclear. In more than 98% of cases, the neoplastic Hodgkin R-S cells are derived from mature B cells at the germinal center stage of differentiation. In very rare cases, they are derived from peripheral T cells. Genetically, the cell is hyperdiploid without recurring karyotypic abnormalities. Two antigenic markers are thought to provide diagnostic information: CD-30 and CD-15. These markers reside on the R-S cells or their variants and not on the background inflammatory cells.

In the World Health Organization (WHO) classification, Hodgkin's disease is termed Hodgkin's lymphoma (to emphasize its clonal B-cell origin) with two major histologic subtypes: nodular lymphocyte-predominant Hodgkin's lymphoma and classic Hodgkin's lymphoma. Within classic Hodgkin's lymphoma are the subcategories of nodular sclerosis, lymphocyte-rich, mixed cellularity, and lymphocyte depletion. Each subtype is based on the number, appearance, and immunostaining characteristics of R-S cells as well as the background milieu. Nodular lymphocyte-predominant Hodgkin's disease (NLPHD) is a rare form of Hodgkin's disease (5% of cases) in which few malignant cells may be identified. The malignant cells are called L & H cells, or popcorn cells (lymphocytic and/or histiocytic R-S cell variants). The origin of the malignant cells in NLPHD is from germinal center B cells at centroblastic stage of differentiation. L&H cells are positive for CD20, CD 45, CD79a, and BCL6, and they lack CD30 and CD15. The cellular background consists primarily of lymphocytes in a nodular or sometimes diffuse pattern, which may be mistaken for a low-grade non-Hodgkin's lymphoma. NLPHD is more often clinically localized in peripheral nodes, and it rarely involves the mediastinum or the spleen. NLPHD is usually effectively treated with limited-field radiation alone; despite occasional late relapses (clinical features reminiscent of low-grade lymphoma), overall prognosis is excellent.

In classic Hodgkin's lymphoma, nodular sclerosis is the most common subcategory (70% of cases) and typically affects young females with early stage supradiaphragmatic presentations that often involve the mediastinum. The number of R-S cells is greater than in NLPHD, and they may sometimes be found in clusters. The distinguishing feature is the presence of broad birefringent bands of collagen that divide the cellular process into macroscopic nodules. The tumors contain large numbers of T lymphocytes, eosinophils, neutrophils, and histiocytes. The cytoplasm of the R-S cells sometimes retracts in formalin fixation so that they seem to be sitting in lacunae; they are called lacunar cells. Sclerosis is not a diagnostic feature limited to nodular sclerosis; it may occur in non-Hodgkin's lymphomas as well, particularly when the mediastinum or retroperitoneum is involved. The most difficult differential diagnosis pathologically is between nodular sclerosis and anaplastic large-cell lymphoma. Both entities may include sclerosis, large binucleated giant cells, and a T-cell lymphocytic infiltrate. Anaplastic large-cell lymphoma (Chapter 195) is a non-Hodgkin's lymphoma in which both the large and small cells are malignant. In such lymphomas, R-S–like cells are CD30 positive but CD15 negative. Moreover, immunostain for ALK protein or detection of gene rearrangement for NPM/ALK or for the T-cell receptor gene is diagnostic of anaplastic large-cell lymphoma. Accurate pathologic diagnosis is critical because the two diseases often affect the same young female population and present as large mediastinal masses, but treatment and prognosis may be decidedly different.

Mixed cellularity is the second most common subcategory (20% of cases). It is diagnosed more often in males, usually presents as generalized lymphadenopathy or as disease in extranodal sites, and produces associated systemic symptoms. R-S cells are frequently identified and bands of collagen are absent, although a fine reticular fibrosis may exist. The cellular background includes lymphocytes, eosinophils, neutrophils, and histiocytes.

Lymphocyte-rich classic Hodgkin's disease is diagnosed in about 5% of cases. It contains typical R-S cells and a nodular (most common) or diffuse background of mostly small lymphocytes. It often involves only peripheral lymph nodes and has a very good prognosis (similar to NLPHD).

Lymphocyte depletion is a rare disorder, particularly so because antigen marker studies have demonstrated that in the past many such cases were misdiagnosed and would now be classified as non-Hodgkin's lymphomas. R-S cells are numerous and may be pleomorphic, the cellular background is sparse, and diffuse fibrosis and necrosis may be present. This is the histologic subcategory that may be associated with HIV infection and is most commonly diagnosed in elderly persons and in underdeveloped countries. By the time of diagnosis, affected patients usually have advanced-stage disease, extranodal involvement, an aggressive clinical course, and poor prognosis.

As a general rule, findings in extranodal tissues should not be used to diagnose Hodgkin's disease unless R-S cells are conclusively identified. Extranodal sites may contain noncaseating granulomas that are neither diagnostic of Hodgkin's nor indicators of active disease. Rather, granulomas appear to be a nonspecific finding in Hodgkin's disease and may denote a favorable prognosis.

Differential Diagnosis

Hodgkin's disease is a lymph node–based malignancy and uniquely consists of lymphadenopathy in predictable clinical locations. More than 80% of patients present with lymphadenopathy above the diaphragm, often involving the anterior mediastinum; less than 10 to 20% present with lymphadenopathy limited to regions below the diaphragm. Therefore, the differential diagnosis is usually not that of generalized lymphadenopathy but, more commonly, that of regional lymphadenopathy in selected sites.

MEDIASTINAL PRESENTATIONS. Hodgkin's disease frequently affects the anterior mediastinum, and this may be the only site of involvement. In this location (Chapter 95), the differential diagnosis is limited to neoplasms (Hodgkin's disease, aggressive non-Hodgkin's lymphomas, germ cell tumors (Chapter 206), thymoma (Chapter 464), infections (tuberculosis; Chapter 341), and sarcoidosis (Chapter 91). Hodgkin's disease is remarkably silent when it involves the mediastinal structures. Masses may reach a large size before patients complain of symptoms such as cough, wheeze, chest discomfort, or tightness. Unlike aggressive non-Hodgkin's lymphomas or other neoplasms, Hodgkin's disease rarely causes superior vena cava obstruction (Chapter 95), phrenic nerve involvement with diaphragmatic paralysis (Chapter 95), or laryngeal nerve compression and hoarseness. A common complaint of patients with large mediastinal masses due to Hodgkin's disease compressing the trachea is a cough or shortness of breath that intensifies when lying supine but is relieved by sitting upright.

REGIONAL LYMPH NODE PRESENTATIONS. Cervical, supraclavicular, axillary, or, uncommonly, inguinal lymphadenopathy may be the initial complaint. Lymph nodes that are unlikely to be involved with Hodgkin's disease at diagnosis include those in Waldeyer's tonsillar ring, as well as at preauricular, occipital, epitrochlear, posterior mediastinal, mesenteric, and popliteal sites. Involvement, if any, of these areas is more likely to occur in non-Hodgkin's lymphomas. In addition, retroperitoneal lymphadenopathy (Chapter 164) rarely occurs as the only site of Hodgkin's disease but rather is accompanied by other supradiaphragmatic presentations and/or inguinal adenopathy. Many conditions can cause regional lymphadenopathy, including infections with reactive lymphadenopathy (particularly frequent in the cervical and inguinal distributions); neoplasms (such as primary head and neck, lung or thyroid, breast, rectum), and autoimmune disorders. Patients with lymphoma may develop superimposed regional reactive lymphadenopathy that may improve partially with a course of antibiotics; however, when residual lymphadenopathy persists, it deserves further investigation.

GENERALIZED LYMPH NODE PRESENTATIONS. Disseminated lymphadenopathy is infrequent in Hodgkin's disease (Chapter 164). When present, it is usually associated with systemic symptoms and often extranodal involvement as well. This presentation is sufficiently uncommon that one must consider other causes of widespread lymphadenopathy: infections (viral, bacterial, fungal, mycobacterial), autoimmune disorders, HIV-associated lymphadenopathy, and non-Hodgkin's lymphomas.

EXTRANODAL INVOLVEMENT. Hodgkin's disease may affect extranodal tissues by direct invasion (contiguity), the so-called E-lesion, or by hematogenous dissemination, that is, stage IV disease. Isolated extranodal presentations (e.g., cutaneous nodules or gastric involvement) without nodal involvement usually denote a non-Hodgkin's lymphoma except when associated with HIV disease. When extranodal involvement is suspected, one must also consider the possibility that the patient has an infection concurrent with regional Hodgkin's disease. Examples include patients who have bulky mediastinal involvement that produces tracheal or bronchial compression and an obstructive pneumonia as well.

Sites of extranodal involvement that suggest a diagnosis other than Hodgkin's disease include meninges, parenchymal brain involvement, nasal sinuses, lung lesions without mediastinal adenopathy,

gastrointestinal tract invasion, ascites or mesenteric nodal disease, and genitourinary structures (kidney, bladder, testis, or ovary). All these areas are more commonly affected by a non-Hodgkin's lymphoma, other neoplasms, or infectious processes.

SYSTEMIC MANIFESTATIONS OF HODGKIN'S DISEASE. Occasionally, patients come to attention because of systemic complaints or findings. These findings include chronic pruritus, which may be intense and produce destructive excoriation; systemic "B" symptoms of fever, night sweats, or weight loss; lymph node pain with alcohol consumption; an abnormal blood profile, such as leukocytosis with neutrophilia (Chapter 163), eosinophilia (Chapter 184), or thrombocytosis (Chapter 183); or rarely hypercalcemia (Chapter 260), nephrotic syndrome (Chapter 119), or pancytopenia (Chapter 174) with a fibrotic bone marrow and splenomegaly.

STAGING. The next step after the diagnosis of Hodgkin's disease is the staging process, that is, the classification of the tumor according to its extent. Precise definition of the extent of nodal and extranodal involvement with Hodgkin's disease is made according to a standard staging classification system and is critical for selection of the proper treatment. Detailed documentation of the extent of disease also provides the baseline for evaluating the response to therapy and for monitoring potential relapse. Accurate delineation of disease sites is mandatory for the design of radiation therapy fields. The use of a standard staging system also allows comparison of the results of therapeutic interventions in different clinical trials.

The Ann Arbor staging classification has been the basis for treatment decisions for Hodgkin's disease patients since 1971. It was originally designed to distinguish patients who would benefit from extended-field radiation therapy from those who would require systemic chemotherapy. The staging system is an anatomic one and describes the sites of tumor in relation to the diaphragm (Fig. 194–1). The Ann Arbor staging classification was revised at a meeting in Cotswolds, England, to recognize the importance of tumor bulk (Table 194–1).

The assignment of stage is based on the number of sites of involvement, whether lymph nodes are involved on both sides of the diaphragm, whether this involvement is bulky (particularly in the mediastinum), whether there is contiguous extranodal involvement (E sites) or disseminated extranodal disease, and whether typical

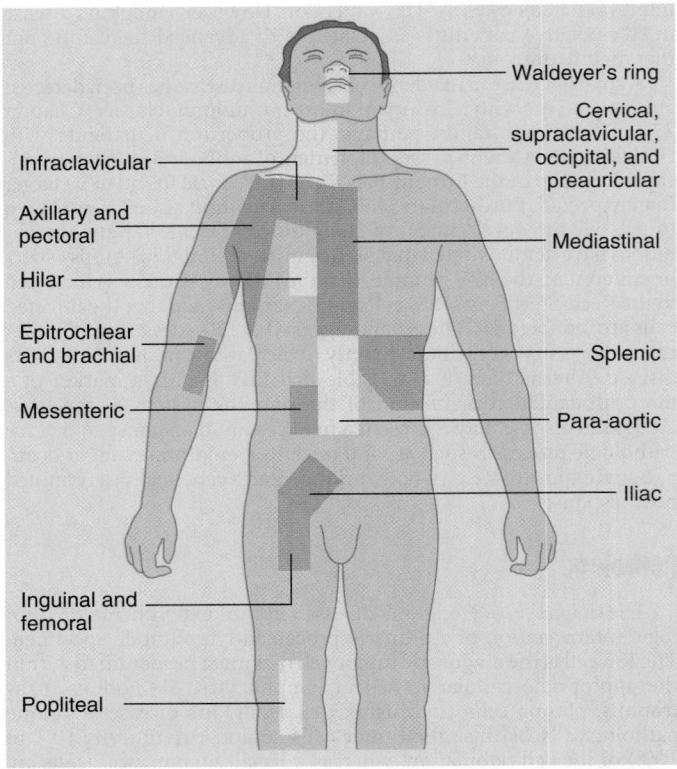

FIGURE 194–1 • Anatomic definition of lymph node regions for staging of Hodgkin's disease. (From Kaplan HS, Rosenberg SA: The treatment of Hodgkin's disease. Med Clin North Am 1966;50:1591–1610.)

Table 194–1 • THE COTSWOLDS STAGING CLASSIFICATION FOR HODGKIN'S DISEASE

Stage I
Involvement of a single lymph node region or a lymphoid structure (e.g., spleen, thymus, Waldeyer's ring)

Stage II
Involvement of two or more lymph node regions on the same side of the diaphragm (i.e., the mediastinum is a single site, hilar lymph nodes are lateralized). The number of anatomic sites should be indicated by a subscript (e.g., II_2).

Stage III
Involvement of lymph node regions or structures on both sides of the diaphragm:
III_1: With or without involvement of splenic, hilar, celiac, or portal nodes
III_2: With involvement of para-aortic, iliac, or mesenteric nodes

Stage IV
Involvement of extranodal sites beyond that designated as E

DESIGNATIONS APPLICABLE TO ANY DISEASE STAGE
A: No symptoms
B: Fever, drenching sweats, weight loss
X: Bulky disease:
  $>\frac{1}{3}$ the width of the mediastinum
  >10 cm maximal dimension of nodal mass
E: Involvement of a single extranodal site, contiguous or proximal to a known nodal site
CS: Clinical stage
PS: Pathologic stage

---

systemic symptoms (B symptoms) are present (Table 194–2). In the past, staging had two designations: clinical staging referred to information that was obtained by initial biopsy, history, physical examination, and radiographic studies only, whereas pathologic staging was determined by more extensive surgical assessment of potentially involved sites, such as by surgical staging laparotomy and splenectomy. Because staging laparotomy is no longer performed, the staging system is now based on clinical criteria unless surgical specimens are available for reasons other than staging.

Even though the Ann Arbor staging system is still universally used, stage I and II are commonly collapsed into an "early stage" category and stages III and IV into an "advanced stage" category. Even more relevant is the distinction between "favorable early stage" and "unfavorable early stage." Although, there is no official consensus for this grouping, most clinicians define an unfavorable early stage by the presence of any of the following: bulky disease (>10 cm), B symptoms, more than three sites of disease, or sedimentation rate greater than 50 mm/hr.

Table 194–2 • RECOMMENDED PROCEDURES IN STAGING HODGKIN'S DISEASE

1. Adequate surgical biopsy reviewed by an experienced pathologist
2. History and physical examination with particular attention to the presence and duration of B symptoms (see Table 194–1) and pruritus
3. *Imaging studies*
   Plain chest radiograph
   Computed tomography (CT) scan of thorax
   CT scan of abdomen and pelvis
   Positron-emission tomography or gallium scan
4. *Hematologic studies*
   Complete blood cell count
   Erythrocyte sedimentation rate
   Bone marrow biopsy (as indicated)
5. *Biochemical studies*
   Liver function tests
   Renal function tests
   Lactate dehydrogenase, albumin, calcium
6. *Cardiac and lung function studies*
7. *Under special circumstances*
   Magnetic resonance imaging
   Technetium bone scan
   Percutaneous or laparoscopic liver biopsy

HISTORY AND PHYSICAL EXAMINATION. The history should pay special attention to the presence or absence of disease-associated symptoms, which may occur in up to one third of patients and include fever, night sweats, weight loss (B symptoms), pruritus, and, less commonly, pain in involved regions after ingestion of alcohol. In each anatomic stage, the presence of B symptoms is an adverse prognostic indicator that may affect the choice of treatment. Unexplained fever is defined as recurrent temperatures above 38° C during the previous month, night sweats are considered present if they are drenching and recurrent, and unexplained weight loss is significant only if at least 10% of body weight is lost within the preceding 6 months. Although pruritus is no longer considered a B symptom, the presence of generalized itching is considered by many to be an adverse prognostic symptom. Certain combinations of B symptoms have been found to be more prognostically significant than others. For example, the combination of fever and weight loss has a more adverse prognosis than night sweats alone. B symptoms probably reflect the end-product manifestation of cytokines produced by the tumor cells.

The physical examination should carefully determine the location and size of all palpable lymph nodes. An inspection of Waldeyer's ring, detection of splenomegaly or hepatomegaly, and evaluation of the cardiac and respiratory status are important.

LABORATORY STUDIES. The initial laboratory studies should include a complete blood cell count with white cell differential and platelet count, an erythrocyte sedimentation rate (ESR), tests for liver and renal function, and assays for serum alkaline phosphatase and lactate dehydrogenase.

Mild to moderate anemia with normal indices of the type often found in patients with other malignancies or chronic disease may accompany Hodgkin's disease and does not necessarily indicate bone marrow involvement or hypersplenism. A moderate to marked leukemoid reaction (Chapter 163) and thrombocytosis (Chapter 183) are common, particularly in symptomatic patients, and usually disappear with treatment. Mild eosinophilia frequently exists, especially in patients with pruritus. Patients with advanced stage disease and those with HIV-related Hodgkin's disease may show absolute lymphopenia (<1000 cells/mm^3), which usually denotes a poor prognosis.

The ESR may provide helpful prognostic information. At some centers, treatment programs for patients with early-stage disease are influenced by the degree of ESR elevation. Changes in the ESR after therapy also may correlate with response and relapse. Other acute-phase reactants, such as serum copper, have been proposed as reliable nonspecific markers of disease activity but have shown no advantage over ESR.

Abnormalities of liver function studies should prompt further evaluation of that organ, with imaging and possible biopsy. An elevated alkaline phosphatase value may be a nonspecific marker, but it also may indicate bone involvement that should be appropriately evaluated by a radionuclide bone scan and directed skeletal radiographs. An appreciably elevated lactate dehydrogenase (LDH) has been associated with a poor prognosis in some studies.

IMAGING STUDIES. Radiologic studies should include a chest radiograph and computed tomographic (CT) scan of the chest, abdomen, and pelvis with intravenous contrast medium enhancement. In most patients, fluorine-18 fluorodeoxyglucose positron-emission tomography (PET) or gallium radionuclide scan provides important information and is highly recommended (Fig. 194–2). PET scanning appears to be superior in terms of sensitivity and number of sites detected, and it may provide better information than gallium scanning. Radionuclide bone scan, magnetic resonance imaging (MRI) of the chest or abdomen, and CT scans of the neck are contributory only under special circumstances.

The standard chest radiograph provides basic information regarding the extent of disease in the chest and offers a simple test for monitoring patients after treatment (see Fig. 194–2). Thoracic CT details the status of intrathoracic lymph node groups, lung parenchyma, pericardium, pleura, and the chest wall. This additional information may alter the treatment recommendation in at least 10% of patients. The information obtained with chest CT also helps in the design of the radiation field and in assessing response. Because chest CT scans may have residual abnormalities long after completion of therapy, a PET or gallium scan assists in the evaluation of pretreatment involvement and response to therapy. A negative PET or gallium scan after completion of treatment supports the supposition that no active disease exists despite residual abnormality on the CT scan.

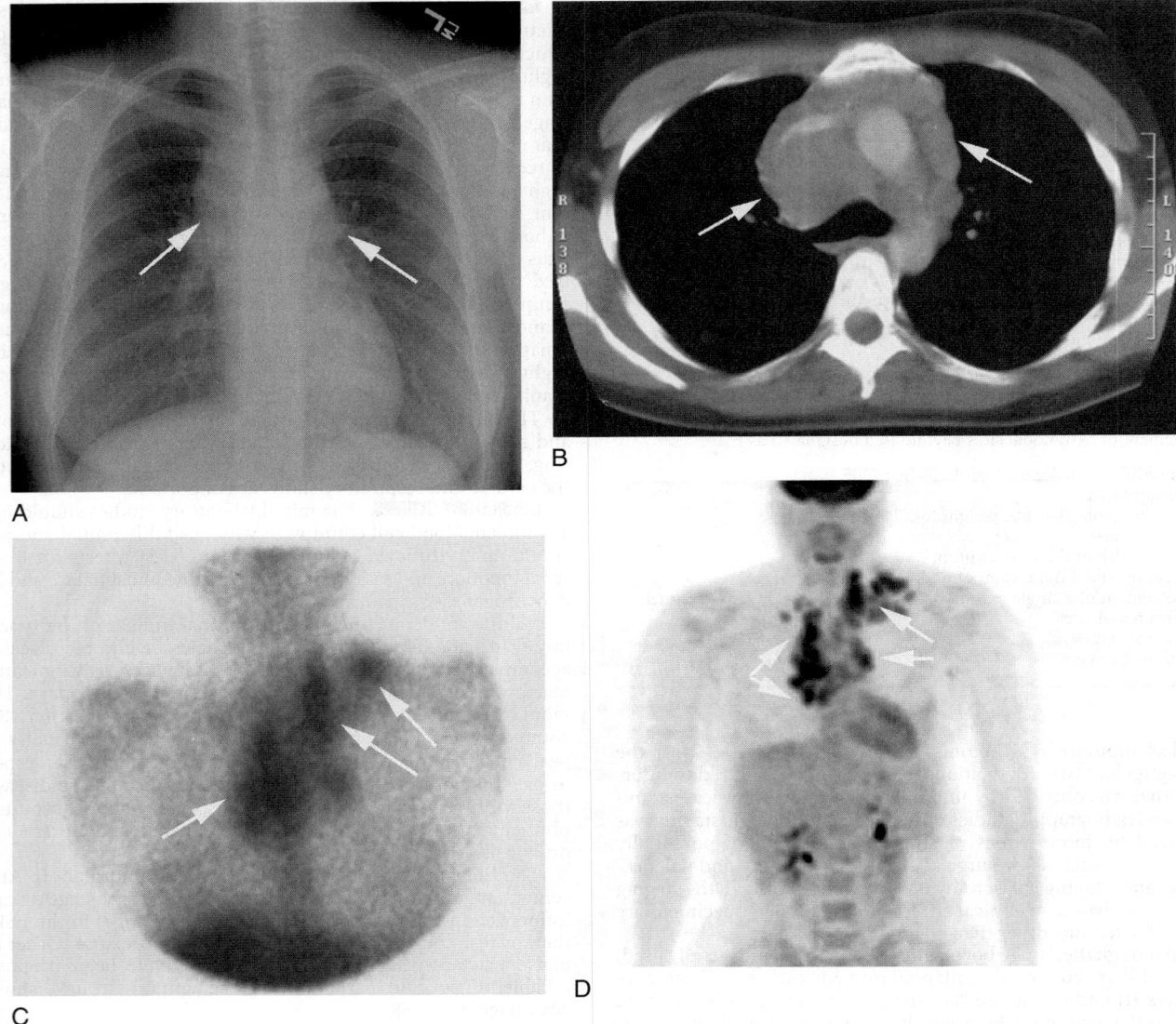

FIGURE 194–2 • Bulky Hodgkin's disease as seen on chest radiograph (*A*), computed tomography (CT) scan of the chest (*B*), gallium scan (*C*), and positron-emission tomography (PET) scan (*D*). The arrows indicate sites of disease. Note that PET and CT scans provide more detailed information compared to chest radiograph and gallium scan, respectively.

CT and PET scanning provide the basic imaging studies for evaluation of the abdomen and pelvis. Gallium scanning is less accurate in these sites. Although the information from CT and PET scanning may be complementary, PET scans are not widely available, and as a result, CT remains the standard study for the abdomen and pelvis. Radionuclide bone scans are appropriate for investigating the nature of bone pain or an elevated serum alkaline phosphatase. MRI may be a sensitive indicator of bone or bone marrow involvement.

BONE MARROW BIOPSY. Bone marrow involvement is relatively uncommon, but because of the impact of a positive biopsy on further staging and treatment, unilateral iliac crest bone marrow biopsy is generally recommended in any patient with systemic symptoms or with abdominal or generalized adenopathy; it is recommended infrequently in patients with nonbulky, early-stage Hodgkin's disease presenting above the diaphragm only ("favorable early stage"). Because the disease involves the marrow inhomogeneously, single biopsies are not always adequate, and bilateral biopsies may be warranted in evaluating the extent of disease in some patients.

STAGING LAPAROTOMY. Staging laparotomy has been abandoned in the management of Hodgkin's disease.

Rx Treatment

Advances in radiation therapy and the development of effective combination chemotherapy have resulted in the cure of more than 75% of all newly diagnosed patients with Hodgkin's disease. All patients, regardless of stage, can and should be treated with curative intent.

The stage of the disease is the most important determinant of treatment options and outcome, so precise definition of the extent of nodal and extranodal involvement during staging is critical to select the proper treatment strategy. Hodgkin's disease is very sensitive to radiation and to many chemotherapy drugs; in most stages, more than one option provides effective treatment. Because most patients are expected to have a normal life expectancy, new treatment programs must pay particular attention to minimizing future toxicity. Any changes must be undertaken without compromising the excellent cure rates obtained by well-established therapies.

Effective treatment of Hodgkin's disease is complex, requiring the expertise of a multidisciplinary team consisting of a hemato-pathologist, diagnostic radiologist, and medical and radiation oncologists during staging of the disease and subsequent treatment. Because radiation plays an important role in the treatment, the use of a modern, high-quality radiation therapy facility staffed with an experienced team yields the best treatment results.

EARLY-STAGE DISEASE

The curative treatment of early-stage Hodgkin's disease was established in the 1960s and 1970s using radiation alone, and this single modality has been the "gold standard" for the management of most patients with early-stage disease. In patients who were pathologically (laparotomy) staged and treated with primary irradiation alone, several large series reported a 15- to 20-year survival of nearly 90% and a relapse-free survival rate of 75 to 80%. Most relapses (75%) occur within the first 3 years after completing therapy; late relapses are uncommon. More than half of the patients who experience relapse after radiation therapy alone have disease that is still curable with standard chemotherapy.

An alternative treatment approach for early-stage disease is the combination of lower dose radiation therapy that is delivered to smaller areas (only clinically involved sites) with chemotherapy using Adriamycin (doxorubicin), bleomycin, vinblastine, and dacarbazine (ABVD; Table 194–3). This combination is considered the new gold standard for favorable early-stage Hodgkin's disease. ABVD alone may be equivalent to ABVD plus radiation therapy in favorable, early-stage Hodgkin's disease; at this time, however, ABVD alone should be used only in the context of a controlled clinical trial. ABVD is less toxic than the combination of nitrogen mustard, vincristine, procarbazine, and prednisone (MOPP) and has replaced MOPP as the standard chemotherapy. [1,2]

Unfavorable early-stage patients are also candidates for combined therapy but with full-dose radiation. A new drug regimen, Stanford V, may be superior to ABVD-based therapy in this setting, but randomized comparisons have not yet been completed (see Table 194–3).

Radiation Therapy

The cure of early-stage Hodgkin's disease with radiation alone requires that all involved sites and adjacent nodal areas be treated with tumoricidal doses. Successful therapy with radiation alone requires treatment of all clinically involved lymph nodes and all nodal and extranodal regions at risk for subclinical involvement (Fig. 194–3). The fields are shaped to include multiple adjacent lymph node sites while accounting for normal tissue tolerance and the technical constraints of field size. The radiation fields are treated sequentially, the total dose is fractionated, and the radiated volumes are carefully tailored with individualized divergent blocks.

Based on the results of randomized trials, however, the radiation field is usually confined to the anatomic regions of the clinically involved lymph nodes ("involved-field") and combined with chemotherapy. This involved-field approach significantly reduces the morbidity of the treatment.

When radiation is used alone, the dose required to eradicate Hodgkin's disease in demonstrably involved nodes is 40 Gy (1 Gy = 100 rad). A standard course of therapy with radiation alone includes treatment of the whole field to a total dose of 36 Gy (in 20 daily fractions of 1.8 Gy each, over a period of 4 weeks), with additional radiation restricted to the clinically apparent disease sites of 4 to 6 Gy. A lower dose of radiation, in the range of 24 to 36 Gy, is used when radiation is administered as adjuvant or consolidation treatment after chemotherapy such as after ABVD for early-stage disease.

Side Effects and Complications of Radiation Therapy

EARLY EFFECTS. These effects depend on the radiated volume, dose administered, and technique employed. They are also influenced by the extent and type of prior chemotherapy, if any, and by the patient's age.

The acute side effects of mantle field radiation are usually mild and transient: they may include mouth dryness, change in taste, pharyngitis, nausea, dry cough, dermatitis, and fatigue. These side effects are managed symptomatically and subside gradually soon after the completion of radiation therapy. The main potential side effects of subdiaphragmatic radiation are loss of appetite, nausea, and increase in bowel movements. These reactions are usually mild and can be minimized with standard antiemetic medications. Irradiation of more than one field, particularly after chemotherapy, can cause myelosuppression, and treatment delays may be required during therapy.

Six weeks to 3 months after completion of mantle therapy, approximately 15% of patients may develop Lhermitte's sign: patients note an electric shock sensation radiating down the backs of both legs when the head is flexed. Lhermitte's sign may be secondary to transient demyelinization of the cervical spinal cord; it resolves spontaneously after a few months and is not associated with late or permanent cord damage. During the same period, radiation pneumonitis and/or acute pericarditis may occur in less than 5% of patients, more often in those who had extensive mediastinal disease. Both inflammatory processes have become rare with modern radiation

Continued

Table 194–3 • COMBINATION CHEMOTHERAPY REGIMENS IN ADVANCED HODGKIN'S DISEASE

ABVD (Adriamycin, bleomycin, vinblastine, dacarbazine)
Doxorubicin (Adriamycin), 25 mg/m² IV
Bleomycin, 10 mg/m² IV
Vinblastine (Velban), 6 mg/m² IV
Dacarbazine, 375 mg/m² IV
ABVD is repeated every 2 weeks; two treatments equal one cycle.

Stanford V
Doxorubicin, 25 mg/m² IV days 1 and 15
Vinblastine 6 mg/m² IV days 1 and 15
Mechlorethamine, 6 mg/m² IV day 1
Vincristine, 1.4 mg/m² (2 mg cap) IV day 8 and 22
Bleomycin 5 mg/m² IV days 8 and 22
Etoposide 60 mg/m² IV days 15 and 16
Prednisone, 40 mg/m² PO every other day, with administration of prophylactic antibiotics
Stanford V is repeated every 28 days; each cycle is one 28-day course of therapy. Three cycles are administered.

BEACOPP (bleomycin, etoposide, doxorubicin, cyclophosphamide, vincristine, procarbazine, prednisone)
Bleomycin, 10 mg/m² IV day 8
Etoposide 100 mg/m² IV days 1, 2, 3
Doxorubicin (Adriamycin), 25 mg/m² IV day 1
Cyclophosphamide 650 mg/m² IV day 1
Vincristine (Oncovin), 1.4 mg/m² IV day 8
Procarbazine, 100 mg/m² PO days 1–7
Prednisone, 40 mg/m² PO days 1–14
BEACOPP is repeated every 21 days.

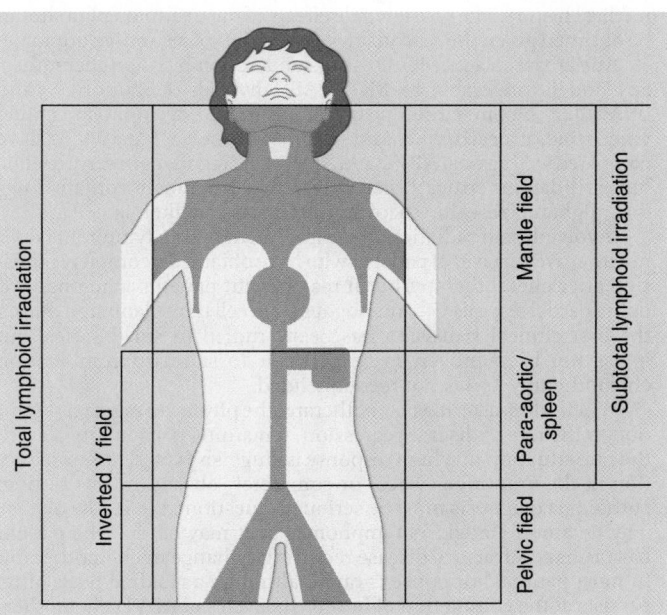

FIGURE 194–3 • Standard radiation fields for Hodgkin's disease.

techniques. Patients with Hodgkin's disease, regardless of treatment type, have a propensity to develop herpes zoster infection (Chapter 369) within 2 years after the onset of therapy. Usually the infection is confined to a single dermatome and is self-limited. If the cutaneous eruption is identified promptly, treatment with systemic acyclovir limits the duration and intensity of the infection.

LATE EFFECTS. Mantle field radiation therapy can induce subclinical hypothyroidism, detected by elevation of the level of thyroid-stimulating hormone, in about one third of patients (Chapter 239). Thyroid replacement with L-thyroxine is recommended, even for asymptomatic patients, to prevent the development of overt hypothyroidism and to decrease the risk of developing benign thyroid nodules. Radiation of the pelvic field may have deleterious effects on fertility; in most patients this effect can be avoided by appropriate gonadal shielding. In females, the ovaries can be moved (oophoropexy) into a shielded area laterally or inferomedially near the uterine cervix. Irradiation of the mantle and para-aortic fields alone does not increase the risk of sterility.

Hodgkin's disease patients who were cured with radiation therapy and/or chemotherapy have an increased risk of developing secondary solid tumors and non-Hodgkin's lymphoma 10 or more years after treatment. Unlike MOPP and similar MOPP-containing chemotherapy combinations, radiation therapy and/or ABVD for Hodgkin's disease is not leukemogenic. The most frequent solid tumors reported after radiation therapy or chemotherapy for Hodgkin's disease are lung cancer, breast cancer, stomach cancer, and melanoma. Patients who smoke should be strongly encouraged to stop because the increase in lung cancer after irradiation or chemotherapy has been detected mostly in smokers. The increase in breast cancer risk is inversely related to the age at treatment of Hodgkin's disease; in women irradiated after the age of 30 years, no increase in the risk of breast cancer has been found. Breast cancer is curable in its early stages, and early detection significantly improves survival. Breast examination should be part of the routine follow-up program for women cured of Hodgkin's disease, and routine mammography should begin about 7 years after treatment of Hodgkin's disease.

A small increase in the risk of coronary artery disease has been reported for patients who have received mediastinal irradiation. To reduce this hazard, patients should be monitored and advised to avoid other established coronary disease risk factors such as smoking, hyperlipidemia, hypertension, and poor dietary and exercise habits. In children, high-dose radiation affects bone and muscle growth and may result in deformities. Current programs for pediatric Hodgkin's disease are chemotherapy based, and radiation therapy is limited to low doses.

ADVANCED-STAGE DISEASE. The mainstay of treatment in advanced Hodgkin's disease (stages IIIB and IV) is combination chemotherapy. Before embarking on a therapeutic regimen, it is important to document carefully the diagnosis, stage, and possible confounding medical history. The possible side effects of the treatment plan should be outlined given the reasonable expectation of a curative outcome.

ABVD has replaced MOPP as the standard combination chemotherapy and is preferable to MOPP/ABV hybrids.[3] Stanford V and BEACOPP (bleomycin, etoposide, doxorubicin, cyclophosphamide, vincristine, procarbazine, and prednisone; see Table 194–3) have compared well against ABVD and ABVD-like regimens in early results, but more data are critical because these newer regimens contain drugs that might increase the risk of myelodysplasia/leukemia.

Involved-field radiation of advanced Hodgkin's lymphoma does not improve survival of patients who have obtained a complete remission after chemotherapy, but it may benefit patients who obtained only a partial response.[4] Autologous stem cell transplantation during the first clinical remission has been studied in small series, but it has not been proven to be superior to standard combination chemotherapy and is not recommended.

When administering chemotherapy, the physician must pay attention to the rate of disease regression, remaining particularly alert to the rare situation in which response is sluggish (<50% tumor reduction in the first three cycles) or completely absent. In this setting, pathologic diagnosis must be seriously questioned (e.g., the disease may be a non-Hodgkin's lymphoma) or it may be that the patient has primary refractory disease requiring a change in chemotherapy. In most patients, response is rapid, although a residual mass often persists at the completion of four to six cycles of ABVD chemother-

apy. It is generally recommended to continue treatment for at least two cycles beyond a clinical complete remission. Response is measured by physical examination, chest radiography, CT (when appropriate), and PET or gallium scanning. If the response remains equivocal at the end of a chemotherapy regimen, it may be appropriate to evaluate the treatment effect with biopsy, particularly if there is residual PET or gallium avidity. Prompt salvage therapy in poorly responsive and refractory patients is important to optimize outcome.

Toxicities of Combination Chemotherapy

ABVD is a well-tolerated drug regimen whose major consistent toxicities include modest hair loss, fatigue, and myelosuppression (particularly neutropenia). Side effects in some patients include nausea and vomiting, not completely controlled even with the routine use of ondansetron; pulmonary toxicity (which must be monitored closely with measures of diffusion capacity and for which bleomycin must be discontinued as soon as symptoms or a significant decrease in diffusion capacity is identified); vinblastine-associated peripheral or autonomic neuropathy; and symptomatic phlebitis. Rarely, patients may develop doxorubicin-induced cardiomyopathy or extravasation necrosis at injection sites.

ABVD causes a transient azoospermia but not permanent infertility in men and only temporarily disrupts menstrual function in most women. Older women, however, may suffer permanent menopause or infertility. Embryo harvesting is occasionally a consideration before treatment in older women who present with favorable disease. In men, sperm banking should be recommended before chemotherapy. Sperm counts generally recover within 1 to 2 years after ABVD or pelvic radiation.

RELAPSED HODGKIN'S DISEASE

Hodgkin's disease may be cured even if the initial treatment fails. The choice of salvage approach depends on the history of prior treatments, considering the relapse sites as well as the patient's age and general medical condition.

For patients who relapse after radiation therapy, combination chemotherapy such as ABVD is the treatment of choice. If the relapse is regional and outside the prior radiation field, involved-field irradiation may be added. The salvage rate in this group is excellent (10-year relapse-free survival of 50 to 60%). The most important prognostic factor after relapse in a patient who has received radiation therapy is the extent of disease at the time of relapse, emphasizing the importance of careful follow-up.

Standard-dose chemotherapy seldom salvages patients who fail to attain a complete response with chemotherapy or who relapse early after completion of combination chemotherapy (or combined-modality therapy). High-dose chemotherapy accompanied by autologous stem cell transplantation (HD-ASCT) has become the preferred therapy in this situation (Chapter 166). Randomized studies have demonstrated the advantage of HD-ASCT over standard-dose salvage in refractory and relapsed patients.[5] Results of transplantation are best in patients who have chemoresponsive disease at relapse. Adverse factors for successful salvage include refractory disease or remission duration shorter than 1 year, B symptoms, and extranodal disease. Favorable patients have a curative potential of 50 to 80% in most series. By contrast, only 10 to 30% of poor-risk patients are cured by HD-ASCT. Less than 2% of patients die of transplant complication. A repeat cycle of standard-dose combination chemotherapy, with or without involved-field irradiation, remains a salvage option for carefully selected patients with a late first relapse (>2 years after completion of standard-dose chemotherapy) and contraindications to HD-ASCT.

HD-ASCT is a cumbersome, toxic, and expensive process, making it important to identify proper candidates accurately. All should have histologic proof of active Hodgkin's disease before initiation of salvage therapy because residual masses are common and may not represent active tumor. Consolidation HD-ASCT is not recommended in first remission. At relapse, there is no standard reinduction chemotherapy, but the regimen generally uses a combination of new agents that are not associated with excessive hematologic stem cell toxicity and that permit peripheral stem cell harvest in responsive patients. The most commonly used HD-ASCT conditioning regimen is CBV (cyclophosphamide, BCNU [carmustine], and VP 16 [etoposide]). Other combinations also have demonstrated efficacy, and some programs also incorporate standard involved-field or intensive large-field radiation therapy. The autologous stem cells are usually harvested from the patient's own peripheral blood or less frequently from bone marrow.

SPECIAL CIRCUMSTANCES

Pregnancy may complicate the management of initial or relapsed Hodgkin's disease (Chapter 252). When the pregnancy is first diagnosed, it is important to stage the patient clinically by history and physical examination, posteroanterior chest radiograph, abdominal ultrasonography, and, in selected patients, bone marrow biopsy; and MRI studies of the chest, abdomen, and pelvis are performed as indicated. Before recommending medical management, it must be kept in mind that Hodgkin's disease is often an indolent tumor and may be clinically silent or asymptomatic for many months. For that reason, it may be possible to monitor a patient and defer treatment during the pregnancy. If treatment is indicated, options include involved-field radiation with shielding of the pregnant uterus, single-agent chemotherapy such as vinblastine, or even combination chemotherapy with ABVD. Treatment selection depends on disease sites at risk, age and size of the developing fetus, tumor bulk, the patient's symptoms, and predicted delivery date. Very rarely it may be necessary to consider therapeutic abortion if the diagnosis of advanced and/or symptomatic Hodgkin's disease is made early in the pregnancy.

HIV-associated Hodgkin's disease is much less frequent than non-Hodgkin's lymphoma; the most important consideration is to establish an accurate diagnosis (Chapter 419). Clinical staging often reveals more advanced disease than in non-HIV patients, and extranodal involvement is more frequent. It is important to distinguish between Hodgkin's disease and infectious causes of apparent extranodal involvement (such as pulmonary nodules) before determining a final treatment plan. Based on clinical stage, ABVD with involved-field radiation is appropriate for early-stage disease, whereas ABVD with or without consolidative radiation is given in advanced disease. ABVD may need to be modified to avoid bleomycin pulmonary toxicity. *Pneumocystis carinii* pneumonia prophylaxis should be instituted routinely. Highly active antiretroviral therapy should be administered during treatment as tolerated. Whenever possible, these patients should be approached with curative intent.

TREATMENT RECOMMENDATIONS

After an accurate histologic diagnosis and staging, the following general guidelines may be used in recommending therapy.

For early-stage, nonbulky presentations (stages I and IIA or B), ABVD (four cycles) with involved-field irradiation is indicated. Radiotherapy alone using subtotal lymphoid irradiation is no longer the treatment of choice for early-stage disease, but it remains a curative option for early-stage patients who are not candidates for ABVD chemotherapy. Primary chemotherapy with ABVD (six cycles) without consolidative radiotherapy is an option for patients who are entered into clinical trials.

Radiotherapy alone is the preferred treatment for patients with nodular lymphocyte-predominant Hodgkin's disease. These patients receive involved- or regional-field radiation therapy alone, almost always excluding the mediastinum.

For bulky early-stage presentations, clinical stage IX or IIX disease, combined-modality therapy is essential. The choice of combination chemotherapy regimen is usually ABVD (six cycles). In this setting, Stanford V has become a reasonable alternative in selected patients. After successful induction of complete clinical remission, consolidative radiation should be administered.

For all patients with clinical stage IIIA disease, ABVD alone (six cycles) or combined with irradiation are acceptable options. For advanced-stage disease (IIIB and IV), combination chemotherapy alone (usually ABVD for six cycles or, in selected patients, Stanford V with involved-field radiation), as indicated, is recommended.

Follow-up studies for successfully treated patients are listed in Table 194–4.

Table 194–4 • RECOMMENDED FOLLOW-UP IN TREATED HODGKIN'S DISEASE

1. End of Therapy
Repeat all studies initially positive for baseline values. If suspicious, consider biopsy.

2. 0 to 2 Years After Therapy
Visits: Every 3 to 4 months
Imaging: Chest radiography each visit, unless computed tomography (CT) scan of chest obtained
CT scan of chest every 6 months × 2, then yearly
CT scan of abdomen and pelvis yearly
Laboratory:
With each visit: Complete blood cell count, platelets, erythrocyte sedimentation rate
Liver and renal function tests
Lactate dehydrogenase
Every 6 months: Thyroid-stimulating hormone

3. 2 to 5 Years After Therapy
Visits: Every 6 months
Imaging: Chest radiography each visit, unless CT scan of chest obtained
CT scan of chest, abdomen, pelvis yearly
Laboratory: As in 2

4. More than 5 Years After Therapy
Visits: Yearly
Imaging: Chest radiography; CT scan only as indicated
Laboratory: As in 2

5. Other Considerations, as Indicated
Mammography
Lipid profile
Pulmonary function studies
Echocardiography
Hormone replacement if prematurely menopausal

1. Canellos GP, Anderson JR, Propert KJ, et al: Chemotherapy of advanced Hodgkin's disease with MOPP, ABVD, or MOPP alternating with ABVD. N Engl J Med 1992;327:1478–1484.
2. Canellos GP, Niedzwiecki D: Long-term follow-up of Hodgkin's disease trial. N Engl J Med 2002;346:1417–1418.
3. Duggan DB, Petroni GR, Johnson JL, et al: Randomized comparison of ABVD and MOPP/ABV hybrid for the treatment of advanced Hodgkin's disease: Report of an Intergroup Trial. J Clin Oncol 2003;21:607–614.
4. Aleman BM, Raemaekers JM, Tirelli U, et al: Involved-field radiotherapy for advanced Hodgkin's lymphoma. N Engl J Med 2003;348:2396–2406.
5. Schmitz N, Pfistner B, Sextro M, et al: Aggressive conventional chemotherapy compared with high-dose chemotherapy with autologous haemopoietic stem-cell transplantation for relapsed chemosensitive Hodgkin's disease: A randomised trial. Lancet 2002;359:2065–2071.

SUGGESTED READINGS
Franklin J, Diehl V: Current clinical trials for the treatment of advanced-stage Hodgkin's disease: BEACOPP. Ann Oncol 2002;13:98–101. *A brief discussion of BEACOPP and ongoing clinical trials comparing this regimen to ABVD.*
Horning SK, Hoppe RT, Breslin S, Bartlett NL, et al: Stanford V and radiotherapy for locally extensive and advanced Hodgkin's disease: Mature results of a prospective clinical trial. J Clin Oncol 2002;20:630–637. *Updated results of the Stanford V. A commonly used program in bulky and advanced-stage patients.*
Kuppers R, Klein U, Schwering I, et al: Identification of Hodgkin and Reed-Sternberg cell-specific genes by gene expression profiling. J Clin Invest 2003;111:529–537. *Of 27 Hodgkin-lymphoma specific genes upregulated in the cell lines studied, five were confirmed in primary tumor specimens.*
Moskowitz CH, Nimer SD, Zelenetz AD, et al: A two-step comprehensive high-dose chemo-radiotherapy second-line program for relapsed and refractory Hodgkin disease: Analysis by intent to treat and development of a prognostic model. Blood 2001;97:616–623. *An example of a successful high-dose therapy and ASCT program for salvage.*
Ng AK, Bernardo MV, Weller E, et al: Second malignancy after Hodgkin disease treated with radiation therapy with or without chemotherapy: Long-term risks and risk factors. Blood 2002;100:1989–1996. *A comprehensive retrospective review of second malignancies as a complication of therapy.*
Weihrauch MR, Re D, Scheidhauer K, et al: Thoracic positron emission tomography using 18F-flurodeoxyglucose for the evaluation of residual mediastinal Hodgkin disease. Blood 2001;98:2930–2934. *An indication for the contribution of PET imaging to staging and response evaluation in Hodgkin's disease.*
Yahalom J, Mauch PM: The involved-field is back: Issues in delineating the radiation field in Hodgkin's disease. Ann Oncol 2002;13:79–83. *Guidelines for designing the radiation field for a combined modality approach.*

195 NON-HODGKIN'S LYMPHOMAS

Philip J. Bierman
Nancy Lee Harris
James O. Armitage

Lymphomas are solid tumors of the immune system. Rapidly increasing knowledge of the biology of the immune system has led to corresponding increases in our understanding of these malignancies. In addition to better systems of classification and clinical evaluation, this new knowledge has led to the development of new therapies. Beneficial treatment is available for essentially every patient with non-Hodgkin's lymphoma, and some patients can be cured.

Epidemiology

In the United States, approximately 55,000 new cases of non-Hodgkin's lymphoma are diagnosed annually, and about 25,000 people die of the disease each year. Non-Hodgkin's lymphomas account for about 4% of new cancers in the United States and result in about 5% of cancer deaths in men and 4% of cancer deaths in women. The U.S. lifetime risk of developing non-Hodgkin's lymphoma is 2.11% for men and 1.79% for women. The age-adjusted incidence rate is about 23.4 per 100,000 for men and 15.6 per 100,000 in women. The incidence rate increases dramatically with age and is higher in whites than in other ethnic groups (Fig. 195–1).

Geographic differences in the incidence of non-Hodgkin's lymphomas vary as much as five-fold. The highest rates are seen in the United States, Europe, and Australia, whereas lower rates are seen in Asia. Even more striking are geographic differences in the incidence of certain types of non-Hodgkin's lymphomas such as Burkitt's lymphoma, follicular lymphoma, extranodal NK/T-cell nasal lymphoma, and adult T-cell leukemia/lymphoma (see later text).

Over the past four decades, the incidence rate for non-Hodgkin's lymphomas increased by about 3 to 4% yearly, but it declined slightly between 1995 and 1999 (Fig. 195–2). Increases have occurred in men and women in all parts of the world. This increase in incidence is largely unexplained. It is partially related to the aging population (see Fig. 195–1) and the acquired immunodeficiency syndrome (AIDS) epidemic (Chapter 409); occupational and environmental exposures may also explain some of the increase. Finally, some of the increase may be explained by improvements in the ability of pathologists to

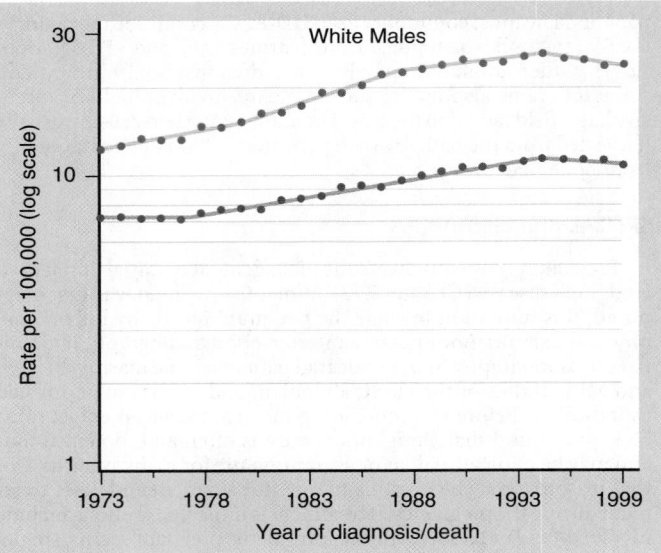

FIGURE 195–2 • Non-Hodgkin's lymphoma incidence (green) and mortality (red), white males. (From the Surveillance, Epidemiology, and End Results Program of the National Cancer Institute: *In* Ries LAG, Eisner MP, Kosary CL, et al [eds]. SEER Cancer Statistics Review, 1973–1999. Bethesda, MD, National Cancer Institute [http://seer.cancer.gov/csr/1973_1999/,2002].)

diagnose lymphoma and by improvements in imaging techniques and in minimally invasive biopsy techniques.

Etiology

For most cases of non-Hodgkin's lymphoma, the etiology is unknown, although genetic, environmental, and infectious agents have been implicated (Table 195–1). Familial clusters have been described, and there may be a slightly higher risk of non-Hodgkin's lymphoma among siblings or first-degree relatives of patients with lymphoma or other hematologic malignancies.

IMMUNE SYSTEM ABNORMALITIES. Several inherited disorders increase the risk of developing non-Hodgkin's lymphoma as much as 250-fold (see Table 195–1). In some of these conditions, the lymphoma may be related to the Epstein-Barr virus (EBV) (Chapter 371); for example, patients with the X-linked lymphoproliferative disorder may develop

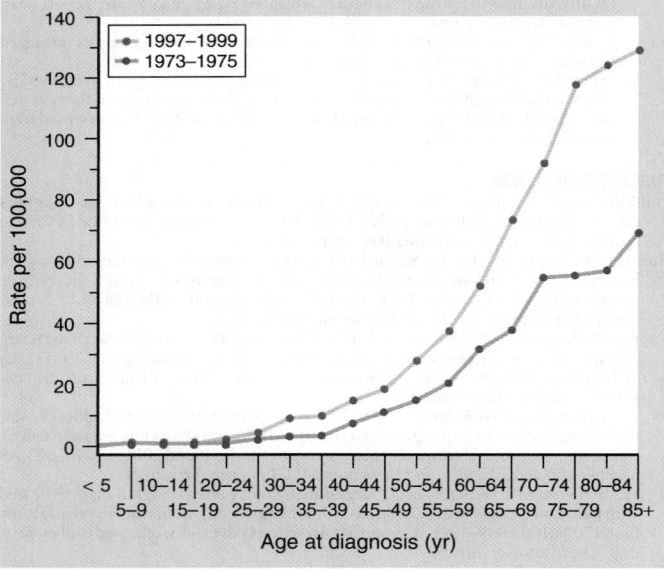

FIGURE 195–1 • Non-Hodgkin's lymphoma incidence by age 1973–1975 vs. 1997–1999, all races, males. (From the Surveillance, Epidemiology, and End Results Program of the National Cancer Institute: *In* Ries LAG, Eisner MP, Kosary CL, et al [eds]. SEER Cancer Statistics Review, 1973–1999. Bethesda, MD, National Cancer Institute [http://seer.cancer.gov/csr/1973_1999/,2002].)

Table 195–1 • FACTORS ASSOCIATED WITH THE DEVELOPMENT OF NON-HODGKIN'S LYMPHOMA

Immune abnormalities
  Inherited disorders
    Common variable immunodeficiency
    Wiskott-Aldrich syndrome
    Ataxia-telangiectasia
    X-linked lymphoproliferative disorder
  Acquired disorders
    Solid organ transplant recipients
    Acquired immunodeficiency syndrome
    Methothrexate therapy for autoimmune disorders
    Rheumatoid arthritis
    Sjögren's syndrome
    Hashimoto's thyroiditis
Infectious agents
  Epstein-Barr virus
  Human T-cell lymphotropic virus type I
  Human herpesvirus 8
  Hepatitis C virus
  Helicobacter pylori
Occupational and environmental exposure
  Herbicides
  Organic solvents
  Hair dyes
  Ultraviolet light

fatal infectious mononucleosis or non-Hodgkin's lymphoma after primary exposure to EBV virus.

Acquired immunodeficiency states are also associated with an increased risk of non-Hodgkin's lymphoma. For example, post-transplant lymphoproliferative disorders occur in as many as 20% of patients who have received solid organ transplants, related to the proliferation of B lymphocytes that have been transformed by EBV immunosuppressive therapy. The risk of non-Hodgkin's lymphoma is also increased more than 100-fold in patients with the human immunodeficiency virus (HIV); almost all central nervous system (CNS) lymphomas and approximately 50% of other lymphomas in patients with AIDS are related to EBV (Chapter 419). Some studies have shown a two-fold increase in the incidence of non-Hodgkin's lymphomas in patients with rheumatoid arthritis (Chapter 278), and the risk of marginal zone lymphomas is increased approximately 30- to 40-fold in patients with Sjögren's syndrome (Chapter 282). Increases in the incidence of thyroid lymphoma are seen in patients with Hashimoto's thyroiditis (Chapter 239). Enteropathy-type T-cell lymphomas are associated with celiac disease (Chapter 141).

INFECTIOUS AGENTS. EBV is associated with the majority of post-transplant lymphoproliferative disorders and many AIDS-associated lymphomas. This viral genome is detectable in more than 95% of cases of endemic Burkitt's lymphoma and in approximately 40% of sporadic cases of Burkitt's lymphoma and AIDS-associated lymphomas.

The human T-cell lymphotropic virus type I (HTLV-I; Chapter 372) is detectable in virtually all cases of adult T-cell leukemia/lymphoma. The risk of lymphoma is approximately 3% in patients infected with HTLV-I; in endemic areas, up to 50% of all non-Hodgkin's lymphomas may be related to HTLV-I.

Human herpesvirus 8 (Kaposi's sarcoma-associated herpesvirus), which is associated with expansion of the B-cell population, is also associated with primary effusion lymphoma (see later text) in immunocompromised patients and with multicentric Castleman's disease. Primary effusion lymphoma is often co-infected with EBV.

Epidemiologic evidence has linked hepatitis C virus (Chapter 152) to lymphoplasmacytic lymphoma and splenic marginal zone lymphoma. Chronic antigenic stimulation from this virus may lead to the emergence of malignant B-cell clones.

Helicobacter pylori is associated with gastric lymphoma (Chapter 199) of extranodal marginal zone/mucosa associated lymphoid tissue (MALT). Colonized patients develop gastritis (Chapter 137) from chronic antigenic stimulation that is mediated by T cells, which respond to *H. pylori*–specific antigens; malignant B-cell clones emerge. *Borrelia burgdorferi* (Chapter 352) has been associated with marginal zone B-cell lymphoma of the skin, particularly in Europe.

ENVIRONMENTAL AND OCCUPATIONAL EXPOSURE. Agricultural chemicals have been associated with an increased risk of developing non-Hodgkin's lymphomas, and the strongest associations have been described with phenoxy herbicides such as 2,4-dichlorophenoxyacetic acid (2,4-D), which was also a component of Agent Orange (Chapter 18). An increased risk has also been associated with ionizing radiation (Chapter 19), organic solvents, hair dyes, and nitrates in drinking water, although contradictory results have been reported. Some studies have also linked non-Hodgkin's lymphomas to high-fat diets and ultraviolet radiation (Chapter 186). The risk of non-Hodgkin's lymphomas is increased approximately 20-fold after treatment for Hodgkin's disease (Chapter 194).

Pathobiology

Non-Hodgkin's lymphomas are derived from cells of the immune system at varying stages of differentiation. In some cases, an understanding of the cell of origin can be used to predict the morphology, immunophenotype, and clinical behavior of the lymphoma (Fig. 195–3). The immunophenotype of the lymphoma reflects the cell of origin (Table 195–2).

The transformation of cells from the normal immune system into malignant lymphoma reflects the acquisition of specific genetic abnormalities. In many cases, cytogenetic studies can identify chromosomal translocations that underlie the development or progression of the lymphoma. In most cases of non-Hodgkin's lymphoma, the activation of proto-oncogenes is the major abnormality, but occasionally chromosomal translocations can lead to fusion genes that code for chimeric proteins. In addition, some cases are associated with deletion of tumor suppressor genes. Specific genetic abnormalities are

Table 195–2 • TYPICAL IMMUNOPHENOTYPE OF COMMON NON-HODGKIN'S LYMPHOMAS

Small lymphocytic	CD20+, CD3–, CD10–, CD5+, CD23+
Lymphoplasmacytic	CD20+, CD3–, CD10–, CD5–, CD23–, cytoplasmic Ig+
Extranodal marginal zone MALT	CD20+, CD3–, CD10–, CD5–, CD23–
Nodal marginal zone	CD20+, CD3–, CD10–, CD5–, CD23–
Follicular	CD20+, CD3–, CD10+, CD5–
Mantle cell	CD20+, CD10–, CD5+, CD23–, Cyclin D1+
Diffuse large B cell	CD20+, CD3–
Mediastinal large B cell	CD20+, CD3–
Burkitt's	CD20+, CD3–, CD10+, CD5–, TdT–
Precursor T lymphoblastic	CD20–, CD3+/–, TdT+, CD1a +/–, CD7+
Anaplastic large T cell	CD20–, CD3+/–, CD30+, CD15–, EMA+, ALK+
Peripheral T cell	CD20–, CD3+/–, (other pan-T variable)

Table 195–3 • CYTOGENETIC ABNORMALITIES MOST FREQUENTLY SEEN IN NON-HODGKIN'S LYMPHOMAS

CYTOGENETIC ABNORMALITY	ASSOCIATED ONCOGENE	TYPICAL LYMPHOMA TYPE
t(8;14), t(2;8), t(8;22)	c-myc + IgH or IgL	Burkitt's
t(14;18)	bcl-2 + IgH	Follicular
t(11;14)	bcl-1 (cyclin D1) + IgH	Mantle cell
t(3;v)	bcl-6 + variable	Diffuse large B cell
t(2;5)	ALK protein + NPN	Anaplastic large T cell
t(11;18)	API2 + MLT	MALT lymphoma

IgH = immunoglobulin heavy chain; IgL = Immunoglobulin light chain; NPN = nucleophosmin; t = translocation.

associated with some specific subtypes of non-Hodgkin's lymphoma (Table 195–3).

Classification

The recognition of the Reed-Sternberg cell approximately 100 years ago made it possible to define Hodgkin's disease (Chapter 194) as a distinct entity, while other lymphomas were included under the heading of non-Hodgkin's lymphomas. In the 1990s, a classification system incorporating morphologic, immunologic, genetic, and clinical information (the Revised European-American Lymphoma Classification [REAL]) was developed to identify distinct clinicopathologic subgroups that represented diseases that could be recognized by clinicians. This system was subsequently adopted as the World Health Organization (WHO) classification of lymphomas in 2001 (Table 195–4).

The WHO classification divides lymphomas on the basis of B-cell or T/NK-cell origin and whether or not the lymphomas are derived from primitive precursor cells or more mature "peripheral" cells. Specific clinical and pathologic entities are recognized within each of these groupings. In the United States and Europe, 85 to 90% of non-Hodgkin's lymphomas are B cell in origin.

The most frequent type is diffuse large B-cell lymphoma, which represents 31% of all non-Hodgkin's lymphomas worldwide. The next most frequent type is follicular lymphoma, which represents 22% of cases; follicular lymphoma is relatively more frequent in North America and Western Europe, and less frequent in Asia. Less common types, each representing between 5 and 10% of all non-Hodgkin's lymphomas, are the extranodal marginal zone/MALT lymphomas, the peripheral T-cell lymphomas, small lymphocytic lymphoma, and mantle cell lymphoma. Rarer types, each of which constitutes more than 1% of cases, include mediastinal large B-cell lymphoma, anaplastic large T-cell lymphoma, and lymphoblastic lymphoma. Other groups such as Burkitt's lymphoma, adult T-cell leukemia/lymphoma, and rare types of T-cell lymphomas each represent less than 1% of non-Hodgkin's lymphomas seen in the United States.

The non-Hodgkin's lymphomas recognized in the WHO classification have clinically distinctive characteristics (Table 195–5) so that

Oncology

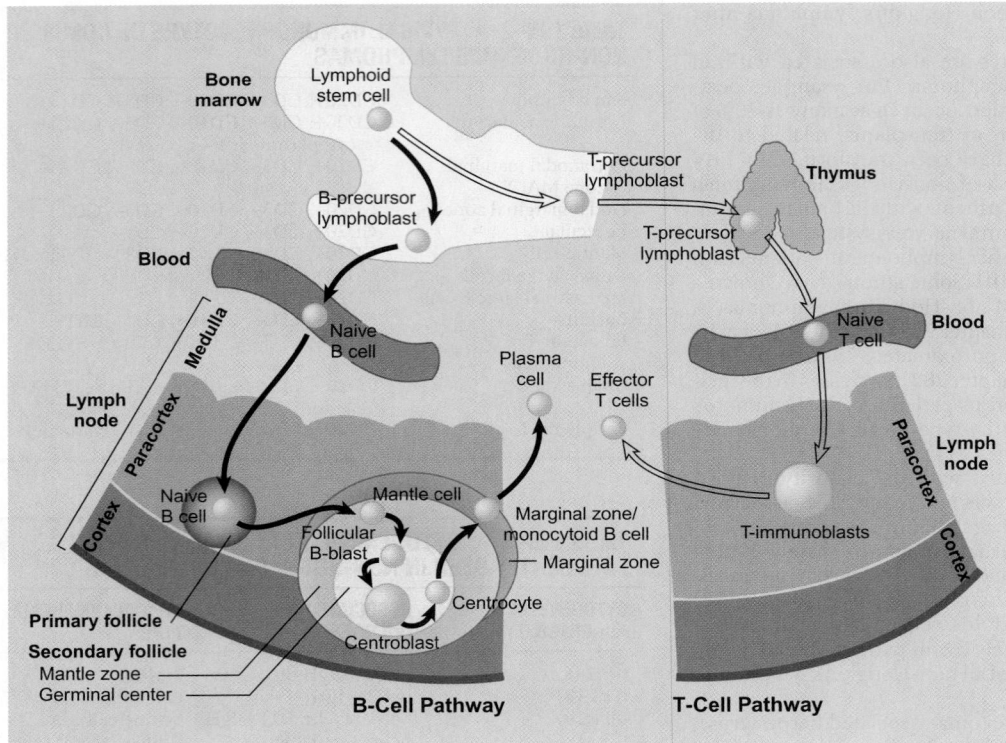

A

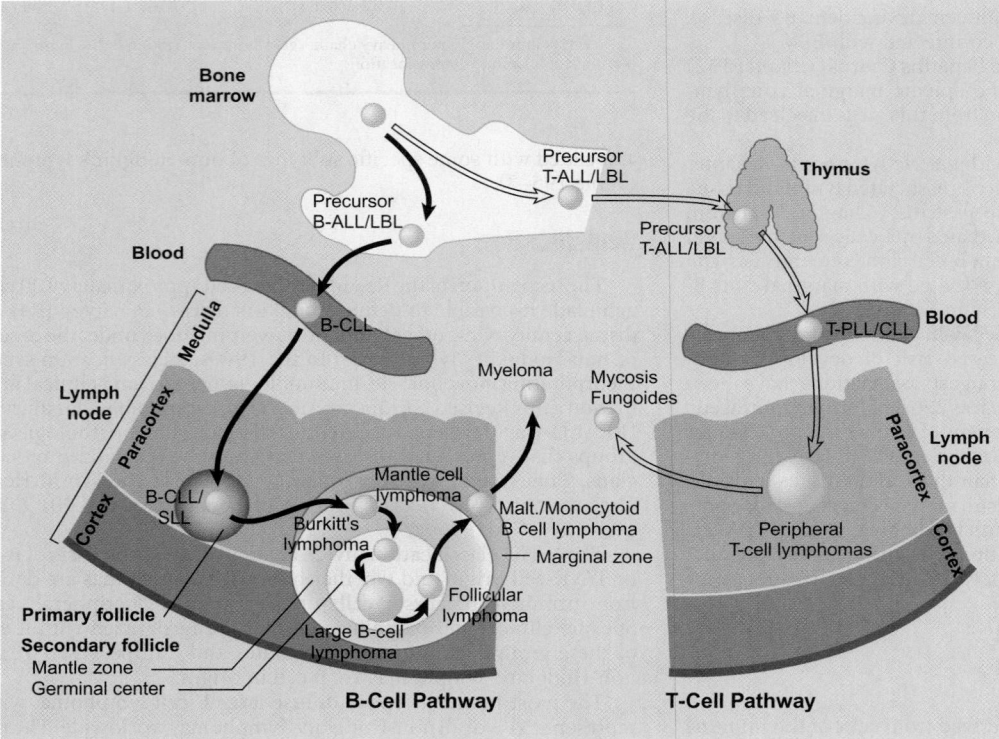

B

FIGURE 195–3 • Postulated normal counterparts of currently recognized B- and T-cell malignancies. *A*, Schema of normal B- and T-cell differentiation. Bone marrow–derived lymphoid stem cells differentiate into committed B-cell precursors or T-cell precursors that undergo further maturation in the thymus. Thereafter, these B- and T-cell precursors mature into naive B- or T-cells that circulate to lymph nodes. After antigen exposure, normal B blasts proliferate and undergo further differentiation in the germinal center of the secondary follicle. The germinal center is surrounded by a mantle zone and marginal zone. Antigen-specific B cells generated in the germinal center leave the follicle and reappear in the marginal zone. Thereafter, immunoglobulin-producing plasma cells accumulate in the lymph node medulla and subsequently exit to the periphery. Antigen-dependent T-cell proliferation occurs in the lymph node paracortex. After antigen exposure, mature T cells become immunoblasts, and subsequently, antigen-specific effector T cells that exit to the periphery. The postulated normal counterparts of many currently recognized T- and B-cell neoplasms are shown. *B*, T- and B-cell malignancies derived from the postulated normal counterparts shown in *A*.

an experienced hematopathologist can accurately classify 85% of patients by WHO criteria when adequate material is available. Some diagnoses, such as follicular lymphoma, can be made with a high degree of accuracy without immunologic or genetic studies. The diagnosis of T-cell lymphomas cannot be made accurately without immunophenotyping. Cytogenetic studies and molecular genetic studies can help resolve difficult differential diagnoses. For example, a t(8;14) would support the diagnosis of a Burkitt's lymphoma, whereas a t(11;14) with cyclin D1 overexpression can confirm the diagnosis of mantle cell lymphoma (see Tables 195–2 and 195–3).

Clinical Manifestations

The most common presentation of non-Hodgkin's lymphoma is lymphadenopathy (Fig. 195–4; Chapter 164). In many cases, patients notice cervical, axillary, or inguinal adenopathy and seek a physician's advice. In general, lymph nodes containing lymphoma are firm, nontender, and not associated with a regional infection. However, patients are frequently treated with a course of antibiotics before a biopsy is performed to confirm the diagnosis of

Table 195–4 • WHO CLASSIFICATION OF NON-HODGKIN'S LYMPHOMA

B-CELL LYMPHOMAS

Precursor B-cell lymphoma	Precursor B lymphoblastic lymphoma/leukemia
Mature B-cell lymphoma	Chronic lymphocytic leukemia/small lymphocytic lymphoma
	Lymphoplasmacytic lymphoma
	Splenic marginal zone lymphoma
	Extranodal marginal zone B-cell lymphoma of mucosa associated lymphoid tissue (MALT-lymphoma)
	Nodal marginal zone B-cell lymphoma
	Follicular lymphoma
	Mantle cell lymphoma
	Diffuse large B-cell lymphoma
	Mediastinal (thymic) large B-cell lymphoma
	Intravascular large B-cell lymphoma
	Primary effusion lymphoma
	Burkitt's lymphoma/leukemia

T/NK-CELL LYMPHOMAS

Precursor T-cell lymphoma	Precursor T-cell lymphoblastic leukemia/lymphoma
	Blastic NK cell lymphoma
Mature T/NK cell lymphoma	Adult T-cell leukemia/lymphoma
	Extranodal NK/T cell lymphoma, nasal type
	Enteropathy-type T-cell lymphoma
	Hepatosplenic T-cell lymphoma
	Subcutaneous panniculitis-like T-cell lymphoma
	Mycosis fungoides
	Sézary syndrome
	Primary cutaneous anaplastic large cell lymphoma
	Peripheral T-cell lymphoma, unspecified
	Angioimmunoblastic T-cell lymphoma
	Anaplastic large cell lymphoma

NK = natural killer.
Adapted from Jaffe ES, Harris NL, Stein H, Vardiman JW (eds): World Health Organization Classification of Tumours. Pathology & Genetics. Tumours of Haematopoietic and Lymphoid Tissues. Lyon, IARC Press, 2001.

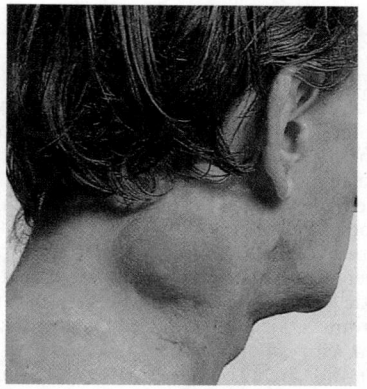

FIGURE 195–4 • Non-Hodgkin's lymphoma. Despite the redness of the skin over the enlarged lymph node in this patient, the lesion was completely painless. (From Forbes CD, Jackson WF: Color Atlas and Text of Clinical Medicine, 3rd ed. London, Mosby, 2003, with permission.)

lymphoma. In other patients, lymphadenopathy occurring in sites such as the mediastinum or retroperitoneum causes symptoms that bring the patient to the physician. Chest pain, cough, superior vena cava syndrome, abdominal pain, back pain, spinal cord compression, and symptoms of renal insufficiency associated with ureteral compression are characteristic.

Non-Hodgkin's lymphomas are often associated with systemic symptoms that may be the complaint that leads to the diagnosis. The most obvious symptoms are fevers, night sweats, and unexplained weight loss. Any of these symptoms without an obvious cause should lead a physician to consider the diagnosis of lymphoma. Other less characteristic symptoms include fatigue, which is frequently present at the time of diagnosis of lymphoma if the patient is questioned carefully, and pruritus.

Non-Hodgkin's lymphomas can involve essentially any organ in the body, and malfunction of that organ can cause symptoms that lead to the diagnosis. Examples include neurologic symptoms with primary brain lymphoma (Chapter 457), shortness of breath with MALT lymphomas in the lung, epigastric pain and vomiting with gastric MALT or diffuse large B-cell lymphomas (Chapter 199), bowel obstruction with small bowel lymphomas (Chapter 200), testicular masses with diffuse large B-cell lymphoma (Chapter 206), and skin lesions with cutaneous lymphomas (Chapter 476). Many lymphomas involve the bone marrow and can occasionally cause extensive myelophthisis (Chapter 174) and

Continued

Table 195–5 • PRESENTING CLINICAL CHARACTERISTICS OF THE MOST COMMON SUBTYPES OF NON-HODGKIN'S LYMPHOMAS

TYPE OF LYMPHOMA	MEDIAN AGE	% MALE	% ANN ARBOR STAGE 1	2	3	4	% B SYMPTOMS	% BONE MARROW INVOLVED	% IPI SCORE 0/1	2/3	4/5	5-YEAR SURVIVAL
B-CELL												
Small lymphocytic	65	53	4	5	8	83	33	72	23	64	13	51%
Lymphoplasmacytic	63	53	7	13	7	73	13	73	16	69	15	59%
Extranodal marginal zone MALT	60	48	39	28	2	31	19	14	44	48	8	74%
Nodal marginal zone	58	42	13	13	34	40	37	32	60	27	13	57%
Follicular	59	42	18	15	16	51	28	42	45	48	7	72%
Mantle cell	63	74	13	7	9	71	28	64	23	54	23	27%
Diffuse large B cell	64	55	25	29	13	33	33	16	35	46	19	46%
Mediastinal large B cell	37	34	10	56	3	31	38	3	52	37	11	50%
Burkitt's	31	89	37	25	0	38	22	33	57	29	14	44%
PRECURSOR B/T CELL												
Precursor T-lymphoblastic	28	64	0	11	14	75	21	50	33	41	26	26%
T-CELL												
Anaplastic large T cell	34	69	19	32	10	39	53	13	61	18	21	77%
Peripheral T cell	61	55	8	12	15	65	50	36	17	52	31	25%

B symptoms = fevers, night sweats, and weight loss; MALT = mucosa associated lymphoid tissue.
Adapted from Armitage JO, Weisenburger DD, for the Non-Hodgkin's Lymphoma Classification Project: New approach to classifying non-Hodgkin's lymphomas: Clinical features of the major histologic subtypes. J Clin Oncol 1998:16:2780–2795.

bone marrow failure; these patients can present with infections, bleeding, and anemia.

Non-Hodgkin's lymphomas can also manifest with a variety of immunologic abnormalities. For example, autoimmune hemolytic anemia (Chapter 169) and immune thrombocytopenia (Chapter 177) can be the presenting manifestations of non-Hodgkin's lymphoma, especially small lymphocytic lymphoma/chronic lymphocytic leukemia but also other subtypes, including diffuse large B-cell lymphoma. Peripheral neuropathies (Chapter 462), often associated with overproduction of a monoclonal protein, can be seen in a variety of subtypes but are most characteristic of lymphoplasmacytic lymphoma and are also sometimes seen with POEMS syndrome associated with Castleman's disease. Although more common with carcinomas, distant effects of cancer on the CNS (Chapter 188) are also rarely seen with lymphomas.

The differential diagnosis in patients who are found to have non-Hodgkin's lymphoma is broad. Any cause of lymphadenopathy or splenomegaly can potentially be confused with non-Hodgkin's lymphoma (Chapter 164). However, this confusion is resolved by appropriate biopsy. It is extremely important to recognize that the diagnosis of non-Hodgkin's lymphoma must be considered in patients with compatible clinical presentations and then confirmed by means of an adequate biopsy that is read by an experienced hematopathologist. The diagnosis should never be inferred, and patients should not be treated until the diagnosis is confirmed by biopsy.

Diagnosis

Each new patient with a non-Hodgkin's lymphoma should be thoroughly evaluated in a systematic manner (Table 195–6). Because subtle pathologic distinctions may alter therapy, the most important issue in managing non-Hodgkin's lymphoma is to establish an accurate diagnosis. Core needle biopsies can occasionally be used for a primary diagnosis if the specimen is handled properly. Fine-needle aspirates are almost never the way to diagnose lymphoma and preclude accurate diagnosis of the specific subtype of non-Hodgkin's lymphoma. In most cases, an excisional biopsy is necessary for the initial diagnosis; another biopsy should be performed if sufficient material is not obtained. Review by an experienced hematopathologist is essential.

Staging

After diagnosis, a meticulous staging evaluation is necessary to estimate prognosis and to determine therapy. The most common staging system is the Ann Arbor classification, which separates patients into four stages based on anatomic sites of disease (Table 195–7). In addition, each stage is subdivided into A (without defined general symptoms) and B (unexplained weight loss of more than 10% in the previous 6 months, unexplained temperature greater than 38° F, or night sweats) categories. Known sites of disease can be reexamined later to evaluate the response to therapy. Gallium scans and positron-emission tomographic scans may sometimes be helpful in distinguishing active disease from residual areas of fibrosis after treatment.

Table 195–6 • TYPICAL EVALUATION OF A NEW PATIENT WITH NON-HODGKIN'S LYMPHOMA

1. Biopsy to establish diagnosis
2. Careful history and physical examination
3. Laboratory evaluation:
   Complete blood count
   Chemistry screen including lactate dehydrogenase level
   β_2-microglobulin
4. Imaging studies:
   Chest radiograph
   Computed tomographic scan of chest, abdomen, and pelvis
   Positron-emission tomographic scan or gallium scan (consider for patients with diffuse large B-cell lymphoma and other aggressive histologic subtypes)
5. Further biopsies:
   Bone marrow
   Any other suspicious site if the results of the biopsy would change therapy

Table 195–7 • NON-HODGKIN'S LYMPHOMA STAGING

Stage I	Involvement of a single lymph node region (I) or a single extralymphatic organ or site (I$_E$)
Stage II	Involvement of 2 or more lymph node regions on the same side of the diaphragm (II) or localized involvement of extralymphatic organ or site and 1 or more lymph node regions on the same side of the diaphragm (II$_E$)
Stage III	Involvement of lymph node regions on both sides of the diaphragm (III), which may also be accompanied by localized involvement of extralymphatic organ or site (III$_E$) or by involvement of spleen (III$_S$), or both (III$_{SE}$)
Stage IV	Diffuse or disseminated involvement of 1 or more extralymphatic organs or tissues with or without associated lymph node enlargement

Adapted from Carbone PP, Kaplan HS, Musshoff K, et al: Report of the Committee on Hodgkin's Disease Staging Classification. Cancer Res 1971;31:1860–1861.

Rx Treatment

Lymphomas may behave in an indolent or aggressive manner. The behavior of many of these neoplasms is distinctive, but within each category the behavior is frequently influenced by sites of disease, bulk of tumor, and the performance status of the patient. Some lymphomas can be managed, at least initially, with observation, whereas other situations, such as spinal cord compression (Chapter 457), are medical emergencies. It is important to consider three questions before starting therapy: (1) Does treatment have curative potential? (2) Can treatment prolong survival? (3) Will treatment alleviate symptoms?

Surgical excision is sometimes curative for patients with localized MALT lymphoma. Sometimes, resection of colon and small bowel lymphoma is appropriate to avoid the potential complications of perforation and hemorrhage with the initiation of chemotherapy. Splenectomy can improve cytopenias and is sometimes used as palliative therapy for symptomatic splenomegaly. Otherwise, surgery has little role in the therapy of non-Hodgkin's lymphoma.

Radiotherapy is frequently used alone or in combination with chemotherapy for localized disease and is sometimes used after chemotherapy to consolidate treatment of bulky disease. Radiation therapy is also used as palliative therapy to treat symptomatic sites of relapse.

Most patients require chemotherapy, which may consist of single agents or combinations of drugs. Two monoclonal antibodies are approved in the United States for the treatment of follicular non-Hodgkin's lymphoma; these are also active for more aggressive histologic subtypes.

Prognostic Factors

Within each category of non-Hodgkin's lymphoma, the prognosis may vary according to factors relating to the patient and the tumor. The International Prognostic Index, which has become the most widely used means to evaluate prognosis for non-Hodgkin's lymphoma (Table 195–8), incorporates five factors (age, performance status, lactate dehydrogenase [LDH] level, number of extranodal sites of disease, and stage). Risk groups are determined according to the number of adverse prognostic characteristics. These risk groups can be used to determine the probability of attaining a complete remission with aggressive combination chemotherapy and the probability of survival. A separate age-adjusted index is used for patients age 60 years or younger. The index is used primarily for diffuse large B-cell lymphomas, but it is also useful for peripheral T-cell lymphomas and follicular lymphomas.

Other factors that influence prognosis include the bulk of the tumor, cytogenetics, the cellular proliferation rate, the β_2-microglobulin level, bcl-2 protein expression, and p53 gene mutations. Recent studies suggest that gene expression profiles identified with cDNA or oligonucleotide microarrays may have the potential to identify genes that could be better predictors of prognosis than currently-used clinical prognostic factors.

Table 195–8 • **THE INTERNATIONAL PROGNOSTIC INDEX**

	NO. OF RISK FACTORS	COMPLETE RESPONSE RATE (%)	5-YR RELAPSE-FREE SURVIVAL (%)	5-YR OVERALL SURVIVAL (%)
All patients				
Adverse factors (age > 60 yr, ↑ LDH, performance status 2–4, >1 extranodal sites, Ann Arbor stage III or IV)				
Low	0 or 1	87	70	73
Low intermediate	2	67	50	51
High intermediate	3	55	49	43
High	4 or 5	44	40	26
Age-adjusted index, patients ≤ 60 yr				
Adverse factors (↑ LDH, performance status 2–4, Ann Arbor stage III or IV)				
Low	0	92	86	83
Low intermediate	1	78	66	69
High intermediate	2	57	53	46
High	3	46	58	32

LDH = lactate dehydrogenase.
Adapted from Shipp M, Harrington D, Anderson J, et al: A predictive model for aggressive non-Hodgkin's lymphoma. N Engl J Med 1993;329:987–994.

SPECIFIC TYPES OF NON-HODGKIN'S LYMPHOMAS

PRECURSOR T-CELL AND B-CELL LYMPHOMAS

PRECURSOR B LYMPHOBLASTIC LYMPHOMA AND PRECURSOR T LYMPHOBLASTIC LYMPHOMA

These tumors are nodal or other solid tissue infiltrates of cells that are morphologically and immunophenotypically identical to the immature cells seen in B-cell or T-cell acute lymphoblastic leukemia (Chapter 193). Patients who have predominantly nodal disease with minimal or no involvement of the bone marrow are frequently classified as having *lymphoblastic lymphoma*, whereas those with more than 25% neoplastic cells in the marrow are classified as having *lymphoblastic leukemia*. These distinctions are arbitrary and reflect the stage of disease rather than different diagnoses. These neoplasms are much more common in children than adults.

B-cell precursor lymphomas are neoplasms that frequently manifest as solid tumors with involvement of the skin and bones, whereas T-cell neoplasms frequently manifest with a mediastinal mass and with involvement of the CNS. Approximately 90% of patients who present with lymphoblastic lymphoma have a T-cell phenotype, whereas about 85% of patients who present with acute lymphoblastic leukemia have a B-cell precursor phenotype. Adverse prognostic characteristics include CNS involvement, stage IV disease, and an elevated LDH level.

 Treatment

Patients with T lymphoblastic lymphoma require treatment with intensive chemotherapy regimens. Patients with precursor B lymphoblastic lymphoma are typically treated with regimens modeled after ones used for acute lymphoblastic leukemia (Chapter 193). These regimens frequently contain cytarabine and high-dose methotrexate, and they often require prolonged maintenance therapy. CNS prophylaxis with intrathecal chemotherapy, high-dose methotrexate, or cranial irradiation is also a component of these regimens.

MATURE B-CELL LYMPHOMAS

SMALL LYMPHOCYTIC LYMPHOMA/CHRONIC LYMPHOCYTIC LEUKEMIA

Small lymphocytic lymphoma is defined as a lymph node or other tissue infiltrate that is morphologically and immunophenotypically identical to chronic lymphocytic leukemia. Patients are frequently asymptomatic, and the diagnosis is often made when blood counts are performed for other reasons. Patients frequently have lymphadenopathy or splenomegaly. Fatigue is common. Hypogammaglobulinemia can occur and lead to an increased susceptibility to infection. Patients may develop autoimmune thrombocytopenia, autoimmune neutropenia, and red blood cell aplasia. These autoimmune disorders may respond to treatment with steroids, intravenous immune globulin, or splenectomy. Some patients may exhibit transformation to diffuse large B-cell lymphoma (Richter's syndrome), which is associated with a poor prognosis. The median survival is more than 10 years for patients without adverse characteristics, and these patients can often be managed with observation. Therapy is necessary for patients who have rapidly progressive or symptomatic lymphadenopathy and for those who develop cytopenias. Management must be individualized because therapy is not curative and patients are often elderly. Single-agent chemotherapy with chlorambucil or cyclophosphamide (Chapter 191) is useful, although fludarabine is associated with higher response rates. Fludarabine may also be administered in combination with cyclophosphamide, monoclonal antibodies, or both. Chemotherapy combinations used for more aggressive lymphomas may also be used. The anti-CD20 antibody rituximab has been used, and another monoclonal antibody, alemtuzumab, which is directed against the CD52 antigen, is also approved for treatment in the United States. Allogeneic hematopoietic stem cell transplantation may be curative, but few patients are candidates for this approach.

EXTRANODAL MARGINAL ZONE LYMPHOMA OF MUCOSA ASSOCIATED LYMPHOID TISSUE (MALT LYMPHOMA)

MALT lymphomas are indolent tumors that originate in association with epithelial cells and are seen most commonly in the gastrointestinal tract, salivary glands, breast, thyroid, orbit, conjunctiva, skin, and lung. These tumors were once thought to represent benign "pseudolymphomas." The majority of cases are stage I or II at diagnosis, although in some series as many as 30% may disseminate to bone marrow or other sites. These lymphomas tend to remain localized for extended periods. Local treatment with surgery or radiotherapy can be used initially and can cure a high proportion of these neoplasms. Other patients, or those who fail to respond, are treated like patients with follicular lymphoma.

Eradication of *H. pylori* with antibiotics leads to regression in more than 50% of gastric MALT lymphomas, although polymerase chain reaction analysis demonstrates minimal residual disease in many of the patients, and the long-term outcome of this approach is unknown. The likelihood of responding to antibiotic therapy is less when invasion is deeper, lymph node metastases are found, or the t(11;18) chromosomal translocation is present. If a MALT lymphoma from a gastric or other site is associated with disseminated nodal metastases, treatment is similar to the therapy for disseminated follicular lymphoma. Bone marrow involvement does not seem to affect the prognosis after treatment of the primary lesion. Patients may have tumors in more than one extranodal site, and these locations can be successfully treated with local therapy. Thus, the usual staging schemes for nodal lymphomas do not seem to predict outcome for MALT lymphomas.

FOLLICULAR LYMPHOMA

Follicular lymphoma comprises the vast majority of indolent or "low-grade" lymphomas in the United States. Follicular lymphoma is divided into three grades based on the proportion of large transformed cells (centroblasts). The clinical behavior and treatment of follicular lymphoma grade 1 and follicular lymphoma grade 2 are the same and are discussed in this section. Grade 3 follicular lymphoma may have a more aggressive clinical course, and patients are frequently treated like patients with diffuse large B-cell lymphoma.

Patients with follicular lymphoma are frequently asymptomatic. The most common presenting complaint is painless lymphadenopathy. Some patients may have cough or dyspnea related to pulmonary or mediastinal involvement or may have pleural effusions. Other patients may have symptoms of abdominal pain or fullness related to subdiaphragmatic or splenic disease. A minority of patients may have systemic symptoms of fevers, night sweats, or weight loss.

Rx Treatment

LOCALIZED DISEASE. Approximately 5 to 15% of patients have localized disease (stage I or minimal stage II disease) at diagnosis. These patients are usually treated with involved-field radiation, and most series report 5-year disease-free survival rates that exceed 50% and overall survival rates of 70 to 100%. Some retrospective series have reported improved outcomes when chemotherapy is combined with radiation.

ADVANCED DISEASE. Most patients with follicular lymphoma have extensive disease at diagnosis. The median survival of these patients is approximately 8 to 10 years. Spontaneous regression has been described, but as many as one third of patients may experience transformation to a more aggressive histology. Transformation is frequently associated with an aggressive clinical course and poor prognosis.

There are numerous options for the initial management of patients with follicular lymphoma. Asymptomatic patients, especially the elderly or patients with other medical illnesses, can frequently be managed with a "watch and wait" approach. Prospective trials have demonstrated that this approach does not influence overall survival, and patients can sometimes be observed for long periods before treatment is required.[1]

Most patients with follicular lymphoma eventually require treatment because of symptomatic or progressive lymphadenopathy, splenomegaly, effusions, or cytopenias. Patients can be treated with single agents such as chlorambucil or cyclophosphamide. In some cases, less aggressive combinations of chemotherapy, such as cyclophosphamide, vincristine, and prednisone (CVP) can be used. In other cases, physicians may prefer to use combinations such as CHOP (cyclophosphamide, doxorubicin, vincristine, prednisone). Fludarabine used alone or in combination with mitoxantrone, is also effective. Although the response rate and duration is usually higher with more aggressive regimens, prospective trials have generally failed to show improved overall survival with any particular chemotherapy regimen for follicular lymphoma.[2]

The CD20 antigen is expressed on virtually all follicular lymphoma cells, and the first monoclonal antibody approved for cancer treatment in humans was the anti-CD20 antibody, rituximab. When added to standard chemotherapy, rituximab may result in complete molecular remissions, disappearance of bcl-2 gene rearrangements from the blood and bone marrow, and improved disease-free survival. When interferon-α is combined with initial chemotherapy, improvements in overall survival have been seen in some trials. The best outcomes are apparently seen when interferon is combined with aggressive anthracycline-based chemotherapy, and when higher doses of interferon are used. Nevertheless, interferon is not commonly used in the primary treatment of follicular lymphoma in the United States because of side effects and contradictory results of efficacy.

SALVAGE THERAPY. Response to initial chemotherapy exceeds 50%, and initial responses generally persist for 1 to 3 years. However, follicular lymphoma eventually progresses in almost all patients with advanced stage disease. Patients with relapse usually respond to additional therapy, often with the same agents, although the duration of response becomes progressively shorter with repeated courses of therapy. Approximately 50% of patients with relapsed follicular lymphoma respond to rituximab; however, fewer than 10% attain a complete response, and the exact role of rituximab has not been defined. Some patients who do not respond to rituximab respond to the yttrium-90 radiolabeled anti-CD20 antibody, ibritumomab tiuxetan, but the proper role for this antibody is also undefined. Some patients with relapsed follicular lymphoma may respond to treatment with interferon-α. Radiation therapy may also be useful for patients with a localized site of symptomatic disease.

Allogeneic hematopoietic stem cell transplantation may cure some patients with relapsed follicular lymphoma, although the transplant-related mortality rate is high. Prolonged remissions have also been observed following autologous hematopoietic stem cell transplantation, but the role of autologous transplantation is unclear.

MANTLE CELL LYMPHOMA

Mantle cell lymphoma is a B-cell neoplasm composed of small lymphoid cells that may resemble small lymphocytic lymphoma or follicular lymphoma. It is most common in elderly patients and is usually at an advanced stage at the time of diagnosis. Male patients are more frequently affected, and extranodal disease, especially involvement of Waldeyer's ring and the gastrointestinal tract, is common. Mantle cell lymphoma is the most common cause of multiple lymphomatous polyposis, and the gastrointestinal tract should be evaluated with endoscopy during the initial evaluation.

Mantle cell lymphoma has a poorer prognosis than any of the common types of non-Hodgkin's lymphoma, with a median survival of about 3 to 4 years. Although there is some evidence that prognosis may be improved with aggressive chemotherapy, mantle cell lymphoma does not appear to be curable with standard chemotherapy regimens. Autologous hematopoietic stem cell transplantation for patients in their first remission may improve survival, but randomized trials have not been performed, and it is unknown whether patients are cured. Allogeneic transplantation is also being evaluated.

DIFFUSE LARGE B-CELL LYMPHOMA

These tumors are the most common type of non-Hodgkin's lymphoma, but their morphology and genetic features are heterogeneous. Signs and symptoms are similar to other subtypes, although patients are more likely to be symptomatic with B symptoms or symptoms from the local tumor than are patients with follicular lymphoma.

Treatment

LOCALIZED DISEASE. As many as 30% of patients with diffuse large B-cell lymphoma have stage I or minimal stage II disease; these patients may occasionally be cured with radiation, but combined modality treatment is most effective. Standard therapy for patients with localized diffuse large B-cell lymphoma is an abbreviated (three to four cycles) course of anthracycline-based chemotherapy, such as CHOP (see earlier text), followed by involved-field radiation; this approach is equivalent to a full eight cycles of chemotherapy.[3] However, a full course of chemotherapy may be used instead for patients who are likely to experience excessive toxicity from the radiation (e.g., loss of teeth or dry mouth following radiation to the salivary glands).

ADVANCED DISEASE. More than 30 prospective randomized trials have compared aggressive combination chemotherapy regimens for diffuse large B-cell lymphoma, and dozens of combination chemotherapy regimens can cure diffuse large B-cell lymphoma. Most regimens are combinations of an alkylating agent, anthracycline, vinca alkaloid, and corticosteroid, but other regimens contain agents such as bleomycin, methotrexate, cytarabine, and etoposide (Table 195–9). All of these regimens yield complete response rates of 60 to 80%, and long-term disease-free survival is seen in 50 to 65% of those who attain a complete response. A large trial conducted by the Southwest Oncology Group compared the first-generation CHOP regimen with other regimens that contained up to eight drugs (Table 195–10). On the basis of this trial, it was concluded that other regimens were not superior to CHOP, and this regimen became the standard of care in the United States, although other anthracycline-containing regimens are still considered superior by some investigators. Recently, a prospective randomized trial conducted in patients 60 to 80 years of age determined that the addition of rituximab to CHOP improved overall survival when compared with CHOP alone (Table 195–11).[4] The combination of CHOP with rituximab is generally considered to be the gold standard for treatment of adults of all ages with diffuse large B-cell lymphoma in the United States.

The use of hematopoietic growth factors permits the use of higher doses of chemotherapeutic drugs and allows chemotherapy cycles to be administered at shorter intervals. Several prospective trials have examined the role of high-dose chemotherapy followed by autologous hematopoietic stem cell transplantation as consolidation therapy after initial chemotherapy for patients with adverse prognostic characteristics. Although there is variability of results, some of the trials have shown benefits for transplantation in first remission, and many investigators recommend early transplantation for selected patients.[5]

Table 195–9 • **COMBINATION CHEMOTHERAPY REGIMENS FOR DIFFUSE LARGE B-CELL LYMPHOMA**

	REGIMEN	DOSE (mg/m²)	DAYS OF ADMINISTRATION	FREQUENCY
CHOP				
	Cyclophosphamide	750 IV	1	q21d
	Doxorubicin	50 IV	1	
	Vincristine*	1.4 IV	1	
	Prednisone fixed dose	100 PO	1–5	
	+/– Rituximab	375 IV	1	
m-BACOD				
	Methotrexate	200 IV	8 and 15	q21d
	Bleomycin†	4 IV	1	
	Doxorubicin	45 IV	1	
	Cyclophosphamide	600 IV	1	
	Vincristine*	1.4 IV	1	
	Dexamethasone	6 PO	1–5	
	Leucovorin	10 PO	24 h after methotrexate, then q6 h for 8 doses	
ProMACE/CytaBOM				
	Prednisone	60 PO	1–14	q28d
	Doxorubicin	25 IV	1	
	Cyclophosphamide	650 IV	1	
	Etoposide	120 IV	1	
	Cytarabine	300 IV	8	
	Bleomycin	5 IV	8	
	Vincristine*	1.4 IV	8	
	Methotrexate	120 IV	8	
	Leucovorin	25 IV	24 h after methotrexate, then q6h for 5 doses	
MACOP-B				
	Methotrexate	400 IV	8	q28d × 3
	Doxorubicin	50 IV	1 and 15	
	Cyclophosphamide	350 IV	1 and 15	
	Vincristine*	1.4 IV	8 and 22	
	Prednisone fixed dose	75 PO	Daily for 12 wk	
	Bleomycin	10 IV	28	
	Leucovorin	15 PO	24 h after methotrexate, then q6h for 6 doses	

*Vincristine dose often capped at 2 mg total.
†Total bleomycin dose, 10 mg.

Table 195–10 • **PROSPECTIVE RANDOMIZED COMPARISON OF REGIMENS FOR ADVANCED AGGRESSIVE NON-HODGKIN'S LYMPHOMA**

	COMPLETE REMISSION (%)	PARTIAL REMISSION (%)	30-YR DISEASE-FREE SURVIVAL (%)	3-YR OVERALL SURVIVAL (%)	FATAL TOXICITY (%)
CHOP	44	36	41	54	1
m-BACOD	48	34	46	52	5
ProMACE/CytaBOM	56	31	46	50	3
MACOP-B	51	32	41	50	6

CHOP = cyclophosphamide, doxorubicin, vincristine, prednisone; MACOP-B = methotrexate, doxorubicin, cyclophosphamide, vincristine, prednisone, bleomycin, leucovorin; m-BACOD = methotrexate, bleomycin, doxorubicin, cyclophosphamide, vincristine, dexamethasone, leucovorin; ProMACE/CytaBOM = prednisone, doxorubicin, cyclophosphamide, etoposide, cytarabine, bleomycin, vincristine, methotrexate, leucovorin.
Adapted from Fisher R, Gaynor ER, Dahlberg S, et al: Comparison of a standard regimen (CHOP) with three intensive chemotherapy regimens for advanced non-Hodgkin's lymphoma. N Engl J Med 1993;328:1002–1006.

SALVAGE THERAPY. A variety of chemotherapy regimens have been developed for patients who relapse after attaining a remission with initial chemotherapy. These regimens commonly contain agents such as cisplatin, cytarabine, etoposide, carboplatin, and ifosfamide. Response rates exceeding 50% can be observed with these combinations, although no more than 10 to 15% of patients achieve long-term disease-free survival. High-dose therapy followed by autologous hematopoietic stem cell transplantation has become accepted therapy for patients with relapsed diffuse large B-cell lymphoma; approximately 40% of these patients attain long-term disease-free survival with transplantation if they are still responsive to conventional salvage chemotherapy. [6]

Table 195–11 • **COMPARISON OF CHOP CHEMOTHERAPY WITH CHOP + RITUXIMAB FOR ELDERLY PATIENTS WITH DIFFUSE LARGE B-CELL LYMPHOMA**

	CHOP	CHOP + RITUXIMAB	P
Complete response	63%	76%	0.005
2-Year event-free survival	38%	57%	<0.001
2-Year overall survival	57%	70%	0.007

CHOP = cyclophosphamide, doxorubicin, vincristine, prednisone.
Adapted from Coiffier B, Lepage E, Briere J, et al: CHOP chemotherapy plus rituximab compared with CHOP alone in elderly patients with diffuse large B-cell lymphoma. N Engl J Med 2002;346:235–242.

MEDIASTINAL LARGE B-CELL LYMPHOMA

Primary mediastinal large B-cell lymphoma originates in the thymus and is most common in young women. This entity is distinguished by the presence of a mediastinal mass, which usually causes symptoms of cough, chest pain, or superior vena cava syndrome.

Disease is confined to the chest and neck in most cases. A very large mass (>10 cm) or the existence of a malignant pleural effusion is associated with worse prognosis. The management of patients with mediastinal large B-cell lymphoma involves initial chemotherapy with regimens used for diffuse large B-cell lymphoma followed, in most cases, by consolidative radiotherapy, and the prognosis is similar to that for other patients with diffuse large B-cell lymphoma. Relapses often occur in extranodal sites such as the CNS, lungs, gastrointestinal tract, liver, ovaries, and kidneys.

BURKITT'S LYMPHOMA

Burkitt's lymphoma is a highly aggressive B-cell lymphoma that is more common in children and immunosuppressed individuals than healthy adults. Widespread extranodal involvement is common. The endemic form of Burkitt's lymphoma is seen most frequently in children who reside in equatorial Africa. Involvement of bones of the jaw is common in this form. The sporadic form of Burkitt's lymphoma is seen most commonly in children in the United States. Males are more frequently affected. Both children and adults frequently have bulky abdominal disease, sometimes with involvement of the kidneys, ovaries, and breast. Bone marrow involvement is seen in about one third of cases.

Tumors may progress extremely rapidly, so therapy should be started as soon as possible. Tumor lysis syndrome may occur because of the frequent presence of bulky disease, the high rate of tumor proliferation, and the extreme sensitivity of the tumor to chemotherapy. Patients are usually treated with specialized high-intensity regimens of relatively short duration. CNS prophylaxis with intrathecal chemotherapy or high-dose methotrexate is required. Cure rates in excess of 50% have been reported.

RARE TYPES OF B-CELL LYMPHOMA

Several rare types of lymphoma have distinct clinical features. *Lymphoplasmacytic lymphoma* is an indolent lymphoma that frequently involves the bone marrow, peripheral blood, and spleen. Patients frequently have an IgM paraprotein (Waldenström's macroglobulinemia) that may lead to symptoms of hyperviscosity, autoimmune phenomena, or neuropathies (Chapter 196). Plasmapheresis can reduce symptoms of hyperviscosity. Chemotherapy with alkylating agents, combination chemotherapy, or fludarabine may be used. Rituximab is also effective. *Splenic marginal zone lymphoma* is an indolent lymphoma that usually manifests with splenomegaly and lymphocytosis. A monoclonal gammopathy is frequently seen. Peripheral lymphadenopathy is unusual. Anemia and thrombocytopenia may respond to splenectomy. Chemotherapy with single agents or anthracycline-based combinations may be useful, and responses to interferon have been described. *Nodal marginal zone B-cell lymphoma* is an indolent disorder that is usually associated with generalized lymphadenopathy. The clinical course and prognosis is similar to chronic lymphocytic leukemia, and patients are generally treated in a similar manner. *Intravascular large B-cell lymphoma* is an aggressive lymphoma caused by cells that infiltrate the lumina of small blood vessels. Widespread extranodal involvement is common. Focal neurologic deficits and mental status changes are frequent. Most cases are diagnosed at autopsy, although durable responses to combination chemotherapy have been described. *Primary effusion lymphoma* is associated with HHV-8 and is seen in HIV-infected and other immunosuppressed patients. Effusions occur in serous body cavities; peripheral lymphadenopathy is not seen. Prognosis is poor despite chemotherapy.

MATURE T-CELL LYMPHOMAS

MYCOSIS FUNGOIDES

Mycosis fungoides (often referred to as cutaneous T-cell lymphoma) is an indolent malignancy that is most common in middle-aged and older adults. The clinical course usually progresses from isolated patches or plaques, to thickened widespread plaques, and then to multiple cutaneous tumors that may ulcerate (Chapter 474). A subset of patients can present with generalized erythroderma and circulating tumor cells, a presentation that is called Sézary syndrome. Lymph node and visceral involvement may occur late in the course of the disease.

 Treatment

> Cutaneous radiotherapy may be curative for patients with limited-stage patch or plaque disease if the radiation fields are not large. Patients with early stage (<10% body surface area) disease are frequently treated with skin-directed therapy that may include ultraviolet radiation, topical steroids, or topical nitrogen mustard.
>
> Patients with more advanced disease frequently benefit from total skin electron beam therapy or extracorporeal photopheresis. Medical treatments include interferon-α, retinoids, monoclonal antibodies, the fusion toxin denileukin diftitox, traditional cytotoxic chemotherapeutic agents, and bone marrow transplantation. However, these treatments are usually palliative.

ADULT T-CELL LYMPHOMA/LEUKEMIA

Adult T-cell lymphoma/leukemia, which is associated with HTLV-I infection (Chapter 372), is most commonly seen in southern Japan and the Caribbean. Most infected patients are asymptomatic, and the lifetime risk of developing adult T-cell lymphoma/leukemia is approximately 3%.

Patients may have acute leukemia, aggressive lymphoma, or an indolent lymphoproliferative disease. Most patients have aggressive disease and present with generalized lymphadenopathy, hepatosplenomegaly, cutaneous infiltration, and hypercalcemia. Many patients have characteristic circulating tumor cells with a "flower" or "clover leaf" nucleus.

Patients with indolent disease can sometimes be followed without therapy. Aggressive disease is usually treated with combination chemotherapy, but there is no consensus on the best regimen, and the 5-year survival is less than 10%.

PRIMARY SYSTEMIC ANAPLASTIC LARGE CELL LYMPHOMA

Anaplastic large cell lymphoma is a CD30+, aggressive T-cell non-Hodgkin's lymphoma that is seen most frequently in young males. B-cell lymphomas with CD30 expression and similar morphology can occur, but they have clinical features identical to other diffuse large B-cell lymphomas and are not considered part of this disease. A morphologically similar but biologically unrelated and clinically distinct neoplasm, primary cutaneous anaplastic large cell lymphoma, occurs predominantly in older adults and represents part of the spectrum of cutaneous CD30+ lymphoproliferative disorders (Chapter 476). Primary systemic anaplastic large T-cell lymphoma typically has a t(2;5) chromosomal translocation leading to overexpression of anaplastic lymphoma kinase (ALK), a protein not normally detectable in lymphoid cells.

Patients usually have lymphadenopathy; involvement of the skin, bone, and gastrointestinal tract may be observed. Patients are usually treated with chemotherapy regimens similar to those used for diffuse large B-cell lymphoma. Patients whose tumors express ALK have an excellent outcome, and 5-year survival rates of 70 to 90% have been observed. Autologous hematopoietic stem cell transplantation may be curative for patients who relapse.

OTHER PERIPHERAL T-CELL LYMPHOMAS

Most patients with peripheral T-cell lymphomas are defined in the WHO classification as having "peripheral T-cell lymphoma, not otherwise categorized." These patients have signs and symptoms that are similar to those of patients with aggressive B-cell lymphomas, although systemic symptoms (fevers, night sweats, and weight loss) and extranodal involvement are more frequent. The diagnosis of peripheral T-cell lymphoma requires immunophenotyping to demonstrate the T-cell origin. Patients are generally treated with the same regimens used for diffuse large B-cell lymphomas, although the outcome for patients with peripheral T-cell lymphoma is substantially worse (see Table 195–5). Patients who relapse after complete remission can sometimes be cured with autologous hematopoietic stem cell transplantation.

UNUSUAL SUBTYPES OF T-CELL LYMPHOMA

As with B-cell lymphomas, rare types of T-cell lymphoma also occur. *Angioimmunoblastic T-cell lymphoma* is associated with generalized lymphadenopathy, fever, weight loss, skin rash, and polyclonal hyper-gammaglobulinemia. Results of therapy are similar to those for peripheral T-cell lymphoma, not otherwise categorized, as described earlier. *Extranodal NK/T-cell lymphoma* usually occurs in extranodal sites, especially the nose, palate, and nasopharynx. Involvement of the nose and face leads to the syndrome that was previously called lethal midline granuloma. This disorder is unusual in the United States, but it is frequent in Southeast Asia and Peru. The prognosis is extremely poor, although patients with localized disease can sometimes be cured with aggressive combination chemotherapy and radiotherapy. *Hepatosplenic T-cell lymphoma* is characterized by sinusoidal infiltration of the spleen, liver, and bone marrow, which lead to hepatosplenomegaly, systemic symptoms, and cytopenias. Lymphadenopathy is unusual. Patients are typically young males, and this disease seems to occur more often in allograft recipients and in the setting of immune dysfunction. Patients have a poor prognosis, and remissions are rarely observed with chemotherapy. *Enteropathy type T-cell lymphoma* is usually seen in patients with gluten-sensitive enteropathy (Chapter 141). Patients typically present with abdominal pain, diarrhea, and sometimes with bowel perforation. Treatment of celiac disease with a gluten-free diet appears to reduce the risk of lymphoma. The prognosis in these often undernourished patients is poor, and large series of uniformly treated patients have not been reported. *Subcutaneous panniculitis-like T-cell lymphoma* manifests with multiple subcutaneous nodules and is often misdiagnosed as panniculitis. Patients with disseminated disease often have a syndrome consisting of fevers, weight loss, hepatosplenomegaly, pancytopenia, and phagocytosis of blood cells (hemophagocytic syndrome). Patients sometimes respond to combination chemotherapy regimens used for diffuse large B-cell lymphoma, interferon, and radiotherapy, but long-term disease-free survival is unusual.

SPECIAL CLINICAL SITUATIONS

Specific Primary Sites of Diffuse Large B-Cell Lymphoma

The diagnosis and management of patients with the various types of non-Hodgkin's lymphoma can be profoundly influenced by the site of origin of the lymphoma or by certain clinical characteristics of the patients. Examples of the latter include pregnant patients with lymphoma, elderly patients with lymphoma, and lymphoma occurring in patients who are severely immunosuppressed.

Approximately 30% of diffuse large B-cell lymphomas originate in extranodal sites. Presentation in certain extranodal sites is associated with unique clinical behaviors that may necessitate diagnostic studies or additional therapy beyond what is used for patients with nodal presentations.

Patients with primary CNS lymphoma (Chapter 457) commonly have ocular involvement, and all patients with this diagnosis should have a slit lamp examination. Surgical resection of primary CNS lymphoma is not beneficial, and the only role for surgery is diagnosis. Primary lymphomas of the CNS are very sensitive to corticosteroids, and the best results have been observed with chemotherapy regimens that use high-dose methotrexate, alone or in combination with other agents such as cytarabine. By comparison, conventional chemotherapy regimens, such as CHOP, are of little benefit. Whole brain irradiation is also effective therapy, although the incidence of leukoencephalopathy is extremely high, especially in elderly patients. Radiation therapy is frequently reserved for relapse rather than being used as adjunctive treatment with primary chemotherapy.

Treatment of primary testicular lymphoma (Chapter 206) generally consists of orchiectomy followed by combination chemotherapy. Relapse in the contralateral testicle is common, and most investigators recommend adjuvant radiation to the scrotum. CNS involvement is common, and prophylactic intrathecal chemotherapy is usually recommended. Late relapses occur frequently.

Diffuse large B-cell lymphoma of the stomach and gastrointestinal tract is treated differently from gastric MALT lymphoma even if a history of prior MALT lymphoma exists. Patients can be cured with surgery and adjunctive radiation or chemotherapy, although surgery is rarely performed because of the morbidity associated with gastric resection. Patients should be treated with chemotherapy regimens used for other patients with diffuse large B-cell lymphoma. Radiation therapy is sometimes used after chemotherapy, although the role of combined modality treatment is not defined.

Lymphoma in Immunocompromised Patients

Non-Hodgkin's lymphoma is an AIDS-defining illnesses in HIV-infected individuals (Chapter 409), and the risk of developing a non-Hodgkin's lymphoma is increased more than 150-fold after the diagnosis of another AIDS-defining illness. Most cases are diffuse large B-cell lymphomas or Burkitt's lymphomas. AIDS-associated lymphomas behave aggressively and frequently involve the CNS and other unusual sites, such as the gastrointestinal tract, anus, rectum, skin, and soft tissue (Chapter 419). Factors associated with poor survival include low CD4 counts, poor performance status, older age, and advanced stage. The prognosis of these lymphomas has generally been poor, with median survival rates of approximately 6 months. More recently, better outcomes have been observed when chemotherapy is given in association with highly active antiretroviral agents in patients with a good performance status. Intrathecal prophylaxis is generally recommended because of a higher risk of CNS involvement.

The risk of developing a non-Hodgkin's lymphoma is also markedly increased in patients who have received solid organ transplants. The histologic appearance of these lymphomas is variable, but they frequently resemble aggressive lymphomas in non-immunocompromised patients. Similar disorders can be seen in patients who are treated with methotrexate for autoimmune disorders and in recipients of allogeneic hematopoietic stem cell transplants, especially if the transplants are T-cell depleted. These post-transplant lymphoproliferative disorders, which may develop within weeks of surgery, are more common in patients who have received more aggressive immunosuppression following transplantation. Involvement of extranodal sites is common, and lymphoma frequently involves the transplanted organ. Post-transplant lymphoproliferative disorders may respond to reduction or withdrawal of immunosuppression. Some investigators have advocated the use of acyclovir or ganciclovir, because these lymphomas are usually related to EBV. Other patients require treatment with combination chemotherapy regimens. Responses have also been described with rituximab.

Non-Hodgkin's Lymphoma in Elderly Patients

More than 50% of patients who develop non-Hodgkin's lymphomas are older than age 60 years, and the prognosis is generally worse for elderly patients. These poorer outcomes are related to increased toxicity of drug therapy, lower remission rates, increased rates of relapse, and higher death rates from cardiovascular disease causes other than the lymphoma itself. Older patients are also more likely to have other adverse prognostic characteristics (see Table 195–8), which also contribute to poorer outcomes.

Several chemotherapy regimens have been developed specifically for elderly patients, but it is unclear whether they yield better outcomes. The practice of arbitrary dose reductions based solely on age should be discouraged if patients have a good performance status and no comorbid illnesses.

Non-Hodgkin's Lymphoma and Pregnancy

Non-Hodgkin's lymphoma in pregnancy involves major clinical and ethical issues, and it requires a multidisciplinary approach (Chapter 252). Although chest radiographs are generally considered to be safe, ultrasound examination is usually used instead of computed tomography for staging the abdomen and pelvis.

Treatment can occasionally be delayed until after delivery; however, most women have a tumor that is potentially curable, and treatment delays may decrease the chance for cure. Other patients may have conditions such as superior vena cava syndrome that require immediate treatment. After the first trimester, full-dose standard therapy such as CHOP may be used; several studies indicate high probabilities of cure without adverse long-term physical or intellectual deficits for the child. Although some investigators have recommended consideration of therapeutic abortion for women in the first trimester, chemotherapy may also be successful in this situation.

DISEASES SOMETIMES CONFUSED WITH LYMPHOMA

The most common atypical lymphoid proliferations that can be confused with lymphoma are florid reactions to immune stimulation. Follicular hyperplasia with diffuse proliferation of B cells and T cells can be seen in a variety of autoimmune diseases (e.g., Sjögren's syndrome, systemic lupus erythematosus, rheumatoid arthritis) and infectious processes (e.g., EBV, cytomegalovirus, cat scratch disease) (Chapter 164). When the definitive diagnosis of lymphoma cannot be made even after immunologic and molecular studies, the patient should be closely observed. The clinical course or subsequent biopsies can usually resolve the confusion.

Several rare lymphoproliferative disorders other than lymphoma have distinctive clinical courses. *Castleman's disease*, or angiofollicular lymph node hyperplasia, usually appears with a hyaline vascular pattern of lymphoid proliferation, but a subset of patients has hyperplastic lymphoid follicles and sheets of plasma cells. Patients with Castleman's disease most often present with a localized lymphoid mass, but some patients have a systemic illness with fevers, night sweats, weight loss, and fatigue. Many of the manifestations of Castleman's disease are related to excessive production of IL-6 associated with HHV-8. Patients with disseminated and plasma cell–rich forms of Castleman's disease may progress to lymphoma. Patients with localized Castleman's disease can be treated with surgical removal or radiotherapy. Patients with systemic disease may respond to treatment with high-dose corticosteroids. Patients who fail to respond to corticosteroid treatment sometimes benefit from combination chemotherapy regimens that are used for diffuse large B-cell lymphoma.

Sinus histiocytosis with massive lymphadenopathy, also known as *Rosai-Dorfman disease*, manifests as bulky lymphadenopathy in children and young adults. Extranodal sites such as the skin, upper airways, gastrointestinal tract, and CNS can be involved. There is a characteristic pattern of lymphoid proliferation with a thick fibrous capsule, distention of lymphoid sinuses, accumulation of plasma cells, and proliferation of large, often atypical, histiocytes. The disease is usually self-limiting, but it has been associated with autoimmune hemolytic anemia.

Lymphomatoid papulosis (Chapter 476) is the most benign of the CD30+ cutaneous lymphoproliferative disorders. On biopsy examination, it can be impossible to distinguish lymphomatoid papulosis from primary cutaneous anaplastic large cell lymphoma. The lesions are often monoclonal. The clinical course typically consists of waxing and waning erythematous papular skin lesions that progress, regress, and heal by scarring. Rare cases may progress to anaplastic large cell lymphoma.

Grade Ⓐ

1. Brice P, Bastion Y, Lepage E, et al: Comparison in low-tumor-burden follicular lymphomas between an initial no-treatment policy, prednimustine, or interferon alfa: A randomized study from the Groupe D'Etude des Lymphomes Folliculaires. J Clin Oncol 1997;15:1110–1117.
2. Ezdinli EZ, Anderson JR, Melvin F, et al: Moderate versus aggressive chemotherapy of nodular lymphocytic poorly differentiated lymphoma. J Clin Oncol 1985;3:769–775.
3. Miller TP, Dahlberg S, Cassady JR, et al: Chemotherapy alone compared with chemotherapy plus radiotherapy for localized intermediate- and high-grade non-Hodgkin's lymphoma. N Engl J Med 1998;339:21–26.
4. Coiffier B, Lepage E, Briere J, et al: CHOP chemotherapy plus rituximab compared with CHOP alone in elderly patients with diffuse large-B-cell lymphoma. N Engl J Med 2002;346:235–242.
5. Haioun C, Lepage E, Gisselbrecht C, et al: Survival benefit of high-dose therapy in poor-risk aggressive non-Hodgkin's lymphoma: Final analysis of the prospective LNH87-2 protocol-a Groupe d'Etude des Lymphomes de l'Adulte study. J Clin Oncol 2000;18:3025–3030.
6. Philip T, Guglielmi C, Hagenbeek A, et al: Autologous bone marrow transplantation as compared with salvage chemotherapy in relapses of chemotherapy-sensitive non-Hodgkin's lymphoma. N Engl J Med 1995;333:1540–1545.

SUGGESTED READINGS
Fisher RI: Overview of non-Hodgkin's lymphoma: Biology, staging, and treatment. Semin Oncol 2003;30(2 Suppl 4):3–9. *Combination chemotherapy remains the initial standard of care, but high-dose therapy with stem cell support may be the treatment of choice for patients with relapsed aggressive lymphomas that remain chemosensitive.*
Kouroukis CT, Browman GP, Esmail R, et al: Chemotherapy for older patients with newly diagnosed, advanced-stage, aggressive-histology non-Hodgkin lymphoma: A systematic review. Ann Intern Med 2002;136:144–152. *For older patients with advanced-stage, aggressive-histology lymphoma who do not have significant comorbid illnesses, an anthracycline-containing regimen provides superior outcomes.*

Rosenwald A, Wright G, Chan WC, et al: The use of molecular profiling to predict survival after chemotherapy for diffuse large-B-cell lymphoma. N Engl J Med 2002;346:1937–1947. *DNA microarrays can be used to formulate a molecular predictor of survival after chemotherapy for diffuse large B-cell lymphoma.*

196 PLASMA CELL DISORDERS

Robert A. Kyle
S. Vincent Rajkumar

The plasma cell disorders, which are neoplastic or potentially neoplastic diseases associated with proliferation of a single clone of immunoglobulin-secreting plasma cells derived from the B-cell series of immunocytes, are characterized by the secretion of electrophoretically and immunologically homogeneous (monoclonal) proteins. Each monoclonal protein (M protein, myeloma protein, or paraprotein) consists of two heavy (H) polypeptide chains of the same class and subclass and two light (L) polypeptide chains of the same type (Chapter 41). The heavy polypeptide chains are designated by Greek letters: γ in immunoglobulin G (IgG), α in immunoglobulin A (IgA), μ in immunoglobulin M (IgM), δ in immunoglobulin D (IgD), and ε in immunoglobulin E (IgE). IgG includes subclasses IgG1, IgG2, IgG3, and IgG4; IgA includes subclasses IgA1 and IgA2; no subclasses have been recognized of IgM, IgD, or IgE. The light-chain types are kappa (κ) and lambda (λ). Both heavy chains and light chains have "constant" and "variable" regions with respect to amino acid sequence. Class specificity of each immunoglobulin is defined by a series of antigenic determinants on the constant regions of the heavy chains (γ, α, μ, δ, and ε) and the two major classes of light chains (κ and λ). The amino acid sequence in the variable regions of the immunoglobulin molecule corresponds to the active antigen-combining site of the antibody, whereas the constant regions convey other biologic properties (Chapter 41).

RECOGNITION OF MONOCLONAL PROTEINS

Agarose gel electrophoresis is preferred for the detection of monoclonal proteins (M proteins). Immunofixation should be used to confirm the presence of an M protein and to distinguish the immunoglobulin class and its light-chain type.

ANALYSIS OF SERUM. Serum protein electrophoresis should be performed when multiple myeloma or Waldenström's macroglobulinemia is suspected because of unexplained weakness or fatigue, anemia, back pain, osteoporosis, osteolytic lesions or spontaneous fracture, increase of the erythrocyte sedimentation rate, hypercalcemia, Bence Jones proteinuria, renal insufficiency, immunoglobulin deficiency, or recurrent infections. It should also be considered in adults with sensorimotor peripheral neuropathy, carpal tunnel syndrome, refractory heart failure, nephrotic syndrome, orthostatic hypotension, or malabsorption because a spike or localized band is strongly suggestive of primary systemic amyloidosis.

An M protein is usually seen as a narrow peak (like a church spire) in the densitometer tracing or as a dense, discrete band on agarose gel (Fig. 196–1). Immunofixation should be performed when a peak or band is seen on protein electrophoresis or when multiple myeloma or related disorders are suspected despite a normal protein electrophoresis. Immunofixation is especially useful for finding a small M protein in primary amyloidosis, solitary plasmacytoma, or extramedullary plasmacytoma or after successful treatment of multiple myeloma or macroglobulinemia (Fig. 196–2). Although the immunoglobulins (IgG, IgA, IgM, IgD, and IgE) compose the γ component, they are also found in the β-γ or β region, and IgG may actually extend to the α_2-globulin area. Consequently, an IgG M protein may range from the slow γ (cathode) to the α_2-globulin region.

In 3% of sera with a monoclonal peak, there is an additional M protein of a different immunoglobulin class; this condition is designated a biclonal (double) gammopathy. In contrast, an excess of polyclonal immunoglobulins (one or more heavy-chain types and both κ and λ light chains, usually limited to the γ region [Fig. 196–3]) produces a broad-based peak or broad band; this finding is associated with a reactive or inflammatory process.

The presence of an M protein is most suggestive of monoclonal gammopathy of undetermined significance (MGUS), multiple myeloma, primary amyloidosis, Waldenström's macroglobulinemia,

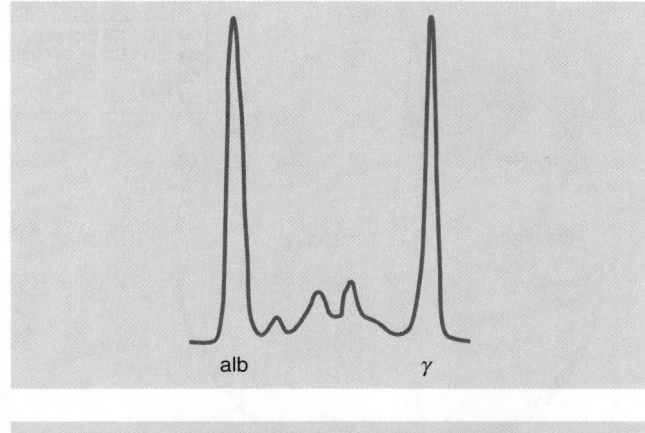

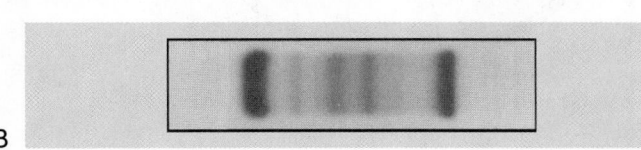

FIGURE 196–1 • *A*, Monoclonal pattern of serum protein as traced by densitometer after electrophoresis on agarose gel: tall, narrow-based peak of γ mobility. *B*, Monoclonal pattern from electrophoresis of serum on agarose gel (anode on left): dense, localized band representing monoclonal protein of γ mobility. (From Kyle RA, Katzmann JA: Immunochemical characterization of immunoglobulins. *In* Rose NR, Conway de Macario E, Folds JD, et al [eds]: Manual of Clinical Laboratory Immunology, 5th ed. Washington, DC, ASM Press, 1997, p 156, with permission of the American Society for Microbiology.)

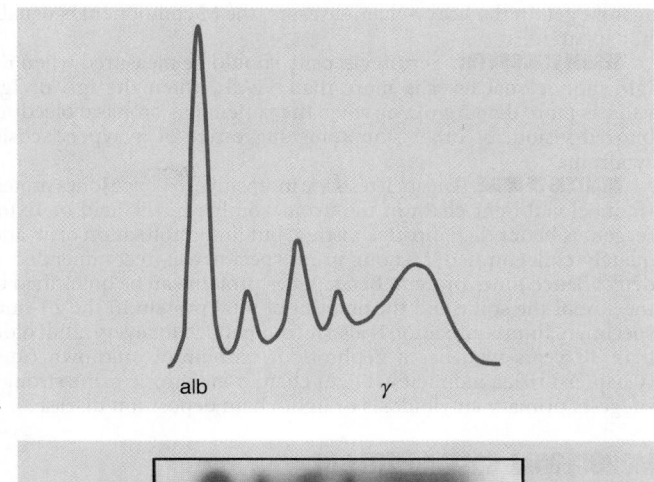

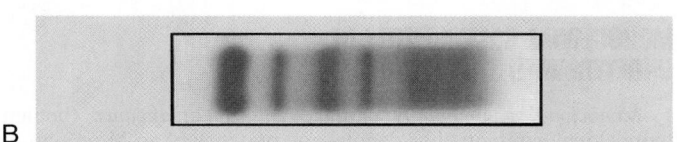

FIGURE 196–3 • *A*, Polyclonal pattern from densitometer tracing of agarose gel: broad-based peak of γ mobility. *B*, Polyclonal pattern from electrophoresis of agarose gel (anode on left). Band at right is broad and extends throughout the γ area. (From Kyle RA, Katzmann JA: Immunochemical characterization of immunoglobulins. *In* Rose NR, Conway de Macario E, Folds JD, et al [eds]: Manual of Clinical Laboratory Immunology, 5th ed. Washington, DC, ASM Press, 1997, p 156, with permission of the American Society for Microbiology.)

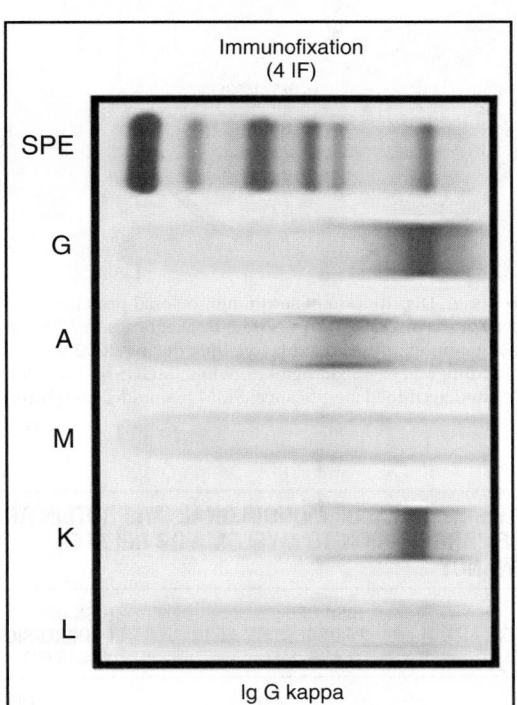

FIGURE 196–2 • Immunofixation depicting an immunoglobulin G κ monoclonal protein.

Table 196–1 • CLASSIFICATION OF PLASMA CELL PROLIFERATIVE DISORDERS

I. Monoclonal gammopathies of undetermined significance (MGUS)
   A. Benign (IgG, IgA, IgD, IgM, and rarely, free light chains)
   B. Associated neoplasms or other diseases not known to produce monoclonal proteins
   C. Biclonal gammopathies
   D. Idiopathic Bence Jones proteinuria
II. Malignant monoclonal gammopathies
   A. Multiple myeloma (IgG, IgA, IgD, IgE, and free light chains)
      1. Overt multiple myeloma
      2. Smoldering multiple myeloma
      3. Plasma cell leukemia
      4. Nonsecretory myeloma
      5. IgD myeloma
      6. Osteosclerotic myeloma (POEMS syndrome)
      7. Solitary plasmacytoma of bone
      8. Extramedullary plasmacytoma
   B. Waldenström's macroglobulinemia
      1. Other lymphoproliferative diseases
III. Heavy-chain diseases (HCDs)
   A. γ-HCD
   B. α-HCD
   C. μ-HCD
IV. Cryoglobulinemia
V. Primary amyloidosis (AL)

Modified from Kyle RA: Classification and diagnosis of monoclonal gammopathies. *In* Rose NR, Friedman H, Fahey JL (eds): Manual of Clinical Laboratory Immunology, 3rd ed. Washington, DC, American Society for Microbiology, 1986, p 152, with permission of the American Society for Microbiology (ASM Press).
IgG = immunoglobulin G; POEMS = polyneuropathy, organomegaly, endocrinopathy, M protein, and skin changes.

or other lymphoproliferative disease (Table 196–1). Rarely, other conditions (e.g., free hemoglobin-haptoglobin complexes resulting from hemolysis, large amounts of transferrin in patients with iron deficiency anemia, or the presence of fibrinogen) may also simulate the presence of an M protein in the serum. Alternatively, an M protein may appear as a rather broad band on agarose gel or as a broad peak in the densitometer tracing as a result of the complexing of an M protein with other plasma components or aggregates of IgG, polymers of IgA, or dimers of IgM.

An M protein can be present when the total protein concentration, β- and γ-globulin levels, and quantitative immunoglobulin values are all within normal limits. A small M protein may be concealed in the normal β or γ areas and may be overlooked. In addition, monoclonal light chains (Bence Jones proteinemia) are rarely seen in the agarose gel. In the heavy-chain diseases, the M component is usually not apparent.

SERUM VISCOMETRY. Serum viscosity should be measured when the IgM monoclonal level is more than 4 g/dL, when the IgA or IgG value is more than 5 g/dL, or when the patient has oronasal bleeding, blurred vision, or other symptoms suggestive of a hyperviscosity syndrome.

ANALYSIS OF URINE. Dipstick tests are insensitive to Bence Jones protein (monoclonal light chain in the urine). Sulfosalicylic acid or Exton reagent is better than dipstick testing, but immunofixation of an adequately concentrated 24-hour urine specimen is recommended to detect Bence Jones protein. Bence Jones protein can be quantified by the size of the spike and the amount of total protein in the 24-hour specimen. Immunofixation is also recommended for every adult older than 40 years who has a nephrotic syndrome of unknown cause (Chapter 119); a monoclonal light chain in nephrotic urine strongly suggests primary amyloidosis or light-chain deposition disease.

MONOCLONAL GAMMOPATHY OF UNDETERMINED SIGNIFICANCE

Monoclonal gammopathy of undetermined significance (benign monoclonal gammopathy) denotes the presence of an M protein in persons without evidence of multiple myeloma, macroglobulinemia, amyloidosis, or other related diseases. The term *benign* should not be used because it is not known whether the process that produces the M protein will remain stable or progress to symptomatic disease. MGUS is characterized by a serum M-protein concentration less than 3 g/dL; fewer than 10% plasma cells in the bone marrow; no or only small amounts of M protein in the urine; absence of lytic bone lesions, anemia, hypercalcemia, and renal insufficiency; and, most important, stability of the amount of the M protein and the failure of other abnormalities to develop.

Incidence

More than 50% of patients with a serum M protein have an initial clinical diagnosis of MGUS (Fig. 196–4). The prevalence of MGUS is 1% in patients older than 50 years and 3% in patients older than 70 years. Because of this high prevalence, it is crucial to determine whether the M protein will remain benign or evolve to multiple myeloma, amyloidosis, macroglobulinemia, or another lymphoproliferative disease.

Prognosis

In one series of 241 patients observed after a diagnosis of apparently benign monoclonal gammopathy (i.e., patients in whom multiple myeloma, macroglobulinemia, amyloidosis, lymphoma, or related diseases were excluded), the incidence of multiple myeloma and related disorders was 33% at 20 years. The interval from the time of recognition of the M protein to the diagnosis of serious disease ranged from 2 to 29 years (median, 10 years).

Among 1384 patients residing in southeastern Minnesota and diagnosed with MGUS from 1960 through 1994, 115 patients progressed to multiple myeloma (relative risk [RR] vs. a control correlation = 25), IgM lymphoma (RR = 2.4), primary amyloidosis (RR = 8.4), macroglobulinemia (RR = 46), chronic lymphocytic leukemia (RR = 0.9), or plasmacytoma (RR = 8.5) during 11,009 person-years of follow-up. The cumulative probability of progression to malignancy (myeloma or related disease) was 12, 25, and 30% at 10, 20, and 25 years, respectively. In 32 additional patients, the M-protein level increased to more than 3 g/dL or the percentage of plasma cells in the bone marrow increased to more than 10% without progression to overt myeloma or a related disorder. Risk of progression was higher with higher M-protein values (Table 196–2). Patients with IgM and IgA M proteins had an increased risk of progression compared with patients who had IgG M proteins. Reductions in uninvolved immunoglobulins and the presence of small monoclonal light chains in the urine did not identify patients who progressed.

Differential Diagnosis

Differentiation of the patient with benign monoclonal gammopathy from one in whom multiple myeloma, macroglobulinemia, or a

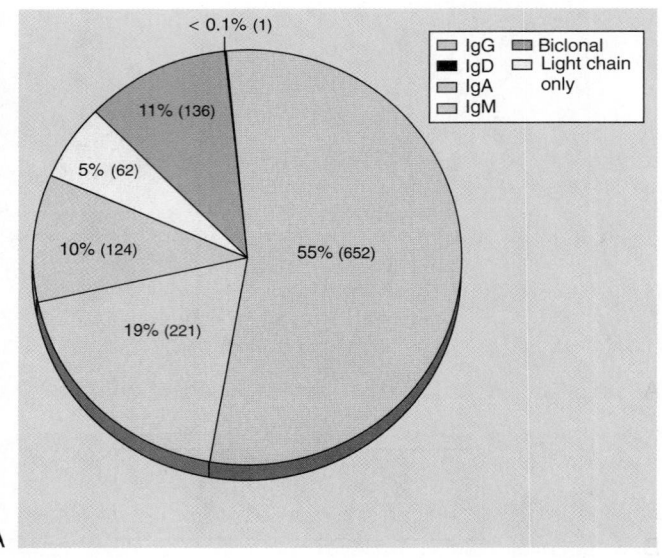

A

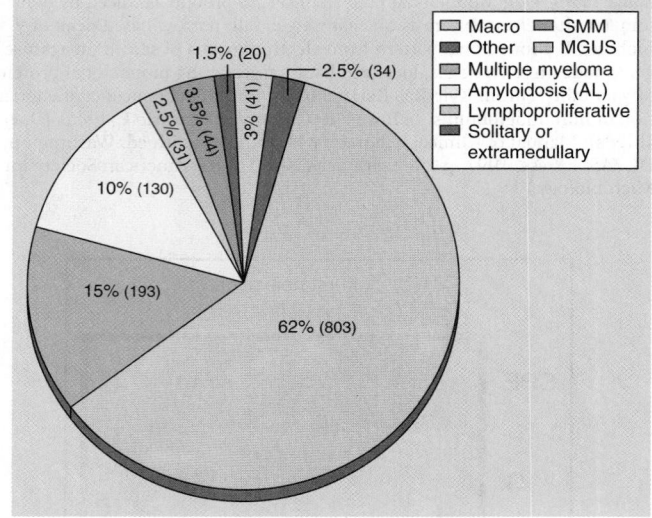

B

FIGURE 196–4 • *A*, Distribution of serum monoclonal proteins in 1196 patients seen at Mayo Clinic during 2000. *B*, Diagnoses in 1296 cases of monoclonal gammopathy seen at Mayo Clinic during 2000. Ig = immunoglobulin; Macro = macroglobulinemia; MGUS = monoclonal gammopathy of undetermined significance; SMM = smoldering multiple myeloma.

Table 196–2 • SIZE OF MONOCLONAL (M) PROTEIN AND RISK OF PROGRESSION TO MYELOMA OR RELATED MALIGNANCY

M-PROTEIN SIZE (g/dL)	RISK OF PROGRESSION AT 10 YEARS (%)	RISK OF PROGRESSION AT 20 YEARS (%)
≤0.5	6	14
1.0	7	16
1.5	11	25
2.0	20	41
2.5	24	49
3.0	34	64

related disorder eventually develops is difficult when the M protein is first recognized. The size of the M protein is of some help; levels greater than 3 g/dL usually indicate overt multiple myeloma or macroglobulinemia, but some exceptions, such as smoldering multiple myeloma, exist. Levels of the immunoglobulin classes other than the M protein (i.e., the normal polyclonal or background immunoglobulins) are usually reduced in multiple myeloma or Waldenström's macroglobulinemia, but a reduction also occurs in almost 40% of patients with MGUS. The association of a monoclonal light chain (Bence Jones proteinuria) with a serum monoclonal gammopathy suggests multiple myeloma or macroglobulinemia, but many patients with small amounts of monoclonal light chain in the urine have stable M-protein levels in the serum for many years. The presence of more than 10% plasma cells in the bone marrow suggests multiple myeloma, but some patients with more plasma cells (smoldering myeloma) have remained stable for long periods without therapy. The presence of osteolytic lesions strongly suggests multiple myeloma, but metastatic carcinoma may produce lytic lesions as well as plasmacytosis and may be associated with an unrelated monoclonal gammopathy.

The plasma cell labeling index measures the synthesis of DNA; when increased, it is good evidence that the patient has multiple myeloma or will soon have symptomatic disease. The presence of circulating plasma cells in the peripheral blood usually indicates active multiple myeloma.

However, no single technique reliably differentiates a patient with a benign monoclonal gammopathy from one who will subsequently have symptomatic multiple myeloma or other malignant disease. The M-protein level in the serum and urine should be serially measured, together with periodic reevaluation of clinical and other laboratory features, to determine whether multiple myeloma or another related disorder is present. In general, if the serum M-protein value is less than 2.0 g/dL, electrophoresis should be repeated at 6 months; if it is stable, it should be rechecked annually. If the serum M-protein value is greater than 2.0 g/dL without evidence of myeloma or related disorders, electrophoresis should be repeated in 3 months; if it is stable, the test should be repeated annually.

Association of Monoclonal Gammopathies with Other Diseases

Monoclonal gammopathy frequently exists without other abnormalities. However, certain diseases are associated with it more often than expected by chance.

LYMPHOPROLIFERATIVE DISORDERS. An M protein is found in 3 to 4% of patients with a diffuse lymphoproliferative process but in fewer than 1% of those with a follicular lymphoma. IgM monoclonal gammopathies are more common than IgG or IgA in lymphoproliferative diseases. In a large series of patients in whom a serum IgM monoclonal gammopathy was identified, more than half were originally considered to have MGUS (Table 196–3). During follow-up, 17% of patients with MGUS of the IgM class developed a malignant lymphoid disease, most frequently Waldenström's macroglobulinemia.

LEUKEMIA. M proteins occur in the sera of some patients with chronic lymphocytic leukemia (Chapter 192) but with no recognizable effect on the clinical course. M proteins have also been recognized in hairy cell, adult T-cell, chronic myelogenous, acute promyelocytic, and acute myelomonocytic leukemias (Chapter 193) but without a documented increased prevalence over that in the normal population. M proteins may also be found after liver, bone marrow, or kidney transplantation.

NEUROLOGIC DISORDERS. Approximately 5% of patients with sensorimotor peripheral neuropathy of unknown cause have an associated monoclonal gammopathy. In half of those with an IgM monoclonal gammopathy and peripheral neuropathy, the M protein binds to myelin-associated glycoprotein. These patients have a slowly progressive sensorimotor neuropathy beginning in the distal extremities and extending proximally. Sensory involvement is more prominent than motor involvement. Cranial nerves and autonomic function are intact. The clinical and electrodiagnostic manifestations resemble those of chronic inflammatory demyelinating polyneuropathy. The relationship of the M protein to the peripheral neuropathy is not clear.

In a patient presenting with MGUS and neuropathy, it is often difficult to determine clinically whether the association is coincidental or whether a causal relationship exists. In younger patients with significant neuropathy, it is likely that the M protein may be playing a role in the pathogenesis. MGUS-associated neuropathy is often diagnosed clinically after excluding other causes. Therapeutic approaches include plasmapheresis and, occasionally, chemotherapy (melphalan and prednisone for IgG and IgA monoclonal proteins, chlorambucil for IgM monoclonal proteins).

DERMATOLOGIC DISEASES. Lichen myxedematosus (papular mucinosis, scleromyxedema) is characterized by papules, macules, and plaques infiltrating the skin and is associated with a cathodal IgG λ protein. Pyoderma gangrenosum and necrobiotic xanthogranuloma have also been associated with an M protein.

Monoclonal Gammopathies with Antibody Activity

In some patients with MGUS, myeloma, or macroglobulinemia, the M protein has exhibited unusual specificity to one of various antigens. Examples include actin, dextran, anti–streptolysin O, antinuclear antibody, riboflavin, von Willebrand factor, thyroglobulin, insulin, double-stranded DNA, and apolipoprotein.

The binding of calcium by an M protein may produce hypercalcemia without symptomatic or pathologic consequences. Affected patients should not be treated for hypercalcemia. M proteins have also been found to bind to copper and to phosphate.

BICLONAL GAMMOPATHIES

Biclonal gammopathies occur in at least 3% of patients with monoclonal gammopathies. Biclonal gammopathy of undetermined significance accounts for about two thirds of patients. The remainder have multiple myeloma, macroglobulinemia, or other lymphoproliferative diseases. Triclonal gammopathies may also occur.

IDIOPATHIC BENCE JONES PROTEINURIA

Bence Jones proteinuria is a recognized feature of multiple myeloma, primary amyloidosis, Waldenström's macroglobulinemia, and other malignant lymphoproliferative disorders. A benign Bence Jones proteinuria may also occur. Patients have been documented to have a stable serum level of M protein and Bence Jones proteinuria for more than 20 years without developing multiple myeloma or related disorders.

MULTIPLE MYELOMA

Multiple myeloma (myelomatosis, plasma cell myeloma, or Kahler's disease) is characterized by the neoplastic proliferation of a single clone of plasma cells engaged in the production of a monoclonal immunoglobulin. This clone of plasma cells proliferates in the bone marrow and frequently invades the adjacent bone, producing extensive skeletal destruction that results in bone pain and fractures. Anemia, hypercalcemia, and renal insufficiency are other important features.

Etiology and Epidemiology

The cause of multiple myeloma is unclear. Exposure to radiation, benzene and other organic solvents, herbicides, and insecticides may play a role. Multiple myeloma has been reported in familial clusters of two or more first-degree relatives and in identical twins.

Table 196–3 • CLASSIFICATION OF IMMUNOGLOBULIN M MONOCLONAL GAMMOPATHIES AMONG 430 PATIENTS

CLASSIFICATION	PERCENTAGE OF PATIENTS
Monoclonal gammopathy of undetermined significance	56
Waldenström's macroglobulinemia	17
Lymphoma	7
Chronic lymphocytic leukemia	5
Primary amyloidosis (AL)	1
Lymphoproliferative disease	14
Total	100

From Kyle RA, Garton JP: The spectrum of IgM monoclonal gammopathy in 430 cases. Mayo Clin Proc 1987;62:719, with permission of Mayo Foundation, Rochester, MN.

Multiple myeloma accounts for 1% of all malignant disease and slightly more than 10% of hematologic malignancies in the United States. The annual incidence of multiple myeloma is 4 per 100,000. An apparent increased incidence in recent years is probably related to increased availability and use of medical facilities, especially for older persons. Multiple myeloma occurs in all races and all geographic locations. Its incidence in blacks is almost twice that in whites. Multiple myeloma is slightly more common in men than in women. The median age of patients at the time of diagnosis is about 65 years; only 2% of patients are younger than 40 years.

Biologic Aspects

Multiple myeloma is a B-cell malignancy with mature plasma cell morphology. In most cases, the plasma cells are cytoplasmic Ig+, CD38+, CD138+, and PCA-1+, only a minority express CD10 and human leukocyte antigen (HLA)–DR, and 20% express CD20. However, the nature of clonogenic cells in myeloma is still unknown. Circulating clonogenic premyeloma cells or long-lived plasma cells, by means of adhesion molecules, may home to the marrow, where they find an appropriate microenvironment (cytokine network) to differentiate and expand further. T cells may play an important role. In patients with multiple myeloma, CD4 T cells are often reduced. Levels of interleukin (IL)-6 are higher in patients with progressive myeloma than in those with MGUS. Both IL-1β and tumor necrosis factor α (TNF-α), each of which has bone-resorbing activity, are over-produced in patients with multiple myeloma.

Lytic bone lesions, osteopenia, hypercalcemia, and pathologic fractures in myeloma are a result of abnormal osteoclast activity induced by the neoplastic plasma cells. Osteoclasts are activated by stimulation of the transmembrane receptor RANK (receptor activator of nuclear factor κB), which belongs to the TNF receptor superfamily. The ligand for this receptor (RANKL) also has a decoy receptor, osteoprotegerin (OPG). Stimulation of RANK is controlled by the ratio of RANKL to OPG. Cytokines secreted by myeloma cells such as IL-6, IL-1β, and TNF-α increase the RANKL/OPG ratio, thereby inducing osteoclast activation (Chapters 187 and 208).

Cytogenetic Abnormalities

Conventional cytogenetic studies show an abnormal karyotype in less than 40% of patients with myeloma. However, fluorescent in situ hybridization (FISH) using chromosome-specific probes reveals chromosome abnormalities in almost 100% of patients. Translocations involving the immunoglobulin heavy-chain loci (chromosome 14q32) are seen in 75% of patients with multiple myeloma and in almost 50% of patients with MGUS. Cytogenetic abnormalities not involving the immunoglobulin loci include complete or partial deletions of chromosome 13, activating mutations of N- and K-ras, inactivating mutations of p53, and dysregulation of c-myc. Deletions of chromosome 13 occur in 15% of myeloma patients in conventional cytogenetic studies and in 50% of patients on FISH, and they are associated with an adverse prognosis.

Flow cytometry studies have shown aneuploidy in about 80% of patients, hyperdiploidy in 70%, and hypodiploidy in the remaining 10%.

Clinical Manifestations

SYMPTOMS (Table 196–4). Bone pain, particularly in the back or chest and less often in the extremities, is present at the time of diagnosis in more than two thirds of patients. The pain is usually induced by movement and does not occur at night except with change of position. The patient's height may be reduced by several inches because of vertebral collapse. Weakness and fatigue are common and are often associated with anemia. Fever is rare and, when present, is usually from an infection. The major symptoms may result from an acute infection, renal insufficiency, hypercalcemia, or amyloidosis.

PHYSICAL FINDINGS. Pallor is the most frequent physical finding. The liver is palpable in about 5% of patients and the spleen in 1%. Occasionally, extramedullary plasmacytomas may appear.

Table 196–4 • CLINICAL MANIFESTATIONS OF MULTIPLE MYELOMA

Skeletal involvement: pain, reduced height, pathologic fractures, hypercalcemia

Anemia: mainly caused by decreased erythropoiesis; produces weakness and fatigue

Renal insufficiency: mainly caused by "myeloma kidney" from light chains or hypercalcemia; rarely from amyloidosis

Recurrent infections: respiratory and urinary tract infections or septicemia caused by gram-positive or gram-negative organisms

Bleeding diathesis: from thrombocytopenia or coating of platelets with M protein

Amyloidosis: develops in 10%

Extramedullary plasmacytomas: occur late in the disease

Cryoglobulinemia type I: rarely symptomatic

Diagnosis

LABORATORY FINDINGS. A normocytic, normochromic anemia (Chapter 173) is present initially in two thirds of patients but eventually occurs in nearly every patient with multiple myeloma. The serum protein electrophoretic pattern shows a peak or localized band in 80% of patients, hypogammaglobulinemia in almost 10%, and no apparent abnormality in the remainder. IgG M protein is found in 53%, IgA in 20%, light chain only (Bence Jones proteinemia) in 17%, IgD in 2%, and biclonal gammopathy in 1%, and 7% have no serum M protein at diagnosis. Immunofixation of the urine reveals an M protein in approximately 75% of patients. The κ/λ ratio is 2:1. At the time of diagnosis, 97% of patients with multiple myeloma have an M protein in the serum or urine.

In the bone marrow, plasma cells usually account for 10% or more of all nucleated cells, but they may range from less than 5% to almost 100% (Fig. 196–5). Bone marrow involvement may be focal rather than diffuse, so repeated bone marrow examinations may be required. Identification of a monoclonal immunoglobulin in the cytoplasm of plasma cells by immunoperoxidase staining is helpful for differentiating monoclonal plasma cell proliferation in multiple myeloma from reactive plasmacytosis related to connective tissue disease, metastatic carcinoma, liver disease, and infections.

RADIOLOGIC FINDINGS. Conventional radiographs reveal abnormalities consisting of punched-out lytic lesions (Fig. 196–6), osteoporosis, or fractures in nearly 80% of patients. The vertebrae, skull, thoracic cage, pelvis, and proximal humeri and femora are the most frequent sites of involvement. Technetium-99m bone scanning is inferior to conventional radiography and should not be used. Computed tomography or magnetic resonance imaging is helpful in patients who have skeletal pain but no abnormality on radiographs.

DIAGNOSTIC CRITERIA. Minimal criteria for the diagnosis of multiple myeloma are a bone marrow containing more than 10% plasma cells or a plasmacytoma plus at least one of the following: (1) M protein in the serum (usually >3 g/dL), (2) M protein in the urine, and (3) lytic bone lesions. These findings must not be from metastatic carcinoma, connective tissue diseases, chronic infection, or lymphoma. Patients with multiple myeloma must be differentiated from those with MGUS and smoldering multiple myeloma (Table 196–5).

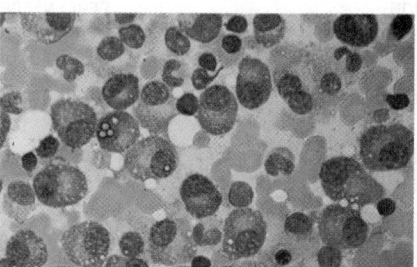

FIGURE 196–5 • Multiple myeloma. Bone marrow aspirate with predominance of plasma cells.

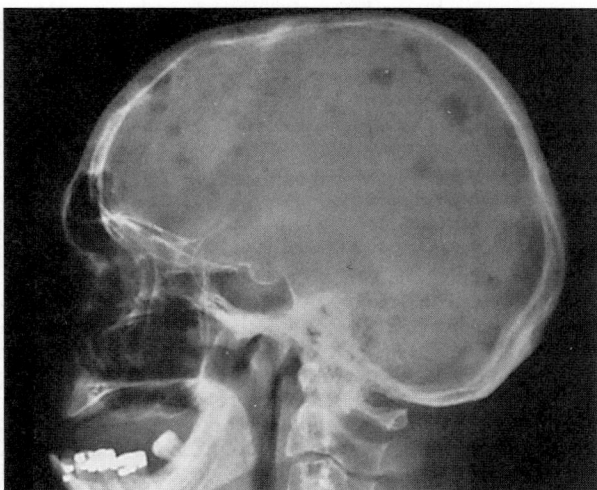

FIGURE 196–6 • Skull radiograph showing multiple lytic lesions.

Table 196–5 • MAYO CLINIC CRITERIA FOR THE DIAGNOSIS OF MGUS, SMM, AND MM

MGUS	Serum monoclonal protein <3 g/dL *and* bone marrow plasma cells <10% *and* absence of anemia, renal failure, hypercalcemia, and lytic bone lesions
SMM	Serum monoclonal protein ≥3 g/dL *and/or* bone marrow plasma cells ≥10% *and* absence of anemia, renal failure, hypercalcemia, and lytic bone lesions
MM	Presence of a serum or urine monoclonal protein, bone marrow plasmacytosis, *and* anemia, renal failure, hypercalcemia, or lytic bone lesions. Patients with primary systemic amyloidosis and ≥30% bone marrow plasma cells are considered to have both multiple myeloma and amyloidosis

MGUS = monoclonal gammopathy of undetermined significance; MM = multiple myeloma; SMM = smoldering multiple myeloma.

From Rajkumar SV, Dispenzieri A, Fonseca R, et al: Thalidomide for previously untreated indolent or smoldering multiple myeloma. Leukemia 2001;15:1274–1276, with permission of Nature Publishing Group.

Organ Involvement

RENAL. Bence Jones proteinuria detected by immunofixation is present in 75%. The serum creatinine value is increased initially in almost half of patients and is greater than 2 mg/dL in 25%.

The two major causes of renal insufficiency are "myeloma kidney" and hypercalcemia. Myeloma kidney is characterized by the presence of large, waxy, laminated casts in the distal and collecting tubules. The casts are composed mainly of precipitated monoclonal light chains. The extent of cast formation correlates directly with the amount of free urinary light chain and with the severity of renal insufficiency. Dehydration may precipitate acute renal failure.

Hypercalcemia, which is present in 15 to 20% of patients initially, is a major and treatable cause of renal insufficiency. It results from destruction of bone. Hyperuricemia may contribute to renal failure. Amyloidosis occurs in 10% of patients and may produce nephrotic syndrome, renal insufficiency, or both. Acquired Fanconi's syndrome, characterized by proximal tubular dysfunction, results in glycosuria, phosphaturia, and aminoaciduria. Deposition of monoclonal light chains in the renal glomerulus (light-chain deposition disease) may produce renal insufficiency and the nephrotic syndrome.

NEUROLOGIC. Radiculopathy, the single most frequent neurologic complication, is usually in the thoracic or lumbosacral area and results from compression of the nerve by the vertebral lesion or by the collapsed bone itself. Compression of the spinal cord occurs in up to 10% of patients. Peripheral neuropathy is uncommon in multiple myeloma and, when present, is usually caused by amyloidosis. Rarely, myeloma cells diffusely infiltrate the meninges. Intracranial plasmacytomas almost always represent extensions of myelomatous lesions of the skull.

Other Systemic Involvement

Hepatomegaly from plasma cell infiltration is uncommon. Plasmacytomas of the ribs are common and arise either as expanding bone lesions or as soft tissue masses. The incidence of infections is increased in multiple myeloma. *Streptococcus pneumoniae* and *Staphylococcus aureus* organisms have been the most frequent pathogens, but gram-negative organisms now account for more than half of all infections. Propensity to infection results from impairment of antibody response, deficiency of normal immunoglobulins, and neutropenia. Bleeding from coating of the platelets by the M protein may occur. Occasionally, a tendency to thrombosis is present.

 Treatment

Patients with MGUS or smoldering multiple myeloma should not be treated, but an increasing level of the M protein in the serum or urine suggests that therapy will be needed in the near future (Fig. 196–7). Indications for therapy include significant anemia, hypercalcemia, or renal insufficiency; the occurrence of lytic bone lesions; and the finding of extramedullary plasmacytomas. If there is doubt in the physician's mind, it is usually better to withhold therapy and to reevaluate the patient in 2 or 3 months.

RADIATION THERAPY. Palliative radiation in a dose of 20 to 30 Gy should be limited to patients who have multiple myeloma with disabling pain and a well-defined focal process that has not responded to chemotherapy. Analgesics in combination with chemotherapy can usually control the pain.

AUTOLOGOUS STEM CELL TRANSPLANTATION. If the patient is younger than 70 years, autologous peripheral blood stem cell transplantation (Chapter 166) with conventional chemotherapy provides a better median survival than conventional chemotherapy.[1] Initial chemotherapy with vincristine, doxorubicin (Adriamycin), and dexamethasone (VAD) is usually preferred for 3 to 4 months to reduce the number of tumor cells in the bone marrow and peripheral blood. Pulsed dexamethasone, alone or in combination with low-dose thalidomide (200 mg), is an alternative. The patient is then given high-dose cyclophosphamide followed by granulocyte colony-stimulating factor, and the peripheral stem cells are collected. The patient is then given melphalan, 200 mg/m^2, followed by infusion of the peripheral blood stem cells.

An alternative approach for patients with newly diagnosed disease is to treat for several months with chemotherapy that is not toxic to stem cells, such as VAD or single-agent dexamethasone, to minimize their tumor burden. Peripheral blood stem cells are then mobilized and cryopreserved for future use. Patients then continue conventional chemotherapy, such as melphalan and prednisone, followed by observation until relapse or progression, at which point transplantation is considered. Data from a randomized trial comparing early versus delayed transplantation indicate no significant difference in survival between the two strategies.[2] The choice between the two options is based on patients' preferences and other clinical conditions, but early transplantation is often preferred because its mortality is low (<1%) and it avoids the inconvenience, cost, and potential side effects of chemotherapy.

Autologous transplantation is applicable for up to 50% of patients with multiple myeloma, but it should not be performed if the patient has received long-term chemotherapy and has refractory multiple myeloma. Transplantation does not eradicate the myeloma, in part because the transplanted cells are usually contaminated by myeloma cells or their precursors even when attempts are made to purge such cells. Preliminary results from one randomized study suggest that patients who had a double transplant with peripheral blood stem cells had a longer event-free survival and a more favorable 5-year survival than those randomly assigned to a single transplant with stem cells from the bone marrow,[3] but early results from three other randomized trials have not yet shown a similar benefit. Final results

Continued

from these studies will determine the need for tandem transplantation.

ALLOGENEIC BONE MARROW TRANSPLANTATION. Ninety to 95% of patients with multiple myeloma cannot have allogeneic bone marrow transplantation because of their age, lack of an HLA-matched sibling donor, or inadequate renal, pulmonary, or cardiac function. Allogeneic transplantation has the advantage that the graft does not contain tumor cells, and it can produce a graft-versus-myeloma effect. Unfortunately, the mortality rate from the procedure is approximately 25%. Although a complete response occurs in 40% of patients, most have a relapse; in long-term follow-up, there is no apparent survival plateau. The use of T-cell–depleted peripheral blood stem cells decreases the incidence of graft-versus-host disease and reduces transplant-related mortality. Donor lymphocyte infusions have produced significant benefit in up to half of patients after allogeneic transplantation. The mortality rate for allogeneic transplantation must be reduced before it can assume a major role in the treatment of multiple myeloma.

CHEMOTHERAPY. Chemotherapy is the preferred initial treatment for overt, symptomatic multiple myeloma in patients older than 70 years or in younger patients in whom transplantation is not feasible. Oral administration of melphalan and prednisone produces an objective response in 50 to 60% of patients. Melphalan can be given daily in a dosage of 0.15 mg/kg for 7 days (8 to 10 mg/day) with 20 mg of prednisone 3 times daily for the same 7 days. Leukocyte and platelet levels should be determined every 3 weeks after beginning each cycle of therapy, and the melphalan and prednisone treatment should be repeated every 6 weeks. The dosage of melphalan must be adjusted until midcycle cytopenia occurs. Unless the disease progresses rapidly, at least three courses of melphalan and prednisone should be given before therapy is discontinued. Because the natural course of multiple myeloma is to progress, alleviation of pain and stabilization of disease usually indicate some therapeutic benefit. An objective improvement may not be achieved for 6 to 12 months or longer. In a large meta-analysis comparing melphalan and prednisone with various combinations of chemotherapy, the objective response rate was higher with a combination of alkylating agents but there was no significant difference in overall survival or evidence that any group of patients benefited from combination chemotherapy.

Chemotherapy should be continued for 1 year or until the patient is in a plateau state. At that point, α_2-interferon may be given; it prolongs the duration of the plateau state but does not generally produce significant survival benefit. If relapse occurs during the plateau state, the initial chemotherapeutic regimen should be reinstituted. Most patients respond, but the duration and quality of response are usually inferior to those of the initial response.

REFRACTORY MULTIPLE MYELOMA. Almost all patients with multiple myeloma eventually relapse. The highest response rates for patients resistant to alkylating agents have been with the VAD regimen. Dexamethasone is administered in a dosage of 40 mg/day on days 1 to 4, 9 to 12, and 17 to 20. The cycles are repeated every 28 days. Dexamethasone is usually given only on days 1 to 4 in even-numbered cycles because of toxicity. Most of the VAD activity is from the corticosteroid effects of dexamethasone. Methylprednisolone, 2 g three times weekly intravenously for a minimum of 4 weeks, is helpful for patients with pancytopenia and may have fewer side effects than dexamethasone. If there is a response, methylprednisolone is reduced to once or twice weekly.

Thalidomide produces an objective response, with a median duration of about 1 year, in about a third of patients with refractory myeloma. Side effects are sedation, constipation, peripheral neuropathy, rash, bradycardia, and thrombotic events. The addition of dexamethasone to thalidomide may produce a response in refractory disease.

Thalidomide analogues, immunomodulatory drugs such as CDC-501, are well tolerated and produce objective benefit. PS-341, an inhibitor of the ubiquitin-proteasome pathway, acts through multiple mechanisms to arrest tumor growth, tumor spread, and angiogenesis. It produces objective responses in about 40% of patients with refractory myeloma. 2-Methoxyestradiol farnesyltransferase inhibitors are also being studied.

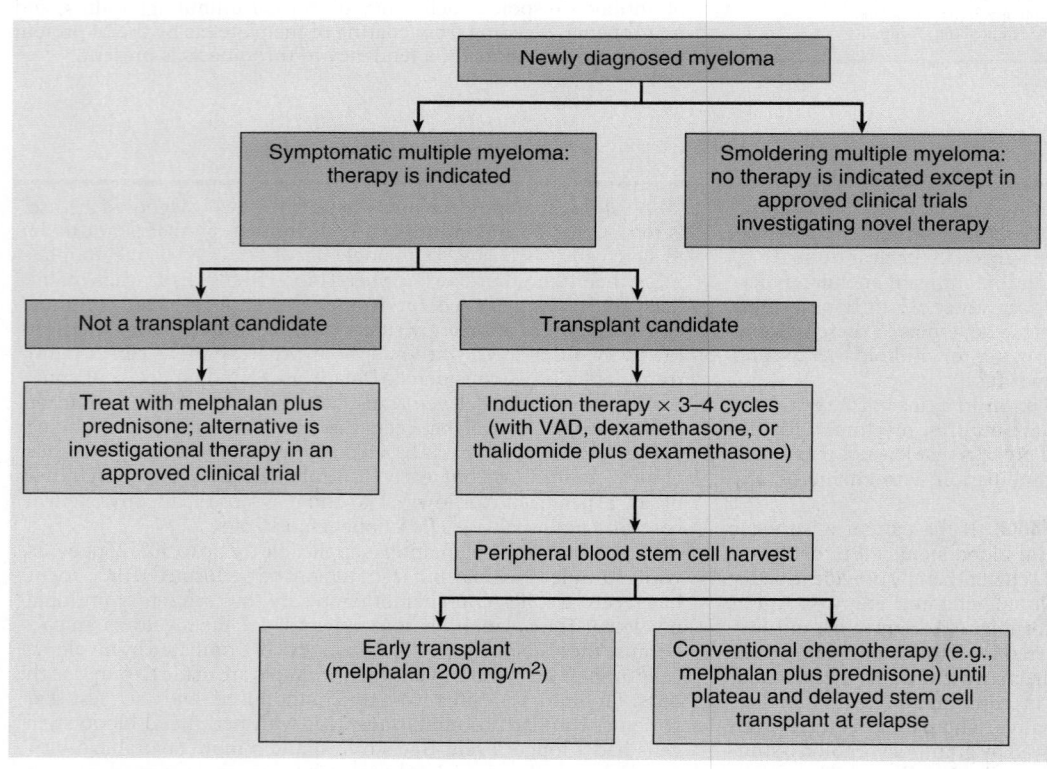

FIGURE 196–7 • Approach to newly diagnosed multiple myeloma. VAD = vincristine, doxorubicin (Adriamycin), and dexamethasone.

Management of Complications

HYPERCALCEMIA. Hypercalcemia, present in 15 to 20% of patients at diagnosis, should be suspected in the presence of anorexia, nausea, vomiting, polyuria, polydipsia, constipation, weakness, confusion, or stupor. If hypercalcemia is untreated, renal insufficiency may develop. Hydration, preferably with isotonic saline plus prednisone (25 mg four times per day), usually relieves hypercalcemia. The dose of prednisone must be reduced and its use discontinued as soon as possible. If these measures fail, bisphosphonates such as zoledronate or pamidronate are beneficial (Chapters 187, 258, and 260). Patients with myeloma should be encouraged to be as active as possible because prolonged bed rest contributes to hypercalcemia.

RENAL INSUFFICIENCY. This complication occurs in half of patients with multiple myeloma and may develop insidiously or rapidly (acute renal failure). Hydration and prednisone are necessary if there is accompanying hypercalcemia. Furosemide is helpful for maintaining a high urine flow rate (100 mL/hour). Hemodialysis is necessary for symptomatic azotemia. Plasmapheresis may be helpful for regaining renal function, but patients with severe myeloma casts or other irreversible changes are unlikely to benefit from plasmapheresis. Allopurinol is necessary if hyperuricemia is present. Renal transplantation for myeloma kidney has been followed by prolonged survival. Maintenance of a high urine output (3 L/day) is important for preventing renal failure in patients with Bence Jones proteinuria.

INFECTION. Prompt, appropriate therapy for bacterial infections is necessary. Prophylactic penicillin often benefits patients with recurrent gram-positive infections. Intravenously administered γ-globulin is helpful but expensive. Pneumococcal and influenza immunizations should be given to all patients.

SKELETAL LESIONS. Patients should be encouraged to be as active as possible but to avoid trauma. Fixation of fractures or impending fractures of long bones with an intramedullary rod and methyl methacrylate has produced good results. In a randomized trial of patients with lytic bone lesions, pamidronate (90 mg intravenously over a 4-hour infusion every 4 weeks) reduced skeletal events (pathologic fractures, need for operation to treat or prevent pathologic fractures, need for radiation to bone, or spinal cord compression) by 50%. Decreased bone pain and improved quality of life were also seen in the pamidronate group. This regimen is now routinely recommended for such patients.

MISCELLANEOUS COMPLICATIONS. Symptomatic hyperviscosity, which is usually manifested by oronasal bleeding, blurred vision, or heart failure, should be treated with plasmapheresis. Serum viscosity levels do not correlate well with the symptoms or clinical findings. Plasmapheresis promptly relieves the symptoms and should be done regardless of the viscosity level if the patient is symptomatic. Anemia often responds to erythropoietin.

Spinal cord compression from an extramedullary plasmacytoma should be suspected in patients who have severe back pain, weakness or paresthesias of the lower extremities, or bladder or bowel dysfunction. Magnetic resonance imaging, computed tomography, or myelography must be performed immediately. Dexamethasone and radiation therapy are usually helpful. If the neurologic deficit increases, surgical decompression is necessary.

Prognosis

Multiple myeloma has a progressive course, and the median survival is approximately 3 years. The bone marrow plasma cell labeling index and β$_2$-microglobulin level are the most important prognostic factors in previously untreated multiple myeloma. Cytogenetic findings contribute important and independent prognostic information: partial or complete deletion of chromosome 13 is a predictor of a poor outcome. Advanced age, plasmablastic morphology, circulating myeloma cells in the peripheral blood, increased myeloma colony growth, and increased levels of IL-6 are all associated with a more aggressive disease. The level of C-reactive protein correlates with the serum IL-6 level and is a useful prognostic factor, as is an increased lactate dehydrogenase level. Twenty to 30% of patients survive 5 or more years, but fewer than 5% survive longer than 10 years. In some patients, an acute or aggressive terminal phase is characterized by rapid tumor growth, pancytopenia, soft tissue subcutaneous masses, decreased M-protein levels, and fever; the survival in this subset is usually only a few months.

VARIANT FORMS OF MULTIPLE MYELOMA (see Table 196-1)

SMOLDERING MULTIPLE MYELOMA. The diagnosis of *smoldering multiple myeloma* depends on the presence of an M-protein level greater than 3 g/dL in the serum and more than 10% plasma cells in the bone marrow but no anemia, renal insufficiency, or skeletal lesions. Often, a small amount of M protein is found in the urine, and the concentration of normal immunoglobulins in the serum is decreased. The plasma cell labeling index is low. Biologically, patients with smoldering multiple myeloma have a benign monoclonal gammopathy (MGUS), but it is difficult to accept that diagnosis because of their M-protein levels and bone marrow findings. These patients must be observed over time because symptomatic multiple myeloma often develops, but smoldering multiple myeloma should not be treated unless progression occurs.

PLASMA CELL LEUKEMIA. Patients with plasma cell leukemia have more than 20% plasma cells in the peripheral blood and an absolute plasma cell count greater than or equal to 2000/μL. Plasma cell leukemia is classified as primary when it is diagnosed in the leukemic phase (60%) or as secondary when there is leukemic transformation of a previously recognized multiple myeloma (40%). Patients with primary plasma cell leukemia are younger and have a greater incidence of hepatosplenomegaly and lymphadenopathy, a higher platelet count, fewer bone lesions, a smaller serum M-protein component, and a longer survival (median, 6.8 vs. 1.3 months) than patients with secondary plasma cell leukemia. Treatment of plasma cell leukemia is unsatisfactory, but partial responses occur with VAD or with alkylating agents. Autologous stem cell transplantation after myeloablative therapy is beneficial for some patients. Secondary plasma cell leukemia rarely responds to chemotherapy because the patients have already received chemotherapy and are resistant.

NONSECRETORY MYELOMA. Patients with nonsecretory myeloma have no M protein in either the serum or the urine and account for only 3% of cases of myeloma. To make the diagnosis, an M protein must be identified in the plasma cells by immunoperoxidase or immunofluorescence methods, but no M protein is found even within the myeloma cell in rare cases. Responses to therapy and survival rates in patients with nonsecretory myeloma are similar to those in patients with a serum or urinary M component, but renal involvement is less.

IMMUNOGLOBULIN D MYELOMA. The M protein is smaller than in IgG and IgA myelomas, and Bence Jones proteinuria of the λ type is more common. Amyloidosis and extramedullary plasmacytomas are more frequent with IgD myeloma. Survival is generally believed to be shorter than with other myeloma types, but IgD myeloma is often not diagnosed until later in its course.

OSTEOSCLEROTIC MYELOMA (POEMS SYNDROME). This syndrome is characterized by *p*olyneuropathy, *o*rganomegaly, *e*ndocrinopathy, *M* protein, and *s*kin changes (POEMS). The major clinical features are a chronic inflammatory-demyelinating polyneuropathy with predominantly motor disability and sclerotic skeletal lesions. Except for the presence of papilledema, the cranial nerves are not involved. The autonomic nervous system is intact. Hepatomegaly occurs in almost 50% of patients, but splenomegaly and lymphadenopathy occur in a minority. Hyperpigmentation and hypertrichosis are usually evident. Gynecomastia and atrophic testes as well as clubbing of the fingers and toes may be seen. In contrast to findings in multiple myeloma, the hemoglobin level is usually normal or increased, and thrombocytosis is common. The bone marrow usually contains fewer than 5% plasma cells, and hypercalcemia and renal insufficiency rarely occur. Most patients have a λ protein. Evidence of Castleman's disease may be found. Diagnosis is confirmed by the identification of monoclonal plasma cells obtained at biopsy of an osteosclerotic lesion.

If the lesions are in a limited area, radiation therapy produces substantial improvement of the neuropathy in more than 50% of patients. If the patient has widespread osteosclerotic lesions, autologous stem cell transplantation or chemotherapy with melphalan and prednisone may be helpful.

SOLITARY PLASMACYTOMA (SOLITARY MYELOMA) OF BONE. Diagnosis of this disease is based on histologic evidence of a tumor consisting of monoclonal plasma cells identical to those in multiple myeloma. In addition, complete skeletal radiographs must show no other lesions of myeloma, the bone marrow aspirate must contain no evidence of multiple myeloma, and immunofixation of the serum and concentrated urine should show no M protein. Exceptions to the last-mentioned criterion occur, but therapy for the solitary lesion usually results in the disappearance of the M protein. Persistence of the M protein after radiation therapy is associated with an increased risk of progression to multiple myeloma. Magnetic resonance imaging of the spine and pelvis is helpful for detecting marrow involvement. Almost 50% of patients who have a solitary plasmacytoma are alive at 10 years, and disease-free survival at 10 years ranges from 15 to 25%. Treatment consists of radiation in the range of 40 to 50 Gy. There is no evidence that chemotherapy affects the rate of conversion to multiple myeloma. Progression, when it occurs, usually appears within 3 to 4 years, but the most uncertain criterion for diagnosis is the duration of observation necessary before deciding that the disease will not become generalized.

EXTRAMEDULLARY PLASMACYTOMA. Extramedullary plasmacytoma is a plasma cell tumor that arises outside the bone marrow. The tumor is found in the upper respiratory tract in approximately 80% of cases, especially in the nasal cavity and sinuses, nasopharynx, and larynx. Extramedullary plasmacytomas may also occur in the gastrointestinal tract, central nervous system, urinary bladder, thyroid, breast, testes, parotid gland, or lymph nodes. The diagnosis is based on the finding of a plasma cell tumor in an extramedullary site and the absence of multiple myeloma on bone marrow examination, radiography, and appropriate studies of blood and urine. Treatment consists of tumoricidal irradiation. The plasmacytoma may recur locally, metastasize to regional nodes, or, rarely, develop into multiple myeloma.

WALDENSTRÖM'S MACROGLOBULINEMIA (PRIMARY MACROGLOBULINEMIA)

Macroglobulinemia is the result of an uncontrolled proliferation of lymphocytes and plasma cells in which a large IgM M protein is produced. The cause is unknown, but it occurs more frequently in certain families. The median age of patients at the time of diagnosis is about 65 years, and about 60% are male.

Clinical Manifestations

Weakness, fatigue, and bleeding (especially oozing from the oronasal area) are common presenting symptoms. Blurred or impaired vision, dyspnea, loss of weight, neurologic symptoms, recurrent infections, and heart failure may occur. In contrast to multiple myeloma, lytic bone lesions, renal insufficiency, and amyloidosis are rare. Physical findings include pallor, hepatosplenomegaly, and lymphadenopathy. Retinal hemorrhages, exudates, and venous congestion with vascular segmentation ("sausage" formation) may occur. Sensorimotor peripheral neuropathy is common. Pulmonary involvement is manifested by diffuse pulmonary infiltrates and isolated masses. Pleural effusion may occur. Diarrhea and steatorrhea are uncommon.

Laboratory Evaluation

Almost all patients have moderate to severe normocytic, normochromic anemia. Coombs-positive hemolytic anemia is uncommon. The serum cholesterol value is often low. The serum electrophoretic pattern is characterized by a tall, narrow peak or dense band and is usually of γ mobility. Seventy-five per cent of the IgM proteins have a κ light chain. Low-molecular-weight IgM (7S) is present and may account for a significant part of the increased IgM level. A monoclonal light chain is present in the urine of 80% of patients. The amount of urinary protein is usually modest.

The bone marrow aspirate is often hypocellular, but the biopsy is hypercellular and extensively infiltrated with lymphoid cells and plasma cells. The number of mast cells is frequently increased. Rouleaux formation is prominent (see Fig. 161–3), and the sedimentation rate is markedly increased unless gelation of the plasma occurs. About 10% of macroglobulins have cryoproperties.

Diagnosis

The lymphoplasmacytic cells express CD19, CD20, and CD22, whereas expression of CD5 and CD10 occurs in a minority. The combination of typical symptoms and physical findings, the presence of a large IgM M protein (usually >3 g/dL), and lymphoid–plasma cell infiltration of the bone marrow provide the diagnosis. Multiple

myeloma, chronic lymphocytic leukemia, and MGUS of the IgM type must be excluded.

Patients with an IgM protein less than 3 g/dL have sometimes been classified as having non-Hodgkin's lymphoma (Chapter 195) with an IgM protein. The clinical picture, therapy, and prognosis for these patients are no different than for patients with typical Waldenström's macroglobulinemia, and the distinction is artificial. Consensus is building that these patients should also be classified as having Waldenström's macroglobulinemia.

 Treatment

Patients should not be treated unless they have anemia; constitutional symptoms such as weakness, fatigue, night sweats, or weight loss; hyperviscosity; or significant hepatosplenomegaly or lymphadenopathy. Rituximab (Rituxan), a chimeric anti-CD20 monoclonal antibody, produces a response in at least 50% of untreated patients. Chlorambucil (Leukeran) is usually given orally in a dosage of 6 to 8 mg/day and is reduced when the leukocyte or platelet value decreases. Patients should be treated until the disease has reached a plateau state; the treatment can be discontinued and the patients observed closely. Chemotherapy should be reinstituted when the disease relapses. Combinations of alkylating agents, such as the M2 protocol (vincristine, BCNU, melphalan, cyclophosphamide, and prednisone), may be beneficial. α_2-Interferon may be of some use. Previously untreated patients may respond to fludarabine or 2-chlorodeoxyadenosine, but cytopenias and immunosuppression may be troublesome. Autologous stem cell transplantation has been performed in some cases, but more data are needed before this therapy can be recommended.

Erythropoietin or transfusions of packed red blood cells should be given for symptomatic anemia. Spuriously low hemoglobin and hematocrit levels may occur because of the increased plasma volume from the large amount of M protein. Consequently, transfusions should not be given solely on the basis of the hemoglobin or hematocrit value. Symptomatic hyperviscosity should be treated with plasmapheresis. The median survival in macroglobulinemia is 5 years.

HYPERVISCOSITY SYNDROME

Chronic nasal bleeding and oozing from the gums are frequent, but postsurgical or gastrointestinal bleeding may also occur. Retinal hemorrhages are common, and papilledema may be seen. The patient occasionally complains of blurring or a loss of vision. Dizziness, headache, vertigo, nystagmus, decreased hearing, ataxia, paresthesias, diplopia, somnolence, and coma may occur. Hyperviscosity can precipitate or exacerbate heart failure. Most patients have symptoms when the relative viscosity is greater than 4 centipoises, but the relationship between serum viscosity and clinical manifestations is not precise. Patients with symptomatic hyperviscosity should be treated with plasmapheresis. Plasma exchange of 3 to 4 L should be performed daily until the patient is asymptomatic. The plasma should be replaced with albumin rather than plasma.

HEAVY-CHAIN DISEASES

The heavy-chain diseases (HCDs) are characterized by the presence of an M protein consisting of a portion of the immunoglobulin heavy chain in the serum or urine or both. These heavy chains are devoid of light chains and represent a lymphoplasma cell proliferative process. There are three major types: γ-HCD, α-HCD, and μ-HCD.

γ-HCD. The abnormal protein consists of monoclonal γ chains with significant deletions of amino acids, including the C_{H1} domain of the constant region. The median age of patients is approximately 60 years, although the condition has been noted in persons younger than age 20. Patients with γ-HCD often present with a lymphoma-like illness, but the clinical findings are diverse and range from an aggressive lymphoproliferative process to an asymptomatic state. Hepatosplenomegaly and lymphadenopathy occur in about 60% of patients. Anemia is found in about 80% initially and in nearly all eventually. A few patients have had a Coombs-positive hemolytic anemia. The electrophoretic pattern often shows a broad-based band more suggestive of a polyclonal increase than an M protein. The urinary protein value ranges from a trace to 20 g/day, but it is usually less than 1 g/day.

The numbers of lymphocytes, plasma cells, or plasmacytoid lymphocytes in the bone marrow and lymph nodes are increased. The histologic pattern varies, usually including generalized or localized lymphoma or myeloma, but in some cases there is no evidence of a lymphoplasmacytic proliferative process.

Treatment is indicated only for symptomatic patients. Many different drugs have been used, but the results have been inconsistent and generally disappointing. Therapy with cyclophosphamide, vincristine, and prednisone is a reasonable choice. If there is no response to this regimen, doxorubicin should be added. The prognosis of γ-HCD is variable and ranges from a rapidly progressive downhill course of a few weeks' duration to the asymptomatic presence of a stable monoclonal heavy chain in the serum or urine.

α-HCD. This most common HCD occurs in patients from the Mediterranean region or Middle East, usually in the second or third decade of life. About 60% are men. Most commonly, the gastrointestinal tract is involved, resulting in severe malabsorption with diarrhea, steatorrhea, and loss of weight (Chapter 141). Plasma cell infiltration of the jejunal mucosa is the most frequent pathologic feature. Immunoproliferative small intestinal disease is restricted to patients with small intestinal lesions who have the same pathologic features as those of α-HCD, but these patients do not synthesize α heavy chains.

The serum protein electrophoretic pattern is normal in half the cases, and in the remainder an unimpressive broad band may appear in the α_2 or β regions. The diagnosis depends on the recognition of a monoclonal α heavy chain. The amount of α heavy chain in the urine is small, and Bence Jones proteinuria has never been reported.

Most often, α-HCD is progressive and fatal, but it may respond to melphalan or to cyclophosphamide and prednisone. Antibiotics such as tetracyclines may also produce a remission.

μ-HCD. This disease is characterized by the demonstration of a monoclonal μ-chain fragment in the serum. The patient may present with chronic lymphocytic leukemia or lymphoma, but it is likely that the clinical spectrum will broaden when more cases are recognized.

The serum protein electrophoretic pattern is usually normal except for hypogammaglobulinemia. Bence Jones proteinuria has been found in two thirds of cases. Lymphocytes, plasma cells, and lymphoplasmacytoid cells are increased in the bone marrow. Vacuolization of the plasma cells is common and should suggest the possibility of HCD. The course of μ-HCD is variable, and survival ranges from a few months to many years. Treatment with corticosteroids and alkylating agents has produced some benefit.

CRYOGLOBULINEMIA

Cryoglobulins are proteins that precipitate when cooled and dissolve when heated. They are designated as idiopathic or essential when they are not associated with any recognizable disease. Cryoglobulins are classified into three types: type I (monoclonal), type II (mixed), and type III (polyclonal).

Type I (monoclonal) cryoglobulinemia is most commonly of the IgM or IgG class, but IgA and Bence Jones cryoglobulins have been reported. Most patients, even with large amounts of type I cryoglobulin, are completely asymptomatic from this source. Others with monoclonal cryoglobulins in the range of 1 to 2 g/dL may have pain, purpura, Raynaud's phenomenon, cyanosis, and even ulceration and sloughing of skin and subcutaneous tissue (Fig. 196–8) on exposure to the cold because their cryoglobulins precipitate at relatively high temperatures. Type I cryoglobulins are associated with macroglobulinemia, multiple myeloma, or MGUS.

Type II (mixed) cryoglobulinemia typically consists of an IgM M protein and polyclonal IgG, although monoclonal IgG or monoclonal IgA may also be seen with polyclonal IgM. Serum protein electrophoresis usually shows a normal pattern or a diffuse, polyclonal hypergammaglobulinemic pattern. The quantity of mixed cryoglobulin is usually less than 0.2 g/dL. Vasculitis, glomerulonephritis, lymphoproliferative disease, and chronic infectious processes are common. Purpura and polyarthralgias are frequently seen. Involvement of the joints is symmetrical, but joint deformities rarely develop. Raynaud's phenomenon, necrosis of the skin, and neurologic involvement may be present. In almost 80% of renal biopsy specimens, glomerular

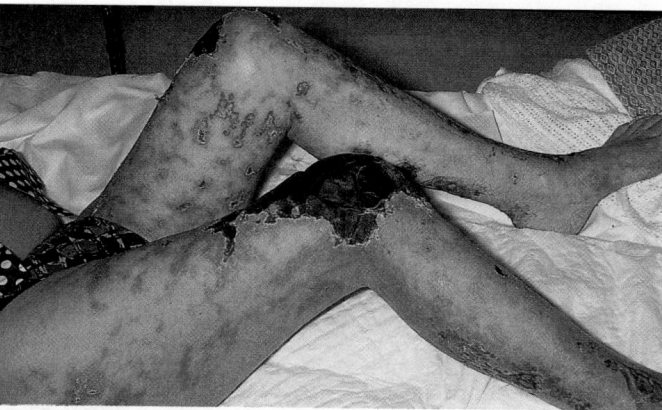

FIGURE 196–8 • Skin infarction in cryoglobulinemia. There is a reticulated pattern to the skin resulting from leakage of red blood cells from damaged skin capillaries. Necrosis and ulceration have occurred in peripheral sites as a result of vessel blockage. This patient eventually required plastic surgery. (From Forbes CD, Jackson WF: Color Atlas and Text of Clinical Medicine, 3rd ed. London, Mosby, 2003.)

damage can be identified. Nephrotic syndrome may result, but severe renal insufficiency is uncommon. Hepatic dysfunction and serologic evidence of infection with hepatitis C virus (Chapter 152) are common.

Early administration of corticosteroids is the most frequent therapy. α_2-Interferon has been of benefit, but relapse is common after cessation of therapy. Cyclophosphamide, chlorambucil, or azathioprine should be used if there is no response. Plasmapheresis has been effective in some instances.

Type III (polyclonal) cryoglobulinemia is not associated with a monoclonal component. Type III cryoglobulins are found in many patients with infections or inflammatory diseases and are of no clinical significance.

PRIMARY AMYLOIDOSIS (Chapter 290)

Amyloid stained with Congo red produces an apple-green birefringence under polarized light. It is a fibrous protein that consists of rigid, linear, nonbranching, aggregated fibrils of 7.5 to 10 nm width and of indefinite length. The type of amyloid cannot be differentiated by organ distribution or by electron microscopy. The amyloid fibrils in amyloidosis consist of the variable portion of a monoclonal light chain or, in some instances, the intact light chain (Table 196–6). The light-chain class is more frequently λ than κ (2:1), with a predominance of the λ_{VI} subclass. Patients with amyloidosis may have aberrant de novo synthesis or abnormal proteolytic processing of light chains. Rarely, the fibril consists of a monoclonal heavy chain. Amyloid

Table 196–6 • CLINICAL CLASSIFICATION OF AMYLOIDOSIS		
AMYLOID TYPE	**CLASSIFICATION**	**MAJOR PROTEIN COMPONENT**
AL	Primary	κ or λ light chain
AA	Secondary	Protein A
AL	Localized	κ or λ light chain
ATTR	Familial	
	Neurologic	Transthyretin mutant (prealbumin)
	Cardiopathic	Transthyretin mutant (prealbumin)
	Nephropathic	
	Familial	
	Mediterranean fever	Protein A
	Fibrinogen α-chain	
	Lysozyme	
	Apolipoprotein A-I	
	Senile systemic amyloidosis	Normal transthyretin (prealbumin)
Aβ_2M	Long-term dialysis	β_2-Microglobulin

P component is a glycoprotein found in all types of amyloid, but its function is unknown. The catabolism, or breakdown, of amyloid fibrils is an important but poorly understood factor in pathogenesis.

Clinical Manifestations

The median age at diagnosis is 65 years, and only 1% of patients are younger than age 40. Two thirds are male. Weakness or fatigue and loss of weight are the most frequent symptoms. Dyspnea, pedal edema, paresthesias, light-headedness, and syncope are frequent in patients with heart failure or peripheral neuropathy. Hoarseness or change of voice as well as jaw claudication may occur.

The liver is palpable in one fourth of patients, but splenomegaly occurs in only 5%. Macroglossia is present in 10%. Purpura often involves the neck, face, and eyes. Ankle edema is common.

Almost one third of patients have nephrotic syndrome. Carpal tunnel syndrome, heart failure, peripheral neuropathy, and orthostatic hypotension are other major presenting syndromes (Fig. 196-9). The presence of one of these syndromes and an M protein in the serum or urine is a strong indication of amyloidosis, for which appropriate biopsy specimens must be taken for diagnosis.

Laboratory Findings

Anemia is not a prominent feature, but, when present, it is usually due to renal insufficiency, multiple myeloma, or gastrointestinal bleeding. Thrombocytosis occurs in 10% of patients. Proteinuria is present initially in 80%, and the serum creatinine level is greater than 2 mg/dL in 20%. The serum alkaline phosphatase level may be increased. Hyperbilirubinemia is infrequent, but, when present, it is an ominous sign. Hypoalbuminemia and increased cholesterol and triglyceride levels are common with the nephrotic syndrome. The factor X level is decreased in more than 10% of patients but is rarely the cause of bleeding. The prothrombin time is increased in about 15% of patients, and the thrombin time is prolonged in 60%.

A localized band or spike in the serum protein electrophoretic pattern is found in about 50% of patients, but it is modest in size (median, 1.4 g/dL). Hypogammaglobulinemia is present in about 20%. Immunofixation reveals an M protein in the serum and in the urine of more than 70% of patients. An M protein is found in the serum or urine in almost 90% of patients at diagnosis.

Bone marrow plasma cells are usually only modestly increased, with a median value of 7%. Less than 20% of patients have more than 20% plasma cells in the marrow. Radiographs of the bones are normal unless the patient has multiple myeloma.

Organ System Involvement

CARDIAC AND CIRCULATORY. Heart failure is present in approximately 20% of patients at diagnosis and develops during the course of the disease in an additional 10% (Chapter 73). The electrocardiogram frequently shows either low voltage in the limb leads or features consistent with an anteroseptal infarction (loss of anterior forces), but there is no evidence of myocardial infarction at autopsy. Atrial fibrillation, atrial or junctional tachycardia, ventricular premature complexes, and heart block are common electrocardiographic features.

Echocardiography is valuable for evaluation of amyloid heart disease. Increased thickness of the ventricular wall and septum correlates with an increased prevalence of heart failure (Chapter 73). Early cardiac amyloidosis is characterized by abnormal relaxation, whereas advanced involvement is characterized by restrictive hemodynamics. Intermittent claudication of the lower extremities, the upper extremities, or the jaw may be a prominent feature. Orthostatic hypotension occurs in about 15%.

OTHER ORGANS. Nephrotic syndrome is present in more than 25% of patients at the time of diagnosis (Chapter 119). The degree of proteinuria does not correlate well with the extent of amyloid deposition in the kidney. Gross hematuria is rare. Sensorimotor peripheral neuropathy characterized by dysesthetic numbness involving the lower extremities occurs in about 15% of patients. Autonomic dysfunction may be a prominent feature and is usually manifested by orthostatic hypotension, diarrhea, or impotence. Amyloidosis can involve the periarticular structures and produce the shoulder pad syndrome. Rarely, osteolytic lesions from amyloid may occur. Pseudohypertrophy of skeletal muscles from amyloid deposition may be impressive. Petechiae, ecchymoses, papules, plaques, nodules, tumors, bullous lesions, thickening of the skin, and dystrophy of the nails may occur.

Diagnosis

The diagnosis of primary amyloidosis requires documentation of positive amyloid staining in addition to evidence that the amyloid is from a plasma cell proliferative disorder. The initial diagnostic procedure should be abdominal fat aspiration, which is positive in 75% of patients. A bone marrow aspiration and biopsy should be performed to determine the degree of plasmacytosis, and results are positive for amyloid in more than 50% of patients. Either abdominal fat or bone marrow biopsy results are positive in 90%; if both are negative, options include a rectal biopsy or biopsy of a suspected organ (Table 196-7).

Specific antisera are helpful for identifying the type of systemic amyloidosis. Antiserum to amyloid-P component, which reacts with all amyloid types, should be used to demonstrate the presence of amyloid.

Prognosis

Currently, the median survival of patients with amyloidosis is 13 months. Survival varies greatly, depending on the associated syndrome; it is 4 months after the onset of heart failure. Patients with only peripheral neuropathy have a median survival of 2 years.

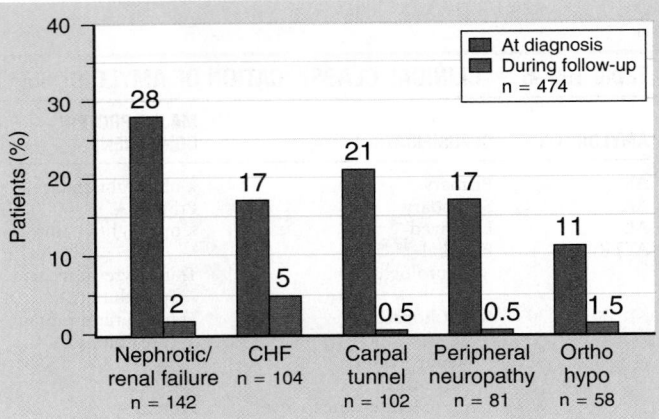

FIGURE 196-9 • Syndromes seen at diagnosis and during follow-up of patients with primary amyloidosis. Some patients had more than two syndromes at presentation. CHF = congestive heart failure; Ortho hypo = orthostatic hypotension. (From Kyle RA, Gertz MA: Primary systemic amyloidosis: Clinical and laboratory features in 474 cases. Semin Hematol 1995;32:45–59.)

Table 196–7 • **DIAGNOSIS OF PRIMARY AMYLOIDOSIS***

I. Evidence of positive amyloid staining by Congo red in one or more of the following sites:
  1. Fat aspirate
  2. Bone marrow biopsy specimen
  3. Organ biopsy (such as kidney, liver, heart, gastrointestinal tract, sural nerve)
II. Evidence that amyloid is light-chain related by the following methods:
  1. Immunoperoxidase staining of amyloid tissue showing positive light-chain staining
  2. Presence of serum or urine (or both) monoclonal protein
  3. Presence of monoclonal plasma cells in bone marrow specimen

*Both I and II must be present for the diagnosis of primary amyloidosis.

Rx Treatment

Therapy of amyloidosis is not satisfactory. In a randomized trial, regimens containing melphalan, prednisone, and colchicine provided better survival (18 vs. 8.5 months) than colchicine alone. [6]

Clinical improvement has also been observed with 4'-iodo-4'-deoxyrubicin (I-DOX), which appears to bind to amyloid fibrils and thus to contribute to the resolution of amyloid deposits. Encouraging results have been reported with high-dose intravenous melphalan (140 to 200 mg/m²) followed by autologous peripheral stem cell rescue. However, because of the short-term follow-up, the impact of this approach is still unknown.

The nephrotic syndrome should be managed with salt restriction and diuretic agents as needed. If symptomatic azotemia develops, chronic dialysis is necessary. Salt restriction and the judicious use of diuretic drugs are helpful for heart failure. Digitalis must be avoided or used with great care because patients are unusually sensitive to the drug, and heart block and arrhythmias are common. Elastic stockings or leotards may be of benefit in patients with orthostatic hypotension; fludrocortisone may also be useful, but it leads to retention of fluids.

FUTURE DIRECTIONS

Future efforts must be directed toward improving the preparative regimen before autologous stem cell transplantation and reducing contamination of the reinfused stem cells by myeloma cells or their precursors. Immunotherapy, using dendritic cell vaccination with the myeloma cell idiotype as a tumor-specific antigen, and monoclonal antibody therapy are under investigation.

1. Child JA, Morgan GJ, Davies FE: High-dose chemotherapy with hematopoietic stem-cell rescue for multiple myeloma. N Engl J Med 2003;348:1875–1883.
2. Fernand JP, Ravaud P, Chevret S, et al: High-dose therapy and autologous peripheral blood stem cell transplantation in multiple myeloma: Up-front or rescue treatment? Results of a multicenter sequential randomized clinical trial. Blood 1998;92:3131–3136.
3. Attal M, Harousseau JL: Randomized trial experience of the Intergroupe Francophone du Myélome. Semin Hematol 2001;38:226–230.
4. Myeloma Trialists' Collaborative Group: Combination chemotherapy versus melphalan plus prednisone as treatment for multiple myeloma: An overview of 6,633 patients from 27 randomized trials. J Clin Oncol 1998;16:3832–3842.
5. Berenson JR, Lichtenstein A, Porter L, et al: Long-term pamidronate treatment of advanced multiple myeloma patients reduces skeletal events. Myeloma Aredia Study Group. J Clin Oncol 1998;16:593–602.
6. Kyle RA, Gertz MA, Greipp PR, et al: A trial of three regimens for primary amyloidosis: Colchicine alone, melphalan and prednisone, and melphalan, prednisone, and colchicine. N Engl J Med 1997;336:1202–1207.

SUGGESTED READINGS

Dimopoulos MA, Moulopoulos LA, Maniatis A, Alexanian R: Solitary plasmacytoma of bone and asymptomatic multiple myeloma. Blood 2000;96:2037–2044. *An excellent review of solitary plasmacytoma of bone.*
Dimopoulos MA, Panayiotidis P, Moulopoulos LA, et al: Waldenström's macroglobulinemia. Clinical features, complications, and management. J Clin Oncol 2000;18:214–226. *Review of the disease, including complications and management.*
Kyle RA, Gertz MA, Witzig TE, et al: Review of 1027 patients with newly diagnosed multiple myeloma. Mayo Clin Proc 2003;78:21–33. *Median survival is 33 months.*
Kyle RA, Therneau TM, Rajkumar SV, et al: Prognosis of monoclonal gammopathy of undetermined significance (MGUS): A long-term study of 1,384 cases. N Engl J Med 2002;346:564–569. *Long-term study of a large MGUS cohort.*

197 HEAD AND NECK CANCER

Marshall Posner

Definition

The principal cancers of the head and neck include squamous cell cancers that arise from the mucosal surfaces of the upper aerodigestive tract and a diverse group of salivary gland neoplasms. Unique cancers of the region include nasopharyngeal carcinoma, thyroid malignancies (Chapter 239), esthesioneuroblastoma, and sinonasal undifferentiated carcinoma. A variety of other cancers arise from structures and tissues in the head and neck, including the more common skin cancers (Chapter 209), lymphomas (Chapters 194 and 195), and sarcomas.

Epidemiology

Squamous cell carcinomas account for 95% of all malignancies of the head and neck, whereas salivary gland cancers are nearly all of the remaining 5%. There are approximately 40,000 cases of squamous cell carcinoma of the head and neck in the United States each year, representing about 4% of all malignancies in the country. The incidence is declining slightly, but the decline has not mirrored the decline in the use of tobacco. Approximately 13,000 deaths are directly attributable each year to squamous cell carcinoma of the head and neck, and the peak incidence is between 55 and 65 years of age, although individuals do present in their mid-40s or earlier. The disease is about three times more common in men than women.

The mucosal surfaces of the head and neck are divided into six anatomic regions: the oral cavity, oropharynx, hypopharynx, larynx, nasopharynx, and paranasal sinuses. The site of anatomic origin for a squamous cell carcinoma of the head and neck has important, albeit imperfect, implications for diagnosis, spread, prognosis, and treatment because of intrinsic biologic differences in the mucosal cells at the sites of origin as well as differences in lymphatic drainage patterns and proximity to other structures in this compact region.

ORAL CAVITY. The oral cavity includes the floor of the mouth, anterior or oral tongue, lips, buccal surfaces, hard palate, retromolar trigone, and gums. The oral cavity is easily appreciable by physical examination and thus tumors in this area can frequently present early in their course. Tumors of the oral cavity, which are strongly related to the use of smokeless tobacco and other oral tobacco products, appear on the buccal and gingival surfaces in the sites where tobacco products are held in contact with the mucosa for long periods of time. Anterior tongue cancers are more common among smokers. Lip cancers are particularly prevalent among transplant patients and can be caused by DNA damage from solar ultraviolet light.

OROPHARYNX. The oropharynx consists of the tongue from the mid-tongue posteriorly to the epiglottis, the tonsils, the associated pharyngeal walls, and the soft palate. The oropharynx has become the most common site of head and neck tumors in the United States and is a common site of origin in Europe. Tumors in this anatomic region are associated with human papillomavirus (HPV), especially in younger, nonsmoking patients.

HYPOPHARYNX. The hypopharynx comprises the pyriform sinuses, the lateral and posterior pharyngeal walls, and the posterior surfaces of the larynx. These structures surround the larynx posteriorly and laterally. Tumors in this region can be difficult to detect because of the recesses and spaces surrounding the larynx. As a result, primary hypopharyngeal tumors may be asymptomatic and, like oropharyngeal tumors, present in an advanced state or as an "unknown primary." These tumors are associated with tobacco and alcohol use.

LARYNX. The larynx includes the vocal cords, the subglottis, and the supraglottic larynx as well as the thyroid, cricoid, and arytenoid cartilages. The supraglottic larynx is composed of several structures including the epiglottis, the surrounding aryepiglottic folds, and the false vocal folds. Tumors arising in the true vocal cords are frequently symptomatic early and rarely spread beyond the confines of the larynx, whereas subglottic and supraglottic cancers can be relatively asymptomatic and have a much higher and earlier risk of spread to lymphatics and to regional sites. Laryngeal cancers are strongly associated with smoking.

NASOPHARYNX. The nasopharynx includes the mucosal surfaces and structures of the cavity behind the nasal passages. Nasopharyngeal cancers are common in the Pacific Rim, Northern Africa, and the Middle East. In some areas of China and Southeast Asia, nasopharyngeal cancers occur with a frequency that rivals lung cancer. In North America, there are about 2000 cases each year. Nasopharyngeal cancers are frequently associated with the presence of latent infection of the epithelial tumor cells by Epstein-Barr virus (EBV), the etiologic agent of infectious mononucleosis (Chapter 371). Nasopharyngeal cancers also are associated with both environmental and genetic factors, in that the second generations of susceptible populations that have migrated to North America remain at high risk for this disease. Unlike other squamous cell carcinomas of the head and neck, nasopharyngeal cancers can occur at an early age, with a distinct peak in adolescents and young adults. Nasopharyngeal cancers are categorized into three histologic subtypes by the World Health Organization (WHO): the undifferentiated (WHO III) and nonkeratinizing forms (WHO II) are latently infected with EBV in 95% of cases and represent the majority of cases in North America and worldwide; the well-differentiated (WHO I) form is more rare, representing about 5% worldwide but about 15 to 25% of all nasopharyngeal cancers in North America, and it is usually associated with traditional risk factors such as smoking. The biologic behavior of nasopharyngeal cancers is similar regardless of differentiation or presence of EBV, with a high risk of early regional lymph node involvement, a prolonged natural history, and a high risk of spread to distant sites.

PARANASAL SINUSES. The paranasal sinuses comprise the maxillary, ethmoid, sphenoid, and frontal sinuses as well as the nasal cavity. These are relatively rare locations for tumors of the head and neck in North America, but there is an unexplained higher rate for malignant sinus disease among the Japanese. Squamous maxillary sinus cancers are more common among smokers. Up to 50% of cancers of the sinuses may be of salivary gland origin, often related to exposure to dusts from woodworking, tanning, or leather working. Occasionally, neuroendocrine tumors (including esthesioneuroblastoma, a neuroendocrine sarcoma deriving from olfactory neural tissue) and the rare sinonasal undifferentiated carcinoma are found. Sinus cancers frequently present late in their course at the time of symptomatic invasion of surrounding structures including the orbit, the nasal cavity, the base of the skull, and cranial nerves.

SALIVARY GLANDS. Salivary glands occur in all of the regions described, as well as in the trachea and esophagus. Tumors can develop in all the major and minor salivary glands with incidence that is roughly proportional to the quantity of the glandular tissue. The most common single site is the parotid. Although tumors can present at any age, including children, the peak incidence is between 55 and 65 years of age. Salivary gland cancers have diverse histologies and manifest different behaviors based on histologic classification. A substantial fraction of parotid salivary tumors can be benign. Among malignant tumors, the three most common histologic types are adenoid cystic carcinoma, mucoepidermoid cancer, and adenocarcinoma. Rare types include acinic cell cancer, salivary duct cancer, carcinoma ex pleomorphic adenoma, and squamous cell cancer. Risk factors for salivary gland cancers are poorly understood, but prior radiotherapy in adjacent areas increases the risk (Chapter 19).

Pathobiology

Tobacco products and alcohol are the most important etiologic and risk factors for squamous cell carcinoma of the head and neck, and both show a clear dose response. Any irritating smoked product increases the risk of local cancer, but nicotine in tobacco as well as other tobacco leaf components directly affect the oral mucosa and increase the risk of squamous cancer (Chapter 14). Alcohol is also a carcinogen, and alcohol consumption (Chapter 17) as well as its direct application in mouthwashes is associated with an increased risk. Alcohol also affects local and systemic detoxification enzymes and may increase the carcinogenic potential of other environmental carcinogens. Other environmental risk factors include radiation exposure and solar radiation; welding, metal refining, diesel exhaust, wood stove, and asbestos exposure; chronic irritants; vitamin A deficiency; and immunosuppression. About 25% of patients have no or only minimal exposure to any risk factors.

Pathogenic HPV subtypes, particularly HPV 16, independently account for approximately 50% of oropharyngeal cancer. Nasopharyngeal cancer is predominantly associated with keratinocyte infection with EBV. The classic nasopharyngeal cancer, which is also called lymphoepithelioma, is associated with a brisk lymphoid infiltrate that can be confused with a lymphoma. Careful examination reveals the malignant epithelial cells in the tumor. EBV is associated with the early development of dysplasia of the nasopharynx and has been linked to the earliest events in neoplastic transformation in nasopharyngeal cancer. EBV is also rarely associated with epithelial tumors of the oropharynx, tonsil, and salivary gland.

Several inherited diseases and genetic abnormalities are associated with the development of head and neck cancer. Fanconi's anemia (Chapter 174), a rare disorder of a family of related gene products, is associated with the development of tongue cancer, as is Cowden's syndrome, which is associated with mutation of the PTEN gene. Recently inherited loss of heterozygosity of the tumor suppressor gene p16 has also been associated with head and neck cancer. Finally, common inherited allelic variants of alcohol dehydrogenase and p450 genes may be associated with increased susceptibility to alcohol and other environmental carcinogens.

The development of squamous cell carcinoma of the head and neck is a multistep process in which early genetic changes evolve into frank malignancy. First, abnormal premalignant clones of mucosal cells may be localized in a single site within the head and neck; they may occur independently in many sites, or they may spread from a single site and evolve at other sites within the head and neck to form distinct but related tumors. Consequently, about 20% of patients develop a second primary in the upper aerodigestive tract, most commonly in the head and neck, lung, and esophagus; 5% of patients present with a synchronous second primary. Tumors frequently show similar, if not identical genetic alterations when compared with the original primary, providing further evidence for the phenomenon of field cancerization. Early changes in mucosal keratinocytes involve alterations in critical molecular pathways. Many of these changes are shared with other malignancies. The cell cycle is dysregulated through the early loss of p16, an inhibitor of cyclin D1, or through cyclin D1 upregulation; p53 is disabled through a number of mechanisms preventing programmed cell death; mitogenic signaling is enhanced by upregulation of EGF receptor function; COX-2 is overexpressed, inhibiting apoptosis and promoting angiogenesis; and chromosomal instability with aneuploidy appears. Many of these early molecular and functional changes occur without obvious alteration in the physical appearance of the oral mucosa, although leukoplakia can occur. Many of these early changes have become targets for novel therapeutics, and molecular changes can be monitored in response to treatment.

Oral premalignancy, which includes leukoplakia and erythroplakia, is a dysplastic state that carries a high risk for the development of squamous cell carcinoma of the head and neck. Leukoplakia (Fig. 197–1), which is diagnosed clinically as a white patch of mucosal tissue in the oral mucosa or larynx, progresses to cancer over a period

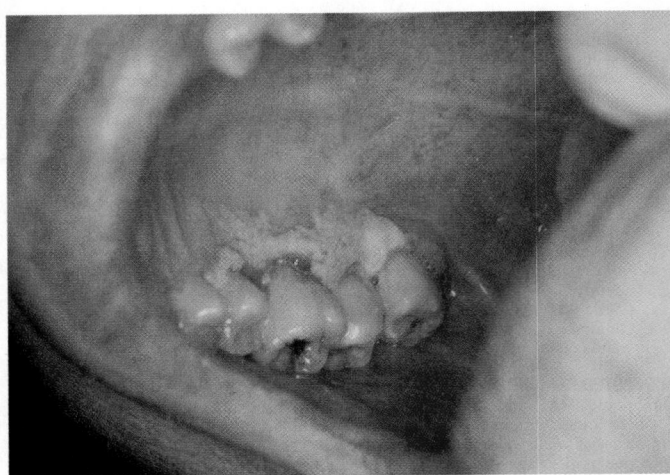

FIGURE 197–1 • Oral leukoplakia.

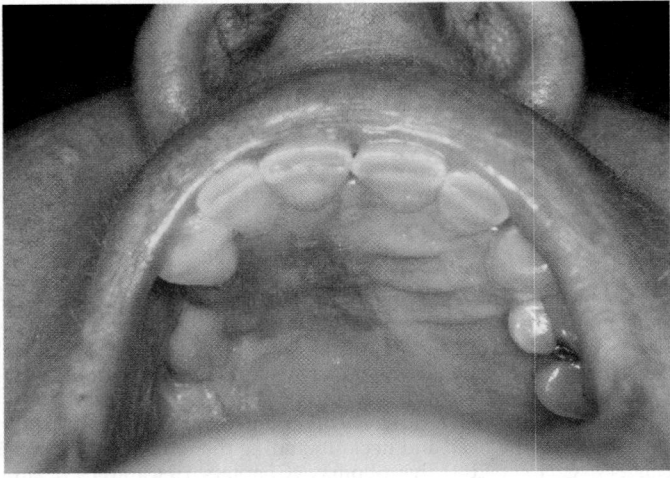

FIGURE 197–2 • Oral erythroplakia.

of several years in approximately 30% of patients; when associated with moderate to severe dysplasia or aneuploidy, however, the rate of progression is much higher. Erythroplakia (Fig. 197–2), which is a red hyperkeratotic change in the mucosa, is an advanced premalignant lesion with an approximately 60% rate of progression to oral cancer. The presence of aneuploidy in dysplastic lesions and leukoplakia has been strongly linked to the development of cancer, whereas other molecular changes, including loss of specific retinoid receptors, have not been as firmly related to the malignant transformation.

There is no proven chemopreventive therapy for persons with oral premalignant lesions. It has, however, been shown that continued smoking or alcohol consumption increases the risk of recurrence and second primaries dramatically.

Patients with squamous cell carcinoma of the head and neck are more at risk for local and regional recurrences and for persistent disease than for distant metastases. In addition, although the physical growth rate of tumors may appear to be slow, the cells within the tumor mass double rapidly. If all the cycling tumor cells survived and remained active, the tumors would have the potential to double every 48 hours. Most early tumors have a high rate of cell loss from apoptosis, senescence, differentiation, and inactivation; as a result, tumors may fluctuate in size early in presentation. Once therapy is instituted, however, surviving cells have an increased capacity to grow and repopulate, with less cell loss and more rapid clinical growth. Therefore, curative therapy should be continuous, brisk, and without interruption.

Clinical Manifestations and Natural History

Symptoms and clinical presentations of tumors in the head and neck can vary broadly and are related to the structures at the site of the primary tumor as well as the regional lymph node drainage. Small tumors can be easily appreciated because of physical self-discovery or early compromise of the function of a critical structure. Because of the propensity for squamous cell carcinoma of the head and neck to remain a local and regional disease, it is unusual for this cancer to present with abnormalities outside the head and neck. Salivary gland malignancies are less constrained and frequently spread distantly; however, because the primary tumors are also frequently accessible to direct physical examination and discovery, it is still uncommon to identify these tumors as a result of metastatic spread outside the region.

Clinical manifestations of *tumors in the oral cavity* include a painless lump, a painful mass or ulcer, or simple thickening of the mucosa. Small lesions in the lateral tongue and the floor of mouth can cause referred pain in the mandible, gums, and ear because of the shared sensory nerves supplying these areas. These symptoms can lead to unnecessary dental procedures or repeated courses of antibiotics if the tumor is not apparent on examination. Antibiotics can relieve symptoms and even reduce the size of a tumor or lymph nodes when superficial infection and inflammation contribute to the pain; however, recurrent or continued pain in an adult should trigger suspicion about more ominous disease. Speech may be affected late if the tumor causes restricted tongue motion or cranial nerve XII dysfunction. Gingival tumors can loosen teeth and invade the mandible along tooth sockets. Tumors originating in minor salivary glands of the oral cavity are submucosal and are less prone to ulceration.

For true vocal cord cancer, hoarseness and other forms of voice change are common and expected early presentations, but they may be later manifestations for *supraglottic and subglottic laryngeal tumors*, which become relatively large without affecting the voice. Tumors of the pyriform sinus can affect voice when they become large, impair the recurrent vagal nerve, or are associated with deep local invasion; pain in the ear or pain on swallowing referred to the ear is also a common and important presentation of these tumors. Adults with ear pain or persistent hoarseness should be referred to an otolaryngologist for evaluation. Because this posterior area is difficult to assess, primary tumors are frequently missed in routine office examinations. *Tumors of the supraglottic region, subglottic cancers, and cancers of the pyriform sinus* can also present with acute, emergent airway obstruction. Frequently patients have a history of wheezing and mild upper airway distress in the period leading up to emergent presentation. Occasionally this presentation is confused with adult-onset asthma.

A middle ear infection or infusion in an adult should also prompt an ear-nose-throat (ENT) evaluation. Nasopharyngeal cancer may present as an ear infection in young adults. Hemoptysis or epistaxis may be the only clue to a nasopharyngeal cancer or a *paranasal sinus tumor*. Cranial nerve findings from deep invasion of the base of skull are late events, including lateral gaze abnormalities, diplopia, facial pain, or facial nerve paralysis. *Sinus tumors* can also present with these later findings, although nasal stuffiness occurs frequently and can be confused with sinusitis. New and persistent symptoms of sinusitis or facial pain should raise suspicions of sinus disease and prompt an evaluation.

Tumors presenting in the tonsil or base of tongue can present with local pain and referred ear pain; however, tumors in these areas are frequently asymptomatic and can reach a large size before becoming manifest because of changes in speech (hot potato voice), a sense of globus, or restriction of tongue movement. Presentation with a painless lump in the neck is also common. Tumors of the tonsil or base of tongue may also lose their mucosal component, not be seen or felt on direct inspection, and present as a solid or cystic neck mass, so-called unknown primary. Isolated neck masses can wax and wane with antibiotics. A mass, especially a cystic mass, in the neck in an adult is cancer until proven otherwise and should prompt an ENT evaluation, before fine needle aspiration (FNA) or excisional biopsy.

The staging of squamous cell carcinoma of the head and neck is based on the TNM (tumor, node, metastasis) staging system, and prognosis is related primarily to N and T stage (Table 197–1). The risk of the cancer spreading to lymph nodes is directly related to the location of the primary and secondarily to the size of the primary. Tumors of the oropharynx have a high risk of nodal metastases, followed in risk by supraglottic larynx and pyriform sinus (hypopharynx), oral tongue, soft palate, oral cavity/floor of mouth, and larynx. Nasopharyngeal cancer is highly associated with extensive nodal spread, whereas paranasal sinus cancers rarely spread to lymph nodes. The location of lymph node spread is determined in part by site. Nasopharyngeal cancer spreads to posterior cervical lymph nodes as well as high cervical nodes. Oropharynx, larynx, and pyriform sinus tumors spread to high cervical nodes. Nodal metastases from these locations can be bilateral. Oral cavity tumors spread to submental nodes and submandibular nodes. Spread tends to be orderly from submandibular nodes to midcervical nodes. Oral cavity cancers can have as high as a 20% risk of clinically unappreciated contralateral spread.

Prognosis for squamous cell carcinoma of the head and neck is directly related to stage and performance status. The recurrence risk drops off dramatically at 2 years after the definitive treatment, and survival and possible cure can be defined after 3 years. N (nodal) status is the most important prognostic indicator of recurrence, with T (tumor) stage being next. Stage I patients (T1N0) have a greater than 90% likelihood of tumor control, whereas stage II patients (T2N0) have greater than 85% tumor control. Cancer control among stage III patients (T1–2N1, T3N0–1) is site dependent and varies from 50 to 75%. Patients with stage IV disease (T1–4, N2–3, or T4N0) have a 20 to 50% tumor-specific 3-year survival. Bad prognostic signs among advanced-stage patients are related to invasion of basic structures (carotid, base of skull, pterygoid muscles) and absolute size of tumor masses. Patients with recurrent disease and no curative options have a median survival of 6 to 9 months. Death can occur as a result of the compromise of local critical structures, including vessels, breathing, and swallowing.

Distant metastases occur in about 15 to 20% of patients. Oropharynx, tonsil, and pyriform sinus tumors have the highest risk of distant metastases. Approximately 5% of patients present with a synchronous lung tumor or metastasis. A single lung metastasis in a patient at presentation or in follow-up can be cured in about 20% of cases. As more patients survive their primary malignancy, late distant metastases may become more common. Nasopharyngeal cancer is associated with a three-fold higher rate of distant metastases than is squamous cell carcinoma of the head and neck.

Salivary gland cancers vary in behavior based on histology. Adenocarcinoma, salivary duct cancers, salivary squamous cell

Continued

cancer, and high-grade mucoepidermoid cancer spread to lymph nodes, but also spread rapidly hematogenously. Except in adenoid cystic carcinoma, the presence of lymph node metastases signals a high risk for distant metastases. Adenoid cystic carcinoma infrequently involves lymph nodes but does spread along nerves. Regional recurrences along cranial nerves are frequent and are associated with "skip" lesions. Adenoid cystic carcinoma is also associated with late development of lung metastases, but these patients can have a prolonged history, lasting more than 20 years. Low-grade mucoepidermoid cancers and acinic cell cancers have little risk of distant spread and are more notable for local recurrence if not completely removed.

Diagnosis and Evaluation

The relative accessibility of the head and neck to direct inspection makes physical examination critical for diagnosis and staging. Patients presenting with localized symptoms or a sign such as an ulcer or small mass should have a thorough head and neck office examination performed by their primary physician and by a specialist, including inspection of the visible structures and palpation of the base of tongue and tonsil areas as well as the neck. Specialized office examinations with fiberoptics should be included in the preliminary assessment by a specialist. Patients with a readily accessible primary can have a diagnostic biopsy performed at first presentation. Whether cancer is suspected or not, excisional biopsies should be discouraged because margins are frequently violated and inadequate, leading to larger re-excisions. A simple punch biopsy is sufficient for diagnosis, particularly in the oral tongue where tumors can spread readily though lymphatics.

When cancer is highly suspected and before definitive surgical intervention, computed tomography (CT) scanning from the base of skull to the clavicles, preferably with the spiral technique, and a chest radiograph should be obtained. Magnetic resonance imaging (MRI) provides added information in evaluating soft tissue involvement, especially in the base of tongue, parapharyngeal spaces, and for sinus tumors. MRI can distinguish between soft tissue masses and retained secretions, whereas CT is more helpful in assessing bone invasion. Positron-emission tomography (PET) scanning is a potential adjunct, but its precise role remains to be defined.

When a biopsy indicates cancer or cancer is highly suspected, an examination under anesthesia with endoscopy should be performed to stage the primary tumor before definitive therapy is undertaken. This procedure, which provides information regarding the extent of disease, the appropriateness of the planned definitive procedure, and the presence of second primaries, is an absolute requirement before definitive therapy can be discussed with a patient. Endoscopy and palpation under anesthesia can identify unexpected local spread or a synchronous second primary (found in about 5% of patients), and the procedure should include esophagoscopy or barium swallow in all patients and bronchoscopy in high-risk patients.

APPROACH TO THE PATIENT WITH AN UNKNOWN PRIMARY. Patients frequently present to their primary physician with an enlarged lymph node or collection of lymph nodes in the upper neck (Fig. 197–3). Unless there is an obvious symptom or sign that leads the clinician to the diagnosis of a head and neck cancer, patients presenting in this

Table 197–1 • AMERICAN JOINT COMMITTEE ON CANCER STAGING FOR HEAD AND NECK SQUAMOUS CELL CARCINOMA

	LARYNX	LIP AND ORAL CAVITY	OROPHARYNX	HYPOPHARYNX
TUMOR				
Tis	Carcinoma in situ	Carcinoma in situ	Carcinoma in situ	Carcinoma in situ
T1	Tumor limited to one subsite of the larynx	Tumor < 2 cm	Tumor < 2 cm	Tumor < 2 cm, limited to one subsite of the hypopharynx
T2	Tumor involving more than one subsite and/or impaired vocal cord mobility	Tumor > 2 cm and ≤ 4 cm	Tumor > 2 cm and ≤ 4 cm	Tumor > 2 cm and < 4 cm, involving more than one subsite
T3	Paralyzed vocal cord; involvement of pre-epiglottic or postcricoid areas (supraglottic primary)	Tumor > 4 cm	Tumor > 4 cm	Tumor > 4 cm, or paralyzed vocal cord
T4	Extension outside the larynx; cartilage invasion	Extension to adjacent structures (soft tissue or bone outside the oral cavity, deep tongue)	Invasion of adjacent structures (larynx, bone, muscle)	Invasion of adjacent structures (bone, muscle, or cartilage)

NODE	**DEFINITION**
N0	No cervical lymph nodes positive
N1	Single ipsilateral lymph node < 3 cm
N2a	Single ipsilateral lymph node > 3 cm and < 6 cm
N2b	Multiple ipsilateral lymph nodes, each < 6 cm
N2c	Bilateral or contralateral lymph nodes, each < 6 cm
N3	Single or multiple lymph nodes < 6 cm

METASTASIS	**DEFINITION**
M0	No distant metastasis
M1	Distant metastasis present
Mx	Distant metastasis cannot be assessed

STAGE	**T**	**N**	**M**
Stage I	T1	N0	M0
Stage II	T2	N0	M0
Stage III	T3	N0	M0
	T1-3	N1	M0
Stage IV	T4	N0–1	M0
	Any T	N2–3	M0
	Any T	Any N	M1

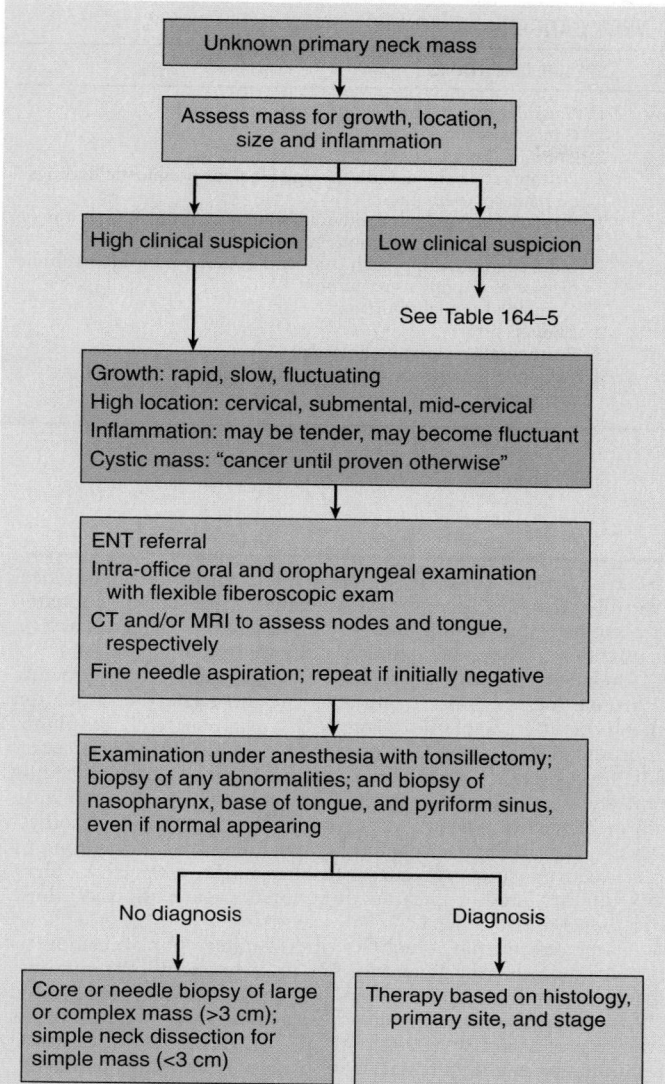

FIGURE 197–3 • Evaluation of an unknown primary neck mass.

Flowchart content:

Unknown primary neck mass

↓

Assess mass for growth, location, size and inflammation

↓

High clinical suspicion | Low clinical suspicion

Low clinical suspicion → See Table 164–5

Growth: rapid, slow, fluctuating
High location: cervical, submental, mid-cervical
Inflammation: may be tender, may become fluctuant
Cystic mass: "cancer until proven otherwise"

↓

ENT referral
Intra-office oral and oropharyngeal examination with flexible fiberoscopic exam
CT and/or MRI to assess nodes and tongue, respectively
Fine needle aspiration; repeat if initially negative

↓

Examination under anesthesia with tonsillectomy; biopsy of any abnormalities; and biopsy of nasopharynx, base of tongue, and pyriform sinus, even if normal appearing

↓

No diagnosis | Diagnosis

No diagnosis → Core or needle biopsy of large or complex mass (>3 cm); simple neck dissection for simple mass (<3 cm)

Diagnosis → Therapy based on histology, primary site, and stage

---

manner are considered to have an unknown primary. Masses in the supraclavicular areas represent primary tumors below the clavicles, and masses in the midneck and cervical regions are rarely metastatic from below the clavicle. Identification of a primary site is critical to focus therapy, reduce morbidity, and determine prognosis.

The most common primary sites for painless lumps are the oropharynx (base of tongue and tonsil) and pyriform sinus. Salivary gland cancers, lymphomas, melanomas, and skin cancers can also present in this manner. Bilateral nodal disease or nodal disease with systemic symptoms may suggest lymphoma. By comparison, pain, warmth, and erythema may suggest an infectious etiology. Intraparotid nodes most likely represent metastases from skin malignancies. Physical examination should include a careful investigation for skin primary cancers. CT and MRI should be part of the initial evaluation. FNA should be performed and repeated if initially negative. CT-guided biopsy may be indicated if the mass is difficult to approach. PET scans may be helpful in this setting, although the data are controversial. If squamous cells are identified in the FNA or CT-guided biopsy, the tumor is most likely a squamous cell carcinoma of the head and neck. A second FNA is indicated if the first is negative. Next, endoscopy under anesthesia should be performed with tonsillectomy. The endoscopy should include directed biopsies of any abnormalities, areas of firmness, and the base of tongue, nasopharynx, and ipsilateral

pyriform sinus even if they appear normal. Core or excisional (single node < 3 cm in size) biopsy of the lymph node should be performed if pathology is equivocal and a primary site is not confirmed. A neck dissection can be accomplished if a primary site is not identified and the patient has an N1 or small N2a/b presentation. Some unknown primaries with squamous histology are never identified. Currently, there are no molecular markers to separate head and neck cancer from skin or salivary gland squamous cancer. EBV positivity suggests a nasopharynx cancer.

In contrast to squamous cell carcinoma of the head and neck, salivary gland cancers are heterogeneous in their natural history and treatment. The three most common histologies are adenoid cystic carcinoma, mucoepidermoid cancer, and adenocarcinoma. Other histologies include the aggressive salivary duct cancer and squamous cell cancers, whereas less aggressive histologies include adenocarcinoma ex pleomorphic adenoma and acinic cell. Because adenoid cystic carcinoma travels along nerves and can spread hematogenously, careful assessment of the cranial nerves and the chest by CT scanning is indicated before major surgery is undertaken. Patients should also be evaluated for bone and liver metastases. A formal lymph node dissection is not indicated. Ethmoid and sphenoid sinus adenoid cystic carcinomas are locally and regionally aggressive and require specialized surgery and radiotherapy techniques for local and regional control. The behavior of mucoepidermoid carcinoma is determined by histology. Low- and intermediate-grade lesions rarely metastasize. Isolated high-grade tumors spread to local lymph nodes and by hematogenous routes with a high risk of lung metastases. Work-up should be similar to that for adenoid cystic carcinoma for high-grade lesions. Local therapy should be directed at local and regional control with lymph node dissection. Radiotherapy is indicated for close microscopic margins or lymph node involvement. Adenocarcinoma, salivary duct cancers, and squamous cell carcinoma are also poor prognosis lesions with aggressive local and distant behaviors. These tumors should be evaluated in the same fashion as aggressive mucoepidermoid carcinomas. Acinic cell carcinomas and carcinoma ex pleomorphic adenoma are relatively rare cancers. They have a propensity for local regional recurrence if they are not removed in toto. Metastases are rare and tend to be slow growing.

OTHER TUMORS OF THE HEAD AND NECK. Lymphomas frequently present in the head and neck as either nodal disease in the neck or as tumor involving the lymphoid tissues of Waldeyer's Ring (Chapters 194 and 195). Unless they are accompanied by systemic symptoms or lymphadenopathy, it can be difficult to distinguish a lymphoma presenting as a tonsillar mass or an isolated neck node from a primary squamous cell cancer of the neck and head. In addition, patients with lymphoma may develop a later primary head and neck cancer as a consequence of past exposures to tobacco, radiation therapy, or immunosuppression. Lymphoma can be distinguished from inflammation by flow cytometry or special stains on a sample obtained by FNA. Any lymphoma can present in the neck or in Waldeyer's ring. The tonsil is a preferred site for mantle cell and undifferentiated lymphomas. Mucosa-associated lymphoid tissue (MALT) lymphomas can affect salivary glands.

In the context of an isolated neck mass, a systematic evaluation (see Fig. 197–3) should be followed, even in young adults without a smoking history. The sinonasal T-cell and NK lymphomas, known also as lethal midline granulomas, represent a unique family of lymphomas of the head and neck. These lymphomas are associated with EBV infection (Chapter 371). Solitary, extramedullary plasmacytoma can also occur in the nasopharynx or paranasal sinuses (Chapter 196).

Sarcomas that present in the head and neck include osteogenic sarcomas (Chapter 208) and nerve sheath tumors. Paragangliomas, which are rare malignant tumors of the chief cells of the nerve paraganglia, can be extensive, multicentric, and vascular. Rhabdomyosarcomas, which have a predilection for the orbit and sinuses, occur in younger persons; prognosis tends to be better for tumors of the head and neck than for other locations. Olfactory neuroblastomas or esthesioneuroblastomas invade the nasal cavity and base of skull.

Many skin tumors can present with adenopathy of the neck or parotid area, including melanoma and squamous cell cancers (Chapter 209). An unusual skin appendage tumor, Merkel cell cancer, can be confused with other neuroendocrine epithelial tumors.

Table 197–2 • GENERAL APPROACH TO SQUAMOUS CELL HEAD AND NECK CANCER

STAGING	TNM	DISEASE-SPECIFIC SURVIVAL	TREATMENT APPROACH	SPECIAL CONDITIONS
Stage I	T1N0	85–95%	Surgery or radiotherapy	1. Consider organ function and long-term toxicity
Stage II	T2N0	75–90%	Surgery or radiotherapy	1. Consider organ function 2. Combined modality for high-volume tumor 3. Postoperative chemoradiotherapy for poor prognostic findings on pathologic staging
Stage III	T3N0 T1–3N1	50–75%	Combined-modality treatment	1. Primary concomitant chemoradiotherapy for organ function 2. Postoperative chemoradiotherapy 3. More aggressive approach (sequential therapy) for high-volume disease or hypopharynx tumors
Stage IV	T1–3N2–3 T4N0–3 Any M1	20–60%	Combined-modality treatment	1. Combined-modality therapy 2. Limited surgery 3. Postoperative chemoradiotherapy 4. Palliative therapy for M1 (curative therapy for isolated lung metastases)

Rx Treatment and Prognosis (Table 197–2)

Selection of a treatment program for an individual patient is based on three factors: the primary site and stage of the tumor, the patient's comorbidities and preferences, and the biology of the tumor. Early-stage lesions, T1N0 and T2N0, are defined by their size, and their prognosis is site specific. For example, early *larynx cancer* involving the true vocal cords has an excellent prognosis and can be treated with local excision. Voice-preserving partial laryngectomy is effective for selected patients. Radiotherapy is equally effective for early cancer. When there is a risk of lymph node spread, radiotherapy must be given postoperatively, and the primary value of surgery is diminished.

Oral tongue, base of tongue, and pyriform sinus tumors have a worse prognosis and are difficult to stage accurately because of submucosal spread or lymphatic involvement. Stage I and II cancers are cured with local and regional surgery or radiotherapy in 80 to 90% of cases. Surgery may be preferred for limited oral cavity and anterior lesions. In surgically staged patients, a positive margin, two or more positive lymph nodes, or extracapsular spread is associated with a poor survival (<30%) over 5 years; postoperative chemoradiotherapy or radiotherapy may improve survival. At present, no molecular or immunohistochemical finding definitively adds to the information gleaned from pathology, staging, and performance status.

When organ preservation and function are an issue or when radiotherapy is required regardless of surgical outcome, primary radiotherapy should be considered. A randomized study has shown improved tumor response rates to hyperfractionated and accelerated radiation treatment, but this response has not translated into improved survival and is associated with a greater short-term morbidity.

The curative treatment of intermediate (stage III—T1–3N1, T3N0) and locally advanced (Stage IV—T1–3N2–3, T4) disease remains controversial. Long-term survival (3 years) in patients with stage III disease is generally between 50 and 75%, whereas only 15 to 50% of stage IV patients survive for 3 years. Intermediate-stage tumors are generally resectable, but organ preservation may be an important consideration. In many of these cases, a combined-modality approach that includes chemotherapy is a standard of care.

Patients with anterior lesions may do better with initial surgical treatment. The oral cavity is easy to assess and is relatively forgiving for surgery and reconstruction; radiotherapy or chemoradiotherapy can be moderated in the absence of bad prognostic features. For intermediate and advanced tumors, radiotherapy or chemoradiotherapy is a necessary adjunct to prevent recurrence. For example, a T3 or N1 lesion of the oropharyngeal tongue or hypopharynx is almost always more extensive then clinically appreciated and may be more suited to a nonsurgical regional and systemic approach. In addition, patients with rapidly growing tumors are more suitable for a combined-modality approach. Patients with extensive N2 or N3 nodal disease (stage IV) should be considered as potentially unresectable because of poor prognosis from regional recurrence and distant metastases. Certain locations such as the nasopharynx and posterior pharynx should also be considered for definitive radiotherapy or chemoradiotherapy.

Radiotherapy is proven by randomized trials to yield better local control and disease-free survival if given in twice-daily fractionated treatments rather than as daily therapy. However, overall survival is no different than with standard daily radiotherapy.

Induction chemotherapy is the delivery of chemotherapy before definitive local/regional treatment. The most effective induction chemotherapy is cisplatin 100 mg/M^2 intravenous (IV) bolus plus 5-fluorouracil 1000 mg/M^2/day for 5 days by IV infusion, repeated every 3 to 4 weeks). This regimen of induction chemotherapy preceding radiotherapy and surgery improves survival in patients with advanced head and neck cancer compared with standard radiotherapy.[1,2] This induction chemotherapy followed by radiotherapy is as effective as surgery for curing oropharynx, larynx, and hypopharynx tumors, and it permits functional preservation of these organs.[3,4]

Chemoradiotherapy, which describes the integration of chemotherapy and radiotherapy given together, provides significant improvements in overall survival in patients with advanced disease compared with radiotherapy alone. For example, in a nasopharynx trial, patients who received cisplatin (100 mg/M^2, IV bolus) every 3 weeks during radiotherapy and then received adjuvant chemotherapy had better survival than those treated with radiotherapy alone.[5] In a trial for oropharyngeal carcinoma, patients treated with carboplatin and 5-fluorouracil plus simultaneous radiotherapy had a significantly better survival compared with radiotherapy alone.[6]

Patients with locally advanced and/or unresectable disease should receive chemotherapy as part of a combined-modality approach. Both induction chemotherapy and chemoradiotherapy prolong survival. A sequential combination of both might be considered as well. Organ preservation should be offered to patients who can tolerate the treatment and participate in the rehabilitation.

The treatment of *tumors of the paranasal sinuses* is a special case. They rarely metastasize, and treatment should focus on surgical resection with postoperative radiotherapy or chemoradiotherapy for resectable stage III and IV disease and on chemoradiotherapy for local and regional control in unresectable disease. Proton beam radiation may be more suited for tumors in and around the base of skull and brain.

FOLLOW-UP. Patients need life-long follow-up. A chest radiograph should be performed at least yearly, and surveillance examinations for second primaries and recurrences should be performed monthly to bimonthly in the first year and then less frequently over time. Treatment failure after 3 years is uncommon, but second primaries can continue to be identified. It is important to counsel patients to avoid tobacco products and any exposure to alcohol.

During therapy and immediately after therapy, patients benefit from pain medications, local anesthetics, mucolytics, and saline mouthwash. Patients must avoid alcohol-containing preparations or irritants. Long-acting agents such as fentanyl or time-released narcotics should be added when needed (Chapter 29). A percutaneous endoscopic gastrostomy feeding tube is effective for maintaining weight, improving healing, and managing nutrition during radiotherapy. Depression is a major problem; psychiatric support and antidepressants may be very helpful (Chapter 426). Salivary function improves over more than 4 years after radiotherapy, but most improvement occurs in the first 2 years. Pilocarpine is an effective stimulant of salivary flow in about 20% of patients.

Long-term sequelae of radiation therapy include hypothyroidism, which occurs in up to 50% of patients and as early as 3 months after treatment. Patients should be monitored with a serum thyroid-stimulating hormone level at regular intervals and then be treated as appropriate (Chapter 239). Patients are at substantial lifelong risk for complications from dental manipulations after radiotherapy. Bone necrosis is painful, can be confused with tumor recurrence, and requires vigorous antibiotic therapy, débridement, and hyperbaric oxygen to promote healing.

Patients with recurrent disease, a second primary, or metastatic disease must be evaluated for potential curability. If patients have a recurrence or second primary, curative treatment options are defined by their current stage, their prior therapy, and the interval from their original therapy. Patients who have been treated with prior surgery but not radiotherapy can receive surgery, radiotherapy, or chemotherapy as part of a curative treatment plan. Patients with a surgically treatable recurrence in an irradiated field should have surgery as appropriate. It is important to recognize that the surgery must encompass the entire recurrence. Symptomatically, persistent pain may be the most important indicator of a recurrence, and rebiopsy should be considered when a suspicious lesion is observed. Surgical salvage

may cure as many as 30% of patients with recurrent oral cavity, larynx, or hypopharyngeal tumors. Re-irradiation is also acceptable in some patients.

Patients who are incurable can be treated effectively with palliative therapy to improve quality of life and improve survival; for example, tracheostomy for airway control, laryngectomy for pain and aspiration, and a percutaneous endoscopic gastrostomy tube for feeding. These maneuvers can improve comfort and care for appropriate patients.

Palliative chemotherapy can provide meaningful benefit to some patients. Response rates for single agents are generally poor, and combination therapy offers higher response rates (30 to 50%), but with limited improvements in median and 1-year survival and more toxicity.

SALIVARY GLAND TUMORS. In contrast to squamous cell carcinomas of the head and neck, salivary gland cancers are heterogeneous in their natural history and treatment; however, the mainstay of therapy for these tumors is surgery. Early symptoms of local/regional recurrence include cranial nerve dysfunction and progressive pain. A PET scan may be useful in distinguishing recurrence from the neuropathy that may result from radiotherapy.

There are no highly active agents or combinations for treatment of metastatic salivary gland tumors. Local therapy can include surgical removal of isolated metastases, radiofrequency ablation, and radiotherapy. Response rates are generally in the 20 to 35% range, but prolonged responses are occasionally seen.

Future Directions

New computer-enhanced radiotherapy techniques can direct radiotherapy treatments more precisely to target tissues and reduce radiation-induced morbidity. Molecular profiling of tumors may enhance diagnosis, monitoring, and prognosis. Vaccines against two viruses associated with head and neck cancer, EBV and HPV, are under development and may prevent malignancy in high-risk populations. New anticancer agents that target dysregulated pathways critical to maintaining tumor viability and growth are in clinical trials.

1. Paccagnella A, Orlando A, Marchiori C, et al: Phase III trial of initial chemotherapy in stage III or IV head and neck cancers: A study by the Gruppo di Studio sui Tumori della Testa e del collo. J Natl Cancer Inst 1994;86:265–272.
2. Domenge C, Hill C, Lefebvre J, et al: Randomized trial of neoadjuvant chemotherapy in oropharyngeal carcinoma. Br J Cancer 2000;83:1594–1598.
3. Veterans Affairs Laryngeal Cancer Study Group: Induction chemotherapy plus radiation compared with surgery plus radiation in patients with advanced laryngeal cancer. N Engl J Med 1991;324:1685–1689.
4. Lefebvre J, Chevalier D, Luboinski B, et al: Larynx preservation in pyriform sinus cancer: Preliminary results of a European organization for research and treatment of cancer phase III trial. J Natl Cancer Inst 1996;88:890–898.
5. Al-Sarraf M, LeBlanc M, Shanker GP, et al: Chemoradiotherapy versus radiotherapy in patients with advanced nasopharyngeal cancer: Phase III randomized Intergroup study 0099. J Clin Oncol 1998;16:1310–1317.
6. Calais G, Alfonsi M, Bardet E, et al: Randomized trial of radiation therapy versus concomitant chemotherapy and radiation therapy for advanced stage oropharynx carcinoma. J Natl Cancer Inst 1999;91:2081–2086.

SUGGESTED READINGS
Braakhuis BJM, Tabor MP, Leemans CR, et al: Second tumors and field cancerization in oral and oropharyngeal cancer: Molecular techniques provide new insights and definitions. Head Neck 2002;24:198–206. *An excellent review of the current state-of-the-art and theories of molecular cancer pathogenesis in the head and neck.*
Forastiere A, Koch W, Trotti A, et al: Head and neck cancer. N Engl J Med 2001;345:1890–1900. *A useful overview.*
Haddad R, Wirth L, Posner M. Integration of chemotherapy in the curative treatment of locally advanced head and neck cancer. Expert Rev Anticancer Ther 2003;3:331–338. *A thorough review of the topic with the most recently published trials.*
Pignon J, Bourhis J, Domenge C, et al: Chemotherapy added to locoregional treatment for head and neck squamous-cell cancer: Three meta-analyses of updated individual data. Lancet 2000;355:949–955. *A definitive meta-analysis of combined modality treatment in locally advanced head and neck cancer.*

198 LUNG CANCER AND OTHER PULMONARY NEOPLASMS

York E. Miller

Definition

Lung cancer is the leading cause of cancer death in both men and women in the United States. More than 99% of malignant lung tumors arise from the respiratory epithelium and are termed *bronchogenic carcinoma*. Primary pulmonary lymphomas (Chapter 195) are the most common nonepithelial pulmonary neoplasm. For practical purposes, bronchogenic carcinoma can be divided into two subgroups: small cell lung cancer (SCLC) and non-small cell lung cancer (NSCLC), which includes the subtypes adenocarcinoma, squamous cell carcinoma, and large cell carcinoma (Table 198–1). A correct tissue diagnosis is crucial, because SCLC has a high response rate to chemotherapy and radiation and is appropriately treated by surgery only in rare situations. Conversely, NSCLC can be cured by surgery in certain stages and is not curable by chemotherapy alone. The overall 5-year survival rate for lung cancer is a disappointing 14%. Smoking is the major risk factor for development of lung cancer (Chapters 14 and 186).

Table 198–1 • MALIGNANT PULMONARY NEOPLASMS

NEOPLASM	INCIDENCE (%)
Common	99
Non-small cell lung cancer	~75
Adenocarcinoma	~35
Squamous cell carcinoma	~30
Large cell carcinoma	~10
Small cell lung cancer	~20
Carcinoids	~5
Rare	<1
Lymphoma, carcinosarcoma, mucoepidemoid carcinoma, malignant fibrous histiocytoma, melanoma, sarcoma, blastoma	

Incidence and Prevalence

In the first decade of the 20th century, lung cancer was a rare disorder. Now, however, approximately 170,000 new cases of lung cancer are diagnosed in the United States each year, and approximately 160,000 patients die annually from the disease. Lung cancer is now the most common cause of cancer death for both men and women and accounts for 28% of the overall cancer death rate. In terms of both cancer deaths and years of life lost, the effect of lung cancer is greater than that of breast, prostate, colon, and rectal cancer combined. Lung cancer incidence for middle-aged white men recently peaked and is now declining slightly. However, trends for women show a continued increase, and in the past decade, lung cancer surpassed breast cancer as the leading cause of cancer death in women. On a worldwide basis, lung cancer will continue to be a major problem into the 21st century, due to cases in ex-smokers, the increasing incidence of smoking in teenagers, and the marketing of cigarettes to developing countries.

Epidemiology

MODIFIABLE RISK FACTORS

TOBACCO PRODUCTS. Tobacco smoking causes approximately 87% of cases of lung cancer in men and 85% in women, with a dose-dependent relationship with mortality of both duration and intensity of smoking. SCLC has the strongest association with smoking, with attributable fractions of 97% and 91% for men and women, respectively. Smoking cessation causes a gradual drop in lung cancer risk, but not a complete normalization of risk, over a number of years. Cigarette smoke contains a number of active carcinogens and procarcinogens, and the pattern of mutations (transversions versus transitions) seen in oncogenes and tumor suppressor genes isolated from smokers with lung cancer is that expected from the mechanism of action of the major cigarette smoke carcinogens (Chapter 185).

PASSIVE SMOKE EXPOSURE. The Environmental Protection Agency has classified passive smoke exposure as carcinogenic. In support of this association, increased levels of carcinogens are measurable in the blood of passive smokers. A number of studies have shown increased risk for lung cancer in the spouses and children of smokers, and passive tobacco smoke exposure in childhood carries a higher risk than exposure during adult life. Exposure to 25 smoker-years in childhood approximately doubles the risk of lung cancer in a nonsmoker.

OCCUPATIONAL AND OTHER EXPOSURES (Chapter 89). In addition to its association with mesothelioma, asbestos exposure also increases the risk for all histologic subtypes of lung cancer. The relative risk of lung cancer in a nonsmoking asbestos worker is approximately 5. The effect of smoking and asbestos exposure is synergistic, with a risk ratio of between 50 and 100. Common sources of asbestos exposure include the shipbuilding industry, nautical engine rooms, automotive (particularly brake-lining) work, painting, and the construction industry. Exposures that may seem trivial can be significant; for example, cases of mesothelioma have been reported in the spouses and children of asbestos workers who brought their workclothes home to be washed. Exposure to asbestos fibers is now closely regulated. Because risk from asbestos exposure and smoking is synergistic, the most important intervention in an individual with both exposures is to stop smoking.

The association between ionizing radiation (Chapter 19) and lung cancer was made in classic studies of uranium miners exposed to radon daughters. Other miners in areas of significant subterranean radioactivity can also be exposed. Some home environments also have significant levels of radon, especially because modern insulation practices lead to increased radon levels. It is estimated that between 5000 and 15,000 excess lung cancer deaths, mostly in smokers, are caused annually in the United States by radon. As with asbestos and smoking, the risks of ionizing radiation exposure and smoking are synergistic. Other environmental or occupational lung carcinogens include arsenic, chromium, chloromethyl ethers, mustard gas, nickel, polycyclic hydrocarbons, vinyl chloride, and possibly silica and certain man-made fibers (Chapter 20).

AIR POLLUTION. Air pollution is associated with a variety of respiratory disorders and has long been suspected as a possible pulmonary carcinogen. A number of studies demonstrate an increased incidence of lung cancer in urban versus rural environments, but other factors could also explain these differences.

CHRONIC OBSTRUCTIVE PULMONARY DISEASE. The presence of chronic obstructive pulmonary disease (Chapter 85), defined as either airflow obstruction on pulmonary function testing or symptoms of chronic bronchitis, increases the risk of lung cancer several-fold. Chronic obstructive pulmonary disease is a risk factor by itself and is not just a reflection of the number of cigarettes smoked. In middle-aged individuals with mild chronic obstructive pulmonary disease, lung cancer has now surpassed cardiovascular disease as a cause of death.

DIET (Chapter 12). Epidemiologic studies demonstrate increased risk for lung cancer in individuals with a diet low in fruits and vegetables. The effect of dietary intervention by increasing fruit and vegetable intake on risk for lung cancer has not been determined.

NONMODIFIABLE RISK FACTORS

GENDER AND RACIAL DIFFERENCES. The largest factor in gender differences in incidence of lung cancer is differences in cigarette smoking habits. The predominant lung cancer incidence and mortality in the United States are currently seen in men, but the incidence rates for women are rising rapidly, whereas those for middle-aged men are reaching a plateau. However, given the same exposures, women may be more susceptible to lung cancer than men. African-American men have the highest incidence of lung cancer, but racial differences are confounded by differences in socioeconomic status and smoking behavior. One study has concluded that African-American men and women have higher rates of lung cancer than do whites, after adjustment for differences in these factors.

GENETIC SUSCEPTIBILITY. A segregation analysis has demonstrated that lung cancer incidence within families is consistent with mendelian inheritance of a major autosomal gene governing susceptibility (Chapter 36). It is estimated that segregation at this locus accounts for 69%, 47%, and 22% of lung cancers diagnosed at ages 50, 60, and 70 years, respectively. However, other studies have suggested that the genetic susceptibility to lung cancer is explained by a large number of genes with low penetrance.

Major categories of genes that potentially determine susceptibility to lung cancer (Chapter 185) include proto-oncogenes, tumor suppressor genes, genes regulating the abundance and action of growth factors, genes encoding enzymes that metabolize procarcinogens to active carcinogens (typified by the p450 enzymes), and genes that detoxify carcinogens (typified by glutathione S transferase μ). Although kindreds with germline abnormalities of either the p53 or the retinoblastoma tumor suppressor genes have higher incidences of lung cancer, these abnormalities do not appear to be a common mechanism in the general population. Two isozymes, CYP2D6 and CYP1A1, of the p450 enzyme system, which metabolizes and in many cases activates carcinogens, have been implicated in susceptibility to lung cancer. Glutathione S-transferase μ has a common null allele that confers an increased risk for lung cancer in some populations. Combinations of susceptibility genes appear to increase lung cancer risk significantly.

Pathogenesis

The respiratory epithelium develops as an outpouching from the endoderm of the primitive foregut. All respiratory epithelial cells differentiate from the primitive respiratory epithelium. Animal studies demonstrate that in the airway epithelium, both the secretory and basal cells can dedifferentiate and subsequently redifferentiate into the various epithelial subtypes. In the alveolar epithelium, the type II cell is the proliferative stem cell. All histologic subtypes of bronchogenic carcinoma are believed to be derived from the respiratory epithelium. The different histologic subtypes are a reflection of the differentiation pathway taken by a particular tumor. The plasticity of this differentiation is demonstrated by the occurrence of mixed tumors expressing differentiation markers for more than one histologic subtype. In addition, experimental expression of specific oncogenes in lung cancer cell lines can alter their differentiation characteristics.

PREMALIGNANT BIOLOGY

Currently, the favored model for the development of bronchogenic carcinoma is that of multistep carcinogenesis with the successive accumulation of mutations in a number of genes involved in regulating growth. For squamous cell carcinoma, premalignant lesions have been described and widely accepted. For peripheral adenocarcinoma, atypical alveolar hyperplasia has been proposed as a precursor lesion; these lesions are clonal and exhibit the mutations commonly found in adenocarcinoma of the lung.

Microdissection of bronchial epithelium with varying degrees of squamous dysplasia has demonstrated alterations, including chromosome 3p, 8p, and 9p deletions, and, more rarely, p53 gene mutations in premalignant lesions. Mutations are also quite common in the bronchial epithelium of smokers and ex-smokers, even after relatively trivial tobacco exposure. While the presence of a single mutation in the epithelium of a smoker is common, multiple mutations, including less common abnormalities such as p53 and Ki-ras mutations, are most often associated with advanced dysplasias.

Increased cellular proliferation is also necessary for carcinogenesis. It is likely that growth factors, derived from inflammatory cells, epithelial cells, and neuroendocrine cells, are elevated in tobacco smokers and play a role in the pathogenesis of lung cancer. Intraepithelial angiogenesis, termed *angiogenic squamous dysplasia*, has been noted in preneoplastic lesions, but it is not known whether this lesion is more likely to progress to invasive carcinoma.

TUMOR BIOLOGY

GENETIC ALTERATIONS. Bronchogenic carcinomas (Chapter 185) have highly abnormal tumor karyotypes, but certain consistent chromosomal abnormalities have been noted both in SCLC and NSCLC, including deletions involving chromosomes 3p, 5q, 9p, 11p, 13q, and 17p (Table 198–2). These abnormalities typically result in loss of heterozygosity but not homozygous deletion of a region. The deleted regions are likely the loci of tumor suppressor genes. Indeed, several tumor suppressor genes, Rb (13q14), p53 (17p13), *CDKN2A* (9p21), and *CDKN2B* (9p21) are in regions typically deleted in lung cancer. The chromosome 3p deletion is quite large and likely contains several tumor suppressor genes, two of which (*FHIT* and *RASSF1A*) have been identified. The *VHL* gene at chromosome 3p25 can also be inactivated in lung cancer. Although Rb and p53 mutations are found in both SCLC and NSCLC, the incidence of both is significantly higher in SCLC.

Transforming oncogenes can be activated by a number of mechanisms, including point mutation, gene amplification, and overexpression (Table 198–3). Abnormalities of the Ki-ras, her2/neu, and myc family oncogenes have been described and reported to affect prognosis adversely. Cyclin D1 overexpression is common in NSCLC and, in conjunction with inactivation of the cyclin-dependent kinase inhibitors *CDK2NA* and *CDK2NB*, represents a nonmutation mechanism inactivation of Rb that leads to loss of cell cycle control. Because abnormalities in tumor suppressor and proto-oncogenes in lung cancer may have prognostic significance, it is likely that in the future treatment plans will be altered on the basis of these abnormalities.

AUTOCRINE GROWTH FACTORS. Bronchogenic carcinomas produce a variety of autocrine growth factors. Multiple neuropeptide growth factors, exemplified by the bombesin-like peptides, acting through G protein-coupled receptors (characterized by possession of seven transmembrane-spanning domains), are particularly dominant in SCLC, although they also drive proliferation in NSCLC. Other autocrine growth factors expressed by bronchogenic carcinomas include insulin-

like growth factor 1, transforming growth factor-α, the c-*kit* ligand (stem cell growth factor), and the heregulins. Clinical trials are underway in humans using strategies either to disrupt stimulation by autocrine growth factors or to bias postreceptor signal transduction pathways to lead to apoptosis rather than proliferation.

PATHOLOGY

NON-SMALL CELL LUNG CANCER. Adenocarcinoma has increased in incidence and is now the most frequent histologic subtype. Adenocarcinomas can be derived from either the periphery of the lung or the central airways. Thyroid transcription factor 1 is expressed by the majority of adenocarcinomas arising in lung and is infrequently expressed by extrapulmonary adenocarcinomas; this marker is useful for assessing the origin of adenocarcinoma of unknown primary site. The hallmark of adenocarcinomas is the tendency to form glands. Special stains demonstrate that the tumor cells contain mucins.

Bronchoalveolar carcinoma, a subcategory of adenocarcinoma, arises in the periphery and tends to spread in a lepidic fashion along preexisting alveolar septa. Bronchoalveolar carcinoma characteristically contains air bronchograms on imaging studies. Localized bronchoalveolar carcinoma has a relatively good prognosis if treated surgically, whereas the multifocal form, presenting as diffuse, bilateral infiltrates has a poor prognosis.

Squamous cell carcinoma tends to originate in the central airways. Histologically, squamous cell carcinomas are characterized by keratinization with keratin "pearl" formation (i.e., flattened cells surrounding central cores of keratin). Squamous carcinomas are also characterized by predominant desmosomes that can be visualized on histologic sections as intercellular bridges.

Large cell carcinoma, often referred to as *large cell undifferentiated carcinoma*, is a group of carcinomas undifferentiated at the light microscopic level. Large cell carcinomas may exhibit neuroendocrine or glandular differentiation markers when studied by immunohistochemistry or electron microscopy. Two rare subtypes of large cell carcinomas are the giant cell carcinomas, associated with peripheral leukocytosis, and clear cell carcinomas, which resemble renal cell carcinomas.

Bronchial carcinoids are well-differentiated neuroendocrine tumors that often cause localized bronchial obstruction and appear in young people (Chapter 245). Although carcinoids tend not to metastasize widely, they can exhibit a spectrum of biologic behavior. Carcinoid syndrome is uncommon in patients with pulmonary carcinoid.

SMALL CELL LUNG CANCER. SCLC is characterized by small, dark-staining cells with little cytoplasm. The nuclear chromatin is finely distributed, and nucleoli are inconspicuous. Biopsies frequently exhibit a "crush artifact," in which the tumor cells are compressed and distorted. Rarely, SCLC tumors comprise a combination of cells with SCLC and NSCLC features and are termed *combined small cell carcinomas* in the recent World Health Organization/International Association for the Study of Lung Cancer classification. When SCLC recurs after chemotherapy, NSCLC elements often increase. The diagnosis of SCLC is not usually difficult to make, but in certain situations, such as fine-needle aspirations of lymph nodes, immuno-

---

Table 198–3 • ONCOGENE ABNORMALITIES

ONCOGENE	ABNORMALITY	
	SCLC	NSCLC
Ki-ras	0	30–50% of adenocarcinomas (activating mutation)
H-ras	0	Rare mutation; overexpression occurs
N-ras	0	Rare mutation; overexpression occurs
myc (c, L, N)	Majority	Gene amplification and overexpression
her2/neu	—	30% (overexpression)
c-kit	Overexpression	—
bcl-2	?	Overexpression
cyclin D1 (prad)	—	Overexpression

SCLC = small cell lung cancer; NSCLC = non-SCLC.

Table 198–2 • CHARACTERISTIC CHROMOSOMAL DELETIONS COMMON IN LUNG CANCER

CHROMOSOMAL REGION DELETED	TUMOR SUPPRESSOR GENES INACTIVATED
3p14-25	Unknown, probably multiple, including *FHIT* and *RASSF1A*
5q	?*APC, MCC*
9p21	*CDKN2A, CDKN2B*, possibly others
13q14	Rb (~100% SCLC, ~20% NSCLC)
17p13	p53 (~90% SCLC, ~60% NSCLC)

FHIT = fragile histidine triad; *RASSF1A* = RAS association domain family 1A gene; *APC* = adenomatous polyposis coli; *MCC* = mutated in colon carcinoma; Rb = retinoblastoma; SCLC = small cell lung cancer; NSCLC = non-SCLC.

Oncology

histochemical markers such as N-CAM or chromogranin A can be helpful in differentiating SCLC from lymphoma.

PRIMARY PULMONARY LYMPHOMA. Primary pulmonary lymphomas are most commonly of B-cell origin and develop from bronchus-associated lymphoid tissue. Other categories of lymphoma can originate in the lung (Chapter 195), however. Surgical biopsy is often necessary for accurate diagnosis and classification of primary pulmonary lymphoma.

Clinical Manifestations

Lung cancer is clinically silent for most of its course. The presence of symptoms is usually accompanied by late disease, and prognosis is worse than with a carcinoma that manifests as an asymptomatic radiographic abnormality. Symptoms can be divided into four categories: (1) those caused by tumor growing locally, (2) those caused by tumor invading adjacent structures, (3) those caused by metastatic disease, and (4) paraneoplastic syndromes.

LOCAL. Either a new cough or a change in the nature of a chronic cough is the most common presenting symptom of bronchogenic carcinoma. This symptom should always cause concern in a smoker, in whom it may be present for several months before a new diagnosis of lung cancer is made. Hemoptysis, either gross or minor, commonly occurs when mucosal lesions ulcerate. Although the most common cause of hemoptysis is bronchitis, this symptom in a high-risk individual should lead to prompt investigation. Tumors that obstruct major airways can produce wheezing, and unilateral wheezing suggests a localized obstruction. Airway obstruction can result in atelectasis or postobstructive pneumonia. Bronchogenic carcinomas are often associated with cavitation and lung abscess formation, due either to airway obstruction with postobstructive pneumonia or to necrosis of a large tumor mass. Clinical signs particularly indicative of malignancy-associated lung abscess include chronicity of symptoms, lack of high fever, and lack of leukocytosis.

LOCAL INVASION. Local invasion can produce chest pain, dyspnea from pleural effusion, and symptoms referable to nerves, heart, and great vessels. Malignant pleural effusions occur in approximately 10 to 20% of patients at the time of diagnosis and are most frequently a sign that the tumor is not surgically resectable. Invasion of the pericardium can lead to cardiac tamponade as well as to arrhythmias.

A number of syndromes have been described in association with locally invasive disease. The superior vena cava syndrome (Chapter 95) is characterized by facial suffusion and swelling due to blockage of the superior vena cava by either tumor or associated thrombosis. Although this syndrome is no longer considered a medical emergency, it should be treated promptly. Horner's syndrome results from disruption of the cervical sympathetic nerves and is characterized by unilateral facial anhidrosis, ptosis, and miosis in its full-blown form. Hoarseness can occur from invasion of the recurrent laryngeal nerve, usually by either tumor directly extending into the mediastinum or by adjacent malignant lymph nodes. The symptom of hoarseness is important because vocal cord paralysis denotes that the tumor is not resectable. The Pancoast syndrome occurs in tumors involving the apex and superior sulcus of the lung and results from local invasion into the brachial plexus as well as the cervical sympathetic nerves. Clinical manifestations are dominated by shoulder and arm pain and may include Horner's syndrome. The tumor may not be readily apparent on plain radiographs, and computed tomographic (CT) scanning or magnetic resonance imaging may be necessary for diagnosis.

METASTATIC DISEASE. Common sites of metastases of bronchogenic carcinomas include brain, bone, adrenal gland, and liver. In smokers who present with space-occupying lesions in these sites, the possibility of bronchogenic carcinoma should be immediately considered. In addition, metastatic carcinoma is a frequent cause of cervical and supraclavicular lymphadenopathy. Metastases to skin are relatively rare but are important to recognize clinically because of the ease of making a diagnosis by biopsy.

PARANEOPLASTIC SYNDROMES. Paraneoplastic syndromes occur in approximately 10% of patients with bronchogenic carcinoma and occasionally are the presenting symptom. Paraneoplastic manifestations can be divided into systemic, endocrine, neurologic, cutaneous, hematologic, and renal categories. Systemic manifestations are often nonspecific and can include weight loss, anorexia, and fever. The endocrine and neurologic manifestations of bronchogenic carcinoma are more specific (Chapter 187).

Digital clubbing is seen in a variety of pulmonary conditions but occurs most commonly in association with bronchogenic carcinoma. Clubbing is caused by soft tissue subungual thickening that most commonly involves the fingernails, resulting in loss of the normal angle between the fingernail and nail bed. In addition, the fingernails are easily compressed against the nail bed and have a spongy feel. Hypertrophic pulmonary osteoarthropathy (Chapter 187) is often associated with clubbing, and patients commonly present with exquisite tenderness over the long bones. Hypercoagulable states can result from bronchogenic carcinoma. Invasion of the bone marrow can produce anemia or leukocytosis with a leukoerythroblastic reaction.

ASYMPTOMATIC RADIOGRAPHIC ABNORMALITY. High-risk individuals (e.g., smokers with chronic obstructive pulmonary disease) receive frequent chest imaging studies for a variety of indications. A significant number of lung cancers are initially detected as an asymptomatic radiographic abnormality, especially a solitary pulmonary nodule (Chapter 81). Lack of symptoms should not delay evaluation, as these patients are the most likely to be cured by appropriate therapy.

Diagnosis and Staging

GENERAL PRINCIPLES AND DIFFERENTIAL DIAGNOSIS

A wide variety of disorders can lead to radiographic abnormalities that could represent a pulmonary neoplasm. Either acute or remote infections can produce infiltrates or nodules indistinguishable from a lung tumor. Congenital lesions, such as bronchogenic cysts, pulmonary sequestrations, or vascular malformations, are often removed because of a concern for lung cancer. In general, if a radiographic abnormality can be shown to resolve or to be stable over a period of several years, then lung cancer is unlikely.

In many cases, the decision of whether to investigate a patient aggressively for lung cancer is obvious (Fig. 198–1). In other situations, such as when a relatively low-risk patient presents with an asymptomatic radiographic abnormality, the decision to initiate an evaluation is less clear. A variety of factors must be considered, including the patient's age, smoking history, exposure to other environmental carcinogens, family history of lung cancer, exposure to fungal and other infectious diseases that might cause pulmonary nodules, general health and operative risk, and personality and tolerance for uncertainty regarding a diagnosis. Once a decision to investigate is made, a firm diagnosis should be obtained. Usually, diagnosis requires a tissue biopsy. Positron-emission tomographic (PET) scanning or contrast nodule enhancement CT can often reliably and noninvasively discriminate between benign and malignant nodules; however, current imaging tests are not infallible. It is imperative that the clinicians directing the patient's evaluation consult closely with the pathologist who is interpreting tissue biopsy and cytologic results. When the cell type is in doubt, additional tissue should be obtained for pathologic study.

IMAGING STUDIES. The chest radiograph is often the most important radiologic study in the evaluation of lung nodules, especially if old films are available. The stability of a lesion over time can be very helpful in suggesting either a benign or a malignant diagnosis (Fig. 198–2). Doubling times of less than 6 weeks or more than 18 months strongly suggest a benign diagnosis (doubling is calculated on the basis of volume, i.e., proportional to the cube of the radius of a lesion). Another reliable sign of benignity is the presence of heavy calcification within a lesion, particularly when present in a concentric, solid, or popcorn pattern. It must be kept in mind, however, that carcino-

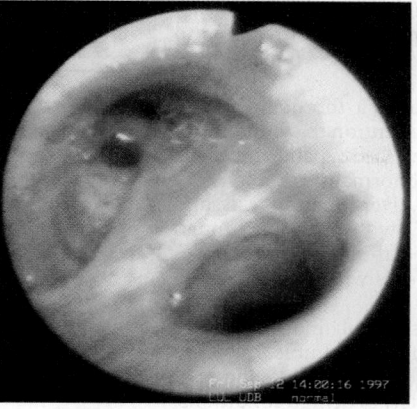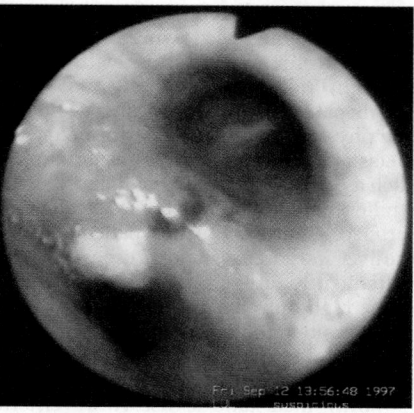

FIGURE 198–1 • Left, Carina between the lingular and upper division bronchus of the left upper lobe. Note the well-defined, sharp features of the carina. Right, Carina between the left upper and lower lobes in the same patient. Note the swollen, red, infiltrated appearance of the mucosa and the white exophytic lesion. In addition, there is subepithelial hemorrhage. A biopsy specimen demonstrates squamous cell carcinoma. The patient presented with increased sputum production, positive sputum cytologic findings, and a nonlocalizing chest radiograph and computed tomography scan.

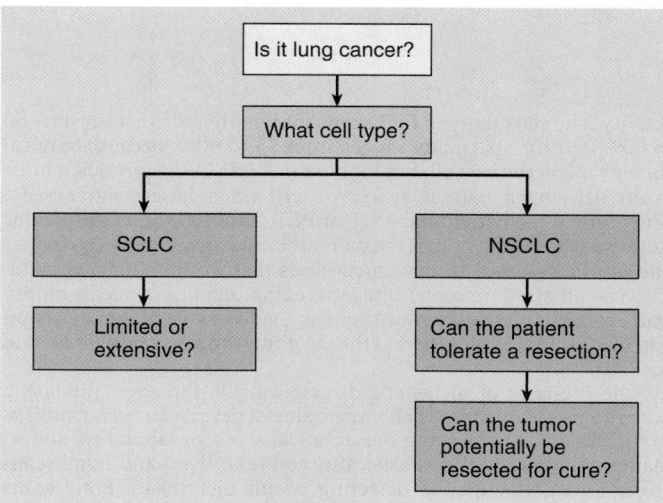

FIGURE 198–2 • Questions to determine therapy for lung cancer. NSCLC = non-small cell lung cancer; SCLC = small cell lung cancer.

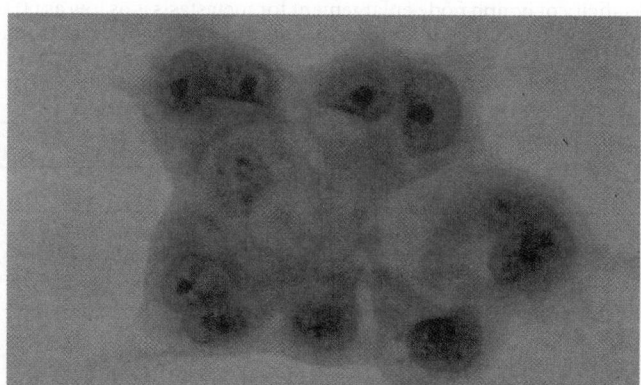

FIGURE 198–3 • Adenocarcinoma cells in a sputum smear. (From Forbes CD, Jackson WF: Color Atlas and Text of Clinical Medicine, 3rd ed. London, Mosby, 2003, with permission.)

mas can arise adjacent to calcified granulomas; therefore, if a lesion that contains a significant amount of calcium enlarges over time, it should be considered likely to be malignant. CT scanning of the thorax is usually undertaken in patients with suspicious nodules. In many cases, dense or diffuse calcification (suggesting a high likelihood that the lesion is a granuloma) or fat (suggesting a hamartoma) can be detected. CT scans also reliably detect enlarged lymph nodes, although biopsy is required to determine whether the lymphadenopathy is due to metastatic tumor. The CT scan can easily be extended to include the liver and adrenal glands to assess common sites of metastatic disease. Magnetic resonance imaging studies are particularly useful to detect vertebral, spinal cord, and mediastinal invasion in selected patients. PET scanning or contrast nodule enhancement CT are highly reliable in differentiating between benign and malignant nodules, although both false-positive findings, which are particularly common in the presence of active inflammation, and false-negative findings occur. Although some uncommon benign lesions, such as hamartomas or amyloid nodules, may enlarge with time, a progressively enlarging lung nodule should be considered to be most likely malignant. PET scans have the advantage of potentially detecting metastatic disease, either in the mediastinal lymph nodes or in extrathoracic sites. ◼

PATHOLOGIC DIAGNOSIS. Sputum cytology (Fig. 198–3) is the least invasive means to establish a tissue diagnosis. Sputum cytology is approximately 60 to 70% sensitive for central lesions but much less accurate for small peripheral lesions. In some instances, the diagnosis of cell type can be difficult on sputum cytologic analysis, and many clinicians believe that it is preferable to obtain biopsies of a tumor if at all possible. Other relatively noninvasive means of establishing a diagnosis include pleural fluid cytologic analysis, biopsy or aspiration cytologic analysis of enlarged cervical and supraclavicular lymph nodes, and biopsies of skin lesions. More invasive means of establishing a tissue diagnosis include bronchoscopy, needle biopsy, video-assisted thoracoscopy, cervical mediastinoscopy, and thoracotomy (Chapter 97). Flexible fiberoptic bronchoscopy to visualize all the central, lobar, segmental, and subsegmental airways (see Fig. 198–1) can be performed on awake patients with local sedation; it has low rates of morbidity and mortality and is highly accurate, with a sensitivity of approximately 95% for diagnosing lesions that can be directly visualized. The sensitivity of fiberoptic bronchoscopy for peripheral lesions is much lower than for directly visualized airway lesions, with a sensitivity dependent on size and location of the lesion. Bronchoscopy also provides important staging information by allowing inspection of potential resection margins for endobronchial tumors and by allowing detection of occult second primary lesions, which are present in 1 to 3% of patients presenting with lung cancer. All patients in whom a resection of a carcinoma is planned should undergo a bronchoscopic examination, either at the time of surgery or prior to it. Needle biopsy of suspicious pulmonary masses under either fluoroscopic or CT guidance is highly accurate, with a sensitivity of 90 to 95%. Video-assisted thoracoscopy is increasingly used to diagnose pulmonary nodules and provides excellent tissue specimens. Lesions that lie close to the visceral pleura are most easily accessible by this technique. Cervical mediastinoscopy with sampling of lymph nodes is also highly accurate in selected patients with lymphadenopathy. Finally, thoracotomy with biopsy of a lesion is often appropriately used when the pretest probability of a malignancy is high, such as when a peripheral nodule has been demonstrated to increase in size on serial chest radiographs. The diagnosis of primary pulmonary lymphoma may be particularly difficult to establish on the basis of limited biopsies or cytology; surgical biopsy is often required.

STAGING AND PROGNOSIS

Accurate staging of lung cancer is necessary to predict prognosis and determine the appropriate therapy. The staging systems for NSCLC and SCLC are different: in NSCLC a TNM (tumor-node-metastasis) staging system is used, whereas in SCLC, patients are divided into those with limited and those with extensive disease (Tables 198–4 through 198–6).

All patients with lung cancer should have a thorough history and physical examination performed, with attention to symptoms of metastatic disease such as weight loss and bone pain and signs such as lymphadenopathy and neurologic abnormalities. Laboratory studies include a complete blood cell count, liver function tests, and serum calcium assay. In most patients, chest CT with extension through the liver and adrenal glands is useful. Imaging of the brain and abdomen is frequently ordered in asymptomatic patients with SCLC because of the high prevalence of metastases.

Computed tomographic scans can suggest lymph node metastases based on the size of the nodes that are seen. For example, intrathoracic lymph nodes that exceed 1 cm in size have a high likelihood of harboring metastatic disease. However, a variety of benign conditions, including pneumonia, healed tuberculous and fungal infection, silicosis, and sarcoidosis, can cause significant lymphadenopathy, so the specificity of lymph node enlargement for metastasis is as low as 60%. PET scans detect lymph node metastasis due to enhanced metabolic

Table 198–4 • STAGING OF SMALL CELL LUNG CANCER

STAGE	DEFINITION
Limited	Tumor confined to chest plus supraclavicular nodes, but excluding cervical, axillary nodes
Extensive	Tumor outside of above confines

Table 198–5 • STAGING DEFINITIONS FOR NON-SMALL CELL LUNG CANCER

STAGE	DEFINITION
	Tumor
T0	No tumor
TX	Primary tumor cannot be assessed; or positive cytology, no apparent tumor
Tis	Carcinoma in situ
T1	Tumor <3 cm in diameter, no visceral pleural or main bronchial involvement
T2	Tumor >3 cm diameter, visceral pleural or main bronchial involvement <2 cm from carina; atelectasis extending to hilum but not involving whole lung
T3	Direct extension to chest wall, diaphragm, mediastinal pleura, parietal pericardium or <2 cm from carina, but not involving carina; atelectasis involving whole lung
T4	Invades heart, great vessels, esophagus, trachea, carina, vertebrae, malignant pleural or pericardial effusion, or satellite tumor nodules within the ipsilateral primary tumor lobe of lung
	Nodes
N0	No involvement
NX	Cannot assess regional lymph nodes
N1	Ipsilateral peribronchial or hilar nodal involvement and intrapulmonary nodes involved by direct extension
N2	Ipsilateral mediastinal or subcarinal nodal metastasis
N3	Contralateral mediastinal or hilar nodal metastasis; any supraclavicular or scalene nodal metastasis
	Metastasis
M0	None detected
M1	Any distant metastasis

From Mountain CF. Revisions in the International System for Staging Lung Cancer. Chest 1997;111:1710.

Table 198–6 • STAGE GROUPING AND SURVIVAL FOR NON-SMALL CELL LUNG CANCER

STAGE	DEFINITION	5-YEAR SURVIVAL (%) Clinical Staging	5-YEAR SURVIVAL (%) Pathologic Staging
0	Carcinoma in situ		
IA	T1N0M0	60	67
IB	T2N0M0	38	57
IIA	T1N1M0	34	55
IIB	T2N1M0, T3N0M0	22–24	38
IIIA	T3N1M0, T1N2M0 T2N2M0, T3N2M0	9–13	25
IIIB	T4, any N, M0 T1–3, N3, M0	3–7	
IV	Any T, any N, M1	1	

T = tumor; N = node; M = metastasis.

activity. The sensitivity of PET scans for lymph node metastasis is 80 to 90%, but the specificity ranges from 75 to 90%. Because surgical therapy offers the best chance for cure in NSCLC, the physician must avoid denying a patient surgery based on a false-positive scan. Therefore, if the patient has a CT or PET scan that shows suspicious intrathoracic lymph nodes, the patient should always undergo biopsy and not be assumed to have metastases that would alter treatment. Cervical mediastinoscopy is the most common option; needle biopsy (either transbronchial or transthoracic), video-assisted thoracoscopy, and mediastinal exploration at thoracotomy are also useful in certain patients.

The presence of metastatic disease outside the chest predicts a poor prognosis, and these patients are almost never referred for surgery. In the absence of any symptoms, clinical signs, or laboratory abnormalities suggesting metastasis, routine brain, liver, and bone scans are not cost-effective for detecting occult metastases. Bone scans are complicated by a high rate of false-positive results due to old fractures. CT of the upper abdomen is often performed in asymptomatic patients to detect occult metastases, particularly silent metastasis involving the adrenal gland. However, a high incidence of adrenal adenomas occurs in the normal population, so the rate of false-positive findings is high; most adrenal lesions should be histologically confirmed to be metastatic disease before treatment plans are altered. A recent randomized trial comparing preoperative PET scan to conventional evaluation showed a significant reduction in futile thoracotomies in patients who had PET scans.∎ As in detection of mediastinal nodal metastases, distant metastases detected by PET should be verified before one denies a patient otherwise potentially curative surgery.

PHYSIOLOGIC ASSESSMENT FOR RESECTION. Before considering a patient for surgical resection of a bronchogenic carcinoma, one must determine that adequate pulmonary reserve exists to permit this therapy. Simple spirometry and an arterial blood gas measurement are the only tests routinely required. Patients with a forced expiratory volume in 1 second (FEV_1) of greater than 60% predicted or more than 2.0 L will likely tolerate a pneumonectomy. When pulmonary function does not appear to be evenly distributed between right and left lungs, perfusion scanning, which correlates well with regional pulmonary function, may help estimate postoperative pulmonary function. CO_2 retention on arterial blood gas analysis, unless solely on the basis of a low respiratory drive, is a predictor of poor postoperative outcome, but hypoxemia is not a strong indicator of poor outcome. The roles of exercise testing and pulmonary artery pressure measurement are unclear.

With the advent of lung-sparing operations, including segmentectomies, sleeve resections, and wedge resections, many patients who previously would not have been considered surgical candidates are now undergoing pulmonary resection. Close collaboration between internists and thoracic surgeons is necessary to determine whether patients with marginal criteria are indeed appropriate candidates for surgical therapy.

Rx Treatment

NON-SMALL CELL LUNG CANCER

SURGERY. Surgery offers the best chance for curing appropriately staged patients with NSCLC. Patients with stages I through IIIA NSCLC are routinely considered for surgery, with 5-year survival rates ranging from 60 to 80% for patients with stage I disease to 15 to 25% for selected patients with stage IIIA disease. Since the late 1960s, operative mortality has dropped from 10 to 20% to approximately 3%. The incidence of "fruitless thoracotomy," in which a lesion is discovered to be inoperable at the time of thoracotomy, has decreased from 25% to approximately 5%. The increased use of lung-sparing resections, including sleeve lobectomy, segmentectomy, wedge resection, and thoracoscopic wedge resection has allowed surgical therapy to be applied to a group of patients with less pulmonary reserve than in the past. Although a prospective trial comparing conventional lobectomy with wedge resection has demonstrated that local recurrence rates are higher with the latter procedure, wedge resection is still an acceptable alternative in patients with diminished pulmonary reserve.

Before a decision for surgical therapy is made in a given patient, three questions must be addressed (see Fig. 198–1). (1) Is the cell type NSCLC? With the exception of peripheral solitary pulmonary nodules without hilar or mediastinal lymphadenopathy, a firm tissue diagnosis should almost always be obtained prior to surgical therapy. Owing to the rarity with which SCLC manifests with stage I disease and the likelihood that surgical therapy benefits stage I patients, it may not be necessary to obtain tissue diagnosis for all patients in this group prior to surgical therapy. (2) Is the patient physiologically capable of tolerating resectional surgery? General medical criteria, such as absence of a recent myocardial infarction, should be considered. In addition, physiologic assessment should determine whether the planned resection will leave the patient with adequate pulmonary reserve. (3) Can the lesion be completely resected? This answer requires adequate staging with detection of both distant metastases and local lymph node involvement. As surgical therapy provides the best hope for long-term survival in NSCLC, physiologic assessment and staging should be accurate and objective.

RADIATION THERAPY. Radiation therapy for NSCLC often effectively controls local disease. Significant physiologic impairment does result, however, so most patients who might be considered for curative radiation therapy are also candidates for curative surgical therapy. Although few trials of radiation therapy have been undertaken in early-stage lung cancer, an estimated 10 to 20% of localized lesions can be cured by radiation. Radiation therapy is often used to palliate symptoms; endobronchial symptoms, including hemoptysis and obstruction, frequently respond to radiation. Distant metastases also are frequently treated primarily with radiation. Radiation therapy is an important component of combined-modality therapy for NSCLC.

CHEMOTHERAPY. A number of drugs are frequently used: cisplatin, carboplatin, paclitaxel, mitomycin, vinca alkaloids, gemcitabine, vinorelbine, ifosfamide, and etoposide. Newer regimens, such as carboplatin and paclitaxel, have improved activity over the regimens with which most controlled trials have been performed. Trials comparing chemotherapy with best supportive care for stage IV NSCLC have yielded conflicting results; however, several recent trials and meta-analyses suggest a small (several weeks to months increased survival) benefit from chemotherapy, and the costs of the chemotherapy option are less than the best supportive care because of lower utilization of palliative treatments. Several trials treating stage IIIB patients with chemotherapy plus radiation have demonstrated a longer survival with chemoradiotherapy than with radiation alone. Further trials are underway.

In selecting patients with NSCLC for chemotherapy, several factors should be kept in mind. Survival is reduced and side effects of chemotherapy are increased in patients who are not fully ambulatory; benefits to this group are likely to be minimal. Response to therapy must be ascertainable. Patients must be fully informed of the limitations of chemotherapy in NSCLC; many physicians discontinue treatment if no clinical response occurs after two or three cycles of chemotherapy. Most patients with NSCLC are not cured by surgery and eventually die with stage IV disease; the disappointing response to chemotherapy for this subgroup emphasizes the major need for new agents and approaches.

MULTIMODALITY THERAPY. In patients with resectable stage II or III NSCLC, surgical therapy often fails because of local, mediastinal, or distant metastatic recurrence; adding adjuvant radiation therapy decreases the risk of mediastinal recurrence but does not improve overall survival. Several prospective randomized controlled trials have demonstrated increased disease-free survival in stage II and III NSCLC patients treated after resection either with chemotherapy or with radiation therapy plus chemotherapy; again, however, overall survival has not increased. Induction chemotherapy, followed by surgery, has shown survival benefit in two relatively small randomized trials and is being evaluated further. Patients are more likely to tolerate a full course of chemotherapy in the preoperative than in the postoperative state, and preoperative adjuvant therapy may favorably affect resection margins.

SMALL CELL LUNG CANCER

Before the development of effective chemotherapy for SCLC, the median survival time was approximately 6 to 12 weeks for extensive disease and approximately 6 months for limited-stage SCLC; the overall 5-year survival rate was less than 1%. With optimal therapy, current median survival for limited-stage SCLC exceeds 1 year, and for extensive-stage disease it is approximately 10 months. The 5-year survival rate has increased to between 5 and 10%.

Chemotherapy is the cornerstone of treatment for both limited- and extensive-stage SCLC. A variety of agents have activity. Many experts believe that regimens containing etoposide or irinotecan and either carboplatin or cisplatin offer the best combination of efficacy and lack of toxicity. A recent prospective randomized trial suggested that irinotecan plus cisplatin is somewhat superior to etoposide plus cisplatin.[2]

A number of trials have examined whether increased duration or intensity of chemotherapy for SCLC is beneficial. At the present time, no data support the efficacy of more than four to six cycles of chemotherapy. Increasing dose intensity above standard results in increased toxicity and is not currently supported.

In patients with limited-stage SCLC, the most frequent site of recurrence is the primary lesion. Therefore, at the present time, either concurrent or alternating chest radiation therapy with chemotherapy is preferred in patients with limited-stage disease. No evidence indicates that prophylactic cranial irradiation improves survival, but it is associated with increased central nervous system morbidity. In patients with extensive-stage SCLC, radiation therapy is generally not used in the initial management because chemotherapy produces initial palliation in 80% or more of cases. The addition of radiation therapy does not seem to increase survival, but it does increase toxicity. Radiation therapy is used as palliation in patients in whom initial chemotherapy fails.

A small proportion (<1%) of patients with SCLC present with stage I disease. This rare subset of patients has a 5-year survival rate of 50 to 70% if treated by surgery followed by chemotherapy with or without radiation therapy. Surgery for patients with SCLC, with the exception of rare stage I disease, is not indicated.

Prognosis

The overall prognosis for patients with lung cancer remains grim, with a 5-year survival rate of 14%. Owing to the high incidence of bronchogenic carcinoma, this 14% survival rate represents a large number of patient years that are potentially salvageable, however. Certain subgroups, including patients with stage I and II NSCLC treated by surgery, have a 50 to 85% 5-year survival rate, making it critical for the physician to recognize and appropriately diagnose and treat these individuals. Long-term survivors of both NSCLC and SCLC are a high-risk group for second primary lung cancers, with an incidence of 3 to 5% per year.

Prevention and Early Intervention

The most important preventive measure is deterring young people from starting to smoke (Chapter 14). This public health issue is mainly a social, economic, and political problem. Increasing the cost of tobacco products, through increased taxes, is an effective strategy for keeping people from starting this habit. Negative advertising and measures that make it less socially acceptable and glamorous to smoke are also effective.

Smoking cessation is also an important strategy and results in a gradual decrease in risk for lung cancer over 10 to 15 years. Approximately 5 to 20% of patients who enter a smoking cessation program are successful over the long term. Physician input is crucial in this process.

Large trials in the 1970s of sputum cytology and chest radiographs as screening tools for lung cancer showed no reduction in lung cancer–specific mortality. Low-dose spiral CT is more sensitive than chest radiography for the detection of early peripheral lung cancer and is currently being evaluated in large randomized trials.

Chemoprevention of lung cancer may be possible. The use of 13-*cis*-retinoic acid in patients with laryngeal cancer has been shown to decrease the incidence of second primary lesions in the aerodigestive system. However, toxicity associated with high doses of this compound is significant. Vitamin A and its derivatives have potent effects on the differentiation of the respiratory epithelium and are logical agents for chemoprevention studies, but several trials have demonstrated that dietary supplementation with β-carotene alone or in combination with vitamin A or vitamin E actually increases rates of lung cancer in susceptible populations. These unexpected results emphasize the need for further controlled trials. Additional agents, including selenium, cyclo-oxygenase-2 inhibitors, inhaled corticosteroids, prostacyclin analogues, epidermal growth factor receptor antagonists, farnesyl transferase inhibitors, and low-dose 13-*cis*-retinoic acid, are under investigation. Owing to the large reservoir of smokers and ex-smokers at risk, chemoprevention has considerable potential.

1. van Tinteren H, Hoekstra OS, Smit EF, et al: Effectiveness of positron emission tomography in the preoperative assessment of patients with suspected non-small-cell lung cancer: The PLUS multicentre randomized trial. Lancet 2002;359:1388–1393.
2. Noda K, Nishiwaki Y, Kawahara M, et al: Irinotecan plus cisplatin compared with etoposide plus cisplatin for extensive small-cell lung cancer. N Engl J Med 2002;346:85–91.

SUGGESTED READINGS

Eton DT, Fairclough DL, Cella D, et al: Early change in patient-reported health during lung cancer chemotherapy predicts clinical outcomes beyond those predicted by baseline report: Results from Eastern Cooperative Oncology Group Study 5592. J Clin Oncol 2003;21:1536–1543. *Health status before and during therapy predicts outcomes.*

Hirsch FR, Franklin WA, Gazdar AF, Bunn PA: Early detection of lung cancer: Clinical perspectives of recent advances in biology and radiology. Clin Cancer Res 2001;7:5–22. *Reviews molecular genetic alterations in lung cancer and premalignancy as well as bronchoscopic and radiologic early detection advances.*

Patz EF, Goodman PC, Bepler G: Screening for lung cancer. N Engl J Med 2000;343:1627–1633. *General review of potential biases that complicate interpretation of screening trials, as well as an overview of past lung cancer screening trials.*

Schiller JH, Harrington D, Belani CP, et al: Comparison of four chemotherapy regimens for advanced non-small-cell lung cancer. N Engl J Med 2002;346:92–98. *Four different chemotherapy regimens yielded similar results for advanced non-small cell lung cancer.*

199 NEOPLASMS OF THE STOMACH

Anil K. Rustgi

Gastric neoplasms are predominantly malignant, and nearly 90 to 95% of cases are adenocarcinomas. Less frequently observed malignancies include lymphomas, especially non-Hodgkin's lymphoma, as well as sarcomas, such as leiomyosarcoma. Benign gastric neoplasms include leiomyomas, carcinoid tumors, and lipomas.

ADENOCARCINOMA OF THE STOMACH

Epidemiology

There is great geographic variation in the incidence of gastric cancer worldwide, strongly indicating that environmental factors influence the pathogenesis of gastric carcinogenesis. Further support for this notion comes from observations that groups emigrating from high-risk to low-risk areas, such as Japanese moving to Hawaii and Brazil, acquire the low risk of the area into which they emigrate, presumably because of adoption of the endogenous lifestyle and exposure to different environmental factors.

Gastric adenocarcinoma was the most frequently observed malignancy in the world until the mid-1980s, and it remains extremely common among males in certain regions, such as tropical South America, some parts of the Caribbean, and Eastern Europe. Regardless of gender, it remains the most common malignancy in Japan and China. It was the first-ranked malignancy in the United States in the 1930s to 1940s, but it has rapidly declined in more recent decades, approaching an incidence rate of less than 10 cases per 100,000. Whereas gastric adenocarcinoma localized to the distal stomach has declined, the incidence rate of proximal gastric and gastroesophageal adenocarcinomas has been steadily increasing in the United States, perhaps reflecting differences in pathogenic factors.

Etiology

Risk factors for the development of gastric adenocarcinoma can be divided into environmental and genetic factors as well as precursor conditions (Table 199–1). For example, *Helicobacter pylori* infection is significantly more common in patients with gastric cancer than in matched control groups. Epidemiologic studies of high-risk populations have also suggested that genotoxic agents such as N-nitroso compounds may play a role in gastric tumorigenesis. N-nitroso compounds can be formed in the human stomach by nitrosation of ingested nitrates, which are common constituents of the diet. High nitrate concentrations in the soil and drinking water have been observed in areas with high death rates from gastric cancer. Atrophic gastritis (Chapter 137) with or without intestinal metaplasia is seen in association with gastric cancer, especially in endemic areas. Pernicious anemia (Chapter 175) is associated with a several-fold increase in gastric cancer. Atrophic gastritis and gastric cancer share a number of common environmental risk factors. It is likely that atrophic gastritis and intestinal metaplasia represent intermediary steps to gastric cancer. The achlorhydria associated with gastritis related to *H. pylori*, pernicious anemia, or other causes favors the growth of bacteria capable of converting nitrates to nitrites. The nitrosamine N-methyl-N'-nitro-N-nitrosoguanidine (MNNG) causes a high rate of induction of adenocarcinoma in the glandular stomach of rats. At the same time, most patients with atrophic gastritis do not develop gastric cancer, suggesting that neither atrophic gastritis nor achlorhydria alone is responsible.

Table 199–1 • CONDITIONS PREDISPOSING TO OR ASSOCIATED WITH GASTRIC CANCER

ENVIRONMENTAL
Helicobacter pylori infection
Dietary: excess of salt (salted pickled foods), nitrates/nitrites, carbohydrates; deficiency of fresh fruit, vegetables, vitamins A and C, refrigeration
Low socioeconomic status
Cigarette smoking

GENETIC
Familial gastric cancer (rare)
Associated with hereditary nonpolyposis colorectal cancer
Blood group A

PREDISPOSING CONDITIONS
Chronic gastritis, especially atrophic gastritis with or without intestinal metaplasia
Pernicious anemia
Intestinal metaplasia
Gastric adenomatous polyps (>2 cm)
Postgastrectomy stumps
Gastric epithelial dysplasia
Ménétrier's disease (hypertrophic gastropathy)
Chronic peptic ulcer

Benign gastric ulcers do not appear to predispose patients to gastric cancer. However, patients who have a gastric remnant after subtotal gastrectomy for benign disorders have a relative risk of gastric cancer of 1.5 to 3.0 by 15 to 20 years after surgery.

Incidence and Prevalence

Whereas gastric cancer was the most common cancer in the United States in the 1930s, its annual incidence rate has steadily decreased; the annual incidence is now fewer than 20,000 new cases per year. The age-adjusted mortality rate for males and females decreased by 25% from 1973 to 1985. Typically, gastric cancer occurs between ages 50 to 70 years and is uncommon before age 30 years. The rates are higher in males than females by 2 to 1. Five-year survival is less than 20%.

Pathology, Pathogenesis, and Genetics

Gastric adenocarcinomas can be divided into two types: intestinal and diffuse. The intestinal type is typically in the distal stomach with ulcerations, is often preceded by premalignant lesions, and is declining in incidence in the United States. In contrast, the diffuse type involves widespread thickening of the stomach, especially in the cardia, and often affects younger patients; this form may present as linitis plastica, a nondistensible stomach with absence of folds and narrowed lumen caused by infiltration of the stomach wall with tumor. Other conditions may result in linitis plastica, such as lymphoma (Chapter 195), tuberculosis (Chapter 341), syphilis (Chapter 349), and amyloidosis (Chapter 290). The prognosis is generally worse in the diffuse type.

Key histopathologic features of gastric cancer include degree of differentiation, invasion through the gastric wall, lymph node involvement, and presence or absence of signet-ring cells within the tumor itself. Other pathologic manifestations include a polypoid mass, which may be difficult to distinguish from a benign polyp. Early gastric cancer, a condition that is not uncommon in Japan and that has a relatively favorable prognosis, consists of superficial lesions with or without lymph node involvement.

The leading hypothesis to explain how H. pylori predisposes to gastric cancer risk is the induction of an inflammatory response, which itself is genotoxic. Chronic H. pylori infection also leads to chronic atrophic gastritis with resulting achlorhydria, which in turn favors bacterial growth that can convert nitrates (dietary components) to nitrites. These nitrites, in combination with genetic factors, promote abnormal cellular proliferation, genetic mutations, and eventually cancer.

It is clear that genetic factors play a role in gastric cancer. For example, blood group A is associated with a higher incidence rate of gastric cancer, even in nonendemic areas. There is a three-fold increase in gastric cancer among first-degree relatives of patients with gastric cancer. Furthermore, germline or inherited mutations in the E-cadherin gene have been described in familial gastric cancer. In addition, in hereditary nonpolyposis colorectal cancer (HNPCC) type II (Chapter 200) there are associated extracolonic cancers, including gastric cancer.

It now appears that several genetic mechanisms are important in gastric cancer: oncogene activation, tumor suppressor gene inactivation, and DNA microsatellite instability. For example, loss of heterozygosity of the *APC* (adenomatous polyposis coli) gene has been observed in gastric cancers. The *p53* tumor suppressor gene product regulates the cell cycle at the G_1/S phase transition and probably also functions in DNA repair and apoptosis (programmed cell death). The *p53* gene is mutated not only in gastric cancer but also in gastric precancerous lesions, suggesting that mutation of the *p53* gene is an early event in gastric carcinogenesis. Microsatellite DNA alterations or instability in dinucleotide repeats that were originally identified in HNPCC also occur frequently in sporadic gastric carcinoma. Mutations in oncogenes and tumor suppressor genes may accumulate as a result of DNA microsatellite instability.

Clinical Manifestations

In its early stages, gastric cancer may often be asymptomatic or produce only nonspecific symptoms, making early diagnosis difficult. Later symptoms include bloating, dysphagia, epigastric pain, or early satiety. Early satiety or vomiting may suggest partial gastric outlet obstruction, although gastric dysmotility may contribute to the vomiting in nonobstructive cases. Epigastric pain, reminiscent of that associated with peptic ulcer (Chapter 138), occurs in about one fourth of patients; but in the majority of patients with gastric cancer, the pain is not relieved by food or antacids. Pain that radiates to the back may indicate that the tumor has penetrated into the pancreas. When dysphagia is associated with gastric cancer, this symptom suggests a more proximal gastric tumor at the gastroesophageal junction (Chapter 136) or in the fundus.

Signs of gastric cancer include bleeding, which can result in anemia that produces the symptoms of weakness, fatigue, and malaise as well as more serious cardiovascular and cerebral consequences. Perforation related to gastric cancer is unusual. Gastric cancer metastatic to the liver can lead to right upper quadrant pain, jaundice, and/or fever. Lung metastases can cause cough, hiccups, and hemoptysis. Peritoneal carcinomatosis can lead to malignant ascites unresponsive to diuretics. Gastric cancer can also metastasize to bone.

In the earliest stages of gastric cancer, the physical examination may be unremarkable. At later stages, patients become cachectic, and an epigastric mass may be palpated. If the tumor has metastasized to the liver, hepatomegaly with jaundice and ascites may be present. Portal or splenic vein invasion can cause splenomegaly. Lymph node involvement in the left supraclavicular area is termed Virchow's node, and periumbilical nodal involvement is called Sister Mary Joseph's node. The fecal occult blood test may be positive.

Paraneoplastic syndromes may precede or occur concurrently with gastric cancer. Examples include Trousseau's syndrome (Chapter 180), which is recurrent migratory superficial thrombophlebitis indicating a possible hypercoagulable state; acanthosis nigricans, which arises in flexor areas with skin lesions that are raised and hyperpigmented; neuromyopathy with involvement of the sensory and motor pathways; and central nervous system involvement with altered mental status and ataxia.

Laboratory studies may reveal iron deficiency anemia. Predisposing pernicious anemia can progress to megaloblastic anemia. Microangiopathic hemolytic anemia has been reported. Abnormalities in liver tests generally indicate metastatic disease. Hypoalbuminemia is a marker of malnourishment. Protein-losing enteropathy is rare but can be seen in Ménétrier's disease (Chapter 137), another predisposing condition. Serologic test results, such as those for carcinoembryonic antigen and CA 72.4, may be abnormal. Although these tests are not recommended for original diagnosis, they may be useful for monitoring disease after surgical resection.

Diagnosis

The diagnostic accuracy of upper endoscopy with biopsy and cytology approaches 95 to 99% for both types of gastric cancer. Cancers may arise as small mucosal ulcerations, a polyp, or a mass (Fig. 199–1). In some patients, gastric ulceration may first be noted in an upper gastrointestinal barium contrast study. A benign gastric ulcer is suggested by a smooth, regular base, whereas a malignant ulcer is manifested by a surrounding mass, irregular folds, and an irregular base. Although these and other radiographic characteristics historically helped to predict benign versus malignant disease, an upper endoscopy with biopsy and cytology is mandatory whenever a gastric ulcer is found in the radiologic study, even if the ulcer has benign characteristics.

Staging of gastric cancer, and at times diagnosis, has been greatly enhanced by the advent of endoscopic ultrasonography. The extent of tumor, including wall invasion and local lymph node involvement, can be assessed by endoscopic ultrasonography (Fig. 199–2), which provides information complementary to that from computed tomographic (CT) scans. Endoscopic ultrasonography can help guide

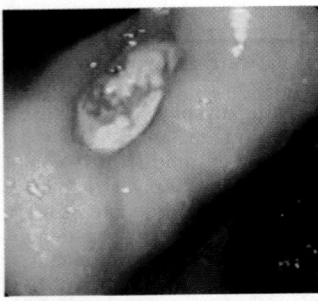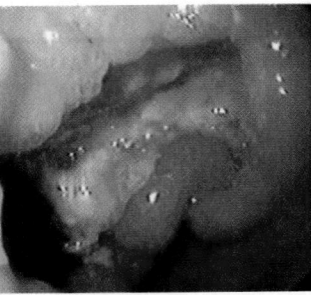

FIGURE 199–1 • Benign (left) and malignant (right) gastric ulcer. Note the shaggy, thickened, and overhanging edges of the cancer. (Courtesy of Pankaj Jay Pasricha, MD.)

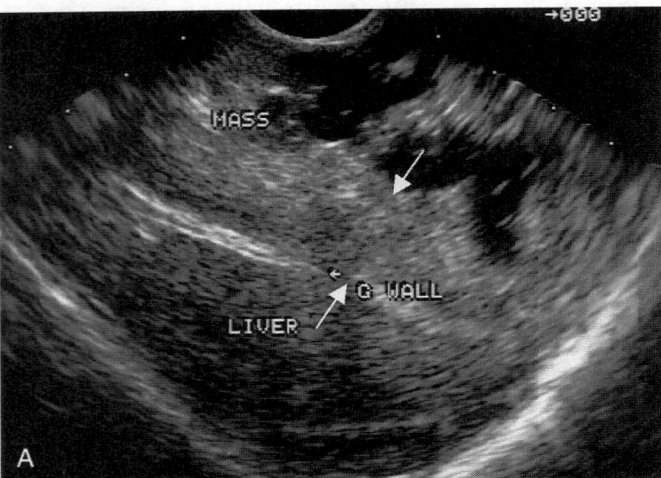

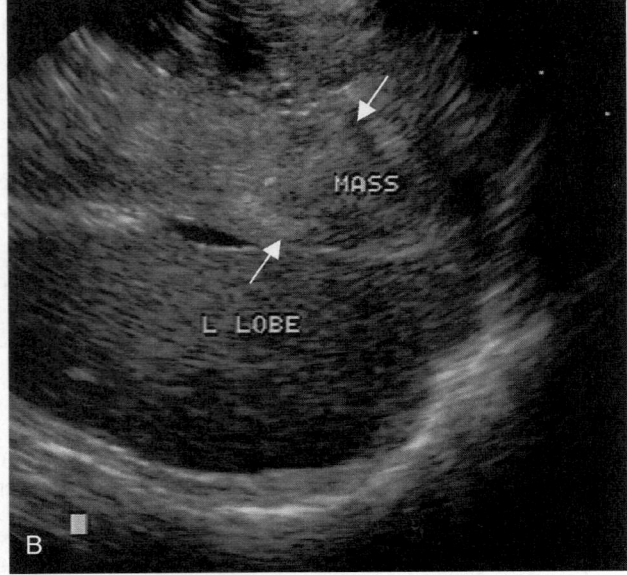

FIGURE 199–2 • Endoscopic ultrasonography depicting a large gastric mass that is compressing the liver and gallbladder wall (A) and, on a different view, the left lobe of the liver (B).

aspiration biopsies of lymph nodes to determine their malignant features, if any. CT scans of the chest and abdomen should be performed to document lymphadenopathy and extragastric organ (especially lung and liver) involvement. In some centers, staging of gastric cancer entails bone scans because of the proclivity of gastric cancer to metastasize to bone.

Rx Treatment

The only chance for cure of gastric cancer remains surgical resection, which is possible in only 25 to 30% of cases. If the tumor is confined to the distal stomach, subtotal gastrectomy is performed with resection of lymph nodes in the porta hepatis and in the pancreatic head. In contrast, tumors of the proximal stomach merit total gastrectomy to obtain an adequate margin and to remove lymph nodes; distal pancreatectomy and splenectomy are usually also performed as part of this procedure, which carries with it higher mortality and morbidity rates. Limited gastric resection is necessary for patients with excessive bleeding or obstruction. If cancer recurs in the gastric remnant, limited resection may again be necessary for palliation. Most recurrences in both types of gastric cancer are in the local or regional area of the original tumor.

Gastric cancer is one of the few gastrointestinal cancers that is somewhat responsive to chemotherapy. Single-agent treatment with 5-fluorouracil, doxorubicin, mitomycin C, or cisplatin provides partial response rates of 20 to 30%. When used in combination, certain chemotherapeutic regimens, such as doxorubicin and mitomycin C, doxorubicin and cisplatin, or doxorubicin and high-dose methotrexate, yield partial response rates of 35 to 50%. Radiation therapy alone is ineffective and generally employed only for palliative purposes in the setting of bleeding, obstruction, or pain. The combination of chemotherapy (fluorouracil plus leucovorin) with radiation therapy has been shown to improve median survival from 27 months to 36 months compared with surgery alone in patients with adenocarcinoma of the stomach or gastroesophageal junction.∎ Gene therapy and immune-based therapy are currently only investigational in animal models.

Implicit in the management of the patient with gastric cancer is meticulous attention to nutrition (jejunal enteral feedings or total parenteral nutrition), correction of metabolic abnormalities that arise from vomiting or diarrhea, and treatment of infection from aspiration or spontaneous bacterial peritonitis. To maintain lumen patency, endoscopic laser treatment or prosthesis placement can be utilized in a palliative fashion.

Prognosis

Approximately one third of patients who undergo a curative resection are alive after 5 years. In the aggregate, the overall 5-year survival rate of gastric cancer is less than 10%. Prognostic factors include anatomic location and nodal status (Table 199–2); distal gastric cancers without lymph node involvement have a better prognosis than proximal gastric cancers with or without lymph node involvement. Other prognostic factors include depth of penetration and tumor cell DNA aneuploidy. Linitis plastica and infiltrating lesions have a much worse prognosis than polypoid disease or exophytic masses. In the subset of mostly Japanese patients with the entity of early gastric cancer that is confined to the mucosa and submucosa, surgical resection may be

Table 199–2 • TUMOR, NODES, AND METASTASIS (TNM) STAGING OF GASTRIC CANCER

TUMOR
T1: Tumor confined to the mucosa or submucosa
T2: Tumor extending into the muscularis propria
T3: Tumor extending through the serosa without involving contiguous structures
T4: Tumor extending through the serosa and involving contiguous structures

NODES
N0: No lymph node metastases
N1: Regional lymph node involvement within 3 cm of the tumor along the greater or lesser curvature
N2: Regional lymph node involvement more than 3 cm from the primary tumor
N3: Involvement of other intra-abdominal lymph nodes not removable at surgery

METASTASES
M0: No distant metastases
M1: Distant metastases

curative and definitely improves the 5-year survival rate to more than 50%. In fact, when early gastric cancer is confined to the mucosa, endoscopic mucosal resection may be an alternative.

LYMPHOMA OF THE STOMACH

Gastric lymphoma represents about 5% of all malignant gastric tumors and is increasing in incidence. The majority of gastric lymphomas are non-Hodgkin's lymphomas (Chapter 195), and the stomach is the most common extranodal site for non-Hodgkin's lymphomas. Patients with gastric lymphoma are generally younger than those with gastric adenocarcinoma but retain the male predominance. Patients commonly present with symptoms and signs similar to those of gastric adenocarcinoma. Lymphoma in the stomach can be a primary tumor or can be due to disseminated lymphoma.

B-cell lymphomas of the stomach are most commonly large cell with a high-grade type. Low-grade variants are noted in the setting of chronic gastritis and are termed mucosa-associated lymphoid tissue (MALT) lymphomas. MALT lesions are strongly associated with *H. pylori* infection.

Radiographically, gastric lymphoma usually arises as ulcers or as exophytic masses; a diffusely infiltrating lymphoma is more suggestive of secondary lymphoma. Thus, upper gastrointestinal barium studies usually show multiple nodules and ulcers for a primary gastric lymphoma and typically have the appearance of linitis plastica with secondary lymphoma. As with gastric adenocarcinoma, however, upper endoscopy with biopsy and cytology are required for diagnosis and have an accuracy of nearly 90%. Apart from conventional histopathologic analysis, immunoperoxidase staining for lymphocyte markers is helpful in diagnosis. As with gastric adenocarcinoma, proper staging of gastric lymphoma involves endoscopic ultrasonography, chest and abdominal CT scans, and bone marrow biopsy as needed.

Treatment of gastric diffuse large B-cell lymphoma is best pursued with combination chemotherapy with or without radiotherapy (Chapter 195). In this context, 5-year survival rates of 40 to 60% have been reported. For MALT lesions, early data suggest that eradication of *H. pylori* infection with antibiotics (Chapter 138) induces regression of the tumor, but longer term follow-up is needed to be confident that such therapy is sufficient. Radiotherapy can be curative for localized MALT lymphomas.

OTHER MALIGNANT TUMORS OF THE STOMACH

Leiomyosarcomas, which constitute about 1% of all gastric cancers, usually occur as an intramural mass with central ulceration. Symptoms may include bleeding accompanied by a palpable mass. Leiomyosarcomas are often relatively indolent; surgical resection yields a 5-year survival rate of about 50%. Metastasis can occur to lymph nodes and the liver. Other gastric sarcomas include liposarcomas, fibrosarcomas, myosarcomas, and neurogenic sarcomas. Some gastrointestinal stromal tumors (GISTs) have been associated with activating mutations in the c-*kit* gene. C-*kit* mutations are also found in chronic myelogenous leukemia (CML) and acute myelogenous leukemia (Chapters 192 and 193), and data suggest that GISTs respond to imatinib mesylate, which is also used in CML. Carcinoid tumors (Chapter 245) may begin in the stomach and are curable by removal if they have not yet spread to the liver.

Primary tumors can also spread to the stomach. In addition to lymphomas, other tumors found in the stomach include primary lung (Chapter 198) and breast (Chapter 204) cancers as well as malignant melanoma (Chapter 209).

LEIOMYOMAS AND BENIGN TUMORS

Leiomyomas, which are smooth muscle tumors of benign origin, occur with equal frequency in men and women and are typically located in the middle and distal stomach. Leiomyomas can grow into the lumen with secondary ulceration and resulting bleeding. Alternatively, they can expand to the serosa with extrinsic compression. Endoscopy may reveal a mass that has overlying mucosa or mucosa replaced by ulceration. On upper gastrointestinal series, leiomyomas are usually smooth with an intramural filling defect, with or without central ulceration. However, benign leiomyomas can be difficult to distinguish from their malignant counterparts radiographically or endoscopically; tissue diagnosis is imperative. Symptomatic leiomyomas should be

removed, but those without associated symptoms do not require therapy.

Other benign gastric tumors include lipoma, neurofibroma (Chapter 459), lymphangioma, ganglioneuroma, and hamartoma, the latter associated with Peutz-Jeghers syndrome (Chapter 200) or juvenile polyposis (restricted to the stomach).

ADENOMAS

Gastric adenomas and hyperplastic polyps are unusual but may be found in middle-aged and elderly patients. Polyps may be sessile or pedunculated and are also found in nearly 50% of patients with familial adenomatosis polyposis or Gardner's syndrome. Gastric adenocarcinoma arising in the antrum has been described in such patients. Although isolated gastric adenomatous polyps are generally asymptomatic, some patients may have dyspepsia, nausea, or bleeding. Gastric adenomas and hyperplastic polyps are smooth and regular on upper gastrointestinal series, but the diagnosis must be confirmed by upper endoscopy with biopsy. Pedunculated polyps that are larger than 2 cm or that have associated symptoms should be removed by endoscopic snare cautery polypectomy, whereas large sessile gastric adenomatous polyps may merit segmental surgical resection. If polyps progress to an intermediary stage of severe dysplasia or culminate in cancer, the treatment is the same as for gastric adenocarcinoma.

1. Macdonald JS, Smalley SR, Benedetti J, et al: Chemoradiotherapy after surgery compared with surgery alone for adenocarcinoma of the stomach or gastroesophageal junction. N Engl J Med 2001;345:725–730.

SUGGESTED READINGS

Demetri GD, von Mehren M, Blanke CD, et al: Efficacy and safety of imatinib mesylate in advanced gastrointestinal stromal tumors. N Engl J Med 2002;347:472–480. *About 50% of these tumors respond to the same therapy as now used for chronic myelogenous leukemia.*

D'Ugo DM, Pende V, Persiani R, et al: Laparoscopic staging of gastric cancer: An overview. J Am Coll Surg 2003;196:965–974. *A useful approach.*

El-Rifai W, Powell SM: Molecular biology of gastric cancer. Semin Radiat Oncol 2002;12:128–140. *Review of the genetic alterations associated with gastric cancer.*

Huntsman DG, Carneiro F, Lewis FR, et al: Early gastric cancer in young, asymptomatic carriers of germ-line E-cadherin mutations. N Engl J Med 2001;344:1904–1909. *Clinical recommendations for patients with a family history of hereditary diffuse gastric cancer and germline E-cadherin mutations.*

Kelley JR, Duggan JM: Gastric cancer epidemiology and risk factors. J Clin Epidemiol 2003;56:1–9. *Estimates that H. pylori accounts for somewhat less than 50% of cases in western societies.*

Uemura N, Okamoto S, Yamamoto S, et al: *Helicobacter pylori* infection and the development of gastric cancer. N Engl J Med 2001;345:784–789. *Persons with H. pylori infection in the setting of severe gastric atrophy, corpus-predominant gastritis, and intestinal metaplasia are at increased risk for gastric cancer.*

200 NEOPLASMS OF THE LARGE AND SMALL INTESTINE

Raymond N. DuBois

NEOPLASMS OF THE LARGE INTESTINE

A person living in North America faces an average lifetime risk of 6% for developing colorectal cancer. Colorectal cancer is the second leading cause of cancer-related deaths after lung cancer and has a 5-year survival rate of approximately 55%. Cancers of the colon and rectum are the most lethal gastrointestinal malignancies in the Western world. Despite these grim statistics, colorectal cancer is preventable and is highly curable if detected early enough, so public health initiatives have emphasized large-scale screening and surveillance.

Major advances in understanding the genetic pathogenesis of colorectal cancer are likely to lead to cell-selective chemotherapeutic agents. By far the two most common and clinically significant neoplastic lesions that appear in the large intestine are adenomatous polyps and adenocarcinomas arising from epithelial cells of the colonic or rectal mucosa. However, the large bowel is also the site of other malignancies including anal carcinoma (squamous or transitional cell types; Chapter 147), lymphoma (Chapter 195), leiomyosarcoma, malignant carcinoid tumor (Chapter 245), and Kaposi's sarcoma. Malignancies from adjacent sites such as the prostate, ovary, uterus, and stomach may also involve the colon and/or rectum by direct invasion.

POLYPS OF THE COLON

A polyp is defined as a grossly visible mass of cells with stroma that protrudes from the mucosal surface into the lumen of the intestine (Fig. 200–1). A polyp may either be sessile or pedunculated when it is attached by a stalk of cells. Polyps are classified as either non-neoplastic or neoplastic and become clinically relevant by causing rectal bleeding or partial bowel obstruction (rare) or because of their potential to develop into a malignancy.

NONADENOMATOUS POLYPS

Nonadenomatous polyps, which account for approximately 90% of all mucosal polyps detected in the large bowel, can be found in more than 50% of people older than 60 years of age. These polyps, which are also termed non-neoplastic polyps, can be further sub-categorized into hyperplastic, inflammatory, lymphoid, and juvenile polyps. The majority of non-neoplastic polyps are hyperplastic polyps, which arise due to abnormal maturation of the mucosal epithelial cells; these polyps are usually small in diameter and found predominantly in the distal sigmoid colon and rectum. Importantly, hyperplastic polyps are not malignant and are not generally associated with any measurable increase in malignant potential, although the cancer-causing genes in some cells in some subsets of hyperplastic polyps can undergo aberrant methylation. Inflammatory polyps, which arise in the setting of chronic ulcerative colitis and are composed of regions of inflamed mucosa surrounded by areas of ulceration, are associated with an increased risk of cancer. Lymphoid polyps are regions of the mucosa that contain exaggerated intramucosal lymphoid tissue. Juvenile polyps usually develop in the rectum of children younger than 5 years of age and are termed *hamartomatous* because they are focal malformations that resemble tumors but are caused by abnormal development of the lamina propria; these polyps require no therapy unless they cause symptoms such as obstruction or severe bleeding.

ADENOMATOUS POLYPS

Definition and Epidemiology

Adenomatous polyps (or adenomas), which are neoplastic polyps with malignant potential, are more common in the distal colon and

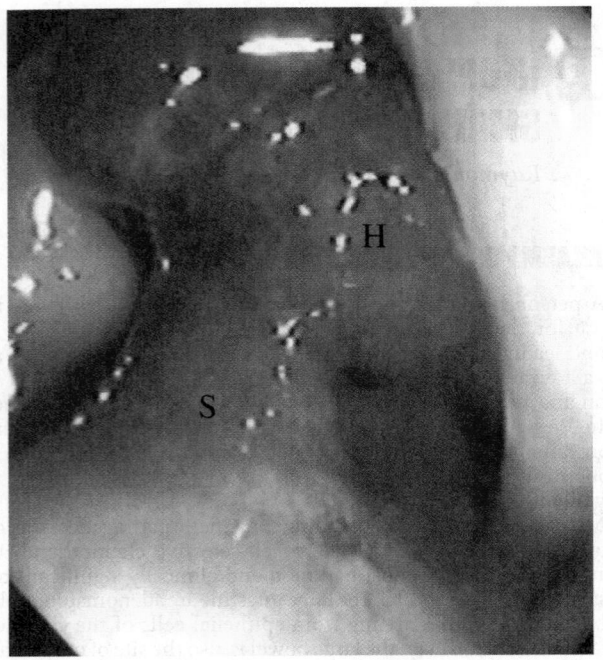

FIGURE 200–1 • Large pedunculated polyp in the rectum. The stalk (S) itself is benign, with the head (H) containing the adenomatous tissue. The polyp was removed safely in a one-step endoscopic procedure. (Courtesy of Pankaj Jay Pasricha.)

rectum, where their anatomic distribution parallels that of colorectal adenocarcinoma. Adenomatous polyps manifest in a range of sizes; smaller lesions are usually pedunculated, whereas larger polyps can be sessile. Convincing evidence that adenomatous polyps are the precursor lesion to colorectal adenocarcinoma comes from humans with the hereditary polyposis syndromes and animal studies in which adenomas are induced by either carcinogens or genetic manipulation. Correlative evidence includes the observations that the epidemiology is similar for adenomas and carcinomas, that both lesions are more common in the same anatomic locations, and that adenomatous tissue can often be found in small adenocarcinomas.

Adenomatous polyps are relatively common, particularly in elderly populations; the prevalence is 20 to 30% in persons in the United States under the age of 40 years and 40 to 50% in individuals over the age of 60 years. The prevalence of adenomas tends to be high in regions of the world where colorectal cancer is common, and most autopsy studies indicate a 30% higher prevalence in men. The importance of genetic risk factors is clear in the hereditary polyposis syndromes (see Inherited Colorectal Cancer Syndromes), and there is a familial component in sporadic adenomas; for example, individuals with a positive first-degree family history are at a four-fold greater risk for developing adenomatous polyps.

Pathobiology

The layer of epithelial cells lining the surface of the normal large bowel undergoes continuous self-renewal with a turnover period of 3 to 8 days. Undifferentiated stem cells located at the base of invaginated crypts give rise to cells that migrate toward the lumen as they further differentiate into specialized enterocytes; these cells are subsequently removed by apoptosis, by extrusion, or by phagocytes underlying the epithelial layer. The development of adenomatous polyps is associated with a sequence-specific accumulation of genetic lesions that cause an imbalance between epithelial cell proliferation and cell death. As a result, cells accumulate at the luminal surface, where they remain undifferentiated and continue to undergo cell division, eventually leading to the abnormal development of a mass of adenomatous tissue.

Adenomas are classified into three main histologic subtypes: (1) tubular adenomas, (2) villous adenomas, and (3) tubulovillous adenomas. Tubular adenomas, which are the most common type of adenoma, account for 70 to 85% of all adenomas removed at colonoscopy. They are often small and pedunculated, and they consist of dysplastic, tubular glands that divide and branch out from the mucosal surface. In contrast, villous adenomas are much more rare (<5% of all adenomas), are generally large and sessile, and are composed of strands of dysplastic epithelium that project, finger-like, into the lumen of the gut. Tubulovillous adenomas (10 to 25% of all adenomas) have a mixture of tubular and villous architecture. Small, tubular adenomas generally have low malignant potential, whereas approximately 40% of large, sessile adenomatous polyps will develop into a cancer.

Clinical Manifestations and Natural History

Patients with adenomatous polyps generally remain asymptomatic but may present with an asymptomatic positive stool occult blood test or with evident hematochezia. The lifetime incidence of additional adenomas in a patient with one known adenoma is 30 to 50%. Less than 5% of all adenomas will eventually develop into carcinomas. Two critical factors that determine the likelihood that a presenting adenoma will eventually develop into an invasive lesion are the size of the polyp and the grade of dysplasia. For polyps less than 1 cm in size, the risk for carcinoma is 1 to 3%; polyps between 1 and 2 cm have a 10% risk or becoming cancer; and more than 40% of polyps that are greater than 2 cm are predicted to transform into an invasive lesion. All adenomatous polyps contain some degree of dysplasia but can be further categorized as low- or high-grade to indicate the degree of dysplasia and corresponding risk for invasive carcinoma. High-grade dysplasia is associated with a 27% rate for eventual transformation into carcinoma.

Diagnosis

Adenomatous polyps in the colon and rectum can be diagnosed by endoscopy (Chapter 132) or barium radiography (Chapter 131), but multiple studies indicate that colonoscopy is the most accurate for diagnosing colorectal polyps. For example, the National Polyp Study reported that barium enema missed 52% of polyps greater than or equal to 1 cm in size. Colonoscopy is thus the preferred method for diagnosing adenomas based on this higher rate of accuracy and because the technique allows for immediate biopsy and resection of most polyps; current evidence supports the use of colonoscopy as a screening tool for the general population over the age of 50 years (Chapter 11). Flexible sigmoidoscopy, which is often used to screen asymptomatic persons at average risk for colorectal adenocarcinoma, will detect 50 to 60% of all polyps and cancers. Generally, patients who have polyps detected by barium radiography or flexible sigmoidoscopy should undergo colonoscopy to remove the lesion and to search for additional polyps. However, colonoscopy may not be adequately performed in patients who have advanced diverticulosis or who have had previous pelvic surgery. In these instances, a combination of double-contrast barium radiography and flexible sigmoidoscopy may be an acceptable alternative. "Virtual colonoscopy," whereby images of the colon can be reconstructed by computer analysis of data generated from a high-resolution computed tomography (CT) scan, has shown promising early results, but the precise clinical role for this technique has not yet been resolved.

Rx Treatment

The major goal of treatment for adenomatous polyps is removal or destruction of the lesion during endoscopy by electrocautery. This recommendation is based on the overwhelming evidence that endoscopic polypectomy reduces the subsequent incidence and mortality of colorectal cancer. Pedunculated adenomas are generally removed by snare polypectomy with subsequent submission of the tissue for pathologic analysis. Piecemeal snare resection may be required to remove sessile polyps. Surgical resection of a polyp is indicated when endoscopic resection of an advanced adenoma is not possible. The biopsied polyp must be evaluated histologically so that the presence or absence of carcinoma can be determined; if a malignant lesion is found, its histologic grade, vascular and lymphatic involvement, and proximity to the margin of resection should be determined. Polypectomy is the definitive therapy for localized cancers that have not spread beyond the muscularis mucosae layer, are not poorly differentiated, do not involve vascular or lymphatic structures, have margins free of carcinoma cells, and have been completely excised by endoscopic inspection. If invasive carcinoma is present in the stalk of a resected polyp and if it is unclear whether any of the stalk remains after polypectomy, then colonic resection might be indicated. The mortality rate associated with colonic resection is less than 2% in patients between the ages of 50 and 69 but rises to 4% in persons older than 70 years of age; it also increases considerably when comorbidities such as chronic liver, renal, or heart disease are present.

Prognosis and Future Directions

Patients who have undergone resection of an adenomatous polyp are at increased risk for subsequent development of adenomas and colorectal adenocarcinoma. In general, a follow-up colonoscopy is recommended in 3 years. Earlier colonoscopies may be warranted in patients who have multiple or large sessile adenomas removed. In contrast, the risk of malignancy is not significantly increased in patients who have had less than three small (<1 cm) tubular adenomas removed; for these individuals, the first follow-up colonoscopy can be delayed to 5 years. If the first follow-up colonoscopy is negative, the second scheduled follow-up can usually be delayed until 5 years.

Intense research has been directed toward identifying agents that may prevent polyps from forming or recurring. Such chemoprevention strategies include dietary supplementation with calcium and folic acid as well as chronic intake of nonsteroidal anti-inflammatory drugs or cyclooxygenase-2 inhibitors. These are currently used for experimental purposes only.

INHERITED SYNDROMES

The inherited colorectal cancer syndromes constitute approximately 6% of all cases of colorectal adenocarcinoma. Genetic analyses of these syndromes have led to major advances in understanding how sporadic colorectal cancer develops. Inherited syndromes can be further divided into inherited polyposis syndromes, which include familial adenomatous polyposis and its variants Gardner's syndrome and Turcot's syndrome; hereditary nonpolyposis colon cancer (HNPCC) or Lynch's syndrome; and hamartomatous polyposis syndromes, which include Peutz-Jeghers syndrome, juvenile polyposis, and the related syndrome of Cowden's disease. Each of these syndromes is characterized by unique genetic lesions, age of onset, and clinical manifestations (Table 200–1).

FAMILIAL ADENOMATOUS POLYPOSIS. The hallmark of familial adenomatous polyposis is the development of hundreds to thousands of adenomatous polyps in the large bowel at a relatively young age (Fig. 200–2). Estimates of disease incidence vary from 1 in 6850 to 1 in 31,250. The disease, which is autosomal dominant with incomplete penetrance, has been mapped to the adenomatous polyposis coli (APC) gene located on the long arm of chromosome 5 (5q21). APC is a tumor suppressor gene that is a critical regulator of intestinal epithelial cell growth. Patients with the familial syndrome inherit one mutant copy of APC; when a loss of function mutation develops in the other APC allele, mucosal epithelial cell growth is no longer controlled normally, and polyps are formed. Variable phenotypes can be partly attributed to differences in the location of the APC mutation.

Adenomas begin to appear early in the second decade of life, and gastrointestinal symptoms begin to appear in the third or fourth decade. Polyps are distributed relatively evenly throughout the colon, although a slight predominance has been noted in the distal

Table 200–1 • GENERAL FEATURES OF THE INHERITED COLORECTAL CANCER SYNDROMES

SYNDROME	POLYP HISTOLOGY	POLYP DISTRIBUTION	AGE OF ONSET	RISK OF COLON CANCER	GENETIC LESION	CLINICAL MANIFESTATIONS	ASSOCIATED LESIONS
Familial adenomatous polyposis	Adenoma	Large intestine	16 yr (range 8–34 yr)	100%	5q (APC gene)	Rectal bleeding, abdominal pain, bowel obstruction	Desmoids, CHRPE
Gardner's syndrome	Adenoma	Large and small intestine	16 yr (range 8–34 yr)	100%	5q (APC gene)	Rectal bleeding, abdominal pain, bowel obstruction	Desmoids, CHRPE
Peutz-Jeghers syndrome	Hamartoma	Large and small intestine	First decade	Slightly above average	19p (STK11)	Possible rectal bleeding, abdominal pain, intussusception	Orocutaneous melanin pigment spots
Juvenile polyposis	Hamartoma (rarely adenoma)	Large and small intestine	First decade	Approximately 9%	PTEN, SMAD4, BMPR1	Possible rectal bleeding, abdominal pain, intussusception	Congenital abnormalities in 20% of the nonfamilial type
Heriditary nonpolyposis colon cancer	Adenoma	Large intestine	40 yr (range 18–65 yr)	30%	Mismatch repair genes*	Rectal bleeding, abdominal pain, bowel obstruction	Other tumors (e.g., ovary, ureter, pancreas, stomach)

*Including hMSH2, hMSH3, hMSH6, hMLH1, hPMS1, and hPMS2.
CHRPE = congenital hypertrophy of the retinal pigment epithelium.

FIGURE 200–2 • A colon lined with hundreds of adenomatous polyps resected from a patient with familial adenomatous polyposis.

colon. Almost all patients with familial adenomatous polyposis will develop frank colorectal carcinoma by the age of 40 years if left untreated. Gastric polyps occur in 30 to 100% of patients, and duodenal adenomas are found in 45 to 90% of patients. Periampullary duodenal cancer develops in approximately 10% of cases. Small bowel lesions that are distal to the duodenum rarely progress into malignancy.

The primary treatment option is total proctocolectomy with conventional ileostomy or ileoanal (pouch) anastomosis. First-degree relatives of afflicted individuals should be screened. A blood test to detect mutations in the APC gene has a sensitivity of 85%, but flexible proctosigmoidoscopy should be performed annually from the ages of 12 to 40 years (and every 3 years after the age of 40 years), even in those who test negative for the APC mutation. A randomized clinical trial showed that therapy with a selective cyclooxygenase-2 inhibitor can reduce the burden of polyps in patients with familial adenomatous polyposis, but this therapy alone does not obviate the need for colectomy.∎

GARDNER'S SYNDROME. Gardner's syndrome, which is also caused by mutations in the APC gene, differs from familial adenomatous polyposis mainly by the presence of extraintestinal manifestations, including osteomas (particularly mandibular), soft tissue tumors (including lipomas, sebaceous cysts, and fibrosarcomas), supernumerary teeth, desmoid tumors, mesenteric fibromatosis, and congenital hypertrophy of the retinal pigment epithelium. The phenotypic differences between Gardner's syndrome and familial adenomatous polyposis appear to be due to differences in the location of the APC mutation, the presence of modifying genes, and environmental factors. Adenomatous polyps in Gardner's syndrome have the same malignant potential as those found in familial adenomatous polyposis; hence, colorectal cancer treatment and screening recommendations are similar.

TURCOT'S SYNDROME. A hallmark of Turcot's syndrome is the combination of colorectal polyposis and central nervous system malignancies. Mutations in the APC gene account for two thirds of cases, and the remaining one third are due to mutations in the DNA mismatch repair genes that are also mutated in HNPCC. The central nervous system manifestations include medulloblastomas, glioblastomas, and ependymomas.

HEREDITARY NONPOLYPOSIS COLORECTAL CANCER. HNPCC, also known as Lynch's syndrome, is the most common hereditary colorectal cancer syndrome and accounts for approximately 5% of all cases of colorectal cancer. It is inherited as an autosomal dominant trait and is highly penetrant. Clinically, HNPCC has been defined by the presence of all three of the following: (1) three or more relatives with histologically verified HNPCC-associated cancer (colorectal cancer, or cancer of the endometrium, small bowel, ureter, or renal pelvis), one of whom is a first-degree relative of the other two in the absence of familial adenomatous polyposis; (2) colorectal cancer involving at least two generations; (3) one or more family members with cancer diagnosed before the age of 50 years.

Hereditary nonpolyposis colorectal cancer is caused by loss-of-function germline mutations in a set of genes involved in the repair of DNA base pair mismatches that occur during DNA replication (also known as the mutation mismatch repair system). Mutation mismatch repair genes include hMSH2, hMSH3, hMSH6, hMLH1, hPMS1, and hPMS2. Mutations in these genes lead to the development of DNA microsatellite instability that can be detected using genomic techniques. Tumor cells displaying microsatellite instability (MSI) have increased mutation rates in genes that contain small nucleotide repeats; one common gene mutated in HNPCC due to the MSI phenotype is the transforming growth factor-β type II receptor, which is an important component of a signaling pathway that regulates normal intestinal epithelial cell growth and differentiation.

The median age for diagnosis of HNPCC is in the mid-40s. Although several adenomas may be present, the diffuse polyposis characteristic of familial adenomatous polyposis is not found, hence the name nonpolyposis. Adenomatous polyps in HNPCC are located predominantly in the right colon proximal to the splenic flexure. These tumors generally have a better prognosis than similar lesions found in sporadic colorectal cancer. Patients with HNPCC also are at high risk for other malignancies, including cancers of the ovary, ureter, pancreas, and stomach, probably partly owing to loss of proper DNA repair. Screening strategies for families with a history suggestive of HNPCC may include the use of genetic testing to identify the MSI phenotype. Persons in families with HNPCC should undergo a colonoscopy every 2 years from the ages of 21 to 40 years and every year after the age of 40 because their risk is quite high and genetic testing is not perfect. Women in HNPCC families should have pelvic examinations every 1 to 3 years beginning at the age of 18; annual pelvic examinations, transvaginal ultrasonography, and endometrial biopsy have been recommended beginning at age 25.

PEUTZ-JEGHERS SYNDROME. The defining clinical presentation of Peutz-Jeghers syndrome is intestinal hamartomatous polyposis in association with characteristic mucocutaneous pigmentation. The average age of diagnosis is in the mid-20s. The syndrome is inherited in an autosomal dominant fashion with high penetrance. It is rare, with an incidence rate one tenth that of familial adenomatous polyposis. The gene responsible for the syndrome is believed to be the serine-threonine kinase STK11 gene located on chromosome 19p. The hamartomatous polyps in Peutz-Jeghers syndrome are located predominantly in the small intestine (64 to 96%), stomach (24 to 49%), and colon (60%). Histologically, these polyps are benign and unique in that a layer of muscle that extends into the submucosa or muscularis propria may surround the glandular tissue. In rare instances, these polyps may become malignant, particularly in the small bowel. Otherwise, the major gastrointestinal symptoms include recurrent bouts of small bowel intussusception, obstruction, and bleeding that may require surgery. Gastrointestinal bleeding may also occur and lead to iron deficiency anemia. Extraintestinal manifestations include ovarian sex cord stromal tumors and polyps of the gallbladder, ureter, and nasal passages. More than 95% of patients have a characteristic pattern of melanin spots on the lips, buccal mucosa, and skin (Fig. 200–3); in one large series, 23% of patients were diagnosed on the basis of this typical cutaneous pigmentation.

JUVENILE POLYPOSIS. Juvenile (non-neoplastic, hamartomatous) polyposis is a rare syndrome characterized by 10 or more non-neoplastic, hamartomatous polyps throughout the gastrointestinal tract or any number of polyps in a patient with a family history of juvenile polyposis. The syndrome is inherited in an autosomal dominant manner and is caused by mutations in the SMAD4, PTEN, or BMPR1A gene. The hamartomas are histologically distinct from Peutz-Jeghers polyps. Patients generally present with rectal bleeding, anemia, abdominal pain, or intussusception in childhood or early adolescence. Extraintestinal symptoms include pulmonary arteriovenous malformations. The risk of malignancy in juvenile polyposis is reported to be 10%; subtotal colectomy may be necessary in patients with severe dysplasia.

COWDEN'S SYNDROME. Cowden's syndrome is a rare, autosomal dominant syndrome of multiple hamartomatous polyps of the skin and mucous membranes, including gastrointestinal polyps, facial tricholemmomas, oral papillomas, and keratoses of the hands and feet. There is a high rate of associated malignancy, particularly in the thyroid and breast. The polyps in Cowden's syndrome are benign. The causative genetic lesion has been mapped to the PTEN tumor suppressor gene.

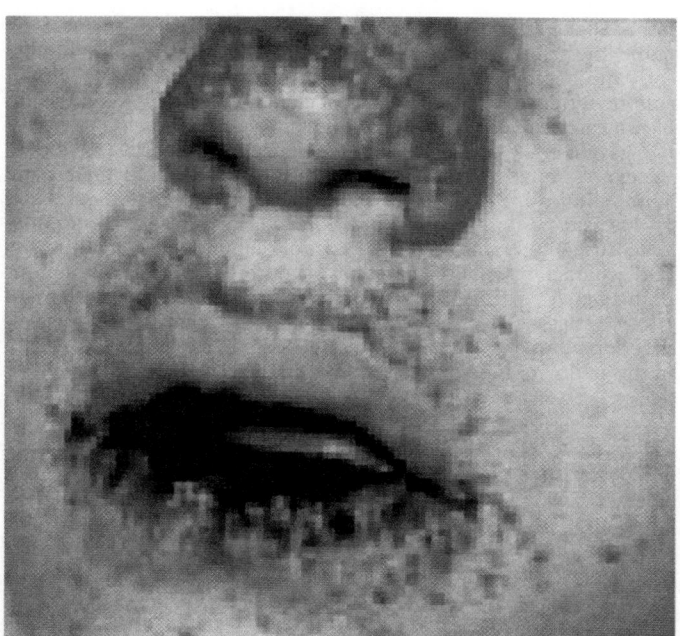

FIGURE 200–3 • Mucosal pigmentation characteristic of a patient with Peutz-Jeghers syndrome.

Table 200–2 • LIFESTYLE AND DIETARY RECOMMENDATIONS FOR THE PRIMARY PREVENTION OF COLORECTAL CANCER

DIETARY RECOMMENDATIONS	LIFESTYLE RECOMMENDATIONS
Limit total fat to below 20–30% total calorie intake	Maintain normal body weight
Increase quantity and variety of fruits and vegetables (at least five servings per day)	Exercise daily
Ingest 20–30 g of fiber per day	Avoid smoking
Consider supplementation with 3 g of calcium carbonate per day	Avoid excessive alcohol

ADENOCARCINOMA OF THE COLON AND RECTUM

Definition and Epidemiology

Adenocarcinomas constitute 98% of the malignancies found in the large bowel. Most adenocarcinomas are believed to arise from adenomatous polyps that progress from severe dysplasia to invasive carcinoma. The peak incidence is from 60 to 79 years of age, with fewer than 10% of all cases arising before the age of 50. The geographic pattern of colorectal cancer worldwide is highly variable. The highest rates are found in industrialized countries, including the United States, Canada, New Zealand, and the countries of northwestern Europe. Most countries in Asia, Africa, and South America (with the exception of Argentina) have a relatively low rate. This geographic distribution is thought to be primarily due to environmental factors, since ethnic groups from low-incidence countries in Asia develop low rates of disease equivalent to white Americans after they migrate to the West. African Americans in the United States also have a much higher risk for disease than black Africans. Population studies have found positive correlations between the risk for colorectal cancer and the dietary intake of red meat.

In the 2001, 135,000 new cases of colorectal cancer were detected in the United States and 57,000 deaths were caused by the disease, making colorectal cancer the second leading cause of cancer-related deaths after lung cancer. The 5-year survival rate for colorectal cancer is approximately 55%, but this varies greatly depending on the stage of disease at the time of diagnosis. Men and women have a similar incidence of adenocarcinoma of the colon, but rectal cancer is more common in men in most parts of the world. The overall rate of deaths due to colorectal cancer has declined in the last 20 years, perhaps owing to increased screening and improved treatment.

ENVIRONMENTAL FACTORS. Recommendations for the primary prevention of colorectal cancer are based on risk factors that are associated with colorectal cancer (Table 200–2); it has been estimated that adoption of these diet and lifestyle changes could reduce the incidence of colorectal cancer by 50%. Total energy intake, irrespective of dietary content, is positively associated with the development of colorectal cancer. Colorectal adenomas are associated with tobacco use, and the increased consumption of ethanol, particularly beer, has been associated with a higher risk for colorectal cancer. The higher rates of colorectal cancer in countries that consume "Western-style" diets high in red meat suggests that high dietary fat and low fiber could promote colorectal cancer. However, recent data show no benefit of low-fat diets on colorectal cancer despite their other health advantages. The role of dietary fiber is controversial, and two major prospective studies have found no correlation between the intake of dietary fiber and the development of colorectal adenomas.[2,3] Whether diets high in fruits and vegetables can prevent colorectal cancer is under investigation.

INHERITED PREDISPOSITION. Individuals who have a first-degree relative with colorectal cancer face a two- to three-fold increase in risk for malignancy, and this risk rises to five- or six-fold if two first-degree relatives are involved. Various genetic studies suggest that a large percentage of the population (up to 50%) is susceptible to colorectal neoplasia on a familial basis.

INFLAMMATORY BOWEL DISEASE. Adenocarcinoma of the colon is 10 to 20 times more common in persons with ulcerative colitis (Chapter 142) as compared with the general population. Between 2 and 4% of all patients with long-term ulcerative colitis develop this malignancy, and the cumulative incidence over a 25-year period is approximately 12%. The two most important predictors for eventual development of carcinoma are the duration of the inflammatory disease and the extent of colonic involvement. Identification of dysplasia in the setting of ulcerative colitis is the best indicator of early cancer, but it is difficult to distinguish true dysplastic lesions from areas of intense mucosal regeneration. Dysplasia in a plaque or elevated mass and high-grade dysplasia warrant consideration of colectomy. Most experts agree that colonoscopy every 2 years with multiple biopsies is warranted after 8 years of symptomatic ulcerative colitis with extensive colonic involvement. The recent evolution of surgical procedures, such as ileoanal pull-through, favors the use of prophylactic colectomy in high-risk patients. Individuals with Crohn's colitis have a four to seven times higher risk of colorectal cancer as compared with the general population. Although this risk is less than that seen with ulcerative colitis, routine surveillance is recommended in patients with extensive colonic disease.

OTHER HIGH-RISK FACTORS. Persons diagnosed with endocarditis or septicemia from *Streptococcus bovis* have a high rate of occult colorectal neoplasias and other upper gastrointestinal malignancies; endoscopic or radiographic screening may be warranted in this setting. There is also a 5 to 10% increase in colorectal cancer rates 15 to 30 years after ureterosigmoidostomy to correct congenital extrophy of the bladder; the lesions are typically distal to the ureteral implant, where the mucosa is chronically exposed to urine and feces.

Pathobiology

PATHOLOGY. The anatomic distribution of carcinoma of the colon (Fig. 200–4) is associated with distinct morphologic patterns. Right-sided tumors commonly grow as polypoid, exophytic masses that bleed, often occultly, and rarely cause obstruction, whereas carcinomas of the distal colon are generally annular, encircling lesions that both bleed and lead to constriction of the bowel ("napkin ring" or "apple core" constriction). Almost all colorectal cancers are adenocarcinomas that exhibit differing degrees of glandular differentiation; most tend to produce mucin that aids in extension of the lesion and worsens prognosis. Lesions spread by direct extension through the wall of the bowel into the pericolonic fat and mesentery, and they can also invade surrounding organs. Alternatively, tumors can enter the lymphatic system and spread to regional lymph nodes, or enter the venous system and drain to the liver via the portal vein. Colorectal cancers can spread throughout the peritoneal cavity and can also metastasize to the lung and bone marrow via the blood stream. Rectal cancers

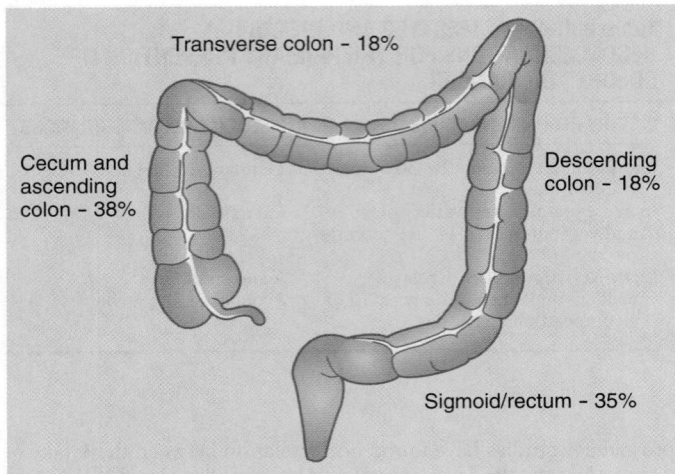

FIGURE 200–4 • Distribution of colorectal cancers in various regions of the large intestine.

can invade the perirectal fat and surrounding structures, including the vagina, prostate, bladder, ureters, and bony pelvis; they may also spread to the lungs and liver.

MOLECULAR GENETICS AND THE ADENOMA TO CARCINOMA SEQUENCE. Colorectal cancer is caused by the accumulation of multiple genetic lesions in a specific sequence over time. Both the tissue architecture and the cellular genotype change as the disease progresses (Fig. 200–5).

Approximately 80 to 85% of sporadic colorectal cancers are aneuploid tumors that exhibit chromosomal instability. The initiating genetic event is often mutations in APC, the causative gene for familial adenomatous polyposis. APC is a multifunctional protein with an essential role in the regulation of the growth of intestinal epithelial cells. One of the important consequences of loss of normal APC is the accumulation of the β-catenin oncogene within the nucleus of cells, where it can participate in the regulation of gene expression that promotes malignancy. Other genomic abnormalities, including gain of function mutations in the k-RAS protooncogene and allelic

loss at 18q21 (where several putative tumor suppressor genes reside), hallmark the progression of the lesion from dysplastic epithelium to early and late adenomas. Loss-of-function mutations in the p53 tumor suppressor gene are commonly associated with progression to full-blown carcinoma and can occur even after transformation to cancer has developed. Other genetic and epigenetic alterations, including the expression of genes capable of cleaving extracellular matrix and a protein tyrosine phosphatase, lead to metastasis.

The remaining 15 to 20% of colorectal cancers without chromosomal instability exhibit the phenotype of genomic microsatellite instability characteristic of the hereditary syndrome HNPCC—mutations in mismatch repair genes and mutations in important growth regulatory genes such as transforming growth factor-β RII. Loss-of-function mutations in p53 commonly occur in carcinomas that arise in the setting of inflammatory bowel disease.

Clinical Manifestations

Colorectal adenocarcinomas can remain clinically silent for years. When present, symptoms often develop insidiously over a period of months and years. The major symptoms suggesting colorectal cancer are rectal bleeding, pain, and a change in bowel habits. Symptoms typically vary depending on where the lesion resides. Neoplasms in the proximal colon, where intestinal contents are relatively liquid, do not generally cause the abdominal pain or change in bowel habits characteristic of obstructive lesions. These lesions often ulcerate and cause chronic blood loss; patients commonly present with complaints of fatigue, palpitations, or even angina pectoris. Physician examination often reveals hemoccult positive stools (Chapter 133), and laboratory testing demonstrates hypochromic, microcytic anemia characteristic of iron deficiency (Chapter 167). Thus, the presence of unexplained iron deficiency anemia in any adult male or postmenopausal female patient should prompt a rigorous evaluation for colorectal cancer, that is, endoscopic and/or radiographic visualization of the entire colon. In contrast to right-sided lesions, cancers in the distal colon may bleed, but they often cause constriction of the gut wall and can manifest with abdominal cramping, stool obstruction, or even perforation (Fig. 200–6). Tumors of the rectosigmoid region may manifest with hematochezia, tenesmus, and narrowing of the caliber

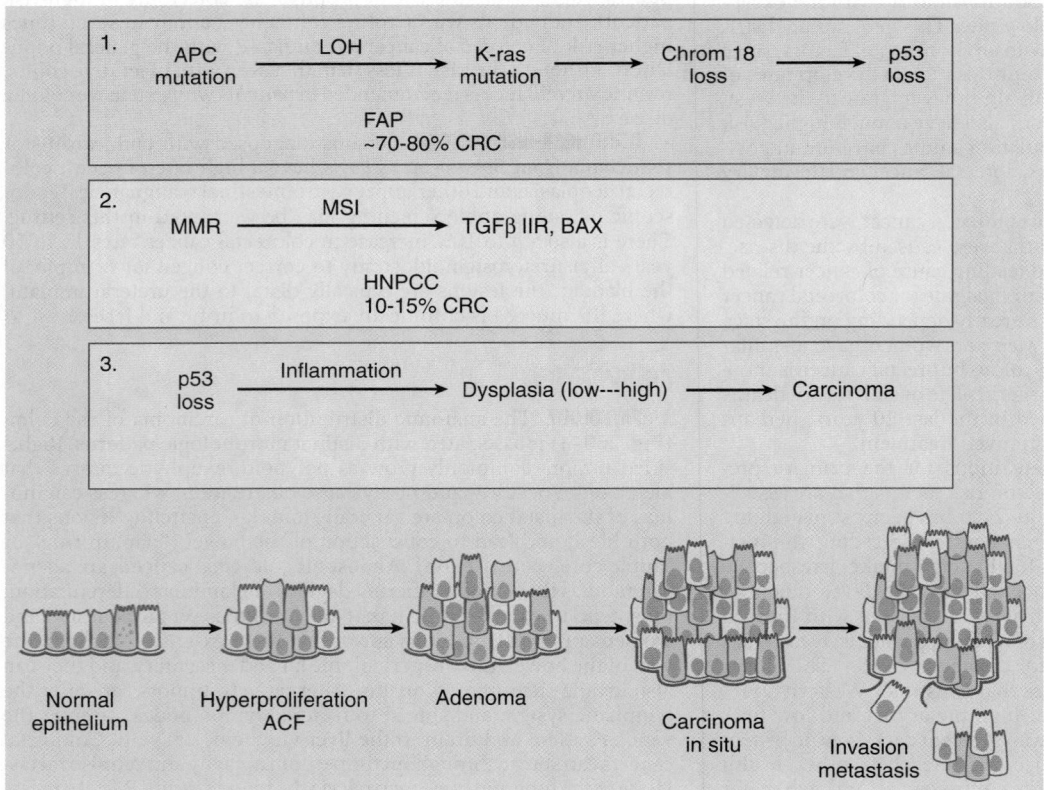

FIGURE 200–5 • The molecular basis of colorectal cancer. Sequence-specific genetic lesions result in the transition from normal large bowel mucosa to invasive carcinoma. BAX = apoptosis-related protein; CRC = colorectal cancer; FAP = familial adenomatous polyposis; HNPCC = hereditary nonpolyposis colon cancer; IIR = Type II receptor; MMR = mutation mismatch repair; MSI = microsatellite instability; TGFβ = transforming growth factor-β.

of the stool. The differential diagnosis for rectal bleeding should include hemorrhoids, angiodysplasia, diverticulosis, and other benign and malignant tumors (Chapter 133).

Clinically apparent metastatic disease may present prior to or after resection of primary colorectal cancer. Symptoms may include pain related to distention of the liver capsule caused by massive hepatomegaly. If disease has spread to the abdomen, both ascites and bowel obstruction may occur. Metastatic spread to the pelvic region may present as bladder dysfunction, sacral or sciatic nerve pain, and vaginal discharge or bleeding. Lesions that have spread to the lung or bone marrow can remain silent until very advanced disease is present.

Diagnosis

The history, physical examination, and judicious use of both laboratory and radiologic tests are important in diagnosing colorectal cancer. Pertinent history should include a prior history of colorectal cancer or adenomatous polyps, inflammatory bowel disease, any inherited colorectal cancer syndromes, and whether the patient has any first-degree relative with colorectal cancer. On physical examination, extraintestinal lesions characteristic of Peutz-Jeghers or Gardner's

syndrome may be noticed. Metastatic disease is suggested by enlargement of the supraclavicular lymph nodes or liver or by the presence of an umbilical mass or ascites. The digital rectal examination may reveal a distal rectal cancer or the spread of tumor to the rectal shelf or pelvis. The stool shows evidence of frank or occult blood in 40 to 80% of advanced cases. Iron deficiency anemia or an elevation in liver enzymes may aid in diagnosis.

Methods for diagnosing colorectal cancer are similar to those used to detect adenomatous polyps. Colonoscopy is the procedure of choice for all patients who have occult blood in their stools or who present with signs and symptoms characteristic of colorectal cancer (Fig. 200–7). Colonoscopy is more accurate than radiographic studies for the detection of colorectal neoplasms of all sizes and has the advantage of being able to detect synchronous (simultaneously present, additional) cancers and obtain tissue for histologic analysis.

The staging of rectal cancers is helped by the use of endoscopic ultrasonography, by which the depth of lesion invasion can be accurately assessed. Patients with colorectal cancers who present with generalized abdominal pain or symptoms characteristic of multiple diseases may be diagnosed initially by CT scanning of the abdomen. A CT scan may also play a role in determining the extent of tumor spread. Both a chest radiograph and a CT scan may detect lung or liver metastases.

TUMOR STAGING. Accurate anatomic staging of colorectal cancer is essential, since the most important predictive factor for postsurgical outcome and the need for adjuvant chemotherapy is the stage of disease at the time surgery. Colorectal cancers are staged using both the Dukes method and the universal TNM classification system (Table 200–3). Stage A tumors (T1N0M0) are superficial lesions that do not

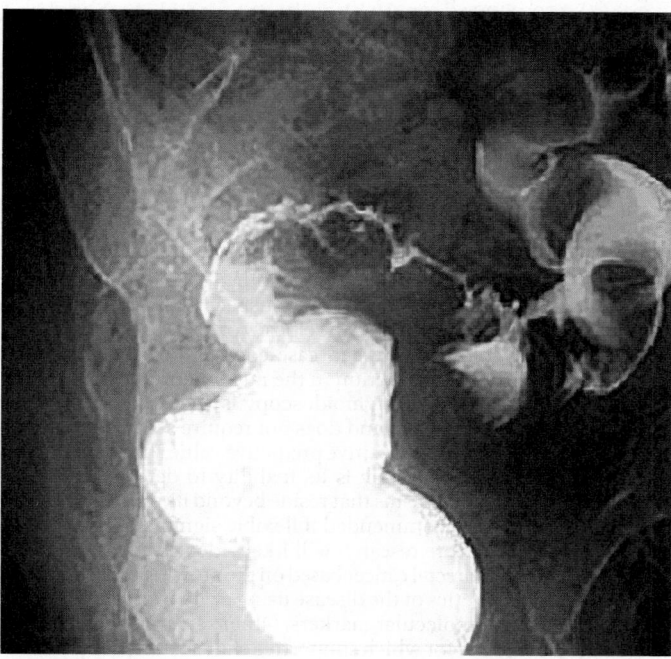

FIGURE 200–6 • A barium enema radiograph in which a colorectal cancer in the distal segment of the large intestine has formed an annular, encircling lesion that leads to constriction of the bowel wall.

Table 200–3 • CLASSIFICATION SYSTEMS USED TO STAGE COLON CANCER AND THEIR CORRELATION TO DISEASE OUTCOME

DUKES	TNM*	STAGE	PATHOLOGY	PROGNOSIS (APPROXIMATE 5-YEAR SURVIVAL RATE, %)
A	T1N0M0	I	No invasion beyond submucosa	>90
B₁	T2N0M0	I	Extension into muscularis	85
B₂	T3N0M0	II	Extension into or through the serosa	70–80
C	TxN1M0	III	Involvement of regional lymph nodes	35–65
D	TxNxM1	IV	Distant metastases present	5

*T is the depth of tumor penetration, N is the presence of lymph node involvement, and M indicates the presence of distant metastases.

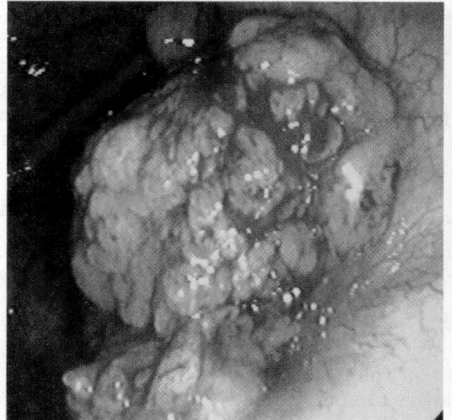
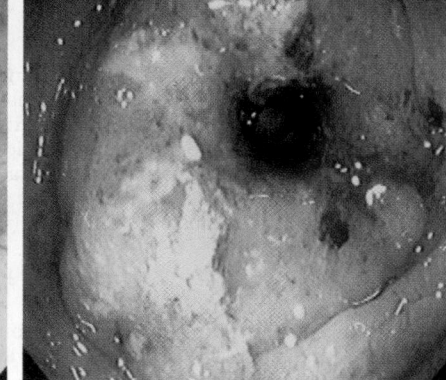

FIGURE 200–7 • Two manifestations of colorectal cancer. *A*, Exophytic growth within the lumen. *B*, "Stricturing" (apple core) lesion.

A
B

Oncology

penetrate the muscularis or involve regional lymph nodes. Neoplasms that are more invasive but have not yet spread to the lymph nodes are categorized as stage B. Stage C cancer involves regional lymph nodes, and stage D indicates distant metastases.

Rx Treatment

SURGERY. Total resection of all malignant tissue is the treatment of choice for most patients with colorectal cancer and is currently the only treatment option that offers a reasonable chance of cure or long-term survival. The primary goal is complete removal of the involved bowel and associated lymphatic drainage. Laparoscopic resection is the most common approach, but its long-term success compared with open resection is still being evaluated. A hemicolectomy is performed when lesions are present in the left or right portions of the colon. Tumors located in the sigmoid region and upper rectum are resected anteriorly, with removal of normal colon both proximal and distal to the lesion; modern stapling techniques allow a sphincter-saving resection to be performed in a high percentage of cases. Lesions within 5 cm of the anal verge are treated by abdominoperineal resection and permanent colostomy; this approach is also used for large tumors that reside deep in the pelvis, for all neoplasms with high-grade histologic type, and when there is marked local spread of rectal lesions.

A palliative colostomy is often helpful in the presence of colonic obstruction caused by a tumor that is unresectable because it is widely metastatic or widely advanced into the peritoneum. Perforated lesions are generally managed by primary resection and colostomy followed by subsequent closure of the colostomy within a few months after the original surgery; in some patients, however, a permanent colostomy may be required. Focal surgical resection of a well-defined single liver metastasis or a wedge resection of a few lesions may be indicated depending on the medical condition of the patient; such procedures are associated with 5-year survival rates of 25 to 30% in patients who do not have advanced liver disease or other significant comorbidities.

RADIATION THERAPY. For rectal cancer, radiation therapy can be combined with 5-fluorouracil (5-FU) and leucovorin preoperatively to minimize local recurrence and metastasis. Radiation therapy is also useful in reducing tumor size and enabling large, otherwise unresectable lesions to be resected. Postoperative radiation and chemotherapy reduce local recurrence and distant metastasis. [4]

CHEMOTHERAPY. The mainstay of adjuvant chemotherapy for colorectal cancer is 5-FU, a compound that targets the enzyme thymidylate synthase. The drug is well tolerated but produces response rates in only 10 to 20% of patients with advanced disease. Leucovorin acts as a biomodulator by enhancing the binding of 5-FU to its target. Regimens combining 5-FU with leucovorin can improve disease-free survival in patients with Dukes type C cancers. [5] Direct infusion of the drug into the hepatic artery can improve response rates in patients with hepatic involvement, but the effect on survival is marginal and may not outweigh the cost and toxicity of this approach. The addition of either irinotecan, which is a topoisomerase inhibitor, or oxaliplatin to 5-FU and leucovorin improves response rates in cases of metastatic disease. [6]

Prognosis

The 5-year survival rate of colorectal cancer directly correlates with the stage of disease at the time of diagnosis (see Table 200–3). Other predictors of poor outcome following surgical resection include poorly differentiated histologic type, perforation, adherence of tumor to adjacent organs, venous invasion, preoperative elevation of carcinoembryonic antigen (CEA) to levels greater than 5.0 ng/mL, aneuploidy, and specific chromosomal deletions.

Follow-up

A primary goal following curative resection for colorectal cancer is to detect curable recurrences or second primary tumors. Patients whose colon cancers have been cured face a 3 to 5% probability of developing an additional cancer of the large intestine during their lifetime and a more than 15% risk of developing an adenomatous polyp. It is also important to detect both synchronous (occurring at the same time) and metachronous (occurring at different times) cancers that may develop later. After curative resection, surveillance colonoscopy should be performed at 3 years and, if negative, at 5-year intervals thereafter. For patients who have had a low anterior resection of a stage B or C rectosigmoid cancer, flexible sigmoidoscopy should be performed to examine the lower bowel every 3 to 6 months for 2 years and a colonoscopy will be required to evaluate bowel beyond 60 cm. Additional follow-up measures include semiannual physical examinations and yearly blood chemistries. No clear consensus exists on the value of obtaining periodic chest radiographs or CT scans of the abdomen and pelvis in the absence of meaningful symptoms or signs. If the serum CEA level was normal after the initial resection, a rising CEA suggests recurrent colorectal cancer; some experts advocate periodic assays for blood CEA levels following curative resection.

Screening

Colorectal cancer is particularly amenable to widespread screening (Chapter 11). First, it is one of the most common and lethal malignancies in many countries, thereby justifying the public health cost associated with a population-wide screening. Second, the natural progression of the lesion from dysplastic mucosa to invasive disease takes on average 10 to 20 years, thereby allowing suitable time to detect the disease before it progresses to an incurable state. Finally, there is clear clinical evidence that early detection of colorectal cancer improves survival. The major approaches to screen for colon cancer are the fecal occult blood test (FOBT), flexible sigmoidoscopy, and colonoscopy.

Controlled prospective clinical trials performed in Minnesota, New York, Denmark, and the United Kingdom indicate that FOBT screening is relatively sensitive and reduces the rate of colorectal cancer mortality by 15 to 43%. [7] However, the FOBT technique has a low sensitivity for detecting precancerous polyps and cancers of the rectosigmoid or distal rectum. Since many other conditions can cause blood in the stool, FOBT is relatively nonspecific. Although no randomized trials have demonstrated the efficacy of flexible sigmoidoscopy for screening of colorectal cancer, case-control and cohort studies have shown a 60 to 85% reduction in the rate of mortality from distal colorectal cancers. Flexible sigmoidoscopy is well tolerated, can be performed relatively quickly, and does not require sedation. It is also highly accurate, with a high positive predictive value. The major drawback of flexible sigmoidoscopy is its inability to detect the 40% or more of large bowel neoplasms that reside beyond its reach; as a result, a full colonoscopy is recommended if flexible sigmoidoscopy reveals a polyp or tumor. Future research will likely identify biomarkers for early detection of colorectal cancer based on the growing understanding of the molecular genetics of the disease using evaluation of stool DNA and other pertinent molecular markers. Other screening options that may be considered but for which supportive clinical evidence is limited include a barium enema plus flexible sigmoidoscopy every 5 years or a colonoscopy every 10 years.

Since colonoscopy is a required part of any screening strategy, an alternative is to screen only with colonoscopy every 10 years in persons over the age of 50 years. Because screening colonoscopy is now covered by Medicare, it is becoming a standard recommendation that is supported by several professional organizations and by formal quantitative analyses, despite the absence of a randomized trial. Screening recommendations for individuals at high risk due to the presence of inflammatory bowel disease or because of a familial disposition are summarized in Table 200–4.

Chemoprevention

Several chemicals, drugs, and nutriceuticals are being evaluated for either primary or secondary prevention of adenomatous polyps and colorectal cancer. In a randomized trial, calcium provided a moderate 15% reduction for colorectal adenomas as early as 1 year after dietary supplementation. [8] The mechanism may be calcium's blockage of the tumor-promoting effects of bile acids. Chronic intake of aspirin and other nonsteroidal anti-inflammatory drugs is associated with a reduction in the relative risk for developing colorectal cancer, likely due to inhibition of the cyclooxygenase

Table 200–4 • SCREENING RECOMMENDATIONS FOR COLORECTAL CANCER

RISK	TEST	INTERVAL	AGE TO BEGIN, yr
Average	FOBT or sigmoidoscopy or colonoscopy	Annually Every 5 years Every 10 years	50
FAP	Sigmoidoscopy	Every 6–12 months	10–12
HNPCC	Colonoscopy	Every 2 years until age 40 and annually thereafter	25
Low familial risk for sporadic cancer	FOBT or sigmoidoscopy or colonoscopy	Annually Every 5 years Every 10 years	40
High familial risk for cancer	Colonoscopy	Every 5 years	40

FAP = familial adenomatous polyposis; FOBT = fecal occult blood testing; HNPCC = hereditary nonpolyposis colorectal cancer.

enzyme. Randomized trials of aspirin indicate a reduction in adenoma formation in the aspirin-treated group, but the preferred dose and duration of aspirin therapy remain uncertain. [9] Patients with familial adenomatous polyposis have a reduced burden of polyps when placed on chronic nonsteroidal anti-inflammatory or cyclooxygenase-2 inhibitor therapy, and prospective trials are evaluating the efficacy of these drugs to prevent polyps. Several cohort and case-control studies indicate that folic acid may prevent colon cancer by unknown mechanisms. Hormone replacement therapy is associated with lower risk for colorectal cancer, but estrogen plus progestin supplementation has thrombogenic side effects that outweigh this benefit. There are no convincing clinical data that supplementation with vitamins or antioxidants reduces the risk for colorectal cancer.

NEOPLASMS OF THE SMALL INTESTINE

Epidemiology and Scope of the Problem

The small intestine represents one of the largest portions of the gastrointestinal tract by tissue mass, but cancer of the small intestine accounts for a very small percentage of gastrointestinal malignancies (~2000 cases per year in the United States). The epithelial and stromal elements can give rise to transformed cells directly, or the small intestine can be the site of metastatic disease. Risk factors for cancer of the small intestine include Crohn's disease (Chapter 142) especially after surgical bypass; Gardner's syndrome, specifically periampullary

adenocarcinoma; and Peutz-Jeghers syndrome, which carries a 16-fold increased risk for small bowel cancer. Patients who have celiac disease or who are chronically immunocompromised have an increased risk of intestinal lymphoma. Immunoproliferative disease of the small intestine (Mediterranean abdominal lymphoma) occurs primarily in individuals of Middle Eastern origin but can also develop sporadically in others. The lower rate of adenocarcinomas in the small bowel as compared with the large intestine is not understood, but the higher rate of programmed cell death and cell proliferation in the small intestine may result in the shedding of abnormal cells before they become fully transformed.

Pathology

Benign lesions of the small intestine include adenomas, leiomyomas, lipomas, and angiomas. Routine upper gastrointestinal endoscopy can detect Brunner's gland adenomas, which are small, benign nodules in the duodenal mucosa that are caused by hyperplasia and hypertrophy of the submucosal duodenal glands. Malignancies of the small intestine include adenocarcinomas, carcinoids tumors, lymphomas, and leiomyosarcomas. Adenocarcinomas, which account for almost 50% of all small intestinal malignancies, occur most frequently in the duodenum. Carcinoid is the most common tumor of the distal small bowel. Lymphomas typically arise in the ileum.

Clinical Manifestations

Most benign small bowel neoplasms do not result in symptoms and are usually found incidentally at laparotomy or autopsy. Since the small intestinal contents are mostly liquid and the bowel wall is highly distensible, these lesions are unlikely to produce symptoms unless they become quite large. Symptoms can occur when the tumors grow large enough to cause intussusception or volvulus, either of which can lead to partial or complete small bowel obstruction.

The symptoms of cancer of the small intestine include abdominal pain (63%), vomiting (48%), weight loss (44%), and bleeding (23%). Patients with tumors distal to the duodenal bulb often present with symptoms similar to those of peptic ulcer disease, whereas lesions located in the periampullary region can cause obstructive jaundice. Carcinomas in the distal small bowel are usually asymptomatic until intestinal obstruction or gastrointestinal hemorrhage occurs.

Small carcinoid neoplasms (Chapter 245) are often asymptomatic, whereas larger carcinoids can obstruct the lumen or cause bleeding (Fig. 200–8). The carcinoid syndrome can develop after the lesion has metastasized to the liver. Peritoneal involvement is common.

Patients with small intestinal lymphoma can present with symptoms similar to those of adenocarcinomas of similar location. Fever and malabsorption are common (Chapter 195). Large sarcomas of the small bowel can perforate or cause massive hemorrhage.

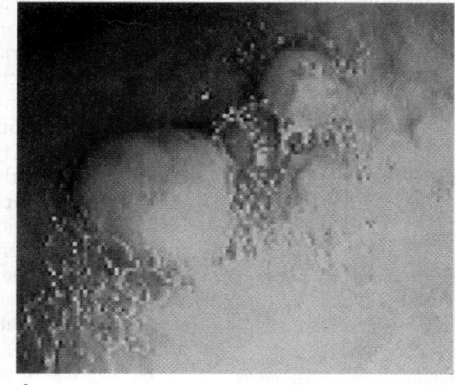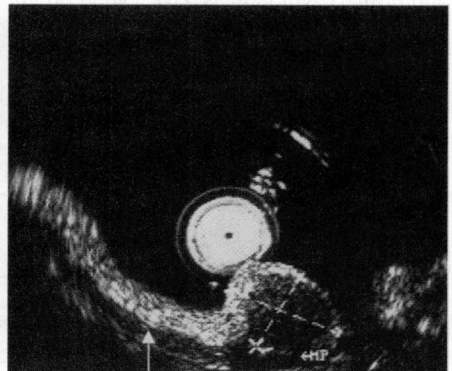

**FIGURE 200–8 • ** *A*, Carcinoid nodule in duodenum. *B*, Endoscopic ultrasonographic image shows that the lesion is confined to the submucosa, because the black stripe (arrow) representing the muscular layer is intact. Based on the endoscopic ultrasonographic findings, the lesion was safely resected endoscopically.

A   B

Diagnosis

Cancer of the small intestine is often associated with an unremarkable or nonspecific physical examination, but patients can also present with obstructive abdominal distention and evidence of augmented peristalsis proximal to the lesion. Patients with advanced cancers may present with cachexia, hepatomegaly, ascites, and jaundice. Advanced lymphomas are commonly accompanied by splenomegaly and/or peripheral lymphadenopathy.

Differential Diagnosis

The same symptoms and signs caused by benign and malignant small bowel tumors are actually more likely to be caused by other conditions. For example, bleeding can be due to peptic ulceration, a Meckel diverticulum, or vascular anomalies. Obstructive jaundice is more commonly caused by common duct stones, pancreatitis, or pancreatic cancer. Small bowel obstruction is most often caused by adhesions (especially in patients who have had prior abdominal surgery), internal hernias, volvulus, or intussusception.

Diagnostic Evaluation

Bleeding from neoplasms of the small intestine can lead to hypochromic, microcytic anemia. Hepatic metastases or periampullary tumors that obstruct the ampulla of Vater may lead to elevation of the alkaline phosphatase and bilirubin levels. Carcinoid syndrome is associated with increases in the plasma serotonin level and the urinary level of 5-hydroxyindoleacetic acid (Chapter 245). Mediterranean lymphoma is characterized by dysproteinemia in which heavy chain fragments of immunoglobulin A are present in the serum and urine (Chapter 196).

Upper gastrointestinal endoscopy, barium radiography, and selective nasoenteric intubation (enteroclysis) can locate tumors of the small bowel. Colonoscopy can visualize the mucosa of the terminal ileum. Endoscopic ultrasonography can determine the depth of invasion of a particular lesion. Abdominal ultrasonography and CT scanning can assess intra-abdominal and retroperitoneal spread.

Rx Treatment

> The primary treatment for neoplasms of the small bowel is surgical resection of the lesion. Whipple's procedure (pancreaticoduodenal resection) is used to treat carcinomas or large villous adenomas in the duodenum. Patients with localized lymphoma can be treated with surgical excision, but chemotherapy is necessary for more extensive disease. Adjuvant radiation therapy is recommended for large tumors or localized recurrences. As with any malignancy, patients with advanced tumors remain at risk for recurrence.

Prognosis

Survival rates and prognosis are good for benign tumors of the intestine if surgical resection is able to treat bleeding and obstruction. The prognosis for adenocarcinomas is poor. Leiomyosarcomas and primary lymphomas have a good prognosis if complete surgical resection is possible, but most such tumors cannot be completely resected. Long-term survival is possible even when hepatic carcinoid tumors involve the liver (Chapter 245).

Mediterranean abdominal lymphoma could be prevented if parasitic infestation could be eliminated. In patients with celiac disease (Chapter 141), early diagnosis and adoption of a gluten-free diet may reduce the incidence of cancer. Rates of periampullary cancers in the hereditary polyposis syndromes may decline with periodic monitoring.

1. Steinbach G, Lynch PM, Phillips RK, et al: The effect of celecoxib, a cyclooxygenase-2 inhibitor, in familial adenomatous polyposis. N Engl J Med 2000;342:1946–1952.
2. Schatzkin A, Lanza E, Corle D, et al: Lack of effect of a low-fat, high-fiber diet on the recurrence of colorectal adenomas. Polyp Prevention Trial Study Group. N Engl J Med 2000;342:1149–1155.
3. Alberts DS, Martinez ME, Roe DJ, et al: Lack of effect of a high-fiber cereal supplement on the recurrence of colorectal adenomas. Phoenix Colon Cancer Prevention Physicians' Network. N Engl J Med 2000;342:1156–1162.
4. Krook JE, Moertel CG, Gunderson LL, et al: Effective surgical adjuvant therapy for high-risk rectal carcinoma. N Engl J Med 1991;324:709–715.
5. O'Connell MJ, Mailliard JA, Kahn MJ, et al: Controlled trial of fluorouracil and low-dose leucovorin given for 6 months as postoperative adjuvant therapy for colon cancer. J Clin Oncol 1997;15:246–250.
6. Saltz LB, Cox JV, Blanke C, et al: Irinotecan plus fluorouracil and leucovorin for metastatic colorectal cancer. Irinotecan Study Group. N Engl J Med 2000;343:905–914.
7. Mandel JS, Bond JH, Church TR, et al: Reducing mortality from colorectal cancer by screening for fecal occult blood. Minnesota Colon Cancer Control Study. N Engl J Med 1993;328:1365–1371.
8. Baron JA, Beach M, Mandel JS, et al: Calcium supplements for the prevention of colorectal adenomas. Calcium Polyp Prevention Study Group. N Engl J Med 1999;340:101–107.
9. Baron JA, Cole BF, Sandler RS, et al: A randomized trial of aspirin to prevent colorectal adenomas. N Engl J Med 2003;348:891–899.

SUGGESTED READINGS

Bond JH: Polyp guideline: Diagnosis, treatment, and surveillance for patients with colorectal polyps. Am J Gastroenterol 2000;95:3053–3063. *A complete set of guidelines on management of polyps with citations to primary literature.*

Chung DC, Rustgi AK: The hereditary nonpolyposis colorectal cancer syndrome: Genetics and clinical implications. Ann Intern Med 2003;138:560–570. *Emphasizes role of counseling and genetic testing.*

Janne PA, Mayer RJ: Chemoprevention of colorectal cancer. N Engl J Med 2000;342:1960–1968. *An excellent review of the progress in the field of colon cancer chemoprevention.*

Pignone M, Rich M, Teutsch SM, et al: Screening for colorectal cancer in adults at average risk: A summary of the evidence for the U.S. Preventive Services Task Force. Ann Intern Med 2002;137:132–141. *The current U.S. consensus favors screening but does not prefer any single approach.*

Pignone M, Saha S, Hoerger T, et al: Cost-effectiveness analyses of colorectal cancer screening: A systematic review for the U.S. Preventive Services Task Force. Ann Intern Med 2002;137:96–104. *Screening is cost-effective.*

Walsh JM, Terdiman JP: Colorectal cancer screening: Scientific review. JAMA 2003;289:1288–1296. *Overview suggesting fecal occult blood testing, sigmoidoscopy, and colonoscopy are of reasonably similar effectiveness.*

Winawer SJ, Stewart ET, Zauber AG, et al: A comparison of colonoscopy and double-contrast barium enema for surveillance after polypectomy. National Polyp Study Work Group. N Engl J Med 2000;342:1766–1772. *Colonoscopy was a better screening test in these patients.*

201 PANCREATIC CANCER

Margaret Tempero
Randall Brand

The term *pancreatic cancer* usually refers to ductal adenocarcinomas, since more than 90% of pancreatic neoplasms are of ductal epithelial origin. Other pancreatic tumors include endocrine tumors (Chapter 140), carcinoid tumors (Chapter 245), lymphomas, and the rare cystic neoplasms, squamous cell carcinomas, giant cell carcinomas, carcinosarcomas, malignant fibrous histiocytomas, solid pseudopapillary neoplasms, sarcomas, and pancreaticoblastomas.

Epidemiology

In the United States, about 30,000 pancreatic neoplasms are diagnosed annually, and nearly the same number of persons die each year from cancer-related causes. Carcinoma of the pancreas is the fourth most common cause of cancer death in men and women. Worldwide, pancreatic cancer accounts for 2% of all malignancies. Its incidence is higher in developed than in developing countries, but there is less than a twofold variation in incidence worldwide. The 5-year survival rate for adenocarcinoma of the pancreas is less than 5%, with most patients dying within the first 2 years. The risk for developing a pancreatic carcinoma increases with age, with a mean age of onset in the seventh and eighth decades of life. The cancer is slightly more common in men than in women.

Pancreatic cancer is more common in African Americans, Maori New Zealanders, and Polynesians. Cigarette smoking, which is the most significant environmental risk factor, results in a 1.5- to 5.5-fold increased rate of pancreatic cancer. Other risk factors include increased body mass index, chronic pancreatitis (Chapter 145), high intake of animal fat, and prolonged contact with petroleum products and wood pulp.

Up to 10% of patients with pancreatic cancer have one or more first- or second-degree relatives with the disease. Recognized inherited syndromes include hereditary pancreatitis (Chapter 145), mutation of the *BRCA2* gene (Chapter 204), familial atypical multiple mole-melanoma syndrome and a p16 germline mutation, hereditary nonpolyposis colorectal cancer (Chapter 200), Peutz-Jeghers polyposis (Chapter 200), and ataxia-telangiectasia.

Intraductal papillary mucinous neoplasms occur more frequently in men and are usually located in the head of the pancreas. Other cystic neoplasms most commonly occur in young to middle-aged women and are located in the body or tail of the pancreas.

Pathobiology

Ductal adenocarcinoma and its variants are characterized by a dense, fibrotic reaction surrounding a compact mass of hard pancreatic tissue that can invade surrounding mesenteric vessels and involve perineuronal tissue and lymphatic channels or nodes. Since about 75% of pancreatic carcinomas are located in the head of the pancreas, the usual clinical presentations are related to invasion or compression of the bile or pancreatic ducts. The duodenum, stomach, and colon may be invaded or compressed. The three common types of cystic neoplasms are serous cystadenomas, mucinous cystic neoplasms, and intraductal papillary mucinous neoplasms. Serous cystadenomas are almost always benign, whereas the other lesions have a high risk of malignancy. Pancreatic cancers other than ductal adenocarcinoma, such as islet-cell tumors or lymphomas, tend to be softer and less fibrotic and thus tend to cause distortion rather than encasement or compression of adjacent structures.

Tumor-suppressor genes that are most frequently mutated in pancreatic adenocarcinoma are *p16* (95%), *p53* (50–75%), and *DPC4* (55%). K-*ras*, which is the most commonly activated oncogene, occurs in about 90% of pancreatic cancers. Pancreatic cancers are thought to progress from precursor duct lesions, termed *pancreatic intraepithelial neoplasms*, which have a typical histology and contain initial genetic alterations, to an invasive adenocarcinoma (Fig. 201–1).

Clinical Manifestations

Early symptoms include nonspecific abdominal discomfort, nausea, vomiting, sleeping difficulties, anorexia, and generalized malaise. Despite the historic perception that a mass in the head of the pancreas presents with painless jaundice, the more common presenting symptoms are epigastric pain, obstructive jaundice, and weight loss. Although these symptoms prompt evaluation of the pancreas and biliary tree, they occur late in the disease and are usually associated with advanced tumor at the time of diagnosis. The finding of a palpably distended, nontender gallbladder as a result of obstruction of the distal common bile duct by a pancreatic cancer has been called Courvoisier's sign. Patients may manifest superficial or deep venous thrombosis (Trousseau's syndrome; Chapter 188).

Diabetes or impaired glucose tolerance is observed in up to 80% of patients with pancreatic cancer at the time of their diagnosis. The diabetes is characterized by insulin resistance. The cause is unknown, but it may be a direct effect of the tumor because it can resolve after treatment. The most common laboratory abnormalities include anemia and elevation of serum levels of alkaline phosphatase, bilirubin, and aminotransferases. About 80% of patients have jaundice related to biliary obstruction.

Tumors of other histologic types arising in the pancreas may also have nonspecific symptoms. Patients with functioning islet cell tumors can present initially with symptoms related to the overproduction of peptides manufactured in the islets (Chapter 140). Cystic neoplasms generally remain asymptomatic until they become quite large, at which point patients can present with a palpable mass, abdominal pain, nausea, emesis, and weight loss. Obstruction of the common bile duct is less common than with ductal adenocarcinoma. Intraductal papillary mucinous tumors may cause symptoms of acute pancreatitis or pancreatic insufficiency owing to obstruction of the pancreatic duct.

Diagnosis

The differential diagnosis of pancreatic ductal cancer includes conditions that can manifest as a solid mass in the pancreas, especially

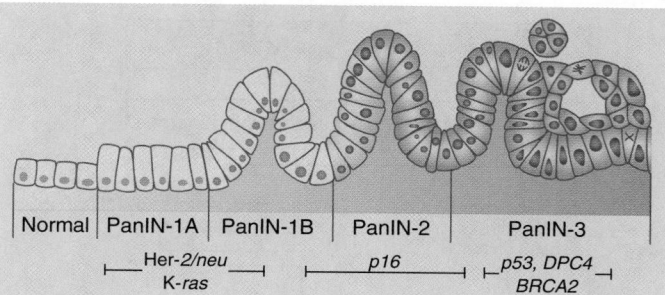

FIGURE 201–1 • Progression model for pancreatic cancer. Normal duct epithelium progresses to infiltrating cancer (left to right) through a series of histologically defined precursors (PanINs). The overexpression of Her-*2/neu* and point mutations in the K-*ras* gene occur early, inactivation of the *p16* gene occurs at an intermediate stage, and the inactivation of *p53*, *DPC4*, and *BRCA2* occur relatively late. (From Hruban RH, Goggins M, Parsons J, Kern SE: Progression model for pancreatic cancer. Clin Cancer Res 2000;6:2969–2972.)

acute or, more commonly, chronic pancreatitis (Chapter 145). Ampullary carcinomas or distal cholangiocarcinomas also manifest with biliary obstruction and jaundice (Chapter 158). It may be difficult to differentiate cystic pancreatic neoplasms from nonneoplastic pancreatic pseudocysts based on noninvasive imaging studies; a cystic neoplasm should always be considered in patients who present with isolated cystic lesions and have no risk factors for pancreatitis, such as alcoholism, abdominal trauma, or a prior history of acute or chronic pancreatitis or biliary tract disease.

For all patients with suspected pancreatic tumors, the preferred imaging study is a helical computed tomographic (CT) scan with thin cuts through the pancreas (Fig. 201–2). The CT scan provides important information about vascular involvement and metastases, and it is approximately 90% accurate in assessing resectability. Endoscopic ultrasonography may be useful in patients with equivocal findings on the CT scan. Patients with potentially resectable disease can proceed directly to surgery. Although a fine-needle aspiration biopsy can be performed under CT or endoscopic ultrasonographic guidance, most patients do not require a definitive preoperative diagnosis. Because of the desmoplastic reaction characteristic of pancreatic ductal adenocarcinoma, false-negative biopsy findings can occur. Patients who present with obstructive jaundice and cholangitis should have a temporary plastic stent placed in the bile duct via endoscopic retrograde cholangiopancreatography or by transhepatic cholangiography. Laparoscopy can identify patients who may have occult metastases in the peritoneum or surface of the liver. Patients whose CT scans indicate an unresectable tumor based on local extension or the presence of metastases should have a definitive diagnosis established by a fine-needle aspiration biopsy of the primary or metastatic site.

The clinical role for tumor markers (Chapter 189) is limited. CA-19-9, a sialylated Lewis[a] antigen associated with circulating mucins, is the most widely used marker for pancreatic disease; its sensitivity and specificity for the diagnosis of pancreas adenocarcinoma are dependent on the cutoff level selected. At the most commonly used cutoff level of 37 U/mL, sensitivity ranges from 81 to 85% and specificity ranges from 81 to 90%. However, this test is not a substitute for a histologic diagnosis, and it does not discriminate between resectable and unresectable disease. Nevertheless, CA-19-9 may be useful in monitoring the response to treatment.

The aforementioned radiographic studies also apply to other pancreatic tumors. Endoscopic ultrasonography with fine-needle aspiration can be useful in the evaluation of cystic lesions, often providing additional detail not seen by CT and permitting sampling of the cystic fluid for tumor marker levels, amylase content, viscosity, and cytology. For obvious reasons, it is important to clarify whether the lesion is a simple cyst, which would suggest a pseudocyst, or a cystic neoplasm.

Oncology

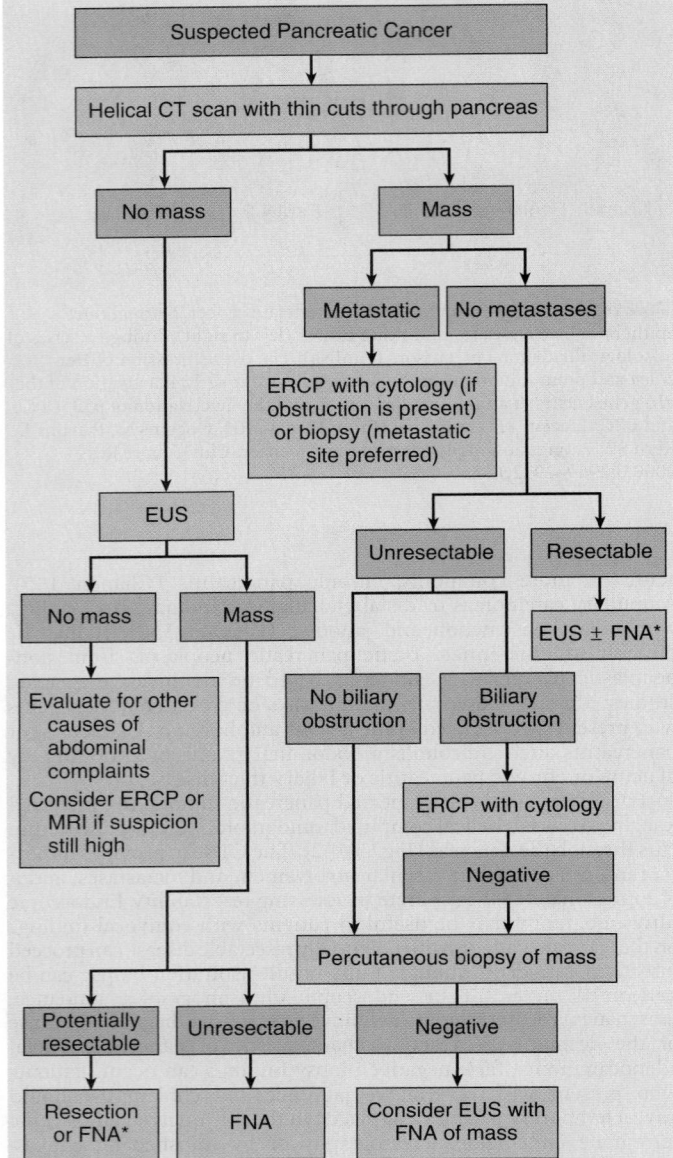

Suspected Pancreatic Cancer

Helical CT scan with thin cuts through pancreas

No mass | Mass

Metastatic | No metastases

ERCP with cytology (if obstruction is present) or biopsy (metastatic site preferred)

EUS

No mass | Mass

Unresectable | Resectable

EUS ± FNA*

Evaluate for other causes of abdominal complaints

Consider ERCP or MRI if suspicion still high

No biliary obstruction | Biliary obstruction

ERCP with cytology

Negative

Percutaneous biopsy of mass

Potentially resectable | Unresectable | Negative

Resection or FNA* | FNA | Consider EUS with FNA of mass

FIGURE 201–2 • Diagnostic algorithm for pancreatic cancer. *Intraoperative fine-needle aspiration (FNA) if found inoperable during surgery. CT = computed tomographic scan; ERCP = endoscopic retrograde cholangiopancreatography; EUS = endoscopic ultrasonography; MRI = magnetic resonance imaging.

Rx Treatment and Prognosis

In the absence of metastatic disease, surgical resection is the initial treatment of choice for all pancreatic adenocarcinomas. The procedure should be performed in centers that have a high volume of pancreatectomies, since surgical outcomes are improved with more volume and experience. For pancreatic ductal cancers, preoperative chemotherapy and radiation can be considered, although this approach has not yet become the standard of care.

Tumors are considered resectable if there is a clear fat plane around the celiac and superior mesenteric arteries and if the mesenteric and portal veins are patent. After successful resection, 2 years of adjuvant chemotherapy using 5-flourouracil (5-FU) has commonly been used, although gemcitabine is being studied as an alternative; radiation may not confer any added value beyond 5-FU alone.[1] In general, successful resection followed by adjuvant therapy results in a 2-year survival rate of approximately 20%.

Surgery can also have an important palliative role. Those patients who are explored but are found not to be resectable may benefit

from a biliary or gastric bypass procedure depending on the clinical setting. In addition, intraoperative chemical splanchnicectomy can provide protracted pain control.

Patients with locally unresectable disease are usually managed with a combination of chemotherapy and radiation followed by additional chemotherapy. The most commonly used approach is 5-FU combined with radiotherapy, but gemcitabine is also being studied. The median survival time for these patients is 10 to 12 months.

For patients with metastatic disease, gemcitabine is preferable to 5-FU.[2] The median survival time for patients with metastatic disease treated with single-agent chemotherapy is 5 to 6 months. For patients with advanced disease, optimal management of pain and of local complications is critical. Biliary obstruction can be managed surgically or with placement of a plastic or expandable metal stent. Narcotic analgesics (Chapter 29) and palliative care (Chapter 3) are cornerstones of therapy.

Most patients with a cystic neoplasm should be considered for surgical resection. The long-term survival rate following resection of malignant pancreatic cystic neoplasms exceeds 70%, and adjuvant therapy is currently not recommended.

Future Directions

Future programs for pancreatic adenocarcinoma will focus on identifying individuals at high risk, developing strategies for early detection, and optimizing treatment. Drugs that interact with tyrosine kinase receptors, downstream signaling events, or tumor-associated angiogenesis and invasion are under active investigation.

Grade A

1. Neoptolemos JP, Dunn JA, Stocken DD, et al: Adjuvant chemoradiotherapy and chemotherapy in resectable pancreatic cancer: A randomised controlled trial. Lancet 2001;358:1576–1585.
2. Burris H, Moore M, Anderson J, et al: Improvements in survival and clinical benefit with gemcitabine as first-line therapy for patients with advanced pancreas cancer: A randomized trial. J Clin Oncol 1997;15:2403–2413.

SUGGESTED READINGS

DiMagno EP, Reber HA, Tempero MA: AGA technical review on the epidemiology, diagnosis, and treatment of pancreatic ductal adenocarcinoma. Gastroenterology 1999;117:1464–1484. *Official recommendations of the American Gastroenterological Association Clinical Practice and Practice Economics Committee.*

Neoptolemos JP, Cunningham D, Friess H, et al: Adjuvant therapy in pancreatic cancer: Historical and current perspectives. Ann Oncol 2003;14:675–692. *Overview of chemotherapeutic options.*

Rocha Lima CM, Centeno B: Update on pancreatic cancer. Curr Opin Oncol 2002;14: 424–430. *A comprehensive review.*

202 HEPATIC TUMORS

Michael Fallon

Tumors of the liver are relatively uncommon but are being increasingly recognized, often incidentally, owing to the frequent use of abdominal radiologic imaging techniques on which they appear as space-occupying lesions. The appropriate diagnostic possibilities are best considered by determining the clinical setting in which the tumor is discovered (Table 202–1). Benign tumors are frequently found incidentally or occur with local symptoms due to mass effect and may be influenced by gender and the use of oral contraceptives. Primary malignant tumors of the liver usually occur in the setting of known chronic liver disease and may be associated with a deterioration in hepatic function. Metastatic liver tumors are most frequently found in patients who have documented primary extrahepatic tumors in the gastrointestinal tract, lung, or breast.

BENIGN HEPATIC TUMORS

HEMANGIOMA. Hemangiomas, which consist of ectatic dilated vascular spaces that usually measure less than 4 cm in diameter, are the most common benign hepatic tumors and do not have malignant potential. Autopsy studies show a prevalence of 2 to 7% in the general

Table 202–1 • SELECTED FEATURES OF BENIGN AND MALIGNANT HEPATIC TUMORS

TUMOR	PATIENTS/RISK FACTORS	DIAGNOSIS	THERAPY
BENIGN			
Hemangioma	Healthy, incidental finding	Red blood cell–labeled scan	Observe: resect if symptoms
Adenoma	Young females on oral contraceptives	US/CT; sulfur-colloid scan: no uptake in lesion	Stop oral contraceptives: consider resection
Focal nodular hyperplasia	Middle-aged females, ± oral contraceptives	US/CT; sulfur-colloid scan: increased uptake in 60%	Stop oral contraceptives: observation
Focal fatty infiltration	Obesity, diabetes, corticosteroids, alcohol, weight changes, total parenteral nutrition	US/CT; sulfur-colloid scan: homogeneous uptake	Observation
MALIGNANT			
Hepatocellular carcinoma	Cirrhosis, chronic viral hepatitis	US/three-phase CT; α-fetoprotein; biopsy	Resection, local ablation, liver transplantation
Fibrolamellar variant	Young, healthy, no risk factors	As above	As above
Cholangiocarcinoma	Sclerosing cholangitis, oriental cholangiopathies	US/CT/cholangiogram; carcinoembryonic antigen/ CA 19-9	Resection, biliary drainage, chemotherapy/ radiation
Metastatic	Extrahepatic malignancy (gastrointestinal, breast, lung)	US/CT, biopsy	Resection (colon cancer); treat underlying tumor
Angiosarcoma	Vinyl chloride, Thorotrast, arsenic exposure	US/CT/angiogram	Resection

CT = computed tomography; US = ultrasonography.

population. Because of hormonal factors, the prevalence is somewhat higher in female patients, in whom the lesions may also be larger. Most patients with hepatic hemangiomas are asymptomatic, and the tumors are usually discovered by chance. When tumors are symptomatic, abdominal pain may occur due to bleeding or thrombosis within the lesion or to stretching of Glisson's capsule. Hemoperitoneum can occur if a hemangioma near the surface of the liver ruptures, but this complication is so uncommon that prophylactic resection is not indicated. Rarely, disseminated intravascular coagulation (Chapter 179) with hypofibrinogenemia and thrombocytopenia (Kasabach-Merritt syndrome) is found in patients with large lesions. Imaging techniques can demonstrate characteristic findings that indicate a space-occupying lesion of the liver is a hepatic hemangioma: ultrasonography (US) generally reveals a well-circumscribed hyperechoic lesion; dynamic computed tomography (CT) with contrast medium enhancement shows peripheral enhancement early after contrast agent administration and homogeneous uptake on later images; and magnetic resonance imaging (MRI) shows a homogeneous high-signal intensity lesion on T2-weighted images. However, technetium-99 m–labeled human red cell scanning is the most specific test in lesions of more than 1.5 cm in diameter. Specific therapy is usually not necessary; in patients with symptoms or complications, surgical resection and/or hepatic artery ligation is recommended.

HEPATIC ADENOMA. Hepatic adenomas arise in normal livers from proliferation of normal-appearing hepatocytes that are arranged in cords or plates devoid of portal tracts. The estimated incidence is 4 per 1000. There is a strong association between the development of adenomas and the use of oral contraceptives, and as many as 90% of these lesions are found in women of reproductive age during estrogen use. Uncommonly, adenomas have been reported in males using anabolic steroids and in patients with hemosiderosis or type I glycogen storage disease. The tumors are of variable size, usually single, and usually located in the right lobe. Patients frequently present with right upper quadrant fullness or pain, and the lesions are less commonly discovered incidentally. Patients may also present with severe abdominal pain and hypovolemic shock when the tumor ruptures and causes hemoperitoneum. This complication is particularly common during pregnancy; it may also be more common in lesions larger than 5 cm in diameter and may have a high morbidity and mortality. Malignant transformation appears to be less common than previously thought, especially if stimulating factors are eliminated. The diagnosis should be suspected in females of child-bearing age using oral contraceptives. A combination of imaging modalities is frequently helpful: US often shows a hyperechoic lesion, CT and MRI demonstrate a solid tumor, occasionally with areas of hemorrhage or necrosis, and sulfur colloid scanning demonstrates a filling defect due to

the absence of Kupffer cells within the tumor. If the clinical and radiologic picture is consistent with hepatic adenoma, oral contraceptives should be discontinued and alternative birth control measures instituted to prevent pregnancy. Surgical resection should be considered for subcapsular and larger lesions because of their increased risk of rupture, when pregnancy is being contemplated, and when diagnostic uncertainty exists. In other patients, monitoring with serial imaging studies over a period of 6 to 12 months may be justified to determine whether the tumor is resolving before consideration of resection.

FOCAL NODULAR HYPERPLASIA. Focal nodular hyperplasia is an uncommon hepatic pseudotumor thought to arise from hamartomatous change within the liver. Classically, there is a central scar with radiating bands of fibrosis surrounded by plates of hepatocytes associated with vessels and bile ducts. The lesion is more common in female patients and usually is found incidentally between the ages of 20 and 50 years. There is no consistent association with the use of oral contraceptives, and it is unclear whether estrogens have a trophic effect on focal nodular hyperplasia. The lesions are usually solitary, measure less than 5 cm, and are often located in the right hepatic lobe. Symptoms are reported by 10% of patients and usually consist of abdominal pain and/or right upper quadrant mass. Hemoperitoneum is rare. US, CT, and MRI detect focal nodular hyperplasia and may be diagnostic when the characteristic central scar is observed. Sulfur colloid scan demonstrates increased uptake in Kupffer cells in 60% of focal nodular hyperplasia lesions and thus may allow distinction from adenoma. Because focal nodular hyperplasia appears to lack malignant potential, asymptomatic lesions may be observed, with surgical intervention reserved for symptomatic or enlarging lesions or when there is diagnostic uncertainty.

BENIGN CYSTIC MASSES. Cystic lesions of the liver may be congenital or acquired. Most hepatic cysts are solitary and idiopathic, but multiple cysts also can occur in adulthood as part of an autosomal dominant disorder involving the liver and kidney. Idiopathic liver cysts are usually asymptomatic but uncommonly may cause right upper quadrant pain, abdominal fullness, and distention. Rare complications include spontaneous bleeding, rupture, and infection. Symptoms and complications are more commonly observed in inherited polycystic syndromes.

OTHER BENIGN TUMORS. A number of other uncommon benign lesions of the liver reported in adults arise from the biliary epithelium (adenomas), vascular endothelium (hemangioendothelioma, lymphangiomas), and mesenchymal cells (lipomas, leiomyomas). Other lesions that have been recognized on radiologic imaging and that should be distinguished from true tumors in the liver include focal fatty infiltration and inflammatory pseudotumors.

Oncology

MALIGNANT HEPATIC TUMORS

HEPATOCELLULAR CARCINOMA

Definition

Hepatocellular carcinoma (HCC) is an epithelial tumor arising from malignant transformation of the hepatocyte. It is the most common primary malignancy of the liver and is observed characteristically as a complication of chronic liver disease and cirrhosis, especially related to chronic viral infection with hepatitis B virus (HBV) and hepatitis C virus (HCV; Chapter 152). Because early detection of HCC is difficult, the prognosis remains poor.

Epidemiology

HCC is a leading cause of death from cancer throughout the world and is especially common in sub-Saharan Africa, Southeast Asia, Japan, and Korea, where its incidence (up to 500/100,000 per year) correlates with the prevalence of chronic HBV infection. In the United States, HCC is infrequent (annual incidence of 1 to 2 cases per 100,000), but the incidence is increasing predominately because of an increase in chronic liver disease from HCV infection. Other important causes of liver disease associated with HCC include alcohol consumption (Chapter 155), genetic hemochromatosis (Chapter 225), and HBV infection. HCC occurs predominantly in males with a male:female ratio 2 to 4:1. The risk increases with age, and in Western countries HCC tends to appear in the fifth to seventh decades of life. In sub-Saharan Africa and Southeast Asia, HCC appears earlier and is likely related to vertical transmission of HBV infection. A rare fibrolamellar variant of HCC occurs in young patients without underlying liver disease and has a favorable prognosis because it often can be successfully resected.

Pathogenesis

HCC usually arises in cirrhotic livers but may also develop rarely in patients without liver disease. The risk of HCC is highest in adult liver disease caused by HBV infection, HCV infection, and hemochromatosis. Cirrhosis results in cell proliferation and increased DNA synthesis in regenerating nodules; these processes may lead to aberrant rearrangements and altered regulatory protein function. Chronic HBV infection may predispose to HCC by integration of HBV DNA at sites within the human genome responsible for the control of the cell cycle, and thus lead to disruption of tumor suppressor genes or activation of oncogenes. The HBV gene product may also result in transactivation of oncogenes. Environmental factors are implicated in the development of HCC. The best understood is the ingestion of aflatoxins (especially aflatoxin B1) elaborated by *Aspergillus* molds, which frequently contaminate peanuts and grains. These toxins cause a mutation that impairs function of the *p53* tumor suppressor gene. Other factors potentially important in the development of HCC include Thorotrast, a radionuclide used in angiographic procedures during the 1930s and 1940s, anabolic steroids, estrogens, and parasitic infection with *Schistosoma* (Chapter 402), *Clonorchis* (Chapter 403), *Echinococcus* (Chapter 403), and *Opisthorchis* (Chapter 403).

Clinical Manifestations

Classically, HCC presents as abdominal pain, a palpable abdominal mass, and/or constitutional symptoms in patients with cirrhosis. More recently, tumors have been increasingly discovered during screening or incidentally during radiologic studies. Other symptoms and signs include fever, early satiety, anorexia, hepatomegaly, ascites, lower extremity edema, jaundice, and a hepatic arterial bruit or friction rub. Many signs and symptoms may be confused with progression of cirrhosis, and the diagnosis must be considered in cirrhotics with sudden decompensation or in those who develop bloody ascites. HCC can also cause obstructive jaundice as a result of invasion or compression of the biliary tract, or it may cause bleeding into the bile ducts. HCC may also invade vascular structures and cause thrombosis of the portal or hepatic veins. Associated paraneoplastic syndromes include erythrocytosis (Chapter 176), thrombocytosis (Chapter 180), hypoglycemia (Chapter 243), hypercholesterolemia (Chapter 211), hypercalcemia

(Chapter 260), dysfibrinogenemia (Chapter 178), cryofibrinogenemia (Chapter 196), porphyria cutanea tarda (Chapter 223), and hypertrophic osteoarthropathy (Chapter 188). The tumor preferentially metastasizes to regional lymph nodes and lung.

Diagnosis

Routine laboratory studies usually reflect abnormalities associated with the underlying chronic liver disease. The alkaline phosphatase may increase with tumor infiltration. α-Fetoprotein (AFP), an α_1-globulin produced in fetal, regenerating, and malignant hepatocytes, is a marker used in screening for HCC and for suggesting the diagnosis. It is elevated in 60 to 80% of patients, and the level is dependent, in part, on the size of the tumor. Levels of more than 400 to 500 ng/mL are virtually diagnostic when associated with a liver mass in a cirrhotic patient. Values greater than 20 ng/mL in cirrhosis have a sensitivity of 39 to 64% and a specificity of 64 to 91% for the presence of HCC. AFP levels may also increase during hepatic regeneration associated with inflammation, so the specificity of the test for the presence of tumor is lower in active hepatitis. Other proposed tumor markers are des-γ-carboxy prothrombin, plasma urokinase-like plasminogen activator, α-L-fucosidase, and transcobalamin I (patients with fibrolamellar variant). Imaging techniques that aid in the diagnosis include US, CT (especially three-phase tomography), and MRI. US generally shows a hypoechoic lesion. Dynamic CT with contrast characteristically demonstrates early diffuse enhancement of the lesion with rapid de-enhancement and a subsequent hypodense appearance relative to the surrounding parenchyma. T1-weighted MR images may reveal high, low, or isointense signals relative to surrounding parenchyma; the characteristic T2-weighted finding is a mosaic pattern of signal intensity within the lesion. Percutaneous fine-needle biopsy may not be needed to confirm the diagnosis in cirrhotic patients with an elevated AFP and a typical liver mass, but tissue diagnosis is reasonable in those without elevated tumor markers or when diagnostic uncertainty is present.

Prevention and Screening

Prevention of HCC has become an important focus, particularly related to viral liver disease, based on the difficulty in eradicating HCC once established. Studies supporting the merits of preventive strategies include data from a neonatal vaccination program for hepatitis B in Taiwan, which resulted in a significant reduction in the rate of childhood HCC.[1] In addition, therapy of hepatitis C cirrhosis with interferon has been shown to decrease the risk for HCC even if virologic clearance is not achieved.[2] These results will likely lead to an expansion of preventive strategies over the next 3 to 5 years. Screening and surveillance for HCC have also been attempted in patients with cirrhosis in the hopes of detecting tumors at earlier and more treatable stages. Studies suggest that tumors of smaller size may be detected by surveillance and that the yield and efficacy of such strategies appear to be highest in areas with an increased prevalence of chronic viral liver disease. However, no controlled screening trials have been performed in the United States, and there is no consensus as to an appropriate surveillance schedule. Surveillance using US and AFP determinations at 6-month intervals is frequently used and is reasonable in high-risk patients for whom treatments are available and would be considered for use if a lesion were discovered.

Rx Treatment

The prognosis of HCC is poor and is related to tumor size, residual liver function, and the presence of extrahepatic disease. For symptomatic unresectable disease, survival is less than 5% at 2 years. Treatment options include resection, transplantation, hepatic arterial chemoembolization, intratumor injection of ethanol, and radiofrequency ablation. Systemic chemotherapy and radiation therapy are of limited value. The choice of a particular therapy must be individualized because no single therapy has emerged as a treatment of choice. Liver transplantation is reserved for patients with small tumors, no extrahepatic disease, and poor liver reserve.

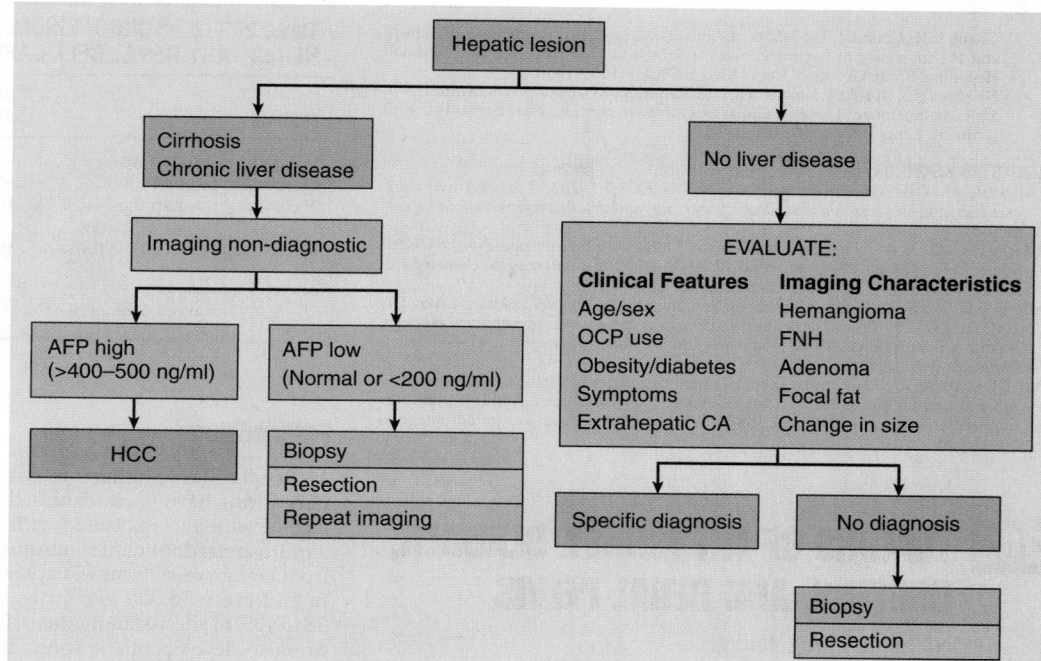

FIGURE 202–1 • Diagnostic approach to space-occupying lesions of the liver. AFP = α-fetoprotein; CA = cancer; FNH = focal nodular hyperplasia; HCC = hepatocellular carcinoma; OCP = oral contraceptives.

ANGIOSARCOMA

Angiosarcoma is an extremely rare malignant endothelial tumor of the liver. It has been associated with exposure to vinyl chloride, Thorotrast, and arsenic compounds. The tumor usually manifests as abdominal pain and a palpable right upper quadrant mass, but progressive liver failure and acute hemoperitoneum have been described. Metastases, usually to the lungs and skeleton, are common at diagnosis. US and CT frequently show markedly heterogeneous single or multiple liver masses, which may be diagnostic in the proper clinical setting. Angiography shows a characteristic blush and persistence of peripheral enhancement with a central hypovascular area. Treatment consists of surgical resection, which is difficult to achieve owing to the advanced stage of the tumor at the time of diagnosis. Radiation therapy and chemotherapy have not been effective. Most patients die within 6 months of diagnosis.

OTHER PRIMARY MALIGNANT TUMORS OF THE LIVER

Other rare hepatic tumors in the adult liver include squamous cell carcinoma (usually arising in congenital cysts), embryonal sarcoma, fibrosarcoma, leiomyosarcoma, liposarcoma, biliary cystadenocarcinoma, mucoepidermoid carcinoma, malignant rhabdoid tumor, and carcinosarcomas. These tumors cause symptoms and signs similar to the more common hepatic malignant neoplasms. Diagnosis is usually made by needle biopsy during evaluation or at the time of resection.

METASTATIC TUMORS

Metastatic tumors are the most common malignant neoplasms of the liver in the United States. The most frequent primary tumors to metastasize to the liver include those originating in the gastrointestinal tract (colon, stomach, pancreas, esophagus, extrahepatic cholangiocarcinoma), lung, and breast. Other solid tumors that metastasize to the liver include neuroendocrine tumors, bladder cancer, melanoma, and renal cell carcinoma. The liver is also an extranodal site of involvement for lymphomas and malignant histiocytosis.

Metastatic tumors usually occur in the setting of known extrahepatic malignancy, and the diagnosis is often suspected before a liver lesion is found. Metastatic tumors may occasionally present as diffuse involvement and cause rapidly progressive hepatic dysfunction and diagnostic uncertainty. Prognosis is poor once tumor metastases have been found, with a mean survival after diagnosis of 6 months. Selected patients may be surgical candidates for resection of isolated metastases, particularly those from colorectal adenocarcinoma. Patients who have unresectable disease may be offered systemic chemotherapy with the specific protocol depending on the origin of the primary tumor.

APPROACH TO SPACE-OCCUPYING LESIONS OF THE LIVER

The diagnostic approach to defining space-occupying lesions of the liver is guided by the clinical setting in which a lesion is identified and by the radiologic characteristics of the lesion (Fig. 202–1; see Table 202–1). In some cases, a period of observation may be combined with repeat imaging at 12- to 16-week intervals to identify whether a lesion is enlarging before considering invasive studies. Biopsy and/or resection are indicated when diagnostic uncertainty, complications, or malignant potential are present.

Once a liver lesion is identified, a primary consideration is whether the patient has underlying cirrhosis or chronic liver disease, particularly related to chronic viral infection, genetic hemochromatosis, or alcohol consumption. If clinical, biochemical, or radiologic studies confirm the presence of cirrhosis and the lesion does not have diagnostic imaging features of a benign process, then the likelihood of HCC is increased. A markedly elevated serum AFP level (>400 to 500 ng/mL) in this setting is essentially diagnostic for HCC, and efforts are focused on the appropriate therapy based on the particular clinical situation of the patient. If the AFP is not diagnostic, then biopsy, resection, or a period of observation with repeat imaging (particularly for small or difficult to reach lesions) is needed.

If there is no evidence of underlying chronic liver disease, then clinical features such as the age and sex of the patient, the presence of symptoms, the use of oral contraceptives, the presence of obesity or diabetes, and a history of extrahepatic malignancy can focus diagnostic considerations. Specific imaging characteristics and/or additional radiologic studies may provide a firm diagnosis of benign lesions such as hemangioma, focal nodular hyperplasia, focal fatty infiltration, and adenoma, as well as define the need for resection. If radiologic studies are nondiagnostic, if the lesion enlarges, if progressive symptoms are present, or if adenoma or metastatic disease is the primary consideration, then biopsy or resection is appropriate.

1. Chang MH, Chen CJ, Lai MS, et al: Universal hepatitis B vaccination in Taiwan and the incidence of hepatocellular carcinoma in children. Taiwan Childhood Hepatoma Study Group. N Engl J Med 1997;336:1855-1859.
2. Nishiguchi S, Kuroki T, Nakatani S, et al: Randomised trial of effects of interferon-alpha on incidence of hepatocellular carcinoma in chronic active hepatitis C with cirrhosis. Lancet 1995;346:1051-1055.

SUGGESTED READINGS
DiBisceglie AM (ed): Liver tumors. Clin Liver Dis 2001;5:1–283. *A focused, well referenced series of chapters that is an ideal reference for more detailed information on hepatic tumors.*
El-Serag HB, Mason AC: The rising incidence of hepatocellular carcinoma in the United States. N Engl J Med 1999;340:745–750. *An important evaluation of the changing epidemiology of HCC in the United States over the last 20 years.*
Federle MP, Brancatelli G: Imaging of benign hepatic masses. Semin Liver Dis 2001;21:237–249. *Provides a detailed and practical approach to the evaluation of benign hepatic tumors with an emphasis on differentiation from malignant lesions and current radiologic techniques.*
Kerr DJ, McArdle CS, Ledermann J, et al: Intrahepatic arterial versus intravenous fluorouracil and folinic acid for colorectal cancer liver metastases: A multicentre randomised trial. Lancet 2003;361:368–373. *Demonstrates there was no advantage to intrahepatic therapy.*

203 TUMORS OF THE KIDNEY, BLADDER, URETERS, AND RENAL PELVIS

Nicholas J. Vogelzang

RENAL CELL CARCINOMA

Definition

Cancers arising in the kidney are a heterogeneous group of renal parenchymal neoplasms. Classic renal cell carcinoma, commonly called *clear cell carcinoma* or *hypernephroma*, represents approximately 80% of adult kidney cancers. The remaining kidney cancers are of other histologic subtypes (Table 203–1) or arise from the transitional epithelium lining the renal collecting ducts, pelvis, and the ureters (see Cancer of the Renal Pelvis and Ureters).

Epidemiology

Approximately 30,000 new renal cell cancers are diagnosed annually, and about 12,000 persons die of this cancer each year. The incidence of renal cell carcinoma has been increasing steadily over the past few decades, partially because of early detection owing to the increased use of computed tomography (CT) scans. The male-to-female ratio is about 2 to 3 : 1, and the incidence is highest in African Americans and lowest in Asians/Pacific Islanders. Other than the genetic predispositions in hereditary cases, the risk factors for sporadic renal cell carcinoma are not well characterized. Obesity, hypertension, cigarette smoking, and the use of diuretics and analgesics have been linked to the development of renal cell carcinoma, and a diet high in fruit and low in fat is reported to be protective. Renal cell carcinoma appears to be more common in patients with certain preexisting renal conditions, such as polycystic disease (Chapter 127), horseshoe kidney, and renal failure on hemodialysis.

Table 203–1 • CLASSIFICATION OF ADULT KIDNEY CANCERS

HISTOLOGY	PERCENT OF CASES
Clear cell renal cell carcinoma	75-80%
Papillary renal cell carcinoma	10%
Chromophobic renal carcinoma	5%
Renal oncocytoma	3%
Collecting duct carcinoma	2%
Transitional cell carcinoma of the ureters and renal pelvis	5%

Modified from Zambrano NR, Lubensky IA, Merino MY, et al: Histopathology and molecular genetics of renal tumors: Toward unification of a classification system. J Urol 1999;162:1246–1258.

Table 203–2 • CHROMOSOMAL ABNORMALITIES IN HEREDITARY RENAL CELL CARCINOMA

DISEASE	CHROMOSOMAL ABNORMALITY	AFFECTED GENE
von Hippel-Lindau disease	−3p	VHL
Hereditary papillary RCC	+7q	c-met
Hereditary nonpapillary RCC	t(3;6), t(3;8), t(3;11)	Not identified
Hereditary renal oncocytoma	t(5;11), t(9;11), −1, −Y,	Birt-Hogg-Dube (BHD)

RCC = renal cell carcinoma.

Pathobiology

Renal cell carcinoma is most commonly sporadic, but four hereditary forms have been identified (Table 203–2), the best characterized of which is associated with von Hippel-Lindau (VHL) disease, an autosomal dominant syndrome in which renal cell carcinoma arises from benign renal cysts (Chapters 127 and 459). VHL disease occurs in 1 of every 36,000 live births, and renal cell carcinoma occurs in 28 to 45% of affected individuals. Benign cystic VHL-associated tumors can also develop in the spine, brain, eye, pancreas, inner ear, and adrenal gland. Certain VHL kindreds also develop pheochromocytomas (Chapter 241).

The VHL gene, mapped to chromosome 3, contains three exons. Wild-type VHL protein is a ubiquitin ligase that causes the degradation of hypoxia-inducible factor-α (HIF-α), a transcription factor that regulates a number of genes involved in angiogenesis and cell growth, such as vascular endothelial growth factor (VEGF), Glut-1, and platelet-derived growth factor. Mutations in the VHL gene variably affect the ability of the protein to form the repressive complex, resulting in an overproduction of HIF-α and downstream upregulation of VEGF and other proteins that contribute to the neoangiogenesis of renal cell carcinoma. About 70% of sporadic clear cell renal cell carcinoma cases contain VHL mutations. Other familial forms of renal cell carcinoma include hereditary papillary and nonpapillary renal cell carcinoma as well as hereditary renal oncocytoma.

Besides the chromosomal abnormalities seen in hereditary tumors, several other genetic alterations have been described in sporadic renal cell carcinoma cases, such as the activation of *ras* and *myc* oncogenes as well as the overexpression of *bcl*-2 antiapoptotic protein. In addition, increased levels of epidermal growth factor and transforming growth factor-α (TGF-α) are found in renal cell carcinomas.

Virtually all renal cell carcinomas arise from the renal tubular epithelium, and they are classified into five histologic types. Approximately 80% are clear cell types arising from the proximal renal tubule; they have vacuolated and empty-appearing cytoplasm owing to the intracellular accumulation of glycogen and lipids. Papillary renal carcinoma (10% of all kidney cancers) is characterized microscopically by chromophilic cytoplasm with overlapping and centrally located small nuclei, tending to manifest with small, multifocal lesions and associated with a favorable prognosis when localized. Chromophobic renal cell carcinoma originates from the cortical collecting ducts, and the tumor, which tends to be low grade and indolent, is composed of large polygonal cells with pale reticular cytoplasm. The rare collecting duct tumors (Bellini's duct tumors) arise from the medullary collecting duct and usually have an aggressive course; this tumor is relatively frequent among young African Americans with sickle cell trait (Chapter 171). Renal oncocytoma is a low-grade tumor and rarely metastasizes. The sarcomatoid variant of clear cell carcinoma usually has high-grade histology and a median survival of only 6.6 months compared with a 19-month median survival for nonsarcomatous renal carcinoma.

Clinical Manifestations

Renal cell carcinoma has been called the "internist tumor" because of its insidious course and various presenting symptoms. The classic triad of flank pain, abdominal mass, and hematuria occur in less than 10% of patients. Instead, low-grade anemia, hematuria, and pain are among the most common presenting symptoms (Table 203–3). Patients may also complain of nonspecific constitutional symptoms, such as weight loss, fatigue, and anorexia. Because of the increased use of radiographic studies, renal cell carcinoma tumors are often found incidentally during evaluations for other medical conditions. Approximately 45% of patients with renal carcinoma present with localized tumors and 25% with locally advanced disease. About 30% of patients have distant metastases at diagnosis. The most common metastatic sites are lung, bone, soft tissue, liver, and central nervous system.

Patients with renal cell carcinoma sometimes develop paraneoplastic syndromes, especially hypercalcemia owing to the secretion of parathyroid hormone–related peptide by the tumor (Chapter 187). Other renal cell carcinoma–associated syndromes include erythrocytosis (from ectopic erythropoietin production), hypertension, and amyloidosis. Stauffer's syndrome (leukocytosis and hepatic dysfunction without tumor involvement of the liver) is a rare, unique syndrome that usually resolves after nephrectomy.

Diagnosis

Ultrasonography and CT scanning can often distinguish the benign lesions, such as renal cysts and angiomas, from malignant tumors and eliminate the need for biopsy. CT scans are also fairly accurate in determining the regional lymph node involvement. Magnetic resonance imaging (MRI), which provides excellent images of the primary tumor and its vasculature, is used for preoperative planning and to evaluate possible vena cava thrombosis. For all patients with suspected metastatic diseases, the evaluation should include routine chemistry panels, a complete blood cell count, a bone scan, and a CT scan of the chest, abdomen, and pelvis. Positron-emission tomography is not routinely used.

The TNM (tumor, node, metastasis) staging system (Table 203–4) is the standard classification scheme. An alternative staging system (Table 203–5) identifies five distinct risk groups based on TNM staging, tumor grade, and the patient's performance status (Fig. 203–1). Group 1 patients closely resemble the asymptomatic TNM stage I patients and have an excellent long-term survival with surgical intervention alone. Group 2 is heterogeneous, with one or more poor prognostic factors, but no metastases. Groups 3, 4, and 5 have metastatic disease with different tumor grades and performance statuses.

Table 203–3 • PRESENTING SYMPTOMS AND SIGNS OF RENAL CELL CARCINOMA

SYMPTOMS AND SIGNS	PERCENT OF PATIENTS
Classic triad	9%
Hematuria	59%
Flank or abdominal mass	45%
Pain	41%
Fatigue	33%
Weight loss	28%
Anemia	21%
Hypertension	20%
Fever	7%
Erythrocytosis	3%
Hypercalcemia	3%
Amyloidosis	3%
Neuropathy	3%

Modified from Skinner DG, Calvin RB, Vermillion CD, et al: Diagnosis and management of renal cell carcinoma. Cancer 1971;28:1165–1177.

Table 203–4 • TNM STAGING OF RENAL CELL CARCINOMA

PRIMARY TUMOR (T)

TX	Primary tumor never assessed pathologically
T0	No evidence of primary tumor
T1	Tumor confined to kidney, <7.0 cm in greatest diameter
T2	Tumor confined to kidney, >7.0 cm in greatest diameter
T3a	Tumor involving perinephric tissues, inside Gerota's fascia
T3b	Tumor involving renal vein or vena cava below the diaphragm
T3c	Tumor involving vena cava and extending above the diaphragm
T4	Tumor invasion of neighboring structures

NODAL INVOLVEMENT (N)

TX	Minimum requirements cannot be met
N0	No evidence of involvement of regional nodes
N1	Single, homolateral regional nodal involvement
N2	Metastases in more than one regional lymph node

DISTANT METASTASIS (M)

MX	Not assessed
M0	No (known) distant metastasis
M1	Distant metastasis

STAGE GROUPING

Stage I	T1	N0	M0
Stage II	T2	N0	M0
Stage III	T1	N1	M0
	T2	N1	M0
	T3	N0,N1	M0
Stage IV	T4	N0,N1	M0
	Any T	N2	M0
	Any T	Any N	M1

Table 203–5 • UCLA INTEGRATED STAGING SYSTEM FOR RENAL CELL CARCINOMA

PROGNOSTIC GROUP	NUMBER OF PATIENTS	TNM STAGE	TUMOR GRADE	PERFORMANCE STATUS	5-YEAR SURVIVAL
1	92	I	1, 2	0	94%
2	81	I	1, 2	1 or more	67%
		I	3, 4	Any	
		II	Any	Any	
		III	Any	0	
		III	1	1 or more	
3	56	III	2–4	1 or more	39%
		IV	1, 2	0	
4	218	IV	3, 4	0	23%
			1–3	1 or more	
5	30	IV	4	1 or more	0%

TNM = tumor, node, metastasis; UCLA = University of California at Los Angeles.
Modified from Zisman A, Pantuck AJ, Dorey F, et al: Improved prognostication of renal cell carcinoma using an integrated staging system. J Clin Oncol 2001;19:1649–1657.

Rx Treatment

LOCALIZED DISEASE. Surgery with en bloc removal of Gerota's fascia and its contents is the treatment of choice for localized renal cell carcinoma. The ipsilateral adrenal gland is often removed as well. If the tumor extends into the inferior vena cava (stage III disease), the tumor thrombus and/or part of the vena cava should also be removed. Regional lymph node dissection is controversial.

Nephron sparing or partial nephrectomy, performed as an open or laparoscopic procedure, is an option in patients with impaired renal function, a single kidney, or small tumors. Laparoscopic nephrectomy is especially attractive for otherwise healthy patients with metastatic disease, for whom nephrectomy slightly improves median survival time.

Renal cell carcinomas are relatively resistant to radiation, which may damage the surrounding vital organs. Stereotatic radiosurgery is an investigational approach for patients not fit for surgery. Adjuvant immunotherapy with interferon (IFN) does not improve overall survival rates for locally advanced disease, and adjuvant chemotherapy also has not shown benefit.

METASTATIC DISEASE. Approximately 30% of renal cell carcinomas present with distant metastases, and about 20 to 30% of patients with surgically resected localized disease eventually relapse with metastatic disease. Cytotoxic chemotherapy provides no better than a 10% overall response rate for metastatic disease, with 5-fluorouracil, floxuridine, and capecitabine as the preferred agents.

Immunomodulatory therapy with high-dose intravenous infusion of interleukin (IL)-2 produces a 15 to 20% response rate in metastatic renal cell carcinoma, with about half of the responders achieving complete responses. Long-term follow-up indicates that a majority of complete responders remain disease free and are potentially cured. The toxicities of high-dose IL-2 (hypotension, pulmonary edema, cardiac and cerebral ischemia, renal failure, and gastrointestinal bleeding) have led to trials of low-dose, subcutaneous IL-2, which has much less toxicity (fever, chills, fatigue, and anorexia). However, high-dose IL-2 provides significantly higher overall and complete response rates than low-dose IL-2 with a trend toward better survival.

IFN-α has moderate activity against renal cell carcinoma as a single agent, with a 10 to 15% overall response rate, and IFN-α is better than oral medroxyprogesterone acetate.[1] IFN-α alone is equivalent to vinblastine plus IFN-α and provides a significantly better median survival than does vinblastine alone (15 months versus 8 months); IL-2 alone is equivalent to the combination of IL-2 and IFN.

Durable regression of metastatic renal cell carcinoma has been reported after nonmyeloablative allogeneic stem cell transplantation (Chapter 166), apparently owing to a graft-versus-tumor effect from the engrafted allogeneic T cells. However, this treatment is associated with major toxicities, mainly from the severe graft-versus-host disease, and further studies are needed to confirm its efficacy. Thalidomide, perhaps because of its antiangiogenic effects, is associated with a 2 to 10% tumor response rate and a 20 to 30% disease stabilization rate. Bevacizumab, an antivascular endothelial growth factor antibody, has shown promising results in a small randomized trial.[2]

Late complications include pain from skeletal metastasis and hematuria from the local tumor. Radiation is useful for the palliative treatment of local symptoms. Palliative nephrectomy provides symptomatic relief and a survival benefit when performed in conjunction with postoperative immunotherapy.[3] This benefit is likely due to the reduced tumor burden and should be considered for patients who have a low volume of systemic metastases and a good performance status and who are eligible for postoperative immunotherapy. A small number of patients present with one or a few metastases and can achieve a 25 to 50% 5-year survival if rendered apparently disease-free by surgery.

Prognosis

Patients with early stage renal cell carcinoma can expect a 60 to 70% 5-year survival after undergoing radical nephrectomy. Five-year survival decreases significantly for stage III patients to 20 to 40%. The prognosis for patients with metastatic disease is dismal, with only 3 to 10% alive at 5 years. Nevertheless, patients with metastatic renal cell carcinoma sometimes remain stable for a prolonged period of time before eventually succumbing to their disease.

Future Directions

Renal cell carcinoma is a model system for tumor immunology, including dendritic cell–based tumor vaccines, and for biologic therapies that target angiogenesis and growth factor receptors.

BLADDER CANCER

Definition

More than 90% of the transitional cell carcinomas arising in the urothelium occur in the urinary bladder. The remaining 10% arise in the renal pelvis (8%) or in the ureter and the proximal two thirds of the urethra (2%). Transitional cell carcinomas in these various locations share a similar natural history; they tend to be multifocal and carry a high recurrence rate.

Epidemiology

Bladder cancer is the fourth most common cancer in men and the tenth in women. Each year in the United States, about 56,000 new cases occur and about 12,000 patients die of the disease. The diagnosis is more common in whites, and the male to female ratio is about 3 : 1 in all racial groups. Bladder cancer increases with age, and the median age at diagnosis is 70. The incidence of bladder cancer has been declining by almost 1% per year overall, and the decline is greater among Hispanics (4.4% per year). The death rate from bladder cancer also has declined significantly by about 0.8% per year in men over the past 25 years, but mortality rates for women have not changed significantly. African-American men have lower incidence rates for bladder cancer than white men but have a higher mortality rate.

The development of bladder cancer is closely related to the length of exposure to a variety of environmental carcinogens. In the Western world, cigarette smoking is the leading cause for bladder cancer, and smokers have about ten-fold increased risk for development of bladder cancer (Chapters 14, 186, and 190). That risk decreases but remains elevated up to 10 years after smoking cessation. Occupational exposure to arylamine among the workers in dye, rubber, or leather manufacturing industries has been linked to the development of bladder cancer. Chronic bladder infections, especially from *Schistosoma haematobium* (Chapter 402), are associated with squamous cell bladder cancer. Other risk factors include high-fat diet, a history of external

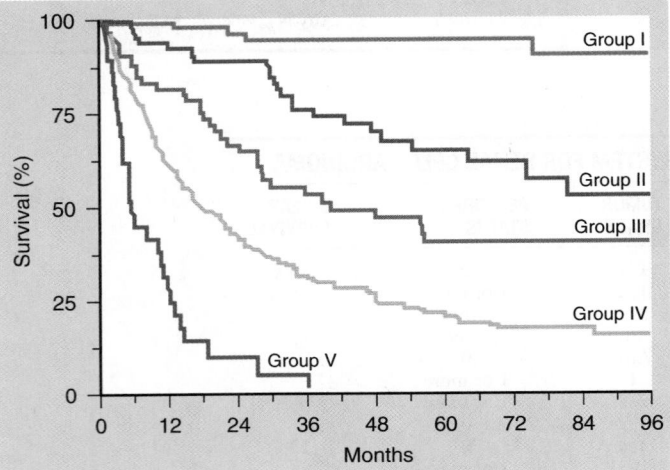

FIGURE 203–1 • Kaplan-Meier survival analysis of renal cell carcinoma according to the UCLA Integrated Staging System categories. (Modified from Zisman A, Pantuck AJ, Wieder J, et al: Risk group assessment and clinical outcome algorithm to predict the natural history of patients with surgically resected renal cell carcinoma. J Clin Oncol 2002;20:4559–4566.)

beam radiation to the pelvis, and drugs, such as cyclophosphamide, phenacetin, and chlornaphazine.

Pathobiology

A unique aspect of bladder cancer is its tendency to recur locally despite optimal control of the initial tumor, probably because chronic exposure to carcinogens results in genetic instability along the entire urothelium. However, whether recurrences represent independent tumorigenesis or are derived from the original neoplastic clone remains controversial.

Deletion in chromosome 9 is the most consistent chromosomal finding and is thought to be an early event in tumorigenesis, whereas deletions in chromosomes 3, 8, 11, and 18 are often associated with high-grade disease. Other genetic changes, including the activation of *ras* oncogene and overexpression of epidermal growth factor genes, have been found frequently in bladder cancers. Mutations or deletions of *p53* (17p) or *RB* (13q24) genes are found in up to 50% of bladder cancers, and this loss of tumor suppression, which is associated with a worse prognosis, presumably contributes to the genetic instability of the urothelium.

In the Western world, more than 90% of tumors in the urinary bladder are transitional cell carcinomas, which can be classified as low grade (G1), intermediate grade (G2), and high grade (G3) based on their differentiation. Pure squamous cell tumors constitute 3% of the cases and are strongly associated with chronic bladder infection. Adenocarcinomas, which represent 2 to 3% of tumors, usually develop at the dome of the bladder (urachal carcinomas) or in the periurethral tissues. Occasionally, lymphomas or melanomas are diagnosed in the urinary bladder. Tumors with mixed histology, consisting of transitional cell with squamous or adenocarcinomatous features, are frequently encountered and should be treated as variants of transitional cell carcinomas because they behave similarly.

Carcinoma in situ of the bladder is a distinct disease entity that usually presents with diffuse erythema in the bladder epithelium and is often associated with a primary exophytic tumor. Carcinoma in situ is generally considered a precursor to invasive tumor; if untreated, at least 50% of carcinomas in situ progress to invasive disease within 5 years.

Clinical Manifestations

The predominant presenting symptom is painless hematuria, either gross or microscopic. The hematuria typically occurs throughout urination, indicating that the blood is from the bladder or above it, not the urethra. Patients may have flank pain from ureteral obstruction or pain in the lower abdomen from a bladder mass. Bladder irritation from invasive disease or carcinoma in situ may manifest as increased urinary frequency, urgency, or dysuria. The physical examination is usually unremarkable, especially among patients with superficial disease. Occasionally, patients with advanced disease may present with fatigue, weight loss, and anorexia. About 15% of patients with hematuria throughout urination are eventually diagnosed with bladder cancer. Although routine screening for microscopic hematuria can increase the sensitivity for detecting early stage bladder cancer, this earlier diagnosis has not been translated into prolonged survival.

Diagnosis

In patients with painless hematuria, the diagnostic evaluation should begin with a CT scan to locate or exclude any tumor above the bladder (Chapter 110). Urine cytology is helpful to confirm the diagnosis, but it is unable to determine the location of the tumor. Flexible cystoscopy, which is the single most important test in diagnosing bladder cancer, is required in adults with unexplained hematuria; it can be performed easily and quickly in the office with local anesthesia. If a bladder tumor or a suspicious lesion is found, the patient should then undergo transurethral resection of the tumor with a resectoscope and have biopsies of the underlying muscle under general anesthesia to ensure that the entire bladder interior is optimally visualized and examined, especially the proximal urethra and bladder neck regions. The locations of the tumors should be recorded

Table 203–6 • TNM STAGING SYSTEM FOR BLADDER CANCER

PRIMARY TUMOR (T)

TX	Primary tumor cannot be assessed
T0	No evidence of primary tumor
Ta	Noninvasive papillary carcinoma
Tis	Carcinoma in situ: flat tumor
T1	Tumor invades lamina propria
T2	Tumor invades muscle
T2a	Tumor invades superficial muscle
T2b	Tumor invades deep muscle (outer half)
T3	Tumor invades perivesical fat
T3a	Microscopically
T3b	Macroscopically (extravesical mass)
T4	Tumor invades prostate, uterus, vagina, pelvic wall, or abdominal wall
T4a	Tumor invades prostate, uterus, vagina
T4b	Tumor invades pelvic or abdominal wall

NODAL INVOLVEMENT (N)

NX	Regional lymph nodes cannot be assessed
N0	No regional lymph node metastasis
N1	Metastasis in a single lymph node, 2 cm or less in greatest dimension
N2	Metastasis in a single lymph node, more than 2 cm but not more than 5 cm in greatest dimension, or multiple lymph nodes, none more than 5 cm in greatest dimension
N3	Metastasis in a lymph node more than 5 cm in greatest dimension

DISTANT METASTASIS (M)

MX	Presence of distant metastasis cannot be assessed
M0	No distant metastasis
M1	Distant metastasis

STAGE GROUPING

0a	Ta, N0, M0
0is	Tis, N0, M0
I	T1, N0, M0
II	T2, N0, M0 T3a, N0, M0
III	T3b, N0, M0 T4a, N0, M0
IV	T4b, N0, M0
	Any T, N1, M0
	Any T, N2, M0
	Any T, N3, M0
	Any T, Any N, M1

for future follow-up. Areas of diffuse erythema should also be biopsied for possible carcinoma in situ. Patients with suspected invasive disease should have a bimanual examination under general anesthesia before or after the cystoscopy because fixed bladders are often unresectable.

When the diagnosis of invasive disease is made, radiographic studies, such as CT scans of chest, abdomen, and pelvis, should be performed to evaluate possible regional and distant metastasis. MRI is more sensitive in evaluating tumors at the base and dome of the bladder as well as in determining whether the tumor is invading the perivesical fat, prostate gland, or seminal vesicles. However, no noninvasive technique is completely reliable in determining the extent of tumor invasion or evaluating regional lymph node involvement, so up to 30% of patients are understaged clinically.

The most commonly used staging system for bladder cancer is the American Joint Committee on Cancer Staging (Table 203–6). At diagnosis, more than 70% of bladder cancers are low-grade papillary tumors that are confined to the mucosa (Ta disease) or invade only the submucosa (T1 disease). Despite complete resection, 50 to 70% of these tumors recur within 5 years in the bladder or in other parts of the urinary tract. Only 5 to 20% of these superficial tumors later progress into muscle invasive disease. Approximately 20% of bladder cancer patients present with disease invading at least into the muscularis propria (T2 disease). These tumors are almost always high grade and can progress to regional and distant metastases. Once nodal or distant metastases are documented, outcomes without systemic therapy are poor, and few patients survive 5 years.

Oncology

Rx Treatment

SUPERFICIAL DISEASE. The standard initial treatment of superficial bladder cancer is a complete transurethral resection with the cystoscope followed by surveillance flexible cystoscopy at 3-month intervals to monitor disease recurrence. Single and low-grade papillary lesions (Ta) have a very low probability of progressing into muscle invasive disease and can be managed by surgical resection only. Vigilant follow-up with cystoscopy, urine cytology, and repeat transurethral resections as needed is performed every 3 to 6 months for at least the first 5 years. Intravesical treatment is rarely indicated for these low-grade Ta tumors. Conversely, patients with T1 disease, frequently recurrent or high-grade Ta disease, multifocal tumors, or large primary tumors should be considered for adjuvant intravesical therapy with bacillus Calmette-Guérin (BCG), which cures about 75% of carcinomas in situ, significantly decreases tumor recurrence, improves progression-free survival, and reduces cancer-related death. **4** Side effects from intravesical BCG include cystitis, flu-like symptoms, and rarely fatal sepsis from disseminated BCG in immunosuppressed patients. Valrubicin chemotherapy has been approved by the Food and Drug Administration for BCG-refractory patients.

Of the patients with muscle-invasive disease on the cystoscopic biopsy, about half are found to have disease extending outside of the bladder at the time of radical cystectomy. When tumor invades the muscle but does not extend beyond it (stage II-T2a/b; see Table 203–6), death from bladder cancer occurs in 20 of 50% of patients; if the disease extends into the fat around the bladder (T3), death from metastatic bladder cancer occurs in 40 to 80% of patients; if the disease has extended into the lymph nodes, 70 to 90% die of the cancer. The precise extent of disease can be determined only after a radical cystectomy. Radical cystectomy is the standard of care in the United States, whereas external beam radiation up to 6800 to 7200 cGy (with salvage cystectomy if the disease persists or relapses) is the standard in many other countries. When chemotherapy (methotrexate, cisplatin, and vinblastine, with or without Adriamycin) is added to either management strategy, the 5-year survival rate improves by 5 to 15%. **5**

In men, radical cystectomy includes removal of the bladder, prostate, and proximal urethra; in women, a hysterectomy, oophorectomy, and partial vaginectomy is required. Urinary diversion is usually via an internal reservoir from either a segment of colon or small bowel, which is then anastomosed to either the abdominal wall (urine being drained from it with a catheter carried by the patient) or to the urethra. Complications include hypochloremic acidosis, oxalate stones, urethral strictures, recurrent urinary infections, nocturnal incontinence, and malignancy in the neobladder. The alternative is aggressive cystoscopic resection of all visible bladder cancer, followed by chemotherapy and radiation; this approach appears to provide comparable survival rates and the preservation of the native bladder in 60 to 70% of patients.

METASTATIC DISEASE. Bladder cancer patients who either present with metastatic disease or who develop systemic relapse after the initial treatment of local disease are managed predominantly by chemotherapy with platinum compounds, taxanes, vinca alkaloids, anthracyclines, and antimetabolites (e.g., methotrexate and gemcitabine). Metastatic bladder cancer patients with poor performance status have a median survival of 6 months, whereas patients with a good performance status have a median survival of 14 to 36+ months, depending upon the extent of the metastatic disease burden. Pure squamous or adenocarcinomas respond poorly to chemotherapy.

Prognosis

Patients with superficial bladder cancer have excellent long-term survival with proper surgical intervention, surveillance, and intravesical therapy. For patients with locally advanced disease, large series have demonstrated 5-year survival rates of 50 to 80% for T2 and T3a disease and 37 to 61% for T3b disease. Once metastases are identified, the disease becomes much less curable; less than 10% of patients with distant metastases and 20% of patients with regional lymph node involvement are alive after 5 years.

CANCER OF THE RENAL PELVIS AND URETERS

Approximately 10% of transitional cell carcinomas occur in the ureters and renal pelvis, with about 500 new cases diagnosed annually in the United States. These tumors closely resemble the transitional cell carcinomas of the bladder. Patients frequently present with painless hematuria, and their tumor locations are usually first determined by an intravenous pyelogram. CT scan, bone scan, and MRI can evaluate the extent of the primary tumor involvement as well as distant metastasis.

For patients with localized tumor, nephroureterectomy provides excellent long-term survival. For patients with inoperable locally advanced disease or with distant metastases, systemic chemotherapy with M-VAC or its equivalent is indicated. The 5-year survival is similar to that of patients with metastatic bladder cancer.

Grade A

1. Medical Research Council Renal Cancer Collaborators: Interferon-alpha and survival in metastatic renal carcinoma: Early results of a randomized controlled trial. Lancet 1999;353:14–17.
2. Yang JC, Haworth L, Sherry RM, et al: A randomized trial of bevacizumab, an anti-vascular endothelial growth factor antibody, for metastatic cancer. N Engl J Med 2003;349:427–434.
3. Flanigan RC, Salmon SE, Blumenstein BA, et al: Nephrectomy followed by interferon alfa-2b compared with interferon alfa-2b alone for metastatic renal-cell cancer. N Engl J Med 2001;345:1655–1659.
4. Grossman HB, Natale RB, Tangen CM, et al: Neoadjuvant chemotherapy plus cystectomy compared with cystectomy alone for locally advanced bladder cancer. N Engl J Med 2003;349:859–866.
5. Herr HW, Wartinger DD, Fair WR, et al: Bacillus Calmette-Guerin therapy for superficial bladder cancer: A 10-year follow-up. J Urol 1992;147:1020–1023.

SUGGESTED READINGS
Childs R, Chernoff A, Contentin N, et al: Regression of metastatic renal-cell carcinoma after nonmyeloablative allogeneic peripheral-blood stem-cell transplantation. N Engl J Med 2000;343:750–758. *Sustained regression was seen in some patients who had not responded to conventional immunotherapy.*

Vogelzang NJ, Scardino PT, Shipley WU, Coffey DS (eds): Comprehensive Textbook of Genitourinary Oncology, 2nd ed. Philadelphia, Lippincott Williams & Wilkins, 2000. *A detailed text.*

204 BREAST CANCER AND DIFFERENTIAL DIAGNOSIS OF BENIGN LESIONS

Hyman B. Muss

Epidemiology/Statistics

Breast cancer is the most common cancer affecting American women. Each year in the United States, about 200,000 new cases of invasive breast cancer are diagnosed and about 40,000 people die of breast cancer. Breast cancer occurs in 12.5% of women, or one in every eight, during their lifetime and accounts for 31% of cases of female cancer; it is the second leading cause of female cancer death, after lung cancer. Male breast cancer accounts for about 1% of all new cases and, stage for stage, has a natural history similar to that of female breast cancer. The incidence of breast cancer continues to increase slowly, but mortality rates are now decreasing. This decrease is probably due to multiple factors, including wider use of mammographic screening, better surgical and radiation therapy, and the use of systemic adjuvant therapy.

It is estimated that worldwide almost 1 million new cases of breast cancer are diagnosed yearly. The incidence and mortality rates for breast cancer differ dramatically among nations. In general, more affluent Western nations have the highest incidence rates, whereas developing nations have the lowest. Although racial factors may play a role in its incidence, the differing rates of breast cancer among nations are more likely related to sociodemographic and dietary factors, including per capita income, nutritional status, and dietary composition.

Pathogenesis and Risk Factors

The causes of breast cancer remain elusive. Numerous risk factors have been defined (Table 204–1). The incidence of breast cancer increases dramatically with increasing age; more than 50% of women with breast cancer in the United States are older than 60 years, and the number of older women with breast cancer is increasing dramatically

Table 204–1 • **RISK FACTORS FOR BREAST CANCER**

RISK FACTOR	RELATIVE RISK
Any benign breast disease	1.5
Postmenopausal hormone replacement (estrogen ± progestin)	1.5
Menarche at <12 yr	1.1–1.9
Moderate alcohol intake (two to three drinks per day)	1.1–1.9
Menopause at >55 yr	1.1–1.9
Increased bone density	1.1–1.9
Sedentary lifestyle and lack of exercise	1.1–1.9
Proliferative breast disease without atypia	2.0
Age at first birth >30 yr or nulliparous	2.0–4.0
First-degree relative with breast cancer	2.0–4.0
Postmenopausal obesity	2.0–4.0
Upper socioeconomic class	2.0–4.0
Personal history of endometrial or ovarian cancer	2.0–4.0
Significant radiation to chest	2.0–4.0
Increased breast density on mammogram	2.0–4.0
Older age	>4.0
Personal history of breast cancer (in situ or invasive)	>4.0
Proliferative breast disease with atypia	>4.0
Two first-degree relatives with breast cancer	5.0
Atypical hyperplasia and first-degree relative with breast cancer	10.0

Table 204–2 • **CHARACTERISTICS OF THE *BRCA1* AND *BRCA2* GENES**

CHARACTERISTIC	*BRCA1*	*BRCA2*
Chromosome location	17	13
Percentage of all breast cancers	<5%	<5%
Contribution to hereditary breast cancer	20–40%	10–30%
Population frequency (U.S.)		
General	1/345	?
Ashkenazi Jewish	1/40	~1/40
Lifetime cancer risk		
Breast cancer	56–85%	56–85%
Second primary breast cancer	~60%	~60%
Ovarian cancer	15–45%	10–20%
Male breast cancer	Low	6%
Other cancers seen in families	Colon Prostate	Prostate Laryngeal Pancreas Gastric Melanoma

as the population ages. Several risk factors, such as younger age at menarche and older age at menopause, are indirect measures of the number of menstrual cycles that a woman has in her lifetime. Increasing the number of cycles might predispose women to greater DNA damage in the proliferating breast ductal tissue and thus increase the risk of mutations that directly lead to breast cancer. The Western and especially the American lifestyle may predispose women to breast cancer by increasing the frequency of known risk factors. Western cultures are characterized by younger age at menarche, older age at menopause, later age of childbearing or being nulliparous, increased obesity, more sedentary lifestyles, and increased use of hormone replacement therapy. A convincing body of data indicates that breast cancer risk directly correlates with serum estradiol concentration. Exposure to environmental pollutants (dichlorodiphenyltrichloroethane [DDT], polychlorinated biphenyls [PCBs], and others) may increase the risk of breast cancer, but such a relationship has not been confirmed.

The available data suggest that the risk of breast cancer is not affected by dietary saturated fat intake during adulthood or by vitamin A, C, and E consumption. Dietary composition, however, may be important; populations with high intake of soy proteins, which are rich sources of plant estrogen-like compounds (phytoestrogens), have lower rates of hormonally related cancers such as breast, endometrial, and prostate cancer. Alcohol intake is also related to breast cancer, with women who have several drinks daily having a moderately higher risk than those who abstain. Oral contraceptive use increases breast cancer risk minimally if at all. The use of hormone replacement therapy for 5 or more years in postmenopausal women increases the risk of breast cancer about 1.5 times, and this risk is higher for estrogen-progestin regimens than for estrogen replacement alone. The greatest increase in risk associated with the use of hormone replacement therapy is in leaner postmenopausal women. Women whose Hodgkin's disease has been treated with chest irradiation have a risk of breast cancer that is at least two- to threefold higher than average, with a cumulative lifetime risk of 30 to 40%.

Twenty per cent of women with breast cancer have a positive family history, and a clear pattern of autosomal dominant inheritance is noted in about 5 to 10% of all breast cancer patients. The majority of these patients have mutations of either the *BRCA1* or the *BRCA2* gene (Table 204–2). The *BRCA1* and *BRCA2* genes can be carried and passed to offspring by males as well as females. Specific genetic abnormalities appear to be characteristic of specific ethnic groups. For example, only three specific mutations account for 95% of *BRCA1* and *BRCA2* carriers among Ashkenazi Jewish women. The Li-Fraumeni syndrome is a rare disorder of the *p53* gene; affected patients have a high incidence of breast cancer, brain tumors, sarcomas, and leukemias. Patients with Cowden's syndrome and germline abnormalities of the *PTEN* gene have a 30 to 50% lifetime risk of breast cancer. Patients who carry the ataxia telangiectasia trait (one abnormal *ATM* gene; Chapter 205) may be at increased risk.

Genetic tests for *BRCA1* and *BRCA2* are now commercially available (Chapter 185). Consideration of genetic testing is appropriate for women in whom breast cancer develops at a young age, women with a family history of breast or ovarian cancer (Chapter 205) in first-degree relatives, and women who are blood relatives of those with known *BRCA1* or *BRCA2* mutations. All women who have testing for genetic abnormalities should have genetic counseling (Chapter 36). In addition to psychosocial issues related to testing, issues concerning insurance coverage and potential job discrimination are unresolved.

Management of women who carry the *BRCA1* and *BRCA2* genes is controversial. Prophylactic mastectomy will eliminate the likelihood of breast cancer in 90% or more of these patients. Prophylactic oophorectomy after completion of childbearing is also recommended and will substantially lower the likelihood of ovarian cancer, although areas of embryonic epithelial tissue in the peritoneal cavity remain a potential source of ovarian cancer even after oophorectomy. Oophorectomy may also lower the risk of breast cancer in these patients. Tamoxifen may lower the risk of breast cancer in patients with *BRCA2* mutations but appears ineffective in lowering risk in patients with *BRCA1* mutations.

Screening and Prevention

The routine use of annual screening mammography in women 40 to 74 years of age reduces the likelihood of dying of breast cancer by 10 to 20%. In women 40 to 49 years of age, the use of screening mammography remains controversial, but data from studies of fair quality or better show about a 15% reduction in the risk of breast cancer death. More extensive data indicate that a similar reduction is seen in older patients. About 15 to 25% of palpable breast cancers are not imaged by mammography; this phenomenon is most common in premenopausal women and in women with dense breasts. The sensitivity and specificity of screening mammography are also lower in postmenopausal women who are taking hormone replacement therapy and in women with dense breast tissue. The U.S. Preventative Task Force (USPTF) found fair evidence (grade B) that mammography every 12 to 33 months in women 40 to 69 years of age significantly reduced mortality from breast cancer (Chapter 11). The USPTF recommends that women 40 years of age and older consider screening mammography every 1 to 2 years. Screening mammography has not been rigorously tested in clinical trials in women over the age of 70 years, but the USPTF recommends mammography for women 70 years of age and older who are in reasonably good health. Newer imaging methods, including digital mammography, magnetic resonance imaging of the breast, radionuclide imaging with sestamibi, and high-resolution ultrasonography are being evaluated in clinical trials but have not yet been shown to be superior to mammography for routine screening.

Physical examination by a health professional should be part of all screening programs. The value of breast self-examination is controversial, and a recent large randomized trial in Chinese women showed no effect of self-examination for reducing breast cancer mor-

Table 204–3 • SCREENING RECOMMENDATIONS (AMERICAN CANCER SOCIETY)

AGE GROUP	EXAMINATION	FREQUENCY
20–39 yr	Breast self-examination	Every month
	Clinical breast examination	Every 3 yr
40 yr and over	Breast self-examination	Every month
	Mammography	Every year
	Clinical breast examination	Every year

tality. Nevertheless, a substantial number of cancerous breast masses are first detected by self-examination. Current screening recommendations of the American Cancer Society are listed in Table 204–3; these recommendations, which include annual mammography and breast self-examinations, serve as a reasonable guideline for breast cancer screening.

Most experts have recommended that women with a strong family history of breast cancer have screening performed at an age 5 to 10 years younger than that of the youngest relative in whom breast cancer has developed, but not before age 25 years. For carriers of mutations in *BRCA1* or *BRCA2*, mammography is recommended beginning at 25 years of age, although no evidence has proved that this strategy saves lives. Newer techniques, such as ductal lavage, in which cytology is performed on aspirated specimens from the breast ducts, show great promise and are being assessed in large clinical trials.

Prevention of breast cancer remains a major goal. The U.S. Breast Cancer Prevention Trial (National Surgical Adjuvant Breast and Bowel Project P-1) randomized 13,388 high-risk women (those with a risk of invasive breast cancer of 1.67% or more over 5 years) to either tamoxifen, 20 mg daily or a placebo and showed that tamoxifen reduced the risk of both invasive and noninvasive breast cancer by about 50%.[1] This risk reduction was seen in all age groups. Two smaller randomized trials similar in design have not shown any benefit for tamoxifen, but these trials had different eligibility criteria. Women at high risk should be informed of the potential benefits and risks of tamoxifen. The benefits of tamoxifen exceed the risk in all premenopausal women whose risk of breast cancer is greater than 1.5% over 5 years. In postmenopausal women who have had a hysterectomy and therefore are not at risk of endometrial cancer, the benefit of tamoxifen exceeds its risk for women ages 50 to 59 years, 60 to 69 years, and 70 to 79 years who have 5-year risks of invasive breast cancer of 1.5%, 3.5%, and 6.0%, respectively. In postmenopausal women with an intact uterus, tamoxifen's benefit exceeds its risk for those 50 to 59 years of age and those 60 to 79 years of age who have 5-year risks of invasive breast cancer of 4.0% and 7.0%, respectively. A prevention trial comparing tamoxifen with raloxifene in postmenopausal women is currently in progress. New retinoic acid derivatives, cyclooxygenase-2 inhibitors, phytochemicals, and aromatase inhibitors are potential preventive agents, and several are currently being evaluated in clinical trials.

Postmenopausal obesity is strongly correlated with an increased risk of breast cancer, probably because it is directly correlated with increased estrogen levels. Maintaining ideal or average body mass decreases risk. Regular exercise may lower estrogen levels and has been associated with a lower risk of breast cancer.

Diagnosis

SIGNS AND SYMPTOMS. Breast cancer is usually first detected as a palpable mass or as a mammographic abnormality, but it can also be manifested by nipple discharge, changes in the skin over the breast, or breast pain. Palpable masses, including discrete masses and areas of asymmetrical thickening of breast glandular tissue, remain the most common manifestation of breast cancer and are often first detected by the patient. Paget's disease of the nipple is a form of adenocarcinoma involving the skin and lactiferous sinuses of the nipple; it usually appears as an eczematous lesion of the skin of the nipple and is frequently associated with excoriation of the skin and discharge.

Spontaneous bloody or watery discharge from the nipple is commonly associated with underlying breast malignancy. Milky discharge almost always has a benign cause. Patients with a clear or bloody discharge require breast examination and mammography. If the results of mammography and breast examination are normal and the discharge is located within a single or a few well-defined ducts, excisional biopsy of the involved ducts is indicated. A bloody discharge is frequently caused by an intraductal papilloma; a ductogram may help locate such lesions. Recently, breast duct endoscopy has been shown to be an effective way to locate such lesions.

Breast pain is a common symptom in many women and is reported in about 10% of patients with breast cancer. In patients with breast cancer, the breast pain typically is associated with a palpable lump or mammographic abnormality. In premenopausal women, breast pain is a common premenstrual symptom. When pain is localized to a specific region of the breast and occurs throughout the menstrual cycle, an underlying lesion should be suspected. All patients with noncyclic breast pain should undergo a breast examination and bilateral mammography. If no abnormalities are found, evaluation of the painful area by ultrasonography or magnetic resonance imaging may help exclude the small possibility of a malignancy.

In a small percentage of patients, breast cancer is manifested as an axillary mass without any breast lesion detected on physical examination, mammography, or other breast imaging modality (Chapter 210); these patients characteristically have axillary node involvement by adenocarcinoma. Such patients are best managed by axillary node dissection, ipsilateral breast irradiation (mastectomy is not mandatory and, even when performed, fails to detect a primary lesion in 30% of patients), and appropriate systemic adjuvant therapy. The natural history of such patients may be somewhat better than that of node-positive patients with palpable breast lesions.

EVALUATING A BREAST MASS. Most breast masses, especially those found in young premenopausal women, are benign. However, all breast masses require evaluation. In a premenopausal woman, if the mass is small and likely to be a cyst, it can be observed for 2 to 4 weeks until after the next menstrual period. If the mass persists, biopsy is indicated; all masses in postmenopausal women require prompt investigation.

Mammograms and ultrasonographic evaluation may help characterize a mass as well as detect abnormalities in noninvolved breast tissues. All persistent masses require biopsy, even when all imaging studies are normal. As many as 15 to 25% of all palpable breast cancers are not detected with mammography. Fine-needle aspiration should be considered for lesions likely to be cysts; aspiration of the fluid with resolution of the mass is adequate treatment. If the cystic fluid is clear, cytologic evaluation is not usually necessary. Core biopsy is preferable to fine-needle aspiration as a diagnostic tool for solid masses. Core biopsies provide larger tissue samples and, most importantly, are usually able to distinguish in situ from invasive lesions. Because management may be quite different for these lesions (i.e., axillary node dissection is not indicated for in situ lesions), treatment can be guided by core biopsy. A negative fine-needle or core biopsy of a persistent breast mass should be followed by a repeat biopsy, preferably an excisional biopsy.

Pathology and Prognostic Factors

PATHOLOGY. Invasive breast cancer accounts for approximately 75 to 85% of breast malignancies, with the remaining 15 to 25% being carcinoma in situ. Infiltrating ductal carcinoma accounts for 85% of invasive lesions, infiltrating lobular carcinoma for 5 to 10%, medullary carcinoma for 5 to 7%, mucinous or colloid carcinoma for 3%, and tubular carcinoma for 2%. When matched for stage, infiltrating ductal and infiltrating lobular carcinoma have a similar prognosis to each other, and both are more likely to metastasize than is medullary carcinoma. Tubular and colloid carcinomas are usually associated with an excellent prognosis. The histologic grade is important in determining the prognosis for women with infiltrating ductal carcinoma; when matched by stage, patients with high-grade lesions are more likely to develop metastatic disease. A small percentage of patients, mainly premenopausal, initially have inflammatory carcinoma. This lesion is associated with an almost 95% risk of distant metastases and is characterized clinically by redness and erythema involving more than half the breast and pathologically by tumor involving the dermal lymphatics of the breast.

Carcinoma in situ is characterized by the proliferation of malignant cells within the ducts or lobules of the breast without invasion of stromal tissue. The two major subtypes are ductal carcinoma in situ (DCIS) and lobular carcinoma in situ (LCIS). Differences in the clinical features of these lesions are noted in Table 204–4.

Metastases from invasive breast cancer probably develop early during growth of the primary lesion, proliferate in distant metastatic sites as occult "micrometastases," and become clinically detectable (about 1 cm^3) after about 30 tumor cell doublings. The axillary lymph nodes are not barriers to metastases; the number of axillary nodes

Table 204–4 • CARCINOMA IN SITU: DUCTAL VERSUS LOBULAR

FEATURE	LOBULAR CARCINOMA IN SITU (LCIS)	DUCTAL CARCINOMA IN SITU (DCIS)
Age	Younger	Older
Palpable mass	No	Uncommon
Mammographic appearance	Not detected on mammography	Microcalcifications, mass
Usual manifestation	Incidental finding on breast biopsy	Microcalcifications on mammography or breast mass
Bilateral involvement	Common	Uncertain
Risk and site of subsequent breast cancer	About 25% risk for invasive breast cancer in either breast	At site of initial lesion; about 0.5% risk per year of invasive breast cancer in noninvolved breast
Prevention	Consider tamoxifen	Consider tamoxifen if estrogen-receptor positive
Treatment	Yearly mammography and breast examination	Lumpectomy alone or with breast radiation; mastectomy for large or multifocal lesions

involved by tumor is directly correlated with the risk of both locoregional and distant metastases.

PROGNOSTIC FACTORS. Numerous prognostic factors have been identified, but few have proved to be independent predictors of outcome when subjected to multivariate analysis. The essential prognostic factors remain (1) invasion—DCIS and other noninvasive tumors have excellent prognoses; (2) the number of involved ipsilateral axillary nodes; and (3) tumor size. Estrogen and progesterone receptor expression is only marginally related to prognosis, although patients whose primary lesions express either estrogen or progesterone receptors generally have a 5 to 10% better survival rate. Estrogen and progesterone receptors also help predict the response to endocrine therapy; women whose breast cancers lack both estrogen and progesterone receptors derive no benefit from adjuvant endocrine therapy.

Axillary dissection, with removal of at least six lymph nodes, should be performed in almost all patients for both therapeutic and prognostic purposes; the exception is patients with a negative sentinel lymph node biopsy finding, in whom further axillary dissection is not indicated. Clinical examination of the axilla correlates poorly with pathologic findings. Patients without palpable ipsilateral axillary nodes on physical examination display pathologic tumor involvement in up to 40% of cases, whereas palpable axillary nodes exhibit no tumor involvement in up to 40% of patients. The risk of recurrence in the axilla is extremely low (<5%) when adequate dissection is performed.

The major use of prognostic factors has been to predict the risk of distant metastases in women with node-negative breast cancer. For node-negative patients, tumor size, estrogen and progesterone receptor status, and histologic grade remain the key prognostic indices. Primary tumors with an invasive component 1 cm or smaller in largest diameter generally have a very good prognosis with an overall survival rate of 90% or more. Poorly differentiated tumors tend to have more aggressive growth patterns and are associated with a poorer prognosis. Calculation of the number of breast cancer cells synthesizing DNA (S phase) is commonly performed on node-negative lesions; tumors with a low percentage of cells in S phase are associated with a more favorable prognosis. A variety of potential predictive factors remain under investigation. The *HER-2/neu* (c-*erb*-b2) oncogene is expressed in about 20% of all breast cancers; patients with *HER-2* expression tend to have a poorer prognosis but may be more likely to respond to anthracycline-containing chemotherapy or trastuzumab (Herceptin), a humanized monoclonal antibody targeted against the transmembrane protein encoded by the *HER-2* oncogene. Most prognostic and predictive factors can be assayed on paraffin-embedded tissue with immunohistochemical or fluorescent in situ hybridization techniques.

Rx **Primary Treatment of Malignant Lesions**

CARCINOMA IN SITU. Most patients with DCIS are best managed with lumpectomy (excision of the tumor mass with a clear margin around the tumor) and irradiation, but selected patients can have lumpectomy alone. Lumpectomy with or without irradiation allows for breast preservation and is preferred by most patients. At present, the best predictor of in-breast recurrence following lumpectomy alone is the extent of the normal tissue margin around the tumor; patients with DCIS in which the closest margin is 1 cm or larger have a local recurrence rate that is 10% or less. Breast irradiation following lumpectomy lowers the risk of breast recurrence, irrespective of the size of the primary lesion, but the major benefits of breast irradiation are in patients with larger lesions. Patients with lesions larger than 2.5 cm in largest diameter or close margins, or both, and those with multifocal DCIS may be best treated with mastectomy. Metastatic disease occurs in only 1 to 3% of patients with DCIS, but DCIS confers a risk of about 0.5% per year for developing contralateral invasive breast cancer. Axillary nodes are rarely involved, so axillary dissection is not indicated. Despite the better prognosis of DCIS than invasive breast cancer, primary treatment of DCIS remains controversial, and such patients should be managed by surgeons and radiation oncologists with expertise in breast cancer.

LCIS is not considered a malignant lesion but rather a marker of increased risk for subsequent breast cancer, a risk that is about a 25% lifetime risk of invasive ductal cancer developing in either breast. Patients with LCIS alone are currently managed by annual physical examination and mammography without additional surgery or irradiation. In patients who have DCIS or LCIS, tamoxifen decreases the risk of both ipsilateral and contralateral invasive breast cancer by 50%.

INVASIVE BREAST CANCER. Patients with tumors less than 5 cm are best managed with lumpectomy followed by radiation therapy to the involved breast. This treatment is as effective as mastectomy, is associated with similar survival, and results in breast preservation.[2] Breast irradiation following lumpectomy reduces the risk of ipsilateral breast tumor recurrence (which usually occurs at the lumpectomy site) from 40% to less than 10% with a minimal effect on cosmetic results.[2] For patients with larger lesions, mastectomy is preferred, but preoperative chemotherapy or endocrine therapy (in patients with estrogen receptor–positive tumors) may shrink the tumor and make the majority of these patients suitable candidates for lumpectomy and irradiation. Patients with large breast cancers or inflammatory breast cancer are best treated with preoperative ("neoadjuvant") chemotherapy, mastectomy, and post-mastectomy chest wall irradiation. Patients with DCIS in addition to invasive breast cancer are managed like patients with invasive breast cancer. In patients with lesions that contain both in situ and invasive components, tumor size is defined as the largest diameter of the invasive lesion.

Axillary node evaluation should be performed on almost all women who are suitable candidates for preventive (adjuvant) therapy (see later discussion). Exceptions include patients with small, well-differentiated primary lesions (5 mm or smaller) or patients with small tubular carcinomas. Newer techniques such as the sentinel node biopsy may minimize the need for extensive axillary dissection in most patients. The sentinel node is identified by injecting a blue dye, a radioactive isotope, or both around the primary lesion or areolar area. The sentinel node is identified visually (blue dye) or by a gamma detector (radioisotope) and is defined as the first node (or nodes) draining the primary lesion. In 95% of breast cancer patients, the sentinel node is in the ipsilateral axilla. Patients whose sentinel node is histologically negative have less than a 5% chance of having histologically positive nodes higher in the axilla. In 60%

Continued

of patients with a positive sentinel node, only the sentinel node is involved by tumor but axillary dissection is recommended to stage these patients' disease. The technique of sentinel node biopsy requires special surgical training and is still considered a research procedure by many physicians.

Preoperative chemotherapy—the use of four to eight courses of an active chemotherapy regimen or a single agent before definitive treatment of the primary tumor—is not superior to postoperative therapy in preventing metastases. It can cause tumor regression in as many as 90% of patients, and 5 to 25% of these patients demonstrate complete regression of the tumor pathologically as well as clinically. Recent data suggest that patients who achieve a complete or nearly complete response to preoperative chemotherapy have better survival rates than do patients who have significant residual disease in the primary site or lymph nodes. This observation suggests that the response to preoperative chemotherapy may be a "predictive factor" for the recurrence of breast cancer. Another use of preoperative chemotherapy is its ability to convert a large primary lesion unsuitable for lumpectomy to a smaller lesion that is amenable to lumpectomy and breast conservation. Recent data suggest that preoperative endocrine therapy may be as effective as chemotherapy in shrinking tumors in patients with estrogen or progesterone receptor–positive lesions.

Adaptation to a diagnosis of breast cancer is frequently difficult. A wealth of information suggests that psychological counseling and support groups can help patients cope better with breast cancer, especially during the first several years after diagnosis. Moreover, a few but not all controlled trials have suggested that such support may be associated with improved survival. Patients should be offered psychosocial support shortly after diagnosis. Many women may wish to become more involved in breast cancer issues through advocacy. The National Alliance of Breast Cancer Organizations (1-800-719-9154, see Table 204–9) is an outstanding resource for information on organizations interested in breast cancer.

RECONSTRUCTION. In many women, mastectomy is associated with a loss of self-esteem and body image, as well as sexual dysfunction. Breast reconstruction provides an opportunity for women to overcome the psychological damage that frequently follows mastectomy and helps relieve the patient's sense of deformity. Several procedures are available, including implants and the use of flaps from autogenous tissue. Implants are less costly and generally easier to perform, whereas flaps eliminate the need for the foreign materials and are more suitable for the repair of large mastectomy defects. There is now excellent evidence that silicone implants do not increase the risk of breast cancer or connective tissue disorders. Reconstruction is usually performed after mastectomy, but concomitant reconstruction at the time of mastectomy has become popular. The remaining breast frequently requires surgery to match its size and configuration to the reconstructed site. Although reconstruction is frequently associated with excellent cosmetic results, the cosmetic results of lumpectomy and breast irradiation are usually far superior.

Staging

A complete history and physical examination, complete blood cell count and chemistry profile, and chest radiography constitute an appropriate preoperative work-up for asymptomatic women with breast cancer. Women with bone pain, abdominal pain, or other symptoms should have appropriate studies of symptomatic sites. Bilateral mammograms should be performed in all women with biopsy-proven breast cancer to look for other lesions in the involved breast as well as the opposite breast.

Staging of breast cancer is based on tumor size, the extent of breast involvement, axillary lymph node involvement, and distant metastases (the TNM system). Determination of tumor size is made by the pathologist on review of biopsy, lumpectomy, or mastectomy specimens. The staging system has been revised for 2003 (Table 204–5). Survival rates based on the TNM stage are listed in Table 204–6. Currently, about 50 to 60% of women with newly diagnosed breast cancer are node negative, and 25 to 40% are node positive; of those who are node positive, about 60% have involvement of only one to three nodes. Fewer than 10% of patients are initially seen with distant metastases. Patients who present with involvement of ipsilateral supraclavicular nodes and are treated with chemotherapy, surgery, radiation, and endocrine therapy have a long-term disease-free survival rate of 20 to 30%.

Table 204–5 • STAGING OF BREAST CANCER: THE TNM SYSTEM

TUMOR SIZE—T (LARGEST DIAMETER)

TX Primary tumor cannot be assessed
T0 No evidence of primary tumor
Tis Carcinoma in situ: intraductal carcinoma, lobular carcinoma in situ, or Paget's disease of the nipple with no tumor
T1 Tumor ≤2 cm in greatest dimension
T2 Tumor >2 cm but not >5 cm in greatest dimension
T3 Tumor >5 cm in greatest dimension
T4 Tumor of any size with direct extension to chest wall* or skin (includes inflammatory carcinoma)

NODAL INVOLVEMENT—N (NODAL STATUS)

NX Regional lymph nodes cannot be assessed (e.g., previously removed, not removed)
N0 No regional lymph node metastases histologically
N1 Metastasis to one to three ipsilateral axillary nodes
N2 Metastases to four to nine ipsilateral axillary nodes or internal mammary lymph nodes in absence of axillary lymph node metastases
N3 Metastases to 10 or more ipsilateral internal mammary lymph nodes, or to internal mammary lymph nodes and axillary lymph nodes, to ipsilateral supraclavicular lymph nodes, or to ipsilateral infraclavicular lymph nodes

METASTASES—M

M0 No evidence of distant metastasis
M1 Distant metastases

*The chest wall includes the ribs, intercostal muscles, and serratus anterior but not the pectoral muscle.
From Singletary SE, Allred C, Ashley P, et al: Revision of the American Joint Committee on Cancer staging system for breast cancer. J Clin Oncol 2002;20:3628–3636.

Table 204–6 • TNM STAGE AND SURVIVAL

STAGE	TNM CATEGORY*	RECURRENCE FREE AT 10 YEARS (NO SYSTEMIC ADJUVANT THERAPY), %
0	Tis, N0, M0	98
I	T1, N0, M0	80 (all stage I patients)
	T < 1 cm	90
	T > 1–2 cm	80–90
IIA	T0, N1, M0; T2, N0, M0	60–80
IIA	T1, N1, M0	50–60
IIB	T2, N1, M0	5–10 worse than IIA above and based on node status
IIB	T3, N0, M0	30–50
IIIA	T0 or T1 or T2, N2, M0; or T3, N1 or N2, M0	10–40
IIIB	T4, N0 or N1 or N2, M0	5–30
IIIC	Any T, N3, M0	15–20
IV	Any T, any N, M1	< 5

*See Table 204–5 for TNM definitions.

Adjuvant Therapy

Adjuvant therapy is defined as the use of chemotherapy, hormonal therapy, radiation therapy, or immunotherapy, or a combination of these, before, during, or after definitive treatment of the primary breast cancer. The objective of adjuvant therapy is to destroy small, clinically occult, distant micrometastases. Breast cancer metastases composed of microscopic distant foci can be eliminated by adjuvant therapy, with a subsequent reduction in the annual odds of dying of breast cancer of about 10 to 50% within each stage, depending on age, presence of hormone receptors, and menopausal status. **3,4** In addition, adjuvant therapy probably delays recurrence for a median of 2 to 3 years in the majority of treated women. The benefits of systemic adjuvant therapy can be accurately estimated using Internet-based programs (*http://www.mhs.mayo.edu/adjuvant* or *http://www.adjuvantonline.com*).

The rationale for adjuvant chemotherapy is based on the observations that (1) smaller tumors have a larger component of dividing cells, (2) most chemotherapeutic agents are most effective in destroying proliferating cells, (3) smaller tumors are less likely to be drug resistant, (4) the immunologic status of patients is most favorable early in the course of their disease when they are asymptomatic, and (5) asymptomatic patients are better able to tolerate therapy than are those who are ill. Response to adjuvant therapy is based on recurrence-free (relapse-free) survival and overall survival. Recurrence in these patients indicates treatment failure. Because micrometastases cannot be detected clinically, both patients who have been cured by their primary treatment and patients who truly have micrometastases will be treated. Careful estimation of the risks versus benefits of therapy, by both the patient and the physician, is mandatory before patients are placed on such treatment regimens.

Recommendations for adjuvant therapy are based on menopausal status, tumor size, the presence of lymph node involvement, and the estrogen and progesterone receptor status of the tumor. It is an area with much controversy, and all patients with primary breast cancer should be seen by a surgical or medical oncologist to discuss the risks and benefits of adjuvant therapy (Table 204–7). The proportional decrease in risk of recurrence is similar for all patients irrespective of the presence of lymph node involvement. For instance, if the risk of dying of breast cancer is 30% and adjuvant therapy decreases this risk by 25%, the overall survival rate for patients given adjuvant therapy is 77.5% (70% survival without adjuvant therapy + 7.5% [0.25 × 30%] with adjuvant therapy). Similarly, if the risk of dying of breast cancer is 80% without adjuvant therapy, the use of adjuvant therapy increases survival to 40% (20% survival without adjuvant therapy + 20% [0.25 × 80%] with adjuvant therapy). Therefore, the absolute benefit of adjuvant therapy will be greater for individuals with greater risk of recurrence.

In general, combinations of several chemotherapeutic agents given concurrently are superior to single-drug treatment, and short courses of chemotherapy (3 to 6 months) are as effective as longer treatments. The most effective chemotherapy regimens include anthracyclines (epirubicin or doxorubicin). Oophorectomy and chemotherapy are equally effective in improving survival in premenopausal women with estrogen or progesterone-positive tumors.

Tamoxifen is the most widely used endocrine agent and, when added to chemotherapy, improves survival in both premenopausal and postmenopausal patients who are estrogen or progesterone-receptor positive. Tamoxifen should be given for 5 years; its estrogen-agonist effects on bone and liver help maintain bone density and lower cholesterol levels in postmenopausal women but may cause bone loss in premenopausal women. Over a period of 5 years, use of tamoxifen results in a 1% risk of endometrial cancer and a 1% incidence of deep venous thrombosis. Tamoxifen can cause or exacerbate hot flashes in 10 to 30% of postmenopausal women because of its estrogen antagonist effects. After 4 years of median follow-up, preliminary results of a randomized trial in 9000 women suggest that anastrozole, an aromatase inhibitor, appears to be more effective than tamoxifen in lowering the frequency of both metastases and new invasive breast cancers in postmenopausal women with estrogen or progesterone receptor–positive invasive breast cancers, but further follow-up is needed to confirm these early results.

Experimental regimens for patients at high risk for recurrence use chemotherapy at more frequent intervals and integrate new biologic agents or other drugs (for example, trastuzumab). High-dose chemotherapy combined with autologous bone marrow or stem cell transplantation is not superior to standard-dose treatments and is not recommended outside of a clinical trial.

Radiation therapy to the chest wall following mastectomy decreases the rate of local recurrence at the mastectomy site and in the regional nodes in node-positive women with early-stage breast cancer, and it improves these women's survival by a few percentage points. Post-mastectomy chest wall irradiation should be offered to all women with large primary lesions (5 cm or larger, irrespective of nodal involvement) and those with extensive nodal involvement (four or more positive lymph nodes). The use of routine post-mastectomy chest wall irradiation in patients with one to three positive nodes is controversial and is currently being tested in a randomized trial. Although routine post-mastectomy chest wall irradiation is generally well tolerated, it increases the risk of lymphedema in the upper extremity on the side of the mastectomy and is associated with a very small risk of radiation-induced malignancy. Breast radiation after lumpectomy also improves survival.

Follow-Up of Early-Stage Patients

Routine follow-up visits provide a forum for patients to discuss their fears and concerns and for physicians to provide reassurance and obtain annual mammograms (Table 204–8). Intensive follow-up of asymptomatic patients after the diagnosis and treatment of early-stage breast cancer does not improve survival. Detection of metastases by routine laboratory tests, tumor marker assessment (carcinoembryonic antigen, CA-15.3, and CA-27.29), and imaging studies (for example, chest radiographs, bone scans, and computed tomography or ultrasonography of the liver) may occasionally precede the development of signs and symptoms of metastases by 3 to 6 months, but early detection by these means has not been translated into improved survival or quality of life. **5**

Even when frequent imaging and laboratory testing are performed, about 75% of recurrences are detected by the physician or the patient from signs and symptoms. Locoregional recurrence on the chest wall or in regional lymph nodes accounts for 19 to 39% of initial recurrences, bone for 16 to 63%, lung for 16 to 25%, liver for 5 to 22%, and the central nervous system for 5 to 15%. Of note, almost a third of initial recurrences occur in soft tissue and nodal areas; physical examination remains the mainstay of such detection.

Treatment of Metastatic Disease

SYSTEMIC THERAPY: ENDOCRINE THERAPY, CHEMOTHERAPY, AND BIOLOGICS

Almost all patients with metastatic breast cancer are incurable. One to 3% of patients treated with standard endocrine therapy or chemotherapy regimens may attain long-term remission and may never have further recurrence, but the median survival for all patients after recurrence remains 2 to 3 years, with a 5-year survival rate less than 20%. Breast cancer may recur in any site; clinically detectable metastatic disease indicates a substantial amount of body tumor burden. Responses are defined as complete (complete disappearance of all metastatic lesions irrespective of location or means of measurement), partial (30% reduction in tumor mass based on the sum of the largest diameters of measurable lesions before and after treatment), stable (less than 30% reduction or a 25% increase in measurable lesions for 3 to 4 months), and progressing (continued

Continued

Table 204–7 • **ADJUVANT TREATMENT GUIDELINES FOR PATIENTS WITH EARLY-STAGE INVASIVE BREAST CANCER**

PATIENT GROUP	TREATMENT
NODE NEGATIVE	
Less than 0.5 cm	No adjuvant therapy
Tubular Colloid, or Medullary	
Less than 1 cm	No adjuvant therapy
>1 cm to <3 cm	Consider adjuvant therapy
≥3 cm	Adjuvant therapy recommended
Invasive Ductal or Lobular	
0.6–1 cm and no unfavorable features*	No adjuvant therapy
0.6–1 cm with any unfavorable feature	Consider adjuvant therapy
>1 cm	
*ER or PR negative	Adjuvant therapy recommended
ER or PR positive	
≤3 cm	Tamoxifen[†] ± chemotherapy
>3 cm	Tamoxifen[†] + chemotherapy
NODE POSITIVE	
ER and PR negative	Adjuvant therapy recommended
ER or PR positive	Tamoxifen[†] + chemotherapy

ER = estrogen receptor; PR = progesterone receptor.
*Unfavorable characteristics include high-grade tumor, blood vessel or lymphatic invasion by tumor, and high tumor proliferation rate (high S-phase by flow cytometry or high Ki-67 value by immunohistochemistry).
[†]For premenopausal patients, ovarian ablation should be considered; for postmenopausal patients, the use of aromatase inhibitors in place of tamoxifen should be considered.
Modified from National Comprehensive Cancer Network guidelines: www.nccn.org.

Table 204–8 • **FOLLOW-UP GUIDELINES FOR PATIENTS WITH EARLY-STAGE BREAST CANCER: AMERICAN SOCIETY OF CLINICAL ONCOLOGY GUIDELINES***

PROCEDURE OR TEST	FREQUENCY
History and physical examination* (eliciting of symptoms of breast cancer)	Every 3–6 mo for first 3 yr, every 6–12 mo for next yr, then yearly
Mammography	
Mastectomy patients	Yearly
Lumpectomy patients	Yearly
Pelvic examination	Yearly
Breast self-examination	Monthly
Complete blood cell counts and chemistry studies	The literature does not support the use of these tests
Chest radiography, bone scans, liver imaging, and tumor marker studies	Not recommended for routine follow-up in asymptomatic patients
Patient education regarding signs and symptoms of recurrence	Each visit

*Limited evaluation: Assess for pain, dyspnea, weight loss, and other major changes in function. The limited examination should include an assessment of nodes, axillae, lumpectomy or mastectomy site, chest, and abdomen. Patients should be instructed regarding symptoms of recurrence.
Modified from Smith TJ, Davidson NE, Schapira DV, et al: American Society of Clinical Oncology 1998 Update of Recommended Breast Cancer Surveillance Guidelines. J Clin Oncol 1999;7:1080.

growth during therapy). New lesions at any time during therapy indicate treatment failure. Tumor reduction must last for at least 1 month to be considered a complete or partial response.

Patients whose tumors are positive for estrogen or progesterone receptors are good candidates for endocrine therapy. Women who are older, who have a long disease-free interval (time from diagnosis to metastases), or who have bone or soft tissue lesions are most likely to respond. Response to endocrine therapy is seen in 30 to 70% of women who are hormone receptor positive and in 10 to 20% who are receptor negative. The antiestrogen tamoxifen is appropriate therapy for both premenopausal and postmenopausal women. In premenopausal women, tamoxifen and oophorectomy are the treatments of choice. Oophorectomy can be done surgically, with external beam irradiation, or medically, with luteinizing hormone-releasing hormone agonists such as goserelin or leuprolide. Recent data suggest that combining oophorectomy with tamoxifen is associated with higher response rates, longer time to tumor progression, and superior survival when compared with treatment with oophorectomy or tamoxifen alone. In postmenopausal women, new aromatase inhibitors (letrozole, anastrozole, and exemestane) are superior to tamoxifen and progestins (megestrol and medroxyprogesterone acetate) and should be considered first-line endocrine therapy. Oophorectomy is not effective in postmenopausal women. In selected postmenopausal patients who have responded to previous endocrine therapy, androgens and estrogens can be used. Responses to initial hormonal therapy last an average of 12 months, and patients who respond to one agent have a fair chance of responding to a second hormonal agent after failure of initial therapy.

Chemotherapy is best reserved for women who have tumor progression on hormonal therapy or whose cancers lack hormone receptors. In general, 40 to 80% of patients have a complete or partial response to their initial chemotherapy regimen. Initial responses generally persist for 6 to 12 months. Responses to second- and third-line chemotherapy are frequent but usually persist for only several months. Single-agent therapy, using taxanes (paclitaxel [Taxol] and docetaxel [Taxotere]) or capecitabine, provides response rates similar to those of combination regimens. High-dose chemotherapy with autologous bone marrow or stem cell transplantation yields results that are generally similar to those of standard chemotherapy [6] and

should not be used in women with metastatic disease, except in the setting of a randomized clinical trial.

Trastuzumab is a humanized mouse monoclonal antibody that reacts with the transmembrane tyrosine kinase receptor protein HER-2, which is overexpressed in 20% of primary breast cancers; about 25% of these patients respond to trastuzumab. Chemotherapy plus trastuzumab provides significantly higher response rates, time to tumor progression, and survival times as compared with standard chemotherapy alone in HER-2–positive patients. Other biologics targeted to epidermal growth factor receptor pathways and to blocking tumor angiogenesis are now in clinical trials. Vaccines targeted against transmembrane glycoproteins coded by the *MUC*-1 oncogene are also being tested in clinical trials.

SPECIFIC ISSUES RELATED TO METASTATIC DISEASE

CENTRALIZED NERVOUS SYSTEM, SPINAL CORD, AND LEPTOMENINGEAL METASTASES. Radiation therapy can be an extremely effective palliative therapy for central nervous system metastases and spinal cord compression. Dexamethasone in doses of 4 to 10 mg every 6 hours should be used in conjunction with irradiation. Spinal cord compression is most commonly seen in patients with bone metastases, and almost all patients have back pain and radiographic evidence of spinal metastases. Magnetic resonance imaging is currently the imaging method of choice to establish the diagnosis. For patients with rapid loss of function or progression of symptoms while receiving radiation therapy, surgical decompression is necessary to lower the probability of paraplegia. Patients with leptomeningeal metastases frequently have headaches and lesions of cranial and peripheral nerves; the diagnosis is best made with lumbar puncture and examination of cerebrospinal fluid for malignant cells. Gadolinium-enhanced magnetic resonance imaging of the brain or spinal cord may show enhancement of the meninges in about 70% of patients with leptomeningeal spread. Intrathecal chemotherapy (methotrexate and other agents) can lead to brief remission, but the general outlook for such patients is exceedingly poor.

SKELETAL METASTASES. The use of bisphosphonates can significantly reduce the complications of skeletal metastases in both premenopausal and postmenopausal patients. Such treatment does not improve survival. Pamidronate and zolendronate given intravenously every 3 or 4 weeks are effective in this setting and can be given at the same time as endocrine therapy or chemotherapy. In addition, radioisotopes that localize in bone, such as strontium-89 and samarium-153 may be effective. External beam irradiation results in significant palliation in patients with moderate to severe bone pain at specific metastatic sites. Hypercalcemia is a common complication of metastatic breast cancer (Chapter 187) and more likely to occur in patients with skeletal metastases. Initial treatment of symptomatic patients includes hydration, bisphosphonates, and diuresis. Calcitonin and glucocorticoids can also be effective in patients who need rapid reduction of their serum calcium level. Ultimate control depends on the response to systemic therapy.

SURGERY. Patients with isolated or minimal metastatic disease (one to three lesions) to the central nervous system, lung, or liver and those who have limited or no other metastatic disease may benefit from surgical resection of metastatic lesions. Also, patients with locoregional recurrence are best managed by surgical resection of chest wall lesions when feasible, followed by external beam irradiation of the involved area. Chest tube drainage and sclerotherapy are successful in about 70% of patients with persistent or recurrent malignant effusions that have not been controlled by systemic therapy. Patients with ipsilateral breast tumor recurrence after lumpectomy alone or with breast irradiation for early-stage breast cancer are usually best managed by mastectomy, although further lumpectomy may be appropriate in patients with smaller recurrences.

Other Issues

GETTING INFORMATION. Never has high-quality medical information been more accessible to the practicing clinician. In addition to journals and textbooks, the Internet has now become a major resource for up-to-date information derived from multiple sources (Table 204–9). The National Cancer Institute Physician Data Query (PDQ) system is a resource for both patients and physicians seeking general or specific information about cancer and available clinical trials. PDQ is updated monthly by an editorial board of physician scientists. Physicians can also contact the National Cancer Institute's Cancer Information Service for access to PDQ by calling 1-888-80-NABCO.

BREAST CANCER IN OLDER WOMEN. The majority of new breast cancers in the United States occur in women 65 years and older. With the number of older people in the population growing dramatically, the number of new breast cancers seen in this older population will continue to increase. Older women are less likely to have mammographic screening, to be offered the opportunity for breast preservation, to receive breast radiation after lumpectomy, to be considered for adjuvant therapy, and to be treated aggressively for metastases. However, older women in reasonably good health are able to tolerate and benefit from treatment similar to younger women, without a higher rate of surgical complications or toxicities to radiation therapy or chemotherapy. Healthy older women should be offered the same prevention, diagnostic, and treatment options as their younger peers.

BREAST CANCER IN MEN. Men account for about 0.8% of cases of breast cancer, and the disease is more common in men with benign breast disease, testicular disease, and a positive family history. Treatment recommendations are similar to those for women.

BREAST CANCER AND PREGNANCY. The diagnosis of breast cancer during pregnancy (Chapter 205) is extremely traumatic. Such patients are usually first seen when their disease is at higher stages, probably because of difficulties in diagnosis. After the first trimester, definitive surgical procedures can usually be performed with minimal risk to the mother and fetus. Chemotherapy administered after the first trimester has not been associated with increased fetal loss or birth defects. Limited data suggest that development is normal in children of mothers who have received chemotherapy during pregnancy. Alkylating agents given during pregnancy frequently cause subsequent infertility. Hormonal agents should be avoided during pregnancy. Pregnancy following breast cancer, especially 2 to 3 years after diagnosis, does not appear to increase the risk of metastatic disease. Major considerations relating to childbearing after breast cancer should be based on the risks of recurrence.

HORMONE REPLACEMENT THERAPY AFTER BREAST CANCER (Chapter 256). The use of hormone replacement therapy in women with a diagnosis of breast cancer is an area of heated controversy. Current data suggest that the use of estrogens alone in patients with hysterectomy or the use of estrogens and progestins in patients with an intact uterus for 5 years or longer is associated with a relative risk of breast cancer 1.5 times greater than that of women who do not use hormone replacement therapy. The major concerns related to the use of hormone replacement therapy after breast cancer are (1) whether such therapy will substantially increase the risk of a new primary breast cancer in patients already at higher risk for breast cancer and (2) whether such therapy might stimulate the growth of occult breast cancer metastases. Given the uncertainties and risks of such therapy (Chapter 256), hormone replacement therapy probably should be considered after early-stage breast cancer only for patients with disabling vasomotor symptoms. The bone and cardiovascular benefits of hormone replacement therapy can be accomplished with nonendocrine agents.

LYMPHEDEMA. Lymphedema develops in the ipsilateral arm in about 15% of women with breast cancer following primary therapy. The

Table 204–9 • INFORMATION RESOURCES

WEB ADDRESS OR PHONE NUMBER	DESCRIPTION
1-800-4-CANCER	Access number for the NCI Cancer Information Service
http://www.cancer.gov	Information service of the NCI. Includes PDQ and summaries on treatment, screening, prevention, supportive care, and ongoing clinical trials. Also access to CANCERLIT, NCI's bibliographic database
http://www.nabco.org 1-888-80-NABCO	National Alliance of Breast Cancer Organizations—The leading nonprofit resource for information about breast cancer events and activities and has links to other key sites
http://www.fda.gov/cder/cancer	U.S. Food and Drug Administration—Variety of information on cancer and approved drug therapies
http://www.ncbi.nlm.nih.gov/entrez/query.fcgi	PubMed—Access to more than 11,000,000 literature citations from the National Library of Medicine
http://www.asco.org	American Society of Clinical Oncology—Rich source of information for providers and patients. Patient follow-up guidelines for breast cancer
http://www.cancer.org/	American Cancer Society—Excellent resources and links for providers and patients
http://www.nccn.org/	National Comprehensive Cancer Network—Treatment guidelines for patients and providers
http://www.mayoclinic.com/calcs/	Mayo Clinic Site—Predicting risk of recurrence in early-stage breast cancer and estimating benefits of adjuvant systemic therapy
http://www.adjuvantonline.com	Excellent site for estimating risks for recurrence and benefits of adjuvant therapy
http://www.breastcancerupdate.com/	Excellent resource for new treatment-related information and references
http://www.y-me.org	Y-me National Breast Cancer Organization—Excellent resource for patients with breast cancer
http://www.komen.org	Susan G. Komen Breast Cancer Foundation—Excellent resource for information about breast cancer

NCI = National Cancer Institute; PDQ = Physician Data Query.

incidence of this complication may be slightly higher in women treated with lumpectomy and radiation and may be less in women whose disease is staged via sentinel lymph node procedures. Symptoms are usually mild, but persistent; slowly progressive edema can lead to functional loss. Early recognition is key, and patients should be asked about this complication at each visit. Affected patients should be referred to physical therapists and other health professionals skilled in the management of lymphedema. Treatment consists of avoidance of trauma, special exercises, elevation of the extremity, and the use of compression pumps and specially fitted compression stockings. Manual lymphatic drainage procedures may be more effective than compression pumping. No effective medications have as yet been identified; diuretics are rarely effective and should be avoided.

Grade A

1. Fisher B, Costantino JP, Wickerham DL, et al: Tamoxifen for prevention of breast cancer: Report of the National Surgical Adjuvant Breast and Bowel Project P-1 Study. J Natl Cancer Inst 1998;90:1371–1388.
2. Fisher B, Anderson S, Bryant J, et al: Twenty-year follow-up of a randomized trial comparing total mastectomy, lumpectomy, and lumpectomy plus irradiation for the treatment of invasive breast cancer. N Engl J Med 2002;347:1233–1241.
3. Early Breast Cancer Trialists' Collaborative Group: Polychemotherapy for early breast cancer: An overview of the randomised trials. Lancet 1998;352:930–942.
4. Cuzick J, Powles T, Veronesi U, et al: Overview of the main outcomes in breast-cancer prevention trials. Lancet 2003;361:296–300.
5. The GIVIO Investigators: Impact of follow-up testing on survival and health-related quality of life in breast cancer patients: A multicenter randomized controlled trial. JAMA 1994;271:1587–1592.
6. Tallman MS, Gray R, Robert NJ, et al: Conventional adjuvant chemotherapy with or without high-dose chemotherapy and autologous stem-cell transplantation in high-risk breast cancer. N Engl J Med 2003;349:17–26.

SUGGESTED READINGS
Burstein HJ, Winer EP: Primary care: Primary care for survivors of breast cancer. N Engl J Med 2000;343:1086–1094. *Review of issues and management of women who have had breast cancer.*
Eifel P, Axelson JA, Costa J, et al: National Institutes of Health Consensus Development Conference Statement. Adjuvant therapy for breast cancer. J Natl Cancer Inst 2001;93:979–989. *Overview of the current status of adjuvant therapy for early stage breast cancer.*
Fletcher SW, Elmore JG: Mammographic screening for breast cancer. N Engl J Med 2003;348:1672–1680. *A succinct yet comprehensive overview.*
Giordano SH, Buzdar AU, Hortobagyi GN: Breast cancer in men. Ann Intern Med 2002;137:678–687. *Overview of the disease in men, who account for 0.8% of cases.*
Humphrey LL, Helfand M, Chan BK, Woolf SH: Breast cancer screening: A summary of the evidence for the U.S. Preventive Services Task Force. Ann Intern Med 2002;137:347–360. *Meticulous meta-analysis of mammography trials and the role of mammography in improving breast cancer survival.*
Kissinger LS, Harris R, Woolf SH, et al: Chemoprevention of breast cancer: A summary of the evidence for the U.S. Preventive Services Task Force. Ann Intern Med 2002;137:59–67. *With accompanying recommendations, it outlines the evidence for when to use chemoprevention.*
The ATAC Trialists Group: Anastrozole alone or in combination with tamoxifen versus tamoxifen alone for adjuvant treatment of postmenopausal women with early breast cancer: First results of the ATAC randomised trial. Lancet 2002;359:2131–2139. *Seminal clinical trial whose preliminary results show that the aromatase inhibitor anastrozole is superior to tamoxifen in the adjuvant setting.*
U.S. Preventative Services Task Force: Screening for breast cancer: Recommendations and rationale. Ann Intern Med 2002;137:344–346. *Screening recommendations of the U.S. Preventative Services Task Force.*

205 GYNECOLOGIC CANCERS

Kelly L. Molpus
Howard W. Jones III

Gynecologic tumors may originate in the vulva, vagina, cervix, uterus, fallopian tubes, ovaries, or peritoneum. Uterine cancers are the most common, frequently arise from the endometrial lining of the uterus, and usually are diagnosed when the disease is confined to the uterus. Ovarian carcinoma is the second most frequent; signs and symptoms are nonspecific, and most ovarian cancers are not diagnosed until disease has spread to the abdomen and/or distant sites. Invasive cervical cancer is one of the most common malignancies in developing countries but is now uncommon in the United States, where cervical intraepithelial neoplasia (CIN) is more common. Vulvar carcinoma arises from the external genitalia (vulva) and accounts for only 1 to 2% of all gynecologic cancers. Primary vaginal tumors are rare and manifest like cervical cancers. Primary peritoneal carcinomas can be indistinguishable from ovarian carcinoma (Chapter 210). Primary fallopian tube carcinomas are rare and share characteristics of ovarian and primary peritoneal tumors. Gestational trophoblastic tumors range from benign to overtly malignant neoplasms that result from abnormal proliferation of trophoblastic tissue associated with a normal or abnormal pregnancy.

UTERINE CANCER

Epidemiology

Uterine malignancies usually arise from the glandular component of the endometrial lining. Infrequently, tumors arise from the endometrial stroma or from the smooth muscle and connective tissue within the wall of the uterus. In the United States each year, approximately 36,100 cases of endometrial cancer are diagnosed and about 6500 patients die from the disease. The lifetime risk is approximately 2% for the general population. Most women with uterine cancer are postmenopausal, but about 5% of patients are diagnosed prior to the age of 40 years. For type I endometrial cancers, excessive estrogenic stimuli is a risk factor, and women taking postmenopausal unopposed estrogen replacement therapy have about a 9.5-fold increased risk. Breast cancer patients on tamoxifen for 5 years have an estimated 1.7- to 4-fold increased relative risk. Women who are 50 pounds above their ideal body weight have an estimated 10-fold increased risk of developing endometrial adenocarcinoma because of prolonged stimulation of the endometrium by estrone, a weak estrogen that is converted from adrenal androstenedione in adipose tissue. Hypertension, diabetes, early menarche, late menopause, and nulliparity are also considered risk factors. In contrast, type II endometrial cancers tend to occur in older, thinner women without exogenous estrogen exposure and tend to be higher grade, clinically aggressive tumors.

Pathobiology

Endometrial hyperplasia with cellular atypia (increased nuclear-to-cytoplasmic ratio, pleomorphism, multinucleated cells) has an approximately 30% chance of malignant transformation, and early adenocarcinomas often arise within a background of atypical endometrial hyperplasia. It is unlikely, however, that all endometrial carcinomas transition through a detectable premalignant phase. Although no genetic cause of uterine cancer has been identified, women with Lynch II/hereditary nonpolyposis colon cancer (Chapter 200) syndrome may have endometrial cancer.

Clinical Manifestations

Endometrial cancer is often diagnosed at an early stage, since more than 90% of patients present with postmenopausal or irregular bleeding. Atrophic changes are the most common cause of postmenopausal bleeding, and only about 10% of women who present with bleeding actually have carcinoma. Nevertheless, any postmenopausal spotting, isolated bleeding episode, or blood-tinged vaginal discharge warrants further evaluation. Younger women commonly present with intermenstrual bleeding (metrorrhagia) and/or heavy menstrual bleeding (menorrhagia).

Diagnosis

Endometrial tissue sampling is the only definitive way to establish the diagnosis. Endometrial biopsy in the office can obtain adequate tissue samples in 90 to 95% of patients, with an accurate diagnosis rendered in 85% (false-negative rate of 15%). All endometrial surfaces should be sampled. If endometrial biopsy results are inconclusive or inconsistent with the clinical presentation, a dilation and curettage may be necessary. Direct visualization of the uterine cavity and removal of lesions via hysteroscopy may be warranted if bleeding persists and/or the cause of the uterine bleeding remains uncertain.

Transvaginal pelvic ultrasonography or sonohysterography are less invasive means to delineate the endometrial anatomy; they may be useful in selected patients who have uterine bleeding due to atrophy and do not require biopsy. Endometrial atrophy is the most likely cause of postmenopausal bleeding and can be reliably diagnosed when the endometrial stripe thickness is 5.0 mm or less. As the stripe thickness increases above 5.0 mm, the risk of significant pathology (atypical hyperplasia, carcinoma) increases proportionally, and an endometrial biopsy is indicated. The Papanicolaou (Pap) smear has no established role in the diagnosis or screening of uterine carcinoma. Women who have breast cancer and are taking tamoxifen are at increased risk and should have an annual pelvic examination, but ultrasonography or endometrial biopsy is not indicated unless they have atypical bleeding.

 Treatment

Women who have simple or complex hyperplasia without cellular atypia may be treated with progestins to offset the estrogenic stimulation. Because of the risk of associated endometrial cancer, atypical hyperplasia is best treated with hysterectomy. In patients who are medically inoperable or who wish to preserve fertility, however, progestins are an alternative if combined with clinical surveillance and follow-up biopsy within 6 months to ensure regression of the hyperplasia.

Endometrial carcinoma is treated with hysterectomy and bilateral salpingo-oophorectomy. Additional surgical staging is individualized based on the tumor's grade, size, and depth of invasion and on whether there is extension into the cervix or there is obvious extrauterine disease. The most common route of extrauterine spread is to the pelvic or para-aortic lymph nodes. Metastases to the ovary are also found in 6 to 10% of women in whom the disease appears to be confined to the uterus, thereby warranting routine salpingo-oophorectomy.

Post-surgical therapy depends on the surgical stage, grade, and extent of disease. Low-grade tumors confined to the uterus have an excellent chance of cure with surgery alone. Positive lymph node metastases are a poor prognostic finding, and most such patients are treated with postoperative radiation therapy to include the affected lymphatics. Women with advanced-stage, metastatic, or recurrent disease require multimodality therapy and should be included in clinical trials when available. Metastatic endometrial adenocarcinoma responds poorly to chemotherapy.

Prognosis

The majority of endometrial cancers can be cured because their presenting symptoms lead to rapid diagnosis and treatment (Table 205–1). Prognosis worsens as the extent of disease is more advanced. If patients with histologically proven pelvic and/or para-aortic lymph nodes are treated with adjunctive radiation therapy, they may have 40 to 50% 5-year survival.

Table 205–1 • DISTRIBUTION AND PROGNOSIS OF GYNECOLOGIC CANCER

STAGE*	PERCENTAGE OF PATIENTS	5-YEAR SURVIVAL RATE (%)
ENDOMETRIAL ADENOCARCINOMA		
I (Corpus only)	70.2	87.4
II (Cervical involvement)	12.4	76.3
III (Pelvic metastases)	13.3	56.6
IV (Distant metastases)	4.1	17.8
EPITHELIAL OVARIAN CANCER		
IA (Ovary only)	12.7	89.9
IIB (Pelvic metastases)	3.2	63.7
IIIC (Abdominal metastases >2 cm)	40.0	28.7
IV (Extra-abdominal metastases)	11.9	16.8
CANCER OF THE CERVIX		
IB1 (Cervix only)	33.2	90.5
IIB (Parametrium)	23.7	73.3
IIIB (Pelvic sidewall)	19.3	46.4
IV (Metastatic)	3.9	25.2

*Note: Not all substages are listed in this table.
From Pecorelli S, Benedet JL, Boyle P, et al: FIGO Annual Report on the Results of Treatment in Gynecological Cancer; vol 24. J Epidemiol Biostat 2001;6:7–43.

OVARIAN CARCINOMA

Epidemiology

Ovarian carcinoma is the most deadly of the gynecologic malignancies. The incidence gradually rises and reaches a peak at about 70 years of age, at which age the incidence is 55 per 100,000 among white women but somewhat lower in African-American women. The lifetime risk of ovarian cancer for women in the United States is about 1.4%, but women with one first-degree relative who has had ovarian cancer appear to have an increased risk of 3 to 5%. The cause of ovarian cancer is unknown. *BRCA 1* or *BRCA 2* (Chapter 204) gene mutations are found in about 10% of women with epithelial ovarian cancer. Rare families with a high incidence of ovarian, breast, endometrial, and colon cancer comprise the hereditary nonpolyposis colon cancer syndrome (Lynch syndrome II) (Chapters 185 and 200). Multiple pregnancies and the use of oral contraceptives exert a protective effect, perhaps because of decreased ovulation.

Pathobiology

There are four types of ovarian tumors. *Common epithelial tumors* of the ovary include serous, mucinous, endometrioid, clear cell, and otherwise unspecified adenocarcinomas; these tumors account for almost 90% of ovarian cancers and are most commonly found in postmenopausal women. *Germ cell tumors*, which arise from the totipotent oocytes, are usually benign ("dermoid cysts"); they often occur in young women and are almost always unilateral. When malignant (e.g., dysgerminoma, teratoma), these tumors are highly aggressive but respond very well to combination chemotherapy. *Stromal tumors* are generally low grade and arise from the granulosa, theca, and Sertoli-Leydig cells of the ovary; they may be hormonally functional. These tumors are usually unilateral and may occur in any age group but most typically occur in the fourth and fifth decades. Surgical excision may be sufficient, but combination chemotherapy is effective for metastatic or recurrent disease. *Metastatic cancer* to the ovary must always be considered in patients with a pelvic mass, which may be the first indication of a primary gastrointestinal, endometrial, or breast carcinoma.

Clinical Manifestations

Early ovarian cancer is usually asymptomatic. Occasionally, ovarian enlargement is found on routine examination, and cancer may be discovered incidentally at the time of abdominal or pelvic surgery for other indications. In two thirds of patients, however, widespread intra-abdominal metastases are present by the time the diagnosis is made. Symptoms of abdominal swelling, bloating, and pelvic fullness or pressure are common. Many patients have vague abdominal complaints or nonspecific gastrointestinal symptoms. Ascites or a palpable abdominopelvic mass may be found on examination. The presence of an irregular mass in the pelvis or nodularity in the cul-de-sac accompanied by ascites is often diagnostic. Malignant pleural effusions may manifest as shortness of breath.

Diagnosis

SCREENING TESTS. Screening tests for ovarian cancer remain controversial. Transvaginal ultrasonography, although quite effective for diagnosing ovarian cysts and tumors, is nonspecific, and its use results in surgical exploration of a large number of women with benign ovarian cysts. Serum levels of the tumor-associated antigen CA-125 above 35 U/mL are present in 80% of postmenopausal women with ovarian cancer (Chapter 189). Unfortunately, many low-stage ovarian tumors do not cause elevated levels of CA-125, whereas endometriosis, pelvic inflammatory disease, and some benign ovarian tumors may do so. The relative rarity of ovarian cancer, combined with the nonspecific nature and relative insensitivity of currently available tests, makes ovarian cancer screening unsatisfactory.

DIFFERENTIAL DIAGNOSIS. A pelvic mass can be caused by either a benign or a malignant tumor of the ovary, as well as by ectopic pregnancy, endometriosis, inflammatory conditions, physiologic cysts, and malignancies of other pelvic organs and structure. After a complete history and physical examination have been performed and the size and character of the mass have been confirmed by ultrasonography, several additional studies may be helpful. A chest radiograph is useful to exclude pulmonary metastases and pleural effusions. An abdominal and pelvic computed tomographic scan can identify evidence of upper abdominal metastases or ureteral obstruction, and a barium enema or colonoscopy is almost always indicated before surgery to exclude a primary lesion or secondary involvement of the colon.

Rx Treatment

SURGERY. In almost all cases of suspected ovarian carcinoma, an exploratory laparotomy is the ultimate diagnostic procedure. Laparoscopy may be used by some surgeons to establish a diagnosis, but laparoscopy may disseminate localized cancer, and most experts feel definitive resection cannot be done via laparoscopy. If the diagnosis is confirmed, tumor debulking, including total abdominal hysterectomy and bilateral salpingo-oophorectomy, should be performed if possible to make a definitive diagnosis and to stage the extent of disease. Aggressive tumor debulking, even when all cancer cannot be removed, improves the length and quality of survival. Ideally, this initial surgery should be done by a gynecologic oncologist whose special training and experience should provide the optimal management.

CHEMOTHERAPY. Except for some patients with stage IA disease, chemotherapy is recommended postoperatively for most women with ovarian cancer.[1] Combined platinum (carboplatin or cisplatin) and paclitaxel is an effective and the most widely used initial chemotherapy regimen for ovarian cancer.[2] Following primary surgery, patients are usually treated with six cycles at 3-week intervals. The mean disease-free interval for women with stage III and IV disease is about 18 months, and 20 to 30% of these patients will be long-term survivors. A large randomized trial suggests that single-agent carboplatin or the combination of cyclophosphamide, doxorubicin, and cisplatin may be equally effective alternatives.[3] Other active drugs include topotecan, gemcitabine, taxotere, etoposide, ifosfamide, and altretamine. Intraperitoneal chemotherapy has sometimes been used for patients with minimal residual disease. Chemotherapy is well tolerated, and quality of life is usually quite satisfactory until late in the course of the disease. Postoperative radiation therapy, which is no better than chemotherapy, is generally more toxic; as a result, chemotherapy is usually preferred.

TREATMENT OF RECURRENT, METASTATIC DISEASE. The overall survival rate of patients treated for ovarian cancer is only about 40%; progressive disease develops in many women despite appropriate primary therapy. Salvage chemotherapy protocols for recurrent disease produce a 20 to 30% response rate. Although almost all women with recurrent disease succumb to cancer, many women live 3 to 5 years with a good quality of life.

Prognosis

The long-term survival rate of patients treated for epithelial ovarian cancer is still disappointing (see Table 205–1). Almost 60% of patients have stage III or IV disease at the time of diagnosis. Although the majority of women with advanced disease live several years with a reasonable qualify of life, recurrent cancer usually becomes symptomatic; only about 25% of patients with advanced disease survive for 5 years. By comparison, almost 80% of women with stage I ovarian cancer survive for 5 years.

Future Directions

Attempts to improve early diagnosis of ovarian cancer via accurate screening tests is perhaps the most important area of future investigation.

CERVICAL CANCER

Epidemiology

Cervical cancers originate from the squamous epithelium of the ectocervix or the glandular lining of the endocervix. Approximately

12,800 new cases of cervical carcinoma are diagnosed annually in the United States, and 4600 women die from the disease each year. The prevalence of invasive cervical cancer is much higher in developing countries where health care is not readily available. In the United States, the incidence of cervical cancer has dramatically declined since the introduction of the Pap smear, and there has been a four- to five-fold reduction in death from cervical cancer. However, even in developed countries, up to 50% of all women diagnosed with cervical cancer have never had a Pap smear.

Pathobiology

Most, if not all, cervical cancers are preceded by a phase of epithelial dysplasia or CIN that progresses slowly over years before stromal invasion occurs. Human papillomavirus (HPV; Chapter 345) DNA can be identified in at least 95% of dysplastic and malignant cervical lesions. HPV subtypes 16 and 18 are isolated most frequently in invasive squamous cell carcinoma and adenocarcinoma, respectively. Additional high-risk subtypes such as 31, 33, 35, and others have been characterized. It is estimated that up to 50% of sexually active women have been exposed to HPV, but only a small fraction of exposed women develop high-grade CIN or invasive cervical cancer. Cofactors for malignant transformation include tobacco use and immunosuppression. For example, cervical cancers manifest at a later stage and are clinically more aggressive in women infected with human immunodeficiency virus, and cervical carcinoma is an acquired immunodeficiency syndrome–defining illness (Chapter 419).

Clinical Manifestations

Early cervical cancers are asymptomatic. Regular Pap smear screening is vital to detect premalignant and early malignant changes. As the cervical cancer progresses, the patient may complain of intermenstrual spotting, postcoital bleeding, postmenopausal bleeding, or bloody vaginal discharge. Advanced cases may present with severe back or pelvic pain, alteration of bowel and bladder function, enlarged lymph nodes, or obstructive uremia.

Diagnosis

The Pap smear is a well-established screening test for abnormalities arising from the cervix. Cervical cytology can detect microscopic changes not visible on physical examination. However, a single Pap test may have a false-negative rate of up to 50% because of problems with sampling, preparation, or interpretation. Despite the low sensitivity of a single Pap test, repeated smears have a high sensitivity, so that a woman with three consecutive negative Pap tests has less than a 1% chance of an undetected cervical lesion. Invasive cancer is usually associated with inflammation, hemorrhage, and necrosis, which may make a Pap test difficult to interpret. Accordingly, any suspicious visible lesion should be biopsied.

Pap smears suggestive of an intraepithelial lesion or carcinoma warrant further investigation via colposcopy and directed biopsy. The management of Pap smears showing atypia remains controversial, but there is increasing evidence to indicate that HPV testing may be the most effective way to evaluate these patients. In patients who have biopsy-confirmed high-grade dysplasia or carcinomas that are not grossly visible, further diagnostic evaluation via cervical conization or a loop electrosurgical excision procedure is recommended. Any woman with evidence of invasive carcinoma should be referred to a gynecologic oncologist.

Prevention

The current screening guidelines for cervical cancer recommend that every woman undergo an annual pelvic examination including Pap smear by the age of 21 or within 3 years of the onset of sexual activity, whichever comes first (Chapter 11). After three consecutive normal annual Pap smears, women at low risk may be screened at 3-year intervals at the discretion of their physician. Women at higher risk (i.e., those with previous history of abnormal Pap smear, HPV infection, dysplasia or carcinoma, tobacco use, multiple sexual partners, or immunosuppression) may not be good candidates for prolonged screening intervals. Screening should be continued to at least the age of 65 years.

Rx Treatment

Women diagnosed with CIN can be treated by loop electro-surgical excision procedure. Some early lesions can be managed by cryotherapy or laser vaporization. Effective treatment for very early stage cancers with depth of invasion of less than 3 mm (stage IA-1) include a hysterectomy or the option of cervical conization in women who wish to preserve fertility. Larger tumors that are confined to the cervix and/or upper vagina (stage IA-2, IB-1, or IIA) can be managed by radical hysterectomy with pelvic lymphadenectomy, or by pelvic radiation therapy. Very large primary cervical cancers (i.e., bulky stage IB-2 or greater) and invasive tumors in patients who are deemed medically inoperable are best treated with a combination of radiation and cisplatin-based chemotherapy. **4** Patients whose tumors have invaded into the bladder or rectum (stage IV-A) or metastasized to distant sites (stage IV-B) require multimodality therapy, preferably in a clinical trial if available. Platinum-based chemotherapy is usually recommended for patients with metastatic or recurrent disease, but the response rates are only 20 to 30% and are of limited duration.

Prognosis

The prognosis is directly related to the clinical stage at the time of diagnosis (see Table 205–1). A large primary tumor, invasion of the lymphovascular space, and lymph node metastases are poor prognostic factors. Overall, patients who are treated when the tumor is confined to the cervix can expect an 85% or better 5-year survival. In contrast, tumors that have spread beyond the cervix to the parametrial tissue and pelvic sidewalls are associated with approximately 70% and 50% 5-year survivals, respectively.

Future Directions

Fluid-based cytology and automated cytology screening techniques may enhance the accuracy of Pap smears. HPV subtyping is being evaluated for screening. Vaccines against HPV have shown promising preliminary results. **5**

VULVAR CANCER

Vulvar cancers arise from the external female genitalia (vulva) and account for 1 to 2% of all gynecologic malignancies. Approximately 3500 new cases are diagnosed annually in the United States, more than 90% of which are squamous cell carcinomas. The second most common vulvar cancer is malignant melanoma (Chapter 209). HPV appears to be involved in some cancers, especially in the younger age group.

Chronic pruritus and a persistent lesion are the most common presentations of vulvar carcinoma. The lesion is usually pale and white, but it may be pigmented and slightly raised. Tumors may arise from any region, including the perineum, labia minora, labia majora, or mons pubis. Many women downplay their symptoms and are reluctant to seek evaluation. Health care providers often treat women with a variety of steroid, hormone, antibacterial, or antifungal creams for prolonged periods without a tissue diagnosis. Immediate biopsy of any suspicious area is crucial.

Wide, local excision is the preferred management of precancerous vulvar intraepithelial neoplasia. The prognosis of vulvar cancer is directly related to the depth of invasion and size of the lesion, both of which predict the chance of lymphatic spread. Small lesions that are confined to the vulva and have less than 1.0 mm of invasion can usually be cured with local surgical excision. More deeply invasive lesions and those greater than 2 cm in diameter require more radical resection and inguinal-femoral lymphadenectomy. Pelvic and groin radiation therapy is usually recommended after surgery if lymph node metastases are identified. Advanced disease (i.e., lesions involving the urethra, vagina, or anus) and metastatic disease should receive multimodality therapy, preferably in a clinical trial.

Lesions that are confined to the vulva and have minimal invasion can usually be cured with surgical excision. If the primary tumor is less than 2 cm in diameter, 5-year survival is 85% or better. Metastases to regional lymph nodes suggest a poor prognosis, especially when more than two lymph nodes are involved or when there is extranodal

extension of disease. Even with postoperative radiation, 5-year survival for patients with multiple nodal metastases is less than 35%.

GESTATIONAL TROPHOBLASTIC DISEASE

Gestational trophoblastic disease (GTD) encompasses an array of disease processes including benign to overtly malignant neoplasms related to pregnancy. GTD is characterized by an abnormal growth of trophoblastic (placental) tissue and most commonly manifests in the form of molar pregnancy. Persistent GTD occurs in 20% of molar pregnancies, despite complete uterine evacuation. GTD may also follow any other pregnancy event, including preterm or term birth, miscarriage, abortion, or ectopic pregnancy. GTD includes complete or partial mole, invasive mole, choriocarcinoma, and placental site trophoblastic tumor (PSTT).

Molar pregnancy commonly manifests as second trimester bleeding in a woman whose uterus is larger than expected for the estimated gestational age. A characteristic heterogeneous echogenic pattern ("snow-storm") is evident on ultrasonogram. Postpregnancy GTD may manifest as persistent bleeding greater than expected subsequent to delivery or uterine evacuation. With metastatic disease, pulmonary symptoms may be present because the lungs are involved in 80% of cases. Distant metastases to other sites are uncommon in the absence of lung metastases. The second most common site of extrauterine disease is the vagina, which occurs in 30% of advanced cases. The characteristic laboratory feature is a persistently elevated serum β-human chorionic gonadotropin (β-hCG) level. Human placental lactogen level may be elevated in PSTT.

Gestational trophoblastic disease was the first metastatic tumor ever cured with systemic chemotherapy. Nonmetastatic GTD and low-risk metastatic disease usually respond well to single-agent chemotherapy with methotrexate or actinomycin-D. High-risk metastatic disease and disease unresponsive to single-agent therapy are treated with combination chemotherapy. Hysterectomy is recommended when the uterus is involved by tumor that is not responding to chemotherapy; it is also recommended for PSTT. The majority of patients with gestational trophoblastic tumors can be placed into complete remission, with cure rates approximating 100% for nonmetastatic and low-risk metastatic disease and 90% for high-risk metastatic disease.

VAGINAL CANCER

Vaginal cancers are rare, accounting for less than 1% of all gynecologic malignancies. The vast majority are squamous cell carcinomas, which are usually treated with primary radiation. Clear cell carcinomas are a vary rare variant that occur significantly more often in women with in utero exposure to diethylstilbestrol. Therapy is individualized based on the extent of disease.

1. Colombo N, Guthrie D, Chiari S, et al: International Collaborative Ovarian Neoplasm trial 1: A randomized trial of adjuvant chemotherapy in women with early-stage ovarian cancer. J Natl Cancer Inst 2003;95:125–132.
2. McGuire WP, Hoskins WJ, Brady MF, et al: Cyclophosphamide and cisplatin versus paclitaxel and cisplatin: A phase III randomized trial in patients with suboptimal stage III/IV ovarian cancer. N Engl J Med 1996;334:1–6.
3. International Collaborative Ovarian Neoplasm Group: Paclitaxel plus carboplatin versus standard chemotherapy with either single-agent carboplatin or cyclophosphamide, doxorubicin, and cisplatin in women with ovarian cancer: The ICON3 randomised trial. Lancet 2002;360:505–515.
4. Rose PG, Bundy BN, Watkins EB, et al: Concurrent cisplatin-based radiotherapy and chemotherapy for locally advanced cervical cancer. N Engl J Med 1999;340:1144–1153.
5. Koutsky LA, Ault KA, Wheeler CM, et al: A controlled trial of a human papillomavirus type 16 vaccine. N Engl J Med 2002;347:1645–1651.

SUGGESTED READINGS
Paley PJ: Screening for the major malignancies affecting women: Current guidelines. Am J Obstet Gynecol 2001;184:1021–1030. *A good review of risk factors and screening techniques for the most common malignancies in women.*
Pecorelli S, Benedet JL, Boyle P, et al: FIGO Annual Report on the Results of Treatment in Gynecological Cancer, vol 24. J Epidemiol Biostat 2001;6:1–184. *This "Annual Report," which is actually published every 3 years by the International Federation of Gynecology and Obstetrics, defines the staging for gynecologic cancers and presents an extensive database on the results of treatment.*
Saslow D, Runowicz CD, Solomon D, et al: American Cancer Society guideline for the early detection of cervical neoplasia and cancer. CA Cancer J Clin 2002;52:342–362. *Consensus guidelines and evidence to support them.*

Oncology

206 **TESTICULAR CANCER**

Lawrence H. Einhorn

Definition and Epidemiology

Testicular tumors are relatively uncommon, accounting for only 1% of male malignancies in the United States. The highest worldwide incidence is in Scandinavian countries; by contrast, testicular cancer is rare in African Americans and Asian Americans. The primary age group is 15 to 35 years for nonseminomatous tumors and a decade older for seminoma.

Male patients with a history of cryptorchidism have a 10- to 40-fold increased risk of developing testicular cancer. The normally descended testis in these men is also at a higher risk, suggesting a dysgenetic abnormality.

Pathobiology

More than 95% of tumors of the testis originate from germ cells. Germ cell tumors can be seminomas or nonseminomatous germ cell tumors. Seminomas are more likely to be confined to the testis (stage I) and are exquisitely sensitive to irradiation. Pure seminomas never have elevated serum α-fetoprotein (AFP) levels. Nonseminomatous germ cell tumors consist of embryonal cell carcinomas, choriocarcinomas, yolk sac tumors, or teratomas, alone or mixed with other elements. Teratomas do not secrete human chorionic gonadotropin (hCG) or AFP and do not metastasize, but they grow by local extension and are completely resistant to radiation and chemotherapy.

Most germ cell testicular cancers in adults are associated with a cytogenetic abnormality, i12p—an isochromosome of the short arm of chromosome 12 that is a highly specific chromosomal finding in germ cell tumors. Sertoli cell tumors, Leydig cell tumors, and lymphomas are the most common non–germ cell tumors. In men older than age 60 years, most tumors are non-Hodgkin's lymphoma (Chapter 195), with a predilection for bilateral involvement.

Clinical Manifestations

Most patients with testicular cancer present because of testicular pain or because of a mass or enlargement of one testis. Others are asymptomatic and are first detected during a routine physical examination. Less commonly, the diagnosis may first be detected during an evaluation for infertility, in part because testicular cancer can cause oligospermia.

Metastatic spread is either lymphatic or hematogenous. Lymphatic metastases usually go initially to the ipsilateral retroperitoneal lymph nodes, where they can produce flank pain. Lymphatic metastases may continue in a superior direction to the posterior mediastinum and eventually to the left supraclavicular lymph nodes. A large retroperitoneal mass or a supraclavicular lymph node may be palpable on physical examination. Hematogenous spread is usually first to the pulmonary parenchyma bilaterally. Pulmonary symptoms such as chest pain, shortness of breath, dyspnea on exertion, cough, or hemoptysis are seen only with extensive pulmonary metastases. Other sites of hematogenous spread include liver, bone, or brain. Significant elevation of the serum hCG level may produce gynecomastia.

Diagnosis and Staging

Patients with a palpable mass in the testis should be suspected of having testicular cancer, especially if there is a history of cryptorchidism. Other causes of testicular and scrotal abnormalities may be in the differential diagnosis. Acute pain in the testis suggests torsion. Painful enlargement may be due to a hydrocele. Pain and tenderness adjacent to the testis may be due to epididymitis or a varicocele. Tenderness of the testis itself on physical examination may reflect orchitis. However, an underlying neoplasm should always be considered.

Any testicular symptoms, including pain or a suspected mass, require evaluation. Testicular ultrasound is the test of choice in all suspicious cases. A hypoechogenic mass within the testis must be presumed to be testicular cancer and requires referral to a urologist.

When an orchiectomy reveals the diagnosis of testicular cancer, a staging evaluation determines the extent of disease and appropriate therapy. Clinical stage I disease is confined to the testis; stage II disease reflects spread to the retroperitoneal lymph nodes; stage III is supradiaphragmatic disease, with either nodal metastases to the posterior mediastinum or supraclavicular region or hematogenous spread, especially to the lungs.

In addition to a full history and physical examination, serum hCG and AFP levels should be obtained. Because the serum half-life is 1 day for hCG and 5 days for AFP, an AFP level of 1000 may take more than a month to normalize after orchiectomy even if the tumor has been fully removed. Imaging studies to define extent of disease include abdominal and pelvic computed tomography (CT) scan, and a chest radiograph. If the chest radiograph does not show pulmonary metastases, a chest CT scan should be performed. Bone scans and head CT scans can be reserved for patients with symptoms suggestive of osseous or central nervous system metastases, respectively.

Table 206–1 • SURVIVAL OF VARIOUS STATES OF GERM CELL TESTICULAR CANCERS

STAGE		5-YEAR SURVIVAL
Stage I	Disease confined to the testis	99%
Stage II	Disease extends to retroperitoneal lymph nodes	98%
Stage III	Disease above the diaphragm	80%

Rx Treatment

SEMINOMA. About 70% of seminomas present with clinical stage I disease. Although the cure rate with orchiectomy alone is 85 to 95% (Table 206–1), most centers prefer to add 2500 cGy of para-aortic irradiation.

Twenty per cent of patients with seminoma present with stage II disease (positive abdominal CT scan). For these patients, radiation therapy has a 90% cure rate; in patients who are not cured by radiation therapy, subsequent cisplatin combination chemotherapy (cisplatin combined with etoposide with or without bleomycin) is usually curative. If the transverse diameter of the tumor is greater than 5 cm, if there are multiple anatomic levels of nodal metastases, or if stage III disease is present, the preferred initial treatment is cisplatin combination chemotherapy without radiation, and the cure rate is 70 to 100%, depending on the extent of the disease.

NONSEMINOMATOUS GERM CELL TUMORS. The management of clinical stage I nonseminomatous germ cell tumors begins with orchiectomy, which has a 70% cure rate, followed either by retroperitoneal lymph node dissection or close surveillance, which can detect metastases early and guide curative chemotherapy. Most relapses occur during the first year, when meticulous surveillance should include monthly history and physical examination, serum markers, and chest radiograph, with an abdominal CT scan every 2 months. The same studies are done every 4 months during the second year, every 6 months during the third to fifth years of surveillance, and annually thereafter. CT scans are discontinued after 5 years. The physical examination should include palpation of the remaining testis because these patients have a 1 to 2% chance of a contralateral primary. The major complication of retroperitoneal lymph node dissection is the inadvertent severing of the sympathetic plexus with resultant retrograde ejaculation or failure of ejaculation. Nerve-sparing retroperitoneal lymph node dissection can retain antegrade ejaculation in more than 95% of patients. Some centers advocate primary chemotherapy for high-risk (embryonal predominant or vascular or lymphatic invasion) clinical stage I disease with two courses of cisplatin combination chemotherapy.

For clinical stage II disease with persistently elevated serum markers or a transverse diameter greater than 3 cm, chemotherapy is preferred. Other stage II patients are treated with retroperitoneal lymph node dissection, often followed by close surveillance

Table 206–2 • DEFINITION OF POOR-RISK DISEASE (ALL NONSEMINOMATOUS TESTICULAR CANCER PATIENTS)

Any of the following:
1. Lactate dehydrogenase >10 times upper limit of normal, human chorionic gonadotropin >50,000 IU/mL, or α-fetoprotein >10,000 ng/mL
2. Any primary mediastinal nonseminomatous germ cell tumor
3. Nonpulmonary visceral metastases (e.g., bone, liver, brain)

(as noted earlier, but without abdominal CT scans) or adjuvant chemotherapy. Testicular cancer has a higher cure rate with surgery alone despite nodal metastases than any other cancer.

CHEMOTHERAPY

The combination of bleomycin, etoposide, and cisplatin repeated every 3 weeks for three to four courses cures 70% of patients with metastatic disease and is the standard chemotherapy for disseminated testicular cancer. In several studies, this regimen has outperformed newer alternatives. Poor-risk disease (Table 206–2), however, has only a 40 to 60% cure rate with standard three-drug therapy.

In the 30% of metastatic germ cell tumors that are not cured by the initial combination chemotherapy, the use of salvage therapy (ifosfamide, cisplatin, and either vinblastine or paclitaxel) can result in cure rates of 20 to 25%. High-dose carboplatin and etoposide therapy followed by peripheral blood stem cell transplantation provides a 50% probability for cure and is currently the preferred approach in many centers.

1. Williams SD, Birch R, Irwin L, et al: Disseminated germ cell tumors: Chemotherapy with cisplatin plus bleomycin plus either vinblastine or etoposide. N Engl J Med 1987;316:1435–1440.
2. Toner GC, Stockler MR, Boyer MJ, et al: Comparison of two standard chemotherapy regimens for good-prognosis germ-cell tumours: A randomised trial. Lancet 2001;357:739–745.

SUGGESTED READINGS
Einhorn LH: Curing cancer: Testicular cancer. Proc Natl Acad Sci U S A 2002;99:4592–4595. *A review of the evolution of therapy and the success rates for current regimens.*
Huyghe E, Matsuda T, Thonneau P: Increasing incidence of testicular cancer worldwide: A review. J Urol 2003;170:5–11. *Incidence varies widely, even in adjacent geographic locations, but is rising in recent birth cohorts throughout Europe and the U.S.*
Vaughn DJ, Gignac GA, Meadows AT: Long-term medical care of testicular cancer survivors. Ann Intern Med 2002;136:463–470. *Emphasis on the role of the primary care physician.*

207 PROSTATE CANCER

Eric J. Small

Definition

Prostate cancer is the most common noncutaneous malignancy in men, with nearly 200,000 new cases per year in the United States. It also causes about 32,000 deaths in the United States each year, thereby making it the second most common cause of cancer death in men. Prostate cancer is a single histologic disease whose marked clinical heterogeneity ranges from indolent, clinically irrelevant disease to a virulent, rapidly lethal phenotype.

Epidemiology and Pathobiology

The incidence of clinically diagnosed prostate cancer reflects the effects of screening using the prostate-specific antigen (PSA) assay. Before PSA testing was available, about 19,000 new cases of prostate cancer were reported per year in the United States; this number reached 84,000 by 1993, and peaked at about 300,000 new cases in 1996.

Since 1996, the reported annual incidence of prostate cancer in the United States has declined to about 200,000, a number that may more closely estimate the true annual incidence of clinically detectable disease. The death rate due to prostate cancer has declined by about 1% per year since 1990. The age-specific decrease in mortality has been greatest in men younger than age 75 years. Men older than 75 years still account for two thirds of all prostate cancer deaths. Whether this decline is due to early detection (screening) or to improved therapy is not proven.

Risk factors for prostate cancer include increasing age, family history, African-American race, and dietary factors. Epidemiologic studies have suggested that nutritional factors such as reduced fat intake and soy protein, lycopene, vitamin E, and selenium supplementation may have a protective effect against the development of prostate cancer, although prospective data are minimal. The incidence of prostate cancer among African Americans is nearly twice that observed among white Americans. Prostate cancer is diagnosed in African Americans at a more advanced stage, and disease-specific survival is lower in African Americans. The relative contributions of biologic, genetic, and environmental differences, as well as differences in health care access, are not well established. Prior vasectomy and benign prostatic hypertrophy (Chapter 129) do not increase the risk. Prostatic intraepithelial neoplasia (PIN), particularly when high grade, is recognized as a premalignant lesion, so its presence on biopsy increases the likelihood of subsequent malignancy.

Prostate cancer appears to be common among relatives of men with early-onset prostate cancer. At the molecular level, there appears to be a susceptibility locus for the development of prostate cancer at an early age on chromosome 1, band Q24, although an abnormality at this locus occurs in less than 10% of prostate cancer patients.

Clinical Manifestations

Most patients with early stage, organ-confined disease are asymptomatic. The development of obstructive voiding symptoms (hesitancy, intermittent urinary stream, decreased force of stream) generally reflects locally advanced disease with growth into the urethra or bladder neck, although these symptoms are indistinguishable from benign prostatic hypertrophy (Chapter 129). Locally advanced tumors can also result in hematuria and hematospermia. Prostate cancer that has spread to the regional pelvic lymph nodes can occasionally cause edema of the lower extremities, or discomfort in the pelvic and perineal areas. Metastasis occurs most commonly to bone, where it is frequently asymptomatic, but can also cause severe and unremitting pain. Bone metastasis can result in pathologic fractures or spinal cord compression. Although visceral metastases are rare as presenting features of prostate cancer, patients can develop pulmonary, hepatic, pleural, peritoneal, and central nervous system metastases late in the natural history or after hormonal therapies fail.

Detection and Diagnosis

Over 60% of patients with prostate cancer are asymptomatic, and the diagnosis is made solely because of an elevated screening PSA level. A palpable nodule on digital rectal examination, which is the next most common clinical presentation, generally prompts biopsy. Much less commonly, prostate cancer is diagnosed because of advanced disease that causes obstructive voiding symptoms, pelvic or perineal discomfort, lower extremity edema, or symptomatic bone lesions.

Although the digital rectal examination has a low sensitivity and specificity for diagnosing prostatic cancer, biopsy of a nodule or area of induration reveals cancer 50% of the time, suggesting that prostate biopsy should be undertaken in all men with palpable nodules. The PSA level has a far better sensitivity but a low specificity because conditions such as benign prostatic hypertrophy and prostatitis can cause false-positive PSA elevations (Chapter 129). Using a PSA threshold of 4 ng/mL, 70 to 80% of tumors are detected. However, cancer rates range from 4 to 9% in patients whose PSA level is less than 4 ng/mL. The positive predictive value for a single PSA level greater than 10 ng/mL is greater than 60% for cancer, but the positive predictive value for a PSA level between 4 and 10 ng/mL is only about 30%.

Oncology

Table 207–1 • APPROACH TO THE TREATMENT OF PROSTATE CANCER

EXTENT OF CANCER	THERAPEUTIC OPTIONS
Organ confined: low risk (usually T1 or 2, GS < 7, PSA < 10)	• Surveillance • Radical prostatectomy • External beam radiotherapy to prostate • Brachytherapy
Organ confined: intermediate risk (usually T2 or GS 7, or PSA 10–20)	• Radical prostatectomy • External beam radiotherapy to prostate, possibly to pelvis, with or without androgen deprivation (AD) • Brachytherapy
Organ confined: high risk (usually T3, or GS > 7, or PSA > 20)	• Radical prostatectomy (with adjuvant radiotherapy, if needed) • External beam radiotherapy to prostate and pelvis (usually with AD) • Brachytherapy plus radiotherapy (usually with AD)
Climbing PSA after local therapy	• AD: antiandrogen monotherapy or combined AD • Salvage radiation therapy (for prior prostatectomy patients) • Salvage radical prostatectomy (for prior radiation patients) • Surveillance • Investigational therapy
Node positive	• Surveillance • AD • Pelvic/prostate radiotherapy + AD • Investigational therapy
Metastatic: untreated	• AD
Hormone-refractory prostate cancer	• Second-line hormones • Chemotherapy • Investigational therapy

GS = Gleason score; PSA = prostate-specific antigen.

Table 207–2 • FOUR-YEAR PROGRESSION-FREE SURVIVAL AFTER RADICAL PROSTATECTOMY AS A FUNCTION OF PERCENTAGE OF POSITIVE BIOPSIES

	≤34% OF BIOPSIES POSITIVE	34–50% OF BIOPSIES POSITIVE	>50% OF BIOPSIES POSITIVE
Good risk (usually T1 or 2, GS < 7, PSA < 10)	95%	88%	74%
Intermediate risk (usually T2, GS 7, or PSA 10-20)	88%	50%	20%
Poor risk (usually T3, GS > 7, or PSA > 20)	68%	25%	18%

Modified from D'Amico AV, Whittington R, Malkowicz SB, et al: Clinical utility of the percentage of positive prostate biopsies in defining biochemical outcome after radical prostatectomy for patients with clinically localized prostate cancer. J Clin Oncol 2000;18:1164–1172. See text for definitions of risk.

GS = Gleason score; PSA = prostate-specific antigen.

Assays of the PSA fraction that circulates unbound (per cent–free PSA) may help distinguish prostate cancer from benign processes: in patients with a PSA level of 4 to 10 ng/mL, the percentage of free PSA appears to be an independent predictor of prostate cancer, and a cutoff value of a free PSA less than 25% can detect 95% of cancers while avoiding 20% of unnecessary biopsies.

Transrectal ultrasound with biopsies is indicated when the PSA level is elevated, when the per cent–free PSA is less than 25%, or when an abnormality is noted on digital rectal examination. Sextant biopsies (base, midgland, and apex on each side) are generally obtained. Seminal vesicles are biopsied in high-risk patients. A bone scan is warranted only in patients with PSA level greater than 10 ng/mL, and abdominal and pelvic computed tomographic (CT) scanning or magnetic resonance imaging (MRI) is usually unrevealing in patients with a PSA level less than 20 ng/mL.

The prognosis of prostate cancer correlates with histologic grade and extent (stage) of disease. More than 95% of prostate cancers are adenocarcinomas, and multifocality is common. Histologic grade ranges from 1 to 5: the Gleason score, which refers to the sum of the two most common histologic patterns seen on each tissue specimen, ranges from 2 (1 + 1) to 10 (5 + 5). In general, tumors are classified as well-differentiated (Gleason scores 2, 3, or 4), of intermediate differentiation (Gleason scores 5, 6, or 7), and poorly differentiated (Gleason scores 8, 9, or 10).

Clinical stage is defined by the extent of disease based on the physical examination, imaging studies, and pathology. Stage T1 is nonpalpable prostate cancer detected only on pathologic examination, either incidentally noted after transurethral resection for benign hypertrophy (T1a and T1b) or on biopsy obtained because of an elevated PSA (T1c—the most common clinical stage at diagnosis). Stage T2 is a palpable tumor that appears to be confined to the prostatic gland (T2a if one lobe, T2b if two lobes), and stage T3 is tumor with extension through the prostatic capsule (T2a if focal, T2b if seminal vesicles are involved). T4 tumors are those with invasion of adjacent structures, such as the bladder neck, the external urinary sphincter, the rectum, the levator muscles, or the pelvic sidewall. Nodal metastases can be microscopic and can be detected only by biopsy or lymphadenectomy, or they can be visible on imaging studies. Distant metastases are predominantly to bone, but occasional visceral metastases occur.

Prevention

There is currently no proven preventive approach to prostate cancer. Epidemiologic studies suggest that a low-fat diet, high soy protein intake, and supplementation with selenium and vitamin E may reduce the incidence of prostate cancer. Prospective randomized trials are underway.

Rx Treatment (Table 207–1)

LOCALIZED PROSTATE CANCER

PRINCIPLES OF THERAPY. The principal therapeutic options for men with localized prostate cancer include (1) watchful waiting, (2) androgen deprivation, (3) retropubic or perineal radical prostatectomy, with or without postoperative radiotherapy to the prostate margins and pelvis; (4) external beam radiotherapy, and (5) brachytherapy (either permanent or temporary radioactive seed implants), with or without external beam radiotherapy to the prostate margins and pelvis.

Treatment options require individualization, taking into account the patient's comorbidity, life expectancy, likelihood of cure, and personal preferences based on an understanding of potential morbidity associated with each treatment. A multidisciplinary approach to integrate surgery, radiation therapy, and androgen deprivation is increasingly recommended. For higher risk patients with a greater likelihood of systemic micrometastases, androgen deprivation is often combined with radiation therapy. In patients at extremely high risk of micrometastatic disease, systemic therapy alone without concurrent local therapy may be appropriate.

PSA screening has led to the early detection of a large number of nonpalpable tumors, for which conventional clinical means of staging are inadequate. Thus, less emphasis is being placed on clinical stage and more emphasis is being placed on PSA and other predictors of outcome. Careful risk assessment is required to identify patients who are appropriate candidates for definitive local treatment.

Several studies have confirmed that serum PSA level, clinical stage, and biopsy Gleason score can be used to predict final pathologic stage after prostatectomy and that they are independent predictors of survival without PSA elevation after external beam radiation therapy or radical prostatectomy. For example, in a radiation therapy series, clinical stage T3 or higher, PSA greater than 10, and biopsy Gleason score of 7 or higher were risk factors for poor outcome (death or PSA elevation): 5-year survival without PSA elevation was 85% for patients with none of these adverse features (good risk), 65% for patients with one adverse feature (intermediate risk), and 35% for patients with two or three adverse features (poor risk). Similar statistics are cited in radical prostatectomy series. The percent of biopsy specimens that are positive is also an independent predictor of outcome after radical prostatectomy and can be used to counsel patients on therapeutic options (Table 207–2).

LOW/INTERMEDIATE RISK DISEASE. In a randomized trial of patients under the age of 75 with clinical stage T1b, T1c, or T2 prostate cancer, radical prostatectomy reduced the relative risk of death from prostate cancer by 50% (a 2% absolute risk reduction) compared with watchful waiting; however, despite a significant reduction in the risk of metastasis, overall mortality was unchanged. The adverse effects on quality of life differ between the two strategies—more dysfunction and urinary leakage after radical prostatectomy, more urinary obstruction with watchful waiting—but are of similar magnitude. [1,2] Nerve-sparing radical prostatectomy was not routinely performed in this study, and many patients already had palpable disease, so the implications for less advanced disease with newer surgical techniques are not known. Nonrandomized data suggest that watchful waiting may be judiciously used in patients with Gleason score 2, 3, or 4 tumors who have a life expectancy of 10 years or less. Watchful waiting is probably not appropriate for young, otherwise healthy men with high-risk features as described earlier (PSA > 10, Gleason sum = 7, or clinical stage T3 or higher). Whether watchful waiting is appropriate for men with intermediate risk tumors remains debated. Androgen deprivation has not been carefully studied as primary therapy for localized disease, but it is becoming a more common approach in men who wish to receive some therapy but are not suited for or decline prostatectomy or radiation therapy.

Men with T1 or T2 prostate cancer who otherwise have a life expectancy of more than 10 years and no significant comorbid illnesses are candidates for definitive local therapy with either surgery or radiation therapy. Long-term survival is excellent. Men with T1 or T2 tumors with Gleason scores of 7 or less have 8-year survival rates of 85 to 95%. Patients with T1 or T2 tumors with Gleason scores of 8 to 10 have 8-year survival rates of about 70%.

Nerve-sparing procedures and careful dissection techniques have decreased the risk of postoperative urinary incontinence and impotence. Postoperative urinary incontinence is reported to occur in less than 10% of cases. Postoperative impotence is dependent on a variety of factors, including the patient's age, preoperative erectile function, extent of cancer, and whether a nerve-sparing procedure was undertaken. In general, impotence rates of 10 to 50% are cited. Following a radical prostatectomy, the PSA should become undetectable; a detectable PSA implies the presence of cancer cells, either locally or at a metastatic site. Adjuvant postoperative radiotherapy is of unproven benefit unless the PSA remains or becomes detectable.

Conventional external beam radiation therapy is being replaced by three-dimensional conformal radiation therapy (3D-CRT), which permits higher doses to the target tissue with less toxicity; randomized trials are required to assess any clinical benefits. Brachytherapy, which is the placement of permanent or temporary radioactive seeds directly into the prostate, is adequate for intracapsular disease with no more than minimal transcapsular extension; otherwise it can be combined with external beam radiation therapy.

HIGH-RISK DISEASE. Patients with adverse risk features (Gleason score 8 to 10, PSA > 10, stage T3) are at high risk of nodal and micrometastatic disease and are generally treated with aggressive local therapy in combination with androgen deprivation, which is synergistic with radiation therapy. Taken in aggregate, these trials have suggested that 4 months of androgen deprivation with radiation therapy can improve local control and prolong progression-free survival in patients with intermediate risk features, whereas long-term androgen deprivation (up to 3 years) prolongs local control, progression-free survival, and overall survival in patients with high-risk features compared with radiation therapy. [1,2] T3 patients with Gleason scores of 7 have intermediate outcomes, with 8-year survival rates of about 70%, whereas T3 patients with Gleason scores of 8 to 10 have an 8-year survival after radiation therapy of about 50%.

RECURRENT DISEASE

Nearly 50% of men treated with radiation therapy or prostatectomy develop evidence of recurrence, as defined by a climbing PSA level. For selected patients with clear local recurrences, local salvage therapy (surgery for patients previously treated with radiation, radiation for patients previously treated with surgery and androgen deprivation) can be considered. However, early hormone therapy appears to be better than hormonal salvage therapy in terms of survival. [3,4]

ADVANCED DISEASE

In patients whose radical prostatectomy surgery reveals microscopic involvement of lymph nodes, immediate androgen deprivation prolongs survival compared with deferring androgen deprivation until osseous metastases are detected. [4] Similarly, patients who are at high risk of nodal invasion and who undergo external beam radiation benefit from concurrent short-term hormonal therapy. [5]

In patients with newly diagnosed metastatic prostate cancer, androgen deprivation is the mainstay of treatment and results in symptomatic improvement and disease regression in approximately 80 to 90% of patients. Androgen deprivation can be achieved by orchiectomy or by medical castration, with a luteinizing hormone–releasing hormone (LHRH) agonist (leuprolide acetate, goserelin acetate), which is safer and as effective as estrogen treatment.

Some LHRH agonists cause a transient worsening of signs and symptoms during the first week of therapy as a result of a surge in LH and testosterone, which peaks within 72 hours; an antiandrogen (flutamide, bicalutamide, or nilutamide) should be given with the first LHRH injection to prevent a tumor flare. Medical castration occurs within 4 weeks. The duration of hormone sensitivity is 5 to 10 years for node-positive or high-risk localized (or recurrent) prostate cancer, but the duration of hormone sensitivity is closer to 18 to 24 months in patients with overt metastatic disease. The most common side effects of androgen ablation are loss of libido, impotence, hot flashes, weight gain, fatigue, anemia, and osteoporosis. Bisphosphonates reduce bone mineral loss associated with androgen deprivation. [6]

HORMONE-RESISTANT PROSTATE CANCER

Typically, the first manifestation of resistance to androgen deprivation is a climbing PSA in the setting of anorchid levels of testosterone. In about 20% of patients, discontinuation of antiandrogen therapy (flutamide, bicalutamide, nilutamide) while continuing with LHRH agonists results in a PSA decline that can be associated with symptomatic improvement and can persist for 4 to 24 months or more. If this approach fails, treatment with secondary hormonal manipulations such as ketoconazole or estrogens is appropriate. Thereafter, treatment with chemotherapeutic regimens, such as mitoxantrone plus corticosteroids or estramustine plus a taxane, may be effective. In general, serial PSA levels are the best, although imperfect, way to follow up patients, and a decline of 50% or more is probably clinically significant.

Palliative Care

Many patients with advanced prostate cancer have bone pain or functional impairments that adversely affect quality of life, and provision of appropriate palliative care is an integral component of their management. In addition to the usual analgesics, glucocorticoids serve as anti-inflammatory agents and can alleviate bone pain. For patients with widespread bony metastases and pain not easily controlled with analgesics or local radiation (Chapter 29), strontium-89 and samarium-153 are selectively concentrated in bone metastases and alleviate pain in 70% or more of treated patients.

Prognosis

In general, the 10-year PSA progression-free survival is 70 to 80% with Gleason scores of 2 to 4, whether treated with radiation therapy or surgery; 50 to 70% for Gleason scores of 5 to 7, and 15 to 30% for Gleason scores of 8 to 10. For patients with a climbing PSA after radical prostatectomy, time to detectable PSA, Gleason score at the time of prostatectomy, and PSA doubling time are important prognostic variables. The likelihood of bone metastases at 7 years ranges from 20% for good-prognosis patients to 80% for poor-prognosis patients.

For patients with microscopic nodal disease, 10-year survival appears to exceed 80% in men treated with androgen deprivation. Median survival in men treated with androgen deprivation for established metastatic disease ranges from 3 to 5 years. The median survival for men with hormone-resistant disease ranges from 20 months if they are minimally symptomatic to 8 to 12 months if they are severely symptomatic.

Future Directions

Molecular markers help not only in identifying patients at risk of developing progressive disease, but also as therapeutic targets. Enhanced understanding of androgen receptor biology may permit the development of specific hormonal therapies and guide the more rational use of existing agents.

1. Holmberg L, Bill-Axelson A, Helgesen F, et al: A randomized trial comparing radical prostatectomy with watchful waiting in early prostate cancer. N Engl J Med 2002;347:781–789.
2. Steineck G, Helgesen F, Adolfsson J, et al: Quality of life after radical prostatectomy or watchful waiting. N Engl J Med 2002;347:790–796.
3. Bolla M, Gonzalez D, Warde P, et al: Improved survival in patients with locally advanced prostate cancer treated with radiotherapy and goserelin. N Engl J Med 1997;337:295–300.
4. Messing EM, Manola J, Saorsdy M, et al: Immediate hormonal therapy compared with observation after radical prostatectomy and pelvic lymphadenectomy in men with node-positive prostate cancer. N Engl J Med 1999;341:1781–1788.
5. Roach M 3rd, DeSilvio M, Lawton C, et al: Phase III trial comparing whole-pelvic versus prostate-only radiotherapy and neoadjuvant versus adjuvant combined androgen suppression: Radiation Therapy Oncology Group 9413. J Clin Oncol 2003;21:1904–1911.
6. Smith MR, McGovern F, Fallon M, et al: Pamidronate to prevent bone loss during androgen deprivation therapy for prostate cancer. N Engl J Med 2001;345:948–955.

SUGGESTED READINGS
Frankel S, Smith GD, Donovan J, et al: Screening for prostate cancer. Lancet 2003;361:1122–1128. *A concise overview.*
Harris R, Lohr KN: Screening for prostate cancer: An update of the evidence for the U.S. Preventive Services Task Force. Ann Intern Med 2002;137:917–929. *The evidence on which U.S. recommendations are based.*
Pound CR, Partin AW, Eisenberger MA, et al: Natural history of progression after PSA elevation following radical prostatectomy. JAMA 1999;281:1591–1597. *This seminal paper describes the natural history of disease progression in patients with PSA recurrence after radical prostatectomy.*
Small EJ, McMillan A, Meyer M, et al: Serum PSA decline as a marker of clinical outcome in hormone refractory prostate cancer patients: Association with progression-free survival, pain endpoints and survival. J Clin Oncol 2001;19:1304–1310. *In patients with hormone-refractory prostate cancer, a 50% or more decline in PSA appears to correlate well with various clinical outcomes.*

208 BONE TUMORS

Daniel I. Rosenthal

Tumors may involve bone as the result of (1) primary neoplastic transformation of bone or bone marrow cells, (2) metastatic dissemination of neoplasms arising in other organs, or (3) local invasion from contiguous tissues. Of these three mechanisms, metastatic involvement is by far the most frequent.

METASTATIC TUMORS

Several common cancers frequently involve the skeleton. In women, breast cancer (Chapter 204) is the most common primary tumor to result in skeletal metastases. Lung cancer (Chapter 198) is a distant second, although increasing in frequency. In men, prostate cancer (Chapter 207) is the most common primary tumor, followed by tumors arising in lung, kidney, gastrointestinal tract, and thyroid.

Whenever a destructive lesion of the skeleton is encountered, an effort should be made to determine whether it is primary or secondary. Metastatic bone lesions usually produce an infiltrative pattern of bone destruction on radiographic or other imaging studies. Compared with primary tumors, metastatic disease is usually accompanied by little or no soft tissue mass. Cancers arising in breast or prostate generally produce mixed lytic and blastic change within bone, whereas lung and renal cancers (see Chapter 203) are purely lytic.

A radioisotope bone scan is recommended to determine whether the lesion is solitary, because metastatic lesions are often multiple at presentation. Isotope bone scans are generally more sensitive than plain films for detecting metastasis. The addition of single-photon emission computed tomography (SPECT) further increases the sensitivity of the isotope scan. For this reason, radiographic surveys are rarely performed to identify skeletal metastasis. An important exception is multiple myeloma (Chapter 196), for which there may be a significant false-negative rate on isotope scans. Recent clinical practice has tended to defer screening for metastases in asymptomatic patients with early stage disease.

Magnetic resonance imaging (MRI) is probably even more sensitive, especially for lesions involving the spine, and some authorities recommend "whole-body" MRI. However, even though there has been progress in rapid-imaging pulse sequences, imaging of the entire skeleton by MRI is time-consuming and cumbersome (Chapter 7).

When more than one focus is present, the primary tumor is probably extraskeletal. Although bone sarcomas may metastasize to other parts of the skeleton, this phenomenon generally occurs late in the course of the disease, after lung metastases are present.

If multiple lesions are present but the primary tumor is not apparent, it may be desirable to consider biopsy for diagnosis rather than to engage in an extended search for the primary lesion (Chapter 210). Needle biopsy is safe and the most direct approach to diagnosis. In some cases of metastatic carcinoma, however, the primary tumor remains unknown despite all appropriate efforts.

Whether chemotherapy or hormonal therapy is useful in treating metastatic disease depends on the primary tumor. Most metastatic lesions can be palliated with radiation. Bisphosphonates can ameliorate symptoms and perhaps slow the progression of disease (Chapter 204). Surgical stabilization should be considered to preserve function when there is important structural compromise and the patient's life expectancy justifies surgery.

DIRECT INVASION

Direct invasion of bone by contiguous visceral or soft tissue tumors is uncommon. The most frequent cause of this complication is lung cancer (Chapter 198) invading ribs or vertebrae. Paraspinal lymphadenopathy may sometimes involve the vertebrae. Deeply situated soft tissue sarcomas may also invade bone, but this event is relatively rare considering the frequent proximity of these lesions to the skeleton. The radioisotope bone scan is useful to exclude bone involvement. However, a positive bone scan must be viewed with caution, because reactive changes at the margins of the tumor may cause the bone scan to be "hot." Confirmation of involvement by computed tomography (CT) or MRI is desirable.

PRIMARY BONE TUMORS

Primary tumors may arise from any of the cellular elements of bone. Tumors may be either benign or malignant, but often are characterized along a spectrum that extends from benign to malignant. For this reason, adequate diagnosis requires not only the type of tumor but also its histologic grade. Furthermore, individual tumors commonly exhibit a variety of cell types and grades. Features on imaging studies reflect the most abundant histologic elements, whereas clinical behavior is shaped by the most aggressive or malignant components. In general, the better differentiated the lesion (lower grade), the more it resembles the tissue from which it arose. Highly malignant lesions exhibit considerable similarity to each other on imaging studies.

Tumors may arise sporadically, as part of a generalized (and sometimes inherited) tendency to neoplasia, or by degeneration of precursor lesions. Almost any condition that causes a prolonged period of accelerated bone remodeling may lead to tumor formation. Examples include Paget's disease (Chapter 263), infections, irradiation, bone infarctions, and benign bone lesions.

Adequate staging requires four pieces of information: tumor type, histologic grade, local extent, and presence of metastases. Tissue type and grade are learned from biopsy. Biopsy should be performed so as to obtain representative tissue, preserve structural integrity, and permit curative resection if needed. Such resection usually requires that the biopsy track be excised along with the tumor.

Local extent can be determined by imaging studies. Plain radiographs are important in all cases. Either CT or MRI may be used to evaluate involvement of soft tissues and bone marrow. If the lesion is suspected to be malignant, a radioisotope bone scan is used to determine whether the lesion is solitary, and either chest radiography or, preferably, CT is used to exclude pulmonary metastases.

Benign bone tumors are usually relatively small and often painless. Of these, the most common (and least significant) is the bone island. These asymptomatic lesions arise during adult life, may enlarge slowly, and eventually regress. They are usually incidental findings on radiographs. Bone islands are not usually detected on isotope scans, although large lesions may show some uptake. Benign cartilage tumors, including osteochondroma and enchondroma, are the next most common. These lesions are not generally painful unless complicated by pathologic fracture, adjacent soft tissue inflammation (bursitis), or malignant degeneration. Some painful benign tumors include osteoid osteoma, chondroblastoma, giant cell tumors, and chondromyxoid fibroma. Treatment by limited resection is adequate for these tumors. If the diagnosis is certain from imaging studies and if resection is not required to relieve symptoms, observation may be adequate.

The most common malignant bone tumor is multiple myeloma (Chapter 196). Osteosarcoma (or osteogenic sarcoma) is next most frequent and much more common than other malignant bone tumors

(Fig. 208–1). Osteosarcoma peaks in the second decade of life and again in the fifth and sixth decades, when it frequently represents a complication of a precursor lesion such as Paget's disease. It is most common in the distal femur and proximal tibia. Although low-grade osteosarcoma exists, most lesions are highly malignant. The alkaline phosphatase level is usually elevated, and levels correlate with prognosis. Contemporary treatment uses combination chemotherapy and amputation or, if possible, limb-sparing surgery. With this approach, survival rates of 85 to 90% are possible. For the 10% of patients with metastases, particularly bone metastases, at the time of presentation, death ensues in less than 1 year if the disease is not treated. A combination of surgery and chemotherapy may produce a 20% long-term survival rate.

Ewing's sarcoma and lymphoma are classified as round cell lesions because of similar histologic and radiographic features. Ewing's sarcoma tends to occur in children and young adults, whereas primary lymphoma of bone (usually non-Hodgkin's lymphoma; Chapter 195) is seen in older individuals. The two entities may be difficult to differentiate from each other. However, recent progress in molecular genetics indicates the presence of a characteristic translocation (usually $t(11;22)$ in cells of the Ewing's family of tumors (Ewing's and primitive neuroectodermal tumor). This translocation leads to production of a chimeric protein (EWS-FLI 1) that may be involved in neoplastic transformation. Ewing's sarcoma is highly malignant, with a tendency to produce both local and systemic symptoms such as fever, malaise, and chills that may simulate infection. Chemotherapy and surgery produce 60% cure rates. Newer regimens that add ifosfamide and etoposide to standard four-drug chemotherapy can improve survival in nonmetastatic disease.∎

Chondrosarcoma usually develops in the fourth, fifth, and sixth decades of life. Unlike osteosarcoma and Ewing's sarcoma, chondrosarcoma is of more variable grade, with most lesions of low or intermediate malignancy. Irradiation and chemotherapy are relatively

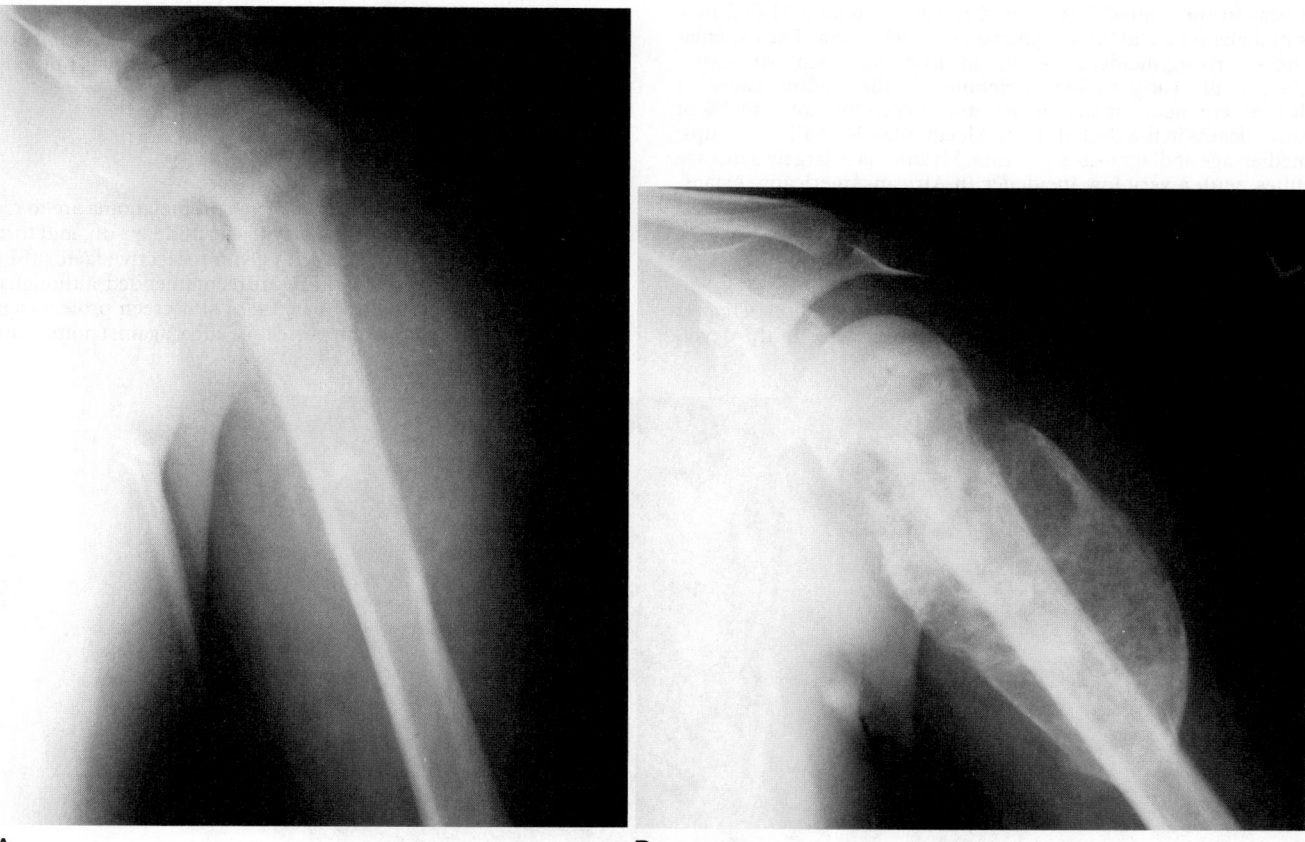

A   B

FIGURE 208–1 • *A,* Osteogenic sarcoma of the humerus. There is a large, destructive lesion of the upper half of the humerus. A circumferential soft tissue mass is present, and faint tumor ossification is seen. At the lower margin of the soft tissue mass, periosteal elevation is seen (Codman's triangle). *B,* After chemotherapy, the soft tissue mass appears slightly smaller, the lesion is much more densely ossified, and the tumor appears almost completely marginated by periosteal bone.

Oncology

ineffective against large lesions of the extremities, but surgery may produce a cure rate of 85%. Excellent results can be achieved for smaller lesions (such as skull base tumors) using proton beam irradiation.

1. Grier HE, Krailo MD, Tarbell NJ, et al: Addition of ifosfamide and etoposide to standard chemotherapy for Ewing's sarcoma and primitive neuroectodermal tumor of bone. N Engl J Med 2003;348:694–701.

SUGGESTED READINGS

Fiorenza F, Abdud A, Grimer RJ, et al: Risk factors for survival and local control in chondrosarcoma of bone. J Bone Joint Surg Br 2002;84:93–99. *Local recurrence is returned to tumor size and inadequate surgical margins; survival depends on tumor grade as well as local recurrence. Local recurrence without lung metastases is associated with a 64% cumulative survival at 5 years.*

Scully SP, Ghert MA, Surakowski D, et al: Pathological fracture in osteosarcoma: Prognostic importance and treatment implications. J Bone Joint Surg Am 2002;84A:49–57. *Pathologic fracture is a poor prognostic factor; limb-salvage surgery and amputation yield similar outcomes in carefully selected patients.*

West DC: Ewing sarcoma family of tumors. Curr Opin Oncol 2000;12:323–329. *An excellent review of recent progress in the cytogenetics of these tumors.*

209 MELANOMA AND NONMELANOMA SKIN CANCERS

Lynn Schuchter

MELANOMA

Epidemiology

Throughout the world, cases of melanoma are increasing at a rate of approximately 5% per year. It is now estimated that 1 in 75 individuals will be diagnosed with melanoma during their lifetime. Each year in the United States, there are an estimated 51,000 new cases of melanoma and 8000 deaths due to melanoma. The explanation for the rising incidence is thought to be increasing sun exposure, especially early in life. Melanoma is the leading cause of death from cutaneous malignancies, and it accounts for 1 to 2% of all cancer deaths in the United States. Melanoma affects all age groups; the median age at diagnosis is 50 years. Melanoma is largely a disease of whites, with a very low incidence in African-Americans, Asians, and Hispanics.

Pathogenesis and Risk Factors

Exposure to sunlight, and especially ultraviolet radiation (Chapter 19), has been strongly implicated as a causative factor in the development of melanoma. Melanomas originate from melanocytes, which are located predominantly in the basal cell layer of the epidermis and use the enzyme tyrosinase to synthesize melanin pigment, which serves to protect against ultraviolet damage (Chapter 471). Worldwide, the incidence of melanoma in whites generally correlates inversely with latitude; that is, rates are generally higher closer to the equator and become progressively lower near the poles. Individuals with fair complexion, blond or red hair, blue eye color, and freckles have a tendency to burn rather than tan when exposed to sunlight and have higher rates of melanoma. The pattern of sun exposure may also be important; intermittent intense exposure, rather than chronic exposure, may carry a higher risk of melanoma. For example, blistering sunburns, particularly in childhood, are associated with an increased risk of melanoma.

Individuals with an increased number of typical or benign moles (melanocytic nevi; Fig. 209–1) also have an increased risk of melanoma. The proportion of melanomas that arise from melanocytic nevi ranges from 18 to 85%. Atypical moles or dysplastic nevi are important precursor lesions of melanoma and also serve as markers for increasing risk. For example, individuals with dysplastic nevi have a 6% lifetime chance of developing melanoma, and this risk increases to as high as 80% in individuals who have dysplastic nevi and a family history of melanoma. At least 5% of the population has at least one dysplastic nevus. Other risk factors for melanoma include a family history of melanoma, a personal history of melanoma, and other skin cancers.

GENETICS. Approximately 10% of patients with melanoma have a family history of melanoma. Some cases occur in the setting of the familial atypical mole and melanoma syndrome, also known as the dysplastic nevus syndrome. This syndrome is defined by the occurrence of melanoma in one or more first- or second-degree relatives and the presence of large numbers of moles (often more than 50), some of which are dysplastic nevi. Persons with this syndrome have a markedly increased risk of developing melanoma, with estimates ranging from 55% to as high as 100%.

Several chromosomal loci determine susceptibility to melanoma, the most important of which is *p16/CDKN2A*, a gene located on chromosome *9p21*. This gene is a member of a class of molecules that play a central role in cell cycle regulation. Testing for mutations in the *p16/CDKN2A* locus is available, but its clinical utility is limited, and therefore testing is not currently recommended.

Prevention and Screening

The most important measures to prevent melanoma are to reduce excessive sun exposure, particularly to the midday sun, and to avoid sunburns. Sunscreen products with a sun protective factor (SPF) of 15 or greater and protective clothing are recommended, although there is no definitive proof that regular use of sunscreen protects against melanoma despite its apparent protective effect against nonmelanoma

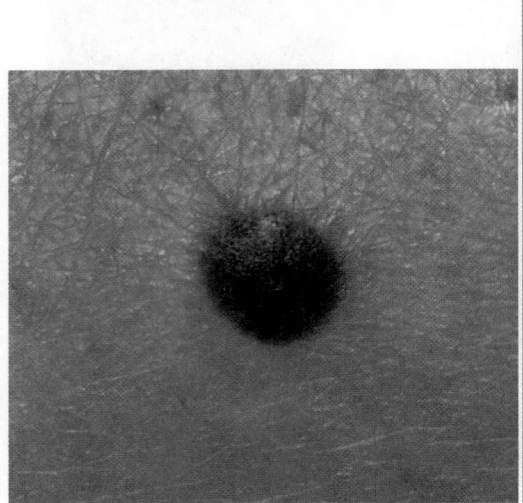

FIGURE 209–1 • *A,* Common benign nevus; *B,* dermal nevus.

Oncology

skin cancer. Sunscreens block primarily ultraviolet (UV) B rays, which are considered to be the major causative agent of cutaneous cancers. Newer sunscreen products also block UVA rays, which may contribute to the risk of melanoma.

Screening for skin cancer, whether by self-examination or by a health care provider, is controversial (Chapter 11). Many public health experts do not recommend screening for adults, but some organizations do. On the basis of the type and number of nevi, family history of melanoma, prior melanoma, and history of severe sunburns, clinicians can identify patients who are at high risk for melanoma and who may benefit from screening programs. In several population studies, screening has detected melanomas at an earlier, curable stage. Physicians, other health care providers, and the public should be educated regarding the early signs of melanoma and the need for prompt biopsy of a suspicious pigmented lesion.

Patients with clinically atypical nevi (Fig. 209–2), particularly if there is family history of melanoma, require a regular surveillance program. Regular skin examinations should be performed every 6 to 12 months, preferably assisted by the use of serial photography.

Clinical Manifestations

Early detection and recognition of melanoma is key to improving survival. The signs of early melanoma are based on the clinical appearance of the pigmented lesion and a change in the shape, color, or surface of an existing mole (Chapters 472 and 476). Most patients report a preexisting mole at the site of the melanoma. Itching, burning, or pain in a pigmented lesion should increase suspicion, although melanomas often are not associated with local discomfort. Bleeding and ulceration are signs of a more advanced melanoma. Most melanomas are varying shades of brown, but black, blue, or pink colors may be found. The ABCDs for the recognition of melanoma are Asymmetry, Border irregularity, Color variation, and Diameter greater than 6 mm.

Cutaneous melanoma has been divided into four subtypes. Superficial spreading melanoma, which accounts for 70% of all melanomas, can be located on any anatomic site (Fig. 209–3). Lentigo maligna melanomas, which represent 4 to 10% of all melanomas, tend to occur more commonly in chronically sun-exposed skin in older patients, frequently on the head and neck (Fig. 209–4); clinically, it appears as a macular (flat) lesion, arising in a lentigo maligna. Nodular melanoma (Fig. 209–5) accounts for 15 to 30% of melanomas and manifests as a rapidly enlarging elevated or polypoid lesion, often blue or black in color. The ABCD rule does not apply to nodular melanomas. Acral lentiginous melanomas manifest as darkly pigmented, flat to nodular lesions on palms, on soles, and subungually; sunlight is not thought to play a causative role in this form of melanoma.

Diagnosis

Any skin lesion suspicious for melanoma should be biopsied with complete excision, including a 1 to 2 mm margin of normal skin and some subcutaneous fat. An incisional biopsy may be necessary for

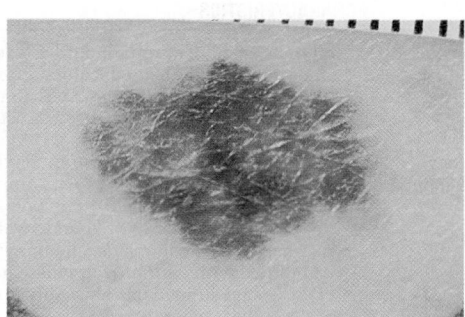

FIGURE 209–3 • Superficial spreading melanoma.

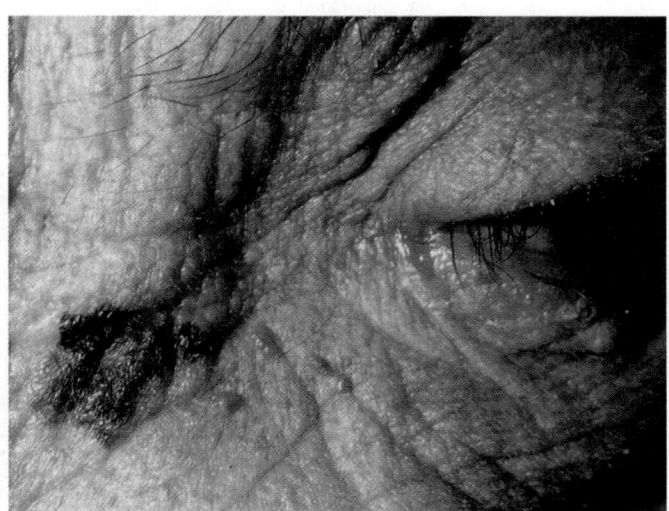

FIGURE 209–4 • Lentigo maligna melanoma.

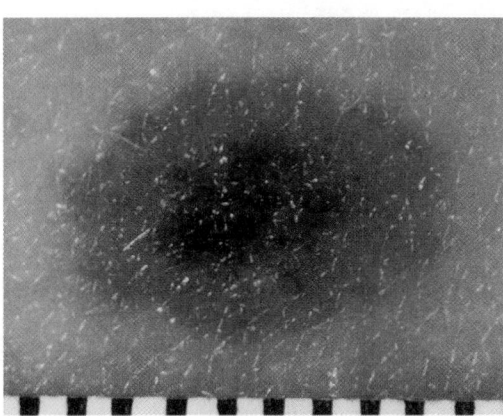

A

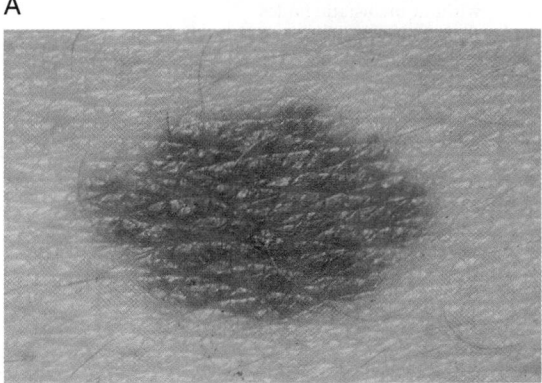

B

FIGURE 209–2 • *A, B,* Dysplastic nevi.

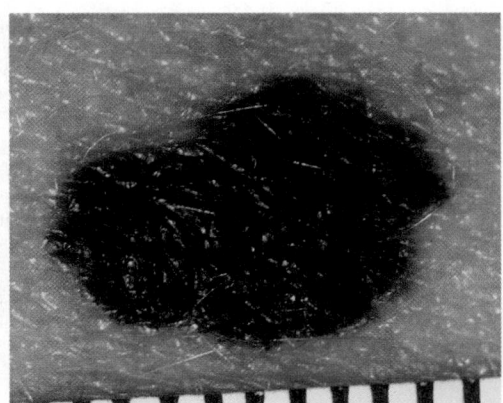

FIGURE 209–5 • Malignant melanoma.

lesions too large for complete excision. Shallow shave biopsies, curettage, cryosurgery, laser, and electrodesiccation are contraindicated in lesions suspicious for melanoma. Other lesions that can be confused with melanoma include blue nevi, pigmented basal cell carcinoma, seborrhea keratosis, and hemangiomas (Table 209–1).

Prognostic Factors and Staging

PROGNOSTIC FACTORS. The single best prognostic factor is the depth of invasion (Breslow thickness) of the original lesion, measured in millimeters from the top of the epidermis to the underlying dermis.

Increasing thickness is associated with an increased risk of recurrence, with microscopic lymph node involvement, and with death from melanoma. Patients whose melanomas are less than 1 mm thick have about an 80 to 90% 10-year survival, whereas patients whose melanomas are greater than 4 mm thick have only a 40 to 50% 10-year survival. The number of involved lymph nodes correlates with risk of distant metastatic disease and therefore survival, independent of the thickness of the primary lesion. For example, patients with multiple lymph nodes positive for melanoma have a 20% 5-year survival rate. Other poor prognostic factors include presence of ulceration, increasing level of invasion (Clark's level), high mitotic rate, and presence of microscopic satellites. Melanomas that arise on the extremity tend to have a better prognosis, and women tend to do better than men.

STAGING SYSTEM FOR MELANOMA. The staging system (Table 209–2) and prognosis (Table 209–3) for melanoma is based on the TNM system, where T refers to tumor, N to nodes, and M to metastasis. Stages I and II indicate clinically localized primary melanoma, stage III melanoma indicates regional involvement (lymph nodes or in-transit metastases), and stage IV is metastatic disease beyond the regional lymph nodes (i.e., lung, liver, brain).

PATIENT EVALUATION. The initial evaluation of a patient with melanoma includes a personal history, a family history, a total skin examination, and palpation of regional (draining) lymph nodes. The focus is to identify risk factors, signs or symptoms of metastases, dysplastic nevi, and additional melanomas. In practice, a chest radiograph and liver enzyme tests are performed, but there are no data to support this common practice. The majority of patients who present with melanoma do not have distant metastatic disease at presentation; therefore, extensive evaluations with computed tomographic scans to search for distant metastases have an extremely low yield and are not indicated in asymptomatic patients. More extensive staging evaluation with computed tomographic scans can be considered in patients with high-risk disease (primary melanoma >4 mm thick or node-positive disease) in whom the risk of distant metastatic disease is higher.

Table 209–1 • CLINICAL FEATURES OF COMMON NEVI, DSYPLASTIC NEVI, AND MELANOMAS

DISEASE	CHARACTERISTICS
Common acquired nevi (moles)	Tend to be small, flat, round; border is regular, smooth, and well defined; coloration is homogeneous, usually no more than two shades of brown; any site affected, usually <6 mm.
Dysplastic nevi (atypical moles)	Occur predominantly on the trunk; tend to be large, usually >5 mm, with a flat component; border is characteristically fuzzy and ill defined. The shape can be round, oval, or misshapen. The color is usually brown but can be mottled with dark brown, pink, and tan colors. Some individuals have only one to five moles, others more than 100.
Melanoma	The border is more irregular; lesions tend to be larger, often >6 mm; substantial heterogeneity of color, ranging from tan-brown, dark brown, black, pink, red, gray, blue, white.

Table 209–2 • MELANOMA TNM CLASSIFICATION

T CLASSIFICATION	THICKNESS	ULCERATION STATUS
T1	≤1.0 mm	a: without ulceration and level II/III b: with ulceration or level IV/V
T2	1.01–2.0 mm	a: without ulceration or level IV/V b: with ulceration
T3	2.01–4.0 mm	a: without ulceration b: with ulceration
T4	>4.0 mm	a: without ulceration b: with ulceration

N CLASSIFICATION	NUMBER OF METASTATIC NODES	NODAL METASTATIC MASS
N1	One node	a: micrometastasis* b: macrometastasis[†]
N2	Two to three nodes	a: micrometastasis* b: macrometastasis[†] c: in transit met(s)/satellite(s) without metastatic nodes
N3	Four or more metastatic nodes, or matted nodes, or in transit met(s)/satellite(s) with metastatic node(s)	

M CLASSIFICATION	SITE	SERUM LACTATE DEHYDROGENASE
M1a	Distant skin, subcutaneous, or nodal metastases	Normal
M1b	Lung metastases	Normal
M1c	All other visceral metastases	Normal
	Any distant metastasis	Elevated

*Micrometastases are diagnosed after sentinel or elective lymphadenectomy.
[†]Macrometastases are defined as clinically detectable nodal metastases confirmed by therapeutic lymphadenectomy or when nodal metastasis exhibits gross extracapsular extension.
From Balch CM, Buzaid AC, Soong ST, et al: Final version of the American Joint Committee on Cancer staging system for cutaneous melanoma. J Clin Oncol 2001;19:3635–3645.

Table 209–3 • SURVIVAL RATES FOR MELANOMA TNM AND STAGING CATEGORIES

PATHOLOGIC STAGE	TNM	THICKNESS (mm)	ULCERATION	NUMBER OF POSITIVE NODES	NODAL SIZE	DISTANT METASTASIS	10-YEAR SURVIVAL ± SE
IA	T1a	1	No	0	—	—	87.9 ± 1.0
IB	T1b	1	Yes or Level IV, V	0	—	—	83.1 ± 1.0
	T2a	1.01–2.0	No	0	—	—	79.2 ± 1.1
IIA	T2b	1.01–2.0	Yes	0	—	—	64.4 ± 2.2
	T3a	2.01–4.0	No	0	—	—	63.8 ± 1.7
IIB	T3b	2.01–4.0	Yes	0	—	—	50.8 ± 1.7
	T4a	>4.0	No	0	—	—	53.9 ± 3.3
IIC	T4b	>4.0	Yes	0	—	—	32.3 ± 2.1
IIIA	N1a	Any	No	1	Micro	—	63.0 ± 4.4
	N2a	Any	No	2–3	Micro	—	56.9 ± 6.8
IIIB	N1a	Any	Yes	1	Micro	—	37.8 ± 4.8
	N2a	Any	Yes	2–3	Micro	—	35.9 ± 7.2
	N1b	Any	No	1	Macro	—	47.7 ± 5.8
	N2b	Any	No	2–3	Macro	—	39.2 ± 5.8
IIIC	N1b	Any	Yes	1	Macro	—	24.4 ± 5.3
	N2b	Any	Yes	2–3	Macro	—	15.0 ± 3.9
	N3	Any	Any	4	Micro/macro	—	18.4 ± 2.5
IV	M1a	Any	Any	Any	Any	Skin, Subcutaneous	15.7 ± 2.9
	M1b	Any	Any	Any	Any	Lung	2.5 ± 1.5
	M1c	Any	Any	Any	Any	Other Visceral	6.0 ± 0.9

From Balch CM, Buzaid AC, Soong ST, et al: Final version of the American Joint Committee on Cancer staging system for cutaneous melanoma. J Clin Oncol 2001;19:3635–3645.

Treatment

TREATMENT OF THE PRIMARY MELANOMA. Once melanoma is diagnosed, the standard treatment is surgical excision. The extent of the surgery depends on the thickness of the primary melanoma. Large surgical excisions are no longer required, and most wide excisions can be performed with primary closure.◘ For melanoma in situ, excision with a 0.5 cm border of clinically normal skin is sufficient. For melanomas less than 1 mm thick, a 1 cm margin is recommended. If the thickness is between 1 and 4 mm, a 2 cm margin is recommended. For melanomas thicker than 4 mm, at least a 2 cm margin should be taken, including underlying subcutaneous tissue down to fascia. In cosmetically sensitive areas (face) or anatomically difficult areas (ear, hands), it may be difficult to achieve the desired margin, but at least a 1-cm margin should be obtained.

MANAGEMENT OF REGIONAL LYMPH NODES

Clinically Normal Regional Lymph Nodes. In about 15 to 20% of patients who do not have clinically apparent lymph node involvement, lymph nodes contain occult micrometastases. The risk of having occult lymph node involvement rises with increasing tumor thickness. Results from randomized trials fail to show a survival benefit from elective or prophylactic lymph node dissections in patients with clinically negative lymph nodes.◙

Sentinel lymph mapping or biopsy is a new technique that accurately evaluates whether occult melanoma cells involve regional lymph nodes. The technique relies on the concept that specific regions of the skin drain specifically to an initial lymph node within the regional nodal basin via an organized pathway of afferent lymphatic channels. This technique is performed by injecting the primary melanoma site with blue dye (isosulfan blue) and/or radiolabeled colloid. Five minutes later, an incision is made over the lymph node basin, and the blue lymphatic channel to the blue "sentinel" node is identified and surgically removed. If the radiolabeled colloid is used, then a hand-held gamma detector is used intraoperatively to identify the sentinel node. When both modalities are used in combination, a sentinel node can be identified in 98% of patients; biopsy of the node accurately determines whether melanoma cells have metastasized to that specific lymph node basin. The sentinel node technique also promotes a more careful histologic examination of lymph nodes because limited amounts of pathologic material are submitted.

Candidates for sentinel lymph node mapping or biopsy include patients with melanomas 1 mm thick or thicker. The use of this technique for patients with thinner melanomas, that is, those less

than 1 mm thick, is controversial. The sentinel lymph mapping or biopsy is generally performed at the same time as the formal wide excision of the primary tumor. If the sentinel lymph node is negative for melanoma, no further lymph node surgery is required. If melanoma is detected in the sentinel lymph node, a complete lymph node dissection is recommended.

Clinically Enlarged Regional Lymph Nodes. Patients with clinically enlarged lymph nodes and no evidence of distant metastatic disease should undergo complete lymph node dissection. The goal is to provide long-term, disease-free survival, and 25 to 50% of patients may be cured by surgery.

ADJUVANT THERAPY. Post-surgical adjuvant therapy can be considered for patients at high risk for recurrence (melanomas >4 mm thick or node-positive disease). These patients have at least a 50 to 75% chance of dying from melanoma. High-dose interferon-α_2 can prolong disease-free survival and may improve overall survival.◙ The treatment is given for 1 year and is associated with considerable toxicity. A number of vaccine studies are ongoing but should be considered experimental at the current time.

TREATMENT AND COURSE OF ADVANCED MELANOMA (STAGE IV). The treatment of a patient with metastatic melanoma emphasizes palliation. There is no evidence that treatment of metastatic melanoma has any impact on survival, which ranges from 5 to 11 months, with a median of 8.5 months. Treatment options include surgery for resection of solitary metastases, single-agent chemotherapy such as DTIC, combination chemotherapy, immunotherapy (vaccines, interleukin-2, interferon), or combined immunotherapy. Melanoma can metastasize to virtually any organ, especially the lung, skin, liver, and brain.

SURVEILLANCE AND FOLLOW-UP. Patients should be educated on the clinical characteristics of melanoma, the importance of safe sun strategies, and the performance of monthly self-examinations of the skin. Patients should be followed regularly for evidence of local or regional recurrence, distant metastatic disease, and a second primary tumor. The intensity of the surveillance and the extent of the investigation are related to the tumor thickness, with more frequent follow-up visits in patients who have thicker tumors and are at greater risk for recurrence.

For low-risk melanoma (<1 mm), visits are recommended every 6 months for 2 years and then annually. The surveillance guidelines for patients with high-risk melanoma include evaluation every 3 to 4 months for 2 years, then every 6 months for 3 years. After 5 years, patients are seen once a year. Patients are generally followed for 10

Continued

years, but patients with dysplastic nevi or a family history of melanoma should continue to be followed annually. In most practices, a history and physical examination are performed at each visit, a chest radiograph is obtained every other visit, and laboratory studies are performed at the discretion of the treating physician. The physical examination should include a thorough skin examination, because at least 3% of patients develop an additional cutaneous melanoma within 3 years. Regional lymph nodes should be thor-

oughly examined, especially in patients without prior nodal surgery. For the remainder of the examination, one should keep in mind the frequency of metastases to lung, liver, and brain. Follow-up studies generally include a complete blood cell count and chemistries, including liver enzyme tests. An elevated lactate dehydrogenase level is suggestive of metastatic melanoma. Periodic chest radiographs are recommended, but routine screening computed tomographic, magnetic resonance imaging, and bone scans are not justified.

BASAL AND SQUAMOUS CELL SKIN CANCER

Nonmelanoma skin cancer is the most common malignancy in the United States. Although national statistics are imprecise, an estimated 900,000 to 1,200,000 nonmelanoma skin cancers are diagnosed annually in the United States. Squamous cell carcinoma accounts for 20%, and the remainder are basal cell carcinomas. Squamous cell carcinoma is associated with a higher absolute mortality rate, with the majority of the 2300 annual deaths from nonmelanoma skin cancer in the United States arising from this tumor.

Epidemiology

Overall, skin cancer incidence rates are increasing due to increased recreational sun exposure, increased life expectancy, and depletion of the ozone layer. More than 99% of nonmelanoma skin cancers occur in whites. These skin cancers are most commonly seen in the elderly, especially those with fair skin and long-standing sun exposure. However nonmelanoma skin cancers are increasingly being seen in people in their 30s and 40s.

Pathogenesis and Risk Factors

The most important risk factor is exposure to ultraviolet radiation from sunlight. Most dangerous is UVB radiation, but increasing evidence suggests that UVA is probably carcinogenic as well (Chapter 19). The timing and pattern of sun exposure are associated with different types of skin cancer. In general, nonmelanoma skin cancers are associated with cumulative sun exposure and occur most frequently in areas maximally exposed to the sun (e.g., the face, back of hands, and forearms). Intermittent, intense exposure to the sun, particularly in childhood, is associated with an increased risk of basal cell carcinoma, whereas cumulative sun exposure seems to be related to the development of squamous cell carcinoma. Individuals who have fair skin, light-colored eyes, red hair, a tendency to burn rather than tan, and a history of severe sunburns are at increased risk for nonmelanoma skin cancers. Other risk factors, particularly for squamous cell carcinoma, include chronic arsenic exposure, therapeutic radiation, chronic inflammatory skin conditions, psoralen plus UVA (PUVA) treatment for psoriasis and other diseases, and immunosuppression. The majority of cases in African-American patients are associated with scarring or burns rather than ultraviolet exposure. Human papillomavirus infection has also been implicated in some squamous cell carcinomas, particularly in the autosomal dominant disorder epidermodysplasia verruciformis.

Basal cell carcinoma can be seen in association with several conditions, including the basal cell nevus syndrome (also called *nevoid basal cell carcinoma syndrome* or *Gorlin's syndrome*), albinism, and xeroderma pigmentosum. The basal cell nevus syndrome is a rare autosomal dominant disorder that is caused by germline mutations in the patched gene (*PTCH*), a tumor suppressor gene in the hedgehog pathway. Acquired mutations in *PTCH* have also been identified in cases of sporadic basal cell carcinoma. Sporadic basal cell carcinomas are also associated with mutations in the genes encoding p53 and ras. Basal cell carcinoma arises from a pluripotential stem cell within the skin.

Squamous cell carcinoma of the skin is a malignancy of epidermal keratinocytes. Many such carcinomas are derived from actinic keratoses, a precursor that appears as a rough, scaly, often erythematous papule that is usually more easily palpated than seen. Estimates of the likelihood of progression of actinic keratoses to squamous cell carcinoma range from 0.025% to as high as 20%. Mutations in the gene encoding the p53 protein and in the *ras* oncogene

have been found in both actinic keratoses and squamous cell carcinomas. Mutations in *p16* have also been reported in squamous cell carcinomas.

Prevention and Screening

Primary prevention strategies are aimed at reducing chronic sun exposure. Public education and patient education should encourage the regular use of sunscreens with an SPF of 15 or greater, especially in childhood, and sun protective clothing (e.g., a broad-brimmed hat). Avoidance of tanning parlors and minimizing total sun exposure, especially to the midday sun, is recommended. The thinning of the ozone layer has been linked to increased ultraviolet radiation and increases in the incidence of nonmelanoma skin cancers. Currently, there is no evidence that total body skin examination is effective at reducing mortality or morbidity from nonmelanoma skin cancer.

Clinical Manifestations

BASAL CELL CARCINOMA. About 90% of basal cell carcinoma occurs on sun-exposed areas such as the face, neck, ears, scalp, and arms. The nose is the most common site. Typical basal cell carcinomas appear as slowly growing, shiny, skin-colored to pink translucent papules with telangiectasia and a "pearly" rolled border (Fig. 209–6). As the tumor grows, the center may become ulcerated and bleed, although there is usually no associated pain or tenderness. Most basal cell carcinomas are diagnosed when they are 2 cm in diameter.

Basal cell carcinoma rarely metastasizes and is usually curable with a variety of treatments. Although the mortality rate is low, these cancers may result in significant morbidity owing to invasive local growth with potential disfigurement and destruction of skin, bone, and cartilage.

SQUAMOUS CELL CARCINOMA. This type of skin cancer usually appears on areas of skin that are heavily damaged by sun exposure. The most common sites include the head or neck, back, forearms, and dorsum of the hand. Clinically, squamous cell carcinoma

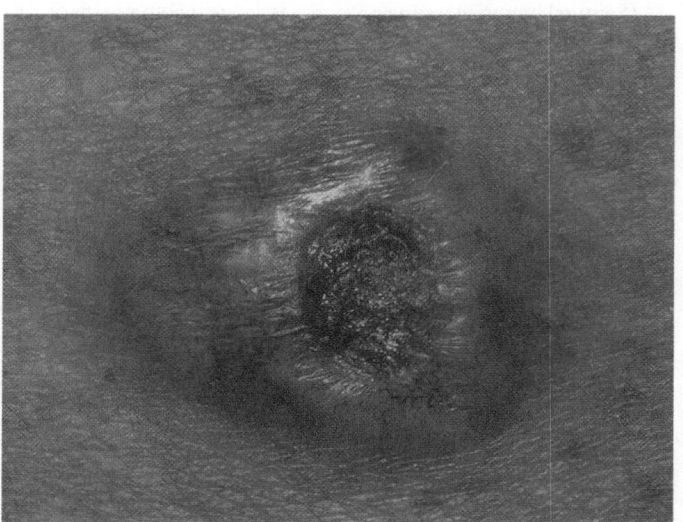

FIGURE 209–6 • Basal cell carcinoma.

Oncology

occurs as a discrete scaly erythematous papule on an indurated base that can develop on normal-appearing skin or on an actinic keratosis (Fig. 209–7). The lesion may grow over time and become ulcerated, itchy, painful, or bleeding. Keratoacanthoma is a variant that is characterized by rapid growth and a crateriform appearance with a central plug. Bowen's disease, or squamous cell carcinoma in situ, manifests as an erythematous, scaly, sharply defined plaque.

Untreated squamous cell carcinoma may cause significant local destruction. However, unlike basal cell carcinoma, squamous cell carcinomas carry a 5% risk of metastasis. Higher risk lesions are those that are larger than 2 cm, are moderately or poorly differentiated, have perineural involvement, are on the ear or the lip, arise in scars, or occur in immunosuppressed patients. Most metastases develop in regional lymph nodes, although metastases may also occur in lung, liver, brain, skin, or bone. For patients with lymph node metastases, the 5-year survival is less than 50%.

Diagnosis

The diagnosis of basal cell carcinoma and squamous cell carcinoma is frequently suspected by inspection alone, but histologic confirmation is usually indicated. Either a shave or a punch biopsy technique is acceptable (Chapter 472). Care should be taken to include the base of the lesion if a shave biopsy technique is used.

 Treatment

BASAL CELL CARCINOMA. The technique with the lowest recurrence rate and using the least tissue is Mohs micrographic surgery, which utilizes frozen tissue mapping of the resection margins in stages to locate residual tumor. Mohs microsurgery should be considered when treating recurrent cases; microscopically aggressive forms, such as the morpheaform subtype; lesions greater than 2 cm in greatest diameter; and tumors of the ears, eyelids, nose, nasolabial folds, and lips. Other options for local lesions include

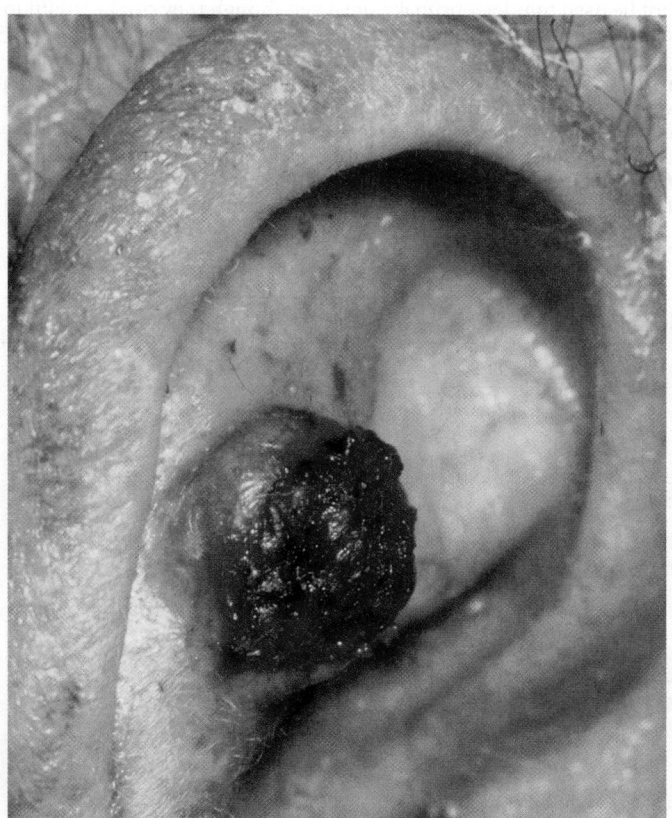

FIGURE 209–7 • Squamous cell carcinoma of the skin.

traditional surgical excision, cryosurgery (liquid nitrogen), electrodesiccation and curettage, and radiation therapy. Retinoids, interferon-α, topical 5-fluorouracil, photodynamic therapy, and imiquimod are also used. Cure rates for basal cell carcinoma range between 90 and 99%.

SQUAMOUS CELL CARCINOMA. As with basal cell carcinoma, Mohs micrographic surgery provides the lowest recurrence rate, with cure rates greater than 90%. Mohs microsurgery is especially useful for recurrent tumors or lesions that have an increased risk of metastasis. Squamous cell carcinoma can also be cured by traditional surgical excision, cryosurgery (liquid nitrogen), electrodesiccation and curettage, and radiation therapy. Topical 5-fluorouracil, photodynamic therapy, or imiquimod may have a role in the management of in situ squamous cell cancers.

FOLLOW-UP. Patients with basal cell carcinoma and squamous cell carcinoma require ongoing follow-up to detect local recurrences and to recognize new skin cancers. The likelihood of developing a second basal cell carcinoma or squamous cell carcinoma is about 40% over 3 years. In addition, these patients have an increased risk for developing cutaneous melanoma. Patient education regarding modification of risk factors (i.e., sun exposure) is an important component of follow-up.

1. Balch CM, Soong S, Ross MI, et al: Long-term results of a multi-institutional randomized trial comparing prognostic factors and surgical results for intermediate thickness melanomas (1.0 to 4.0 mm). Intergroup Melanoma Surgical Trial. Ann Surg Oncol 2000;7:87–97.
2. Cascinelli N, Morabito A, Santinami M, et al: Immediate or delayed dissection of regional lymph nodes in patients with melanoma of the trunk: A randomized trial. WHO Melanoma Programme. Lancet 1998;351:793–796.
3. Kirkwood JM, Ibrahim JG, Sosman JA, et al: High dose interferon alfa-2b significantly prolongs relapse free and overall survival compared with the GM2-KLH/QS21 vaccine in patients with resected stage IIB/III melanoma: Results of intergroup Trial E1694/S9512/C509801. J Clin Oncol 2001;19:2370–2380.

SUGGESTED READINGS

Balch CM, Buzaid AC, Soong SJ, et al: Final version of the American Joint Committee on Cancer staging system for cutaneous melanoma. J Clin Oncol 2001;19:3635–3648. *Summary of the new staging system for melanoma, with useful information regarding prognostic factors.*

Khayat D, Rixe O, Martin G, et al: Surgical margins in cutaneous melanoma (2 cm versus 5 cm for lesions measuring less than 2.1-mm thick). Cancer 2003;97:1941–1946. *For melanoma less than 2.1 mm thick, a margin of excision of 2 cm is sufficient.*

Marcil I, Stern RS: Risk of developing a subsequent nonmelanoma skin cancer in patients with a history of nonmelanoma skin cancer: A critical review of the literature and meta-analysis. Arch Dermatol 2000;136:1524–1530. *Risk factors for a second cancer in patients with melanoma.*

Sober AJ, Chuang TY, Duvic M, et al: Guidelines of care for primary cutaneous melanoma. J Am Acad Dermatol 2001;45:579–586. *Good guidelines for treatment and follow-up of patients with melanoma.*

210 CANCER OF UNKNOWN PRIMARY ORIGIN

John D. Hainsworth
F. Anthony Greco

Definition

The first signs or symptoms of cancer are frequently due to metastases to visceral or nodal sites. In most such patients, routine clinical evaluation with a comprehensive history, physical examination, complete blood cell count, screening chemistries, and directed radiologic evaluation of specific symptoms or signs identifies the primary tumor. Patients who have no primary tumor located after this routine clinical evaluation are defined as having cancer of unknown primary site. Further clinical and pathologic evaluation will identify the primary site in only a small minority of patients, and about 80% will never have a primary site identified during their subsequent clinical course.

Etiology

In patients whose primary site of cancer remains undetectable, the primary site presumably has remained small or, less likely, has regressed spontaneously. Large autopsy series before the routine use of computed tomographic scans or magnetic resonance imaging identified small primary sites of cancer in 85% of patients with previously unidentified primary tumors, usually in the pancreas, lung, and various other gastrointestinal sites; with current use of computed tomography and magnetic resonance imaging, however, autopsy series have identified primary sites in only 50 to 70% of patients.

Incidence

About 3% of all patients with cancer have metastatic disease without a known primary site, accounting for about 50,000 to 60,000 cases per year in the United States. Cancer of unknown primary site occurs with approximately equal frequency in men and women, and it increases in incidence with advancing age.

Clinical and Pathologic Evaluation

Since all patients with cancer of unknown primary site have advanced disease, therapeutic nihilism has been common. However, it is now evident that this heterogeneous group contains subsets of patients with widely diverse prognoses; some cancers are highly responsive to treatment, and some patients may have a substantial chance of achieving long-term survival with appropriate treatment. The initial clinical and pathologic evaluation should therefore focus on identifying a primary site when possible and on identifying patients for whom specific treatment is indicated.

In the majority of patients with cancer of unknown primary site, the diagnosis of advanced cancer is strongly suspected after the initial history and physical examination. A brief additional evaluation, including complete blood cell counts, chemistry profile, and computed tomography of the chest and abdomen should be performed. In addition, specific symptoms or signs should be evaluated with appropriate radiologic and endoscopic studies. If a primary site is located, management should follow guidelines for the specific cancer identified. In patients with no obvious primary site, the most accessible metastatic site should be biopsied.

Fine needle aspiration may or may not provide sufficient material for optimal histologic examination and special pathologic procedures. If tissue is inadequate, a larger biopsy sample should be obtained so that all necessary stains and procedures can be performed.

PATHOLOGIC EVALUATION. Optimal pathologic evaluation can identify subsets of patient who have chemotherapy-responsive tumors and sometimes can identify a primary site. The initial light microscopic evaluation identifies an adenocarcinoma in approximately 60% of patients with cancer of unknown primary site. Other diagnoses obtained by initial light microscopic examination include poorly differentiated carcinoma (25%), squamous carcinoma (10%), and poorly differentiated neoplasm (inability to distinguish among carcinoma, lymphoma, melanoma, and sarcoma; 5%).

In patients with adenocarcinoma, it is seldom possible for the pathologist to identify a primary site either by light microscopic characteristics or with additional pathologic techniques. Specific exceptions include immunoperoxidase staining for prostate-specific antigen (PSA), which is relatively specific for adenocarcinoma of the prostate (Chapter 207); for estrogen/progesterone receptors, which are suggestive of breast cancer (Chapter 204); and for leukocyte common antigen, which can identify non-Hodgkin's lymphoma (Chapter 195) as the primary tumor in up to 50% of patients with poorly differentiated neoplasms. Other diagnoses suggested by immunoperoxidase staining include neuroendocrine carcinomas, melanomas (Chapter 209), and sarcomas. Electron microscopy should be considered when light microscopy and immunoperoxidase staining fail to identify the tumor, especially in young patients with anaplastic tumors, for which specific ultrastructural features may suggest neuroendocrine carcinoma (neurosecretory granules), melanoma (premelanosomes), and certain sarcomas.

Occasionally, detection of a tumor-specific chromosomal abnormality can provide a definitive diagnosis. Cancers with recognized specific chromosomal abnormalities include germ cell tumors (i12p; Chapter 206), peripheral neuroepithelioma and Ewing's tumor (t11;22; Chapter 208), and non-Hodgkin's lymphoma (Chapter 195). Chromosomal analysis should therefore be considered, especially in young men who have poorly differentiated mediastinal or retroperitoneal tumors and in whom other pathologic studies have been inconclusive.

SEARCH FOR THE PRIMARY SITE. After completion of the brief and directed initial evaluation outlined above, further diagnostic studies should be limited (Table 210–1). Routine radiologic and endoscopic evaluation of asymptomatic areas are not useful in the identification of a primary site and therefore are not recommended. Whether positron emission tomography is useful in identifying the primary site in a fraction of these patients is unproven. Levels of serum tumor markers, including carcinoembryonic antigen, CA-125, CA-19-9, and CA-15-3, are frequently elevated in patients with carcinoma of unknown primary site; however, these elevations are nonspecific and should not be used to infer a primary site, even though they can be useful in monitoring response to treatment.

All men with metastatic adenocarcinoma should have measurement of serum PSA. Mammograms should be considered in women with metastatic adenocarcinoma, particularly if clinical features are consistent with metastatic breast cancer (e.g., axillary node involvement, pleural effusion, lytic/blastic bone metastases). Patients younger than 50 years of age with poorly differentiated carcinoma should have measurement of serum human chorionic gonadotropin and

---

Table 210–1 • RECOMMENDED EVALUATION FOLLOWING INITIAL LIGHT MICROSCOPIC DIAGNOSIS

DIAGNOSIS	CLINICAL EVALUATION*	SPECIAL PATHOLOGIC STUDIES
Adenocarcinoma (or poorly differentiated adenocarcinoma)	CT scans of chest, abdomen Men: serum PSA Women: Mammograms Additional directed radiologic/endoscopic studies to evaluate abnormal symptoms, signs, laboratory values	Men: PSA stain Women: estrogen, and progesterone receptor stain (if clinical features suggest metastatic breast cancer)
Poorly differentiated carcinoma	CT scans of chest, abdomen Serum hCG, AFP Additional directed radiologic/endoscopic studies to evaluate abnormal symptoms, signs, laboratory values	Immunoperoxidase staining Electron microscopy (if immunoperoxidase stains indeterminate) Molecular genetic analysis (consider in young men with features of extragonadal germ cell tumor)
Squamous carcinoma, cervical nodes	Direct laryngoscopy with visualization/biopsy of nasopharynx, pharynx, hypopharynx, larynx Fiberoptic bronchoscopy (if laryngoscopy is negative)	—
Squamous carcinoma inguinal nodes	Complete examination of perineal area (including pelvic examination) Anoscopy Cystoscopy	

*In addition to a history, physical examination, complete blood cell counts, chemistry profile, and chest radiograph.
AFP = α-fetoprotein; CT = computed tomography; hCG = human chorionic gonadotropin; PSA = prostate-specific antigen.

α-fetoprotein levels. Patients with metastatic squamous carcinoma involving cervical lymph nodes should have thorough endoscopic evaluation of the head and neck, including visualization of the structures from the nasopharynx to the larynx and biopsy of any suspicious areas (Chapter 197). Fiberoptic bronchoscopy should also be considered in patients who have low cervical adenopathy and who do not have a head or neck primary site established by endoscopic examination (Chapter 198). Patients with metastatic squamous carcinoma involving inguinal lymph nodes should have careful inspection of all perineal structures, including anoscopy, a urologic evaluation, and a pelvic examination in women.

Rx Treatment

MANAGEMENT OF SPECIFIC TREATABLE SUBSETS

Several subsets of patients who benefit from specific treatment can be identified on the basis of clinical and pathologic features (Table 210–2). These patients are important to recognize and treat appropriately, since some patients in each group have potential for long-term survival.

Adenocarcinoma

WOMEN WITH AXILLARY LYMPH NODE METASTASES. Metastatic breast cancer should be suspected in women who have axillary lymph node involvement with adenocarcinoma, particularly when other metastatic sites are not evident. In these patients, pathologic evaluation of the initial lymph node biopsy should include staining for estrogen and progesterone receptors; elevated levels provide strong evidence for the diagnosis of breast cancer. When no other metastases are identified, these women should be treated as if they had stage II breast cancer, which is potentially curable with appropriate therapy (Chapter 204). Modified radical mastectomy identifies a breast primary site in 44 to 82% of women, even when the breast examination and mammographic findings are normal. Axillary lymph node dissection followed by empiric radiation therapy to the breast appears to give results similar to those of mastectomy, although these two options for primary therapy have not been compared directly. Adjuvant systemic therapy should follow standard guidelines for treatment of patients with stage II breast cancer.

WOMEN WITH PERITONEAL CARCINOMATOSIS. Adenocarcinoma involving the peritoneum in women usually originates from the ovary (Chapter 205), although carcinomas arising in the gastrointestinal tract or breast can occasionally produce this syndrome. However, diffuse peritoneal carcinomatosis occasionally occurs in women who have histologically normal ovaries, or who have had previous bilateral oophorectomy. The peritoneum is frequently the only site of tumor involvement,

and serum CA-125 levels are usually elevated. When histologic features suggest ovarian cancer, this syndrome has been called *peritoneal papillary serous carcinoma* or *primary extraovarian serous carcinoma*.

Even when the histology is not typical, women with adenocarcinoma of unknown primary site involving the peritoneum often have cancers with a biology that is similar to ovarian cancer (Chapter 205). Treatment of these patients should follow guidelines for stage III ovarian cancer. When feasible, a full laparotomy with maximal surgical cytoreduction should be performed, followed by combination chemotherapy with a taxane/platinum-containing regimen. Measurement of serial serum CA-125 levels provides an accurate assessment of the efficacy of treatment. A minority of these patients may have complete responses and long-term survival, particularly when initial surgical cytoreduction leaves minimal residual disease. A similar syndrome of peritoneal carcinomatosis that is responsive to chemotherapy for ovarian cancer has occasionally been reported in men.

MEN WITH SKELETAL METASTASES AND/OR ELEVATED SERUM PSA LEVEL. Metastatic prostate cancer (Chapter 207) should be suspected in men with adenocarcinoma predominantly involving bone, particularly if the metastases are blastic. An elevated serum level of PSA or tumor immunostaining for PSA provides confirmatory evidence for the diagnosis of prostate cancer. Occasionally, men with adenocarcinoma of unknown primary site and patterns of metastasis unusual for prostate cancer (e.g., lung metastases, mediastinal lymph node metastases) are found to have elevated serum PSA levels. These patients should be treated according to guidelines for advanced prostate cancer. Androgen ablation produces excellent responses and substantial palliation in a majority of patients.

SINGLE METASTATIC LESION. Occasionally, a single metastatic lesion containing adenocarcinoma or poorly differentiated carcinoma is identified, and a complete evaluation reveals no other evidence of disease. Such presentations can include a single lymph node or subcutaneous site, or single lesions at various visceral sites, including bone, liver, lung, brain, and adrenal gland. The possibility of an unusual primary site mimicking a metastatic lesion should be considered (e.g., a subcutaneous nodule from a primary apocrine or sebaceous carcinoma rather than a metastasis), but this possibility can usually be excluded on the basis of clinical or pathologic features. For patients with a single lesion, definitive local therapy should be used, as guided by the site of tumor involvement. Such therapy may include surgical resection, radiation therapy, or a combination of these modalities. Although the majority of these patients eventually develop other metastatic sites, a significant disease-free interval is often experienced, and local treatment provides substantial palliation. The role of systemic chemotherapy in addition to definitive local therapy is not well defined; younger patients with poorly differentiated carcinoma or poorly differentiated adenocarcinoma are often treated with a short course of a taxane/platinum-based regimen (see Empiric Chemotherapy).

Table 210–2 • SPECIFIC PATIENT SUBSETS AND RECOMMENDED TREATMENT

SPECIFIC SUBSET—IDENTIFYING FEATURES		
Histologic	**Clinical**	**TREATMENT RECOMMENDATIONS**
Adenocarcinoma	Women, isolated axillary adenopathy	Treat as stage II breast cancer
Adenocarcinoma	Women, peritoneal carcinomatosis (?occasionally men)	Treat as stage III ovarian cancer
Adenocarcinoma	Men, elevated PSA and/or blastic bone metastases	Treat as advanced prostate cancer
Adenocarcinoma, poorly differentiated carcinoma	Single metastatic lesion	Definitive local therapy (resection and/or radiation therapy) with or without chemotherapy
Squamous	Cervical adenopathy	Treat as locally advanced head/neck cancer
Squamous	Inguinal adenopathy	Definitive local therapy (node dissection with or without radiation therapy) with or without chemotherapy
Poorly differentiated carcinoma	Young men with midline tumor and/or elevated hCG, AFP	Treat as extragonadal germ cell tumor
Poorly differentiated carcinoma	Diverse clinical features	Empiric chemotherapy with paclitaxel/platinum/etoposide
Neuroendocrine carcinoma, poorly differentiated	Diverse clinical presentations	Treat with platinum/etoposide or paclitaxel/platinum/etoposide
Neuroendocrine carcinoma, well differentiated	Usually liver metastases	Treat as metastatic carcinoid tumor

AFP = α-fetoprotein; hCG = human chorionic gonadotropin; PSA = prostate-specific antigen.

Squamous Carcinoma

CERVICAL ADENOPATHY. Squamous carcinoma of unknown primary site is relatively uncommon. The large majority of patients with this syndrome have involvement of cervical lymph nodes, usually in the upper or mid-cervical area. Often, patients with this syndrome are middle-aged or elderly and have a history of substantial tobacco or alcohol use, or both. A primary site in the head and neck region should be suspected (Chapter 197); however, complete endoscopic evaluation fails to identify a primary site in approximately 15% of these patients.

Even when no primary site is identified, management of these patients should follow standard guidelines for treatment of locally advanced squamous carcinoma arising in head and neck regions. Many reports have documented long-term survival rates of 30 to 60% following definitive local treatment, which should include radiation therapy or combined radiation and cervical lymph node dissection. Outcome of treatment depends on the size and number of involved cervical lymph nodes. Combined radiation and chemotherapy is also reasonable for patients with cervical adenopathy and unknown primary site, particularly if the bulk of tumor is large.

Inguinal Adenopathy. Occasionally, metastatic squamous cancer is found in inguinal lymph nodes. In most of these patients, a primary site can be located in the perineal or anorectal area. For the occasional patient in whom no primary site is identified, long-term survival can result from local therapy with inguinal lymph node dissection, with or without radiation therapy. Recently, combined modality treatment with concurrent chemotherapy and radiation therapy has improved the cure rates of several squamous cancers arising in this region (e.g., cervix, anus, bladder). Although data are incomplete for the uncommon patient without an identified primary site, the addition of chemotherapy with a platinum/5-fluorouracil regimen is reasonable.

Poorly Differentiated Carcinoma

EXTRAGONADAL GERM CELL CANCER SYNDROME. Young men with clinical features of extragonadal germ cell tumors, including tumors that are in the mediastinum or retroperitoneum or are associated with elevated serum levels of human chorionic gonadotropin or α-fetoprotein, should be treated according to guidelines for extragonadal germ cell tumors (Chapter 206). Some of these patients have proven germ cell tumors by molecular genetic analysis, even when the diagnosis is not possible with other standard pathologic techniques. About 30 to 40% of these patients may achieve complete responses and long-term survival following chemotherapy with cisplatin, etoposide, and bleomycin, as used for advanced germ cell tumors.

ANAPLASTIC LYMPHOMA. Appropriate initial pathologic evaluation should identify most histologically atypical lymphomas. Occasionally, immunoperoxidase staining for leukocyte common antigen is negative or cannot be adequately performed in patients with anaplastic lymphoma. Some of these patients can be recognized using other immunoperoxidase stains (e.g., Ki-1 or CD-30) or molecular genetic analysis (detection of immunoglobulin gene rearrangements). All lymphomas identified by special pathologic studies should be treated using standard guidelines for aggressive non-Hodgkin's lymphoma (Chapter 195).

NEUROENDOCRINE CARCINOMA. In approximately 10% of poorly differentiated carcinomas, neuroendocrine features are identified either by immunoperoxidase staining or by electron microscopy. Treatment of these patients is discussed later (see Neuroendocrine Carcinoma).

OTHER POORLY DIFFERENTIATED CARCINOMAS. Most patients with poorly differentiated carcinoma do not have clinical or pathologic features that enable them to be assigned to any one of these three subsets. However, this heterogeneous group contains some patients whose carcinomas are highly sensitive to platinum-based chemotherapy. Clinical factors predictive of sensitivity to chemotherapy include site of tumor involvement (lymph nodes as compared with visceral metastases), fewer sites of metastatic disease, and younger age. In patients with one or more of these favorable clinical features,

treatment with cisplatin-based chemotherapy can produce a greater than 60% response rate, with about 15% of patients remaining disease-free more than 8 years after completing treatment. Therefore, a brief trial of empiric chemotherapy (see later) is recommended for all patients with poorly differentiated carcinoma, unless they are extremely debilitated at the time of diagnosis. Patients with highly sensitive tumors can be identified within the first 4 to 6 weeks of treatment, and ineffective treatment can be discontinued in the remainder.

Neuroendocrine Carcinoma

POORLY DIFFERENTIATED NEUROENDOCRINE CARCINOMA, OR SMALL CELL ANAPLASTIC CARCINOMA. These high-grade neuroendocrine tumors are now reliably identified using widely available immunoperoxidase stains. Although the origin of these tumors remains unknown, they are often highly sensitive to combination chemotherapy; with platinum/etoposide chemotherapy, the overall response rate is about 75%, and 25% of patients have complete responses. More recently, excellent activity has been documented with a three-drug regimen containing paclitaxel, carboplatin, and etoposide. In patients with locoregional disease, the addition of radiation therapy following chemotherapy is reasonable.

LOW-GRADE (CARCINOID TYPE) NEUROENDOCRINE TUMORS. Occasionally, low-grade neuroendocrine tumors are found at a metastatic site. In almost all cases, the liver is the site of involvement, and the histology suggests a carcinoid (Chapter 245) or islet cell tumor of gastrointestinal origin (Chapter 140). Various clinical syndromes caused by secretion of vasoactive peptides (e.g., serotonin, vasoactive intestinal peptide, gastrin) have been described. Like other carcinoid tumors, these tumors often have indolent biology, and patients can frequently survive for several years despite multiple liver metastases. Unlike poorly differentiated neuroendocrine tumors, these tumors are relatively resistant to chemotherapy, and intensive combination regimens should usually be avoided. Management of these patients should follow guidelines for metastatic carcinoid tumors (Chapter 245) and may include the use of somatostatin analogues, local ablative procedures (e.g., surgical resection, radiofrequency ablation, chemoembolization), or fluorouracil-based chemotherapy regimens.

EMPIRIC CHEMOTHERAPY

Approximately 60 to 70% of patients with carcinoma of unknown primary site do not fit into any of these defined clinical subsets. In these patients, earlier reports of empiric chemotherapy were discouraging, with overall response rates of only 20 to 25% and short median survival times (5 to 7 months). More recently, several taxane-containing chemotherapy regimens have appeared to produce better results, although no randomized clinical data are available. The combination of paclitaxel and carboplatin, with or without etoposide, produces objective responses in 30 to 45% of patients, with median survival in the 9- to 12-month range. In addition, a minority of patients receive a major benefit from treatment; the 2-year survival rate with taxane-containing regimens is 20 to 25%.

At present, patients with carcinoma of unknown primary site who have reasonable performance status should be considered for an empiric trial of combination chemotherapy. Patients with responsive tumors can be identified after 4 to 6 weeks of treatment, and they should continue treatment for a standard 4- to 5-month course. Patients who do not respond to initial combination chemotherapy are unlikely to respond to further treatment; palliative care is appropriate in these patients (Chapter 3). For patients who have poor performance status at the time of diagnosis, palliative care alone is an appropriate approach.

SUGGESTED READINGS

Greco FA, Burris HA 3rd, Erland JB, et al: Carcinoma of unknown primary site. Cancer 2000;89:2655–2660. *Multicenter experience documents improved outcome with empiric chemotherapy.*

Mantaka P, Baum RP, Hertel A, et al: PET with 2-[F-18]-fluoro-2-deoxy-D-glucose (FDG) in patients with cancer of unknown primary (CUP): Influence on patients' diagnostic and therapeutic management. Cancer Biother Radiopharm 2003;18:47–58. *PET scanning was better than CT for detecting unknown primary cancers.*

Note: Page numbers followed by the letter f refer to figures; those followed by the letter t refer to tables. **Boldface** page numbers refer to main discussions.